THE AUTHORITY SINCE 1868

# THE WORLD ALMANAC®

## AND BOOK OF FACTS

# 1994

WORLD ALMANAC

AN IMPRINT OF FUNK & WAGNALLS CORPORATION

# THE WORLD ALMANAC®
## AND BOOK OF FACTS
## 1994

**Editor:** Robert Famighetti
**Senior Editor:** June Foley    **Senior Editor:** Thomas McGuire
**Associate Editor:** Christina Cheddar    **Assistant Editor:** Michael Northrop
**Chronology Editor:** Donald Young    **Index:** Aris Georgiadis

### Funk & Wagnalls
**Editorial Director:** Leon L. Bram
**Director of Manufacturing:** Sally McCravey
**Director of Editorial Production:** Andrea J. Pitluk
**Copy Editor:** Matthew Friedlander
**Keyboard Input:** Melissa Humbert

### World Almanac Books
**Publisher:** Richard W. Eiger
**Sales Manager:** James R. Keenley    **Publicity Manager:** Joyce H. Stein

---

The editors acknowledge with thanks the many letters of helpful comment and criticism from readers of THE WORLD ALMANAC. Because of the volume of mail directed to the editorial offices, it is not possible to reply to each letter writer. However, every communication is read by the editors and all comments and suggestions receive careful attention. THE WORLD ALMANAC does not decide wagers.

The first edition of THE WORLD ALMANAC, a 120-page volume with 12 pages of advertising, was published by the New York World in 1868. Annual publication was suspended in 1876. Joseph Pulitzer, publisher of the New York World, revived THE WORLD ALMANAC in 1886 with the goal of making it a "compendium of universal knowledge." It has been published annually since then.

---

---

**WORLD ALMANAC**
An Imprint of Funk & Wagnalls
One International Boulevard, Suite 444
Mahwah, New Jersey 07495-0017

# 1994 HIGHLIGHTS

# GENERAL INDEX

3

# The World Almanac

## and Book of Facts 1994

## The Top 10 News Stories

Bill Clinton was inaugurated as the 42d U.S. president on January 20; he brought to the presidency a lengthy agenda of domestic policy initiatives.

Clinton proposed to Congress in September a complex and controversial plan to provide health insurance to all Americans and hold down health-care costs; the plan was largely the work of a task force headed by First Lady Hillary Rodham Clinton.

By the narrowest of margins, Clinton won congressional passage in August of a bill designed to reduce federal budget deficits by $496 billion over five years, through federal spending cuts and new taxes.

Although many issues remained unresolved, dramatic steps were taken in September to end 45 years of conflict in the Middle East, when Israel and the Palestine Liberation Organization exchanged letters of recognition and signed an agreement on Palestinian autonomy in Israeli-occupied territories.

Russian President Boris Yeltsin continued to press for economic and political reforms and, after a bloody confrontation in October, succeeded in dissolving a legislature dominated by hard-line opponents of his program.

During the year, negotiators repeatedly attempted to devise an acceptable partition plan to end the slaughter in Bosnia and Herzegovina.

The "Great Flood of 1993" left at least 50 dead, over 70,000 homeless, and some $12 billion in property damage in 9 midwestern states in the summer.

Clearing the way for black majority rule, South Africa announced that elections open to all races would be held in 1994.

Massive starvation in Somalia had ended by May; however, a deadly confrontation then developed between U.N. and U.S. peacekeeping forces and a fugitive Somali warlord.

A terrorist bomb exploded in New York City's World Trade Center in February, killing 6, and just a few months later, another bombing and assassination plot was uncovered.

## America's Role in the Post-Cold War World

### By Arthur M. Schlesinger, Jr.

The Cold War is history. Those grim days of Soviet-American confrontation, once so frightening, now seem remote, even improbable. Who today remembers bomb shelters, and teachers drilling schoolchildren to hide under desks, and loyalty oaths, and the blacklisting of movie stars, and SAC planes on 24-hour alert, and academics moving to Australia to flee nuclear war? The Great Fear is finally over. Communism is an extinct ideology, the Soviet Union a fading memory. A historical epoch has come to an end.

But the end of the epoch leaves American foreign policy all dressed up and nowhere to go. For the half-century of the Cold War, the United States had a supreme objective in the world: to stop Soviet expansionism. Containment, the diplomat George Kennan predicted in 1947, would lead to "the break-up or the gradual mellowing of Soviet power." In the end, it led to both, and the Western democracies under creative American leadership, expressed in such initiatives as the Marshall Plan, were victorious. Today, mission accomplished, the next question arises: Where do we go from here? What is America's role in the post-Cold War world?

"We have slain a large dragon," James Woolsey, President Bill Clinton's director of the Central Intelligence Agency, told Congress, "but we live now in a jungle filled with a bewildering variety of poisonous snakes. And in many ways, the dragon was easier to keep track of."

The zoological metaphor is catchy. Still, it would be a mistake to look back on the Cold War with nostalgia. For in those dark times nuclear war threatened civilization with total extinction. We lived for forty years on the edge of apocalypse. Poisonous snakes may do local harm, but they do not menace the future of humanity—or even the national security of the United States. Let us rejoice that the Cold War is behind us.

Mr. Woolsey launched his metaphor to strengthen the argument that, even though the Cold War is over,

the republic must maintain national security spending at more or less Cold War levels. Such a reaction is predictable. The Cold War conferred power and money on the national security establishment—the intelligence community and the Pentagon. Giant bureaucracies in any case prefer to keep on doing what they have been doing. Cold War habits are bound to persist until we think through the role of the United States in the post-Cold War world and replace the containment of Soviet power with a new strategic objective.

#### Does America Need an Enemy?

Some say that Americans need an enemy to give focus and coherence to foreign policy. Americans had Germany as the enemy in two world wars, then the Soviet Union as the enemy in the Cold War. Who will be the designated enemy now? Some nominate Japan; some nominate Islamic fundamentalism; in due course other potential enemies will no doubt be proclaimed.

But this needing-an-enemy hypothesis is a demeaning idea for a great nation, especially one founded, like the American republic, on lofty ideals. Self-preservation must be the mainspring of a country's foreign policy, but no mature country wants an enemy to define its world role. Surely the republic of Jefferson and Lincoln and Wilson has something affirmative to offer suffering humanity. Moreover, history shows that the United States got along quite comfortably without an obsessive enemy in the century from 1815, the end of America's last war with Great Britain, to 1917, the year of America's entry into the First World War. Who needs an enemy now?

No, the search for a new enemy cannot save Americans from the much harder job of rethinking the U.S. role in the new era. The task is to construct a strategic design consistent with the perils and possibilities of the epoch into which the world is now moving.

31

## Ethnic and National Hostility

The 20th century was an epoch defined above all by the warfare of ideologies. The liberal democratic idea was under siege by two mortal foes: fascism in the first half of the century, Communism in the second. Democracy finally succeeded in defeating both totalitarian creeds: fascism perishing with a bang, Communism with a whimper.

But the end of the warfare of ideologies does not mean, as some sages have optimistically forecast, the "end of history." One set of hatreds replaces another. Lifting the iron grip of ideological repression in Eastern Europe and the ex-Soviet Union releases pent-up ethnic, nationalist, religious, and linguistic antagonisms deeply rooted in history and in memory. The evaporation of the Cold War removes superpower restraints on national and tribal conflicts in the Third World.

At the same time, the collapse of Communism, the bankruptcy of Marxism-Leninism, have left behind, in the words of President Vaclav Havel of the Czech Republic, "a great unsettling void that had to be filled at any cost." It is a void of belief, a void of belonging—and the void is rendered the more acute by the spread of a world market, in which peoples, at the mercy of economic developments beyond their control, feel beleaguered and vulnerable and seek the reassurance of identity. It is this void that ethnicity and nationalism rush to fill. Tribal instincts are surging back, and the hostility of one tribe for another is a primordial human reaction. The tragedy of Yugoslavia is only the most murderous portent of the century to come.

The situation is intensified by the increase in mass migrations across national frontiers. As the 20th century staggers to a close, a number of factors—not just the end of the Cold War but, more fundamentally, the development of swifter modes of communication and transport, the growth of population, the breakdown of traditional structures, the flight from chaos, from tyranny, from poverty, from ethnic cleansing, from ecological disaster—drive people as never before from one country to another in the quest for a better life. Already 100 million people around the world today live outside the countries in which they were born.

What happens when people of different ethnic origins, speaking different languages, professing different religions, settle in the same geographical locality and live under the same political sovereignty? Unless a common purpose binds them together, tribal fears and enmities will drive them apart. On every side the potent mix of nationalism and ethnicity is tearing nations into pieces. Look around the globe. From India to Ireland, from Sri Lanka to Sudan, from Angola to Zaire, you will find growing ethnic and racial tensions. During the summer of 1993 in what used to be the Soviet Union, seven separate wars were going on in the Transcaucasus region. Even nations as stable as Canada and Britain and France, Belgium and Spain and Germany and Italy, face internal threats of secession. "The virus of tribalism," in the words of the British magazine The Economist, "...risks becoming the AIDS of international politics—lying dormant for years, then flaring up to destroy nations." If the 20th century has been the century of the warfare of ideologies, the 21st century begins as the century of the warfare of ethnicities.

## A Parade of International Imperatives

And other troubles loom ahead: economic stagnation; overpopulation; environmental degradation; proliferation of nuclear, biological, and chemical weapons; terrorism; drugs; AIDS. The 21st century presents humankind with a formidable agenda.

The priority, indeed the condition for tackling nearly everything else, must be peace among nations. This means most urgently the completion of the task of bringing weapons of mass destruction under control. No one can rest happily at the thought of nuclear bombs in the hands of leaders like Saddam Hussein of Iraq and Kim Il Sung of North Korea. It means too the development of international means to prevent future Somalias and future Bosnias. The ultimate aim must be the evolution from a world of war to a world of law.

There follows a parade of international imperatives. There is the need to promote the spread of human rights. There is the need to protect the planet against toxic wastes, acid rain, ozone depletion, global warming, and other environmental scourges. There is the need for a global energy policy that will ensure both efficient use in rich countries and adequate supply in poor countries. There is the need to check the population explosion and to restrain mass migrations. There is the need to stop the sale of arms to unstable governments around the world—an area in which the United States has been a particular offender. There is the need to regulate the swarm of global corporations that float across frontiers and are unaccountable to national governments. There is the need to end terrorism and the international drug traffic.

## Where Does America Fit In?

Where does the United States fit in? What should be the American objective? The goal of any country's foreign policy is to protect and advance its own national interest. Now the phrase "national interest" worries some goodhearted people, who fear that it implies egoistic concern with one's own country at the expense of other countries and thereby nourishes a nation's baser self. Yet national interest properly construed implies concern with the long-term international environment—and it implies respect for the national interests of other countries. Without the compass of national interest, moreover, there would be no order or predictability in international affairs. As George Washington said, "No nation is to be trusted farther than it is bound by its interest."

National interest is not, however, a self-executing formula. Historically, the United States has always had bedrock strategic interests—ensuring balances of power in Europe and Asia, guaranteeing the freedom of the seas, preventing extracontinental aggression in the western hemisphere. In recent times, it has developed economic and political interests—a freely trading world to be made safe for democracy and human rights. Though Americans argue endlessly over the best way to pursue those goals, a relationship to the national interest is necessary in a democracy to win public support for a sustainable foreign policy.

Some people these days propose that America, as the only remaining superpower, king of the hill, should simply impose a pax Americana on the fractious world. It is true that the United States is the world's only military superpower, but military power will not suffice without economic power behind it. The United States achieved a swift military victory in the Persian Gulf War of 1991, but it had to pass a begging bowl among its allies to meet the economic costs. Superpowers that cannot pay for their own wars won't stay in the superpower business very long.

Even if it should have the money, one wonders whether America has the power or the wisdom to rule the world. "We must face the fact," President John F.

Kennedy said a third of a century ago, "that the United States is neither omnipotent nor omniscient— that we are only 6 percent of the world's population— that we cannot impose our will upon the other 94 percent of mankind—that we cannot right every wrong or reverse each adversity—and that therefore there cannot be an American solution to every world problem."

What was true thirty years ago when the United States was at the height of its power is even more true today when a vast literature has arisen to chart America's relative decline. It seems essential for the new strategic conception to recognize the limits of American capacity to regenerate a corrupt world. How can the United States hope to disarm Somalia when it cannot disarm Los Angeles or Washington, D.C.? Nor do the American people have the inclination to be the world's policeman, rushing to arrest or occupy other countries every time the alarm bell rings. The notion of a world to be ordered unilaterally by the United States is fantasy.

#### A Need for Collective Action

If none of the parade of international imperatives is susceptible to solution by a single nation, the key to the future is collective action through the building of international institutions. Of course every nation will continue to advance its own interests, but nations will increasingly discover that joint action may be the best way to safeguard those interests. The end of the Cold War at last liberates the United Nations to do what its founders intended it should do: to get countries of the world to work together in keeping the peace, extending the rule of law, and promoting economic growth, human rights, environmental protection, and cultural dignity.

The world ahead will be turbulent, chaotic, and dangerous for a long time to come—a world of inconceivable poverty, exploding population, desperate inequalities, mass migrations, fanatic ethnic and religious animosities, artificial frontiers, continuing arms flows, angry competition for resources, disintegration of traditional structures, and instantaneous communication of hopes and grievances. In such a world, as the respected international civil servant Sir Brian Urquhart has said, "No one nation, or even a partnership of two or three powerful nations, is going to be able to assume the role of world arbitrator and policeman, even if we suppose the other nations would accept it, which they are most unlikely to do. The United Nations, therefore, must be brought to maturity to take that role."

This is not to suggest that the UN is capable of providing solutions to every world problem. At the moment it is an imperfect organization, underfunded, incompetently staffed, and overbureaucratized. Nor is it to suggest that the control of U.S. foreign policy be handed over to the UN. The existence of the UN does not abolish the basic dynamics of international politics—national interest and the search for a balance of power. The United States, and other nations, must retain the freedom to protect vital interests. But the UN

and regional organizations like the European Community, the Organization of American States, and the Organization of African Unity supply arenas where clashes of interest and power can be contained, refined, and harmonized. International organization offers the means by which the collective wisdom and force of humankind might be brought to bear on the problems that assail all humanity.

Yet collective action is not easy. The impotence of the European Community in the face of the torment of Yugoslavia illustrates the difficulty of getting countries to act in unison, especially when the situation calls for sending ground forces into battle in countries that do not present a direct threat to the vital interests of one's own country.

While the UN Charter affirms the inherent right of unilateral self-defense against armed attack, military intervention for other purposes is more likely to be acceptable if it is multilateral in character. Still, even if the UN gets the stand-by military force requested by Boutros Boutros-Ghali, the UN Secretary-General, in his 1992 "Agenda for Peace," or the UN volunteer foreign legion proposed by Brian Urquhart, questions will remain about the timing, duration, and utility of military action. Hit-and-run raids rarely change conditions abroad; sustained military occupation is unpopular both in foreign lands and at home.

The Third World in particular is periodically convulsed by what the novelist V. S. Naipaul calls "movements of rage" directed against Western styles of modernity. Collective intervention by Western powers may only intensify resentments without solving problems: consider the case of Somalia. Moreover, most post-Cold War problems are simply not amenable to military solutions.

The persistence of economic stagnation, for example, makes all global troubles worse. Poverty feeds the movements of rage, embitters the competition for scarce resources, impedes the development of democratic institutions in ex-Communist countries, and reduces the freedom of maneuver in democratic countries. Never in history has global economic interdependence been so inclusive; never has a growing world economy been so vital for humanity's future.

The agenda for the 21st century is formidable. Surely the role of American leadership is to mobilize international institutions for the challenges ahead. Nor is such leadership alien to American traditions. It is rather the fulfillment of an American hope. Despite the republic's isolationist past, the vision of a new world order had its first great prophet in Woodrow Wilson after the First World War and its first great architects in the men who organized the Marshall Plan after the Second World War.

It is now time for American foreign policy once again to come in from the cold.

*Arthur M. Schlesinger, Jr., the Pulitzer Prize-winning historian and writer, is Albert Schweitzer Professor in the Humanities at the City University of New York. He served as Special Assistant to the President in the Kennedy Administration.*

## The Great Flood of 1993

### By Donald Young

The United States experienced a number of frightful natural calamities in the late 1980s and early 1990s: droughts, blizzards, several of the hottest summers on record, an earthquake in central California, and hurricanes in the Southeast. During the winter of 1992-1993, along the East Coast, 2 onslaughts of wind

and precipitation had each been proclaimed the storm of the century.

As tragic and destructive as these events were, none could quite compare with the Great Flood of 1993 along the Mississippi and Missouri rivers and their tributaries. The flood did not rank first, among recent disasters, in the number of deaths or in the total amount of property damage. Compared with the other misfortunes, however, the flood disrupted more lives and put more stress on human spirit and endurance and gave promise of setting back agricultural production for a longer time.

Stated just in bloodless numbers, the deluge was impressive. Eight million acres were flooded and 12 million more were too wet to produce crops. Damage was put at $12 billion, with $8 billion of that suffered by farmers. Fifty people died. Almost 70,000 were left homeless. In 9 states—Illinois, Iowa, Kansas, Minnesota, Missouri, Nebraska, North Dakota, South Dakota, and Wisconsin—a total of 421 counties were declared federal disaster areas.

In human terms, the cost was nearly incalculable. Thousands lost all their possessions, fleeing to higher ground when levees collapsed, often without warning. Children were reported to be especially traumatized by their experiences. With whole towns underwater, often for weeks, many workers lost their sources of income as well as their homes. In Hardin, Mo., the ferocious waters tore away most of a cemetery and dropped 900 caskets into the maelstrom.

### Endless Rainfall

The Midwestern flood appears to have had its origin, in part at least, in El Niño, the pool of warm water that develops every few years in the eastern Pacific Ocean off South America. El Niño spawned a strong subtropical jet stream that brought heavy winter 1992-1993 rains to the upper Mississippi valley, saturating the ground. The cool summer of 1992 had resulted in less evaporation, so the land could hardly absorb more water. The mild summer, in turn, was attributed to the sun-blocking haze caused by fallout from the volcanic eruption of Mt. Pinatubo in the Philippines.

Another apparent villain in this story was a high pressure system that formed over the eastern United States in the spring and summer of 1993. The high pressure produced dry conditions throughout the East—including drought in the Southeast—and intense heat in the Northeast during the summer.

A strong jet stream, moving from west to east in typical fashion, and causing cooler and wetter weather, bumped into the high pressure system and was diverted to the north. The moisture it created, beginning in April, almost all came down in the upper Midwest.

The rain not only seemed to fall almost steadily for weeks, it also came down in often prodigious amounts. A foot of rain fell in southern Minnesota, beginning June 11, and 4 days later 11 more inches were recorded. Morris, Minn., reported 5.9 inches on the night of July 3-4. In Iowa, on July 9, 5 to 8 inches of rain were reported at a number of locations. Not until late July did the stubborn weather pattern in the Midwest and East begin to break up.

### Dams and Levees

The Mississippi River and its tributaries drain one-third of the United States, 1.25 million square miles, covering all or parts of 31 states. Native Americans called the Mississippi the Father of Waters, and the river's historical and contemporary importance to the agriculture and commerce of the nation can hardly be overstated.

In 1927, 214 people died in a flood that also caused extensive damage in the lower Mississippi Valley. In the next year Congress passed the Mississippi River flood control act, directing the U.S. Army Corps of Engineers to confine the river to a prescribed channel.

Some 300 dams were built on the river's tributaries. The government also constructed levees and flood walls along the major rivers of the system. Cities and towns put up their own levees. In 1993 levees, some rising to 50 feet or more, lined almost 3,600 miles of Mississippi River system riverbanks—the world's most extensive flood-control program.

Controlling the Mississippi and its tributaries proved, however, to be a most challenging task. Flooding is a recurring phenomenon, and the river has always responded to floods by widening its channel and eroding its banks to make room for the heavier volume of water to be transported south to the Gulf of Mexico. It has often changed its channel here and there, sometimes adding loops and cutting off others.

Throughout the years, the rich alluvial soil left by receding floodwaters proved irresistible to farmers. Elsewhere, settlements—some of which grew into major cities—occupied the banks of the Mississippi and its tributaries, which had become major arteries of transportation by the mid-19th century.

While dams could be built to control the flow of water downstream, the construction of levees on floodplains to shelter humans and farmlands proved to be a mixed blessing. By denying the river its ability to expand in many places, the engineers simply guaranteed that floodwaters would climb higher and would move more swiftly and with more force. Where levees were breached or nonexistent, the impact could be even more severe. Record crests of the rivers, reported in many places in 1993, would not have been set if they could have spread out into the floodplains. Furthermore, because sediments being transported downriver could not be deposited in floodplains, they tended to settle in the main channels, thus raising the rivers more.

The Corps of Engineers asserts that the investment of billions of dollars in flood control has been well worthwhile, and that the amount of damage averted since the 1920s far outweighs the cost of construction. In 1937, Cairo, Ill., which is situated on the Mississippi River where the channel narrows between high bluffs, was spared during a flood because a floodway had been constructed that redirected much of the water several miles to the west before returning it to the main channel.

The avalanche of 1993, however, could fairly be described as a "100-year flood," that is, one that was of a magnitude that would likely be seen only once in a century. The result was unfortunate: of about 1,400 levees along the paths of the raging waters, some 800 were breached, damaged, or demolished outright.

Most Corps levees, and most levees in larger cities, were concrete, and relatively few of these gave way. On the other hand, earthen levees built to protect many small towns and farmlands fared less well. Typically, they became saturated and ultimately succumbed to the pressures of the water.

Sandbags were another element in the line of defense against the roiling waters. The National Guard, prisoners, and countless volunteers filled—by one estimate—75 million sandbags during the flood. The bags fortified the levees and raised them higher where needed.

### Course of the Flood

In 1992, Hurricane Andrew had swept through the Caribbean, Florida, and Louisiana in about 72 hours. But the Great Flood of 1993 (apparently it has not occurred to anyone to give human names to floods) rolled on and on for about 2 months, affording the prudent a chance to evacuate, but also leaving muck-filled streets and houses that required additional weeks to clean up.

Photographs taken from boats and aircraft illustrated the depth of the water. The rounded domes of grain silos barely broke above the water, and farm animals were seen crowding onto the sloped roofs of farm buildings.

Satellite photos, however, provided some of the most dramatic testimony to the scope of the flood. Rivers shown in older photos to be one-fourth to one-half of a mile in width had now spread out to a width of several miles. East of Kansas City, Mo., the width of the Missouri River was estimated to be as much as 10 miles. And beyond the rivers, patches of low ground had disappeared. After studying satellite photographs, Vice Pres. Al Gore observed, "It's as if another Great Lake has been added to the map of the United States."

At each town and city along the rivers, people asked similar questions. On what day would the river reach its crest here? What would be the height of the crest? How does that compare with the height of our levees? They also sought to estimate the flood stage, or the number of feet the river would rise above its banks.

On the Mississippi, the most destructive flooding occurred on the stretch of river from Davenport, in northeastern Iowa, down to the confluence with the Ohio River. On the Missouri River, the most devastation occurred from the region of Omaha, Neb., to the river's confluence with the Mississippi north of St. Louis. On July 19, the Mississippi was flooded for 464 miles (from McGregor, Iowa, to St. Louis) and the Missouri for 616 miles (from Omaha to St. Louis).

The drama played itself out in each city and community, but with variations on the main theme.

The story in Davenport, Iowa (population 96,000), was that the city had decided not to build any flood-control system. Davenport had missed the opportunity for full federal financing in the 1970s, and thereafter residents were reluctant to accept high construction costs. Furthermore, they didn't want to lose their excellent view of the river. In 1993, Davenport suffered extensive urban flooding.

Des Moines, Iowa, the state capital, suffered great disruption. Situated at the confluence of the Raccoon River with the Des Moines River, which flows southeast to the Mississippi, the city had levees, but one of them broke on July 11. The water treatment plant that provides the city's water was flooded. Pumps and generators were under 9 feet of water, and the filtration and purification system was contaminated. As a result, 250,000 people had to turn to outside sources for drinking water for almost 3 weeks. With no water available from hydrants, the danger of catastrophic fire was high.

Hannibal, Mo., on the Mississippi, had been the boyhood home of Mark Twain, whose writing reflected his fascination with the big river. He once wrote, "Except for the fact that the streets are quiet of kids and drays, there's really nothing good to say about a flood." In 1993, on the July 4 weekend, Hannibal went defiantly ahead with its National Tom Sawyer Days, featuring the usual boat races, picket-fence painting, and mud volleyball tournament. Hannibal had calculated that once every 500 years the river would crest at 30 feet, so it had built a levee of 31 feet. As the waters rose in July, 3 feet of sandbags were added to the top of the levee. The sandbags proved to be the difference . . . the river crested at 32 feet.

Jefferson City, Missouri's capital, on the Missouri River in the middle of the state, suffered its biggest blows on July 29. Flooding knocked out the city's sewage treatment plant, and the city began pumping raw sewage into the river. Route 54, the principal access route to the capital from the north, was closed when water overrode the sandbag walls along the road.

The Mississippi and Missouri rivers unite about 20 miles north of downtown St. Louis. Before the confluence, for about 20 miles, they run parallel to each other, just a few miles apart, as they arc around the city's northern suburbs. The peninsula of land between these 2 mighty tides of water, which contains a dozen villages and hundreds of farms, virtually vanished. Indeed, the rivers met 20 miles above their usual point of confluence. All of the peninsula's residents were evacuated.

As the largest city in harm's way, and the first to witness the combined flow of the Missouri and Mississippi, St. Louis was a center of attention. Predictions as to the ultimate crest there were revised upward frequently. More than 400 million gallons of water per minute swept past the graceful Gateway Arch on the St. Louis waterfront. In South St. Louis, a levee along the River des Peres, a drainage channel, collapsed, July 20. Water in the vicinity floated 51 propane gas tanks off their concrete moorings, and city officials, fearing a fiery explosion, evacuated a 40-square-block area. Divers sought to anchor the tanks. At the airport, planes were pushed about by the water until they wedged against trees. The Mississippi crested at St. Louis, Aug. 1, at 49.4 feet, a record, and the city's 11-mile concrete floodwall held firm.

Downriver, the historic towns of St. Genevieve, Mo., and Prairie du Rocher, Ill., across the divide, braced for the crest. Both had been founded by the French in the 18th century. St. Genevieve, with its houses built with logs stuck together with clay, animal hair, and straw, contained the nation's best examples of French colonial architecture. It had no government-issue, Corps of Engineers levee, however, because the town's 4,500 people couldn't afford their share of the cost, $10 million. Makeshift barriers were unable to prevent some flooding. After the town's plight was reported in the media, help began to arrive from afar. A busload of people came from Memphis, Tenn. Others traveled even greater distances. In 90-degree heat, volunteers filled 750,000 sandbags and backed them up with 100,000 tons of rock. Water lapped at the base of the 1789 Green Tree Inn, but the historic buildings were saved.

Prairie du Rocher, population 700, founded by the French in 1722, was saved by a bold gamble. The Army Corps of Engineers punched a 400-foot hole in a levee north of town in order to divert some of the water into farmland and ease the pressure on the town itself. On their own, at 4 A.M., town officials dynamited the levee in 2 more places, then put out a call for help on the main levee, to which hundreds of people responded. They raised the levee by another 18 inches, and the river was turned back.

At Cairo, at the southern tip of Illinois, the Ohio River joins the Mississippi. From Cairo south, the river opens up dramatically. Because the Ohio was low in 1993, the broad lower river easily absorbed the massive contribution from the upper Mississippi, and the South was spared the Midwest's agony.

It seemed almost a miracle that only 50 people perished in the flood. Most of the deaths were by drowning, and there were several electrocutions. In the most tragic accident, 4 boys and 2 adult counselors drowned in a cave in Missouri when water from a thunderstorm poured into its mouth.

## The Damage and the Cleanup

For 2 months, the flood trapped 3,000 of the 25,000 barges that carry corn, wheat, soybeans, petroleum, and coal downriver. Many bridges, roads, and rail lines were knocked out. Most affected farmers lost their crops for 1993. But further east, in Indiana and Ohio, ideal weather was producing bumper crops. Initial government estimates of the trend in food prices and of the size of national crop harvests suggested that changes would be minimal. In fact, some analysts saw the flood and Southeastern drought, taken together, contributing only a 1 percent increase to the price of food.

Amid the devastation, some animal life benefited. Plants fertilized by river sediment flourished and provided abundant food for ducks and other waterfowl. Fish occupied new ground, so to speak, and eagles and hawks who search them out had new targets of opportunity.

Long after the national television crews had packed up, citizens went about the physically and emotionally stressful task of cleaning out homes and neighborhoods. Violet Merrigan, postmaster of Pattonsburg, Mo., told the *New York Times*: "There's the diarrhea and the nausea and the mold, which kind of makes you lightheaded.... There's the stench of hundreds of dead night-crawlers, and other dead animals all over the sidewalks."

No one could know all of the chemical pollutants the river water might have picked up, not to mention oil; the presence of human sewage meant that anyone working in the water had to get a tetanus shot. Potential damage to electrical systems and to roadbeds represented accidents waiting to happen and had to be investigated carefully.

Pres. Bill Clinton visited the flood area 4 times. One citizen of Des Moines who shook his hand said later, "We need some divine intervention. He has a lot of power, but he doesn't have that kind of power. He can't make the rain end."

The organizations most active in flood relief were the Federal Emergency Management Agency (FEMA), the Salvation Army, and the Red Cross. FEMA, stung by criticism of its slow response to Hurricane Andrew, got high marks in 1993, at least at first, for its well-organized relief effort. In locations declared to be disaster areas, residents could receive rental payments for temporary housing and unemployment payments for lost jobs. In addition, low-interest loans were made available for farmers and businesses. FEMA did come under some criticism, however, because of its tight regulations and overwhelming paperwork. The U.S. Small Business Administration was also on the scene, offering loans of up to $100,000 for homeowners and up to $500,000 for businesses. (Private insurance companies do not offer flood insurance, and while the federal government does offer flood insurance, only about 20 percent of eligible persons buy it.)

Congress approved $6.2 billion in flood relief. Clinton signed the bill in St. Louis, Aug. 12. The principal payouts would be to farmers who had lost crops and to people who had lost property, as well as for the restoration of public buildings.

Mike Espy, the secretary of agriculture, started a debate about the future when he recommended that some towns be moved to higher ground. Levees would then be dismantled so that the Mississippi River could reclaim its original floodplain. The extent to which that might happen—or to which breached and broken levees would be rebuilt—was not immediately clear.

Reflecting the stubborn optimism of Americans, developers in Davenport announced, while the waters were still rising, that a block that was then partially underwater would be the site of a new 220-room hotel.

*Donald Young is a writer and editor specializing in current affairs and environmental issues.*

# The Clinton Presidency

### By Bruce Drake

Bill Clinton came to the White House with an ambitious domestic agenda. The sheer volume of proposals and policy initiatives he set in motion stood in sharp contrast to the previous eight years of relative inactivity on the domestic front under the Bush administration and the second term of Ronald Reagan.

The two most important issues Clinton had promised to tackle —the economy and health-care reform— by themselves would have required of any new administration an enormous investment of political will and energy. But Clinton also chose to press ahead quickly on a wide range of issues: lifting the ban on gays in the military, seeking passage of a highly controversial U.S.-Mexico-Canada free trade agreement, pressing campaign finance reform and welfare reform, enacting a national service program to let young people repay federal education loans through community service, proposing an anticrime program, devising a timber policy for the Northwest that balanced economic and environmental interests, and launching a program to streamline government—or what Vice President Al Gore, put in charge of the effort by Clinton, called "reinventing government."

It was not surprising, therefore, that Clinton had a difficult first year in office. He was elected with a less than overwhelming mandate for so sweeping an agenda, having won only 43 percent of the vote in a three-way race against incumbent George Bush and maverick billionaire Ross Perot. And, to carry out his program, he first had to take control of the government—no small challenge after 12 years in which Republicans were in charge of the executive branch.

Ultimately, Clinton won a hard-fought victory on his initial top priority, a deficit-reduction package. But the narrowness of that victory, and the fact that it inspired little enthusiasm among many Americans, raised questions about the strength of his presidency.

On foreign affairs, Clinton was confronted with a more complicated geopolitical map than his predecessors. The competition with the Soviet Union and the Communist world, which had been the central focus of American policymaking for more than four decades, had given way to less clear-cut questions about what role the U.S. should play in restoring order or keeping the peace in countries like Bosnia and Herzegovina or Somalia.

### First Days in Office

William Jefferson Clinton took the oath of office as the nation's 42d president on January 20, 1993. At 46, the former Arkansas governor represented a generational shift in the White House, having been born after World War II and having come of age during the turbulent era of the civil rights battles and Vietnam.

Clinton used his brief inaugural address and his first days in office to set a new tone now that the Democrats had control of both the White House and Congress. He promised "an end to the era of deadlock and drift and a new season of American renewal."

He underlined the break with recent Republican administrations by signing a series of executive orders. One imposed higher ethical standards on top officials of the executive branch. Another overturned five restrictions on abortions that had been imposed under the previous Republican administrations.

The first legislation he signed as president was a bill providing workers up to 12 weeks of unpaid leave in order to tend to family needs and crises. The signing of the family leave bill on February 5 was a symbolic moment for Clinton and fellow Democrats because the legislation was a key part of their agenda that had been stymied under the previous Republican administration.

Clinton had promised to be ready with an economic package and health-care reform plan within his first 100 days, but it was immediately clear that the magnitude of the economic and political challenges facing his new administration would force Clinton to alter some of his economic goals and force him to delay for several months tackling the health-care issue.

## Battle of the Budget

A series of reports before he took office pointed to a steadily worsening federal budget deficit. The deficit threat increasingly drove Clinton's decision-making because, as he later told the nation's governors in August, "unless we did something about it, we would not have the capacity to deal with a whole range of other issues" during his term in office. One casualty of his rising concern about the deficit was his campaign promise to enact a middle-class tax cut—a promise that had helped his cause during the Democratic presidential primaries.

Speaking to a joint session of Congress on Feb. 17, Clinton outlined a package of tax hikes and spending reductions totaling $493 billion. Key elements were higher tax rates for corporations and those individuals in the highest income brackets, but there was also a broad-based energy tax based on the heat content of fuels as measured in British thermal units (Btu's), which would have meant increased costs for all Americans.

As he did during the campaign, Clinton also called for new government spending to make up for what he called the "investment" deficit in America. Mostly through a $16.3 billion economic stimulus bill, Clinton proposed government spending that he said would create jobs, fund public works projects, aid education, and increase important social welfare services.

Clinton said his program represented "a new direction" and an end to Republican economic policies under Reagan and Bush. Clinton did, in fact, turn the nation away from the low-tax policies of the Reagan-Bush years. But in putting the emphasis on deficit reduction, he set in motion the political forces that removed much of the "new Democrat" imprint he sought to put on the economic package, such as his domestic "investment" initiatives.

The first casualty was his economic stimulus bill. Republicans, despite their minority status, found new strength in their use of the filibuster in the Senate and succeeded in killing Clinton's economic stimulus package. The GOP critics skewered the bill as one that would worsen the deficit and do little to spur the economy. Senate Democrats tried and failed four times to muster the 60 votes necessary to break the filibuster and gave up on April 21.

Emboldened by their victory over the economic stimulus bill, Republicans turned to Clinton's deficit-reduction package and assailed Democrats for once again pursuing policies that resulted in more taxes on Americans. Another persistent source of criticism was Perot, the independent presidential candidate who had received 18.9 percent of the vote in the 1992 election. Perot began a new round of public appearances and advertising in late January, criticizing the proposed tax increases and what he saw as inadequate spending cuts. He also reincarnated his former campaign organization, United We Stand, America, as a citizen's advocacy group in order to actively raise funds and sponsor membership drives without being subjected to laws governing campaign organizations.

All in all Perot and the Republicans appeared to have been more successful than Clinton and the Democrats in putting their spin on the deficit-reduction plan. A *Washington Post* poll in August showed that two out of three Americans agreed with the charge that the package was too tax heavy, and many congressional Democrats feared they would pay the price in the next elections if the economy failed to show new strength.

Ultimately, Republicans voted as a block against the plan in both the House and the Senate, and Clinton had to struggle to hold the support of enough Democrats to win passage. He faced revolts from liberal and conservative wings of the party. In the House, conservative Democrats wanted more spending cuts, tighter caps on entitlement programs like Medicare, and fewer taxes, and in the Senate, Democrats like Oklahoma's David Boren not only wanted to steer the plan away from tax increases to spending cuts, but opposed the broad-based Btu tax. Liberals exerted counterpressure on Clinton as members of the increasingly influential Congressional Black Caucus and others decried the move toward more domestic cutbacks.

The final package was put together after painstaking negotiations and compromises. It kept to Clinton's original target of almost $500 billion in deficit reduction, relying on $255 billion in spending cuts and $241 billion in tax increases. But Clinton's Btu tax, which he had proposed as the fairest approach, gave way to a much more modest 4.3-cents-a-gallon gasoline tax; his "investment"proposals were cut roughly by half; a tax break aimed at encouraging business investment in new equipment was greatly whittled down; and increases he had sought in social spending were cut back.

In the final votes in early August the House approved the plan by the bare margin of 218-216, and, in the Senate, Vice President Gore had to cast a tie-breaking vote to get a 51-to-50 victory.

In assessing why the budget battle turned into such a cliffhanger, critics said Clinton made several mistakes that indicated he had lessons to learn as a new president. They said he failed to mount an effective public campaign for the package, letting the Republicans and Perot instead define it as a Democratic tax hike; that important elements of the original plan, like the Btu tax, were lost because Clinton was seen as too willing to bargain away parts of the package for votes; and that Clinton had erred by believing he could prevail with Democratic votes alone, rather than bolstering his support by courting moderate Republicans earlier in the process.

## Taking on Health-Care Reform

Health care, with all the competing interests involved, promised to be another tough political battle for an administration that had already gone through the political wringer on the budget. However, supporters hoped that different dynamics would be at work, in part because the immediate benefit of reform would be more apparent to Americans than the results of the deficit-reduction plan and in part because the Clinton administration had learned the hard way about the importance of laying the political groundwork early with Congress.

The plan, to be fully in place by 1997, was aimed at providing a standard package of health benefits for all U.S. citizens and legal aliens, including the estimated 37 million Americans who currently had no insurance. The benefits were designed to be comparable to the kind of coverage that employees of big corporations commonly received. In general, insurance coverage would be provided through state-controlled regional insurance purchasing groups (health alliances)—creating a "managed competition" system intended to hold down costs.

Under the Clinton proposal, the Medicare and Medicaid programs would continue; however, there would be changes. Medicare recipients would see their premiums rise, but would receive coverage for prescription drugs and long-term home- and community-based care. While some Medicaid recipients would remain in the program, others would be privately insured through the health alliances.

Having realized during the deficit-reduction fight the extent to which new taxes were anathema to lawmakers and the public, administration officials tried to avoid measures that would be seen as tax increases. However, the initial package did contain higher levies on tobacco and a surtax on large corporations electing to become their own insurance provider. The major share of the cost would be borne largely by requiring all employers to pick up 80 percent of their full-time workers' health-care premiums and a portion of their part-time workers' premiums (which some Republicans said was tantamount to a tax) and from cost savings in Medicare and Medicaid. In addition, the plan depended on other measures to sharply curb the steady increase in health-care costs, including reduced paperwork and curbs on medical malpractice suits and health insurance fraud. The price of prescription drugs would also be investigated and monitored.

Employees would generally pay 20 percent of their health-insurance costs, and individuals not insured through an employer would have to pay for all or part of their own health insurance. The plan included subsidies for low-income people, as well as for small businesses.

Clinton unveiled the program in a nationally televised address before a joint session of Congress on September 22, but because it was presented so late in the year and the draft legislation was not available for some weeks following Clinton's speech, significant congressional action on the plan was not expected until 1994.

## North American Free Trade

Clinton began another major fight in the fall—attempting to secure passage of the North American Free Trade Agreement (NAFTA) originally negotiated with Mexico and Canada during the Bush administration. The pact would erase tariffs and other barriers to trade among the three nations.

Clinton's support for the agreement was one of the ways he separated himself during the campaign from traditional Democrats, many of whom sided with organized labor, which feared a loss of jobs to Mexico, in opposing NAFTA. Clinton sought to make the pact more palatable to fellow Democrats by negotiating side agreements aimed at ensuring tighter enforcement of each nation's labor and environmental standards, but a number of important Democrats still refused to back him. With the lack of support from within his own party—and more vocal criticism from Perot, who released an anti-NAFTA book in September—the

Clinton administration's political skills were put to the test.

## Gays in the Military

Faced with these major battles, the new administration could ill afford to get sidetracked by protracted controversies or political miscues, but Clinton and his aides proved during the administration's opening months in office to be less surefooted than they had been during the presidential campaign.

The president's political judgment was questioned by many in Washington when he turned almost immediately after his inauguration to the issue of gays in the military. Clinton announced his intention to lift the ban despite intense opposition from the Joint Chiefs of Staff and many on Capitol Hill, including the influential chairman of the Senate Armed Services Committee, Democrat Sam Nunn of Georgia.

The firestorm over the issue distracted public attention from the focus Clinton wanted to put on the economy. In order to get it off the front burner, Clinton announced at the end of January an interim plan under which he would wait six months while Congress held hearings and a compromise could be reached.

In mid-July, after difficult negotiations with the Joint Chiefs and on Capitol Hill, Clinton announced what he called "an honorable compromise" that allowed homosexuals to serve as long as they were discreet about their orientation. The compromise, dubbed "don't ask, don't tell, don't pursue," permitted gays to serve in the military as long as they kept their orientation to themselves. Applicants for military service would no longer be asked to reveal their sexual orientation. The compromise also prohibited commanders from investigating military personnel on suspicion or hearsay of homosexual activity, but did allow them to discharge gay soldiers if such behavior were proved.

## Controversial Nominations

At about the same time that the issue of gays in the military erupted, Clinton was faced with an uproar over his first choice for attorney general—an insurance company executive named Zoe Baird—who had employed an illegal alien couple at her Connecticut home in violation of a 1986 immigration law. Baird withdrew as a nominee, only to give way to another embarrassing controversy when Clinton's next choice, U.S. District Court Judge Kimba Wood, was reported to have employed an illegal alien as a babysitter (although, unlike Baird, she had done so at a time when it was not illegal). The White House decided not to formally nominate her. (In the end, Clinton's choice of Janet Reno, who had been the Florida state chief prosecutor in Miami, proved to be a popular one.)

Clinton ran into even more serious trouble over his nomination of University of Pennsylvania law professor Lani Guinier to be assistant attorney general in charge of civil rights enforcement. Conservatives launched a well-honed campaign to publicize articles in which Guinier discussed ways of strengthening minority influence under the Voting Rights Act both in elections and in legislatures. Critics dubbed her a "quota queen," saying her views were antidemocratic and a rejection of the concept of one-person, one-vote. Guinier and supporters said her writings were being distorted.

As Democratic senators began to waver, Guinier was left in limbo while the White House wrestled with whether to stand by her. Clinton was caught between two political crosscurrents: the desire to maintain his image as a "new" centrist Democrat and the angry warnings of blacks, particularly important members of the Congressional Black Caucus, against dropping her. Clinton abandoned the nomination on June 3, saying he had not previously read her writings but now that he had, he found them "difficult to defend."

After several nomination mishaps, Clinton was eager to strike the right note when a resignation gave him the opportunity to name a Supreme Court justice, the first such nomination by a Democratic president in 26 years. In mid-June, Clinton announced his choice, Judge Ruth Bader Ginsburg of the U.S. Court of Appeals for the District of Columbia. Ginsburg, considered a judicial moderate, easily won confirmation by the Senate, 96-3, in August.

## Political Miscues

There were a number of other miscues that undermined Clinton's image and distracted from important issues at hand. In May, press reports that Clinton got a $200 haircut from Christophe of Beverly Hills while Air Force One sat on a runway and delayed flights at Los Angeles International Airport dominated media coverage of his administration for days and gave the president a huge public relations black eye.

White House staffers also triggered an unnecessary controversy in May when they moved to dismiss the staff of the White House Travel Office, whose most visible job was arranging charters for journalists who accompanied Clinton on trips. The firings prompted charges that the ouster came at the behest of friends and relatives of Clinton who either wanted a share of the travel business or jobs in the office. There were also accusations that the FBI had been misused by Clinton aides to support its case against the fired staffers. The White House backed down and ultimately issued a report in July saying its own staff had acted inappropriately.

While Clinton often expressed irritation with press focus on his administration's difficulties, he and other aides conceded by late spring that the White House needed "tighter coordination." Clinton bolstered his staff by bringing in as counselor David Gergen, a former adviser to Republican presidents who was reputed to have great skills in helping his bosses get their message across. The addition of Gergen and other changes in key staff positions added up to a far more extensive shake-up of the White House staff than usually took place so early in an administration.

## Foreign Policy Challenges

Foreign challenges also presented difficulties for Clinton in his first year. He was criticized by some for failing to develop a coherent foreign policy framework. Whether or not the criticism was valid, Clinton did come to the presidency less versed in foreign policy than many of his predecessors. He was also determined to keep his focus on domestic affairs and make U.S. economic security a priority in foreign policy considerations.

Clinton's most consistent policy effort was his determination to help Russia through its transition to political and economic democracy. He firmly supported Russian President Boris Yeltsin, with whom he met in Vancouver on April 3 and 4, and helped engineer increased economic aid to Russia on the part of the U.S. and its allies.

The U.S. did not play a pivotal role in the breakthrough that resulted in a peace agreement between Israel and the Palestine Liberation Organization in September. But Clinton presided at the September 13 White House signing ceremony for the framework accord and indicated the U.S. would play a more active role in assisting the two parties in working out a final agreement. Clinton also promised that the U.S. would do everything possible to make the pact politically viable in the Mideast.

His most visible foreign policy problems during the first year were precisely the kind of post-Cold War situations that proved so vexing for American policymakers—namely, the bloody war in Bosnia and the effort to restore order in Somalia. Both of these were areas where there was little public enthusiasm for major U.S. commitments and where administration officials were confronted by an array of unappetizing choices.

During the presidential campaign, Clinton had freely criticized President Bush for not taking a more aggressive American role in stopping the bloodshed in Bosnia, where the republic's Serbs had made huge territorial gains at the expense of the outgunned Muslim population. But after Clinton took office, the administration's policy wavered several times between threatening possible U.S. military action against the Serbs and following the European Community's lead in seeking to bring about a negotiated solution to the conflict.

In September, after yielding to European resistance to military measures, Clinton made clear to Bosnian President Alija Izetbegovic that the U.S. was unlikely to use force and indicated that the Bosnian Muslims should try to get the best deal they could through negotiations even though their bargaining position had greatly worsened since the beginning of the year.

Clinton took more assertive action on Somalia, as the humanitarian mission there to safeguard the supply line of food increasingly took on the form of a police action to put down powerful warlords as a step toward enabling the country to reconstitute itself. When the United Nations peacekeeping contingent found itself unable to cope with Mohammed Farah Aidid, the most powerful warlord, Clinton approved the use of U.S. forces to break Aidid's power. Administration officials found themselves caught between the belief that the U.N. mission might collapse if the U.S. withdrew and the fact that there was not the same kind of public support for an American commitment to restore order as there was earlier for the largely humanitarian mission that ensured the supply of food. Defense Secretary Les Aspin said in September the U.S. would remain until there was order in Somalia, but many on Capitol Hill openly questioned the extent of U.S. involvement and appeared ready to challenge the legality of Clinton's unilaterally committing American troops, especially as U.S. casualties mounted in bloody clashes with Aidid's forces. On October 7, after more than a dozen Americans had been killed in a single firefight, Clinton ordered that the number of U.S. troops in the region be doubled. But he also appointed a special envoy to pursue a political settlement in Somalia and promised to have all U.S. forces out of the country by March 31, 1994.

## The Public Verdict

The public verdict on the first act of the Clinton presidency seemed to indicate that Clinton had not yet accomplished one of the most important political tasks before him—significantly broadening his base of support from the 43 percent of Americans who elected him. A *Washington Post*/ABC News poll in August found his overall approval rating after roughly 200 days in office to be 51 percent negative and 45 percent positive, generally in line with other major polls. His biggest triumph to that point—the budget victory—did not improve these standings because Americans were so evenly divided about whether they supported or opposed the economic plan. However, with many of his programs still untested and the effects of his economic program—whether good or bad—yet to be seen, there was time for public opinion to sway in many directions.

*Bruce Drake is Managing Editor of National Public Radio in Washington, D.C.*

# CHRONOLOGY OF THE YEAR'S EVENTS

Reported Month by Month in 3 Categories: National, International, and General
Nov. 1, 1992 to Oct. 15, 1993

## NOVEMBER

### National

**Clinton Elected 42d President** — Gov. Bill Clinton of Arkansas was elected 42d president of the U.S. on Nov. 3. His running mate on the Democratic ticket, Sen. Al Gore, Jr., of Tennessee, was elected vice president. Clinton and Gore carried 32 states and the District of Columbia and thereby won 370 electoral votes. Pres. George Bush, the Republican candidate, and his running mate, Vice Pres. Dan Quayle, carried 18 states for a total of 168 electoral votes. In the nationwide popular vote, the official tally gave Clinton 44,908,254 (43 percent), Bush 39,102,343 (37.4 percent), independent candidate H. Ross Perot 19,741,065 (18.9 percent), and all other candidates 666,744 (0.7 percent). Communist governments had collapsed in many countries during the Bush years, and the president had enjoyed great popularity after the Persian Gulf War. But many voters felt that Bush had not responded aggressively enough to an economic recession that triggered a big increase in the ranks of the unemployed. Clinton, who took moderate positions on economic and social issues, was the biggest beneficiary of the desire for change, but Perot, a Texas billionaire with a folksy manner, won a large following with his pledge to eliminate the large annual federal budget deficits in just 5 years. The Democrats held control of both houses of Congress. After a final Senate seat was determined in a runoff election on Nov. 24, Democrats retained the 57-43 margin they had held prior to the Nov. 3 election. In the House, the Republicans gained 10 seats, but the Democrats still held a 258-176 majority, with 1 independent. Altogether, there would be 110 new faces in the House, representing the biggest turnover since 1948. The new House would contain record numbers of women (47), blacks (38), and Hispanics (17). Reapportionment after the 1990 census accounted, in part, for the upheaval, but voters were in a mood for change and voted out a number of representatives in both parties during the primaries and general election. The new Senate would have a record number of women members, 6. Two women Democrats won Senate elections in California, and Carol Moseley Braun of Illinois would become the first black woman to serve in the Senate. The Democrats picked up 2 governorships, for a 30-18 major over the Republicans. Independents held 2 state houses. Nationwide, Republicans gained ground in voting for state legislators. Fourteen states approved term limits for members of Congress, and 13 of these states also set limits of service for members of their state legislatures.

**Court Rejects 'Gag Rule' on Abortions** — A panel of the U.S. Circuit Court of Appeals for the District of Columbia rejected, Nov. 3, a regulation issued by the Bush administration that forbade anyone at federally funded family-planning clinics, except doctors, from discussing abortion with patients. In May, U.S. District Court Judge Charles Richey had ruled in favor of family-planning groups that had challenged the regulation. In upholding Richey, the appeals court panel held that the administration had improperly bypassed federal provisions requiring that proposed regulations be published in the Federal Register and that the public be allowed to comment on them for up to 90 days.

**Decline Reported in Economic Indicators** — The Commerce Dept. reported, Nov. 3, that the index of leading economic indicators, a gauge of future economic activity, had declined 0.3 percent in September. The Federal Reserve Board said, Nov. 4, that the economy was improving at a slow and uneven rate nationwide. The Labor Dept. reported, Nov. 6, that the unemployment rate had edged downward to 7.4 percent from 7.5 percent in October. The department said, Nov. 10, that prices charged by producers for finished goods had risen by 0.1 percent in October. On Nov. 13, the department said that consumer prices had risen 0.4 percent in October.

**Court Reinstates Homosexual Sailor** — A U.S. District Court judge reinstated a homosexual Naval officer who had been discharged because of his sexual orientation. In May, Petty Officer 1st Class Keith Meinhold, who had served in the Navy for 12 years, had stated on a television program that he was a homosexual. In August, in accord with a policy barring gay men and lesbians from military services, he received an honorable discharge. Meinhold sued for reinstatement, and on Nov. 6, Judge Terry Hatter, Jr., ordered the Navy to reinstate Meinhold until the case was resolved. On Nov. 12, the Navy swore Meinhold back into service. He became the first homosexual to be reinstated in the military as the result of a court challenge.

**Clinton Prepares to Assume Presidency** — Pres.-elect Bill Clinton announced, Nov. 6, that his transition team would be headed by Vernon Jordan, a Washington, D.C., attorney and former president of the National Urban League, and by Warren Christopher, a deputy secretary of state under Pres. Jimmy Carter. On Nov. 12, Clinton named 48 people to conduct the transition. Their principal task would be to help Clinton assemble his cabinet.

**Report Issued on Search of Passport Files** — The State Dept. issued a report on the search of passport files in the presidential campaign. *The Washington Post*, which had reported in October that the files of Democratic presidential candidate Bill Clinton and his mother had been searched, also reported, Nov. 9, that State Dept. officials had searched the files of independent presidential candidate H. Ross Perot. On Nov. 10, Elizabeth Tamposi was dismissed as assistant secretary of state for consular affairs. In his report of Nov. 18, Sherman Funk, inspector general for the State Dept., said that department personnel had searched the files of the Clintons and Perot in September in an effort to get politically damaging information. Funk placed primary responsibility on Tamposi and Steven Berry, acting assistant secretary of state for legislative affairs. Lawrence Eagleburger, the acting secretary of state, deplored the searches, Nov. 18, and said the department should never be in the political arena.

**10 Women Accuse Senator of Harassment** — It was reported, Nov. 22, that 10 women had accused Sen. Robert Packwood (R, Ore.) of sexual harassment. Packwood, who had been reelected to the Senate, was a strong supporter of issues of concern to women's rights groups. (By February, 23 women had made allegations against him.) Most of the women had been employed by Packwood or had worked with him. Packwood said he was sorry if anything he had done had caused anyone discomfort or embarrassment. On Nov. 27, he suggested that an alcohol problem might have been related to his conduct, and he entered an alcohol-treatment program.

**Auditor of S&Ls Pays $400 Million U.S. Claim** — Ernst & Young, the firm that had audited at least 300

40

thrifts that ultimately went bankrupt, reached a costly settlement with federal regulators. The regulators charged that the auditing firm had committed mistakes and was careless in many audits, and failed to identify weaknesses in real-estate portfolios that led to bankruptcies. On Nov. 23, Ernst & Young agreed to pay $400 million to settle the government's claims.

**Senators Report on 'October Surprise'** — A Senate subcommittee reported, Nov. 23, that it had found no evidence that the Reagan-for-president campaign in 1980 had sought to delay release of U.S. hostages in Iran until after the election. Reagan campaign managers had feared that then-Pres. Jimmy Carter would succeed in arranging for the release of the hostages just before the election—an "October surprise." Rumors had circulated for years that Reagan supporters had sought to make a deal with Iran not to free the captives until after the election, by promising to provide weapons if Ronald Reagan were elected. In its report, the Senate Foreign Relations subcommittee on Near Eastern and South Asian affairs found no evidence of any meetings or other actions in support of such a scheme. However, it did say members of the Reagan campaign had operated "on the outer limits of propriety."

### International

**U.N. Authorizes Blockade of Yugoslavia** — The U.N. Security Council authorized a naval blockade as a means of enforcing its economic sanctions against Yugoslavia. On Nov. 9, the ethnic Serb leader in Bosnia and Herzegovina proposed a partition of Bosnia along ethnic lines. Much of Bosnia's territory had already been divided up by Serbs and Croats, and the Serb leader, Radovan Karadzic, recommended that the permanent partition be based on how the territory was then controlled. The U.N. Council adopted its blockade resolution, Nov. 16, by a 13-0 vote with 2 abstentions. Ships of all nations were empowered to halt and inspect vessels entering or leaving Yugoslav waters. The Council, however, did not act on an appeal from Muslim states that Bosnia be exempted from an arms embargo imposed in 1991 on Yugoslavia and all former Yugoslav republics.

**Germany Confronts Neo-Nazis** — Neo-Nazi violence, which had been on the rise in Germany, claimed more victims in November. Extreme right-wing organizations had focused their anger on a provision in Germany's constitution that guaranteed that any refugee could seek political asylum in Germany. Although most applicants were ultimately rejected, they were allowed to remain in Germany and receive extensive benefits while their status was being considered. Some 1,800 acts of violence against those seeking asylum had been reported in 1992. In Berlin, Nov. 8, 350,000 persons demonstrated against right-wing violence, and a similar protest drew 100,000 in Bonn, Nov. 14. Police in Halbe, south of Berlin, blocked an attempted march by neo-Nazis, Nov. 15. A Turkish woman and 2 Turkish girls, members of a family of "guest workers" who had lived in Germany for 2 decades, were killed in Moelln, Nov. 23, by a firebomb. Their deaths brought to 16 the number of people killed in right-wing attacks in 1992. Under a provision of the constitution, the government announced, Nov. 27, that it was banning the Nationalist Front, a neo-Nazi group.

**Ex-Communists Win Lithuanian Election** — On Nov. 15, in the second round of Lithuania's parliamentary elections, former communists of the Democratic Labor Party secured a majority in the Supreme Council. The DLP won at least 79 of the 141 seats to 35 for

the Sajudis nationalist movement, which had run the government.

**Czechs, Slovaks Move Toward Separation** — The Czech and Slovak regional parliaments adopted a joint resolution, Nov. 17, authorizing the separation of Czechoslovakia into 2 separate, independent republics. The Czechoslovak Federal Assembly (parliament) approved a constitutional amendment, Nov. 25, permitting the dissolution without a national referendum.

**Senators in Vietnam for MIA Inquiry** — Three U.S. senators and a general traveled to Southeast Asia to seek information on 2,265 American servicemen who were missing in action during the Vietnam war. The delegation, headed by Sen. John Kerry (D, Mass.), met with Vietnamese Pres. Le Duc Anh in Hanoi, Nov. 18, and visited Laos, Nov. 19. Members of the delegation also traveled to the Mekong River Delta and Danang province, Nov. 20, to investigate reports of American MIAs living there. The Vietnamese gave their visitors personal effects of dead or captured Americans, including photographs, letters, diaries, wallets, and uniforms.

**U.S., Europe Reach Compromise on Trade** — Negotiators from the U.S. and the European Community achieved a breakthrough in trade talks, Nov. 20. For years, the U.S. had pressed European countries to reduce their subsidies on farm products. Subsidies for oilseed products had been a particular sticking point. Oilseed trade was relatively insignificant, but farm lobbies from France and the U.S. had prevented agreement. In the compromise, the U.S. accepted more modest limits on subsidies than it had sought, and the Europeans agreed to across-the-board limits. French negotiators, however, objected strongly to the agreement.

**Nations Act Again on Ozone Threat** — Delegates from 87 nations met in Copenhagen and agreed to accelerate their schedules for phasing out chemicals that damaged the Earth's ozone layer. Under the agreement of Nov. 25, some chemicals would be regulated for the first time. Chlorofluorocarbons (CFCs), chemicals thought to be most harmful to the ozone, would be phased out by 1996 rather than 2000.

**U.S. Offers to Intervene in Somalia** — The U.S. moved toward a humanitarian intervention in Somalia, where thieves had seized most of the food and other supplies being shipped from other countries to starving people. Lawrence Eagleburger, the acting U.S. secretary of state, meeting with U.N. Secretary General Boutros Boutros-Ghali in New York, Nov. 26, offered the use of as many as 30,000 American troops. The U.N. force in Somalia consisted of 500 Pakistani peacekeepers, and 3,000 from other countries were due to arrive soon. On Nov. 30, Boutros-Ghali endorsed immediate military action in Somalia.

**Another Coup Thwarted in Venezuela** — For the second time in less than a year, military rebels sought to overthrow the government of Venezuela. On Nov. 27, the rebels, aided by some civilians, seized a television station and 2 air bases. Planes bombed the presidential palace and other sites in Caracas, the capital. The insurgents denounced Pres. Carlos Andres Perez for his alleged disregard for poor people, and they pledged to install a "real democracy." Forces supporting the government overcame the rebellion by the afternoon of Nov. 27. The death toll from the brief conflict was reported to be at least 169.

### General

**Magic Johnson Retires a Second Time** — Just 5 weeks after he said he would resume his career in the National Basketball Association, Earvin (Magic) Johnson of the Los Angeles Lakers issued a statement,

**Nov. 2,** that he was retiring for good. Johnson had retired the first time in 1991 as he announced that he had contracted the virus that causes AIDS. In his latest statement, Johnson noted that "various controversies" had surrounded his comeback. Some players had said they feared they might contract the virus from minor skin cuts that could occur during a game.

**Fischer Defeats Spassky in Chess** — Former world chess champion Bobby Fischer, playing in public for the first time in 2 decades, defeated Boris Spassky, from whom he had won the title in 1972, in a match in Yugoslavia. Their contest, sponsored by a Yugoslav businessman, ended, **Nov. 5.** Fischer, as the winner, received $3.35 million, and Spassky received $1.65 million. On **Dec. 15,** Fischer was indicted by a federal grand jury in Washington, D.C., on a charge that he had violated sanctions against Yugoslavia by playing there.

**Catholic Church Issues New Catechism** — A new universal catechism of the Roman Catholic Church was issued, **Nov. 16,** by a commission that had devoted 6 years to the task of revising the 400-year-old text. The compilation of teachings embraced many modern-day issues. For example, the catechism warned drivers against alcohol and "an immoderate taste for speed" that put themselves and others in danger. Economic sins cited for the first time included embezzlement, tax fraud, and forgery. The catechism remained conservative on social issues, declaring, for example, "Human life must be totally respected and protected from the moment of conception." It asserted that homosexuals "do not choose their homosexual condition" and urged that they be "treated with respect, compassion and sensitivity," but it also called on gays to remain chaste. The document declared that "Jews were not collectively responsible for the death of Jesus . . . All sinners were responsible for Christ's Passion."

## DECEMBER

### National

**Economic Recovery Appears Underway** — The index of leading economic indicators rose 0.4 percent in October, the Commerce Dept. reported, **Dec. 1.** The Labor Dept. said, **Dec. 4,** that the unemployment rate had declined by 0.2 of a point to 7.2 percent in November. The Federal Reserve Board reported, **Dec. 9,** "a slight to moderate pickup in some or all sectors of the economy." Prices charged by producers for finished goods declined by 0.2 percent in November, the Labor Dept. said, **Dec. 10.** The department reported, **Dec. 11,** that consumer prices had risen 0.2 percent in November. The Commerce Dept. reported, **Dec. 17,** that the merchandise trade deficit had shrunk substantially in October to $7.03 billion. In a final revision issued **Dec. 22,** the department said third-quarter gross domestic product had grown at a 3.4 percent annual rate. This was the 6th consecutive quarterly increase. The department reported, **Dec. 30,** that the leading economic indicators had jumped 0.8 percent in November. On Wall Street, the Dow Jones Industrial average closed, **Dec. 31,** at 3301.11, an increase of 4.2 percent for the year.

**Clinton Selects His Cabinet** — Pres.-elect Bill Clinton chose the members of his cabinet in December. They would be subject to approval by the Senate. On **Dec. 10,** Clinton named Sen. Lloyd Bentsen (D, Tex.), a fiscal conservative who had been the 1988 Democratic nominee for vice president, as secretary of the Treasury. He chose Rep. Leon Panetta (D, Cal.) to head the Office of Management and Budget. On **Dec. 11,** Clinton chose Robert Reich, a Harvard lecturer

and adviser to Clinton, as secretary of Labor, and Laura D'Andrea Tyson, an economist at the Univ. of California at Berkeley, as head of the Council of Economic Advisers. He also named Donna Shalala, chancellor of the Univ. of Wisconsin, to be secretary of Health and Human Services, and Carol Browner, head of Florida's Dept. of Environmental Regulation, to be administrator of the Environmental Protection Agency. Thomas McLarty, a friend of Clinton since childhood, was named, **Dec. 12,** as his White House chief of staff, and Ron Brown, a Washington, D.C., lobbyist and chairman of the Democratic National Committee, was chosen as secretary of Commerce. On **Dec. 17,** Clinton named Henry Cisneros, former mayor of San Antonio, to be secretary of Housing and Urban Development, and Jesse Brown, director of the Disabled Veterans of America, as head of the Veterans Affairs Dept. On **Dec. 21,** Clinton chose Hazel O'Leary, a Minnesota power company executive, and Richard Riley, former governor of South Carolina, as secretary of Energy and secretary of Education, respectively. Warren Christopher, a lawyer and diplomat, was tapped, **Dec. 22,** to be secretary of State. Rep. Les Aspin (D, Wis.) was named secretary of Defense. Also on **Dec. 22,** Clinton named W. Anthony Lake as his national security adviser, R. James Woolsey as director of the CIA, and Madeleine Albright as ambassador to the U.N. On **Dec. 24,** Clinton chose Zoe Baird, a corporate lawyer who had worked in the Justice Dept. under Pres. Jimmy Carter, as attorney general. She was the first woman nominated to head the Justice Dept. (Baird withdrew on **Jan. 22,** after it became known that she and her husband had employed illegal aliens in their household.) Clinton rounded out his team, **Dec. 24,** by naming Rep. Mike Espy (D, Miss.) as secretary of Agriculture, former Denver Mayor Federico Pena as secretary of Transportation, former Arizona Gov. Bruce Babbitt as secretary of the Interior, Mickey Kantor as U.S. trade representative, and Joycelyn Elders as surgeon general.

**Bush Pardons 6 in Iran-Contra Case** — Pres. George Bush pardoned 6 former public officials involved in the Iran-contra case. In the final judicial action prior to the pardons, former CIA Director of Operations Clair George was convicted, **Dec. 9,** on 2 felony counts for giving false testimony to congressional committees. Acting under authority granted by the U.S. Constitution, Bush announced his pardons, **Dec. 24.** He said that the 6 men, "whether their actions were right or wrong," had been motivated by patriotism rather than by personal gain. He said that their prosecution represented an attempt to resolve "policy differences" through criminal trials. Former Defense Sec. Caspar Weinberger was the most prominent figure to receive a pardon. He had been facing a trial in January 1993 on charges relating to a diary he had withheld from prosecutors after having been asked to provide any notes he had taken on the arms-for-hostages deal with Iran. Three former CIA officials were pardoned: George, who had just been convicted; Duane Clarridge, who was awaiting trial in March 1993; and Alan Fiers, who had pleaded guilty to misdemeanor charges of withholding information from Congress. Robert McFarlane, a former national security adviser, and Elliott Abrams, a former assistant secretary of state, who had also pleaded guilty to withholding information, were also pardoned. Lawrence Walsh, the independent counsel who had conducted the prosecutions, denounced the pardons, **Dec. 24.** He said Bush was a "subject" of the investigation and that he was guilty of "misconduct" for withholding notes relevant to the Iran-contra investigation. Bush, **Dec. 30,**

retained former Attorney Gen. Griffin Bell to represent him in the ongoing inquiry.

**Inquiry Into Iraq Loans Rejected** — Attorney Gen. William Barr said, **Dec. 9**, that he would not request appointment of an independent counsel to pursue allegations that the Bush administration had mishandled a bank fraud case involving loans to Iraq. The loans to Iraq, prior to the Gulf War, had been made by the Atlanta branch of Italy's Banca Nazionale del Lavaro. Barr's own investigator, retired Federal Judge Frederick Lacey said, **Dec. 9**, he had found no evidence that the U.S. government had sought to obstruct prosecution of the BNL case, and was certain that Italian bank officials were unaware of the illegal loans.

**Independent Counsel Named in Passport Case** — Attorney Gen. William Barr requested that an independent counsel be appointed to investigate a search, during the campaign, of the passport files of Pres.-elect Bill Clinton, his mother, and H. Ross Perot. A 3-judge panel, responded by naming Joseph di Genova, a former U.S. attorney, as independent counsel on **Dec. 14**.

**Facing Losses, IBM to Cut 25,000 Jobs** — (IBM) said that it would reduce its work force again. Still the world's largest computer manufacturer, IBM had once dominated the industry but had fallen behind in the development of personal computers. The company had cut 40,000 jobs in 1992 through voluntary retirements. IBM said, **Dec. 15**, that it would eliminate 25,000 jobs in 1993, through dismissals if necessary. The company also projected a $5.25 billion net loss for the 4th quarter. The value of IBM's shares plunged sharply on this news, and by **Dec. 16** its stock had declined by nearly 50 percent in 5 months.

### International

**Yeltsin Accepts a New Premier** — Russian Pres. Boris Yeltsin, **Dec. 1**, appealed for an extension of his emergency powers, which would allow him to choose the government and control economic policy. A motion by conservative deputies to impeach Yeltsin, **Dec. 1**, received fewer than 400 votes in the 1,041-member Congress of People's Deputies. Yeltsin's opponents failed, **Dec. 5**, to pass constitutional amendments that would have put the cabinet under parliamentary control. The conservatives were more successful, **Dec. 9**, narrowly rejecting the confirmation as premier of Yegor Gaidar, Yeltsin's choice, who had served as acting premier since June. Gaidar had designed Yeltsin's economic-reform program, which had not yet produced many positive results. After vowing, **Dec. 10**, that he would keep Gaidar as acting premier, Yeltsin, **Dec. 14**, joined with the Congress in supporting the confirmation of Deputy Premier Viktor Chernomyrdin as the new premier. Yeltsin, **Dec. 19**, cut short a visit to China when he heard Chernomyrdin was being pressured to choose a conservative cabinet. However, the cabinet list, approved by Yeltsin, **Dec. 23**, contained mostly economic reformers who had served under Gaidar.

**German Parties Agree to Curb Refugees** — A German prosecutor said, **Dec. 1**, that 2 young men had admitted to a fire-bombing in Moelln in November that had killed a Turkish woman and 2 Turkish girls. They had been among the victims of violent neo-Nazi protests against the law allowing any foreigner to seek refuge or asylum in Germany. On **Dec. 6**, Germany's 2 major parties, the Christian Democratic Union and the Social Democrats, reached an agreement to modify the law, under which 400,000 had entered Germany in 1992. Would-be refugees would now be turned back if they were citizens of countries deemed by Parliament to be free of political persecution. The government,

**Dec. 10**, banned a 2d right-wing party for inciting racial hatred.

**U.S.-Led Force Enters Somalia** — A U.N.-sanctioned military force, led by American troops, arrived in Somalia to ensure the delivery of food to starving people. The U.N. Security Council, voting unanimously, **Dec. 3**, authorized the intervening forces to use "all necessary means" to deliver the food, and the Council also called on warring factions to cease fighting. Some 1,800 Marines entered the capital, Mogadishu, **Dec. 9**, and began to restore the airport runway so that it could receive planes carrying food and supplies. Armed Somalis had fled elsewhere. On **Dec. 10**, Marines and French Legionnaires killed 2 Somalis in a van that was speeding toward a roadblock. The nation's 2 principal warlords signed a peace agreement, **Dec. 11**, in Mogadishu. U.S. and French troops entered Baidoa, a city hard-hit by famine, **Dec. 16**. Marines, **Dec. 20**, occupied the southern coastal city of Kismayu, following a massacre of more than 100 of its citizens by the forces of the local warlord. A civilian employee of the U.S. Army was killed, **Dec. 23**, when his truck struck a mine. Within the next few days, U.S., French, and Italian troops occupied other towns that needed food. Pres. Bush arrived in Somalia, **Dec. 31**, visited the U.S. Embassy in Mogadishu, and toured a schoolhouse where he greeted children recovering from hunger and illness.

**Razing of Mosque Ignites Violence in India** — Hindus in India destroyed a Muslim mosque and provoked new sectarian conflict. The mosque, built in 1528 in the northern Indian city of Ayodhia, stood on a site that Hindus said was the birthplace of the Hindu diety Ram. They wanted to build a temple there in his honor. On **Dec. 6**, militant Hindus tore down the mosque, using sledgehammers and bare hands. Violent clashes followed. On **Dec. 13**, the government said 1,210 people had been killed and 4,600 wounded.

**Israel Deports 415 Palestinians** — An Israeli border policeman was kidnapped, **Dec. 13**, by Hamas, a fundamentalist Muslim organization, and his body was found **Dec. 15**. The Israeli cabinet voted unanimously, **Dec. 16**, to expel 415 Palestinians who were Hamas sympathizers. They were rounded up and taken to the Lebanese border, **Dec. 17**, and, after the Israeli Supreme Court declined to block the expulsion, they were sent into Lebanese territory controlled by Israel. The Bush administration, **Dec. 17**, deplored the expulsions, which were illegal under international law. Lebanon barred the Palestinians from proceeding beyond the border area, forcing them to camp without food and supplies. The U.N. Security Council, **Dec. 18**, unanimously condemned the expulsion.

**Ex-Dissident Wins Korean Presidency** — Kim Young Sam, a longtime opponent of Korean governments, won the presidency of South Korea, **Dec. 18**, as the candidate of the ruling Democratic Liberal Party. He won with 42 percent in a large field. His principal challenger, Kim Dae Jung, was also a prominent dissident. Kim Young Sam would succeed Pres. Roh Tae Woo in February.

**President of Serbia Reelected** — Pres. Slobodan Milosevic of Serbia was reelected, **Dec. 20**. Official results, reported **Dec. 23**, gave him 56 percent of the vote to 35 percent for his principal challenger, Premier Milan Panic. Panic had blamed Milosevic for the civil war with Bosnia. U.S. Sec. of State Lawrence Eagleburger had charged that Milosevic bore some of the responsibility for Serbian atrocities committed in Bosnia. One of Milosevic's political allies charged in parliament, **Dec. 29**, that Panic was a foreign agent. Panic had come from California in 1992 to assume the premiership. In a no-confidence vote, **Dec. 29**, parliament ousted Panic as premier.

**U.S. Downs Iraqi Plane in 'No-Fly Zone'** — An Iraqi warplane was shot down, **Dec. 27**, by a U.S. fighter plane after it entered the so-called no-fly zone in southern Iraq. The U.S., Britain, and France had created the zone in August to help protect Shiite Muslims in the area from Iraqi attack.

**U.S., Russia Agree on Nuclear Arms Treaty** — The U.S. and Russia announced an agreement, **Dec. 29**, on the terms of a treaty that would reduce their strategic nuclear arms by two thirds. The details of the agreement, the second Strategic Arms Reduction Treaty (START), were worked out by Sec. of State Lawrence Eagleburger and Foreign Minister Andrei Kozyrev. The broad outlines of the treaty had been determined at a summit meeting of presidents George Bush and Boris Yeltsin in June.

**President of Brazil Resigns** — Pres. Fernando Collor de Mello of Brazil resigned in December. Vice Pres. Itamar Franco had been serving as acting president since October, pending outcome of a Senate trial of Collor on corruption charges. Collor resigned, **Dec. 29**, within hours after the Senate convened an impeachment trial. Franco was sworn in as president. At the trial, witnesses testified that they had had to pay large bribes to win government contracts. The Senate voted, **Dec. 30**, 76-3 to convict Collor. Collor and some of his relatives also faced criminal charges that they had received millions of dollars illegally.

## General

**Guidelines Announced for Food Labels** — Implementation of the Nutrition Labeling and Education Act of 1990 advanced, **Dec. 2**, when the Bush administration announced guidelines for the manufacturers of packaged foods. The rules, to be fully in effect by May 1994, required that the amount of fat, sodium, protein, cholesterol, and carbohydrates be printed on the packaging for every product. A number of terms used in advertising, such as "light" and "low fat," could only be used if certain criteria were met.

**Letterman Accepts $16 Million From CBS** — David Letterman, host of NBC's popular "Late Night With David Letterman" show, announced, **Dec. 8**, he would leave NBC to accept an offer from CBS to host a show beginning at 11:30 P.M. Eastern time each week night and would receive an annual salary of $16 million. He also said he would give NBC until Jan. 15 to make another offer; however, NBC, **Jan. 14**, announced that Letterman would not return next season.

**Prince, Princess of Wales Separate** — Prince Charles, heir to the British throne, and his wife, Diana, separated in December. In making the announcement to Parliament, **Dec. 9**, Prime Minister John Major said the couple had no plans to divorce, would both participate fully in the upbringing of their 2 sons, and would continue their schedule of public appearances. On **Dec. 12**, Charles's sister, Princess Anne, married Timothy Laurence, a naval commander. She had been divorced from Capt. Mark Phillips in April.

## JANUARY

### National

**Transition to New Leadership Continues** — The 103d Congress convened, **Jan. 5**. The Senate and House contained 123 new faces, an unusually high number. Congress, **Jan. 6**, formally counted the votes cast by the members of the Electoral College, and Bill Clinton and Al Gore were declared elected as presi-

dent and vice president. The Senate, **Jan. 6**, began confirmation hearings for those chosen by Clinton for cabinet positions and other top jobs in his administration. Clinton, **Jan. 8**, met in Austin, Tex., with Pres. Carlos Salinas de Gortari of Mexico. Clinton said he supported the North American Free Trade Agreement but would not press for its ratification by the Senate until Mexico gave assurances on matters of concern to U.S. labor leaders and environmentalists.

**Economic Data Issued** — The Office of Management and Budget, **Jan. 6**, issued projections for immense budget deficits through the next 6 years. The deficit for 1993 was put at $327.3 billion, and the shortfalls for 1994 through 1998 were foreseen as nearly as large. The Labor Dept. reported, **Jan. 8**, that the unemployment rate had held steady at 7.3 percent in December. The Commerce Dept. reported, **Jan. 14**, that a strong Christmas buying season had helped retail sales post a 5.1 percent increase in 1992. The department said, **Jan. 15**, that the merchandise trade deficit had widened in November 1992 to $7.59 billion. The Labor Dept. reported, **Jan. 15**, that consumer prices had risen 2.9 percent in 1992, the lowest annual inflation rate since 1986. Food and clothing costs had held nearly steady, but medical expenses had jumped 6.6 percent. The Commerce Dept. said, **Jan. 28**, that the gross national product had grown 2.1 percent in 1992, following a 1.2 percent decline in 1991. The growth rate had been accelerating toward the end of 1992.

**Keating Guilty on More S&L Charges** — Charles H. Keating, Jr., former chairman of the parent company of the failed Lincoln Savings & Loan Association, was convicted on more charges. On **Jan. 6**, a federal jury in Los Angeles found him guilty on 73 counts of fraud and racketeering. His son, Charles H. Keating, 3d, was found guilty on 64 counts. Prosecutors had accused the Keatings of defrauding investors and regulators and of diverting Lincoln's profits for their own use. The elder Keating, **July 8**, was sentenced to 12 years and 7 months in prison. He was currently serving a previous sentence for violations of California security laws.

**Senators Report on POW-MIA Inquiry** — The Senate Select Committee on POW-MIA Affairs reported, **Jan. 13**, that it had found "no compelling evidence" that any U.S. service personnel were being held in Indochina (although the committee determined that 305 POWs might have survived for a while in captivity after the peace agreement was signed in 1973). The committee rejected any suggestion that U.S. government officials had sought to conceal evidence that Americans were being held long after the war.

**Attorney-General Rebukes FBI Director** — Attorney-Gen. William Barr, **Jan. 15**, wrote to William Sessions, director of the FBI, and accused him of "a pattern of abuse." A report released by the FBI's Office of Professional Responsibility on **Jan. 19**, charged that Sessions had failed to pay income tax on his government limousine, used government funds for personal travel, assigned his security personnel to non-FBI work, and billed the government $10,000 for a fence around his house. Sessions, **Jan. 19**, denied the allegations. Barr left office with the installation of a new administration, but Sessions continued to serve.

**Clinton Becomes 42d President** — Bill Clinton (officially William Jefferson Clinton) was inaugurated in January as the 42d president of the U.S. The president-elect and Vice President-elect Al Gore began the celebration with a visit, **Jan. 17**, to the home of Pres. Thomas Jefferson in Charlottesville, Va. Clinton and Gore then traveled by bus to the capital, following the approximate route Jefferson had taken to his inaugural in 1801. They joined some 300,000 spectators at a musical program at the Lincoln Memorial that afternoon, then led a procession across the Potomac River to ring a replica of the Liberty Bell. Clinton addressed the diplomatic corps at Georgetown University, **Jan. 18**, then attended a service at Howard University in honor of the Rev. Martin Luther King, Jr. On **Jan. 19**, Clinton visited the gravesite of former Pres. John Kennedy and attended a Celebration for Children at the Kennedy Center and the Presidential Gala at the Capital Centre. On the morning of Inauguration Day, **Jan. 20**, Clinton and his wife and daughter attended an interfaith church service and were welcomed to the White House by Pres. George Bush and Barbara Bush. The two first families then traveled to the Capitol. Before a large throng of dignitaries and citizens, Gore and then Clinton took the oath for their respective offices. In his inaugural address, Clinton said, "This ceremony is held in the depth of winter, but by the words we speak and the faces we show the world, we force the spring." He asserted, "There is nothing wrong with America that cannot be cured by what is right with America." George and Barbara Bush left Washington immediately for Houston, where they were renting a home. The Clintons led the inaugural parade down Pennsylvania Avenue to the White House, walking the last 2 blocks. That evening, the president, vice president, and their wives attended 11 inaugural balls. On **Jan. 21**, the Clintons held an open house at the White House for 3,000 visitors. The White House announced, **Jan. 21**, that First Lady Hillary Clinton would have an office in the West Wing of the White House, the section usually reserved for high government officials. Meanwhile, the Senate, acting quickly, confirmed on **Jan. 20** and **21** most of Clinton's nominees for administration offices.

**Large Corporations Face Turmoil** — January was a difficult month for some major U.S. corporations. IBM, **Jan. 19**, announced that it had lost $4.97 billion in 1992, the largest one-year loss ever for any U.S. corporation. McDonnell Douglas, the largest U.S. defense contractor, announced, **Jan. 25**, that it would cut 8,700 jobs. Sears, Roebuck & Co., the nation's 3d largest retailer, said, **Jan. 25**, that it would eliminate 50,000 jobs, close 113 of 859 stores, and cease publication of its catalog, a marketing tool since 1896. Boeing, the world's largest airplane manufacturer, **Jan. 26**, announced production cutbacks that appeared likely to trigger 20,000 dismissals. The Pratt & Whitney unit of United Technologies said, **Jan. 26**, that it would eliminate 6,700 jobs.

**Clinton Reverses Restrictions on Abortion** — Pres. Bill Clinton, **Jan. 22**, issued executive orders overturning restrictions on abortion imposed during the administrations of Ronald Reagan and George Bush. Clinton canceled the rule barring anyone (except doctors) at federally funded family-planning clinics from discussing abortion; lifted the ban on fetal tissue use in federally funded medical research; ordered a review of the prohibition on RU-486, a French-made abortion pill; killed the policy barring U.S. aid to foreign family-planning programs that included abortion counseling; and ended a ban on abortions in U.S. military hospitals overseas if they were paid for by private funds.

**Ban on Gays in Military Debated** — During his presidential campaign, Bill Clinton had said he would end the policy of the armed forces that barred homosexuals from enlisting and that required the discharge of any service personnel found to be gay. At a meeting, **Jan. 25**, with Pres. Clinton, Gen. Colin Powell, chairman of the Joint Chiefs of Staff, and the other chiefs made clear their opposition to lifting the ban. The chiefs and others who supported the ban acknowledged that many homosexuals were serving secretly in the armed forces. But they contended that if gays could make their sexual orientation publicly known, the services would see a decline in morale and recruitment. Supporters of homosexual rights contended that the ban was a violation of gays' civil rights and that only actual misconduct should be the basis of disciplinary action or dismissal. On **Jan. 28**, U.S. District Judge Terry Hatter, ruling in the case of Petty Officer 1st Class Keith Meinhold, held that the ban on homosexuals was unconstitutional. An appeal was later filed. Clinton, **Jan. 29**, announced a 6-month interim policy: The armed forces would no longer ask recruits about their sexual orientation, and openly gay personnel would be placed on standby reserve status rather than receive a discharge.

**Hillary Rodham Clinton to Head Health Task Force** — On **Jan. 25**, Pres. Bill Clinton appointed his wife, Hillary Rodham Clinton, as head of the Task Force on National Health Care Reform. The task force would seek to find ways to provide medical coverage for all Americans and to control the costs of medical care. No other first lady had ever assumed such a major public responsibility.

**Republicans Elect New Leader** — The Republican National Committee, **Jan. 29**, elected Haley Barbour of Mississippi as its new chairman. Barbour, a lawyer and lobbyist, had once made an unsuccessful bid for a U.S. Senate seat. In a speech to the committee the retiring chairman, Rich Bond, warned that social conservatives in the GOP were driving away voters by making opposition to abortion a leading issue.

## International

**Czech, Slovak States Established** — On **Jan. 1**, 2 independent states—the Czech Republic and Slovakia—were founded as a result of the division of Czechoslovakia. Slovaks generally celebrated, but Czechs were reported to have mixed feelings about the amicable divorce. Vaclav Havel, a former president of Czechoslovakia, was elected president of the Czech Republic, **Jan. 26**. Michal Kovac, an economist, was elected president of Slovakia, **Feb. 15**.

**U.N. Forces in Somalia** — Pres. George Bush concluded his trip to Somalia, **Jan. 1**, with a visit to an orphanage in Baidoa. After snipers fired on U.S. Marines in Mogadishu, the Marines, **Jan. 7**, raided the compound of one of the Somali warlords. No Americans were injured in the exchange of fire, but many Somalis fled or were killed or captured. Representatives of 14 Somali factions, meeting in Addis Ababa, the capital of Ethiopia, **Jan. 15**, signed a nationwide cease-fire. They agreed to relinquish their heavy artillery to the U.S.-led forces until a government was established. Militias were to be disarmed. On **Jan. 19**, planes flew 556 Marines from Somalia to their base in California. They were the first American service personnel to leave Somalia. U.S. and Belgian troops, **Jan. 25**, enforced the cease-fire by routing Somali guerrillas advancing on the city of Kismayu. A U.S. Marine, shot on patrol in Mogadishu, **Jan. 25**, became the 3d American to be killed in the U.S.-led relief operation.

**Division of Bosnia Proposed** — Talks aimed at ending the devastating civil war in Bosnia and Herzegovina opened in Geneva, **Jan. 2**. The conference cochairmen, Cyrus Vance and Lord Owen, representing the U.N. and the European Community, respectively, proposed to split Bosnia into 10 semiautonomous provinces. Pres. Alija Izetbegovic of Bosnia visited the U.S., **Jan. 7** and **8**, seeking Western military aid. A European Community investigation found, **Jan. 8**, that Bosnian Serbs had raped up to 20,000 Muslim women and girls. Deputy Premier Hakija Turajlic of Bosnia was assassinated, **Jan. 8**, by Serbian militiamen even though he was traveling under U.N. protection. The Croatian army, **Jan. 22**, attacked a Serbian-held enclave on the Adriatic Sea; the Serbians launched a counterattack, **Jan. 27**.

**Bush, Yeltsin Sign Arms Treaty** — Pres. George Bush and Russian Pres. Boris Yeltsin signed the 2d Strategic Arms Reduction Treaty (START II) in Moscow, **Jan. 3**. It required the signatories to cut their long-range nuclear arsenals by about two-thirds from existing levels. Land-based multiple-warhead missiles would be eliminated entirely. START II would not be implemented until the other signatories to START I —Ukraine, Belarus, and Kazakhstan—honored the terms of that treaty. Ukraine and Belarus had yet to ratify START I.

**Allies Launch Air Attacks in Iraq** — U.S., French, and British warplanes attacked missile batteries and radar stations in Iraq, **Jan. 13**. The White House said, **Jan. 13**, that Iraq had attempted to position anti-aircraft surface-to-air missiles in the southern no-fly zone created to protect Shiite Muslims from Iraqi attack. Pres. George Bush also sent 1,250 Army troops to Kuwait to guard against Iraqi incursions. In the northern no-fly zone, established to protect the Kurdish population, a U.S. fighter plane, **Jan. 17**, downed an Iraqi fighter. The Iraqi government said, **Jan. 19**, after more Allied attacks, that it would no longer harass Allied planes patrolling the no-fly zones and that it would guarantee the safety of U.N. arms experts conducting inspections in Iraq. The ruling council said its action was a gesture of goodwill toward the incoming Clinton administration. U.S. planes again attacked air-defense installations, **Jan. 22** and **23**.

**Israel Drops Ban on Contacts With PLO** — The Israeli parliament, **Jan. 19**, overturned the law barring Israelis from contact with members of the Palestine Liberation Organization. Although the government of Prime Minister Yitzhak Rabin remained opposed to direct contacts with the PLO, the law's repeal represented an attempt to revive the Middle East peace negotiations. Israel's deportation in December of more than 400 Palestinians remained a source of controversy. U.N. Secretary-Gen. Boutros Boutros-Ghali urged the Security Council, **Jan. 26**, to do whatever was necessary to force Israel to take back the deportees. The Israeli Supreme Court ruled, **Jan. 28**, that the expulsions were legal.

## General

**Nations Sign Chemical-Weapons Ban** — After 24 years of negotiations, more than 120 countries began to sign, at a ceremony in Paris, **Jan. 13**, a treaty that would forbid the manufacture, stockpiling, and use of chemical weapons. Twenty-nine toxic chemicals and 14 "families" of compounds would be banned outright or controlled tightly if they had both military and civilian uses. Countries were given 10 years to destroy any existing stockpiles of chemical weapons. The U.S., Russia, and Iraq openly possessed chemical weapons, but 20 other nations were suspected to have them as well. Although the U.S. and Russia agreed to sign the treaty, Iraq did not.

**EPA Issues Warning on Second-Hand Smoke** — A U.S. Environmental Protection Agency report, **Jan. 7**, said that nonsmokers were at risk when they inhaled the smoke from other people's tobacco products. The EPA said that so-called passive smoking caused 3,000 cases of lung cancer in nonsmokers annually, up to 300,000 cases of bronchitis and other respiratory infections in small children, and a higher frequency of asthma attacks in up to 1 million children. Tobacco industry representatives said that studies on secondhand smoke were scientifically unsound.

**Subway Opens in Los Angeles** — Los Angeles, long notorious for its maze of highways and glut of private cars, got its first subway service, **Jan. 30**. The only route available linked 5 stations, from Union Station to MacArthur Park. The 4.4-mile route could be covered in 7 minutes. A 22.7-mile system, connecting 20 stations, was projected by 2001.

**Cowboys Win Super Bowl** — Before 98,374 fans at the Rose Bowl in Pasadena, Calif., **Jan. 31**, the Dallas Cowboys trounced the Buffalo Bills, 52-17, in Super Bowl XXVII. The victory gave the Cowboys their first championship in 15 years, while the Bills suffered their 3d straight Super Bowl loss, a new record. Dallas quarterback Troy Aikman, who completed 22 of 30 passes for 273 yards and 4 touchdowns, was voted the game's most valuable player.

## FEBRUARY

### National

**Data Suggest Improving Economy** — The index of leading economic indicators rose 1.9 percent in December, the Commerce Dept. reported, **Feb. 2**. That was the largest monthly increase in almost 10 years. The Labor Dept. reported, **Feb. 5**, that the unemployment rate had fallen from 7.3 percent to 7.1 percent in January. On Wall Street, **Feb. 5**, the Dow Jones industrial average closed at 3,442.14, an all-time high. The Labor Dept. reported, **Feb. 12**, that the prices charged by producers for finished goods had risen 0.2 percent in January. Concern among investors over Pres. Bill Clinton's economic program caused the Dow Jones average to tumble 82.94 points, **Feb. 16**, to 3,309.49, but stock prices soon resumed an upward trend. Consumer prices jumped 0.5 percent in January, the Labor Dept. reported, **Feb. 18**. The Commerce Dept. reported, **Feb. 18**, that the deficit in merchandise trade had been $84.34 billion for all of 1992, a 29 percent jump over 1991. In New York trading, **Feb. 22**, the Japanese yen closed at 116.40 to the U.S. dollar, a record high for the yen since World War II.

**Reno Nominated for Attorney General** — Pres. Bill Clinton in February nominated Janet Reno, a Florida state attorney, for the office of attorney general in his cabinet. Clinton's first announced choice for the position, Zoe Baird, had withdrawn her name from consideration in January, after it became known that she and her husband had hired illegal aliens when it was not legal to do so, and had also failed to pay Social Security taxes on their wages. White House officials reportedly learned, **Feb. 4**, that U.S. District Judge Kimba Wood of New York City, who was then thought to be in line for the appointment, had also employed an illegal alien as a babysitter, although at a time when such employment was not illegal. Wood, **Feb. 5**, withdrew her name from consideration. On **Feb. 11**, Clinton nominated Reno, who had been the chief state prosecutor in Miami since 1978.

**GM's Pickup Truck, Financial Woes** — A statecourt jury in Atlanta, **Feb. 4**, found General Motors negligent and ordered the company to pay $105.2 million in damages to the parents of Shannon Moseley, 17, who had been killed in 1989 when his GM pickup truck burst into flames after being struck by another vehicle. The plaintiffs had argued that the placement of dual fuel tanks outside the truck's steel internal frame had increased the likelihood of a fire after a collision. One witness had testified that GM knew the design was flawed. GM charged, **Feb. 8**, that in November of

1992, NBC had shown rigged crash tests of GM pickup trucks on television. GM said NBC had ordered the company that had conducted the crash tests to place toy rocket engines under a truck to ensure that it caught fire when struck. NBC agreed, **Feb. 9,** to issue a televised apology that night and to pay GM $2 million, the cost of GM's investigation into the crash tests. GM, **Feb. 11,** reported a loss of $23.5 billion in 1992, by far the largest one-year loss in the U.S. corporate history, although most of the deficit was the result of a one-time charge to cover future costs of retirees' health benefits.

**Family-Leave Act 1st Victory for Clinton** — Pres. Bill Clinton claimed his first legislative victory when the Senate and House, **Feb. 4,** both passed the Family and Medical Leave Act. Clinton, who strongly supported the measure, signed it into law, **Feb. 5.** The bill, which applied to government workers and to employees of companies having 50 or more workers, permitted anyone employed at least one year to take up to 12 weeks of unpaid leave a year to deal with the birth or adoption of a child or with an illness suffered by the employee or another family member. Employers would be required to provide health-care benefits during the leave and to guarantee that employees on leave could reclaim their jobs. Pres. George Bush had vetoed similar bills twice.

**Weinberger's Diaries Made Public** — Lawrence Walsh, the independent prosecutor in the Iran-contra case, released excerpts from the diaries of Caspar Weinberger, **Feb. 8.** Walsh said that the diaries, which Weinberger had kept while serving as secretary of defense, showed that he had been involved in a cover-up of the scandal. Pres. George Bush had pardoned Weinberger in December, just before he was to go on trial. Walsh said that a Weinberger trial would have brought new evidence to light that members of the Reagan administration had sought to conceal facts from Congress and the public. In his interim report, Walsh suggested that Bush had pardoned Weinberger to avoid being called as a witness at the trial.

**Clinton Announces Economic Program** — Pres. Bill Clinton presented his economic program to Congress and the American people in February. The plan sought to add impetus to the economic recovery and at the same time cut deeply into the size of the annual federal budget deficits. In his first step to create a climate of shared sacrifice, Clinton announced, **Feb. 9,** that the White House staff would be reduced by 25 percent, with the elimination of 350 positions. He issued executive orders, **Feb. 10,** to phase out 100,000 federal jobs in 4 years and to reduce federal administrative expenses by 14 percent. The president unveiled the broad outlines of his program in a nationally televised address to a joint session of Congress, **Feb. 17.** The program, if enacted, was expected to reduce the aggregate budget deficit by $325 billion over 4 years. Clinton proposed to increase the personal income tax rate to 36 percent from 31 percent for those couples with taxable incomes of $140,000 or more and individuals with taxable incomes of $115,000 or more. He would also add a 10 percent surtax on family income above $250,000. For couples with total income of more than $32,000 receiving Social Security benefits, the portion of benefits subject to taxation would rise from 50 percent to 85 percent. The top corporate income-tax rate would rise from 34 percent to 36 percent, and the deductible portion of business meals and entertainment would be reduced from 80 percent to 50 percent. Taxes on gasoline and other forms of energy would be imposed, possibly increasing a family's annual fuel bill by $100 to $150. In an effort to cut federal spending under Clinton's plan, federal workers would forgo one annual

raise; the Defense Dept. would cut expenditures on new weapons and reduce troop levels; and spending on over 150 civil projects, including a space station and the superconducting supercollider, would be slashed. Also, new limits would be imposed on Medicare payments to doctors, hospitals, and laboratories. On the other hand, Clinton endorsed a short-term economic stimulus plan with increased spending on education, mass transit, highway construction, and summer jobs.

**Explosion Shuts Down World Trade Center** — A powerful bomb exploded in an underground parking garage beneath the World Trade Center in New York City, **Feb. 26,** killing 6 people and forcing the temporary closing of the complex. The twin towers of the World Trade Center are the world's second and third tallest buildings. The lower Manhattan complex also includes a hotel, a building housing commodity exchanges, and a shopping arcade. The explosion, at 12:18 P.M. on a Friday, left a crater 200 feet wide and several stories deep within the garage. The Port Authority of New York and New Jersey operates the complex, including an underground train station where many people were trapped for awhile under rubble. Four Port Authority employees were killed as they ate lunch in their underground office. A 5th victim died of a heart attack after the explosion. The 6th victim's body was not recovered until **Mar. 15.** About 50,000 people evacuated the buildings. Most of the occupants of the 110-story towers had to walk down stairwells through dense smoke. More than 1,000 suffered injuries, mostly smoke inhalation.

**Four Agents Die in Shootout With Cult** — Four federal agents were killed, **Feb. 28,** during an unsuccessful raid on the compound of a religious cult near Waco, Tex. At least 2 cultists were killed and 16 agents were wounded. The Branch Davidians, a Christian group, had broken away from the Davidians, who in turn had left the Seventh-Day Adventist church. The leader of the Branch Davidians, David Koresh, had said that he was the messiah and that he believed the apocalypse would occur soon. Koresh claimed more than 100 people lived in the compound, named Mount Carmel, including Koresh's many wives and children. After an investigation, 100 agents of the U.S. Bureau of Alcohol, Tobacco, and Firearms attempted to approach the compound by surprise, **Feb. 28,** carrying warrants to search the premises for illegal guns and explosives and to arrest Koresh. But Koresh had apparently been warned of the ATF's plans, and the exchange of fire occurred. ATF agents were allowed to retrieve their comrades who had been hit. Then, ATF personnel, joined by hundreds of officers from federal, state, and local agencies, surrounded and laid siege to the compound.

### International

**Israel Offers Compromise on Deportees** — Israeli Prime Minister Yitzhak Rabin made a proposal, **Feb. 1,** to defuse the controversy over some 400 Palestinians it had deported. Israel would allow 100 of the deportees to return right away, though most of them would be imprisoned, and the remaining exiles could return home in a year. But the deportees declared, **Feb. 2,** that they would all remain in no-man's land between Israel and Lebanon until all could return to Israel.

**Fighting Resumes in Somalia** — Sec. of State Warren Christopher reported, **Feb. 1,** that he and U.N. Secretary Gen. Boutros Boutros-Ghali had agreed that U.S. soldiers in Somalia should soon be replaced by a U.N. peace-keeping force. The American withdrawal from the southern port city of Kismayu was delayed, **Feb. 22,** by fighting between Somali factions. Rioting and demonstrations against foreigners erupted in Mogadishu, the capital, **Feb. 24.** Protesters fired on U.N. offices, the U.S. diplomatic mission, and hotels where foreigners stayed. Four Americans were wounded. An attacking clan leader was warned to pull out of Kismayu and on **Feb. 26,** 71 of his soldiers surrendered to international forces.

**President, Premier Clash in Zaire; 1,000 Killed** — Fighting erupted in Zaire in late January and early February after soldiers and shopkeepers protested the introduction of a new high-denomination banknotes. Soldiers loyal to Pres. Mobutu Sese Seko fought with rebel soldiers, and about 1,000 people were killed. Premier Etienne Tshisekedi declared the new paper money to be worthless, and on **Feb. 4** he called for foreign military intervention to restore order. Mobutu, **Feb. 5,** rejected appeals from foreign diplomats that he step down as president, and he dismissed Tshisekedi, who refused to leave office. On **Feb. 24,** soldiers and tanks surrounded the legislature in the capital, Kinshasa, and Mobutu insisted that the lawmakers accept the banknotes. The legislators agreed, **Feb. 26,** to cooperate with Mobutu.

**U.S. Drops Food, Medicine Over Bosnia** — The United States began parachuting food and medical supplies into Muslim-held areas of Bosnia and Herzegovina in February. On **Feb. 10,** Sec. of State Warren Christopher said that the Clinton administration would actively engage in the Vance-Owen negotiations and would "tighten the enforcement of economic sanctions, increase political pressure on Serbia and deter Serbia from widening the war." By a unanimous vote, the U.N. Security Council, **Feb. 22,** approved creation of an international court to prosecute war crimes in the former Yugoslavia. Operating under the 1949 Geneva Convention, the court would be the first of its kind since those who judged accused war criminals after World War II. In a statement issued **Feb. 25,** Pres. Bill Clinton said he had ordered air drops over Bosnia to proceed, "strictly for humanitarian purposes." The action represented the first unilateral U.S. military involvement in the Yugoslav conflict. The supplies were to be dropped by unarmed transport flying at high altitude without fighter escorts. The first mission, to aid the besieged Muslims of Cerska, took place **Feb. 28.**

**South African Transition Approved** — The government of South Africa and the African National Congress reached agreement, **Feb. 12,** on a plan that would lead to black-majority rule in 1999. In the first step, South Africans of all races would elect a 400-seat assembly in 1994. The assembly would serve as a parliament until 1999 and would write a new constitution. A new president, chosen from the most successful party, would need cabinet approval for all major decisions. Not all blacks welcomed the plan. Mangosuthu Gatsha Buthelezi, president of the Inkatha Freedom Party, objected vigorously, **Feb. 13,** and he appeared to support greater regional autonomy. The left-wing Pan African Congress also protested, **Feb. 15.** The ANC, **Feb. 18,** approved the transition plan, although some ANC leaders said the transition period was too long.

**Mulroney Steps Down in Canada** — Prime Minister Brian Mulroney of Canada announced, **Feb. 24,** he would resign as leader of the Progressive Conservative Party and as prime minister when a successor was chosen. Given Mulroney's popularity rating of only 17 percent, his resignation was seen as likely to enhance the chances of his party in the national election that would take place in late 1993. Canada's economy was in a deep recession, and the 7 percent value-added tax adopted by the government in 1991 was unpopular. Mulroney's tenure of 8½ years had been noteworthy for the establishment of free trade with the U.S. and

for his failure to resolve conflicts between Canadians of English and French descent.

### General

**Owner of Baseball Team Suspended** — Marge Schott, the only woman who owned a major league baseball team, was suspended for one year, **Feb. 3,** by baseball's executive council. Schott, owner of the Cincinnati Reds, had been accused of making racist and anti-Semitic remarks. She was fined $25,000 and barred from the team's day-to-day operations for one year. She would continue as general partner of the Reds.

**Impact of AIDS on Society Studied** — In a report issued **Feb. 4,** the National Research Council said that AIDS had little impact on most Americans because the epidemic had struck mostly "marginalized" groups—homosexuals, drug users, the poor, and the undereducated. As a result, the report said, AIDS "may be ignored by the general population and by public policy."

## MARCH

### National

**Standoff With Texas Cult Continues** — The armed confrontation between federal authorities and the Branch Davidian religious cult continued in March. Many Davidians remained inside their compound near Waco, Tex; however, more than 30 people, mostly children, left or were freed from the compound by the cult leader, David Koresh. Fewer than 100, including at least 17 children, remained. Koresh said, **Mar. 2,** that he and his followers would surrender if his 58-minute taped monologue were broadcast on the radio. Although several stations played the tape, Koresh then said that God had told him to wait. Agents cut off the compound's electricity, **Mar. 12,** and concentrated floodlights on the compound at night, beginning **Mar. 14.** Two cultists came out, **Mar. 15,** to meet with federal officials, but negotiations made no headway. Three cult members who had left the compound earlier were indicted, **Mar. 30,** for conspiracy to murder federal officers. Four agents had been killed in an unsuccessful assault on the compound in February.

**Data Suggest Inflationary Pressures** — Statistics released in March suggested that inflation might become a problem for the U.S. economy. The Commerce Dept. reported, **Mar. 2,** that the index of leading economic indicators had risen 0.1 percent in January. The Labor Dept. said, **Mar. 5,** that the unemployment rate in February had edged downward from 7.1 percent to 7.0 percent and that 365,000 new jobs had been created. On Wall Street, the Dow Jones industrial average closed, **Mar. 10,** at 3478.34, a new all-time high. The Labor Dept. reported, **Mar. 12,** that prices charged by producers for finished goods had jumped 0.4 percent in February. The department said, **Mar. 17,** that consumer prices had risen 0.3 percent in February. The Federal Reserve Board said, **Mar. 17,** that the output of the nation's factories, mines, and utilities had risen 0.4 percent in February. The U.S. merchandise trade deficit had widened in January, to $7.3 billion, the Commerce Dept. reported, **Mar. 18.** The department said, **Mar. 26,** that after-tax profits of U.S. corporations had risen by 10 percent, to $231.8 billion, in 1992. On **Mar. 31,** the department reported that the index of leading economic indicators had jumped 0.5 percent in February.

**Aid to Jobless Extended** — The Senate, **Mar. 3,** and the House, **Mar. 4,** approved a bill extending through

October a program giving unemployed workers who had exhausted their benefits up to 6 months in additional aid. In a provision reflecting Pres. Bill Clinton's call for federal employees to forgo salary increases, the bill also froze the pay of members of Congress. On **Mar. 4,** Clinton signed the bill.

**Suspects Held in New York Bombing** — Five men were arrested in March in connection with the February bombing at the World Trade Center in New York City. In Jersey City, N.J., **Mar. 4,** FBI agents arrested Mohammed Salameh, a Jordanian-born Palestinian who lived in Jersey City. According to authorities, Salameh was a follower of Sheikh Omar Abdel Rahman, described as a spiritual leader of radical Islamic groups. Investigators had found fragments of a yellow Ford van at the site of the explosion and believed it had carried the bomb. They traced its vehicle identification number to a van rented by Salameh in Jersey City 3 days before the explosion. Salameh had notified the Ryder truck-rental agency that the van had been stolen, and when he returned to the agency to get a refund on a $400 deposit, he was arrested. The FBI said that his apartment contained evidence that he had been involved in making a bomb. A 2d man, Ibrahim Elgabrowny, was arrested, **Mar. 4,** in Brooklyn, N.Y. after resisting authorities as they searched his apartment in connection with the investigation. A chemical engineer, Nidal Ayyad, was arrested, **Mar. 10,** at his Maplewood, N.J. apartment. The FBI said he had had contacts with Salameh and had the expertise to make explosives. The 3 suspects were indicted in New York City, **Mar. 17.** Abdel Rahman denied, **Mar. 18,** that he had been involved in the bombing. While repair work continued, some tenants returned to the World Trade Center, **Mar. 18.** Mahmud Abouhalima was turned over to U.S. authorities by the Egyptian government and arrested on the plane, **Mar. 24,** upon arrival in the U.S. Abouhalima was reported to have been seen with Salameh the morning of the bombing. A fifth suspect, Bilal Alkaisi, was arrested on **Mar. 25,** the day after he turned himself in at FBI offices in Newark, N.J. Allegedly, Alkaisi was sighted at a N.J. storage shed containing materials to make explosives. Later, a timing mechanism was found in Alkaisi's apartment. A sixth man, Ramzi Ahmed Yousef, was indicted, **Mar. 31,** in connection with the bombing. Yousef, who shared an apartment with Salameh, was at large, and it was not known whether he was still in the U.S.

**First Woman Attorney General Confirmed** — In March, Janet Reno became the first woman to serve as attorney general of the U.S. Reno, a Florida state attorney, had been nominated for the office by Pres. Bill Clinton in February. At her confirmation hearings before the Senate Judiciary Committee, **Mar. 9** and **10,** Reno said that she would resist political pressures on the Justice Dept. and act forcefully against violent crime and drug trafficking. The committee, **Mar. 10,** and the full Senate, **Mar. 11,** approved her nomination unanimously. Reno took the oath of office **Mar. 12.**

**Health Task Force Hears Many Opinions** — The Task Force on National Health Care Reform, established by Pres. Bill Clinton and headed by First Lady Hillary Rodham Clinton, conducted its first public meeting in March. A U.S. District Court judge held, **Mar. 10,** that any hearing in which the task force gathered information must be open to the public, since the Federal Advisory Committee Act required that federal advisory bodies conduct open meetings. During a 13-hour public meeting, **Mar. 29,** the task force heard from more than 60 witnesses, including doctors, nurses, social workers, and representatives from insurance companies, small businesses, and nursing homes.

**Doctor Killed by Opponent of Abortion** — A doctor was shot dead, **Mar. 10,** outside an abortion clinic in Pensacola, Fla. The gunman, Michael Griffin, surrendered to police and accepted responsibility for the shooting. The victim, David Gunn, had performed many abortions in Pensacola and elsewhere. Demonstrations, sometimes becoming violent, had become commonplace at abortion clinics across the United States. Griffin was a member of Rescue America, an antiabortion organization. Don Teshman, national director of Rescue America, said, **Mar. 10,** that Dr. Gunn's death was unfortunate but that "it's also true that quite a number of babies' lives will be saved."

**Clinton Economic Program Advances** — Congress approved a budget resolution supporting Pres. Bill Clinton's plan to reduce the federal budget deficits. The budget resolution sets broad guidelines, which need to be fleshed out later in more specific implementing legislation before they can take effect. The House first passed its version, **Mar. 18,** providing for spending cuts and tax increases designed to achieve a net deficit reduction of $496 billion over 5 years. The House, **Mar. 19,** also approved the president's short-term economic-stimulus package, which included benefits for the long-term unemployed and outlays for highway construction, small business loans, community development, college loans, and summer jobs for youths. The Senate passed its version of the budget resolution, **Mar. 25,** which projected deficit reductions totaling $502 billion over 5 years. In conference committee, **Mar. 30,** Senate and House negotiators agreed to a budget reduction over 5 years. To secure the support of Senate and House Democrats from western states, the compromise conference resolution omitted cuts in crop subsidies and also eliminated increased fees on mining, grazing, and logging on public lands. The House, **Mar. 31,** and the Senate, **Apr. 1,** gave final approval to budget resolution.

**Justice White Announces Retirement** — Associate Justice Byron White announced, **Mar. 19,** that he would retire from the U.S. Supreme Court at the conclusion of the court's 1992-1993 term. Appointed by Pres. John Kennedy in 1962, White had served longer than any other justice currently on the court and had been the only sitting justice nominated by a Democratic president. White's voting record on the court generally placed him with the advocates of judicial restraint. At a press conference, **Mar. 23,** Pres. Bill Clinton was asked if the abortion issue would be considered in the search for a successor to White. Clinton said he would not seek to ascertain a candidate's views on a specific case but that he would seek someone who supported "the constitutional rights to privacy."

### International

**Search for Peace in Bosnia Stalls** — Efforts to bring peace to Bosnia and Herzegovina enjoyed only limited success in March. Peace talks resumed, **Mar. 1,** at U.N. headquarters in New York. U.S. officials said, **Mar. 1,** that Pres. Bill Clinton had warned Pres. Slobodan Milosevic of Serbia that the U.S. would take military action if Serbia permitted civil war to spread to its Kosovo region, which was populated mostly by Muslim ethnic Albanians. In the first days of March the U.S. continued to airdrop food and supplies into Bosnia. In a letter released **Mar. 2,** the Bosnian Serb leader, Radovan Karadzic, warned that the "ill-advised American humanitarian" effort could cause the local conflict to expand even to a world war. Reports from Bosnia indicated that the Serbs were continuing to advance and to block U.N. truck convoys seeking to provide humanitarian aid. Gen. Philippe Morillon, the

U.N. commander in Bosnia, went to the besieged Muslim town of Srebrenica, **Mar. 12**, and residents persuaded him to stay to protect them from massacre at the hands of the Serbs. A U.N. effort to airlift sick and wounded Muslims from Srebrenica was suspended, **Mar. 24**, when Serbs shelled the landing zone. In New York, **Mar. 25**, Bosnian Muslims joined Croat leaders in endorsing the Vance-Owen plan to divide Bosnia into 10 semi-autonomous provinces, but Karadzic rejected the plan because most natural and industrial resources would remain in Muslim and Croat control. A U.N. truck convoy reached Srebrenica, **Mar. 28**, and the trucks took out several thousand refugees, **Mar. 29-31**.

**U.N. Peace Force Approved for Somalia** — U.N. Secretary-Gen. Boutros Boutros-Ghali proposed, **Mar. 3**, that a U.N. peacekeeping force replace the U.S.-led coalition forces in Somalia. The U.N. Security Council, **Mar. 26**, approved unanimously a resolution to send 28,000 soldiers and 2,800 civilians to Somalia. The troops would come from about 24 countries, and the civilians would run Somalia, which currently lacked a government. U.N.-sponsored talks in Ethiopia resulted in agreement, **Mar. 27**, by Somali leaders to the creation of a transitional government. Under the plan, a council of 74 representatives would lead the country until a national government could be formed.

**Yeltsin Struggles to Keep His Powers** — For several weeks during March, Russian Pres. Boris Yeltsin resisted attempts by his adversaries in the Congress of People's Deputies to curtail his powers. The congress, elected in 1989, was dominated by former Communists. On **Mar. 12**, the congress repudiated an agreement of December 1992 extending the president's powers to rule by decree. It also canceled an April referendum in which the people were to vote on the relative powers of congress and the president. While most of Russia was undergoing a painful adjustment to a market economy, the congress, **Mar. 13**, called for a slower transition to a market system. At a press conference in Moscow, **Mar. 16**, with French Pres. François Mitterrand, Yeltsin said a serious threat hung over democracy and reforms in Russia. Mitterrand said the West would continue to support the reform process in Russia. Yeltsin announced, **Mar. 20**, that he had signed a decree asserting "special powers" and that there would be a referendum **Apr. 25** on his presidency as well as a vote on a new constitution. Yeltsin's major cabinet ministers rallied behind him, **Mar. 21**, but the vice president, Gen. Aleksandr Rutskoi, said Yeltsin's decree was unconstitutional. On **Mar. 21** the Supreme Soviet, Russia's smaller standing parliament, asked the Constitutional Court to rule on Yeltsin's assumption of special powers. On **Mar. 23**, the court found, by a 10-3 vote, that Yeltsin had violated 9 provisions of the constitution. The court said Yeltsin could not ask the public to choose between presidential and parliamentary control. Ruslan Khasbulatov, chairman of the Congress of People's Deputies, called **Mar. 23**, for Yeltsin's impeachment. Pres. Bill Clinton, **Mar. 23**, publicly backed Yeltsin and "the historic movement toward democratic political reform in Russia." Yeltsin's decree was published, **Mar. 24**, with softer language containing no reference to special powers. Yeltsin and other leaders then sought to avoid further confrontation. On **Mar. 26**, the chairman of the Constitutional Court, Valery Zorkin, offered a compromise plan for government, and Yeltsin acknowledged that mistakes had been made in his economic reform program. But congress deputies responded negatively to a comprise plan between Yeltsin and Khasbulatov, and on **Mar. 28** a vote to impeach Yeltsin fell just 72 votes short—689 were needed. On **Mar. 29**, the Congress of

People's Deputies approved an **Apr. 25** referendum but also terminated Yeltsin's powers to rule by decree.

**North Korea to Exit From Nuclear Treaty** — North Korea announced its withdrawal, **Mar. 12**, from the Nuclear Nonproliferation Treaty. More than 150 countries had signed the treaty, which sought to restrict the spread of nuclear-weapons technology and sales. North Korea gave, as reasons for its withdrawal, joint military exercises by U.S. and South Korean forces in South Korea as well as "unjust acts" by the International Atomic Energy Agency. The agency had asked to inspect suspicious sites in North Korea. South Korea's Foreign Ministry states, **Mar. 12**, that North Korea's withdrawal "heightens the suspicion that it is developing nuclear arms."

**Bombs Kill 300 in India** — Bombs that exploded in Bombay and Calcutta in March killed more than 300 people and left 1,100 injured. An explosion at the Bombay Stock Exchange, **Mar. 12**, killed about 50 people, and within 90 minutes 10 more bombs had claimed additional lives at banks, government offices, hotels, an airline office, and a shopping complex. Bombay police charged 2 men in the bombings, **Mar. 15**. At least 80 people were killed in Calcutta, **Mar. 17**, when an explosion destroyed 2 apartment buildings. Another bomb exploded in a Calcutta train station, **Mar. 19**. Bombay police said, **Mar. 19**, that a Muslim family in Bombay with links to organized crime had played a role in that city's bombings.

**China's Parliament Elects New President** — The National People's Congress, the parliament of China, convened **Mar. 15**. Major actions taken by the 2,977 delegates reflected decisions already made by Deng Xiaoping, China's paramount ruler, and other leaders. Premier Li Peng, **Mar. 15**, called for continued economic reform under the leadership of the Communist party. Jiang Zemin, the general secretary of the party, was elected president, **Mar. 27**. Li was reelected as premier, **Mar. 28**, but in something of a surprise more than 10 percent of the delegates voted against him or abstained. On **Mar. 29**, the delegates approved a new constitution that used the phrase "socialist market economy" to characterize the regime's capitalist-style reforms.

**Salvadoran Army Blamed in Atrocities** — A U.N. commission reported, **Mar. 15**, that it had concluded that most of the human-rights abuses during El Salvador's civil war had been committed by the U.S.-supported Salvadoran army. The commission had interviewed almost 20,000 Salvadorans. The commission linked some leaders of the Nationalist Republican Alliance (ARENA) party, which now ruled El Salvador, to death squads that operated during the 12-year-long war, which ended in 1992. The commission declared that no current members of the country's Supreme Court were capable of fairness in dealing with those accused of human-rights abuses. Defense Minister Gen. René Emilio Ponce, linked by the commission to the killing in 1989 of 6 Jesuit priests and 2 women, had already offered to resign. The report by the commission also said that the late Roberto D'Aubuisson, founder of ARENA, had probably ordered the slaying of Archbishop Oscar Arnulfo Romero in 1980. The report blamed the left-wing Farabundo Martí National Liberation Front for the assassination of many public officials. On **Mar. 20**, ARENA and other right-wing factions successfully supported approval by the National Assembly of an amnesty for those who had committed atrocities during the war, ending any prospects for prosecutions for human-rights abuses.

**Clinton Meets Exiled President of Haiti** — The Rev. Jean-Bertrand Aristide, who had been elected president of Haiti and then ousted in a military coup, met with Pres. Bill Clinton in Washington, **Mar. 16.** Clinton said he would seek to restore Aristide to power and that the U.S. would not support "continuation of an illegal government in Haiti."

**Conservatives Win French Election** — Conservative parties won an overwhelming majority of the seats in the French National Assembly in elections held in March. A trend toward the right was apparent in the first round of voting, **Mar. 21,** and after the runoff elections, **Mar. 28,** the conservatives had won 484 of the 577 seats. Scandals and an unemployment rate of 10.5 percent had turned many voters against the governing Socialist party. The results meant that Premier Pierre Beregovoy would have to step down. On **Mar. 29,** Pres. François Mitterrand, a Socialist, named as premier Edouard Balladur, a member of the neo-Gaullist Rally for the Republic party.

**Israel's Likud Bloc Names New Leader** — The Likud bloc, the principal opposition party in Israel, elected a new leader in March. After Likud was defeated by the Labor party in the 1992 election, the outgoing prime minister, Yitzhak Shamir, announced that he would step down as party leader. On **Mar. 25,** Likud members chose Benjamin Netanyahu, a former deputy foreign minister, as their new leader in a nationwide primary. At age 43, he was a generation younger than most prominent Israeli political leaders.

### General

**Gene Linked to Lou Gehrig's Disease** — The British journal *Nature* reported, **Mar. 4,** that the gene whose mutation caused amyotrophic lateral sclerosis (ALS) had been identified. The disorder, also known as Lou Gehrig's disease for the baseball player who was one of its most prominent victims, causes muscles to waste away and leads to death for most patients within 5 years. Dr. Robert Horovitz of the Massachusetts Institute of Technology, one of the authors of the report, called the discovery "a major breakthrough," but he added, "at this point we do not have a therapy."

**Eastern U.S. Storm Claims 200 Lives** — A massive storm swept through the Southeast and up the East Coast, **Mar. 13** and **14.** Described by the National Weather Service as one of the worst storms of the century, the onslaught left 13 inches of snow in Birmingham, Ala., and 36 inches in Syracuse, N.Y. Dozens of tornadoes were reported in the South. Power was cut off to millions of homes, thousands of families fled coastal flooding, and most forms of transportation were brought to a near-halt in many states. More than 200 deaths were attributed to the storm.

**Huntington's Disease Gene Identified** — In a report published in the journal *Cell,* **Mar. 26,** scientists from the U.S., England, and Wales said that they had identified the gene responsible for Huntington's disease. The disease, which afflicts about 30,000 Americans every year, involves degeneration of the basal ganglia, 2 nerve clusters in the brain. Symptoms include rapid and involuntary motion, dementia, personality changes, and memory loss. Huntington's is incurable and is usually fatal within 20 years. Researchers said that although the discovery was a major breakthrough, no treatment for the disease was imminent.

### APRIL

#### National

**Texas Cult's Compound Burns, 72 Die**— The confrontation between the Branch Davidians and law-enforcement officials ended tragically in April when the religious cult's compound near Waco, Tex., burned to the ground. At least 72 died in the inferno. A lawyer, Dick DeGuerin, visited the compound, **Mar. 29-Apr. 1,** to meet with his client, David Koresh, the leader of the cult. DeGuerin said that Koresh had been wounded in the initial federal assault on the compound in February and appeared to need medical treatment. Hopes, sometimes based on assurances by Koresh, that he would lead his followers out of the compound peacefully were repeatedly dashed. On **Apr. 14,** he said they would come out after he had completed a manuscript on the seven seals mentioned in the Book of Revelations in the Bible. On the morning of **Apr. 19,** the 51st day of the siege, Koresh said that there were 95 people in the compound. A total of 37 others had left since the confrontation began. On that day, the FBI decided to make a move. Bob Ricks, a senior FBI agent, said that an aide to Koresh had been told that the FBI intended to pump tear gas into the compound. Shortly after 6 a.m., armored vehicles moved forward, knocked holes in the walls of the compound, and released tear gas inside. The FBI said that those inside responded with gunfire. Shortly after 12 p.m., flames appeared at a window. The fire spread rapidly, and the compound was leveled within 30 minutes. Nine persons fled from the compound during the fire. When the site cooled, no one else was found alive. Two cultists who had escaped claimed that there had been no plans for a mass suicide and that the fire had been started when one of the armored vehicles had knocked over a container of fuel. Attorney Gen. Janet Reno said, **Apr. 19,** that she made the decision to move on the compound because agents surrounding it lacked adequate replacements, negotiations with Koresh had proved frustrating, and the FBI reported that babies in the compound were being beaten. Pres. Bill Clinton said, **Apr. 19,** that he stood by Reno's decision, and he said, **Apr. 20,** that he bore "full responsibility" for the result. Arson investigators concluded, **Apr. 26,** that the fire had been deliberately set by those inside the compound. Authorities said, **Apr. 29,** that 72 had died in the fire based on remains that had been found. They said it was possible other bodies had been completely incinerated. It was believed that 17 of the victims were children. The remains of 5 cultists killed in the February assault on the compound were also found.

**Clinton Stimulus Plan Fails in Senate** — Pres. Bill Clinton's $16.3 billion economic stimulus package was defeated by a filibuster by Senate Republicans in April. Republicans complained that the package, part of the president's economic-recovery program, emphasized low-priority projects, including aid to cities, summer jobs, and highway construction, without providing financing. Clinton charged, **Apr. 2,** that the Republican Senate minority was perpetuating gridlock. By **Apr. 6,** when the Senate began a recess, the Democrats had failed 3 times to end the filibuster. Clinton, **Apr. 8,** submitted to Congress a $1.52 trillion budget for the 1994 fiscal year (Oct. 1, 1993-Sept. 30, 1994) that reflected proposals in his February address to Congress. His budget projected a deficit of $264.1 billion in 1994, down from a likely deficit of $322 billion in 1993. The budget called for additional revenue of $296.2 billion over 5 years, mostly from increased income taxes on wealthy individuals and on corporations and an energy tax. Military spending would be reduced. Senate Democrats, **Apr. 21,** gave up their efforts to cut off the Republican filibuster on the stimulus package. However, the Senate did then give its approval, by voice vote, to one part of the plan, which provided $4 billion in extended jobless benefits for the long-term unemployed. The House also approved the benefits, **Apr. 22.**

**Economic Growth Rate Slows** — A report issued in late April suggested that the economic recovery was losing momentum. The Labor Dept. reported, **Apr. 2,** that the unemployed rate in March was 7 percent for the second consecutive month. The department said, **Apr. 8,** that the prices charged by producers for finished goods had risen 0.4 percent in March. Consumer prices rose only 0.1 percent in March, the department reported, **Apr. 9.** The Commerce Dept. said, **Apr. 16,** that the U.S. trade deficit had been $7.2 billion in February. The Japanese yen, which had appreciated by 12 percent in relation to the U.S. dollar since January, reached a record high, **Apr. 22,** when it stood at 109.95 to the dollar. The weaker dollar had the potential advantage of making U.S. products more attractive to Japanese buyers. To prevent the dollar from tumbling further, however, the Federal Reserve Bank of New York reportedly sold yen for dollars, **Apr. 27,** and brought the yen's surge to a halt, at least temporarily.

**Clinton Attends Summit on Forests** — Pres. Bill Clinton convened a meeting in Portland, Ore., **Apr. 2,** that sought to determine what should be done with the remaining old-growth forests occupying portions of Washington, Oregon, and northern California. In 1991, a federal court decided in favor of environmentalists, in a suit against the Interior Dept. The court held that the government had failed to protect the habitat of the northern spotted owl, an endangered species, and thus ordered a halt to all logging in the area. Loggers and their families, appearing at the summit in Portland, pleaded with Clinton, Vice Pres. Al Gore, and 4 cabinet secretaries who were present to devise a plan to permit cutting of the forests to resume. Representatives of environmental organizations argued that the loggers would soon run out of the old trees and that what was left should be saved. Spokespeople for the salmon industry said that logging had caused so much environmental damage to streams that their livelihood was also at risk. Clinton said he would seek a balanced solution to the controversy.

**Ten Die at Ohio Prison** — Nine inmates and a hostage died in April during an outbreak of violence at the Southern Ohio Correctional Facility near Lucasville, Ohio's only maximum security prison. On **Apr. 11,** 8 guards were taken hostage after they sought to break up a fight among inmates in the prison's recreational yard. Prison officials, police, and the National Guard began an 11-day siege of 450 barricaded prisoners, who demanded improvements in conditions within the prison. On **Apr. 12,** the prisoners released the bodies of 6 inmates who appeared to have been fatally beaten by other inmates. Another inmate was found dead the following day in an adjoining cell block. On **Apr. 14,** the prisoners warned they would kill a hostage if their demands were ignored, and the body of a slain guard was left outside the cell block, **Apr. 15.** In an agreement signed **Apr. 21,** Warden Arthur Tate promised to review inmate complaints. The prisoners then surrendered. The bodies of 2 more inmates were found inside the prison.

**Gay-Rights Advocates March in Capital** — A gay-rights march and rally in Washington, D.C., in April drew at least several hundred thousand demonstrators. Earlier, on **Apr. 16,** Pres. Bill Clinton met with gay and lesbian leaders in the White House in the first meeting of its kind involving an incumbent president. Clinton reportedly reaffirmed his commitment to lifting the ban on service by homosexuals in the U.S. military. Attendance at the **Apr. 25** march in Washington was put at 300,000 to 1 million. Participants called for an end to the military ban, more money to fight AIDS, and a civil-rights bill for gays.

**L.A. Calm After Verdicts in King Case** — Los Angeles remained quiet in April after a federal jury found 2 police officers guilty and two others not guilty of violating the civil rights of Rodney King, a black motorist whom they had arrested and beaten in 1991. In April 1992 the 4 Los Angeles policemen, all white, had been acquitted of all but one of the state charges brought as a result of the beating of King. That verdict had been followed by widespread urban rioting that left 52 dead and caused $1 billion in property damages. In the second trial, prosecutors had to prove that the accused had intended to deny King his constitutional rights. As in 1992, the principal evidence was an 81-second videotape, made by a man who lived near the site of the incident, which showed that the policemen struck King with their batons more than 50 times and kicked him as he lay on the ground. The defense contended that the blows were appropriate because King was putting up resistance. King testified, **Mar. 9,** that an officer had threatened to kill him and that in resisting, "I was just trying to stay alive, sir." Sgt. Stacey Koon, one of the defendants, testified, **Mar. 24,** that every blow struck had complied with police department policy. The jury, which included 2 blacks and 1 Hispanic, returned its verdict **Apr. 17.** They found Officer Laurence Powell, who had delivered most of the blows, guilty of violating King's right to be free from an arrest made with unreasonable force. Koon, the ranking officer present, was convicted of allowing the violation to occur. The other defendants, Theodore Briseno and Timothy Wind, were acquitted. After the verdict was reached, but before it was announced, 6,500 police officers, supported by National Guard troops, were mobilized throughout Los Angeles. They were not needed, however, and it appeared that most people accepted the split verdict.

**Alabama Governor Convicted** — Gov. Guy Hunt of Alabama, a Republican, was convicted, **Apr. 22,** of diverting money from an inaugural fund to his personal use, a felony. A circuit court jury in Montgomery delivered the verdict. The case involved $200,000 from Hunt's nonprofit inaugural fund that he had transferred to personal bank accounts and then spent. Hunt denied wrongdoing, and his lawyers planned an appeal based on the vagueness of the law; however, it was unlikely that the Alabama Court of Criminal Appeals would rule on the case before Hunt's term expires in January 1995. Required by state law to resign after his conviction, Hunt did so, **Apr. 22,** and he was succeeded as governor by Lt. Gov. Jim Folsom, Jr., a Democrat. Hunt was sentenced, **May 7,** to pay $211,000 in fines and restitution and perform 1,000 hours of community service.

**Tailhook Report Says 90 Were Assaulted** — A report released by the Defense Dept., **Apr. 23,** said that 83 women and 7 men were assaulted during the 1991 Tailhook Association convention at the Las Vegas Hilton. (The association's members are present and former Navy fliers.) The 300-page report, prepared by acting Pentagon Deputy Inspector General Derek Vander Schaaf, was based on more than 2,900 interviews. Up to 175 officers could face disciplinary action as a result of their conduct. The report said that victims were "groped, pinched, fondled" and "bitten" by their assailants and that oral sex and sexual intercourse performed in front of others contributed to a "general atmosphere of debauchery." In its latest report on the scandal, the Pentagon said that "Tailhook '91 is the culmination of a long-term failure of leadership in naval aviation."

**Women Eligible for Aerial Combat** — Women became eligible in April to pilot combat aircraft and to serve on fighter and bomber crews in all 4 branches of the U.S. armed forces. On **Apr. 28,** Defense Sec. Les Aspin, rejecting recommendations by a presidential panel in 1992 that a ban be continued, removed restrictions on aerial combat roles by women in the Air Force, Army, Marines, and Navy. He said he would also recommend that Congress lift a prohibition on participation in combat by women on most ships in the Navy.

## International

**Foreign Aid, Russian Voters Give Yeltsin a Lift** — Russia's beleaguered president, Boris Yeltsin, strengthened his hand in April by obtaining promises of international financial assistance and by getting a vote of confidence in a national referendum. Pres. Bill Clinton said, **Apr. 1**, that support for the Yeltsin government was related to continued domestic U.S. economic growth. Yeltsin was embroiled in a power struggle with conservatives sympathetic with the former communist regime. Great Britain, **Apr. 1**, and Canada, **Apr. 2**, announced packages of financial aid to Russia. Representatives of Russia and its creditor nations agreed in Paris, **Apr. 2**, to reschedule about 75 percent of the $20 billion Russia owed in principal and interest in 1993. Clinton and Yeltsin met at a summit in Vancouver, Canada, **Apr. 3** and **4**. Clinton pledged $1.6 billion in aid. Of this, $894 million consisted of credits and grants for food. Other large sums would help Russia launch investment initiatives and dismantle and store elements of its nuclear arsenal. The Group of 7 nations—the world's leading industrial democracies—announced a $28.4 billion package of aid at a meeting in Tokyo, **Apr. 15**. In their communiqué, the G7 nations stated that continued democratic reform in Russia was "essential to world peace." The U.S. and Japan also announced separate commitments of $1.8 billion, the U.S. pledge being in addition to Clinton's previous promise of support. In the **Apr. 25** referendum, 58 percent of the voters declared that they had confidence in Yeltsin, and 53 percent said they approved of his social and economic policies. A court had held that a simple majority of those voters actually participating in the referendum would be sufficient to decide those 2 questions. Proposals for early parliamentary and presidential elections failed. Yeltsin, **Apr. 29**, proposed a new constitution that would abolish the Congress of People's Deputies and create a 2-chamber parliament. Under Yeltsin's draft, the president would have the power to disband parliament and call new elections in certain circumstances.

**Macedonia Joins U.N.** — On **Apr. 8**, Macedonia became a member of the U.N. under the formal, but temporary, designation as The Former Yugoslav Republic of Macedonia. A permanent name would be the subject of negotiations with Greece, which had expressed concerns that the use of the name "Macedonia" indicated that the new country was eyeing the territory of the Greek province of Macedonia.

**U.S. Planes Bomb Iraqi Positions** — Four U.S. planes patrolling the no-fly zone in northern Iraq, **Apr. 9**, were fired on by Iraqi antiaircraft guns, U.S. officials reported. The U.S. planes then bombed the Iraqi positions. Iraq denied initiating the exchange. No U.S. planes were damaged.

**Black South African Leader Assassinated** — Chris Hani, a secretary general of the South African Communist Party and a leader of the African National Congress, was shot fatally in the driveway of his home in a Johannesburg suburb, **Apr. 10**. Januzu Walus, a Pole who had become a South African citizen, was seized by police, and a pistol in his possession was identified as the weapon used in the assassination. On **Apr. 14**, designated as a day of mourning for Hani, as many as 8 people were killed and hundreds injured as demonstrations turned violent. Clive Derby-Lewis, a

leader of the Conservative Party, was arrested, **Apr. 17**, in connection with Hani's death. More than 80,000 attended Hani's funeral, **Apr. 19**, and 4 million black workers went on strike for the day. On **Apr. 21**, 5 more people were held in connection with the assassination. Two were questioned and released.

**Bosnian Serbs Reject Peace Plan** — The self-proclaimed Bosnian Serb parliament in Bijeljina rejected in late April the U.N.-supported peace plan that would divide Bosnia and Herzegovina into regions based on ethnic makeup. The military situation in Bosnia had grown more complex, **Apr. 16**, when an alliance between Muslims and Croats broke down and they began to fight each other. The U.N. Security Council, **Apr. 17**, reaffirmed sanctions against the Yugoslav Federation—Serbia and Montenegro—for its support of the Bosnian Serb forces. A ceasefire agreement signed, **Apr. 18**, by Serbs and the Muslim defenders of Srebrenica provided that the town become a "safe area" for civilians under U.N. auspices. Yugoslav leaders, **Apr. 26**, urged the Bosnian Serbs to endorse the U.N. peace plan, but the Bosnian Serb parliament voted unanimously that day not to approve it. Pres. Bill Clinton, **Apr. 26**, committed the U.S. to the support of the U.N. sanctions, which went into effect **Apr. 27**. The sanctions froze Yugoslav assets abroad and banned shipment in or out of Yugoslavia, by land or water, of most products. The Serbian parliament in Belgrade, **Apr. 28**, endorsed the U.N. peace plan.

**Clinton, Miyazawa Disagree on Trade** — Pres. Bill Clinton and Japanese Prime Minister Kiichi Miyazawa failed to see eye to eye on trade issues when they met at the White House, **Apr. 16**. Clinton supported a policy of managed trade, in which market-share goals would be established in the Japanese market for products from the U.S. and other countries. Miyazawa rejected this concept and said later at a news conference that free trade "cannot be realized with managed trade . . . " Clinton had also asserted during their meeting that Japan did not have an open market and that hidden barriers turned away exports to Japan.

**Italians Vote for Government Reforms** — Allegations of corruption involving many leading Italian politicians produced a backlash in April. In a referendum held **Apr. 18** and **19**, 82 percent of voters endorsed an end to strict proportional representation in the Senate, the upper parliamentary chamber. Proportionality meant that even very small parties could gain representation. Weak and unstable coalition governments were the result. Legislation would be required to end proportional representation in the Chamber of Deputies, the lower parliamentary body. In other referendum results, voters also supported, overwhelmingly, an end to state financing for political parties. Premier Giuliano Amato, a Socialist, submitted his resignation, **Apr. 22**. Seven of his ministers had been touched by scandal. Pres. Oscar Luigi Scalfaro, **Apr. 26**, chose Carlo Azeglio Ciampi, the central bank governor and a political independent, as Amato's successor. Ciampi's broad-based government took office **Apr. 29**. Ciampi's government was immediately threatened when the Chamber of Deputies resisted lifting the immunity of former Socialist Premier Bettino Craxi, so he could be charged in 6 separate corruption cases. The Chamber eventually relented and lifted immunity for the least serious of the allegations.

**IRA Bomb Rocks London Financial District** — The Irish Republican Army claimed responsibility for a bomb that exploded, **Apr. 24**, in the financial district of London. One man was killed and 45 other people were injured. A 500-year-old church was destroyed, and many buildings were damaged. Despite the displacement of over 20,000 workers, the financial markets reopened Monday, Apr. 26. Later that day the police announced that more than 10 people had been arrested in connection with the bombing.

## General

**Doubt Cast on Value of AIDS Drug** — A report published Apr. 3 called into question the value of the drug AZT in combatting the onset of AIDS symptoms. The U.S. government had recommended the use of AZT by persons infected with the AIDS virus who had not yet developed any symptoms. But the new study showed that the drug did not slow the rate of progression to AIDS or death, when groups who did and did not take AZT were compared. The survey was sponsored by the Medical Research Council of Britain and the National AIDS Research Agency of France.

**Parasite Blamed for Illnesses in Milwaukee** — Many thousands of people became ill in Milwaukee in March and April, and city health officials said, Apr. 7, that a parasite was apparently the culprit. They believed that the parasite, cryptosporidium, had contaminated the city's water supply. It appeared that the protozoan was contained in animal feces washed into Lake Michigan, the city's reservoir. City residents were advised to boil drinking water. Symptoms, including nausea and diarrhea, usually lasted 7 to 10 days, but 6 deaths were attributed to the parasite. Estimates of those who became ill ran as high as 281,000.

**Queen Opens Palace to Tourists** — Queen Elizabeth II announced, Apr. 29, that for 8 weeks beginning in Aug. tourists would be able to enter parts of Buckingham Palace, her residence in London. Admission fees would help pay the cost—put as high as $62 million—of repairing Windsor Castle, which had been damaged by a fire in 1992.

## MAY

### National

**Body of Cult Leader Identified** — Investigators said, May 2, that they had identified the body of David Koresh, leader of the Branch Davidian cult who had died with scores of his followers when a fire destroyed their compound near Waco, Tex., in April. Aside from being badly burned, the body had a bullet wound in the middle of the forehead. It appeared that Koresh was fatally shot prior to the fire's destruction of the compound. A team of therapists reported, May 3, on their interviews with 19 of the 21 children who had left the compound during the 7 weeks it was under siege. (Two children, ages 7 months and 3 years, were too young to be interviewed.) The therapists said that the children had been beaten and deprived of food as a means of discipline. Children said Koresh had "wives" as young as 11. Investigators of the fire reported, May 4, at least 24 of the victims' bodies had bullet wounds.

**Gay Issues Remain in Public Focus** — Issues involving homosexuality remained prominent in May. On May 3, Airman Apprentice Terry Helvey pleaded guilty to murder with intent to do great bodily harm in the death, in October 1992, of a shipmate, Allen Schindler. At that time, both were serving on the *Belleau Wood*. Schindler had made it known that he was gay, and he was due to be discharged. While the ship was anchored in Sasebo, Japan, Helvey and another shipmate, Charles Vins, encountered Schindler in a public toilet, and Schindler was beaten to death. Vins pleaded guilty to reduced charges and testified against Helvey. Gay-rights leaders denounced the death of Schindler as a bias crime and charged that the Navy was trying to cover up the incident. Helvey gave different accounts of his motivation. His trial was held at the Yokosuko Naval Base near Tokyo. Meanwhile, Sen. Sam Nunn (D, Ga.), chairman of the Armed Services Committee, was conducting hearings on Pres. Bill Clinton's proposal to lift the ban on homosexuals serving in the U.S. military. He and other senators visited the Norfolk Naval Base, May 10, and Nunn said that the close quarters in which sailors had to live on ships would cause tense situations between heterosexuals and homosexuals. On May 24 the Senate approved, 58-31, Clinton's appointment of Roberta Achtenberg as assistant secretary for fair housing and equal opportunity in the Dept. of Housing and Urban Development. She was the first open homosexual to be appointed to a position requiring Senate approval. Helvey, May 27, was sentenced to life in prison.

**Data Raise Concerns on Inflation** — Government statistics released in May helped revise concerns about inflation. The Commerce Dept. reported, May 4, that the index of leading economic indicators had declined by 1 percent in March, the sharpest drop since November 1990. The Labor Dept. said, May 7, that the unemployment rate had remained at an even 7 percent in April, for the 3d straight month. The department reported, May 12, that prices charged by producers for finished goods had jumped 0.6 percent in April. This increase, the largest for any month since October 1990, was attributed in part to the inclement weather that had driven up the cost of fruit and vegetables. The Labor Dept. announced, May 13, that consumer prices had risen 0.4 percent in April. On Wall Street, the Dow Jones industrial average broke through a new barrier and closed, May 19, at an all-time high of 3500.03. By May 27 the average stood at 3554.83.

**Congress Approves 'Motor-Voter' Bill** — The House, May 5, and the Senate, May 11, approved a bill establishing new opportunities for citizens to register to vote. Under the bill, often called the "motor-voter" bill, citizens would be able, in any state, to register to vote when applying for a driver's license. They could also register at welfare and disability benefits offices, and could obtain registration forms at military recruitment stations. Registration by mail would be allowed in any state. Clinton signed the bill May 20.

**7th Man Charged in Trade Center Bombing** — A 7th man was charged, May 6, in connection with the bombing in February at the World Trade Center in New York City. Authorities said that the latest suspect, Mohammad Ahmad Ajaj, had arrived in the U.S. in September 1992 carrying instructions on how to construct a bomb like the one used in New York. Five other suspects linked to the bombing were also in custody, and one remained at large.

**'Star Wars' Defense Plan Abandoned** — Defense Sec. Les Aspin announced, May 13, that research on the Strategic Defense Initiative—better known as Star Wars—would be discontinued. Pres. Ronald Reagan had proposed SDI in 1983. The program envisioned creation of a defensive shield against incoming missiles, and $30 billion had been spent on research over 10 years. Aspin said that the study of ground-based defenses against missiles would continue under a scaled-down Ballistic Missile Defense Organization.

**Ex-Reagan Aide to Advise Clinton** — Pres. Bill Clinton in May appointed David Gergen, who was once an assistant to Pres. Ronald Reagan, to an advisory position in the White House. Clinton had found it difficult to keep public attention focused on his economic and other major policy initiatives, while peripheral controversies seemed to dominate news out of his administration. The dismissal of 7 staff members in the White House travel office had proved to be embarrassing. On May 18, Clinton received a haircut, which reportedly cost $200, while Air Force One sat on a runway at the Los Angeles International Airport for an hour, tying up other planes. The president's approval ratings had declined sharply. On **May 29**, Clinton announced that Gergen would serve as an adviser with the title of counselor to the president. Gergen had served as Reagan's communications director in the early 1980s and was, at the time of his appointment, an editor for *U.S. News and World Report* and a television commentator. Gergen was registered as an independent and had known Clinton for some time. Clinton also announced that George Stephanopoulos would step aside as his communications director and concentrate on development of policy.

**White House Travel Office Center of Furor** — The White House announced, **May 19**, that the 7 staff members of the White House travel office had been dismissed. Dee Dee Myers, White House press secretary, said that an accounting firm had found evidence of "gross mismanagement" in the office and that the FBI was investigating. The White House said, **May 19**, that a distant cousin of Pres. Bill Clinton, Catherine Cornelius, would assume temporary control of the office. The White House acknowledged, **May 21**, that Cornelius had sought in February to have herself put in charge of the travel office. It was also acknowledged that a partner of Harry Thomason, a television producer and a friend of the president, had sought without success to get White House business for a charter airplane consulting firm. On **May 21**, the White House also announced that World Wide Travel Inc., a company based in Little Rock, had voluntarily withdrawn as coordinator of operations at the travel office. Three executives of the company, which had been brought in after the dismissals, had contributed to Clinton's 1992 campaign. It was learned, **May 24**, that members of the White House staff had asked the FBI to rewrite a report on the travel office to make it supportive of the firings. The White House announced, **May 25**, that 5 of those dismissed would be placed on paid leave pending completion of the investigation.

**House OKs Deficit-Reduction Package** — The U.S. House of Representatives gave a boost to Pres. Bill Clinton's deficit-reduction program in May, passing the so-called budget reconciliation bill. The legislation, which projected a total reduction in the federal government's anticipated budget deficits of about $500 billion by 1998, was debated intensely throughout the month. Many Democrats insisted on strict controls on spending entitlement programs and a mechanism was incorporated into the bill requiring Congress and the president to act if entitlement spending significantly exceeded targets set in annual budget resolutions. The text of the bill did not specify some of the spending cuts that would be made in order for the deficit-reduction goals to be met. A key feature of the bill was an energy tax, which would be levied on all fuels based on their energy content in British thermal units (Btu's). A group of senators from both parties, led by David Boren (D, Okla.), signaled that the bill would face difficulty in the Senate when they insisted, **May 20**, on deeper spending cuts and fewer tax increases. Boren also opposed the Btu tax. With vigorous lobbying by Clinton and his aides, the bill barely got approval in the House, **May 27**, by a vote of 219 to 213; 38 Democrats and all voting Republicans opposed it. Ross Perot, an independent candidate for president in 1992, also opposed what he called Clinton's "tax and spend" program, and on **May 30** he also ran a 30-minute commercial on television denouncing the North American Free Trade Agreement, which Clinton supported. Perot said if NAFTA was approved, millions of U.S. jobs would be lost to Mexico.

**Ex-Policeman Acquitted in Deaths of 2 Blacks** — A former Miami police officer was acquitted in Orlando, Fla., **May 28**, on 2 manslaughter counts in the deaths of 2 men in 1989. The policeman, William Lozano, was Hispanic, and the 2 men who were killed were black. The victims were on a motorcycle being chased by a police car. Lozano shot and killed the driver, and the passenger was injured fatally in the subsequent crash of the cycle. The deaths had triggered serious rioting in Miami. Lozano was convicted of manslaughter in 1989, but an appeals court overturned the result in 1991, contending that the jury might have feared that more rioting would have followed an acquittal. At the second trial, the defense contended that Lozano had acted in self-defense. The acquittal in Orlando resulted in only sporadic violence in Miami; 5 people were reported injured, and more than 60 were arrested.

### International

**President of Sri Lanka Assassinated** — Pres. Ranasinghe Premadasa of Sri Lanka was assassinated in May. Earlier, on **Apr. 23**, opposition leader Lalith Athulathmudali had also been assassinated, during a campaign rally. The gunman fled, but police, **Apr. 24**, produced the body of a man they said was the killer. On May Day, **May 1**, during a parade in Colombo, the capital, a suicide bomber riding a bicycle set off explosives strapped to his body that killed a total of 24 people, including the president and the bomber. Within hours, Prime Minister Dingiri Banda Wijetunge was sworn in as president. Although the Liberation Tigers of Tamil Eelam denied responsibility, the government blamed the Tamil separatist organization.

**Bosnian Serb Voters Defiant in Referendum** — The Bosnian Serb parliament—for the 3d time—and Bosnian Serb voters, in a referendum, rejected a U.N. peace plan for Bosnia and Herzegovina in May. Radovan Karadzic, leader of the Bosnian Serbs, signed the Vance-Owen peace plan, **May 2**, but said his assent was subject to the approval of the self-proclaimed Bosnian Serb parliament. The parliament turned down the plan, **May 6**, but voted to submit it to a referendum of all Bosnian Serbs. Pres. Slobodan Milosevic of Serbia, **May 6**, ordered a halt to the delivery of arms and fuel to the Bosnian Serbs. The U.N. Security Council, **May 6**, declared Sarajevo, the Bosnian capital, and 5 other cities that were Muslim strongholds to be "safe areas" where noncombatants could seek safety from Serb forces. The Council voted to send 50 military monitors to each city. European foreign ministers, meeting in Brussels, **May 10**, turned down Pres. Bill Clinton's proposal to increase pressure on the Bosnian Serbs, including air strikes on Serb positions and the rearming of the Muslims. Milosevic, **May 11**, urged cancellation of the forthcoming referendum and attempted to call a meeting of legislators from all the Serbian populated areas of the Balkans. In the **May 15-16** referendum, 96 percent of the 1.1 million Bosnian Serbs polled voted against the peace plan and, according to the announced results, the same percentage favored the creation of an independent Serb state within Bosnia. Karadzic, **May 16**, declared the peace plan to be dead and declared that he now represented Republic Srpska—the new Serb state. On **May 18**, however, Muslims and Croats in Bosnia agreed to a cease-fire and to some of the terms of the peace plan. On **May 22**, France, Great Britain, Russia, Spain, and the U.S. approved a joint policy calling for a negotiated settlement of the war. Alija Izetbegovic, the Muslim president of Bosnia, rejected negotiations, **May 23**. The U.N. Security Council, **May 25**, voted unanimously to establish a war-crimes tribunal, capable of imposing prison terms, to deal with atrocities in the war.

**U.S. Gives U.N. Control in Somalia** — May 4 saw the conclusion of the first phase of the relief mission in Somalia. Lieut. Gen. Robert Johnston of the U.S. Marine Corps handed authority to Lieut. Gen. Cevik Bir of Turkey, the U.N. military commander. This was the first time U.S. troops served under U.N. leadership. The U.S.-led mission, begun in December, had essentially cleared the streets of the cities of weapons, and the distribution of food had brought an end to mass starvation. Clan warfare, starvation, and disease had claimed 350,000 lives in Somalia in 1992. The U.N.-controlled force was projected to reach 28,000 troops, including 5,000 Americans.

**State-Owned Enterprises Privatized in Poland** — The Polish parliament completed action, May 7, on legislation to transfer control of 600 state-owned enterprises to investment funds. Shares in the funds would be distributed to adult Poles at a nominal charge. At the insistence of former Communist deputies and some members of the right-wing National Christian Union, distribution would be free to pensioners and to civil servants who had not gotten pay increases in 1991. Financiers from Western countries would manage the funds. With the legislation's approval, the World Bank authorized $750 million in new loans to Poland.

**Denmark Approves European Union Treaty** — Danish citizens, voting in a referendum May 18, reversed a position they had taken a year earlier and ratified, by a 57 percent majority, the Maastricht treaty on greater European unity. The Danish government had won concessions from its partners in the European Community, allowing Denmark to opt out of closer cooperation on defense and monetary matters. The treaty, previously given final ratification by 9 other of the EC's 12 members, still awaited final approval in Great Britain and faced potential legal challenges in Germany.

**Venezuelan President Faces Corruption Trial** — The Supreme Court of Venezuela ruled, May 20, that grounds existed to try Pres. Carlos Andrés Pérez for misappropriating $17 million in government funds. The Senate, May 21, authorized the Court to try Pérez, who was suspended from office. The president of the Senate, Octavio Lepage, became acting president. The Venezuelan Congress had 30 days to elect a president to serve until Feb. 2, 1994, the end of Pérez's term.

**Cardinal Shot to Death in Mexico** — Cardinal Juan Jesús Posadas Ocampo, the archbishop of Guadalajara, Mex., was shot to death at Guadalajara's international airport, May 24. He had been driven to the airport in a limousine, and was to welcome a representative from the Vatican. His car was caught in a shootout between members of 2 drug cartels, and he may have been mistaken for a leader of a cartel. Six other people were killed. Police detained 2 suspects, but most of the gunmen got away.

**Bomb Kills 5 at Museum in Florence** — A car bomb exploded, May 27, near the renowned Uffizi Gallery in Florence, Italy, one of Europe's greatest art museums. Five people were killed and about two dozen injured. Three paintings by relatively minor artists were destroyed and about 30 were damaged. Masterpieces by Botticelli and Michelangelo survived behind shatterproof glass. Authorities believed that the Florence explosion and other recent terrorist acts were the work of the Mafia, which might be signaling that it had not been crippled by the recent roundup of hundreds of alleged mobsters.

**British Leader Shakes Up Cabinet** — British Prime Minister John Major made changes in his cabinet, May 27, in the face of continued national economic stress. More than 10 percent of the work force was unemployed, and Major's popularity ratings were low. The prime minister replaced Chancellor of the Exchequer Norman Lamont with Kenneth Clarke, the former home secretary. Michael Howard, former secretary of state for the environment, would succeed Clarke at the Home Office. Major announced several other changes among his ministers.

**Germany Tightens Asylum Policy** — Germany's parliament completed action, May 28, on constitutional changes that would restrict access to persons seeking asylum in Germany. More than 1 million persons seeking asylum had entered Germany in the past 4 years, and about 1.8 million Turks had been admitted as "guest workers." Under the changed policy, Germany would rebuff would-be immigrants from nations that Germany deemed free of persecution, and asylum-seekers crossing Germany's land borders would be turned back. On May 29, 5 members of a Turkish family in Solingen were killed when their home was firebombed. Attacks on foreigners in Germany were reportedly up sharply in 1993.

**Clinton Compromises on China Trade** — Pres. Bill Clinton, May 28, extended most-favored-nation trading status for China for one year. Most U.S. trading partners are granted MFN, which provides relatively low tariffs for imports into the U.S. In a compromise that sought to mollify both U.S. business interests and human-rights advocates, Clinton conditioned MFN on improvement in China's human rights record, including the release of political prisoners and better treatment for prisoners. China's trading status would be reviewed again in 1994.

### General

**Man Convicted in Assault With Condom** — In a decision that advocates of women's rights hailed as a victory, a Texas man was found guilty of aggravated sexual assault, May 13, despite his claims that a woman had consented, in effect, to having sex when she gave him 2 condoms. The defendant, Joel Rene Valdez, admitted that he entered her bedroom without permission and that he was carrying a knife. He testified that he had consumed a case of beer. The woman testified that there was little that she could do to prevent an attack and that she asked him to use a condom because she feared for her life and feared that she might contract the virus that causes AIDS. The trial was held in Travis County Court in Austin.

**Defender of Home Freed in Killing** — A Louisiana man who said he was defending his home against someone he perceived to be an intruder was acquitted, May 23, by a jury in Baton Rouge in the shooting death of a 16-year-old Japanese exchange student. The youth, Yoshihiro Hattori, and his American host had come to the home of Rodney Peairs, seeking the location of a party, and had rung the doorbell. Peairs answered the door armed with a gun, and when Hattori, who spoke little English, failed to respond to Peairs' command to freeze, Peairs shot him. Peairs' lawyer contended that his client had the "absolute right" to answer a door holding a gun. The verdict provoked anger in Japan, where shootings were rare.

**Mystery Illness Fatal to 10 in Southwest** — An unidentified illness with no known cause had taken 10 lives on or near the Navajo Reservation by May 29. Victims lived in Arizona, Colorado, and New Mexico. Eight of those who had died were Navajo. Twenty-three persons were being treated at hospitals in New Mexico. Symptoms were flulike and progressed quickly to a severe respiratory ailment. Four who became ill recovered after treatment with antibiotics.

## JUNE

### National

**Economic Data 'Flat' in June** — Statistics released by the government in June showed little improvement in the economy. The Commerce Dept. said, **June 2**, that the index of leading economic indicators had risen 0.1 percent in April. The Labor Dept., **June 4**, put the unemployment rate at 6.9 percent in May, a decline of 0.1 percent. The department said, **June 11**, that prices charged by producers for finished goods remained unchanged in May. More encouraging news on inflation came, **June 15**, when the department said that consumer prices had risen only 0.1 percent in May. The Commerce Dept. said, **June 17**, that the merchandise trade deficit in April had been $10.49 billion, a 4-year high. Further discouraging news came with the department's announcement, **June 23**, of the final revision to the growth rate of the gross domestic product for the 1st quarter of 1993. The revision placed GDP growth at an annual rate of 0.7 percent, substantially lower than had been reported in April. Also, the department reported, **June 29**, that the index of leading economic indicators had dipped by 0.3 percent in May.

**Clinton Drops Justice Dept. Nominee** — On **June 3**, Pres. Bill Clinton withdrew his nomination of Lani Guinier to head the civil rights division of the Justice Dept. Guinier, whose father was black and whose mother was Jewish, was a professor of law at the Univ. of Pennsylvania and a friend of Bill and Hillary Rodham Clinton. After she had been nominated, conservatives had criticized her past discussion of means by which black voters could increase their influence in elections. In announcing his withdrawal of the nomination, **June 3**, Clinton said he had just read Guinier's articles and found them "difficult to defend." Guinier expressed frustration, **June 4**, at not being able to defend herself before the Senate. Black civil rights leaders sharply criticized Clinton's decision.

**Republicans Win 2 Key Elections** — Republicans took 2 major offices from the Democrats in June. On **June 5**, Texas state Treasurer Kay Bailey Hutchison was elected to the U.S. Senate. She defeated the incumbent Democrat, Bob Krueger, who had been appointed to the Senate by Gov. Ann Richards after Lloyd Bentsen resigned to become secretary of the Treasury. Hutchison, who won by a 2-1 margin, campaigned against Pres. Bill Clinton's economic program, particularly his proposed tax increases. On **June 8**, Richard Riordan, a businessman, defeated Michael Woo, a Democrat, and became the first Republican mayor of Los Angeles since 1961. Riordan, who spent $6 million of his own money in the campaign, ran as a tough opponent of crime. He would succeed Tom Bradley, a Democrat, who was retiring after 20 years as mayor.

**Clinton and Press Exchange Salvos** — Pres. Bill Clinton responded forcefully to tough questions from the press in June. On **June 7**, the White House announced that Mark Gearan, Clinton's deputy chief of staff, would become communications director. As part of an effort to mend fences with the press, which had given heavy coverage to administration misfortunes, the Clintons entertained 300 political journalists at a picnic at the White House, **June 13**. On **June 14**, Clinton rebuked a reporter who raised the issue of why it had taken so long for Clinton to fill a Supreme Court vacancy. During a **June 15** press conference, Clinton was asked if he could be accused of "wavering" on important policies, and he called his presidency "the most decisive . . . you've had in a very long time on all the big issues."

**Judge Ginsburg Nominated for Supreme Court** — Pres. Bill Clinton announced, **June 14**, that he was nominating Judge Ruth Bader Ginsburg of the U.S. Court of Appeals for the District of Columbia for a seat on the U.S. Supreme Court. If approved by the Senate, Ginsburg would succeed Justice Byron White, who had announced in March that he would retire at the end of the current court term. Since March, Clinton had reportedly come close to making other choices, and the selection of Ginsburg came as something of a surprise. A graduate of Columbia Law School, she had served as director of the Women's Rights Project of the American Civil Liberties Union. Ginsburg had won 5 of 6 gender-equality cases that she had argued before the Supreme Court. Pres. Jimmy Carter nominated her for the Court of Appeals in 1980. As a judge, she had taken generally moderate positions. On confirmation by the Senate, Ginsburg would become the high court's second woman justice and the first Jewish justice in 24 years.

**Senate Approves Clinton Budget Bill** — The Senate in June narrowly approved the budget bill that incorporated Pres. Bill Clinton's deficit-reduction program. The Democratic members of the Senate Finance Committee, **June 16**, abandoned the broad-based energy tax, the Btu tax, which Clinton had supported and which had been included in the bill approved by the House. The committee Democrats substituted a 4.3-cents-per-gallon tax increase on transportation fuels, which would yield far less revenue than the Btu tax. On **June 25** the Senate divided, 49-49, on the bill, with 2 Senators absent. All voting Republicans opposed it, and they were joined by 6 Democrats. The bill passed on the tie-breaking vote cast by Vice Pres. Al Gore. A conference committee would reconcile differences between the Senate and House versions of the bill.

**FBI Arrests 9 in 2d New York Bomb Plot** — On **June 24** the FBI arrested 8 men who, it was alleged, were plotting to bomb several sites in New York City and to assassinate the secretary general of the U.N., among others. The men were charged, **June 24**, with conspiracy in federal court in Manhattan, and 5 of them were charged with attempted bombing. Five of the men had come to the U.S. carrying Sudanese passports, and 6 worshipped at the mosque of Sheikh Omar Abdel Rahman. The sheikh had ties with several of the suspects charged in the bombing of the World Trade Center in February. Emad Salem, who had been a translator and bodyguard for the sheikh, was identified, **June 25**, as an informer who had secretly taped conversations among the alleged plotters. A 9th suspect was arrested and charged with conspiracy to transport explosives on **June 30**.

**More Military Bases Face Closure** — Concluding 5 days of deliberations, the Defense Base Closure and Realignment Commission recommended, **June 27**, that 33 major military installations be closed. Nearly 100 smaller bases would also be closed, and 45 others would be reduced in scale. The Defense Dept. estimated that the proposed closings and cutbacks would cause the loss of 120,000 jobs. Pres. Bill Clinton, **July 2**, approved the recommendations and proposed to spend $5 billion to assist communities affected by the commission's recommendations. Congressional approval was still needed.

**Judge's Ruling Delays Trade Pact** — U.S. Federal District Court Judge Charles Richey ruled, **June 30**, that the U.S. government must submit an environmental impact statement for the North American Free Trade Agreement. NAFTA, which had been ratified by Canada in early June, was to take effect in January 1994, assuming approval by the U.S. Congress and Mexican legislature, but the judge's ruling, if upheld on appeal, was expected to delay the approval process by several months. Many organizations opposed NAFTA because of concern about the loss of jobs in the U.S. and because of potential negative impacts on natural resources and human health.

## International

**Military Ousts Guatemala President** — Pres. Jorge Serrano Elías was forced from office in June. On May 25, he had instituted executive rule and imprisoned opponents to "purge the state of . . . corruption." International criticism followed, and Guatemala's business, labor, and academic communities united in opposition to the president's move. On June 1, the constitutional court urged implementation of its earlier ruling that the action by the president was unconstitutional. Later on June 1, Defense Minister Jose Domingo Garcia Samayoa announced that the armed forces, acting in response to appeals from the judiciary and the public, had forced Serrano out. On June 2, Serrano flew to El Salvador. On the night of June 5-6, Congress elected as president the nation's human rights ombudsman, Ramiro de Leon Carpio. On June 7 he dismissed the defense minister and reassigned several military commanders in an apparent effort to confirm civilian authority over the armed forces. Meanwhile, Serrano sought and received, asylum in Panama.

**Moderate Yugoslav President Ousted** — Pres. Dobrica Cosic of Yugoslavia was voted out of office by Parliament, June 1. Pres. Slobodan Milosevic of Serbia, the principal component of what was left of Yugoslavia, was a leader in the move to remove Cosic, who had angered Serbian hard-liners by urging Bosnian Serbs to accept an international peace plan. Eight U.S. military officers arrived, June 18, in The Former Yugoslav Republic of Macedonia to help plan the deployment of a U.N. force that would seek to prevent the Bosnian conflict from spreading into Macedonia. Representatives of the 3 factions in Bosnia and Herzegovina met in Geneva, June 23, to consider a Serb-Croat plan to divide the country into 3 autonomous areas based on ethnicity.

**Cambodia Parties to Share Power** — Two Cambodian parties that had received the most support in a U.N.-sponsored election agreed in June to share power. The election was the key element in the 1991 peace accord, under which the nation's 4 leading factions agreed to end their 14-year civil war. The voting for a constituent assembly was completed on May 28, and by early June tabulations showed that Funcinpec, the French acronym for the royalist party, had received more than 45 percent of the vote. The incumbent Cambodian People's Party (CPP) had 39 percent. On June 3, Prince Norodom Sihanouk, the nation's dominant political figure and former monarch, installed himself as prime minister and sought to form a coalition government between Funcinpec and the Vietnamese-installed CPP. Sihanouk named his son, Prince Norodom Ranariddh, the Funcinpec leader, and Hun Sen, the CPP leader, as co-equal deputy premiers. His son, however, balked at the arrangement in a message made public June 4, in which he said he could not work with those who, he charged, had assassinated members of the royalist party. The new constituent assembly, June 14, granted Prince Sihanouk the powers he deemed necessary to "save our nation." Ranariddh said, June 14, that the Khmer Rouge, a Communist faction that had imposed brutal rule on Cambodia in the past, was willing to give up the territory it controlled and drop its demand for a place in the government. On June 18, Ranariddh and Hun Sen agreed to serve as co-presidents and to divide up cabinet posts.

**U.S. Attacks Iraq Because of Plot to Kill Bush** — The U.S. fired missiles at Iraq's intelligence headquarters in Baghdad in June in retaliation for an Iraqi plot to kill former Pres. George Bush. Fourteen men charged in the plot went on trial in Kuwait, June 5. One testified, June 5, that Iraqi intelligence had trained them and ordered them to kill Bush during his visit to Kuwait in April. On June 26, in a televised speech, Pres. Bill Clinton said, "The Iraqi attack against President Bush was an attack against our country," and he announced that the U.S. had launched an attack on Iraq's intelligence complex. Early on June 27, Iraq time, 23 Tomahawk missiles had been fired from 2 U.S. ships in the Persian Gulf. The main headquarters building was badly damaged. Iraq said, June 27, that 8 people had been killed in the attack and a dozen wounded, and it denied the existence of a plot. On June 29, a U.S. plane fired on an Iraqi antiaircraft battery in the southern no-fly zone after it reportedly locked its radar on a U.S. squadron.

**U.S., Allies Attack Somali Warlord** — The level of conflict between U.N. peacekeeping forces and a Somali warlord escalated rapidly in June. On June 5, 23 Pakistani members of the peacekeeping force were killed in a series of attacks in Mogadishu, the capital, after the U.N. troops had inspected munitions depots controlled by Gen. Mohammed Farah Aidid. Aidid was the strongest of the warlords in the city and a key figure in the Somali civil war. Americans came to the rescue of the Pakistanis, and 3 were wounded. Although Aidid denied responsibility for the deaths of the peacekeepers, U.S. helicopters bombed 3 of his arms caches. The U.N. Security Council, June 6, condemned the attacks on the peacekeepers and demanded that those responsible be punished. On June 12, U.S. helicopters and gunships destroyed 4 of Aidid's arms depots. Ground troops from several countries then moved in to seize heavy weapons, ammunition, and 200 of Aidid's men. U.S. planes, June 13, attacked a compound owned by a financial supporter of Aidid. These actions were overshadowed, June 13, when Pakistanis fired into a crowd of demonstrators protesting the attacks on Aidid, killing 20 and wounding 50. On June 14 and 16, U.S. planes attacked other targets linked to Aidid, and on June 17, U.N. troops stormed his headquarters, but Aidid was not present.

**North Korea Reverses Itself on Nuclear Treaty** — North Korea announced in June that it would suspend its withdrawal from the Nuclear Nonproliferation Treaty. Although North Korea and the U.S. did not have diplomatic relations, delegations from the 2 nations met at the U.N. in early June. In a joint statement, issued June 11, they said that North Korea had decided to suspend its withdrawal. North Korea, however, did not agree to allow inspection of its nuclear-energy facilities, as mandated by the treaty. The statement said the 2 nations had pledged not to threaten or use force against each other and had promised not to interfere in each other's internal affairs.

**Woman Becomes Canada's Prime Minister** — Kim Campbell became Canada's 19th prime minister in June, and she also became the first woman to hold the office. Prime Minister Brian Mulroney had announced his retirement, and on June 13 his Progressive Conservative Party, which held a majority in Parliament, voted on a successor as party leader at a convention in Ottawa. The leading contenders were Campbell, 46, the defense minister, and Jean Charest, 34, the environment minister. Campbell defeated Charest, 53 percent to 47 percent, on the second ballot. Campbell, who was from British Columbia, was sworn in as prime minister June 25. She reduced the number of ministers in her cabinet from 39 to 25 and the number of government departments from 32 to 23. Charest was named deputy prime minister.

**U.N. Imposes Oil Ban on Haiti** — The U.N. Security Council, **June 16**, voted to impose a worldwide ban on oil shipments to Haiti and also voted to ban arms shipments and freeze Haitian assets abroad. The object was to force Haitian military leaders to accept the return of the Rev. Jean-Bertrand Aristide, Haiti's elected president. The sanctions became effective **June 23**. Talks sponsored by the U.N. opened in New York, **June 27**, between Aristide and Lt. Gen. Raoul Cedras, representing Haiti's military government.

**Japan's Government Falls** — Premier Kiichi Miyazawa lost a no-confidence vote in the Japanese parliament, **June 18**. The vote was 255-220, with 39 members of his own Liberal Democratic Party (LDP) voting against the government. Miyazawa had served as premier since 1991, a period of serious economic recession. He had been criticized for failing to move forcefully against widespread corruption in Japanese politics. As a result of the vote in parliament, new elections would be held on July 18th. On **June 22**, more than 40 LDP dissidents resigned from the party and on **June 23** they announced they had formed a new party, the Renaissance Party.

**Kurdish Militants Attack Turks in Europe** — Kurdish militants, seeking to call attention to their 9-year struggle to establish an independent Kurdish state, attacked Turkish diplomatic missions and businesses in more than two dozen European cities, **June 24**. Twenty people were taken hostage, then released, at the Turkish consulate in Munich. Hostages were also taken in Marseille. One Kurdish demonstrator was shot to death in Bern.

### General

**Pessimism Voiced at AIDS Conference** — More than 14,000 people attended the 9th International Conference on AIDS, which opened in Berlin, **June 7**. Reports indicated that the number of people infected with the AIDS virus continued to rise worldwide, with especially sharp increases in Africa and Southeast Asia. Confirming a report first published in April, scientists said, **June 8**, that the antiviral drug AZT provided no long-term benefit in delaying the onset of symptoms and the death of AIDS patients. A research team headed by Dr. Jonas Salk said, **June 9**, that use of an experimental AIDS vaccine, on which much hope had been focused, had not slowed the course of the disease or lessened its severity. On **June 25**, Pres. Bill Clinton appointed the first AIDS-policy coordinator for the federal government. She was Kristine Gebbie, who had chaired the Centers for Disease Control and Prevention committee on HIV infection. In a final report before disbanding, **June 28**, the White House's National Commission on AIDS criticized the Bush administration's response to the epidemic as inadequate and challenged Pres. Clinton to do more to halt the spread of the disease.

**Japan's Crown Prince Marries** — Crown Prince Naruhito of Japan and Masako Owada were married, **June 9**, in a traditional Shinto ceremony at the Imperial Palace in Tokyo. The bride had been educated at Harvard and Oxford universities and had been a trade negotiator in the Japanese foreign service. She was the first woman with a career to join the royal family.

**Mystery Illness Blamed on Rodents** — Health officials concluded in early June that a mysterious illness in the Southwest was caused by microbes belonging to a family of viruses called hantaviruses that are found in the urine and droppings of rodents. On **June 9**, New Mexico state health officials began trapping rodents in an attempt to identify the virus. By late June at least 19 deaths had been linked to the disease.

**'Jurassic Park' Stomps Box-Office Records** — Universal Studios' long-awaited film "Jurassic Park," directed by Steven Spielberg, opened on **June 11**, setting a record for the largest opening day box-office earnings with $18.2 million in first-day gross ticket sales. Based on a novel by Michael Crichton, the movie tells the story of a former sideshow owner who exploits scientific technology to clone dinosaurs and develops a theme park to show off his creations. Spielberg spent over 2 years in preproduction creating the movie. In addition to using traditional clay models and stop-action photography, Spielberg utilized the groundbreaking computer-generated images of Industrial Light and Magic in more than half of the dinosaur scenes. The movie, which cost over $60 million to make, quickly went on to set records for the largest 3-day gross box-office earnings ($50.2 million) and the largest full-week gross earnings ($81.7 million). "Jurassic Park" had passed the $100 million and $200 million marks faster than any previous film.

**Chicago Wins 3d Straight NBA Title** — The Chicago Bulls won their 3d straight National Basketball Association championship, **June 20**, when they defeated the Phoenix Suns, 99-98, to take the final series, 4 games to 2. In the last seconds of the game the Bulls were down by 2 points, but John Paxson scored a 3-point basket, the final points of the game, with 3.9 seconds to play. For the 3d straight year, Michael Jordan of the Bulls was named the most valuable player in the finals. In the 6 games with the Suns, he averaged 41 points per game, a record for the final series. No team had won 3 straight titles since the Boston Celtics won their 8th straight championship in 1966.

## JULY

### National

**Congress OKs Reduced Stimulus Program** — Congress, **July 1**, completed action on an economic-stimulus package that fell far short of what Pres. Bill Clinton had wanted. In April, a Republican filibuster in the Senate had killed a bill that would have provided $16.3 billion for short-term economic assistance. The bill adopted by Congress provided only $3.5 billion, for summer jobs, expanded Small Business Administration loans, and the employment of police officers by communities. In signing the bill, **July 3**, Clinton expressed disappointment.

**Clinton Offers Plan on Northwest Logging** — Pres. Bill Clinton, **July 1**, presented a plan for logging on federal old-growth forests in the Northwest and for the protection of the northern spotted owl, an endangered species. A federal court had suspended logging in the Northwest in 1991 until the government devised a plan to protect the owl. At a forest summit in April 1993, Clinton had heard presentations from timber companies, environmentalists, and others on what to do. Clinton's plan would limit logging to 1.2 billion board feet per year in the U.S. forests of the Pacific Northwest, about one-fourth what the government had allowed in the 1980s. Reserves for the owl would be established. It was estimated that 6,000 jobs, mostly in Oregon, would be lost under the plan, and Clinton proposed to spend $1.2 billion over 5 years to aid the region economically, retrain workers, and restore rivers damaged by logging. The plan was subject to the court's approval.

**U.S. Detains Radical Muslim Sheikh** — Sheikh Omar Abdel Rahman, whose Muslim followers had been linked to 2 bombing plots, was taken into federal custody, **July 2**. Abdel Rahman had entered the U.S. in 1990. His residency status had been revoked in March 1992, and an immigration judge had held in March 1993 that he could be deported. The sheikh had appealed that ruling and had been free pending the outcome of the case.

**White House Travel Office Report Issued** — The White House issued a report, **July 2**, on the controversy involving the White House Travel Office. Chief of Staff Thomas McLarty and Budget Dir. Leon Panetta were the authors of the report. The report reprimanded 4 officials, but McLarty assumed ultimate responsibility. Those reprimanded included Catherine Cornelius, a distant cousin of Pres. Bill Clinton who had been appointed head of the travel office, and David Watkins, the White House director of administration. Cornelius was reprimanded for attempting to find evidence of wrongdoing by the travel staff, and the report said that she and Watkins had reported rumors of wrongdoing to the FBI to help prompt an investigation of the staff. The report confirmed that Harry Thomason, a friend of the Clintons, had pressed the White House to investigate the office. He had sought without success to bid for White House travel business. McLarty said 5 former travel office employees who had been cleared of wrongdoing would be given other government jobs.

**Economic Indicators, Layoffs Announced** — The Labor Dept., **July 2**, put the unemployment rate at 7.0 percent for June, an increase of 0.1 percent over May. The department said, **July 13**, that an index of prices charged by producers for finished goods had declined 0.3 percent in June. It reported, **July 14**, that the consumer price index was unchanged in June. Procter & Gamble Co., **July 15**, announced that it would close 30 factories and cut 13,000 jobs. The Commerce Dept. reported, **July 16**, that the merchandise trade deficit in May was $8.37 billion. Federal Reserve Board Chairman Alan Greenspan told a House subcommittee, **July 20**, that the rate of inflation had not eased as much as expected, and he testified, **July 22**, that "at some point" interest rates "are going to have to move up." IBM announced, **July 27**, that 35,000 jobs would be eliminated as part of a restructuring program.

**Flood Devastates Parts of Midwest** — A flood that was worse than anyone in the Midwest could remember surged down the Mississippi River and its tributaries in the summer of 1993. Fifty people died, and the lives of tens of thousands of others were disrupted. Heavy rains in the winter, spring, and summer left the ground saturated, and the excess water formed lakes. Ultimately, all of the overflow found its way downstream. Many record flood crests were set, and hundreds of levees collapsed or were overrun. All of Iowa and large portions of 8 other states were declared federal disaster areas. Pres. Bill Clinton, **July 4**, visited Davenport, Iowa, in the first of 4 trips to the impacted region. The Mississippi River, a major commercial artery for the Midwest, was closed to barge traffic, **July 6**, from Sioux City, Iowa, to St. Louis. The collapse of a levee, **July 11**, flooded Des Moines' water treatment plant and left 250,000 people without any drinking water from their taps. In St. Louis, **July 14**, Clinton said he would ask Congress to provide funds for flood relief. On **July 16**, the rising Missouri and Mississippi rivers converged near St. Charles, Mo., 20 miles upstream from their normal confluence. The flood, **July 17**, knocked out the Bayview Bridge, connecting Quincy, Ill., and West Quincy, Mo., the only crossing on the Mississippi for about 200 miles. Clinton, Vice Pres. Al Gore, 8 governors, and other officials met in Arnold, Mo., **July 17**, to map strategy to overcome the disaster. Tap water became available in Des Moines,

**July 22**, but was not yet safe to drink. By **July 26**, disaster areas had been declared in Illinois, Iowa, Kansas, Minnesota, Missouri, Nebraska, North Dakota, South Dakota, and Wisconsin. In Kansas City, Mo., **July 28**, the Missouri River crested at 48.9 feet, 17 feet above flood stage. In Des Moines, **July 30**, tap water was declared safe to drink.

**Clinton Dismisses FBI Director** — Pres. Bill Clinton dismissed FBI Dir. William Sessions in July. Sessions, a former federal judge, had been appointed FBI director by Pres. Ronald Reagan in 1987. In January 1993 the Justice Dept.'s Office of Professional Responsibility sharply criticized Sessions and his wife for various alleged abuses, including failure to pay taxes for perquisites provided by the government. Sessions denied any wrongdoing and resisted pressure from Attorney Gen. Janet Reno that he resign. He rejected her July 17 demand that he resign or be fired. Clinton dismissed Sessions, **July 19**, and on **July 20** he nominated U.S. District Judge Louis J. Freeh of New York City to succeed him. Freeh had served in the FBI and had been a U.S. attorney. He had gained plaudits for his prosecution of the "pizza connection" drug-smuggling ring in 1987. The Senate, **Aug. 6**, confirmed Freeh's nomination unanimously.

**Ex-House Postmaster Pleads Guilty** — Robert Rota, former postmaster for the U.S. House, pleaded guilty, **July 19**, to one count of conspiring to embezzle public funds and 2 counts of helping embezzlement by House members. Rota had resigned in 1992 during an investigation into alleged irregularities at the House Post Office. In his plea agreement, in U.S. District Court in Washington, D.C., Rota was said to have given lawmakers cash, directly or indirectly, in transactions ostensibly involving stamps. Rota admitted giving $30,000 to 2 unidentified House members. Press reports said that the 2 beneficiaries in the transactions were Rep. Dan Rostenkowski (D, Ill.) and former Rep. Joe Kolter (D, Pa.). Prosecutors said Rota had not profited personally from the transactions.

**Policy on Gays in the Military Announced** — Pres. Bill Clinton, **July 19**, announced the circumstances under which homosexual men and women could serve in the U.S. military. The directive issued by Defense Sec. Les Aspin endorsed the "don't ask, don't tell, don't pursue" approach. Clinton had once promised to repeal outright the 50-year-old ban on homosexuals in the military, and the members of the joint chiefs of staff had initially opposed any modification in it. The administration's policy provided that enlistees would not be asked about their sexual orientation. Once in the service, they could visit bars or read publications that catered to homosexuals, and they could attend rallies in behalf of homosexual rights if they wore civilian clothes. Commission of homosexual acts, however, would be the basis for dismissal from the service. Commanding officers could not initiate investigations on the basis of rumors or hearsay, but only if there was credible information. The order would take effect in October. The joint chiefs supported the policy, but some gay rights leaders said Clinton had reneged on his earlier commitment.

**Aide to Clinton Found Dead** — Vincent Foster, the deputy White House counsel, was found shot to death in a park in northern Virginia, **July 20**. Foster had been a friend of Pres. Bill Clinton and Thomas McLarty, the White House chief of staff, since childhood. The White House counsel's office had come under criticism for the handling of presidential nominations and the White House travel office controversy. Investigators believed that Foster had taken his own life.

**Committee Approves Court Nominee** — Judge Ruth Bader Ginsburg appeared before the Senate Judiciary Committee, **July 20-23**, as it considered her nomination to serve on the U.S. Supreme Court. She said she believed that the courts had a role to play on social issues when the political process faltered. Ginsburg said a woman's right to an abortion was based on the equal protection clause of the 14th Amendment. On **July 29**, the committee unanimously approved her nomination, which went to the full Senate.

### International

**Date Set for Open South Africa Election** — Negotiators announced, **July 2**, in Johannesburg that South Africa's first election open to all races would be held on Apr. 27, 1994. The announcement was also made in Washington, D.C., by Pres. F. W. de Klerk and Nelson Mandela, president of the African National Congress. Pres. Bill Clinton met separately at the White House, **July 2**, with de Klerk and Mandela. While in the U.S., de Klerk and Mandela criticized each other's policies, but both promoted South Africa as a stable country worthy of foreign investment.

**Haitian Leader to Return to Power** — The Rev. Jean-Bertrand Aristide, the deposed president of Haiti, and Lt. Gen. Raoul Cedras, who led the coup in 1991 that ousted him, reached an agreement, **July 3**, that would put Aristide back in power by October. The agreement, brokered by the U.N. and signed in New York City, provided for an end to embargoes that the U.N. and the Organization of American States had imposed on Haiti. Pres. Bill Clinton, **July 4**, backed the agreement and pledged financial support to Haiti.

**Leaders of 'G7' Nations Attend Summit** — The heads of government of the world's 7 leading industrial nations, the so-called Group of 7, met in Tokyo in July. The 7 nations are the U.S., Canada, France, Germany, Great Britain, Italy, and Japan. On **July 7**, the opening date of the summit, trade ministers from the U.S., Canada, Japan, and the European Community announced an agreement that, if implemented, would eliminate tariffs on a wide range of manufactured products, including construction equipment, furniture, farm equipment, and pharmaceuticals. The leaders, **July 8**, declared their commitment to "the territorial integrity" of Bosnia and Herzegovina and said they could not accept a settlement dictated by Serbs and Croats at the expense of Bosnian Muslims. Pres. Boris Yeltsin of Russia joined the meeting, **July 8**, and on **July 9** the G7 nations announced a $3 billion loan package for Russia. The leaders declared, **July 9**, that their highest priority was the conclusion of trade talks being conducted under auspices of the General Agreement on Tariffs and Trade. Pres. Bill Clinton and Premier Kiichi Miyazawa announced a bilateral trade agreement, **July 10**. Japan said it would take steps to reduce its large trade surplus with the U.S.; however, the U.S. agreed not to insist on Japan's acceptance of numerical market-share goals for foreign products.

**Clinton Visits South Korea** — Pres. Bill Clinton visited South Korea in July. He addressed the parliament, **July 10**, and on **July 11** visited U.S. military personnel guarding the demilitarized zone between North and South Korea. Clinton warned North Korea that any use of nuclear weapons would mean the end of their country, and he said he would support tougher sanctions against North Korea if it did not open its nuclear-energy sites to international inspection. He said the U.S. would not remove any of its 36,000 troops from South Korea.

**Bosnian Factions Support Federation** — Ethnic leaders in Bosnia and Herzegovina agreed in July to support creation of a loose federation in the embattled state. Seven of the 10 members of Bosnia's collective presidency, meeting in Zagreb, Croatia, **July 11**, said that they had agreed that Bosnia's government "should be along the lines of a federal state" in which Muslims, Croats, and Serbs would have equal rights as citizens. Serb, Croat, and Muslim leaders met in Geneva in late July under the cloud of increased fighting around the capital city of Sarajevo. On **July 30** they agreed to the establishment of ethnically based republics in a loose federation. The central government would be responsible only for trade and external relations. Each republic would have its own currency and armed forces. The Serbs would get 60 percent of Bosnia's territory even though they constituted only about 31 percent of the prewar population. The Muslims, who made up 44 percent of the prewar population, would receive 25 to 30 percent of Bosnia's land area. The remaining 10 to 15 percent would become Croat-controlled. The Croats composed 17 percent of the prewar population.

**U.N. Removes Italian General in Somalia** — Four journalists were killed in Mogadishu, **July 12**, by Somalis when they went to the scene of an attack by an American helicopter on a stronghold of Somali warlord Mohammed Farah Aidid. On **July 14**, the U.N. announced the removal of Gen. Bruno Loi, commander of the Italian force participating in the Somali operation, because he had refused to engage his troops in the conflict with Aidid.

**Voters Desert Japan's Ruling Party** — Japan's voters went to the polls, **July 18**, to elect members of the lower house of the Diet (parliament), and no political party emerged with a majority of the seats. The Liberal Democratic Party had held a majority in the Diet since the party's founding in 1955, but many of its leaders had been implicated in corrupt activities in recent years, and the party had seemed unable or unwilling to institute political reform. The LDP had won 275 of the 511 seats in the 1990 election, but in July it took only 223 seats. The strength of the Social Democratic Party also declined, from 136 to 70 seats. Three centrist parties recently organized by LDP defectors captured 103 seats with their reform platforms. Prime Minister Kiichi Miyazawa resigned as LDP leader, **July 22**. On **July 28**, 7 parties formed a coalition that excluded the LDP, and on **July 29** they chose as their candidate for prime minister Morihiro Hosokawa, who had bolted the LDP in 1992 and formed the Japan New Party.

**Britain Ratifies European Union Treaty** — Britain in July completed ratification of the so-called Maastricht Treaty on greater European unity. Prime Minister John Major as well as the treaty, which he supported, suffered a defeat, **July 22**, on a key vote in the House of Commons when 23 members of his Conservative Party deserted him. In a tactical maneuver, they opposed Major's desire to "opt out" of the treaty's "social chapter," which would subject British industry to European Community regulation of labor relations and working conditions. In a shrewd, but politically risky move, Major called for a vote of confidence on his government's handling of the treaty, **July 23**. Tory rebels returned to the fold to uphold the government in the two-step confidence motion that cleared the way for ratification, pending court approval. First, the Tories defeated the Labor Party amendment to accept the "social chapter," with the vote falling along party lines, 339 to 301. The second vote, 339 to 299, supported Major's government. Had the government lost, the Conservatives would have had to face the electorate at a time when its standing in opinion polls was low. Britain's High Court, **July 30**, rejected a court challenge to the treaty. After an announcement, **Aug. 2**, that there would be no appeal, Britain notified the EC of its ratification of Maastricht. Eleven of the EC's 12 member countries had now completed ratification. In Germany, the treaty faced a court challenge.

**Israeli Attacks Kill 130 in Lebanon** — Two guerrilla groups, Hizballah and the Popular Front for the Liberation of Palestine, launched attacks on Israeli soldiers in the Israeli "security zone" in southern Lebanon in July. By late July, 7 Israelis had been killed. Beginning **July 25**, Israeli forces struck back at guerrilla bases and towns in southern Lebanon with air raids and artillery. Hizballah guerrillas, **July 25**, then shelled towns in northern Israel, causing 2 fatalities. A cease-fire went into effect, **July 31**, after Lebanon and Syria reportedly said they would take steps to stop the guerrilla attacks. The Israeli bombardment of 70 villages had killed about 130, mostly civilians, wounded approximately 500, destroyed up to 10,000 homes, and driven as many as 300,000 people from their homes.

**Court Overturns War Crimes Conviction** — The Supreme Court of Israel, **July 29**, overturned the conviction and death sentence of John Demjanjuk. Born in Ukraine, he had served in the Soviet army and claimed that he had been captured by the Germans in World War II. After the war, he moved to the U.S. He was stripped of his U.S. citizenship in 1986 when the government concluded he had lied about his Nazi past. In 1986 he was extradited to Israel and in 1988 found guilty of brutal mistreatment of Jews at the Nazi death camp at Treblinka. Evidence showed that he had been trained by his Nazi captors as a death-camp guard, and survivors of the camp identified him as a guard known as Ivan the Terrible. Subsequently, evidence from the Soviet KGB files indicated that the notorious Ivan was another Ukrainian, Ivan Marchenko. The KGB files also indicated that Demjanjuk had been a guard at 2 other camps, but the Israeli Supreme Court threw out the conviction because he had been tried as Ivan the Terrible, not for crimes committed elsewhere. The court also said it would be unreasonable to initiate new charges against Demjanjuk.

**Mystery Illness Afflicts 46,000 Cubans** — An illness of unknown origin had afflicted 46,000 Cubans by early July. The illness became apparent during the winter, and by spring as many as 4,000 new cases were being reported each week. Two patterns of symptoms had emerged. One involved impairment of vision, though not blindness. The second affected the nerves and was characterized by a tingling sensation in the hands and feet, muscle cramps, and weakness in the legs. Some of those with nerve damage suffered hearing loss and difficulty swallowing, speaking, and urinating. Delegations of scientists had come to Cuba to study the problem. Possible causes included nutritional deficiency, viral infection, cyanide poisoning, and an unidentified toxin. Dr. Jorge Antelo, Cuba's deputy health minister, said, **July 1**, that the number of reported cases had declined soon after the government had begun to distribute multivitamin pills to the national population. He said 25,000 people had been hospitalized, usually for up to 20 days, and that "much evidence points to a new disease."

**Biological Parents Win Custody Fight** — The biological parents of a 2-year-old girl won legal custody in July after a protracted dispute with adoptive parents. After the girl's birth in 1991 her mother, Cara Clausen, gave her up for adoption. She named as the father a man who in fact was not the baby's father, and he signed consent forms for adoption. Clausen lived in Iowa. The girl was adopted by Jan and Roberta DeBoer, who lived in Michigan. They named the girl Jessica. Clausen and the girl's natural father, Daniel

Schmidt, later decided to fight for custody and subsequently married. They argued that the adoption was not final because Clausen had named the wrong father. An Iowa court supported them. The Michigan Supreme Court, **July 2**, decided, 6-1, to defer to the Iowa ruling. It ordered the DeBoers to surrender the child to the Schmidts by Aug. 2. Justice John Paul Stevens of the U.S. Supreme Court, **July 26**, refused the DeBoers' appeal to block the order. The full court, **July 30**, did the same, 7-2. As an attorney carried the girl from the DeBoers' Ann Arbor, Mich., home, **Aug. 2**, she cried and screamed "Mommy!"

## AUGUST

### National

**'Great Flood' Leaves Heavy Damage** — "The Great Flood of 1993," as it was now being called, receded in August, leaving considerable damage in 9 states. In St. Louis, the Mississippi River finally crested at a record 49.4 feet, **Aug. 1**, about 2.5 feet below the top of the flood wall. Although portions of South St. Louis were flooded, the central city was spared. In Alton, Ill., **Aug. 1**, 60,000 people lost their drinking water when floodwaters crashed into the city's water-treatment plant. On **Aug. 2**, the U.S. Army Corps of Engineers deliberately opened a levee outside the historic town of Prairie du Rocher, Ill., in order to channel floodwaters into farmlands and ease pressure on the levees at the town. Town officials dynamited the levee again, **Aug. 4**, and the strategy worked. On **Aug. 6**, Congress completed action on a $6.2 billion flood-relief package. It was reported, **Aug. 9**, that Agriculture Sec. Mike Espy had estimated that 8 million acres had been flooded and 12 million more acres were too wet to grow crops. State and federal officials put total damage estimates at $12 billion, with nearly $8 billion of this suffered by farmers. The final death toll appeared to be 50, and nearly 70,000 people were made homeless. In St. Louis, **Aug. 12**, Clinton signed the flood-relief bill.

**Ginsburg Sworn In as Justice** — The Senate, **Aug. 3**, approved the nomination of Judge Ruth Bader Ginsburg for the U.S. Supreme Court, by a vote of 96-3. She was sworn in, **Aug. 10**, as the court's 107th justice.

**Unemployment Rate Declines** — The Commerce Dept. reported, **Aug. 3**, that the index of leading economic indicators had risen by 0.1 percent in June. The Labor Dept. said, **Aug. 6**, that the unemployment rate in July stood at 6.8 percent, a drop of 0.2 percentage point from June. This was the lowest monthly rate since October 1991. The department said, **Aug. 12**, that the index of prices charged by producers for finished goods fell 0.2 percent in July, and it reported, **Aug. 15**, that the consumer price index rose 0.1 percent in July. June's deficit in merchandise trade, $12.06 billion, was the widest since February 1988, the Commerce Dept. announced **Aug. 19**. On Wall Street, the Dow Jones Industrial Average closed, **Aug. 25**, at an all-time high of 3652.09.

**Two in Rodney King Case Sentenced** — Federal Judge John Davies, **Aug. 4**, sentenced 2 police officers to 2½ years in prison for violating Rodney King's civil rights. The 1992 state court acquittal of the 2 officers and 2 other policemen in the beating of King had resulted in widespread protests and violence in Los Angeles and elsewhere that had taken more than 50 lives. In 1993, Stacey Koon and Laurence Powell were tried in federal court, and they were convicted in April. Although many in the black community in Los Angeles objected to the relatively lenient sentences, the city remained calm.

**Congress Passes Bill to Reduce Deficits** — After a long and acrimonious debate, Congress in August narrowly approved a bill, supported by Pres. Bill Clinton, that was designed to reduce federal budget deficits by $496 billion over 5 years. The bill, the centerpiece in Clinton's economic-recovery program, was modified many times during the spring and summer as supporters sought to pick up votes for it. The Senate and House had approved different versions of the bill in June, and conferees from both houses had spent weeks reconciling the differences. The votes in August were on the conference committee's final version. This final bill raised taxes on taxable incomes above $115,000 for individuals and $140,000 for couples from 31 percent to 36 percent. All taxable incomes over $250,000 would be subject to an additional tax of 3.6 percent. All salary income would be subject to a 2.9 percent Medicare tax. The federal tax on all transportation fuels would be increased by 4.3-cents-per-gallon. For individuals earning more than $34,000 (couples, $44,000), the portion of Social Security benefits subject to income tax would rise from 50 percent to 85 percent. On the spending side, total discretionary federal spending would be frozen at 1993 levels, with details of the cuts to be determined each year. Payments to health care providers under Medicare and Medicaid would be subject to new formulas and limits, with total savings of $63 billion anticipated. In the principal spending increase under the bill, the earned income tax credit for the working poor would be extended to families earning up to $27,000 a year. Public-opinion surveys showed Americans about equally divided on the bill. Republican leaders denounced the tax increases and called the spending cuts inadequate, and all Republicans in both houses voted against the bill. The House, **Aug. 5**, approved the bill by a bare 218-216 margin. The Senate, **Aug. 6**, divided 50-50, and the legislation passed with the tie-breaking vote of Vice Pres. Al Gore. Clinton signed the bill on **Aug. 10**.

**White House Suicide Left Bitter Note** — Investigators said, **Aug. 5**, that an autopsy indicated that Vincent Foster, the deputy White House counsel who had been found shot to death in July, had committed suicide. On **Aug. 10**, the Justice Dept. made public the contents of a note Foster wrote before his death. He said he was not meant for "the spotlight of public life in Washington. Here ruining people is considered sport."

**Grazing Fees Raised on Public Lands** — The Clinton administration announced, **Aug. 9**, that it was more than doubling the fees the federal government charges ranchers who graze their animals on public lands. Fees would still be lower than those generally charged on private lands. Pres. Bill Clinton had included a fee increase in his deficit-reduction plan but had dropped it to avoid defections in Congress. The administration also announced stricter environmental controls on grazing practices.

**Clinton Announces Anticrime Measures** — Pres. Bill Clinton, **Aug. 11**, endorsed legislation aimed at combating crime. He backed the so-called Brady bill, which would require a 5-day waiting period for the purchase of handguns. He proposed to spend $3.4 billion over 5 years to hire 50,000 more police officers. Clinton also favored extending the federal death penalty to almost 50 crimes. Clinton issued executive orders, **Aug. 11**, that required stricter licensing of gun dealers and that banned the import of semiautomatic assault-style handguns.

**Polish-Born General to Head Joint Chiefs** — Pres. Bill Clinton, **Aug. 11**, named an Army general, John Shalikashvili, to be the next chairman of the Joint Chiefs of Staff. He would succeed Gen. Colin Powell on the latter's retirement at the end of September. The appointment was subject to Senate approval. Born in Poland of Georgian descent, Shalikashvili came to the U.S. at age 16. Drafted into the Army, he served in Vietnam and Korea, rising rapidly in rank. He commanded the international relief effort for the Iraqi Kurds in 1991 and, at the time of his appointment by Clinton, he was supreme allied commander, Europe, NATO's top military officer.

**Altman Acquitted in BCCI Case** — Robert Altman, a Washington, D.C., lawyer, was acquitted in August on 4 charges related to the notorious Bank of Credit and Commerce International. Altman and his mentor, Clark Clifford, a prominent figure for many years in Democratic politics, had been indicted in both federal and New York state courts. Federal charges were later dropped, and Clifford was deemed unable to face trial in New York because of illness. The case involved the relationship between BCCI and First American Bancshares Inc., a Washington, D.C., bank in which Clifford and Altman were officers. Five of 9 state charges against Altman had also been dropped, and on **Aug. 14** he was found not guilty of misleading bank regulators and filing false documents.

**Wetlands Policy Announced by Clinton** — In a package of legislative and administrative measures announced **Aug. 24**, the Clinton administration made a commitment to "no net loss" of wetlands. The Bush administration had made a similar commitment, but environmentalists pointed out that wetlands acreage throughout the U.S. continued to disappear under farmland and development. Under the Clinton plan, a Bush administration proposal to open 1.7 million acres of wetlands in Alaska to development would be dropped. Also, owners allowed to develop wetlands would pay a fee to help protect or create wetlands elsewhere. Drainage projects would be subject to more stringent federal review. However, 53 million acres that had been drained and converted to farmland since 1985 would be exempted from new regulations.

**Muslim Cleric Indicted in Bomb Plots** — Sheikh Omar Abdel Rahman was indicted by a federal grand jury in New York City, **Aug. 25**, on conspiracy charges in connection with a number of terrorist activities. These included the February bombing of the World Trade Center, a foiled plot to bomb other targets in New York City, and the 1990 assassination of Rabbi Meir Kahane. The indictment said that Abdel Rahman had instructed and advised other conspirators. In all, 15 men were named in the indictment. Evidence included 150 hours of taped conversations recorded by a government informer. One of those indicted was El Sayyid Nosair, who had been acquitted in a New York state court of killing Kahane but now faced a federal charge of committing a murder to promote a larger conspiracy.

### International

**Demjanjuk Remains in Israeli Custody** — Although John Demjanjuk's conviction in the "Ivan the Terrible" case was overturned in July, he remained in detention in Israel in August. On **Aug. 1**, an Israeli Supreme Court panel issued a restraining order keeping him in custody until prosecutors decided whether to try him for other alleged concentration camp activities during World War II. The 6th U.S. Circuit Court of Appeals held, **Aug. 3**, that he should be allowed to return to the U.S. while other charges were under review. Israel's Supreme Court, **Aug. 18**, ordered that Demjanjuk be set free, but then heard arguments that the decision be delayed.

**Israel, Palestinians Near Agreement** — A tense month in Middle East negotiations took a dramatically encouraging turn at the end of August, and it appeared that a plan for limited Palestinian self-rule might soon be approved. Yasir Arafat, chairman of the Palestine Liberation Organization, caused a rift in his ranks, **Aug. 3,** when he asked his negotiation delegation to offer more concessions to Israel than they were prepared to accept. For one thing, Arafat was willing to postpone discussion of the status of Jerusalem. The Palestinian delegates rejected Arafat's terms and presented their own proposal to U.S. Sec. of State Warren Christopher. The PLO announced, **Aug. 5,** that Arafat had ordered a restructuring of the PLO bureaucracy in order to overcome serious financial problems. Israeli and Palestinian officials reported, **Aug. 5,** that an Israeli cabinet minister and a senior adviser to Arafat had met, an historic initial contact between the old enemies. In January 1993, the Israeli Knesset (parliament) had repealed a law prohibiting contacts between Israeli citizens and PLO members. Two Palestinian delegates to the peace talks had reportedly decided, **Aug. 7,** to resign in protest over Arafat's direct intervention in the negotiations. But then, a compromise was announced, **Aug. 12.** Seven delegates were made a formal part of the PLO decision-making process and were appointed to the PLO committee that directed peace-talk strategy. Foreign Minister Shimon Peres of Israel announced, **Aug. 13,** that even though the delegates representing the Palestinians were now officially part of the PLO, Israel would continue to negotiate with them. Never before had Israel publicly been willing to negotiate in any manner with the PLO. Deploring this shift, former Israeli Prime Minister Yitzhak Shamir called the PLO a "murderous organization." On **Aug. 15,** about 400 Palestinian men who had been deported from Israel to southern Lebanon in 1992 agreed to Israel's terms for their return. Some would be returned to prison. Norway's Foreign Minister Johan Joergan Holst confirmed, **Aug. 30,** reports that he had mediated talks between the PLO and the Israeli government, beginning in April, that were separate from the publicly known peace talks. Most of the meetings had taken place in Norway. While much of the world rejoiced at the news, hard-liners on both sides were outraged as details of a tentative agreement came out, and one radical Palestinian leader appeared to call for Arafat's assassination. Peres told the Knesset, **Aug. 30,** "This is the beginning of the end" of Israel's dispute with the Palestinians. The Israeli government, **Aug. 31,** approved in principle a plan for interim Palestinian self-rule. Self-rule would be established in the Gaza Strip and in the historic biblical town of Jericho on the West Bank within a few months. Later, self-rule would be extended to the rest of the West Bank, excepting the Israeli settlements. Internationally supervised elections would be held in the occupied territories. Negotiations on the status of Jerusalem would begin within 2 years. In areas obtaining self-rule, Israel would control overall security and border crossings, but the Palestinians would control taxation, education, health, welfare, and the police.

**Italy Reforms Electoral System** — Reacting to public outrage over widespread political scandals, Italy's parliament gave final approval, **Aug. 4,** to a new means for electing its members. Previously, seats had been allocated according to proportional representation. With many parties winning seats, it had proved difficult to form stable coalition governments. Under the new electoral system, 75 percent of the seats in both parliamentary houses would be awarded to the candidate in each district who received the most votes. The remaining 25 percent of the seats would be distributed according to proportional representation.

**Reformer Becomes Premier of Japan** — Morihiro Hosokawa, who had left the ruling Liberal Democratic Party (LDP) in 1992, was elected premier of Japan in August as head of a coalition of reform-minded parties. The July election for seats in the lower house of the Diet (parliament) had proved inconclusive, and Hosokawa became the candidate of 7 parties for premier. In the 511-member house, **Aug. 6,** Hosokawa received a majority, 262 votes, to 224 for the new LDP leader, Yohei Kono. Hosokawa, at 55, was much younger than most recent Japanese premiers. He had quit the LDP to protest political and bureaucratic corruption. With Hosokawa's help, **Aug. 6,** Takako Doi, former head of the Socialist Party, became the first woman elected speaker of the lower house. In addition, Hosokawa's cabinet, announced **Aug. 9,** included 3 women, the most ever in a Japanese cabinet. Hosokawa said he would seek quick enactment of political-reform laws. He pledged, **Aug. 10,** to take steps to reduce Japan's large trade surplus with the U.S. and other nations. He also stated that World War II was, for Japan, "a war of aggression, a war that was wrong." His acknowledgment of Japanese guilt went beyond that made by any previous government official.

**Four U.S. Soldiers Killed in Somalia** — Four U.S. soldiers were killed, **Aug. 8,** in Mogadishu, the capital of Somalia, when a land mine exploded under their jeep. The soldiers were part of the U.N. peacekeeping force. In all, 12 U.S. troops had been killed in combat in Somalia since December.

**Fed Acts to Halt Rise in Value of Yen** — The U.S. dollar, **Aug. 17,** fell in value to 100.40 Japanese yen in trading in New York City. At the beginning of 1993, the dollar had been worth about 125 yen, but it was now at a post-World War II low against the Japanese currency. The dollar rebounded, **Aug. 19,** to 105.85 yen after the U.S. Federal Reserve Board intervened in world currency markets in an effort to reverse the trend.

**U.S. Labels Sudan a Terrorist Supporter** — The U.S. State Dept. informed the government of Sudan, **Aug. 18,** that the country would be added to the list of nations that the U.S. regarded as supporters of international terrorism, making the nation ineligible for all U.S. aid, except humanitarian relief. The department had concluded that Sudan had trained Islamic militants who had committed terrorist acts and acted as a "safe harbor" for alleged terrorists.

**Political Hostages Freed in Nicaragua** — Two rival political groups seized hostages in Nicaragua in August, but all of them were freed without harm. On **Aug. 19,** a band of rearmed former contra rebels seized a 38-member government delegation visiting their mountain camp. They demanded that Gen. Humberto Ortega Saavedra, a Marxist Sandinista, be ousted as defense minister. In retaliation, former Sandinista soldiers, **Aug. 20,** seized 34 conservative political leaders in Managua, the capital. The vice president and the president of the national assembly were among the captives. Some of the original hostages were released by both sides, **Aug. 21** and **22,** but then, on **Aug. 22,** leftists seized 9 journalists who had been covering the story. On **Aug. 25,** all of the remaining hostages were released.

## General

**Pope Attends Youth Festival in Colorado** — Pope John Paul II visited the U.S. in August to participate in a Roman Catholic youth festival. Before his arrival, he visited Mexico, **Aug. 11.** During one speech in

# 1993 IN
# PICTURES

*President Clinton and the First Lady in the inaugural parade along Pennsylvania Avenue, January 20.*

# THE NEW ADMINISTRATION

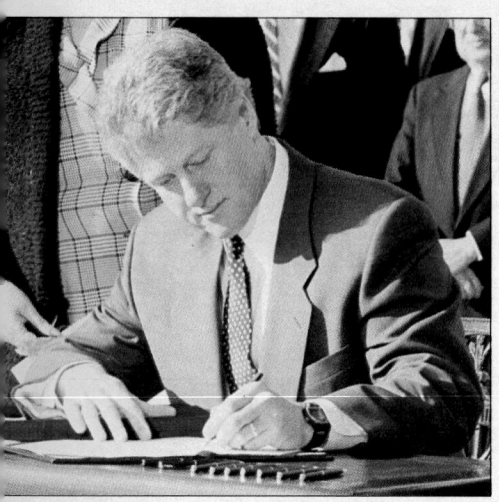

AP/WIDE WORLD PHOTOS

President Clinton signs the family-leave bill, his first legislative victory, in a February Rose Garden ceremony.

Hillary Rodham Clinton, head of the administration's health care reform task force, visits a Philadelphia hospital.

AP/WIDE WORLD PHOTOS

In May, ex-Reagan aide David Gergen is hired to help refocus Clinton's message.

Clinton stresses U.S.-Japanese trade issues
during a July economic summit in Tokyo.

REUTERS/BETTMANN

The commander in chief at
Ft. McNair July 19, after
announcing his policy on
gays in the military.

AP/WIDE WORLD PHOTOS

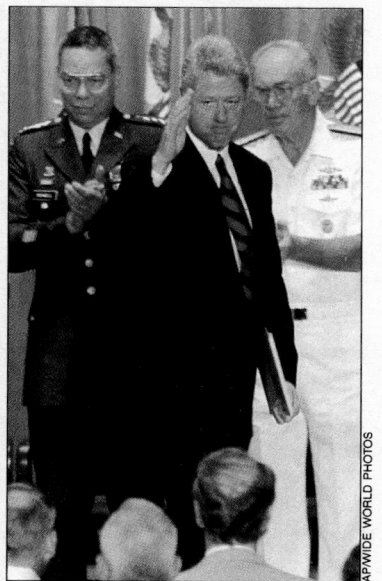

AP/WIDE WORLD PHOTOS

Ruth Bader Ginsburg, Clinton's first
Supreme Court nominee, is sworn in
August 10; to her right, her husband
and Chief Justice William Rehnquist.

President Clinton discusses
his deficit reduction bill
with Illinois congressman
Dan Rostenkowski.

ROBERT GIROUX/AFP

67

# ON THE WORLD SCENE

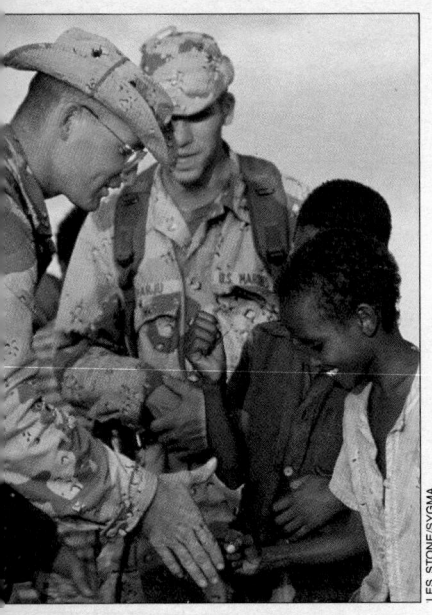

Both friendship (left) and brutal hostility greeted U.S. troops on a peacekeeping mission in Somalia. Below: Cambodians vote in May elections aimed at ending civil war.

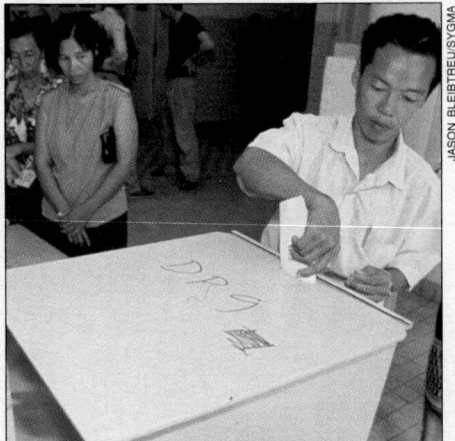

LES STONE/SYGMA

JASON BLEIBTREU/SYGMA

Russian President Boris Yeltsin campaigning for support during another turbulent year in the former Soviet republics.

MALCOLM LINTON/BLACK STAR

*Historic handshake: Israeli leader Yitzhak Rabin and Palestine Liberation Organization head Yasir Arafat at the September 13 signing of a peace accord in Washington.*

*Nelson Mandela, president of South Africa's African National Congress, visits the Liberty Bell July 3.*

*A mass burial of Muslims April 28 attests to the continued horrors of ethnic warfare in Bosnia.*

*Opposition leader Tsutomu Hata celebrates, in a traditional way, big gains by his party in July 18 Japanese elections.*

# CONFRONTATION IN WACO

KWTX-TV/SYGMA

*Four federal agents are killed in a February shoot-out with Branch Davidians in Waco, Texas (above). A two-month standoff ends April 19 as the compound goes up in flames (below); inset: the cult's leader, David Koresh.*

AP/WIDE WORLD PHOTOS; INSET: ROD AYDELOTTE/WACO TRIBUNE HERALD/SYGMA

# MIDWEST UNDER WATER

Davenport, Iowa, was one of many
places hit hard by massive floods
in the Midwest in the summer.

CHRIS STEWART/BLACK STAR

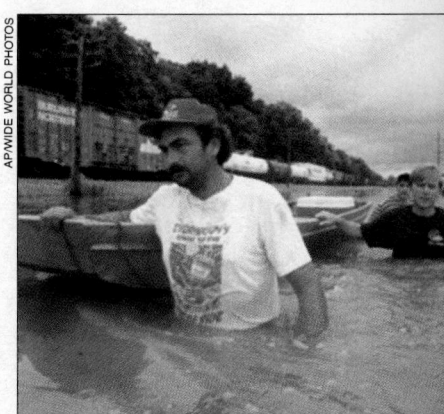

AP/WIDE WORLD PHOTOS

In St. Joseph, Missouri, a
boat is used to help wade
through chest-high waters.

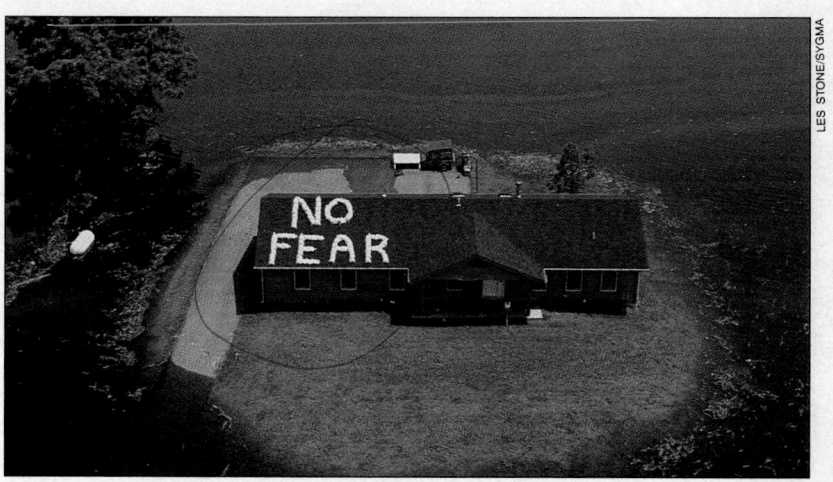

LES STONE/SYGMA

NO
FEAR

A message of determination, written with sandbags,
tops a St. Charles County, Missouri, home.

# TERRORISTS STRIKE

*A woman is helped from the scene after a bombing at New York City's World Trade Center February 26.*

*Mahmud Abouhalima, turned over by Egypt, is taken into custody in connection with the bombing.*

*New York police search for evidence in the underground garage where the blast occurred.*

Yucatan, the Pontiff condemned the mistreatment of native peoples. Pres. Bill Clinton welcomed the Pope to Denver, **Aug. 12**. The Pope addressed 90,000 young people in Denver's stadium, **Aug. 12**. In an address, **Aug. 14**, he deplored sexual abuse of children by priests, which had become a subject of great concern in the U.S. On **Aug. 15**, in the main event of the World Youth Day festival, the Pope conducted a mass south of Denver for up to 400,000 people.

**Spacecraft Falls Silent Near Mars** — The *Mars Observer* spacecraft ceased communicating from space in August as it approached Mars, its destination. The *Observer*, which cost $980 million, had been launched in September 1992. Contact with ground controllers was lost **Aug. 21**, 3 days before the spacecraft was to orbit the red planet and map the surface of Mars to obtain information on its geology in anticipation of a possible visit by a crewed spacecraft.

## SEPTEMBER

### National

**Jobless Rate Down Again** — The unemployment rate continued to edge downward in August, to 6.7 percent, the Labor Dept. reported, **Sept. 3**. The Commerce Dept. said, **Sept. 3**, that the index of indicators of future economic trends fell by 0.1 percent in July. Good news on inflation came, **Sept. 10**, when the Labor Dept. reported that prices charged by producers for finished goods declined 0.6 percent in August. This was the biggest monthly decline since February 1991, and the trend, based on revised data, had now been downward for 4 months. The Commerce Dept. reported, **Sept. 16**, that the U.S. trade deficit had fallen to $10.34 billion in August.

**Clinton Seeks to 'Reinvent Government'** — Pres. Bill Clinton and Vice Pres. Al Gore announced a broad program, **Sept. 7**, that had as its goal the streamlining of the federal government to make it leaner, more efficient, and more responsive. The program to "reinvent government," which included more than 800 recommendations, had been put together under Gore's leadership. Projected savings under the plan, if implemented, were put at $108 billion over 5 years. Under the plan, budgets and appropriations would be made for a 2-year period. Agencies could carry unspent funds into the next fiscal year. It would be easier to dismiss employees, and the number of government reports would be reduced. Mid-level managers would have more decision-making control. The federal work force would be cut by 252,000. Many regional offices of federal departments would be closed. Similar sweeping proposals had been offered during previous administrations, but with little effect. Many of the recommendations would require congressional approval.

**National-Service Bill Approved** — The Senate, **Sept. 8**, approved, 57-40, the national-service bill supported by Pres. Bill Clinton. Participants in the program would receive grants for up to 2 years, for as much as $4,725 a year, by performing community service administered at the state level through nonprofit organizations, state and federal agencies, colleges, and other groups. Grants would be applied toward study at a college, university, or technical school. Twenty thousand students would be funded the first year, and over 3 years the program would cost $1.5 billion. The House had already approved the bill in early August. On **Sept. 21**, nearly 1,000 people gathered at a White House ceremony to watch Clinton sign the bill.

**Clinton Signs NAFTA Side Agreements** — On **Sept. 14**, Pres. Bill Clinton signed 3 supplemental agreements to the North American Free Trade Agreement.

Negotiators from Canada, Mexico, and the U.S. had concluded the side agreements as a means of firming up labor and environmental standards and to guard against the negative impact of a sudden flood of imports. Former Presidents Gerald Ford, Jimmy Carter, and George Bush joined Clinton at the White House signing ceremony and endorsed NAFTA. (Separately, the heads of government of Canada and Mexico also signed the side agreements on **Sept. 13** and **14**, respectively.) Richard Gephardt (D, Mo.), the House Majority Leader, announced his opposition to NAFTA, **Sept. 21**. Overruling a district court decision, a federal appeals court held, **Sept. 24**, that the administration could submit NAFTA to Congress without an environmental impact statement.

**Vietnam War-Era Radical Surrenders** — Katherine Ann Power, an opponent of the Vietnam War who had been sought for more than 20 years in the death of a police officer, surrendered in September. She had driven a getaway car in 1970 following a bank robbery in Boston in which a police officer was killed. She later moved to Oregon and had married. Deciding to abandon her life as a fugitive, Power appeared in State Superior Court in Boston, **Sept. 15**, and pleaded guilty to armed robbery and manslaughter. On **Sept. 24**, she pleaded guilty to an earlier burglary at a National Guard armory. She was sentenced, **Oct. 7**, to 8 to 12 years in a Massachusetts prison for the 1970 bank robbery.

**Over 130 Military Bases to Close** — Congress made little effort to overturn the recommendations of the Base Closure and Realignment Commission in September. The commission's recommendations were announced in June and approved by Pres. Bill Clinton in July, but they were subject to congressional veto. Subsequently, no measure was introduced in the House to overturn the decision to close 130 domestic military bases and scale down 45 others. On **Sept. 20**, the Senate, 83-12, rejected a motion to disapprove the commission's work, and the commission's recommendations became final.

**Clinton Announces Health-Care Program** — Pres. Bill Clinton announced his health-care reform package in September. For months, the president's health-care task force, headed by First Lady Hillary Rodham Clinton, had listened to recommendations for change from health-care professionals, insurers, and citizens. The particulars of the president's sweeping reforms had been openly debated for months, but his appearance before a joint session of Congress, **Sept. 22**, was nonetheless awaited with great anticipation. In his address, Clinton noted the immense cost of health care and the fact that millions of Americans had inadequate insurance or no insurance at all. Under his reform plan, all American citizens and legal immigrants would receive health-care coverage. Under the concept of "managed competition", regional alliances, each representing thousands of consumers, would negotiate with insurance companies (or possibly directly with networks of health-care providers) for lower-cost premiums. All employers would be required to cover at least 80 percent of the health-insurance costs of all their full-time employees (with small businesses being eligible for subsidies). All consumers would get an ID card establishing their eligibility for a standard package of benefits. Medicare would still cover senior citizens, but they would have the option to turn to the regional alliances. To reduce bureaucracy and paperwork, all health plans would use the same standard claim form. The reform program was projected to cost the federal government $350 billion over 7 years, to be funded largely out of savings from Medicare, Medicaid, and other health programs and by a tax on tobacco. Clinton projected that his plan would reduce the federal deficit by $91 billion over 7 years (the figure was later revised). The scope and complexity of the plan suggested that its progress through Congress would be slow. Appearing before congressional committees, **Sept. 28,** Hillary Clinton was the administration's lead witness in behalf of the health-care program. The American Medical Association, **Sept. 29,** declared its opposition to federal regulation of health insurance premiums and cuts in Medicare and Medicaid.

**Newly Elected Senator Indicted** — Kay Bailey Hutchison, who had been elected to a U.S. Senate seat from Texas earlier in 1993, was indicted, **Sept. 27,** on charges that she had used state workers, computers, and supplies for her "personal benefit" during her Senate campaign. Hutchison had been State Treasurer before her election to the Senate. Two of her aides were also charged. Hutchison denied that she had done anything wrong.

**Report Rebukes Agency on Its Attack on Cult** — The U.S. Treasury Dept. issued a report, **Sept. 30,** that sharply criticized top officials of its Bureau of Alcohol, Tobacco, and Firearms for their handling of the February raid on the Branch Davidian complex near Waco, Tex. In this initial raid, 4 agents and 6 cultists were killed. The report contended that ATF officials had subsequently deceived investigators and Congress and had sought to blame the failure of the raid on an undercover agent, who in fact had warned that the raid should be called off because the element of surprise had been lost. Treasury Sec. Lloyd Bentsen announced that he had replaced the head of the agency, Stephen Higgins, and had suspended 5 other ATF officials. Higgins had announced his resignation on Sept. 27.

### International

**Bosnian Diplomatic Deadlock Continues** — Bosnian Muslims refused, **Sept. 1,** to accept a draft U.N. peace agreement unless Serbs and Croats ceded them more land. Leaders of the 3 factions broke off their negotiations, **Sept. 20,** aboard a British aircraft carrier in the Adriatic Sea. In an address and press conference, **Sept. 27,** during a visit to the U.N., Pres. Bill Clinton said that the U.S. would no longer support U.N. peacekeeping operations unless the U.N. became more selective in the tasks it undertook, defined missions more clearly, and reduced American dues. Clinton said that if there was to be a U.S. commitment to Bosnia, he would want "a clear political strategy along with a military strategy," and he would want to know "exactly what our financial responsibilities were." Bosnia's Muslim-dominated parliament joined, **Sept. 29,** in rejecting the U.N. peace plan.

**Power Struggle in Russia Intensifies** — The confrontation between Pres. Boris Yeltsin and the Russian parliament became more intense in September. On **Sept. 1,** Yeltsin suspended from office Vice Pres. Aleksandr Rutskoi, one of his adversaries, and First Deputy Premier Vladimir Shumeiko, a Yeltsin ally. A presidential spokesman said they had been suspended because of "reciprocal accusations of corruption." The Supreme Soviet (the standing legislature), **Sept. 3,** rejected Yeltsin's suspension of Rutskoi and referred the question to the Constitutional Court. Rutskoi, elected on the same ticket as Yeltsin in 1991, was the president's automatic successor. On **Sept. 18,** Yeltsin named former Premier Yegor Gaidar, the architect of Russia's market liberalizations who had been forced out of office by parliamentary opposition in 1992, as first deputy premier for economic affairs. Yeltsin, **Sept. 21,** suspended parliament and announced parliamentary elections for December. Rutskoi called this step a

coup d'etat, and his supporters in the Supreme Soviet voted to depose Yeltsin and elected Rutskoi acting president. The Constitutional Court, **Sept. 22,** held that Yeltsin had violated the constitution and could be impeached. Yeltsin, **Sept. 23,** announced presidential elections for June 1994. On **Sept. 24,** the Congress of People's Deputies (the country's highest legislative body, from which the Supreme Soviet members are drawn) voted to hold simultaneous parliamentary and presidential elections by March 1994. Moscow authorities cut off electricity, phone service, and hot water to the parliament building, **Sept. 25.** Yeltsin, **Sept. 27,** ruled out simultaneous elections. The Interior Ministry moved, **Sept. 28,** to seal off the parliament building. Barricades and wire were put around the building.

**Israel, PLO Sign Accord in Washington** — In a dramatic ceremony at the White House in September, representatives of Israel and the Palestine Liberation Organization signed a declaration of principles for interim Palestinian self-rule. The broad outlines of the agreement had become known in August. PLO Chairman Yasir Arafat, **Sept. 4,** obtained the endorsement of the accord by Fatah, the PLO's largest and most moderate faction. During early September, a number of moderate Arab regimes endorsed the accord, but Iraq, Libya, Sudan, and Iran opposed it. Syria appeared cautious, while seeking to make its own peace with Israel. The PLO Executive Committee, though not unanimously, endorsed the accord, **Sept. 9.** In a letter to Israeli Prime Minister Yitzhak Rabin, Arafat declared, **Sept. 9,** "The PLO recognizes the right of the State of Israel to exist in peace and security." He renounced terrorism and other acts of violence. In reply, **Sept. 9,** Rabin stated, "The Government of Israel has decided to recognize the PLO as the representative of the Palestinian people." Some 3,000 invited guests attended the signing of the interim accord on the lawn of the White House, **Sept. 13.** Foreign Minister Shimon Peres signed for Israel and Mahmoud Abbas, a negotiator in the secret talks leading to the agreement, signed for the PLO. Rabin and Arafat made generous and conciliatory statements. The prime minister said, "Enough of blood and tears. Enough." Those present applauded as Rabin and Arafat shook hands, with some coaxing from Pres. Bill Clinton. The accord said the parties would strive to "achieve a just, lasting and comprehensive peace settlement." Demonstrations for and against the agreement occurred in Israel and the occupied territories. Benjamin Netanyahu, Israel's opposition leader, deplored the agreement. On **Sept. 14,** in Washington, representatives of Israel and Jordan signed an "agenda for peace," but Jordanian officials said a formal agreement awaited normalization of relations between Israel and other countries. Rabin met with King Hassan of Morocco, **Sept. 14,** in Morocco, the first official visit by an Israeli prime minister to any Arab country other than Egypt. On **Sept. 23,** the Israeli parliament approved the peace agreement, 61-50.

**Shift of Power in South Africa Nears** — South Africa's ruling National Party agreed, **Sept. 7,** to share power with a multiparty council that would be established within 2 months. The Transitional Executive Council, which would consist of a member from each of South Africa's two dozen political parties, would oversee preparations for the nation's first universal-suffrage election, to be held in April 1994. The council would organize a multiracial peacekeeping force. In an address at the U.N., **Sept. 24,** Nelson Mandela, leader of the African National Congress, said that the "countdown to democracy" had begun in South Africa, and he called for the lifting of remaining international economic sanctions.

**Casualties Rise in Somalia** — As many as 100 Somalis were killed, **Sept. 9**, in a clash with U.N. peacekeepers in Mogadishu. Somali soldiers had fired on the U.N. forces. The response included attacks from Pakistani tanks and 2 U.S. helicopters. Somali victims included women and children, who either joined in the attack or were used as shields. Three U.S. soldiers were killed, **Sept. 25**, when their helicopter was shot down.

**Sihanouk Restored to Cambodian Throne** — On **Sept. 17**, Cambodia's 2 leading political parties resolved the question of who should lead the nation. They agreed that Prince Norodom Sihanouk would be restored as king. Sihanouk had reigned, 1941-1955, and then had served as Cambodia's civilian leader, until ousted in a coup in 1970. The parties also agreed that Prince Norodom Ranariddh, a son of Sihanouk, would serve as First Prime Minister, and Hun Sen, leader of the opposition party who had been co-president with Ranariddh since June, would serve as Second Prime Minister. Sihanouk was installed as king on **Sept. 24**.

**Georgian Rebels Take Provincial Capital** — Rebels in the breakaway province of Abkhazia gained ground in September in their fight against the government of Georgia. In mid-September they began a siege of the provincial capital of Sukhumi. Pres. Eduard Shevardnadze of Georgia went to Sukhumi and, on **Sept. 17**, appealed to civilians with arms to join government troops in its defense. On **Sept. 27**, the rebels captured the city, with Shevardnadze fleeing at the last minute.

**Demjanjuk Returns to U.S.** — John Demjanjuk returned to the U.S. in September, nearly 2 months after his conviction for war crimes was overturned in Israel. An Israeli Supreme Court justice, **Sept. 19**, rejected appeals that he be tried on other charges relating to his conduct during World War II. He left Israel **Sept. 22**.

### General

**China's Bid for Olympics Rebuffed** — The International Olympic Committee met in Monte Carlo, **Sept. 23**, to choose the site for the Summer Olympics to be held in the year 2000. China had vigorously promoted Beijing as the site, but many argued that a country with such a poor human rights record should not be chosen. Five cities competed for the honor. On the 4th ballot, Sydney, Australia, in an upset, edged out Beijing by a vote of 45-43.

**Participants Complete 2 Years in Biosphere** — Four men and 4 women emerged, **Sept. 26**, from the 3.15-acre, glass-enclosed "Biosphere 2" in the desert near Tucson. For 2 years, they shared their space with more than 3,800 species of plants and animals in recreated ecosystems that included a rain forest, a marsh, and a desert. Air and drinking water were recycled, although air had to be pumped in when the oxygen level fell. Most food was grown inside the biosphere.

### OCTOBER

### National

**Tailhook Nearly Sinks Top Admiral** — It was reported, **Oct. 1**, that Navy Secretary John Dalton had recommended that Adm. Frank Kelso be removed as Chief of Naval Operations. Kelso, the Navy's top officer, was one of 35 admirals and Marine Corps generals who had attended the Tailhook Association convention in Las Vegas in 1991 during which scores of women had been subjected to abuse and indignities by junior officers, and he had been nearby when such behavior was occurring. On **Oct. 4**, Defense Sec. Les Aspin decided to keep Kelso as CNO. A Pentagon spokesman said that Aspin did not agree with Dalton's view that Kelso should be judged by a higher or different standard than would be applied to other top officers. The Pentagon, **Oct. 15**, censured 3 admirals who had organized the 1991 convention. One of them had retired, and it was believed that the censure would effectively end the careers of the other 2. Twenty-nine other admirals, including Kelso, and one Marine general received letters of caution, which were not placed in their files.

**Economic Indicators Rise Sharply** — The Commerce Dept. reported, **Oct. 1**, that the index of leading economic indicators had risen 1 percent in August, the biggest advance of the year. The Census Bureau said, **Oct. 4**, that, despite the end of the recession, the number of poor people in the U.S. had risen in 1992 by 1.2 million, to 36.9 million. This total represented 14.5 percent of the population. The Labor Dept. reported, **Oct. 8**, that the unemployment rate remained at 6.7 percent in September.

**Ex-House Official Admits Guilt** — In a plea agreement with the federal government, made public **Oct. 5**, Jack Russ, former House sergeant-at-arms, admitted committing 3 felonies. Russ's plea came after 2 years of an ongoing Justice Dept. investigation into practices at the House bank. Russ agreed to plead guilty to embezzlement by a custodian of public funds, wire fraud, and making a false statement on his financial disclosure form. Russ agreed to cooperate with prosecutors.

**Justice Dept. Issues Report on Waco Cult** — The U.S. Justice Dept., **Oct. 8**, released a report on its handling of the 51-day siege of the Branch Davidian compound near Waco, Tex. At least 75 cult members died when federal agents attacked the compound in April. The report concluded that the department and Attorney Gen. Janet Reno had made no mistakes and that the cult bore the blame for the climactic fire that destroyed the compound. Investigators, however, found no evidence of child abuse by cultists, which Reno had cited as one reason for the assault on the compound. The report said nothing about Reno's assertion that the attack went forward because agents were exhausted and there was no one to replace them. According to the report, once tear gas had been fired into the buildings the cultists not only set the compound afire, but also killed children with knives, guns, and clubs.

**Social Security Payment Increase Announced** — The U.S. government announced, **Oct. 15**, that, based on the rate of increase in consumer prices, Social Security and other federal benefit recipients would receive a cost-of-living increase of 2.6 percent for 1994. The increase was the second-smallest annual rise since benefit payments were linked to inflation in 1975.

### International

**Yeltsin Routs Foes in Bloody Confrontation** — Russian Pres. Boris Yeltsin delivered a crushing blow to adversaries in parliament in October, but not without a considerable loss of life. On **Oct. 1**, the Interior Ministry estimated that 600 fighting men with a large cache of arms had joined Yeltsin's political opponents in the parliament building, called the White House. On **Oct. 2**, anti-Yeltsin demonstrators built street barricades in Moscow. Ousted Vice Pres. Aleksandr Rutskoi called for people to take to the streets against Yeltsin's "dictatorship." On the afternoon of **Oct. 3**, armed opponents of Yeltsin marched to the White House, overrunning government forces. Yeltsin declared a state of emergency in Moscow. With some people already dead on the streets below, Rutskoi appeared on the White House balcony and urged the crowd to seize the mayor's office and television center. The mayor's office was taken, but the rebels, advancing under both Soviet and Czarist flags, were met at the TV complex by Interior Ministry units. In the ensuing fight, the stations went off the air and 62 people were killed. Before midnight, Interior forces had turned back the attackers. Meanwhile, thousands of Yeltsin supporters also demonstrated in the streets. By sunrise, **Oct. 5**, army armored personnel carriers were surrounding the parliament building. Fighting broke out on the streets nearby and, after an appeal to occupants of the building to surrender went unheeded, tanks fired into the building, portions of which began to burn. Troops entered the White House and began to occupy it, floor by floor. By mid-afternoon, organized resistance dwindled to occasional sniper's fire. Many in the building, including Rutskoi and the speaker of parliament, Ruslan Khasbulatov, surrendered and were taken away in buses. Yeltsin, **Oct. 5**, banned opposition parties and newspapers, notably those of Communist or extreme nationalist views. He also dismissed regional officials who had opposed his moves against the parliament. In an address to the nation, **Oct. 6**, Yeltsin called for a purge of regional councils and new local elections. Police said, **Oct. 8**, that 187 had died in the conflict and 437 had been wounded. Yeltsin decreed, **Oct. 12**, that both houses of parliament would be elected in December. On **Oct. 15**, he ordered that a popular referendum be held in December on a new constitution. Rutskoi and Khasbulatov were charged, **Oct. 15**, with organizing mass disorders.

**Clinton Beefs Up U.S. Force in Somalia** — Responding to more U.S. combat deaths, Pres. Bill Clinton in October moved to build up American military forces in Somalia. On **Oct. 3**, 3 U.S. marines were killed when a mine blew up their vehicle in Mogadishu, the capital. Later that day a U.N. force, principally American, launched an air and ground attack on a crowded market area in south Mogadishu, where aides to Somali warlord Gen. Mohammed Farah Aidid were hiding. About 20 Somalis were seized, but Aidid's forces counterattacked. A total of 18 Americans, 2 Pakistanis, and a Malaysian were killed in the fighting and rescue effort. Somali casualties were unknown, but they were believed to be high and to include civilians. The Pentagon reported that some 75 Americans were wounded. Television coverage showed Somalis interrogating a wounded U.S. Army officer, Michael Durant, and other Somalis dragging 2 dead Americans through the streets. The U.S. role in Somalia was hotly debated in Congress and across the country. Clinton, **Oct. 4**, ordered several hundred new troops to Somalia, as well as tanks, helicopters, and gunships. Clinton, **Oct. 7**, announced that U.S. forces in Somalia and offshore would be increased from the present 4,700 to about 20,000. He indicated that the Americans would operate more independently from the U.N. command. Robert Oakley, a former State Department official, was appointed as a special envoy to Somalia. The president said all U.S. forces would be out of Somalia by March 31, 1994. On **Oct. 14**, Aidid freed Durant.

**U.S. Confronts Haiti's Military** — The international effort to restore democratic government to Haiti faltered in October. It was reported, **Oct. 4**, that Col. Joseph Michel François, commander of Haiti's military policy, would defy an internationally brokered agreement that called for him to step down. The agreement also provided that, in return for the ending of the international oil embargo of Haiti, the ousted elected president, the Rev. Jean-Bertrand Aristide, would return from exile by the end of October and be restored to power. The settlement provided as well for creation of a 1,300-member international force that would separate the military from the police. On **Oct. 11**, however, armed demonstrators prevented U.S. and Canadian troops from landing at Port-au-Prince, the capital. A

U.S. ship carrying the Americans and Canadians withdrew from Haitian waters, **Oct. 12**, and Pres. Bill Clinton said the U.S. soldiers would not return until Haitian authorities guaranteed their safety and that of Father Aristide. The U.N. Security Council voted, **Oct. 13**, to reimpose an oil and arms embargo on Haiti. On **Oct. 14**, gunmen in Port-au-Prince shot and killed the justice minister, Guy Malary, and 2 of his aides. Six weeks earlier, Aristide had appointed Malary and other members of a transitional cabinet. Clinton, **Oct. 15**, ordered 6 U.S. warships into the waters off Haiti, where they were to stop any ship that appeared to be violating the embargo. Leaders of Haiti's military and police did not step down as scheduled **Oct. 15**.

**China Breaks Nuclear Moratorium** — China exploded a nuclear weapon beneath its western desert, **Oct. 5**, breaking an informal moratorium on testing. Pres. Bill Clinton, **Oct. 5**, ordered preparations for a resumption of American tests.

**Bhutto Returns as Pakistan's Prime Minister** — In Pakistan's parliamentary election, **Oct. 6**, former Prime Minister Benazir Bhutto's Pakistan People's Party captured the largest bloc of seats, 86 of 217. The Pakistan Muslim League, headed by another former prime minister, Nawaz Sharif, won 72 seats. The new parliament chose Bhutto as prime minister, **Oct. 19**.

**Greek Voters Restore Former Leader** — In a national election held **Oct. 10**, Greeks returned former Prime Minister Andreas Papandreou and his Pan-Hellenic Socialist Movement to power. Papandreou had fallen from power in 1989 as a result of political scandals and accusations of inept management. Since then, however, voters had apparently grown tired of the economic austerity program of Prime Minister Constantine Mitsotakis.

**Death Toll Announced for Indian Quake** — Government officials, **Oct. 12**, announced an official death toll from September's earthquake in southern India. Chief Minister Sharad Pawar of the Maharashtra state government said 9,748 people died in the disaster, based upon the number of bodies that Army units leading the relief effort had removed from the rubble.

**German Court Rejects Appeal to Block European Unity Treaty** — The last obstacle blocking final ratification of the European Community's so-called Maastricht Treaty on greater economic and political unity was removed in October. In Germany, the only EC country that had not completed its ratification, the constitutional court rejected, **Oct. 12**, a legal challenge contending that the treaty would surrender national power in violation of the German constitution.

## General

**Superstar Michael Jordan Retires** — Michael Jordan, acclaimed by many as the greatest basketball player ever, announced his retirement, **Oct. 6**. After leading North Carolina to the NCAA championship in 1982, Jordan had starred for 9 years with the Chicago Bulls of the NBA. Jordan said he had nothing more to accomplish in basketball. He said his decision was not based on the murder of his father, to whom he was greatly devoted, during the summer.

**Phone-Cable Merger Valued at $33 Billion** — The Bell Atlantic Corporation and Tele-Communications Inc. announced plans for a merger, **Oct. 13**, that was seen as a $33 billion deal. Bell Atlantic would buy Tele-Communications, the nation's largest cable operator, and the Liberty Media Corporation, its cable programming company, for $23 billion and assume $10 billion in debt. The new company would be well positioned to develop and deliver a variety of new programming to American homes. The merger was subject to federal approval.

## Notable Decisions of the U.S. Supreme Court, 1992-1993 Term

The Supreme Court's 1992-1993 term began Oct. 5, 1992, and ended June 28, 1993. The Court issued 107 decisions, the same number as in the previous term, but a decrease from the average of 150 rulings per term during the mid-1980s. Forty percent of the decisions were unanimous, far more than in recent years, yet the Court remained divided in such important areas as civil rights and religion. The triad of Chief Justice William H. Rehnquist, Justice Anthony M. Kennedy, and Justice Antonin Scalia was in the majority more than 90 percent of the time, the highest figure among the justices. The most frequent dissenter was Justice David H. Souter. Among the major decisions were:

**Abortion:** The Court declined to hear a challenge by abortion-rights advocates to a Mississippi law requiring a 24-hour waiting period, a provision similar to one in Pennsylvania that had been upheld by the Court during the previous term (Dec. 7). The Court also declined to hear appeals from Louisiana and Guam, where laws banning abortions, except to save a woman's life or in some cases of rape or incest, had been declared unconstitutional by lower federal courts (Mar. 8). The Court ruled, 6-3, that federal courts could not prohibit antiabortion protesters from blocking access to abortion clinics by invoking the Civil Rights Act of 1871, which had been designed to protect former slaves from conspiracies to deprive them of their civil rights (Jan. 13).

**Animal Sacrifice:** The Court ruled unanimously that a ban imposed by the city of Hialeah, Florida, on ritual animal sacrifice was unconstitutional. The Court held that, because the ban was clearly directed only at members of the Santeria faith, a Caribbean religion combining Yoruba African traditions with Roman Catholicism, it violated the First Amendment guarantee of the free exercise of religion (June 11).

**Employee Bias Suits:** Shifting the burden of proof to the employee, the Court ruled, 5-4, that workers must provide explicit evidence that they had been discriminated against on the basis of race, religion, or other status in order to qualify for protection under civil rights legislation (June 25).

**Hate Crimes:** The Court ruled unanimously that states could impose harsher sentences on defendants convicted of so-called hate crimes—those motivated by religious, racial, or other biases—because those crimes could inflict great harm on victims and society in general. More than 20 states and the District of Columbia, as well as federal sentencing guidelines, permitted stricter sentencing for bias-motivated crimes (June 11).

**"Minority-Majority" Voting Districts:** The Court ruled, 5-4, that states that designed voting districts to increase black representation to compensate for past discrimination could not violate the constitutional rights of white voters to equal protection under the law. The shape of the North Carolina district in question was "bizarre," the Court said, resembling "the most egregious racial gerrymanders of the past," and the state must demonstrate a "compelling interest" for such design over one with compact and contiguous districts (June 28).

**Refugees:** The Court ruled, 8-1, that a U.S. policy in which boats carrying Haitian refugees were intercepted on the high seas and the refugees returned to Haiti without receiving asylum hearings did not violate U.S. law. The Court held that U.S. refugee law applied only when aliens were in U.S. territory (June 21).

**Religion and Schools:** The Court ruled unanimously that schools must allow church groups the same after-hours access to their facilities as secular community organizations were given (June 7). The Court ruled, 5-4, that local governments could comply with a federal law requiring equal educational opportunities for disabled children by paying for special services in parochial schools (June 18).

**Rights of Suspects, Defendants, and Prisoners:** In a unanimous decision the Court expanded the "plain view" doctrine, under which police do not need a warrant to seize narcotics or other illegal objects that are clearly visible. If such items are recognized by "plain feel" while a suspect is frisked for concealed weapons, the Court said, no warrant is needed for their seizure (June 7). The Court ruled unanimously that the government holds only limited power under the Constitution to seize the assets of convicted criminals by using civil forfeiture law. Such a seizure could be considered an "excessive fine" under the Eighth Amendment, applicable to both criminal and civil penalties (June 28). The Court ruled, 7-2, that confining a nonsmoking prisoner in a cell with a chain-smoking cellmate could constitute "cruel and unusual punishment" under the Eighth Amendment (June 18). The Court ruled, 5-4, that federal courts should refuse to grant habeas corpus review of violations of a defendant's rights during a trial unless the violation had a "substantial and injurious effect" or influence in determining the jury's verdict" (April 21). The Court ruled, 7-2, that the conclusions of an expert witness need not be "generally accepted" within the scientific community, but the "methods and procedures" involved in reaching such conclusions must be valid (June 28).

**Tax Deductions for Home Offices:** The Court ruled, 8-1, that self-employed people maintaining offices in their homes could claim housing costs as business deductions only if their home office was their "primary" place of business, not if they did their most important work or most of their work elsewhere (Jan. 12).

## The 1993 Nobel Prizes

Each of the 1993 Nobel Prizes, awarded in October, consisted of a large solid gold medal and a cash award of more than $800,000.

**Chemistry:** Kary B. Mullis, an American, and Michael Smith, a British-born Canadian, shared the award. Dr. Mullis invented a method to "amplify" (or copy) DNA; Dr. Smith designed one to splice foreign components into genetic material.

**Memorial Prize in Economic Science:** Robert W. Fogel and Douglass C. North, both Americans, shared the prize, the first ever awarded for work in economic history.

**Literature:** Toni Morrison, an American novelist and essayist whose works include *Song of Solomon, Be-* loved, and *Jazz,* won the award. She was the first African-American to do so.

**Peace:** Frederik W. de Klerk, president of South Africa, and Nelson Mandela, leader of the African National Congress, shared the prize, for their efforts to end apartheid and to institute majority rule in South Africa.

**Physics:** Two Americans, Joseph H. Taylor and Russell A. Hulse, shared the prize for discovering the first known binary pulsar.

**Physiology or Medicine:** Philip A. Sharp and Richard J. Roberts shared the prize for their independent discovery of "split genes." Dr. Sharp is an American; Dr. Roberts, born in Britain, works in the U.S.

# Notable Quotes in 1993

"I pray that I may be all that she would have been had she lived in an age when women could aspire and achieve, and daughters are cherished as much as sons."
Supreme Court Justice *Ruth Bader Ginsburg,* invoking the memory of her mother

"Vast sections of society are confused about what is right and what is wrong."
*Pope John Paul II*

"I love the game, but I don't need that kind of turmoil."
*George Bush,* on whether he had any interest in being commissioner of baseball

"To forget would mean to kill the victims a second time. We could not prevent their first death; we must not allow them to be killed again."
*Elie Wiesel,* at the dedication of the Holocaust Memorial Museum in Washington, D.C.

"We want a guy who's amiable and doesn't cause any trouble."
Rolling Stone *Mick Jagger,* on what the aging band was looking for in a replacement for retiring bass player Bill Wyman

"He ate everything but the drapes. . . . He's a man who does like to put it down."
NBC's *Tom Brokaw,* on a lunch held by President Bill Clinton with network news anchors

"That's the president of the United States you're talking about, pinhead."
Vice President *Al Gore* to David Letterman after Letterman joked: "What does (Clinton) love to hear all the time? 'Would you like fries with that?' "

"I don't think you're going to see a great, great uproar in this country about the Republican committee trying to bug the Democratic headquarters."
*Richard Nixon,* four days after the 1972 Watergate burglary, as recorded on a White House tape released in 1993

"If Thomas Jefferson was alive today, I would appoint him secretary of state, and then suggest to [Vice President Al] Gore that we both resign so he could become president."
*President Bill Clinton,* asked if Jefferson would merit a job in his administration

"I was not meant for the job or the spotlight of public life in Washington. Here ruining people is considered sport."
Note left by White House lawyer *Vincent Foster,* an apparent suicide

"I love Charles [Oakley]. . . . He'll push me, shove me, scratch me, hit me, bite me, but never an elbow."
*Horace Grant,* Chicago Bulls forward

"Fifty guys standing around in their little posing trunks with oil slapped on their body. Showing off and posing in front of 5,000 people. It's a joke."
*Arnold Schwarzenegger* on bodybuilding competitions

"It's just like Pepsi-Cola!"
Georgia's President *Eduard Shevardnadze,* after sampling Coca-Cola at the opening of a new Coke bottling plant in Tbilisi

"If that happens, I'll just buy a new audience."
*David Letterman* on whether his $14 million salary and new time slot might alienate his audience

"If he wants me as a character witness, I'll be there."
Senator *Bob Packwood,* while under an ethics committee investigation of sexual misconduct, referring to Representative Dan Rostenkowski, who was implicated in the House post office scandal

"If he starts sleeping through cabinet meetings, you'll know the transformation is complete."
*Marlin Fitzwater,* former press secretary to George Bush, on ex-Reagan aide David Gergen's efforts to reshape Bill Clinton's image

"Left to their own devices, the three networks would televise live executions. Except Fox—they'd televise live naked executions."
TV producer *Gary David Goldberg*

"Now she knows how most women in America feel every day. She's got an impossible job, she's underpaid and every night her boss wants to sleep with her."
*Jay Leno* on Hillary Rodham Clinton's appointment as head of the Clinton administration's health care task force

"Well, they look so much alike I get them confused."
*Barry Manilow,* after referring to the wedding of Lyle Lovett and Julia Child, rather than Julia Roberts

"There's a lot to be said for superficiality."
TV producer *Linda Bloodworth-Thomason,* calling Washington a more trivial town than Hollywood

"When I started doing screenplays, I described it as work for idiots, but it's really work for strong, passionate idiots."
Author *Stephen King*

"They're failures. Well, that's a little strong. But if $120,000 a year is the best job you've ever had, you haven't really done much."
Author *Tom Clancy,* on what's wrong with Congress

"You don't need to be 'straight' to fight and die for your country. You just need to shoot straight."
*Barry Goldwater,* on whether gays should be allowed to serve in the military

"What is so important about having Chicago schools open on a specific date? . . . We just add it on to the end of the school year, another 10 days or two weeks. I don't see anything wrong with that. Half the kids aren't going to graduate anyway"
*James (Pate) Philip,* president of the Illinois Senate

"We who have fought against you, the Palestinians, we say to you today in a loud and a clear voice: 'Enough of blood and tears. Enough!' "
Israeli Prime Minister *Yitzhak Rabin,* speaking at the White House signing of a peace accord with the Palestine Liberation Organization

"Although not a lawyer, Mr. Burr strove for such authenticity . . . that we regard his passing as though we lost one of our own."
*R. William Ide III,* president of the American Bar Association, on the death of actor Raymond Burr, who portrayed TV lawyer Perry Mason

"I can't really say I ever sat around and fantasized about how I would have liked to have ended my career. But I think if I had, it certainly would have been with a strong performance in a pennant race. I guess by striking out the last hitter."
Pitcher *Nolan Ryan,* whose career ended in Sept. 1993 when he tore a ligament in his right elbow.

# Historical Anniversaries

## 1894—100 Years Ago

Economic depression continued in the U.S.

The U.S. Treasury offered a $50 million bond issue to restore the declining gold reserve, **Jan. 17,** but public response was poor; a 2nd issue was offered **Nov. 13.**

Labor unrest was widespread all year, with strikes for higher wages, shorter hours, and safer conditions involving some 750,000 U.S. workers, including 136,000 coal miners in Columbus, Oh. and 12,000 garment workers in New York City. The strike by workers of the Pullman Palace Car Co. was joined by Eugene Debs's American Railway Union. U.S. troops sent to Chicago to enforce a federal injunction against the strikers opened fire, killing two men and injuring several; mob violence brought extensive damage. A federal grand jury sentenced Debs to 6 months in prison, but he was successfully defended by Clarence Darrow, who resigned his position as a railroad counsel to do so.

A Chinese Exclusion Treaty, by which China agreed to keep its laborers from the U.S., was signed **Mar. 17.**

Coxey's Army, some 400 unemployed men led by Jacob S. Coxey, marched from Ohio to Washington, D.C. to protest unemployment and demand public work programs. Coxey and 2 other leaders were arrested for trespassing at the Capitol, **Apr. 30.**

The Democratic Silver Convention was held in Omaha, Neb. **June 21,** and William Jennings Bryan came to national prominence for his eloquence in leading 1,000 delegates to the adoption of a free-coinage plank on a silver-to-gold ratio of 16 to 1.

Congress made Labor Day a legal holiday, **June 28.**

Following controversy surrounding the overthrow of Hawaii's Queen Liliuokalani by proannexation sugar interests headed by Sanford B. Dole and aided by the U.S. Minister, the Republic of Hawaii was proclaimed **July 4.** Dole became president and a progressive constitution was adopted. U.S. recognition came **Aug. 7.**

The Bureau of Immigration was created by an Act of Congress **Aug. 18.**

The Carey Act, adopted **Aug. 18,** promised each state up to a million acres of public lands, if the state would agree to irrigate.

The controversial Wilson-Gorman Tariff Act, which became law **Aug. 27,** without Pres. Grover Cleveland's signature, reduced U.S. tariff duties and levied the first graduated tax on incomes over $4,000. One senator termed the income tax "socialism, communism, devilism," and in 1895 the Supreme Court would declare it unconstitutional.

The U.S. and Japan signed a commercial treaty, **Nov. 22.**

Radcliffe College for Women, affiliated with Harvard Univ., opened at Cambridge, Mass. Elizabeth Cary Agassiz, influential in its founding, became its first president.

William Ramsay and John Rayleigh discovered the inert gas they named argon.

**Literature:** *Pudd'nhead Wilson* by Mark Twain; *Trilby,* featuring the hypnotic "Svengali," by George du Maurier; *The Memoirs of Sherlock Holmes* by Arthur Conan Doyle; *The Jungle Book* by Rudyard Kipling.

**Journalism:** *Wealth Against Commonwealth,* a study of the Standard Oil Co. by Henry Demarest Lloyd, one of the first "muckrakers"; *The Yellow Book,* a London periodical, which gained fame through art director Aubrey Beardsley's provocative drawings.

**Art:** Edgar Degas's "Femme à sa toilette" and American artist Mary Cassatt's "La toilette" were exhibited at Paris. Louis Comfort Tiffany invented and trademarked a process for staining glass to achieve radiantly iridescent colors, which he used to create "art nouveau" style lamps, vases, jewelry, and windows.

**Theater:** *Arms and the Man* by George Bernard Shaw, in London.

**Ballet:** *Afternoon of a Faun,* with music by French composer Claude Debussy, in Paris.

**Popular songs:** "Humoresque" by Anton Dvorák; "The Sidewalks of New York" by Charles B. Lawlor and James W. Blake; "I've Been Working on the Railroad," published as "Levee Song."

**Sports:** The first U.S. Open golf tournament was held at St. Andrew Golf Club in Yonkers, N.Y. The first Penn Relays were held in Philadelphia.

**Miscellaneous:** Pêche Melba—a scoop of vanilla ice cream on a cooked peach half with a purée of raspberries topped by almond slivers—was created by Auguste Escoffier at London's Savoy Hotel. The dessert honored Nellie Melba, the Australian diva. The Hershey Bar was introduced by Milton S. Hershey, whose family would found Hershey, Pa., to be populated mainly by company employees, in 1903.

## 1944—50 Years Ago

On D-Day, **June 6,** some 176,000 Allied troops landed at 5 beachheads along a 50-mile Normandy coastline under the command of Gen. Dwight D. Eisenhower. The date marked the start of the reconquest of France, and the beginning of the end for the Axis forces in World War II. The Battle of the Bulge in the Ardennes Forest of Belgium, **Dec. 16–27,** was the last major counteroffensive.

In the Pacific, Japanese forces were retreating. U.S. forces headed by Gen. Douglas MacArthur returned to the Philippines, **Oct. 20,** and 4 separate operations of a 6-day naval battle in Leyte Gulf marked the effective end of the Japanese fleet. The kamikaze, or suicide plane, was first used during the Leyte campaign.

The Supreme Court ruled, **April 3,** that an American could not be denied the right to vote because of race.

Jacob Coxey, age 90, stood on the Capitol steps, **May 1,** and delivered the speech he had attempted to make 50 years earlier. (See *1894—100 Years Ago.*)

Meat rationing was ended **May 3,** except for steak and choice cuts of beef.

The Servicemen's Readjustment Act, or "G.I. Bill of Rights," was passed by Congress **June 22,** and would finance college educations and low-interest, no-down-payment home loans for millions of veterans.

The United Nations Monetary and Financial Conference took place at Bretton Woods, New Hampshire, **July 1–22.** Forty-four countries attended to develop plans for mutual assistance, including the establishment of the International Monetary Fund for currency stabilization.

Representatives of the U.S., Britain, China, and the USSR met at Dumbarton Oaks, Washington, D.C. to discuss postwar world organization, **Aug. 21–Oct. 7.** Proposals would become the basis for the United Nations charter.

Pres. Franklin D. Roosevelt was reelected to a 4th term, **Nov. 7,** and would be the only U.S. president to do so. Votes included several million absentee ballots sent by members of the armed forces. FDR won 36 states with 432 electoral votes, while New York governor Thomas E. Dewey won only 12 states with 99 electoral votes, failing to carry his home state. Vice Pres. Henry A. Wallace had been replaced on the Democratic ticket by Harry S. Truman, U.S. senator from Missouri.

A Federal Highway Act was passed by Congress, **Nov. 29,** creating a new U.S. national system of interstate highways, covering 40,000 miles.

Congress created, **Dec. 15,** the rank of General of the Army—"5-star general"—for Dwight D. Eisenhower, Douglas MacArthur, George C. Marshall, and Henry Arnold.

The first large-scale automatic digital computer was built by the IBM Corporation at Harvard Univ. to the specifications of Harvard prof. Howard H. Aiken. The Harvard-IBM Automatic Sequence Controlled Calculator, or Mark I, had more than 750,000 parts, was 51 feet long, and weighed 5 tons. It performed a multiplication in about 6 seconds.

**Literature:** *Winter Tales* by Isak Dinesen; *Dangling Man* by Saul Bellow; *A Bell for Adano* by John Hersey; *Strange Fruit* by Lillian Smith; *The Lost Weekend* by Charles Jackson; *The Razor's Edge* by W. Somerset Maugham.

**Art:** "Three Studies for Figures at the Base of a Crucifix" by Francis Bacon; "Effervescence" by Hans Hoffman; "Plantation Road" by Thomas Hart Benton; "Pelvis III" by Georgia O'Keeffe.

**Theater:** *Antigone* by Jean Anouilh, and *No Exit* by Jean-Paul Sartre, both in Paris; *Harvey* by Mary Coyle; *I Remember Mama* by John Van Druten—with young Marlon Brando.

**Musicals:** *On the Town*, with Betty Comden, Adolph Green, and Nancy Walker; music by Leonard Bernstein, lyrics by Comden and Green; dances derived from the ballet *Fancy Free* by Jerome Robbins.

**Movies:** *Henry V*, with Laurence Olivier; *Thirty Seconds Over Tokyo*, with Clark Gable, Walter Pidgeon; Sergei Eisenstein's *Ivan the Terrible, Part I*; Alfred Hitchcock's *Lifeboat*, with Tallulah Bankhead, William Bendix, John Hodiak, Canada Lee; Preston Sturges's *Hail the Conquering Hero*, with Eddie Bracken, Ella Raines; Otto Preminger's *Laura*, with Clifton Webb, Gene Tierney, Dana Andrews; Billy Wilder's *Double Indemnity*, with Barbara Stanwyck,

Fred MacMurray, Edward G. Robinson; George Cukor's *Gaslight*, with Ingrid Bergman, Charles Boyer; Howard Hawks's *To Have and Have Not*, with Humphrey Bogart, Lauren Bacall; *National Velvet*, with Mickey Rooney and 12-year-old Elizabeth Taylor.

**Musicals:** Vincente Minelli's *Meet Me in St. Louis*, with Judy Garland, songs including "The Trolley Song" and "The Boy Next Door"; Leo McCarey's *Going My Way*, with Bing Crosby, Barry Fitzgerald, songs including "Would You Like to Swing on a Star?"; Charles Vidor's *Cover Girl*, with Rita Hayworth, Gene Kelly, songs including "Long Ago (and Far Away)".

**Pop Songs:** "I'll Walk Alone"; "Don't Fence Me In"; "Nancy (with the Laughing Face)"; "Rum and Coca-Cola"; "You're Nobody Till Somebody Loves You"; "You Always Hurt the One You Love".

**Sports:** The St. Louis Cardinals won the World Series over the St. Louis Braves, 4 games to 2.

**Miscellaneous:** Chiquita Banana was introduced by the United Fruit Company.

## 1969—25 Years Ago

A human walked on the moon for the first time, July 20, when U.S. astronaut Neil A. Armstrong left the lunar module of Apollo 11. He announced, "That's one small step for man, one giant leap for mankind." Armstrong was joined by Edwin E. "Buzz" Aldrin Jr.; the two astronauts deposited a lunar capsule and an American flag on the moon.

Richard M. Nixon was inaugurated as the 37th U.S. president, Spiro T. Agnew as vice president, Jan. 20.

U.S. combat deaths in Vietnam since Jan. 1, 1961 topped those of the Korean War, reaching 33,641 Apr. 1.

The world's first entirely artificial heart, made of Dacron and plastic, was implanted into a human, Apr. 4, by Dr. Denton A. Cooley in Houston, Tex., and the patient lived until Apr. 8.

The Supreme Court ruled unanimously, Apr. 7, that laws prohibiting the reading or viewing of obscene material in the privacy of a home were unconstitutional.

Several hundred students, mostly members of the militant Students for a Democratic Society (SDS), occupied Harvard Univ.'s administration building, Apr. 9; student protests followed at many other institutions.

U.S. B-52s dropped almost 3,000 tons of bombs on enemy positions near the Cambodian border, Apr. 24, the heaviest bombing raid in the war.

Pres. Nixon met with South Vietnam Pres. Nguyen Van Thieu, June 8, and announced the start of U.S. troop withdrawal and a "Vietnamization" policy.

Chief Justice Earl Warren retired from the Supreme Court, June 23, after swearing in Warren Burger as his successor.

The body of 28-year-old Mary Jo Kopechne was retrieved, July 19, from a car that had plunged off Chappaquiddick Island, near Martha's Vineyard, Mass. Sen. Edward M. Kennedy had been driving the car, and had failed to report the accident to police for 10 hours.

Actress Sharon Tate and 4 others were found murdered, Aug. 9, in Los Angeles; Charles Manson and several members of his cult were arrested.

The Woodstock Music and Art Fair at Bethel, New York brought an estimated 300,000–400,000 young people for 4 days in mid-Aug. Performers included Jimi Hendrix, Richie Havens, Joan Baez, the Jefferson Airplane, the Who, and the Grateful Dead. Despite traffic jams, inadequate food, water, and medical supplies, heavy rains and heavy drug use, the general atmosphere was one of peaceful celebration.

North Vietnamese leader Ho Chi Minh died, Sept. 3, at age 79 after 15 years as president.

The Concorde supersonic jet made its first supersonic flight, Oct. 1.

The first Vietnam Moratorium Day took place, Oct. 15, millions wearing black armbands, many meeting or marching to protest the war. Huge peace demonstrations took place in several major cities in Oct. and Nov., the largest involving 250,000 people in Wash., D.C., Nov. 15.

Pres. Nixon appealed for the first time, Nov. 3, to "the great Silent Majority."

News reports, Nov. 16, charged a U.S. infantry unit with the massacre at My Lai, a village in South Vietnam on Mar. 16, 1968; said to have been slain were more than 450 villagers, including women and children.

Public Television's "Sesame Street" began in Nov. to teach preschool children letters and numbers using the same techniques as commercial TV. The stars that were born included Bert and Ernie, Cookie Monster, Oscar the Grouch, and Big Bird.

The federal government announced the relaxation of trade restrictions with China, Dec. 19.

A far-reaching tax reform bill was signed by Pres. Nixon, Dec. 30. It reduced individual tax rates and removed some 9 million poor from federal tax rolls, but was criticized as mainly benefiting the rich.

**Literature:** *Ada* by Vladimir Nabokov; *Portnoy's Complaint* by Philip Roth; *Slaughterhouse Five* by Kurt Vonnegut Jr.; *Bullet Park* by John Cheever; *The Godfather* by Mario Puzo.

**Art:** "The Finn" by Andrew Wyeth; "Orange Yellow Orange" by Mark Rothko.

**Theater:** *To Be Young, Gifted and Black* by Lorraine Hansberry, adapted by Robert Nemiroff; *Ceremonies in Dark Old Men* by Lonnie Elder III; *No Place to Be Somebody* by Charles Gordone; *Last of the Red Hot Lovers* by Neil Simon.

**Movies:** Dennis Hopper's *Easy Rider*, with Hopper, Peter Fonda, Jack Nicholson; John Schlesinger's *Midnight Cowboy*, with Dustin Hoffman, Jon Voight; Sam Peckinpah's *The Wild Bunch*, with William Holden, Robert Ryan, Ernest Borgnine; George Roy Hill's *Butch Cassidy and the Sundance Kid*, with Paul Newman, Robert Redford, Katharine Ross; Karel Reisz's *The Loves of Isadora Duncan*, with Vanessa Redgrave; Sidney Pollack's *They Shoot Horses, Don't They?* with Jane Fonda; Henry Hathaway's *True Grit*, with John Wayne; Woody Allen's *Take the Money and Run*.

**Sports:** On the 100th anniversary of major league baseball, the Natl. League added San Diego and Montreal; the American League, Kansas City and Seattle. Each league was split into divisions, playoffs for league pennants began; changes were also made in ballpark outfields, strike zones, and pitchers' mounds. Willie Mays hit his 600th home run, Sept. 22, the San Francisco Giants outfielder joining Babe Ruth as the only players to do so. Outfielder Mickey Mantle retired after 18 years with the New York Yankees. The New York Mets won their first World Series. Rod Laver won the Grand Slam of tennis—Australian, French, Wimbledon, and U.S. singles titles—for the second time. The NCAA basketball championship was won by UCLA, whose center Lew Alcindor was the first player to win the tournament's MVP award 3 successive years.

**Miscellaneous:** *The Saturday Evening Post* ended publication after 148 years. *Penthouse*, a more explicit competitor of Hugh Hefner's *Playboy*, began publication.

# UNITED STATES GOVERNMENT

| LEGISLATIVE BRANCH | EXECUTIVE BRANCH | JUDICIAL BRANCH |
|---|---|---|
| **CONGRESS** | **PRESIDENT** | **Supreme Court of the United States** |
| Senate   House | Vice President   Cabinet | Courts of Appeals |
| | | District Courts |
| Architect of the Capitol | **Executive Office of the President** | Claims Court |
| U.S. Botanic Garden | | Court of Appeals for the Federal Circuit |
| General Accounting Office | White House Office | Court of International Trade |
| Government Printing Office | Office of Management and Budget | Territorial Courts |
| Library of Congress | Council of Economic Advisers | Court of Military Appeals |
| Office of Technology Assessment | National Economic Council | Court of Veterans Appeals |
| Congressional Budget Office | National Security Council | Administrative Office of the Courts |
| Copyright Royalty Tribunal | Office of Policy Development | Federal Judicial Center |
| U.S. Tax Court | Office of the U.S. Trade Representative | |
| | Council on Environmental Quality | |
| | Office of Science and Technology Policy | |
| | Office of Administration | |
| | Office of National Drug Control Policy | |
| | National Critical Materials Council | |
| | National Space Council | |

## The Clinton Administration

As of mid-1993

Terms of office of the president and vice president: Jan. 20, 1993, to Jan. 20, 1997. No person may be elected president of the United States for more than two 4-year terms.

**President** — Bill Clinton of Arkansas receives salary of $200,000 a year taxable; in addition an expense allowance of $50,000 to assist in defraying expenses resulting from his official duties. Also there may be expended not exceeding $100,000, nontaxable, a year for travel expenses and $20,000 for official entertainment available for allocation within the Executive Office of the President.

**Vice President** — Albert Gore, Jr., of Tennessee receives salary of $171,500 a year and $10,000 for expenses, all of which is taxable.

### The Cabinet

(Salary: $148,400 per annum)

Secretary of State — Warren M. Christopher.
Secretary of Treasury — Lloyd Bentsen.
Secretary of Defense — Les Aspin.
Attorney General — Janet Reno.
Secretary of Interior — Bruce Babbitt.
Secretary of Agriculture — Mike Espy.
Secretary of Commerce — Ronald H. Brown.
Secretary of Labor — Robert B. Reich.
Secretary of Health and Human Services — Donna E. Shalala.
Secretary of Housing and Urban Development — Henry G. Cisneros.
Secretary of Transportation — Federico F. Pena.
Secretary of Energy — Hazel R. O'Leary.
Secretary of Education — Richard W. Riley.
Secretary of Veterans Affairs — Jesse Brown.

### The White House Staff

1600 Pennsylvania Ave. NW 20500

Chief of Staff — Thomas F. McLarty 3d.
Asst. to the President & Deputy Chief of Staff — Roy Neel.
Counselor to the President — David Gergen.
Adviser on Policy and Strategy — George Stephanopoulos.
Assistants to the President:
  Counsel to the President — Bernard W. Nussbaum.
  Counsel to the President on Domestic Policy — Carol Rasco.
  Presidential Personnel — Bruce Lindsay.
  Public Events & Initiatives — Marcia Hale.
  Science & Technology — Dr. John H. Gibbons.
  Press Secretary — Dee Dee Myers.

  Legislative Affairs — Howard Paster.
  Communications — Mark Gearan.
  Economic & Domestic Affairs — Robert Rubin.
  Management & Admin. — David Watkins.
  Cabinet Secy. — Christine A. Varney.
  National Security — W. Anthony Lake.
  Staff Secretary — John Podesta.
  National Service — Eli Segal.
  Media Affairs — Jeff Eller.
AIDS Policy Coordinator — Kristine M. Gebbie.

### Executive Agencies

Council of Economic Advisers — Laura D'Andrea Tyson, chmn.
National Economic Council — Robert Rubin, dir.
Central Intelligence Agency — R. James Woolsey, dir.
Office of National Drug Control Policy — Lee P. Brown.
Office of Management and Budget — Leon E. Panetta, dir.
U.S. Trade Representative — Michael Kantor.
Council on Environmental Quality — vacant.

### Department of State

2201 C St. NW 20520

Secretary of State — Warren M. Christopher.
Deputy Secretary — Clifton R. Wharton, Jr.
Under Sec. for Political Affairs — Peter Tarnoff.
Under Sec. for International Security Affairs — Lynn Davis.
Under Secretary for Management — Richard Moose.
Under Sec. for Global Affairs — Timothy Wirth.
Legal Advisor — Sherman M. Funk.
Assistant Secretaries for:
  Administration — Patrick F. Kennedy.
  African Affairs — George E. Moose.
  Consular Affairs — Mary A. Ryan.
  Diplomatic Security — Tony Quainton.
  East Asian & Pacific Affairs — Winston Lord.
  Economic & Business Affairs — Daniel Tarullo.
  European & Canadian Affairs — Stephen Oxman.
  Human Rights & Humanitarian Affairs — John H. F. Shattuck.
  Intelligence & Research — Tobi Gati.
  Inter-American Affairs — Alexander Watson.
  International Narcotics Matters — vacant.

International Organization Affairs — Douglas J. Bennett, Jr.
Legislative Affairs — Wendy R. Sherman.
Near-Eastern & S. Asian Affairs — Edward Djerejian.
Oceans, International Environmental & Scientific Affairs — Elinor G. Constable.
Politico-Military Affairs — Robert L. Galucci.
Public Affairs — Thomas Dinilon.
South Asian Affairs — Robin Raphel.

## Department of the Treasury
1500 Pennsylvania Ave. NW 20220
Secretary of the Treasury — Lloyd Bentsen.
Deputy Sec. of the Treasury — Roger Altman.
Under Sec. for Domestic Finance — Frank N. Newman.
Under Sec. for International Affairs — Lawrence Summers.
General Counsel — Jean Hanson.
Assistant Secretaries for:
  Economic Policy — Alicia Hancock Munnell.
  Enforcement — Ronald K. Noble.
  Fiscal Affairs — vacant.
  International Affairs — Jeffrey Shafer.
  Legislative Affairs — Mary B. Levy.
  Policy Management — vacant.
  Public Affairs & Public Liaison — Jack R. DeVore.
  Tax Policy — Leslie B. Samuels.
Bureaus:
  Alcohol, Tobacco & Firearms — vacant.
  Comptroller of the Currency — Eugene A. Ludwig.
  Customs — George J. Weise, comm.
  Engraving & Printing — Peter H. Daley, dir.
  Federal Law Enforcement Training Center — Charles F. Rinkevich, dir.
  Financial Management Service — vacant.
  Internal Revenue Service — Margaret Richardson, comm.
  Mint — David Ryder, dir.
  Public Debt — Richard L. Gregg, comm.
  Treasurer of the U.S. — vacant.
  U.S. Savings Bond Division — vacant.
  U.S. Secret Service — Guy Caputo, act.

## Department of Defense
The Pentagon 20301
Secretary of Defense — Les Aspin.
Deputy Secretary — William Perry.
Under Secy. for Acquisition — John Deutch.
Under Secy. for Policy — Frank Wisner.
Asst. Secretaries for:
  Command, Control, Communications & Intelligence — vacant.
  Force Management & Personnel — vacant.
  Health Affairs — vacant.
  International Security Policy — vacant.
  Legislative Affairs — vacant.
  Policy & Plans — Graham T. Allison.
  Products & Logistics — vacant.
  Program Analysis & Evaluation — vacant.
  Public Affairs — Kathleen DeLaski.
  Reserve Affairs — Deborah Lee.
  Special Operations & Low Intensity Conflict— vacant.
Comptroller— John Hamre.
General Counsel — Jamie Gorelick.
Administration — Ann Reese, dir.
Operational Test & Evaluation — vacant.
Chairman, Joint Chiefs of Staff — Gen. John Shalikashvili.
Secretary of the Army — Togo West.
Secretary of the Navy — John Dalton.
Secretary of the Air Force — Sheila Widnall.

## Department of Justice
Constitution Ave. & 10th St. NW 20530
Attorney General — Janet Reno.
Deputy Attorney General — Philip B. Heymann.
Associate Attorney General — Webster L. Hubbell.

Solicitor General — Drew Days 3d.
Intelligence Policy & Review — vacant.
Professional Responsibility —vacant.
Assistants:
  Antitrust Division — Anne Bingaman.
  Civil Division — Frank Hunger.
  Civil Rights Division — James Turner, act.
  Criminal Division — vacant.
  Environment & Natural Resources Division — Gerald Torres.
  Justice Management Division — vacant.
  Legal Counsel — Walter Dellinger.
  Legal Policy — Eleanor Acheson.
  Legislative Affairs — Sheila Foster.
  Policy & Communications — vacant.
  Tax Division — vacant.
Fed. Bureau of Investigation — Louis J. Freeh, dir.
Exec. Off. for Immigration Review — vacant.
Bureau of Prisons — Kathleen M. Hawk, dir.
Comm. Relations Service — Jeffrey Weiss, act. dir.
Office of Inspector General — vacant.
Office of Justice Programs — vacant.
Drug Enforcement Adm. — Robert C. Bonner.
Office of Special Counsel for Immigration-Related Unfair Employment Practices — vacant.
Exec. Off. for U.S. Trustees — John Logan, dir.
Exec. Off. for U.S. Attorneys — Anthony C. Moscato, dir.
Immigration and Naturalization Service — Gene McNary.
Pardon Attorney — Margaret Love.
U.S. Parole Commission — Edward F. Reilly, Jr., chmn.
U.S. Marshals Service — Eduardo Gonzalez, dir.
U.S. Natl. Central Bureau of Interpol — Shelley G. Altenstadtero, chief.

## Department of the Interior
C St. between 18th & 19th Sts. NW 20240
Secretary of the Interior — Bruce Babbitt.
Deputy Secretary — Robert Hattoy, act.
Assistant Secretaries for:
  Fish, Wildlife, and Parks — George T. Framton, Jr.
  Indian Affairs — Ada Deer.
  Land & Minerals — Robert Armstrong.
  Policy, Budget, and Management — Bonnie R. Cohen.
  Territorial & Intl. Affairs — Leslie Turner.
  Water & Science — Elizabeth A. Reike.
Bureau of Land Management — Jim Baca, dir.
Bureau of Mines — Herman Enzer, act. dir.
Bureau of Reclamation — Daniel T. Beard, comm.
Fish & Wildlife Service — Mollie Beattie, dir.
Geological Survey — Robert Hirsch, act. dir.
National Park Service — Roger Kennedy, dir.
Public Affairs — Kevin Sweeney, dir.
Office of Congressional and Legislative Affairs — Stephanie Solien.
Solicitor — John D. Leshy.

## Department of Agriculture
The Mall, 12th & 14th Sts. 20250
Secretary of Agriculture — Mike Espy.
Deputy Secretary — vacant.
Assistant Secretaries for:
  Administration — Wardell Townsend, Jr.
  Congressional Relations — Robin Rorapaugh.
  Economics — Keith Collins, act.
  Food & Consumer Services — Ellen Haas.
  Internatl. Affairs & Commodity Programs — Eugene Moos.
  Marketing & Inspection Services — Eugene Branstool.
  Natural Resources & Environment — James Lyons.
  Science & Education — R. D. Plowman, act.
General Counsel — James Gilliland.
Inspector General — Charles Gillum, act.
Public Affairs — Ali Webb.
Press Secretary — Steve Kinsella.

## Department of Commerce
14th St. between Constitution & E St. NW 20230
Secretary of Commerce — Ronald H. Brown.
Deputy Secretary — vacant.
Chief of Staff — Carole Timble.
General Counsel — vacant.
Assistant Secretaries for:
  Chief Financial Officer & Asst. for Administration — vacant.
  Economic Development Adm. — vacant.
  Export Enforcement — Douglas Lavin.
  Import Administration — Loretta Dunn.
  Intl. Economic Policy — vacant.
  Legislative Affairs — vacant.
  Natl. Telecommunications Information Adm. — vacant.
  Oceans & Atmosphere — Douglas K. Hall.
  Patent & Trademark Office & Act. Asst. Comm. — vacant.
  Trade Development — vacant.
Bureau of the Census — vacant.
Bureau of Economic Analysis — Carol Carson, dir.
Under Secy. for International Trade — Jeffrey Garten.
Under Secy. for Econ. Affairs — Everett Ehrlich.
Under Secy. for Technology — Mary Lowe Good.
Natl. Technical Info. Service — vacant.
Natl. Institute for Standards & Technology — Arati Prabhakar, dir.
Minority Business Development Agency — Joe Lira.
Public Affairs — Eric Ruff, dir.

## Department of Labor
200 Constitution Ave. NW 20210

Secretary of Labor — Robert B. Reich.
Deputy Secretary — Thomas P. Glynn.
Chief of Staff — Kathryn Higgins.
Assistant Secretaries for:
  Administration and Management — vacant.
  Congressional & Intergovernmental Affairs — Geri Palast.
  Employment & Training — Doug Ross.
  Employment Standards — vacant.
  Labor-Management Standards — vacant.
  Occupational Safety & Health — Joseph Dear.
  Pension & Welfare Benefits — Olena Berg.
  Policy — John Donahue.
  Public Affairs — Anne Lewis.
Solicitor of Labor — Thomas S. Williamson.
Bureau of International Affairs — vacant.
Dep. Under Secy. for Labor-Management Relations & Co-operative Programs — vacant.
Women's Bureau — Karen Nussbaum, dir.
Inspector General — vacant.
Bureau of Labor Statistics — Katharine Abraham.

## Department of Health and Human Services
200 Independence Ave. SW 20201

Secretary of HHS — Donna E. Shalala.
Under Secretary — vacant.
Assistant Secretaries for:
  Children & Families — Mary Jo Bane.
  Health — James Mason, M.D.
  Legislation — Jerry D. Klepner.
  Management & Budget — Kenneth Apfel.
  Personnel Administration — Thomas McFee.
  Planning & Evaluation — David T. Ellwood.
  Public Affairs — Avis LaVelle.
General Counsel — Harriet Rabb.
Inspector General — June Gibbs Brown.
Office of Civil Rights — vacant.
Surgeon General — Joycelyn Elders.
Social Security Adm. — Shirley Sears Chater.
Office of Consumer Affairs — vacant.
Health Care Financing Adm. — vacant.

## Department of Housing and Urban Development
451 7th St. SW 20410

Secretary of Housing & Urban Development — Henry G. Cisneros.
Deputy Secretary — Terrence Duvernay.
Assistant Secretaries for:
  Administration — vacant.
  Community Planning & Development — Andrew Cuomo.
  Fair Housing & Equal Opportunity — Robert A. Achtenberg.
  Field Mgt. — Frank Wing.
  Housing & Federal Housing Commissioner — Nicolas P. Retsinas.
  Labor Relations — Joseph A. Scudero.
  Congressional & Intergovernmental Relations — William J. Gilmartin.
  Policy Development & Research — Michael Stegman.
  Public Affairs — Jean Nolan.
  Public & Indian Housing — Joseph Shuldiner.
General Counsel — Nelson Diaz.
Inspector General — Susan Gaffney.

## Department of Transportation
400 7th St. SW 20590

Secretary of Transportation — Federico F. Pena.
Deputy Secretary — Mortimer L. Downey.
Assistant Secretaries for:
  Administration — Jon H. Seymour.
  Budget & Programs — Louise Stoll.
  Governmental Affairs — vacant.
  Policy & International Affairs — vacant.
  Public Affairs — Richard I. Mintz.
U. S. Coast Guard Commandant — Adm. J. W. Kime.
Federal Aviation Admin. — David Hinson.
Federal Highway Admin. — Rodney Slater.
Federal Railroad Admin. — Jolene Molitoris.
Maritime Admin. — Albert Herberger.
Federal Transit Admin. — Gordon J. Linton.
Research & Special Programs Admin. — vacant.
Saint Lawrence Seaway Development Corp. — Stan E. Parris.

## Department of Energy
1000 Independence Ave. SW 20585

Secretary of Energy — Hazel R. O'Leary.
Deputy Secy. — William H. White.
Under Secretary — vacant.
General Counsel — Robert Nordhaus.
Inspector General — John C. Layton.
Assistant Secretaries for:
  Congressional & Intergovernmental Affairs — William Taylor.
  Conservation & Renewable Energy — vacant.
  Defense Programs — Victor Reis.
  Domesic & International Energy Policy — Susan Tierney.
  Environment, Safety & Health — Tara Jeanne O'Toole.
  Fossil Energy — vacant.
  Nuclear Energy — vacant.
Energy Information Adm. — Jay Hakes. adm.
Economic Regulatory Adm. — Jay Thompson, act. adm.
Federal Energy Regulatory Comm. — Elizabeth Moler, chair.
Hearings & Appeals — vacant.
Energy Research — Martha Krebs.
Civilian Radioactive Waste Management — vacant.
Minority Economic Impact — vacant.
Board of Contract Appeals — vacant.
Public Affairs — vacant.

## Department of Education
400 Maryland Ave. SW 20202
Secretary of Education — Richard W. Riley.
Under Secretary — Marshall S. Smith.

Deputy Secretary — Madeleine Kunin.
Chief of Staff — Polly Gault.
Inspector General — James B. Thomas, Jr.
General Counsel — Judith Winston.
Assistant Secretaries for:
  Adult & Vocational Education — Augusta Kappner.
  Bilingual & Minority Language Affairs — vacant.
  Civil Rights — Norma V. Cantu.
  Educational Research and Improvement — Porter Robinson.
  Elementary and Secondary Education — Thomas W. Payzant.
  Human Resources & Administration — vacant.
  Intergovernmental & Interagency Affairs — vacant.
  Legislation & Congressional Affairs — Kay Casstevens.
  Management & Budget — vacant.
  Postsecondary Education — David Longanecker.
  Special Education and Rehabilitative Services — Judith Heumann.

## Department of Veterans Affairs

810 Vermont Ave. NW 20420

Secretary of Veterans Affairs — Jesse Brown.
Deputy — Hershel W. Gober.
Assistant Secretaries for:
  Acquisition & Facilities — Gary Krump, act.
  Congressional Affairs — Edward P. Scott.
  Finance & Information Resources Mgmt. — D. Mark Catlett.
  Human Resources & Adm. — Eugene Brickhouse.
  Policy & Planning — Victor P. Raymond.
  Public & Intergovernmental Affairs — Kathy E. Jurado.
Inspector General — Stephen Trodden.
Under Secy. for Benefits — vacant.
Under Secy. for Health — vacant.
National Cemetery System — Jerry W. Bowen, dir.
General Counsel — Mary Lou Keener.
Board of Veterans Appeals — Charles L. Cragin, chmn.

# Judiciary of the U.S.

Data as of mid-1993

## Justices of the United States Supreme Court

The Supreme Court comprises the chief justice of the United States and 8 associate justices, all appointed by the president with advice and consent of the Senate. Salaries: chief justice $171,500 annually, associate justice $164,100. The Supreme Court is located at the U.S. Supreme Court Bldg., 1 First St. NE, Wash., DC 20543.

Members of the Supreme Court at the start of the 1993–1994 term (Oct. 4, 1993): *Chief justice:* William H. Rehnquist; *associate justices:* Harry A. Blackmun, Ruth Bader Ginsburg, Anthony M. Kennedy, Sandra Day O'Connor, Antonin Scalia, David H. Souter, John Paul Stevens, Clarence Thomas.

| Name; apptd from Chief Justices in italics | Service Term | Yrs. | Born | Died |
|---|---|---|---|---|
| John Jay, N. Y. | 1789-1795 | 5 | 1745 | 1829 |
| John Rutledge, S. C. | 1789-1791 | 1 | 1739 | 1800 |
| William Cushing, Mass. | 1789-1810 | 20 | 1732 | 1810 |
| James Wilson, Pa. | 1789-1798 | 8 | 1742 | 1798 |
| John Blair, Va. | 1789-1796 | 6 | 1732 | 1800 |
| James Iredell, N. C. | 1790-1799 | 9 | 1751 | 1799 |
| Thomas Johnson, Md. | 1791-1793 | 1 | 1732 | 1819 |
| William Paterson, N. J. | 1793-1806 | 13 | 1745 | 1806 |
| John Rutledge, S.C. | 1795(a) | — | 1739 | 1800 |
| Samuel Chase, Md. | 1796-1811 | 15 | 1741 | 1811 |
| Oliver Ellsworth, Conn. | 1796-1800 | 4 | 1745 | 1807 |
| Bushrod Washington, Va. | 1798-1829 | 31 | 1762 | 1829 |
| Alfred Moore, N. C. | 1799-1804 | 4 | 1755 | 1810 |
| John Marshall, Va. | 1801-1835 | 34 | 1755 | 1835 |
| William Johnson, S. C. | 1804-1834 | 30 | 1771 | 1834 |
| Henry B. Livingston, N. Y. | 1806-1823 | 16 | 1757 | 1823 |
| Thomas Todd, Ky. | 1807-1826 | 18 | 1765 | 1826 |
| Joseph Story, Mass. | 1811-1845 | 33 | 1779 | 1845 |
| Gabriel Duval, Md. | 1811-1835 | 22 | 1752 | 1844 |
| Smith Thompson, N. Y. | 1823-1843 | 20 | 1768 | 1843 |
| Robert Trimble, Ky. | 1826-1828 | 2 | 1777 | 1828 |
| John McLean, Oh. | 1829-1861 | 32 | 1785 | 1861 |
| Henry Baldwin, Pa. | 1830-1844 | 14 | 1780 | 1844 |
| James M. Wayne, Ga. | 1835-1867 | 32 | 1790 | 1867 |
| Roger B. Taney, Md. | 1836-1864 | 28 | 1777 | 1864 |
| Philip P. Barbour, Va. | 1836-1841 | 4 | 1783 | 1841 |
| John Catron, Tenn. | 1837-1865 | 28 | 1786 | 1865 |
| John McKinley, Ala. | 1837-1852 | 15 | 1780 | 1852 |
| Peter V. Daniel, Va. | 1841-1860 | 19 | 1784 | 1860 |
| Samuel Nelson, N. Y. | 1845-1872 | 27 | 1792 | 1873 |
| Levi Woodbury, N. H. | 1845-1851 | 5 | 1789 | 1851 |
| Robert C. Grier, Pa. | 1846-1870 | 23 | 1794 | 1870 |
| Benjamin R. Curtis, Mass. | 1851-1857 | 6 | 1809 | 1874 |
| John A. Campbell, Ala. | 1853-1861 | 8 | 1811 | 1889 |
| Nathan Clifford, Me. | 1858-1881 | 23 | 1803 | 1881 |
| Noah H. Swayne, Oh. | 1862-1881 | 18 | 1804 | 1884 |
| Samuel F. Miller, Ia. | 1862-1890 | 28 | 1816 | 1890 |
| David Davis, Ill. | 1862-1877 | 14 | 1815 | 1886 |
| Stephen J. Field, Cal. | 1863-1897 | 34 | 1816 | 1899 |
| Salmon P. Chase, Oh. | 1864-1873 | 8 | 1808 | 1873 |
| William Strong, Pa. | 1870-1880 | 10 | 1808 | 1895 |
| Joseph P. Bradley, N. J. | 1870-1892 | 21 | 1813 | 1892 |
| Ward Hunt, N. Y. | 1872-1882 | 9 | 1810 | 1886 |

| Name; apptd from Chief Justices in italics | Service Term | Yrs. | Born | Died |
|---|---|---|---|---|
| Morrison R. Waite, Oh. | 1874-1888 | 14 | 1816 | 1888 |
| John M. Harlan, Ky. | 1877-1911 | 34 | 1833 | 1911 |
| William B. Woods, Ga. | 1880-1887 | 6 | 1824 | 1887 |
| Stanley Matthews, Oh. | 1881-1889 | 7 | 1824 | 1889 |
| Horace Gray, Mass. | 1881-1902 | 20 | 1828 | 1902 |
| Samuel Blatchford, N. Y. | 1882-1893 | 11 | 1820 | 1893 |
| Lucius Q. C. Lamar, Miss. | 1888-1893 | 5 | 1825 | 1893 |
| Melville W. Fuller, Ill. | 1888-1910 | 21 | 1833 | 1910 |
| David J. Brewer, Kan. | 1889-1910 | 20 | 1837 | 1910 |
| Henry B. Brown, Mich. | 1890-1906 | 15 | 1836 | 1913 |
| George Shiras Jr., Pa. | 1892-1903 | 10 | 1832 | 1924 |
| Howell E. Jackson, Tenn. | 1893-1895 | 2 | 1832 | 1895 |
| Edward D. White, La. | 1894-1910 | 16 | 1845 | 1921 |
| Rufus W. Peckham, N. Y. | 1895-1909 | 13 | 1838 | 1909 |
| Joseph McKenna, Cal. | 1898-1925 | 26 | 1843 | 1926 |
| Oliver W. Holmes, Mass. | 1902-1932 | 29 | 1841 | 1935 |
| William R. Day, Oh. | 1903-1922 | 19 | 1849 | 1923 |
| William H. Moody, Mass. | 1906-1910 | 3 | 1853 | 1917 |
| Horace H. Lurton, Tenn. | 1909-1914 | 4 | 1844 | 1914 |
| Charles E. Hughes, N. Y. | 1910-1916 | 5 | 1862 | 1948 |
| Willis Van Devanter, Wy. | 1910-1937 | 26 | 1859 | 1941 |
| Joseph R. Lamar, Ga. | 1910-1916 | 5 | 1857 | 1916 |
| Edward D. White, La. | 1910-1921 | 10 | 1845 | 1921 |
| Mahlon Pitney, N. J. | 1912-1922 | 10 | 1858 | 1924 |
| James C. McReynolds, Tenn. | 1914-1941 | 26 | 1862 | 1946 |
| Louis D. Brandeis, Mass. | 1916-1939 | 22 | 1856 | 1941 |
| John H. Clarke, Oh. | 1916-1922 | 5 | 1857 | 1945 |
| William H. Taft, Conn. | 1921-1930 | 8 | 1857 | 1930 |
| George Sutherland, Ut. | 1922-1938 | 15 | 1862 | 1942 |
| Pierce Butler, Minn. | 1922-1939 | 16 | 1866 | 1939 |
| Edward T. Sanford, Tenn. | 1923-1930 | 7 | 1865 | 1930 |
| Harlan F. Stone, N. Y. | 1925-1941 | 16 | 1872 | 1946 |
| Charles E. Hughes, N. Y. | 1930-1941 | 11 | 1862 | 1948 |
| Owen J. Roberts, Pa. | 1930-1945 | 15 | 1875 | 1955 |
| Benjamin N. Cardozo, N.Y. | 1932-1938 | 6 | 1870 | 1938 |
| Hugo L. Black, Ala. | 1937-1971 | 34 | 1886 | 1971 |
| Stanley F. Reed, Ky. | 1938-1957 | 19 | 1884 | 1980 |
| Felix Frankfurter, Mass. | 1939-1962 | 23 | 1882 | 1965 |
| William O. Douglas, Conn. | 1939-1975 | 36 | 1898 | 1980 |
| Frank Murphy, Mich. | 1940-1949 | 9 | 1890 | 1949 |
| Harlan F. Stone, N. Y. | 1941-1946 | 5 | 1872 | 1946 |

| Name; apptd from Chief Justices in italics | Service Term | Yrs. | Born | Died |
|---|---|---|---|---|
| James F. Byrnes, S. C. | 1941-1942 | 1 | 1879 | 1972 |
| Robert H. Jackson, N. Y. | 1941-1954 | 12 | 1892 | 1954 |
| Wiley B. Rutledge, la. | 1943-1949 | 6 | 1894 | 1949 |
| Harold H. Burton, Oh. | 1945-1958 | 13 | 1888 | 1964 |
| Fred M. Vinson, Ky. | 1946-1953 | 7 | 1890 | 1953 |
| Tom C. Clark, Tex. | 1949-1967 | 18 | 1899 | 1977 |
| Sherman Minton, Ind. | 1949-1956 | 7 | 1890 | 1965 |
| Earl Warren, Cal. | 1953-1969 | 16 | 1891 | 1974 |
| John Marshall Harlan, N. Y. | 1955-1971 | 16 | 1899 | 1971 |
| William J. Brennan Jr., N. J. | 1956-1990 | 33 | 1906 | — |
| Charles E. Whittaker, Mo. | 1957-1962 | 5 | 1901 | 1973 |
| Potter Stewart, Oh. | 1958-1981 | 23 | 1915 | 1985 |
| Byron R. White, Col. | 1962-1993 | 31 | 1917 | — |
| Arthur J. Goldberg, Ill. | 1962-1965 | 3 | 1908 | 1990 |
| Abe Fortas, Tenn. | 1965-1969 | 4 | 1910 | 1982 |

(a) Rejected Dec. 15, 1795.

| Name; apptd from Chief Justices in italics | Service Term | Yrs. | Born | Died |
|---|---|---|---|---|
| Thurgood Marshall, N.Y. | 1967-1991 | 24 | 1908 | 1993 |
| Warren E. Burger, Va. | 1969-1986 | 17 | 1907 | — |
| Harry A. Blackmun, Minn. | 1970 — | — | 1908 | — |
| Lewis F. Powell Jr., Va. | 1972-1987 | 15 | 1907 | — |
| William H. Rehnquist, Ariz. | 1972-1986 | 14 | 1924 | — |
| John Paul Stevens, Ill. | 1975 — | — | 1920 | — |
| Sandra Day O'Connor, Ariz. | 1981 — | — | 1930 | — |
| William H. Rehnquist, Ariz. | 1986 — | — | 1924 | — |
| Antonin Scalia, Va. | 1986 — | — | 1936 | — |
| Anthony M. Kennedy, Cal. | 1988 — | — | 1936 | — |
| David H. Souter, N.H. | 1990 — | — | 1939 | — |
| Clarence Thomas, Va. | 1991 — | — | 1948 | — |
| Ruth Bader Ginsburg, D.C. | 1993 — | — | 1933 | — |

## U.S. Court of International Trade

New York, NY 10007 (Salaries, $133,600)

**Chief Judge** — Dominick L. DeCarlo.

**Judges** — Jane A. Restani, Gregory W. Carmen, Thomas J. Aquilino Jr., Nicholas Tsoucalas, R. Kenton Musgrave, Richard W. Goldberg.

## U.S. Claims Court

Washington, D.C. 20005 (Salaries, $133,600)

**Chief Judge** — Loren A. Smith.

**Judges** — James F. Merow, John P. Wiese, Robert J. Yock, Reginald W. Gibson, Lawrence S. Margolis, Christine C. Nettesheim, Moody R. Tidwell 3d, Marian Blank Horn, Eric G. Bruggink, Bohdan A. Futey, Wilkes C. Robinson, Roger B. Andewelt, James T. Turner, Robert H. Hodges Jr., Diane G. Weinstein.

## U.S. Tax Court

Washington DC 20217 (Salaries, $133,600)

**Chief Judge** — Lapsley W. Hamblen Jr.

**Judges** — Renato Beghe, Herbert L. Chabot, Edna G. Parker, Mary Ann Cohen, John O. Colvin, Perry Shields, Charles E. Clapp 2d, Joel Gerber, Julien I. Jacobs, Carolyn Miller Parr, Robert P. Ruwe, James S. Halpern, Carolyn P. Chiechi.

## U.S. Courts of Appeals

(Salaries, $141,700. CJ means Chief Judge)

**Federal Circuit** — Helen W. Nies, CJ; Giles S. Rich, Pauline Newman, Glenn L. Archer Jr., H. Robert Mayer, Paul R. Michel, S. Jay Pfager; Alan D. Lourie, Raymond C. Clevenger 3d, Randall F. Rader, Alvin A. Schall; Clerk's Office, Washington, DC 20439.

**District of Columbia** — Abner J. Mikva, CJ; Patricia M. Wald, Harry T. Edwards, Laurence H. Silberman; James L. Buckley, Stephen F. Williams, Douglas Ginsburg, David B. Sentelle; Karen LeCraft Henderson, A. Raymond Randolph; Clerk's Office, Washington, DC 20001.

**First Circuit** (Me., Mass., N.H., R.I., Puerto Rico) — Stephen Breyer, CJ; Juan R. Torruella, Bruce M. Selya, Conrad K. Cyr, Michael Boudin, Norman H. Stahl; Clerk's Office, Boston, MA 02109.

**Second Circuit** (Conn., N.Y., Vt.) — Thomas J. Meskill, CJ; James L. Oakes, Jon O. Newman, Amalya Lyle Kearse, Richard J. Cardamone, Ralph K. Winter Jr., George C. Pratt, Roger J. Miner, Frank X. Altimari, J. Daniel Mahoney, John M. Walker; Joseph M. McLaughlin, Dennis G. Jacobs; Clerk's Office, New York, NY 10007.

**Third Circuit** (Del., N.J., Pa., Virgin Is.) — Dolores K. Sloviter, CJ; Edward R. Becker, Carol Los Mansmann, Walter K. Stapleton, Morton I. Greenberg, Anthony J. Scirica, William D. Hutchinson, Robert E. Cowen, Richard L. Nygaard, Samuel A. Alito Jr., Jane R. Roth, Timothy K. Lewis; Clerk's Office, Philadelphia, PA 19106.

**Fourth Circuit** (Md., N.C., S.C., Va., W.Va.) — Sam J. Ervin 3d, CJ; Kenneth K. Hall, Donald Stuart Russell, H. Emory Widener Jr., James D. Phillips Jr., Francis D. Murnaghan Jr., J. Harvie Wilkinson 3d, William W. Wilkins Jr., Paul V. Niemeyer, Clyde H. Hamilton, J. Michael Luttig, Karen J. Williams; Clerk's Office, Richmond, VA 23219.

**Fifth Circuit** (La., Miss., Tex.) — Henry A. Politz, CJ; Carolyn D. King, Will Garwood, E. Grady Jolly, Patrick E. Higginbotham, W. Eugene Davis, Jerry E. Smith, Edith Hollan Jones, John M. Duhe Jr., Rhesa H. Barksdale, Jacques L. Wiener Jr., Emilio M. Garza, Harold R. DeMoss Jr.; Clerk's Office, New Orleans, LA 70130.

**Sixth Circuit** (Ky., Mich., Ohio, Tenn.) — Gilbert S. Merritt, CJ; Damon J. Keith, Boyce F. Martin Jr., Nathaniel R. Jones, Cornelia G. Kennedy, H. Ted Milburn, Ralph B. Guy Jr., David A. Nelson, James L. Ryan, Danny J. Boggs, Alan E. Norris, Richard H. Suhrheinrich, Eugene E. Siler Jr., Alice M. Batchelder; Clerk's Office, Cincinnati, OH 45202.

**Seventh Circuit** (Ill., Ind., Wis.) — William J. Bauer, CJ; Walter J. Cummings, Richard D. Cudahy, Richard A. Posner, John L. Coffey, Joel M. Flaum, Frank H. Easterbrook, Kenneth F. Ripple, Daniel A. Manion, Michael S. Kanne, Ilana D. Rovner; Clerk's Office, Chicago, IL 60604.

**Eighth Circuit** (Ark., Ia., Minn., Mo., Neb., N.D., S.D.) — Richard S. Arnold, CJ; Theodore McMillian, John R. Gibson, George C. Fagg, Pasco M. Bowman 2d, Roger L. Wollman, Frank J. Magill, C. Arlen Beam, James B. Loken, David R. Hanson, Morris S. Arnold; Clerk's Office, St. Louis, MO 63101.

**Ninth Circuit** (Alaska, Ariz., Cal., Ha., Ida., Mont., Nev., Ore., Wash., Guam, N. Mariana Islands) — J. Clifford Wallace, CJ; James R. Browning, Procter Hug Jr., Thomas Tang, Jerome Farris, Betty B. Fletcher, Mary M. Schroeder, Harry Pregerson, Cecil F. Poole, Dorothy W. Nelson, William C. Canby Jr., William A. Norris, Stephen Reinhardt, Robert R. Beezer, Cynthia M. Hall, Charles E. Wiggins, Melvin Brunetti, Alex Kozinski, David R. Thompson, John T. Noonan, Diarmuid F. O'Scannlain, Edward Leavy, Stephen S. Trott, Ferdinand F. Fernandez, Pamela Ann Rymer, Thomas G. Nelson, Andrew J. Kleinfeld; Clerk's Office, San Francisco, CA 94119.

**Tenth Circuit** (Col., Kan., N.M., Okla., Ut., Wy.) — Monroe G. McKay, CJ; James K. Logan, Stephanie K. Seymour, John P. Moore, Stephen H. Anderson, Deanell R. Tacha, Bobby R. Baldock, Wade Brorby, David M. Ebel, Paul J. Kelly Jr.; Clerk's Office, Denver, CO 80294.

**Eleventh Circuit** (Ala. Fla., Ga.) — Gerald B. Tjoflat, CJ; Peter T. Fay, Phyllis A. Kravitch, Joseph W. Hatchett, R. Lanier Anderson 3d, J.L. Edmondson, Emmett R. Cox, Stanley F. Birch Jr., Joel F. Dubina, Susan H. Black, Edward E. Carnes; Clerk's Office, Atlanta GA 30303.

**Temporary Emergency Court of Appeals** — Reynaldo G. Garza, CJ; Robert A. Grant, Charles M. Metzner, John W. Peck, Frederick A. Daugherty, Wesley E. Brown, Stanley A. Weigel; Clerk's Office, Washington, DC 20001.

## U.S. District Courts

(Salaries, $133,600. CJ means Chief Judge)

**Alabama — Northern:** Sam C. Pointer Jr., CJ; James Hughes Hancock, Robert B. Propst, U. W. Clemon, William M. Acker Jr., Edwin L. Nelson, Sharon Lovelace Blackburn; Clerk's Office, Birmingham 35203. **Middle:** Myron H. Thompson, CJ; William H. Albritton, Ira Dement; Clerk's Office, Montgomery 36101. **Southern:** Alex T. Howard Jr., CJ; Charles R. Butler Jr., Richard W. Vollmer Jr.; Clerk's Office, Mobile 36602.

**Alaska** — H. Russel Holland, CJ; John K. Singleton, John W. Sedwick; Clerk's Office, Anchorage 99513.

**Arizona** — William D. Browning, CJ; Richard M. Bilby, Earl H. Carroll, Paul G. Rosenblat, Robert C. Bloomfield, Roger G. Strand, Stephen M. McNamee, John M. Roll; Clerk's Office, Phoenix 85025.

**Arkansas — Eastern:** Samuel R. Reasoner, CJ; Henry Woods, George Howard Jr., Susan Weber Wright; Clerk's Office, Little Rock 72203. **Western:** H. Franklin Waters, CJ; George Howard Jr., Jimm Larry Hendren; Clerk's Office, Fort Smith 72902.

California — Northern: Thelton E. Henderson, CJ; Robert P. Aguilar, Marilyn H. Patel, Eugene F. Lynch, John P. Vukasin Jr, Charles A. Legge, D. Lowell Jensen, Fern M. Smith, Vaughn R. Walker, James Ware, Susan B. Armstrong, Barbara A. Caulfield, Ronald J. Whyte; Clerk's Office, San Francisco 94102. Eastern: Robert E. Coyle, CJ; Lawrence K. Karlton, Edward J. Garcia, William B. Shubb, David F. Levi, Oliver W. Wanger, Garland E. Burrell Jr.; Clerk's Office, Sacramento 95814. Central: Manuel L. Real, CJ; Wm. Matthew Byrne Jr., Robert M. Takasugi, Mariana R. Pfaelzer, Terry J. Hatter Jr., A. Wallace Tashima, Consuelo Bland Marshall, David V. Kenyon, Richard A. Gadbois, Edward Rafeedie, Harry L. Hupp, Alicemarie H. Stotler, James M. Ideman, William J. Rea, William D. Keller, Stephen W. Wilson, J. Spencer Letts, Dickran M. Tevrizian Jr., John G. Davies, Ronald S.W. Lew, Gary L. Taylor, Linda Hodge McLaughlin, Lourdes G. Baird; Clerk's Office, Los Angeles 90012. Southern: Judith N. Keep, CJ; Gordon Thompson Jr., Earl B. Gilliam, Rudi M. Brewster, John S. Rhoades Sr., Marilyn L. Huff, Irma E. Gonzalez; Clerk's Office, San Diego 92101.

Colorado — Sherman G. Finesilver, CJ; Richard P. Matsch, Jim R. Carrigan, Zita L. Weinshienk, Lewis T. Babcock, Edward W. Nottingham, Daniel B. Sparr; Clerk's Office, Denver 80294.

Connecticut — Jose A. Cabranes, CJ; T.F. Gilroy Daly, Peter C. Dorsey, Alan H. Nevas, Alfred V. Covello; Clerk's Office, New Haven 06510.

Delaware — Joseph J. Longobardi, CJ; Joseph J. Farnan Jr., Sue L. Robinson, Roderick R. McKelvie; Clerk's Office, Wilmington 19801.

District of Columbia — John Garrett Penn, CJ; Charles R. Richey, Harold H. Greene, Joyce Hens Green, Norma H. Johnson, Thomas P. Jackson, Thomas F. Hogan, Stanley S. Harris, George H. Revercomb, Stanley Sporkin, Royce C. Lamberth; Clerk's Office, Washington DC 20001.

Florida — Northern: Maurice M. Paul, CJ; C. Roger Vinson, Lacey A. Collier, William H. Stafford; Clerk's Office, Tallahassee 32301. Middle: John H. Moore 2d, CJ; William Terrell Hodges, Elizabeth A. Kovachevich, George K. Sharp, Patricia C. Fawsett, Harvey E. Schlesinger, Ralph W. Nimmons Jr., Anne C. Conway, Steven D. Merry Day; Clerk's Office, Jacksonville 32201. Southern: Norman C. Roettger Jr., CJ; Jose A. Gonzalez Jr., Edward B. Davis, Lenore C. Nesbitt, Stanley Marcus, William J. Zloch, Kenneth L. Ryskamp, Federico A. Moreno, Shelby Highsmith, Donald L. Graham, K. Kenneth Moore, Ursula Ungaro-Benages; Clerk's Office, Miami 33128.

Georgia — Northern: William C. O'Kelley, CJ; Harold L. Murphy, G. Ernest Tidwell, Orinda Dale Evans, Robert L. Vining Jr., Harold T. Ward, J. Owen Forrester, Jack T. Camp, Julie E. Carnes; Clerk's Office, Atlanta 30335. Middle: Wilbur D. Owens Jr., CJ; J. Robert Elliott, Duross Fitzpatrick; Clerk's Office, Macon 31202. Southern: B. Avant Edenfield, CJ; Dudley H. Bowen Jr.; Clerk's Office, Savannah 31412.

Hawaii — Alan C. Kay, CJ; Harold M. Fong, David A. Ezra; Clerk's Office, Honolulu 96850.

Idaho — Edward J. Lodge, CJ; Clerk's Office, Boise 83724.

Illinois — Northern: James B. Moran, CJ; John F. Grady, Marvin E. Aspen, Milton I. Shadur, Charles P. Kocoras, John A. Nordberg, William T. Hart, Paul E. Plunkett, Charles R. Norgle Sr., James F. Holderman Jr., Ann C. Williams, Brian Barnett Duff, Harry D. Lienenweber, James B. Zagel, James H. Alesia, Suzanne B. Conlon, George M. Marovich, George W. Lindberg, Wayne R. Anderson, Philip G. Reinhard; Clerk's Office, Chicago 60604. Central: Michael M. Mihm, CJ; Harold Albert Baker, Richard Mills, Joe Billy McDade; Clerk's Office, Springfield 62705. Southern: William D. Stiehl, CJ; J. Phil Gilbert; Clerk's Office, E. St. Louis 62202.

Indiana — Northern: Allen Sharp, CJ; William C. Lee, James T. Moody, Robert L. Miller Jr., Rudy Lozano; Clerk's Office, South Bend 46601. Southern: Gene E. Brooks, CJ; S. Hugh Dillin, Sarah E. Barker, Larry J. McKinney, John D. Tinder; Clerk's Office, Indianapolis 46204.

Iowa — Northern: Michael J. Melloy, CJ; Clerk's Office, Cedar Rapids 52401. Southern: Charles R. Wolle, CJ; Harold D. Victor, R. E. Longstaff; Clerk's Office, Des Moines 50309.

Kansas — Patrick F. Kelly, CJ; Sam A. Crow, C. Thomas Van Bebber, John W. Lungstrum, Monti L. Belot, Kathryn H. Vritil; Clerk's Office, Wichita 67202.

Kentucky — Eastern: William Bertelsman, CJ; Henry R. Wilhoit Jr., Karl S. Forester, Joseph M. Hood; Clerk's Office, Lexington 40586. Western: Ronald E. Meredith, CJ; Charles R. Simpson 3d, Edward H. Johnstone, John G. Heyburn 3d; Clerk's Office, Louisville 40202.

Louisiana — Eastern: Morley L. Sear, CJ; Adrian A. Duplantier, Robert F. Collins, George Arceneaux Jr., Veronica D. Wicker, Peter Beer, A J. McNamara, Martin L. C. Feldman, Marcel Livaudais Jr., Edith Brown Clement; Clerk's Office, New Orleans 70130. Middle: John V. Parker, CJ; Frank J. Polozola; Clerk's Office, Baton Rouge 70821. Western: John M. Shaw, CJ; F. A. Little Jr., Donald E. Walter, Richard Haiks, James T. Trimble, Rebecca F. Doherty; Clerk's Office, Shreveport 71101.

Maine — Gene Carter, CJ; D. Brock Hornby, Martin A. Brody; Clerk's Office, Portland 04112.

Maryland — William E. Black Jr., CJ; John R. Hargrove, J. Frederick Motz, Frederic N. Smalkin, William M. Nickerson, Marvin J. Garbis, Benson Everett Legg; Clerk's Office, Baltimore 21201.

Massachusetts — Joseph L. Tauro, CJ; A. David Mazzone, Robert E. Keeton, Rya W. Zobel, William G. Young, Mark L. Wolf, Douglas P. Woodlock, Edward F. Harrington; Clerk's Office, Boston 02109.

Michigan — Eastern: Julian A. Cook Jr., CJ; Stewart A. Newblatt, Avern Cohn, Anna Diggs Taylor, George E. Woods, George La Plata, Barbara K. Hackett, Lawrence P. Zatkoff, Patrick J. Duggan, Bernard A. Friedman, Paul V. Gadola, Gerald E. Rosen, Robert H. Cleland, Nancy G. Edmunds; Clerk's Office, Detroit 48226. Western: Benjamin F. Gibson, CJ; Richard A. Enslen, Robert H. Bell, David W. McKeague; Clerk's Office, Grand Rapids 49503.

Minnesota — Diana E. Murphy, CJ; Paul A. Magnuson, James M. Rosenbaum, David S. Doty, Richard H. Kyle; Clerk's Office, St. Paul 55101.

Mississippi — Northern: L. T. Senter Jr., CJ; Neal Biggers, Glen H. Davidson; Clerk's Office, Oxford 38655. Southern: William H. Barbour Jr., CJ; Harry T. Wingate, Tom S. Lee, Walter J. Gex 3d, Charles W. Pickering Sr., David Bramlette; Clerk's Office, Jackson 39201.

Missouri — Eastern: Edward D. Filippine, CJ; Stephen N. Limbaugh, George F. Gunn Jr., Jean Hamilton, Donald J. Stohr, Carol E. Jackson; Clerk's Office, St. Louis 63101. Western: Joseph E. Stevens Jr., CJ; D. Brook Bartlett, Dean Whipple, Fernando J. Gaitan Jr.; Clerk's Office, Kansas City 64106.

Montana — Paul G. Hatfield, CJ; Charles C. Lovell, Jack D. Shanstrom; Clerk's Office, Billings 59101.

Nebraska — Lyle E. Strom, CJ; William G. Cambridge, Richard G. Kopf; Clerk's Office, Omaha 68101.

Nevada — Lloyd D. George, CJ; Howard D. McKibben, Philip M. Pro; Clerk's Office, Las Vegas 89101.

New Hampshire — Joseph A. DiClerico, CJ; Paul J. Barbadaro, Steven J. McAuliffe; Clerk's Office, Concord 03301.

New Jersey — John F. Gerry, CJ; Anne E. Thompson, Dickinson R. Debevoise, H. Lee Sarokin, Harold A. Ackerman, John W. Bissell, Maryanne Trump Barry, Joseph H. Rodriguez, Garrett E. Brown Jr., Alfred J. Lechner Jr., Nicholas H. Politan, Alfred M. Wolin, John C. Lifland, William G. Bassler, Mary Little Parell, Jerome E. Simandle, Joseph E. Irenas; Clerk's Office, Newark 07102.

New Mexico — Juan G. Burciaga, CJ; John E. Conway, James A. Parker, C. Leroy Hansen; Clerk's Office, Albuquerque 87103.

New York — Northern: Thomas J. McAvoy, CJ; Con G. Cholakis, Frederick J. Scullin Jr.; Clerk's Office, Albany 12201. Eastern: Thomas C. Platt Jr., CJ; Charles P. Sifton, Eugene H. Nickerson, Israel Leo Glasser, Raymond J. Dearie, Leonard D. Wexler, Edward R. Korman, Reena Raggi; Arthur D. Spatt, Carol Bagley Amon, Sterling Johnson Jr., Denis R. Hurley; Clerk's Office, Brooklyn 11201. Southern: Thomas P. Criesa, CJ; David N. Edelstein, Charles L. Brieant, Kevin Thomas Duffy, Leonard B. Sand, Gerard L. Goettel, Charles S. Haight Jr., Pierre N. Leval, John E. Sprizzo, Shirley Wohl Kram, John F. Keenan, Peter K. Leisure, Louis L. Stanton, Miriam G. Cedarbaum, Michael B. Mukasey, Kenneth Conboy, Kimba Wood, Robert P. Patterson Jr., Lawrence McKenna, John S. Martin Jr., Loretta A. Preska, Sonia Sotomayer; Clerk's Office N. Y. City 10007. Western: Michael A. Telesca, CJ; Richard J. Arcara, David G. Larimer, William M. Skretny; Clerk's Office, Buffalo 14202.

**North Carolina — Eastern:** James C. Fox, CJ; W. Earl Britt, Terrence W. Boyle, Malcolm J. Howard; Clerk's Office, Raleigh 27611. **Middle:** Frank W. Bullock, CJ; N. Carlton Tilley Jr., William L. Osteen Sr.; Clerk's Office, Greensboro 27402. **Western:** Richard L. Voorhees, CJ; Robert D. Potter, Graham C. Mullen; Clerk's Office, Asheville 28801.

**North Dakota —** Rodney S. Webb, CJ; Patrick A. Conmy; Clerk's Office, Bismarck 58502.

**Ohio — Northern:** Thomas D. Lambros, CJ; Frank J. Battisti, George W. White, Ann Aldrich, David D. Dowd Jr., Sam H. Bell, Paul R. Matia; Clerk's Office, Cleveland 44114. **Southern:** John D. Holschuh, CJ; Carl B. Rubin, Walter H. Rice, S. Arthur Spiegel, Herman J. Weber, James L. Graham, George C. Smith, Sandra S. Beckwith; Clerk's Office, Columbus 43215.

**Oklahoma — Northern:** James O. Ellison, CJ; Thomas R. Brett; Clerk's Office, Tulsa 74103. **Eastern:** Frank H. Shey, CJ; Clerk's Office, Muskogee 74401. **Western:** Ralph G. Thompson, CJ; Wayne Alley, Lee R. West, David L. Russell, Robin Cauthron, Timothy D. Leonard; Clerk's Office, Oklahoma City 73102.

**Oregon —** James A. Redden, CJ; Helen J. Frye, Malcolm F. Marsh, Robert E. Jones, Michael R. Hogan; Clerk's Office, Portland 97205.

**Pennsylvania — Eastern:** Louis Charles Bechtle, CJ; Edward N. Cahn, Norma L. Shapiro, James T. Giles, James McGirr Kelly, Thomas N. O'Neill Jr., Marvin Katz, Edmund V. Ludwig, Robert F. Kelly, Franklin S. Van Antwerpen, Robert S. Gawthrop, Lowell A. Reed Jr., Jan E. Dubois, Herbert J. Hutton, Jay C. Waldman, Ronald L. Buckwalter, Stewart Dalzell, William H. Yohn Jr., Harvey Battle 3d, John R. Padova, J. Curtis Joyner, Eduardo C. Robreno; Clerk's Office, Philadelphia 19106. **Middle:** Sylvia H. Rambo, CJ; William W. Caldwell, Edward M. Kosik, James F. McClure Jr.; Clerk's Office, Scranton 18501. **Western:** Maurice B. Cohill Jr., CJ; Gustave Diamond, Donald E. Ziegler, Alan N. Bloch, Glenn E. Mencer, William L. Standish, D. Brooks Smith, Donald J. Lee; Clerk's Office, Pittsburgh 15230.

**Rhode Island —** Ronald R. Lagueux, CJ; Ernest C. Torres; Clerk's Office, Providence 02903.

**South Carolina —** Falcon B. Hawkins, CJ; C. Weston Houck, Matthew J. Perry Jr., George R. Anderson Jr., Joseph F. Anderson Jr., David C. Norton, Dennis W. Shedd, Henry M. Herlong Jr., William B. Traxler; Clerk's Office, Columbia 29202.

**South Dakota —** John Baily Jones, CJ; Richard H. Battey; Clerk's Office, Sioux Falls 57102.

**Tennessee — Eastern:** James H. Jarvis, CJ; Thomas G. Hill, R. Allan Edgar, Leon Jordan; Clerk's Office, Knoxville 37901. **Middle:** John T. Nixon, CJ; Thomas A. Wiseman Jr., Thomas A. Higgins, Robert L. Echols; Clerk's Office, Nashville 37203. **Western:** Odell Horton, CJ; Julia S. Gibbons, James D. Todd, Jerome Turner, John Phipps McCalla; Clerk's Office, Memphis 38103.

**Texas — Northern:** Barefoot Sanders, CJ; Mary Lou Robinson, Jerry Buchmeyer, A. Joe Fish, Robert B. Maloney, Sidney A. Fitzwater, Samuel R. Cummings, John H. McBryde, Jorge A. Solis,

Terry Means, Joe Kendall; Clerk's Office, Dallas 75242. **Southern:** Norman W. Black, CJ; George P. Kazen, Filemon B. Vela, Hayden W. Head Jr., Ricardo H. Hinojosa, Lynn N. Hughes, David Hittner, Kenneth M. Hoyt, Simeon T. Lake 3d, Melinda Harmon, John Rainey, Samuel B. Kent, Ewing Werlein Jr., Lee H. Rosenthal; Clerk's Office, Houston 77208. **Eastern:** Robert M. Parker, CJ; William Wayne Justice, Howell Cobb, Sam B. Hall Jr., Paul N. Brown, Richard A. Schell; Clerk's Office, Tyler 75702. **Western:** Harry Lee Hudspeth, CJ; Hipolito F. Garcia, James R. Nowlin, Edward C. Prado, Walter S. Smith Jr., Sam Sparks; Clerk's Office, San Antonio 78206.

**Utah —** Bruce S. Jenkins, CJ; J. Thomas Greene, David Sam, David K. Winder, Dee V. Benson; Clerk's Office, Salt Lake City 84101.

**Vermont —** Fred I. Parker, CJ; Franklin S. Billings Jr.; Clerk's Office, Burlington 05402.

**Virginia — Eastern:** James C. Cacheris, CJ; Robert G. Doumar, Claude M. Hilton, James R. Spencer, Thomas S. Ellis 3d, Rebecca Beach Smith, Henry Coke Morgan Jr., Robert E. Payne; Clerk's Office, Alexandria 22320. **Western:** James C. Turk, CJ; James H. Michael Jr., Jackson L. Kiser, Samuel G. Wilson; Clerk's Office, Roanoke 24006.

**Washington — Eastern:** Justin L. Quackenbush, CJ; Alan A. McDonald; Fred Van Sickle, W. Fremming Nielsen; Clerk's Office, Spokane 99210. **Western:** Barbara J. Rothstein, CJ; John C. Coughenour, Carolyn R. Dimmick, Robert J. Bryan, William L. Dwyer, Thomas Zilly; Clerk's Office, Seattle 98104.

**West Virginia — Northern:** Robert Earl Maxwell, CJ; Frederick P. Stamp Jr., Irene M. Keeley; Clerk's Office, Elkins 26241. **Southern:** Charles H. Haden 2d, CJ; Robert J. Staker, John T. Copenhaver Jr., Elizabeth V. Hallanan, David A. Faber; Clerk's Office, Charleston 25329.

**Wisconsin — Eastern:** Terence T. Evans, CJ; Thomas J. Curran, J.P. Stadtmueller, Rudolph T. Randa; Clerk's Office, Milwaukee 53202. **Western:** Barbara B. Crabb, CJ; John C. Shabaz; Clerk's Office, Madison 53701.

**Wyoming —** Alan B. Johnson, CJ; Clarence A. Brimmer; Clerk's Office, Cheyenne 82001.

## U.S. Territorial District Courts

**Guam —** John S. Unpingco; Clerk's Office, Agana 96910.

**Puerto Rico —** Gilberto Gierbolini, CJ; Juan M. Perez-Gimenez, Carmen Consuelo Cerezo, Jaime Pieras Jr., Raymond L. Acosta, Hector M. Laffitte, Jose Antonio Fuste; Clerk's Office, San Juan 00904.

**Virgin Islands —** Thomas K. Moore, CJ; Clerk's Office, Charlotte Amalie, St. Thomas 00801.

## U.S. Court of Veterans Appeals

Washington, D.C. 20004 (Salaries, $133,600)
**Chief Judge —** Frank Q. Nebeker.
**Judges —** Kenneth B. Kramer, John J. Farley 3d, Hart T. Mankin, Ronald M. Holdaway, Donald L. Ivers, Jonathan R. Steinberg.

# U.S. Government Independent Agencies

Source: National Archives & Records Administration Address: Washington, DC. Location and ZIP codes of agencies in parentheses; as of mid-1993.

**ACTION —** John Seal, act. dir. (1100 Vermont Ave., NW, 20525).

**Administrative Conference of the United States —** Brian C. Griffin, chmn. (Suite 500, 2120 L St. NW, 20037).

**African Development Foundation —** Gregory Robeson Smith, pres. (1400 Eye St. NW, 20005).

**Central Intelligence Agency —** R. James Woolsey, dir. (Wash., DC 20505).

**Commission on Civil Rights —** Arthur A. Fletcher, chmn. (624 9th St. NW, 20425).

**Commodity Futures Trading Commission —** William P. Albrecht, act. chmn. (2033 K St. NW, 20581).

**Consumer Product Safety Commission —** Jacqueline Jones-Smith, chmn. (East West Towers, 4340 East West Hwy., Bethesda, MD 20814).

**Environmental Protection Agency —** Carol M. Browner, adm. (401 M St., SW, 20460).

**Equal Employment Opportunity Commission —** Tony E. Gallegos, act. chmn. (1801 L St. NW, 20507).

**Export-Import Bank of the United States —** Kenneth D. Brody, pres. and chmn. (811 Vermont Ave. NW 20571).

**Farm Credit Administration —** Harold B. Steele, chmn., Farm Credit Administration Board (1501 Farm Credit Drive, McLean, VA 22102).

**Federal Communications Commission —** James H. Quello, chmn. (1919 M St. NW, 20554).

**Federal Deposit Insurance Corporation —** Andrew C. Hove Jr., chmn. (550 17th St. NW, 20429).

**Federal Election Commission —** Scott E. Thomas, chmn. (999 E St. NW, 20463).

**Federal Emergency Management Agency —** James Lee Witt, dir. (500 C St. SW, 20472).

**Federal Housing Finance Board —** Daniel F. Evans Jr., chmn. (1777 F St. NW., 20006).

**Federal Labor Relations Authority —** Jean McKee, chmn. (607 14th St. NW, 20424).

**Federal Maritime Commission —** William D. Hathaway, chmn. (800 N. Capitol St. NW, 20573).

**Federal Mediation and Conciliation Service —** Bernard E. DeLury, dir. (2100 K St. NW, 20427).

**Federal Mine Safety & Health Review Commission —** Arlene Holen, chmn. (1730 K St. NW, 20006).

**Federal Reserve System** — Chairman, board of governors: Alan Greenspan. (20th St. & Constitution Ave. NW, 20551).

**Federal Retirement Thrift Investment Board** — Roger W. Mehle, chmn. (1250 H St. NW, 20005).

**Federal Trade Commission** — Janet D. Steiger, chmn. (Pennsylvania Ave. at 6th St. NW, 20580).

**General Accounting Office** — Comptroller General of the U.S.; Charles A. Bowsher (441 G St. NW, 20548).

**General Services Administration** — Roger W. Johnson, adm. (18th & F Sts. NW, 20405).

**Government Printing Office** — Public printer: Michael F. Di-Mario, act. (North Capitol and H Sts. NW, 20401).

**Inter-American Foundation** — Frank D. Yturria, chmn. (901 N. Stuart St., Arlington, VA 22203).

**Interstate Commerce Commission** — Gail C. McDonald, chmn. (12th St. & Constitution Ave. NW, 20423).

**Library of Congress** — James H. Billington, librarian of Congress (101 Independence Ave. SE, 20540).

**Merit Systems Protection Board** — Benjamin L. Erdreich, chmn. (1120 Vermont Ave. NW, 20419).

**National Aeronautics and Space Administration** — Daniel S. Goldin, adm. (300 E St. SW, 20546).

**National Archives & Records Administration** — Trudy H. Peterson, act. archivist (7th St. & Pennsylvania Ave. NW, 20408).

**National Credit Union Administration** — Roger W. Jepsen, chmn. (1776 G St. NW, 20456).

**National Foundation on the Arts and the Humanities** — Jane Alexander, chmn. (arts) 1100 Pennsylvania Ave. NW, 20506; Donald Gibson, act. chmn. (humanities) same address. Institute of Museum Services: Linda Bell, act. dir., same address.

**National Labor Relations Board** — James M. Stephens, chmn. (1099 14th St. NW, 20570).

**National Mediation Board** — Kimberly A. Madigan, chmn. (Suite 250 East, 1301 K St. NW, 20572).

**National Railroad Passenger Corporation (Amtrak)** — W. Graham Claytor Jr., chmn. (60 Massachusetts Ave. NE, 20002).

**National Science Foundation** — James J. Duderstadt, chmn., National Science Board (1800 G St. NW, 20550).

**National Transportation Safety Board** — Carl W. Vogt, chmn. (490 L'Enfant Plaza SW, 20594).

**Nuclear Regulatory Commission** — Ivan Selin, chmn. (1717 H St. NW, 20555).

**Occupational Safety and Health Review Commission** — Edwin G. Foulke Jr., chmn. (1120 20th St. NW, 20036).

**Office of Personnel Management** — James B. King, dir. (1900 E St. NW, 20415).

**Peace Corps** — Carol Bellamy, dir. (1990 K St. NW, 20526).

**Postal Rate Commission** — George W. Haley, chmn. (1333 H St. NW, 20268-0001).

**Railroad Retirement Board** — Glen L. Bower, chmn. (Suite 558, 2000 L St. NW, 20036). Main Office (844 N. Rush St., Chicago, IL 60611).

**Securities and Exchange Commission** — Richard C. Breeden, chmn. (450 5th St. NW, 20549).

**Selective Service System** — Robert W. Gambino, dir. (National Headquarters, 20435).

**Small Business Administration** — Erskine B. Bowles, adm. (409 Third St. SW, 20416).

**Smithsonian Institution** — Robert McC. Adams, secy. (1000 Jefferson Dr. SW, 20560).

**Tennessee Valley Authority** — Chairman, board of directors: Craven Crowell (400 W. Summit Hill Dr., Knoxville, TN 37902 and Room 300, 412 1st St. SE, Washington, DC 20444).

**United States Arms Control & Disarmament Agency** — Thomas Graham, Jr., dir. (320 21st St. NW 20451).

**United States Information Agency** — Joseph D. Duffey, dir. (301 4th St. SW, 20547).

**United States International Development Cooperation Agency** — James H. Michel, act. dir. (320 21st St. NW, 20523).

**United States International Trade Commission** — Don E. Newquist, chmn. (500 E St. SW, 20436).

**United States Postal Service** — Marvin Runyon, postmaster general (475 L'Enfant Plaza SW, 20260).

## Other Notable U.S. Agencies

| Agency | Cabinet Department |
|---|---|
| Bureau of Alcohol, Tobacco, and Firearms | Treasury |
| Federal Aviation Administration | Transportation |
| Bureau of the Census | Commerce |
| U.S. Coast Guard | Transportation |
| Office of Consumer Affairs | Health & Human Services |
| U.S. Customs Service | Treasury |
| Centers for Disease Control & Prevention | Health & Human Services |
| Bureau of Economic Analysis | Commerce |
| Federal Bureau of Investigation | Justice |
| Fish & Wildlife Service | Interior |
| Food & Drug Administration | Health & Human Services |
| Foreign Service | State |
| Forest Service | Agriculture |
| National Institutes of Health | Health & Human Services |
| Federal Highway Administration | Transportation |
| Immigration & Naturalization Service | Justice |
| Bureau of Indian Affairs | Interior |
| U.S. Mint | Treasury |
| National Oceanic & Atmospheric Administration | Commerce |
| National Park Service | Interior |
| Bureau of Prisons | Justice |
| Internal Revenue Service | Treasury |
| U.S. Secret Service | Treasury |
| Social Security Administration | Health & Human Services |
| Surgeon General | Health & Human Services |

## Governors of States and Possessions

(as of mid-1993)

| State | Capital, Zip Code | Governor | Party | Term years | Term expires | Annual salary |
|---|---|---|---|---|---|---|
| Alabama | Montgomery 36130 | Jim Folsom Jr. | Dem. | 4 | Jan. 1995 | $87,913 |
| Alaska | Juneau 99811 | Walter Hickel | Ind. | 4 | Dec. 1994 | 81,648 |
| Arizona | Phoenix 85007 | Fife Symington | Rep. | 4 | Jan. 1995 | 75,000 |
| Arkansas | Little Rock 72201 | Jim Guy Tucker | Dem. | 4 | Jan. 1995 | 60,000 |
| California | Sacramento 95814 | Pete Wilson | Rep. | 4 | Jan. 1995 | 120,000 |
| Colorado | Denver 80203 | Roy Romer | Dem. | 4 | Jan. 1995 | 70,000 |
| Connecticut | Hartford 06106 | Lowell Weicker | Ind. | 4 | Jan. 1995 | 78,000 |
| Delaware | Dover 19901 | Thomas R. Carper | Dem. | 4 | Jan. 1997 | 95,000 |
| Florida | Tallahassee 32399 | Lawton Chiles | Dem. | 4 | Jan. 1995 | 95,000 |
| Georgia | Atlanta 30334 | Zell Miller | Dem. | 4 | Jan. 1995 | 91,092 |
| Hawaii | Honolulu 96813 | John Waihee | Dem. | 4 | Dec. 1994 | 94,780 |
| Idaho | Boise 83720 | Cecil D. Andrus | Dem. | 4 | Jan. 1995 | 75,000 |
| Illinois | Springfield 62706 | Jim Edgar | Rep. | 4 | Jan. 1995 | 100,681 |
| Indiana | Indianapolis 46204 | Evan Bayh | Dem. | 4 | Jan. 1997 | 77,200 |
| Iowa | Des Moines 50319 | Terry E. Branstad | Rep. | 4 | Jan. 1995 | 76,900 |
| Kansas | Topeka 66612 | Joan Finney | Dem. | 4 | Jan. 1995 | 74,235 |
| Kentucky | Frankfort 40601 | Brereton C. Jones | Dem. | 4 | Dec. 1995 | 79,255 |
| Louisiana | Baton Rouge 70804 | Edwin W. Edwards | Dem. | 4 | May 1996 | 73,440 |
| Maine | Augusta 04333 | John McKernan Jr. | Rep. | 4 | Jan. 1995 | 70,000 |
| Maryland | Annapolis 21401 | William Donald Schaefer | Dem. | 4 | Jan. 1995 | 120,000 |
| Massachusetts | Boston 02113 | William Weld | Rep. | 4 | Jan. 1995 | 75,000 |
| Michigan | Lansing 48913 | John Engler | Rep. | 4 | Jan. 1995 | 106,700 |

| State | Capital, Zip Code | Governor | Party | Term years | Term expires | Annual salary |
|---|---|---|---|---|---|---|
| Minnesota | St. Paul 55155 | Arne Carlson | Rep. | 4 | Jan. 1995 | 109,053 |
| Mississippi | Jackson 39205 | Kirk Fordice | Rep. | 4 | Jan. 1996 | 75,600 |
| Missouri | Jefferson City 65101 | Mel Carnahan | Dem. | 4 | Jan. 1997 | 90,312 |
| Montana | Helena 59620 | Marc Racicot | Rep. | 4 | Jan. 1997 | 55,502 |
| Nebraska | Lincoln 68509 | Ben Nelson | Dem. | 4 | Jan. 1995 | 65,000 |
| Nevada | Carson City 89710 | Robert Miller | Dem. | 4 | Jan. 1995 | 90,000 |
| New Hampshire | Concord 03301 | Stephen Merrill | Rep. | 2 | Jan. 1995 | 71,587 |
| New Jersey | Trenton 08625 | James Florio | Dem. | 4 | Jan. 1994 | 85,000 |
| New Mexico | Santa Fe 07503 | Bruce King | Dem. | 4 | Jan. 1995 | 90,000 |
| New York | Albany 12224 | Mario M. Cuomo | Dem. | 4 | Jan. 1995 | 130,000 |
| North Carolina | Raleigh 27603 | James B. Hunt Jr. | Dem. | 4 | Jan. 1997 | 123,300 |
| North Dakota | Bismarck 58505 | Edward T. Schafer | Rep. | 4 | Jan. 1997 | 68,280 |
| Ohio | Columbus 43215 | George Voinovich | Rep. | 4 | Jan. 1995 | 110,250 |
| Oklahoma | Oklahoma City 73105 | David Walters | Dem. | 4 | Jan. 1995 | 70,000 |
| Oregon | Salem 97310 | Barbara Roberts | Dem. | 4 | Jan. 1995 | 80,000 |
| Pennsylvania | Harrisburg 17120 | Robert Casey | Dem. | 4 | Jan. 1995 | 105,000 |
| Rhode Island | Providence 02903 | Bruce Sundlun | Dem. | 4 | Jan. 1995 | 69,000 |
| South Carolina | Columbia 29201 | Carroll A. Campbell Jr. | Rep. | 4 | Jan. 1995 | 101,959 |
| South Dakota | Pierre 57501 | Walter Dale Miller | Rep. | 4 | Jan. 1995 | 65,761 |
| Tennessee | Nashville 37219 | Ned Ray McWherter | Dem. | 4 | Jan. 1995 | 85,000 |
| Texas | Austin 78711 | Ann Richards | Dem. | 4 | Jan. 1995 | 93,432 |
| Utah | Salt Lake City 84114 | Michael O. Leavitt | Rep. | 4 | Jan. 1997 | 70,000 |
| Vermont | Montpelier 05602 | Howard Dean | Dem. | 2 | Jan. 1995 | 85,977 |
| Virginia | Richmond 23219 | L. Douglas Wilder | Dem. | 4 | Jan. 1994 | 108,000 |
| Washington | Olympia 98504 | Mike Lowry | Dem. | 4 | Jan. 1997 | 121,000 |
| West Virginia | Charleston 25305 | Gaston Caperton | Dem. | 4 | Jan. 1997 | 72,000 |
| Wisconsin | Madison 53703 | Tommy G. Thompson | Rep. | 4 | Jan. 1995 | 92,283 |
| Wyoming | Cheyenne 82002 | Mike Sullivan | Dem. | 4 | Jan. 1995 | 70,000 |
| Puerto Rico | San Juan 00936 | Pedro J. Rosselló | — | 4 | Jan. 1995 | — |

## State Officials, Salaries, Party Membership

As of mid-1993; † Ind. or other party.

### Alabama

Governor — Jim Folsom Jr., D., $87,913.
Lt. Gov. — vacant.
Sec. of State — Billy Joe Camp, D., $57,203.
Atty. Gen. — Jimmy Evans, D., $90,474.
Treasurer — George Wallace Jr., D., $57,203.
Legislature: meets annually the 3d Tuesday in Apr. (first year of term of office), first Tuesday in Feb. (2d and 3d years), 2d Tuesday in Jan. (4th year) at Montgomery. Members receive $60 a day salary, plus $2,280 per month expenses and mileage of 10¢ per mile.
Senate — Dem., 26; Rep., 8; 1 vac. Total, 35.
House — Dem., 82; Rep., 23. Total, 105.

### Alaska

Governor — Walter Hickel, †, $81,648.
Lt. Gov. — John B. Coghill, †, $76,188.
Atty. General — Charles Cole, R., $79,860.
Legislature: meets annually in January at Juneau, for 120 days with a 10-day extension possible upon ⅔ vote. First session in odd years. Members receive $22,872 per year plus $80 a day per diem.
Senate — Dem., 10; Rep., 10. Total, 20.
House — Dem., 20; Rep., 18; 2 other. Total, 40.

### Arizona

Governor — Fife Symington, R., $75,000.
Sec. of State — Richard Mahoney, D., $54,600.
Atty. Gen. — Grant Woods, R., $76,440.
Treasurer — Tony West, R., $54,600.
Legislature: meets annually in January at Phoenix. Each member receives an annual salary of $15,000.
Senate — Dem., 12; Rep., 18. Total, 30.
House — Dem., 25; Rep., 35. Total, 60.

### Arkansas

Governor — Jim Guy Tucker, D., $60,000.
Lt. Gov. — vacant.
Sec. of State — W. J. "Bill" McCuen, D., $37,000.
Atty. Gen. — Winston Bryant, D., $50,000.
Treasurer — Jimmie Lou Fisher Lumpkin, D., $37,000.
Auditor — Julia Hughes Jones, D., $37,000.
General Assembly: meets odd years in January at Little Rock. Members receive $12,500 per year, $77 a day while in regular session, plus travel expenses.
Senate — Dem., 30; Rep., 5. Total, 35.
House — Dem., 89; Rep. 10; 1 ind. Total, 100.

### California

Governor — Pete Wilson, R., $70,000.
Lt. Gov. — Leo T. McCarthy, D., $90,000.
Sec. of State — Marsh Fong Eu, D., $90,000.
Controller — Gray Davis, D., $90,000.
Atty. Gen. — Dan Lungren, R., $102,000.
Legislature: meets at Sacramento; regular sessions commence on the first Monday in Dec. of every even-numbered year; each session lasts 2 years. Members receive $52,500 per year plus mileage and $100 per diem.
Senate — Dem., 23; Rep., 14, 2 ind., 1 vac.; Total, 40.
Assembly — Dem., 48; Rep. 32; Total, 80.

### Colorado

Governor — Roy Romer, D., $70,000.
Lt. Gov. — Mike Callihan, D., $48,500.
Secy. of State — Natalie Meyer, R., $48,500.
Atty. Gen. — Gale Norton, R., $60,000.
Treasurer — Gail Schoettler, D., $48,500.
General Assembly: meets annually in January at Denver. Members receive $17,500 annually.
Senate — Dem., 19. Total, 35.
House — Dem., 31; Rep., 34. Total, 65.

### Connecticut

Governor — Lowell Weicker, †, $78,000.
Lt. Gov. — Eunice S. Groark, †, $55,000.
Sec. of State — Pauline R. Kezer, R., $50,000.
Treasurer — Francisco Borges, D., $50,000.
Comptroller — William E. Curry Jr., D., $50,000.
Atty. Gen. — Richard Blumenthal, D., $60,000.
General Assembly: meets annually odd years in January and even years in February at Hartford. Salary $15,200 per year plus $4,500 (senator), $3,500 (representative) per year for expenses, plus travel allowance.
Senate — Dem., 19; Rep., 16; 1 vac. Total, 36.
House — Dem., 86; Rep., 64; 1 vac. Total, 151.

### Delaware

Governor — Thomas R. Carper, D., $95,000.
Lt. Gov. — Ruth Ann Minner, D., $36,500.
Sec. of State — William P. Quillen, D., $73,700.
Atty. Gen. — Charles Oberly 3d, D., $84,700.
Treasurer — Janet C. Rzewnicki, R., $68,200.
General Assembly: 55 day session beginning the 2d Tuesday in January until June 30. Members receive $24,213 base salary, plus $5,500 expense account.

Senate — Dem., 15; Rep., 6. Total, 21.
House — Dem., 18; Rep., 23. Total, 41.

## Florida

Governor — Lawton Chiles, D., $95,000.
Lt. Gov. — Buddy McKay, D., $91,000.
Sec. of State — Jim Smith, R., $94,040.
Comptroller — Gerald Lewis, D., $94,040.
Atty. Gen. — Robert Butterworth, D., $94,040.
Treasurer — Tom Gallagher. R., $94,040.
Legislature: meets annually at Tallahassee. Members receive $22,560 per year plus expense allowance while on official business.
Senate — Dem., 20; Rep., 20. Total, 40.
House — Dem., 71; Rep., 49. Total, 120.

## Georgia

Governor — Zell Miller, D., $91,092.
Lt. Gov. — Pierre Howard, D., $59,145.
Sec. of State — Max Cleland, D., $72,966.
Insurance Comm. — Tim Ryles, D., $72,954.
Atty. Gen. — Michael J. Bowers, $74,645.
General Assembly: meets annually at Atlanta. Members receive $10,509 per year, $59 per diem, and $4,800 expense reimbursement. During session $59 per day for expenses.
Senate — Dem., 45; Rep., 11. Total, 56.
House — Dem., 145; Rep. 35. Total, 180.

## Hawaii

Governor — John Waihee, D., $94,780.
Lt. Gov. — Benjamin Cayetano, D., $90,041.
Atty. Gen. — Robert Marks, $85,302.
Comptroller — Robert Takushi, $85,302.
Dir. of Budget & Finance — Yukio Takemoto, $85,302.
Legislature: meets annually on 3d Wednesday in January at Honolulu. Members receive $27,000 per year plus expenses.
Senate — Dem., 22. Rep., 3. Total, 25.
House — Dem., 47. Rep. 4. Total, 51.

## Idaho

Governor — Cecil D. Andrus, D., $75,000.
Lt. Gov. — C. L. "Butch" Otter, R., $20,000.
Sec. of State — Pete T. Cenarrusa, R., $62,500.
Treasurer — Lydia Justice Edwards, R., $62,500.
Atty. Gen. — Larry EchoHawk, D., $67,500.
Legislature: meets the Monday on or nearest the 9th of January at Boise. Members receive $12,000 per year plus $70 per day during session if required to maintain a 2d residence; $40 if no 2d residence, plus $50.00 per day when engaged in legislative business when legislature is not in session.
Senate — Dem., 12; Rep., 23. Total, 35.
House — Dem., 20; Rep., 50. Total, 70.

## Illinois

Governor — Jim Edgar, R., $100,681.
Lt. Gov. — Bob Kustra, R., $71,069.
Sec. of State — George H. Ryan, R., $88,836.
Comptroller — Dawn Clark Netsch, D., $76,991.
Atty. Gen. — Roland W. Burris, D., $88,836.
Treasurer — Patrick Quinn, D., $76,991.
General Assembly: meets annually in January at Springfield. Members receive $38,496 per annum.
Senate — Dem., 27; Rep., 32. Total, 59.
House — Dem., 67; Rep., 51. Total, 118.

## Indiana

Governor — Evan Bayh, D., $77,200 plus discretionary expenses.
Lt. Gov. — Frank O'Bannon, D., $64,000 plus discretionary expenses.
Sec. of State — Joseph Hogsett, D., $46,000.
Atty. Gen. — Pamela Carter, D., $59,200.
Treasurer — Marjorie H. O'Laughlin, R., $46,000.
Auditor — Ann G. DeVore, R., $46,000.
General Assembly: meets annually in January. Members receive $11,600 per year plus $92 per day while in session, $25 per day while not in session.
Senate — Dem., 22; Rep., 28. Total, 50.
House — Dem., 55; Rep., 45. Total, 100.

## Iowa

Governor — Terry E. Branstad, R., $76,900.
Lt. Gov. — Joy Corning, R., $60,000.
Sec. of State — Elaine Baxter, D., $60,000.
Atty. Gen. — Bonnie Campbell, D., $73,600.
Treasurer — Michael L. Fitzgerald, D., $60,000.
Auditor — Richard D. Johnson, R., $60,000.
Secy. of Agriculture — Dale M. Cochran, D., $60,000.
General Assembly: meets annually in January at Des Moines. Members receive $18,100 annually plus maximum expense allow-

ance of $50 per day for first 110 days of first session, and first 100 days of 2d session (except for Polk Co. legislators); mileage expenses at 21¢ a mile.
Senate — Dem., 27; Rep., 23. Total. 50.
House — Dem., 49; Rep., 51. Total, 100.

## Kansas

Governor — Joan Finney, D., $74,235.
Lt. Gov. — James Francisco, D., $20,998.
Sec. of State — Bill Graves. R., $57,668.
Atty. Gen. — Robert T. Stephan, R., $66,324.
Treasurer — Sally Thompson, D., $57,668.
Legislature: meets annually in January at Topeka. Members receive $60 a day plus $70 a day expenses while in session, plus $600 per month while not in session.
Senate — Dem., 18; Rep., 22. Total, 40.
House — Dem., 63; Rep., 62. Total, 125.

## Kentucky

Governor — Brereton C. Jones, D., $79,255.
Lt. Gov. — Paul Patton, D., $67,378.
Sec. of State — Bob Babbage, D., $67,378.
Atty. Gen. — Chris Gorman, D., $67,378.
Treasurer — Francis J. Mills, D., $67,378.
Auditor — Ben Chandler, D., $67,378.
General Assembly: meets even years in January at Frankfort. Members receive $100 per day and $75 per day during session and $950 per month for expenses for interim.
Senate — Dem., 27; Rep., 11. Total, 38.
House — Dem., 68; Rep., 32. Total, 100.

## Louisiana

Governor — Edwin W. Edwards, D., $73,440.
Lt. Gov. — Melinda Schwegmann, D., $63,367.
Sec. of State — Fox McKeithen, R., $60,169.
Atty. Gen. — Richard Ieyoub, D., $60,169.
Treasurer — Mary Landrieu, D., $60,169.
Legislature: meets annually for 60 legislative days commencing on the last Monday in March. Members receive $75 per day and mileage plus annual salary of $16,800.
Senate — Dem., 33; Rep., 6. Total, 39.
House — Dem., 88; Rep., 16, 1 ind. Total, 105.

## Maine

Governor — John R. McKernan Jr., R., $70,000.
Sec. of State — G. William Diamond, D., $48,152.
Atty. Gen. — Michael E. Carpenter, D., $61,152.
Treasurer — Samuel Shapiro, D., $61,200.
Legislature: meets annually the first Wednesday in December at Augusta, and the Wednesday after the first Tuesday in Jan. in even numbered years. Members receive $10,500 for first regular sessions, $7,500 for second regular session plus expenses; presiding officers receive 50% more.
Senate — Dem., 20; Rep., 15. Total, 35.
House — Dem., 90; Rep., 61. Total, 151.

## Maryland

Governor — William Donald Schaefer, D., $120,000.
Lt. Gov. — Melvin Steinberg, D., $100,000.
Comptroller — Louis L. Goldstein, D., $100,000.
Atty. Gen. — J. Joseph Curran Jr., D., $100,000.
Sec. of State — Winfield M. Kelly Jr., D., $70,000.
Treasurer — Lucille Maurer, D., $100,000.
General Assembly: meets 90 consecutive days annually beginning on the 2d Wednesday in January at Annapolis. Members receive $27,000 per year plus expenses.
Senate — Dem., 38; Rep., 9. Total, 47.
House — Dem., 117; Rep., 24. Total, 141.

## Massachusetts

Governor — William Weld, R., $75,000.
Lt. Gov. — A. Paul Cellucci, R., $60,000.
Sec. of State — Michael Joseph Connolly, D., $60,000.
Atty. Gen. — L. Scott Harshbarger, D., $65,000.
Treasurer — Joseph Malone. R., $60,000.
Auditor — A. Joseph DeNucci, D., $60,000.
General Court (Legislature): meets each January in Boston. Salaries $30,000 per annum.
Senate — Dem., 31; Rep., 9. Total, 40.
House — Dem., 124; Rep., 35; ind., 1. Total, 160.

## Michigan

Governor — John Engler, R., $106,700.
Lt. Gov. — Connie Binsfeld. R., $80,300.
Sec. of State — Richard H. Austin, D., $109,000.
Atty. Gen. — Frank J. Kelley, D., $109,000.
Treasurer — Doug Roberts, N-P, $83,100.
Legislature: meets annually in January at Lansing. Members receive $45,450 per year, plus $8,500 expense allowance.

Senate — Dem., 16; Rep., 20; 2 vac. Total, 38.
House — Dem., 55; Rep., 55. Total, 110.

## Minnesota

Governor — Arne Carlson, R., $109,053.
Lt. Gov. — Joanell Dyrstad, IR, $59,981.
Sec. of State — Joan Anderson Growe, DFL., $59,981.
Atty. Gen. — Hubert H. Humphrey 3d, DFL., $85,194.
Treasurer — Michael McGrath, DFL., $59,981.
Auditor — Mark Dayton, IR, $65,437.
Legislature: meets for a total of 120 days within every 2 years at St. Paul. Members receive $27,979 per year, plus expense allowance during session.
Senate — DFL., 45; IR, 22. Total, 67.
House — DFL., 86; IR, 48. Total, 134.
(DFL means Democratic-Farmer-Labor. IR means Independent Republican.)

## Mississippi

Governor — Kirk Fordice, R., $75,600.
Lt. Gov. — Eddie Briggs, R., $40,800.
Sec. of State — Dick Molpus, D., $54,000.
Atty. Gen. — Mike Moore, D., $61,200.
Treasurer — Marshall Bennett, D., $54,000.
Legislature: meets annually in January at Jackson. Members receive $10,100 per regular session plus travel allowance, and $500 per month while not in session.
Senate — Dem., 39; Rep., 13. Total, 52.
House — Dem., 93; Rep., 27, 2 ind. Total, 122.

## Missouri

Governor — Mel Carnahan, D., $90,312.
Lt. Gov. — Roger Wilson, D., $54,343.
Sec. of State — Judith Moriarty, D., $72,327.
Atty. Gen. — Jeremiah W. Nixon, D., $78,322.
Treasurer — Bob Holden, D., $72,327.
State Auditor — Margaret Kelly, R., $72,327.
General Assembly: meets annually in Jefferson City on the first Wednesday after first Monday in January. Members receive $22,862 annually.
Senate — Dem., 18; Rep., 14, 2 vac. Total, 34.
House — Dem., 101; Rep., 61, 1 vac. Total, 163.

## Montana

Governor — Marc Racicot, R., $55,502.
Lt. Gov. — Dennis Rehberg, R., $40,466.
Sec. of State — Mike Cooney, D., $37,526.
Atty. Gen. — Joe Mazurek, D., $50,841.
Legislative Assembly: meets odd years in January at Helena. Members receive $55.50 per legislative day plus $50 per day for expenses while in session.
Senate — Dem., 30; Rep., 20. Total, 50.
House — Dem., 53; Rep., 47. Total, 100.

## Nebraska

Governor — Ben Nelson, D., $65,000.
Lt. Gov. — Maxine Moul, D., $47,000.
Sec. of State — Allen J. Beermann, R., $52,000.
Atty. Gen. — Don Stenberg, R., $64,500.
Treasurer — Dawn Rockey, D., $49,500.
Legislature: meets annually in January at Lincoln. Members receive salary of $12,000 annually plus expenses.
Unicameral body composed of 49 members who are elected on a nonpartisan ballot and are called senators.

## Nevada

Governor — Robert Miller, D., $90,000.
Lt. Gov. — Sue Wagner, R., $20,000.
Sec. of State — Cheryl Lau, R., $62,500.
Comptroller — Darrel Daines, R., $62,500.
Atty. Gen. — Frankie Sue Del Papa, D., $85,000.
Treasurer — Bob Seale, R., $62,500.
Legislature: meets odd years in January at Carson City. Members receive $130 per day for 60 days (20 days for special sessions).
Senate — Dem., 10; Rep., 11. Total, 21.
Assembly — Dem., 29; Rep., 13. Total, 42.

## New Hampshire

Governor — Stephen Merrill, R., $71,587.
Sec. of State — William M. Gardner, D., $63,430.
Atty. Gen. — Jeffrey Howard, R., $71,007.
Treasurer — Georgie A. Thomas, R., $63,430.
General Court (Legislature): meets every year in January at Concord. Members receive $200; presiding officers $250.
Senate — Dem., 11; Rep., 13. Total, 24.
House — Rep., 257; Dem., 137, ind. & other 5, vac. 1. Total, 400.

## New Jersey

Governor — James J. Florio, D., $85,000.
Sec. of State — Daniel Dalton, D., $100,225.
Atty. Gen. — Robert J. Dei Tufo, D., $100,225.
Treasurer — Samuel Crane, D., $100,225.
Legislature: meets throughout the year at Trenton. Members receive $25,000 per year, except president of Senate and speaker of Assembly who receive ⅓ more.
Senate — Dem., 13; Rep., 27. Total, 40.
Assembly — Dem., 22; Rep. 58. Total, 80.

## New Mexico

Governor — Bruce King, D., $90,000.
Lt. Gov. — Casey Luna, D., $65,000.
Sec. of State — Stephanie Gonzales, D., $65,000.
Atty. Gen. — Tom Udall, D., $72,500.
Treasurer — David King, D., $65,000.
Legislature: meets on the 3d Tuesday in January at Santa Fe; odd years for 60 days, even years for 30 days. Members receive $75 per day while in session.
Senate — Dem., 26; Rep., 16. Total, 42.
House — Dem., 45; Rep., 25. Total, 70.

## New York

Governor — Mario M. Cuomo, D., $130,000.
Lt. Gov. — Stan Lundine, D., $110,000.
Sec. of State — Gail S. Shaffer, D., $87,338.
Comptroller — Edward V. Regan, R., $110,000.
Atty. Gen. — Robert Abrams, D., $110,000.
Legislature: meets annually in January at Albany. Members receive $57,500 per year.
Senate — Dem., 26; Rep., 35. Total, 61.
Assembly — Dem., 101; Rep., 48; 1 vac. Total, 150.

## North Carolina

Governor — James B. Hunt Jr., D., $123,300 plus $11,500 per year expenses.
Lt. Gov. — Dennis Wicker, D., $75,774 plus expenses.
Sec. of State — Rufus L. Edmisten, D., $75,252.
Atty. Gen. — Michael Easley, D., $75,252.
Treasurer — Harlan E. Boyles, D., $75,252.
General Assembly: meets odd years in January at Raleigh. Members receive $12,504 annual salary and $6,624 annual expense allowance, plus $81 per diem subsistence and travel allowance while in session.
Senate — Dem., 39; Rep., 11. Total, 50.
House — Dem., 78; Rep., 42. Total, 120.

## North Dakota

Governor — Edward T. Schafer, R., $68,280.
Lt. Gov. — Rosemarie Myrdal, R., $56,112.
Sec. of State — Alvin A. Jaeger, R., $51,752.
Atty. Gen. — Heidi Heitkamp, D., $57,936.
Treasurer — Kathi Gilmore, D., $51,744.
Legislative Assembly: meets odd years in January at Bismarck. Members receive $90 per day expenses during session and $180 per month.
Senate — Dem., 25; Rep., 24. Total, 49.
House — Dem., 33; Rep., 65. Total, 98.

## Ohio

Governor — George Voinovich, R., $110,250.
Lt. Gov. — Michael DeWine, R., $57,011.
Sec. of State — Bob Taft, R., $81,444.
Atty. Gen. — Lee Fisher, D., $81,444.
Treasurer — Mary Ellen Withrow, D., $81,444.
Auditor — Thomas E. Ferguson, D., $81,444.
General Assembly: meets odd years at Columbus on first Monday in January; no limit on session. Members receive $43,833 per annum.
Senate — Dem., 13; Rep., 20. Total, 33.
House — Dem., 54; Rep., 45. Total, 99.

## Oklahoma

Governor — David Walters, D., $70,000.
Lt. Gov. — Jack Mildren, D., $40,000.
Sec. of State — John Kennedy, D., $42,500.
Atty. Gen. — Susan Loving, D., $55,000.
Treasurer — Claudette Henry, R., $50,000.
Auditor — Clifton Scott, D., $50,000.
Legislature: meets annually the first Monday in Feb. at Oklahoma City. Members receive $32,000 annually.
Senate — Dem., 37; Rep., 11. Total, 48.
House — Dem., 68; Rep., 33. Total, 101.

## Oregon

Governor — Barbara Roberts, D., $80,000.
Sec. of State — Phil Keisling, D., $61,500.
Atty. Gen. — Ted Kulongosk, D., $66,000.

Treasurer — Jim Hill, D., $61,500.
**Legislative Assembly:** meets odd years in January at Salem. Members receive $1,029 monthly and $73 expenses per day both during & out of session.
Senate — Dem., 16; Rep., 14. Total, 30.
House — Dem., 32; Rep., 28. Total, 60.

## Pennsylvania

**Governor** — Robert Casey, D., $105,000.
**Lt. Gov.** — Mark S. Singel, D., $83,000.
**Sec. of the Commonwealth** — Brenda K. Mitchell, D., $72,000.
**Atty. Gen.** — Ernest R. Preate, R., $84,000.
**Treasurer** — Catherine Baker Knoll, D., $84,000.
**General Assembly** — convenes annually in January at Harrisburg. Members receive $47,000 per year plus expenses.
Senate — Dem., 25; Rep., 24; 1 vacancy. Total, 50.
House — Dem., 105; Rep., 98. Total, 203.

## Rhode Island

**Governor** — Bruce Sundlun, D., $69,000.
**Lt. Gov.** — Robert A. Weygand, D., $52,000.
**Sec. of State** — Barbara M. Leonard, R., $52,000.
**Atty. Gen.** — Jeffrey B. Pine, R., $55,000.
**Treasurer** — Nancy J. Mayer, R., $52,000.
**General Assembly:** meets annually in January at Providence. Members receive $5 per day for 60 days, and travel allowance of 8¢ per mile.
Senate — Dem., 39; Rep., 11. Total, 50.
House — Dem., 85; Rep., 15. Total, 100.

## South Carolina

**Governor** — Carroll A. Campbell Jr., R., $101,959.
**Lt. Gov.** — Nick Theodore, D., $44,737.
**Sec. of State** — Jim Miles, R., $88,434.
**Comptroller Gen.** — Earle E. Morris Jr., D., $88,434.
**Atty. Gen.** — T.T. Medlock, D., $88,434.
**Treasurer** — G.L. Patterson Jr., D., $85,000.
**General Assembly:** meets annually in January at Columbia. Members receive $10,400 per year and expense allowance of $79 per day, plus travel and postage allowance.
Senate — Dem., 30; Rep., 16. Total, 46.
House — Dem. 73; Rep., 50; 1 ind. Total, 124.

## South Dakota

**Governor** — Walter Dale Miller, R., $65,761.
**Lt. Gov.** — vacant.
**Sec. of State** — Joyce Hazeltine, R., $44,681.
**Treasurer** — G. Homer Harding, R., $44,681.
**Atty. Gen.** — Mark Barnett, R., $55,853.
**Auditor** — Vernon Larson, R., $44,681.
**Legislature:** meets annually in January at Pierre. Members receive $4,267 for 40-day session in odd-numbered years, and $3,733 for 35-day session in even-numbered years, plus $75 per legislative day.
Senate — Dem., 20; Rep., 15. Total, 35.
House — Dem., 29; Rep., 41. Total, 70.

## Tennessee

**Governor** — Ned Ray McWherter, D., $85,000.
**Lt. Gov.** — John S. Wilder, D., $49,500.
**Sec. of State** — Riley C. Darnell, D., $76,068.
**Comptroller** — William Snodgrass D., $76,068.
**Atty. Gen.** — Charles W. Burson, D., $93,540.
**General Assembly:** meets annually in January at Nashville. Members receive $16,500 yearly plus $78.00 per diem plus office expenses.
Senate — Dem., 19; Rep., 14. Total, 33.
House — Dem., 63; Rep., 36. Total, 99.

## Texas

**Governor** — Ann Richards, D., $99,122.
**Lt. Gov.** — Bob Bullock, D., $7,200.
**Sec. of State** — John Hannah, D., $76,966.
**Comptroller** — John Sharp, D., $79,246.
**Atty. Gen.** — Dan Morales, D., $79,246.
**Treasurer** — Martha Whitehead, D., $79,246.
**Legislature:** meets odd years in January at Austin. Members receive annual salary not exceeding $7,200, per diem while in session, and travel allowance.
Senate — Dem., 18; Rep., 13. Total, 31.
House — Dem., 92; Rep., 58. Total, 150.

## Utah

**Governor** — Michael O. Leavitt, R., $70,000.
**Lt. Gov.** — Olene S. Walker, R., $52,500.
**Atty. Gen.** — Jan Graham, D., $56,000.
**Treasurer** — Edward T. Alter, R., $53,000.

**Legislature:** convenes for 45 days on 2d Monday in January each year; members receive $25 per day, $15 daily expenses, and mileage.
Senate — Dem., 11; Rep., 18. Total, 29.
House — Dem., 26; Rep., 49. Total, 75.

## Vermont

**Governor** — Howard Dean, D., $85,977.
**Lt. Gov.** — Barbara W. Snelling, R., $35,842.
**Sec. of State** — Dennis M. Hooper, D., $54,102.
**Atty. Gen.** — Jeffrey Amestoy, R., $64,991.
**Treasurer** — Paul W. Ruse Jr., D., $54,102.
**Auditor of Accounts** — Edward S. Flanagan, D., $54,102.
**General Assembly:** meets odd years in January at Montpelier. Members receive $510 per week while in session plus $100 per day for special session, plus specified expenses.
Senate — Dem., 14; Rep., 16. Total, 30.
House — Dem., 87; Rep., 59., ind. 2, Prog. Coalition 2. Total, 150.

## Virginia

**Governor** — L. Douglas Wilder, D., $108,000.
**Lt. Gov.** — Donald S. Beyer Jr., D. $29,550.
**Atty. Gen.** — Mary Sue Terry, D., $95,000.
**Sec. of the Commonwealth** — Pamela Womack, D., $57,735.
**Treasurer** — Eddie N. Moore Jr., $85,881.
**General Assembly:** meets annually in January at Richmond. Members receive $18,000 annually plus expense and mileage allowances.
Senate — Dem., 22; Rep., 18. Total, 40.
House — Dem., 58; Rep., 41; ind., 1. Total, 100.

## Washington

**Governor** — Mike Lowry, D., $121,000.
**Lt. Gov.** — Joel Pritchard, R., $62,700.
**Sec. of State** — Ralph Munro, R., $64,300.
**Atty. Gen.** — Christine Gregoire, D., $92,000.
**Treasurer** — Daniel K. Grimm, D., $79,500.
**Legislature:** meets annually in January at Olympia. Members receive $25,900 annually plus $66 per diem and 28¢ per mile while in session, and $66 per diem for attending meetings during interim.
Senate — Dem., 28; Rep., 21. Total, 49.
House — Dem., 65; Rep., 33. Total, 98.

## West Virginia

**Governor** — Gaston Caperton, D., $72,000.
**Sec. of State** — Ken Hechler, D., $43,200.
**Atty. Gen.** — Darrell McGraw, D., $50,400.
**Treasurer** — Larrie Bailey, D., $50,400.
**Comm. of Agric.** — Gus Douglass, D., $46,800.
**Auditor** — Glen B. Gainer 3d, D., $46,800.
**Legislature:** meets annually in January at Charleston. Members receive $6,500.
Senate — Dem., 32; Rep., 2. Total, 34.
House — Dem., 79; Rep., 21. Total, 100.

## Wisconsin

**Governor** — Tommy G. Thompson, R., $92,283.
**Lt. Gov.** — Scott McCallum, R., $49,673.
**Sec. of State** — Douglas La Follette, D., $45,088.
**Treasurer** — Cathy S. Zeuske, R., $45,088.
**Atty. Gen.** — James E. Doyle, D., $82,706.
**Superintendent of Public Instruction** — Herbert J. Grover, $72,337.
**Legislature:** meets in January at Madison. Members receive $35,070 annually plus $64 per day expenses.
Senate — Dem., 15; Rep., 15, 3 vac. Total, 33.
Assembly — Dem., 52; Rep., 47. Total, 99.

## Wyoming

**Governor** — Mike Sullivan, D., $70,000.
**Sec. of State** — Kathy Karpan, D., $52,500.
**Atty. Gen.** — Joseph Meyer, $52,500.
**Treasurer** — Stan Smith, R., $52,500.
**Auditor** — Dave Ferrari, R., $52,500.
**Legislature:** meets odd years in January, even years in February, at Cheyenne. Members receive $75 per day while in session, plus $60 per day for expenses.
Senate — Dem., 10; Rep., 20. Total, 30.
House — Dem., 19; Rep. 45. Total, 64.

## Puerto Rico

**Governor** — Pedro J. Rosselló.
**Legislature:** composed of a Senate of 27 members and a House of Representatives of 53 members. Majority of the members of both chambers belongs to the New Progressive Party. They meet annually on the 2d Monday in January in San Juan.

# CABINETS OF THE U. S.

## Secretaries of State

The Department of Foreign Affairs was created by act of Congress July 27, 1789, and the name changed to Department of State on Sept. 15.

| President | Secretary | Home | Apptd. | President | Secretary | Home | Apptd. |
|---|---|---|---|---|---|---|---|
| Washington | Thomas Jefferson | Va. | 1789 | Harrison, B. | Thomas F. Bayard | Del. | 1889 |
| " | Edmund Randolph | " | 1794 | " | James G. Blaine | Me. | 1889 |
| " | Timothy Pickering | Pa. | 1795 | " | John W. Foster | Ind. | 1892 |
| Adams, J. | Timothy Pickering | Pa. | 1797 | Cleveland | Walter Q. Gresham | Ind. | 1893 |
| " | John Marshall | Va. | 1800 | " | Richard Olney | Mass. | 1895 |
| Jefferson | James Madison | " | 1801 | McKinley | Richard Olney | Mass. | 1897 |
| Madison | Robert Smith | Md. | 1809 | " | John Sherman | Oh. | 1897 |
| " | James Monroe | Va. | 1811 | " | William R. Day | Oh. | 1898 |
| Monroe | John Quincy Adams | Mass. | 1817 | " | John Hay | D.C. | 1898 |
| Adams, J.Q. | Henry Clay | Ky. | 1825 | Roosevelt, T. | John Hay | D.C. | 1901 |
| Jackson | Martin Van Buren | N.Y. | 1829 | " | Elihu Root | N.Y. | 1905 |
| " | Edward Livingston | La. | 1831 | " | Robert Bacon | N.Y. | 1909 |
| " | Louis McLane | Del. | 1833 | Taft | Robert Bacon | N.Y. | 1909 |
| " | John Forsyth | Ga. | 1834 | " | Philander C. Knox | Pa. | 1909 |
| Van Buren | John Forsyth | Ga. | 1837 | Wilson | Philander C. Knox | Pa. | 1913 |
| Harrison, W.H. | Daniel Webster | Mass. | 1841 | " | William J. Bryan | Neb. | 1913 |
| Tyler | Daniel Webster | Mass. | 1841 | " | Robert Lansing | N.Y. | 1915 |
| " | Abel P. Upshur | Va. | 1843 | " | Bainbridge Colby | N.Y. | 1920 |
| " | John C. Calhoun | S.C. | 1844 | Harding | Charles E. Hughes | N.Y. | 1921 |
| Polk | John C. Calhoun | S.C. | 1845 | Coolidge | Charles E. Hughes | N.Y. | 1923 |
| " | James Buchanan | Pa. | 1845 | " | Frank B. Kellogg | Minn. | 1925 |
| Taylor | James Buchanan | Pa. | 1849 | Hoover | Frank B. Kellogg | Minn. | 1929 |
| " | John M. Clayton | Del. | 1849 | " | Henry L. Stimson | N.Y. | 1929 |
| Fillmore | John M. Clayton | Del. | 1850 | Roosevelt, F.D. | Cordell Hull | Tenn. | 1933 |
| " | Daniel Webster | Mass. | 1850 | " | E.R. Stettinius Jr. | Va. | 1944 |
| " | Edward Everett | " | 1852 | Truman | E.R. Stettinius Jr. | Va. | 1945 |
| Pierce | William L. Marcy | N.Y. | 1853 | " | James F. Byrnes | S.C. | 1945 |
| Buchanan | William L. Marcy | N.Y. | 1857 | " | George C. Marshall | Pa. | 1947 |
| " | Lewis Cass | Mich. | 1857 | " | Dean G. Acheson | Conn. | 1949 |
| " | Jeremiah S. Black | Pa. | 1860 | Eisenhower | John Foster Dulles | N.Y. | 1953 |
| Lincoln | Jeremiah S. Black | Pa. | 1861 | " | Christian A. Herter | Mass. | 1959 |
| " | William H. Seward | N.Y. | 1861 | Kennedy | Dean Rusk | N.Y. | 1961 |
| Johnson, A. | William H. Seward | N.Y. | 1865 | Johnson, L.B. | Dean Rusk | N.Y. | 1963 |
| Grant | Elihu B. Washburne | Ill. | 1869 | Nixon | William P. Rogers | N.Y. | 1969 |
| " | Hamilton Fish | N.Y. | 1869 | " | Henry A. Kissinger | D.C. | 1973 |
| Hayes | Hamilton Fish | N.Y. | 1877 | Ford | Henry A. Kissinger | D.C. | 1974 |
| " | William M. Evarts | N.Y. | 1877 | Carter | Cyrus R. Vance | N.Y. | 1977 |
| Garfield | William M. Evarts | N.Y. | 1881 | " | Edmund S. Muskie | Me. | 1980 |
| " | James G. Blaine | Me. | 1881 | Reagan | Alexander M. Haig Jr. | Conn. | 1981 |
| Arthur | James G. Blaine | Me. | 1881 | " | George P. Shultz | Cal. | 1982 |
| " | F.T. Frelinghuysen | N.J. | 1881 | Bush | James A. Baker 3d | Tex. | 1989 |
| Cleveland | F.T. Frelinghuysen | N.J. | 1885 | " | Lawrence S. Eagleburger | Mich. | 1992 |
| " | Thomas F. Bayard | Del. | 1885 | Clinton | Warren M. Christopher | Cal. | 1993 |

## Secretaries of the Treasury

The Treasury Department was organized by act of Congress Sept. 2, 1789.

| President | Secretary | Home | Apptd. | President | Secretary | Home | Apptd. |
|---|---|---|---|---|---|---|---|
| Washington | Alexander Hamilton | N.Y. | 1789 | Lincoln | Hugh McCulloch | Ind. | 1865 |
| " | Oliver Wolcott | Conn. | 1795 | Johnson, A. | Hugh McCulloch | Ind. | 1865 |
| Adams, J. | Oliver Wolcott | Conn. | 1797 | Grant | George S. Boutwell | Mass. | 1869 |
| " | Samuel Dexter | Mass. | 1801 | " | William A. Richardson | Mass. | 1873 |
| Jefferson | Samuel Dexter | Mass. | 1801 | " | Benjamin H. Bristow | Ky. | 1874 |
| " | Albert Gallatin | Pa. | 1801 | " | Lot M. Morrill | Me. | 1876 |
| Madison | Albert Gallatin | Pa. | 1809 | Hayes | John Sherman | Oh. | 1877 |
| " | George W. Campbell | Tenn. | 1814 | Garfield | William Windom | Minn. | 1881 |
| " | Alexander J. Dallas | Pa. | 1814 | Arthur | Charles J. Folger | N.Y. | 1881 |
| " | William H. Crawford | Ga. | 1816 | " | Walter Q. Gresham | Ind. | 1884 |
| Monroe | William H. Crawford | Ga. | 1817 | " | Hugh McCulloch | Ind. | 1884 |
| Adams, J.Q. | Richard Rush | Pa. | 1825 | Cleveland | Daniel Manning | N.Y. | 1885 |
| Jackson | Samuel D. Ingham | Pa. | 1829 | " | Charles S. Fairchild | N.Y. | 1887 |
| " | Louis McLane | Del. | 1831 | Harrison, B. | William Windom | Minn. | 1889 |
| " | William J. Duane | Pa. | 1833 | " | Charles Foster | Oh. | 1891 |
| " | Roger B. Taney | Md. | 1833 | Cleveland | John G. Carlisle | Ky. | 1893 |
| " | Levi Woodbury | N.H. | 1834 | McKinley | Lyman J. Gage | Ill. | 1897 |
| Van Buren | Levi Woodbury | N.H. | 1837 | Roosevelt, T. | Lyman J. Gage | Ill. | 1901 |
| Harrison, W.H. | Thomas Ewing | Oh. | 1841 | " | Leslie M. Shaw | Ia. | 1902 |
| Tyler | Thomas Ewing | Oh. | 1841 | " | George B. Cortelyou | N.Y. | 1907 |
| " | Walter Forward | Pa. | 1841 | Taft | Franklin MacVeagh | Ill. | 1909 |
| " | John C. Spencer | N.Y. | 1843 | Wilson | William G. McAdoo | N.Y. | 1913 |
| " | George M. Bibb | Ky. | 1844 | " | Carter Glass | Va. | 1918 |
| Polk | Robert J. Walker | Miss. | 1845 | " | David F. Houston | Mo. | 1920 |
| Taylor | William M. Meredith | Pa. | 1849 | Harding | Andrew W. Mellon | Pa. | 1921 |
| Fillmore | Thomas Corwin | Oh. | 1850 | Coolidge | Andrew W. Mellon | Pa. | 1923 |
| Pierce | James Guthrie | Ky. | 1853 | Hoover | Andrew W. Mellon | Pa. | 1929 |
| Buchanan | Howell Cobb | Ga. | 1857 | " | Ogden L. Mills | N.Y. | 1932 |
| " | Phillip F. Thomas | Md. | 1860 | Roosevelt, F.D. | William H. Woodin | N.Y. | 1933 |
| " | John A. Dix | N.Y. | 1861 | " | Henry Morgenthau, Jr. | N.Y. | 1934 |
| Lincoln | Salmon P. Chase | Oh. | 1861 | Truman | Fred M. Vinson | Ky. | 1945 |
| " | William P. Fessenden | Me. | 1864 | " | John W. Snyder | Mo. | 1946 |

| President | Secretary | Home | Apptd. | President | Secretary | Home | Apptd. |
|---|---|---|---|---|---|---|---|
| Eisenhower .. | George M. Humphrey | Oh. | 1953 | Nixon | William E. Simon | N.J. | 1974 |
| " | Robert B. Anderson | Conn. | 1957 | Ford | William E. Simon | N.J. | 1974 |
| Kennedy | C. Douglas Dillon | N.J. | 1961 | Carter | W. Michael Blumenthal | Mich. | 1977 |
| Johnson, L.B. | C. Douglas Dillon | N.J. | 1963 | " | G. William Miller | R.I. | 1979 |
| " | Henry H. Fowler | Va. | 1965 | Reagan | Donald T. Regan | N.Y. | 1981 |
| " | Joseph W. Barr | Ind. | 1968 | " | James A. Baker 3d | Tex. | 1985 |
| Nixon | David M. Kennedy | Ill. | 1969 | " | Nicholas F. Brady | N.J. | 1988 |
| " | John B. Connally | Tex. | 1971 | Bush | Nicholas F. Brady | N.J. | 1989 |
| " | George P. Shultz | Ill. | 1972 | Clinton | Lloyd Bentsen | Tex. | 1993 |

## Secretaries of Defense

The Department of Defense, originally designated the National Military Establishment, was created Sept. 18, 1947. It is headed by the secretary of defense, who is a member of the president's cabinet.

The departments of the army, of the navy, and of the air force function within the Department of Defense, and since 1947 their respective secretaries are not members of the president's cabinet.

| President | Secretary | Home | Apptd. | President | Secretary | Home | Apptd. |
|---|---|---|---|---|---|---|---|
| Truman | James V. Forrestal | N.Y. | 1947 | Nixon | Melvin R. Laird | Wis. | 1969 |
| " | Louis A. Johnson | W.Va. | 1949 | " | Elliot L. Richardson | Mass. | 1973 |
| " | George C. Marshall | Pa. | 1950 | " | James R. Schlesinger | Va. | 1973 |
| " | Robert A. Lovett | N.Y. | 1951 | Ford | James R. Schlesinger | Va. | 1974 |
| Eisenhower | Charles E. Wilson | Mich. | 1953 | " | Donald H. Rumsfeld | Ill. | 1975 |
| " | Neil H. McElroy | Oh. | 1957 | Carter | Harold Brown | Cal. | 1977 |
| " | Thomas S. Gates Jr. | Pa. | 1959 | Reagan | Caspar W. Weinberger | Cal. | 1981 |
| Kennedy | Robert S. McNamara | Mich. | 1961 | " | Frank C. Carlucci | Pa. | 1987 |
| Johnson, L.B. | Robert S. McNamara | Mich. | 1963 | Bush | Richard B. Cheney | Wyo. | 1989 |
| " | Clark M. Clifford | Md. | 1968 | Clinton | Les Aspin | Wis. | 1993 |

## Secretaries of War

The War Department (which included jurisdiction over the navy until 1798) was created by act of Congress Aug. 7, 1789, and Gen. Henry Knox was commissioned secretary of war under that act Sept. 12, 1789.

| President | Secretary | Home | Apptd. | President | Secretary | Home | Apptd. |
|---|---|---|---|---|---|---|---|
| Washington .. | Henry Knox | Mass. | 1789 | Grant | John A. Rawlins | Ill. | 1869 |
| " | Timothy Pickering | Pa. | 1795 | " | William T. Sherman | Oh. | 1869 |
| " | James McHenry | Md. | 1796 | " | William W. Belknap | Ia. | 1869 |
| Adams, J. | James McHenry | Md. | 1797 | " | Alphonso Taft | Oh. | 1876 |
| " | Samuel Dexter | Mass. | 1800 | " | James D. Cameron | Pa. | 1876 |
| Jefferson | Henry Dearborn | Mass. | 1801 | Hayes | George W. McCrary | Ia. | 1877 |
| Madison | William Eustis | Mass. | 1809 | " | Alexander Ramsey | Minn. | 1879 |
| " | John Armstrong | N.Y. | 1813 | Garfield | Robert T. Lincoln | Ill. | 1881 |
| " | James Monroe | Va. | 1814 | Arthur | Robert T. Lincoln | Ill. | 1881 |
| " | William H. Crawford | Ga. | 1815 | Cleveland | William C. Endicott | Mass. | 1885 |
| Monroe | John C. Calhoun | S.C. | 1817 | Harrison, B. | Redfield Proctor | Vt. | 1889 |
| Adams, J.Q. | James Barbour | Va. | 1825 | " | Stephen B. Elkins | W.Va. | 1891 |
| " | Peter B. Porter | N.Y. | 1828 | Cleveland | Daniel S. Lamont | N.Y. | 1893 |
| Jackson | John H. Eaton | Tenn. | 1829 | McKinley | Russel A. Alger | Mich. | 1897 |
| " | Lewis Cass | Mich. | 1831 | " | Elihu Root | N.Y. | 1899 |
| " | Benjamin F. Butler | N.Y. | 1837 | Roosevelt, T. | Elihu Root | N.Y. | 1901 |
| Van Buren | Joel R. Poinsett | S.C. | 1837 | " | William H. Taft | Oh. | 1904 |
| Harrison, W.H. | John Bell | Tenn. | 1841 | " | Luke E. Wright | Tenn. | 1908 |
| Tyler | John Bell | Tenn | 1841 | Taft | Jacob M. Dickinson | Tenn. | 1909 |
| " | John C. Spencer | N.Y. | 1841 | " | Henry L. Stimson | N.Y. | 1911 |
| " | James M. Porter | Pa. | 1843 | Wilson | Lindley M. Garrison | N.J. | 1913 |
| " | William Wilkins | Pa. | 1844 | " | Newton D. Baker | Oh. | 1916 |
| Polk | William L. Marcy | N.Y. | 1845 | Harding | John W. Weeks | Mass. | 1921 |
| Taylor | George W. Crawford | Ga. | 1849 | Coolidge | John W. Weeks | Mass. | 1923 |
| Fillmore | Charles M. Conrad | La. | 1850 | " | Dwight F. Davis | Mo. | 1925 |
| Pierce | Jefferson Davis | Miss. | 1853 | Hoover | James W. Good | Ill. | 1929 |
| Buchanan | John B. Floyd | Va. | 1857 | " | Patrick J. Hurley | Okla. | 1929 |
| " | Joseph Holt | Ky. | 1861 | Roosevelt, F.D. | George H. Dern | Ut. | 1933 |
| Lincoln | Simon Cameron | Pa. | 1861 | " | Harry H. Woodring | Kan. | 1937 |
| " | Edwin M. Stanton | Pa. | 1862 | " | Henry L. Stimson | N.Y. | 1940 |
| Johnson, A. | Edwin M. Stanton | Pa. | 1865 | Truman | Robert P. Patterson | N.Y. | 1945 |
| " | John M. Schofield | Ill. | 1868 | " | *Kenneth C. Royall | N.C. | 1947 |

## Secretaries of the Navy

The Navy Department was created by act of Congress Apr. 30, 1798.

| President | Secretary | Home | Apptd. | President | Secretary | Home | Apptd. |
|---|---|---|---|---|---|---|---|
| Adams, J. | Benjamin Stoddert | Md. | 1798 | Tyler | Abel P. Upshur | Va. | 1841 |
| Jefferson | Benjamin Stoddert | Md. | 1801 | " | David Henshaw | Mass. | 1843 |
| " | Robert Smith | Md. | 1801 | " | Thomas W. Gilmer | Va. | 1844 |
| Madison | Paul Hamilton | S.C. | 1809 | " | John Y. Mason | Va. | 1844 |
| " | William Jones | Pa. | 1813 | Polk | George Bancroft | Mass. | 1845 |
| " | Benjamin W. Crowninshield | Mass. | 1814 | " | John Y. Mason | Va. | 1846 |
| Monroe | Benjamin W. Crowninshield | Mass. | 1817 | Taylor | William B. Preston | Va. | 1849 |
| " | Smith Thompson | N.Y. | 1818 | Fillmore | William A. Graham | N.C. | 1850 |
| " | Samuel L. Southard | N.J. | 1823 | " | John P. Kennedy | Md. | 1852 |
| Adams, J.Q. | Samuel L. Southard | N.J. | 1825 | Pierce | James C. Dobbin | N.C. | 1853 |
| Jackson | John Branch | N.C. | 1829 | Buchanan | Isaac Toucey | Conn. | 1857 |
| " | Levi Woodbury | N.H. | 1831 | Lincoln | Gideon Welles | Conn. | 1861 |
| " | Mahlon Dickerson | N.J. | 1834 | Johnson, A. | Gideon Welles | Conn. | 1865 |
| Van Buren | Mahlon Dickerson | N.J. | 1837 | Grant | Adolph E. Borie | Pa. | 1869 |
| " | James K. Paulding | N.Y. | 1838 | " | George M. Robeson | N.J. | 1869 |
| Harrison, W.H. | George E. Badger | N.C. | 1841 | Hayes | Richard W. Thompson | Ind. | 1877 |
| Tyler | George E. Badger | N.C. | 1841 | " | Nathan Goff Jr. | W.Va. | 1881 |

| President | Secretary | Home | Apptd. | President | Secretary | Home | Apptd. |
|---|---|---|---|---|---|---|---|
| Garfield | William H. Hunt | La. | 1881 | Taft | George von L. Meyer | Mass. | 1909 |
| Arthur | William E. Chandler | N.H. | 1882 | Wilson | Josephus Daniels | N.C. | 1913 |
| Cleveland | William C. Whitney | N.Y. | 1885 | Harding | Edwin Denby | Mich. | 1921 |
| Harrison, B. | Benjamin F. Tracy | N.Y. | 1889 | Coolidge | Edwin Denby | Mich. | 1923 |
| Cleveland | Hilary A. Herbert | Ala. | 1893 | " | Curtis D. Wilbur | Cal. | 1924 |
| McKinley | John D. Long | Mass. | 1897 | Hoover | Charles Francis Adams | Mass. | 1929 |
| Roosevelt, T. | John D. Long | Mass. | 1901 | Roosevelt, F.D. | Claude A. Swanson | Va. | 1933 |
| " | William H. Moody | Mass. | 1902 | " | Charles Edison | N.J. | 1940 |
| " | Paul Morton | Ill. | 1904 | " | Frank Knox | Ill. | 1940 |
| " | Charles J. Bonaparte | Md. | 1905 | " | James V. Forrestal | N.Y. | 1944 |
| " | Victor H. Metcalf | Cal. | 1906 | Truman | *James V. Forrestal | N.Y. | 1945 |
| " | Truman H. Newberry | Mich. | 1908 | | | | |

* Last members of Cabinet. The War Department became the Department of the Army and it and the Navy Department became branches of the Department of Defense, created Sept. 18, 1947.

## Attorneys General

The office of attorney general was organized by act of Congress Sept. 24, 1789. The Department of Justice was created June 22, 1870.

| President | Attorney General | Home | Apptd. | President | Attorney General | Home | Apptd. |
|---|---|---|---|---|---|---|---|
| Washington | Edmund Randolph | Va. | 1789 | Harrison, B. | William H. H. Miller | Ind. | 1889 |
| " | William Bradford | Pa. | 1794 | Cleveland | Richard Olney | Mass. | 1893 |
| " | Charles Lee | Va. | 1795 | " | Judson Harmon | Oh. | 1895 |
| Adams, J. | Charles Lee | Va. | 1797 | McKinley | Joseph McKenna | Cal. | 1897 |
| Jefferson | Levi Lincoln | Mass. | 1801 | " | John W. Griggs | N.J. | 1898 |
| " | John Breckenridge | Ky. | 1805 | " | Philander C. Knox | Pa. | 1901 |
| " | Caesar A. Rodney | Del. | 1807 | Roosevelt, T. | Philander C. Knox | Pa. | 1901 |
| Madison | Caesar A. Rodney | Del. | 1797 | " | William H. Moody | Mass. | 1904 |
| " | William Pinkney | Md. | 1811 | " | Charles J. Bonaparte | Md. | 1906 |
| " | Richard Rush | Pa. | 1814 | Taft | George W. Wickersham | N.Y. | 1909 |
| Monroe | Richard Rush | Pa. | 1817 | Wilson | J.C. McReynolds | Tenn. | 1913 |
| " | William Wirt | Va. | 1817 | " | Thomas W. Gregory | Tex. | 1914 |
| Adams, J.Q. | William Wirt | Va. | 1825 | " | A. Mitchell Palmer | Pa. | 1919 |
| Jackson | John M. Berrien | Ga. | 1829 | Harding | Harry M. Daugherty | Oh. | 1921 |
| " | Roger B. Taney | Md. | 1831 | Coolidge | Harry M. Daugherty | Oh. | 1923 |
| " | Benjamin F. Butler | N.Y. | 1833 | " | Harlan F. Stone | N.Y. | 1924 |
| Van Buren | Benjamin F. Butler | N.Y. | 1837 | " | John G. Sargent | Vt. | 1925 |
| " | Felix Grundy | Tenn. | 1838 | Hoover | William D. Mitchell | Minn. | 1929 |
| " | Henry D. Gilpin | Pa. | 1840 | Roosevelt, F.D. | Homer S. Cummings | Conn. | 1933 |
| Harrison, W.H. | John J. Crittenden | Ky. | 1841 | " | Frank Murphy | Mich. | 1939 |
| Tyler | John J. Crittenden | Ky. | 1841 | " | Robert H. Jackson | N.Y. | 1940 |
| " | Hugh S. Legare | S.C. | 1841 | " | Francis Biddle | Pa. | 1941 |
| " | John Nelson | Md. | 1843 | Truman | Thomas C. Clark | Tex. | 1945 |
| Polk | John Y. Mason | Va. | 1845 | " | J. Howard McGrath | R.I. | 1949 |
| " | Nathan Clifford | Me. | 1846 | " | J.P. McGranery | Pa. | 1952 |
| " | Isaac Toucey | Conn. | 1848 | Eisenhower | Herbert Brownell Jr. | N.Y. | 1953 |
| Taylor | Reverdy Johnson | Md. | 1849 | " | William P. Rogers | Md. | 1957 |
| Fillmore | John J. Crittenden | Ky. | 1850 | Kennedy | Robert F. Kennedy | Mass. | 1961 |
| Pierce | Caleb Cushing | Mass. | 1853 | Johnson, L.B. | Robert F. Kennedy | Mass. | 1963 |
| Buchanan | Jeremiah S. Black | Pa. | 1857 | " | N. de B. Katzenbach | Ill. | 1964 |
| " | Edwin M. Stanton | Pa. | 1860 | " | Ramsey Clark | Tex. | 1967 |
| Lincoln | Edward Bates | Mo. | 1861 | Nixon | John N. Mitchell | N.Y. | 1969 |
| " | James Speed | Ky. | 1864 | " | Richard G. Kleindienst | Ariz. | 1972 |
| Johnson, A. | James Speed | Ky. | 1865 | " | Elliot L. Richardson | Mass. | 1973 |
| " | Henry Stanbery | Oh. | 1866 | " | William B. Saxbe | Oh. | 1974 |
| " | William M. Evarts | N.Y. | 1868 | Ford | William B. Saxbe | Oh. | 1974 |
| Grant | Ebenezer R. Hoar | Mass. | 1869 | " | Edward H. Levi | Ill. | 1975 |
| " | Amos T. Akerman | Ga. | 1870 | Carter | Griffin B. Bell | Ga. | 1977 |
| " | George H. Williams | Ore. | 1871 | " | Benjamin R. Civiletti | Md. | 1979 |
| " | Edwards Pierrepont | N.Y. | 1875 | Reagan | William French Smith | Cal. | 1981 |
| " | Alphonso Taft | Oh. | 1876 | " | Edwin Meese 3d | Cal. | 1985 |
| Hayes | Charles Devens | Mass. | 1877 | " | Richard Thornburgh | Pa | 1988 |
| Garfield | Wayne MacVeagh | Pa. | 1881 | Bush | Richard Thornburgh | Pa. | 1989 |
| Arthur | Benjamin H. Brewster | " | 1881 | " | William P. Barr | N.Y. | 1991 |
| Cleveland | Augustus Garland | Ark. | 1885 | Clinton | Janet Reno | Fla. | 1993 |

## Secretaries of the Interior

The Department of the Interior was created by act of Congress Mar. 3, 1849.

| President | Secretary | Home | Apptd. | President | Secretary | Home | Apptd. |
|---|---|---|---|---|---|---|---|
| Taylor | Thomas Ewing | Oh. | 1849 | Grant | Jacob D. Cox | Oh. | 1869 |
| Fillmore | Thomas M. T. McKennan | Pa. | 1850 | " | Columbus Delano | Oh. | 1870 |
| " | Alex H. H. Stuart | Va. | 1850 | " | Zachariah Chandler | Mich. | 1875 |
| Pierce | Robert McClelland | Mich. | 1853 | Hayes | Carl Schurz | Mo. | 1877 |
| Buchanan | Jacob Thompson | Miss. | 1857 | Garfield | Samuel J. Kirkwood | Ia. | 1881 |
| Lincoln | Caleb B. Smith | Ind. | 1861 | Arthur | Henry M. Teller | Col. | 1882 |
| " | John P. Usher | Ind. | 1863 | Cleveland | Lucius Q.C. Lamar | Miss. | 1885 |
| Johnson, A. | John P. Usher | Ind. | 1865 | " | William F. Vilas | Wis. | 1888 |
| " | James Harlan | Ia. | 1865 | Harrison, B. | John W. Noble | Mo. | 1889 |
| " | Orville H. Browning | Ill. | 1866 | Cleveland | Hoke Smith | Ga. | 1893 |

| President | Secretary | Home | Apptd. |
|---|---|---|---|
| Cleveland | David R. Francis | Mo. | 1896 |
| McKinley | Cornelius N. Bliss | N.Y. | 1897 |
| " | Ethan A. Hitchcock | Mo. | 1898 |
| Roosevelt, T. | Ethan A. Hitchcock | Mo. | 1901 |
| " | James R. Garfield | Oh. | 1907 |
| Taft | Richard A. Ballinger | Wash. | 1909 |
| " | Walter L. Fisher | Ill. | 1911 |
| Wilson | Franklin K. Lane | Cal. | 1913 |
| " | John B. Payne | Ill. | 1920 |
| Harding | Albert B. Fall | N.M. | 1921 |
| " | Hubert Work | Col. | 1923 |
| Coolidge | Hubert Work | Col. | 1923 |
| " | Roy O. West | Ill. | 1929 |
| Hoover | Ray Lyman Wilbur | Cal. | 1929 |
| Roosevelt, F.D. | Harold L. Ickes | Ill. | 1933 |
| Truman | Harold L. Ickes | Ill. | 1945 |
| " | Julius A. Krug | Wis. | 1946 |
| Truman | Oscar L. Chapman | Col. | 1949 |
| Eisenhower | Douglas McKay | Ore. | 1953 |
| " | Fred A Seaton | Neb. | 1956 |
| Kennedy | Stewart L. Udall | Ariz. | 1961 |
| Johnson, L.B. | Stewart L. Udall | Ariz. | 1963 |
| Nixon | Walter J. Hickel | Alas. | 1969 |
| " | Rogers C.B. Morton | Md. | 1971 |
| Ford | Rogers C.B. Morton | Md. | 1971 |
| " | Stanley K. Hathaway | Wyo. | 1975 |
| " | Thomas S. Kleppe | N.D. | 1975 |
| Carter | Cecil D. Andrus | Ida. | 1977 |
| Reagan | James G. Watt | Col. | 1981 |
| " | William P. Clark | Cal. | 1983 |
| " | Donald P. Hodel | Ore. | 1985 |
| Bush | Manuel Lujan | N.M. | 1989 |
| Clinton | Bruce Babbitt | Ariz. | 1993 |

## Secretaries of Agriculture

The Department of Agriculture was created by act of Congress May 15, 1862. On Feb. 8, 1889, its commissioner was re-named secretary of agriculture and became a member of the cabinet.

| President | Secretary | Home | Apptd. |
|---|---|---|---|
| Cleveland | Norman J. Colman | Mo. | 1889 |
| Harrison, B. | Jeremiah M. Rusk | Wis. | 1889 |
| Cleveland | J. Sterling Morton | Neb. | 1893 |
| McKinley | James Wilson | Ia. | 1897 |
| Roosevelt, T. | James Wilson | Ia. | 1901 |
| Taft | James Wilson | Ia. | 1909 |
| Wilson | David F. Houston | Mo. | 1913 |
| " | Edwin T. Meredith | Ia. | 1920 |
| Harding | Henry C. Wallace | Ia. | 1921 |
| Coolidge | Henry C. Wallace | Ia. | 1923 |
| " | Howard M. Gore | W.Va. | 1924 |
| " | William M. Jardine | Kan. | 1925 |
| Hoover | Arthur M. Hyde | Mo. | 1929 |
| Roosevelt, F.D. | Henry A. Wallace | Ia. | 1933 |
| " | Claude R. Wickard | Ind. | 1940 |
| Truman | Clinton P. Anderson | N.M. | 1945 |
| " | Charles F. Brannan | Col. | 1948 |
| Eisenhower | Ezra Taft Benson | Ut. | 1953 |
| Kennedy | Orville L. Freeman | Minn. | 1961 |
| Johnson, L.B. | Orville L. Freeman | Minn. | 1963 |
| Nixon | Clifford M. Hardin | Ind. | 1969 |
| " | Earl L. Butz | Ind. | 1971 |
| Ford | Earl L. Butz | Ind. | 1974 |
| " | John A. Knebel | Va. | 1976 |
| Carter | Bob Bergland | Minn. | 1977 |
| Reagan | John R. Block | Ill. | 1981 |
| " | Richard E. Lyng | Cal. | 1986 |
| Bush | Clayton K. Yeutter | Neb. | 1989 |
| " | Edward Madigan | Ill. | 1991 |
| Clinton | Mike Espy | Miss. | 1993 |

## Secretaries of Commerce and Labor

The Department of Commerce and Labor, created by Congress Feb. 14, 1903, was divided by Congress Mar. 4, 1913, into separate departments of Commerce and Labor. The secretary of each was made a cabinet member.

### Secretaries of Commerce and Labor

| President | Secretary | Home | Apptd. |
|---|---|---|---|
| Roosevelt, T. | George B. Cortelyou | N.Y. | 1903 |
| " | Victor H. Metcalf | Cal. | 1904 |
| " | Oscar S. Straus | N.Y. | 1906 |
| Taft | Charles Nagel | Mo. | 1909 |

### Secretaries of Labor

| President | Secretary | Home | Apptd. |
|---|---|---|---|
| Wilson | William B. Wilson | Pa. | 1913 |
| Harding | James J. Davis | Pa. | 1921 |
| Coolidge | James J. Davis | Pa. | 1923 |
| Hoover | James J. Davis | Pa. | 1929 |
| " | William N. Doak | Va. | 1930 |
| Roosevelt, F.D. | Frances Perkins | N.Y. | 1933 |
| Truman | L.B. Schwellenbach | Wash. | 1945 |
| " | Maurice J. Tobin | Mass. | 1949 |
| Eisenhower | Martin P. Durkin | Ill. | 1953 |
| " | James P. Mitchell | N.J. | 1953 |
| Kennedy | Arthur J. Goldberg | Ill. | 1961 |
| " | W. Willard Wirtz | Ill. | 1962 |
| Johnson, L.B. | W. Willard Wirtz | Ill. | 1963 |
| Nixon | George P. Shultz | Ill | 1969 |
| " | James D. Hodgson | Cal. | 1970 |
| " | Peter J. Brennan | N.Y. | 1973 |
| Ford | Peter J. Brennan | N.Y. | 1974 |
| " | John T. Dunlop | Cal. | 1975 |
| " | W.J. Usery Jr. | Ga. | 1976 |
| Carter | F. Ray Marshall | Tex. | 1977 |
| Reagan | Raymond J. Donovan | N.J. | 1981 |
| " | William E. Brock | Tenn. | 1985 |
| " | Ann D. McLaughlin | D.C. | 1987 |
| Bush | Elizabeth Hanford Dole | N.C. | 1989 |
| " | Lynn Martin | Ill. | 1991 |
| Clinton | Robert B. Reich | Mass. | 1993 |

### Secretaries of Commerce

| President | Secretary | Home | Apptd. |
|---|---|---|---|
| Wilson | William C. Redfield | N.Y. | 1913 |
| " | Joshua W. Alexander | Mo. | 1919 |
| Harding | Herbert C. Hoover | Cal. | 1921 |
| Coolidge | Herbert C. Hoover | Cal. | 1923 |
| " | William F. Whiting | Mass. | 1928 |
| Hoover | Robert P. Lamont | Ill. | 1929 |
| " | Roy D. Chapin | Mich. | 1932 |
| Roosevelt, F.D. | Daniel C. Roper | S.C. | 1933 |
| " | Harry L. Hopkins | N.Y. | 1939 |
| " | Jesse Jones | Tex. | 1940 |
| " | Henry A. Wallace | Ia. | 1945 |
| Truman | Henry A. Wallace | Ia. | 1945 |
| " | W. Averell Harriman | N.Y. | 1947 |
| " | Charles Sawyer | Oh. | 1948 |
| Eisenhower | Sinclair Weeks | Mass. | 1953 |
| " | Lewis L. Strauss | N.Y. | 1958 |
| " | Frederick H. Mueller | Mich. | 1959 |
| Kennedy | Luther H. Hodges | N.C. | 1961 |
| Johnson, L.B. | Luther H. Hodges | N.C. | 1963 |
| " | John T. Connor | N.J. | 1965 |
| " | Alex B. Trowbridge | N.J. | 1967 |
| " | Cyrus R. Smith | N.Y. | 1968 |
| Nixon | Maurice H. Stans | Ill. | 1969 |
| " | Peter G. Peterson | Ill. | 1972 |
| " | Frederick B. Dent | S.C. | 1973 |
| Ford | Frederick B. Dent | S.C. | 1974 |
| " | Rogers C.B. Morton | Md. | 1975 |
| " | Elliot L. Richardson | Mass. | 1975 |
| Carter | Juanita M. Kreps | N.C. | 1977 |
| " | Philip M. Klutznick | Ill. | 1979 |
| Reagan | Malcolm Baldrige | Conn. | 1981 |
| " | C. William Verity Jr. | Oh. | 1987 |
| Bush | Robert A. Mosbacher | Tex. | 1989 |
| " | Barbara H. Franklin | Pa. | 1992 |
| Clinton | Ronald H. Brown | D.C. | 1993 |

## Secretaries of Housing and Urban Development

The Department of Housing and Urban Development was created by act of Congress Sept. 9, 1965.

| President | Secretary | Home | Apptd. | President | Secretary | Home | Apptd. |
|---|---|---|---|---|---|---|---|
| Johnson, L.B. | Robert C. Weaver | Wash. | 1966 | Carter | Patricia Roberts Harris | D.C. | 1977 |
| " | Robert C. Wood | Mass. | 1969 | " | Moon Landrieu | La. | 1979 |
| Nixon | George W. Romney | Mich. | 1969 | Reagan | Samuel R. Pierce Jr. | N.Y. | 1981 |
| " | James T. Lynn | Oh. | 1973 | Bush | Jack F. Kemp | N.Y. | 1989 |
| Ford | James T. Lynn | Oh. | 1974 | Clinton | Henry G. Cisneros | Tex. | 1993 |
| Ford | Carla Anderson Hills | Cal. | 1975 | | | | |

## Secretaries of Transportation

The Department of Transportation was created by act of Congress Oct. 15, 1966.

| President | Secretary | Home | Apptd. | President | Secretary | Home | Apptd. |
|---|---|---|---|---|---|---|---|
| Johnson, L.B. | Alan S. Boyd | Fla. | 1966 | Reagan | Andrew L. Lewis Jr. | Pa. | 1981 |
| Nixon | John A. Volpe | Mass. | 1969 | " | Elizabeth Hanford Dole | N.C. | 1983 |
| " | Claude S. Brinegar | Cal. | 1973 | " | James H. Burnley | N.C. | 1987 |
| Ford | Claude S. Brinegar | Cal. | 1974 | Bush | Samuel K. Skinner | Ill. | 1989 |
| " | William T. Coleman Jr. | Pa. | 1975 | " | Andrew H. Card Jr. | Mass. | 1992 |
| Carter | Brock Adams | Wash. | 1977 | Clinton | Federico F. Pena | Col. | 1993 |
| " | Neil E. Goldschmidt | Ore. | 1979 | | | | |

## Secretaries of Energy

The Department of Energy was created by federal law Aug. 4, 1977.

| President | Secretary | Home | Apptd. | President | Secretary | Home | Apptd. |
|---|---|---|---|---|---|---|---|
| Carter | James R. Schlesinger | Va. | 1977 | Reagan | Donald P. Hodel | Ore. | 1982 |
| " | Charles Duncan Jr. | Wyo. | 1979 | " | John S. Herrington | Cal. | 1985 |
| Reagan | James B. Edwards | S.C. | 1981 | Bush | James D. Watkins | Cal. | 1989 |
| | | | | Clinton | Hazel R. O'Leary | Minn. | 1993 |

## Secretaries of Health, Education, and Welfare

The Department of Health, Education, and Welfare, created by Congress Apr. 11, 1953, was divided by Congress Sept. 27, 1979, into separate departments of Education and of Health and Human Services. The secretary of each is a cabinet member.

| President | Secretary | Home | Apptd. | President | Secretary | Home | Apptd. |
|---|---|---|---|---|---|---|---|
| Eisenhower | Oveta Culp Hobby | Tex. | 1953 | Nixon | Robert H. Finch | Cal. | 1969 |
| " | Marion B. Folsom | N.Y. | 1955 | " | Elliot L. Richardson | Mass. | 1970 |
| " | Arthur S. Flemming | Oh. | 1958 | " | Caspar W. Weinberger | Cal. | 1973 |
| Kennedy | Abraham A. Ribicoff | Conn. | 1961 | Ford | Caspar W. Weinberger | Cal. | 1974 |
| " | Anthony J. Celebrezze | Oh. | 1962 | " | Forrest D. Mathews | Ala. | 1975 |
| Johnson, L.B. | Anthony J. Celebrezze | Oh. | 1963 | Carter | Joseph A. Califano, Jr. | D.C. | 1977 |
| " | John W. Gardner | N.Y. | 1965 | " | Patricia Roberts Harris | D.C. | 1979 |
| " | Wilbur J. Cohen | Mich. | 1968 | | | | |

## Secretaries of Health and Human Services

| President | Secretary | Home | Apptd. | President | Secretary | Home | Apptd. |
|---|---|---|---|---|---|---|---|
| Carter | Patricia Roberts Harris | D.C. | 1979 | Reagan | Otis R. Bowen | Ind. | 1985 |
| Reagan | Richard S. Schweiker | Pa. | 1981 | Bush | Louis W. Sullivan | Ga. | 1989 |
| " | Margaret M. Heckler | Mass. | 1983 | Clinton | Donna E. Shalala | Wis. | 1993 |

## Secretaries of Education

| President | Secretary | Home | Apptd. | President | Secretary | Home | Apptd. |
|---|---|---|---|---|---|---|---|
| Carter | Shirley Hufstedler | Cal. | 1979 | Bush | Lauro F. Cavazos | Tex. | 1989 |
| Reagan | Terrel Bell | Ut. | 1981 | " | Lamar Alexander | Tenn. | 1991 |
| " | William J. Bennett | N.Y. | 1985 | Clinton | Richard W. Riley | S.C. | 1993 |
| " | Lauro F. Cavazos | Tex. | 1988 | | | | |

## Secretaries of Veterans Affairs

The Department of Veterans Affairs was created Oct. 25, 1988, when Pres. Reagan signed a bill that made the Veterans Administration into a cabinet post as of Mar. 15, 1989.

| President | Secretary | Home | Apptd. | President | Secretary | Home | Apptd. |
|---|---|---|---|---|---|---|---|
| Bush | Edward J. Derwinski | Ill. | 1989 | Clinton | Jesse Brown | Ill. | 1993 |

# Role of the Cabinet

The Cabinet as a governmental institution is not provided for in the U.S. Constitution. It developed as an advisory body out of the desire of presidents to consult the heads of the executive departments on policy issues and problems. Aside from its role as a consultative and advisory body, the cabinet has no function and wields no executive authority. The president may or may not consult the cabinet and is not bound by its advice. Most presidents also consult numerous advisers outside the cabinet. A group of regular informal advisers to the president has been known in American history as a "kitchen cabinet." The formal cabinet meets at times set by the president, often once a week.

# Speakers of the House of Representatives

Party designations: A, American; D, Democratic; DR, Democratic-Republican; F, Federalist; R, Republican; W, Whig.

| Name | Party | State | Tenure | Name | Party | State | Tenure |
|------|-------|-------|--------|------|-------|-------|--------|
| Frederick Muhlenberg | F | Pa. | 1789-1791 | Theodore M. Pomeroy | R | N.Y. | 1869-1869 |
| Jonathan Trumbull | F | Conn. | 1791-1793 | James G. Blaine | R | Me. | 1869-1875 |
| Frederick Muhlenberg | F | Pa. | 1793-1795 | Michael C. Kerr | D | Ind. | 1875-1876 |
| Jonathan Dayton | F | N.J. | 1795-1799 | Samuel J. Randall | D | Pa. | 1876-1881 |
| Theodore Sedgwick | F | Mass. | 1799-1801 | Joseph W. Keifer | R | Oh. | 1881-1883 |
| Nathaniel Macon | DR | N.C. | 1801-1807 | John G. Carlisle | D | Ky. | 1883-1889 |
| Joseph B. Varnum | DR | Mass. | 1807-1811 | Thomas B. Reed | R | Me. | 1889-1891 |
| Henry Clay | DR | Ky. | 1811-1814 | Charles F. Crisp | D | Ga. | 1891-1895 |
| Langdon Cheves | DR | S.C. | 1814-1815 | Thomas B. Reed | R | Me. | 1895-1899 |
| Henry Clay | DR | Ky. | 1815-1820 | David B. Henderson | R | Ia. | 1899-1903 |
| John W. Taylor | DR | N.Y. | 1820-1821 | Joseph G. Cannon | R | Ill. | 1903-1911 |
| Philip P. Barbour | DR | Va. | 1821-1823 | Champ Clark | D | Mo. | 1911-1919 |
| Henry Clay | DR | Ky. | 1823-1825 | Frederick H. Gillett | R | Mass. | 1919-1925 |
| John W. Taylor | D | N.Y. | 1825-1827 | Nicholas Longworth | R | Oh. | 1925-1931 |
| Andrew Stevenson | D | Va. | 1827-1834 | John N. Garner | D | Tex. | 1931-1933 |
| John Bell | D | Tenn. | 1834-1835 | Henry T. Rainey | D | Ill. | 1933-1935 |
| James K. Polk | D | Tenn. | 1835-1839 | Joseph W. Byrns | D | Tenn. | 1935-1936 |
| Robert M. T. Hunter | D | Va. | 1839-1841 | William B. Bankhead | D | Ala. | 1936-1940 |
| John White | W | Ky. | 1841-1843 | Sam Rayburn | D | Tex. | 1940-1947 |
| John W. Jones | D | Va. | 1843-1845 | Joseph W. Martin Jr. | R | Mass. | 1947-1949 |
| John W. Davis | D | Ind. | 1845-1847 | Sam Rayburn | D | Tex. | 1949-1953 |
| Robert C. Winthrop | W | Mass. | 1847-1849 | Joseph W. Martin Jr. | R | Mass. | 1953-1955 |
| Howell Cobb | D | Ga. | 1849-1851 | Sam Rayburn | D | Tex. | 1955-1961 |
| Linn Boyd | D | Ky. | 1851-1855 | John W. McCormack | D | Mass. | 1962-1971 |
| Nathaniel P. Banks | A | Mass. | 1856-1857 | Carl Albert | D | Okla. | 1971-1977 |
| James L. Orr | D | S.C. | 1857-1859 | Thomas P. O'Neill Jr. | D | Mass. | 1977-1987 |
| William Pennington | R | N.J. | 1860-1861 | James Wright | D | Tex. | 1987-1989 |
| Galusha A. Grow | R | Pa. | 1861-1863 | Thomas S. Foley | D | Wash. | 1989- |
| Schuyler Colfax | R | Ind. | 1863-1869 | | | | |

# Floor Leaders in the U.S. Senate

## Majority Leaders

| Name | Party | State | Tenure |
|------|-------|-------|--------|
| Charles Curtis | R | Kan. | 1925-1929 |
| James E. Watson | R | Ind. | 1929-1933 |
| Joseph T. Robinson | D | Ark. | 1933-1937 |
| Alben W. Barkley | D | Ky. | 1937-1947 |
| Wallace H. White | R | Me. | 1947-1949 |
| Scott W. Lucas | D | Ill. | 1949-1951 |
| Ernest W. McFarland | D | Ariz. | 1951-1953 |
| Robert A. Taft | R | Oh. | 1953 |
| William F. Knowland | R | Cal. | 1953-1955 |
| Lyndon B. Johnson | D | Tex | 1955-1961 |
| Mike Mansfield | D | Mont. | 1961-1977 |
| Robert C. Byrd | D | W.Va. | 1977-1981 |
| Howard H. Baker Jr. | R | Tenn. | 1981-1985 |
| Robert J. Dole | R | Kan. | 1985-1987 |
| Robert C. Byrd | D | W.Va. | 1987-1989 |
| George J. Mitchell | D | Me. | 1989- |

## Minority Leaders

| Name | Party | State | Tenure |
|------|-------|-------|--------|
| Oscar W. Underwood | D | Ala | 1920-1923 |
| Joseph T. Robinson | D | Ark. | 1923-1933 |
| Charles L. McNary | R | Ore. | 1933-1944 |
| Wallace H. White | R | Me. | 1944-1947 |
| Alben W. Barkley | D | Ky. | 1947-1949 |
| Kenneth S. Wherry | R | Neb. | 1949-1951 |
| Henry Styles Bridges | R | N.H. | 1952-1953 |
| Lyndon B. Johnson | D | Tex. | 1953-1955 |
| William F. Knowland | R | Cal. | 1955-1959 |
| Everett M. Dirksen | R | Ill. | 1959-1969 |
| Hugh D. Scott | R | Penn. | 1969-1977 |
| Howard H. Baker Jr. | R | Tenn. | 1977-1981 |
| Robert C. Byrd | D | W.Va. | 1981-1987 |
| Robert J. Dole | R | Kan. | 1987- |

# Federal Bureau of Investigation

The Federal Bureau of Investigation was created July 26, 1908, and was referred to as Office of Chief Examiner. It became the Bureau of Investigation (Mar. 26, 1909), United States Bureau of Investigation (July 1, 1932), Division of Investigation (Aug. 10, 1933), and Federal Bureau of Investigation (July 1, 1935).

| Director | Assumed office | Director | Assumed office |
|----------|----------------|----------|----------------|
| Stanley W. Finch | July 26, 1908 | William D. Ruckelshaus, act. | Apr. 27, 1973 |
| A(lexander) Bruce Bielaski | Apr. 30, 1912 | Clarence M. Kelley | July 9, 1973 |
| William E. Allen, act. | Feb. 10, 1919 | William H. Webster | Feb. 23, 1978 |
| William J. Flynn | July 1, 1919 | John E. Otto, act. | May 26, 1987 |
| William J. Burns | Aug. 22, 1921 | William S. Sessions | Nov. 2, 1987 |
| J. Edgar Hoover, act. | May 10, 1924 | Floyd I. Clarke, act. | July 19, 1993 |
| J. Edgar Hoover | Dec. 10, 1924 | Louis J. Freeh | Sept. 1, 1993 |
| L. Patrick Gray, act. | May 3, 1972 | | |

# Central Intelligence Agency

On June 13, 1942, President Roosevelt established the Office of Strategic Services (OSS) and named William J. Donovan as its director. The OSS was disbanded Oct. 1, 1945, and its functions absorbed by the State and War departments. President Truman, Jan. 22, 1946, established the Central Intelligence Agency Group (CIG) to operate under the direction of the National Intelligence Authority (NIA). The National Security Act of 1947 replaced the NIA with the National Security Council and the CIG with the Central Intelligence Agency.

| Director | Served | Appointed by President | Director | Served | Appointed by President |
|----------|--------|------------------------|----------|--------|------------------------|
| Adm. Sidney W. Souers | 1946 | Truman | James R. Schlesinger | 1973 | Nixon |
| Gen. Hoyt S. Vandenberg | 1946-1947 | Truman | William E. Colby | 1973-1976 | Nixon |
| Adm. Roscoe H. Hillenkoetter | 1947-1950 | Truman | George Bush | 1976-1977 | Ford |
| Gen. Walter Bedell Smith | 1950-1953 | Truman | Adm. Stansfield Turner | 1977-1981 | Carter |
| Allen W. Dulles | 1953-1961 | Eisenhower | William J. Casey | 1981-1987 | Reagan |
| John A. McCone | 1961-1965 | Kennedy | William H. Webster | 1987-1991 | Reagan |
| Adm. William F. Raborn Jr. | 1965-1966 | Johnson | Robert M. Gates | 1991-1993 | Bush |
| Richard Helms | 1966-1973 | Johnson | R. James Woolsey | 1993- | Clinton |

# ECONOMICS

## U.S. Budget Receipts and Outlays—1989-1992

Source: Financial Management Service, U.S. Dept. of the Treasury
(Fiscal year ends Sept. 30)
(millions of dollars; some figures may not add due to independent rounding)
(outlays incl. selected departments and agencies)

| Classification | Fiscal 1989 | Fiscal 1990 | Fiscal 1991 | Fiscal 1992 |
|---|---|---|---|---|
| **Net Receipts** | | | | |
| Individual income taxes.............. | $445,690 | $466,884 | $467,827 | $476,465 |
| Corporation income taxes ............ | 103,291 | 93,507 | 98,086 | 100,270 |
| Social insurance taxes and contributions: | | | | |
| Federal old-age and survivors insurance .... | 240,595 | 255,031 | 265,503 | 273,137 |
| Federal disability insurance ........... | 23,071 | 26,625 | 28,382 | 29,289 |
| Federal hospital insurance ........... | 65,396 | 68,556 | 72,842 | 79,109 |
| Railroad retirement fund ........... | 3,798 | 3,679 | 3,799 | 3,957 |
| Total employment taxes and contributions .. | 332,859 | 353,891 | 370,526 | 385,491 |
| Other insurance and retirement: | | | | |
| Unemployment................ | 22,011 | 21,635 | 20,922 | 23,410 |
| Federal employees retirement .......... | 4,428 | 4,405 | 4,459 | 4,683 |
| Non-federal employees ............. | 119 | 117 | 108 | 105 |
| Total social insurance taxes and contributions ................... | 359,416 | 380,047 | 396,016 | 413,689 |
| Excise taxes .................... | 34,386 | 35,345 | 42,402 | 45,570 |
| Estate and gift taxes ............... | 8,745 | 11,500 | 11,138 | 11,143 |
| Customs duties .................. | 16,334 | 16,607 | 15,949 | 17,359 |
| Deposits of earnings-Federal Reserve Banks .... | 19,604 | 24,319 | 19,158 | 22,920 |
| All other miscellaneous receipts......... | 3,235 | 2,997 | 3,688 | 4,275 |
| Net Budget Receipts.............. | $990,701 | $1,031,308 | $1,054,265 | $1,091,692 |
| **Net Outlays** | | | | |
| Legislative Branch................. | $2,095 | $2,244 | $2,296 | $2,677 |
| The Judiciary.................... | 1,492 | 1,641 | 1,989 | 2,295 |
| Executive Office of the President: | | | | |
| The White House Office........... | 27 | 30 | 32 | 36 |
| Office of Management and Budget........ | 42 | 44 | 53 | 54 |
| Total Executive Office ............ | 124 | 157 | 193 | 190 |
| Funds appropriated to the President: | | | | |
| International security assistance ......... | 1,012 | 8,352 | 9,531 | 7,203 |
| Multinational assistance ............ | 1,492 | 1,695 | 1,520 | 1,717 |
| Agency for International Development...... | 1,215 | 1,773 | 1,835 | 2,142 |
| International Development Assistance...... | 2,780 | 3,528 | 3,444 | 4,029 |
| Total funds appropriated to the President... | 4,257 | 10,086 | 11,724 | 11,108 |
| Agriculture Department: | | | | |
| Food stamp program ............ | 13,725 | 15,923 | 19,649 | 22,800 |
| Farmer's Home Admin............. | 7,608 | 6,713 | 6,629 | 4,455 |
| Forest service ............... | 2,944 | 2,934 | 3,001 | 3,293 |
| Total Agriculture Department........... | 48,316 | 46,012 | 54,119 | 56,436 |
| Commerce Department ............. | | | | |
| Total Commerce Department........... | 2,571 | 3,734 | 2,585 | 2,567 |
| Bureau of the Census ............. | 557 | 1,575 | 451 | 302 |
| Defense Department: | | | | |
| Military personnel ............... | 80,676 | 75,622 | 83,439 | 81,171 |
| Operation and maintenance ........... | 87,001 | 88,340 | 101,769 | 92,042 |
| Procurement .................. | 81,620 | 80,972 | 82,028 | 74,881 |
| Research, development, test, evaluation .... | 37,002 | 37,458 | 34,589 | 34,632 |
| Military construction ............. | 5,275 | 5,080 | 3,497 | 4,262 |
| Total Defense Department (military)....... | 294,881 | 289,755 | 261,925 | 286,632 |
| Defense Department (civil) ............ | 23,450 | 24,975 | 26,543 | 28,265 |
| Education Department ............... | 21,608 | 23,109 | 25,339 | 26,047 |
| Energy Department ................ | 11,387 | 12,023 | 12,459 | 15,439 |
| Health and Human Services Department: | | | | |
| Food and Drug Administration .......... | 510 | 553 | 648 | 752 |
| National Institutes of Health........... | 6,992 | 7,492 | 7,677 | 8,376 |
| Public Health Service ............. | 12,250 | 14,007 | 15,348 | 17,447 |
| Health Care Financing Adm............ | 163,028 | 184,893 | 205,776 | 239,366 |
| Total Health and Human Services Dept...... | 172,301 | 193,679 | 217,969 | 257,961 |
| Social Security (Off Budget) .......... | 227,473 | 244,998 | 266,395 | 281,418 |
| Housing and Urban Development Department.... | 19,680 | 20,167 | 22,751 | 24,470 |
| Interior Department ............... | 5,308 | 5,795 | 6,096 | 6,555 |
| Justice Department: | | | | |
| Federal Bureau of Investigation ......... | 1,528 | 1,473 | 1,695 | 1,832 |
| Total Justice Department ............. | 6,232 | 6,507 | 8,244 | 9,826 |
| Labor Department: | | | | |
| Unemployment Trust Fund ........... | 18,730 | 20,250 | 28,434 | 41,294 |
| Total Labor Department.............. | 22,657 | 25,316 | 34,040 | 47,193 |
| State Department ................. | 3,722 | 3,979 | 4,252 | 5,007 |
| Transportation Department: | | | | |
| Federal Aviation Adm.............. | 5,740 | 6,391 | 7,241 | 8,155 |
| Total Transportation Department ........ | 26,607 | 28,637 | 30,503 | 32,560 |
| Treasury Department: | | | | |
| Internal Revenue Service ........... | 11,049 | 12,053 | 13,689 | 17,904 |
| Interest on the public debt........... | 240,863 | 264,853 | 285,472 | 292,330 |
| Total Treasury Department ............ | 230,566 | 255,264 | 276,352 | 293,428 |
| Veterans Affairs Department........... | 30,041 | 28,998 | 31,214 | 33,737 |
| Environmental Protection Agency ......... | 4,906 | 5,108 | 5,770 | 5,932 |
| General Services Administration........... | −462 | −123 | 487 | 469 |
| National Aeronautics and Space Administration .... | 11,036 | 12,429 | 13,878 | 13,961 |

| Classification | Fiscal 1989 | Fiscal 1990 | Fiscal 1991 | Fiscal 1992 |
|---|---|---|---|---|
| Office of Personnel Management . . . . . . . . . . | $29,073 | $31,949 | $34,808 | $35,596 |
| Small Business Administration . . . . . . . . . . . . . | 85 | 692 | 613 | 394 |
| Selected independent agencies: | | | | |
|   Action . . . . . . . . . . . . . . . . . . . . . . . . . . . . . . | 163 | 169 | 192 | 194 |
|   Board for International Broadcasting . . . . . . . | 199 | 208 | 228 | 210 |
|   Corporation for Public Broadcasting . . . . . . . | 228 | 229 | 299 | 327 |
|   District of Columbia . . . . . . . . . . . . . . . . . . | 538 | 578 | 671 | 691 |
|   Equal Employment Opportunity Commission . . | 182 | 181 | 192 | 209 |
|   Export-Import Bank of the United States . . . . | 47 | 357 | −88 | −119 |
|   Federal Communications Commission . . . . . . | 49 | 79 | 66 | 78 |
|   Federal Deposit Insurance Corporation . . . . . | 2,847 | 6,429 | 7,363 | 3,666 |
|   Federal Trade Commission . . . . . . . . . . . . . | 65 | 57 | 60 | 71 |
|   Interstate Commerce Comm. . . . . . . . . . . . . | 44 | 43 | 45 | 40 |
|   Legal Services Corporation . . . . . . . . . . . . . | 309 | 291 | 344 | 329 |
|   National Archives & Record Adm. . . . . . . . . | 71 | 157 | 172 | 226 |
|   National Foundation on the Arts and Humanities | 309 | 307 | 325 | 331 |
|   National Labor Relations Board . . . . . . . . . . | 136 | 141 | 143 | 155 |
|   National Science Foundation . . . . . . . . . . . . | 1,752 | 1,838 | 2,081 | 2,249 |
|   Nuclear Regulatory Commission . . . . . . . . . | 189 | 221 | −1 | 50 |
|   Railroad Retirement Board . . . . . . . . . . . . . | 4,315 | 4,477 | 4,358 | 4,843 |
|   Securities and Exchange Commission . . . . . . | 140 | 129 | 143 | 117 |
|   Smithsonian Institution . . . . . . . . . . . . . . . . | 288 | 302 | 340 | 378 |
|   Tennessee Valley Authority . . . . . . . . . . . . . | 348 | −312 | 740 | 1,469 |
|   U.S. Information Agency . . . . . . . . . . . . . . . | 888 | 888 | 1,001 | 1,050 |
| Total independent agencies . . . . . . . . . . . . | 33,770 | 73,666 | 81,217 | 18,876 |
| Undistributed offsetting receipts . . . . . . . . . . . . | −89,155 | −99,025 | −110,005 | −117,118 |
| Net Budget Outlays . . . . . . . . . . . . . . . . | 1,144,020 | 1,251,776 | 1,323,757 | 1,381,895 |
| Less net receipts . . . . . . . . . . . . . . . . . . | 990,701 | 1,031,308 | 1,054,265 | 1,091,692 |
| Deficit . . . . . . . . . . . . . . . . . . . . . . . . . | S−153,319 | S−220,469 | S−269,492 | S−290,204 |

## Summary of Receipts, Outlays, and Surpluses or Deficits, 1936-1988

Source: Financial Management Service, U.S. Dept. of the Treasury

(millions of dollars)

| Year | Receipts | Total Outlays | Surplus or Deficit (−) | Year | Receipts | Total Outlays | Surplus or Deficit (−) |
|---|---|---|---|---|---|---|---|
| 1936 . . . . . . . . . | $3,923 | $8,228 | S−4,304 | 1963 . . . . . . . . . | $106,560 | $111,316 | S−4,756 |
| 1937 . . . . . . . . . | 5,387 | 7,580 | −2,193 | 1964 . . . . . . . . . | 112,613 | 118,528 | −5,915 |
| 1938 . . . . . . . . . | 6,751 | 6,840 | −89 | 1965 . . . . . . . . . | 116,817 | 118,228 | −1,411 |
| 1939 . . . . . . . . . | 6,295 | 9,141 | −2,846 | 1966 . . . . . . . . . | 130,835 | 134,532 | −3,698 |
| 1940 . . . . . . . . . | 6,548 | 9,468 | −2,920 | 1967 . . . . . . . . . | 148,822 | 157,464 | −8,643 |
| 1941 . . . . . . . . . | 8,712 | 13,653 | −4,941 | 1968 . . . . . . . . . | 152,973 | 178,134 | −25,161 |
| 1942 . . . . . . . . . | 14,634 | 35,137 | −20,503 | 1969 . . . . . . . . . | 186,882 | 183,640 | 3,242 |
| 1943 . . . . . . . . . | 24,001 | 78,555 | −54,554 | 1970 . . . . . . . . . | 192,807 | 195,649 | −2,842 |
| 1944 . . . . . . . . . | 43,747 | 91,304 | −47,557 | 1971 . . . . . . . . . | 187,139 | 210,172 | −23,033 |
| 1945 . . . . . . . . . | 45,159 | 92,712 | −47,553 | 1972 . . . . . . . . . | 207,309 | 230,681 | −23,373 |
| 1946 . . . . . . . . . | 39,296 | 55,232 | −15,936 | 1973 . . . . . . . . . | 230,799 | 245,707 | −14,908 |
| 1947 . . . . . . . . . | 38,514 | 34,496 | 4,018 | 1974 . . . . . . . . . | 263,224 | 269,359 | −6,135 |
| 1948 . . . . . . . . . | 41,560 | 29,764 | 11,796 | 1975 . . . . . . . . . | 279,090 | 332,332 | −53,242 |
| 1949 . . . . . . . . . | 39,415 | 38,835 | 580 | 1976 . . . . . . . . . | 298,060 | 371,779 | −73,719 |
| 1950 . . . . . . . . . | 39,443 | 42,562 | −3,119 | Transition quarter[1] | 81,232 | 95,973 | −14,741 |
| 1951 . . . . . . . . . | 51,616 | 45,514 | 6,102 | 1977 . . . . . . . . . | 355,559 | 409,203 | −53,644 |
| 1952 . . . . . . . . . | 66,167 | 67,686 | −1,519 | 1978 . . . . . . . . . | 399,561 | 458,729 | −59,168 |
| 1953 . . . . . . . . . | 69,608 | 76,101 | −6,493 | 1979 . . . . . . . . . | 463,302 | 503,464 | −40,162 |
| 1954 . . . . . . . . . | 69,701 | 70,855 | −1,154 | 1980 . . . . . . . . . | 517,112 | 590,920 | −73,808 |
| 1955 . . . . . . . . . | 65,451 | 68,444 | −2,993 | 1981 . . . . . . . . . | 599,272 | 678,209 | −78,936 |
| 1956 . . . . . . . . . | 74,587 | 70,640 | 3,947 | 1982 . . . . . . . . . | 617,766 | 745,706 | −127,940 |
| 1957 . . . . . . . . . | 79,990 | 76,578 | 3,412 | 1983 . . . . . . . . . | 600,562 | 808,327 | −207,764 |
| 1958 . . . . . . . . . | 79,636 | 82,405 | −2,769 | 1984 . . . . . . . . . | 666,457 | 851,781 | −185,324 |
| 1959 . . . . . . . . . | 79,249 | 92,098 | −12,849 | 1985 . . . . . . . . . | 734,057 | 946,316 | −212,260 |
| 1960 . . . . . . . . . | 92,492 | 92,191 | 301 | 1986 . . . . . . . . . | 769,091 | 990,231 | −221,140 |
| 1961 . . . . . . . . . | 94,388 | 97,723 | −3,335 | 1987 . . . . . . . . . | 854,143 | 1,003,804 | −149,661 |
| 1962 . . . . . . . . . | 99,676 | 106,821 | −7,146 | 1988 . . . . . . . . . | 908,166 | 1,063,318 | −155,151 |

(1) Effective fiscal year 1977, fiscal year is reckoned Oct. 1-Sept. 30; Transition Quarter covers July 1, 1976-Sept. 30, 1976.

## Net Receipts and Outlays, 1789-1935

Source: U.S. Dept. of the Treasury; annual statements for year ending June 30

(thousands of dollars)

| Yearly average | Receipts | Outlays | Yearly average | Receipts | Outlays | Yearly average | Receipts | Outlays |
|---|---|---|---|---|---|---|---|---|
| 1789-1800[1] . . . . . | $5,717 | $5,776 | 1866-1870 . . . . . | $447,301 | $377,642 | 1901-1905 . . . . . | $559,481 | $535,559 |
| 1801-1810[2] . . . . . | 13,056 | 9,086 | 1871-1875 . . . . . | 336,830 | 287,460 | 1906-1910 . . . . . | 628,507 | 639,178 |
| 1811-1820[2] . . . . . | 21,032 | 23,943 | 1876-1880 . . . . . | 288,124 | 255,598 | 1911-1915 . . . . . | 710,227 | 720,252 |
| 1821-1830[2] . . . . . | 21,928 | 16,162 | 1881-1885 . . . . . | 366,961 | 257,691 | 1916-1920 . . . . . | 3,483,652 | 8,065,333 |
| 1831-1840[2] . . . . . | 30,461 | 24,495 | 1886-1890 . . . . . | 375,448 | 279,134 | 1921-1925 . . . . . | 4,306,673 | 3,578,989 |
| 1841-1850[2] . . . . . | 28,545 | 34,097 | 1891-1895 . . . . . | 352,891 | 363,599 | 1926-1930 . . . . . | 4,069,138 | 3,182,807 |
| 1851-1860 . . . . . | 60,237 | 60,163 | 1896-1900 . . . . . | 434,877 | 457,451 | 1931-1935 . . . . . | 2,770,973 | 5,214,874 |
| 1861-1865 . . . . . | 160,907 | 683,785 | | | | | | |

(1) Average for period March 4, 1789, to Dec. 31, 1800. (2) Years ended Dec. 31, 1801 to 1842; average for 1841-1850 is for the period Jan. 1, 1841, to June 30, 1850.

# The Federal Budget Process

Source: Executive Office of the President, Office of Management and Budget.

CBO = Congressional Budget Office; GRH = Gramm-Rudman-Hollings (*Balanced Budget and Emergency Deficit Control Act of 1985*); OMB = Office of Management and Budget.

| Executive budget process | Timing | Congressional budget process |
|---|---|---|
| Agencies subject to executive branch review submit initial budget request materials. | Sept. 1 | |
| Fiscal year begins. President's initial GRH sequester order takes effect (amounts are withheld from obligation pending issuance of final order). | Oct. 1 | Fiscal year begins. |
| | Oct. 10 | CBO issues revised GRH report to OMB and Congress. |
| OMB reports on changes in initial GRH estimates and determinations resulting from legislation enacted and regulations promulgated after its initial report to Congress. President issues final GRH sequester order, effective immediately, and transmits message to Congress within 15 days of final order. Agencies not subject to executive branch review submit budget request materials. | Oct. 15 | |
| | Nov. 15 | Comptroller General issues GRH compliance report. |
| Legislative branch and the judiciary submit budget request materials. | Nov.-Dec. | |
| President transmits budget to Congress. | 1st Mon. after Jan. 3 | Congress receives the President's budget. |
| OMB sends allowance letters to agencies. | Jan.-Feb. | |
| | Feb. 15 | CBO reports to the Budget Committees on the President's budget. |
| | Feb. 25 | Committees submit views and estimates to Budget Committee in their own house. |
| OMB and the President conduct reviews to establish presidential policy to guide agencies in developing the next budget. | Apr.-June | |
| | Apr. 1 | Senate Budget Committee reports concurrent resoluion on the budget. |
| | Apr. 15 | Congress completes action on concurrent resolution. |
| | May 15 | House may consider appropriations bills in the absence of a concurrent resolution on the budget. |
| | June 10 | House Appropriations Committee reports last appropriations bill. |
| | June 15 | Congress completes action on reconciliation legislation. |
| | June 30 | House completes action on annual appropriations bills. |
| President transmits the mid-session review, updating the budget estimates. | July 15 | Congress receives mid-session review of the budget. |
| OMB provides agencies with policy guidance for the upcoming budget. | July-Aug. | |
| Date of "snapshot" of projected deficits for the upcoming fiscal year for initial OMB and CBO GRH reports. | Aug. 15 | |
| OMB issues its initial GRH report providing estimates and determinations to the President and Congress. President issues initial GRH sequester order and sends message to Congress within 15 days. | Aug. 20 Aug. 25 | CBO issues its initial GRH report to OMB and Congress. |

# Public Debt of the U.S.

Source: Bureau of Public Debt, U.S. Dept. of the Treasury

| Fiscal year | Debt (billions) | Per. cap. (dollars) | Interest paid (billions) | % of federal outlays | Fiscal year | Debt (billions) | Per. cap. (dollars) | Interest paid (billions) | % of federal outlays |
|---|---|---|---|---|---|---|---|---|---|
| 1870 | $2.4 | $61.06 | — | — | 1977 | $698.8 | $3,170 | $41.9 | 10.2 |
| 1880 | 2.0 | 41.60 | — | — | 1978 | 771.5 | 3,463 | 48.7 | 10.6 |
| 1890 | 1.1 | 17.80 | — | — | 1979 | 826.5 | 3,669 | 59.8 | 11.9 |
| 1900 | 1.2 | 16.60 | — | — | 1980 | 907.7 | 3,985 | 74.9 | 12.7 |
| 1910 | 1.1 | 12.41 | — | — | 1981 | 997.9 | 4,338 | 95.6 | 14.1 |
| 1920 | 24.2 | 228 | — | — | 1982 | 1,142.0 | 4,913 | 117.4 | 15.7 |
| 1930 | 16.1 | 131 | — | — | 1983 | 1,377.2 | 5,870 | 128.8 | 15.9 |
| 1940 | 43.0 | 325 | $1.0 | 10.5 | 1984 | 1,572.3 | 6,640 | 153.8 | 18.1 |
| 1945 | 258.7 | 1,849 | 3.8 | 4.1 | 1985 | 1,823.1 | 7,598 | 178.9 | 18.9 |
| 1950 | 256.1 | 1,688 | 5.7 | 13.4 | 1986 | 2,125.3 | 8,774 | 190.2 | 19.2 |
| 1955 | 272.8 | 1,651 | 6.4 | 9.4 | 1987 | 2,350.3 | 9,615 | 195.4 | 19.5 |
| 1960 | 284.1 | 1,572 | 9.2 | 10.0 | 1988 | 2,602.3 | 10,534 | 214.1 | 20.1 |
| 1965 | 313.8 | 1,613 | 11.3 | 9.6 | 1989 | 2,857.4 | 11,545 | 240.9 | 21.0 |
| 1970 | 370.1 | 1,814 | 19.3 | 9.9 | 1990 | 3,233.3 | 13,000 | 264.8 | 21.1 |
| 1975 | 533.2 | 2,475 | 32.7 | 9.8 | 1991 | 3,665.3 | 14,436 | 285.4 | 21.5 |
| 1976 | 620.4 | 2,852 | 37.1 | 10.0 | 1992 | 4,064.6 | 15,846 | 292.3 | 21.1 |

Note: Through 1976 the fiscal year ended June 30. From 1977 on, fiscal year ends Sept. 30.

## Consumer Price Index

The Consumer Price Index (CPI) is a measure of the average change in prices over time of basic consumer goods and services. From Jan. 1978, the Bureau of Labor Statistics began publishing CPI's for two population groups: (1) a CPI for all urban consumers (CPI-U), which covers about 80% of the total population; and (2) a CPI for urban wage earners and clerical workers (CPI-W), which covers about 32% of the total population. The CPI-U includes, in addition to wage earners and clerical workers, groups such as professional, managerial, and technical workers, the self-employed, short-term workers, the unemployed, retirees, and others not in the labor force.

The CPI is based on prices of food, clothing, shelter, and fuels, transportation fares, charges for doctors' and dentists' services, drugs, and prices of the other goods and services bought for day-to-day living. The index measures price changes from a designated reference period, 1982-84, which equals 100.0.

Use of this reference period began in January 1988.

### Consumer Price Indexes, 1993

Source: Bureau of Labor Statistics, U.S. Dept. of Labor

| (1982-84 = 100) | CPI-U Unadjusted indexes July 1993 | CPI-U Unadjusted percent change to July 1993 from- July 1992 | CPI-U Unadjusted percent change to July 1993 from- June 1993 | Seasonally adjusted percent change from- June to July | CPI-W Unadjusted indexes July 1993 | CPI-W Unadjusted percent change to July 1993 from- July 1992 | CPI-W Unadjusted percent change to July 1993 from- June 1993 | Seasonally adjusted percent change from- June to July |
|---|---|---|---|---|---|---|---|---|
| Food, beverages | 141.1 | 2.2 | 0 | 0 | 140.8 | 2.2 | 0 | 0.1 |
| Housing | 141.9 | 2.6 | 0.3 | 0 | 139.1 | 2.5 | 0.2 | 0 |
| Apparel, upkeep | 129.4 | 0.2 | −1.9 | 0 | 128.4 | 0.2 | −1.8 | 0 |
| Transportation | 130.3 | 2.4 | 0 | 0.2 | 129.4 | 2.1 | −0.1 | 0.2 |
| Medical care | 202.2 | 6.0 | 0.5 | 0.4 | 201.7 | 6.0 | 0.5 | 0.4 |
| Entertainment | 145.3 | 2.0 | −1 | 0 | 143.7 | 1.9 | −0.1 | −0.1 |
| Other goods, services | 193.7 | 6.3 | 0.3 | 0.4 | 193.8 | 6.1 | 0.3 | 0.3 |
| Services | 158.4 | 3.9 | 0.4 | 0.2 | 156.0 | 3.7 | 0.3 | 0.1 |
| **Special Indexes** | | | | | | | | |
| All items less food | 145.2 | 2.9 | 0.1 | 0.4 | 142.4 | 2.7 | 0 | 0.1 |
| Commodities less food | 125.5 | 1.0 | −0.6 | 0 | 125.5 | 1.2 | −0.5 | 0 |
| Nondurables | 134.2 | 1.3 | −0.6 | −0.6 | 134.1 | 1.3 | −0.5 | −0.5 |
| Energy | 105.8 | −0.2 | −0.7 | 0 | 105.2 | −0.4 | −0.8 | −0.1 |
| All items less energy | 149.7 | 3.0 | 0.1 | 0.1 | 147.3 | 2.9 | 0.1 | 0.1 |

### Consumer Price Indexes for Selected Items and Groups

Source: Bureau of Labor Statistics, U.S. Dept. of Labor

(all urban consumers = CPI-U)

(1982-84 = 100. Annual averages of monthly figures)

| | 1970 | 1975 | 1980 | 1985 | 1989 | 1990 | 1991 | 1992 |
|---|---|---|---|---|---|---|---|---|
| **All Items** | 38.8 | 53.8 | 82.4 | 107.6 | 124.0 | 130.7 | 136.2 | 140.3 |
| **Food and beverages** | 40.1 | 60.2 | 86.7 | 105.6 | 124.9 | 132.1 | 136.8 | 138.7 |
| Food | 39.2 | 59.8 | 86.8 | 105.6 | 125.1 | 132.4 | 136.3 | 137.9 |
| Food at home | 39.9 | 61.8 | 88.4 | 104.3 | 124.2 | 132.3 | 135.8 | 136.8 |
| Cereals, bakery prods. | 37.1 | 62.9 | 83.9 | 107.9 | 132.4 | 140.0 | 145.8 | 151.5 |
| Meats, poultry, fish, eggs | 44.6 | 67.0 | 92.0 | 100.1 | 121.3 | 130.0 | 132.6 | 130.9 |
| Dairy prods. | 44.7 | 62.6 | 90.9 | 103.2 | 115.6 | 126.5 | 125.1 | 128.5 |
| Fruits, vegetables | 37.8 | 56.9 | 82.1 | 106.4 | 138.0 | 149.0 | 155.8 | 155.4 |
| Sugar, sweets | 30.5 | 65.3 | 90.5 | 105.8 | 119.4 | 124.7 | 129.3 | 133.1 |
| Fats, oils | 39.2 | 73.5 | 89.3 | 106.9 | 121.2 | 126.3 | 131.7 | 129.8 |
| Nonalcoholic beverages | 27.1 | 41.3 | 91.4 | 104.3 | 111.3 | 113.5 | 114.1 | 114.3 |
| Other prepared foods | 39.6 | 58.9 | 83.6 | 106.4 | 125.5 | 131.2 | 137.1 | 140.1 |
| Food away from home | 37.5 | 54.5 | 83.4 | 108.3 | 127.4 | 133.4 | 137.9 | 140.7 |
| Alcoholic beverages | 52.1 | 65.9 | 86.4 | 106.4 | 123.5 | 129.3 | 142.8 | 147.3 |
| **Housing** | 36.4 | 50.7 | 81.1 | 107.7 | 123.0 | 128.5 | 133.6 | 137.5 |
| Shelter | 35.5 | 48.8 | 81.0 | 109.8 | 132.8 | 140.0 | 146.3 | 151.2 |
| Rent | 46.5 | 58.0 | 80.9 | 111.8 | 132.8 | 146.7 | 155.6 | 160.9 |
| Maintenance, repairs | 35.8 | 54.1 | 82.4 | 106.5 | 118.0 | 122.2 | 126.3 | 128.6 |
| Fuel, other utilities | 29.1 | 45.4 | 75.4 | 106.5 | 107.8 | 111.6 | 115.3 | 117.8 |
| Energy services | 31.8 | 50.0 | 75.8 | 106.9 | 114.7 | 117.4 | 112.6 | 114.8 |
| Household furnishings & operation | 46.8 | 63.4 | 86.3 | 103.8 | 111.2 | 113.3 | 116.0 | 118.0 |
| House furnishings | 55.5 | 69.8 | 88.5 | 101.7 | 105.5 | 106.7 | 107.5 | 109.0 |
| **Apparel & upkeep** | 59.2 | 72.5 | 90.9 | 105.0 | 118.6 | 124.1 | 128.7 | 131.9 |
| Apparel commodities | 63.3 | 76.7 | 92.9 | 104.0 | 116.7 | 122.0 | 126.4 | 129.4 |
| Men's & boys' | 62.2 | 75.5 | 89.4 | 105.0 | 117.0 | 120.4 | 124.2 | 126.5 |
| Women's & girls' | 71.8 | 85.5 | 96.0 | 104.9 | 116.4 | 122.6 | 127.6 | 130.4 |
| Footwear | 56.8 | 69.6 | 91.8 | 102.3 | 114.4 | 117.4 | 120.9 | 125.0 |
| **Transportation** | 37.5 | 50.1 | 83.1 | 106.4 | 114.1 | 120.5 | 123.8 | 126.5 |
| Private | 37.5 | 50.6 | 84.2 | 106.2 | 112.9 | 118.8 | 121.9 | 124.6 |
| New cars | 53.0 | 62.9 | 88.4 | 106.1 | 119.2 | 121.4 | 126.0 | 128.4 |
| Used cars | 31.2 | 43.8 | 62.3 | 113.7 | 120.4 | 117.6 | 118.1 | 123.2 |
| Gasoline | 27.9 | 45.1 | 97.5 | 98.6 | 88.5 | 101.0 | 99.2 | 99.0 |
| Public | 35.2 | 43.5 | 69.0 | 110.5 | 129.5 | 142.6 | 148.9 | 151.4 |
| **Medical care** | 34.0 | 47.5 | 74.9 | 113.5 | 149.3 | 162.8 | 177.0 | 190.1 |
| **Entertainment** | 47.5 | 62.0 | 83.6 | 107.9 | 126.5 | 132.4 | 138.4 | 142.3 |
| **Other goods & services** | 40.9 | 53.9 | 75.2 | 114.5 | 147.7 | 159.0 | 171.6 | 183.3 |
| Tobacco products | 43.1 | 54.7 | 72.0 | 116.7 | 164.4 | 181.5 | 202.7 | 219.8 |
| Personal care | 43.5 | 57.9 | 81.9 | 106.3 | 125.0 | 130.4 | 134.9 | 138.3 |
| Toilet goods | 42.7 | 58.0 | 79.6 | 107.6 | 123.2 | 128.2 | 132.8 | 136.5 |
| Personal care services | 44.2 | 57.7 | 83.7 | 108.9 | 126.8 | 132.8 | 137.0 | 140.0 |
| Personal, educational expenses | 35.5 | 48.7 | 70.9 | 119.1 | 158.1 | 170.2 | 183.7 | 197.4 |

## Consumer Price Indexes[1] Annual Percent Change

Source: Bureau of Labor Statistics, U.S. Dept. of Labor

| | 1981[2] | 1982 | 1983 | 1984 | 1985 | 1986 | 1987 | 1988 | 1989 | 1990 | 1991 | 1992 |
|---|---|---|---|---|---|---|---|---|---|---|---|---|
| All items. . . . . . . . | 10.3 | 6.2 | 3.2 | 4.3 | 3.6 | 1.9 | 3.6 | 4.1 | 4.8 | 5.4 | 4.2 | 3.0 |
| Food. . . . . . . . . . | 7.8 | 4.1 | 2.1 | 3.8 | 2.3 | 3.2 | 4.1 | 4.1 | 5.8 | 5.8 | 2.9 | 1.2 |
| Shelter. . . . . . . . . | 11.7 | 7.1 | 2.3 | 4.9 | 5.6 | 5.5 | 4.7 | 4.8 | 4.5 | 5.4 | 4.5 | 3.3 |
| Rent, residential . . . . | 8.7 | 7.6 | 5.8 | 5.2 | 6.2 | 5.8 | 4.1 | 3.8 | 3.9 | 5.6 | 6.1 | 2.5 |
| Fuel & other utilities . . | 14.6 | 9.8 | 5.6 | 4.6 | 1.6 | −2.3 | −1.1 | −1.4 | 3.3 | 3.5 | 3.3 | 2.2 |
| Apparel and upkeep . . | 4.8 | 2.6 | 2.5 | 1.9 | 2.8 | 0.9 | 4.4 | 4.3 | 2.8 | 4.6 | 3.7 | 2.5 |
| Private transportation . | 11.4 | 3.5 | 2.3 | 4.3 | 2.5 | −4.7 | −3.0 | 3.3 | 4.9 | 5.2 | 2.6 | 2.2 |
| New cars . . . . . . . | 6.0 | 3.9 | 2.6 | 2.9 | 3.2 | 4.2 | 3.6 | 2.0 | 2.0 | 1.8 | 3.8 | 2.5 |
| Gasoline. . . . . . . . | 11.3 | −5.3 | −3.3 | −1.6 | .8 | −21.9 | −4.0 | 0.9 | 9.5 | 14.1 | −1.8 | −0.2 |
| Public transportation . . | 24.1 | 10.9 | 4.8 | 6.2 | 4.5 | 5.9 | 3.5 | 1.8 | 5.0 | 10.1 | 4.4 | 1.7 |
| Medical care . . . . . . | 10.7 | 11.6 | 8.8 | 6.2 | 6.3 | 7.5 | 6.6 | 6.5 | 7.7 | 9.0 | 8.7 | 7.4 |
| Entertainment . . . . . . | 7.8 | 6.5 | 4.3 | 3.7 | 3.9 | 3.4 | 3.3 | 4.3 | 5.2 | 4.7 | 4.5 | 2.8 |
| Commodities . . . . . . | 8.4 | 4.1 | 2.9 | 3.4 | 2.1 | −0.9 | 3.2 | 3.5 | 4.7 | 5.2 | 4.2 | 2.0 |

(1) The Consumer Price Index (CPI-U) measures the average change in prices of goods and services purchased by all urban consumers. (2) Change from 1980.

## Consumer Price Index by Region and Selected Cities

Source: Bureau of Labor Statistics, U.S. Dept. of Labor

| Area (1982-84 = 100) | CPI-U Indexes May 1993 | CPI-U Indexes June 1993 | CPI-U Indexes July 1993 | Percent change: July 1992–July 1993 | CPI-W Indexes May 1993 | CPI-W Indexes June 1993 | CPI-W Indexes July 1993 | Percent change: July 1992–July 1993 |
|---|---|---|---|---|---|---|---|---|
| U.S. city average . . . . . . . . | 144.2 | 144.4 | 144.4 | 2.8 | 141.9 | 142.0 | 142.1 | 2.7 |
| Northeast urban . . . . . . . . | 150.8 | 151.2 | 151.4 | 2.6 | 148.7 | 149.0 | 149.1 | 2.5 |
| More than 1,200,000. . . . . | 151.2 | 151.7 | 151.9 | 2.7 | 148.0 | 148.5 | 148.6 | 2.6 |
| 500,000 to 1,200,000. . . . | 150.3 | 150.3 | 150.4 | 2.0 | 148.3 | 148.4 | 148.4 | 2.0 |
| 50,000 to 500,000 . . . . . | 149.2 | 149.5 | 149.7 | 2.8 | 151.0 | 151.2 | 151.2 | 2.7 |
| North Central urban. . . . . . | 139.8 | 140.0 | 140.0 | 2.7 | 137.2 | 137.3 | 137.2 | 2.6 |
| More than 1,200,000. . . . . | 141.0 | 141.1 | 141.3 | 2.8 | 137.5 | 137.6 | 137.8 | 2.8 |
| 360,000 to 1,200,000. . . . | 137.8 | 138.6 | 138.2 | 3.0 | 134.7 | 135.5 | 135.0 | 2.8 |
| 50,000 to 360,000 . . . . . | 141.9 | 141.4 | 141.1 | 2.4 | 139.9 | 139.3 | 138.9 | 2.2 |
| Less than 50,000 . . . . . . | 134.4 | 134.9 | 134.9 | 2.5 | 133.5 | 133.8 | 133.9 | 2.1 |
| South urban . . . . . . . . . . | 140.7 | 140.8 | 140.9 | 3.0 | 139.3 | 139.6 | 139.6 | 2.9 |
| More than 1,200,000. . . . . | 141.1 | 141.0 | 141.0 | 2.5 | 139.4 | 139.6 | 139.5 | 2.4 |
| 450,000 to 1,200,000. . . . | 142.1 | 142.6 | 142.7 | 3.2 | 138.9 | 139.4 | 139.5 | 3.2 |
| 50,000 to 450,000 . . . . . | 140.0 | 140.2 | 140.1 | 3.0 | 140.1 | 140.2 | 140.2 | 2.9 |
| Less than 50,000 . . . . . . | 138.7 | 138.8 | 139.0 | 3.7 | 138.8 | 138.9 | 139.2 | 3.5 |
| West urban . . . . . . . . . . . | 146.0 | 146.0 | 146.0 | 2.9 | 143.5 | 143.4 | 143.4 | 2.6 |
| More than 1,250,000. . . . . | 148.1 | 147.8 | 147.7 | 2.6 | 143.9 | 143.7 | 143.6 | 2.5 |
| 50,000 to 330,000 . . . . . | 143.6 | 144.0 | 144.9 | 4.2 | 141.8 | 142.1 | 142.8 | 3.8 |
| **Selected areas** | | | | | | | | |
| Chicago, Ill.–Gary-Lake County, Ill., Ind., Wis.. . . . . . . . | 145.7 | 145.6 | 145.5 | 2.9 | 141.4 | 141.2 | 141.1 | 3.0 |
| L.A.–Anaheim, Riverside, Cal. . | 150.1 | 149.7 | 149.8 | 2.1 | 145.1 | 144.8 | 144.8 | 1.8 |
| New York, N.Y.–Northern N.J., Long Island, N.Y. . . . . . . . | 153.8 | 154.2 | 154.3 | 2.9 | 150.4 | 150.7 | 150.7 | 2.8 |
| Philadelphia, Wilmington, Trenton, Pa., Del., N.J., Md. . . . . | 149.4 | 150.5 | 150.7 | 2.3 | 149.3 | 150.4 | 150.6 | 2.2 |
| San Francisco–Oakland, San Jose, Cal. . . . . . . . . . . . | 146.9 | 146.1 | 146.1 | 2.7 | 144.8 | 144.0 | 144.1 | 2.6 |
| Baltimore, Md. . . . . . . . . . . | 142.8 | — | 143.7 | 2.2 | 142.1 | — | 143.0 | 2.0 |
| Boston, Lawrence, Salem, Mass., N.H. . . . . . . . . . . | 151.8 | — | 152.4 | 2.4 | 151.2 | — | 151.5 | 2.2 |
| Cleveland, Akron, Lorain, Oh. . | 139.6 | — | 140.9 | 2.8 | 132.7 | — | 133.9 | 2.6 |
| Miami, Ft. Lauderdale, Fla. . . . | 139.0 | — | 139.0 | 3.9 | 137.2 | — | 137.2 | 3.9 |
| St. Louis, E. St. Louis, Mo., Ill. . | 136.8 | — | 138.8 | 2.3 | 136.4 | — | 138.3 | 2.1 |
| Washington, D.C.–Md.–Va. . . | 149.2 | — | 149.2 | 3.0 | 147.0 | — | 147.0 | 2.6 |
| Dallas–Fort Worth, Tex. . . . . | — | 136.2 | — | — | — | 136.5 | — | — |
| Detroit, Ann Arbor, Mich. . . . . | — | 139.1 | — | — | — | 135.1 | — | — |
| Houston, Galveston, Brazoria, Tex. . . . . . . . . . . . . . . . | — | 132.9 | — | — | — | 132.4 | — | — |
| Pittsburgh, Beaver Valley, Pa. . | — | 139.5 | — | — | — | 133.7 | — | — |

## Percent Change in Consumer Prices in Selected Countries

Source: International Monetary Fund

| Country | 1975-1980, avg. | 1980-1985, avg. | 1987-1988, avg. | 1988-1989, avg. | 1989-1990, avg. | 1990-1991, avg. | 1991-1992, avg. |
|---|---|---|---|---|---|---|---|
| Canada . . . . . . . . . . . . . | 8.7 | 7.4 | 4.0 | 5.0 | 4.8 | 5.6 | 1.5 |
| France. . . . . . . . . . . . . . | 10.5 | 9.6 | 2.7 | 3.5 | 3.4 | 3.1 | 2.4 |
| Germany . . . . . . . . . . . . | 4.1 | 3.9 | 1.3 | 2.8 | 2.7 | 3.5 | 4.0 |
| Italy . . . . . . . . . . . . . . . | 16.3 | 13.7 | 5.1 | 6.3 | 6.5 | 6.4 | 5.6 |
| Japan . . . . . . . . . . . . . . | 6.5 | 2.7 | 0.7 | 2.3 | 3.1 | 3.3 | 1.7 |
| Spain . . . . . . . . . . . . . . | 18.6 | 12.2 | 4.8 | 6.8 | 6.7 | 5.9 | 5.8 |
| Sweden . . . . . . . . . . . . . | 10.5 | 9.0 | 5.8 | 6.4 | 10.5 | 9.3 | 2.3 |
| Switzerland . . . . . . . . . . . | 2.3 | 4.3 | 1.9 | 3.2 | 5.4 | 5.8 | 4.0 |
| United Kingdom . . . . . . . . | 14.4 | 7.2 | 4.9 | 7.8 | 9.5 | 5.9 | 3.7 |
| United States . . . . . . . . . . | 8.9 | 5.5 | 4.0 | 4.8 | 5.4 | 4.2 | 3.0 |

## Index of Leading Economic Indicators

Source: Bureau of Economic Analysis, U.S. Dept. of Commerce

The index of leading economic indicators is used to project the U.S. economy's performance six months or a year ahead. The index is made up of 11 measurements of economic activity that tend to change direction long before the overall economy does.

**Components**
Average work week of production workers in manufacturing
Average weekly claims for state unemployment insurance
New orders for consumer goods and materials, adjusted for inflation
Vendor performance (companies receiving slower deliveries from suppliers)
Contracts and orders for plant and equipment, adjusted for inflation

**Components**
New building permits issued
Change in manufacturers unfilled orders, durable goods
Change in sensitive materials prices
Index of stock prices
Money supply: M-2, adjusted for inflation
Index of consumer expectations

## Gross Domestic Product, Gross National Product, Net National Product, National Income, and Personal Income

Source: Bureau of Economic Analysis, U.S. Dept. of Commerce

(billions of dollars)

|  | 1960 | 1970 | 1980 | 1990 | 1991 | 1992 |
|---|---|---|---|---|---|---|
| Gross domestic product . . . . . . . . . . | — | — | — | $5,513.8 | $5,677.5 | $5,950.7 |
| Gross national product . . . . . . . . . . . . | $515.3 | $1,015.5 | $2,732.0 | $5,524.5 | 5,694.9 | 5,961.9 |
| Less: Capital consumption allowances. . . . . . | 46.4 | 88.8 | 303.8 | 594.8 | 626.1 | 653.4 |
| Equals: Net national product . . . . . . . . . | 468.9 | 926.6 | 2,428.1 | 4,929.8 | 5,068.8 | 5,308.5 |
| Less: Indirect business tax and nontax liability . | 45.3 | 94.0 | 213.3 | 439.2 | 475.2 | 504.2 |
|   Business transfer payments . . . . . . . . . . | 2.0 | 4.1 | 12.1 | 27.7 | 28.1 | 29.7 |
|   Statistical discrepancy . . . . . . . . . . . . . | −2.8 | −1.1 | 4.9 | 8.1 | 21.9 | 34.1 |
| Plus: Subsidies less current surplus of | | | | | | |
|   government enterprises . . . . . . . . . . | .4 | 2.9 | 5.7 | 4.8 | 0.5 | 2.9 |
| Equals: National income . . . . . . . . . . . . | 424.9 | 832.6 | 2,203.5 | 4,459.6 | 4,544.2 | 4,743.4 |
| Less: Corporate profits with inventory | | | | | | |
|   valuation and capital consumption adjustment | 49.5 | 74.7 | 177.2 | 319.0 | 346.3 | 393.8 |
|   Net interest . . . . . . . . . . . . . . . . . . . | 11.3 | 41.2 | 200.9 | 490.1 | 449.5 | 415.2 |
|   Contributions for social insurance . . . . . . . | 21.9 | 62.2 | 216.5 | 501.7 | 528.8 | 553.5 |
|   Wage accruals less disbursement . . . . . . . | .0 | .0 | .0 | −0.1 | −0.1 | −1.5 |
| Plus: Government transfer payment to persons. | 27.5 | 81.8 | 312.6 | 661.7 | 748.3 | 841.6 |
|   Personal interest income . . . . . . . . . . . . | 24.9 | 69.3 | 271.9 | 721.3 | 700.6 | 670.2 |
|   Personal dividend income . . . . . . . . . . . | 12.9 | 22.2 | 52.9 | 124.8 | 137.0 | 139.3 |
|   Business transfer payments . . . . . . . . . . | 2.0 | 4.1 | 12.1 | 23.2 | 22.8 | 24.5 |
| Equals: Personal income . . . . . . . . . . . | 409.4 | 831.8 | 2,258.5 | 4,679.8 | 4,828.3 | 5,058.1 |

## Gross Domestic Product

Source: Bureau of Economic Analysis, U.S. Dept. of Commerce

(billions of dollars)

|  | 1991 | 1992 | 1993 (1st Quarter) |  | 1991 | 1992 | 1993 (1st Quarter) |
|---|---|---|---|---|---|---|---|
| Gross domestic product . | 5,677.5 | 5,950.7 | 6,145.8 | Nonfarm . . . . . . . . . | −10.3 | 2.2 | 32.6 |
| Personal consumption | | | | Farm . . . . . . . . . | 0 | 2.2 | 2.3 |
|   expenditures . . . . . . . | 3,887.7 | 4,095.8 | 4,234.7 | Net exports of goods and | | | |
|   Durable goods . . . . . . | 446.1 | 480.4 | 498.8 |   services . . . . . . . . . . | −21.8 | −30.4 | −49.4 |
|   Nondurable goods . . . . | 1,251.5 | 1,290.7 | 1,320.8 |   Exports . . . . . . . . . | 598.2 | 636.3 | 649.4 |
|   Services . . . . . . . . . | 2,190.1 | 2,324.7 | 2,415.1 |   Imports . . . . . . . . . | 620.0 | 666.7 | 698.9 |
| Gross private domestic | | | | Government purchases . | 1,090.5 | 1,114.9 | 1,116.6 |
|   investment . . . . . . . . | 721.1 | 770.4 | 844.0 |   Federal . . . . . . . . . . | 447.3 | 449.1 | 441.1 |
|   Fixed investment . . . . . | 731.3 | 766.0 | 809.0 |     National defense . . . | 323.8 | 315.8 | 304.2 |
|   Nonresidential . . . . . | 541.1 | 548.2 | 573.8 |     Nondefense . . . . . . | 123.6 | 133.4 | 136.9 |
|   Structures . . . . . | 180.1 | 168.4 | 168.0 |   State and local . . . . . . | 643.2 | 665.8 | 675.4 |
|   Producers' durable | | | | | | | |
|     equipment . . . . . | 390.9 | 379.9 | 405.8 | | | | |
|   Residential . . . . . . . | 190.3 | 217.7 | 235.2 | | | | |
| Change in business | | | | | | | |
|   inventories . . . . . . . | −10.2 | 4.4 | 34.9 | | | | |

## Notable Bankruptcy Filings Since 1970

| Year | Company | Year | Company | Year | Company |
|---|---|---|---|---|---|
| 1970 | Penn Central | 1989 | Southmark | 1991 | America West Airlines |
| 1982 | Manville | 1989 | Lomas Financial | 1991 | Orion Pictures |
| 1983 | Baldwin-United | 1989 | American Continental | 1991 | Maxwell Communications |
| 1985 | Wheeling-Pittsburgh Steel | 1990 | Drexel Burnham Lambert | 1991 | Carter Hawley Hale |
| 1986 | LTV Corp. | 1990 | Allied/Federal | 1992 | R.H. Macy |
| 1987 | Texaco | 1990 | Ames Department Stores | 1992 | Zale Corp. |
| 1988 | Financial Corp. of America | 1990 | Continental Airlines | 1992 | T.W.A. |
| 1989 | MCorp | 1990 | Pan Am | | |

# Chapter 11

Chapter 11 refers to the provisions in the Federal Bankruptcy Act for court-supervised reorganization of debtor companies. A company files for Chapter 11 protection when it can no longer pay its creditors or when it expects future liabilities it cannot hope to pay, like product liability damage awards. In 1991, the U.S. Supreme Court ruled that the provision of Federal bankruptcy law that permits corporations to reorganize while continuing to operate was also available for use by individuals.

## Process

**1. Judge issues automatic stay**
• Creditors cannot press suits for repayment.
• Debts are frozen.
• Company's day-to-day operations continue.
• Significant spending must have judge's approval.
• Secured creditors can ask court for hardship exemption from debt freeze.
**2. Unsecured creditors form a committee**
• Representatives are chosen to deal with the company.
• Creditors can ask the court to appoint an examiner to investigate possible fraud or mismanagement.
• Court can name a trustee to run the company.

**3. The committee and company negotiate a reorganization plan.**
• Parties negotiate a repayment plan for frozen debts. This step can take months or years.
**4. Creditors approve the plan**
• Must have assent of majority of creditors as well as creditors who are owed two-thirds of the debt.
**5. Judge approves the plan**

## Reorganized Company Emerges

• It must meet the terms of the agreed repayment plan.
• It operates as a normal company.

# State Finances
## Revenue, Expenditures, Debt, and Taxes

Source: Census Bureau, U.S. Dept. of Commerce (fiscal year 1992)

| State | Revenue (millions) | Expenditures (millions) | Debt (millions) | Per cap.[1] debt | Per cap.[1] taxes | Per cap.[1] expenditures |
|---|---|---|---|---|---|---|
| Alabama | $10,536 | $9,651 | $4,129 | $998 | $1,019 | $2,333 |
| Alaska | 6,327 | 5,255 | 4,942 | 8,418 | 2,730 | 8,952 |
| Arizona | 9,551 | 9,096 | 2,849 | 743 | 1,259 | 2,373 |
| Arkansas | 5,864 | 5,478 | 1,942 | 809 | 1,145 | 2,283 |
| California | 100,154 | 97,079 | 37,824 | 1,225 | 1,494 | 3,145 |
| Colorado | 9,079 | 7,492 | 2,977 | 857 | 1,018 | 2,159 |
| Connecticut | 11,784 | 11,627 | 11,957 | 3,644 | 1,846 | 3,543 |
| Delaware | 2,848 | 2,504 | 3,542 | 5,140 | 1,944 | 3,634 |
| Florida | 28,311 | 27,089 | 12,295 | 911 | 1,068 | 2,008 |
| Georgia | 14,761 | 14,054 | 4,471 | 662 | 1,076 | 2,081 |
| Hawaii | 5,299 | 5,301 | 4,687 | 4,040 | 2,335 | 4,570 |
| Idaho | 2,902 | 2,604 | 1,292 | 1,210 | 1,303 | 2,440 |
| Illinois | 27,865 | 26,832 | 18,742 | 1,611 | 1,157 | 2,306 |
| Indiana | 13,490 | 12,341 | 5,172 | 913 | 1,143 | 2,179 |
| Iowa | 7,520 | 7,227 | 1,884 | 669 | 1,280 | 2,569 |
| Kansas | 5,794 | 5,484 | 486 | 192 | 1,110 | 2,173 |
| Kentucky | 10,640 | 10,154 | 6,619 | 1,762 | 1,353 | 2,704 |
| Louisiana | 11,842 | 11,750 | 9,994 | 2,331 | 991 | 2,740 |
| Maine | 3,755 | 3,722 | 2,637 | 2,135 | 1,347 | 3,013 |
| Maryland | 13,730 | 13,004 | 8,335 | 1,698 | 1,324 | 2,649 |
| Massachusetts | 20,456 | 20,368 | 24,008 | 4,002 | 1,651 | 3,395 |
| Michigan | 26,298 | 25,509 | 10,357 | 1,097 | 1,195 | 2,703 |
| Minnesota | 15,090 | 13,526 | 4,143 | 924 | 1,662 | 3,019 |
| Mississippi | 6,177 | 5,762 | 1,626 | 621 | 954 | 2,204 |
| Missouri | 11,619 | 10,446 | 6,301 | 1,213 | 988 | 2,011 |
| Montana | 2,661 | 2,460 | 1,868 | 2,266 | 1,153 | 2,984 |
| Nebraska | 3,751 | 3,624 | 1,754 | 1,092 | 1,176 | 2,256 |
| Nevada | 3,948 | 3,826 | 1,934 | 1,457 | 1,369 | 2,883 |
| New Hampshire | 2,727 | 2,871 | 4,313 | 3,882 | 770 | 2,584 |
| New Jersey | 28,922 | 29,316 | 19,786 | 2,540 | 1,643 | 3,763 |
| New Mexico | 5,582 | 4,972 | 1,605 | 1,015 | 1,415 | 3,144 |
| New York | 74,931 | 73,153 | 55,868 | 3,083 | 1,661 | 4,037 |
| North Carolina | 17,664 | 16,046 | 3,819 | 558 | 1,316 | 2,344 |
| North Dakota | 2,072 | 2,001 | 1,027 | 1,615 | 1,186 | 3,145 |
| Ohio | 35,590 | 30,425 | 12,193 | 1,106 | 1,099 | 2,761 |
| Oklahoma | 8,379 | 8,183 | 3,657 | 1,138 | 1,206 | 2,547 |
| Oregon | 10,025 | 7,979 | 6,295 | 2,114 | 1,113 | 2,680 |
| Pennsylvania | 36,699 | 33,622 | 12,962 | 1,079 | 1,354 | 2,799 |
| Rhode Island | 3,609 | 3,968 | 5,151 | 5,125 | 1,270 | 3,948 |
| South Carolina | 9,897 | 9,428 | 4,685 | 1,300 | 1,092 | 2,616 |
| South Dakota | 1,756 | 1,565 | 1,889 | 2,657 | 794 | 2,200 |
| Tennessee | 11,126 | 10,406 | 2,806 | 558 | 900 | 2,071 |
| Texas | 36,763 | 33,894 | 8,001 | 453 | 964 | 1,919 |
| Utah | 4,917 | 4,481 | 2,153 | 1,187 | 1,096 | 2,471 |
| Vermont | 1,898 | 1,841 | 1,543 | 2,706 | 1,339 | 3,230 |
| Virginia | 15,292 | 13,921 | 7,403 | 1,160 | 1,101 | 2,182 |
| Washington | 17,366 | 17,316 | 7,192 | 1,400 | 1,648 | 3,371 |
| West Virginia | 5,452 | 5,262 | 2,594 | 1,431 | 1,297 | 2,903 |
| Wisconsin | 17,131 | 13,596 | 7,299 | 1,457 | 1,380 | 2,715 |
| Wyoming | 2,007 | 1,925 | 895 | 1,920 | 1,386 | 4,131 |
| **United States** | **$741,857** | **$699,432** | **$371,901** | **$1,461** | **$1,288** | **$2,748** |

(1) Per capita amounts are based on population figures of the resident U.S. population (excluding the District of Columbia) as of July 1, 1992.

## State and Local Government Receipts and Expenditures

Source: Bureau of Economic Analysis, U.S. Dept. of Commerce

(billions of dollars)

| | 1991 | 1992 | First Quarter 1993[1] | | 1991 | 1992 | First Quarter 1993[1] |
|---|---|---|---|---|---|---|---|
| **Receipts** | $777.9 | $837.7 | $863.3 | Other | $207.6 | $210.8 | $207.6 |
| Personal tax and nontax receipts | 145.4 | 153.2 | 156.9 | Transfer payments to persons | 198.0 | 233.6 | 253.5 |
| Income taxes | 110.3 | 115.8 | 118.1 | Net interest paid | −48.4 | −43.8 | −41.3 |
| Nontaxes | 16.7 | 17.9 | 18.6 | Interest paid | 63.7 | 66.5 | 68.1 |
| Other | 18.4 | 19.5 | 20.2 | Less: Interest received by | | | |
| Corporate profits tax accruals | 21.5 | 25.2 | 26.8 | government | 112.1 | 110.3 | 109.5 |
| Indirect business tax and nontax | | | | Less: Dividends received by | | | |
| accruals | 397.0 | 422.7 | 435.9 | government | 9.5 | 10.0 | 10.4 |
| Sales taxes | 189.0 | 200.8 | 207.1 | Subsidies less current surplus of | | | |
| Property taxes | 167.7 | 180.5 | 188.0 | government enterprises | −22.6 | −23.3 | −24.1 |
| Other | 40.4 | 41.4 | 40.9 | Subsidies | .4 | .4 | .4 |
| Contributions for social insurance | 60.6 | 63.7 | 65.4 | Less: Current surplus of | | | |
| Federal grants-in-aid | 153.3 | 173.0 | 178.2 | government enterprises | 23.0 | 23.7 | 24.5 |
| **Expenditures** | 760.7 | 822.3 | 853.2 | Less: Wage accruals less | | | |
| Purchases | 643.2 | 665.8 | 675.4 | disbursements | 0 | 0 | 0 |
| Compensation of employees | 435.6 | 454.9 | 467.8 | Surplus or deficit (−), national | | | |
| | | | | income and product accounts | 17.1 | 15.5 | 10.1 |

(1) Seasonally adjusted at annual rates

## Federal Grants to State and Local Governments

Source: Office of Management and Budget

(millions of dollars)

| | 1980 | 1985 | 1990 | 1991 | 1992 |
|---|---|---|---|---|---|
| National defense | $93 | $157 | $241 | $185 | $318 |
| Energy | 499 | 529 | 461 | 457 | 448 |
| Natural resources and environment | 5,363 | 4,069 | 3,745 | 4,040 | 3,929 |
| Agriculture | 569 | 2,420 | 1,285 | 1,220 | 1,142 |
| Commerce and housing credit | 3 | 2 | 0 | 0 | 11 |
| Transportation | 13,087 | 17,055 | 19,225 | 19,878 | 20,608 |
| Community and regional development | 6,486 | 5,221 | 4,965 | 4,273 | 4,539 |
| Education, employment, training, and social services | 21,862 | 17,817 | 23,359 | 26,566 | 28,795 |
| Health | 15,758 | 24,451 | 43,890 | 55,783 | 71,416 |
| Income security | 18,495 | 27,153 | 35,189 | 38,864 | 43,486 |
| Veterans benefits and services | 90 | 91 | 134 | 141 | 164 |
| Administration of justice | 529 | 95 | 574 | 940 | 987 |
| General government[1] | 8,616 | 6,838 | 2,309 | 2,224 | 2,274 |
| **Total** | $91,451 | $105,897 | $135,377 | $154,570 | $178,117 |

(1) Includes general purpose fiscal assistance.

## All Banks in U.S.—Number, Deposits

Source: Federal Reserve System

Comprises all national banks in the United States and all state commercial banks, trust companies, mutual stock savings banks, private and industrial banks, and special types of institutions that are treated as banks by the federal bank supervisory agencies. Data as of June 30 prior to 1975.

| Year | Number of banks | | | | | Total deposits (millions of dollars) | | | | | |
|---|---|---|---|---|---|---|---|---|---|---|---|
| | Total all banks | F.R.S. members | | | Nonmembers | | Total all banks | F.R.S. members | | | Nonmembers | |
| | | Total | Nat'l | State | Mutual savings | Other | | Total | Nat'l | State | Mutual savings | Other |
| 1925 | 26,479 | 9,538 | 8,066 | 1,472 | 621 | 18,320 | $51,641 | $32,457 | $19,912 | $12,546 | $7,089 | $12,095 |
| 1930 | 23,855 | 8,315 | 7,247 | 1,068 | 604 | 14,936 | 59,828 | 38,069 | 23,235 | 14,834 | 9,117 | 12,642 |
| 1935 | 16,047 | 6,410 | 5,425 | 985 | 569 | 9,068 | 51,149 | 34,938 | 22,477 | 12,461 | 9,830 | 6,381 |
| 1940 | 14,955 | 6,398 | 5,164 | 1,234 | 551 | 8,008 | 70,770 | 51,729 | 33,014 | 18,715 | 10,631 | 8,410 |
| 1945 | 14,542 | 6,840 | 5,015 | 1,825 | 539 | 7,163 | 151,033 | 118,378 | 76,534 | 41,844 | 14,413 | 18,242 |
| 1950 | 14,674 | 6,885 | 4,971 | 1,914 | 527 | 7,262 | 163,770 | 122,707 | 82,430 | 40,277 | 19,927 | 21,137 |
| 1955 | 14,309 | 6,611 | 4,744 | 1,867 | 525 | 7,173 | 208,850 | 154,670 | 98,636 | 56,034 | 27,310 | 26,870 |
| 1960 | 14,006 | 6,217 | 4,542 | 1,675 | 513 | 7,276 | 249,163 | 179,519 | 116,178 | 63,341 | 35,316 | 34,328 |
| 1965 | 14,295 | 6,235 | 4,803 | 1,432 | 504 | 7,556 | 362,611 | 259,743 | 171,528 | 88,215 | 50,980 | 51,889 |
| 1970 | 14,167 | 5,805 | 4,638 | 1,167 | 496 | 7,866 | 502,542 | 346,289 | 254,322 | 91,967 | 69,285 | 86,968 |
| 1975 | 15,108 | 5,787 | 4,741 | 1,046 | 475 | 8,846 | 896,879 | 590,999 | 447,590 | 143,409 | 110,569 | 195,311 |
| 1980 | 15,145 | 5,422 | 4,425 | 997 | 460 | 9,263 | 1,333,399 | 843,030 | 651,848 | 191,182 | 150,000 | 340,369 |
| 1985 | 14,713 | 6,044 | 4,964 | 1,080 | 344 | 8,325 | 1,973,816 | 1,285,562 | 1,033,631 | 251,931 | 137,535 | 500,179 |
| 1990 | 12,736 | 5,034 | 4,012 | 1,022 | 361 | 7,341 | 2,522,492 | 1,679,654 | 1,374,004 | 305,650 | 183,522 | 659,316 |
| 1991 | 12,312 | 4,808 | 3,823 | 985 | 358 | 7,146 | 2,546,753 | 1,694,124 | 1,380,379 | 313,745 | 178,231 | 674,398 |
| 1992 | 11,927 | 4,598 | 3,631 | 967 | 428 | 6,901 | 2,573,682 | 1,721,979 | 1,370,564 | 351,415 | 177,832 | 673,871 |

# Largest U.S. Commercial Banks

Source: *American Banker* (as of Dec. 31, 1992)

| Bank | Assets (millions) | Bank | Assets (millions) |
|---|---|---|---|
| Citicorp, New York | $213,701.0 | National City Corp., Cleveland | $28,963.5 |
| BankAmerica Corp., San Francisco | 180,646.0 | Comerica, Detroit | 26,586.8 |
| Chemical Banking Corp., New York | 139,655.0 | Shawmut National Corp., Hartford | 25,288.3 |
| Nationsbank Corp., Charlotte, N.C. | 118,059.3 | Society Corp., Cleveland | 24,978.3 |
| J.P. Morgan & Co., New York | 102,941.0 | Corestates Financial Corp., Philadelphia | 23,699.1 |
| Chase Manhattan Corp., New York | 95,862.0 | First Bank System, Minneapolis | 23,527.0 |
| Bankers Trust New York Corp., New York | 72,448.0 | Boatmen's Bancshares, St. Louis | 23,386.7 |
| Banc One Corp., Columbus, Oh. | 61,417.4 | National Westminster Bancorp, Jersey City, N.J. | 22,714.6 |
| Wells Fargo & Co., San Francisco | 52,537.0 | Continental Bank Corp., Chicago | 22,467.0 |
| PNC Bank Corp., Pittsburgh | 51,379.9 | U.S. Bancorp, Portland, Ore. | 20,741.1 |
| First Union Corp., Charlotte, N.C. | 51,326.7 | First of America Bank Corp., Kalamazoo, Mich. | 20,146.8 |
| First Interstate Bancorp, Los Angeles | 50,863.1 | Marine Midland Banks, Buffalo | 17,109.2 |
| First Chicago Corp., Chicago | 49,281.0 | MNC Financial, Baltimore | 16,985.5 |
| Fleet Financial Group, Providence | 46,938.5 | Union Bank, San Francisco | 16,843.5 |
| Norwest Corp., Minneapolis | 44,557.1 | State Street Boston Corp., Boston | 16,489.8 |
| NBD Bancorp, Detroit | 40,937.2 | Northern Trust Corp., Chicago | 14,959.6 |
| Bank of New York Co., New York | 40,909.0 | Midlantic Corp., Edison, N.J. | 14,421.8 |
| Barnett Banks, Jacksonville, Fla. | 39,464.8 | Huntington Bancshares, Columbus, Oh. | 13,894.9 |
| Republic New York Corp., New York | 37,146.4 | UJB Financial, Princeton, N.J. | 13,770.9 |
| Suntrust Banks, Atlanta | 36,648.6 | Firstar Corp., Milwaukee | 13,168.9 |
| Wachovia Corp., Winston-Salem, N.C. | 33,366.5 | Harris Bankcorp, Chicago | 12,729.2 |
| Bank of Boston Corp., Boston | 32,346.1 | Southtrust Corp., Birmingham, Ala. | 12,714.4 |
| Mellon Bank Corp., Pittsburgh | 31,574.0 | Bancorp Hawaii, Honolulu | 12,713.1 |
| First Fidelity Bancorp, Lawrenceville, N.J. | 31,480.3 | Crestar Financial Corp., Richmond | 12,674.7 |
| Keycorp, Albany, N.Y. | 30,114.1 | Meridian Bancorp, Reading, Pa. | 12,208.3 |

# Bank Failures

Source: Federal Deposit Insurance Corp.

| Year | Closed or Assisted | Year | Closed or Assisted | Year | Closed or Assisted | Year | Closed or Assisted |
|---|---|---|---|---|---|---|---|
| 1934 | 61 | 1961 | 9 | 1973 | 6 | 1984 | 72 |
| 1935 | 32 | 1963 | 2 | 1975 | 14 | 1985 | 120 |
| 1936 | 72 | 1964 | 8 | 1976 | 17 | 1986 | 145 |
| 1937 | 84 | 1965 | 9 | 1978 | 7 | 1987 | 184 |
| 1938 | 81 | 1966 | 8 | 1979 | 10 | 1988 | 221 |
| 1939 | 72 | 1967 | 4 | 1980 | 10 | 1989 | 207 |
| 1940 | 48 | 1969 | 9 | 1981 | 10 | 1990 | 169 |
| 1955 | 5 | 1970 | 8 | 1982 | 42 | 1991 | 127 |
| 1959 | 3 | 1971 | 6 | 1983 | 48 | 1992 | 122 |
| 1960 | 2 | 1972 | 3 | | | | |

# Federal Deposit Insurance Corporation (FDIC)

The primary purpose of the Federal Deposit Insurance Corporation (FDIC) is to insure deposits in all banks approved for insurance coverage benefits under the Federal Deposit Insurance Act. The major functions of the FDIC are to protect depositors of insured banks, to act as receiver for all national banks placed in receivership and for state banks placed in receivership when appointed receiver by state authorities, and to ensure the continuance or development of safe and sound banking practices. The FDIC's income consists of assessments on insured banks and income from investments; it receives no appropriations from Congress. It may borrow from the U.S. Treasury not to exceed $30 billion outstanding, but has made no such borrowings since it was organized in 1933. The FDIC deficit (Deposit Insurance Fund) as of Mar. 31, 1993, was $1.2 billion.

# The Savings and Loan Crisis

As of September 1993, the Congressional Budget Office estimated that handling losses in failed savings and loan institutions would cost $120 billion from 1990 through 1998. This does not include $60 billion spent before 1989.

# Federal Reserve Board Discount Rate

The discount rate is the rate of interest set by the Federal Reserve that member banks are charged when borrowing money through the Federal Reserve System.

| Effective Date | Rate | Effective Date | Rate | Effective Date | Rate | Effective Date | Rate |
|---|---|---|---|---|---|---|---|
| **1980:** Feb. 15 | 13 | Dec. 4 | 12 | Nov. 21 | 8½ | **1989:** Feb. 24 | 7 |
| May 30 | 12 | **1982:** July 20 | 11½ | Dec. 24 | 8 | **1990:** Dec. 18 | 6½ |
| June 13 | 11 | Aug. 2 | 11 | **1985:** May 20 | 7½ | **1991:** Feb. 1 | 6 |
| July 28 | 10 | Aug. 16 | 10½ | **1986:** March 7 | 7 | **1991:** Apr. 30 | 5½ |
| Sept. 26 | 11 | Aug. 27 | 10 | April 21 | 6½ | Sept. 13 | 5 |
| Nov. 17 | 12 | Oct. 12 | 9½ | July 11 | 6 | Nov. 6 | 4½ |
| Dec. 5 | 13 | Nov. 22 | 9 | Aug. 21 | 5½ | Dec. 20 | 3½ |
| **1981:** May 5 | 14 | Dec. 15 | 8½ | **1987:** Sept. 4 | 6 | **1992:** July 3 | 3 |
| Nov. 2 | 13 | **1984:** April 9 | 9 | **1988:** Aug. 9 | 6½ | | |

## Federal Reserve System

(as of Aug. 1993)

The Federal Reserve System is the central bank for the United States. The system was established on December 23, 1913, originally to give the country an elastic currency, to provide facilities for discounting commercial paper, and to improve the supervision of banking. Since then, the System's responsibilities have been broadened. Over the years, stability and growth of the economy, a high level of employment, stability in the purchasing power of the dollar, and reasonable balance in transactions with foreign countries have come to be recognized as primary objectives of governmental economic policy.

The Federal Reserve System consists of the Board of Governors, the 12 District Reserve Banks and their branch offices, and the Federal Open Market Committee. Several advisory councils help the Board meet its varied responsibilities.

The hub of the System is the seven member Board of Governors in Washington. The members of the Board are appointed by the President and confirmed by the Senate, to serve 14-year terms. The President also appoints the Chairman and Vice-Chairman of the Board from among the Board members for 4-year terms that may be renewed. Currently, the board members are: Alan Greenspan, Chairman; David W. Mullins Jr., Vice Chairman; Edward W. Kelley Jr.; Wayne D. Angell; John P. La Ware; Lawrence B. Lindsey; Susan M. Phillips.

The Board is the policy-making body. In addition to its policy-making responsibilities, it supervises the budget and operations of the Reserve Banks, approves the appointments of their presidents, and appoints 3 of each District Bank's directors, including the chairman and vice chairman of each Reserve Bank's board.

The 12 Reserve Banks and their branch offices serve as the decentralized portion of the System, carrying out day-to-day operations such as circulating currency and coin, providing fiscal agency functions and payments mechanism services. The District Banks are located in Boston, New York, Philadelphia, Cleveland, Richmond, Atlanta, Chicago, St. Louis, Minneapolis, Kansas City, Dallas, and San Francisco.

The System's principal function is monetary policy, which it controls using three tools: reserve requirements, the discount rate, and open market operations. Uniform reserve requirements, set by the Board, are applied to the transaction accounts and nonpersonal time deposits of all depository institutions. Responsibility for setting the discount rate (the interest rate at which depository institutions can borrow money from the Reserve Banks) is shared by the Board of Governors and the Reserve Banks. Changes in the discount rate are recommended by the individual Boards of Directors of the Reserve Banks and are subject to approval by the Board of Governors. The most important tool of monetary policy is open market operations (the purchase and sale of government securities). Responsibility for influencing the cost and availability of money and credit through the purchase and sale of government securities lies with the Federal Open Market Committee (FOMC). This committee is composed of the 7 members of the Board of Governors, the president of the Federal Reserve Bank of New York, and 4 other Federal Reserve Bank presidents, who serve one-year terms on a rotating basis. The committee bases its decisions on current economic and financial developments and outlook, setting yearly growth objectives for key measures of money supply and credit. The decisions of the committee are carried out by the Domestic Trading Desk of the Federal Reserve Bank of New York.

The Federal Reserve Act prescribes a Federal Advisory Council, consisting of one member from each Federal Reserve District, elected annually by the Board of Directors of each of the 12 Federal Reserve Banks. They meet with the Federal Reserve Board four times a year to discuss business and financial conditions and to make advisory recommendations.

The Consumer Advisory Council is a statutory body, including both consumer and creditor representatives, which advises the Board of Governors on its implementation of consumer regulations and other consumer-related matters.

Following the passage of the Monetary Control Act of 1980, the Board of Governors established the Thrift Institutions Advisory Council to provide information and views on the special needs and problems of thrift institutions. The group is comprised of representatives of mutual savings banks, savings and loan associations, and credit unions.

## U.S. Corporate Profits by Industry

Source: Bureau of Economic Analysis, U.S. Dept. of Commerce

(billions of dollars)

| | 1991 | 1992 | First[1] Quarter 1993 | | 1991 | 1992 | First[1] Quarter 1993 |
|---|---|---|---|---|---|---|---|
| Corporate profits with inventory valuation and capital consumption adjustments... | 346.3 | 393.8 | 424.2 | Manufacturing............ | 89.3 | 113.8 | 110.7 |
| Domestic industries......... | 279.8 | 329.8 | 357.0 | Durable goods...... | 25.8 | 41.0 | 40.7 |
| Financial................ | 49.9 | 46.8 | 54.5 | Primary metal industries.... | 1.1 | .4 | −.8 |
| Nonfinancial.............. | 229.9 | 283.0 | 302.6 | Fabricated metal prods...... | 5.4 | 7.1 | 4.7 |
| Rest of the world.......... | 66.5 | 64.0 | 67.2 | Industrial machinery and equip. | 8.9 | 9.4 | 7.3 |
| Receipts from the rest of the world. | 62.5 | 66.4 | 73.4 | Electronic and other electric equip............ | 6.6 | 9.3 | 10.6 |
| Less: Payments to the rest of the world................ | −4.0 | 2.5 | 6.2 | Motor vehicles and equip.... | −6.9 | 3.1 | 4.7 |
| Corporate profits with inventory valuation adjustment...... | 337.8 | 364.2 | 383.6 | Other............... | 10.8 | 11.7 | 14.3 |
| | | | | Nondurable goods........ | 63.5 | 72.9 | 70.0 |
| Domestic industries......... | 271.3 | 300.2 | 316.4 | Food and kindred prods..... | 16.6 | 16.6 | 15.7 |
| Financial................ | 60.9 | 56.8 | 64.1 | Chemicals and allied prods... | 16.1 | 18.1 | 19.6 |
| Federal Reserve banks...... | 20.2 | 17.8 | 16.6 | Petroleum and coal prods.... | 7.7 | 9.4 | 8.9 |
| Other.................. | 40.7 | 38.9 | 47.5 | Other................ | 23.1 | 28.7 | 25.8 |
| | | | | Transportation and public utilities. | 46.1 | 44.4 | 47.0 |
| | | | | Wholesale and retail trade..... | 44.0 | 47.7 | 51.9 |
| Nonfinancial.............. | 210.4 | 243.5 | 252.3 | Other................. | 31.1 | 37.5 | 42.7 |
| | | | | Rest of the world........... | 66.5 | 64.0 | 67.2 |

(1) Seasonally adjusted at annual rates.

# United States Mint

Source: United States Mint, U.S. Dept. of the Treasury

The United States Mint was created by an act of Congress on April 2, 1792, which established the U.S. national coinage system. Supervision of the Mint was a function of the Secretary of State, but in 1799, the Mint became an independent agency reporting directly to the President. The Mint was made a statutory bureau of the Treasury Department in 1873, with a director appointed by the President to oversee its operations.

The Mint manufactures and ships all U.S. coins for circulation to the Federal Reserve banks and branches, which issue coins to the public and the business community through depository institutions. The Mint also safeguards the Treasury Department's stored gold and silver and other monetary assets.

The composition of dimes, quarters, and half dollars, traditionally produced from silver, was changed by the Coinage Act of 1965, which mandated that these coins be minted from a cupronickel-clad alloy and reduced the silver content of the half dollar to 40 percent. In 1970, legislative action mandated that the half dollar, and a dollar coin, be minted from the same cupronickel-clad alloy.

The Eisenhower dollar was minted from 1971 through 1978, when legislation called for the minting of the smaller Susan B. Anthony dollar coin. The Anthony dollar, which was minted from 1979 through 1981, marked the first time that a woman, other than a mythical figure, appeared on a U.S. circulating coin.

Mint headquarters is located in Washington, D.C. Mint production facilities are located in Philadelphia, PA; Denver, CO; San Francisco, CA; and West Point, NY. In addition, the Mint is responsible for the U.S. Bullion Depository at Fort Knox, KY.

Proof coin sets, silver proof coin sets, and uncirculated coin sets are available annually from the Mint. The Mint also produces ongoing series of national and historic medals in honor of outstanding persons or events and sites of special meaning to the American people.

Since 1982, the Mint has produced the following congressionally authorized commemorative coins: the 1982 George Washington commemorative half dollar; 1984 U.S. Olympic coins; 1986 U.S. Statue of Liberty coins; 1987 bicentennial of the U.S. Constitution coins; 1988 U.S. Olympic coins; 1989 U.S. Congress coins; 1990 Eisenhower centennial coin; 1991 United Services Organization 50th anniversary coin; 1991 Korean War Memorial coin; 1991 Mount Rushmore anniversary coins; 1992 U.S. Olympic coins; 1992 White House 200th anniversary coin; and 1992 Christopher Columbus quincentenary coins.

The Mint in 1993 offered the Bill of Rights commemorative coins in gold and silver. Surcharges from sales of these coins support teaching and graduate study of the Constitution of the United States. The World War II 50th anniversary coins also were available in gold, silver, and clad. Surcharges from sales of these coins help fund the creation of World War II memorials in the United States and France.

Designs for clad, silver, and gold 1994 World Cup coins have been selected, with sales of these coins to help fund scholarships and staging of the 1994 World Cup in the United States. In addition, the 1996 Atlanta centennial Olympic Games commemorative coins, scheduled to go on sale in 1995 and 1996, will help support the staging of the 1996 Olympic Games in Atlanta, GA.

The congressionally authorized American eagle gold and silver bullion coins produced by the Mint are available through dealers worldwide. The gold eagles are sold in one-ounce, half-ounce, quarter-ounce, and one-tenth-ounce sizes; the price of the coins fluctuates with the daily market value of gold. The American eagle silver bullion coin contains one troy ounce of .999 fine silver and is priced according to the daily market value of silver. These coins also are available in proof condition, separately priced.

The Mint offers free public tours and operates sales centers at the U.S. Mints in Denver and Philadelphia. The Mint also operates a museum and sales center at the Old Mint in San Francisco and a sales center at Union Station in Washington, D.C.

Information about Mint programs and products is available from the United States Mint, Customer Service Center, 10001 Aerospace Road, Lanham, MD 20706. Telephone: (301) 436-7400.

## Portraits on U.S. Treasury Bills, Bonds, Notes, and Savings Bonds

| Denomination | Savings bonds | Treas. bills | Treas. bonds | Treas. notes |
|---|---|---|---|---|
| 50 | Washington | | Jefferson | |
| 75 | Adams | | | |
| 100 | Jefferson | | Jackson | |
| 200 | Madison | | | |
| 500 | Hamilton | | Washington | |
| 1,000 | Franklin | H. McCulloch | Lincoln | Lincoln |
| 5,000 | Revere | J.G. Carlisle | Monroe | Monroe |
| 10,000 | J. Wilson | J. Sherman | Cleveland | Cleveland |
| 50,000 | | C. Glass | | |
| 100,000 | | A. Gallatin | Grant | Grant |
| 1,000,000 | | O. Wolcott | T. Roosevelt | T. Roosevelt |
| 100,000,000 | | | | Madison |
| 500,000,000 | | | | McKinley |

## Large Denominations of U.S. Currency Discontinued

The largest denomination of United States currency now being issued is the $100 bill. Issuance of currency in denominations larger than $100 was discontinued in 1969.

As large denomination bills reach the Federal Reserve Bank they are removed from circulation.

Because some of the discontinued currency is expected to be in the hands of holders for many years, the description of the various denominations below is continued:

| Amt. | Portrait | Embellishment on back |
|---|---|---|
| $ 1 | Washington | Great Seal of U.S. |
| 2 | Jefferson | Signers of Declaration |
| 5 | Lincoln | Lincoln Memorial |
| 10 | Hamilton | U.S. Treasury |
| 20 | Jackson | White House |
| 50 | Grant | U.S. Capitol |
| 100 | Franklin | Independence Hall |

| Amt. | Portrait | Embellishment on back |
|---|---|---|
| $ 500 | McKinley | Ornate denominational marking |
| 1,000 | Cleveland | Ornate denominational marking |
| 5,000 | Madison | Ornate denominational marking |
| 10,000 | Chase | Ornate denominational marking |
| 100,000* | W. Wilson | Ornate denominational marking |

* For use only in transactions between Federal Reserve System and Treasury Department.

# U.S. Currency and Coin

Source: Financial Management Service, U.S. Dept. of the Treasury (Mar. 31, 1993)

## Amounts Outstanding and in Circulation

|  | Total currency and coin | Total currency | Federal Reserve notes[1] | U.S. notes | Currency no longer issued |
|---|---|---|---|---|---|
| **Currency** |  |  |  |  |  |
| Amounts outstanding . . . . . | $395,458,605,364 | $374,471,288,466 | $373,886,055,293 | $322,539,016 | $262,694,157 |
| Less amounts held by: |  |  |  |  |  |
| Treasury . . . . . . . . . . . | 509,126,491 | 41,848,106 | 4,530,288 | 37,112,039 | 205,779 |
| Federal Reserve banks. . . | 62,126,759,101 | 61,623,603,315 | 61,623,599,799 | 300 | 3,216 |
| **Amounts in circulation. . . .** | **$332,822,719,772** | **$312,805,837,045** | **$312,257,925,206** | **$285,426,677** | **$262,485,162** |

|  | Total | Dollars[3] | Fractional coin |
|---|---|---|---|
| **Coin[2]** |  |  |  |
| Amounts outstanding . . . . . | $20,987,316,898 | $2,024,703,898 | $18,962,613,000 |
| Less amounts held by: |  |  |  |
| Treasury . . . . . . . . . . . | 467,278,385 | 305,182,245 | 162,096,140 |
| Federal Reserve banks. . . | 503,155,786 | 118,873,015 | 384,282,771 |
| **Amounts in circulation . . .** | **$20,016,882,727** | **$1,600,648,638** | **$18,416,234,089** |

## Currency in Circulation by Denominations

| Denomination | Total currency in circulation | Federal Reserve notes[1] | U.S. notes | Currency no longer issued |
|---|---|---|---|---|
| 1 Dollar | $5,304,356,907 | $5,154,336,328 | $143,481 | $149,877,098 |
| 2 Dollars | 917,111,492 | 784,359,718 | 132,738,966 | 12,808 |
| 5 Dollars | 6,332,792,210 | 6,186,740,170 | 111,285,810 | 34,766,230 |
| 10 Dollars | 12,133,540,290 | 12,109,938,660 | 5,950 | 23,595,680 |
| 20 Dollars | 70,202,720,044 | 70,182,595,780 | 3,380 | 20,120,884 |
| 50 Dollars | 37,661,467,850 | 37,649,949,450 | — | 11,518,400 |
| 100 Dollars | 179,932,145,750 | 179,868,854,100 | 41,249,000 | 22,042,650 |
| 500 Dollars | 146,619,900 | 146,431,000 | — | 188,900 |
| 1,000 Dollars | 169,852,000 | 169,645,000 | — | 207,000 |
| 5,000 Dollars | 1,780,000 | 1,725,000 | — | 55,000 |
| 10,000 Dollars | 3,450,000 | 3,350,000 | — | 100,000 |
| Fractional parts | 487 | — | — | 487 |
| Partial notes[4] | 115 | — | 90 | 25 |
| **Total currency** | **$312,805,837,045** | **$312,257,925,206** | **$285,426,677** | **$262,485,162** |

## Comparative Totals of Money in Circulation — Selected Dates

| Date | Dollars (in millions) | Per capita[5] | Date | Dollars (in millions) | Per capita[5] | Date | Dollars (in millions) | Per capita[5] |
|---|---|---|---|---|---|---|---|---|
| Mar. 31, 1993 | 332,822.7 | 1,293.58 | June 30, 1975 | 81,196.4 | 380.08 | June 30, 1940 | 7,847.5 | 59.40 |
| Mar. 31, 1992 | 303,215.0 | 1,219.15 | June 30, 1970 | 54,351.0 | 265.39 | June 30, 1935 | 5,567.1 | 43.75 |
| Mar. 31, 1991 | 286,675.0 | 1,138.62 | June 30, 1965 | 39,719.8 | 204.14 | June 30, 1930 | 4,522.0 | 36.74 |
| Mar. 31, 1990 | 257,664.4 | 1,028.71 | June 30, 1960 | 32,064.6 | 177.47 | June 30, 1925 | 4,815.2 | 41.56 |
| June 30, 1989 | 249,182.7 | 1,002.54 | June 30, 1955 | 30,229.3 | 182.90 | June 30, 1920 | 5,467.6 | 51.36 |
| June 30, 1985 | 185,890.7 | 778.58 | June 30, 1950 | 27,156.3 | 179.03 | June 30, 1915 | 3,319.6 | 33.01 |
| June 30, 1980 | 127,097.2 | 558.28 | June 30, 1945 | 26,746.4 | 191.14 | June 30, 1910 | 3,148.7 | 34.07 |

(1) Issued on and after July 1, 1929. (2) Excludes coin sold to collectors at premium prices. (3) Includes $481,781,898 in standard silver dollars. (4) Represents value of certain partial denominations not presented for redemption. (5) Based on Bureau of the Census estimates of population.

The requirement for a gold reserve against U.S. notes was repealed by Public Law 90-269 approved Mar. 18, 1968. Silver certificates issued on and after July 1, 1929, became redeemable from the general fund on June 24, 1968. The amount of security after those dates has been reduced accordingly.

# Consumer Credit Outstanding, 1970 to 1992

Source: Federal Reserve System

(billions of dollars)

Estimated amounts of credit outstanding as of end of year. Not seasonally adjusted (unless noted).

| Type of Credit | 1970 | 1975 | 1980 | 1985 | 1988 | 1989 | 1990 | 1991 | 1992 |
|---|---|---|---|---|---|---|---|---|---|
| Credit outstanding. . . . . . . | 133.8 | 207.5 | 355.4 | 601.6 | 742.1 | 799.5 | 813.0 | 799.9 | 809.2 |
| Ratio to disposable personal income[1] (percent) . . . . . | 18.5 | 18.0 | 18.2 | 20.4 | 20.9 | 20.6 | 19.5 | 18.5 | 17.8 |
| Installment . . . . . . . . . . . | 105.5 | 168.7 | 302.1 | 526.2 | 673.5 | 736.3 | 752.9 | 749.0 | 756.9 |
| Automobile paper. . . . . . . | 36.3 | 57.2 | 111.9 | 210.4 | 285.4 | 292.4 | 284.9 | 261.2 | 260.0 |
| Revolving. . . . . . . . . . . . | 5.1 | 15.0 | 58.5 | 128.9 | 184.0 | 209.4 | 234.8 | 256.9 | 267.9 |
| All other loans[2] . . . . . . . . | 64.1 | 99.7 | 131.6 | 213.8 | 181.3 | 239.2 | 238.4 | 236.5 | 229.0 |
| Commercial banks . . . . . . | 48.7 | 82.9 | 147.0 | 245.1 | 324.8 | 342.8 | 347.1 | 340.7 | 331.9 |
| Finance companies. . . . . . | 27.6 | 32.7 | 62.3 | 111.7 | 144.7 | 138.9 | 133.3 | 121.9 | 117.1 |
| Credit unions . . . . . . . . . | 13.0 | 25.7 | 44.0 | 72.7 | 88.3 | 93.1 | 93.1 | 92.7 | 97.6 |
| Retailers[3] . . . . . . . . . . . | 13.9 | 18.2 | 28.7 | 43.0 | 48.4 | 44.2 | 43.5 | 39.8 | 42.1 |
| Other[4] . . . . . . . . . . . . . | 2.3 | 9.2 | 20.1 | 53.8 | 67.1 | 67.2 | 57.0 | 50.3 | 47.8 |
| Noninstallment . . . . . . . . . | 28.3 | 38.8 | 53.3 | 75.3 | 68.7 | 63.2 | 60.1 | 50.9 | 52.3 |

(1) Based on fourth quarter seasonally adjusted disposable personal income at annual rates as published by the U.S. Bureau of Economic Analysis. (2) Comprises mobile home loans and all other installment loans not incl. in automobile or revolving credit, such as loans for education, boats, trailers, or vacations. (3) Excludes 30-day charge credit held by travel and entertainment companies. (4) Comprises savings institutions and gasoline companies.

## Leading U.S. Businesses in 1992

Source: FORTUNE Magazine; World Almanac Research

(millions of dollars in sales, unless otherwise noted)

### Aerospace

| | |
|---|---|
| Boeing | $30,184 |
| United Technologies | 22,032 |
| McDonnell-Douglas | 17,513 |
| Allied-Signal | 12,089 |
| Lockheed | 10,138 |
| General Dynamics | 8,731 |
| Textron | 8,348 |
| Martin Marietta | 5,970 |
| Northrop | 5,550 |
| Grumman | 3,504 |

### Apparel

| | |
|---|---|
| Levi Strauss | $5,570 |
| VF | 3,865 |
| Fruit of the Loom | 1,855 |
| Hartmarx | 1,054 |
| Kellwood | 917 |
| Russell | 899 |
| Gitano Group | 826 |
| Leslie Fay | 777 |
| Crystal Brands | 736 |
| Warnaco Group | 627 |

### Beverages

| | |
|---|---|
| Pepsico | $22,084 |
| Coca-Cola | 13,238 |
| Anheuser-Busch | 11,401 |
| Coca-Cola Enterprises | 5,127 |
| J.E. Seagram | 4,130 |
| Whitman | 2,397 |
| Adolph Coors | 1,806 |
| Brown-Forman | 1,264 |
| Dr Pepper/Seven-Up | 663 |
| Coca-Cola Bottling Cons. | 656 |

### Building Materials

| | |
|---|---|
| American Standard | $3,801 |
| Corning | 3,744 |
| Owens-Illinois | 3,718 |
| Owens-Corning | 2,878 |
| Armstrong World Ind. | 2,550 |
| USG | 1,777 |
| Lafarge | 1,511 |
| Anchor Glass | 1,163 |
| Holnam | 946 |

### Chemicals

| | |
|---|---|
| E.I. Du Pont De Nemours | $37,643 |
| Dow Chemical | 19,177 |
| Occidental Petroleum | 8,940 |
| Monsanto | 8,485 |
| Hoechst Celanese | 7,044 |
| Miles | 6,499 |
| W.R. Grace | 6,330 |
| Union Carbide | 6,167 |
| PPG Industries | 5,858 |
| BASF | 5,042 |

### Computers, Office Equip.

| | |
|---|---|
| IBM | $65,096 |
| Hewlett-Packard | 16,427 |
| Digital Equipment | 14,027 |
| Unisys | 8,422 |
| Apple Computer | 7,087 |
| Compaq Computer | 4,132 |
| Sun Microsystems | 3,628 |
| Pitney Bowes | 3,460 |
| Seagate Technology | 2,889 |
| Amdahl | 2,554 |

### Electronics, Electrical Equip.

| | |
|---|---|
| General Electric | $62,202 |
| Motorola | 13,341 |
| Westinghouse Electric | 12,100 |
| Rockwell International | 10,995 |
| Raytheon | 9,119 |
| Emerson Electric | 7,706 |
| Texas Instruments | 7,470 |
| Whirlpool | 7,309 |
| Cooper Industries | 6,159 |
| North American Philips | 6,138 |

### Food

| | |
|---|---|
| Philip Morris | $50,157 |
| Conagra | 21,219 |
| Sara Lee | 13,321 |
| IBP | 11,130 |
| Archer Daniels | 9,344 |
| General Mills | 7,796 |
| Ralston Purina | 7,768 |
| Borden | 7,143 |
| H.J. Heinz | 6,628 |
| CPC International | 6,599 |

### Forest Products

| | |
|---|---|
| International Paper | $13,600 |
| Georgia-Pacific | 11,847 |
| Weyerhaeuser | 9,260 |
| Kimberly-Clark | 7,091 |
| Stone Container | 5,533 |
| Champion International | 4,950 |
| Scott Paper | 4,886 |
| James River | 4,748 |
| Mead | 4,703 |
| Boise Cascade | 3,732 |

### Furniture

| | |
|---|---|
| Interco | $1,472 |
| Leggett & Platt | 1,170 |
| Herman Miller | 810 |
| Hon Industries | 712 |
| Sealy | 654 |
| Kimball International | 624 |
| La-Z-Boy Chair | 621 |

### Industrial and Farm Equip.

| | |
|---|---|
| Tenneco | $13,606 |
| Caterpillar | 10,194 |
| Deere | 6,961 |
| Black & Decker | 4,790 |
| Dresser Industries | 4,283 |
| Ingersoll-Rand | 3,784 |
| Cummins Engine | 3,749 |
| Baker Hughes | 2,545 |
| Parker Hannifin | 2,382 |
| Dover | 2,291 |

### Life Insurance[1]

| | |
|---|---|
| Prudential of America | $154,780 |
| Metropolitan Life | 118,178 |
| Teachers Insurance & Annuity | 61,778 |
| Aetna Life | 50,897 |
| New York Life | 46,925 |
| Equitable Life Assurance | 46,624 |
| Connecticut General Life | 44,076 |
| Northwestern Mutual Life | 39,666 |
| John Hancock Mutual Life | 39,146 |
| Principal Mutual Life | 35,125 |

### Metal Products

| | |
|---|---|
| Gillette | $5,190 |
| Crown Cork & Seal | 3,781 |
| Masco | 3,554 |
| Tyco Laboratories | 3,066 |
| Illinois Tool Works | 2,821 |
| Ball | 2,446 |
| McDermott | 2,373 |
| Stanley Works | 2,218 |
| Masco Industries | 1,678 |
| Harsco | 1,633 |

### Metals

| | |
|---|---|
| Aluminum Co. of America | $9,588 |
| Reynolds Metals | 5,620 |
| LTV | 5,425 |
| Bethlehem Steel | 4,013 |
| Amax | 3,703 |
| Inland Steel Ind. | 3,494 |
| Phelps Dodge | 2,594 |
| National Steel | 2,373 |
| Maxxam | 2,254 |
| Armco | 2,084 |

### Motor Vehicles and Parts

| | |
|---|---|
| General Motors | $132,775 |
| Ford Motor | 100,786 |
| Chrysler | 36,897 |
| TRW | 8,311 |
| Dana | 5,036 |
| Eaton | 4,109 |
| Navistar International | 3,892 |
| Varity | 3,186 |
| Paccar | 2,761 |
| Arvin Industries | 1,893 |

### Petroleum Refining

| | |
|---|---|
| Exxon | $103,547 |
| Mobil | 57,389 |
| Chevron | 37,464 |
| Texaco | 37,130 |
| Amoco | 25,543 |
| Shell Oil | 21,702 |
| Atlantic Richfield | 18,061 |
| USX | 16,186 |
| Phillips Petroleum | 11,933 |
| Coastal | 10,063 |

### Pharmaceuticals

| | |
|---|---|
| Johnson & Johnson | $13,846 |
| Bristol-Myers Squibb | 11,805 |
| Merck | 9,801 |
| Abbott Laboratories | 7,894 |
| American Home Products | 7,874 |
| Pfizer | 7,415 |
| Eli Lilly | 6,282 |
| Warner-Lambert | 5,598 |
| American Cyanamid | 5,348 |
| Rhône-Poulenc Rorer | 4,096 |

### Publishing & Printing

| | |
|---|---|
| R.R. Donnelley | $4,193 |
| Times Mirror | 3,702 |
| Gannett | 3,469 |
| Berkshire Hathaway | 3,029 |
| Reader's Digest | 2,667 |
| Knight-Ridder | 2,335 |
| Tribune | 2,109 |
| McGraw-Hill | 2,050 |
| Dow Jones | 1,825 |
| New York Times | 1,774 |

### Retailing[2]

| | |
|---|---|
| Sears Roebuck | $59,101 |
| Wal-Mart Stores | 55,484 |
| K Mart | 37,724 |
| Kroger | 22,145 |
| J.C. Penney | 19,085 |
| American Stores | 19,051 |
| Dayton Hudson | 17,927 |
| Safeway | 15,152 |
| Great Atlantic & Pacific Tea | 11,593 |
| May Department Stores | 11,170 |

### Rubber and Plastic Prods.

| | |
|---|---|
| Goodyear Tire | $11,924 |
| Premark International | 2,954 |
| Rubbermaid | 1,810 |
| M.A. Hanna | 1,338 |
| Cooper Tire & Rubber | 1,176 |
| Mark IV Industries | 1,146 |
| A. Schulman | 739 |
| Insilco | 725 |
| Standard Products | 658 |
| Bandag | 602 |

### Scientific and Photographic Equip.

| | |
|---|---|
| Eastman Kodak | $20,577 |
| Xerox | 18,261 |
| Minnesota Mining | 13,883 |
| Baxter International | 8,471 |
| Honeywell | 6,254 |
| Johnson Controls | 5,165 |
| EG&G | 2,789 |
| Becton Dickinson | 2,365 |
| Polaroid | 2,168 |
| Bausch & Lomb | 1,722 |

### Soaps, Cosmetics

| | |
|---|---|
| Procter & Gamble | $29,890 |
| Unilever U.S. | 9,217 |
| Colgate-Palmolive | 7,035 |
| Avon Products | 3,848 |
| Clorox | 1,717 |
| International Flavors | 1,126 |
| Alberto-Culver | 1,091 |
| Helene Curtis | 1,023 |
| Safety-Kleen | 796 |
| Stanhome | 744 |

### Textiles

| | |
|---|---|
| Collins & Aikman Group | $2,227 |
| Burlington Ind. Equity | 2,066 |
| Springs Industries | 1,976 |

| | | | | | |
|---|---|---|---|---|---|
| Shaw Industries | 1,751 | Mattel | 1,880 | Union Pacific | 7,294 |
| West Point-Pepperell | 1,500 | Tyco Toys | 769 | USAir Group | 6,696 |
| DWG | 1,279 | Fisher-Price | 696 | Continental Airlines | 5,575 |
| Amoskeag | 1,248 | **Transportation Equip.** | | **Utilities[1]** | |
| Unifi | 1,091 | Brunswick | $2,228 | GTE | $42,144 |
| JPS Textile Group | 852 | Coltec Industries | 1,369 | BellSouth | 31,463 |
| Cone Mills | 770 | Trinity Industries | 1,194 | Bell Atlantic | 28,100 |
| | | Harley-Davidson | 1,106 | US West | 27,964 |
| **Tobacco** | | Huffy | 704 | NYNEX | 27,714 |
| RJR Nabisco Holdings | $15,734 | Avondale Industries | 592 | Pacific Gas & Electric | 24,188 |
| American Brands | 8,840 | | | Southwestern Bell | 23,810 |
| Universal | 2,989 | **Transportation[3]** | | Ameritech | 22,818 |
| Standard Commercial | 1,185 | United Parcel Service | $16,541 | Pacific Telesis Group | 22,516 |
| Dibrell Brothers | 1,085 | AMR | 14,495 | Southern | 20,038 |
| UST | 1,013 | UAL | 12,890 | | |
| Brooke Group | 929 | Delta Air Lines | 10,837 | | |
| | | CSX | 8,734 | | |
| **Toys, Sporting Goods** | | Northwest Airlines | 7,964 | | |
| Hasbro | $2,541 | Federal Express | 7,550 | | |

(1) Millions of dollars of assets as of Dec. 31, 1992. (2) Incl. revenue from nonretailing activities. (3) Incl. revenue from nontransportation activities.

## U.S. Industrial Corporations with Largest Sales in 1992

Source: FORTUNE Magazine

(millions of dollars)

| Company, headquarters | Sales | Company, headquarters | Sales |
|---|---|---|---|
| General Motors, Detroit, Mich. | $132,775 | Chrysler, Highland Park, Mich. | $36,897 |
| Exxon, Irving, Tex. | 103,547 | Boeing, Seattle, Wash. | 30,184 |
| Ford Motor, Dearborn, Mich. | 100,786 | Procter & Gamble, Cincinnati, Oh. | 29,890 |
| IBM, Armonk, N.Y. | 65,096 | Amoco, Chicago, Ill. | 25,543 |
| General Electric, Fairfield, Conn. | 62,202 | Pepsico, Purchase, N.Y. | 22,084 |
| Mobil, Fairfax, Va. | 57,389 | United Technologies, Hartford, Conn. | 22,032 |
| Philip Morris, New York, N.Y. | 50,157 | Shell Oil, Houston, Tex. | 21,702 |
| E.I. du Pont de Nemours, Wilmington, Del. | 37,643 | Conagra, Omaha, Neb. | 21,219 |
| Chevron, San Francisco, Cal. | 37,464 | Eastman Kodak, Rochester, N.Y. | 20,577 |
| Texaco, White Plains, N.Y. | 37,130 | Dow Chemical, Midland, Mich. | 19,177 |

## Largest Corporate Mergers or Acquisitions in U.S.

(as of mid-1993)

| Company | Acquirer | Dollars | Year | Company | Acquirer | Dollars | Year |
|---|---|---|---|---|---|---|---|
| Tele-Communi-cations Inc., Liberty Media[1] [2] | Bell Atlantic | $33.0 bln. | 1993 | Borg-Warner | AV Holdings | 4.2 bln. | 1987 |
| | | | | Texasgulf | Elf Aquitaine | 4.2 bln. | 1981 |
| RJR Nabisco | Kohlberg Kravis Roberts | 24.9 bln. | 1988 | Cities Service | Occidental Petroleum | 4.0 bln. | 1982 |
| | | | | Security Pacific | BankAmerica | 4.0 bln. | 1991 |
| Warner Communica-tions | Time | 13.9 bln. | 1989 | Travelers[1] | Primerica | 4.0 bln.[4] | 1993 |
| | | | | Dome Petroleum | Amoco | 3.8 bln. | 1987 |
| Gulf Oil | Chevron | 13.3 bln. | 1984 | R.H. Macy | various investors | 3.7 bln. | 1986 |
| Kraft | Philip Morris | 13.1 bln. | 1988 | American Hospital | Baxter Travenol | 3.7 bln. | 1986 |
| McCaw Cellular[1] | AT&T | 12.6 bln. | 1993 | Owens-Illinois | Kohlberg Kravis Roberts | 3.6 bln. | 1987 |
| Squibb | Bristol-Myers | 11.5 bln. | 1989 | | | | |
| Getty Oil | Texaco | 10.1 bln. | 1984 | Belridge Oil | Shell Oil | 3.6 bln. | 1979 |
| Conoco | DuPont | 8.0 bln. | 1981 | NWA | Checchi Group | 3.6 bln. | 1988 |
| Standard Oil | British Petroleum | 7.9 bln.* | 1987 | Allied Stores | Campeau | 3.5 bln. | 1986 |
| Federated Dept. Stores | Campeau | 7.4 bln. | 1988 | Fort Howard Paper | Morgan Stanley Group | 3.5 bln. | 1988 |
| | | | | ABC Broadcasting | Capital Cities Comm. | 3.5 bln. | 1985 |
| NCR | AT&T | 7.4 bln. | 1991 | Columbia Pictures | Sony | 3.4 bln. | 1989 |
| MCA | Matsushita | 6.5 bln. | 1990 | Viacom | National Amusements | 3.4 bln. | 1987 |
| Marathon Oil | U.S. Steel | 6.5 bln. | 1981 | LIN Broadcasting | McCaw Cellular | 3.3 bln.[3] | 1989 |
| Contel | GTE | 6.2 bln. | 1990 | Panhandle Eastern | Texas Eastern | 3.2 bln. | 1989 |
| Beatrice | Kohlberg Kravis Roberts | 6.2 bln. | 1986 | Chesebrough-Ponds | Unilever N.V. | 3.1 bln. | 1987 |
| | | | | MidCon | Occidental Petroleum | 3.0 bln. | 1986 |
| RCA | General Electric | 6.2 bln. | 1986 | American Medical Intl. | IMA Holdings | 3.0 bln. | 1989 |
| Medco | Merck | 6.0 bln. | 1993 | Texas Oil and Gas | USX Corp. | 3.0 bln. | 1986 |
| Superior Oil | Mobil Oil | 5.7 bln. | 1984 | Emhart | Black & Decker | 2.8 bln. | 1989 |
| Pillsbury | Grand Metropolitan | 5.7 bln. | 1988 | Carnation | Nestle | 2.8 bln. | 1984 |
| General Foods | Philip Morris | 5.6 bln. | 1986 | Celanese | American Hoechst | 2.7 bln. | 1987 |
| Safeway Stores | Kohlberg Kravis Roberts | 5.3 bln. | 1986 | Esmark | Beatrice Foods | 2.7 bln. | 1984 |
| | | | | G.D. Searle | Monsanto | 2.7 bln. | 1986 |
| Farmers Group | B.A.T. Industries | 5.2 bln. | 1988 | Continental Group | Kiewit-Murdock | 2.7 bln. | 1984 |
| Southern Pacific | Santa Fe Railroad | 5.2 bln. | 1983 | St. Joe Minerals | Fluor | 2.6 bln. | 1981 |
| Southland | J.T. Acquisition | 5.1 bln. | 1987 | Electronic Data Systems | General Motors | 2.6 bln. | 1984 |
| Hughes Aircraft | General Motors | 5.0 bln. | 1985 | Firestone Tire | Bridgestone | 2.6 bln. | 1988 |
| Nabisco | R.J. Reynolds | 4.9 bln. | 1985 | Macmillan | Maxwell Comm. | 2.6 bln. | 1988 |
| Signal Cos. | Allied Corp. | 4.9 bln. | 1986 | Associated Dry Goods | May Dept. Stores | 2.5 bln. | 1986 |
| Sperry | Burroughs | 4.8 bln. | 1986 | | | | |
| Connecticut General | INA | 4.3 bln. | 1981 | | | | |

* For the 45% of Standard Oil that British Petroleum did not already own. (1) Proposed. (2) Includes $10 billion in assumed debt. (3) For about 42% of LIN's shares. (4) For the 73% of Travelers that Primerica did not already own.

## Fastest Growing Franchises in 1992[1]

Source: *Entrepreneur* magazine

| Company | Business | Minimum start-up cost[2] | Company | Business | Minimum start-up cost[2] |
|---|---|---|---|---|---|
| Subway | submarine sandwiches | $38,000 | Jazzercise Inc. | fitness centers | $2,000 |
| 7-Eleven Convenience Stores | convenience stores | 12,500 | Worldwide Refinishing Systems Inc. | porcelain, marble restoration | 6,500 |
| Jani-King | commercial cleaning | 1,500 | | | |
| Burger King Corp. | hamburgers | 274,400 | Travelodge | hotels and motels | 500,000 |
| Dunkin' Donuts | donuts | 175,000 | Merry Maids | residential cleaning | 7,500 |
| McDonald's | hamburgers | varies | Futurekids Inc. | computer learning centers | 19,600 |
| Coverall North America Inc. | commercial cleaning | 350 | | | |
| CleanNet | commercial cleaning | 0 | GNC Franchising Inc. | health food, vitamin stores | 37,700 |
| Little Caesars Pizza | pizza | 170,000 | | | |
| Mail Boxes Etc. | packaging, mailing, and shipping services | 27,700 | Play It Again Sports | sports equipment and apparel | 68,000 |
| Chem-Dry | carpet, upholstery, and drapery services | 6,600 | H & R Block | income tax services | 5,000 |
| | | | Howard Johnson Franchise Sys. Inc. | hotels and motels | varies |
| Domino's Pizza Inc. | pizza | 76,500 | Decorating Den | miscellaneous decorative products and services | 8,600 |
| O.P.E.N. Cleaning Systems | commercial cleaning | 500 | | | |
| Miracle Ear | health-care equipment | 35,000 | | | |
| Choice Hotels Int'l. | hotels and motels | 1,500,000 | | | |
| MicroAge Computer Centers Inc. | misc. computer-related products and services | 56,000 | Re/Max Int'l. Inc. | real estate services | 50,000 |
| | | | Valet Park | miscellaneous services | 3,750 |
| Blockbuster Video | videocassette rentals | 365,000 | Super 8 Motels Inc. | hotels and motels | 150,000 |

(1) Based on the number of new franchise units added. (2) Not including franchise fee, which varies.

## Largest U.S. Black-Owned Companies in 1992

Source: *Black Enterprise* Magazine

| Company (Business) | Location | Sales (millions) | Company (Business) | Location | Sales (millions) |
|---|---|---|---|---|---|
| TLC Beatrice International Holdings (food distributor and processor, primarily in Europe) | New York, N.Y. | $1,665.0 | Pavilion Lincoln-Mercury | Austin, Tex. | $223.8 |
| | | | H. J. Russell and Co. (construction) | Altanta, Ga. | 145.6 |
| Johnson Publishing Co. (Ebony, Jet) | Chicago, Ill. | 274.2 | Mel Farr Automotive Group (Ford and Toyota) | Oak Park, Mich. | 118.0 |
| Philadelphia Coca-Cola Bottling Co. | Philadelphia, Pa. | 266.0 | | | |
| Trainer Oldsmobile-Cadillac-Pontiac-GM Truck | Warner Robins, Ga. | 254.6 | S and J Enterprises (Ford and Subaru) | Charlotte, N.C. | 112.2 |
| Shack-Woods and Associates (Ford and Volkswagen) | Long Beach, Cal. | 228.3 | Anderson-Dubose Co. (food distributor) | Solon, Ohio | 110.0 |

## Capital Gains Tax

Source: U.S. Chamber of Commerce

The following shows how the top effective tax rate on capital gains has changed since 1960.

| Year | Effective rate (percent) | Year | Effective rate (percent) | Year | Effective rate (percent) | Year | Effective rate (percent) |
|---|---|---|---|---|---|---|---|
| 1960 | 25.0 | 1971 | 34.4 | 1979 | 28.0 | 1988 | 33.0 |
| 1968 | 26.9 | 1972 | 45.5 | 1981 | 20.0 | 1991 | 28.0 |
| 1969 | 27.5 | 1976 | 49.1 | 1987 | 28.0 | | |
| 1970 | 32.2 | | | | | | |

## Global Stock Markets

Source: Morgan Stanley Capital International Perspective

(in local currencies)

| Index[1] | Aug. 26, 1993 | 52-week Range | Index[1] | Aug. 26, 1993 | 52-week Range |
|---|---|---|---|---|---|
| **The World** | 456.7 | 456.9- 367.3 | Italy | 533.0 | 533.0- 266.0 |
| E.A.F.E.[2] | 566.3 | 570.2- 427.6 | Japan | 962.5 | 982.3- 719.1 |
| Australia | 400.3 | 400.3- 289.8 | Malaysia | 289.9 | 289.9- 181.8 |
| Austria | 427.1 | 427.1- 315.6 | Netherlands | 418.6 | 422.2- 318.4 |
| Belgium | 458.0 | 469.5- 358.1 | New Zealand | 99.2 | 100.8- 62.3 |
| Canada | 421.5 | 422.7- 355.5 | Norway | 748.5 | 782.3- 461.4 |
| Denmark | 768.8 | 795.7- 556.5 | Singapore | 974.7 | 974.7- 718.3 |
| Finland | 109.0 | 114.0- 37.5 | Spain | 264.8 | 264.8- 144.9 |
| France | 638.2 | 638.2- 471.0 | Sweden | 1,640.6 | 1,763.0- 787.2 |
| Germany | 281.1 | 285.1- 213.1 | Switzerland | 311.5 | 314.1- 216.1 |
| Hong Kong | 5,172.1 | 5,294.1- 3,589.8 | United Kingdom | 934.2 | 934.8- 677.1 |
| Ireland | 178.8 | 181.0- 104.4 | United States | 431.7 | 431.7- 376.7 |

(1) Base: Jan. 1, 1970 = 100. (2) Europe, Australia, Far East Index.

## Foreign Exchange Rates: 1970 to 1992

Source: International Monetary Fund

(National currency units per dollar except as indicated; data are annual averages)

| Year | Australia[1] (dollar) | Austria (schilling) | Belgium (franc) | Canada (dollar) | Denmark (krone) | France (franc) | Germany[2] (deutsche mark) | Greece (drachma) |
|---|---|---|---|---|---|---|---|---|
| 1970 | 1.1136 | 25.880 | 49.680 | 1.0103 | 7.489 | 5.5200 | 3.6480 | 30.00 |
| 1975 | 1.3077 | 17.443 | 36.799 | 1.0175 | 5.748 | 4.2876 | 2.4613 | 32.29 |
| 1980 | 1.1400 | 12.945 | 29.237 | 1.1693 | 5.634 | 4.2250 | 1.8175 | 42.62 |
| 1984 | .8794 | 20.009 | 57.784 | 1.2951 | 10.357 | 8.7391 | 2.8454 | 112.73 |
| 1985 | .7003 | 20.690 | 59.378 | 1.3655 | 10.596 | 8.9852 | 2.9440 | 138.12 |
| 1987 | .7009 | 12.643 | 37.334 | 1.3260 | 6.840 | 6.0107 | 1.7974 | 135.43 |
| 1988 | .7842 | 12.243 | 36.768 | 1.2307 | 6.732 | 5.9569 | 1.7562 | 141.89 |
| 1989 | .7925 | 13.231 | 39.404 | 1.1840 | 7.310 | 6.3801 | 1.8800 | 162.42 |
| 1990 | .7813 | 11.370 | 33.418 | 1.1668 | 6.189 | 5.4453 | 1.6157 | 158.51 |
| 1991 | .7791 | 11.676 | 34.148 | 1.1457 | 6.396 | 5.6421 | 1.6595 | 182.27 |
| 1992 | .7353 | 10.989 | 32.150 | 1.2087 | 6.036 | 5.2938 | 1.5617 | 190.62 |

| Year | India (rupee) | Ireland[1] (pound) | Italy (lira) | Japan (yen) | Malaysia (ringgit) | Netherlands (guilder) | Norway (kroner) | Portugal (escudo) |
|---|---|---|---|---|---|---|---|---|
| 1970 | 7.576 | 2.3959 | 623 | 357.60 | 3.0900 | 3.5970 | 7.1400 | 28.75 |
| 1975 | 8.409 | 2.2216 | 653 | 296.78 | 2.4030 | 2.5293 | 5.2282 | 25.51 |
| 1980 | 7.887 | 2.0577 | 856 | 226.63 | 2.1767 | 1.9875 | 4.9381 | 50.08 |
| 1984 | 11.363 | 1.0871 | 1,756 | 237.52 | 2.3436 | 3.2087 | 8.1615 | 146.39 |
| 1985 | 12.369 | 1.0656 | 1,909 | 238.54 | 2.4830 | 3.3214 | 8.5972 | 170.39 |
| 1987 | 12.962 | 1.4881 | 1,296 | 144.64 | 2.5196 | 2.0257 | 6.7375 | 140.88 |
| 1988 | 13.917 | 1.5261 | 1,301 | 128.15 | 2.6188 | 1.9766 | 6.5170 | 143.95 |
| 1989 | 16.226 | 1.4190 | 1,372 | 137.96 | 2.7088 | 2.1207 | 6.9045 | 157.46 |
| 1990 | 17.504 | 1.6585 | 1,198 | 144.79 | 2.7048 | 1.8209 | 6.2597 | 142.55 |
| 1991 | 22.742 | 1.6155 | 1,240 | 134.71 | 2.7501 | 1.8697 | 6.4829 | 144.48 |
| 1992 | 25.918 | 1.7053 | 1,232 | 126.65 | 2.5474 | 1.7885 | 6.2145 | 135.00 |

| Year | Singapore (dollar) | South Korea (won) | Spain (peseta) | Sweden (krona) | Switzerland (franc) | Thailand (baht) | United[1] Kingdom (pound) |
|---|---|---|---|---|---|---|---|
| 1970 | 3.0800 | 310.57 | 69.72 | 5.1700 | 4.3160 | 21.000 | 2.3959 |
| 1975 | 2.3713 | 484.00 | 57.43 | 4.1530 | 2.5839 | 20.379 | 2.2216 |
| 1980 | 2.1412 | 607.43 | 71.76 | 4.2309 | 1.6772 | 20.476 | 2.3243 |
| 1984 | 2.1331 | 805.69 | 160.78 | 8.2718 | 2.3497 | 23.639 | 1.3366 |
| 1985 | 2.2002 | 870.02 | 170.04 | 8.6039 | 2.4571 | 27.159 | 1.2963 |
| 1987 | 2.1059 | 822.57 | 123.48 | 6.3404 | 1.4912 | 25.723 | 1.6389 |
| 1988 | 2.0124 | 731.57 | 116.49 | 6.1272 | 1.4633 | 25.294 | 1.7813 |
| 1989 | 1.9508 | 671.46 | 118.38 | 6.4469 | 1.6359 | 25.702 | 1.6897 |
| 1990 | 1.8125 | 707.76 | 101.93 | 5.9188 | 1.3892 | 25.585 | 1.7847 |
| 1991 | 1.7276 | 733.35 | 103.91 | 6.0475 | 1.4340 | 25.517 | 1.7694 |
| 1992 | 1.6290 | 780.65 | 102.38 | 5.8238 | 1.4062 | 25.400 | 1.7655 |

(1) Value of one unit of foreign currency in dollars. (2) W. Germany prior to 1991.

## Foreign Direct Investment[1] in the U.S. by Selected Countries

Source: Bureau of Economic Analysis; U.S. Dept. of Commerce

(millions of dollars)

| | 1991 | 1992 | | 1991 | 1992 |
|---|---|---|---|---|---|
| All countries[2] | $414,358 | $419,526 | Mexico | $708 | $1,184 |
| Canada | 37,301 | 36,997 | Panama | 4,841 | 4,732 |
| Europe[2] | 251,248 | 248,461 | Venezuela | 538 | 502 |
| Austria | 488 | 387 | Other Western Hemisphere[2] | 10,646 | 11,518 |
| Belgium | 3,089 | 4,066 | Bahamas | 1,194 | 989 |
| Denmark | 1,301 | 1,308 | Bermuda | 1,261 | 1,577 |
| Finland | 1,305 | 1,385 | Middle East[2] | 4,771 | 4,813 |
| France | 24,155 | 23,808 | Israel | 1,147 | 1,131 |
| Germany | 28,618 | 29,205 | Kuwait | 1,891 | 1,893 |
| Ireland | 1,823 | 2,273 | Saudi Arabia | 1,598 | 1,642 |
| Italy | 2,705 | 571 | United Arab Emirates | 99 | 121 |
| Netherlands | 59,355 | 61,341 | Asia and Pacific[2] | 102,730 | 107,725 |
| Spain | 1,155 | 1,290 | Australia | 6,083 | 7,140 |
| Sweden | 5,684 | 6,923 | Hong Kong | 1,763 | 1,714 |
| Switzerland | 19,189 | 19,562 | Japan | 92,896 | 96,743 |
| United Kingdom | 100,386 | 94,718 | Singapore | 870 | 847 |
| South and Central America[2] | 7,020 | 7,378 | Taiwan | 1,142 | 1,154 |
| Brazil | 478 | 502 | | | |

(1) The book value of foreign direct investors' equity in, and net outstanding loans to, their U.S. affiliates. A U.S. affiliate is a U.S. business enterprise in which a single foreign direct investor owns at least 10 percent of the voting securities or the equivalent. (2) Totals include countries not shown.

## U.S. International Transactions

Source: Bureau of Economic Analysis, U.S. Dept. of Commerce

(millions of dollars)

| | 1965 | 1970 | 1975 | 1980 | 1985 | 1990 | 1991 | 1992 |
|---|---|---|---|---|---|---|---|---|
| **Exports of goods, services, and income**[1] | $42,722 | $68,387 | $157,936 | $344,440 | $380,051 | $680,890 | $708,489 | $730,460 |
| Merchandise, adjusted, excluding military[2] | 26,461 | 42,469 | 107,088 | 224,250 | 215,915 | 388,705 | 416,937 | 440,138 |
| Services | 8,824 | 14,171 | 25,497 | 47,584 | 73,026 | 148,638 | 164,260 | 179,710 |
| Income receipts on U.S. assets abroad: | 7,437 | 11,748 | 25,351 | 71,388 | 82,282 | 143,547 | 127,292 | 110,612 |
| **Imports of goods, services, and income** | -32,708 | -59,901 | -33,745 | -333,774 | -473,998 | -738,401 | -723,388 | -763,965 |
| Merchandise, adjusted, excluding military[2] | -21,510 | -39,866 | -98,185 | -249,750 | -338,088 | -497,558 | -490,739 | -536,276 |
| Services | -9,111 | -14,520 | -4,795 | -21,996 | -41,491 | -116,583 | -118,378 | -123,299 |
| Income payments on foreign assets in the U.S. | -2,088 | -5,515 | -12,564 | -45,532 | -67,875 | -124,261 | -114,272 | -104,391 |
| **Unilateral transfers, net** | -4,583 | -6,156 | -7,075 | -8,349 | -22,950 | -32,916 | 6,575 | -32,895 |
| **U.S. assets abroad, net (increase/capital outflow [-])** | -5,716 | -9,337 | -39,703 | -86,967 | -34,069 | -56,321 | -59,974 | -50,961 |
| U.S. official reserve assets, net | 1,225 | 2,481 | -849 | -8,155 | -3,858 | -2,158 | 5,763 | 3,901 |
| U.S. Government assets, other than official reserve assets, net | -1,605 | -1,589 | -3,474 | -5,162 | -2,821 | -2,304 | 2,905 | -1,609 |
| U.S. private assets, net | -5,336 | -10,229 | -35,380 | -73,651 | -27,391 | -56,467 | -68,643 | -53,253 |
| **Foreign assets in U.S., net (increase/capital inflow [+])** | 742 | 6,359 | 15,670 | 58,112 | 130,012 | 99,379 | 83,439 | 129,579 |
| Statistical discrepancy (sum of above items with sign reversed) | -457 | -219 | 5,917 | 25,386 | 24,825 | 47,370 | -15,140 | -12,216 |
| **Memorandum:** | | | | | | | | |
| Balance on current account | 5,431 | 2,331 | 18,116 | 2,317 | -121,721 | -90,428 | -8,324 | -66,400 |

(1) Excludes transfers of goods and services under U.S. military grant programs. (2) Excludes exports of goods under U.S. military agency sales contracts identified in Census export documents, excludes imports of goods under direct defense expenditures identified in Census import documents, and reflects various other adjustments.

## North American Free Trade Agreement

The United States, Canada, and Mexico announced a comprehensive plan for free trade across North America on Aug. 12, 1992, and portrayed it as an opportunity for greater economic growth for all three nations. The North American Free Trade Agreement (NAFTA) was greeted enthusiastically by business groups generally, but U.S. labor unions, long opposed to opening the southern border, contended that the accord would send jobs to Mexico, where labor costs were lower and environmental regulations laxer than in the United States.

The three countries attempted to satisfy some of the NAFTA opposition by concluding side agreements, announced on Aug. 13, 1993. These additional agreements called for the establishment of a 5-step procedure to enforce existing labor and environmental laws in the U.S., Canada, and Mexico. Secretariats to process, investigate, and enforce this procedure would be established, one in Canada to handle environmental complaints and the other in Washington to deal with labor issues. Failure to comply with a decision of a secretariat could result in fines of up to $20 million on national governments and limited trade sanctions. The side agreements were signed (separately) by Canada on Sept. 13, 1993, and by the U.S. and Mexico on Sept. 14, 1993.

NAFTA would bring together 360 million consumers in a $6.6 trillion market and would create the world's richest and largest trading bloc. The agreement must be ratified by the legislatures of the three nations. Canada ratified the agreement June 23, 1993. The Clinton administration said, after conclusion of the side agreements, that it would submit NAFTA to Congress for approval.

### Key Provisions

**Agriculture**—Tariffs on all farm products would be eliminated over 15 years. All three countries agreed to allow domestic price-support systems, provided that they did not distort trade.

**Automobiles**—After eight years, at least 62.5% of an automobile's value must have been produced in North America for it to qualify for duty-free status. Tariffs would be phased out over 10 years.

**Banking**—U.S. and Canadian banks would be allowed to acquire Mexican banks accounting for as much as 8 percent of the industry's capital. All limits on bank ownership would end Jan. 1, 2000.

**Disputes**—Special judges would be empaneled to resolve disagreements.

**Energy**—Mexico would not alter its constitution, which prohibited foreign ownership of its oil fields, but after 10 years U.S. and Canadian companies would be allowed to bid on all contracts offered by Mexican oil and electricity monopolies.

**Environment**—The agreement could not be used to override national and state environmental, health or safety laws.

**Immigration**—All three countries would ease restrictions on the movement of business executives and professionals.

**Jobs**—Visa restrictions would be reduced for business executives and professionals. Current barriers designed to limit Mexican migration to the U.S. would remain in force.

**Patent and Copyright protection**—Mexico would strengthen its laws providing protection to intellectual property. It would honor foreign patents for pharmaceuticals for 20 years.

**Textiles**—A strict "rule of origin" provision would require garments to be made from yarn and fabric also produced in North America. Tariffs would be phased out over five years.

**Tariffs**—Tariffs on 10,000 customs goods would be eliminated over 15 years. One-half of U.S. exports to Mexico would be considered duty-free within five years.

**Trucking**—Trucks would be allowed free access on cross-border routes and throughout the three countries by the end of 1999.

## National Income by Industry

Source: Bureau of Economic Analysis, U.S. Dept. of Commerce

(billions of dollars)

| | 1960 | 1970 | 1975 | 1980 | 1990 | 1991 | 1992 |
|---|---|---|---|---|---|---|---|
| National income without capital consumption adjustment | $428.6 | $835.1 | $1,315.0 | $2,263.9 | $4,497.5 | $4,587.5 | $4,769.0 |
| Domestic industries | 425.1 | 827.8 | 1,297.4 | 2,216.3 | 4,486.7 | 4,570.1 | 4,757.7 |
| Private industries | 371.6 | 695.4 | 1,088.3 | 1,894.5 | 3,828.9 | 3,870.6 | 4,029.3 |
| Agriculture, forestry, fisheries | 17.8 | 25.9 | 46.5 | 61.4 | 97.1 | 90.9 | 95.6 |
| Mining | 5.6 | 8.4 | 21.2 | 43.8 | 38.1 | 36.7 | 36.1 |
| Construction | 22.5 | 47.4 | 69.9 | 126.6 | 234.4 | 210.1 | 219.6 |
| Manufacturing | 125.3 | 215.6 | 317.5 | 532.1 | 846.9 | 841.0 | 873.8 |
| Durable goods | 73.4 | 127.7 | 185.0 | 313.7 | 484.3 | 464.2 | 480.5 |
| Nondurable goods | 52.0 | 87.9 | 132.5 | 218.4 | 362.6 | 376.7 | 393.5 |
| Transportation, public utilities | 35.8 | 64.4 | 101.1 | 177.3 | 328.7 | 335.2 | 337.2 |
| Transportation | 18.5 | 31.5 | 48.0 | 85.8 | 139.4 | 140.8 | 144.8 |
| Communications | 8.2 | 17.6 | 26.8 | 48.1 | 96.4 | 95.3 | 98.6 |
| Electric, gas, and sanitary services | 9.1 | 86.8 | 90.2 | 43.4 | 92.9 | 99.0 | 93.9 |
| Wholesale trade | 25.0 | 47.5 | 83.0 | 143.3 | 263.6 | 266.0 | 272.9 |
| Retail trade | 41.3 | 79.9 | 123.1 | 189.4 | 392.1 | 403.3 | 418.3 |
| Finance, insurance, and real estate | 51.3 | 96.4 | 143.9 | 279.5 | 679.8 | 685.0 | 703.2 |
| Services | 46.9 | 109.8 | 182.1 | 341.0 | 948.3 | 1,002.4 | 1,072.5 |
| Government | 53.5 | 132.4 | 209.1 | 321.8 | 657.9 | 699.4 | 728.4 |

## National Income by Type of Income

Source: Bureau of Economic Analysis, U.S. Dept. of Commerce

(billions of dollars)

| | 1960 | 1970 | 1975 | 1980 | 1990 | 1991 | 1992 |
|---|---|---|---|---|---|---|---|
| National income[1] | $424.9 | $832.6 | $1,289.1 | $2,203.5 | $4,459.6 | $4,544.2 | $4,743.4 |
| Compensation of employees | 296.7 | 618.3 | 948.7 | 1,638.2 | 3,290.3 | 3,390.8 | 3,525.2 |
| Wages and salaries | 272.8 | 551.5 | 814.7 | 1,372.0 | 2,738.9 | 2,812.2 | 2,916.6 |
| Government | 49.2 | 117.1 | 176.1 | 260.1 | 514.0 | 543.5 | 562.5 |
| Other | 223.7 | 434.3 | 638.6 | 1,111.8 | 2,224.9 | 2,268.7 | 2,354.1 |
| Supplements to wages, salary | 23.8 | 66.8 | 134.0 | 266.3 | 551.4 | 578.7 | 608.6 |
| Employer contrib. for social ins. | 12.6 | 34.3 | 68.0 | 127.9 | 277.3 | 290.4 | 302.9 |
| Other labor income | 11.2 | 32.5 | 65.9 | 138.4 | 274.0 | -288.3 | 305.7 |
| Proprietors' income | 52.1 | 80.2 | 124.4 | 180.7 | 373.2 | 368.0 | 404.5 |
| Farm | 11.6 | 14.7 | 25.4 | 20.5 | 42.5 | 35.8 | 39.5 |
| Nonfarm | 40.5 | 65.4 | 100.0 | 160.1 | 330.7 | 332.2 | 364.9 |
| Rental income of persons with capital consump. adjust. | 15.3 | 18.2 | 13.5 | 6.6 | -12.9 | -10.4 | 4.7 |
| Corp. profits with inventory adjustment | 49.8 | 69.5 | 123.9 | 194.0 | 319.0 | 346.3 | 393.8 |
| Corp. profits before tax | 49.9 | 76.0 | 134.8 | 237.1 | 332.3 | 334.7 | 371.6 |
| Corp. profits tax liability | 22.7 | 34.4 | 50.9 | 84.8 | 135.3 | 124.0 | 140.2 |
| Corp. profits after tax | 27.2 | 41.7 | 83.9 | 152.3 | 197.0 | 210.7 | 231.4 |
| Dividends | 12.9 | 22.5 | 29.6 | 54.7 | 133.7 | 146.5 | 149.3 |
| Undistributed profits | 14.3 | 19.2 | 54.3 | 97.6 | 63.3 | 64.2 | 82.1 |
| Inventory valuation adjustment | -.2 | -6.6 | -11.0 | -43.1 | -14.2 | 3.1 | -7.4 |
| Net interest | 11.3 | 41.2 | 83.8 | 200.9 | 490.1 | 449.5 | 415.2 |

(1) National income is the aggregate of labor and property earnings that arises in the current production of goods and services. It is the sum of employee compensation, proprietors' income, rental income, corporate profits, and net interest. It measures the total factor costs of the goods and services produced by the economy. Income is measured before deduction of taxes on income.

## Distribution of Total Personal Income[1]

Source: Bureau of Economic Analysis; U.S. Dept. of Commerce

(billions of dollars)

| Year | Personal income | Personal taxes | Disposable Personal income | Personal outlays | Personal Savings Amount | Personal Savings As pct. of disposable income |
|---|---|---|---|---|---|---|
| 1960 | $ 402.3 | $ 50.4 | $ 352.0 | $ 332.3 | $ 19.7 | 5.6% |
| 1965 | 540.7 | 64.9 | 475.8 | 442.1 | 33.7 | 7.1 |
| 1970 | 811.1 | 115.8 | 695.3 | 639.5 | 55.8 | 8.0 |
| 1975 | 1,265.0 | 168.9 | 1,096.1 | 1,001.8 | 94.3 | 8.6 |
| 1980 | 2,165.3 | 336.5 | 1,828.9 | 1,718.7 | 110.2 | 6.0 |
| 1981 | 2,429.5 | 387.7 | 2,041.7 | 1,904.3 | 137.4 | 6.7 |
| 1982 | 2,584.6 | 404.1 | 2,180.5 | 2,044.5 | 136.0 | 6.2 |
| 1983 | 2,838.6 | 410.5 | 2,428.1 | 2,297.4 | 130.6 | 5.4 |
| 1984 | 3,108.7 | 440.2 | 2,668.6 | 2,504.5 | 164.1 | 6.1 |
| 1985 | 3,325.3 | 486.6 | 2,838.7 | 2,713.3 | 125.4 | 4.4 |
| 1986 | 3,526.2 | 512.9 | 3,013.3 | 2,888.5 | 124.9 | 4.1 |
| 1987 | 3,776.6 | 571.7 | 3,205.9 | 3,104.1 | 101.8 | 3.2 |
| 1988 | 4,070.8 | 591.6 | 3,479.2 | 3,333.6 | 145.6 | 4.2 |
| 1989 | 4,384.3 | 658.8 | 3,725.5 | 3,553.7 | 171.8 | 4.6 |
| 1990 | 4,679.8 | 621.0 | 4,058.8 | 3,853.1 | 205.8 | 5.1 |
| 1991 | 4,828.4 | 618.7 | 4,209.6 | 4,009.9 | 199.6 | 4.7 |
| 1992 | 5,058.1 | 627.3 | 4,430.6 | 4,218.1 | 212.6 | 4.8 |

(1) Figures may not add because of rounding.

## U.S. Direct Investment[1] Abroad in Selected Countries

Source: Bureau of Economic Analysis, U.S. Dept. of Commerce

(millions of dollars)

| | 1990 | 1991 | 1992 |
|---|---|---|---|
| All countries | $424,096 | $460,955 | $486,670 |
| Africa | | | |
| Egypt | 1,465 | 1,239 | 922 |
| Nigeria | 161 | 611 | 274 |
| S. Africa | 956 | 857 | 871 |
| Asia and Pacific (excl. Japan) | | | |
| China | — | 431 | 469 |
| Hong Kong | 6,187 | 6,516 | 8,544 |
| India | 513 | 410 | 479 |
| Indonesia | 3,226 | 3,783 | 4,278 |
| Malaysia | 1,384 | 1,711 | 1,714 |
| Philippines | 1,629 | 1,377 | 1,565 |
| Singapore | 3,385 | 5,294 | 6,631 |
| South Korea | 2,178 | 2,862 | 2,779 |
| Taiwan | 2,014 | 2,626 | 2,870 |
| Thailand | 1,585 | 2,038 | 2,459 |
| Australia | 14,846 | 15,795 | 16,697 |
| Bermuda | 21,737 | 23,059 | 25,799 |
| Canada | 67,033 | 68,853 | 68,432 |
| European Communities | | | |
| Belgium | 9,050 | 10,607 | 10,771 |
| Denmark | 1,597 | 1,813 | 1,707 |
| France | 18,874 | 20,798 | 23,257 |
| Germany | 27,259 | 34,027 | 35,393 |
| Greece | 288 | 363 | 429 |
| Ireland | 6,880 | 6,634 | 7,229 |
| Italy | 13,117 | 14,775 | 13,605 |
| Luxembourg | 1,390 | 1,782 | 1,863 |
| Netherlands | 22,658 | 19,772 | 19,114 |
| Portugal | 598 | 1,026 | 1,160 |
| Spain | 7,704 | 7,992 | 8,165 |
| United Kingdom | 68,224 | 78,072 | 77,842 |
| Other Europe | | | |
| Austria | 889 | 1,258 | 1,365 |
| Finland | 551 | 359 | 322 |
| Norway | 3,815 | 4,349 | 4,047 |
| Sweden | 1,600 | 2,242 | 2,033 |
| Switzerland | 25,199 | 25,604 | 28,662 |
| Turkey | 494 | 529 | 705 |
| Japan | 20,997 | 24,938 | 26,213 |
| South America | | | |
| Argentina | 2,956 | 2,767 | 3,353 |
| Brazil | 14,918 | 14,882 | 16,114 |
| Chile | 1,368 | 1,916 | 2,446 |
| Colombia | 1,728 | 1,627 | 2,077 |
| Ecuador | 387 | 296 | 310 |
| Peru | 410 | 522 | 466 |
| Venezuela | 1,490 | 1,424 | 1,725 |
| Central America | | | |
| Mexico | 9,398 | 12,257 | 13,330 |
| Panama | 7,409 | 10,427 | 11,457 |
| Middle East | | | |
| Israel | 756 | 1,014 | 1,543 |
| Saudi Arabia | 1,981 | 2,163 | 2,503 |
| United Arab Emirates | 519 | 466 | 480 |

(1) The book value of U.S. direct investors' equity in, and net outstanding loans to, their foreign affiliates. A foreign affiliate is a foreign business enterprise in which a single U.S. investor owns at least 10% of the voting securities or the equivalent.

## Gold Reserves of Central Banks and Governments

Source: IMF, *International Financial Statistics*; million fine troy ounces

| Year end | All countries[1] | United States | Canada | Japan | Belgium | France | Germany | Italy | Netherlands | Switzerland | United Kingdom |
|---|---|---|---|---|---|---|---|---|---|---|---|
| 1975 | 1,018.71 | 274.71 | 21.95 | 21.11 | 42.17 | 100.93 | 117.61 | 82.48 | 54.33 | 83.20 | 21.03 |
| 1976 | 1,014.23 | 274.68 | 21.62 | 21.11 | 42.17 | 101.02 | 117.61 | 82.48 | 54.33 | 83.28 | 21.03 |
| 1977 | 1,029.19 | 277.55 | 22.01 | 21.62 | 42.45 | 101.67 | 118.30 | 82.91 | 54.63 | 83.28 | 22.23 |
| 1978 | 1,036.82 | 276.41 | 22.13 | 23.97 | 42.59 | 101.99 | 118.64 | 83.12 | 54.78 | 83.28 | 22.83 |
| 1979 | 944.44 | 264.60 | 22.18 | 24.23 | 34.21 | 81.92 | 95.25 | 66.71 | 43.97 | 83.28 | 18.25 |
| 1980 | 952.99 | 264.32 | 20.98 | 24.23 | 34.18 | 81.85 | 95.18 | 66.67 | 43.94 | 83.28 | 18.84 |
| 1981 | 953.72 | 264.11 | 20.46 | 24.23 | 34.18 | 81.85 | 95.18 | 66.67 | 43.94 | 83.28 | 19.03 |
| 1982 | 949.16 | 264.03 | 20.26 | 24.23 | 34.18 | 81.85 | 95.18 | 66.67 | 43.94 | 83.28 | 19.01 |
| 1983 | 947.84 | 263.39 | 20.17 | 24.23 | 34.18 | 81.85 | 95.18 | 66.67 | 43.94 | 83.28 | 19.03 |
| 1984 | 946.79 | 262.79 | 20.14 | 24.23 | 34.18 | 81.85 | 95.18 | 66.67 | 43.94 | 83.28 | 19.03 |
| 1985 | 949.39 | 262.65 | 20.11 | 24.33 | 34.18 | 81.85 | 95.18 | 66.67 | 43.94 | 83.28 | 19.03 |
| 1986 | 949.11 | 262.04 | 19.72 | 24.23 | 34.18 | 81.85 | 95.18 | 66.67 | 43.94 | 83.28 | 19.01 |
| 1987 | 944.49 | 262.38 | 18.52 | 24.23 | 33.63 | 81.85 | 95.18 | 66.67 | 43.94 | 83.28 | 19.01 |
| 1988 | 944.92 | 261.87 | 17.14 | 24.23 | 33.67 | 81.85 | 95.18 | 66.67 | 43.94 | 83.28 | 19.00 |
| 1989 | 938.95 | 261.93 | 16.10 | 24.23 | 30.23 | 81.85 | 95.18 | 66.67 | 43.94 | 83.28 | 18.99 |
| 1990 | 940.29 | 261.91 | 14.76 | 24.23 | 30.23 | 81.85 | 95.18 | 66.67 | 43.94 | 83.28 | 18.94 |
| 1991 | 939.58 | 261.91 | 12.96 | 24.23 | 30.23 | 81.85 | 95.18 | 66.67 | 43.94 | 83.28 | 18.89 |
| 1992 | 930.30 | 261.91 | 9.94 | 24.23 | 25.04 | 81.85 | 95.18 | 66.67 | 43.94 | 83.28 | 18.61 |

(1) Covers IMF members with reported gold holdings. For countries not listed above, see *International Financial Statistics*, a monthly publication of the International Monetary Fund.

## Industrial Production Indexes,[1] by Industry Groups

Source: Bureau of Economic Analysis, U.S. Dept. of Commerce; billions of dollars

| Industry Groups | 1991 | 1992 | May 1993 |
|---|---|---|---|
| Mining | 100.4 | 97.6 | 96.9 |
| Metal mining | 156.7 | 161.8 | 163.8 |
| Coal | 109.3 | 105.5 | 106.0 |
| Oil and gas extraction | 96.0 | 92.6 | 91.4 |
| Crude oil | 89.1 | 85.7 | 82.6 |
| Natural gas | 107.0 | 106.7 | ..... |
| Stone and earth minerals | 94.2 | 93.8 | 94.6 |
| Utilities | 111.9 | 111.9 | 113.4 |
| Electric | 112.7 | 111.6 | 112.7 |
| Gas | 109.0 | 112.9 | 116.2 |
| Manufacturing | 103.7 | 106.9 | 111.4 |
| Durable | 103.9 | 108.2 | 114.8 |
| Lumber and products | 90.5 | 96.4 | 98.1 |
| Furniture and fixtures | 94.0 | 98.9 | 106.9 |
| Clay, glass, and stone products | 92.6 | 95.9 | 99.5 |
| Primary metals | 98.5 | 101.2 | 106.5 |
| Iron and steel | 100.7 | 104.8 | 112.0 |
| Nonferrous | 95.5 | 96.2 | 98.9 |
| Fabricated metal products | 95.0 | 96.8 | 100.1 |
| Machinery and computer equipment | 113.8 | 124.9 | 143.4 |
| Electrical machinery | 112.8 | 120.0 | 129.4 |
| Transportation equipment | 102.0 | 102.7 | 105.7 |
| Motor vehicles and parts | 94.8 | 105.0 | 119.0 |
| Instruments | 105.4 | 104.3 | 102.2 |
| Nondurable | 103.5 | 105.4 | 107.3 |
| Foods | 105.3 | 106.0 | 106.4 |
| Tobacco products | 96.7 | 99.6 | 100.9 |
| Textile mill products | 96.9 | 104.7 | 105.8 |
| Apparel products | 91.8 | 92.6 | 91.9 |
| Paper and products | 106.2 | 108.2 | 112.9 |
| Printing and publishing | 96.8 | 95.0 | 95.0 |
| Chemicals and products | 111.3 | 115.0 | 119.0 |
| Petroleum products | 101.6 | 102.0 | 105.9 |
| Rubber and plastics products | 104.5 | 109.7 | 112.6 |
| Leather and products | 87.9 | 92.5 | 98.4 |

(1) 1987 = 100.

## Average Yields of Long-Term Treasury, Corporate, and Municipal Bonds

Source: Office of Market Finance. U.S. Dept. of the Treasury

| Period | Treasury 30-Year Bonds | New Aa Corporate Bonds[1] | New Aa Municipal Bonds[2] | Period | Treasury 30-Year Bonds | New Aa Corporate Bonds[1] | New Aa Municipal Bonds[2] |
|---|---|---|---|---|---|---|---|
| **1982** | | | | **1990** | | | |
| June . . . . | 13.92 | 15.96 | 12.14 | June . . . . | 8.46 | 9.69 | 6.98 |
| Dec. . . . . | 10.54 | 12.15 | 9.84 | Dec. . . . . | 8.24 | 9.55 | 6.85 |
| **1983** | | | | **1991** | | | |
| June . . . . | 10.93 | 11.90 | 9.08 | Jan. . . . . | 8.27 | 9.60 | 7.00 |
| Dec. . . . . | 11.88 | 12.87 | 9.77 | Apr. . . . . | 8.21 | 9.07 | 6.81 |
| **1984** | | | | Sept. . . . | 7.95 | 8.79 | 6.58 |
| June . . . . | 13.44 | 14.49 | 10.44 | Dec. . . . . | 7.70 | 8.55 | 6.43 |
| Dec. . . . . | 11.52 | 12.47 | 9.65 | **1992** | | | |
| **1985** | | | | Jan. . . . . | 7.58 | 8.36 | 6.29 |
| June . . . . | 10.45 | 11.33 | 8.46 | Feb. . . . . | 7.85 | 8.63 | 6.42 |
| Dec. . . . . | 9.54 | 10.42 | 8.44 | Mar. . . . . | 7.97 | 8.62 | 6.59 |
| **1986** | | | | Apr. . . . . | 7.96 | 8.59 | 6.54 |
| June . . . . | 7.57 | 9.39 | 7.75 | May . . . . | 7.89 | 8.57 | 6.39 |
| Dec. . . . . | 7.37 | 8.87 | 6.70 | June . . . . | 7.84 | 8.45 | 6.32 |
| **1987** | | | | July . . . . | 7.60 | 8.19 | 5.90 |
| June . . . . | 8.57 | 9.64 | 7.69 | Aug. . . . . | 7.39 | 7.96 | 5.81 |
| Dec. . . . . | 9.12 | 10.22 | 7.83 | Sept. . . . | 7.34 | 7.99 | 6.05 |
| **1988** | | | | Oct. . . . . | 7.53 | 8.17 | 6.18 |
| June . . . . | 9.00 | 10.08 | 7.67 | Nov. . . . . | 7.61 | 8.25 | 6.22 |
| Dec. . . . . | 9.01 | 10.05 | 7.40 | Dec. . . . . | 7.44 | 8.12 | 6.02 |
| **1989** | | | | **1993** | | | |
| June . . . . | 8.27 | 9.24 | 6.94 | Jan. . . . . | 7.34 | 7.91 | 6.05 |
| Dec. . . . . | 7.90 | 9.23 | 6.76 | Feb. . . . . | 7.09 | 7.73 | 5.74 |
| | | | | Mar. . . . . | 6.82 | 7.39 | 5.54 |

(1) Treasury series based on 3-week moving average of reoffering yields of new corporate bonds rated Aa by Moody's Investors Service with an original maturity of at least 20 years. (2) Index of new reoffering yields on 20-year general obligations rated Aa by Moody's Investors Service. Source: U.S. Treasury, 1982-1990; Moody's, 1991-1993.

## Top Mutual Funds in 1992

Source: Lipper Analytical Services Inc.

| Fund | Total Return | Fund | Total Return | Fund | Total Return |
|---|---|---|---|---|---|
| Fidelity Sel. Saving & Loan | 57.8% | PaineWebber Reg. Fin.; B | 37.8% | Main Street: Income & Growth | 31.1% |
| Harris Oakmark | 48.9 | Parnassus | 36.8 | J. Hancock Spec. Equities | 30.4 |
| Fidelity Sel. Reg. Banks | 48.5 | Fidelity Sel. Software | 35.5 | Thomson Opportunity; A | 29.6 |
| J. Hancock Reg. Bank; B | 47.4 | Sife Trust Fund | 33.9 | Royce Fund: OTC | 29.4 |
| Fidelity Sel. Financial | 42.8 | Ret. Plan Amer.: Global Value | 33.8 | Pioneer Capital Growth | 29.0 |
| Heartland: Value | 42.5 | Crabbe Huson Growth | 33.4 | Fidelity Low-Priced Stock | 29.0 |
| Skyline Special Equities | 42.4 | Regis: ICM Small Company | 32.3 | Capstone PBHG Growth | 28.5 |
| Fidelity Sel. Automotive | 41.6 | GT Global America | 31.7 | Thomson Opportunity; B | 28.5 |
| PaineWebber Reg. Fin.; A | 38.7 | | | | |

## Performance of Mutual Funds by Type

Source: Lipper Analytical Services Inc.

| Fund type | 1992 Results No. of funds | Best | Return Average | Worst | Five-Year Results No. of funds | Best | Return Average | Worst |
|---|---|---|---|---|---|---|---|---|
| Capital Appreciation | 122 | +29.57 | +8.28 | −19.94 | 101 | +26.23 | +14.67 | −9.38 |
| Growth | 305 | +48.90 | +7.79 | −25.36 | 204 | +26.56 | +14.86 | −8.08 |
| Small Company Growth | 119 | +42.48 | +12.54 | −11.08 | 70 | +34.24 | +17.24 | +2.54 |
| Growth and Income | 252 | +31.08 | +8.61 | −8.22 | 168 | +32.14 | +13.88 | +6.73 |
| Equity Income | 69 | +21.10 | +9.46 | −2.86 | 40 | +17.99 | +12.68 | +6.07 |
| Health/Biotechnology | 10 | +18.36 | −8.28 | −22.88 | 7 | +31.01 | +24.78 | +18.01 |
| Natural Resources | 19 | +13.34 | +1.95 | −13.23 | 14 | +13.57 | +7.23 | −1.65 |
| Environmental | 7 | +4.92 | −6.18 | −18.72 | 1 | +13.70 | +13.70 | +13.70 |
| Science and Technology | 18 | +35.54 | +13.54 | −4.03 | 16 | +25.91 | +16.29 | +8.34 |
| Specialty/Miscellaneous | 27 | +41.57 | +11.52 | −11.54 | 22 | +28.50 | +14.12 | −12.91 |
| Utility | 28 | +21.00 | +9.16 | +0.43 | 13 | +16.85 | +14.52 | +13.12 |
| Financial Services | 12 | +57.83 | +35.18 | +5.12 | 10 | +26.85 | +21.52 | +16.77 |
| Real Estate | 6 | +21.04 | +12.83 | +4.15 | 2 | +13.78 | +12.44 | +11.09 |
| Option Income | 5 | +14.13 | +10.05 | +4.97 | 5 | +13.54 | +10.73 | +8.64 |
| Gold Oriented | 32 | +2.90 | −14.58 | −60.71 | 22 | +6.70 | −7.65 | −29.95 |
| Global | 43 | +9.01 | −0.27 | −14.20 | 20 | +13.52 | +7.63 | +1.11 |
| Global Small Company | 8 | +11.44 | +1.49 | −5.58 | 2 | +13.12 | +10.32 | +7.52 |
| International | 86 | +5.85 | −5.05 | −26.63 | 39 | +15.57 | +5.90 | +0.60 |
| European Region | 27 | +7.53 | −8.02 | −33.60 | 7 | +6.66 | +4.65 | −1.55 |
| Pacific Region | 19 | +26.42 | +0.40 | −18.17 | 7 | +13.43 | +5.95 | −1.41 |
| Japanese | 5 | −13.40 | −21.33 | −28.88 | 3 | +1.27 | −0.10 | −0.88 |
| Latin American | 3 | +2.15 | +0.39 | −2.32 | 0 | N/A | N/A | N/A |
| Canadian | 3 | −2.87 | −6.55 | −9.21 | 3 | +10.39 | +2.96 | −4.63 |
| Flexible-Portfolio | 54 | +21.09 | +7.51 | −15.36 | 18 | +17.75 | +10.88 | +4.60 |
| Global Flexible Portfolio | 14 | +12.19 | +2.86 | −6.18 | 5 | +11.13 | +6.74 | +2.79 |
| Balanced | 69 | +19.99 | +7.17 | −6.06 | 43 | +17.78 | +12.63 | +8.70 |
| Balanced Target Maturity | 7 | +9.54 | +5.31 | +1.91 | 1 | +12.41 | +12.41 | +12.41 |
| Convertible Securities | 25 | +31.17 | +13.56 | +3.79 | 17 | +19.19 | +12.85 | +7.55 |
| Income | 13 | +21.76 | +8.77 | +2.27 | 11 | +14.26 | +11.76 | +9.04 |

## Dow Jones Industrial Average Since 1961

| High | | Year | Low | | High | | Year | Low | |
|---|---|---|---|---|---|---|---|---|---|
| Dec. 13 | 734.91 | 1961 | Jan. 3 | 610.25 | Sept. 8 | 907.74 | 1978 | Feb. 28 | 742.12 |
| Jan. 3 | 726.01 | 1962 | June 26 | 535.76 | Oct. 5 | 897.61 | 1979 | Nov. 7 | 796.67 |
| Dec. 18 | 767.21 | 1963 | Jan. 2 | 646.79 | Nov. 20 | 1000.17 | 1980 | Apr. 21 | 759.13 |
| Nov. 18 | 891.71 | 1964 | Jan. 2 | 766.08 | Apr. 27 | 1024.05 | 1981 | Sept. 25 | 824.01 |
| Dec. 31 | 969.26 | 1965 | June 28 | 840.59 | Dec. 27 | 1070.55 | 1982 | Aug. 12 | 776.92 |
| Feb. 9 | 995.15 | 1966 | Oct. 7 | 744.32 | Nov. 29 | 1287.20 | 1983 | Jan. 3 | 1027.04 |
| Sept. 25 | 943.08 | 1967 | Jan. 3 | 786.41 | Jan. 6 | 1286.64 | 1984 | July 24 | 1086.57 |
| Dec. 3 | 985.21 | 1968 | Mar. 21 | 825.13 | Dec. 16 | 1553.10 | 1985 | Jan. 4 | 1184.96 |
| May 14 | 968.85 | 1969 | Dec. 17 | 769.93 | Dec. 2 | 1955.57 | 1986 | Jan. 22 | 1502.29 |
| Dec. 29 | 842.00 | 1970 | May 6 | 631.16 | Aug. 25 | 2722.42 | 1987 | Oct. 19 | 1738.74 |
| Apr. 28 | 950.82 | 1971 | Nov. 23 | 797.97 | Oct. 21 | 2183.50 | 1988 | Jan. 20 | 1879.14 |
| Dec. 11 | 1036.27 | 1972 | Jan. 26 | 889.15 | Oct. 9 | 2791.41 | 1989 | Jan. 3 | 2144.64 |
| Jan. 11 | 1051.70 | 1973 | Dec. 5 | 788.31 | July 16 | 2999.75 | 1990 | Oct. 11 | 2365.10 |
| Mar. 13 | 891.66 | 1974 | Dec. 6 | 577.60 | Dec. 31 | 3168.83 | 1991 | Jan. 9 | 2470.30 |
| July 15 | 881.81 | 1975 | Jan. 2 | 632.04 | June 1 | 3413.21 | 1992 | Jan. 9 | 3136.58 |
| Sept. 21 | 1014.79 | 1976 | Jan. 2 | 858.71 | Aug. 26 | 3652.37 | 1993* | Jan. 20 | 3241.95 |
| Jan. 3 | 999.75 | 1977 | Nov. 2 | 800.85 | | | | *As of | Oct.1 |

## Components of Dow Jones Industrial Average

| | | |
|---|---|---|
| Allied-Signal | Eastman Kodak | Morgan (J.P.) |
| Aluminum Co. of Amer. | Exxon | Philip Morris |
| American Express | General Electric | Procter & Gamble |
| AT&T | General Motors | Sears |
| Bethlehem Steel | Goodyear | Texaco |
| Boeing | IBM | Union Carbide |
| Caterpillar | International Paper | United Technologies |
| Chevron | McDonald's | Westinghouse |
| Coca-Cola | Merck | Woolworth |
| Disney (Walt) | Minn. Mining & Manuf. | |
| DuPont | | |

## Components of Dow Jones Transportation Average

| | | |
|---|---|---|
| AMR Corp. | Consolidated Freightways | Santa Fe Pacific |
| Airborne Freight | Consolidated Rail | Southwest Air Lines |
| Alaska Air | Delta Air Lines | UAL |
| American President | Federal Express | Union Pacific |
| Burlington Northern | Norfolk Southern | USAir Group |
| CSX | Roadway Services | XTRA Corp |
| Carolina Freight | Ryder System | |

## Components of Dow Jones Utility Average

| | | |
|---|---|---|
| American Electric Power | Consolidated Natural Gas | Panhandle Eastern |
| Arkla | Detroit Edison | Peoples Energy |
| Centerior Energy | Houston Industries | Philadelphia Electric |
| Commonwealth Edison | Niagara Mohawk Power | Public Service Enterprises |
| Consolidated Edison | Pacific Gas & Electric | SCE |

## Milestones of the Dow Jones Industrial Average

| First close over... | | First close over... | | First close over... | |
|---|---|---|---|---|---|
| 100 | Jan. 12, 1906 | 2,000 | Jan. 8, 1987 | 3,400 | June 1, 1992 |
| 500 | March 12, 1956 | 2,500 | July 17, 1987 | 3,500 | May 19, 1993 |
| 1,000 | Nov. 14, 1972 | 3,000 | April 17, 1991 | 3,600 | Aug. 18, 1993 |
| 1,500 | Dec. 11, 1985 | | | | |

## Most Active Common Stocks in 1992

| New York Exchange | Volume (millions of shares) | American Exchange | Volume (millions of shares) | NASDAQ | Volume (millions of shares) |
|---|---|---|---|---|---|
| Glaxo | 569.39 | Chambers Devel. "A" | 105.82 | Intel | 553.72 |
| RJR Nabisco | 543.23 | Amdahl | 102.89 | Tele-Commun. "A" | 443.85 |
| General Motors | 537.62 | U.S. Bioscience | 81.66 | Novell | 434.32 |
| IBM | 512.98 | Echo Bay Mines Ltd. | 72.33 | Microsoft | 402.46 |
| Philip Morris | 472.41 | Sulcus Computer | 71.97 | Seagate Technology | 390.22 |
| Téléfonos de México | 464.88 | Exploration Co. of La. | 68.77 | Sun Microsystems | 384.36 |
| Citicorp | 453.48 | Hillhaven | 66.60 | Apple Computer | 367.89 |
| AT & T | 428.89 | Ivax | 66.28 | Oracle Systems | 343.86 |
| Chrysler | 427.79 | Fruit of the Loom | 62.49 | Téléfonos de México | 339.40 |
| Merck | 406.01 | Interdigital Communic. | 51.04 | Amgen | 329.46 |
| Ford Motor | 395.74 | Hasbro | 47.71 | Medco Containment | 305.99 |
| Unisys | 346.20 | Energy Service Co. | 37.99 | MCI Communications | 299.99 |
| Bristol-Myers Squibb | 334.12 | Nabors Industries | 36.01 | Comverse Technol. | 290.44 |
| Coca-Cola | 331.88 | American Exploration | 33.36 | Costco Wholesale | 277.82 |
| American Express | 324.73 | New York Times Co. | 32.13 | Dell Computer | 268.54 |

# Who Owns Stocks?

**Source:** Federal Reserve

(as of Mar. 31, 1993)

| Stockholder | Percent | Stockholder | Percent | Stockholder | Percent |
|---|---|---|---|---|---|
| Households | 45.8 | State, Local Govt. Retirement | | Other Insurance Cos. | 2.6 |
| Private Pension Funds | 22.0 |   Funds | 9.3 | Brokers & Dealers | 0.3 |
| Mutual Funds | 10.3 | Foreign | 6.6 | Mutual Savings Banks | 0.2 |
| | | Life Insurance Cos. | 2.7 | Commercial Banks | 0.1 |

# Selected Personal Consumption Expenditures in the U.S.

**Source:** Bureau of Economic Analysis, U.S. Dept. of Commerce

(billions of dollars)

| | 1986 | 1987 | 1988 | 1989 | 1990 | 1991 | 1992 |
|---|---|---|---|---|---|---|---|
| **Personal consumption expenditures** | $2,797.4 | $3,009.4 | $3,296.1 | $3,523.1 | $3,761.2 | $3,906.4 | $4,139.9 |
| **Food & Tobacco** | 533.7 | 566.4 | 569.8 | 605.6 | 648.2 | 666.8 | 684.5 |
| Food purchased for off-premise consumption | 339.1 | 353.7 | 351.7 | 373.7 | 400.2 | 411.1 | 418.0 |
| Purchased meals and beverages | 151.6 | 165.5 | 171.7 | 180.6 | 193.1 | 198.5 | 203.5 |
| Tobacco products | 33.6 | 35.6 | 36.2 | 40.5 | 43.4 | 45.4 | 50.9 |
| **Clothing, accessories, jewelry** | 207.5 | 223.3 | 231.8 | 248.7 | 259.3 | 264.3 | 282.4 |
| Shoes | 24.3 | 25.9 | 27.4 | 30.1 | 31.4 | 31.3 | 32.3 |
| Clothing and accessories less shoes | 142.4 | 152.5 | 158.9 | 170.1 | 175.7 | 181.6 | 195.7 |
| Jewelry and watches | 22.8 | 24.7 | 28.8 | 29.7 | 31.3 | 31.6 | 34.0 |
| **Personal care** | 41.4 | 44.4 | 51.4 | 55.8 | 59.2 | 60.9 | 63.2 |
| Toilet articles, preparations | 24.6 | 26.3 | 31.8 | 34.1 | 36.8 | 38.2 | 39.3 |
| Barbershops, beauty parlors, baths, health clubs | 16.8 | 18.2 | 19.6 | 21.6 | 22.4 | 22.6 | 23.9 |
| **Housing** | 434.2 | 468.9 | 484.2 | 514.4 | 547.5 | 574.4 | 600.0 |
| Owner-occupied nonfarm dwellings space rent | 293.7 | 316.9 | 334.1 | 355.8 | 379.5 | 399.1 | 417.8 |
| Tenant-occupied nonfarm dwellings rent | 114.3 | 123.6 | 125.3 | 132.6 | 141.1 | 147.7 | 153.8 |
| Rental value of farm dwellings | 9.7 | 10.3 | 4.9 | 5.0 | 5.2 | 5.3 | 5.3 |
| **Household operation** | 347.5 | 363.3 | 398.9 | 422.6 | 437.3 | 452.7 | 475.2 |
| Furniture, incl. bedding | 30.4 | 31.8 | 34.0 | 36.9 | 36.7 | 36.8 | 40.0 |
| Kitchen, other household appliances | 25.5 | 26.7 | 24.1 | 25.7 | 26.4 | 27.1 | 29.2 |
| China, glassware, tableware, utensils | 14.3 | 15.3 | 16.4 | 17.9 | 18.7 | 19.4 | 21.0 |
| Other durable house furnishings | 30.6 | 33.5 | 37.7 | 40.2 | 42.0 | 41.9 | 45.2 |
| Semidurable house furnishings | 15.2 | 16.0 | 19.4 | 20.4 | 21.2 | 21.9 | 23.6 |
| Household utilities | 122.4 | 125.8 | 127.3 | 134.1 | 136.7 | 145.3 | 149.9 |
| Telephone, telegraph | 42.7 | 44.1 | 50.2 | 51.7 | 53.8 | 56.2 | 58.7 |
| **Medical care** | 357.6 | 399.0 | 487.7 | 536.4 | 597.8 | 651.7 | 704.6 |
| Drug preparations, sundries | 30.2 | 32.3 | 50.8 | 55.0 | 60.6 | 64.4 | 65.9 |
| Physicians | 80.6 | 94.0 | 110.6 | 121.6 | 133.8 | 144.0 | 153.1 |
| Dentists | 22.8 | 25.0 | 27.9 | 30.0 | 31.6 | 32.9 | 36.4 |
| Hospitals and nursing homes | 152.4 | 166.3 | 190.9 | 209.5 | 231.3 | 255.3 | 279.6 |
| Health insurance | 22.4 | 25.3 | 26.4 | 31.2 | 36.6 | 40.0 | 45.9 |
| **Personal business** | 192.5 | 215.4 | 255.0 | 272.2 | 296.0 | 323.4 | 356.0 |
| Brokerage charges, investment counseling | 19.7 | 20.5 | 19.3 | 21.6 | 22.0 | 24.3 | 28.5 |
| Bank service charges, trust services, safe deposit box | 13.0 | 14.6 | 19.8 | 22.0 | 23.7 | 25.2 | 27.6 |
| Legal services | 30.9 | 35.0 | 41.7 | 45.5 | 49.2 | 49.9 | 54.0 |
| Funeral, burial expenses | 6.6 | 7.0 | 7.8 | 7.9 | 8.5 | 9.0 | 9.6 |
| **Transportation** | 366.3 | 379.7 | 413.2 | 437.3 | 453.9 | 434.6 | 463.1 |
| User-operated transportation | 335.9 | 346.3 | 376.9 | 399.6 | 414.0 | 395.5 | 423.9 |
| New autos | 101.3 | 93.5 | 101.0 | 99.9 | 96.6 | 79.5 | 87.3 |
| Used autos | 33.6 | 38.5 | 30.5 | 32.5 | 33.1 | 36.7 | 39.5 |
| Repair, greasing, washing, parking, storage, rental, leasing | 52.0 | 55.9 | 73.5 | 79.1 | 82.6 | 82.4 | 89.5 |
| Gasoline and oil | 73.5 | 75.3 | 86.9 | 96.2 | 108.4 | 102.9 | 103.4 |
| Tolls | 1.7 | 1.9 | 1.8 | 2.1 | 2.0 | 2.0 | 2.1 |
| Insurance premiums less claims paid | 12.6 | 15.4 | 16.8 | 16.8 | 18.1 | 22.7 | 24.6 |
| Purchased local transportation | 7.8 | 8.2 | 8.3 | 8.1 | 8.9 | 9.1 | 9.2 |
| Mass transit systems | 3.8 | 4.0 | 5.4 | 5.3 | 5.7 | 5.7 | 5.9 |
| Taxicab | 3.3 | 3.5 | 2.9 | 2.8 | 3.2 | 3.4 | 3.3 |
| Purchased intercity transportation | 22.6 | 25.5 | 28.0 | 29.5 | 30.9 | 30.0 | 30.0 |
| Railway (excl. commutation) | .7 | .7 | .6 | .7 | .7 | .7 | .7 |
| Bus | 1.1 | 1.4 | 2.2 | 1.7 | 1.4 | 1.5 | 1.5 |
| Airline | 18.8 | 20.8 | 23.0 | 24.7 | 26.4 | 25.6 | 25.7 |
| **Recreation** | 201.2 | 223.2 | 246.8 | 266.0 | 285.7 | 299.4 | 318.8 |
| Books, maps | 8.6 | 9.5 | 14.6 | 15.8 | 17.5 | 18.3 | 20.2 |
| Magazines, newspapers, sheet music | 13.9 | 15.4 | 20.8 | 22.0 | 23.8 | 24.7 | 25.4 |
| Nondurable toys and sport supplies | 23.1 | 26.2 | 27.5 | 30.0 | 32.1 | 33.5 | 35.2 |
| Wheel goods, durable toys, sports equipment, boats, pleasure aircraft | 29.7 | 33.2 | 30.0 | 31.0 | 31.3 | 31.4 | 34.0 |
| Video & audio prods., computers, musical instruments | — | — | 44.5 | 47.3 | 50.4 | 55.4 | 59.1 |
| Flowers, seeds, potted plants | 5.8 | 7.0 | 9.3 | 10.1 | 10.3 | 10.4 | 11.0 |
| Admissions to specified spectator amusements | 10.2 | 11.3 | 11.1 | 12.1 | 14.0 | 14.9 | 16.1 |
| Motion picture theaters | 3.9 | 4.2 | 3.6 | 3.9 | 4.7 | 5.0 | 5.5 |
| Legitimate theater, opera | 3.3 | 4.0 | 3.6 | 3.9 | 4.5 | 4.7 | 5.1 |
| Spectator sports | 2.9 | 3.0 | 3.9 | 4.3 | 4.9 | 5.2 | 5.5 |
| Clubs, fraternal organizations | 5.0 | 5.5 | 7.6 | 8.0 | 8.4 | 8.6 | 9.0 |
| Commerical participant amusements | 16.0 | 17.1 | 19.1 | 20.5 | 23.1 | 23.8 | 25.7 |
| **Education & Research** | 46.6 | 50.9 | 71.6 | 79.4 | 86.2 | 91.8 | 98.2 |
| Higher education | 16.9 | 17.7 | 36.7 | 40.3 | 44.0 | 47.3 | 50.8 |
| Nursery, elementary and secondary schools | 14.5 | 15.5 | 17.1 | 19.2 | 19.8 | 20.6 | 21.6 |
| **Religious and welfare activities** | 62.9 | 68.1 | 86.0 | 92.7 | 101.6 | 105.7 | 116.2 |

# AGRICULTURE
## The U.S. Farm Population
Source: Bureau of the Census, U.S. Dept. of Commerce

The total estimated number of persons living on U.S. farms in 1991 was 4,632,000, about the same as in 1990. As late as 1950, there were 23 million farm residents in the U.S. The farm population peaked at about 32 million in the 1910-1920 period. When the first reports of farm population were published in 1945, 20 percent of Americans were farm residents. In 1991, only about 2 percent of Americans were farm residents. In 1991, farm residence was no longer a reliable indication of whether someone was involved in farming:

32 percent of farm managers were not farm residents and 86 percent of farm workers lived elsewhere. The Midwest was home to a larger proportion of the nation's farm population—49.3 percent—than any other region of the country in 1991. Whites comprised most of the U.S. farm population (97 percent). Approximately 29 percent of men living on farms had some college education, compared with 43 percent of men who did not live on farms.

## Persons in Farm Occupations, 1820-1991
Source: Economic Research Service, U.S. Dept. of Agriculture; Bureau of the Census, U.S. Dept. of Commerce
(in thousands)

| Year | Total workers[1] | Farm occupations Number | Farm occupations % of total | Year | Total workers[1] | Farm occupations Number | Farm occupations % of total |
|---|---|---|---|---|---|---|---|
| 1820 | 2,881 | 2,069 | 71.8 | 1950 | 59,230 | 6,858 | 11.6 |
| 1850 | 7,697 | 4,902 | 63.7 | 1960 | 67,990 | 4,132 | 6.1 |
| 1870 | 12,925 | 6,850 | 53.0 | 1970 | 79,802 | 2,881 | 3.6 |
| 1900 | 29,030 | 10,888 | 37.5 | 1980 | 104,058 | 2,818 | 2.7 |
| 1920 | 42,206 | 11,390 | 27.0 | 1985 (March) | 106,214 | 2,949 | 2.8 |
| 1930 | 48,686 | 10,321 | 21.2 | 1990 (March) | 117,491 | 2,864 | 2.4 |
| 1940 | 51,742 | 8,995 | 17.4 | 1991 (March) | 116,000 | 2,848 | 2.5 |

(1) Total workers for 1985 to 1991 are employed workers 15 years and over; total workers for 1970 and 1980 are members of the experienced civilian labor force 16 years and over; total workers for 1900 to 1960 are members of the experienced civilian labor force 14 years and over; and total workers for 1820 to 1890 are gainfully employed workers 10 years and over.

## Farms—Number and Acreage by State, 1980 & 1992
Source: Natl. Agricultural Statistics Service, U.S. Dept. of Agriculture

| State | Farms (1,000) 1980 | Farms (1,000) 1992 | Acreage (mil.) 1980 | Acreage (mil.) 1992 | Acreage per Farm 1980 | Acreage per Farm 1992 | State | Farms (1,000) 1980 | Farms (1,000) 1992 | Acreage (mil.) 1980 | Acreage (mil.) 1992 | Acreage per Farm 1980 | Acreage per Farm 1992 |
|---|---|---|---|---|---|---|---|---|---|---|---|---|---|
| U.S. | 2,437 | 2,094 | 1,039 | 980 | 426 | 468 | Nebraska | 65 | 56 | 48 | 47 | 734 | 841 |
| Alabama | 59 | 46 | 12 | 10 | 207 | 213 | Nevada | 3 | 3 | 9 | 9 | 3,100 | 3,560 |
| Alaska | (z) | 1 | 2 | 1 | 3,378 | 1,778 | New Hampshire | 3 | 3 | 1 | (z) | 160 | 162 |
| Arizona | 7 | 8 | 38 | 36 | 5,080 | 4,500 | New Jersey | 10 | 9 | 1 | 1 | 109 | 104 |
| Arkansas | 58 | 46 | 17 | 16 | 280 | 337 | New Mexico | 13 | 14 | 47 | 44 | 3,467 | 3,274 |
| California | 79 | 80 | 34 | 30 | 417 | 373 | New York | 48 | 38 | 9 | 8 | 200 | 216 |
| Colorado | 26 | 26 | 36 | 33 | 1,358 | 1,286 | North Carolina | 92 | 60 | 12 | 10 | 126 | 158 |
| Connecticut | 4 | 4 | (z) | (z) | 117 | 103 | North Dakota | 41 | 33 | 42 | 40 | 1,043 | 1,224 |
| Delaware | 4 | 3 | 1 | 1 | 186 | 207 | Ohio | 96 | 78 | 16 | 15 | 171 | 197 |
| Florida | 38 | 39 | 13 | 11 | 344 | 269 | Oklahoma | 72 | 71 | 35 | 34 | 481 | 479 |
| Georgia | 59 | 46 | 15 | 12 | 254 | 263 | Oregon | 34 | 38 | 18 | 18 | 517 | 467 |
| Hawaii | 4 | 5 | 2 | 2 | 458 | 380 | Pennsylvania | 61 | 52 | 9 | 8 | 145 | 154 |
| Idaho | 24 | 21 | 15 | 14 | 623 | 643 | Rhode Island | 1 | 1 | (z) | (z) | 87 | 90 |
| Illinois | 108 | 81 | 29 | 28 | 269 | 351 | South Carolina | 35 | 25 | 6 | 5 | 188 | 212 |
| Indiana | 88 | 65 | 17 | 16 | 193 | 246 | South Dakota | 39 | 35 | 45 | 44 | 1,169 | 1,263 |
| Iowa | 121 | 102 | 34 | 33 | 284 | 327 | Tennessee | 96 | 88 | 14 | 13 | 142 | 143 |
| Kansas | 75 | 67 | 48 | 48 | 644 | 713 | Texas | 192 | 183 | 138 | 130 | 715 | 710 |
| Kentucky | 103 | 91 | 15 | 14 | 143 | 155 | Utah | 13 | 13 | 12 | 11 | 919 | 856 |
| Louisiana | 37 | 30 | 10 | 9 | 273 | 290 | Vermont | 7 | 7 | 2 | 2 | 226 | 219 |
| Maine | 8 | 7 | 2 | 1 | 195 | 200 | Virginia | 59 | 44 | 10 | 9 | 169 | 198 |
| Maryland | 17 | 16 | 3 | 2 | 157 | 141 | Washington | 37 | 37 | 16 | 16 | 429 | 432 |
| Massachusetts | 6 | 7 | 1 | 1 | 116 | 99 | West Virginia | 20 | 20 | 4 | 4 | 191 | 185 |
| Michigan | 66 | 54 | 11 | 11 | 175 | 200 | Wisconsin | 94 | 79 | 19 | 17 | 200 | 219 |
| Minnesota | 104 | 88 | 30 | 30 | 291 | 339 | Wyoming | 9 | 9 | 35 | 35 | 3,846 | 3,783 |
| Mississippi | 56 | 38 | 15 | 13 | 265 | 337 | | | | | | | |
| Missouri | 121 | 107 | 31 | 30 | 261 | 283 | | | | | | | |
| Montana | 24 | 25 | 62 | 60 | 2,601 | 2,439 | | | | | | | |

(z) Less than 500 farms or 500,000 acres

## Livestock on Farms in the U.S.
Source: Natl. Agricultural Statistics Service, U.S. Dept. of Agriculture (in thousands)

| Year (On Jan. 1) | All cattle | Milk cows | Sheep | Hogs[3] | Year (On Jan. 1) | All cattle | Milk cows | Sheep | Hogs[3] |
|---|---|---|---|---|---|---|---|---|---|
| 1890 | 60,014 | 15,000 | 44,518 | 48,130 | 1955 | 96,592 | 23,462 | 31,582 | 50,474 |
| 1900 | 59,739 | 16,544 | 48,105 | 51,055 | 1960 | 96,236 | 19,527 | 33,170 | 59,026 |
| 1910 | 58,993 | 19,450 | 50,239 | 48,072 | 1965 | 109,000 | 16,981[2] | 25,127 | 56,106 |
| 1920 | 70,400 | 21,455 | 40,743 | 60,159 | 1970 | 112,369 | 12,091 | 20,423 | 57,046 |
| 1925 | 63,373 | 22,575 | 38,543 | 55,770 | 1980 | 111,242 | 10,758 | 12,699 | 67,318 |
| 1930 | 61,003 | 23,032 | 51,565 | 55,705 | 1985 | 109,582 | 10,777 | 10,716 | 54,073 |
| 1935 | 68,846 | 26,082 | 51,808 | 39,066 | 1990 | 98,162 | 10,153 | 11,363 | 53,821 |
| 1940 | 68,309 | 24,940 | 52,107 | 61,165 | 1991 | 98,896 | 10,156 | 11,200 | 54,477 |
| 1945 | 85,573 | 27,770 | 46,520 | 59,373 | 1992 | 99,559 | 9,913 | 10,750 | 57,684 |
| 1950 | 77,963 | 23,853 | 29,826 | 58,937 | 1993[1] | 100,892 | 9,844 | 10,174 | 59,016 |

(1) Total estimated value on farms as of Jan. 1, 1993, was (avg. value per head in parentheses): cattle & calves $65,481,884 ($649.00) sheep & lambs $715,834 ($70.20); hogs & pigs $4,281,213 ($71.60). (2) From 1965, milk cows and heifers that have calved. (3) As of Dec. 1 of preceding year.

## U.S. Farms, 1940-1992

Source: U.S. Dept. of Agriculture

## Eggs: U.S. Production, Price, and Value, 1991-92[1]

Source: Economic Research Service, U.S. Dept. of Agriculture

| State | Eggs Produced[2] 1991 (million) | Eggs Produced[2] 1992 (million) | Price Per Dozen 1991 (cents) | Price Per Dozen 1992 (cents) | Value of Production 1991 (1,000 dollars) | Value of Production 1992 (1,000 dollars) | State | Eggs Produced[2] 1991 (million) | Eggs Produced[2] 1992 (million) | Price Per Dozen 1991 (cents) | Price Per Dozen 1992 (cents) | Value of Production 1991 (1,000 dollars) | Value of Production 1992 (1,000 dollars) |
|---|---|---|---|---|---|---|---|---|---|---|---|---|---|
| AL | 2,417 | 2,512 | 91.4 | 81.3 | 184,095 | 170,188 | NE | 1,400 | 1,777 | 48.9 | 36.0 | 57,050 | 53,310 |
| AK | 0.7 | 0.5 | 149.0 | 169.0 | 87 | 70 | NV | 1.8 | 1.5 | 52.7 | 38.8 | 79 | 49 |
| AZ | 85 | 85 | 56.0 | 49.7 | 3,967 | 3,520 | NH | 52 | 63 | 104.0 | 104.0 | 4,507 | 5,460 |
| AR | 3,737 | 3,601 | 91.8 | 88.3 | 285,881 | 264,974 | NJ | 491 | 515 | 83.0 | 70.0 | 33,961 | 30,042 |
| CA | 7,444 | 7,007 | 58.4 | 47.6 | 362,275 | 277,944 | NM | 302 | 303 | 70.0 | 58.0 | 17,617 | 14,645 |
| CO | 873 | 837 | 73.0 | 61.4 | 53,108 | 42,827 | NY | 987 | 1,040 | 64.0 | 53.9 | 52,640 | 46,713 |
| CT | 947 | 940 | 104.0 | 96.9 | 82,073 | 75,905 | NC | 3,045 | 3,026 | 78.7 | 71.4 | 199,701 | 180,047 |
| DE | 165 | 164 | 113.0 | 107.0 | 15,538 | 14,623 | ND | 45 | 41 | 48.0 | 41.0 | 1,800 | 1,401 |
| FL | 2,537 | 2,341 | 57.2 | 46.7 | 120.903 | 91.104 | OH | 4,637 | 5,021 | 54.7 | 40.7 | 211,370 | 170,296 |
| GA | 4,301 | 4,326 | 80.8 | 74.8 | 289,601 | 269.654 | OK | 830 | 873 | 100.0 | 96.0 | 69,167 | 69,840 |
| HI | 224.5 | 222.4 | 85.5 | 85.5 | 15,996 | 15,846 | OR | 686 | 686 | 74.6 | 76.6 | 42,646 | 43,790 |
| ID | 203 | 214 | 72.9 | 62.6 | 12,332 | 11,164 | PA | 5,130 | 5,513 | 52.0 | 42.9 | 222,300 | 197,090 |
| IL | 809 | 801 | 70.5 | 48.0 | 47,529 | 32,040 | RI | 50 | 57 | 99.0 | 91.0 | 4,125 | 4,323 |
| IN | 5,290 | 5,207 | 60.1 | 48.8 | 264,941 | 211,751 | SC | 1,420 | 1,447 | 65.9 | 57.3 | 77,982 | 69,094 |
| IA | 2,247 | 2,902 | 53.0 | 39.4 | 99,243 | 95,282 | SD | 602 | 690 | 45.8 | 32.5 | 22,976 | 18,688 |
| KS | 389 | 355 | 47.8 | 38.3 | 15,495 | 11,330 | TN | 279 | 262 | 80.7 | 72.8 | 18,763 | 15,895 |
| KY | 507 | 578 | 73.5 | 61.7 | 31,054 | 29,719 | TX | 3,356 | 3,462 | 72.6 | 63.0 | 203,038 | 181,755 |
| LA | 254 | 316 | 115.0 | 97.0 | 24,342 | 25,543 | UT | 486 | 493 | 59.0 | 53.0 | 23,895 | 21,774 |
| ME | 1,070 | 1,078 | 97.0 | 89.5 | 86,492 | 80,401 | VT | 30 | 31 | 102.0 | 98.0 | 2,550 | 2,532 |
| MD | 903 | 855 | 75.4 | 62.2 | 56,739 | 44,318 | VA | 988 | 1,008 | 81.2 | 75.3 | 66,855 | 63,252 |
| MA | 237 | 213 | 102.0 | 97.0 | 20,145 | 17,218 | WA | 1,313 | 1,305 | 71.5 | 63.4 | 78,233 | 68,948 |
| MI | 1,396 | 1,398 | 53.8 | 40.4 | 62,587 | 47,066 | WV | 174 | 180 | 109.0 | 104.0 | 15,805 | 15,600 |
| MN | 2,697 | 2,805 | 54.0 | 41.0 | 121,365 | 95,838 | WI | 896 | 831 | 54.0 | 42.5 | 40,320 | 29,431 |
| MS | 1,478 | 1,408 | 86.7 | 82.1 | 106,786 | 96,331 | WY | 1.7 | 1.7 | 83.0 | 65.5 | 118 | 93 |
| MO | 1,622 | 1,575 | 51.5 | 41.0 | 69,611 | 53,813 | U.S. | 69,196 | 70,528 | 67.8 | 57.7 | 3,908,730 | 3,389,070 |
| MT | 164 | 160 | 66.0 | 49.0 | 9,020 | 6,533 | | | | | | | |

(1) Estimates cover the 12 month period from Dec. 1, of the previous year through Nov. 30. (2) States may not add to U.S. total due to rounding.

## U.S. Meat Production and Consumption

Source: Economic Research Service, U.S. Dept. of Agriculture; in millions of pounds

| Year | Beef Production | Beef Consumption[1] | Veal Production | Veal Consumption[1] | Lamb and mutton Production | Lamb and mutton Consumption[1] | Pork (exclud. lard) Production | Pork (exclud. lard) Consumption[1] | All meats[3] Production | All meats[3] Consumption[1] | Lard Production | Lard Consumption[2] |
|---|---|---|---|---|---|---|---|---|---|---|---|---|
| 1940 . . . . | 7,175 | 7,257 | 981 | 981 | 876 | 873 | 10,044 | 9,701 | 19,076 | 18,812 | 2,288 | 1,901 |
| 1950 . . . . | 9,534 | 9,529 | 1,230 | 1,206 | 597 | 596 | 10,714 | 10,390 | 22,075 | 21,721 | 2,631 | 1,891 |
| 1960 . . . . | 14,728 | 15,465 | 1,109 | 1,118 | 769 | 857 | 13,905 | 14,057 | 30,511 | 31,497 | 2,562 | 1,358 |
| 1970 . . . . | 21,684 | 23,451 | 588 | 613 | 551 | 669 | 14,699 | 14,957 | 37,522 | 39,689 | 1,913 | 939 |
| 1980 . . . . | 21,643 | 23,560 | 400 | 420 | 318 | 351 | 16,617 | 16,838 | 38,978 | 41,701 | 1,207 | 588 |
| 1990 . . . . | 22,743 | 24,031 | 327 | 325 | 363 | 397 | 15,354 | 16,030 | 38,787 | 40,784 | (4) | (4) |
| 1991 . . . . | 22,917 | 24,113 | 306 | 305 | 363 | 396 | 15,999 | 16,399 | 39,585 | 41,214 | (4) | (4) |
| 1992 . . . . | 23,086 | 24,261 | 310 | 312 | 348 | 348 | 17,234 | 17,475 | 40,978 | 42,436 | (4) | (4) |

(1) Includes shipments. (2) Direct use. Excludes lard used in such products as table spreads and shortenings. (3) Meats may not add to total. (4) Data collection discontinued.

## Government Agricultural Payments by State, 1992[1]

Source: Economic Research Service. U.S. Dept. of Agriculture; in thousands of dollars

| State | Feed Grain | Wheat | Rice | Cotton | Wool Act | Conservation[2] | Miscellaneous[3] | Total |
|---|---|---|---|---|---|---|---|---|
| Alabama | $4,086 | $4,165 | $0 | $28,731 | $101 | $29,144 | $52,905 | $119,132 |
| Alaska | 118 | 0 | 0 | 0 | 10 | 1,095 | 471 | 1,694 |
| Arizona | 2,330 | 4,813 | 0 | 46,592 | 2,074 | 1,481 | 18,290 | 75,580 |
| Arkansas | 6,969 | 25,758 | 198,861 | 45,173 | 303 | 17,658 | 115,304 | 410,026 |
| California | 10,643 | 23,134 | 103,570 | 91,232 | 10,794 | 13,479 | 177,530 | 430,382 |
| Colorado | 36,381 | 54,185 | 0 | 0 | 7,625 | 84,998 | 20,045 | 203,234 |
| Connecticut | 438 | 0 | 0 | 0 | 41 | 582 | 1,156 | 2,217 |
| Delaware | 1,819 | 237 | 0 | 0 | 7 | 537 | 376 | 2,976 |
| Florida | 2,327 | 560 | 273 | 2,457 | 15 | 14,569 | 32,884 | 53,085 |
| Georgia | 14,791 | 13,197 | 0 | 25,525 | 41 | 32,954 | 95,792 | 182,300 |
| Hawaii | 0 | 0 | 0 | 0 | 15 | 731 | 1,076 | 1,822 |
| Idaho | 16,101 | 50,781 | 0 | 0 | 4,752 | 42,514 | 23,247 | 137,395 |
| Illinois | 345,505 | 23,974 | 0 | 0 | 670 | 62,406 | 48,096 | 480,651 |
| Indiana | 157,033 | 10,982 | 0 | 0 | 336 | 35,245 | 28,922 | 232,518 |
| Iowa | 449,568 | 319 | 0 | 0 | 2,816 | 175,822 | 33,753 | 662,278 |
| Kansas | 123,952 | 249,608 | 0 | 39 | 2,272 | 157,719 | 58,555 | 592,145 |
| Kentucky | 28,989 | 6,209 | 0 | 0 | 192 | 29,615 | 7,120 | 72,125 |
| Louisiana | 4,070 | 4,339 | 78,784 | 60,908 | 27 | 10,389 | 112,318 | 270,835 |
| Maine | 503 | 1 | 0 | 0 | 97 | 4,635 | 5,017 | 10,253 |
| Maryland | 7,549 | 1,054 | 0 | 0 | 130 | 2,864 | 4,470 | 16,067 |
| Massachusetts | 145 | 0 | 0 | 0 | 72 | 836 | 3,708 | 4,761 |
| Michigan | 74,688 | 14,569 | 0 | 0 | 890 | 20,733 | 31,629 | 142,509 |
| Minnesota | 208,034 | 63,480 | 0 | 0 | 2,180 | 106,692 | 41,637 | 422,023 |
| Mississippi | 3,568 | 6,649 | 40,763 | 103,746 | 9 | 39,696 | 85,473 | 279,904 |
| Missouri | 67,963 | 31,481 | 15,027 | 14,174 | 1,306 | 100,132 | 53,562 | 293,645 |
| Montana | 34,840 | 105,910 | 0 | 0 | 11,541 | 108,749 | 37,733 | 298,773 |
| Nebraska | 305,962 | 53,412 | 0 | 0 | 1,620 | 83,662 | 34,573 | 478,729 |
| Nevada | 237 | 603 | 0 | 0 | 1,118 | 837 | 8,449 | 11,244 |
| New Hampshire | 125 | 0 | 0 | 0 | 57 | 798 | 570 | 1,550 |
| New Jersey | 2,020 | 360 | 0 | 0 | 44 | 671 | 7,600 | 10,695 |
| New Mexico | 7,854 | 7,372 | 0 | 4,224 | 8,173 | 21,106 | 11,538 | 60,267 |
| New York | 21,096 | 3,018 | 0 | 0 | 407 | 7,487 | 15,864 | 47,872 |
| North Carolina | 21,048 | 5,400 | 0 | 9,964 | 85 | 10,809 | 27,499 | 74,805 |
| North Dakota | 75,561 | 202,923 | 0 | 0 | 2,933 | 109,955 | 51,784 | 443,156 |
| Ohio | 96,457 | 19,087 | 0 | 0 | 1,331 | 28,335 | 20,912 | 166,122 |
| Oklahoma | 8,063 | 126,992 | 187 | 18,202 | 2,648 | 54,841 | 37,389 | 248,322 |
| Oregon | 4,677 | 30,395 | 0 | 0 | 3,919 | 29,882 | 18,601 | 87,474 |
| Pennsylvania | 13,335 | 968 | 0 | 0 | 568 | 10,008 | 23,886 | 48,765 |
| Rhode Island | 1 | 0 | 0 | 0 | 5 | 121 | 181 | 308 |
| South Carolina | 10,892 | 6,792 | 0 | 11,717 | 5 | 13,859 | 29,323 | 72,588 |
| South Dakota | 88,340 | 58,450 | 0 | 0 | 10,348 | 73,891 | 40,870 | 271,899 |
| Tennessee | 12,221 | 6,728 | 92 | 28,911 | 92 | 27,603 | 40,219 | 115,866 |
| Texas | 107,439 | 89,920 | 74,743 | 259,358 | 81,655 | 179,671 | 369,253 | 1,162,039 |
| Utah | 2,344 | 4,016 | 0 | 0 | 7,820 | 11,212 | 10,580 | 35,972 |
| Vermont | 413 | 1 | 0 | 0 | 168 | 2,057 | 2,911 | 5,550 |
| Virginia | 9,525 | 2,971 | 0 | 224 | 755 | 7,331 | 8,266 | 29,072 |
| Washington | 17,636 | 82,019 | 0 | 0 | 799 | 56,594 | 31,695 | 188,743 |
| West Virginia | 1,254 | 75 | 0 | 0 | 408 | 2,100 | 3,025 | 6,862 |
| Wisconsin | 88,977 | 1,742 | 0 | 0 | 541 | 48,774 | 25,993 | 166,027 |
| Wyoming | 1,886 | 4,039 | 0 | 0 | 14,267 | 12,542 | 3,929 | 36,663 |
| United States | $2,499,273 | $1,402,688 | $512,300 | $751,177 | $188,082 | $1,899,421 | $1,915,979 | $9,168,920 |

(1) Includes both cash payments and payment-in-kind (PIK). (2) Includes amount paid under agriculture and conservation programs (Conservation Reserve, Agriculture Conservation, Emergency Conservation, and Great Plains Program). (3) The programs included are Rural Clean Water, Forest Incentive, Water Bank, Dairy Indemnity, Dairy Termination, Extended Warehouse Storage, Extended Farm Storage, Colorado River Salinity, Livestock Emergency Assistance, Interest Penalty Payments, Disaster, Loan Deficiency, Market Gains, Naval Stores Conservation, Milk Marketing Fee, Animal Waste Management, and interest.

## Federal Food Assistance Programs[1]

Source: Food and Nutrition Service, U.S. Dept. of Agriculture; in millions of dollars

| Program | 1983 | 1984 | 1985 | 1986 | 1987 | 1988 | 1989 | 1990 | 1991 | 1992 |
|---|---|---|---|---|---|---|---|---|---|---|
| Food Stamps[2] | $11,847 | $11,579 | $11,703 | $11,638 | $11,605 | $12,317 | $12,932 | $15,491 | $18,769 | $22,460 |
| P.R. Nutr. Asst.[3] | 825 | 825 | 825 | 820 | 853 | 879 | 908 | 937 | 963 | 1,002 |
| Natl. School Lunch[4] | 3,203 | 3,335 | 3,380 | 3,537 | 3,685 | 3,730 | 3,770 | 3,834 | 4,215 | 4,566 |
| School Breakfast | 344 | 364 | 379 | 406 | 447 | 482 | 513 | 596 | 685 | 787 |
| WIC[5] | 1,126 | 1,388 | 1,489 | 1,583 | 1,680 | 1,798 | 1,911 | 2,122 | 2,301 | 2,597 |
| Summer Food Svc.[4] | 93 | 96 | 112 | 115 | 129 | 133 | 146 | 164 | 176 | 204 |
| Child/Adult Care[4] | 356 | 407 | 452 | 496 | 548 | 628 | 703 | 820 | 950 | 1,099 |
| Special Milk | 17 | 16 | 16 | 16 | 15 | 19 | 18 | 19 | 20 | 20 |
| Nutrition for the Elderly[4] | 120 | 127 | 134 | 137 | 139 | 146 | 146 | 142 | 140 | 145 |
| Food Distrib. to Indian Reserv. | 44 | 51 | 60 | 60 | 63 | 62 | 65 | 66 | 65 | 62 |
| Commodity Supp. Food[4,6] | 42 | 48 | 48 | 48 | 56 | 62 | 73 | 85 | 93 | 105 |
| Food Dist.—Charitable Instit.[7] | 154 | 190 | 170 | 240 | 158 | 159 | 136 | 104 | 90 | 115 |
| Emergency Food Assistance | 998 | 1,075 | 1,026 | 895 | 895 | 645 | 276 | 257 | 256 | 236 |
| Soup Kitchens/Food Banks | 0 | 0 | 0 | 0 | 0 | 0 | 34 | 70 | 44 | 35 |
| Other Costs[8] | 53 | 52 | 56 | 60 | 62 | 58 | 66 | 76 | 72 | 88 |
| Total[9] | $19,222 | $19,552 | $19,851 | $20,051 | $20,335 | $21,118 | $21,696 | $24,782 | $28,841 | $33,520 |

(1) Data are for fiscal (not calendar) years. (2) Includes the federal share of state administrative expenses and other federal costs. (3) Puerto Rico participated in the Food Stamp Program from FY 1975 until July 1982, when it initiated a separate grant program. (4) Includes the value of commodities (entitlement, bonus, and cash in lieu). (5) Special Supplemental Pgm. for Women, Infants, and Children includes program studies and farmers market demonstration projects. (6) Includes elderly feeding projects. (7) Includes summer camps. (8) Includes child nutrition state admin. expenses, nutrition studies, nutrition education and training, and nutrition assistance to the Northern Marianas. (9) Excludes food program administration (FPA) costs.

## Farm Marketings by State, 1991 and 1992

Source: Economic Research Service, U.S. Dept. of Agriculture; in thousands of dollars

| State/Rank | 1991 Farm marketings Total | Crops | Livestock and products | 1992 Farm marketings Total | Crops | Livestock and products |
|---|---|---|---|---|---|---|
| Alabama (25) | $3,006,747 | $769,639 | $2,237,108 | $2,830,062 | $767,503 | $2,062,559 |
| Alaska (50) | 26,559 | 20,173 | 6,386 | 25,478 | 19,631 | 5,847 |
| Arizona (32) | 1,867,235 | 1,081,013 | 786,222 | 1,835,250 | 942,787 | 892,463 |
| Arkansas (11) | 4,241,502 | 1,577,632 | 2,663,870 | 4,602,230 | 1,900,501 | 2,701,729 |
| California (1) | 17,776,785 | 12,522,600 | 5,254,185 | 18,234,014 | 13,179,284 | 5,054,730 |
| Colorado (17) | 3,762,245 | 1,098,989 | 2,663,256 | 4,038,389 | 1,083,185 | 2,955,204 |
| Connecticut (44) | 472,178 | 263,957 | 208,221 | 488,746 | 249,113 | 239,633 |
| Delaware (40) | 621,954 | 183,784 | 438,170 | 635,762 | 184,436 | 451,326 |
| Florida (8) | 6,124,957 | 4,953,331 | 1,171,626 | 6,144,508 | 4,984,913 | 1,159,595 |
| Georgia (16) | 3,933,768 | 1,772,025 | 2,161,743 | 4,073,125 | 1,763,842 | 2,309,283 |
| Hawaii (41) | 561,873 | 474,272 | 87,601 | 564,151 | 475,722 | 88,429 |
| Idaho (26) | 2,651,430 | 1,586,238 | 1,065,192 | 2,815,512 | 1,642,545 | 1,172,967 |
| Illinois (5) | 7,534,410 | 5,181,365 | 2,353,045 | 7,633,692 | 5,431,346 | 2,202,346 |
| Indiana (12) | 4,500,353 | 2,583,245 | 1,917,108 | 4,505,292 | 2,683,849 | 1,821,443 |
| Iowa (3) | 10,249,590 | 4,529,154 | 5,720,436 | 10,329,712 | 4,715,624 | 5,614,088 |
| Kansas (7) | 7,076,365 | 2,275,897 | 4,800,468 | 7,000,307 | 2,442,242 | 4,558,065 |
| Kentucky (22) | 3,196,220 | 1,490,870 | 1,705,350 | 3,221,305 | 1,580,236 | 1,641,069 |
| Louisiana (31) | 1,728,110 | 1,091,798 | 636,312 | 1,846,181 | 1,258,928 | 587,253 |
| Maine (42) | 483,586 | 192,052 | 291,534 | 513,187 | 212,686 | 300,501 |
| Maryland (35) | 1,352,025 | 563,821 | 788,204 | 1,390,765 | 586,792 | 803,973 |
| Massachusetts (43) | 485,376 | 356,021 | 129,355 | 491,234 | 356,298 | 134,936 |
| Michigan (20) | 3,209,894 | 1,922,219 | 1,287,675 | 3,286,329 | 1,961,720 | 1,324,609 |
| Minnesota (6) | 7,378,091 | 3,785,567 | 3,592,524 | 7,082,069 | 3,459,768 | 3,622,301 |
| Mississippi (27) | 2,383,299 | 1,107,762 | 1,275,537 | 2,601,966 | 1,246,850 | 1,355,116 |
| Missouri (15) | 3,910,867 | 1,642,464 | 2,268,403 | 4,123,300 | 1,934,931 | 2,188,369 |
| Montana (33) | 1,514,382 | 704,411 | 809,971 | 1,742,408 | 821,096 | 921,312 |
| Nebraska (4) | 9,044,459 | 3,111,126 | 5,933,333 | 8,782,653 | 3,109,062 | 5,673,591 |
| Nevada (47) | 296,946 | 88,220 | 208,726 | 272,795 | 71,147 | 201,648 |
| New Hampshire (48) | 142,474 | 79,135 | 63,339 | 143,983 | 78,975 | 65,008 |
| New Jersey (39) | 658,186 | 465,203 | 192,983 | 656,888 | 464,505 | 192,383 |
| New Mexico (34) | 1,452,294 | 474,405 | 977,889 | 1,530,425 | 490,324 | 1,040,101 |
| New York (24) | 2,873,699 | 1,081,117 | 1,792,582 | 2,946,039 | 1,031,986 | 1,914,053 |
| North Carolina (10) | 4,955,786 | 2,338,602 | 2,617,184 | 5,181,017 | 2,386,168 | 2,794,849 |
| North Dakota (23) | 2,546,552 | 1,876,863 | 669,689 | 3,093,612 | 2,338,761 | 754,851 |
| Ohio (14) | 4,164,857 | 2,483,541 | 1,681,316 | 4,167,316 | 2,587,323 | 1,579,993 |
| Oklahoma (18) | 3,856,406 | 1,068,129 | 2,788,277 | 3,634,931 | 1,137,254 | 2,497,677 |
| Oregon (28) | 2,524,544 | 1,699,026 | 825,518 | 2,489,821 | 1,694,516 | 795,305 |
| Pennsylvania (19) | 3,401,890 | 996,834 | 2,405,056 | 3,618,490 | 1,064,239 | 2,554,251 |
| Rhode Island (49) | 69,293 | 56,904 | 12,389 | 72,218 | 59,527 | 12,691 |
| South Carolina (36) | 1,226,129 | 677,414 | 548,715 | 1,176,746 | 631,500 | 545,246 |
| South Dakota (21) | 3,313,596 | 1,188,465 | 2,125,131 | 3,229,480 | 1,263,112 | 1,966,368 |
| Tennessee (30) | 1,936,439 | 892,657 | 1,043,782 | 2,103,471 | 1,042,225 | 1,061,246 |
| Texas (2) | 12,216,963 | 4,336,062 | 7,880,901 | 11,619,842 | 4,096,754 | 7,523,088 |
| Utah (38) | 720,860 | 171,254 | 549,606 | 738,338 | 181,976 | 556,362 |
| Vermont (45) | 434,044 | 64,437 | 369,607 | 451,898 | 63,396 | 388,502 |
| Virginia (29) | 2,115,662 | 752,685 | 1,362,977 | 2,134,353 | 781,438 | 1,352,915 |
| Washington (13) | 4,143,238 | 2,844,292 | 1,298,946 | 4,454,223 | 2,922,152 | 1,532,071 |
| West Virginia (46) | 323,901 | 70,787 | 253,114 | 342,548 | 75,476 | 267,072 |
| Wisconsin (9) | 5,416,533 | 1,225,460 | 4,191,073 | 5,499,038 | 1,185,676 | 4,313,362 |
| Wyoming (37) | 836,923 | 168,850 | 668,073 | 773,312 | 167,127 | 606,185 |
| United States | $168,721,475 | $81,941,767 | $86,779,708 | $171,168,411 | $84,810,447 | $86,357,964 |

## Value of U.S. Agricultural Exports and Imports, 1970-1990

Source: Economic Research Service, U.S. Dept. of Agriculture; in billions of dollars, except percent

| Year | Trade balance | Exports, domestic products | Percent of all exports | Imports for consumption | Percent of all imports | Year | Trade balance | Exports, domestic products | Percent of all exports | Imports for consumption | Percent of all imports |
|---|---|---|---|---|---|---|---|---|---|---|---|
| 1970 . . . | $1.5 | $7.3 | 17 | $5.8 | 15 | 1981 . . . | 26.6 | 43.3 | 18 | 16.8 | 6 |
| 1972 . . . | 2.9 | 9.4 | 19 | 6.5 | 12 | 1982 . . . | 21.2 | 36.6 | 17 | 15.4 | 6 |
| 1973 . . . | 9.3 | 17.7 | 25 | 8.4 | 12 | 1983 . . . | 19.5 | 36.1 | 18 | 16.6 | 7 |
| 1974 . . . | 11.7 | 21.9 | 23 | 10.2 | 10 | 1984 . . . | 18.5 | 37.8 | 17 | 19.3 | 6 |
| 1975 . . . | 12.6 | 21.9 | 21 | 9.3 | 10 | 1985 . . . | 9.1 | 29.0 | 13 | 20.0 | 6 |
| 1976 . . . | 12.0 | 23.0 | 20 | 11.0 | 9 | 1986 . . . | 4.8 | 26.2 | 13 | 21.5 | 6 |
| 1977 . . . | 10.2 | 23.6 | 20 | 13.4 | 9 | 1987 . . . | 8.3 | 28.7 | 12 | 20.4 | 5 |
| 1978 . . . | 14.6 | 29.4 | 21 | 14.8 | 9 | 1988 . . . | 16.1 | 37.1 | 12 | 21.0 | 5 |
| 1979 . . . | 18.0 | 34.7 | 19 | 16.7 | 8 | 1989 . . . | 18.2 | 39.9 | 11 | 21.7 | 5 |
| 1980 . . . | 23.9 | 41.2 | 18 | 17.4 | 7 | 1990 . . . | 16.6 | 39.3 | 10 | 22.8 | 5 |

## Farm Real Estate Debt Outstanding by Lender Groups[1]

Source: Economic Research Service, U.S. Dept. of Agriculture; in thousands of dollars

| Dec. 31 | Total farm real estate debt[2] | Federal land banks[2] | Farmers Home Adminis-tration[3] | Life in-surance com-panies[4] | All commer-cial banks | Other[5] |
|---|---|---|---|---|---|---|
| | | | Amounts held by principal lender groups | | | |
| 1960............ | $12,867,524 | $2,539,000 | $723,000 | $2,975,000 | $1,592,000 | $5,039,000 |
| 1970............ | 30,492,357 | 7,145,363 | 2,440,043 | 5,610,300 | 3,772,377 | 11,524,000 |
| 1980............ | 97,486,996 | 36,196,103 | 8,163,270 | 12,927,800 | 8,563,457 | 31,636,000 |
| 1985............ | 105,739,201 | 44,583,842 | 10,426,971 | 11,830,400 | 11,384,920 | 27,507,000 |
| 1986............ | 95,879,799 | 37,757,626 | 10,348,597 | 10,940,200 | 12,710,650 | 24,123,000 |
| 1987............ | 87,717,601 | 32,637,687 | 10,083,239 | 9,895,800 | 14,455,162 | 20,646,000 |
| 1988............ | 82,952,518 | 30,326,707 | 9,606,796 | 9,581,700 | 15,416,700 | 18,020,000 |
| 1989............ | 80,476,478 | 28,501,000 | 8,719,822 | 9,597,900 | 16,646,179 | 17,011,577 |
| 1990............ | 78,398,009 | 26,885,056 | 8,092,982 | 10,186,300 | 17,227,171 | 16,006,500 |
| 1991............ | 79,133,192 | 26,700,747 | 7,462,411 | 10,029,300 | 18,436,918 | 16,503,786 |
| 1992............ | 79,759,547 | 26,907,316 | 6,779,546 | 9,208,000 | 19,862,622 | 17,001,963 |

(1) Includes operator households. (2) Includes data for joint stock land banks and real estate loans by Agricultural Credit Assn. (3) Includes loans made directly by FmHA for farm ownership, soil and water loans to individuals, Indian tribe land acquisition, grazing associations, and half of economic emergency loans. Also includes loans for rural housing on farm tracts and labor housing. (4) American Council of Life Insurance. (5) Estimated by ERS, USDA. Includes Commodity Credit Corporation storage and drying facility loans.

## Grain, Hay, Potato, Cotton, Soybean, Tobacco Production, by State, 1992

Source: Economic Research Service, U.S. Dept. of Agriculture

| 1992 State | Barley (1,000 bushels) | Corn, grain (1,000 bushels) | Cotton lint (1,000 bales) | All Hay (1,000 tons) | Oats (1,000 bushels) | Potatoes (1,000 cwt.) | Soybeans (1,000 bushels) | Tobacco (1,000 pounds) | All Wheat (1,000 bushels) |
|---|---|---|---|---|---|---|---|---|---|
| Alabama | — | 30,080 | 621 | 1,491 | 1,500 | 1,733 | 7,830 | — | 4,180 |
| Alaska | — | — | — | — | — | — | — | — | — |
| Arizona | 2,205 | 1,870 | 863 | 1,224 | — | 1,800 | — | — | 7,700 |
| Arkansas | — | 12,350 | 1,681 | 2,796 | 1,600 | — | 104,280 | — | 39,100 |
| California | 11,160 | 23,925 | 3,111 | 7,755 | 2,800 | 15,592 | — | — | 46,365 |
| Colorado | 9,000 | 123,580 | — | 3,961 | 2,100 | 24,120 | — | — | 72,619 |
| Connecticut | — | — | — | 194 | — | — | — | 2,320 | — |
| Delaware | 2,590 | 19,159 | — | 52 | — | 1,380 | 6,880 | — | 4,060 |
| Florida | — | 8,250 | 72 | 875 | — | 9,370 | 1,350 | 19,575 | 840 |
| Georgia | — | 69,000 | 744 | 1,624 | 3,685 | — | 18,560 | 100,980 | 16,100 |
| Hawaii | — | — | — | — | — | — | — | — | — |
| Idaho | 54,000 | 4,290 | — | 3,655 | 1,440 | 127,050 | — | — | 100,000 |
| Illinois | — | 1,646,450 | — | 3,316 | 7,930 | 1,320 | 405,490 | — | 62,100 |
| Indiana | — | 877,590 | — | 1,971 | 2,800 | 989 | 194,360 | 18,900 | 22,500 |
| Iowa | — | 1,903,650 | — | 6,615 | 25,125 | 280 | 363,880 | — | 1,560 |
| Kansas | 680 | 259,500 | 0 | 6,670 | 7,840 | — | 68,450 | — | 363,800 |
| Kentucky | 1,188 | 171,600 | — | 4,935 | — | — | 44,080 | 524,378 | 23,100 |
| Louisiana | — | 37,080 | 1,299 | 644 | — | — | 35,100 | — | 6,120 |
| Maine | — | — | — | 417 | 1,650 | 24,300 | — | — | — |
| Maryland | 4,672 | 58,280 | — | 648 | 594 | 320 | 17,985 | 11,931 | 12,760 |
| Massachusetts | — | — | — | 248 | — | 825 | — | 678 | — |
| Michigan | 1,736 | 241,500 | — | 4,640 | 8,400 | 13,920 | 47,520 | — | 35,280 |
| Minnesota | 50,625 | 741,000 | — | 6,550 | 35,000 | 18,388 | 172,800 | — | 139,860 |
| Mississippi | — | 27,000 | 2,131 | 2,025 | — | — | 59,500 | — | 10,500 |
| Missouri | — | 324,000 | 541 | 7,030 | 2,430 | 1,764 | 161,500 | 3,298 | 64,800 |
| Montana | 52,800 | 2,750 | — | 4,650 | 3,920 | 2,465 | — | — | 139,581 |
| Nebraska | 1,500 | 1,066,500 | — | 8,023 | 15,400 | 3,298 | 103,320 | — | 55,500 |
| Nevada | 550 | — | — | 1,062 | — | 2,925 | — | — | 800 |
| New Hampshire | — | — | — | 181 | — | — | — | — | — |
| New Jersey | 448 | 9,840 | — | 333 | — | 840 | 4,224 | — | 1,400 |
| New Mexico | — | 11,360 | 67 | 1,401 | — | 3,247 | — | — | 11,220 |
| New York | — | 61,640 | — | 3,590 | 7,700 | 7,808 | — | — | 6,160 |
| North Carolina | 1,980 | 98,800 | 468 | 1,234 | 3,000 | 3,614 | 36,450 | 609,873 | 27,750 |
| North Dakota | 172,250 | 36,540 | — | 3,515 | 37,400 | 27,690 | 17,250 | — | 469,850 |
| Ohio | — | 507,650 | — | 4,550 | 12,070 | 1,440 | 147,200 | 21,840 | 59,095 |
| Oklahoma | 396 | 17,550 | 210 | 4,940 | 2,250 | — | 5,940 | — | 171,100 |
| Oregon | 9,450 | 2,250 | — | 2,440 | 4,230 | 21,075 | — | — | 47,800 |
| Pennsylvania | 6,390 | 118,800 | — | 4,900 | 13,735 | 4,940 | 11,115 | 21,030 | 10,175 |
| Rhode Island | — | — | — | 18 | — | 377 | — | — | — |
| South Carolina | 558 | 30,800 | 226 | 450 | 2,205 | — | 14,740 | 112,320 | 12,925 |
| South Dakota | 20,520 | 277,200 | — | 7,020 | 42,900 | 1,500 | 63,000 | — | 119,590 |
| Tennessee | — | 79,360 | 834 | 3,465 | — | — | 33,250 | 146,556 | 13,440 |
| Texas | 270 | 202,500 | 3,322 | 9,800 | 5,720 | 2,459 | 12,870 | — | 129,200 |
| Utah | 8,970 | 3,240 | — | 2,240 | 1,050 | 1,650 | — | — | 6,256 |
| Vermont | — | — | — | 835 | — | — | — | — | — |
| Virginia | 7,110 | 40,020 | 28 | 2,905 | — | 1,980 | 15,500 | 111,459 | 15,105 |
| Washington | 19,800 | 15,840 | — | 2,962 | 1,800 | 69,300 | — | — | 119,640 |
| West Virginia | — | 5,400 | — | 1,070 | 360 | — | — | 3,623 | 539 |
| Wisconsin | 4,160 | 306,800 | — | 6,090 | 34,410 | 25,160 | 22,080 | 12,837 | 2,640 |
| Wyoming | 11,340 | 3,920 | — | 2,131 | 1,560 | 448 | — | — | 5,720 |
| United States | 456,348 | 9,478,914 | 16,219 | 149,141 | 294,604 | 425,367 | 2,196,504 | 1,721,598 | 2,458,830 |

## Production of Chief U.S. Crops

Source: National Agricultural Statistics Service: U.S. Dept. of Agriculture

| Year | Corn for grain (1,000 bushels) | Oats (1,000 bushels) | Barley (1,000 bushels) | Sorghum for grain (1,000 bushels) | All Wheat (1,000 bushels) | Rye (1,000 bushels) | Flax-seed (1,000 bushels) | Cotton lint (1,000 bales) | Cotton seed (1,000 tons) |
|---|---|---|---|---|---|---|---|---|---|
| 1970 .. | 4,152,243 | 915,236 | 416,091 | 683,179 | 1,351,558 | 36,840 | 29,416 | 10,192 | 4,068 |
| 1975 .. | 5,828,961 | 638,960 | 379,162 | 754,354 | 2,126,927 | 15,924 | 15,553 | 8,302 | 3,218 |
| 1980 .. | 6,639,396 | 458,792 | 361,135 | 579,343 | 2,380,934 | 15,958 | 7,728 | 11,122 | 4,470 |
| 1982 .. | 8,235,101 | 592,630 | 515,935 | 835,083 | 2,764,967 | 19,533 | 10,278 | 11,963 | 4,744 |
| 1985 .. | 8,875,453 | 518,490 | 590,213 | 1,120,271 | 2,424,115 | 20,373 | 8,293 | 13,432 | 5,279 |
| 1986 .. | 8,225,764 | 384,996 | 608,532 | 938,869 | 2,090,570 | 19,067 | 11,538 | 9,731 | 3,801 |
| 1987 .. | 7,131,300 | 373,713 | 521,499 | 730,809 | 2,107,685 | 19,526 | 7,444 | 14,760 | 5,769 |
| 1988 .. | 4,928,681 | 217,600 | 289,994 | 576,686 | 1,812,201 | 14,689 | 1,615 | 15,412 | 6,062 |
| 1989 .. | 7,525,493 | 373,587 | 404,203 | 615,420 | 2,036,618 | 13,647 | 1,215 | 12,196 | 4,677 |
| 1990 .. | 7,934,028 | 357,524 | 422,196 | 573,303 | 2,736,428 | 10,176 | 3,812 | 15,505 | 5,969 |
| 1991 .. | 7,475,480 | 243,451 | 464,326 | 584,860 | 1,981,129 | 9,761 | 6,200 | 17,614 | 6,926 |
| 1992 .. | 9,478,914 | 294,604 | 456,348 | 884,010 | 2,458,830 | 11,952 | 3,288 | 16,260 | 6,265 |

| Year | Tobacco (1,000 lbs.) | All Hay (1,000 tons) | Beans dry edible (1,000 cwt.) | Peas dry edible (1,000 cwt.) | Peanuts (1,000 lbs.) | Soybeans (1,000 bushels) | Potatoes (1,000 cwt.) | Sweet potatoes (1,000 cwt.) |
|---|---|---|---|---|---|---|---|---|
| 1970 ..... | 1,906,453 | 126,969 | 17,399 | 3,315 | 2,983,121 | 1,127,100 | 325,716 | 13,164 |
| 1975 ..... | 2,182,304 | 132,397 | 17,442 | 2,731 | 3,846,722 | 1,548,344 | 321,978 | 12,891 |
| 1980 ..... | 1,786,225 | 130,740 | 26,729 | 3,285 | 2,302,762 | 1,797,543 | 303,905 | 10,953 |
| 1982 ..... | 1,994,494 | 149,241 | 25,563 | NA | 3,440,255 | 2,190,297 | 355,131 | 14,833 |
| 1985 ..... | 1,511,638 | 148,719 | 22,298 | NA | 4,122,787 | 2,099,056 | 407,109 | 14,573 |
| 1986 ..... | 1,161,940 | 155,385 | 22,960 | 3,196 | 3,697,085 | 1,942,558 | 361,511 | 12,368 |
| 1987 ..... | 1,188,868 | 147,319 | 26,031 | 3,385 | 3,616,010 | 1,938,087 | 385,774 | 11,611 |
| 1988 ..... | 1,369,500 | 126,010 | 19,253 | 3,868 | 3,980,917 | 1,548,841 | 356,438 | 10,945 |
| 1989 ..... | 1,367,188 | 145,512 | 23,729 | 3,883 | 3,989,995 | 1,923,666 | 370,444 | 11,358 |
| 1990 ..... | 1,626,380 | 146,820 | 32,379 | 2,372 | 3,602,770 | 1,925,947 | 402,110 | 12,594 |
| 1991 ..... | 1,664,372 | 153,325 | 33,765 | 3,715 | 4,926,570 | 1,986,539 | 417,622 | 11,203 |
| 1992 ..... | 1,683,831 | 149,140 | 22,047 | 2,535 | 4,284,390 | 2,196,504 | 411,636 | 11,760 |

| Year | Rice (1,000 cwt.) | Sugar-cane (1,000 tons) | Sugar beets (1,000 tons) | Pecans (1,000 tons) | Al-monds (1,000 tons) | Wal-nuts (1,000 tons) | Hazel-nuts[1] (1,000 tons) | Oranges[2] (1,000 boxes) | Grape-fruit[2] (1,000 boxes) |
|---|---|---|---|---|---|---|---|---|---|
| 1970 ...... | NA | 23,996 | 26,378 | NA | NA | 111.8 | 9.3 | 185,770 | 53,910 |
| 1975 ...... | NA | 28,344 | 29,704 | NA | NA | 199.3 | 12.1 | 237,810 | 61,610 |
| 1980 ...... | 146,150 | 26,963 | 23,502 | 91.8 | 264.4 | 197.0 | 15.4 | 273,630 | 73,200 |
| 1982 ...... | 153,637 | 29,770 | 20,894 | 109.3 | 283.5 | 234.0 | 18.8 | 176,690 | 70,550 |
| 1985 ...... | 134,913 | 28,213 | 22,529 | 122.2 | 375.6 | 219.0 | 24.6 | 158,350 | 56,150 |
| 1986 ...... | 133,356 | 30,311 | 25,150 | 136.4 | 201.3 | 180.0 | 15.1 | 175,440 | 57,870 |
| 1987 ...... | 129,603 | 29,218 | 28,072 | 131.1 | 519.0 | 247.0 | 21.8 | 181,175 | 63,775 |
| 1988 ...... | 159,897 | 29,904 | 24,810 | 154.1 | 451.9 | 209.0 | 16.5 | 200,250 | 68,700 |
| 1989 ...... | 154,487 | 29,426 | 25,131 | 125.3 | 394.7 | 229.0 | 13.0 | 209,050 | 69,500 |
| 1990 ...... | 156,088 | 28,136 | 27,513 | 102.5 | 519.7 | 227.0 | 21.7 | 186,075 | 48,600 |
| 1991 ...... | 157,457 | 30,252 | 28,203 | 149.5 | 385.8 | 259.0 | 25.5 | 178,950 | 55,500 |
| 1992 ...... | 179,088 | 30,852 | 28,848 | 89.8 | 451.9 | 200.0 | 27.5 | 209,610 | 55,265 |

NA = Not available. (1) Formerly called filberts. (2) Crop year ending in year cited.

## Principal U.S. Crops: Area Planted and Harvested, 1990-92

Source: Natl. Agricultural Statistics Service, U.S. Dept. of Agriculture; in thousand acres

| State | Area Planted[1] 1990 | 1991 | 1992 | Area Harvested[2] 1990 | 1991 | 1992 | State | Area Planted[1] 1990 | 1991 | 1992 | Area Harvested[2] 1990 | 1991 | 1992 |
|---|---|---|---|---|---|---|---|---|---|---|---|---|---|
| AL | 2,516 | 2,354 | 2,246 | 2,338 | 2,229 | 2,130 | NE | 18,732 | 19,009 | 19,276 | 18,044 | 18,366 | 18,330 |
| AZ | 809 | 778 | 744 | 802 | 770 | 736 | NV | 525 | 502 | 407 | 520 | 495 | 403 |
| AR | 8,320 | 8,180 | 8,310 | 8,080 | 7,863 | 8,110 | NH | 93 | 94 | 105 | 91 | 92 | 103 |
| CA | 5,289 | 4,872 | 4,899 | 4,789 | 4,396 | 4,433 | NJ | 419 | 431 | 446 | 361 | 380 | 391 |
| CO | 6,131 | 6,023 | 5,867 | 5,862 | 5,591 | 5,394 | NM | 1,200 | 1,287 | 1,302 | 880 | 1,042 | 1,053 |
| CT | 133 | 132 | 134 | 129 | 125 | 128 | NY | 3,630 | 3,541 | 3,325 | 3,538 | 3,443 | 3,185 |
| DE | 506 | 568 | 531 | 496 | 556 | 515 | NC | 4,618 | 4,666 | 4,757 | 4,336 | 4,397 | 4,519 |
| FL | 1,115 | 1,104 | 1,152 | 1,076 | 1,048 | 1,093 | ND | 22,119 | 21,338 | 21,732 | 21,014 | 20,655 | 21,011 |
| GA | 4,405 | 4,185 | 4,039 | 3,788 | 3,777 | 3,690 | OH | 10,348 | 10,229 | 10,479 | 10,132 | 9,972 | 10,137 |
| HI | 79 | 74 | 71 | 79 | 74 | 71 | OK | 11,067 | 11,185 | 11,112 | 9,688 | 8,518 | 9,397 |
| ID | 4,273 | 4,311 | 4,177 | 4,175 | 4,079 | 4,006 | OR | 2,375 | 2,367 | 2,233 | 2,290 | 2,260 | 2,145 |
| IL | 23,608 | 23,695 | 23,940 | 22,759 | 22,906 | 23,237 | PA | 4,203 | 4,182 | 4,176 | 4,094 | 4,067 | 4,065 |
| IN | 11,731 | 11,813 | 12,219 | 11,485 | 11,527 | 11,709 | RI | 10 | 10 | 11 | 10 | 10 | 11 |
| IA | 24,182 | 23,877 | 24,372 | 23,276 | 23,356 | 23,816 | SC | 2,225 | 1,945 | 1,989 | 2,046 | 1,824 | 1,887 |
| KS | 21,937 | 21,901 | 21,903 | 20,978 | 20,712 | 20,255 | SD | 16,359 | 16,328 | 17,047 | 15,528 | 15,606 | 15,858 |
| KY | 5,748 | 5,770 | 5,643 | 5,505 | 5,495 | 5,415 | TN | 4,639 | 4,567 | 4,517 | 4,477 | 4,379 | 4,324 |
| LA | 4,485 | 4,010 | 4,150 | 4,346 | 3,665 | 4,029 | TX | 23,002 | 23,501 | 23,872 | 18,544 | 17,714 | 18,772 |
| ME | 379 | 369 | 385 | 361 | 351 | 374 | UT | 1,042 | 1,040 | 1,050 | 992 | 973 | 990 |
| MD | 1,626 | 1,626 | 1,680 | 1,551 | 1,562 | 1,620 | VT | 451 | 442 | 473 | 441 | 434 | 463 |
| MA | 142 | 141 | 140 | 135 | 136 | 135 | VA | 2,897 | 2,833 | 2,858 | 2,725 | 2,656 | 2,705 |
| MI | 6,756 | 6,918 | 7,044 | 6,510 | 6,733 | 6,797 | WA | 4,171 | 5,469 | 4,226 | 3,999 | 3,861 | 3,950 |
| MN | 19,488 | 19,294 | 19,905 | 18,765 | 18,692 | 19,301 | WV | 677 | 630 | 652 | 668 | 615 | 639 |
| MS | 4,491 | 4,716 | 4,900 | 4,719 | 4,478 | 4,855 | WI | 8,885 | 8,830 | 8,668 | 8,550 | 8,449 | 8,096 |
| MO | 12,989 | 13,204 | 13,201 | 12,685 | 12,900 | 12,904 | WY | 1,789 | 1,960 | 1,777 | 1,735 | 1,899 | 1,706 |
| MT | 9,798 | 9,680 | 9,320 | 8,926 | 8,848 | 8,369 | U.S.[3] | 326,913 | 326,032 | 327,612 | 308,318 | 303,864 | 307,314 |

(1) Crops included in area planted are corn, sorghum, oats, barley, winter wheat, rye, durum wheat, other spring wheat, rice, soybeans, peanuts, sunflower, cotton, dry edible beans, potatoes, and sugarbeets. The harvested acreage is used for all hay, tobacco, and sugarcane in computing total area planted. (2) Crops included in area harvested are listed in footnote 1. (3) State figures do not add to U.S. totals due to sunflower and sugarbeet unallocated acreage.

## Average Prices Received by U.S. Farmers

Source: Natl. Agricultural Statistics Service, U.S. Dept. of Agriculture

The figures represent dollars per 100 lbs. for hogs, beef cattle, veal calves, sheep, lamb, and milk (wholesale); dollars per head for milk cows; cents per lb. for chickens, broilers, turkeys, and wool; cents per dozen for eggs.

Weighted calendar year prices for livestock and livestock products other than wool. For 1943 through 1963, wool prices are weighted on marketing year basis. The marketing year was changed in 1964 from a calendar year to a Dec.-Nov. basis for hogs, chickens, broilers, and eggs.

| Year | Hogs | Cattle (beef) | Calves (veal) | Sheep | Lambs | Milk cows | Milk | Chickens (excl. broilers) | Broilers | Turkeys | Eggs | Wool |
|------|------|------|------|------|------|------|------|------|------|------|------|------|
| 1930 | 8.84 | 7.71 | 9.68 | 4.74 | 7.76 | 74 | 2.21 | ... | ... | 20.2 | 23.7 | 19.5 |
| 1940 | 5.39 | 7.56 | 8.83 | 3.95 | 8.10 | 61 | 1.82 | 13.0 | 17.3 | 15.2 | 18.0 | 28.4 |
| 1950 | 18.00 | 23.30 | 26.30 | 11.60 | 25.10 | 198 | 3.89 | 22.2 | 27.4 | 32.8 | 36.3 | 62.1 |
| 1960 | 15.30 | 20.40 | 22.90 | 5.61 | 17.90 | 223 | 4.21 | 12.2 | 16.9 | 25.4 | 36.1 | 42.0 |
| 1970 | 22.70 | 27.10 | 34.50 | 7.51 | 26.40 | 332 | 5.71 | 9.1 | 13.6 | 22.6 | 39.1 | 35.4 |
| 1975 | 46.10 | 32.20 | 27.20 | 11.30 | 42.10 | 412 | 8.75 | 9.9 | 26.3 | 34.8 | 54.5 | 44.8 |
| 1979 | 41.80 | 66.10 | 88.80 | 26.30 | 66.70 | 1,040 | 12.00 | 14.4 | 25.9 | 41.3 | 58.3 | 86.3 |
| 1980 | 38.00 | 62.40 | 76.80 | 21.30 | 63.60 | 1,190 | 13.05 | 11.0 | 27.7 | 41.3 | 56.3 | 88.1 |
| 1984 | 47.10 | 57.30 | 59.90 | 16.40 | 60.10 | 895 | 13.46 | 15.9 | 33.7 | 46.9 | 72.3 | 79.5 |
| 1985 | 44.00 | 53.70 | 62.10 | 23.90 | 67.70 | 860 | 12.76 | 14.8 | 30.1 | 49.1 | 57.1 | 63.3 |
| 1986 | 49.30 | 52.60 | 61.10 | 25.60 | 69.00 | 820 | 12.51 | 15.2 | 34.5 | 47.1 | 61.6 | 66.8 |
| 1987 | 51.20 | 61.10 | 78.50 | 29.50 | 77.60 | 920 | 12.54 | 11.0 | 28.7 | 34.8 | 54.9 | 91.7 |
| 1988 | 42.30 | 66.60 | 89.20 | 25.60 | 69.10 | 990 | 12.26 | 9.2 | 33.1 | 38.6 | 52.8 | 1.38 |
| 1989 | 42.50 | 69.50 | 90.80 | 24.40 | 66.10 | 1,030 | 13.56 | 14.9 | 36.6 | 40.9 | 68.9 | 1.24 |
| 1990 | 53.70 | 74.60 | 95.60 | 23.20 | 55.50 | 1,160 | 13.74 | 9.3 | 32.6 | 39.4 | 70.9 | 80.0 |
| 1991 | 49.10 | 72.70 | 98.00 | 19.70 | 52.20 | 1,100 | 12.27 | 7.1 | 30.8 | 38.4 | 67.6 | 55.0 |
| 1992 | 41.60 | 71.30 | 89.00 | 25.80 | 59.50 | 1,130 | 13.15 | 8.6 | 31.8 | 37.7 | 57.7 | 74.0 |

The figures represent cents per lb. for cotton, apples, and peanuts; dollars per bushel for oats, wheat, corn, barley, and soybeans; dollars per 100 lbs. for rice, sorghum, and potatoes; dollars per ton for cottonseed and baled hay.

Weighted crop year prices. Crop years are as follows: apples, June-May; wheat, oats, barley, hay, and potatoes, July-June; cotton, rice, peanuts, and cottonseed, August-July; soybeans, September-August; and corn and sorghum grain, October-September.

|  | Corn | Wheat | Upland cotton[1] | Oats | Barley | Rice | Soybeans | Sorghum | Peanuts | Cottonseed | Hay | Potatoes | Apples |
|------|------|------|------|------|------|------|------|------|------|------|------|------|------|
| 1930 | .598 | .663 | 9.46 | 0.311 | .420 | 1.74 | 1.34 | 1.02 | 5.01 | 22.00 | 11.00 | 1.47 | ... |
| 1940 | .618 | .674 | 9.83 | 0.298 | .393 | 1.80 | .892 | .873 | 3.72 | 21.70 | 9.78 | .850 | ... |
| 1950 | 1.52 | 2.00 | 39.90 | 0.788 | 1.19 | 5.09 | 2.47 | 1.88 | 10.9 | 86.60 | 21.10 | 1.50 | ... |
| 1960 | 1.00 | 1.74 | 30.08 | 0.599 | .840 | 4.55 | 2.13 | 1.49 | 10.0 | 42.50 | 21.70 | 2.00 | 2.72 |
| 1970 | 1.33 | 1.33 | 21.86 | 0.623 | .973 | 5.17 | 2.85 | 2.04 | 12.8 | 56.40 | 26.10 | 2.21 | 6.52 |
| 1975 | 2.54 | 3.55 | 51.10 | 1.45 | 2.42 | 8.35 | 4.92 | 4.21 | 19.6 | 97.00 | 52.10 | 4.48 | 8.80 |
| 1979 | 2.52 | 3.78 | 62.3 | 1.36 | 2.29 | 10.50 | 6.28 | 4.18 | 20.6 | 121.00 | 59.50 | 3.43 | 15.40 |
| 1980 | 3.11 | 3.91 | 74.4 | 1.79 | 2.86 | 12.80 | 7.57 | 5.25 | 25.1 | 129.00 | 71.00 | 6.55 | 12.1 |
| 1984 | 2.63 | 3.39 | 58.7 | 1.67 | 2.29 | 8.04 | 5.84 | 4.15 | 27.9 | 99.50 | 72.70 | 5.69 | 15.5 |
| 1985 | 2.23 | 3.08 | 56.8 | 1.23 | 1.98 | 6.53 | 5.05 | 3.45 | 24.4 | 66.00 | 67.60 | 3.92 | 17.3 |
| 1986 | 1.50 | 2.42 | 51.5 | 1.21 | 1.61 | 3.75 | 4.78 | 2.45 | 29.2 | 80.00 | 59.70 | 5.03 | 19.1 |
| 1987 | 1.94 | 2.57 | 63.7 | 1.56 | 1.81 | 7.27 | 5.88 | 3.04 | 28.0 | 82.50 | 65.00 | 4.38 | 12.7 |
| 1988 | 2.54 | 3.72 | 55.6 | 2.61 | 2.79 | 6.83 | 7.42 | 4.05 | 28.0 | 118.00 | 85.20 | 6.02 | 17.4 |
| 1989 | 2.36 | 3.72 | 63.6 | 1.49 | 2.42 | 7.35 | 5.69 | 3.75 | 28.0 | 105.00 | 85.40 | 7.36 | 13.9 |
| 1990 | 2.28 | 2.61 | 67.1 | 1.14 | 2.14 | 6.70 | 5.74 | 2.12 | 34.7 | 121.00 | 80.60 | 6.08 | 20.9 |
| 1991 | 2.37 | 3.00 | 56.8 | 1.21 | 2.10 | 7.58 | 5.58 | 2.25 | 28.3 | 71.00 | 71.20 | 4.96 | 25.1 |
| 1992 | 2.05 | 3.25 | 53.1 | 1.30 | 2.05 | 6.20 | 5.40 | 1.90 | 3.00 | 97.00 | 72.10 | 5.28 | 19.2 |

(1) Beginning in 1964, 480 lb. net weight bales.

## Grain Storage Capacity at Principal U.S. Grain Centers

Source: Chicago Board of Trade Market Information Department, Aug. 1993

(bushels)

| Cities | Capacity |
|------|------|
| **Atlantic Coast** | 16,000,000 |
| **Great Lakes** | |
| Toledo | 63,100,000 |
| Buffalo | 15,200,000 |
| Chicago | 52,400,000 |
| Milwaukee | 6,600,000 |
| Duluth | 58,200,000 |
| **River Points** | |
| Minneapolis | 82,300,000 |
| Peoria | 3,300,000 |
| St. Louis | 17,700,000 |
| Sioux City | 3,800,000 |
| Omaha-Council Bluffs | 7,800,000 |
| Atchison | 16,900,000 |
| St. Joseph | 22,300,000 |
| Kansas City, Mo. | 95,200,000 |

| Cities | Capacity |
|------|------|
| **Southwest** | |
| Fort Worth | 68,000,000 |
| Texas High Plains | 72,700,000 |
| Enid | 79,700,000 |
| **Gulf Points** | |
| South Mississippi | 47,300,000 |
| Texas Gulf | 45,800,000 |
| **Plains** | |
| Wichita | 37,400,000 |
| Topeka | 55,500,000 |
| Salina | 49,500,000 |
| Hutchinson | 42,000,000 |
| Hastings-Grand Island | 25,100,000 |
| Lincoln | 33,700,000 |
| **Pacific N.W.** | |
| Puget Sound (incl. Portland) | 35,100,000 |
| California Ports | NA |

**Atlantic Coast** — Albany, N.Y., Philadelphia, Pa., Baltimore, Md., Norfolk, Va. **Gulf Points** — New Orleans, Baton Rouge, Ama, Belle Chasse, La., Mobile, Ala. **Texas Gulf** — Houston, Galveston, Beaumont, Port Arthur, Corpus Christi, Brownsville. **Pacific N.W.** — Seattle, Tacoma, Wash., Portland, Ore., Columbia River. **Texas High Plains** — Amarillo, Lubbock, Hereford, Plainview. NA = not available.

## World Wheat, Rice, and Corn Production, 1990

Source: U.N. Food and Agriculture Organization

(thousands of metric tons)

| Country | Wheat | Rice | Corn | Country | Wheat | Rice | Corn |
|---|---|---|---|---|---|---|---|
| **World, total** | **595,149** | **518,508** | **475,429** | Japan | 952 | 13,124 | 1 |
| Afghanistan | 1,925 | 430 | 800 | Korea, North | 220 | 5,500 | 4,400 |
| Argentina | 10,800 | 467 | 5,049 | Korean, South | 1 | 7,786 | 2 |
| Australia | 15,712 | 923 | 202 | Laos | — | 1,491 | 67 |
| Austria | 1,370 | — | 1,400 | Madagascar | 1 | 2,400 | 170 |
| Bangladesh | 890 | 28,140 | 3 | Malaysia | — | 1,650 | 35 |
| Belgium-Lux. | 1,527 | — | 60 | Mexico | 3,899 | — | |
| Brazil | 3,140 | 7,425 | 21,298 | Nepal | 855 | 3,300 | 950 |
| Bulgaria | 5,095 | 23 | 1,241 | Netherlands | 1,076 | — | 5 |
| Burma (Myanmar) | 124 | 13,965 | 186 | New Zealand | 220 | — | 160 |
| Cambodia | — | 2,400 | 55 | Pakistan | 14,315 | 4,713 | 1,279 |
| Canada | 31,798 | — | 7,033 | Panama | — | — | 115 |
| Chile | 1,718 | 136 | 823 | Peru | 95 | 966 | 621 |
| China | 96,004 | 188,403 | 87,345 | Philippines | — | 9,319 | 4,854 |
| Colombia | 105 | 2,117 | 1,213 | Poland | 9,026 | — | 290 |
| Cuba | — | 500 | 95 | Portugal | 268 | 153 | 643 |
| Czechoslovakia | 6,707 | — | 468 | Romania | 7,320 | 67 | 6,810 |
| Denmark | 4,101 | — | — | South Africa | 1,794 | — | 9,442 |
| Ecuador | 22 | 760 | 400 | Soviet Union | 108,000 | 2,473 | 16,000 |
| Egypt | 4,267 | 2,800 | 4,400 | Spain | 4,760 | 569 | 3,051 |
| Ethiopia | 870 | — | 2,000 | Sri Lanka | — | 2,200 | 36 |
| Finland | 627 | — | — | Sweden | 2,173 | — | — |
| France | 33,363 | 109 | 8,996 | Switzerland | 572 | — | 231 |
| Germany | 15,787 | — | 1,546 | Syria | 2,069 | — | 132 |
| Greece | 1,580 | 100 | 1,700 | Thailand | — | 19,000 | 3,675 |
| Hungary | 6,159 | 35 | 4,500 | Turkey | 20,000 | 235 | 2,000 |
| India | 49,652 | 112,500 | 9,500 | United Kingdom | 13,900 | — | |
| Indonesia | — | 44,490 | 6,741 | United States | 74,534 | 7,027 | 201,509 |
| Iran | 7,000 | 1,400 | 7 | Uruguay | 420 | 517 | 101 |
| Iraq | 805 | 200 | 110 | Venezuela | — | 400 | 1,150 |
| Ireland | 603 | — | — | Vietnam | — | 18,400 | 850 |
| Israel | 160 | — | 22 | Yugoslavia | 6,359 | 40 | 6,270 |
| Italy | 8,109 | 1,282 | 5,864 | | | | |

Note: Some figures are FAO estimates. Where production is small or nonexistent, — is indicated.

## Wheat, Rice, and Corn—Exports and Imports of 10 Leading Countries

Source: U.N. Food and Agriculture Organization

(thousands of metric tons)

| Leading Exporters Wheat | Exports[1] | | | Leading Importers Wheat | Imports[1] | | |
|---|---|---|---|---|---|---|---|
| | 1980 | 1990 | 1991P | | 1980 | 1990 | 1991P |
| U.S. | 41,199 | 29,064 | 34,869 | Soviet Union | 16,000 | 15,650 | 21,000 |
| Canada | 16,262 | 21,731 | 24,500 | China | 13,789 | 9,500 | 15,500 |
| France | 13,423 | 18,600 | 18,000 | Italy | 3,028 | 5,500 | 7,300 |
| Australia | 9,577 | 11,760 | 7,600 | Egypt | 5,423 | 5,668 | 6,000 |
| Turkey | 530 | 544 | 5,000 | Japan | 5,840 | 5,622 | 5,750 |
| Argentina | 3,845 | 5,592 | 4,600 | Brazil | 3,910 | 4,444 | 4,672 |
| United Kingdom | 1,100 | 4,165 | 4,600 | South Korea | 2,095 | 4,200 | 4,396 |
| Germany, Fed. Rep.[2] | 1,502 | 3,295 | 4,400 | Algeria | 2,294 | 4,600 | 4,000 |
| Italy | 1,620 | 2,700 | 3,600 | Iran | 1,896 | 4,000 | 2,500 |
| Saudi Arabia | 27 | 1,661 | 2,425 | Indonesia | 1,474 | 2,300 | 2,300 |
| **Rice** | 1980 | 1990 | 1991P | **Rice** | 1980 | 1990 | 1991P |
| Thailand | 3,049 | 3,993 | 4,600 | Iran | 583 | 565 | 800 |
| U.S. | 3,028 | 2,317 | 2,123 | Soviet Union | 1,283 | 400 | 800 |
| Pakistan | 1,163 | 1,320 | 1,200 | Saudi Arabia | 356 | 525 | 550 |
| Vietnam | 5 | 1,000 | 1,200 | Senegal | 340 | 430 | 400 |
| China | 580 | 689 | 750 | Hong Kong | 362 | 368 | 400 |
| Australia | 468 | 443 | 600 | Malaysia | 167 | 355 | 400 |
| Italy | 475 | 580 | 593 | South Africa | 126 | 346 | 375 |
| India | 900 | 500 | 450 | Brazil | 0 | 800 | 350 |
| Uruguay | 184 | 270 | 334 | Turkey | 32 | 161 | 350 |
| Spain | 45 | 210 | 210 | Ivory Coast | 275 | 310 | 325 |
| **Corn** | 1980 | 1990 | 1991P | **Corn** | 1980 | 1990 | 1991P |
| United States | 60,737 | 43,807 | 40,007 | Japan | 13,989 | 16,042 | 16,200 |
| China | 125 | 6,571 | 10,000 | Soviet Union | 11,800 | 8,720 | 12,200 |
| Argentina | 9,098 | 4,000 | 6,400 | South Korea | 2,355 | 5,571 | 6,800 |
| France | 2,380 | 5,300 | 5,700 | Taiwan | 2,703 | 5,250 | 5,700 |
| Hungary | 300 | 500 | 1,400 | South Africa | 0 | 375 | 5,000 |
| Canada | 1,056 | 142 | 1,000 | Netherlands | 2,638 | 1,869 | 1,800 |
| Thailand | 2,142 | 1,193 | 800 | Zimbabwe | 0 | 100 | 1,800 |
| Greece | 0 | 400 | 700 | Malaysia | 717 | 1,490 | 1,750 |
| Yugoslavia | 300 | 21 | 600 | Spain | 4,251 | 1,523 | 1,600 |
| Belgium-Luxembourg | 1,742 | 16 | 200 | United Kingdom | 2,349 | 1,250 | 1,575 |

(1) Marketing years. (2) Data for total Germany not available. p = preliminary.

# EMPLOYMENT

## U.S. Labor Force, Employment and Unemployment

Source: Bureau of Labor Statistics, U.S. Dept. of Labor; seasonally adjusted

### Selected Unemployment Indicators

| Category Characteristic | 1990 II | 1990 III | 1990 IV | 1991 I | 1991 II | 1991 III | 1991 IV | 1992 I | 1992 II | 1992 III | 1992 IV | 1993 I | 1993 II |
|---|---|---|---|---|---|---|---|---|---|---|---|---|---|
| Total (all civilian workers).. | 5.3 | 5.6 | 6.0 | 6.5 | 6.7 | 6.8 | 6.9 | 7.2 | 7.5 | 7.5 | 7.3 | 7.0 | 7.0 |
| Men, 20 years and over... | 4.7 | 5.0 | 5.5 | 6.1 | 6.4 | 6.5 | 6.5 | 6.9 | 7.2 | 7.2 | 7.0 | 6.5 | 6.5 |
| Women, 20 years and over. | 4.6 | 4.9 | 5.1 | 5.4 | 5.7 | 5.6 | 6.0 | 6.0 | 6.2 | 6.4 | 6.3 | 6.0 | 5.9 |
| Both sexes, 16 to 19 years . | 14.9 | 15.9 | 16.6 | 18.0 | 18.7 | 19.0 | 19.0 | 19.6 | 21.0 | 20.3 | 19.4 | 19.6 | 20.1 |
| White | 4.6 | 4.8 | 5.1 | 5.8 | 6.0 | 6.1 | 6.2 | 6.4 | 6.5 | 6.6 | 6.4 | 6.1 | 6.1 |
| Black and other ....... | 9.4 | 10.5 | 10.9 | 10.9 | 11.2 | 11.0 | 11.4 | 12.4 | 13.0 | 12.8 | 12.7 | 12.3 | 12.1 |
| Black | 10.5 | 11.7 | 12.1 | 12.1 | 12.7 | 12.2 | 12.6 | 13.9 | 14.5 | 14.2 | 14.1 | 13.6 | 13.3 |
| Hispanic origin ........ | 7.7 | 8.1 | 8.7 | 9.6 | 9.6 | 10.1 | 10.1 | 11.5 | 11.2 | 11.6 | 11.8 | 11.4 | 10.1 |
| Married men, spouse present . . . . . . . . . . . . | 3.2 | 3.5 | 3.7 | 4.2 | 4.4 | 4.4 | 4.5 | 4.9 | 5.0 | 5.3 | 4.9 | 4.6 | 4.5 |
| Married women, spouse present. . . . . . . . . . | 3.6 | 3.8 | 4.1 | 4.3 | 4.5 | 4.5 | 4.7 | 4.8 | 5.1 | 5.1 | 5.0 | 4.5 | 4.7 |
| Women who maintain families . . . . . . . . . . . . | 7.7 | 8.5 | 8.7 | 9.1 | 9.3 | 9.0 | 9.2 | 9.5 | 10.1 | 9.9 | 10.0 | 9.9 | 9.8 |
| Full-time workers ...... | 4.9 | 5.3 | 5.7 | 6.2 | 6.5 | 6.5 | 6.6 | 7.0 | 7.2 | 7.3 | 7.0 | 6.7 | 6.6 |
| Part-time workers ...... | 7.3 | 7.6 | 7.4 | 8.0 | 8.5 | 8.3 | 8.5 | 9.0 | 9.2 | 9.2 | 9.4 | 9.1 | 9.0 |
| Unemployed 15 weeks and over[1] | 1.1 | 1.3 | 1.4 | 1.6 | 1.8 | 1.9 | 2.1 | 2.5 | 2.6 | 2.8 | 2.8 | 2.5 | 2.3 |
| Labor force time lost[2] .... | 6.0 | 6.3 | 6.8 | 7.4 | 7.6 | 7.7 | 7.9 | 8.2 | 8.3 | 8.4 | 8.2 | 7.9 | 7.8 |
| **Industry** | | | | | | | | | | | | | |
| Nonagricultural private wage and salary workers. | 5.4 | 5.7 | 6.2 | 6.8 | 7.1 | 7.0 | 7.2 | 7.6 | 7.8 | 7.9 | 7.6 | 7.2 | 7.2 |
| Goods-producing industries. | 6.5 | 6.9 | 7.9 | 8.7 | 9.1 | 9.0 | 9.2 | 9.5 | 9.9 | 10.1 | 9.4 | 8.8 | 9.0 |
| Mining. . . . . . . . . . . . . | 4.2 | 4.3 | 5.2 | 6.5 | 7.7 | 8.7 | 8.6 | 7.6 | 8.2 | 9.2 | 6.4 | 6.8 | 8.8 |
| Construction . . . . . . . . | 10.6 | 11.2 | 13.5 | 14.6 | 15.1 | 15.8 | 16.2 | 17.3 | 17.1 | 17.1 | 15.4 | 14.4 | 15.1 |
| Manufacturing . . . . . . . | 5.4 | 5.8 | 6.4 | 7.1 | 7.5 | 7.1 | 7.2 | 7.3 | 7.8 | 8.1 | 7.8 | 7.2 | 7.2 |
| Durable goods . . . . . | 5.3 | 5.9 | 6.6 | 7.6 | 7.9 | 7.2 | 7.2 | 7.4 | 7.8 | 8.4 | 8.3 | 7.1 | 7.2 |
| Nondurable goods . . . | 5.5 | 5.6 | 6.0 | 6.4 | 6.9 | 6.9 | 7.2 | 7.2 | 7.9 | 7.7 | 7.2 | 7.5 | 7.2 |
| Service-producing industries | 5.0 | 5.2 | 5.5 | 5.9 | 6.2 | 6.2 | 6.4 | 6.8 | 6.9 | 7.0 | 6.9 | 6.6 | 6.5 |
| Transportation and public utilities . . . . . . . . . | 3.5 | 3.9 | 4.3 | 5.0 | 5.3 | 5.1 | 5.9 | 5.5 | 5.0 | 5.6 | 5.9 | 4.8 | 5.0 |
| Wholesale and retail trade | 6.2 | 6.3 | 6.8 | 7.4 | 7.5 | 7.8 | 7.7 | 8.3 | 8.5 | 8.7 | 8.0 | 7.9 | 8.1 |
| Finance and service industries . . . . . . . . . . . | 4.4 | 4.6 | 4.8 | 5.1 | 5.4 | 5.4 | 5.7 | 6.0 | 6.2 | 6.0 | 6.3 | 6.0 | 5.6 |
| Government workers. . . . . | 2.5 | 2.8 | 2.8 | 3.2 | 3.1 | 3.2 | 3.5 | 3.9 | 3.5 | 3.4 | 3.5 | 3.6 | 3.3 |
| Agricultural wage and salary workers . . . . . . . . . . . | 9.6 | 9.7 | 10.2 | 12.0 | 11.2 | 11.5 | 11.9 | 10.7 | 12.4 | 13.2 | 12.8 | 12.3 | 11.1 |

(1) Unemployment as a percent of the civilian labor force. (2) Aggregate hours lost by the unemployed and persons on part time for economic reasons as a percent of potentially available labor force hours.

## Employed Persons by Occupation, Sex, and Age

Source: Bureau of Labor Statistics, U.S. Dept. of Labor

(in thousands)

| Occupation | Total 16 years and over 1991 | Total 16 years and over 1992 | Men 16 years and over 1991 | Men 16 years and over 1992 | Women 16 years and over 1991 | Women 16 years and over 1992 |
|---|---|---|---|---|---|---|
| Total . . . . . . . . . . . . | 116,877 | 117,598 | 63,593 | 63,805 | 53,284 | 53,793 |
| Managerial and professional specialty . . . . . . . . . . . . . . . . | 31,012 | 31,153 | 16,656 | 16,416 | 14,356 | 14,736 |
| Executive, administrative, and managerial . . . . . . . . . . . . . . . | 14,954 | 14,767 | 8,890 | 8,641 | 6,064 | 6,126 |
| Officials and administrators, public administration . . . . . . . . . | 591 | 619 | 336 | 361 | 255 | 258 |
| Other executive, administrative, and managerial . . . . . . . . . | 10,412 | 10,187 | 6,611 | 6,384 | 3,801 | 3,802 |
| Management-related occupations . . . . . . . . . . . . . . . . . . . | 3,951 | 3,961 | 1,943 | 1,896 | 2,008 | 2,065 |
| Professional specialty . . . . . . . . . . . . . . . . . . . . . . . . | 16,058 | 16,386 | 7,767 | 7,775 | 8,292 | 8,611 |
| Engineers. . . . . . . . . . . . . . . . . . . . . . . . . . . . . . | 1,846 | 1,751 | 1,694 | 1,603 | 152 | 148 |
| Mathematical and computer scientists . . . . . . . . . . . . . | 923 | 935 | 583 | 622 | 339 | 313 |
| Natural scientists . . . . . . . . . . . . . . . . . . . . . . . . | 438 | 459 | 324 | 334 | 114 | 125 |
| Health diagnosing occupations. . . . . . . . . . . . . . . . . . | 849 | 914 | 696 | 747 | 153 | 167 |
| Health assessment and treating occupations. . . . . . . . . . | 2,376 | 2,517 | 328 | 332 | 2,048 | 2,184 |
| Teachers, college and university. . . . . . . . . . . . . . . . . | 773 | 737 | 457 | 435 | 316 | 302 |
| Teachers, except college and university . . . . . . . . . . . . | 4,029 | 4,216 | 1,038 | 1,062 | 2,992 | 3,154 |
| Lawyers and judges. . . . . . . . . . . . . . . . . . . . . . . | 772 | 788 | 626 | 620 | 146 | 167 |
| Other professional specialty occupations . . . . . . . . . . . | 4,051 | 4,068 | 2,020 | 2,018 | 2,031 | 2,050 |
| Technical, sales, and administrative support . . . . . . . . . . . . . | 36,086 | 36,808 | 12,734 | 13,269 | 23,352 | 23,539 |
| Technicians and related support . . . . . . . . . . . . . . . . . . | 3,794 | 4,253 | 1,921 | 2,169 | 1,873 | 2,084 |
| Sales occupations . . . . . . . . . . . . . . . . . . . . . . . . . . | 13,958 | 13,919 | 7,142 | 7,252 | 6,816 | 6,667 |
| Administrative support, including clerical . . . . . . . . . . . . . . | 18,334 | 18,636 | 3,671 | 3,848 | 14,663 | 14,788 |
| Service occupations . . . . . . . . . . . . . . . . . . . . . . . . . . | 15,986 | 16,096 | 6,429 | 6,494 | 9,557 | 9,602 |
| Precision production, craft, and repair. . . . . . . . . . . . . . . . . | 13,162 | 13,128 | 12,030 | 12,000 | 1,132 | 1,128 |
| Mechanics and repairers . . . . . . . . . . . . . . . . . . . . . . | 4,427 | 4,441 | 4,264 | 4,293 | 163 | 147 |
| Construction trades . . . . . . . . . . . . . . . . . . . . . . . . | 4,808 | 4,790 | 4,721 | 4,702 | 88 | 89 |
| Other precision production, craft, and repair . . . . . . . . . . | 3,927 | 3,897 | 3,045 | 3,005 | 881 | 892 |
| Operators, fabricators, and laborers . . . . . . . . . . . . . . . . . | 17,172 | 16,957 | 12,842 | 12,720 | 4,330 | 4,237 |
| Machine operators, assemblers, and inspectors . . . . . . . . . . | 7,696 | 7,524 | 4,610 | 4,535 | 3,086 | 2,989 |
| Transportation and material moving occupations . . . . . . . . . | 4,878 | 4,878 | 4,441 | 4,451 | 437 | 427 |
| Handlers, equipment cleaners, helpers, and laborers . . . . . . | 4,597 | 4,556 | 3,791 | 3,734 | 806 | 821 |
| Farming, forestry, and fishing . . . . . . . . . . . . . . . . . . . . . | 3,459 | 3,456 | 2,903 | 2,905 | 557 | 551 |

Note: Data for 1992 are not fully comparable with data for prior years because of the introduction of the occupational classification system used in the 1990 census.

## Selected Unemployment Insurance Data by State

Calendar year 1992. state programs only

Source: Employment and Training Admin.. U.S. Dept. of Labor

| State | Insured Claimants | First Payments | Final Payments | Initial Claims | Benefits Paid | Average Weekly Benefit Amount | Employers Subject to State Law |
|---|---|---|---|---|---|---|---|
| AK . . . . . | 46,940 | 44,094 | 23,502 | 96,387 | $117,356,159 | $169.92 | 13,595 |
| AL . . . . . | 179,501 | 157,084 | 40,255 | 357,722 | 208,562,138 | 120.95 | 77,517 |
| AR . . . . . | 144,378 | 99,922 | 36,484 | 240,416 | 185,383,263 | 150.63 | 51,070 |
| AZ . . . . . | 124,770 | 90,486 | 38,791 | 197,204 | 211,218,020 | 146.75 | 81,011 |
| CA . . . . . | 1,398,923 | 1,443,782 | 657,585 | 3,718,795 | 3,851,818,253 | 152.07 | 772,499 |
| CO . . . . . | 115,076 | 79,360 | 35,629 | 161,297 | 178,798,392 | 177.54 | 93,169 |
| CT . . . . . | 157,275 | 157,319 | 70,569 | 320,842 | 587,162,128 | 210.78 | 93,387 |
| DC . . . . . | 32,423 | 26,831 | 18,358 | 43,789 | 127,890,580 | 227.72 | 21,087 |
| DE . . . . . | 33,445 | 28,787 | 7,868 | 62,734 | 72,263,852 | 181.02 | 19,697 |
| FL . . . . . | 427,156 | 339,288 | 191,037 | 627,518 | 860,664,948 | 158.01 | 318,565 |
| GA . . . . . | 310,731 | 231,957 | 97,785 | 455,754 | 381,474,993 | 148.17 | 145,515 |
| HI . . . . . | 50,159 | 39,381 | 10,980 | 81,903 | 137,717,882 | 239.80 | 26,990 |
| IA . . . . . | 103,379 | 88,604 | 27,502 | 158,477 | 194,800,426 | 170.38 | 63,360 |
| ID . . . . . | 51,716 | 46,156 | 16,010 | 111,601 | 83,533,355 | 156.22 | 27,793 |
| IL . . . . . | 472,014 | 390,904 | 175,163 | 883,168 | 1,338,706,871 | 183.21 | 250,759 |
| IN . . . . . | 217,854 | 149,845 | 45,226 | 356,070 | 216,750,547 | 125.98 | 110,146 |
| KS . . . . . | 84,746 | 70,823 | 27,518 | 146,014 | 188,709,911 | 179.06 | 58,780 |
| KY . . . . . | 142,470 | 127,034 | 30,142 | 310,284 | 227,500,554 | 144.43 | 72,650 |
| LA . . . . . | 132,700 | 109,968 | 36,948 | 243,626 | 209,629,877 | 118.06 | 81,730 |
| MA . . . . . | 309,384 | 249,341 | 131,636 | 485,500 | 1,035,951,213 | 226.31 | 146,851 |
| MD . . . . . | 200,277 | 144,626 | 32,250 | 305,466 | 460,715,268 | 180.25 | 113,289 |
| ME . . . . . | 67,322 | 58,640 | 25,826 | 136,741 | 145,515,586 | 166.73 | 33,827 |
| MI . . . . . | 672,589 | 487,246 | 159,494 | 1,197,825 | 1,287,583,689 | 211.29 | 187,666 |
| MN . . . . . | 140,221 | 133,506 | 47,410 | 237,288 | 409,170,477 | 198.09 | 102,972 |
| MO . . . . . | 243,793 | 184,467 | 73,148 | 517,986 | 380,203,456 | 146.07 | 128,605 |
| MS . . . . . | 109,982 | 79,145 | 26,353 | 208,404 | 128,545,059 | 122.62 | 45,820 |
| MT . . . . . | 30,238 | 25,147 | 9,507 | 56,115 | 44,845,680 | 134.62 | 24,607 |
| NC . . . . . | 349,452 | 243,700 | 58,903 | 780,541 | 378,479,337 | 158.50 | 136,775 |
| ND . . . . . | 17,936 | 14,936 | 6,147 | 31,965 | 29,707,904 | 146.22 | 17,865 |
| NE . . . . . | 43,507 | 33,436 | 10,433 | 71,638 | 50,394,676 | 132.95 | 39,391 |
| NH . . . . . | 52,832 | 39,915 | 6,875 | 67,353 | 61,112,771 | 135.55 | 31,400 |
| NJ . . . . . | 375,463 | 339,837 | 201,575 | 631,750 | 1,428,882,933 | 224.88 | 200,420 |
| NM . . . . . | 39,398 | 31,702 | 12,681 | 68,619 | 72,762,929 | 138.28 | 34,336 |
| NV . . . . . | 97,078 | 60,268 | 24,916 | 123,522 | 154,800,311 | 167.89 | 29,708 |
| NY . . . . . | 726,608 | 673,398 | 365,156 | 1,353,373 | 2,634,623,256 | 197.42 | 431,276 |
| OH . . . . . | 417,429 | 357,397 | 120,629 | 823,073 | 971,732,545 | 179.87 | 211,093 |
| OK . . . . . | 81,277 | 65,969 | 28,834 | 159,409 | 147,771,561 | 159.50 | 66,189 |
| OR . . . . . | 150,441 | 141,756 | 52,363 | 358,642 | 382,072,229 | 171.81 | 80,110 |
| PA . . . . . | 610,759 | 517,810 | 194,509 | 1,251,135 | 1,751,434,187 | 200.92 | 233,178 |
| PR . . . . . | 118,619 | 112,984 | 67,601 | 248,073 | 179,349,935 | 83.50 | 50,006 |
| RI . . . . . | 65,195 | 60,746 | 30,009 | 137,756 | 196,453,246 | 206.09 | 31,646 |
| SC . . . . . | 186,655 | 125,030 | 39,721 | 375,209 | 215,450,616 | 142.89 | 72,060 |
| SD . . . . . | 10,965 | 8,868 | 1,119 | 22,479 | 12,040,598 | 127.84 | 19,262 |
| TN . . . . . | 246,856 | 189,667 | 68,157 | 475,802 | 288,504,996 | 123.85 | 95,338 |
| TX . . . . . | 569,160 | 429,726 | 220,997 | 888,525 | 1,181,146,078 | 176.11 | 331,008 |
| UT . . . . . | 47,823 | 37,685 | 13,000 | 67,330 | 82,164,098 | 174.49 | 34,899 |
| VA . . . . . | 219,104 | 137,598 | 50,060 | 369,577 | 288,440,500 | 164.15 | 132,219 |
| VI . . . . . | 3,604 | 2,660 | 1,083 | 4,873 | 6,306,143 | 160.58 | 2,899 |
| VT . . . . . | 28,342 | 26,477 | 7,650 | 47,483 | 65,877,963 | 155.31 | 19,027 |
| WA . . . . . | 248,165 | 219,217 | 73,267 | 545,753 | 661,184,886 | 175.62 | 141,151 |
| WI . . . . . | 235,061 | 215,669 | 49,764 | 478,927 | 462,783,556 | 175.46 | 105,933 |
| WV . . . . . | 68,483 | 60,922 | 18,621 | 105,070 | 147,535,478 | 162.74 | 35,715 |
| WY . . . . . | 16,927 | 12,222 | 4,042 | 32,491 | 29,332,631 | 163.42 | 15,628 |
| U.S.. . . . . | 11,026,601 | 9,243,338 | 3,821,088 | 21,239,294 | 25,152,817,940 | 165.14 | 5,761,484 |

## Employment and Unemployment in the U.S.

Source: Bureau of Labor Statistics. U.S. Dept. of Labor

Civilian labor force, persons 16 years of age and over (in thousands)

| Year* | Employed | Unemployed | Unemployment Rate | Year* | Employed | Unemployed | Unemployment Rate |
|---|---|---|---|---|---|---|---|
| 1940[1] . . . . . | 47,520 | 8,120 | 14.6% | 1984 . . . . . | 105,005 | 8,539 | 7.5 |
| 1950 . . . . . | 58,918 | 3,288 | 5.0 | 1985 . . . . . | 107,150 | 8,312 | 7.2 |
| 1960 . . . . . | 65,778 | 3,852 | 5.5 | 1986[2] . . . . . | 109,597 | 8,237 | 7.0 |
| 1970 . . . . . | 78,678 | 4,093 | 4.9 | 1987 . . . . . | 112,440 | 7,425 | 6.2 |
| 1975 . . . . . | 85,846 | 7,929 | 8.5 | 1988 . . . . . | 114,988 | 6,701 | 5.5 |
| 1980 . . . . . | 99,303 | 7,637 | 7.1 | 1989 . . . . . | 117,342 | 6,528 | 5.3 |
| 1981 . . . . . | 100,397 | 8,273 | 7.6 | 1990 . . . . . | 117,914 | 6,874 | 5.5 |
| 1982 . . . . . | 99,526 | 10,678 | 9.7 | 1991 . . . . . | 116,877 | 8,426 | 6.7 |
| 1983 . . . . . | 100,834 | 10,717 | 9.6 | 1992 . . . . . | 117,598 | 9,384 | 7.4 |

(1) Persons 14 years of age and over; (2) Not strictly comparable with prior years.
* **Early unemployment rates:** 1915, 9.7; 1916, 4.8; 1917, 4.8; 1918, 1.4; 1919, 2.3; 1920, 4.0; 1921, 11.9; 1922, 7.6; 1923, 3.2; 1924, 5.5; 1925, 4.0; 1926, 1.9; 1927, 4.1; 1928, 4.4; 1929, 3.2; 1930, 8.7; 1931, 15.9; 1932, 23.6; 1933, 24.9; 1934, 21.7; 1935, 20.1; 1936, 16.9; 1937, 14.3; 1938, 19.0; 1939, 17.2.

# Employment and Training Services and Unemployment Insurance

Source: Employment and Training Administration, U.S. Dept. of Labor; September 1993.

## Employment Service

The Federal-State Employment Service consists of the United States Employment Service and affiliated state employment services that make up the nation's public employment service system. From July 1, 1991, to June 30, 1992, the public employment service listed 5.6 million job openings and placed more than 2.6 million people in jobs.

The employment service refers employable applicants to job openings that use their highest skills and helps the unemployed obtain services or training to make them employable. It also provides special attention to handicapped workers, migrants and seasonal farmworkers, workers who lose their jobs because of foreign trade competition, and other worker groups. Veterans receive priority services including referral to jobs and training. During program year 1991, 382,000 veterans were placed in jobs.

## Job Training

The Job Training Partnership Act (JTPA), which became fully operational on October 1, 1983, provides job training and employment services for economically disadvantaged youths and adults, dislocated workers, and others who face significant employment barriers. The goal of the Act is to move as many jobless workers as possible into permanent, unsubsidized, self-sustaining employment.

As at the end of program year 1991, JTPA had provided approximately 8 million Americans with training and employment services since its inception. Its placement rate is almost 69 percent, making it one of the most successful job and training efforts ever undertaken.

Title I of the Act's five titles basically establishes an administrative structure for the delivery of job and training services. Generally, state governors receive bloc grants from the Labor Department, and the funds are then distributed to Service Delivery Areas — areas of 200,000 population or more where local elected officials work with Private Industry Councils to plan and conduct local training projects.

Title II is in two parts, with Title II-A spelling out the Act's provision of employment and training projects for the economically disadvantaged. In program year 1991 (July 1, 1991, to Sept. 30, 1992), these projects served more than 1 million people.

Title II-B outlines a summer youth program offering basic and remedial education, institutional and on-the-job training, work experience, and supportive services. This program had nearly 550,000 participants in program year 1990. Beginning July 1, 1993, a new Title II-C provided for a year-round youth training program.

Title III, Economic Dislocation and Worker Adjustment Assistance, provides for job and training help for dislocated workers — workers who lose jobs and are unlikely to return to their previous industries or occupations. This includes workers who lose their jobs because of plant closings or mass layoffs; long-term unemployed persons with limited local opportunities for jobs in their fields; farmers, ranchers, and other self-employed persons who become jobless due to general economic conditions or natural disasters; and, under certain circumstances, displaced homemakers. Such assistance benefitted 330,643 workers in program year 1991.

Title IV authorizes programs to address the employment and training needs of specific groups facing significant barriers to productive employment, including Native Americans, migrant and seasonal farmworkers, and the disabled. In program year 1991, these programs served 11,310 Native Americans; 10,123 migrant and seasonal farmworkers; and more than 2,600 disabled workers.

In addition, Title IV includes the Job Corps, which each year enrolls approximately 100,000 young people between the ages of 16 and 21 in 107 residential job training centers throughout the United States; the National Commission for Employment Policy; and nationally administered programs for technical assistance, labor market information, research and evaluation, and pilots and demonstrations.

With recent amendments to JTPA, Title V is now the Jobs for Employable Dependent Individuals (JEDI) Incentive Bonus Program. Title VI provides for new State human resources investment councils, and Title VII covers transition provisions and technical conforming amendments.

## Trade Adjustment Assistance for Workers

The Trade Adjustment Assistance (TAA) is available to workers who lose their jobs or whose hours of work and wages are reduced as a result of increased imports. TAA includes a variety of benefits and reemployment services to help unemployed workers prepare for and obtain suitable employment. Workers may be eligible for training, job search, relocation, and other reemployment services. Additionally, weekly trade readjustment allowances (TRA) may be payable to eligible workers following their exhaustion of unemployment insurance benefits. In fiscal year 1992, about 8,727 workers received $42.7 million in TRA payments; 18,582 workers entered training; 594 workers were involved in job search visits; and 751 workers relocated in order to obtain long term jobs.

The TAA program is administered by the Employment and Training Administration's Office of Trade Adjustment Assistance. State employment security agencies serve as agents of the U.S., under an agreement with the Secretary of Labor, for administering the TAA benefit provisions in the Trade Act of 1974, as amended.

## Unemployment Insurance

Unlike old-age and survivors insurance, entirely a federal program, the unemployment insurance program is a Federal-State system that provides insured wage earners with partial replacement of wages lost during involuntary unemployment. The program protects most workers. During calendar year 1992, an estimated 105 million workers in commerce, industry, agriculture, and government, including the armed forces, were covered under the Federal-State system.

Each state, as well as the District of Columbia, Puerto Rico, and the Virgin Islands, has its own law and operates its own program. The amount and duration of the weekly benefits are determined by state laws, based on prior wages and length of employment. States are required to extend the duration of benefits when unemployment rises to and remains above specified state levels; costs of extended benefits are shared by the state and federal governments.

Under the Federal Unemployment Tax Act, as amended in 1985, the tax rate is 6.2% on the first $7,000 paid to each employee of employers with one or more employees in 20 weeks of the year or a quarterly payroll of $1,500. A credit of up to 5.4% is allowed for taxes paid under state unemployment insurance laws that meet certain criteria, leaving the federal share at 0.8% of taxable wages.

## Social Security Requirement

The Social Security Act requires, as a condition of such grants, prompt payment of due benefits. The Federal Unemployment Tax Act provides safeguards for workers' right to benefits if they refuse jobs that fail to meet certain labor standards. Through the Unemployment Insurance Service of the Employment and Training Administration, the Secretary of Labor determines whether states qualify for grants and for tax offset credit from employers.

Benefits are financed solely by employer contributions, except in Alaska, Pennsylvania, and New Jersey where employees also contribute. Benefits are paid through the states' public employment offices, at which unemployed workers must register for work and to which they must report regularly for referral to a possible job during the time when they are drawing weekly benefit payments. During the fiscal year 1992, $25.61 billion in benefits was paid under state unemployment insurance programs to 9.6 million beneficiaries. They received an average weekly payment of $172.77 for total unemployment for an average of 15.9 weeks.

## 10 Facts About Women Workers

Source: Women's Bureau, U.S. Dept. of Labor

1. Of the 100 million women 16 and older in the U.S., 58 million were labor force participants (working or looking for work) during 1992. Women accounted for 60 percent of labor force growth between 1982 and 1992.
2. Women represented 45 percent of all persons in the civilian labor force in 1992. Women are projected to comprise 47 percent of the labor force by the year 2005.
3. Teenage women (16-19 years old) are not as active in the labor force as adult women (20 years of age and over). Only 49 percent were in the labor force, compared with 58 percent of adult women. In addition, teenage women's unemployment rate was three times as high as that of adult women—18.5 percent and 6.3 percent, respectively.
4. The unemployment rate for all women in the labor force was 6.9 percent in 1992. Teenage black and Hispanic women continued to experience very high unemployment rates —37.2 percent and 26.4 percent, respectively.
5. Of the 54 million employed women in the United States in 1992, 40 million worked full time (35 or more hours per week); nearly 14 million, or 25 percent of all women workers, held part-time jobs. Two-thirds (66 percent) of all part-time workers were women.
6. Women have made substantial progress in obtaining jobs in virtually all managerial and professional specialty occupations. In 1983 they held 40 percent (9.7 million) of these high-paying jobs; in 1992 they held 47 percent (14.7 million). Women employed in managerial and professional specialty occupations had 1992 median weekly earnings between $357 and $917.
7. Women are still overrepresented in low-paying jobs. Almost half (44 percent) of employed women work in technical, sales, and administrative support jobs—23.5 million women. Even though the earnings gap between

men and women is slowly closing, women earn only 75 cents for every dollar earned by men when comparing 1992 median weekly earnings of full-time workers ($381 for women and $505 for men). The five most lucrative occupations for women are lawyer, physician, pharmacist, engineer, and computer systems analyst and scientist. (This list excludes any occupation at which fewer than 50,000 females are employed.)

8. Median earnings for female high school graduates (with no college) working year-round, full time in 1991 were less than those of fully employed men who were high school dropouts—$18,042 and $20,944, respectively. In addition, men with an associate's degree working year-round, full time earned nearly the same as similarly employed women with a master's degree—$32,221 and $33,122, respectively.
9. Of the approximately 67 million families in the United States in 1992, 12 million (18 percent) were maintained by women. In black families, women maintained 47 percent; in Hispanic families, 24 percent; and in white families, 14 percent. The median weekly earnings of families maintained by women in 1992 was $385, compared with $779 for married-couple families and $519 for families maintained by men.
10. In 1991 women represented 63 percent of all persons 18 years old and over who were living below the poverty level. The poverty rate for families maintained by women with no husband present was six times as high as for married-couple families—35.6 percent and 6.0 percent, respectively. Women maintained 54 percent of all poor families in 1991. Women maintained 78 percent of poor black families, about 46 percent of poor Hispanic families, and 44 percent of poor white families.

## The Family and Medical Leave Act of 1993

Source: Women's Bureau, U.S. Dept. of Labor; effective Aug. 5, 1993.

### Employee Rights

- Public and private sector employees who have been employed by the employer for one year and worked at least 1,250 hours can take up to 12 weeks of unpaid leave in any 12-month period for the birth or adoption of a child; acquiring a foster child; the serious illness of a child, spouse, or parent; or the serious illness of the employee.
- The right to take leave applies equally to male and female workers who are employed at or within 75 miles of the work place by an employer of 50 or more workers.
- Leave can be taken intermittently or on a schedule that reduces the usual number of hours per workday or workweek to care for an ill child, spouse, or parent or because of the employee's illness. Intermittent or reduced leave schedules because of the birth of a child, adoption, or fos-

ter care are subject to employer approval. Such a reduced or intermittent leave schedule does not reduce the total amount of leave to which the employee is entitled.

- An employee may elect or an employer may require the employee to substitute categories of paid leave for any part of the 12-week period.
- The employee maintains any preexisting health insurance for the duration of the leave and at the level and under the same conditions coverage was provided prior to commencement of the leave.
- At the end of the leave, the employee must be restored to the original or an equivalent position with equivalent benefits, pay, and all other terms of employment.

### Other Requirements

- When husband and wife work for the same employer, the total amount of leave that they may take is limited to 12 weeks if they are taking leave for the birth or adoption of a child or to care for a sick parent.
- An employer may require certification from a health care provider to support a claim for leave.

- When the need for leave is foreseeable, an employee is required to provide at least 30 days advance notice.
- A new Commission on Leave will conduct a comprehensive study of existing and proposed leave policies, including the potential costs, benefits, and impact on productivity, and report its findings to Congress within 2 years of its first meeting.

### Exclusions

- The law excludes any person employed at a worksite with fewer than 50 total employees at the worksite and employed by the employer within 75 miles of the worksite. Where employees have no fixed worksite, as is the case for many construction workers, transportation workers, and salespersons, such employees' "worksite" should be construed to mean the single site of employment to which they are assigned as their home base.

- An employer may deny job restoration to salaried employees who are among the highest paid 10 percent of the persons employed by the employer within 75 miles of the facility at which the employee works, if such denial is necessary to prevent substantial and grievous economic injury to the employer's operation.

### Relationship to State Laws and Employer Policies

The Act does not supersede any state or local law, collective bargaining agreement, or employment benefit plan providing greater employee family leave rights, nor does it diminish the capacity to adopt more generous family leave policies.

## Median Weekly Earnings of Full-Time Wage and Salary Workers by Age, Sex, and Union Affiliation

Source: Bureau of Labor Statistics, U.S. Dept. of Labor

| Sex and Age | 1991 | | | | 1992 | | | |
|---|---|---|---|---|---|---|---|---|
| | Total | Members of unions[1] | Represented by unions[2] | Non-union | Total | Members of unions[1] | Represented by unions[2] | Non-union |
| Total, 16 years and over | $430 | $526 | $522 | $404 | $445 | $547 | $541 | $413 |
| 16 to 24 years | 278 | 356 | 347 | 272 | 277 | 352 | 346 | 272 |
| 25 years and over | 468 | 539 | 535 | 436 | 480 | 559 | 554 | 450 |
| 25 to 34 years | 417 | 496 | 491 | 403 | 424 | 506 | 499 | 410 |
| 35 to 44 years | 499 | 557 | 555 | 479 | 504 | 576 | 572 | 484 |
| 45 to 54 years | 507 | 581 | 580 | 480 | 523 | 601 | 601 | 496 |
| 55 to 64 years | 469 | 534 | 529 | 427 | 483 | 552 | 549 | 447 |
| 65 years and over | 381 | 522 | 526 | 348 | 378 | 495 | 493 | 354 |
| Men, 16 years and over | 497 | 568 | 567 | 473 | 505 | 589 | 586 | 480 |
| 16 to 24 years | 286 | 377 | 368 | 279 | 285 | 374 | 367 | 279 |
| 25 years and over | 525 | 579 | 579 | 508 | 539 | 597 | 596 | 515 |
| 25 to 34 years | 462 | 520 | 518 | 440 | 470 | 535 | 528 | 449 |
| 35 to 44 years | 578 | 591 | 592 | 567 | 584 | 609 | 608 | 570 |
| 45 to 54 years | 614 | 613 | 615 | 612 | 636 | 636 | 638 | 633 |
| 55 to 64 years | 562 | 579 | 580 | 543 | 578 | 597 | 598 | 557 |
| 65 years and over | 465 | 601 | 607 | 404 | 421 | 571 | 557 | 400 |
| Women, 16 years and over | 368 | 467 | 462 | 348 | 381 | 484 | 481 | 361 |
| 16 to 24 years | 267 | 321 | 317 | 263 | 267 | 319 | 322 | 263 |
| 25 years and over | 388 | 477 | 473 | 369 | 400 | 491 | 489 | 383 |
| 25 to 34 years | 372 | 440 | 432 | 360 | 383 | 451 | 445 | 374 |
| 35 to 44 years | 408 | 491 | 490 | 389 | 419 | 504 | 503 | 399 |
| 45 to 54 years | 398 | 499 | 497 | 375 | 417 | 519 | 518 | 391 |
| 55 to 64 years | 363 | 448 | 445 | 337 | 376 | 461 | 460 | 355 |
| 65 years and over | 319 | 388 | 392 | 306 | 328 | 409 | 419 | 310 |

(1) Data refer to members of a labor union or an employee association similar to a union. (2) Data refer to members of a labor union or an employee association similar to a union as well as workers who report no union affiliation but whose jobs are covered by a union or an employee association contract. **Note:** Data refer to the sole or principal job of full-time workers. Excluded are self-employed workers whose businesses are incorporated although they technically qualify as wage and salary workers. Detail for the above race and Hispanic-origin groups will not sum to totals because data for the "other races" group are not presented and Hispanics are included in both the white and black population groups.

## Employment Status of Persons in Families by Family Relationship, 1992

Source: Bureau of Labor Statistics, U.S. Dept. of Labor; in thousands

| Family Relationship | Civilian Labor Force | | | | | Not in Labor Force | | | | |
|---|---|---|---|---|---|---|---|---|---|---|
| | Total | Percent of Population | Employed | Unemployed Number | Percent | Total | Home-makers | Students | Unable to Work | Other Reasons |
| Total, 16 years and over [1] | 101,215 | 66.8 | 93,754 | 7,461 | 7.4 | 50,388 | 20,292 | 6,998 | 2,643 | 20,455 |
| Husbands | 40,193 | 77.5 | 38,274 | 1,918 | 4.8 | 11,641 | 212 | 175 | 990 | 10,264 |
| With employed wife | 26,813 | 91.5 | 25,656 | 1,157 | 4.3 | 2,500 | 101 | 103 | 408 | 1,889 |
| With unemployed wife | 1,328 | 90.6 | 1,147 | 181 | 13.6 | 137 | 5 | 5 | 26 | 101 |
| With wife not in labor force | 12,052 | 57.2 | 11,471 | 580 | 4.8 | 9,004 | 107 | 68 | 556 | 8,274 |
| Wives | 30,778 | 59.4 | 29,313 | 1,465 | 4.8 | 21,056 | 15,460 | 366 | 449 | 4,781 |
| With employed husband | 26,803 | 70.0 | 25,656 | 1,147 | 4.3 | 11,471 | 9,757 | 305 | 165 | 1,244 |
| With unemployed husband | 1,338 | 69.7 | 1,157 | 181 | 13.5 | 580 | 478 | 18 | 22 | 63 |
| With husband not in labor force | 2,637 | 22.7 | 2,500 | 137 | 5.2 | 9,004 | 5,225 | 44 | 262 | 3,473 |
| Relatives in married-couple families | 12,833 | 63.1 | 11,075 | 1,758 | 13.7 | 7,493 | 729 | 4,419 | 360 | 1,984 |
| 16 to 19 years | 4,358 | 51.6 | 3,621 | 738 | 16.9 | 4,084 | 128 | 3,256 | 10 | 689 |
| 20 to 24 years | 4,747 | 75.7 | 4,197 | 550 | 11.6 | 1,527 | 148 | 1,025 | 44 | 311 |
| 25 years and over | 3,727 | 66.4 | 3,257 | 470 | 12.6 | 1,882 | 453 | 138 | 306 | 984 |
| Women who maintain families | 7,303 | 62.3 | 6,582 | 721 | 9.9 | 4,423 | 2,744 | 231 | 291 | 1,156 |
| Relatives in families maintained by women | 5,689 | 59.0 | 4,598 | 1,092 | 19.2 | 3,947 | 771 | 1,478 | 364 | 1,335 |
| 16 to 19 years | 1,240 | 44.6 | 859 | 381 | 30.7 | 1,541 | 95 | 1,126 | 12 | 309 |
| 20 to 24 years | 1,602 | 72.1 | 1,302 | 300 | 18.7 | 620 | 142 | 267 | 27 | 185 |
| 25 years and over | 2,848 | 61.5 | 2,437 | 411 | 14.4 | 1,786 | 534 | 85 | 325 | 841 |
| Men who maintain families | 2,514 | 77.9 | 2,288 | 226 | 9.0 | 711 | 44 | 40 | 92 | 535 |
| Relatives in families maintained by men | 1,905 | 63.0 | 1,624 | 281 | 14.7 | 1,117 | 332 | 289 | 97 | 399 |
| 16 to 19 years | 288 | 51.4 | 218 | 70 | 24.3 | 272 | 22 | 193 | 1 | 56 |
| 20 to 24 years | 479 | 77.0 | 412 | 68 | 14.1 | 143 | 31 | 69 | 6 | 37 |
| 25 years and over | 1,137 | 61.8 | 994 | 143 | 12.6 | 702 | 279 | 27 | 90 | 306 |

(1) Excludes persons living alone or with nonrelatives, persons in married-couple families where the husband or wife is in the Armed Forces, and persons in unrelated subfamilies. **Note:** Estimates shown in this table for husbands, wives, and women who maintain families are somewhat different from marital status estimates shown in other tables in this publication because of differences in definitions and weighting patterns used in aggregating the data.

## Work Stoppages (Strikes) in the U.S., 1955-1992

Source: Bureau of Labor Statistics. U.S. Dept. of Labor

(involving 1,000 workers or more)

| | Number stoppages[1] | Workers involved[1] (thousands) | Work days idle[1] (thousands) | | Number stoppages[1] | Workers involved[1] (thousands) | Work days idle[1] (thousands) |
|---|---|---|---|---|---|---|---|
| 1955 | 363 | 2,055 | 21,100 | 1978 | 219 | 1,006 | 23,774 |
| 1960 | 222 | 896 | 13,260 | 1979 | 235 | 1,021 | 20,409 |
| 1965 | 268 | 999 | 15,140 | 1980 | 187 | 795 | 20,844 |
| 1966 | 321 | 1,300 | 16,000 | 1981 | 145 | 729 | 16,908 |
| 1967 | 381 | 2,192 | 31,320 | 1982 | 96 | 656 | 9,061 |
| 1968 | 392 | 1,855 | 35,567 | 1983 | 81 | 909 | 17,461 |
| 1969 | 412 | 1,576 | 29,397 | 1984 | 62 | 376 | 8,499 |
| 1970 | 381 | 2,468 | 52,761 | 1985 | 54 | 324 | 7,079 |
| 1971 | 298 | 2,516 | 35,538 | 1986 | 69 | 533 | 11,861 |
| 1972 | 250 | 975 | 16,764 | 1987 | 46 | 174 | 4,481 |
| 1973 | 317 | 1,400 | 16,260 | 1988 | 40 | 118 | 4,364 |
| 1974 | 424 | 1,796 | 31,809 | 1989 | 51 | 452 | 16,996 |
| 1975 | 235 | 965 | 17,563 | 1990 | 44 | 185 | 5,926 |
| 1976 | 231 | 1,519 | 23,962 | 1991 | 40 | 392 | 4,584 |
| 1977 | 298 | 1,212 | 21,258 | 1992 | 35 | 364 | 3,989 |

(1) The number of stoppages and workers relate to stoppages that began in the year. Days of idleness include all stoppages in effect. Workers are counted more than once if they were involved in more than one stoppage during the year.

## Work Stoppages Involving 5,000 Workers or More Beginning in 1992

Source: Bureau of Labor Statistics. U.S. Labor Dept.

| Employer, location, and union | Began | Ended | Workers involved[1] | Estimated days idle in 1992[1] |
|---|---|---|---|---|
| Kroger Co., Michigan, Food and Commercial Workers .... | 4/13 | 6/19 | 7,800 | 388,200 |
| Railroad industry, interstate, various unions ......... | 6/24 | 6/25 | 230,000 | 460,000 |
| General Motors, Lordstown, OH, Automobile Workers .... | 8/27 | 9/5 | 45,100 | 217,600 |
| Board of Education, Detroit, MI, teachers (AFT). ....... | 8/31 | 9/26 | 10,500 | 199,500 |
| General Motors, Lansing, MI, Automobile Workers ...... | 9/25 | 9/28 | 7,200 | 14,400 |
| USAir, interstate, Machinists .................. | 10/5 | 10/10 | 8,300 | 41,500 |

(1) Workers and days idle are rounded to the nearest 100.

## Unemployed Jobseekers, 1992

Source: Bureau of Labor Statistics. U.S. Dept. of Labor

| Sex, Age, and Race | Thousands of Persons | | Methods Used as a Percent of Total Jobseekers | | | | | | Average Number of Methods Used |
|---|---|---|---|---|---|---|---|---|---|
| | Total Unemployed | Total Jobseekers | Public Employment Agency | Private Employment Agency | Employer Directly | Placed or Answered Ads | Friends or Relatives | Other | |
| Total, 16 years and over | 9,384 | 8,027 | 22.6 | 9.3 | 74.3 | 41.7 | 23.7 | 5.3 | 1.77 |
| 16 to 19 years | 1,352 | 1,283 | 11.6 | 4.0 | 81.5 | 27.5 | 18.1 | 3.5 | 1.46 |
| 20 to 24 years | 1,546 | 1,365 | 21.8 | 8.7 | 74.8 | 42.1 | 22.2 | 3.8 | 1.73 |
| 25 to 34 years | 2,662 | 2,258 | 26.2 | 9.9 | 73.2 | 45.6 | 24.4 | 4.5 | 1.84 |
| 35 to 44 years | 1,941 | 1,602 | 25.9 | 11.4 | 72.9 | 45.0 | 25.7 | 6.6 | 1.87 |
| 45 to 54 years | 1,145 | 933 | 25.3 | 12.4 | 71.7 | 44.8 | 26.6 | 8.2 | 1.89 |
| 55 to 64 years | 603 | 473 | 22.4 | 10.2 | 70.7 | 43.9 | 26.4 | 7.4 | 1.81 |
| 65 years and over | 135 | 112 | 15.2 | 6.9 | 68.6 | 37.6 | 24.0 | 7.4 | 1.60 |
| Men, 16 years and over | 5,380 | 4,444 | 24.7 | 9.8 | 74.8 | 40.4 | 26.6 | 6.2 | 1.82 |
| 16 to 19 years | 761 | 720 | 12.3 | 3.8 | 81.7 | 26.1 | 20.0 | 3.4 | 1.47 |
| 20 to 24 years | 884 | 759 | 23.3 | 9.0 | 75.3 | 41.5 | 25.7 | 4.2 | 1.79 |
| 25 to 34 years | 1,508 | 1,217 | 29.1 | 10.5 | 74.1 | 44.8 | 28.7 | 5.0 | 1.92 |
| 35 to 44 years | 1,095 | 857 | 28.9 | 12.4 | 72.9 | 43.9 | 28.8 | 8.2 | 1.95 |
| 45 to 54 years | 675 | 535 | 27.6 | 12.9 | 71.2 | 42.2 | 28.2 | 10.8 | 1.93 |
| 55 to 64 years | 387 | 299 | 23.7 | 11.3 | 72.2 | 42.2 | 27.7 | 8.8 | 1.86 |
| 65 years and over | 69 | 57 | 15.0 | 6.0 | 72.0 | 31.1 | 24.3 | 6.9 | 1.55 |
| Women, 16 years and over | 4,005 | 3,582 | 20.0 | 8.7 | 73.8 | 43.3 | 20.0 | 4.1 | 1.70 |
| 16 to 19 years | 591 | 563 | 10.8 | 4.2 | 81.2 | 29.4 | 15.7 | 3.5 | 1.45 |
| 20 to 24 years | 662 | 606 | 19.9 | 8.3 | 74.1 | 42.9 | 17.7 | 3.3 | 1.66 |
| 25 to 34 years | 1,154 | 1,041 | 22.8 | 9.3 | 72.1 | 46.6 | 19.4 | 3.9 | 1.74 |
| 35 to 44 years | 845 | 744 | 22.3 | 10.3 | 72.9 | 46.2 | 22.2 | 4.8 | 1.79 |
| 45 to 54 years | 470 | 398 | 22.1 | 11.7 | 72.3 | 48.2 | 24.4 | 4.7 | 1.83 |
| 55 to 64 years | 216 | 174 | 20.2 | 8.4 | 68.2 | 46.8 | 24.2 | 5.1 | 1.73 |
| 65 years and over | 66 | 55 | 15.4 | 7.8 | 65.2 | 44.4 | 23.7 | 7.8 | 1.64 |
| White, 16 years and over | 7,047 | 5,896 | 21.9 | 9.0 | 74.8 | 43.3 | 23.9 | 5.7 | 1.79 |
| Men | 4,121 | 3,320 | 24.4 | 9.6 | 75.3 | 41.6 | 26.8 | 6.8 | 1.84 |
| Women | 2,926 | 2,576 | 18.8 | 8.2 | 74.1 | 45.5 | 20.3 | 4.3 | 1.71 |
| Black, 16 years and over | 1,958 | 1,787 | 25.0 | 10.3 | 73.9 | 35.4 | 21.5 | 4.0 | 1.70 |
| Men | 1,046 | 933 | 26.2 | 10.3 | 74.2 | 34.9 | 24.9 | 4.3 | 1.75 |
| Women | 912 | 854 | 23.6 | 10.3 | 73.4 | 35.9 | 17.8 | 3.7 | 1.65 |

Note: The jobseekers total is less than the total unemployed because it does not include persons on layoff or waiting to begin a new job within 30 days, groups for whom jobseeking information is not collected. The percent using each method will always total more than 100 because many jobseekers use more than one method.

## Absences from Work of Employed, Full-Time Wage and Salary Workers, 1992

Source: Bureau of Labor Statistics. U.S. Dept. of Labor

(in thousands)

| Industry | Total Employed | Absence Rate[1] | | | Lost Worktime Rate[2] | | |
|---|---|---|---|---|---|---|---|
| | | Total | Illness | Other Reasons | Total | Illness | Other Reasons |
| Agricultural wage and salary workers | 1,200 | 3.8 | 1.9 | 2.0 | 2.8 | 1.6 | 1.2 |
| Private nonagricultural wage and salary workers | 67,570 | 4.7 | 2.6 | 2.1 | 2.7 | 1.6 | 1.2 |
| Mining | 605 | 4.7 | 2.4 | 2.3 | 3.7 | 1.5 | 2.2 |
| Construction | 4,081 | 5.0 | 2.6 | 2.4 | 3.4 | 1.8 | 1.6 |
| Manufacturing | 18,197 | 4.6 | 2.9 | 1.7 | 2.7 | 1.8 | .9 |
| Durable goods | 10,608 | 4.6 | 3.0 | 1.6 | 2.8 | 1.8 | .9 |
| Nondurable goods | 7,589 | 4.6 | 2.8 | 1.9 | 2.7 | 1.7 | 1.0 |
| Transportation and public utilities | 5,658 | 4.5 | 2.7 | 1.8 | 3.1 | 1.8 | 1.3 |
| Transportation | 3,033 | 4.7 | 2.6 | 2.1 | 3.7 | 2.0 | 1.7 |
| Communications and other public utilities | 2,625 | 4.2 | 2.7 | 1.5 | 2.4 | 1.6 | .8 |
| Wholesale and retail trade | 14,346 | 4.3 | 2.2 | 2.2 | 2.4 | 1.3 | 1.1 |
| Wholesale trade | 3,781 | 3.8 | 2.1 | 1.7 | 2.2 | 1.3 | .9 |
| Retail trade | 10,565 | 4.5 | 2.2 | 2.3 | 2.4 | 1.3 | 1.2 |
| Finance, insurance, and real estate | 5,850 | 3.8 | 2.1 | 1.7 | 2.0 | 1.1 | .9 |
| Services | 18,832 | 5.2 | 2.7 | 2.5 | 2.8 | 1.5 | 1.3 |
| Government workers | 15,373 | 5.5 | 2.9 | 2.7 | 3.2 | 1.7 | 1.5 |

(1) Absences refer to work missed due to illnesses or other personal reasons. Excluded is work missed due to vacation, holiday, labor-management dispute, or bad weather resulting in an employer temporarily curtailing business activity. The absence rate is the ratio of workers with absences to total full-time employment. To be counted as having had an absence, a person who usually works 35 hours or more per week must have been at work fewer than 35 hours or have not been at work at all during the survey reference week. (2) Hours absent as a percent of total hours usually worked. **Note:** Data for 1992 are not fully comparable with data for prior years because of the introduction of the occupational and industrial classification systems used in the 1990 census.

## Federal Minimum Hourly Wage Rates Since 1950

Source: U.S. Dept. of Labor

The Fair Labor Standards Act of 1938 and subsequent amendments provide for minimum wage coverage applicable to specified nonsupervisory employment categories. Exempt from coverage are executives and administrators or professionals.

| Minimum Rates for Nonfarm Workers | | | | Minimum Rates for Nonfarm Workers | | | |
|---|---|---|---|---|---|---|---|
| Effective date | Laws prior to 1966[1] | Percent, avg earnings[2] | 1966 and later[3] | Minimum rates for farm workers[4] | Effective date | Laws prior to 1966[1] | Percent, avg earnings[2] | 1966 and later[3] | Minimum rates for farm workers[4] |

| Effective date | Laws prior to 1966[1] | Percent, avg earnings[2] | 1966 and later[3] | Minimum rates for farm workers[4] |
|---|---|---|---|---|
| Jan. 25, 1950 | $.75 | 54 | (X) | (X) |
| Mar. 1, 1956 | 1.00 | 52 | (X) | (X) |
| Sept. 3, 1961 | 1.15 | 50 | (X) | (X) |
| Sept. 3, 1963 | 1.25 | 51 | (X) | (X) |
| Feb. 1, 1967 | 1.40 | 50 | $1.00 | $1.00 |
| Feb. 1, 1968 | 1.60 | 54 | 1.15 | 1.15 |
| Feb. 1, 1969 | (5) | (5) | 1.30 | 1.30 |
| Feb. 1, 1970 | (5) | (5) | 1.45 | (5) |
| Feb. 1, 1971 | (5) | (5) | 1.60 | (5) |
| May 1, 1974 | 2.00 | 46 | 1.90 | 1.60 |
| Jan. 1, 1975 | 2.10 | 45 | 2.00 | 1.80 |
| Jan. 1, 1976 | 2.30 | 46 | 2.20 | 2.00 |
| Jan. 1, 1977 | (5) | (5) | 2.30 | 2.20 |
| Jan. 1, 1978 | 2.65 | 44 | 2.65 | 2.65 |
| Jan. 1, 1979 | 2.90 | 45 | 2.90 | 2.90 |
| Jan. 1, 1980 | 3.10 | 43 | 3.10 | 3.10 |
| Jan. 1, 1981 | 3.35 | 42 | 3.35 | 3.35 |
| Apr. 1, 1990 | 3.80[6] | 35 | 3.80[6] | 3.80[6] |
| Apr. 1, 1991 | 4.25[6] | 38 | 4.25[6] | 4.25[6] |

(X) Not applicable. (1) Applies to workers covered prior to 1961 Amendments and, after Sept. 1965, to workers covered by 1961 Amendments. Rates set by 1961 Amendments were: Sept. 1961, $1.00; Sept. 1964, $1.15; and Sept. 1965, $1.25. (2) Percent of gross average hourly earnings of production workers in manufacturing. (3) Applies to workers newly covered by Amendments of 1966, 1974, and 1977, and Title IX of Education Amendments of 1972. (4) Included in coverage as of 1966, 1974, and 1977 Amendments. (5) No change in rate. (6) Training wage for workers age 16-19 in first six months of first job: 1990, $3.35; 1991, $3.62 and from Apr. 1, 1991 additional requirements re subsequent employment by a different employer for an additional 90 days. The training wage expired Mar. 31, 1993.

## Part-Time Workers, 1992

Source: Bureau of Labor Statistics. U.S. Dept. of Labor

(in thousands)

| Reason for Working Less Than 35 Hours | All industries | | | Nonagricultural industries | | |
|---|---|---|---|---|---|---|
| | Total | Usually Work Full-Time | Usually Work Part-Time | Total | Usually Work Full-Time | Usually Work Part-Time |
| Total, 16 years and over | 30,147 | 11,029 | 19,118 | 29,245 | 10,710 | 18,535 |
| Economic reasons | 6,385 | 2,026 | 4,359 | 6,116 | 1,910 | 4,206 |
| Slack work | 3,220 | 1,728 | 1,492 | 3,037 | 1,623 | 1,414 |
| Material shortages or repairs to plant and equipment | 39 | 39 | — | 38 | 38 | — |
| New job started during week | 188 | 188 | — | 180 | 180 | — |
| Job terminated during week | 71 | 71 | — | 69 | 69 | — |
| Could find only part-time work | 2,867 | — | 2,867 | 2,792 | — | 2,792 |
| Other reasons | 23,762 | 9,003 | 14,759 | 23,129 | 8,800 | 14,329 |
| Does not want, or unavailable for, full-time work | 12,054 | — | 12,054 | 11,732 | — | 11,732 |
| Vacation | 1,716 | 1,716 | — | 1,696 | 1,696 | — |
| Illness | 1,500 | 1,326 | 174 | 1,473 | 1,310 | 163 |
| Bad weather | 557 | 557 | — | 462 | 462 | — |
| Industrial dispute | 10 | 10 | — | 10 | 10 | — |
| Legal or religious holiday | 3,856 | 3,856 | — | 3,837 | 3,837 | — |
| Full time for this job | 1,650 | — | 1,650 | 1,613 | — | 1,613 |
| All other reasons | 2,419 | 1,538 | 881 | 2,306 | 1,485 | 821 |
| **Average hours:** | | | | | | |
| Economic reasons | 22.2 | 24.4 | 21.2 | 22.3 | 24.5 | 21.3 |
| Other reasons | 22.7 | 27.8 | 19.5 | 22.7 | 27.9 | 19.6 |
| **Worked 30 to 34 hours:** | | | | | | |
| Economic reasons | 2,065 | 924 | 1,141 | 1,994 | 883 | 1,111 |
| Other reasons | 8,905 | 6,001 | 2,904 | 8,750 | 5,914 | 2,836 |

## Distribution of Wage and Salary Workers Paid Hourly Rates

Source: Bureau of Labor Statistics. U.S. Dept. of Labor; unpublished tabulations from Current Population Survey. 1992.

(in thousands)

| | Total paid hourly rates | $4.25* or less | Less than $10.00 | $10.00 or more |
|---|---|---|---|---|
| **Sex and age** | | | | |
| Total, 16 years and over. . . . . . . . . . . . . . . . | 62,683 | 4,762 | 41,295 | 21,388 |
| 16 to 24 years . . . . . . . . . . . . . . . | 14,173 | 2,479 | 13,090 | 1,083 |
| 20 to 24 years . . . . . . . . . . . . . . . . . . . . | 9,300 | 1,065 | 8,293 | 1,007 |
| 25 years and over . . . . . . . . . . . . . . . . | 48,511 | 2,283 | 28,207 | 20,304 |
| 25 to 54 years . . . . . . . . . . . . . . . . . | 42,054 | 1,854 | 24,073 | 17,981 |
| 25 to 34 years . . . . . . . . . . . . . | 17,835 | 912 | 11,411 | 6,424 |
| 35 to 44 years . . . . . . . . . . . . . | 15,005 | 602 | 7,801 | 7,124 |
| 45 to 54 years . . . . . . . . . . . . . | 9,215 | 340 | 4,782 | 4,433 |
| 55 years and over . . . . . . . . . . . . . | 6,456 | 429 | 4,114 | 2,324 |
| 55 to 64 years . . . . . . . . . . . . . | 5,076 | 252 | 3,018 | 2,058 |
| 65 years and over . . . . . . . . . . . . . | 1,380 | 177 | 1,114 | 266 |
| Men, 16 years and over . . . . . . . . . . . . . | 31,510 | 1,792 | 17,849 | 13,661 |
| 16 to 24 years . . . . . . . . . . . . . | 7,399 | 1,093 | 6,695 | 704 |
| 20 to 24 years . . . . . . . . . . . . . | 4,909 | 444 | 4,259 | 650 |
| 25 years and over . . . . . . . . . . . . | 24,111 | 699 | 11,155 | 12,956 |
| Women, 16 years and over . . . . . . . . . . . . . | 31,173 | 2,970 | 23,446 | 7,727 |
| 16 to 24 years . . . . . . . . . . . . . | 6,773 | 1,386 | 6,394 | 379 |
| 20 to 24 years . . . . . . . . . . . . . | 4,397 | 621 | 4,041 | 356 |
| 25 years and over . . . . . . . . . . . . | 24,400 | 1,584 | 17,053 | 7,347 |
| **Family relationship** | | | | |
| Husbands . . . . . . . . . . . . . . . . . . . . . . . . | 16,400 | 310 | N/A | N/A |
| Wives . . . . . . . . . . . . . . . . . . . . . . . . | 15,701 | 895 | N/A | N/A |
| Women who maintain families . . . . . . . . . . . . . | 4,061 | 386 | N/A | N/A |
| Men who maintain families . . . . . . . . . . . . . | 1,289 | 52 | N/A | N/A |
| **Race and Hispanic origin** | | | | |
| White | | | | |
| Total, 16 years and over . . . . . . . . . . . . . | 52,452 | 3,872 | 33,960 | 18,492 |
| Men . . . . . . . . . . . . . . . . . . . . | 26,508 | 1,431 | 14,538 | 11,970 |
| Women . . . . . . . . . . . . . . . . . . . . | 25,944 | 2,442 | 19,423 | 6,521 |
| Black | | | | |
| Total, 16 years and over . . . . . . . . . . . . . | 8,054 | 719 | 5,859 | 2,195 |
| Men . . . . . . . . . . . . . . . . . . . . | 3,926 | 288 | 2,640 | 1,286 |
| Women . . . . . . . . . . . . . . . . . . . . | 4,129 | 432 | 3,220 | 909 |
| Hispanic origin | | | | |
| Total, 16 years and over . . . . . . . . . . . . . | 5,984 | 590 | 4,528 | 1,456 |
| Men . . . . . . . . . . . . . . . . . . . . | 3,638 | 298 | 2,580 | 1,058 |
| Women . . . . . . . . . . . . . . . . . . . . | 2,346 | 292 | 1,946 | 400 |
| **Full- and part-time status and sex** | | | | |
| Full-time workers | | | | |
| Total, 16 years and over . . . . . . . . . . . . . | 46,645 | 1,742 | 27,579 | 19,066 |
| Men . . . . . . . . . . . . . . . . . . . . | 26,426 | 731 | 13,331 | 13,095 |
| Women . . . . . . . . . . . . . . . . . . . . | 20,219 | 1,011 | 14,249 | 5,970 |
| Part-time workers | | | | |
| Total, 16 years and over . . . . . . . . . . . . . | 16,037 | 3,020 | 13,715 | 2,322 |
| Men . . . . . . . . . . . . . . . . . . . . | 5,084 | 1,061 | 4,520 | 564 |
| Women . . . . . . . . . . . . . . . . . . . . | 10,953 | 1,959 | 9,198 | 1,755 |

Note: Data exclude the incorporated self-employed. * $4.25 = minimum wage from April 1, 1991. N/A = Not available.

## Average Hours and Earnings of Production Workers, 1964-1992

Source: Bureau of Labor Statistics. U.S. Dept. of Labor

(annual averages)

| | Weekly hours | Total private[1] Hourly earnings | Weekly earnings | | Weekly hours | Total private[1] Hourly earnings | Weekly earnings |
|---|---|---|---|---|---|---|---|
| 1964 . . . . | 38.7 | $2.36 | $91.33 | 1979 . . . . | 35.7 | 6.16 | 219.91 |
| 1965 . . . . | 38.8 | 2.46 | 95.45 | 1980 . . . . | 35.3 | 6.66 | 235.10 |
| 1966 . . . . | 38.6 | 2.56 | 98.82 | 1981 . . . . | 35.2 | 7.25 | 255.20 |
| 1967 . . . . | 38.0 | 2.68 | 101.84 | 1982 . . . . | 34.8 | 7.68 | 267.26 |
| 1968 . . . . | 37.8 | 2.85 | 107.73 | 1983 . . . . | 35.0 | 8.02 | 280.70 |
| 1969 . . . . | 37.7 | 3.04 | 114.61 | 1984 . . . . | 35.2 | 8.32 | 292.86 |
| 1970 . . . . | 37.1 | 3.23 | 119.83 | 1985 . . . . | 34.9 | 8.57 | 299.09 |
| 1971 . . . . | 36.9 | 3.45 | 127.31 | 1986 . . . . | 34.8 | 8.76 | 304.85 |
| 1972 . . . . | 37.0 | 3.70 | 136.90 | 1987 . . . . | 34.8 | 8.98 | 312.50 |
| 1973 . . . . | 36.9 | 3.94 | 145.39 | 1988 . . . . | 34.7 | 9.28 | 322.02 |
| 1974 . . . . | 36.5 | 4.24 | 154.76 | 1989 . . . . | 34.6 | 9.66 | 334.24 |
| 1975 . . . . | 36.1 | 4.53 | 163.53 | 1990 . . . . | 34.5 | 10.01 | 345.35 |
| 1976 . . . . | 36.1 | 4.86 | 175.45 | 1991 . . . . | 34.3 | 10.32 | 353.98 |
| 1977 . . . . | 36.0 | 5.25 | 189.00 | 1992 . . . . | 34.4 | 10.58 | 363.95 |
| 1978 . . . . | 35.8 | 5.69 | 203.70 | | | | |

(1) Data relate to production workers in mining and manufacturing; construction workers in construction; and nonsupervisory workers in transportation and public utilities; wholesale and retail trade; finance, insurance, and real estate; and services.

## Workers Paid Hourly Rates, 1979-1992

Source: Bureau of Labor Statistics, U.S. Dept. of Labor; unpublished tabulations from the Current Population Survey.

(in thousands)

| Year | Total Wage and Salary Workers | Workers paid hourly rates | | |
|---|---|---|---|---|
| | | Total | Percent of Wage and Salary Workers | Paid Below Prevailing Minimum Wage | Paid at Prevailing Minimum Wage |
| **Both sexes** | | | | | |
| 1979 | 85,773 | 50,637 | 59.0 | 2,846 | 3,907 |
| 1980 | 85,780 | 50,210 | 58.5 | 3,017 | 4,581 |
| 1981 (end 1970 weights) | 86,651 | 50,770 | 58.6 | 3,440 | 4,201 |
| 1981 (begin 1980 weights) | 88,516 | 51,869 | 58.6 | 3,513 | 4,311 |
| 1982 | 87,368 | 50,846 | 58.2 | 2,348 | 4,148 |
| 1983 | 88,290 | 51,820 | 58.7 | 2,077 | 4,261 |
| 1984 | 92,194 | 54,143 | 58.7 | 1,838 | 4,125 |
| 1985 | 94,521 | 55,762 | 59.0 | 1,639 | 3,899 |
| 1986 | 96,903 | 57,529 | 59.4 | 1,599 | 3,461 |
| 1987 | 99,303 | 59,552 | 60.0 | 1,468 | 3,229 |
| 1988 | 101,407 | 60,878 | 60.0 | 1,319 | 2,608 |
| 1989 | 103,480 | 62,389 | 60.3 | 1,372 | 1,790 |
| 1990 (2nd quarter - 1st quarter 1991)* | 103,587 | 62,112 | 60.0 | 2,221 | 968 |
| 1991 (2nd quarter - 1st quarter 1992) | 102,872 | 61,782 | 60.1 | 2,351 | 3,365 |
| 1992 | 103,688 | 62,683 | 60.5 | 1,896 | 2,866 |
| **Men** | | | | | |
| 1979 | 48,389 | 27,771 | 57.4 | 820 | 1,318 |
| 1980 | 47,641 | 27,075 | 56.8 | 957 | 1,654 |
| 1981 (end 1970 weights) | 47,769 | 26,936 | 56.4 | 1,090 | 1,489 |
| 1981 (begin 1980 weights) | 48,844 | 27,576 | 56.5 | 1,119 | 1,533 |
| 1982 | 47,591 | 26,481 | 55.6 | 697 | 1,587 |
| 1983 | 47,856 | 26,831 | 56.1 | 585 | 1,658 |
| 1984 | 50,022 | 28,140 | 56.3 | 490 | 1,626 |
| 1985 | 51,015 | 28,893 | 56.6 | 440 | 1,544 |
| 1986 | 51,942 | 29,666 | 57.1 | 408 | 1,336 |
| 1987 | 52,938 | 30,474 | 57.6 | 364 | 1,283 |
| 1988 | 53,912 | 31,058 | 57.6 | 311 | 1,066 |
| 1989 | 54,789 | 31,687 | 57.8 | 379 | 733 |
| 1990 (2nd quarter - 1st quarter 1991) | 54,573 | 31,355 | 57.5 | 732 | 318 |
| 1991 (2nd quarter - 1st quarter 1992) | 53,879 | 31,010 | 57.6 | 781 | 1,301 |
| 1992 | 54,135 | 31,510 | 58.2 | 628 | 1,164 |
| **Women** | | | | | |
| 1979 | 37,384 | 22,866 | 61.2 | 2,026 | 2,589 |
| 1980 | 38,140 | 23,135 | 60.7 | 2,060 | 2,927 |
| 1981 (end 1970 weights) | 38,882 | 23,834 | 61.3 | 2,350 | 2,711 |
| 1981 (begin 1980 weights) | 39,672 | 24,294 | 61.2 | 2,394 | 2,778 |
| 1982 | 39,777 | 24,365 | 61.3 | 1,651 | 2,561 |
| 1983 | 40,433 | 24,989 | 61.8 | 1,492 | 2,603 |
| 1984 | 42,172 | 26,003 | 61.7 | 1,348 | 2,499 |
| 1985 | 43,506 | 26,869 | 61.8 | 1,198 | 2,356 |
| 1986 | 44,961 | 27,863 | 62.0 | 1,192 | 2,125 |
| 1987 | 46,365 | 29,078 | 62.7 | 1,105 | 1,946 |
| 1988 | 47,495 | 29,820 | 62.8 | 1,008 | 1,542 |
| 1989 | 48,691 | 30,702 | 63.1 | 994 | 1,056 |
| 1990 (2nd quarter - 1st quarter 1991) | 49,014 | 30,757 | 62.8 | 1,489 | 650 |
| 1991 (2nd quarter - 1st quarter 1992) | 48,993 | 30,771 | 62.8 | 1,570 | 2,064 |
| 1992 | 49,554 | 31,173 | 62.9 | 1,268 | 1,702 |

* The prevailing federal minimum wage was $2.90 in 1979, $3.10 in 1980, and $3.35 in 1981-89. The minimum wage rose to $3.80 in April 1990, and to $4.25 in April 1991. **NOTE:** Data exclude the incorporated self-employed. Estimates based on sample weights applicable to 1970 census population controls are not strictly comparable to those weights applicable to 1980 controls. Data for 1981 are shown both ways. Although the new weights caused the number of wage and salary workers to rise by 1.9 million, hourly paid workers to rise by 1.1 million, and those at or below the minimum wage to rise by 183,000, percentages and medians changed very little or not at all.

## Employment Status of the Civilian Noninstitutional Population in Poverty and Nonpoverty Areas, 1992

Source: Bureau of Labor Statistics, U.S. Dept. of Labor

(in thousands)

| | Total U.S. | | Metropolitan Areas | | Nonmetropolitan Areas | |
|---|---|---|---|---|---|---|
| | Poverty Areas | Nonpoverty Areas | Poverty Areas | Nonpoverty Areas | Poverty Areas | Nonpoverty Areas |
| Civilian noninstitutional population | 26,797 | 164,778 | 17,122 | 131,998 | 9,676 | 32,780 |
| Civilian labor force | 15,364 | 111,618 | 9,666 | 90,393 | 5,698 | 21,226 |
| Percent of population | 57.3 | 67.7 | 56.5 | 68.5 | 58.9 | 64.8 |
| Employed | 13,520 | 104,078 | 8,313 | 84,283 | 5,207 | 19,795 |
| Unemployed | 1,844 | 7,540 | 1,353 | 6,110 | 491 | 1,431 |
| Unemployment rate | 12.0 | 6.8 | 14.0 | 6.8 | 8.6 | 6.7 |
| Men, 20 years and over | 11.2 | 6.5 | 13.2 | 6.5 | 7.8 | 6.3 |
| Women, 20 years and over | 10.5 | 5.7 | 12.2 | 5.7 | 7.6 | 5.6 |
| Both sexes, 16 to 19 years | 30.5 | 18.4 | 34.7 | 18.7 | 23.4 | 17.5 |
| Men | 30.6 | 20.0 | 35.4 | 20.5 | 23.2 | 18.3 |
| Women | 30.3 | 16.7 | 33.9 | 16.7 | 23.7 | 16.7 |
| Not in labor force | 11,434 | 53,160 | 7,456 | 41,605 | 3,977 | 11,555 |

## Employer-Provided Pension Plans

Source: Bureau of the Census, Economics and Statistics Administration, U.S. Dept. of Commerce; April 1993

- **Coverage rates rise slightly.** In 1991, 68 percent of workers were covered by employer-provided pension plans, up from 66 percent in 1987 but not significantly different from 1984. These plans may include 401(k) plans. Covered workers are those whose employer offered a retirement plan for any employees. However, not every covered worker was a participant. In 1991, 53 percent of all workers participated in pension plans, the same as in 1987 but lower than the 55 percent who did so in 1984. Covered workers did not participate in 1991 for the following reasons: 33 percent had not worked for the firm long enough; 23 percent chose not to participate; 22 percent did not work sufficient hours per year; 11 percent were in an ineligible job category; and 11 percent started the job too close to retirement age or had another, unspecified reason.
- **Who is covered?** Many factors affect coverage rates. *Size of company:* Many of larger firms have a much higher pension coverage rate than those in smaller firms. Coverage rates in 1991 ranged from 90 percent in firms with more than 1,000 employees to 23 percent in those with fewer than 25 employees. *Level of earnings:* Highly paid workers were more likely to be covered by pension plans. Coverage rates ranged from 82 percent for those with monthly earnings of $2,000 or more to 43 percent for those who earned less than $500 per month. Employees covered by employer-sponsored plans had much higher median monthly earnings than those not covered: $2,003 versus $1,253. *Union status:* Union members had a higher coverage rate than nonmembers (89 versus 62 percent). By industry, pension coverage ranged from 100 percent in the armed forces and 92 percent in public administration to 37 percent in personal services and 34 percent in agriculture, forestry, and fisheries.

- **More workers are vested.** In 1991, 47 percent of all workers were vested in a pension plan, an increase from the 1984 and 1987 rates of 45 percent. These workers were eligible to receive a lump-sum distribution at retirement or continuing payments during retirement. Since vesting is usually linked to the length of service on the job, young workers are less likely to be vested than older workers. Vesting rates ranged from 33 percent of workers under age 30 to 55 percent of those 50 to 59 years of age.
- **IRA ownership down, 401(k) plan participation up.** Individual Retirement Accounts (IRA's) were established in 1974 as a means of building savings for retirement for workers not covered by an employer-provided pension plan. In 1982, eligibility was extended to all workers. IRA's thus became a popular way to supplement pension income: 77 percent of workers who had IRA's in 1991 were also covered by employer-sponsored pension plans, about the same as in 1987 and 1984. However, ownership of IRA's, which had increased from 21 to 24 percent of all workers between 1984 and 1987, fell to 20 percent in 1991. This drop probably reflects both the effect of the Tax Reform Act of 1986, which limited the tax deductibility of IRA contributions, and the growing popularity of 401(k) and other types of thrift savings plans. The percentage of workers participating in employer-sponsored thrift plans, known as 401(k)'s, tripled between 1984 and 1991, from 6 to 19 percent. Larger firms were likelier to offer 401(k)'s: participation in 1991 ranged from 3 percent at firms employing fewer than 25 people to 28 percent at those employing 1,000 or more. Increasing numbers of workers are both IRA and 401(k) plan participants: 6 percent in 1991, up from 4 percent in 1987 and 2 percent in 1984.

## Employer Costs for Employee Compensation, March 1993

Source: Bureau of Labor Statistics, U.S. Dept. of Labor; dollar figures are costs per hour worked.

| | Total Compensation | Wages and Salaries | Total[1] | Benefit Costs | | | | |
|---|---|---|---|---|---|---|---|---|
| | | | | Paid Leave | Supplemental Pay | Insurance | Retirement and Savings | Legally Required Benefits |
| **Civilian workers** . . . . . . . . . . . . | $17.88 | $12.68 | $5.20 | $1.22 | $0.39 | $1.32 | $0.70 | $1.53 |
| Occupational group: | | | | | | | | |
| White-collar occupations . . . . . . | 21.23 | 15.38 | 5.86 | 1.55 | 0.38 | 1.48 | 0.87 | 1.54 |
| Professional specialty and technical . . . . . . . . . . . . . | 29.33 | 21.41 | 7.92 | 2.05 | 0.42 | 1.94 | 1.51 | 1.96 |
| Executive, administrative, and managerial . . . . . . . . . . . | 30.48 | 21.98 | 8.50 | 2.65 | 0.67 | 1.76 | 1.19 | 2.13 |
| Administrative support including clerical . . . . . . . . . . . . . | 14.36 | 10.05 | 4.31 | 1.08 | 0.25 | 1.35 | 0.50 | 1.12 |
| Blue-collar occupations . . . . . . . . | 16.58 | 11.08 | 5.50 | 1.02 | 0.55 | 1.42 | 0.61 | 1.84 |
| Service occupations . . . . . . . . . | 10.04 | 7.25 | 2.79 | 0.58 | 0.17 | 0.69 | 0.35 | 1.00 |
| Industry group: | | | | | | | | |
| Services . . . . . . . . . . . . . . | 18.91 | 13.80 | 5.11 | 1.26 | 0.27 | 1.29 | 0.83 | 1.43 |
| Health services . . . . . . . . . . | 17.55 | 12.66 | 4.88 | 1.36 | 0.44 | 1.16 | 0.49 | 1.42 |
| Hospitals . . . . . . . . . . . . | 19.74 | 13.83 | 5.91 | 1.69 | 0.60 | 1.54 | 0.56 | 1.51 |
| Educational services . . . . . . . . | 26.87 | 19.56 | 7.32 | 1.63 | 0.08 | 2.09 | 1.95 | 1.53 |
| Elementary and secondary education . . . . . . . . . . | 27.24 | 19.78 | 7.46 | 1.54 | 0.08 | 2.25 | 2.09 | 1.47 |
| Higher education . . . . . . . . | 27.39 | 20.02 | 7.37 | 1.86 | 0.10 | 1.91 | 1.81 | 1.68 |
| | | | | **Percent of Total Compensation** | | | | |
| **Civilian workers** . . . . . . . . . . . . | 100.0 | 70.9 | 29.1 | 6.8 | 2.2 | 7.4 | 3.9 | 8.6 |
| Occupational group: | | | | | | | | |
| White-collar occupations . . . . . . | 100.0 | 72.4 | 27.6 | 7.3 | 1.8 | 7.0 | 4.1 | 7.3 |
| Professional specialty and technical . . . . . . . . . . . . . | 100.0 | 73.0 | 27.0 | 7.0 | 1.4 | 6.6 | 5.1 | 6.7 |
| Executive, administrative, and managerial . . . . . . . . . . . | 100.0 | 72.1 | 27.9 | 8.7 | 2.2 | 5.8 | 3.9 | 7.0 |
| Administrative support including clerical . . . . . . . . . . . . . | 100.0 | 70.0 | 30.0 | 7.5 | 1.7 | 9.4 | 3.4 | 7.8 |
| Blue-collar occupations . . . . . . . . | 100.0 | 66.8 | 33.2 | 6.1 | 3.3 | 8.6 | 3.7 | 11.1 |
| Service occupations . . . . . . . . . | 100.0 | 72.2 | 27.8 | 5.8 | 1.7 | 6.8 | 3.5 | 10.0 |
| Industry group: | | | | | | | | |
| Services . . . . . . . . . . . . . . | 100.0 | 73.0 | 27.0 | 6.7 | 1.4 | 6.8 | 4.4 | 7.6 |
| Health services . . . . . . . . . . | 100.0 | 72.2 | 27.8 | 7.8 | 2.5 | 6.6 | 2.8 | 8.1 |
| Hospitals . . . . . . . . . . . . | 100.0 | 70.0 | 30.0 | 8.6 | 3.0 | 7.8 | 2.8 | 7.7 |
| Educational services . . . . . . . . | 100.0 | 72.8 | 27.2 | 6.1 | 0.3 | 7.8 | 7.3 | 5.7 |
| Elementary and secondary education . . . . . . . . . . | 100.0 | 72.6 | 27.4 | 5.7 | 0.3 | 8.3 | 7.7 | 5.4 |
| Higher education . . . . . . . . | 100.0 | 73.1 | 26.9 | 6.8 | 0.4 | 7.0 | 6.6 | 6.2 |

(1) Includes severance pay and supplemental unemployment benefits.

## Civilian Employment of the Federal Government in May 1993

Source: Workforce Analysis and Statistics Division. U.S. Office of Personnel Management
(Payroll in thousands of dollars, for the month of May, 1993)

| Agency | All Areas Employment | All Areas Payroll | United States Employment | United States Payroll | Wash., D.C. MSA Employment | Wash., D.C. MSA Payroll | Overseas Employment | Overseas Payroll |
|---|---|---|---|---|---|---|---|---|
| Total, all agencies[1] . . . . . . . . | 3,033,215 | $10,323,268 | 2,918,308 | $9,917,094 | 380,442 | $1,717,767 | 114,907 | $406,174 |
| Legislative Branch . . . . . . . . | 38,779 | 157,762 | 38,721 | 157,390 | 36,508 | 145,240 | 58 | 372 |
| Congress. . . . . . . . . . . . . | 20,695 | 66,417 | 20,695 | 66,417 | 20,695 | 66,417 | — | — |
| U.S. Senate . . . . . . . . . | 7,723 | 24,698 | 7,723 | 24,698 | 7,723 | 24,698 | — | — |
| House of Rep Summary. . . . | 12,954 | 41,633 | 12,954 | 41,633 | 12,954 | 41,633 | — | — |
| Comm. on Scty & Coop in Eur | 18 | 86 | 18 | 86 | 18 | 86 | — | — |
| Architect of the Capitol . . . . . . | 2,334 | 9,238 | 2,334 | 9,238 | 2,334 | 9,238 | — | — |
| Botanic Garden . . . . . . . . . | 51 | 216 | 51 | 216 | 51 | 216 | — | — |
| Competit Policy Council . . . . . | 6 | 28 | 6 | 28 | 6 | 28 | — | — |
| Congressional Budget Ofc. . . . | 239 | 1,631 | 239 | 1,631 | 239 | 1,631 | — | — |
| Copyright Royalty Tribunal. . . . | 8 | 65 | 8 | 65 | 8 | 65 | — | — |
| General Accounting Ofc . . . . . | 5,109 | 31,747 | 5,058 | 31,445 | 3,349 | 21,166 | 51 | 302 |
| Government Printing Ofc. . . . . | 4,775 | 22,350 | 4,775 | 22,350 | 4,302 | 20,585 | — | — |
| John C Stennis Ctr Pub Dev . . . | 6 | 16 | 6 | 16 | — | — | — | — |
| Library of Congress. . . . . . . | 4,999 | 23,358 | 4,992 | 23,288 | 4,973 | 23,220 | 7 | 70 |
| Nat Comm on AIDS Syndrome . | 11 | 44 | 11 | 44 | 11 | 44 | — | — |
| Nat Comm Prev Infant Mort . . . | 10 | 27 | 10 | 27 | 10 | 27 | — | — |
| Ofc Technology Assessment . . | 217 | 1,301 | 217 | 1,301 | 217 | 1,301 | — | — |
| U.S. Tax Court. . . . . . . . . . | 319 | 1,324 | 319 | 1,324 | 313 | 1,302 | — | — |
| Judicial Branch . . . . . . . . . . | 28,075 | 133,183 | 27,769 | 131,727 | 2,070 | 11,006 | 306 | 1,456 |
| Supreme Court . . . . . . . . . | 371 | 1,094 | 371 | 1,094 | 371 | 1,094 | — | — |
| U.S. Courts . . . . . . . . . . . | 27,618 | 131,639 | 27,312 | 130,183 | 1,613 | 9,462 | 306 | 1,456 |
| U.S. Court of Vets Appeals . . . | 86 | 450 | 86 | 450 | 86 | 450 | — | — |
| Executive Branch . . . . . . . . . | 2,966,361 | 10,032,323 | 2,851,818 | 9,627,977 | 341,864 | 1,561,521 | 114,543 | 404,346 |
| Exec Ofc of the President . . . . | 1,991 | 7,598 | 1,983 | 7,557 | 1,983 | 7,557 | 8 | 41 |
| White House Office . . . . . . | 559 | 1,798 | 559 | 1,798 | 559 | 1,798 | — | — |
| Ofc of Vice President . . . . . | 23 | 105 | 23 | 105 | 23 | 105 | — | — |
| Ofc of Mgt & Budget . . . . . . | 564 | 2,456 | 564 | 2,456 | 564 | 2,456 | — | — |
| Office of Administration . . . . | 241 | 715 | 241 | 715 | 241 | 715 | — | — |
| Council Economic Advisors . . | 33 | 133 | 33 | 133 | 33 | 133 | — | — |
| Council on Environ Qual . . . . | 23 | 83 | 23 | 83 | 23 | 83 | — | — |
| Ofc of Policy Development . . . | 52 | 190 | 52 | 190 | 52 | 190 | — | — |
| Exec Residence at WH . . . . . | 93 | 581 | 93 | 581 | 93 | 581 | — | — |
| Natl Crit Materials Coun . . . . | 2 | 8 | 2 | 8 | 2 | 8 | — | — |
| National Security Council . . . | 65 | 240 | 65 | 240 | 65 | 240 | — | — |
| National Space Council . . . | 7 | 5 | 7 | 5 | 7 | 5 | — | — |
| Ofc of Natl Drug Control. . . . | 90 | 351 | 90 | 351 | 90 | 351 | — | — |
| Ofc of Sci and Tech Policy . . | 39 | 110 | 39 | 110 | 39 | 110 | — | — |
| Ofc of U.S. Trade Rep . . . . . | 200 | 823 | 192 | 782 | 192 | 782 | 8 | 41 |
| Executive Departments . . . . . | 2,001,621 | 6,968,252 | 1,906,940 | 6,629,080 | 259,118 | 1,157,252 | 94,681 | 339,172 |
| State. . . . . . . . . . . . . . | 26,220 | 153,086 | 9,852 | 54,772 | 8,852 | 48,150 | 16,368 | 98,314 |
| Treasury. . . . . . . . . . . . | 165,530 | 743,467 | 164,373 | 736,703 | 24,523 | 138,892 | 1,157 | 6,764 |
| Defense, Total . . . . . . . . . | 941,608 | 2,731,443 | 873,639 | 2,532,490 | 89,692 | 282,341 | 67,969 | 198,953 |
| Dept of the Army. . . . . . . | 306,562 | 827,905 | 276,610 | 742,534 | 26,493 | 56,125 | 29,952 | 85,371 |
| Army, Mil Func Total . . . . | 275,857 | 751,411 | 245,996 | 666,321 | 25,314 | 52,599 | 29,861 | 85,090 |
| Army, Civil Func Total . . . | 30,705 | 76,494 | 30,614 | 76,213 | 1,179 | 3,526 | 91 | 281 |
| Corps of Engineers. . . | 30,565 | 76,170 | 30,474 | 75,889 | 1,039 | 3,202 | 91 | 281 |
| Cemeterial Expenses . | 140 | 324 | 140 | 324 | 140 | 324 | — | — |
| Dept of the Navy. . . . . . . | 285,079 | 898,000 | 273,357 | 863,786 | 37,394 | 124,463 | 11,722 | 34,214 |
| Dept of the Air Force . . . . | 196,074 | 557,131 | 186,662 | 532,198 | 5,892 | 20,795 | 9,412 | 24,933 |
| Defense Log Agcy. . . . . . | 64,120 | 178,758 | 63,603 | 177,237 | 2,993 | 12,281 | 517 | 1,521 |
| Other Defense Activities . . | 89,773 | 269,649 | 73,407 | 216,735 | 16,920 | 68,677 | 16,366 | 52,914 |
| Justice. . . . . . . . . . . . . | 98,022 | 463,622 | 96,105 | 453,637 | 21,981 | 101,927 | 1,917 | 9,985 |
| Interior. . . . . . . . . . . . | 84,736 | 335,269 | 84,341 | 333,498 | 9,780 | 48,816 | 395 | 1,771 |
| Agriculture. . . . . . . . . . . | 123,057 | 464,622 | 121,550 | 459,343 | 13,467 | 68,851 | 1,507 | 5,279 |
| Commerce . . . . . . . . . . | 38,651 | 177,589 | 37,734 | 172,925 | 20,479 | 106,950 | 917 | 4,664 |
| Labor . . . . . . . . . . . . . | 17,609 | 88,358 | 17,567 | 88,102 | 6,170 | 32,860 | 42 | 256 |
| Health and Human Services . | 132,406 | 585,517 | 131,706 | 582,495 | 31,443 | 161,902 | 700 | 3,022 |
| Housing & Urban Dev . . . . | 13,208 | 65,684 | 13,095 | 65,104 | 3,404 | 20,202 | 113 | 580 |
| Transportation . . . . . . . . | 69,922 | 302,919 | 69,349 | 300,318 | 10,776 | 47,158 | 573 | 2,601 |
| Energy. . . . . . . . . . . . . | 20,637 | 124,146 | 20,633 | 124,109 | 7,298 | 50,722 | 4 | 37 |
| Education . . . . . . . . . . . | 5,001 | 26,508 | 4,996 | 26,480 | 3,451 | 19,050 | 5 | 28 |
| Veterans Affairs . . . . . . . | 265,014 | 706,022 | 262,000 | 699,104 | 7,802 | 29,431 | 3,014 | 6,918 |
| Independent Agencies[1]. . . . . . | 962,749 | 3,056,473 | 942,895 | 2,991,340 | 80,763 | 396,712 | 19,854 | 65,133 |
| Action. . . . . . . . . . . . . . | 418 | 2,196 | 416 | 2,182 | 159 | 939 | 2 | 14 |
| Environmtl Protect Agcy . . . . | 18,478 | 98,110 | 18,457 | 97,994 | 6,050 | 35,857 | 21 | 116 |
| Equal Employ Opp Comm . . . . | 2,938 | 14,475 | 2,938 | 14,475 | 765 | 4,253 | — | — |
| Federal Deposit Ins Corp. . . . | 21,889 | 123,339 | 21,880 | 123,280 | 3,802 | 26,359 | 9 | 59 |
| Fed Emergency Mgmt Agcy . . . | 4,117 | 18,265 | 4,025 | 17,941 | 1,556 | 8,266 | 92 | 324 |
| General Svcs Admin. . . . . . | 20,780 | 95,503 | 20,677 | 95,031 | 6,795 | 37,554 | 103 | 472 |
| Natl Archives & Recds Admin. . . | 3,133 | 9,270 | 3,133 | 9,270 | 1,298 | 5,080 | — | — |
| Natl Aero Space Admin . . . . . | 25,149 | 148,159 | 25,141 | 148,097 | 5,754 | 36,474 | 8 | 62 |
| Nuclear Regulatory Comm. . . . | 3,542 | 17,195 | 3,542 | 17,195 | 2,356 | 11,815 | — | — |
| Office of Personnel Mgmt . . . . | 6,842 | 24,985 | 6,818 | 24,928 | 2,913 | 13,415 | 24 | 57 |
| Panama Canal Commission . . . | 8,495 | 27,934 | 19 | 115 | 7 | 66 | 8,476 | 27,819 |
| Securities & Exchnge Comm . . | 2,697 | 16,381 | 2,697 | 16,381 | 1,762 | 10,589 | — | — |
| Small Business Admin . . . . . . | 5,363 | 25,461 | 5,251 | 25,016 | 988 | 5,614 | 112 | 445 |
| Smithsonian, Summary. . . . . . | 5,491 | 22,862 | 5,320 | 22,233 | 4,923 | 20,498 | 171 | 629 |
| Tennessee Valley Auth. . . . . . | 19,145 | 75,470 | 19,145 | 75,470 | 9 | 39 | — | — |
| U.S. Information Agency . . . . . | 8,298 | 33,960 | 4,335 | 24,638 | 4,072 | 22,504 | 3,963 | 9,322 |
| U.S. Intnatl Dev Coop Agcy . . . | 4,385 | 26,413 | 2,292 | 13,990 | 2,285 | 13,951 | 2,093 | 12,423 |
| U.S. Postal Service . . . . . . | 779,606 | 2,166,456 | 775,817 | 2,155,088 | 21,115 | 67,329 | 3,789 | 11,368 |

(1) Included in total are other independent agencies with fewer than 2,500 employees.

# Labor Union Directory

Source: Bureau of Labor Statistics, U.S. Dept. of Labor; World Almanac questionnaire

(*) Independent union; all others affiliated with AFL-CIO.

**American Federation of Labor & Congress of Industrial Organizations (AFL-CIO)**, 815 16th St. NW, Washington, DC 20006; founded 1955; Lane Kirkland, Pres. (since 1979); 14 mln. members.

**Actors and Artistes of America, Associated (AAAA)**, 165 W. 46th St., New York, NY 10036; founded 1919; Theodore Bikel, Pres.; no individual members, 7 National Performing Arts Unions are affiliates; approx. 220,000 combined membership.

**Actors' Equity Association**, 165 W. 46th St., New York, NY 10036; founded 1913; Ron Silver, Pres.; 36,000 active members.

**Air Line Pilots Association**, 1625 Massachusetts Ave. NW, Washington, DC 20036; J. Randolph Babbitt, Pres.; 43,000 members.

**Aluminum, Brick & Glass Workers International Union (ABGWIU)**, 3362 Hollenberg Drive, Bridgeton, MO 63044; founded 1953; Ernie Labaff, Pres. (since 1985); 45,000 members, 390 locals.

**Automobile, Aerospace & Agricultural Implement Workers of America, International Union, United (UAW)**, 8000 E. Jefferson Ave., Detroit, MI 48214; founded 1935; Owen Bieber, Pres. (since 1983); 1,000,000 members, 1,194 locals.

**Bakery, Confectionery & Tobacco Workers International Union (BC&T)**, 10401 Connecticut Ave., Kensington, MD 20895; founded 1886; Frank Hurt, Pres. (since 1992); 125,000 members.

**Boilermakers, Iron Ship Builders, Blacksmiths, Forgers and Helpers, International Brotherhood of (IBBISB/BF&H)**, 570 New Brotherhood Bldg., 753 State Ave., Kansas City, KS 66101; founded 1880; Charles W. Jones, Pres. (since 1983); 80,000 members.

**Bricklayers and Allied Craftsmen, International Union of**, 815 15th St. NW, Washington, DC 20005; John T. Joyce, Pres.; 100,000 members, 430 locals.

**Carpenters and Joiners of America, United Brotherhood of**, 101 Constitution Ave. NW, Washington, DC 20001; founded 1881; Sigurd Lucassen, Gen. Pres. (since 1988); 500,000 members, 1,500 locals.

**Chemical Workers Union, International (ICWU)**, 1655 West Market St., Akron, OH 44313; founded 1944; Frank D. Martino, Pres. (since 1975); 50,000 members, 350 locals.

**Clothing and Textile Workers Union, Amalgamated (ACTWU)**, 15 Union Square, New York, NY 10003; founded 1976 (by merger of 2 unions); Jack Sheinkman, Pres. (since 1987); 234,000 members, 1,400 locals.

**Communications Workers of America**, 501 3rd St. NW, Washington, DC 20001-2797; Morton Bahr, Pres.; 700,000 members, 1,200 locals.

**Distillery, Wine & Allied Workers International Union (DWU)**, 66 Grand Ave., Englewood, NJ 07631; founded 1940; George J. Orlando, Pres. (since 1984); 15,500 members, 57 locals.

***Education Association, National**, 1201 16th St. NW, Washington, DC 20036; Keith Geiger, Pres. (since 1989); 2,000,000 members, 12,000 affiliates.

**Electrical Workers, International Brotherhood of (IBEW)**, 1125 15th St. NW, Washington, DC 20005; founded 1891; J.J. Barry, Int'l Pres. (since 1986); 750,000 members.

**Electronic, Electrical, Salaried, Machine and Furniture Workers, International Union of (IUE)**, 1126 16th St. NW, Washington, DC 20036; founded 1949; William H. Bywater, Pres. (since 1982); 150,000 members, 500 locals.

**Farm Workers of America, United (UFW)**, P.O. Box 62, Keene, CA 93531; founded 1962; Arturo Rodriguez, Pres. (since 1993); 20,000 members.

***Federal Employees, National Federation of (NFFE)**, 1016 16th St. NW, Washington, DC 20036; founded 1917; Sheila K. Velazco, Pres.; 60,000+ members, 487 locals.

**Fire Fighters, International Association of**, 1750 New York Ave. NW, Washington, DC 20006; founded 1918; Alfred K. Whitehead, Pres. (since 1988); 195,000 members, 1,943 locals.

**Firemen and Oilers, International Brotherhood of**, 1100 Circle 75 Parkway, Suite 350, Atlanta, GA 30339; Jimmy L. Walker, Pres.; 25,000 members.

**Food and Commercial Workers International Union, United (UFCW)**, 1775 K St. NW, Washington, DC 20006; founded 1979 following merger; William H. Wynn, Int'l Pres. (since 1979); 1,224,840 members, 600 locals.

**Garment Workers of America, United (UGWA)**, 4207 Lebanon Rd., Hermitage, TN 37076; founded 1891; Dave Johnson, Gen. Pres. (since 1991); 20,000 members, 120 locals.

**Glass, Molders, Pottery, Plastics & Allied Workers Intl. Union (GMP)**, 608 E. Baltimore Pike, P.O. Box 607, Media, PA 19063; founded 1842; James E. Hatfield, Int'l Pres. (since 1977); 90,000 members, 435 locals.

**Government Employees, American Federation of (AFGE)**, 80 F St. NW, Washington, DC 20001; founded 1932; John N. Sturdivant, Natl. Pres. (since 1988); 200,000 members, 1,300 locals.

**Grain Millers, American Federation of (AFGM)**, 4949 Olson Memorial Hwy., Minneapolis, MN 55422; founded 1936; Larry R. Jackson, Gen. Pres. (since 1991); 28,000 members, 210 locals.

**Graphic Communications International Union (GCIU)**, 1900 L St., NW, Washington, DC 20036; founded 1983; James J. Norton, Pres. (since 1985); 182,706 members, 520 locals.

**Hotel Employees and Restaurant Employees International Union**, 1219 28th St. NW, Washington, DC 20007; Edward T. Henley, Gen. Pres.; 330,000 members, 190 locals.

**Industrial Workers of America, International Union, Allied (AIW)**, 3520 W. Oklahoma Ave., Milwaukee, WI 53215; founded 1935; Dominick D'Ambrosio, Intl. Pres. (since 1975); 61,000 members, 330 locals.

**Iron Workers, International Association of Bridge, Structural and Ornamental**, 1750 New York Ave. NW, Washington, DC 20006; founded 1896; Jake West, Gen. Pres. (since 1989); 140,000 members, 300 locals.

**Laborers' International Union of North America (LIUNA)**, 905 16th St. NW, Washington, DC 20006; founded 1903; Arthur A. Coia, Gen. Pres. (since 1993); 700,000 members.

**Ladies Garment Workers Union, International (ILGWU)**, 1710 Broadway, New York, NY 10019; founded 1900; Jay Mazur, Pres. (since 1986); 150,000 members, 340 locals.

**Leather Goods, Plastic and Novelty Workers' Union, International**, 265 W. 14th St., New York, NY 10011; Andrew McKenzie, Gen. Pres.; 20,000 members, 85 locals.

**Letter Carriers, National Association of (NALC)**, 100 Indiana Ave. NW, Washington, DC 20001; founded 1889; Vincent R. Sombrotto, Pres. (since 1978); 311,202 members, 3,466 locals.

***Locomotive Engineers, Brotherhood of (BLE)**, The Standard Bldg., 1370 Ontario Ave., Cleveland, OH 44113-1702; founded 1863; Ronald P. McLaughlin, Pres. (since 1991); 55,000 members, 650 divisions.

**Longshoremen's Association, International**, 17 Battery Pl., New York, NY 10004; John Bowers, Pres.; 76,579 members, 331 locals.

***Longshoremen's & Warehousemen's Union, International (ILWU)**, 1188 Franklin St., San Francisco, CA 94109; founded 1937; David Arian, Pres. (since 1991); 55,000 members, 58 locals.

**Machinists and Aerospace Workers, International Association of (IAM)**, 9000 Machinist Pl., Upper Marlboro, MD 20772-2687; founded 1888; George J. Kourpias, Int'l Pres.; 826,875 members, 1,700 locals.

**Maintenance of Way Employees, Brotherhood of (BMWE)**, 12050 Woodward Ave., Detroit, MI 48203; founded 1887; Mac. A. Fleming, Pres.; 75,000 members, 827 locals.

**Marine & Shipbuilding Workers of America, Industrial Union of (IUMSWA)**, 5101 River Rd., #110, Bethesda, MD 20816; founded 1934 (merged with Machinists and Aerospace Workers, Dec. 1, 1990).

**Marine Engineer Beneficial Assn./National Maritime Union (MEBA/NMU)**, 444 N. Capitol St. NW, Suite 800, Washington, DC 20001; C.E. DeFries, Pres.; 50,000 members.

***Mine Workers of America, United (UMWA)**, 900 15th St. NW, Washington, DC 20005; founded 1890; Richard Trumka, Int'l Pres. (since 1982); 186,000 members, 800 locals.

**Musicians of the United States and Canada, American Federation of (AF of M)**, 1501 Broadway, Suite 600, New York, NY 10036; founded 1896; Mark Tully Massagli, Pres.; 160,000 members.

**Newspaper Guild, The (TNG)**, 8611 Second Ave., Silver Spring, MD 20910; founded 1933; Charles Dale, Pres. (since 1987); 33,000 members, 80 locals.

**Novelty & Production Workers, Intl. Union of Allied**, 1815 Franklin Ave., Valley Stream, NY 11581; Julius Isaacson, Pres.; 30,000 members, 18 locals.

**\*Nurses Association, American,** 600 Maryland Ave. SW, Washington, DC 20024-2571; Virginia Trotter Betts, J.D., R.N., Pres.; 53 constituent state assns.

**Office and Professional Employees International Union (OPEIU),** 265 W. 14th St., New York, NY 10011; founded 1945 (AFL Charter); John Kelly, Int'l Pres. (since 1979); 135,000 members, 300 locals.

**Oil, Chemical and Atomic Workers International Union (OCAW),** PO Box 2812, Denver, CO 80201; Robert E. Wages, Pres.; 100,000 members, 400 locals.

**Operating Engineers, International Union of (IUOE),** 1125 17th St. NW, Washington, DC 20036; founded 1896; Frank Hanley, Gen. Pres.; 375,000 members, 200 locals.

**Painters and Allied Trades, International Brotherhood of (IBPAT),** 1750 New York Ave. NW, Washington, DC 20006; founded 1887; A. L. "Mike" Monroe, Gen. Pres.; 149,177 members, 626 locals.

**Paperworkers International Union, United (UPIU),** 3340 Perimeter Hill Dr., Nashville, TN 37211; founded 1884; Wayne E. Glenn, Pres. (since 1978); 229,000 members, 1,100 locals.

**\*Plant Guard Workers of America, International Union, United (UPGWA),** 25510 Kelly Rd., Roseville, MI 48066; founded 1948; Gene McConville, Pres.; 28,000 members, 176 locals.

**Plasterers' and Cement Mason's International Association of the United States & Canada; Operative,** 1125 17th St. NW, Washington, DC 20036; Dominic A. Martell, Gen. Pres.; 65,000 members, 365 locals.

**Plumbing and Pipe Fitting Industry of the United States and Canada, United Association of Journeymen and Apprentices of the,** 901 Massachusetts Ave. NW, Washington, DC 20001; founded 1889; Marvin J. Boede, Pres. (since 1982); 303,000 members.

**\*Police, Fraternal Order of,** 2100 Gardiner Lane, Louisville, KY 40205; Dewey R. Stokes, Natl. Pres. and Charles R. Orms, Natl. Secy.; 225,000 members, 1,860 affiliates.

**\*Postal Supervisors, National Association of,** 490 L'Enfant Plaza SW, Suite 3200, Washington, DC 20024-2120; Rubin Handelman, Pres.; 44,000 members, 443 locals.

**Postal Workers Union, American (APWU),** 1300 L St. NW, Washington, DC 20005; founded 1971; Moe Biller, Pres. (since 1980); 330,000 members, 2,000 locals.

**Railway Carmen Division of Transportation Communications Int'l. Union (BRC Division/TCU),** 3 Research Pl., Rockville, MD 20850; founded 1888; R. P. Wojtowicz, Gen. Pres. (since 1992); 50,000 members, 310 locals.

**Retail, Wholesale and Department Store Union,** 30 E. 29th St., New York, NY 10016; Lenore Miller, Pres.; 200,000 members, 250 locals.

**Roofers, Waterproofers & Allied Workers, United Union of,** 1125 17th St. NW, Washington, DC 20036; Earl J. Kruse, Pres.; 27,000 members, 138 locals.

**Rubber, Cork, Linoleum and Plastic Workers of America, United (URW),** 570 White Pond Dr., Akron, OH 44320-1156; founded 1935; Kenneth L. Coss, Int'l Pres.; 100,000 members, 400 locals.

**\*Rural Letter Carriers' Association, National,** 4th floor, 1630 Duke St., Alexandria, VA 22314; founded 1903; Vernon H. Meier, Pres. (since 1989); 80,000 members; 47 state organizations.

**Seafarers International Union of North America (SIUNA),** 5201 Auth Way, Camp Springs, MD 20746; founded 1938; Michael Sacco, Pres.; 85,000 members.

**Service Employees International Union (SEIU),** 1313 L St. NW, Washington, DC 20005; founded 1921; John J. Sweeney, Pres. (since 1980); 950,000 members, 300 locals.

**Sheet Metal Workers' International Association (SMWIA),** 1750 New York Ave. NW, Washington, DC 20006; founded 1888; Edward J. Carlough, Gen. Pres. (since 1970); 150,000 members, 245 locals.

**State, County and Municipal Employees, American Federation of,** 1625 L St. NW, Washington, DC 20036; Gerald McEntee, Pres.; 1.2 mln. members, 2,991 locals.

**Steelworkers of America, United (USWA),** 5 Gateway Center, Pittsburgh, PA 15222; founded 1936; Lynn Williams, Int'l Pres. (since 1984); 750,000 members, 3,500 locals.

**Teachers, American Federation of (AFT),** 555 New Jersey Ave. NW, Washington, DC 20001; founded 1916; Albert Shanker, Pres. (since 1974); 850,000 members.

**Teamsters, Chauffeurs, Warehousemen and Helpers of America, International Brotherhood of (IBT),** 25 Louisiana Ave. NW, Washington, DC 20001; founded 1903; Ronald R. Carey, Pres. (since 1992); 1.5 mln. members, 700 locals.

**Television and Radio Artists, American Federation of,** 260 Madison Ave., New York, NY 10016; founded 1937; Reed Farrell, Pres.; 67,000 members, 38 locals.

**Textile Workers of America, United (UTWA),** 2 Echelon Plaza, Laurel Rd., P.O. Box 749, Voorhees, NJ 08043-0749; founded 1901; Ron Mysiowka, Intl. Pres. (since 1992); 20,000 members, 180 locals.

**Theatrical Stage Employees, International Alliance of,** 1515 Broadway, New York, NY 10036; founded 1893; Alfred W. Di Tolla, Pres. (since 1986); 70,000 members, 750 locals.

**Transit Union, Amalgamated (ATU),** 5025 Wisconsin Ave. NW, Washington, DC 20016; founded 1892; James La Sala, Intl. Pres. (since 1986); 160,000 members, 275 locals.

**Transport Workers Union of America,** 80 West End Ave., New York, NY 10023; founded 1934; George Leitz, Int'l Pres. (since 1985); 100,000 members, 94 locals.

**Transportation Communications International Union (TCU),** 3 Research Place, Rockville, MD 20850; founded 1899; Robert A. Scardelletti, Int'l Pres. (since 1991); 127,725 members, 750 locals.

**\*Transportation Union, United (UTU),** 14600 Detroit Ave., Cleveland, OH 44107; founded 1969; G. Thomas DuBose, Pres. (since 1979); 100,000 members, 769 locals.

**\*Treasury Employees Union, National (NTEU),** 901 E. St. NW Suite 600, Washington, DC 20004; founded 1938; Robert M. Tobias, Natl. Pres. (since 1983); 140,000 represented, 250 chapters.

**\*University Professors, American Association of (AAUP),** 1012-14th St., Washington, DC 20005; founded 1915; Carol Simpson Stern, Pres.; 40,000 members, 600 chapters.

**Upholstery Division - United Steelworkers of America,** 25 N. 4th St., Philadelphia, PA 19106; founded 1882; Ernest F. Shock, dir.; approx. 18,000 members, 91 locals.

**Utility Workers Union of America (UWUA),** 815 16th St. NW, Washington, DC 20006; founded 1938; Marshall M. Hicks, Natl. Pres. (since 1991); 55,000 members, 220 locals.

**International Woodworkers of America —U.S. (IWA—U.S.),** 25 Cornell Ave., Gladstone, OR 97027; founded 1937; Wilson J. Hubbell, Natl. Pres.; 20,000 members.

# U.S. Union Membership, 1930-1992

Source: Bureau of Labor Statistics, U.S. Dept. of Labor

| Year | Labor[1] force (thousands) | Union[2] members (thousands) | Percent | Year | Labor[1] force (thousands) | Union[2] members (thousands) | Percent |
|---|---|---|---|---|---|---|---|
| 1930 | 29,424 | 3,401 | 11.6 | 1983 | 88,290 | 17,717 | 20.1 |
| 1935 | 27,053 | 3,584 | 13.2 | 1984 | 92,194 | 17,340 | 18.8 |
| 1940 | 32,376 | 8,717 | 26.9 | 1985 | 94,521 | 16,996 | 18.0 |
| 1945 | 40,394 | 14,322 | 35.5 | 1986 | 96,903 | 16,975 | 17.5 |
| 1950 | 45,222 | 14,267 | 31.5 | 1987 | 99,303 | 16,913 | 17.0 |
| 1955 | 50,675 | 16,802 | 33.2 | 1988 | 101,407 | 17,002 | 16.8 |
| 1960 | 54,234 | 17,049 | 31.4 | 1989 | 103,480 | 16,960 | 16.4 |
| 1965 | 60,815 | 17,299 | 28.4 | 1990 | 103,905 | 16,740 | 16.1 |
| 1970 | 70,920 | 19,381 | 27.3 | 1991 | 102,786 | 16,568 | 16.1 |
| 1975 | 76,945 | 19,611 | 25.5 | 1992 | 103,688 | 16,390 | 15.8 |
| 1980 | 90,564 | 19,843 | 21.9 | | | | |

(1) Does not include agricultural employment; from 1983 data do not include self-employed or unemployed persons. (2) From 1930 to 1980 data are the number of dues-paying members of traditional trade unions with members counted regardless of employment status; from 1983 members include employee associations that engage in collective bargaining with employers.

# TAXES

## Federal Income Tax

Source: George W. Smith III, CPA, Nationally Syndicated Tax Author and Columnist

On August 10, President Bill Clinton signed the Omnibus Budget Reconciliation Act of 1993, legislation intended—through a combination of $241 billion in tax increases and $255 billion in spending cuts—to reduce the federal government's budget deficits by a total of $496 billion over five years. Many of the tax provisions of the act were retroactive to January 1, 1993, and therefore will affect some Americans when they file their 1993 income tax returns. Other portions of the legislation will take effect in 1994 or later.

## Tax Highlights of the Omnibus Budget Reconciliation Act of 1993

**Individual Income Taxes.** The act increases the top tax rate to 36% for joint filers with taxable income over $140,000, heads of households with taxable income over $127,500, and singles with taxable income of more than $115,000. Congress also added a 10% surtax on taxable income of more than $250,000 ($125,000 for married individuals filing separately). This provision creates a marginal top tax rate of 39.6% and is retroactive to January 1, 1993.

**Social Security Benefits.** Effective January 1, 1994, retirees whose incomes, including half their Social Security benefits, exceed $34,000 for singles or $44,000 for married couples filing jointly will pay income tax on up to 85% of their benefits. The current law, taxing up to 50% of Social Security benefits, will continue to apply for retirees whose incomes, including half their Social Security benefits, exceed $25,000 for singles or $32,000 for married taxpayers filing jointly.

**Estate and Gift Taxes.** The act reinstates the 1992 top tax rate of 53% on estates between $2.5 million and $3 million, and 55% on estates of more than $3 million. On taxable estates between $10 million and $21.04 million, an additional tax of 5% of the transfer above $10 million will continue to be imposed as well. The effective date is retroactive to January 1, 1993.

**Corporate Tax Rates.** The act increases the top tax rate for corporations with taxable income over $10 million per year from 34% to 35%. The tax rate for qualified personal service corporations also increases from 34% to 35%. The effective date is January 1, 1993.

**Moving Expense Deductions.** For expenses incurred after 1993, moving expense deductions associated with a new job will be limited. Deductions for meals while traveling, living expenses in temporary quarters, pre-move house-hunting trips, and the costs of selling an old residence or buying or renting a new residence will no longer be deductible. In addition, the job distance test to qualify for a deduction has been increased to 50 miles from 35 miles. A taxpayer will no longer need to itemize deductions to take a qualified moving expense deduction.

**Business Meals and Entertainment.** The act reduces the proportion of qualified business meals and entertainment costs that can be deducted as business expenses to 50% starting in 1994. For 1993, the deduction remains at 80%. Also beginning in 1994, Congress eliminated the deduction as a business expense of dues in business, social, athletic, luncheon, sporting, and country clubs, including airport and hotel clubs.

**Lobbying Expenses.** The act eliminates the business deduction for lobbying Congress and federal, state, and local government agencies, beginning in 1994.

**Energy Tax.** The act imposes a 4.3-cents-per-gallon tax on transportation fuels, including gasoline and diesel fuel. Commercial airline fuel is exempt for 2 years. The effective date is October 1, 1993.

**Medicare Tax.** Effective in 1994, Congress repealed the $135,000 limit on earned income subject to the payroll tax for Medicare. Therefore, *all* wages will be subject to the Medicare tax of 1.45% for both employers and employees. Self-employed individuals will pay a 2.9% Medicare tax on their net self-employed income.

**Earned Income Tax Credit.** The tax credit rate increases for low-income working taxpayers starting in 1994. Also new is a credit of up to $300 that is extended to childless low-income workers over age 25 and below age 65. The Young Child Care Credit and Supplemental Health Insurance Credit are repealed as of 1994.

**Rental Passive Losses.** The act allows certain real estate professionals to use losses from rental real estate to offset other nonpassive income, such as wages and self-employment profits. The effective date is January 1, 1994.

**Charitable Contributions.** Effective January 1, 1994, taxpayers deducting charitable contributions of $250 or more will have to obtain written substantiation from the charity before filing a tax return.

**Equipment Write-off.** Congress elected to allow small businesses to deduct as an expense up to $17,500 of the cost of new equipment. Previously, the maximum was $10,000. The change is effective for property placed in service for tax years beginning in 1993.

**Retirement Plans.** The new law reduces from $235,840 to $150,000 the level of compensation for which tax-deferred contributions can be made to retirement plans. The effective date is January 1, 1994.

**Nonresidential Real Estate.** For property placed in service on or after May 13, 1993, the depreciation recovery period has been increased to 39 years. Under prior law it was 31.5 years.

**Alternative Minimum Tax (AMT).** Retroactive to January 1, 1993, the 24% AMT rate has been replaced with a two-tier tax rate of 26% and 28%.

**Estates and Trusts.** Retroactive to January 1, 1993, the tax rates for the taxable income of estates and trusts increased as follows:

| Taxable Income Amount | Tax Rate |
|---|---|
| 0 to $1,500 | 15% |
| $1,501 to $3,500 | 28% |
| $3,501 to $5,500 | 31% |
| $5,501 to $7,500 | 36% |

In addition, there is a 10% surtax on taxable income over $7,500. This provision creates a marginal top rate of 39.6%.

## Other Tax Law Changes and Recent Tax Developments

- The highest income tax rate for individuals, estates, and trusts was changed for 1993. There are currently four tax rates: 15%, 28%, 31%, and 36%. In addition, for individuals there is a 10% surtax on taxable incomes over $250,000 ($125,000 for married individuals filing separately). For estates and trusts, the surtax starts at $7,500. This provision creates a marginal top tax rate of 39.6% for individuals, estates, and trusts.
- The maximum income tax rate on capital gains for individuals, estates, and trusts remains at 28%.
- Effective January 1, 1993, the limitation on elective deferrals to 401(k) plans is increased to $8,994 from $8,728.
- An individual may not claim an exemption for a dependent child in 1993 who qualifies as a full time student and is over age 23 at the end of the year unless the child's gross income is less than $2,350.
- Interest earned on Series EE bonds issued in 1990 or later may be exempt from federal income tax if used to pay tuition and fees for a taxpayer, spouse, or dependents to attend a college, university, or qualified technical school during the year the bonds are redeemed. This exclusion is subject to an income phase-out in 1993 starting when adjusted gross income exceeds $45,500 for a single taxpayer; $68,250 for taxpayers filing jointly. The full phase-out occurs at $60,500 for a single taxpayer and $98,250 for taxpayers filing jointly.
- Parents may elect to include on their income tax return the unearned income of a dependent child under age 14

whose unearned income is more than $500 but less than $5,000. The income must consist solely of interest and dividends. Form 8814, Parent's Election to Report Child's Interest and Dividends, is required to report this income. This election is not available if estimated tax payments were made in the child's name.

- For individuals age 55 or over, the 3 out of 5 year home use rule for the sale of a principal residence has been expanded. Certain incapacitated individuals who reside in state-licensed facilities may exclude from gross income up to $125,000 of gain resulting from the sale of their home if the house was used as their principal residence for at least one year out of the last five years. This is a once-in-a-life-time exclusion.

- Interest on Veterans Affairs (VA) dividends left on deposit with the Department of Veterans Affairs is not taxable.

- Face-lifts, tummy tucks, liposuction, and many other elective cosmetic surgeries are no longer a deductible medical expense.

- Starting in 1993, the Unemployment Compensation Amendment Act of 1992 made three important changes to the treatment of distributions from qualified pension plans and annuities.
  (1) It made all pension plan distributions eligible for rollovers except certain periodic payments, minimum distributions, and amounts not excluded from gross income.
  (2) It required plans to permit direct rollovers.
  (3) It imposed a mandatory 20 percent income tax withholding on distributions that are not directly rolled over.

- For a taxpayer to be eligible for the child and dependent care credit, the dependent must be under age 13. The taxpayer must also report the name, address, and identification number of the child care provider on his or her income tax return or the taxpayer will not be entitled to the credit.

- A taxpayer must list the Social Security number of any dependent claimed on his or her income tax return who is at least 1 year old by the end of the tax year. The penalty for noncompliance can be $50 per omitted number.

- A business deduction is not allowed for the base rate charged on the first telephone line into a personal residence. This disallowance does not affect the deductibility of long distance calls or optional services such as call waiting, call forwarding, three-way calling, or extra directory listings as long as they are business related.

- For 1993, the Social Security tax base (the maximum amount of earnings on which the Social Security tax can apply) increased to $57,600. The Medicare tax base increased to $135,000. For Social Security, the tax rate is 6.2% for employees and the same for employers. For Medicare, the rate is 1.45% for both employees and employers. Thus, the maximum an employee and an employer each will pay is 6.2% of $57,605 plus 1.45% of

$135,000, or $5,528.70 each. Starting in 1994, the $135,000 maximum tax base for Medicare has been eliminated. Consequently, all wages will be subject to the Medicare tax.

- IRA investments are allowed for certain gold and silver coins issued by the U.S. government. Investments also may include certain coins issued by a state government.

- Jury duty pay returned by an employee to an employer in exchange for his or her normal salary is deductible as an adjustment to income.

- The business use of a cellular phone must be for the convenience of the employer and a condition of employment to be an allowable business deduction for employees. All phone calls must be substantiated and business related.

- Self-employed persons are entitled to an income tax adjustment of one-half of their Social Security self-employment tax liabiliity. The self-employment tax rate for 1993 is 15.3%. The maximum Social Security tax a self-employed individual will pay in 1993 is $11,057.40.

- To be deductible, points paid for the purchase of a taxpayer's principal residence must meet the following requirements:
  (1) The purchase must be for the taxpayer's *principal* residence.
  (2) The amount paid must be clearly designated as "points," "loan origination fees," "loan discount," or "discount points."
  (3) Points must be computed as a percentage of the taxpayer's stated principal loan amount.
  (4) The payment of points must be an established business practice in the area.
  (5) The points must be paid from the taxpayer's own funds. The points may not be borrowed.
  (6) FHA and VA loan origination fees paid by a home buyer may be treated as "points".

- A sole proprietor claiming a home office deduction on Schedule C, Profit or Loss From Business, must file Form 8829, Expenses for Business Use of Your Home, with his or her income tax return.

- For 1993, the standard mileage rate for business use of an automobile remains at 28 cents per mile. This rate applies to all business miles driven. U.S. Postal Service employees who collect or deliver mail on a rural route can use a special standard mileage rate of 42 cents per mile.

- Travel expenses reimbursed to employees that include an additional Saturday night's lodging and meals in order to take advantage of lower air fares for roundtrip tickets are deductible by the company and excludable from employees' gross income. The reimbursements are not subject to employment taxes and withholding.

- The maximum earned income that retirees under the age of 65 can receive in 1993 without losing all or part of their Social Security benefits is $7,680. For individuals age 65 through age 69, the maximum amount is $10,560. Individuals receiving Social Security benefits who are age 70 or over can receive full benefits regardless of earnings.

## 1993 Individual Tax Rates

There are four tax rates for 1993: 15%, 28%, 31%, and 36%. The dollar bracket amounts are adjusted each year for inflation.

### Single

| Tax Rates | Taxable Income |
| --- | --- |
| 15% | $0 to $22,100 |
| 28% | $22,101 to $53,500 |
| 31% | $53,501 to $115,000 |
| 36% | $115,001 to $250,000 |

### Married Filing Jointly or Qualifying Widow(er)

| Tax Rates | Taxable Income |
| --- | --- |
| 15% | $0 to $36,900 |
| 28% | $36,901 to $89,150 |
| 31% | $89,151 to $140,000 |
| 36% | $140,001 to $250,000 |

### Married Filing Separately

| Tax Rate | Taxable Income |
| --- | --- |
| 15% | $0 to $18,450 |
| 28% | $18,451 to $44,575 |
| 31% | $44,576 to $70,000 |
| 36% | $70,001 to $125,000 |

### Head of Household

| Tax Rate | Taxable Income |
| --- | --- |
| 15% | $0 to $29,600 |
| 28% | $29,601 to $76,400 |
| 31% | $76,401 to $127,500 |
| 36% | $127,501 to $250,000 |

Please note, however, there is also a 10% surtax on taxable incomes over $250,000 ($125,000 for married individuals filing separately). This provision creates a marginal top tax rate of 39.6%.

The maximum tax rate on net capital gains for an individual, estate, or trust is 28%.

The alternative minimum tax rate for noncorporate taxpayers is 26% for alternative minimum taxable income less the exemption amount up to $175,000 ($87,500 for married individuals filing separately). Above that dollar level, a 28% rate applies.

## Standard Deduction

The standard deduction is a flat dollar amount that is subtracted from the adjusted gross income of taxpayers who do not itemize their deductions. The amount of the basic standard deduction depends upon the taxpayer's filing status and is adjusted annually for inflation. The standard deductions for 1993 are as follows:

### 1993 Basic Standard Deduction

| | |
|---|---|
| Single | $3,700 |
| Married filing jointly or qualifying widow(er) | $6,200 |
| Married filing separately | $3,100 |
| Head of household | $5,450 |

Taxpayers with itemized deductions such as medical expenses, property taxes, investment and home mortgage interest, charitable contributions, moving expenses, and gambling losses totaling more than the standard deduction amount should not use the standard deduction. Instead, they should itemize their deductions.

An individual claimed as a dependent on another person's income tax return may claim on his or her own tax return only the larger of $600 or the amount of earned income up to the amount of the basic standard deduction that the taxpayer would normally be allowed. Earned income includes wages, salaries, commissions, and tips. It also includes net profit from self-employment received as compensation for personal services rendered. Any part of a scholarship or fellowship grant that must be included in gross income is also earned income.

**Example 1:** During 1993, a dependent parent, age 60, had unearned income (interest and dividends) of $1,700. She had no earned income. Her basic standard deduction would be $600. She would have taxable income of $1,100. A dependent cannot claim his or her own personal exemption.

**Example 2:** A dependent son had $10,000 of unearned income and $100 of earned income. He is entitled to a $600 standard deduction. He is limited to this amount because he is a dependent and his earned income is less than $600. The taxpayer would, therefore, have $9,500 in taxable income.

**Example 3:** A dependent daughter with $4,000 of earned income and $600 of unearned income would claim a maximum $3,700 standard deduction because her earned income of $4,000 is greater than the standard deduction. She would have taxable income of $900.

## Additional Standard Deduction for Age and Blindness

Elderly or blind taxpayers may claim an additional standard deduction in addition to the basic standard deduction. Taxpayers who are age 65 or over or blind at the end of 1993 qualify. Individuals who claim the additional standard deduction because of blindness must attach a doctor's statement to their income tax return.

### 1993 Additional Standard Deduction

| | |
|---|---|
| Single or head of household, age 65 or over OR blind | $ 900 |
| Single or head of household, age 65 or over AND blind | $1,800 |
| Married filing jointly or qualifying widow(er), age 65 or over OR blind (per person) | $ 700 |
| Married filing jointly or qualifying widow(er), age 65 or over AND blind (per person) | $1,400 |
| Married filing separately, age 65 or over OR blind | $ 700 |
| Married filing separately, age 65 or over AND blind | $1,400 |

**Example 1:** A single, sixty-five-year-old individual would have a standard deduction of $4,600 computed as follows:

| | |
|---|---|
| Basic standard deduction for a single person | $3,700 |
| Additional standard deduction for age | 900 |
| Total | $4,600 |

**Example 2:** A seventy-year-old husband and a fifty-eight-year old blind wife filing jointly would be entitled to a standard deduction totaling $7,600 computed as follows:

| | |
|---|---|
| Basic standard deduction for married filing jointly | $6,200 |
| Additional standard deduction for (husband's) age | 700 |
| Additional standard deduction for (wife's) blindness | 700 |
| Total | $7,600 |

The additional and basic standard deductions are adjusted each year for inflation. However, the additional standard deduction for 1993 remains the same as 1992. Taxpayers who itemize their deductions cannot claim the additional or basic standard deductions.

## Dependent and Personal Exemptions

The exemption amount for 1993 has been increased to $2,350. This amount is adjusted each year for inflation.

The deduction for exemptions is phased out for certain higher income taxpayers. The exemption amount is reduced by 2% for each $2,500 ($1,250 for married filing separately) or a fraction thereof by which the adjusted gross income exceeds the threshold amount.

The 1993 threshold amount for the phase-out of the personal exemption begins as follows:

| | |
|---|---|
| Married filing jointly | $162,700 |
| Qualifying widow(er) | $162,700 |
| Head of household | $135,600 |
| Single | $108,450 |
| Married filing separately | $ 81,350 |

The exemption amount is fully phased out when adjusted gross income is more than $122,500 ($61,250 for married filing separately) over the threshold amount.

## Adjustments to Income

### Individual Retirement Accounts (IRAs)

Taxpayers who are not covered by a qualified employer retirement plan may take an IRA deduction up to the lesser of $2,000, or the amount of their earned income, regardless of their total income. Income earned from IRAs will remain tax-free until the taxpayer withdraws it.

Taxpayers may still make contributions to their IRAs even if they are covered by a qualified retirement plan of their employer. However, there are limits as to the amount that can be deducted on their income tax return if they are covered by a qualified retirement plan. If either husband or wife participates in a qualified retirement plan, *both* spouses are subject to these limitations.

For 1993, married taxpayers filing jointly with adjusted gross income of $40,000 or less may take an IRA deduction whether or not either one is an active participant in a qualified retirement plan. Single taxpayers in a qualified retirement plan may also deduct IRA contributions if their adjusted gross income is $25,000 or less.

The IRA deduction is phased out over the next $10,000 of adjusted gross income if taxpayers are active participants in a qualified retirement plan. Consequently, married couples filing jointly with adjusted gross income of $50,000 or more, or single filers with adjusted gross income of $35,000 or more, may not deduct any contributions to their IRAs.

A qualified retirement plan generally includes: (1) a qualified pension, profit-sharing, or stock bonus plan; (2) a qualified annuity plan; (3) a simplified employee pension plan; or (4) a plan established for its employees by federal, state, or local government or by an agency of these entities.

## Itemized Deductions

- Many elective cosmetic surgeries, including hair transplants and other similar procedures, are no longer a deductible medical expense. Only cosmetic surgery for congenital abnormality, personal injury resulting from an accident or trauma, or a disfiguring disease is allowed as a medical deduction. In general, medical expenses are deductible, but only the amount that exceeds 7.5 percent of the taxpayer's adjusted gross income.

- Consumer interest, such as finance charges on personal credit cards and installment interest paid on personal automobile loans, is no longer deductible.
- Investment interest is deductible only to the extent of net investment income. Any excess is carried over to future years.
- Most mortgage interest on a taxpayer's first and second home remains fully deductible; however, there are limitations.
- Interest on home equity loans is deductible, but only up to the first $100,000 in equity debt.
- State and local income taxes, real estate taxes, and personal property taxes remain fully deductible. Sales taxes are not deductible.
- Casualty and theft losses are deductible subject to the $100 limitation rule and the 10% of adjusted gross income provision.
- Miscellaneous deductions, such as union and professional dues, tax preparation fees, safe deposit box rental expense, and employee business expenses, are deductible, but only the amount that exceeds 2 percent of the taxpayer's adjusted gross income.
- An individual can deduct gambling losses such as the cost of lottery tickets, but only up to the amount of the winnings reported on page 1, Form 1040.

## Moving Expenses

Taxpayers who change jobs during the year can usually deduct part of their moving expenses. These expenses include the cost of moving household goods, travel to the new home, house-hunting trips, temporary living quarters, and other related expenses. To qualify, the move must be job-related and it must meet several other requirements, including distance and time tests. The expenses for moving household goods and traveling to a new home have some limitations. All other deductible moving expenses, such as house-hunt-

ing trips or temporary living quarters, are subject to a $3,000 ceiling. Meal expenses are only 80% deductible. Moving expenses are deductible only if the taxpayer itemizes deductions on Schedule A of Form 1040. Moves within the U.S. are reported on Form 3903, Moving Expenses.

Effective January 1, 1994, the new 1993 tax law makes 4 modifications:
(1) The distance test is extended from 35 to 50 miles.
(2) Pre-move house-hunting trips, temporary living expenses, and the closing costs of selling the old home and buying a new one are nondeductible. Meals while traveling to the new location are not deductible.
(3) Moving expenses paid or reimbursed by the taxpayer's employer are excludable from gross income.
(4) Moving expenses are deductible as an adjustment to income and not as an itemized deduction on Schedule A.

### Employee Business Expenses

All employee business expenses including travel, automobile, telephone, gifts, and entertainment are deductible only as itemized miscellaneous deductions. Only 80% (50% for 1994) of the cost of customer meals and entertainment is deductible. These expenses are then subject to the 2% of the taxpayer's adjusted gross income limitation for miscellaneous deductions. Beginning in 1994, country club dues will no longer be deductible.

### Itemized Deduction Reduction

Many itemized deductions otherwise allowed are reduced by the lesser of 3% of a taxpayer's adjusted gross income in excess of $108,450 ($54,225 for married taxpayers filing separately) or 80% of the amount of these itemized deductions otherwise allowable for the year. These amounts are adjusted each year for inflation. This provision does not affect medical expenses, investment interest expense, casualty losses, or gambling losses to the extent of gambling gains.

## Earned Income Credit, Young Child Credit, and Health Insurance Credit

Low income workers who have dependent children and maintain a household are eligible for a refundable earned income credit. The credit for 1993 is calculated on earned income such as wages and tips. For a taxpayer with one qualifying child, the maximum credit is $1,434. For a taxpayer with two or more qualifying children, it is $1,511. The credit begins to be phased out when the taxpayer's adjusted gross income is more than $12,200.

In addition to the basic earned income credit, a supplemental young child care credit is also available to low income workers with a qualifying child who has not attained the age of one by the close of the calendar year. The maximum credit is $388. If this supplemental credit is claimed, the dependent care credit may not be claimed. This credit is repealed effective in 1994.

A supplemental credit for health insurance premium costs that cover one or more qualifying children is also available. The maximum credit for 1993 is $465. If medical expenses

are itemized on Schedule A, these amounts must be reduced dollar for dollar by the amount of the allowable supplemental health insurance credit. This credit is also repealed for 1994.

If an individual qualifies, these credits are refundable even if the taxpayer is not required to file an income tax return. However, a tax return must be filed in order to receive these credits. Taxpayers must fill out Schedule EIC and attach it to their tax return to receive these credits. To assist individuals, the IRS publishes a table showing the earned income credit at various levels of income. This chart is available free at any IRS office. The IRS will also assist individuals with the preparation of this form.

Effective for years beginning after 1993, the earned income tax credit (EITC) has been increased and extended to include low-income childless workers over age 25 and below age 65.

## Taxing Children's Income

A child who may be claimed as a dependent by another taxpayer may not claim his or her own personal exemption on a tax return. Children under age 14 with at least one living parent may use up to $600 of their standard deduction against unearned income. Unearned income includes dividend and interest income. If the child's unearned income is more than $1,200, that income will be taxed at the child's tax rate or the parent's rate, whichever is higher.

Parents have the option of including a child's unearned income on their tax return. However, when this income is included on the parents' tax return, all the income over $1,000 is subject to the higher tax rate. Therefore, if the child includes the unearned income on his or her tax return, the child could receive the benefit of a lower tax rate on an additional $200 of unearned income.

## When to File

U.S. individual income tax returns for 1993 are required to be filed with the Internal Revenue Service no later than Friday, April 15, 1994.

What if you can't file on time? File Form 4868, Application for Automatic Extension of Time to File U.S. Individual Income Tax Return. This gives the taxpayer an auto-

matic four-month extension of time to file, until Monday, August 15, 1994. However, this is not an extension of time to pay the tax. Any federal income tax owed must be paid to the Internal Revenue Service by midnight April 15, 1994; otherwise, penalties and interest may be assessed for any income tax balance not paid. Form 4868 provides space for you to estimate your tax obligation, if any.

## Who Must File

Whether a U.S. citizen or resident alien living in the U.S. must file an income tax return depends on the person's gross income, filing status, and age.

Generally, a U.S. citizen or resident alien will have to file an income tax return if the person's gross income for the year is at least as much as the amount shown in the following table.

| Filing Status | 1993 Gross Income |
|---|---|
| Single | |
| • Under 65 | $ 6,050 |
| • 65 or older | 6,950 |
| Married filing jointly | |
| • Both spouses under 65 | 10,900 |
| • One spouse 65 or older | 11,600 |
| • Both spouses 65 or older | 12,300 |
| Married filing separately | 2,350 |
| Head of household | |
| • Under 65 | 7,800 |
| • 65 or older | 8,700 |
| Qualifying widow(er) | |
| • Under 65 | 8,500 |
| • 65 or older | 9,250 |

**Example 1:** John and Mary Smith intend to file a joint return for 1993. John's income is entirely from wages. Mary receives no income subject to tax. Neither John nor Mary is blind. John is 67 years old, but Mary will not be 65 until next year. For 1993, their combined gross income subject to tax will be $11,900. They will have to file a tax return because their gross income will be at least $11,600.

If Mary were age 65, they would not have to file a 1993 tax return because their gross income would be less than $12,300 as shown in the table.

**Some Exceptions to Filing Requirements.** A tax return must be filed if:

• Net earnings from self-employment for the year are $400 or more.
• Advance earned income credit payments were received during the year from an employer.
• Taxpayers file for the earned income credit, young child credit, or health insurance credit.
• A taxpayer wishes to receive an income tax refund.
• Gross income is less than the filing requirement amount, but additional taxes are owed for:
  – Social security tax on unreported tips.
  – Alternative minimum tax.
  – Recapture of investment credit.
  – Tax attributable to qualified retirement distributions (including IRAs), annuities, and modified endowment contracts.

## Which Form to File

Use either Form 1040EZ or Form 1040A unless the filing of Form 1040 allows you to pay a lower tax, or the rules say you must file Form 1040. The 1040EZ and 1040A are generally easier to complete than the longer Form 1040.

**You may be able to use the short Form 1040EZ if:**

• You are single and do not claim any dependents. In 1993 married couples filing jointly with no dependents may also use Form 1040EZ.
• You are not 65 or older or blind.
• You have income only from wages, salaries, tips, taxable scholarships or fellowships, and not more than $400 of interest income.
• Your taxable income is less than $50,000.
• You do not itemize deductions, claim any adjustments to income, or have tax credits.
• You did not receive any advanced earned income credit payments.
• You did not make estimated tax payments.
• You file on or before April 15th. You cannot use Form 1040EZ if you apply for an extension.

**You may be able to use Form 1040A if:**

• You have income from wages, salaries, tips, taxable scholarships or fellowships, interest, and dividends.
• You have income from Individual Retirement Account (IRA) distributions, pensions, annuities, unemployment compensation, and Social Security or railroad retirement benefits.
• Your taxable income is less than $50,000.
• You do not itemize deductions.
• You claim a deduction for qualified contributions to an IRA.
• You claim a credit for child and dependent care expenses, credit for the elderly or the disabled, earned income credit, supplemental young child credit, or the health insurance credit.
• You have made estimated tax payments.
• You filed for an extension of time to file.

**Even if you do meet the above tests, you will have to file the longer Form 1040 if any of the following situations apply:**

• Your taxable income is $50,000 or more.
• You itemize deductions.
• You receive any nontaxable dividends or capital gain distributions.
• You have foreign bank accounts and/or foreign trusts.
• You have taxable refunds of state or local income taxes.
• You have business, farm, or rental income.
• You have miscellaneous income not allowed on Form 1040EZ or 1040A such as alimony or lottery winnings.
• You have other adjustments to income such as alimony paid.
• You can claim a foreign tax credit or certain other credits to which you are entitled.
• You have other taxes such as self-employment tax or the alternative minimum tax.
• You file any additional required forms, such as:

Form 2555, Foreign Earned Income.

Form 3903, Moving Expenses.

Form 4972, Tax on Lump-Sum Distributions.

Form 5329, Return for Additional Taxes Attributable to Qualified Retirement Plans (including IRAs), Annuities, and Modified Endowment Contracts.

Form 8814, Parent's Election to Report Child's Interest and Dividends.

## 1993 Corporate Tax Rates

| Taxable Income Amount | Tax Rate |
|---|---|
| Not over $50,000 | 15% |
| $50,001 to $75,000 | 25% |
| $75,001 to $10,000,000 | 34% |
| over $10,000,000 | 35% |

An additional 5% tax, up to $11,750, applies to corporate taxable income over $100,000 and up to $335,000. There is an additional 3% tax, up to $100,000, that applies to corporate taxable income over $15 million and up to $18,333,333. Corporations with taxable income over $18,333,333, and personal service corporations (used by professional individuals such as attorneys and doctors), pay a flat rate of 35%.

## Internal Revenue Service Audit

Although fewer than one out of every hundred individual tax returns will probably be audited this year, the IRS is good at selecting returns for audit that will yield additional income taxes.

If your return is audited and you feel you are not being treated fairly, or that proper attention is not being paid to your statements, you have a right to ask for a hearing at the IRS appellate level. If you are still dissatisfied, you can take your case to the United States Tax Court. If the total amount in question is less than $10,000, your case can be handled under the Small Tax Case procedures. If you are still dissatisfied, your next move would be the United States Circuit Court of Appeals.

## Your Rights As a Taxpayer

Congress responded to complaints that taxpayers were not being treated fairly by the IRS and passed a comprehensive law to force the IRS to explain, in easy to understand language, the actions it proposes to take against a taxpayer and to relax some of its audit and collection procedures. This law is called, "The Taxpayer Bill of Rights."

You can learn more about this law by obtaining a free copy of IRS Publication 1, "Your Rights As a Taxpayer." Call 1-800-TAX-FORM for a copy.

## Some Frequently Used Federal Tax Forms

**706**
**U.S. Estate (and Generation-Skipping Transfer) Tax Return**
Used for the estate of a deceased U.S. resident or citizen.

**709-A**
**U.S. Short Form Gift Tax Return**
Used by married couples to report nontaxable gifts of more than $10,000 but less than $20,000.

**1040**
**U.S. Individual Income Tax Return**
Used by citizens and residents of the U.S. to report their income tax. Certain taxpayers may also use the shorter 1040A or 1040EZ.

**1040-ES**
**Estimated Tax for Individuals**
Used to make estimated income tax payments that may be required during the year (including self-employment tax and the alternative minimum tax).

**1040NR**
**U.S. Nonresident Alien Income Tax Return**
Used by all nonresident alien individuals who file a U.S. tax return, whether or not engaged in a trade or business within the U.S. Also used when required for filing nonresident alien fiduciary (estate and trust) returns.

**1040X**
**Amended U.S. Individual Income Tax Return**
Used to correct errors, omissions, and other adjustments on Forms 1040, 1040A, or 1040EZ tax returns that have already been filed.

**1041**
**U.S. Fiduciary Income Tax Return**
Used by a fiduciary for a domestic estate or domestic trust.

**1065**
**U.S. Partnership Return of Income**
Used by partnerships as an information return.

**1116**
**Foreign Tax Credit—Individual, Fiduciary, or Nonresident Alien Individual**
Used to figure and support the foreign tax credit claimed for the amount of any income, war profits, and excess profits taxes paid or accrued during the tax year to any foreign country or U.S. possession.

**1120**
**U.S. Corporation Income Tax Return**
Used by a corporation to report their income, deductions, and payment of taxes.

**1120S**
**U.S. Income Tax Return for an S Corporation**
Used by S corporations to report income and deductions under Subchapter S of the IRS code. Stockholders' share of taxable income is reported on their individual 1040.

**1139**
**Corporation Application for Tentative Refund**
Used by corporations that have certain loss and credit carrybacks and desire a quick refund of taxes.

**1310**
**Statement of Person Claiming Refund Due a Deceased Taxpayer**
Used by a claimant to secure payment of refund on behalf of a deceased taxpayer.

**2106**
**Employee Business Expenses**
For use by employees and outside salespersons to support deductions from income for travel, transportation, and other business expenses.

**2119**
**Sale of Your Home**
For use by individuals who sold their principal residence. Also used by those individuals age 55 or older who elect to exclude gain on the sale of their principal residence.

**2120**
**Multiple Support Declaration**
Used as a statement to disclaim as an income tax exemption an individual to whose support the taxpayer and others have jointly contributed.

**2441**
**Child and Dependent Care Expenses**
Used to figure the credit for child and dependent care expenses.

**2848**
**Power of Attorney and Declaration of Representative**
Used as an authorization for one person to act for another in any tax matter (except alcohol and tobacco taxes and firearms activities).

**3903**
**Moving Expenses**
For optional use to support deductions from income for expenses of travel, transportation (including meals and lodging), and certain expenses of selling an old residence and buying a new residence for employees or self-employed individuals moving to a new job location in the U.S. or its possessions.

**4562**
**Depreciation and Amortization**
For use by individuals, estates and trusts, partnerships, and corporations claiming depreciation, amortization, and section 179 expense deduction. Also used to provide required information for automobiles and all other "listed property."

**4684**
**Casualties and Thefts**
For use by all taxpayers for reporting gains and losses from casualties and thefts.

**4868**
**Application for Automatic Extension of Time to File U.S. Individual Income Tax Return**
Used to apply for an automatic 4-month extension of time to file Form 1040 or 1040A.

**5329**
**Return for Additional Taxes Attributable to Qualified Retirement Plans (including IRAs), Annuities, and Modified Endowment Contracts**
Used to report tax on excess contributions, premature distributions, excess distributions, and excess accumulations.

**5500EZ**
**Annual Return of One-Participant (Owners and Their Spouses) Pension Benefit Plan**
Used to report on a pension, profit-sharing, etc., plan covering an individual, partner, or an individual and spouse, or partners and spouses who wholly own a business.

**6251**
**Alternative Minimum Tax—Individuals**
Used by individuals to report tax preference items and to figure their alternative minimum tax liability.

**7004**
**Application for Automatic Extension of Time to File Corporation Income Tax Return**
Used by corporations and certain exempt organizations to request an automatic extension of 6 months to file their returns.

**8283**
**Noncash Charitable Contributions**
Used by taxpayers to report noncash contributions of property in which the total claimed fair market value of all property contributed exceeds $500.

**8582**
**Passive Activity Loss Limitations**
Used to determine limitations on passive activity losses.

**8606**
**Nondeductible IRA Contributions, IRA Basis, and Nontaxable IRA Distributions**
Used to report the nondeductible amount of IRA contributions and distributions. It is also used to determine IRA basis.

**8615**
**Tax for Children Under Age 14 Who Have Investment Income of More Than $1,200**
Used to figure the tax on unearned income of more than $1,200 belonging to a child under age 14.

**8815**
**Exclusion of Interest from Series EE U.S. Savings Bonds Issued After 1989.**
Used to figure the amount of interest on post-1989 Series EE U.S. Savings Bonds that can be excluded from income when the bonds are cashed and qualified higher education expenses are paid.

# State Government Individual Income Taxes

Source: U.S. Advisory Commission on Intergovernmental Relations

As of November 1992. Only basic rates, brackets, and exemptions are shown. Local income tax rates, even those mandated by the state, are not included. Taxable income rates and brackets listed below apply to single taxpayers and married taxpayers filing "combined separate" returns in states where this is permitted.

| State | Tax Rates (range in percent) | Taxable Income Brackets Lowest: Amount Under | Taxable Income Brackets Highest: Amount Over | Personal Exemptions Single | Personal Exemptions Married-Joint Return | Personal Exemptions Dependents | Standard Deduction[a] Percent | Standard Deduction[a] Single | Standard Deduction[a] Married-Joint Return | Federal Income Tax Deductible[b] |
|---|---|---|---|---|---|---|---|---|---|---|
| AL·* | 2.0-5.0% | $500 | $3,000 | $1,500 | $3,000 | $300 | 20% | $2,000 | $4,000 | yes |
| AK | | | | | No state income tax | | | | | |
| AZ[c] | 3.8-7.0 | 10,000 | 150,000 | 2,100 | 4,200 | 2,100 | NA | 3,500 | 7,000 | no |
| AR* | 1.0-7.0 | 3,000 | 25,000 | 20[d] | 40[d] | 20[d] | 10 | 1,000 | 1,000 | no |
| CAC* | 1.0-11.0 | 4,552 | 207,200 | 62[d] | 124[d] | 62[d] | NA | 2,343 | 4,686 | no |
| CO | 4.5 | Flat rate | | 5 percent of federal taxable income | | | | | | no |
| CT* | | | | 12,000 | 24,000 | 0 | NA | NA | NA | NA |
| DE·* | 3.2-7.7 | 2,000 | 40,000 | 1,250 | 2,500 | 1,250 | NA | 1,300 | 1,600 | no |
| DC | 6.0-9.5 | 10,000 | 20,000 | 1,370 | 2,740 | 1,370 | NA | 2,000 | 2,000 | no |
| FL | | | | | No state income tax | | | | | |
| GA | 1.0-6.0 | 750 | 7,000 | 1,500 | 3,000 | 1,500 | NA | 2,300 | 3,000 | no |
| HI* | 2.0-10.0 | 1,500 | 20,500 | 1,040 | 2,080 | 1,040 | NA | 1,000 | 1,700 | no |
| ID* | 2.0-8.2 | 1,000 | 20,000 | | Same as federal | | | | | no |
| IL* | 3.0 | Flat rate | | 1,000 | 2,000 | 1,000 | NA | NA | NA | no |
| IN* | 3.4 | Flat rate | | 1,000 | 2,000 | 1,000 | NA | NA | NA | no |
| IAC* | 0.4-9.98 | 1,060 | 47,700 | 20[d] | 40[d] | 15[d] | NA | 1,310 | 3,220 | yes |
| KS* | 4.5-7.75 | 20,000 | 30,000 | 2,000 | 4,000 | 2,000 | NA | 3,000 | 5,000 | no |
| KY·* | 2.0-6.0 | 3,000 | 8,000 | 20[d] | 40[d] | 20[d] | NA | 650 | 650 | no |
| LA | 2.0-6.0 | 10,000 | 50,000 | 4,500 | 9,000 | 1,000 | Combined with exemptions | | | yes |
| MEC* | 2.1-9.89 | 4,150 | 37,500 | 2,100 | 4,200 | 2,100 | NA | 3,600 | 6,000 | no |
| MD·* | 2.0-6.0 | 1,000 | 100,000 | 1,200 | 2,400 | 1,200 | 15 | 2,000 | 4,000 | no |
| MA* | 5.95-12.0 | Flat rate | | 2,200 | 4,400 | 1,000 | NA | NA | NA | no |
| MI·* | 4.6 | Flat rate | | 2,100 | 4,200 | 2,100 | NA | NA | NA | no |
| MN | 6.0-8.5 | 14,340 | 47,110 | | Same as federal | | | | | no |
| MS | 3.0-5.0 | 5,000 | 10,000 | 6,000 | 9,500 | 1,500 | NA | 2,300 | 3,400 | no |
| MO·* | 1.5-6.0 | 1,000 | 9,000 | 1,200 | 2,400 | 400 | NA | Same as federal | | yes |
| MTC* | 2.0-11.0 | 1,700 | 59,400 | 1,360 | 2,720 | 1,360 | 20 | 2,540 | 5,080 | yes |
| NEC* | 2.37-6.92 | 1,800 | 27,000 | 1,360 | 2,720 | 1,360 | NA | Same as federal | | no |
| NV | | | | | No state income tax | | | | | |
| NH* | | | | | Limited income tax | | | | | |
| NJ* | 2.0-7.0 | 20,000 | 75,000 | 1,000 | 2,000 | 1,500 | NA | NA | NA | no |
| NM | 1.8-8.5 | 5,200 | 41,600 | | Same as federal | | NA | Same as federal | | no |
| NY·* | 4.0-7.875 | 5,500 | 13,000 | 0 | 0 | 1,000 | NA | 6,000 | 9,500 | no |
| NC* | 6.0-7.75 | 12,750 | 60,000 | 2,000 | 4,000 | 2,000 | NA | 3,000 | 5,000 | no |
| ND* | | | | | 14 percent of federal income tax liability | | | | | yes |
| OH·* | 0.743-6.9 | 5,000 | 100,000 | 650 | 1,300 | 650 | NA | NA | NA | no |
| OK* | 0.5-7.0 | 1,000 | 9,950 | 1,000 | 2,000 | 1,000 | 15 | 2,000 | 2,000 | yes |
| ORC* | 5.0-9.0 | 2,000 | 5,000 | 109 | 218 | 109 | NA | 1,800 | 3,000 | yes |
| PA·* | 2.95 | Flat rate | | NA | NA | NA | NA | NA | NA | no |
| RI* | | | | | 27.5 percent of federal income tax liability | | | | | no |
| SC[c] | 2.5-7.0 | 2,120 | 10,600 | 2,300 | 4,600 | 2,300 | | Same as federal | | no |
| SD | | | | | No state income tax | | | | | |
| TN* | | | | | Limited income tax | | | | | |
| TX | | | | | No state income tax | | | | | |
| UT* | 2.55-7.2 | 750 | 3,750 | 1,725 | 3,450 | 1,725 | | Same as federal | | partial |
| VT* | | | | | 28-34 percent of federal income tax liability | | | | | no |
| VA | 2.0-5.75 | 3,000 | 17,000 | 800 | 1,600 | 800 | NA | 3,000 | 5,000 | no |
| WA | | | | | No state income tax | | | | | |
| WV | 3.0-6.5 | 10,000 | 60,000 | 2,000 | 4,000 | 2,000 | NA | NA | NA | no |
| WI* | 4.9-6.93 | 7,500 | 15,000 | 0 | 0 | 50[d] | NA | 5,200 | 8,900 | no |
| WY | | | | | No state income tax | | | | | |

**Notes:** (NA) = not applicable. (+) = states in which one or more local governments levy a local income tax. (a) The lesser of (1) the percentage indicated, multiplied by adjusted gross income (AGI), or (2) the dollar value listed. In some states, when a standard deduction computed using a percentage of AGI is less than the fixed amount shown above, a minimum dollar deduction is allowed. Maryland and Utah have a minimum deduction as well. (b) A state provision that allows the taxpayer to deduct fully the federal income tax reduces the effective marginal tax rate for persons in the highest state and federal tax brackets by approximately 30% of the nominal tax rate—the deduction is of a lesser benefit to other taxpayers with lower federal and state top tax brackets. (c) Elements of income tax are indexed by an inflation factor. (d) Exemption is a tax credit.

**\*State Notes:**

**Alabama:** Social Security taxes are included in itemized deductions. Taxable income brackets for married filing joint over $6,000, taxed at highest rate.

**Arkansas:** Tax credit per dependent. Taxpayers 65 or older, or blind or deaf, receive a $20 credit. No tax is imposed on (1) a single taxpayer whose gross income is less than $5,000; (2) a married couple with gross income less than $10,000; and (3) a head of household with gross income less than $7,150.

**California:** Taxpayers 65 and older receive an additional $62 credit.

**Connecticut:** Personal exemption amount is reduced by $1,000 for each $1,000, or fraction thereof, by which the taxpayer's Connecticut AGI exceeds $24,000 (single, married filing separately), $38,000 (head of household), $48,000 (married filing jointly).

**Delaware:** Lowest personal income tax rate (3.2%) applies to income in the $2,000-5,000 bracket. Taxable income under $2,000 is not subject to tax and is referred to as the "zero bracket" amount.

**Hawaii:** A refundable food/excise tax credit of at least $55 per exemption is granted; a refundable medical services excise tax credit of 4% of qualified medical expenses, subject to limitation, is granted.

**Idaho:** Idaho allows a refundable $15 per exemption credit.

**Illinois:** Effective 1/1/90, an additional $1,000 exemption for taxpayer or spouse 65 years of age or older. An additional $1,000 exemption for taxpayer or spouse who is blind.

**Indiana:** Additional $1,000 exemption if taxpayer or spouse is over 65 or blind.

**Iowa:** Tax may not reduce after-tax income of taxpayer below $7,500 (single) or $11,500 (married filing jointly, head of household, surviving spouse). Only limitation for the standard deduction is that the deduction otherwise allowable of $1,310 or $3,220 may not exceed the amount of income remaining after the federal tax deduction. Additional $20 personal exemption is allowed for each blind taxpayer age 65 years and older. Voters within a school district may approve a school district income surtax, which is computed as a percentage of regular state tax liability before refundable credits.

**Kansas:** A child care credit equal to 25% of the federal child care credit is allowed to taxpayers claiming the federal credit.

**Kentucky:** Tax credit per dependent. Taxpayers 65 or older receive a $60 credit.

**Maine:** Rates include a variable surcharge that is imposed for tax years 1991 and 1992. A 5% surcharge will be imposed on tax liabilities arising from the first $75,000 of taxable income for married taxpayers filing a joint return ($37,500 for single filers or married filing separately and $56,250 for head of household filers). Any taxpayer with taxable income in excess of these amounts will pay a top marginal rate of 8.6% and a 15% surcharge.

**Maryland:** For tax years 1992-1994 only, the state's income tax rate is 6% for taxable income $100,000 or over for single, married filing separately, and dependent taxpayers; $150,000 for all others. All counties have a local income tax surcharge of at least 20% of the state tax liability; most counties have a surcharge of 50%. The maximum local income tax rate is 60% (50% for income taxed at the 6% state rate). Single taxpayers have a minimum standard deduction of $1,500; married taxpayers a minimum standard deduction of $3,000. Blind and elderly get an additional exemption of $1,000. An additional $1,200 exemption is allowed for elderly dependents.

**Massachusetts:** 12% (flat rate) imposed on net capital gains, interest, and dividends of residents, and Massachusetts business income of nonresidents. All other net income taxed at 5.95%. No tax is imposed on a single person whose gross income is $8,000 or less ($12,000 married). Social Security taxes are deducted from taxable income up to $2,000 per taxpayer.

**Michigan:** Persons who can be claimed as a dependent on someone else's return get an exception of $1,000. If their AGI is $1,500 or less, they owe no tax.

**Missouri:** For taxpayers itemizing deductions, Social Security taxes are deductible.

**Montana:** Standard deductions are 20% of the taxpayer's AGI. Maximum amounts are given.

**Nebraska:** Taxable income brackets will vary by filing status. Married individuals filing separate returns: lowest amount under $1,500; highest amount over $22,500.

**New Hampshire:** There is a 5% tax on taxable interest and dividends in excess of $1,200 ($2,400 married). There is no filing requirement for an individual whose total interest and dividend income, after deducting all interest from U.S. obligations, New Hampshire and Vermont banks or credit unions, and dividends from New Hampshire non-holding company bonds, is less than $1,200 ($2,400 for joint filers) for a taxable period.

**New Jersey:** No taxpayer is subject to tax if gross income is $3,000 or less ($1,500 married, filing separately).

**New York:** A supplemental tax is imposed on taxpayers with New York adjusted gross income in excess of $100,000. Taxpayers must add back the benefit of the lower tax brackets (i.e., 4%, 5%, 6%, and 7%). Taxpayers with New York AGI in excess of $150,000 are taxed at a flat rate of 7.875%.

**North Carolina:** Breaking points for higher marginal tax rates vary according to filing status. Taxable income brackets shown are for single taxpayers. North Carolina taxable income reflects federal reductions of personal exemptions and itemized deductions for higher income brackets.

**North Dakota:** Information in table applies to the short-form method, which is used by 95% of taxpayers. As an alternative, taxpayers may use the long-form method with tax ranging from 2.67% to 12.0% applied to income brackets ranging from $3,000 to over $50,000.

**Ohio:** Taxpayers take a $20 tax credit per exemption.

**Oklahoma:** These rates and brackets apply to single persons not deducting federal income tax. For individuals deducting the tax, rates range from 0.5% of the first $1,000 to 10% on income over $16,000 (single rate).

**Oregon:** Federal tax deduction limited to $3,000 ($1,500 if married filing separately).

**Pennsylvania:** There are eight classes of income: (1) compensation; (2) net profits; (3) interest; (4) dividends; (5) sale or exchange of property; (6) rents, royalties, patents, and copyrights; (7) income derived through estates or trusts; and (8) gambling and lottery winnings in excess of $1,250 ($2,500 married).

**Rhode Island:** For 1992, if a taxpayer's federal income tax liability is greater than $15,000, the effective tax rate is 29.75% of federal income tax liability in excess of $15,000. For 1993, the effective tax rate on federal income tax liability in excess of $15,000 is 32%. For the period 1/1/94 and thereafter, the tax rate is equal to 27.5% of the taxpayer's federal income tax liability.

**Tennessee:** Interest and dividends taxed at 6%. Persons over 65 having total annual gross income derived from any and all sources of $9,000 or less are exempt. Blindness is a basis for total exemption.

**Utah:** One-half of federal tax liability is deductible. In determining Utah taxable income, 25% of federal personal exemptions are added back. Exemptions reflect this add-back.

**Vermont:** Refundable state earned income tax credit (28% of federal credit, maximum $619). Three percent surtax of liability between $3,400 and $13,100 and 6% liability over $13,100 are reflected in rates.

**Wisconsin:** The standard deduction is gradually phased out as income increases; deduction is completely phased out at $50,830 of AGI for single filers and $55,000 of AGI for joint filers. Taxpayers age 65 and older receive additional $25 exemption.

# ENERGY

## World Energy Production and Consumption Trends

Source: Energy Information Administration, U.S. Dept. of Energy, *International Energy Annual 1991*

Since 1982, the world's total output of primary energy—petroleum, natural gas, coal, hydroelectricity, and nuclear electricity—has increased steadily at an average annual rate of 2.4 percent. World production increased from 279 quadrillion Btu in 1982 to 346 quadrillion Btu in 1991. In 1991 world production of petroleum was more than 66 million barrels per day, or 136 quadrillion Btu. Over the past 10 years, petroleum has been the world's most heavily used source of energy. Between 1982 and 1991, petroleum production increased by more than 8 million barrels per day. In that period, production by OPEC (Organization of Petroleum Exporting Countries) increased by 5.4 million barrels per day.

In 1991 three countries—the U.S., the former U.S.S.R., and China—were the leading producers and consumers of energy. These three countries produced 47 percent and consumed 48 percent of the world totals. The former U.S.S.R. and the U.S. were the world's largest producers of energy in 1991, supplying 39 percent of the world total. The United States accounted for 23 percent of the world's total energy consumption—more than any other country. The U.S. consumed 20 percent more than it produced—an imbalance of 13.6 quadrillion Btu.

## U.S. Energy Summary

Source: Energy Information Administration, U.S. Dept. of Energy, *Annual Energy Review 1992*

In 1992 a gradually reviving domestic economy, low energy prices, and mild weather had the combined effect of producing modest growth in U.S. total energy consumption, which rose to a record 82 quadrillion Btu. The increase, which was the first since 1989, came as a result of increases in the consumption of petroleum, natural gas, coal, and nuclear electric power. Total sales of electricity, however, declined—for only the second time in 44 years. This decline was probably the result of a combination of factors: mild summer weather that held down residential and commercial demand for electricity for air conditioning; the growing prevalence of electric utilities' demand-side management practices, which attempt to reduce electricity use, particularly during periods of peak demand; and increasing electricity generation by nonutility power producers, which may have counteracted, to some extent, an increase in industrial demand attributable to gradually improving economy. Electricity sales of 2.8 trillion kilowatt-hours were 0.2 percent below 1991 sales.

Energy consumption per dollar of gross domestic product (GDP) declined slightly in 1992. About 17,000 Btu of energy were consumed for each dollar in 1992, compared with 23,000 Btu per dollar in the early 1970s (1987 dollars used throughout). However, energy consumption per capita rose from 322 million Btu in 1991 to 323 million Btu in 1992.

U.S. total energy production declined in 1992 for the second consecutive year, down 1.2 percent to 67 quadrillion Btu. Essentially all of the decline was attributed to lower crude oil production, which fell 0.5 quadrillion Btu from the 1991 level to 15 quadrillion Btu, and lower hydroelectric power production, which fell 0.4 quadrillion Btu to 2.5 quadrillion Btu. Crude oil production dropped to 7.2 million barrels per day, down 3.6 percent from the level in 1991. Hydroelectric power production fell 13 percent to 239 billion kilowatt-hours, the lowest level since 1988. The decline was attributable to persistent drought in western states.

U.S. net imports of energy rose to 14 quadrillion Btu in 1992, an increase of 7.9 percent from the 1991 level and the highest net import volume since 1979. Petroleum net imports rose 4.6 percent to 15 quadrillion Btu, natural gas net imports rose 10 percent to 1.8 quadrillion Btu, and coal net exports declined 0.5 percent to 2.6 quadrillion Btu. U.S. net imports of petroleum totaled 6.9 million barrels per day in 1992. Members of OPEC supplied 4.1 million barrels per day, well over half the total. Despite a decline from the 1991 level, coal remained the primary U.S. energy export. Coal exports totaled 103 million short tons in 1992.

## U.S. Energy Overview, 1960-1992

Source: Energy Information Administration, U.S. Dept. of Energy; *Annual Energy Review 1992*; in quadrillion Btu

| Activity and Energy Source | 1960 | 1965 | 1970 | 1975 | 1980 | 1985 | 1990 | 1991 | 1992P |
|---|---|---|---|---|---|---|---|---|---|
| Production | 41.49 | 49.34 | 62.07 | 59.86 | 64.76 | 64.87R | 67.85 | 67.54R | 66.72 |
| Coal | 10.82 | 13.06 | 14.61 | 14.99 | 18.60 | 19.33 | 22.46 | 21.59R | 21.56 |
| Natural Gas (Dry) | 12.66 | 15.78 | 21.67 | 19.64 | 19.91 | 16.98 | 18.36 | 18.28R | 18.27 |
| Crude Oil[1] | 14.93 | 16.52 | 20.40 | 17.73 | 18.25 | 18.99 | 15.57 | 15.70R | 15.19 |
| Natural Gas Plant Liquids | 1.46 | 1.88 | 2.51 | 2.37 | 2.25 | 2.24 | 2.17 | 2.31R | 2.36 |
| Nuclear Electric Power | 0.01 | 0.04 | 0.24 | 1.90 | 2.74 | 4.15 | 6.16 | 6.58R | 6.65 |
| Hydroelectric Power[2] | 1.61 | 2.06 | 2.63 | 3.15 | 2.90 | 2.97R | 2.93 | 2.88 | 2.51 |
| Other[3] | (4) | 0.01 | 0.02 | 0.07 | 0.11 | 0.21 | 0.20 | 0.19 | 0.19 |
| Imports | 4.23 | 5.92 | 8.39 | 14.11 | 15.97 | 12.10 | 18.99 | 18.58R | 19.45 |
| Natural Gas | 0.16 | 0.47 | 0.85 | 0.98 | 1.01 | 0.95 | 1.55 | 1.80R | 2.09 |
| Crude Oil[5] | 2.20 | 2.65 | 2.81 | 8.72 | 11.19 | 6.81 | 12.77 | 12.55 | 13.19 |
| Petroleum Products[6] | 1.80 | 2.75 | 4.66 | 4.23 | 3.46 | 3.80 | 4.35 | 3.79R | 3.68 |
| Other[7] | 0.07 | 0.04 | 0.07 | 0.19 | 0.31 | 0.54 | 0.32 | 0.43R | 0.49 |
| Exports | 1.48 | 1.85 | 2.66 | 2.36 | 3.72 | 4.23 | 4.91 | 5.22R | 5.03 |
| Coal | 1.02 | 1.38 | 1.94 | 1.76 | 2.42 | 2.44 | 2.77 | 2.85 | 2.68 |
| Crude Oil | 0.43 | 0.39 | 0.55 | 0.44 | 1.16 | 1.66 | 1.82 | 2.13 | 2.01 |
| Other[8] | 0.03 | 0.09 | 0.18 | 0.16 | 0.14 | 0.14 | 0.31 | 0.24R | 0.34 |
| Adjustments[9] | -0.43 | -0.72 | -1.37 | -1.07 | -1.05 | 1.24 | -0.67R | 0.24R | 1.21 |
| Consumption | 43.80 | 52.68 | 66.43 | 70.55 | 75.96 | 73.98R | 81.26R | 81.14R | 82.36 |
| Coal | 9.84 | 11.58 | 12.26 | 12.66 | 15.42 | 17.48 | 19.10R | 18.77R | 18.92 |
| Natural Gas[10] | 12.39 | 15.77 | 21.79 | 19.95 | 20.39 | 17.83 | 19.30 | 19.63R | 20.32 |
| Petroleum[11] | 19.92 | 23.25 | 29.52 | 32.73 | 34.20 | 30.92 | 33.55 | 32.85R | 33.47 |
| Nuclear Electric Power | 0.01 | 0.04 | 0.24 | 1.90 | 2.74 | 4.15 | 6.16 | 6.58R | 6.65 |
| Hydroelectric Power[12] | 1.66 | 2.06 | 2.65 | 3.22 | 3.12 | 3.40R | 2.95 | 3.12R | 2.79 |
| Other[13] | (4) | -0.01 | -0.04 | 0.09 | 0.08 | 0.20 | 0.21 | 0.20 | 0.22 |

(1) Includes lease condensate. (2) Electric utility and industrial generation. (3) "Other" production is electricity generated for distribution from wood, waste, geothermal, wind, photovoltaic, and solar thermal energy. (4) Less than 0.005 quadrillion Btu. (5) Includes imports of crude oil for the Strategic Petroleum Reserve, which began in 1977. (6) Includes imports of unfinished oils and natural gas plant liquids. (7) "Other" imports are coal, electricity, and coal coke. (8) "Other" exports are natural gas, petroleum products, electricity, and coal coke. (9) A balancing item. Includes stock changes, losses, gains, miscellaneous blending components, and unaccounted for supply. (10) Includes supplemental gaseous fuels. (11) Petroleum products supplied, including natural gas plant liquids and crude oil burned as fuel. (12) Electric utility and industrial generation, and net imports of electricity. (13) "Other" consumption is net imports of coal coke and electricity generated for distribution from wood, waste, geothermal, wind, photovoltaic, and solar thermal energy. R = Revised data. P = Preliminary data. **Notes:** Due to a lack of consistent historical data, some renewable energy sources are not included. For 1991 consumption, 3.3 quadrillion Btu of renewable energy consumed by U.S. electric utilities to generate electricity for distribution is included, but an estimated 3.4 quadrillion Btu of renewable energy used by other sectors in the United States is not included. Sum of components may not equal total due to independent rounding.

# World's Major Producers of Primary Energy, 1991

| | |
|---|---|
| United States | 67.35 |
| Former U.S.S.R. | 66.00 |
| China | 30.19 |
| Saudi Arabia | 19.98 |
| Canada | 13.66 |
| United Kingdom | 9.13 |
| Iran | 8.44 |
| Mexico | 7.88 |
| India | 7.15 |
| Venezuela | 7.11 |

SOURCE: Energy Information Administration; International Energy Annual 1991; Quadrillion Btu

# World's Major Consumers of Primary Energy, 1991

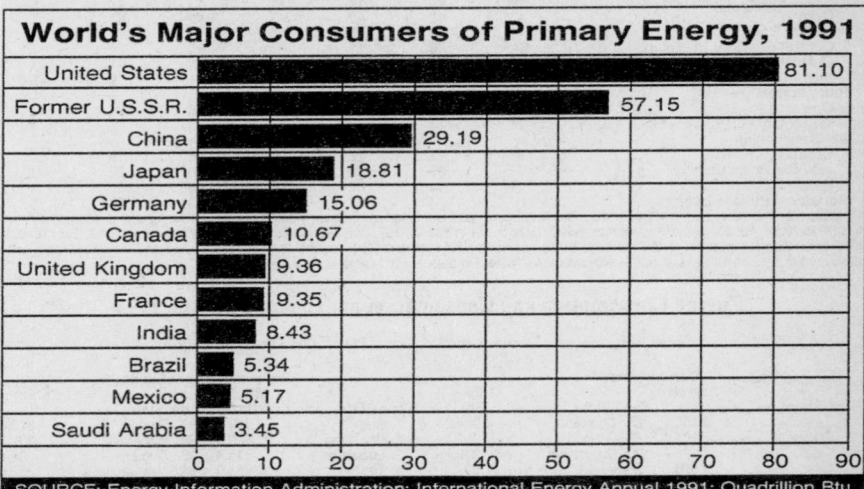

| | |
|---|---|
| United States | 81.10 |
| Former U.S.S.R. | 57.15 |
| China | 29.19 |
| Japan | 18.81 |
| Germany | 15.06 |
| Canada | 10.67 |
| United Kingdom | 9.36 |
| France | 9.35 |
| India | 8.43 |
| Brazil | 5.34 |
| Mexico | 5.17 |
| Saudi Arabia | 3.45 |

SOURCE: Energy Information Administration; International Energy Annual 1991; Quadrillion Btu

## U.S. Net Imports of Petroleum, 1973-1992

Source: Energy Information Administration, U.S. Dept. of Energy, *Monthly Energy Review,* June 1993; thousand barrels per day

| Average Annual Rate | Net Imports[1] | | | Petroleum Products Supplied | Average Annual Rate | Net Imports[1] | | | Petroleum Products Supplied |
| | From Arab OPEC[2] | From OPEC[3] | From All Countries | | | From Arab OPEC[2] | From OPEC[3] | From All Countries | |
|---|---|---|---|---|---|---|---|---|---|
| 1973 . . . . | 914 | 2,991 | 6,025 | 17,308 | 1983 . . . . | 630 | 1,843 | 4,312 | 15,231 |
| 1974 . . . . | 752 | 3,277 | 5,892 | 16,653 | 1984 . . . . | 817 | 2,037 | 4,715 | 15,726 |
| 1975 . . . . | 1,382 | 3,599 | 5,846 | 16,322 | 1985 . . . . | 470 | 1,821 | 4,286 | 15,726 |
| 1976 . . . . | 2,423 | 5,063 | 7,090 | 17,461 | 1986 . . . . | 1,160 | 2,828 | 5,439 | 16,281 |
| 1977 . . . . | 3,184 | 6,190 | 8,565 | 18,431 | 1987 . . . . | 1,272 | 3,053 | 5,914 | 16,665 |
| 1978 . . . . | 2,962 | 5,747 | 8,002 | 18,847 | 1988 . . . . | 1,837 | 3,513 | 6,587 | 17,283 |
| 1979 . . . . | 3,054 | 5,633 | 7,985 | 18,513 | 1989 . . . . | 2,128 | 4,124 | 7,202 | 17,325 |
| 1980 . . . . | 2,549 | 4,293 | 6,365 | 17,056 | 1990 . . . . | 2,243 | 4,285 | 7,161 | 16,988 |
| 1981 . . . . | 1,844 | 3,315 | 5,401 | 16,058 | 1991 . . . . | 2,057R | 4,064R | 6,626R | 16,714R |
| 1982 . . . . | 852 | 2,136 | 4,298 | 15,296 | 1992 . . . . | 1,972R | 4,071R | 6,938R | 17,033R |

R = Revised. (1) Net Imports is imports minus exports. Imports from members of the Organization of Petroleum Exporting Countries (OPEC) exclude indirect imports, which are petroleum products primarily from Caribbean and West European areas and refined from crude oil produced by OPEC. (2) The Arab members of OPEC are Algeria, Iraq, Kuwait, Libya, Qatar, Saudi Arabia, and the United Arab Emirates. Net imports from the Neutral Zone between Kuwait and Saudi Arabia are included in net imports from Arab OPEC. (3) OPEC currently consists of Gabon, Indonesia, Iran, Nigeria, and Venezuela, as well as the Arab members; prior to 1993, it also included Ecuador. **Notes:** Beginning in October 1977, Strategic Petroleum Reserves are included. Geographic coverage is the 50 States and the District of Columbia. Annual averages may not equal average of quarters due to independent rounding.

## Appliance Use in U.S. Households, 1978-1990

Source: Energy Information Administration, U.S. Dept. of Energy, *Annual Energy Review 1992*

(percent of households)

| Appliance | 1978 | 1980 | 1982 | 1984 | 1987 | 1990 | Change 1980-1990 |
|---|---|---|---|---|---|---|---|
| **Total Households** | 100 | 100 | 100 | 100 | 100 | 100 | — |
| **Type of Appliances** | | | | | | | |
| **Electric Appliances** | | | | | | | |
| Television Set (Color) | NA | 82 | 85 | 88 | 93 | 96 | 14 |
| Television Set (B/W) | NA | 51 | 47 | 43 | 36 | 31 | −20 |
| Clothes Washer | 75 | 75 | 72 | 74 | 76 | 76 | 1 |
| Range (Stove-Top Burner) | 53 | 54 | 53 | 54 | 57 | 58 | 4 |
| Oven, Regular or Microwave | 54 | 59 | 59 | 63 | 79 | 88 | 29 |
| Oven, Microwave | 8 | 14 | 21 | 34 | 61 | 79 | 65 |
| Clothes Dryer | 45 | 47 | 45 | 46 | 51 | 53 | 6 |
| Separate Freezer | 35 | 38 | 37 | 37 | 34 | 35 | −3 |
| Dishwasher | 35 | 37 | 36 | 38 | 43 | 45 | 8 |
| Dehumidifier | NA | 9 | 9 | 9 | 10 | 12 | 3 |
| Waterbed Heaters | NA | NA | NA | 10 | 14 | 15 | NA |
| Window or Ceiling Fan | NA | NA | 28 | 35 | 46 | 51 | NA |
| Whole House Fan | NA | NA | 8 | 8 | 9 | 10 | NA |
| Evaporative Cooler | NA | 4 | 4 | 4 | 3 | 4 | (1) |
| Personal Computer | NA | NA | NA | NA | NA | 16 | NA |
| Pump for Well Water | NA | NA | NA | NA | NA | 15 | NA |
| Swimming-Pool Pump[2] | NA | 4 | 3 | NA | NA | 5 | 1 |
| **Gas Appliances[3]** | | | | | | | |
| Range (Stove-Top Burner) | 48 | 46 | 47 | 45 | 43 | 42 | −4 |
| Oven | 47 | 42 | 42 | 42 | 41 | 41 | −1 |
| Clothes Dryer | 14 | 14 | 15 | 16 | 15 | 16 | 2 |
| Outdoor Gas Grill | NA | 9 | 11 | 13 | 20 | 26 | 17 |
| Outdoor Gas Light | 2 | 2 | 2 | 1 | 1 | 1 | −1 |
| Swimming Pool Heater[4] | NA | NA | NA | 1 | 1 | 2 | NA |
| **Refrigerators[5]** | | | | | | | |
| One | 86 | 86 | 86 | 88 | 86 | 84 | −2 |
| Two or More | 14 | 14 | 13 | 12 | 14 | 15 | 1 |
| **Air Conditioning** | | | | | | | |
| Central[6] | 23 | 27 | 28 | 30 | 36 | 39 | 12 |
| Individual Room Units[6] | 33 | 30 | 30 | 30 | 30 | 29 | −1 |
| None | 44 | 43 | 42 | 40 | 36 | 32 | −11 |
| **Portable Kerosene Heaters** | (1) | (1) | 3 | 6 | 6 | 5 | 5 |

(1) Less than 0.5 percent. (2) All reported swimming pools were assumed to have an electric pump for filtering and circulating the water. (3) Includes natural gas or liquefied petroleum gases. (4) In 1984, 1987, and 1990, also includes heaters for jacuzzis and hot tubs. (5) Fewer than 0.5 percent of the households do not have a refrigerator. (6) Households with both central and individual room units are counted only under central. NA = Not available. **Note:** No data are available for years not shown.

## Energy Consumption and Consumption per Capita by State, 1991

Source: Energy Information Administration, U.S. Dept. of Energy, *Annual Energy Review 1992*

| | Consumption Trillion Btu | | | Consumption Trillion Btu | | | Consumption per Capita Million Btu | | | Consumption per Capita Million Btu |
|---|---|---|---|---|---|---|---|---|---|---|
| **Rank State** | | **Rank State** | | | **Rank State** | | **Rank State** | | | |
| 1. Texas | 9,785.1 | 27. Colorado | 964.2 | | 1. Alaska | 1,030.9 | 27. Georgia | 310.6 | | |
| 2. California | 7,161.9 | 28. Oregon | 953.4 | | 2. Wyoming | 849.5 | 28. Minnesota | 307.7 | | |
| 3. Ohio | 3,686.9 | 29. Mississippi | 949.6 | | 3. Louisiana | 815.4 | 29. Illinois | 304.4 | | |
| 4. New York | 3,558.5 | 30. Iowa | 937.4 | | 4. Texas | 564.0 | 30. New Jersey | 296.6 | | |
| 5. Illinois | 3,513.0 | 31. Arizona | 923.6 | | 5. North Dakota | 504.4 | 31. Virginia | 294.3 | | |
| 6. Pennsylvania | 3,491.6 | 32. West Virginia | 782.9 | | 6. West Virginia | 434.2 | 32. District of | | | |
| 7. Louisiana | 3,468.9 | 33. Arkansas | 769.6 | | | | Columbia | 294.3 | | |
| 8. Florida | 3,021.9 | 34. Connecticut | 732.0 | | 7. Indiana | 431.5 | 33. Maine | 293.6 | | |
| 9. Michigan | 2,753.9 | 35. New Mexico | 588.0 | | 8. Montana | 422.9 | 34. Michigan | 293.6 | | |
| 10. Indiana | 2,421.0 | 36. Alaska | 587.6 | | 9. Kansas | 416.4 | 35. Missouri | 293.3 | | |
| 11. New Jersey | 2,299.7 | 37. Utah | 566.3 | | 10. Oklahoma | 404.1 | 36. Pennsylvania | 292.0 | | |
| 12. Georgia | 2,057.0 | 38. Nebraska | 522.0 | | 11. Kentucky | 397.7 | 37. North Carolina | 291.2 | | |
| 13. Washington | 1,965.1 | 39. Nevada | 400.2 | | 12. Washington | 392.1 | 38. South Dakota | 291.2 | | |
| 14. North Carolina | 1,961.6 | 40. Wyoming | 390.8 | | 13. Alabama | 388.8 | 39. Colorado | 285.4 | | |
| 15. Virginia | 1,848.4 | 41. Idaho | 387.7 | | 14. New Mexico | 379.6 | 40. Wisconsin | 284.8 | | |
| 16. Tennessee | 1,746.5 | 42. Maine | 362.3 | | 15. Idaho | 372.7 | 41. Maryland | 250.1 | | |
| 17. Alabama | 1,590.7 | 43. Montana | 342.1 | | 16. Mississippi | 366.2 | 42. Arizona | 246.4 | | |
| 18. Missouri | 1,512.6 | 44. North Dakota | 320.3 | | 17. Tennessee | 352.6 | 43. Hawaii | 238.9 | | |
| 19. Kentucky | 1,476.5 | 45. Hawaii | 271.6 | | 18. Delaware | 347.9 | 44. California | 235.7 | | |
| 20. Wisconsin | 1,411.7 | 46. New Hampshire | 238.7 | | 19. South Carolina | 339.7 | 45. Vermont | 233.7 | | |
| 21. Minnesota | 1,363.7 | 47. Delaware | 236.6 | | 20. Ohio | 337.0 | 46. Florida | 227.8 | | |
| 22. Massachusetts | 1,313.1 | 48. Rhode Island | 214.5 | | 21. Iowa | 335.4 | 47. Connecticut | 222.6 | | |
| 23. Oklahoma | 1,283.0 | 49. South Dakota | 205.0 | | 22. Nebraska | 327.7 | 48. Massachusetts | 219.0 | | |
| 24. Maryland | 1,215.3 | 50. District of | | | 23. Oregon | 326.3 | 49. New Hampshire | 216.2 | | |
| | | Columbia | 175.1 | | 24. Arkansas | 324.3 | 50. Rhode Island | 213.4 | | |
| 25. South Carolina | 1,209.3 | 51. Vermont | 132.5 | | 25. Utah | 320.0 | 51. New York | 197.1 | | |
| 26. Kansas | 1,038.9 | **Total United States** | **81,119.0** | | 26. Nevada | 311.9 | **Total United States** | **321.7** | | |

## World's Largest Capacity Hydro Plants

Source: U.S. Committee on Large Dams of the Intl. Commission on Large Dams, Sept. 1993

| Rank order | Name | Country | Rated capacity now (MW) | Rated capacity planned (MW) | Rank order | Name | Country | Rated capacity now (MW) | Rated capacity planned (MW) |
|---|---|---|---|---|---|---|---|---|---|
| 1 | Turukhansk (Lower Tunguska)* | former USSR | | 20,000 | 13= | Bratsk | former USSR | 4,500 | 4,500 |
| | | | | | 13= | Ust-Ilim | former USSR | 3,675 | 4,500 |
| 2 | Itaipu | Brazil/Paraguay | 7,400 | 13,320 | 15 | Cabora Bassa | Mozambique | 2,425 | 4,150 |
| 3 | Grand Coulee | USA | 6,495 | 10,830 | 16 | Boguchany | former USSR | | 4,000 |
| 4 | Guri (Raúl Leoni) | Venezuela | 10,300 | 10,300 | 17= | Rogun* | former USSR | | 3,600 |
| 5 | Tucuruí | Brazil | 2,640 | 7,260 | 17= | Oak Creek | USA | 3,600 | 3,600 |
| 6 | Sayano Shu-shensk* | former USSR | 6,400 | 6,400 | 19 | Paulo Afonso I | Brazil | 1,524 | 3,409 |
| 7= | Corpus Posadas | Argentina/ Paraguay | 4,700 | 6,000 | 20 | Pati* | Argentina | | 3,300 |
| | | | | | 21= | Ilha Solteira | Brazil | 3,200 | 3,200 |
| 7= | Krasnoyarsk | former USSR | 6,000 | 6,000 | 21= | Brumley Gap* | USA | 3,200 | 3,200 |
| 9 | La Grande 2 | Canada | 5,328 | 5,328 | 23 | Chapetón* | Argentina | | 3,000 |
| 10 | Churchill Falls | Canada | 5,225 | 5,225 | 24 | Gezhouba | China | 2,715 | 2,715 |
| 11 | Xingo | Brazil | 3,012 | 5,020 | 25 | John Day | USA | 2,160 | 2,700 |
| 12 | Tarbela | Pakistan | 1,750 | 4,678 | 25 | Nurek | former USSR | 900 | 2,700 |
| | | | | | 25= | Yaciretá* | Argentina/ Paraguay | | 2,700 |

* Planned or under construction.

## Major Dams of the World

Source: U.S. Committee on Large Dams of the Intl. Commission of Large Dams, Sept. 1993

### World's Highest Dams

| Rank order | Name | Country | Height above lowest formation (m) | Rank order | Name | Country | Height above lowest formation (m) |
|---|---|---|---|---|---|---|---|
| 1 | Rogun* | former USSR | 335 | 11 | Mica | Canada | 242 |
| 2 | Nurek | former USSR | 300 | 12 | Mauvoisin | Switzerland | 237 |
| 3 | Grand Dixence | Switzerland | 285 | 13 | Chivor | Colombia | 237 |
| 4 | Inguri | former USSR | 272 | 14 | El Cajón | Honduras | 234 |
| 5 | Chicoasén | Mexico | 261 | 15 | Chirkei | former USSR | 233 |
| 6 | Tehri* | India | 261 | 16 | Oroville | USA | 230 |
| 7 | Kishau* | India | 253 | 17 | Bhakra | India | 226 |
| 8= | Ertan | China | 245 | 18 | Hoover | USA | 221 |
| 9= | Sayano-Shushensk* | former USSR | 245 | 19 | Contra | Switzerland | 220 |
| 10 | Guavio* | Colombia | 243 | 20 | Mratinje | Yugoslavia | 220 |

* Under construction.

### World's Largest Volume Embankment Dams

| Rank order | Name | Country | Volume cubic meters × 1000 | Rank order | Name | Country | Volume cubic meters × 1000 |
|---|---|---|---|---|---|---|---|
| 1 | Tarbela | Pakistan | 148,500 | 11 | Gardiner | Canada | 65,000 |
| 2 | Fort Peck | USA | 96,050 | 12 | Afsluitdijk | Netherlands | 63,400 |
| 3 | Tucurui | Brazil | 85,200 | 13 | Mangla | Pakistan | 63,379 |
| 4 | Ataturk* | Turkey | 85,000 | 14 | Oroville | USA | 59,635 |
| 5 | Yaciretá* | Argentina | 81,000 | 15 | San Luis | USA | 59,559 |
| 6 | Rogun* | former USSR | 75,500 | 16 | Nurek | former USSR | 58,000 |
| 7 | Oahe | USA | 70,339 | 17 | Tanda | Pakistan | 57,250 |
| 8 | Guri | Venezuela | 70,000 | 18 | Garrison | USA | 50,843 |
| 9 | Parambikulam | India | 69,165 | 19 | Chochiti | USA | 50,228 |
| 10 | High Island West | Hong Kong | 67,000 | 20 | Oosterschelde | Netherlands | 50,000 |

* Under construction.

### World's Largest Capacity Manmade Reservoirs

| Rank order | Name | Country | Capacity cubic meters × 1000 | Rank order | Name | Country | Capacity cubic meters × 1000 |
|---|---|---|---|---|---|---|---|
| 1 | Owen Falls | Uganda | 204,800 | 11 | Cabora Bassa | Mozambique | 63,000 |
| 2 | Bratsk | former USSR | 169,000 | 12 | La Grande 2 | Canada | 61,715 |
| 3 | Aswan (High) | Egypt | 162,000 | 13 | La Grande 3 | Canada | 60,020 |
| 4 | Kariba | Zimbabwe/Zambia | 160,368 | 14 | Ust-Ilim | former USSR | 59,300 |
| 5 | Akosombo | Ghana | 147,960 | 15 | Boguchany* | former USSR | 58,200 |
| 6 | Daniel Johnson | Canada | 141,851 | 16 | Kuibyshev | former USSR | 58,000 |
| 7 | Guri | Venezuela | 135,000 | 17 | Serra de Mesa | Brazil | 54,400 |
| 8 | Krasnoyarsk | former USSR | 73,300 | 18 | Caniapiscau Barrage KA 3 | Canada | 53,790 |
| 9 | W A C Bennett (Portage Mt.) | Canada | 70,309 | 19 | Bukhtarma | former USSR | 49,800 |
| 10 | Zeya | former USSR | 68,400 | 20 | Ataturk | Turkey | 48,700 |

* Under construction

## Major U.S. Dams and Reservoirs

Source: Committee on Register of Dams, Corps of Engineers, U.S. Army, Sept. 1993

### Highest Dams

| | | | | | Height | | Year |
|---|---|---|---|---|---|---|---|
| Order | Dam Name | River | State | Type | Feet | Meters | Complete |
| 1 | Oroville | Feather | California | E | 754 | 230 | 1968 |
| 2 | Hoover | Colorado | Nevada | A | 725 | 221 | 1936 |
| 3 | Dworshak | N Fork Clearwater | Idaho | G | 718 | 219 | 1973 |
| 4 | Glen Canyon | Colorado | Arizona | A | 708 | 216 | 1966 |
| 5 | New Bullards Bar | North Yuba | California | A | 636 | 194 | 1970 |
| 6 | New Melones | Stanislaus | California | R | 626 | 191 | 1979 |
| 7 | Swift | Lewis | Washington | E | 610 | 186 | 1958 |
| 8 | Mossyrock | Cowlitz | Washington | A | 607 | 185 | 1968 |
| 9 | Shasta | Sacramento | California | G | 600 | 183 | 1945 |
| 10 | Hungry Horse | S Fork Flathead | Montana | A | 564 | 172 | 1953 |
| 11 | Grand Coulee | Columbia | Washington | G | 551 | 168 | 1942 |
| 12 | Ross | Skagit | Washington | A | 541 | 165 | 1949 |

E = Embankment, Earthfill; R = Embankment, Rockfill; G = Gravity; A = Arch.

### Largest Embankment Dams

| | | | | | Volume | | Year |
|---|---|---|---|---|---|---|---|
| | | | | | Cubic yards | Cubic Meters | |
| Order | Dam Name | River | State | Type | X 1000 | X 1000 | Complete |
| 1 | Fort Peck | Missouri | Montana | E | 125,624 | 96,050 | 1937 |
| 2 | Oahe | Missouri | South Dakota | E | 91,996 | 70,339 | 1958 |
| 3 | Oroville | Feather | California | E | 77,997 | 59,635 | 1968 |
| 4 | San Luis | San Luis Creek | California E | | 77,897 | 59,559 | 1967 |
| 5 | Garrison | Missouri | North Dakota | E | 66,498 | 50,843 | 1953 |
| 6 | Cochiti | Rio Grande | New Mexico | E | 65,693 | 50,228 | 1975 |
| 7 | Earthquake Lake | Madison | Montana | E-G | 49,998 | 38,228 | 1959 |
| 8 | Fort Randall | Missouri | South Dakota | E | 49,962 | 38,200 | 1952 |
| 9 | Castaic | Castaic Creek | California | E | 43,998 | 33,640 | 1973 |
| 10 | Ludington P/S | Lake Michigan | Michigan | E | 37,699 | 28,824 | 1973 |
| 11 | Kingsley | N. Platte | Nebraska | E | 31,999 | 24,466 | 1941 |
| 12 | Warm Springs | Dry Creek | California | E | 29,977 | 22,920 | 1982 |

E = Embankment, Earthfill; G = Gravity.

### Largest Man-Made Reservoirs

| | | | | Reservoir Capacity | | Year |
|---|---|---|---|---|---|---|
| | | | | | Cubic Meters | |
| Order | Dam Name | Reservoir | Location | Acre-Feet | x 1000 | Completed |
| 1 | Hoover | Lake Mead | Nevada | 28,253,000 | 34,850,000 | 1936 |
| 2 | Glen Canyon | Lake Powell | Arizona | 26,997,000 | 33,300,000 | 1966 |
| 3 | Garrison | Lake Sakakawea | North Dakota | 22,635,000 | 27,920,000 | 1953 |
| 4 | Oahe | Lake Oahe | South Dakota | 22,238,000 | 27,430,000 | 1958 |
| 5 | Fort Peck | Fort Peck Lake | Montana | 17,933,000 | 22,120,000 | 1937 |
| 6 | Grand Coulee | F D Roosevelt Lake | Washington | 9,558,000 | 11,790,000 | 1942 |
| 7 | Libby | Lake Koocanusa | Montana | 5,813,000 | 7,170,000 | 1973 |
| 8 | Fort Randall | Lake Francis Case | South Dakota | 4,621,000 | 5,700,000 | 1952 |
| 9 | Shasta | Lake Shasta | California | 4,548,000 | 5,610,000 | 1945 |
| 10 | Toledo Bend | Toledo Bend Lake | Louisiana | 4,475,000 | 5,520,000 | 1968 |
| 11 | Wolf Creek | Cumberland Lake | Kentucky | 3,997,000 | 4,930,000 | 1951 |
| 12 | Flaming Gorge | Flaming Gorge Reservoir | Utah | 3,786,000 | 4,670,000 | 1964 |

1 acre foot = 1 acre of water, 1 foot deep

## Gasoline Retail Prices, U.S. City Average, 1973-1992

Source: Energy Information Administration, U.S. Dept. of Energy, *Monthly Energy Review*, June 1993

(cents per gallon, including taxes)

| Average | Leaded Regular | Unleaded Regular | Unleaded Premium | All Types[1] | Average | Leaded Regular | Unleaded Regular | Unleaded Premium | All Types[1] |
|---|---|---|---|---|---|---|---|---|---|
| 1973 .. | 38.8 | NA | NA | NA | 1983 .. | 115.7 | 124.1 | 138.3 | 122.5 |
| 1974 .. | 53.2 | NA | NA | NA | 1984 .. | 112.9 | 121.2 | 136.6 | 119.8 |
| 1975 .. | 56.7 | NA | NA | NA | 1985 .. | 111.5 | 120.2 | 134.0 | 119.6 |
| 1976 .. | 59.0 | 61.4 | NA | NA | 1986 .. | 85.7 | 92.7 | 108.5 | 93.1 |
| 1977 .. | 62.2 | 65.6 | NA | NA | 1987 .. | 89.7 | 94.8 | 109.3 | 95.7 |
| 1978 .. | 62.6 | 67.0 | NA | 65.2 | 1988 .. | 89.9 | 94.6 | 110.7 | 96.3 |
| 1979 .. | 85.7 | 90.3 | NA | 88.2 | 1989 .. | 99.8 | 102.1 | 119.7 | 106.0 |
| 1980 .. | 119.1 | 124.5 | NA | 122.1 | 1990 .. | 114.9 | 116.4 | 134.9 | 121.7 |
| 1981 .. | 131.1 | 137.8 | 147.0[3] | 135.3 | 1991 .. | NA | 114.0 | 132.1 | 119.6 |
| 1982 .. | 122.2 | 129.6 | 141.5 | 128.1 | 1992 .. | NA | 112.7 | 131.6 | 119.0 |

(1) Also includes types of motor gasoline not shown separately. (2) In Sept. 1981, the Bureau of Labor Statistics changed the weights used in the calculation of average motor gasoline prices. From Sept. 1981 forward, gasohol is included in the average for all types, and unleaded premium is weighted more heavily. (3) Based on Sept. through Dec. data only. **Notes:** Geographic coverage for 1973-1977 is 56 urban areas; for 1978 forward, 85 urban areas. NA = Not available.

## World Crude Oil and Natural Gas Reserves, January 1, 1992

Source: Energy Information Administration, U.S. Dept. of Energy, *Annual Energy Review 1992*

| Region and Country | Crude Oil (billion barrels) Oil and Gas Journal | World Oil | Natural Gas (trillion cubic feet) Oil and Gas Journal | World Oil | Region and Country | Crude Oil (billion barrels) Oil and Gas Journal | World Oil | Natural Gas (trillion cubic feet) Oil and Gas Journal | World Oil |
|---|---|---|---|---|---|---|---|---|---|
| North America. . . . | 81.6 | 81.7 | 335.3 | 334.0 | Iran . . . . . . . . . | 92.9 | 62.5 | 600.4 | 600.0 |
| Canada . . . . . . . | 5.6 | 6.1 | 96.7 | 96.0 | Iraq . . . . . . . . . | 100.0 | 100.0 | 95.0 | 109.4 |
| Mexico . . . . . . . . | 51.3 | 50.9 | 71.5 | 71.0 | Kuwait . . . . . . . . | 96.5 | 95.2 | 48.5 | 51.8 |
| United States . . . . | 24.7 | 24.7 | 167.1 | 167.1 | Oman . . . . . . . . | 4.3 | 4.4 | 9.9 | 13.0 |
| Central and South | | | | | Qatar . . . . . . . . | 3.7 | 2.9 | 162.0 | 162.0 |
| America . . . . . . | 68.5 | 73.1 | 167.0 | 186.9 | Saudi Arabia . . . . . | 260.3 | 261.9 | 184.5 | 184.5 |
| Argentina . . . . . . | 1.6 | 1.5 | 20.4 | 22.7 | United Arab Emirates | 98.1 | 65.8 | 199.3 | 195.7 |
| Bolivia . . . . . . . . | 0.1 | 0.1 | 4.5 | 4.1 | Other . . . . . . . . | 5.7 | 3.8 | 13.5 | 22.6 |
| Brazil . . . . . . . . . | 2.8 | 3.0 | 4.0 | 4.4 | Africa . . . . . . . . . | 60.5 | 75.5 | 310.2 | 334.0 |
| Colombia . . . . . . . | 1.9 | 1.7 | 3.9 | 3.6 | Algeria . . . . . . . . | 9.2 | 9.9 | 116.5 | 128.1 |
| Ecuador . . . . . . . | 1.6 | 1.7 | 3.9 | 3.9 | Cameroon . . . . . . | 0.4 | 0.4 | 3.9 | 3.9 |
| Trinidad and Tobago | 0.5 | 0.6 | 8.9 | 8.7 | Egypt . . . . . . . . . | 4.5 | 3.5 | 12.4 | 12.0 |
| Venezuela . . . . . . | 59.1 | 62.7 | 110.0 | 128.5 | Libya . . . . . . . . . | 22.8 | 38.4 | 43.0 | 43.5 |
| Other . . . . . . . . . | 0.9 | 1.8 | 11.4 | 11.0 | Nigeria . . . . . . . . | 17.9 | 17.9 | 104.7 | 120.1 |
| Western Europe. . . | 14.7 | 22.2 | 181.4 | 215.5 | Tunisia . . . . . . . . | 1.7 | 1.8 | 3.0 | 3.2 |
| Denmark . . . . . . . | 0.8 | 0.7 | 4.1 | 4.0 | Other . . . . . . . . . | 4.0 | 3.6 | 26.7 | 23.2 |
| Germany . . . . . . . | 0.4 | 0.3 | 8.8 | 8.2 | Far East and Oceania | 44.1 | 56.4 | 299.3 | 389.3 |
| Italy . . . . . . . . . . | 0.7 | 0.7 | 11.4 | 11.4 | Australia . . . . . . . | 1.5 | 2.1 | 15.1 | 75.4 |
| Netherlands . . . . . | 0.1 | 0.1 | 69.6 | 68.9 | Brunei . . . . . . . . | 1.3 | 1.1 | 11.2 | 11.9 |
| Norway . . . . . . . . | 7.6 | 15.3 | 60.7 | 96.7 | China . . . . . . . . . | 24.0 | 30.0 | 35.4 | 35.0 |
| United Kingdom. . . . | 4.0 | 4.1 | 19.2 | 19.2 | India . . . . . . . . . | 6.1 | 6.1 | 25.8 | 25.8 |
| Other . . . . . . . . . | 1.1 | 1.0 | 7.6 | 7.1 | Indonesia . . . . . . . | 6.6 | 11.8 | 64.8 | 104.3 |
| Eastern Europe and | | | | | Malaysia . . . . . . . | 3.0 | 3.6 | 59.1 | 59.1 |
| Former U.S.S.R. . . | 58.5 | 61.8 | 1,763.5 | 1,871.3 | New Zealand . . . . | 0.2 | 0.2 | 3.4 | 3.4 |
| Former U.S.S.R. . . | 57.0 | 59.9 | 1,750.0 | 1,853.4 | Pakistan . . . . . . . | 0.2 | 0.4 | 22.6 | 26.7 |
| Other[1] . . . . . . . . | 1.5 | 1.9 | 13.5 | 17.9 | Thailand . . . . . . . | 0.3 | 0.3 | 13.6 | 14.7 |
| Middle East. . . . . . | 661.6 | 596.6 | 1,319.1 | 1,344.9 | Other . . . . . . . . . | 0.9 | 0.8 | 48.3 | 33.0 |
| Bahrain . . . . . . . . | 0.1 | 0.1 | 6.0 | 5.9 | World . . . . . . . . . | 989.4 | 967.1 | 4,375.8 | 4,675.9 |

(1) Albania, Bulgaria, Czechoslovakia, Hungary, Poland, and Romania. **Notes:** Data for Kuwait and Saudi Arabia include one-half of the reserves in the Neutral Zone between Kuwait and Saudi Arabia. All reserve figures except those for the former U.S.S.R. and natural gas reserves in Canada are proved reserves recoverable with present technology and prices. Former U.S.S.R. figures are "explored reserves," which include proved, probable, and some possible. The Canadian natural gas figure includes proved and some probable. The latest Energy Information Administration data for the United States are for December 31, 1991. Sum of components may not equal total due to rounding.

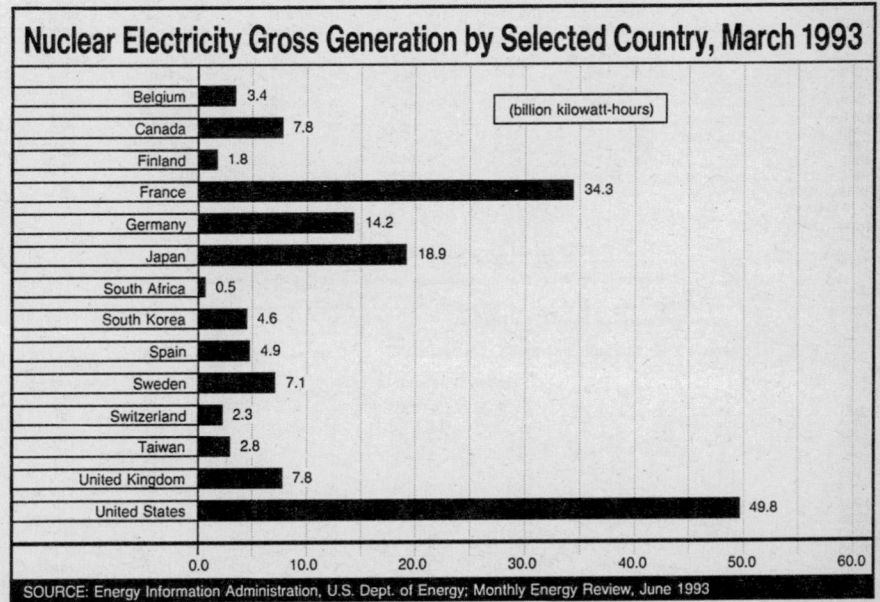

# Nuclear Electricity Gross Generation by Selected Country, March 1993

(billion kilowatt-hours)

| Country | |
|---|---|
| Belgium | 3.4 |
| Canada | 7.8 |
| Finland | 1.8 |
| France | 34.3 |
| Germany | 14.2 |
| Japan | 18.9 |
| South Africa | 0.5 |
| South Korea | 4.6 |
| Spain | 4.9 |
| Sweden | 7.1 |
| Switzerland | 2.3 |
| Taiwan | 2.8 |
| United Kingdom | 7.8 |
| United States | 49.8 |

## World Nuclear Power

Source: International Atomic Energy Agency, Dec. 31, 1992

| Country | Reactors in Operation No. of Units | Reactors in Operation Total MW(e)[1] | Reactors under Construction No. of Units | Reactors under Construction Total MW(e)[1] | Nuclear Electricity Supplied in 1992 TW(e).h | Nuclear Electricity Supplied in 1992 % of Total | Total Operating Experience to 31 December 1992 Years | Total Operating Experience to 31 December 1992 Months |
|---|---|---|---|---|---|---|---|---|
| Argentina | 2 | 935 | 1 | 692 | 6.6 | 14.4 | 28 | 7 |
| Belgium | 7 | 5,484 | — | — | 40.9 | 59.9 | 114 | 7 |
| Brazil | 1 | 626 | 1 | 1,245 | 1.8 | 0.7 | 10 | 9 |
| Bulgaria | 6 | 3,538 | — | — | 11.6 | 32.5 | 65 | 6 |
| Canada | 21 | 14,874 | 1 | 881 | 76.0 | 15.2 | 283 | 2 |
| China | 1 | 288 | 2 | 1,812 | 0.5 | 0.1 | 1 | 1 |
| Cuba | — | — | 2 | 816 | — | — | — | — |
| Czechoslovakia | 4 | 1,632 | 2 | 1,784 | 12.3 | 20.7 | 26 | 8 |
| Finland | 4 | 2,310 | — | — | 18.2 | 33.2 | 55 | 4 |
| France | 56 | 57,688 | 5 | 7,125 | 321.7 | 72.9 | 709 | 10 |
| Germany | 21 | 22,559 | — | — | 150.0 | 30.1 | 448 | 0 |
| Hungary | 4 | 1,729 | — | — | 13.1 | 48.4 | 30 | 2 |
| India | 9 | 1,593 | 5 | 1,010 | 5.6 | 3.3 | 101 | 3 |
| Iran | — | — | 2 | 2,392 | — | — | — | — |
| Italy | — | — | — | — | — | — | 81 | 0 |
| Japan | 44 | 34,238 | 9 | 8,129 | 217.0 | 27.7 | 556 | 11 |
| Kazakhstan | 1 | 135 | — | — | 0.5 | 0.6 | 19 | 6 |
| Korea, South | 9 | 7,220 | 3 | 2,550 | 58.5 | 43.2 | 72 | 1 |
| Lithuania | 2 | 2,760 | 1 | 1,380 | 15.6* | 80.0* | 14 | 6 |
| Mexico | 1 | 654 | 1 | 654 | 3.0 | 3.2 | 3 | 4 |
| Netherlands | 2 | 504 | — | — | 3.8 | 4.9 | 43 | 9 |
| Pakistan | 1 | 125 | — | — | 0.5 | 1.2 | 21 | 3 |
| Romania | — | — | 5 | 3,155 | — | — | — | — |
| Russia | 28 | 18,893 | 18 | 14,175 | 119.6 | 11.8 | 439 | 9 |
| S. Africa | 2 | 1,842 | — | — | 9.3 | 6.0 | 16 | 2 |
| Spain | 9 | 7,101 | — | — | 53.4 | 36.4 | 119 | 8 |
| Sweden | 12 | 10,002 | — | — | 60.8 | 43.2 | 183 | 2 |
| Switzerland | 5 | 2,952 | — | — | 22.1 | 39.6 | 88 | 10 |
| Ukraine | 15 | 13,020 | 6 | 5,700 | 71.0* | 25.0* | 128 | 11 |
| United Kingdom | 37 | 12,066 | 1 | 1,188 | 69.1 | 23.2 | 962 | 10 |
| United States | 109 | 98,729 | 3 | 3,480 | 618.8 | 22.3 | 1,702 | 4 |
| Total[2] | 424 | 330,651 | 72 | 59,720 | 2,027.4 | — | 6,479 | 9 |

(1) 1 terawatt-hour (TW(e).h) = $10^6$ megawatt-hour (MW(e).h). For an average power plant, 1 TW(e).h = 0.39 megatonnes of coal equivalent (input) and 0.23 megatonnes of oil equivalent (input). (2) Includes Taiwan data. * IAEA estimate.

## U.S. Nuclear Power Plant Operations

Source: Energy Information Administration, *Monthly Energy Review*, June 1993

| | Operable Reactors Number | Nuclear-Based Electricity Generation Million Net Kilowatthours | Nuclear Portion of Domestic Electricity Generation Percent | | Operable Reactors Number | Nuclear-Based Electricity Generation Million Net Kilowatthours | Nuclear Portion of Domestic Electricity Generation Percent |
|---|---|---|---|---|---|---|---|
| 1976 | 61 | 191,104 | 9.4 | 1985 | 95 | 383,691 | 15.5 |
| 1977 | 65 | 250,883 | 11.8 | 1986 | 100 | 414,038 | 16.6 |
| 1978 | 70 | 276,403 | 12.5 | 1987 | 107 | 455,270 | 17.7 |
| 1979 | 68 | 255,155 | 11.4 | 1988 | 108 | 526,973 | 19.5 |
| 1980 | 70 | 251,116 | 11.0 | 1989 | 110 | 529,355 | 19.0 |
| 1981 | 74 | 272,674 | 11.9 | 1990 | 111 | 576,862R | 20.5R |
| 1982 | 77 | 282,773 | 12.6 | 1991 | 111 | 612,565R | 21.7 |
| 1983 | 80 | 293,677 | 12.7 | 1992 | 109 | 618,776 | 22.1 |
| 1984 | 86 | 327,634 | 13.6 | | | | |

R = Revised

## Status of U.S. Nuclear Reactor Units

Source: Energy Information Administration, *Monthly Energy Review*, June 1993

| | Licensed for Operation Operable | Licensed for Operation In Startup | Construction Permits Granted | Construction Permits Pending | On Order | Announced | Total | Total Design Capacity Million Net Kilowatts |
|---|---|---|---|---|---|---|---|---|
| | | | | Number of Reactor Units | | | | |
| 1980 | 70 | 2 | 82 | 12 | 3 | 0 | 169 | 163 |
| 1981 | 74 | 0 | 75 | 11 | 3 | 0 | 163 | 157 |
| 1982 | 77 | 2 | 60 | 3 | 2 | 0 | 144 | 135 |
| 1983 | 80 | 3 | 53 | 0 | 2 | 0 | 138 | 129 |
| 1984 | 86 | 6 | 38 | 0 | 2 | 0 | 132 | 123 |
| 1985 | 95 | 3 | 30 | 0 | 2 | 0 | 130 | 121 |
| 1986 | 100 | 7 | 19 | 0 | 2 | 0 | 128 | 119 |
| 1987 | 107 | 4 | 14 | 0 | 2 | 0 | 127 | 119 |
| 1988 | 108 | 3 | 12 | 0 | 0 | 0 | 123 | 115 |
| 1989 | 110 | 1 | 10 | 0 | 0 | 0 | 121 | 113 |
| 1990 | 111 | 0 | 8R | 0 | 0 | 0 | 119R | 111R |
| 1991 | 111 | 0 | 8 | 0 | 0 | 0 | 119 | 111 |
| 1992 | 109 | 0 | 8 | 0 | 0 | 0 | 117 | 111 |

R = Revised

# SCIENCE AND TECHNOLOGY
## Computer Glossary

Source: *Electronic Computer Glossary* by Alan Freedman, The Computer Language Co. Inc., 1992

**access:** to store data on and retrieve data from a disk or other device connected to the computer.

**analog:** of or relating to the representation of an object that resembles the original. For example, the telephone system converts sound waves into electrical impulses.

**arithmetic logic unit (ALU):** a part of the *central processing unit (CPU)* that performs arithmetic operations and logical comparisons.

**artificial intelligence (AI):** a broad range of computer applications that resemble human intelligence and behavior, such as understanding speech, making judgments, and learning.

**ASCII:** an acronym for American Standard Code for Information Interchange; a widely-used binary code for storing data, often used to transfer data from one system to an incompatible system.

**assembly language:** a low-level, machine-oriented language, specific to a CPU, using mnemonics to represent each machine-language instruction.

**authorization code:** an identification number or password used to gain access to a computer system.

**back up:** to make a copy of important data to be used if the current file is destroyed.

**BASIC:** an acronym for Beginner's All-purpose Symbolic Instruction Code; a computer language used by many small and personal computer systems.

**baud rate:** the number of changes in an electrical line per second. Often used as measurement of printer or modem speed.

**binary code:** a representation of the base-2 number system in which the only allowable digits are 0 and 1.

**bit:** short for binary digit; a single binary digit (0 or 1) or the smallest unit of information stored in a computer, such as a memory cell.

**board:** short for printed circuit board; a flat board that holds chips and other electronic components connected by electronically conductive pathways.

**boot:** to start the computer.

**buffer:** a temporary place to put information for processing when it is being transferred between devices.

**bug:** a mistake that occurs in a program within a computer or in the unit's electrical system.

**bus:** a common channel, or pathway, between hardware devices.

**byte:** an 8-bit sequence of binary digits. Each byte corresponds to 1 character of data, representing a single letter, number, or symbol.

**C:** a high-level programming language often used to write commercial products due to its transportability to many different computer systems.

**C++:** an object-oriented version of C.

**cache:** a memory unit between the main memory and the CPU that accelerates retrieval of data.

**CAD/CAM:** abbreviation for computer-aided design/computer-aided manufacturing.

**cathode ray tube (CRT):** a vacuum tube used as a display screen in a terminal or TV. Term usually used to refer to the entire terminal.

**CD-ROM:** an acronym for Compact Disk-Read Only Memory; general term applied to a variety of storage formats by which audio, text, and graphics are retrieved by a laser beam that scans tracks of microscopic holes in a rotating compact disk. The disk can store over 600 million characters, but the user cannot store new information or alter the existing information.

**central processing unit (CPU):** the part within the computer that interprets and executes the instructions the user gives the system. It is composed of an arithmetic logic unit, a control unit, and some memory.

**chip:** short for integrated circuit chip, a collection of interconnected microminiature electronic components.

**COBOL:** an acronym for Common Business Oriented Language; widely used programming language.

**code:** a set of machine symbols that represents data or instructions; also to write a program.

**computer:** a programmable machine that accepts, processes, and displays data.

**connect time:** the time a user at a workstation is logged-on to a computer system.

**cursor:** the movable symbol on the computer monitor that marks the place where the operator is working.

**cybernetics:** the comparative study of human and machine processes in order to understand the similarities and differences.

**database:** a large amount of data stored in a well-organized format and managed by a program that allows access to the information.

**Data Encryption Standard (DES):** the U.S. National Institute of Standards and Technology system for encryption of commercial data.

**data glove:** a glove used to report the position of a user's hand in *virtual reality* systems.

**debug:** to eliminate a mistake within a computer program or in the unit's electrical system.

**desktop publishing:** the use of a personal computer to produce high-quality output (camera-ready hard copy or digital files) ready for commercial printing.

**digital:** of or relating to the representation, manipulation, or transmission of data by discrete signals.

**disk:** a revolving magnetized plate on which information and programs are stored. See also *floppy disk*.

**disk drive:** a peripheral machine that rotates a storage disk in order to read or record information.

**DOS:** stands for disk operating system; a single-user operating system used on IBM-compatible PCs.

**download:** to transmit data from a central to a remote computer, from a file server to a workstation, or from a computer to a floppy disk.

**dump:** a printout of the contents of memory or a file.

**electronic mail:** transmission of memos and messages over a *network*. Also called e-mail.

**encryption:** the encoding of data for security purposes.

**field:** the physical unit of data in a record.

**file:** any collection data treated as a single unit.

**file server:** a computer that stores data and programs that are shared by many users in a network.

**floppy disk:** a small, inexpensive removable disk used to record and store information.

**font:** a set of type characters of a particular design.

**format:** the arrangement by which data are stored or displayed.

**FORTRAN:** an acronym for Formula Translator; a high-level computer language widely used for scientific, engineering, or mathematical purposes.

**global memory:** the shared central memory of a multiple-processor system.

**groupware:** interactive software designed for several users working together on one project.

**hard copy:** printed computer output.

**hard disk:** a metal disk covered with a magnetic recording surface. Hard disks are often installed inside PCs for increased storage capacity.

**hardware:** the physical apparatus that makes up a computer: chips, transformers, boards, and wires. Also used to describe various pieces of equipment including the CPU, printer, modem, and CRT.

**hexadecimal:** refers to the base-16 number system, which is used to condense binary-based codes, such as bytes, for more efficient computer processing.

**integrated circuit (IC):** the formal name for a *chip*.

**interface:** a connection and interaction between hardware, software, and the user.

**Internet:** a network of computer networks involving millions of scientists and other users.

**joystick:** a hand-held lever that can be tilted in different directions to control the movement of the cursor on the terminal screen.

**K:** abbreviation for kilobyte, used to denote 1,024 units of stored matter.

**keyboard:** a set of input keys; also used as a verb meaning to type data into a computer for processing.

**language:** any set of related commands or instructions that are understandable to a computer.

**light pen:** an input device in which directions are given to the computer by touching the terminal screen with a light-sensitive stylus.

**load:** the actual operation of putting information and data into the computer or memory.

**local area network (LAN):** a computer system that links computers, printers, and other peripheral devices in a network for transmitting data between users situated near one another.

**machine language:** a set of binary-code instructions capable of being directly understood by a computer.

**machine readable:** any paper form or storage medium that can be automatically read by the computer.

**mainframe computer:** the largest type of computer, usually capable of processing data quickly and able to serve many users simultaneously.

**memory:** the computer's internal storage capacity.

**menu:** programs, functions, or other choices displayed on the monitor for user selection.

**microcomputer:** a computer that uses a microprocessor for its CPU. Personal computers are microcomputers.

**microprocessor:** a complete CPU on a single chip.

**minicomputer:** an intermediate computer system sized between the very small microcomputer and the large mainframe computer.

**modem:** an acronym for modulator-demodulator; a device that enables data to be transmitted between computers, generally over telephone lines, but sometimes via fiber-optic cable or wireless radio frequency.

**monitor:** a high-resolution screen used to display the output of a computer.

**mouse:** a hand-held object that when rolled across a flat surface is used as an input device.

**multitasking:** the ability to run more than one program on one computer at the same time.

**network:** in communications, terminals and computers linked together with the ability to interact with each other. In database management, a database design.

**nibble:** half a byte, or four bits.

**noise:** extraneous, random disturbances that degrade or disrupt data communications.

**object-oriented programming:** a programming method with formalized rules for developing self-contained software routines that can be reused in other program applications, allowing greater programming flexibility.

**on-line:** immediately accessible by a computer's CPU.

**operating system:** a master control program that runs the computer and acts as a scheduler and traffic cop.

**optical character reader (OCR):** a device capable of recognizing characters in a special typeface.

**optical fiber:** an ultrathin strand of glass with the ability to carry billions of bits of encoded data per second when pulses of laser light are beamed through it.

**optoelectronics:** a technology that joins light and electricity. OCRs, laser printers, and CD-ROMs are examples of optoelectronic devices.

**Pascal:** a popular high-level programming language.

**PC:** an abbreviation for personal computer; a microcomputer that serves one user.

**peripheral:** any hardware device connected to a computer, such as keyboards, printers, or joy sticks.

**pixel:** an acronym for picture element; the smallest display element on a video display screen.

**printer:** a device that converts computer output into printed images.

**program:** a sequence of detailed, coded instructions telling a computer how to perform a specific function.

**RAM:** an abbreviation for Random Access Memory; same as *memory*. Contents of RAM may be retrieved and altered by the user.

**random access:** the ability to retrieve records in a file directly without reading any previous records.

**record:** a group of related fields that are used to store data about a subject.

**ROM:** an abbreviation for Read Only Memory; a permanent memory.

**sector:** a defined portion of concentric track on a disk.

**software:** the programs, or sets of instructions, that tell the computer what to do.

**supercomputer:** a term applied to the fastest, most powerful computers at a given time; typically used to manipulate large amounts of data.

**telecommuting:** working at home and communicating via computer with the office.

**teleconferencing:** to communicate with a number of people simultaneously via telephone lines with audio, video, or computer connections.

**terminal:** a keyboard and display unit (usually a CRT) that allows a person to communicate with a computer.

**timesharing:** the simultaneous use of a computer by more than one person, as in a *local area network*.

**track:** a concentric band on a magnetic disk that contains a specified amount of data.

**user-friendly:** easy to learn and use.

**UNIX:** a multi-user operating system that runs on a wide variety of computers.

**virtual memory:** the use of hard disk storage to expand effective memory capability.

**virtual reality:** interaction with a computer to create an artificial reality that projects the user into a 3-dimensional space.

**virus:** a destructive program that is secretly attached to an existing program, once run it alters or deletes data, or causes other computer system malfunctions, whenever the preexisting program is run.

**window:** a separate viewing area on a display screen.

**word:** a computer's basic storage unit; a sequence of bits—8 to 32—occupying a single storage location and processed as a unit by the computer.

**word processor:** a text creation and editing program or system that allows electronic writing and correcting of documents.

**workstation:** a high-performance, single-user microcomputer or minicomputer; or in a *local area network*, a PC that serves a single user.

**worm:** a destructive program that reproduces itself and deletes data from a computer's memory.

**write-access:** authorization to record or alter data stored in a computer.

## The Internet

The Internet links people together via computer terminals and telephone lines (and in some cases wireless radio connections) in a web of networks and shared software, allowing users in one area to reach other users anywhere in the "net." Among the services available through the Internet are telnet, granting users access to more powerful computers; usenet newsgroups, allowing open discussion between users; archives with access to scientific and government research; and electronic mail. Originally created by the Pentagon, the Internet is now subsidized by the National Science Foundation, which controls the Internet's core computer network. It is thought that 15 million people in the U.S. and 25 million worldwide access the Internet regularly. Despite the increasing accessibility through some public libraries, computer bulletin boards, and software packages, the primary users remain government officials, scientists, and corporate researchers.

## Inventions and Discoveries

| Invention | Date | Inventor | Nation. |
|---|---|---|---|
| Adding machine | 1642 | Pascal | French |
| Adding machine | 1885 | Burroughs | U.S. |
| Aerosol spray | 1926 | Rotheim | Norwegian |
| Air brake | 1868 | Westinghouse | U.S. |
| Air conditioning | 1911 | Carrier | U.S. |
| Air pump | 1654 | Guericke | German |
| Airplane, automatic pilot | 1912 | Sperry | U.S. |
| Airplane, experimental | 1896 | Langley | U.S. |
| Airplane jet engine | 1939 | Ohain | German |
| Airplane with motor | 1903 | Wright bros. | U.S. |
| Airplane, hydro. | 1911 | Curtiss | U.S. |
| Airship | 1852 | Giffard | French |
| Airship, rigid dirigible | 1900 | Zeppelin | German |
| Arc welder | 1919 | Thomson | U.S. |
| Aspartame | 1965 | Schlatter | U.S. |
| Autogyro | 1920 | de la Cierva | Spanish |
| Automobile, differential gear | 1885 | Benz | German |
| Automobile, electric | 1892 | Morrison | U.S. |
| Automobile, exp'mtl | 1864 | Marcus | Austrian |
| Automobile, gasoline | 1889 | Daimler | German |
| Automobile, gasoline | 1892 | Duryea | U.S. |
| Automobile magneto | 1897 | Bosch | German |
| Automobile muffler | ... | Maxim, H.P. | U.S. |
| Automobile self-starter | 1911 | Kettering | U.S. |
| Babbitt metal | 1839 | Babbitt | U.S. |
| Bakelite | 1907 | Baekeland | Belg., U.S. |
| Balloon | 1783 | Montgolfier | French |
| Barometer | 1643 | Torricelli | Italian |
| Bicycle, modern | 1885 | Starley | English |
| Bifocal lens | 1780 | Franklin | U.S. |
| Block signals, railway | 1867 | Hall | U.S. |
| Bomb, depth | 1916 | Tait | U.S. |
| Bottle machine | 1895 | Owens | U.S. |
| Braille printing | 1829 | Braille | French |
| Burner, gas | 1855 | Bunsen | German |
| Calculating machine | 1833 | Babbage | English |
| Calculator, electronic pocket | 1972 | Merryman, Van Tassel | U.S. |
| Camera, Kodak | 1888 | Eastman, Walker | U.S. |
| Camera, Polaroid Land | 1948 | Land | U.S. |
| Car coupler | 1873 | Janney | U.S. |
| Carburetor, gasoline | 1893 | Maybach | German |
| Card time recorder | 1894 | Cooper | U.S. |
| Carding machine | 1797 | Whittemore | U.S. |
| Carpet sweeper | 1876 | Bissell | U.S. |
| Cassette, audio | 1963 | Philips Co. | Dutch |
| Cassette, videotape | 1969 | Sony | Japanese |
| Cash register | 1879 | Ritty | U.S. |
| Cathode ray oscilloscope | 1897 | Braun | German |
| Cathode ray tube | 1878 | Crookes | English |
| CAT, or CT, scan (computerized tomography) | 1973 | Hounsfield | English |
| Cellophane | 1908 | Brandenberger | Swiss |
| Celluloid | 1870 | Hyatt | U.S. |
| Cement, Portland | 1824 | Aspdin | English |
| Chronometer | 1761 | Harrison | English |
| Circuit breaker | 1925 | Hilliard | U.S. |
| Circuit, integrated | 1959 | Kilby, Noyce, Texas Instr. | U.S. |
| Clock, pendulum | 1657 | Huygens | Dutch |
| Coaxial cable system | 1929 | Affel, Espensched | U.S. |
| Coke oven | 1893 | Hoffman | Austrian |
| Compressed air rock drill | 1871 | Ingersoll | U.S. |
| Comptometer | 1887 | Felt | U.S. |
| Computer, automatic sequence | 1944 | Aiken, et al. | U.S. |
| Computer, mini. | 1960 | Digital Corp. | U.S. |
| Condenser microphone (telephone) | 1916 | Wente | U.S. |
| Contraceptive, oral | 1954 | Pincus, Rock | U.S. |
| Corn, hybrid | 1917 | Jones | U.S. |

| Invention | Date | Inventor | Nation. |
|---|---|---|---|
| Cotton gin | 1793 | Whitney | U.S. |
| Cream separator | 1878 | DeLaval | Swedish |
| Cultivator, disc | 1878 | Mallon | U.S. |
| Cystoscope | 1878 | Nitze | German |
| Diesel engine | 1895 | Diesel | German |
| Disk, compact | 1972 | RCA | U.S. |
| Disk, floppy | 1970 | IBM | U.S. |
| Disk player, compact | 1979 | Sony, Philips Co. | Japan., Dutch |
| Disk, video | 1972 | Philips Co. | Dutch |
| Dynamite | 1866 | Nobel | Swedish |
| Dynamo, continuous current | 1871 | Gramme | Belgian |
| Dynamo, hydrogen cooled | 1915 | Schuler | U.S. |
| Electric battery | 1800 | Volta | Italian |
| Electric fan | 1882 | Wheeler | U.S. |
| Electrocardiograph | 1903 | Einthoven | Dutch |
| Electroencephalograph | 1929 | Berger | German |
| Electromagnet | 1824 | Sturgeon | English |
| Electron spectrometer | 1944 | Deutsch, Elliott, Evans | U.S. |
| Electron tube multigrid | 1913 | Langmuir | U.S. |
| Electroplating | 1805 | Brugnatelli | Italian |
| Electrostatic generator | 1929 | Van de Graaff | U.S. |
| Elevator brake | 1852 | Otis | U.S. |
| Elevator, push button | 1922 | Larson | U.S. |
| Engine, automatic transmission | 1910 | Fottinger | German |
| Engine, coal-gas 4-cycle | 1876 | Otto | German |
| Engine, compression ignition | 1883 | Daimler | German |
| Engine, electric ignition | 1883 | Benz | German |
| Engine, gas, compound | 1926 | Eickemeyer | U.S. |
| Engine, gasoline | 1872 | Brayton, Geo. | U.S. |
| Engine, gasoline | 1889 | Daimler | German |
| Engine, jet | 1930 | Whittle | English |
| Engine, steam, piston | 1705 | Newcomen | English |
| Engine, steam, piston | 1769 | Watt | Scottish |
| Engraving, half-tone | 1852 | Talbot | U.S. |
| Fiberglass | 1938 | Owens-Corning | U.S. |
| Fiber optics | 1955 | Kapany | English |
| Filament, tungsten | 1913 | Coolidge | U.S. |
| Flanged rail | 1831 | Stevens | U.S. |
| Flatiron, electric | 1882 | Seely | U.S. |
| Food, frozen | 1924 | Birdseye | U.S. |
| Freon (low-boiling fluorine compounds) | 1930 | Midgley, et al. | U.S. |
| Furnace (for steel) | 1858 | Siemens | German |
| Galvanometer | 1820 | Sweigger | German |
| Gas discharge tube | 1922 | Hull | U.S. |
| Gas lighting | 1792 | Murdoch | Scottish |
| Gas mantle | 1885 | Welsbach | Austrian |
| Gasoline (lead ethyl) | 1922 | Midgley | U.S. |
| Gasoline, cracked | 1913 | Burton | U.S. |
| Gasoline, high octane | 1930 | Ipatieff | Russian |
| Geiger counter | 1913 | Geiger | German |
| Glass, laminated safety | 1909 | Benedictus | French |
| Glider | 1853 | Cayley | English |
| Gun, breechloader | 1811 | Thornton | U.S. |
| Gun, Browning | 1897 | Browning | U.S. |
| Gun, magazine | 1875 | Hotchkiss | U.S. |
| Gun, silencer | 1908 | Maxim, H.P. | U.S. |
| Guncotton | 1847 | Schoenbein | German |
| Gyrocompass | 1911 | Sperry | U.S. |
| Gyroscope | 1852 | Foucault | French |
| Harvester-thresher | 1818 | Lane | U.S. |
| Heart, artificial | 1982 | Jarvik | U.S. |
| Helicopter | 1939 | Sikorsky | U.S. |
| Hydrometer | 1768 | Baume | French |

(continued)

| Invention | Date | Inventor | Nation. |
|---|---|---|---|
| Hydrogen bomb | 1952 | U.S. government scientists | U.S. |
| Ice-making machine | 1851 | Gorrie | U.S. |
| Iron lung | 1928 | Drinker, Slaw. | U.S. |
| Kaleidoscope | 1817 | Brewster | Scottish |
| Kinetoscope | 1889 | Edison | U.S. |
| Lacquer, nitrocellulose | 1921 | Flaherty | U.S. |
| Lamp, arc | 1847 | Staite | English |
| Lamp, flourescent | 1938 | General Electric, Westinghouse | U.S. |
| Lamp, incandescent | 1879 | Edison | U.S. |
| Lamp, incand., frosted | 1924 | Pipkin | U.S. |
| Lamp, incand., gas. | 1913 | Langmuir | U.S. |
| Lamp, Klieg | 1911 | Kliegl, A.&J. | U.S. |
| Lamp, mercury vapor | 1912 | Hewitt | U.S. |
| Lamp, miner's safety | 1816 | Davy | English |
| Lamp, neon | 1909 | Claude | French |
| Lathe, turret | 1845 | Fitch | U.S. |
| Launderette | 1934 | Cantrell | U.S. |
| Lens, achromatic | 1758 | Dollond | English |
| Lens, fused bifocal | 1908 | Borsch | U.S. |
| Leyden jar (condenser) | 1745 | von Kleist | German |
| Lightning rod | 1752 | Franklin | U.S. |
| Linoleum | 1860 | Walton | English |
| Linotype | 1884 | Mergenthaler | U.S. |
| Lock, cylinder | 1851 | Yale | U.S. |
| Locomotive, electric | 1851 | Vail | U.S. |
| Locomotive, exp'mtl | 1802 | Trevithick | English |
| Locomotive, exp'mtl | 1812 | Fenton et al. | English |
| Locomotive, exp'mtl | 1813 | Hedley | English |
| Locomotive, exp'mtl | 1814 | Stephenson | English |
| Locomotive practical | 1829 | Stephenson | English |
| Locomotive, 1st U.S. | 1830 | Cooper, P. | U.S. |
| Loom, power | 1785 | Cartwright | English |
| Loudspeaker, dynamic | 1924 | Rice, Kellogg | U.S. |
| Machine gun | 1861 | Gatling | U.S. |
| Machine gun, improved | 1872 | Hotchkiss | U.S. |
| Machine gun (Maxim) | 1883 | Maxim, H.S. | U.S., Eng. |
| Magnet, electro | 1828 | Henry | U.S. |
| Mantle, gas | 1885 | Welsbach | Austrian |
| Mason jar | 1858 | Mason, J. | U.S. |
| Match, friction | 1827 | John Walker | English |
| Mercerized textiles | 1843 | Mercer, J. | English |
| Meter, induction | 1888 | Shallenberg | U.S. |
| Metronome | 1816 | Malezel | German |
| Microcomputer | 1973 | Truong, et al. | French |
| Micrometer | 1636 | Gascoigne | English |
| Microphone | 1877 | Berliner | U.S. |
| Microprocessor | 1971 | Intel Corp. | U.S. |
| Microscope, compound | 1590 | Janssen | Dutch |
| Microscope, electronic | 1931 | Knoll, Ruska | German |
| Microscope, field ion. | 1951 | Mueller | German |
| Monitor, warship | 1861 | Ericsson | U.S. |
| Monotype | 1887 | Lanston | U.S. |
| Motor, AC | 1892 | Tesla | U.S. |
| Motor, DC | 1837 | Davenport | U.S. |
| Motor, induction | 1887 | Tesla | U.S. |
| Motorcycle | 1885 | Daimler | German |
| Movie machine | 1894 | Jenkins | U.S. |
| Movie, panoramic | 1952 | Waller | U.S. |
| Movie, talking | 1927 | Warner Bros. | U.S. |
| Mower, lawn | 1831 | Budding, Ferrabee | English |
| Mowing machine | 1822 | Bailey | U.S. |
| Neoprene | 1930 | Carothers | U.S. |
| Nylon synthetic | 1930 | Carothers | U.S. |
| Nylon | 1937 | Du Pont lab. | U.S. |
| Oil cracking furnace | 1891 | Gavrilov | Russian |
| Oil filled power cable | 1921 | Emanueli | Italian |
| Oleomargarine | 1869 | Mege-Mouries | French |
| Ophthalmoscope | 1851 | Helmholtz | German |
| Paper | 105 | Lun | Chinese |
| Paper machine | 1809 | Dickinson | U.S. |
| Parachute | 1785 | Blanchard | French |
| Pen, ballpoint | 1938 | Biro | Hungarian |
| Pen, fountain | 1884 | Waterman | U.S. |
| Pen, steel | 1780 | Harrison | English |
| Pendulum | 1583 | Galileo | Italian |
| Percussion cap | 1807 | Forsythe | Scottish |
| Phonograph | 1877 | Edison | U.S. |
| Photo, color | 1892 | Ives | U.S. |
| Photo film, celluloid | 1893 | Reichenbach | U.S. |
| Photo film, transparent | 1884 | Eastman, Goodwin | U.S. |
| Photoelectric cell | 1895 | Elster | German |
| Photographic paper | 1835 | Talbot | U.S. |
| Photography | 1835 | Talbot | English |

| Invention | Date | Inventor | Nation. |
|---|---|---|---|
| Photography | 1835 | Daguerre | French |
| Photography | 1816 | Niepce | French |
| Photophone | 1880 | Bell | U.S.-Scot. |
| Phototelegraphy | 1925 | Bell Labs | U.S. |
| Piano | 1709 | Cristofori | Italian |
| Piano, player | 1863 | Fourneaux | French |
| Pin, safety | 1849 | Hunt | U.S. |
| Pistol (revolver) | 1836 | Colt | U.S. |
| Plow, cast iron | 1785 | Ransome | English |
| Plow, disc | 1896 | Hardy | U.S. |
| Pneumatic hammer | 1890 | King | U.S. |
| Powder, smokeless | 1884 | Vieille | French |
| Printing press, rotary | 1845 | Hoe | U.S. |
| Printing press, web | 1865 | Bullock | U.S. |
| Propeller, screw | 1804 | Stevens | U.S. |
| Propeller, screw | 1837 | Ericsson | Swedish |
| Pulsars | 1967 | Bell | English |
| Punch card accounting | 1889 | Hollerith | U.S. |
| Quasars | 1963 | Schmidt | U.S. |
| Radar | 1940 | Watson-Watt | Scottish |
| Radio amplifier | 1906 | De Forest | U.S. |
| Radio beacon | 1928 | Donovan | U.S. |
| Radio crystal oscillator | 1918 | Nicolson | U.S. |
| Radio receiver, cascade tuning | 1913 | Alexanderson | U.S. |
| Radio receiver, heterodyne | 1913 | Fessenden | U.S. |
| Radio transmitter triode modulation | 1914 | Alexanderson | U.S. |
| Radio tube-diode | 1905 | Fleming | English |
| Radio tube oscillator | 1915 | De Forest | U.S. |
| Radio tube triode | 1906 | De Forest | U.S. |
| Radio, signals | 1895 | Marconi | Italian |
| Radio, magnetic detector | 1902 | Marconi | Italian |
| Radio FM 2-path | 1933 | Armstrong | U.S. |
| Rayon (acetate) | 1895 | Cross | English |
| Rayon (cuprammonium) | 1890 | Despeissis | French |
| Rayon (nitrocellulose) | 1884 | Chardonnet | French |
| Razor, electric | 1917 | Schick | U.S. |
| Razor, safety | 1895 | Gillette | U.S. |
| Reaper | 1834 | McCormick | U.S. |
| Record, cylinder | 1887 | Bell, Tainter | U.S. |
| Record, disc | 1887 | Berliner | U.S. |
| Record, long playing | 1947 | Goldmark | U.S. |
| Record, wax cylinder | 1888 | Edison | U.S. |
| Refrigerator car | 1868 | David | U.S. |
| Resin, synthetic | 1931 | Hill | English |
| Richter scale | 1935 | Richter | U.S. |
| Rifle, repeating | 1860 | Spencer | U.S. |
| Rocket engine | 1926 | Goddard | U.S. |
| Rubber, vulcanized | 1839 | Goodyear | U.S. |
| Saccharin | 1879 | Remsen, Fahlberg | U.S. |
| Saw, band | 1808 | Newberry | English |
| Saw, circular | 1777 | Miller | English |
| Sewing machine | 1846 | Howe | U.S. |
| Shoe-sewing machine | 1860 | McKay | U.S. |
| Shrapnel shell | 1784 | Shrapnel | English |
| Shuttle, flying | 1733 | Kay | English |
| Sleeping-car | 1865 | Pullman | U.S. |
| Slide rule | 1620 | Oughtred | English |
| Soap, hardwater | 1928 | Bertsch | German |
| Spectroscope | 1859 | Kirchoff, Bunsen | German |
| Spectroscope (mass) | 1918 | Dempster | U.S. |
| Spinning jenny | 1767 | Hargreaves | English |
| Spinning mule | 1779 | Crompton | English |
| Steamboat, exp'mtl | 1778 | Jouffroy | French |
| Steamboat, exp'mtl | 1785 | Fitch | U.S. |
| Steamboat, exp'mtl | 1787 | Rumsey | U.S. |
| Steamboat, exp'mtl | 1788 | Miller | Scottish |
| Steamboat, exp'mtl | 1803 | Fulton | U.S. |
| Steamboat, exp'mtl | 1804 | Stevens | U.S. |
| Steamboat, practical | 1802 | Symington | Scottish |
| Steamboat, practical | 1807 | Fulton | U.S. |
| Steam car | 1770 | Cugnot | French |
| Steam turbine | 1884 | Parsons | English |
| Steel (converter) | 1856 | Bessemer | English |
| Steel alloy | 1891 | Harvey | U.S. |
| Steel alloy, high-speed | 1901 | Taylor, White | U.S. |
| Steel, electric | 1900 | Heroult | French |
| Steel, manganese | 1884 | Hadfield | English |
| Steel, stainless | 1916 | Brearley | English |
| Stereoscope | 1838 | Wheatstone | English |
| Stethoscope | 1819 | Laennec | French |
| Stethoscope, binaural | 1840 | Cammann | U.S. |
| Stock ticker | 1870 | Edison | U.S. |
| Storage battery, rechargeable | 1859 | Plante | French |
| Stove, electric | 1896 | Hadaway | U.S. |
| Submarine | 1891 | Holland | U.S. |
| Submarine, even keel | 1894 | Lake | U.S. |
| Submarine, torpedo | 1776 | Bushnell | U.S. |

(continued )

| Invention | Date | Inventor | Nation. |
|---|---|---|---|
| Superconductivity (BCS | | Bardeen, Cooper, | |
| theory) | 1957 | Schreiffer | U.S. |
| | | | |
| Tank, military | 1914 | Swinton | English |
| Tape recorder, magnetic | 1899 | Poulsen | Danish |
| Teflon | 1938 | Du Pont | U.S. |
| Telegraph, magnetic | 1837 | Morse | U.S. |
| Telegraph, quadruplex | 1864 | Edison | U.S. |
| Telegraph, railroad | 1887 | Woods | U.S. |
| Telegraph, wireless | | | |
| high frequency | 1895 | Marconi | Italian |
| Telephone | 1876 | Bell | U.S.-Scot. |
| Telephone amplifier | 1912 | De Forest | U.S. |
| Telephone, automatic | 1891 | Stowger | U.S. |
| Telephone, radio | 1900 | Poulsen, | |
| | | Fessenden | Danish |
| Telephone, radio | 1906 | De Forest | U.S. |
| Telephone, radio, l. d. | 1915 | AT&T | U.S. |
| Telephone, recording | 1898 | Poulsen | Danish |
| Telephone, wireless | 1899 | Collins | U.S. |
| Telescope | 1608 | Lippershey | Neth. |
| Telescope | 1609 | Galileo | Italian |
| Telescope, astronomical | 1611 | Kepler | German |
| Teletype | 1928 | Morkrum, | |
| | | Kleinschmidt | U.S. |
| Television, iconoscope | 1923 | Zworykin | U.S. |
| Television, electronic | 1927 | Farnsworth | U.S. |
| Television, mech. | | | |
| scanner | 1923 | Baird | Scottish |
| Thermometer | 1593 | Galileo | Italian |
| Thermometer | 1730 | Reaumur | French |
| Thermometer, mercury | 1714 | Fahrenheit | German |
| Time recorder | 1890 | Bundy | U.S. |
| Time, self-regulator | 1918 | Bryce | U.S. |
| Tire, double-tube | 1845 | Thomson | Scottish |
| Tire, pneumatic | 1888 | Dunlop | Scottish |
| Toaster, automatic | 1918 | Strite | U.S. |

| Invention | Date | Inventor | Nation. |
|---|---|---|---|
| Tool, pneumatic | 1865 | Law | English |
| Torpedo, marine | 1804 | Fulton | U.S. |
| Tractor, crawler | 1904 | Holt | U.S. |
| Transformer AC. | 1885 | Stanley | U.S. |
| Transistor | 1947 | Shockley, | |
| | | Brattain, | |
| | | Bardeen | U.S. |
| Trolley car, electric | 1884 | Van DePoele, | |
| | -87 | Sprague | U.S. |
| Tungsten, ductile | 1912 | Coolidge | U.S. |
| Tupperware | 1945 | Tupper | U.S. |
| Turbine, gas | 1849 | Bourdin | French |
| Turbine, hydraulic | 1849 | Francis | U.S. |
| Turbine, steam | 1884 | Parsons | English |
| Type, movable | 1447 | Gutenberg | German |
| Typewriter | 1867 | Sholes, Soule, | |
| | | Glidden | U.S. |
| | | | |
| Vacuum cleaner, electric | 1907 | Spangler | U.S. |
| Velcro | 1948 | de Mestral | Swiss |
| Video game ("Pong") | 1972 | Buschnel | U.S. |
| Video home system (VHS) | 1975 | Matsushita, JVC | Japanese |
| | | | |
| Washer, electric | 1901 | Fisher | U.S. |
| Welding, atomic | | Langmuir, | |
| hydrogen | 1924 | Palmer | U.S. |
| Welding, electric | 1877 | Thomson | U.S. |
| Wind tunnel | 1912 | Eiffel. | French |
| Wire, barbed | 1874 | Glidden | U.S. |
| Wire, barbed | 1875 | Haisn | U.S. |
| Wrench, double-acting | 1913 | Owen | U.S. |
| | | | |
| X-ray tube | 1913 | Coolidge | U.S. |
| | | | |
| Zipper | 1891 | Judson | U.S. |

## Discoveries and Innovations: Chemistry, Physics, Biology, Medicine

| | Date | Discoverer | Nation. |
|---|---|---|---|
| Acetylene gas | 1862 | Berthelot | French |
| ACTH | 1927 | Evans, Long | U.S. |
| Adrenalin | 1901 | Takamine | Japanese |
| Aluminum, electro- | | | |
| lytic process | 1886 | Hall | U.S. |
| Aluminum, isolated | 1825 | Oersted | Danish |
| Anesthesia, ether | 1842 | Long | U.S. |
| Anesthesia, local | 1885 | Koller | Austrian |
| Anesthesia, spinal | 1898 | Bier | German |
| Aniline dye | 1856 | Perkin | English |
| Anti-rabies | 1885 | Pasteur | French |
| Antiseptic surgery | 1867 | Lister | English |
| Antitoxin, diphtheria | 1891 | Von Behring | German |
| Argyrol | 1897 | Bayer | German |
| Arsphenamine | 1910 | Ehrlich | German |
| Aspirin | 1889 | Dresser | German |
| Atabrine | ... | Mietzsch, et al. | German |
| Atomic numbers | 1913 | Moseley | English |
| Atomic theory | 1803 | Dalton | English |
| Atomic time clock | 1947 | Libby | U.S. |
| Atom-smashing | | | |
| theory | 1919 | Rutherford | English |
| | | | |
| Bacitracin | 1945 | Johnson, et al. | U.S. |
| Bacteria (described) | 1676 | Leeuwenhoek | Dutch |
| Barbital | 1903 | Fischer | German |
| Bleaching powder | 1798 | Tennant | English |
| Blood, circulation | 1628 | Harvey | English |
| Bordeaux mixture | 1885 | Millardet | French |
| Bromine from sea | 1924 | Edgar Kramer | U.S. |
| | | | |
| Calcium carbide | 1888 | Wilson | U.S. |
| Calculus | 1670 | Newton | English |
| Camphor synthetic | 1896 | Haller | French |
| Canning (food) | 1804 | Appert | French |
| Carbomycin | 1952 | Tanner | U.S. |
| Carbon oxides | 1925 | Fisher | German |
| Chloamphenicol | 1947 | Burkholder | U.S. |
| Chlorine | 1774 | Scheele | Swedish |
| Chloroform | 1831 | Guthrie, S. | U.S. |
| Chlortetracycline | 1948 | Duggen | U.S. |
| Classification of | | | |
| plants and animals | 1735 | Linnaeus | Swedish |
| Cocaine | 1860 | Niermann | German |
| Combustion explained | 1777 | Lavoisier | French |
| Conditioned reflex | 1914 | Pavlov | Russian |
| Cortisone | 1936 | Kendall | U.S. |
| Cortisone, synthesis | 1946 | Sarett | U.S. |
| Cosmic rays | 1910 | Gockel | Swiss |
| Cyanamide | 1905 | Frank, Caro. | German |
| Cyclotron | 1930 | Lawrence | U.S. |
| | | | |
| DDT | 1874 | Zeidler | German |
| (not applied as insecticide until 1939) | | | |

| | Date | Discoverer | Nation. |
|---|---|---|---|
| Deuterium | 1932 | Urey, Brickwedde, | |
| | | Murphy | U.S. |
| DNA (structure) | 1951 | Crick | English |
| | | Watson | U.S. |
| | | Wilkins | English |
| Electric resistance | | | |
| (law) | 1827 | Ohm | German |
| Electric waves | 1888 | Hertz | German |
| Electrolysis | 1852 | Faraday | English |
| Electromagnetism | 1819 | Oersted | Danish |
| Electron | 1897 | Thomson, J. | English |
| Electron diffraction | 1936 | Thomson, G. | English |
| | | Davisson | U.S. |
| Electroshock treat- | | | |
| ment | 1938 | Cerletti, Bini | Italian |
| Erythromycin | 1952 | McGuire | U.S. |
| Evolution, natural | | | |
| selection | 1858 | Darwin | English |
| Falling bodies, law | 1590 | Galileo | Italian |
| Gases, law of | | | |
| combining volumes | 1808 | Gay-Lussac | French |
| Geometry, analytic | 1619 | Descartes | French |
| Gold (cyanide process | | MacArthur, | |
| for extraction) | 1887 | Forest | British |
| Gravitation, law | 1687 | Newton | English |
| | | | |
| Holograph | 1948 | Gabor | British |
| Human heart | | | |
| transplant | 1967 | Barnard | S. African |
| Human immunodeficiency | | Montagnier, | |
| virus identified | 1984 | Gallo | French, U.S. |
| Indigo, synthesis of | 1880 | Baeyer | German |
| Induction, electric | 1830 | Henry | U.S. |
| Insulin | 1922 | Banting, Best, | Canadian, |
| | | Macleod | Scottish |
| Intelligence testing | 1905 | Binet, Simon | French |
| In vitro fertilization | 1978 | Steptoe, | |
| | | Edwards | English |
| Isoniazid | 1952 | Hoffman- | |
| | | La-Roche | U.S. |
| | | Domagk | German |
| Isotopes, theory | 1912 | Soddy | English |
| Laser (light amplification by | | | |
| stimulated emission | | Townes, Schaw- | |
| of radiation) | 1958 | low | U.S. |
| Light, velocity | 1675 | Roemer | Danish |
| Light, wave theory | 1690 | Huygens | Dutch |

*(continued )*

| | Date | Discoverer | Nation. |
|---|---|---|---|
| Lithography | 1796 | Senefelder | Bohemian |
| Lobotomy | 1935 | Egas Moniz | Portuguese |
| LSD-25 | 1943 | Hoffman | Swiss |
| | | | |
| Mendelian laws | 1866 | Mendel | Austrian |
| Mercator projection (map) | 1568 | Mercator (Kremer) | Flemish |
| Methanol | 1661 | Boyle | Irish |
| Milk condensation | 1853 | Borden | U.S. |
| Molecular hypothesis | 1811 | Avogadro | Italian |
| Motion, laws of | 1687 | Newton | English |
| | | | |
| Neomycin | 1949 | Waksman, Lechevalier | U.S. |
| Neutron | 1932 | Chadwick | English |
| Nitric acid | 1648 | Glauber | German |
| Nitric oxide | 1772 | Priestley | English |
| Nitroglycerin | 1846 | Sobrero | Italian |
| | | | |
| Oil cracking process | 1891 | Dewar | U.S. |
| Oxygen | 1774 | Priestley | English |
| Oxytetracycline | 1950 | Finlay, et al. | U.S. |
| Ozone | 1840 | Schonbein | German |
| | | | |
| Paper, sulfite process | 1867 | Tilghman | U.S. |
| Paper, wood pulp, sulfate process | 1884 | Dahl | German |
| Penicillin | 1929 | Fleming | Scottish |
| practical use | 1941 | Florey, Chain. | English |
| Periodic law and table of elements | 1869 | Mendeleyev | Russian |
| Planetary motion, laws | 1609 | Kepler | German |
| Plutonium fission | 1940 | Kennedy, Wahl, Seaborg, Segre | U.S. |
| | | | |
| Polymyxin | 1947 | Ainsworth | English |
| Positron | 1932 | Anderson | U.S. |
| Proton | 1919 | Rutherford | N. Zealand |
| Psychoanalysis | 1900 | Freud | Austrian |
| | | | |
| Quantum theory | 1900 | Planck | German |
| Quasars | 1963 | Matthews, Sandage | U.S. |
| Quinine synthetic | 1946 | Woodward, Doering | U.S. |
| | | | |
| Radioactivity | 1896 | Becquerel | French |
| Radium | 1898 | Curie, Pierre | French |
| | | Curie, Marie | Pol.-Fr. |
| Relativity theory | 1905 | Einstein | German |
| Reserpine | 1949 | Jal Vaikl. | Indian |

| | Date | Discoverer | Nation. |
|---|---|---|---|
| Schick test | 1913 | Schick | U.S. |
| Silicon | 1823 | Berzelius | Swedish |
| Smallpox eradication | 1979 | World Health Organization | United Nations |
| Streptomycin | 1945 | Waksman | U.S. |
| Sulfadiazine | 1940 | Roblin | U.S. |
| Sulfanilamide | 1935 | Bovet, Trefouel. | French |
| Sulfanilamide theory | 1908 | Gelmo | German |
| Sulfapyridine | 1938 | Ewins, Phelps | English |
| Sulfathiazole | ... | Fosbinder, Walter. | U.S. |
| Sulfuric acid | 1831 | Phillips | English |
| Sulfuric acid, lead | 1746 | Roebuck | English |
| | | | |
| Thiacetazone | 1950 | Belmisch, Mietzsch, Domagk. | German |
| Tuberculin | 1890 | Koch. | German |
| | | | |
| Uranium fission (theory) | 1939 | Hahn, Meitner, Strassmann | German |
| | | Bohr. | Danish |
| | | Fermi | Italian |
| | | Einstein, Pegram, Wheeler. | U.S. |
| Uranium fission, atomic reactor | 1942 | Fermi, Szilard | U.S. |
| Vaccine, measles | 1954 | Enders, Peebles | U.S. |
| Vaccine, meningitis (first conjugate) | 1987 | Gordon, et. al., Connaught Lab., Inc. | U.S. |
| Vaccine, polio | 1955 | Salk | U.S. |
| Vaccine, polio, oral | 1955 | Sabin | U.S. |
| Vaccine, rabies | 1885 | Pasteur | French |
| Vaccine, smallpox | 1796 | Jenner | English |
| Vaccine, typhus | 1909 | Nicolle. | French |
| Van Allen belts, radiation | 1958 | Van Allen | U.S. |
| Vitamin A | 1913 | McCollum, Davis. | U.S. |
| Vitamin B | 1916 | McCollum. | U.S. |
| Vitamin C | 1928 | Szent-Gyorgyi, King | U.S. |
| Vitamin D | 1922 | McCollum. | U.S. |
| Wassermann test | 1906 | Wassermann. | German |
| Xerography | 1938 | Carlson | U.S. |
| X-ray | 1895 | Roentgen | German |

## Chemical Elements, Atomic Weights, Discoverers

Atomic weights, based on the exact number 12 as the assigned atomic mass of the principal isotope of carbon, carbon 12, are provided through the courtesy of the International Union of Pure and Applied Chemistry and Butterworth Scientific Publications.

For the radioactive elements, with the exception of uranium and thorium, the mass number of either the isotope of longest half-life (*) or the better known isotope (**) is given.

| Chemical element | Symbol | Atomic number | Atomic weight | Year discov. | Discoverer |
|---|---|---|---|---|---|
| Actinium | Ac | 89 | 227* | 1899 | Debierne |
| Aluminum | Al | 13 | 26.9815 | 1825 | Oersted |
| Americium | Am | 95 | 243* | 1944 | Seaborg, et al. |
| Antimony | Sb | 51 | 121.75 | 1450 | Valentine |
| Argon | Ar | 18 | 39.948 | 1894 | Rayleigh, Ramsay |
| Arsenic | As | 33 | 74.9216 | 13th c. | Albertus Magnus |
| Astatine | At | 85 | 210* | 1940 | Corson, et al. |
| Barium | Ba | 56 | 137.34 | 1808 | Davy |
| Berkelium | Bk | 97 | 249** | 1949 | Thompson, Ghiorso, Seaborg |
| Beryllium | Be | 4 | 9.0122 | 1798 | Vauquelin |
| Bismuth | Bi | 83 | 208.980 | 15th c. | Valentine |
| Boron | B | 5 | 10.811a | 1808 | Gay-Lussac, Thenard |
| Bromine | Br | 35 | 79.904b | 1826 | Balard |
| Cadmium | Cd | 48 | 112.40 | 1817 | Stromeyer |
| Calcium | Ca | 20 | 40.08 | 1808 | Davy |
| Californium | Cf | 98 | 251* | 1950 | Thompson, et al. |
| Carbon | C | 6 | 12.01115a | B.C. | unknown |
| Cerium | Ce | 58 | 140.12 | 1803 | Klaproth |
| Cesium | Cs | 55 | 132.905 | 1860 | Bunsen, Kirchhoff |
| Chlorine | Cl | 17 | 35.453b | 1774 | Scheele |
| Chromium | Cr | 24 | 51.996b | 1797 | Vauquelin |
| Cobalt | Co | 27 | 58.9332 | 1735 | Brandt |
| Copper | Cu | 29 | 63.546b | B.C. | unknown |
| Curium | Cm | 96 | 247* | 1944 | Seaborg, James, Ghiorso |
| Dysprosium | Dy | 66 | 162.50 | 1886 | Boisbaudran |
| Einsteinium | Es | 99 | 254* | 1952 | Ghiorso, et al. |
| Erbium | Er | 68 | 167.26 | 1843 | Mosander |
| Europium | Eu | 63 | 151.96 | 1901 | Demarcay |

| Chemical element | Symbol | Atomic number | Atomic weight | Year discov. | Discoverer |
|---|---|---|---|---|---|
| Fluorine | F | 9 | 18.9984 | 1771 | Scheele |
| Francium | Fr | 87 | 223* | 1939 | Perey |
| Gadolinium | Gd | 64 | 157.25 | 1886 | Marignac |
| Gallium | Ga | 31 | 69.72 | 1875 | Boisbaudran |
| Germanium | Ge | 32 | 72.59 | 1886 | Winkler |
| Gold | Au | 79 | 196.967 | B.C. | unknown |
| Hafnium | Hf | 72 | 178.49 | 1923 | Coster, Hevesy |
| Hahnium | Ha | 105 | 262* | 1970 | Ghiorso, et al. |
| Hassium | Hs | 108 | 265* | 1984 | Münzenberg, et al. |
| Helium | He | 2 | 4.0026 | 1868 | Janssen, Lockyer |
| Holmium | Ho | 67 | 164.930 | 1878 | Soret, Delafontaine |
| Hydrogen | H | 1 | 1.00797a | 1766 | Cavendish |
| Indium | In | 49 | 114.82 | 1863 | Reich, Richter |
| Iodine | I | 53 | 126.9044 | 1811 | Courtois |
| Iridium | Ir | 77 | 192.2 | 1804 | Tennant |
| Iron | Fe | 26 | 55.847b | B.C. | unknown |
| Krypton | Kr | 36 | 83.80 | 1898 | Ramsay, Travers |
| Lanthanum | La | 57 | 138.91 | 1839 | Mosander |
| Lawrencium | Lr | 103 | 262* | 1961 | Ghiorso, T. Sikkeland, A.E. Larsh, and R.M. Latimer |
| Lead | Pb | 82 | 207.19 | B.C. | unknown |
| Lithium | Li | 3 | 6.939 | 1817 | Arfvedson |
| Lutetium | Lu | 71 | 174.97 | 1907 | Welsbach, Urbain |
| Magnesium | Mg | 12 | 24.312 | 1829 | Bussy |
| Manganese | Mn | 25 | 54.9380 | 1774 | Gahn |
| Meitnerium | Mt | 109 | 266* | 1982 | Münzenberg, et al. |
| Mendelevium | Md | 101 | 258* | 1955 | Ghiorso, et al. |
| Mercury | Hg | 80 | 200.59 | B.C. | unknown |
| Molybdenum | Mo | 42 | 95.94 | 1782 | Hjelm |
| Neodymium | Nd | 60 | 144.24 | 1885 | Welsbach |
| Neon | Ne | 10 | 20.183 | 1898 | Ramsay, Travers |
| Neptunium | Np | 93 | 237* | 1940 | McMillan, Abelson |
| Nickel | Ni | 28 | 58.71 | 1751 | Cronstedt |
| Nielsbohrium | Ns | 107 | 262* | 1981 | Münzenberg, et al. |
| Niobium[1] | Nb | 41 | 92.906 | 1801 | Hatchett |
| Nitrogen | N | 7 | 14.0067 | 1772 | Rutherford |
| Nobelium | No | 102 | 259* | 1958 | Ghiorso, et al. |
| Osmium | Os | 76 | 190.2 | 1804 | Tennant |
| Oxygen | O | 8 | 15.9994a | 1774 | Priestley, Scheele |
| Palladium | Pd | 46 | 106.4 | 1803 | Wollaston |
| Phosphorus | P | 15 | 30.9738 | 1669 | Brand |
| Platinum | Pt | 78 | 195.09 | 1735 | Ulloa |
| Plutonium | Pu | 94 | 242** | 1940 | Seaborg, et al. |
| Polonium | Po | 84 | 210** | 1898 | P. and M. Curie |
| Potassium | K | 19 | 39.102 | 1807 | Davy |
| Praseodymium | Pr | 59 | 140.907 | 1885 | Welsbach |
| Promethium | Pm | 61 | 147** | 1945 | Glendenin, Marinsky, Coryell |
| Protactinium | Pa | 91 | 231* | 1917 | Hahn, Meitner |
| Radium | Ra | 88 | 226* | 1898 | P. & M. Curie, Bemont |
| Radon | Rn | 86 | 222* | 1900 | Dorn |
| Rhenium | Re | 75 | 186.2 | 1925 | Noddack, Tacke, Berg |
| Rhodium | Rh | 45 | 102.905 | 1803 | Wollaston |
| Rubidium | Rb | 37 | 85.47 | 1861 | Bunsen, Kirchhoff |
| Ruthenium | Ru | 44 | 101.07 | 1845 | Klaus |
| Rutherfordium | Rf | 104 | 261* | 1969 | Ghiorso, et al. |
| Samarium | Sm | 62 | 150.35 | 1879 | Boisbaudran |
| Scandium | Sc | 21 | 44.956 | 1879 | Nilson |
| Selenium | Se | 34 | 78.96 | 1817 | Berzelius |
| Silicon | Si | 14 | 28.086a | 1823 | Berzelius |
| Silver | Ag | 47 | 107.868b | B.C. | unknown |
| Sodium | Na | 11 | 22.9898 | 1807 | Davy |
| Strontium | Sr | 38 | 87.62 | 1790 | Crawford |
| Sulfur | S | 16 | 32.064 a | B.C. | unknown |
| Tantalum | Ta | 73 | 180.948 | 1802 | Ekeberg |
| Technetium | Tc | 43 | 99** | 1937 | Perrier and Segre |
| Tellurium | Te | 52 | 127.60 | 1782 | Von Reichenstein |
| Terbium | Tb | 65 | 158.924 | 1843 | Mosander |
| Thallium | Tl | 81 | 204.37 | 1861 | Crookes |
| Thorium | Th | 90 | 232.038 | 1828 | Berzelius |
| Thulium | Tm | 69 | 168.934 | 1879 | Cleve |
| Tin | Sn | 50 | 118.69 | B.C. | unknown |
| Titanium | Ti | 22 | 47.90 | 1791 | Gregor |
| Tungsten (Wolfram) | W | 74 | 183.85 | 1783 | d'Elhujar |
| Uranium | U | 92 | 238.03 | 1789 | Klaproth |
| Vanadium | V | 23 | 50.942 | 1830 | Sefstrom |
| Xenon | Xe | 54 | 131.30 | 1898 | Ramsay, Travers |
| Ytterbium | Yb | 70 | 173.04 | 1878 | Marignac |
| Yttrium | Y | 39 | 88.905 | 1794 | Gadolin |
| Zinc | Zn | 30 | 65.37 | B.C. | unknown |
| Zirconium | Zr | 40 | 91.22 | 1789 | Klaproth |

(1) Formerly Columbium. (a) Atomic weights so designated are known to be variable because of natural variations in isotopic composition. The observed ranges are: hydrogen±0.0001; boron±0.003; carbon±0.005; oxygen±0.0001; silicon±0.001; sulfur±0.003. (b) Atomic weights so designated are believed to have the following experimental uncertainties: chlorine±0.001; chromium±0.001; iron±0.003; bromine±0.001; silver±0.001; copper±0.001.

# METEOROLOGY

## National Weather Service Watches and Warnings

Source: National Weather Service, NOAA, U.S. Dept. of Commerce; *Glossary of Meteorology*, American Meteorological Society

National Weather Service forecasters issue a Severe Thunderstorm or Tornado Watch for a specific area where threatening weather is most likely to occur during the valid time of the watch. A Severe Thunderstorm Watch is issued for a specific area where severe thunderstorms are most likely. A Tornado Watch is issued when severe thunderstorms that produce tornados are likely to occur in a specific area. A Watch alerts people to check for threatening weather, make plans for action, and listen for a Tornado Warning. A Tornado Warning means that a tornado has been sighted or indicated by radar, and that safety precautions should be taken at once. A Hurricane Watch means that an existing hurricane poses a threat to coastal and inland communities, within 24-36 hours, in the area specified by the Watch. A Hurricane Warning means hurricane force winds and/or dangerously high water and exceptionally high waves are expected in a specified coastal area within 24 hours.

**Tornado**—A violent rotating column of air in contact with the ground and pendant from a thundercloud, usually recognized as a funnel-shaped vortex accompanied by a loud roar. With rotating winds est. up to 300 mph., on a local scale, it is the most destructive storm. Tornado paths have varied in length from a few feet to nearly 300 miles (avg. 5 mi.); diameter from a few feet to over a mile (average 220 yards); average forward speed, 30 mph.

**Cyclone**—An atmospheric circulation of winds rotating counterclockwise in the northern hemisphere and clockwise in the southern hemisphere. Tornadoes, hurricanes, and the lows shown on weather maps are all examples of cyclones having various sizes and intensities. Cyclones are usually accompanied by precipitation or stormy weather.

**Hurricane**—A severe cyclone originating over tropical ocean waters and having winds 74 miles an hour or higher. (In the western Pacific, such storms are known as typhoons.) The area of strong winds takes the form of a circle or an oval, sometimes as much as 500 miles in diameter. In the lower latitudes hurricanes usually move toward the west or northwest at 10 to 15 mph. When the center approaches 25° to 30° North Latitude, direction of motion often changes to northeast, with increased forward speed.

**Blizzard**—A severe weather condition characterized by strong winds bearing a great amount of snow. The National Weather Service specifies winds of 35-miles an hour or higher, and sufficient falling and/or blowing snow to frequently reduce visibility to less than ¼ mile for a duration of at least three hours.

**Severe Thunderstorm**—A thunderstorm with winds of 58 mph. or greater and/or hail three-fourths of an inch or larger in diameter.

**Flood**—The condition that occurs when water overflows the natural or artificial confines of a stream or other body of water, or accumulates by drainage over low-lying areas.

## National Weather Service Marine Warnings and Advisories

**Small Craft Advisory:** A Small Craft Advisory alerts mariners to sustained (exceeding two hours) weather and/or sea conditions either present or forecast, potentially hazardous to small boats. Although there is no definition of a small craft, hazardous conditions generally include winds of 18 to 33 knots and/or dangerous wave conditions. It is the responsibility of the mariner, based on his experience, location and size or type of boat, to determine if the conditions are hazardous. When a mariner becomes aware of a Small Craft Advisory, he should immediately obtain the latest marine forecast to determine the reason for the Advisory.

**Gale Warning** indicates that winds within the range 34 to 47 knots, not directly associated with a tropical storm, are forecast for the area.

**Tropical Storm Warning** indicates that winds of 34 to 63 knots are forecast in a specified coastal area in 24 hours or less. Only issued for winds of tropical weather systems.

**Storm Warning** indicates that winds 48 knots and above, no matter how high the speed, not directly associated with a tropical storm, are forecast for the area.

**Hurricane Warning** indicates that winds 64 knots or greater are forecast for the area. Only issued for winds produced by tropical weather systems.

**Special Marine Warning:** A warning for potentially hazardous weather conditions, usually of short duration (2 hours or less) and producing wind speeds of 34 knots or more, not adequately covered by existing marine warnings.

Primary sources of dissemination are commercial radio, TV, U.S. Coast Guard radio stations, and NOAA VHF-FM broadcasts. These broadcasts on 162.40 to 162.55 MHz can usually be received 20-40 miles from the transmitting antenna site, depending on terrain and quality of the receiver used. Where transmitting antennas are on high ground, the range may be somewhat greater, reaching 60 miles or more.

## Speed of Winds in the U.S.

Source: National Climatic Data Center, NESDIS, NOAA, U.S. Dept. of Commerce
Miles per hour — average through 1991. High through 1991. Wind velocities in true values.

| Station | Avg. | High | Station | Avg. | High | Station | Avg. | High |
|---|---|---|---|---|---|---|---|---|
| Albuquerque, N.M. | 9.1 | (b)90 | Helena, Mont. | 7.8 | 73 | Mt. Washington, N.H. | 35.3 | 231 |
| Anchorage, Alas. | 7.0 | 75 | Honolulu, Ha. | 11.4 | (b)67 | New Orleans, La. | 8.2 | (b)98 |
| Atlanta, Ga. | 9.1 | 60 | Houston, Tex. | 7.9 | 51 | New York, N.Y.(c) | 9.4 | (b)70 |
| Baltimore, Md. | 9.2 | 80 | Indianapolis, Ind. | 9.6 | 46 | Omaha, Neb. | 10.6 | (b)109 |
| Bismarck, N.D. | 10.2 | (b)72 | Jacksonville, Fla. | 8.0 | (b)82 | Philadelphia, Pa. | 9.5 | 73 |
| Boston, Mass. | 12.5 | (b)61 | Kansas City, Mo. | 10.8 | (b)70 | Phoenix, Ariz. | 6.3 | (b)86 |
| Buffalo, N.Y. | 12.0 | 91 | Lexington, Ky. | 9.2 | 46 | Pittsburgh, Pa. | 9.1 | 58 |
| Cape Hatteras, N.C. | 11.1 | (b)110 | Little Rock, Ark. | 7.8 | 65 | Portland, Ore. | 7.9 | 88 |
| Casper, Wyo. | 12.9 | 81 | Los Angeles, Cal. | 6.2 | 49 | St. Louis, Mo. | 9.7 | (b)60 |
| Chicago, Ill. | 10.4 | 58 | Louisville, Ky. | 8.4 | (b)61 | Salt Lake City, Ut. | 8.8 | 71 |
| Cleveland, Oh. | 10.6 | (b)74 | Memphis, Tenn. | 8.9 | 46 | San Diego, Cal. | 6.9 | 56 |
| Dallas, Tex. | 10.8 | 73 | Miami, Fla. | 9.3 | (a)74 | San Francisco, Cal. | 8.7 | 47 |
| Denver, Col. | 8.7 | (b)56 | Milwaukee, Wis. | 11.6 | 54 | Seattle, Wash. | 9.0 | 66 |
| Detroit, Mich. | 10.4 | 48 | Minneapolis, Minn. | 10.6 | (b)92 | Spokane, Wash. | 8.9 | 59 |
| Galveston, Tex. | 11.0 | (d)100 | Mobile, Ala. | 9.0 | 63 | Washington, D.C. | 9.3 | (b)78 |

(a) Highest velocity ever recorded in Miami area was 132 mph, at former station in Miami Beach in September 1926. (b) Previous location. (c) Data for Central Park; Battery Place data through 1960, avg. 14.5, high 113. (d) Recorded before anemometer blew away. Estimated high 120.

## Monthly Normal Temperature and Precipitation

**Source:** National Climatic Data Center, NESDIS, NOAA, U.S. Dept. of Commerce

The normal temperatures below are based on records for the 30-year period 1951 to 1980 inclusive. For stations that did not have continuous records from the same instrument site for the entire 30 years, the means have been adjusted to the record at the present site.

Airport station; *city office stations. T, temperature in Fahrenheit; P, precipitation in inches; L, less than .05 inch.

| Station | Jan. T | Jan. P | Feb. T | Feb. P | Mar. T | Mar. P | Apr. T | Apr. P | May T | May P | June T | June P | July T | July P | Aug. T | Aug. P | Sept. T | Sept. P | Oct. T | Oct. P | Nov. T | Nov. P | Dec. T | Dec. P |
|---|---|---|---|---|---|---|---|---|---|---|---|---|---|---|---|---|---|---|---|---|---|---|---|---|
| Albany, N.Y. | 21 | 2.4 | 23 | 2.3 | 34 | 3.0 | 47 | 2.9 | 58 | 3.3 | 67 | 3.3 | 71 | 3.0 | 69 | 3.3 | 61 | 3.2 | 51 | 2.9 | 39 | 3.0 | 26 | 3.0 |
| Albuquerque, N.M. | 35 | 0.4 | 39 | 0.4 | 46 | 0.5 | 55 | 0.4 | 64 | 0.5 | 75 | 0.5 | 79 | 1.3 | 76 | 1.5 | 69 | 0.9 | 57 | 0.9 | 44 | 0.4 | 36 | 0.5 |
| Anchorage, Alas. | 13 | 0.8 | 18 | 0.9 | 24 | 0.7 | 35 | 0.7 | 46 | 0.6 | 54 | 1.1 | 58 | 2.0 | 56 | 2.1 | 48 | 2.5 | 35 | 1.7 | 22 | 1.1 | 14 | 1.1 |
| Asheville, N.C. | 37 | 3.5 | 39 | 3.6 | 46 | 5.1 | 56 | 3.8 | 63 | 4.2 | 70 | 4.2 | 73 | 4.4 | 73 | 4.8 | 70 | 4.0 | 56 | 3.3 | 46 | 3.3 | 39 | 3.5 |
| Atlanta, Ga. | 42 | 4.9 | 45 | 4.4 | 53 | 5.9 | 62 | 4.4 | 69 | 4.0 | 76 | 3.4 | 79 | 4.7 | 78 | 3.4 | 73 | 3.2 | 62 | 2.5 | 52 | 3.4 | 45 | 4.2 |
| Atlantic City, N.J. | 34 | 3.3 | 35 | 3.2 | 42 | 3.7 | 51 | 3.1 | 60 | 2.9 | 69 | 2.9 | 74 | 3.9 | 74 | 4.5 | 68 | 2.7 | 58 | 2.8 | 48 | 3.5 | 38 | 3.5 |
| Baltimore, Md. | 33 | 3.0 | 35 | 3.0 | 43 | 3.7 | 54 | 3.4 | 63 | 3.4 | 72 | 3.8 | 77 | 3.9 | 76 | 4.6 | 69 | 3.5 | 57 | 3.1 | 46 | 3.1 | 37 | 3.4 |
| Barrow, Alas. | -14 | 0.2 | -20 | 0.2 | -16 | 0.2 | -2 | 0.2 | 19 | 0.2 | 33 | 0.4 | 39 | 0.9 | 38 | 1.0 | 31 | 0.6 | 14 | 0.6 | -1 | 0.3 | -13 | 0.2 |
| Birmingham, Ala. | 42 | 5.2 | 46 | 4.7 | 54 | 6.6 | 63 | 5.0 | 70 | 4.5 | 77 | 3.7 | 80 | 5.4 | 80 | 3.9 | 74 | 4.3 | 62 | 2.7 | 52 | 3.6 | 45 | 5.0 |
| Bismarck, N.D. | 7 | 0.5 | 15 | 0.5 | 26 | 0.7 | 43 | 1.5 | 55 | 2.2 | 64 | 3.0 | 70 | 2.0 | 69 | 1.7 | 57 | 1.4 | 46 | 0.8 | 29 | 0.5 | 15 | 0.5 |
| Boise, Ida. | 30 | 1.6 | 36 | 1.1 | 41 | 1.0 | 49 | 1.2 | 57 | 1.2 | 66 | 1.0 | 75 | 0.3 | 72 | 0.4 | 63 | 0.6 | 52 | 0.8 | 40 | 1.3 | 32 | 1.3 |
| Boston, Mass. | 30 | 4.0 | 31 | 3.7 | 38 | 4.1 | 49 | 3.7 | 59 | 3.5 | 68 | 2.9 | 74 | 2.7 | 72 | 3.7 | 65 | 3.4 | 55 | 3.4 | 45 | 4.2 | 34 | 4.9 |
| Buffalo, N.Y. | 24 | 3.0 | 25 | 2.4 | 33 | 3.0 | 45 | 3.0 | 56 | 2.9 | 66 | 2.7 | 71 | 3.0 | 69 | 4.2 | 62 | 3.4 | 52 | 2.9 | 40 | 3.6 | 29 | 3.4 |
| Burlington, Vt. | 17 | 1.9 | 18 | 1.7 | 29 | 2.2 | 43 | 2.8 | 55 | 3.0 | 65 | 3.6 | 70 | 3.4 | 67 | 3.9 | 59 | 3.2 | 48 | 2.8 | 37 | 2.8 | 23 | 2.4 |
| Caribou, Me. | 11 | 2.4 | 13 | 2.1 | 24 | 2.4 | 37 | 2.6 | 50 | 2.9 | 60 | 3.2 | 65 | 4.0 | 63 | 4.0 | 54 | 3.5 | 43 | 3.1 | 31 | 3.2 | 16 | 3.1 |
| Charleston, S.C. | 49 | 3.3 | 51 | 3.4 | 57 | 4.4 | 66 | 2.6 | 73 | 4.4 | 79 | 6.5 | 82 | 7.3 | 81 | 6.5 | 77 | 4.9 | 68 | 2.9 | 59 | 2.2 | 52 | 3.1 |
| Chicago, Ill. | 21 | 1.6 | 26 | 1.3 | 36 | 2.6 | 49 | 3.7 | 59 | 4.1 | 73 | 3.6 | 72 | 3.5 | 70 | 3.4 | 65 | 3.4 | 54 | 2.3 | 40 | 2.1 | 28 | 2.1 |
| Cleveland, Oh. | 26 | 2.5 | 27 | 2.2 | 37 | 3.0 | 48 | 3.3 | 58 | 3.5 | 68 | 3.5 | 72 | 3.4 | 70 | 3.4 | 64 | 2.9 | 53 | 2.5 | 42 | 2.8 | 31 | 2.8 |
| Columbus, Oh. | 27 | 2.8 | 30 | 2.2 | 40 | 3.2 | 51 | 3.4 | 61 | 3.8 | 70 | 4.0 | 74 | 4.0 | 72 | 3.7 | 66 | 2.8 | 54 | 1.9 | 42 | 2.6 | 32 | 2.6 |
| Dallas-Ft. Worth, Tex. | 44 | 1.7 | 49 | 1.9 | 56 | 2.4 | 66 | 3.6 | 74 | 4.3 | 82 | 2.6 | 86 | 2.0 | 86 | 1.8 | 79 | 3.3 | 68 | 2.5 | 56 | 1.8 | 48 | 1.7 |
| Denver, Col. | 30 | 0.5 | 34 | 0.7 | 38 | 1.2 | 47 | 1.8 | 57 | 2.5 | 67 | 1.6 | 73 | 1.9 | 71 | 1.5 | 63 | 1.2 | 52 | 1.0 | 39 | 0.8 | 33 | 0.6 |
| Des Moines, Ia. | 19 | 1.0 | 25 | 1.1 | 35 | 2.2 | 51 | 3.2 | 62 | 4.0 | 72 | 4.2 | 76 | 3.2 | 74 | 4.1 | 65 | 3.1 | 54 | 2.2 | 39 | 1.5 | 26 | 1.5 |
| Detroit, Mich. | 23 | 1.9 | 26 | 1.7 | 35 | 2.5 | 47 | 3.2 | 58 | 2.8 | 68 | 3.4 | 72 | 3.1 | 71 | 3.2 | 63 | 2.3 | 52 | 2.1 | 40 | 2.3 | 29 | 2.5 |
| Dodge City, Kan. | 30 | 0.5 | 35 | 0.5 | 42 | 1.5 | 54 | 1.8 | 64 | 3.3 | 75 | 3.0 | 80 | 3.1 | 78 | 2.5 | 69 | 1.9 | 58 | 1.3 | 43 | 0.8 | 34 | 0.5 |
| Duluth, Minn. | 6 | 1.2 | 12 | 0.9 | 23 | 1.8 | 38 | 2.2 | 50 | 3.2 | 59 | 4.0 | 65 | 4.0 | 63 | 4.1 | 54 | 3.3 | 44 | 2.2 | 28 | 1.7 | 14 | 1.3 |
| Eureka, Cal.* | 47 | 7.0 | 49 | 5.2 | 48 | 5.1 | 49 | 2.9 | 52 | 1.6 | 55 | 0.6 | 56 | 0.1 | 57 | 0.4 | 57 | 0.9 | 54 | 2.7 | 51 | 5.9 | 48 | 6.2 |
| Fairbanks, Alas. | -13 | 0.5 | -4 | 0.5 | 9 | 0.4 | 30 | 0.3 | 48 | 0.6 | 59 | 1.3 | 62 | 1.8 | 57 | 1.9 | 45 | 1.1 | 25 | 0.7 | 4 | 0.7 | -10 | 0.7 |
| Fresno, Cal. | 46 | 2.0 | 51 | 1.9 | 54 | 1.6 | 60 | 1.2 | 68 | 0.3 | 75 | 0.1 | 81 | L | 79 | L | 74 | 0.2 | 65 | 0.4 | 53 | 1.2 | 45 | 1.6 |
| Galveston, Tex.* | 54 | 3.0 | 56 | 2.3 | 62 | 2.1 | 69 | 2.6 | 76 | 3.3 | 81 | 3.5 | 83 | 3.8 | 83 | 4.4 | 80 | 5.8 | 73 | 2.6 | 63 | 3.2 | 57 | 3.6 |
| Grand Junction, Col. | 26 | 0.6 | 34 | 0.5 | 42 | 0.8 | 52 | 0.7 | 62 | 0.8 | 72 | 0.4 | 79 | 0.5 | 76 | 0.9 | 67 | 0.7 | 55 | 0.9 | 40 | 0.6 | 28 | 0.6 |
| Gr. Rapids, Mich. | 22 | 1.9 | 24 | 1.5 | 33 | 2.5 | 46 | 3.6 | 58 | 3.0 | 67 | 3.9 | 71 | 3.0 | 70 | 3.5 | 62 | 3.1 | 51 | 2.9 | 39 | 2.9 | 27 | 2.6 |
| Hartford, Conn. | 25 | 3.5 | 28 | 3.2 | 37 | 4.2 | 49 | 4.0 | 59 | 3.4 | 69 | 3.4 | 73 | 3.1 | 71 | 4.0 | 63 | 3.9 | 52 | 3.5 | 42 | 4.1 | 29 | 4.2 |
| Helena, Mon. | 18 | 0.7 | 26 | 0.4 | 32 | 0.7 | 42 | 1.0 | 52 | 1.7 | 60 | 2.0 | 68 | 1.0 | 66 | 1.2 | 56 | 0.8 | 45 | 0.7 | 31 | 0.5 | 23 | 0.6 |
| Honolulu, Hi. | 73 | 3.8 | 73 | 2.7 | 74 | 3.5 | 76 | 1.5 | 78 | 1.2 | 79 | 0.5 | 80 | 0.5 | 81 | 0.6 | 81 | 0.6 | 80 | 1.9 | 77 | 3.2 | 74 | 3.4 |
| Houston, Tex. | 51 | 3.2 | 55 | 3.3 | 61 | 2.7 | 69 | 4.2 | 75 | 4.7 | 81 | 4.0 | 83 | 3.3 | 83 | 3.7 | 78 | 4.9 | 70 | 3.7 | 60 | 3.4 | 54 | 3.7 |
| Huron, S.D. | 11 | 0.4 | 18 | 0.8 | 29 | 1.2 | 46 | 2.0 | 57 | 2.7 | 68 | 3.3 | 74 | 2.3 | 72 | 2.0 | 61 | 1.4 | 49 | 1.4 | 32 | 0.7 | 19 | 0.5 |
| Indianapolis, Ind. | 26 | 2.7 | 30 | 2.5 | 40 | 3.6 | 52 | 3.7 | 63 | 3.7 | 72 | 4.0 | 75 | 4.3 | 73 | 3.5 | 67 | 2.7 | 55 | 2.5 | 42 | 3.0 | 32 | 3.0 |
| Jackson, Miss. | 46 | 5.0 | 49 | 4.9 | 56 | 5.9 | 65 | 5.9 | 73 | 4.8 | 79 | 2.9 | 82 | 4.4 | 81 | 3.7 | 76 | 3.6 | 65 | 2.6 | 55 | 4.2 | 49 | 5.4 |
| Jacksonville, Fla. | 53 | 3.1 | 55 | 3.5 | 61 | 3.7 | 68 | 3.3 | 74 | 4.9 | 79 | 5.4 | 81 | 6.5 | 81 | 7.2 | 78 | 7.3 | 70 | 3.4 | 61 | 1.9 | 55 | 2.6 |
| Juneau, Alas. | 22 | 3.7 | 28 | 3.7 | 31 | 3.3 | 39 | 2.9 | 46 | 3.4 | 53 | 3.0 | 56 | 4.1 | 55 | 5.0 | 49 | 6.4 | 42 | 7.7 | 33 | 5.2 | 27 | 4.7 |
| Kansas City, Mo. | 26 | 1.0 | 32 | 1.0 | 42 | 2.1 | 55 | 2.7 | 65 | 3.4 | 74 | 4.1 | 79 | 3.5 | 77 | 3.2 | 68 | 3.3 | 58 | 2.5 | 43 | 1.2 | 32 | 1.1 |
| Knoxville, Tenn. | 38 | 4.7 | 42 | 4.2 | 50 | 5.5 | 60 | 3.9 | 67 | 3.7 | 74 | 4.0 | 78 | 4.3 | 77 | 3.0 | 72 | 3.0 | 60 | 2.7 | 49 | 3.8 | 41 | 4.6 |
| Lander, Wyo. | 20 | 0.5 | 26 | 0.6 | 32 | 1.1 | 42 | 2.2 | 53 | 2.7 | 62 | 1.5 | 71 | 0.7 | 69 | 0.5 | 58 | 0.9 | 47 | 1.2 | 31 | 0.8 | 23 | 0.5 |
| Lexington, Ky. | 32 | 3.6 | 35 | 3.3 | 44 | 4.8 | 55 | 4.0 | 64 | 4.2 | 72 | 4.3 | 76 | 5.0 | 75 | 4.0 | 69 | 3.3 | 57 | 2.3 | 45 | 3.3 | 36 | 3.8 |
| Little Rock, Ark. | 40 | 3.9 | 44 | 3.8 | 52 | 4.7 | 62 | 5.4 | 71 | 5.3 | 79 | 3.7 | 82 | 3.6 | 81 | 3.1 | 74 | 4.3 | 63 | 2.8 | 51 | 4.4 | 43 | 4.2 |
| Los Angeles, Cal.* | 57 | 3.7 | 59 | 3.0 | 60 | 2.4 | 62 | 1.2 | 65 | 0.2 | 69 | L | 74 | L | 75 | 0.1 | 73 | 0.3 | 69 | 0.2 | 63 | 1.9 | 58 | 2.0 |
| Louisville, Ky. | 33 | 3.4 | 36 | 3.2 | 45 | 4.7 | 57 | 4.1 | 65 | 4.2 | 74 | 3.6 | 78 | 4.1 | 76 | 3.3 | 70 | 3.6 | 58 | 2.6 | 46 | 3.5 | 37 | 3.5 |
| Marquette, Mich.* | 12 | 2.0 | 14 | 1.9 | 23 | 2.8 | 37 | 3.6 | 50 | 4.0 | 60 | 3.9 | 65 | 3.2 | 63 | 3.3 | 54 | 3.9 | 44 | 3.3 | 30 | 2.9 | 18 | 2.4 |
| Memphis, Tenn. | 40 | 4.6 | 44 | 4.3 | 52 | 5.4 | 63 | 5.8 | 71 | 5.1 | 79 | 3.6 | 82 | 4.0 | 81 | 3.7 | 74 | 3.6 | 63 | 2.4 | 51 | 4.2 | 43 | 4.9 |
| Miami, Fla. | 67 | 2.1 | 68 | 2.1 | 72 | 1.9 | 75 | 3.1 | 79 | 6.5 | 81 | 9.2 | 83 | 6.1 | 83 | 7.0 | 82 | 8.1 | 78 | 7.1 | 73 | 2.7 | 69 | 1.9 |
| Milwaukee, Wis. | 19 | 1.6 | 23 | 1.3 | 32 | 2.6 | 45 | 3.4 | 55 | 2.6 | 65 | 3.6 | 71 | 3.5 | 69 | 3.1 | 62 | 2.9 | 51 | 2.3 | 37 | 2.0 | 25 | 2.0 |
| Minneapolis, Minn. | 11 | 0.8 | 18 | 0.9 | 29 | 1.7 | 46 | 2.1 | 59 | 3.2 | 68 | 4.1 | 73 | 3.5 | 71 | 3.6 | 61 | 2.5 | 50 | 1.9 | 33 | 1.3 | 19 | 0.9 |
| Mobile, Ala. | 51 | 4.6 | 54 | 4.9 | 60 | 6.5 | 68 | 5.4 | 75 | 5.5 | 81 | 5.1 | 82 | 7.7 | 82 | 6.8 | 78 | 6.6 | 69 | 2.6 | 59 | 3.7 | 53 | 5.4 |
| Moline, Ill. | 20 | 1.6 | 25 | 1.3 | 36 | 2.8 | 50 | 4.0 | 61 | 4.2 | 71 | 4.3 | 75 | 3.9 | 73 | 4.3 | 64 | 3.7 | 53 | 2.4 | 39 | 2.0 | 26 | 1.9 |
| Nashville, Tenn. | 37 | 4.5 | 40 | 4.0 | 49 | 5.6 | 60 | 4.8 | 68 | 4.6 | 76 | 3.7 | 79 | 3.8 | 78 | 3.4 | 72 | 3.7 | 60 | 2.6 | 49 | 3.5 | 41 | 4.6 |
| Newark, N.J. | 31 | 3.1 | 33 | 3.1 | 41 | 4.2 | 52 | 3.6 | 62 | 3.6 | 72 | 2.9 | 77 | 3.9 | 76 | 4.3 | 68 | 3.5 | 57 | 3.1 | 47 | 3.6 | 36 | 3.4 |
| New Orleans, La. | 52 | 5.0 | 55 | 5.2 | 61 | 4.7 | 69 | 4.5 | 75 | 5.1 | 80 | 4.6 | 82 | 6.7 | 82 | 6.0 | 79 | 5.9 | 69 | 2.7 | 60 | 4.1 | 55 | 5.3 |
| New York, N.Y.* | 32 | 3.2 | 33 | 3.1 | 41 | 4.2 | 53 | 3.8 | 62 | 3.8 | 71 | 3.2 | 77 | 3.8 | 75 | 4.0 | 68 | 3.7 | 58 | 3.4 | 47 | 4.1 | 36 | 3.8 |
| Nome, Alas.* | 9 | 0.8 | 3 | 0.5 | 7 | 0.6 | 18 | 0.6 | 40 | 0.5 | 45 | 1.2 | 51 | 2.2 | 50 | 3.1 | 42 | 2.3 | 28 | 1.3 | 16 | 0.9 | 4 | 0.7 |
| Norfolk, Va. | 40 | 3.7 | 41 | 3.3 | 49 | 3.9 | 58 | 2.9 | 67 | 3.8 | 76 | 3.5 | 78 | 5.2 | 78 | 5.3 | 72 | 4.4 | 61 | 3.4 | 52 | 2.9 | 44 | 3.2 |
| Okla. City, Okla. | 36 | 1.0 | 41 | 1.3 | 49 | 2.1 | 60 | 2.9 | 68 | 5.5 | 77 | 3.9 | 82 | 3.0 | 81 | 2.7 | 73 | 3.4 | 62 | 2.7 | 49 | 1.5 | 40 | 1.2 |
| Omaha, Neb. | 19 | 0.8 | 25 | 0.9 | 35 | 1.9 | 50 | 2.9 | 62 | 4.3 | 71 | 4.1 | 76 | 3.6 | 74 | 4.1 | 64 | 2.5 | 54 | 2.1 | 38 | 1.3 | 26 | 0.8 |
| Pago Pago, Amer. Samoa. | 81 | 13 | 81 | 13 | 81 | 11 | 81 | 11 | 80 | 11 | 80 | 8.6 | 79 | 6.5 | 79 | 7.1 | 79 | 9.7 | 80 | 11 | 80 | 11 | 81 | 14 |
| Philadelphia, Pa. | 31 | 3.2 | 33 | 2.8 | 42 | 3.9 | 53 | 3.5 | 63 | 3.2 | 72 | 3.9 | 77 | 4.1 | 68 | 3.4 | 57 | 3.2 | 46 | 3.6 | 45 | 2.8 | 36 | 3.5 |
| Phoenix, Ariz. | 52 | 0.7 | 56 | 0.6 | 61 | 0.8 | 68 | 0.3 | 77 | 0.1 | 87 | 0.2 | 92 | 0.7 | 90 | 1.0 | 85 | 0.6 | 73 | 0.6 | 61 | 0.5 | 53 | 0.8 |
| Pittsburgh, Pa. | 27 | 2.9 | 29 | 2.4 | 39 | 3.6 | 50 | 3.3 | 60 | 3.5 | 68 | 3.3 | 72 | 3.8 | 71 | 3.3 | 64 | 2.8 | 53 | 2.5 | 42 | 2.3 | 31 | 2.6 |
| Portland, Me. | 22 | 3.8 | 23 | 3.6 | 32 | 4.0 | 43 | 3.9 | 53 | 3.2 | 63 | 3.2 | 68 | 2.8 | 67 | 2.6 | 59 | 3.3 | 48 | 3.8 | 38 | 4.7 | 26 | 4.5 |
| Portland, Ore. | 39 | 6.2 | 43 | 3.9 | 46 | 3.6 | 50 | 2.3 | 57 | 2.1 | 63 | 1.5 | 68 | 0.5 | 67 | 1.1 | 63 | 1.6 | 54 | 3.0 | 46 | 5.2 | 41 | 6.4 |
| Providence, R.I. | 28 | 4.1 | 29 | 3.7 | 37 | 4.2 | 48 | 3.8 | 57 | 3.6 | 67 | 2.8 | 73 | 3.0 | 71 | 4.0 | 64 | 3.4 | 54 | 3.6 | 44 | 4.6 | 32 | 4.5 |
| Raleigh, N.C. | 40 | 3.6 | 42 | 3.4 | 49 | 3.7 | 59 | 2.9 | 67 | 3.7 | 74 | 3.6 | 78 | 4.4 | 77 | 4.4 | 71 | 3.3 | 60 | 2.7 | 50 | 2.9 | 42 | 3.1 |
| Rapid City, S.D. | 21 | 0.4 | 26 | 0.6 | 33 | 1.0 | 45 | 2.0 | 56 | 2.8 | 66 | 3.2 | 74 | 2.1 | 71 | 1.4 | 61 | 1.0 | 50 | 0.8 | 35 | 0.5 | 26 | 0.5 |
| Reno, Nev. | 32 | 1.2 | 37 | 1.0 | 41 | 0.7 | 46 | 0.5 | 54 | 0.7 | 62 | 0.5 | 69 | 0.3 | 68 | 0.3 | 60 | 0.3 | 50 | 0.4 | 40 | 0.5 | 34 | 0.9 |
| Richmond, Va. | 37 | 3.2 | 39 | 3.1 | 47 | 3.6 | 58 | 3.0 | 67 | 3.7 | 74 | 3.5 | 78 | 5.3 | 76 | 4.9 | 70 | 3.4 | 59 | 3.3 | 49 | 3.0 | 40 | 3.4 |
| St. Louis, Mo. | 29 | 1.7 | 34 | 2.1 | 43 | 3.1 | 56 | 3.7 | 66 | 3.9 | 75 | 4.2 | 79 | 3.6 | 78 | 2.8 | 70 | 2.7 | 59 | 2.8 | 45 | 2.0 | 34 | 1.9 |
| Salt Lake City, Ut. | 29 | 1.4 | 34 | 1.3 | 41 | 1.7 | 49 | 2.1 | 59 | 1.5 | 69 | 1.0 | 78 | 0.7 | 76 | 0.9 | 65 | 0.9 | 53 | 1.1 | 40 | 1.3 | 30 | 1.4 |
| San Antonio, Tex. | 50 | 1.6 | 54 | 1.9 | 62 | 1.3 | 70 | 2.7 | 76 | 3.7 | 82 | 3.0 | 85 | 1.9 | 85 | 2.4 | 79 | 3.2 | 70 | 3.0 | 61 | 1.9 | 54 | 1.4 |
| San Diego, Cal. | 57 | 2.1 | 58 | 1.6 | 59 | 1.6 | 61 | 0.8 | 64 | 0.2 | 66 | 0.1 | 70 | L | 72 | 0.1 | 70 | 0.2 | 67 | 0.3 | 61 | 1.1 | 57 | 1.4 |
| San Francisco, Cal. | 49 | 4.7 | 52 | 3.2 | 53 | 2.6 | 55 | 1.5 | 58 | 0.3 | 61 | 0.1 | 62 | L | 63 | 0.1 | 64 | 0.2 | 61 | 1.1 | 55 | 2.4 | 49 | 3.6 |
| San Juan, P.R. | 77 | 3.0 | 77 | 2.0 | 78 | 2.3 | 80 | 3.6 | 79 | 5.9 | 80 | 4.7 | 82 | 4.9 | 82 | 6.0 | 82 | 6.0 | 82 | 5.4 | 80 | 5.6 | 78 | 4.7 |
| Sault Ste. Marie, Mich.* | 13 | 2.2 | 14 | 1.7 | 24 | 2.0 | 38 | 2.4 | 50 | 2.9 | 58 | 3.3 | 64 | 3.0 | 63 | 3.5 | 55 | 3.8 | 45 | 3.2 | 30 | 2.6 | 18 | 2.8 |
| Savannah, Ga. | 49 | 3.1 | 52 | 3.2 | 58 | 3.8 | 66 | 3.2 | 73 | 4.6 | 79 | 5.7 | 81 | 7.4 | 81 | 6.7 | 77 | 5.2 | 67 | 2.3 | 58 | 1.9 | 51 | 2.8 |
| Seattle, Wash. | 39 | 6.0 | 43 | 4.2 | 46 | 3.6 | 50 | 2.4 | 56 | 1.6 | 61 | 1.4 | 65 | 0.7 | 65 | 1.1 | 60 | 2.0 | 53 | 4.0 | 45 | 5.6 | 41 | 6.3 |
| Spokane, Wash. | 26 | 2.5 | 32 | 1.6 | 38 | 1.4 | 46 | 1.1 | 54 | 1.4 | 62 | 1.2 | 70 | 0.5 | 68 | 0.7 | 60 | 0.7 | 48 | 1.1 | 35 | 2.1 | 29 | 2.5 |
| Springfield, Mo. | 32 | 1.6 | 36 | 2.1 | 45 | 3.5 | 58 | 4.0 | 65 | 4.3 | 74 | 3.8 | 78 | 3.6 | 77 | 2.8 | 69 | 4.0 | 58 | 2.9 | 45 | 2.9 | 36 | 2.6 |
| Syracuse, N.Y. | 23 | 2.6 | 24 | 2.7 | 33 | 3.1 | 46 | 3.3 | 57 | 3.2 | 66 | 3.6 | 71 | 3.8 | 69 | 3.8 | 62 | 3.3 | 51 | 3.1 | 41 | 3.5 | 29 | 3.2 |
| Tampa, Fla. | 60 | 2.2 | 61 | 3.0 | 66 | 3.5 | 72 | 1.8 | 77 | 3.4 | 81 | 5.3 | 82 | 7.4 | 82 | 7.6 | 81 | 6.2 | 74 | 2.3 | 67 | 1.9 | 61 | 2.1 |
| Washington, D.C. | 31 | 2.8 | 34 | 2.6 | 42 | 3.2 | 53 | 3.1 | 62 | 3.6 | 71 | 4.2 | 76 | 3.8 | 74 | 4.2 | 67 | 3.3 | 55 | 3.0 | 45 | 3.0 | 35 | 3.3 |
| Wilmington, Del. | 31 | 3.1 | 33 | 3.0 | 42 | 3.7 | 53 | 3.1 | 62 | 3.6 | 71 | 3.5 | 76 | 4.5 | 73 | 4.2 | 68 | 3.6 | 56 | 2.9 | 46 | 3.3 | 36 | 3.5 |

## Normal Temperatures, Highs, Lows, Precipitation

Source: National Climatic Data Center, NESDIS, NOAA, U.S. Dept. of Commerce

The normal temperatures below are based on records for the thirty-year period 1951-1980. The extreme temperatures (through 1990) are listed for the stations shown and may not agree with the states records shown on pages 168-169.

Airport stations; * designates city office stations. The minus (−) sign indicates temperatures below zero. Fahrenheit thermometer registration.

| State | Station | Normal temperature January Max. | Min. | July Max. | Min. | Extreme temperature Highest | Lowest | Normal annual precipitation (inches) |
|---|---|---|---|---|---|---|---|---|
| Alabama | Mobile | 61 | 41 | 91 | 73 | 104 | 3 | 64.64 |
| Alabama | Montgomery | 57 | 36 | 92 | 72 | 105 | 0 | 49.16 |
| Alaska | Juneau | 27 | 16 | 64 | 47 | 90 | −22 | 53.15 |
| Arizona | Phoenix | 65 | 39 | 105 | 80 | 118 | 17 | 7.11 |
| Arkansas | Little Rock | 50 | 30 | 93 | 71 | 112 | −5 | 49.20 |
| California | Los Angeles* | 67 | 48 | 84 | 64 | 110 | 28 | 14.85 |
| California | San Francisco | 55 | 42 | 71 | 53 | 106 | 20 | 19.71 |
| Colorado | Denver | 43 | 16 | 88 | 59 | 104 | −30 | 15.31 |
| Connecticut | Hartford | 34 | 17 | 85 | 62 | 102 | −26 | 44.39 |
| Delaware | Wilmington | 39 | 23 | 86 | 66 | 102 | −14 | 41.38 |
| Dist. of Col. | Washington | 43 | 28 | 88 | 70 | 104 | −5 | 39.00 |
| Florida | Jacksonville | 65 | 42 | 91 | 72 | 105 | 7 | 52.76 |
| Florida | Key West | 72 | 66 | 89 | 80 | 95 | 41 | 39.42 |
| Florida | Miami | 75 | 59 | 89 | 76 | 98 | 30 | 57.55 |
| Georgia | Atlanta | 51 | 33 | 88 | 69 | 105 | −8 | 48.61 |
| Hawaii | Honolulu | 80 | 65 | 87 | 73 | 94 | 53 | 23.47 |
| Idaho | Boise | 37 | 23 | 91 | 59 | 111 | −23 | 11.71 |
| Illinois | Chicago | 29 | 14 | 83 | 63 | 104 | −27 | 33.34 |
| Indiana | Indianapolis | 34 | 18 | 85 | 65 | 104 | −23 | 39.12 |
| Iowa | Des Moines | 27 | 10 | 86 | 66 | 108 | −24 | 30.83 |
| Iowa | Dubuque | 24 | 7 | 82 | 62 | 101 | −28 | 38.59 |
| Kansas | Wichita | 40 | 19 | 93 | 70 | 113 | −21 | 28.61 |
| Kentucky | Louisville | 41 | 24 | 88 | 68 | 105 | −20 | 43.56 |
| Louisiana | New Orleans | 62 | 43 | 91 | 74 | 102 | 11 | 59.74 |
| Maine | Portland | 31 | 12 | 79 | 57 | 103 | −39 | 43.52 |
| Maryland | Baltimore | 41 | 24 | 87 | 67 | 105 | −7 | 41.84 |
| Massachusetts | Boston | 36 | 23 | 82 | 65 | 102 | −12 | 43.84 |
| Michigan | Detroit | 31 | 16 | 83 | 61 | 104 | −21 | 30.97 |
| Michigan | Sault Ste. Marie* | 21 | 5 | 75 | 52 | 98 | −36 | 33.48 |
| Minnesota | Minn.-St. Paul | 20 | 2 | 83 | 63 | 105 | −34 | 26.36 |
| Mississippi | Jackson | 57 | 35 | 93 | 68 | 106 | 2 | 52.82 |
| Missouri | St. Louis | 38 | 20 | 89 | 69 | 107 | −18 | 33.91 |
| Montana | Helena | 28 | 8 | 84 | 52 | 105 | −42 | 11.37 |
| Nebraska | Omaha | 30 | 10 | 89 | 67 | 114 | −23 | 30.34 |
| Nevada | Las Vegas | 55 | 33 | 105 | 76 | 116 | 8 | 4.19 |
| New Hampshire | Concord | 31 | 9 | 83 | 56 | 102 | −37 | 36.53 |
| New Jersey | Atlantic City | 41 | 23 | 84 | 65 | 106 | −11 | 41.93 |
| New Mexico | Albuquerque | 47 | 22 | 93 | 65 | 105 | −17 | 8.12 |
| New Mexico | Roswell | 55 | 27 | 94 | 65 | 109 | −9 | 9.70 |
| New York | Albany | 30 | 12 | 83 | 60 | 100 | −28 | 35.74 |
| New York | New York-La Guardia | 37 | 26 | 84 | 69 | 107 | −3 | 42.82 |
| No. Carolina | Charlotte | 50 | 31 | 88 | 69 | 104 | −5 | 43.16 |
| No. Carolina | Raleigh | 50 | 29 | 88 | 67 | 105 | −9 | 41.76 |
| No. Dakota | Bismarck | 18 | −4 | 84 | 56 | 109 | −44 | 15.36 |
| Ohio | Cincinnati-Greater | 37 | 20 | 86 | 65 | 102 | −25 | 40.14 |
| Ohio | Cleveland | 33 | 19 | 82 | 61 | 104 | −19 | 35.40 |
| Oklahoma | Oklahoma City | 47 | 25 | 94 | 71 | 110 | −8 | 30.89 |
| Oregon | Portland | 44 | 34 | 80 | 56 | 107 | −3 | 37.39 |
| Pennsylvania | Harrisburg | 37 | 22 | 86 | 65 | 107 | −9 | 39.09 |
| Pennsylvania | Philadelphia | 39 | 24 | 86 | 67 | 104 | −7 | 41.42 |
| Rhode Island | Block Island | 37 | 25 | 76 | 64 | 92 | −4 | 41.91 |
| So. Carolina | Charleston | 59 | 37 | 89 | 72 | 104 | 6 | 51.59 |
| So. Dakota | Huron | 22 | 0 | 87 | 61 | 112 | −39 | 18.66 |
| So. Dakota | Rapid City | 32 | 9 | 87 | 59 | 110 | −29 | 16.27 |
| Tennessee | Nashville | 46 | 28 | 90 | 69 | 107 | −17 | 48.49 |
| Texas | Amarillo | 49 | 22 | 91 | 66 | 108 | −14 | 19.10 |
| Texas | Galveston* | 59 | 48 | 87 | 79 | 101 | 8 | 40.24 |
| Texas | Houston | 62 | 41 | 94 | 73 | 107 | 7 | 44.76 |
| Utah | Salt Lake City | 37 | 20 | 93 | 62 | 107 | −30 | 15.31 |
| Vermont | Burlington | 25 | 8 | 81 | 59 | 101 | −30 | 33.69 |
| Virginia | Norfolk | 48 | 32 | 90 | 70 | 104 | −3 | 45.22 |
| Washington | Seattle-Tacoma | 44 | 34 | 75 | 54 | 99 | 0 | 38.60 |
| Washington | Spokane | 31 | 20 | 84 | 55 | 108 | −25 | 16.71 |
| West Virginia | Huntington | 41 | 25 | 86 | 65 | 102 | −16 | 40.74 |
| Wisconsin | Madison | 25 | 7 | 83 | 58 | 104 | −37 | 30.84 |
| Wisconsin | Milwaukee | 26 | 11 | 80 | 61 | 103 | −26 | 30.94 |
| Wyoming | Cheyenne | 37 | 15 | 83 | 55 | 100 | −34 | 13.31 |
| Puerto Rico | San Juan | 83 | 70 | 88 | 76 | 98 | 60 | 53.99 |

**Mean Annual Snowfall** (inches) based on record through 1980: Boston, Mass., 42; Sault Ste. Marie, Mich., 113; Albany, N.Y., 65.2; Rochester, N.Y., 89.2; Burlington, Vt., 78.6; Cheyenne, Wyo., 53.3; Juneau, Alas., 105.8.

**Wettest Spot:** Mount Waialeale, Ha., on the island of Kauai, is the rainiest place in the world, according to the National Geographic Society, with an average annual rainfall of 460 inches.

**Highest Temperature:** A temperature of 136° F. observed at Azizia, Tripolitania in northern Africa on Sept. 13, 1922, is generally accepted as the world's highest temperature recorded under standard conditions.

The record high in the United States was 134° F. in Death Valley, Cal., July 10, 1913.

**Lowest Temperature:** A record low temperature of −128.6° F. was recorded at the Soviet Antarctica station Vostok on July 21, 1983.

The record low in the United States was −80° F. at Prospect Creek, Alas., Jan. 23, 1971.

The lowest official temperature on the North American continent was recorded at −81° F. in February 1947, at a lonely airport in the Yukon called Snag.

These are the meteorological champions—the official temperature extremes—but there are plenty of other claimants to thermometer fame. However, sun readings are unofficial records, since meteorological data to qualify officially must be taken on instruments in a sheltered and ventilated location.

# Annual Climatological Data

Source: National Climatic Data Center, NESDIS, NOAA, U.S. Dept. of Commerce

| 1992 Station | Elev. ft. | Highest | Date | Lowest | Date | Temp Total (in.) | Greatest 24 hours | Date | Precip Total (in.) | Greatest 24 hours | Sleet/snow Date | Wind MPH | Date | Clear* | Cloudy* | Prec. .01 in. or more | Snow, sleet 1 in. or more |
|---|---|---|---|---|---|---|---|---|---|---|---|---|---|---|---|---|---|
| Albany, N.Y. | 275 | 90 | 8/27 | −3 | 2/10 | 31.38 | 1.47 | 5/30 | 31.9 | 5.6 | 12/11 | 38 | 12/24 | 67 | 190 | 145 | 12 |
| Albuquerque, N.M. | 5311 | 100 | 7/6 | 10 | 12/17 | 12.08 | 0.84 | 8/11 | 20.1 | 4.8 | 11/20 | 40 | 12/4 | 144 | 120 | 88 | 9 |
| Anchorage, Alas. | 114 | 74 | 7/1 | −16 | 3/5 | 14.44 | 1.16 | 9/5 | 79.8 | 11.1 | 10/26 | 32 | 10/22 | 64 | 238 | 113 | 21 |
| Asheville, N.C. | 2140 | 92 | 7/13 | 11 | 1/17 | 54.04 | 2.47 | 5/7 | 0.5 | 0.4 | 3/11 | 35 | 12/11 | 92 | 165 | 136 | 0 |
| Atlanta, Ga. | 1010 | 96 | 7/12 | 18 | 1/16 | 60.11 | 5.87 | 9/4 | 5.0 | 5.0 | 1/18 | 39 | 7/5 | 110 | 156 | 130 | 1 |
| Atlantic City, N.J. | 11 | 94 | 7/14 | 13 | 1/19 | 37.49 | 2.12 | 12/10 | — | — | — | 45 | 12/11 | — | — | 123 | — |
| Baltimore, Md. | 148 | 98 | 7/14 | 9 | 1/19 | 38.93 | 2.62 | 9/25 | 5.6 | 2.2 | 1/25 | 35 | 4/24 | 87 | 174 | 128 | 3 |
| Barrow, Alas. | 31 | 62 | 8/29 | −44 | 1/31 | 2.70 | 0.20 | 8/7 | 43.3 | 2.7 | 9/12 | 46 | 12/3 | 117 | 196 | 87 | 10 |
| Birmingham, Ala. | 678 | 95 | 8/10 | 17 | 1/16 | 55.60 | 2.71 | 8/20 | 4.4 | 4.4 | 1/18 | — | — | — | 130 | 1 | — |
| Bismarck, N.D. | 1647 | 99 | 8/8 | −23 | 12/31 | 12.70 | 1.38 | 6/14 | 48.6 | 5.1 | 3/20 | 45 | 12/24 | 90 | 161 | 89 | 19 |
| Boise, Ida. | 2838 | 106 | 7/31 | 0 | 12/6 | 7.67 | 0.82 | 6/12 | 9.6 | 2.0 | 11/27 | 40 | 4/8 | 111 | 153 | 73 | 3 |
| Boston, Mass. | 15 | 92 | 5/23 | 7 | 2/10 | 43.72 | 5.14 | 12/11 | 26.5 | 9.3 | 12/12 | 51 | 12/12 | 90 | 179 | 132 | 7 |
| Buffalo, N.Y. | 705 | 90 | 6/17 | −6 | 2/12 | 47.56 | 2.30 | 7/14 | 84.0 | 15.1 | 3/11 | 51 | 11/12 | 58 | 209 | 190 | 22 |
| Burlington, Vt. | 332 | 91 | 5/23 | −17 | 2/10 | 30.85 | 2.36 | 9/22 | 67.6 | 8.0 | 2/4 | 35 | 5/17 | 68 | 207 | 161 | 23 |
| Caribou, Me. | 624 | 93 | 5/22 | −21 | 3/1 | 36.27 | 2.21 | 8/27 | 86.6 | 14.0 | 2/28 | 32 | 12/24 | — | — | 163 | 26 |
| Charleston, S.C. | 40 | 98 | 7/11 | 25 | 1/17 | 53.87 | 3.44 | 10/3 | 0.0 | 0.0 | — | 30 | 3/27 | 89 | 177 | 128 | 0 |
| Chicago, Ill. | 658 | 93 | 8/9 | −12 | 1/16 | 30.12 | 1.82 | 11/1 | 25.8 | 8.8 | 3/21 | 41 | 7/2 | 81 | 197 | 125 | 7 |
| Cleveland, Oh. | 777 | 91 | 8/10 | −2 | 1/16 | 48.53 | 2.81 | 12/30 | 67.0 | 8.3 | 1/15 | 37 | 6/18 | 58 | 224 | 167 | 23 |
| Columbus, Oh. | 812 | 91 | 8/10 | −3 | 1/19 | 39.60 | 5.16 | 7/12 | 22.1 | 4.5 | 1/25 | 39 | 11/12 | 57 | 231 | 151 | 6 |
| Dallas-Ft. Worth, Tex. | 551 | 100 | 8/10 | 17 | 1/16 | 42.19 | 2.66 | 12/13 | T | T | 12/15 | 44 | 10/15 | 118 | 154 | 92 | 0 |
| Denver, Co. | 5283 | 99 | 7/6 | −5 | 1/15 | 15.68 | 1.99 | 8/23 | 71.14 | 14.5 | 1/7 | 40 | 3/8 | 113 | 135 | 90 | 18 |
| Des Moines, Ia. | 938 | 92 | 7/7 | −7 | 1/15 | 33.51 | 2.58 | 7/12 | 20.4 | 9.3 | 11/25 | 40 | 7/2 | 92 | 169 | 123 | 6 |
| Detroit, Mich. | 633 | 92 | 6/17 | −3 | 1/19 | 37.33 | 1.86 | 9/9 | 39.0 | 11.1 | 1/14 | 35 | 11/12 | 66 | 205 | 149 | 9 |
| Dodge City, Kan. | 2582 | 102 | 7/7 | 5 | 12/20 | 21.66 | 1.90 | 6/27 | — | — | — | — | — | — | — | 85 | — |
| Duluth, Minn. | 1428 | 86 | 8/8 | −23 | 2/12 | 28.67 | 2.11 | 7/1 | 80.3 | 8.6 | 11/2 | 32 | 12/25 | 75 | 196 | 135 | 21 |
| Fairbanks, Alas. | 436 | 91 | 6/29 | −45 | 12/26 | 12.73 | 0.95 | 7/6 | 146.2 | 9.4 | 5/12 | 31 | 5/15 | 78 | 212 | 121 | 41 |
| Fresno, Cal. | 328 | 108 | 8/18 | 29 | 12/19 | 14.08 | 1.76 | 10/29 | T | 2/15 | | 28 | 6/12 | 170 | 115 | 38 | 0 |
| Galveston, Tex. | 7 | 95 | 8/26 | 31 | 1/16 | 52.63 | 4.04 | 2/3 | T | T | 4/19 | 37 | 1/13 | — | — | 97 | 0 |
| Grand Rapids, Mich. | 784 | 95 | 6/17 | 1 | 2/12 | 42.36 | 3.38 | 6/8 | 55.0 | 10.0 | 3/21 | 39 | 6/17 | 64 | 223 | 153 | 16 |
| Hartford, Conn. | 169 | 95 | 5/22 | 2 | 2/13 | 41.98 | 3.48 | 6/5 | 23.6 | 4.6 | 3/19 | 39 | 12/24 | 93 | 177 | 134 | 8 |
| Helena, Mont. | 3828 | 98 | 8/14 | −21 | 12/31 | 9.33 | 0.67 | 10/3 | 36.3 | 6.2 | 8/22 | 54 | 8/19 | 94 | 153 | 83 | 12 |
| Honolulu, Ha. | 7 | 92 | 9/10 | 58 | 2/9 | 19.00 | 2.90 | 12/25 | 0.0 | 0.0 | — | 38 | 9/11 | 108 | 74 | 98 | 0 |
| Houston, Tex. | 96 | 97 | 8/26 | 27 | 11/28 | 52.33 | 4.56 | 3/4 | T | T | 5/28 | 48 | 8/31 | 76 | 164 | 109 | 0 |
| Huron, S.D. | 1281 | 95 | 4/30 | −13 | 1/15 | 22.49 | 1.62 | 6/30 | 31.0 | 6.5 | 2/11 | 64 | 7/7 | 101 | 164 | 93 | 9 |
| Indianapolis, Ind. | 792 | 91 | 6/17 | −6 | 1/16 | 44.18 | 2.72 | 7/6 | 16.7 | 3.9 | 1/14 | 37 | 6/18 | 67 | 222 | 150 | 7 |
| Jackson, Miss. | 291 | 97 | 8/10 | 20 | 1/16 | 48.41 | 4.79 | 8/26 | 0.2 | 0.2 | 1/18 | 35 | 6/29 | 98 | 144 | 111 | 0 |
| Jacksonville, Fla. | 26 | 98 | 7/12 | 24 | 1/17 | 63.18 | 7.90 | 10/3 | T | T | 3/30 | 46 | 4/25 | 62 | 174 | 126 | 0 |
| Kansas City, Mo. | 1014 | 93 | 8/8 | 4 | 1/15 | 50.63 | 3.79 | 7/9 | 10.2 | 2.8 | 4/20 | 38 | 10/7 | 105 | 158 | 119 | 3 |
| Knoxville, Tenn. | 979 | 93 | 7/13 | 9 | 1/16 | 44.23 | 2.03 | 8/6 | 0.3 | 0.3 | 12/25 | 30 | 3/10 | 87 | 174 | 135 | 0 |
| Lander, Wyo. | 5557 | 95 | 8/9 | −20 | 12/5 | 13.22 | 0.90 | 7/1 | 76.4 | 15.4 | 11/22 | 40 | 5/19 | 117 | 133 | 67 | 16 |
| Lexington, Ky. | 966 | 90 | 8/9 | 2 | 1/16 | 49.09 | 4.99 | 6/18 | 7.3 | 1.9 | 12/25 | 38 | 6/18 | 69 | 198 | 145 | 2 |
| Little Rock, Ark. | 257 | 97 | 8/10 | 16 | 1/16 | 41.91 | 2.38 | 3/9 | T | T | 12/5 | — | — | — | — | 119 | 0 |
| Los Angeles, Cal. | 97 | 92 | 7/8 | 40 | 12/20 | 16.59 | 2.31 | 12/6 | 0.0 | 0.0 | — | — | — | 154 | 112 | 43 | 0 |
| Louisville, Ky. | 477 | 94 | 7/13 | 5 | 1/16 | 40.79 | 3.13 | 8/7 | 4.5 | 0.9 | 12/25 | 29 | 10/8 | 76 | 198 | 140 | 0 |
| Marquette, Mich. | 1415 | 88 | 6/12 | −17 | 2/12 | 31.27 | 2.46 | 7/1 | 190.1 | 17.2 | 2/7 | — | — | — | — | 168 | 54 |
| Memphis, Tenn. | 258 | 95 | 7/13 | 14 | 1/16 | 47.15 | 3.86 | 3/9 | T | T | 12/25 | 32 | 11/12 | 100 | 160 | 111 | 0 |
| Miami, Fla. | 7 | 97 | 7/5 | 46 | 1/16 | 57.82 | 8.01 | 11/17 | 0.0 | 0.0 | — | 86 | 8/24 | 79 | 109 | 128 | 0 |
| Milwaukee, Wis. | 672 | 90 | 8/25 | −5 | 1/16 | 33.95 | 1.82 | 11/1 | 31.5 | 6.6 | 3/21 | 35 | 11/1 | 77 | 201 | 139 | 8 |
| Minneapolis, Minn. | 834 | 92 | 6/12 | −14 | 1/15 | 29.67 | 3.39 | 9/15 | 45.0 | 6.5 | 11/1 | 35 | 6/17 | 78 | 192 | 113 | 17 |
| Mobile, Ala. | 211 | 99 | 7/8 | 25 | 1/20 | 70.46 | 3.79 | 11/11 | T | T | 7/8 | 60 | 7/8 | 92 | 157 | 127 | 0 |
| Moline, Ill. | 582 | 93 | 8/9 | −9 | 1/19 | 39.94 | 2.43 | 9/9 | 18.0 | 6.1 | 12/9 | 46 | 4/10 | 97 | 189 | 126 | 5 |
| Nashville, Tenn. | 590 | 96 | 8/9 | 9 | 1/16 | 39.84 | 4.32 | 7/2 | 1.3 | 1.0 | 3/12 | 35 | 11/12 | 88 | 161 | 119 | 1 |
| Newark, N.J. | 7 | 98 | 5/22 | 10 | 1/19 | 36.74 | 2.97 | 6/5 | 13.9 | 7.3 | 3/18 | 39 | 12/11 | 84 | 188 | 126 | 3 |
| New Orleans, La. | 4 | 97 | 7/11 | 27 | 1/21 | 81.87 | 4.96 | 8/25 | T | T | 3/25 | 39 | 8/26 | 83 | 162 | 134 | 0 |
| New York, N.Y. | 132 | 93 | 7/14 | 11 | 1/19 | 43.35 | 2.90 | 6/5 | 12.3 | 6.2 | 3/18 | 39 | 12/11 | — | — | 128 | 4 |
| Norfolk, Va. | 24 | 102 | 7/10 | 19 | 1/20 | 47.28 | 3.14 | 1/3 | T | T | 4/5 | 37 | 3/27 | 83 | 170 | 118 | 0 |
| Oklahoma City, Okla. | 1285 | 98 | 7/2 | 14 | 1/16 | 39.85 | 2.31 | 9/5 | — | — | — | 43 | 10/7 | — | — | 103 | — |
| Omaha, Neb. | 997 | 92 | 7/1 | −4 | 1/15 | 34.69 | 1.92 | 10/7 | 21.5 | 9.9 | 4/20 | 37 | 12/23 | 79 | 192 | 118 | 5 |
| Philadelphia, Pa. | 5 | 97 | 7/14 | 11 | 1/19 | 30.41 | 3.03 | 12/10 | 4.7 | 2.1 | 3/22 | 44 | 12/11 | 86 | 176 | 119 | 1 |
| Phoenix, Ariz. | 1110 | 113 | 8/17 | 36 | 12/20 | 14.24 | 1.80 | 7/23 | T | T | 10/24 | 35 | 5/23 | 187 | 80 | 61 | 0 |
| Pittsburgh, Pa. | 1137 | 89 | 7/14 | −1 | 1/19 | 36.65 | 2.31 | 8/27 | 45.6 | 8.4 | 12/10 | 36 | 11/12 | 55 | 217 | 147 | 15 |
| Portland, Me. | 43 | 90 | 5/22 | −7 | 2/13 | 38.51 | 2.40 | 6/5 | 41.0 | 11.4 | 3/20 | 36 | 1/23 | 89 | 180 | 133 | 11 |
| Portland, Ore. | 21 | 101 | 8/11 | 27 | 12/18 | 29.50 | 1.63 | 11/20 | 4.6 | 2.5 | 12/31 | 35 | 12/16 | 73 | 189 | 126 | 2 |
| Providence, R.I. | 51 | 94 | 5/22 | 5 | 1/17 | 47.48 | 3.02 | 12/11 | 21.1 | 4.8 | 3/19 | 39 | 3/27 | 90 | 187 | 133 | 7 |
| Raleigh, N.C. | 434 | 96 | 7/13 | 19 | 12/25 | 43.18 | 3.78 | 8/12 | T | T | 12/27 | 35 | 3/11 | 93 | 167 | 120 | 0 |
| Rapid City, S.D. | 3162 | 103 | 8/8 | −13 | 12/31 | 13.50 | 1.01 | 7/20 | 36.4 | 7.3 | 12/12 | 51 | 4/19 | 123 | 130 | 94 | 12 |
| Reno, Nev. | 4404 | 102 | 8/11 | 5 | 12/5 | 5.36 | 0.95 | 12/28 | 16.0 | 11.3 | 12/28 | 41 | 12/10 | 134 | 114 | 45 | 4 |
| Richmond, Va. | 164 | 98 | 7/14 | 16 | 1/20 | 41.55 | 3.43 | 3/6 | 0.8 | 0.8 | 2/8 | 40 | 7/31 | 83 | 179 | 127 | 0 |
| Scottsbluff, Neb. | 3957 | 98 | 8/8 | −13 | 12/5 | 15.83 | 1.03 | 5/21 | 40.2 | 6.8 | 1/7 | 46 | 6/3 | 115 | 133 | 86 | 14 |
| St. Louis, Mo. | 535 | 97 | 7/2 | 8 | 1/16 | 33.49 | 2.88 | 8/26 | 9.9 | 3.5 | 1/13 | 37 | 9/9 | 69 | 202 | 113 | 3 |
| Salt Lake City, Ut. | 4221 | 103 | 8/2 | 1 | 1/20 | 12.07 | 1.10 | 11/1 | 48.6 | 7.5 | 11/19 | 54 | 11/22 | 114 | 134 | 84 | 13 |
| San Antonio, Tex. | 788 | 100 | 8/26 | 24 | 11/27 | 46.49 | 3.59 | 3/3 | T | T | 11/4 | 32 | 6/11 | 91 | 152 | 102 | 0 |
| San Diego, Cal. | 13 | 91 | 9/23 | 38 | 12/20 | 12.81 | 2.04 | 3/2 | 0.0 | 0.0 | — | 29 | 3/26 | 150 | 123 | 49 | 0 |
| San Francisco, Cal. | 8 | 92 | 10/6 | 35 | 12/18 | 20.69 | 1.76 | 12/26 | T | T | 12/29 | 38 | 6/14 | 143 | 104 | 63 | 0 |
| Sault Ste. Marie, Mich. | 721 | 86 | 5/22 | −17 | 2/9 | 35.81 | 1.46 | 4/21 | 125.7 | 9.9 | 12/25 | 33 | 12/25 | 69 | 213 | 158 | 37 |
| Savannah, Ga. | 46 | 100 | 7/10 | 25 | 1/17 | 58.36 | 3.82 | 6/25 | 0.0 | 0.0 | — | 35 | 7/1 | 100 | 164 | 110 | 0 |
| Seattle, Wash. | 400 | 92 | 6/24 | 25 | 1/7 | 32.78 | 1.80 | 1/27 | 6.7 | 2.8 | 12/10 | 42 | 4/16 | 67 | 192 | 141 | 3 |
| Spokane, Wash. | 2356 | 101 | 8/14 | 3 | 12/6 | 14.52 | 1.01 | 6/12 | 61.7 | 10.9 | 12/19 | 38 | 4/17 | 62 | 192 | 105 | 21 |
| Springfield, Mo. | 1268 | 93 | 8/10 | 4 | 1/15 | 48.04 | 2.89 | 7/4 | 8.6 | 4.6 | 1/13 | 46 | 7/2 | 103 | 178 | 120 | 2 |
| Syracuse, N.Y. | 410 | 88 | 8/26 | −8 | 2/12 | 43.61 | 1.97 | 5/30 | 154.8 | 21.5 | 1/18 | 35 | 1/18 | 66 | 211 | 197 | 46 |
| Tampa, Fla. | 19 | 96 | 7/9 | 36 | 1/17 | 34.98 | 3.68 | 8/28 | 0.0 | 0.0 | — | 29 | 6/25 | 93 | 111 | 93 | 0 |
| Washington, D.C. | 19 | 99 | 7/14 | 14 | 1/19 | 36.38 | 1.84 | 1/4 | 7.6 | 3.8 | 1/25 | 38 | 12/11 | 70 | 188 | 122 | 3 |
| Wilmington, Del. | 74 | 97 | 7/14 | 10 | 1/19 | 37.04 | 2.33 | 12/10 | 3.4 | 1.4 | 1/25 | 39 | 12/24 | 86 | 179 | 115 | 0 |

\* To get partly cloudy days deduct the total of clear and cloudy days from 365 (1 yr.). T—trace. (1) Date shown is the starting date of the storm (in some cases it lasted more than one day). (2) Sustained for at least 1 minute, not peak gust.

## Record Temperatures by States Through 1992

Source: National Climatic Data Center, NESDIS, NOAA, U.S. Dept. of Commerce

| State | Lowest °F | Highest | Latest date | Station | Approximate elevation in feet |
|---|---|---|---|---|---|
| Alabama | −27 | | Jan. 30, 1966 | New Market | 760 |
| | | 112 | Sept. 5, 1925 | Centerville | 345 |
| Alaska | −80 | | Jan. 23, 1971 | Prospect Creek Camp | 1,100 |
| | | 100 | June 27, 1915 | Fort Yukon | 420 |
| Arizona | −40 | | Jan. 7, 1971 | Hawley Lake | 8,180 |
| | | 127 | July 7, 1905 [1] | Parker | 345 |
| Arkansas | −29 | | Feb. 13, 1905 | Pond | 1,250 |
| | | 120 | Aug. 10, 1936 | Ozark | 396 |
| California | −45 | | Jan. 20, 1937 | Boca | 5,532 |
| | | 134 | July 10, 1913 | Greenland Ranch | −178 |
| Colorado | −61 | | Feb. 1, 1985 | Maybell | 5,920 |
| | | 118 | July 11, 1888 | Bennett | 5,484 |
| Connecticut | −32 | | Feb. 16, 1943 | Falls Village | 585 |
| | | 105 | July 21, 1991 [1] | Danbury | 450 |
| Delaware | −17 | | Jan. 17, 1893 | Millsboro | 20 |
| | | 110 | July 21, 1930 | Millsboro | 20 |
| Dist. of Col. | −15 | | Feb. 11, 1899 | Washington | 112 |
| | | 106 | July 20, 1930 | Washington | 112 |
| Florida | −2 | | Feb. 13, 1899 | Tallahassee | 193 |
| | | 109 | June 29, 1931 | Monticello | 207 |
| Georgia | −17 | | Jan. 27, 1940 | CCC Camp F-16 | 1,000 |
| | | 112 | Jul. 24, 1952 | Louisville | 132 |
| Hawaii | 12 | | May 17, 1979 | Mauna Kea | 13,770 |
| | | 100 | Apr. 27, 1931 | Pahala | 850 |
| Idaho | −60 | | Jan. 18, 1943 | Island Park Dam | 6,285 |
| | | 118 | July 28, 1934 | Orofino | 1,027 |
| Illinois | −35 | | Jan. 22, 1930 | Mount Carroll | 817 |
| | | 117 | July 14, 1954 | E. St. Louis | 410 |
| Indiana | −35 | | Feb. 2, 1951 | Greensburg | 954 |
| | | 116 | July 14, 1936 | Collegeville | 672 |
| Iowa | −47 | | Jan. 12, 1912 | Washta | 1,157 |
| | | 118 | July 20, 1934 | Keokuk | 614 |
| Kansas | −40 | | Feb. 13, 1905 | Lebanon | 1,812 |
| | | 121 | July 24, 1936 [1] | Alton (near) | 1,651 |
| Kentucky | −34 | | Jan. 28, 1963 | Cynthiana | 684 |
| | | 114 | July 28, 1930 | Greensburg | 581 |
| Louisiana | −16 | | Feb. 13, 1899 | Minden | 194 |
| | | 114 | Aug. 10, 1936 | Plain Dealing | 268 |
| Maine | −48 | | Jan. 19, 1925 | Van Buren | 510 |
| | | 105 | July 10, 1911 [1] | North Bridgton | 450 |
| Maryland | −40 | | Jan. 13, 1912 | Oakland | 2,461 |
| | | 109 | July 10, 1936 [1] | Cumberland and Frederick | 623; 325 |
| Massachusetts | −35 | | Jan. 12, 1981 | Chester | 640 |
| | | 107 | Aug. 2, 1975 | Chester and New Bedford | 120; 640 |
| Michigan | −51 | | Feb. 9, 1934 | Vanderbilt | 785 |
| | | 112 | July 13, 1936 | Mio | 963 |
| Minnesota | −59 | | Feb. 16, 1903 [1] | Pokegama Dam | 1,280 |
| | | 114 | July 6, 1936 [1] | Moorhead | 904 |
| Mississippi | −19 | | Jan. 30, 1966 | Corinth | 420 |
| | | 115 | July 29, 1930 | Holly Springs | 600 |
| Missouri | −40 | | Feb. 13, 1905 | Warsaw | 700 |
| | | 118 | July 14, 1954 [1] | Warsaw and Union | 687; 560 |
| Montana | −70 | | Jan. 20, 1954 | Rogers Pass | 5,470 |
| | | 117 | July 5, 1937 | Medicine Lake | 1,950 |
| Nebraska | −47 | | Feb. 12, 1899 | Camp Clarke | 3,700 |
| | | 118 | July 24, 1936 [1] | Minden | 2,169 |
| Nevada | −50 | | Jan. 8, 1937 | San Jacinto | 5,200 |
| | | 122 | June 26, 1990 [1] | Laughlin | 680 |
| New Hampshire | −46 | | Jan. 28 1925 | Pittsburgh | 1,575 |
| | | 106 | July 4, 1911 | Nashua | 125 |
| New Jersey | −34 | | Jan. 5, 1904 | River Vale | 70 |
| | | 110 | July 10, 1936 | Runyon | 18 |
| New Mexico | −50 | | Feb. 1, 1951 | Gavilan | 7,350 |
| | | 116 | July 14, 1934 [1] | Orogrande | 4,171 |
| New York | −52 | | Feb. 18, 1979 | Old Forge | 1,720 |
| | | 108 | July 22, 1926 | Troy | 35 |
| North Carolina | −34 | | Jan. 21, 1985 | Mt. Mitchell | 6,525 |
| | | 110 | Aug. 21, 1983 | Fayetteville | 213 |
| North Dakota | −60 | | Feb. 15, 1936 | Parshall | 1,929 |
| | | 121 | July 6, 1936 | Steele | 1,857 |
| Ohio | −39 | | Feb. 10, 1899 | Milligan | 800 |
| | | 113 | July 21, 1934 [1] | Gallipolis (near) | 673 |
| Oklahoma | −27 | | Jan. 18, 1930 | Watts | 958 |
| | | 120 | July 26, 1943 [1] | Tishomingo | 670 |
| Oregon | −54 | | Feb. 10, 1933 [1] | Seneca | 4,700 |
| | | 119 | Aug. 10, 1898 | Pendleton | 1,074 |
| Pennsylvania | −42 | | Jan. 5, 1904 | Smethport | 1,500 |
| | | 111 | July 10, 1936 [1] | Phoenixville | 100 |
| Rhode Island | −23 | | Jan. 11, 1942 | Kingston | 100 |
| | | 104 | Aug. 2, 1975 | Providence | 51 |
| South Carolina | −19 | | Jan. 21, 1985 | Caesar's Head | 3,100 |
| | | 111 | June 28, 1954 [1] | Camden | 170 |
| South Dakota | −58 | | Feb. 17, 1936 | McIntosh | 2,277 |
| | | 120 | July 5, 1936 | Gannvalley | 1,750 |

| State | Lowest °F | Highest | Latest date | Station | Approximate elevation in feet |
|---|---|---|---|---|---|
| Tennessee | −32 | | Dec. 30, 1917 | Mountain City | 2,471 |
| | | 113 | Aug. 9, 1930 [1] | Perryville | 377 |
| Texas | −23 | | Feb. 8, 1933 | Seminole | 3,275 |
| | | 120 | Aug. 12, 1936 | Seymour | 1,291 |
| Utah | −69 | | Feb. 1, 1985 | Peter's Sink | 8,092 |
| | | 117 | Jul. 5, 1985 | Saint George | 2,880 |
| Vermont | −50 | | Dec. 30, 1933 | Bloomfield | 915 |
| | | 105 | July 4, 1911 | Vernon | 310 |
| Virginia | −30 | | Jan. 22, 1985 | Mountain Lake Bio. Station | 3,870 |
| | | 110 | July 15, 1954 | Balcony Falls | 725 |
| Washington | −48 | | Dec. 30, 1968 | Mazama and Winthrop | 2,120; 1,765 |
| | | 118 | Aug. 5, 1961 [1] | Ice Harbor Dam | 475 |
| West Virginia | −37 | | Dec. 30, 1917 | Lewisburg | 2,200 |
| | | 112 | July 10, 1936 [1] | Martinsburg | 435 |
| Wisconsin | −54 | | Jan. 24, 1922 | Danbury | 908 |
| | | 114 | July 13, 1936 | Wisconsin Dells | 900 |
| Wyoming | −63 | | Feb. 9, 1933 | Moran | 6,770 |
| | | 114 | July 12, 1900 | Basin | 3,500 |

(1) Also on earlier dates at the same or other places.

## International Temperature and Precipitation

Source: Environmental Data Service. U.S. Dept. of Commerce

A standard period of 30 years has been used to obtain the average daily maximum and minimum temperatures and precipitation. The length of record of extreme maximum and minimum temperatures includes all available years of data for a given location and is usually for a longer period.

| Station | Elev. Feet | Average Daily January Max. | Average Daily January Min. | Average Daily July Max. | Average Daily July Min. | Extreme Max. | Extreme Min. | Average annual precipitation (inches) |
|---|---|---|---|---|---|---|---|---|
| Addis Ababa, Ethiopia | 8,038 | 75 | 43 | 69 | 50 | 94 | 32 | 48.7 |
| Algiers, Algeria | 194 | 59 | 49 | 83 | 70 | 107 | 32 | 30.0 |
| Amsterdam, Netherlands | 5 | 40 | 34 | 69 | 59 | 95 | 3 | 25.6 |
| Athens, Greece | 351 | 54 | 42 | 90 | 72 | 109 | 20 | 15.8 |
| Auckland, New Zealand | 23 | 73 | 60 | 56 | 46 | 90 | 33 | 49.1 |
| Bangkok, Thailand | 53 | 89 | 67 | 90 | 76 | 104 | 50 | 57.8 |
| Beirut, Lebanon | 111 | 62 | 51 | 87 | 73 | 107 | 30 | 35.1 |
| Berlin, Germany | 187 | 35 | 26 | 74 | 55 | 96 | −15 | 23.1 |
| Bogotá, Colombia | 8,355 | 67 | 48 | 64 | 50 | 75 | 30 | 41.8 |
| Bombay, India | 27 | 88 | 62 | 88 | 75 | 110 | 46 | 71.2 |
| Bucharest, Romania | 269 | 33 | 20 | 86 | 61 | 105 | −18 | 22.8 |
| Budapest, Hungary | 394 | 35 | 26 | 82 | 61 | 103 | −10 | 24.2 |
| Buenos Aires, Argentina | 89 | 85 | 63 | 57 | 42 | 104 | 22 | 37.4 |
| Cairo, Egypt | 381 | 65 | 47 | 96 | 70 | 117 | 34 | 1.1 |
| Capetown, South Africa | 56 | 78 | 60 | 63 | 45 | 103 | 28 | 20.0 |
| Caracas, Venezuela | 3,418 | 75 | 56 | 78 | 61 | 91 | 45 | 32.9 |
| Casablanca, Morocco | 164 | 63 | 45 | 79 | 65 | 110 | 31 | 15.9 |
| Copenhagen, Denmark | 43 | 36 | 29 | 72 | 55 | 91 | −3 | 23.3 |
| Damascus, Syria | 2,362 | 53 | 36 | 96 | 64 | 113 | 21 | 8.6 |
| Dublin, Ireland | 155 | 47 | 35 | 67 | 51 | 86 | 8 | 29.7 |
| Geneva, Switzerland | 1,329 | 39 | 29 | 77 | 58 | 101 | −1 | 33.9 |
| Havana, Cuba | 80 | 79 | 65 | 89 | 75 | 104 | 43 | 48.2 |
| Hong Kong | 109 | 64 | 56 | 87 | 78 | 97 | 32 | 85.1 |
| Istanbul, Turkey | 59 | 45 | 36 | 81 | 65 | 100 | 17 | 31.5 |
| Jerusalem, Israel | 2,654 | 55 | 41 | 87 | 63 | 107 | 26 | 19.7 |
| Lagos, Nigeria | 10 | 88 | 74 | 83 | 74 | 104 | 60 | 72.3 |
| La Paz, Bolivia | 12,001 | 63 | 43 | 62 | 33 | 80 | 26 | 22.6 |
| Lima, Peru | 394 | 82 | 66 | 67 | 57 | 93 | 49 | 1.6 |
| London, England | 149 | 44 | 35 | 73 | 55 | 99 | 9 | 22.9 |
| Madrid, Spain | 2,188 | 47 | 33 | 87 | 62 | 102 | 14 | 16.5 |
| Manila, Philippines | 49 | 86 | 69 | 88 | 75 | 101 | 58 | 82.0 |
| Mexico City, Mexico | 7,340 | 66 | 42 | 74 | 54 | 92 | 24 | 23.0 |
| Montreal, Canada | 187 | 21 | 6 | 78 | 61 | 97 | −35 | 40.8 |
| Moscow, Russia | 505 | 21 | 9 | 76 | 55 | 96 | −27 | 24.8 |
| Nairobi, Kenya | 5,971 | 77 | 54 | 69 | 51 | 87 | 41 | 37.7 |
| Oslo, Norway | 308 | 30 | 20 | 73 | 56 | 93 | −21 | 26.9 |
| Paris, France | 164 | 42 | 32 | 76 | 55 | 105 | 1 | 22.3 |
| Prague, Czech Republic | 662 | 34 | 25 | 74 | 58 | 98 | −16 | 19.3 |
| Reykjavik, Iceland | 92 | 36 | 28 | 58 | 48 | 74 | 4 | 33.9 |
| Rome, Italy | 377 | 54 | 39 | 88 | 64 | 104 | 20 | 29.5 |
| San Salvador, El Salvador | 2,238 | 90 | 60 | 89 | 65 | 105 | 45 | 70.0 |
| Santiago, Chile | 1,706 | 85 | 53 | 59 | 37 | 99 | 24 | 14.2 |
| Sao Paolo, Brazil | 2,628 | 77 | 63 | 66 | 53 | 100 | 32 | 57.3 |
| Shanghai, China | 16 | 47 | 32 | 91 | 75 | 104 | 10 | 45.0 |
| Singapore | 33 | 86 | 73 | 88 | 75 | 97 | 66 | 95.0 |
| Stockholm, Sweden | 146 | 31 | 23 | 70 | 55 | 97 | −26 | 22.4 |
| Sydney, Australia | 62 | 78 | 65 | 60 | 46 | 114 | 35 | 46.5 |
| Teheran, Iran | 3,937 | 45 | 27 | 99 | 72 | 109 | −5 | 9.7 |
| Tokyo, Japan | 19 | 47 | 29 | 83 | 70 | 101 | 17 | 61.6 |
| Toronto, Canada | 379 | 30 | 16 | 79 | 59 | 105 | −26 | 32.2 |
| Tripoli, Libya | 72 | 61 | 47 | 85 | 71 | 114 | 33 | 15.1 |
| Vienna, Austria | 664 | 34 | 26 | 75 | 59 | 98 | −14 | 25.6 |
| Warsaw, Poland | 294 | 30 | 21 | 75 | 56 | 98 | −22 | 22.0 |

# Tides and Their Causes

Source: U.S. Dept. of Commerce, (NOAA) Natl. Oceanic & Atmospheric Admin., (NOS) Natl. Ocean Service

The tides are a natural phenomenon involving the alternating rise and fall in the large fluid bodies of the earth caused by the combined gravitational attraction of the sun and moon. The combination of these two variable force influences produces the complex recurrent cycle of the tides. Tides may occur in both oceans and seas, to a limited extent in large lakes, the atmosphere, and, to a very minute degree, in the earth itself. The period between succeeding tides varies as the result of many factors and force influences.

The tide-generating force represents the difference between (1) the centrifugal force produced by the revolution of the earth around the common center-of-gravity of the earth-moon system and (2) the gravitational attraction of the moon acting upon the earth's overlying waters. Since, on the average, the moon is only 238,852 miles from the earth compared with the sun's much greater distance of 92,956,000 miles, this closer distance outranks the much smaller mass of the moon compared with that of the sun, and the moon's tide-raising force is, accordingly, $2^1/_2$ times that of the sun.

The effect of the tide-generating forces of the moon and sun acting tangentially to the earth's surface (the so-called "tractive force") tends to cause a maximum accumulation of the waters of the oceans at two diametrically opposite positions on the surface of the earth and to withdraw compensating amounts of water from all points 90° removed from the positions of these tidal bulges. As the earth rotates beneath the maxima and minima of these tide-generating forces, a sequence of two high tides, separated by two low tides, ideally is produced each day (semidiurnal tide).

Twice in each lunar month, when the sun, moon, and earth are directly aligned, with the moon between the earth and the sun (at new moon) or on the opposite side of the earth from the sun (at full moon), the sun and the moon exert their gravitational force in a mutual or additive fashion. The highest high tides and lowest low tides are produced. These are called *spring* tides. At two positions 90° in between, the gravitational forces of the moon and sun — imposed at right angles—tend to counteract each other to the greatest extent, and the range between high and low tides is reduced. These are called *neap* tides. This semi-monthly variation between the spring and neap tides is called the *phase inequality.*

The inclination of the moon's monthly orbit to the equator and the inclination of the sun during the earth's yearly orbit to the equator produce a difference in the height of succeeding high tides and in the extent of depression of succeeding low tides that is known as the diurnal inequality. In most cases, this produces a type of tide called a mixed tide. In extreme cases, these phenomena can result in only one high tide and one low each tide (diurnal tide). There are also other monthly and yearly variations in the tide due to the elliptical shape of the orbits themselves.

The datum for Charting and Predictions is (MLLW) Mean Lower Low Water. This became effective January 1989 according to the convention of 1980 which prescribed that datums on all United States coastlines would be the same. Namely (MHHW) Mean Higher High Water, (MHW) Mean High Water, (MTL) Mean Tide Level, (MSL) Mean Sea Level, (MLW) Mean Low Water, (MLLW) Mean Lower Low Water. Diurnal range of tide is the difference in height between mean higher high water and mean lower low water. Mean range of tide is the difference in height between mean high water and mean low water.

The actual range of tide in the waters of the open oceans may amount to only one to three feet. However, as the ocean tide approaches shoal waters and its effects are augmented the tidal range may be greatly increased. In Nova Scotia along the narrow channel of the Bay of Fundy, the range of tides, or difference between high and low waters, may reach 43 1/2 feet or more (under spring tide conditions) due to resonant amplification.

At New Orleans, the periodic rise and fall of the diurnal tide is affected by the seasonal stages of the Mississippi River, being about 10 inches at low stage and zero at high. The Canadian Tide Tables for 1972 gave a maximum range of nearly 50 feet at Leaf Basin, Ungava Bay, Quebec.

In every case, actual high or low tide can vary considerably from the average, due to weather conditions such as strong winds, abrupt barometric pressure changes, or prolonged periods of extreme high or low pressure.

## The Average Rise and Fall of Tides[1]

| Places | Ft. | In. | Places | Ft. | In. | Places | Ft. | In. |
|---|---|---|---|---|---|---|---|---|
| Baltimore, Md. | 1 | 8 | Mobile, Ala. | 1 | 6 | San Diego, Cal. | 5 | 9 |
| Boston, Mass. | 10 | 4 | New London, Conn. | 3 | 1 | Sandy Hook, N.J. | 5 | 2 |
| Charleston, S.C. | 5 | 10 | Newport, R.I. | 3 | 11 | San Francisco, Cal. | 5 | 10 |
| Cristobal, Panama | 1 | 1 | New York, N.Y. | 5 | 1 | Savannah, Ga. | 8 | 3 |
| Eastport, Me. | 19 | 4 | Old Pt. Comfort, Va. | 3 | 0 | Seattle, Wash. | 11 | 4 |
| Galveston, Tex. | 1 | 5 | Philadelphia, Pa. | 6 | 9 | Tampa, Fla. | 2 | 10 |
| Halifax, N.S. | 4 | 5[2] | Portland, Me. | 9 | 11 | Vancouver, B.C. | 10 | 6 |
| Key West, Fla. | 1 | 10 | St. John's, Nfld. | 2 | 7[2] | Washington, D.C. | 3 | 2 |

(1) Diurnal range. (2) Mean range.

## Hurricane Names in 1994

Names assigned to Atlantic hurricanes, 1994 — Alberto, Beryl, Chris, Debby, Ernesto, Florence, Gordon, Helene, Isaac, Joyce, Keith, Leslie, Michael, Nadine, Oscar, Patty, Rafael, Sandy, Tony, Valerie, William.

Names assigned to Eastern Pacific hurricanes, 1994 — Aletta, Bud, Carlotta, Daniel, Emilia, Fabio, Gilma, Hector, Ileana, John, Kristy, Lane, Miriam, Norman, Olivia, Paul, Rosa, Sergio, Tara, Vicente, Willa, Xavier, Yolanda, Zeke.

## Historic Floods of the Mississippi River Region

Source: U.S. Army Corps of Engineers, Vicksburg, Miss.

| Year | Location | Volume (cu. ft./ sec.) | Damage (1993 dollars) | Year | Location | Volume (cu. ft./ sec.) | Damage (1993 dollars) |
|---|---|---|---|---|---|---|---|
| 1844 | upper Mississippi | 1.3 million | NA | 1945 | upper and lower Mississippi | 1.9 million | NA |
| 1913 | lower Mississippi | 1.97 million | NA | 1950 | lower Mississippi | 1.96 million | NA |
| 1927 | upper and lower Mississippi | 2.3 million | $4.4 billion | 1973 | upper and lower Mississippi | 1.9 million | $11.54 billion |
| 1937 | lower Mississippi and Ohio valleys | 2.0 million | $150 million | 1983 | upper and lower Mississippi | 1.8 million | $1.15 billion |
| | | | | 1993 | upper Mississippi | 1.0 million | $12 billion* |

* Preliminary figure based on World Almanac research. NA = not available.

# Glossary of Inland Flood Terms

Source: U.S. Army Corps of Engineers

**Crest:** The highest level that a river reaches. National Weather Service river gauges, automatic measuring devices stationed every few miles along large rivers, record not only the water level every six hours but also the precise time and height at which the river crests at that gauge. Mathematical formulas based on the historical record then predict how long the crest will take to reach the next gauge. The crest is measured from the river's deepest point.

**Cubic Feet per Second (cfs):** Engineers measure the flow of water past a given point as the volume per second, in cubic feet. This figure is essentially calculated by multiplying the width of the stream or river by the average depth and then by the speed of the water. For example, if a stream is 10 feet wide, has an average depth of 1 foot, and has a speed of 5 feet per second, then the stream is flowing at 50 cubic feet per second (10 times 1 times 5). One cubic foot of water equals about 7.5 gallons and weighs 62 pounds.

**Flood Stage:** The height of a river above which damage begins to occur, typically because the river begins to overflow its banks.

**100-Year Flood:** More accurately referred to as a "1 percent chance flood," a flood that, based on the historical record, has 1 chance in 100 of occurring in any given year. Of course, if a location has a 100-year flood, that does not mean that it is safe from another such flood for 99 years.

**Levee:** A structure of earth, stone, or concrete built parallel to a river to protect land from flooding.

**Saturation:** A soil condition in which all the spaces between soil particles are filled with water. The soil is therefore unable to absorb any additional rainfall or snow melt. Earthen levees may weaken if they become saturated.

**Spillway:** A feature in a dam that allows the release of large volumes of excess water from the reservoir to prevent water from flowing over the top of the dam. The spillway is usually a gap in the top of a dam that the water reaches only during floods.

**Stage:** The height of a river above a given level or the river bottom, as measured by a gauge.

## Wind Chill Table

Source: National Weather Service, NOAA, U.S. Dept. of Commerce

Both temperature and wind cause heat loss from body surfaces. A combination of cold and wind makes a body feel colder than the actual temperature. The table shows, for example, that a temperature of 20 degrees Fahrenheit, plus a wind of 20 miles per hour, causes a body heat loss equal to that in minus 10 degrees with no wind. In other words, the wind makes 20 degrees feel like minus 10.

Top line of figures shows actual temperatures in degrees Fahrenheit. Column at left shows wind speeds.

| MPH | 35 | 30 | 25 | 20 | 15 | 10 | 5 | 0 | −5 | −10 | −15 | −20 | −25 | −30 | −35 | −40 | −45 |
|---|---|---|---|---|---|---|---|---|---|---|---|---|---|---|---|---|---|
| 5 | 33 | 27 | 21 | 16 | 12 | 7 | 0 | −5 | −10 | −15 | −21 | −26 | −31 | −36 | −42 | −47 | −52 |
| 10 | 22 | 16 | 10 | 3 | −3 | −9 | −15 | −22 | −27 | −34 | −40 | −46 | −52 | −58 | −64 | −71 | −77 |
| 15 | 16 | 9 | 2 | −5 | −11 | −18 | −25 | −31 | −38 | −45 | −51 | −58 | −65 | −72 | −78 | −85 | −92 |
| 20 | 12 | 4 | −3 | −10 | −17 | −24 | −31 | −39 | −46 | −53 | −60 | −67 | −74 | −81 | −88 | −95 | −103 |
| 25 | 8 | 1 | −7 | −15 | −22 | −29 | −36 | −44 | −51 | −59 | −66 | −74 | −81 | −88 | −96 | −103 | −110 |
| 30 | 6 | −2 | −10 | −18 | −25 | −33 | −41 | −49 | −56 | −64 | −71 | −79 | −86 | −93 | −101 | −109 | −116 |
| 35 | 4 | −4 | −12 | −20 | −27 | −35 | −43 | −52 | −58 | −67 | −74 | −82 | −89 | −97 | −105 | −113 | −120 |
| 40 | 3 | −5 | −13 | −21 | −29 | −37 | −45 | −53 | −60 | −69 | −76 | −84 | −92 | −100 | −107 | −115 | −123 |
| 45 | 2 | −6 | −14 | −22 | −30 | −38 | −46 | −54 | −62 | −70 | −78 | −85 | −93 | −102 | −109 | −117 | −125 |

*(Wind speeds greater than 45 mph have little additional chilling effect.)*

## Heat Index

The index is a measure of the contribution that high humidity makes with abnormally high temperatures in reducing the body's ability to cool itself. For example, the index shows that for an actual air temperature of 100 degrees Fahrenheit and a relative humidity of 50 percent, the effect on the human body would be same as 120 degrees. Sunstroke and heat exhaustion are likely when the heat index reaches 105. This index is a measure of what hot weather "feels like" to the average person for various temperatures and relative humidities.

| Relative Humidity | Air Temperature* 70 | 75 | 80 | 85 | 90 | 95 | 100 | 105 | 110 | 115 | 120 |
|---|---|---|---|---|---|---|---|---|---|---|---|
| | Apparent Temperature* | | | | | | | | | | |
| 0% | 64 | 69 | 73 | 78 | 83 | 87 | 91 | 95 | 99 | 103 | 107 |
| 10% | 65 | 70 | 75 | 80 | 85 | 90 | 95 | 100 | 105 | 111 | 116 |
| 20% | 66 | 72 | 77 | 82 | 87 | 93 | 99 | 105 | 112 | 120 | 130 |
| 30% | 67 | 73 | 78 | 84 | 90 | 96 | 104 | 113 | 123 | 135 | 148 |
| 40% | 68 | 74 | 79 | 86 | 93 | 101 | 110 | 123 | 137 | 151 | |
| 50% | 69 | 75 | 81 | 88 | 96 | 107 | 120 | 135 | 150 | | |
| 60% | 70 | 76 | 82 | 90 | 100 | 114 | 132 | 149 | | | |
| 70% | 70 | 77 | 85 | 93 | 106 | 124 | 144 | | | | |
| 80% | 71 | 78 | 86 | 97 | 113 | 136 | | | | | |
| 90% | 71 | 79 | 88 | 102 | 122 | | | | | | |
| 100% | 72 | 80 | 91 | 108 | | | | | | | |

*Degrees Fahrenheit.

# ENVIRONMENT

## U.S. Environmental Quality Index, 1992

Source: Feb.-Mar. 1993 issue of *National Wildlife* magazine; World Almanac research.

In 1993, *National Wildlife* magazine published the twenty-fifth in its series of annual reports on the environment. According to the report, conflict continued to increase in 1992 over whether economic or ecological concerns should be of primary importance in the allocation of America's natural resources. The continued sluggishness of the U.S. economy rendered this debate increasingly political, as the environment once again became a theme in the presidential election.

**Wildlife:** The Endangered Species Act expired in 1992 and, while it would continue to be enforced, the controversy surrounding reauthorizing the law centered on a few publicized conflicts between economic development and species survival. One example was provided by a controversy in the Southeast over the use of turtle excluder devices (TEDs), which allow endangered sea turtles to escape from shrimping nets. In December, the National Marine Fisheries Service extended mandatory use of TEDs to year round, despite industry fears that the devices might reduce catches. Meanwhile, the decline in duck populations, a traditional indicator of the health of North America's ecosystems, was the worst recorded since the 1930s. This decline prompted calls for increased protection, that is to say decreased development, of wetlands, which play roles in the life cycles of ducks and many other endangered and threatened animals.

**Air:** In mid-1992, a change in the regulations of the Clean Air Act was made that allowed large companies, citing a change in production methods, to increase pollutant emissions by up to 245 tons a year. The presidential council recommending this change contended that obtaining permits for such "minor" changes would be a costly process, while critics charged that the move would gut the Clean Air Act. The Clean Air Act also authorized the trading of pollution credits and debits, in an attempt to use market incentives to lower pollution. The first sales of credits for unused pollution capacity were made by Wisconsin Power and Light in 1992. The purchaser, the Tennessee Valley Authority, paid $2.5–4 million for the credits, which would allow it to discharge as many as 25,000 tons of sulfur dioxide. Meanwhile, the California Air Resources Board reported continued declines in hazardous air pollution for locations in the California basin, though current levels remained unhealthy. Smog levels in Southern California were the lowest ever recorded. Reductions in pollution were reported elsewhere in the U.S. as well. The Environmental Protection Agency (EPA) announced stricter testing for some cities and metropolitan areas, as a way to further reduce air pollution, but carbon dioxide emissions remained high in 1992.

**Water:** As congress began considering the rewrite of the Clean Water Act, an EPA study reported that U.S. water pollution had decreased in the two decades since the law's original passage. The study noted that two-thirds of surface water meets water-quality standards, despite continued problems with contaminated runoff from farms, streets, and lawns. Agricultural runoff figured prominently in an EPA analysis that found nearly half of more than 500,000 miles of rivers tested to be too polluted for their intended uses. There was also bad news concerning U.S. coastal waters, where pollution had closed a third of all shellfish fisheries, and where there were more than 2,000 beach closings because of sewage contamination in 1991. The beach closings were spread among 14 states; another 10 coastal states did not regularly test for contamination.

A Florida study found that, rather than dispersing, wastewater can concentrate in coastal waters into something resembling "underwater smog."

**Energy:** A federal energy bill passed in 1992 set new standards for such things as lighting and electric motors, imposed safeguards for fish and other wildlife at hydroelectric plants, and established incentives for producers of renewable energies, such as solar and wind. Meanwhile, states and electric utilities appeared to be making some progress with conservation efforts. One example of this was the increased emphasis electric utilities placed on "demand-side management," an approach that attempts to reduce demand for electricity by such methods as giving away high-efficiency light bulbs and helping customers weatherize their homes. With the cooperation of regulators, utilities can potentially make more money by encouraging conservation than they can by continuing to build generating capacity. While the energy bill stated that the federal government should try to stay out of the way of such efforts by utilities and states, federal authorities drew the line at fuel efficiency standards, with the National Highway Traffic Safety Administration preempting a Maryland law giving sales-tax rebates for more fuel-efficient cars, on the grounds that allowing states to set their own standards would unduly burden U.S. automakers. Meanwhile, with one quarter of the nation's electricity going to lighting, the EPA began a program to encourage corporations and government agencies to use high-efficiency light bulbs.

**Forests:** In 1992, U.S. courts continued to halt logging of Pacific Northwest old-growth forests, the habitat of the endangered northern spotted owl. The situation was complicated, though, by the third meeting in 14 years of a committee made up mainly of high-ranking federal officials and empowered to overrule the Endangered Species Act for extremely compelling economic reasons. Their ruling to open up approximately 1,700 acres of public old-growth forests had no immediate effect, however, because of court challenges. Meanwhile, the logging industry appeared to be moving from the Northwest to the South, where a longer growing season and cheaper land offered incentives unrelated to wildlife protection. The U.S. Forest Service formalized its approach of ecosystem management, implying an increased emphasis on recreational and wildlife uses of public forests.

**Soil:** In a highly significant change in farming practices, an increasing number of farmers were using conservation tillage, or "no-till," methods. A survey found that in 1991 the technique, which involves avoiding plowing and leaving at least a third of a field's plant residues intact, was used in more than 28 percent of the 281 million planted acres in the U.S. Conservation tillage was developed as a way to control erosion and is required in some cases by the 1990 U.S. farm bill; it has demonstrated other potential benefits, such as lowering the cost of some crop yields and reducing the need for pesticides and fertilizers. A study by the World Resources Institute acknowledged that the U.S. soil conservation program was among the world's best but cited continued problems, especially in such areas as the Central Valley of California and the watersheds of the Mississippi and Missouri rivers. The topic of grazing cattle on public rangelands in the West was again contentious in 1992. Supporters of a failed bill to raise grazing fees on these lands charged that U.S. taxpayers were subsidizing overgrazing.

# Hazardous Waste Sites

Source: Environmental Protection Agency, Natl. Priorities List Fact Book. Feb. 1992

| State/Territory | General | Final Federal | Total* | State/Territory | General | Final Federal | Total* |
|---|---|---|---|---|---|---|---|
| Alabama | 10 | 2 | 12 | New Hampshire | 15 | 1 | 17 |
| Alaska | 2 | 4 | 6 | New Jersey | 102 | 6 | 108 |
| Arizona | 7 | 3 | 10 | New Mexico | 8 | 2 | 10 |
| Arkansas | 10 | 0 | 12 | New York | 79 | 4 | 84 |
| California | 67 | 20 | 95 | North Carolina | 21 | 1 | 23 |
| Colorado | 13 | 3 | 17 | North Dakota | 2 | 0 | 2 |
| Connecticut | 14 | 1 | 15 | Ohio | 30 | 3 | 33 |
| Delaware | 19 | 1 | 20 | Oklahoma | 9 | 1 | 10 |
| District of Columbia | 0 | 0 | 0 | Oregon | 7 | 1 | 9 |
| Florida | 47 | 4 | 55 | Pennsylvania | 90 | 4 | 100 |
| Georgia | 11 | 2 | 13 | Rhode Island | 9 | 2 | 12 |
| Hawaii | 0 | 1 | 2 | South Carolina | 22 | 1 | 24 |
| Idaho | 7 | 2 | 9 | South Dakota | 2 | 1 | 4 |
| Illinois | 32 | 4 | 37 | Tennessee | 12 | 2 | 15 |
| Indiana | 32 | 0 | 33 | Texas | 25 | 3 | 29 |
| Iowa | 19 | 1 | 20 | Utah | 7 | 4 | 13 |
| Kansas | 9 | 1 | 11 | Vermont | 8 | 0 | 8 |
| Kentucky | 17 | 0 | 19 | Virginia | 19 | 1 | 22 |
| Louisiana | 10 | 1 | 12 | Washington | 31 | 14 | 49 |
| Maine | 7 | 2 | 9 | West Virginia | 5 | 0 | 5 |
| Maryland | 8 | 2 | 10 | Wisconsin | 39 | 0 | 40 |
| Massachusetts | 22 | 3 | 26 | Wyoming | 2 | 1 | 3 |
| Michigan | 77 | 0 | 77 | American Samoa | 0 | 0 | 0 |
| Minnesota | 39 | 2 | 41 | Guam | 1 | 0 | 2 |
| Mississippi | 2 | 0 | 2 | Northern Marianas | 0 | 0 | 0 |
| Missouri | 19 | 3 | 23 | Palau | 0 | 0 | 0 |
| Montana | 8 | 0 | 8 | Puerto Rico | 8 | 1 | 9 |
| Nebraska | 5 | 1 | 8 | Virgin Islands | 0 | 0 | 1 |
| Nevada | 1 | 0 | 1 | Total | 1067 | 116 | 1235* |

* Includes previously proposed sites

## Toxics Release Inventory, 1991

Source: Environmental Protection Agency

Pollutants discharged into the nation's air, water, and land and injected underground by major manufacturing facilities (excluding power plants and mining facilities) continued to decrease nationally in 1991, according to the EPA's Toxics Release Inventory (TRI). The pollutants reported released in 1991 represented a decrease of 9% from the 1990 figure and a decrease of 31% from the figure in 1988, the baseline year. In addition, new data became available in 1991, as required by the Pollution Prevention Act of 1990: major manufacturing facilities reported that some 38 billion pounds of wastes were "managed," that is, sent to treatment facilities or recycled.

| | | | |
|---|---|---|---|
| 1991 pollutant releases | 3,385 million pounds | Ohio | 171 million pounds |
| Air releases | 2,010 million pounds | Indiana | 136 million pounds |
| Water releases | 244 million pounds | Top industries, total releases | |
| Underground injection | 710 million pounds | Chemicals | 1,550 million pounds |
| Land releases | 421 million pounds | Primary metals | 433 million pounds |
| 1991 pollutant transfers | 3,865 million pounds | Paper | 242 million pounds |
| To publicly owned treatment works | 412 million pounds | Plastics | 152 million pounds |
| To treatment/disposal/other | 661 million pounds | Transportation equipment | 149 million pounds |
| To recycling | 2,354 million pounds | Top chemicals, total releases | |
| To energy recovery | 438 million pounds | Ammonia | 485 million pounds |
| Top states, total releases | | Hydrochloric acid | 288 million pounds |
| (air, water, land, and underground injection): | | Methanol | 252 million pounds |
| Louisiana | 459 million pounds | Toluene | 200 million pounds |
| Texas | 411 million pounds | Acetone | 165 million pounds |
| Tennessee | 215 million pounds | | |

## Releases of Toxic Substances, 1988-1991

Source: Environmental Protection Agency

| | Percent Change 1990-1991 | Percent Change 1988-1991 | | Percent Change 1990-1991 | Percent Change 1988-1991 |
|---|---|---|---|---|---|
| Total releases | −9 | −31 | Transfers for treatment/ | | |
| Air releases | −13 | −26 | disposal | −19 | −34 |
| Water releases* | +24 | −22 | To publicly owned treatment works | −12 | −28 |
| Underground injection | −5 | −47 | To other treatment facilities | −6 | −28 |
| Land releases | −9 | −20 | To disposal facilities | −32 | −39 |

* The net increase in water releases from 1990 to 1991 is largely attributable to increased runoff from four fertilizer facilities in Louisiana. Excluding those increases, reported water releases would have decreased about 7% from 1990 to 1991.

## "Urban Air": Soot in Selected Cities, 1990

Source: Environmental Protection Agency

(Micrograms per cubic meter of air of suspended particles that are 10 microns or less in diameter)

| Area | High* | Average | Area | High* | Average |
|---|---|---|---|---|---|
| Anaheim-Santa Ana, Calif. | 108 | 48 | New York | 103 | 37 |
| Atlanta, Ga. | 110 | 51 | Oakland, Calif. | 118 | 33 |
| Chicago | 149 | 45 | Pittsburgh | 191 | 43 |
| Detroit | 114 | 35 | Riverside-San Bernardino, Calif. | 278 | 80 |
| Los Angeles-Long Beach | 132 | 55 | St. Louis | 164 | 82 |
| Minneapolis-St. Paul, Minn.-Wis. | 140 | 34 | | | |

* The EPA treats the reading from the highest day as a statistical anomaly and reports the reading for the second highest day of the year. Note: Figures are for metropolitan areas.

# Some Endangered Species

Source: Fish and Wildlife Service, U.S. Dept. of Interior; as of June 3, 1993. For a complete list of threatened and endangered species, write to: Publications Unit, U.S. Fish and Wildlife Service (110 WEBB), Washington, DC 20240.

| Common name | Scientific name | Range |
| --- | --- | --- |
| **Mammals** | | |
| Asian wild ass | Equus hemianus. | Southwestern & Central Asia |
| Point Arena mountain beaver | Aplodontia rufa nigra. | U.S. (Cal.) |
| Bobcat | Felis rufus escuinapae. | Central Mexico |
| Ozark big-eared bat | Plecotus townsendii ingens. | U.S. (Mo., Okla., Ariz.) |
| Brown or grizzly bear | Ursus arctos horribilis | U.S. (48 conterminous states) |
| Cheetah | Acinonyx jubatus. | Africa to India |
| Eastern cougar | Felis concolor cougar. | Eastern N.A. |
| Columbian white-tailed deer | Odocoileus virginianus leucurus | U.S. (Wash., Ore.) |
| Chinese river dolphin | Lipotes vexillifer | China |
| Asian elephant. | Elephas maximus. | Southcentral, Southeast Asia |
| San Joaquin kit fox | Vulpes macrotis mutica. | U.S. (Cal.) |
| Gorilla | Gorilla gorilla. | Central & W. Africa |
| Leopard | Panthera pardus. | Africa, Asia |
| Asiatic lion | Panthera leo persica. | Turkey to India |
| Howler monkey | Alouatta pigra. | Mexico to S. America |
| Southeastern beach mouse | Peromyscus polionotus phasma | U.S. (Fla.) |
| Ocelot | Felis pardalis | U.S. (Tex., Ariz.) |
| Southern sea otter | Enhydra lutris hereis | U.S. (Wash., Ore., Cal.) |
| Giant panda | Ailuropoda melanoleuca | China |
| Florida panther | Felis concolor coryi. | U.S. (La., Ark. east to S.C., Fla.) |
| Utah prairie dog. | Cynomys parvidens | U.S. (Ut.) |
| Morro Bay kangaroo rat | Dipodomys heermanni morroensis. | U.S. (Cal.) |
| Black rhinoceros. | Diceros bicornis. | Sub-Saharan Africa |
| Carolina northern flying squirrel | Glaucomys sabrinus coloratus | U.S. (N.C., Tenn.) |
| Tiger | Panthera tigris | Asia |
| Hualapai Mexican vole | Microtus mexicanus hualpaiensis | U.S. (Ariz.) |
| Gray whale | Eschrichtius robustus. | N. Pacific Ocean |
| Wild yak | Bos grunniens | China (Tibet), India |
| Mountain zebra | Equus zebra zebra | South Africa |
| Red wolf | Canis rufus | U.S. (Southeast to central Tex.) |
| **Birds** | | |
| Masked bobwhite (quail) | Colinus virginianus ridgwayi | U.S. (Ariz.) |
| California condor | Gymnogyps californianus | U.S. (Ore., Cal.) |
| Hooded crane | Grus monacha | Japan, USSR |
| White-necked crow | Corvus leucognaphalus | U.S. (P.R.), Dominican Rep., Haiti |
| Eskimo curlew. | Numenius borealis | Alaska and N. Canada |
| Bald eagle | Haliaeetus leucocephalus | U.S. (most states), Canada |
| American peregrine falcon | Falco peregrinus anatum | Canada to Mexico |
| Hawaiian hawk | Buteo solitarius | U.S. (Hi.) |
| Indigo macaw | Anodorhynchus leari | Brazil |
| West African ostrich | Struthio camelus spatzi | Spanish Sahara |
| Golden parakeet | Aratinga guarouba | Brazil |
| Australian parrot | Geopsittacus occidentalis. | Australia |
| Attwater's greater prairie-chicken | Tympanuchus cupido attwateri | U.S. (Tex.) |
| Bachman's warbler (wood) | Vermivora bachmanii | U.S. (Southeast), Cuba |
| Kirtland's warbler (wood) | Dendroica kirtlandii | U.S., Canada, Bahama Is. |
| Ivory-billed woodpecker | Campephilus principalis | U.S. (Southcentral and Southeast), Cuba |
| **Reptiles** | | |
| American alligator | Alligator mississippiensis. | U.S (Southeastern) |
| American crocodile | Crocodylus acutus | U.S. (Fla.) |
| Atlantic salt marsh snake | Nerodia fasciatia taeniata. | U.S. (Fla.) |
| Plymouth red-bellied turtle | Pseudemys rubiventris bangsi | U.S. (Mass.) |
| **Fishes** | | |
| Bonytail chub | Gila elegans | U.S. (Ariz., Cal., Col., Nev., Ut., Wyo.) |
| Cave crayfish | Cambarus aculabrum | U.S. (Ariz.) |
| Gila trout | Salmo gilae | U.S. (Ariz., N.M.) |
| **Plants** | | |
| Florida golden aster | Chrysopsis floridana | U.S. (Fla.) |
| Autumn buttercup | Ranunculus acriformis | U.S. (Ut.) |
| Bakersfield cactus | Opuntia treleasei | U.S. (Cal.) |
| Santa Cruz cypress | Cypressus abramsiana | U.S. (Cal.) |
| Maguire daisy | Erigeron maguireivar masguirei | U.S. (Ut.) |
| Short's goldenrod | Solidago shortii | U.S. (Ky.) |
| Tennessee yellow-eyed grass | Xyris tennesseensis | U.S. (Ala., Ga., Tenn.) |
| Mountain golden heather | Hudsonia montana | U.S. (N.C.) |
| Cooley's meadowrue | Thalictrum cooleyi | U.S. (N.C., Fla.) |
| Wheeler's peperomia | Peperomia wheeleri | U.S. (P.R.) |
| Chapman rhododendron | Rhododendron chapmanii | U.S. (Fla.) |
| Texas wild-rice | Zizania texana. | U.S. (Tex.) |

## U.S. List of Endangered and Threatened Species

Source: Fish and Wildlife Service, U.S. Dept. of Interior; as of June 3, 1993.

| | Endangered | | | Threatened | | | |
|---|---|---|---|---|---|---|---|
| Group | U.S. Only | U.S. & Foreign | Foreign Only | U.S. Only | U.S. & Foreign | Foreign Only | Total Listed Species |
| Mammals | 37 | 19 | 249 | 6 | 3 | 22 | 336 |
| Birds | 57 | 16 | 153 | 8 | 9 | 0 | 243 |
| Reptiles | 8 | 8 | 64 | 14 | 4 | 14 | 112 |
| Amphibians | 6 | 0 | 8 | 4 | 1 | 0 | 19 |
| Fishes | 55 | 3 | 11 | 31 | 6 | 0 | 106 |
| Snails | 12 | 0 | 1 | 7 | 0 | 0 | 20 |
| Clams | 50 | 0 | 2 | 5 | 0 | 0 | 57 |
| Crustaceans | 10 | 0 | 0 | 2 | 0 | 0 | 12 |
| Insects | 13 | 2 | 4 | 9 | 0 | 0 | 28 |
| Arachnids | 3 | 0 | 0 | 0 | 0 | 0 | 3 |
| Animals, Total | 251 | 48 | 492 | 86 | 23 | 36 | 936 |
| Plants | 301 | 7 | 1 | 67 | 9 | 2 | 387 |
| Total | 552 | 55 | 493 | 153 | 32 | 38 | 1323 |

Note: When separate populations of a species are listed as endangered and as threatened, those species are tallied twice. The 10 species so counted are chimpanzee, grizzly bear, leopard, gray wolf, bald eagle, piping plover, roseate tern, Nile crocodile, green sea turtle, and olive ridley sea turtle. In addition, 9 species of lemurs; 9 of gibbons; 2 each of musk deer, sifakas, and uakaris; and 29 to 41 of Oahu tree snails are each counted as 1 species above.

## Gestation, Longevity, and Incubation of Animals

Average longevity figures were supplied by Ronald T. Reuther. They refer to animals in captivity; the potential life span of animals is rarely attained in nature. Maximum longevity figures are from the Biology Data Book, 1972. Figures on gestation and incubation are averages based on estimates by leading authorities.

| Animal | Gestation (days) | Average longevity (years) | Maximum longevity (yrs., mos.) | Animal | Gestation (days) | Average longevity (years) | Maximum longevity (yrs., mos.) |
|---|---|---|---|---|---|---|---|
| Ass | 365 | 12 | 35-10 | Leopard | 98 | 12 | 19-4 |
| Baboon | 187 | 20 | 35-7 | Lion | 100 | 15 | 25-1 |
| Bear: Black | 219 | 18 | 36-10 | Monkey (rhesus) | 164 | 15 | — |
| Grizzly | 225 | 25 | — | Moose | 240 | 12 | — |
| Polar | 240 | 20 | 34-8 | Mouse (meadow) | 21 | 3 | — |
| Beaver | 122 | 5 | 20-6 | Mouse (dom. white) | 19 | 3 | 3-6 |
| Bison | 278 | 15 | — | Opossum (American) | 14-17 | 1 | — |
| Camel (Bactrian) | 406 | 12 | 29-5 | Pig (domestic) | 112 | 10 | 27 |
| Cat (domestic) | 63 | 12 | 28 | Puma | 90 | 12 | 19 |
| Chimpanzee | 231 | 20 | 44-6 | Rabbit (domestic) | 31 | 5 | 13 |
| Chipmunk | 31 | 6 | 8 | Rhinoceros (black) | 450 | 15 | — |
| Cow | 284 | 15 | 30 | Rhinoceros (white) | — | 20 | — |
| Deer (white-tailed) | 201 | 8 | 17-6 | Sea lion (California) | 350 | 12 | 28 |
| Dog (domestic) | 61 | 12 | 20 | Sheep (domestic) | 154 | 12 | 20 |
| Elephant (African) | — | 35 | 60 | Squirrel (gray) | 44 | 10 | — |
| Elephant (Asian) | 645 | 40 | 70 | Tiger | 105 | 16 | 26-3 |
| Elk | 250 | 15 | 26-6 | Wolf (maned) | 63 | 5 | — |
| Fox (red) | 52 | 7 | 14 | Zebra (Grant's) | 365 | 15 | — |
| Giraffe | 425 | 10 | 33-7 | | | | |
| Goat (domestic) | 151 | 8 | 18 | **Incubation time (days)** | | | |
| Gorilla | 257 | 20 | 39-4 | Chicken . . . . . . . . . . . . . . . . . . . . . . | | | 21 |
| Guinea pig | 68 | 4 | 7-6 | Duck . . . . . . . . . . . . . . . . . . . . . . . | | | 30 |
| Hippopotamus | 238 | 25 | — | Goose . . . . . . . . . . . . . . . . . . . . . . | | | 30 |
| Horse | 330 | 20 | 46 | Pigeon . . . . . . . . . . . . . . . . . . . . . . | | | 18 |
| Kangaroo | 42 | 7 | — | Turkey . . . . . . . . . . . . . . . . . . . . . . | | | 26 |

## Speeds of Animals

Source: Natural History magazine, March 1974. Copyright © The American Museum of Natural History, 1974.

| Animal | Mph | Animal | Mph | Animal | Mph |
|---|---|---|---|---|---|
| Cheetah | 70 | Mongolian wild ass | 40 | Human | 27.89 |
| Pronghorn antelope | 61 | Greyhound | 39.35 | Elephant | 25 |
| Wildebeest | 50 | Whippet | 35.50 | Black mamba snake | 20 |
| Lion | 50 | Rabbit (domestic) | 35 | Six-lined race runner | 18 |
| Thomson's gazelle | 50 | Mule deer | 35 | Wild turkey | 15 |
| Quarterhorse | 47.5 | Jackal | 35 | Squirrel | 12 |
| Elk | 45 | Reindeer | 32 | Pig (domestic) | 11 |
| Cape hunting dog | 45 | Giraffe | 32 | Chicken | 9 |
| Coyote | 43 | White-tailed deer | 30 | Spider (Tegenaria atrica) | 1.17 |
| Gray fox | 42 | Wart hog | 30 | Giant tortoise | 0.17 |
| Hyena | 40 | Grizzly bear | 30 | Three-toed sloth | 0.15 |
| Zebra | 40 | Cat (domestic) | 30 | Garden snail | 0.03 |

Most of these measurements are for maximum speeds over approximate quarter-mile distances. Exceptions are the lion and elephant, whose speeds were clocked in the act of charging; the whippet, which was timed over a 200-yard course; the cheetah, timed over a 100-yard distance; the human, timed for a 15-yard segment of a 100-yard run (of 13.6 seconds); and the black mamba, six-lined race runner, spider, giant tortoise, three-toed sloth, and garden snail, which were measured over various small distances.

# Major Venomous Animals

## Snakes

**Coral snake** - 2 to 4 ft. long, in Americas south of Canada; bite is nearly painless; very slow onset of paralysis, difficulty breathing; mortality high without antivenin.

**Rattlesnake** - 2 to 8 ft. long, throughout W. Hemisphere. Rapid onset of symptoms of severe pain, swelling; mortality low, but amputation of affected limb is sometimes necessary; antivenin. Probably higher mortality rate for Mojave rattler.

**Cottonmouth water moccasin** - up to 5 ft. long, wetlands of southern U.S. from Virginia to Texas. Rapid onset of symptoms of severe pain, swelling; mortality low, but tissue destruction can be extensive; antivenin.

**Copperhead** - less than 4 ft. long, from New England to Texas; pain and swelling; very seldom fatal; antivenin seldom needed.

**Bushmaster** - up to 12 ft. long, wet tropical forests of C. and S. America; few bites occur, but mortality rate is high.

**Barba Amarilla** or **Fer-de-lance** - up to 7 ft. long, from tropical Mexico to Brazil; severe tissue damage common; moderate mortality; antivenin.

**Asian pit vipers** - from 2 to 5 ft. long throughout Asia; reactions and mortality vary but most bites cause tissue damage and mortality is generally low.

**Sharp-nosed pit viper** or **One Hundred Pace Snake** - up to 5 ft. long, in southern Vietnam and Taiwan, China; the most toxic of Asian pit vipers; very rapid onset of swelling and tissue damage, internal bleeding; moderate mortality; antivenin.

**Boomslang** - under 6 ft. long, in African savannahs; rapid onset of nausea and dizziness, often followed by slight recovery and then sudden death from internal hemorrhaging; bites rare, mortality high; antivenin.

**European vipers** - from 1 to 3 ft. long; bleeding and tissue damage; mortality low; antivenins.

**Puff adder** - up to 5 ft. long, fat; south of the Sahara and throughout the Middle East; rapid large swelling, great pain, dizziness; moderate mortality often from internal bleeding; antivenin.

**Gaboon viper** - over 6 ft. long, fat; 2-inch fangs; south of the Sahara; massive tissue damage, internal bleeding; few recorded bites.

**Saw-scaled** or **carpet viper** - up to 2 ft. long, in dry areas from India to Africa; severe bleeding, fever; high mortality, causes more human fatalities than any other snake; antivenin.

**Desert horned viper** - in dry areas of Africa and western Asia; swelling and tissue damage; low mortality; antivenin.

**Russell's viper** or **tic-polonga** - over 5 ft. long, throughout Asia; internal bleeding; moderate mortality rate; bite reports common; antivenin.

**Black mamba** - up to 14 ft. long, fast-moving; S. and C. Africa; rapid onset of dizziness, difficulty breathing, erratic heart-beat; mortality high, nears 100% without antivenin.

**Kraits** - in S. Asia; rapid onset of sleepiness; numbness; up to 50% mortality even with antivenin treatment.

**Common or Asian cobra** - 4 to 8 ft. long, throughout S. Asia; considerable tissue damage, sometimes paralysis; mortality probably not more than 10%; antivenin.

**King cobra** - up to 16 ft. long, throughout S. Asia; rapid swelling, dizziness, loss of consciousness, difficulty breathing, erratic heart-beat; mortality varies sharply with amount of venom involved, most bites involve non-fatal amounts; antivenin.

**Yellow or Cape cobra** - 7 ft. long, in southern Africa; most toxic venom of any cobra; rapid onset of swelling, breathing and cardiac difficulties; mortality high without treatment; antivenin.

**Ringhals, or spitting, cobra** - 5 ft. and 7 ft. long; southern Africa; squirt venom through holes in front of fangs as a defense; venom is severely irritating and can cause blindness.

**Australian brown snakes** - very slow onset of symptoms of cardiac or respiratory distress; moderate mortality; antivenin.

**Tiger snake** - 2 to 6 ft. long, S. Australia; pain, numbness, mental disturbances with rapid onset of paralysis; may be the most deadly of all land snakes though antivenin is quite effective.

**Death adder** - less than 3 ft. long, Australia; rapid onset of faintness, cardiac and respiratory distress; at least 50% mortality without antivenin.

**Taipan** - up to 11 ft. long, in Australia and New Guinea; rapid paralysis with severe breathing difficulty; mortality nears 100% without antivenin.

**Sea snakes** - throughout Pacific, Indian oceans except NE Pacific; almost painless bite, variety of muscle pain, paralysis; mortality rate low, many bites are not envenomed; some antivenins.

*Notes:* Not all snake bites by venomous snakes are actually envenomed. Any animal bite, however, carries the danger of tetanus and anyone suffering a venomous snake bite should seek medical attention. Antivenins are not certain cures; they are only an aid in the treatment of bites. Mortality rates above are for envenomed bites; low mortality, up to 2% result in death; moderate, 2–5%; high, 5–15%. Even when the victim recovers fully, prolonged hospitalization and extensive medical procedures are usually required.

## Lizards

**Gila monster** - up to 24 inches long with heavy body and tail, in high desert in southwest U.S. and N. Mexico; immediate severe pain followed by vomiting, thirst, difficulty swallowing, weakness approaching paralysis; no recent mortality.

**Mexican beaded lizard** - similar to Gila monster, Mexican west-coast; reaction and mortality rate similar to Gila monster.

## Insects

**Ants, bees, wasps, hornets, etc.** Global distribution. Usual reaction is piercing pain in area of sting. Not directly fatal, except in cases of massive multiple stings. Many people suffer allergic reactions - swelling, rashes, partial paralysis - and a few may die within minutes from severe sensitivity to the venom (anaphylactic shock).

## Spiders, scorpions

**Black widow** - small, round-bodied with hour-glass marking; the widow and its relatives are found around the world in tropical and temperate zones; sharp pain, weakness, clammy skin, muscular rigidity, breathing difficulty and, in small children, convulsions; low mortality; antivenin.

**Recluse or fiddleback and brown spiders** - small, oblong body; throughout U.S.; pain with later ulceration at place of bite; in severe cases fever, nausea, and stomach cramps; ulceration may last months; very low mortality.

**Atrax spiders** - several varieties, often large, in Australia; slow onset of breathing, circulation difficulties; low mortality.

**Tarantulas** - large, hairy spiders found around the world; American tarantulas, and probably all others, are **harmless**, though their bite may cause some pain and swelling.

**Scorpions** - crab-like body with stinger in tail, various sizes, many varieties throughout tropical and subtropical areas; various symptoms may include severe pain spreading from the wound, numbness, severe emotional agitation, cramps; severe reactions include vomiting, diarrhea, respiratory failure; low mortality, usually in children; antivenins.

## Sea Life

**Sea wasps** - jellyfish, with tentacles up to 30 ft. long, in the S. Pacific; very rapid onset of circulatory problems; high mortality largely because of speed of toxic reaction; antivenin.

**Portuguese man-of-war** - jellyfish-like, with tentacles up to 70 ft. long, in most warm water areas; immediate severe pain; not fatal, though shock may cause death in a rare case.

**Octopi** - global distribution, usually in warm waters; all varieties produce venom but only a few can cause death; rapid onset of paralysis with breathing difficulty.

**Stingrays** - several varieties of differing sizes, found in tropical and temperate seas and some fresh water; severe pain, rapid onset of nausea, vomiting, breathing difficulties; wound area may ulcerate, gangrene may appear; seldom fatal.

**Stonefish** - brownish fish that lies motionless as a rock on bottom in shallow water; throughout S. Pacific and Indian oceans; extraordinary pain, rapid paralysis; low mortality.

**Cone-shells** - molluscs in small, beautiful shells in the S. Pacific and Indian oceans; shoot barbs into victims; paralysis; low mortality.

# How Much Water Is Used . . . ?

Source: American Water Works Assn.

1. In the average residence during a year? **107,000 gallons**
2. By an average person daily? **168 gallons**
3. To flush a toilet? **5-7 gallons**
4. To take a shower? **25-50 gallons**
5. To brush your teeth (water running)? **2 gallons**
6. To shave (water running)? **10-15 gallons**
7. To wash dishes by hand? **20 gallons**
8. To run a dishwasher? **10 gallons**

## Mammals: Orders and Major Families

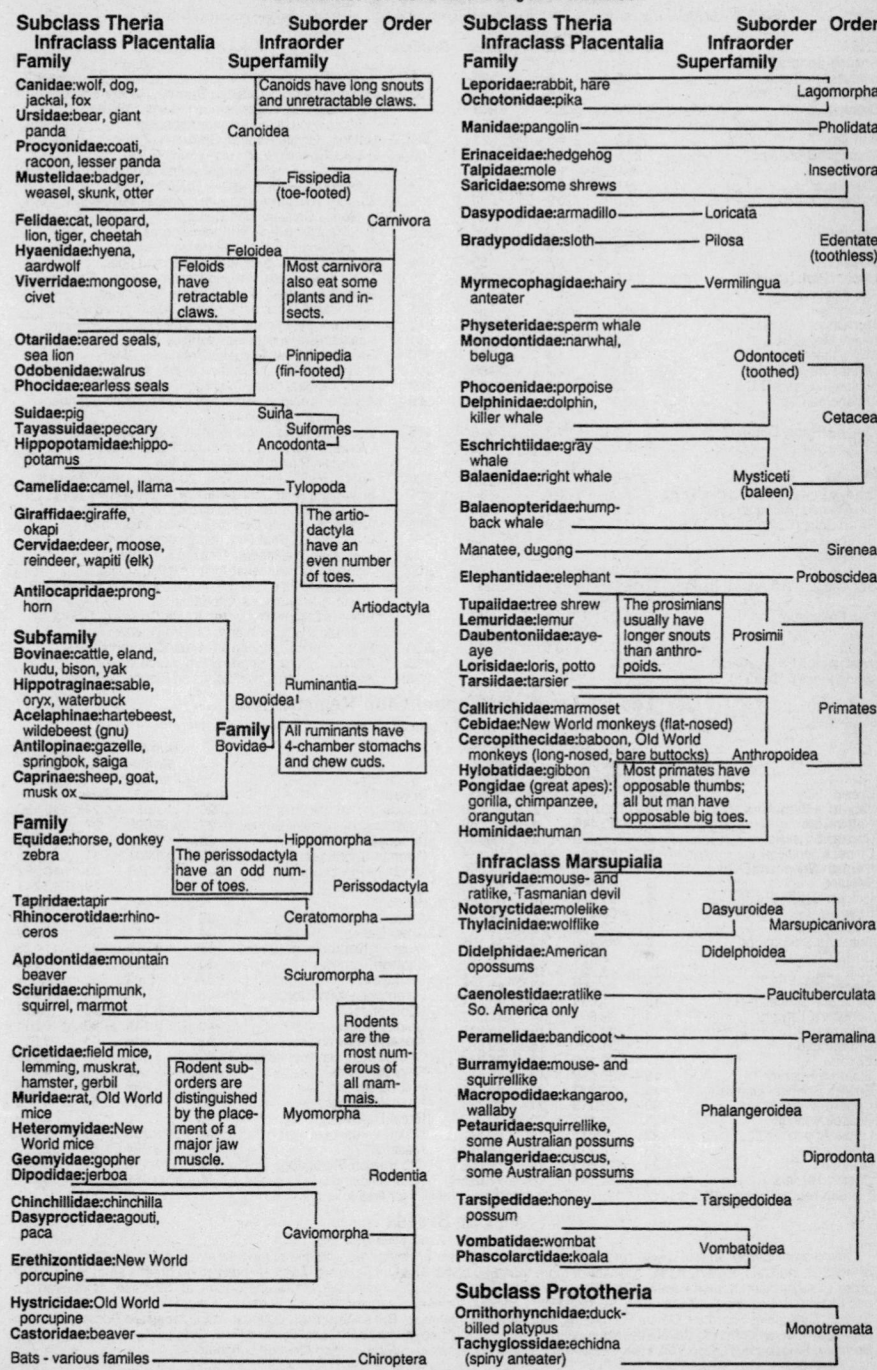

**Subclass Theria**
**Infraclass Placentalia**
**Family** / **Suborder** / **Order**
**Infraorder**
**Superfamily**

Canidae:wolf, dog, jackal, fox
Ursidae:bear, giant panda
Procyonidae:coati, racoon, lesser panda
Mustelidae:badger, weasel, skunk, otter
— Canoidea — Canoids have long snouts and unretractable claws.

Fissipedia (toe-footed)

Felidae:cat, leopard, lion, tiger, cheetah
Hyaenidae:hyena, aardwolf
Viverridae:mongoose, civet
— Feloidea — Feloids have retractable claws.

Carnivora — Most carnivora also eat some plants and insects.

Otariidae:eared seals, sea lion
Odobenidae:walrus
Phocidae:earless seals
— Pinnipedia (fin-footed)

Suidae:pig
Tayassuidae:peccary
Hippopotamidae:hippopotamus
— Suina — Suiformes — Ancodonta

Camelidae:camel, llama — Tylopoda

Giraffidae:giraffe, okapi
Cervidae:deer, moose, reindeer, wapiti (elk)

Antilocapridae:pronghorn

The artiodactyla have an even number of toes.

Artiodactyla

**Subfamily**
Bovinae:cattle, eland, kudu, bison, yak
Hippotraginae:sable, oryx, waterbuck
Acelaphinae:hartebeest, wildebeest (gnu)
Antilopinae:gazelle, springbok, saiga
Caprinae:sheep, goat, musk ox
— Ruminantia — Bovoidea¹

**Family**
Bovidae — All ruminants have 4-chamber stomachs and chew cuds.

**Family**
Equidae:horse, donkey, zebra — Hippomorpha
The perissodactyla have an odd number of toes.
Tapiridae:tapir
Rhinocerotidae:rhinoceros — Ceratomorpha
Perissodactyla

Aplodontidae:mountain beaver
Sciuridae:chipmunk, squirrel, marmot
— Sciuromorpha

Cricetidae:field mice, lemming, muskrat, hamster, gerbil
Muridae:rat, Old World mice
Heteromyidae:New World mice
Geomyidae:gopher
Dipodidae:jerboa
— Rodent suborders are distinguished by the placement of a major jaw muscle. — Myomorpha

Rodents are the most numerous of all mammals.

Rodentia

Chinchillidae:chinchilla
Dasyproctidae:agouti, paca
Erethizontidae:New World porcupine
Hystricidae:Old World porcupine
Castoridae:beaver
— Caviomorpha

Bats - various families — Chiroptera

---

**Subclass Theria**
**Infraclass Placentalia**
**Family** / **Suborder** / **Order**
**Infraorder**
**Superfamily**

Leporidae:rabbit, hare
Ochotonidae:pika
— Lagomorpha

Manidae:pangolin — Pholidata

Erinaceidae:hedgehog
Talpidae:mole
Saricidae:some shrews
— Insectivora

Dasypodidae:armadillo — Loricata
Bradypodidae:sloth — Pilosa
Edentate (toothless)

Myrmecophagidae:hairy anteater — Vermilingua

Physeteridae:sperm whale
Monodontidae:narwhal, beluga
Phocoenidae:porpoise
Delphinidae:dolphin, killer whale
— Odontoceti (toothed)

Cetacea

Eschrichtiidae:gray whale
Balaenidae:right whale
Balaenopteridae:humpback whale
— Mysticeti (baleen)

Manatee, dugong — Sirenea

Elephantidae:elephant — Proboscidea

Tupaiidae:tree shrew
Lemuridae:lemur
Daubentoniidae:aye-aye
Lorisidae:loris, potto
Tarsiidae:tarsier
— The prosimians usually have longer snouts than anthropoids. — Prosimii

Callitrichidae:marmoset
Cebidae:New World monkeys (flat-nosed)
Cercopithecidae:baboon, Old World monkeys (long-nosed, bare buttocks)
Hylobatidae:gibbon
Pongidae (great apes): gorilla, chimpanzee, orangutan
Hominidae:human
— Anthropoidea — Most primates have opposable thumbs; all but man have opposable big toes.

Primates

### Infraclass Marsupialia
Dasyuridae:mouse- and ratlike, Tasmanian devil
Notoryctidae:molelike
Thylacinidae:wolflike
— Dasyuroidea — Marsupicanivora

Didelphidae:American opossums — Didelphoidea

Caenolestidae:ratlike So. America only — Paucituberculata

Peramelidae:bandicoot — Peramalina

Burramyidae:mouse- and squirrellike
Macropodidae:kangaroo, wallaby
Petauridae:squirrellike, some Australian possums
Phalangeridae:cuscus, some Australian possums
— Phalangeroidea

Diprodonta

Tarsipedidae:honey possum — Tarsipedoidea

Vombatidae:wombat
Phascolarctidae:koala
— Vombatoidea

### Subclass Prototheria
Ornithorhynchidae:duck-billed platypus
Tachyglossidae:echidna (spiny anteater)
— Monotremata

## Major U.S. Public Zoological Parks

Source: World Almanac questionnaire, 1993; budget and attendance in millions. (*) park has not provided up-to-date data.

| Zoo | Budget | Attend-ance | Acres | Species | Major attractions |
|---|---|---|---|---|---|
| Arizona-Sonora Desert Museum (Tucson) | $4.3 | 0.6 | 198 | 200 | "Living" museum, 90% outdoors, hummingbird aviary |
| Audubon (New Orleans) | 7.8 | 0.9 | 58 | 500 | White alligators, Louisiana Swamp, Reptile Encounter |
| Bronx (N.Y.C.) | 24.6 | 2.1 | 265 | 670 | Himalayan Highlands, African Plains, Wild Asia, MouseHouse, endangered species |
| Buffalo | 4.0 | 0.5+ | 23 | 206 | Habicat, Gorilla Habitat, Children's Zoo |
| Chicago (Brookfield) | 27.0 | 2.0 | 215 | 400+ | 7 Seas Seascape, Tropic World, Africa! |
| Cincinnati | 12.0 | 1.3 | 67 | 761 | Gorilla World, white bengal tigers, Jungle Trails |
| Cleveland | 2.9 | 0.9 | 165 | 563 | Rain Forest—600 animals, 10,000 plants |
| Dallas | 6.0 | 0.5 | 70 | 329 | 25-acre Wilds of Africa with monorail, nature trail, Gorilla Conservation Center |
| Denver | 6.8 | 1.3 | 76 | 310 | Tropical Discovery, Northern Shores |
| Detroit | 8.8 | 1.0 | 125 | 413 | Penguinarium, Chimps of Harambee |
| Houston | 5.7 | 1.5 | 50 | 596 | Bird Garden, white tigers, African lion pride |
| Lincoln Park (Chicago) | 14.0 | 4.0 | 35 | 339 | Great Ape House, Bird House, Lion House, Farm-in-Zoo |
| Los Angeles | 7.2 | 1.8 | 113 | 500+ | Adventure Island, World of Birds, Tiger Falls |
| Louisville | 4.5 | 0.6 | 133 | 395 | American wildcat, polar bears, Black-footed ferret |
| Memphis | 5.7 | 0.7 | 70 | 445 | Cat Country, Primate World, The Forest |
| Miami Metrozoo | 7.0 | 0.8 | 290 | 281 | Koalas, Aviary, cageless exhibits, Asian River Life |
| Milwaukee* | 12.0 | 1.4 | 200 | 350 | Sea Lion Exhibit, Predator Prey, new Aviary |
| Minnesota | 12.0 | 1.2 | 485 | 311 | Malayan sun bear, Siberian tigers, World of Birds |
| National (Wash. D.C.)* | 13.0 | 3.0 | 163 | 509 | Giant pandas, Komodo dragon lizards, gorillas |
| Oklahoma City | 12.0 | 0.6 | 110 | 500+ | Aquaticus dolphin & sea lion shows, Great EscApe, Children's Discovery |
| Omaha/Henry Doorly Zoo | 4.5 | 1.3 | 110 | 475 | Indoor rainforest, free-flight aviary, cat complex |
| Philadelphia | 16.0 | 1.2 | 42 | 560 | World of Primates, Treehouse, Rare Animal House, African Plains, female white lion |
| Phoenix | 8.0 | 1.0 | 125 | 324 | African Veldt, Arizona Trail, 200 endangered animals |
| Gladys Porter (Brownsville, Tex.) | 2.0 | 0.4 | 31 | 450 | Free-flight aviary, Herpetarium, 4 geographic areas |
| Rio Grande (Albuquerque)* | 3.2 | 0.5 | 60 | 292 | Ape Country, Free-flying bird show, rainforest |
| Riverbanks (Columbia, S.C.) | 3.9 | 0.9 | 39 | 483 | Aquarium Reptile Complex, Riverbanks Farm |
| St. Louis | 14.7 | 2.7 | 83 | 665 | Living World, Bear Pits, Jungle of the Apes |
| San Antonio | 7.3 | 1.0 | 40 | 700 | Australian Walkabout, Amazonia, Aquarium |
| San Diego* | 40.0 | 3.5 | 100 | 800 | Tiger River, Southeast Asian exhibit, koalas |
| San Diego (Wild Animal Park)* | 15.0 | 1.4 | 2,200 | 450 | Mixed-species enclosures; exotic species, monorail with 50-minute, narrated tour |
| San Francisco | 11.0 | 1.0 | 140 | 270 | Primate Discovery Center, Koala Crossing, Gorilla World, Penguin Island, Children's Zoo |
| Toledo* | 7.8 | 0.8 | 30 | 400 | Hippoquarium, African savanna, Children's Zoo |
| Washington Pk (Portland) | 15.0 | 1.1 | 64 | 166 | Alaska Tundra, Penguinarium, Africa exhibit |
| Woodland Pk (Seattle)* | 7.5 | 0.9 | 92 | 300 | African savanna, gorillas, Asian Elephant Forest |

## Top 50 American Kennel Club Registrations

Source: American Kennel Club, New York, N.Y.; dogs registered Jan. 1, 1992, to Dec. 31, 1992.

| Breed | Rank | Number Registered 1992 | Rank | Number Registered 1991 | Breed | Rank | Number Registered 1992 | Rank | Number Registered 1991 |
|---|---|---|---|---|---|---|---|---|---|
| Labrador Retrievers | 1 | 120,879 | 1 | 105,876 | Collies | 26 | 17,081 | 24 | 18,129 |
| Rottweilers | 2 | 95,445 | 4 | 76,889 | Pugs | 27 | 16,008 | 27 | 15,387 |
| Cocker Spaniels | 3 | 91,925 | 2 | 98,937 | Brittanys | 28 | 14,901 | 28 | 14,282 |
| Chinese Shar-Pei | * | 90,081 | — | — | German Shorthaired Pointers | 29 | 13,737 | 31 | 12,158 |
| German Shepherd Dogs | 4 | 76,941 | 5 | 68,844 | Miniature Pinschers | 30 | 13,353 | 33 | 10,772 |
| Poodles | 5 | 73,449 | 3 | 77,709 | Bichons Frises | 31 | 12,172 | 29 | 12,245 |
| Golden Retrievers | 6 | 69,850 | 6 | 67,284 | Bulldogs | 32 | 12,046 | 30 | 12,186 |
| Beagles | 7 | 60,661 | 7 | 56,956 | Akitas | 33 | 11,383 | 35 | 9,949 |
| Dachshunds | 8 | 50,046 | 8 | 48,713 | Great Danes | 34 | 11,067 | 34 | 10,159 |
| Shetland Sheepdogs | 9 | 43,449 | 10 | 44,106 | West Highland White Terriers | 35 | 10,015 | 32 | 11,128 |
| Chow Chows | 10 | 42,670 | 9 | 45,131 | Scottish Terriers | 36 | 7,914 | 36 | 8,724 |
| Shih Tzu | 11 | 42,561 | 12 | 41,367 | Samoyeds | 37 | 7,267 | 37 | 7,649 |
| Pomeranians | 12 | 42,488 | 13 | 41,034 | Pembroke Welsh Corgis | 38 | 6,501 | 40 | 6,039 |
| Miniature Schnauzers | 13 | 41,058 | 11 | 42,404 | Keeshonden | 39 | 6,177 | 38 | 7,017 |
| Yorkshire Terriers | 14 | 39,904 | 14 | 39,772 | Cairn Terriers | 40 | 6,141 | 39 | 6,911 |
| Dalmatians | 15 | 38,927 | 15 | 30,225 | Alaskan Malamutes | 41 | 5,644 | 41 | 5,631 |
| Chihuahuas | 16 | 31,301 | 16 | 29,860 | Chesapeake Bay Retrievers | 42 | 5,295 | 42 | 4,738 |
| Boxers | 17 | 30,123 | 17 | 26,722 | Saint Bernards | 43 | 4,863 | 43 | 4,637 |
| Siberian Huskies | 18 | 26,057 | 19 | 23,436 | Weimaraners | 44 | 4,758 | 45 | 4,136 |
| English Springer Spaniels | 19 | 22,183 | 20 | 22,448 | Airedale Terriers | 45 | 4,236 | 44 | 4,328 |
| Doberman Pinschers | 20 | 22,113 | 21 | 20,734 | Great Pyrenees | 46 | 3,776 | 48 | 3,269 |
| Basset Hounds | 21 | 21,137 | 22 | 20,497 | Schipperkes | 47 | 3,752 | 46 | 3,705 |
| Lhasa Apsos | 22 | 20,616 | 18 | 23,543 | Mastiffs | 48 | 3,294 | 54 | 2,886 |
| Pekingese | 23 | 18,218 | 23 | 18,843 | Old English Sheepdogs | 49 | 3,178 | 47 | 3,417 |
| Maltese | 24 | 17,615 | 25 | 17,502 | Newfoundlands | 50 | 3,153 | 50 | 3,180 |
| Boston Terriers | 25 | 17,271 | 26 | 17,075 | | | | | |

* Breed recognized by AKC only as of 1992; will not be officially ranked for first time until 1993.

## Cat Breeds

Source: Cat Fanciers' Assn., Manasquan, N.J.

Only a small percentage of house cats in the U.S. are pedigreed, or registered with one of the official registering bodies, the largest of which is the Cat Fanciers' Assn., sponsor of more than 600 clubs. The Cat Fanciers' Assn. recognized 40 breeds as of mid-1993 (in order of registration totals): Persian (Traditional, Pointed Pattern, and Colorpoint Carrier), Maine Coon Cat, Siamese, Abyssinian, Exotic Shorthair, Scottish Fold Shorthair, Scottish Fold Longhair, Oriental Shorthair, Birman, Burmese, Ocicat, Tonkinese, Cornish Rex, Somali, Colorpoint Shorthair, Devon Rex, Manx, Russian Blue, Balinese, British Shorthair, Egyptian Mau, Japanese Bobtail Shorthair, Japanese Bobtail Longhair, Javanese, Norwegian Forest Cat, Cartreux, American Curl, Highland Fold, Cymric, Korat, Turkish Angora, Bombay, Singapura, Turkish Van, Havana Brown, Selkirk Rex, American Wirehair, and Oriental Longhair.

# Giant Trees of the U.S.

Source: The American Forestry Assn., Washington, D.C.

Approximately 850 native and naturalized species of trees are grown in the U.S. The oldest living thing on earth is believed to be a bristlecone pine tree in California named Methusalah, estimated to be 4,700 years old. The world's largest living thing, the General Sherman giant sequoia in California, weighs more than 1,400 tons—as much as 9 blue whales or 360 elephants.

Recognition as the National Champion of each species is determined by total mass of each tree, based on this formula: the circumference in inches as measured at a point 4½ feet above the ground plus the total height of the tree in feet plus ¼ of the average crown spread in feet. Trees within 5 points of each other are declared co-champions. Of all the trees nominated at the beginning of AFA's Big Tree program in 1940, only 4 trees have never lost their title—the giant sequoia (Sequoia Natl. Park, Cal.), white oak (Wye Mills State Park, Md.), western juniper (Stanislaus Natl. Forest, Cal.), and Rocky Mountain juniper (Cache Natl. Forest, Ut.). The coast redwood Dyerville Giant (Dyerville, Cal.) was also one of the original champs until it fell in March 1991. Florida has more national champs (113) than any other state. No champions have been identified for nearly 200 species, including white fir, papaya, eucalyptus, California sycamore, and saguaro.

Anyone can nominate candidates for the National Register of Big Trees. For information, write to American Forestry Assn., P.O. Box 2000, Washington, DC 20013. The following is a small selection of the trees registered.

**(Figure in parentheses is year of most recent measurement; * = co-champion)**

| Species | Height (ft.) | Location |
|---|---|---|
| Alder, Hazel (1989) | 35 | Norfolk, Va. |
| Allthorn (1989)* | 13 | Midland, Tex. |
| Anacahuite (1992) | 25 | Mercedes, Tex. |
| Anise, Florida (1991) | 29 | Perry County, Ala. |
| Apple, Common (1986) | 70 | East End, Va. |
| Ash, Carolina (1988) | 48 | Chesapeake, Va. |
| Ash, Texas (1989) | 66 | Lost Maples State Natl. Area, Tex. |
| Ash, Velvet (1991) | 81 | Modesto, Cal. |
| Aspen, Bigtooth (1989)* | 66 | Caroline Co., Md. |
| Avocado (1991) | 60 | Whittier, Cal. |
| Bald Cypress, Montezuma (1991) | 45 | Hidalgo Co., Tex. |
| Basswood, White (1986) | 75 | Henderson Co., N.C. |
| Beech, American (1984) | 130 | Ashtabula Co., Oh. |
| Birch, Gray (1989) | 77 | Somers, Ct. |
| Birch, River (1988)* | 90 | Appleton Comm., Tenn. |
| Birch, Water (1973) | 53 | Wallowa Co., Ore. |
| Blackbead, Ebony (1986) | 40 | Hidalgo Co., Tex. |
| Bladdernut, Sierra (1986) | 28 | Fresno, Co., Cal. |
| Bluewood (1989) | 30 | San Juan, Tex. |
| Box elder (1991)* | 98 | Livingston Co., Mich. |
| Buckeye, Bottlebrush (1989) | 20 | Cashiers, N.C. |
| Buffaloberry, Silver (1975) | 22 | Malheur Co., Ore. |
| Bumelia, Tough (1987) | 41 | Amelia Is., Fla. |
| Butternut (1989)* | 88 | Eugene, Ore. |
| California Laurel (1978) | 88 | Siskiyou Natl. For., Ore. |
| Camphor-Tree (1977) | 72 | Hardee Co., Fla. |
| Catalpa, Southern (1981) | 80 | Henderson Co., Ill. |
| Catclaw, Wright (1986) | 36 | Uvalde Co., Tex. |
| Cedar, Atlantic white (1985) | 88 | Escambia Co., Ala. |
| Cherry, Bitter (1985) | 104 | Vashon Is., Wash. |
| Chestnut, American (1992) | 110 | Grand Traverse, Mich. |
| Coconut, Palm (1979) | 92 | Hilo, Hi. |
| Crab Apple, Southern (1992) | 36 | Swannanoa, N.C. |
| Cranberrybush, American (1989)* | 25 | Trenton, Mich. |
| Cypress, Monterey (1991)* | 93 | Mendocino Co., Cal. |
| Dahoon, Myrtle (1972) | 46 | Lawtey, Fla. |
| Devilwood (1989) | 36 | Perry, Fla. |
| Dogwood, Blackfruit (1986) | 18 | Shasta Co., Cal. |
| Dogwood, Swamp (1989)* | 23 | Chesapeake, Va. |
| Douglas-Fir, Coast (1991) | 329 | Coos Co., Ore. |
| Elder, American (1987) | 16 | Jefferson Natl. For., Va. |
| Elder, Pacific Red (1989) | 30 | Lincoln Co., Ore. |
| Elm, American (1991) | 100 | Louisville, Kan. |
| Elm, Siberian (1991) | 146 | Detroit, Mich. |
| Fiddlewood, Florida (1988) | 39 | Dade Co., Fla. |
| Fig, Shortleaf (1986) | 41 | Monroe Co., Fla. |
| Fir, Grand (1987) | 251 | Olympic Natl. Park, Wash. |
| Fringetree (1992)* | 32 | Fairfax Co., Va. |
| Geiger Tree (1988) | 25 | Lee Co., Fla. |
| Guajillo (1989) | 15 | Starr Co., Tex. |
| Guiana Plum (1976) | 31 | Coral Gables, Fla. |
| Gumbo-Limbo (1984)* | 36 | Miami Shores, Fla. |
| Hackberry, Common (1989) | 111 | Rock Co., Wis. |
| Haw, May (1989) | 12 | Williamsburg, Va. |
| Hawthorne, Fleshy (1988) | 8 | Kirkwood, Mo. |
| Hazel, California (1984) | 47 | Seattle, Wash. |
| Hemlock, Western (1991)* | 227 | Olympic Natl. Park, Wash. |
| Hickory, Mockernut (1985)* | 125 | Monroe Co., Ala. |
| Hickory, Shellbark (1986) | 105 | Rixeyville, Va. |
| Holly, Carolina (1986) | 25 | Jacksonville, Fla. |
| Honeylocust (1972) | 115 | Wayne Co., Mich. |
| Huisache (1989) | 33 | Big Bend Natl. Park, Tex. |
| Jerusalem-thorn (1969) | 36 | Florence, Ariz. |
| Jujube, Common (1989) | 43 | Fort Worth, Tex. |
| Juniper, Western (1945) | 86 | Stanislaus Natl. Forest, Cal. |
| Larch, European (1989) | 83 | Greenwich, Ct. |
| Laurelcherry, English (1987) | 32 | Seattle, Wash. |
| Lidflower, Pale (1991) | 33 | Monroe Co., Fla. |
| Loblolly Bay (1963) | 94 | Ocala Natl. Forest, Fla. |
| Locust, Black (1974) | 96 | Dansville, N.Y. |
| Magnolia, Umbrella (1969) | 50 | Bucks Co., Pa. |
| Mahogany, W. Indies (1988) | 70 | Lee Co., Fla. |
| Mango (1991) | 40 | Pompano Beach, Fla. |
| Manzanita, Common (1989) | 22 | Guerneville, Cal. |
| Maple, Black (1976) | 118 | Allegan Co., Mich. |
| Maple, Douglas (1985)* | 65 | Ahsahka, Ida. |
| Mesquite, Honey (1984) | 52 | Real County, Tex. |
| Mountain Laurel (1991) | 25 | Asheville, N.C. |
| Mulberry, Black (1971) | 68 | Westminster, Md. |
| Nannyberry (1989) | 40 | Oakland Co., Mich. |
| Oak, Bluejack (1985) | 64 | Cherokee Co., Tex. |
| Oak, Cherrybark (1991) | 124 | Sussex Co., Va. |
| Oak, Harvard (1986) | 30 | Yoakum Co., Tex. |
| Oysterwood (1986) | 24 | Monroe Co., Fla. |
| Palm, Texas Sabal (1989) | 45 | Hidalgo Co., Tex. |
| Palmetto, Cabbage (1991) | 62 | Brunswick, Ga. |
| Paper-Mulberry (1989) | 34 | Yorktown, Va. |
| Pawpaw, Common (1986) | 60 | Newton Co., Miss. |
| Peach (1986) | 18 | Morrisville, Va. |
| Pear, Common (1991) | 59 | Waitsburg, Wash. |
| Pecan (1980) | 143 | Cocke Co., Tenn. |
| Persimmon, Texas (1965) | 26 | Uvalde Co., Tex. |
| Pine, Bishop (1986) | 112 | Mendocino Co., Cal. |
| Pine, Digger (1991)* | 114 | Bar 71 Ranch, Cal. |
| Pine, Virginia (1989) | 120 | Chambers Co., Ala. |
| Pistache, Texas (1976) | 39 | Val Verde Co., Tex. |
| Plum, Chicasaw (1988) | 32 | Henderson Co., N.C. |
| Plum, Wildgoose (1989) | 26 | New Salem Village, Ill. |
| Poison-Sumac (1972) | 16 | Robins Is., N.Y. |
| Poplar, Balsam (1984) | 138 | Marquette, Mich. |
| Portiatree (1968) | 42 | Kekaha, Ha. |
| Privet, California (1989)* | 28 | Yorktown, Va. |
| Redbud, Eastern (1989) | 36 | Nashville, Tenn. |
| Redwood, Coast (1972) | 362 | Humboldt Redwoods State Park, Cal. |
| Ribbonbush (1977) | 23 | No. Warner Springs, Cal. |
| Russian-Olive (1982) | 58 | Cortez, Col. |
| Saffron-Plum (1987) | 31 | Santa Ana, Tex. |
| Sassafras (1954) | 76 | Owensboro, Ky. |
| Sequoia, Giant (1975) | 275 | Sequoia Natl. Park, Cal. |
| Serviceberry, Downy (1986) | 60 | Burkes Garden, Va. |
| Silktree, Mimosa (1986)* | 54 | Webster Parish, La. |
| Sophora, Mescalbean (1983) | 27 | Comal Co., Tex. |
| Spruce, Norway (1989) | 94 | Susquehanna City, Pa. |
| Stewartia, Virginia (1987) | 15 | Chesapeake, Va. |
| Sparkleberry Tree (1991)* | 29 | Evergreen, Ala. |
| Sweetgum, American (1986) | 136 | Craven Co., N.C. |
| Sycamore, Arizona (1981) | 114 | Sierra Co., N.M. |
| Tamarisk (1981) | 34 | Columbus, N.M. |
| Thatchpalm, Florida (1986) | 23 | Monroe Co., Fla. |
| Walnut, Arizona (1987) | 85 | Mimbres Valley, N.M. |
| Walnut, Black (1991) | 105 | Southhampton Co., Va. |
| Willow, Sitka (1988) | 34 | Coupeville, Wash. |
| Willow, Weeping (1982)* | 114 | Asheville, N.C. |
| Yew, Florida (1986) | 20 | Torreya State Park, Fla. |
| Yucca, Mojave (1987) | 24 | Needles Res. Area, Cal. |
| Yucca, Torrey (1987) | 23 | Lincoln Natl. Forest, N.M. |

## Minerals

Source: Bureau of Mines, U.S. Dept. of the Interior, as of mid-1993.

**Aluminum:** the second most abundant metal element in the Earth's crust. Bauxite is the main source of aluminum; convert to aluminum equivalent by multiplying by 0.211. Guinea and Australia have 49 percent of the world's reserves. Aluminum is used in the U.S. principally in packaging (35%), transportation (20%), and building (17%).

**Chromium:** some two-thirds of the world's chromite production is in Kazakhstan and South Africa. The chemical and metallurgical industries use about 80% of the chromite consumed in the world.

**Cobalt:** used in superalloys for jet engines; chemicals (paint driers, catalysts, magnetic coatings); permanent magnets; and cemented carbides for cutting tools. Principal cobalt-producing countries include Zaire, Zambia, and the former USSR. The U.S. uses about one-third of total world consumption. Although its resources are relatively large, the U.S. has produced no cobalt since 1971; most cobalt resources are low grade, and production from these deposits is not economically feasible.

**Columbium:** used mostly as an additive in steelmaking and in superalloys. Brazil and Canada are the world's leading producers. There is no U.S. columbium mining industry.

**Copper:** main uses of copper in the U.S. are in building construction (41%), electrical and electronic products (24%), industrial machinery and equipment (13%), transportation (12%), and consumer and general products (10%). The leading producer is Chile, followed by the U.S., Poland, Russia, Peru, Kazakhstan, Australia, and China. Principal mining states are Arizona, New Mexico, and Utah.

**Gold:** used in the U.S. in jewelry and the arts (70%), the electronics and other industries (23%), and in dentistry (7%). South Africa has about half of the world's resources; significant quantities are also present in the U.S., Canada, the former USSR, and Brazil. Gold mining in the U.S. takes place in nearly all of the western states and Alaska.

**Iron ore:** the source of primary iron for the world's iron and steel industries. Major iron ore producers include the former USSR, Brazil, Australia, and China.

**Lead:** the U.S., Australia, China, and the former USSR are the world's largest producers of lead. Transportation accounted for the major end use in the U.S., with 75% used in batteries, gasoline additives, and other applications. Other uses include emergency power supply batteries, construction sheeting, sporting ammunition, and TV tubes. The U.S. produces and consumes more than 20% of the world's lead metal.

**Manganese:** essential to iron and steel production. The U.S., Japan, and Western Europe are all nearly deficient in economically minable manganese. South Africa and the former USSR have over 80% of the world's reserves.

**Nickel:** vital to the stainless steel industry and played a key role in the development of the chemical and aerospace industries. Leading producers include the former USSR, Canada, Australia, and New Caledonia.

**Platinum-Group Metals:** the platinum group comprises 6 closely related metals: platinum, palladium, rhodium, ruthenium, iridium, and osmium. They commonly occur together in nature and are among the scarcest of the metallic elements. They are consumed in the U.S. by the following industries: automotive (38%), electrical and electronic (29%), dental (9%), and other (24%). The former USSR and South Africa have nearly all the world's reserves.

**Silver:** used in the following U.S. industries: photography; electrical and electronic products; sterlingware, electroplated ware, and jewelry. Silver is mined in more than 60 countries. Nevada produces over 34% of U.S. silver, Idaho 14%.

**Tantalum:** a refractory metal with unique electrical, chemical, and physical properties; it is used in the U.S. mostly to produce electronic components, mainly tantalum capacitors. Australia, Brazil, Canada, and Thailand are the leading producers. There is no U.S. tantalum mining industry.

**Titanium:** a metal that is mostly used in jet engines, airframes, and space and missile applications. It is produced in Ukraine, Russia, Kazakhstan, Japan, the western and central U.S., the United Kingdom, and China.

**Vanadium:** used as an alloying element in steel, as an alloying agent in aerospace titanium alloys, and as a catalyst in the production of sulfuric acid and maleic anhydride. The former USSR and South Africa are the world's largest producers.

**Zinc:** used as a protective coating on steel, as diecastings, as an alloying metal with copper to make brass, and as a component of chemical compounds in rubber and paints. It is mined in over 50 countries, with Canada the leading producer, followed by Australia, the former USSR, Peru, China, and the U.S. In the U.S., mine production comes mostly from Tennessee, Missouri, New York, and Alaska.

## World Mineral Reserve Base

Source: Bureau of Mines, U.S. Dept. of the Interior, as of mid-1993.

| Mineral | Reserve Base[1] | Mineral | Reserve Base[1] |
|---|---|---|---|
| Aluminum | 28,000 mln. metric tons[2] | Nickel | 110,000 thousand metric tons |
| Chromium | 6,800 mln. metric tons | Platinum— | |
| Cobalt | 8,800 thou. metric tons | Group Metals | 66 mln. kilograms |
| Columbium | 4,200 kilograms | Silver | 420,000 metric tons |
| Copper | 590 mln. metric tons | Tantalum | 35 mln. kilograms |
| Gold | 51,000 metric tons | Titanium | 595 mln. metric tons |
| Iron | 230,000 mln. metric tons[3] | Vanadium | 27,000 thousand metric tons |
| Lead | 125 mln. metric tons | Zinc | 325 mln. metric tons |
| Manganese | 4,800,000 thousand metric tons | | |

(1) Includes demonstrated resources that are currently economic (reserves), marginally economic (marginal reserves), and some of those that are currently subeconomic. (2) Bauxite. (3) Crude ore.

## U.S. Nonfuel Mineral Production—10 Leading States in 1991

Source: Bureau of Mines, U.S. Dept. of the Interior

| Rank/State | Value (millions) | Percent of U.S. total | Principal minerals |
|---|---|---|---|
| 1. California | $3,017 | 9.80 | Cement, boron minerals, sand & gravel (construction), stone (crushed) |
| 2. Arizona | 3,791 | 9.06 | Copper, gold, sand and gravel |
| 3. Nevada | 2,510 | 8.15 | Gold, sand & gravel (construction), silver |
| 4. Florida | 1,422 | 4.62 | Stone (crushed), cement, phosphate rock |
| 5. Michigan | 1,398 | 4.54 | Iron ore, cement, sand & gravel, stone |
| 6. Georgia | 1,392 | 4.52 | Clays, stone (crushed) |
| 7. Minnesota | 1,389 | 4.51 | Iron ore, sand & gravel (construction), stone (crushed) |
| 8. Texas | 1,379 | 4.48 | Cement, stone (crushed), sand & gravel (construction), salt |
| 9. Utah | 1,182 | 3.84 | Cement, lime, sand & gravel (construction), salt, copper |
| 10. New Mexico | 976 | 3.17 | Potassium salts, copper |

## U.S. Nonfuel Mineral Production

Source: Bureau of Mines, U.S. Dept. of the Interior

Production as measured by mine shipments, sales, or marketable production (including consumption by producers)

| | 1987 | 1988 | 1989 | 1990 | 1991[1] | 1992[1] |
|---|---|---|---|---|---|---|
| Antimony (ore and concentrate) . . . . . . . . . . . . . . . . . | — | W | W | W | W | W |
| Bauxite . . . . . . . . . . thousand metric tons, dried equivalent | 576 | 588 | W | W | W | W |
| Beryllium (metal equivalent) . . . . . . . . . . . . . . metric tons | 220 | 212 | 184 | 182 | 174 | 193 |
| Copper (recoverable content of ores, etc.) . thousand metric tons | 1,244 | 1,417 | 1,498 | 1,588 | 1,631 | 1,720[E] |
| Gold (recoverable content of ores, etc.) . . . . . . . metric tons | 153.9 | 200.9 | 265.7 | 294.3 | 289.9 | 320.0[E] |
| Iron ore, usable (includes byproduct material) . . . . . . . . . . . . . . . . . . . million metric tons | 47.6 | 57.5 | 59.0 | 56.4 | 56.8 | 56.7[E] |
| Lead (in concentrate) . . . . . . . . . . . . thousand metric tons | 319 | 394 | 420 | 495 | 477 | 410[E] |
| Magnesium metal (primary) . . . . . . . . thousand metric tons | 124 | 142 | 152 | 139 | 131 | 135[E] |
| Molybdenum (content of ore and concentrate) . . . . . . . . . . . . . . . . . . . . metric tons | 34,073 | 43,051 | 63,105 | 61,611 | 53,364 | 45,400[E] |
| Nickel (content of ore and concentrate) . . . . . . . metric tons | — | — | 330 | 5,523 | 6,671 |
| Silver (recoverable content of ores, etc.) . . . . . . metric tons | 1,241 | 1,661 | 2,007 | 2,125 | 1,848 | 1,800[E] |
| Tungsten (content of ore and concentrate) . . . . . metric tons | 34 | W | W | W | W | W |
| Zinc (recoverable content of ores, etc.) . . thousand metric tons | 216 | 244 | 276 | 515 | 518 | 520[E] |
| Asbestos . . . . . . . . . . . . . . . . . . . thousand metric tons | 51 | 18 | 17 | W | 20 | 16 |
| Barite . . . . . . . . . . . . . . . . . . . . . thousand metric tons | 406 | 404 | 290 | 430 | 448 | 326 |
| Boron minerals . . . . . . . . . . . . . . . thousand metric tons | 625 | 578 | 562 | 608 | 626 | 521[E] |
| Bromine . . . . . . . . . . . . . . . . . . . . . million kilograms | 152 | 163 | 175 | 177 | 170 | 166[E] |
| Cement: (portland, masonry, etc.) . . . . . . thousand short tons | 78,198 | 76,867 | 77,189 | 77,111 | 71,300 | 76,484[E] |
| Clays . . . . . . . . . . . . . . . . . . . . . . thousand short tons | 43,234 | 44,515 | 42,254 | 42,904 | 41,017 | 40,712 |
| Diatomite . . . . . . . . . . . . . . . . . . . thousand metric tons | 596 | 629 | 617 | 631 | 610 | 595 |
| Feldspar . . . . . . . . . . . . . . . . . . . . thousand metric tons | 655 | 650 | 655 | 630 | 580 | 725 |
| Fluorspar . . . . . . . . . . . . . . . . . . . thousand metric tons | 64 | 64 | 64 | 64 | 58 | 50[E] |
| Garnet (industrial) . . . . . . . . . . . . . . . . . . . metric tons | 38,353 | 42,506 | 42,605 | 47,009 | 50,860 | 54,304[E] |
| Gem stones . . . . . . . . . . . . . . . . . . . . million dollars | 21.4 | 43.5 | 42.9 | 52.9 | 84.4 | 51.2 |
| Gypsum . . . . . . . . . . . . . . . . . . . . thousand short tons | 15,612 | 16,390 | 17,624 | 16,406 | 15,456 | 16,300[E] |
| Helium (extracted from natural gas) . . . . . million cubic meters | 54.6 | 63.3 | 66.3 | 64.6 | 86.4 | 88.2[E] |
| Helium (Grade A) . . . . . . . . . . . . . . . . million cubic meters | 61.9 | 71.4 | 79.9 | 84.8 | 88.1 | 90.7[E] |
| Iodine . . . . . . . . . . . . . . . . . . . . . . thousand kilograms | W | 1,015 | 1,508 | 1,973 | 1,999 | 1,995 |
| Lime . . . . . . . . . . . . . . . . . . . . . . thousand metric tons | 15,577 | 17,052 | 17,152 | 17,452 | 17,270 | 18,000[E] |
| Mica (scrap & flake) . . . . . . . . . . . . . thousand metric tons | 146 | 130 | 119 | 109 | 103 | 93[E] |
| Peat . . . . . . . . . . . . . . . . . . . . . . . thousand short tons | 955 | 844 | 761 | 763 | 697 | 719 |
| Perlite (sold and used by producers) . . . . thousand short tons | 484 | 523 | 545 | 576 | 514 | 541 |
| Phosphate rock (marketable product) . . . thousand metric tons | 40,954 | 45,389 | 49,817 | 46,343 | 48,096 | 46,965 |
| Pumice and pumicite . . . . . . . . . . . . . thousand short tons | 356 | 353 | 424 | 443 | 401 | 481 |
| Salt . . . . . . . . . . . . . . . . . . . . . . . thousand short tons | 36,943 | 39,170 | 39,278 | 40,558 | 40,031 | 39,800[E] |
| Sand and gravel (construction) . . . . . . . thousand short tons | 895,200[E] | 923,400 | 897,300[E] | 910,600 | 780,300[E] | 805,700[E] |
| Sand and gravel (industrial) . . . . . . . . . thousand short tons | 28,010 | 28,480 | 29,205 | 28,406 | 25,600 | 26,967 |
| Sodium sulfate (natural) . . . . . . . . . . . thousand metric tons | 346 | 361 | 340 | 349 | 354 | 350[E] |
| Stone (crushed) . . . . . . . . . . . . . . . . . million short tons | 1,200 | 1,248[E] | 1,213 | 1,222[E] | 1,103 | 1,162 |
| Stone (dimension)[1] . . . . . . . . . . . . . . thousand metric tons | 1,179 | 1,159[E] | 1,238 | 1,186 | 1,139 | 1,086[E] |
| Sulfur . . . . . . . . . . . . . . . . . . . . . . thousand metric tons | 10,539 | 10,746 | 11,592 | 11,560 | 10,820 | 10,600[E] |
| Talc and pyrophyllite . . . . . . . . . . . . . thousand metric tons | 1,163 | 1,234 | 1,253 | 1,267 | 1,037* | 997* |
| Vermiculite . . . . . . . . . . . . . . . . . . . thousand metric tons | 275 | 276 | 249 | 209[E] | 168 | 170[E] |

(E) Estimated. (W) Withheld to avoid disclosing company proprietary data. (—) No production. * Talc only. (1) 1991 and 1992 production includes Puerto Rico.

## U.S. Reliance on Foreign Supplies of Minerals

Source: Bureau of Mines, U.S. Dept. of the Interior

| Mineral | Percent imported in 1992 | Major sources (1988-91) | Major uses |
|---|---|---|---|
| Columbium | 100% | Brazil, Canada, Germany | Steelmaking and aerospace alloys |
| Graphite | 100 | Mexico, China, Brazil, Madagascar | Metallurgical processes |
| Manganese | 100 | S. Africa, France, Gabon | Steelmaking |
| Mica (sheet) | 100 | India, Belgium, Brazil, Japan | Electronic and electrical equipment |
| Strontium (celestite) | 100 | Mexico, Spain, Germany | Television picture tubes, pyrotechnics |
| Bauxite and alumina | 100 | Australia, Guinea, Jamaica, Brazil | Aluminum production |
| Diamonds (industrial) | 98 | Ireland, Zaire, Britain, South Africa | Machinery for grinding and cutting |
| Fluorspar | 87 | Mexico, South Africa, China, Canada | Raw material for metallurgical and chemical industries |
| Platinum group | 94 | South Africa, Britain, USSR and former USSR | Catalytic converters for autos, electrical and electronic equipment |
| Cobalt | 76 | Zaire, Zambia, Canada, Norway | Aerospace alloys, magnets, cutting tools, chemicals |
| Tantalum | 87 | Germany, Thailand, Australia | Electronic components |
| Nickel | 64 | Canada, Norway, Australia, Dominican Rep. | Stainless steel and other alloys |
| Chromium | 74 | South Africa, Turkey, Zimbabwe, Yugoslavia | Stainless steel |
| Tin | 73 | Brazil, Bolivia, China, Indonesia, Malaysia | Cans, electrical construction |
| Tungsten | 85 | China, Bolivia, Germany, Peru | Lamp filaments |
| Barite | 53 | China, India, Mexico, Morocco | Oil drilling fluids |
| Potash | 67 | Canada, Israel, USSR and former USSR, Germany | Fertilizer |
| Cadmium | 49 | Canada, Mexico, Australia, Germany | Batteries, plating and coating of metals |
| Silver | NA | Mexico, Canada, Britain, Peru | Photography, electrical and electronic prods. |

## U.S. Copper, Lead, and Zinc Production, 1950-1992

Source: Bureau of Mines, U.S. Dept. of the Interior

| Year | Copper Quantity (metric tons) | Copper Value ($1,000) | Lead Quantity (metric tons) | Lead Value ($1,000) | Zinc Quantity (metric tons) | Zinc Value ($1,000) | Year | Copper Quantity (metric tons) | Copper Value ($1,000) | Lead Quantity (metric tons) | Lead Value ($1,000) | Zinc Quantity (metric tons) | Zinc Value ($1,000) |
|---|---|---|---|---|---|---|---|---|---|---|---|---|---|
| 1950 | 827 | 379,122 | 390,839 | 113,078 | 565,516 | 167,000 | 1987 | 1,244 | 2,262,000 | 311,381 | 246,720 | 216,281 | 200,529 |
| 1960 | 1,037 | 733,706 | 223,774 | 57,722 | 395,013 | 112,365 | 1988 | 1,417 | 3,764,000 | 384,983 | 315,222 | 244,314 | 324,249 |
| 1965 | 1,226 | 957,028 | 273,196 | 93,959 | 554,429 | 178,284 | 1989 | 1,497 | 4,323,000 | 410,915 | 356,476 | 275,883 | 499,103 |
| 1970 | 1,560 | 1,984,484 | 518,698 | 178,609 | 484,560 | 163,650 | 1990 | 1,586 | 4,310,000 | 483,704 | 490,750 | 515,355 | 847,485 |
| 1975 | 1,282 | 1,814,763 | 563,783 | 267,230 | 425,792 | 366,097 | 1991 | 1,631 | 3,931,000 | 465,931 | 343,907 | 517,804 | 602,426 |
| 1980 | 1,181 | 2,666,931 | 550,366 | 515,189 | 317,103 | 261,671 | 1992 | 1,705 | 4,180,000 | 397,923 | 307,922 | 523,430 | 673,800 |
| 1985 | 1,105 | 1,631,000 | 413,955 | 174,008 | 226,545 | 201,607 | | | | | | | |

## U.S. Pig Iron and Raw Steel Output, 1940-1992

Source: American Iron and Steel Institute (net tons)

| Year | Total pig iron | Raw steel | Year | Total pig iron | Raw steel |
|---|---|---|---|---|---|
| 1940 | 46,071,666 | 66,982,686 | 1985 | 50,446,000 | 88,259,000 |
| 1945 | 53,223,169 | 79,701,648 | 1986 | 43,952,000 | 81,606,000 |
| 1950 | 64,586,907 | 96,836,075 | 1987 | 48,410,000 | 89,151,000 |
| 1955 | 76,857,417 | 117,036,085 | 1988 | 55,745,000 | 99,924,000 |
| 1960 | 66,480,648 | 99,281,601 | 1989 | 55,873,000 | 97,943,000 |
| 1965 | 88,184,901 | 131,461,601 | 1990 | 54,750,000 | 98,906,000 |
| 1970 | 91,435,000 | 131,514,000 | 1991 | 48,637,000 | 87,896,000 |
| 1975 | 101,208,000 | 116,642,000 | 1992 | 52,224,000 | 92,949,000 |
| 1980 | 68,721,000 | 111,835,000 | | | |

Steel figures include only that portion of the capacity and production of steel for castings used by foundries that were operated by companies producing steel ingots.

## World Gold Production, 1972-1992

Source: Bureau of Mines, U.S. Dept. of the Interior

(Troy Ounces)

| Year | World prod. | Africa South Africa | Africa Ghana | Africa Zaire[r] | North and South America United States | North and South America Canada | North and South America Mexico | North and South America Colombia | Other Australia | Other China | Other Philippines | Other USSR |
|---|---|---|---|---|---|---|---|---|---|---|---|---|
| 1972 | 44,843,374 | 29,245,273 | 724,051 | 80,377 | 1,449,943 | 2,078,567 | 146,061 | 188,137 | 754,866 | NA | 606,730 | NA |
| 1975 | 38,476,371 | 22,937,820 | 523,889 | 115,743 | 1,052,252 | 1,653,611 | 144,710 | 308,864 | 526,821 | NA | 502,577 | NA |
| 1977 | 38,906,145 | 22,501,886 | 480,884 | 96,452 | 1,100,347 | 1,733,609 | 212,709 | 257,070 | 624,270 | NA | 558,554 | NA |
| 1978 | 38,983,019 | 22,648,558 | 402,034 | 32,151 | 998,832 | 1,735,077 | 202,003 | 246,446 | 647,579 | NA | 586,531 | NA |
| 1979 | 38,768,978 | 22,617,179 | 362,000 | 73,947 | 964,390 | 1,644,265 | 190,364 | 269,369 | 596,910 | NA | 535,166 | NA |
| 1980 | 39,197,315 | 21,669,468 | 353,000 | 96,452 | 969,782 | 1,627,477 | 195,991 | 510,439 | 547,591 | NA | 753,452 | 8,425,000 |
| 1982 | 43,082,814 | 21,355,111 | 331,000 | 135,033 | 1,465,686 | 2,081,230 | 214,349 | 472,674 | 866,815 | 1,800,000 | 834,439 | 8,550,000 |
| 1984 | 46,929,444 | 21,860,933 | 287,000 | 321,507 | 2,084,615 | 2,682,786 | 270,998 | 730,670 | 1,295,963 | 1,900,000 | 827,149 | 8,650,000 |
| 1985 | 49,283,691 | 21,565,230 | 299,363 | 257,206 | 2,427,232 | 2,815,118 | 265,693 | 1,142,385 | 1,881,491 | 1,950,000 | 1,062,997 | 8,700,000 |
| 1986 | 51,534,056 | 20,513,665 | 287,127 | 257,206 | 3,739,015 | 3,364,700 | 250,615 | 1,285,878 | 2,413,842 | 2,100,000 | 1,296,400 | 8,850,000 |
| 1987 | 53,033,614 | 19,176,500 | 327,598 | 385,809 | 4,947,040 | 3,724,000 | 256,822 | 853,600 | 3,558,954 | 2,300,000 | 1,048,081 | 8,850,000 |
| 1988 | 60,308,973 | 19,965,611 | 355,620 | 401,884 | 6,459,534 | 4,334,338 | 292,508 | 932,822 | 5,046,059 | 2,507,758 | 980,019 | 8,925,046 |
| 1989 | 65,335,998 | 19,530,290 | 429,470 | 340,798 | 8,543,449 | 5,127,850 | 276,914 | 940,646 | 6,544,702 | 2,893,567 | 964,265 | 9,773,826 |
| 1990 | 68,632,896 | 19,454,414 | 541,419 | 299,002 | 9,458,395 | 5,381,166 | 268,073 | 943,689 | 7,849,186 | 3,215,074 | 790,619 | 9,709,524 |
| 1991 | 69,083,682 | 19,323,014 | 845,886 | 282,927 | 9,542,501 | 5,676,278 | 287,331 | 1,120,267 | 7,530,283 | 3,858,089 | 801,775 | 8,359,193 |
| 1992 | 72,269,724 | 19,737,341 | 997,670 | 257,206 | 10,581,581 | 5,081,393 | 321,507 | 1,189,578 | 7,716,178 | 4,501,104 | 771,618 | 8,101,987[*] |

NA = not available. r = revised to reflect improved data. * = USSR as constituted prior to Dec. 1991.

## U.S. and World Silver Production, 1930-1992

Source: Bureau of Mines, U.S. Dept. of the Interior

(metric tons)

Largest production of silver in the United States in 1915—2,332 metric tons.

| Year | United States | World | Year | United States | World | Year | United States | World |
|---|---|---|---|---|---|---|---|---|
| 1930 .. | 1,578 | 7,736 | 1965 .. | 1,238 | 8,007 | 1987 .. | 1,241 | 14,019 |
| 1935 .. | 1,428 | 6,865 | 1970 .. | 1,400 | 9,670 | 1988 .. | 1,661 | 15,484 |
| 1940 .. | 2,164 | 8,565 | 1975 .. | 1,087 | 9,428 | 1989 .. | 2,008 | 16,041 |
| 1945 .. | 904 | 5,039 | 1980 .. | 1,006 | 10,556 | 1990 .. | 2,121 | 16,216 |
| 1950 .. | 1,347 | 6,323 | 1985 .. | 1,227 | 13,051 | 1991 .. | 1,855 | 15,692 |
| 1955 .. | 1,134 | 6,967 | 1986 .. | 1,074 | 12,970 | 1992 .. | 1,804 | 15,345 |
| 1960 .. | 1,120 | 7,505 | | | | | | |

## Aluminum Summary, 1980 to 1992

Source: Bureau of Mines, U.S. Dept. of the Interior

| Item | Unit | 1980 | 1985 | 1988 | 1989 | 1990 | 1991 | 1992 |
|---|---|---|---|---|---|---|---|---|
| U.S. production . . . . . . . . . | 1,000 metric ton . . | 5,914 | 5,262 | 6,066 | 6,084 | 6,441 | 6,407 | 6,799 |
| Primary aluminum . . . . . . . | 1,000 metric ton . . | 4,654 | 3,500 | 3,944 | 4,030 | 4,048 | 4,121 | 4,042 |
| Secondary aluminum[1] . . . . . | 1,000 metric ton . . | 1,260 | 1,762 | 2,122 | 2,054 | 2,393 | 2,286 | 2,757 |
| Primary aluminum value . . . . | Bil. dol . . . . . . . | 7.3 | 6.3 | 9.5 | 7.8 | 6.6 | 5.4 | 5.1 |
| Price (Primary alum.)[2] . . . . | Cents/lb . . . . . . | 71.6 | 81.0 | 110.1 | 87.8 | 74.0 | 59.5 | 57.5 |
| Imports for consumption[3] . . . | 1,000 metric ton . . | 647 | 1,420 | 1,620 | 1,470 | 1,514 | 1,490 | 1,725 |
| Exports[3] . . . . . . . . . . . . | 1,000 metric ton . . | 1,346 | 908 | 1,247 | 1,613 | 1,659 | 1,762 | 1,453 |
| World production . . . . . . . . | 1,000 metric ton . . | 15,383 | 15,398 | 18,495 | 19,104 | 19,292 | 19,528 | 19,219 |

(1) Recoverable metal content from purchased scrap, old and new; (2) Average prices for primary aluminum, quoted by *Metals Week;* (3) Crude and semicrude (including metal and alloys, plates, bars, etc., and scrap).

# TRADE AND TRANSPORTATION

## U.S. Foreign Trade with Leading Countries and Areas, 1992

Source: Office of Trade and Economic Analysis, U.S. Dept. of Commerce

(millions of dollars; not seasonally adjusted)

| Country/Area | Trade Balance | Rank | Exports | Rank | Imports | Rank |
|---|---|---|---|---|---|---|
| Total | $ −84,501.2 | (X) | $488,163.6 | (X) | $532,664.8 | (X) |
| Japan | −49,600.9 | 1 | 47,812.8 | 2 | 97,413.8 | 2 |
| China | −18,309.2 | 2 | 7,418.4 | 15 | 25,727.6 | 5 |
| Taiwan | −9,345.7 | 3 | 15,250.3 | 6 | 24,596.0 | 6 |
| Canada | −8,035.7 | 4 | 90,594.3 | 1 | 98,630.0 | 1 |
| Germany | −7,571.8 | 5 | 21,248.6 | 5 | 28,820.4 | 4 |
| Nigeria | −4,101.4 | 6 | 1,001.1 | 49 | 5,102.5 | 20 |
| Malaysia | −3,931.2 | 7 | 4,362.9 | 21 | 8,294.1 | 14 |
| Italy | −3,593.0 | 8 | 8,721.3 | 14 | 12,314.4 | 10 |
| Thailand | −3,539.7 | 9 | 3,989.2 | 23 | 7,528.9 | 17 |
| Saudi Arabia | −3,204.5 | 10 | 7,166.8 | 16 | 10,371.3 | 12 |
| Venezuela | −2,737.4 | 11 | 5,443.7 | 19 | 8,181.1 | 15 |
| Angola | −2,145.1 | 12 | 157.7 | 91 | 2,302.8 | 31 |
| South Korea | −2,043.4 | 13 | 14,638.8 | 7 | 16,682.2 | 8 |
| Sweden | −1,871.2 | 14 | 2,844.9 | 28 | 4,716.2 | 21 |
| India | −1,862.7 | 15 | 1,917.1 | 36 | 3,779.8 | 26 |
| Brazil | −1,858.2 | 16 | 5,751.1 | 17 | 7,609.3 | 16 |
| Indonesia | −1,750.0 | 17 | 2,779.5 | 29 | 4,529.5 | 22 |
| Singapore | −1,686.8 | 18 | 9,625.8 | 11 | 11,312.6 | 11 |
| Philippines | −1,596.4 | 19 | 2,758.5 | 30 | 4,354.9 | 24 |
| Switzerland | −1,104.5 | 20 | 4,540.2 | 20 | 5,644.7 | 18 |
| Algeria | −898.2 | 21 | 687.9 | 59 | 1,586.1 | 36 |
| Gabon | −866.2 | 22 | 54.7 | 120 | 920.9 | 46 |
| Hong Kong | −715.9 | 23 | 9,077.1 | 12 | 9,793.1 | 13 |
| Macao | −701.5 | 24 | 19.6 | 151 | 721.2 | 54 |
| Norway | −689.7 | 25 | 1,278.9 | 42 | 1,968.6 | 33 |
| North America | −2,654.7 | (X) | 131,186.5 | (X) | 133,841.2 | (X) |
| Western Europe | 6,373.6 | (X) | 117,100.3 | (X) | 110,726.7 | (X) |
| European Community (EC) | 8,964.9 | (X) | 102,958.1 | (X) | 93,993.2 | (X) |
| European Free Trade Association | −4,184.9 | (X) | 10,836.5 | (X) | 15,021.4 | (X) |
| Eastern Europe | 2,517.8 | (X) | 4,069.2 | (X) | 1,551.4 | (X) |
| Former Soviet Republics | 2,105.3 | (X) | 2,763.5 | (X) | 658.2 | (X) |
| Organization for Economic Cooperation & Development (OECD) in Europe | 6,399.3 | (X) | 116,536.5 | (X) | 110,137.2 | (X) |
| Pacific Rim Countries | −83,972.3 | (X) | 124,451.3 | (X) | 208,423.6 | (X) |
| Asia—Near East | 1,146.7 | (X) | 16,872.8 | (X) | 15,726.1 | (X) |
| Asia—(NICS) | −13,791.9 | (X) | 48,592.0 | (X) | 62,383.9 | (X) |
| Asia—South | −3,169.0 | (X) | 3,172.3 | (X) | 6,341.2 | (X) |
| Assn. of Southeast Asian Nations (ASEAN) | −12,080.6 | (X) | 23,968.9 | (X) | 36,049.5 | (X) |
| South/Central America | 1,673.1 | (X) | 35,204.0 | (X) | 33,530.9 | (X) |
| Twenty Latin American Republics | 5,857.7 | (X) | 71,346.8 | (X) | 65,489.0 | (X) |
| Central American Common Market | 572.4 | (X) | 4,299.8 | (X) | 3,727.3 | (X) |
| Latin American Free Trade Association (LAFTA) | 4,605.2 | (X) | 63,633.4 | (X) | 59,028.3 | (X) |
| North Atlantic Treaty Organization (NATO) | 1,219.4 | (X) | 194,823.7 | (X) | 193,604.3 | (X) |
| Organization of Petroleum Exporting Countries (OPEC) | −11,240.2 | (X) | 21,959.6 | (X) | 33,199.8 | (X) |
| Unidentified[1] | 300.9 | (X) | 300.9 | (X) | (X) | (X) |

Definitions of Areas:

**North America** - Canada, Mexico.

**Western Europe** - Andorra, Austria, Belgium, Bosnia and Herzegovina, Croatia, Cyprus, Denmark, Faroe Islands, Fed. Rep. of Yugoslavia, Finland, France, Germany, Gibraltar, Greece, Iceland, Ireland, Italy, Liechtenstein, Luxembourg, Malta and Gozo, Macedonia, Monaco, Netherlands, Norway, Portugal, San Marino, Slovenia, Spain, Svalbard, Jan Mayen Island, Sweden, Switzerland, Turkey, United Kingdom, Vatican City.

**European Community** - Belgium, Denmark, France, Germany, Greece, Ireland, Italy, Luxembourg, Netherlands, Portugal, Spain, United Kingdom.

**European Free Trade Association** - Austria, Finland, Iceland, Liechtenstein, Norway, Sweden, Switzerland.

**Eastern Europe** - Albania, Armenia, Azerbaijan, Belarus, Bulgaria, Czech Republic, Estonia, Georgia, Hungary, Kazakhstan, Kyrgyzstan, Latvia, Lithuania, Moldova, Poland, Romania, Russia, Slovakia, Tajikistan, Turkmenistan, Ukraine, Uzbekistan.

**Former Soviet Republics** - Armenia, Azerbaijan, Belarus, Estonia, Georgia, Kazakhstan, Kyrgyzstan, Latvia, Lithuania, Moldova, Russia, Tajikistan, Turkmenistan, Ukraine, Uzbekistan.

**OECD** - Austria, Belgium, Denmark, Finland, France, Germany, Greece, Iceland, Ireland, Italy, Liechtenstein, Luxembourg, Monaco, Netherlands, Norway, Portugal, San Marino, Spain, Svalbard, Jan Mayen Island, Sweden, Switzerland, Turkey, United Kingdom.

**Pacific Rim Countries** - Australia, Brunei, China, Hong Kong, Indonesia, Japan, South Korea, Macao, Malaysia, New Zealand, Papua New Guinea, Philippines, Singapore, Taiwan.

**Asia Near East** - Bahrain, Iran, Iraq, Israel, Jordan, Kuwait, Lebanon, Oman, Qatar, Saudi Arabia, Syria, United Arab Emirates, Yemen.

**Asia NICS** - Hong Kong, South Korea, Singapore, Taiwan.

**Asia South** - Afghanistan, Bangladesh, India, Nepal, Pakistan, Sri Lanka.

**ASEAN** - Brunei, Indonesia, Malaysia, Philippines, Singapore, Thailand.

**South/Central America** - Anguilla, Antigua and Barbuda, Argentina, Aruba, Bahamas, Barbados, Belize, Bermuda, Bolivia, Brazil, British Virgin Islands, Cayman Islands, Chile, Colombia, Costa Rica, Cuba, Dominica, Dominican Republic, Ecuador, El Salvador, Falkland Islands, French Guiana, Grenada, Guadeloupe, Guatemala, Guyana, Haiti, Honduras, Jamaica, Martinique, Montserrat, Netherlands Antilles, Nicaragua, Panama, Paraguay, Peru, St. Kitts and Nevis, St. Lucia, St. Vincent and the Grenadines, Suriname, Trinidad and Tobago, Turks and Caicos Islands, Uruguay, Venezuela.

**Twenty Latin American Republics** - Argentina, Bolivia, Brazil, Chile, Colombia, Costa Rica, Cuba, Dominican Republic, Ecuador, El Salvador, Guatemala, Haiti, Honduras, Mexico, Nicaragua, Panama, Paraguay, Peru, Uruguay, Venezuela.

**Central American Common Market** - Costa Rica, El Salvador, Guatemala, Honduras, Nicaragua.

**LAFTA** - Argentina, Bolivia, Brazil, Chile, Colombia, Ecuador, Mexico, Paraguay, Peru, Uruguay, Venezuela.

**NATO** - Belgium, Canada, Denmark, France, Germany, Greece, Iceland, Italy, Luxembourg, Netherlands, Norway, Portugal, Spain, Turkey, United Kingdom.

**OPEC** - Algeria, Ecuador, Gabon, Indonesia, Iran, Iraq, Kuwait, Libya, Nigeria, Qatar, Saudi Arabia, United Arab Emirates, Venezuela.

(1) The export totals reflect shipments of certain grains, oilseeds, and satellites that are not included in the country/area totals.
(X) Not applicable. **Note:** Details may not equal totals due to rounding.

## U.S. Exports and Imports by Principal Commodity Groupings, 1992

Source: Office of Trade and Economic Analysis, U.S. Dept. of Commerce

(millions of dollars, not seasonally adjusted, current dollar basis)

| Item | Exports | Imports | Item | Exports | Imports |
|---|---|---|---|---|---|
| **Total** . . . . . . . . . . . . . | **$448,163.6** | **$532,664.8** | Metal manufactures. . . . . . | $5,513.1 | $6,727.0 |
| **Agricultural commodities.** . . . | **42,237.7** | **23,374.9** | Metalworking machinery . . . . | 3,033.9 | 3,187.0 |
| Animal feeds. . . . . . . . . . | 3,550.2 | 337.0 | Motorcycles, bicycles. . . . . | 1,439.2 | 1,912.9 |
| Bulbs . . . . . . . . . . . . | 111.8 | 200.8 | Nickel. . . . . . . . . . . . . . | 195.6 | 797.0 |
| Cereal flour . . . . . . . . . . | 924.4 | 723.9 | Optical goods . . . . . . . . . | 766.4 | 1,645.1 |
| Cocoa . . . . . . . . . . . . | 30.6 | 774.4 | Paper and paperboard . . . . | 6,347.8 | 7,998.2 |
| Coffee . . . . . . . . . . . . | 17.7 | 1,562.8 | Photographic equipment . . . . | 2,950.1 | 3,843.5 |
| Corn . . . . . . . . . . . . | 4,965.8 | 68.5 | Plastic articles. . . . . . . . . | 2,776.9 | 3,571.9 |
| Cotton, raw and linters . . . . | 2,014.6 | 11.4 | Platinum . . . . . . . . . . . | 291.5 | 1,428.6 |
| Dairy products; eggs . . . . . | 710.5 | 506.3 | Pottery . . . . . . . . . . . . | 103.4 | 1,404.2 |
| Fur skins, raw . . . . . . . . | 95.4 | 61.3 | Power generating mach. . . . . | 17,994.7 | 15,888.1 |
| Grains, unmilled . . . . . . . . | 893.6 | 121.6 | Printed materials . . . . . . . | 3,803.3 | 1,875.3 |
| Hides and skins . . . . . . . . | 1,252.8 | 124.0 | Records/magnetic media . . . | 4,846.1 | 3,105.7 |
| Live animals . . . . . . . . . . | 608.6 | 1,437.3 | Rubber articles . . . . . . . . | 621.8 | 877.7 |
| Meat and preparations . . . . . | 4,207.9 | 2,711.5 | Rubber tires and tubes . . . . | 1,409.0 | 2,511.7 |
| Oils/fats, animal. . . . . . . . | 496.8 | 17.5 | Scientific instruments . . . . . | 14,374.5 | 7,602.0 |
| Oils/fats, vegetable. . . . . . . | 725.0 | 954.5 | Ships, boats . . . . . . . . . | 1,421.0 | 319.4 |
| Plants. . . . . . . . . . . . . | 135.3 | 102.4 | Silver and bullion . . . . . . . | 209.4 | 449.2 |
| Rice. . . . . . . . . . . . . | 725.8 | 91.6 | Spacecraft . . . . . . . . . . | 269.6 | 91.8 |
| Seeds . . . . . . . . . . . . | 302.4 | 152.8 | Specialized ind. mach. . . . . | 16,688.6 | 11,814.4 |
| Soybeans . . . . . . . . . . . | 4,462.8 | 15.8 | Telecommunications equip. . . | 11,247.8 | 25,802.8 |
| Sugar. . . . . . . . . . . . . | 5.6 | 662.0 | Textile yarn, fabric . . . . . . | 5,778.0 | 7,843.9 |
| Tobacco, unmanufactured . . . | 1,649.1 | 950.8 | Toys/games/sporting goods . | 2,437.2 | 10,749.0 |
| Vegetables and fruit . . . . . . | 5,736.3 | 5,697.6 | Travel goods. . . . . . . . . . | 193.9 | 2,508.6 |
| Wheat . . . . . . . . . . . . | 4,503.2 | 191.1 | Vehicles/new cars - Canada . | 5,930.5 | 13,890.4 |
| Other agricultural . . . . . . . | 4,111.6 | 5,897.9 | Vehicles/new cars - Japan . . | 694.1 | 20,801.1 |
| **Manufactured goods** . . . . . . | **347,493.7** | **434,348.8** | Vehicles/new cars - other . . . | 5,095.3 | 11,561.3 |
| ADP equipment; office mach. . | 26,999.9 | 36,377.1 | Vehicles/trucks . . . . . . . . | 3,706.1 | 9,771.9 |
| Airplanes . . . . . . . . . . . | 26,285.7 | 3,859.8 | Vehicles/chassis/bodies. . . . | 309.7 | 338.1 |
| Airplane parts . . . . . . . . . | 9,366.4 | 3,358.1 | Vehicles/parts. . . . . . . . . | 16,753.1 | 15,838.3 |
| Aluminum . . . . . . . . . . . | 2,666.5 | 2,539.6 | Watches/clocks/parts . . . . . | 207.6 | 2,320.1 |
| Artwork/antiques . . . . . . . | 1,075.8 | 2,086.9 | Wood manufactures . . . . . . | 1,389.4 | 2,409.7 |
| Basketware, etc. . . . . . . . | 1,522.0 | 2,188.8 | Zinc. . . . . . . . . . . . . . | 37.8 | 854.7 |
| Chemicals - cosmetics . . . . | 2,631.5 | 1,711.4 | Other manufactured goods . . | 27,030.7 | 32,923.9 |
| Chemicals - dyeing . . . . . . | 1,871.2 | 1,623.4 | **Mineral fuel** . . . . . . . . . . . | **11,254.1** | **55,255.6** |
| Chemicals - fertilizers. . . . . | 2,371.3 | 951.5 | Coal . . . . . . . . . . . . . | 4,427.0 | 419.1 |
| Chemicals - inorganic. . . . . | 4,122.8 | 3,305.0 | Crude oil . . . . . . . . . . . | 32.4 | 38,553.1 |
| Chemicals - medicinal . . . . . | 5,357.3 | 3,809.8 | Petroleum preparations . . . . | 4,011.3 | 11,277.1 |
| Chemicals - organic. . . . . . | 10,992.6 | 9,408.1 | Liquefied propane/butane . . . | 257.2 | 707.1 |
| Chemicals - plastics . . . . . . | 10,257.9 | 4,292.0 | Natural gas . . . . . . . . . . | 352.5 | 3,030.0 |
| Chemicals - other . . . . . . . | 6,264.6 | 2,622.4 | Electricity. . . . . . . . . . . | 62.9 | 589.8 |
| Clothing . . . . . . . . . . . | 4,091.5 | 31,226.5 | Other mineral fuels . . . . . . | 2,110.8 | 679.5 |
| Copper. . . . . . . . . . . . | 1,171.9 | 1,641.7 | **Selected commodities:** | | |
| Electrical machinery . . . . . . | 32,172.4 | 39,710.4 | Fish and preparations. . . . . | 3,382.9 | 5,657.3 |
| Footwear. . . . . . . . . . . | 603.4 | 10,163.4 | Cork, wood, lumber. . . . . . | 5,314.1 | 3,970.0 |
| Furniture and parts . . . . . . | 2,553.0 | 5,502.5 | Pulp and waste paper . . . . | 3,859.2 | 2,129.4 |
| Gem diamonds . . . . . . . . | 368.7 | 4,147.8 | Metal ores; scrap . . . . . . | 3,470.4 | 3,339.8 |
| General industrial mach. . . . . | 18,479.6 | 15,519.7 | Crude fertilizers . . . . . . . . | 1,387.8 | 894.0 |
| Glass . . . . . . . . . . . . . | 1,213.1 | 849.7 | Cigarettes . . . . . . . . . . | 4,192.5 | 270.8 |
| Glassware . . . . . . . . . . | 495.5 | 1,015.4 | Alcoholic bev., distilled . . . . | 343.9 | 1,827.4 |
| Gold, nonmonetary . . . . . . | 4,109.4 | 1,898.7 | **All other** . . . . . . . . . . . . . | **2,800.6** | **1,596.9** |
| Iron and steel mill products . . | 3,606.1 | 8,327.7 | | | |
| Lighting, plumbing. . . . . . . | 976.7 | 1,546.9 | | | |

Note: Details may not equal totals due to rounding.

## U.S. Exports, Imports, and Merchandise Trade Balance, 1950-1992

Source: Office of Trade and Economic Analysis, U.S. Dept. of Commerce

(millions of dollars)

| | Principal Census trade totals | | | | | Other Census totals | | |
|---|---|---|---|---|---|---|---|---|
| Year | U.S. exports and reexports excluding military grant-aid | U.S. general imports f.a.s. transaction values[1] | U.S. merchandise balance f.a.s.[1] | U.S. general imports c.i.f. | U.S. balance exports f.a.s. imports c.i.f. | Military grant-aid shipments | Exports of domestic merchandise | Re-exports |
| 1950 | $9,997 | $8,954 | $1,043 | $ — | $ — | $282 | $10,146 | $133 |
| 1955 | 14,298 | 11,566 | 2,732 | — | — | 1,256 | 15,426 | 128 |
| 1960 | 19,659 | 15,073 | 4,586 | — | — | 949 | 20,408 | 201 |
| 1965 | 26,742 | 21,520 | 5,222 | — | — | 779 | 27,178 | 343 |
| 1970 | 42,681 | 40,356 | 2,325 | 42,833 | −152 | 565 | 42,612 | 634 |
| 1975 | 107,652 | 98,503 | 9,149 | 105,935 | 1,716 | 461 | 106,622 | 1,490 |
| 1980 | 220,626 | 244,871 | −24,245 | 256,984 | −36,358 | 156 | 216,668 | 4,115 |
| 1985 | 213,133 | 345,276[2] | −132,143 | 361,626 | −148,493 | 13 | 206,925 | 6,221 |
| 1990 | 394,030 | 495,042[2] | −101,012 | 516,987 | −122,957 | 15 | 375,606 | 18,439 |
| 1991 | 421,730 | 485,453[2] | −66,723 | 508,363 | −86,633 | NA | 401,109 | 20,621 |
| 1992 | 448,164 | 532,665[2] | −84,501 | 554,023 | −105,859 | NA | 425,737 | 22,427 |

Note: Export values include both commercially financed shipments and shipments under government-financed programs such as AID and PL-480. (1) Prior to 1974, imports are customs values, i.e., generally at prices in principal foreign markets. (2) In 1981 import value changes back to customs value. NA = Not available.

## New Passenger Cars Imported into the U.S., by Country of Origin,[1] 1964-1990

Source: Bureau of the Census, U.S. Dept. of Commerce

| | Japan | West Germany | Italy | United Kingdom | Sweden | France | South Korea | Mexico | Canada | Total[2] |
|---|---|---|---|---|---|---|---|---|---|---|
| 1964... | 16,023 | 364,683 | 10,843 | 77,548 | 18,562 | 39,532 | N.A. | N.A. | 9,201 | 536,725 |
| 1965... | 25,538 | 376,950 | 9,509 | 66,565 | 26,010 | 24,941 | N.A. | N.A. | 33,378 | 563,673 |
| 1966... | 56,050 | 527,137 | 14,110 | 81,870 | 34,632 | 33,122 | N.A. | N.A. | 152,333 | 899,895 |
| 1967... | 70,304 | 472,360 | 16,928 | 67,928 | 43,371 | 25,454 | N.A. | N.A. | 323,638 | 1,020,618 |
| 1968... | 169,849 | 707,972 | 33,843 | 96,787 | 52,515 | 39,551 | N.A. | N.A. | 500,881 | 1,620,452 |
| 1969... | 260,005 | 642,157 | 41,569 | 104,050 | 41,008 | 24,457 | N.A. | N.A. | 691,146 | 1,846,717 |
| 1970... | 381,338 | 674,945 | 42,523 | 76,257 | 57,844 | 37,114 | N.A. | N.A. | 692,783 | 2,013,420 |
| 1971... | 703,672 | 770,807 | 51,469 | 106,710 | 61,925 | 23,316 | N.A. | 0 | 802,281 | 2,587,484 |
| 1972... | 697,788 | 676,967 | 64,614 | 72,038 | 64,541 | 14,713 | N.A. | 9 | 842,300 | 2,485,901 |
| 1973... | 624,805 | 677,465 | 56,102 | 64,140 | 58,626 | 8,219 | N.A. | 4,469 | 871,557 | 2,437,345 |
| 1974... | 791,791 | 619,757 | 107,071 | 72,512 | 60,817 | 21,331 | N.A. | 3,914 | 817,559 | 2,572,557 |
| 1975... | 695,573 | 370,012 | 102,344 | 67,106 | 51,993 | 15,647 | N.A. | 0 | 733,766 | 2,074,653 |
| 1976... | 1,128,936 | 349,804 | 82,500 | 77,190 | 37,466 | 21,916 | N.A. | 0 | 825,590 | 2,536,749 |
| 1977... | 1,341,530 | 423,492 | 55,437 | 56,889 | 39,370 | 19,215 | N.A. | N.A. | 849,814 | 2,790,144 |
| 1978... | 1,563,047 | 416,231 | 69,689 | 54,478 | 56,140 | 28,502 | N.A. | 6 | 833,061 | 3,024,982 |
| 1979... | 1,617,328 | 495,565 | 72,456 | 46,911 | 65,907 | 27,887 | N.A. | 4 | 677,008 | 3,005,523 |
| 1980... | 1,991,502 | 338,711 | 46,899 | 32,517 | 61,496 | 47,386 | N.A. | 1 | 594,770 | 3,116,448 |
| 1981... | 1,911,525 | 234,052 | 21,635 | 12,728 | 68,042 | 42,477 | N.A. | 1 | 563,943 | 2,856,286 |
| 1982... | 1,801,185 | 259,385 | 9,402 | 13,023 | 89,231 | 50,032 | N.A. | 27 | 702,495 | 2,926,407 |
| 1983... | 1,871,192 | 239,807 | 5,442 | 17,261 | 114,726 | 40,823 | N.A. | 2 | 835,665 | 3,133,836 |
| 1984... | 1,948,714 | 335,032 | 8,582 | 19,833 | 114,854 | 37,788 | N.A. | N.A. | 1,073,425 | 3,559,427 |
| 1985... | 2,527,467 | 473,110 | 8,689 | 24,474 | 142,640 | 42,882 | N.A. | 13,647 | 1,144,805 | 4,397,679 |
| 1986... | 2,618,711 | 451,699 | 11,829 | 27,506 | 148,700 | 10,869 | 169,309 | 41,983 | 1,162,226 | 4,691,297 |
| 1987... | 2,417,509 | 377,542 | 8,648 | 50,059 | 138,565 | 26,707 | 399,856 | 126,266 | 926,927 | 4,589,010 |
| 1988... | 2,123,051 | 264,249 | 6,053 | 31,636 | 108,006 | 15,990 | 455,741 | 148,065 | 1,191,357 | 4,450,213 |
| 1989... | 2,051,525 | 216,881 | 9,319 | 29,378 | 101,571 | 4,885 | 270,609 | 133,049 | 1,151,122 | 4,042,728 |
| 1990... | 1,867,794 | 245,286 | 11,045 | 27,271 | 93,084 | 1,976 | 201,475 | 215,986 | 1,220,221 | 3,944,602 |

(1) Excludes passenger cars assembled in U.S. foreign trade zones. (2) Includes countries not shown separately.

## 50 Busiest United States Ports, 1991

Source: Corps of Engineers, Dept. of the Army, U.S. Dept. of Defense

(ports ranked by tonnage handled, all figures in tons)

| Rank | Port | Total | Domestic | Foreign | Imports | Exports |
|---|---|---|---|---|---|---|
| 1 | South Louisiana, LA, Port of | 189,374,451 | 100,252,774 | 89,121,677 | 25,859,022 | 63,262,655 |
| 2 | Houston, TX | 131,233,876 | 62,943,241 | 68,290,635 | 41,065,418 | 27,225,217 |
| 3 | New York, NY | 126,860,940 | 83,082,893 | 43,778,047 | 36,076,481 | 7,701,566 |
| 4 | Valdez, AK | 99,616,158 | 99,576,371 | 39,787 | 23,986 | 15,801 |
| 5 | Baton Rouge, LA | 87,630,227 | 49,341,472 | 38,288,755 | 19,891,036 | 18,397,719 |
| 6 | New Orleans, LA | 60,897,696 | 31,784,891 | 29,112,805 | 13,190,037 | 15,922,768 |
| 7 | Corpus Christi, TX | 59,052,232 | 22,886,556 | 36,165,676 | 30,545,740 | 5,619,936 |
| 8 | Plaquemine, LA, Port of | 53,781,692 | 37,163,309 | 16,618,383 | 2,888,779 | 13,729,604 |
| 9 | Norfolk Harbor, VA | 53,472,834 | 9,514,842 | 43,957,992 | 4,749,565 | 39,208,427 |
| 10 | Long Beach, CA | 52,890,856 | 26,775,954 | 26,114,902 | 10,852,590 | 15,262,312 |
| 11 | Tampa, FL | 49,548,191 | 28,185,229 | 21,362,962 | 5,699,268 | 15,663,694 |
| 12 | Los Angeles, CA | 47,007,818 | 21,766,328 | 25,241,490 | 13,104,955 | 12,136,535 |
| 13 | Texas City, TX | 43,289,659 | 19,260,752 | 24,028,907 | 20,894,862 | 3,134,045 |
| 14 | Mobile, AL | 41,260,410 | 20,638,650 | 20,621,760 | 7,041,682 | 13,580,078 |
| 15 | Lake Charles, LA | 41,241,080 | 17,506,750 | 23,734,330 | 17,826,283 | 5,908,047 |
| 16 | Baltimore, MD | 37,744,610 | 14,394,950 | 23,349,660 | 8,905,761 | 14,443,899 |
| 17 | Duluth-Superior, MN | 37,715,527 | 31,516,232 | 6,199,295 | 720,502 | 5,478,793 |
| 18 | Philadelphia, PA | 37,256,505 | 13,798,731 | 23,457,774 | 22,269,992 | 1,187,782 |
| 19 | Pittsburgh, PA | 31,277,381 | 31,277,381 | 0 | 0 | 0 |
| 20 | Port Arthur, TX | 29,835,115 | 9,322,861 | 20,512,254 | 17,540,467 | 2,971,787 |
| 21 | Pascagoula, MS | 29,567,012 | 10,152,815 | 19,414,197 | 16,015,036 | 3,399,161 |
| 22 | Portland, OR | 29,299,132 | 12,487,795 | 16,811,337 | 2,957,439 | 13,853,898 |
| 23 | St. Louis, Metro., MO | 29,262,653 | 29,262,653 | 0 | 0 | 0 |
| 24 | Newport News, VA | 29,168,022 | 3,352,965 | 25,815,057 | 1,166,447 | 24,648,610 |
| 25 | Paulsboro, NJ | 23,712,833 | 10,868,539 | 12,844,294 | 12,651,940 | 192,354 |
| 26 | Beaumont, TX | 22,383,039 | 16,023,672 | 6,359,367 | 4,415,802 | 1,943,565 |
| 27 | Marcus Hook, PA | 22,337,153 | 13,560,809 | 8,776,344 | 8,493,382 | 282,962 |
| 28 | Chicago, IL | 21,767,354 | 19,975,150 | 1,792,204 | 1,529,071 | 263,133 |
| 29 | Seattle, WA | 20,897,097 | 6,972,843 | 13,924,254 | 6,129,956 | 7,794,298 |
| 30 | Richmond, CA | 19,919,081 | 14,501,561 | 5,417,520 | 2,123,441 | 3,294,079 |
| 31 | Tacoma, WA | 19,544,196 | 5,091,025 | 14,453,171 | 4,896,733 | 9,556,438 |
| 32 | Boston, MA | 18,562,490 | 9,144,085 | 9,418,405 | 8,772,215 | 646,190 |
| 33 | Huntington, WV | 18,042,588 | 18,042,588 | 0 | 0 | 0 |
| 34 | Jacksonville, FL | 15,780,263 | 8,226,322 | 7,553,941 | 4,866,254 | 2,687,687 |
| 35 | Freeport, TX | 15,665,993 | 7,966,433 | 7,699,560 | 6,522,710 | 1,176,850 |
| 36 | Port Everglades, FL | 14,498,908 | 9,966,821 | 4,532,087 | 3,481,434 | 1,050,653 |
| 37 | Anacortes, WA | 14,480,734 | 12,858,072 | 1,622,662 | 404,258 | 1,218,404 |
| 38 | Detroit, MI | 14,320,909 | 11,938,978 | 2,381,931 | 1,886,256 | 495,675 |
| 39 | San Juan, PR | 14,163,380 | 8,762,131 | 5,401,249 | 4,761,348 | 639,901 |
| 40 | Indiana Harbor, IN | 13,767,044 | 13,709,364 | 57,680 | 38,224 | 19,456 |
| 41 | Lorain, OH | 13,631,998 | 13,523,439 | 108,559 | 105,270 | 3,289 |
| 42 | Cleveland, OH | 13,405,999 | 10,609,015 | 2,796,984 | 2,716,169 | 80,815 |
| 43 | Savannah, GA | 13,325,692 | 2,427,463 | 10,898,229 | 4,921,284 | 5,976,945 |
| 44 | Toledo, OH | 12,537,683 | 6,417,750 | 6,119,933 | 783,926 | 5,336,007 |
| 45 | Two Harbors, MN | 12,500,967 | 12,500,967 | 0 | 0 | 0 |
| 46 | Memphis, TN | 12,297,780 | 12,297,757 | 23 | 0 | 23 |
| 47 | Cincinnati, OH | 11,717,298 | 11,717,298 | 0 | 0 | 0 |
| 48 | Ashtabula, OH | 11,276,068 | 6,808,618 | 4,467,450 | 398,424 | 4,069,026 |
| 49 | Honolulu, HI | 11,208,056 | 10,603,204 | 604,852 | 422,602 | 182,250 |
| 50 | Galveston, TX | 10,858,221 | 3,326,998 | 7,531,223 | 3,621,711 | 3,909,512 |

## Commerce on U.S. Inland Waterways

Source: Corps of Engineers, Dept. of the Army, U.S. Dept. of Defense, 1991

### Mississippi River System and Gulf Intracoastal Waterway

| Waterway | Tons |
|---|---|
| Mississippi River, Minneapolis to the Gulf | 462,735,996 |
| Mississippi River, Minneapolis to St. Louis | 79,356,272 |
| Mississippi River, St. Louis to Cairo | 101,799,998 |
| Mississippi River, Cairo to Baton Rouge | 181,802,058 |
| Mississippi River, Baton Rouge to New Orleans | 331,655,147 |
| Mississippi River, New Orleans to the Gulf | 281,225,303 |
| Gulf Intracoastal Waterway | 112,739,177 |
| Mississippi River System | 626,384,122 |

### Ton-Mileage of Freight Carried on Inland Waterways

| System | Ton-miles |
|---|---|
| Atlantic Coast Waterways | 28,204,948 |
| Gulf Coast Waterways | 42,545,820 |
| Pacific Coast Waterways | 23,999,523 |
| Mississippi River System, including Ohio River and tributaries | 268,089,639 |
| Great Lakes System, U.S. commerce only | 85,847,239 |
| Total: | 448,687,169 |

**Note:** Tons are for calendar year 1989; all tons are in U.S. short tons (2,000 lbs. per ton); ton-miles(000) have been omitted.

## Important Waterways and Canals

The St. Lawrence & Great Lakes Waterway, the largest inland navigation system on the North American continent, extends from the Atlantic Ocean to Duluth at the western end of Lake Superior, a distance of 2,342 miles. With the deepening of channels and locks to 27 ft., ocean carriers are able to penetrate to ports in the Canadian interior and the American midwest.

The major canals are those of the St. Lawrence Great Lakes waterway — the 3 canals of the St. Lawrence Seaway, with their 7 locks, providing navigation for vessels of 26-foot draft from Montreal to Lake Ontario; the Welland Ship Canal, with its 8 locks, by-passing the Niagara River between Lake Ontario and Lake Erie; and the Sault Ste. Marie Canal and lock between Lake Huron and Lake Superior. These 16 locks overcome a drop of 580 ft. from the head of the lakes to Montreal. From Montreal to Lake Ontario the former bottleneck of narrow, shallow canals and of slow passage through 22 locks has been overcome, giving faster and safer movement for larger vessels. The current locks and linking channels now accommodate all but the largest ocean-going vessels and the upper St. Lawrence and Great Lakes are open to 80% of the world's saltwater fleet.

Subsidiary Canadian canals or branches include the St. Peters Canal between Bras d'Or Lakes and the Atlantic Ocean in Nova Scotia; the St. Ours and Chambly Canals on the Richelieu River, Quebec; the Ste. Anne and Carillon Canals on the Ottawa River; the Rideau Canal between the Ottawa River and Lake Ontario; the Trent and Murray Canals between Lake Ontario and Georgian Bay in Ontario; and the St. Andrew's Canal on the Red River. The commercial value of these canals is not great but they are maintained to control water levels and permit the passage of small vessels and pleasure craft. The Canso Canal permits shipping to pass through the causeway connecting Cape Breton Island with the Nova Scotia mainland.

The Welland Canal overcomes the 326-ft. drop of Niagara Falls and the rapids of the Niagara River. It has 8 locks, each 859 ft. long, 80 ft. wide, and 30 ft. deep. Regulations permit ships of 730-ft. length and 75-ft. beam to transit.

## Shortest Navigable Distances Between Ports

Source: *Distances Between Ports* (Pub. 151, 7th Edition, 1993), Defense Mapping Agency Hydrographic/Topographic Center

Distances shown are in nautical miles (1,852 meters or about 6,076.115 feet). For statute miles, multiply by 1.15.

| From | To | Distance | From | To | Distance |
|---|---|---|---|---|---|
| New York, New York | Barcelona, Spain | 3,714 | " | Copenhagen, Denmark | 5,233 |
| " | Cape Town, South Africa | 6,786 | " | Galveston, Texas | 1,508 |
| " | Cherbourg, France | 3,134 | " | Gibraltar[3] | 4,332 |
| " | Copenhagen, Denmark | 3,826 | " | Hamburg, Germany | 5,061 |
| " | Galveston, Texas | 1,935 | " | Helsinki, Finland | 5,696 |
| " | Glasgow, Scotland | 3,210 | " | Lagos, Nigeria | 5,049 |
| " | Hamburg, Germany | 3,654 | " | Lisbon, Portugal | 4,152 |
| " | Havana, Cuba | 1,186 | " | Oslo, Norway | 5,053 |
| " | Helsinki, Finland | 4,289 | " | Piraeus, Greece | 5,759 |
| " | Oslo, Norway | 3,704 | " | Port Said, Egypt | 6,251 |
| " | Piraeus, Greece | 4,688 | " | St. John's, New- foundland | 2,695 |
| " | Southampton, England | 3,169 | " | Southampton, England | 4,576 |
| Montreal, Canada | Algiers, Algeria | 3,842 | San Francisco, Calif. | Bombay, India | 9,794 |
| " | Barcelona, Spain | 3,959 | " | Calcutta, India | 9,384 |
| " | Cape Town, South Africa | 7,118 | " | Colón, Panama | 3,264 |
| " | Gibraltar[3] | 3,429 | Vancouver, Canada | Calcutta, India | 8,727 |
| " | Halifax, Nova Scotia | 895 | " | Melbourne, Australia | 7,365 |
| " | Havana, Cuba | 2,528 | Panama, Panama | Jakarta, Indonesia | 10,603 |
| " | Istanbul, Turkey | 5,226 | Port Said, Egypt | Ho Chi Minh City, Vietnam | 5,684 |
| " | Kingston, Jamaica | 3,269 | " | Hong Kong | 6,489 |
| " | Lagos, Nigeria | 5,170 | " | Manila, Philippines | 6,365 |
| " | Marseille, France | 4,116 | " | Melbourne, Australia | 7,886 |
| " | Naples, Italy | 4,406 | " | Singapore | 5,035 |
| " | Oslo, Norway | 3,165 | " | Yokohama, Japan | 7,024 |
| " | Piraeus, Greece | 4,856 | Cape Town,[2] South Africa | Jakarta, Indonesia | 5,276 |
| " | Port Said, Egypt | 5,348 | " | Melbourne, Australia | 5,719 |
| " | Southampton, England | 2,913 | " | Singapore | 5,614 |
| Colón,[1] Panama | Buenos Aires, Argentina | 5,385 | Singapore | Jakarta, Indonesia | 525 |

(1) Colón on the Atlantic is 44 nautical miles from Panamá (port) on the Pacific; (2) Cape Town is 35 nautical miles northwest of the Cape of Good Hope. (3) Gibraltar (port) is 24 nautical miles east of the Strait of Gibraltar.

## Major Merchant Fleets of the World

Source: Maritime Administration, U.S. Dept. of Commerce (tonnage in thousands)

Fleets of oceangoing steam and motor ships totaling 1 million gross tons or over as of Jan. 1, 1993. Excludes ships operating exclusively on the Great Lakes and inland waterways and special types such as channel ships, icebreakers, cable ships, and merchant ships owned by any military force. Gross tonnage is a volume measurement; each cargo gross ton represents 100 cubic ft. of enclosed space. Deadweight tonnage is the carrying capacity of a ship in long tons (2,240 lbs.). Tonnage figures may not add, due to rounding.

| | Total | | | Freighters | | | Type of Vessel Bulk Carriers | | | Tankers | | |
|---|---|---|---|---|---|---|---|---|---|---|---|---|
| | No. of Ships | Gross Tons | Dwt. Tons | No. of Ships | Gross Tons | Dwt. Tons | No. of Ships | Gross Tons | Dwt. Tons | No. of Ships | Gross Tons | Dwt. Tons |
| All Countries[1] | 23,753 | 402,217 | 656,591 | 12,339 | 101,635 | 123,179 | 5,420 | 138,712 | 246,983 | 5,642 | 156,683 | 285,009 |
| United States[2] | 603 | 15,406 | 22,500 | 349 | 6,824 | 7,232 | 23 | 574 | 991 | 220 | 7,825 | 14,180 |
| Privately owned[3] | 384 | 12,611 | 18,774 | 167 | 4,648 | 4,498 | 21 | 536 | 929 | 193 | 7,349 | 13,320 |
| Government owned | 219 | 2,795 | 3,726 | 182 | 2,176 | 2,734 | 2 | 38 | 62 | 27 | 476 | 860 |
| Australia | 74 | 2,313 | 3,495 | 21 | 241 | 271 | 30 | 1,007 | 1,685 | 23 | 1,065 | 1,539 |
| Bahamas | 818 | 19,412 | 32,173 | 380 | 4,003 | 5,213 | 147 | 4,343 | 7,690 | 242 | 10,062 | 19,034 |
| Bermuda | 62 | 3,150 | 5,369 | 18 | 177 | 200 | 9 | 204 | 347 | 35 | 2,769 | 4,822 |
| Brazil | 220 | 5,131 | 8,783 | 59 | 543 | 698 | 77 | 2,434 | 4,250 | 83 | 2,153 | 3,834 |
| *Bulgaria | 117 | 1,266 | 1,880 | 59 | 371 | 463 | 37 | 603 | 949 | 19 | 290 | 468 |
| *China | 1,231 | 12,631 | 19,388 | 752 | 5,364 | 7,438 | 285 | 5,433 | 9,181 | 170 | 1,661 | 2,685 |
| Cyprus | 1,251 | 20,050 | 35,630 | 616 | 4,085 | 5,996 | 488 | 10,858 | 19,840 | 140 | 5,046 | 9,766 |
| Denmark | 281 | 4,335 | 6,309 | 189 | 2,294 | 2,563 | 14 | 555 | 1,029 | 78 | 1,486 | 2,717 |
| France | 106 | 3,020 | 4,742 | 45 | 1,003 | 1,084 | 6 | 103 | 153 | 48 | 1,853 | 3,485 |
| Germany | 419 | 4,462 | 5,672 | 351 | 3,475 | 4,263 | 22 | 522 | 853 | 39 | 327 | 513 |
| Greece | 904 | 24,431 | 46,101 | 193 | 1,540 | 2,258 | 458 | 11,834 | 22,134 | 231 | 10,898 | 21,639 |
| Hong Kong | 200 | 7,085 | 11,981 | 64 | 1,135 | 1,286 | 104 | 4,821 | 8,839 | 31 | 1,039 | 1,853 |
| India | 296 | 6,029 | 10,036 | 97 | 914 | 1,339 | 119 | 2,928 | 4,994 | 77 | 2,162 | 3,693 |
| Indonesia | 365 | 1,588 | 2,514 | 247 | 842 | 1,310 | 19 | 181 | 268 | 92 | 549 | 922 |
| Iran | 124 | 4,421 | 8,228 | 38 | 385 | 533 | 50 | 1,058 | 1,757 | 36 | 2,978 | 5,938 |
| Isle of Man | 68 | 1,498 | 2,583 | 28 | 275 | 314 | 12 | 311 | 543 | 28 | 912 | 1,726 |
| Italy | 468 | 6,411 | 9,737 | 172 | 1,346 | 1,355 | 60 | 2,317 | 4,208 | 217 | 2,473 | 4,110 |
| Japan | 913 | 21,109 | 32,562 | 351 | 3,849 | 3,077 | 251 | 8,653 | 15,992 | 296 | 8,407 | 13,437 |
| Korea, South | 422 | 6,383 | 10,238 | 225 | 1,996 | 2,307 | 130 | 3,869 | 7,013 | 67 | 518 | 918 |
| Kuwait | 43 | 2,208 | 3,792 | 13 | 281 | 370 | 0 | 0 | 0 | 30 | 1,927 | 3,422 |
| Latvia | 118 | 1,023 | 1,316 | 75 | 431 | 425 | 0 | 0 | 0 | 43 | 592 | 891 |
| Liberia | 1,568 | 55,139 | 97,173 | 367 | 5,911 | 6,363 | 540 | 17,333 | 32,001 | 639 | 31,143 | 58,679 |
| Luxembourg | 51 | 1,609 | 2,605 | 16 | 199 | 225 | 17 | 881 | 1,630 | 17 | 496 | 745 |
| Malaysia | 185 | 1,865 | 2,779 | 107 | 666 | 926 | 24 | 468 | 842 | 54 | 731 | 1,011 |
| Malta | 752 | 10,569 | 17,971 | 343 | 2,286 | 3,313 | 255 | 5,209 | 9,163 | 147 | 3,002 | 5,468 |
| Marshall Islands | 31 | 2,031 | 4,002 | 4 | 86 | 102 | 18 | 625 | 1,163 | 9 | 1,320 | 2,737 |
| Netherlands | 367 | 3,240 | 4,265 | 285 | 1,950 | 2,403 | 19 | 393 | 638 | 58 | 766 | 1,206 |
| Norway | 737 | 20,230 | 35,371 | 193 | 1,860 | 2,049 | 219 | 6,114 | 11,079 | 311 | 11,866 | 22,173 |
| Panama | 3,171 | 49,589 | 79,414 | 1,719 | 13,966 | 16,325 | 717 | 17,115 | 29,587 | 704 | 18,169 | 33,375 |
| Philippines | 534 | 7,979 | 13,420 | 239 | 1,382 | 1,833 | 251 | 6,202 | 10,871 | 39 | 360 | 699 |
| Poland | 212 | 2,780 | 4,046 | 119 | 980 | 1,111 | 85 | 1,671 | 2,740 | 5 | 109 | 185 |
| Romania | 255 | 2,701 | 4,135 | 193 | 1,147 | 1,535 | 50 | 1,110 | 1,820 | 12 | 444 | 780 |
| Russia | 1,363 | 10,036 | 13,370 | 1,006 | 5,509 | 6,369 | 135 | 2,092 | 3,209 | 211 | 2,378 | 3,781 |
| Saint Vincent | 431 | 4,344 | 7,114 | 285 | 1,625 | 2,313 | 97 | 1,881 | 3,286 | 47 | 823 | 1,503 |
| Singapore | 493 | 9,525 | 15,377 | 227 | 2,706 | 3,168 | 82 | 2,514 | 4,480 | 184 | 4,305 | 7,729 |
| Spain | 222 | 2,116 | 3,904 | 130 | 350 | 558 | 30 | 530 | 959 | 61 | 1,234 | 2,384 |
| Sweden | 172 | 2,467 | 3,157 | 90 | 1,079 | 1,035 | 10 | 220 | 374 | 67 | 1,011 | 1,723 |
| Taiwan | 215 | 5,955 | 9,146 | 134 | 2,444 | 2,852 | 60 | 2,537 | 4,622 | 21 | 974 | 1,672 |
| Turkey | 339 | 3,817 | 6,583 | 189 | 715 | 1,039 | 93 | 2,239 | 3,987 | 54 | 849 | 1,551 |
| United Kingdom | 154 | 2,749 | 3,081 | 58 | 1,062 | 1,032 | 19 | 139 | 209 | 59 | 1,159 | 1,731 |
| Vanuatu | 119 | 2,018 | 3,021 | 55 | 644 | 599 | 52 | 1,115 | 1,948 | 11 | 253 | 472 |

(1) Includes combination passenger & cargo ships. (2) Excludes nonmerchant type and/or Navy-owned vessels that are currently in the National Reserve Fleet. (3) Includes 18 integrated tug/barge vessels of 637,000 deadweight tons. (*) = Source material limited.

## Fastest Scheduled Passenger Train Runs in the U.S. and Canada

Source: Darrell J. Smith, Natl. Railroad Passenger Corp.; 1993 timetables

| Railroad | Train | From | To | Mi. | Min. | MPH |
|---|---|---|---|---|---|---|
| Amtrak | Eight Metroliner Service trains | Wilmington | Baltimore | 68.4 | 42 | 97.7 |
| Amtrak | 16 Metroliner Service trains | Baltimore | Wilmington | 68.4 | 43 | 95.0 |
| Amtrak | Express Metroliner Service train 203 | Metropark | Baltimore | 160.0 | 103 | 93.0 |
| Amtrak | Express Metroliner Service train 202 | New Carrollton | New York City | 216.0 | 141 | 91.9 |
| Amtrak | Express Metroliner Service train 220 | Washington | Philadelphia | 135.0 | 88 | 91.8 |
| Amtrak | Express Metroliner Service train 223 | New York | Baltimore | 185.0 | 123 | 90.2 |
| Amtrak | Two Metroliner Service trains | Newark | Philadelphia | 80.7 | 55 | 87.7 |
| Amtrak | Nine Metroliner Service trains | Newark | Philadelphia | 80.7 | 56 | 86.8 |
| VIA | Renaissance | Dorval | Kingston | 165.0 | 117 | 84.6 |
| VIA | York | Kingston | Cornwall | 108.0 | 77 | 84.4 |
| Amtrak | Three Metroliner Service trains | Philadelphia | Newark | 80.7 | 58 | 83.2 |
| VIA | York | Cornwall | Kingston | 108.0 | 78 | 83.1 |
| VIA | Renaissance | Kingston | Dorval | 165.0 | 120 | 82.5 |

**Notes:** The fastest scheduled passenger train runs in the world are those of France's TGV Atlantique, between Paris and various cities in western France, at 186.4 mph. On Dec. 12, 1992, Amtrak operated the Swedish X-2000 train at 155 mph, and on July 18, 1993, operated the German ICE train at 162 mph, both on a portion (in northern New Jersey) of the Northeast Corridor. The runs were part of Amtrak's program to test high-speed equipment for use on the Washington-Boston Northeast Corridor.

## Top 50 U.S. Industrial Exporters

Source: FORTUNE magazine; June 14, 1993.

| Rank 1992 | 1991 | Company | Export sales 1992 $ millions | % change from 1991 | As % of total sales % | Rank | Rank 1992 | 1991 | Company | Export sales 1992 $ millions | % change from 1991 | As % of total sales % | Rank |
|---|---|---|---|---|---|---|---|---|---|---|---|---|---|
| 1 | 1 | Boeing | $17,486.0 | -2.1 | 57.5 | 1 | 26 | * | IBP | 1,300.0 | 30.3 | 11.7 | 30 |
| 2 | 2 | General Motors | 14,045.1[1] | -6.8 | 10.6 | 35 | 27 | 33 | Xerox | 1,292.0 | 24.2 | 7.1 | 46 |
| 3 | 3 | General Electric | 8,200.0 | -4.8 | 13.2 | 27 | 28 | 23 | Dow Chemical | 1,247.0 | -9.4 | 6.5 | 47 |
| 4 | 4 | IBM | 7,524.0 | -1.9 | 11.6 | 31 | 29 | 29 | Textron | 1,244.0 | 6.2 | 14.9 | 22 |
| 5 | 5 | Ford | 7,220.0[2] | -1.6 | 7.2 | 45 | 30 | 27 | International Paper | 1,200.0[2] | — | 8.8 | 40 |
| 6 | 6 | Chrysler | 7,051.8 | 14.3 | 19.1 | 14 | 31 | * | RJR Nabisco | 1,171.0 | 16.9 | 7.4 | 43 |
| 7 | 7 | McDonnell Douglas | 4,983.0 | -19.1 | 28.5 | 6 | 32 | 28 | Union Carbide | 1,125.0 | -6.3 | 18.2 | 15 |
| 8 | 12 | Philip Morris | 3,797.0 | 24.0 | 7.6 | 42 | 33 | 37 | Compaq Computer | 1,104.0[3] | 16.2 | 26.7 | 7 |
| 9 | 11 | Hewlett-Packard | 3,720.0 | 15.4 | 22.6 | 10 | 34 | 30 | Hoechst Celanese | 1,072.0 | -7.4 | 15.2 | 19 |
| 10 | 8 | du Pont | 3,509.0 | -7.9 | 9.4 | 38 | 35 | 38 | FMC | 997.7 | 9.3 | 25.0 | 9 |
| 11 | 14 | Motorola | 3,460.0 | 18.2 | 25.9 | 8 | 36 | 35 | Abbott Laboratories | 996.7 | 4.1 | 12.6 | 29 |
| 12 | 10 | United Technologies | 3,451.0 | -3.8 | 15.7 | 17 | 37 | 39 | Miles | 956.0[4] | 9.0 | 14.7 | 23 |
| 13 | 9 | Caterpillar | 3,341.0 | -9.9 | 32.8 | 4 | 38 | * | Apple Computer | 934.7 | 20.8 | 13.2 | 26 |
| 14 | 13 | Eastman Kodak | 3,220.0 | 6.6 | 15.6 | 18 | 39 | 32 | Monsanto | 927.0 | -17.8 | 10.9 | 34 |
| 15 | 15 | Archer Daniels Midland | 2,700.0 | 3.8 | 28.9 | 5 | 40 | 43 | Bristol-Myers Squibb | 915.0[1] | 13.4 | 7.8 | 41 |
| 16 | 17 | Intel | 2,339.0 | 21.3 | 39.1 | 3 | 41 | 45 | Exxon | 906.0 | 21.8 | 0.9 | 50 |
| 17 | 16 | Digital Equipment | 1,900.0 | -13.6 | 13.5 | 24 | 42 | 34 | Aluminum Co. of America | 886.0 | -8.4 | 9.2 | 39 |
| 18 | 18 | Allied-Signal | 1,810.0 | 4.7 | 15.0 | 21 | 43 | * | Georgia Pacific | 859.0 | 30.0 | 7.3 | 44 |
| 19 | 20 | Unisys | 1,795.8 | 12.4 | 21.3 | 11 | 44 | 44 | Lockheed | 831.0 | 24.8 | 10.0 | 37 |
| 20 | 19 | Sun Microsystems | 1,783.6 | 11.1 | 49.2 | 2 | 45 | 42 | Honeywell | 830.0 | 2.7 | 13.3 | 25 |
| 21 | 21 | Raytheon | 1,760.0 | 13.1 | 19.3 | 13 | 46 | 40 | Cooper Industries | 805.0 | -3.6 | 13.1 | 28 |
| 22 | 22 | Weyerhaeuser | 1,500.0 | -3.2 | 16.2 | 16 | 47 | * | Cummins Engine | 781.0 | 48.5 | 20.8 | 12 |
| 23 | 25 | Merck | 1,489.8 | 11.0 | 15.2 | 20 | 48 | 46 | Deere | 778.0 | 9.1 | 11.2 | 33 |
| 24 | 26 | Minnesota Mining & Mfg. | 1,433.0 | 12.4 | 10.3 | 36 | 49 | 48 | Tenneco | 702.0 | 1.4 | 5.2 | 49 |
| 25 | 31 | Westinghouse Electric | 1,360.0 | 19.2 | 11.2 | 32 | 50 | 41 | Rockwell Intl. | 701.0 | -15.3 | 6.4 | 48 |
| | | | | | | | | | **Total** | **$135,440.2** | | | |

* Not on last year's list. [1] FORTUNE estimate. [2] Excludes some U.S. exports. [3] Exports from U.S. and Canada. [4] Owned by Bayer AG, Germany.

## Passenger Car Production, U.S. Plants

Source: American Automobile Manufacturers Assn.

| | 1991 | 1992 | | 1991 | 1992 |
|---|---|---|---|---|---|
| **Chrysler Corp.** | | | Custom Cruiser | 7,811 | 1,984 |
| Horizon | — | — | Delta 88 | 93,051 | 66,620 |
| Acclaim | 82,358 | 70,768 | Oldsmobile 98 | 75,362 | 26,154 |
| Sundance | 61,605 | 64,953 | Toronado | 5,934 | 3,553 |
| **Total Plymouth** | **143,963** | **135,721** | Calais | 34,616 | 296 |
| Concorde | — | 9,755 | Achieva | 6,199 | 87,372 |
| LeBaron | — | 9,755 | Cutless Supreme | 105,151 | 76,855 |
| LeBaron J | 29,388 | 45,235 | Ciera | 111,628 | 133,140 |
| Fifth Avenue (Y) | 36,706 | 40,436 | **Total Oldsmobile** | **439,752** | **359,974** |
| Imperial | 9,335 | 6,635 | LeSabre | 111,232 | 157,790 |
| New Yorker (C) | 15,142 | 21,339 | Roadmaster | 60,259 | 50,566 |
| **Total Chrysler-Plymouth** | **234,534** | **259,121** | Park Avenue | 93,700 | 58,587 |
| Shadow | 69,463 | 93,920 | Riviera | 10,314 | 11,801 |
| Daytona | 11,492 | 14,544 | Century | 98,670 | 88,820 |
| Spirit | 80,216 | 68,068 | Skylark | 61,537 | 60,351 |
| Dynasty | 114,439 | 86,697 | Reatta | 1,210 | — |
| Viper | 3 | 310 | **Total Buick** | **436,922** | **427,915** |
| **Total Dodge** | **275,613** | **263,539** | DeVille | 160,223 | 122,844 |
| **Total Chrysler Corp.** | **510,147** | **522,660** | Fleetwood | — | 17,384 |
| **Ford Motor Co.** | | | Brougham | 22,234 | 2,170 |
| Thunderbird | 71,395 | 97,822 | Eldorado | 16,276 | 29,866 |
| Taurus | 317,810 | 427,621 | Seville | 26,786 | 46,440 |
| Tempo | 112,105 | 129,334 | Allante | 2,900 | 2,408 |
| Escort | 188,450 | 179,143 | **Total Cadillac** | **228,419** | **221,112** |
| Mustang | 81,594 | 88,568 | Saturn | 95,821 | 212,122 |
| **Total Ford** | **771,354** | **922,488** | **Total General Motors Corp.** | **2,496,006** | **2,466,290** |
| Cougar | 52,157 | 61,042 | **Diamond Star** | | |
| Sable | 110,619 | 123,531 | Mitsubishi Eclipse | 57,926 | 72,367 |
| Topaz | 49,493 | 57,961 | Mitsubishi Mirage | 24,192 | 10,140 |
| Town Car | 126,354 | 117,789 | Plymouth Laser | 27,778 | 21,993 |
| Mark | 9,297 | 11,468 | Eagle Talon | 34,923 | 31,802 |
| Continental | 52,406 | 39,299 | Eagle Summit | 9,117 | 3,481 |
| **Total Lincoln-Mercury** | **400,326** | **411,090** | **Total Diamond Star** | **153,936** | **139,783** |
| **Total Ford Motor Co.** | **1,171,680** | **1,333,578** | **Honda** | | |
| **General Motors Corp.** | | | Accord | 366,231 | 356,382 |
| Caprice | 124,224 | 103,594 | Civic | 84,968 | 101,872 |
| Corvette | 21,082 | 20,839 | **Total Honda** | **451,199** | **458,254** |
| Beretta-Corsica | 240,745 | 187,441 | **Mazda** | 165,314 | 167,940 |
| Camaro | 52,177 | 47,757 | **Nissan** | | |
| Cavalier | 252,857 | 212,117 | Altima | — | 52,166 |
| Geo Prizm | 94,927 | 75,479 | Sentra | 133,505 | 119,238 |
| **Total Chevrolet** | **786,012** | **647,227** | **Total Nissan** | **133,505** | **171,404** |
| Grand Prix | 114,718 | 110,485 | Subaru Legacy | 57,945 | 57,623 |
| 6000 | 19,603 | — | **Toyota** | | |
| Grand Am | 147,467 | 251,822 | Corolla | 111,139 | 105,370 |
| Firebird | 20,322 | 14,786 | Camry | 187,708 | 240,382 |
| Bonneville H. | 88,355 | 98,748 | **Total Toyota** | **298,847** | **345,752** |
| Sunbird | 118,615 | 86,119 | **Total Passenger Cars** | **5,438,579** | **5,663,284** |
| **Total Pontiac** | **509,080** | **561,940** | | | |

## Selected Motor Vehicle Statistics

Source: Federal Highway Administration; U.S. Dept. of Transportation; Insurance Institute for Highway Safety; 1991 figures unless otherwise specified.

| State | Driver's age Jan. 1, 1993 (1) Regular | (2) Juvenile | State gas tax cents/gal. (Oct.1, 1992) | Safety belt use law[3] (Aug. 1, 1993) | Licensed drivers per 1,000 resident population | Registered motor vehicles per 1,000 resident population | Licensed drivers per registered motor vehicle | Gallons of fuel used per vehicle | Miles per gallon | Annual miles driven per vehicle | Vehicle miles per licensed driver |
|---|---|---|---|---|---|---|---|---|---|---|---|
| Alabama.... | 16 | — | 18 | S | 673 | 905 | 0.74 | 704 | 16.48 | 11,605 | 15,594 |
| Alaska.... | 16 | — | 8 | S | 551 | 826 | 0.67 | 509 | 16.78 | 8,539 | 12,794 |
| Arizona .... | 16 | — | 18 | S | 638 | 760 | 0.84 | 695 | 17.64 | 12,262 | 14,599 |
| Arkansas ... | 16 | — | 18.7 | S | 726 | 624 | 1.16 | 1,068 | 13.89 | 14,824 | 12,737 |
| California ... | 16/18 | 14 | 16 | P | 653 | 732 | 0.89 | 638 | 18.18 | 11,593 | 12,999 |
| Colorado ... | 18 | 16 | 22 | S | 605 | 902 | 0.67 | 554 | 16.45 | 9,111 | 13,580 |
| Connecticut .. | 16/18 | — | 26 | P | 673 | 787 | 0.86 | 570 | 18.04 | 10,286 | 12,026 |
| Delaware ... | 16/18 | — | 19 | S | 713 | 785 | 0.91 | 697 | 18.07 | 12,596 | 13,863 |
| Dist. of Col... | 18 | 16 | 20 | S | 689 | 412 | 1.67 | 764 | 18.23 | 13,921 | 8,319 |
| Florida .... | 16 | — | 11.6 | S | 695 | 752 | 0.92 | 656 | 17.33 | 11,371 | 12,293 |
| Georgia .... | 16 | — | 7.5 | S* | 676 | 863 | 0.78 | 757 | 16.88 | 12,776 | 16,302 |
| Hawaii..... | 15 | — | 16 | P | 597 | 692 | 0.86 | 505 | 20.53 | 10,373 | 12,017 |
| Idaho .... | 17 | 15 | 21 | S | 678 | 1,016 | 0.67 | 551 | 17.75 | 9,777 | 14,652 |
| Illinois .... | 16/18 | — | 19 | S | 632 | 710 | 0.89 | 639 | 16.33 | 10,428 | 11,711 |
| Indiana .... | 16/18 | — | 15 | S | 642 | 787 | 0.82 | 756 | 16.27 | 12,295 | 15,068 |
| Iowa ...... | 16/18 | — | 20 | P | 670 | 955 | 0.70 | 604 | 14.28 | 8,627 | 12,294 |
| Kansas .... | 16 | 14 | 18 | S | 687 | 753 | 0.91 | 760 | 16.23 | 12,337 | 13,523 |
| Kentucky ... | 16 | — | 15.4 | No | 647 | 798 | 0.81 | 749 | 15.88 | 11,885 | 14,662 |
| Louisiana ... | 15/17 | 15 | 20 | S | 606 | 716 | 0.85 | 686 | 16.60 | 11,396 | 13,477 |
| Maine ..... | 16/17 | 16 | 19 | No | 718 | 793 | 0.91 | 695 | 17.41 | 12,105 | 13,358 |
| Maryland ... | 16/18 | 16 | 23.5 | S | 692 | 747 | 0.93 | 639 | 17.83 | 11,390 | 12,299 |
| Massachusetts | 17/18 | 16½ | 21 | No | 705 | 611 | 1.15 | 683 | 18.60 | 12,702 | 11.003 |
| Michigan ... | 16/18 | 14 | 15 | S | 687 | 773 | 0.89 | 649 | 17.42 | 11,309 | 12,722 |
| Minnesota .. | 16/18 | 15 | 20 | S | 571 | 739 | 0.77 | 708 | 16.95 | 11,993 | 15,522 |
| Mississippi .. | 15 | — | 18.2 | P | 727 | 728 | 1.00 | 819 | 16.10 | 13,191 | 13,211 |
| Missouri .... | 16 | — | 13.03 | S | 715 | 766 | 0.93 | 823 | 15.68 | 12,906 | 13,823 |
| Montana ... | 15/16 | 13 | 21.4 | S | 747 | 948 | 0.79 | 687 | 15.80 | 10,857 | 13,774 |
| Nebraska ... | 16 | 14 | 24.3 | S | 683 | 882 | 0.78 | 664 | 15.12 | 10,036 | 12,947 |
| Nevada .... | 16 | 14 | 24 | S | 659 | 686 | 0.96 | 887 | 13.45 | 11,926 | 12,417 |
| New Hampshire . | 16/18 | 16 | 18.6 | No | 763 | 820 | 0.93 | 611 | 17.95 | 10,960 | 11,779 |
| New Jersey . | 17 | 16 | 10.5 | S | 720 | 711 | 1.01 | 670 | 16.04 | 10,743 | 10,616 |
| New Mexico . | 15/16 | — | 17 | P | 694 | 853 | 0.81 | 769 | 16.53 | 12,702 | 15,620 |
| New York ... | 17/18 | 16 | 22.89 | P | 568 | 541 | 1.05 | 650 | 16.96 | 11,018 | 10,499 |
| North Carolina | 16/18 | — | 21.9 | P | 675 | 774 | 0.87 | 724 | 17.18 | 12,439 | 14,258 |
| North Dakota . | 16 | 14 | 17 | No** | 669 | 990 | 0.68 | 654 | 14.47 | 9,466 | 14,006 |
| Ohio ...... | 16/18 | 14 | 21 | S | 679 | 794 | 0.86 | 630 | 17.00 | 10,709 | 12,521 |
| Oklahoma ... | 16 | — | 17 | S | 717 | 841 | 0.85 | 727 | 17.65 | 12,827 | 15,034 |
| Oregon .... | 16 | 14 | 22 | P | 757 | 858 | 0.88 | 662 | 15.53 | 10,276 | 11,649 |
| Pennsylvania . | 17/18 | 16 | 22.4 | S | 660 | 672 | 0.98 | 672 | 16.15 | 10,859 | 11,050 |
| Rhode Island . | 16/18 | — | 26 | S | 668 | 626 | 1.07 | 623 | 18.26 | 11,381 | 10,664 |
| South Carolina | 16 | 15 | 16 | S | 667 | 694 | 0.96 | 837 | 16.66 | 13,943 | 14,521 |
| South Dakota | 16 | 14 | 18 | No | 700 | 999 | 0.70 | 661 | 14.46 | 9,560 | 13,630 |
| Tennessee .. | 16 | 14 | 20 | S | 673 | 917 | 0.73 | 638 | 16.30 | 10,407 | 14,175 |
| Texas ..... | 16/18 | 15 | 20 | P | 642 | 732 | 0.88 | 763 | 16.38 | 12,504 | 14,255 |
| Utah ...... | 16/18 | — | 19 | S | 591 | 695 | 0.85 | 720 | 17.37 | 12,516 | 14,713 |
| Vermont ... | 18 | 16 | 16 | S*** | 726 | 788 | 0.92 | 734 | 17.91 | 13,137 | 14,250 |
| Virginia .... | 16/19 | — | 17.5 | S | 698 | 799 | 0.87 | 693 | 17.55 | 12,166 | 13,922 |
| Washington . | 16/18 | — | 23 | S | 673 | 878 | 0.77 | 591 | 17.85 | 10,548 | 13,756 |
| West Virginia . | 16/18 | 16 | 20.35 | S*** | 713 | 707 | 1.01 | 765 | 16.44 | 12,585 | 12,484 |
| Wisconsin .. | 16/18 | 14 | 22.2 | S | 672 | 744 | 0.90 | 673 | 18.32 | 12,336 | 13,660 |
| Wyoming ... | 16 | 14 | 9 | S | 725 | 1,019 | 0.71 | 938 | 13.65 | 12,801 | 17,983 |
| Average ... | | | | | 662 | 747 | 0.89 | 683 | 16.89 | 11,532 | 13,006 |

(1) Unrestricted operation of private passenger car. When 2 ages are shown, license is issued at lower age upon completion of approved driver education course. (2) Juvenile license issued with consent of parent or guardian. (3) P = an officer may stop a vehicle for a violation (primary); S = an officer may only issue a seat belt citation when the vehicle is stopped for another moving violation (secondary); *Although the Georgia law is secondary, for persons 4-18 years of age it is enforced primarily. **North Dakota enacted a seat belt law to be enforced secondarily; however, the law may not go into effect depending on the outcome of a referendum in the June 1994 election. ***The Vermont law is effective 1/1/94; the West Virginia law is effective 9/1/93.

## U.S. Car Sales by Vehicle Size and Type, 1983-1992

Source: American Automobile Manufacturers Assn.

| Year | Small | Midsize | Large | Luxury | Total |
|---|---|---|---|---|---|
| 1992 ........... | 32.9% | 44.5% | 9.2% | 13.4% | 100.0% |
| 1991 ........... | 35.7 | 42.6 | 8.3 | 13.4 | 100.0 |
| 1990 ........... | 35.2 | 42.8 | 9.5 | 12.5 | 100.0 |
| 1989 ........... | 38.6 | 41.9 | 9.9 | 11.8 | 100.0 |
| 1988 ........... | 37.6 | 42.5 | 10.0 | 9.9 | 100.0 |
| 1987 ........... | 38.4 | 42.3 | 9.1 | 10.2 | 100.0 |
| 1986 ........... | 37.6 | 42.5 | 9.8 | 10.1 | 100.0 |
| 1985 ........... | 37.9 | 42.1 | 9.8 | 10.2 | 100.0 |
| 1984 ........... | 39.1 | 39.6 | 11.6 | 9.7 | 100.0 |
| 1983 ........... | 38.8 | 40.6 | 10.7 | 9.9 | 100.0 |

## U.S. Car Sales by Type of Buyer, 1980-1992

Source: American Automobile Manufacturers Assn.

| Year | Consumer | Sales in Thousands Business | Government | Total | % of Total Sales Consumer | Business |
|---|---|---|---|---|---|---|
| 1992 | 4,569 | 3,679 | 104 | 8,352 | 54.7% | 44.0% |
| 1991 | 4,538 | 3,752 | 97 | 8,387 | 54.1 | 44.8 |
| 1990 | 5,768 | 3,567 | 149 | 9,484 | 60.8 | 37.6 |
| 1989 | 6,375 | 3,402 | 136 | 9,913 | 64.3 | 34.3 |
| 1988 | 6,802 | 3,699 | 138 | 10,639 | 63.9 | 34.8 |
| 1987 | 6,748 | 3,395 | 135 | 10,278 | 65.7 | 33.0 |
| 1986 | 7,658 | 3,666 | 127 | 11,450 | 66.9 | 32.0 |
| 1985 | 7,083 | 3,822 | 134 | 11,039 | 64.2 | 34.6 |
| 1984 | 6,590 | 3,669 | 135 | 10,394 | 63.4 | 35.3 |
| 1983 | 6,054 | 3,006 | 119 | 9,179 | 66.0 | 32.7 |
| 1982 | 5,285 | 2,593 | 102 | 7,980 | 66.2 | 32.5 |
| 1981 | 5,623 | 2,787 | 116 | 8,535 | 66.0 | 32.7 |
| 1980 | 6,062 | 2,791 | 126 | 8,979 | 67.5 | 31.1 |

## Domestic and Imported Retail Car Sales in the U.S., 1980-1992

Source: American Automobile Manufacturers Assn.

| Calendar Year | Domestic | Imports From Japan | From Germany | Other Countries | Total Imports | Total U.S. Sales | Import Percent Total | Japan | U.S. Sponsored Imports |
|---|---|---|---|---|---|---|---|---|---|
| 1980 | 6,581,307 | 1,905,968 | 305,219 | 186,700 | 2,397,887 | 8,979,194 | 26.7 | 21.2 | 223,310 |
| 1981 | 6,208,760 | 1,858,896 | 282,881 | 185,502 | 2,327,279 | 8,536,039 | 27.3 | 21.8 | 174,665 |
| 1982 | 5,758,586 | 1,801,969 | 247,080 | 174,508 | 2,223,557 | 7,982,143 | 27.9 | 22.6 | 139,767 |
| 1983 | 6,795,295 | 1,915,621 | 279,748 | 191,403 | 2,386,772 | 9,182,067 | 26.0 | 20.9 | 138,798 |
| 1984 | 7,951,523 | 1,906,206 | 344,416 | 188,220 | 2,438,842 | 10,390,365 | 23.5 | 18.3 | 116,965 |
| 1985 | 8,204,542 | 2,217,837 | 423,983 | 195,925 | 2,837,745 | 11,042,287 | 25.7 | 20.1 | 206,252 |
| 1986 | 8,214,897 | 2,382,614 | 443,721 | 418,286 | 3,244,621 | 11,459,518 | 28.3 | 20.8 | 314,358 |
| 1987 | 7,080,858 | 2,190,405 | 347,881 | 657,465 | 3,195,751 | 10,276,609 | 31.1 | 21.3 | 348,154 |
| 1988 | 7,526,038 | 2,022,602 | 280,099 | 700,991 | 3,003,692 | 10,529,730 | 28.5 | 19.2 | 393,412 |
| 1989 | 7,072,902 | 1,897,143 | 248,561 | 553,660 | 2,699,364 | 9,772,266 | 27.6 | 19.4 | 340,425 |
| 1990 | 6,896,888 | 1,719,384 | 265,116 | 418,823 | 2,403,323 | 9,300,211 | 25.8 | 18.5 | 296,778 |
| 1991 | 6,136,757 | 1,500,309 | 192,776 | 344,814 | 2,037,899 | 8,174,656 | 24.9 | 18.4 | 254,572 |
| 1992 | 6,276,557 | 1,452,737 | 200,851 | 283,939 | 1,937,527 | 8,214,084 | 23.6 | 17.7 | 228,927 |

## World Motor Vehicle Production, 1950-1992

Source: American Automobile Manufacturers Assn.

(in thousands)

| Year | United States | Canada | Europe | Japan | Other | World Total | U.S. % of World Total |
|---|---|---|---|---|---|---|---|
| 1992 | 9,702 | 1,968 | 17,244 | 12,499 | 5,964 | 47,377 | 20.5 |
| 1991 | 8,811 | 1,873 | 17,527 | 13,245 | 5,040 | 46,496 | 19.0 |
| 1990 | 9,783 | 1,928 | 18,651 | 13,487 | 4,496 | 48,345 | 20.2 |
| 1989 | 10,874 | 2,002 | 18,979 | 13,026 | 4,220 | 49,101 | 22.1 |
| 1988 | 11,214 | 1,949 | 18,234 | 12,700 | 4,113 | 48,210 | 23.3 |
| 1987 | 10,925 | 1,635 | 17,548 | 12,249 | 3,546 | 45,903 | 23.8 |
| 1986 | 11,335 | 1,854 | 16,727 | 12,260 | 3,121 | 45,297 | 25.0 |
| 1985 | 11,653 | 1,933 | 16,015 | 12,271 | 2,939 | 44,811 | 26.0 |
| 1984 | 10,925 | 1,829 | 15,290 | 11,465 | 2,549 | 42,058 | 26.0 |
| 1983 | 9,225 | 1,525 | 15,706 | 11,112 | 2,187 | 39,755 | 23.2 |
| 1982 | 6,986 | 1,276 | 14,808 | 10,732 | 2,311 | 36,113 | 19.3 |
| 1981 | 7,943 | 1,289 | 14,439 | 11,180 | 2,379 | 37,230 | 21.3 |
| 1980 | 8,010 | 1,324 | 15,445 | 11,043 | 2,692 | 38,514 | 20.8 |
| 1970 | 8,284 | 1,160 | 13,033 | 5,289 | 1,637 | 29,403 | 28.2 |
| 1960 | 7,905 | 398 | 6,837 | 482 | 866 | 16,488 | 47.9 |
| 1950 | 8,006 | 388 | 6,837 | 32 | 160 | 10,577 | 75.7 |

Note: As far as can be determined, production refers to vehicles locally manufactured.

## World Motor Vehicle Production, 1992

Source: American Automobile Manufacturers Assn.

| Country | Passenger Cars | Commercial Vehicles | Total | Country | Passenger Cars | Commercial Vehicles | Total |
|---|---|---|---|---|---|---|---|
| Argentina | 220,498 | 41,445 | 261,943 | Italy | 1,476,627 | 209,860 | 1,686,487 |
| Australia | 279,550 | 4,858 | 284,408 | Japan | 9,378,694 | 3,120,590 | 12,499,284 |
| Austria | 23,479 | 4,491 | 27,970 | Korea, South | 1,306,752 | 422,944 | 1,729,696 |
| Belgium | 222,680 | 75,392 | 298,072 | Malaysia | 117,773 | 11,414 | 129,187 |
| Brazil | 814,423 | 257,141 | 1,071,564 | Mexico | 778,413 | 304,678 | 1,083,091 |
| Canada | 1,024,739 | 943,758 | 1,968,497 | Netherlands | 94,019 | 23,973 | 117,992 |
| China | 180,000 | 900,000 | 1,080,000 | Poland | 200,000 | 30,000 | 230,000 |
| Commonwealth of Independent States | 930,000 | 600,000 | 1,530,000 | Spain | 1,790,615 | 331,272 | 2,121,887 |
| Czechoslovakia | 202,450 | 26,608 | 229,058 | Sweden | 293,499 | 63,096 | 356,595 |
| France | 3,329,490 | 438,310 | 3,767,800 | United Kingdom | 1,291,880 | 248,453 | 1,540,333 |
| Germany | 4,863,721 | 330,221 | 5,193,942 | United States | 5,663,284 | 4,038,218 | 9,701,502 |
| Hungary | 12,000 | 6,000 | 18,000 | Yugoslavia | 116,391 | 9,250 | 125,641 |
| India | 153,867 | 170,518 | 324,385 | Total | 34,764,844 | 12,612,490 | 47,377,334 |

Note: As far as can be determined, production in this table refers to vehicles locally manufactured.

## Top Selling Passenger Cars in the U.S. by Calendar Year, 1989-1992
### (Domestic and Import)

Source: American Automobile Manufacturers Assn.

**1992**

| | | | | | |
|---|---|---|---|---|---|
| 1. Ford Taurus | 409,751 | 8. Pontiac Grand Am | 210,332 | 15. Cadillac DeVille/Fleetwood | 127,766 |
| 2. Honda Accord | 393,477 | 9. Ford Tempo | 207,173 | 16. Oldsmobile Ciera | 117,292 |
| 3. Toyota Camry | 286,602 | 10. Saturn | 196,126 | 17. Mercury Sable | 116,623 |
| 4. Ford Escort | 236,622 | 11. Toyota Corolla | 196,118 | 18. Lincoln Town Car | 115,075 |
| 5. Honda Civic/CRX | 219,228 | 12. Chevrolet Corsica/Beretta | 166,625 | 19. Buick Century | 114,273 |
| 6. Chevrolet Lumina | 218,114 | 13. Nissan Sentra | 158,909 | 20. Pontiac Grand Prix | 103,517 |
| 7. Chevrolet Cavalier | 212,374 | 14. Buick LeSabre | 138,409 | | |

| **1991** | | **1990** | | **1989** | |
|---|---|---|---|---|---|
| 1. Honda Accord | 399,297 | 1. Honda Accord | 417,179 | 1. Honda Accord | 362,707 |
| 2. Ford Taurus | 299,659 | 2. Ford Taurus | 313,274 | 2. Ford Taurus | 348,081 |
| 3. Toyota Camry | 263,818 | 3. Chevrolet Cavalier | 295,123 | 3. Ford Escort | 333,535 |
| 4. Chevrolet Cavalier | 259,385 | 4. Ford Escort | 288,727 | 4. Chevrolet Corsica/Beretta | 328,006 |
| 5. Ford Escort | 247,864 | 5. Toyota Camry | 284,595 | 5. Chevrolet Cavalier | 295,715 |
| 6. Chevrolet Corsica/Beretta | 231,227 | 6. Chevrolet Corsica/Beretta | 277,176 | 6. Toyota Camry | 257,466 |
| 7. Chevrolet Lumina | 217,555 | 7. Toyota Corolla | 228,211 | 7. Ford Tempo | 228,426 |
| 8. Honda Civic | 205,715 | 8. Honda Civic | 220,852 | 8. Nissan Sentra | 221,292 |
| 9. Toyota Corolla | 199,083 | 9. Chevrolet Lumina | 218,288 | 9. Pontiac Grand Am | 202,185 |
| 10. Ford Tempo | 189,457 | 10. Ford Tempo | 215,290 | 10. Toyota Corolla | 199,975 |

## Licensed Drivers, by Age

Source: Federal Highway Administration, U.S. Dept. of Transportation

| Age | 1991 | | | | Estimated 1992 | | | Percent change total drivers 1981-1991 |
|---|---|---|---|---|---|---|---|---|
| | Male | Female | Total | Percent male | Male (1,000) | Female (1,000) | Total (1,000) | |
| Under 16 | 34,738 | 30,372 | 65,110 | 53.35 | 35,335 | 30,750 | 66,085 | −36.79 |
| 16 | 738,889 | 654,916 | 1,393,806 | 53.01 | 751,593 | 663,057 | 1,414,650 | −18.30 |
| 17 | 1,098,120 | 970,474 | 2,068,595 | 53.09 | 1,117,000 | 982,538 | 2,099,538 | −23.81 |
| 18 | 1,310,554 | 1,155,524 | 2,466,078 | 53.14 | 1,333,086 | 1,169,888 | 2,502,974 | −22.74 |
| 19 | 1,490,071 | 1,330,268 | 2,820,339 | 52.83 | 1,515,689 | 1,346,804 | 2,862,493 | −19.42 |
| (19 and under) | 4,672,373 | 4,141,555 | 8,813,928 | 53.01 | 4,752,703 | 4,193,037 | 8,945,740 | −21.42 |
| 20 | 1,658,907 | 1,510,566 | 3,169,472 | 52.34 | 1,687,427 | 1,529,343 | 3,216,770 | −12.54 |
| 21 | 1,749,527 | 1,604,432 | 3,353,959 | 52.16 | 1,779,606 | 1,624,376 | 3,403,982 | −10.66 |
| 22 | 1,739,128 | 1,602,800 | 3,341,927 | 52.04 | 1,769,028 | 1,622,724 | 3,391,752 | −12.68 |
| 23 | 1,770,181 | 1,625,316 | 3,395,497 | 52.13 | 1,800,615 | 1,645,521 | 3,446,136 | −12.85 |
| 24 | 1,799,897 | 1,654,267 | 3,454,164 | 52.11 | 1,830,841 | 1,674,831 | 3,505,672 | −12.64 |
| (20-24) | 8,717,640 | 7,997,380 | 16,715,020 | 52.15 | 8,867,517 | 8,096,795 | 16,964,312 | −12.28 |
| 25-29 | 10,077,882 | 9,474,395 | 19,552,277 | 51.54 | 10,251,144 | 9,592,169 | 19,843,313 | 1.76 |
| 30-34 | 10,602,820 | 10,166,862 | 20,769,681 | 51.05 | 10,785,108 | 10,293,245 | 21,078,353 | 17.88 |
| 35-39 | 9,909,582 | 9,598,466 | 19,508,047 | 50.80 | 10,079,951 | 9,717,783 | 19,797,734 | 35.68 |
| 40-44 | 8,853,965 | 8,625,425 | 17,479,390 | 50.65 | 9,006,186 | 8,732,646 | 17,738,832 | 53.01 |
| 45-49 | 6,984,470 | 6,712,628 | 13,697,098 | 50.99 | 7,104,550 | 6,796,072 | 13,900,622 | 35.27 |
| 50-54 | 5,533,913 | 5,282,952 | 10,816,865 | 51.16 | 5,629,055 | 5,348,624 | 10,977,679 | 7.99 |
| 55-59 | 4,873,679 | 4,628,134 | 9,501,813 | 51.29 | 4,957,469 | 4,685,666 | 9,643,135 | −2.54 |
| 60-64 | 4,710,051 | 4,492,971 | 9,203,022 | 51.18 | 4,791,028 | 4,548,823 | 9,339,851 | 8.74 |
| 65-69 | 4,294,243 | 4,166,932 | 8,461,175 | 50.75 | 4,368,071 | 4,218,731 | 8,586,802 | 25.89 |
| 70 and over | 7,434,760 | 7,041,999 | 14,476,759 | 51.36 | 7,562,581 | 7,129,537 | 14,692,118 | 59.21 |
| Total | 86,665,378 | 82,329,699 | 168,995,077 | 51.28 | 88,155,363 | 83,353,128 | 171,508,491 | 14.90 |

## Some Countries with Safety Belt Use Laws

Source: American Automobile Manufacturers Assn.

| Country | Effective Date | Country | Effective Date |
|---|---|---|---|
| Australia | 1/72 | Hungary | 7/77 |
| Austria | 7/76 | Iceland | 10/81 |
| Belgium | 6/75 | Ireland | 2/79 |
| Brazil | 6/72 | Israel | 7/75 |
| Bulgaria | 1976 | Ivory Coast | 1970 |
| Canadian Provinces | | Japan | 12/71 |
| Alberta | 7/87 | Jordan | 12/83 |
| British Columbia | 10/77 | Luxembourg | 6/75 |
| Manitoba | 4/84 | Malaysia | 4/79 |
| Newfoundland | 7/82 | Netherlands | 6/75 |
| New Brunswick | 11/83 | New Zealand | 6/72 |
| Nova Scotia | 1/85 | Norway | 9/75 |
| Ontario | 1/76 | Poland | 1/84 |
| Prince Edward Island | 1/88 | Portugal | 1/78 |
| Quebec | 7/76 | Singapore | 7/81 |
| Saskatchewan | 7/77 | South Africa | 12/77 |
| Denmark | 1/76 | Spain | 10/74 |
| Finland | 7/75 | Sweden | 1/75 |
| France | 10/79 | Switzerland | 1/76 |
| Greece | 12/79 | Turkey | 10/84 |
| Hong Kong | 10/83 | | |

## Tips for Fuel-Efficient Driving

Source: U.S. Environmental Protection Agency

**When Buying a New Vehicle**

• Buy the type of vehicle that best suits your needs. Check the federal *Gas Mileage Guide*, available free at all auto dealerships, to compare the fuel economy of similar models. In general, *larger displacement engines and higher horsepower ratings will result in lower fuel economy.* The additional power and torque may be useful for mountain driving or trailer towing situations, but your fuel economy will suffer during almost all types of driving. *Avoid unnecessary optional equipment* (especially heavy options such as four-wheel drive and options such as air conditioning that tax the engine). Extra equipment adds weight and decreases fuel economy. Beware of "sport" packages, which often include fuel-guzzling features (such as energy robbing tires) not reflected by *Guide* mileage values.

**Conserving Fuel with Your Current Vehicle:**

• Drive your vehicle wisely. *Avoid idles* of more than one minute (turn off your engine in traffic jams, limit vehicle warm-ups in winter, park and go instead of using drive-up lanes at restaurants and banks). Go easy on the brakes and gas pedal (anticipate stops and avoid "jack-rabbit" starts). Pay attention to speed. *You can improve your fuel economy about 15 percent by driving 55 mph rather than*

*65 mph.* Put your vehicle's transmission into overdrive or a "fuel economy" position when cruising on the highway. If you have manual transmission, follow recommended shift guidelines or heed your shift indicator light. *Do not carry unneeded items* that add weight. Reduce drag by placing items inside the vehicle or trunk rather than on roof racks. *Use air conditioning only when necessary.*

• Maintain your vehicle regularly. *Periodic tune-ups improve vehicle fuel economy and performance.* Dragging brakes, low transmission fluid levels, out of tune engines, and old plugged fuel or air filters all hurt fuel economy. *Inflate tires* to maximum recommended pressure and perform periodic *wheel alignments.* Use energy conserving oils which increase fuel economy by reducing internal engine friction (the best are labeled "Energy Conserving II").

• Keep track of your vehicle's fuel economy. A marked increase in the amount of fuel you use could indicate the need for a tune-up or for necessary repairs.

• Use your vehicle effectively. *Use your vehicle only when necessary.* Combine errands into one trip. If you have access to more than one vehicle, drive the one that's most fuel efficient whenever possible. Consider carpooling, bicycling, walking, or public transportation.

## How Americans Get to Work[1]

Source: Bureau of the Census, U.S. Dept. of Commerce

| Means of Transportation | 1990 Number | 1990 Percent | 1980 Number | 1980 Percent |
|---|---|---|---|---|
| Workers 16 years and over | 115,070,274 | 100.0 | 96,617,296 | 100.0 |
| Car, truck, or van | 99,592,932 | 86.5 | 81,258,496 | 84.1 |
| Drove alone | 84,215,298 | 73.2 | 62,193,449 | 64.4 |
| Carpool | 15,377,634 | 13.4 | 19,065,047 | 19.7 |
| Public transportation | 6,069,589 | 5.3 | 6,175,061 | 6.4 |
| Bus or trolley bus[2] | 3,445,000 | 3.0 | 3,924,787 | 4.1 |
| Streetcar or trolley car[2] | 78,130 | 0.1 | — | — |
| Subway or elevated | 1,755,476 | 1.5 | 1,528,852 | 1.6 |
| Railroad | 574,052 | 0.5 | 554,089 | 0.6 |
| Ferryboat | 37,497 | 0.0 | — | — |
| Taxicab | 179,434 | 0.2 | 167,133 | 0.2 |
| Motorcycle | 237,404 | 0.2 | 419,007 | 0.4 |
| Bicycle | 466,856 | 0.4 | 468,348 | 0.5 |
| Walked | 4,488,886 | 3.9 | 5,413,248 | 5.6 |
| Other means | 808,582 | 0.7 | 703,273 | 0.7 |
| Worked at home | 3,406,025 | 3.0 | 2,179,863 | 2.3 |

(1) Means of transportation used to commute to and from work. (2) This category was "Bus or streetcar" in 1980.

## Personal Consumption Expenditures for Transportation

Source: American Automobile Manufacturers Assn.; Bureau of Economic Analysis, U.S. Dept. of Commerce; in millions of dollars

| | 1980 | 1982 | 1984 | 1986 | 1988 | 1990 | 1991 | 1992 |
|---|---|---|---|---|---|---|---|---|
| **User-Operated Transportation** | | | | | | | | |
| New Autos | $46,395 | $53,336 | $77,560 | $100,328 | $101,041 | $96,692 | $79,500 | $85,374 |
| Net Purchases of Used Autos | 10,848 | 13,551 | 21,152 | 25,356 | 30,532 | 33,663 | 35,782 | 38,464 |
| Other Motor Vehicles[1] | 11,489 | 15,605 | 28,589 | 40,818 | 45,577 | 49,586 | 47,155 | 55,923 |
| Tires, Tubes, and Accessories and Parts | 14,889 | 15,230 | 17,302 | 18,353 | 20,685 | 22,483 | 23,006 | 23,948 |
| Repair, Greasing, Washing, Parking, Storage, and Rental | 33,662 | 37,903 | 49,723 | 60,695 | 73,531 | 82,538 | 83,678 | 87,511 |
| Gasoline and Oil | 86,689 | 94,125 | 94,532 | 79,699 | 86,899 | 108,471 | 105,459 | 105,446 |
| Bridge, Tunnel, Ferry, and Road Tolls | 1,104 | 1,306 | 1,387 | 1,794 | 1,774 | 2,024 | 2,021 | 2,115 |
| Insurance Premiums, Less Claims Paid | 9,443 | 9,150 | 10,099 | 12,724 | 16,842 | 18,066 | 21,826 | 25,200 |
| **Total User-Operated Transportation** | $214,879 | $240,205 | $300,344 | $339,767 | $376,881 | $413,523 | $398,427 | $423,979 |
| **Purchased Local Transportation** | | | | | | | | |
| Transit Systems | $2,927 | $3,839 | $4,244 | $4,913 | $5,377 | $5,707 | $5,707 | $5,696 |
| Taxicabs | 1,866 | 1,513 | 2,498 | 2,998 | 2,935 | 3,209 | 3,358 | 3,394 |
| **Total Purchased Local Transportation** | $4,793 | $5,352 | $6,742 | $7,911 | $8,312 | $8,916 | $9,065 | $9,090 |
| **Purchased Intercity Transportation** | | | | | | | | |
| Railway Excluding Commutation | $300 | $317 | $415 | $472 | $588 | $708 | $722 | $699 |
| Bus | 1,403 | 1,665 | 1,632 | 1,469 | 2,181 | 1,396 | 1,521 | 1,378 |
| Airline | 13,454 | 14,708 | 17,721 | 18,993 | 22,993 | 26,467 | 25,842 | 25,867 |
| Other | 910 | 1,173 | 1,380 | 1,737 | 2,229 | 2,644 | 2,651 | 2,672 |
| **Total Purchased Intercity Transportation** | $15,057 | $17,861 | $21,128 | $22,671 | $27,991 | $31,215 | $30,736 | $30,616 |
| **Total Transportation** | $235,739 | $263,416 | $328,214 | $370,349 | $413,184 | $453,654 | $438,228 | $463,685 |
| **Total Personal Consumption Expenditures** | $1,748,077 | $2,059,179 | $2,460,288 | $2,850,553 | $3,296,126 | $3,748,417 | $3,887,689 | $4,095,823 |

(1) New and used trucks, recreation vehicles, etc.

# Road Mileage Between Selected U.S. Cities

| | Atlanta | Boston | Chicago | Cincinnati | Cleveland | Dallas | Denver | Des Moines | Detroit | Houston |
|---|---|---|---|---|---|---|---|---|---|---|
| Atlanta, Ga. . . . . | ... | 1,037 | 674 | 440 | 672 | 795 | 1,398 | 870 | 699 | 789 |
| Boston, Mass. . . . | 1,037 | ... | 963 | 840 | 628 | 1,748 | 1,949 | 1,280 | 695 | 1,804 |
| Chicago, Ill. . . . . | 674 | 963 | ... | 287 | 335 | 917 | 996 | 327 | 266 | 1,067 |
| Cincinnati, Oh. . . | 440 | 840 | 287 | ... | 244 | 920 | 1,164 | 571 | 259 | 1,029 |
| Cleveland, Oh. . . | 672 | 628 | 335 | 244 | ... | 1,159 | 1,321 | 652 | 170 | 1,273 |
| Dallas Tex. . . . . | 795 | 1,748 | 917 | 920 | 1,159 | ... | 781 | 684 | 1,143 | 243 |
| Denver, Col. . . . | 1,398 | 1,949 | 996 | 1,164 | 1,321 | 781 | ... | 669 | 1,253 | 1,019 |
| Detroit, Mich. . . | 699 | 695 | 266 | 259 | 170 | 1,143 | 1,253 | 584 | ... | 1,265 |
| Houston, Tex. . . . | 789 | 1,804 | 1,067 | 1,029 | 1,273 | 243 | 1,019 | 905 | 1,265 | ... |
| Indianapolis, Ind. . | 493 | 906 | 181 | 106 | 294 | 865 | 1,058 | 465 | 278 | 987 |
| Kansas City, Mo. . | 798 | 1,391 | 499 | 591 | 779 | 489 | 600 | 195 | 743 | 710 |
| Los Angeles, Cal. | 2,182 | 2,979 | 2,054 | 2,179 | 2,367 | 1,387 | 1,059 | 1,727 | 2,311 | 1,538 |
| Memphis, Tenn. . | 371 | 1,296 | 530 | 468 | 712 | 452 | 1,040 | 599 | 713 | 561 |
| Milwaukee, Wis. . | 761 | 1,050 | 87 | 374 | 422 | 991 | 1,029 | 361 | 353 | 1,142 |
| Minneapolis, Minn. | 1,068 | 1,368 | 405 | 692 | 740 | 936 | 841 | 252 | 671 | 1,157 |
| New Orleans, La.. | 479 | 1,507 | 912 | 786 | 1,030 | 496 | 1,273 | 978 | 1,045 | 356 |
| New York, N.Y. . . | 841 | 206 | 802 | 647 | 473 | 1,552 | 1,771 | 1,119 | 637 | 1,608 |
| Omaha, Neb. . . . | 986 | 1,412 | 459 | 693 | 784 | 644 | 537 | 132 | 716 | 865 |
| Philadelphia, Pa. . | 741 | 296 | 738 | 567 | 413 | 1,452 | 1,691 | 1,051 | 573 | 1,508 |
| Pittsburgh, Pa. . . | 687 | 561 | 452 | 287 | 129 | 1,204 | 1,411 | 763 | 287 | 1,313 |
| Portland Ore. . . . | 2,601 | 3,046 | 2,083 | 2,333 | 2,418 | 2,009 | 1,238 | 1,786 | 2,349 | 2,205 |
| St. Louis, Mo. . . . | 541 | 1,141 | 289 | 340 | 529 | 630 | 857 | 333 | 513 | 779 |
| San Francisco . . | 2,496 | 3,095 | 2,142 | 2,362 | 2,467 | 1,753 | 1,235 | 1,815 | 2,399 | 1,912 |
| Seattle, Wash. . . | 2,618 | 2,976 | 2,013 | 2,300 | 2,348 | 2,078 | 1,307 | 1,749 | 2,279 | 2,274 |
| Tulsa, Okla. . . . . | 772 | 1,537 | 683 | 736 | 925 | 257 | 681 | 443 | 909 | 478 |
| Wash., D.C. . . . . | 608 | 429 | 671 | 481 | 346 | 1,319 | 1,616 | 984 | 506 | 1,375 |

| | Indianapolis | Kansas City | Los Angeles | Louisville | Memphis | Milwaukee | Minneapolis | New Orleans | New York | Omaha |
|---|---|---|---|---|---|---|---|---|---|---|
| Atlanta, Ga. . . . . | 493 | 798 | 2,182 | 382 | 371 | 761 | 1,068 | 479 | 841 | 986 |
| Boston, Mass. . . . | 906 | 1,391 | 2,979 | 941 | 1,296 | 1,050 | 1,368 | 1,507 | 206 | 1,412 |
| Chicago, Ill. . . . . | 181 | 499 | 2,054 | 292 | 530 | 87 | 405 | 912 | 802 | 459 |
| Cincinnati, Oh. . . | 106 | 591 | 2,179 | 101 | 468 | 374 | 692 | 786 | 647 | 693 |
| Cleveland Oh. . . | 294 | 779 | 2,367 | 345 | 712 | 422 | 740 | 1,030 | 473 | 784 |
| Dallas, Tex. . . . . | 865 | 489 | 1,387 | 819 | 452 | 991 | 936 | 496 | 1,552 | 644 |
| Denver, Col. . . . | 1,058 | 600 | 1,059 | 1,120 | 1,040 | 1,029 | 841 | 1,273 | 1,771 | 537 |
| Detroit, Mich. . . . | 278 | 743 | 2,311 | 360 | 713 | 353 | 671 | 1,045 | 637 | 716 |
| Houston, Tex. . . . | 987 | 710 | 1,538 | 928 | 561 | 1,142 | 1,157 | 356 | 1,608 | 865 |
| Indianapolis, Ind. . | ... | 485 | 2,073 | 111 | 435 | 268 | 586 | 796 | 713 | 587 |
| Kansas City, Mo. . | 485 | ... | 1,589 | 520 | 451 | 537 | 447 | 806 | 1,198 | 201 |
| Los Angeles, Cal. | 2,073 | 1,589 | ... | 2,108 | 1,817 | 2,087 | 1,889 | 1,883 | 2,786 | 1,595 |
| Memphis, Tenn. . | 435 | 451 | 1,817 | 367 | ... | 612 | 826 | 390 | 1,100 | 652 |
| Milwaukee, Wis. . | 268 | 537 | 2,087 | 379 | 612 | ... | 332 | 994 | 889 | 493 |
| Minneapolis, Minn. | 586 | 447 | 1,889 | 697 | 826 | 332 | ... | 1,214 | 1,207 | 357 |
| New Orleans, La.. | 796 | 806 | 1,883 | 685 | 390 | 994 | 1,214 | ... | 1,311 | 1,007 |
| New York, N.Y. . . | 713 | 1,198 | 2,786 | 748 | 1,100 | 889 | 1,207 | 1,311 | ... | 1,251 |
| Omaha, Neb. . . . | 587 | 201 | 1,595 | 687 | 652 | 493 | 357 | 1,007 | 1,251 | ... |
| Philadelphia, Pa. . | 633 | 1,118 | 2,706 | 668 | 1,000 | 825 | 1,143 | 1,211 | 100 | 1,183 |
| Pittsburgh, Pa. . . | 353 | 838 | 2,426 | 388 | 752 | 539 | 857 | 1,070 | 368 | 895 |
| Portland, Ore. . . . | 1,227 | 1,809 | 959 | 2,320 | 2,259 | 2,010 | 1,678 | 2,505 | 2,885 | 1,654 |
| St. Louis, Mo. . . . | 235 | 257 | 1,845 | 263 | 285 | 363 | 552 | 673 | 948 | 449 |
| San Francisco . . | 2,256 | 1,835 | 379 | 2,349 | 2,125 | 2,175 | 1,940 | 2,249 | 2,934 | 1,683 |
| Seattle, Wash. . . | 2,194 | 1,839 | 1,131 | 2,305 | 2,290 | 1,940 | 1,608 | 2,574 | 2,815 | 1,638 |
| Tulsa, Okla. . . . . | 631 | 248 | 1,452 | 659 | 401 | 757 | 695 | 647 | 1,344 | 387 |
| Washington, D.C.. | 558 | 1,043 | 2,631 | 582 | 867 | 758 | 1,076 | 1,078 | 233 | 1,116 |

| | Philadelphia | Pittsburgh | Portland | St. Louis | Salt Lake City | San Francisco | Seattle | Toledo | Tulsa | Wash., D.C. |
|---|---|---|---|---|---|---|---|---|---|---|
| Atlanta, Ga. . . . . | 741 | 687 | 2,601 | 541 | 1,878 | 2,496 | 2,618 | 640 | 772 | 608 |
| Boston, Mass. . . . | 296 | 561 | 3,046 | 1,141 | 2,343 | 3,095 | 2,976 | 739 | 1,537 | 429 |
| Chicago, Ill. . . . . | 738 | 452 | 2,083 | 289 | 1,390 | 2,142 | 2,013 | 232 | 683 | 671 |
| Cincinnati, Oh. . . | 567 | 287 | 2,333 | 340 | 1,610 | 2,362 | 2,300 | 200 | 736 | 481 |
| Cleveland Oh. . . | 413 | 129 | 2,418 | 529 | 1,715 | 2,467 | 2,348 | 111 | 925 | 346 |
| Dallas, Tex. . . . . | 1,452 | 1,204 | 2,009 | 630 | 1,242 | 1,753 | 2,078 | 1,084 | 257 | 1,319 |
| Denver, Col. . . . | 1,691 | 1,411 | 1,238 | 857 | 504 | 1,235 | 1,307 | 1,218 | 681 | 1,616 |
| Detroit, Mich. . . . | 576 | 287 | 2,349 | 513 | 1,647 | 2,399 | 2,279 | 59 | 909 | 506 |
| Houston, Tex. . . . | 1,508 | 1,313 | 2,205 | 779 | 1,438 | 1,912 | 2,274 | 1,206 | 478 | 1,375 |
| Indianapolis, Ind. . | 633 | 353 | 2,227 | 235 | 1,504 | 2,256 | 2,194 | 219 | 631 | 558 |
| Kansas City, Mo. . | 1,118 | 838 | 1,809 | 257 | 1,086 | 1,835 | 1,839 | 687 | 248 | 1,043 |
| Los Angeles, Cal. | 2,706 | 2,426 | 959 | 1,845 | 715 | 379 | 1,131 | 2,276 | 1,452 | 2,631 |
| Memphis, Tenn. . | 1,000 | 752 | 2,259 | 285 | 1,535 | 2,125 | 2,290 | 654 | 401 | 867 |
| Milwaukee, Wis. . | 825 | 539 | 2,010 | 363 | 1,423 | 2,175 | 1,940 | 319 | 757 | 758 |
| Minneapolis, Minn. | 1,143 | 857 | 1,678 | 552 | 1,186 | 1,940 | 1,608 | 637 | 695 | 1,076 |
| New Orleans, La.. | 1,211 | 1,070 | 2,505 | 673 | 1,738 | 2,249 | 2,574 | 986 | 647 | 1,078 |
| New York, N.Y.. . | 100 | 368 | 2,885 | 948 | 2,182 | 2,934 | 2,815 | 578 | 1,344 | 233 |
| Omaha, Neb. . . . | 1,183 | 895 | 1,654 | 449 | 931 | 1,683 | 1,638 | 681 | 387 | 1,116 |
| Philadelphia, Pa. . | ... | 288 | 2,821 | 868 | 2,114 | 2,866 | 2,751 | 514 | 1,264 | 133 |
| Pittsburgh, Pa. . . | 288 | ... | 2,535 | 588 | 1,826 | 2,578 | 2,465 | 228 | 984 | 221 |
| Portland, Ore. . . . | 2,821 | 2,535 | ... | 2,060 | 767 | 636 | 172 | 2,315 | 1,913 | 2,754 |
| St. Louis, Mo. . . . | 868 | 588 | 2,060 | ... | 1,337 | 2,089 | 2,081 | 454 | 396 | 793 |
| San Francisco . . | 2,866 | 2,578 | 636 | 2,089 | 752 | ... | 808 | 2,364 | 1,760 | 2,799 |
| Seattle, Wash. . . | 2,751 | 2,465 | 172 | 2,081 | 836 | 808 | ... | 2,245 | 1,982 | 2,684 |
| Tulsa, Okla. . . . . | 1,264 | 984 | 1,913 | 396 | 1,172 | 1,760 | 1,982 | 850 | ... | 1,189 |
| Washington, D.C.. | 133 | 221 | 2,754 | 793 | 2,047 | 2,799 | 2,684 | 447 | 1,189 | ... |

## Air Distances Between Selected World Cities in Statute Miles

Point-to-point measurements are usually from City Hall.

| | Bangkok | Beijing | Berlin | Cairo | Cape Town | Caracas | Chicago | Hong Kong | Honolulu | Lima |
|---|---|---|---|---|---|---|---|---|---|---|
| Bangkok | ... | 2,046 | 5,352 | 4,523 | 6,300 | 10,555 | 8,570 | 1,077 | 6,609 | 12,244 |
| Beijing | 2,046 | ... | 4,584 | 4,698 | 8,044 | 8,950 | 6,604 | 1,217 | 5,077 | 10,349 |
| Berlin | 5,352 | 4,584 | ... | 1,797 | 5,961 | 5,238 | 4,414 | 5,443 | 7,320 | 6,896 |
| Cairo | 4,523 | 4,698 | 1,797 | ... | 4,480 | 6,342 | 6,141 | 5,066 | 8,848 | 7,726 |
| Cape Town | 6,300 | 8,044 | 5,961 | 4,480 | ... | 6,366 | 8,491 | 7,376 | 11,535 | 6,072 |
| Caracas | 10,555 | 8,950 | 5,238 | 6,342 | 6,366 | ... | 2,495 | 10,165 | 6,021 | 1,707 |
| Chicago | 8,570 | 6,604 | 4,414 | 6,141 | 8,491 | 2,495 | ... | 7,797 | 4,256 | 3,775 |
| Hong Kong | 1,077 | 1,217 | 5,443 | 5,066 | 7,376 | 10,165 | 7,797 | ... | 5,556 | 11,418 |
| Honolulu | 6,609 | 5,077 | 7,320 | 8,848 | 11,535 | 6,021 | 4,256 | 5,556 | ... | 5,947 |
| London | 5,944 | 5,074 | 583 | 2,185 | 5,989 | 4,655 | 3,958 | 5,990 | 7,240 | 6,316 |
| Los Angeles | 7,637 | 6,250 | 5,782 | 7,520 | 9,969 | 3,632 | 1,745 | 7,240 | 2,557 | 4,171 |
| Madrid | 6,337 | 5,745 | 1,165 | 2,087 | 5,308 | 4,346 | 4,189 | 6,558 | 7,872 | 5,907 |
| Melbourne | 4,568 | 5,643 | 9,918 | 8,675 | 6,425 | 9,717 | 9,673 | 4,595 | 5,505 | 8,059 |
| Mexico City | 9,793 | 7,753 | 6,056 | 7,700 | 8,519 | 2,234 | 1,690 | 8,788 | 3,789 | 2,639 |
| Montreal | 8,338 | 6,519 | 3,740 | 5,427 | 7,922 | 2,438 | 745 | 7,736 | 4,918 | 3,970 |
| Moscow | 4,389 | 3,607 | 1,006 | 1,803 | 6,279 | 6,177 | 4,987 | 4,437 | 7,047 | 7,862 |
| New York | 8,669 | 6,844 | 3,979 | 5,619 | 7,803 | 2,120 | 714 | 8,060 | 4,969 | 3,639 |
| Paris | 5,877 | 5,120 | 548 | 1,998 | 5,786 | 4,732 | 4,143 | 5,990 | 7,449 | 6,370 |
| Rio de Janeiro | 9,994 | 10,768 | 6,209 | 6,143 | 3,781 | 2,804 | 5,282 | 11,009 | 8,288 | 2,342 |
| Rome | 5,494 | 5,063 | 737 | 1,326 | 5,231 | 5,195 | 4,824 | 5,774 | 8,040 | 6,750 |
| San Francisco | 7,931 | 5,918 | 5,672 | 7,466 | 10,248 | 3,902 | 1,859 | 6,905 | 2,398 | 4,518 |
| Singapore | 883 | 2,771 | 6,164 | 5,137 | 6,008 | 11,402 | 9,372 | 1,605 | 6,726 | 11,689 |
| Stockholm | 5,089 | 4,133 | 528 | 2,096 | 6,423 | 5,471 | 4,331 | 5,063 | 6,875 | 7,166 |
| Tokyo | 2,865 | 1,307 | 5,557 | 5,958 | 9,154 | 8,808 | 6,314 | 1,791 | 3,859 | 9,631 |
| Warsaw | 5,033 | 4,325 | 322 | 1,619 | 5,935 | 5,559 | 4,679 | 5,147 | 7,366 | 7,215 |
| Washington, D.C. | 8,807 | 6,942 | 4,181 | 5,822 | 7,895 | 2,047 | 596 | 8,155 | 4,838 | 3,509 |

| | London | Los Angeles | Madrid | Melbourne | Mexico City | Montreal | Moscow | New Delhi | New York | Paris |
|---|---|---|---|---|---|---|---|---|---|---|
| Bangkok | 5,944 | 7,637 | 6,337 | 4,568 | 9,793 | 8,338 | 4,389 | 1,813 | 8,669 | 5,877 |
| Beijing | 5,074 | 6,250 | 5,745 | 5,643 | 7,753 | 6,519 | 3,607 | 2,353 | 6,844 | 5,120 |
| Berlin | 583 | 5,782 | 1,165 | 9,918 | 6,056 | 3,740 | 1,006 | 3,598 | 3,979 | 548 |
| Cairo | 2,185 | 7,520 | 2,087 | 8,675 | 7,700 | 5,427 | 1,803 | 2,758 | 5,619 | 1,998 |
| Cape Town | 5,989 | 9,969 | 5,308 | 6,425 | 8,519 | 7,922 | 6,279 | 5,769 | 7,803 | 5,786 |
| Caracas | 4,655 | 3,632 | 4,346 | 9,717 | 2,234 | 2,438 | 6,177 | 8,833 | 2,120 | 4,732 |
| Chicago | 3,958 | 1,745 | 4,189 | 9,673 | 1,690 | 745 | 4,987 | 7,486 | 714 | 4,143 |
| Hong Kong | 5,990 | 7,240 | 6,558 | 4,595 | 8,788 | 7,736 | 4,437 | 2,339 | 8,060 | 5,990 |
| Honolulu | 7,240 | 2,557 | 7,872 | 5,505 | 3,789 | 4,918 | 7,047 | 7,412 | 4,969 | 7,449 |
| London | ... | 5,439 | 785 | 10,500 | 5,558 | 3,254 | 1,564 | 4,181 | 3,469 | 214 |
| Los Angeles | 5,439 | ... | 5,848 | 7,931 | 1,542 | 2,427 | 6,068 | 7,011 | 2,451 | 5,601 |
| Madrid | 785 | 5,848 | ... | 10,758 | 5,643 | 3,448 | 2,147 | 4,530 | 3,593 | 655 |
| Melbourne | 10,500 | 7,931 | 10,758 | ... | 8,426 | 10,395 | 8,950 | 6,329 | 10,359 | 10,430 |
| Mexico City | 5,558 | 1,542 | 5,643 | 8,426 | ... | 2,317 | 6,676 | 9,120 | 2,090 | 5,725 |
| Montreal | 3,254 | 2,427 | 3,448 | 10,395 | 2,317 | ... | 4,401 | 7,012 | 331 | 3,432 |
| Moscow | 1,564 | 6,068 | 2,147 | 8,950 | 6,676 | 4,401 | ... | 2,698 | 4,683 | 1,554 |
| New York | 3,469 | 2,451 | 3,593 | 10,359 | 2,090 | 331 | 4,683 | 7,318 | ... | 3,636 |
| Paris | 214 | 5,601 | 655 | 10,430 | 5,725 | 3,432 | 1,554 | 4,102 | 3,636 | ... |
| Rio de Janeiro | 5,750 | 6,330 | 5,045 | 8,226 | 4,764 | 5,078 | 7,170 | 8,753 | 4,801 | 5,684 |
| Rome | 895 | 6,326 | 851 | 9,929 | 6,377 | 4,104 | 1,483 | 3,684 | 4,293 | 690 |
| San Francisco | 5,367 | 347 | 5,803 | 7,856 | 1,887 | 2,543 | 5,885 | 7,691 | 2,572 | 5,577 |
| Singapore | 6,747 | 8,767 | 7,080 | 3,759 | 10,327 | 9,203 | 5,228 | 2,571 | 9,534 | 6,673 |
| Stockholm | 942 | 5,454 | 1,653 | 9,630 | 6,012 | 3,714 | 716 | 3,414 | 3,986 | 1,003 |
| Tokyo | 5,959 | 5,470 | 6,706 | 5,062 | 7,035 | 6,471 | 4,660 | 3,638 | 6,757 | 6,053 |
| Warsaw | 905 | 5,922 | 1,427 | 9,598 | 6,337 | 4,022 | 721 | 3,277 | 4,270 | 852 |
| Washington, D.C. | 3,674 | 2,300 | 3,792 | 10,180 | 1,885 | 489 | 4,876 | 7,500 | 205 | 3,840 |

| | Rio de Janiero | Rome | San Francisco | Singapore | Stockholm | Teheran | Tokyo | Vienna | Warsaw | Wash., D.C. |
|---|---|---|---|---|---|---|---|---|---|---|
| Bangkok | 9,994 | 5,494 | 7,931 | 883 | 5,089 | 3,391 | 2,865 | 5,252 | 5,033 | 8,807 |
| Beijing | 10,768 | 5,063 | 5,918 | 2,771 | 4,133 | 3,490 | 1,307 | 4,648 | 4,325 | 6,942 |
| Berlin | 6,209 | 737 | 5,672 | 6,164 | 528 | 2,185 | 5,557 | 326 | 322 | 4,181 |
| Cairo | 6,143 | 1,326 | 7,466 | 5,137 | 2,096 | 1,234 | 5,958 | 1,481 | 1,619 | 5,822 |
| Cape Town | 3,781 | 5,231 | 10,248 | 6,008 | 6,423 | 5,241 | 9,154 | 5,656 | 5,935 | 7,895 |
| Caracas | 2,804 | 5,195 | 3,902 | 11,402 | 5,471 | 7,320 | 8,808 | 5,372 | 5,559 | 2,047 |
| Chicago | 5,282 | 4,824 | 1,859 | 9,372 | 4,331 | 6,502 | 6,314 | 4,698 | 4,679 | 596 |
| Hong Kong | 11,009 | 5,774 | 6,905 | 1,605 | 5,063 | 3,843 | 1,791 | 5,431 | 5,147 | 8,155 |
| Honolulu | 8,288 | 8,040 | 2,398 | 6,726 | 6,875 | 8,070 | 3,859 | 7,632 | 7,366 | 4,838 |
| London | 5,750 | 895 | 5,367 | 6,747 | 942 | 2,743 | 5,959 | 771 | 905 | 3,674 |
| Los Angeles | 6,330 | 6,326 | 347 | 8,767 | 5,454 | 7,682 | 5,470 | 6,108 | 5,922 | 2,300 |
| Madrid | 5,045 | 851 | 5,803 | 7,080 | 1,653 | 2,978 | 6,706 | 1,128 | 1,427 | 3,792 |
| Melbourne | 8,226 | 9,929 | 7,856 | 3,759 | 9,630 | 7,826 | 5,062 | 9,790 | 9,598 | 10,180 |
| Mexico City | 4,764 | 6,377 | 1,887 | 10,327 | 6,012 | 8,184 | 7,035 | 6,320 | 6,337 | 1,885 |
| Montreal | 5,078 | 4,104 | 2,543 | 9,203 | 3,714 | 5,880 | 6,471 | 4,009 | 4,022 | 489 |
| Moscow | 7,170 | 1,483 | 5,885 | 5,228 | 716 | 1,532 | 4,660 | 1,043 | 721 | 4,876 |
| New York | 4,801 | 4,293 | 2,572 | 9,534 | 3,986 | 6,141 | 6,757 | 4,234 | 4,270 | 205 |
| Paris | 5,684 | 690 | 5,577 | 6,673 | 1,003 | 2,625 | 6,053 | 645 | 852 | 3,840 |
| Rio de Janeiro | ... | 5,707 | 6,613 | 9,785 | 6,683 | 7,374 | 11,532 | 6,127 | 6,455 | 4,779 |
| Rome | 5,707 | ... | 6,259 | 6,229 | 1,245 | 2,127 | 6,142 | 477 | 820 | 4,497 |
| San Francisco | 6,613 | 6,259 | ... | 8,448 | 5,399 | 7,362 | 5,150 | 5,994 | 5,854 | 2,441 |
| Singapore | 9,785 | 6,229 | 8,448 | ... | 5,936 | 4,103 | 3,300 | 6,035 | 5,843 | 9,662 |
| Stockholm | 6,683 | 1,245 | 5,399 | 5,936 | ... | 2,173 | 5,053 | 780 | 494 | 4,183 |
| Tokyo | 11,532 | 6,142 | 5,150 | 3,300 | 5,053 | 4,775 | ... | 5,689 | 5,347 | 6,791 |
| Warsaw | 6,455 | 820 | 5,854 | 5,843 | 494 | 1,879 | 5,689 | 347 | ... | 4,472 |
| Washington, D.C. | 4,779 | 4,497 | 2,441 | 9,662 | 4,183 | 6,341 | 6,791 | 4,438 | 4,472 | ... |

# EDUCATION

## Historical Summary of Public Elementary and Secondary Schools

Source: National Center for Education Statistics, U.S. Dept. of Education

| | 1909-10 | 1919-20 | 1929-30 | 1939-40 | 1949-50 | 1959-60[1] | 1969-70[1] | 1979-80 | 1989-90 | 1990-91 |
|---|---|---|---|---|---|---|---|---|---|---|
| **Pupils and teachers (thousands)** . | | | | | | | | | | |
| Total U.S. population . . . . . . . . | 90,492 | 104,512 | 121,770 | 130,880 | 148,665 | 179,323 | 203,212 | 224,567 | 246,819 | 249,415 |
| Population 5-17 years of age . . . . | 24,009 | 27,556 | 31,417 | 30,150 | 30,168 | 43,881 | 52,490 | 48,041 | 44,949 | 45,311 |
| Percent aged 5-17 years. . . . . . . | 26.5 | 26.4 | 25.8 | 23.0 | 20.3 | 24.5 | 25.8 | 21.4 | 18.2 | 18.2 |
| **Enrollment (thousands)** | | | | | | | | | | |
| Elementary and secondary . . . . | 17,814 | 21,578 | 25,678 | 25,434 | 25,111 | 36,087 | 45,619 | 41,645 | 40,543 | 41,217 |
| Percent pop. 5-17 enrolled . . . . | 74.2 | 78.3 | 81.7 | 84.4 | 83.2 | 82.2 | 86.9 | 86.7 | 90.2 | 91.0 |
| Percent in high schools . . . . . . | 5.1 | 10.2 | 17.1 | 26.0 | 22.7 | 23.5 | 28.5 | 32.9 | 28.1 | 27.5 |
| High school graduates | | | | | | | | | | |
| (thousands) . . . . . . . . . . . | 111 | 231 | 592 | 1,143 | 1,063 | 1,627 | 2,589 | 2,748 | 2,320 | 2,237 |
| Average school term (in days). . . . | 157.5 | 161.9 | 172.7 | 175.0 | 177.9 | 178.0 | 178.9 | 178.5 | — | 179.8 |
| Total instructional staff . . . . . . . . | — | 678 | 880 | 912 | 962 | 1,464 | 2,253 | 2,441 | — | — |
| Teachers, librarians: Men . . . . . . | 110 | 93 | 140 | 195 | 195 | 402 | 691 | 782 | — | — |
| Women . . . . | 413 | 565 | 703 | 681 | 719 | 985 | 1,440 | 1,518 | — | — |
| Percent men . . . . . . . . . . . | 21.1 | 14.1 | 16.6 | 22.2 | 21.3 | 29.0 | 33.4 | 34.0 | — | — |
| **Revenue & expenditures (millions)** | | | | | | | | | | |
| Total revenue . . . . . . . . . . . . . | $433 | $970 | $2,088 | $2,260 | $5,437 | $14,746 | $40,267 | $96,881 | $207,753 | $222,823 |
| Total expenditures . . . . . . . . . . | 426 | 1,036 | 2,316 | 2,344 | 5,837 | 15,613 | 40,683 | 95,962 | 212,100 | 228,933 |
| Current elem. and secondary. . . | 356 | 861 | 1,843 | 1,941 | 4,687 | 12,239 | 34,218 | 86,984 | 187,558 | 201,550 |
| Capital outlay. . . . . . . . . . . . | 69 | 153 | 370 | 257 | 1,014 | 2,661 | 4,659 | 6,506 | 17,788 | 19,771 |
| Interest on school debt . . . . . . | — | 18 | 92 | 130 | 100 | 489 | 1,171 | 1,874 | 3,770 | 4,314 |
| Other . . . . . . . . . . . . . . . . | — | 3 | 9 | 13 | 35 | 132 | 636 | 598 | 2,985 | 3,298 |
| **Salaries and pupil cost** | | | | | | (Data in unadjusted dollars) | | | | |
| Average annual teacher salary[2]. . | $485 | $871 | $1,420 | $1,441 | $3,010 | $5,174 | $8,840 | $16,715 | $32,723 | $34,385 |
| Expenditure per capita total pop. . | 4.71 | 9.91 | 19.03 | 17.91 | 39 | 87 | 200 | 427 | 859 | 918 |
| Current expenditure per pupil ADA[3] | 27.85 | 53.32 | 86.70 | 88.09 | 209 | 375 | 816 | 2,272 | 4,962 | 5,245 |

(1) Because of a modification of the scope, "current expenditures for elementary and secondary schools" data for 1959-60 and later years are not entirely comparable with data for prior years. (2) Includes supervisors, principals, teachers and other non-supervisory instructional staff. (3) "ADA" means average daily attendance in elementary and secondary day schools.

## 1992 High School Graduates, 1991-1992 High School Drop-Outs

Source: Bureau of the Census, U.S. Dept. of Commerce; numbers in table in thousands

The proportion of the most recent high school graduates who had enrolled in colleges or universities was at an all-time high of 63 percent in the fall of 1992. In 1980 about half the most recent high school graduates had enrolled in college by the fall. Young women continued to be more likely than young men to enter colleges and universities—65 versus 60 percent. There also continued to be wide gaps in the college enrollment rates by race and ethnic group. Whereas 64 percent of the white high school graduates entered college, the enrollment rates for black and Hispanic youths were much lower—49 and 47 percent, respectively. The majority of the 1992 college freshmen (63 percent) were enrolled in 4-year institutions. Among these students, about two-fifths were combining school with some labor force activity. Among the youths enrolled in 2-year colleges, the proportion in the labor force was much higher—two-thirds. The labor force participation rate was still higher—78 percent—among the high school graduates who had not enrolled in college. The unemployment rate for this group, at 19.4 percent, was well below the jobless rate for 1991 graduates, at 25.3 percent the group's highest in 8 years. As for school dropouts, of the 400,000 youths who had dropped out of high school between October 1991 and October 1992, only about 60 percent were in the labor force. Their unemployment rate of 39.1 percent was double the rate for the year's high school graduates.

| | Civilian Non-institutional Population | Number | Participation Rate | Number | Percent of Population | Number | Percent of Labor Force | Not in Labor Force |
|---|---|---|---|---|---|---|---|---|
| | | | | Employed | | Unemployed | | |
| Characteristic | | | | | | | | |
| **Total 1992 high school** | | | | | | | | |
| graduates . . . . . . . . . | 2,461 | 1,475 | 60.0 | 1,225 | 49.8 | 251 | 17.0 | 986 |
| Men . . . . . . . . . . . . . | 1,240 | 785 | 63.3 | 656 | 52.9 | 129 | 16.5 | 455 |
| Women . . . . . . . . . . . | 1,221 | 690 | 56.5 | 569 | 46.6 | 121 | 17.6 | 531 |
| White . . . . . . . . . . . . | 1,954 | 1,220 | 62.4 | 1,060 | 54.3 | 159 | 13.1 | 734 |
| Black . . . . . . . . . . . . | 359 | 172 | 47.8 | 104 | 28.9 | 68 | 39.6 | 188 |
| Hispanic origin . . . . . . . | 210 | 133 | 63.6 | 97 | 46.1 | 37 | 27.4 | 76 |
| **Enrolled in college** . . . . . | 1,542 | 761 | 49.3 | 649 | 42.1 | 112 | 14.7 | 781 |
| Enrolled in 2-year college . | 571 | 384 | 67.2 | 333 | 58.3 | 51 | 13.2 | 188 |
| Enrolled in 4-year college . | 971 | 377 | 38.8 | 315 | 32.5 | 61 | 16.3 | 594 |
| Full-time students . . . . . | 1,429 | 665 | 46.6 | 567 | 39.7 | 98 | 14.8 | 763 |
| Part-time students . . . . . | 113 | 95 | 84.1 | 82 | 71.9 | 14 | 14.5 | 18 |
| Men . . . . . . . . . . . . . | 749 | 367 | 49.0 | 317 | 42.4 | 49 | 13.5 | 382 |
| Women . . . . . . . . . . . | 793 | 394 | 49.7 | 331 | 41.8 | 63 | 15.9 | 399 |
| White . . . . . . . . . . . . | 1,258 | 646 | 51.4 | 573 | 45.6 | 73 | 11.3 | 612 |
| Black . . . . . . . . . . . . | 175 | 58 | 32.8 | 35 | 20.1 | 22 | (1) | 118 |
| Hispanic origin . . . . . . . | 120 | 69 | 57.4 | 48 | 40.2 | 21 | (1) | 51 |
| **Not enrolled in college** . . . | 919 | 714 | 77.8 | 576 | 62.7 | 138 | 19.4 | 204 |
| Men . . . . . . . . . . . . . | 491 | 418 | 85.2 | 339 | 69.0 | 80 | 19.1 | 73 |
| Women . . . . . . . . . . . | 428 | 296 | 69.2 | 237 | 55.5 | 59 | 19.8 | 132 |
| White . . . . . . . . . . . . | 696 | 574 | 82.5 | 487 | 70.0 | 86 | 15.1 | 122 |
| Black . . . . . . . . . . . . | 184 | 114 | 62.0 | 69 | 37.2 | 46 | 40.0 | 70 |
| Hispanic origin . . . . . . . | 90 | 64 | 71.8 | 48 | 54.1 | 16 | (1) | 25 |
| **Total 1991-1992 high** | | | | | | | | |
| **school dropouts**[2] . . . . | 406 | 242 | 59.6 | 147 | 36.3 | 95 | 39.1 | 164 |
| Men . . . . . . . . . . . . . | 189 | 130 | 69.1 | 85 | 45.2 | 45 | 34.7 | 58 |
| Women . . . . . . . . . . . | 218 | 112 | 51.4 | 62 | 28.6 | 50 | 44.3 | 106 |
| White . . . . . . . . . . . . | 319 | 190 | 59.7 | 128 | 40.3 | 62 | 32.5 | 129 |
| Black . . . . . . . . . . . . | 66 | 35 | 52.5 | 7 | (1) | 28 | (1) | 31 |
| Hispanic origin . . . . . . . | 80 | 40 | 49.9 | 23 | 28.4 | 17 | (1) | 40 |

(1) Data not shown where base is less than 75,000. (2) Data refer to persons who dropped out of school between October 1991 and October 1992. Note: Detail for the above race and Hispanic-origin groups will not sum to totals because data for the "other races" group are not presented and Hispanics are included in both the white and black population groups. Because of rounding, sum of individual items may not equal totals.

## Fall Enrollment and Teachers in Full-time Day Schools
### Elementary and Secondary Day Schools, Fall 1991

Source: National Center for Education Statistics, U.S. Dept. of Education; National Education Assn.

| | Local school districts | Classroom teachers | Total enrollment | Pupils per teacher | Teacher's average pay (1991-1992) | Instructional aides | Expenditure per pupil |
|---|---|---|---|---|---|---|---|
| United States . . . . . | 15,173 | 2,431,622 | 42,000,343 | 17.3 | $34,098 | 410,498 | $5,245 |
| Alabama . . . . . . . . | 129 | 40,480 | 722,004 | 17.8 | 26,951 | 3,543 | 3,627 |
| Alaska . . . . . . . . | 56 | 7,118 | 118,680 | 16.7 | 44,718 | 1,626 | 8,330 |
| Arizona . . . . . . . . | 229 | 33,978 | 656,980 | 19.3 | 31,176 | 5,489 | 4,309 |
| Arkansas . . . . . . . | 325 | 25,785 | 438,518 | 17.0 | 27,070 | 4,511 | 3,700 |
| California . . . . . . . | 1,005 | 224,000 | 5,107,145 | 22.8 | 40,192 | 55,290 | 4,491 |
| Colorado . . . . . . . | 176 | 33,093 | 593,030 | 17.9 | 33,072 | 4,441 | 5,064 |
| Connecticut . . . . . . | 166 | 34,383 | 481,050 | 14.0 | 46,971 | 5,547 | 7,602 |
| Delaware . . . . . . . | 19 | 6,095 | 102,196 | 16.8 | 34,548 | 732 | 5,865 |
| District of Columbia . . | 1 | 6,087 | 80,618 | 13.2 | 38,798 | 308 | 9,259 |
| Florida . . . . . . . . . | 69 | 109,939 | 1,932,131 | 17.6 | 31,070 | 21,384 | 5,276 |
| Georgia . . . . . . . . | 183 | 63,816 | 1,177,569 | 18.5 | 29,509 | 17,534 | 4,466 |
| Hawaii . . . . . . . . . | 1 | 9,451 | 174,747 | 18.5 | 34,528 | 1,049 | 5,166 |
| Idaho . . . . . . . . . . | 114 | 11,626 | 225,680 | 19.4 | 26,334 | 1,402 | 3,386 |
| Illinois . . . . . . . . . | 942 | 110,143 | 1,848,166 | 16.8 | 36,461 | 15,607 | 5,520 |
| Indiana . . . . . . . . . | 296 | 54,546 | 956,994 | 17.5 | 34,809 | 11,912 | 4,930 |
| Iowa . . . . . . . . . . | 435 | 31,395 | 491,363 | 15.7 | 29,202 | 4,536 | 4,679 |
| Kansas . . . . . . . . | 304 | 29,324 | 445,390 | 15.2 | 30,731 | 3,150 | 4,874 |
| Kentucky . . . . . . . | 176 | 37,571 | 646,024 | 17.2 | 30,870 | 7,652 | 4,354 |
| Louisiana . . . . . . . | 66 | 46,118 | 765,589 | 16.6 | 25,948 | 8,433 | 4,146 |
| Maine . . . . . . . . . | 283 | 15,416 | 216,400 | 14.0 | 30,097 | 3,386 | 5,458 |
| Maryland . . . . . . . | 24 | 43,616 | 736,238 | 16.9 | 38,728 | 6,231 | 6,566 |
| Massachusetts . . . . | 352 | 55,963 | 846,155 | 15.1 | 37,256 | 9,009 | 6,366 |
| Michigan . . . . . . . | 561 | 82,967 | 1,591,120 | 19.2 | 41,149 | 12,969 | 5,883 |
| Minnesota. . . . . . . | 434 | 44,903 | 773,571 | 17.2 | 34,451 | 7,888 | 5,239 |
| Mississippi. . . . . . . | 150 | 28,111 | 504,127 | 17.9 | 24,367 | 9,788 | 3,187 |
| Missouri . . . . . . . . | 543 | 52,306 | 827,404 | 15.8 | 28,895 | 5,009 | 4,754 |
| Montana . . . . . . . | 539 | 9,883 | 155,779 | 15.8 | 27,590 | 1,373 | 5,204 |
| Nebraska . . . . . . . | 777 | 19,069 | 279,552 | 14.7 | 27,231 | 3,065 | 5,038 |
| Nevada . . . . . . . . | 17 | 11,409 | 211,810 | 18.6 | 33,857 | — | 4,653 |
| New Hampshire . . . . | 174 | 11,464 | 177,138 | 15.5 | 33,170 | 2,253 | 5,672 |
| New Jersey. . . . . . . | 608 | 80,515 | 1,109,796 | 13.8 | 41,027 | 10,000 | 8,645 |
| New Mexico. . . . . . | 88 | 17,498 | 308,667 | 17.6 | 26,389 | 4,080 | 3,895 |
| New York . . . . . . . | 717 | 171,914 | 2,643,993 | 15.4 | 43,335 | 24,110 | 8,565 |
| North Carolina . . . . | 133 | 65,326 | 1,097,598 | 16.8 | 28,791 | 19,407 | 4,488 |
| North Dakota . . . . . | 276 | 7,733 | 118,376 | 15.3 | 24,495 | 1,135 | 4,199 |
| Ohio . . . . . . . . . . | 613 | 103,372 | 1,783,767 | 17.3 | 33,243 | 9,229 | 5,245 |
| Oklahoma. . . . . . . | 593 | 37,650 | 588,263 | 15.6 | 25,339 | 5,746 | 3,791 |
| Oregon . . . . . . . . | 296 | 26,745 | 498,614 | 18.6 | 34,100 | 4,746 | 5,683 |
| Pennsylvania . . . . . | 503 | 100,475 | 1,692,797 | 16.8 | 38,715 | 11,316 | 6,541 |
| Rhode Island . . . . . | 37 | 9,709 | 142,144 | 14.6 | 36,417 | 1,217 | 6,343 |
| South Carolina . . . . | 95 | 37,115 | 627,470 | 16.9 | 28,068 | 6,597 | 4,351 |
| South Dakota . . . . . | 189 | 8,868 | 131,576 | 14.8 | 23,291 | 1,205 | 3,965 |
| Tennessee . . . . . . | 140 | 43,062 | 833,651 | 19.4 | 28,621 | 7,963 | 3,782 |
| Texas . . . . . . . . . | 1,051 | 219,192 | 3,464,371 | 15.8 | 29,041 | 33,976 | 4,438 |
| Utah . . . . . . . . . . | 40 | 18,305 | 456,430 | 24.9 | 26,339 | 3,812 | 2,960 |
| Vermont. . . . . . . . | 279 | 7,031 | 97,137 | 13.8 | 33,646 | 2,052 | 6,738 |
| Virginia . . . . . . . . | 141 | 64,537 | 1,016,204 | 15.7 | 31,657 | 10,283 | 4,836 |
| Washington . . . . . . | 296 | 42,931 | 869,327 | 20.2 | 34,823 | 6,797 | 5,000 |
| West Virginia . . . . . | 55 | 20,997 | 320,249 | 15.3 | 27,366 | 2,748 | 4,911 |
| Wisconsin . . . . . . . | 428 | 52,028 | 814,671 | 15.7 | 35,227 | 7,741 | 5,871 |
| Wyoming . . . . . . . | 49 | 6,564 | 102,074 | 15.6 | 30,425 | 1,221 | 5,723 |

## Programs for the Disabled

Source: Office of Special Educ. and Rehabilitative Services, U.S. Dept. of Education

Number of children 0 to 21 years old served annually in educational programs for the disabled; in thousands.

| Type of Disability | 1982-83 | 1983-84 | 1984-85 | 1985-86 | 1986-87 | 1987-88 | 1988-89 | 1989-90 | 1990-91 |
|---|---|---|---|---|---|---|---|---|---|
| All disabilities . . . . . . . | 4,255 | 4,298 | 4,315 | 4,317 | 4,374 | 4,446 | 4,544 | 4,641 | 4,771 |
| Learning disabilities. . . . . . . . | 1,741 | 1,806 | 1,832 | 1,862 | 1,914 | 1,928 | 1,987 | 2,050 | 2,130 |
| Speech impairments . . . . . . . | 1,131 | 1,128 | 1,126 | 1,125 | 1,136 | 953 | 967 | 973 | 987 |
| Mental retardation . . . . . . . | 757 | 727 | 694 | 660 | 643 | 582 | 564 | 548 | 536 |
| Serious emotional disturbance . | 352 | 361 | 372 | 375 | 383 | 373 | 376 | 381 | 391 |
| Hearing impairments . . . . . . . | 73 | 72 | 69 | 66 | 65 | 56 | 56 | 57 | 58 |
| Orthopedic impairments . . . . . | 57 | 56 | 56 | 57 | 57 | 47 | 47 | 48 | 49 |
| Visual impairments . . . . . . . . | 28 | 29 | 28 | 27 | 26 | 22 | 23 | 22 | 23 |
| Deaf-blindness . . . . . . . . . . | 2 | 2 | 2 | 2 | 2 | 12 | 2 | 2 | 1 |

Note: Counts are based on reports from the 50 States, District of Columbia and Puerto Rico (i.e., figures from U.S. territories are not included). Details may not add to totals because of rounding.

## Microcomputer Use by Public Elementary and Secondary Schools, 1981 to 1990[1]

Source: Digest of Education Statistics 1992, National Center for Education Statistics, U.S. Dept. of Education; in percent.

| | All Schools | Elementary | Junior High | Senior High | K-12 | Other | | All Schools | Elementary | Junior High | Senior High | K-12 | Other |
|---|---|---|---|---|---|---|---|---|---|---|---|---|---|
| 1981 | 18.2 | 11.1 | 25.6 | 42.7 | — | — | 1986 | 95.6 | 94.9 | 98.5 | 98.7 | — | — |
| 1982 | 30.0 | 20.2 | 39.8 | 57.8 | — | — | 1987 | 96.4 | 96.0 | 98.6 | 99.0 | — | — |
| 1983 | 68.4 | 62.4 | 80.5 | 86.1 | — | — | 1988 | 97.1 | 96.8 | 98.8 | 99.1 | — | — |
| 1984 | 85.1 | 82.2 | 93.1 | 94.6 | — | — | 1989 | 97.0 | 96.8 | 98.5 | 99.1 | — | — |
| 1985 | 92.2 | 91.0 | 97.3 | 97.4 | — | — | 1990 | 97.2 | 97.3 | 98.4 | 98.8 | 98.7 | 86.4 |

Notes: (1) Schools were surveyed in the Fall. — Data not available. Some data have been revised from previously published figures.

## Preprimary School Enrollment: 1970 to 1992

Source: Bureau of the Census, U.S. Dept. of Commerce

As of October. Civilian noninstitutional population. Includes public and nonpublic nursery school and kindergarten programs. Excludes 5 year olds enrolled in elementary school.

| Item | 1970 | 1975 | 1980 | 1985 | 1986 | 1987 | 1988 | 1989 | 1990 | 1991 | 1992 |
|---|---|---|---|---|---|---|---|---|---|---|---|
| **Number of Children (1,000)** | | | | | | | | | | | |
| Population, 3 to 5 years old . . | 10,949 | 10,183 | 9,284 | 10,733 | 10,866 | 10,872 | 10,894 | 11,038 | 11,207 | 11,370 | 11,544 |
| Total Enrolled[1] . . . . . . . | 4,104 | 4,954 | 4,878 | 5,865 | 5,971 | 5,932 | 5,977 | 6,026 | 6,659 | 6,334 | 6,403 |
| Nursery school . . . . . . . . . | 1,094 | 1,745 | 1,981 | 2,477 | 2,545 | 2,555 | 2,621 | 2,825 | 3,378 | 2,824 | 2,857 |
| Public . . . . . . . . . . . . . | 332 | 570 | 628 | 848 | 829 | 819 | 852 | 930 | 1,202 | 996 | 1,074 |
| Private . . . . . . . . . . . | 762 | 1,174 | 1,353 | 1,631 | 1,715 | 1,736 | 1,770 | 1,894 | 2,177 | 1,827 | 1,784 |
| Kindergarten . . . . . . . . . . | 3,010 | 3,211 | 2,897 | 3,388 | 3,426 | 3,377 | 3,356 | 3,201 | 3,281 | 3,510 | 3,546 |
| Public . . . . . . . . . . . . | 2,498 | 2,682 | 2,438 | 2,847 | 2,859 | 2,842 | 2,875 | 2,704 | 2,767 | 2,968 | 2,996 |
| Private . . . . . . . . . . . | 511 | 528 | 459 | 541 | 567 | 535 | 481 | 496 | 513 | 543 | 550 |
| White . . . . . . . . . . . . . | 3,443 | 4,105 | 3,994 | 4,757 | 4,851 | 4,748 | 4,891 | 4,911 | 5,389 | 5,104 | 5,137 |
| Black . . . . . . . . . . . . . | 586 | 731 | 725 | 919 | 892 | 893 | 814 | 872 | 964 | 928 | 966 |
| Hispanic[2] . . . . . . . . . . . | (NA) | (NA) | 370 | 496 | 593 | 587 | 544 | 520 | 642 | 675 | 728 |
| 3 years old . . . . . . . . . . | 454 | 683 | 857 | 1,035 | 1,041 | 1,022 | 1,028 | 1,005 | 1,205 | 1,075 | 1,081 |
| 4 years old . . . . . . . . . . | 1,007 | 1,418 | 1,423 | 1,765 | 1,772 | 1,717 | 1,768 | 1,882 | 2,086 | 1,993 | 1,982 |
| 5 years old . . . . . . . . . . | 2,643 | 2,852 | 2,598 | 3,065 | 3,157 | 3,192 | 3,183 | 3,139 | 3,367 | 3,266 | 3,340 |
| **Enrollment Rate** | | | | | | | | | | | |
| Total enrolled[1] . . . . . . . | 37.5 | 48.6 | 52.5 | 54.6 | 55.0 | 54.6 | 54.4 | 54.6 | 59.4 | 55.7 | 55.5 |
| White . . . . . . . . . . . . . | 37.8 | 48.6 | 52.7 | 54.7 | 55.2 | 54.1 | 55.4 | 55.0 | 59.7 | 56.2 | 55.8 |
| Black . . . . . . . . . . . . . | 34.9 | 48.1 | 51.8 | 55.8 | 54.1 | 54.2 | 48.2 | 54.2 | 57.8 | 53.1 | 55.1 |
| Hispanic[2] . . . . . . . . . . . | (NA) | (NA) | 43.3 | 43.3 | 47.8 | 45.5 | 44.2 | 41.6 | 49.0 | 46.4 | 48.4 |
| 3 years old . . . . . . . . . . | 12.9 | 21.5 | 27.3 | 28.8 | 28.9 | 28.6 | 27.6 | 27.1 | 32.6 | 28.2 | 27.7 |
| 4 years old . . . . . . . . . . | 27.8 | 40.5 | 46.3 | 49.1 | 49.0 | 47.7 | 49.1 | 51.0 | 56.0 | 53.0 | 52.1 |
| 5 years old . . . . . . . . . . | 69.3 | 81.3 | 84.7 | 86.5 | 86.7 | 86.1 | 86.6 | 86.4 | 88.8 | 86.0 | 87.2 |

(NA) Not available. (1) Includes races not shown separately. (2) Persons of Hispanic origin may be of any race. The method of identifying Hispanic children was changed in 1980 from allocation based on status of mother to status reported for each child. Using the new method, the number of Hispanic children is larger.

## Number of Private Schools and Their Enrollment in Grades K Through 12, 1990-1991

Source: National Center for Education Statistics, U.S. Dept. of Education

| Selected Characteristics | Number of Schools | | | | Kindergarten through 12th grade enrollment[1] | | | |
|---|---|---|---|---|---|---|---|---|
| | Total | Catholic | Other religious | Non-sectarian | Total | Catholic | Other religious | Non-sectarian |
| Total . . . . . . . . . . | 24,690 | 8,731 | 11,476 | 4,483 | 4,673,878 | 2,555,930 | 1,468,534 | 649,414 |
| **School enrollment** | | | | | | | | |
| Less than 150 . . . . . | 13,072 | 1,703 | 8,217 | 3,152 | 824,438 | 175,995 | 461,852 | 186,591 |
| 150 to 299 . . . . . . . | 7,027 | 4,148 | 2,082 | 797 | 1,499,516 | 904,563 | 430,038 | 164,915 |
| 300 to 499 . . . . . . . | 2,923 | 1,824 | 775 | 324 | 1,112,661 | 692,766 | 291,324 | 128,571 |
| 500 to 749 . . . . . . . | 1,122 | 700 | 301 | 121 | 682,309 | 420,341 | 184,861 | 77,107 |
| 750 or more . . . . . . | 546 | 357 | 101 | 88 | 554,956 | 362,266 | 100,460 | 92,230 |
| **Minority status** | | | | | | | | |
| Less than 5% . . . . . | 9,885 | 3,343 | 5,620 | 922 | 1,680,489 | 871,541 | 659,317 | 149,631 |
| 5-19% . . . . . . . . | 7,115 | 2,474 | 2,962 | 1,679 | 1,492,350 | 757,822 | 462,148 | 272,380 |
| 20-49% . . . . . . . . | 4,176 | 1,355 | 1,708 | 1,113 | 824,003 | 456,891 | 207,049 | 160,063 |
| 50% or more . . . . . . | 3,515 | 1,559 | 1,187 | 769 | 677,035 | 469,677 | 140,019 | 67,339 |
| **Community** | | | | | | | | |
| Urban/central city. . . . | 9,411 | 4,027 | 3,610 | 1,774 | 2,299,025 | 1,402,887 | 623,994 | 272,144 |
| Suburban ringe . . . . . | 7,694 | 3,001 | 3,209 | 1,484 | 1,553,338 | 842,895 | 493,451 | 216,992 |
| Small city/rural . . . . . | 7,585 | 1,703 | 4,657 | 1,225 | 821,516 | 310,150 | 351,088 | 160,278 |

(1) Includes only prekindergarten and kindergarten pupils who attend schools that offer first grade. Note: Details may not add to totals due to rounding.

## Education and Income, 1993

Source: Bureau of the Census, U.S. Dept. of Commerce

Mean monthly income was notably different at all levels of educational attainment between whites and blacks, with whites earning more at all levels. Note: at the master's degree level, because of the sample size, the difference in mean monthly income levels was not statistically significant. Between men and women, mean monthly income was significantly different at all educational levels, with men earning more than women. The figures in the following table are based upon a sample population survey that includes a representative sample of all people, including those without a monthly income.

| Level of Education | Mean Monthly Income | | | | |
|---|---|---|---|---|---|
| | White | Black | Hispanic[1] | Male | Female |
| Doctorate | $4,679 | N.A.[2] | N.A.[2] | $4,915 | $3,162 |
| Master's degree | 3,248 | $2,786 | $2,840 | 3,748 | 2,614 |
| Bachelor's degree | 2,552 | 2,002 | 1,895 | 3,235 | 1,698 |
| Some college | 1,595 | 1,204 | 1,298 | 2,002 | 1,115 |
| High school graduate | 1,405 | 1,009 | 1,092 | 1,853 | 943 |
| Some high school | 909 | 652 | 760 | 1,116 | 579 |

N.A.= Not available. [1] Hispanic people may be of any race. [2] There were too few black and Hispanic recipients of doctoral degrees to determine monthly income.

## Percent of Public School Teachers Who Are Men, 1991-1992

Source: National Education Association

| Rank/State | Pct. Men | Rank/State | Pct. Men | Rank/State | Pct. Men |
|---|---|---|---|---|---|
| 1. Massachusetts | 37.9 | 18. Indiana | 30.0* | 36. Maryland | 23.8 |
| 2. Minnesota | 36.8* | 20. Wisconsin | 29.9 | 37. Missouri | 23.7 |
| 3. Pennsylvania | 36.4 | 21. Kansas | 29.8* | 38. Florida | 23.1 |
| 4. Oregon | 36.2 | 22. Connecticut | 29.7 | 39. Arkansas | 22.0 |
| 5. Montana | 35.4 | 23. Nebraska | 29.4 | 39. Tennessee | 22.0 |
| 6. Wyoming | 35.3 | 24. Ohio | 29.3 | 41. Texas | 21.7 |
| 7. Washington | 34.6 | 25. Arizona | 28.8* | 42. Dist. of Col. | 21.6 |
| 8. Vermont | 32.5* | 26. Rhode Island | 28.4 | 43. Hawaii | 21.5 |
| 9. Iowa | 32.2 | 26. South Dakota | 28.4 | 44. Kentucky | 21.2 |
| 9. Alaska | 32.2 | 28. New Jersey | 28.0 | 45. Alabama | 20.5 |
| 11. North Dakota | 31.6 | 29. New Hampshire | 27.7 | 46. North Carolina | 19.0 |
| 12. Utah | 31.4 | 30. New Mexico | 27.2 | 47. Louisiana | 18.9* |
| 12. Maine | 31.4 | 31. Nevada | 27.1 | 47. Virginia | 18.9* |
| 14. New York | 31.0 | 32. West Virginia | 26.8 | 49. Mississippi | 18.4 |
| 15. Idaho | 30.8 | 33. Delaware | 26.7 | 50. South Carolina | 17.0 |
| 16. California | 30.3 | 34. Oklahoma | 25.2 | 51. Georgia | 16.9 |
| 17. Colorado | 30.1 | 35. Michigan | 24.3* | U.S. Average | 27.1 |
| 18. Illinois | 30.0 | | | | |

* Estimated

## Public High School Graduation Rates, 1991

Source: National Center for Education Statistics, U.S. Dept. of Education

| | Graduation Rate | Rank | | Graduation Rate | Rank | | Graduation Rate | Rank |
|---|---|---|---|---|---|---|---|---|
| U.S. | 71.2% | | Kansas | 81.1 | (10) | North Dakota | 86.7 | (2) |
| Alabama | 65.6 | (44) | Kentucky | 70.0 | (36) | Ohio | 72.3 | (33) |
| Alaska | 72.3 | (33) | Louisiana | 54.3 | (51) | Oklahoma | 75.5 | (24) |
| Arizona | 72.4 | (32) | Maine | 79.0 | (14) | Oregon | 71.6 | (35) |
| Arkansas | 76.6 | (21) | Maryland | 73.1 | (29) | Pennsylvania | 78.5 | (17) |
| California | 67.7 | (42) | Massachusetts | 79.7 | (12) | Rhode Island | 73.6 | (27) |
| Colorado | 74.5 | (26) | Michigan | 69.9 | (37) | South Carolina | 61.2 | (48) |
| Connecticut | 78.6 | (16) | Minnesota | 89.5 | (1) | South Dakota | 84.2 | (6) |
| Delaware | 68.0 | (40) | Mississippi | 61.7 | (47) | Tennessee | 67.8 | (41) |
| D.C. | 59.5 | (50) | Missouri | 72.5 | (31) | Texas | 65.9 | (43) |
| Florida | 61.2 | (48) | Montana | 84.9 | (5) | Utah | 79.0 | (14) |
| Georgia | 64.0 | (46) | Nebraska | 86.3 | (3) | Vermont[1] | 80.9 | (11) |
| Hawaii | 76.1 | (23) | Nevada | 77.4 | (20) | Virginia | 73.6 | (27) |
| Idaho | 79.7 | (12) | New Hampshire | 76.2 | (22) | Washington | 73.1 | (29) |
| Illinois | 77.5 | (18) | New Jersey | 82.1 | (8) | West Virginia | 77.5 | (18) |
| Indiana | 75.3 | (25) | New Mexico | 69.5 | (38) | Wisconsin | 82.5 | (7) |
| Iowa | 85.9 | (4) | New York | 64.4 | (45) | Wyoming | 81.7 | (9) |
| | | | North Carolina | 68.4 | (39) | | | |

## Scholastic Aptitude Test (SAT) Mean Scores and Characteristics of College Bound Seniors: 1970 to 1993

Source: College Entrance Examination Board

(For school year ending in year shown)

| Type of Test and Characteristic Test Scores[1] | Unit | 1970 | 1975 | 1980 | 1985 | 1987 | 1988 | 1989 | 1990 | 1991 | 1992 | 1993 |
|---|---|---|---|---|---|---|---|---|---|---|---|---|
| Verbal, total[1] | Point | 460 | 434 | 424 | 431 | 430 | 428 | 427 | 424 | 422 | 423 | 424 |
| Male | Point | 459 | 437 | 428 | 437 | 435 | 435 | 434 | 429 | 426 | 428 | 428 |
| Female | Point | 461 | 431 | 420 | 425 | 425 | 422 | 421 | 419 | 418 | 419 | 420 |
| Math, total[2] | Point | 488 | 472 | 466 | 475 | 476 | 476 | 476 | 476 | 474 | 476 | 478 |
| Male | Point | 509 | 495 | 491 | 499 | 500 | 498 | 500 | 499 | 497 | 499 | 502 |
| Female | Point | 465 | 449 | 443 | 452 | 453 | 455 | 454 | 455 | 453 | 456 | 457 |
| **Participants (thousands)** | | | | | | | | | | | | |
| Total | | 996 | 992 | 989 | 1,080 | 1,134 | 1,088 | 1,025 | 1,033 | NA | 1,034 | 1,109 |
| Male | Percent | NA | 49.9 | 48.2 | 48.3 | 48.0 | 48.0 | 48.0 | 48 | 48 | 48 | 47 |
| White | Percent | NA | 86.0 | 82.1 | 80.0 | 78.0 | 77.0 | 75.0 | 73 | 72 | 71 | 70 |
| Black | Percent | NA | 7.9 | 9.1 | 8.9 | 9.0 | 9.0 | 10.0 | 10 | 10 | 10 | 11 |
| Obtaining scores[1] of—600 or above: | | | | | | | | | | | | |
| Verbal | Percent | NA | 7.9 | 7.2 | 7.0 | 8.0 | 7.0 | 7.8 | 7 | 7 | 7 | 7 |
| Math | Percent | NA | 15.6 | 15.1 | 17.0 | 18.0 | 17.0 | 18.0 | 18 | 17 | 18 | 19 |
| Below 400: | | | | | | | | | | | | |
| Verbal | Percent | NA | 37.8 | 41.8 | 40.0 | 40.0 | 42.0 | 40.5 | 41 | 43 | 42 | 42 |
| Math | Percent | NA | 28.5 | 30.2 | 28.0 | 29.0 | 27.0 | 28.0 | 28 | 29 | 27 | 28 |

(NA) Not available. (1) Minimum score, 200; maximum score, 800. (2) 1970 is an estimate based on total number of persons taking SAT.

## American College Testing (ACT) Program Mean Scores and Characteristics of College-Bound Students: 1970 to 1992

Source: The American College Testing Program

Data for academic year ending in year shown.

| Type of Test and Mean Test Scores[1] | Unit | 1970 | 1975 | 1980 | 1985 | 1986 | 1987* | 1988* | 1989* | 1990* | 1991* | 1992* |
|---|---|---|---|---|---|---|---|---|---|---|---|---|
| Composite | Point ... | 19.9 | 18.6 | 18.5 | 18.6 | 20.8 | 20.8 | 20.8 | 20.6 | 20.6 | 20.6 | 20.6 |
| Male | Point ... | 20.3 | 19.5 | 19.3 | 19.4 | 19.6 | 19.5 | 19.6 | 19.3 | 21.0 | 20.9 | 20.9 |
| Female | Point ... | 19.4 | 17.8 | 17.9 | 17.9 | 17.9 | 18.1 | 18.1 | 18.0 | 20.3 | 20.4 | 20.5 |
| English | Point ... | 18.5 | 17.7 | 17.9 | 18.1 | 18.5 | 18.4 | 18.5 | 18.4 | 20.5 | 20.3 | 20.2 |
| Male | Point ... | 17.6 | 17.1 | 17.3 | 17.6 | 17.9 | 17.9 | 18.0 | 17.8 | 20.1 | 19.8 | 19.8 |
| Female | Point ... | 19.4 | 18.3 | 18.3 | 18.6 | 18.9 | 18.9 | 19.0 | 18.9 | 20.9 | 20.7 | 20.6 |
| Math | Point ... | 20.0 | 17.6 | 17.4 | 17.2 | 17.3 | 17.2 | 17.2 | 17.1 | 19.9 | 20.0 | 20.0 |
| Male | Point ... | 21.1 | 19.3 | 18.9 | 18.6 | 18.8 | 18.6 | 18.4 | 18.3 | 20.7 | 20.6 | 20.7 |
| Female | Point ... | 18.8 | 16.2 | 16.2 | 16.0 | 16.0 | 16.1 | 16.1 | 16.1 | 19.3 | 19.4 | 19.5 |
| Participants | | | | | | | | | | | | |
| Total | 1,000 ... | 788 | 714 | 822 | 739 | 730 | 777 | 842 | 855 | 817 | 796 | 832 |
| Male | Percent . | 52 | 46 | 45 | 46 | 46 | 46 | 46 | 46 | 46 | 45 | 45 |
| White | Percent . | (NA) | 77 | 83 | 82 | 82 | 81 | 81 | 80 | 79 | 79 | 79 |
| Black | Percent . | 4 | 7 | 8 | 8 | 8 | 8 | 9 | 9 | 9 | 9 | 9 |
| Obtaining composite scores of— | | | | | | | | | | | | |
| 27 or above | Percent . | 14 | 14 | 13 | 14 | 14 | 14 | 14 | 14 | 12 | 11 | 12 |
| 18 or below | Percent . | 21 | 33 | 33 | 32 | 31 | 31 | 31 | 31 | 32 | 35 | 35 |

* Beginning with the October 1989 test (1990 scores), an entirely new ACT Assessment was introduced. The Enhanced ACT Assessment increases the emphasis on rhetorical skills in the measurement of writing proficiency, increases the number of advanced math items, and includes a new reading test which features inferential and reasoning skills and a test designed to measure science reasoning. The Enhanced ACT also provides subscores in English, Mathematics, and Reading. The "Composite" scores for 1986-1989 have been converted to provide a basis of comparison; all 1990, 1991, and 1992 scores are for the Enhanced ACT. It is not possible to make direct comparisons between these data and data from earlier years.
(NA) Not available. Minimum score, 1; maximum score, 36. Test scores and characteristics of college-bound students based on a 10% sample prior to 1985. Beginning in 1985, these data are based on the performance of all ACT-tested students who graduated in the spring of a given school year and who took the ACT Assessment during junior or senior year of high school.

## SAT Mean Scores by State 1983-1993

Source: College Entrance Examination Board

| | 1983 Verbal | 1983 Math | 1990 Verbal | 1990 Math | 1991 Verbal | 1991 Math | 1992 Verbal | 1992 Math | 1993 Verbal | 1993 Math | % Graduates Taking SAT* |
|---|---|---|---|---|---|---|---|---|---|---|---|
| Alabama | 466 | 508 | 470 | 514 | 476 | 515 | 476 | 520 | 480 | 526 | 9 |
| Alaska | 437 | 468 | 438 | 476 | 439 | 481 | 433 | 475 | 438 | 477 | 42 |
| Arizona | 465 | 505 | 445 | 497 | 442 | 490 | 440 | 493 | 444 | 497 | 28 |
| Arkansas | 482 | 518 | 470 | 511 | 482 | 523 | 474 | 516 | 478 | 519 | 6 |
| California | 421 | 474 | 419 | 484 | 415 | 482 | 416 | 484 | 415 | 484 | 47 |
| Colorado | 469 | 520 | 456 | 513 | 453 | 506 | 453 | 507 | 454 | 509 | 28 |
| Connecticut | 433 | 465 | 430 | 471 | 429 | 468 | 430 | 470 | 430 | 474 | 88 |
| Delaware | 433 | 467 | 433 | 470 | 428 | 464 | 432 | 463 | 429 | 465 | 68 |
| Dist. of Columbia | 399 | 427 | 409 | 441 | 405 | 435 | 405 | 437 | 405 | 441 | 76 |
| Florida | 423 | 464 | 418 | 466 | 416 | 466 | 416 | 468 | 416 | 466 | 52 |
| Georgia | 390 | 428 | 401 | 443 | 400 | 444 | 398 | 444 | 399 | 445 | 65 |
| Hawaii | 393 | 471 | 404 | 481 | 405 | 478 | 401 | 477 | 401 | 478 | 56 |
| Idaho | 479 | 513 | 466 | 502 | 463 | 505 | 460 | 503 | 465 | 507 | 18 |
| Illinois | 462 | 517 | 466 | 528 | 471 | 535 | 473 | 537 | 475 | 541 | 15 |
| Indiana | 410 | 454 | 408 | 459 | 408 | 457 | 409 | 459 | 409 | 460 | 61 |
| Iowa | 520 | 573 | 511 | 577 | 515 | 578 | 512 | 584 | 520 | 583 | 5 |
| Kansas | 498 | 540 | 492 | 548 | 493 | 546 | 487 | 546 | 494 | 548 | 9 |
| Kentucky | 475 | 513 | 473 | 521 | 473 | 520 | 470 | 518 | 476 | 522 | 11 |
| Louisiana | 469 | 502 | 476 | 517 | 476 | 518 | 471 | 520 | 481 | 527 | 9 |
| Maine | 427 | 464 | 423 | 463 | 421 | 458 | 422 | 460 | 422 | 463 | 69 |
| Maryland | 427 | 466 | 430 | 478 | 429 | 475 | 431 | 476 | 431 | 478 | 66 |
| Massachusetts | 427 | 463 | 427 | 473 | 426 | 470 | 428 | 474 | 427 | 476 | 81 |
| Michigan | 458 | 511 | 454 | 514 | 461 | 519 | 464 | 523 | 469 | 528 | 11 |
| Minnesota | 482 | 538 | 477 | 542 | 480 | 543 | 492 | 561 | 489 | 556 | 10 |
| Mississippi | 474 | 507 | 477 | 519 | 477 | 520 | 478 | 526 | 481 | 521 | 4 |
| Missouri | 466 | 510 | 473 | 522 | 476 | 526 | 475 | 529 | 481 | 532 | 11 |
| Montana | 480 | 535 | 464 | 523 | 464 | 518 | 465 | 523 | 459 | 516 | 24 |
| Nebraska | 494 | 546 | 484 | 546 | 481 | 543 | 478 | 540 | 479 | 544 | 10 |
| Nevada | 441 | 480 | 434 | 487 | 435 | 484 | 434 | 488 | 432 | 488 | 28 |
| New Hampshire | 444 | 481 | 442 | 486 | 440 | 481 | 440 | 483 | 442 | 487 | 78 |
| New Jersey | 418 | 455 | 418 | 473 | 417 | 469 | 420 | 471 | 419 | 473 | 76 |
| New Mexico | 484 | 519 | 480 | 527 | 474 | 522 | 475 | 521 | 478 | 525 | 11 |
| New York | 422 | 466 | 412 | 470 | 413 | 468 | 416 | 466 | 416 | 471 | 74 |
| North Carolina | 394 | 431 | 401 | 440 | 400 | 444 | 405 | 450 | 406 | 453 | 60 |
| North Dakota | 505 | 560 | 505 | 564 | 502 | 571 | 501 | 567 | 518 | 583 | 6 |
| Ohio | 458 | 504 | 450 | 499 | 450 | 496 | 450 | 501 | 454 | 505 | 22 |
| Oklahoma | 489 | 521 | 478 | 523 | 476 | 521 | 480 | 527 | 482 | 530 | 9 |

| | 1983 Verbal | Math | 1990 Verbal | Math | 1991 Verbal | Math | 1992 Verbal | Math | 1993 Verbal | Math | % Graduates Taking SAT* |
|---|---|---|---|---|---|---|---|---|---|---|---|
| Oregon | 432 | 469 | 439 | 484 | 439 | 483 | 439 | 486 | 441 | 492 | 56 |
| Pennsylvania | 425 | 461 | 420 | 463 | 417 | 459 | 418 | 459 | 418 | 460 | 70 |
| Rhode Island | 422 | 459 | 422 | 461 | 421 | 459 | 421 | 460 | 419 | 464 | 71 |
| South Carolina | 383 | 415 | 397 | 437 | 395 | 437 | 394 | 437 | 396 | 442 | 61 |
| South Dakota | 517 | 560 | 506 | 555 | 496 | 551 | 490 | 550 | 502 | 558 | 6 |
| Tennessee | 483 | 519 | 483 | 525 | 487 | 528 | 484 | 529 | 486 | 531 | 13 |
| Texas | 412 | 453 | 413 | 461 | 411 | 463 | 410 | 466 | 413 | 472 | 45 |
| Utah | 508 | 545 | 492 | 539 | 494 | 537 | 496 | 545 | 500 | 549 | 4 |
| Vermont | 434 | 472 | 431 | 466 | 424 | 466 | 429 | 468 | 426 | 467 | 68 |
| Virginia | 427 | 463 | 425 | 470 | 424 | 466 | 425 | 468 | 425 | 469 | 63 |
| Washington | 463 | 510 | 437 | 486 | 433 | 480 | 432 | 484 | 435 | 486 | 52 |
| West Virginia | 466 | 512 | 443 | 490 | 441 | 485 | 440 | 484 | 439 | 485 | 17 |
| Wisconsin | 473 | 533 | 476 | 543 | 481 | 542 | 481 | 548 | 485 | 551 | 10 |
| Wyoming | 492 | 530 | 458 | 519 | 466 | 514 | 462 | 516 | 463 | 507 | 13 |
| National Average | 425 | 468 | 424 | 476 | 422 | 474 | 423 | 476 | 424 | 478 | 43 |

* Based on number of high school graduates in 1993 as projected by the Western Interstate Commission for Higher Education, and number of students in the Class of 1993 who took the SAT. Note: Making comparison of states, or ranking them, on the basis of SAT scores alone is invalid and strongly discouraged by the College Board.

## Tuition and College Costs 1993-1994

Based on the *Peterson's Guides* Annual Survey of Undergraduate Institutions, the average cost of tuition, mandatory fees, and college room and board at four-year private colleges is $14,176. The average cost at four-year public colleges is $6,083 for state residents and $9,961 for nonresidents. Two-year public colleges are the least expensive group of institutions; tuition and fees average $1,679 for state residents and $3,938 for nonresidents. Tuition and fees at two-year private colleges average $5,813.

The most expensive four-year institutions, including tuition, mandatory fees, and college room and board, are Sarah Lawrence College ($25,900); Brandeis University ($25,655); Barnard College ($25,492); Bard College ($25,184); Yale University ($25,110); Tufts University ($24,962); Hampshire College ($24,930); Bennington College ($24,850); Tulane University ($24,830); Massachusetts Institute of Technology ($24,800). The least expensive four-year undergraduate institutions are the United States service academies, which are all free.

## Institutions of Higher Education—Charges: 1970 to 1992

Source: National Center for Education Statistics, U.S. Dept. of Education

Data are for the entire academic year ending in year shown. Figures for 1970 are average charges for full-time resident degree-credit students; figures for later years are average charges per full-time equivalent student. Room and board are based on full-time students.

| Academic Control and Year | Tuition and Required Fees All institutions | 2-yr. colleges | 4-yr. universities | Board Rates All institutions | 2-yr. colleges | 4-yr. universities | Dormitory Charges All institutions | 2-yr. colleges | 4-yr. universities |
|---|---|---|---|---|---|---|---|---|---|
| **Public:** | | | | | | | | | |
| 1970 . . . . . | $323 | $178 | $427 | $511 | $465 | $540 | $369 | $308 | $395 |
| 1980 . . . . . | 583 | 355 | 840 | 867 | 894 | 898 | 715 | 572 | 749 |
| 1990 . . . . . | 1,356 | 756 | 2,035 | 1,635 | 1,581 | 1,728 | 1,513 | 962 | 1,561 |
| 1991 . . . . . | 1,454 | 824 | 2,159 | 1,691 | 1,594 | 1,767 | 1,612 | 1,050 | 1,658 |
| 1992 . . . . . | 1,624 | 937 | 2,410 | 1,780 | 1,612 | 1,852 | 1,731 | 1,074 | 1,789 |
| **Private:** | | | | | | | | | |
| 1970 . . . . . | 1,533 | 1,034 | 1,809 | 561 | 546 | 608 | 436 | 413 | 503 |
| 1980 . . . . . | 3,130 | 2,062 | 3,811 | 955 | 924 | 1,078 | 827 | 769 | 999 |
| 1990 . . . . . | 8,147 | 5,196 | 10,348 | 1,948 | 1,811 | 2,339 | 1,923 | 1,663 | 2,411 |
| 1991 . . . . . | 8,772 | 5,570 | 11,379 | 2,074 | 1,989 | 2,470 | 2,063 | 1,744 | 2,654 |
| 1992 . . . . . | 9,434 | 5,752 | 12,192 | 2,252 | 2,090 | 2,727 | 2,221 | 1,789 | 2,860 |

## Colleges and Universities Offering Remedial Instruction or Tutoring

Source: National Center for Education Statistics, U.S. Dept. of Education.

| Type of institution | Percent of Colleges Offering Remedial Instruction or Tutoring 1980-81 | 1984-85 | 1988-89 | 1989-90 | 1990-91 | 1991-92 | Change in Percentage Points 1980-81 to 1988-89 | 1984-85 to 1988-89 | 1988-89 to 1990-91 | 1990-91 to 1991-92 |
|---|---|---|---|---|---|---|---|---|---|---|
| All 4-year colleges . . . . | 78.9 | 85.8 | 89.0 | 90.2 | 89.0 | 88.6 | 6.9 | 3.2 | 0.0 | -0.5 |
| All 2-year colleges . . . . | 83.8 | 93.4 | 93.8 | 94.9 | 94.1 | 90.9 | 9.6 | 0.4 | 0.3 | -3.2 |
| **Public institutions** | | | | | | | | | | |
| 4-year colleges . . . . . . | 89.8 | 92.9 | 94.7 | 99.5 | 95.5 | 95.0 | 3.1 | 1.8 | 0.8 | -0.5 |
| 2-year colleges . . . . . . | 89.6 | 97.2 | 98.9 | 99.0 | 98.8 | 96.0 | 7.6 | 1.7 | -0.1 | -2.8 |
| **Private institutions** | | | | | | | | | | |
| 4-year colleges . . . . . . | 73.8 | 82.5 | 86.3 | 85.9 | 86.0 | 85.6 | 8.7 | 3.8 | -0.3 | -0.4 |
| 2-year colleges . . . . . . | 61.9 | 78.9 | 77.8 | 79.8 | 79.8 | 76.1 | 17.0 | -1.1 | 2.0 | -3.6 |

## Salaries of College Professors, 1992-1993

Source: American Association of University Professors

| Type of Institution (by highest degree offered) | Public | Private/ Indepen- dent | Church- Related | Type of Institution (by highest degree offered) | Public | Private/ Indepen- dent | Church- Related |
|---|---|---|---|---|---|---|---|
| **Doctoral Degrees** | | | | **Four-Year Liberal Arts Degrees** | | | |
| Professor | $63,250 | $80,280 | $70,770 | Professor | $48,600 | $54,620 | $43,210 |
| Associate Professor | 45,840 | 53,860 | 50,640 | Associate Professor | 40,180 | 41,710 | 36,220 |
| Assistant Professor | 38,880 | 45,510 | 42,090 | Assistant Professor | 33,430 | 34,400 | 30,500 |
| **Master's Degrees** | | | | **Two-Year Degrees** | | | |
| Professor | $54,240 | $57,060 | $55,970 | Professor | $47,820 | $36,710 | $32,010 |
| Associate Professor | 43,430 | 44,020 | 44,800 | Associate Professor | 39,760 | 31,800 | 29,290 |
| Assistant Professor | 36,160 | 35,360 | 37,090 | Assistant Professor | 34,300 | 27,100 | 24,850 |

## Public Libraries

Source: World Almanac questionnaire (1992)

| City | No. bound Volumes | Circulation | Annual Acquisi- tions Expend. | City | No. bound Volumes | Circulation | Annual Acquisi- tions Expend. |
|---|---|---|---|---|---|---|---|
| Akron, Oh. (17) | 1,498,836 | 3,191,088 | $1,900,000 | Mesa, Ariz. (2) | 556,416 | 2,064,658 | $768,638 |
| Albuquerque, N.M. (12) | 810,871 | 2,830,979 | 1,150,000 | Miami, Fla.[a] (28) | 2,386,204 | 4,200,000 | 2,200,000 |
| Anaheim, Cal. (5) | 393,231 | 1,550,000 | 450,000 | Milwaukee, Wis. (12) | 2,306,006 | 3,057,442 | 1,788,125 |
| Anchorage, Alas.[a] (5) | 395,700 | 1,099,780 | 662,790 | Minneapolis, Minn. (14) | 1,977,573 | 3,065,032 | 2,026,182 |
| Arlington, Tex. (5) | 246,125 | 1,211,662 | 280,533 | Mobile, Ala. (6) | 415,000 | 1,323,318 | 700,000 |
| Atlanta, Ga.[a] (33) | 1,678,750 | 2,303,681 | 3,011,362 | Nashville, Tenn. (16) | 665,249 | 1,849,973 | 820,310 |
| Baltimore, Md. (28) | 2,217,508 | 1,673,310 | 1,904,681 | New Orleans, La. (15) | 928,871 | 1,251,366 | 892,728 |
| Baton Rouge, La. (10) | 815,467 | 2,276,247 | 1,146,850 | New York, N.Y. (research) | 10,700,000 | — | 9,400,000 |
| Birmingham, Ala. (19) | 889,000 | 2,000,000 | 1,200,000 | Branches (82) | 4,000,000 | 9,908,640 | 6,650,000 |
| Boston, Mass. (26) | 6,000,000 | 1,600,000 | 2,000,000 | Brooklyn[a] (58) | 4,637,167 | 8,610,459 | 5,133,434 |
| Buffalo, N.Y. (53) | 2,494,000 | 7,587,811 | 2,629,489 | Queens[a] (61) | 5,500,000 | 11,320,000 | 5,500,000 |
| Charlotte, N.C.[a] (19) | 1,200,000 | 2,700,000 | 1,400,000 | Norfolk, Va. (11) | 901,775 | 767,110 | 500,626 |
| Chicago, Ill. (Main) | 1,700,000 | 950,000 | 3,600,000 | Oklahoma City, | | | |
| Branches (82) | 4,600,000 | 8,400,000 | 4,600,000 | Okla.[a] (11) | 933,241 | 4,184,437 | 1,346,726 |
| Cincinnati, Oh. (42) | 4,281,202 | 10,413,286 | 5,561,019 | Oakland, Cal. (16) | 1,300,000 | 1,580,000 | 762,000 |
| Cleveland, Oh. (28) | 2,734,894 | 5,624,099 | 6,098,471 | Omaha, Neb. (9) | 613,472 | 1,985,822 | 933,050 |
| Colorado Springs, Col. (13) | 867,906 | 2,470,986 | 1,998,445 | Philadelphia, Pa.[a] (53) | 3,458,700 | 4,800,000 | 6,200,000 |
| Columbus, Oh. (20) | 1,928,603 | 8,341,885 | 5,178,015 | Phoenix, Az. (11) | 1,783,410 | 5,962,000 | 2,200,000 |
| Corpus Christi, Tex. (4) | 362,433 | 1,153,718 | 520,756 | Pittsburgh, Pa. (19) | 1,934,390 | 2,925,154 | 1,300,000 |
| Dallas, Tex.[a] (19) | 2,409,864 | 4,364,027 | 17,201,527 | Portland, Ore.[a] (15) | 4,000,000 | 2,000,000 | 1,400,000 |
| Dayton, Oh. (20) | 1,555,475 | 6,224,061 | 2,316,854 | Richmond, Va. (8) | 785,023 | 842,143 | 427,734 |
| Denver, Col.[a] (21) | 2,239,106 | 3,396,268 | 1,856,485 | Rochester, N.Y. (11) | 1,542,038 | 1,597,407 | 1,029,258 |
| Des Moines, Ia. (5) | 549,544 | 1,241,800 | 267,050 | Sacramento, Cal.[a] (24) | 1,663,893 | 3,977,515 | 2,045,262 |
| Detroit, Mich. (25) | 2,763,442 | 1,494,160 | 1,932,650 | St. Louis, Mo. (12) | 1,400,000 | 1,830,302 | 1,670,000 |
| District of Columbia[a] (25) | 1,507,556 | 1,843,098 | 1,530,000 | St. Paul, Minn. (12) | 599,048 | 2,628,951 | 894,113 |
| El Paso, Tex.[a] (10) | 600,000 | 1,300,000 | 3,500,000 | San Diego, Cal. (32) | 2,030,185 | 5,364,276 | 2,480,597 |
| Fairfax, Va.[a] (22) | 1,761,264 | 8,454,714 | 3,387,721 | San Francisco, Cal. (27) | 2,000,000 | 3,300,000 | 1,015,855 |
| Ft. Worth, Tex. (10) | 1,693,975 | 2,238,871 | 1,266,213 | Shreveport, La. (19) | 475,685 | 1,081,232 | 400,000 |
| Fresno, Cal. (36) | 1,192,409 | 2,003,511 | 500,000 | Syracuse, N.Y. (8) | 650,080 | 1,911,930 | 1,281,088 |
| Honolulu, Ha. (49) | 2,389,153 | 6,290,173 | 3,579,085 | Tampa, Fla.[a] (17) | 1,100,600 | 3,200,000 | 1,800,000 |
| Houston, Tex. (34) | 3,982,539 | 6,342,340 | 4,038,166 | Toledo, Oh. (18) | 1,793,735 | 5,849,356 | 2,968,076 |
| Indianapolis, Ind.[a] (21) | 1,500,000 | 5,376,388 | 2,170,167 | Tucson, Ariz. (17) | 1,200,000 | 5,100,000 | 1,355,000 |
| Jersey City, N.J. (11) | 792,423 | 285,549 | 139,412 | Tulsa, Okla. (20) | 874,272 | 3,344,153 | 1,550,000 |
| Kansas City, Mo. (8) | 1,817,937 | 2,032,835 | 1,589,306 | Wichita, Kan. (11) | 875,558 | 1,718,806 | 464,630 |
| Los Angeles, Cal.[a] (62) | 5,663,240 | 10,382,321 | 4,469,364 | Yonkers, N.Y.[a] (3) | 233,532 | 865,901 | 481,286 |
| Louisville, Ky. (14) | 700,000 | 2,603,723 | 1,575,340 | | | | |
| Memphis, Tenn.[a] (23) | 1,700,000 | 2,700,000 | 3,228,007 | | | | |

(a) Has not provided up-to-date information. Figure in parentheses denotes number of branches.

## Funding of Public Libraries, 1991

Source: National Center for Education Statistics, U.S. Dept. of Education; per capita spending

| | | | | | |
|---|---|---|---|---|---|
| United States | $17.83 | Kentucky | $9.16 | North Dakota | $8.70 |
| Alabama | $9.88 | Louisiana | $12.62 | Ohio | $28.34 |
| Alaska | $28.64 | Maine | $15.40 | Oklahoma | $12.37 |
| Arizona | $16.16 | Maryland | $25.52 | Oregon | $17.86 |
| Arkansas | $6.75 | Massachusetts | $21.36 | Pennsylvania | $12.92 |
| California | $17.54 | Michigan | $15.51 | Rhode Island | $18.63 |
| Colorado | $20.51 | Minnesota | $20.58 | South Carolina | $9.67 |
| Connecticut | $27.20 | Mississippi | $7.62 | South Dakota | $13.59 |
| Delaware | $9.48 | Missouri | $15.50 | Tennessee | $7.44 |
| District of Columbia | $35.62 | Montana | $9.02 | Texas | $9.53 |
| Florida | $15.09 | Nebraska | $15.38 | Utah | $15.71 |
| Georgia | $11.62 | Nevada | $16.41 | Vermont | $13.24 |
| Hawaii | $19.39 | New Hampshire | $17.40 | Virginia | $18.79 |
| Idaho | $13.62 | New Jersey | $27.40 | Washington | $23.79 |
| Illinois | $22.72 | New Mexico | $10.71 | West Virginia | $8.38 |
| Indiana | $22.80 | New York | $30.36 | Wisconsin | $19.10 |
| Iowa | $14.67 | North Carolina | $12.01 | Wyoming | $22.40 |
| Kansas | $17.41 | | | | |

# American Colleges and Universities

### General Information for the 1992-93 Academic Year

### Source: Peterson's Guides

These listings include all accredited undergraduate degree-granting institutions in the United States and U.S. territories that have a total institutional enrollment of 1,000 or more. Four-year colleges (those that award a bachelor's as their highest undergraduate degree) are listed first, followed by two-year colleges (those that award an associate as their highest or primary undergraduate degree).

All institutions are coeducational except those where the zip code is directly followed by: (1)–men only, (2)–primarily men, (3)–women only, (4)–primarily women.

Year is that of founding.

Governing official is the chief executive officer.

Institutional control: 1–independent (nonprofit), 2–independent-religious, 3–proprietary (profit making), 4–federal, 5–state, 7–commonwealth (Puerto Rico), 8–territory (U.S. territories), 9–county, 10–district, 11–city, 12–state and local, 13–state related.

Highest degree offered: B–bachelor's, M–master's, F–first professional, D–doctorate.

Enrollment is the total number of matriculated undergraduate and (if applicable) graduate students.

Faculty is the total number of faculty members teaching undergraduate courses and (if available) graduate courses.

Any data not reported are indicated as NR.

## Four-Year Colleges

| Name, address | Year | Governing official, control, and highest degree offered | | Enroll-ment | Faculty |
|---|---|---|---|---|---|
| Abilene Christian U, Abilene, TX 79699 | 1906 | Dr. Royce Money | 2-M | 4,055 | 227 |
| Acad of Art Coll, San Francisco, CA 94105 | 1929 | Dr. Andrew Jameson | 3-M | 2,318 | 140 |
| Adams State Coll, Alamosa, CO 81102 | 1921 | Dr. William M. Fulkerson, Jr. | 5-M | 2,482 | 120 |
| Adelphi U, Garden City, NY 11530 | 1896 | Dr. Peter Diamandopoulos | 1-D | 8,261 | 663 |
| Adrian Coll, Adrian, MI 49221 | 1859 | Dr. Stanley P. Caine | 2-B | 1,145 | 134 |
| Alabama A&M U, Normal, AL 35762 | 1875 | Dr. David B. Henson | 5-D | 5,069 | 337 |
| Alabama State U, Montgomery, AL 36101 | 1874 | Dr. C. C. Baker | 5-M | 5,800 | 270 |
| Albany State Coll, Albany, GA 31705 | 1903 | Dr. Billy C. Black | 5-M | 3,106 | 150 |
| Albertson Coll, Caldwell, ID 83605 | 1891 | Mr. Robert L. Hendren, Jr. | 1-M | 1,062 | 118 |
| Albion Coll, Albion, MI 49224 | 1835 | Dr. Melvin L. Vulgamore | 2-B | 1,677 | 131 |
| Albright Coll, Reading, PA 19612 | 1856 | Dr. Ellen S. Hurwitz | 2-B | 1,260 | 112 |
| Alfred U, Alfred, NY 14802 | 1836 | Dr. Edward G. Coll, Jr. | 1-D | 2,258 | 197 |
| Allegheny Coll, Meadville, PA 16335 | 1815 | Dr. Daniel F. Sullivan | 2-B | 1,783 | 202 |
| Allentown Coll of St Francis de Sales, Center Valley, PA 18034-9568 | 1962 | Rev. Daniel Gambet, OSFS | 2-M | 2,100 | 98 |
| Alma Coll, Alma, MI 48801-1599 | 1886 | Dr. Alan J. Stone | 2-B | 1,295 | 110 |
| Alvernia Coll, Reading, PA 19607-1799 | 1958 | Dr. Daniel N. DeLucca | 2-B | 1,332 | 106 |
| Alverno Coll, Milwaukee, WI 53234-3922 (3) | 1887 | Sr. Joel Read | 2-B | 2,514 | 208 |
| Amber U, Garland, TX 75041 | 1971 | Dr. Douglas W. Warner | 1-M | 1,610 | 65 |
| American International Coll, Springfield, MA 01109-3189 | 1885 | Dr. Harry J. Courniotes | 1-M | 1,815 | 122 |
| American Tech Inst, Brunswick, TN 38014 (2) | 1985 | NR | 1-B | 1,500 | 8 |
| American U, Washington, DC 20016 | 1893 | Mr. Elliott Milstein | 2-D | 10,153 | 1,335 |
| Amherst Coll, Amherst, MA 01002 | 1821 | Dr. Peter R. Pouncey | 1-B | 1,575 | 191 |
| Anderson Coll, Anderson, SC 29621 | 1911 | Dr. Mark L. Hopkins | 2-B | 1,172 | 73 |
| Anderson U, Anderson, IN 46012 | 1917 | Dr. James L. Edwards | 2-M | 2,249 | 184 |
| Andrews U, Berrien Springs, MI 49104 | 1874 | Dr. W. Richard Lesher | 2-D | 2,979 | 329 |
| Angelo State U, San Angelo, TX 76909 | 1928 | Dr. Lloyd Drexell Vincent | 5-M | 6,102 | 240 |
| Anna Maria Coll, Paxton, MA 01612 | 1946 | Sr. Bernadette Madore | 2-M | 1,486 | 92 |
| Appalachian State U, Boone, NC 28608 | 1899 | Dr. John E. Thomas | 5-D | 11,650 | 688 |
| Aquinas Coll, Grand Rapids, MI 49506-1799 | 1886 | Mr. R. Paul Nelson | 2-M | 2,544 | 197 |
| Arizona State U, Tempe, AZ 85287 | 1885 | Dr. Lattie F. Coor | 5-D | 43,635 | 1,822 |
| Arkansas State U, State University, AR 72467 | 1909 | Dr. John N. Mangieri | 5-D | 10,177 | 449 |
| Arkansas Tech U, Russellville, AR 72801-2222 | 1909 | Dr. Robert C. Brown | 5-M | 4,790 | 230 |
| Armstrong State Coll, Savannah, GA 31419 | 1935 | Dr. Robert A. Burnett | 5-B | 4,839 | 179 |
| Art Ctr Coll of Design, Pasadena, CA 91103 | 1930 | Mr. David R. Brown | 1-M | 1,275 | 310 |
| Asbury Coll, Wilmore, KY 40390-1198 | 1890 | Dr. David J. Gyertson | 2-B | 1,129 | 102 |
| Ashland U, Ashland, OH 44805 | 1878 | Mr. G. William Benz | 2-M | 5,652 | 202 |
| Assumption Coll, Worcester, MA 01615-0005 | 1904 | Dr. Joseph H. Hagan | 2-M | 2,896 | 189 |
| Athens State Coll, Athens, AL 35611 | 1822 | Dr. Jerry F. Bartlett | 5-B | 3,234 | 182 |
| Atlantic Union Coll, South Lancaster, MA 01561 | 1882 | Dr. Lawrence T. Geraty | 2-M | 1,273 | 87 |
| Auburn U, Auburn University, AL 36849 | 1856 | Dr. William V. Muse | 5-D | 21,551 | 1,181 |
| Auburn U at Montgomery, Montgomery, AL 36117-3596 | 1967 | Dr. James O. Williams | 5-M | 6,386 | 383 |
| Audrey Cohen Coll, New York, NY 10014 | 1964 | Dr. Audrey C. Cohen | 1-M | 1,096 | 66 |
| Augsburg Coll, Minneapolis, MN 55454 | 1869 | Dr. Charles S. Anderson | 2-M | 2,924 | 189 |
| Augusta Coll, Augusta, GA 30904-2200 | 1925 | Dr. Martha Farmer | 5-M | 5,579 | 237 |
| Augustana Coll, Rock Island, IL 61201 | 1860 | Dr. Thomas Tredway | 2-B | 2,080 | 173 |
| Augustana Coll, Sioux Falls, SD 57197 | 1860 | Dr. Ralph H. Wagoner | 2-M | 1,929 | 156 |
| Aurora U, Aurora, IL 60506 | 1893 | Dr. Thomas H. Zarle | 1-M | 2,025 | 240 |
| Austin Coll, Sherman, TX 75091 | 1849 | Dr. Harry E. Smith | 2-M | 1,174 | 96 |
| Austin Peay State U, Clarksville, TN 37044 | 1927 | Dr. Oscar Page | 5-M | 7,670 | 469 |
| Averett Coll, Danville, VA 24541 | 1859 | Dr. Frank R. Campbell | 2-M | 1,674 | 63 |
| Avila Coll, Kansas City, MO 64145 | 1916 | Dr. Larry Kramer | 2-M | 1,409 | 135 |
| Azusa Pacific U, Azusa, CA 91702 | 1899 | Dr. Richard E. Felix | 2-M | 3,651 | 319 |
| Babson Coll, Babson Park, MA 02157-0310 | 1919 | Mr. William F. Glavin | 1-M | 3,157 | 168 |
| Baker Coll of Flint, Flint, MI 48507 | 1911 | Mr. Edward J. Kurtz | 1-B | 4,179 | 127 |
| Baker Coll of Muskegon, Muskegon, MI 49442 | 1888 | Mr. Robert D. Jewell | 1-B | 1,860 | 60 |
| Baker Coll of Owosso, Owosso, MI 48867 | 1984 | NR | 1-B | 1,274 | 67 |
| Baker U, Baldwin City, KS 66006 | 1858 | Dr. Daniel M. Lambert | 2-M | 1,840 | 74 |
| Baldwin-Wallace Coll, Berea, OH 44017 | 1845 | Dr. Neal Malicky | 2-M | 4,736 | 374 |
| Ball State U, Muncie, IN 47306 | 1918 | Dr. John E. Worthen | 5-D | 20,333 | 1,123 |
| Bard Coll, Annandale-on-Hudson, NY 12504 | 1860 | Dr. Leon Botstein | 1-M | 1,178 | 135 |
| Barnard Coll, New York, NY 10027-6598 (3) | 1889 | Ms. Ellen V. Futter | 1-B | 2,190 | 249 |
| Barry U, Miami Shores, FL 33161 | 1940 | Sr. Jeanne O'Laughlin, OP | 2-D | 6,466 | 376 |
| Barton Coll, Wilson, NC 27893 | 1902 | Dr. James B. Hemby | 2-B | 1,720 | 106 |

| Name, address | Year | Governing official, control, and highest degree offered | Enroll-ment | Faculty |
|---|---|---|---|---|
| Baruch Coll of the City U of New York, New York, NY 10010 | 1919 | Dr. Matthew Goldstein . . . . .12-D | 15,030 | 820 |
| Bates Coll, Lewiston, ME 04240 | 1855 | Dr. Donald W. Harward . . . . . 1-B | 1,515 | 176 |
| Bayamón Central U, Bayamón, PR 00960-1725 | 1970 | Rev. Vincent A. M. Van Rooij, OP . . . . . 2-M | 2,921 | 112 |
| Baylor U, Waco, TX 76798 | 1845 | Dr. Herbert H. Reynolds . . . 2-D | 12,185 | 636 |
| Beaver Coll, Glenside, PA 19038-3295 | 1853 | Dr. Bette E. Landman . . . . . 2-M | 2,220 | 184 |
| Belhaven Coll, Jackson, MS 39202-1789 | 1883 | Dr. Newton Wilson . . . . . . 2-B | 1,056 | 73 |
| Bellarmine Coll, Louisville, KY 40205-0671 | 1950 | Dr. Joseph J. McGowan, Jr. . 2-M | 2,326 | 175 |
| Bellevue Coll, Bellevue, NE 68005-3039 | 1965 | Dr. John B. Muller . . . . . . 1-M | 2,157 | 83 |
| Belmont Abbey Coll, Belmont, NC 28012 | 1876 | Dr. Joseph Brosnan . . . . . 2-B | 1,016 | 84 |
| Belmont U, Nashville, TN 37212 | 1951 | Dr. William E. Troutt . . . . . 2-M | 2,866 | 298 |
| Beloit Coll, Beloit, WI 53511 | 1846 | Mr. Victor E. Ferrall, Jr. . . . 1-M | 1,187 | 136 |
| Bemidji State U, Bemidji, MN 56601 | 1919 | Dr. Linda Baer . . . . . . . . 5-M | 4,816 | 220 |
| Benedict Coll, Columbia, SC 29204 | 1870 | Dr. Ruby W. Watts . . . . . . 2-B | 1,207 | 100 |
| Benedictine Coll, Atchison, KS 66002 | 1859 | Dr. Thomas O. James . . . . . 2-M | 1,130 | 91 |
| Bentley Coll, Waltham, MA 02154-4705 | 1917 | Dr. Joseph M. Cronin . . . . . 1-M | 5,577 | 374 |
| Berea Coll, Berea, KY 40404 | 1855 | Dr. John B. Stephenson . . . . 1-B | 1,563 | 128 |
| Berklee Coll of Music, Boston, MA 02215 | 1945 | Dr. Lee Eliot Berk . . . . . . 1-B | 2,555 | 263 |
| Berry Coll, Mount Berry, GA 30149-0159 | 1902 | Dr. Gloria M. Shatto . . . . . 1-M | 1,745 | 126 |
| Bethel Coll, St Paul, MN 55112 | 1871 | Dr. George K. Brushaber . . . 2-M | 1,963 | 177 |
| Bethune-Cookman Coll, Daytona Beach, FL 32115 | 1904 | Dr. Oswald P. Bronson, Sr. . . 2-B | 2,301 | 199 |
| Biola U, La Mirada, CA 90639 | 1908 | Dr. Clyde Cook . . . . . . . 2-D | 2,883 | 216 |
| Birmingham-Southern Coll, Birmingham, AL 35254 | 1856 | Dr. Neal R. Berte . . . . . . 2-M | 1,763 | 141 |
| Black Hills State U, Spearfish, SD 57799-9501 | 1883 | Dr. Clifford M. Trump . . . . . 5-M | 2,814 | 103 |
| Bloomfield Coll, Bloomfield, NJ 07003 | 1868 | Dr. John F. Noonan . . . . . 2-B | 2,036 | 180 |
| Bloomsburg U of Pennsylvania, Bloomsburg, PA 17815 | 1839 | Dr. Harry Ausprich . . . . . 5-M | 7,551 | 398 |
| Bluefield State Coll, Bluefield, WV 24701 | 1895 | Dr. Leonard C. Nelson . . . . 5-B | 2,931 | 178 |
| Boise State U, Boise, ID 83725 | 1932 | Dr. Charles Ruch . . . . . . 5-M | 13,231 | 878 |
| Boricua Coll, New York, NY 10032 | 1974 | Dr. Victor G. Alicea . . . . . 1-B | 1,146 | 128 |
| Boston Coll, Chestnut Hill, MA 02167 | 1863 | Rev. J. Donald Monan, SJ . . 2-D | 14,455 | 957 |
| Boston U, Boston, MA 02215 | 1839 | Dr. John Silber . . . . . . . 1-D | 28,364 | 2,556 |
| Bowdoin Coll, Brunswick, ME 04011 | 1794 | Mr. Robert H. Edwards . . . . 1-B | 1,445 | 132 |
| Bowie State U, Bowie, MD 20715 | 1865 | Dr. Nathanael Pollard, Jr. . . 5-M | 4,437 | 234 |
| Bowling Green State U, Bowling Green, OH 43403 | 1910 | Dr. Paul J. Olscamp . . . . . 5-D | 17,502 | 852 |
| Bradley U, Peoria, IL 61625 | 1897 | Dr. John R. Brazil . . . . . . 1-M | 6,191 | 428 |
| Brandeis U, Waltham, MA 02254-9110 | 1948 | Dr. Samuel O. Thier . . . . . 1-D | 3,829 | 468 |
| Brenau U, Gainesville, GA 30501-3697 (4) | 1878 | Dr. John S. Burd . . . . . . 1-M | 1,987 | 159 |
| Brewton-Parker Coll, Mt Vernon, GA 30445 | 1904 | Dr. Y. Lynn Holmes . . . . . 2-B | 1,974 | 229 |
| Briar Cliff Coll, Sioux City, IA 51104 | 1930 | Sr. Margaret Wick . . . . . . 2-B | 1,144 | 72 |
| Bridgewater State Coll, Bridgewater, MA 02325 | 1840 | Dr. Adrian Tinsley . . . . . . 5-M | 8,350 | 334 |
| Brigham Young U, Provo, UT 84602 | 1875 | Dr. Rex E. Lee . . . . . . . 2-D | 31,108 | 1,652 |
| Brigham Young U–Hawaii Cmps, Laie, Oahu, HI 96762 | 1955 | Dr. Alton L. Wade . . . . . . 2-B | 2,064 | 149 |
| Brooklyn Coll of the City U of New York, Brooklyn, NY 11210 | 1930 | Dr. Vernon E. Lattin . . . . .12-M | 17,218 | 850 |
| Brown U, Providence, RI 02912 | 1764 | Dr. Vartan Gregorian . . . . . 1-D | 7,593 | 663 |
| Bryant Coll, Smithfield, RI 02917 | 1863 | Dr. William E. Trueheart . . . 1-M | 4,598 | 216 |
| Bryn Mawr Coll, Bryn Mawr, PA 19010 (4) | 1885 | Dr. Mary Patterson McPherson . . . . . . . . . 1-D | 1,847 | 209 |
| Bucknell U, Lewisburg, PA 17837 | 1846 | Dr. Gary A. Sojka . . . . . . 1-M | 3,603 | 268 |
| Butler U, Indianapolis, IN 46208 | 1855 | Dr. Geoffrey Bannister . . . . 1-M | 3,825 | 368 |
| Cabrini Coll, Radnor, PA 19087-3699 | 1957 | Dr. Antoinette Iadarola . . . . 2-M | 1,760 | 141 |
| Caldwell Coll, Caldwell, NJ 07006-6195 | 1939 | Sr. Vivien Jennings . . . . . 2-M | 1,339 | 89 |
| California Coll for Health Sciences, National City, CA 91950 | 1977 | NR . . . . . . . . . . . . . 3-M | 4,200 | 9 |
| California Coll of Arts and Crafts, Oakland, CA 94618 | 1907 | Mr. Neil J. Hoffman . . . . . 1-M | 1,146 | 167 |
| California Inst of Tech, Pasadena, CA 91125 | 1891 | Dr. Thomas E. Everhart . . . . 1-D | 2,009 | 270 |
| California Lutheran U, Thousand Oaks, CA 91360 | 1959 | Dr. Luther S. Luedtke . . . . 2-M | 2,970 | 261 |
| California Polytechnic State U, San Luis Obispo, San Luis Obispo, CA 93407 | 1901 | Dr. Warren J. Baker . . . . . 5-M | 16,377 | 953 |
| California State Polytechnic U, Pomona, Pomona, CA 91768 | 1938 | Dr. Bob Suzuki . . . . . . . 5-M | 18,297 | 916 |
| California State U, Bakersfield, Bakersfield, CA 93311 | 1970 | Dr. Tomas A. Arciniega . . . . 5-M | 5,422 | 337 |
| California State U, Chico, Chico, CA 95929-0720 | 1887 | Dr. Manuel Esteban . . . . . 5-M | 15,172 | 873 |
| California State U, Dominguez Hills, Carson, CA 90747 | 1960 | Dr. Robert Detweiler . . . . . 5-M | 10,477 | 401 |
| California State U, Fresno, Fresno, CA 93740 | 1911 | Dr. John D. Welty . . . . . . 5-D | 18,902 | 1,220 |
| California State U, Fullerton, Fullerton, CA 92634-9480 | 1957 | Dr. Milton A. Gordon . . . . . 5-M | 24,411 | 1,245 |
| California State U, Hayward, Hayward, CA 94542 | 1957 | Dr. Norma Rees . . . . . . . 5-M | 12,986 | 578 |
| California State U, Long Beach, Long Beach, CA 90840-0119 | 1949 | Dr. Karl W. E. Anatol . . . . . 5-M | 30,071 | 1,441 |
| California State U, Northridge, Northridge, CA 91330 | 1958 | Dr. Blenda J. Wilson . . . . . 5-M | 29,084 | 1,292 |
| California State U, Sacramento, Sacramento, CA 95819-6048 | 1947 | Dr. Donald R. Gerth . . . . . 5-M | 24,468 | 1,171 |
| California State U, San Bernardino, San Bernardino, CA 92407 | 1965 | Dr. Anthony H. Evans . . . . . 5-M | 12,483 | 626 |
| California State U, San Marcos, San Marcos, CA 92096 | 1990 | NR . . . . . . . . . . . . . 5-M | 1,904 | 121 |
| California State U, Stanislaus, Turlock, CA 95380 | 1957 | Dr. John W. Moore . . . . . . 5-M | 5,907 | 335 |
| California U of Pennsylvania, California, PA 15419-1394 | 1852 | Dr. John Pierce Watkins . . . 5-M | 6,484 | 375 |
| Calumet Coll of Saint Joseph, Whiting, IN 46394 | 1951 | Dr. Dennis C. Rittenmeyer . . 2-B | 1,086 | 110 |
| Calvin Coll, Grand Rapids, MI 49546 | 1876 | Dr. Anthony J. Diekema . . . 2-M | 3,725 | 282 |
| Cameron U, Lawton, OK 73505 | 1908 | Dr. Don Davis . . . . . . . . 5-M | 5,988 | 306 |
| Campbellsville Coll, Campbellsville, KY 42718-2799 | 1906 | Dr. Kenneth W. Winters . . . 2-B | 1,042 | 72 |
| Campbell U, Buies Creek, NC 27506 | 1887 | Dr. Norman A. Wiggins . . . . 2-F | 5,806 | 261 |
| Canisius Coll, Buffalo, NY 14208 | 1870 | Rev. James M. Demske, SJ . 2-M | 4,859 | 361 |
| Capital U, Columbus, OH 43209-2394 | 1830 | NR . . . . . . . . . . . . . 2-F | 3,680 | 161 |
| Cardinal Stritch Coll, Milwaukee, WI 53217-3985 | 1937 | Sr. Mary Lea Schneider . . . 2-M | 5,150 | 518 |
| Carleton Coll, Northfield, MN 55057 | 1866 | Dr. Stephen R. Lewis, Jr. . . 1-B | 1,662 | 163 |
| Carlow Coll, Pittsburgh, PA 15213 (4) | 1929 | Dr. Grace Ann Geibel, RSM . 2-M | 1,668 | 200 |
| Carnegie Mellon U, Pittsburgh, PA 15213 | 1900 | Dr. Robert Mehrabian . . . . . 1-D | 7,131 | 722 |
| Carroll Coll, Helena, MT 59625 | 1909 | Dr. Matthew Quinn . . . . . . 2-B | 1,382 | 114 |
| Carroll Coll, Waukesha, WI 53186 | 1846 | Dr. Frank Falcone . . . . . . 2-M | 2,108 | 117 |
| Carson-Newman Coll, Jefferson City, TN 37760 | 1851 | Dr. J. Cordell Maddox . . . . 2-M | 2,022 | 182 |
| Carthage Coll, Kenosha, WI 53140 | 1847 | Dr. F. Gregory Campbell . . . 2-M | 2,092 | 151 |
| Case Western Reserve U, Cleveland, OH 44106 | 1826 | Dr. Agnar Pytte . . . . . . . 1-D | 9,156 | 1,742 |
| Castleton State Coll, Castleton, VT 05735 | 1787 | Dr. Lyle A. Gray . . . . . . . 5-M | 2,028 | 165 |
| Catholic U of America, Washington, DC 20064 | 1887 | Br. F. Patrick Ellis . . . . . . 2-D | 6,464 | 694 |
| Cedar Crest Coll, Allentown, PA 18104 (4) | 1867 | Dr. Dorothy G. Blaney . . . . 2-B | 1,342 | 137 |

| Name, address | Year | Governing official, control, and highest degree offered | Enrollment | Faculty |
|---|---|---|---|---|
| Cedarville Coll, Cedarville, OH 45314 | 1887 | Dr. Paul H. Dixon ... 2-B | 2,172 | 163 |
| Centenary Coll of Louisiana, Shreveport, LA 71134 | 1825 | Dr. Kenneth L. Schwab ... 2-M | 1,048 | 95 |
| Central Connecticut State U, New Britain, CT 06050-4010 | 1849 | Dr. John W. Shumaker ... 5-M | 10,655 | 774 |
| Central Michigan U, Mount Pleasant, MI 48859 | 1892 | Dr. Leonard E. Plachta ... 5-D | 16,349 | 858 |
| Central Missouri State U, Warrensburg, MO 64093 | 1871 | Dr. Ed Elliott ... 5-M | 11,631 | 524 |
| Central State U, Wilberforce, OH 45384 | 1887 | Dr. Arthur E. Thomas ... 5-M | 3,279 | 147 |
| Central U of Iowa, Pella, IA 50219 | 1853 | Dr. William M. Wiebenga ... 2-B | 1,520 | 135 |
| Central Washington U, Ellensburg, WA 98926 | 1891 | Dr. Ivory V. Nelson ... 5-M | 7,697 | 344 |
| Central Wesleyan Coll, Central, SC 29630-1020 | 1906 | Dr. John M. Newby ... 2-M | 1,091 | 132 |
| Chadron State Coll, Chadron, NE 69337 | 1911 | Dr. Samuel H. Rankin ... 5-M | 3,693 | 137 |
| Chapman U, Orange, CA 92666 | 1861 | Dr. James Doti ... 2-M | 2,568 | 220 |
| Charleston Southern U, Charleston, SC 29411 | 1964 | Dr. Jairy C. Hunter, Jr. ... 2-M | 2,491 | 131 |
| Charter Oak State Coll, Farmington, CT 06032-1934 | 1973 | Dr. Merle W. Harris ... 5-B | 1,145 | NR |
| Chestnut Hill Coll, Philadelphia, PA 19118-2695 (3) | 1924 | Dr. Carol J. Vale, SSJ ... 2-M | 1,351 | 120 |
| Cheyney U of Pennsylvania, Cheyney, PA 19319 | 1837 | Dr. Douglas Covington ... 5-M | 1,550 | 91 |
| Chicago State U, Chicago, IL 60628 | 1867 | Dr. Dolores Cross ... 5-M | 8,675 | 397 |
| Christian Brothers U, Memphis, TN 38104-5581 | 1871 | Br. Stanislaus Sobczyk, FSC ... 2-M | 1,736 | 149 |
| Christopher Newport U, Newport News, VA 23606 | 1961 | Dr. Anthony Santoro ... 5-M | 4,880 | 279 |
| The Citadel, The Military Coll of South Carolina, Charleston, SC 29409 (1) | 1842 | Lt. Gen. Claudius E. Watts, III 5-M | 3,600 | 166 |
| City Coll of the City U of New York, New York, NY 10031 | 1847 | Dr. Augusta Sousa Kappner .12-D | 14,783 | 1,140 |
| City U, Bellevue, WA 98004 | 1973 | Dr. Michael A. Pastore ... 1-M | 3,520 | 811 |
| Clarion U of Pennsylvania, Clarion, PA 16214 | 1867 | Dr. Diane L. Reinhard ... 5-M | 6,159 | 373 |
| Clark Atlanta U, Atlanta, GA 30314 | 1869 | NR ... 2-D | 4,480 | 321 |
| Clarkson U, Potsdam, NY 13699 | 1896 | Dr. Richard H. Gallagher ... 1-D | 2,978 | 203 |
| Clark U, Worcester, MA 01610-1477 | 1887 | Dr. Richard P. Traina ... 1-D | 2,866 | NR |
| Clayton State Coll, Morrow, GA 30260 | 1969 | NR ... 5-B | 4,861 | 191 |
| Cleary Coll, Ypsilanti, MI 48197 | 1883 | Mr. Thomas Sullivan ... 1-B | 1,100 | 67 |
| Clemson U, Clemson, SC 29634 | 1889 | Dr. Max Lennon ... 5-D | 17,666 | 1,266 |
| Cleveland State U, Cleveland, OH 44115 | 1964 | Dr. Claire A. Van Ummersen 5-D | 18,199 | 686 |
| Clinch Valley Coll of the U of Virginia, Wise, VA 24293 | 1954 | Dr. L. Jay Lemons ... 5-B | 1,729 | 90 |
| Coastal Carolina U, Myrtle Beach, SC 29578 | 1954 | Dr. Ronald R. Ingle ... 5-B | 4,023 | 253 |
| Coe Coll, Cedar Rapids, IA 52402 | 1851 | Dr. John E. Brown ... 2-B | 1,285 | 109 |
| Colby Coll, Waterville, ME 04901 | 1813 | Dr. William R. Cotter ... 1-B | 1,716 | 172 |
| Colgate U, Hamilton, NY 13346 | 1819 | Dr. Neil R. Grabois ... 1-M | 2,691 | 273 |
| Coll Misericordia, Dallas, PA 18612-1098 | 1924 | Dr. Carol A. Jobe ... 2-M | 1,689 | 120 |
| Coll of Aeronautics, Flushing, NY 11371 (2) | 1932 | Dr. Richard B. Goetze, Jr. ... 1-B | 1,230 | 88 |
| Coll of Charleston, Charleston, SC 29424 | 1770 | Dr. Alexander M. Sanders, Jr. ... 5-M | 9,660 | 538 |
| Coll of Great Falls, Great Falls, MT 59405 | 1932 | Dr. Frederick W. Gilliard ... 2-M | 1,328 | 139 |
| Coll of Insurance, New York, NY 10007 | 1962 | Dr. Ellen Thrower ... 1-M | 2,379 | 93 |
| Coll of Mount St Joseph, Cincinnati, OH 45233-1670 | 1920 | Ms. Francis Marie Thrailkill, OSU ... 2-M | 2,592 | 218 |
| Coll of Mount Saint Vincent, Riverdale, NY 10471 | 1911 | Dr. Mary C. Stuart ... 1-M | 1,060 | 95 |
| Coll of New Rochelle, New Rochelle, NY 10805-2308 (4) | 1904 | Sr. Dorothy A. Kelly, OSU ... 1-M | 2,445 | 92 |
| Coll of New Rochelle, New Resources Division, New Rochelle, NY 10805-2308 | 1972 | NR ... 1-B | 3,242 | 468 |
| Coll of Notre Dame, Belmont, CA 94002 | 1851 | Sr. Veronica Skillin ... 2-M | 1,497 | 147 |
| Coll of Notre Dame of Maryland, Baltimore, MD 21210 (3) | 1873 | Sr. Rosemarie Nassif ... 2-M | 1,019 | 81 |
| Coll of Saint Benedict, Saint Joseph, MN 56374 (3) | 1887 | Dr. Colman O'Connell, OSB 2-B | 1,787 | 147 |
| Coll of St Catherine, St Paul, MN 55105 (3) | 1905 | Dr. Anita Pampusch ... 2-B | 2,638 | 231 |
| Coll of Saint Elizabeth, Morristown, NJ 07960-6989 (4) | 1899 | Sr. Jacqueline Burns ... 2-B | 1,298 | 129 |
| Coll of St Francis, Joliet, IL 60435 | 1920 | Dr. John C. Orr ... 2-M | 1,888 | 124 |
| Coll of Saint Mary, Omaha, NE 68124 (4) | 1923 | Dr. Kenneth Nielsen ... 2-B | 1,322 | 134 |
| Coll of Saint Rose, Albany, NY 12203 | 1920 | Dr. Louis C. Vaccaro ... 2-M | 3,715 | 241 |
| Coll of St Scholastica, Duluth, MN 55811 | 1912 | Dr. Daniel H. Pilon ... 2-M | 1,988 | 122 |
| Coll of Santa Fe, Santa Fe, NM 87501 | 1947 | Dr. James A. Fries ... 1-M | 1,472 | 129 |
| Coll of Staten Island of the City U of New York, Staten Island, NY 10314-6600 | 1955 | Dr. Edmond L. Volpe ... 12-M | 12,123 | 734 |
| Coll of the Holy Cross, Worcester, MA 01610 | 1843 | Rev. John E. Brooks, SJ ... 2-B | 2,742 | 265 |
| Coll of the Ozarks, Point Lookout, MO 65726 | 1906 | Dr. Jerry C. Davis ... 2-B | 1,524 | 109 |
| The Coll of West Virginia, Beckley, WV 25802 | 1933 | Dr. Charles Polk ... 1-B | 1,847 | 115 |
| Coll of William and Mary, Williamsburg, VA 23187-8795 | 1693 | Mr. Timothy J. Sullivan ... 5-D | 7,732 | 656 |
| The Coll of Wooster, Wooster, OH 44691 | 1866 | Dr. Henry J. Copeland ... 2-B | 1,686 | 155 |
| Colorado Christian U, Lakewood, CO 80226 | 1914 | Dr. Ronald Schmidt ... 2-M | 1,000 | 81 |
| The Colorado Coll, Colorado Springs, CO 80903 | 1874 | Dr. Kathryn Mohrman ... 1-M | 1,945 | 199 |
| Colorado Sch of Mines, Golden, CO 80401 | 1874 | Dr. George S. Ansell ... 5-D | 2,957 | 200 |
| Colorado State U, Fort Collins, CO 80523 | 1862 | Dr. Albert C. Yates ... 5-D | 21,210 | 1,021 |
| Colorado Tech Coll, Colorado Springs, CO 80907 | 1965 | Mr. David D. O'Donnell ... 3-M | 1,540 | 80 |
| Columbia Coll, Chicago, IL 60605 | 1890 | Dr. John B. Duff ... 1-M | 7,133 | 791 |
| Columbia Coll, New York, NY 10027 | 1754 | Mr. Steven Marcus ... 1-B | 3,422 | 475 |
| Columbia Coll, Columbia, SC 29203 (3) | 1854 | Dr. Peter T. Mitchell ... 2-M | 1,228 | 77 |
| Columbia Union Coll, Takoma Park, MD 20912 | 1904 | Dr. Charles Scriven ... 2-B | 1,121 | 56 |
| Columbia U, Sch of Engineering & Applied Sci, New York, NY 10027 | 1864 | Mr. David H. Auston ... 1-D | 1,832 | 101 |
| Columbia U, Sch of General Studies, New York, NY 10027 | 1754 | Ms. Caroline W. Bynum ... 1-M | 1,196 | 450 |
| Columbia U, Sch of Nursing, New York, NY 10032 (4) | 1892 | NR ... 1-M | 498 | 40 |
| Columbus Coll, Columbus, GA 31907-2079 | 1958 | Dr. Frank D. Brown ... 5-M | 5,009 | 228 |
| Columbus Coll of Art and Design, Columbus, OH 43215-1758 | 1879 | Mr. Joseph V. Canzani ... 1-B | 1,667 | 108 |
| Concord Coll, Athens, WV 24712 | 1872 | Dr. Jerry L. Beasley ... 5-B | 2,960 | 145 |
| Concordia Coll, Moorhead, MN 56562 | 1891 | Dr. Paul J. Dovre ... 2-B | 2,942 | 253 |
| Concordia Coll, St Paul, MN 55104 | 1893 | Dr. Robert Holst ... 2-M | 1,265 | 116 |
| Concordia Coll, Portland, OR 97211 | 1905 | Dr. Charles E. Schlimpert ... 2-B | 1,066 | 83 |
| Concordia U, River Forest, IL 60305-1499 | 1864 | Dr. Eugene L. Krentz ... 2-M | 1,726 | 157 |
| Concordia U Wisconsin, Mequon, WI 53092-7699 | 1881 | Dr. R. John Buuck ... 2-M | 2,370 | 135 |
| Connecticut Coll, New London, CT 06320 | 1911 | Ms. Claire L. Gaudiani ... 1-M | 1,838 | 180 |
| Converse Coll, Spartanburg, SC 29302 (3) | 1889 | Dr. Ellen Wood Hall ... 1-M | 1,120 | 100 |
| Cooper Union for the Advancement of Science & Art, New York, NY 10003 | 1859 | Mr. John Jay Iselin ... 1-M | 1,062 | 167 |
| Coppin State Coll, Baltimore, MD 21216 | 1900 | Dr. Calvin W. Burnett ... 5-M | 2,816 | 153 |
| Cornell Coll, Mount Vernon, IA 52314-1098 | 1853 | Dr. David G. Marker ... 2-B | 1,162 | 125 |
| Cornell U, Ithaca, NY 14853 | 1865 | Dr. Frank H. T. Rhodes ... 1-D | 18,450 | 1,593 |
| Creighton U, Omaha, NE 68178 | 1878 | Rev. Michael G. Morrison, SJ 2-D | 5,600 | 1,261 |
| Culver-Stockton Coll, Canton, MO 63435-1299 | 1853 | Dr. Edwin B. Strong, Jr. ... 2-B | 1,145 | 66 |
| Cumberland Coll, Williamsburg, KY 40769-1372 | 1889 | Dr. James Taylor ... 2-M | 1,498 | 100 |
| Curry Coll, Milton, MA 02186 | 1879 | Dr. Catherine W. Ingold ... 1-M | 1,143 | 178 |

| Name, address | Year | Governing official, control, and highest degree offered | | Enroll-ment | Faculty |
|---|---|---|---|---|---|
| Daemen Coll, Amherst, NY 14226 | 1947 | Dr. Robert S. Marshall | 1-M | 1,625 | 152 |
| Dakota State U, Madison, SD 57042 | 1881 | Dr. Jerald Tunheim | 5-B | 1,504 | 68 |
| Dallas Baptist U, Dallas, TX 75211-9288 | 1965 | Dr. Gary R. Cook | 2-M | 2,712 | 175 |
| Dartmouth Coll, Hanover, NH 03755 | 1769 | Mr. James O. Freedman | 1-D | 5,475 | 468 |
| Davenport Coll of Business, Grand Rapids, MI 49503 | 1866 | Mr. Donald W. Maine | 1-B | 4,500 | 188 |
| Davenport Coll of Business, Kalamazoo Cmps, Kalamazoo, MI 49006 (4) | 1866 | Mr. C. Dexter Rohm | 1-B | 1,942 | 106 |
| Davenport Coll of Business, Lansing Cmps, Lansing, MI 48933 | 1979 | Mr. Don Colizzi | 1-B | 1,512 | 86 |
| David Lipscomb U, Nashville, TN 37204 | 1891 | Dr. Harold Hazelip | 2-M | 2,272 | 178 |
| Davidson Coll, Davidson, NC 28036 | 1837 | Dr. John W. Kuykendall | 2-B | 1,550 | 127 |
| Delaware State Coll, Dover, DE 19901 | 1891 | Dr. William B. DeLauder | 5-M | 2,935 | 182 |
| Delaware Valley Coll, Doylestown, PA 18901-2697 | 1896 | Mr. George F. West | 1-B | 1,286 | 106 |
| Delta State U, Cleveland, MS 38733 | 1925 | Dr. F. Kent Wyatt | 5-D | 3,665 | 225 |
| Denison U, Granville, OH 43023 | 1831 | Dr. Michele Tolela Myers | 1-B | 2,003 | 162 |
| DePaul U, Chicago, IL 60604 | 1898 | Rev. John T. Richardson, CM | 2-D | 16,499 | 1,170 |
| DePauw U, Greencastle, IN 46135 | 1837 | Dr. Robert G. Bottoms | 2-B | 2,058 | 217 |
| Detroit Coll of Business, Dearborn, MI 48126 | 1962 | Dr. James Mendola | 1-B | 2,872 | 142 |
| Detroit Coll of Business, Warren Cmps, Warren, MI 48092 | 1975 | Ms. Janet Guggenheim | 1-B | 1,397 | 106 |
| DeVry Inst of Tech, Phoenix, AZ 85021 | 1967 | Mr. James A. Dugan | 3-B | 2,583 | 86 |
| DeVry Inst of Tech, Pomona, CA 91768-2642 | 1983 | Mr. David G. Moore | 3-B | 2,112 | 71 |
| DeVry Inst of Tech, Decatur, GA 30030 | 1969 | Dr. Ronald Bush | 3-B | 2,801 | 81 |
| DeVry Inst of Tech, Addison, IL 60101-6106 | 1982 | Mr. Jerry R. Dill | 3-B | 2,687 | 102 |
| DeVry Inst of Tech, Chicago, IL 60518 | 1931 | Dr. E. Arthur Stunnard | 3-B | 3,192 | 112 |
| DeVry Inst of Tech, Kansas City, MO 64131 | 1931 | Mr. Charles R. Levalley | 3-B | 1,781 | 76 |
| DeVry Inst of Tech, Columbus, OH 43209-2705 | 1952 | Mr. Richard A. Czerniak | 3-B | 2,752 | 91 |
| DeVry Inst of Tech, Irving, TX 75038-2440 | 1969 | Dr. Francis V. Cannon | 3-B | 2,141 | 99 |
| Dickinson Coll, Carlisle, PA 17013-2896 | 1773 | Dr. A. Lee Fritschler | 1-B | 2,047 | 188 |
| Dickinson State U, Dickinson, ND 58601-4896 | 1918 | Dr. Albert A. Watrel | 5-B | 1,605 | 98 |
| Dillard U, New Orleans, LA 70122 | 1869 | Dr. Samuel DuBois Cook | 2-B | 1,625 | 124 |
| Dominican Coll of Blauvelt, Orangeburg, NY 10962 | 1952 | Sr. Kathleen Sullivan | 1-B | 1,500 | 162 |
| Dordt Coll, Sioux Center, IA 51250-1697 | 1955 | Dr. John B. Hulst | 2-B | 1,077 | 90 |
| Dowling Coll, Oakdale, NY 11769 | 1955 | Dr. Victor P. Meskill | 1-M | 5,146 | 387 |
| Drake U, Des Moines, IA 50311 | 1881 | Dr. Michael R. Ferrari | 1-D | 6,333 | 278 |
| Drew U, Madison, NJ 07940 | 1867 | Mr. Thomas H. Kean | 2-D | 2,045 | 220 |
| Drexel U, Philadelphia, PA 19104-2875 | 1891 | Dr. Richard D. Breslin | 1-D | 11,038 | 841 |
| Drury Coll, Springfield, MO 65802 | 1873 | Dr. John E. Moore, Jr. | 2-M | 1,406 | 129 |
| Duke U, Durham, NC 27708-0586 | 1838 | Dr. Nannerl O. Keohane | 2-D | 11,426 | 2,304 |
| Duquesne U, Pittsburgh, PA 15282 | 1878 | Dr. John E. Murray, Jr. | 2-D | 8,359 | 638 |
| Dyke Coll, Cleveland, OH 44115 | 1848 | Dr. John C. Corfias | 1-B | 1,426 | 92 |
| D'Youville Coll, Buffalo, NY 14201 | 1908 | Dr. Denise A. Roche, GNSH | 1-M | 1,650 | 128 |
| Earlham Coll, Richmond, IN 47374 | 1847 | Dr. Richard J. Wood | 2-M | 1,106 | 108 |
| East Carolina U, Greenville, NC 27858-4353 | 1907 | Dr. Richard Eakin | 5-D | 17,757 | 1,188 |
| East Central U, Ada, OK 74820 | 1909 | Dr. Bill S. Cole | 5-M | 4,388 | 200 |
| Eastern Coll, St Davids, PA 19087-3696 | 1932 | Dr. Roberta Hestenes | 2-M | 1,745 | 141 |
| Eastern Connecticut State U, Willimantic, CT 06226 | 1889 | Mr. David G. Carter | 5-M | 4,328 | 195 |
| Eastern Illinois U, Charleston, IL 61920-3099 | 1895 | Mr. David L. Jorns | 5-M | 11,411 | 676 |
| Eastern Kentucky U, Richmond, KY 40475 | 1906 | Dr. Hanly Funderburk | 5-M | 16,866 | 829 |
| Eastern Mennonite Coll, Harrisonburg, VA 22801 | 1917 | Dr. Joseph L. Lapp | 2-M | 1,070 | 104 |
| Eastern Michigan U, Ypsilanti, MI 48197 | 1849 | Dr. William E. Shelton | 5-D | 25,620 | 1,081 |
| Eastern Montana Coll, Billings, MT 59101 | 1927 | Dr. Bruce H. Carpenter | 5-M | 3,761 | 192 |
| Eastern Nazarene Coll, Quincy, MA 02170-2999 | 1918 | Dr. Kent R. Hill | 2-M | 1,283 | 66 |
| Eastern New Mexico U, Portales, NM 88130 | 1934 | Dr. Everett L. Frost | 5-M | 3,916 | 224 |
| Eastern Oregon State Coll, La Grande, OR 97850 | 1929 | Mr. David E. Gilbert | 5-M | 2,171 | 145 |
| Eastern Washington U, Cheney, WA 99004-2496 | 1882 | Dr. Marshall Drummond | 5-M | 8,363 | 423 |
| East Stroudsburg U of Pennsylvania, East Stroudsburg, PA 18301-2999 | 1893 | Dr. James Gilbert | 5-M | 5,352 | 273 |
| East Tennessee State U, Johnson City, TN 37614 | 1911 | Dr. Roy S. Nicks | 5-D | 12,055 | 629 |
| East Texas Baptist U, Marshall, TX 75670-1498 | 1912 | Dr. Bob E. Riley | 2-M | 1,187 | 75 |
| East Texas State U, Commerce, TX 75429-3011 | 1889 | Dr. Jerry D. Morris | 5-D | 8,344 | 360 |
| East Texas State U at Texarkana, Texarkana, TX 75505-0518 | 1971 | Dr. John F. Moss | 5-M | 1,399 | 59 |
| Eckerd Coll, St Petersburg, FL 33733 | 1958 | Dr. Peter H. Armacost | 2-B | 1,368 | 113 |
| Edgewood Coll, Madison, WI 53711 | 1927 | Dr. James A. Ebben | 2-M | 1,692 | 111 |
| Edinboro U of Pennsylvania, Edinboro, PA 16444 | 1857 | Mr. Foster F. Diebold | 5-M | 8,202 | 417 |
| Elizabeth City State U, Elizabeth City, NC 27909 | 1891 | Dr. Jimmy R. Jenkins | 5-B | 2,100 | 133 |
| Elizabethtown Coll, Elizabethtown, PA 17022-2298 | 1899 | Dr. Gerhard E. Spiegler | 2-B | 1,864 | 157 |
| Elmhurst Coll, Elmhurst, IL 60126-3296 | 1871 | Dr. Ivan E. Frick | 2-B | 2,725 | 140 |
| Elmira Coll, Elmira, NY 14901 | 1855 | Dr. Thomas K. Meier | 1-M | 1,076 | 75 |
| Elms Coll, Chicopee, MA 01013 (3) | 1928 | Sr. Mary A. Dooley | 2-M | 1,150 | 94 |
| Elon Coll, Elon College, NC 27244 | 1889 | Dr. J. Fred Young | 2-M | 3,227 | 238 |
| Embry-Riddle Aeronautical U, Daytona Beach, FL 32114-3900 | 1926 | Dr. Steven M. Sliwa | 1-M | 4,508 | 232 |
| Embry-Riddle Aeronautical U, Coll of Continuing Ed, Daytona Beach, FL 32114 | 1970 | NR | 1-M | 4,707 | 1,782 |
| Embry-Riddle Aeronautical U, Western Cmps, Prescott, AZ 86301 | 1978 | Mr. Paul S. Daly | 1-B | 1,661 | 86 |
| Emerson Coll, Boston, MA 02116 | 1880 | Dr. Jacqueline W. Liebergott | 1-D | 2,776 | 246 |
| Emmanuel Coll, Boston, MA 02115 (3) | 1919 | Sr. Janet Eisner, SND | 2-M | 1,393 | 100 |
| Emory U, Atlanta, GA 30322 | 1836 | Dr. James T. Laney | 2-D | 9,958 | 1,929 |
| Emporia State U, Emporia, KS 66801-5087 | 1863 | Dr. Robert E. Glennen | 5-M | 6,006 | 244 |
| Eugene Lang Coll, New Sch for Social Research, New York, NY 10011 | 1985 | Dr. Beatrice Banu | 1-B | 320 | 60 |
| Evangel Coll, Springfield, MO 65802 | 1955 | Dr. Robert H. Spence | 2-B | 1,420 | 115 |
| Evergreen State Coll, Olympia, WA 98505 | 1967 | Dr. Jane Jervis | 5-M | 3,410 | 179 |
| Fairfield U, Fairfield, CT 06430 | 1942 | Rev. Aloysius P. Kelley, SJ | 2-M | 4,873 | 319 |
| Fairleigh Dickinson U, Madison, NJ 07940 | 1942 | Dr. Francis J. Mertz | 1-D | 8,451 | 606 |
| Fairmont State Coll, Fairmont, WV 26554 | 1865 | Dr. Robert J. Dillman | 5-B | 6,615 | 349 |
| Fashion Inst of Tech, New York, NY 10001-5992 | 1944 | Mr. Allan F. Hershfield | 12-M | 12,121 | 820 |
| Faulkner U, Montgomery, AL 36109-3398 | 1942 | Dr. Billy D. Hilyer | 2-D | 1,990 | 125 |
| Fayetteville State U, Fayetteville, NC 28301 | 1867 | Dr. Lloyd V. Hackley | 5-M | 3,902 | 220 |
| Felician Coll, Lodi, NJ 07644 | 1942 | Sr. Theresa Martin | 2-B | 1,002 | 99 |
| Ferris State U, Big Rapids, MI 49307 | 1884 | Dr. Helen Popovich | 5-M | 12,461 | 751 |
| Ferrum Coll, Ferrum, VA 24088 | 1913 | Dr. Jerry M. Boone | 2-B | 1,234 | 102 |
| Fitchburg State Coll, Fitchburg, MA 01420-2697 | 1894 | Dr. Vincent J. Mara | 5-M | 5,317 | 243 |
| Flagler Coll, St Augustine, FL 32085 | 1968 | Dr. William L. Proctor | 1-B | 1,275 | 112 |

| Name, address | Year | Governing official, control, and highest degree offered | Enrollment | Faculty |
|---|---|---|---|---|
| Florida A&M U, Tallahassee, FL 32307 | 1887 | Dr. Frederick Humphries ... 5-D | 9,508 | 670 |
| Florida Atlantic U, Boca Raton, FL 33431 | 1961 | Dr. Anthony James Catanese 5-D | 14,778 | 563 |
| Florida Inst of Tech, Melbourne, FL 32901-6988 | 1958 | Dr. Lynn E. Weaver ... 1-D | 5,826 | 459 |
| Florida International U, Miami, FL 33199 | 1965 | Dr. Modesto A. Maidique ... 5-D | 19,142 | 1,143 |
| Florida Memorial Coll, Miami, FL 33054 | 1879 | Dr. Albert E. Smith ... 2-B | 1,489 | NR |
| Florida Southern Coll, Lakeland, FL 33801 | 1885 | Dr. Robert A. Davis ... 2-M | 2,604 | 120 |
| Florida State U, Tallahassee, FL 32306 | 1857 | Dr. Dale W. Lick ... 5-D | 28,512 | 1,526 |
| Fontbonne Coll, St Louis, MO 63105 | 1917 | Dr. Meneve Dunham ... 2-M | 1,989 | 131 |
| Fordham U, New York, NY 10458 | 1841 | Rev. Joseph A. O'Hare, SJ . 2-D | 14,612 | 759 |
| Fort Hays State U, Hays, KS 67601 | 1902 | Dr. Edward H. Hammond . 5-M | 5,603 | 265 |
| Fort Lauderdale Coll, Fort Lauderdale, FL 33304 | 1940 | Mr. William P. Bedard ... 3-M | 1,120 | 34 |
| Fort Lewis Coll, Durango, CO 81301-3999 | 1911 | Mr. Joel M. Jones ... 5-B | 4,096 | 230 |
| Fort Valley State Coll, Fort Valley, GA 31030 | 1895 | Dr. Oscar L. Prater ... 5-M | 2,368 | 154 |
| Framingham State Coll, Framingham, MA 01701 | 1839 | Dr. Paul F. Weller ... 5-M | 5,146 | 220 |
| Franciscan U of Steubenville, Steubenville, OH 43952 | 1946 | Rev. Michael Scanlan, TOR . 2-M | 1,812 | 128 |
| Francis Marion U, Florence, SC 29501-0547 | 1970 | Dr. Thomas C. Stanton ... 5-M | 3,975 | 209 |
| Franklin and Marshall Coll, Lancaster, PA 17604-3003 | 1787 | Dr. A. Richard Kneedler ... 1-B | 1,800 | 197 |
| Franklin Pierce Coll, Rindge, NH 03461-0060 | 1962 | Dr. Walter Peterson ... 1-B | 1,235 | 106 |
| Franklin U, Columbus, OH 43215 | 1902 | Dr. Paul J. Otte ... 1-B | 3,852 | 196 |
| Freed-Hardeman U, Henderson, TN 38340 | 1869 | Dr. Milton R. Sewell ... 2-M | 1,236 | 91 |
| Fresno Pacific Coll, Fresno, CA 93702 | 1944 | Dr. Richard Kriegbaum ... 2-M | 1,530 | 157 |
| Friends U, Wichita, KS 67213 | 1898 | Dr. Biff Green ... 2-M | 1,540 | 88 |
| Frostburg State U, Frostburg, MD 21532 | 1898 | Dr. Catherine R. Gira ... 5-M | 5,295 | 305 |
| Furman U, Greenville, SC 29613 | 1826 | Dr. John E. Johns ... 1-M | 2,936 | 204 |
| Gallaudet U, Washington, DC 20002-3625 | 1856 | Dr. I. King Jordan ... 1-M | 2,287 | 330 |
| Gannon U, Erie, PA 16541 | 1925 | Msgr. David Rubino, PhD ... 2-M | 4,384 | 331 |
| Gardner-Webb U, Boiling Springs, NC 28017 | 1905 | Dr. M. Christopher White ... 2-M | 2,053 | 163 |
| Geneva Coll, Beaver Falls, PA 15010 | 1848 | Dr. John H. White ... 2-M | 1,438 | 102 |
| George Fox Coll, Newberg, OR 97132 | 1891 | Dr. Edward F. Stevens ... 2-D | 1,439 | 133 |
| George Mason U, Fairfax, VA 22030 | 1957 | Dr. George W. Johnson ... 5-D | 20,829 | 1,114 |
| Georgetown Coll, Georgetown, KY 40324-1696 | 1829 | Dr. William H. Crouch, Jr. . 2-M | 1,476 | 94 |
| Georgetown U, Washington, DC 20057 | 1789 | Rev. Leo J. O'Donovan, SJ . 2-D | 12,084 | 1,740 |
| George Washington U, Washington, DC 20052 | 1821 | Mr. Stephen J. Trachtenberg 1-D | 16,293 | 2,308 |
| Georgia Coll, Milledgeville, GA 31061 | 1889 | Dr. Edwin G. Speir ... 5-M | 5,501 | 264 |
| Georgia Inst of Tech, Atlanta, GA 30332 | 1885 | Dr. John P. Crecine ... 5-D | 12,891 | 658 |
| Georgian Court Coll, Lakewood, NJ 08701-2697 (4) | 1908 | Sr. Barbara Williams ... 2-M | 2,503 | 182 |
| Georgia Southern U, Statesboro, GA 30460 | 1906 | Dr. Nicholas Henry ... 5-M | 13,411 | 615 |
| Georgia Southwestern Coll, Americus, GA 31709 | 1906 | Dr. William H. Capitan ... 5-M | 2,533 | 155 |
| Georgia State U, Atlanta, GA 30303 | 1913 | Dr. Carl V. Patton ... 5-D | 24,101 | 1,221 |
| Gettysburg Coll, Gettysburg, PA 17325 | 1832 | Dr. Gordon A. Haaland ... 2-B | 1,950 | 174 |
| Glenville State Coll, Glenville, WV 26351 | 1872 | Dr. William K. Simmons ... 5-B | 2,358 | 152 |
| GMI Engineering & Management Inst, Flint, MI 48504-4898 | 1919 | Dr. James E. A. John ... 1-M | 3,141 | 130 |
| Golden Gate U, San Francisco, CA 94105 | 1901 | Dr. Thomas M. Stauffer ... 1-D | 7,490 | 826 |
| Goldey-Beacom Coll, Wilmington, DE 19808 | 1886 | Mr. William R. Baldt ... 1-M | 1,757 | 70 |
| Gonzaga U, Spokane, WA 99258 | 1887 | Rev. Bernard J. Coughlin, SJ 2-D | 5,214 | 230 |
| Gordon Coll, Wenham, MA 01984 | 1889 | Dr. R. Judson Carlberg ... 2-B | 1,234 | 101 |
| Governors State U, University Park, IL 60466 | 1969 | Dr. Paula Wolff ... 5-M | 5,194 | 307 |
| Graceland Coll, Lamoni, IA 50140 | 1895 | Dr. William T. Higdon ... 2-B | 1,058 | 77 |
| Grambling State U, Grambling, LA 71245 | 1901 | Dr. Harold Lundy ... 5-M | 7,533 | 224 |
| Grand Canyon U, Phoenix, AZ 85017 | 1949 | Dr. Bill Williams ... 2-M | 1,747 | 164 |
| Grand Valley State U, Allendale, MI 49401 | 1960 | Mr. Arend D. Lubbers ... 5-M | 12,867 | 599 |
| Grand View Coll, Des Moines, IA 50316-1599 | 1896 | Dr. Arthur E. Puotinen ... 2-B | 1,478 | 120 |
| Greensboro Coll, Greensboro, NC 27401 | 1838 | Dr. Craven E. Williams ... 2-B | 1,000 | 81 |
| Grinnell Coll, Grinnell, IA 50112 | 1846 | Dr. Pamela A. Ferguson ... 1-B | 1,240 | 151 |
| Grove City Coll, Grove City, PA 16127-2104 | 1876 | Dr. Jerry H. Combee ... 2-B | 2,217 | 141 |
| Guilford Coll, Greensboro, NC 27410 | 1837 | Dr. William R. Rogers ... 2-B | 1,202 | 111 |
| Gustavus Adolphus Coll, St Peter, MN 56082 | 1862 | Dr. Axel D. Steuer ... 2-B | 2,275 | 217 |
| Gwynedd-Mercy Coll, Gwynedd Valley, PA 19437 | 1948 | Sr. Isabelle Keiss, RSM ... 2-M | 1,653 | 173 |
| Hahnemann U, Philadelphia, PA 19102 | 1848 | Mr. Iqbal F. Paroo ... 1-D | 1,551 | 430 |
| Hamilton Coll, Clinton, NY 13323 | 1812 | Dr. Harry C. Payne ... 1-B | 1,710 | 192 |
| Hamline U, St Paul, MN 55104 | 1854 | Dr. Larry G. Osnes ... 2-F | 2,465 | 230 |
| Hampshire Coll, Amherst, MA 01002 | 1965 | Dr. Gregory S. Prince, Jr. . 1-B | 1,173 | 99 |
| Hampton U, Hampton, VA 23668 | 1868 | Dr. William R. Harvey ... 1-D | 5,704 | 390 |
| Hanover Coll, Hanover, IN 47243 | 1827 | Dr. Russell L. Nichols ... 2-B | 1,071 | 103 |
| Harding U, Searcy, AR 72149 | 1924 | Dr. David B. Burks, Jr. ... 2-M | 3,463 | 201 |
| Hardin-Simmons U, Abilene, TX 79698-0001 | 1891 | Dr. Lanny Hall ... 2-M | 1,950 | 90 |
| Harris-Stowe State Coll, St Louis, MO 63103 | 1857 | Dr. Henry Givens, Jr. ... 5-B | 1,945 | 99 |
| Hartwick Coll, Oneonta, NY 13820 | 1797 | Dr. Richard A. Detweiler ... 1-B | 1,470 | 139 |
| Harvard U, Cambridge, MA 02138 | 1636 | Dr. Neil Rudenstine ... 1-D | 18,273 | 2,278 |
| Hastings Coll, Hastings, NE 68902 | 1882 | Dr. Thomas J. Reeves ... 2-M | 1,016 | 86 |
| Haverford Coll, Haverford, PA 19041-1392 | 1833 | Dr. Tom G. Kessinger ... 1-B | 1,138 | 107 |
| Hawaii Pacific U, Honolulu, HI 96813 | 1965 | Mr. Chatt Wright ... 1-M | 6,976 | 381 |
| Heidelberg Coll, Tiffin, OH 44883 | 1850 | Dr. William C. Cassell ... 2-M | 1,182 | 113 |
| Henderson State U, Arkadelphia, AR 71999-0001 | 1890 | Dr. Charles D. Dunn ... 5-M | 3,742 | 173 |
| High Point U, High Point, NC 27262-3598 | 1924 | Dr. Jacob C. Martinson, Jr. . 2-B | 2,326 | 108 |
| Hillsdale Coll, Hillsdale, MI 49242 | 1844 | Dr. George C. Roche, III ... 1-B | 1,080 | 108 |
| Hobart Coll, Geneva, NY 14456 (1) | 1822 | Dr. Richard H. Hersh ... 2-B | 1,061 | 177 |
| Hofstra U, Hempstead, NY 11550 | 1935 | Dr. James M. Shuart ... 1-D | 11,998 | 984 |
| Holy Family Coll, Philadelphia, PA 19114-2094 | 1954 | Sr. Francesca Onley ... 2-M | 2,465 | 224 |
| Hood Coll, Frederick, MD 21701-8575 (4) | 1893 | Dr. Martha E. Church ... 2-M | 2,005 | 94 |
| Hope Coll, Holland, MI 49422-9000 | 1862 | Dr. John H. Jacobson, Jr. . 2-B | 2,755 | 233 |
| Houghton Coll, Houghton, NY 14744 | 1883 | Dr. Daniel R. Chamberlain . 2-M | 1,140 | 100 |
| Houston Baptist U, Houston, TX 77074 | 1960 | Dr. E. Douglas Hodo ... 2-M | 2,200 | 145 |
| Howard Payne U, Brownwood, TX 76801 | 1889 | Dr. Don Newbury ... 2-B | 1,427 | 108 |
| Howard U, Washington, DC 20059 | 1867 | Dr. Franklyn G. Jenifer ... 1-D | 11,941 | 780 |
| Humboldt State U, Arcata, CA 95521-8299 | 1913 | Dr. Alistair W. McCrone ... 5-M | 7,851 | 551 |
| Hunter Coll of the City U of New York, New York, NY 10021 | 1870 | Dr. Paul Le Clerc ... 12-M | 18,390 | 696 |
| Huron U, Huron, SD 57350 | 1883 | NR ... 3-M | 1,076 | 78 |
| Husson Coll, Bangor, ME 04401 | 1898 | Dr. William H. Beardsley ... 1-M | 2,080 | 67 |
| Idaho State U, Pocatello, ID 83209 | 1901 | Dr. Richard Bowen ... 5-D | 10,755 | 601 |
| Illinois Benedictine Coll, Lisle, IL 60532-0900 | 1887 | Dr. Richard C. Becker ... 2-M | 2,982 | 245 |
| Illinois Inst of Tech, Chicago, IL 60616 | 1890 | Mr. Lewis Collens ... 1-D | 6,693 | 498 |
| Illinois State U, Normal, IL 61761 | 1857 | Dr. Thomas P. Wallace ... 5-D | 21,765 | 947 |
| Illinois Wesleyan U, Bloomington, IL 61702 | 1850 | Dr. Minor Myers, Jr. ... 2-B | 1,822 | 180 |

| Name, address | Year | Governing official, control, and highest degree offered | | Enroll-ment | Faculty |
|---|---|---|---|---|---|
| Immaculata Coll, Immaculata, PA 19345-0900 (4) | 1920 | Sr. Marie Roseanne Bonfini | 2-M | 2,522 | 167 |
| Incarnate Word Coll, San Antonio, TX 78209 | 1881 | Dr. Louis J. Agnese, Jr. | 2-M | 2,801 | 196 |
| Indiana Inst of Tech, Fort Wayne, IN 46803 | 1930 | Mr. Donald J. Andorfer | 1-B | 1,150 | 42 |
| Indiana State U, Terre Haute, IN 47809 | 1865 | Dr. John W. Moore | 5-D | 12,271 | 718 |
| Indiana U at South Bend, South Bend, IN 46634 | 1922 | Dr. H. Daniel Cohen | 5-M | 7,801 | 557 |
| Indiana U Bloomington, Bloomington, IN 47405 | 1820 | Dr. Kenneth R. R. Gros Louis | 5-D | 36,076 | 1,575 |
| Indiana U East, Richmond, IN 47374 | 1971 | Dr. Charlie Nelms | 5-B | 2,411 | 179 |
| Indiana U Kokomo, Kokomo, IN 46904 | 1945 | Dr. Ernita B. Hill | 5-M | 3,522 | 195 |
| Indiana U Northwest, Gary, IN 46408 | 1959 | Dr. Hilda Richards | 5-M | 5,963 | 372 |
| Indiana U of Pennsylvania, Indiana, PA 15705 | 1875 | Dr. Lawrence K. Pettit | 5-D | 14,357 | 758 |
| Indiana U–Purdue U at Fort Wayne, Fort Wayne, IN 46805-1499 | 1917 | Dr. Joanne B. Lantz | 5-M | 12,090 | 667 |
| Indiana U–Purdue U at Indianapolis, Indianapolis, IN 46202-2896 | 1969 | Mr. Gerald L. Bepko | 5-D | 28,345 | 2,065 |
| Indiana U Southeast, New Albany, IN 47150 | 1941 | Dr. Leon Rand | 5-M | 5,942 | 335 |
| Indiana Wesleyan U, Marion, IN 46953 | 1920 | Dr. James Barnes | 2-M | 3,450 | 105 |
| Inter American U of PR, Arecibo Cmps, Arecibo, PR 00613 | 1957 | Dr. Zaida Vega | 1-B | 4,509 | 231 |
| Inter Amer U of PR, Barranquitas Regional Coll, Barranquitas, PR 00618 | 1957 | Mr. Vidal Rivera Garcia | 1-B | 1,424 | 75 |
| Inter American U of PR, San Germán Cmps, San Germán, PR 00683 | 1912 | Prof. Agnes Mojica | 1-M | 5,553 | 277 |
| International Correspondence Inst, Irving, TX 75063 | 1967 | NR | 2-B | 11,800 | NR |
| Iona Coll, New Rochelle, NY 10801 | 1940 | Br. John G. Driscoll, CFC | 1-M | 7,397 | 511 |
| Iowa State U of Science and Tech, Ames, IA 50011 | 1858 | Dr. Martin C. Jischke | 5-D | 25,263 | 1,759 |
| Ithaca Coll, Ithaca, NY 14850 | 1892 | Dr. James J. Whalen | 1-M | 6,058 | 597 |
| ITT Tech Inst, Indianapolis, IN 46268 | 1966 | Mr. Larry L. Graphman | 3-B | 1,035 | 44 |
| Jackson State U, Jackson, MS 39217 | 1877 | Dr. James E. Lyons, Sr. | 5-D | 6,203 | 380 |
| Jacksonville State U, Jacksonville, AL 36265-9982 | 1883 | Dr. Harold J. McGee | 5-M | 8,022 | 349 |
| Jacksonville U, Jacksonville, FL 32211 | 1934 | Dr. James J. Brady | 1-M | 2,567 | 245 |
| James Madison U, Harrisonburg, VA 22807 | 1908 | Dr. Ronald E. Carrier | 5-M | 11,203 | 777 |
| Jamestown Coll, Jamestown, ND 58405 | 1883 | Dr. James Walker | 2-B | 1,083 | 68 |
| Jersey City State Coll, Jersey City, NJ 07305 | 1927 | Dr. Carlos Hernandez | 5-M | 7,193 | 434 |
| John Brown U, Siloam Springs, AR 72761 | 1919 | Dr. John E. Brown, III | 2-B | 1,018 | 88 |
| John Carroll U, University Heights, OH 44118 | 1886 | Rev. Michael J. Lavelle, SJ | 2-M | 4,488 | 333 |
| John F Kennedy U, Orinda, CA 94563 | 1964 | Mr. Charles E. Glasser | 1-F | 1,753 | 86 |
| John Jay Coll of Criminal Justice of City U of NY, New York, NY 10019 | 1964 | Dr. Gerald Lynch | 12-M | 8,500 | 496 |
| Johns Hopkins U, Baltimore, MD 21218 | 1876 | Dr. William C. Richardson | 1-D | 4,613 | 473 |
| Johnson & Wales U, Providence, RI 02903 | 1914 | Dr. John A. Yena | 1-M | 7,920 | 312 |
| Johnson C Smith U, Charlotte, NC 28216 | 1867 | Dr. Robert L. Albright | 1-B | 1,266 | 96 |
| Johnson State Coll, Johnson, VT 05656 | 1828 | Dr. Robert Hahn | 5-M | 1,758 | 140 |
| Jones Coll, Jacksonville, FL 32211 | 1918 | Mrs. Dorothy D. Jones | 1-B | 1,000 | 57 |
| Juniata Coll, Huntingdon, PA 16652-2119 | 1876 | Dr. Robert W. Neff | 1-B | 1,050 | 104 |
| Kalamazoo Coll, Kalamazoo, MI 49006 | 1833 | Dr. Lawrence Bryan | 1-B | 1,245 | 109 |
| Kansas Newman Coll, Wichita, KS 67213 | 1933 | Sr. Tarcisia Roths | 2-B | 1,618 | 170 |
| Kansas State U, Manhattan, KS 66506 | 1863 | Dr. Jon Wefald | 5-D | 21,224 | 1,083 |
| Kean Coll of New Jersey, Union, NJ 07083 | 1855 | Dr. Elsa Gomez | 5-M | 12,497 | 824 |
| Keene State Coll, Keene, NH 03431 | 1909 | Dr. Judith A. Sturnick | 5-M | 3,987 | 350 |
| Kennesaw State Coll, Marietta, GA 30061 | 1963 | Dr. Betty L. Siegel | 5-M | 11,670 | 449 |
| Kent State U, Kent, OH 44242-0001 | 1910 | Dr. Carol A. Cartwright | 5-D | 24,100 | 1,340 |
| Kentucky State U, Frankfort, KY 40601 | 1886 | Dr. Mary L. Smith | 13-M | 2,545 | 158 |
| Kenyon Coll, Gambier, OH 43022-9623 | 1824 | Dr. Philip H. Jordan, Jr. | 1-B | 1,488 | 164 |
| King's Coll, Wilkes-Barre, PA 18711-0801 | 1946 | Rev. James Lackenmier, CSC | 2-M | 2,356 | 162 |
| Kutztown U of Pennsylvania, Kutztown, PA 19530 | 1866 | Dr. David E. McFarland | 5-M | 7,791 | 400 |
| Lafayette Coll, Easton, PA 18042 | 1826 | Dr. Robert I. Rotberg | 2-B | 2,225 | 228 |
| Lakeland Coll, Sheboygan, WI 53082-0359 | 1862 | Dr. David R. Black | 2-M | 2,656 | 165 |
| Lake Superior State U, Sault Sainte Marie, MI 49783 | 1946 | Dr. Robert D. Arbuckle | 5-M | 3,384 | 179 |
| Lamar U–Beaumont, Beaumont, TX 77705 | 1923 | Dr. Rex Cottle | 5-D | 11,295 | 725 |
| Lambuth U, Jackson, TN 38301 | 1843 | Dr. Thomas F. Boyd | 2-B | 1,153 | 87 |
| Lander U, Greenwood, SC 29649-2099 | 1872 | Dr. William C. Moran | 5-M | 2,521 | 162 |
| La Roche Coll, Pittsburgh, PA 15237 | 1963 | Msgr. William Kerr | 2-M | 1,763 | 123 |
| La Salle U, Philadelphia, PA 19141 | 1863 | Br. Joseph Burke | 2-M | 5,900 | 324 |
| La Sierra U, Riverside, CA 92515 | 1922 | Dr. Fritz Guy | 2-D | 1,524 | 102 |
| Lawrence Tech U, Southfield, MI 48075 | 1932 | Dr. Richard E. Marburger | 1-M | 4,886 | 307 |
| Lawrence U, Appleton, WI 54912 | 1847 | Dr. Richard Warch | 1-M | 1,202 | 136 |
| Lebanon Valley Coll, Annville, PA 17003 | 1866 | Mr. John A. Synodinos | 2-M | 1,535 | 89 |
| Lee Coll, Cleveland, TN 37311 | 1918 | Dr. Paul Conn | 2-B | 1,922 | 157 |
| Lehigh U, Bethlehem, PA 18015-3094 | 1865 | Dr. Peter Likins | 1-D | 6,550 | 484 |
| Lehman Coll of the City U of New York, Bronx, NY 10468 | 1931 | Dr. Ricardo R. Fernandez | 12-M | 9,956 | NR |
| Le Moyne Coll, Syracuse, NY 13214 | 1946 | Rev. Kevin G. O'Connell, SJ | 2-B | 2,403 | 205 |
| LeMoyne-Owen Coll, Memphis, TN 38126 | 1862 | Dr. Doris W. Weathers | 2-B | 1,200 | 100 |
| Lenoir-Rhyne Coll, Hickory, NC 28603 | 1891 | Dr. John E. Trainer, Jr. | 2-M | 1,522 | 120 |
| Lesley Coll, Cambridge, MA 02138 (3) | 1909 | Ms. Margaret A. McKenna | 1-D | 5,129 | 39 |
| LeTourneau U, Longview, TX 75607-7001 | 1946 | Dr. Alvin O. Austin | 1-M | 1,600 | 119 |
| Lewis & Clark Coll, Portland, OR 97219 | 1867 | Dr. Michael J. Mooney | 1-F | 3,453 | 302 |
| Lewis-Clark State Coll, Lewiston, ID 83501 | 1894 | Dr. Lee A. Vickers | 5-B | 3,029 | 120 |
| Lewis U, Romeoville, IL 60441 | 1932 | Br. James Gaffney, FSC | 2-M | 4,102 | 160 |
| Liberty U, Lynchburg, VA 24506-8001 | 1971 | Dr. A. Pierre Guillermin | 2-D | 3,834 | 216 |
| Lincoln Memorial U, Harrogate, TN 37752 | 1897 | Dr. Scott D. Miller | 1-M | 1,860 | 139 |
| Lincoln U, Jefferson City, MO 65102 | 1866 | Dr. Wendell G. Rayburn, Sr. | 13-M | 4,031 | 246 |
| Lincoln U, Lincoln University, PA 19352 | 1854 | Dr. Niara Sudarkasa | 13-M | 1,477 | 138 |
| Lindenwood Coll, St Charles, MO 63301 | 1927 | Dr. Dennis Spellmann | 2-M | 2,825 | 162 |
| Lindsey Wilson Coll, Columbia, KY 42728 | 1903 | Dr. John B. Begley | 2-B | 1,099 | 55 |
| Linfield Coll, McMinnville, OR 97128 | 1849 | Dr. Vivian A. Bull | 2-M | 1,528 | 150 |
| Livingston U, Livingston, AL 35470 | 1835 | Dr. Asa N. Green | 5-M | 1,977 | 110 |
| Lock Haven U of Pennsylvania, Lock Haven, PA 17745-2390 | 1870 | Dr. Craig Dean Willis | 5-M | 3,895 | 226 |
| Long Island U, Brooklyn Cmps, Brooklyn, NY 11201 | 1926 | Dr. David J. Steinberg | 1-F | 6,838 | 507 |
| Long Island U, C W Post Cmps, Brookville, NY 11548 | 1954 | NR | 1-D | 8,220 | 722 |
| Long Island U, Southampton Cmps, Southampton, NY 11968 | 1963 | Dr. David J. Steinberg | 1-M | 1,458 | 120 |
| Longwood Coll, Farmville, VA 23909 | 1839 | Dr. William F. Dorrill | 5-M | 3,202 | 211 |
| Loras Coll, Dubuque, IA 52004 | 1839 | Rev. Msgr. James Barta | 2-M | 1,776 | 133 |
| Louisiana Coll, Pineville, LA 71359 | 1906 | Dr. Robert L. Lynn | 2-B | 1,026 | 77 |

| Name, address | Year | Governing official, control, and highest degree offered | Enrollment | Faculty |
|---|---|---|---|---|
| Louisiana State U and A&M Coll, Baton Rouge, LA 70803 | 1860 | Dr. William E. Davis ...... 5-D | 26,607 | 1,340 |
| Louisiana State U in Shreveport, Shreveport, LA 71115-2399 | 1965 | Dr. John R. Darling, Jr. ..... 5-M | 4,665 | 234 |
| Louisiana State U Medical Ctr, New Orleans, LA 70112 | 1931 | Dr. Perry G. Rigby ...... 5-D | 2,908 | NR |
| Louisiana Tech U, Ruston, LA 71272 | 1894 | Dr. Daniel D. Reneau ...... 5-D | 10,263 | 482 |
| Lourdes Coll, Sylvania, OH 43560 | 1958 | Sr. Ann Francis Klimkowski, OSF ............. 2-B | 1,469 | 119 |
| Loyola Coll, Baltimore, MD 21210-2699 | 1852 | NR .......... 2-M | 6,221 | 406 |
| Loyola Marymount U, Los Angeles, CA 90045-2699 | 1911 | Rev. Thomas P. O'Malley, SJ 2-F | 6,397 | 438 |
| Loyola U Chicago, Chicago, IL 60611 | 1870 | Rev. Raymond C. Baumhart, SJ .......... 2-D | 15,298 | 876 |
| Loyola U, New Orleans, New Orleans, LA 70118 | 1912 | Rev. James C. Carter, SJ .. 2-M | 5,582 | 391 |
| Lubbock Christian U, Lubbock, TX 79407 | 1957 | Dr. Ken Jones ........ 2-M | 1,141 | 97 |
| Luther Coll, Decorah, IA 52101 | 1861 | Dr. H. George Anderson .. 2-B | 2,327 | 193 |
| Lycoming Coll, Williamsport, PA 17701 | 1812 | Dr. James E. Douthat ..... 2-B | 1,478 | 125 |
| Lynchburg Coll, Lynchburg, VA 24501-3199 | 1903 | Dr. Charles O. Warren, Jr. .. 2-M | 2,379 | 186 |
| Lyndon State Coll, Lyndonville, VT 05851 | 1911 | Dr. Margaret R. Williams .. 5-M | 1,195 | 111 |
| Lynn U, Boca Raton, FL 33431 | 1962 | Dr. Donald E. Ross ...... 1-M | 1,200 | 75 |
| Macalester Coll, St Paul, MN 55105-1899 | 1874 | Dr. Robert M. Gavin, Jr. ... 2-B | 1,838 | 187 |
| Madonna U, Livonia, MI 48150-1173 | 1947 | Sr. Mary Francilene ...... 2-M | 4,419 | 241 |
| Malone Coll, Canton, OH 44709 | 1892 | Dr. E. Arthur Self ....... 2-M | 1,801 | 125 |
| Manchester Coll, North Manchester, IN 46962 | 1889 | Dr. Edgar C. Butterbaugh .. 2-M | 1,080 | 102 |
| Manhattan Coll, Riverdale, NY 10471 | 1853 | Br. Thomas J. Scanlan .... 2-B | 3,616 | 276 |
| Manhattanville Coll, Purchase, NY 10577 | 1841 | Dr. Marcia A. Savage ..... 1-M | 1,502 | 207 |
| Mankato State U, Mankato, MN 56002-8400 | 1867 | Dr. Richard R. Rush ...... 5-M | 13,925 | 552 |
| Mannes Coll of Music, New Sch for Social Research, New York, NY 10024 | 1916 | Dr. Charles Kaufman ..... 1-M | 230 | 216 |
| Mansfield U of Pennsylvania, Mansfield, PA 16933 | 1857 | Mr. Rod C. Kelchner ...... 5-M | 3,223 | 188 |
| Marian Coll, Indianapolis, IN 46222 | 1851 | Dr. Daniel A. Felicetti .... 2-B | 1,288 | 138 |
| Marian Coll of Fond du Lac, Fond du Lac, WI 54935 | 1936 | Mr. Matthew G. Flanigan .. 2-M | 2,271 | 103 |
| Marietta Coll, Marietta, OH 45750 | 1835 | Dr. Patrick D. McDonough .. 1-M | 1,379 | 110 |
| Marist Coll, Poughkeepsie, NY 12601 | 1929 | Dr. Dennis J. Murray ..... 1-M | 4,294 | 352 |
| Marquette U, Milwaukee, WI 53233 | 1881 | Rev. Albert J. DiUlio, SJ ... 2-D | 11,017 | 975 |
| Marshall U, Huntington, WV 25755 | 1837 | Dr. J. Wade Gilley ...... 5-D | 12,744 | 589 |
| Mars Hill Coll, Mars Hill, NC 28754 | 1856 | Dr. Fred B. Bentley ...... 2-B | 1,070 | 122 |
| Marygrove Coll, Detroit, MI 48221-2599 | 1910 | Dr. John E. Shay, Jr. ..... 2-M | 1,300 | 60 |
| Marylhurst Coll, Marylhurst, OR 97036 | 1893 | Ms. Nancy A. Wilgenbusch .. 2-M | 1,238 | 223 |
| Marymount Coll, Tarrytown, NY 10591-3796 (4) | 1907 | Dr. Brigid Driscoll, RSHM .. 1-B | 1,142 | 129 |
| Marymount Manhattan Coll, New York, NY 10021 (4) | 1936 | Dr. Regina Peruggi ...... 1-B | 1,600 | 155 |
| Marymount U, Arlington, VA 22207 | 1950 | Sr. M. Majella Berg, RSHM .. 2-M | 3,839 | 333 |
| Maryville Coll of St Louis, St Louis, MO 63141 | 1872 | Dr. Keith Lovin ........ 1-M | 3,722 | 280 |
| Mary Washington Coll, Fredericksburg, VA 22401 | 1908 | Dr. William M. Anderson, Jr. .. 5-M | 3,432 | 228 |
| Marywood Coll, Scranton, PA 18509 | 1915 | Sr. Mary Reap, IHM ..... 2-M | 2,902 | 216 |
| Massachusetts Coll of Art, Boston, MA 02115 | 1873 | Dr. William F. O'Neil ..... 5-M | 1,206 | 92 |
| Mass Coll of Pharmacy and Allied Health Sciences, Boston, MA 02115 | 1823 | Dr. Louis P. Jeffrey ...... 1-D | 1,325 | 122 |
| Massachusetts Inst of Tech, Cambridge, MA 02139 | 1861 | Dr. Charles M. Vest ...... 1-D | 9,798 | 975 |
| McKendree Coll, Lebanon, IL 62254 | 1828 | Dr. Gerrit J. TenBrink .... 2-B | 1,450 | 74 |
| McMurry U, Abilene, TX 79697 | 1923 | Dr. Robert E. Shimp ..... 2-B | 1,518 | 121 |
| McNeese State U, Lake Charles, LA 70609 | 1939 | Dr. Robert D. Hebert ..... 5-M | 8,474 | 342 |
| Medaille Coll, Buffalo, NY 14214 | 1875 | Mr. Kevin I. Sullivan ..... 1-B | 1,215 | 88 |
| Medgar Evers Coll of the City U of New York, Brooklyn, NY 11225 | 1969 | Dr. Edison O. Jackson ... 12-B | 5,000 | 272 |
| Medical Coll of Georgia, Augusta, GA 30912 | 1828 | Dr. Francis J. Tedesco .... 5-D | 2,058 | 751 |
| Medical U of South Carolina, Charleston, SC 29425 | 1824 | Dr. James B. Edwards .... 5-D | 2,290 | 2,435 |
| Memphis State U, Memphis, TN 38152 | 1912 | Dr. V. Lane Rawlins ...... 5-D | 20,578 | 1,120 |
| Mercer U, Macon, GA 31207 | 1833 | Dr. R. Kirby Godsey ..... 2-F | 6,348 | 670 |
| Mercer U, Cecil B Day Cmps, Atlanta, GA 30341 | 1968 | Dr. R. Kirby Godsey ..... 2-M | 1,599 | 44 |
| Mercy Coll, Dobbs Ferry, NY 10522 | 1951 | Dr. Jay Sexter ........ 1-M | 6,211 | 480 |
| Mercyhurst Coll, Erie, PA 16546 | 1926 | Dr. William P. Garvey .... 2-M | 2,308 | 145 |
| Meredith Coll, Raleigh, NC 27607-5298 (3) | 1891 | Dr. John E. Weems ...... 2-M | 2,049 | 200 |
| Merrimack Coll, North Andover, MA 01845 | 1947 | Rev. John E. Deegan, OSA .. 2-B | 2,952 | 169 |
| Messiah Coll, Grantham, PA 17027 | 1909 | Dr. D. Ray Hostetter ..... 2-B | 2,263 | 182 |
| Methodist Coll, Fayetteville, NC 28311 | 1956 | Dr. M. Elton Hendricks ... 2-B | 1,508 | 85 |
| Metropolitan State Coll of Denver, Denver, CO 80217 | 1963 | Dr. Sheila Kaplan ...... 5-B | 17,570 | 908 |
| Metropolitan State U, St Paul, MN 55106-5000 | 1971 | Mr. Richard Green ...... 5-M | 5,390 | 522 |
| Miami U, Oxford, OH 45056 | 1809 | Dr. Paul G. Risser ...... 5-D | 16,104 | 1,027 |
| Michigan State U, East Lansing, MI 48824 | 1855 | Dr. Gordon Guyer ...... 5-D | 40,047 | 4,006 |
| Michigan Tech U, Houghton, MI 49931 | 1885 | Dr. Curtis J. Tompkins ... 5-D | 6,961 | 365 |
| MidAmerica Nazarene Coll, Olathe, KS 66062-1899 | 1966 | Dr. Richard Spindle ..... 2-M | 1,446 | 105 |
| Middlebury Coll, Middlebury, VT 05753 | 1800 | Dr. John McCardell ..... 1-M | 1,960 | 220 |
| Middle Tennessee State U, Murfreesboro, TN 37132 | 1911 | Dr. James E. Walker ..... 5-D | 16,780 | 877 |
| Midwestern State U, Wichita Falls, TX 76308 | 1922 | Dr. Louis J. Rodriguez ... 5-M | 5,764 | 213 |
| Millersville U of Pennsylvania, Millersville, PA 17551-0302 | 1854 | Dr. Joseph A. Caputo .... 5-M | 6,545 | 398 |
| Millikin U, Decatur, IL 62522 | 1901 | Dr. Curtis L. McCray .... 2-B | 1,892 | 187 |
| Millsaps Coll, Jackson, MS 39210 | 1890 | Dr. George M. Harmon ... 2-M | 1,329 | 106 |
| Mills Coll, Oakland, CA 94613 (3) | 1852 | Dr. Janet H. McKay ..... 1-M | 1,083 | 143 |
| Milwaukee Sch of Engineering, Milwaukee, WI 53202-3109 | 1903 | Dr. Hermann Viets ...... 1-M | 3,166 | 253 |
| Minot State U, Minot, ND 58707 | 1913 | Dr. H. Erik Shaar ...... 5-M | 3,797 | 192 |
| Mississippi Coll, Clinton, MS 39058 | 1826 | Dr. Lewis Nobles ...... 2-M | 3,771 | 234 |
| Mississippi State U, Mississippi State, MS 39762 | 1878 | Dr. Donald W. Zacharias .. 5-D | 14,619 | 824 |
| Mississippi U for Women, Columbus, MS 39701 (4) | 1884 | Dr. Clyda S. Rent ...... 5-M | 2,652 | 160 |
| Mississippi Valley State U, Itta Bena, MS 38941 | 1946 | Dr. William W. Sutton ... 5-M | 2,222 | 137 |
| Missouri Baptist Coll, St Louis, MO 63141 | 1968 | Dr. Thomas S. Field ..... 2-B | 1,429 | 79 |
| Missouri Southern State Coll, Joplin, MO 64801-1595 | 1937 | Dr. Julio Leon ........ 5-D | 5,640 | 278 |
| Missouri Valley Coll, Marshall, MO 65340 | 1889 | Dr. Earl J. Reeves ...... 2-B | 1,153 | 68 |
| Missouri Western State Coll, St Joseph, MO 64507-2294 | 1915 | Dr. Janet Gorman Murphy .. 5-B | 5,093 | 296 |
| Molloy Coll, Rockville Centre, NY 11570-1199 | 1955 | Dr. Janet A. Fitzgerald, OP .. 1-M | 1,549 | 188 |
| Monmouth Coll, West Long Branch, NJ 07764-1898 | 1933 | Dr. Rebecca Stafford ..... 1-M | 4,201 | 321 |
| Montana Coll of Mineral Science and Tech, Butte, MT 59701-8997 | 1895 | Dr. Lindsay D. Norman, Jr. .. 5-M | 1,975 | 139 |
| Montana State U, Bozeman, MT 59717 | 1893 | Dr. Michael P. Malone ... 5-D | 10,540 | 663 |
| Montclair State Coll, Upper Montclair, NJ 07043-1624 | 1908 | Dr. Irvin D. Reid ....... 5-M | 13,657 | 816 |
| Moody Bible Inst, Chicago, IL 60610 | 1886 | Dr. Joseph M. Stowell, III .. 2-M | 1,495 | 78 |
| Moorhead State U, Moorhead, MN 56563 | 1885 | Dr. Roland Dille ....... 5-M | 8,723 | 435 |
| Moravian Coll, Bethlehem, PA 18018-8650 | 1742 | Dr. Roger Harry Martin ... 2-M | 1,332 | 129 |
| Morehead State U, Morehead, KY 40351 | 1922 | Dr. Ronald Eaglin ...... 5-M | 9,169 | 391 |

| Name, address | Year | Governing official, control, and highest degree offered | | Enrollment | Faculty |
|---|---|---|---|---|---|
| Morehouse Coll, Atlanta, GA 30314 (1) | 1867 | Dr. Leroy Keith, Jr. | 1-B | 2,990 | 178 |
| Morgan State U, Baltimore, MD 21239 | 1867 | Dr. Earl Richardson | 5-D | 5,307 | 297 |
| Morningside Coll, Sioux City, IA 51106-1751 | 1894 | Dr. Jerry Israel | 2-M | 1,288 | 100 |
| Mount Aloysius Coll, Cresson, PA 16630 | 1939 | Dr. Edward F. Pierce | 2-B | 1,045 | 88 |
| Mount Holyoke Coll, South Hadley, MA 01075 (3) | 1837 | Mrs. Elizabeth T. Kennan | 1-M | 1,932 | 240 |
| Mount Marty Coll, Yankton, SD 57078-3724 | 1936 | Sr. Jacquelyn Ernster | 2-M | 1,104 | 81 |
| Mount Mary Coll, Milwaukee, WI 53222 (3) | 1913 | Sr. Ruth Hollenbach | 2-M | 1,526 | 155 |
| Mount Mercy Coll, Cedar Rapids, IA 52402 | 1928 | Dr. Thomas R. Feld | 2-B | 1,398 | 110 |
| Mount Saint Mary Coll, Newburgh, NY 12550 | 1960 | Sr. Ann Sakac | 1-M | 1,721 | 149 |
| Mount St Mary's Coll, Los Angeles, CA 90049 (4) | 1925 | Sr. Karen Kennelly | 2-M | 1,491 | 177 |
| Mount Saint Mary's Coll, Emmitsburg, MD 21727 | 1808 | Rev. James N. Loughran, SJ | 2-M | 1,723 | 165 |
| Mount Union Coll, Alliance, OH 44601 | 1846 | Dr. Harold M. Kolenbrander | 2-B | 1,410 | 96 |
| Mount Vernon Nazarene Coll, Mount Vernon, OH 43050 | 1964 | Dr. E. LeBron Fairbanks | 2-M | 1,126 | 69 |
| Muhlenberg Coll, Allentown, PA 18104 | 1848 | Mr. Arthur R. Taylor | 2-B | 1,641 | 161 |
| Murray State U, Murray, KY 42071 | 1922 | Dr. Ronald J. Kurth | 5-M | 8,190 | 371 |
| Muskingum Coll, New Concord, OH 43762 | 1837 | Dr. Samuel W. Speck, Jr. | 2-M | 1,135 | 102 |
| National–Louis U, Evanston, IL 60201 | 1886 | NR | 1-D | 7,600 | 243 |
| National U, San Diego, CA 92108 | 1971 | Dr. Jerry C. Lee | 1-M | 8,972 | 1,281 |
| Nazareth Coll of Rochester, Rochester, NY 14618-3790 | 1924 | Dr. Rose Marie Beston | 2-M | 2,673 | 185 |
| Nebraska Wesleyan U, Lincoln, NE 68504 | 1887 | Dr. John W. White, Jr. | 2-B | 1,694 | 151 |
| Neumann Coll, Aston, PA 19014 | 1965 | Dr. Nan B. Hechenberger | 2-M | 1,214 | 111 |
| New Hampshire Coll, Manchester, NH 03106-1045 | 1932 | Dr. Richard A. Gustafson | 1-M | 2,513 | 179 |
| New Jersey Inst of Tech, Newark, NJ 07102 | 1881 | Dr. Saul K. Fenster | 13-D | 7,697 | 452 |
| New Mexico Highlands U, Las Vegas, NM 87701 | 1893 | Dr. Gilbert Sanchez | 5-M | 2,807 | 134 |
| New Mexico Inst of Mining and Tech, Socorro, NM 87801 | 1889 | Dr. Laurence H. Lattman | 5-D | 1,592 | 101 |
| New Mexico State U, Las Cruces, NM 88003 | 1888 | Dr. James E. Halligan | 5-D | 15,500 | 794 |
| New Sch Bach of Arts, New Sch for Social Research, New York, NY 10011 | 1919 | NR | 1-B | 233 | 545 |
| New York Inst of Tech, Old Westbury, NY 11568-8000 | 1955 | Dr. Matthew Schure | 1-F | 10,221 | 1,253 |
| New York U, New York, NY 10011 | 1831 | Dr. L. Jay Oliva | 1-D | 33,973 | 4,110 |
| Niagara U, Niagara University, NY 14109 | 1856 | Rev. Brian J. O'Connell, CM | 1-M | 3,002 | 214 |
| Nicholls State U, Thibodaux, LA 70310 | 1948 | Dr. Donald J. Ayo | 5-M | 7,605 | 265 |
| Nichols Coll, Dudley, MA 01571 | 1815 | Dr. Lowell C. Smith | 1-M | 1,865 | 49 |
| Norfolk State U, Norfolk, VA 23504 | 1935 | Dr. Harrison B. Wilson | 5-M | 8,624 | 526 |
| North Adams State Coll, North Adams, MA 01247 | 1894 | Dr. Thomas D. Aceto | 5-M | 1,694 | 127 |
| North Carolina Ag and Tech State U, Greensboro, NC 27411 | 1891 | Dr. Edward B. Fort | 5-M | 7,580 | 424 |
| North Carolina Central U, Durham, NC 27707 | 1910 | Mr. Julius L. Chambers | 5-M | 5,385 | 376 |
| North Carolina State U, Raleigh, NC 27695 | 1887 | Dr. Larry K. Monteith | 5-D | 27,156 | 1,431 |
| North Central Bible Coll, Minneapolis, MN 55404 | 1930 | Dr. Don H. Argue | 2-B | 1,042 | 68 |
| North Central Coll, Naperville, IL 60566-7063 | 1861 | Dr. Harold R. Wilde | 2-M | 2,535 | 178 |
| North Dakota State U, Fargo, ND 58105 | 1890 | Dr. Jim Ozbun | 5-D | 9,307 | 536 |
| Northeastern Illinois U, Chicago, IL 60625-4699 | 1961 | Dr. Gordon Lamb | 5-M | 10,820 | 496 |
| Northeastern State U, Tahlequah, OK 74464-2399 | 1846 | Dr. W. Roger Webb | 5-M | 9,023 | 329 |
| Northeastern U, Boston, MA 02115 | 1898 | Mr. John A. Curry | 1-D | 27,619 | 2,206 |
| Northeast Louisiana U, Monroe, LA 71209 | 1931 | Mr. Lawson L. Swearingen, Jr. | 5-M | 11,732 | 527 |
| Northeast Missouri State U, Kirksville, MO 63501 | 1867 | Dr. Russell G. Warren | 5-M | 5,941 | 470 |
| Northern Arizona U, Flagstaff, AZ 86011 | 1899 | Dr. Patsy Reed | 5-D | 18,491 | 722 |
| Northern Illinois U, De Kalb, IL 60115-2864 | 1895 | Dr. John E. LaTourette | 5-D | 24,052 | 1,233 |
| Northern Kentucky U, Highland Heights, KY 41099 | 1968 | Dr. Leon E. Boothe | 5-F | 11,218 | 609 |
| Northern Michigan U, Marquette, MI 49855 | 1899 | Dr. William E. Vandament | 5-M | 8,897 | 359 |
| Northern Montana Coll, Havre, MT 59501 | 1929 | Dr. William Daehling | 5-M | 1,742 | 113 |
| Northern State U, Aberdeen, SD 57401 | 1901 | Dr. John Hutchinson | 5-M | 2,667 | 121 |
| North Georgia Coll, Dahlonega, GA 30597 | 1873 | Dr. Delmas J. Allen | 5-M | 2,794 | 147 |
| North Park Coll, Chicago, IL 60625 | 1891 | Dr. David G. Horner | 2-M | 1,107 | 80 |
| Northwestern Coll, Orange City, IA 51041-1996 | 1882 | Dr. James E. Bultman | 2-B | 1,055 | 84 |
| Northwestern Coll, St Paul, MN 55113-1598 | 1902 | Dr. Donald Ericksen | 2-B | 1,244 | 110 |
| Northwestern Oklahoma State U, Alva, OK 73717-9898 | 1897 | Dr. Joe J. Struckle | 5-M | 2,106 | 121 |
| Northwestern State U of Louisiana, Natchitoches, LA 71497 | 1884 | Dr. Robert A. Alost | 5-M | 8,412 | 200 |
| Northwestern U, Evanston, IL 60208 | 1851 | Dr. Arnold R. Weber | 1-D | 12,032 | 1,079 |
| Northwest Missouri State U, Maryville, MO 64468-6001 | 1905 | Dr. Dean L. Hubbard | 5-M | 5,865 | 274 |
| Northwest Nazarene Coll, Nampa, ID 83686 | 1913 | Dr. Gilbert Ford | 2-M | 1,248 | 101 |
| Northwood U, Midland, MI 48640 | 1959 | Dr. David E. Fry | 1-M | 1,701 | 62 |
| Norwich U, Northfield, VT 05663 | 1819 | Dr. Richard Schneider | 1-M | 2,620 | 194 |
| Notre Dame Coll, Manchester, NH 03104 | 1950 | Dr. Carol J. Descoteaux, CSC | 2-M | 1,300 | 98 |
| Nova U, Fort Lauderdale, FL 33314 | 1964 | Dr. Stephen Feldman | 1-D | 10,879 | 435 |
| Oakland U, Rochester, MI 48309 | 1957 | Dr. Sandra Packard | 5-D | 13,068 | 616 |
| Oakwood Coll, Huntsville, AL 35896 | 1896 | Dr. Benjamin F. Reaves | 2-B | 1,225 | 110 |
| Oberlin Coll, Oberlin, OH 44074 | 1833 | Mr. S. Frederick Starr | 1-M | 2,902 | 232 |
| Occidental Coll, Los Angeles, CA 90041 | 1887 | Dr. John B. Slaughter | 1-M | 1,649 | 184 |
| Oglethorpe U, Atlanta, GA 30319 | 1835 | Dr. Donald S. Stanton | 1-M | 1,195 | 102 |
| Ohio Dominican Coll, Columbus, OH 43219 | 1911 | Sr. Mary Andrew Matesich | 2-B | 1,510 | 99 |
| Ohio Northern U, Ada, OH 45810 | 1871 | Dr. DeBow Freed | 2-F | 2,872 | 227 |
| Ohio State U, Columbus, OH 43210 | 1870 | Dr. E. Gordon Gee | 5-D | 52,183 | 3,823 |
| Ohio State U–Lima Cmps, Lima, OH 45804 | 1960 | Dr. Violet I. Meek | 5-B | 1,410 | 74 |
| Ohio State U–Mansfield Cmps, Mansfield, OH 44906 | 1958 | Dr. John O. Riedl, Jr. | 5-B | 1,465 | 75 |
| Ohio State U–Marion Cmps, Marion, OH 43302 | 1957 | Dr. Dominic Dottavio | 5-B | 1,066 | 86 |
| Ohio State U–Newark Cmps, Newark, OH 43055 | 1957 | Dr. Julius S. Greenstein | 5-B | 1,732 | 93 |
| Ohio U, Athens, OH 45701 | 1804 | Dr. Charles J. Ping | 5-D | 18,248 | 920 |
| Ohio U–Chillicothe, Chillicothe, OH 45601 | 1946 | Dr. Delbert Meyer | 5-B | 1,738 | 81 |
| Ohio U–Lancaster, Lancaster, OH 43130 | 1968 | Dr. Raymond Wilkes | 5-M | 1,554 | 127 |
| Ohio U–Zanesville, Zanesville, OH 43701 | 1946 | Dr. Craig D. Laubenthal | 5-M | 1,232 | 49 |
| Ohio Wesleyan U, Delaware, OH 43015 | 1842 | Dr. David L. Warren | 2-B | 2,037 | 179 |
| Oklahoma Baptist U, Shawnee, OK 74801 | 1910 | Dr. Bob R. Agee | 2-B | 2,260 | 155 |
| Oklahoma Christian U of Science and Arts, Oklahoma City, OK 73136 | 1950 | Dr. J. Terry Johnson | 2-M | 1,636 | 124 |
| Oklahoma City U, Oklahoma City, OK 73106 | 1904 | Dr. Jerald C. Walker | 2-F | 4,450 | 263 |
| Oklahoma Panhandle State U, Goodwell, OK 73939 | 1909 | Dr. Ray Brown | 5-B | 1,209 | 83 |
| Oklahoma State U, Stillwater, OK 74078 | 1890 | Dr. John Campbell | 5-D | 19,477 | 896 |
| Old Dominion U, Norfolk, VA 23529 | 1930 | Dr. James V. Koch | 5-D | 16,561 | 1,040 |
| Olivet Nazarene U, Kankakee, IL 60901 | 1907 | Dr. John C. Bowling | 2-M | 1,996 | 115 |
| Oral Roberts U, Tulsa, OK 74171 | 1963 | Mr. Richard Roberts | 2-D | 4,054 | 211 |
| Oregon Health Sciences U, Portland, OR 97201 | 1974 | Dr. Peter O. Kohler | 5-D | 1,388 | 76 |
| Oregon Inst of Tech, Klamath Falls, OR 97601-8801 | 1947 | Dr. Lawrence J. Wolf | 5-B | 2,757 | 182 |

| Name, address | Year | Governing official, control, and highest degree offered | Enrollment | Faculty |
|---|---|---|---|---|
| Oregon State U, Corvallis, OR 97331 | 1868 | Dr. John V. Byrne ...... 5-D | 14,336 | 2,285 |
| Orlando Coll, Orlando, FL 32810 | 1918 | Mrs. Ouida B. Kirby ..... 3-M | 2,127 | 106 |
| Otterbein Coll, Westerville, OH 43081 | 1847 | Dr. C. Brent DeVore ..... 2-M | 2,531 | 186 |
| Ouachita Baptist U, Arkadelphia, AR 71998 | 1886 | Dr. Ben M. Elrod ........ 2-B | 1,296 | 103 |
| Our Lady of Holy Cross Coll, New Orleans, LA 70131 | 1916 | Rev. Thomas E. Chambers, CSC ............. 2-M | 1,145 | 63 |
| Our Lady of the Lake U of San Antonio, San Antonio, TX 78207-4689 | 1911 | Sr. Elizabeth Anne Sueltenfuss ......... 2-M | 2,947 | 171 |
| Pace U, New York, NY 10038 | 1906 | Dr. Patricia Ewers ...... 1-D | 13,567 | 1,053 |
| Pacific Lutheran U, Tacoma, WA 98447 | 1890 | Dr. Loren J. Anderson .... 2-M | 3,451 | 320 |
| Pacific Union Coll, Angwin, CA 94508 | 1882 | Dr. D. Malcolm Maxwell ... 2-M | 1,512 | 134 |
| Pacific U, Forest Grove, OR 97116 | 1849 | Dr. Robert F. Duvall ..... 1-F | 1,575 | 199 |
| Palm Beach Atlantic Coll, West Palm Beach, FL 33416-4708 | 1968 | Dr. Paul R. Corts ....... 2-M | 1,715 | 121 |
| Palmer Coll of Chiropractic, Davenport, IA 52803 | 1895 | Dr. Donald P. Kern ...... 1-F | 1,700 | 129 |
| Parks Coll of Saint Louis U, Cahokia, IL 62206 | 1927 | Dr. Margaret J. Baty ..... 2-B | 1,070 | 109 |
| Parsons Sch of Design, New Sch for Social Research, New York, NY 10011 | 1896 | Mr. Charles S. Olton ..... 1-M | 1,777 | 332 |
| Pembroke State U, Pembroke, NC 28372 | 1887 | Dr. Joseph Oxendine .... 5-M | 3,041 | 193 |
| Pennsylvania Coll of Optometry, Philadelphia, PA 19141 | 1919 | Dr. Thomas L. Lewis ..... 1-F | 5,913 | 75 |
| Penn State U at Erie, The Behrend Coll, Erie, PA 16563 | 1948 | Dr. John M. Lilley ...... 13-M | 3,159 | 140 |
| Penn State U at Harrisburg—The Capital Coll, Middletown, PA 17057-4898 | 1966 | Dr. Ruth Leventhal ..... 13-D | 3,646 | 203 |
| Penn State U Univ Park Cmps, University Park, PA 16802 | 1855 | Dr. Joab L. Thomas ..... 13-D | 38,446 | 2,108 |
| Pepperdine U, Malibu, CA 90263 | 1937 | Dr. David Davenport ..... 2-D | 7,011 | 297 |
| Peru State Coll, Peru, NE 68421 | 1867 | Dr. Robert L. Burns ..... 5-M | 1,592 | 77 |
| Philadelphia Coll of Pharmacy and Science, Philadelphia, PA 19104-4495 | 1821 | Dr. Allen Misher ........ 1-D | 1,786 | 198 |
| Philadelphia Coll of Textiles and Science, Philadelphia, PA 19144 | 1884 | Dr. James P. Gallagher .... 1-M | 3,357 | 113 |
| Pittsburg State U, Pittsburg, KS 66762 | 1903 | Dr. Donald W. Wilson .... 5-M | 6,515 | 289 |
| Plymouth State Coll of the U System of NH, Plymouth, NH 03264 | 1871 | Dr. Theodora J. Kalikow .. 5-M | 4,000 | 263 |
| Point Loma Nazarene Coll, San Diego, CA 92106 | 1902 | Dr. Jim L. Bond ........ 2-M | 2,450 | 138 |
| Point Park Coll, Pittsburgh, PA 15222 | 1960 | Dr. J. Matthew Simon .... 1-M | 2,834 | 194 |
| Polytechnic U, Brooklyn Cmps, Brooklyn, NY 11201-2999 | 1854 | Dr. George Bugliarello ... 1-D | 2,173 | 393 |
| Pomona Coll, Claremont, CA 91711 | 1887 | Dr. Peter W. Stanley ..... 1-B | 1,389 | 188 |
| Pontifical Catholic U of Puerto Rico, Ponce, PR 00732 | 1948 | Rev. F. Tosello Giangiacomo 2-M | 12,366 | 577 |
| Prairie View A&M U, Prairie View, TX 77446 | 1878 | Lt. Gen. Julius W. Becton, Jr. 5-M | 5,660 | 303 |
| Pratt Inst, Brooklyn, NY 11205 | 1887 | Dr. Warren F. Tichman ... 1-M | 2,898 | 447 |
| Presbyterian Coll, Clinton, SC 29325 | 1880 | Dr. Kenneth B. Orr ...... 2-B | 1,167 | 109 |
| Princeton U, Princeton, NJ 08544 | 1746 | Mr. Harold T. Shapiro .... 1-D | 6,438 | 935 |
| Providence Coll, Providence, RI 02918 | 1917 | Rev. John F. Cunningham, OP ............. 2-D | 6,387 | 303 |
| Purdue U, West Lafayette, IN 47907 | 1869 | Dr. Steven C. Beering .... 5-D | 36,163 | 2,269 |
| Purdue U Calumet, Hammond, IN 46323-2094 | 1951 | Dr. James Yackel ....... 5-M | 8,285 | 457 |
| Purdue U North Central, Westville, IN 46391 | 1967 | Dr. Dale W. Alspaugh .... 5-M | 3,588 | 218 |
| Queens Coll, Charlotte, NC 28274 | 1857 | Dr. Billy O. Wireman ..... 2-M | 1,602 | 115 |
| Queens Coll of the City U of New York, Flushing, NY 11367-1597 | 1937 | Dr. Shirley Strum Kenny .. 12-M | 17,921 | 1,274 |
| Quincy U, Quincy, IL 62301 | 1860 | Rev. James Toal, OFM .... 2-M | 1,223 | 98 |
| Quinnipiac Coll, Hamden, CT 06518 | 1929 | Dr. John L. Lahey ....... 1-F | 4,658 | 333 |
| Radford U, Radford, VA 24142 | 1910 | Dr. Donald N. Dedmon ... 5-M | 9,432 | 392 |
| Ramapo Coll of New Jersey, Mahwah, NJ 07430 | 1969 | Dr. Robert A. Scott ..... 5-B | 4,636 | 309 |
| Randolph-Macon Coll, Ashland, VA 23005-5505 | 1830 | Dr. Ladell Payne ....... 2-B | 1,118 | 142 |
| Reed Coll, Portland, OR 97202-8199 | 1909 | Dr. Steven Koblik ....... 1-M | 1,230 | 133 |
| Regis Coll, Weston, MA 02193 (3) | 1927 | Sr. Sheila Megley, RSM ... 1-M | 1,121 | 104 |
| Regis U, Denver, CO 80221 | 1877 | Rev. Michael J. Sheeran, SJ 2-M | 6,471 | 67 |
| Rensselaer Polytechnic Inst, Troy, NY 12180 | 1824 | Dr. R. Byron Pipes ...... 1-D | 6,839 | 465 |
| Rhode Island Coll, Providence, RI 02908 | 1854 | Dr. John Nazarian ...... 5-M | 9,838 | 502 |
| Rhode Island Sch of Design, Providence, RI 02903-2784 | 1877 | Mr. Louis A. Fazzano .... 1-M | 1,986 | 286 |
| Rhodes Coll, Memphis, TN 38112 | 1848 | Dr. James H. Daughdrill, Jr. 2-M | 1,414 | 154 |
| Rice U, Houston, TX 77251 | 1912 | Dr. Malcolm Gillis ...... 1-D | 4,033 | 542 |
| Rider Coll, Lawrenceville, NJ 08648 | 1865 | Dr. J. Barton Luedeke .... 1-M | 5,484 | 448 |
| Rivier Coll, Nashua, NH 03060 | 1933 | Sr. Jeanne Perreault ..... 2-M | 2,765 | 202 |
| Roanoke Coll, Salem, VA 24153 | 1842 | Dr. David M. Gring ...... 2-B | 1,677 | 150 |
| Robert Morris Coll, Coraopolis, PA 15108 | 1921 | Dr. Edward A. Nicholson .. 1-M | 5,566 | 238 |
| Rochester Inst of Tech, Rochester, NY 14623-0887 | 1829 | Dr. Albert J. Simone ..... 1-D | 13,004 | 1,087 |
| Rockford Coll, Rockford, IL 61108-2393 | 1847 | Dr. Bill Shields ........ 1-M | 1,491 | 123 |
| Rockhurst Coll, Kansas City, MO 64110 | 1910 | Rev. Thomas J. Savage, SJ 2-M | 2,702 | 203 |
| Roger Williams U, Bristol, RI 02809 | 1948 | Dr. Malcolm H. Forbes ... 1-B | 2,111 | 229 |
| Rollins Coll, Winter Park, FL 32789-4499 | 1885 | Dr. Rita Bornstein ...... 1-M | 2,093 | 284 |
| Roosevelt U, Chicago, IL 60605 | 1945 | Dr. Theodore L. Gross .... 1-M | 6,444 | 508 |
| Rosary Coll, River Forest, IL 60305 | 1901 | Dr. Jean Murray, OP ..... 2-M | 1,766 | 116 |
| Rose-Hulman Inst of Tech, Terre Haute, IN 47803 (1) | 1874 | Dr. Samuel F. Hulbert .... 1-M | 1,420 | 97 |
| Rowan Coll of New Jersey, Glassboro, NJ 08028 | 1923 | Dr. Herman D. James .... 5-M | 7,983 | 323 |
| Rush U, Chicago, IL 60612 | 1969 | Dr. Leo M. Henikoff ..... 1-M | 1,301 | 170 |
| Rust Coll, Holly Springs, MS 38635 | 1866 | Dr. David L. Beckley ..... 2-B | 1,129 | 61 |
| Rutgers, State U of NJ, Camden Coll of Arts & Scis, Camden, NJ 08102 | 1927 | NR ............... 5-B | 2,672 | NR |
| Rutgers, State U of NJ, Coll of Engineering, Piscataway, NJ 08855-0909 | 1864 | Dr. Ellis H. Dill ........ 5-B | 2,454 | NR |
| Rutgers, State U of NJ, Coll of Nursing, Newark, NJ 07102 | 1956 | Ms. Dorothy J. DeMaio ... 5-D | 391 | NR |
| Rutgers, State U of NJ, Coll of Pharmacy, New Brunswick, NJ 08903-2101 | 1927 | Dr. John Louis Colaizzi ... 5-D | 858 | NR |
| Rutgers, State U of NJ, Cook Coll, New Brunswick, NJ 08903-2101 | 1921 | Mr. Daryl B. Lund ...... 5-B | 2,908 | NR |
| Rutgers, State U of NJ, Douglass Coll, New Brunswick, NJ 08903-0270 (3) | 1918 | Dr. Mary S. Hartman .... 5-B | 3,181 | NR |
| Rutgers, State U of NJ, Livingston Coll, New Brunswick, NJ 08903-2101 | 1969 | NR ............... 5-B | 3,645 | NR |
| Rutgers, State U of NJ, Mason Gross Sch of Arts, New Brunswick, NJ 08903-2101 | 1976 | Dr. Marilyn F. Somville ... 5-M | 630 | NR |

| Name, address | Year | Governing official, control, and highest degree offered | | Enrollment | Faculty |
|---|---|---|---|---|---|
| Rutgers, State U of NJ, Newark Coll of Arts & Scis, Newark, NJ 07102 | 1946 | Dr. David Hosford | 5-B | 3,782 | NR |
| Rutgers, State U of NJ, Rutgers Coll, New Brunswick, NJ 08903-2101 | 1766 | Dr. James W. Reed | 5-B | 8,550 | NR |
| Rutgers, State U of NJ, U Coll–Camden, Camden, NJ 08102 | 1950 | Dr. Robert A. Catlin | 5-B | 851 | NR |
| Rutgers, State U of NJ, U Coll–Newark, Newark, NJ 07102-1896 | 1934 | NR | 5-B | 2,000 | NR |
| Rutgers, State U of NJ, U Coll–New Brunswick, New Brunswick, NJ 08903 | 1934 | NR | 5-B | 3,249 | NR |
| Sacred Heart U, Fairfield, CT 06432 | 1963 | Dr. Anthony J. Cernera | 2-M | 5,185 | 303 |
| The Sage Colleges, Troy, NY 12180-4115 (3) | 1916 | Dr. Sara Chapman | 1-M | 1,250 | 212 |
| Saginaw Valley State U, University Center, MI 48710 | 1963 | Dr. Eric R. Gilbertson | 5-M | 6,869 | 386 |
| St Ambrose U, Davenport, IA 52803 | 1882 | Dr. Edward J. Rogalski | 2-M | 2,417 | 197 |
| Saint Anselm Coll, Manchester, NH 03102 | 1889 | Rev. Jonathan DeFelice, OSB | 2-B | 1,857 | 160 |
| Saint Augustine's Coll, Raleigh, NC 27610-2298 | 1867 | Dr. Prezell R. Robinson | 2-B | 1,918 | 92 |
| St Bonaventure U, St Bonaventure, NY 14778-2284 | 1858 | Sr. Alice Gallin, OSU | 2-M | 2,797 | 231 |
| St Cloud State U, St Cloud, MN 56301-4498 | 1869 | Dr. Robert Bess | 5-M | 16,047 | 761 |
| St Edward's U, Austin, TX 78704 | 1885 | Dr. Patricia Hayes | 2-M | 3,047 | 211 |
| St Francis Coll, Brooklyn Heights, NY 11201 | 1884 | Br. Donald Sullivan, OSF | 1-B | 2,099 | 132 |
| Saint Francis Coll, Loretto, PA 15940 | 1847 | Rev. Christian R. Oravec | 2-M | 1,508 | 93 |
| St John Fisher Coll, Rochester, NY 14618 | 1948 | Dr. William L. Pickett | 2-M | 2,401 | 213 |
| Saint John's U, Collegeville, MN 56321 (1) | 1857 | Br. Dietrich Reinhart, OSB | 2-M | 1,902 | 165 |
| St John's U, Jamaica, NY 11439 | 1870 | Rev. Donald J. Harrington, CM | 2-D | 18,813 | 1,037 |
| Saint Joseph Coll, West Hartford, CT 06117 (3) | 1932 | Ms. Winifred E. Coleman | 2-M | 2,007 | 155 |
| Saint Joseph's Coll, Rensselaer, IN 47978 | 1889 | Dr. Albert J. Shannon | 2-M | 1,000 | 87 |
| St Joseph's Coll, Brooklyn, NY 11205-3688 | 1916 | Sr. George Aquin O'Connor | 1-B | 1,004 | 98 |
| St Joseph's Coll, Suffolk Cmps, Patchogue, NY 11772 | 1916 | Sr. George Aquin O'Connor | 1-B | 1,933 | 168 |
| Saint Joseph's U, Philadelphia, PA 19131 | 1851 | Rev. Nicholas S. Rashford, SJ | 2-M | 6,909 | 350 |
| St Lawrence U, Canton, NY 13617 | 1856 | Dr. Patti McGill Peterson | 1-M | 2,137 | 185 |
| Saint Louis U, St Louis, MO 63103 | 1818 | Rev. Lawrence Biondi, SJ | 2-D | 11,747 | 2,868 |
| Saint Mary Coll, Leavenworth, KS 66048-5082 | 1923 | Dr. Peter Clifford, FSC | 2-B | 1,023 | 108 |
| Saint Mary-of-the-Woods Coll, Saint Mary-of-the-Woods, IN 47876 (3) | 1840 | Dr. Barbara Doherty, SP | 2-M | 1,258 | 55 |
| Saint Mary's Coll, Notre Dame, IN 46556 (3) | 1844 | Dr. William A. Hickey | 2-B | 1,576 | 196 |
| Saint Mary's Coll of California, Moraga, CA 94556 | 1863 | Br. Mel Anderson, FSC | 2-M | 4,112 | 167 |
| St Mary's Coll of Maryland, St Mary's City, MD 20686 | 1840 | Dr. Edward T. Lewis | 5-B | 1,301 | 146 |
| Saint Mary's Coll of Minnesota, Winona, MN 55987-1399 | 1912 | Br. Louis DeThomasis, FSC | 2-M | 6,186 | 298 |
| St Mary's U of San Antonio, San Antonio, TX 78228-8507 | 1852 | Rev. John Moder, SM | 2-D | 4,007 | 281 |
| Saint Michael's Coll, Colchester, VT 05439 | 1904 | Dr. Paul J. Reiss | 2-M | 2,555 | 168 |
| St Norbert Coll, De Pere, WI 54115 | 1898 | Dr. Thomas A. Manion | 2-M | 1,981 | 143 |
| St Olaf Coll, Northfield, MN 55057-1098 | 1874 | Dr. Melvin George | 2-B | 3,015 | 329 |
| Saint Peter's Coll, Jersey City, NJ 07306 | 1872 | NR | 2-M | 3,567 | 420 |
| St Thomas Aquinas Coll, Sparkill, NY 10976 | 1958 | Dr. Donald T. McNelis | 1-M | 1,454 | 115 |
| St Thomas U, Miami, FL 33054 | 1961 | Rev. Edward McCarthy, OSA | 2-F | 2,703 | 149 |
| Saint Vincent Coll, Latrobe, PA 15650 | 1846 | Rev. John F. Murtha, OSB | 2-B | 1,248 | 103 |
| Saint Xavier U, Chicago, IL 60655 | 1847 | Dr. Ronald Champagne | 2-M | 3,850 | 226 |
| Salem State Coll, Salem, MA 01970 | 1854 | Dr. Nancy D. Harrington | 5-M | 10,132 | 300 |
| Salisbury State U, Salisbury, MD 21801-6837 | 1925 | Dr. Thomas E. Bellavance | 5-M | 6,022 | 323 |
| Salve Regina U, Newport, RI 02840-4192 | 1934 | Dr. M. Lucille McKillop, RSM | 2-M | 2,314 | 212 |
| Samford U, Birmingham, AL 35229 | 1841 | Dr. Thomas E. Corts | 2-F | 4,248 | 323 |
| Sam Houston State U, Huntsville, TX 77341 | 1879 | Dr. Martin J. Anisman | 5-D | 12,412 | 498 |
| San Diego State U, San Diego, CA 92182 | 1897 | Dr. Thomas B. Day | 5-D | 30,369 | 2,139 |
| San Francisco State U, San Francisco, CA 94132 | 1899 | Dr. Robert A. Corrigan | 5-D | 26,530 | 1,429 |
| Sangamon State U, Springfield, IL 62794-9243 | 1969 | Dr. Naomi B. Lynn | 5-M | 4,536 | 236 |
| San Jose State U, San Jose, CA 95192 | 1857 | Mr. J. Handel Evans | 5-M | 29,626 | 1,522 |
| Santa Clara U, Santa Clara, CA 95053 | 1851 | Rev. Paul L. Locatelli, SJ | 2-D | 7,802 | 577 |
| Sarah Lawrence Coll, Bronxville, NY 10708 | 1926 | Dr. Alice Stone Ilchman | 1-M | 1,255 | 211 |
| Savannah Coll of Art and Design, Savannah, GA 31402-3146 | 1978 | Mr. Richard G. Rowan | 1-M | 2,330 | 127 |
| Savannah State Coll, Savannah, GA 31404 | 1890 | NR | 5-B | 3,100 | 149 |
| Sch of the Art Inst of Chicago, Chicago, IL 60603 | 1866 | Mr. Peter Brown | 1-M | 1,729 | 304 |
| Sch of Visual Arts, New York, NY 10010 | 1947 | Mr. David Rhodes | 3-M | 2,571 | 599 |
| Seattle Pacific U, Seattle, WA 98119 | 1891 | NR | 2-M | 3,531 | 244 |
| Seattle U, Seattle, WA 98122 | 1891 | Rev. William J. Sullivan, SJ | 2-D | 4,864 | 451 |
| Seton Hall U, South Orange, NJ 07079 | 1856 | Rev. Thomas R. Peterson, OP | 2-D | 9,970 | 640 |
| Seton Hill Coll, Greensburg, PA 15601 (4) | 1883 | Ms. JoAnne W. Boyle | 2-B | 1,027 | 113 |
| Shawnee State U, Portsmouth, OH 45662 | 1986 | NR | 5-B | 3,636 | 266 |
| Shaw U, Raleigh, NC 27601 | 1865 | Dr. Talbert O. Shaw | 2-M | 2,491 | 242 |
| Shenandoah U, Winchester, VA 22601 | 1875 | Dr. James A. Davis | 2-M | 1,467 | 180 |
| Shepherd Coll, Shepherdstown, WV 25443 | 1871 | Dr. Michael P. Riccards | 5-B | 3,559 | 246 |
| Shippensburg U of Pennsylvania, Shippensburg, PA 17257 | 1871 | Dr. Anthony F. Ceddia | 5-M | 6,688 | 359 |
| Siena Coll, Loudonville, NY 12211-1462 | 1937 | Fr. William McConville, OFM | 2-B | 3,492 | 260 |
| Siena Heights Coll, Adrian, MI 49221-1796 | 1919 | Sr. Cathleen Real, CHM | 2-M | 1,141 | 110 |
| Simmons Coll, Boston, MA 02115 (3) | 1899 | Dr. Jean A. Dowdall | 1-D | 3,079 | 337 |
| Simpson Coll, Indianola, IA 50125 | 1860 | Dr. Stephen G. Jennings | 2-B | 1,690 | 146 |
| Skidmore Coll, Saratoga Springs, NY 12866 | 1903 | Dr. David H. Porter | 1-M | 2,158 | 211 |
| Slippery Rock U of Pennsylvania, Slippery Rock, PA 16057 | 1889 | Dr. Robert Aebersold | 5-M | 7,777 | 408 |
| Smith Coll, Northampton, MA 01063 (3) | 1871 | Ms. Mary Maples Dunn | 1-D | 2,879 | 276 |
| Sonoma State U, Rohnert Park, CA 94928 | 1961 | Dr. Ruben Arminana | 5-M | 7,405 | 422 |
| South Carolina State U, Orangeburg, SC 29117 | 1896 | Dr. Barbara R. Hatton | 5-D | 5,024 | 241 |
| South Dakota Sch of Mines and Tech, Rapid City, SD 57701-3995 | 1885 | Dr. Richard J. Gowen | 5-D | 2,444 | 131 |
| South Dakota State U, Brookings, SD 57007 | 1881 | Dr. Robert T. Wagner | 5-D | 8,550 | 500 |
| Southeastern Coll of the Assemblies of God, Lakeland, FL 33801 | 1935 | Dr. James Hennesy | 2-B | 1,209 | 79 |
| Southeastern Louisiana U, Hammond, LA 70402 | 1925 | Dr. G. Warren Smith | 5-M | 12,847 | 425 |
| Southeastern Oklahoma State U, Durant, OK 74701 | 1909 | Dr. Larry Williams | 5-M | 4,109 | 193 |
| Southeastern U of the Health Sciences, North Miami Beach, FL 33162 | | Dr. Morton Terry | 1-F | 1,343 | NR |
| Southeast Missouri State U, Cape Girardeau, MO 63701 | 1873 | Dr. Kala M. Stroup | 5-M | 8,704 | 436 |
| Southern Arkansas U, Magnolia, AR 71753 | 1909 | Dr. Steven G. Gamble | 5-M | 2,742 | 130 |

212 Education—Colleges and Universities

| Name, address | Year | Governing official, control, and highest degree offered | Enrollment | Faculty |
|---|---|---|---|---|
| Southern Coll of Seventh-day Adventists, Collegedale, TN 37315 | 1892 | Dr. Donald R. Sahly ..... 2-B | 1,494 | 99 |
| Southern Coll of Tech, Marietta, GA 30060-2896 | 1948 | Dr. Stephen R. Cheshier ... 5-M | 3,922 | 199 |
| Southern Connecticut State U, New Haven, CT 06515 | 1893 | Mr. Michael J. Adanti ..... 5-M | 12,420 | 747 |
| Southern Illinois U at Carbondale, Carbondale, IL 62901 | 1869 | Dr. John C. Guyon ....... 5-D | 24,766 | 1,399 |
| Southern Illinois U at Edwardsville, Edwardsville, IL 62026 | 1957 | Dr. Earl E. Lazerson ...... 5-D | 11,670 | 724 |
| Southern Methodist U, Dallas, TX 75275 | 1911 | Mr. A. Kenneth Pye ...... 2-D | 8,538 | 643 |
| Southern Nazarene U, Bethany, OK 73008 | 1899 | Dr. Loren P. Gresham ..... 2-M | 1,591 | 103 |
| Southern Oregon State Coll, Ashland, OR 97520 | 1926 | Dr. Joseph Cox ......... 5-M | 4,478 | 300 |
| Southern U and A&M Coll, Baton Rouge, LA 70813 | 1880 | Dr. Marvin L. Yates ...... 5-D | 10,000 | 603 |
| Southern U at New Orleans, New Orleans, LA 70126 | 1959 | Dr. Robert B. Gex ....... 5-M | 4,556 | 235 |
| Southern Utah U, Cedar City, UT 84720 | 1897 | Mr. Gerald R. Sherratt .... 5-M | 4,434 | 155 |
| Southwest Baptist U, Bolivar, MO 65613 | 1878 | Dr. Roy Blunt .......... 2-M | 3,087 | 208 |
| Southwestern Baptist Theological Sem, Fort Worth, TX 76122-0150 | 1908 | Dr. Russell H. Dilday ..... 2-D | 3,364 | 183 |
| Southwestern Oklahoma State U, Weatherford, OK 73096 | 1901 | Dr. Joe Anna Hibler ...... 5-M | 4,953 | 223 |
| Southwestern U, Georgetown, TX 78626 | 1840 | Dr. Roy B. Shilling, Jr. .... 2-B | 1,204 | 133 |
| Southwest Missouri State U, Springfield, MO 65804 | 1905 | Dr. John H. Keiser ....... 5-M | 19,002 | 844 |
| Southwest State U, Marshall, MN 56258 | 1963 | Dr. Oliver Ford, III ...... 5-B | 2,742 | 131 |
| Southwest Texas State U, San Marcos, TX 78666 | 1899 | Dr. Jerome Supple ....... 5-M | 25,249 | 874 |
| Spalding U, Louisville, KY 40203 | 1814 | Dr. Eileen M. Egan ...... 2-D | 1,141 | 112 |
| Spelman Coll, Atlanta, GA 30314 (3) | 1881 | Dr. Johnnetta B. Cole ..... 1-B | 2,026 | 174 |
| Springfield Coll, Springfield, MA 01109 | 1885 | Dr. Randolph W. Bromery .. 1-D | 3,468 | 232 |
| Spring Hill Coll, Mobile, AL 36608 | 1830 | Rev. William J. Rewak, SJ .. 2-M | 1,273 | 84 |
| Stanford U, Stanford, CA 94305 | 1891 | Dr. Gerhard Casper ...... 1-D | 13,893 | 1,408 |
| State U of NY at Binghamton, Binghamton, NY 13902-6000 | 1946 | Dr. Lois B. DeFleur ...... 5-D | 11,966 | 687 |
| State U of NY at Buffalo, Buffalo, NY 14260 | 1846 | Mr. William R. Greiner .... 5-D | 23,470 | 1,915 |
| State U of NY at Stony Brook, Stony Brook, NY 11794 | 1957 | Dr. John H. Marburger, III .. 5-D | 17,233 | 1,577 |
| State U of NY Coll at Brockport, Brockport, NY 14420 | 1867 | Dr. John E. Van de Wetering 5-M | 7,994 | 530 |
| State U of NY Coll at Buffalo, Buffalo, NY 14222 | 1867 | Dr. F. C. Richardson ..... 5-M | 11,211 | 577 |
| State U of NY Coll at Fredonia, Fredonia, NY 14063 | 1826 | Dr. Donald A. MacPhee .... 5-M | 4,889 | 271 |
| State U of NY Coll at Geneseo, Geneseo, NY 14454 | 1867 | Dr. Carol C. Harter ...... 5-M | 5,578 | 323 |
| State U of NY Coll at New Paltz, New Paltz, NY 12561-2449 | 1828 | Dr. Alice Chandler ....... 5-M | 8,141 | 504 |
| State U of NY Coll at Old Westbury, Old Westbury, NY 11568 | 1965 | Dr. L Eudora Pettigrew .... 5-B | 4,200 | 259 |
| State U of NY Coll at Oneonta, Oneonta, NY 13820 | 1889 | Dr. Alan B. Donovan ..... 5-M | 5,963 | 306 |
| State U of NY Coll at Oswego, Oswego, NY 13126 | 1861 | Dr. Stephen Weber ...... 5-M | 8,235 | 388 |
| State U of NY Coll at Plattsburgh, Plattsburgh, NY 12901 | 1889 | Dr. Charles Warren ...... 5-M | 6,161 | 388 |
| State U of NY Coll at Potsdam, Potsdam, NY 13676 | 1816 | Dr. William Merwin ...... 5-M | 4,579 | 273 |
| State U of NY Coll at Purchase, Purchase, NY 10577 | 1967 | Dr. Sheldon Grebstein .... 5-M | 2,494 | 298 |
| State U of NY Coll of Environ Sci and Forestry, Syracuse, NY 13210-2779 | 1911 | Dr. Ross S. Whaley ...... 5-D | 1,844 | 122 |
| State U of NY Empire State Coll, Saratoga Springs, NY 12866-4391 | 1971 | Dr. James W. Hall ....... 5-M | 10,000 | 360 |
| State U of NY Health Science Ctr at Brooklyn, Brooklyn, NY 11203 | 1858 | Dr. Donald J. Scherl ..... 5-D | 1,641 | 156 |
| State U of NY Health Science Ctr at Syracuse, Syracuse, NY 13210 | 1950 | Dr. Gregory L. Eastwood ... 5-D | 1,100 | 45 |
| State U of NY Inst of Tech at Utica/Rome, Utica, NY 13504 | 1966 | Dr. Peter J. Cayan ...... 5-M | 2,550 | 138 |
| Stephen F Austin State U, Nacogdoches, TX 75962 | 1923 | Dr. Daniel D. Angel ...... 5-D | 12,721 | 667 |
| Stephens Coll, Columbia, MO 65215 (3) | 1833 | Dr. Patsy H. Sampson ..... 1-B | 1,045 | 95 |
| Stetson U, DeLand, FL 32720 | 1883 | Dr. H. Douglas Lee ...... 2-F | 3,069 | 188 |
| Stevens Inst of Tech, Hoboken, NJ 07030 | 1870 | Dr. Harold J. Raveche .... 1-D | 3,240 | 250 |
| Stockton State Coll, Pomona, NJ 08240-9988 | 1971 | Dr. Vera King Farris ..... 5-B | 5,054 | 293 |
| Stonehill Coll, North Easton, MA 02357 | 1948 | Rev. Bartley MacPhaidin, CSC ............. 2-B | 1,925 | 179 |
| Strayer Coll, Washington, DC 20005 | 1892 | Mr. Ron K. Bailey ....... 3-M | 5,566 | 178 |
| Suffolk U, Boston, MA 02108 | 1906 | Mr. David J. Sargent ..... 1-F | 6,076 | 378 |
| Sullivan Coll, Louisville, KY 40232 | 1864 | NR ............... 3-B | 1,990 | 68 |
| Sul Ross State U, Alpine, TX 79832 | 1920 | Dr. R. Vic Morgan ...... 5-M | 2,706 | 165 |
| Susquehanna U, Selinsgrove, PA 17870 | 1858 | Dr. Joel L. Cunningham ... 2-B | 1,447 | 136 |
| Swarthmore Coll, Swarthmore, PA 19081 | 1864 | Dr. Alfred H. Bloom ..... 1-B | 1,267 | 171 |
| Syracuse U, Syracuse, NY 13244 | 1870 | Dr. Kenneth A. Shaw ..... 1-D | 15,421 | 1,568 |
| Tampa Coll, Tampa, FL 33614 | 1890 | Mr. David Zorn ......... 3-M | 1,527 | 57 |
| Tarleton State U, Stephenville, TX 76402 | 1899 | Dr. Dennis P. McCabe .... 5-M | 6,425 | 223 |
| Taylor U, Upland, IN 46989-1001 | 1846 | Dr. Jay L. Kesler ....... 1-B | 1,817 | 139 |
| Teikyo Marycrest U, Davenport, IA 52804-4096 | 1939 | Dr. Joseph D. Olander .... 1-M | 1,264 | 83 |
| Teikyo Post U, Waterbury, CT 06723-2540 | 1890 | Dr. Norman L. Stewart .... 1-B | 1,964 | 166 |
| Temple U, Philadelphia, PA 19122 | 1884 | Mr. Peter J. Liacouras .... 13-D | 27,736 | 2,374 |
| Tennessee State U, Nashville, TN 37209-1561 | 1912 | Dr. James A. Hefner ..... 5-M | 7,591 | 430 |
| Tennessee Tech U, Cookeville, TN 38505 | 1915 | Dr. Angelo A. Volpe ..... 5-D | 8,244 | 393 |
| Texas A&I U, Kingsville, TX 78363 | 1925 | Dr. Manuel L. Ibanez ..... 5-D | 6,414 | 324 |
| Texas A&M International U, Laredo, TX 78040 | 1969 | Dr. Leo Sayavedra ...... 5-M | 1,573 | 57 |
| Texas A&M U, College Station, TX 77843 | 1876 | Dr. William H. Mobley .... 5-D | 41,710 | 2,424 |
| Texas A&M U at Galveston, Galveston, TX 77553 | 1962 | Dr. David J. Schmidly .... 5-B | 1,278 | 86 |
| Texas A&M U-Corpus Christi, Corpus Christi, TX 78412 | 1971 | Dr. Robert R. Furgason ... 5-D | 3,557 | 279 |
| Texas Christian U, Fort Worth, TX 76129 | 1873 | Dr. William E. Tucker .... 2-D | 6,728 | 375 |
| Texas Lutheran Coll, Seguin, TX 78155 | 1891 | Dr. Charles H. Oestreich .. 2-B | 1,072 | 90 |
| Texas Southern U, Houston, TX 77004 | 1947 | Dr. William H. Harris ..... 5-D | 10,800 | 400 |
| Texas Tech U, Lubbock, TX 79409 | 1923 | Dr. Robert W. Lawless .... 5-D | 24,215 | 944 |
| Texas Wesleyan U, Fort Worth, TX 76105 | 1890 | Dr. Jake B. Schrum ...... 2-M | 1,772 | 120 |
| Texas Woman's U, Denton, TX 76204-1925 (4) | 1901 | Dr. Shirley Sears Chater ... 5-D | 9,636 | 538 |
| Thomas Edison State Coll, Trenton, NJ 08608-1176 | 1972 | Dr. George A. Pruitt ..... 5-B | 8,612 | NR |
| Thomas Jefferson U, Philadelphia, PA 19107 | 1824 | Dr. Paul C. Brucker ..... 1-M | 1,560 | 83 |
| Thomas More Coll, Crestview Hills, KY 41017 | 1921 | Rev. William F. Cleves .... 2-B | 1,308 | 110 |
| Tiffin U, Tiffin, OH 44883 | 1888 | Dr. George Kidd, Jr. ..... 1-M | 1,014 | 70 |
| Tougaloo Coll, Tougaloo, MS 39174 | 1869 | Dr. Adib A. Shakir ...... 2-B | 1,131 | 91 |
| Touro Coll, New York, NY 10010 | 1971 | NR ............... 1-F | 8,942 | 894 |
| Towson State U, Towson, MD 21204-7097 | 1866 | Dr. Hoke L. Smith ...... 5-M | 15,232 | 903 |
| Trenton State Coll, Trenton, NJ 08650-4700 | 1855 | Dr. Harold Eickhoff ..... 5-M | 6,170 | 526 |
| Trevecca Nazarene Coll, Nashville, TN 37210 | 1901 | Dr. Millard Reed ....... 2-M | 1,386 | 131 |
| Trinity Coll, Hartford, CT 06106 | 1823 | Mr. Tom Gerety, Jr. ..... 1-M | 2,027 | 214 |
| Trinity Coll, Washington, DC 20017-1094 (3) | 1897 | NR ............... 2-M | 1,164 | 110 |
| Trinity Coll of Vermont, Burlington, VT 05401 (4) | 1925 | Sr. Janice Ryan ........ 2-M | 1,115 | 103 |
| Trinity U, San Antonio, TX 78212 | 1869 | Dr. Ronald K. Calgaard ... 2-M | 2,518 | 261 |

| Name, address | Year | Governing official, control, and highest degree offered | Enroll-ment | Faculty |
|---|---|---|---|---|
| Tri-State U, Angola, IN 46703 | 1884 | Dr. R. John Reynolds ..... 1-B | 1,051 | 92 |
| Troy State U, Troy, AL 36082 | 1887 | Dr. Jack Hawkins, Jr. .... 5-M | 4,750 | 205 |
| Troy State U at Dothan, Dothan, AL 36304 | 1961 | Dr. Thomas Harrison .... 5-M | 2,319 | 62 |
| Troy State U in Montgomery, Montgomery, AL 36103-4419 | 1957 | Dr. Glenda S. McGaha ... 5-M | 3,331 | 168 |
| Tufts U, Medford, MA 02155 | 1852 | Dr. John A. DiBiaggio .... 1-D | 7,642 | 1,660 |
| Tulane U, New Orleans, LA 70118 | 1834 | Dr. Eamon M. Kelly ..... 1-D | 11,345 | 717 |
| Tusculum Coll, Greeneville, TN 37743 | 1794 | Dr. Robert E. Knott ..... 2-M | 1,040 | 88 |
| Tuskegee U, Tuskegee, AL 36088 | 1881 | Dr. Benjamin F. Payton ... 1-M | 3,598 | 267 |
| Union Coll, Schenectady, NY 12308 | 1795 | Dr. Roger H. Hull ...... 1-M | 2,309 | 194 |
| Union Inst, Cincinnati, OH 45206 | 1964 | Mr. Robert T. Conley .... 1-D | 1,440 | 739 |
| Union U, Jackson, TN 38305 | 1823 | Dr. Hyran E. Barefoot .... 2-M | 2,009 | 120 |
| United States Air Force Acad, USAF Academy, CO 80840-5025 | 1954 | Lt. Gen. Bradley C. Hosmer . 4-B | 4,000 | 517 |
| United States International U, San Diego, CA 92131-1799 | 1952 | Dr. Garry D. Hays ...... 1-D | 3,489 | 84 |
| United States Merchant Marine Acad, Kings Point, NY 11024 | 1943 | Rear Adm. P. L. Krinsky, USMS ......... 4-B | 1,001 | 80 |
| United States Military Acad, West Point, NY 10996 | 1802 | Lt. Gen. Howard D. Graves . 4-B | 4,340 | 491 |
| United States Naval Acad, Annapolis, MD 21402 (2) | 1845 | Rear Adm. Thomas Lynch .. 4-B | 4,265 | 650 |
| Universidad del Turabo, Gurabo, PR 00778 | 1972 | Dr. Dennis Alicea ...... 1-M | 7,796 | 363 |
| Universidad Politécnica de Puerto Rico, Hato Rey, PR 00919 | 1966 | Mr. Ernesto Vazquez-Barquet 1-B | 4,720 | 186 |
| U at Albany, State U of NY, Albany, NY 12222 | 1844 | Dr. H. Patrick Swygert ... 5-D | 15,168 | 902 |
| U of Akron, Akron, OH 44325-0001 | 1870 | Dr. Peggy Gordon Elliott .. 5-D | 27,079 | 1,722 |
| U of Alabama, Tuscaloosa, AL 35487-0132 | 1831 | Dr. E. Roger Sayers ..... 5-D | 18,784 | 995 |
| U of Alabama at Birmingham, Birmingham, AL 35294 | 1969 | Dr. Charles A. McCallum .. 5-D | 16,658 | 1,830 |
| U of Alabama in Huntsville, Huntsville, AL 35899 | 1950 | Dr. Frank Franz ....... 5-D | 8,026 | 441 |
| U of Alaska Anchorage, Anchorage, AK 99508 | 1954 | Dr. Donald F. Behrend ... 5-M | 17,126 | 1,162 |
| U of Alaska Fairbanks, Fairbanks, AK 99775-0660 | 1917 | Dr. Joan K. Wadlow .... 5-D | 5,072 | 717 |
| U of Arizona, Tucson, AZ 85721 | 1885 | Dr. Manuel T. Pacheco ... 5-D | 35,129 | 1,652 |
| U of Arkansas, Fayetteville, AR 72701 | 1871 | Dr. Daniel E. Ferritor ... 5-D | 14,582 | 837 |
| U of Arkansas at Little Rock, Little Rock, AR 72204 | 1927 | Dr. Charles E. Hathaway .. 5-D | 12,419 | 786 |
| U of Arkansas at Pine Bluff, Pine Bluff, AR 71601-2799 | 1873 | Dr. Lawrence A. Davis, Jr. . 5-M | 3,709 | 193 |
| U of Arkansas for Medical Sciences, Little Rock, AR 72205 | 1879 | Dr. Harry P. Ward ..... 5-D | 1,734 | NR |
| U of Baltimore, Baltimore, MD 21201 | 1925 | Dr. H. Mebane Turner ... 5-F | 5,844 | 275 |
| U of Bridgeport, Bridgeport, CT 06601 | 1927 | Dr. Edwin G. Eigel, Jr. ... 1-M | 1,500 | 150 |
| U of California at Berkeley, Berkeley, CA 94720 | 1868 | Dr. Chang-Lin Tien ..... 5-D | 30,622 | 1,512 |
| U of California, Davis, Davis, CA 95616 | 1906 | Dr. Theodore L. Hullar ... 5-D | 22,889 | 1,612 |
| U of California, Irvine, Irvine, CA 92717 | 1965 | Ms. Laurel L. Wilkening .. 5-D | 17,189 | 785 |
| U of California, Los Angeles, Los Angeles, CA 90024 | 1919 | Dr. Charles E. Young .... 5-D | 35,407 | 3,280 |
| U of California, Riverside, Riverside, CA 92521 | 1954 | Dr. Raymond L. Orbach ... 5-D | 8,805 | 739 |
| U of California, San Diego, La Jolla, CA 92093 | 1959 | Dr. Richard C. Atkinson .. 5-D | 18,241 | 1,384 |
| U of California, Santa Barbara, Santa Barbara, CA 93106 | 1891 | Dr. Barbara S. Uehling ... 5-D | 18,655 | 853 |
| U of California, Santa Cruz, Santa Cruz, CA 95064 | 1965 | Dr. Karl S. Pister ...... 5-D | 10,256 | 559 |
| U of Central Arkansas, Conway, AR 72035 | 1907 | Dr. Winfred L. Thompson .. 5-M | 9,473 | 566 |
| U of Central Florida, Orlando, FL 32816 | 1963 | Dr. John C. Hitt ...... 5-D | 21,590 | 910 |
| U of Central Oklahoma, Edmond, OK 73034-0172 | 1890 | Mr. George Nigh ...... 5-M | 15,839 | 640 |
| U of Charleston, Charleston, WV 25304 | 1888 | Dr. Edwin H. Welch ..... 1-M | 1,479 | 238 |
| U of Chicago, Chicago, IL 60637 | 1891 | Mr. Hugo R. Sonneschein . 1-D | 10,231 | 1,843 |
| U of Cincinnati, Cincinnati, OH 45221 | 1819 | Dr. Joseph A. Steger .... 5-D | 17,931 | 968 |
| U of Colorado at Boulder, Boulder, CO 80309 | 1876 | NR ........... 5-D | 25,089 | 1,193 |
| U of Colorado at Colorado Springs, Colorado Springs, CO 80933-7150 | 1965 | Dr. Linda Bunnell Jones .. 5-D | 5,751 | 361 |
| U of Colorado at Denver, Denver, CO 80217 | 1912 | Mr. John Buechner ..... 5-D | 11,188 | 516 |
| U of Colorado Health Sciences Ctr, Denver, CO 80262 | 1883 | Dr. Vincent A. Fulginiti ... 5-D | 2,167 | NR |
| U of Connecticut, Storrs, CT 06269 | 1881 | Dr. Harry J. Hartley .... 5-D | 18,399 | 1,250 |
| U of Connecticut at Hartford, West Hartford, CT 06117 | 1946 | Dr. Russell F. Farnen .... 5-B | 1,183 | 91 |
| U of Connecticut at Stamford, Stamford, CT 06903 | 1951 | NR ........... 5-M | 1,600 | 93 |
| U of Dallas, Irving, TX 75062-4799 | 1956 | Dr. Robert F. Sasseen ... 2-D | 2,869 | 136 |
| U of Dayton, Dayton, OH 45469-1611 | 1850 | Dr. Raymond L. Fitz, SM .. 2-D | 10,658 | 794 |
| U of Delaware, Newark, DE 19716 | 1743 | Dr. David P. Roselle .... 13-D | 17,489 | 954 |
| U of Denver, Denver, CO 80208 | 1864 | Dr. Daniel Ritchie ..... 1-D | 8,213 | 392 |
| U of Detroit Mercy, Detroit, MI 48221 | 1877 | Sr. Maureen A. Fay, OP .. 2-D | 7,774 | 495 |
| U of Dubuque, Dubuque, IA 52001 | 1852 | Dr. John J. Agria ...... 2-M | 1,264 | 86 |
| U of Evansville, Evansville, IN 47722 | 1854 | Dr. James S. Vinson .... 2-M | 2,928 | 165 |
| The U of Findlay, Findlay, OH 45840 | 1882 | Dr. Kenneth E. Zirkle .... 2-M | 3,136 | 235 |
| U of Florida, Gainesville, FL 32611-2073 | 1853 | Dr. John V. Lombardi .... 5-D | 34,361 | 2,660 |
| U of Georgia, Athens, GA 30602 | 1785 | Dr. Charles B. Knapp .... 5-D | 28,493 | 2,538 |
| U of Hartford, West Hartford, CT 06117 | 1877 | Dr. Humphrey Tonkin .... 1-D | 7,340 | 730 |
| U of Hawaii at Hilo, Hilo, HI 96720 | 1970 | Dr. Edward J. Kormondy .. 5-B | 2,675 | 235 |
| U of Hawaii at Manoa, Honolulu, HI 96822 | 1907 | Dr. Kenneth P. Mortimer .. 5-D | 19,810 | 1,526 |
| U of Health Sciences/Chicago Medical Sch, North Chicago, IL 60064 | 1912 | Mr. Herman M. Finch .... 1-D | 1,070 | 18 |
| U of Houston-Clear Lake, Houston, TX 77058 | 1971 | Dr. Glenn A. Goerke .... 5-M | 7,281 | 374 |
| U of Houston-Downtown, Houston, TX 77002 | 1974 | Dr. George Magner ..... 5-B | 8,702 | 361 |
| U of Houston-Victoria, Victoria, TX 77901 | 1973 | Dr. Lesta Van Der Wert Turchen ........ 5-M | 1,223 | 74 |
| U of Idaho, Moscow, ID 83843-4140 | 1889 | Dr. Elisabeth Zinser .... 5-D | 10,790 | 570 |
| U of Illinois at Chicago, Chicago, IL 60680 | 1965 | Dr. James J. Stukel .... 5-D | 24,985 | 2,529 |
| U of Illinois at Urbana-Champaign, Champaign, IL 61820 | 1867 | Dr. Michael J. Aiken .... 5-D | 35,815 | 2,203 |
| U of Indianapolis, Indianapolis, IN 46227-3697 | 1902 | Dr. G. Benjamin Lantz, Jr. . 2-M | 3,729 | 276 |
| The U of Iowa, Iowa City, IA 52242 | 1847 | Dr. Hunter R. Rawlings, III . 5-D | 27,463 | 1,729 |
| U of Kansas, Lawrence, KS 66045 | 1866 | Dr. Gene A. Budig ..... 5-D | 29,161 | 2,002 |
| U of Kentucky, Lexington, KY 40506-0032 | 1865 | Dr. Charles T. Wethington, Jr. ........... 5-D | 24,197 | 2,081 |
| U of La Verne, La Verne, CA 91750 | 1891 | Dr. Stephen Morgan .... 1-D | 7,047 | 840 |
| U of Louisville, Louisville, KY 40292 | 1798 | Dr. Donald C. Swain .... 5-D | 22,633 | 1,191 |
| U of Maine, Orono, ME 04469 | 1865 | Dr. Frederick E. Hutchinson 5-D | 12,313 | 781 |
| U of Maine at Farmington, Farmington, ME 04938 | 1864 | Dr. Michael J. Orendulf .. 5-B | 2,267 | 148 |
| U of Maine at Presque Isle, Presque Isle, ME 04769 | 1903 | Dr. W. Michael Easton ... 5-B | 1,577 | 105 |
| U of Mary, Bismarck, ND 58504 | 1959 | Sr. Thomas Welder ..... 2-M | 1,851 | 100 |
| U of Mary Hardin-Baylor, Belton, TX 76513 | 1845 | Dr. Jerry G. Bawcom .... 2-M | 1,904 | 113 |
| U of Maryland Baltimore County, Baltimore, MD 21228-5398 | 1966 | Dr. Freeman A. Hrabowski . 5-D | 10,654 | 623 |
| U of Maryland Coll Park, College Park, MD 20742 | 1856 | Dr. William E. Kirwan ... 5-D | 32,858 | 1,803 |
| U of Maryland Eastern Shore, Princess Anne, MD 21853 | 1886 | Dr. William P. Hytche ... 5-D | 2,430 | 154 |
| U of Maryland U Coll, College Park, MD 20742-1628 | 1947 | Dr. T. Benjamin Massey .. 5-M | 38,567 | 1,641 |

| Name, address | Year | Governing official, control, and highest degree offered | Enroll- ment | Faculty |
|---|---|---|---|---|
| U of Massachusetts at Amherst, Amherst, MA 01003 | 1863 | Dr. David K. Scott ...... 5-D | 21,834 | 1,254 |
| U of Massachusetts at Boston, Boston, MA 02125-3393 | 1964 | Dr. Sherry H. Penney ..... 5-D | 10,590 | 820 |
| U of Massachusetts Dartmouth, North Dartmouth, MA 02747 | 1895 | Dr. Peter H. Cressy ...... 5-M | 5,525 | 413 |
| U of Massachusetts Lowell, Lowell, MA 01854 | 1894 | Dr. William T. Hogan ..... 5-D | 13,618 | 604 |
| U of Miami, Coral Gables, FL 33124 | 1925 | Mr. Edward T. Foote, II ... 1-D | 13,857 | 1,615 |
| U of Michigan, Ann Arbor, MI 48109 | 1817 | Dr. James J. Duderstadt ... 5-D | 36,626 | 3,374 |
| U of Michigan–Dearborn, Dearborn, MI 48128 | 1959 | Dr. James C. Renick ...... 5-M | 7,318 | 385 |
| U of Michigan–Flint, Flint, MI 48502-2186 | 1956 | Dr. Clinton B. Jones ...... 5-M | 6,652 | 211 |
| U of Minnesota, Duluth, Duluth, MN 55812 | 1947 | Dr. Lawrence A. Ianni ..... 5-M | 7,680 | 510 |
| U of Minnesota, Morris, Morris, MN 56267 | 1959 | Dr. David C. Johnson ..... 5-B | 1,923 | 142 |
| U of Minnesota, Twin Cities Cmps, Minneapolis, MN 55455-0213 | 1851 | Dr. Nils Hasselmo ....... 5-D | 38,019 | 2,953 |
| U of Mississippi, University, MS 38677 | 1844 | Dr. R. Gerald Turner ..... 5-D | 10,704 | 461 |
| U of Mississippi Medical Ctr, Jackson, MS 39216 | 1955 | Dr. Norman Crooks Nelson . 5-D | 1,631 | 617 |
| U of Missouri–Columbia, Columbia, MO 65211 | 1839 | Dr. Charles A. Kiesler .... 5-D | 23,346 | 1,517 |
| U of Missouri–Kansas City, Kansas City, MO 64110 | 1929 | Dr. Eleanor B. Schwartz ... 5-D | 10,489 | 540 |
| U of Missouri–Rolla, Rolla, MO 65401 | 1870 | Dr. John T. Park ........ 5-D | 5,657 | 345 |
| U of Missouri–St Louis, St Louis, MO 63121-4499 | 1963 | Dr. Blanche M. Touhill .... 5-D | 11,774 | 635 |
| U of Mobile, Mobile, AL 36663-0220 | 1961 | Dr. Michael A. Magnoli .... 2-M | 1,703 | 106 |
| U of Montana, Missoula, MT 59812 | 1893 | Dr. George M. Dennison ... 5-D | 10,614 | 520 |
| U of Montevallo, Montevallo, AL 35115 | 1896 | Dr. Robert M. McChesney . 5-M | 3,254 | 172 |
| U of Nebraska at Kearney, Kearney, NE 68849 | 1903 | Dr. William R. Nester ..... 5-M | 8,775 | 415 |
| U of Nebraska at Omaha, Omaha, NE 68182 | 1908 | Dr. Del D. Weber ........ 5-M | 17,045 | 750 |
| U of Nebraska–Lincoln, Lincoln, NE 68588 | 1869 | Dr. Graham B. Spanier .... 5-D | 24,573 | 1,516 |
| U of Nebraska Medical Ctr, Omaha, NE 68198 | 1869 | Dr. Carol A. Aschenbrener . 5-D | 2,757 | 489 |
| U of Nevada, Las Vegas, Las Vegas, NV 89154 | 1957 | Dr. Robert Maxson ....... 5-D | 19,504 | 1,001 |
| U of Nevada, Reno, Reno, NV 89557 | 1874 | Dr. Joseph N. Crowley .... 5-D | 11,909 | 545 |
| U of New England, Biddeford, ME 04005-9526 | 1939 | Dr. Thomas Hedley Reynolds 1-F | 1,287 | 154 |
| U of New Hampshire, Durham, NH 03824 | 1866 | Dr. Dale F. Nitzschke .... 5-D | 12,257 | 900 |
| U of New Haven, West Haven, CT 06516 | 1920 | Dr. Lawrence J. DeNardis .. 1-D | 5,916 | 401 |
| U of New Mexico, Albuquerque, NM 87131-2039 | 1889 | Dr. Richard E. Peck ...... 5-D | 25,009 | 1,315 |
| U of New Orleans, New Orleans, LA 70148 | 1958 | Dr. Gregory M. O'Brien .... 5-D | 16,308 | 819 |
| U of North Alabama, Florence, AL 35632-0001 | 1872 | Mr. Robert L. Potts ...... 5-M | 5,523 | 239 |
| U of North Carolina at Asheville, Asheville, NC 28804 | 1927 | Dr. Samuel Schuman ..... 5-M | 3,277 | 235 |
| U of North Carolina at Chapel Hill, Chapel Hill, NC 27599 | 1795 | Mr. Paul Hardin, III ...... 5-D | 23,944 | 2,430 |
| U of North Carolina at Charlotte, Charlotte, NC 28223 | 1946 | Dr. James H. Woodward, Jr. 5-M | 15,363 | 872 |
| U of North Carolina at Greensboro, Greensboro, NC 27412 | 1891 | Dr. William E. Moran ..... 5-D | 12,117 | 724 |
| U of North Carolina at Wilmington, Wilmington, NC 28403 | 1947 | Dr. James R. Leutze ..... 5-M | 7,898 | 419 |
| U of North Dakota, Grand Forks, ND 58202 | 1883 | Dr. Kendall Baker ....... 5-D | 12,438 | 752 |
| U of Northern Colorado, Greeley, CO 80639 | 1890 | Dr. Herman D. Lujan ..... 5-D | 10,328 | 548 |
| U of Northern Iowa, Cedar Falls, IA 50614 | 1876 | Dr. Constantine W. Curris . 5-D | 13,045 | 810 |
| U of North Florida, Jacksonville, FL 32224 | 1965 | Dr. Adam W. Herbert ..... 5-D | 9,073 | 214 |
| U of North Texas, Denton, TX 76203 | 1890 | Dr. Alfred F. Hurley ...... 5-D | 26,433 | 1,088 |
| U of Notre Dame, Notre Dame, IN 46556 | 1842 | Rev. Edward A. Malloy, CSC 2-D | 10,000 | 820 |
| U of Oklahoma, Norman, OK 73019 | 1890 | Dr. Richard L. Van Horn ... 5-D | 20,015 | 957 |
| U of Oklahoma Health Sciences Ctr, Oklahoma City, OK 73190 | 1890 | Dr. Jay H. Stein ........ 5-D | 3,016 | 838 |
| U of Oregon, Eugene, OR 97403 | 1872 | Dr. Myles Brand ........ 5-D | 16,719 | 1,464 |
| U of Osteopathic Medicine and Health Sciences, Des Moines, IA 50312 | 1898 | Dr. J. Leonard Azneer .... 1-F | 1,090 | 108 |
| U of Pennsylvania, Philadelphia, PA 19104 | 1740 | Dr. Claire Fagin ........ 1-D | 22,418 | 3,916 |
| U of Phoenix, Phoenix, AZ 85072-9382 | 1976 | Mr. William Gibbs ....... 3-M | 15,341 | 1,500 |
| U of Pittsburgh, Pittsburgh, PA 15260 | 1787 | Dr. J. Dennis O'Connor ... 13-D | 27,852 | 3,312 |
| U of Pittsburgh at Bradford, Bradford, PA 16701 | 1963 | Dr. Richard E. McDowell .. 13-B | 1,309 | 95 |
| U of Pittsburgh at Greensburg, Greensburg, PA 15601 | 1963 | Dr. George F. Chambers ... 13-B | 1,465 | 89 |
| U of Pittsburgh at Johnstown, Johnstown, PA 15904 | 1927 | Dr. Frank H. Blackington, III 13-B | 3,243 | 192 |
| U of Portland, Portland, OR 97203 | 1901 | Rev. David T. Tyson, CSC . 2-M | 2,716 | 200 |
| U of Puerto Rico at Ponce, Ponce, PR 00732 | 1970 | Mr. Pedro E. Laboy ...... 7-B | 2,263 | 124 |
| U of Puerto Rico, Cayey U Coll, Cayey, PR 00737 | 1967 | Dr. Margarita Benítez ..... 7-B | 3,236 | 182 |
| U of Puerto Rico, Humacao U Coll, Humacao, PR 00791 | 1962 | Dr. Félix Castrodad ...... 7-B | 3,884 | 243 |
| U of Puerto Rico Medical Sciences Cmps, San Juan, PR 00936-5067 | 1950 | Dr. Francisco H. Oquendo . 7-D | 2,981 | 719 |
| U of Puget Sound, Tacoma, WA 98416 | 1888 | Dr. Susan Resneck Pierce . 2-M | 3,162 | 230 |
| U of Redlands, Redlands, CA 92373-0999 | 1907 | Dr. James R. Appleton .... 1-M | 3,950 | 156 |
| U of Rhode Island, Kingston, RI 02881 | 1892 | Dr. Robert L. Carothers ... 5-D | 12,360 | 750 |
| U of Richmond, Richmond, VA 23173 | 1830 | Dr. Richard L. Morrill .... 2-F | 4,579 | 360 |
| U of Rio Grande, Rio Grande, OH 45674 | 1876 | Dr. Barry M. Dorsey ...... 1-M | 2,072 | 114 |
| U of Rochester, Rochester, NY 14627-0001 | 1850 | Mr. G. Dennis O'Brien .... 1-D | 9,539 | 1,376 |
| U of St Thomas, St Paul, MN 55105 | 1885 | Rev. Dennis Dease ...... 2-F | 10,423 | 636 |
| U of St Thomas, Houston, TX 77006 | 1947 | Mr. Joseph M. McFadden .. 2-D | 2,079 | 172 |
| U of San Diego, San Diego, CA 92110-2492 | 1949 | Dr. Author E. Hughes ..... 2-F | 6,083 | 466 |
| U of San Francisco, San Francisco, CA 94117-1080 | 1855 | Rev. John P. Schlegel, SJ . 2-D | 7,328 | 713 |
| U of Science and Arts of Oklahoma, Chickasha, OK 73018-0001 | 1908 | Dr. Roy Troutt ......... 5-B | 1,619 | 75 |
| U of Scranton, Scranton, PA 18510-4501 | 1888 | Rev. J. A. Panuska, SJ .... 2-M | 5,061 | 387 |
| U of South Alabama, Mobile, AL 36688 | 1963 | Dr. Frederick P. Whiddon .. 5-D | 12,311 | 802 |
| U of South Carolina, Columbia, SC 29208 | 1801 | Dr. John M. Palms ...... 5-D | 26,138 | 1,466 |
| U of South Carolina–Aiken, Aiken, SC 29801 | 1961 | Dr. Robert E. Alexander ... 5-B | 3,208 | 232 |
| U of South Carolina at Spartanburg, Spartanburg, SC 29303 | 1967 | Dr. Olin B. Sansbury, Jr. .. 5-B | 3,536 | 237 |
| U of South Dakota, Vermillion, SD 57069-2390 | 1862 | Dr. Betty Turner Asher .... 5-D | 7,591 | 354 |
| U of Southern California, Los Angeles, CA 90089 | 1880 | Dr. Steven B. Sample .... 1-D | 27,353 | 3,086 |
| U of Southern Colorado, Pueblo, CO 81001 | 1933 | Dr. Robert Shirley ....... 5-M | 4,488 | 278 |
| U of Southern Indiana, Evansville, IN 47712 | 1965 | Dr. David L. Rice ....... 5-M | 7,430 | 359 |
| U of Southern Maine, Portland, ME 04103 | 1878 | Dr. Richard L. Pattenaude . 5-M | 10,077 | 574 |
| U of Southern Mississippi, Hattiesburg, MS 39406 | 1910 | Dr. Aubrey K. Lucas ..... 5-D | 11,680 | 646 |
| U of South Florida, Tampa, FL 33620 | 1956 | Dr. Francis T. Borkowski .. 5-D | 34,161 | 1,504 |
| U of Southwestern Louisiana, Lafayette, LA 70504 | 1898 | Dr. Ray P. Authement .... 5-D | 15,677 | 631 |
| U of Tampa, Tampa, FL 33606 | 1931 | Dr. David G. Ruffer ...... 1-M | 2,506 | 182 |
| U of Tennessee at Chattanooga, Chattanooga, TN 37403 | 1886 | Dr. Frederick W. Obear ... 5-M | 8,147 | 495 |
| U of Tennessee at Martin, Martin, TN 38238 | 1927 | Dr. Margaret N. Perry .... 5-M | 5,660 | 283 |
| U of Tennessee, Knoxville, Knoxville, TN 37996 | 1794 | Dr. William T. Snyder .... 5-D | 25,998 | 1,155 |
| U of Tennessee, Memphis, Memphis, TN 38163 | 1911 | NR | 2,001 | 992 |
| U of Texas at Arlington, Arlington, TX 76019 | 1895 | Dr. Ryan C. Amacher ..... 5-D | 24,727 | 863 |
| U of Texas at Austin, Austin, TX 78712 | 1883 | Mr. Robert M. Berdahl .... 5-D | 49,253 | 2,358 |
| The U of Texas at Brownsville, Brownsville, TX 78520-4991 | 1973 | NR ............... 5-M | 1,675 | 390 |
| U of Texas at Dallas, Richardson, TX 75083-0688 | 1969 | Dr. Robert H. Rutford .... 5-D | 8,993 | NR |

| Name, address | Year | Governing official, control, and highest degree offered | Enroll- ment | Faculty |
|---|---|---|---|---|
| U of Texas at El Paso, El Paso, TX 79968 | 1913 | Dr. Diana Natalicio .... 5-D | 17,209 | 724 |
| U of Texas at San Antonio, San Antonio, TX 78249 | 1969 | Dr. Samuel A. Kirkpatrick . 5-D | 16,767 | 660 |
| U of Texas at Tyler, Tyler, TX 75701 | 1971 | Dr. George F. Hamm .... 5-M | 3,988 | 219 |
| U of Texas Health Science Ctr at Houston, Houston, TX 77225 | 1943 | Dr. M. David Low ....... 5-D | 3,204 | 200 |
| U of Texas Health Science Ctr at San Antonio, San Antonio, TX 78284 | 1976 | Dr. John P. Howe, III ..... 5-D | 2,573 | 1,213 |
| U of Texas Medical Branch at Galveston, Galveston, TX 77555 | 1891 | Dr. Thomas N. James .... 5-D | 2,112 | 118 |
| U of Texas of the Permian Basin, Odessa, TX 79762-0001 | 1969 | Dr. Charles A. Sorber .... 5-M | 2,224 | 78 |
| U of Texas–Pan American, Edinburg, TX 78539 | 1927 | Dr. Miguel A. Nevarez .... 5-M | 13,298 | 478 |
| U of Texas Southwestern Medical Ctr at Dallas, Dallas, TX 75235-9096 | 1943 | Dr. C. Kern Wildenthal .... 5-D | 1,582 | 272 |
| U of the Arts, Philadelphia, PA 19102 | 1870 | NR ............... 1-M | 1,420 | 294 |
| U of the District of Columbia, Washington, DC 20008 | 1976 | Dr. Tilden J. LeMelle .... 10-M | 11,578 | 612 |
| U of the Pacific, Stockton, CA 95211 | 1851 | Dr. Bill L. Atchley ....... 1-D | 5,694 | 309 |
| U of the Sacred Heart, Santurce, PR 00914 | 1935 | Dr. Jose Jaime Rivera .... 2-M | 5,030 | 366 |
| U of the South, Sewanee, TN 37375-1000 | 1857 | Dr. Samuel R. Williamson . 2-D | 1,214 | 141 |
| U of the State of NY, Regents Coll, Albany, NY 12203 | 1970 | Mr. C. Wayne Williams .... 1-B | 14,464 | NR |
| U of the Virgin Islands, Charlotte Amalie, St Thomas, VI 00802 | 1962 | Dr. Orville Kean ........ 8-M | 2,924 | 266 |
| U of Toledo, Toledo, OH 43606-3398 | 1872 | Mr. Frank E. Horton ..... 5-D | 24,541 | 1,391 |
| U of Tulsa, Tulsa, OK 74104 | 1894 | Dr. Robert H. Donaldson .. 2-D | 4,922 | 439 |
| U of Utah, Salt Lake City, UT 84112 | 1850 | Dr. Arthur K. Smith ..... 5-D | 25,549 | 1,343 |
| U of Vermont, Burlington, VT 05405 | 1791 | Mr. Thomas P. Salmon ... 5-D | 9,532 | 1,014 |
| U of Virginia, Charlottesville, VA 22906 | 1819 | Dr. John T. Casteen, III ... 5-D | 17,604 | 1,887 |
| U of Washington, Seattle, WA 98195 | 1861 | Dr. William P. Gerberding . 5-D | 34,598 | 4,067 |
| U of West Florida, Pensacola, FL 32514-5750 | 1963 | Dr. Morris L. Marx ...... 5-M | 7,941 | 255 |
| U of Wisconsin–Eau Claire, Eau Claire, WI 54702-4004 | 1916 | Dr. Larry Schnack ...... 5-M | 10,431 | 572 |
| U of Wisconsin–Green Bay, Green Bay, WI 54311-7001 | 1968 | Dr. David L. Outcalt ..... 5-M | 4,801 | 241 |
| U of Wisconsin–La Crosse, La Crosse, WI 54601 | 1909 | Dr. Judith L. Kuipers .... 5-M | 8,362 | 450 |
| U of Wisconsin–Madison, Madison, WI 53706 | 1848 | Dr. David Ward ........ 5-D | 43,196 | 2,325 |
| U of Wisconsin–Milwaukee, Milwaukee, WI 53201 | 1956 | Dr. John H. Schroeder, Jr. . 5-D | 24,341 | 1,302 |
| U of Wisconsin–Oshkosh, Oshkosh, WI 54901 | 1871 | Dr. John E. Kerrigan .... 5-M | 11,039 | 524 |
| U of Wisconsin–Parkside, Kenosha, WI 53141 | 1968 | Dr. Sheila Kaplan ...... 5-M | 4,993 | 293 |
| U of Wisconsin–Platteville, Platteville, WI 53818 | 1866 | Dr. Lee A. Halgren ...... 5-M | 5,225 | 280 |
| U of Wisconsin–River Falls, River Falls, WI 54022 | 1874 | Dr. Gary A. Thibodeau ... 5-M | 5,440 | 295 |
| U of Wisconsin–Stevens Point, Stevens Point, WI 54481 | 1894 | Dr. Keith R. Sanders .... 5-M | 8,545 | 462 |
| U of Wisconsin–Stout, Menomonie, WI 54751 | 1891 | Dr. Charles Sorensen .... 5-M | 7,343 | 415 |
| U of Wisconsin–Superior, Superior, WI 54880 | 1893 | Dr. Betty J. Youngblood ... 5-M | 2,891 | 162 |
| U of Wisconsin–Whitewater, Whitewater, WI 53190 | 1868 | Dr. H. Gaylon Greenhill ... 5-M | 10,512 | 475 |
| U of Wyoming, Laramie, WY 82071 | 1886 | Dr. Terry P. Roark ...... 5-D | 12,052 | 754 |
| Upper Iowa U, Fayette, IA 52142 | 1857 | Dr. James R. Rocheleau .. 1-B | 2,641 | 230 |
| Upsala Coll, East Orange, NJ 07019-1186 | 1893 | Dr. Robert E. Karsten .... 2-M | 1,163 | 116 |
| Ursinus Coll, Collegeville, PA 19426 | 1869 | Dr. Richard P. Richter .... 2-B | 1,113 | 120 |
| Ursuline Coll, Pepper Pike, OH 44124 (4) | 1871 | Sr. Anne Marie Diederich, OSU, PhD ........... 2-M | 1,600 | 135 |
| Utah State U, Logan, UT 84322 | 1888 | Dr. George H. Emert .... 5-D | 15,425 | 784 |
| Utica Coll of Syracuse U, Utica, NY 13502-4892 | 1946 | Dr. Michael K. Simpson ... 1-B | 1,707 | 141 |
| Valdosta State Coll, Valdosta, GA 31698 | 1906 | Dr. Hugh C. Bailey ..... 5-M | 7,898 | 390 |
| Valley City State U, Valley City, ND 58072 | 1890 | Dr. Charles B. House, Jr. .. 5-B | 1,003 | 68 |
| Valparaiso U, Valparaiso, IN 46383 | 1859 | Dr. Alan F. Harre ....... 2-F | 3,757 | 346 |
| Vanderbilt U, Nashville, TN 37240 | 1873 | Mr. Joe B. Wyatt ....... 1-D | 9,724 | 1,861 |
| Vassar Coll, Poughkeepsie, NY 12601 | 1861 | Dr. Frances D. Fergusson . 1-M | 2,272 | 234 |
| Villanova U, Villanova, PA 19085 | 1842 | Rev. Edmund J. Dobbin, OSA 2-D | 11,413 | 886 |
| Virginia Commonwealth U, Richmond, VA 23284 | 1838 | Dr. Eugene P. Trani .... 5-D | 21,939 | 2,401 |
| Virginia Military Inst, Lexington, VA 24450 (1) | 1839 | Maj. Gen. John W. Knapp . 5-B | 1,265 | 111 |
| Virginia Polytechnic Inst and State U, Blacksburg, VA 24061-0202 | 1872 | Dr. James D. McComas ... 5-D | 23,637 | 1,909 |
| Virginia State U, Petersburg, VA 23806 | 1882 | Mr. Eddie N. Moore, Jr. ... 5-M | 4,435 | 224 |
| Virginia Union U, Richmond, VA 23220 | 1865 | Dr. S. Dallas Simmons ... 2-M | 1,511 | 122 |
| Virginia Wesleyan Coll, Norfolk, VA 23502-5599 | 1961 | Dr. William T. Greer, Jr. ... 2-B | 1,513 | 91 |
| Viterbo Coll, La Crosse, WI 54601 | 1890 | Dr. William J. Medland ... 2-M | 1,392 | 107 |
| Wagner Coll, Staten Island, NY 10301 | 1883 | Dr. Norman R. Smith .... 1-M | 1,501 | 155 |
| Wake Forest U, Winston-Salem, NC 27109 | 1834 | Dr. Thomas K. Hearn, Jr. .. 1-D | 5,624 | 1,507 |
| Walla Walla Coll, College Place, WA 99324 | 1892 | Dr. Niels-Erik Andreasen .. 1-M | 1,789 | 169 |
| Walsh Coll of Accountancy and Business Admin, Troy, MI 48007-7006 | 1922 | Mr. David A. Spencer .... 1-M | 3,578 | 102 |
| Walsh U, North Canton, OH 44720 | 1958 | Rev. Richard Mucowski ... 2-M | 1,550 | 113 |
| Wartburg Coll, Waverly, IA 50677 | 1852 | Dr. Robert Vogel ....... 2-B | 1,445 | 136 |
| Washburn U of Topeka, Topeka, KS 66621 | 1865 | Dr. Hugh Thompson ... 11-F | 6,630 | 400 |
| Washington and Jefferson Coll, Washington, PA 15301 | 1781 | Dr. Howard J. Burnett ... 1-B | 1,144 | 110 |
| Washington and Lee U, Lexington, VA 24450 | 1749 | Dr. John D. Wilson ...... 1-D | 1,985 | 167 |
| Washington State U, Pullman, WA 99164 | 1890 | Dr. Samuel H. Smith .... 5-D | 17,882 | 1,112 |
| Washington U, St Louis, MO 63130 | 1853 | Dr. William H. Danforth ... 1-D | 9,429 | 3,284 |
| Waynesburg Coll, Waynesburg, PA 15370 | 1849 | Mr. Timothy R. Thyreen ... 2-M | 1,351 | 99 |
| Wayne State Coll, Wayne, NE 68787 | 1910 | Dr. Donald J. Mash ..... 5-M | 3,761 | 209 |
| Wayne State U, Detroit, MI 48202 | 1868 | Mr. David Adamany ..... 5-M | 34,945 | 2,533 |
| Weber State U, Ogden, UT 84408 | 1889 | Dr. Paul H. Thompson ... 5-M | 14,993 | 457 |
| Webster U, St Louis, MO 63119 | 1915 | Dr. Daniel H. Perlman ... 1-M | 9,699 | 1,149 |
| Wellesley Coll, Wellesley, MA 02181 (3) | 1870 | Dr. Luella G. Goldberg ... 1-B | 2,340 | 313 |
| Wentworth Inst of Tech, Boston, MA 02115 | 1904 | Dr. John F. Van Domelen .. 1-B | 2,601 | 231 |
| Wesleyan U, Middletown, CT 06459 | 1831 | Mr. William M. Chace .... 1-D | 3,331 | 321 |
| Wesley Coll, Dover, DE 19901 | 1873 | Dr. Reed M. Stewart .... 2-B | 1,294 | 103 |
| West Chester U of Pennsylvania, West Chester, PA 19383 | 1871 | Dr. Madeleine Wing Adler . 5-M | 11,806 | 659 |
| West Coast U, Los Angeles, CA 90020-1765 | 1909 | Dr. Robert M. L. Baker, Jr. . 1-M | 1,600 | 250 |
| Western Carolina U, Cullowhee, NC 28723 | 1889 | Dr. Myron L. Coulter .... 5-M | 6,576 | 430 |
| Western Illinois U, Macomb, IL 61455 | 1899 | Dr. Ralph H. Wagoner ... 5-M | 13,377 | 703 |
| Western International U, Phoenix, AZ 85021 | 1978 | Dr. Robert S. Webber .... 1-M | 1,552 | 80 |
| Western Kentucky U, Bowling Green, KY 42101-3576 | 1906 | Dr. Thomas C. Meredith .. 5-M | 15,750 | 768 |
| Western Maryland Coll, Westminster, MD 21157-4390 | 1867 | Dr. Robert H. Chambers .. 1-M | 2,143 | 194 |
| Western Michigan U, Kalamazoo, MI 49008 | 1903 | Dr. Diether H. Haenicke .. 5-D | 27,282 | 1,115 |
| Western New England Coll, Springfield, MA 01119 | 1919 | Dr. Beverly W. Miller .... 1-F | 4,242 | 259 |
| Western New Mexico U, Silver City, NM 88061 | 1893 | Dr. Jerry L. Gallentine ... 5-M | 2,240 | 113 |
| Western Oregon State Coll, Monmouth, OR 97361 | 1856 | Dr. Richard S. Meyers ... 5-M | 3,936 | 282 |
| Western State Coll of Colorado, Gunnison, CO 81231 | 1911 | Dr. Kaye Howe ........ 5-B | 2,668 | 143 |

| Name, address | Year | Governing official, control, and highest degree offered | Enroll- ment | Faculty |
|---|---|---|---|---|
| Western State U Coll of Law of Orange County, Fullerton, CA 92631 | 1966 | NR . . . . . . . . . . . . . . . 3-F | 1,804 | 78 |
| Western Washington U, Bellingham, WA 98225 | 1893 | Dr. Roland L. DeLorme . . . 5-M | 10,150 | 525 |
| Westfield State Coll, Westfield, MA 01086 | 1838 | Dr. Ronald L. Applbaum . . 5-M | 5,103 | 365 |
| West Georgia Coll, Carrollton, GA 30118 | 1933 | Dr. Maurice K. Townsend . . 5-M | 7,717 | 309 |
| West Liberty State Coll, West Liberty, WV 26074 | 1837 | Dr. Clyde D. Campbell . . . . 5-B | 2,377 | 153 |
| Westminster Coll, New Wilmington, PA 16172-0001 | 1852 | Dr. Oscar E. Remick . . . . . 2-M | 1,554 | 140 |
| Westminster Coll of Salt Lake City, Salt Lake City, UT 84105 | 1875 | Dr. Charles H. Dick . . . . . 1-M | 2,141 | 201 |
| Westmont Coll, Santa Barbara, CA 93108 | 1940 | Dr. David K. Winter . . . . . 2-B | 1,317 | 110 |
| West Texas A&M U, Canyon, TX 79016-0001 | 1909 | Dr. Barry B. Thompson . . . 5-M | 6,405 | 312 |
| West Virginia Inst of Tech, Montgomery, WV 25136 | 1895 | Dr. John P. Carrier . . . . . 5-M | 3,051 | 214 |
| West Virginia State Coll, Institute, WV 25112 | 1891 | NR . . . . . . . . . . . . . . . 5-B | 4,896 | 233 |
| West Virginia U, Morgantown, WV 26506 | 1867 | Dr. Neil S. Bucklew . . . . . 5-D | 22,712 | 1,543 |
| West Virginia Wesleyan Coll, Buckhannon, WV 26201 | 1890 | Dr. Thomas B. Courtice . . . 2-M | 1,655 | 126 |
| Wheaton Coll, Wheaton, IL 60187 | 1860 | Dr. A. Duane Litfin . . . . . 2-M | 2,606 | 259 |
| Wheaton Coll, Norton, MA 02766 | 1834 | Dr. Dale Rogers Marshall . . 1-B | 1,319 | 110 |
| Wheeling Jesuit Coll, Wheeling, WV 26003-6233 | 1954 | Fr. Thomas S. Acker, SJ . . 2-M | 1,438 | 80 |
| Wheelock Coll, Boston, MA 02215 (4) | 1888 | Dr. Gerald N. Tirozzi . . . . 1-M | 1,343 | 203 |
| Whitman Coll, Walla Walla, WA 99362 | 1859 | Mr. Charles Anderson . . . 1-B | 1,198 | 129 |
| Whittier Coll, Whittier, CA 90608 | 1887 | Dr. James L. Ash, Jr. . . . . 1-F | 1,957 | 101 |
| Whitworth Coll, Spokane, WA 99251 | 1890 | Dr. William P. Robinson . . 2-M | 1,676 | 95 |
| Wichita State U, Wichita, KS 67260 | 1895 | Dr. Eugene Morgan Hughes . 5-D | 15,120 | 488 |
| Widener U, Chester, PA 19013 | 1821 | Dr. Robert J. Bruce . . . . . 1-D | 8,938 | 312 |
| Wilkes U, Wilkes-Barre, PA 18766 | 1933 | Dr. Christopher N. Breiseth . 1-M | 3,200 | 228 |
| Willamette U, Salem, OR 97301 | 1842 | Dr. Jerry E. Hudson . . . . . 2-F | 2,332 | 247 |
| William Carey Coll, Hattiesburg, MS 39401 | 1906 | Dr. James W. Edwards . . . 2-M | 2,032 | 156 |
| William Jewell Coll, Liberty, MO 64068 | 1849 | Dr. J. Gordon Kingsley . . . 2-B | 1,384 | 146 |
| William Paterson Coll of New Jersey, Wayne, NJ 07470 | 1855 | Dr. Arnold Speert . . . . . . 5-M | 9,391 | 320 |
| Williams Coll, Williamstown, MA 01267 | 1793 | Dr. Francis C. Oakley . . . . 1-M | 2,064 | 267 |
| Wilmington Coll, New Castle, DE 19720 | 1967 | Dr. Audrey K. Doberstein . . 1-D | 2,500 | 253 |
| Wingate Coll, Wingate, NC 28174 | 1895 | Dr. Jerry E. McGee . . . . . 2-M | 1,434 | 97 |
| Winona State U, Winona, MN 55987 | 1858 | Dr. Darrell Krueger . . . . . 5-M | 7,500 | 400 |
| Winston-Salem State U, Winston-Salem, NC 27110 | 1892 | Dr. Cleon F. Thompson, Jr. . 5-B | 2,655 | 179 |
| Winthrop U, Rock Hill, SC 29733 | 1886 | Dr. Anthony DiGiorgio . . . 5-M | 5,025 | 420 |
| Wittenberg U, Springfield, OH 45501 | 1845 | Dr. William A. Kinnison . . . 2-B | 2,250 | 182 |
| Wofford Coll, Spartanburg, SC 29303-3663 | 1854 | Dr. Joab M. Lesesne . . . . 2-B | 1,127 | 94 |
| Woodbury U, Burbank, CA 91510 | 1884 | Dr. Paul E. Sago . . . . . . 1-M | 1,106 | 125 |
| Worcester Polytechnic Inst, Worcester, MA 01609 | 1865 | Dr. Jon C. Strauss . . . . . 1-D | 3,171 | 345 |
| Worcester State Coll, Worcester, MA 01602 | 1874 | Dr. Kalyan K. Ghosh . . . . 5-M | 4,418 | 194 |
| Wright State U, Dayton, OH 45435 | 1964 | Dr. Paige E. Mulhollan . . . 5-D | 17,657 | 950 |
| Xavier U, Cincinnati, OH 45207-5311 | 1831 | Rev. James E. Hoff, SJ . . . 2-M | 6,383 | 411 |
| Xavier U of Louisiana, New Orleans, LA 70125 | 1925 | Dr. Norman C. Francis . . . 2-F | 3,330 | 253 |
| Yale U, New Haven, CT 06520 | 1701 | Mr. Richard C. Levin . . . . 1-D | 11,129 | 712 |
| Yeshiva U, New York, NY 10033-3201 | 1886 | Dr. Norman Lamm . . . . . 1-D | 4,899 | 1,092 |
| York Coll of Pennsylvania, York, PA 17405-7199 | 1787 | Dr. George W. Waldner . . . 1-M | 4,942 | 286 |
| York Coll of the City U of New York, Jamaica, NY 11451 | 1967 | Dr. Josephine D. Davis . . .12-B | 6,480 | 200 |
| Youngstown State U, Youngstown, OH 44555 | 1908 | Dr. Leslie H. Cochran . . . . 5-D | 14,806 | 889 |

## Two-Year Colleges

The highest undergraduate degree offered for all two-year colleges is the associate degree.

| Name, address | Year | Governing official, control | Enroll- ment | Faculty |
|---|---|---|---|---|
| Abraham Baldwin Ag Coll, Tifton, GA 31794-2601 | 1933 | Dr. Harold J. Loyd . . . . . . . .5 | 2,851 | 135 |
| Adirondack Comm Coll, Queensbury, NY 12804 | 1960 | Dr. Roger Andersen . . . . . . 12 | 3,778 | 224 |
| Aiken Tech Coll, Aiken, SC 29802 | 1972 | Dr. Paul L. Blowers . . . . . . 12 | 2,373 | 124 |
| Aims Comm Coll, Greeley, CO 80632 | 1967 | Dr. George R. Conger . . . . . 10 | 9,035 | 434 |
| Alabama Southern Comm Coll, Monroeville, AL 36460 | 1965 | Dr. John A. Johnson . . . . . . . .5 | 1,898 | 107 |
| Alabama Southern Comm Coll, Thomasville, AL 36784 | 1965 | Dr. Hoyt Jones . . . . . . . . . .5 | 1,225 | 119 |
| Alamance Comm Coll, Graham, NC 27253 | 1958 | Dr. W. Ronald McCarter . . . . .5 | 3,775 | 145 |
| Albuquerque Tech Vocational Inst, Albuquerque, NM 87106 | 1965 | NR . . . . . . . . . . . . . . . . .5 | 12,806 | 746 |
| Allan Hancock Coll, Santa Maria, CA 93454 | 1920 | Dr. Ann F. Stephenson . . . . 12 | 8,221 | 417 |
| Allegany Comm Coll, Cumberland, MD 21502 | 1961 | Dr. Donald L. Alexander . . . 12 | 2,915 | 210 |
| Allen County Comm Coll, Iola, KS 66749 | 1923 | Mr. John Masterson . . . . . . 12 | 1,717 | 125 |
| Alpena Comm Coll, Alpena, MI 49707 | 1952 | Dr. Donald L. Newport . . . . 12 | 2,118 | 128 |
| Alvin Comm Coll, Alvin, TX 77511-4898 | 1949 | Dr. A. Rodney Allbright . . . . 12 | 4,085 | 141 |
| Amarillo Coll, Amarillo, TX 79178 | 1929 | Dr. Luther Bud Joyner . . . . 12 | 6,547 | 374 |
| American Inst of Business, Des Moines, IA 50321 | 1921 | Mr. Keith Fenton . . . . . . . . .1 | 1,040 | 55 |
| American River Coll, Sacramento, CA 95841 | 1955 | Dr. Queen F. Randall . . . . . 10 | 20,824 | 700 |
| Angelina Coll, Lufkin, TX 75902 | 1968 | Dr. Larry M. Phillips . . . . . 12 | 3,398 | 151 |
| Anne Arundel Comm Coll, Arnold, MD 21012 | 1961 | Dr. Thomas E. Florestano . . 12 | 11,749 | 590 |
| Anoka-Ramsey Comm Coll, Coon Rapids, MN 55433 | 1965 | Dr. Patrick M. Johns . . . . . 12 | 6,250 | 228 |
| Antelope Valley Coll, Lancaster, CA 93536 | 1929 | Dr. Allan W. Kurki . . . . . . . 12 | 10,751 | 400 |
| Arapahoe Comm Coll, Littleton, CO 80160-9002 | 1965 | Dr. James F. Weber . . . . . . .5 | 7,165 | 298 |
| Arizona Western Coll, Yuma, AZ 85366-0929 | 1962 | Dr. James R. Carruthers . . . 12 | 5,400 | 334 |
| Arkansas State U–Beebe Branch, Beebe, AR 72012 | 1927 | Dr. William H. Owen, Jr. . . . .5 | 1,872 | 79 |
| Art Inst of Atlanta, Atlanta, GA 30326 | 1949 | Mr. Hal R. Griffith . . . . . . . .3 | 1,386 | 106 |
| Art Inst of Dallas, Dallas, TX 75231 | 1978 | Dr. Pat DeCoursey . . . . . . . .3 | 1,000 | 84 |
| Art Inst of Fort Lauderdale, Fort Lauderdale, FL 33316 | 1968 | Mr. David P. Higley . . . . . . . .3 | 2,100 | 150 |
| The Art Inst of Houston, Houston, TX 77056 | 1978 | NR . . . . . . . . . . . . . . . . .3 | 1,083 | 91 |
| The Art Inst of Philadelphia, Philadelphia, PA 19103-5198 | 1966 | Dr. Max R. Tudor . . . . . . . . .3 | 1,200 | 90 |
| Art Inst of Pittsburgh, Pittsburgh, PA 15222 | 1921 | Ms. Saundra M. Van Dyke . . .3 | 2,500 | 106 |
| Art Inst of Seattle, Seattle, WA 98121 | 1982 | Mr. David J. Pauldine . . . . . .3 | 1,605 | 101 |
| Asnuntuck Comm Coll, Enfield, CT 06082 | 1972 | Dr. Harvey S. Irlen . . . . . . . .5 | 2,122 | 79 |
| Atlanta Metropolitan Coll, Atlanta, GA 30310 | 1974 | Dr. Edwin A. Thompson . . . . .5 | 1,700 | 100 |
| Atlantic Comm Coll, Mays Landing, NJ 08330 | 1966 | Dr. John May . . . . . . . . . . .9 | 5,687 | 215 |
| Austin Comm Coll, Austin, MN 55912 | 1940 | Dr. Vicky R. Smith . . . . . . . .5 | 1,373 | 73 |
| Austin Comm Coll, Austin, TX 78752 | 1972 | Mr. Roland K. Smith . . . . . . 10 | 25,275 | 1,388 |
| Bainbridge Coll, Bainbridge, GA 31717 | 1972 | Dr. Edward D. Mobley . . . . . .5 | 1,023 | 39 |
| Bakersfield Coll, Bakersfield, CA 93305 | 1913 | Dr. Richard Wright . . . . . . . 12 | 12,267 | 496 |
| Baltimore City Comm Coll, Baltimore, MD 21215 | 1947 | Dr. James D. Tschichtelin . . .5 | 6,856 | 493 |
| Barstow Coll, Barstow, CA 92311 | 1959 | Dr. Joseph A. Clark, Jr. . . . . 12 | 3,569 | 128 |
| Barton County Comm Coll, Great Bend, KS 67530 | 1969 | Dr. Jimmie L. Downing . . . . 12 | 4,460 | 205 |
| Bay de Noc Comm Coll, Escanaba, MI 49829 | 1963 | Dr. Dwight E. Link . . . . . . . .9 | 2,238 | 143 |

| Name, address | Year | Governing official, control | Enrollment | Faculty |
|---|---|---|---|---|
| Beaufort County Comm Coll, Washington, NC 27889 | 1967 | Dr. Ron Champion . . . . . . . . .5 | 1,281 | 95 |
| Bee County Coll, Beeville, TX 78102 | 1965 | Dr. Norman Wallace . . . . . . . .9 | 2,520 | 116 |
| Belleville Area Coll, Belleville, IL 62221 | 1946 | Dr. Joseph Cipfl . . . . . . . . .10 | 15,440 | 842 |
| Bellevue Comm Coll, Bellevue, WA 98007-6484 | 1966 | Dr. B. Jean Floten . . . . . . . . .5 | 10,543 | 670 |
| Belmont Tech Coll, St Clairsville, OH 43950 | 1971 | Dr. Wesley R. Channell . . . . . .5 | 1,750 | 133 |
| Bergen Comm Coll, Paramus, NJ 07652 | 1965 | Dr. Jose Lopez-Isa . . . . . . . .9 | 8,659 | 613 |
| Berkeley Coll of Business, West Paterson, NJ 07424 | 1931 | Mr. Kevin L. Luing . . . . . . . .3 | 1,608 | 110 |
| Berkshire Comm Coll, Pittsfield, MA 01201 | 1960 | Dr. Cathryn L. Addy . . . . . . .5 | 2,641 | 126 |
| Bessemer State Tech Coll, Bessemer, AL 35021 | 1966 | Dr. W. Michael Bailey . . . . . . .5 | 1,868 | 102 |
| Bevill State Comm Coll, Fayette, AL 35555 | 1969 | Dr. Wayland DeWitt . . . . . . . .5 | 1,145 | 63 |
| Big Bend Comm Coll, Moses Lake, WA 98837-3299 | 1962 | Dr. Greg Fitch . . . . . . . . . .5 | 1,850 | 147 |
| Bishop State Comm Coll, Mobile, AL 36603 | 1965 | NR . . . . . . . . . . . . . . . .5 | 2,757 | 90 |
| Bismarck State Coll, Bismarck, ND 58501 | 1939 | Dr. Kermit Lidstrom . . . . . . . .5 | 2,472 | 117 |
| Black Hawk Coll, Moline, IL 61265 | 1946 | Dr. Charles E. Laws . . . . . . .12 | 5,881 | 305 |
| Blackhawk Tech Coll, Janesville, WI 53547 | 1968 | Dr. James C. Catania . . . . . .10 | 2,700 | 293 |
| Blinn Coll, Brenham, TX 77833 | 1883 | Mr. Walter C. Schwartz . . . . .12 | 8,105 | 326 |
| Blue Mountain Comm Coll, Pendleton, OR 97801 | 1962 | Mr. Ronald L. Daniels . . . . . .12 | 5,588 | 189 |
| Blue Ridge Comm Coll, Flat Rock, NC 28731 | 1969 | Dr. David W. Sink . . . . . . . .12 | 1,514 | 98 |
| Blue Ridge Comm Coll, Weyers Cave, VA 24486 | 1965 | Dr. James R. Perkins . . . . . . .5 | 2,950 | 141 |
| Borough of Manhattan Comm Coll of City U of NY, New York, NY 10007 | 1963 | Dr. Steven M. Curtis . . . . . .12 | 15,677 | 995 |
| Bossier Parish Comm Coll, Bossier City, LA 71111 | 1967 | Mr. James M. Conerly . . . . . .12 | 4,356 | 134 |
| Bowling Green State U–Firelands Coll, Huron, OH 44839 | 1968 | Dr. R. Darby Williams . . . . . . .5 | 1,451 | 75 |
| Brainerd Comm Coll, Brainerd, MN 56401 | 1938 | Ms. Sally Jane Ihne . . . . . . . .5 | 1,856 | 97 |
| Bramson ORT Tech Inst, Forest Hills, NY 11375 | 1977 | Dr. Howard J. Friedman . . . . . .1 | 1,360 | 57 |
| Brazosport Coll, Lake Jackson, TX 77566 | 1948 | Dr. John R. Grable . . . . . . .12 | 3,346 | 157 |
| Brevard Comm Coll, Cocoa, FL 32922 | 1960 | Dr. Maxwell C. King . . . . . . .5 | 14,083 | 976 |
| Briarcliffe–The Coll for Bus/Data Systems Inst, Woodbury, NY 11797 | 1966 | Mr. Richard Turan . . . . . . . . .3 | 1,400 | 114 |
| Bristol Comm Coll, Fall River, MA 02720 | 1965 | Ms. Eileen Farley . . . . . . . . .9 | 3,143 | 183 |
| Brookdale Comm Coll, Lincroft, NJ 07738 | 1967 | Dr. Peter Burnham . . . . . . . .9 | 12,809 | 443 |
| Brookhaven Coll, Farmers Branch, TX 75244 | 1978 | Dr. Walter G. Bumphus . . . . . .9 | 9,060 | 525 |
| Broome Comm Coll, Binghamton, NY 13902 | 1946 | Dr. Donald A. Dellow . . . . . .12 | 5,685 | 451 |
| Broward Comm Coll, Fort Lauderdale, FL 33301 | 1960 | Dr. Willis N. Holcombe . . . . . .5 | 28,433 | 775 |
| Brunswick Coll, Brunswick, GA 31523 | 1961 | Dr. Dorothy L. Lord . . . . . . . .5 | 1,841 | 75 |
| Bryant and Stratton Business Inst, Buffalo, NY 14202 | 1854 | Mr. William Schatt . . . . . . . .3 | 1,009 | 26 |
| Bucks County Comm Coll, Newtown, PA 18940 | 1964 | Dr. James J. Linksz . . . . . . .9 | 11,348 | 375 |
| Bunker Hill Comm Coll, Boston, MA 02129 | 1973 | NR . . . . . . . . . . . . . . . .5 | 6,120 | 145 |
| Burlington County Comm Coll, Pemberton, NJ 08068 | 1969 | Dr. Robert Messina . . . . . . . .9 | 7,085 | 150 |
| Butler County Comm Coll, El Dorado, KS 67042 | 1927 | Dr. Rodney V. Cox, Jr. . . . . . .12 | 6,627 | 473 |
| Butler County Comm Coll, Butler, PA 16003 | 1965 | Dr. Thaddeus H. Penar . . . . . .9 | 3,290 | 135 |
| Camden County Coll, Blackwood, NJ 08012 | 1967 | Dr. Bob Barringer . . . . . . . .12 | 15,713 | 385 |
| Cañada Coll, Redwood City, CA 94061 | 1968 | NR . . . . . . . . . . . . . . . .10 | 6,936 | 263 |
| Cape Cod Comm Coll, West Barnstable, MA 02668 | 1961 | NR . . . . . . . . . . . . . . . . .5 | 4,009 | 258 |
| Cape Fear Comm Coll, Wilmington, NC 28401 | 1959 | Dr. Richard C. Conrath . . . . . .5 | 3,150 | 153 |
| Capital Comm Tech Coll, Hartford, CT 06105 | 1946 | NR . . . . . . . . . . . . . . . . .5 | 3,773 | 130 |
| Carl Albert State Coll, Poteau, OK 74953 | 1934 | NR . . . . . . . . . . . . . . . . .5 | 1,979 | 160 |
| Carl Sandburg Coll, Galesburg, IL 61401 | 1967 | NR . . . . . . . . . . . . . . . . .5 | 3,397 | 234 |
| Carteret Comm Coll, Morehead City, NC 28557 | 1963 | Dr. Donald W. Bryant . . . . . . .5 | 1,602 | 93 |
| Casper Coll, Casper, WY 82601 | 1945 | Dr. LeRoy Strausner . . . . . . .10 | 2,400 | 185 |
| Catawba Valley Comm Coll, Hickory, NC 28602-9699 | 1960 | Dr. Cuyler A. Dunbar . . . . . .12 | 3,566 | 175 |
| Catonsville Comm Coll, Catonsville, MD 21228 | 1957 | Dr. Frederick J. Walsh . . . . . .9 | 10,731 | 534 |
| Cayuga County Comm Coll, Auburn, NY 13021-3099 | 1953 | Dr. Lawrence H. Poole . . . . . .12 | 2,924 | 212 |
| Cazenovia Coll, Cazenovia, NY 13035 | 1824 | Dr. Stephen M. Schneeweiss . . .1 | 1,042 | 145 |
| Cecil Comm Coll, North East, MD 21901 | 1968 | Dr. Robert L. Gell . . . . . . . . .9 | 1,033 | 108 |
| Cedar Valley Coll, Lancaster, TX 75134 | 1977 | Dr. Carol J. Spencer . . . . . . .5 | 3,281 | 130 |
| Central Alabama Comm Coll, Alexander City, AL 35010 | 1965 | Dr. James H. Cornell . . . . . . .5 | 2,092 | 139 |
| Central Arizona Coll, Coolidge, AZ 85228 | 1961 | Dr. John J. Klein . . . . . . . . .5 | 14,724 | NR |
| Central Carolina Comm Coll, Sanford, NC 27330 | 1962 | Dr. Marvin R. Joyner . . . . . .12 | 3,050 | 189 |
| Central Carolina Tech Coll, Sumter, SC 29150 | 1963 | Dr. Herbert C. Robbins . . . . . .5 | 2,232 | 144 |
| Central Comm Coll–Grand Island Cmps, Grand Island, NE 68802 | 1976 | Dr. William Giddings . . . . . . .12 | 2,510 | 198 |
| Central Comm Coll–Hastings Cmps, Hastings, NE 68902 | 1966 | Dr. Judy Dresser . . . . . . . .12 | 3,063 | 144 |
| Central Comm Coll–Platte Cmps, Columbus, NE 68602 | 1968 | Dr. Peter Rush . . . . . . . . .12 | 2,524 | 118 |
| Central Florida Comm Coll, Ocala, FL 34478 | 1957 | NR . . . . . . . . . . . . . . . . .5 | 5,616 | 178 |
| Central Ohio Tech Coll, Newark, OH 43055 | 1971 | Dr. Julius S. Greenstein . . . . . .5 | 1,860 | 99 |
| Central Oregon Comm Coll, Bend, OR 97701 | 1949 | Dr. Robert L. Barber . . . . . . .10 | 3,138 | 184 |
| Central Piedmont Comm Coll, Charlotte, NC 28235 | 1963 | Mr. Paul A. Zeiss . . . . . . . .12 | 15,871 | 1,220 |
| Central Texas Coll, Killeen, TX 76540 | 1967 | Dr. James R. Anderson . . . . .12 | 6,825 | 300 |
| Central Virginia Comm Coll, Lynchburg, VA 24502-4907 | 1966 | Dr. Belle S. Wheelan . . . . . . .5 | 4,105 | 120 |
| Central Wyoming Coll, Riverton, WY 82501 | 1966 | Dr. JoAnne McFarland . . . . . .12 | 1,607 | 147 |
| Cerritos Coll, Norwalk, CA 90650 | 1956 | Dr. Ernest Martinez . . . . . . .12 | 21,067 | 683 |
| Cerro Coso Comm Coll, Ridgecrest, CA 93555 | 1973 | Dr. Raymond A. McCue . . . . . .5 | 4,118 | 282 |
| Chabot Coll, Hayward, CA 94545 | 1961 | Dr. Raul J. Cardoza . . . . . . .12 | 15,290 | 957 |
| Chaffey Coll, Rancho Cucamonga, CA 91737-3002 | 1883 | Dr. Jerry W. Young . . . . . . .10 | 15,000 | 540 |
| Champlain Coll, Burlington, VT 05401 | 1878 | Dr. Roger H. Perry . . . . . . . .1 | 1,966 | 117 |
| Charles County Comm Coll, La Plata, MD 20646 | 1958 | Dr. John Sine . . . . . . . . . .12 | 5,769 | 247 |
| Charles Stewart Mott Comm Coll, Flint, MI 48503 | 1923 | Dr. Charles R. Donnelly . . . . .10 | 11,222 | 454 |
| Chattahoochee Valley State Comm Coll, Phenix City, AL 36869 | 1974 | Mr. Bob Boothe . . . . . . . . .5 | 1,763 | 77 |
| Chattanooga State Tech Comm Coll, Chattanooga, TN 37406 | 1965 | Dr. James L. Catanzaro . . . . .5 | 8,943 | 358 |
| Chemeketa Comm Coll, Salem, OR 97309 | 1955 | Dr. Gerard Berger . . . . . . . .12 | 10,757 | 881 |
| Chesapeake Coll, Wye Mills, MD 21679 | 1965 | Dr. John R. Kotula . . . . . . . .12 | 2,131 | 95 |
| Chipola Jr Coll, Marianna, FL 32446 | 1947 | Dr. Jerry W. Kandzer . . . . . . .5 | 2,949 | 142 |
| Chippewa Valley Tech Coll, Eau Claire, WI 54701 | 1912 | Mr. Norbert K. Wurtzel . . . . . .10 | 3,800 | 400 |
| Cincinnati Tech Coll, Cincinnati, OH 45223 | 1966 | Dr. James P. Long . . . . . . . .5 | 5,562 | 317 |
| Cisco Jr Coll, Cisco, TX 76437 | 1940 | Dr. Roger C. Schustereit . . . . .12 | 2,559 | 98 |
| City Coll of San Francisco, San Francisco, CA 94112 | 1935 | Dr. Evans S. Dobelle . . . . . .12 | 34,000 | 1,117 |
| City Colls of Chicago, Harold Washington Coll, Chicago, IL 60601 | 1962 | Dr. Wayne Watson . . . . . . . .12 | 6,804 | 197 |
| City Colls of Chicago, Harry S Truman Coll, Chicago, IL 60640 | 1956 | Dr. Wallace B. Appelson . . . .12 | 5,078 | 160 |
| City Colls of Chicago, Kennedy-King Coll, Chicago, IL 60621 | 1935 | Dr. Harold Pates . . . . . . . .12 | 2,680 | 106 |
| City Colls of Chicago, Malcolm X Coll, Chicago, IL 60612 | 1911 | Ms. Zerrie D. Campbell . . . . .12 | 2,670 | 142 |
| City Colls of Chicago, Olive-Harvey Coll, Chicago, IL 60628 | 1970 | Mr. Homer D. Franklin . . . . . .12 | 3,698 | 123 |

| Name, address | Year | Governing official, control | Enroll-ment | Faculty |
|---|---|---|---|---|
| City Colls of Chicago, Richard J Daley Coll, Chicago, IL 60652 | 1960 | Mr. William P. Conway ..... 12 | 5,557 | NR |
| City Colls of Chicago, Wilbur Wright Coll, Chicago, IL 60634 | 1934 | Mr. Raymond F. LeFevour ... 12 | 6,188 | 161 |
| Clackamas Comm Coll, Oregon City, OR 97045 | 1966 | Dr. John S. Keyser .........9 | 6,621 | 512 |
| Clark Coll, Vancouver, WA 98663 | 1933 | Dr. Earl P. Johnson ........5 | 9,100 | 320 |
| Clark State Comm Coll, Springfield, OH 45501 | 1962 | Mr. Albert A. Salerno ......5 | 3,113 | 131 |
| Clatsop Comm Coll, Astoria, OR 97103 | 1958 | Dr. John W. Wubben ........9 | 2,265 | 165 |
| Cleveland Inst of Electronics, Cleveland, OH 44114 (2) | 1934 | Mr. John R. Drinko .........3 | 2,700 | 6 |
| Cleveland State Comm Coll, Cleveland, TN 37320-3570 | 1967 | Dr. James W. Ford .........5 | 3,596 | 184 |
| Clinton Comm Coll, Clinton, IA 52732 | 1946 | Dr. Desna L. Wallin ........5 | 1,274 | 75 |
| Clinton Comm Coll, Plattsburgh, NY 12901 | 1969 | Dr. Jay L. Fennell .........12 | 2,080 | 156 |
| Cloud County Comm Coll, Concordia, KS 66901-1002 | 1965 | Dr. James P. Ihrig ........12 | 3,018 | 225 |
| Clovis Comm Coll, Clovis, NM 88101 | 1971 | Dr. Jay Gurley ............5 | 3,328 | NR |
| Coastal Carolina Comm Coll, Jacksonville, NC 28546-6877 | 1964 | Dr. Ronald K. Lingle, Jr. .. 12 | 3,590 | 192 |
| Coastline Comm Coll, Fountain Valley, CA 92708 | 1976 | Dr. William M. Vega .......12 | 15,562 | 505 |
| Cochise Coll, Douglas, AZ 85607 | 1962 | Dr. Walter S. Patton .......12 | 4,938 | 342 |
| Coffeyville Comm Coll, Coffeyville, KS 67337 | 1923 | Dr. Dan Kinney ...........12 | 2,300 | 86 |
| Colby Comm Coll, Colby, KS 67701 | 1964 | Dr. Mikel Ary .............12 | 1,023 | 80 |
| Coll of Alameda, Alameda, CA 94501 | 1970 | Dr. Marie B. Smith ........12 | 5,962 | NR |
| Coll of DuPage, Glen Ellyn, IL 60137 | 1967 | Dr. Harold D. McAninch ... 12 | 31,625 | 1,808 |
| Coll of Eastern Utah, Price, UT 84501 | 1937 | Dr. Michael A. Petersen ....5 | 2,746 | 96 |
| Coll of Lake County, Grayslake, IL 60030-1198 | 1967 | Dr. Daniel J. La Vista ..... 10 | 15,644 | 677 |
| Coll of Marin, Kentfield, CA 94904 | 1926 | Dr. John D. Randall ........12 | 9,604 | 464 |
| Coll of Southern Idaho, Twin Falls, ID 83303-1238 | 1964 | Dr. Gerald R. Meyerhoeffer . 12 | 3,804 | 244 |
| Coll of The Albemarle, Elizabeth City, NC 27906-2327 | 1960 | Dr. Larry R. Donnithorne ....5 | 2,038 | 117 |
| Coll of the Canyons, Santa Clarita, CA 91355 | 1969 | Dr. Dianne G. Van Hook ... 12 | 6,250 | 229 |
| Coll of the Desert, Palm Desert, CA 92260 | 1959 | Dr. David A. George .......12 | 10,975 | 419 |
| Coll of the Mainland, Texas City, TX 77591 | 1967 | Mr. Larry L. Stanley .......12 | 3,883 | 180 |
| Coll of the Redwoods, Eureka, CA 95501 | 1964 | Dr. Cedric A. Sampson .....12 | 7,222 | 379 |
| Coll of the Sequoias, Visalia, CA 93277 | 1925 | Dr. Robert A. Lombardi ....12 | 9,499 | 479 |
| Coll of the Siskiyous, Weed, CA 96094 | 1957 | Dr. Martha Romero ........12 | 2,441 | 146 |
| Collin County Comm Coll, McKinney, TX 75070 | 1985 | NR .....................12 | 9,590 | 528 |
| Colorado Inst of Art, Denver, CO 80203 | 1952 | Dr. W. C. Bottoms .........3 | 1,328 | 77 |
| Columbia Coll, Columbia, CA 95310 | 1968 | Dr. Kenneth White .........12 | 3,618 | 119 |
| Columbia-Greene Comm Coll, Hudson, NY 12534 | 1969 | Dr. Terry A. Cline .........12 | 1,778 | 115 |
| Columbia State Comm Coll, Columbia, TN 38401 | 1966 | Dr. Paul Sands ...........5 | 3,721 | 197 |
| Columbus State Comm Coll, Columbus, OH 43216 | 1963 | Dr. Harold M. Nestor .......5 | 16,510 | 842 |
| Comm Coll of Allegheny County Allegheny Cmps, Pittsburgh, PA 15212 | 1966 | Dr. J. David Griffin ........9 | 13,831 | 274 |
| Comm Coll of Allegheny County Boyce Cmps, Monroeville, PA 15146 | 1966 | Dr. Carl A. Di Sibio .......9 | 4,635 | 190 |
| Comm Coll of Allegheny County, North Cmps, Pittsburgh, PA 15237 | 1972 | Dr. Fred F. Bartok .........9 | 4,336 | 1,398 |
| Comm Coll of Allegheny County South Cmps, West Mifflin, PA 15122 | 1967 | Dr. Thomas A. Juravich .....9 | 5,688 | 760 |
| Comm Coll of Aurora, Aurora, CO 80011-9036 | 1983 | Dr. Larry Carter ..........5 | 4,695 | 197 |
| Comm Coll of Beaver County, Monaca, PA 15061 | 1966 | Ms. Margaret Williams-Betlyn .5 | 2,800 | 150 |
| Comm Coll of Denver, Denver, CO 80217-3363 | 1970 | Dr. Byron McClenney .......5 | 7,021 | 271 |
| Comm Coll of Philadelphia, Philadelphia, PA 19130 | 1964 | Dr. Bob Barringer .........12 | 19,476 | 1,170 |
| Comm Coll of Rhode Island, Warwick, RI 02886-1807 | 1964 | Mr. Edward Liston .........5 | 12,365 | 720 |
| Comm Coll of Southern Nevada, North Las Vegas, NV 89030 | 1971 | Dr. Paul E. Meacham .......5 | 17,747 | 730 |
| Comm Coll of the Air Force, Maxwell Air Force Base, AL 36112-6655 | 1972 | Col. Paul A. Reid ..........4 | 478,245 | 11,000 |
| Comm Coll of Vermont, Waterbury, VT 05676 | 1970 | Dr. Michael Holland ........5 | 2,358 | 591 |
| Compton Comm Coll, Compton, CA 90221-5393 | 1927 | Dr. Warren A. Washington .. 12 | 5,700 | 347 |
| Connors State Coll, Warner, OK 74469 | 1908 | Dr. Carl O. Westbrook ......5 | 2,379 | 110 |
| Contra Costa Coll, San Pablo, CA 94806 | 1948 | Dr. D. Candy Rose .........12 | 8,242 | 244 |
| Cooke County Coll, Gainesville, TX 76240 | 1924 | Dr. Luther Bud Joyner ......9 | 4,068 | 175 |
| Copiah-Lincoln Comm Coll, Wesson, MS 39191 | 1928 | Dr. Billy B. Thames ........12 | 1,531 | 116 |
| Corning Comm Coll, Corning, NY 14830 | 1956 | Dr. Donald H. Hangen ......12 | 3,512 | 147 |
| Cosumnes River Coll, Sacramento, CA 95823 | 1970 | Dr. Marc E. Hall ..........10 | 11,525 | 398 |
| County Coll of Morris, Randolph, NJ 07869 | 1966 | Dr. Edward J. Yaw .........9 | 10,568 | 553 |
| Cowley County Comm Coll and Voc-Tech Sch, Arkansas City, KS 67005 | 1922 | Dr. Patrick J. McAtee ......12 | 3,059 | 184 |
| Crafton Hills Coll, Yucaipa, CA 92399 | 1972 | Dr. Luis S. Gomez .........12 | 5,136 | 190 |
| Crowder Coll, Neosho, MO 64850 | 1963 | Dr. Kent A. Farnsworth .....12 | 1,895 | 147 |
| Cuesta Coll, San Luis Obispo, CA 93403-8106 | 1964 | Dr. Grace N. Mitchell ......10 | 8,004 | 298 |
| Culinary Inst of America, Hyde Park, NY 12538-1499 | 1946 | Mr. Ferdinand E. Metz ......1 | 1,923 | 101 |
| Cumberland County Coll, Vineland, NJ 08360 | 1963 | Dr. Roland J. Chapdelaine .. 12 | 2,783 | 118 |
| Cuyahoga Comm Coll, Eastern Cmps, Highland Hills, OH 44122 | 1971 | Mr. Paul E. Shumaker ..... 12 | 5,858 | 225 |
| Cuyahoga Comm Coll, Metropolitan Cmps, Cleveland, OH 44115 | 1963 | Dr. Ronald R. Zambetti .....12 | 7,004 | 474 |
| Cuyahoga Comm Coll, Western Cmps, Parma, OH 44130 | 1966 | Mr. Ronald M. Sobel .......12 | 12,961 | 596 |
| Cuyamaca Coll, El Cajon, CA 92019 | 1978 | Dr. Samuel M. Ciccati .....12 | 4,945 | NR |
| Cypress Coll, Cypress, CA 90630 | 1966 | Dr. Kirk Avery ............12 | 14,672 | 434 |
| Dabney S Lancaster Comm Coll, Clifton Forge, VA 24422 | 1964 | Dr. John F. Backels ........5 | 1,653 | NR |
| Dalton Coll, Dalton, GA 30720 | 1963 | Dr. Derrell C. Roberts ......5 | 2,884 | 108 |
| Danville Area Comm Coll, Danville, IL 61832 | 1946 | Dr. Harry J. Braun ........12 | 3,429 | 143 |
| Danville Comm Coll, Danville, VA 24541 | 1967 | Dr. B. Carlyle Ramsey ......5 | 4,045 | 152 |
| Darton Coll, Albany, GA 31707 | 1965 | Dr. Peter J. Sireno ........5 | 2,633 | 136 |
| Davidson County Comm Coll, Lexington, NC 27293 | 1958 | Dr. J. Bryan Brooks ........12 | 2,252 | 149 |
| Daytona Beach Comm Coll, Daytona Beach, FL 32120-2811 | 1958 | NR .....................5 | 10,807 | 704 |
| Dean Jr Coll, Franklin, MA 02038 | 1865 | Mr. John A. Dunn ..........1 | 1,000 | 126 |
| DeKalb Coll, Decatur, GA 30034 | 1964 | Dr. Marvin M. Cole ........5 | 15,976 | 1,010 |
| Delaware County Comm Coll, Media, PA 19063-1094 | 1967 | Dr. Richard D. De Cosmo .. 12 | 10,269 | 486 |
| Delaware Tech & Comm Coll, Southern Cmps, Georgetown, DE 19947 | 1967 | Mr. Jack F. Owens .........5 | 3,563 | 159 |
| Delaware Tech & Comm Coll, Stanton/Wilmington Cmps, Newark, DE 19702 | 1968 | Dr. Orlando J. George, Jr. ...5 | 6,273 | 348 |
| Delaware Tech & Comm Coll, Terry Cmps, Dover, DE 19901 | 1972 | Mr. Wayne N. Dabson .......5 | 1,997 | 105 |
| Delgado Comm Coll, New Orleans, LA 70119 | 1921 | Dr. Ione Elioff ...........5 | 15,115 | 1,029 |
| Del Mar Coll, Corpus Christi, TX 78404 | 1935 | Mr. B. R. Venters .........12 | 11,659 | 480 |

| Name, address | Year | Governing official, control | Enroll-ment | Faculty |
|---|---|---|---|---|
| Delta Coll, University Center, MI 48710 | 1961 | Dr. Peter D. Boyse ... 10 | 11,228 | 508 |
| Des Moines Area Comm Coll, Ankeny, IA 50021 | 1966 | Dr. Joseph Borgen ... 12 | 11,040 | NR |
| DeVry Inst of Tech, Woodbridge, NJ 07095 | 1969 | NR ... 3 | 2,202 | 75 |
| Diablo Valley Coll, Pleasant Hill, CA 94523 | 1949 | Dr. Phyllis L. Peterson ... 12 | 23,000 | 800 |
| Dixie Coll, St George, UT 84770 | 1911 | Dr. Douglas Alder ... 5 | 2,347 | 107 |
| Dodge City Comm Coll, Dodge City, KS 67801 | 1935 | Dr. Thomas E. Gamble ... 12 | 2,601 | 161 |
| Doña Ana Branch Comm Coll, Las Cruces, NM 88003-0001 | 1973 | NR ... 12 | 3,615 | 158 |
| Dundalk Comm Coll, Baltimore, MD 21222 | 1970 | Dr. Martha A. Smith ... 9 | 3,383 | 237 |
| Durham Tech Comm Coll, Durham, NC 27703 | 1961 | Dr. Phail Wynn, Jr. ... 5 | 5,003 | 271 |
| Dutchess Comm Coll, Poughkeepsie, NY 12601 | 1957 | Dr. D. David Conklin ... 12 | 7,693 | 415 |
| Dyersburg State Comm Coll, Dyersburg, TN 38025-0648 | 1969 | Dr. Karen A. Bowyer ... 5 | 2,100 | 132 |
| East Arkansas Comm Coll, Forrest City, AR 72335 | 1974 | Dr. Tom Spencer ... 5 | 1,804 | 89 |
| East Central Coll, Union, MO 63084 | 1968 | Dr. Dale Gibson ... 10 | 3,216 | 155 |
| East Central Comm Coll, Decatur, MS 39327 | 1928 | Dr. Eddie M. Smith ... 12 | 1,402 | 56 |
| Eastern Arizona Coll, Thatcher, AZ 85552-0769 | 1888 | Mr. Gherald L. Hoopes, Jr. ... 12 | 1,819 | 268 |
| Eastern New Mexico U-Roswell, Roswell, NM 88202 | 1958 | Dr. Loyd R. Hughes ... 5 | 2,085 | 140 |
| Eastern Oklahoma State Coll, Wilburton, OK 74578 | 1907 | NR ... 5 | 2,474 | 54 |
| Eastern Wyoming Coll, Torrington, WY 82240 | 1948 | Dr. Roy Mason ... 12 | 2,024 | 136 |
| Eastfield Coll, Mesquite, TX 75150 | 1970 | Dr. Robert Aguero ... 12 | 9,526 | 399 |
| East Los Angeles Coll, Monterey Park, CA 91754 | 1945 | Dr. Omero Suarez ... 12 | 13,423 | 450 |
| East Mississippi Comm Coll, Scooba, MS 39358 | 1927 | Dr. Thomas L. Davis ... 12 | 1,381 | 175 |
| Edgecombe Comm Coll, Tarboro, NC 27886 | 1968 | Mr. Charles B. McIntyre ... 12 | 2,018 | 168 |
| Edison Comm Coll, Fort Myers, FL 33906-6210 | 1962 | Dr. Kenneth Walker ... 12 | 9,120 | 724 |
| Edison State Comm Coll, Piqua, OH 45356 | 1973 | Dr. Kenneth A. Yowell ... 5 | 3,297 | 183 |
| Edmonds Comm Coll, Lynnwood, WA 98036 | 1967 | Mr. Thomas C. Nielsen ... 12 | 8,140 | 381 |
| Elaine P Nunez Comm Coll, Chalmette, LA 70043 | 1967 | Dr. Carol S. Hopson ... 12 | 1,887 | 47 |
| El Centro Coll, Dallas, TX 75202 | 1966 | Dr. Wright L. Lassiter, Jr. ... 9 | 6,328 | 331 |
| Elgin Comm Coll, Elgin, IL 60123 | 1949 | Dr. Paul Heath ... 12 | 9,031 | 400 |
| El Paso Comm Coll, El Paso, TX 79998 | 1969 | Dr. Leonardo de la Garza ... 9 | 18,474 | 1,539 |
| Enterprise State Jr Coll, Enterprise, AL 36331 | 1965 | Dr. Joseph D. Talmadge ... 5 | 2,285 | 125 |
| Erie Comm Coll, City Cmps, Buffalo, NY 14203-2601 | 1971 | Dr. Louis M. Ricci ... 12 | 4,034 | 256 |
| Erie Comm Coll, North Cmps, Williamsville, NY 14221-7095 | 1946 | Dr. Louis M. Ricci ... 12 | 7,131 | 391 |
| Erie Comm Coll, South Cmps, Orchard Park, NY 14127-2199 | 1974 | Dr. Louis M. Ricci ... 12 | 3,545 | 282 |
| Essex Comm Coll, Baltimore, MD 21237 | 1957 | Dr. Donald J. Slowinski ... 12 | 10,767 | 599 |
| Essex County Coll, Newark, NJ 07102 | 1966 | Dr. Zachary Yamba ... 9 | 8,500 | 270 |
| Everett Comm Coll, Everett, WA 98201 | 1941 | Ms. Susan C. Carroll ... 5 | 7,726 | 252 |
| Evergreen Valley Coll, San Jose, CA 95135 | 1975 | NR ... 12 | 11,255 | 275 |
| Fairleigh Dickinson U, Edward Williams Coll, Hackensack, NJ 07601 | 1964 | Mr. Kenneth T. Vehrkens ... 1 | 1,158 | 62 |
| Fashion Inst of Design & Merchandising, LA Cmps, Los Angeles, CA 90015 | 1969 | Ms. Tonian Hohberg ... 3 | 2,934 | 180 |
| Fayetteville Tech Comm Coll, Fayetteville, NC 28303-0236 | 1961 | Dr. Craig Allen ... 5 | 6,975 | 317 |
| Feather River Comm Coll District, Quincy, CA 95971 | 1968 | Dr. Donald Donato ... 5 | 1,300 | 92 |
| Fergus Falls Comm Coll, Fergus Falls, MN 56537 | 1960 | Mr. Dan F. True ... 5 | 1,300 | 60 |
| Finger Lakes Comm Coll, Canandaigua, NY 14424-8395 | 1965 | Dr. Daniel T. Hayes ... 12 | 4,002 | 234 |
| Fiorello H LaGuardia Comm Coll of City U of NY, Long Island City, NY 11101 | 1970 | Dr. Raymond C. Bowen ... 12 | 9,702 | 585 |
| Flathead Valley Comm Coll, Kalispell, MT 59901 | 1967 | Dr. Howard L. Fryett ... 12 | 1,719 | 105 |
| Florence-Darlington Tech Coll, Florence, SC 29501-0548 | 1963 | Dr. Michael B. McCall ... 5 | 2,639 | 201 |
| Florida Comm Coll at Jacksonville, Jacksonville, FL 32202 | 1963 | Dr. Charles C. Spence ... 5 | 19,734 | 1,575 |
| Florida Keys Comm Coll, Key West, FL 33040 | 1965 | Dr. William A. Seeker ... 5 | 2,200 | 94 |
| Floyd Coll, Rome, GA 30162 | 1970 | Dr. H. Lynn Cundiff ... 5 | 2,825 | 66 |
| Foothill Coll, Los Altos Hills, CA 94022 | 1958 | Dr. Thomas H. Clements ... 12 | 17,162 | 578 |
| Forsyth Tech Comm Coll, Winston-Salem, NC 27103 | 1964 | Dr. Bob H. Greene ... 5 | 5,175 | 574 |
| Fort Scott Comm Coll, Fort Scott, KS 66701 | 1919 | Dr. Laura Meeks ... 12 | 1,815 | 141 |
| Fox Valley Tech Coll, Appleton, WI 54913 | 1967 | Dr. H. Victor Baldi ... 12 | 6,500 | 1,241 |
| Frederick Comm Coll, Frederick, MD 21702 | 1957 | Dr. Lee J. Betts ... 12 | 4,336 | 267 |
| Fresno City Coll, Fresno, CA 93741 | 1910 | Dr. Brice W. Harris ... 10 | 18,598 | 832 |
| Front Range Comm Coll, Westminster, CO 80030 | 1968 | Dr. Thomas Gonzales ... 5 | 11,547 | 450 |
| Fullerton Coll, Fullerton, CA 92632 | 1913 | Dr. Philip W. Borst ... 12 | 21,211 | 678 |
| Fulton-Montgomery Comm Coll, Johnstown, NY 12095 | 1964 | Dr. Jacqueline D. Taylor ... 12 | 1,953 | 122 |
| Gadsden State Comm Coll, Gadsden, AL 35902-0227 | 1985 | NR ... 5 | 6,210 | 303 |
| Gainesville Coll, Gainesville, GA 30503 | 1964 | Dr. J. Foster Watkins ... 12 | 2,942 | 118 |
| Galveston Coll, Galveston, TX 77550 | 1967 | Dr. Marc A. Nigliazzo ... 12 | 2,331 | 122 |
| Garden City Comm Coll, Garden City, KS 67846 | 1919 | Dr. James H. Tangeman ... 10 | 2,111 | 101 |
| Garland County Comm Coll, Hot Springs, AR 71913 | 1973 | NR ... 12 | 2,313 | 111 |
| Gaston Coll, Dallas, NC 28034 | 1963 | Dr. W. Wayne Scott ... 12 | 4,047 | 309 |
| Gateway Comm Coll, Phoenix, AZ 85034 | 1968 | Dr. Phil Randolph ... 12 | 6,617 | 253 |
| Gateway Comm-Tech Coll, New Haven, CT 06511 | 1968 | Dr. Antonio Perez ... 5 | 5,207 | 259 |
| Gateway Tech Coll, Kenosha, WI 53144 | 1911 | Mr. William P. Nickolai ... 12 | 12,741 | 755 |
| Gavilan Coll, Gilroy, CA 95020 | 1919 | Dr. Glenn E. Mayle ... 12 | 4,029 | 164 |
| Genesee Comm Coll, Batavia, NY 14020-9704 | 1966 | Dr. Stuart Steiner ... 12 | 3,648 | 214 |
| George Corley Wallace State Comm Coll, Selma, AL 36702 | 1966 | Dr. Julius Ray Brown ... 5 | 1,800 | 78 |
| George C Wallace State Comm Coll, Dothan, AL 36303 | 1949 | Dr. Larry Beaty ... 5 | 4,060 | 180 |
| Georgia Military Coll, Milledgeville, GA 31061 | 1879 | NR ... 12 | 2,549 | 179 |
| Germanna Comm Coll, Locust Grove, VA 22508 | 1970 | Dr. Francis S. Turnage ... 5 | 2,500 | 83 |
| Glendale Comm Coll, Glendale, AZ 85302 | 1965 | Dr. John R. Waltrip ... 12 | 17,936 | 680 |
| Glendale Comm Coll, Glendale, CA 91208 | 1927 | Dr. John A. Davitt ... 12 | 15,337 | 345 |
| Glen Oaks Comm Coll, Centreville, MI 49032 | 1965 | Dr. Philip G. Ward ... 12 | 1,387 | 89 |
| Gloucester County Coll, Sewell, NJ 08080 | 1967 | Dr. Richard H. Jones ... 9 | 5,266 | 264 |
| Gogebic Comm Coll, Ironwood, MI 49938 | 1932 | Dr. James R. Grote ... 12 | 1,376 | 91 |
| Golden West Coll, Huntington Beach, CA 92647-0592 | 1966 | NR ... 12 | 15,295 | 462 |
| Gordon Coll, Barnesville, GA 30204 | 1852 | Dr. Jerry M. Williamson ... 5 | 1,913 | 105 |
| Grand Rapids Comm Coll, Grand Rapids, MI 49503 | 1914 | Mr. Richard Calkins ... 11 | 14,200 | 535 |
| Grays Harbor Coll, Aberdeen, WA 98520 | 1930 | Dr. Jewell Manspeaker ... 5 | 2,815 | 140 |
| Grayson County Coll, Denison, TX 75020 | 1964 | Dr. Jim M. Williams ... 12 | 3,400 | 176 |
| Great Lakes Jr Coll of Business, Saginaw, MI 48607 | 1907 | NR ... 1 | 2,097 | 150 |
| Greenfield Comm Coll, Greenfield, MA 01301 | 1962 | Dr. Katherine H. Sloan ... 5 | 1,954 | 124 |
| Green River Comm Coll, Auburn, WA 98002 | 1965 | Mr. Richard A. Rutkowski ... 5 | 7,955 | 253 |
| Greenville Tech Coll, Greenville, SC 29606 | 1962 | Dr. Thomas E. Barton, Jr. ... 5 | 8,814 | 480 |
| Grossmont Coll, El Cajon, CA 92020-1799 | 1961 | Dr. Richard M. Sanchez ... 12 | 15,004 | 572 |
| Gulf Coast Comm Coll, Panama City, FL 32401 | 1957 | Dr. Robert L. McSpadden ... 5 | 8,053 | 338 |

| Name, address | Year | Governing official, control | Enroll-ment | Faculty |
|---|---|---|---|---|
| Hagerstown Jr Coll, Hagerstown, MD 21742-6590 | 1946 | Dr. Norman P. Shea ....... 9 | 3,189 | 180 |
| Harford Comm Coll, Bel Air, MD 21015 | 1957 | Dr. Richard J. Pappas .... 12 | 5,508 | 364 |
| Harrisburg Area Comm Coll, Harrisburg, PA 17110 | 1964 | Dr. Mary L. Fifield ....... 12 | 11,561 | 485 |
| Hartnell Coll, Salinas, CA 93901 | 1920 | Dr. James R. Hardt ....... 10 | 7,772 | 356 |
| Hawkeye Comm Coll, Waterloo, IA 50704 | 1967 | Dr. Phillip O. Barry ...... 12 | 2,467 | 151 |
| Haywood Comm Coll, Clyde, NC 28721 | 1964 | Dr. Dan W. Moore ........ 12 | 1,255 | 126 |
| Henry Ford Comm Coll, Dearborn, MI 48128 | 1938 | Dr. Andrew A. Mazzara .... 10 | 14,975 | 1,005 |
| Herkimer County Comm Coll, Herkimer, NY 13350 | 1966 | Dr. Ronald F. Williams .... 12 | 2,391 | 109 |
| Hesser Coll, Manchester, NH 03103 | 1900 | Mr. Linwood W. Galeucia ... 3 | 3,000 | 60 |
| Hibbing Comm Coll, Hibbing, MN 55746 | 1916 | Dr. Anthony Kuznik ....... 12 | 1,115 | 65 |
| Highland Comm Coll, Freeport, IL 61032 | 1962 | Dr. Ruth Mercedes Smith .. 12 | 3,181 | 159 |
| Highland Comm Coll, Highland, KS 66035 | 1858 | Dr. Eric M. Priest ....... 12 | 2,160 | 182 |
| Highline Comm Coll, Des Moines, WA 98198 | 1961 | Dr. Edward M. Command .... 5 | 10,300 | 432 |
| Hill Coll of the Hill Jr Coll District, Hillsboro, TX 76645 | 1923 | Dr. W. R. Auvenshine ..... 10 | 2,000 | 80 |
| Hillsborough Comm Coll, Tampa, FL 33631-3127 | 1968 | Dr. Andreas A. Paloumpis .. 5 | 20,838 | 343 |
| Hinds Comm Coll, Raymond, MS 39154 | 1917 | NR ................... 12 | 9,288 | 725 |
| Hocking Tech Coll, Nelsonville, OH 45764 | 1968 | Dr. John J. Light ....... 5 | 5,948 | 252 |
| Holmes Comm Coll, Goodman, MS 39079 | 1928 | NR ................... 12 | 2,317 | 125 |
| Holyoke Comm Coll, Holyoke, MA 01040 | 1946 | Dr. David M. Bartley ..... 5 | 3,646 | 222 |
| Horry-Georgetown Tech Coll, Conway, SC 29526 | 1965 | Dr. D. Kent Sharples ..... 12 | 2,404 | 113 |
| Housatonic Comm-Tech Coll, Bridgeport, CT 06608 | 1966 | Dr. Vincent S. Darnowski .. 5 | 2,658 | 105 |
| Houston Comm Coll System, Houston, TX 77270 | 1971 | Dr. Charles Green ....... 12 | 37,410 | 2,277 |
| Howard Coll, Big Spring, TX 79720 | 1945 | Dr. Cheryl T. Sparks ..... 12 | 2,399 | 147 |
| Howard Comm Coll, Columbia, MD 21044 | 1966 | Dr. Dwight A. Burrill ..... 12 | 4,961 | 312 |
| Hudson County Comm Coll, Jersey City, NJ 07306 | 1974 | NR ................... 12 | 3,076 | 198 |
| Hudson Valley Comm Coll, Troy, NY 12180 | 1953 | Dr. Joseph J. Bulmer ..... 12 | 10,647 | 514 |
| Hutchinson Comm Coll, Hutchinson, KS 67501 | 1928 | Dr. Edward E. Berger .... 12 | 3,888 | 264 |
| ICS Ctr for Degree Studies, Scranton, PA 18515 | 1975 | Mr. Gary Keisling ....... 3 | 20,363 | 5 |
| Illinois Central Coll, East Peoria, IL 61635 | 1967 | Dr. Thomas K. Thomas .... 12 | 13,632 | 626 |
| Illinois Eastern Comm Colls, Frontier Comm Coll, Fairfield, IL 62837 | 1976 | Mr. Richard Mason ...... 12 | 1,907 | 148 |
| Illinois Eastern Comm Colls, Lincoln Trail Coll, Robinson, IL 62454 | 1969 | Dr. Donald E. Donnay ..... 12 | 1,085 | 67 |
| Illinois Eastern Comm Colls, Olney Central Coll, Olney, IL 62450 | 1962 | Dr. Judith M. Hansen ..... 12 | 1,550 | 92 |
| Illinois Eastern Comm Colls, Wabash Valley Coll, Mount Carmel, IL 62863 | 1960 | Dr. Harry K. Benson ..... 12 | 2,562 | 94 |
| Illinois Valley Comm Coll, Oglesby, IL 61348 | 1924 | Dr. Alfred E. Wisgoski .... 10 | 4,497 | 176 |
| Imperial Valley Coll, Imperial, CA 92251-2663 | 1922 | Dr. John A. DePaoli ...... 12 | 5,226 | 290 |
| Independence Comm Coll, Independence, KS 67301 | 1925 | Dr. Don Schoening ....... 10 | 1,605 | 153 |
| Indiana Business Coll, Indianapolis, IN 46204 | 1902 | Mr. Kenneth J. Konesco ... 3 | 1,700 | 70 |
| Indiana Vocational Tech Coll–Central Indiana, Indianapolis, IN 46206 | 1963 | Dr. Meredith L. Carter .... 5 | 5,767 | 363 |
| Indiana Vocational Tech Coll–Columbus, Columbus, IN 47203 | 1963 | NR .................... 5 | 2,612 | 198 |
| Indiana Vocational Tech Coll–Eastcentral, Muncie, IN 47302 | 1968 | Dr. Luanne G. Pruens .... 5 | 2,315 | 169 |
| Indiana Vocational Tech Coll–Kokomo, Kokomo, IN 46901 | 1968 | Dr. Shanon Christiansen ... 5 | 1,739 | 125 |
| Indiana Vocational Tech Coll–Lafayette, Lafayette, IN 47903 | 1968 | Dr. Elizabeth J. Doversberger . 5 | 1,830 | 128 |
| Indiana Vocational Tech Coll–Northcentral, South Bend, IN 46619 | 1968 | Dr. Carl F. Lutz ........ 5 | 2,686 | 219 |
| Indiana Vocational Tech Coll–Northeast, Fort Wayne, IN 46805 | 1969 | Mr. Jon L. Rupright ...... 5 | 4,197 | 290 |
| Indiana Vocational Tech Coll–Northwest, Gary, IN 46409 | 1963 | Dr. Rob Jeffs ........... 5 | 2,503 | 213 |
| Indiana Vocational Tech Coll–Southcentral, Sellersburg, IN 47172 | 1968 | Mr. Jonathan W. Thomas ... 5 | 2,092 | 124 |
| Indiana Vocational Tech Coll–Southwest, Evansville, IN 47710 | 1963 | Dr. H. Victor Baldi ...... 5 | 2,092 | 185 |
| Indiana Vocational Tech Coll–Wabash Valley, Terre Haute, IN 47802 | 1966 | Dr. Sam E. Borden ...... 5 | 2,310 | 181 |
| Indiana Vocational Tech Coll–Whitewater, Richmond, IN 47374 | 1963 | Mr. James Steck ........ 5 | 1,186 | 108 |
| Indian Hills Comm Coll, Ottumwa, IA 52501 | 1966 | Dr. Lyle A. Hellyer ...... 12 | 3,279 | 137 |
| Indian River Comm Coll, Fort Pierce, FL 34981-5599 | 1960 | Dr. Edwin R. Massey ..... 5 | 13,156 | 821 |
| Inver Hills Comm Coll, Inver Grove Heights, MN 55076 | 1969 | Dr. Steve Wallace ....... 5 | 5,383 | 237 |
| Iowa Central Comm Coll, Fort Dodge, IA 50501 | 1966 | Dr. Jack L. Bottenfield ... 12 | 2,500 | 155 |
| Iowa Lakes Comm Coll, Estherville, IA 51334 | 1967 | Dr. Richard H. Blacker ... 12 | 1,574 | 40 |
| Iowa Western Comm Coll, Council Bluffs, IA 51502 | 1966 | Dr. Carl L. Heinrich ..... 10 | 3,623 | 152 |
| Irvine Valley Coll, Irvine, CA 92720 | 1979 | Dr. Anna L. McFarlin .... 12 | 10,007 | 223 |
| Itasca Comm Coll, Grand Rapids, MN 55744 | 1922 | Dr. Lawrence N. Dukes .... 5 | 1,169 | 75 |
| Itawamba Comm Coll, Fulton, MS 38843 | 1947 | Dr. David Cole ......... 12 | 3,500 | 102 |
| ITT Tech Inst, Fort Wayne, IN 46825 | 1967 | Mr. Jack B. Cozad ...... 3 | 1,114 | 34 |
| Jackson Comm Coll, Jackson, MI 49201 | 1928 | Dr. Clyde LeTarte ....... 9 | 8,100 | 435 |
| Jackson State Comm Coll, Jackson, TN 38301 | 1967 | Dr. Walter L. Nelms ..... 5 | 3,461 | 177 |
| James H Faulkner State Jr Coll, Bay Minette, AL 36507 | 1965 | Dr. Gary L. Branch ...... 5 | 3,496 | 173 |
| James Sprunt Comm Coll, Kenansville, NC 28349 | 1964 | Dr. Donald L. Reichard ... 5 | 1,051 | 71 |
| Jamestown Comm Coll, Jamestown, NY 14701 | 1950 | Dr. Timothy G. Davies .... 12 | 4,664 | 316 |
| Jefferson Coll, Hillsboro, MO 63050-2441 | 1963 | Dr. Gery Hochanadel .... 12 | 4,220 | 199 |
| Jefferson Comm Coll, Watertown, NY 13601 | 1961 | Dr. John W. Deans ...... 12 | 2,100 | 180 |
| Jefferson Davis Comm Coll, Brewton, AL 36427 | 1965 | NR .................... 5 | 1,832 | 44 |
| Jefferson State Comm Coll, Birmingham, AL 35215 | 1965 | Dr. Judy M. Merritt ..... 12 | 7,440 | 301 |
| Jefferson Tech Coll, Steubenville, OH 43952 | 1966 | Dr. Edward L. Florak .... 12 | 1,691 | 98 |
| John A Logan Coll, Carterville, IL 62918 | 1967 | Dr. Ray Hancock ....... 12 | 4,971 | 193 |
| John C Calhoun State Comm Coll, Decatur, AL 35609 | 1965 | Dr. Richard Carpenter ... 12 | 8,070 | 404 |
| Johnston Comm Coll, Smithfield, NC 27577 | 1969 | Dr. John L. Tart ........ 5 | 2,850 | 235 |
| John Tyler Comm Coll, Chester, VA 23831 | 1967 | Dr. Marshall W. Smith .... 5 | 5,562 | 226 |
| John Wood Comm Coll, Quincy, IL 62301 | 1974 | Dr. Robert C. Keys ...... 10 | 3,950 | 143 |
| Joliet Jr Coll, Joliet, IL 60436 | 1901 | Dr. Raymond A. Pietak ... 12 | 10,427 | 591 |
| Jones County Jr Coll, Ellisville, MS 39437 | 1928 | Dr. T. Terrell Tisdale .... 12 | 4,400 | 153 |
| Jordan Coll, Cedar Springs, MI 49319 | 1967 | Dr. Lexie K. Coxon ...... 2 | 2,118 | 176 |
| J Sargeant Reynolds Comm Coll, Richmond, VA 23285-5622 | 1972 | Dr. S. A. Burnette ....... 5 | 12,739 | 580 |
| Kalamazoo Valley Comm Coll, Kalamazoo, MI 49009 | 1966 | Dr. Marilyn J. Schlack .... 12 | 9,637 | 406 |
| Kankakee Comm Coll, Kankakee, IL 60901 | 1966 | Dr. Larry D. Huffman .... 12 | 4,000 | 213 |
| Kansas City Kansas Comm Coll, Kansas City, KS 66112 | 1923 | Dr. Thomas R. Burke ..... 9 | 5,876 | 367 |
| Kaskaskia Coll, Centralia, IL 62801 | 1966 | Mr. Raymond D. Woods ... 12 | 3,498 | 192 |

| Name, address | Year | Governing official, control | Enroll-ment | Faculty |
|---|---|---|---|---|
| Kellogg Comm Coll, Battle Creek, MI 49017 | 1956 | Dr. Paul R. Ohm . . . . . . . . . 12 | 7,662 | 268 |
| Kelsey Jenney Coll, San Diego, CA 92101 | 1863 | NR . . . . . . . . . . . . . . . . .1 | 1,000 | 50 |
| Kent State U, Ashtabula Cmps, Ashtabula, OH 44004 | 1958 | Dr. John K. Mahan . . . . . . . .5 | 1,025 | 69 |
| Kent State U, Salem Cmps, Salem, OH 44460 | 1966 | Dr. James F. Cooney . . . . . .5 | 1,010 | 62 |
| Kent State U, Stark Cmps, Canton, OH 44720 | 1967 | Dr. William G. Bittle . . . . . . .5 | 2,531 | 124 |
| Kent State U, Trumbull Cmps, Warren, OH 44483 | 1954 | Dr. David A. Allen, Jr. . . . . . .5 | 1,869 | 95 |
| Kent State U, Tuscarawas Cmps, New Philadelphia, OH 44663 | 1962 | NR . . . . . . . . . . . . . . . . .5 | 1,246 | 83 |
| Keystone Jr Coll, La Plume, PA 18440 | 1868 | Dr. Robert E. Mooney, Jr. . . . .1 | 1,008 | 88 |
| Kilgore Coll, Kilgore, TX 75662 | 1935 | NR . . . . . . . . . . . . . . . . 12 | 4,540 | 240 |
| Kings River Comm Coll, Reedley, CA 93654 | 1926 | Mr. Richard J. Giese . . . . . 12 | 6,722 | 221 |
| Kirkwood Comm Coll, Cedar Rapids, IA 52406 | 1966 | Dr. Norm Nielsen . . . . . . . 12 | 9,612 | 450 |
| Kirtland Comm Coll, Roscommon, MI 48653 | 1966 | Dr. Dorothy N. Franke . . . . 10 | 1,309 | 95 |
| Kishwaukee Coll, Malta, IL 60150 | 1967 | Dr. Norman L. Jenkins . . . . 12 | 3,388 | NR |
| Labette Comm Coll, Parsons, KS 67357 | 1923 | Mr. Joseph C. Birmingham . . 12 | 2,598 | 261 |
| Lake City Comm Coll, Lake City, FL 32055 | 1962 | Dr. Muriel Kay Heimer . . . . .5 | 2,551 | 186 |
| Lake Land Coll, Mattoon, IL 61938 | 1966 | Dr. Robert K. Luther . . . . . 12 | 4,543 | 361 |
| Lakeland Comm Coll, Mentor, OH 44060 | 1967 | Dr. Ralph R. Doty . . . . . . . 12 | 9,174 | 434 |
| Lake Michigan Comm Coll, Benton Harbor, MI 49022 | 1946 | Dr. Anne E. Mulder . . . . . . 10 | 3,816 | 240 |
| Lakeshore Tech Coll, Cleveland, WI 53015 | 1967 | Dr. Dennis Ladwig . . . . . . 12 | 2,678 | 344 |
| Lake-Sumter Comm Coll, Leesburg, FL 34788 | 1962 | Dr. Robert Westrick . . . . . . 12 | 2,394 | 117 |
| Lake Tahoe Comm Coll, South Lake Tahoe, CA 96151 | 1975 | Dr. Guy F. Lease . . . . . . . 12 | 3,000 | 121 |
| Lakewood Comm Coll, White Bear Lake, MN 55110 | 1967 | Dr. Neil Christenson . . . . . .5 | 6,414 | 215 |
| Lamar U–Orange, Orange, TX 77630 | 1969 | Dr. Steve Maradian . . . . . . .5 | 1,550 | 63 |
| Lamar U–Port Arthur, Port Arthur, TX 77641 | 1909 | Dr. Sam Monroe . . . . . . . . .5 | 2,109 | 109 |
| Lane Comm Coll, Eugene, OR 97405-0640 | 1964 | Dr. Jerry Moskus . . . . . . . 12 | 9,350 | 553 |
| Lansing Comm Coll, Lansing, MI 48901 | 1957 | Dr. Abel B. Sykes, Jr. . . . . 12 | 21,828 | 1,236 |
| Laramie County Comm Coll, Cheyenne, WY 82007 | 1968 | Dr. Charles Bohlen . . . . . . .9 | 4,300 | 220 |
| Laredo Jr Coll, Laredo, TX 78040 | 1946 | Dr. Roger L. Worsley . . . . . 12 | 5,944 | 297 |
| Las Positas Coll, Livermore, CA 94550 | 1988 | NR . . . . . . . . . . . . . . . . .5 | 5,722 | NR |
| Lassen Coll, Susanville, CA 96130 | 1925 | Dr. Larry J. Blake . . . . . . . 12 | 2,825 | 204 |
| Lawson State Comm Coll, Birmingham, AL 35221 | 1965 | Dr. Perry W. Ward . . . . . . . .5 | 2,044 | 89 |
| Lee Coll, Baytown, TX 77522-0818 | 1934 | Dr. Jackson N. Sasser . . . . 10 | 5,481 | 236 |
| Lehigh County Comm Coll, Schnecksville, PA 18078-2598 | 1967 | Mr. James R. Davis . . . . . . 12 | 5,200 | 155 |
| Lewis and Clark Comm Coll, Godfrey, IL 62035 | 1970 | NR . . . . . . . . . . . . . . . . 10 | 5,853 | 305 |
| Lima Tech Coll, Lima, OH 45804 | 1971 | Dr. James J. Countryman . . .5 | 2,750 | 167 |
| Lincoln Land Comm Coll, Springfield, IL 62794-9256 | 1967 | Dr. Norman Stephens, Jr. . . 10 | 10,012 | 401 |
| Linn-Benton Comm Coll, Albany, OR 97321 | 1966 | Mr. Jon Carnahan . . . . . . . 12 | 6,357 | 479 |
| Long Beach City Coll, Long Beach, CA 90808 | 1927 | Miss Barbara A. Adams . . . 12 | 27,000 | 850 |
| Longview Comm Coll, Lee's Summit, MO 64081 | 1969 | Mr. Aldo W. Leker . . . . . . . 12 | 9,414 | 385 |
| Lorain County Comm Coll, Elyria, OH 44035 | 1963 | Dr. Roy Church . . . . . . . . . 12 | 7,681 | 333 |
| Lord Fairfax Comm Coll, Middletown, VA 22645 | 1969 | Dr. Marilyn C. Beck . . . . . . .5 | 3,200 | 158 |
| Los Angeles City Coll, Los Angeles, CA 90029 | 1929 | Dr. Jose Robledo . . . . . . . 10 | 17,500 | 614 |
| Los Angeles Harbor Coll, Wilmington, CA 90744 | 1949 | Mr. James L. Heinselman . . 12 | 9,200 | 350 |
| Los Angeles Mission Coll, Sylmar, CA 91342-3244 | 1974 | Dr. Jack Fujimoto . . . . . . . 12 | 7,380 | 115 |
| Los Angeles Pierce Coll, Woodland Hills, CA 91371 | 1947 | Mr. Lowell J. Erickson . . . . 12 | 18,314 | 519 |
| Los Angeles Southwest Coll, Los Angeles, CA 90047 | 1967 | Dr. Carolyn G. Williams . . . 12 | 6,557 | 250 |
| Los Angeles Trade-Tech Coll, Los Angeles, CA 90015 | 1925 | Mr. Thomas L. Stevens . . . . 12 | 13,713 | 259 |
| Los Angeles Valley Coll, Van Nuys, CA 91401 | 1949 | Dr. Mary E. Lee . . . . . . . . 12 | 17,768 | 482 |
| Los Medanos Coll, Pittsburg, CA 94565 | 1974 | Mr. Stanley H. Chin . . . . . . 10 | 7,493 | 223 |
| Louisiana State U at Alexandria, Alexandria, LA 71302 | 1960 | Dr. Ben F. Martin . . . . . . . .5 | 2,771 | 91 |
| Louisiana State U at Eunice, Eunice, LA 70535 | 1967 | Dr. Michael Smith . . . . . . . .5 | 2,861 | 120 |
| Lurleen B Wallace State Jr Coll, Andalusia, AL 36420 | 1969 | Dr. Seth Hammett . . . . . . . .5 | 1,263 | 39 |
| Luzerne County Comm Coll, Nanticoke, PA 18634-9804 | 1966 | Mr. Donald R. Bronsard . . . .9 | 7,285 | 406 |
| Macomb Comm Coll, Warren, MI 48093 | 1954 | Dr. Albert L. Lorenzo . . . . . 10 | 28,165 | 841 |
| Macon Coll, Macon, GA 31297 | 1968 | Dr. S. Aaron Hyatt . . . . . . . .5 | 5,080 | 129 |
| Madison Area Tech Coll, Madison, WI 53704 | 1911 | Dr. Beverly S. Simone . . . . 10 | 11,622 | 1,960 |
| Manatee Comm Coll, Bradenton, FL 34206 | 1957 | Dr. Stephen J. Korcheck . . . .5 | 8,726 | 314 |
| Manchester Comm-Tech Coll, Manchester, CT 06040 | 1963 | Dr. Jonathan M. Daube . . . . .5 | 6,686 | 205 |
| Maple Woods Comm Coll, Kansas City, MO 64156 | 1969 | Dr. Stephen R. Brainard . . . 12 | 5,167 | 186 |
| Marion Tech Coll, Marion, OH 43302-5694 | 1971 | Dr. John Richard Bryson . . . 13 | 1,697 | 105 |
| Marshalltown Comm Coll, Marshalltown, IA 50158 | 1927 | Dr. William Simpson . . . . . . 10 | 1,245 | 100 |
| Marymount Coll, Palos Verdes, California, Rancho Palos Verdes, CA 90274-6299 | 1932 | Dr. Thomas M. McFadden . . .2 | 1,074 | 91 |
| Massachusetts Bay Comm Coll, Wellesley Hills, MA 02181 | 1961 | Mr. Roger A. Van Winkle . . . .5 | 5,233 | 278 |
| Massasoit Comm Coll, Brockton, MA 02402 | 1966 | Dr. Gerard F. Burke . . . . . . .5 | 6,502 | 427 |
| McCook Comm Coll, McCook, NE 69001 | 1926 | Dr. Robert G. Smallfoot . . . 12 | 1,100 | 64 |
| McLennan Comm Coll, Waco, TX 76708 | 1965 | Dr. Dennis F. Michaelis . . . .9 | 6,006 | 259 |
| Mendocino Coll, Ukiah, CA 95482 | 1973 | Dr. Carl J. Ehmann . . . . . . 12 | 4,810 | 169 |
| Merced Coll, Merced, CA 95348 | 1962 | Dr. E. Jan Moser . . . . . . . . 12 | 7,803 | 421 |
| Mercer County Comm Coll, Trenton, NJ 08690 | 1966 | Dr. Thomas Sepe . . . . . . . 12 | 9,053 | 356 |
| Meridian Comm Coll, Meridian, MS 39307 | 1937 | Dr. William F. Scaggs . . . . 12 | 3,081 | 236 |
| Mesa Comm Coll, Mesa, AZ 85202 | 1965 | Dr. Larry K. Christiansen . . 12 | 19,879 | 736 |
| Metropolitan Comm Coll, Omaha, NE 68103-0777 | 1974 | Dr. J. Richard Gilliland . . . . 12 | 10,301 | 373 |
| Miami-Dade Comm Coll, Miami, FL 33132 | 1960 | Dr. Robert H. McCabe . . . . 12 | 53,824 | 2,189 |
| Miami U–Hamilton Cmps, Hamilton, OH 45011 | 1968 | Dr. Harriet V. Taylor . . . . . . .5 | 2,182 | 160 |
| Miami U–Middletown Cmps, Middletown, OH 45042 | 1966 | Dr. Michael P. Governanti . . .5 | 2,329 | 165 |
| Middle Georgia Coll, Cochran, GA 31014 | 1884 | Dr. Joe Ben Welch . . . . . . . .5 | 1,878 | 82 |
| Middlesex Comm Coll, Middletown, CT 06457 | 1966 | Dr. Leila Gonzalez Sullivan . .5 | 3,230 | 130 |
| Middlesex Comm Coll, Bedford, MA 01730 | 1970 | Dr. Carole A. Cowan . . . . . .5 | 7,190 | 295 |
| Middlesex County Coll, Edison, NJ 08818 | 1964 | Dr. Flora M. Edwards . . . . . .9 | 12,500 | 287 |
| Midland Coll, Midland, TX 79705 | 1969 | Dr. David E. Daniel . . . . . . 12 | 3,789 | 192 |
| Midlands Tech Coll, Columbia, SC 29202 | 1974 | Dr. James L. Hudgins . . . . 12 | 8,729 | 655 |
| Mid Michigan Comm Coll, Harrison, MI 48625-9447 | 1965 | Dr. Charles J. Corrigan . . . 12 | 2,134 | 199 |
| Mid-Plains Comm Coll, North Platte, NE 69101 | 1965 | Dr. William A. Griffin, Jr. . . 10 | 1,947 | 87 |
| Mid-State Tech Coll, Wisconsin Rapids, WI 54494 | 1917 | Dr. M. H. Schneeberg . . . . 12 | 2,808 | 86 |
| Mineral Area Coll, Flat River, MO 63601 | 1922 | Dr. Dixie A. Kohn . . . . . . . 10 | 3,064 | 128 |
| Minneapolis Comm Coll, Minneapolis, MN 55403-1779 | 1965 | Dr. Jacquelyn Belcher . . . . .5 | 4,310 | 189 |
| MiraCosta Coll, Oceanside, CA 92056 | 1934 | Dr. H. Deon Holt . . . . . . . . .5 | 8,389 | 376 |
| Mississippi County Comm Coll, Blytheville, AR 72316-1109 | 1975 | Dr. John P. Sullins . . . . . . . .5 | 1,745 | 128 |
| Mississippi Delta Comm Coll, Moorhead, MS 38761 | 1926 | Dr. Bobby Garvin . . . . . . . 10 | 2,472 | 128 |
| Mississippi Gulf Coast Comm Coll, Perkinston, MS 39573 | 1911 | Dr. Richard Miller . . . . . . . 10 | 8,827 | 527 |
| Mitchell Comm Coll, Statesville, NC 28677 | 1852 | Dr. Douglas O. Eason . . . . .5 | 1,526 | 90 |
| Moberly Area Comm Coll, Moberly, MO 65270 | 1927 | Dr. Andrew Komar, Jr. . . . . .5 | 1,846 | 95 |
| Modesto Jr Coll, Modesto, CA 95350 | 1921 | Dr. Stanley L. Hodges . . . . 12 | 8,300 | 454 |
| Mohave Comm Coll, Kingman, AZ 86401 | 1971 | Dr. Charles W. Hall . . . . . . .5 | 5,329 | 241 |

| Name, address | Year | Governing official, control | Enrollment | Faculty |
|---|---|---|---|---|
| Mohawk Valley Comm Coll, Utica, NY 13501 | 1946 | Dr. Michael I. Schafer .... 12 | 6,500 | 340 |
| Monroe Coll, Bronx, NY 10468 | 1933 | Mr. Stephen J. Jerome ..... 3 | 2,400 | 100 |
| Monroe Comm Coll, Rochester, NY 14623 | 1961 | Dr. Peter A. Spina ..... 12 | 13,312 | 660 |
| Monroe County Comm Coll, Monroe, MI 48161 | 1964 | Mr. Gerald D. Welch ..... 9 | 3,924 | 178 |
| Montcalm Comm Coll, Sidney, MI 48885-0300 | 1965 | Dr. Donald C. Burns ..... 12 | 1,693 | 112 |
| Monterey Peninsula Coll, Monterey, CA 93940-4799 | 1947 | Dr. David W. Hopkins, Jr. ... 5 | 8,500 | 390 |
| Montgomery Coll–Germantown Cmps, Germantown, MD 20874 | 1975 | Dr. Robert E. Parilla ..... 12 | 3,930 | 176 |
| Montgomery Coll–Rockville Cmps, Rockville, MD 20850 | 1965 | Dr. Robert E. Parilla ..... 12 | 14,355 | 705 |
| Montgomery Coll–Takoma Park Cmps, Takoma Park, MD 20912 | 1946 | Dr. Robert E. Parilla ..... 12 | 4,830 | 219 |
| Montgomery County Comm Coll, Blue Bell, PA 19422 | 1964 | Dr. Edward M. Sweitzer ..... 9 | 9,411 | 412 |
| Moorpark Coll, Moorpark, CA 93021 | 1967 | Dr. James W. Walker ..... 9 | 12,078 | 450 |
| Moraine Park Tech Coll, Fond du Lac, WI 54936 | 1967 | Dr. John J. Shanahan ..... 12 | 6,074 | 290 |
| Moraine Valley Comm Coll, Palos Hills, IL 60465 | 1967 | Dr. Vernon O. Crawley ..... 12 | 14,074 | 636 |
| Morgan Comm Coll, Fort Morgan, CO 80701 | 1967 | Dr. Richard Bond ..... 5 | 1,002 | 132 |
| Morton Coll, Cicero, IL 60650 | 1924 | Mr. Charles P. Ferro ..... 12 | 4,695 | 275 |
| Motlow State Comm Coll, Tullahoma, TN 37388 | 1969 | Dr. A. Frank Glass ..... 5 | 3,211 | 245 |
| Mountain Empire Comm Coll, Big Stone Gap, VA 24219 | 1972 | Dr. Robert H. Sandel ..... 5 | 2,641 | 133 |
| Mountain View Coll, Dallas, TX 75211-6599 | 1970 | Dr. Rodger A. Pool ..... 9 | 6,600 | 268 |
| Mt Hood Comm Coll, Gresham, OR 97030 | 1966 | Dr. Paul Kreider ..... 12 | 7,960 | 501 |
| Mount Ida Coll, Newton Centre, MA 02159 | 1899 | Dr. Bryan E. Carlson ..... 1 | 1,750 | 177 |
| Mt San Antonio Coll, Walnut, CA 91789 | 1946 | Dr. William H. Feddersen ..... 10 | 23,294 | 821 |
| Mt San Jacinto Coll, San Jacinto, CA 92583 | 1963 | Dr. Richard H. Lowe ..... 12 | 7,010 | 181 |
| Mount Wachusett Comm Coll, Gardner, MA 01440 | 1963 | Dr. Daniel M. Asquino ..... 5 | 2,200 | 112 |
| Murray State Coll, Tishomingo, OK 73460-3130 | 1908 | Dr. Clyde R. Kindell ..... 5 | 1,674 | 69 |
| Muscatine Comm Coll, Muscatine, IA 52761 | 1929 | Dr. Victor G. McAvoy ..... 5 | 1,203 | 68 |
| Muskegon Comm Coll, Muskegon, MI 49442 | 1926 | Dr. James L. Stevenson ..... 12 | 5,169 | 150 |
| Muskingum Area Tech Coll, Zanesville, OH 43701-2694 | 1969 | Dr. Lynn H. Willett ..... 12 | 2,701 | 104 |
| Napa Valley Coll, Napa, CA 94558 | 1942 | Dr. Diane E. Carey ..... 12 | 7,102 | 297 |
| Nash Comm Coll, Rocky Mount, NC 27804 | 1967 | Dr. J. Reid Parrott, Jr. ..... 5 | 1,911 | 175 |
| Nashville State Tech Inst, Nashville, TN 37209 | 1970 | Dr. George H. Van Allen ..... 5 | 6,082 | 294 |
| Nassau Comm Coll, Garden City, NY 11530 | 1959 | Dr. Sean A. Fanelli ..... 12 | 18,641 | 1,440 |
| National Ed Ctr–Bauder Coll Cmps, Fort Lauderdale, FL 33334 | 1964 | NR ..... 3 | 1,000 | 41 |
| National Ed Ctr–Brown Inst Cmps, Minneapolis, MN 55407 | 1946 | Mr. Steve Marks ..... 3 | 1,197 | 79 |
| National Ed Ctr–Spartan Sch of Aeronautics Cmps, Tulsa, OK 74158-2833 (2) | 1928 | Mr. Ross L. Alloway ..... 3 | 1,773 | 150 |
| Navajo Comm Coll, Tsaile, AZ 86556 | 1968 | Dr. Tommy Lewis, Jr. ..... 4 | 1,804 | 155 |
| Navarro Coll, Corsicana, TX 75110 | 1946 | Dr. Gerald Burson ..... 12 | 3,202 | 198 |
| Neosho County Comm Coll, Chanute, KS 66720 | 1936 | Mr. Jim Stringer ..... 12 | 1,920 | 117 |
| Newbury Coll, Brookline, MA 02146 | 1962 | Mr. Edward J. Tassinari ..... 1 | 1,001 | 81 |
| The New England Banking Inst, Boston, MA 02111 | 1909 | NR ..... 1 | 1,046 | 360 |
| New England Inst of Tech, Warwick, RI 02886 | 1940 | Dr. Richard I. Gouse ..... 1 | 1,950 | 134 |
| New Hampshire Tech Inst, Concord, NH 03302-2039 | 1964 | Dr. David E. Larrabee, Sr. ..... 5 | 1,522 | 145 |
| New Mexico Jr Coll, Hobbs, NM 88240 | 1965 | Dr. Charles D. Hays ..... 12 | 2,438 | 109 |
| New Mexico State U–Carlsbad, Carlsbad, NM 88220 | 1950 | Dr. Shelton W. Marlow ..... 5 | 1,214 | 72 |
| New Orleans Baptist Theological Sem, New Orleans, LA 70126 | 1917 | Dr. Landrum P. Leavell, II ..... 2 | 1,917 | 18 |
| New River Comm Coll, Dublin, VA 24084 | 1969 | Dr. Edwin L. Barnes ..... 5 | 2,003 | 200 |
| Niagara County Comm Coll, Sanborn, NY 14132 | 1962 | Mr. Gerald L. Miller ..... 12 | 5,610 | 455 |
| Nicolet Area Tech Coll, Rhinelander, WI 54501 | 1968 | Dr. Adrian Lorbetske ..... 12 | 1,700 | 84 |
| Normandale Comm Coll, Bloomington, MN 55431 | 1968 | Dr. Thomas J. Horak ..... 5 | 9,221 | 300 |
| Northampton County Area Comm Coll, Bethlehem, PA 18017 | 1967 | Dr. Robert J. Kopecek ..... 12 | 6,725 | 372 |
| North Arkansas Comm/Tech Coll, Harrison, AR 72601 | 1974 | Dr. Bill Baker ..... 12 | 1,415 | 84 |
| North Central Michigan Coll, Petoskey, MI 49770 | 1958 | Mr. Robert B. Graham ..... 9 | 2,230 | 102 |
| North Central Missouri Coll, Trenton, MO 64683 | 1925 | Dr. James Selby ..... 10 | 1,050 | 70 |
| North Central Tech Coll, Mansfield, OH 44901 | 1961 | Dr. Byron E. Kee ..... 12 | 2,971 | 181 |
| Northcentral Tech Coll, Wausau, WI 54401 | 1912 | Mr. Dean Dietrich ..... 10 | 4,881 | 211 |
| North Country Comm Coll, Saranac Lake, NY 12983 | 1967 | Dr. Gail Rogers Rice ..... 12 | 1,823 | 140 |
| North Dakota State Coll of Science, Wahpeton, ND 58076 | 1903 | Dr. Jerry Olson ..... 5 | 2,147 | 146 |
| Northeast Alabama State Jr Coll, Rainsville, AL 35986 | 1963 | Dr. Charles M. Pendley ..... 5 | 1,787 | 53 |
| Northeast Comm Coll, Norfolk, NE 68702 | 1973 | Dr. Robert P. Cox ..... 12 | 3,257 | 122 |
| Northeastern Jr Coll, Sterling, CO 80751 | 1941 | Dr. Henry M. Milander ..... 12 | 1,743 | 79 |
| Northeastern Oklahoma A&M Coll, Miami, OK 74354 | 1919 | Dr. Jerry D. Carroll ..... 5 | 2,600 | 133 |
| Northeast Iowa Comm Coll, Peosta Cmps, Peosta, IA 52068 | 1970 | Ms. Karla Berns ..... 12 | 1,450 | 66 |
| Northeast Mississippi Comm Coll, Booneville, MS 38829 | 1948 | Mr. Joe M. Childers ..... 10 | 2,775 | NR |
| Northeast State Tech Comm Coll, Blountville, TN 37617 | 1966 | Dr. R. Wade Powers ..... 12 | 3,464 | 166 |
| Northeast Texas Comm Coll, Mount Pleasant, TX 75456-1307 | 1985 | NR ..... 12 | 2,024 | 85 |
| Northeast Wisconsin Tech Coll, Green Bay, WI 54307 | 1913 | Dr. Gerald D. Prindiville ..... 12 | 7,614 | 310 |
| Northern Essex Comm Coll, Haverhill, MA 01830 | 1960 | Dr. John R. Dimitry ..... 5 | 6,609 | 457 |
| Northern Nevada Comm Coll, Elko, NV 89801 | 1967 | Dr. Ronald K. Remington ..... 5 | 2,500 | 188 |
| Northern New Mexico Comm Coll, Española, NM 87532 | 1909 | Ms. Connie A. Valdez ..... 5 | 1,832 | 163 |
| Northern Oklahoma Coll, Tonkawa, OK 74653-0310 | 1901 | Dr. Joe Kinzer ..... 5 | 2,100 | 80 |
| Northern Virginia Comm Coll, Annandale, VA 22003 | 1965 | Dr. Richard J. Ernst ..... 5 | 39,250 | 1,314 |
| North Florida Jr Coll, Madison, FL 32340 | 1958 | Dr. William H. McCoy ..... 5 | 1,050 | 30 |
| North Harris Montgomery Comm Coll District, Houston, TX 77060 | 1972 | Dr. John E. Pickelman ..... 12 | 3,080 | 196 |
| North Idaho Coll, Coeur d'Alene, ID 83814 | 1933 | Dr. Carl R. Bennett ..... 12 | 3,068 | 168 |
| North Iowa Area Comm Coll, Mason City, IA 50401 | 1918 | Dr. David Buettner ..... 12 | 3,074 | 107 |
| North Lake Coll, Irving, TX 75038 | 1977 | Dr. James F. Horton, Jr. ..... 12 | 6,835 | 280 |
| Northland Pioneer Coll, Holbrook, AZ 86025 | 1974 | Dr. John H. Anderson ..... 12 | 4,350 | 400 |
| North Seattle Comm Coll, Seattle, WA 98103 | 1970 | Dr. Peter Ku ..... 12 | 8,990 | 290 |
| Northwest Alabama Comm Coll, Phil Campbell, AL 35581 | 1961 | NR ..... 5 | 2,049 | 83 |
| NorthWest Arkansas Comm Coll, Bentonville, AR 72712 | 1989 | NR ..... 5 | 1,889 | 124 |
| Northwest Coll, Powell, WY 82435 | 1946 | Dr. John P. Hanna ..... 12 | 1,930 | 173 |
| Northwestern Coll, Lima, OH 45805 | 1920 | Mr. Loren R. Jarvis ..... 1 | 1,400 | 59 |
| Northwestern Connecticut Comm Coll, Winsted, CT 06098 | 1965 | Dr. Booker T. DeVaughn ..... 5 | 2,053 | 87 |
| Northwestern Michigan Coll, Traverse City, MI 49684 | 1951 | Dr. Timothy G. Quinn ..... 12 | 4,275 | 231 |
| Northwest Mississippi Comm Coll, Senatobia, MS 38668 | 1927 | Dr. David M. Haraway ..... 12 | 4,000 | 180 |
| Northwest State Comm Coll, Archbold, OH 43502 | 1968 | Dr. Larry G. McDougle ..... 12 | 2,054 | 121 |
| Norwalk Comm-Tech Coll, Norwalk, CT 06854 | 1961 | Dr. William H. Schwab ..... 5 | 4,943 | 135 |
| Oakland Comm Coll, Bloomfield Hills, MI 48304 | 1964 | Dr. Patsy J. Fulton ..... 12 | 29,333 | 788 |

| Name, address | Year | Governing official, control | Enrollment | Faculty |
|---|---|---|---|---|
| Oakton Comm Coll, Des Plaines, IL 60016 | 1969 | Dr. Thomas TenHoeve . . . . . 10 | 11,253 | 495 |
| Ocean County Coll, Toms River, NJ 08754-2001 | 1964 | Dr. Milton Shaw . . . . . . . . . .9 | 8,353 | 375 |
| Odessa Coll, Odessa, TX 79764 | 1946 | Dr. Philip T. Speegle . . . . . . 12 | 4,800 | 255 |
| Ohio U–Southern Cmps, Ironton, OH 45638 | 1956 | Dr. Bill Dingus . . . . . . . . . . .5 | 2,358 | 122 |
| Ohlone Coll, Fremont, CA 94539 | 1967 | Dr. Peter Blomerley . . . . . . . 12 | 9,827 | 434 |
| Okaloosa-Walton Comm Coll, Niceville, FL 32578 | 1963 | Dr. James R. Richburg . . . . . 12 | 5,820 | 265 |
| Oklahoma City Comm Coll, Oklahoma City, OK 73159 | 1969 | Dr. Bobby Gaines . . . . . . . . .5 | 10,875 | 340 |
| Oklahoma State U, Oklahoma City, Oklahoma City, OK 73107 | 1961 | Dr. James Hooper . . . . . . . . .5 | 4,357 | 205 |
| Oklahoma State U, Tech Branch, Okmulgee, Okmulgee, OK 74447 | 1946 | Dr. Robert Klabenes . . . . . . .5 | 2,300 | 138 |
| Olympic Coll, Bremerton, WA 98310-1699 | 1946 | Dr. Wallace A. Simpson . . . . .5 | 6,605 | 415 |
| Onondaga Comm Coll, Syracuse, NY 13215 | 1962 | Dr. Bruce H. Leslie . . . . . . . 12 | 8,517 | 494 |
| Orangeburg-Calhoun Tech Coll, Orangeburg, SC 29115 | 1968 | Mr. M. Rudolph Groomes . . . 12 | 1,848 | 120 |
| Orange Coast Coll, Costa Mesa, CA 92628-5005 | 1947 | Mr. David A. Grant . . . . . . . 12 | 27,960 | 880 |
| Orange County Comm Coll, Middletown, NY 10940 | 1950 | Dr. William F. Messner . . . . . 12 | 6,027 | 349 |
| Owensboro Comm Coll, Owensboro, KY 42303 | 1986 | NR . . . . . . . . . . . . . . . . . . .5 | 2,980 | 124 |
| Owens Tech Coll, Toledo, OH 43699-1947 | 1966 | NR . . . . . . . . . . . . . . . . . . .5 | 8,860 | 370 |
| Owens Tech Coll, Findlay Cmps, Findlay, OH 45840 | 1983 | NR . . . . . . . . . . . . . . . . . . .5 | 1,299 | 83 |
| Oxnard Coll, Oxnard, CA 93033 | 1975 | Dr. Elise D. Schneider . . . . . .9 | 6,500 | 288 |
| Palm Beach Comm Coll, Lake Worth, FL 33461 | 1933 | Dr. Edward M. Eissey . . . . . .5 | 16,543 | 656 |
| Palo Alto Coll, San Antonio, TX 78224 | 1987 | NR . . . . . . . . . . . . . . . . . . 12 | 6,666 | 317 |
| Palomar Coll, San Marcos, CA 92069 | 1946 | Dr. George R. Boggs . . . . . . 12 | 24,335 | 1,097 |
| Palo Verde Coll, Blythe, CA 92225 | 1947 | Dr. Wilford J. Beumel . . . . . . 12 | 1,200 | 69 |
| Panola Coll, Carthage, TX 75633 | 1947 | Dr. W. F. Edmondson . . . . . . 12 | 1,381 | 62 |
| Paradise Valley Comm Coll, Phoenix, AZ 85032 | 1985 | NR . . . . . . . . . . . . . . . . . . 12 | 5,313 | 222 |
| Paris Jr Coll, Paris, TX 75460 | 1924 | Mr. Bobby R. Walters . . . . . . 12 | 2,389 | 117 |
| Parkland Coll, Champaign, IL 61821 | 1967 | Dr. Zelema M. Harris . . . . . . 10 | 9,343 | 549 |
| Pasadena City Coll, Pasadena, CA 91106 | 1924 | Dr. Jack A. Scott . . . . . . . . . 10 | 24,209 | 946 |
| Pasco-Hernando Comm Coll, Dade City, FL 33525-7599 | 1972 | Dr. Milton O. Jones . . . . . . . .5 | 4,954 | 204 |
| Passaic County Comm Coll, Paterson, NJ 07505-1179 | 1968 | Mr. Elliott Collins . . . . . . . . . .9 | 3,776 | 225 |
| Patrick Henry Comm Coll, Martinsville, VA 24115 | 1962 | NR . . . . . . . . . . . . . . . . . . .5 | 2,570 | 88 |
| Paul D Camp Comm Coll, Franklin, VA 23851-0737 | 1971 | Mr. Jerome J. Friga . . . . . . . .5 | 1,464 | 59 |
| Pearl River Comm Coll, Poplarville, MS 39470 | 1909 | Dr. Ted J. Alexander . . . . . . 12 | 2,786 | 160 |
| Pellissippi State Tech Comm Coll, Knoxville, TN 37933-0990 | 1974 | Dr. Fred Martin . . . . . . . . . . .5 | 7,838 | 428 |
| Peninsula Coll, Port Angeles, WA 98362-2779 | 1961 | Ms. Joyce M. Helens . . . . . . .5 | 2,904 | 149 |
| Pennsylvania Coll of Tech, Williamsport, PA 17701 | 1965 | Dr. Robert Breuder . . . . . . . 13 | 4,781 | 330 |
| Penn State U Altoona Cmps, Altoona, PA 16601-3760 | 1929 | Dr. Kiell Meling . . . . . . . . . . 13 | 2,502 | 134 |
| Penn State U Berks Cmps, Reading, PA 19610-6009 | 1924 | Dr. Frederick H. Gaige . . . . . 13 | 1,773 | 103 |
| Penn State U Delaware County Cmps, Media, PA 19063-5596 | 1966 | Dr. Edward S. J. Tomezsko . . 13 | 1,565 | 91 |
| Penn State U DuBois Cmps, DuBois, PA 15801-3199 | 1935 | Dr. Donald T. Hartman . . . . . 13 | 1,047 | 55 |
| Penn State U Hazleton Cmps, Hazleton, PA 18201-1291 | 1934 | Dr. James J. Staudenmeier . . 13 | 1,248 | 78 |
| Penn State U McKeesport Cmps, McKeesport, PA 15132-7698 | 1947 | Dr. Joanne E. Burley . . . . . . 13 | 1,015 | 79 |
| Penn State U New Kensington Cmps, New Kensington, PA 15068-1798 | 1958 | Dr. Roy Myers . . . . . . . . . . . 13 | 1,095 | 83 |
| Penn State U Ogontz Cmps, Abington, PA 19001 | 1950 | Dr. Anthony Fusaro . . . . . . . 13 | 3,455 | 168 |
| Penn State U Schuylkill Cmps, Schuylkill Haven, PA 17972-2208 | 1934 | Dr. Wayne Lammie . . . . . . . . 13 | 1,140 | 65 |
| Penn State U Shenango Cmps, Sharon, PA 16146-1537 | 1965 | Dr. Albert N. Skomra . . . . . . 13 | 1,118 | 79 |
| Penn State U Worthington Scranton Cmps, Dunmore, PA 18512-1699 | 1923 | Dr. James D. Gallagher . . . . 13 | 1,270 | 89 |
| Penn State U York Cmps, York, PA 17403-3298 | 1926 | Dr. John J. Romano . . . . . . . 13 | 2,052 | 132 |
| Penn Valley Comm Coll, Kansas City, MO 64111 | 1969 | Dr. E. Paul Williams . . . . . . . 12 | 5,822 | 311 |
| Pensacola Jr Coll, Pensacola, FL 32504-8998 | 1948 | Dr. Horace E. Hartsell . . . . . .5 | 13,000 | 950 |
| Phillips Jr Coll, New Orleans, LA 70123 | 1970 | NR . . . . . . . . . . . . . . . . . . .3 | 1,100 | NR |
| Phillips Jr Coll, Condie Cmps, Campbell, CA 95008 | 1968 | Ms. Sylvia Karp . . . . . . . . . . .3 | 1,000 | 45 |
| Piedmont Tech Coll, Greenwood, SC 29648 | 1966 | Dr. Lex D. Walters . . . . . . . . .5 | 2,747 | 127 |
| Piedmont Virginia Comm Coll, Charlottesville, VA 22902 | 1972 | Dr. Deborah M. DiCroce . . . . .5 | 4,316 | 262 |
| Pierce Coll, Tacoma, WA 98498 | 1967 | Dr. Frank Brouillet . . . . . . . . .5 | 9,340 | 499 |
| Pikes Peak Comm Coll, Colorado Springs, CO 80906-5498 | 1969 | Dr. Marijane Axtell Paulsen . . .5 | 6,841 | 430 |
| Pima Comm Coll, Tucson, AZ 85702-3010 | 1966 | Dr. Johnas F. Hockaday . . . . .5 | 30,172 | 1,632 |
| Pitt Comm Coll, Greenville, NC 27835-7007 | 1961 | Dr. Charles E. Russell . . . . . 12 | 4,501 | 233 |
| Polk Comm Coll, Winter Haven, FL 33881-4299 | 1964 | Dr. Maryly VanLeer Peck . . . .5 | 6,100 | 260 |
| Porterville Coll, Porterville, CA 93257 | 1927 | Dr. John McCuen . . . . . . . . . .5 | 2,886 | 128 |
| Portland Comm Coll, Portland, OR 97219 | 1961 | Dr. Daniel F. Moriarty . . . . . . 12 | 34,028 | 1,215 |
| Potomac State Coll of West Virginia U, Keyser, WV 26726 | 1901 | Dr. Joseph M. Gratto . . . . . . .5 | 1,205 | 83 |
| Prairie State Coll, Chicago Heights, IL 60411 | 1958 | Dr. T. Lightfield . . . . . . . . . . 12 | 5,834 | 289 |
| Prince George's Comm Coll, Largo, MD 20772 | 1958 | Dr. Robert I. Bickford . . . . . . .9 | 13,318 | 600 |
| Pueblo Comm Coll, Pueblo, CO 81004 | 1979 | Dr. Joe May . . . . . . . . . . . . .5 | 3,200 | 396 |
| Queensborough Comm Coll of City U of NY, Bayside, NY 11364 | 1958 | Dr. Kurt R. Schmeller . . . . . . 12 | 12,300 | 563 |
| Quincy Coll, Quincy, MA 02169 | 1958 | Dr. O. Clayton Johnson . . . . . 11 | 2,280 | 69 |
| Quinebaug Valley Comm-Tech Coll, Danielson, CT 06239 | 1971 | Ms. Dianne E. Williams . . . . . .5 | 1,178 | 55 |
| Quinsigamond Comm Coll, Worcester, MA 01606 | 1963 | Dr. Clifford S. Peterson . . . . . .5 | 5,044 | 239 |
| Randolph Comm Coll, Asheboro, NC 27204 | 1962 | Dr. Larry K. Linker . . . . . . . . .5 | 1,548 | 80 |
| Rappahannock Comm Coll, Glenns, VA 23149 | 1970 | Dr. John H. Upton . . . . . . . . 12 | 2,089 | 129 |
| Raritan Valley Comm Coll, Somerville, NJ 08876 | 1965 | Dr. S. Charles Irace . . . . . . . .9 | 5,882 | 276 |
| Reading Area Comm Coll, Reading, PA 19603 | 1971 | Dr. Gust Zogas . . . . . . . . . . .9 | 3,418 | 159 |
| Redlands Comm Coll, El Reno, OK 73036 | 1938 | Dr. Larry F. Devane . . . . . . . .5 | 1,908 | 101 |
| Red Rocks Comm Coll, Lakewood, CO 80401 | 1969 | Dr. Dorothy A. Horrell . . . . . . .5 | 6,831 | 276 |
| Rend Lake Coll, Ina, IL 62846 | 1967 | Dr. Mark S. Kern . . . . . . . . . .5 | 4,322 | 201 |
| Richard Bland Coll of the Coll of William and Mary, Petersburg, VA 23805 | 1961 | Dr. Clarence Maze, Jr. . . . . . .5 | 1,264 | 49 |
| Richland Coll, Dallas, TX 75243-2199 | 1972 | Dr. Stephen Mittelstet . . . . . 12 | 13,391 | 665 |
| Richland Comm Coll, Decatur, IL 62521 | 1971 | Dr. Charles R. Novak . . . . . . 10 | 4,000 | 194 |
| Richmond Comm Coll, Hamlet, NC 28345 | 1964 | Mr. Joseph W. Grimsley . . . . .2 | 1,092 | 100 |
| Ricks Coll, Rexburg, ID 83460 | 1888 | Dr. Steven D. Bennion . . . . . .5 | 7,943 | 384 |
| Rio Hondo Coll, Whittier, CA 90608 | 1960 | Dr. Alex A. Sanchez . . . . . . . 12 | 14,500 | 710 |
| Rio Salado Comm Coll, Phoenix, AZ 85003 | 1978 | Dr. Linda Thor . . . . . . . . . . . 12 | 8,931 | 467 |
| Riverside Comm Coll, Riverside, CA 92506 | 1916 | Dr. Salvatore Rotella . . . . . . 12 | 23,000 | 480 |
| Roane State Comm Coll, Harriman, TN 37748 | 1971 | Dr. Sherry L. Hoppe . . . . . . . .5 | 5,840 | 333 |
| Robert Morris Coll, Chicago Cmps, Chicago, IL 60601 | 1913 | Mr. Richard D. Pickett . . . . . . .1 | 1,733 | 95 |

| Name, address | Year | Governing official, control | Enroll-ment | Faculty |
|---|---|---|---|---|
| Rochester Comm Coll, Rochester, MN 55904 | 1915 | Dr. Karen E. Nagle ... 5 | 4,001 | 186 |
| Rockingham Comm Coll, Wentworth, NC 27375 | 1964 | Dr. N. J. Owens, Jr. ... 5 | 2,020 | 111 |
| Rockland Comm Coll, Suffern, NY 10901 | 1959 | Dr. Neal A. Raisman ... 12 | 8,044 | 792 |
| Rock Valley Coll, Rockford, IL 61114-5699 | 1964 | Dr. Karl J. Jacobs ... 10 | 7,960 | 226 |
| Rogers State Coll, Claremore, OK 74017-2099 | 1909 | Dr. Richard H. Mosier ... 5 | 3,875 | 270 |
| Rogue Comm Coll, Grants Pass, OR 97527 | 1970 | Dr. Harvey Bennett ... 12 | 2,785 | 334 |
| Rose State Coll, Midwest City, OK 73110-2799 | 1971 | Dr. Larry Nutter ... 12 | 9,800 | 341 |
| Rowan-Cabarrus Comm Coll, Salisbury, NC 28145 | 1963 | Dr. Richard L. Brownell ... 5 | 3,500 | 130 |
| Roxbury Comm Coll, Roxbury Crossing, MA 02120 | 1973 | Dr. Grace C. Brown ... 5 | 2,500 | NR |
| Sacramento City Coll, Sacramento, CA 95822 | 1916 | Dr. Robert M. Harris ... 12 | 16,403 | 420 |
| Saddleback Coll, Mission Viejo, CA 92692 | 1967 | NR ... 12 | 19,274 | 651 |
| Saint Augustine Coll, Chicago, IL 60640 | 1980 | Fr. Carlos A. Plazas ... 1 | 1,341 | 150 |
| Saint Charles County Comm Coll, St Peters, MO 63376 | 1986 | NR ... 5 | 4,631 | 201 |
| St Clair County Comm Coll, Port Huron, MI 48061 | 1923 | Dr. R. Ernest Dear ... 9 | 4,914 | 241 |
| St Cloud Tech Coll, St Cloud, MN 56303-1240 | 1948 | NR ... 12 | 1,977 | 100 |
| St Johns River Comm Coll, Palatka, FL 32177 | 1958 | Dr. R. L. McLendon, Jr. ... 5 | 3,391 | 157 |
| St Louis Comm Coll at Florissant Valley, St Louis, MO 63135-1499 | 1963 | Dr. Michael T. Murphy ... 10 | 9,923 | 416 |
| St Louis Comm Coll at Forest Park, St Louis, MO 63110 | 1962 | Dr. Henry D. Shannon ... 10 | 7,521 | 368 |
| St Louis Comm Coll at Meramec, Kirkwood, MO 63122 | 1963 | Mr. Richard A. Black ... 10 | 14,764 | 577 |
| St Mary's Cmps of the Coll of St Catherine, Minneapolis, MN 55454 | 1964 | Dr. Anita M. Pampusch ... 2 | 1,057 | 88 |
| St Paul Tech Coll, St Paul, MN 55102 | 1922 | Dr. Donovan Schwichtenberg ... 12 | 3,570 | 565 |
| St Petersburg Jr Coll, St Petersburg, FL 33733-3489 | 1927 | Dr. Carl M. Kuttler, Jr. ... 12 | 23,488 | 569 |
| Salem Comm Coll, Carneys Point, NJ 08069-2799 | 1971 | Ms. Linda C. Jolly ... 9 | 1,553 | 74 |
| Salt Lake Comm Coll, Salt Lake City, UT 84130 | 1948 | Dr. Frank W. Budd ... 5 | 17,029 | 849 |
| Sampson Comm Coll, Clinton, NC 28328 | 1965 | Dr. Clifton W. Paderick ... 12 | 1,049 | 99 |
| San Antonio Coll, San Antonio, TX 78212-4299 | 1925 | Dr. Ruth Burgos-Sasscer ... 12 | 19,908 | 847 |
| Sandhills Comm Coll, Pinehurst, NC 28374 | 1963 | Dr. John Dempsey ... 12 | 2,301 | 130 |
| San Diego City Coll, San Diego, CA 92101 | 1914 | Dr. Jerome Hunter ... 12 | 13,200 | 250 |
| San Diego Mesa Coll, San Diego, CA 92111-4998 | 1962 | Dr. Constance Carroll ... 10 | 24,460 | 768 |
| San Diego Miramar Coll, San Diego, CA 92126-2999 | 1969 | Dr. Jerome Hunter ... 12 | 6,998 | 180 |
| San Jacinto Coll–Central Cmps, Pasadena, TX 77501-2007 | 1961 | Dr. Monte Blue ... 12 | 10,562 | 539 |
| San Jacinto Coll–North Cmps, Houston, TX 77049 | 1974 | Dr. Edwin E. Lehr ... 12 | 4,291 | 212 |
| San Jacinto Coll–South Cmps, Houston, TX 77089 | 1979 | Dr. Parker Williams ... 12 | 5,635 | 213 |
| San Joaquin Delta Coll, Stockton, CA 95207 | 1935 | Dr. L. H. Horton, Jr. ... 10 | 17,199 | 579 |
| San Jose City Coll, San Jose, CA 95128 | 1921 | Ms. Del M. Anderson ... 10 | 10,856 | 390 |
| San Juan Coll, Farmington, NM 87402-4699 | 1958 | Dr. James C. Henderson ... 9 | 3,963 | 165 |
| Santa Barbara City Coll, Santa Barbara, CA 93109 | 1908 | Dr. Peter R. MacDougall ... 10 | 11,481 | 500 |
| Santa Fe Comm Coll, Gainesville, FL 32606 | 1966 | Dr. Larry W. Tyree ... 12 | 11,813 | 539 |
| Santa Fe Comm Coll, Santa Fe, NM 87502 | 1983 | Dr. Bill J. Priest ... 12 | 3,296 | 294 |
| Santa Monica Coll, Santa Monica, CA 90405 | 1929 | Dr. Richard L. Moore ... 12 | 23,203 | 664 |
| Santa Rosa Jr Coll, Santa Rosa, CA 95401 | 1918 | Dr. Robert F. Agrella ... 12 | 28,223 | 1,387 |
| Sauk Valley Comm Coll, Dixon, IL 61021 | 1965 | Dr. Richard I. Behrendt ... 12 | 2,870 | 185 |
| Schenectady County Comm Coll, Schenectady, NY 12305 | 1968 | Dr. Gabriel J. Basil ... 12 | 3,824 | 239 |
| Schoolcraft Coll, Livonia, MI 48152 | 1961 | Dr. Richard W. McDowell ... 12 | 10,057 | 446 |
| Scott Comm Coll, Bettendorf, IA 52722-6804 | 1966 | Dr. Lenny E. Stone ... 12 | 3,850 | 185 |
| Seattle Central Comm Coll, Seattle, WA 98122 | 1966 | Dr. Charles H. Mitchell ... 5 | 9,673 | 388 |
| Seminole Comm Coll, Sanford, FL 32773 | 1966 | Dr. Earl S. Weldon ... 12 | 6,404 | 512 |
| Seminole Jr Coll, Seminole, OK 74818-0351 | 1931 | Dr. James J. Cook ... 5 | 1,844 | 76 |
| Seward County Comm Coll, Liberal, KS 67905-1137 | 1969 | Mr. Donald E. Guild ... 12 | 1,609 | 147 |
| Shasta Coll, Redding, CA 96049 | 1948 | Mr. George C. Kutras ... 12 | 12,820 | 397 |
| Shawnee Comm Coll, Ullin, IL 62992 | 1967 | NR ... 12 | 2,500 | 194 |
| Shelby State Comm Coll, Memphis, TN 38174-0568 | 1970 | Dr. Lawrence M. Cox ... 5 | 6,988 | 354 |
| Shelton State Comm Coll, Tuscaloosa, AL 35405 | 1979 | Dr. Tom Umphrey ... 5 | 7,000 | NR |
| Sheridan Coll, Sheridan, WY 82801 | 1948 | Dr. Stephen Maier ... 12 | 2,998 | 156 |
| Shoreline Comm Coll, Seattle, WA 98133 | 1964 | Dr. Ronald E. Bell ... 5 | 8,092 | 253 |
| Sierra Coll, Rocklin, CA 95677 | 1936 | Dr. Kevin M. Ramirez ... 5 | 15,057 | 503 |
| Sinclair Comm Coll, Dayton, OH 45402 | 1887 | Dr. David H. Ponitz ... 12 | 20,800 | 933 |
| Skyline Coll, San Bruno, CA 94066-1698 | 1969 | Ms. Linda Graef Salter ... 9 | 9,144 | 268 |
| Snead State Jr Coll, Boaz, AL 35957 | 1935 | Dr. William H. Osborn ... 5 | 1,715 | 78 |
| Snow Coll, Ephraim, UT 84627 | 1888 | Dr. Gerald Day ... 5 | 2,344 | 93 |
| Solano Comm Coll, Suisun City, CA 94585 | 1945 | Dr. Virginia L. Holton ... 9 | 11,370 | 402 |
| South Arkansas Comm Coll, El Dorado, AR 71731-7010 | 1975 | Dr. Ben Whitfield ... 5 | 1,200 | 81 |
| Southeast Comm Coll, Lincoln Cmps, Lincoln, NE 68520 | 1973 | NR ... 10 | 4,168 | 538 |
| Southeastern Comm Coll, Whiteville, NC 28472 | 1964 | Dr. Stephen C. Scott ... 5 | 1,750 | 145 |
| Southeastern Comm Coll, North Cmps, West Burlington, IA 52655-0605 | 1968 | Dr. R. Gene Gardner ... 12 | 2,166 | 94 |
| Southeastern Illinois Coll, Harrisburg, IL 62946 | 1960 | Dr. Harry W. Abell ... 12 | 3,763 | 152 |
| Southern Arkansas U Tech, Camden, AR 71701 | 1968 | Dr. George J. Brown ... 5 | 1,197 | 114 |
| Southern Maine Tech Coll, South Portland, ME 04106 | 1946 | Dr. Wayne H. Ross ... 5 | 1,359 | 148 |
| Southern State Comm Coll, Hillsboro, OH 45133 | 1975 | Dr. George R. McCormick ... 5 | 1,654 | 114 |
| Southern Union State Jr Coll, Wadley, AL 36276 | 1922 | Dr. Richard J. Federinko ... 5 | 3,334 | 167 |
| Southern U, Shreveport–Bossier City Cmps, Shreveport, LA 71107 | 1964 | Dr. Robert H. Smith ... 5 | 1,054 | 75 |
| Southern West Virginia Comm Coll, Logan, WV 25601 | 1971 | Dr. Harry J. Boyer ... 5 | 3,115 | 198 |
| South Florida Comm Coll, Avon Park, FL 33825 | 1965 | Dr. Catherine P. Cornelius ... 5 | 1,500 | 266 |
| South Georgia Coll, Douglas, GA 31533-5098 | 1906 | Dr. Edward D. Jackson, Jr. ... 5 | 1,495 | 57 |
| South Mountain Comm Coll, Phoenix, AZ 85040 | 1979 | Dr. John A. Cordova ... 12 | 3,061 | 173 |
| South Plains Coll, Leveland, TX 79336 | 1958 | Dr. Marvin L. Baker ... 12 | 5,960 | 339 |
| South Puget Sound Comm Coll, Olympia, WA 98512-6218 | 1970 | Dr. Kenneth Minnaert ... 5 | 5,200 | 201 |
| South Seattle Comm Coll, Seattle, WA 98106-1499 | 1970 | Mr. Jerry M. Brockey ... 5 | 3,421 | 292 |
| Southside Virginia Comm Coll, Alberta, VA 23821 | 1970 | Dr. John J. Cavan ... 5 | 1,996 | 169 |
| South Suburban Coll, South Holland, IL 60473 | 1927 | Dr. Richard Fonte ... 12 | 7,589 | 323 |
| Southwestern Coll, Chula Vista, CA 91910-7299 | 1961 | Mr. Joseph M. Conte ... 12 | 17,222 | 672 |
| Southwestern Comm Coll, Creston, IA 50801 | 1966 | NR ... 5 | 1,372 | 65 |
| Southwestern Comm Coll, Sylva, NC 28779 | 1964 | Dr. Barry W. Russell ... 5 | 1,544 | 197 |
| Southwestern Michigan Coll, Dowagiac, MI 49047 | 1964 | Mr. David C. Briegel ... 12 | 2,873 | 182 |
| Southwestern Oregon Comm Coll, Coos Bay, OR 97420 | 1961 | Dr. Stephen J. Kridelbaugh ... 12 | 1,924 | 161 |
| Southwest Mississippi Comm Coll, Summit, MS 39666 | 1918 | NR ... 10 | 1,520 | 89 |
| Southwest State Tech Coll, Mobile, AL 36605 | 1954 | Dr. Thomas A. McLeod ... 5 | 1,039 | 98 |
| Southwest Texas Jr Coll, Uvalde, TX 78801 | 1946 | Mr. Billy Word ... 12 | 2,859 | 147 |
| Southwest Virginia Comm Coll, Richlands, VA 24641 | 1968 | Dr. Charles R. King ... 5 | 4,896 | 235 |
| Southwest Wisconsin Tech Coll, Fennimore, WI 53809 | 1967 | Dr. Richard A. Rogers ... 12 | 1,550 | 101 |
| Spartanburg Methodist Coll, Spartanburg, SC 29301 | 1911 | Dr. George D. Fields ... 2 | 1,050 | 32 |
| Spartanburg Tech Coll, Spartanburg, SC 29305 | 1961 | Dr. Jack A. Powers ... 5 | 2,500 | NR |
| Spokane Comm Coll, Spokane, WA 99207 | 1963 | Dr. Joseph Rich ... 5 | 8,000 | 481 |

| Name, address | Year | Governing official, control | Enroll-ment | Faculty |
|---|---|---|---|---|
| Spokane Falls Comm Coll, Spokane, WA 99204 | 1967 | Dr. Vern Loland .........5 | 6,431 | 656 |
| Spoon River Coll, Canton, IL 61520 | 1959 | Dr. Felix T. Haynes .......5 | 2,300 | 133 |
| Springfield Tech Comm Coll, Springfield, MA 01105 | 1967 | Mr. Andrew M. Scibelli ......5 | 3,810 | 234 |
| Stark Tech Coll, Canton, OH 44720 | 1970 | Dr. John J. McGrath .......12 | 4,537 | 188 |
| State Comm Coll of East St Louis, East St Louis, IL 62201 | 1969 | NR .............5 | 1,268 | 83 |
| State Fair Comm Coll, Sedalia, MO 65301 | 1966 | Dr. Marvin Fielding .......10 | 2,369 | 98 |
| State Tech Inst at Memphis, Memphis, TN 38134 | 1967 | Dr. Charles Temple .......5 | 10,519 | 527 |
| State U of NY Coll of A&T at Cobleskill, Cobleskill, NY 12043 | 1916 | Dr. Kenneth E. Wing ......5 | 2,797 | 164 |
| State U of NY Coll of A&T at Morrisville, Morrisville, NY 13408 | 1908 | Dr. Frederick W. Woodward . .5 | 3,449 | 171 |
| State U of NY Coll of Tech at Alfred, Alfred, NY 14802 | 1908 | Dr. William Rezak ........5 | 3,518 | 176 |
| State U of NY Coll of Tech at Canton, Canton, NY 13617 | 1906 | Dr. Joseph L. Kennedy ......5 | 2,278 | 107 |
| State U of NY Coll of Tech at Farmingdale, Farmingdale, NY 11735 | 1912 | Dr. Frank A. Cipriani ......5 | 8,800 | 393 |
| Suffolk County Comm Coll–Ammerman Cmps, Selden, NY 11784 | 1962 | Dr. John F. Cooper .......12 | 13,154 | 782 |
| Suffolk County Comm Coll–Eastern Cmps, Riverhead, NY 11901 | 1977 | Mr. Steven T. Kenny ......12 | 2,680 | 216 |
| Suffolk County Comm Coll–Western Cmps, Brentwood, NY 11717 | 1974 | Mr. Salvatore J. LaLima ....12 | 6,097 | 349 |
| Sullivan County Comm Coll, Loch Sheldrake, NY 12759-4002 | 1962 | Dr. Jeffrey B. Willens ......12 | 2,093 | 167 |
| Surry Comm Coll, Dobson, NC 27017 | 1965 | Dr. Swanson Richards ......5 | 3,036 | 98 |
| Tacoma Comm Coll, Tacoma, WA 98465 | 1965 | Dr. Raymond Needham .....5 | 5,012 | 284 |
| Tallahassee Comm Coll, Tallahassee, FL 32304-2895 | 1966 | Dr. James H. Hinson, Jr. . . .12 | 9,800 | 370 |
| Tarrant County Jr Coll, Fort Worth, TX 76102 | 1967 | Mr. C. A. Roberson .......9 | 28,515 | 1,019 |
| Tech Coll of the Lowcountry, Beaufort, SC 29901-1288 | 1972 | Dr. Anne S. McNutt .......5 | 1,424 | 66 |
| Temple Jr Coll, Temple, TX 76504-7435 | 1926 | Dr. Marvin R. Felder ......10 | 2,363 | 122 |
| Terra Tech Coll, Fremont, OH 43420-9670 | 1968 | Dr. Charlotte J. Lee ........5 | 2,940 | 148 |
| Texarkana Coll, Texarkana, TX 75599 | 1927 | Dr. Carl M. Nelson ......12 | 4,099 | 188 |
| Texas Southmost Coll, Brownsville, TX 78520-4991 | 1926 | Dr. Juliet V. Garcia .......10 | 6,429 | 390 |
| Texas State Tech Coll–Harlingen Cmps, Harlingen, TX 78550-3697 | 1967 | Dr. J. Gilbert Leal ........5 | 3,236 | 195 |
| Texas State Tech Coll–Waco Cmps, Waco, TX 76705 | 1965 | Mr. Don E. Goodwin .......5 | 3,108 | 332 |
| Thomas Nelson Comm Coll, Hampton, VA 23670 | 1968 | Dr. Robert G. Templin, Jr. . . .5 | 7,815 | 318 |
| Three Rivers Comm Coll, Poplar Bluff, MO 63901 | 1966 | Dr. Stephen M. Poort .......5 | 3,061 | 67 |
| Three Rivers Comm-Tech Coll, Norwich, CT 06360 | 1969 | Dr. Booker T. DeVaughn ....5 | 4,275 | 128 |
| Tidewater Comm Coll, Portsmouth, VA 23703 | 1968 | Dr. Larry Whitworth .......5 | 16,943 | 708 |
| Tomball Coll, Tomball, TX 77375-4036 | 1988 | NR .............12 | 3,604 | 187 |
| Tompkins Cortland Comm Coll, Dryden, NY 13053 | 1968 | Dr. Eduardo J. Marti .......12 | 2,899 | 196 |
| Treasure Valley Comm Coll, Ontario, OR 97914 | 1962 | NR .............12 | 2,231 | 117 |
| Tri-County Tech Coll, Pendleton, SC 29670 | 1962 | Dr. Don C. Garrison ........5 | 3,155 | 250 |
| Trident Tech Coll, Charleston, SC 29411 | 1964 | Dr. Mary Dellamura Thornley . 12 | 9,120 | 375 |
| Trinidad State Jr Coll, Trinidad, CO 81082 | 1925 | Dr. Harold Deselms ........5 | 2,322 | 111 |
| Trinity Valley Comm Coll, Athens, TX 75751 | 1946 | Mr. Ron Baugh .........12 | 4,796 | 224 |
| Triton Coll, River Grove, IL 60171 | 1964 | Dr. George Jorndt .........5 | 12,968 | 635 |
| Trocaire Coll, Buffalo, NY 14220 | 1958 | Ms. Barbara Ciarico, RSM . . .1 | 1,123 | 101 |
| Truckee Meadows Comm Coll, Reno, NV 89512 | 1971 | Dr. John Gwaltney .......6 | 9,551 | 489 |
| Tulsa Jr Coll, Tulsa, OK 74135 | 1968 | Dr. Dean P. VanTrease ......5 | 22,702 | 700 |
| Tunxis Comm Coll, Farmington, CT 06032 | 1969 | Ms. Marilyn Menack .......5 | 2,465 | 175 |
| Tyler Jr Coll, Tyler, TX 75711 | 1926 | Dr. Raymond M. Hawkins . . .12 | 7,984 | 364 |
| Ulster County Comm Coll, Stone Ridge, NY 12484 | 1961 | Mr. Robert T. Brown ......12 | 2,319 | 194 |
| Umpqua Comm Coll, Roseburg, OR 97470 | 1964 | Dr. James Kraby ........12 | 2,112 | 120 |
| Union County Coll, Cranford, NJ 07016 | 1933 | Dr. Thomas H. Brown .....12 | 10,476 | 424 |
| U of Akron–Wayne Coll, Orrville, OH 44667 | 1972 | Dr. Peggy Gordon Elliott . . . .5 | 1,461 | 109 |
| U of Alaska Anchorage, Kenai Peninsula Coll, Soldotna, AK 99669 | 1964 | NR .............5 | 1,673 | 85 |
| U of Alaska Anchorage, Matanuska-Susitna Coll, Palmer, AK 99645 | 1958 | Mr. Ted Berry ..........5 | 1,689 | 114 |
| U of Alaska Southeast, Sitka Cmps, Sitka, AK 99835 | 1962 | Ms. Elaine Sunde ........5 | 1,200 | 91 |
| U of Cincinnati Clermont Coll, Batavia, OH 45103 | 1972 | Dr. Roger J. Barry ........5 | 1,651 | 106 |
| U of Cincinnati Raymond Walters Coll, Cincinnati, OH 45236 | 1967 | Dr. Roger J. Barry ........5 | 4,300 | 195 |
| U of Hawaii–Kapiolani Comm Coll, Honolulu, HI 96816 | 1957 | Mr. John F. Morton ........5 | 7,116 | 239 |
| U of Hawaii–Kauai Comm Coll, Lihue, HI 96766 | 1965 | Mr. David Iha ..........5 | 1,563 | 84 |
| U of Kentucky, Ashland Comm Coll, Ashland, KY 41101-3683 | 1937 | Mr. Charles Dassance ......5 | 3,267 | 142 |
| U of Kentucky, Elizabethtown Comm Coll, Elizabethtown, KY 42701 | 1964 | Dr. Charles E. Stebbins . . . . .5 | 4,297 | 136 |
| U of Kentucky, Hazard Comm Coll, Hazard, KY 41701 | 1968 | Dr. G. Edward Hughes ......5 | 1,695 | 85 |
| U of Kentucky, Henderson Comm Coll, Henderson, KY 42420 | 1963 | Dr. Patrick R. Lake .......5 | 1,479 | 96 |
| U of Kentucky, Hopkinsville Comm Coll, Hopkinsville, KY 42241-2100 | 1965 | Dr. Jim Kerley .........5 | 3,000 | 113 |
| U of Kentucky, Jefferson Comm Coll, Louisville, KY 40202 | 1968 | Dr. Ronald J. Horvath ......5 | 11,861 | 365 |
| U of Kentucky, Lexington Comm Coll, Lexington, KY 40506 | 1965 | Dr. Allen G. Edwards ......5 | 4,862 | 302 |
| U of Kentucky, Madisonville Comm Coll, Madisonville, KY 42431 | 1968 | Dr. Arthur D. Stumpf ......5 | 2,312 | 127 |
| U of Kentucky, Maysville Comm Coll, Maysville, KY 41056 | 1967 | Dr. James C. Shires .......5 | 1,325 | 111 |
| U of Kentucky, Paducah Comm Coll, Paducah, KY 42002 | 1932 | Dr. Leonard O'Hara .......5 | 3,133 | 102 |
| U of Kentucky, Prestonsburg Comm Coll, Prestonsburg, KY 41653 | 1964 | Dr. Deborah Lee Floyd ......5 | 2,887 | 124 |
| U of Kentucky, Somerset Comm Coll, Somerset, KY 42501 | 1965 | Dr. Rollin J. Watson .......5 | 2,528 | 153 |
| U of Kentucky, Southeast Comm Coll, Cumberland, KY 40823-1099 | 1960 | Dr. W. Bruce Ayers .......5 | 2,453 | 107 |
| U of Maine at Augusta, Augusta, ME 04330 | 1965 | Dr. George P. Connick ......5 | 4,972 | 172 |
| U of Minnesota, Crookston, Crookston, MN 56716 | 1966 | Dr. Donald G. Sargeant .....5 | 1,352 | 71 |
| U of New Mexico–Gallup Branch, Gallup, NM 87301 | 1968 | Dr. John M. Phillips .......5 | 2,650 | 117 |
| U of New Mexico–Valencia Cmps, Los Lunas, NM 87031 | 1981 | Dr. Ralph Sigala .........5 | 1,367 | 93 |
| U of Puerto Rico, Carolina Regional Coll, Carolina, PR 00984-4800 | 1974 | Prof. Marta Arroyo .......7 | 1,751 | 87 |
| U of South Carolina at Beaufort, Beaufort, SC 29902 | 1959 | Dr. Chris P. Plyler .......5 | 1,070 | 64 |
| U of South Carolina at Salkehatchie, Allendale, SC 29810 | 1965 | Dr. Carl A. Clayton ........5 | 1,006 | 40 |
| U of South Carolina at Sumter, Sumter, SC 29150 | 1966 | Mr. J. C. Anderson, Jr. ......5 | 1,627 | 98 |
| U of Wisconsin Ctr–Fox Valley, Menasha, WI 54952 | 1933 | Dr. James W. Perry .......5 | 1,447 | 55 |

| Name, address | Year | Governing official, control | Enroll-ment | Faculty |
|---|---|---|---|---|
| U of Wisconsin Ctr–Waukesha County, Waukesha, WI 53188 | 1966 | Dr. Mary S. Knudten ...... 5 | 2,140 | 86 |
| Utah Valley Comm Coll, Orem, UT 84058 | 1941 | Dr. Kerry D. Romesburg ..... 5 | 9,623 | 425 |
| Valencia Comm Coll, Orlando, FL 32802 | 1967 | Dr. Paul C. Gianini, Jr. ..... 5 | 22,094 | 893 |
| Vance-Granville Comm Coll, Henderson, NC 27536 | 1969 | Dr. Ben F. Currin ......... 5 | 2,670 | 153 |
| Ventura Coll, Ventura, CA 93003 | 1925 | Dr. Jesus Carreon ....... 12 | 12,158 | 541 |
| Vernon Regional Jr Coll, Vernon, TX 76384-4092 | 1972 | Dr. Wade Kirk .......... 12 | 1,780 | 115 |
| Victoria Coll, Victoria, TX 77901 | 1925 | Dr. Jimmy Goodson ........ 9 | 3,411 | 120 |
| Victor Valley Coll, Victorville, CA 92392-9699 | 1961 | Dr. Edward O. Gould ....... 5 | 8,000 | 325 |
| Vincennes U, Vincennes, IN 47591 | 1801 | Dr. Phillip M. Summers ...... 5 | 7,211 | 400 |
| Vincennes U–Jasper Ctr, Jasper, IN 47546 | 1970 | NR ................. 5 | 1,274 | 62 |
| Virginia Western Comm Coll, Roanoke, VA 24038 | 1966 | Dr. Charles L. Downs ...... 5 | 6,895 | 202 |
| Volunteer State Comm Coll, Gallatin, TN 37066 | 1970 | Dr. Hal R. Ramer ......... 5 | 5,218 | 276 |
| Wake Tech Comm Coll, Raleigh, NC 27603 | 1958 | Dr. Bruce I. Howell ....... 12 | 6,850 | 325 |
| Wallace State Comm Coll, Hanceville, AL 35077-2000 | 1966 | Dr. James C. Bailey ....... 5 | 5,953 | 266 |
| Walla Walla Comm Coll, Walla Walla, WA 99362 | 1967 | Dr. Steven L. VanAusdle .... 5 | 5,674 | 278 |
| Walters State Comm Coll, Morristown, TN 37813 | 1970 | Dr. Jack E. Campbell ...... 5 | 5,427 | 253 |
| Washington State Comm Coll, Marietta, OH 45750 | 1971 | Dr. Carson K. Miller ....... 5 | 2,138 | 122 |
| Washtenaw Comm Coll, Ann Arbor, MI 48106 | 1965 | Dr. Gunder A. Myran ...... 12 | 10,954 | 757 |
| Waubonsee Comm Coll, Sugar Grove, IL 60554 | 1966 | Dr. John J. Swalec ....... 10 | 7,550 | 542 |
| Waukesha County Tech Coll, Pewaukee, WI 53072 | 1923 | Dr. Richard T. Anderson .... 12 | 4,700 | 520 |
| Wayne Comm Coll, Goldsboro, NC 27533-8002 | 1957 | Dr. Edward H. Wilson, Jr. ... 12 | 2,752 | 153 |
| Wayne County Comm Coll, Detroit, MI 48226 | 1967 | Dr. Rafael L. Cortada ..... 12 | 9,577 | 417 |
| Weatherford Coll, Weatherford, TX 76086 | 1869 | Dr. Jim Boyd ........... 5 | 2,277 | 94 |
| Wenatchee Valley Coll, Wenatchee, WA 98801 | 1939 | Dr. Arnie Heuchert ....... 12 | 3,419 | 168 |
| Westark Comm Coll, Fort Smith, AR 72913 | 1928 | Mr. Joel R. Stubblefield .... 12 | 5,472 | 234 |
| Westchester Comm Coll, Valhalla, NY 10595-1698 | 1946 | Dr. Joseph N. Hankin ..... 12 | 11,870 | 574 |
| Western Iowa Tech Comm Coll, Sioux City, IA 51102-0265 | 1966 | Dr. Robert E. Dunker ...... 5 | 2,575 | 157 |
| Western Nebraska Comm Coll–Scottsbluff Cmps, Scottsbluff, NE 69361 | 1926 | Dr. John N. Harms ........ 5 | 1,656 | 56 |
| Western Nevada Comm Coll, Carson City, NV 89703 | 1971 | Dr. Anthony D. Calabro ..... 5 | 4,847 | 358 |
| Western Oklahoma State Coll, Altus, OK 73521 | 1926 | Dr. Stephen R. Hensley ..... 5 | 1,803 | 78 |
| Western Texas Coll, Snyder, TX 79549 | 1969 | Dr. Harry L. Krenek ...... 12 | 1,095 | 55 |
| Western Wisconsin Tech Coll, La Crosse, WI 54602 | 1911 | Dr. James Lee Rasch ...... 10 | 4,006 | 185 |
| Western Wyoming Comm Coll, Rock Springs, WY 82902 | 1959 | Dr. T. L. Boggs ......... 12 | 2,572 | 112 |
| West Hills Coll, Coalinga, CA 93210 | 1932 | Dr. Lincoln H. Hall ....... 5 | 3,500 | 160 |
| West Los Angeles Coll, Culver City, CA 90230-3500 | 1969 | Dr. Evelyn C. Wong ...... 12 | 8,958 | 320 |
| Westmoreland County Comm Coll, Youngwood, PA 15697 | 1970 | Dr. Daniel C. Krezenski ..... 9 | 6,845 | 390 |
| West Shore Comm Coll, Scottville, MI 49454 | 1967 | Dr. William M. Anderson ... 10 | 1,430 | 71 |
| West Valley Coll, Saratoga, CA 95070 | 1963 | Dr. Leo Chavez ........ 12 | 14,224 | 560 |
| West Virginia Northern Comm Coll, Wheeling, WV 26003 | 1972 | Dr. Ron Hutkin ......... 12 | 2,991 | 165 |
| Wharton County Jr Coll, Wharton, TX 77488 | 1946 | Dr. Elbert C. Hutchins .... 12 | 3,361 | 161 |
| Whatcom Comm Coll, Bellingham, WA 98226 | 1970 | Dr. Harold G. Heiner ...... 5 | 2,234 | 104 |
| Wilkes Comm Coll, Wilkesboro, NC 28697 | 1965 | Dr. James R. Randolph .... 5 | 1,962 | 102 |
| William Rainey Harper Coll, Palatine, IL 60067-7398 | 1965 | Dr. Paul N. Thompson .... 12 | 15,842 | 1,004 |
| Willmar Comm Coll, Willmar, MN 56201 | 1961 | Mr. Harold G. Conradi ...... 5 | 1,383 | 61 |
| Willmar Tech Coll, Willmar, MN 56201 | 1961 | NR ................ 12 | 1,275 | 91 |
| Wilson Tech Comm Coll, Wilson, NC 27893 | 1958 | Dr. Frank L. Eagles ....... 5 | 1,292 | 89 |
| Wisconsin Indianhead Tech Coll, New Richmond Cmps, New Richmond, WI 54017 | 1972 | Ms. Marilyn McCarty ...... 10 | 1,102 | 65 |
| Wisconsin Indianhead Tech Coll, Rice Lake Cmps, Rice Lake, WI 54868 | 1941 | Ms. Mary Ellen Filkins ..... 10 | 1,136 | 79 |
| Wood Coll, Mathiston, MS 39752 | 1886 | Dr. Doyce W. Gunter ....... 2 | 1,500 | 35 |
| Wor-Wic Tech Comm Coll, Salisbury, MD 21801 | 1976 | NR ................ 12 | 1,834 | 94 |
| Wytheville Comm Coll, Wytheville, VA 24382 | 1967 | Dr. William F. Snyder ...... 5 | 2,460 | 137 |
| Yakima Valley Comm Coll, Yakima, WA 98907 | 1928 | Dr. V. Philip Tullar ....... 5 | 5,500 | 410 |
| Yavapai Coll, Prescott, AZ 86301 | 1966 | Dr. Doreen Dailey ....... 12 | 5,739 | 364 |
| York Tech Coll, Rock Hill, SC 29730 | 1961 | Mr. Dennis F. Merrell ...... 5 | 3,187 | 218 |
| Yuba Coll, Marysville, CA 95901 | 1927 | Dr. Patricia L. Wirth ...... 12 | 12,373 | 267 |

## College Freshman Attitudes

The 27th annual survey of college freshmen conducted by the American Council on Education and the Univ. of California at Los Angeles reported an increased interest in activism, racial understanding, and social change. A record two out of every five freshmen participated in organized demonstrations in 1992 (40.5 percent, up from 39.0 percent in 1991); and more than double the levels recorded during the late 1960s); a record percentage of students said "helping to promote racial understanding" was an "essential" or "very important" goal (42.0 percent, up from 33.7 percent in 1991), and a record percentage of students said that "influencing social values" was an "essential" or "very important" goal (43.3 percent, up from 39.6 percent in 1991).

The trend of strong interest in careers in the health professions continued, with the percentage of new college freshmen indicating an interest in majoring in that area reaching a new high in 1992 (15.6 percent, up from 12.9 percent in 1991). This trend began five years earlier, and the latest figure represented a doubling of interest since 1987. In contrast, the percentage of students planning business careers continued to decline; the figure, 14.3 percent in 1992, decreased by almost one-half in just five years.

Economic constraints continued to affect students, with record numbers of freshmen indicating that they selected their college on the basis of low tuition (30.0 percent, up from 27.7 in 1991), because of the offer of financial assistance (28.3 percent, up from 27.8 in 1991), or because they wanted to live near home (23.6 percent, up from 21.3 percent in 1991). A record one in six freshmen (17.4 percent, compared with 13.1 percent in 1989) indicated a "major concern" about their ability to finance college, while the percentage who said they decided to attend college because they "could not find a job" reached an all-time high (8.2 percent, up from 7.3 percent in 1991). A record 3.3 percent reported their father's occupation as "unemployed."

Regarding life goals, the commitment of freshmen to "being very well off financially" dropped for the fifth straight year (from 75.6 percent in 1987 to 73.0 percent in 1992), while the percentage of students who wanted to "develop a meaningful philosophy of life" increased for the fifth straight year (to 45.6 percent).

# ASTRONOMY AND CALENDAR

Edited by Dr. Kenneth L. Franklin, Astronomer Emeritus
American Museum of Natural History-Hayden Planetarium

## Celestial Events Summary, 1994

(Greenwich Mean Time, or GMT)

This year begins with 3 of the planets conjoined with the sun, and on January 11, the moon is new. Thus 4 of the naked eye planetary bodies are invisible, leaving only Jupiter in the morning and Saturn in the evening for us to view. In March, Saturn has 2 close encounters, once with Mars, the other, Mercury. In April, Mars and Mercury brush each other. Venus gives a fine evening show from mid-spring to mid-autumn. From late spring to the end of the year, first Jupiter then Saturn liven our nights, and Mars increasingly dominates the morning sky from late summer to year's end. In early October, Venus and Jupiter give us a bit of a show in the southwest twilight, but never get much closer than about 7°.

For North America, The Event is the annular solar eclipse of May 10. The entire continent will see at least a bite taken from the solar disk by the moon. In a narrow band starting from Scammon's Lagoon in Baja California, Mexico, through El Paso, central Missouri, Lakes Erie and Ontario, central NY state, almost all of Vermont and New Hampshire, southern Maine, and most of Nova Scotia, observers will see a ring, or an annulus, of the sun surrounding the dark obscuring disk of the moon. In a total solar eclipse all of the bright photosphere of the sun is hidden by the moon. During totality, the sun's corona may be safely observed with the naked eye and even with powerful binoculars or telescopes with no danger to the eye. Not so in an annular eclipse, however. The ring of the sun still unhidden provides a strong danger to the eye, even without use of a light collector. For this reason, the viewer is strongly advised to use adequate eye protection at all times while observing this eclipse. It is not the eclipse, itself, but the exposed solar surface that the source of danger to the eye. Of course, that surface, and the danger, is exposed to view every clear day. We don't usually have a need or desire to stare at the sun, but an eclipse offers the opportunity for a prolonged gaze, thus the danger during an eclipse. The next central eclipse whose path crosses the United States will be total, August 21, 2017.

Watchers of meteor showers will again stay up late for the Perseid shower, which usually peaks about August 11-12. The swift streaks of light crossing the sky are caused by chunks—meteoroids—of comet Swift-Tuttle as they crash into our upper atmosphere. That comet passed our way in 1992 after an absence from our neighborhood of 130 years, so the region behind it should be much more cluttered with debris than the region in front of it. Avid observers will watch the skies all week surrounding this date, because the cloud of meteoroids is somewhat stretched out along the comet's path and beside it, thus giving us a protracted viewing period, perhaps even greater than this shower's usual 4-5 day duration.

Whenever notice is given in the following listing of some celestial object passing close to another, we may not see the actual event, but regard the notice that the evenings before and after that time will be good times to see the relative movements in our ever-changing, dramatic sky.

## Celestial Events Highlights, 1994

(GMT, or as indicated)

### January

**Mercury** begins this year lost in the sun's glare, passing superior conjunction, beyond the sun, on the 3rd.

**Venus** follows Mercury to superior conjunction on the 17th, also lost in the sun's light, coming to easy view in mid-spring in evening twilight.

**Mars**, in conjunction last December 27, is mingling with the inferior planets at this time, but will be visible in the morning sky in early March.

**Jupiter**, the brightest planet to be seen until mid-spring, can be seen these mornings in Libra, becoming an evening object after passing opposition April 30.

**Saturn** looks like a first magnitude star low in the evening twilight all this month.

**Moon** passes Jupiter on the 6th, Saturn on the 15th, the other planets too close to the sun to observe the moon's passage.

**Jan. 2**—Earth at perihelion, 91.4 million miles from the sun.

**Jan. 3**—Mercury at superior conjunction entering the evening sky, nearly 134 million miles from us, beyond the sun.

**Jan. 4**—Quadrantid meteor shower.

**Jan. 6**—Moon passes 3° south of Jupiter.

**Jan. 11**—Neptune in conjunction with the sun, about 2,900 million miles away.

**Jan. 12**—Uranus in conjunction with the sun, over 1,900 million miles away.

**Jan. 15**—Moon passes 7° north of Saturn.

**Jan. 17**—Venus in superior conjunction beyond the sun, 159 million miles from us, entering the evening sky.

**Jan. 19**—Sun enters Capricornus.

### February

**Mercury** may be briefly visible in the southwest evening twilight early this month, passing very close to Saturn on the evening of the 1st.

**Venus**, while technically in the evening sky, is too deep in the evening twilight to be seen.

**Mars** is similarly invisible, until late in the month, but in the morning sky.

**Jupiter** is stationary on the 28th, thus beginning its retrograde motion, westward among the stars, prior to opposition April 30.

**Saturn** may be visible for the first few days of the month, perhaps pointing out Mercury on the evening of the 1st, but soon thereafter enters the evening twilight to be lost to view until mid-March.

**Moon** passes Jupiter on the 3rd, Neptune and Uranus on the 8th.

**Feb. 2**—Mercury passes 1.3° north of Saturn, seen close the evening of the 1st.

**Feb. 3**—Moon passes 3° south of Jupiter.

**Feb. 4**—Mercury at greatest elongation, 18° east of the sun.

**Feb. 8**—Moon passes 3° north of Neptune and 5° north of Uranus.

**Feb. 10**—Mercury stationary, beginning its retrograde motion, westward against the background stars, prior to inferior conjunction.

**Feb. 16**—Sun enters Aquarius.

**Feb. 20**—Mercury in inferior conjunction, between the earth and the sun, less than 60 million miles away, entering the morning sky.

**Feb. 21**—Saturn in conjunction with the sun, beyond it, to enter our morning sky, 999 million miles away.

**Feb. 27**—Mercury passes 4° north of Mars.

**Feb. 28**—Jupiter stationary, beginning its retrograde, westward, motion.

### March

**Mercury** rises southeast of the sun all month, passing just 0.3° south of Saturn about 3 AM EST, on the morning of the 24th.

**Venus** may become visible very low in the evening twilight after mid-month.

**Mars,** looking like a star a bit fainter than 1st magnitude in Aquarius for most of this year, passes only 0.4° north of slightly brighter Saturn in the dawn sky of the 14th, about 5 AM EST.

**Jupiter,** in Libra, is 2° north of the moon on the 2nd and the 29th.

**Saturn** has close encounters this month with Mars on the 14th, and Mercury on the 24th, its passing of the moon on the 11th being a distant 7°.

**Moon** passes Jupiter on the 2nd, Neptune and Uranus on the 7th, Mercury and Mars on the 10th, Saturn on the 11th, Venus on the 13th, and Jupiter on the 29th.

**Mar. 2**—Moon passes 2° south of Jupiter.

**Mar. 4**—Pluto stationary, beginning retrograde, westward, motion; Mercury stationary, resuming direct, eastward, motion.

**Mar. 7**—Moon passes 4° south of Uranus and 5° south of Neptune.

**Mar. 10**—Moon passes 5° south of Mercury and 7° south of Mars.

**Mar. 11**—Moon passes 7° south of Saturn; sun enters Pisces.

**Mar. 13**—Moon passes 5° south of Venus.

**Mar. 14**—Mars passes 0.4° north of Saturn.

**Mar. 19**—Mercury at greatest elongation, 28° west of the sun.

**Mar. 20**—Vernal equinox; spring begins in the northern hemisphere at 20:28 GMT, 3:28 PM EST.

**Mar. 24**—Mercury 0.3° south of Saturn.

**Mar. 29**—Moon passes 2° south of Jupiter.

### April

**Mercury,** nearly 1.5 magnitudes brighter, passes close to Mars on the 4th, but soon moves into the morning twilight, thus lost to view.

**Venus** is becoming more prominent in the western evening sky, so close to the thin crescent moon on the evening of the 12th as to be occulted, its shadow passing across our Arctic regions, a good photo opportunity.

**Mars,** in Pisces after the 1st week, passes close to Mercury on the 4th.

**Jupiter,** at magnitude minus 2.5, coming to opposition on the 30th, still dominates the night sky, but evenings belong to Venus at magnitude minus 3.9.

**Saturn** continues to take over the morning sky in Aquarius, about as bright as Mars.

**Moon** passes Neptune on the 3rd, Uranus on the 4th, Saturn on the 7th, Mars and Mercury on the 9th, occults Venus on the 12th, and passes Jupiter on the 26th.

**Apr. 3**—Moon passes 4° north of Neptune.

**Apr. 4**—Mercury passes 1.5° south of Mars; moon passes 5° north of Uranus.

**Apr. 9**—Moon passes 6° north of Mars and 7° north of Mercury.

**Apr. 12**—Moon passes 1° north of Venus, occulting it for viewers in the Arctic regions.

**Apr. 18**—Sun enters Aries.

**Apr. 25**—Neptune stationary, beginning its retrograde motion.

**Apr. 26**—Moon passes 3° south of Jupiter.

**Apr. 30**—Jupiter at opposition, 411 million miles away; Mercury in superior conjunction, 123 million miles away.

### May

**Mercury,** by the 20th, may become easily visible in the northwest twilight after sunset, lower and fainter than brilliant Venus, which sets over an hour later.

**Venus,** in Taurus, may be seen north of Aldebaran on the 4th, and is north of the thin crescent moon on the evening of the 12th.

**Mars** continues to linger in the low morning sky, as it slides across constellations, in Aries before the end of the month.

**Jupiter,** now in the sky all night, is the brightest object continuously visible, surpassed only by the fleeting moon, and by Venus, who leaves the sky early for her beauty sleep.

**Saturn** is slowly brightening, heading for its late summer opposition when its turn to patrol the sky all night comes around the 1st of September.

**Moon** passes Neptune and Uranus on the 1st, Saturn on the 5th, Mars on the 8th, eclipses the sun on the 10th, passes Venus on the 13th, Jupiter on the 23rd, partially enters the earth's shadow on the 25th, and on the 28th, again passes Uranus and Neptune.

**May 1**—Uranus stationary; moon passes 4° north of Neptune; moon passes 5° north of Uranus.

**May 5**—Venus passes 6° north of Aldebaran; moon passes 6° south of Saturn.

**May 8**—Moon passes 4° north of Mars.

**May 10**—Annular eclipse of the sun.

**May 13**—Moon passes 4° south of Venus; sun enters Taurus.

**May 15**—Mercury passes 8° north of Aldebaran.

**May 17**—Pluto at opposition, 2,723 million miles from us.

**May 23**—Moon passes 3° south of Jupiter.

**May 25**—Partial eclipse of the moon.

**May 28**—Moon passes 4° north of Neptune and 5° north of Uranus.

**May 30**—Mercury at greatest elongation, 23° east of the sun.

### June

**Mercury,** although fairly well placed for viewing, is turning its dark side toward us as it heads for inferior conjunction on the 25th, thus becoming fainter in our sky.

**Venus,** passing Pollux and the moon this month at unspectacular distances, is becoming more spectacular by just being in our western evening sky well after sunset.

**Mars'** most exciting adventure this month, other than entering Taurus about the 22nd, is being about 2° from the thin crescent moon in the dawn sky of the 6th.

**Jupiter,** in Virgo, is brighter and yellower than Spica to its west.

**Saturn** is a bright 1st magnitude object in Aquarius, not known for bright objects.

**Moon** passes Saturn on the 1st, Mars on the 6th, Mercury on the 11th, Venus on the 12th, Jupiter on the 19th, Neptune on the 24th, Uranus on the 25th, and Saturn, again, on the 28th.

**June 1**—Moon passes 7° north of Saturn.

**June 6**—Moon passes 2° north of Mars.

**June 10**—Venus passes 5° south of Pollux.

**June 11**—Moon passes 3° south of Mercury.

**June 12**—Mercury stationary, beginning its retrograde motion; moon passes 7° south of Venus.

**June 19**—Moon passes 3° south of Jupiter.

**June 20**—Sun enters Gemini.

**June 21**—Summer solstice at 14:48 GMT (9:48 EST); summer begins in the northern hemisphere.

**June 24**—Saturn stationary, beginning its retrograde motion; moon passes 4° north of Neptune.

**June 25**—Moon passes 5° north of Uranus; Mercury at inferior conjunction, 51.7 million miles away.

**June 28**—Moon passes 7° north of Saturn.

### July

**Mercury** is in the morning sky virtually the entire month, but not easy to see.

**Venus** passes Regulus, the bright star of Leo, by a little over 2 moon diameters on the 10th.

**Mars**, in Taurus all month, is occulted by the moon on the 5th, but for us in North America we see them only close together that morning.

**Jupiter** is stationary on the 2nd, resuming its direct motion, again heading for Libra.

**Saturn** continues to lurk in Aquarius, passed only by the moon on the 26th.

**Moon** occults Mars on the 5th, passes Mercury on the 7th, Venus on the 12th, Jupiter on the 16th, Neptune and Uranus on the 22nd, and Saturn on the 26th.

**July 2**—Jupiter stationary, resuming its direct motion.

**July 5**—Moon occults Mars; earth at aphelion, 94.4 million miles from the sun.

**July 6**—Mercury stationary, resuming its direct motion.

**July 7**—Moon passes 1.3° south of Mars, occulting it.

**July 10**—Venus passes 1.1° north of Regulus.

**July 12**—Moon passes 7° south of Venus.

**July 14**—Neptune at opposition, 2,710 million miles away.

**July 16**—Moon passes 3° south of Jupiter.

**July 17**—Uranus at opposition, almost 1,734 million miles away; Mercury at greatest elongation, 21° west of the sun.

**July 18**—Mars passes 5° north of Aldebaran.

**July 20**—Sun enters Cancer.

**July 22**—Moon passes 4° north of Neptune, and 5° north of Uranus.

**July 26**—Moon passes 7° north of Saturn.

**July 30**—Mercury 3° north of Pollux.

### August

**Mercury** is lost in the sun all month.

**Venus** is at greatest elongation, 46° east of the sun on the 24th, appearing like a half moon in telescopes.

**Mars** continues its dogged round of the sky all month, moving into Gemini about the 15th.

**Jupiter** decreases its distance from Venus, fading slightly as Venus grows still brighter.

**Saturn** attains its greatest brilliancy this year, but never getting brighter than 0.5 magnitude.

**Moon** passes Mars on the 3rd, Venus on the 10th, Jupiter on the 13th, Neptune and Uranus on the 18th, and Saturn on the 22nd.

**Aug. 3**—Moon passes 3° south of Mars.

**Aug. 9**—Pluto stationary.

**Aug. 10**—Moon passes 3° south of Venus; sun enters Leo.

**Aug. 11**—Watch for Perseid meteor shower tonight and tomorrow night.

**Aug. 13**—Mercury in superior conjunction, over 125 million miles away; moon passes 2° south of Jupiter.

**Aug. 18**—Moon passes 4° north of Neptune and 5° north of Uranus.

**Aug. 22**—Moon passes 7° north of Saturn.

**Aug. 24**—Venus at greatest elongation, 46° east of the sun.

**Aug. 31**—Venus 0.7° south of Spica.

### September

**Mercury** is in the evening sky all month and half of October, appearing as a zero magnitude star to the left of the set sun in the evening twilight, passing 0.1° south of Spica on the 21st, a binocular and telescope photo opportunity.

**Venus** achieves greatest brilliancy on the 28th, minus 4.6 magnitude, putting nearby Jupiter in his place, after a pleasant encounter with the crescent moon on the evening of the 8th.

**Mars** begins to brighten almost imperceptibly in preparation for its show at the end of the year, sneaking into Cancer just as the month ends.

**Jupiter** closes in on Venus, just to lose the spectacle to the traditional evening star, but providing a pleasant supporting role to the passing moon on the evenings of the 9th and 10th.

**Saturn**, at opposition on the 1st, has the whole night to itself, after the evening show in the west, and before the challenging Mars to the east.

**Moon** passes Mars on the 1st, Mercury on the 7th, Venus and Jupiter on the 9th, Neptune and Uranus on the 14th, Saturn on the 18th, and Mars, again, on the 29th.

**Sep. 1**—Moon passes 4° south of Mars; Saturn at opposition, about 808 million miles from us.

**Sep. 7**—Moon passes 3° south of Mercury.

**Sep. 9**—Moon passes 2° north of Venus, and 1.4° south of Jupiter.

**Sep. 14**—Moon passes 4° north of Neptune and 5° north of Uranus.

**Sep. 16**—Sun enters Virgo.

**Sep. 18**—Moon passes 7° north of Saturn.

**Sep. 21**—Mercury passes 0.1° south of Spica.

**Sep. 23**—Autumnal equinox; autumn begins in the northern hemisphere at 6:19 GMT (1:19 AM EST).

**Sep. 24**—Mars passes 6° south of Pollux.

**Sep. 26**—Mercury at greatest elongation, 26° east of the sun.

**Sep. 28**—Venus at greatest brilliancy.

**Sep. 29**—Moon passes 6° south of Mars.

### October

**Mercury**, except for the 1st week, and then only for very dedicated observers, is lost to view in the solar glare.

**Venus** and **Jupiter** are about 7° apart in the N-S direction, Venus considerably more to the left in the evening twilight, and it will plunge into the brighter parts of the twilight before Jupiter.

**Mars**, in Cancer all month, continues to brighten during the rest of the year.

**Jupiter** plays with a standoffish Venus for the rest of the month, but remains visible with some difficulty into November.

**Saturn** takes over the night sky as Venus and Jupiter leave, but Mars is becoming a serious contender.

**Moon** passes Mercury on the 6th, Venus and Jupiter on the 7th, occulting Jupiter, passes Neptune and Uranus on the 12th, Saturn on the 15th, and Mars on the 28th.

**Oct. 2**—Uranus and Neptune stationary, resuming their direct motions.

**Oct. 6**—Moon passes 3° north of Mercury.

**Oct. 7**—Moon passes 7° north of Venus, 0.7° south of Jupiter, occulting it; Venus is 34 million miles away, Jupiter, over 578 million miles.

**Oct. 9**—Mercury stationary, beginning its retrograde motion.

**Oct. 12**—Moon passes 4° north of Neptune, 5° north of Uranus; Venus stationary, beginning its retrograde motion.

**Oct. 15**—Moon passes 7° north of Saturn.

**Oct. 21**—Mercury at inferior conjunction, 62 million miles from us; Orionid meteor shower.

**Oct. 28**—Moon passes 7° south of Mars.

**Oct. 29**—Mercury stationary, resuming its direct motion.

**Oct. 30**—Sun enters Libra.

### November

**Mercury** is a morning object early in the month, passing Venus on the 12th.

**Venus** emerges into the morning sky, taking charge by mid-November, passing Mercury on the 12th.

**Mars** leaves Cancer for Leo on the 6th, brightening by half a magnitude this month.

**Jupiter** is lost to view all month, passing through conjunction on the 17th.

**Saturn** is alone in the evening sky, still faithful to Aquarius.

**Moon** passes Mercury on the 2nd, totally eclipses the sun on the 3rd, passes Neptune and Uranus on the 8th, Saturn on the 11th, has a penumbral eclipse on the 18th, passes Mars on the 25th, and Venus on the 30th.

**Nov. 2**—Moon passes 4° south of Mercury; Venus in inferior conjunction.

**Nov. 3**—Mercury passes 4° north of Spica; total solar eclipse.

**Nov. 6**—Mercury at greatest elongation, 10° west of the sun.

**Nov. 8**—Moon passes 4° north of Neptune and 6° north of Uranus.

**Nov. 9**—Saturn stationary, resuming its direct motion.

**Nov. 11**—Moon passes 7° north of Saturn.

**Nov. 12**—Mercury 5° north of Venus.

**Nov. 17**—Jupiter in conjunction with the sun, 593 million miles away; Leonid meteor shower.

**Nov. 18**—Moon in penumbral eclipse.

**Nov. 20**—Pluto in conjunction with the sun, nearly 2,851 million miles from earth.

**Nov. 22**—Sun enters Scorpius.

**Nov. 25**—Moon passes 8° south of Mars.

**Nov. 29**—Sun enters Ophiuchus.

**Nov. 30**—Moon passes 2° south of Venus.

### December

**Mercury** is lost to view all month, passing superior conjunction on the 14th.

**Venus** is at greatest brilliancy in the dawn sky on the 9th.

**Mars** stays in Leo, slowing its direct motion, passing 2° north of Regulus on the 8th, and brightening over a half magnitude during the month.

**Jupiter** emerges from the dawn solar glare early in the month, quickly moving into Scorpius from Libra, where it has spent the year.

**Saturn**, prominent in our western sky after sunset, remains in Aquarius.

**Moon** passes Neptune on the 5th, Uranus on the 6th, Saturn on the 9th, Mars on the 23rd, Venus on the 29th, and occults Jupiter on the 30th.

**Dec. 5**—Moon passes 4° north of Neptune.

**Dec. 6**—Moon passes 6° north of Uranus.

**Dec. 8**—Mars passes 2° north of Regulus.

**Dec. 9**—Moon passes 7° north of Saturn; Venus at greatest brilliancy.

**Dec. 13**—Geminid meteor shower.

**Dec. 14**—Mercury in superior conjunction, nearly 135 million miles away.

**Dec. 16**—Sun enters Sagittarius.

**Dec. 22**—Winter solstice; winter begins in the northern hemisphere at 2:23 GMT (10:23 PM EST, Dec. 21).

**Dec. 23**—Moon passes 9° south of Mars.

**Dec. 29**—Moon passes 3° south of Venus.

**Dec. 30**—Moon occults Jupiter.

## Planets and the Sun

The planets of the solar system, in order of their mean distance from the sun, are Mercury, Venus, the earth, Mars, Jupiter, Saturn, Uranus, Neptune and Pluto. Both Uranus and Neptune are visible through good field glasses, but Pluto is so distant and so small that only large telescopes or long exposure photographs can make it visible.

Since Mercury and Venus are nearer to the sun than is the earth, their motions about the sun are seen from the earth as wide swings first to one side of the sun and then to the other, although they are both passing continuously around the sun in orbits that are almost circular. When their passage takes them either between the earth and the sun, or beyond the sun as seen from the earth, they are invisible to us. Because of the laws that govern the motions of planets about the sun, both Mercury and Venus require much less time to pass between the earth and the sun than around the far side of the sun, so their periods of visibility and invisibility are unequal.

The planets that lie farther from the sun than does the earth may be seen for longer periods of time and are invisible only when they are so located in our sky that they rise and set about the same time as the sun when, of course, they are overwhelmed by the sun's great brilliance. None of the planets has any light of its own but each shines only by reflecting sunlight from its surface. Mercury and Venus, because they are between the earth and the sun, show phases very much as the moon does. The planets farther from the sun are always seen as full, although Mars does occasionally present a slightly gibbous phase — like the moon when not quite full.

The planets move rapidly among the stars because they are very much nearer to us. The stars are also in motion, some of them at tremendous speeds, but they are so far away that their motion does not change their apparent positions in the heavens sufficiently for anyone to perceive that change in a single lifetime. The very nearest star is about 7,000 times as far away as the most distant planet.

# Planets of the Solar System

## Mercury

Mercury, nearest planet to the sun, is the second smallest of the nine planets known to be orbiting the sun. Its diameter is 3,100 miles and its mean distance from the sun is 36,000,000 miles.

Mercury moves with great speed in its journey about the sun, averaging about 30 miles a second to complete its circuit in 88 of our days. Mercury rotates upon its axis over a period of nearly 59 days, thus exposing all of its surface periodically to the sun. It is believed that the surface passing before the sun may have a temperature of about 800° F., while the temperature on the side turned temporarily away from the sun does not fall as low as might be expected. This night temperature has been described by Russian astronomers as "room temperature" — possibly about 70° F. This would contradict the former belief that Mercury did not possess an atmosphere, for some sort of atmosphere would be needed to retain the fierce solar radiation that strikes Mercury. A shallow but dense layer of carbon dioxide would produce the "greenhouse" effect, in which heat accumulated during exposure to the sun would not completely escape at night. The actual presence of a carbon dioxide atmosphere is in dispute. Other research, however, has indicated a nighttime temperature approaching −300° F.

This uncertainty about conditions upon Mercury and its motion arise from its shorter angular distance from the sun as seen from the earth, for Mercury is always too much in line with the sun to be observed against a dark sky, but is always seen during either morning or evening twilight.

Mariner 10 made 3 passes by Mercury in 1974 and 1975. A large fraction of the surface was photographed from varying distances, revealing a degree of cratering similar to that of the moon. An atmosphere of hydrogen and helium may be made up of gases of the solar wind temporarily concentrated by the presence of Mercury. The discovery of a weak but permanent magnetic field was a surprise. It has been held that both a fluid core and rapid rotation were necessary for the generation of a planetary magnetic field. Mercury may demonstrate these conditions to be unnecessary, or the field may reveal something about the history of Mercury.

## Venus

Venus, slightly smaller than the earth, moves about the sun at a mean distance of 67,000,000 miles in 225 of our days. Its synodical revolution — its return to the same relationship with the earth and the sun, which is a result of the combination of its own motion and that of the earth — is 584 days. Every 19 months, then, Venus will be nearer to the earth than any other planet of the solar system. The planet is covered with a dense, white, cloudy atmosphere that conceals whatever is below it. This same cloud reflects sunlight efficiently so that when Venus is favorably situated, it is the third brightest object in the sky, exceeded only by the sun and the moon.

Spectral analysis of sunlight reflected from Venus' cloud tops has shown features that can best be explained by identifying the material of the clouds as sulphuric acid (oil of vitriol). Infrared spectroscopy from a balloon-borne telescope nearly 20 miles above the earth's surface gave indications of a small amount of water vapor present in the same region of the atmosphere of Venus. In 1956, radio astronomers at the Naval Research Laboratories in Washington, D.C., found a temperature for Venus of about 600° F., in marked contrast to minus 125° F., previously found at the cloud tops. Subsequent radio work confirmed a high temperature and produced evidence for this temperature to be associated with the solid body of Venus. With this peculiarity in mind, space scientists devised experiments for the U.S. space probe Mariner 2 to perform when it flew by in 1962. Mariner 2 confirmed the high temperature and the fact that it pertained to the ground rather than to some special activity of the atmosphere. In addition, Mariner 2 was unable to detect any radiation belts similar to the earth's so-called Van Allen belts. Nor was it able to detect the existence of a magnetic field even as weak as 1/100,000 of that of the earth.

In 1967, a Russian space probe, Venera 4, and the American Mariner 5 arrived at Venus within a few hours of each other. Venera 4 was designed to allow an instrument package to land gently on the planet's surface via parachute. It ceased transmission of information in about 75 minutes when the temperature it read went above 500° F. After considerable controversy, it was agreed that it still had 20 miles to go to reach the surface. The U.S. probe, Mariner 5, went around the dark side of Venus at a distance of about 6,000 miles. Again, it detected no significant magnetic field but its radio signals passed to earth through Venus' atmosphere twice — once on the night side and once on the day side. The results are startling. Venus' atmosphere is nearly all carbon dioxide and must exert a pressure at the planet's surface of up to 100 times the earth's normal sea-level pressure of one atmosphere. Since the earth and Venus are about the same size, and were presumably formed at the same time by the same general process from the same mixture of chemical elements, one is faced with the question: Which is the planet with the unusual history — earth or Venus?

Radar astronomers using powerful transmitters as well as sensitive receivers and computers have succeeded in determining the rotation period of Venus. It turns out to be 243 days clockwise — in other words, contrary to the spin of most of the other planets and to its own motion around the sun. If it were exactly 243.16 days, Venus would always present the same face toward the earth at every inferior conjunction. This rate and sense of rotation allows a "day" on Venus of 117.4 earth days. Any part of Venus will receive sunlight on its clouds for over 58 days and will be in darkness for 58 days. Recent radar observations have shown surface features below the clouds. Large craters, continent-sized highlands, and extensive, dry "ocean" basins have been identified.

Mariner 10 passed Venus before traveling on to Mercury in 1974. The carbon dioxide molecule found in such abundance in the atmosphere is rather opaque to certain ultraviolet wavelengths, enabling sensitive television cameras to take pictures of the Venusian cloud cover. Photos radioed to earth show a spiral pattern in the clouds from equator to the poles.

In December, 1978, two U.S. Pioneer probes arrived at Venus. One went into orbit about Venus, the other split into 5 separate probes targeted for widely spaced entry points to sample different conditions. The instrumentation ensemble was selected on the basis of previous missions that had shown the range of conditions to be studied. The probes confirmed expected high surface temperatures and high winds aloft. Winds of about 200 miles per hour, there, may account for the transfer of heat into the night side in spite of the low rotation speed of the planet. Surface winds were light at the time, however. Atmosphere and cloud chemistries were examined in detail, providing much data for continued analysis. The probes detected 4 layers of clouds and more light on the surface than expected solely from sunlight. This light allowed Russian scientists to obtain at least two photos showing rocks on the surface. Sulphur seems to play a large role in the chemistry of Venus, and reactions involving sulphur may be responsible for the glow. To learn more about the weather and atmospheric circulation on Venus, the orbiter takes daily photos of the daylight side cloud cover. It confirms the cloud pattern and its circulation shown by Mariner 10. The ionosphere shows large variability. The orbiter's radar operates in 2 modes: one for ground elevation variability, and the second for ground reflectivity in 2 dimensions, thus "imaging" the surface. Radar maps of the entire planet that show the features mentioned above have been produced.

The Venus orbiter Magellan was launched May 5, 1989. It was equipped to observe Venus by a side-scanning radar system, together with one to gather data on variations in elevations directly beneath the craft. Magellan has mapped all but a small fraction of the planet. The side-looking radar illuminates the surface and its features with radio waves and records the strength and distance of returning echoes. Computer processing produces what seems to be a view of the landscape as if seen through a clear atmosphere from above, near sunset, with a resolution better than about a mile on Venus.

Craters over 20 miles wide are believed to have been caused by impacting bodies. One 150-mile-wide crater, the largest found to date, has been named for Margaret Mead. Smaller craters are probably due to volcanic action. The largest such caldera has been named Sakajawea. Many lava flows have been seen, and some old craters and plains seem to be filled with lava.

Most of the surface is believed to be younger than 1000 to 500 million years old. Modifications of previously existing surface features have been due to tectonic actions such as faulting, and to weathering. Tectonic actions in general are distinctly different from such actions on earth. The intense heat at the surface of Venus can prevent the surface materials from cooling to the same brittle condition as on earth. The same actions on earth, thus, may produce somewhat different results on Venus. Although there are deep regions, somewhat similar to our ocean basins, there is no water to fill them. There seems to be no activity on Venus similar to our moving tectonic plates, but there may be local stretching and compressing that produce rift valleys and higher plains and mountains. Although there is no weathering due to water on Venus, the action of winds is in evidence. Extensive sand dunes have been seen, and windblown deposits indicate stable wind patterns for very long periods of time.

Despite deterioration in the physical condition of the orbiter, Magellan continues to function in adapted capacities.

## Mars

Mars is the first planet beyond the earth, away from the sun. Mars' diameter is about 4,200 miles, although a determination of the radius and mass of Mars by the space-probe Mariner 4, which flew by Mars on July 14, 1965, at a distance of less than 6,000 miles, indicated that these dimensions were slightly larger than had been previously estimated. While Mars' orbit is also nearly circular, it is somewhat more eccentric than the orbits of many of the other planets, and Mars is more than 30 million miles farther from the sun in some parts of its year than it is at others. Mars takes 687 of our days to make one circuit of the sun, traveling at about 15 miles a second. Mars rotates upon its axis in almost the same period of time that the earth does — 24 hours and 37 minutes. Mars' mean distance from the sun is 141 million miles, so that the temperature on Mars would be lower than that on the earth even if Mars' atmosphere were about the same as ours. The atmosphere is not, however, for Mariner 4 reported that atmospheric pressure on Mars is between 1% and 2% of the earth's atmospheric pressure. This thin atmosphere appears to be largely carbon dioxide. No evidence of free water was found.

There appears to be no magnetic field about Mars. This would eliminate the previous conception of a dangerous radiation belt around Mars. The same lack of a magnetic field would expose the surface of Mars to an influx of cosmic radiation about 100 times as intense as that on earth.

Deductions from years of telescopic observation indicate that 5/8ths of the surface of Mars is a desert of reddish rock, sand, and soil. The rest of Mars is covered by irregular patches that appear generally green in hues that change through the Martian year. These were formerly held to be some sort of primitive vegetation, but with the findings of Mariner 4 of a complete lack of water and oxygen, such growth does not appear possible. The nature of the green areas is now unknown. They may be regions covered with volcanic salts whose color changes with changing temperatures and atmospheric conditions, or they may be gray, rather than green. When large gray areas are placed beside large red areas, the gray areas will appear green to the eye.

Mars' axis of rotation is inclined from a vertical to the plane of its orbit about the sun by about 25° and therefore Mars has seasons as does the earth, except that the Martian seasons are longer because Mars' year is longer. White caps form about the winter pole of Mars, growing through the winter and shrinking in summer. These polar caps are now believed to be both water ice and carbon dioxide ice. It is the carbon dioxide that is seen to come and go with the seasons. The water ice is apparently in many layers with dust between them, indicating climatic cycles.

The canals of Mars have become more of a mystery than they were before the voyage of Mariner 4. Markings forming a network of fine lines crossing much of the surface of Mars have been seen there by men who have devoted much time to the study of the planet, but no canals have shown clearly enough in previous photographs to be universally accepted. A few of the 21 photographs sent back to earth by Mariner 4 covered areas crossed by canals. The pictures show faint, ill-defined, broad, dark markings, but no positive identification of the nature of the markings.

Mariners 6 & 7 in 1969 sent back many more photographs of higher quality than those of the pioneering Mariner 4. These pictures showed cratering similar to the earlier views, but in addition showed 2 other types of terrain. Some regions seemed featureless for many square miles, but others were chaotic, showing high relief without apparent organization into mountain chains or craters.

Mariner 9, the first artificial body to be placed in an orbit about Mars, has transmitted over 10,000 photographs covering 100% of the planet's surface. Preliminary study of these photos and other data shows that Mars resembles no other planet we know. Using terrestrial terms, however, scientists describe features that seem to be clearly of volcanic origin. One of these features is Nix Olympica (now called Olympus Mons), apparently a shield volcano whose caldera is over 50 miles wide, whose outer slopes are over 300 miles in diameter, and which stands about 90,000 feet above the surrounding plain. Some features may have been produced by cracking (faulting) of the surface and the sliding of one region over or past another. Many craters seem to have been produced by impacting bodies such as may have come from the nearby asteroid belt. Features near the south pole may have been produced by glaciers that are no longer present. Flowing water, nonexistent on Mars at the present time, probably carved canyons, one 10 times longer and 3 times deeper than the Grand Canyon.

Although the Russians landed a probe on the Martian surface, it transmitted for only 20 seconds. In 1976, the U.S. landed 2 Viking spacecraft on the Martian surface. The landers had devices aboard to perform chemical analyses of the soil in search of evidence of life. The results have been inconclusive. The 2 Viking orbiters have returned the best pictures yet of Martian topographic features. Many features can be explained only if Mars once had large quantities of flowing water.

Mars' position in its orbit and its speed around that orbit in relation to the earth's position and speed bring Mars fairly close to the earth on occasions about two years apart and then move Mars and the earth too far apart for accurate observation and photography. Every 15-17 years, the close approaches are especially favorable to close observation.

Mars has 2 satellites, discovered in 1877 by Asaph Hall. The outer satellite, Deimos, revolves around Mars in about 31 hours. The inner satellite, Phobos, whips around Mars in a little more than 7 hours, making 3 trips around the planet each Martian day. Mariner and Viking photos show these bodies to be irregularly shaped and pitted with numerous craters. Phobos also shows a system of linear grooves, each about 1/3-mile across and roughly parallel. Phobos measures about 8 by 12 miles and Deimos about 5 by 7.5 miles in size.

## Jupiter

Jupiter is the largest of the planets. Its equatorial diameter is 88,000 miles, 11 times the diameter of the earth. Its polar diameter is about 6,000 miles shorter. This is an equilibrium condition resulting from the liquidity of the planet and its extremely rapid rate of rotation: a Jupiter day is only 10 earth hours long. For a planet this size, this rotational speed is amazing, and it moves a point on Jupiter's equator at a speed of 22,000 miles an hour, as compared with 1,000 miles an hour for a point on the earth's equator. Jupiter is at an average distance of 480 million miles from the sun and takes almost 12 of our years to make one complete circuit of the sun.

The only directly observable chemical constituents of Jupiter's atmosphere are methane ($CH_4$) and ammonia ($NH_3$), but it is reasonable to assume the same mixture of elements available to make Jupiter as to make the sun. This would mean a large fraction of hydrogen and helium must be present also, as well as water ($H_2O$). The temperature at the tops of the clouds

may be about minus 260° F. The clouds are probably ammonia ice crystals, becoming ammonia droplets lower down. There may be a space before water ice crystals show up as clouds: in turn, these become water droplets near the bottom of the entire cloud layer. The total atmosphere may be only a few hundred miles in depth, pulled down by the surface gravity (= 2.64 times earth's) to a relatively thin layer. Of course, the gases become denser with depth until they may turn into a slush or a slurry. Perhaps there is no surface — no real interface between the gaseous atmosphere and the body of Jupiter. Pioneers 10 and 11 provided evidence for considering Jupiter to be almost entirely liquid hydrogen. Long before a rocky core about the size of the earth is reached, hydrogen mixed with helium becomes a liquid metal at very high temperature and pressure. Jupiter's cloudy atmosphere is a fairly good reflector of sunlight and makes it appear far brighter than any of the stars.

Fourteen of Jupiter's 17 or more satellites have been found through earth-based observations. Four of the moons are large and bright, rivaling our own moon and the planet Mercury in diameter, and may be seen through a field glass. They move rapidly around Jupiter and their change of position from night to night is extremely interesting to watch. The other satellites are much smaller and in all but one instance much farther from Jupiter and cannot be seen except through powerful telescopes. The 4 outermost satellites are revolving around Jupiter clockwise as seen from the north, contrary to the motions of the great majority of the satellites in the solar system and to the direction of revolution of the planets around the sun. The reason for this retrograde motion is not known, but one theory is that Jupiter's tremendous gravitational power may have captured 4 of the minor planets or asteroids that move about the sun between Mars and Jupiter, and that these would necessarily revolve backward. At the great distance of these bodies from Jupiter — some 14 million miles — direct motion would result in decay of the orbits, while retrograde orbits would be stable. Jupiter's mass is more than twice the mass of all the other planets put together, and accounts for Jupiter's tremendous gravitational field and so, probably, for its numerous satellites and its dense atmosphere.

In December 1973, Pioneer 10 passed about 80,000 miles from the equator of Jupiter and was whipped into a path that would take it beyond the system of planets on June 13, 1983, and out of our solar system in about 50 years. In December 1974, Pioneer 11 passed within 30,000 miles of Jupiter, moving roughly from south to north, over the poles.

Photographs from both encounters were useful at the time but were far surpassed by those of Voyagers I and II. Thousands of high resolution multi-color pictures show rapid variations of features both large and small. The Great Red Spot exhibits internal counterclockwise rotation. Much turbulence is seen in adjacent material passing north or south of it. The satellites Amalthea, Io, Europa, Ganymede, and Callisto were photographed, some in great detail. Each is individual and unique, with no similarities to other known planets or satellites. Io has active volcanoes that probably have ejected material into a doughnut-shaped ring enveloping its orbit about Jupiter. This is not to be confused with the thin flat disk-like ring closer to Jupiter's surface. Now that such a ring has been seen by the Voyagers, older uncertain observations from earth can be reinterpreted as early sightings of this structure.

## Saturn

Saturn, last of the planets visible to the unaided eye, is almost twice as far from the sun as Jupiter, almost

900 million miles. It is second in size to Jupiter but its mass is much smaller. Saturn's specific gravity is less than that of water. Its diameter is about 71,000 miles at the equator; its rotational speed spins it completely around in a little more than 10 hours, and its atmosphere is much like that of Jupiter, except that its temperature at the top of its cloud layer is at least 100° F. lower. At about 300° F. below zero, the ammonia would be frozen out of Saturn's clouds. The theoretical construction of Saturn resembles that of Jupiter; it is either all gas, or it has a small dense center surrounded by a layer of liquid and a deep atmosphere.

Until Pioneer 11 passed Saturn in September 1979 only 10 satellites of the planet were known. Data retrieved since that time have confused scientists. Added to data interpretations from the fly-by are earth-based observations using techniques employed while the rings were edge-on and virtually invisible. It was hoped that the Voyager I and II fly-bys would help scientists sort out the satellite system, but it is still not entirely understood. It is now believed that Saturn has at least 22 satellites, some sharing orbits.

Saturn's ring system begins about 7,000 miles above the visible disk of Saturn, lying above its equator and extending about 35,000 miles into space. The diameter of the ring system visible from earth is about 170,000 miles; the rings are estimated to be no thicker than 10 miles. In 1973, radar observation showed the ring particles to be large chunks of material averaging a meter on a side.

Voyager I and II observations showed the rings to be considerably more complex than had been believed, so much so that interpretation will take much time. To the untrained eye, the Voyager photographs could be mistaken for pictures of a colorful phonograph record.

## Uranus

Voyager II, after passing Saturn in August 1981, headed for a rendezvous with Uranus culminating in a fly-by January 24, 1986. This encounter answered many questions, and raised others.

Uranus, discovered by Sir William Herschel on Mar. 13, 1781, lies at a distance of 1.8 billion miles from the sun, taking 84 years to make its circuit around our star. Uranus has a diameter of about 32,000 miles and spins once in some 16.8 hours, according to fly-by data. One of the most fascinating features of Uranus is how far it is tipped over. Its north pole lies 98° from being directly up and down to its orbit plane. Thus, its seasons are extreme. When the sun rises at the north pole, it stays up for 42 years; then it sets and the north pole will be in darkness (and winter) for 42 years.

The satellite system of Uranus consists of at least 15 moons (the 5 largest having been known before the fly-by), which have orbits lying in the plane of the planet's equator. In that plane there is also a complex of rings, 9 of which were discovered in 1978. Invisible from earth, the 9 original rings were found by observers watching Uranus pass before a star. As they waited, they saw their photoelectric equipment register several short eclipses of the star. Then the planet occulted the star as expected. After the star came out from behind Uranus, the star winked out several more times. Subsequent observations and analyses indicated the 9 narrow, nearly opaque rings circling Uranus. Evidence from the Voyager II fly-by has shown the ring particles to be predominantly a yard or so in diameter.

In addition to the 10 new, very small satellites, Voyager II returned detailed photos of the 5 large satellites. As in the case of other satellites newly observed in the Voyager program, these bodies proved to be entirely different from each other and any others. Miranda has grooved markings, reminiscent of Jupiter's Ganymede, but often arranged in a chevron pattern. Ariel shows rifts and channels. Umbriel is extremely dark, prompting some observers to regard its surface as among the oldest in the system. Titania has rifts and fractures, but not the evidence of flow found on Ariel. Oberon's main feature is its surface saturated with craters, unrelieved by other formations.

The structure of Uranus is subject to some debate. Basically, however, it may have a rocky core surrounded by a thick icy mantle on top of which is a crust of hydrogen and helium that gradually becomes an atmosphere. Perhaps continued analysis of the wealth of data returned by Voyager II will shed some light on this problem.

## Neptune

Neptune, currently the most distant planet from the sun (until 1999), lies at an average distance of 2.8 billion miles. It was the last planet visited in Voyager II's epic 12 year trek from earth. While much new information was immediately perceived, much more must await further analysis of the tremendous amount of data returned from the spacecraft.

As with the other giant planets, there may be no solid surface to give real meaning to a measure of a diameter. However, a mean value of 30,600 miles may be assigned to a diameter between atmosphere levels where the pressure is about the same as sea level on earth, as determined by radio experimenters. A different radio observational technique gave evidence of a rotation period for the bulk of Neptune of 16.1 hours, a shorter value than the 18.2 hours given by the clouds seen in the blue atmosphere. Neptune orbits the sun in 164 years in nearly a circular orbit.

Voyager II, which passed 3000 miles from Neptune's north pole, found a magnetic field that is considerably asymmetric to the planet's structure, similar, but not so extreme, to that found at Uranus.

Neptune's atmosphere was seen to be quite blue, with quickly changing white clouds often suspended high above an apparent surface. In that apparent surface were found features, one of which was reminiscent of the Great Red Spot of Jupiter, even to the counterclockwise rotation expected in a high-pressure system in the southern hemisphere. Atmospheric constituents are mostly hydrocarbon compounds. Although lightning and auroras have been found on other giant planets, only the aurora phenomenon has been seen on Neptune.

Six new satellites were discerned around Neptune, one confirming a 1981 sighting that was then difficult to recover for proper identification. Five of these satellites orbit Neptune in a half day or less. Of the eight satellites of Neptune, the largest, Triton, is in a retrograde orbit suggesting that it was captured rather than being coeval with Neptune. Triton's large size, sufficient to raise significant tides on Neptune, will one day, say 100 million years from now, cause Triton to come close enough to Neptune for it to be torn apart. Nereid was found in 1949, and is in a long looping orbit suggesting it, too, was captured. Each of the satellites that has been photographed by the two Voyagers in the planetary encounters has been different from any of the other planetary satellites, and certainly from any of the planets. Only about half of Triton has been observed, but its terrain shows cratering and a strange regional feature described as resembling the skin of a cantaloupe. Triton has a tenuous atmosphere of nitrogen with a trace of hydrocarbons, and evidence of active geysers injecting material into it. At minus 238 degrees Celsius, Triton is one of the coldest objects in the solar system observed by Voyager II.

In addition to the satellite system, Voyager II confirmed the existence of at least three rings composed of very fine particles. There may some clumpiness in their structure, but the known satellites may not contribute to the formation or maintenance of the rings, as they have in other systems.

As with the other giant planets, Neptune is emitting more energy than it receives from the sun, Voyager finding the excess to be 2.7 times the solar contribution. These excesses are thought to be cooling from internal heat sources and from the heat of formation of the planets.

## Pluto

Although Pluto on the average stays about 3.6 billion miles from the sun, its orbit is so eccentric that its minimum distance of 2.7 billion miles is less than the current distance of Neptune. Thus Pluto, until 1999, is temporarily planet number 8 from the sun. At its mean distance, Pluto takes 247.7 years to circumnavigate the sun, a 3/2 resonance with Neptune. Until recently that was about all that was known of Pluto.

About a century ago, a hypothetical planet was believed to lie beyond Neptune and Uranus because neither planet followed the paths predicted by astronomers even when all known gravitational influences were considered. Little more than a guess, a mass of one earth was assigned to the mysterious body and mathematical searches were begun. Amid some controversy about the validity of the predictive process, Pluto was found nearly where it was predicted to be. It was found by Clyde Tombaugh at the Lowell Observatory in Flagstaff, Ariz., in 1930.

At the U.S. Naval Observatory, also in Flagstaff, on July 2, 1978, James Christy obtained a photograph of Pluto that was distinctly elongated. Repeated observations of this shape and its variation were convincing evidence of the discovery of a satellite of Pluto, now named Charon. Subsequent observations show it to be 750 miles across, at a distance of over 12,000 miles

from Pluto, and taking 6.4 days to move around Pluto. In this same length of time Pluto and Charon each rotate once around their individual axes. The Pluto-Charon system thus appears to rotate as virtually a ridged body. Gravitational laws allow these interactions to give us the mass of Pluto as 0.0020 of the earth. This mass, together with a new diameter for Pluto of 1,430 miles makes the density about twice that of water. Theorists predict a rocky core for Pluto surrounded by a thick mantle of ice.

It is now clear that Pluto, the body found by Tombaugh, could not have influenced Neptune and Uranus to go astray. Theorists are again at work looking for a new planet X.

Because the rotational axis of the system is tipped from the reference plane of the solar system by about 98°.3, similar to that of Uranus, there is only a short interval every half solar period when Pluto and Charon alternately eclipse each other. Analysis of the variations in light in and out of the recent eclipses has led to the diameters quoted above, and to interesting knowledge of other aspects of the system. Each component is approximately spherical, but they are otherwise different. Pluto is red, Charon grey. Charon has a surface identified as water ice; Pluto's surface is frozen methane. There are large regions on Pluto that are dark, others light; Pluto has spots, and, perhaps, polar caps. Although extremely cold, Pluto's methane surface produces a tenuous atmosphere that may be slowly escaping into space, perhaps going to Charon. When Pluto occulted a star, the star's light faded in such a way as to have passed through a haze layer lying above the planet's surface, indicating an inversion of temperatures, 110°K above, and 50°K below, suggesting Pluto has primitive weather.

There are tentative plans for a spacecraft reconnaissance of the Pluto system, thus completing direct, close-up observation of each of the planets of the solar system.

## Greenwich Sidereal Time for 0ʰ GMT, 1994

(Add 12 hours to obtain Right Ascension of Mean Sun)

| Date | | h | m | Date | | h | m | Date | | h | m | Date | | h | m |
|------|---|---|---|------|---|---|---|------|---|---|---|------|---|---|---|
| Jan. | 1 | 06 | 41.7 | Apr. | 1 | 12 | 36.5 | July | 10 | 19 | 10.8 | Oct. | 8 | 01 | 05.6 |
| | 11 | 07 | 21.1 | | 11 | 13 | 15.9 | | 20 | 19 | 50.2 | | 18 | 01 | 45.0 |
| | 21 | 08 | 0.5 | | 21 | 13 | 55.4 | | 30 | 20 | 29.6 | | 28 | 02 | 24.4 |
| | 31 | 08 | 40.0 | May | 1 | 14 | 34.8 | Aug. | 9 | 21 | 09.0 | Nov. | 7 | 03 | 03.9 |
| Feb. | 10 | 09 | 19.4 | | 11 | 15 | 14.2 | | 19 | 21 | 48.5 | | 17 | 03 | 43.3 |
| | 20 | 09 | 58.8 | | 21 | 15 | 53.6 | | 29 | 22 | 27.9 | | 27 | 04 | 22.7 |
| Mar. | 2 | 10 | 38.2 | | 31 | 16 | 33.1 | Sept. | 8 | 23 | 07.3 | Dec. | 7 | 05 | 02.1 |
| | 12 | 11 | 17.7 | June | 10 | 17 | 12.5 | | 18 | 23 | 46.7 | | 17 | 05 | 41.6 |
| | 22 | 11 | 57.1 | | 20 | 17 | 51.9 | | 28 | 00 | 26.2 | | 27 | 06 | 21.0 |
| | | | | | 30 | 18 | 31.3 | | | | | | | | |

## Astronomical Signs and Symbols

| | | | | | | | |
|---|---|---|---|---|---|---|---|
| ☉ | The Sun | ⊕ | The Earth | ♅ | Uranus | ⊓ | Quadrature |
| ☽ | The Moon | ♂ | Mars | ♆ | Neptune | ♂ | Opposition |
| ☿ | Mercury | ♃ | Jupiter | ♇ | Pluto | ☊ | Ascending Node |
| ♀ | Venus | ♄ | Saturn | ☌ | Conjunction | ☋ | Descending Node |

Two heavenly bodies are in "conjunction" ( ☌ ) when they are due north and south of each other, either in Right Ascension (with respect to the north celestial pole) or in Celestial Longitude (with respect to the north ecliptic pole). If the bodies are seen near each other, they will rise and set at nearly the same time. They are in "opposition" ( ☍ ) when their Right Ascensions differ by exactly 12 hours, or their Celestial Longitudes differ by 180°. One of the two objects in opposition will rise while the other is setting. "Quadrature" ( ⊓ ) refers to the arrangement when the coordinates of two bodies differ by exactly 90°. These terms may refer to the relative positions of any two bodies as seen from the earth, but one of the bodies is so fre-

quently the sun that mention of the sun is omitted; otherwise both bodies are named. The geocentric angular separation between sun and object is termed "elongation." Elongation is limited only for Mercury and Venus; the "greatest elongation" for each of these bodies is noted in the appropriate tables and is approximately the time for longest observation. When a planet is in its "ascending" ( ☊ ) or "descending" ( ☋ ) node, it is passing northward or southward, respectively, through the plane of the earth's orbit, across the celestial circle called the ecliptic. The term "perihelion" means nearest to the sun, and "aphelion," farthest from the sun. An "occultation" of a planet or star is an eclipse of it by some other body, usually the moon.

# Planetary Configurations, 1994

Greenwich Mean Time (0 designates midnight; 12 designates noon; * = star; ☽ = moon)

| Mo. | d. h. m. | | Event |
|---|---|---|---|
| Jan. | 2 06 | - | ⊕ closest to ☉; Perihelion |
| | 3 20 | ☌ ☿ ☉ | Superior Conj. |
| | 6 22 | ☌ ♃ ☽ | ♃ 3° N |
| | 11 08 | ☌ ♆ ☉ | |
| | 12 17 | ☌ ♅ ☉ | |
| | 15 00 | ☌ ♄ ☉ | ♄ 7° S |
| | 17 02 | ☌ ♀ ☉ | |
| Feb. | 2 04 | ☌ ☿ ♄ | ☿ 1°.3 N |
| | 3 08 | ☌ ♃ ☽ | ♃ 3° N |
| | 4 21 | | ☿ Gr Elong; 18° E of ☉ |
| | 8 08 | ☌ ♆ ☽ | ♆ 3° S |
| | 8 12 | ☌ ♅ ☽ | ♅ 5° S |
| | 10 18 | | ☿ Stationary |
| | 20 08 | ☌ ☿ ☉ | Inferior Conj. |
| | 21 17 | ☌ ♄ ☉ | |
| | 27 01 | ☌ ☿ ♂ | ☿ 4° N |
| | 28 21 | | ♃ Stationary |
| Mar. | 2 16 | ☌ ♃ ☽ | ♃ 2° N |
| | 4 01 | | P Stationary |
| | 4 12 | | ☿ Stationary |
| | 7 16 | ☌ ♆ ☽ | ♆ 4° S |
| | 7 21 | ☌ ♅ ☽ | ♅ 5° S |
| | 10 04 | ☌ ☿ ☽ | ☿ 5° S |
| | 10 23 | ☌ ♂ ☽ | ♂ 7° S |
| | 11 04 | ☌ ♄ ☽ | ♄ 7° S |
| | 13 17 | ☌ ♀ ☽ | ♀ 5° S |
| | 14 10 | ☌ ♂ ♄ | ♂ 0°.4 N |
| | 19 02 | | ☿ Gr Elong; 28° W of ☉ |
| | 20 28 | | Vernal Equinox; Spring begins in Northern Hemisphere |
| | 24 08 | ☌ ☿ ☽ | ☿ 0°.3 S |
| | 29 23 | ☌ ♃ ☽ | ♃ 2° N |
| Apr. | 3 22 | ☌ ♆ ☽ | ♆ 4° S |
| | 4 02 | ☌ ☿ ☽ | ☿ 1°.5 S |
| | 4 04 | ☌ ♅ ☽ | ♅ 5° S |
| | 7 16 | ☌ ♄ ☽ | ♄ 7° S |
| | 9 02 | ☌ ♂ ☽ | ♂ 6° S |
| | 9 11 | ☌ ☿ ☽ | ☿ 7° S |
| | 12 23 | ☌ ♀ ☽ | ♀ 1°.0 S; Occultation |
| | 25 09 | | ♆ Stationary |
| | 26 05 | ☌ ♃ ☽ | ♃ 3° N |
| | 30 09 | ☍ ♃ ☉ | |
| | 30 10 | ☌ ☿ ☉ | Superior Conj. |
| May | 1 01 | | ♅ Stationary |
| | 1 06 | ☌ ♆ ☽ | ♆ 4° S |
| | 1 12 | ☌ ♅ ☽ | ♅ 5° S |
| | 5 00 | ☌ ♀ * | ♀ 6° N of Aldebaran |
| | 5 03 | ☌ ♄ ☽ | ♄ 7° S |
| | 8 04 | ☌ ♂ ☽ | ♂ 4° S |
| | 10 17 | ☌ ☽ ☉ | Annular Solar Eclipse |
| | 13 06 | ☌ ♀ ☽ | ♀ 4° N |
| | 15 11 | ☌ ☿ * | ☿ 8° N of Aldebaran |
| | 17 20 | ☍ P ☉ | |
| | 23 11 | ☌ ♄ ☽ | ♃ 3° N |
| | 25 04 | ☍ ♃ ☉ | Partial Lunar Eclipse |
| | 28 14 | ☌ ♆ ☽ | ♆ 4° S |
| | 28 20 | ☌ ♅ ☽ | ♅ 5° S |
| | 30 07 | | ☿ Gr Elong; 23° E of ☉ |
| June | 1 12 | ☌ ♄ ☽ | ♄ 7° S |
| | 6 05 | ☌ ♂ ☽ | ♂ 2° S |
| | 10 05 | ☌ ♀ * | ♀ 5° S of Pollux |
| | 11 00 | ☌ ☿ ☽ | ☿ 3° N |
| | 12 12 | | ☿ Stationary |
| | 12 13 | ☌ ♀ ☽ | ♀ 7° N |
| | 19 16 | ☌ ♃ ☽ | ♃ 3° N |
| | 21 14 48 | | Summer Solstice; Summer begins in Northern Hemisphere |
| | 24 04 | | ♄ Stationary |
| | 24 23 | ☌ ♆ ☽ | ♆ 4° S |
| | 25 05 | ☌ ♅ ☽ | ♅ 5° S |
| | 25 10 | ☌ ☿ ☉ | Inferior Conj. |
| | 28 21 | ☌ ♄ ☽ | ♄ 7° S |
| July | 2 16 | | ♃ Stationary |
| | 5 05 | ☌ ♂ ☽ | ♂ 0°.3 N; Occultation |
| | 5 19 | | ⊕ farthest from ☉; Aphelion |
| | 6 20 | | ☿ Stationary |
| | 7 13 | ☌ ☿ ☽ | ☿ 1°.3 S |
| | 10 17 | ☌ ♀ ☽ | ♀ 1°.1 N of Regulus |
| | 12 12 | ☌ ♀ ☽ | ♀ 7° N |
| | 14 16 | ☍ ♅ ☉ | |
| | 16 23 | ☌ ♃ ☽ | ♃ 3° N |
| | 17 04 | ☍ ♅ ☉ | |
| | 17 14 | | ☿ Gr Elong; 21° W of ☉ |
| | 18 21 | ☌ ♂ * | ♂ 5° N of Aldebaran |
| | 22 07 | ☌ ♆ ☽ | ♆ 4° S |
| | 22 12 | ☌ ♅ ☽ | ♅ 5° S |
| | 26 04 | ☌ ♄ ☽ | ♄ 7° S |
| | 31 07 | ☌ ♀ * | ♀ 6° S of Pollux |
| Aug. | 3 04 | ☌ ♂ ☽ | ♂ 3° N |
| | 9 14 | | P Stationary |
| | 10 23 | ☌ ♀ ☽ | ♀ 3° N |
| | 13 01 | ☌ ☿ ☉ | Superior Conj. |
| | 13 07 | ☌ ♃ ☽ | ♃ 2° N |
| | 18 14 | ☌ ♆ ☽ | ♆ 4° S |
| | 18 18 | ☌ ♅ ☽ | ♅ 5° S |
| | 22 10 | ☌ ♄ ☽ | ♄ 7° S |
| | 24 23 | | ♀ Gr Elong; 46° E of ☉ |
| | 31 21 | ☌ ♀ * | ♀ 0°.7 S of Spica |
| Sept. | 1 03 | ☌ ♂ ☽ | ♂ 4° N |
| | 1 17 | ☍ ♄ ☉ | |
| | 7 09 | ☌ ☿ ☽ | ☿ 3° N |
| | 9 01 | ☌ ♀ ☽ | ♀ 2° S |
| | 9 20 | ☌ ♃ ☽ | ♃ 1°.4 N |
| | 14 19 | ☌ ♆ ☽ | ♆ 4° S |
| | 14 23 | ☌ ♅ ☽ | ♅ 5° S |
| | 18 13 | ☌ ♄ ☽ | ♄ 7° S |
| | 21 13 | ☌ ☿ * | ☿ 0°.1 S of Spica |
| | 23 06 19 | | Autumnal Equinox; Autumn begins in Northern Hemisphere |
| | 24 15 | ☌ ♂ * | ♂ 6° S of Pollux |
| | 26 16 | | ☿ Gr Elong; 26° E of ☉ |
| | 28 22 | | ♀ Gr Brilliancy |
| | 29 22 | ☌ ♂ ☽ | ♂ 6° N |
| Oct. | 2 03 | | ♅ Stationary |
| | 2 14 | | ♆ Stationary |
| | 6 18 | ☌ ☿ ☽ | ☿ 3° S |
| | 7 10 | ☌ ♀ ☽ | ♀ 7° S |
| | 7 12 | ☌ ♃ ☽ | ♃ 0°.7 N; Occultation |
| | 9 09 | | ☿ Stationary |
| | 12 01 | ☌ ♆ ☽ | ♆ 4° S |
| | 12 04 | ☌ ♅ ☽ | ♅ 5° S |
| | 12 23 | | ♀ Stationary |
| | 15 16 | ☌ ♄ ☽ | ♄ 7° S |
| | 21 05 | ☌ ☿ ☉ | Inferior Conj. |
| | 28 13 | ☌ ♂ ☽ | ♂ 7° N |
| | 29 17 | | ☿ Stationary |
| Nov. | 2 10 | ☌ ☿ ☽ | ☿ 4° N |
| | 2 23 | ☌ ♀ ☉ | Inferior Conj. |
| | 3 01 | ☌ ♀ * | ♀ 4° N of Spica |
| | 3 14 | ☌ ♂ ☉ | Total Solar Eclipse |
| | 6 01 | | ☿ Gr Elong; 19° W of ☉ |
| | 8 08 | ☌ ♆ ☽ | ♆ 4° S |
| | 8 12 | ☌ ♅ ☽ | ♅ 6° S |
| | 9 21 | | ♄ Stationary |
| | 11 21 | ☌ ♄ ☽ | ♄ 7° S |
| | 12 18 | ☌ ☿ ☽ | ☿ 5° N |
| | 17 20 | ☍ ♃ ☉ | |
| | 18 07 | ☍ ☽ ☉ | Penumbral Lunar Eclipse |
| | 20 13 | ☌ P ☉ | |
| | 25 20 | ☌ ♂ ☽ | ♂ 8° N |
| | 30 14 | ☌ ♀ ☽ | ♀ 2° N |
| Dec. | 5 19 | ☌ ♆ ☽ | ♆ 4° S |
| | 6 00 | ☌ ♅ ☽ | ♅ 6° S |
| | 8 08 | ☌ ♂ * | ♂ 2° N of Regulus |
| | 9 05 | ☌ ♄ ☽ | ♄ 7° S |
| | 9 11 | | ♀ Gr Brilliancy |
| | 14 03 | ☌ ☿ ☉ | Superior Conj. |
| | 22 02 23 | | Winter Solstice; Winter begins in Northern Hemisphere |
| | 23 15 | ☌ ♂ ☽ | ♂ 9° N |
| | 29 05 | ☌ ♀ ☽ | ♀ 3° N |
| | 30 00 | ☌ ♃ ☽ | ♃ 1°.1 S; Occultation |

# Rising and Setting of Planets, 1994

Greenwich Mean Time (0 designates midnight)

## Venus, 1994

| | | 20° N. Latitude | | 30° N. Latitude | | 40° N. Latitude | | 50° N. Latitude | | 60° N. Latitude | |
|---|---|---|---|---|---|---|---|---|---|---|---|
| | | Rise | Set | Rise | Set | Rise | Set | Rise | Set | Rise | Set |
| Jan. | 1 | 6:21 | 17:14 | 6:43 | 16:52 | 7:10 | 16:25 | 7:48 | 15:47 | 8:57 | 14:38 |
| | 11 | 6:35 | 17:31 | 6:56 | 17:10 | 7:21 | 16:44 | 7:58 | 16:08 | 9:02 | 15:04 |
| | 21 | 6:46 | 17:48 | 7:04 | 17:30 | 7:27 | 17:07 | 8:00 | 16:35 | 8:54 | 15:40 |
| | 31 | 6:53 | 18:05 | 7:08 | 17:50 | 7:28 | 17:31 | 7:54 | 17:05 | 8:37 | 16:22 |
| Feb. | 10 | 6:57 | 18:22 | 7:09 | 18:10 | 7:23 | 17:55 | 7:43 | 17:36 | 8:14 | 17:05 |
| | 20 | 6:58 | 18:37 | 7:06 | 18:29 | 7:16 | 18:20 | 7:28 | 18:07 | 7:48 | 17:48 |
| Mar. | 2 | 6:58 | 18:51 | 7:01 | 18:47 | 7:06 | 18:43 | 7:11 | 18:38 | 7:20 | 18:30 |
| | 12 | 6:56 | 19:04 | 6:56 | 19:05 | 6:55 | 19:07 | 6:53 | 19:08 | 6:50 | 19:12 |
| | 22 | 6:55 | 19:18 | 6:50 | 19:23 | 6:43 | 19:30 | 6:34 | 19:39 | 6:21 | 19:53 |
| Apr. | 1 | 6:54 | 19:31 | 6:45 | 19:41 | 6:33 | 19:53 | 6:17 | 20:10 | 5:51 | 20:36 |
| | 11 | 6:55 | 19:46 | 6:41 | 20:00 | 6:24 | 20:17 | 6:01 | 20:41 | 5:23 | 21:20 |
| | 21 | 6:58 | 20:02 | 6:41 | 20:19 | 6:19 | 20:41 | 5:48 | 21:12 | 4:57 | 22:05 |
| May | 1 | 7:04 | 20:18 | 6:43 | 20:39 | 6:18 | 21:05 | 5:41 | 21:42 | 4:35 | 22:48 |
| | 11 | 7:13 | 20:34 | 6:50 | 20:57 | 6:21 | 21:26 | 5:40 | 22:08 | 4:22 | 23:26 |
| | 21 | 7:25 | 20:49 | 7:01 | 21:13 | 6:31 | 21:43 | 5:47 | 22:27 | 4:23 | 23:51 |
| | 31 | 7:39 | 21:01 | 7:15 | 21:25 | 6:46 | 21:54 | 6:02 | 22:37 | 4:40 | 23:59 |
| June | 10 | 7:53 | 21:11 | 7:32 | 21:32 | 7:04 | 22:00 | 6:24 | 22:39 | 5:12 | 23:50 |
| | 20 | 8:08 | 21:16 | 7:49 | 21:35 | 7:25 | 21:59 | 6:50 | 22:33 | 5:51 | 23:30 |
| | 30 | 8:21 | 21:18 | 8:05 | 21:34 | 7:45 | 21:53 | 7:18 | 22:20 | 6:33 | 23:04 |
| July | 10 | 8:32 | 21:16 | 8:20 | 21:28 | 8:06 | 21:42 | 7:45 | 22:02 | 7:13 | 22:34 |
| | 20 | 8:42 | 21:12 | 8:34 | 21:19 | 8:24 | 21:29 | 8:11 | 21:41 | 7:50 | 22:01 |
| | 30 | 8:49 | 21:05 | 8:46 | 21:08 | 8:41 | 21:12 | 8:35 | 21:18 | 8:26 | 21:27 |
| Aug. | 9 | 8:55 | 20:56 | 8:56 | 20:55 | 8:56 | 20:54 | 8:57 | 20:53 | 8:59 | 20:51 |
| | 19 | 8:59 | 20:45 | 9:04 | 20:40 | 9:10 | 20:34 | 9:18 | 20:26 | 9:30 | 20:13 |
| | 29 | 9:01 | 20:33 | 9:10 | 20:24 | 9:21 | 20:13 | 9:36 | 19:57 | 9:59 | 19:34 |
| Sept. | 8 | 9:00 | 20:19 | 9:13 | 20:06 | 9:29 | 19:50 | 9:51 | 19:28 | 10:25 | 18:53 |
| | 18 | 8:55 | 20:02 | 9:11 | 19:45 | 9:32 | 19:25 | 10:00 | 18:56 | 10:47 | 18:09 |
| | 28 | 8:42 | 19:40 | 9:02 | 19:20 | 9:26 | 18:56 | 10:00 | 18:22 | 10:59 | 17:23 |
| Oct. | 8 | 8:19 | 19:10 | 8:40 | 18:48 | 9:07 | 18:21 | 9:45 | 17:43 | 10:53 | 16:35 |
| | 18 | 7:40 | 18:29 | 8:01 | 18:07 | 8:28 | 17:40 | 9:07 | 17:01 | 10:16 | 15:52 |
| | 28 | 6:42 | 17:37 | 7:02 | 17:18 | 7:27 | 16:53 | 8:01 | 16:19 | 9:01 | 15:19 |
| Nov. | 7 | 5:36 | 16:43 | 5:52 | 16:27 | 6:12 | 16:08 | 6:39 | 15:40 | 7:24 | 14:56 |
| | 17 | 4:37 | 15:57 | 4:49 | 15:44 | 5:04 | 15:29 | 5:25 | 15:09 | 5:58 | 14:36 |
| | 27 | 3:55 | 15:22 | 4:05 | 15:12 | 4:18 | 15:00 | 4:35 | 14:42 | 5:01 | 14:16 |
| Dec. | 7 | 3:29 | 14:58 | 3:39 | 14:48 | 3:51 | 14:36 | 4:07 | 14:20 | 4:32 | 13:55 |
| | 17 | 3:15 | 14:42 | 3:26 | 14:31 | 3:39 | 14:18 | 3:56 | 14:00 | 4:24 | 13:32 |
| | 27 | 3:09 | 14:32 | 3:22 | 14:19 | 3:37 | 14:04 | 3:57 | 13:43 | 4:30 | 13:11 |

## Mars, 1994

| | | 20° N. Latitude | | 30° N. Latitude | | 40° N. Latitude | | 50° N. Latitude | | 60° N. Latitude | |
|---|---|---|---|---|---|---|---|---|---|---|---|
| | | Rise | Set | Rise | Set | Rise | Set | Rise | Set | Rise | Set |
| Jan. | 1 | 6:32 | 17:23 | 6:54 | 17:01 | 7:22 | 16:34 | 8:01 | 15:55 | 9:11 | 14:44 |
| | 11 | 6:25 | 17:18 | 6:46 | 16:57 | 7:13 | 16:31 | 7:50 | 15:53 | 8:57 | 14:47 |
| | 21 | 6:17 | 17:14 | 6:37 | 16:54 | 7:02 | 16:29 | 7:37 | 15:54 | 8:38 | 14:53 |
| | 31 | 6:08 | 17:10 | 6:26 | 16:51 | 6:49 | 16:28 | 7:21 | 15:57 | 8:15 | 15:03 |
| Feb. | 10 | 5:57 | 17:06 | 6:14 | 16:49 | 6:34 | 16:29 | 7:02 | 16:01 | 7:49 | 15:14 |
| | 20 | 5:46 | 17:01 | 6:00 | 16:47 | 6:18 | 16:29 | 6:42 | 16:05 | 7:21 | 15:26 |
| Mar. | 2 | 5:33 | 16:57 | 5:45 | 16:45 | 6:00 | 16:30 | 6:20 | 16:10 | 6:51 | 15:39 |
| | 12 | 5:20 | 16:51 | 5:29 | 16:42 | 5:41 | 16:31 | 5:56 | 16:15 | 6:21 | 15:51 |
| | 22 | 5:06 | 16:46 | 5:12 | 16:39 | 5:21 | 16:31 | 5:32 | 16:20 | 5:49 | 16:03 |
| Apr. | 1 | 4:51 | 16:40 | 4:55 | 16:36 | 5:00 | 16:31 | 5:07 | 16:24 | 5:17 | 16:14 |
| | 11 | 4:35 | 16:34 | 4:37 | 16:32 | 4:39 | 16:31 | 4:41 | 16:29 | 4:45 | 16:25 |
| | 21 | 4:20 | 16:27 | 4:19 | 16:29 | 4:17 | 16:30 | 4:15 | 16:33 | 4:12 | 16:36 |
| May | 1 | 4:04 | 16:21 | 4:01 | 16:25 | 3:56 | 16:30 | 3:50 | 16:36 | 3:40 | 16:47 |
| | 11 | 3:49 | 16:14 | 3:43 | 16:21 | 3:35 | 16:29 | 3:24 | 16:40 | 3:07 | 16:57 |
| | 21 | 3:34 | 16:07 | 3:25 | 16:16 | 3:14 | 16:27 | 2:59 | 16:43 | 2:35 | 17:07 |
| | 31 | 3:19 | 16:01 | 3:07 | 16:12 | 2:53 | 16:26 | 2:34 | 16:46 | 2:04 | 17:17 |
| June | 10 | 3:04 | 15:54 | 2:51 | 16:07 | 2:34 | 16:24 | 2:11 | 16:48 | 1:33 | 17:26 |
| | 20 | 2:50 | 15:47 | 2:35 | 16:03 | 2:15 | 16:22 | 1:48 | 16:50 | 1:03 | 17:35 |
| | 30 | 2:37 | 15:40 | 2:20 | 15:57 | 1:58 | 16:19 | 1:27 | 16:50 | 0:35 | 17:43 |
| July | 10 | 2:24 | 15:32 | 2:05 | 15:52 | 1:41 | 16:16 | 1:07 | 16:50 | 0:09 | 17:49 |
| | 20 | 2:12 | 15:25 | 1:52 | 15:45 | 1:26 | 16:11 | 0:50 | 16:48 | 23:43 | 17:53 |
| | 30 | 2:01 | 15:16 | 1:39 | 15:37 | 1:12 | 16:05 | 0:34 | 16:43 | 23:22 | 17:53 |
| Aug. | 9 | 1:49 | 15:07 | 1:28 | 15:29 | 1:00 | 15:57 | 0:20 | 16:37 | 23:05 | 17:50 |
| | 19 | 1:38 | 14:56 | 1:16 | 15:19 | 0:48 | 15:47 | 0:07 | 16:27 | 22:52 | 17:42 |
| | 29 | 1:27 | 14:45 | 1:05 | 15:07 | 0:37 | 15:35 | 23:56 | 16:15 | 22:42 | 17:30 |
| Sept. | 8 | 1:16 | 14:32 | 0:54 | 14:54 | 0:27 | 15:21 | 23:46 | 16:01 | 22:34 | 17:13 |
| | 18 | 1:04 | 14:18 | 0:43 | 14:39 | 0:16 | 15:06 | 23:37 | 15:44 | 22:29 | 16:52 |
| | 28 | 0:51 | 14:02 | 0:31 | 14:22 | 0:06 | 14:48 | 23:28 | 15:24 | 22:25 | 16:28 |
| Oct. | 8 | 0:38 | 13:45 | 0:18 | 14:04 | 23:53 | 14:28 | 23:19 | 15:02 | 22:21 | 16:01 |
| | 18 | 0:23 | 13:27 | 0:05 | 13:45 | 23:41 | 14:07 | 23:09 | 14:39 | 22:15 | 15:33 |
| | 28 | 0:06 | 13:06 | 23:48 | 13:23 | 23:27 | 13:44 | 22:58 | 14:13 | 22:09 | 15:03 |
| Nov. | 7 | 23:47 | 12:44 | 23:31 | 13:00 | 23:12 | 13:19 | 22:44 | 13:47 | 22:00 | 14:31 |
| | 17 | 23:26 | 12:21 | 23:12 | 12:35 | 22:54 | 12:53 | 22:29 | 13:18 | 21:48 | 13:59 |
| | 27 | 23:04 | 11:55 | 22:50 | 12:09 | 22:33 | 12:25 | 22:10 | 12:49 | 21:32 | 13:27 |
| Dec. | 7 | 22:38 | 11:27 | 22:25 | 11:40 | 22:09 | 11:56 | 21:47 | 12:18 | 21:12 | 12:53 |
| | 17 | 22:09 | 10:56 | 21:56 | 11:09 | 21:41 | 11:24 | 21:20 | 11:45 | 20:46 | 12:19 |
| | 27 | 21:35 | 10:22 | 21:23 | 10:35 | 21:08 | 10:50 | 20:47 | 11:11 | 20:13 | 11:44 |

## Jupiter, 1994

| | | 20° N. Latitude | | 30° N. Latitude | | 40° N. Latitude | | 50° N. Latitude | | 60° N. Latitude | |
|---|---|---|---|---|---|---|---|---|---|---|---|---|
| | | Rise | Set | Rise | Set | Rise | Set | Rise | Set | Rise | Set |
| Jan. | 1 | 2:07 | 13:30 | 2:18 | 13:18 | 2:33 | 13:03 | 2:52 | 12:44 | 3:23 | 12:13 |
| | 11 | 1:34 | 12:55 | 1:46 | 12:43 | 2:01 | 12:28 | 2:21 | 12:08 | 2:53 | 11:36 |
| | 21 | 1:00 | 12:20 | 1:12 | 12:08 | 1:27 | 11:52 | 1:48 | 11:32 | 2:21 | 10:59 |
| | 31 | 0:25 | 11:44 | 0:37 | 11:32 | 0:53 | 11:16 | 1:14 | 10:55 | 1:48 | 10:21 |
| Feb. | 10 | 23:45 | 11:07 | *0:01 | 10:55 | 0:17 | 10:39 | 0:39 | 10:17 | 1:13 | 9:43 |
| | 20 | 23:07 | 10:30 | 23:20 | 10:17 | 23:36 | 10:01 | *0:02 | 9:39 | 0:36 | 9:04 |
| Mar. | 2 | 22:28 | 9:51 | 22:41 | 9:38 | 22:57 | 9:22 | 23:19 | 9:00 | 23:53 | 8:26 |
| | 12 | 21:48 | 9:11 | 22:01 | 8:58 | 22:17 | 8:42 | 22:38 | 8:20 | 23:12 | 7:46 |
| | 22 | 21:06 | 8:30 | 21:19 | 8:17 | 21:34 | 8:01 | 21:56 | 7:40 | 22:29 | 7:06 |
| Apr. | 1 | 20:23 | 7:48 | 20:36 | 7:35 | 20:51 | 7:20 | 21:12 | 6:59 | 21:45 | 6:26 |
| | 11 | 19:40 | 7:05 | 19:52 | 6:53 | 20:07 | 6:38 | 20:27 | 6:17 | 20:59 | 5:45 |
| | 21 | 18:55 | 6:21 | 19:07 | 6:10 | 19:21 | 5:55 | 19:41 | 5:35 | 20:12 | 5:04 |
| May | 1 | 18:10 | 5:38 | 18:22 | 5:26 | 18:36 | 5:12 | 18:55 | 4:53 | 19:25 | 4:23 |
| | 11 | 17:25 | 4:54 | 17:37 | 4:43 | 17:50 | 4:29 | 18:09 | 4:11 | 18:38 | 3:42 |
| | 21 | 16:41 | 4:11 | 16:52 | 4:00 | 17:05 | 3:47 | 17:23 | 3:29 | 17:51 | 3:01 |
| | 31 | 15:57 | 3:28 | 16:08 | 3:18 | 16:21 | 3:05 | 16:38 | 2:47 | 17:06 | 2:20 |
| June | 10 | 15:15 | 2:46 | 15:25 | 2:36 | 15:38 | 2:23 | 15:55 | 2:06 | 16:22 | 1:39 |
| | 20 | 14:33 | 2:05 | 14:44 | 1:55 | 14:56 | 1:42 | 15:13 | 1:25 | 15:39 | 0:59 |
| | 30 | 13:53 | 1:25 | 14:03 | 1:15 | 14:16 | 1:02 | 14:33 | 0:45 | 14:59 | 0:19 |
| July | 10 | 13:14 | 0:46 | 13:25 | 0:35 | 13:37 | 0:23 | 13:54 | 0:06 | 14:21 | 23:35 |
| | 20 | 12:37 | 0:08 | 12:47 | 23:53 | 13:00 | 23:41 | 13:17 | 23:23 | 13:44 | 22:56 |
| | 30 | 12:00 | 23:27 | 12:11 | 23:16 | 12:24 | 23:03 | 12:42 | 22:45 | 13:09 | 22:17 |
| Aug. | 9 | 11:25 | 22:50 | 11:36 | 22:39 | 11:50 | 22:26 | 12:08 | 22:08 | 12:36 | 21:39 |
| | 19 | 10:51 | 22:15 | 11:02 | 22:04 | 11:16 | 21:50 | 11:35 | 21:31 | 12:05 | 21:01 |
| | 29 | 10:18 | 21:40 | 10:29 | 21:28 | 10:44 | 21:14 | 11:04 | 20:54 | 11:35 | 20:23 |
| Sept. | 8 | 9:45 | 21:06 | 9:57 | 20:54 | 10:12 | 20:39 | 10:33 | 20:18 | 11:05 | 19:46 |
| | 18 | 9:13 | 20:33 | 9:26 | 20:20 | 9:42 | 20:04 | 10:03 | 19:43 | 10:37 | 19:09 |
| | 28 | 8:42 | 20:00 | 8:56 | 19:47 | 9:12 | 19:30 | 9:34 | 19:08 | 10:10 | 18:32 |
| Oct. | 8 | 8:12 | 19:27 | 8:26 | 19:14 | 8:43 | 18:56 | 9:06 | 18:33 | 9:44 | 17:55 |
| | 18 | 7:42 | 18:55 | 7:56 | 18:41 | 8:14 | 18:23 | 8:38 | 17:59 | 9:18 | 17:19 |
| | 28 | 7:12 | 18:24 | 7:27 | 18:09 | 7:45 | 17:50 | 8:11 | 17:25 | 8:52 | 16:43 |
| Nov. | 7 | 6:42 | 17:52 | 6:58 | 17:37 | 7:17 | 17:17 | 7:43 | 16:51 | 8:26 | 16:08 |
| | 17 | 6:13 | 17:21 | 6:29 | 17:05 | 6:49 | 16:45 | 7:16 | 16:17 | 8:01 | 15:32 |
| | 27 | 5:43 | 16:50 | 6:00 | 16:33 | 6:20 | 16:13 | 6:49 | 15:44 | 7:36 | 14:57 |
| Dec. | 7 | 5:14 | 16:19 | 5:31 | 16:02 | 5:52 | 15:40 | 6:21 | 15:11 | 7:10 | 14:22 |
| | 17 | 4:44 | 15:48 | 5:01 | 15:30 | 5:23 | 15:08 | 5:54 | 14:38 | 6:44 | 13:48 |
| | 27 | 4:14 | 15:16 | 4:32 | 14:58 | 4:54 | 14:36 | 5:25 | 14:05 | 6:17 | 13:13 |
| | | | | *2nd Rise | | | | *2nd Set | | | |
| | | | | 23:58 | | | | 23:58 | | | |

## Saturn, 1994

| | | 20° N. Latitude | | 30° N. Latitude | | 40° N. Latitude | | 50° N. Latitude | | 60° N. Latitude | |
|---|---|---|---|---|---|---|---|---|---|---|---|---|
| | | Rise | Set | Rise | Set | Rise | Set | Rise | Set | Rise | Set |
| Jan. | 1 | 9:34 | 20:56 | 9:46 | 20:44 | 10:00 | 20:30 | 10:20 | 20:10 | 10:51 | 19:39 |
| | 11 | 8:58 | 20:21 | 9:09 | 20:10 | 9:24 | 19:55 | 9:43 | 19:36 | 10:13 | 19:06 |
| | 21 | 8:22 | 19:47 | 8:33 | 19:35 | 8:47 | 19:22 | 9:06 | 19:03 | 9:35 | 18:34 |
| | 31 | 7:47 | 19:12 | 7:57 | 19:01 | 8:11 | 18:48 | 8:29 | 18:30 | 8:57 | 18:02 |
| Feb. | 10 | 7:11 | 18:38 | 7:22 | 18:28 | 7:34 | 18:15 | 7:52 | 17:58 | 8:19 | 17:30 |
| | 20 | 6:36 | 18:04 | 6:46 | 17:54 | 6:58 | 17:42 | 7:15 | 17:25 | 7:41 | 16:59 |
| Mar. | 2 | 6:00 | 17:30 | 6:10 | 17:20 | 6:22 | 17:08 | 6:38 | 16:53 | 7:03 | 16:28 |
| | 12 | 5:25 | 16:56 | 5:34 | 16:47 | 5:46 | 16:35 | 6:01 | 16:20 | 6:25 | 15:56 |
| | 22 | 4:49 | 16:22 | 4:58 | 16:13 | 5:09 | 16:02 | 5:24 | 15:47 | 5:47 | 15:24 |
| Apr. | 1 | 4:14 | 15:47 | 4:22 | 15:38 | 4:33 | 15:28 | 4:47 | 15:14 | 5:09 | 14:52 |
| | 11 | 3:38 | 15:12 | 3:46 | 15:04 | 3:56 | 14:54 | 4:10 | 14:40 | 4:31 | 14:19 |
| | 21 | 3:02 | 14:37 | 3:10 | 14:29 | 3:19 | 14:19 | 3:32 | 14:06 | 3:53 | 13:46 |
| May | 1 | 2:25 | 14:01 | 2:33 | 13:54 | 2:42 | 13:44 | 2:55 | 13:32 | 3:14 | 13:12 |
| | 11 | 1:48 | 13:25 | 1:56 | 13:18 | 2:05 | 13:08 | 2:17 | 12:56 | 2:36 | 12:37 |
| | 21 | 1:11 | 12:48 | 1:18 | 12:41 | 1:27 | 12:32 | 1:39 | 12:20 | 1:58 | 12:02 |
| | 31 | 0:33 | 12:11 | 0:40 | 12:04 | 0:49 | 11:55 | 1:01 | 11:43 | 1:19 | 11:25 |
| June | 10 | 23:51 | 11:33 | *0:02 | 11:26 | 0:11 | 11:17 | 0:22 | 11:05 | 0:40 | 10:47 |
| | 20 | 23:12 | 10:54 | 23:19 | 10:47 | 23:28 | 10:38 | 23:40 | 10:27 | *0:01 | 10:09 |
| | 30 | 22:33 | 10:15 | 22:40 | 10:07 | 22:49 | 9:59 | 23:00 | 9:47 | 23:18 | 9:29 |
| July | 10 | 21:53 | 9:34 | 22:00 | 9:27 | 22:09 | 9:18 | 22:21 | 9:06 | 22:39 | 8:48 |
| | 20 | 21:13 | 8:54 | 21:20 | 8:46 | 21:29 | 8:37 | 21:41 | 8:25 | 22:00 | 8:06 |
| | 30 | 20:32 | 8:12 | 20:39 | 8:05 | 20:49 | 7:55 | 21:01 | 7:43 | 21:20 | 7:24 |
| Aug. | 9 | 19:51 | 7:30 | 19:58 | 7:22 | 20:08 | 7:13 | 20:21 | 7:00 | 20:41 | 6:40 |
| | 19 | 19:09 | 6:48 | 19:17 | 6:40 | 19:27 | 6:30 | 19:40 | 6:17 | 20:01 | 5:56 |
| | 29 | 18:28 | 6:05 | 18:36 | 5:57 | 18:46 | 5:47 | 19:00 | 5:33 | 19:21 | 5:12 |
| Sept. | 8 | 17:46 | 5:23 | 17:54 | 5:14 | 18:05 | 5:04 | 18:19 | 4:50 | 18:41 | 4:28 |
| | 18 | 17:04 | 4:40 | 17:13 | 4:31 | 17:24 | 4:21 | 17:38 | 4:06 | 18:01 | 3:44 |
| | 28 | 16:23 | 3:58 | 16:32 | 3:49 | 16:43 | 3:38 | 16:58 | 3:23 | 17:21 | 3:00 |
| Oct. | 8 | 15:42 | 3:16 | 15:51 | 3:07 | 16:02 | 2:56 | 16:17 | 2:41 | 16:41 | 2:17 |
| | 18 | 15:01 | 2:35 | 15:10 | 2:26 | 15:22 | 2:14 | 15:37 | 1:59 | 16:01 | 1:35 |
| | 28 | 14:20 | 1:55 | 14:30 | 1:45 | 14:42 | 1:33 | 14:57 | 1:18 | 15:21 | 0:54 |
| Nov. | 7 | 13:41 | 1:15 | 13:50 | 1:05 | 14:02 | 0:54 | 14:17 | 0:38 | 14:42 | 0:14 |
| | 17 | 13:02 | 0:36 | 13:11 | 0:26 | 13:23 | 0:15 | 13:38 | 23:55 | 14:02 | 23:31 |
| | 27 | 12:23 | 23:53 | 12:32 | 23:44 | 12:44 | 23:33 | 12:59 | 23:17 | 13:23 | 22:53 |
| Dec. | 7 | 11:45 | 23:16 | 11:54 | 23:07 | 12:05 | 22:55 | 12:20 | 22:40 | 12:44 | 22:17 |
| | 17 | 11:07 | 22:39 | 11:16 | 22:30 | 11:27 | 22:19 | 11:42 | 22:04 | 12:05 | 21:41 |
| | 27 | 10:30 | 22:03 | 10:39 | 21:54 | 10:50 | 21:43 | 11:04 | 21:29 | 11:26 | 21:07 |
| | | | | *2nd Rise | | | | | | *2nd Rise | |
| | | | | 23:58 | | | | | | 23:57 | |

## Calculation of Risetimes

The *Daily Calendar* pages contain rise and set times for the sun and moon for the Greenwich Meridian at north latitudes 20°, 30°, 40°, 50°, and 60°. You probably live somewhere west of the Greenwich meridian, 0° longitude, and within the range of latitudes in the table. Notice that from day to day, the values for the sun at any particular latitude do not change very much. This slow variation for the sun means that no important correction needs to be made from one day to the next, once a proper correction for your latitude has been made. Thus, whenever it rises or sets at the 0° meridian, that will also be the time of that phenomenon at your Standard Time meridian. Any correction necessary for you to be able to observe that phenomenon from your location will be to account for your distance from the Standard Time meridian, and for your latitude.

The moon, however, moves its own diameter, about a half degree, in an hour, or about 12°.5 in one complete turn of the earth—one day. Most of this is eastward against the background stars of the sky, but some is also north or south of the equator. If there is little change on the same day of the times over the range of latitudes, the moon is near the celestial equator. All of this motion considerably affects the times of rise or set, as you can see from the adjacent entries in the table. Thus, it is necessary also to take your longitude into account in addition to your latitude. If you have no need for total accuracy, simply note that the time will be between the four values you find surrounding your location and the dates of interest.

The process of finding more accurate corrections is called interpolation. In the example, linear interpolation involving simple differences is used. In extreme cases, higher order interpolation should be used. If such cases are important to you, it is suggested that you make a plot of the times, draw smooth curves through the plots, and interpolate by eye between the relevant curves. Some people find this exercise fun.

Let's find the time of the June Full Moon in Brandon, Manitoba.

First, where is Brandon? Find Brandon's latitude and longitude on page 262.

I. Brandon, Manitoba 49° 51' 00" N
99° 57' 00" W

IA. Convert these values to decimals:
51 / 60 = 0°.85
49 + .85 = 49°.85
57 / 60 = 0°.95
99 + .95 = 99°.95

IB. Fraction Brandon lies between 50° and 60°:
49°.85 − 40° = 9.85; 9.85 / 10 = .985

IC. Fraction world must turn between Greenwich and Brandon:
99.95 / 360 = .278

ID. The CST meridian is 90°, thus 99°.95 is 99.95 − 90 = 9.95 degrees west of the CST. In 24 hours, there are 24 × 60 = 1440 minutes; 1440 / 360 = 4 minutes for every degree around the earth. So events happen
4 × 9.95 = 40
minutes later for Brandon than on the CST meridian of 90°.

IE. The values IB and IC are interpolates for Brandon; ID is the time correction from local to Standard time for Brandon. These values need never be calculated for Brandon again.

IIA. We need the Greenwich times for moonrise at latitudes 50° and 60°, and for June 23 and 24, the day of Full Moon and the next day.

|         | 50°   | Diff. | 60°   |
|---------|-------|-------|-------|
| June 23 | 20:04 | 55    | 20:59 |
| June 24 | 20:48 | 45    | 21:33 |

IIB. We want IB and the June 23 time difference:
.985 × 55 = 54
Add this to the June 23 time:
20:04 + 54 = 20:58
And for June 24:
.985 × 45 = 44
Add this to the June 24 rise time:
20:48 + 44 = 21:32
These two times are for the latitude of Brandon, but for the Greenwich meridian.

IIC. To get the time for Brandon, take the difference in the times just determined,
21:32 − 20:58 = 34
and find what fraction of this one day difference occurred while the earth turned from Greenwich to Brandon, .278:
.278 × 34 = 9.4 minutes after 20:58
Thus, 20:58 + 9 = 21:07, the time the moon will rise at the 90° CST meridian, at the latitude of Brandon.

IID. Events happen at Brandon 40 later than at the 90° meridian, therefore
21:07 + 40 = 21:47 CST at Brandon on June 23. However, the date is in the Daylight Time period, so we must add a 1 hour correction. Finally, Brandon's moonrise is 22:47 CDT on June 23, 1994.

## Star Tables

These tables include stars of visual magnitude 2.5 and brighter. Coordinates are for mid-1994. Where no parallax figures are given, the trigonometric parallax figure is smaller than the margin for error and the distance given is obtained by indirect methods. Stars of variable magnitude designated by v.

To find the time when the star is on meridian, subtract Right Ascension of Mean Sun from the sidereal time table on page 235 from the star's right ascension, first adding 24h to the latter, if necessary. Mark this result P.M., if less than 12h; but if greater than 12, subtract 12h and mark the remainder A.M.

| Star                    | Magnitude | Parallax " | Light yrs. | Right ascension h. m. | Declination ° ' | Star          | Magnitude | Parallax " | Light yrs. | Right ascension h. m. | Declination ° ' |
|-------------------------|-----------|------------|------------|-----------------------|-----------------|---------------|-----------|------------|------------|-----------------------|-----------------|
| α Andromedae (Alpheratz) | 2.06      | 0.02       | 90         | 0 08.1                | 29 04           | β Cassiopeiae | 2.27v     | 0.07       | 45         | 0 08.9                | 59 07           |
|                         |           |            |            |                       |                 | α Phoenicis   | 2.39      | 0.04       | 93         | 0 26.0                | −42 20          |

| Star | Magnitude | Parallax " | Light yrs. | Right ascen. h. m. | Declination ° ' |
|---|---|---|---|---|---|
| α Cassiopeiae (Schedir) | 2.23 | 0.01 | 150 | 0 40.2 | 56 30 |
| β Ceti | 2.04 | 0.06 | 57 | 0 43.3 | −18 01 |
| γ Cassiopeiae | 2.47v | 0.03 | 96 | 0 56.4 | 60 41 |
| β Andromedae | 2.06 | 0.04 | 76 | 1 09.4 | 35 35 |
| α Eridani (Achernar) | 0.46 | 0.02 | 118 | 1 37.5 | −57 16 |
| γ Andromedae | 2.26 | | 260 | 2 03.5 | 42 18 |
| α Arietis | 2.00 | 0.04 | 76 | 2 06.9 | 23 26 |
| o Ceti | 2.00v | 0.01 | 103 | 2 19.1 | −3 00 |
| α Ursae Min. (Pole Star) | 2.02v | | 680 | 2 25.8 | 89 14 |
| β Persei (Algol) | 2.12v | 0.03 | 105 | 3 07.8 | 40 56 |
| α Persei | 1.80 | 0.03 | 570 | 3 23.9 | 49 51 |
| α Tauri (Aldebaran) | 0.85v | 0.05 | 68 | 4 35.6 | 16 30 |
| β Orionis (Rigel) | 0.12v | | 900 | 5 14.3 | −8 12 |
| α Aurigae (Capella) | 0.08 | 0.07 | 45 | 5 16.3 | 46 00 |
| γ Orionis (Bellatrix) | 1.64 | 0.03 | 470 | 5 24.8 | 6 21 |
| β Tauri (El Nath) | 1.65 | 0.02 | 300 | 5 25.9 | 28 36 |
| δ Orionis | 2.23v | | 1500 | 5 31.7 | −0 18 |
| ε Orionis | 1.70 | | 1600 | 5 35.9 | −1 12 |
| ζ Orionis | 2.05 | 0.02 | 1600 | 5 40.5 | −1 57 |
| κ Orionis | 2.06 | 0.01 | 2100 | 5 47.5 | −9 40 |
| α Orionis (Betelgeuse) | 0.50v | | 520 | 5 54.9 | 7 24 |
| β Aurigae | 1.90 | 0.04 | 88 | 5 59.1 | 44 57 |
| β Canis Majoris | 1.98 | 0.01 | 750 | 6 22.5 | −17 57 |
| α Carinae (Canopus) | −0.72 | 0.02 | 98 | 6 23.8 | −52 42 |
| γ Geminorum | 1.93 | 0.03 | 105 | 6 37.4 | 16 24 |
| α Canis Majoris (Sirius) | −1.46 | 0.38 | 8.7 | 6 44.9 | −16 42 |
| ε Canis Majoris | 1.50 | | 680 | 6 58.4 | −28 58 |
| δ Canis Majoris | 1.86 | | 2100 | 7 08.2 | −26 23 |
| η Canis Majoris | 2.44 | | 2700 | 7 23.9 | −29 18 |
| α Geminorum (Castor) | 1.99 | 0.07 | 45 | 7 34.2 | 31 54 |
| α Canis Minoris (Procyon) | 0.38 | 0.29 | 11.3 | 7 39.0 | 5 14 |
| β Geminorum (Pollux) | 1.14 | 0.09 | 35 | 7 45.0 | 28 02 |
| ζ Puppis | 2.25 | | 2400 | 8 03.4 | −39 59 |
| γ Velorum | 1.82 | | 520 | 8 09.4 | −47 19 |
| ε Carinae | 1.86 | | 340 | 8 22.4 | −59 30 |
| δ Velorum | 1.96 | 0.04 | 76 | 8 44.6 | −54 41 |
| λ Velorum | 2.21 | 0.02 | 750 | 9 07.8 | −43 25 |
| β Carinae | 1.68 | 0.04 | 86 | 9 13.1 | −69 42 |
| ι Carinae | 2.25 | | 750 | 9 16.9 | −59 15 |
| κ Velorum | 2.50 | 0.01 | 470 | 9 21.9 | −54 59 |
| α Hydrae | 1.98 | 0.02 | 94 | 9 27.3 | −8 38 |
| α Leonis (Regulus) | 1.35 | 0.04 | 84 | 10 08.1 | 12 00 |
| γ Leonis | 1.90 | 0.02 | 90 | 10 19.7 | 19 55 |
| β Ursae Majoris (Merak) | 2.37 | 0.04 | 78 | 11 01.5 | 56 25 |
| α Ursae Majoris (Dubhe) | 1.79 | 0.03 | 105 | 11 03.4 | 61 47 |
| β Leonis (Denebola) | 2.14 | 0.08 | 43 | 11 48.8 | 14 36 |
| γ Ursae Majoris (Phecda) | 2.44 | 0.02 | 90 | 11 53.5 | 53 44 |
| α Crucis | 1.58 | | 370 | 12 26.3 | −63 04 |
| γ Crucis | 1.63 | | 220 | 12 30.9 | −57 05 |
| α Centauri | 2.17 | | 160 | 12 41.2 | −48 56 |
| β Crucis | 1.25v | | 490 | 12 47.4 | −59 40 |
| ε Ursae Majoris (Alioth) | 1.77v | 0.01 | 68 | 12 53.8 | 55 59 |
| ζ Ursae Majoris (Mizar) | 2.05 | 0.04 | 88 | 13 23.7 | 54 57 |
| α Virginis (Spica) | 0.97v | 0.02 | 220 | 13 24.9 | −11 08 |
| ε Centauri | 2.30v | | 570 | 13 39.5 | −53 26 |
| η Ursae Majoris (Alkaid) | 1.86 | | 210 | 13 47.3 | 49 20 |
| β Centauri | 0.61v | 0.02 | 490 | 14 03.4 | −60 21 |
| θ Centauri | 2.06 | 0.06 | 55 | 14 06.4 | −36 21 |
| α Bootis (Arcturus) | −0.04 | 0.09 | 36 | 14 15.4 | 19 13 |
| η Centauri | 2.31v | | 390 | 14 35.2 | −42 08 |
| α Centauri | −0.01 | 0.75 | 4.3 | 14 39.2 | −60 49 |
| β Lupi | 2.30v | | 430 | 14 41.6 | −47 22 |
| ε Bootis | 2.40 | 0.01 | 103 | 14 44.7 | 27 06 |
| β Ursae Minoris | 2.08 | 0.03 | 105 | 14 50.7 | 74 11 |
| α Coronae Borealis | 2.23v | 0.04 | 76 | 15 34.5 | 26 44 |
| δ Scorpii | 2.32 | | 590 | 16 00.0 | −22 36 |
| α Scorpii (Antares) | 0.96v | 0.02 | 520 | 16 29.1 | −26 25 |
| α Trianguli Australis | 1.92 | 0.02 | 82 | 16 48.1 | −69 01 |
| ε Scorpii | 2.29 | 0.05 | 66 | 16 49.8 | −34 17 |
| η Ophiuchi | 2.43 | 0.05 | 69 | 17 10.1 | −15 43 |
| λ Scorpii | 1.63v | | 310 | 17 33.2 | −37 06 |
| θ Ophiuchi | 2.08 | 0.06 | 58 | 17 34.7 | 12 34 |
| θ Scorpii | 1.87 | 0.02 | 650 | 17 36.9 | −43 00 |
| κ Scorpii | 2.41v | | 470 | 17 42.1 | −39 02 |
| γ Draconis | 2.23 | 0.02 | 108 | 17 56.5 | 51 29 |
| ε Sagittarii | 1.85 | 0.02 | 124 | 18 23.8 | −34 23 |
| α Lyrae (Vega) | 0.03 | 0.12 | 26.5 | 18 36.8 | 38 47 |
| σ Sagittarii | 2.02 | | 300 | 18 54.9 | −26 18 |
| α Aquilae (Altair) | 0.77 | 0.20 | 16.5 | 19 50.5 | 8 51 |
| γ Cygni | 2.20 | | 750 | 20 22.0 | 40 14 |
| α Pavonis | 1.94 | | 310 | 20 25.2 | −56 45 |
| α Cygni (Deneb) | 1.25 | | 1600 | 20 41.2 | 45 16 |
| ε Cygni | 2.46 | 0.04 | 74 | 20 46.0 | 33 57 |
| α Cephei | 2.44 | 0.06 | 52 | 21 18.4 | 62 34 |
| ε Pegasi | 2.39 | | 780 | 21 43.9 | 9 51 |
| α Gruis | 1.74 | 0.05 | 64 | 22 07.9 | −46 59 |
| β Gruis | 2.11v | | 280 | 22 42.3 | −46 55 |
| α Piscis Austrini (Fomalhaut) | 1.16 | 0.14 | 22.6 | 22 57.3 | −29 39 |
| β Pegasi | 2.42v | 0.02 | 210 | 23 03.5 | 28 03 |
| α Pegasi | 2.49 | 0.03 | 109 | 23 04.5 | 15 11 |

## Astronomical Constants; Speed of Light

The following were adopted in 1968, in accordance with the resolutions and recommendations of the International Astronomical Union (Hamburg 1964): Speed of light, 299,792.5 kilometers per second, or about 186,282.3976 statute miles per second; solar parallax, 8".794; constant of nutation, 9".210; and constant of aberration, 20".496.

## Constellations

Culturally, constellations are imagined patterns among the stars that, in some cases, have been recognized through millenia of tradition. In the early days of astronomy, knowledge of the constellations was necessary in order to function as an astronomer. For today's astronomers, constellations are simply areas on the entire sky in which interesting objects await observation and interpretation.

Because western culture has prevailed in establishing modern science, equally viable and interesting constellations and celestial traditions of other cultures (of Asia or Africa, for example) are not well known outside of their regions of origin. Even the patterns with which we are most familiar today have undergone considerable change over the centuries, because the west-

ern heritage embraces teachings of cultures disparate in time as well as place.

Today, students of the sky the world over recognize 88 constellations that cover the entire celestial sphere. Many of these have their origins in ancient days; many are "modern," contrived out of unformed stars by astronomers a few centuries ago. Unformed stars were those usually too faint or inconveniently placed to be included in depicting the more prominent constellations. When astronomers began to travel to South Africa in the 16th and 17th centuries, they found a sky that itself was unformed, and showing numerous brilliant stars. Thus, we find constellations in the southern hemisphere like the "air pump," the "microscope," the "furnace," and other technological marvels of the time, as well as some arguably traditional forms, such as the "fly."

Many of the commonly recognized constellations had their origins in ancient Asia Minor—Syria, Babylon, etc. These were adopted by the Greeks and Romans who translated their names and stories into their own languages, some details being modified in the process. After the declines of these cultures, most such knowledge entered oral tradition, or remained hidden in monastic libraries. Beginning in the 8th century, the Moslem explosion spread through the Mediterranean world. Wherever possible, everything was translated into Arabic to be taught in the universities of the Moslems established all over their new-found world.

In the 13th century, Alphonsus XX of Spain, an avid student of astronomy, succeeded in having Claudius Ptolemy's *Almagest*, as its Arabian title was known, translated into Latin. It thus became widely available to European scholars. In the process, the constellation names were translated, but the star names were retained in their Arabic forms. Transliterating Arabic into the Roman alphabet has never been an exact art, so many of the star names we use today only "seem" Arabic to all but scholars.

Names of stars often indicated what parts of the traditional figures they represented: Deneb, the tail of the swan; Betelgeuse, the armpit of the giant. Thus, the names were an indication of the position in the sky of a particular star, provided one recognized the traditional form of the mythic figure.

In English, usage of the Latin names for the constellations couples often inconceivable creatures, represented in unimaginable configurations, with names that often seem unintelligible. Avoiding traditional names, astronomers may designate the brighter stars in a constellation with Greek letters, usually in order of brightness. Thus, the "alpha star" is often the brightest star of that constellation. The "of" implies possession, so the genetive (possessive) form of the constellation name is used, as in Alpha Orionis, the first star of Orion (Betelgeuse). Astronomers usually use a 3-letter form for the constellation name, understanding it to be read as either the nominative or genitive case of the name.

Until the 1920's, astronomers used curved boundaries for the constellation areas. As these were rather arbitrary at best, the International Astronomical Union adopted boundaries that ran due north-south and east-west, filling the sky much as the contiguous states fill up the area of the "lower 48" United States.

Within these boundaries, and occasionally crossing them, popular "asterisms" are recognized: the Big Dipper is a small part of Ursa Major, the big bear; the Sickle is the traditional head and mane of Leo, the lion; one of the horntips of Taurus, the bull, properly belongs to Auriga, the charioteer; the northeast star of the Great Square of Pegasus is Alpha Andromedae.

It is unlikely that further change will occur in the realm of the celestial constellations.

| Name | Genitive | Abbreviation | Meaning |
|---|---|---|---|
| Andromeda | Andromedae | And | Chained Maiden |
| Antlia | Antliae | Ant | Air Pump |
| Apus | Apodis | Aps | Bird of Paradise |
| Aquarius | Aquarii | Aqr | Water Bearer |
| Aquila | Aquilae | Aql | Eagle |
| Ara | Arae | Ara | Altar |
| Aries | Arietis | Ari | Ram |
| Auriga | Aurigae | Aur | Charioteer |
| Bootes | Bootis | Boo | Herdsmen |
| Caelum | Caeli | Cae | Chisel |
| Camelopardalis | Camelopardalis | Cam | Giraffe |
| Cancer | Cancri | Cnc | Crab |
| Canes Venatici | Canum Venaticorum | CVn | Hunting Dogs |
| Canis Major | Canis Majoris | CMa | Great Dog |
| Canis Minor | Canis Minoris | CMi | Little Dog |
| Capricornus | Capricorni | Cap | Sea-goat |
| Carina | Carinae | Car | Keel |
| Cassiopeia | Cassiopeiae | Cas | Queen |
| Centaurus | Centauri | Cen | Centaur |
| Cepheus | Cephei | Cep | King |
| Cetus | Ceti | Cet | Whale |
| Chamaeleon | Chamaeleontis | Cha | Chameleon |
| Circinus | Circini | Cir | Compasses (art) |
| Columba | Columbae | Col | Dove |
| Coma Berenices | Comae Berenices | Com | Berenice's Hair |
| Corona Australis | Coronae Australis | CrA | Southern Crown |
| Corona Borealis | Coronae Borealis | CrB | Northern Crown |
| Corvus | Corvi | Crv | Crow |
| Crater | Crateris | Crt | Cup |
| Crux | Crucis | Cru | Cross (southern) |
| Cygnus | Cygni | Cyg | Swan |
| Delphinus | Delphini | Del | Dolphin |
| Dorado | Doradus | Dor | Goldfish |
| Draco | Draconis | Dra | Dragon |
| Equuleus | Equulei | Equ | Little Horse |
| Eridanus | Eridani | Eri | River |
| Fornax | Fornacis | For | Furnace |
| Gemini | Geminorum | Gem | Twins |
| Grus | Gruis | Gru | Crane (bird) |
| Hercules | Herculis | Her | Hercules |
| Horologium | Horologii | Hor | Clock |
| Hydra | Hydrae | Hya | Water Snake (female) |
| Hydrus | Hydri | Hyi | Water Snake (male) |
| Indus | Indi | Ind | Indian |
| Lacerta | Lacertae | Lac | Lizard |
| Leo | Leonis | Leo | Lion |
| Leo Minor | Leonis Minoris | LMi | Little Lion |
| Lepus | Leporis | Lep | Hare |
| Libra | Librae | Lib | Balance |
| Lupus | Lupi | Lup | Wolf |
| Lynx | Lyncis | Lyn | Lynx |
| Lyra | Lyrae | Lyr | Lyre |
| Mensa | Mensae | Men | Table Mountain |
| Microscopium | Microscopii | Mic | Microscope |
| Monoceros | Monocerotis | Mon | Unicorn |
| Musca | Muscae | Mus | Fly |
| Norma | Normae | Nor | Square (rule) |
| Octans | Octantis | Oct | Octant |
| Ophiuchus | Ophiuchi | Oph | Serpent Bearer |
| Orion | Orionis | Ori | Hunter |
| Pavo | Pavonis | Pav | Peacock |
| Pegasus | Pegasi | Peg | Flying Horse |
| Perseus | Persei | Per | Hero |
| Phoenix | Phoenicis | Phe | Phoenix |
| Pictor | Pictoris | Pic | Painter |
| Pisces | Piscium | Psc | Fishes |
| Piscis Austrinius | Piscis Austrini | PsA | Southern Fish |
| Puppis | Puppis | Pup | Stern (deck) |
| Pyxis | Pyxidis | Pyx | Compass (sea) |
| Reticulum | Reticuli | Ret | Reticle |
| Sagitta | Sagittae | Sge | Arrow |
| Sagittarius | Sagittarii | Sgr | Archer |
| Scorpius | Scorpii | Sco | Scorpion |
| Sculptor | Sculptoris | Scl | Sculptor |
| Scutum | Scuti | Sct | Shield |
| Serpens | Serpentis | Ser | Serpent |
| Sextans | Sextantis | Sex | Sextant |
| Taurus | Tauri | Tau | Bull |
| Telescopium | Telescopii | Tel | Telescope |
| Triangulum | Trianguli | Tri | Triangle |
| Triangulum Australe | Trianguli Australis | TrA | Southern Triangle |
| Tucana | Tucanae | Tuc | Toucan |
| Ursa Major | Ursae Majoris | UMa | Great Bear |
| Ursa Minor | Ursae Minoris | UMi | Little Bear |
| Vela | Velorum | Vel | Sail |
| Virgo | Virginis | Vir | Maiden |
| Volans | Volantis | Vol | Flying Fish |
| Vulpecula | Vulpeculae | Vul | Fox |

## Aurora Borealis and Aurora Australis

The Aurora Borealis, also called the Northern Lights, is a broad display of rather faint light in the northern skies at night. The Aurora Australis, a similar phenomenon, appears at the same time in southern skies. The aurora appears in a wide variety of forms. Sometimes it is seen as a quiet glow, almost foglike in character; sometimes as vertical streamers in which there may be considerable motion; sometimes as a series of luminous expanding arcs. There are many colors, with white, yellow, and red predominating.

The auroras are most vivid and most frequently seen at about 20 degrees from the magnetic poles, along the northern coast of the North American continent and the eastern part of the northern coast of Europe. They have been seen as far south as Key West and as far north as Australia and New Zealand, but rarely.

While the cause of the auroras is not known beyond question, there does seem to be a definite correlation between auroral displays and sun-spot activity. It is thought that atomic particles expelled from the sun by the forces that cause solar flares speed through space at velocities of 400 to 600 miles per second. These particles are entrapped by the earth's magnetic field, forming what are termed the Van Allen belts. The encounter of these clouds of the solar wind with the earth's magnetic field weakens the field so that previously trapped particles are allowed to impact the upper atmosphere. The collisions between solar and terrestrial atoms result in the glow in the upper atmosphere called the aurora. The glow may be vivid where the lines of magnetic force converge near the magnetic poles.

The auroral displays appear at heights ranging from 50 to about 600 miles and have given us a means of estimating the extent of the earth's atmosphere.

The auroras are often accompanied by magnetic storms whose forces, also guided by the lines of force of the earth's magnetic field, disrupt electrical communication.

## Eclipses, 1994

There are four eclipses, two of the sun and two of the moon.

### I. Annular eclipse of the sun, May 10.

The partial phases of this eclipse are visible throughout North America, from south of Panama to beyond the North Pole, including far eastern Siberia, Bering Strait, Greenland, Iceland, the Scandinavian Peninsula, and as a sunset phenomenon in parts of western Europe and western Africa; the Hawaiian Islands experience a partial phase at sunrise.

The path of annularity begins in the eastern Pacific Ocean, southeast of Hawaii, passes over the middle of the Baja Peninsula, enters the United States at El Paso, passes through central Missouri, over Lakes Erie and Ontario, central New York state, portions of New England, and portions of the Canadian Maritime Provinces.

#### Circumstances of the Eclipse

| Event | Date | | h | m |
|---|---|---|---|---|
| Eclipse begins | May | 10 | 14 | 12.2 |
| Central Eclipse begins | | 10 | 15 | 23.3 |
| Central Eclipse at local noon | | 10 | 17 | 19.8 |
| Central Eclipse ends | | 10 | 18 | 59.5 |
| Eclipse ends | | 10 | 20 | 10.6 |

Maximum Duration: 6 min 08.5 sec.

### II. Partial eclipse of the moon, May 25.

The beginning of the umbral phase is generally visible in the United States (except for the far west, Alaska, and Hawaii), southeastern and central Canada, Mexico, Central America, South America, the southern tip of Greenland, Iceland, most of Antarctica, most of Africa, most of Europe, the southeastern North Pacific Ocean, the eastern South Pacific Ocean, the Atlantic Ocean, and the southwestern Indian Ocean. The end of the umbral phase is generally visible in the United States (except Alaska and Hawaii), Canada (except for the northwest), Mexico, Central America, South America, the southern tip of Greenland, most of Antarctica, southern and western Africa, the southern United Kingdom, southern and western France, the Iberian Peninsula, the southeastern North Pacific Ocean, the eastern South Pacific Ocean, and the Atlantic Ocean.

#### Circumstances of the Eclipse

| Event | Date | | h | m |
|---|---|---|---|---|
| Moon enters penumbra | May | 25 | 1 | 17.9 |
| Moon enters umbra | | 25 | 2 | 37.3 |
| Middle of eclipse | | 25 | 3 | 30.3 |
| Moon leaves umbra | | 25 | 4 | 23.3 |
| Moon leaves penumbra | | 25 | 5 | 42.7 |

Magnitude of the eclipse: 0.249

### III. Total eclipse of the sun, November 3.

The partial phases are visible in South America, parts of Antarctica including the Palmer Peninsula, and parts of southern Africa.

The path of totality begins in the eastern Pacific Ocean, enters South America in southern Peru, crosses northern Chile, parts of Argentina, Paraguay, and southern Brazil, and the South Atlantic Ocean. The path of totality ends south of Madagascar.

#### Circumstances of the Eclipse

| Event | Date | | h | m |
|---|---|---|---|---|
| Eclipse begins | Nov. | 3 | 11 | 05.0 |
| Central Eclipse begins | | 3 | 12 | 02.7 |
| Central Eclipse at local noon | | 3 | 13 | 47.1 |
| Central Eclipse ends | | 3 | 15 | 15.4 |
| Eclipse ends | | 3 | 16 | 13.1 |

Maximum duration: 4 min 27.6 sec.

### IV. Penumbral eclipse of the moon, November 18.

The beginning of the penumbral phases generally visible in North America, Greenland, Iceland, the Arctic regions, Central America, South America, Hawaii, western Africa, Europe, extreme western Asia, the Palmer Peninsula of Antarctica, the eastern Pacific Ocean, and most of the Atlantic Ocean. The end is generally visible in North America, Greenland, Iceland, the Arctic regions, Central America, western South America, Hawaii, northeastern Asia, eastern Australia, New Zealand, the Pacific Ocean, and the western North Atlantic Ocean.

### Circumstances of the Eclipse

| Event | Date | h | m |
|---|---|---|---|
| Moon enters penumbra | Nov. 18 | 4 | 25.7 |
| Middle of eclipse | 18 | 6 | 43.9 |
| Moon leaves penumbra | 18 | 9 | 02.1 |

Penumbral magnitude of the eclipse: 0.908.

## Transit of Mercury, 1993

A transit of Mercury over the face of the sun will occur on November 6.

The beginning of the transit will be generally visible in the Hawaiian Islands, the Aleutians Islands except the eastern end, Siberia except the northeastern tip, western Pacific Ocean, New Zealand, Australia, the Indian Ocean, Asia, Antarctica except the Palmer Peninsula, the southeastern Arabian Peninsula, and extreme eastern Africa. The end is generally visible in Asia, Siberia except the eastern end, the western Pacific Ocean, New Zealand, Australia, Antarctica except the Palmer Peninsula, the Indian Ocean, Africa east of the South Atlantic coast, Turkey, and the southern former USSR from the western Black Sea.

### Geocentric Circumstances of the Transit

| Event | Date | h | m |
|---|---|---|---|
| Ingress, exterior contact | Nov. 6 | 3 | 05.9 |
| Ingress, interior contact | 6 | 3 | 11.8 |
| Least angular distance from Sun's center | 6 | 3 | 56.6 |
| Egress, interior contact | 6 | 4 | 41.4 |
| Egress, exterior contact | 6 | 4 | 47.2 |

Least angular distance: 15'16".7

## The Planets and the Solar System

| Planet | Mean daily motion " | Orbital velocity miles per sec. | Sidereal revolution days | Synodical revolution days | Dist. from sun in millions of mi. Max. | Min. | Dist. from Earth in millions of mi. Max. | Min. | Light at[1] perihelion | aphelion |
|---|---|---|---|---|---|---|---|---|---|---|
| Mercury .. | 14732 | 29.75 | 88.0 | 115.9 | 43.4 | 28.6 | 136 | 50 | 10.58 | 4.59 |
| Venus ... | 5768 | 21.76 | 224.7 | 583.9 | 67.7 | 66.8 | 161 | 25 | 1.94 | 1.89 |
| Earth.... | 3548 | 18.51 | 365.3 | — | 94.6 | 91.4 | — | 1.03 | 0.97 | |
| Mars .... | 1886 | 14.99 | 687.0 | 779.9 | 155.0 | 128.5 | 248 | 35 | 0.524 | 0.360 |
| Jupiter ... | 299 | 8.12 | 4331.8 | 398.9 | 507.0 | 460.6 | 600 | 368 | 0.0408 | 0.0336 |
| Saturn ... | 120 | 5.99 | 10760.0 | 378.1 | 937.5 | 838.4 | 1031 | 745 | 0.01230 | 0.00984 |
| Uranus... | 42 | 4.23 | 30684.0 | 369.7 | 1859.7 | 1669.3 | 1953 | 1606 | 0.00300 | 0.00250 |
| Neptune .. | 21 | 3.38 | 60188.3 | 367.5 | 2821.7 | 2760.4 | 2915 | 2667 | 0.00114 | 0.00109 |
| Pluto .... | 14 | 2.95 | 90466.8 | 366.7 | 4551.4 | 2756.4 | 4644 | 2663 | 0.00114 | 0.00042 |

1. Light at perihelion and aphelion is solar illumination in units of mean illumination at Earth.

| Planet | Mean longitude of:[*] ascending node ° ' " | perihelion ° ' " | Inclination[*] of orbit to ecliptic ° ' " | Mean[*] distance[**] | Eccentricity[*] of orbit | Mean longitude at the epoch[*] ° ' " |
|---|---|---|---|---|---|---|
| Mercury.... | 48 16 4 | 77 22 24 | 7 0 18 | .387098 | .205307 | 214 37 25 |
| Venus..... | 76 37 55 | 131 29 21 | 3 23 41 | .732333 | .006774 | 306 33 46 |
| Earth ..... | 0 0 0 | 102 50 45 | 0 0 0 | 1.000001 | .016711 | 343 52 31 |
| Mars ..... | 49 31 1 | 335 57 44 | 1 50 59 | 1.523679 | .093396 | 232 42 23 |
| Jupiter .... | 100 24 36 | 14 14 44 | 1 18 13 | 5.202603 | .048486 | 344 56 27 |
| Saturn .... | 113 37 8 | 92 57 8 | 2 29 21 | 9.554910 | .055527 | 291 10 12 |
| Uranus .... | 73 58 42 | 172 55 34 | 0 46 23 | 19.218450 | .046297 | 292 38 33 |
| Neptune ... | 131 43 31 | 48 2 52 | 1 46 14 | 30.110390 | .008988 | 229 37 8 |
| Pluto[***] ... | 110 13 37 | 224 0 32 | 17 8 9 | 39.810100 | .254949 | 229 37 8 |

* Consistent for the standard Epoch: 1994 September 5 Ephemeris Time. ** Astronomical units *** Consistent for the standard Epoch: 1993 August 1 Ephemeris Time.

| Sun and planets | Semi-diameter at unit distance ' " | at mean least dist. ' " | in miles mean s.d. | Volume ⊕=1. | Mass. ⊕=1. | Density ⊕=1. | Sidereal period of rotation d. | h. | m. | s. | Gravity at surface ⊕=1. | Reflecting power Pct. | Probable temperature °F. |
|---|---|---|---|---|---|---|---|---|---|---|---|---|---|
| Sun...... | 959.62 | — | 432449 | 1299370 | 332946 | 0.26 | 24 | 16 | 48 | 27.9 | — | +10,000 | |
| Mercury ... | 3.37 | 5.5 | 1515 | 0.0559 | 0.0553 | 1.00 | 58 | 15 | 30 | 0.37 | 0.11 | + | 620 |
| Venus .... | 8.34 | 30.1 | 3760 | 0.8541 | 0.8150 | 0.97 | 243 | R | | 0.88 | 0.65 | + | 900 |
| Earth..... | — | — | 3963 | 1.000 | 1.000 | 1.00 | 23 | 56 | 6.7 | 1.00 | 0.37 | + | 72 |
| Moon ..... | 2.40 | 932.4 | 1080 | 0.020 | 0.0123 | 0.62 | 27 | 7 | 43 | 0.17 | 0.12 | — | 10 |
| Mars ..... | 4.69 | 8.95 | 2108.5 | 0.1506 | 0.1074 | 0.73 | | 24 | 37 | 26 | 0.38 | 0.15 | — | 10 |
| Jupiter .... | 98.35 | 23.4 | 44419 | 1403 | 317.89 | 0.25 | | 9 | 3 | 30 | 2.64 | 0.52 | — | 240 |
| Saturn .... | 82.83 | 9.7 | 37448 | 832 | 95.18 | 0.13 | | 10 | 39 | 22 | 1.15 | 0.47 | — | 300 |
| Uranus .... | 35.4 | 1.9 | 15881 | 63 | 14.54 | 0.23 | | 17 | 14 | R | 1.15 | 0.40 | — | 340 |
| Neptune ... | 33.4 | 1.2 | 15387 | 55 | 17.15 | 0.30 | | 16 | 6 | | 1.12 | 0.35 | ? | 370 |
| Pluto ..... | 1.9 | 0.05 | 714 | 0.006 | 0.0020 | 0.37 | 6 | 9 | 17 | 0.04 | 0.5 | ? | ? |

(R) retrograde of Venus and Uranus.

## The Sun

The sun, the controlling body of our solar system, is a star whose dimensions cause it to be classified among stars as average in size, temperature, and brightness. Its proximity to the earth makes it appear to us as tremendously large and bright. A series of thermo-nuclear reactions involving the atoms of the elements of which it is composed produces the heat and light that make life possible on earth.

The sun has a diameter of 864,000 miles and is distant, on the average, 92,900,000 miles from the earth. It is 1.41 times as dense as water. The light of the sun reaches the earth in 499.012 seconds or slightly more than 8 minutes. The average solar surface temperature has been measured by several indirect methods that agree closely on a value of 6,000° Kelvin or about 10,000° F. The interior temperature of the sun is about 35,000,000° F.

When sunlight is analyzed with a spectroscope, it is found to consist of a continuous spectrum composed of all the colors of the rainbow in order, crossed by many dark lines. The "absorption lines" are produced by gaseous materials in the atmosphere of the sun. More than 60 of the natural terrestrial elements have been identified in the sun, all in gaseous form because of the intense heat of the sun.

### Spheres and Corona

The radiating surface of the sun is called the **photosphere**, and just above it is the **chromosphere**. The chromosphere is visible to the naked eye only at times of total solar eclipses, appearing then to be a pinkish-violet layer with occasional great prominences projecting above its general level. With proper instruments the chromosphere can be seen or photographed whenever the sun is visible without waiting for a total eclipse. Above the chromosphere is the **corona**, also visible to the naked eye only at times of total eclipse. Instruments also permit the brighter portions of the corona to be studied whenever conditions are favorable. The pearly light of the corona surges millions of miles from the sun. Iron, nickel, and calcium are believed to be principal contributors to the composition of the corona, all in a state of extreme attenuation and high ionization that indicates temperatures on the order of a million degrees Fahrenheit.

### Sunspots

There is an intimate connection between sunspots and the corona. At times of low sunspot activity, the fine streamers of the corona will be much longer above the sun's equator than over the polar regions of the sun, while during high sunspot activity, the corona extends fairly evenly outward from all regions of the sun, but to a much greater distance in space. Sunspots are dark, irregularly-shaped regions whose diameters may reach tens of thousands of miles. The average life of a sunspot group is from two to three weeks, but there have been groups that have lasted for more than a year, being carried repeatedly around as the sun rotated upon its axis. The record for the duration of a sunspot is 18 months. Sunspots reach a low point every 11.3 years, with a peak of activity occurring irregularly between two successive minima.

The sun is 400,000 times as bright as the full moon and gives the earth 6 million times as much light as do all the other stars put together. Actually, most of the stars that can be easily seen on any clear night are brighter than the sun.

## The Zodiac

The sun's apparent yearly path among the stars is known as the **ecliptic**. The zone, 16° wide, 8° on each side of the ecliptic, is known as the **zodiac**. Inside of this zone are the apparent paths of the sun, moon, earth, and major planets. Beginning at the point on the ecliptic that marks the position of the sun at the vernal equinox, and thence proceeding eastward, the zodiac is divided into twelve signs of 30° each, as shown herewith.

These signs are named from the twelve constellations of the zodiac with which the signs coincided in the time of the astronomer Hipparchus, about 2,000 years ago. Owing to the precession of the equinoxes, that is to say, to the retrograde motion of the equinoxes along the ecliptic, each sign in the zodiac has, in the course of 2,000 years, moved backward 30° into the constellation west of it; so that the sign Aries is now in the constellation Pisces, and so on. The vernal equinox will move from Pisces into Aquarius about the middle of the 26th century. The signs of the zodiac with their Latin and English names are as follows:

| | | | |
|---|---|---|---|
| Spring | 1. | ♈ Aries. | The Ram. |
| | 2. | ♉ Taurus. | The Bull. |
| | 3. | ♊ Gemini. | The Twins. |
| Summer | 4. | ♋ Cancer. | The Crab. |
| | 5. | ♌ Leo. | The Lion. |
| | 6. | ♍ Virgo. | The Virgin. |
| Autumn | 7. | ♎ Libra. | The Balance. |
| | 8. | ♏ Scorpius. | The Scorpion. |
| | 9. | ♐ Sagittarius. | The Archer. |
| Winter | 10. | ♑ Capricorn. | The Goat. |
| | 11. | ♒ Aquarius. | The Water Bearer. |
| | 12. | ♓ Pisces. | The Fishes. |

## Twilight

Twilight is that evening period of waning light from the time of sunset to dark, often termed dusk. Morning twilight, a time of increasing light, is called dawn. The source of this light is the sun shining on the atmosphere above the observer. Twilight is a time of very slowly changing sky illumination with no abrupt variations. Nevertheless, there are three commonly accepted divisions in this smooth continuum defined by the distance the sun lies below the astronomical horizon: civil twilight, nautical twilight, and astronomical twilight. The astronomical horizon is that great circle lying 90° from the zenith, the point directly over the observer's head. Twilight ends in the evening or begins in the morning at a particular time. Nominally, evening events are repeated in reverse order in the morning.

Civil twilight is the time between the moment of sunset, when the sun's apparent upper edge is just at the horizon until the center of the sun is 6° directly below the horizon. In many states, this is the time in the evening when automobile headlights must be turned on, not to see better, but to be seen by other drivers. After this time, a newspaper becomes increasingly difficult to read.

Nautical twilight ends when the sun's center is 12° below the horizon. By this time in the evening, the bright stars used by navigators have appeared and the horizon may still be seen. After this time, the horizon is more difficult to perceive, preventing navigators from making star sights.

Astronomical twilight ends in the evening when the sun is 18° below the horizon, and the sky is dark enough, at least away from the sun's location, to allow astronomical work to proceed. Sunlight, however, is still shining on the higher levels of the atmosphere from the observer's zenith to the horizon toward the sun. Although not named as a period of twilight, when the sun is 24° below the horizon, no part of the observer's atmosphere, even toward the sun, receives any sunlight.

In the tropics, the sun moves nearly vertically accomplishing its 6°, 12°, or 18° depression very quickly.

In the polar regions, the sun's diurnal motion may actually be nearly along the horizon, prolonging the twilight period, or even not permitting darkness to fall at all. In mid-latitudes, civil twilight may last about a half hour, nautical, an hour, and astronomers can go to work in about 90 minutes.

The twilight tables given in The World Almanac are for astronomical twilight, and presented for reference only. Although the instant of the sun's horizontal depression may be calculated precisely, the phenomena associated with the event are sufficiently imprecise that the table is not recalculated each year.

## Moon's Perigee and Apogee, 1994

### Perigee

| Month | Day | h | Month | Day | h |
|-------|-----|---|-------|-----|---|
| Jan.... | 6 | 1 | July .... | 18 | 18 |
| Jan.... | 31 | 4 | Aug...... | 12 | 23 |
| Feb.... | 27 | 22 | Sept. .... | 8 | 14 |
| Mar. .. | 28 | 6 | Oct. .... | 6 | 14 |
| Apr... | 25 | 17 | Nov...... | 4 | 0 |
| May.. | 24 | 3 | Dec. ..... | 2 | 12 |
| June .. | 21 | 7 | Dec. ..... | 30 | 23 |

### Apogee

| Month | Day | h | Month | Day | h |
|-------|-----|---|-------|-----|---|
| Jan. ..... | 19 | 5 | July .... | 30 | 23 |
| Feb...... | 16 | 2 | Aug...... | 27 | 18 |
| Mar...... | 15 | 17 | Sept. .... | 24 | 12 |
| Apr...... | 12 | 0 | Oct...... | 22 | 2 |
| May...... | 9 | 2 | Nov...... | 18 | 5 |
| June..... | 5 | 13 | Dec...... | 15 | 8 |
| July .... | 3 | 5 | | | |

### Perihelion

| | Day | h |
|---|-----|---|
| Jan. | 2 | 6 |

### Aphelion

| | Day | h |
|---|-----|---|
| July | 5 | 16 |

## Moon Phases, 1994
Greenwich Mean Time

### New Moon

| Month | Day | h | m |
|-------|-----|---|---|
| Jan. | 11 | 23 | 10 |
| Feb. | 10 | 14 | 30 |
| Mar. | 12 | 07 | 05 |
| Apr. | 11 | 00 | 17 |
| May | 10 | 17 | 07 |
| June | 9 | 08 | 26 |
| July | 8 | 21 | 37 |
| Aug. | 7 | 08 | 45 |
| Sept. | 5 | 18 | 33 |
| Oct. | 5 | 03 | 55 |
| Nov. | 3 | 13 | 35 |
| Dec. | 2 | 23 | 54 |

### First Q

| Month | Day | h | m |
|-------|-----|---|---|
| Jan. | 19 | 20 | 27 |
| Feb. | 18 | 17 | 47 |
| Mar. | 20 | 12 | 14 |
| Apr. | 19 | 02 | 34 |
| May | 18 | 12 | 50 |
| June | 16 | 19 | 56 |
| July | 16 | 01 | 12 |
| Aug. | 14 | 05 | 57 |
| Sept. | 12 | 11 | 34 |
| Oct. | 11 | 19 | 17 |
| Nov. | 10 | 06 | 14 |
| Dec. | 9 | 21 | 06 |

### Full Moon

| Month | Day | h | m |
|-------|-----|---|---|
| Jan. | 27 | 13 | 23 |
| Feb. | 26 | 01 | 15 |
| Mar. | 27 | 11 | 09 |
| Apr. | 25 | 19 | 45 |
| May | 25 | 03 | 39 |
| June | 23 | 11 | 33 |
| July | 22 | 22 | 16 |
| Aug. | 21 | 06 | 47 |
| Sept. | 19 | 20 | 00 |
| Oct. | 19 | 12 | 18 |
| Nov. | 18 | 06 | 57 |
| Dec. | 18 | 02 | 17 |

### Last Q

| Month | Day | h | m |
|-------|-----|---|---|
| Jan. | 5 | 00 | 00 |
| Feb. | 3 | 08 | 06 |
| Mar. | 4 | 16 | 53 |
| Apr. | 3 | 02 | 55 |
| May | 2 | 14 | 32 |
| June | 1 | 04 | 02 |
| June | 30 | 19 | 31 |
| July | 30 | 12 | 40 |
| Aug. | 29 | 06 | 41 |
| Sept. | 28 | 00 | 23 |
| Nov. | 27 | 16 | 44 |
| Nov. | 26 | 07 | 04 |
| Dec. | 25 | 19 | 06 |

## The Moon

The moon completes a circuit around the earth in a period whose mean or average duration is 27 days 7 hours 43.2 minutes. This is the moon's sidereal period. Because of the motion of the moon in common with the earth around the sun, the mean duration of the lunar month — the period from one new moon to the next new moon — is 29 days 12 hours 44.05 minutes. This is the moon's synodical period.

The mean distance of the moon from the earth according to the American Ephemeris is 238,857 miles. Because the orbit of the moon about the earth is not circular but elliptical, however, the maximum distance from the earth that the moon may reach is 252,710 miles and the least distance is 221,463 miles. All distances are from the center of one object to the center of the other.

The moon's diameter is 2,160 miles. If we deduct the radius of the moon, 1,080 miles, and the radius of the earth, 3,963 miles from the minimum distance or perigee, given above, we shall have for the nearest approach of the bodies' surfaces 216,420 miles.

The moon rotates on its axis in a period of time exactly equal to its sidereal revolution about the earth — 27.321666 days. The moon's revolution about the earth is irregular because of its elliptical orbit. The moon's rotation, however, is regular and this, together with the irregular revolution, produces what is called "libration in longitude," which permits us to see first farther around the east side and then farther around the west side of the moon. The moon's variation north or south of the ecliptic permits us to see farther over first one pole and then the other of the moon; this is called "libration in latitude." These two libration effects permit us to see a total of about 60% of the moon's surface over a period of time. The hidden side of the moon was photographed in 1959 by the Soviet space vehicle Lunik III. Since then many excellent pictures of nearly all of the moon's surface have been transmitted to earth by Lunar Orbiters launched by the U.S.

The tides are caused mainly by the moon, because of its proximity to the earth. The ratio of the tide-raising power of the moon to that of the sun is 11 to 5.

### Harvest Moon and Hunter's Moon

The Harvest Moon, the full moon nearest the Autumnal Equinox, ushers in a period of several successive days when the moon rises soon after sunset. This phenomenon gives farmers in temperate latitudes extra hours of light in which to harvest their crops before frost and winter come. The 1993 Harvest Moon falls on Sept. 19 GMT. Harvest Moon in the south temperate latitudes falls on Mar. 27.

The next full moon after Harvest Moon is called the Hunter's Moon, accompanied by a similar phenomenon but less marked; — Oct. 19, northern hemisphere; May 25, southern hemisphere.

## The Earth: Size, Computation of Time, Seasons

### Size and Dimensions

The earth is the fifth largest planet and the third from the sun. Its mass is 6 sextillion, 588 quintillion short tons. Using the parameters of an ellipsoid adopted by the International Astronomical Union in 1964 and recognized by the International Union of Geodesy and Geophysics in 1967, the length of the equator is 24,901.55 miles, the length of a meridian is 24,859.82 miles, the equatorial diameter is 7,926.41 miles, and the area of this reference ellipsoid is approximately 196,938,800 square miles.

The earth is considered a solid, rigid mass with a dense core of magnetic, probably metallic material. The outer part of the core is probably liquid. Around the core is a thick shell or mantle of heavy crystalline rock that in turn is covered by a thin crust forming the solid granite and basalt base of the continents and ocean basins. Over broad areas of the earth's surface the crust has a thin cover of sedimentary rock such as sandstone, shale, and limestone formed by weathering of the earth's surface and deposition of sands, clays, and plant and animal remains.

The temperature in the earth increases about 1° F. with every 100 to 200 feet in depth, in the upper 100 kilometers of the earth, and the temperature near the core is believed to be near the melting point of the core materials under the conditions at that depth. The heat of the earth is believed to be derived from radioactivity in the rocks, pressures developed within the earth, and original heat (if the earth in fact was formed at high temperatures).

### Atmosphere of the Earth

The earth's atmosphere is a blanket composed of nitrogen, oxygen, and argon, in amounts of about 78%, 21%, and 1% by volume. Also present in minute quantities are carbon dioxide, hydrogen, neon, helium, krypton, and xenon.

Water vapor displaces other gases and varies from nearly zero to about 4% by volume. The height of the ozone layer varies from approximately 12 to 21 miles above the earth. Traces exist as low as 6 miles and as high as 35 miles. Traces of methane have been found.

The atmosphere rests on the earth's surface with the weight equivalent to a layer of water 34 ft. deep. For about 300,000 ft. upward the gases remain in the proportions stated. Gravity holds the gases to the earth. The weight of the air compresses it at the bottom, so that the greatest density is at the earth's surface. Pressure, as well as density, decreases as height increases because the weight pressing upon any layer is always less than that pressing upon the layers below.

The temperature of the air drops with increased height until the **tropopause** is reached. This may vary from 25,000 to 60,000 ft. The atmosphere below the tropopause is the **troposphere;** the atmosphere for about twenty miles above the tropopause is the **stratosphere,** where the temperature generally increases with height except at high latitudes in winter. A temperature maximum near the 30-mile level is called the **stratopause.** Above this boundary is the **mesosphere,** where the temperature decreases with height to a minimum, the **mesopause,** at a height of 50 miles. Extending above the mesosphere to the outer fringes of the atmosphere is the **thermosphere,** a region where temperature increases with height to a value measured in thousands of degrees Fahrenheit. The lower portion of this region, extending from 50 to about 400 miles in altitude, is characterized by a high ion density, and is thus called the **ionosphere.** The outer region is called **exosphere;** this is the region where gas molecules traveling at high speed may escape into outer space, above 600 miles.

### Latitude, Longitude

Position on the globe is measured by means of meridians and parallels. Meridians, which are imaginary lines drawn around the earth through the poles, determine **longitude.** The meridian running through Greenwich, England, is the **prime meridian of longitude,** and all others are either east or west. Parallels, which are imaginary circles parallel with the equator, determine **latitude.** The length of a degree of longitude varies as the cosine of the latitude. At the equator a degree is 69.171 statute miles; this is gradually reduced toward the poles. Value of a longitude degree at the poles is zero.

**Latitude** is reckoned by the number of degrees north or south of the equator, an imaginary circle on the earth's surface everywhere equidistant between the two poles. According to the International Astronomical Union ellipsoid of 1964, the length of a degree of latitude is 68.708 statute miles at the equator and varies slightly north and south because of the oblate form of the globe; at the poles it is 69.403 statute miles.

### Definitions of Time

The earth rotates on its axis and follows an elliptical orbit around the sun. The rotation makes the sun appear to move across the sky from East to West. It determines day and night and the complete rotation, in relation to the sun, is called the **apparent** or **true solar day.** This varies but an average determines the **mean solar day** of 24 hours.

The mean solar day is in universal use for civil purposes. It may be obtained from apparent solar time by correcting observations of the sun for the equation of time, but when high precision is required, the mean solar time is calculated from its relation to sidereal time. These relations are extremely complicated, but for most practical uses, they may be considered as follows:

**Sidereal time** is the measure of time defined by the diurnal motion of the vernal equinox, and is determined from observation of the meridian transits of stars. One complete rotation of the earth relative to the equinox is called the **sidereal day. The mean sidereal day** is 23 hours, 56 minutes, 4.091 seconds of mean solar time.

The **Calendar Year** begins at 12 o'clock midnight precisely local clock time, on the night of Dec. 31-Jan. 1. The day and the calendar month also begin at midnight by the clock. The interval required for the earth to make one absolute revolution around the sun is a sidereal year; it consisted of 365 days, 6 hours, 9 minutes, and 9.5 seconds of mean solar time (approximately 24 hours per day) in 1900, and is increasing at the rate of 0.0001-second annually.

The **Tropical Year,** on which the return of the seasons depends, is the interval between two consecutive returns of the sun to the vernal equinox. The tropical year consisted of 365 days, 5 hours, 48 minutes, and 46 seconds in 1900. It is decreasing at the rate of 0.530 seconds per century.

In 1956 the unit of time interval was defined to be identical with the second of **Ephemeris Time,** 1/31,556,925.9747 of the tropical year for 1900 January Od 12th hour E.T. A physical definition of the second based on a quantum transition of cesium (atomic second) was adopted in 1964. The atomic second is equal to 9,192,631,770 cycles of the emitted radiation. In 1967 this atomic second was adopted as the unit of time interval for the Intern'l System of Units.

## The Zones and Seasons

The five zones of the earth's surface are Torrid, lying between the Tropics of Cancer and Capricorn; North Temperate, between Cancer and the Arctic Circle; South Temperate, between Capricorn and the Antarctic Circle; the Frigid Zones, between the polar Circles and the Poles.

The inclination or tilt of the earth's axis with respect to the sun determines the seasons. These are commonly marked in the North Temperate Zone, where spring begins at the vernal equinox, summer at the summer solstice, autumn at the autumnal equinox and winter at the winter solstice.

In the South Temperate Zone, the seasons are reversed. Spring begins at the autumnal equinox, summer at the winter solstice, etc.

If the earth's axis were perpendicular to the plane of the earth's orbit around the sun there would be no change of seasons. Day and night would be of nearly constant length and there would be equable conditions of temperature. But the axis is tilted 23° 27' away from a perpendicular to the orbit and only in March and September is the axis at right angles to the sun.

The points at which the sun crosses the equator are the equinoxes, when day and night are most nearly equal. The points at which the sun is at a maximum distance from the equator are the solstices. Days and nights are then most unequal.

In June the North Pole is tilted 23° 27' toward the sun and the days in the northern hemisphere are longer than the nights, while the days in the southern hemisphere are shorter than the nights. In December the North Pole is tilted 23° 27' away from the sun and the situation is reversed.

### The Seasons in 1994

In 1994 the 4 seasons will begin as follows: add one hour to EST for Atlantic Time; subtract one hour for Central, two hours for Mountain, 3 hours for Pacific, 4 hours for Yukon, 5 hours for Alaska-Hawaii and six hours for Bering Time. Also shown in Greenwich Mean Time.

|  |  | Date | GMT | EST |
|---|---|---|---|---|
| Vernal Equinox | Spring | Mar. 20 | 20:28 | 15:28 |
| Summer Solstice | Summer | June 21 | 14:48 | 9:48 |
| Autumnal Equinox | Autumn | Sept. 23 | 6:19 | 1:19 |
| Winter Solstice | Winter | Dec. 21 | 2:23 | 21:23* |

\* Previous Day

### Poles of the Earth

The geographic (rotation) poles, or points where the earth's axis of rotation cuts the surface, are not absolutely fixed in the body of the earth. The pole of rotation describes an irregular curve about its mean position.

Two periods have been detected in this motion: (1) an annual period due to seasonal changes in barometric pressure, load of ice and snow on the surface and to other phenomena of seasonal character; (2) a period of about 14 months due to the shape and constitution of the earth.

In addition there are small but as yet unpredictable irregularities. The whole motion is so small that the actual pole at any time remains within a circle of 30 or 40 feet in radius centered at the mean position of the pole.

The pole of rotation for the time being is of course the pole having a latitude of 90° and an indeterminate longitude.

## Magnetic Poles

The **north magnetic pole** of the earth is that region where the magnetic force is vertically downward and the **south magnetic pole** that region where the magnetic force is vertically upward. A compass placed at the magnetic poles experiences no directive force in azimuth.

There are slow changes in the distribution of the earth's magnetic field. These changes were at one time attributed in part to a periodic movement of the magnetic poles around the geographical poles, but later evidence refutes this theory and points, rather, to a slow migration of "disturbance" foci over the earth.

There appear shifts in position of the magnetic poles due to the changes in the earth's magnetic field. The center of the area designated as the north magnetic pole was estimated to be in about latitude 70.5° N and longitude 96° W in 1905; from recent nearby measurements and studies of the secular changes, the position in 1970 is estimated as latitude 76.2° N and longitude 101° W. Improved data rather than actual motion account for at least part of the change.

The position of the south magnetic pole in 1912 was near 71° S and longitude 150° E; the position in 1970 is estimated at latitude 66° S and longitude 139.1° E.

The direction of the horizontal components of the magnetic field at any point is known as magnetic north at that point, and the angle by which it deviates east or west of true north is known as the magnetic declination, or in the mariner's terminology, the **variation of the compass.**

A compass without error points in the direction of magnetic north. (In general this is *not* the direction of the magnetic north pole.) If one follows the direction indicated by the north end of the compass, he will travel along a rather irregular curve that eventually reaches the north magnetic pole (though not usually by a great-circle route). However, the action of the compass should not be thought of as due to any influence of the distant pole, but simply as an indication of the distribution of the earth's magnetism at the place of observation.

## Rotation of the Earth

The speed of rotation of the earth about its axis has been found to be slightly variable. The variations may be classified as:

(A) **Secular.** Tidal friction acts as a brake on the rotation and causes a slow secular increase in the length of the day, about 1 millisecond per century.

(B) **Irregular.** The speed of rotation may increase for a number of years, about 5 to 10, and then start decreasing. The maximum difference from the mean in the length of the day during a century is about 5 milliseconds. The accumulated difference in time has amounted to approximately 44 seconds since 1900. The cause is probably motion in the interior of the earth.

(C) **Periodic.** Seasonal variations exist with periods of one year and six months. The cumulative effect is such that each year the earth is late about 30 milliseconds near June 1 and is ahead about 30 milliseconds near Oct. 1. The maximum seasonal variation in the length of the day is about 0.5 millisecond. It is believed that the principal cause of the annual variation is the seasonal change in the wind patterns of the northern and southern hemispheres. The semiannual variation is due chiefly to tidal action of the sun, which distorts the shape of the earth slightly.

The secular and irregular variations were discovered by comparing time based on the rotation of the earth with time based on the orbital motion of the moon about the earth and of the planets about the sun. The periodic variation was determined largely with the aid of quartz-crystal clocks. The introduction of the ce-sium-beam atomic clock in 1955 made it possible to determine in greater detail than before the nature of the irregular and periodic variations.

## Morning and Evening Stars, 1994

(GMT)

| | Morning | Evening |
|---|---|---|
| Jan. | Mercury, Jan. 1 to 3 | Mercury, from Jan. 3 |
| | Venus, Jan. 1 to Jan. 17 | Venus, from Jan. 17 |
| | Mars, Jan. 1 | Saturn, Jan. 1 |
| | Jupiter, Jan. 1 | Uranus, Jan. 1 to Jan. 12 |
| | Uranus, from Jan. 12 | Neptune, Jan. 1 to Jan. 11 |
| | Neptune, from Jan. 11 | |
| | Pluto, Jan. 1 | |
| Feb. | Mercury, from Feb. 20 | Mercury, to Feb. 20 |
| | Mars | Venus |
| | Jupiter | Saturn, to Feb. 21 |
| | Saturn, from Feb. 21 | |
| | Uranus | |
| | Neptune | |
| | Pluto | |
| Mar. | Mercury | Venus |
| | Mars | |
| | Jupiter | |
| | Saturn | |
| | Uranus | |
| | Neptune | |
| | Pluto | |
| Apr. | Mercury, to Apr. 30 | Mercury, from Apr. 30 |
| | Mars | Venus |
| | Jupiter, to Apr. 30 | Jupiter, from Apr. 30 |
| | Saturn | |
| | Uranus | |
| | Neptune | |
| | Pluto | |
| May | Mars | Mercury |
| | Saturn | Venus |
| | Uranus | Jupiter |
| | Neptune | Pluto, from May 17 |
| | Pluto, to May 17 | |
| June | Mercury, from Jun. 25 | Mercury, to Jun. 25 |
| | Mars | Venus |
| | Saturn | Jupiter |
| | Uranus | Pluto |
| | Neptune | |

| | Morning | Evening |
|---|---|---|
| July | Mercury | Venus |
| | Mars | Jupiter |
| | Saturn | Uranus, from July 17 |
| | Uranus, to July 17 | Neptune, from July 14 |
| | Neptune, to July 14 | Pluto |
| Aug. | Mercury, to Aug. 13 | Mercury, from Aug. 13 |
| | Mars | Jupiter |
| | Saturn | Uranus |
| | | Neptune |
| | | Pluto |
| Sept. | Mars | Mercury |
| | Saturn, to Sept. 1 | Venus |
| | | Jupiter |
| | | Saturn, from Sept. 1 |
| | | Uranus |
| | | Neptune |
| | | Pluto |
| Oct. | Mercury, from Oct. 21 | Mercury, to Oct. 21 |
| | Mars | Venus |
| | | Jupiter |
| | | Saturn |
| | | Uranus |
| | | Neptune |
| | | Pluto |
| Nov. | Mercury | Venus, to Nov. 2 |
| | Venus, from Nov. 2 | Jupiter, to Nov. 17 |
| | Mars | Saturn |
| | Jupiter, from Nov. 17 | Uranus |
| | Pluto, from Nov. 20 | Neptune |
| | | Pluto, to Nov. 20 |
| Dec. | Mercury, to Dec. 14 | Mercury, from Dec. 14 |
| | Venus | Saturn |
| | Jupiter | Uranus |
| | Pluto | Neptune |

## Chronological Eras, 1994

The year 1994 of the Christian Era comprises the latter part of the 218th and the beginning of the 219th year of the independence of the United States of America.

| Era | Year | Begins in 1994 | | Era | Year | Begins in 1994 | |
|---|---|---|---|---|---|---|---|
| Byzantine | 7503 | Sept. | 14 | Grecian | 2306 | Sept. | 14 |
| Jewish | 5755 | Sept. | 5 (sunset) | (Seleucidae) | | or Oct. | 14 |
| Roman (Ab Urbe Condita) | 2747 | Jan. | 14 | Diocletian | 1711 | Sept. | 11 |
| Nabonassar (Babylonian) | 2743 | Apr. | 25 | Indian (Saka) | 1916 | Mar. | 22 |
| Japanese | 2654 | Jan. | 1 | Mohammedan (Hegira) | 1415 | June | 9 |

## Chronological Cycles, 1994

| | | | | | | |
|---|---|---|---|---|---|---|
| Dominical Letter | B | Golden Number (Lunar Cycle) | XIX | Roman Indiction | | 2 |
| Epact | 17 | Solar Cycle | 15 | Julian Period (year of) | | 6707 |

## Astronomical Twilight—Meridian of Greenwich

| Date 1993[1] | 20° Begin | 20° End | 30° Begin | 30° End | 40° Begin | 40° End | 50° Begin | 50° End | 60° Begin | 60° End |
|---|---|---|---|---|---|---|---|---|---|---|
| | h m | h m | h m | h m | h m | h m | h m | h m | h m | h m |
| Jan.   1 | 5 16 | 6 50 | 5 30 | 6 35 | 5 45 | 6 21 | 6 00 | 6 07 | 6 18 | 5 49 |
|     11 | 5 19 | 6 56 | 5 33 | 6 43 | 5 46 | 6 30 | 6 00 | 6 17 | 6 15 | 6 01 |
|     21 | 5 21 | 7 01 | 5 32 | 6 51 | 5 43 | 6 40 | 5 55 | 6 30 | 6 06 | 6 18 |

| Date 1993[1] | 20° Begin | 20° End | 30° Begin | 30° End | 40° Begin | 40° End | 50° Begin | 50° End | 60° Begin | 60° End |
|---|---|---|---|---|---|---|---|---|---|---|
| | h m | h m | h m | h m | h m | h m | h m | h m | h m | h m |
| Feb. 1 | 5 21 | 7 07 | 5 29 | 6 58 | 5 38 | 6 51 | 5 45 | 6 44 | 5 51 | 6 38 |
| 11 | 5 18 | 7 11 | 5 24 | 7 05 | 5 29 | 7 01 | 5 32 | 6 59 | 5 32 | 7 01 |
| 21 | 5 13 | 7 15 | 5 17 | 7 12 | 5 17 | 7 12 | 5 16 | 7 14 | 5 09 | 7 23 |
| Mar. 1 | 5 08 | 7 18 | 5 08 | 7 19 | 5 06 | 7 21 | 4 59 | 7 29 | 4 44 | 7 45 |
| 11 | 5 00 | 7 21 | 4 58 | 7 24 | 4 50 | 7 32 | 4 38 | 7 44 | 4 12 | 8 12 |
| 21 | 4 52 | 7 24 | 4 45 | 7 32 | 4 33 | 7 44 | 4 14 | 8 04 | 3 37 | 8 43 |
| Apr. 1 | 4 42 | 7 28 | 4 31 | 7 39 | 4 14 | 7 57 | 3 47 | 8 25 | 2 53 | 9 21 |
| 11 | 4 32 | 7 32 | 4 18 | 7 47 | 3 56 | 8 09 | 3 20 | 8 47 | 2 03 | 10 10 |
| 21 | 4 23 | 7 36 | 4 04 | 7 54 | 3 37 | 8 23 | 2 52 | 9 11 | 0 37 | 11 47 |
| May 1 | 4 14 | 7 41 | 3 52 | 8 04 | 3 19 | 8 37 | 2 22 | 9 39 | | |
| 11 | 4 08 | 7 46 | 3 41 | 8 13 | 3 03 | 8 53 | 1 49 | 10 09 | | |
| 21 | 4 02 | 7 52 | 3 32 | 8 22 | 2 48 | 9 07 | 1 13 | 10 46 | | |
| June 1 | 3 58 | 7 58 | 3 26 | 8 30 | 2 36 | 9 20 | 0 21 | 11 52 | | |
| 11 | 3 56 | 8 03 | 3 22 | 8 36 | 2 29 | 9 30 | | | | |
| 21 | 3 57 | 8 06 | 3 22 | 8 40 | 2 28 | 9 35 | | | | |
| July 1 | 3 59 | 8 07 | 3 25 | 8 41 | 2 30 | 9 35 | | | | |
| 11 | 4 03 | 8 06 | 3 30 | 8 39 | 2 40 | 9 30 | | | | |
| 21 | 4 08 | 8 03 | 3 39 | 8 33 | 2 52 | 9 18 | 1 12 | 11 23 | | |
| Aug. 1 | 4 15 | 7 56 | 3 48 | 8 23 | 3 09 | 9 01 | 1 49 | 10 20 | | |
| 11 | 4 20 | 7 50 | 3 56 | 8 13 | 3 22 | 8 46 | 2 21 | 9 46 | | |
| 21 | 4 24 | 7 41 | 4 05 | 8 01 | 3 34 | 8 27 | 2 47 | 9 15 | | |
| Sept. 1 | 4 29 | 7 31 | 4 14 | 7 46 | 3 51 | 8 08 | 3 13 | 8 43 | 1 40 | 10 02 |
| 11 | 4 32 | 7 20 | 4 20 | 7 33 | 4 02 | 7 50 | 3 33 | 8 16 | 2 36 | 9 12 |
| 21 | 4 35 | 7 11 | 4 26 | 7 19 | 4 14 | 7 31 | 3 52 | 7 52 | 3 11 | 8 31 |
| Oct. 1 | 4 38 | 7 02 | 4 33 | 7 05 | 4 25 | 7 13 | 4 10 | 7 28 | 3 41 | 7 54 |
| 11 | 4 40 | 6 53 | 4 40 | 6 53 | 4 35 | 6 58 | 4 26 | 7 05 | 4 07 | 7 23 |
| 21 | 4 43 | 6 47 | 4 46 | 6 44 | 4 45 | 6 43 | 4 41 | 6 46 | 4 32 | 6 55 |
| Nov. 1 | 4 46 | 6 41 | 4 52 | 6 34 | 4 56 | 6 30 | 4 58 | 6 27 | 4 56 | 6 27 |
| 11 | 4 50 | 6 38 | 4 59 | 6 28 | 5 06 | 6 21 | 5 13 | 6 14 | 5 17 | 6 08 |
| 21 | 4 55 | 6 36 | 5 06 | 6 25 | 5 16 | 6 15 | 5 26 | 6 04 | 5 37 | 5 52 |
| Dec. 1 | 5 00 | 6 37 | 5 13 | 6 24 | 5 25 | 6 11 | 5 38 | 5 58 | 5 53 | 5 42 |
| 11 | 5 06 | 6 40 | 5 20 | 6 26 | 5 34 | 6 12 | 5 48 | 5 57 | 6 06 | 5 38 |
| 21 | 5 11 | 6 45 | 5 25 | 6 30 | 5 39 | 6*16 | 5 55 | 6 00 | 6 15 | 5 40 |
| 31 | 5 15 | 6 50 | 5 30 | 6 35 | 5 44 | 6 21 | 6 00 | 6 06 | 6 18 | 5 48 |

(1) Although the instant of the sun's horizontal depression may be calculated precisely, the phenomena associated with astronomical twilight are sufficiently imprecise that the table is not recalculated each year.

## Total Eclipses, 1940-2000

| Date | Duration m | s | Width miles | Path of Totality |
|---|---|---|---|---|
| 1940 Oct. 1 | 5 | 35 | 135 | Colombia, Brazil, Atlantic Ocean, S. Africa |
| 1941 Sept. 21 | 3 | 21 | 88 | Soviet Union, China, Pacific Ocean |
| 1943 Feb. 4 | 2 | 39 | 142 | Japan, Pacific Ocean, Alaska |
| 1944 Jan. 25 | 4 | 08 | 90 | Peru, Brazil, W. Africa |
| 1945 July 9 | 1 | 15 | 57 | US, Canada, Greenland, Scandinavia, USSR |
| 1947 May 20 | 5 | 13 | 121 | S. America, Atlantic Ocean, Africa |
| 1948 Nov. 1 | 1 | 55 | 52 | Africa, Indian Ocean |
| 1950 Sept. 12 | 1 | 13 | 83 | Arctic Ocean, Siberia, Pacific Ocean |
| 1952 Feb. 25 | 3 | 09 | 85 | Africa, Middle East, Soviet Union |
| 1954 June 30 | 2 | 35 | 95 | US, Canada, Iceland, Europe, Middle East |
| 1955 June 20 | 7 | 07 | 157 | SE Asia, Philippines, Pacific Ocean |
| 1956 June 8 | 4 | 44 | 266 | South Pacific Ocean |
| 1958 Oct. 12 | 5 | 10 | 129 | Pacific Ocean, Chile, Argentina |
| 1959 Oct. 2 | 3 | 01 | 75 | New England, Atlantic Ocean, Africa |
| 1961 Feb. 15 | 2 | 45 | 160 | Europe, Soviet Union |
| 1962 Feb. 5 | 4 | 08 | 91 | Borneo, New Guinea, Pacific Ocean |
| 1963 July 20 | 1 | 39 | 63 | Pacific Ocean, Alaska, Canada, Maine |
| 1965 May 30 | 5 | 15 | 123 | New Zealand, Pacific Ocean |
| 1966 Nov. 12 | 1 | 57 | 52 | Pacific Ocean, S. America, Atlantic Ocean |
| 1968 Sept. 22 | 0 | 39 | 64 | Soviet Union, China |
| 1970 Mar. 7 | 3 | 27 | 95 | Pacific Ocean, Mexico, Eastern US, Canada |
| 1972 July 10 | 2 | 35 | 109 | Siberia, Alaska, Canada |
| 1973 June 30 | 7 | 03 | 159 | Atlantic Ocean, Central Africa, Indian Ocean |
| 1974 June 20 | 5 | 08 | 214 | Indian Ocean, Australia |
| 1976 Oct. 23 | 4 | 46 | 123 | Africa, Indian Ocean, Australia |
| 1977 Oct. 12 | 2 | 37 | 61 | Pacific Ocean, Colombia, Venezuela |
| 1979 Feb. 26 | 2 | 49 | 185 | NW US, Canada, Greenland |
| 1980 Feb. 16 | 4 | 08 | 92 | Africa, Indian Ocean, India, Burma, China |
| 1981 July 31 | 2 | 02 | 67 | Soviet Union, Pacific Ocean |
| 1983 June 11 | 5 | 10 | 123 | Indian Ocean, Indonesia, New Guinea |
| 1984 Nov. 22 | 1 | 59 | 53 | New Guinea, Pacific Ocean |
| 1985 Nov. 12 | 1 | 58 | 430 | Antarctica |
| 1986 Oct. 3h[1] | 0 | 01 | 1 | North Atlantic Ocean |
| 1987 Mar. 29h | 0 | 07 | 3 | South Atlantic Ocean, Africa |
| 1988 Mar. 18 | 3 | 46 | 104 | Sumatra, Borneo, Philippines, Pacific Ocean |
| 1990 July 22 | 2 | 32 | 125 | Finland, Soviet Union, Aleutian Islands |
| 1991 July 11 | 6 | 53 | 160 | Hawaii, Mexico, C. America, Colombia, Brazil |
| 1992 June 30 | 5 | 20 | 182 | South Atlantic Ocean |
| 1994 Nov. 3 | 4 | 23 | 117 | Peru, Bolivia, Paraguay, Brazil |
| 1995 Oct. 24 | 2 | 09 | 48 | Iran, India, SE Asia |
| 1997 Mar. 9 | 2 | 50 | 221 | Mongolia, Siberia |
| 1998 Feb. 26 | 4 | 08 | 94 | Galapagos Islands, Panama, Colombia, Venezuela |
| 1999 Aug. 11 | 2 | 22 | 69 | Europe, Middle East, India |

(1) "h" indicates annular-total hybrid eclipse.

# 1st Month      January 1994      31 days

### Greenwich Mean Time

**NOTE:** Light numbers indicate Sun. **Dark** numbers indicate **Moon.** *Degrees are North Latitude.*

FM = full moon; LQ = last quarter; NM = new moon; FQ = first quarter.

**CAUTION:** Must be converted to local time. For instructions see page 239.

| Day of month week year | Sun on Meridian Moon phase h m s | Sun's Declination ° ' | 20° Rise Sun/Moon h m | 20° Set Sun/Moon h m | 30° Rise Sun/Moon h m | 30° Set Sun/Moon h m | 40° Rise Sun/Moon h m | 40° Set Sun/Moon h m | 50° Rise Sun/Moon h m | 50° Set Sun/Moon h m | 60° Rise Sun/Moon h m | 60° Set Sun/Moon h m |
|---|---|---|---|---|---|---|---|---|---|---|---|---|
| 1 Sa | 12 3 32 | −23 2 | 6 35 | 17 32 | 6 56 | 17 11 | 7 22 | 16 45 | 7 59 | 16 09 | 9 02 | 15 05 |
| 1 | | | 21 09 | 9 06 | 21 03 | 9 14 | 20 56 | 9 23 | 20 47 | 9 36 | 20 32 | 9 55 |
| 2 Su | 12 4 00 | −22 57 | 6 35 | 17 33 | 6 56 | 17 12 | 7 22 | 16 46 | 7 59 | 16 10 | 9 02 | 15 06 |
| 2 | | | 22 07 | 9 48 | 22 06 | 9 52 | 22 05 | 9 56 | 22 03 | 10 01 | 22 01 | 10 09 |
| 3 Mo | 12 4 28 | −22 52 | 6 36 | 17 33 | 6 56 | 17 13 | 7 22 | 16 47 | 7 58 | 16 11 | 9 01 | 15 08 |
| 3 | | | 23 05 | 10 30 | 23 09 | 10 29 | 23 13 | 10 27 | 23 20 | 10 25 | 23 30 | 10 22 |
| 4 Tu | 12 4 56 | −22 46 | 6 36 | 17 34 | 6 57 | 17 13 | 7 22 | 16 48 | 7 58 | 16 12 | 9 01 | 15 10 |
| 4 | | | – – | 11 13 | – – | 11 07 | – – | 11 00 | – – | 10 50 | – – | 10 35 |
| 5 We | 12 5 23 | −22 40 | 6 36 | 17 35 | 6 57 | 17 14 | 7 22 | 16 49 | 7 58 | 16 13 | 9 00 | 15 11 |
| 5 | 00 00 LQ | | 0 04 | 11 57 | 0 12 | 11 47 | 0 23 | 11 34 | 0 37 | 11 17 | 1 00 | 10 50 |
| 6 Th | 12 5 49 | −22 33 | 6 37 | 17 35 | 6 57 | 17 15 | 7 22 | 16 50 | 7 58 | 16 14 | 8 59 | 15 13 |
| 6 | | | 1 04 | 12 44 | 1 17 | 12 30 | 1 33 | 12 12 | 1 55 | 11 48 | 2 30 | 11 09 |
| 7 Fr | 12 6 15 | −22 26 | 6 37 | 17 36 | 6 57 | 17 16 | 7 22 | 16 51 | 7 57 | 16 15 | 8 58 | 15 15 |
| 7 | | | 2 05 | 13 35 | 2 22 | 13 17 | 2 42 | 12 55 | 3 11 | 12 25 | 3 59 | 11 34 |
| 8 Sa | 12 6 41 | −22 18 | 6 37 | 17 36 | 6 57 | 17 17 | 7 22 | 16 52 | 7 57 | 16 17 | 8 57 | 15 17 |
| 8 | | | 3 07 | 14 29 | 3 26 | 14 09 | 3 50 | 13 44 | 4 24 | 13 10 | 5 22 | 12 10 |
| 9 Su | 12 7 06 | −22 10 | 6 37 | 17 37 | 6 57 | 17 17 | 7 22 | 16 53 | 7 57 | 16 18 | 8 56 | 15 19 |
| 9 | | | 4 07 | 15 26 | 4 27 | 15 06 | 4 53 | 14 40 | 5 29 | 14 04 | 6 32 | 13 01 |
| 10 Mo | 12 7 31 | −22 1 | 6 37 | 17 38 | 6 57 | 17 18 | 7 22 | 16 54 | 7 56 | 16 19 | 8 55 | 15 21 |
| 10 | | | 5 05 | 16 25 | 5 25 | 16 06 | 5 50 | 15 41 | 6 26 | 15 06 | 7 27 | 14 06 |
| 11 Tu | 12 7 55 | −21 52 | 6 37 | 17 38 | 6 57 | 17 19 | 7 21 | 16 55 | 7 56 | 16 21 | 8 54 | 15 23 |
| 11 | 23 10 NM | | 5 59 | 17 24 | 6 17 | 17 07 | 6 40 | 16 45 | 7 12 | 16 15 | 8 05 | 15 23 |
| 12 We | 12 8 18 | −21 43 | 6 38 | 17 39 | 6 57 | 17 20 | 7 21 | 16 56 | 7 55 | 16 22 | 8 52 | 15 25 |
| 12 | | | 6 48 | 18 22 | 7 03 | 18 08 | 7 22 | 17 50 | 7 49 | 17 26 | 8 32 | 16 45 |
| 13 Th | 12 8 41 | −21 33 | 6 38 | 17 40 | 6 57 | 17 21 | 7 21 | 16 57 | 7 54 | 16 23 | 8 51 | 15 27 |
| 13 | | | 7 32 | 19 17 | 7 44 | 19 07 | 7 59 | 18 54 | 8 19 | 18 36 | 8 51 | 18 08 |
| 14 Fr | 12 9 03 | −21 23 | 6 38 | 17 40 | 6 57 | 17 21 | 7 21 | 16 58 | 7 54 | 16 25 | 8 50 | 15 29 |
| 14 | | | 8 13 | 20 10 | 8 21 | 20 04 | 8 31 | 19 56 | 8 45 | 19 45 | 9 06 | 19 28 |
| 15 Sa | 12 9 25 | −21 12 | 6 38 | 17 41 | 6 57 | 17 22 | 7 20 | 16 59 | 7 53 | 16 26 | 8 48 | 15 31 |
| 15 | | | 8 51 | 21 01 | 8 55 | 20 59 | 9 01 | 20 56 | 9 07 | 20 53 | 9 18 | 20 47 |
| 16 Su | 12 9 46 | −21 01 | 6 38 | 17 42 | 6 57 | 17 23 | 7 20 | 17 00 | 7 52 | 16 28 | 8 46 | 15 34 |
| 16 | | | 9 28 | 21 51 | 9 28 | 21 53 | 9 28 | 21 55 | 9 28 | 21 58 | 9 29 | 22 03 |
| 17 Mo | 12 10 06 | −20 50 | 6 38 | 17 42 | 6 56 | 17 24 | 7 19 | 17 01 | 7 51 | 16 29 | 8 45 | 15 36 |
| 17 | | | 10 03 | 22 40 | 9 59 | 22 45 | 9 55 | 22 53 | 9 49 | 23 02 | 9 39 | 23 17 |
| 18 Tu | 12 10 25 | −20 38 | 6 38 | 17 43 | 6 56 | 17 25 | 7 19 | 17 02 | 7 50 | 16 31 | 8 43 | 15 38 |
| 18 | | | 10 39 | 23 28 | 10 31 | 23 38 | 10 22 | 23 50 | 10 10 | – – | 9 51 | – – |
| 19 We | 12 10 44 | −20 25 | 6 38 | 17 44 | 6 56 | 17 26 | 7 18 | 17 03 | 7 50 | 16 32 | 8 41 | 15 41 |
| 19 | 20 27 FQ | | 11 16 | – – | 11 04 | – – | 10 51 | – – | 10 32 | 0 06 | 10 04 | 0 32 |
| 20 Th | 12 11 02 | −20 13 | 6 38 | 17 44 | 6 56 | 17 27 | 7 18 | 17 05 | 7 49 | 16 34 | 8 40 | 15 43 |
| 20 | | | 11 55 | 0 18 | 11 40 | 0 31 | 11 23 | 0 47 | 10 58 | 1 09 | 10 20 | 1 45 |
| 21 Fr | 12 11 19 | −19 60 | 6 38 | 17 45 | 6 55 | 17 27 | 7 17 | 17 06 | 7 48 | 16 36 | 8 38 | 15 45 |
| 21 | | | 12 36 | 1 08 | 12 19 | 1 24 | 11 58 | 1 44 | 11 29 | 2 12 | 10 41 | 2 58 |
| 22 Sa | 12 11 35 | −19 46 | 6 38 | 17 46 | 6 55 | 17 28 | 7 17 | 17 07 | 7 47 | 16 37 | 8 36 | 15 48 |
| 22 | | | 13 22 | 2 00 | 13 03 | 2 18 | 12 39 | 2 41 | 12 06 | 3 14 | 11 10 | 4 08 |
| 23 Su | 12 11 51 | −19 33 | 6 38 | 17 46 | 6 55 | 17 29 | 7 16 | 17 08 | 7 45 | 16 39 | 8 34 | 15 50 |
| 23 | | | 14 11 | 2 52 | 13 51 | 3 12 | 13 26 | 3 37 | 12 50 | 4 12 | 11 50 | 5 12 |
| 24 Mo | 12 12 06 | −19 19 | 6 37 | 17 47 | 6 54 | 17 30 | 7 15 | 17 09 | 7 44 | 16 40 | 8 32 | 15 53 |
| 24 | | | 15 04 | 3 44 | 14 45 | 4 04 | 14 20 | 4 30 | 13 44 | 5 05 | 12 44 | 6 06 |
| 25 Tu | 12 12 20 | −19 4 | 6 37 | 17 48 | 6 54 | 17 31 | 7 15 | 17 10 | 7 43 | 16 42 | 8 30 | 15 55 |
| 25 | | | 16 01 | 4 36 | 15 42 | 4 55 | 15 19 | 5 19 | 14 47 | 5 52 | 13 52 | 6 49 |
| 26 We | 12 12 33 | −18 49 | 6 37 | 17 48 | 6 54 | 17 32 | 7 14 | 17 12 | 7 42 | 16 44 | 8 28 | 15 58 |
| 26 | | | 16 59 | 5 26 | 16 44 | 5 43 | 16 24 | 6 04 | 15 57 | 6 33 | 15 12 | 7 20 |
| 27 Th | 12 12 45 | −18 34 | 6 37 | 17 49 | 6 53 | 17 33 | 7 13 | 17 13 | 7 41 | 16 45 | 8 26 | 16 01 |
| 27 | 13 23 FM | | 17 59 | 6 14 | 17 47 | 6 28 | 17 32 | 6 45 | 17 12 | 7 08 | 16 39 | 7 44 |
| 28 Fr | 12 12 57 | −18 19 | 6 37 | 17 49 | 6 53 | 17 34 | 7 12 | 17 14 | 7 39 | 16 47 | 8 23 | 16 03 |
| 28 | | | 18 59 | 7 01 | 18 51 | 7 10 | 18 42 | 7 22 | 18 29 | 7 38 | 18 09 | 8 02 |
| 29 Sa | 12 13 08 | −18 3 | 6 36 | 17 50 | 6 52 | 17 34 | 7 12 | 17 15 | 7 38 | 16 49 | 8 21 | 16 06 |
| 29 | | | 19 58 | 7 45 | 19 55 | 7 50 | 19 52 | 7 56 | 19 47 | 8 05 | 19 40 | 8 17 |
| 30 Su | 12 13 18 | −17 47 | 6 36 | 17 51 | 6 52 | 17 35 | 7 11 | 17 16 | 7 37 | 16 50 | 8 19 | 16 08 |
| 30 | | | 20 58 | 8 29 | 21 00 | 8 29 | 21 03 | 8 29 | 21 06 | 8 30 | 21 11 | 8 31 |
| 31 Mo | 12 13 27 | −17 30 | 6 36 | 17 51 | 6 51 | 17 36 | 7 10 | 17 18 | 7 35 | 16 52 | 8 17 | 16 11 |
| 31 | | | 21 58 | 9 12 | 22 05 | 9 08 | 22 13 | 9 02 | 22 25 | 8 55 | 22 43 | 8 45 |

## 2nd Month · February 1994 · 28 days

Greenwich Mean Time

**NOTE:** Light numbers indicate Sun. **Dark** numbers indicate **Moon**. *Degrees are North Latitude.*

FM = full moon; LQ = last quarter; NM = new moon; FQ = first quarter.

**CAUTION:** Must be converted to local time. For instructions see page 239.

| Day of month / week / year | Sun on Meridian / Moon phase h m s | Sun's Declina-tion ° ' | 20° Rise Sun/Moon h m | 20° Set Sun/Moon h m | 30° Rise Sun/Moon h m | 30° Set Sun/Moon h m | 40° Rise Sun/Moon h m | 40° Set Sun/Moon h m | 50° Rise Sun/Moon h m | 50° Set Sun/Moon h m | 60° Rise Sun/Moon h m | 60° Set Sun/Moon h m |
|---|---|---|---|---|---|---|---|---|---|---|---|---|
| 1 Tu  32 | 12 13 35 | − 17 13 | 6 36 | 17 52 | 6 51 | 17 37 | 7 09 | 17 19 | 7 34 | 16 54 | 8 14 | 16 14 |
|  |  |  | 22 59 | 9 57 | 23 10 | 9 48 | 23 24 | 9 37 | 23 43 | 9 22 | – – | 9 00 |
| 2 We  33 | 12 13 43 | − 16 56 | 6 35 | 17 52 | 6 50 | 17 38 | 7 08 | 17 20 | 7 33 | 16 56 | 8 12 | 16 16 |
|  |  |  | 23 59 | 10 43 | – – | 10 30 | – – | 10 14 | – – | 9 52 | 0 14 | 9 17 |
| 3 Th  34 | 12 13 50  8 6 LQ | − 16 39 | 6 35 | 17 53 | 6 49 | 17 39 | 7 07 | 17 21 | 7 31 | 16 57 | 8 10 | 16 19 |
|  |  |  | – – | 11 32 | 0 15 | 11 16 | 0 34 | 10 55 | 1 00 | 10 27 | 1 44 | 9 41 |
| 4 Fr  35 | 12 13 56 | − 16 21 | 6 35 | 17 53 | 6 49 | 17 40 | 7 06 | 17 22 | 7 30 | 16 59 | 8 07 | 16 21 |
|  |  |  | 1 00 | 12 25 | 1 19 | 12 06 | 1 41 | 11 42 | 2 14 | 11 09 | 3 08 | 10 13 |
| 5 Sa  36 | 12 14 01 | − 16 3 | 6 34 | 17 54 | 6 48 | 17 40 | 7 05 | 17 24 | 7 28 | 17 01 | 8 05 | 16 24 |
|  |  |  | 2 00 | 13 20 | 2 20 | 13 00 | 2 45 | 12 34 | 3 21 | 11 59 | 4 22 | 10 57 |
| 6 Su  37 | 12 14 05 | − 15 45 | 6 34 | 17 55 | 6 47 | 17 41 | 7 04 | 17 25 | 7 26 | 17 02 | 8 02 | 16 27 |
|  |  |  | 2 58 | 14 17 | 3 18 | 13 57 | 3 43 | 13 32 | 4 19 | 12 57 | 5 21 | 11 56 |
| 7 Mo  38 | 12 14 09 | − 15 27 | 6 33 | 17 55 | 6 47 | 17 42 | 7 03 | 17 26 | 7 25 | 17 04 | 8 00 | 16 29 |
|  |  |  | 3 51 | 15 15 | 4 10 | 14 57 | 4 34 | 14 34 | 5 08 | 14 01 | 6 04 | 13 07 |
| 8 Tu  39 | 12 14 12 | − 15 8 | 6 33 | 17 56 | 6 46 | 17 43 | 7 02 | 17 27 | 7 23 | 17 06 | 7 57 | 16 32 |
|  |  |  | 4 41 | 16 12 | 4 58 | 15 56 | 5 19 | 15 37 | 5 47 | 15 10 | 6 34 | 14 25 |
| 9 We  40 | 12 14 14 | − 14 49 | 6 32 | 17 56 | 6 45 | 17 44 | 7 01 | 17 28 | 7 22 | 17 08 | 7 55 | 16 35 |
|  |  |  | 5 27 | 17 07 | 5 40 | 16 55 | 5 57 | 16 40 | 6 20 | 16 19 | 6 56 | 15 46 |
| 10 Th  41 | 12 14 15  14 30 NM | − 14 29 | 6 32 | 17 57 | 6 44 | 17 45 | 6 59 | 17 30 | 7 20 | 17 09 | 7 52 | 16 37 |
|  |  |  | 6 09 | 18 01 | 6 19 | 17 52 | 6 31 | 17 42 | 6 47 | 17 29 | 7 13 | 17 07 |
| 11 Fr  42 | 12 14 15 | − 14 10 | 6 32 | 17 57 | 6 44 | 17 45 | 6 58 | 17 31 | 7 18 | 17 11 | 7 50 | 16 40 |
|  |  |  | 6 48 | 18 52 | 6 54 | 18 48 | 7 01 | 18 43 | 7 11 | 18 36 | 7 26 | 18 25 |
| 12 Sa  43 | 12 14 15 | − 13 50 | 6 31 | 17 58 | 6 43 | 17 46 | 6 57 | 17 32 | 7 16 | 17 13 | 7 47 | 16 43 |
|  |  |  | 7 25 | 19 42 | 7 27 | 19 43 | 7 29 | 19 43 | 7 33 | 19 42 | 7 38 | 19 42 |
| 13 Su  44 | 12 14 14 | − 13 30 | 6 30 | 17 58 | 6 42 | 17 47 | 6 56 | 17 33 | 7 15 | 17 15 | 7 44 | 16 45 |
|  |  |  | 8 01 | 20 32 | 7 59 | 20 36 | 7 57 | 20 41 | 7 53 | 20 47 | 7 49 | 20 58 |
| 14 Mo  45 | 12 14 12 | − 13 10 | 6 30 | 17 59 | 6 41 | 17 48 | 6 55 | 17 34 | 7 13 | 17 16 | 7 42 | 16 48 |
|  |  |  | 8 37 | 21 21 | 8 31 | 21 29 | 8 24 | 21 38 | 8 14 | 21 52 | 8 00 | 22 12 |
| 15 Tu  46 | 12 14 10 | − 12 50 | 6 29 | 17 59 | 6 40 | 17 49 | 6 53 | 17 36 | 7 11 | 17 18 | 7 39 | 16 51 |
|  |  |  | 9 13 | 22 10 | 9 04 | 22 21 | 8 52 | 22 36 | 8 37 | 22 55 | 8 13 | 23 26 |
| 16 We  47 | 12 14 06 | − 12 29 | 6 29 | 18 00 | 6 39 | 17 49 | 6 52 | 17 37 | 7 09 | 17 20 | 7 36 | 16 53 |
|  |  |  | 9 51 | 23 00 | 9 39 | 23 14 | 9 23 | 23 32 | 9 01 | 23 58 | 8 27 | – – |
| 17 Th  48 | 12 14 02 | − 12 8 | 6 28 | 18 00 | 6 38 | 17 50 | 6 51 | 17 38 | 7 07 | 17 21 | 7 33 | 16 56 |
|  |  |  | 10 32 | 23 50 | 10 16 | – – | 9 56 | – – | 9 30 | – – | 8 46 | 0 39 |
| 18 Fr  49 | 12 13 58  17 47 FQ | − 11 47 | 6 28 | 18 01 | 6 37 | 17 51 | 6 49 | 17 39 | 7 06 | 17 23 | 7 31 | 16 58 |
|  |  |  | 11 15 | – – | 10 57 | 0 07 | 10 34 | 0 29 | 10 03 | 0 59 | 9 11 | 1 49 |
| 19 Sa  50 | 12 13 52 | − 11 26 | 6 27 | 18 01 | 6 37 | 17 52 | 6 48 | 17 40 | 7 04 | 17 25 | 7 28 | 17 01 |
|  |  |  | 12 02 | 0 41 | 11 42 | 1 00 | 11 18 | 1 24 | 10 43 | 1 58 | 9 45 | 2 55 |
| 20 Su  51 | 12 13 46 | − 11 5 | 6 26 | 18 01 | 6 36 | 17 52 | 6 47 | 17 41 | 7 02 | 17 27 | 7 25 | 17 04 |
|  |  |  | 12 52 | 1 32 | 12 32 | 1 52 | 12 07 | 2 17 | 11 32 | 2 52 | 10 32 | 3 53 |
| 21 Mo  52 | 12 13 39 | − 10 43 | 6 26 | 18 02 | 6 35 | 17 53 | 6 45 | 17 42 | 7 00 | 17 28 | 7 22 | 17 06 |
|  |  |  | 13 46 | 2 24 | 13 27 | 2 43 | 13 03 | 3 07 | 12 29 | 3 42 | 11 32 | 4 40 |
| 22 Tu  53 | 12 13 32 | − 10 21 | 6 25 | 18 02 | 6 34 | 17 54 | 6 44 | 17 44 | 6 58 | 17 30 | 7 19 | 17 09 |
|  |  |  | 14 42 | 3 14 | 14 25 | 3 32 | 14 04 | 3 54 | 13 34 | 4 25 | 12 45 | 5 16 |
| 23 We  54 | 12 13 24 | − 9 59 | 6 24 | 18 03 | 6 33 | 17 55 | 6 43 | 17 45 | 6 56 | 17 32 | 7 17 | 17 11 |
|  |  |  | 15 41 | 4 02 | 15 27 | 4 18 | 15 10 | 4 36 | 14 46 | 5 02 | 14 08 | 5 44 |
| 24 Th  55 | 12 13 15 | − 9 37 | 6 24 | 18 03 | 6 32 | 17 55 | 6 41 | 17 46 | 6 54 | 17 33 | 7 14 | 17 14 |
|  |  |  | 16 41 | 4 50 | 16 31 | 5 01 | 16 19 | 5 15 | 16 02 | 5 35 | 15 36 | 6 05 |
| 25 Fr  56 | 12 13 06 | − 9 15 | 6 23 | 18 03 | 6 31 | 17 56 | 6 40 | 17 47 | 6 52 | 17 35 | 7 11 | 17 16 |
|  |  |  | 17 42 | 5 35 | 17 36 | 5 43 | 17 30 | 5 52 | 17 21 | 6 04 | 17 08 | 6 22 |
| 26 Sa  57 | 12 12 56  1 15 FM | − 8 53 | 6 22 | 18 04 | 6 30 | 17 57 | 6 38 | 17 48 | 6 50 | 17 37 | 7 08 | 17 19 |
|  |  |  | 18 43 | 6 20 | 18 43 | 6 23 | 18 42 | 6 26 | 18 42 | 6 31 | 18 41 | 6 37 |
| 27 Su  58 | 12 12 46 | − 8 31 | 6 22 | 18 04 | 6 28 | 17 57 | 6 37 | 17 49 | 6 48 | 17 38 | 7 05 | 17 22 |
|  |  |  | 19 45 | 7 05 | 19 50 | 7 03 | 19 55 | 7 01 | 20 03 | 6 57 | 20 16 | 6 52 |
| 28 Mo  59 | 12 12 35 | − 8 8 | 6 21 | 18 05 | 6 27 | 17 58 | 6 35 | 17 50 | 6 46 | 17 40 | 7 02 | 17 24 |
|  |  |  | 20 47 | 7 51 | 20 57 | 7 44 | 21 09 | 7 36 | 21 25 | 7 24 | 21 51 | 7 07 |

**3rd Month**      **March 1994**      **31 days**

Greenwich Mean Time

**NOTE:** Light numbers indicate Sun. **Dark** numbers indicate **Moon.** *Degrees are North Latitude.*

FM = full moon; LQ = last quarter; NM = new moon; FQ = first quarter.

**CAUTION:** Must be converted to local time. For instructions see page 239.

| Day of month / week / year | Sun on Meridian Moon phase h m s | Sun's Declina-tion ° ' | 20° Rise Sun/Moon h m | 20° Set Sun/Moon h m | 30° Rise Sun/Moon h m | 30° Set Sun/Moon h m | 40° Rise Sun/Moon h m | 40° Set Sun/Moon h m | 50° Rise Sun/Moon h m | 50° Set Sun/Moon h m | 60° Rise Sun/Moon h m | 60° Set Sun/Moon h m |
|---|---|---|---|---|---|---|---|---|---|---|---|---|
| 1 Tu 60 | 12 12 23 | − 7 45 | 6 20 | 18 05 | 6 26 | 17 59 | 6 34 | 17 51 | 6 44 | 17 42 | 6 59 | 17 27 |
|  |  |  | 21 50 | 8 39 | 22 04 | 8 27 | 22 21 | 8 13 | 22 45 | 7 54 | 23 24 | 7 25 |
| 2 We 61 | 12 12 11 | − 7 23 | 6 19 | 18 05 | 6 25 | 18 00 | 6 32 | 17 53 | 6 42 | 17 43 | 6 56 | 17 29 |
|  |  |  | 22 53 | 9 29 | 23 10 | 9 13 | 23 32 | 8 55 | — — | 8 29 | — — | 7 47 |
| 3 Th 62 | 12 11 59 | − 6 60 | 6 19 | 18 06 | 6 24 | 18 00 | 6 31 | 17 54 | 6 40 | 17 45 | 6 53 | 17 32 |
|  |  |  | 23 54 | 10 21 | — — | 10 03 | — — | 9 41 | 0 02 | 9 09 | 0 52 | 8 17 |
| 4 Fr 63 | 12 11 46 | − 6 37 | 6 18 | 18 06 | 6 23 | 18 01 | 6 29 | 17 55 | 6 38 | 17 47 | 6 51 | 17 34 |
|  | 16 53 LQ |  | — — | 11 16 | 0 14 | 10 57 | 0 38 | 10 32 | 1 12 | 9 57 | 2 11 | 8 58 |
| 5 Sa 64 | 12 11 32 | − 6 14 | 6 17 | 18 06 | 6 22 | 18 02 | 6 28 | 17 56 | 6 36 | 17 48 | 6 48 | 17 37 |
|  |  |  | 0 53 | 12 13 | 1 13 | 11 53 | 1 38 | 11 28 | 2 14 | 10 53 | 3 15 | 9 52 |
| 6 Su 65 | 12 11 19 | − 5 50 | 6 16 | 18 07 | 6 21 | 18 02 | 6 26 | 17 57 | 6 34 | 17 50 | 6 45 | 17 39 |
|  |  |  | 1 48 | 13 10 | 2 07 | 12 52 | 2 31 | 12 28 | 3 05 | 11 55 | 4 02 | 10 59 |
| 7 Mo 66 | 12 11 05 | − 5 27 | 6 15 | 18 07 | 6 20 | 18 03 | 6 25 | 17 58 | 6 32 | 17 52 | 6 42 | 17 42 |
|  |  |  | 2 38 | 14 07 | 2 56 | 13 50 | 3 17 | 13 30 | 3 47 | 13 02 | 4 36 | 12 14 |
| 8 Tu 67 | 12 10 50 | − 5 4 | 6 15 | 18 07 | 6 19 | 18 04 | 6 23 | 17 59 | 6 29 | 17 53 | 6 39 | 17 44 |
|  |  |  | 3 25 | 15 02 | 3 39 | 14 49 | 3 57 | 14 32 | 4 22 | 14 10 | 5 01 | 13 33 |
| 9 We 68 | 12 10 35 | − 4 40 | 6 14 | 18 08 | 6 17 | 18 04 | 6 22 | 18 00 | 6 27 | 17 55 | 6 36 | 17 47 |
|  |  |  | 4 07 | 15 55 | 4 18 | 15 45 | 4 32 | 15 34 | 4 50 | 15 18 | 5 19 | 14 52 |
| 10 Th 69 | 12 10 20 | − 4 17 | 6 13 | 18 08 | 6 16 | 18 05 | 6 20 | 18 01 | 6 25 | 17 56 | 6 33 | 17 49 |
|  |  |  | 4 47 | 16 46 | 4 54 | 16 41 | 5 03 | 16 34 | 5 15 | 16 25 | 5 34 | 16 10 |
| 11 Fr 70 | 12 10 04 | − 3 53 | 6 12 | 18 08 | 6 15 | 18 06 | 6 19 | 18 02 | 6 23 | 17 58 | 6 30 | 17 52 |
|  |  |  | 5 24 | 17 37 | 5 28 | 17 35 | 5 32 | 17 33 | 5 37 | 17 31 | 5 46 | 17 27 |
| 12 Sa 71 | 12 9 49 | − 3 30 | 6 11 | 18 09 | 6 14 | 18 06 | 6 17 | 18 03 | 6 21 | 18 00 | 6 27 | 17 54 |
|  | 7 5 NM |  | 6 00 | 18 26 | 6 00 | 18 28 | 6 01 | 18 31 | 5 59 | 18 36 | 5 57 | 18 42 |
| 13 Su 72 | 12 9 32 | − 3 6 | 6 10 | 18 09 | 6 13 | 18 07 | 6 15 | 18 04 | 6 19 | 18 01 | 6 24 | 17 57 |
|  |  |  | 6 36 | 19 15 | 6 32 | 19 21 | 6 27 | 19 29 | 6 20 | 19 40 | 6 09 | 19 56 |
| 14 Mo 73 | 12 9 16 | − 2 42 | 6 10 | 18 09 | 6 12 | 18 07 | 6 14 | 18 05 | 6 17 | 18 03 | 6 21 | 17 59 |
|  |  |  | 7 12 | 20 04 | 7 04 | 20 14 | 6 55 | 20 26 | 6 41 | 20 43 | 6 21 | 21 10 |
| 15 Tu 74 | 12 8 59 | − 2 19 | 6 09 | 18 10 | 6 10 | 18 08 | 6 12 | 18 06 | 6 14 | 18 04 | 6 18 | 18 02 |
|  |  |  | 7 50 | 20 53 | 7 39 | 21 07 | 7 24 | 21 23 | 7 05 | 21 46 | 6 36 | 22 23 |
| 16 We 75 | 12 8 42 | − 1 55 | 6 08 | 18 10 | 6 09 | 18 09 | 6 11 | 18 08 | 6 12 | 18 06 | 6 15 | 18 04 |
|  |  |  | 8 29 | 21 43 | 8 15 | 22 00 | 7 57 | 22 20 | 7 32 | 22 48 | 6 53 | 23 34 |
| 17 Th 76 | 12 8 25 | − 1 31 | 6 07 | 18 10 | 6 08 | 18 09 | 6 09 | 18 09 | 6 10 | 18 08 | 6 12 | 18 07 |
|  |  |  | 9 11 | 22 34 | 8 54 | 22 52 | 8 33 | 23 15 | 8 04 | 23 47 | 7 16 | — — |
| 18 Fr 77 | 12 8 08 | − 1 8 | 6 06 | 18 10 | 6 07 | 18 10 | 6 07 | 18 10 | 6 08 | 18 09 | 6 09 | 18 09 |
|  |  |  | 9 56 | 23 24 | 9 37 | 23 44 | 9 14 | — — | 8 41 | — — | 7 46 | 0 41 |
| 19 Sa 78 | 12 7 50 | − 0 44 | 6 05 | 18 11 | 6 06 | 18 11 | 6 06 | 18 11 | 6 06 | 18 11 | 6 06 | 18 11 |
|  |  |  | 10 44 | — — | 10 24 | — — | 10 00 | 0 08 | 9 25 | 0 42 | 8 27 | 1 41 |
| 20 Su 79 | 12 7 33 | − 0 20 | 6 04 | 18 11 | 6 04 | 18 11 | 6 04 | 18 12 | 6 04 | 18 12 | 6 03 | 18 14 |
|  |  |  | 11 35 | 0 14 | 11 16 | 0 34 | 10 52 | 0 58 | 10 18 | 1 33 | 9 20 | 2 31 |
| 21 Mo 80 | 12 7 15 | 0 3 | 6 04 | 18 11 | 6 03 | 18 12 | 6 02 | 18 13 | 6 01 | 18 14 | 6 00 | 18 16 |
|  | 12 14 FQ |  | 12 29 | 1 03 | 12 11 | 1 22 | 11 49 | 1 45 | 11 18 | 2 17 | 10 25 | 3 11 |
| 22 Tu 81 | 12 6 57 | 0 27 | 6 03 | 18 12 | 6 02 | 18 12 | 6 01 | 18 14 | 5 59 | 18 16 | 5 57 | 18 19 |
|  |  |  | 13 25 | 1 51 | 13 10 | 2 08 | 12 51 | 2 28 | 12 24 | 2 56 | 11 41 | 3 42 |
| 23 We 82 | 12 6 39 | 0 51 | 6 02 | 18 12 | 6 01 | 18 13 | 5 59 | 18 15 | 5 57 | 18 17 | 5 54 | 18 21 |
|  |  |  | 14 23 | 2 38 | 14 11 | 2 51 | 13 56 | 3 08 | 13 36 | 3 30 | 13 04 | 4 05 |
| 24 Th 83 | 12 6 21 | 1 14 | 6 01 | 18 12 | 5 59 | 18 14 | 5 58 | 18 16 | 5 55 | 18 19 | 5 50 | 18 24 |
|  |  |  | 15 22 | 3 24 | 15 14 | 3 33 | 15 05 | 3 45 | 14 52 | 4 00 | 14 32 | 4 24 |
| 25 Fr 84 | 12 6 02 | 1 38 | 6 00 | 18 12 | 5 58 | 18 14 | 5 56 | 18 17 | 5 53 | 18 20 | 5 47 | 18 26 |
|  |  |  | 16 22 | 4 08 | 16 19 | 4 13 | 16 16 | 4 20 | 16 11 | 4 28 | 16 04 | 4 40 |
| 26 Sa 85 | 12 5 44 | 2 2 | 5 59 | 18 13 | 5 57 | 18 15 | 5 54 | 18 18 | 5 50 | 18 22 | 5 44 | 18 28 |
|  |  |  | 17 24 | 4 53 | 17 26 | 4 54 | 17 29 | 4 54 | 17 32 | 4 55 | 17 38 | 4 55 |
| 27 Su 86 | 12 5 26 | 2 25 | 5 58 | 18 13 | 5 56 | 18 15 | 5 53 | 18 19 | 5 48 | 18 24 | 5 41 | 18 31 |
|  | 11 9 FM |  | 18 28 | 5 39 | 18 35 | 5 35 | 18 43 | 5 29 | 18 55 | 5 22 | 19 14 | 5 11 |
| 28 Mo 87 | 12 5 08 | 2 49 | 5 57 | 18 13 | 5 55 | 18 16 | 5 51 | 18 20 | 5 46 | 18 25 | 5 38 | 18 33 |
|  |  |  | 19 32 | 6 27 | 19 44 | 6 18 | 19 59 | 6 07 | 20 19 | 5 52 | 20 51 | 5 28 |
| 29 Tu 88 | 12 4 49 | 3 12 | 5 57 | 18 13 | 5 53 | 18 17 | 5 49 | 18 21 | 5 44 | 18 27 | 5 35 | 18 36 |
|  |  |  | 20 38 | 7 18 | 20 53 | 7 04 | 21 13 | 6 48 | 21 40 | 6 25 | 22 25 | 5 49 |
| 30 We 89 | 12 4 31 | 3 35 | 5 56 | 18 14 | 5 52 | 18 17 | 5 48 | 18 22 | 5 42 | 18 28 | 5 32 | 18 38 |
|  |  |  | 21 42 | 8 11 | 22 00 | 7 54 | 22 24 | 7 33 | 22 56 | 7 04 | 23 51 | 6 17 |
| 31 Th 90 | 12 4 13 | 3 59 | 5 55 | 18 14 | 5 51 | 18 18 | 5 46 | 18 23 | 5 40 | 18 30 | 5 29 | 18 41 |
|  |  |  | 22 44 | 9 08 | 23 04 | 8 49 | 23 29 | 8 25 | — — | 7 51 | — — | 6 55 |

# 4th Month   April 1994   30 days

Greenwich Mean Time

**NOTE:** Light numbers indicate Sun. **Dark** numbers indicate **Moon**. *Degrees are North Latitude.*

FM = full moon; LQ = last quarter; NM = new moon; FQ = first quarter.

**CAUTION:** Must be converted to local time. For instructions see page 239.

| Day of month / week / year | Sun on Meridian Moon phase h m s | Sun's Declination ° ' | 20° Rise Sun/Moon h m | 20° Set Sun/Moon h m | 30° Rise Sun/Moon h m | 30° Set Sun/Moon h m | 40° Rise Sun/Moon h m | 40° Set Sun/Moon h m | 50° Rise Sun/Moon h m | 50° Set Sun/Moon h m | 60° Rise Sun/Moon h m | 60° Set Sun/Moon h m |
|---|---|---|---|---|---|---|---|---|---|---|---|---|
| 1 Fr 91 | 12 3 55 | 4 22 | 5 54 | 18 14 | 5 50 | 18 18 | 5 45 | 18 24 | 5 37 | 18 31 | 5 26 | 18 43 |
|  |  |  | 23 42 | 10 06 | – – | 9 46 | – – | 9 21 | 0 03 | 8 46 | 1 03 | 7 46 |
| 2 Sa 92 | 12 3 37 | 4 45 | 5 53 | 18 14 | 5 49 | 18 19 | 5 43 | 18 25 | 5 35 | 18 33 | 5 23 | 18 46 |
|  |  |  | – – | 11 05 | 0 01 | 10 46 | 0 26 | 10 22 | 1 00 | 9 48 | 1 58 | 8 51 |
| 3 Su 93 | 12 3 20 / 2 55 LQ | 5 8 | 5 52 | 18 15 | 5 47 | 18 20 | 5 41 | 18 26 | 5 33 | 18 35 | 5 20 | 18 48 |
|  |  |  | 0 35 | 12 02 | 0 53 | 11 45 | 1 15 | 11 24 | 1 46 | 10 54 | 2 37 | 10 05 |
| 4 Mo 94 | 12 3 02 | 5 31 | 5 51 | 18 15 | 5 46 | 18 20 | 5 40 | 18 27 | 5 31 | 18 36 | 5 17 | 18 50 |
|  |  |  | 1 23 | 12 58 | 1 38 | 12 44 | 1 57 | 12 27 | 2 23 | 12 02 | 3 05 | 11 23 |
| 5 Tu 95 | 12 2 45 | 5 54 | 5 50 | 18 15 | 5 45 | 18 21 | 5 38 | 18 28 | 5 29 | 18 38 | 5 14 | 18 53 |
|  |  |  | 2 07 | 13 52 | 2 19 | 13 41 | 2 34 | 13 28 | 2 54 | 13 10 | 3 25 | 12 42 |
| 6 We 96 | 12 2 27 | 6 17 | 5 50 | 18 16 | 5 44 | 18 22 | 5 37 | 18 29 | 5 27 | 18 39 | 5 11 | 18 55 |
|  |  |  | 2 47 | 14 43 | 2 55 | 14 37 | 3 06 | 14 28 | 3 19 | 14 17 | 3 41 | 13 59 |
| 7 Th 97 | 12 2 11 | 6 39 | 5 49 | 18 16 | 5 43 | 18 22 | 5 35 | 18 30 | 5 25 | 18 41 | 5 08 | 18 58 |
|  |  |  | 3 25 | 15 33 | 3 29 | 15 31 | 3 35 | 15 27 | 3 42 | 15 23 | 3 54 | 15 15 |
| 8 Fr 98 | 12 1 54 | 7 2 | 5 48 | 18 16 | 5 42 | 18 23 | 5 34 | 18 31 | 5 22 | 18 42 | 5 05 | 19 00 |
|  |  |  | 4 01 | 16 22 | 4 02 | 16 24 | 4 03 | 16 25 | 4 04 | 16 27 | 4 06 | 16 30 |
| 9 Sa 99 | 12 1 37 | 7 24 | 5 47 | 18 16 | 5 40 | 18 23 | 5 32 | 18 32 | 5 20 | 18 44 | 5 02 | 19 03 |
|  |  |  | 4 37 | 17 11 | 4 34 | 17 16 | 4 30 | 17 22 | 4 25 | 17 31 | 4 17 | 17 44 |
| 10 Su 100 | 12 1 21 | 7 47 | 5 46 | 18 17 | 5 39 | 18 24 | 5 30 | 18 33 | 5 18 | 18 45 | 4 59 | 19 05 |
|  |  |  | 5 13 | 18 00 | 5 06 | 18 09 | 4 58 | 18 20 | 4 47 | 18 34 | 4 30 | 18 58 |
| 11 Mo 101 | 12 1 05 / 0 17 NM | 8 9 | 5 45 | 18 17 | 5 38 | 18 25 | 5 29 | 18 34 | 5 16 | 18 47 | 4 56 | 19 08 |
|  |  |  | 5 50 | 18 49 | 5 39 | 19 01 | 5 27 | 19 16 | 5 10 | 19 37 | 4 43 | 20 10 |
| 12 Tu 102 | 12 0 50 | 8 31 | 5 45 | 18 17 | 5 37 | 18 25 | 5 27 | 18 35 | 5 14 | 18 49 | 4 53 | 19 10 |
|  |  |  | 6 29 | 19 39 | 6 15 | 19 54 | 5 58 | 20 13 | 5 36 | 20 39 | 5 00 | 21 22 |
| 13 We 103 | 12 0 34 | 8 53 | 5 44 | 18 18 | 5 36 | 18 26 | 5 26 | 18 36 | 5 12 | 18 50 | 4 50 | 19 12 |
|  |  |  | 7 10 | 20 29 | 6 54 | 20 47 | 6 33 | 21 08 | 6 06 | 21 39 | 5 21 | 22 30 |
| 14 Th 104 | 12 0 19 | 9 15 | 5 43 | 18 18 | 5 35 | 18 26 | 5 24 | 18 37 | 5 10 | 18 52 | 4 47 | 19 15 |
|  |  |  | 7 53 | 21 19 | 7 35 | 21 38 | 7 13 | 22 02 | 6 41 | 22 36 | 5 49 | 23 32 |
| 15 Fr 105 | 12 0 05 | 9 36 | 5 42 | 18 19 | 5 34 | 18 27 | 5 23 | 18 38 | 5 08 | 18 53 | 4 44 | 19 17 |
|  |  |  | 8 40 | 22 09 | 8 21 | 22 29 | 7 57 | 22 53 | 7 23 | 23 27 | 6 26 | – – |
| 16 Sa 106 | 11 59 50 | 9 58 | 5 42 | 18 19 | 5 33 | 18 28 | 5 21 | 18 39 | 5 06 | 18 55 | 4 41 | 19 20 |
|  |  |  | 9 30 | 22 58 | 9 10 | 23 17 | 8 46 | 23 40 | 8 12 | – – | 7 14 | 0 26 |
| 17 Su 107 | 11 59 36 | 10 19 | 5 41 | 18 19 | 5 31 | 18 28 | 5 20 | 18 40 | 5 04 | 18 56 | 4 38 | 19 22 |
|  |  |  | 10 21 | 23 45 | 10 03 | – – | 9 40 | – – | 9 08 | 0 13 | 8 14 | 1 08 |
| 18 Mo 108 | 11 59 23 | 10 40 | 5 40 | 18 19 | 5 30 | 18 29 | 5 18 | 18 41 | 5 02 | 18 58 | 4 36 | 19 25 |
|  |  |  | 11 15 | – – | 10 59 | 0 03 | 10 39 | 0 24 | 10 11 | 0 53 | 9 24 | 1 42 |
| 19 Tu 109 | 11 59 09 / 2 34 FQ | 11 1 | 5 39 | 18 19 | 5 29 | 18 29 | 5 17 | 18 42 | 5 00 | 19 00 | 4 33 | 19 27 |
|  |  |  | 12 10 | 0 31 | 11 57 | 0 46 | 11 41 | 1 04 | 11 18 | 1 28 | 10 42 | 2 07 |
| 20 We 110 | 11 58 56 | 11 22 | 5 38 | 18 20 | 5 28 | 18 30 | 5 15 | 18 43 | 4 58 | 19 01 | 4 30 | 19 30 |
|  |  |  | 13 07 | 1 15 | 12 57 | 1 27 | 12 46 | 1 40 | 12 30 | 1 59 | 12 05 | 2 27 |
| 21 Th 111 | 11 58 44 | 11 42 | 5 38 | 18 20 | 5 27 | 18 31 | 5 14 | 18 44 | 4 56 | 19 03 | 4 27 | 19 32 |
|  |  |  | 14 05 | 1 59 | 14 00 | 2 06 | 13 53 | 2 15 | 13 45 | 2 26 | 13 32 | 2 44 |
| 22 Fr 112 | 11 58 32 | 12 3 | 5 37 | 18 20 | 5 26 | 18 31 | 5 13 | 18 45 | 4 54 | 19 04 | 4 24 | 19 35 |
|  |  |  | 15 04 | 2 42 | 15 04 | 2 45 | 15 03 | 2 48 | 15 03 | 2 53 | 15 02 | 2 59 |
| 23 Sa 113 | 11 58 20 | 12 23 | 5 36 | 18 21 | 5 25 | 18 32 | 5 11 | 18 46 | 4 52 | 19 06 | 4 21 | 19 37 |
|  |  |  | 16 05 | 3 27 | 16 10 | 3 25 | 16 15 | 3 22 | 16 23 | 3 19 | 16 35 | 3 14 |
| 24 Su 114 | 11 58 09 | 12 43 | 5 36 | 18 21 | 5 24 | 18 33 | 5 10 | 18 47 | 4 50 | 19 07 | 4 18 | 19 40 |
|  |  |  | 17 09 | 4 13 | 17 18 | 4 06 | 17 30 | 3 58 | 17 46 | 3 47 | 18 11 | 3 30 |
| 25 Mo 115 | 11 57 58 / 19 45 FM | 13 3 | 5 35 | 18 21 | 5 23 | 18 33 | 5 08 | 18 48 | 4 48 | 19 09 | 4 15 | 19 42 |
|  |  |  | 18 15 | 5 02 | 18 28 | 4 51 | 18 45 | 4 37 | 19 09 | 4 18 | 19 47 | 3 49 |
| 26 Tu 116 | 11 57 48 | 13 22 | 5 34 | 18 22 | 5 22 | 18 34 | 5 07 | 18 49 | 4 46 | 19 10 | 4 13 | 19 45 |
|  |  |  | 19 21 | 5 55 | 19 38 | 5 39 | 19 59 | 5 21 | 20 30 | 4 55 | 21 20 | 4 13 |
| 27 We 117 | 11 57 39 | 13 41 | 5 34 | 18 22 | 5 21 | 18 35 | 5 06 | 18 50 | 4 44 | 19 12 | 4 10 | 19 47 |
|  |  |  | 20 26 | 6 51 | 20 46 | 6 33 | 21 10 | 6 10 | 21 44 | 5 39 | 22 42 | 4 47 |
| 28 Th 118 | 11 57 29 | 14 0 | 5 33 | 18 22 | 5 20 | 18 35 | 5 04 | 18 51 | 4 42 | 19 14 | 4 07 | 19 50 |
|  |  |  | 21 29 | 7 51 | 21 48 | 7 31 | 22 13 | 7 07 | 22 48 | 6 32 | 23 47 | 5 33 |
| 29 Fr 119 | 11 57 21 | 14 19 | 5 32 | 18 23 | 5 19 | 18 36 | 5 03 | 18 52 | 4 41 | 19 15 | 4 04 | 19 52 |
|  |  |  | 22 26 | 8 52 | 22 44 | 8 32 | 23 08 | 8 08 | 23 40 | 7 33 | – – | 6 35 |
| 30 Sa 120 | 11 57 13 | 14 38 | 5 32 | 18 23 | 5 18 | 18 36 | 5 02 | 18 53 | 4 39 | 19 17 | 4 02 | 19 55 |
|  |  |  | 23 18 | 9 52 | 23 34 | 9 34 | 23 54 | 9 12 | – – | 8 41 | 0 34 | 7 48 |

# 5th Month

# May 1994

# 31 days

Greenwich Mean Time

**NOTE:** Light numbers indicate Sun. **Dark** numbers indicate **Moon**. *Degrees are North Latitude.*

FM = full moon; LQ = last quarter; NM = new moon; FQ = first quarter.

**CAUTION:** Must be converted to local time. For instructions see page 239.

Each day has two rows: the first (light) row gives Sun Rise/Set; the second (dark) row gives Moon Rise/Set.

| Day of month / week / year | Sun on Meridian Moon phase h m s | Sun's Declination ° ' | 20° Rise h m | 20° Set h m | 30° Rise h m | 30° Set h m | 40° Rise h m | 40° Set h m | 50° Rise h m | 50° Set h m | 60° Rise h m | 60° Set h m |
|---|---|---|---|---|---|---|---|---|---|---|---|---|
| 1 Su 121 | 11 57 05 | 14 56 | 5 31 | 18 23 | 5 17 | 18 37 | 5 01 | 18 54 | 4 37 | 19 18 | 3 59 | 19 57 |
|  |  |  | – – | 10 50 | – – | 10 35 | – – | 10 17 | 0 22 | 9 50 | 1 07 | 9 08 |
| 2 Mo 122 | 11 56 58 / 14 32 LQ | 15 14 | 5 30 | 18 24 | 5 17 | 18 38 | 4 59 | 18 55 | 4 35 | 19 20 | 3 56 | 20 00 |
|  |  |  | 0 04 | 11 46 | 0 17 | 11 34 | 0 33 | 11 20 | 0 55 | 11 00 | 1 30 | 10 28 |
| 3 Tu 123 | 11 56 51 | 15 32 | 5 30 | 18 24 | 5 16 | 18 38 | 4 58 | 18 56 | 4 33 | 19 21 | 3 53 | 20 02 |
|  |  |  | 0 46 | 12 39 | 0 56 | 12 31 | 1 07 | 12 22 | 1 23 | 12 08 | 1 48 | 11 47 |
| 4 We 124 | 11 56 46 | 15 50 | 5 29 | 18 24 | 5 15 | 18 39 | 4 57 | 18 57 | 4 32 | 19 23 | 3 51 | 20 05 |
|  |  |  | 1 25 | 13 30 | 1 31 | 13 26 | 1 38 | 13 21 | 1 47 | 13 15 | 2 02 | 13 04 |
| 5 Th 125 | 11 56 40 | 16 7 | 5 29 | 18 25 | 5 14 | 18 40 | 4 56 | 18 58 | 4 30 | 19 24 | 3 48 | 20 07 |
|  |  |  | 2 02 | 14 19 | 2 04 | 14 19 | 2 06 | 14 19 | 2 09 | 14 19 | 2 14 | 14 19 |
| 6 Fr 126 | 11 56 35 | 16 24 | 5 28 | 18 25 | 5 13 | 18 40 | 4 55 | 18 59 | 4 28 | 19 26 | 3 45 | 20 09 |
|  |  |  | 2 38 | 15 08 | 2 36 | 15 12 | 2 33 | 15 17 | 2 30 | 15 23 | 2 26 | 15 33 |
| 7 Sa 127 | 11 56 31 | 16 41 | 5 28 | 18 26 | 5 12 | 18 41 | 4 53 | 19 00 | 4 27 | 19 27 | 3 43 | 20 12 |
|  |  |  | 3 14 | 15 57 | 3 08 | 16 04 | 3 01 | 16 14 | 2 52 | 16 27 | 2 38 | 16 47 |
| 8 Su 128 | 11 56 28 | 16 58 | 5 27 | 18 26 | 5 12 | 18 42 | 4 52 | 19 01 | 4 25 | 19 29 | 3 40 | 20 14 |
|  |  |  | 3 50 | 16 46 | 3 41 | 16 57 | 3 30 | 17 11 | 3 14 | 17 29 | 2 51 | 17 59 |
| 9 Mo 129 | 11 56 25 | 17 14 | 5 27 | 18 26 | 5 11 | 18 42 | 4 51 | 19 02 | 4 24 | 19 30 | 3 38 | 20 17 |
|  |  |  | 4 28 | 17 35 | 4 16 | 17 49 | 4 00 | 18 07 | 3 39 | 18 32 | 3 07 | 19 11 |
| 10 Tu 130 | 11 56 22 / 17 7 NM | 17 30 | 5 26 | 18 27 | 5 10 | 18 43 | 4 50 | 19 03 | 4 22 | 19 32 | 3 35 | 20 19 |
|  |  |  | 5 09 | 18 25 | 4 53 | 18 42 | 4 34 | 19 03 | 4 08 | 19 32 | 3 26 | 20 21 |
| 11 We 131 | 11 56 20 | 17 46 | 5 26 | 18 27 | 5 09 | 18 44 | 4 49 | 19 04 | 4 20 | 19 33 | 3 33 | 20 22 |
|  |  |  | 5 52 | 19 16 | 5 34 | 19 34 | 5 12 | 19 58 | 4 42 | 20 30 | 3 52 | 21 26 |
| 12 Th 132 | 11 56 19 | 18 1 | 5 25 | 18 28 | 5 09 | 18 44 | 4 48 | 19 05 | 4 19 | 19 35 | 3 30 | 20 24 |
|  |  |  | 6 38 | 20 06 | 6 19 | 20 26 | 5 55 | 20 50 | 5 22 | 21 24 | 4 26 | 22 22 |
| 13 Fr 133 | 11 56 18 | 18 16 | 5 25 | 18 28 | 5 08 | 18 45 | 4 47 | 19 06 | 4 17 | 19 36 | 3 28 | 20 26 |
|  |  |  | 7 26 | 20 55 | 7 07 | 21 14 | 6 43 | 21 38 | 6 09 | 22 12 | 5 10 | 23 08 |
| 14 Sa 134 | 11 56 18 | 18 31 | 5 24 | 18 28 | 5 07 | 18 46 | 4 46 | 19 07 | 4 16 | 19 38 | 3 25 | 20 29 |
|  |  |  | 8 17 | 21 43 | 7 59 | 22 01 | 7 35 | 22 23 | 7 02 | 22 53 | 6 07 | 23 44 |
| 15 Su 135 | 11 56 18 | 18 45 | 5 24 | 18 29 | 5 07 | 18 46 | 4 45 | 19 08 | 4 15 | 19 39 | 3 23 | 20 31 |
|  |  |  | 9 10 | 22 29 | 8 53 | 22 44 | 8 32 | 23 03 | 8 03 | 23 29 | 7 14 | – – |
| 16 Mo 136 | 11 56 19 | 18 60 | 5 24 | 18 29 | 5 06 | 18 47 | 4 44 | 19 09 | 4 13 | 19 40 | 3 21 | 20 34 |
|  |  |  | 10 04 | 23 13 | 9 50 | 23 25 | 9 32 | 23 40 | 9 08 | – – | 8 28 | 0 11 |
| 17 Tu 137 | 11 56 21 | 19 13 | 5 23 | 18 30 | 5 06 | 18 47 | 4 43 | 19 10 | 4 12 | 19 42 | 3 18 | 20 36 |
|  |  |  | 10 59 | 23 55 | 10 48 | – – | 10 35 | – – | 10 17 | 0 01 | 9 48 | 0 33 |
| 18 We 138 | 11 56 23 / 12 50 FQ | 19 27 | 5 23 | 18 30 | 5 05 | 18 48 | 4 42 | 19 11 | 4 11 | 19 43 | 3 16 | 20 38 |
|  |  |  | 11 55 | – – | 11 48 | 0 04 | 11 40 | 0 14 | 11 28 | 0 29 | 11 11 | 0 50 |
| 19 Th 139 | 11 56 25 | 19 40 | 5 23 | 18 30 | 5 04 | 18 49 | 4 42 | 19 12 | 4 09 | 19 44 | 3 14 | 20 40 |
|  |  |  | 12 51 | 0 37 | 12 49 | 0 42 | 12 46 | 0 47 | 12 42 | 0 54 | 12 36 | 1 05 |
| 20 Fr 140 | 11 56 29 | 19 53 | 5 22 | 18 31 | 5 04 | 18 49 | 4 41 | 19 13 | 4 08 | 19 46 | 3 12 | 20 43 |
|  |  |  | 13 50 | 1 19 | 13 52 | 1 19 | 13 55 | 1 19 | 13 58 | 1 20 | 14 05 | 1 19 |
| 21 Sa 141 | 11 56 32 | 20 5 | 5 22 | 18 31 | 5 03 | 18 50 | 4 40 | 19 14 | 4 07 | 19 47 | 3 10 | 20 45 |
|  |  |  | 14 50 | 2 03 | 14 57 | 1 58 | 15 06 | 1 53 | 15 17 | 1 45 | 15 36 | 1 34 |
| 22 Su 142 | 11 56 36 | 20 18 | 5 22 | 18 32 | 5 03 | 18 51 | 4 39 | 19 14 | 4 06 | 19 48 | 3 08 | 20 47 |
|  |  |  | 15 53 | 2 49 | 16 04 | 2 40 | 16 18 | 2 29 | 16 38 | 2 14 | 17 10 | 1 51 |
| 23 Mo 143 | 11 56 41 | 20 29 | 5 22 | 18 32 | 5 03 | 18 51 | 4 39 | 19 15 | 4 04 | 19 50 | 3 06 | 20 49 |
|  |  |  | 16 58 | 3 39 | 17 13 | 3 25 | 17 32 | 3 09 | 17 59 | 2 47 | 18 44 | 2 12 |
| 24 Tu 144 | 11 56 46 | 20 41 | 5 21 | 18 32 | 5 02 | 18 52 | 4 38 | 19 16 | 4 03 | 19 51 | 3 04 | 20 51 |
|  |  |  | 18 04 | 4 33 | 18 22 | 4 16 | 18 45 | 3 55 | 19 17 | 3 26 | 20 12 | 2 40 |
| 25 We 145 | 11 56 52 / 3 39 FM | 20 52 | 5 21 | 18 33 | 5 02 | 18 52 | 4 37 | 19 17 | 4 02 | 19 52 | 3 02 | 20 54 |
|  |  |  | 19 08 | 5 31 | 19 28 | 5 12 | 19 53 | 4 48 | 20 28 | 4 15 | 21 27 | 3 19 |
| 26 Th 146 | 11 56 58 | 21 3 | 5 21 | 18 33 | 5 01 | 18 53 | 4 37 | 19 18 | 4 01 | 19 53 | 3 00 | 20 56 |
|  |  |  | 20 10 | 6 32 | 20 29 | 6 12 | 20 53 | 5 48 | 21 27 | 5 13 | 22 24 | 4 13 |
| 27 Fr 147 | 11 57 04 | 21 13 | 5 21 | 18 34 | 5 01 | 18 53 | 4 36 | 19 18 | 4 00 | 19 55 | 2 58 | 20 58 |
|  |  |  | 21 06 | 7 34 | 21 23 | 7 16 | 21 45 | 6 52 | 22 15 | 6 19 | 23 05 | 5 23 |
| 28 Sa 148 | 11 57 11 | 21 23 | 5 20 | 18 34 | 5 01 | 18 54 | 4 35 | 19 19 | 3 59 | 19 56 | 2 56 | 21 00 |
|  |  |  | 21 56 | 8 36 | 22 11 | 8 19 | 22 29 | 7 59 | 22 53 | 7 30 | 23 33 | 6 42 |
| 29 Su 149 | 11 57 19 | 21 33 | 5 20 | 18 34 | 5 00 | 18 55 | 4 35 | 19 20 | 3 58 | 19 57 | 2 55 | 21 01 |
|  |  |  | 22 42 | 9 35 | 22 53 | 9 21 | 23 06 | 9 05 | 23 25 | 8 42 | 23 53 | 8 06 |
| 30 Mo 150 | 11 57 27 | 21 42 | 5 20 | 18 35 | 5 00 | 18 55 | 4 34 | 19 21 | 3 57 | 19 58 | 2 53 | 21 03 |
|  |  |  | 23 23 | 10 30 | 23 30 | 10 21 | 23 39 | 10 09 | 23 51 | 9 53 | – – | 9 28 |
| 31 Tu 151 | 11 57 36 | 21 51 | 5 20 | 18 35 | 5 00 | 18 56 | 4 34 | 19 22 | 3 57 | 19 59 | 2 51 | 21 05 |
|  |  |  | – – | 11 23 | – – | 11 18 | – – | 11 11 | – – | 11 02 | 0 09 | 10 48 |

# 6th Month | June 1994 | 30 days

### Greenwich Mean Time

**NOTE:** Light numbers indicate Sun. **Dark** numbers indicate **Moon.** *Degrees are North Latitude.*

FM = full moon; LQ = last quarter; NM = new moon; FQ = first quarter.

**CAUTION:** Must be converted to local time. For instructions see page 239.

| Day of month week year | Sun on Meridian Moon phase h m s | Sun's Declina- tion ° ' | 20° Rise Sun Moon h m | 20° Set Sun Moon h m | 30° Rise Sun Moon h m | 30° Set Sun Moon h m | 40° Rise Sun Moon h m | 40° Set Sun Moon h m | 50° Rise Sun Moon h m | 50° Set Sun Moon h m | 60° Rise Sun Moon h m | 60° Set Sun Moon h m |
|---|---|---|---|---|---|---|---|---|---|---|---|---|
| 1 We 152 | 11 57 44 / 4 2 LQ | 21 59 | 5 20 / 0 01 | 18 36 / 12 14 | 4 59 / 0 04 | 18 56 / 12 13 | 4 33 / 0 08 | 19 22 / 12 11 | 3 56 / 0 14 | 20 00 / 12 09 | 2 50 / 0 22 | 21 07 / 12 05 |
| 2 Th 153 | 11 57 54 | 22 8 | 5 20 / 0 38 | 18 36 / 13 04 | 4 59 / 0 37 | 18 57 / 13 06 | 4 33 / 0 36 | 19 23 / 13 09 | 3 55 / 0 36 | 20 01 / 13 14 | 2 48 / 0 34 | 21 09 / 13 20 |
| 3 Fr 154 | 11 58 04 | 22 15 | 5 20 / 1 14 | 18 36 / 13 53 | 4 59 / 1 09 | 18 57 / 13 59 | 4 33 / 1 04 | 19 24 / 14 07 | 3 55 / 0 57 | 20 02 / 14 17 | 2 47 / 0 46 | 21 10 / 14 34 |
| 4 Sa 155 | 11 58 14 | 22 23 | 5 20 / 1 50 | 18 37 / 14 41 | 4 59 / 1 42 | 18 58 / 14 51 | 4 32 / 1 32 | 19 25 / 15 04 | 3 54 / 1 19 | 20 03 / 15 20 | 2 46 / 0 59 | 21 12 / 15 47 |
| 5 Su 156 | 11 58 24 | 22 30 | 5 20 / 2 27 | 18 37 / 15 31 | 4 59 / 2 16 | 18 58 / 15 44 | 4 32 / 2 02 | 19 25 / 16 00 | 3 53 / 1 43 | 20 04 / 16 23 | 2 44 / 1 13 | 21 13 / 16 59 |
| 6 Mo 157 | 11 58 35 | 22 36 | 5 20 / 3 07 | 18 37 / 16 21 | 4 59 / 2 53 | 18 59 / 16 37 | 4 32 / 2 35 | 19 26 / 16 57 | 3 53 / 2 10 | 20 05 / 17 24 | 2 43 / 1 31 | 21 15 / 18 10 |
| 7 Tu 158 | 11 58 46 | 22 42 | 5 20 / 3 49 | 18 38 / 17 11 | 4 58 / 3 32 | 18 59 / 17 29 | 4 31 / 3 11 | 19 26 / 17 52 | 3 52 / 2 42 | 20 05 / 18 24 | 2 42 / 1 55 | 21 16 / 19 17 |
| 8 We 159 | 11 58 57 | 22 48 | 5 20 / 4 34 | 18 38 / 18 02 | 4 58 / 4 16 | 19 00 / 18 21 | 4 31 / 3 52 | 19 27 / 18 45 | 3 52 / 3 20 | 20 06 / 19 19 | 2 41 / 2 26 | 21 18 / 20 17 |
| 9 Th 160 | 11 59 09 / 8 26 NM | 22 54 | 5 20 / 5 23 | 18 39 / 18 52 | 4 58 / 5 03 | 19 00 / 19 11 | 4 31 / 4 39 | 19 28 / 19 36 | 3 52 / 4 05 | 20 07 / 20 10 | 2 40 / 3 07 | 21 19 / 21 07 |
| 10 Fr 161 | 11 59 21 | 22 58 | 5 20 / 6 13 | 18 39 / 19 41 | 4 58 / 5 54 | 19 01 / 19 59 | 4 31 / 5 30 | 19 28 / 20 22 | 3 51 / 4 57 | 20 08 / 20 54 | 2 39 / 4 00 | 21 20 / 21 47 |
| 11 Sa 162 | 11 59 33 | 23 3 | 5 20 / 7 06 | 18 39 / 20 28 | 4 58 / 6 49 | 19 01 / 20 44 | 4 31 / 6 27 | 19 29 / 21 04 | 3 51 / 5 56 | 20 08 / 21 32 | 2 39 / 5 04 | 21 21 / 22 17 |
| 12 Su 163 | 11 59 46 | 23 7 | 5 20 / 8 00 | 18 40 / 21 12 | 4 58 / 7 45 | 19 01 / 21 26 | 4 31 / 7 26 | 19 29 / 21 42 | 3 51 / 7 00 | 20 09 / 22 05 | 2 38 / 6 17 | 21 22 / 22 40 |
| 13 Mo 164 | 11 59 58 | 23 11 | 5 20 / 8 55 | 18 40 / 21 55 | 4 58 / 8 43 | 19 02 / 22 05 | 4 31 / 8 28 | 19 30 / 22 17 | 3 51 / 8 08 | 20 10 / 22 33 | 2 37 / 7 35 | 21 23 / 22 58 |
| 14 Tu 165 | 12 0 11 | 23 14 | 5 20 / 9 50 | 18 40 / 22 37 | 4 58 / 9 42 | 19 02 / 22 43 | 4 31 / 9 32 | 19 30 / 22 50 | 3 50 / 9 18 | 20 11 / 22 59 | 2 37 / 8 57 | 21 24 / 23 14 |
| 15 We 166 | 12 0 24 | 23 17 | 5 20 / 10 45 | 18 40 / 23 18 | 4 58 / 10 42 | 19 02 / 23 20 | 4 31 / 10 37 | 19 31 / 23 22 | 3 50 / 10 30 | 20 11 / 23 24 | 2 36 / 10 20 | 21 25 / 23 28 |
| 16 Th 167 | 12 0 36 / 19 56 FQ | 23 20 | 5 21 / 11 42 | 18 41 / 24 00 | 4 59 / 11 42 | 19 03 / 23 57 | 4 31 / 11 43 | 19 31 / 23 54 | 3 50 / 11 44 | 20 12 / 23 49 | 2 36 / 11 46 | 21 26 / 23 42 |
| 17 Fr 168 | 12 0 49 | 23 22 | 5 21 / 12 40 | 18 41 / -- -- | 4 59 / 12 45 | 19 03 / -- -- | 4 31 / 12 51 | 19 31 / -- -- | 3 50 / 13 00 | 20 12 / -- -- | 2 36 / 13 13 | 21 26 / 23 57 |
| 18 Sa 169 | 12 1 02 | 23 24 | 5 21 / 13 39 | 18 41 / 0 43 | 4 59 / 13 49 | 19 03 / 0 36 | 4 31 / 14 01 | 19 31 / 0 27 | 3 50 / 14 17 | 20 12 / 0 15 | 2 36 / 14 43 | 21 27 / -- -- |
| 19 Su 170 | 12 1 15 | 23 25 | 5 21 / 14 41 | 18 41 / 1 30 | 4 59 / 14 55 | 19 04 / 1 18 | 4 31 / 15 12 | 19 32 / 1 04 | 3 50 / 15 36 | 20 13 / 0 45 | 2 36 / 16 14 | 21 27 / 0 15 |
| 20 Mo 171 | 12 1 28 | 23 26 | 5 21 / 15 45 | 18 42 / 2 20 | 4 59 / 16 02 | 19 04 / 2 05 | 4 31 / 16 23 | 19 32 / 1 46 | 3 50 / 16 53 | 20 13 / 1 20 | 2 36 / 17 43 | 21 27 / 0 39 |
| 21 Tu 172 | 12 1 41 | 23 26 | 5 21 / 16 49 | 18 42 / 3 14 | 4 59 / 17 08 | 19 04 / 2 56 | 4 31 / 17 32 | 19 32 / 2 34 | 3 51 / 18 06 | 20 13 / 2 03 | 2 36 / 19 04 | 21 28 / 1 11 |
| 22 We 173 | 12 1 54 | 23 26 | 5 22 / 17 51 | 18 42 / 4 13 | 5 00 / 18 11 | 19 04 / 3 54 | 4 31 / 18 36 | 19 32 / 3 29 | 3 51 / 19 10 | 20 13 / 2 55 | 2 36 / 20 10 | 21 28 / 1 56 |
| 23 Th 174 | 12 2 07 / 11 33 FM | 23 26 | 5 22 / 18 50 | 18 42 / 5 15 | 5 00 / 19 09 | 19 04 / 4 55 | 4 31 / 19 32 | 19 32 / 4 31 | 3 51 / 20 04 | 20 13 / 3 56 | 2 36 / 20 59 | 21 28 / 2 57 |
| 24 Fr 175 | 12 2 20 | 23 25 | 5 22 / 19 44 | 18 43 / 6 17 | 5 00 / 20 00 | 19 05 / 5 59 | 4 32 / 20 20 | 19 33 / 5 37 | 3 52 / 20 48 | 20 13 / 5 06 | 2 37 / 21 33 | 21 28 / 4 13 |
| 25 Sa 176 | 12 2 33 | 23 24 | 5 22 / 20 33 | 18 43 / 7 18 | 5 01 / 20 46 | 19 05 / 7 03 | 4 33 / 21 01 | 19 33 / 6 45 | 3 52 / 21 23 | 20 13 / 6 19 | 2 37 / 21 57 | 21 28 / 5 36 |
| 26 Su 177 | 12 2 45 | 23 22 | 5 23 / 21 17 | 18 43 / 8 17 | 5 01 / 21 26 | 19 05 / 8 05 | 4 33 / 21 37 | 19 33 / 7 51 | 3 52 / 21 52 | 20 13 / 7 32 | 2 38 / 22 15 | 21 27 / 7 01 |
| 27 Mo 178 | 12 2 58 | 23 20 | 5 23 / 21 57 | 18 43 / 9 12 | 5 01 / 22 02 | 19 05 / 9 05 | 4 33 / 22 09 | 19 33 / 8 56 | 3 53 / 22 17 | 20 13 / 8 44 | 2 38 / 22 30 | 21 27 / 8 24 |
| 28 Tu 179 | 12 3 10 | 23 18 | 5 23 / 22 36 | 18 43 / 10 05 | 5 01 / 22 37 | 19 05 / 10 02 | 4 33 / 22 38 | 19 33 / 9 58 | 3 53 / 22 40 | 20 13 / 9 53 | 2 39 / 22 43 | 21 27 / 9 44 |
| 29 We 180 | 12 3 22 | 23 15 | 5 23 / 23 12 | 18 43 / 10 56 | 5 02 / 23 10 | 19 05 / 10 57 | 4 34 / 23 06 | 19 33 / 10 58 | 3 54 / 23 02 | 20 13 / 11 00 | 2 40 / 22 55 | 21 26 / 11 02 |
| 30 Th 181 | 12 3 34 / 19 31 LQ | 23 12 | 5 24 / 23 49 | 18 43 / 11 46 | 5 02 / 23 42 | 19 05 / 11 51 | 4 34 / 23 34 | 19 33 / 11 57 | 3 54 / 23 24 | 20 13 / 12 05 | 2 41 / 23 07 | 21 26 / 12 17 |

# 7th Month      July 1994      31 days

Greenwich Mean Time

**NOTE:** Light numbers indicate Sun. **Dark** numbers indicate **Moon**. *Degrees are North Latitude.*

FM = full moon; LQ = last quarter; NM = new moon; FQ = first quarter.

**CAUTION:** Must be converted to local time. For instructions see page 239.

| Day of month / week / year | Sun on Meridian / Moon phase (h m s) | Sun's Declination (° ') | 20° Rise Sun / Moon | 20° Set Sun / Moon | 30° Rise Sun / Moon | 30° Set Sun / Moon | 40° Rise Sun / Moon | 40° Set Sun / Moon | 50° Rise Sun / Moon | 50° Set Sun / Moon | 60° Rise Sun / Moon | 60° Set Sun / Moon |
|---|---|---|---|---|---|---|---|---|---|---|---|---|
| 1 Fr 182 | 12 3 46 | 23 8 | 5 24 / – – | 18 43 / 12 35 | 5 02 / – – | 19 05 / 12 44 | 4 35 / – – | 19 33 / 12 54 | 3 55 / 23 47 | 20 12 / 13 09 | 2 42 / 23 21 | 21 25 / 13 31 |
| 2 Sa 183 | 12 3 57 | 23 4 | 5 24 / 0 26 | 18 43 / 13 25 | 5 03 / 0 16 | 19 05 / 13 37 | 4 35 / 0 04 | 19 33 / 13 51 | 3 55 / – – | 20 12 / 14 12 | 2 43 / 23 38 | 21 24 / 14 44 |
| 3 Su 184 | 12 4 09 | 23 0 | 5 25 / 1 05 | 18 43 / 14 14 | 5 03 / 0 51 | 19 05 / 14 29 | 4 36 / 0 35 | 19 32 / 14 48 | 3 56 / 0 13 | 20 12 / 15 14 | 2 44 / 23 59 | 21 23 / 15 56 |
| 4 Mo 185 | 12 4 20 | 22 55 | 5 25 / 1 46 | 18 44 / 15 05 | 5 04 / 1 30 | 19 05 / 15 22 | 4 36 / 1 10 | 19 32 / 15 44 | 3 57 / 0 43 | 20 11 / 16 14 | 2 45 / – – | 21 22 / 17 04 |
| 5 Tu 186 | 12 4 30 | 22 50 | 5 25 / 2 30 | 18 44 / 15 55 | 5 04 / 2 12 | 19 05 / 16 14 | 4 37 / 1 49 | 19 32 / 16 38 | 3 58 / 1 18 | 20 11 / 17 11 | 2 47 / 0 26 | 21 21 / 18 07 |
| 6 We 187 | 12 4 40 | 22 44 | 5 26 / 3 17 | 18 44 / 16 46 | 5 04 / 2 58 | 19 05 / 17 05 | 4 37 / 2 34 | 19 32 / 17 30 | 3 58 / 2 00 | 20 10 / 18 04 | 2 48 / 1 03 | 21 20 / 19 02 |
| 7 Th 188 | 12 4 50 | 22 38 | 5 26 / 4 07 | 18 44 / 17 36 | 5 05 / 3 48 | 19 05 / 17 55 | 4 38 / 3 23 | 19 31 / 18 18 | 3 59 / 2 49 | 20 10 / 18 51 | 2 49 / 1 51 | 21 19 / 19 46 |
| 8 Fr 189 | 12 5 00 / 21 37 NM | 22 31 | 5 26 / 5 00 | 18 43 / 18 24 | 5 05 / 4 41 | 19 04 / 18 41 | 4 39 / 4 18 | 19 31 / 19 02 | 4 00 / 3 46 | 20 09 / 19 32 | 2 51 / 2 52 | 21 18 / 20 20 |
| 9 Sa 190 | 12 5 09 | 22 25 | 5 27 / 5 54 | 18 43 / 19 10 | 5 06 / 5 38 | 19 04 / 19 25 | 4 39 / 5 18 | 19 31 / 19 43 | 4 01 / 4 49 | 20 09 / 20 07 | 2 52 / 4 03 | 21 17 / 20 46 |
| 10 Su 191 | 12 5 18 | 22 17 | 5 27 / 6 49 | 18 43 / 19 55 | 5 06 / 6 36 | 19 04 / 20 06 | 4 40 / 6 20 | 19 30 / 20 19 | 4 02 / 5 57 | 20 08 / 20 38 | 2 54 / 5 21 | 21 16 / 21 06 |
| 11 Mo 192 | 12 5 26 | 22 10 | 5 28 / 7 45 | 18 43 / 20 37 | 5 07 / 7 36 | 19 04 / 20 44 | 4 41 / 7 24 | 19 30 / 20 53 | 4 03 / 7 08 | 20 07 / 21 05 | 2 56 / 6 43 | 21 14 / 21 23 |
| 12 Tu 193 | 12 5 34 | 22 2 | 5 28 / 8 41 | 18 43 / 21 19 | 5 07 / 8 36 | 19 03 / 21 22 | 4 41 / 8 29 | 19 29 / 21 26 | 4 04 / 8 21 | 20 07 / 21 30 | 2 58 / 8 07 | 21 12 / 21 38 |
| 13 We 194 | 12 5 42 | 21 53 | 5 28 / 9 38 | 18 43 / 22 00 | 5 08 / 9 37 | 19 03 / 21 59 | 4 42 / 9 36 | 19 29 / 21 57 | 4 05 / 9 34 | 20 06 / 21 55 | 2 59 / 9 32 | 21 11 / 21 52 |
| 14 Th 195 | 12 5 49 | 21 45 | 5 29 / 10 35 | 18 43 / 22 43 | 5 08 / 10 38 | 19 03 / 22 37 | 4 43 / 10 43 | 19 28 / 22 30 | 4 06 / 10 49 | 20 05 / 22 21 | 3 01 / 10 58 | 21 09 / 22 07 |
| 15 Fr 196 | 12 5 55 | 21 36 | 5 29 / 11 33 | 18 43 / 23 27 | 5 09 / 11 41 | 19 03 / 23 17 | 4 43 / 11 51 | 19 28 / 23 05 | 4 07 / 12 05 | 20 04 / 22 49 | 3 03 / 12 26 | 21 07 / 22 23 |
| 16 Sa 197 | 12 6 01 / 1 12 FQ | 21 26 | 5 29 / 12 33 | 18 43 / – – | 5 09 / 12 45 | 19 02 / – – | 4 44 / 13 00 | 19 27 / 23 44 | 4 08 / 13 21 | 20 03 / 23 21 | 3 05 / 13 55 | 21 06 / 22 44 |
| 17 Su 198 | 12 6 06 | 21 16 | 5 30 / 13 34 | 18 42 / 0 15 | 5 10 / 13 50 | 19 02 / 0 01 | 4 45 / 14 09 | 19 27 / – – | 4 09 / 14 37 | 20 02 / 23 59 | 3 07 / 15 22 | 21 04 / 23 11 |
| 18 Mo 199 | 12 6 11 | 21 6 | 5 30 / 14 36 | 18 42 / 1 06 | 5 11 / 14 54 | 19 02 / 0 49 | 4 46 / 15 17 | 19 26 / 0 28 | 4 11 / 15 50 | 20 01 / – – | 3 09 / 16 44 | 21 02 / 23 50 |
| 19 Tu 200 | 12 6 15 | 20 56 | 5 30 / 15 37 | 18 42 / 2 01 | 5 11 / 15 57 | 19 01 / 1 42 | 4 47 / 16 21 | 19 25 / 1 19 | 4 12 / 16 56 | 20 00 / 0 46 | 3 11 / 17 55 | 21 00 / – – |
| 20 We 201 | 12 6 19 | 20 45 | 5 31 / 16 36 | 18 42 / 3 00 | 5 12 / 16 56 | 19 01 / 2 41 | 4 47 / 17 20 | 19 25 / 2 16 | 4 13 / 17 53 | 19 59 / 1 41 | 3 13 / 18 50 | 20 58 / 0 42 |
| 21 Th 202 | 12 6 22 | 20 33 | 5 31 / 17 32 | 18 41 / 4 01 | 5 12 / 17 49 | 19 00 / 3 42 | 4 48 / 18 11 | 19 24 / 3 19 | 4 14 / 18 41 | 19 58 / 2 46 | 3 15 / 19 31 | 20 56 / 1 50 |
| 22 Fr 203 | 12 6 24 / 20 16 FM | 20 22 | 5 32 / 18 23 | 18 41 / 5 02 | 5 13 / 18 37 | 19 00 / 4 45 | 4 49 / 18 55 | 19 23 / 4 25 | 4 15 / 19 20 | 19 57 / 3 56 | 3 17 / 19 59 | 20 54 / 3 09 |
| 23 Sa 204 | 12 6 26 | 20 10 | 5 32 / 19 09 | 18 41 / 6 01 | 5 13 / 19 20 | 18 59 / 5 48 | 4 50 / 19 33 | 19 22 / 5 32 | 4 17 / 19 52 | 19 55 / 5 09 | 3 19 / 20 20 | 20 52 / 4 33 |
| 24 Su 205 | 12 6 28 | 19 58 | 5 32 / 19 52 | 18 40 / 6 59 | 5 14 / 19 59 | 18 59 / 6 49 | 4 51 / 20 07 | 19 22 / 6 38 | 4 18 / 20 19 | 19 54 / 6 22 | 3 22 / 20 37 | 20 50 / 5 57 |
| 25 Mo 206 | 12 6 29 | 19 45 | 5 33 / 20 31 | 18 40 / 7 53 | 5 15 / 20 34 | 18 58 / 7 48 | 4 52 / 20 38 | 19 21 / 7 42 | 4 19 / 20 43 | 19 53 / 7 33 | 3 24 / 20 51 | 20 47 / 7 19 |
| 26 Tu 207 | 12 6 29 | 19 32 | 5 33 / 21 09 | 18 40 / 8 46 | 5 15 / 21 08 | 18 57 / 8 45 | 4 53 / 21 07 | 19 20 / 8 44 | 4 21 / 21 06 | 19 51 / 8 42 | 3 26 / 21 03 | 20 45 / 8 39 |
| 27 We 208 | 12 6 28 | 19 19 | 5 33 / 21 46 | 18 39 / 9 37 | 5 16 / 21 42 | 18 57 / 9 40 | 4 53 / 21 36 | 19 19 / 9 44 | 4 22 / 21 28 | 19 50 / 9 49 | 3 28 / 21 16 | 20 43 / 9 56 |
| 28 Th 209 | 12 6 27 | 19 5 | 5 34 / 22 24 | 18 39 / 10 27 | 5 16 / 22 15 | 18 56 / 10 34 | 4 54 / 22 05 | 19 18 / 10 43 | 4 23 / 21 51 | 19 49 / 10 54 | 3 31 / 21 29 | 20 41 / 11 12 |
| 29 Fr 210 | 12 6 26 | 18 51 | 5 34 / 23 02 | 18 38 / 11 17 | 5 17 / 22 50 | 18 55 / 11 27 | 4 55 / 22 36 | 19 17 / 11 40 | 4 25 / 22 16 | 19 47 / 11 58 | 3 33 / 21 45 | 20 38 / 12 26 |
| 30 Sa 211 | 12 6 24 / 12 40 LQ | 18 37 | 5 35 / 23 42 | 18 38 / 12 07 | 5 18 / 23 27 | 18 55 / 12 20 | 4 56 / 23 09 | 19 16 / 12 37 | 4 26 / 22 44 | 19 46 / 13 00 | 3 35 / 22 04 | 20 36 / 13 38 |
| 31 Su 212 | 12 6 21 | 18 23 | 5 35 / – – | 18 38 / 12 57 | 5 18 / – – | 18 54 / 13 13 | 4 57 / 23 46 | 19 15 / 13 33 | 4 27 / 23 17 | 19 44 / 14 01 | 3 38 / 22 29 | 20 33 / 14 48 |

## 8th Month                    August 1994                    31 days
### Greenwich Mean Time

**NOTE:** Light numbers indicate Sun. **Dark** numbers indicate **Moon**. *Degrees are North Latitude.*

FM = full moon; LQ = last quarter; NM = new moon; FQ = first quarter.

**CAUTION:** Must be converted to local time. For instructions see page 239.

| Day of month / week / year | Sun on Meridian / Moon phase (h m s) | Sun's Declination (° ') | 20° Rise | 20° Set | 30° Rise | 30° Set | 40° Rise | 40° Set | 50° Rise | 50° Set | 60° Rise | 60° Set |
|---|---|---|---|---|---|---|---|---|---|---|---|---|
| 1 Mo | 12 6 18 | 18 8 | 5 35 | 18 37 | 5 19 | 18 53 | 4 58 | 19 14 | 4 29 | 19 43 | 3 40 | 20 31 |
| 213 | | | 0 25 | 13 47 | 0 07 | 14 05 | – – | 14 28 | 23 55 | 15 00 | 23 01 | 15 53 |
| 2 Tu | 12 6 14 | 17 53 | 5 36 | 18 37 | 5 19 | 18 53 | 4 59 | 19 13 | 4 30 | 19 41 | 3 42 | 20 28 |
| 214 | | | 1 10 | 14 38 | 0 51 | 14 57 | 0 28 | 15 21 | – – | 15 54 | 23 44 | 16 52 |
| 3 We | 12 6 09 | 17 37 | 5 36 | 18 36 | 5 20 | 18 52 | 5 00 | 19 12 | 4 32 | 19 40 | 3 45 | 20 26 |
| 215 | | | 1 59 | 15 27 | 1 39 | 15 47 | 1 15 | 16 10 | 0 41 | 16 44 | – – | 17 40 |
| 4 Th | 12 6 04 | 17 22 | 5 36 | 18 36 | 5 21 | 18 51 | 5 01 | 19 11 | 4 33 | 19 38 | 3 47 | 20 23 |
| 216 | | | 2 50 | 16 16 | 2 31 | 16 34 | 2 08 | 16 57 | 1 35 | 17 28 | 0 39 | 18 19 |
| 5 Fr | 12 5 59 | 17 6 | 5 37 | 18 35 | 5 21 | 18 50 | 5 02 | 19 10 | 4 34 | 19 36 | 3 49 | 20 21 |
| 217 | | | 3 44 | 17 04 | 3 27 | 17 20 | 3 05 | 17 39 | 2 36 | 18 06 | 1 46 | 18 48 |
| 6 Sa | 12 5 52 | 16 49 | 5 37 | 18 34 | 5 22 | 18 50 | 5 03 | 19 08 | 4 36 | 19 35 | 3 52 | 20 18 |
| 218 | | | 4 39 | 17 50 | 4 25 | 18 02 | 4 07 | 18 18 | 3 42 | 18 39 | 3 01 | 19 11 |
| 7 Su | 12 5 45 | 16 33 | 5 37 | 18 34 | 5 22 | 18 49 | 5 04 | 19 07 | 4 37 | 19 33 | 3 54 | 20 16 |
| 219 | 8 45 NM | | 5 36 | 18 34 | 5 25 | 18 43 | 5 11 | 18 53 | 4 53 | 19 08 | 4 23 | 19 30 |
| 8 Mo | 12 5 38 | 16 16 | 5 38 | 18 33 | 5 23 | 18 48 | 5 05 | 19 06 | 4 39 | 19 31 | 3 57 | 20 13 |
| 220 | | | 6 33 | 19 17 | 6 26 | 19 22 | 6 18 | 19 27 | 6 06 | 19 35 | 5 48 | 19 46 |
| 9 Tu | 12 5 30 | 15 59 | 5 38 | 18 33 | 5 24 | 18 47 | 5 06 | 19 05 | 4 40 | 19 30 | 3 59 | 20 10 |
| 221 | | | 7 31 | 19 59 | 7 28 | 20 00 | 7 25 | 20 00 | 7 21 | 20 00 | 7 14 | 20 01 |
| 10 We | 12 5 21 | 15 42 | 5 38 | 18 32 | 5 24 | 18 46 | 5 06 | 19 04 | 4 42 | 19 28 | 4 01 | 20 08 |
| 222 | | | 8 29 | 20 43 | 8 31 | 20 38 | 8 33 | 20 33 | 8 37 | 20 26 | 8 42 | 20 16 |
| 11 Th | 12 5 12 | 15 24 | 5 39 | 18 31 | 5 25 | 18 45 | 5 07 | 19 02 | 4 43 | 19 26 | 4 04 | 20 05 |
| 223 | | | 9 27 | 21 27 | 9 34 | 21 18 | 9 42 | 21 08 | 9 53 | 20 54 | 10 11 | 20 32 |
| 12 Fr | 12 5 02 | 15 6 | 5 39 | 18 31 | 5 25 | 18 44 | 5 08 | 19 01 | 4 45 | 19 24 | 4 06 | 20 02 |
| 224 | | | 10 27 | 22 14 | 10 38 | 22 01 | 10 51 | 21 46 | 11 10 | 21 25 | 11 40 | 20 52 |
| 13 Sa | 12 4 52 | 14 48 | 5 39 | 18 30 | 5 26 | 18 43 | 5 09 | 19 00 | 4 46 | 19 23 | 4 09 | 19 59 |
| 225 | | | 11 28 | 23 04 | 11 43 | 22 48 | 12 01 | 22 28 | 12 26 | 22 01 | 13 07 | 21 17 |
| 14 Su | 12 4 41 | 14 30 | 5 40 | 18 30 | 5 27 | 18 42 | 5 10 | 18 58 | 4 48 | 19 21 | 4 11 | 19 57 |
| 226 | 5 57 FQ | | 12 29 | 23 57 | 12 47 | 23 39 | 13 09 | 23 16 | 13 39 | 22 44 | 14 30 | 21 51 |
| 15 Mo | 12 4 30 | 14 11 | 5 40 | 18 29 | 5 27 | 18 41 | 5 11 | 18 57 | 4 49 | 19 19 | 4 13 | 19 54 |
| 227 | | | 13 30 | – – | 13 49 | – – | 14 13 | – – | 14 47 | 23 36 | 15 44 | 22 38 |
| 16 Tu | 12 4 17 | 13 53 | 5 40 | 18 28 | 5 28 | 18 40 | 5 12 | 18 56 | 4 51 | 19 17 | 4 16 | 19 51 |
| 228 | | | 14 28 | 0 53 | 14 48 | 0 34 | 15 12 | 0 10 | 15 46 | – – | 16 44 | 23 38 |
| 17 We | 12 4 05 | 13 34 | 5 40 | 18 27 | 5 28 | 18 39 | 5 13 | 18 54 | 4 52 | 19 15 | 4 18 | 19 48 |
| 229 | | | 15 24 | 1 52 | 15 42 | 1 33 | 16 04 | 1 09 | 16 36 | 0 35 | 17 28 | – – |
| 18 Th | 12 3 52 | 13 15 | 5 41 | 18 27 | 5 29 | 18 38 | 5 14 | 18 53 | 4 54 | 19 13 | 4 21 | 19 45 |
| 230 | | | 16 15 | 2 51 | 16 31 | 2 34 | 16 50 | 2 12 | 17 17 | 1 42 | 18 00 | 0 51 |
| 19 Fr | 12 3 38 | 12 55 | 5 41 | 18 26 | 5 29 | 18 37 | 5 15 | 18 52 | 4 55 | 19 11 | 4 23 | 19 42 |
| 231 | | | 17 02 | 3 50 | 17 15 | 3 35 | 17 30 | 3 17 | 17 51 | 2 52 | 18 24 | 2 11 |
| 20 Sa | 12 3 24 | 12 36 | 5 41 | 18 25 | 5 30 | 18 36 | 5 16 | 18 50 | 4 57 | 19 09 | 4 25 | 19 40 |
| 232 | | | 17 46 | 4 47 | 17 55 | 4 36 | 18 06 | 4 23 | 18 20 | 4 04 | 18 43 | 3 34 |
| 21 Su | 12 3 09 | 12 16 | 5 42 | 18 24 | 5 31 | 18 35 | 5 17 | 18 49 | 4 58 | 19 07 | 4 28 | 19 37 |
| 233 | 6 47 FM | | 18 27 | 5 42 | 18 32 | 5 35 | 18 38 | 5 27 | 18 46 | 5 15 | 18 58 | 4 56 |
| 22 Mo | 12 2 54 | 11 56 | 5 42 | 18 24 | 5 31 | 18 34 | 5 18 | 18 47 | 5 00 | 19 05 | 4 30 | 19 34 |
| 234 | | | 19 06 | 6 36 | 19 06 | 6 33 | 19 08 | 6 29 | 19 09 | 6 24 | 19 11 | 6 17 |
| 23 Tu | 12 2 39 | 11 36 | 5 42 | 18 23 | 5 32 | 18 33 | 5 19 | 18 46 | 5 01 | 19 03 | 4 33 | 19 31 |
| 235 | | | 19 43 | 7 28 | 19 40 | 7 29 | 19 37 | 7 30 | 19 32 | 7 32 | 19 24 | 7 35 |
| 24 We | 12 2 23 | 11 15 | 5 42 | 18 22 | 5 32 | 18 32 | 5 20 | 18 44 | 5 03 | 19 01 | 4 35 | 19 28 |
| 236 | | | 20 21 | 8 18 | 20 14 | 8 24 | 20 06 | 8 30 | 19 55 | 8 38 | 19 38 | 8 51 |
| 25 Th | 12 2 07 | 10 55 | 5 43 | 18 21 | 5 33 | 18 31 | 5 21 | 18 43 | 5 04 | 18 59 | 4 37 | 19 25 |
| 237 | | | 20 59 | 9 09 | 20 49 | 9 17 | 20 36 | 9 28 | 20 19 | 9 43 | 19 53 | 10 06 |
| 26 Fr | 12 1 50 | 10 34 | 5 43 | 18 21 | 5 33 | 18 30 | 5 22 | 18 41 | 5 06 | 18 57 | 4 40 | 19 22 |
| 238 | | | 21 38 | 9 59 | 21 25 | 10 11 | 21 09 | 10 26 | 20 46 | 10 46 | 20 10 | 11 20 |
| 27 Sa | 12 1 33 | 10 13 | 5 43 | 18 20 | 5 34 | 18 29 | 5 23 | 18 40 | 5 07 | 18 55 | 4 42 | 19 19 |
| 239 | | | 22 20 | 10 49 | 22 04 | 11 04 | 21 44 | 11 22 | 21 17 | 11 48 | 20 33 | 12 30 |
| 28 Su | 12 1 15 | 9 52 | 5 43 | 18 19 | 5 35 | 18 27 | 5 24 | 18 38 | 5 08 | 18 53 | 4 45 | 19 16 |
| 240 | | | 23 04 | 11 39 | 22 46 | 11 56 | 22 24 | 12 17 | 21 53 | 12 47 | 21 01 | 13 37 |
| 29 Mo | 12 0 57 | 9 31 | 5 44 | 18 18 | 5 35 | 18 26 | 5 25 | 18 37 | 5 10 | 18 51 | 4 47 | 19 13 |
| 241 | 6 41 LQ | | 23 50 | 12 29 | 23 32 | 12 47 | 23 08 | 13 10 | 22 35 | 13 43 | 21 39 | 14 38 |
| 30 Tu | 12 0 39 | 9 10 | 5 44 | 18 17 | 5 36 | 18 25 | 5 25 | 18 35 | 5 11 | 18 49 | 4 49 | 19 10 |
| 242 | | | – – | 13 18 | – – | 13 37 | 23 58 | 14 01 | 23 24 | 14 34 | 22 28 | 15 31 |
| 31 We | 12 0 21 | 8 48 | 5 44 | 18 16 | 5 36 | 18 24 | 5 26 | 18 34 | 5 13 | 18 47 | 4 52 | 19 07 |
| 243 | | | 0 40 | 14 07 | 0 21 | 14 25 | – – | 14 48 | – – | 15 20 | 23 29 | 16 13 |

# 9th Month     September 1994     30 days

### Greenwich Mean Time

**NOTE:** Light numbers indicate Sun. **Dark** numbers indicate **Moon**. *Degrees are North Latitude.*

FM = full moon; LQ = last quarter; NM = new moon; FQ = first quarter.

**CAUTION:** Must be converted to local time. For instructions see page 239.

| Day of month / week / year | Sun on Meridian / Moon phase (h m s) | Sun's Declination (° ') | 20° Rise Sun/Moon | 20° Set Sun/Moon | 30° Rise Sun/Moon | 30° Set Sun/Moon | 40° Rise Sun/Moon | 40° Set Sun/Moon | 50° Rise Sun/Moon | 50° Set Sun/Moon | 60° Rise Sun/Moon | 60° Set Sun/Moon |
|---|---|---|---|---|---|---|---|---|---|---|---|---|
| 1 Th 244 | 12 0 02 | 8 27 | 5 44 | 18 15 | 5 37 | 18 23 | 5 27 | 18 32 | 5 14 | 18 45 | 4 54 | 19 04 |
|  |  |  | 1 32 | 14 55 | 1 14 | 15 11 | 0 52 | 15 32 | 0 21 | 16 00 | – – | 16 47 |
| 2 Fr 245 | 11 59 43 | 8 5 | 5 45 | 18 15 | 5 37 | 18 22 | 5 28 | 18 30 | 5 16 | 18 42 | 4 56 | 19 01 |
|  |  |  | 2 26 | 15 41 | 2 11 | 15 55 | 1 51 | 16 12 | 1 24 | 16 35 | 0 40 | 17 13 |
| 3 Sa 246 | 11 59 24 | 7 43 | 5 45 | 18 14 | 5 38 | 18 20 | 5 29 | 18 29 | 5 17 | 18 40 | 4 59 | 18 58 |
|  |  |  | 3 22 | 16 26 | 3 10 | 16 36 | 2 54 | 16 49 | 2 33 | 17 07 | 1 58 | 17 34 |
| 4 Su 247 | 11 59 04 | 7 21 | 5 45 | 18 13 | 5 38 | 18 19 | 5 30 | 18 27 | 5 19 | 18 38 | 5 01 | 18 55 |
|  |  |  | 4 19 | 17 10 | 4 11 | 17 16 | 4 00 | 17 24 | 3 45 | 17 35 | 3 22 | 17 51 |
| 5 Mo 248 | 11 58 44 / 18 33 NM | 6 59 | 5 45 | 18 12 | 5 39 | 18 18 | 5 31 | 18 26 | 5 20 | 18 36 | 5 04 | 18 52 |
|  |  |  | 5 17 | 17 53 | 5 13 | 17 56 | 5 07 | 17 58 | 5 00 | 18 02 | 4 48 | 18 07 |
| 6 Tu 249 | 11 58 24 | 6 36 | 5 45 | 18 11 | 5 39 | 18 17 | 5 32 | 18 24 | 5 22 | 18 34 | 5 06 | 18 49 |
|  |  |  | 6 17 | 18 37 | 6 17 | 18 35 | 6 17 | 18 32 | 6 17 | 18 29 | 6 17 | 18 23 |
| 7 We 250 | 11 58 04 | 6 14 | 5 46 | 18 10 | 5 40 | 18 16 | 5 33 | 18 22 | 5 23 | 18 32 | 5 08 | 18 46 |
|  |  |  | 7 17 | 19 23 | 7 21 | 19 16 | 7 27 | 19 08 | 7 35 | 18 57 | 7 47 | 18 39 |
| 8 Th 251 | 11 57 43 | 5 52 | 5 46 | 18 09 | 5 41 | 18 14 | 5 34 | 18 21 | 5 25 | 18 30 | 5 11 | 18 43 |
|  |  |  | 8 18 | 20 10 | 8 27 | 19 59 | 8 38 | 19 46 | 8 54 | 19 27 | 9 19 | 18 59 |
| 9 Fr 252 | 11 57 23 | 5 29 | 5 46 | 18 08 | 5 41 | 18 13 | 5 35 | 18 19 | 5 26 | 18 27 | 5 13 | 18 40 |
|  |  |  | 9 20 | 21 00 | 9 33 | 20 46 | 9 50 | 20 27 | 10 12 | 20 03 | 10 49 | 19 23 |
| 10 Sa 253 | 11 57 02 | 5 6 | 5 46 | 18 08 | 5 42 | 18 12 | 5 36 | 18 18 | 5 28 | 18 25 | 5 15 | 18 37 |
|  |  |  | 10 23 | 21 53 | 10 39 | 21 36 | 10 59 | 21 14 | 11 28 | 20 44 | 12 16 | 19 55 |
| 11 Su 254 | 11 56 41 | 4 44 | 5 46 | 18 07 | 5 42 | 18 11 | 5 37 | 18 16 | 5 29 | 18 23 | 5 18 | 18 34 |
|  |  |  | 11 24 | 22 49 | 11 43 | 22 30 | 12 06 | 22 07 | 12 38 | 21 34 | 13 34 | 20 38 |
| 12 Mo 255 | 11 56 20 / 11 34 FQ | 4 21 | 5 47 | 18 06 | 5 43 | 18 09 | 5 38 | 18 14 | 5 31 | 18 21 | 5 20 | 18 31 |
|  |  |  | 12 24 | 23 47 | 12 43 | 23 28 | 13 07 | 23 04 | 13 40 | 22 31 | 14 38 | 21 34 |
| 13 Tu 256 | 11 55 59 | 3 58 | 5 47 | 18 05 | 5 43 | 18 08 | 5 39 | 18 13 | 5 32 | 18 19 | 5 22 | 18 28 |
|  |  |  | 13 20 | – – | 13 38 | – – | 14 01 | – – | 14 33 | 23 35 | 15 26 | 22 42 |
| 14 We 257 | 11 55 38 | 3 35 | 5 47 | 18 04 | 5 44 | 18 07 | 5 40 | 18 11 | 5 34 | 18 16 | 5 25 | 18 25 |
|  |  |  | 14 11 | 0 46 | 14 28 | 0 28 | 14 48 | 0 06 | 15 16 | – – | 16 02 | 23 59 |
| 15 Th 258 | 11 55 16 | 3 12 | 5 47 | 18 03 | 5 44 | 18 06 | 5 41 | 18 09 | 5 35 | 18 14 | 5 27 | 18 22 |
|  |  |  | 14 59 | 1 44 | 15 13 | 1 28 | 15 29 | 1 09 | 15 52 | 0 43 | 16 28 | – – |
| 16 Fr 259 | 11 54 55 | 2 49 | 5 48 | 18 02 | 5 45 | 18 04 | 5 42 | 18 08 | 5 37 | 18 12 | 5 29 | 18 19 |
|  |  |  | 15 43 | 2 40 | 15 53 | 2 28 | 16 06 | 2 13 | 16 22 | 1 53 | 16 48 | 1 19 |
| 17 Sa 260 | 11 54 33 | 2 26 | 5 48 | 18 01 | 5 45 | 18 03 | 5 42 | 18 06 | 5 38 | 18 10 | 5 32 | 18 16 |
|  |  |  | 16 24 | 3 35 | 16 31 | 3 27 | 16 38 | 3 16 | 16 49 | 3 02 | 17 04 | 2 40 |
| 18 Su 261 | 11 54 12 | 2 3 | 5 48 | 18 00 | 5 46 | 18 02 | 5 43 | 18 04 | 5 40 | 18 08 | 5 34 | 18 13 |
|  |  |  | 17 03 | 4 28 | 17 06 | 4 24 | 17 09 | 4 18 | 17 12 | 4 11 | 17 18 | 3 59 |
| 19 Mo 262 | 11 53 50 / 20 0 FM | 1 39 | 5 48 | 17 59 | 5 46 | 18 01 | 5 44 | 18 03 | 5 41 | 18 05 | 5 36 | 18 10 |
|  |  |  | 17 41 | 5 20 | 17 40 | 5 20 | 17 38 | 5 19 | 17 35 | 5 18 | 17 32 | 5 17 |
| 20 Tu 263 | 11 53 29 | 1 16 | 5 48 | 17 58 | 5 47 | 17 58 | 5 45 | 18 01 | 5 43 | 18 03 | 5 39 | 18 07 |
|  |  |  | 18 19 | 6 11 | 18 13 | 6 15 | 18 07 | 6 19 | 17 58 | 6 25 | 17 45 | 6 34 |
| 21 We 264 | 11 53 08 | 0 53 | 5 49 | 17 57 | 5 48 | 17 58 | 5 46 | 17 59 | 5 44 | 18 01 | 5 41 | 18 04 |
|  |  |  | 18 57 | 7 01 | 18 48 | 7 09 | 18 37 | 7 18 | 18 22 | 7 30 | 18 00 | 7 49 |
| 22 Th 265 | 11 52 46 | 0 30 | 5 49 | 17 57 | 5 48 | 17 57 | 5 47 | 17 58 | 5 46 | 17 59 | 5 43 | 18 01 |
|  |  |  | 19 36 | 7 51 | 19 24 | 8 02 | 19 09 | 8 15 | 18 48 | 8 34 | 18 17 | 9 03 |
| 23 Fr 266 | 11 52 25 | 0 6 | 5 49 | 17 56 | 5 49 | 17 56 | 5 48 | 17 56 | 5 47 | 17 57 | 5 46 | 17 58 |
|  |  |  | 20 16 | 8 41 | 20 01 | 8 55 | 19 43 | 9 12 | 18 18 | 9 36 | 18 37 | 10 14 |
| 24 Sa 267 | 11 52 04 | – 0 17 | 5 49 | 17 55 | 5 49 | 17 54 | 5 49 | 17 54 | 5 49 | 17 54 | 5 48 | 17 55 |
|  |  |  | 20 59 | 9 31 | 20 42 | 9 48 | 20 21 | 10 08 | 19 52 | 10 36 | 19 04 | 11 23 |
| 25 Su 268 | 11 51 44 | – 0 41 | 5 49 | 17 54 | 5 50 | 17 53 | 5 50 | 17 53 | 5 50 | 17 51 | 5 51 | 17 52 |
|  |  |  | 21 44 | 10 21 | 21 26 | 10 39 | 21 03 | 11 02 | 20 31 | 11 33 | 19 38 | 12 26 |
| 26 Mo 269 | 11 51 23 | – 1 4 | 5 50 | 17 53 | 5 50 | 17 52 | 5 51 | 17 51 | 5 52 | 17 50 | 5 53 | 17 49 |
|  |  |  | 22 32 | 11 10 | 22 13 | 11 29 | 21 50 | 11 53 | 21 17 | 12 25 | 20 22 | 13 21 |
| 27 Tu 270 | 11 51 02 | – 1 27 | 5 50 | 17 52 | 5 50 | 17 51 | 5 51 | 17 50 | 5 52 | 17 49 | 5 55 | 17 46 |
|  |  |  | 23 22 | 11 59 | 23 04 | 12 17 | 22 42 | 12 40 | 22 10 | 13 13 | 21 16 | 14 07 |
| 28 We 271 | 11 50 42 / 00 23 LQ | – 1 51 | 5 50 | 17 51 | 5 51 | 17 50 | 5 53 | 17 48 | 5 55 | 17 46 | 5 58 | 17 42 |
|  |  |  | – – | 12 46 | 23 58 | 13 03 | 23 37 | 13 25 | 23 09 | 13 54 | 22 21 | 14 43 |
| 29 Th 272 | 11 50 22 | – 2 14 | 5 50 | 17 50 | 5 52 | 17 48 | 5 54 | 17 46 | 5 56 | 17 43 | 6 00 | 17 39 |
|  |  |  | 0 14 | 13 32 | – – | 13 47 | – – | 14 05 | – – | 14 31 | 23 35 | 15 12 |
| 30 Fr 273 | 11 50 02 | – 2 37 | 5 51 | 17 49 | 5 53 | 17 47 | 5 55 | 17 45 | 5 58 | 17 41 | 6 02 | 17 36 |
|  |  |  | 1 08 | 14 16 | 0 54 | 14 28 | 0 37 | 14 43 | 0 13 | 15 03 | – – | 15 35 |

## 10th Month  October 1994  31 days

Greenwich Mean Time

**NOTE:** Light numbers indicate Sun. **Dark** numbers indicate **Moon.** *Degrees are North Latitude.*

FM = full moon; LQ = last quarter; NM = new moon; FQ = first quarter.

**CAUTION:** Must be converted to local time. For instructions see page 239.

| Day of month week year | Sun on Meridian Moon phase h m s | Sun's Declina- tion ° ' | 20° Rise Sun/Moon h m | 20° Set Sun/Moon h m | 30° Rise Sun/Moon h m | 30° Set Sun/Moon h m | 40° Rise Sun/Moon h m | 40° Set Sun/Moon h m | 50° Rise Sun/Moon h m | 50° Set Sun/Moon h m | 60° Rise Sun/Moon h m | 60° Set Sun/Moon h m |
|---|---|---|---|---|---|---|---|---|---|---|---|---|
| 1 Sa | 11 49 43 | − 3 1 | 5 51 | 17 48 | 5 53 | 17 46 | 5 56 | 17 43 | 5 59 | 17 39 | 6 05 | 17 33 |
| 274 | | | 2 04 | 15 00 | 1 53 | 15 08 | 1 40 | 15 19 | 1 22 | 15 33 | 0 54 | 15 54 |
| 2 Su | 11 49 24 | − 3 24 | 5 51 | 17 47 | 5 54 | 17 45 | 5 57 | 17 41 | 6 01 | 17 37 | 6 07 | 17 30 |
| 275 | | | 3 00 | 15 43 | 2 54 | 15 48 | 2 46 | 15 53 | 2 35 | 16 00 | 2 17 | 16 11 |
| 3 Mo | 11 49 05 | − 3 47 | 5 51 | 17 47 | 5 54 | 17 43 | 5 58 | 17 40 | 6 03 | 17 35 | 6 09 | 17 27 |
| 276 | | | 3 59 | 16 27 | 3 57 | 16 27 | 3 54 | 16 27 | 3 50 | 16 27 | 3 45 | 16 27 |
| 4 Tu | 11 48 47 | − 4 10 | 5 52 | 17 46 | 5 55 | 17 42 | 5 59 | 17 38 | 6 04 | 17 33 | 6 12 | 17 24 |
| 277 | | | 4 59 | 17 12 | 5 01 | 17 08 | 5 04 | 17 02 | 5 08 | 16 55 | 5 15 | 16 43 |
| 5 We | 11 48 29 | − 4 34 | 5 52 | 17 45 | 5 55 | 17 41 | 6 00 | 17 36 | 6 06 | 17 30 | 6 14 | 17 21 |
| 278 | 3 55 NM | | 6 01 | 18 00 | 6 08 | 17 51 | 6 16 | 17 40 | 6 28 | 17 25 | 6 47 | 17 02 |
| 6 Th | 11 48 11 | − 4 57 | 5 52 | 17 44 | 5 56 | 17 40 | 6 01 | 17 35 | 6 07 | 17 28 | 6 17 | 17 18 |
| 279 | | | 7 04 | 18 50 | 7 16 | 18 37 | 7 30 | 18 21 | 7 49 | 17 59 | 8 21 | 17 25 |
| 7 Fr | 11 47 53 | − 5 20 | 5 52 | 17 43 | 5 57 | 17 39 | 6 02 | 17 33 | 6 09 | 17 26 | 6 19 | 17 15 |
| 280 | | | 8 09 | 19 44 | 8 24 | 19 28 | 8 43 | 19 08 | 9 09 | 18 40 | 9 52 | 17 54 |
| 8 Sa | 11 47 36 | − 5 43 | 5 53 | 17 42 | 5 57 | 17 38 | 6 03 | 17 32 | 6 10 | 17 24 | 6 22 | 17 12 |
| 281 | | | 9 13 | 20 41 | 9 31 | 20 23 | 9 53 | 20 00 | 10 24 | 19 28 | 11 16 | 18 34 |
| 9 Su | 11 47 20 | − 6 5 | 5 53 | 17 42 | 5 58 | 17 36 | 6 04 | 17 30 | 6 12 | 17 22 | 6 24 | 17 10 |
| 282 | | | 10 15 | 21 40 | 10 34 | 21 21 | 10 58 | 20 58 | 11 31 | 20 24 | 12 28 | 19 28 |
| 10 Mo | 11 47 04 | − 6 28 | 5 53 | 17 41 | 5 58 | 17 35 | 6 05 | 17 29 | 6 13 | 17 20 | 6 26 | 17 07 |
| 283 | | | 11 14 | 22 40 | 11 33 | 22 22 | 11 56 | 21 59 | 12 28 | 21 27 | 13 23 | 20 34 |
| 11 Tu | 11 46 48 | − 6 51 | 5 53 | 17 40 | 5 59 | 17 34 | 6 06 | 17 27 | 6 15 | 17 18 | 6 29 | 17 04 |
| 284 | 19 17 FQ | | 12 08 | 23 39 | 12 25 | 23 23 | 12 46 | 23 03 | 13 15 | 22 35 | 14 03 | 21 49 |
| 12 We | 11 46 33 | − 7 14 | 5 54 | 17 39 | 6 00 | 17 33 | 6 07 | 17 26 | 6 17 | 17 16 | 6 31 | 17 01 |
| 285 | | | 12 57 | − − | 13 12 | − − | 13 29 | − − | 13 54 | 23 45 | 14 32 | 23 09 |
| 13 Th | 11 46 18 | − 7 36 | 5 54 | 17 38 | 6 00 | 17 32 | 6 08 | 17 24 | 6 18 | 17 14 | 6 34 | 16 58 |
| 286 | | | 13 42 | 0 36 | 13 53 | 0 23 | 14 07 | 0 07 | 14 25 | − − | 14 54 | − − |
| 14 Fr | 11 46 04 | − 7 59 | 5 54 | 17 37 | 6 01 | 17 31 | 6 09 | 17 22 | 6 20 | 17 12 | 6 36 | 16 55 |
| 287 | | | 14 24 | 1 31 | 14 31 | 1 22 | 14 40 | 1 10 | 14 52 | 0 54 | 15 11 | 0 29 |
| 15 Sa | 11 45 50 | − 8 21 | 5 55 | 17 37 | 6 02 | 17 30 | 6 10 | 17 21 | 6 21 | 17 10 | 6 39 | 16 52 |
| 288 | | | 15 03 | 2 24 | 15 07 | 2 19 | 15 11 | 2 12 | 15 17 | 2 02 | 15 26 | 1 48 |
| 16 Su | 11 45 37 | − 8 43 | 5 55 | 17 36 | 6 02 | 17 29 | 6 11 | 17 20 | 6 23 | 17 07 | 6 41 | 16 49 |
| 289 | | | 15 41 | 3 16 | 15 41 | 3 14 | 15 40 | 3 12 | 15 40 | 3 09 | 15 39 | 3 05 |
| 17 Mo | 11 45 25 | − 9 5 | 5 55 | 17 35 | 6 03 | 17 27 | 6 12 | 17 18 | 6 25 | 17 05 | 6 44 | 16 46 |
| 290 | | | 16 18 | 4 06 | 16 14 | 4 09 | 16 09 | 4 11 | 16 03 | 4 15 | 15 53 | 4 21 |
| 18 Tu | 11 45 13 | − 9 27 | 5 56 | 17 34 | 6 04 | 17 26 | 6 13 | 17 17 | 6 26 | 17 03 | 6 46 | 16 43 |
| 291 | | | 16 56 | 4 56 | 16 48 | 5 02 | 16 39 | 5 10 | 16 26 | 5 20 | 16 07 | 5 35 |
| 19 We | 11 45 01 | − 9 49 | 5 56 | 17 34 | 6 04 | 17 25 | 6 14 | 17 15 | 6 28 | 17 01 | 6 49 | 16 40 |
| 292 | 12 18 FM | | 17 34 | 5 46 | 17 23 | 5 56 | 17 10 | 6 07 | 16 51 | 6 23 | 16 23 | 6 49 |
| 20 Th | 11 44 50 | − 10 11 | 5 56 | 17 33 | 6 05 | 17 24 | 6 15 | 17 14 | 6 29 | 16 59 | 6 51 | 16 38 |
| 293 | | | 18 14 | 6 36 | 18 00 | 6 49 | 17 43 | 7 03 | 17 20 | 7 26 | 16 42 | 8 01 |
| 21 Fr | 11 44 40 | − 10 32 | 5 57 | 17 32 | 6 06 | 17 23 | 6 16 | 17 12 | 6 31 | 16 58 | 6 54 | 16 35 |
| 294 | | | 18 56 | 7 26 | 18 40 | 7 41 | 18 20 | 8 00 | 17 52 | 8 27 | 17 07 | 9 11 |
| 22 Sa | 11 44 31 | − 10 53 | 5 57 | 17 32 | 6 06 | 17 22 | 6 18 | 17 11 | 6 33 | 16 56 | 6 56 | 16 32 |
| 295 | | | 19 41 | 8 16 | 19 23 | 8 33 | 19 01 | 8 55 | 18 30 | 9 25 | 17 38 | 10 16 |
| 23 Su | 11 44 22 | − 11 15 | 5 58 | 17 31 | 6 07 | 17 21 | 6 19 | 17 10 | 6 34 | 16 54 | 6 59 | 16 29 |
| 296 | | | 20 27 | 9 05 | 20 09 | 9 24 | 19 46 | 9 47 | 19 13 | 10 19 | 18 18 | 11 13 |
| 24 Mo | 11 44 14 | − 11 36 | 5 58 | 17 30 | 6 08 | 17 20 | 6 20 | 17 08 | 6 36 | 16 52 | 7 01 | 16 26 |
| 297 | | | 21 16 | 9 54 | 20 58 | 10 12 | 20 35 | 10 35 | 20 03 | 11 08 | 19 09 | 12 02 |
| 25 Tu | 11 44 07 | − 11 56 | 5 58 | 17 30 | 6 08 | 17 19 | 6 21 | 17 07 | 6 38 | 16 50 | 7 04 | 16 24 |
| 298 | | | 22 07 | 10 40 | 21 50 | 10 58 | 21 28 | 11 20 | 20 58 | 11 51 | 20 09 | 12 42 |
| 26 We | 11 44 00 | − 12 17 | 5 59 | 17 29 | 6 09 | 17 18 | 6 22 | 17 06 | 6 39 | 16 48 | 7 06 | 16 21 |
| 299 | | | 22 59 | 11 26 | 22 44 | 11 42 | 22 25 | 12 02 | 21 59 | 12 29 | 21 17 | 13 13 |
| 27 Th | 11 43 54 | − 12 38 | 5 59 | 17 28 | 6 10 | 17 17 | 6 23 | 17 04 | 6 41 | 16 46 | 7 09 | 16 18 |
| 300 | | | 23 52 | 12 10 | 23 40 | 12 23 | 23 25 | 12 39 | 23 05 | 13 02 | 22 32 | 13 37 |
| 28 Fr | 11 43 49 | − 12 58 | 6 00 | 17 28 | 6 11 | 17 17 | 6 24 | 17 03 | 6 43 | 16 44 | 7 11 | 16 15 |
| 301 | | | − − | 12 52 | − − | 13 02 | − − | 13 15 | − − | 13 31 | 23 51 | 13 57 |
| 29 Sa | 11 43 45 | − 13 18 | 6 00 | 17 27 | 6 11 | 17 16 | 6 25 | 17 02 | 6 44 | 16 43 | 7 14 | 16 13 |
| 302 | | | 0 46 | 13 34 | 0 38 | 13 41 | 0 27 | 13 48 | 0 13 | 13 59 | − − | 14 14 |
| 30 Su | 11 43 41 | − 13 38 | 6 00 | 17 27 | 6 12 | 17 15 | 6 26 | 17 00 | 6 46 | 16 41 | 7 16 | 16 10 |
| 303 | | | 1 42 | 14 17 | 1 38 | 14 19 | 1 32 | 14 21 | 1 25 | 14 25 | 1 14 | 14 30 |
| 31 Mo | 11 43 38 | − 13 58 | 6 01 | 17 26 | 6 13 | 17 14 | 6 28 | 16 59 | 6 47 | 16 39 | 7 19 | 16 07 |
| 304 | | | 2 39 | 15 00 | 2 40 | 14 58 | 2 40 | 14 55 | 2 40 | 14 52 | 2 40 | 14 46 |

# 11th Month     November 1994     30 days

Greenwich Mean Time

**NOTE:** Light numbers indicate Sun. **Dark** numbers indicate **Moon.** *Degrees are North Latitude.*

FM = full moon; LQ = last quarter; NM = new moon; FQ = first quarter.

**CAUTION:** Must be converted to local time. For instructions see page 239.

| Day of month / week / year | Sun on Meridian Moon phase h m s | Sun's Declination ° ' | 20° Rise Sun h m | 20° Set Sun h m | 30° Rise Sun h m | 30° Set Sun h m | 40° Rise Sun h m | 40° Set Sun h m | 50° Rise Sun h m | 50° Set Sun h m | 60° Rise Sun h m | 60° Set Sun h m |
|---|---|---|---|---|---|---|---|---|---|---|---|---|
| 1 Tu / 305 | 11 43 37 | −14 17 | 6 01 | 17 26 | 6 14 | 17 13 | 6 29 | 16 58 | 6 49 | 16 37 | 7 21 | 16 05 |
| *Moon* | | | 3 39 | 15 46 | 3 44 | 15 39 | 3 50 | 15 31 | 3 57 | 15 20 | 4 10 | 15 03 |
| 2 We / 306 | 11 43 35 | −14 36 | 6 02 | 17 25 | 6 14 | 17 12 | 6 30 | 16 57 | 6 51 | 16 36 | 7 24 | 16 02 |
| *Moon* | | | 4 42 | 16 35 | 4 51 | 16 24 | 5 02 | 16 10 | 5 18 | 15 52 | 5 42 | 15 23 |
| 3 Th / 307 | 11 43 35  13 35 NM | −14 55 | 6 02 | 17 25 | 6 15 | 17 12 | 6 31 | 16 56 | 6 52 | 16 34 | 7 27 | 16 00 |
| *Moon* | | | 5 46 | 17 28 | 6 00 | 17 13 | 6 16 | 16 55 | 6 39 | 16 30 | 7 16 | 15 50 |
| 4 Fr / 308 | 11 43 36 | −15 14 | 6 03 | 17 24 | 6 16 | 17 11 | 6 32 | 16 55 | 6 54 | 16 32 | 7 29 | 15 57 |
| *Moon* | | | 6 53 | 18 25 | 7 09 | 18 07 | 7 30 | 17 45 | 7 59 | 17 15 | 8 47 | 16 25 |
| 5 Sa / 309 | 11 43 37 | −15 32 | 6 03 | 17 24 | 6 17 | 17 10 | 6 33 | 16 53 | 6 56 | 16 31 | 7 32 | 15 55 |
| *Moon* | | | 7 58 | 19 25 | 8 17 | 19 06 | 8 40 | 18 43 | 9 13 | 18 10 | 10 08 | 17 14 |
| 6 Su / 310 | 11 43 39 | −15 51 | 6 04 | 17 23 | 6 18 | 17 09 | 6 34 | 16 52 | 6 57 | 16 29 | 7 34 | 15 52 |
| *Moon* | | | 9 01 | 20 27 | 9 20 | 20 09 | 9 44 | 19 45 | 10 17 | 19 13 | 11 13 | 18 17 |
| 7 Mo / 311 | 11 43 42 | −16 9 | 6 04 | 17 23 | 6 18 | 17 09 | 6 36 | 16 51 | 6 59 | 16 28 | 7 37 | 15 50 |
| *Moon* | | | 9 59 | 21 29 | 10 17 | 21 12 | 10 39 | 20 51 | 11 10 | 20 21 | 12 01 | 19 32 |
| 8 Tu / 312 | 11 43 46 | −16 26 | 6 05 | 17 23 | 6 19 | 17 08 | 6 37 | 16 50 | 7 01 | 16 26 | 7 39 | 15 47 |
| *Moon* | | | 10 52 | 22 29 | 11 08 | 22 15 | 11 27 | 21 57 | 11 53 | 21 33 | 12 35 | 20 53 |
| 9 We / 313 | 11 43 50 | −16 44 | 6 05 | 17 22 | 6 20 | 17 07 | 6 38 | 16 49 | 7 02 | 16 25 | 7 42 | 15 45 |
| *Moon* | | | 11 40 | 23 26 | 11 52 | 23 15 | 12 07 | 23 02 | 12 27 | 22 44 | 12 59 | 22 15 |
| 10 Th / 314 | 11 43 56  6 14 FQ | −17 1 | 6 06 | 17 22 | 6 21 | 17 07 | 6 39 | 16 48 | 7 04 | 16 23 | 7 45 | 15 42 |
| *Moon* | | | 12 23 | – – | 12 32 | – – | 12 42 | – – | 12 56 | 23 54 | 13 18 | 23 36 |
| 11 Fr / 315 | 11 44 02 | −17 18 | 6 06 | 17 21 | 6 22 | 17 06 | 6 40 | 16 47 | 7 06 | 16 22 | 7 47 | 15 40 |
| *Moon* | | | 13 04 | 0 20 | 13 08 | 0 13 | 13 14 | 0 05 | 13 22 | – – | 13 34 | – – |
| 12 Sa / 316 | 11 44 09 | −17 34 | 6 07 | 17 21 | 6 22 | 17 06 | 6 41 | 16 47 | 7 07 | 16 20 | 7 50 | 15 38 |
| *Moon* | | | 13 42 | 1 12 | 13 43 | 1 10 | 13 44 | 1 06 | 13 45 | 1 01 | 13 47 | 0 54 |
| 13 Su / 317 | 11 44 17 | −17 50 | 6 08 | 17 21 | 6 23 | 17 05 | 6 42 | 16 46 | 7 09 | 16 19 | 7 52 | 15 36 |
| *Moon* | | | 14 19 | 2 03 | 14 16 | 2 04 | 14 12 | 2 05 | 14 08 | 2 07 | 14 01 | 2 10 |
| 14 Mo / 318 | 11 44 26 | −18 6 | 6 08 | 17 21 | 6 24 | 17 05 | 6 44 | 16 45 | 7 11 | 16 18 | 7 55 | 15 33 |
| *Moon* | | | 14 56 | 2 53 | 14 49 | 2 58 | 14 41 | 3 04 | 14 31 | 3 12 | 14 15 | 3 24 |
| 15 Tu / 319 | 11 44 35 | −18 22 | 6 09 | 17 20 | 6 25 | 17 04 | 6 45 | 16 44 | 7 12 | 16 16 | 7 57 | 15 31 |
| *Moon* | | | 15 34 | 3 42 | 15 24 | 3 51 | 15 12 | 4 01 | 14 55 | 4 15 | 14 30 | 4 38 |
| 16 We / 320 | 11 44 46 | −18 37 | 6 09 | 17 20 | 6 26 | 17 04 | 6 46 | 16 43 | 7 14 | 16 15 | 8 00 | 15 29 |
| *Moon* | | | 16 13 | 4 32 | 16 00 | 4 44 | 15 44 | 4 58 | 15 22 | 5 18 | 14 48 | 5 50 |
| 17 Th / 321 | 11 44 57 | −18 52 | 6 10 | 17 20 | 6 26 | 17 03 | 6 47 | 16 42 | 7 16 | 16 14 | 8 02 | 15 27 |
| *Moon* | | | 16 54 | 5 22 | 16 39 | 5 36 | 16 20 | 5 54 | 15 53 | 6 20 | 15 10 | 7 00 |
| 18 Fr / 322 | 11 45 09  6 57 FM | −19 7 | 6 10 | 17 20 | 6 27 | 17 03 | 6 48 | 16 42 | 7 17 | 16 13 | 8 05 | 15 25 |
| *Moon* | | | 17 38 | 6 12 | 17 21 | 6 28 | 16 59 | 6 49 | 16 29 | 7 19 | 15 39 | 8 07 |
| 19 Sa / 323 | 11 45 22 | −19 21 | 6 11 | 17 20 | 6 28 | 17 02 | 6 49 | 16 41 | 7 17 | 16 12 | 8 07 | 15 23 |
| *Moon* | | | 18 24 | 7 01 | 18 06 | 7 20 | 17 43 | 7 42 | 17 10 | 8 14 | 16 16 | 9 08 |
| 20 Su / 324 | 11 45 36 | −19 35 | 6 12 | 17 19 | 6 29 | 17 02 | 6 50 | 16 40 | 7 20 | 16 10 | 8 10 | 15 21 |
| *Moon* | | | 19 12 | 7 50 | 18 54 | 8 09 | 18 31 | 8 32 | 17 58 | 9 05 | 17 03 | 10 00 |
| 21 Mo / 325 | 11 45 50 | −19 49 | 6 12 | 17 19 | 6 30 | 17 02 | 6 52 | 16 40 | 7 22 | 16 09 | 8 12 | 15 19 |
| *Moon* | | | 20 02 | 8 38 | 19 45 | 8 56 | 19 23 | 9 18 | 18 52 | 9 50 | 18 00 | 10 42 |
| 22 Tu / 326 | 11 46 06 | −20 2 | 6 13 | 17 19 | 6 31 | 17 01 | 6 53 | 16 39 | 7 23 | 16 08 | 8 14 | 15 17 |
| *Moon* | | | 20 54 | 9 24 | 20 38 | 9 40 | 20 18 | 10 01 | 19 51 | 10 29 | 19 06 | 11 16 |
| 23 We / 327 | 11 46 22 | −20 15 | 6 13 | 17 19 | 6 31 | 17 01 | 6 54 | 16 39 | 7 25 | 16 07 | 8 17 | 15 15 |
| *Moon* | | | 21 46 | 10 07 | 21 32 | 10 22 | 21 16 | 10 39 | 20 54 | 11 04 | 20 18 | 11 42 |
| 24 Th / 328 | 11 46 39 | −20 27 | 6 14 | 17 19 | 6 32 | 17 01 | 6 55 | 16 38 | 7 26 | 16 06 | 8 19 | 15 14 |
| *Moon* | | | 22 38 | 10 50 | 22 28 | 11 01 | 22 16 | 11 15 | 22 00 | 11 34 | 21 34 | 12 03 |
| 25 Fr / 329 | 11 46 57 | −20 39 | 6 15 | 17 19 | 6 33 | 17 01 | 6 56 | 16 38 | 7 28 | 16 06 | 8 21 | 15 12 |
| *Moon* | | | 23 32 | 11 31 | 23 26 | 11 39 | 23 18 | 11 48 | 23 08 | 12 01 | 22 53 | 12 20 |
| 26 Sa / 330 | 11 47 15  7 4 LQ | −20 51 | 6 15 | 17 19 | 6 34 | 17 00 | 6 57 | 16 37 | 7 29 | 16 05 | 8 24 | 15 10 |
| *Moon* | | | – – | 12 11 | – – | 12 15 | – – | 12 20 | – – | 12 26 | – – | 12 36 |
| 27 Su / 331 | 11 47 35 | −21 2 | 6 16 | 17 19 | 6 35 | 17 00 | 6 58 | 16 37 | 7 31 | 16 04 | 8 26 | 15 09 |
| *Moon* | | | 0 26 | 12 53 | 0 24 | 12 52 | 0 22 | 12 52 | 0 19 | 12 52 | 0 14 | 12 51 |
| 28 Mo / 332 | 11 47 55 | −21 13 | 6 17 | 17 19 | 6 36 | 17 00 | 6 59 | 16 36 | 7 32 | 16 03 | 8 28 | 15 07 |
| *Moon* | | | 1 23 | 13 35 | 1 25 | 13 31 | 1 28 | 13 25 | 1 32 | 13 18 | 1 39 | 13 07 |
| 29 Tu / 333 | 11 48 15 | −21 24 | 6 17 | 17 19 | 6 36 | 17 00 | 7 00 | 16 36 | 7 34 | 16 03 | 8 30 | 15 06 |
| *Moon* | | | 2 22 | 14 21 | 2 29 | 14 12 | 2 37 | 14 01 | 2 49 | 13 47 | 3 07 | 13 24 |
| 30 We / 334 | 11 48 37 | −21 34 | 6 18 | 17 19 | 6 37 | 17 00 | 7 01 | 16 36 | 7 35 | 16 02 | 8 32 | 15 04 |
| *Moon* | | | 3 23 | 15 10 | 3 35 | 14 58 | 3 48 | 14 42 | 4 07 | 14 20 | 4 38 | 13 47 |

# 12th Month     December 1994     31 days

Greenwich Mean Time

**NOTE:** Light numbers indicate Sun. **Dark** numbers indicate **Moon**. *Degrees are North Latitude.*

FM = full moon; LQ = last quarter; NM = new moon; FQ = first quarter.

**CAUTION:** Must be converted to local time. For instructions see page 239.

| Day of month week year | Sun on Meridian Moon phase h m s | Sun's Declination ° ' | 20° Rise Sun/Moon | 20° Set Sun/Moon | 30° Rise Sun/Moon | 30° Set Sun/Moon | 40° Rise Sun/Moon | 40° Set Sun/Moon | 50° Rise Sun/Moon | 50° Set Sun/Moon | 60° Rise Sun/Moon | 60° Set Sun/Moon |
|---|---|---|---|---|---|---|---|---|---|---|---|---|
| 1 Th | 11 48 59 | −21 44 | 6 18 | 17 19 | 6 38 | 17 00 | 7 02 | 16 35 | 7 36 | 16 01 | 8 34 | 15 03 |
| 335 | | | 4 28 | 16 04 | 4 43 | 15 48 | 5 01 | 15 28 | 5 27 | 15 01 | 6 09 | 14 16 |
| 2 Fr | 11 49 22 | −21 53 | 6 19 | 17 20 | 6 39 | 17 00 | 7 03 | 16 35 | 7 38 | 16 01 | 8 36 | 15 02 |
| 336 | 23 54 NM | | 5 34 | 17 03 | 5 51 | 16 45 | 6 13 | 16 22 | 6 44 | 15 50 | 7 36 | 14 57 |
| 3 Sa | 11 49 45 | −22 2 | 6 20 | 17 20 | 6 40 | 17 00 | 7 04 | 16 35 | 7 39 | 16 00 | 8 38 | 15 01 |
| 337 | | | 6 39 | 18 06 | 6 58 | 17 47 | 7 22 | 17 23 | 7 55 | 16 49 | 8 52 | 15 53 |
| 4 Su | 11 50 09 | −22 10 | 6 20 | 17 20 | 6 40 | 17 00 | 7 05 | 16 35 | 7 40 | 16 00 | 8 40 | 15 00 |
| 338 | | | 7 42 | 19 10 | 8 00 | 18 52 | 8 23 | 18 29 | 8 56 | 17 57 | 9 50 | 17 04 |
| 5 Mo | 11 50 34 | −22 18 | 6 21 | 17 20 | 6 41 | 17 00 | 7 06 | 16 35 | 7 41 | 15 59 | 8 42 | 14 59 |
| 339 | | | 8 39 | 20 13 | 8 56 | 19 57 | 9 17 | 19 38 | 9 45 | 19 11 | 10 32 | 18 26 |
| 6 Tu | 11 50 59 | −22 26 | 6 22 | 17 20 | 6 42 | 17 00 | 7 07 | 16 35 | 7 43 | 15 59 | 8 44 | 14 58 |
| 340 | | | 9 31 | 21 13 | 9 45 | 21 01 | 10 02 | 20 46 | 10 25 | 20 25 | 11 02 | 19 51 |
| 7 We | 11 51 25 | −22 33 | 6 22 | 17 20 | 6 43 | 17 00 | 7 08 | 16 35 | 7 44 | 15 59 | 8 46 | 14 57 |
| 341 | | | 10 18 | 22 11 | 10 28 | 22 03 | 10 41 | 21 52 | 10 58 | 21 38 | 11 24 | 21 16 |
| 8 Th | 11 51 51 | −22 40 | 6 23 | 17 21 | 6 43 | 17 00 | 7 09 | 16 35 | 7 45 | 15 59 | 8 47 | 14 56 |
| 342 | | | 11 01 | 23 06 | 11 07 | 23 01 | 11 15 | 22 56 | 11 25 | 22 49 | 11 41 | 22 37 |
| 9 Fr | 11 52 17 | −22 46 | 6 23 | 17 21 | 6 44 | 17 00 | 7 10 | 16 35 | 7 46 | 15 58 | 8 49 | 14 55 |
| 343 | 21 6 FQ | | 11 41 | 23 58 | 11 43 | 23 58 | 11 46 | 23 57 | 11 50 | 23 56 | 11 56 | 23 55 |
| 10 Sa | 11 52 44 | −22 52 | 6 24 | 17 21 | 6 45 | 17 01 | 7 11 | 16 35 | 7 47 | 15 58 | 8 50 | 14 55 |
| 344 | | | 12 19 | – – | 12 17 | – – | 12 16 | – – | 12 13 | – – | 12 09 | – – |
| 11 Su | 11 53 12 | −22 57 | 6 25 | 17 22 | 6 45 | 17 01 | 7 11 | 16 35 | 7 48 | 15 58 | 8 52 | 14 54 |
| 345 | | | 12 56 | 0 49 | 12 51 | 0 52 | 12 45 | 0 57 | 12 36 | 1 02 | 12 23 | 1 11 |
| 12 Mo | 11 53 40 | −23 2 | 6 25 | 17 22 | 6 46 | 17 01 | 7 12 | 16 35 | 7 49 | 15 58 | 8 53 | 14 54 |
| 346 | | | 13 34 | 1 38 | 13 25 | 1 46 | 13 14 | 1 55 | 13 00 | 2 07 | 12 38 | 2 25 |
| 13 Tu | 11 54 08 | −23 7 | 6 26 | 17 22 | 6 47 | 17 01 | 7 13 | 16 35 | 7 50 | 15 58 | 8 55 | 14 54 |
| 347 | | | 14 12 | 2 28 | 14 01 | 2 39 | 13 46 | 2 52 | 13 26 | 3 10 | 12 55 | 3 38 |
| 14 We | 11 54 36 | −23 11 | 6 26 | 17 23 | 6 47 | 17 02 | 7 14 | 16 35 | 7 51 | 15 58 | 8 56 | 14 53 |
| 348 | | | 14 53 | 3 18 | 14 38 | 3 31 | 14 20 | 3 48 | 13 55 | 4 11 | 13 15 | 4 49 |
| 15 Th | 11 55 05 | −23 14 | 6 27 | 17 23 | 6 48 | 17 02 | 7 14 | 16 36 | 7 52 | 15 58 | 8 57 | 14 53 |
| 349 | | | 15 36 | 4 07 | 15 19 | 4 23 | 14 58 | 4 43 | 14 29 | 5 11 | 13 41 | 5 57 |
| 16 Fr | 11 55 34 | −23 18 | 6 28 | 17 23 | 6 49 | 17 02 | 7 15 | 16 36 | 7 53 | 15 59 | 8 58 | 14 53 |
| 350 | | | 16 21 | 4 57 | 16 03 | 5 15 | 15 40 | 5 37 | 15 08 | 6 08 | 14 15 | 7 01 |
| 17 Sa | 11 56 03 | −23 20 | 6 28 | 17 24 | 6 49 | 17 03 | 7 16 | 16 36 | 7 53 | 15 59 | 8 59 | 14 53 |
| 351 | | | 17 09 | 5 47 | 16 50 | 6 05 | 16 27 | 6 29 | 15 54 | 7 01 | 14 59 | 7 56 |
| 18 Su | 11 56 32 | −23 22 | 6 29 | 17 24 | 6 50 | 17 03 | 7 16 | 16 37 | 7 54 | 15 59 | 9 00 | 14 53 |
| 352 | 2 17 FM | | 17 59 | 6 35 | 17 40 | 6 53 | 17 18 | 7 16 | 16 46 | 7 49 | 15 53 | 8 43 |
| 19 Mo | 11 57 02 | −23 24 | 6 29 | 17 25 | 6 50 | 17 04 | 7 17 | 16 37 | 7 55 | 15 59 | 9 01 | 14 53 |
| 353 | | | 18 50 | 7 22 | 18 33 | 7 39 | 18 13 | 8 01 | 17 44 | 8 30 | 16 56 | 9 19 |
| 20 Tu | 11 57 31 | −23 25 | 6 30 | 17 25 | 6 51 | 17 04 | 7 18 | 16 37 | 7 55 | 16 00 | 9 01 | 14 54 |
| 354 | | | 19 42 | 8 07 | 19 28 | 8 22 | 19 10 | 8 41 | 18 46 | 9 07 | 18 07 | 9 48 |
| 21 We | 11 58 01 | −23 26 | 6 30 | 17 26 | 6 52 | 17 04 | 7 18 | 16 38 | 7 56 | 16 00 | 9 02 | 14 54 |
| 355 | | | 20 34 | 8 50 | 20 23 | 9 02 | 20 10 | 9 17 | 19 51 | 9 38 | 19 21 | 10 11 |
| 22 Th | 11 58 31 | −23 26 | 6 31 | 17 26 | 6 52 | 17 05 | 7 19 | 16 38 | 7 56 | 16 01 | 9 02 | 14 55 |
| 356 | | | 21 27 | 9 31 | 21 20 | 9 40 | 21 11 | 9 51 | 20 58 | 10 06 | 20 39 | 10 29 |
| 23 Fr | 11 59 01 | −23 26 | 6 31 | 17 27 | 6 53 | 17 06 | 7 19 | 16 39 | 7 57 | 16 01 | 9 03 | 14 55 |
| 357 | | | 22 21 | 10 11 | 22 17 | 10 17 | 22 13 | 10 23 | 22 07 | 10 32 | 21 59 | 10 45 |
| 24 Sa | 11 59 31 | −23 25 | 6 32 | 17 27 | 6 53 | 17 06 | 7 20 | 16 39 | 7 57 | 16 02 | 9 03 | 14 56 |
| 358 | | | 23 15 | 10 52 | 23 16 | 10 53 | 23 17 | 10 54 | 23 18 | 10 57 | 23 20 | 11 00 |
| 25 Su | 12 0 00 | −23 24 | 6 32 | 17 28 | 6 53 | 17 07 | 7 20 | 16 40 | 7 58 | 16 03 | 9 03 | 14 57 |
| 359 | 19 6 LQ | | – – | 11 32 | – – | 11 30 | – – | 11 26 | – – | 11 22 | – – | 11 15 |
| 26 Mo | 12 0 30 | −23 23 | 6 33 | 17 28 | 6 54 | 17 07 | 7 20 | 16 41 | 7 58 | 16 03 | 9 04 | 14 58 |
| 360 | | | 0 11 | 12 15 | 0 16 | 12 08 | 0 22 | 12 00 | 0 31 | 11 48 | 0 44 | 11 31 |
| 27 Tu | 12 0 60 | −23 21 | 6 33 | 17 29 | 6 54 | 17 08 | 7 21 | 16 41 | 7 58 | 16 04 | 9 04 | 14 59 |
| 361 | | | 1 09 | 13 01 | 1 18 | 12 50 | 1 30 | 12 36 | 1 45 | 12 18 | 2 10 | 11 50 |
| 28 We | 12 1 29 | −23 18 | 6 34 | 17 30 | 6 55 | 17 08 | 7 21 | 16 42 | 7 58 | 16 05 | 9 04 | 15 00 |
| 362 | | | 2 10 | 13 50 | 2 23 | 13 36 | 2 39 | 13 18 | 3 02 | 12 53 | 3 38 | 12 14 |
| 29 Th | 12 1 59 | −23 15 | 6 34 | 17 30 | 6 55 | 17 09 | 7 21 | 16 43 | 7 58 | 16 06 | 9 03 | 15 01 |
| 363 | | | 3 13 | 14 45 | 3 29 | 14 27 | 3 49 | 14 06 | 4 18 | 13 36 | 5 05 | 12 47 |
| 30 Fr | 12 2 28 | −23 12 | 6 34 | 17 31 | 6 55 | 17 10 | 7 22 | 16 44 | 7 59 | 16 07 | 9 03 | 15 02 |
| 364 | | | 4 17 | 15 44 | 4 35 | 15 25 | 4 58 | 15 02 | 5 31 | 14 29 | 6 25 | 13 33 |
| 31 Sa | 12 2 57 | −23 8 | 6 35 | 17 31 | 6 56 | 17 10 | 7 22 | 16 44 | 7 59 | 16 07 | 9 03 | 15 03 |
| 365 | | | 5 20 | 16 46 | 5 39 | 16 28 | 6 03 | 16 04 | 6 36 | 15 31 | 7 32 | 14 35 |

## Latitude, Longitude, and Altitude of U.S. and Canadian Cities

Source for U.S. geographic positions: National Oceanic and Atmospheric Administration. U.S. Dept. of Commerce.

Source for Canadian cities: Geodetic Survey of Canada. Dept. of Energy, Mines, and Resources.

Source for altitudes: U.S. Geological Survey and World Almanac research.

\* Approx. altitude at downtown business area U.S.; in Canada at city hall except where (a),
in which case altitude is at tower of major airport.

| City | Lat. N ° | ′ | ″ | Long. W ° | ′ | ″ | Alt.* feet |
|---|---|---|---|---|---|---|---|
| Abilene, Tex. | 32 | 27 | 05 | 99 | 43 | 51 | 1,710 |
| Akron, Oh. | 41 | 05 | 00 | 81 | 30 | 44 | 874 |
| Albany, N.Y. | 42 | 39 | 01 | 73 | 45 | 01 | 20 |
| Albuquerque, N.M. | 35 | 05 | 01 | 106 | 39 | 05 | 4,945 |
| Allentown, Pa. | 40 | 36 | 11 | 75 | 28 | 06 | 255 |
| Alert, N.W.T. | 82 | 29 | 50 | 62 | 21 | 15 | 95 |
| Amarillo, Tex. | 35 | 12 | 27 | 101 | 50 | 04 | 3,685 |
| Anchorage, Alas. | 61 | 10 | 00 | 149 | 59 | 00 | 118 |
| Ann Arbor, Mich. | 42 | 16 | 59 | 83 | 44 | 52 | 880 |
| Asheville, N.C. | 35 | 35 | 42 | 82 | 33 | 26 | 1,985 |
| Ashland, Ky. | 38 | 28 | 36 | 82 | 38 | 23 | 536 |
| Atlanta, Ga. | 33 | 45 | 10 | 84 | 23 | 37 | 1,050 |
| Atlantic City, N.J. | 39 | 21 | 32 | 74 | 25 | 53 | 10 |
| Augusta, Ga. | 33 | 28 | 20 | 81 | 58 | 00 | 143 |
| Augusta, Me. | 44 | 18 | 53 | 69 | 46 | 29 | 45 |
| Austin, Tex. | 30 | 16 | 09 | 97 | 44 | 37 | 505 |
| Bakersfield, Cal. | 35 | 22 | 31 | 119 | 01 | 18 | 400 |
| Baltimore, Md. | 39 | 17 | 26 | 76 | 36 | 45 | 20 |
| Bangor, Me. | 44 | 48 | 13 | 68 | 46 | 18 | 20 |
| Baton Rouge, La. | 30 | 26 | 58 | 91 | 11 | 00 | 57 |
| Battle Creek, Mich. | 42 | 18 | 58 | 85 | 10 | 48 | 820 |
| Bay City, Mich. | 43 | 36 | 04 | 83 | 53 | 15 | 595 |
| Beaumont, Tex. | 30 | 05 | 20 | 94 | 06 | 09 | 20 |
| Belleville, Ont. | 44 | 09 | 42 | 77 | 23 | 11 | 257 |
| Bellingham, Wash. | 48 | 45 | 34 | 122 | 28 | 36 | 60 |
| Berkeley, Cal. | 37 | 52 | 10 | 122 | 16 | 17 | 40 |
| Billings, Mont. | 45 | 47 | 00 | 108 | 30 | 04 | 3,120 |
| Biloxi, Miss. | 30 | 23 | 48 | 88 | 53 | 00 | 20 |
| Binghamton, N.Y. | 42 | 06 | 03 | 75 | 54 | 47 | 865 |
| Birmingham, Ala. | 33 | 31 | 01 | 86 | 48 | 36 | 600 |
| Bismarck, N.D. | 46 | 48 | 23 | 100 | 47 | 17 | 1,674 |
| Bloomington, Ill. | 40 | 28 | 58 | 88 | 59 | 36 | 800 |
| Boise, Ida. | 43 | 37 | 07 | 116 | 11 | 58 | 2,704 |
| Boston, Mass. | 42 | 21 | 24 | 71 | 03 | 25 | 21 |
| Bowling Green, Ky. | 36 | 59 | 41 | 86 | 26 | 33 | 510 |
| Brandon, Man. | 49 | 51 | 00 | 99 | 57 | 00 | 1,265(a) |
| Brantford, Ont. | 43 | 08 | 34 | 80 | 15 | 39 | 705(a) |
| Brattleboro, Vt. | 42 | 51 | 06 | 72 | 33 | 48 | 300 |
| Bridgeport, Conn. | 41 | 10 | 49 | 73 | 11 | 22 | 10 |
| Brockton, Mass. | 42 | 05 | 02 | 71 | 01 | 25 | 130 |
| Brownsville, Tex. | 25 | 54 | 07 | 97 | 29 | 58 | 35 |
| Buffalo, N.Y. | 42 | 52 | 52 | 78 | 52 | 21 | 585 |
| Burlington, Ont. | 43 | 19 | 33 | 79 | 47 | 57 | 284 |
| Burlington, Vt. | 44 | 28 | 34 | 73 | 12 | 46 | 110 |
| Butte, Mon. | 46 | 01 | 06 | 112 | 32 | 11 | 5,765 |
| Calgary, Alta. | 51 | 02 | 46 | 114 | 03 | 24 | 3,427 |
| Cambridge, Mass. | 42 | 22 | 01 | 71 | 06 | 22 | 20 |
| Canton, Oh. | 40 | 47 | 50 | 81 | 22 | 37 | 1,030 |
| Carson City, Nev. | 39 | 10 | 00 | 119 | 46 | 00 | 4,680 |
| Cedar Rapids, Ia. | 41 | 58 | 01 | 91 | 39 | 53 | 730 |
| Central Islip, N.Y. | 40 | 47 | 24 | 73 | 12 | 00 | 80 |
| Champaign, Ill. | 40 | 07 | 05 | 88 | 14 | 48 | 740 |
| Charleston, S.C. | 32 | 46 | 35 | 79 | 55 | 53 | 9 |
| Charleston, W.Va. | 38 | 21 | 01 | 81 | 37 | 52 | 601 |
| Charlotte, N.C. | 35 | 13 | 44 | 80 | 50 | 45 | 720 |
| Charlottetown, P.E.I. | 46 | 14 | 07 | 63 | 07 | 49 | 31 |
| Chattanooga, Tenn. | 35 | 02 | 41 | 85 | 18 | 32 | 675 |
| Cheyenne, Wy. | 41 | 08 | 09 | 104 | 49 | 07 | 6,100 |
| Chicago, Ill. | 41 | 52 | 28 | 87 | 38 | 22 | 595 |
| Churchill, Man. | 58 | 45 | 15 | 94 | 10 | 00 | 94(a) |
| Cincinnati, Oh. | 39 | 06 | 07 | 84 | 30 | 35 | 550 |
| Cleveland, Oh. | 41 | 29 | 51 | 81 | 41 | 50 | 660 |
| Colorado Springs | 38 | 50 | 07 | 104 | 49 | 16 | 5,980 |
| Columbia, Mo. | 38 | 57 | 03 | 92 | 19 | 46 | 730 |
| Columbia, S.C. | 34 | 00 | 02 | 81 | 02 | 00 | 190 |
| Columbus, Ga. | 32 | 28 | 07 | 84 | 59 | 24 | 265 |
| Columbus, Oh. | 39 | 57 | 47 | 83 | 00 | 17 | 780 |
| Concord, N.H. | 43 | 12 | 22 | 71 | 32 | 25 | 290 |
| Corpus Christi, Tex. | 27 | 47 | 51 | 97 | 23 | 45 | 35 |
| Dallas, Tex. | 32 | 47 | 09 | 96 | 47 | 37 | 435 |
| Dartmouth, N.S. | 44 | 39 | 50 | 63 | 34 | 08 | 24 |
| Dawson, Yukon | 64 | 03 | 30 | 139 | 26 | 00 | 1,211(a) |
| Dayton, Oh. | 39 | 45 | 32 | 84 | 11 | 43 | 574 |
| Daytona Beach, Fla. | 29 | 12 | 44 | 81 | 01 | 10 | 7 |
| Decatur, Ill. | 39 | 50 | 42 | 88 | 56 | 47 | 682 |
| Denver, Col. | 39 | 44 | 58 | 104 | 59 | 22 | 5,280 |
| Des Moines, Ia. | 41 | 35 | 14 | 93 | 37 | 00 | 803 |
| Detroit, Mich. | 42 | 19 | 48 | 83 | 02 | 57 | 585 |
| Dodge City, Kan. | 37 | 45 | 17 | 100 | 01 | 09 | 2,480 |
| Dubuque, Ia. | 42 | 29 | 55 | 90 | 40 | 08 | 620 |
| Duluth, Minn. | 46 | 46 | 56 | 92 | 06 | 24 | 610 |
| Durham, N.C. | 36 | 00 | 00 | 78 | 54 | 45 | 405 |
| Eau Claire, Wis. | 44 | 48 | 31 | 91 | 29 | 49 | 790 |
| Edmonton, Alta. | 53 | 32 | 43 | 113 | 29 | 21 | 2,186 |
| El Paso, Tex. | 31 | 45 | 36 | 106 | 29 | 11 | 3,695 |
| Elizabeth, N.J. | 40 | 39 | 43 | 74 | 12 | 59 | 21 |
| Enid, Okla. | 36 | 23 | 40 | 97 | 52 | 35 | 1,240 |
| Erie, Pa. | 42 | 07 | 15 | 80 | 04 | 57 | 685 |
| Eugene, Ore. | 44 | 03 | 16 | 123 | 05 | 30 | 422 |
| Eureka, Cal. | 40 | 48 | 08 | 124 | 09 | 46 | 45 |
| Evansville, Ind. | 37 | 58 | 20 | 87 | 34 | 21 | 385 |
| Fairbanks, Alas. | 64 | 48 | 00 | 147 | 51 | 00 | 448 |
| Fall River, Mass. | 41 | 42 | 06 | 71 | 09 | 18 | 40 |
| Fargo, N.D. | 46 | 52 | 30 | 96 | 47 | 18 | 900 |
| Flagstaff, Ariz. | 35 | 11 | 36 | 111 | 39 | 06 | 6,900 |
| Flint, Mich. | 43 | 00 | 50 | 83 | 41 | 33 | 750 |
| Ft. Smith, Ark. | 35 | 23 | 10 | 94 | 25 | 36 | 440 |
| Ft. Wayne, Ind. | 41 | 04 | 21 | 85 | 08 | 26 | 790 |
| Ft. Worth, Tex. | 32 | 44 | 55 | 97 | 19 | 44 | 670 |
| Fredericton, N.B. | 45 | 57 | 47 | 66 | 38 | 38 | 29 |
| Fresno, Cal. | 36 | 44 | 12 | 119 | 47 | 11 | 285 |
| Gadsden, Ala. | 34 | 00 | 57 | 86 | 00 | 41 | 555 |
| Gainesville, Fla. | 29 | 38 | 56 | 82 | 19 | 19 | 175 |
| Gallup, N.M. | 35 | 31 | 30 | 108 | 44 | 30 | 6,540 |
| Galveston, Tex. | 29 | 18 | 10 | 94 | 47 | 43 | 5 |
| Gary, Ind. | 41 | 36 | 12 | 87 | 20 | 19 | 590 |
| Grand Junction, Col. | 39 | 04 | 06 | 108 | 33 | 54 | 4,590 |
| Grand Rapids, Mich. | 42 | 58 | 03 | 85 | 40 | 13 | 610 |
| Great Falls, Mon. | 47 | 29 | 33 | 111 | 18 | 23 | 3,340 |
| Green Bay, Wis. | 44 | 30 | 48 | 88 | 00 | 50 | 590 |
| Greensboro, N.C. | 36 | 04 | 17 | 79 | 47 | 25 | 839 |
| Greenville, S.C. | 34 | 50 | 50 | 82 | 24 | 01 | 966 |
| Guelph, Ont. | 43 | 32 | 35 | 80 | 14 | 54 | 1,065 |
| Gulfport, Miss. | 30 | 22 | 04 | 89 | 05 | 36 | 20 |
| Halifax, N.S. | 44 | 38 | 54 | 63 | 34 | 30 | 60 |
| Hamilton, Ont. | 43 | 15 | 20 | 79 | 52 | 30 | 329 |
| Hamilton, Oh. | 39 | 23 | 59 | 84 | 33 | 47 | 600 |
| Harrisburg, Pa. | 40 | 15 | 43 | 76 | 52 | 59 | 365 |
| Hartford, Conn. | 41 | 46 | 12 | 72 | 40 | 49 | 40 |
| Helena, Mon. | 46 | 35 | 33 | 112 | 02 | 24 | 4,155 |
| Hilo, Ha. | 19 | 43 | 30 | 155 | 05 | 24 | 40 |
| Honolulu, Ha. | 21 | 18 | 22 | 157 | 51 | 35 | 21 |
| Houston, Tex. | 29 | 45 | 26 | 95 | 21 | 37 | 40 |
| Hull, Que. | 45 | 25 | 42 | 75 | 42 | 41 | 185 |
| Huntsville, Ala. | 34 | 44 | 18 | 86 | 35 | 19 | 640 |
| Indianapolis, Ind. | 39 | 46 | 07 | 86 | 09 | 46 | 710 |
| Iowa City, Ia. | 41 | 39 | 37 | 91 | 31 | 53 | 685 |
| Jackson, Mich. | 42 | 14 | 43 | 84 | 24 | 22 | 940 |
| Jackson, Miss. | 32 | 17 | 56 | 90 | 11 | 06 | 298 |
| Jacksonville, Fla. | 30 | 19 | 44 | 81 | 39 | 42 | 20 |
| Jersey City, N.J. | 40 | 43 | 50 | 74 | 03 | 56 | 20 |
| Johnstown, Pa. | 40 | 19 | 35 | 78 | 55 | 03 | 1,185 |
| Joplin, Mo. | 37 | 05 | 26 | 94 | 30 | 00 | 990 |
| Juneau, Alas. | 58 | 18 | 12 | 134 | 24 | 30 | 50 |
| Kalamazoo, Mich. | 42 | 17 | 29 | 85 | 35 | 14 | 755 |
| Kansas City, Kan. | 39 | 07 | 04 | 94 | 38 | 24 | 750 |
| Kansas City, Mo. | 39 | 04 | 56 | 94 | 35 | 20 | 750 |
| Kenosha, Wis. | 42 | 35 | 43 | 87 | 50 | 11 | 610 |
| Key West, Fla. | 24 | 33 | 30 | 81 | 48 | 12 | 5 |
| Kingston, Ont. | 44 | 13 | 53 | 76 | 28 | 48 | 264 |
| Kitchener, Ont. | 43 | 26 | 58 | 80 | 29 | 12 | 1,100 |
| Knoxville, Tenn. | 35 | 57 | 39 | 83 | 55 | 07 | 890 |
| Lafayette, Ind. | 40 | 25 | 11 | 86 | 53 | 39 | 550 |
| Lancaster, Pa. | 40 | 02 | 25 | 76 | 18 | 29 | 355 |
| Lansing, Mich. | 42 | 44 | 01 | 84 | 33 | 15 | 830 |
| Laredo, Tex. | 27 | 30 | 22 | 99 | 30 | 30 | 440 |
| La Salle, Que. | 45 | 25 | 30 | 73 | 39 | 30 | 110 |
| Las Vegas, Nev. | 36 | 10 | 20 | 115 | 08 | 37 | 2,030 |
| Laval, Que. | 45 | 33 | 05 | 73 | 44 | 42 | 142 |
| Lawrence, Mass. | 42 | 42 | 16 | 71 | 10 | 08 | 65 |
| Lethbridge, Alta. | 49 | 41 | 38 | 112 | 49 | 58 | 2,985 |
| Lexington, Ky. | 38 | 02 | 50 | 84 | 29 | 46 | 955 |
| Lihue, Ha. | 21 | 58 | 48 | 159 | 22 | 30 | 210 |
| Lima, Oh. | 40 | 44 | 35 | 84 | 06 | 20 | 865 |
| Lincoln, Neb. | 40 | 48 | 59 | 96 | 42 | 15 | 1,150 |
| Little Rock, Ark. | 34 | 44 | 42 | 92 | 16 | 37 | 286 |
| London, Ont. | 42 | 59 | 17 | 81 | 14 | 03 | 822 |
| Long Beach, Cal. | 33 | 46 | 14 | 118 | 11 | 18 | 35 |
| Los Angeles, Cal. | 34 | 03 | 15 | 118 | 14 | 28 | 340 |
| Louisville, Ky. | 38 | 14 | 47 | 85 | 45 | 49 | 450 |
| Lowell, Mass. | 42 | 38 | 25 | 71 | 19 | 14 | 100 |
| Lubbock, Tex. | 33 | 35 | 05 | 101 | 50 | 33 | 3,195 |
| Macon, Ga. | 32 | 50 | 12 | 83 | 37 | 36 | 335 |
| Madison, Wis. | 43 | 04 | 23 | 89 | 22 | 55 | 860 |
| Manchester, N.H. | 42 | 59 | 28 | 71 | 27 | 41 | 175 |
| Marshall, Tex. | 32 | 33 | 00 | 94 | 23 | 00 | 410 |
| Memphis, Tenn. | 35 | 08 | 46 | 90 | 03 | 13 | 275 |
| Meriden, Conn. | 41 | 32 | 06 | 72 | 47 | 30 | 190 |
| Miami, Fla. | 25 | 46 | 37 | 80 | 11 | 32 | 10 |
| Milwaukee, Wis. | 43 | 02 | 19 | 87 | 54 | 15 | 635 |

| City | Lat. N ° | ' | " | Long. W ° | ' | " | Alt.* feet |
|---|---|---|---|---|---|---|---|
| Minneapolis, Minn. | 44 | 58 | 57 | 93 | 15 | 43 | 815 |
| Minot, N.D. | 48 | 14 | 09 | 101 | 17 | 38 | 1,550 |
| Mississauga, Ont. | 43 | 33 | 00 | 79 | 35 | 00 | 260(a) |
| Mobile, Ala. | 30 | 41 | 36 | 88 | 02 | 33 | 5 |
| Moncton, N.B. | 46 | 05 | 18 | 64 | 46 | 41 | 38 |
| Montgomery, Ala. | 32 | 22 | 33 | 86 | 18 | 31 | 160 |
| Montpelier, Vt. | 44 | 15 | 36 | 72 | 34 | 41 | 485 |
| Montréal, Que. | 45 | 30 | 33 | 73 | 33 | 14 | 90 |
| Moose Jaw, Sask. | 50 | 23 | 34 | 105 | 32 | 04 | 1,784 |
| Muncie, Ind. | 40 | 11 | 28 | 85 | 23 | 16 | 950 |
| Nashville, Tenn. | 36 | 09 | 33 | 86 | 46 | 55 | 450 |
| Natchez, Miss. | 31 | 33 | 48 | 91 | 23 | 30 | 210 |
| Newark, N.J. | 40 | 44 | 14 | 74 | 10 | 19 | 55 |
| New Britain, Conn. | 41 | 40 | 08 | 72 | 46 | 59 | 200 |
| New Haven, Conn. | 41 | 18 | 25 | 72 | 55 | 30 | 40 |
| New Orleans, La. | 29 | 56 | 53 | 90 | 04 | 10 | 5 |
| New York, N.Y. | 40 | 45 | 06 | 73 | 59 | 39 | 55 |
| Niagara Falls, N.Y. | 43 | 05 | 34 | 79 | 03 | 26 | 570 |
| Niagara Falls, Ont. | 43 | 06 | 22 | 79 | 03 | 51 | 590 |
| Nome, Alas. | 64 | 30 | 00 | 165 | 25 | 00 | 25 |
| Norfolk, Va. | 36 | 51 | 10 | 76 | 17 | 21 | 10 |
| North Bay, Ont. | 46 | 18 | 35 | 79 | 27 | 45 | 670 |
| Oakland, Cal. | 37 | 48 | 03 | 122 | 15 | 54 | 25 |
| Ogden, Ut. | 41 | 13 | 31 | 111 | 58 | 21 | 4,295 |
| Oklahoma City | 35 | 28 | 26 | 97 | 31 | 04 | 1,195 |
| Omaha, Neb. | 41 | 15 | 42 | 95 | 56 | 14 | 1,040 |
| Orlando, Fla. | 28 | 32 | 42 | 81 | 22 | 38 | 70 |
| Ottawa, Ont. | 45 | 26 | 24 | 75 | 41 | 42 | 185 |
| Paducah, Ky. | 37 | 05 | 13 | 88 | 35 | 56 | 345 |
| Pasadena, Cal. | 34 | 08 | 44 | 118 | 08 | 41 | 830 |
| Paterson, N.J. | 40 | 55 | 01 | 74 | 10 | 21 | 100 |
| Pensacola, Fla. | 30 | 24 | 51 | 87 | 12 | 56 | 15 |
| Peoria, Ill. | 40 | 41 | 42 | 89 | 35 | 33 | 470 |
| Peterborough, Ont. | 44 | 18 | 32 | 78 | 19 | 01 | 673 |
| Philadelphia, Pa. | 39 | 56 | 58 | 75 | 09 | 21 | 100 |
| Phoenix, Ariz. | 33 | 27 | 12 | 112 | 04 | 28 | 1,090 |
| Pierre, S.D. | 44 | 22 | 18 | 100 | 20 | 54 | 1,480 |
| Pittsburgh, Pa. | 40 | 26 | 19 | 80 | 00 | 00 | 745 |
| Pittsfield, Mass. | 42 | 26 | 53 | 73 | 15 | 11 | 1,015 |
| Pocatello, Ida. | 42 | 51 | 38 | 112 | 27 | 01 | 4,460 |
| Pt. Arthur, Tex. | 29 | 52 | 30 | 93 | 56 | 15 | 10 |
| Portland, Me. | 43 | 39 | 33 | 70 | 15 | 19 | 25 |
| Portland, Ore. | 45 | 31 | 06 | 122 | 40 | 35 | 77 |
| Portsmouth, N.H. | 43 | 04 | 30 | 70 | 45 | 24 | 20 |
| Portsmouth, Va. | 36 | 50 | 07 | 76 | 18 | 14 | 10 |
| Prince Rupert, B.C. | 54 | 19 | 00 | 130 | 19 | 00 | 125(a) |
| Providence, R.I. | 41 | 49 | 32 | 71 | 24 | 41 | 80 |
| Provo, Ut. | 40 | 14 | 06 | 111 | 39 | 24 | 4,550 |
| Pueblo, Col. | 38 | 16 | 17 | 104 | 36 | 33 | 4,690 |
| Québec City, Que. | 46 | 48 | 51 | 71 | 12 | 30 | 163 |
| Racine, Wis. | 42 | 43 | 49 | 87 | 47 | 12 | 630 |
| Rapid City, S.D. | 44 | 04 | 52 | 103 | 13 | 11 | 3,230 |
| Raleigh, N.C. | 35 | 46 | 38 | 78 | 38 | 21 | 365 |
| Reading, Pa. | 40 | 20 | 09 | 75 | 55 | 40 | 265 |
| Regina, Sask. | 50 | 26 | 55 | 104 | 36 | 50 | 1,894(a) |
| Reno, Nev. | 39 | 31 | 27 | 119 | 48 | 40 | 4,490 |
| Richmond, Va. | 37 | 32 | 15 | 77 | 26 | 09 | 160 |
| Roanoke, Va. | 37 | 16 | 13 | 79 | 56 | 44 | 905 |
| Rochester, Minn. | 44 | 01 | 21 | 92 | 28 | 03 | 990 |
| Rochester, N.Y. | 43 | 09 | 41 | 77 | 36 | 21 | 515 |
| Rockford, Ill. | 42 | 16 | 07 | 89 | 05 | 48 | 715 |
| Sacramento, Cal. | 38 | 34 | 57 | 121 | 29 | 41 | 30 |
| Saginaw, Mich. | 43 | 25 | 52 | 83 | 56 | 05 | 595 |
| St. Catharines, Ont. | 43 | 09 | 33 | 79 | 14 | 50 | 362(a) |
| St. Cloud, Minn. | 45 | 34 | 00 | 94 | 10 | 24 | 1,040 |
| St. John, N.B. | 45 | 16 | 22 | 66 | 03 | 48 | 27 |
| St. John's, Nfld. | 47 | 33 | 42 | 52 | 42 | 48 | 200(a) |
| St. Joseph, Mo. | 39 | 45 | 57 | 94 | 51 | 02 | 850 |
| St. Louis, Mo. | 38 | 37 | 45 | 90 | 12 | 22 | 455 |
| St. Paul, Minn. | 44 | 57 | 19 | 93 | 06 | 07 | 780 |
| St. Petersburg, Fla. | 27 | 46 | 18 | 82 | 38 | 19 | 20 |
| Salem, Ore. | 44 | 56 | 24 | 123 | 01 | 59 | 155 |
| Salina, Kan. | 38 | 50 | 36 | 97 | 36 | 46 | 1,229 |
| Salt Lake City, Ut. | 40 | 45 | 23 | 111 | 53 | 26 | 4,390 |
| San Antonio, Tex. | 29 | 25 | 37 | 98 | 29 | 06 | 650 |
| San Bernardino, Cal. | 34 | 06 | 30 | 117 | 17 | 28 | 1,080 |
| San Diego, Cal. | 32 | 42 | 53 | 117 | 09 | 21 | 20 |
| San Francisco, Cal. | 37 | 46 | 39 | 122 | 24 | 40 | 65 |
| San Jose, Cal. | 37 | 20 | 16 | 121 | 53 | 24 | 90 |
| San Juan, P.R. | 18 | 27 | 00 | 66 | 04 | 15 | 35 |
| Santa Barbara, Cal. | 34 | 25 | 18 | 119 | 41 | 55 | 100 |
| Santa Cruz, Cal. | 36 | 58 | 18 | 122 | 01 | 18 | 20 |
| Santa Fe, N.M. | 35 | 41 | 11 | 105 | 56 | 10 | 6,950 |
| Sarasota, Fla. | 27 | 20 | 05 | 82 | 32 | 30 | 20 |
| Saskatoon, Sask. | 52 | 07 | 49 | 106 | 39 | 35 | 1,587 |
| Sault Ste. Marie, Ont. | 46 | 30 | 24 | 84 | 20 | 04 | 589 |
| Savannah, Ga. | 32 | 04 | 42 | 81 | 05 | 37 | 20 |
| Schenectady, N.Y. | 42 | 48 | 42 | 73 | 55 | 42 | 245 |
| Seattle, Wash. | 47 | 36 | 32 | 122 | 20 | 12 | 10 |
| Sheboygan, Wis. | 43 | 45 | 03 | 87 | 42 | 52 | 630 |
| Sherbrooke, Que. | 45 | 24 | 27 | 71 | 51 | 07 | 535(a) |
| Sheridan, Wy. | 44 | 47 | 55 | 106 | 57 | 10 | 3,740 |
| Shreveport, La. | 32 | 30 | 46 | 93 | 44 | 58 | 204 |
| Sioux City, Ia. | 42 | 29 | 46 | 96 | 24 | 30 | 1,110 |
| Sioux Falls, S.D. | 43 | 32 | 35 | 96 | 43 | 35 | 1,395 |
| South Bend, Ind. | 41 | 40 | 33 | 86 | 15 | 01 | 710 |
| Spartanburg, S.C. | 34 | 57 | 03 | 81 | 56 | 06 | 875 |
| Spokane, Wash. | 47 | 39 | 32 | 117 | 25 | 33 | 1,890 |
| Springfield, Ill. | 39 | 47 | 58 | 89 | 38 | 51 | 610 |
| Springfield, Mass. | 42 | 06 | 21 | 72 | 35 | 32 | 85 |
| Springfield, Mo. | 37 | 13 | 03 | 93 | 17 | 32 | 1,300 |
| Springfield, Oh. | 39 | 55 | 38 | 83 | 48 | 29 | 980 |
| Stamford, Conn. | 41 | 03 | 09 | 73 | 32 | 24 | 35 |
| Steubenville, Oh. | 40 | 21 | 42 | 80 | 36 | 53 | 660 |
| Stockton, Cal. | 37 | 57 | 30 | 121 | 17 | 16 | 20 |
| Sudbury, Ont. | 46 | 29 | 24 | 80 | 59 | 24 | 850(a) |
| Superior, Wis. | 46 | 43 | 14 | 92 | 06 | 07 | 630 |
| Sydney, N.S. | 46 | 08 | 15 | 60 | 11 | 48 | 15 |
| Syracuse, N.Y. | 43 | 03 | 04 | 76 | 09 | 14 | 400 |
| Tacoma, Wash. | 47 | 14 | 59 | 122 | 26 | 15 | 110 |
| Tallahassee, Fla. | 30 | 26 | 30 | 84 | 16 | 56 | 150 |
| Tampa, Fla. | 27 | 56 | 58 | 82 | 27 | 25 | 15 |
| Terre Haute, Ind. | 39 | 28 | 03 | 87 | 24 | 26 | 496 |
| Texarkana, Tex. | 33 | 25 | 48 | 94 | 02 | 30 | 324 |
| Thunder Bay, Ont. | 48 | 22 | 54 | 89 | 14 | 42 | 616 |
| Toledo, Oh. | 41 | 39 | 14 | 83 | 32 | 39 | 585 |
| Topeka, Kan. | 39 | 03 | 16 | 95 | 40 | 23 | 930 |
| Toronto, Ont. | 43 | 39 | 10 | 79 | 23 | 00 | 300 |
| Trenton, N.J. | 40 | 13 | 14 | 74 | 46 | 13 | 35 |
| Trois-Rivières, Que. | 46 | 20 | 36 | 72 | 32 | 37 | 115(a) |
| Troy, N.Y. | 42 | 43 | 45 | 73 | 40 | 58 | 35 |
| Tucson, Ariz. | 32 | 13 | 15 | 110 | 58 | 08 | 2,390 |
| Tulsa, Okla. | 36 | 09 | 12 | 95 | 59 | 34 | 804 |
| Urbana, Ill. | 40 | 06 | 42 | 88 | 12 | 06 | 725 |
| Utica, N.Y. | 43 | 06 | 12 | 75 | 13 | 33 | 415 |
| Vancouver, B.C. | 49 | 18 | 56 | 123 | 04 | 44 | 141 |
| Victoria, B.C. | 48 | 25 | 43 | 123 | 21 | 49 | 57 |
| Waco, Tex. | 31 | 33 | 12 | 97 | 08 | 00 | 405 |
| Walla Walla, Wash. | 46 | 04 | 08 | 118 | 20 | 24 | 936 |
| Washington, D.C. | 38 | 53 | 51 | 77 | 00 | 33 | 25 |
| Waterloo, Ia. | 42 | 29 | 40 | 92 | 20 | 20 | 850 |
| West Palm Beach, Fla. | 26 | 42 | 36 | 80 | 03 | 07 | 15 |
| Wheeling, W. Va. | 40 | 04 | 03 | 80 | 43 | 20 | 650 |
| Whitehorse, Yukon | 60 | 43 | 17 | 135 | 03 | 03 | 2,305(a) |
| White Plains, N.Y. | 41 | 02 | 00 | 73 | 45 | 48 | 220 |
| Wichita, Kan. | 37 | 41 | 30 | 97 | 20 | 16 | 1,290 |
| Wilkes-Barre, Pa. | 41 | 14 | 32 | 75 | 53 | 17 | 640 |
| Wilmington, Del. | 39 | 44 | 46 | 75 | 32 | 51 | 135 |
| Wilmington, N.C. | 34 | 14 | 14 | 77 | 56 | 58 | 35 |
| Windsor, Ont. | 42 | 18 | 56 | 83 | 02 | 10 | 603 |
| Winnipeg, Man. | 49 | 53 | 56 | 97 | 08 | 23 | 762 |
| Winston-Salem, N.C. | 36 | 05 | 52 | 80 | 14 | 42 | 860 |
| Worcester, Mass. | 42 | 15 | 37 | 71 | 48 | 17 | 475 |
| Yakima, Wash. | 46 | 36 | 00 | 120 | 30 | 39 | 1,060 |
| Yellowknife, N.W.T. | 62 | 27 | 16 | 114 | 22 | 33 | 674(a) |
| Yonkers, N.Y. | 40 | 55 | 55 | 73 | 53 | 54 | 10 |
| Youngstown, Oh. | 41 | 05 | 57 | 80 | 39 | 02 | 840 |
| Yuma, Ariz. | 32 | 42 | 54 | 114 | 37 | 24 | 160 |
| Zanesville, Oh. | 39 | 56 | 18 | 82 | 00 | 30 | 720 |

## World Cities

Source: Defense Mapping Agency and World Almanac Research.

| City | Lat. N ° | ' | " | Long. W ° | ' | " | Alt.* feet |
|---|---|---|---|---|---|---|---|
| Athens, Greece | 37 | 58 | 00N | 23 | 44 | 00E | 300 |
| Beijing, China | 39 | 54 | 00N | 116 | 28 | 00E | 600 |
| Berlin, Germany | 52 | 32 | 00N | 13 | 25 | 00E | 110 |
| Bangkok, Thailand | 13 | 45 | 00N | 100 | 30 | 00E | 0 |
| Bogotá, Colombia | 04 | 35 | 00N | 74 | 05 | 00W | 11,490 |
| Buenos Aires, Argentina | 34 | 36 | 00S | 58 | 22 | 00W | 90 |
| Jerusalem, Israel | 31 | 47 | 00N | 35 | 13 | 00E | 2,500 |
| Johannesburg, So. Afr. | 26 | 10 | 00S | 28 | 02 | 00E | 5,740 |
| Kathmandu, Nepal | 27 | 40 | 00N | 86 | 30 | 00E | 4,500 |
| Kiev, Ukraine | 50 | 26 | 00N | 30 | 31 | 00E | 0 |
| London, UK (Greenwich) | 51 | 30 | 00N | 00 | 00 | 00 | 245 |
| Manila, Philippines | 14 | 35 | 00N | 120 | 58 | 00E | 0 |
| Mecca, Saudi Arabia | 21 | 25 | 00N | 39 | 50 | 00E | 6,562 |
| Mexico City, Mexico | 19 | 25 | 45 | 99 | 07 | 00 | 7,347 |
| Moscow, Russia | 55 | 45 | 00N | 37 | 42 | 00E | 394 |
| New Delhi, India | 28 | 38 | 00N | 77 | 12 | 00E | 770 |
| Panama City, Panama | 30 | 24 | 00N | 87 | 13 | 00W | 0 |
| Paris, France | 48 | 50 | 14N | 02 | 20 | 14E | 300 |
| Rio de Janeiro, Brazil | 22 | 53 | 43S | 43 | 13 | 22W | 30 |
| Rome, Italy | 41 | 53 | 00N | 12 | 30 | 00E | 95 |
| Santiago, Chile | 33 | 29 | 00S | 70 | 38 | 00W | 4,921 |
| Syndey, Australia | 33 | 52 | 00S | 151 | 12 | 00E | 25 |
| Tokyo, Japan | 35 | 45 | 00N | 139 | 45 | 00E | 30 |
| Tripoli, Libya | 32 | 54 | 00N | 13 | 11 | 00E | 0 |
| Warsaw, Poland | 52 | 15 | 00N | 21 | 00 | 00E | 360 |
| Wellington, New Zealand | 41 | 17 | 00S | 174 | 47 | 00E | 0 |

# Perpetual Calendar

The number shown for each year indicates which Gregorian calendar to use. For 1583-1802, or for Julian calendar, see page 266. For years 1803-1820, use numbers for 1983-2000, respectively.

1994   7   8   9   10   11   12   13   14

JANUARY  FEBRUARY  MARCH  APRIL  MAY  JUNE  JULY  AUGUST  SEPTEMBER  OCTOBER  NOVEMBER  DECEMBER

# Julian and Gregorian Calendars; Leap Year; Century

Calendars based on the movements of sun and moon have been used since ancient times, but none has been perfect. The Julian calendar, under which Western nations measured time until A.D. 1582, was authorized by Julius Caesar in 46 B.C., the year 709 of Rome. His expert was a Greek, Sosigenes. The Julian calendar, on the assumption that the true year was 365 1/4 days long, gave every fourth year 366 days. The Venerable Bede, an Anglo-Saxon monk, announced in A.D. 730 that the 365 1/4-day Julian year was 11 min., 14 sec. too long, making a cumulative error of about a day every 128 years, but nothing was done about it for over 800 years.

By 1582 the accumulated error was estimated to have amounted to 10 days. In that year Pope Gregory XIII decreed that the day following Oct. 4, 1582, should be called Oct. 15, thus dropping 10 days.

However, with common years 365 days and a 366-day leap year every fourth year, the error in the length of the year would have recurred at the rate of a little more than 3 days every 400 years. So 3 of every 4 centesimal years (ending in 00) were made common years, not leap years. Thus 1600 was a leap year, 1700, 1800 and 1900 were not, but 2000 will be. **Leap years** are those divisible by 4 except centesimal years, which are common unless divisible by 400.

The Gregorian calendar was adopted at once by France, Italy, Spain, Portugal and Luxembourg. Within 2 years most German Catholic states, Belgium and parts of Switzerland and the Netherlands were brought under the new calendar, and Hungary followed in 1587. The rest of the Netherlands, along with Denmark and the German Protestant states made the change in 1699-1700 (German Protestants retained the old reckoning of Easter until 1776).

The British government imposed the Gregorian calendar on all its possessions, including the American colonies, in 1752. The British decreed that the day following Sept. 2, 1752, should be called Sept. 14, a loss of 11 days. All dates preceding were marked O.S., for Old Style. In addition, New Year's Day was moved to Jan. 1 from Mar. 25 (e.g., under the old reckoning, Mar. 24, 1700, had been followed by Mar. 25, 1701). George Washington's birth date, which was Feb. 11, 1731, O.S., became Feb. 22, 1732, N.S. In 1753 Sweden too went Gregorian, retaining the old Easter rules until 1844.

In 1793 the French revolutionary government adopted a calendar of 12 months of 30 days each with 5 extra days in September of each common year and a 6th extra day every 4th year. Napoleon reinstated the Gregorian calendar in 1806.

The Gregorian system later spread to non-European regions, first in the European colonies, then in the independent countries, replacing traditional calendars at least for official purposes. Japan in 1873, Egypt in 1875, China in 1912 and Turkey in 1917 made the change, usually in conjunction with political upheavals. In China, the republican government began reckoning years from its 1911 founding — e.g., 1948 was designated the year 37. After 1949, the Communists adopted the Common, or Christian Era, year count, even for the traditional lunar calendar.

In 1918 the revolutionary government in Russia decreed that the day after Jan. 31, 1918, Old Style, would become Feb. 14, 1918, New Style. Greece followed in 1923. (In Russia the Orthodox Church has retained the Julian calendar, as have various Middle Eastern Christian sects.) For the first time in history, all major cultures have one calendar.

To change from the Julian to the Gregorian calendar, add 10 days to dates Oct. 5, 1582, through Feb. 28, 1700; after that date add 11 days through Feb. 28, 1800; 12 days through Feb. 28, 1900; and 13 days through Feb. 28, 2100.

A century consists of 100 consecutive calendar years. The 1st century A.D. consisted of the years 1 through 100. The 20th century consists of the years 1901 through 2000 and will end Dec. 31, 2000. The 21st century will begin Jan. 1, 2001.

## Julian Calendar

To find which of the 14 calendars printed on pages 264-265 applies to any year, starting Jan. 1, under the Julian system, find the century for the desired year in the three left-hand columns below; read across. Then find the year in the four top rows; read down. The number in the intersection is the calendar designation for that year.

| **Year** (last two figures of desired year) | | | | | | | | | | | | | | | | | | | | | | | | | | | |
|---|---|---|---|---|---|---|---|---|---|---|---|---|---|---|---|---|---|---|---|---|---|---|---|---|---|---|---|
| 01 02 | 03 | 04 | | 05 | 06 | 07 | 08 | | 09 | 10 | 11 | 12 | | 13 | 14 | 15 | 16 | | 17 | 18 | 19 | 20 | | 21 | 22 | 23 | 24 | | 25 | 26 | 27 | 28 |
| 29 30 | 31 | 32 | | 33 | 34 | 35 | 36 | | 37 | 38 | 39 | 40 | | 41 | 42 | 43 | 44 | | 45 | 46 | 47 | 48 | | 49 | 50 | 51 | 52 | | 53 | 54 | 55 | 56 |
| 57 58 | 59 | 60 | | 61 | 62 | 63 | 64 | | 65 | 66 | 67 | 68 | | 69 | 70 | 71 | 72 | | 73 | 74 | 75 | 76 | | 77 | 78 | 79 | 80 | | 81 | 82 | 83 | 84 |
| **Century** 00 | 85 | 86 | 87 | 88 | | 89 | 90 | 91 | 92 | | 93 | 94 | 95 | 96 | | 97 | 98 | 99 | | | | | | | | | |

| Century | | | 00 29 57 85 | 02 30 58 86 | 03 31 59 87 | 04 32 60 88 | 05 33 61 89 | 06 34 62 90 | 07 35 63 91 | 08 36 64 92 | 09 37 65 93 | 10 38 66 94 | 11 39 67 95 | 12 40 68 96 | 13 41 69 97 | 14 42 70 98 | 15 43 71 99 | 16 44 72 | 17 45 73 | 18 46 74 | 19 47 75 | 20 48 76 | 21 49 77 | 22 50 78 | 23 51 79 | 24 52 80 | 25 53 81 | 26 54 82 | 27 55 83 | 28 56 84 |
|---|---|---|---|---|---|---|---|---|---|---|---|---|---|---|---|---|---|---|---|---|---|---|---|---|---|---|---|---|---|---|---|
| 0 | 700 | 1400 | 12 | 7 | 1 | 2 | 10 | 5 | 6 | 7 | 8 | 3 | 4 | 5 | 13 | 1 | 2 | 3 | 11 | 6 | 7 | 1 | 9 | 4 | 5 | 6 | 14 | 2 | 3 | 4 | 12 |
| 100 | 800 | 1500 | 11 | 6 | 7 | 1 | 9 | 4 | 5 | 6 | 14 | 2 | 3 | 4 | 12 | 7 | 1 | 2 | 10 | 5 | 6 | 7 | 8 | 3 | 4 | 5 | 13 | 1 | 2 | 3 | 11 |
| 200 | 900 | 1600 | 10 | 5 | 6 | 7 | 8 | 3 | 4 | 5 | 13 | 1 | 2 | 3 | 11 | 6 | 7 | 1 | 9 | 4 | 5 | 6 | 14 | 2 | 3 | 4 | 12 | 7 | 1 | 2 | 10 |
| 300 | 1000 | 1700 | 9 | 4 | 5 | 6 | 14 | 2 | 3 | 4 | 12 | 7 | 1 | 2 | 10 | 5 | 6 | 7 | 8 | 3 | 4 | 5 | 13 | 1 | 2 | 3 | 11 | 6 | 7 | 1 | 9 |
| 400 | 1100 | 1800 | 8 | 3 | 4 | 5 | 13 | 1 | 2 | 3 | 11 | 6 | 7 | 1 | 9 | 4 | 5 | 6 | 14 | 2 | 3 | 4 | 12 | 7 | 1 | 2 | 10 | 5 | 6 | 7 | 8 |
| 500 | 1200 | 1900 | 14 | 2 | 3 | 4 | 12 | 7 | 1 | 2 | 10 | 5 | 6 | 7 | 8 | 3 | 4 | 5 | 13 | 1 | 2 | 3 | 11 | 6 | 7 | 1 | 9 | 4 | 5 | 6 | 14 |
| 600 | 1300 | 2000 | 13 | 1 | 2 | 3 | 11 | 6 | 7 | 1 | 9 | 4 | 5 | 6 | 14 | 2 | 3 | 4 | 12 | 7 | 1 | 2 | 10 | 5 | 6 | 7 | 8 | 3 | 4 | 5 | 13 |

## Gregorian Calendar

Pick desired year from table below or on page 264 (for years 1803 to 2080). The number shown with each year shows which calendar to use for that year, as shown on pages 264-265. (The Gregorian calendar was inaugurated Oct. 15, 1582. From that date to Dec. 31, 1582, use calendar 6.)

### 1583-1802

| | | | | | | | | | | | |
|---|---|---|---|---|---|---|---|---|---|---|---|
| 1583 . . 7 | 1603 . . 4 | 1623 . . 1 | 1643 . . 5 | 1663 . . 2 | 1683 . . 6 | 1703 . . 2 | 1723 . . 6 | 1743 . . 3 | 1763 . . 7 | 1783 . . 4 |
| 1584 . . 8 | 1604 . 12 | 1624 . . 9 | 1644 . 13 | 1664 . 10 | 1684 . 14 | 1704 . 10 | 1724 . 14 | 1744 . 11 | 1764 . . 8 | 1784 . 12 |
| 1585 . . 3 | 1605 . . 7 | 1625 . . 4 | 1645 . . 1 | 1665 . . 5 | 1685 . . 2 | 1705 . . 5 | 1725 . . 2 | 1745 . . 6 | 1765 . . 3 | 1785 . . 7 |
| 1586 . . 4 | 1606 . . 1 | 1626 . . 5 | 1646 . . 2 | 1666 . . 6 | 1686 . . 3 | 1706 . . 6 | 1726 . . 3 | 1746 . . 7 | 1766 . . 4 | 1786 . . 1 |
| 1587 . . 5 | 1607 . . 2 | 1627 . . 6 | 1647 . . 3 | 1667 . . 7 | 1687 . . 4 | 1707 . . 7 | 1727 . . 4 | 1747 . . 1 | 1767 . . 5 | 1787 . . 2 |
| 1588 . 13 | 1608 . 10 | 1628 . 14 | 1648 . 11 | 1668 . . 8 | 1688 . 12 | 1708 . . 8 | 1728 . 12 | 1748 . . 9 | 1768 . 13 | 1788 . 10 |
| 1589 . . 1 | 1609 . . 5 | 1629 . . 2 | 1649 . . 6 | 1669 . . 3 | 1689 . . 7 | 1709 . . 3 | 1729 . . 7 | 1749 . . 4 | 1769 . . 1 | 1789 . . 5 |
| 1590 . . 2 | 1610 . . 6 | 1630 . . 3 | 1650 . . 7 | 1670 . . 4 | 1690 . . 1 | 1710 . . 4 | 1730 . . 1 | 1750 . . 5 | 1770 . . 2 | 1790 . . 6 |
| 1591 . . 3 | 1611 . . 7 | 1631 . . 4 | 1651 . . 1 | 1671 . . 5 | 1691 . . 2 | 1711 . . 5 | 1731 . . 2 | 1751 . . 6 | 1771 . . 3 | 1791 . . 7 |
| 1592 . 11 | 1612 . . 8 | 1632 . 12 | 1652 . . 9 | 1672 . 13 | 1692 . 10 | 1712 . 13 | 1732 . 10 | 1752 . 14 | 1772 . 11 | 1792 . . 8 |
| 1593 . . 6 | 1613 . . 3 | 1633 . . 7 | 1653 . . 4 | 1673 . . 1 | 1693 . . 5 | 1713 . . 1 | 1733 . . 5 | 1753 . . 2 | 1773 . . 6 | 1793 . . 3 |
| 1594 . . 7 | 1614 . . 4 | 1634 . . 1 | 1654 . . 5 | 1674 . . 2 | 1694 . . 6 | 1714 . . 2 | 1734 . . 6 | 1754 . . 3 | 1774 . . 7 | 1794 . . 4 |
| 1595 . . 1 | 1615 . . 5 | 1635 . . 2 | 1655 . . 6 | 1675 . . 3 | 1695 . . 7 | 1715 . . 3 | 1735 . . 7 | 1755 . . 4 | 1775 . . 1 | 1795 . . 5 |
| 1596 . . 9 | 1616 . 13 | 1636 . 10 | 1656 . 14 | 1676 . 11 | 1696 . . 8 | 1716 . 11 | 1736 . . 8 | 1756 . 12 | 1776 . . 9 | 1796 . 13 |
| 1597 . . 4 | 1617 . . 1 | 1637 . . 5 | 1657 . . 2 | 1677 . . 6 | 1697 . . 3 | 1717 . . 6 | 1737 . . 3 | 1757 . . 7 | 1777 . . 4 | 1797 . . 1 |
| 1598 . . 5 | 1618 . . 2 | 1638 . . 6 | 1658 . . 3 | 1678 . . 7 | 1698 . . 4 | 1718 . . 7 | 1738 . . 4 | 1758 . . 1 | 1778 . . 5 | 1798 . . 2 |
| 1599 . . 6 | 1619 . . 3 | 1639 . . 7 | 1659 . . 4 | 1679 . . 1 | 1699 . . 5 | 1719 . . 1 | 1739 . . 5 | 1759 . . 2 | 1779 . . 6 | 1799 . . 3 |
| 1600 . 14 | 1620 . 11 | 1640 . . 8 | 1660 . 12 | 1680 . . 9 | 1700 . . 7 | 1720 . . 9 | 1740 . 13 | 1760 . 10 | 1780 . 14 | 1800 . . 4 |
| 1601 . . 2 | 1621 . . 6 | 1641 . . 3 | 1661 . . 7 | 1681 . . 4 | 1701 . . 1 | 1721 . . 4 | 1741 . . 1 | 1761 . . 5 | 1781 . . 2 | 1801 . . 5 |
| 1602 . . 3 | 1622 . . 7 | 1642 . . 4 | 1662 . . 1 | 1682 . . 5 | 1702 . . 2 | 1722 . . 5 | 1742 . . 2 | 1762 . . 6 | 1782 . . 3 | 1802 . . 6 |

# The Julian Period

How many days have you lived? To determine this, you must multiply your age by 365, add the number of days since your last birthday until today, and account for all leap years. Chances are your answer would be wrong. Astronomers, however, find it convenient to express dates and long time intervals in days rather than in years, months and days. This is done by placing events within the Julian period.

The Julian period was devised in 1582 by Joseph Scaliger and named after his father Julius (not after the Julian calendar). Scaliger had Julian Day (JD) #1 begin at noon, Jan. 1, 4713 B.C., the most recent time that three major chronological cycles began on the same day — 1) the 28-year solar cycle, after which dates in the Julian calendar (e.g., Feb. 11) return to the same days of the week (e.g., Monday); 2) the 19-year lunar cycle, after which the phases of the moon return to the same dates of the year; and 3) the 15-year indiction cycle, used in ancient Rome to regulate taxes. It will take 7980 years to complete the period, the product of 28, 19, and 15.

Noon of Dec. 31, 1993, marks the beginning of JD 2,449,353; that many days will have passed since the start of the Julian period. The JD at noon of any date in 1994 may be found by adding to this figure the day of the year for that date, which is given in the left hand column in the chart below. Simple JD conversion tables are used by astronomers.

## Days Between Two Dates

Table covers period of two ordinary years. Example—Days between Feb. 10, 1989 and Dec. 15, 1990; subtract 41 from 714; answer is 673 days. For leap year, such as 1992, one day must be added: final answer is 674.

| Date | Jan. | Feb. | Mar. | April | May | June | July | Aug. | Sept. | Oct. | Nov. | Dec. | Date | Jan. | Feb. | Mar. | April | May | June | July | Aug. | Sept. | Oct. | Nov. | Dec. |
|---|---|---|---|---|---|---|---|---|---|---|---|---|---|---|---|---|---|---|---|---|---|---|---|---|---|
| 1 | 1 | 32 | 60 | 91 | 121 | 152 | 182 | 213 | 244 | 274 | 305 | 335 | 1 | 366 | 397 | 425 | 456 | 486 | 517 | 547 | 578 | 609 | 639 | 670 | 700 |
| 2 | 2 | 33 | 61 | 92 | 122 | 153 | 183 | 214 | 245 | 275 | 306 | 336 | 2 | 367 | 398 | 426 | 457 | 487 | 518 | 548 | 579 | 610 | 640 | 671 | 701 |
| 3 | 3 | 34 | 62 | 93 | 123 | 154 | 184 | 215 | 246 | 276 | 307 | 337 | 3 | 368 | 399 | 427 | 458 | 488 | 519 | 549 | 580 | 611 | 641 | 672 | 702 |
| 4 | 4 | 35 | 63 | 94 | 124 | 155 | 185 | 216 | 247 | 277 | 308 | 338 | 4 | 369 | 400 | 428 | 459 | 489 | 520 | 550 | 581 | 612 | 642 | 673 | 703 |
| 5 | 5 | 36 | 64 | 95 | 125 | 156 | 186 | 217 | 248 | 278 | 309 | 339 | 5 | 370 | 401 | 429 | 460 | 490 | 521 | 551 | 582 | 613 | 643 | 674 | 704 |
| 6 | 6 | 37 | 65 | 96 | 126 | 157 | 187 | 218 | 249 | 279 | 310 | 340 | 6 | 371 | 402 | 430 | 461 | 491 | 522 | 552 | 583 | 614 | 644 | 675 | 705 |
| 7 | 7 | 38 | 66 | 97 | 127 | 158 | 188 | 219 | 250 | 280 | 311 | 341 | 7 | 372 | 403 | 431 | 462 | 492 | 523 | 553 | 584 | 615 | 645 | 676 | 706 |
| 8 | 8 | 39 | 67 | 98 | 128 | 159 | 189 | 220 | 251 | 281 | 312 | 342 | 8 | 373 | 404 | 432 | 463 | 493 | 524 | 554 | 585 | 616 | 646 | 677 | 707 |
| 9 | 9 | 40 | 68 | 99 | 129 | 160 | 190 | 221 | 252 | 282 | 313 | 343 | 9 | 374 | 405 | 433 | 464 | 494 | 525 | 555 | 586 | 617 | 647 | 678 | 708 |
| 10 | 10 | 41 | 69 | 100 | 130 | 161 | 191 | 222 | 253 | 283 | 314 | 344 | 10 | 375 | 406 | 434 | 465 | 495 | 526 | 556 | 587 | 618 | 648 | 679 | 709 |
| 11 | 11 | 42 | 70 | 101 | 131 | 162 | 192 | 223 | 254 | 284 | 315 | 345 | 11 | 376 | 407 | 435 | 466 | 496 | 527 | 557 | 588 | 619 | 649 | 680 | 710 |
| 12 | 12 | 43 | 71 | 102 | 132 | 163 | 193 | 224 | 255 | 285 | 316 | 346 | 12 | 377 | 408 | 436 | 467 | 497 | 528 | 558 | 589 | 620 | 650 | 681 | 711 |
| 13 | 13 | 44 | 72 | 103 | 133 | 164 | 194 | 225 | 256 | 286 | 317 | 347 | 13 | 378 | 409 | 437 | 468 | 498 | 529 | 559 | 590 | 621 | 651 | 682 | 712 |
| 14 | 14 | 45 | 73 | 104 | 134 | 165 | 195 | 226 | 257 | 287 | 318 | 348 | 14 | 379 | 410 | 438 | 469 | 499 | 530 | 560 | 591 | 622 | 652 | 683 | 713 |
| 15 | 15 | 46 | 74 | 105 | 135 | 166 | 196 | 227 | 258 | 288 | 319 | 349 | 15 | 380 | 411 | 439 | 470 | 500 | 531 | 561 | 592 | 623 | 653 | 684 | 714 |
| 16 | 16 | 47 | 75 | 106 | 136 | 167 | 197 | 228 | 259 | 289 | 320 | 350 | 16 | 381 | 412 | 440 | 471 | 501 | 532 | 562 | 593 | 624 | 654 | 685 | 715 |
| 17 | 17 | 48 | 76 | 107 | 137 | 168 | 198 | 229 | 260 | 290 | 321 | 351 | 17 | 382 | 413 | 441 | 472 | 502 | 533 | 563 | 594 | 625 | 655 | 686 | 716 |
| 18 | 18 | 49 | 77 | 108 | 138 | 169 | 199 | 230 | 261 | 291 | 322 | 352 | 18 | 383 | 414 | 442 | 473 | 503 | 534 | 564 | 595 | 626 | 656 | 687 | 717 |
| 19 | 19 | 50 | 78 | 109 | 139 | 170 | 200 | 231 | 262 | 292 | 323 | 353 | 19 | 384 | 415 | 443 | 474 | 504 | 535 | 565 | 596 | 627 | 657 | 688 | 718 |
| 20 | 20 | 51 | 79 | 110 | 140 | 171 | 201 | 232 | 263 | 293 | 324 | 354 | 20 | 385 | 416 | 444 | 475 | 505 | 536 | 566 | 597 | 628 | 658 | 689 | 719 |
| 21 | 21 | 52 | 80 | 111 | 141 | 172 | 202 | 233 | 264 | 294 | 325 | 355 | 21 | 386 | 417 | 445 | 476 | 506 | 537 | 567 | 598 | 629 | 659 | 690 | 720 |
| 22 | 22 | 53 | 81 | 112 | 142 | 173 | 203 | 234 | 265 | 295 | 326 | 356 | 22 | 387 | 418 | 446 | 477 | 507 | 538 | 568 | 599 | 630 | 660 | 691 | 721 |
| 23 | 23 | 54 | 82 | 113 | 143 | 174 | 204 | 235 | 266 | 296 | 327 | 357 | 23 | 388 | 419 | 447 | 478 | 508 | 539 | 569 | 600 | 631 | 661 | 692 | 722 |
| 24 | 24 | 55 | 83 | 114 | 144 | 175 | 205 | 236 | 267 | 297 | 328 | 358 | 24 | 389 | 420 | 448 | 479 | 509 | 540 | 570 | 601 | 632 | 662 | 693 | 723 |
| 25 | 25 | 56 | 84 | 115 | 145 | 176 | 206 | 237 | 268 | 298 | 329 | 359 | 25 | 390 | 421 | 449 | 480 | 510 | 541 | 571 | 602 | 633 | 663 | 694 | 724 |
| 26 | 26 | 57 | 85 | 116 | 146 | 177 | 207 | 238 | 269 | 299 | 330 | 360 | 26 | 391 | 422 | 450 | 481 | 511 | 542 | 572 | 603 | 634 | 664 | 695 | 725 |
| 27 | 27 | 58 | 86 | 117 | 147 | 178 | 208 | 239 | 270 | 300 | 331 | 361 | 27 | 392 | 423 | 451 | 482 | 512 | 543 | 573 | 604 | 635 | 665 | 696 | 726 |
| 28 | 28 | 59 | 87 | 118 | 148 | 179 | 209 | 240 | 271 | 301 | 332 | 362 | 28 | 393 | 424 | 452 | 483 | 513 | 544 | 574 | 605 | 636 | 666 | 697 | 727 |
| 29 | 29 | — | 88 | 119 | 149 | 180 | 210 | 241 | 272 | 302 | 333 | 363 | 29 | 394 | — | 453 | 484 | 514 | 545 | 575 | 606 | 637 | 667 | 698 | 728 |
| 30 | 30 | — | 89 | 120 | 150 | 181 | 211 | 242 | 273 | 303 | 334 | 364 | 30 | 395 | — | 454 | 485 | 515 | 546 | 576 | 607 | 638 | 668 | 699 | 729 |
| 31 | 31 | — | 90 | — | 151 | — | 212 | 243 | — | 304 | — | 365 | 31 | 396 | — | 455 | — | 516 | — | 577 | 608 | — | 669 | — | 730 |

## Lunar Calendar, Chinese New Year, Vietnamese Tet

The ancient Chinese lunar calendar is divided into 12 months of either 29 or 30 days (compensating for the fact that the mean duration of the lunar month is 29 days, 12 hours, 44.05 minutes). The calendar is synchronized with the solar year by the addition of extra months at fixed intervals.

The Chinese calendar runs on a sexagenary cycle, i.e., 60 years. The cycles 1876-1935 and 1936-1995, with the years grouped under their twelve animal designations, are printed below. A new cycle will begin in 1996 and last until 2055. The Year 1994 (Lunar Year 4692) is found in the eleventh column, under Dog, and is known as a "Year of the Dog." Readers can find the animal name for the year of their birth, marriage, etc., in the same chart. (Note: the first 3-7 weeks of each of the Western years belong to the previous Chinese year and animal designation.)

Both the Western (Gregorian) and traditional lunar calendars are used publicly in China and North and South Korea, and two New Year's celebrations are held. On Taiwan, in overseas Chinese communities, and in Vietnam, the lunar calendar has been used only to set the dates for traditional festivals, with the Gregorian system in general use.

The four-day Chinese New Year, Hsin Nien, the three-day Vietnamese New Year festival, Tet, and the three-to-four-day Korean festival, Suhl, begin at the first new moon after the sun enters Aquarius. The day may fall, therefore, between Jan. 21 and Feb. 19 of the Gregorian calendar. Feb. 10, 1994 marks the start of the new Chinese year. The date is fixed according to the date of the new moon in the Far East. Since this is west of the International Date Line, the date may be one day later than that of the new moon in the United States.

| Rat | Ox | Tiger | Hare (Rabbit) | Dragon | Snake | Horse | Sheep (Goat) | Monkey | Rooster | Dog | Pig |
|---|---|---|---|---|---|---|---|---|---|---|---|
| 1876 | 1877 | 1878 | 1879 | 1880 | 1881 | 1882 | 1883 | 1884 | 1885 | 1886 | 1887 |
| 1888 | 1889 | 1890 | 1891 | 1892 | 1893 | 1894 | 1895 | 1896 | 1897 | 1898 | 1899 |
| 1900 | 1901 | 1902 | 1903 | 1904 | 1905 | 1906 | 1907 | 1908 | 1909 | 1910 | 1911 |
| 1912 | 1913 | 1914 | 1915 | 1916 | 1917 | 1918 | 1919 | 1920 | 1921 | 1922 | 1923 |
| 1924 | 1925 | 1926 | 1927 | 1928 | 1929 | 1930 | 1931 | 1932 | 1933 | 1934 | 1935 |
| 1936 | 1937 | 1938 | 1939 | 1940 | 1941 | 1942 | 1943 | 1944 | 1945 | 1946 | 1947 |
| 1948 | 1949 | 1950 | 1951 | 1952 | 1953 | 1954 | 1955 | 1956 | 1957 | 1958 | 1959 |
| 1960 | 1961 | 1962 | 1963 | 1964 | 1965 | 1966 | 1967 | 1968 | 1969 | 1970 | 1971 |
| 1972 | 1973 | 1974 | 1975 | 1976 | 1977 | 1978 | 1979 | 1980 | 1981 | 1982 | 1983 |
| 1984 | 1985 | 1986 | 1987 | 1988 | 1989 | 1990 | 1991 | 1992 | 1993 | 1994 | 1995 |
| 1996 | 1997 | 1998 | 1999 | 2000 | 2001 | 2002 | 2003 | 2004 | 2005 | 2006 | 2007 |

## Standard Time, Daylight Saving Time, and Others
Source: Defense Mapping Agency Hydrographic/Topographic Center; U.S. Dept. of Transportation

### Standard Time

Standard Time is reckoned from Greenwich, England, recognized as the Prime Meridian of Longitude. The world is divided into 24 zones, each 15° of arc, or one hour in time apart. The Greenwich meridian (0°) extends through the center of the initial zone, and the zones to the east are numbered from 1 to 12 with the prefix "minus" indicating the number of hours to be subtracted to obtain Greenwich Time. Each zone extends 7½° on either side of its central meridian.

Westward zones are similarly numbered, but prefixed "plus" showing the number of hours that must be added to get Greenwich Time. While these zones apply generally to sea areas, it should be noted that the Standard Time maintained in many countries does not coincide with zone time. A graphical representation of the zones is shown on the Standard Time Zone Chart of the World published by the Defense Mapping Agency, Attn: PR, 8613 Lee Highway, Fairfax, VA 22031-2137.

The United States and possessions are divided into eight Standard Time zones, as set forth by the Uniform Time Act of 1966, which also provides for the use of Daylight Saving Time therein. Each zone is approximately 15° of longitude in width. All places in each zone use, instead of their own local time, the time counted from the transit of the "mean sun" across the Standard Time meridian which passes near the middle of that zone.

These time zones are designated as Atlantic, Eastern, Central, Mountain, Pacific, Yukon, Alaska-Hawaii, and Bering (Samoa), and the time in these zones is basically reckoned from the 60th, 75th, 90th, 105th, 120th, 135th, 150th and 165th meridians west of Greenwich. The time wanders to conform to local geographical regions. The time in the various zones is earlier than Greenwich Time by 4, 5, 6, 7, 8, 9, 10, and 11 hours respectively.

### 24-Hour Time

24-hour time is widely used in scientific work throughout the world. In the United States it is used also in operations of the Armed Forces. In Europe it is frequently used by the transportation networks in preference to the 12-hour a.m. and p.m. system. With the 24-hour system the day begins at midnight and is designated 0000 through 2359.

### International Date Line

The Date Line is a zig-zag line that approximately coincides with the 180th meridian, and it is where the calendar dates are separated. The date must be advanced one day when crossing in a westerly direction and set back one day when crossing in an easterly direction.

The line is deflected eastward through the Bering Strait and westward of the Aleutians to prevent separating these areas by date. The line is again deflected eastward of the

Tonga and New Zealand Islands in the South Pacific for the same reason.

### Daylight Saving Time

Daylight Saving Time is achieved by advancing the clock one hour. Under the Uniform Time Act, which became effective in 1967, all states, the District of Columbia, and U.S. possessions were to observe Daylight Saving Time beginning at 2 a.m. on the last Sunday in April and ending at 2 a.m. on the last Sunday in October. Any state could, by law, exempt itself; a 1972 amendment to the act authorized states split by time zones to take that into consideration in exempting themselves. Arizona, Hawaii, Puerto Rico, the Virgin Islands, American Samoa, and part of Indiana are now exempt. Some local zone boundaries in Kansas, Texas, Florida, Michigan, and Alaska have been modified by the Dept. of Transportation, which oversees the act. To conserve energy Congress put most of the nation on year-round Daylight Saving Time for two years effective Jan. 6, 1974 through Oct. 26, 1975, but another bill, signed in October 1974, restored Standard Time from the last Sunday in that month to the last Sunday in February 1975. At the end of 1975, Congress failed to renew this temporary legislation and the nation returned to the older end-of-April to end-of-October DST system.

On July 8, 1986, Pres. Ronald Reagan signed legislation moving up the start of Daylight Saving Time to the first Sunday in April. Daylight Saving Time, which used to start the last Sunday in April, still ends the last Sunday in October. The Transportation Dept. estimated that the earlier starting date would help save more than $28 million in traffic accident costs and prevent more than 1,500 injuries and 20 deaths annually. The law, opposed by some farm state lawmakers, took effect in 1987.

### International

Adjusting clock time to be able to use the added daylight on summer evenings is common throughout the world.

Western Europe is on Daylight Saving Time generally from the last Sunday in March to the last Sunday in September; however, the United Kingdom continues until the last Sunday in October.

Russia, which lies over 11 time zones, maintains its Standard Time 1 hour fast of the zone designation. Additionally, it proclaims Daylight Saving Time as does Europe.

China, which lies across 5 time zones, has decreed that the entire country be placed on Greenwich Time plus 8 hours, with Daylight Saving Time from April 12 to September 12.

Many of the countries in the Southern Hemisphere maintain Daylight Saving Time generally from October to March; however, most countries near the equator do not deviate from Standard Time.

## Standard Time Differences—World Cities

The time indicated in the table is fixed by law and is called the legal time, or, more generally, Standard Time. Use of Daylight Saving Time varies widely. * Indicates morning of the following day. At 12:00 noon, Eastern Standard Time, the Standard Time (in 24-hour time) in foreign cities is as follows:

| City | | City | | City | | City | |
|---|---|---|---|---|---|---|---|
| Addis Ababa | 20 00 | Cape Town | 19 00 | Lima | 12 00 | Santiago (Chile) | 13 00 |
| Alexandria | 19 00 | Caracas | 13 00 | Lisbon | 17 00 | Seoul | 2 00* |
| Amsterdam | 18 00 | Casablanca | 17 00 | Liverpool | 17 00 | Shanghai | 1 00* |
| Athens | 19 00 | Copenhagen | 18 00 | London | 17 00 | Singapore | 1 00* |
| Auckland | 5 00* | Delhi | 22 30 | Madrid | 18 00 | Stockholm | 18 00 |
| Baghdad | 20 00 | Dhaka | 23 00 | Manila | 1 00* | Sydney (Australia) | 3 00* |
| Bangkok | 0 00 | Dublin | 17 00 | Mecca (Saudi Arabia) | 20 00 | Tashkent | 23 00 |
| Beijing | 1 00* | Gdańsk | 18 00 | Melbourne | 3 00* | Teheran | 20 30 |
| Belfast | 17 00 | Geneva | 18 00 | Mexico City | 11 00 | Tel Aviv | 19 00 |
| Berlin | 18 00 | Havana | 12 00 | Montevideo | 14 00 | Tokyo | 2 00* |
| Bogotá | 12 00 | Helsinki | 19 00 | Moscow | 20 00 | Valparaiso | 13 00 |
| Bombay | 22 30 | Ho Chi Minh City | 0 00 | Nagasaki | 2 00* | Vladivostok | 3 00* |
| Bremen | 18 00 | Hong Kong | 1 00* | Oslo | 18 00 | Vienna | 18 00 |
| Brussels | 18 00 | Istanbul | 19 00 | Paris | 18 00 | Warsaw | 18 00 |
| Bucharest | 19 00 | Jakarta | 0 00 | Prague | 18 00 | Wellington (N.Z.) | 5 00* |
| Budapest | 18 00 | Jerusalem | 19 00 | Rio de Janeiro | 14 00 | Yangon (Rangoon) | 23 30 |
| Buenos Aires | 14 00 | Johannesburg | 19 00 | Rome | 18 00 | Yokohama | 2 00* |
| Cairo | 19 00 | Karachi | 22 00 | St. Petersburg | 20 00 | Zürich | 18 00 |
| Calcutta | 22 30 | Le Havre | 18 00 | | | | |

## Standard Time Differences — North American Cities

At 12 o'clock noon, Eastern Standard Time, the Standard Time in N.A. cities is as follows:

| City | Time | | City | Time | | City | Time | |
|---|---|---|---|---|---|---|---|---|
| Akron, Oh. | 12 00 | Noon | Frankfort, Ky. | 12 00 | Noon | *Phoenix, Ariz. | 10 00 | A.M. |
| Albuquerque, N.M. | 10 00 | A.M. | Galveston, Tex. | 11 00 | A.M. | Pierre, S.D. | 11 00 | A.M. |
| Atlanta, Ga. | 12 00 | Noon | Grand Rapids, Mich. | 12 00 | Noon | Pittsburgh, Pa. | 12 00 | Noon |
| Austin, Tex. | 11 00 | A.M. | Halifax, N.S. | 1 00 | P.M. | Portland, Me. | 12 00 | Noon |
| Baltimore, Md. | 12 00 | Noon | Hartford, Conn. | 12 00 | Noon | Portland, Ore. | 9 00 | A.M. |
| Birmingham, Ala. | 11 00 | A.M. | Helena, Mon. | 10 00 | A.M. | Providence, R.I. | 12 00 | Noon |
| Bismarck, N.D. | 11 00 | A.M. | *Honolulu, Ha. | 7 00 | A.M. | *Regina, Sask. | 11 00 | A.M. |
| Boise, Ida. | 10 00 | A.M. | Houston, Tex. | 11 00 | A.M. | Reno, Nev. | 9 00 | A.M. |
| Boston, Mass. | 12 00 | Noon | *Indianapolis, Ind. | 12 00 | Noon | Richmond, Va. | 12 00 | Noon |
| Buffalo, N.Y. | 12 00 | Noon | Jacksonville, Fla. | 12 00 | Noon | Rochester, N.Y. | 12 00 | Noon |
| Butte, Mon. | 10 00 | A.M. | Juneau, Alas. | 8 00 | A.M. | Sacramento, Cal. | 9 00 | A.M. |
| Calgary, Alta. | 10 00 | A.M. | Kansas City, Mo. | 11 00 | A.M. | St. John's, Nfld. | 1 30 | P.M. |
| Charleston, S.C. | 12 00 | Noon | Knoxville, Tenn. | 12 00 | Noon | St. Louis, Mo. | 11 00 | A.M. |
| Charleston, W.Va. | 12 00 | Noon | Lexington, Ky. | 12 00 | Noon | St. Paul, Minn. | 11 00 | A.M. |
| Charlotte, N.C. | 12 00 | Noon | Lincoln, Neb. | 11 00 | A.M. | Salt Lake City, Ut. | 10 00 | A.M. |
| Charlottetown, P.E.I. | 1 00 | P.M. | Little Rock, Ark. | 11 00 | A.M. | San Antonio, Tex. | 11 00 | A.M. |
| Chattanooga, Tenn. | 12 00 | Noon | Los Angeles, Cal. | 9 00 | A.M. | San Diego, Cal. | 9 00 | A.M. |
| Cheyenne, Wy. | 10 00 | A.M. | Louisville, Ky. | 12 00 | Noon | San Francisco, Cal. | 9 00 | A.M. |
| Chicago, Ill. | 11 00 | A.M. | *Mexico City | 11 00 | A.M. | Santa Fe, N.M. | 10 00 | A.M. |
| Cleveland, Oh. | 12 00 | Noon | Memphis, Tenn. | 11 00 | A.M. | Savannah, Ga. | 12 00 | Noon |
| Colorado Spr., Col. | 10 00 | A.M. | Miami, Fla. | 12 00 | Noon | Seattle, Wash. | 9 00 | A.M. |
| Columbus, Oh. | 12 00 | Noon | Milwaukee, Wis. | 11 00 | A.M. | Shreveport, La. | 11 00 | A.M. |
| Dallas, Tex. | 11 00 | A.M. | Minneapolis, Minn. | 11 00 | AM. | Sioux Falls, S.D. | 11 00 | A.M. |
| *Dawson, Yuk. | 9 00 | A.M. | Mobile, Ala. | 11 00 | A.M. | Spokane, Wash. | 9 00 | A.M. |
| Dayton, Oh. | 12 00 | Noon | Montreal, Que. | 12 00 | Noon | Tampa, Fla. | 12 00 | Noon |
| Denver, Col. | 10 00 | A.M. | Nashville, Tenn. | 11 00 | A.M. | Toledo, Oh. | 12 00 | Noon |
| Des Moines, Ia. | 11 00 | A.M. | New Haven, Conn. | 12 00 | Noon | Topeka, Kan. | 11 00 | A.M. |
| Detroit, Mich. | 12 00 | Noon | New Orleans, La. | 11 00 | A.M. | Toronto, Ont. | 12 00 | Noon |
| Duluth, Minn. | 11 00 | A.M. | New York, N.Y. | 12 00 | Noon | *Tucson, Ariz. | 10 00 | A.M. |
| El Paso, Tex. | 10 00 | A.M. | Nome, Alas. | 8 00 | A.M. | Tulsa, Okla. | 11 00 | A.M. |
| Erie, Pa. | 12 00 | Noon | Norfolk, Va. | 12 00 | Noon | Vancouver, B.C. | 9 00 | A.M. |
| Evansville, Ind. | 11 00 | A.M. | Okla. City, Okla. | 11 00 | A.M. | Washington, D.C. | 12 00 | Noon |
| Fairbanks, Alas. | 8 00 | A.M. | Omaha, Neb. | 11 00 | A.M. | Wichita, Kan. | 11 00 | A.M. |
| Flint, Mich. | 12 00 | Noon | Peoria, Ill. | 11 00 | A.M. | Wilmington, Del. | 12 00 | Noon |
| *Fort Wayne, Ind. | 12 00 | Noon | Philadelphia, Pa. | 12 00 | Noon | Winnipeg, Man. | 11 00 | A.M. |
| Fort Worth, Tex. | 11 00 | A.M. | | | | | | |

* Cities with an asterisk do not observe Daylight Saving Time. During much of the year, it is necessary to add one hour to the cities which do observe Daylight Saving Time to get the proper time relation.

## Legal or Public Holidays, 1994

Technically there are no national holidays in the United States; each state has jurisdiction over its holidays, which are designated by legislative enactment or executive proclamation. In practice, however, most states observe the federal legal public holidays, even though the President and Congress can legally designate holidays only for the District of Columbia and for federal employees. Federal legal public holidays are New Year's Day, Martin Luther King Day, Washington's Birthday, Memorial Day, Independence Day, Labor Day, Columbus Day, Veterans' Day, Thanksgiving, and Christmas.

### Chief Legal or Public Holidays

When a holiday falls on a Sunday or a Saturday it is usually observed on the following Monday or the preceding Friday. For some holidays, government and business closing practices vary. In most states, the office of the Secretary of State can provide details for holiday closings. The following will be legal or public holidays in most states in 1994:

Jan. 1 (Sat.) — New Year's Day.

Jan. 17 (3d Mon. in Jan.) — Martin Luther King Day.

Feb. 12 (Sat.) — Lincoln's Birthday.

Feb. 21 (3d Mon. in Feb.) — Washington's Birthday, or Presidents' Day, or Washington-Lincoln Day.

May 30 (last Mon. in May) — Memorial Day, or Decoration Day.

July 4 (Mon.) — Independence Day.

Sept. 5 (1st Mon. in Sept.) — Labor Day.

Oct. 10 (2d Monday in Oct.) — Columbus Day, or Discoverers' Day, or Pioneers' Day.

Nov. 11 (Fri.) — Veterans' Day.

Nov. 24 (4th Thurs. in Nov.) — Thanksgiving Day.

Dec. 26 (Mon.) — Christmas Day, obsvd.

In some states, the following will be legal or public holidays in 1994:

Apr. 1 (Fri.) — Good Friday. In some states, observed for half or part of day.

Nov. 8 (1st Tues. after 1st Mon. in Nov.) — Election Day.

### Selected Foreign Holidays

Jan. 2 — Ancestors Day, Haiti.

Jan. 6 — La Befana, Italy.

Jan. 31 — Australia Day obsvd., Australia.

Feb. 1 — Vinegrower's Day, Bulgaria.

Feb. 11 — National Foundation Day, Japan.

Mar. 8 — International Women's Day, UN nations.

Mar. 17 — St. Patrick's Day, Ireland.

Mar. 26 — Fiesta del Arbol (Arbor Day), Spain.

Apr. 7 — World Health Day, UN nations.

Apr. 8 — Buddha's Birthday, Korea, Japan.

Apr. 22 — Independence Day, Israel.

Apr. 26 — ANZAC Day, Australia, New Zealand, and Western Samoa.

May 5 — Cinco de Mayo, Mexico.

May 25 — African Freedom Day, Chad, Zambia.

July 1 — Canada Day, Canada.

July 14 — Bastille Day, France.

Aug. 2 — Picnic Day, Australia.

Aug. 10 — Independence Day, Ecuador.

Sept. 15 — Respect for the Aged Day, Japan.

Sept. 19 — St. Gennaro, Italy.

Oct. 2 — Mahatma Gandi's Birthday, India.

Oct. 10 — Thanksgiving Day, Canada.

Nov. 1-2 — Day of the Dead, Mexico.

Nov. 11 — Remembrance Day, Canada.

Dec. 26 — Boxing Day, Australia, Canada, United Kingdom.

# AEROSPACE

## Notable Crewed Space Flights

Sources: National Aeronautics and Space Administration and The World Almanac

The following table does not include aerospacecraft, such as the U.S. Space Shuttle.

| Crew, date | Mission name | Orbits[1] | Duration | | Remarks |
|---|---|---|---|---|---|
| Yuri A. Gagarin (4/12/61) | Vostok 1 | 1 | 1h 48m | | 1st manned orbital flight. |
| Alan B. Shepard Jr. (5/5/61) | Mercury-Redstone 3 | (2) | 15m 22s | | 1st American in space. |
| Virgil I. Grissom (7/21/61) | Mercury-Redstone 4 | (2) | 15m 37s | | Spacecraft sank. Grissom rescued. |
| Gherman S. Titov (8/6-7/61) | Vostok 2 | 16 | 25h 18m | | 1st space flight of more than 24 hrs. |
| John H. Glenn Jr. (2/20/62) | Mercury-Atlas 6 | 3 | 4h 55m 23s | | 1st American in orbit. |
| M. Scott Carpenter (5/24/62) | Mercury-Atlas 7 | 3 | 4h 56m 05s | | Manual retrofire error caused 250 mi. landing overshoot. |
| Andrian G. Nikolayev (8/11-15/62) | Vostok 3 | 64 | 94h 22m | | Vostok 3 and 4 made first group flight. |
| Pavel R. Popovich (8/12-15/62) | Vostok 4 | 48 | 70h 57m | | On 1st orbit it came within 3 miles of Vostok 3. |
| Walter M. Schirra Jr. (10/3/62) | Mercury-Atlas 8 | 6 | 9h 13m 11s | | Then-closest splashdown to recovery vessel (9,000 yds.). |
| L. Gordon Cooper (5/15-16/63) | Mercury-Atlas 9 | 22 | 34h 19m 49s | | 1st U.S. evaluation of effects on man of one day in space. |
| Valery F. Bykovsky (6/14-19/63) | Vostok 5 | 81 | 119h 06m | | Vostok 5 and 6 made 2d group flight. |
| Valentina V. Tereshkova (6/16-19/63) | Vostok 6 | 48 | 70h 50m | | 1st woman in space. |
| Vladimir M. Komarov, Konstantin P. Feoktistov, Boris B. Yegorov (10/12/64) | Voskhod 1 | 16 | 24h 17m | | 1st 3-man orbital flight, first without space suits. |
| Pavel I. Belyayev, Aleksei A. Leonov (3/18/65) | Voskhod 2 | 17 | 26h 02m | | Leonov made 1st "space walk" (10 min.). |
| Virgil I. Grissom, John W. Young (3/23/65) | Gemini-Titan III | 3 | 4h 53m 00s | | 1st manned spacecraft to change its orbital path. |
| James A. McDivitt, Edward H. White 2d, (6/3-7/65) | Gemini-Titan IV | 62 | 97h 56m 11s | | White was 1st American to "walk in space" (20 min.). |
| L. Gordon Cooper Jr., Charles Conrad Jr. (8/21-29/65) | Gemini-Titan V | 120 | 190h 55m 14s | | 1st use of fuel cells for electric power; evaluated guidance and navigation system. |
| Frank Borman, James A. Lovell Jr. (12/4-18/65) | Gemini-Titan VII | 206 | 330h 35m 31s | | Longest duration Gemini flight. |
| Walter M. Schirra Jr., Thomas P. Stafford (12/15-16/65) | Gemini-Titan VI-A | 16 | 25h 51m 24s | | Completed world's first space rendezvous with Gemini VII. |
| Neil A. Armstrong, David R. Scott (3/16-17/66) | Gemini-Titan VIII | 6.5 | 10h 41m 26s | | 1st docking of one space vehicle with another; mission aborted, control malfunction. |
| Thomas P. Stafford, Eugene A. Cernan (6/3-6/66) | Gemini-Titan IX-A | 45 | 72h 21m | | Closest splashdown to recovery vessel (769.9 yds.). |
| John W. Young, Michael Collins (7/18-21/66) | Gemini-Titan X | 43 | 70h 46m 39s | | 1st use of Agena target vehicle's propulsion systems. |
| Charles Conrad Jr., Richard F. Gordon Jr. (9/12-15/66) | Gemini-Titan XI | 44 | 71h 17m 08s | | Docked, made 2 revolutions of earth tethered; set Gemini altitude record (739.2 mi.). |
| James A. Lovell Jr., Edwin E. Aldrin Jr. (11/11-15/66) | Gemini-Titan XII | 59 | 94h 34m 31s | | Final Gemini mission; record 5½ hrs. of extravehicular activity. |
| Vladimir M. Komarov (4/23/67) | Soyuz 1 | 17 | 26h 40m | | Crashed after re-entry killing Komarov. |
| Walter M. Schirra Jr., Donn F. Eisele, R. Walter Cunningham (10/11-22/68) | Apollo-Saturn 7 | 163 | 260h 09m 03s | | 1st manned flight of Apollo spacecraft command-service module only. |
| Georgi T. Beregovoi (10/26-30/68) | Soyuz 3 | 64 | 94h 51m | | Made rendezvous with unmanned Soyuz 2. |
| Frank Borman, James A. Lovell Jr., William A. Anders (12/21-27/68) | Apollo-Saturn 8 | 10[3] | 147h 00m 42s | | 1st flight to moon (command-service module only); views of lunar surface televised to earth. |
| Vladimir A. Shatalov (1/14-17/69) | Soyuz 4 | 45 | 71h 14m | | Docked with Soyuz 5. |

| Crew, date | Mission name | Orbits[1] | Duration | Remarks |
|---|---|---|---|---|
| Boris V. Volyanov, Aleksei S. Yeliseyev, Yevgeny V. Khrunov (1/15-18/69) | Soyuz 5 | 46 | 72h 46m | Docked with Soyuz 4; Yeliseyev and Khrunov transferred to Soyuz 4. |
| James A. McDivitt, David R. Scott, Russell L. Schweickart (3/3-13/69) | Apollo-Saturn 9 | 151 | 241h 00m 54s | 1st manned flight of lunar module. |
| Thomas P. Stafford, Eugene A. Cernan, John W. Young (5/18-26/69) | Apollo-Saturn 10 | 31[4] | 192h 03m 23s | 1st lunar module orbit of moon. |
| Neil A. Armstrong, Edwin E. Aldrin Jr., Michael Collins (7/16-24/69) | Apollo-Saturn 11 | 30[3] | 195h 18m 35s | 1st lunar landing made by Armstrong and Aldrin; collected 48.5 lbs. of soil, rock samples; lunar stay time 21 h, 36m, 21 s. |
| Georgi S. Shonin, Valery N. Kubasov (10/11-16/69) | Soyuz 6 | 79 | 118h 42m | 1st welding of metals in space. |
| Anatoly V. Filipchenko, Vladislav N. Volkov, Viktor V. Gorbatko (10/12-17/69) | Soyuz 7 | 79 | 118h 41m | Space lab construction tests made; Soyuz 6, 7 and 8 — 1st time 3 spacecraft 7 crew orbited earth at once. |
| Charles Conrad Jr., Richard F. Gordon, Alan L. Bean (11/14-24/69) | Apollo-Saturn 12 | 45[3] | 244h 36m 25s | Conrad and Bean made 2d moon landing; collected 74.7 lbs. of samples, lunar stay time 31 h, 31 m. |
| James A. Lovell Jr., Fred W. Haise Jr., John L. Swigart Jr. (4/11-17/70) | Apollo-Saturn 13 | ... | 142h 54m 41s | Aborted after service module oxygen tank ruptured; crew returned safely using lunar module oxygen and power. |
| Alan B. Shepard Jr., Stuart A. Roosa, Edgar D. Mitchell (1/31-2/9/71) | Apollo-Saturn 14 | 34[3] | 216h 01m 57s | Shepard and Mitchell made 3d moon landing, collected 96 lbs. of lunar samples; lunar stay 33 h, 31 m. |
| Georgi T. Dobrovolsky, Vladislav N. Volkov, Viktor I. Patsayev (6/6-30/71) | Soyuz 11 | 360 | 569h 40m | Docked with Salyut space station; and orbited in Salyut for 23 days; crew died during re-entry from loss of pressurization. |
| David R. Scott, Alfred M. Worden, James B. Irwin (7/26-8/7/71) | Apollo-Saturn 15 | 74[3] | 295h 11m 53s | Scott and Irwin made 4th moon landing; first lunar rover use; first deep space walk; 170 lbs. of samples; 66 h, 55 m, stay. |
| Charles M. Duke Jr., Thomas K. Mattingly, John W. Young (4/16-27/72) | Apollo-Saturn 16 | 64[3] | 265h 51m 05s | Young and Duke made 5th moon landing; collected 213 lbs. of lunar samples; lunar stay line 71 h, 2 m. |
| Eugene A. Cernan, Ronald E. Evans, Harrison H. Schmitt (12/7-19/72) | Apollo-Saturn 17 | 75[3] | 301h 51m 59s | Cernan and Schmitt made 6th manned lunar landing; collected 243 lbs. of samples; record lunar stay of 75 h. |
| Charles Conrad Jr., Joseph P. Kerwin, Paul J. Weitz (5/25-6/22/73) | Skylab 2 | ... | 672h 49m 49s | 1st American manned orbiting space station; made long-flights tests, crew repaired damage caused during boost. |
| Alan L. Bean, Jack R. Lousma, Owen K. Garriott (7/28-9/25/73) | Skylab 3 | ... | 1,427h 09m 04s | Crew systems and operational tests, exceeded pre-mission plans for scientific activities; space walk total 13h, 44 m. |
| Gerald P. Carr, Edward G. Gibson, William Pogue (11/16/73-2/8/74) | Skylab 4 | ... | 2,017h 15m 32s | Final Skylab mission; record space walk of 7 h, 1 m., record space walks total for a mission 22 h, 21 m. |
| Alexi Leonov, Valeri Kubasov (7/15-21/75) | Soyuz 19 | 96 | 143h 31m | U.S.-USSR joint flight. Crews linked-up in space, conducted experiments, shared meals, and held a joint news conference. |
| Vance Brand, Thomas P. Stafford, Donald K. Slayton (7/15-24/75) | Apollo 18 | 136 | 217h 28m 23s | |
| Leonid Kizim, Vladmir Solovyov, Oleg Atkov (2/8-10/2/84). | Soyuz T-10/Salyut 7 | ... | 5,868h 50m | Set space endurance record (since broken). |
| Vladimir Titov, Muso Manarov, Anatoly Levchenko (12/21/87-12/21/88) | Soyuz TM-4/Mir | ... | 8,782h 39m 47s | Set space endurance record. |

(1) The U.S. measures orbital flights in revolutions while the Soviets use "orbits." (2) Suborbital. (3) Moon orbits in command module. (4) Moon orbits.
Fire aboard spacecraft Apollo I on the ground at Cape Kennedy, Fla., killed Virgil I. Grissom, Edward H. White, and Roger B. Chaffee on Jan. 27, 1967. They were the only U.S. astronauts killed in space tests.

# U.S. Space Shuttle Missions

Source: National Aeronautics and Space Administration and the World Almanac; as of Aug. 1993

| Name, date | Crew |
|---|---|
| Columbia (4/12-14/81) . . . . . | Robert L. Crippen, John W. Young. |
| Columbia (11/12-14/81) . . . . | Joe Engle, Richard Truly. |
| Columbia (3/22-30/82) . . . . . | Jack Lousma, C. Gordon Fullerton. |
| Columbia (6/27-7/4/82) . . . . | Thomas Mattingly 2d, Henry Hartsfield Jr. |
| Columbia (11/11-16/82) . . . . | Vance Brand, Robert Overmyer, William Lenoir, Joseph Allen. |
| Challenger (4/4-9/83) . . . . . | Paul Weitz, Karol Bobko, Story Musgrave, Donald Peterson. |
| Challenger (6/18-24/83) . . . . | Robert L. Crippen, Norman Thagard, John Fabian, Frederick Hauck, Sally K. Ride (first U.S. woman in space). |
| Challenger (8/30-9/5/83). . . . | Richard Truly, Daniel Brandenstein, William Thornton, Guion Bluford (first U.S. black in space), Dale Gardner. |
| Columbia (11/28-12/8/83) . . . | John Young, Brewster Shaw Jr., Robert Parker, Owen Garriott, Byron Lichtenberg, Ulf Merbold. |
| Challenger (2/3-11/84) . . . . . | Vance Brand, Robert Gibson, Ronald McNair, Bruce McCandless, Robert Stewart. |
| Challenger (4/6-13/84) . . . . . | Robert L. Crippen, Francis R. Scobee, George D. Nelson, Terry J. Hart, James D. Van Hoften. |
| Discovery (8/30-9/5/84) . . . . | Henry W. Hartsfield Jr., Michael L. Coats, Steven A. Hawley, Judith A. Resnik, Richard M. Mullane, Charles D. Walker. |
| Challenger (10/5-13/84) . . . . | Robert L. Crippen, Jon A. McBride, Kathryn D. Sullivan, Sally K. Ride, Marc Garneau (first Canadian), David C. Leestma, Paul D. Scully-Power. |
| Discovery (11/8-16/84) . . . . . | Frederick H. Hauck, David M. Walker, Dr. Anna L. Fisher, Joseph P. Allen, Dale A. Gardner. |
| Discovery (1/24-27/85) . . . . . | Thomas K. Mattingly, Loren J. Shriver, James F. Buchli, Ellison S. Onizuka, Gary E. Payton. |
| Discovery (4/12-19/85) . . . . . | Karol J. Bobko, Donald E. Williams, Sen. Jake Garn, Charles D. Walker, Jeffrey A. Hoffman, S. David Griggs, M. Rhea Seddon. |
| Challenger (4/29-5/6/85). . . . | Robert F. Overmyer, Frederick D. Gregory, Don L. Lind, Taylor G. Wang, Lodewijk van den Berg, Norman Thagard, William Thornton. |
| Discovery (6/17-24/85) . . . . . | John O. Creighton, Shannon W. Lucid, Steven R. Nagel, Daniel C. Brandenstein, John W. Fabian, Prince Sultan Salman al-Saud (first Arab), Patrick Baudry. |
| Challenger (7/29-8/6/85). . . . | Roy D. Bridges Jr., Anthony W. England, Karl G. Henize, F. Story Musgrave, C. Gordon Fullerton, Loren W. Acton, John-David F. Bartoe. |
| Discovery (8/27-9/3/85) . . . . | John M. Lounge, James D. van Hoften, William F. Fisher, Joe H. Engle, Richard O. Covey. |
| Atlantis (10/4-7/85). . . . . . . | Karol J. Bobko, Ronald J. Grabe, David C. Hilmers, William A. Pailes, Robert C. Stewart. |
| Challenger (10/30-11/6/85) . . | Henry W. Hartsfield Jr., Steven R. Nagel, Bonnie J. Dunbar, James F. Buchli, Guion S. Bluford Jr., Ernst Messerschmid, Reinhard Furrer, Wubbo J. Ockels. |
| Atlantis (11/26-12/3/85) . . . . | Brewster H. Shaw Jr., Bryan D. O'Connor, Charles Walker, Rodolfo Neri (first Mexican), Jerry L. Ross, Sherwood C. Spring, Mary L. Cleave. |
| Columbia (1/12-18/86) . . . . . | Robert L. Gibson, Charles F. Bolden Jr., George D. Nelson, Rep. Bill Nelson (first congressperson), Franklin R. Chang-Diaz, Steven A. Hawley, Robert J. Cenker. |
| Challenger (1/28/86- exploded after takeoff) | Francis R. Scobee, Michael J. Smith, Ronald E. McNair, Ellison S. Onizuka, Judith A. Resnik, Gregory B. Jarvis, Sharon Christa McAuliffe. |
| Discovery (9/29-10/3/88) . . . | Frederick H. Hauck, Richard O. Covey, Michael C. Hilmers, George D. Nelson, John M. Lounge. |
| Atlantis (12/3-6/88) . . . . . . . | Robert L. Gibson, Guy S. Gardner, Richard M. Mullane, Jerry L. Ross, William M. Shepherd. |
| Discovery (3/13-18/89) . . . . . | Michael L. Coats, John E. Blaha, James F. Buchli, Robert C. Springer, James F. Bagian. |
| Atlantis (5/4-8/89) . . . . . . . . | David M. Walker, Ronald J. Grabe, Mary L. Cleave, Norman E. Thagard, Mark C. Lee. |
| Columbia (8/8-13/89) . . . . . . | Brewster H. Shaw Jr., Richard N. Richards, David C. Leestma, James C. Adamson, Mark N. Brown. |
| Atlantis (10/18-23/89) . . . . . | Donald E. Williams, Michael J. McCulley, Shannon W. Lucid, Ellen S. Baker, Franklin R. Chang-Diaz. |
| Discovery (11/22-27/89) . . . . | Frederick D. Gregory, John E. Blaha, Manley L. Carter, F. Story Musgrave, Katherine C. Thornton. |
| Columbia (1/9-20/90) . . . . . . | Daniel C. Brandenstein, Bonnie J. Dunbar, James D. Wetherbee, Marsha S. Ivins, G. David Low. |
| Atlantis (2/28-3/4/90). . . . . . | John O. Creighton, John H. Casper, David C. Hilmers, Richard M. Mullane, Pierre J. Thuot. |
| Discovery (4/24-29/90) . . . . . | Bruce McCandless 2d, Kathryn D. Sullivan, Loren J. Shriver, Charles F. Bolden Jr., Steven A. Hawley. |
| Discovery (10/6-10/90) . . . . . | Richard N. Richards, Robert D. Cabana, Bruce E. Melnick, William M. Shepherd, Thomas D. Akers. |
| Atlantis (11/15-20/90) . . . . . | Richard O. Covey, Frank L. Culbertson, Robert C. Springer, Carl J. Meade, Charles D. Gemar. |
| Columbia (12/2-10/90) . . . . . | Vance D. Brand, Guy S. Gardner, Jeffrey A. Hoffman, John M. Lounge, Robert A.R. Parker, Samuel T. Durrance, Ronald A. Parise. |
| Atlantis (4/5-11/91) . . . . . . . | Stephen R. Nagel, Kenneth D. Cameron, Linda M. Godwin, Jerry L. Ross, Jerome Apt. |
| Discovery (4/28-5/6/91) . . . . | Michael L. Coats, L. Blaine Hammond Jr., Guion S. Bluford Jr., Gregory J. Harbaugh, Richard J. Hieb, Donald R. McMonagle, Charles L. Veach. |
| Columbia (6/5-14/91) . . . . . . | Byron O. O'Connor, Sidney M. Gutierrez, James P. Bagian, Margaret Rhea Seddon, Francis A. Gaffney, Millie Hughes-Fulford, Tamara E. Jernigan. |
| Atlantis (8/2-11/91) . . . . . . . | John E. Blaha, Michael A. Baker, Shannon W. Lucid, G. David Low, James C. Adamson. |
| Discovery (9/12-18/91) . . . . . | John O. Creighton, Kenneth S. Reightler Jr., Charles D. Gemar, James F. Buchli, Mark N. Brown. |
| Atlantis (11/24-12/1/91) . . . . | Frederick D. Gregory, Terrence T. Hendricks, F. Story Musgrave, James S. Voss, Mario Runco Jr., Thomas J. Hennen. |
| Discovery (1/22-30/92) . . . . . | Ronald J. Grabe, Stephen S. Oswald, Norman E. Thagard, William E. Readdy, David Hilmers, Roberta L. Bondar, Ulf Merbold. |
| Atlantis (3/24-4/2/92) . . . . . . | Charles F. Bolden Jr., Brian Duffy, Michael Foale, David C. Leestma, Kathryn D. Sullivan, Bryon K. Lichtenberg, Dirk D. Frimout. |
| Endeavour (5/7-16/92) . . . . . | Daniel C. Brandenstein, Kevin C. Chilton, Thomas D. Akers, Richard J. Hieb, Kathryn C. Thornton, Bruce E. Melnick, Pierre J. Thout. *Set extravehicular duration in space record.* |
| Columbia (6/25-7/9/92) . . . . | Richard N. Richards, Kenneth D. Bowersox, Bonnie J. Dunbar, Ellen S. Baker, Lawrence J. DeLucas, Carl J. Meade, Eugene H. Trinh. *Set Duration Record for Shuttle Flight.* |
| Atlantis (7/31-8/8/92) . . . . . . | Jeffrey A. Hoffman, Loren J. Shriver, Franco Malerda, Franklin R. Chang-Diaz, Andrew M. Allen, Marsha S. Ivins, Claude Nicollier. |
| Endeavour (9/12-21/92) . . . . | Robert L. Gibson, Curtis L. Brown Jr., Jay Apt, N. Jan Davis, Mae Carol Jemison (first black woman), Mark C. Lee, Mamoru Mohri (first Japanese national). |
| Columbia (10/22-11/1/92) . . . | James D. Wetherbee, Michael A. Baker, Charles L. Veach, William M. Shepherd, Tamara E. Jernigan, Steven G. MacLean. |
| Discovery (12/2-9/92) . . . . . . | David M. Walker, Robert D. Cabana, Guion S. Bluford Jr., James S. Voss, Michael R. Clifford. |
| Endeavour (1/13-19/93) . . . . | Gregory Harbaugh, Mario Runco Jr., John H. Casper, Donald R. McMonagle, Susan J. Helms. |
| Discovery (4/8-17/93) . . . . . . | Kenneth D. Cameron, Stephen S. Oswald, Michael Foale, Ellen Ochoa (first Hispanic woman), Kenneth D. Cockrell. |
| Columbia (4/26-5/6/93) . . . . | Stephen R. Nagel, Terrence T. Henricks, Jerry L. Ross, Bernard A. Harris Jr., Charles J. Precourt, Ulrich Walter, Hans William Schlegel. |
| Endeavour (6/21-7/1/93) . . . . | Ronald J. Grabe, Brian Duffy, G. David Low, Nancy J. Sherlock, Janice E. Voss, Peter J.K. Wisoff. |

## Notable U.S. Uncrewed and Planetary Missions

Source: National Aeronautics and Space Administration

| Spacecraft | Launch date (GMT) | Mission | Remarks |
|---|---|---|---|
| Mariner 2 | Aug. 27, 1962 | Venus | Passed within 22,000 miles from Venus 12/14/62; contact lost 1/3/63 at 54 million miles |
| Ranger 7 | July 28, 1964 | Moon | Yielded over 4,000 photos |
| Mariner 4 | Nov. 28, 1964 | Mars | Passed behind Mars 7/14/65; took 22 photos from 6,000 miles |
| Ranger 8 | Feb. 17, 1965 | Moon | Yielded over 7,000 photos |
| Surveyor 3 | Apr. 17, 1967 | Moon | Scooped and tested lunar soil |
| Mariner 5 | June 14, 1967 | Venus | In solar orbit; closest Venus fly-by 10/19/67 |
| Mariner 6 | Feb. 24, 1969 | Mars | Came within 2,000 miles of Mars 7/31/69; sent back data, photos |
| Mariner 7 | Mar. 27, 1969 | Mars | Came within 2,000 miles of Mars 8/5/69 |
| Mariner 9 | May 30, 1971 | Mars | First craft to orbit Mars 11/13/71; sent back over 7,000 photos |
| Pioneer 10 | Mar. 2, 1972 | Jupiter | Passed Jupiter 12/3/73; exited the solar system 6/14/83; still operating in outer solar system |
| Mariner 10 | Nov. 3, 1973 | Venus, Mercury | Passed Venus 2/5/74; arrived Mercury 3/29/74. First time gravity of one planet (Venus) used to whip spacecraft toward another (Mercury) |
| Viking 1 | Aug. 20, 1975 | Mars | Landed on Mars 7/20/76; did scientific research, sent photos; functioned 6 1/2 years |
| Viking 2 | Sept. 9, 1975 | Mars | Landed on Mars 9/3/76; functioned 3 1/2 years |
| Voyager 1 | Sept. 5, 1977 | Jupiter, Saturn | Encountered Jupiter 3/5/79, provided evidence of Jupiter ring; passed near Saturn 11/12/80 |
| Voyager 2 | Aug. 20, 1977 | Jupiter, Saturn, Uranus, Neptune | Encountered Jupiter 7/9/79; Saturn 8/26/81; Uranus 1/8 and 1/27/86; Neptune 8/24/89 |
| Pioneer Venus 1 | May 20, 1978 | Venus | Entered Venus orbit 12/4/78; spent 14 years studying planet; ceased operating 10/19/92 |
| Pioneer Venus 2 | Aug. 8, 1978 | Venus | Encountered Venus 12/9/78; probes impacted on surface |
| Magellan | May 4, 1989 | Venus | Orbit and map Venus; monitoring geological activity on surface; still operating in outer solar system |
| Titan IV | June 14, 1989 | Orbit Earth | First of 41 such rockets whose primary purpose is defense |
| Galileo | Oct. 18, 1989 | Jupiter | Used Earth's gravity to propel it toward Jupiter; encountered Venus Feb. 1991 |

## Notable Proposed U.S. Space Missions

Source: National Aeronautics and Space Administration

| Year, Month | Mission | Purpose |
|---|---|---|
| 1994 Feb. | Wind (a) | Will determine solar wind input to Earth's magnetosphere |
| 1994 | International Microgravity Laboratory - 2 (b) | Spacelab mission to study materials, fluid, and life sciences |
| 1996 | Mars Environmental Survey Pathfinder (a) | Technical demonstration of Mars Environmental Survey |
| 1996 | X-ray Timing Explorer (a) | Study temporal variability in compact x-ray emitting objects |
| 1997 | Cassini (a) | Study of Saturn's atmosphere, rings, magnetosphere and moons |
| 1998 | Earth Observing System (a) | Provide long-term data sets of interactions between Earth's land, atmosphere, water, and life |
| 1998, 1999 | Advanced X-ray Astrophysics Facility (2 spacecraft) (a) | Study of dark matter, stellar evolution, galactic clusters |
| TBD | Pluto Fast Flyby (a) | First fly-by of Pluto for photographic survey and other studies |
| 2001 | Space Infrared Telescope Facility (a) | High sensitivity observations of celestial sources |

(a) Launched by expendable rocket. (b) Carried aboard Shuttle. TBD=To Be Determined.

## Aircraft Operating Statistics, 1992

Source: Air Transport Association of America; figures are averages for most commonly used models

| | Number of Seats | Speed Airborne | Flight Length | Fuel (Gallons Per Hour) | Aircraft Operating Cost Per Hour |
|---|---|---|---|---|---|
| B747-400 | 403 | 534 | 4,375 | 3,361 | $7,098 |
| B747-100 | 399 | 520 | 3,094 | 3,507 | 5,905 |
| L-1011-100/200 | 293 | 495 | 1,519 | 2,362 | 4,072 |
| DC-10-10 | 282 | 488 | 1,387 | 2,189 | 4,056 |
| A300-600 | 266 | 474 | 1,206 | 1,686 | 3,917 |
| DC-10-30 | 265 | 522 | 2,962 | 2,607 | 4,595 |
| B767-300 | 224 | 489 | 2,087 | 1,485 | 3,384 |
| B757-200 | 188 | 458 | 1,105 | 996 | 2,293 |
| B767-200 | 187 | 483 | 2,064 | 1,434 | 2,956 |
| A320-100/200 | 149 | 441 | 944 | 757 | 1,868 |
| B727-200 | 148 | 430 | 689 | 1,242 | 2,263 |
| B737-400 | 145 | 400 | 564 | 769 | 1,743 |
| MD-80 | 142 | 419 | 662 | 889 | 1,842 |
| B737-300 | 131 | 415 | 633 | 739 | 1,768 |
| DC-9-50 | 122 | 387 | 453 | 890 | 1,640 |
| B727-100 | 117 | 429 | 638 | 1,137 | 2,220 |
| B737-100/200 | 112 | 387 | 444 | 793 | 1,735 |
| DC-9-30 | 102 | 381 | 441 | 794 | 1,658 |
| F-100 | 99 | 361 | 388 | 690 | 1,445 |
| DC-9-10 | 77 | 361 | 359 | 727 | 1,439 |

## Summary of Worldwide Payloads, 1986-1992

Source: National Aeronautics and Space Administration

(A payload is something carried into space by a rocket)

| Year | Total[1] | USSR/CIS[2] | United States | Japan | European Space Agency | India | China |
|------|----------|-------------|---------------|-------|----------------------|-------|-------|
| 1986 | 132 | 114 | 9 | 3 | 0 | — | 3 |
| 1987 | 133 | 116 | 9 | 3 | 1 | — | 1 |
| 1988 | 136 | 107 | 15 | 2 | 2 | 2 | 3 |
| 1989 | 129 | 95 | 22 | 4 | 2 | 0 | 0 |
| 1990 | 160 | 96 | 31 | 7 | 1 | 1 | 5 |
| 1991 | 156 | 101 | 30 | 2 | 4 | 1 | 1 |
| 1992 | 128 | 77 | 27 | 3 | 1 | 2 | 2 |
| Total | 4,300[3] | 2,838 | 1,158 | 56 | 31 | 15 | 32 |

(1) Incl. launches in countries not shown. (2) Figures for 1986-1991 are for the Soviet Union; 1992 figure is for the Commonwealth of Independent States. (3) Incl. launches in prior years not shown.

## Traffic at U.S. Airports, 1992

Source: Air Transport Association of America

| Airport | Passenger Arrivals and Departures | Airport | Passenger Arrivals and Departures |
|---------|-----------------------------------|---------|-----------------------------------|
| Chicago (O'Hare) | 64,441,087 | Minneapolis/St. Paul | 22,907,490 |
| Dallas/Ft. Worth | 51,943,567 | Detroit | 22,840,643 |
| Los Angeles | 46,032,988 | Honolulu | 22,608,188 |
| Atlanta | 42,032,988 | Phoenix | 22,111,555 |
| San Francisco | 31,789,021 | Orlando | 21,147,888 |
| Denver | 30,877,180 | St. Louis | 20,984,782 |
| New York (JFK) | 27,760,912 | Las Vegas | 20,913,054 |
| Miami | 26,483,717 | New York (La Guardia) | 19,662,521 |
| Newark | 24,286,986 | Houston | 19,354,013 |
| Boston | 22,988,717 | Pittsburgh | 18,748,884 |

## U.S. Scheduled Airline Traffic, 1990-1992

Source: Air Transport Association of America; in thousands

| Passenger traffic | 1990 | 1991 | 1992 |
|-------------------|------|------|------|
| Revenue passengers enplaned | 465,560 | 452,301 | 473,305 |
| Revenue passenger miles | 457,926,286 | 447,954,829 | 478,081,118 |
| Available seat miles | 733,374,893 | 715,199,140 | 751,815,137 |
| Revenue passenger load factor (%) | 62.4 | 62.6 | 63.6 |
| **Cargo traffic** (ton miles) | 12,549,104 | 12,129,963 | 13,053,681 |
| Revenue freight and express (ton miles) | 10,546,329 | 10,225,199 | 10,989,344 |
| Revenue U.S. Mail (ton miles) | 2,002,775 | 1,904,764 | 2,064,337 |
| **Financial** | | | |
| Passenger revenue | $58,453,215 | $57,091,625 | $59,747,693 |
| Net profit | − $3,921,002 | − $1,940,157 | − $4,028,452 |

## Leading Passenger Airlines, 1992

Source: Air Transport Association of America; in thousands

| Airline | Passengers | Airline | Passengers | Airline | Passengers |
|---------|-----------|---------|-----------|---------|-----------|
| American | 85,955 | Trans World | 22,292 | Simmons | 2,341 |
| Delta | 82,911 | America West | 15,118 | West Air | 1,947 |
| United | 66,596 | Alaska | 6,167 | USAir Shuttle | 1,472 |
| USAir | 54,654 | Aloha | 4,662 | Trans States | 1,322 |
| Northwest | 43,443 | Hawaiian | 4,645 | Executive Airlines | 912 |
| Continental | 38,359 | Air Wisconsin | 2,864 | Midwest Express | 808 |
| Southwest | 31,023 | Horizon Air | 2,380 | | |

## U.S. Airline Safety, Scheduled Commercial Carriers

Source: National Transportation Safety Board

| | Departures (millions) | Fatal accidents | Fatalities | Fatal accidents per 100,000 departures | | Departures (millions) | Fatal accidents | Fatalities | Fatal accidents per 100,000 departures |
|------|------|------|------|------|------|------|------|------|------|
| 1977 | 4.9 | 3 | 78 | 0.061 | 1985 | 5.8 | 4 | 197 | 0.069 |
| 1978 | 5.0 | 5 | 160 | 0.100 | 1986 | 6.4 | 2 | 5 | 0.016 |
| 1979 | 5.4 | 4 | 351 | 0.074 | 1987 | 6.6 | 4[1] | 231 | 0.046[1] |
| 1980 | 5.4 | 0 | 0 | 0.000 | 1988 | 6.7 | 3[1] | 285 | 0.030[1] |
| 1981 | 5.2 | 4 | 4 | 0.077 | 1989 | 6.6 | 11 | 278 | 0.166 |
| 1982 | 5.0 | 4 | 233 | 0.060 | 1990 | 6.9 | 6 | 39 | 0.087 |
| 1983 | 5.0 | 4 | 15 | 0.079 | 1991 | 6.8 | 4 | 62 | 0.059 |
| 1984 | 5.4 | 1 | 4 | 0.018 | 1992 | 6.9 | 4 | 33 | 0.058 |

(1) Sabotage-caused accidents are included in the number of fatal accidents, but not in the calculation of accident rates.

## National Aviation Hall of Fame

The National Aviation Hall of Fame at Dayton, Oh., is dedicated to honoring the outstanding pioneers of air and space.

Allen, William M.
Andrews, Frank M.
Armstrong, Neil A.
Arnold, Henry H. "Hap"
Atwood, John Leland

Balchen, Bernt
Baldwin, Thomas S.
Beachey, Lincoln
Beech, Olive A.
Beech, Walter H.
Bell, Alexander Graham
Bell, Lawrence D.
Bellanca, Giuseppe Mario
Bendix, Vincent T.
Boeing, William E.
Bong, Richard I.
Borman, Frank
Boyd, Albert
Bradley, Mark E.
Brown, George "Scratchley"
Byrd, Richard E.

Cessna, Clyde V.
Chamberlin, Clarence D.
Chanute, Octave
Chennault, Claire L.
Cochran (Odlum), Jacqueline
Collins, Michael
Conrad Jr., Charles
Crawford, Frederick C.
Crossfield, A. Scott
Cunningham, Alfred A.
Curtiss, Glenn H.

deSeversky, Alexander P.
Doolittle, James H.
Douglas, Donald W.
Draper, Charles S.

Eaker, Ira C.
Earhart (Putnam), Amelia
Eielson, C. Benjamin
Ellyson, Theodore G.
Ely, Eugene B.
Everest, Frank K.

Fairchild, Sherman M.
Fleet, Reuben H.
Fokker, Anthony H.G.
Ford, Henry
Foss, Joseph
Foulois, Benjamin D.
Frye, Jack

Gabreski, Francis S.
Glenn Jr., John H.
Goddard, George W.
Goddard, Robert H.
Godfrey, Arthur
Goldwater, Barry M.
Grissom, Virgil I.
Gross, Robert E.
Grumman, Leroy R.
Guggenheim, Harry F.

Haughton, Daniel J.
Hegenberger, Albert F.
Heinemann, Edward H.
Hoover, Robert A.
Hughes, Howard R.

Ingalls, David S.

James Jr., Daniel "Chappie"
Jeppesen, Elrey B.
Johnson, Clarence L.
Johnston, Alvin M. "Tex"
Jones, Thomas V.

Kenney, George C.
Kettering, Charles F.

Kindelberger, James H.
Knabenshue, A. Roy
Knight, William J.

Lahm, Frank P.
Langley, Samuel P.
Lear Sr., William P.
LeMay, Curtis E.
LeVier, Anthony W.
Lindbergh, Anne M.
Lindbergh, Charles A.
Link, Edwin A.
Lockheed, Allan H.
Loening, Grover
Luke Jr., Frank

Macready, Carl B.
Macready, John A.
Martin, Glenn L.
McDonnell, James S.
Mitscher, Marc A.
Meyer, John C.
Mitchell, William "Billy"
Montgomery, John J.
Moorer, Thomas H.
Moss, Sanford A.

Neumann, Gerhard
Nichols, Ruth R.
Northrop, John K.

Patterson, William A.
Piper Sr., William T.
Post, Wiley H.

Read, Albert C.
Reeve, Robert C.
Rentschler, Frederick B.
Richardson, Holden C.
Rickenbacker, Edward V.
Rodgers, Calbraith P.

Rogers, Will
Rushworth, Robert A.
Ryan, T. Claude

Schirra, Walter M.
Schriever, Bernard A.
Selfridge, Thomas E.
Shepard Jr., Alan B.
Sikorsky, Igor I.
Six, Robert F.
Smith, C.R.
Spaatz, Carl A.
Sperry Sr., Elmer A.
Sperry Sr., Lawrence B.
Stanley, Robert M.
Stapp, John P.
Stearmam, Lloyd C.

Taylor, Charles E.
Thomas, Lowell
Towers, John H.
Trippe, Juan T.
Turner, Roscoe
Twining, Nathan F.

Vandenberg, Hoyt
von Braun, Wernher
von Karman, Theodore
von Ohain, Hans P.
Vought, Chance M.

Wade, Leigh
Walden, Henry W.
Wells, Edward
Wilson, Thornton A.
Wright, Orville
Wright, Wilbur

Yeager, Charles E.
Young, John W.

## International Aviation and Space Records

The National Aeronautic Association of the USA, 1815 North Fort Myer Dr., Arlington, VA 22209, representative in the United States of the Fédération Aéronautique Internationale, is the certifying agency for world aviation and space records. The International Aeronautical Federation was formed in 1905 by representatives from Belgium, France, Germany, Great Britain, Spain, Italy, Switzerland, and the United States, with headquarters in Paris. Regulations for the control of official records were signed Oct. 14, 1905.

World absolute records are defined as maximum performance, regardless of class or type of aircraft used. Absolute records for space flight (Class K, spacecraft, and Class P, aerospacecraft) are kept separately. All other records, also international in scope, are termed "World Class" records and are divided into 17 classes, including: Class A, free balloons; Class B, airships; Class C-1, airplanes; Class C-2, seaplanes; Class C-3, amphibians; Class D, gliders; and Class E, rotorcrafts, such as helicopters. Classes are subdivided into four groups based on their power source: Group I—piston engine, Group II—turboprop, Group III—jet engine, Group IV—rocket engine. Sometimes there are also further divisions for weight subclasses, such as Class C-1d, which is a light airplane weighing 3,858 to 6,614 pounds. All FAI course records listed here were accomplished in Class C-1 landplanes. A partial listing of world records follows (records to Jan. 1, 1993):

### World Absolute Records—Maximum Performance in Any Class

**Speed over a straight course** — 2,193.16 mph — Capt. Elden W. Joersz, USAF, U.S., Lockheed SR-71A; Beale AFB, Cal., July 28, 1976.
**Speed over a closed circuit** — 2,092.294 mph — Maj. Adolphus H. Bledsoe Jr., USAF, U.S.; Voyager; Edwards AFB, Cal., Dec. 14-23, 1986.
**Altitude** — 123,523.58 feet — Alexander Fedotov, USSR; MiG-25 E-266M; Pomoskovnoye, USSR, Aug. 31, 1977.
**Altitude in horizontal flight** — 85,068.997 ft. — Capt. Robert C. Helt, USAF, U.S.; Lockheed SR-71; Beale AFB, Cal., July 28, 1976.

### Spacecraft (Class K)

**Duration** — 365 days, 22 hours, 39 minutes, 47 seconds — Vladimir B. Titov, Musa H. Manarov, USSR; Soyuz TM4; Dec. 21, 1987-Dec. 21, 1988.
**Altitude** — 234,672.5 mi. — Frank Borman, James A. Lovell Jr., William Anders, U.S.; Apollo 8; Dec. 21-27, 1968.
**Greatest mass lifted** — 282,197 lbs. — Frank Borman, James A. Lovell Jr., William Anders, U.S.; Apollo 8; Dec. 21-27, 1968.
**Distance** — 87,436,800 mi. — Anatoly N. Beresovoy, Valentin V. Lebedev, USSR; Salyut 7, Soyuz T-5, Soyuz T-7; May 13-Dec. 10, 1982.

## "World Class" Records

### Free Balloons-Class A

**Altitude** — 113,739.9 ft. — Cmdr. Malcolm D. Ross, USNR, U.S.; Lee Lewis Memorial Winzen Research Balloon; Gulf of Mexico, May 4, 1961.

**Distance** — 5,208.67 — Ben Abruzzo, Larry M. Newman, Rocky Aoki, Ron Clark, U.S.; Raven Experimental; Nagashima, Japan to Covello, Cal., Nov. 9-12, 1981.

**Duration** — 144 hrs. 16 min — Richard Abruzzo, Troy Bradley, U.S.; Cameron R-77; Bangor, Maine to Ben Slimane, Morocco, Sept. 16-22, 1992.

### Airplanes (Class C-1, Group I)

**Distance, closed circuit** — 24,986.727 mi — Richard Rutan, Jeana Yeager, U.S.; Voyager; Edwards AFB, Cal., Dec. 14-23, 1986.

**Speed for 100 kilometers (62.137 miles) without payload, closed circuit** — 469.549 mph — Jacqueline Cochran, U.S.; North American P-51 Mustang; Coachella Valley, Cal., Dec. 10, 1947.

**Speed for 1,000 kilometers (621.369 miles) without payload, closed circuit** — 431.09 mph — Jacqueline Cochran, U.S.; North American P-51 Mustang; Santa Rosa Summit, Cal.-Santa Fe, N.Mex.-Flagstaff, Ariz. course, May 24, 1948.

**Speed for 5,000 kilometers (3,106.849 miles) without payload, closed circuit** — 338.39 mph — Capt. James Bauer, USAF, Boeing B-29 Superfortress; Dayton, Oh., June 28, 1946.

**Speed around the world, eastbound** — 203.64 mph — D.N. Dalton, Australia; Beechcraft Duke; Brisbane, Aust.; elapsed time: 5 days 2 hrs. 19 min. 57 sec., July 20-25, 1975.

### Light Airplanes—(Class C-1d, Group I)

**Great Circle distance without landing** — 7,929.71 mi. — Peter Wilkins, Australia; Piper Malibu; Sydney, Aust. to Phoenix, Ariz., Mar. 30-Apr. 1, 1987.

**Speed for 100 kilometers (62.137 miles) without payload, closed circuit** — 322.780 mph — Ms. R. M. Sharpe, Great Britain; Vickers Supermarine Spitfire 5-B; Wolverhampton, Eng., June 17, 1950.

### Airplanes (Class C-1, Group II)

**Great Circle distance without landing** — 8,732.09 mi. — Lt. Col. Edgar L. Allison, USAF, U.S.; Lockheed HC-130 Hercules; Ching-Chuan Kang, Taiwan to Scott AFB, Ill., Feb. 20, 1972.

**Altitude** — 51,014 ft. — Donald R. Wilson, U.S.; LTV L450F; Greenville, Tex., Mar. 27, 1972.

**Speed for 1,000 kilometers (621.369 miles) without payload, closed circuit** — 541.449 mph — Ivan Soukhomlin, USSR; Tupolev Tu-114; Sternberg, USSR, Mar. 24, 1960.

**Speed for 5,000 kilometers (3,106.849 miles) without payload, closed circuit** — 545.072 mph — Ivan Soukhomlin, USSR; Tupolev Tu-114; Sternberg, USSR, Apr. 9, 1960.

**Speed around the world, eastbound** — 304.80 mph — Joe Harnish, David B. Webster, U.S.; Gulfstream Commander 695A; Elkhart, Ind.; elapsed time: 75 hrs. 54 min. 25 sec., Mar. 21-24, 1983.

### Airplanes (Class C-1, Group III)

**Great Circle distance without landing** — 12,532.28 mi. — Maj. Clyde P. Evely, USAF, U.S.; Boeing B- 52H; Kadena, Okinawa, Japan to Madrid, Spain, Jan. 10-11, 1962.

**Distance, closed circuit** — 12,521.78 mi. — Vladimir Tersky, Yuri Resnitsky, USSR; AN-124; Podmoskovnoye, USSR, May 6-7, 1987.

**Altitude** — 123,523.58 ft. — Alexander Fedotov, USSR; E-226M; Podmoskovnoye, USSR, Aug. 31, 1977.

**Speed for 100 kilometers (62.137 miles) without payload, closed circuit** — 1,618.7 mph — Alexander Fedotov, USSR; E-266, Apr. 8, 1973.

**Speed for 500 kilometers (310.68 miles) without payload, closed circuit** — 1,852.61 mph — Mikhail Komarov, USSR; E-266, Oct. 5, 1967.

**Speed for 1,000 kilometers (621.369 miles) without payload, closed circuit** — 2,092.294 mph — Maj. Adolphus H. Bledsoe, USAF, U.S.; Lockheed SR-71 Blackbird; Beale AFB, Cal., July 27, 1976.

**Speed for 2,000 kilometers (1,242.7 miles) without payload, closed circuit** — 1,250.42 mph — S. Agapov, B. Veremey, USSR; Aircraft "101"; Podmoskovnoye, USSR, July 20, 1983.

**Speed around the world, eastbound** — 637.71 mph — Allen E. Paulson, Robert K. Smyth, John Salamanaks, Jeff Bailey, U.S.; Gulfstream IV N400GA; Houston, Tex., Feb. 26-28, 1988.

### Gliders (Class D-1—single seater)

**Distance, straight line** — 907.7 mi. — Hans Werner Grosse, West Germany; ASK12; Luebeck, W. Germany-Biarritz, France, Apr. 25, 1972.

**Distance to a goal & return** — 1,023.25 mi. — Thomas L. Knauff, U.S.; Nimbus II; Williamsport, Pa., Apr. 25, 1983.

### Helicopters (Class E-I)

**Great Circle distance without landing** — 2,213.04 mi — Robert G. Ferry, U.S.; Hughes YOH-6A No. 24213; Culver City, Cal. to Ormond Beach, Fla., Apr. 6-7, 1966.

**Speed around the world** — 35.40 mph — H. Ross Perot Jr., J.W. Coburn, U.S.; Bell 206 L-II Long Ranger No. 3911Z; Dallas, Texas; elapsed time: 29 days 3 hrs. 8 min. 13 sec., Sept. 1-30, 1982.

### FAI Course Records

**Los Angeles to New York** — 1,214.65 mph — Capt. Robert G. Sowers, USAF, U.S.; Convair B-58 Hustler; elapsed time: 2 hrs. 58.71 sec., Mar. 5, 1962.

**New York to Los Angeles** — 1,081.80 mph — Capt. Robert G. Sowers, USAF, U.S.; Convair B-58 Hustler; elapsed time: 2 hrs. 15 min. 50.08 sec., Mar. 5, 1962.

**London to New York** — 1,021.54 mph — Capt. Peter Horton, U.S.; British Airways Concorde G-BOAF; Mar. 14, 1990.

**Baltimore to Moscow, USSR** — 563.36 mph — Col. James B. Swindal, USAF, U.S.; Boeing VC-137 (707); elapsed time: 8 hrs. 33 min. 45.4 sec., May 19, 1963.

**New York to London** — 1,806.964 mph — Maj. James V. Sullivan, USAF, U.S.; Lockheed SR-71; elapsed time 1 hr. 54 min. 56.4 sec., Sept. 1, 1974.

**London to Los Angeles** — 1,435.587 mph — Capt. Harold B. Adams, USAF, U.S.; Lockheed SR-71; elapsed time: 3 hrs. 47 min. 39 sec., Sept. 13, 1974.

## Notable Around the World and Intercontinental Trips

| | From/To | Miles | Time | Date |
|---|---|---|---|---|
| Nellie Bly | New York/New York | | 72d 06h 11m | 1889 |
| George Francis Train | New York/New York | | 67d 12h 03m | 1890 |
| Charles Fitzmorris | Chicago/Chicago | | 60d 13h 29m | 1901 |
| J. W. Willis Sayre | Seattle/Seattle | | 54d 09h 42m | 1903 |
| J. Alcock-A.W. Brown[1] | Newfoundland/Ireland | 1,960 | 16h 12m | June 14-15, 1919 |
| Two U.S. Army airplanes | Seattle/Seattle | 26,103 | 35d 01h 11m | 1924 |
| Richard E. Byrd[2] | Spitsbergen/N. Pole | 1,545 | 15h 30m | May 9, 1926 |
| Amundsen-Ellsworth-Nobile Expedition | Spitsbergen/Teller, Alaska | | 80h | May 11-14,1926 |
| E.S. Evans and L. Wells (N.Y.World)[3] | New York/New York | 18,410 | 28d 14h 36m 05s | June 16-July 14, 1926 |
| Charles Lindbergh[4] | New York/Paris | 3,610 | 33h 29m 30s | May 20-21, 1927 |
| Amelia Earhart, W. Stultz, L. Gordon | Newfoundland/Wales | | 20h 40m | June 17-18, 1928 |
| Graf Zeppelin | Friedrichshafen, Ger./Lakehurst, N.J. | 6,630 | 4d 15h 46m | Oct. 11-15, 1928 |
| Graf Zeppelin | Friedrichshafen, Ger./Lakehurst, N.J. | 21,700 | 20d 04h | Aug. 14-Sept. 4, 1929 |
| Wiley Post and Harold Gatty (Monoplane Winnie Mae) | New York/New York | 15,474 | 8d 15h 51m | July 1, 1931 |
| C. Pangborn-H. Herndon Jr.[5] | Misawa, Japan/Wenatchee, Wash. | 4,458 | 41h 34m | Oct. 3-5, 1931 |
| Amelia Earhart[6] | Newfoundland/Ireland | 2,026 | 14h 56m | May 20-21, 1932 |
| Wiley Post (Monoplane Winnie Mae)[7] | New York/New York | 15,596 | 115h 36m 30s | July 15-22, 1933 |
| Hindenburg Zeppelin | Lakehurst, N.J./Frankfort, Ger. | | 42h 53m | Aug. 9-11, 1936 |
| H. R. Ekins (Scripps-Howard Newspapers in race) (Zeppelin Hindenburg to Germany, airplanes from Frankfurt) | Lakehurst, N.J./Lakehurst, N.J. | 25,654 | 18d 11h 14m 33s | Sept, 30-Oct. 19, 1936 |
| Howard Hughes and 4 assistants | New York/New York | 14,824 | 3d 19h 08m 10s | July 10-13, 1938 |
| Douglas Corrigan | New York/Dublin | | 28h 13m | July 17-18, 1938 |
| Mrs. Clara Adams (Pan American Clipper) | Port Washington, N.Y./Newark, N.J. | | 16d 19h 04m | June 28-July 15, 1939 |
| Globester, U.S. Air Transport Command | Wash., D.C./Wash., D.C. | 23,279 | 149h 44m | Oct. 4, 1945 |
| Capt. William P. Odom (A-26 Reynolds Bombshell) | New York/New York | 20,000 | 78h 55m 12s | Apr. 12-16, 1947 |
| America, Pan American 4-engine Lockheed Constellation[8] | New York/New York | 22,219 | 101h 32m | June 17-30, 1947 |
| Col. Edward Eagan | New York/New York | 20,559 | 147h 15m | Dec. 13, 1948 |
| USAF B-50 Lucky Lady II (Capt. James Gallagher)[9] | Ft. Worth, Tex./Ft. Worth, Tex. | 23,452 | 94h 01m | Feb. 26-Mar. 2, 1949 |
| Col. D. Schilling, USAF[10] | England/Limestone, Me. | 3,300 | 10h 01m | Sept. 22, 1950 |
| C.F. Blair Jr. | Norway/Alaska | 3,300 | 10h 29m | May 29, 1951 |
| Two U.S. S-55. | Massachusetts/Scotland | 3,410 | 42h 30m | July 15-31, 1952 |
| Canberra Bomber[11] | N. Ireland/Newfoundland | 2,073 | 04h 34m | Aug. 26, 1952 |
| | Newfoundland/N. Ireland | 2,073 | 03h 25m | Aug. 26, 1952 |
| Three USAF B-52 Stratofortresses[12] | Merced, Cal./Cal. | 24,325 | 45h 19m | Jan. 15-18, 1957 |
| Max Conrad | Chicago/Rome | 5,000 | 34h 03m | Mar. 5-6, 1959 |
| USSR TU-114[13] | Moscow/New York | 5,092 | 11h 06m | June 28, 1959 |
| Boeing 707-320 | New York/Moscow | c.5090 | 08h 54m | July 23, 1959 |
| Peter Gluckmann (solo) | San Francisco/San Francisco | 22,800 | 29d | Aug. 22-Sept. 20, 1959 |
| Sue Snyder | Chicago/Chicago | 21,219 | 62h 59m | June 22-24, 1960 |
| Max Conrad (solo) | Miami/Miami | 25,946 | 8d 18h 35m 57s | Feb. 28-Mar. 8, 1961 |
| Sam Miller & Louis Fodor | New York/New York | | 46h 28m | Aug. 3-4, 1963 |
| Robert & Joan Wallick | Manila/Manila | 23,129 | 5d 06h 17m 10s | June 2-7, 1966 |
| Arthur Godfrey, Richard Merrill Fred Austin, Karl Keller | New York/New York | 23,333 | 86h 9m 01s | June 4-7, 1966 |
| Trevor K. Brougham | Darwin, Australia/Darwin | 24,800 | 5d 05h 57m | Aug. 5-10, 1972 |
| Walter H. Mullikin, Albert Frink, Lyman Watt, Frank Cassaniti, Edward Shields | New York/New York | 23,137 | 1d 22h 50s | May 1-3,1976 |
| David Kunst[14] | Waseca, Minn./Waseca, Minn. | 14,500 | 4yrs 3mos 16d | June 10, 1970-Oct. 5, 1974 |
| Arnold Palmer | Denver/Denver | 22,985 | 57h 25m 42s | May 17-19, 1976 |
| Boeing 747[15] | San Francisco/San Francisco | 26,382 | 54h 7m 12s | Oct. 28-31, 1977 |
| Concorde | London/Wash., D.C. | 1,023 mph | 03h 34m 48s | May 29, 1976 |
| Concorde | Paris/New York | 1,037.50 mph | 03h 30m 11s | Aug. 22, 1978 |
| Richard Rutan & Jeana Yeager[16] | Edwards AFB, Cal. | 24,986 | 09d 03m 44s | Dec. 14-23, 1986 |

(1) Non-stop transatlantic flight. (2) Polar flight. (3) Mileage by train and auto, 4,110; by plane, 6,300; by steamship, 8,000. (4) Solo transatlantic flight in the Ryan monoplane the "Spirit of St. Louis". (5) Non-stop Pacific flight. (6) Women's transoceanic solo flight. (7) First to fly solo around northern circumference of the world, also first to fly twice around the world. (8) Inception of regular commercial global air service. (9) First non-stop round-the-world flight, refueled 4 times in flight. (10) Non-stop jet transatlantic flight. (11) Transatlantic round trip on same day. (12) First non-stop global flight by jet planes; refueled in flight by KC-97 aerial tankers; average speed approx. 525 mph. (13) Non-stop between Moscow and New York. (14) First to circle the earth on foot. (15) Speed record around the world over both the earth's poles. (16) Circled the earth non-stop without refueling.

# WEIGHTS AND MEASURES

Source: National Institute of Standards and Technology, U.S. Dept. of Commerce

## The International System of Units

Two systems of weights and measures exist side by side in the United States today, with roughly equal but separate legislative sanction: the U.S. Customary System and the International (Metric) System. Throughout U.S. history, the Customary System (inherited from, but now different from, the British Imperial System) has been, as its name implies, customarily used; a plethora of federal and state legislation has given it, through implication, standing as our primary weights and measures system. However, the Metric System (incorporated in the scientists' new SI or Systeme International d'Unites) is the only system that has ever received specific legislative sanction by Congress. The "Law of 1866" reads:

It shall be lawful throughout the United States of America to employ the weights and measures of the metric system; and no contract or dealing, or pleading in any court, shall be deemed invalid or liable to objection because the weights or measures expressed or referred to therein are weights or measures of the metric system.

Over the last 100 years, the Metric System has seen slow, steadily increasing use in the United States. In science and also in the pharmaceutical industry, the use of metrics has

for many years been predominant; today, the manufacturing industry is steadily increasing its use of the metric system largely motivated by the automotive industry, which is now predominantly metric.

On Feb. 10, 1964, the National Bureau of Standards issued the following bulletin:

Henceforth it shall be the policy of the National Bureau of Standards to use the units of the International System (SI), as adopted by the 11th General Conference on Weights and Measures (October 1960), except when the use of these units would obviously impair communication or reduce the usefulness of a report.

The Trade Act of 1988, and other legislation, calls for the federal government to adopt metric specifications and mandates the Commerce Dept. to oversee the program. The conversion process is currently underway.

What had been the Metric System became the International System (SI), a more complete scientific system.

Seven units have been adopted to serve as the base for the International System as follows: **length**—meter; **mass**—kilogram; **time**—second; **electric current**—ampere; **thermodynamic temperature**—kelvin; **amount of substance**—mole; and **luminous intensity**—candela.

### Prefixes

The following prefixes, in combination with the basic unit names, provide the multiples and submultiples in the International System. For example, the unit name "meter," with the prefix "kilo" added, produces "kilometer," meaning "1,000 meters."

| Prefix | Symbol | Multiples | Equivalent | Prefix | Symbol | Submultiples | Equivalent |
|--------|--------|-----------|------------|--------|--------|--------------|------------|
| exa | E | $10^{18}$ | quintillionfold | deci | d | $10^{-1}$ | tenth part |
| peta | P | $10^{15}$ | quadrillionfold | centi | c | $10^{-2}$ | hundredth part |
| tera | T | $10^{12}$ | trillionfold | milli | m | $10^{-3}$ | thousandth part |
| giga | G | $10^{9}$ | billionfold | micro | $\mu$ | $10^{-6}$ | millionth part |
| mega | M | $10^{6}$ | millionfold | nano | n | $10^{-9}$ | billionth part |
| kilo | k | $10^{3}$ | thousandfold | pico | p | $10^{-12}$ | trillionth part |
| hecto | h | $10^{2}$ | hundredfold | femto | f | $10^{-15}$ | quadrillionth part |
| deka | da | 10 | tenfold | atto | a | $10^{-18}$ | quintillionth part |

## Tables of Metric Weights and Measures

### Linear Measure

| | |
|---|---|
| 10 millimeters (mm) | = 1 centimeter (cm) |
| 10 centimeters | = 1 decimeter (dm) = 100 millimeters |
| 10 decimeters | = 1 meter (m) = 1,000 millimeters |
| 10 meters | = 1 dekameter (dam) |
| 10 dekameters | = 1 hectometer (hm) = 100 meters |
| 10 hectometers | = 1 kilometer (km) = 1,000 meters |

### Area Measure

| | |
|---|---|
| 100 square millimeters (mm²) | = 1 square centimeter (cm²) |
| 10,000 square centimeters | = 1 square meter (m²) = 1,000,000 square millimeters |
| 100 square meters | = 1 are (a) |
| 100 ares | = 1 hectare (ha) = 10,000 square meters |
| 100 hectares | = 1 square kilometer (km²) = 1,000,000 square meters |

### Fluid Volume Measure

| | |
|---|---|
| 10 milliliters (mL) | = 1 centiliter (cL) |
| 10 centiliters | = 1 deciliter (dL) = 100 milliliters |
| 10 deciliters | = 1 liter (L) = 1,000 milliliters |
| 10 liters | = 1 dekaliter (daL) |
| 10 dekaliters | = 1 hectoliter (hL) = 100 liters |
| 10 hectoliters | = 1 kiloliter (kL) = 1,000 liters |

### Cubic Measure

| | |
|---|---|
| 1,000 cubic millimeters (mm³) | = 1 cubic centimeter (cm³) |
| 1,000 cubic centimeters | = 1 cubic decimeter (dm³) = 1,000,000 cubic millimeters |
| 1,000 cubic decimeters | = 1 cubic meter (m³) = 1 stere = 1,000,000 cubic centimeters = 1,000,000,000 cubic millimeters |

### Weight

| | |
|---|---|
| 10 milligrams (mg) | = 1 centigram (cg) |
| 10 centigrams | = 1 decigram (dg) = 100 milligrams |
| 10 decigrams | = 1 gram (g) = 1,000 milligrams |
| 10 grams | = 1 dekagram (dag) |
| 10 dekagrams | = 1 hectogram (hg) = 100 grams |
| 10 hectograms | = 1 kilogram (kg) = 1,000 grams |
| 1,000 kilograms | = 1 metric ton (t) |

## Table of U.S. Customary Weights and Measures

### Linear Measure

| | |
|---|---|
| 12 inches (in) | = 1 foot (ft) |
| 3 feet | = 1 yard (yd) |
| 5 ½ yards | = 1 rod (rd), pole, or perch (16 ½ feet) |
| 40 rods | = 1 furlong (fur) = 220 yards = 660 feet |
| 8 furlongs | = 1 statute mile (mi) = 1,760 yards = 5,280 feet |
| 3 miles | = 1 league = 5,280 yards = 15,840 feet |
| 6076.11549 feet | = 1 International Nautical Mile |

## Liquid Measure

When necessary to distinguish the liquid pint or quart from the dry pint or quart, the word "liquid" or the abbreviation "liq" should be used in combination with the name or abbreviation of the liquid unit.

| | |
|---|---|
| 4 gills | = 1 pint (pt) = 28.875 cubic inches |
| 2 pints | = 1 quart (qt) = 57.75 cubic inches |
| 4 quarts | = 1 gallon (gal) = 231 cubic inches = 8 pints = 32 gills |

## Area Measure

Squares and cubes of units are sometimes abbreviated by using "superior" figures. For example. ft² means square foot, and ft³ means cubic foot.

| | |
|---|---|
| 144 square inches | = 1 square foot (ft²) |
| 9 square feet | = 1 square yard (yd²) = 1,296 square inches |
| 30 ¼ square yards | = 1 square rod (rd²) = 272 ¼ square feet |
| 160 square rods | = 1 acre = 4,840 square yards = 43,560 square feet |
| 640 acres | = 1 square mile (mi²) |
| 1 mile square | = 1 section (of land) |
| 6 miles square | = 1 township = 36 sections = 36 square miles |

## Cubic Measure

| | |
|---|---|
| 1 cubic foot (ft³) | = 1,728 cubic inches (in³) |
| 27 cubic feet | = 1 cubic yard (yd³) |

## Gunter's or Surveyors' Chain Measure

| | |
|---|---|
| 7.92 inches (in) | = 1 link |
| 100 links | = 1 chain (ch) = 4 rods = 66 feet |
| 80 chains | = 1 survey mile (mi) = 320 rods = 5,280 feet |

## Troy Weight

| | |
|---|---|
| 24 grains | = 1 pennyweight (dwt) |
| 20 pennyweights | = 1 ounce troy (oz t) = 480 grains |
| 12 ounces troy | = 1 pound troy (lb t) = 240 pennyweights = 5,760 grains |

## Dry Measure

When necessary to distinguish the dry pint or quart from the liquid pint or quart, the word "dry" should be used in combination with the name or abbreviation of the dry unit.

| | |
|---|---|
| 2 pints (pt) | = 1 quart (qt) = 67.2006 cubic inches |
| 8 quarts | = 1 peck (pk) = 537.605 cubic inches = 16 pints |
| 4 pecks | = 1 bushel (bu) = 2,150.42 cubic inches = 32 quarts |

## Avoirdupois Weight

When necessary to distinguish the avoirdupois ounce or pound from the troy ounce or pound, the word "avoirdupois" or the abbreviation "avdp" should be used in combination with the name or abbreviation of the avoirdupois unit.

(The "grain" is the same in avoirdupois and troy weight.)

| | |
|---|---|
| 27 11/32 grains | = 1 dram (dr) |
| 16 drams | = 1 ounce (oz) = 437 ½ grains |
| 16 ounces | = 1 pound (lb) = 256 drams = 7,000 grains |
| 100 pounds | = 1 hundredweight (cwt)* |
| 20 hundredweights | = 1 ton = 2,000 pounds* |

In "gross" or "long" measure, the following values are recognized.

| | |
|---|---|
| 112 pounds | = 1 gross or long hundredweight* |
| 20 gross or long hundredweights | = 1 gross or long ton = 2,240 pounds* |

*When the terms "hundredweight" and "ton" are used unmodified, they are commonly understood to mean the 100-pound hundredweight and the 2,000-pound ton, respectively: these units may be designated "net" or "short" when necessary to distinguish them from the corresponding units in gross or long measure.

# Tables of Equivalents

In this table it is necessary to distinguish between the "international" and the "survey" foot. The international foot, defined in 1959 as exactly equal to 0.3048 meter, is shorter than the old survey foot by exactly 2 parts in one million. The survey foot is still used in data expressed in feet in geodetic surveys within the U.S. In this table the survey foot is italicized.

When the name of a unit is enclosed in brackets thus, [1 hand], this indicates (1) that the unit is not in general current use in the United States, or (2) that the unit is believed to be based on "custom and usage" rather than on formal definition.

Equivalents involving decimals are, in most instances, rounded off to the third decimal place except where they are exact, in which cases these exact equivalents are so designated.

### Lengths

| | |
|---|---|
| 1 angstrom (A) | 0.1 nanometer (exactly)<br>0.000 1 micrometer (exactly)<br>0.000 000 1 millimeter (exactly)<br>0.000 000 004 inch |
| 1 cable's length | 120 fathoms (exactly)<br>720 *feet* (exactly)<br>219 meters |
| 1 centimeter (cm) | 0.3937 inch |
| 1 chain (ch) (Gunter's or surveyors) | 66 *feet* (exactly)<br>20.1168 meters |
| 1 chain (engineers) | 100 feet<br>30.48 meters (exactly) |
| 1 decimeter (dm) | 3.937 inches |
| 1 degree (geographical) | 364,566.929 feet<br>69.047 miles (avg.)<br>111.123 kilometers (avg.) |
| -of latitude | 68.708 miles at equator<br>69.403 miles at poles |
| -of longitude | 69.171 miles at equator |
| 1 dekameter (dam) | 32.808 feet |
| 1 fathom | 6 *feet* (exactly)<br>1.8288 meters (exactly) |
| 1 foot (ft) | 0.3048 meter (exactly) |
| 1 furlong (fur) | 10 chains (surveyors) (exactly)<br>660 *feet* (exactly)<br>⅛ statute mile (exactly)<br>201.168 meters |
| [1 hand] (height measure for horses from ground to top of shoulders) | 4 inches |
| 1 inch (in) | 2.54 centimeters (exactly) |
| 1 kilometer (km) | 0.621 mile<br>3,281.5 feet |

| | |
|---|---|
| 1 league (land) | 3 survey miles (exactly)<br>4.828 kilometers |
| 1 link (Gunter's or surveyors) | 7.92 inches (exactly)<br>0.201 meter |
| 1 link engineers | 1 foot<br>0.305 meter |
| 1 meter (m) | 39.37 inches<br>1.094 yards |
| 1 micrometer (μm) [the Greek letter mu] | 0.001 millimeter (exactly)<br>0.000 039 37 inch |
| 1 mil | 0.001 inch (exactly)<br>0.025 4 millimeter (exactly) |
| 1 mile (mi) (statute or land) | 5,280 feet (exactly)<br>1.609 kilometers |
| 1 international nautical mile (nmi) | 1.852 kilometers (exactly)<br>1.150779 survey miles<br>6,076.11549 feet |
| 1 millimeter (mm) | 0.039 37 inch |
| 1 nanometer (nm) | 0.001 micrometer (exactly)<br>0.000 000 039 37 inch |
| 1 pica (typography) | 12 points |
| 1 point (typography) | 0.013 837 inch (exactly)<br>0.351 millimeter |
| 1 rod (rd), pole, or perch | 16 ½ *feet* (exactly)<br>5.029 meters |
| 1 yard (yd) | 0.9144 meter (exactly) |

### Areas or Surfaces

| | |
|---|---|
| 1 acre | 43,560 square *feet* (exactly)<br>4,840 square yards<br>0.405 hectare |
| 1 are (a) | 119.599 square yards<br>0.025 acre |

1 bolt (cloth measure):
- length . . . . . . . . . . . . 100 yards (on modern looms)
- width . . . . . . . . . . . . { 42 inches (usually, for cotton)
{ 60 inches (usually, for wool)

1 hectare (ha) . . . . . . . . . . . . . . . . . . . . . 2.471 acres
[1 square (building)] . . . . . . . . . . . . . . . 100 square feet
1 square centimeter (cm²) . . . . . . . . . . . 0.155 square inch
1 square decimeter (dm²) . . . . . . . . . . . 15.500 square inches
1 square foot (ft²) . . . . . . . . . . . 929.030 square centimeters
1 square inch (in²) . . . . . . . 6.4516 square centimeters (exactly)
1 square kilometer (km²) . . . { 247.104 acres
{ 0.386 square mile
1 square meter (m²) . . . . . . { 1.196 square yards
{ 10.764 square feet
1 square mile (mi²) . . . . . . . . . . . . . . . 258.999 hectares
1 square millimeter (mm²) . . . . . . . . . . . 0.002 square inch
1 square rod (rd²) sq. pole, or
sq. perch . . . . . . . . . . . . . . . . . 25.293 square meters
1 square yard (yd²) . . . . . . . . . . . . . . 0.836 square meter

## Capacities or Volumes

1 barrel (bbl) liquid . . . . . . . . . . . . . . . . 31 to 42 gallons*

*There are a variety of "barrels," established by law or usage. For example: federal taxes on fermented liquors are based on a barrel of 31 gallons: many state laws fix the "barrel for liquids" as 31 1/2 gallons; one state fixes a 36-gallon barrel for cistern measurement; federal law recognizes a 40-gallon barrel for "proof spirits"; by custom, 42 gallons comprise a barrel of crude oil or petroleum products for statistical purposes, and this equivalent is recognized "for liquids" by 4 states.

1 barrel (bbl), standard, { 7,056 cubic inches
for fruits, vegetables, { 105 dry quarts
and other dry com- {
modities except dry { 3.281 bushels, struck
cranberries . . . . . . . . . . { measure

1 barrel (bbl), standard, { 5,826 cubic inches
cranberry { 86⁴⁵/₆₄ dry quarts
{ 2.709 bushels, struck
{ measure
1 board foot (lumber measure) . . a foot-square board 1 inch thick

1 bushel (bu) (U.S.) { 2,150.42 cubic inches
(struck measure) { (exactly)
{ 35.239 liters

[1 bushel, heaped (U.S.)] { 2,747.715 cubic inches
{ 1.278 bushels, struck
{ measure*

*Frequently recognized as 1¼ bushels, struck measure.
[1 bushel (bu) (British { 1.032 U.S. bushels
Imperial) (struck { measure
measure)] { 2,219.36 cubic inches

1 cord (cd) firewood . . . . . . . . . . . . 128 cubic feet (exactly)
1 cubic centimeter (cm³) . . . . . . . . . . . 0.061 cubic inch
1 cubic decimeter (dm³) . . . . . . . . . . . 61.024 cubic inches

1 cubic inch (in³) { 0.554 fluid ounce
{ 4.433 fluid drams
{ 16.387 cubic centimeters

1 cubic foot (ft³) . . . . . . . { 7.481 gallons
{ 28.317 cubic decimeters
1 cubic meter (m³) . . . . . . . . . . . . . 1.308 cubic yards
1 cubic yard (yd³) . . . . . . . . . . . . . 0.765 cubic meter

1 cup, measuring { 8 fluid ounces (exactly)
{ ½ liquid pint (exactly)

[1 dram, fluid (fl dr) { 0.961 U.S. fluid dram
(British)] . . . . . . . . . { 0.217 cubic inch
{ 3.552 milliliters

1 dekaliter (daL) . . . . . . . . . . . . . . { 2.642 gallons
{ 1.135 pecks

{ 231 cubic inches (exactly)
1 gallon (gal) (U.S.) . . . . . { 3.785 liters
{ 0.833 British gallon
{ 128 U.S. fluid ounces (exactly)

{ 277.42 cubic inches
[1 gallon (gal) { 1.201 U.S. gallons
British Imperial] . . . . . { 4.546 liters
{ 160 British fluid ounces (exactly)

1 gill (gi) . . . . . . . . . . . . . { 7.219 cubic inches
{ 4 fluid ounces (exactly)
{ 0.118 liter

1 hectoliter (hL) . . . . . . . . . . . . . . { 26.418 gallons
{ 2.838 bushels

1 liter (L) (1 cubic decimeter exactly) . . . . { 1.057 liquid quarts
{ 0.908 dry quart
{ 61.025 cubic inches

1 milliliter (mL) (1 cu cm exactly) . . . . . { 0.271 fluid dram
{ 16.231 minims
{ 0.061 cubic inch

1 ounce, liquid { 1.805 cubic inches
(U.S.) . . . . . . . . . . . . { 29.573 milliliters
{ 1.041 British fluid ounces

[1 ounce, fluid (fl oz) (British)] { 0.961 U.S. fluid ounce
{ 1.734 cubic inches
{ 28.412 milliliters

1 peck (pk) . . . . . . . . . . . . . . . . . . . . . . 8.810 liters

1 pint (pt), dry . . . . . . . { 33.600 cubic inches
{ 0.551 liter

1 pint (pt), liquid . . . . . . . { 28.875 cubic inches (exactly)
{ 0.473 liter

1 quart (qt) dry (U.S.) . . . . { 67.201 cubic inches
{ 1.101 liters
{ 0.969 British quart

1 quart (qt) liquid (U.S.) . . . { 57.75 cubic in (exactly)
{ 0.946 liter
{ 0.833 British quart

[1 quart (qt) (British)] . . . . { 69.354 cubic inches
{ 1.032 U.S. dry quarts
{ 1.201 U.S. liquid quarts

1 tablespoon . . . . . . . . . . . { 3 teaspoons*(exactly)
{ 4 fluid drams
{ ½ fluid ounce (exactly)

1 teaspoon . . . . . . . . . . . { ⅓ tablespoon*(exactly)
{ 1⅓ fluid drams*

*The equivalent "1 teaspoon—1⅓ fluid drams" has been found by the bureau to correspond more closely with the actual capacities of "measuring" and silver teaspoons than the equivalent "1 teaspoon—1 fluid dram" which is given by many dictionaries.

## Weights or Masses

1 assay ton*** (AT) . . . . . . . . . . . . . . . . . 29.167 grams

***Used in assaying. The assay ton bears the same relation to the milligram that a ton of 2,000 pounds avoirdupois bears to the ounce troy; hence the weight in milligrams of precious metal obtained from one assay ton of ore gives directly the number of troy ounces to the net ton.

1 bale (cotton measure) . . . . { 500 pounds in U.S.
{ 750 pounds in Egypt
1 carat (c) . . . . . . . . . . . . . . { 200 milligrams (exactly)
{ 3.086 grains
1 dram avoirdupois (dr avdp) { 27¹¹/₃₂ (=27.344) grains
gamma, see microgram { 1.772 grams
1 grain . . . . . . . . . . . . . . . . . . . . . 64.799 milligrams
1 gram . . . . . . . . . . . . . . { 15.432 grains
{ 0.035 ounce, avoirdupois
1 hundredweight, gross or { 112 pounds (exactly)
long*** (gross cwt) . . . . { 50.802 kilograms
1 hundredweight, net or short . { 100 pounds (exactly)
(cwt. or net cwt.) . . . . . { 45.359 kilograms
1 kilogram (kg) . . . . . . . . . . . . . . . . . 2.205 pounds
1 microgram (µg [The Greek letter mu in
combination with the letter g]) . . 0.000001 gram (exactly)
1 milligram (mg) . . . . . . . . . . . . . . . . 0.015 grain
1 ounce, avoirdupois { 437.5 grains (exactly)
(oz avdp) . . . . . . . . . . { 0.911 troy ounce
{ 28.350 grams
1 ounce, troy (oz t) . . . . . . { 480 grains (exactly)
{ 1.097 avoirdupois ounces
{ 31.103 grams
1 pennyweight (dwt) . . . . . . 1.555 grams
1 pound, avoirdupois { 7,000 grains (exactly)
(lb avdp) . . . . . . . . . . { 1.215 troy pounds
{ 453.592 37 grams (exactly)
1 pound, troy (lb t) . . . . . . { 5,760 grains (exactly)
{ 0.823 avoirdupois pound
{ 373.242 grams
1 ton, gross or long*** { 2,240 pounds (exactly)
(gross ton) . . . . . . . . . { 1.12 net tons (exactly)
{ 1.016 metric tons

***The gross or long ton and hundredweight are used commercially in the United States to only a limited extent, usually in restricted industrial fields. These units are the same as British "ton" and "hundredweight."

1 ton, metric (t) . . . . . . . { 2,204.623 pounds
{ 0.984 gross ton
{ 1.102 net tons
1 ton, net or short (sh ton) . . { 2,000 pounds (exactly)
{ 0.893 gross ton
{ 0.907 metric ton

# Tables of Interrelation of Units of Measurement

Units of length and area of the international and survey measures are included in the following tables. Units unique to the survey measure are italicized. See p. 279, Tables of Equivalents, 1st para.

| | |
|---|---|
| 1 international foot | = 0.999 998 survey foot (exactly) |
| 1 survey foot | = 1200/3937 meter (exactly) |
| 1 international foot | = 12 × 0.0254 meter (exactly) |

**Bold face type indicates exact values**

## Units of Length

| Units | Inches | Links | Feet | Yards | Rods | Chains | Miles | cm | Meters |
|---|---|---|---|---|---|---|---|---|---|
| 1 inch= | 1 | 0.126 263 | 0.083 333 | 0.027 778 | 0.005 051 | 0.001 263 | 0.000 016 | 2.54 | 0.025 4 |
| 1 link= | 7.92 | 1 | 0.66 | 0.22 | 0.04 | 0.01 | 0.000 125 | 20.117 | 0.201 168 |
| 1 foot= | 12 | 1.515 152 | 1 | 0.333 333 | 0.060 606 | 0.015 152 | 0.000 189 | 30.48 | 0.304 8 |
| 1 yard= | 36 | 4.545 45 | 3 | 1 | 0.181 818 | 0.045 455 | 0.000 568 | 91.44 | 0.914 4 |
| 1 rod= | 198 | 25 | 16.5 | 5.5 | 1 | 0.25 | 0.003 125 | 502.92 | 5.029 2 |
| 1 chain= | 792 | 100 | 66 | 22 | 4 | 1 | 0.012 5 | 2011.68 | 20.116 8 |
| 1 mile= | 63 360 | 8000 | 5280 | 1760 | 320 | 80 | 1 | 160 934.4 | 1609.344 |
| 1 cm= | 0.3937 | 0.049 710 | 0.032 808 | 0.010 936 | 0.001 988 | 0.000 497 | 0.000 006 | 100 | 0.01 |
| 1 meter= | 39.37 | 4.970 960 | 3.280 840 | 1.093 613 | 0.198 838 | 0.049 710 | 0.000 621 | 100 | 1 |

## Units of Area

| Units | Sq. inches | Sq. links | Sq. feet | Sq. yards | Sq. rods | Sq. chains |
|---|---|---|---|---|---|---|
| 1 sq. inch= | 1 | .015 942 3 | 0.006 944 | 0.000 771 605 | 0.000 025 5 | 0.000 001 594 |
| 1 sq. link= | 62.726 4 | 1 | 0.435 6 | 0.0484 | 0.0016 | 0.000 1 |
| 1 sq. foot= | 144 | 2.295 684 | 1 | 0.111 111 1 | 0.003 673 09 | 0.000 229 568 |
| 1 sq. yard= | 1296 | 20.661 16 | 9 | 1 | 0.033 057 85 | 0.002 066 12 |
| 1 sq. rod= | 39 204 | 625 | 272.25 | 30.25 | 1 | 0.062 5 |
| 1 sq. chain= | 627 264 | 10 000 | 4 356 | 484 | 16 | 1 |
| 1 acre= | 6 272 640 | 100 000 | 43 560 | 4 840 | 160 | 10 |
| 1 sq. mile= | 4 014 489 600 | 64 000 000 | 27 878 400 | 3 097 600 | 102 400 | 6400 |
| 1 sq. cm= | 0.155 000 3 | 0.002 471 05 | 0.001 076 | 0.000 119 599 | 0.000 003 954 | 0.000 000 247 |
| 1 sq. meter= | 1550.003 | 24.710 44 | 10.763 91 | 1.195 990 | 0.039 536 70 | 0.002 471 044 |
| 1 hectare= | 15 500 031 | 247 104 | 107 639.1 | 11 959.90 | 395.367 0 | 24.710 44 |

| Units | Acres | Sq. miles | Sq. cm | Sq. meters | Hectares |
|---|---|---|---|---|---|
| 1 sq. inch= | 0.000 000 159 423 | 0.000 000 000 249 10 | 6.451 6 | 0.000 645 16 | 0.000 000 065 |
| 1 sq. link= | 0.000 01 | 0.000 000 015 625 | 404.685 642 24 | 0.040 468 56 | 0.000 004 047 |
| 1 sq. foot= | 0.000 022 956 84 | 0.000 000 035 870 06 | 929.034 1 | 0.092 903 41 | 0.000 009 290 |
| 1 sq. yard= | 0.000 206 611 6 | 0.000 000 322 830 6 | 8 361.273 6 | 0.836 127 36 | 0.000 083 613 |
| 1 sq. rod= | 0.006 25 | 0.000 009 765 625 | 252 929.5 | 25.292 95 | 0.002 529 295 |
| 1 sq. chain= | 0.1 | 0.000 156 25 | 4 046 873 | 404.687 3 | 0.040 468 73 |
| 1 acre= | 1 | 0.001 562 5 | 40 468 73 | 4 046.873 | 0.404 687 3 |
| 1 sq. mile= | 640 | 1 | 25 899 881 103 | 2 589 988.11 | 258.998 811 034 |
| 1 sq. cm= | 0.000 000 024 711 | 0.000 000 000 038 610 | 1 | 0.000 1 | 0.000 000 01 |
| 1 sq. meter= | 0.000 247 104 4 | 0.000 000 386 102 2 | 10 000 | 1 | 0.0001 |
| 1 hectare= | 2.471 044 | 0.003 861 006 | 100 000 000 | 10 000 | 1 |

## Units of Mass Not Greater than Pounds and Kilograms

| Units | Grains | Pennyweights | Avdp drams | Avdp ounces |
|---|---|---|---|---|
| 1 grain= | 1 | 0.041 666 67 | 0.036 571 43 | 0.002 285 71 |
| 1 pennyweight= | 24 | 1 | 0.877 714 3 | 0.054 857 14 |
| 1 dram avdp= | 27.343 75 | 1.139 323 | 1 | 0.062 5 |
| 1 ounce avdp= | 437.5 | 18.229 17 | 16 | 1 |
| 1 ounce troy= | 480 | 20 | 17.554 29 | 1.097 143 |
| 1 pound troy= | 5760 | 240 | 210.651 4 | 13.165 71 |
| 1 pound avdp= | 7000 | 291.666 7 | 256 | 16 |
| 1 milligram= | 0.015 432 | 0.000 643 015 | 0.000 564 383 | 0.000 035 274 |
| 1 gram= | 15.432 36 | 0.643 014 9 | 0.564 383 4 | 0.035 273 96 |
| 1 kilogram= | 15 432.36 | 643.014 9 | 564.383 4 | 35.273 96 |

| Units | Troy ounces | Troy pounds | Avdp pounds | Milligrams | Grams | Kilograms |
|---|---|---|---|---|---|---|
| 1 grain= | 0.002·083 33 | 0.000 173 611 | 0.000 142 857 | 64.798 91 | 0.064 798 91 | 0.000 064 799 |
| 1 pennyw't.= | 0.05 | 0.004 166 667 | 0.003 428 571 | 1555.173 84 | 1.555 173 84 | 0.001 555 174 |
| 1 dram avdp= | 0.056 966 15 | 0.004 747 179 | 0.003 906 25 | 1771.845 195 | 1.771 845 195 | 0.001 771 845 |
| 1 oz avdp= | 0.911 458 3 | 0.075 954 86 | 0.062 5 | 28 349.523 125 | 28.349 523 125 | 0.028 349 52 |
| 1 oz troy= | 1 | 0.083 333 333 | 0.068 571 43 | 31 103.476 8 | 31.103 476 8 | 0.031 103 48 |
| 1 lb troy= | 12 | 1 | 0.822 857 1 | 373 241.721 6 | 373.241 721 6 | 0.373 241 722 |
| 1 lb avdp= | 14.583 33 | 1.215 278 | 1 | 453 592.37 | 453.592 37 | 0.453 592 37 |
| 1 milligram= | 0.000 032 151 | 0.000 002 679 | 0.000 002 205 | 1 | 0.001 | 0.000 001 |
| 1 gram= | 0.032 150 75 | 0.002 679 229 | 0.002 204 623 | 1000 | 1 | 0.001 |
| 1 kilogram= | 32.150 75 | 2.679 229 | 2.204 623 | 1 000 000 | 1000 | 1 |

## Units of Mass Not Less than Avoirdupois Ounces

| Units | Avdp oz | Avdp lb | Short cwt | Short tons | Long tons | Kilograms | Metric tons |
|---|---|---|---|---|---|---|---|
| 1 oz av= | 1 | 0.0625 | 0.000 625 | 0.000 031 25 | 0.000 027 902 | 0.028 349 523 | 0.000 028 350 |
| 1 lb av= | 16 | 1 | 0.01 | 0.000 5 | 0.000 446 429 | 0.453 592 37 | 0.000 453 592 |
| 1 sh cwt= | 1 600 | 100 | 1 | 0.05 | 0.044 642 86 | 45.359 237 | 0.045 359 237 |
| 1 sh ton= | 32 000 | 2000 | 20 | 1 | 0.892 857 1 | 907.184 74 | 0.907 184 74 |
| 1 long ton= | 35 840 | 2240 | 22.4 | 1.12 | 1 | 1016.046 908 8 | 1.016 046 909 |
| 1 kg= | 35.273 96 | 2.204 623 | 0.022 046 23 | 0.001 102 311 | 0.000 984 207 | 1 | 0.001 |
| 1 metric ton= | 35 273.96 | 2 204.623 | 22.046 23 | 1.102 311 | 0.984 206 5 | 1000 | 1 |

## Units of Volume

| Units | Cubic inches | Cubic feet | Cubic yards | Cubic cm | Cubic dm | Cubic meters |
|---|---|---|---|---|---|---|
| 1 cubic inch= | 1 | 0.000 578 704 | 0.000 021 433 | 16.387 064 | 0.016 387 | 0.000 016 387 |
| 1 cubic foot= | 1728 | 1 | 0.037 037 04 | 28 316.846 592 | 28.316 847 | 0.028 316 847 |
| 1 cubic yard= | 46 656 | 27 | 1 | 764 554.857 984 | 764.554 858 | 0.764 554 858 |
| 1 cubic cm= | 0.061 023 74 | 0.000 035 315 | 0.000 001 308 | 1 | 0.001 | 0.000 001 |
| 1 cubic dm= | 61.023 74 | 0.035 314 67 | 0.001 307 951 | 1 000 | 1 | 0.001 |
| 1 cubic meter | 61 023.74 | 35.314 67 | 1.307 951 | 1 000 000 | 1000 | 1 |

## Units of Capacity (Liquid Measure)

| Units | Minims | Fluid drams | Fluid ounces | Gills | Liquid pt |
|---|---|---|---|---|---|
| 1 minim= | 1 | 0.016 666 7 | 0.002 083 33 | 0.000 520 833 | 0.000 130 208 |
| 1 fluid dram= | 60 | 1 | 0.125 | 0.031 25 | 0.007 812 5 |
| 1 fluid ounce= | 480 | 8 | 1 | 0.25 | 0.062 5 |
| 1 gill= | 1920 | 32 | 4 | 1 | 0.25 |
| 1 liquid pint= | 7680 | 128 | 16 | 4 | 1 |
| 1 liquid quart= | 15 360 | 256 | 32 | 8 | 2 |
| 1 gallon= | 61 440 | 1024 | 128 | 32 | 8 |
| 1 cubic inch= | 265.974 | 4.432 900 | 0.554 112 6 | 0.138 528 1 | 0.034 632 03 |
| 1 cubic foot= | 459 603.1 | 7 660.052 | 957.506 5 | 239.376 6 | 59.844 16 |
| 1 milliliter= | 16.230 73 | 0.270 512 18 | 0.033 814 02 | 0.008 453 506 | .002 113 376 |
| 1 liter= | 16 230.73 | 270.512 18 | 33.814 02 | 8.453 506 | 2.113 376 |

| Units | Liquid quarts | Gallons | Cubic inches | Cubic feet | Liters |
|---|---|---|---|---|---|
| 1 minim= | 0.000 065 104 17 | 0.000 016 276 04 | 0.003 759 766 | 0.000 002 175 790 | 0.000 061 611 52 |
| 1 flu. dram= | 0.003 906 25 | 0.000 976 562 5 | 0.225 585 9 | 0.000 130 547 4 | 0.003 696 691 |
| 1 fluid oz= | 0.031 25 | 0.007 812 5 | 1.804 687 5 | 0.001 044 379 | 0.029 573 53 |
| 1 gill= | 0.125 | 0.031 25 | 7.218 75 | 0.004 177 517 | 0.118 294 118 |
| 1 liquid pt= | 0.5 | 0.125 | 28.875 | 0.016 710 07 | 0.473 176 473 |
| 1 liquid qt= | 1 | 0.25 | 57.75 | 0.033 420 14 | 0.946 352 946 |
| 1 gallon= | 4 | 1 | 231 | 0.133 680 6 | 3.785 411 784 |
| 1 cubic in.= | 0.017 316 02 | 0.004 329 004 | 1 | 0.000 578 703 7 | 0.016 387 064 |
| 1 cubic foot= | 29.922 08 | 7.480 519 | 1728 | 1 | 28.316 846 592 |
| 1 liter= | 1.056 688 | 0.264 172 05 | 61.023 74 | 0.035 314 67 | 1 |

## Units of Capacity (Dry Measure)

| Units | Dry pints | Dry quarts | Pecks | Bushels | Cubic in. | Liters |
|---|---|---|---|---|---|---|
| 1 dry pint= | 1 | 0.5 | 0.062 5 | 0.015 625 | 33.600 312 5 | 0.550 610 47 |
| 1 dry quart= | 2 | 1 | 0.125 | 0.031 25 | 67.200 625 | 1.101 220 9 |
| 1 peck= | 16 | 8 | 1 | 0.25 | 537.605 | 8.809 767 5 |
| 1 bushel= | 64 | 32 | 4 | 1 | 2150.42 | 35.239 07 |
| 1 cubic inch= | 0.029 761 6 | 0.014 880 8 | 0.001 860 10 | 0.000 465 025 | 1 | 0.016 387 06 |
| 1 liter= | 1.816 166 | 0.908 083 | 0.113 510 37 | 0.028 377 59 | 61.023 74 | 1 |

## Miscellaneous Measures

**Caliber**—the diameter of a gun bore. In the U.S., caliber is traditionally expressed in hundredths of inches, eg. .22 or .30. In Britain, caliber is often expressed in thousandths of inches, eg. .270 or .465. Now, it is commonly expressed in millimeters, eg. the 5.56 mm. M16 rifle. Heavier weapons' caliber has long been expressed in millimeters, eg. the 81 mm. mortar, the 105 mm. howitzer (light), the 155 mm. howitzer (medium or heavy).

Naval guns' caliber refers to the barrel length as a multiple of the bore diameter. A 5-inch, 50-caliber naval gun has a 5-inch bore and a barrel length of 250 inches.

**Carat, karat**—a measure of the amount of alloy per 24 parts in gold. Thus 24-carat gold is pure; 18-carat gold is one-fourth alloy.

**Decibel (dB)**—a measure of the relative loudness or intensity of sound. A 20-decibel sound is 10 times louder than a 10-decibel sound; 30 decibels is 100 times louder; 40 decibels is 1,000 times louder, etc. One decibel is the smallest difference between sounds detectable by the human ear. A 120-decibel sound is painful.

| | |
|---|---|
| 10 decibels | – a light whisper |
| 20 | – quiet conversation |
| 30 | – normal conversation |
| 40 | – light traffic |
| 50 | – typewriter, loud conversation |
| 60 | – noisy office |
| 70 | – normal traffic, quiet train |
| 80 | – rock music, subway |
| 90 | – heavy traffic, thunder |
| 100 | – jet plane at takeoff |

**Em**—a printer's measure designating the square width of any given type size. Thus, an em of 10-point type is 10 points. An en is half an em.

**Gauge**—a measure of shotgun bore diameter. Gauge numbers originally referred to the number of lead balls of the gun barrel diameter in a pound. Thus, a 16 gauge shotgun's bore was smaller than a 12-gauge shotgun's. Today, an international agreement assigns millimeter measures to each gauge, eg:

| Gauge | Bore diameter in mm |
|---|---|
| 6 | 23.34 |
| 10 | 19.67 |
| 12 | 18.52 |
| 14 | 17.60 |
| 16 | 16.81 |
| 20 | 15.90 |

**Horsepower**—the power needed to lift 550 pounds one foot in one second, or to lift 33,000 pounds one foot in one minute. Equivalent to 746 watts or 2,546.0756 Btu/h.

**Quire**—25 sheets of paper

**Ream**—500 sheets of paper

**Knot**—a measure of the speed of ships. A knot equals 1 nautical mile per hour.

## Electrical Units

The **watt** is the unit of power (electrical, mechanical, thermal, etc.). Electrical power is given by the product of the voltage and the current.

Energy is sold by the **joule**, but in common practice the billing of electrical energy is expressed in terms of the kilowatt-hour, which is 3,600,000 joules or 3.6 megajoules.

The **horsepower** is a non-metric unit sometimes used in mechanics. It is equal to 746 watts.

The **ohm** is the unit of electrical resistance and represents the physical property of a conductor that offers a resistance to the flow of electricity, permitting just 1 ampere to flow at 1 volt of pressure.

# Compound Interest
## Compounded Annually

| Principal | Period | 4% | 5% | 6% | 7% | 8% | 9% | 10% | 12% | 14% | 16% |
|---|---|---|---|---|---|---|---|---|---|---|---|
| $100 | 1 day | 0.011 | 0.014 | 0.016 | 0.019 | 0.022 | 0.025 | 0.027 | 0.033 | 0.038 | 0.044 |
| | 1 week | 0.077 | 0.096 | 0.115 | 0.134 | 0.153 | 0.173 | 0.192 | 0.230 | 0.268 | 0.307 |
| | 6 mos. | 2.00 | 2.50 | 3.00 | 3.50 | 4.00 | 4.50 | 5.00 | 6.00 | 7.00 | 8.00 |
| | 1 year | 4.00 | 5.00 | 6.00 | 7.00 | 8.00 | 9.00 | 10.00 | 12.00 | 14.00 | 16.00 |
| | 2 years | 8.16 | 10.25 | 12.36 | 14.49 | 16.64 | 18.81 | 21.00 | 25.44 | 29.96 | 34.56 |
| | 3 years | 12.49 | 15.76 | 19.10 | 22.50 | 25.97 | 29.50 | 33.10 | 40.49 | 48.15 | 56.09 |
| | 4 years | 16.99 | 21.55 | 26.25 | 31.08 | 36.05 | 41.16 | 46.41 | 57.35 | 68.90 | 81.06 |
| | 5 years | 21.67 | 27.63 | 33.82 | 40.26 | 46.93 | 53.86 | 61.05 | 76.23 | 92.54 | 110.03 |
| | 6 years | 26.53 | 34.01 | 41.85 | 50.07 | 58.69 | 67.71 | 77.16 | 97.38 | 119.50 | 143.64 |
| | 7 years | 31.59 | 40.71 | 50.36 | 60.58 | 71.38 | 82.80 | 94.87 | 121.07 | 150.23 | 182.62 |
| | 8 years | 36.86 | 47.75 | 59.38 | 71.82 | 85.09 | 99.26 | 114.36 | 147.60 | 185.26 | 227.84 |
| | 9 years | 42.33 | 55.13 | 68.95 | 83.85 | 99.90 | 117.19 | 135.79 | 177.31 | 225.19 | 280.30 |
| | 10 years | 48.02 | 62.89 | 79.08 | 96.72 | 115.89 | 136.74 | 159.37 | 210.58 | 270.72 | 341.14 |
| | 12 years | 60.10 | 79.59 | 101.22 | 125.22 | 151.82 | 181.27 | 213.84 | 289.60 | 381.79 | 493.60 |
| | 15 years | 80.09 | 107.89 | 139.66 | 175.90 | 217.22 | 264.25 | 317.72 | 447.36 | 613.79 | 826.55 |
| | 20 years | 119.11 | 165.33 | 220.71 | 286.97 | 366.10 | 460.44 | 572.75 | 864.63 | 1,274.35 | 1,846.08 |

# Ancient Measures

| Biblical | | | Greek | | | Roman | | |
|---|---|---|---|---|---|---|---|---|
| Cubit | = | 21.8 inches | Cubit | = | 18.3 inches | Cubit | = | 17.5 inches |
| Omer | = | 0.45 peck | Stadion | = | 607.2 or 622 feet | Stadium | = | 202 yards |
| | | 3.964 liters | Obolos | = | 715.38 milligrams | As, libra, | = | 325.971 grams, |
| Ephah | = | 10 omers | Drachma | = | 4.2923 grams | pondus | | .71864 pounds |
| Shekel | = | 0.497 ounce | Mina | = | 0.9463 pounds | | | |
| | | 14.1 grams | Talent | = | 60 mina | | | |

# Weight of Water

| 1 | cubic inch | .0360 pound | 1 | imperial gallon | 10.0 pounds |
|---|---|---|---|---|---|
| 12 | cubic inches | .433 pound | 11.2 | imperial gallons | 112.0 pounds |
| 1 | cubic foot | 62.4 pounds | 224 | imperial gallons | 2240.0 pounds |
| 1 | cubic foot | 7.48052 U.S. gal | 1 | U.S. gallon | 8.33 pounds |
| 1.8 | cubic feet | 112.0 pounds | 13.45 | U.S. gallons | 112.0 pounds |
| 35.96 | cubic feet | 2240.0 pounds | 269.0 | U.S. gallons | 2240.0 pounds |

# Density of Gases and Vapors
## at 0°C and 760 mmHg
### Source: National Institute of Standards and Technology (kilograms per cubic meter)

| Gas | Wgt. | Gas | Wgt. | Gas | Wgt. |
|---|---|---|---|---|---|
| Acetylene | 1.171 | Ethylene | 1.260 | Methyl fluoride | 1.545 |
| Air | 1.293 | Fluorine | 1.696 | Mono methylamine | 1.38 |
| Ammonia | .759 | Helium | .178 | Neon | .900 |
| Argon | 1.784 | Hydrogen | .090 | Nitric oxide | 1.341 |
| Arsine | 3.48 | Hydrogen bromide | 3.50 | Nitrogen | 1.250 |
| Butane-iso | 2.60 | Hydrogen chloride | 1.639 | Nitrosyl chloride | 2.99 |
| Butane-n | 2.519 | Hydrogen iodide | 5.724 | Nitrous oxide | 1.997 |
| Carbon dioxide | 1.977 | Hydrogen selenide | 3.66 | Oxygen | 1.429 |
| Carbon monoxide | 1.250 | Hydrogen sulfide | 1.539 | Phosphine | 1.48 |
| Carbon oxysulfide | 2.72 | Krypton | 3.745 | Propane | 2.020 |
| Chlorine | 3.214 | Methane | .717 | Silicon tetrafluoride | 4.67 |
| Chlorine monoxide | 3.89 | Methyl chloride | 2.25 | Sulfur dioxide | 2.927 |
| Ethane | 1.356 | Methyl ether | 2.091 | Xenon | 5.897 |

# Temperature Conversion Table

The numbers in bold face type refer to the temperature either in degrees Celsius or Fahrenheit which are to be converted. If converting from degrees Fahrenheit to Celsius, the equivalent will be found in the column on the left, while if converting from degrees Celsius to Fahrenheit the answer will be found in the column on the right.

For temperatures not shown. To convert Fahrenheit to Celsius subtract 32 degrees and multiply by 5, divide by 9; to convert Celsius to Fahrenheit, multiply by 9, divide by 5 and add 32 degrees.

| Celsius | Fahrenheit | | Celsius | | Fahrenheit | Celsius | | Fahrenheit |
|---|---|---|---|---|---|---|---|---|
| − 273.2 | − 459.7 | ...... | − 17.8 | 0 | 32 | 35.0 | 95 | 203 |
| − 184 | − 300 | ...... | − 12.2 | 10 | 50 | 36.7 | 98 | 208.4 |
| − 169 | − 273 | − 459.4 | − 6.67 | 20 | 68 | 37.8 | 100 | 212 |
| − 157 | − 250 | − 418 | − 1.11 | 30 | 86 | 43 | 110 | 230 |
| − 129 | − 200 | − 328 | 4.44 | 40 | 104 | 49 | 120 | 248 |
| − 101 | − 150 | − 238 | 10.0 | 50 | 122 | 54 | 130 | 266 |
| − 73.3 | − 100 | − 148 | 15.6 | 60 | 140 | 60 | 140 | 284 |
| − 45.6 | − 50 | − 58 | 21.1 | 70 | 158 | 66 | 150 | 302 |
| − 40.0 | − 40 | − 40 | 23.9 | 75 | 167 | 93 | 200 | 392 |
| − 34.4 | − 30 | − 22 | 26.7 | 80 | 176 | 121 | 250 | 482 |
| − 28.9 | − 20 | − 4 | 29.4 | 85 | 185 | 149 | 300 | 572 |
| − 23.3 | − 10 | 14 | 32.2 | 90 | 194 | | | |

# Boiling and Freezing Points of Water

Water boils at 212°F at sea level. For every 550 feet above sea level, boiling point of water is lower by about 1°F. Methyl alcohol boils at 148°F. Average human oral temperature, 98.6°F. Water freezes at 32°F. Although "Centigrade" is still frequently used, the International Committee on Weights and Measures and the National Institute of Standards have recommended since 1948 that this scale be called "Celsius."

## Breaking the Sound Barrier; Speed of Sound

The prefix Mach is used to describe supersonic speed. It derives from Ernst Mach, a Czech-born German physicist, who contributed to the study of sound. When a plane moves at the speed of sound it is Mach 1. When twice the speed of sound it is Mach 2. When it is near but below the speed of sound its speed can be designated at less than Mach 1, for example, Mach .90. Mach is defined as "in jet propulsion, the ratio of the velocity of a rocket or a jet to the velocity of sound in the medium being considered."

When a plane passes the sound barrier—flying faster than sound travels—listeners in the area hear thunderclaps, but pilots do not hear them.

Sound is produced by vibrations of an object and is transmitted by alternate increase and decrease in pressures that radiate outward through a material media of molecules —somewhat like waves spreading out on a pond after a rock has been tossed into it.

The frequency of sound is determined by the number of times the vibrating waves undulate per second, and is measured in cycles per second. The slower the cycle of waves, the lower the frequency. As frequencies increase, the sound is higher in pitch.

Sound is audible to human beings only if the frequency falls within a certain range. The human ear is usually not sensitive to frequencies of less than 20 vibrations per second, or more than about 20,000 vibrations per second—although this range varies among individuals. Anything at a pitch higher than the human ear can hear is termed ultrasonic.

Intensity or loudness is the strength of the pressure of these radiating waves, and is measured in decibels. The human ear responds to intensity in a range from zero to 120 decibels. Any sound with pressure over 120 decibels is painful.

The speed of sound is generally placed at 1,088 feet per second at sea level at 32°F. It varies in other temperatures and in different media. Sound travels faster in water than in air, and even faster in iron and steel. If in air it travels a mile in 5 seconds, it does a mile under water in 1 second, and through iron in ⅓ of a second. It travels through ice cold vapor at approximately 4,708 feet per second; ice-cold water, 4,938; granite, 12,960; hardwood, 12,620; brick, 11,960; glass, 16,410 to 19,690; silver, 8,658; gold, 5,717.

## Colors of the Spectrum

Color, an electromagnetic wave phenomenon, is a sensation produced through the excitation of the retina of the eye by rays of light. The colors of the spectrum may be produced by viewing a light beam refracted by passage through a prism, which breaks the light into its wave lengths.

Customarily, the primary colors of the spectrum are thought of as those 6 monochromatic colors that occupy relatively large areas of the spectrum: red, orange, yellow, green, blue, and violet. However, Sir Isaac Newton named a 7th, indigo, situated between blue and violet on the spectrum. Aubert estimated (1865) the solar spectrum to contain approximately 1,000 distinguishable hues of which according to Rood (1881) 2 million tints and shades can be distinguished; Luckiesh stated (1915) that 55 distinctly different hues have been seen in a single spectrum.

Many physicists recognize only 3 primary colors: red, yellow, and blue (Mayer, 1775); red, green, and violet (Thomas Young, 1801); red, green, and blue (Clerk Maxwell, 1860).

The color sensation of black is due to complete lack of stimulation of the retina, that of white to complete stimulation. The infra-red and ultra-violet rays, below the red (long) end of the spectrum and above the violet (short) end respectively, are invisible to the naked eye. Heat is the principal effect of the infrared rays and chemical action that of the ultraviolet rays.

## Common Fractions Reduced to Decimals

| 8ths | 16ths | 32ds | 64ths | | 8ths | 16ths | 32ds | 64ths | | 8ths | 16ths | 32ds | 64ths | |
|---|---|---|---|---|---|---|---|---|---|---|---|---|---|---|
| | | | 1 | .015625 | | | | 23 | .359375 | | | | 45 | .703125 |
| | | 1 | 2 | .03125 | 3 | 6 | 12 | 24 | .375 | | | | 46 | .71875 |
| | | | 3 | .046875 | | | | 25 | .390625 | | | | 47 | .734375 |
| | 1 | 2 | 4 | .0625 | | | | 13 | 26 | .40625 | 6 | 12 | 24 | 48 | .75 |
| | | | 5 | .078125 | | | | 27 | .421875 | | | | 49 | .765625 |
| | | 3 | 6 | .09375 | | 7 | 14 | 28 | .4375 | | | | 25 | 50 | .78125 |
| | | | 7 | .109375 | | | | 29 | .453125 | | | | 51 | .796875 |
| 1 | 2 | 4 | 8 | .125 | | | | 15 | 30 | .46875 | | 13 | 26 | 52 | .8125 |
| | | | 9 | .140625 | | | | 31 | .484375 | | | | 53 | .828125 |
| | | 5 | 10 | .15625 | 4 | 8 | 16 | 32 | .5 | | | 27 | 54 | .84375 |
| | | | 11 | .171875 | | | | 33 | .515625 | | | | 55 | .859375 |
| | 3 | 6 | 12 | .1875 | | | 17 | 34 | .53125 | 7 | 14 | 28 | 56 | .875 |
| | | | 13 | .203125 | | | | 35 | .546875 | | | | 57 | .890625 |
| | | 7 | 14 | .21875 | | 9 | 18 | 36 | .5625 | | | 29 | 58 | .90625 |
| | | | 15 | .234375 | | | | 37 | .578125 | | | | 59 | .921875 |
| 2 | 4 | 8 | 16 | .25 | | | 19 | 38 | .59375 | | 15 | 30 | 60 | .9375 |
| | | | 17 | .265625 | | | | 39 | .609375 | | | | 61 | .953125 |
| | | 9 | 18 | .28125 | 5 | 10 | 20 | 40 | .625 | | | 31 | 62 | .96875 |
| | | | 19 | .296875 | | | | 41 | .640625 | | | | 63 | .984375 |
| | 5 | 10 | 20 | .3125 | | | 21 | 42 | .65625 | 8 | 16 | 32 | 64 | 1. |
| | | | 21 | .328125 | | | | 43 | .671875 | | | | | |
| | | 11 | 22 | .34375 | | | 11 | 22 | 44 | .6875 | | | | | |

## Spirits Measures

| | | |
|---|---|---|
| Pony | 0.5 jigger | |
| Shot | { 0.666 jigger | |
| | { 1.0 ounce | |
| Jigger | 1.5 shot | |
| Pint | { 16 shots | |
| | { 0.625 fifth | |
| Fifth | { 25.6 shots | |
| | { 1.6 pints | |
| | { 0.8 quart | |
| | { 0.75706 liter | |

| | | |
|---|---|---|
| Quart | { 32 shots | |
| | { 1.25 fifth | |
| Magnum | { 2 quarts | |
| | { 2.49797 bottles (wine) | |

For champagne and brandy only:

| | | |
|---|---|---|
| Jeroboam | { 6.4 pints | |
| | { 1.6 magnum | |
| | { 0.8 gallon | |

For champagne only:

| | |
|---|---|
| Rehoboam | 3 magnums |
| Methuselah | 4 magnums |
| Salmanazar | 6 magnums |
| Balthazar | 8 magnums |
| Nebuchadnezzar | 10 magnums |

Wine bottle (standard):

| | |
|---|---|
| | { 0.800633 quart |
| | { 0.7576778 liter |

# Mathematical Formulas

### To find the CIRCUMFERENCE of a:

Circle — Multiply the diameter by 3.14159265 (usually 3.1416).

### To find the AREA of a:

Circle — Multiply the square of the diameter by .785398 (usually .7854).

Rectangle — Multiply the length of the base by the height.

Sphere (surface) — Multiply the square of the radius by 3.1416 and multiply by 4.

Square — Square the length of one side.

Trapezoid — Add the two parallel sides, multiply by the height and divide by 2.

Triangle — Multiply the base by the height and divide by 2.

### To find the VOLUME of a:

Cone — Multiply the square of the radius of the base by 3.1416, multiply by the height, and divide by 3.

Cube — Cube the length of one edge.

Cylinder — Multiply the square of the radius of the base by 3.1416 and multiply by the height.

Pyramid — Multiply the area of the base by the height and

divide by 3.

Rectangular Prism — Multiply the length by the width by the height.

Sphere — Multiply the cube of the radius by 3.1416, multiply by 4 and divide by 3.

## Playing Cards and Dice Chances

### Poker Hands

| Hand | Number possible | Odds against |
|---|---|---|
| Royal flush | 4 | 649,739 to 1 |
| Other straight flush | 36 | 72,192 to 1 |
| Four of a kind | 624 | 4,164 to 1 |
| Full house | 3,744 | 693 to 1 |
| Flush | 5,108 | 508 to 1 |
| Straight | 10,200 | 254 to 1 |
| Three of a kind | 54,912 | 46 to 1 |
| Two pairs | 123,552 | 20 to 1 |
| One pair | 1,098,240 | 4 to 3 (1.37 to 1) |
| Nothing | 1,302,540 | 1 to 1 |
| **Total** | **2,598,960** | |

### Dice
(probabilities on 2 dice)

| Total | Odds against (Single toss) | Total | Odds against (Single toss) |
|---|---|---|---|
| 2 | 35 to 1 | 8 | 31 to 5 |
| 3 | 17 to 1 | 9 | 8 to 1 |
| 4 | 11 to 1 | 10 | 11 to 1 |
| 5 | 8 to 1 | 11 | 17 to 1 |
| 6 | 31 to 5 | 12 | 35 to 1 |
| 7 | 5 to 1 | | |

### Dice
(Probabilities of consecutive winning plays)

| No. consecutive wins | By 7, 11 or point | No. consecutive wins | By 7, 11 or point |
|---|---|---|---|
| 1 | 244 in 495 | 6 | 1 in 70 |
| 2 | 6 in 25 | 7 | 1 in 141 |
| 3 | 3 in 25 | 8 | 1 in 287 |
| 4 | 1 in 17 | 9 | 1 in 582 |
| 5 | 1 in 34 | | |

### Pinochle Auction
(Odds against finding in "widow" of 3 cards)

| Open places | Odds against | Open places | Odds against |
|---|---|---|---|
| 1 | 5 to 1 | 4 | 3 to 2 for |
| 2 | 2 to 1 | 5 | 2 to 1 for |
| 3 | Even | | |

### Bridge

The odds—against suit distribution in a hand of 4-4-3-2 are about 4 to 1, against 5-4-2-2 about 8 to 1, against 6-4-2-1 about 20 to 1, against 7-4-1-1 about 254 to 1, against 8-4-1-0 about 2,211 to 1, and against 13-0-0-0 about 158,753,389,899 to 1.

## Measures of Force and Pressure

Dyne = force necessary to accelerate a 1-gram mass 1 centimeter per second squared = 0.000072 poundal

Poundal = force necessary to accelerate a 1-pound mass 1 foot per second squared = 13,825.5 dynes = 0.138255 newtons

Newton = force needed to accelerate a 1-kilogram mass 1 meter per second squared

Pascal (pressure) = 1 newton per square meter = 0.020885 pound per square foot

Atmosphere (air pressure at sea level) = 2,116.102 pounds per square foot = 14.6952 pounds per square inch = 1.0332 kilograms per square centimeter = 101,323 newtons per square meter.

## Large Numbers

| U.S. | Number of zeros | French British, German | U.S. | Number of zeros | French British, German |
|---|---|---|---|---|---|
| million | 6 | million | sextillion | 21 | 1,000 trillion |
| billion | 9 | milliard | septillion | 24 | quadrillion |
| trillion | 12 | billion | octillion | 27 | 1,000 quadrillion |
| quadrillion | 15 | 1,000 billion | nonillion | 30 | quintillion |
| quintillion | 18 | trillion | decillion | 33 | 1,000 quintillion |

## Roman Numerals

| | | | | | | | | | | | | |
|---|---|---|---|---|---|---|---|---|---|---|---|---|
| I | – | 1 | VI | – | 6 | XI | – | 11 | L | – | 50 | CD | – | 400 | $\overline{X}$ | – | 10,000 |
| II | – | 2 | VII | – | 7 | XIX | – | 19 | LX | – | 60 | D | – | 500 | $\overline{L}$ | – | 50,000 |
| III | – | 3 | VIII | – | 8 | XX | – | 20 | XC | – | 90 | CM | – | 900 | $\overline{C}$ | – | 100,000 |
| IV | – | 4 | IX | – | 9 | XXX | – | 30 | C | – | 100 | M | – | 1,000 | $\overline{D}$ | – | 500,000 |
| V | – | 5 | X | – | 10 | XL | – | 40 | CC | – | 200 | $\overline{V}$ | – | 5,000 | $\overline{M}$ | – | 1,000,000 |

# ARTS AND MEDIA

## Notable Movies of the Year (Sept. 1992 to Aug. 1993)

| Movie | Stars | Director |
|---|---|---|
| A Few Good Men | Tom Cruise, Jack Nicholson, Demi Moore, Kevin Bacon | Rob Reiner |
| Aladdin | Robin Williams, Jonathan Freeman, Gilbert Gottfried | John Musker, Ron Clements |
| Benny and Joon | Johnny Depp, Mary Stuart Masterson, Aiden Quinn | Jeremiah Chechik |
| Bob Roberts | Tim Robbins, Giancarlo Esposito, Gore Vidal | Tim Robbins |
| Bram Stoker's Dracula | Gary Oldman, Winona Ryder, Anthony Hopkins | Francis Ford Coppola |
| Chaplin | Robert Downey, Jr., Dan Aykroyd, Anthony Hopkins | Richard Attenborough |
| Cliffhanger | Sylvester Stallone, John Lithgow, Janine Turner | Renny Harlin |
| Dave | Kevin Kline, Sigourney Weaver | Ivan Reitman |
| Damage | Jeremy Irons, Juliette Binoche, Miranda Richardson | Louis Malle |
| Dennis the Menace | Walter Matthau, Mason Gamble, Christopher Lloyd | Nick Castle |
| Falling Down | Michael Douglas, Robert Duvall, Barbara Hershey | Joel Schumacher |
| Glengarry Glen Ross | Al Pacino, Jack Lemmon, Ed Harris, Alec Baldwin | James Foley |
| Groundhog Day | Bill Murray, Andie McDowell | Harold Ramis |
| Hero | Dustin Hoffman, Geena Davis, Andy Garcia | Stephen Frears |
| Hoffa | Jack Nicholson, Danny DeVito, Armand Assante | Danny DeVito |
| Home Alone 2 | Macaulay Culkin, Joe Pesci, Daniel Stern | John Hughes |
| Honeymoon in Vegas | James Caan, Nicolas Cage, Sarah Jessica Parker | Andrew Bergman |
| Hot Shots! Part Deux | Charlie Sheen, Lloyd Bridges, Valeria Golina | Jim Abrahams |
| Husbands and Wives | Woody Allen, Mia Farrow, Judy Davis, Blythe Danner | Woody Allen |
| Indecent Proposal | Robert Redford, Demi Moore, Woody Harrelson | Adrian Lyne |
| In the Line of Fire | Clint Eastwood, John Malkovich, Rene Russo | Wolfgang Peterson |
| Jurassic Park | Sam Neill, Laura Dern, Jeff Goldblum | Steven Spielberg |
| Last Action Hero | Arnold Schwarzenegger, Austin O'Brien | John McTiernan |
| Lorenzo's Oil | Susan Sarandon, Nick Nolte | George Miller |
| Lost in Yonkers | Richard Dreyfuss, Mercedes Ruehl, Irene Worth | Martha Coolidge |
| Mad Dog and Glory | Robert De Niro, Uma Thurman, Bill Murray | John NcNaughton |
| Made in America | Whoopi Goldberg, Ted Danson | Richard Benjamin |
| Malcolm X | Denzel Washington, Angela Bassett, Al Freeman, Jr. | Spike Lee |
| Map of the Human Heart | Patrick Bergin, Ann Parillaud | Vincent Ward |
| Matinee | John Goodman, Cathy Moriarty | Joe Dante |
| Mr. Saturday Night | Billy Crystal, David Paymer | Billy Crystal |
| Much Ado About Nothing | Kenneth Branagh, Emma Thompson, Michael Keaton | Kenneth Branagh |
| Night and the City | Robert De Niro, Jessica Lange | Irwin Winkler |
| Of Mice and Men | Gary Sinise, John Malkovich, Sherilyn Fenn | Gary Sinise |
| Passion Fish | Mary McDonnell, Alfre Woodard | John Sayles |
| Point of No Return | Bridget Fonda, Gabriel Byrne, Harvey Keitel | John Badham |
| Posse | Mario Van Peebles, Charles Lane, Big Daddy Kane | Mario Van Peebles |
| Rising Sun | Sean Connery, Wesley Snipes | Philip Kaufman |
| Scent of a Woman | Al Pacino, Chris O'Donnell | Martin Brest |
| Sliver | Sharon Stone, William Baldwin, Tom Berenger | Phillip Noyce |
| Sniper | Tom Berenger, Billy Zane | Luis Llosa |
| Sleepless in Seattle | Tom Hanks, Meg Ryan | Nora Ephron |
| The Bodyguard | Kevin Costner, Whitney Houston | Mike Jackson |
| The Crying Game | Stephen Rea, Miranda Richardson, Jaye Davidson | Neil Jordan |
| The Firm | Tom Cruise, Ed Harris, Holly Hunter, Hal Holbrook | Sidney Pollack |
| The Fugitive | Harrison Ford, Tommy Lee Jones | Andrew Davis |
| The Last of the Mohicans | Daniel Day-Lewis, Madeleine Stowe | Michael Mann |
| Under Siege | Steven Seagal, Tommy Lee Jones, Gary Busey | Andrew Davis |
| Unforgiven | Clint Eastwood, Gene Hackman, Morgan Freeman | Clint Eastwood |
| What's Love Got to Do With It? | Angela Bassett, Laurence Fishburne | Brian Gibson |

## Notable New York Theater Openings, 1992-1993 Season

**Ain't Broadway Grand,** musical by Mitch Leigh and Lee Adams about showman Mike Todd; with Mike Burstyn.

**Angels in America: Millennium Approaches,** play by Tony Kushner; with Ron Leibman, Joe Mantello, and Stephen Spinella.

**Anna Christie,** revival of the 1922 Eugene O'Neill drama; with Natasha Richardson, Liam Neeson, Rip Torn, and Anne Meara.

**Blood Brothers,** musical by Willy Russell; with Stephanie Lawrence, Barbara Walsh, and Warwick Evans.

**Camelot,** revival of the Alan Jay Lerner and Frederick Loewe 1960 musical; with Robert Goulet.

**Fool Moon,** an evening of clowning with Bill Irwin and David Shiner.

**Kiss of the Spider Woman,** musical by John Kander and Fred Ebb based on Manuel Puig's novel; with Chita Rivera, Brent Carver, and Anthony Crivello.

**Putting It Together,** revue based on the music and lyrics of Stephen Sondheim; with Julie Andrews and Stephen Collins.

**Redwood Curtain,** play by Lanford Wilson; with Jeff Daniels, Sung Yun Cho, and Debra Monk.

**Saint Joan,** revival of the George Bernard Shaw classic; with Maryann Plunkett, Nicholas Kepros, and Remak Ramsay.

**Shakespeare for My Father,** reminiscences conceived and written by Lynn Redgrave; with Lynn Redgrave.

**Someone to Watch Over Me,** drama by Frank McGuinness; with Stephen Rea, Alec McCowen, and James McDaniel.

**The Goodbye Girl,** musical by Marvin Hamlisch and David Zippel based on Neil Simon's play; with Bernadette Peters and Martin Short.

**The Last Yankee,** play by Arthur Miller; with John Heard, Frances Conroy, and Tom Aldredge.

**The Seagull,** revival of the Chekhov classic; with Tyne Daly, Jon Voight, Tony Roberts, Ethan Hawke, and Maryann Plunkett.

**The Show-Off,** revival of George Kelly's 1924 play; with Sophie Hayden and Pat Carroll.

**The Sisters Rosensweig,** drama by Wendy Wasserstein; with Jane Alexander, Frances McDormand, Robert Klein, and Madeline Kahn.

**The Song of Jacob Zula,** play by Tug Yourgrau; with K. Todd Freeman, Danny Johnson, and Zakes Mokae.

**Three Men on a Horse,** revival of the John Cecil Holm and George Abbott comedy; with Tony Randall, Jack Klugman, Julie Hagerty, Jerry Stiller, and Ellen Greene.

**Tommy,** revival of the 1969 Peter Townsend rock opera; with Michael Cerveris, Marcia Mitzman, and Paul Kandel.

**Wrong Turn at Lungfish,** comedy by Garry Marshall; with George C. Scott, Jami Gertz, and Tony Danza.

# Record Long Run Broadway Plays[1]

Source: *Variety*

| | | | | | |
|---|---|---|---|---|---|
| Chorus Line | 6,137 | Dancin' | 1,774 | Funny Girl | 1,348 |
| Oh, Calcutta (revival) | 5,959 | La Cage aux Folles | 1,761 | Mumenschanz | 1,326 |
| *Cats | 4,485 | Hair | 1,750 | Oh! Calcutta! (original) | 1,314 |
| 42d Street | 3,486 | The Wiz | 1,672 | Brighton Beach Memoirs | 1,299 |
| Grease | 3,388 | Born Yesterday | 1,642 | Angel Street | 1,295 |
| Fiddler on the Roof | 3,242 | Ain't Misbehavin' | 1,604 | Lightnin' | 1,291 |
| Life With Father | 3,224 | Best Little Whorehouse in Texas | 1,584 | Promises, Promises | 1,281 |
| Tobacco Road | 3,182 | Mary, Mary | 1,572 | The King and I | 1,246 |
| Hello Dolly | 2,844 | Evita | 1,567 | Cactus Flower | 1,234 |
| My Fair Lady | 2,717 | Voice of the Turtle | 1,557 | Sleuth | 1,222 |
| *Les Miserables | 2,572 | Barefoot in the Park | 1,530 | Torch Song Trilogy | 1,222 |
| Annie | 2,377 | Dreamgirls | 1,521 | "1776" | 1,217 |
| Man of La Mancha | 2,328 | Mame | 1,508 | Equus | 1,209 |
| Abie's Irish Rose | 2,327 | Same Time, Next Year | 1,453 | Sugar Babies | 1,208 |
| *Phantom of the Opera | 2,271 | Arsenic and Old Lace | 1,444 | Guys and Dolls | 1,200 |
| Oklahoma! | 2,212 | The Sound of Music | 1,443 | Amadeus | 1,181 |
| Pippin | 1,944 | How To Succeed in Business | | Cabaret | 1,165 |
| South Pacific | 1,925 | Without Really Trying | 1,417 | Mister Roberts | 1,157 |
| Magic Show | 1,920 | Me and My Girl | 1,412 | Annie Get Your Gun | 1,147 |
| Deathtrap | 1,792 | Hellzapoppin | 1,404 | Seven Year Itch | 1,141 |
| Gemini | 1,788 | The Music Man | 1,375 | Butterflies Are Free | 1,128 |
| Harvey | 1,775 | | | | |

(1) Number of performances through July 4, 1993. * Still running July 4, 1993.

# All-Time Top 50 American Movies

Source: *Variety*, Jan. 1993

Rental figures are in absolute dollars, reflecting actual amounts received by the distributors (estimated for movies in current release). Ticket price inflation favors recent films, but older films have the advantage of numerous reissues.

| Rank/Title/Date | Rentals (millions) | Rank/Title/Date | Rentals (millions) | Rank/Title/Date | Rentals (millions) |
|---|---|---|---|---|---|
| 1. E.T. The Extra-Terrestrial (1982) | $228.6 | 19. Tootsie (1982) | $94.9 | 35. Gone With the Wind (1939) | $79.4 |
| 2. Star Wars* (1977) | 193.8 | 20. The Exorcist (1973) | 89.0 | 37. Rambo: First Blood Part II (1985) | 78.9 |
| 3. Return of the Jedi* (1983) | 169.2 | 21. Rain Man (1989) | 86.8 | 38. The Sting (1973) | 78.2 |
| 4. Batman (1989) | 150.5 | 22. The Godfather (1972) | 86.3 | 39. Rocky IV (1985) | 76.0 |
| 5. The Empire Strikes Back* (1980) | 141.7 | 23. Robin Hood: Prince of Thieves (1991) | 86.0 | 40. Saturday Night Fever (1977) | 74.1 |
| 6. Home Alone* (1990) | 140.1 | 24. Superman (1978) | 82.8 | 41. Back to the Future, Part II (1989) | 72.3 |
| 7. Ghostbusters (1984) | 132.7 | 24. Close Encounters of the Third Kind (1977/1980) | 82.8 | 42. Honey, I Shrunk the Kids (1989) | 72.0 |
| 8. Jaws (1975) | 129.5 | 26. Pretty Woman* (1990) | 81.9 | 43. National Lampoon's Animal House (1978) | 70.8 |
| 9. Raiders of the Lost Ark (1981) | 115.6 | 27. Dances with Wolves (1990) | 81.5 | 44. Crocodile Dundee (1986) | 70.2 |
| 10. Indiana Jones and the Last Crusade (1989) | 115.5 | 28. Three Men and a Baby (1987) | 81.4 | 45. Fatal Attraction (1987) | 70.0 |
| 11. Terminator 2* (1991) | 112.0 | 29. Who Framed Roger Rabbit (1988) | 81.2 | 46. Platoon (1986) | 69.9 |
| 12. Indiana Jones and the Temple Of Doom (1984) | 109.0 | 30. Beverly Hills Cop II (1987) | 80.9 | 47. Beauty and the Beast (1991) | 69.4 |
| 13. Beverly Hills Cop (1984) | 108.0 | 31. Lethal Weapon 3 (1992) | 80.0 | 48. Look Who's Talking (1989) | 68.9 |
| 14. Back to the Future (1985) | 105.5 | 32. The Sound of Music* (1965) | 79.9 | 49. 101 Dalmatians (1961) | 68.7 |
| 15. Home Alone 2 (1992) | 102.0 | 33. Gremlins (1984) | 79.5 | 50. Teenage Mutant Ninja Turtles (1990) | 67.7 |
| 16. Batman Returns (1992) | 100.1 | 33. Lethal Weapon 2 (1989) | 79.5 | | |
| 17. Ghost (1990) | 98.2 | 35. Top Gun (1986) | 79.4 | | |
| 18. Grease (1978) | 96.3 | | | | |

Note: Boldface print = film new to list or significant improvement since previous year; * rentals adjusted since last report.

# Top 50 Movies, 1992

Source: *Variety*, Jan. 1993

Figures represent U.S. and Canadian rentals accruing to distributors, not total ticket sales receipts taken in at theaters.

| Rank/Title/Month Released | Rentals (millions) | Rank/Title/Month Released | Rentals (millions) | Rank/Title/Month Released | Rentals (millions) |
|---|---|---|---|---|---|
| 1. Home Alone 2; Nov. | $102.0 | 18. Under Seige; Oct. | $33.0 | 35. Medicine Man; Feb. | $20.9 |
| 2. Batman Returns; June | 100.1 | 19. Alien 3; May | 31.8 | 36. Forever Young; Dec. | 20.0 |
| 3. Lethal Weapon 3; May | 80.0 | 20. The Last of the Mohicans; Sept. | 31.5 | 36. The Mighty Ducks; Oct. | 20.0 |
| 4. Sister Act; May | 62.4 | | | 36. JFK; continuing | 20.0 |
| 5. Aladdin; Nov. | 60.0 | 21. Death Becomes Her; July | 30.4 | 39. Mo' Money; July | 19.2 |
| 6. Wayne's World; Feb. | 54.0 | 21. Beauty and the Beast; continuing | 30.4 | 40. The Distinguished Gentleman; Dec. | 19.0 |
| 7. A League of Their Own; July | 53.1 | 21. Housesitter; June | 30.4 | 41. Passenger 57; Nov. | 18.0 |
| 8. Basic Instinct; March | 53.0 | 24. Far and Away; May | 28.9 | 42. Encino Man; May | 17.6 |
| 9. The Bodyguard; Nov. | 52.9 | 25. Honey, I Blew Up the Kid; July | 27.4 | 43. Honeymoon in Vegas; Aug. | 16.1 |
| 10. A Few Good Men; Dec. | 52.0 | 26. Beethoven; April | 26.5 | 44. Universal Soldier; July | 16.0 |
| 11. Bram Stoker's Dracula; Nov. | 47.2 | 27. Unlawful Entry; June | 26.4 | 45. A River Runs Through It; Oct. | 15.6 |
| 12. The Hand That Rocks the Cradle; Jan. | 39.3 | 28. My Cousin Vinny; March | 25.6 | 46. Grand Canyon; Dec. 91. | 15.1 |
| 13. Patriot Games; June | 37.5 | 29. Malcolm X; Nov. | 25.0 | 47. The Lawnmower Man; March | 13.6 |
| 14. Fried Green Tomatoes; Dec. 1991 | 37.4 | 29. Hook; continuing | 25.0 | 48. Sleepwalkers; April | 13.2 |
| | | 30. Father of the Bride; continuing | 24.0 | 49. Final Analysis; Feb. | 12.7 |
| 15. Unforgiven; Aug. | 36.0 | 32. Sneakers; Sept. | 23.4 | 49. Stop! or My Mom Will Shoot; Feb. | 12.7 |
| 16. White Men Can't Jump; March | 34.1 | 33. Single White Female; Aug. | 21.1 | | |
| 17. Boomerang; July | 34.0 | 33. The Prince of Tides; continuing | 21.1 | | |

# National Film Registry

"Culturally, historically, or esthetically significant" films placed on the National Film Registry, Library of Congress.

## Films Chosen in 1989
The Best Years of Our Lives (1946)
Casablanca (1942)
Citizen Kane (1941)
The Crowd (1928)
Dr. Strangelove (or, How I Learned to Stop
    Worrying and Love the Bomb) (1964)
The General (1927)
Gone With the Wind (1939)
The Grapes of Wrath (1940)
High Noon (1952)
Intolerance (1916)
The Learning Tree (1969)
The Maltese Falcon (1941)
Mr. Smith Goes to Washington (1939)
Modern Times (1936)
Nanook of the North (1921)
On the Waterfront (1954)
The Searchers (1956)
Singin' in the Rain (1952)
Snow White and the Seven Dwarfs (1937)
Some Like It Hot (1959)
Star Wars (1977)
Sunrise (1927)
Sunset Boulevard (1950)
Vertigo (1958)
The Wizard of Oz (1939)

## Films Chosen in 1990
All About Eve (1950)
All Quiet on the Western Front (1930)
Bringing Up Baby (1938)
Dodsworth (1936)
Duck Soup (1933)
Fantasia (1940)
The Freshman (1925)
The Godfather (1972)
The Great Train Robbery (1903)
Harlan County, U. S. A. (1976)
How Green Was My Valley (1941)
It's a Wonderful Life (1946)
Killer of Sheep (1977)
Love Me Tonight (1932)
Meshes of the Afternoon (1943)
Ninotchka (1939)
Primary (1960)
Raging Bull (1980)
Rebel Without a Cause (1955)
Red River (1948)
The River (1937)
Sullivan's Travels (1941)
Top Hat (1935)
The Treasure of the Sierra Madre (1948)
A Woman under the Influence (1974)

## Films Chosen in 1991
The Battle of San Pietro (1945)
The Blood of Jesus (1941)
Chinatown (1974)
City Lights (1931)
David Holzman's Diary (1968)
Frankenstein (1931)
Gertie the Dinosaur (1914)
Gigi (1958)
Greed (1924)
High School (1968)
I Am a Fugitive from a Chain Gang (1932)
The Italian (1915)
King Kong (1933)
Lawrence of Arabia (1962)
The Magnificent Ambersons (1942)
My Darling Clementine (1946)
Out of the Past (1947)
A Place in the Sun (1951)
The Poor Little Rich Girl (1917)
The Prisoner of Zenda (1937)
Shadow of a Doubt (1943)
Sherlock, Jr. (1924)
Tevya (1939)
Trouble in Paradise (1932)
2001: A Space Odyssey (1968)

## Films Chosen in 1992
Adam's Rib (1949)
Annie Hall (1977)
The Bank Dick (1940)
Big Business (1929)
The Big Parade (1925)
The Birth of a Nation (1915)
Bonnie and Clyde (1967)
Carmen Jones (1954)
Castro Street (1966)
Detour (1946)
Dog Star Man (1964)
Double Indemnity (1944)
Footlight Parade (1933)
The Gold Rush (1925)
Letter from an Unknown Woman (1948)
Morocco (1930)
Nashville (1975)
The Night of the Hunter (1955)
Paths of Glory (1957)
Psycho (1960)
Ride the High Country (1962)
Salesman (1969)
Salt of the Earth (1954)
What's Opera, Doc? (1957)
Within Our Gates (1920)

# Most Popular Movie Videos, 1992

Source: Alexander & Associates/Video Flash

### Top 10 Rentals
1. Terminator 2
2. Home Alone
3. The Silence of the Lambs
4. The Boyz N the Hood
5. The Hand That Rocks the Cradle
6. City Slickers
7. Robin Hood: Prince of Thieves
8. Thelma and Louise
9. Cape Fear
10. 101 Dalmatians

### Top 10 Sales
1. Beauty and the Beast
2. 101 Dalmatians
3. Dances with Wolves
4. Fantasia
5. Hook
6. Sister Act
7. Home Alone
8. Robin Hood: Prince of Thieves
9. The Great Mouse Detective
10. Rescuers Down Under

## Notable Books of 1992

Source: American Library Association

### Fiction

Leviathan, Paul Auster
Before and After, Rosellen Brown
A Good Scent from a Strange Mountain, Robert Olen Butler
The Brothers K., David James Duncan
Turtle Moon, Alice Hoffman
Let the Dead Bury Their Dead and Other Stories, Randall Kenan
Billie Dyer and Other Stories, William Maxwell
All the Pretty Horses, Cormac McCarthy
Small Spaces Between Emergencies, Alison Moore
Jazz, Toni Morrison
Bailey's Cafe, Gloria Naylor
The English Patient, Michael Ondaatje
The Patron Saint of Liars, Ann Patchett
A Thousand Acres, Jane Smiley

### Poetry

Judeville: The Complete Poems, 1970-1990, David Budbill
Moon Crossing Bridge, Tess Gallagher

### Nonfiction

Eleanor Roosevelt, Blanche Wiesen Cook
The Meadow, James Galvin
Who Will Tell the People, William B. Greider
Young Men and Fire, Norman MacLean
Truman, David McCullough
Talking to High Monks in the Snow, Lydia Yuri Minatoya
Becoming a Man, Paul Monette
Technopoly, Neil Postman
Down from Troy: Richard Selzer
Going Back to Bisbee, Richard Shelton
Lincoln at Gettysburg: Garry Wills

## Bestselling Books of 1992

Source: *Publishers Weekly*, Mar. 1, 1993. Rankings are determined by sales figures provided by publishers; numbers generally reflect reports of copies "shipped and billed" in 1992 but not final net sales.

### Hardcover Fiction

1. Dolores Claiborne, Stephen King
2. The Pelican Brief, John Grisham
3. Gerald's Game, Stephen King
4. Mixed Blessings, Danielle Steel
5. Jewels, Danielle Steel
6. The Stars Shine Down, Sidney Sheldon
7. Tale of the Body Thief, Anne Rice
8. Mexico, James A. Michener
9. Waiting to Exhale, Terry McMillan
10. All Around the Town, Mary Higgins Clark
11. Scruples Two, Judith Krantz
12. Sahara, Clive Cussler
13. Hideaway, Dean R. Koontz
14. The Road to Omaha, Robert Ludlum
15. Star Wars: Dark Force Rising, Timothy Zahn

### Hardcover Nonfiction

1. The Way Things Ought to Be, Rush Limbaugh
2. It Doesn't Take a Hero, H. Norman Schwarzkopf
3. How to Satisfy a Woman Every Time, Naura Hayden
4. Every Living Thing, James Herriot
5. A Return to Love, Marianne Williamson
6. Sam Walton, Sam Walton
7. Diana, Andrew Morton
8. Truman, David McCullough
9. Silent Passage, Gail Sheehy
10. Sex, Madonna
11. The Juiceman's Power of Juicing, Ray Kordich
12. Harvey Penick's Little Red Book, Harvey Penick
13. More Wealth Without Risk, Charles Givens
14. I Can't Believe I Said That, Kathie Lee Gifford
15. Creating Love, John Bradshaw

### Trade Paperback

1. Life's Little Instruction Book, H. Jackson Brown, Jr.
2. Forever in Your Embrace, Kathleen Woodiwiss
3. Live and Learn and Pass It On, H. Jackson Brown, Jr.
4. The T-Factor Fat Gram Counter, Dr. Martin Katahn and Jamie Pope-Cordle
5. Attack of the Deranged Mutant Killer Monster Snow Goons, Bill Watterson

6. The Indispensable Calvin and Hobbes, Bill Watterson
7. Mrs. Fields Cookie Book, Debbie Fields and the editors of Time-Life Books
8. Cows of Our Planet, Gary Larson
9. Prophet, Frank Peretti
10. Juicing for Life, Cherie Clabom and Maureen Keane
11. The Complete & Up-to-Date Fat Book, Karen J. Bellerson
12. Daisy Faye and the Miracle Man, Fannie Flagg
13. You Just Don't Understand, Deborah Tannen
14. America: What Went Wrong, Donald L. Barlett and James B. Steele
15. Don't Know Much About History, Kenneth Davis

### Mass-Market Paperback

1. The Firm, John Grisham
2. The Silence of the Lambs, Thomas Harris
3. A Time to Kill, John Grisham
4. Scarlett, Alexandra Ripley
5. Heartbeat, Danielle Steel
6. Message from Nam, Danielle Steel
7. The Sum of All Fears, Tom Clancy
8. Four Past Midnight, Stephen King
9. Needful Things, Stephen King
10. No Greater Love, Danielle Steel
11. Secrets of the Morning, V. C. Andrews
12. September, Rosamunde Pilcher
13. Jurassic Park, Michael Crichton
14. Stand, Stephen King
15. Loves Music, Loves to Dance, Mary Higgins Clark

### Almanacs, Atlases, and Annuals

1. The World Almanac and Book of Facts, 1993, ed. Mark Hoffman
2. The World Almanac and Book of Facts, 1992, ed. Mark Hoffman
3. J.K. Lasser's Your Income Tax, 1993
4. 1993 Information Please Almanac, ed. Otto Johnson
5. The Ernst & Young Tax Guide 1992, ed. Peter Bernstein

## Notable Children's Books of 1992

Source: American Library Association

### All Ages

Red Dragonfly on My Shoulder, Sylvia Cassedy, illus. Molly Bang
The World in 1492, Jean Fritz and others, illus. Stefano Vitale
Gonna Sing My Head Off! ed. Kathleen Krull, illus. Allen Garns
I Saw Esau, ed. Iona Opie and Peter Opie, illus. Maurice Sendak

Charlie Parker Played Be Bop, Chris Raschka
An Angel for Solomon Singer, Cynthia Rylant, ed. Peter Catalanatto
The Stinky Cheese Man and Other Fairly Stupid Tales, Jon Scieszka, illus. Lane Smith
Talking with Artists, ed. Pat Cummings
The Widow's Broom, Chris Van Allsburg

## Younger Readers

The Fortune-Tellers, Lloyd Alexander, illus. Trina Schart Hyman
Hugh Can Do, Jennifer Armstrong, illus. Kimberley Bulcken Root
Old Black Fly, Jim Aylesworth, illus. Stephen Gammell
Emily, Michael Bedard, illus. Barbara Cooney
Moon Rope, Lois Ehlert, trans. Amy Prince
Lunch, Denise Fleming
My Great-Aunt Arizona, Gloria Houston, illus. Susan Condie Lamb
Bently and Egg, William Joyce
Soap Soup and Other Verses, Karla Kuskin
The Moonbow of Mr. B. Bones, J. Patrick Lewis, illus. Dirk Zimmer

Mirette on the High Wire, Emily Arnold McCully
Martha Speaks, Susan Meddaugh
The Life and Times of the Apple, Charles Micucci
Back Home, Gloria Jean Pinkney, illus. Jerry Pinkney
Chicken Sunday, illus. Patricia Polacco
Don't You Know There's a War On? James Stevenson
Talking Like the Rain, ed. X. J. Kennedy and Dorothy M. Kennedy, illus. Jane Dyer
Farmer Duck, Martin Waddell, illus. Helen Oxenbury
June 29, 1999, Davis Wiesner
Working Cotton, Sherley Anne Williams, illus. Carole Byard
Letting a Swift River Go, Jane Yoken, illus. Barbara Cooney
Seven Blind Mice, Ed Young

## Middle-Grade Readers

"Who Was That Masked Man, Anyway?", Avi
Wings Along the Waterway, Mary Barrett Brown
The Moon and I, Betsy Byars
Loop the Loop, Barbara Dugan, illus. James Stevenson
Who Shrank My Grandmother's House? Barbara Esbensen, illus. Eric Beddows
Li'l Sis and Uncle Willie, Gwen Everett
Jim Ugly, Sid Fleischman, illus. Jos. A. Smith
Love Flute, Paul Goble
Words of Stone, Kevin Henkes

Surtsey, Kathryn Lasky, photos Christopher C. Knight
Underruners, Margaret Mahy
The Dark-Thirty, Patricia McKissack, illus. Brian Pinkney
The Amazing Potato, Milton Meltzer
All but Alice, Phyllis Reynolds Naylor
Life's a Funny Proposition, Horatio, Barbara Garland Polikoff
Antarctica, Laurence Pringle
Sukey and the Mermaid, Robert D. San Souci, illus. Brian Pinkney

## Junior High School-Age Readers

Steal Away, Jennifer Armstrong
What's Your Story? Marion Dane Bauer
No Place to Be, Judith Berck
Ajeemah and His Son, James Berry
What Hearts, Bruce Brooks
An Indian Winter, Russell Freedman, illus. Karl Bodmer
A Twilight Struggle, Barbara Harrison and Daniel Terris
Letters from Rifka, Karen Hesse
Against the Storm, Gaye Hicyilmaz
The Harmony Arms, Ron Koertge
Letters from a Slave Girl, Mary E. Lyons

Sojourner Truth, Patricia McKissack and Frederick McKissack
Somewhere in the Darkness, Walter Dean Myers
The Beggar's Ride, Theresa Nelson
Rosa Parks, Rosa Parks and Jim Haskins
Missing May, Cynthia Rylant
Children of the Dust Bowl, Jerry Stanley
When the Road Ends, Jean Thesman
The Same Sky, ed. Naomi Shihab Nye
The Leaving, Budge Wilson
The Pigman and Me, Paul Zindel

## Young Adults (Teenagers)—Fiction

Steal Away, Jennifer Armstrong
What You Don't Know Can Kill You, Fran Arrick
Blue Heron, Avi
Ajeemah and His Son, James Berry
Cherokee Bat and the Goat Guys, Francesca Lia Block
Lily, Cindy Bonner
What Hearts, Bruce Brooks
Two Moons in August, Martha Brooks
Jumping the Nail, Eve Bunting
The Place of Lions, Eric Campbell
My Father, the Nutcase, Judith Casely
Flight #116 Is Down, Caroline B. Cooney
The Sleep of Stone, Louise Cooper
Tunes for Bears to Dance To, Robert Cormier
Gone, Kit Craig
If Rock and Roll Were a Machine, Terry Davis
AK, Peter Dickinson
Dear Nobody, Berlie Doherty
Binge, Charles Ferry
Becca's Story, James D. Forman
Song of the Buffalo Boy, Sherry Garland
Jumper, Steven Gould
The Pelican Brief, John Grisham
Dinotopia: A Land Apart from Time, James Gurney
The Music of Summer, Rosa Guy
Fool's Hill, Barbara Hall
Letters from Rifka, Karen Hesse
The Big Wander, Will Hobbs
Turtle Moon, Alice Hoffman
Acquaintance with the Night, Sollace Holtze
One of the Boys, Scott Johnson
A Sudden Wild Magic, Diana Wynne Jones
Someone Else's Baby, Geraldine Kaye
Crossing Blood, Nanci Kincaid
The Harmony Arms, Ron Koertge
The Primrose Way, Jackie French Koller
Bardic Voices: The Lark and the Wren, Mercedes Lackey
Kiss the Dust, Elizabeth Laird

Letters from a Slave Girl, Mary E. Lyons
Not a Swan, Michelle Magorian
When the Broken Heart Still Beats, Carolyn Meyer
Way Past Cool, Jess Mowry
The Righteous Revenge of Artemis Bonner, Walter Dean Myers
Somewhere in the Darkness, Walter Dean Myers
The Beggar's Ride, Theresa Nelson
The Haymeadow, Gary Paulsen
Family of Strangers, Susan Beth Pfeffer
Is Kissing a Girl Who Smokes Like Licking an Ashtray? Randy Powell
A Little Bit Dead, Chap Reaver
Time Windows, Kathryn Reiss
The Last Pendragon, Robert Rice
A Break with Charity, Ann Rinaldi
Missing May, Cynthia Rylant
Blue Skin of the Sea, Graham Salisbury
The Stinky Cheese Man and Other Fairly Stupid Tales, Jon Scieszka
Child of Faerie, Child of Earth, Joseph Sherman
River Rats, Carolyn Stevermer
Crosses, Shelley Stoehr
The Weirdo, Theodore Taylor
When the Road Ends, Jean Thesman
Plague, Jean Ure
Stormsearch, Robert Westall
Yaxley's Cat, Robert Westall
Weeping Willow, Ruth White
Bad Boy, Diana Wieler
Crocodile Burning, Michael Williams
The Leaving, Budge Wilson
Lockie Leonard, Human Torpedo, Tim Winton
Maizon at Blue Gill, Jacqueline Woodson
Searching for Dragons, Patricia C. Wrede
Briar Rose, Jane Yolen
A Plague of Sorcerers, Mary Frances Zambreno

# Top 100 Daily Newspapers in the U.S.

Source: *1993 Editor & Publisher International Yearbook*
(circulation as of Sept. 30, 1992; m=morning, e=evening)

In 1992, another year of sluggish economic growth brought the discontinuation or merging of 26 daily newspapers. The addition of 10 new dailies during the year brought the total number of daily newspapers published in the U.S. as of Feb. 1, 1993, to 1,570, a loss of 16 when compared with the same date in 1992. There was also a circulation drop of 522,626, when comparing the average daily circulation for the 6-month period ending Sept. 30, 1992, with the average for the same period in 1991, from 60,687,125 to 60,164,499. The trend toward morning distribution that began in the mid-1970s continued, 26 evening dailies switching to morning distribution, to bring the total number of morning papers up to 596 over 1991's count of 571, while the number of evening papers dropped from 1,042 to 996. Another trend continued: the number of daily newspapers publishing Sunday editions increased from 875 to 891; total Sunday circulation increased from 62,067,820 to 62,159,971.

| Newspaper | | Circulation |
|---|---|---|
| 1. Wall Street Journal (New York, NY) | (m) | 1,795,206 |
| 2. USA Today (Arlington, VA) | (m) | 1,506,708 |
| 3. Times (Los Angeles, CA) | (m) | 1,146,631 |
| 4. Times (New York, NY) | (m) | 1,145,890 |
| 5. Post (Washington, DC) | (m) | 802,057 |
| 6. Daily News (New York, NY) | (m) | 777,129 |
| 7. Newsday (Long Island/New York, NY) | (all day) | 758,358 |
| 8. Tribune (Chicago, IL) | (m) | 724,257 |
| 9. Free Press (Detroit, MI) | (m) | 580,372 |
| 10. Chronicle (San Francisco, CA) | (m) | 556,765 |
| 11. Sun-Times (Chicago, IL) | (m) | 528,324 |
| 12. Globe (Boston, MA) | (m) | 508,867 |
| 13. Inquirer (Philadelphia, PA) | (m) | 502,149 |
| 14. Star-Ledger (Newark, NJ) | (m) | 481,027 |
| 15. Morning News (Dallas, TX) | (m) | 479,215 |
| 16. Post (New York, NY) | (m) | 437,962 |
| 17. Chronical (Houston, TX) | (all day) | 419,759 |
| 18. Star Tribune (Minneapolis, MN) | (m) | 410,920 |
| 19. Plain Dealer (Cleveland, OH) | (m) | 410,237 |
| 20. Herald (Miami, FL) | (m) | 404,679 |
| 21. News (Detroit, MI) | (e) | 398,630 |
| 22. Union-Tribune (San Diego, CA) | (all day) | 373,453 |
| 23. Times (St. Petersburg, FL) | (m) | 358,051 |
| 24. Rocky Mountain News (Denver, CO) | (m) | 356,577 |
| 25. Arizona Republic (Phoenix, AZ) | (m) | 342,341 |
| 26. Post-Dispatch (St. Louis, MO) | (m) | 339,545 |
| 27. Oregonian (Portland, OR) | (all day) | 336,087 |
| 28. Register (Orange County, CA) | (all day) | 332,164 |
| 29. Herald (Boston, MA) | (m) | 330,614 |
| 30. News (Buffalo, NY) | (all day) | 305,482 |
| 31. Constitution (Atlanta, GA) | (m) | 302,616 |
| 32. Post (Houston, TX) | (m) | 300,121 |
| 33. Tribune (Tampa, FL) | (m) | 295,436 |
| 34. Star (Kansas City, MO) | (m) | 287,119 |
| 35. Sentinel (Orlando, FL) | (all day) | 285,172 |
| 36. Mercury News (San Jose, CA) | (all day) | 270,174 |
| 37. Times-Picayune (New Orleans, LA) | (all day) | 269,639 |
| 38. Post (Denver, CO) | (m) | 269,020 |
| 39. Dispatch (Columbus, OH) | (m) | 264,601 |
| 40. Bee (Sacramento, CA) | (m) | 264,259 |
| 41. Star-Telegram (Fort Worth, TX) | (all day) | 256,199 |
| 42. Sun-Sentinel (Fort Lauderdale, FL) | (m) | 252,158 |
| 43. Times (Seattle, WA) | (e) | 239,476 |
| 44. Journal (Milwaukee, WI) | (e) | 236,943 |
| 45. Courier-Journal (Louisville, KY) | (m) | 236,103 |
| 46. Observer (Charlotte, NC) | (m) | 231,027 |
| 47. Star (Indianapolis, IN) | (m) | 230,041 |
| 48. Courant (Hartford, CT) | (m) | 229,284 |
| 49. Sun (Baltimore, MD) | (m) | 227,706 |
| 50. Times-Dispatch (Richmond, VA) | (m) | 214,227 |
| 51. Pioneer Press (St. Paul, MN) | (m) | 212,057 |
| 52. Daily Oklahoman (Oklahoma City, OK) | (m) | 210,004 |
| 53. Daily News (Los Angeles, CA) | (m) | 207,421 |
| 54. Post-Intelligencer (Seattle, WA) | (m) | 207,299 |
| 55. Enquirer (Cincinnati, OH) | (m) | 199,257 |
| 56. Journal (Providence, RI) | (all day) | 194,880 |
| 57. Daily News (Philadelphia, PA) | (m) | 193,192 |
| 58. Register (Des Moines, IA) | (m) | 191,511 |
| 59. Times-Union (Jacksonville, FL) | (m) | 180,619 |
| 60. Daily News (Dayton, OH) | (m) | 179,405 |
| 61. Palm Beach Post (West Palm Beach, FL) | (m) | 178,412 |
| 62. Democrat-Gazette (Little Rock, AR) | (m) | 176,741 |
| 63. Commercial Appeal (Memphis, TN) | (m) | 176,411 |
| 64. Express-News (San Antonio, TX) | (all day) | 175,611 |
| 65. American-Statesman (Austin, TX) | (m) | 170,798 |
| 66. Sentinel (Milwaukee, WI) | (m) | 169,961 |
| 67. Press (Asbury Park, NJ) | (e) | 164,756 |
| 68. News (Birmingham, AL) | (e) | 163,380 |
| 69. Record (Hackensack, NJ) | (m) | 160,086 |
| 70. Beacon Journal (Akron, OH) | (m) | 158,605 |
| 71. Journal (Atlanta, GA) | (e) | 156,199 |
| 72. Virginian-Pilot (Norfolk, VA) | (m) | 155,362 |
| 73. Post-Gazette (Pittsburgh, PA) | (m) | 155,307 |
| 74. Press-Enterprise (Riverside, CA) | (m) | 154,790 |
| 75. Press (Grand Rapids, MI) | (e) | 150,702 |
| 76. Blade (Toledo, OH) | (m) | 146,334 |
| 77. Bee (Fresno, CA) | (m) | 146,183 |
| 78. News & Observer (Raleigh, NC) | (m) | 145,988 |
| 79. Tennessean (Nashville, TN) | (m) | 139,086 |
| 80. Democrat and Chronicle (Rochester, NY) | (m) | 137,556 |
| 81. Morning Call (Allentown, PA) | (m) | 137,108 |
| 82. The State (Columbia, SC) | (m) | 134,945 |
| 83. Examiner (San Francisco, CA) | (e) | 134,821 |
| 84. Review-Journal (Las Vegas, NV) | (m) | 131,769 |
| 85. World-Herald (Omaha, NE) | (m) | 129,259 |
| 86. World (Tulsa, OK) | (m) | 127,467 |
| 87. Morning News Tribune (Tacoma, WA) | (m) | 126,303 |
| 88. News-Sentinel (Knoxville, TN) | (m) | 125,965 |
| 89. News Journal (Wilmington, DE) | (all day) | 124,091 |
| 90. Herald-Leader (Lexington, KY) | (m) | 123,474 |
| 91. Press-Telegram (Long Beach, CA) | (m) | 122,716 |
| 92. Herald-Tribune (Sarasota, FL) | (m) | 121,438 |
| 93. Spokesman-Review (Spokane, WA) | (m) | 120,022 |
| 94. Daily Herald (Chicago, IL) | (m) | 119,878 |
| 95. Evening Sun (Baltimore, MD) | (e) | 119,302 |
| 96. Tribune (Salt Lake City, UT) | (m) | 117,858 |
| 97. Eagle (Wichita, KS) | (m) | 117,399 |
| 98. Telegram & Gazette (Worcester, MA) | (m) | 115,129 |
| 99. Journal (Albuquerque, NM) | (m) | 115,094 |
| 100. Times & World-News (Roanoke, VA) | (m) | 114,872 |

## 100 Bestselling U.S. Magazines

Source: Audit Bureau of Circulations, Schaumburg, Ill.

General magazines, exclusive of groups and comics; also exclusive of magazines that failed to file reports to ABC by press time. Based on total average paid circulation during the 6 months prior to Dec. 31, 1992.

| Magazine | Circulation | Magazine | Circulation | Magazine | Circulation |
|---|---|---|---|---|---|
| 1. Modern Maturity . . . . | 22,879,886 | 33. Seventeen . . . . . . . | 1,915,426 | 68. Travel & Leisure. . . . | 1,092,414 |
| 2. NRTA/AARP Bulletin. | 22,746,026 | 34. Home & Away. . . . . | 1,912,160 | 69. Family Handyman. . . | 1,047,679 |
| 3. Reader's Digest. . . . | 16,258,476 | 35. Country Living . . . . | 1,839,363 | 70. Scouting . . . . . . . . | 1,030,194 |
| 4. TV Guide. . . . . . . . | 14,498,341 | 36. Popular Science. . . . | 1,812,019 | 71. Cooking Light . . . . . | 1,025,511 |
| 5. National Geographic . | 9,708,254 | 37. Ebony . . . . . . . . . | 1,791,536 | 72. Conde Nast Traveler . | 1,020,592 |
| 6. Better Homes & | | 38. Life . . . . . . . . . . | 1,777,087 | 73. Car and Driver. . . . . | 1,019,630 |
|    Gardens . . . . . . | 8,002,585 | 39. Parents. . . . . . . . . | 1,749,322 | 74. Discover. . . . . . . . | 1,014,152 |
| 7. Family Circle . . . . . | 5,283,660 | 40. Popular Mechanics . . | 1,642,081 | 75. Home Mechanix. . . . | 1,013,963 |
| 8. Good Housekeeping . | 5,139,355 | 41. Outdoor Life . . . . . | 1,502,542 | 76. Health . . . . . . . . . | 1,013,428 |
| 9. Ladies Home Journal. | 5,041,143 | 42. American Rifleman . . | 1,485,190 | 77. Home. . . . . . . . . . | 1,013,182 |
| 10. Woman's Day . . . . | 4,810,445 | 43. Sunset . . . . . . . . . | 1,452,086 | 78. Weight Watchers . . . | 1,006,397 |
| 11. McCall's . . . . . . . . | 4,704,772 | 44. Golf Digest. . . . . . . | 1,421,883 | 79. PC Magazine . . . . . | 1,004,235 |
| 12. Time . . . . . . . . . . | 4,203,991 | 45. Self . . . . . . . . . . | 1,408,975 | 80. Consumer's Digest . . | 1,003,558 |
| 13. People . . . . . . . . | 3,506,816 | 46. Soap Opera Digest. . | 1,396,346 | 81. House Beautiful . . . . | 1,002,458 |
| 14. Sports Illustrated . . . | 3,432,044 | 47. Elks. . . . . . . . . . | 1,383,318 | 82. Michigan Living . . . . | 983,194 |
| 15. Playboy . . . . . . . . | 3,402,630 | 48. YM . . . . . . . . . . | 1,340,415 | 83. Motor Trend . . . . . . | 943,441 |
| 16. National Enquirer . . . | 3,401,263 | 49. American Hunter . . . | 1,329,124 | 84. Gourmet . . . . . . . . | 915,171 |
| 17. Redbook . . . . . . . . | 3,395,029 | 50. New Woman. . . . . . | 1,313,181 | 85. Jet . . . . . . . . . . . | 909,014 |
| 18. Newsweek . . . . . . . | 3,240,131 | 51. Boys' Life . . . . . . . | 1,288,545 | 86. Essence . . . . . . . . | 906,034 |
| 19. Prevention . . . . . . . | 3,234,901 | 52. Vogue . . . . . . . . . | 1,284,193 | 87. Elle . . . . . . . . . . . | 901,619 |
| 20. AAA World. . . . . . . | 3,107,468 | 53. First for Women . . . . | 1,258,595 | 88. American Health . . . . | 895,668 |
| 21. American Legion . . . | 2,953,941 | 54. Penthouse . . . . . . | 1,254,207 | 89. The Workbasket . . . . | 890,006 |
| 22. Star. . . . . . . . . . . | 2,931,305 | 55. Bon Appetit . . . . . . | 1,231,327 | 90. Victoria. . . . . . . . . | 886,661 |
| 23. Cosmopolitan . . . . | 2,705,224 | 56. True Story Plus . . . . | 1,225,347 | 91. Business Week, NA. . | 886,229 |
| 24. Southern Living . . . . | 2,374,530 | 57. Mademoiselle . . . . . | 1,219,159 | 92. Endless Vacation . . . | 885,604 |
| 25. U.S. News & World | | 58. Sesame Street . . . . | 1,218,722 | 93. Working Woman . . . . | 866,816 |
|    Report. . . . . . . | 2,307,569 | 59. Rolling Stone . . . . . | 1,211,586 | 94. Entertainment Weekly | 866,431 |
| 26. Smithsonian . . . . . . | 2,211,552 | 60. Woman's World . . . . | 1,204,042 | 95. Nation's Business . . . | 861,581 |
| 27. Money . . . . . . . . . | 2,146,140 | 61. Teen . . . . . . . . . . | 1,188,257 | 96. Hot Rod . . . . . . . . | 856,774 |
| 28. Glamour . . . . . . . . | 2,083,849 | 62. Golf. . . . . . . . . . | 1,183,684 | 97. Workbench . . . . . . . | 831,751 |
| 29. Motorland . . . . . . . | 2,072,359 | 63. Kiplingers . . . . . . . | 1,166,539 | 98. American Legion | |
| 30. VFW . . . . . . . . . . | 2,062,914 | 64. Vanity Fair . . . . . . . | 1,151,887 |    Auxiliary . . . . . | 828,855 |
| 31. NEA Today . . . . . . | 2,059,728 | 65. Us. . . . . . . . . . . | 1,102,783 | 99. Mature Outlook . . . . | 824,559 |
| 32. Field & Stream . . . . | 2,007,234 | 66. Globe. . . . . . . . . . | 1,102,335 | 100. Sport . . . . . . . . . | 816,990 |
| | | 67. Country Home. . . . | 1,095,721 | | |

## Some Notable U.S. Dance Companies

Source: Dance/USA, July 1993

African-American Dance Ensemble, Durham, NC
Alvin Ailey American Dance Theater, New York, NY
Aman Folk Ensemble, Los Angeles, CA
American Ballet Theatre, New York, NY
American Repertory Ballet Company, Princeton, NJ
Atlanta Ballet, GA
Avaz International Dance Theatre, Los Angeles, CA
Ballet Arizona, Phoenix, AZ
Ballet Austin, Austin, TX
Ballet Chicago, IL
Ballet Florida, West Palm Beach, FL
Ballet Hispanico of New York, New York, NY
BalletMet, Columbus, OH
Ballet Omaha, NE
Ballet West, Salt Lake City, UT
Tandy Beal and Company, Santa Cruz, CA
Maria Benitez Teatro Flamenco, Santa Fe, NM
Boston Ballet, Boston, MA
Trisha Brown Company, New York, NY
Donald Byrd/The Group, New York, NY
Caribbean Dance Company, St. Croix, VI
Chen & Dancers, New York, NY
Lucinda Childs Dance Company, New York, NY
Cincinnati Ballet, Cincinnati, OH
Cleveland/San Jose Ballet, Cleveland, OH
Colorado Ballet, Denver, CO
Contraband, San Francisco, CA
Cunningham Dance Foundation, New York, NY
Dallas Black Dance Theatre, Dallas, TX
Dance Alloy, Pittsburgh, PA
Dance Exchange, Washington, DC
Dance Theatre of Harlem, New York, NY

DanceBrazil, New York, NY
Danceteller, Philadelphia, PA
Della Davidson Dance Company, San Francisco, CA
Dayton Ballet Association, Dayton, OH
Dayton Contemporary Dance Company, Dayton, OH
Laura Dean Musicians and Dancers, New York, NY
Douglas Dunn & Dancers, New York, NY
Eiko & Koma, New York, NY
Eugene Ballet Company, Eugene, OR
Garth Fagan's Dance, Rochester, NY
Feld Ballet, New York, NY
Fort Worth Ballet, Fort Worth, TX
Joe Goode Performance Group, San Francisco, CA
David Gordon Pick Up Co., New York, NY
Martha Graham Dance Co., New York, NY
Hartford Ballet, Hartford, CT
Erick Hawkins Dance Co., New York, NY
Joseph Holmes Dance Theater, Chicago, IL
Houston Ballet, Houston, TX
Hubbard Street Dance, Chicago, IL
Indianapolis Ballet Theatre, Indianapolis, IN
Isaacs, McCaleb & Dancers, San Diego, CA
Jazz Tap Ensemble, Los Angeles, CA
Margaret Jenkins Dance Company, San Francisco, CA
Joffrey Ballet, New York, NY
Bill T. Jones/Arnie Zane Company, New York, NY
Rebecca Kelly Dance Company, New York, NY
KHADRA International Folk Ballet, San Francisco, CA
Ko-Thi Dance Company, Bronx, NY
Lula Washington's L.A. Contemporary Dance Theatre, Los Angeles, CA
Ralph Lemon Company, New York, NY

Lewitzky Dance Company, Los Angeles, CA
Jose Limon Dance Company, New York, NY
LINES Contemporary Ballet, San Francisco, CA
Loretta Livingston & Dancers, Los Angeles, CA
Los Angeles Chamber Ballet, CA
Louisville Ballet, Louisville, KY
Lar Lubovitch Dance Company, New York, NY
Susan Marshall & Company, New York, NY
Miami City Ballet, Miami Beach, FL
Bebe Miller and Company, New York, NY
Milwaukee Ballet, Milwaukee, WI
Elisa Monte Dance Company, New York, NY
Montgomery Ballet, Montgomery, AL
Mordine & Company, Chicago, IL
Mark Morris Dance Group, New York, NY
Jennifer Muller/The Works, New York, NY
Muntu Dance Theater, Chicago, IL
New Dance, Minneapolis, MN
New York City Ballet, New York, NY
Rosalind Newman and Dancers, New York, NY
Nikolais and Louis Dance, New York, NY
North Carolina Dance Theatre, Winston-Salem, NC
Oakland Ballet, Oakland, CA
ODC/San Francisco, San Francisco, CA
Ohio Ballet, Akron, OH
Oregon Ballet Theater, Portland, OR
Pacific Northwest Ballet, Seattle, WA
Parsons Dance Company, New York, NY
Pennsylvania Ballet, Philadelphia, PA

Pepatian, Bronx, NY
Philadanco, Philadelphia, PA
Pilobolus Dance Theater, Washington, CT
Stuart Pimsler Dance & Theater, Columbus, OH
Pittsburgh Ballet Theatre, Pittsburgh, PA
Pittsburgh Dance Alloy, Pittsburgh, PA
Repertory Dance Theatre, Salt Lake City, UT
Richmond Ballet, Richmond, VA
Elizabeth Streb Ringside, New York, NY
Ririe-Woodbury Dance Company, Salt Lake City, UT
Cleo Parker Robinson Dance Theater, Denver, CO
Nicholas Rodriguez and DanceCompass, Montclair, NJ
San Francisco Ballet, San Francisco, CA
Carlota Santana Spanish Dance Arts Co., New York, NY
Sarasota Ballet, FL
Solomons Company/Dance, New York, NY
Southern Ballet Theater, Winter Park, FL
State Ballet of Missouri, Kansas City, MO
Paul Taylor Dance Company, New York, NY
Joyce Trisler Danscompany, New York, NY
Tulsa Ballet Theatre, Tulsa, OK
Urban Bush Women, New York, NY
Dan Wagoner and Dancers, New York, NY
Washington Ballet, Washington, DC
June Watanabe and Company, San Rafael, CA
Nina Wiener Dance Company, New York, NY
Zenon Dance Company, Minneapolis, MN
ZeroMoving Dance Company, Philadelphia, PA
Zivili Kolo Ensemble, Granville, OH

# Symphony Orchestras of the U.S.

Source: American Symphony Orchestra League, 777 14th St., N.W., Washington, DC 20005
(All orchestras listed had budgets in excess of $1.05 million in fiscal 1992.)

| Symphony Orchestra[1] | Music Director[2] |
|---|---|
| Alabama (Birmingham) | Paul Polivnick |
| Atlanta (Ga.) | Yoel Levi |
| Austin (Tex.) | Sung Kwak |
| Baltimore (Md.) | David Zinman |
| Boston (Mass.) | Seiji Ozawa |
| Brooklyn Philharmonic (N.Y.) | Dennis Russell Davies |
| Buffalo Philharmonic (N.Y.) | Maximiano Valdez |
| Cedar Rapids (Ia.) | Christian Tiemeyer |
| Charleston (S.C.) | David Stahl |
| Charlotte (N.C.) | Leo B. Driehuys |
| Chattanooga, & Opera Assn. (Tenn.) | Robert Bernhardt |
| Chicago (Ill.) | Daniel Barenboim |
| Cincinnati (Oh.) | Jesus Lopez-Cobos |
| Cleveland (Oh.) | Christoph von Dohnanyi |
| Colorado (Denver) | David T. Abosch |
| Colorado Springs (Col.) | Christopher P. Wilkins |
| Columbus (Oh.) | Alessandro Siciliani |
| Dallas (Tex.) | Andrew Litton |
| Dayton Philharmonic (Oh.) | Isaiah Jackson |
| Delaware (Wilmington) | Stephen Gunzenhauser |
| Detroit (Mich.) | Neeme Jarvi |
| Florida Philharmonic (Fort Lauderdale) | James Judd |
| The Florida Orchestra (Tampa) | Jahja Ling |
| Florida Symphonic Pops (Boca Raton) | Derek Stannard |
| Fort Wayne Philharmonic (Ind.) | Edward Chivzel |
| Fort Worth (Tex.) | John Giordano |
| Grand Rapids (Mich.) | Catherine Comet |
| Grant Park (Chicago, Ill.) | Catherine M. Cahill |
| Hartford (Conn.) | Michael Lankester |
| Honolulu (Ha.) | Donald Johanos |
| Houston (Tex.) | Christoph Eschenbach |
| Hudson Valley Philharmonic (Poughkeepsie, N.Y.) | Randall Craig Fleischer |
| Indianapolis (Ind.) | Raymond Leppard |
| Jacksonville (Fla.) | Roger Nierenberg |
| Kansas City (Mo.) | William McGlaughlin |
| Knoxville (Tenn.) | Kirk Trevor |
| Long Beach (Cal.) | JoAnn Falletta |
| Long Island Philharmonic (N.Y.) | Marin Alsop |
| Los Angeles Chamber Or. (Cal.) | Christof Perick |

| Symphony Orchestra[1] | Music Director[2] |
|---|---|
| Los Angeles Philharmonic (Cal.) | Esa-Pekka Salonen |
| The Louisville Orchestra (Ky.) | Lawrence Leighton Smith |
| Memphis (Tenn.) | Alan Balter |
| Milwaukee (Wis.) | Zdenek Macal |
| The Minnesota Orchestra (Minneapolis) | Edo de Waart |
| Mississippi (Jackson) | Colman Pearce |
| Naples Philharmonic (Fla.) | Timothy W. Russell |
| The Nashville Symphony (Tenn.) | Kenneth S. Schermerhorn |
| National (Washington, D.C.) | Mstislav Rostropovich |
| New Haven (Conn.) | Michael Palmer |
| New Jersey (Newark) | Zdenek Macal |
| New Mexico (Albuquerque) | Neal H. Stulberg |
| New World Symphony (Miami Beach, Fla.) | Michael Tilson Thomas |
| New York Chamber Sym. of the 92nd St. Y (N.Y.C.) | Gerard Schwarz |
| New York Philharmonic (N.Y.C.) | Kurt Masur |
| North Carolina (Raleigh) | Gerhardt Zimmermann |
| Ohio Chamber Orchestra (Cleveland) | Vacant |
| Oklahoma City Philharmonic (Okla.) | Joel A. Levine |
| Omaha (Neb.) | Bruce B. Hangen |
| Oregon (Portland) | James DePreist |
| Pacific Symphony (Irvine, Cal.) | Carl St. Clair |
| The Philadelphia Orchestra (Pa.) | Wolfgang Sawallisch |
| Phoenix (Ariz.) | James L. Sedares |
| Pittsburgh (Pa.) | Lorin Maazel |
| Portland (Me.) | Toshiyuki Shimada |
| Puerto Rico (Santurce) | Roselin Pabon |
| Rhode Island Philharmonic Or. (Providence) | Zuohuang Chen |
| The Richmond Symphony (Va.) | George Manahan |
| Rochester Philharmonic Or. (N.Y.) | Mark Elder |
| Sacramento (Cal.) | Alasdair P. Neale |
| St. Louis (Mo.) | Leonard Slatkin |
| St. Paul Chamber Or. (Minn.) | Hugh Wolff |
| San Antonio (Tex.) | Christopher P. Wilkins |
| San Diego (Cal.) | Yoav Talmi |
| San Francisco (Cal.) | Herbert Blomstedt |
| San Jose (Cal.) | Leonid Grin |
| Savannah (Ga.) | Philip B. Greenberg |

| Symphony Orchestra[1] | Music Director[2] | Symphony Orchestra[1] | Music Director[2] |
|---|---|---|---|
| Seattle (Wash.) | Gerard Schwarz | The Virginia Symphony (Norfolk). | JoAnn Falletta |
| Shreveport (La) | Peter Leonard | West Virginia (Charleston) | Thomas B. Conlin |
| Spokane (Wash.) | Vakhtang Jordania | Wichita (Kan.) | Zuohuang Chen |
| Springfield (Mass.). | Raymond C. Harvey | Winston-Salem Piedmont | |
| Syracuse (N.Y.) | Kazuyoshi Akiyama | Triad Symphony (N.C.) | Peter J. Perret |
| Toledo (Oh.) | Andrew Massey | | |
| Tucson (Ariz.) | Robert E. Bernhardt | | |
| Tulsa Philharmonic Or. (Okla.). | Bernard Rubenstein | | |
| Utah (Salt Lake City) | Joseph Silverstein | | |

(1) Orchestra name=place name + Symphony Orchestra, unless otherwise noted; (2) General title; listed is highest-ranking member of conducting personnel.

## U.S. Opera Companies with Budgets of $500,000 or More

Source: OPERA America; July 1993
(Companies listed in state order.)

Anchorage Opera; Margaret Wood, gen. dir.

Arizona Opera Co. (Tucson); Glynn Ross, gen. dir.

Opera Theatre at Wildwood (Ariz.); Ann Chotard, art. dir.

Fullerton Civic Light Opera (Calif.); Griff Duncan, gen. mgr.

Long Beach Opera (Calif.); Michael Milenski, gen. dir.

Long Beach Civic Light Opera (Calif.); Pegge Logefeil, mng. dir.

Los Angeles Music Center Opera Assn.; Peter Hemmings, exec. dir.

Opera Pacific (Costa Mesa, Calif.); David DiChiera, gen. dir.

Sacramento Opera Assn. (Calif.); Marianne H. Oaks, gen. dir.

San Diego Civic Light Opera; C. E. Franks, exec. dir.

San Diego Opera Assn.; Ian Campbell, gen. dir.

San Francisco Opera; Lotfi Mansouri, gen. dir.

San Francisco Opera Center (inc. Western Opera Theater)

Opera San José (Calif.); Irene Dalis, art. dir.

San José Civic Light Opera (Calif.); Dianna Shuster, dir.

Central City Opera (Denver); Daniel Rule, gen. mgr.

Opera Colorado (Denver); Nathaniel Merrill, art. dir.

Connecticut Grand Opera & Stamford State Opera, Laurence Gilgore, art. dir.

Connecticut Opera (Hartford); George Osborne, gen. dir.

Goodspeed Opera House (E. Haddam, Conn.); Michael Price, exec. dir.

Washington Opera (D.C.); Martin Feinstein, gen. dir.

Fort Lauderdale Opera; William H. Martin, gen. mgr.

Greater Miami Opera Assn.; Robert Heuer, gen. mgr.

Orlando Opera Co. (Fla.); Robert Swedberg, gen. dir.

Palm Beach Opera; Herbert P. Benn, gen. mgr.

Sarasota Opera Assn. (Fla.); Deane Allyn, exec. dir.

The Atlanta Opera (Ga.); William Fred Scott, art. dir.; Alfred Kennedy, gen. mgr.

Augusta Opera (Ga.); Edward Bradberry, gen. dir.

Hawaii Opera Theatre; J. Mario Ramos, gen. dir.

Chicago Opera Theater; Alan Stone, art. dir.

Lyric Opera of Chicago; Ardis Krainik, gen. mgr.

Indianapolis Opera; Nando Scheller, gen. dir.

Des Moines Metro Opera (Indianola); Robert Larsen, art. dir.

Kentucky Opera Assn. (Louisville); Thomson Smillie, gen. dir.

New Orleans Opera Assn.; Arthur Cosenza, gen. dir.

Baltimore Opera Co.; Michael Harrison, gen. dir.

Opera Company of Boston; Sarah Caldwell, art. dir.

Boston Opera Theatre; Robert Canon, exec. dir.

Michigan Opera Theatre (Detroit); David DiChiera, gen. dir.

Opera Grand Rapids (Mich.); Robert Lyall, gen. dir.

Minnesota Opera Co. (St. Paul); Kevin Smith, gen. dir.

Lyric Opera of Kansas City (Missouri); Russell Patterson, gen. dir. & art. dir.

Opera Theatre of St. Louis (Missouri); Charles MacKay, gen. dir.

Opera/Omaha (Neb.); Mary Robert, gen. dir.

Nevada Opera (Reno); Ted Puffer, gen. dir.

Opera Festival of N.J. (Princeton Junction); Deborah S. Sandler, exec. dir.

Metro Lyric Opera (Allenhurst, N.J.); Era M. Tognoli, gen. & art. dir.

New Jersey State Opera (Newark); Alfredo Silipigni, gen. dir.

Albuquerque Civic Light Opera; Linda E. McVey, exec. dir.

Santa Fe Opera (New Mexico); John Crosby, gen. dir.

Tri-Cities Opera (Binghamton, N.Y.); Richard Hood, exec. dir.

St. Ann Center for Restoration and the Arts (Brooklyn, N.Y.); Susan Feldman, art. dir.

Greater Buffalo Opera (N.Y.); Judith Wolf, exec. dir.

Chautauqua Opera (N.Y.); Linda Jackson, gen. mgr.

Glimmerglass Opera (Cooperstown, N.Y.); Paul Kellogg, gen. mgr.

Lake George Opera Festival (N.Y.); John Balme, art. dir.; Susan T. Danis, exec. dir.

Syracuse Opera; Julie Richard, mng. dir.

Light Opera of Manhattan; Raymond Allen, Jerry Gotham, art. dir.

Metropolitan Opera Assn. (N.Y.C.); Joseph Volpe, gen. mgr.

Music-Theatre Group (N.Y. & Stockbridge, Mass.); Lyn Austin, prod. dir.

New York City Opera; Christopher Keene, gen. dir.

New York City Opera Natl. Co.; Nancy Kelly, adm. dir.

Opera Orchestra of N.Y. (N.Y.C.); Eve Queler, art. dir.

Opera Carolina (Charlotte, N.C.); James Wright, gen. dir.

Cincinnati Opera Assn.; James deBlasis, art. dir.

Cleveland Opera; David Bamberger, gen. dir.

Lyric Opera Cleveland (Oh.); Michael McConnell, exec. dir.

Opera/Columbus (Oh.); John Gage, gen. dir.

Dayton Opera Assn. (Oh.); Jane Nelson, mng. dir.

Lyric Theatre of Oklahoma; Gayle Pearson, gen. mgr.

Tulsa Opera (Oklahoma); Myrna S. Ruffner, gen. dir.

Portland Opera Assn. (Oregon); Robert Bailey, exec. dir.

American Music Theater Festival (Phila.); Marjorie Samoff, prod. dir.

Opera Company of Philadelphia; Robert B. Driver, gen. dir.

Pennsylvania Opera Theater (Phila.); Barbara Silverstein, art. dir. & gen. mgr.

Pittsburgh Civic Light Opera; Charles Gray, exec. dir.

Pittsburgh Opera; Tito Capobianco, gen. dir.

Knoxville Opera (Tenn.); Robert Lyall, gen. dir.

Nashville Opera (Tenn.); Kyle Rideout, gen. dir.

Opera Memphis (Tenn.); Michael Ching, art. dir.; Bert Adler Wolff, gen. dir.

Austin Lyric Opera (Tex.) Walter Ducloux, art. dir.

Dallas Opera; Plato Karayanis, gen. dir.

Lyric Opera of Dallas (Tex.); John Burrows, art. dir.

Fort Worth Opera; William Walker, gen. dir.

Houston Grand Opera Assn.; R. David Gockley, gen. dir.

Texas Opera Theater (Houston); James Ireland, gen. mgr.

Utah Opera (Salt Lake City); Anne Ewers, gen. dir.

Virginia Opera (Norfolk); Peter Mark, gen. dir.

Wolf Trap Opera (Vienna, Va.); Peter Russell, gen. dir.

Seattle Opera Assn.; Speight Jenkins, gen. dir.

Florentine Opera of Milwaukee; Dennis Hanthorn, gen. mgr.

Skylight Opera Theatre (Milwaukee); Chas Rader-Shieber, art. dir.

## Top 20 Cable Video Networks

Source: *Cable Television Developments*, June 1993; Natl. Cable Television Assn. Ranked by number of subscribers.

| Rank | Network[1] | Systems | Subscribers (millions) | Rank | Network[1] | Systems | Subscribers (millions) |
|---|---|---|---|---|---|---|---|
| 1 | ESPN (1979) | 26,200[2] | 61.6 | 11 | MTV: Music Television (1981) | 8,096 | 57.3 |
| 2 | CNN (1980) | 11,325 | 61.0 | 12 | Lifetime (1984) | 5,800 | 57.0 |
| 3 | USA Network (1980) | 12,000[2] | 60.1 | 13 | Arts & Entertainment Network (1984) | 8,000 | 56.0 |
| 4 | TBS (1976) | 14,954[2] | 60.0 | 14 | The Weather Channel (1982) | 4,925 | 53.4 |
| 5 | The Discovery Channel (1985) | 9,300 | 59.0 | 15 | Headline News (1982) | 6,700 | 51.4 |
| 6 | Nickelodeon (1979) | 9,171 | 59.0 | 16 | CNBC (1989) | 4,000[2] | 48.3 |
|  | Nick At Nite (1985) | 4,381 |  | 17 | VH-1 (Video Hits One) (1985) | 5,304 | 47.4 |
| 7 | C-Span (1979) | 4,336 | 58.7 | 18 | QVC Network (1986) | 4,197 | 44.6 |
| 8 | TNT (Turner Network Television) (1988) | 8,731 | 58.4 | 19 | AMC (American Movie Classics) (1984) | 4,100 | 44.5 |
| 9 | The Family Channel (1977) | 10,102 | 57.4 | 20 | WGN/UVI (1978) | 14,354 | 38.1 |
| 10 | TNN: The Nashville Network (1983) | 13,391 | 57.4 | | | | |

(1) Date in parentheses is year service began. (2) Includes non-cable affiliates.

## U.S. Households With Cable Television, 1975-1992

Source: *Cable Television Developments*, June 1993

| Year | Basic Cable Subscribers | Percent of Households With TVs | Year | Basic Cable Subscribers | Percent of Households With TVs |
|---|---|---|---|---|---|
| 1975 | 9,196,690 | 13.2 | 1984 | 37,290,870 | 43.7 |
| 1976 | 10,787,970 | 15.1 | 1985 | 39,872,520 | 46.2 |
| 1977 | 12,168,450 | 16.6 | 1986 | 42,237,140 | 48.1 |
| 1978 | 13,391,910 | 17.9 | 1987 | 44,970,880 | 50.5 |
| 1979 | 14,814,380 | 19.4 | 1988 | 48,636,520 | 53.8 |
| 1980 | 17,671,490 | 22.6 | 1989 | 52,564,470 | 57.1 |
| 1981 | 23,219,200 | 28.3 | 1990 | 54,871,330 | 59.0 |
| 1982 | 29,340,570 | 35.0 | 1991 | 55,786,390 | 60.6 |
| 1983 | 34,113,790 | 40.5 | 1992 | 57,211,600 | 61.5 |

## Number of Cable TV Systems: 1970-1993

Source: *Cable Television Developments*, June 1993

| Year | Systems | Year | Systems | Year | Systems | Year | Systems |
|---|---|---|---|---|---|---|---|
| 1970 | 2,490 | 1976 | 3,681 | 1982 | 4,825 | 1988 | 8,500 |
| 1971 | 2,639 | 1977 | 3,832 | 1983 | 5,600 | 1989 | 9,050 |
| 1972 | 2,841 | 1978 | 3,875 | 1984 | 6,200 | 1990 | 9,575 |
| 1973 | 2,991 | 1979 | 4,150 | 1985 | 6,600 | 1991 | 10,704 |
| 1974 | 3,158 | 1980 | 4,225 | 1986 | 7,500 | 1992 | 11,075 |
| 1975 | 3,506 | 1981 | 4,375 | 1987 | 7,900 | 1993 | 11,385 |

## TV Viewing Shares: Broadcast Years 1983/1984-1991/1992[1]

Source: *Cable Television Developments*, June 1993

|  | Total Television Households '83/'84 | '84/'85 | '85/'86 | '86/'87 | '87/'88 | '88/'89 | '89/'90 | '90/'91 | '91/'92 | All Cable Households '83/'84 | '84/'85 | '85/'86 | '86/'87 | '87/'88 | '88/'89 | '89/'90 | '90/'91 | '91/'92 | Pay Cable Households '83/'84 | '84/'85 | '85/'86 | '86/'87 | '87/'88 | '88/'89 | '89/'90 | '90/'91 | '91/'92 |
|---|---|---|---|---|---|---|---|---|---|---|---|---|---|---|---|---|---|---|---|---|---|---|---|---|---|---|---|
| Broadcast Network Affiliates | 69 | 66 | 66 | 64 | 61 | 58 | 55 | 53 | 54 | 58 | 56 | 56 | 53 | 52 | 49 | 46 | 46 | 47 | 53 | 51 | 51 | 48 | 48 | 45 | 43 | 41 | 43 |
| Independent TV Stations[2] | 19 | 18 | 18 | 20 | 20 | 20 | 20 | 21 | 20 | 17 | 17 | 17 | 17 | 17 | 16 | 16 | 17 | 16 | 17 | 17 | 17 | 16 | 17 | 16 | 16 | 16 | 16 |
| Public TV Stations | 3 | 3 | 3 | 4 | 4 | 3 | 3 | 3 | 3 | 3 | 3 | 3 | 3 | 3 | 3 | 3 | 2 | 3 | 3 | 3 | 3 | 3 | 3 | 2 | 2 | 2 | 2 |
| Basic Cable Networks[2] |  |  |  |  |  |  |  |  |  | 9 | 11 | 11 | 13 | 15 | 17 | 21 | 24 | 24 | 17 | 19 | 19 | 23 | 25 | 28 | 32 | 35 | 35 |
| Pay Cable Services | 5 | 6 | 5 | 4 | 7 | 7 | 6 | 6 | 6 | 11 | 11 | 10 | 10 | 11 | 11 | 10 | 9 | 8 | 18 | 18 | 17 | 17 | 18 | 18 | 18 | 17 | 17 |

(1) For all television viewing Monday-Sunday, 24 hours/day. Due to multiset use and rounding off of numbers, totals are over 100. (2) For broadcast years 1983/1984-1985/1986, superstation shares are divided between independent stations and basic cable networks categories; for broadcast years 1986/1987-1991/1992, TBS has been counted in the basic cable networks category.

## Average Television Viewing Time, 1993

Source: Nielsen Media Research, May 1993 (Hours:Minutes per week)

| | | Mon.-Fri. 10am-4:30pm | Mon.-Fri. 4:30pm-7:30pm | Mon.-Sun. 8-11pm | Sat. 7am-1pm | Mon.-Fri. 11:30pm-1am |
|---|---|---|---|---|---|---|
| Total Persons | | 3:58 | 3:19 | 7:58 | :41 | 1:11 |
| Total Women | 18+ | 5:34 | 3:57 | 9:14 | :36 | 1:26 |
| | 18-24 | 4:55 | 2:56 | 6:32 | :32 | 1:12 |
| | 25-54 | 4:33 | 3:09 | 8:32 | :34 | 1:24 |
| | 55+ | 7:48 | 5:55 | 11:46 | :42 | 1:35 |
| Total Men | 18+ | 3:09 | 2:54 | 8:22 | :34 | 1:24 |
| | 18-24 | 3:04 | 2:18 | 5:54 | :29 | 1:20 |
| | 25-54 | 2:28 | 2:19 | 7:54 | :35 | 1:28 |
| | 55+ | 4:50 | 4:38 | 10:49 | :35 | 1:19 |
| Total Teens | 12-17 | 1:57 | 2:58 | 6:10 | :44 | :44 |
| Children | 2-5 | 4:47 | 2:52 | 4:19 | 1:11 | :20 |
| | 6-11 | 1:40 | 2:56 | 4:58 | 1:06 | :19 |

## America's Favorite Prime-Time Television Programs, 1992-1993

Source: Nielsen Media Research

(Nielsen People Meter Average Audience Estimates)

Regularly Scheduled Network Programs (Sept. 21, 1992-Apr. 18, 1993)

Percent of TV households and persons in TV households

| Rank | Program | TV Households | Women | Men | Teens | Children |
|------|---------|---------------|-------|-----|-------|----------|
| 1. | 60 Minutes | 21.9 | 16.5 | 16.1 | 2.8 | 2.9 |
| 2. | Roseanne | 20.7 | 15.3 | 10.6 | 15.3 | 12.2 |
| 3. | Home Improvement | 19.2 | 14.1 | 12.0 | 13.4 | 11.8 |
| 4. | Murphy Brown | 17.9 | 14.7 | 9.6 | 6.6 | 4.9 |
| 5. | Murder, She Wrote | 17.7 | 16.0 | 10.1 | 2.6 | 2.4 |
| 6. | Coach | 17.5 | 13.1 | 10.7 | 10.4 | 8.4 |
| 7. | NFL Monday Night Football | 16.7 | 7.6 | 15.3 | 7.5 | 4.1 |
| 8. | CBS Sunday Movie | 16.1 | 14.3 | 8.4 | 3.9 | 2.6 |
| 8. | Cheers | 16.1 | 11.6 | 10.4 | 7.0 | 5.1 |
| 10. | Full House | 15.8 | 10.7 | 6.4 | 13.0 | 16.9 |
| 11. | Northern Exposure | 15.2 | 11.8 | 9.0 | 3.9 | 2.0 |
| 12. | Rescue: 911 | 15.1 | 11.7 | 9.2 | 6.4 | 7.2 |
| 12. | 20/20 | 15.1 | 11.6 | 9.0 | 4.6 | 4.8 |
| 14. | CBS Tuesday Movie | 14.8 | 11.8 | 8.3 | 5.9 | 4.2 |
| 15. | Love and War | 14.7 | 11.9 | 7.7 | 4.5 | 3.1 |
| 16. | Fresh Prince of Bel Air | 14.6 | 9.5 | 6.6 | 17.1 | 12.4 |
| 16. | Hangin' With Mr. Cooper | 14.6 | 9.9 | 6.1 | 13.2 | 14.0 |
| 16. | Jackie Thomas Show | 14.6 | 10.5 | 7.8 | 10.3 | 7.0 |
| 19. | Evening Shade | 14.5 | 12.4 | 8.2 | 3.6 | 3.7 |
| 20. | Hearts Afire | 14.2 | 12.1 | 7.7 | 3.8 | 3.6 |
| 20. | Unsolved Mysteries | 14.2 | 11.2 | 8.8 | 4.7 | 4.5 |
| 22. | Primetime Live | 14.1 | 10.7 | 9.1 | 2.5 | 1.6 |
| 23. | NBC Monday Night Movies | 13.9 | 11.2 | 6.4 | 7.6 | 4.6 |
| 24. | Dr. Quinn Medicine Woman | 13.7 | 12.3 | 8.0 | 5.3 | 5.0 |
| 25. | Seinfeld | 13.6 | 9.9 | 8.7 | 5.0 | 3.2 |
| 26. | Blossom | 13.5 | 8.7 | 5.6 | 17.1 | 11.5 |
| 26. | 48 Hours | 13.5 | 10.2 | 8.4 | 3.0 | 2.0 |
| 28. | ABC Sunday Night Movie | 13.3 | 10.2 | 8.2 | 6.9 | 4.9 |
| 29. | Matlock | 13.2 | 11.6 | 7.8 | 2.5 | 2.2 |
| 30. | Simpsons | 13.0 | 6.3 | 7.2 | 15.5 | 16.2 |
| 30. | Wings | 13.0 | 9.5 | 8.1 | 5.3 | 4.0 |
| 32. | Family Matters | 12.6 | 8.4 | 6.0 | 10.3 | 14.7 |
| 33. | NFL Post 1 | 12.4 | 6.3 | 10.7 | 4.9 | 4.1 |
| 34. | America's Funniest Home Videos | 12.2 | 8.9 | 7.6 | 7.5 | 10.2 |
| 34. | Step By Step | 12.2 | 8.0 | 5.5 | 10.9 | 16.1 |
| 36. | NBC Sunday Night Movie | 12.1 | 8.9 | 8.2 | 5.6 | 3.6 |
| 37. | ABC Monday Night Movie | 11.9 | 8.7 | 7.2 | 4.9 | 3.2 |
| 37. | In the Heat of the Night | 11.9 | 9.9 | 7.4 | 2.5 | 2.5 |
| 39. | Getting By | 11.8 | 7.7 | 4.9 | 10.7 | 15.0 |
| 39. | Laurie Hill | 11.8 | 8.8 | 6.4 | 6.8 | 5.9 |
| 41. | L.A. Law | 11.6 | 8.8 | 6.8 | 3.7 | 2.0 |
| 42. | America's Funniest People | 11.5 | 8.0 | 7.1 | 8.7 | 10.6 |
| 42. | Knots Landing | 11.5 | 10.2 | 4.9 | 3.6 | 2.7 |
| 44. | Married . . .With Children | 11.4 | 6.0 | 7.7 | 12.0 | 6.9 |
| 45. | How'd They Do That? | 11.2 | 8.2 | 7.5 | 4.0 | 3.8 |
| 46. | American Detective | 11.1 | 7.7 | 8.1 | 3.0 | 2.9 |
| 46. | Martin | 11.1 | 5.6 | 5.3 | 15.4 | 12.3 |
| 48. | Street Stories | 11.0 | 8.4 | 6.9 | 2.6 | 2.5 |
| 49. | Dateline NBC | 10.8 | 8.0 | 6.7 | 2.6 | 1.5 |
| 49. | Empty Nest | 10.8 | 8.7 | 5.4 | 5.3 | 4.8 |

## Favorite Syndicated Programs, 1992-1993

Source: Nielsen Media Research, Aug. 31, 1992-Apr. 18, 1993

(Ratings based on Designated Market Area coverage as reported by Nielsen's Cassandra Report)

| Rank | Program | TV Households | Women | Men | Teens | Children |
|------|---------|---------------|-------|-----|-------|----------|
| 1. | Wheel of Fortune | 13.9 | 11.8 | 8.0 | 3.3 | 3.4 |
| 2. | Jeopardy | 12.0 | 9.9 | 6.9 | 3.0 | 2.3 |
| 2. | Star Trek | 12.0 | 7.1 | 9.2 | 6.4 | 5.1 |
| 4. | Star Trek: Deep Space 9 | 10.9 | 6.5 | 8.2 | 5.8 | 4.8 |
| 5. | Oprah Winfrey | 10.4 | 8.4 | 3.4 | 2.7 | 1.7 |
| 6. | Entertainment Tonight | 8.7 | 6.4 | 5.0 | 2.1 | 1.9 |
| 7. | Magic II | 8.2 | 4.9 | 4.7 | 4.6 | 5.8 |
| 8. | Married . . .With Children | 7.8 | 4.1 | 4.5 | 6.8 | 4.7 |
| 9. | Wheel of Fortune-Wknd | 7.6 | 6.3 | 4.5 | 1.7 | 1.6 |
| 10. | Current Affair | 7.5 | 5.1 | 4.2 | 2.3 | 1.8 |
| 10. | Inside Edition | 7.5 | 5.6 | 4.0 | 1.8 | 1.6 |
| 12. | Tri Star Showcase III | 7.3 | 4.8 | 4.7 | 3.1 | 2.9 |
| 13. | Buena Vista I | 7.0 | 4.4 | 4.1 | 3.4 | 3.8 |
| 14. | Warner Bros. Vol. 29 | 6.9 | 4.2 | 4.2 | 4.0 | 3.4 |
| 15. | Imagination I | 6.8 | 4.1 | 3.2 | 4.6 | 7.4 |
| 15. | Roseanne | 6.8 | 4.4 | 3.1 | 5.8 | 4.3 |
| 17. | Kung Fu | 6.7 | 3.7 | 4.9 | 3.4 | 3.2 |
| 18. | Designing Women | 6.3 | 4.3 | 2.7 | 3.4 | 2.2 |
| 18. | National Geographic on Assignment | 6.3 | 3.3 | 4.6 | 2.1 | 2.2 |
| 18. | World Wrestling Fed. | 6.3 | 2.5 | 4.0 | 5.2 | 5.6 |

## All-Time Top Television Programs

Source: A.C. Nielsen estimates, Jan. 1961 through May 20, 1993, excluding unsponsored or joint network telecasts or programs under 30 minutes long.

Ranked by rating (percent of average TV audience).

| Rank | Program | Telecast Date | Network | Rating (%) | Households (000) |
|---|---|---|---|---|---|
| 1. | M*A*S*H (last episode) | 2/28/83 | CBS | 60.2 | 50,150 |
| 2. | Dallas (Who shot J.R.?) | 11/21/80 | CBS | 53.3 | 41,470 |
| 3. | Roots-Pt. 8 | 1/30/77 | ABC | 51.1 | 36,380 |
| 4. | Super Bowl XVI | 1/24/82 | CBS | 49.1 | 40,020 |
| 5. | Super Bowl XVII | 1/30/83 | NBC | 48.6 | 40,480 |
| 6. | Super Bowl XX | 1/26/86 | NBC | 48.3 | 41,490 |
| 7. | Gone With the Wind-Pt. 1 | 11/7/76 | NBC | 47.7 | 33,960 |
| 8. | Gone With the Wind-Pt. 2 | 11/8/76 | NBC | 47.4 | 33,750 |
| 9. | Super Bowl XII | 1/15/78 | CBS | 47.2 | 34,410 |
| 10. | Super Bowl XIII | 1/21/79 | NBC | 47.1 | 35,090 |
| 11. | Bob Hope Christmas Show | 1/15/70 | NBC | 46.6 | 27,260 |
| 12. | Super Bowl XVIII | 1/22/84 | CBS | 46.4 | 38,800 |
| 12. | Super Bowl XIX | 1/20/85 | ABC | 46.4 | 39,390 |
| 14. | Super Bowl XIV | 1/20/80 | CBS | 46.3 | 35,330 |
| 15. | ABC Theater (The Day After) | 11/20/83 | ABC | 46.0 | 38,550 |
| 16. | Roots-Pt. 6 | 1/28/77 | ABC | 45.9 | 32,680 |
| 16. | The Fugitive | 8/29/67 | ABC | 45.9 | 25,700 |
| 18. | Super Bowl XXI | 1/25/87 | CBS | 45.8 | 40,030 |
| 19. | Roots-Pt. 5 | 1/27/77 | ABC | 45.7 | 32,540 |
| 20. | Cheers (last episode) | 5/20/93 | NBC | 45.5 | 42,360 |
| 21. | Ed Sullivan | 2/9/64 | CBS | 45.3 | 23,240 |
| 22. | Super Bowl XXVII | 1/31/93 | NBC | 45.1 | 41,990 |
| 23. | Bob Hope Christmas Show | 1/14/71 | NBC | 45.0 | 27,050 |
| 24. | Roots-Pt. 3 | 1/25/77 | ABC | 44.8 | 31,900 |
| 25. | Super Bowl XI | 1/9/77 | NBC | 44.4 | 31,610 |
| 25. | Super Bowl XV | 1/25/81 | NBC | 44.4 | 34,540 |
| 27. | Super Bowl VI | 1/16/72 | CBS | 44.2 | 27,450 |
| 28. | Roots-Pt. 2 | 1/24/77 | ABC | 44.1 | 31,400 |
| 29. | Beverly Hillbillies | 1/8/64 | CBS | 44.0 | 22,570 |
| 30. | Roots-Pt. 4 | 1/26/77 | ABC | 43.8 | 31,190 |
| 30. | Ed Sullivan | 2/16/64 | CBS | 43.8 | 22,445 |
| 32. | Super Bowl XXIII | 1/22/89 | NBC | 43.5 | 39,320 |
| 33. | Academy Awards | 4/7/70 | ABC | 43.4 | 25,390 |
| 34. | Thorn Birds-Pt. 3 | 3/29/83 | ABC | 43.2 | 35,990 |
| 35. | Thorn Birds-Pt. 4 | 3/30/83 | ABC | 43.1 | 35,900 |
| 36. | CBS NFC Championship | 1/10/82 | CBS | 42.9 | 34,960 |
| 37. | Beverly Hillbillies | 1/15/64 | CBS | 42.8 | 21,960 |
| 38. | Super Bowl VII | 1/14/73 | NBC | 42.7 | 27,670 |
| 39. | Thorn Birds-Pt. 2 | 3/28/83 | ABC | 42.5 | 35,400 |
| 40. | Super Bowl IX | 1/12/75 | NBC | 42.4 | 29,040 |
| 40. | Beverly Hillbillies | 2/26/64 | CBS | 42.4 | 21,750 |

## Top-Rated TV Shows of the Past

Source: A.C. Nielsen

| 1950s Program | Network | Rating* | 1960s Program | Network | Rating* | 1970s Program | Network | Rating* |
|---|---|---|---|---|---|---|---|---|
| 1. A. Godfrey's Talent Scouts | CBS | 32.9 | 1. Bonanza | NBC | 29.6 | 1. All in the Family | CBS | 23.1 |
| 2. I Love Lucy | CBS | 31.6 | 2. The Red Skelton Show | CBS | 26.4 | 2. M*A*S*H | CBS | 17.6 |
| 3. You Bet Your Life | NBC | 30.1 | 3. The Andy Griffith Show | CBS | 22.4 | 3. Hawaii Five-O | CBS | 16.5 |
| 4. Dragnet | NBC | 24.6 | 4. The Beverly Hillbillies | CBS | 21.9 | 4. Happy Days | ABC | 15.9 |
| 5. The Jack Benny Show | CBS | 22.3 | 5. The Ed Sullivan Show | CBS | 21.7 | 5. The Waltons | CBS | 14.0 |
| 6. A. Godfrey and Friends | CBS | 19.5 | 6. The Lucy Show/Here's Lucy | CBS | 21.3 | 6. The Mary Tyler Moore Show | CBS | 13.7 |
| 7. Gunsmoke | CBS | 15.6 | 7. The Jackie Gleason Show | CBS | 16.5 | 7. Sanford & Son | NBC | 13.4 |
| 8. The Red Skelton Show | NBC | 15.2 | 8. Bewitched | ABC | 14.8 | 8. One Day at a Time | CBS | 11.4 |
| 9. December Bride | CBS | 13.8 | 9. Gomer Pyle | CBS | 13.4 | 9. Three's Company | ABC | 10.8 |
| 10. I've Got a Secret | CBS | 12.9 | 10. Candid Camera | CBS | 11.2 | 10. 60 Minutes | CBS | 10.0 |
| 11. $64,000 Question | CBS | 11.2 | 11. The Dick Van Dyke Show | CBS | 11.1 | 11. Maude | CBS | 9.8 |
| 12. Disneyland | ABC | 10.8 | 12. The Danny Thomas Show | CBS | 10.7 | 12. Gunsmoke | CBS | 9.7 |
| 13. The Ed Sullivan Show | CBS | 10.6 | 13. Family Affair | CBS | 9.8 | 13. Charlie's Angels | ABC | 9.6 |
| 14. Have Gun—Will Travel | CBS | 10.3 | 14. Laugh-In | NBC | 7.9 | 14. The Jeffersons | CBS | 9.4 |
| 15. The Danny Thomas Show | CBS | 9.9 | 15. Rawhide | CBS | 7.5 | 15. Laverne & Shirley | ABC | 9.3 |

* Avg. rating over decade

## U.S. Television Set Ownership

Source: A.C. Nielsen; Jan. 1, 1993

**Total Households with TV: 93,100,000** (98% of U.S. households own at least one TV set)

**Homes with:**

| | | | | | |
|---|---|---|---|---|---|
| Color TV sets | 91,238,000 | 98% | 2 or more sets | 59,584,000 | 64% |
| B&W only | 1,862,000 | 2% | One set | 33,516,000 | 36% |

# Recordings & Music Videos

## Gold & Platinum Awards Certification Levels

(Audio and Video)

Source: Recording Industry Assn. of America, *Inside the Recording Industry: A Statistical Overview*, 1992

| | Gold | Platinum | Multi-Platinum |
|---|---|---|---|
| Single | 500,000 units; EP counts as two units | 1 million units; EP counts as two units | 2 million units; EP counts as two units |
| Album | 500,000 units; manufacturers' $ volume at least $1 million based at 33⅓% of list price | 1 million units; manufacturers' $ volume at least $2 million based at 33⅓% of list price | 2 million units; manufacturers' $ volume at least $4 million based at 33⅓% of list price |
| Short Form | 250,000 units; max. running time of 30 minutes | 500,000 units; max. running time of 30 minutes | 1 million units; max. running time of 30 minutes |
| Multi-Box | 250,000 units; min. running time of 120 minutes | 500,000 units; min. running time of 120 minutes | 1 million units; min. running time of 120 minutes |
| Video Single | 25,000 units; max. running time of 15 minutes; two songs per title | 50,000 units; max. running time of 15 minutes; two songs per title | 100,000 units; max. running time of 15 minutes; two songs per title |
| Video Long Form | 50,000 units | 100,000 units | 200,000 units |
| Video Multi-Box | 50,000 units | 100,000 units | 200,000 units |

## Multi-Platinum and Platinum Awards

Awards in 1992 for albums and singles released in 1992, music videos released at any time.

### Albums, Multi-Platinum
(Number in parentheses = millions sold)

Bryan Adams; Waking Up the Neighbours (2)
Michael Bolton; Timeless (The Classics) (3)
Garth Brooks; Beyond the Season (2)
Garth Brooks; The Chase (5)
Mariah Carey; MTV Unplugged EP (1)
Eric Clapton; Unplugged (3)
Billy Ray Cyrus; Some Gave All (5)
Def Leppard; Adrenalize (3)
En Vogue; Funky Divas (2)
Whitney Houston; I Will Always Love You (3)
Wynonna Judd; Wynonna (2)
Kriss Kross; Totally Krossed Out (3)
R.E.M.; Automatic for the People (2)
Soundtrack: Boomerang (2)
Randy Travis; Storms of Life (3)
Megadeth; Countdown to Extinction
Nine Inch Nails; Broken
Prince & New Power Generation;
   Prince & New Power Generation
Queen; Classic Queen
Lionel Richie; Back to Front
Jon Secada; Jon Secada
Sir Mix-a-Lot; Mack Daddy
Soundtrack: Mo' Money
Soundtrack: Singles
Soundtrack: Wayne's World
Bruce Springsteen; Human Touch
Bruce Springsteen; Lucky Town
George Strait; Pure Country (Soundtrack)
TLC; Ooooooooohhh . . . On the TLC Tip
Various; A Very Special Christmas 2
Wilson Phillips; Shadows and Light
ZZ Top; Greatest Hits

### Singles, Multi-Platinum
(Number in parentheses = millions sold)

Kriss Kross; Jump (2)
Sir Mix-a-Lot; Baby Got Back (2)

### Albums, Platinum

AC/DC; Live
Alice in Chains; Dirt
John Anderson; Seminole Wind
Arrested Development; 3 Years, 5 Months and 2 Days in the Life of . . .
The Black Crowes; Southern Harmony and Musical Companion
Clint Black; The Hard Way
Mary J. Blige; What's the 411?
Bobby Brown; Bobby
Jimmy Buffett; Boats, Beaches, Bars & Ballads
The Cure; Wish
Peter Gabriel; Us
Vince Gill; I Still Believe in You
Amy Grant; Home for Christmas
House of Pain; House of Pain
Alan Jackson; A Lot about Livin'
Elton John; The One
Annie Lennox; Diva
Bob Marley; Songs of Freedom
MC Ren; Kizz My Black Azz

### Singles, Platinum

Boyz II Men; End of the Road
Eric Clapton; Tears in Heaven
Billy Ray Cyrus; Achy Breaky Heart
House of Pain; Jump Around
Nirvana; Smells Like Teen Spirit
Shai; If I Ever Fall in Love
TLC; Ain't 2 Proud 2 Beg
TLC; Baby Baby Baby
Wreckx 'N' Effect; Rump Shaker

### Music Videos, Multi-Platinum
(Number in parentheses = units sold)

Garth Brooks; Garth Brooks (400,000)
Garth Brooks; This Is Garth Brooks (400,000)
Carreras, Domingo, Pavarotti in Concert (400,000)
Billy Ray Cyrus; Billy Ray Cyrus (300,000)
Kidsongs; A Day with the Animals (300,000)
Kidsongs; A Day at the Circus (200,000)
Kidsongs; A Day at Old MacDonald's Farm (400,000)
Kidsongs; I'd Like to Teach the World to Sing (200,000)
Kidsongs; Cars, Boats, Trains and Planes (200,000)
Queensryche; Operation Livecrime (200,000)

### Music Video Singles, Multi-Platinum
(Number in parentheses = units sold)

Kriss Kross; Jump (100,000)

## 100 Leading U.S. Advertisers, 1990-1991

Source: *Advertising Age*, Sept. 23, 1992 © Crain Communications Inc. 1992

| Rank '91 | '90 | Advertiser | Ad spending 1991 | Rank '91 | '90 | Advertiser | Ad spending 1991 | Rank '91 | '90 | Advertiser | Ad spending 1991 |
|---|---|---|---|---|---|---|---|---|---|---|---|
| 1. | 1. | Procter & Gamble | $2,149.0 | 36. | 38. | Sara Lee | $273.0 | 69. | 78. | Marriott | $139.7 |
| 2. | 2. | Philip Morris | 2,045.6 | 37. | 27. | Nissan | 268.9 | 70. | * | MCI Comm. | 139.5 |
| 3. | 4. | General Motors | 1,442.1 | 38. | 42. | Mars | 253.9 | 71. | 85. | Thompson | |
| 4. | 3. | Sears, Roebuck | 1,179.4 | 39. | 39. | U.S. Government | 253.0 | | | Medical/Slim-Fast | |
| 5. | 6. | PepsiCo | 903.4 | 40. | 46. | ConAgra | 249.7 | | | Food | 137.5 |
| 6. | 5. | Grand Metropolitan | 744.7 | 41. | 34. | Quaker Oats | 237.7 | 72. | 88. | News Corp. | 135.8 |
| 7. | 12. | Johnson & Johnson | 733.0 | 42. | 44. | Colgate-Palmolive | 227.5 | 73. | 60. | Philips NV | 133.1 |
| 8. | 8. | McDonald's | 694.8 | 43. | 35. | Dayton Hudson | 226.5 | 74. | * | Dr. Pepper/Seven-Up | 131.4 |
| 9. | 16. | Ford | 676.6 | 44. | 50. | American Express | 226.4 | 75. | 80. | CPC International | 131.4 |
| 10. | 11. | Eastman Kodak | 661.4 | 45. | 58. | Nike | 223.3 | 76. | * | Sprint | 131.4 |
| 11. | 15. | Warner Lambert | 656.5 | 46. | 41. | Federated Dept. | | 77. | 59. | Goodyear Tire & | |
| 12. | 17. | Toyota | 632.2 | | | Stores | 222.8 | | | Rubber | 130.7 |
| 13. | 7. | AT&T | 617.3 | 47. | 49. | American Brands | 217.5 | 78. | 65. | Levi Strauss | 129.4 |
| 14. | 14. | Nestle SA | 600.5 | 48. | 45. | Mazda | 215.0 | 79. | 56. | Loews | 129.0 |
| 15. | 19. | Unilever NV | 593.7 | 49. | 69. | Circuit City Stores | 213.7 | 80. | 74. | Revlon | 128.0 |
| 16. | 10. | Time Warner | 587.5 | 50. | 47. | Tandy | 213.3 | 81. | 84. | Bell Atlantic | 127.5 |
| 17. | 18. | Kellogg | 577.7 | 51. | 55. | SmithKline Beecham | 208.3 | 82. | 76. | Dow Chemical | 127.1 |
| 18. | 13. | RJR Nabisco | 571.0 | 52. | 53. | Adolph Coors | 206.9 | 83. | 51. | Montgomery Ward | 126.7 |
| 19. | 20. | General Mills | 555.6 | 53. | 52. | American Stores | 201.6 | 84. | * | Reebok International | 126.5 |
| 20. | 21. | Chrysler | 531.1 | 54. | 54. | Hasbro | 201.4 | 85. | 81. | Seagram | 126.3 |
| 21. | 9. | Kmart | 527.2 | 55. | 48. | General Electric | 198.8 | 86. | 87. | Wm. Wrigley Jr. | 125.4 |
| 22. | 22. | Anheuser-Busch | 508.4 | 56. | 91. | Schering-Plough | 198.4 | 87. | 96. | Wendy's International | 124.1 |
| 23. | 23. | Walt Disney | 489.1 | 57. | 70. | Wal-Mart | 189.8 | 88. | 92. | Daimler-Benz AG | 122.2 |
| 24. | 25. | American Home | | 58. | 63. | Clorox | 182.6 | 89. | 72. | Hallmark Cards | 121.8 |
| | | Products | 447.1 | 59. | 57. | Gillette | 182.5 | 90. | 77. | Mobil | 120.0 |
| 25. | 26. | Sony | 438.6 | 60. | 64. | Paramount | 179.4 | 91. | 82. | Hyundai | 119.5 |
| 26. | 37. | H.J. Heinz | 403.1 | 61. | 66. | S.C. Johnson & Son | 174.0 | 92. | 99. | Upjohn | 119.3 |
| 27. | 31. | Ralston Purina | 393.5 | 62. | 61. | U.S. dairy farmers | 167.9 | 93. | 93. | UAL | 119.2 |
| 28. | 29. | Coca-Cola | 367.4 | 63. | 89. | Delta Air Lines | 164.5 | 94. | 97. | Canon | 117.6 |
| 29. | 28. | J.C. Penney | 362.6 | 64. | 62. | Campbell Soup | 164.1 | 95. | * | Ciba-Geigy | 115.4 |
| 30. | 24. | Bristol-Myers Squibb | 352.5 | 65. | 73. | Helene Curtis | | 96. | 95. | U.S. Shoe | 113.3 |
| 31. | 36. | Honda | 333.1 | | | Industries | 157.4 | 97. | * | B.A.T. | 113.0 |
| 32. | 32. | Hershey Foods | 298.9 | 66. | 67. | Carter Hawley Hale | | 98. | * | Kimberley-Clark | 107.7 |
| 33. | 33. | Matsushita Electric | | | | Stores | 151.9 | 99. | * | American Cyanamid | 105.2 |
| | | Industrial | 292.3 | 67. | 75. | AMR | 150.1 | 100. | 100. | Monsanto | 100.8 |
| 34. | 43. | R.H. Macy | 289.4 | 68. | 83. | ITT | 141.5 | | | | |
| 35. | 30. | May Dept. Stores | 277.3 | | | | | | | | |

* Did not rank among 100 leading advertisers in 1990.

## Total U.S. Ad Spending by Category and Medium, 1991

Source: *Advertising Age*, Sept. 23, 1992 © Crain Communications Inc. 1992

(in millions)

| Category | Total ad spending | Magazine | Sunday magazines | Newspaper | Network TV | Spot TV | Syndicated TV | Cable TV | Network radio |
|---|---|---|---|---|---|---|---|---|---|
| Automotive | $5,259.1 | $940.3 | $38.3 | $746.2 | $1,559.5 | $1,480.6 | $120.7 | $117.7 | $72.2 |
| Retail | 5,125.9 | 197.1 | 93.0 | 2,491.9 | 351.7 | 1,528.0 | 40.1 | 42.9 | 92.1 |
| Business, consumer svcs. | 3,582.8 | 443.3 | 28.4 | 1,207.2 | 598.3 | 811.2 | 72.8 | 112.2 | 77.2 |
| Food | 3,551.9 | 433.4 | 29.1 | 36.5 | 1,443.8 | 974.0 | 346.1 | 141.0 | 41.9 |
| Entertainment | 2,913.2 | 58.5 | 35.7 | 387.3 | 802.3 | 1,196.0 | 196.1 | 83.0 | 15.6 |
| Toiletries & cosmetics | 2,249.3 | 631.8 | 21.9 | 6.8 | 958.6 | 293.3 | 215.3 | 92.5 | 8.2 |
| Travel & hotels * | 2,123.2 | 335.4 | 49.1 | 1,064.5 | 212.7 | 233.6 | 8.6 | 49.1 | 33.4 |
| Drugs & remedies | 1,807.9 | 164.8 | 19.5 | 78.2 | 851.6 | 341.4 | 171.3 | 80.2 | 56.3 |
| Direct response cos. | 1,192.9 | 555.7 | 302.3 | 65.1 | 39.7 | 76.6 | 33.6 | 53.2 | 62.1 |
| Candy, snacks & soft drinks | 1,146.2 | 55.2 | 2.4 | 13.5 | 434.3 | 318.3 | 185.1 | 72.2 | 20.5 |
| Apparel, footwear | 904.8 | 416.0 | 21.5 | 7.0 | 235.4 | 88.5 | 58.9 | 41.0 | 7.5 |
| Beer & wine | 839.6 | 51.6 | 5.4 | 12.8 | 347.0 | 209.2 | 60.1 | 43.5 | 1.5 |
| Insurance & real estate | 705.3 | 141.6 | 8.9 | 187.3 | 171.5 | 106.2 | 9.1 | 19.0 | 19.1 |
| Publishing & media | 700.4 | 195.7 | 11.8 | 194.1 | 40.3 | 137.7 | 12.1 | 19.1 | 21.9 |
| Sporting goods, toys | 688.1 | 146.0 | 2.3 | 4.6 | 159.7 | 204.5 | 115.6 | 51.1 | 0.8 |
| Household equipment | 610.3 | 113.1 | 10.6 | 20.8 | 272.0 | 96.1 | 58.5 | 28.7 | 6.9 |
| Soaps & cleansers | 599.0 | 71.5 | 2.6 | 3.0 | 269.9 | 161.8 | 56.8 | 25.5 | 0.9 |
| Computers, office equip. | 529.0 | 287.0 | 9.7 | 44.7 | 118.5 | 17.0 | 7.0 | 19.3 | 12.9 |
| Cigarettes | 494.7 | 265.7 | 29.0 | 12.7 | 0.0 | 0.2 | 0.0 | 0.1 | 2.1 |
| Electronic entertainment | 371.5 | 91.8 | 1.8 | 16.2 | 116.7 | 71.4 | 29.3 | 31.9 | 9.1 |
| Jewelry, optical | 345.9 | 156.9 | 11.5 | 6.0 | 103.9 | 23.4 | 21.2 | 16.5 | 2.3 |
| Gasoline & lubricants | 303.4 | 27.8 | 0.5 | 15.2 | 48.4 | 152.3 | 1.9 | 8.9 | 0.0 |
| Building materials | 299.0 | 79.7 | 7.1 | 36.0 | 71.7 | 63.7 | 5.3 | 21.6 | 0.5 |
| Liquor | 283.5 | 228.9 | 8.2 | 7.7 | 0.0 | 5.0 | 0.7 | 0.3 | 1.4 |
| Household furnishings | 240.2 | 116.8 | 11.0 | 28.3 | 41.2 | 35.3 | 2.9 | 2.8 | 0.0 |
| Horticulture & farming | 204.9 | 21.0 | 8.9 | 48.5 | 30.1 | 50.1 | 2.0 | 12.6 | 9.1 |
| Pets & pet foods | 197.9 | 39.0 | 4.5 | 5.4 | 82.0 | 28.4 | 19.0 | 14.6 | 2.9 |
| Freight, courier svcs | 152.2 | 42.8 | 0.2 | 6.6 | 61.7 | 34.3 | 0.0 | 4.1 | 0.2 |
| Industrial materials | 106.7 | 57.6 | 0.5 | 5.8 | 27.5 | 10.0 | 0.0 | 3.8 | 0.0 |
| Business propositions | 34.9 | 27.5 | 0.6 | 2.9 | 1.3 | 1.2 | 0.0 | 0.6 | 0.0 |
| Airplanes, aviation | 12.6 | 10.1 | 0.0 | 1.5 | 0.1 | 0.7 | 0.0 | 0.1 | 0.0 |
| Miscellaneous | 243.9 | 111.5 | 17.6 | 73.2 | 4.8 | 1.2 | 0.1 | 2.4 | 0.1 |
| Total | 37,820.2 | 6,515.2 | 794.0 | 6,837.3 | 9,456.2 | 8,751.2 | 1,850.4 | 1,211.6 | 578.7 |

* Includes airline travel.

# AWARDS — MEDALS — PRIZES

## The Alfred B. Nobel Prize Winners

Alfred B. Nobel (1833-1896), inventor of dynamite, bequeathed $9,000,000, the interest to be distributed yearly to those who had most benefited humankind in physics, chemistry, medicine-physiology, literature, and peace. Prizes in these five areas were first awarded in 1901. The first Nobel Memorial Prize in Economic Science was awarded in 1969, funded by the central bank of Sweden. No awards given for years omitted. In 1992, each prize was worth approximately $1.2 million.

### Physics

1992 Georges Charpak, Pol.-Fr.
1991 Pierre-Giles de Gennes, French
1990 Richard E. Taylor, Can.; Jerome I. Friedman, Henry W. Kendall, both U.S.
1989 Norman F. Ramsey, U.S.; Hans G. Dehmelt, German-U.S. & Wolfgang Paul, German
1988 Leon M. Lederman, Melvin Schwartz, Jack Steinberger, all U.S.
1987 K. Alex Muller, Swiss; J. Georg Bednorz, W. German
1986 Ernest Ruska, German; Gerd Binnig, W. German; Heinrich Rohrer, Swiss
1985 Klaus von Klitzing, W. German
1984 Carlo Rubbia, Italian; Simon van der Meere, Dutch
1983 Subrahmanyan Chandrasekhar, William A. Fowler, both U.S.
1982 Kenneth G. Wilson, U.S.
1981 Nicolass Bloembergen, Arthur Schaalow, both U.S.; Kai M. Siegbahn, Swedish
1980 James W. Cronin, Val L. Fitch, U.S.
1979 Steven Weinberg, Sheldon L. Glashow, both U.S.; Abdus Salam, Pakistani
1978 Pyotr Kapitsa, USSR; Arno Penzias, Robert Wilson, both U.S.
1977 John H. Van Vleck, Philip W. Anderson, both U.S.; Nevill F. Mott, British
1976 Burton Richter, U.S. Samuel C.C. Ting, U.S.
1975 James Rainwater, U.S. Ben Mottelson, U.S.-Danish Aage Bohr, Danish
1974 Martin Ryle, British Antony Hewish, British
1973 Ivar Giaever, U.S. Leo Esaki, Japanese Brian D. Josephson, British
1972 John Bardeen, U.S. Leon N. Cooper, U.S. John R. Schrieffer, U.S.
1971 Dennis Gabor, British

1970 Louis Neel, French Hannes Alfven, Swedish
1969 Murray Gell-Mann, U.S.
1968 Luis W. Alvarez, U.S.
1967 Hans A. Bethe, U.S.
1966 Alfred Kastler, French
1965 Richard P. Feynman, U.S. Julian S. Schwinger, U.S. Shinichiro Tomonaga, Japanese
1964 Nikolai G. Basov, USSR Aleksander M. Prochorov, USSR Charles H. Townes, U.S.
1963 Maria Goeppert-Mayer, U.S. J. Hans D. Jensen, German Eugene P. Wigner, U.S.
1962 Lev. D. Landau, USSR
1961 Robert Hofstadter, U.S. Rudolf L. Mossbauer, German
1960 Donald A. Glaser, U.S.
1959 Owen Chamberlain, U.S. Emilio G. Segre, U.S.
1958 Pavel Cherenkov, Ilya Frank, Igor Y. Tamm, all USSR
1957 Tsung-dao Lee, Chen Ning Yang, both U.S.
1956 John Bardeen, U.S. Walter H. Brattain, U.S. William Shockley, U.S.
1955 Polykarp Kusch, U.S. Willis E. Lamb, U.S.
1954 Max Born, British Walter Bothe, German
1953 Frits Zernike, Dutch
1952 Felix Bloch, U.S. Edward M. Purcell, U.S.
1951 Sir John D. Cockcroft, British Ernest T. S. Walton, Irish
1950 Cecil F. Powell, British
1949 Hideki Yukawa, Japanese
1948 Patrick M. S. Blackett, British
1947 Sir Edward V. Appleton, British
1946 Percy Williams Bridgman, U.S.
1945 Wolfgang Pauli, U.S.
1944 Isidor Isaac Rabi, U.S.
1943 Otto Stern, U.S.
1939 Ernest O. Lawrence, U.S.
1938 Enrico Fermi, U.S.

1937 Clinton J. Davisson, U.S. Sir George P. Thomson, British
1936 Carl D. Anderson, U.S. Victor F. Hess, Austrian
1935 Sir James Chadwick, British
1933 Paul A. M. Dirac, British Erwin Schrodinger, Austrian
1932 Werner Heisenberg, German
1930 Sir Chandrasekhara V. Raman, Indian
1929 Prince Louis-Victor de Broglie, French
1928 Owen W. Richardson, British
1927 Arthur H. Compton, U.S. Charles T. R. Wilson, British
1926 Jean B. Perrin, French
1925 James Franck, Gustav Hertz, both German
1924 Karl M. G. Siegbahn, Swedish
1923 Robert A. Millikan, U.S.
1922 Niels Bohr, Danish
1921 Albert Einstein, Ger.-U.S.
1920 Charles E. Guillaume, French
1919 Johannes Stark, German
1918 Max K. E. L. Planck, German
1917 Charles G. Barkla, British
1915 Sir William H. Bragg, British Sir William L. Bragg, British
1914 Max von Laue, German
1913 Heike Kamerlingh-Onnes, Dutch
1912 Nils G. Dalen, Swedish
1911 Wilhelm Wien, German
1910 Johannes D. van der Waals, Dutch
1909 Carl F. Braun, German Guglielmo Marconi, Italian
1908 Gabriel Lippmann, French
1907 Albert A. Michelson, U.S.
1906 Sir Joseph J. Thomson, British
1905 Philipp E. A. von Lenard, Ger.
1904 John W. Strutt, Lord Rayleigh, British
1903 Antoine Henri Becquerel, French Marie Curie, Polish-French Pierre Curie, French
1902 Hendrik A. Lorentz, Pieter Zeeman, both Dutch
1901 Wilhelm C. Roentgen, German

### Chemistry

1992 Rudolph A. Marcus, Can.-U.S.
1991 Richard R. Ernst, Swiss
1990 Elias James Corey, U.S.
1989 Thomas R. Cech, Sidney Altman, both U.S.
1988 Johann Deisenhofer, Robert Huber, Hartmut Michel, all W. German
1987 Donald J. Cram, Charles J. Pederson, both U.S.; Jean-Marie Lehn, French
1986 Dudley Herschbach, Yuan T. Lee, both U.S.; John C. Polanyi, Canadian
1985 Herbert A. Hauptman, Jerome Karle, both U.S.
1984 Bruce Merrifield, U.S.
1983 Henry Taube, Canadian
1982 Aaron Klug, S. African
1981 Kenichi Fukui, Japan., Roald Hoffmann, U.S.
1980 Paul Berg, U.S.; Walter Gilbert, U.S., Frederick Sanger, U.K.

1979 Herbert C. Brown, U.S. George Wittig, German
1978 Peter Mitchell, British
1977 Ilya Prigogine, Belgian
1976 William N. Lipscomb, U.S.
1975 John Cornforth, Austral.-Brit. Vladimir Prelog, Yugo.-Swiss.
1974 Paul J. Flory, U.S.
1973 Ernst Otto Fischer, W. German Geoffrey Wilkinson, British
1972 Christian B. Anfinsen, U.S. Stanford Moore, U.S. William H. Stein, U.S.
1971 Gerhard Herzberg, Canadian
1970 Luis F. Leloir, Arg.
1969 Derek H. R. Barton, British Odd Hassel, Norwegian
1968 Lars Onsager, U.S.
1967 Manfred Eigen, German Ronald G. W. Norrish, British George Porter, British
1966 Robert S. Mulliken, U.S.
1965 Robert B. Woodward, U.S.

1964 Dorothy C. Hodgkin, British
1963 Giulio Natta, Italian Karl Ziegler, German
1962 John C. Kendrew, British Max F. Perutz, British
1961 Melvin Calvin, U.S.
1960 Willard F. Libby, U.S.
1959 Jaroslav Heyrovsky, Czech.
1958 Frederick Sanger, British
1957 Sir Alexander R. Todd, British
1956 Sir Cyril N. Hinshelwood, British Nikolai N. Semenov, USSR
1955 Vincent du Vigneaud, U.S.
1954 Linus C. Pauling, U.S.
1953 Hermann Staudinger, German
1952 Archer J. P. Martin, British Richard L. M. Synge, British
1951 Edwin M. McMillan, U.S. Glenn T. Seaborg, U.S.
1950 Kurt Alder, German Otto P. H. Diels, German
1949 William F. Giauque, U.S.
1948 Arne W. K. Tiselius, Swedish

1947 Sir Robert Robinson, British
1946 James B. Sumner, John H. Northrop, Wendell M. Stanley, U.S.
1945 Artturi I. Virtanen, Finnish
1944 Otto Hahn, German
1943 Georg de Hevesy, Hungarian
1939 Adolf F. J. Butenandt, German Leopold Ruzicka, Swiss
1938 Richard Kuhn, German
1937 Walter N. Haworth, British Paul Karrer, Swiss
1936 Peter J. W. Debye, Dutch
1935 Frederic Joliot-Curie, French Irene Joliot-Curie, French
1934 Harold C. Urey, U.S.
1932 Irving Langmuir, U.S.

1931 Friedrich Bergius, German Karl Bosch, German
1930 Hans Fischer, German
1929 Sir Arthur Harden, British Hans von Euler-Chelpin, Swed.
1928 Adolf O. R. Windaus, German
1927 Heinrich O. Wieland, German
1926 Theodor Svedberg, Swedish
1925 Richard A. Zsigmondy, German
1923 Fritz Pregl, Austrian
1922 Francis W. Aston, British
1921 Frederick Soddy, British
1920 Walther H. Nernst, German
1918 Fritz Haber, German
1915 Richard M. Willstatter, German

1914 Theodore W. Richards, U.S.
1913 Alfred Werner, Swiss
1912 Victor Grignard, French Paul Sabatier, French
1911 Marie Curie, Polish-French
1910 Otto Wallach, German
1909 Wilhelm Ostwald, German
1908 Ernest Rutherford, British
1907 Eduard Buchner, German
1906 Henri Moissan, French
1905 Adolf von Baeyer, German
1904 Sir William Ramsay, British
1903 Svante A. Arrhenius, Swedish
1902 Emil Fischer, German
1901 Jacobus H. van't Hoff, Dutch

## Physiology or Medicine

1992 Edmond H. Fisher, Edwin G. Krebs, both U.S.
1991 Edwin Neher, Bert Sakmann, both German
1990 Joseph E. Murray, E. Donnall Thomas, both U.S.
1989 J. Michael Bishop, Harold E. Varmus, both U.S.
1988 Gertrude B. Elion, George H. Hitchings, both U.S; Sir James Black, Brit.
1987 Susumu Tonegawa, Japanese
1986 Rita Levi-Montalcini, It.-U.S., Stanley Cohen, U.S.
1985 Michael S. Brown, Joseph L. Goldstein, both U.S.
1984 Cesar Milstein, Brit.-Argentine; Georges J. F. Koehler, German; Niels K. Jerne, Brit.-Danish
1983 Barbara McClintock, U.S.
1982 Sune Bergstrom, Bengt Samuelsson, both Swedish; John R. Vane, British
1981 Roger W. Sperry, David H. Hubel, Tosten N. Wiesel, all U.S.
1980 Baruj Benacerraf, George Snell, both U.S.; Jean Dausset, France
1979 Alian M. Cormack, U.S. Geoffrey N. Hounsfield, British
1978 Daniel Nathans, Hamilton O. Smith, both U.S.; Werner Arber, Swiss
1977 Rosalyn S. Yalow, Roger C.L. Guillemin, Andrew V. Schally, U.S.
1976 Baruch S. Blumberg, U.S. Daniel Carleton Gajdusek, U.S.
1975 David Baltimore, Howard Temin, both U.S.; Renato Dulbecco, Ital.-U.S.
1974 Albert Claude, Lux.-U.S.; George Emil Palade, Rom.-U.S.; Christian Rene de Duve, Belg.
1973 Karl von Frisch, Ger.; Konrad Lorenz, Ger.-Austrian; Nikolaas Tinbergen, Brit.
1972 Gerald M. Edelman, U.S. Rodney R. Porter, British
1971 Earl W. Sutherland Jr., U.S.
1970 Julius Axelrod, U.S. Sir Bernard Katz, British Ulf von Euler, Swedish

1969 Max Delbruck, Alfred D. Hershey, Salvador Luria, all U.S.
1968 Robert W. Holley, H. Gobind Khorana, Marshall W. Nirenberg, all U.S.
1967 Ragnar Granit, Swedish Haldan Keffer Hartline, U.S. George Wald, U.S.
1966 Charles B. Huggins, Francis Peyton Rous, both U.S.
1965 Francois Jacob, Andre Lwoff, Jacques Monod, all French
1964 Konrad E. Bloch, U.S. Feodor Lynen, German
1963 Sir John C. Eccles, Australian Alan L. Hodgkin, British Andrew F. Huxley, British
1962 Francis H. C. Crick, British James D. Watson, U.S. Maurice H. F. Wilkins, British
1961 Georg von Bekesy, U.S.
1960 Sir F. MacFarlane Burnet, Australian Peter B. Medawar, British
1959 Arthur Kornberg, U.S. Severo Ochoa, U.S.
1958 George W. Beadle, U.S. Edward L. Tatum, U.S. Joshua Lederberg, U.S.
1957 Daniel Bovet, Italian
1956 Andre F. Cournand, U.S. Werner Forssmann, German Dickinson W. Richards Jr., U.S.
1955 Alex H. T. Theorell, Swedish
1954 John F. Enders, Frederick C. Robbins, Thomas H. Weller, all U.S.
1953 Hans A. Krebs, British Fritz A. Lipmann, U.S.
1952 Selman A. Waksman, U.S.
1951 Max Theiler, U.S.
1950 Philip S. Hench, Edward C. Kendall, both U.S. Tadeus Reichstein, Swiss
1949 Walter R. Hess, Swiss Antonio Moniz, Portuguese
1948 Paul H. Müller, Swiss
1947 Carl F. Cori, Gerty T. Cori, both U.S.

Bernardo A. Houssay, Arg.
1946 Hermann J. Muller, U.S.
1945 Ernst B. Chain, British Sir Alexander Fleming, British Sir Howard W. Florey, British
1944 Joseph Erlanger, U.S. Herbert S. Gasser, U.S.
1943 Henrik C. P. Dam, Danish Edward A. Doisy, U.S.
1939 Gerhard Domagk, German
1938 Corneille J. F. Heymans, Belg.
1937 Albert Szent-Gyorgyi, Hung.-U.S.
1936 Sir Henry H. Dale, British Otto Loewi, U.S.
1935 Hans Spemann, German
1934 George R. Minot, Wm. P. Murphy, G. H. Whipple, all U.S.
1933 Thomas H. Morgan, U.S.
1932 Edgar D. Adrian, British Sir Charles S. Sherrington, Brit.
1931 Otto H. Warburg, German
1930 Karl Landsteiner, U.S.
1929 Christiaan Eijkman, Dutch Sir Frederick G. Hopkins, British
1928 Charles J. H. Nicolle, French
1927 Julius Wagner-Jauregg, Austria
1926 Johannes A. G. Fibiger, Danish
1924 Willem Einthoven, Dutch
1923 Frederick G. Banting, Canadian John J. R. Macleod, Scottish
1922 Archibald V. Hill, British Otto F. Meyerhof, German
1920 Schack A. S. Krogh, Danish
1919 Jules Bordet, Belgian
1914 Robert Barany, Austrian
1913 Charles R. Richet, French
1912 Alexis Carrel, French
1911 Allvar Gullstrand, Swedish
1910 Albrecht Kossel, German
1909 Emil T. Kocher, Swiss
1908 Paul Ehrlich, German Elie Metchnikoff, French
1907 Charles L. A. Laveran, French
1906 Camillo Golgi, Italian Santiago Ramon y Cajal, Sp.
1905 Robert Koch, German
1904 Ivan P. Pavlov, Russian
1903 Niels R. Finsen, Danish
1902 Sir Ronald Ross, British
1901 Emil A. von Behring, German

## Literature

1992 Derek Walcott, West Indian
1991 Nadine Gordimer, South African
1990 Octavio Paz, Mexican
1989 Camilo José Cela, Spanish
1988 Naguib Mahfouz, Egyptian
1987 Joseph Brodsky, USSR-U.S.
1986 Wole Soyinka, Nigerian
1985 Claude Simon, French
1984 Jaroslav Siefert, Czech.
1983 William Golding, British
1982 Gabriel Garcia Marquez, Colombian-Mex.
1981 Elias Canetti, Bulgarian-British
1980 Czeslaw Milosz, Polish-U.S.
1979 Odysseus Elytis, Greek
1978 Isaac Basnevis Singer, U.S. (Yiddish)

1977 Vicente Aleixandre, Spanish
1976 Saul Bellow, U.S.
1975 Eugenio Montale, Ital.
1974 Eyvind Johnson, Harry Edmund Martinson, both Swedish
1973 Patrick White, Australian
1972 Heinrich Boll, W. German
1971 Pablo Neruda, Chilean
1970 Aleksandr I. Solzhenitsyn, Russ.
1969 Samuel Beckett, Irish
1968 Yasunari Kawabata, Japanese
1967 Miguel Angel Asturias, Guate.
1966 Samuel Joseph Agnon, Israeli Nelly Sachs, Swedish
1965 Mikhail Sholokhov, Russian
1964 Jean Paul Sartre, French (Prize declined)

1963 Giorgos Seferis, Greek
1962 John Steinbeck, U.S.
1961 Ivo Andric, Yugoslavian
1960 Saint-John Perse, French
1959 Salvatore Quasimodo, Italian
1958 Boris L. Pasternak, Russian (Prize declined)
1957 Albert Camus, French
1956 Juan Ramon Jimenez, Span.
1955 Halldor K. Laxness, Icelandic
1954 Ernest Hemingway, U.S.
1953 Sir Winston Churchill, British
1952 Francois Mauriac, French
1951 Par F. Lagerkvist, Swedish
1950 Bertrand Russell, British
1949 William Faulkner, U.S.

| | | |
|---|---|---|
| 1948 T.S. Eliot, British | 1928 Sigrid Undset, Norwegian | 1912 Gerhart Hauptmann, German |
| 1947 Andre Gide, French | 1927 Henri Bergson, French | 1911 Maurice Maeterlinck, Belgian |
| 1946 Hermann Hesse, Swiss | 1926 Grazia Deledda, Italian | 1910 Paul J. L. Heyse, German |
| 1945 Gabriela Mistral, Chilean | 1925 George Bernard Shaw, British | 1909 Selma Lagerlof, Swedish |
| 1944 Johannes V. Jensen, Danish | 1924 Wladyslaw S. Reymont, Polish | 1908 Rudolf C. Eucken, German |
| 1939 Frans E. Sillanpaa, Finnish | 1923 William Butler Yeats, Irish | 1907 Rudyard Kipling, British |
| 1938 Pearl S. Buck, U.S. | 1922 Jacinto Benavente, Spanish | 1906 Giosue Carducci, Italian |
| 1937 Roger Martin du Gard, French | 1921 Anatole France, French | 1905 Henryk Sienkiewicz, Polish |
| 1936 Eugene O'Neill, U.S. | 1920 Knut Hamsun, Norwegian | 1904 Frederic Mistral, French |
| 1934 Luigi Pirandello, Italian | 1919 Carl F. G. Spitteler, Swiss | Jose Echegaray, Spanish |
| 1933 Ivan A. Bunin, Russian | 1917 Karl A. Gjellerup, Danish | 1903 Bjornsterne Bjornson, Norw. |
| 1932 John Galsworthy, British | Henrik Pontoppidan, Danish | 1902 Theodor Mommsen, German |
| 1931 Erik A. Karlfeldt, Swedish | 1916 Verner von Heidenstarn, Swed. | 1901 Rene F. A Sully Prudhomme, |
| 1930 Sinclair Lewis, U.S. | 1915 Romain Rolland, French | French |
| 1929 Thomas Mann, German | 1913 Rabindranath Tagore, Indian | |

## Peace

| | | |
|---|---|---|
| 1992 Rigoberta Menchú, Guatemalan | 1965 U.N. Children's Fund (UNICEF) | 1929 Frank B. Kellogg, U.S. |
| 1991 Daw Aung San Suu Kyi, | 1964 Martin Luther King Jr., U.S. | 1927 Ferdinand E. Buisson, French |
| Myanmarese | 1963 International Red Cross, | Ludwig Quidde, German |
| 1990 Mikhail S. Gorbachev, USSR | League of Red Cross Societies | 1926 Aristide Briand, French |
| 1989 Dalai Lama, Tibetan | 1962 Linus C. Pauling, U.S. | Gustav Stresemann, German |
| 1988 United Nations Peacekeeping | 1961 Dag Hammarskjold, Swedish | 1925 Sir J. Austen Chamberlain, Brit. |
| Forces | 1960 Albert J. Luthuli, South African | Charles G. Dawes, U.S. |
| 1987 Oscar Arias Sanchez, Costa Rican | 1959 Philip J. Noel-Baker, British | 1922 Fridtjof Nansen, Norwegian |
| 1986 Elie Wiesel, Romanian-U.S. | 1958 Georges Pire, Belgian | 1921 Karl H. Branting, Swedish |
| 1985 Intl. Physicians for the Prevention of | 1957 Lester B. Pearson, Canadian | Christian L. Lange, Norwegian |
| Nuclear War, U.S. | 1954 Office of the UN High | 1920 Leon V.A. Bourgeois, French |
| 1984 Bishop Desmond Tutu, So. African | Commissioner for Refugees | 1919 Woodrow Wilson, U.S. |
| 1983 Lech Walesa, Polish | 1953 George C. Marshall, U.S. | 1917 International Red Cross |
| 1982 Alva Myrdal, Swedish; Alfonso | 1952 Albert Schweitzer, French | 1913 Henri La Fontaine, Belgian |
| Garcia Robles, Mexican | 1951 Leon Jouhaux, French | 1912 Elihu Root, U.S. |
| 1981 Office of U.N. High Commissioner | 1950 Ralph J. Bunche, U.S. | 1911 Tobias M.C. Asser, Dutch |
| for Refugees | 1949 Lord John Boyd Orr of Brechin | Alfred H. Fried, Austrian |
| 1980 Adolfo Perez Esquivel, Argentine | Mearns, British | 1910 Permanent Intl. Peace Bureau |
| 1979 Mother Teresa of Calcutta, | 1947 Friends Service Council, Brit. | 1909 Auguste M. F. Beernaert, Belg. |
| Albanian-Indian | Amer. Friends Service Com. | Paul H. B. B. d'Estournelles de |
| 1978 Anwar Sadat, Egyptian | 1946 Emily G. Balch, | Constant, French |
| Menachem Begin, Israeli | John R. Mott, both U.S. | 1908 Klas P. Arnoldson, Swedish |
| 1977 Amnesty International | 1945 Cordell Hull, U.S. | Fredrik Bajer, Danish |
| 1976 Mairead Corrigan, Betty Williams, | 1944 International Red Cross | 1907 Ernesto T. Moneta, Italian |
| N. Irish | 1938 Nansen International Office | Louis Renault, French |
| 1975 Andrei Sakharov, USSR | for Refugees | 1906 Theodore Roosevelt, U.S. |
| 1974 Eisaku Sato, Japanese, Sean | 1937 Viscount Cecil of Chelwood, Brit. | 1905 Baroness Bertha von Suttner, |
| MacBride, Irish | 1936 Carlos de Saavedra Lamas, Arg. | Austrian |
| 1973 Henry Kissinger, U.S. | 1935 Carl von Ossietzky, German | 1904 Institute of International Law |
| Le Duc Tho, N. Vietnamese | 1934 Arthur Henderson, British | 1903 Sir William R. Cremer, British |
| (Tho declined) | 1933 Sir Norman Angell, British | 1902 Elie Ducommun, |
| 1971 Willy Brandt, W. German | 1931 Jane Addams, U.S. | Charles A. Gobat, both Swiss |
| 1970 Norman E. Borlaug, U.S. | Nicholas Murray Butler, U.S. | 1901 Jean H. Dunant, Swiss |
| 1969 Intl. Labor Organization | 1930 Nathan Soderblom, Swedish | Frederic Passy, French |
| 1968 Rene Cassin, French | | |

## Nobel Memorial Prize in Economic Science

| | | |
|---|---|---|
| 1992 Gary S. Becker, U.S. | 1982 George J. Stigler, U.S. | Leonid Kantorovich, USSR |
| 1991 Ronald H. Coase, Br.-U.S. | 1981 James Tobin, U.S. | 1974 Gunnar Myrdal, Swed. |
| 1990 Harry M. Markowitz, William F. | 1980 Lawrence R. Klein, U.S. | Friedrich A. von Hayek, Austrian |
| Sharpe, Merton H. Miller, all U.S. | 1979 Theodore W. Schultz, U.S. | 1973 Wassily Leontief, U.S. |
| 1989 Trygve Haavelmo, Norwegian | Sir Arthur Lewis, British | 1972 Kenneth J. Arrow, U.S. |
| 1988 Maurice Allais, French | 1978 Herbert A. Simon, U.S. | John R. Hicks, British |
| 1987 Robert M. Solow, U.S. | 1977 Bertil Ohlin, Swedish | 1971 Simon Kuznets, U.S. |
| 1986 James M. Buchanan, U.S. | James E. Meade, British | 1970 Paul A. Samuelson, U.S. |
| 1985 Franco Modigliani, It.-U.S. | 1976 Milton Friedman, U.S. | 1969 Ragnar Frisch, Norwegian |
| 1984 Richard Stone, British | 1975 Tjalling Koopmans, Dutch-U.S. | Jan Tinbergen, Dutch |
| 1983 Gerard Debreu, Fr.-U.S. | | |

# Pulitzer Prizes in Journalism, Letters, and Music

The Pulitzer Prizes were endowed by Joseph Pulitzer (1847-1911), publisher of the New York World, in a bequest to Columbia University and are awarded annually by the president of the university on recommendation of the Pulitzer Prize
Board for work done during the preceding year. The administrator is Seymour Topping of Columbia Univ. All prizes are
$3,000 (originally $500) in each category, except Meritorious Public Service for which a gold medal is given.

## Journalism

### Meritorious Public Service

For distinguished and meritorious public service by a United
States newspaper.
1918—New York Times. Also special award to Minna Lewinson
  and Henry Beetle Hough.
1919—Milwaukee Journal.
1921—Boston Post.
1922—New York World.
1923—Memphis (Tenn.) Commercial Appeal.
1924—New York World.

1926—Enquirer-Sun, Columbus, Ga.
1927—Canton (Oh.) Daily News.
1928—Indianapolis Times.
1929—Evening World, New York.
1931—Atlanta (Ga.) Constitution.
1932—Indianapolis (Ind.) News.
1933—New York World-Telegram.
1934—Medford (Ore.) Mail-Tribune.
1935—Sacramento (Cal.) Bee.
1936—Cedar Rapids (Ia.) Gazette.
1937—St.Louis Post-Dispatch.

1938—Bismarck (N.D.) Tribune.
1939—Miami (Fla.) Daily News.
1940—Waterbury (Conn.) Republican and American.
1941—St.Louis Post-Dispatch.
1942—Los Angeles Times.
1943—Omaha World Herald.
1944—New York Times.
1945—Detroit Free Press.
1946—Scranton (Pa.) Times.
1947—Baltimore Sun.
1948—St. Louis Post-Dispatch.
1949—Nebraska State Journal.
1950—Chicago Daily News; St. Louis Post-Dispatch.
1951—Miami (Fla.) Herald and Brooklyn Eagle.
1952—St. Louis Post-Dispatch.
1953—Whiteville (N.C.) News Reporter; Tabor City (N.C.) Tribune.
1954—Newsday (Long Island, N.Y.)
1955—Columbus (Ga.) Ledger and Sunday Ledger-Enquirer.
1956—Watsonville (Cal.) Register-Pajaronian.
1957—Chicago Daily News.
1958—Arkansas Gazette, Little Rock.
1959—Utica (N.Y.) Observer-Dispatch and Utica Daily Press.
1960—Los Angeles Times.
1961—Amarillo (Tex.) Globe-Times.
1962—Panama City (Fla.) News-Herald.
1963—Chicago Daily News.
1964—St.Petersburg (Fla.) Times.
1965—Hutchinson (Kan.) News.
1966—Boston Globe.
1967—Louisville Courier-Journal; Milwaukee Journal.
1968—Riverside (Cal.) Press-Enterprise.
1969—Los Angeles Times.
1970—Newsday (Long Island, N.Y.).
1971—Winston Salem (N.C.) Journal & Sentinel.
1972—New York Times.
1973—Washington Post.
1974—Newsday (Long Island, N.Y.).
1975—Boston Globe.
1976—Anchorage Daily News.
1977—Lufkin (Tex.) News.
1978—Philadelphia Inquirer.
1979—Point Reyes (Cal.) Light.
1980—Gannett News Service.
1981—Charlotte (N.C.) Observer.
1982—Detroit News.
1983—Jackson (Miss.) Clarion-Ledger.
1984—Los Angeles Times.
1985—Ft. Worth (Tex.) Star-Telegram.
1986—Denver Post.
1987—Pittsburgh Press.
1988—Charlotte Observer.
1989—Anchorage Daily News.
1990—Philadelphia Inquirer, Gilbert M. Gaul; Washington (N.C.) Daily News.
1991—Des Moines Register, Jane Schorer.
1992—Sacramento Bee, Tom Knudson.
1993—Miami Herald.

## Reporting

This category originally embraced all fields, local, national, and international. Later separate categories were created for national and international reporting.

1917—Herbert Bayard Swope, New York World.
1918—Harold A. Littledale, New York Evening Post.
1920—John J. Leary Jr., New York World.
1921—Louis Seibold, New York World.
1922—Kirke L. Simpson, Associated Press.
1923—Alva Johnston, New York Times.
1924—Magner White, San Diego Sun.
1925—James W. Mulroy and Alvin H. Goldstein, Chicago Daily News.
1926—William Burke Miller, Louisville Courier-Journal.
1927—John T. Rogers, St. Louis Post-Dispatch.
1929—Paul Y. Anderson, St. Louis Post-Dispatch.
1930—Russell D. Owens, New York Times. Also $500 to W.O. Dapping, Auburn (N.Y.) Citizen.
1931—A.B. MacDonald, Kansas City (Mo.) Star.
1932—W.C. Richards, D.D. Martin, J.S. Pooler, F.D. Webb, J.N.W. Sloan, Detroit Free Press.
1933—Francis A. Jamieson, Associated Press.
1934—Royce Brier, San Francisco Chronicle.
1935—William H. Taylor, New York Herald Tribune.
1936—Lauren D. Lyman, New York Times.
1937—John J. O'Neill, N.Y.Herald Tribune; William L. Laurence, N.Y Times; Howard W. Blakeslee, A.P.; Gobind Behari Lal, Universal Service; and David Dietz, Scripps-Howard Newspapers.

1938—Raymond Sprigle, Pittsburgh Post-Gazette.
1939—Thomas L. Stokes, Scripps-Howard Newspaper Alliance.
1940—S.Burton Heath, New York World-Telegram.
1941—Westbrook Pegler, New York World-Telegram.
1942—Stanton Delaplane, San Francisco Chronicle.
1943—George Weller, Chicago Daily News.
1944—Paul Schoenstein, New York Journal-American.
1945—Jack S. McDowell, San Francisco Call-Bulletin.
1946—William L. Laurence, New York Times.
1947—Frederick Woltman, New York World-Telegram.
1948—George E. Goodwin, Atlanta Journal.
1949—Malcolm Johnson, New York Sun.
1950—Meyer Berger, New York Times.
1951—Edward S. Montgomery, San Francisco Examiner.
1952—Geo. de Carvalho, San Francisco Chronicle.

*(1) General or Spot; (2) Special or Investigative*

1953—(1) Providence (R.I.) Journal and Evening Bulletin; (2) Edward J. Mowery, New York World-Telegram & Sun.
1954—(1) Vicksburg (Miss.) Sunday Post-Herald; (2) Alvin Scott McCoy, Kansas City (Mo.) Star.
1955—(1) Mrs. Caro Brown, Alice (Tex.) Daily Echo; (2) Roland K. Towery, Cuero (Tex.) Record.
1956—(1) Lee Hills, Detroit Free Press; (2) Arthur Daley, New York Times.
1957—(1) Salt Lake Tribune, Salt Lake City, Ut.; (2) Wallace Turner and William Lambert, Portland Oregonian.
1958—(1) Fargo, (N.D.) Forum; (2) George Beveridge, Evening Star, Washington, D.C.
1959—(1) Mary Lou Werner, Washington Evening Star; (2) John Harold Brislin, Scranton (Pa.) Tribune, and The Scrantonian.
1960—(1) Jack Nelson, Atlanta Constitution; (2) Miriam Ottenberg, Washington Evening Star.
1961—(1) Sanche de Gramont, New York Herald Tribune; (2) Edgar May, Buffalo Evening News.
1962—(1) Robert D.Mullins, Deseret News, Salt Lake City; (2) George Bliss, Chicago Tribune.
1963—(1) Shared by Sylvan Fox, William Longgood, and Anthony Shannon, New York World-Telegram & Sun; (2) Oscar Griffin Jr., Pecos (Tex.) Independent and Enterprise.
1964—(1) Norman C. Miller, Wall Street Journal; (2) Shared by James V. Magee, Albert V. Gaudiosi, and Frederick A. Meyer, Philadelphia Bulletin.
1965—(1) Melvin H. Ruder, Hungry Horse News (Columbia Falls, Mon.); (2) Gene Goltz, Houston Post.
1966—(1) Los Angeles Times Staff; (2) John A. Frasca, Tampa (Fla.) Tribune.
1967—(1) Robert V. Cox, Chambersburg (Pa.) Public Opinion; (2) Gene Miller, Miami Herald.
1968—Detroit Free Press Staff; (2) J. Anthony Lukas, New York Times.
1969—(1) John Fetterman, Louisville Courier-Journal and Times; (2) Albert L. Delugach, St. Louis Globe Democrat, and Denny Walsh, Life.
1970—(1) Thomas Fitzpatrick, Chicago Sun-Times; (2) Harold Eugene Martin, Montgomery Advertiser & Alabama Journal.
1971—(1) Akron Beacon Journal Staff, (2) William Hugh Jones, Chicago Tribune.
1972—(1) Richard Cooper and John Machacek, Rochester Times-Union; (2) Timothy Leland, Gerard M. O'Neill, Stephen A. Kurkjian and Anne De Santis, Boston Globe.
1973—(1) Chicago Tribune; (2) Sun Newspapers of Omaha.
1974—(1) Hugh F. Hough, Arthur M. Petacque, Chicago Sun-Times; (2) William Sherman, New York Daily News.
1975—(1) Xenia (Oh.) Daily Gazette; (2) Indianapolis Star.
1976—(1) Gene Miller, Miami Herald; (2) Chicago Tribune.
1977—(1) Margo Huston, Milwaukee Journal; (2) Acel Moore, Wendell Rawls Jr., Philadelphia Inquirer.
1978—(1) Richard Whitt, Louisville Courier-Journal; (2) Anthony R. Dolan, Stamford (Conn.) Advocate.
1979—(1) San Diego (Cal.) Evening Tribune; (2) Gilbert M. Gaul, Elliot G. Jaspin, Pottsville (Pa.) Republican.
1980—(1) Philadelphia Inquirer; (2) Stephen A. Kurkjian, Alexander B. Hawes Jr., Nils Bruzelius, Joan Vennochi, Robert M. Porterfield, Boston Globe.
1981—(1) Longview (Wash.) Daily News staff; (2) Clark Hallas and Robert B. Lowe, Arizona Daily Star.
1982—(1) Kansas City Star, Kansas City Times; (2) Paul Henderson, Seattle Times.
1983—(1) Fort Wayne (Ind.) News-Sentinel; (2) Loretta Tofani, Washington Post.
1984—(1) Newsday (N.Y.); (2) Boston Globe.
1985—(1) Thomas Turcol, Virginian-Pilot and Ledger-Star, Norfolk, Va.; (2) William K. Marimow, Philadelphia Inquirer; Lucy Morgan & Jack Reed, St. Petersburg (Fla.) Times.
1986—(1) Edna Buchanan, Miami Herald; (2) Jeffrey A. Marx & Michael M. York, Lexington (Ky.) Herald-Leader.
1987—(1) Akron Beacon Journal; (2) Daniel R. Biddle, H.G. Bissinger, Fredric N. Tulsky, Philadelphia Inquirer; John Woestendiek, Philadelphia Inquirer.

1988—(1) Alabama Journal; Lawrence (Mass.) Eagle-Tribune; (2) Walt Bogdanich, Wall Street Journal.
1989—(1) Louisville Courier-Journal; (2) Bill Dedman, Atlanta Journal and Constitution.
1990—(1) San Jose Mercury News; (2) Lon Kilzer, Chris Ison, Star Tribune, Minneapolis-St. Paul.
1991—(1) Miami Herald; (2) Joseph T. Hallinan, Susan M. Headden, Indianapolis Star.
1992—(1) New York Newsday; (2) Lorraine Adams, Dan Malone, Dallas Morning News.
1993—(1) Los Angeles Times; Jeff Brazil, Steve Berry, Orlando Sentinel.

## Criticism or Commentary

*(1) Criticism; (2) Commentary*

1970—(1) Ada Louise Huxtable, New York Times; (2) Marquis W. Childs, St. Louis Post-Dispatch.
1971—(1) Harold C. Schonberg, New York Times; (2) William A. Caldwell, The Record, Hackensack, N.J.
1972—(1) Frank Peters Jr., St. Louis Post-Dispatch; (2) Mike Royko, Chicago Daily News.
1973—(1) Ronald Powers, Chicago Sun-Times; (2) David S. Broder, Washington Post.
1974—(1) Emily Genauer, Newsday, (N.Y.); (2) Edwin A. Roberts Jr., National Observer.
1975—(1) Roger Ebert, Chicago Sun Times; (2) Mary McGrory, Washington Star.
1976—(1) Alan M. Kriegsman, Washington Post; (2) Walter W. (Red) Smith, New York Times.
1977—(1) William McPherson, Washington Post; (2) George F. Will, Wash. Post Writers Group.
1978—(1) Walter Kerr, New York Times; (2) William Safire, New York Times.
1979—(1) Paul Gapp, Chicago Tribune; (2) Russell Baker, New York Times.
1980—(1) William A. Henry III, Boston Globe; (2) Ellen Goodman, Boston Globe.
1981—(1) Jonathan Yardley, Washington Star; (2) Dave Anderson, New York Times.
1982—(1) Martin Bernheimer, Los Angeles Times; (2) Art Buchwald, Los Angeles Times Syndicate.
1983—(1) Manuela Hoelterhoff, Wall St. Journal; (2) Claude Sitton, Raleigh (N.C.) News & Observer.
1984—(1) Paul Goldberger, New York Times; (2) Vermont Royster, Wall St. Journal
1985—(1) Howard Rosenberg, Los Angeles Times; (2) Murray Kempton, Newsday (N.Y.).
1986—(1) Donal J. Henahan, New York Times; (2) Jimmy Breslin, New York Daily News.
1987—(1) Richard Eder, Los Angeles Times; (2) Charles Krauthammer, Washington Post.
1988—(1) Tom Shales, Washington Post; (2) Dave Barry, Miami Herald.
1989—(1) Michael Skube, News and Observer, Raleigh, N.C.; (2) Clarence Page, Chicago Tribune.
1990—(1) Allan Temko, San Francisco Chronicle; (2) Jim Murray, Los Angeles Times
1991—(1) David Shaw, Los Angeles Times; (2) Jim Hoagland, Washington Post.
1992—(1) No award; (2) Anna Quindlen, New York Times.
1993—(1) Michael Dirda, Washington Post; (2) Liz Balmaseda, Miami Herald.

## National Reporting

1942—Louis Stark, New York Times.
1944—Dewey L. Fleming, Baltimore Sun.
1945—James B. Reston, New York Times.
1946—Edward A. Harris, St. Louis Post-Dispatch.
1947—Edward T. Folliard, Washington Post.
1948—Bert Andrews, New York Herald Tribune; Nat S. Finney, Minneapolis Tribune.
1949—Charles P. Trussell, New York Times.
1950—Edwin O. Guthman, Seattle Times.
1952—Anthony Leviero, New York Times.
1953—Don Whitehead, Associated Press.
1954—Richard Wilson, Des Moines Register.
1955—Anthony Lewis, Washington Daily News.
1956—Charles L. Bartlett, Chattanooga Times.
1957—James Reston, New York Times.
1958—Relman Morin, AP; Clark Mollenhoff, Des Moines Register & Tribune.
1959—Howard Van Smith, Miami (Fla.) News.
1960—Vance Trimble, Scripps-Howard, Washington, D.C.
1961—Edward R. Cony, Wall Street Journal.
1962—Nathan G. Caldwell and Gene S. Graham, Nashville Tennessean.
1963—Anthony Lewis, New York Times.

1964—Merriman Smith, UPI.
1965—Louis M. Kohlmeier, Wall Street Journal.
1966—Haynes Johnson, Washington Evening Star.
1967—Monroe Karmin and Stanley Penn, Wall Street Journal.
1968—Howard James, Christian Science Monitor; Nathan K. Kotz, Des Moines Register.
1969—Robert Cahn, Christian Science Monitor.
1970—William J. Eaton, Chicago Daily News.
1971—Lucinda Franks & Thomas Powers, UPI.
1972—Jack Anderson, United Feature Syndicate.
1973—Robert Boyd and Clark Hoyt, Knight Newspapers.
1974—James R. Polk, Washington Star-News; Jack White, Providence Journal-Bulletin.
1975—Donald L. Barlett and James B. Steele, Philadelphia Inquirer.
1976—James Risser, Des Moines Register.
1977—Walter Mears, Associated Press.
1978—Gaylord D. Shaw, Los Angeles Times.
1979—James Risser, Des Moines Register.
1980—Charles Stafford, Bette Swenson Orsini, St. Petersburg (Fla.) Times.
1981—John M. Crewdson, New York Times.
1982—Rick Atkinson, Kansas City Times.
1983—Boston Globe.
1984—John Noble Wilford, New York Times.
1985—Thomas J. Knudson, Des Moines (Ia.) Register.
1986—Craig Flournoy & George Rodrigue, Dallas Morning News; Arthur Howe, Philadelphia Inquirer.
1987—Miami Herald; New York Times.
1988—Tim Weiner, Philadelphia Inquirer.
1989—Donald L. Barlett & James B. Steele, Philadelphia Inquirer.
1990—Ross Anderson, Bill Dietrich, Mary Ann Gwinn, Eric Nalder, Seattle Times.
1991—Marjie Lundstrom, Rochelle Sharpe, Gannett News Service.
1992—Jeff Taylor, Mike McGraw, Kansas City Star.
1993—David Maraniss, Washington Post.

## International Reporting

1942—Laurence Edmund Allen, Associated Press.
1943—Ira Wolfert, No. Am. Newspaper Alliance.
1944—Daniel DeLuce, Associated Press.
1945—Mark S. Watson, Baltimore Sun.
1946—Homer W. Bigart, New York Herald Tribune.
1947—Eddy Gilmore, Associated Press.
1948—Paul W. Ward, Baltimore Sun.
1949—Price Day, Baltimore Sun.
1950—Edmund Stevens, Christian Science Monitor.
1951—Keyes Beech and Fred Sparks, Chicago Daily News; Homer Bigart and Marguerite Higgins, New York Herald Tribune; Relman Morin and Don Whitehead, AP.
1952—John M. Hightower, Associated Press.
1953—Austin C. Wehrwein, Milwaukee Journal.
1954—Jim G. Lucas, Scripps-Howard Newspapers.
1955—Harrison Salisbury, New York Times.
1956—William Randolph Hearst Jr., Frank Conniff, Hearst Newspapers; Kingsbury Smith, INS.
1957—Russell Jones, United Press.
1958—New York Times.
1959—Joseph Martin and Philip Santora, New York Daily News.
1960—A.M. Rosenthal, New York Times.
1961—Lynn Heinzerling, Associated Press.
1962—Walter Lippmann, New York Herald Tribune Synd.
1963—Hal Hendrix, Miami (Fla.) News.
1964—Malcolm W. Browne, AP; David Halberstam, New York Times.
1965—J.A. Livingston, Philadelphia Bulletin.
1966—Peter Arnett, AP.
1967—R. John Hughes, Christian Science Monitor.
1968—Alfred Friendly, Washington Post.
1969—William Tuohy, Los Angeles Times.
1970—Seymour M. Hersh, Dispatch News Service.
1971—Jimmie Lee Hoagland, Washington Post.
1972—Peter R. Kann, Wall Street Journal.
1973—Max Frankel, New York Times.
1974—Hedrick Smith, New York Times.
1975—William Mullen and Ovie Carter, Chicago Tribune.
1976—Sydney H. Schanberg, New York Times.
1978—Henry Kamm, New York Times.
1979—Richard Ben Cramer, Philadelphia Inquirer.
1980—Joel Brinkley, Jay Mather, Louisville (Ky.) Courier-Journal.
1981—Shirley Christian, Miami Herald.
1982—John Darnton, New York Times.
1983—Thomas L. Friedman, New York Times; Loren Jenkins, Washington Post.
1984—Karen Elliot House, Wall St. Journal

1985—Josh Friedman, Dennis Bell, Ozler Muhammad, Newsday (N.Y.).
1986—Lewis M. Simons, Pete Carey, Katherine Ellison, San Jose (Calif.) Mercury News.
1987—Michael Parks, Los Angeles Times.
1988—Thomas L. Friedman, New York Times.
1989—Glenn Frankel, Washington Post; Bill Keller, New York Times.
1990—Nicholas D. Kirstof, Sheryl WuDunn, New York Times.
1991—Caryle Murphy, Washington Post; Serge Schmemann, New York Times.
1992—Patrick J. Sloyan, Newsday (N.Y.).
1993—John F. Burns, New York Times; Roy Gutman, Newsday (N.Y.)

## Correspondence

For Washington or foreign correspondence. Category was merged with those in national and international reporting in 1948.
1929—Paul Scott Mowrer, Chicago Daily News.
1930—Leland Stowe, New York Herald Tribune.
1931—H.R. Knickerbocker, Philadelphia Public Ledger and New York Evening Post.
1932—Walter Duranty, New York Times, and Charles G. Ross, St. Louis Post-Dispatch.
1933—Edgar Ansel Mowrer, Chicago Daily News.
1934—Frederick T. Birchall, New York Times.
1935—Arthur Krock, New York Times.
1936—Wilfred C. Barber, Chicago Tribune.
1937—Anne O'Hare McCormick, New York Times.
1938—Arthur Krock, New York Times.
1939—Louis P. Lochner, Associated Press.
1940—Otto D. Tolischus, New York Times.
1941—Bronze plaque to commemorate work of American correspondents on war fronts.
1942—Carlos P. Romulo, Philippines Herald.
1943—Hanson W. Baldwin, New York Times.
1944—Ernest Taylor Pyle, Scripps-Howard Newspaper Alliance.
1945—Harold V. (Hal) Boyle, Associated Press.
1946—Arnaldo Cortesi, New York Times.
1947—Brooks Atkinson, New York Times.

## Editorial Writing

1917—New York Tribune.
1918—Louisville (Ky.) Courier-Journal.
1920—Harvey E. Newbranch, Omaha Evening World-Herald.
1922—Frank M. O'Brien, New York Herald.
1923—William Allen White, Emporia Gazette.
1924—Frank Buxton, Boston Herald, Special Prize. Frank I. Cobb, New York World.
1925—Robert Lathan, Charleston (S.C.) News and Courier.
1926—Edward M. Kingsbury, New York Times.
1927—F. Lauriston Bullard, Boston Herald.
1928—Grover C. Hall, Montgomery Advertiser.
1929—Louis Isaac Jaffe, Norfolk Virginian-Pilot.
1931—Chas. Ryckman, Fremont (Neb.) Tribune.
1933—Kansas City (Mo.) Star.
1934—E. P. Chase, Atlantic (Ia.) News Telegraph.
1936—Felix Morley, Washington Post. George B. Parker, Scripps-Howard Newspapers.
1937—John W. Owens, Baltimore Sun.
1938—W.W. Waymack, Des Moines (Ia.) Register and Tribune.
1939—Ronald G. Callvert, Portland Oregonian.
1940—Bart Howard, St. Louis Post-Dispatch.
1941—Reuben Maury, Daily News, N.Y.
1942—Geoffrey Parsons, New York Herald Tribune.
1943—Forrest W. Seymour, Des Moines (Ia.) Register and Tribune.
1944—Henry J. Haskell, Kansas City (Mo.) Star.
1945—George W. Potter, Providence (R.I.) Journal-Bulletin.
1946—Hodding Carter, Greenville (Miss.) Delta Democrat-Times.
1947—William H. Grimes, Wall Street Journal.
1948—Virginius Dabney, Richmond (Va.) Times-Dispatch.
1949—John H. Crider, Boston (Mass.) Herald, Herbert Elliston, Washington Post.
1950—Carl M. Saunders, Jackson (Mich.) Citizen-Patriot.
1951—William H. Fitzpatrick, New Orleans States.
1952—Louis LaCoss, St. Louis Globe Democrat.
1953—Vermont C. Royster, Wall Street Journal.
1954—Don Murray, Boston Herald.
1955—Royce Howes, Detroit Free Press.
1956—Lauren K. Soth, Des Moines (Ia.) Register and Tribune.
1957—Buford Boone, Tuscaloosa (Ala.) News.
1958—Harry S. Ashmore, Arkansas Gazette.
1959—Ralph McGill, Atlanta Constitution.
1960—Lenoir Chambers, Norfolk Virginian-Pilot.
1961—William J. Dorvillier, San Juan (Puerto Rico) Star.

1962—Thomas M. Storke, Santa Barbara (Cal.) News-Press.
1963—Ira B. Harkey Jr., Pascagoula (Miss.) Chronicle.
1964—Hazel Brannon Smith, Lexington (Miss.) Advertiser.
1965—John R. Harrison, Gainesville (Fla.) Sun.
1966—Robert Lasch, St. Louis Post-Dispatch.
1967—Eugene C. Patterson, Atlanta Constitution.
1968—John S. Knight, Knight Newspapers.
1969—Paul Greenberg, Pine Bluff (Ark.) Commercial.
1970—Philip L. Geyelin, Washington Post.
1971—Horance G. Davis Jr., Gainesville (Fla.) Sun.
1972—John Strohmeyer, Bethlehem (Pa.) Globe-Times.
1973—Roger B. Linscott, Berkshire Eagle, Pittsfield, Mass.
1974—F. Gilman Spencer, Trenton (N.J.) Trentonian.
1975—John D. Maurice, Charleston (W.Va.) Daily Mail.
1976—Philip Kerby, Los Angeles Times.
1977—Warren L. Lerude, Foster Church, and Norman F. Cardoza, Reno (Nev.) Evening Gazette and Nevada State Journal.
1978—Meg Greenfield, Washington Post.
1979—Edwin M. Yoder, Washington Star.
1980—Robert L. Bartley, Wall Street Journal.
1982—Jack Rosenthal, New York Times.
1983—Editorial board, Miami Herald.
1984—Albert Scardino, Georgia Gazette.
1985—Richard Aregood, Philadelphia Daily News.
1986—Jack Fuller, Chicago Tribune.
1987—Jonathan Freedman, Tribune (San Diego).
1988—Jane Healy, Orlando Sentinel.
1989—Lois Wille, Chicago Tribune.
1990—Thomas J. Hylton, Pottstown (Pa.) Mercury.
1991—Ron Casey, Harold Jackson, Joey Kennedy, Birmingham (Ala.) News.
1992—Maria Henson, Lexington (Ky.) Herald-Leader.
1993—No award.

## Editorial Cartooning

1922—Rollin Kirby, New York World.
1924—Jay N. Darling, Des Moines Register.
1925—Rollin Kirby, New York World.
1926—D. R. Fitzpatrick, St. Louis Post-Dispatch.
1927—Nelson Harding, Brooklyn Eagle.
1928—Nelson Harding, Brooklyn Eagle.
1929—Rollin Kirby, New York World.
1930—Charles Macauley, Brooklyn Eagle.
1931—Edmund Duffy, Baltimore Sun.
1932—John T. McCutcheon, Chicago Tribune.
1933—H. M. Talburt, Washington Daily News.
1934—Edmund Duffy, Baltimore Sun.
1935—Ross A. Lewis, Milwaukee Journal.
1937—C. D. Batchelor, New York Daily News.
1938—Vaughn Shoemaker, Chicago Daily News.
1939—Charles G. Werner, Daily Oklahoman.
1940—Edmund Duffy, Baltimore Sun.
1941—Jacob Burck, Chicago Times.
1942—Herbert L. Block, Newspaper Enterprise Assn.
1943—Jay N. Darling, Des Moines Register.
1944—Clifford K. Berryman, Washington Star.
1945—Bill Mauldin, United Feature Syndicate.
1946—Bruce Alexander Russell, Los Angeles Times.
1947—Vaughn Shoemaker, Chicago Daily News.
1948—Reuben L. (Rube) Goldberg, N. Y. Sun.
1949—Lute Pease, Newark (N.J.) Evening News.
1950—James T. Berryman, Washington Star.
1951—Reginald W. Manning, Arizona Republic.
1952—Fred L. Packer, New York Mirror.
1953—Edward D. Kuekes, Cleveland Plain Dealer.
1954—Herbert L. Block, Washington Post & Times-Herald.
1955—Daniel R. Fitzpatrick, St. Louis Post-Dispatch.
1956—Robert York, Louisville (Ky.) Times.
1957—Tom Little, Nashville Tennessean.
1958—Bruce M. Shanks, Buffalo Evening News.
1959—Bill Mauldin, St. Louis Post-Dispatch.
1961—Carey Orr, Chicago Tribune.
1962—Edmund S. Valtman, Hartford Times.
1963—Frank Miller, Des Moines Register.
1964—Paul Conrad, Denver Post.
1966—Don Wright, Miami News.
1967—Patrick B. Oliphant, Denver Post.
1968—Eugene Gray Payne, Charlotte Observer.
1969—John Fischetti, Chicago Daily News.
1970—Thomas F. Darcy, Newsday.
1971—Paul Conrad, L. A. Times.
1972—Jeffrey K. MacNelly, Richmond News-Leader.
1974—Paul Szep, Boston Globe.
1975—Garry Trudeau, Universal Press Syndicate.
1976—Tony Auth, Philadelphia Inquirer.
1977—Paul Szep, Boston Globe.
1978—Jeffrey K. MacNelly, Richmond News Leader.

1979—Herbert L. Block, Washington Post.
1980—Don Wright, Miami (Fla.) News.
1981—Mike Peters, Dayton (Oh.) Daily News.
1982—Ben Sargent, Austin American-Statesman.
1983—Richard Lochner, Chicago Tribune.
1984—Paul Conrad, Los Angeles Times.
1985—Jeffrey K. MacNelly, Chicago Tribune.
1986—Jules Feiffer, Village Voice (N.Y. City).
1987—Berke Breathed, Washington Post.
1988—Doug Marlette, Atlanta Constitution, Charlotte Observer.
1989—Jack Higgins, Chicago Sun-Times.
1990—Tom Toles, Buffalo News.
1991—Jim Borgman, Cincinnati Enquirer.
1992—Signe Wilkinson, Philadelphia Daily News.
1993—Stephen R. Benson, Arizona Republic.

## Spot News Photography

1942—Milton Brooks, Detroit News.
1943—Frank Noel, Associated Press.
1944—Frank Filan, AP; Earl L. Bunker, Omaha World-Herald.
1945—Joe Rosenthal, Associated Press, for photograph of planting American flag on Iwo Jima.
1947—Arnold Hardy, amateur, Atlanta, Ga.
1948—Frank Cushing, Boston Traveler.
1949—Nathaniel Fein, New York Herald Tribune.
1950—Bill Crouch, Oakland (Cal.) Tribune.
1951—Max Desfor, Associated Press.
1952—John Robinson and Don Ultang, Des Moines Register and Tribune.
1953—William M. Gallagher, Flint (Mich.) Journal.
1954—Mrs. Walter M. Schau, amateur.
1955—John L. Gaunt Jr., Los Angeles Times.
1956—New York Daily News.
1957—Harry A. Trask, Boston Traveler.
1958—William C. Beall, Washington Daily News.
1959—William Seaman, Minneapolis Star.
1960—Andrew Lopez, UPI.
1961—Yasushi Nagao, Mainichi Newspapers, Tokyo.
1962—Paul Vathis, Associated Press.
1963—Hector Rondon, La Republica, Caracas, Venezuela.
1964—Robert H. Jackson, Dallas Times-Herald.
1965—Horst Faas, Associated Press.
1966—Kyoichi Sawada, UPI.
1967—Jack R. Thornell, Associated Press.
1968—Rocco Morabito, Jacksonville Journal.
1969—Edward Adams, AP.
1970—Steve Starr, AP.
1971—John Paul Filo, Valley Daily News & Daily Dispatch of Tarentum & New Kensington, Pa.
1972—Horst Faas and Michel Laurent, AP.
1973—Huynh Cong Ut, AP.
1974—Anthony K. Roberts, AP.
1975—Gerald H. Gay, Seattle Times.
1976—Stanley Forman, Boston Herald American.
1977—Neal Ulevich, Associated Press; Stanley Forman, Boston Herald American.
1978—John H. Blair, UPI.
1979—Thomas J. Kelly III, Pottstown (Pa.) Mercury.
1980—UPI.
1981—Larry C. Price, Ft. Worth (Tex.) Star-Telegram.
1982—Ron Edmonds, Associated Press.
1983—Bill Foley, AP.
1984—Stan Grossfeld, Boston Globe.
1985—The Register, Santa Ana, Calif.
1986—Carol Guzy & Michel duCille, Miami Herald.
1987—Kim Komenich, San Francisco Examiner.
1988—Scott Shaw, Odessa (Tex.) American.
1989—Ron Olshwanger, St. Louis Post-Dispatch.
1990—Oakland (Calif.) Tribune photo staff.
1991—Greg Marinovich, Associated Press.
1992—Associated Press staff.
1993—Ken Geiger, William Snyder, Dallas Morning News.

## Feature Photography

1968—Toshio Sakai, UPI.
1969—Moneta Sleet Jr., Ebony.
1970—Dallas Kinney, Palm Beach Post.
1971—Jack Dykinga, Chicago Sun-Times.
1972—Dave Kennerly, UPI.
1973—Brian Lanker, Topeka Capitol-Journal.
1974—Slava Veder, AP.
1975—Matthew Lewis, Washington Post.
1976—Louisville Courier-Journal and Louisville Times.
1977—Robin Hood, Chattanooga News-Free Press.
1978—J. Ross Baughman, AP.
1979—Staff photographers, Boston Herald American.
1980—Erwin H. Hagler, Dallas Times-Herald.

1981—Taro M. Yamasaki, Detroit Free Press.
1982—John H. White, Chicago Sun-Times.
1983—James B. Dickman, Dallas Times-Herald.
1984—Anthony Suad, Denver Post.
1985—Stan Grossfeld, Boston Globe; Larry C. Price, Philadelphia Inquirer.
1986—Tom Gralish, Philadelphia Inquirer.
1987—David Peterson, Des Moines Register.
1988—Michel duCille, Miami Herald.
1989—Manny Crisostomo, Detroit Free Press.
1990—David C. Turnley, Detroit Free Press.
1991—William Snyder, Dallas Morning News.
1992—John Kaplan, Block Newspapers (Toledo, Oh.).
1993—Associated Press staff.

## Special Citation

1938—Edmonton (Alberta) Journal, bronze plaque.
1941—New York Times.
1944—Byron Price and Mrs. William Allen White. Also to Richard Rodgers and Oscar Hammerstein 2d, for musical, Oklahoma!
1945—Press cartographers for war maps.
1947—(Pulitzer centennial year.) Columbia Univ. and the Graduate School of Journalism, and St. Louis Post-Dispatch.
1948—Dr. Frank Diehl Fackenthal.
1951—Cyrus L. Sulzberger, New York Times.
1952—Max Kase, New York Journal-American, Kansas City Star.
1953—New York Times; Lester Markel.
1957—Kenneth Roberts, for his historical novels.
1958—Walter Lippmann, New York Herald Tribune.
1960—Garrett Mattingly, for The Armada.
1961—American Heritage Picture History of the Civil War.
1964—Gannett Newspapers.
1973—James T. Flexner, for biography of George Washington.
1976—John Hohenberg, for services to American journalism.
1977—Alex Haley, for Roots.
1978—Richard Lee Strout, Christian Science Monitor and New Republic.
    —E.B. White.
1984—Theodore Geisel ("Dr. Seuss").
1985—William Schuman, composer, educational leader.
1987—Joseph Pulitzer Jr.
1992—Art Spiegelman, Maus.

## Feature Writing

1979—Jon D. Franklin, Baltimore Evening Sun.
1980—Madeleine Blais, Miami Herald Tropic Magazine. Janet Cooke, Washington Post.
1981—Teresa Carpenter, Village Voice, New York City.
1982—Saul Pett, Associated Press.
1984—Peter M. Rinearson, Seattle Times.
1985—Alice Steinbach, Baltimore Sun.
1986—John Camp, St. Paul Pioneer Press & Dispatch.
1987—Steve Twomey, Philadelphia Inquirer.
1988—Jacqui Banaszynski, St. Paul Pioneer Press Dispatch.
1989—David Zucchino, Philadelphia Inquirer.
1990—Dave Curtin, Colorado Springs Gazette Telegraph.
1991—Sheryl James, St. Petersburg Times.
1992—Howell Raines, New York Times.
1993—George Lardner Jr., Washington Post.

## Explanatory Journalism

1985—Jon Franklin, Baltimore Evening Sun.
1986—New York Times staff.
1987—Jeff Lyon & Peter Gorner, Chicago Tribune.
1988—Daniel Hertzberg, James B. Stewart, Wall Street Journal.
1989—David Hanners, William Snyder, Karen Blessen, Dallas Morning News.
1990—David A. Vise, Steve Coll, Washington Post.
1991—Susan C. Faludi, Wall Street Journal.
1992—Robert S. Capers, Eric Lipton, Hartford (Conn.) Courant.
1993—Mike Toner, Atlanta Journal-Constitution.

## Specialized Reporting

1985—Randall Savage, Jackie Crosby, Macon (Ga.) Telegraph and News.
1986—Andrew Schneider & Mary Pat Flaherty, Pittsburgh Press.
1987—Alex S. Jones, New York Times.
1988—Dean Baquet, William Gaines, Ann Marie Lipinski, Chicago Tribune.
1989—Edward Humes, Orange County (Calif.) Register.
1990—Tamar Stieber, Albuquerque Journal.
1991—Natalie Angier, New York Times.
1992—Deborah Blum, Sacramento Bee.
1993—Paul Ingrassia, Joseph B. White, Wall Street Journal.

# Letters

## Fiction

For fiction in book form by an American author, preferably dealing with American life.

1918—Ernest Poole, His Family.
1919—Booth Tarkington, The Magnificent Ambersons.
1921—Edith Wharton, The Age of Innocence.
1922—Booth Tarkington, Alice Adams.
1923—Willa Cather, One of Ours.
1924—Margaret Wilson, The Able McLaughlins.
1925—Edna Ferber, So Big.
1926—Sinclair Lewis, Arrowsmith. (Refused prize.)
1927—Louis Bromfield, Early Autumn.
1928—Thornton Wilder, Bridge of San Luis Rey.
1929—Julia M. Peterkin, Scarlet Sister Mary.
1930—Oliver LaFarge, Laughing Boy.
1931—Margaret Ayer Barnes, Years of Grace.
1932—Pearl S. Buck, The Good Earth.
1933—T. S. Stribling, The Store.
1934—Caroline Miller, Lamb in His Bosom.
1935—Josephine W. Johnson, Now in November.
1936—Harold L. Davis, Honey in the Horn.
1937—Margaret Mitchell, Gone with the Wind.
1938—John P. Marquand, The Late George Apley.
1939—Marjorie Kinnan Rawlings, The Yearling.
1940—John Steinbeck, The Grapes of Wrath.
1942—Ellen Glasgow, In This Our Life.
1943—Upton Sinclair, Dragon's Teeth.
1944—Martin Flavin, Journey in the Dark.
1945—John Hersey, A Bell for Adano.
1947—Robert Penn Warren, All the King's Men.
1948—James A. Michener, Tales of the South Pacific.
1949—James Gould Cozzens, Guard of Honor.
1950—A. B. Guthrie Jr., The Way West.
1951—Conrad Richter, The Town.
1952—Herman Wouk, The Caine Mutiny.
1953—Ernest Hemingway, The Old Man and the Sea.
1955—William Faulkner, A Fable.
1956—MacKinlay Kantor, Andersonville.
1958—James Agee, A Death in the Family.
1959—Robert Lewis Taylor, The Travels of Jaimie McPheeters.
1960—Allen Drury, Advise and Consent.
1961—Harper Lee, To Kill a Mockingbird.
1962—Edwin O'Connor, The Edge of Sadness.
1963—William Faulkner, The Reivers.
1965—Shirley Ann Grau, The Keepers of the House.
1966—Katherine Anne Porter, Collected Stories of Katherine Anne Porter.
1967—Bernard Malamud, The Fixer.
1968—William Styron, The Confessions of Nat Turner.
1969—N. Scott Momaday, House Made of Dawn.
1970—Jean Stafford, Collected Stories.
1972—Wallace Stegner, Angle of Repose.
1973—Eudora Welty, The Optimist's Daughter.
1975—Michael Shaara, The Killer Angels.
1976—Saul Bellow, Humboldt's Gift.
1978—James Alan McPherson, Elbow Room.
1979—John Cheever, The Stories of John Cheever.
1980—Norman Mailer, The Executioner's Song.
1981—John Kennedy Toole, A Confederacy of Dunces.
1982—John Updike, Rabbit Is Rich.
1983—Alice Walker, The Color Purple.
1984—William Kennedy, Ironweed.
1985—Alison Lurie, Foreign Affairs.
1986—Larry McMurtry, Lonesome Dove.
1987—Peter Taylor, A Summons to Memphis.
1988—Toni Morrison, Beloved.
1989—Anne Tyler, Breathing Lessons.
1990—Oscar Hijuelos, The Mambo Kings Play Songs of Love.
1991—John Updike, Rabbit at Rest.
1992—Jane Smiley, A Thousand Acres.
1993—Robert Olen Butler, A Good Scent from a Strange Mountain.

## Drama

For an American play, preferably original and dealing with American life.

1918—Jesse Lynch Williams, Why Marry?
1920—Eugene O'Neill, Beyond the Horizon.
1921—Zona Gale, Miss Lulu Bett.
1922—Eugene O'Neill, Anna Christie.
1923—Owen Davis, Icebound.
1924—Hatcher Hughes, Hell-Bent for Heaven.

1925—Sidney Howard, They Knew What They Wanted.
1926—George Kelly, Craig's Wife.
1927—Paul Green, In Abraham's Bosom.
1928—Eugene O'Neill, Strange Interlude.
1929—Elmer Rice, Street Scene.
1930—Marc Connelly, The Green Pastures.
1931—Susan Glaspell, Alison's House.
1932—George S. Kaufman, Morrie Ryskind, and Ira Gershwin, Of Thee I Sing.
1933—Maxwell Anderson, Both Your Houses.
1934—Sidney Kingsley, Men in White.
1935—Zoe Akins, The Old Maid.
1936—Robert E. Sherwood, Idiot's Delight.
1937—George S. Kaufman and Moss Hart, You Can't Take It With You.
1938—Thornton Wilder, Our Town.
1939—Robert E. Sherwood, Abe Lincoln in Illinois.
1940—William Saroyan, The Time of Your Life.
1941—Robert E. Sherwood, There Shall Be No Night.
1943—Thornton Wilder, The Skin of Our Teeth.
1945—Mary Chase, Harvey.
1946—Russel Crouse and Howard Lindsay, State of the Union.
1948—Tennessee Williams, A Streetcar Named Desire.
1949—Arthur Miller, Death of a Salesman.
1950—Richard Rodgers, Oscar Hammerstein 2d, and Joshua Logan, South Pacific.
1952—Joseph Kramm, The Shrike.
1953—William Inge, Picnic.
1954—John Patrick, Teahouse of the August Moon.
1955—Tennessee Williams, Cat on a Hot Tin Roof.
1956—Frances Goodrich and Albert Hackett, The Diary of Anne Frank.
1957—Eugene O'Neill, Long Day's Journey Into Night.
1958—Ketti Frings, Look Homeward, Angel.
1959—Archibald MacLeish, J. B.
1960—George Abbott, Jerome Weidman, Sheldon Harnick, and Jerry Bock, Fiorello.
1961—Tad Mosel, All the Way Home.
1962—Frank Loesser and Abe Burrows, How To Succeed In Business Without Really Trying.
1965—Frank D. Gilroy, The Subject Was Roses.
1967—Edward Albee, A Delicate Balance.
1969—Howard Sackler, The Great White Hope.
1970—Charles Gordone, No Place to Be Somebody.
1971—Paul Zindel, The Effect of Gamma Rays on Man-in-the-Moon Marigolds.
1973—Jason Miller, That Championship Season.
1975—Edward Albee, Seascape.
1976—Michael Bennett, James Kirkwood, Nicholas Dante, Marvin Hamlisch and Edward Kleban, A Chorus Line.
1977—Michael Cristofer, The Shadow Box.
1978—Donald L. Coburn, The Gin Game.
1979—Sam Shepard, Buried Child.
1980—Lanford Wilson, Talley's Folly.
1981—Beth Henley, Crimes of the Heart.
1982—Charles Fuller, A Soldier's Play.
1983—Marsha Norman, 'night, Mother.
1984—David Mamet, Glengarry Glen Ross.
1985—Stephen Sondheim and James Lapine, Sunday in the Park with George.
1987—August Wilson, Fences.
1988—Alfred Uhry, Driving Miss Daisy.
1989—Wendy Wasserstein, The Heidi Chronicles.
1990—August Wilson, The Piano Lesson.
1991—Neil Simon, Lost in Yonkers.
1992—Robert Schenkkan, The Kentucky Cycle.
1993—Tony Kushner, Angels in America: Millennium Approaches.

## History

For a book on the history of the United States.
1917—J. J. Jusserand, With Americans of Past and Present Days.
1918—James Ford Rhodes, History of the Civil War.
1920—Justin H. Smith, The War with Mexico.
1921—William Sowden Sims, The Victory at Sea.
1922—James Truslow Adams, The Founding of New England.
1923—Charles Warren, The Supreme Court in United States History.
1924—Charles Howard McIlwain, The American Revolution: A Constitutional Interpretation.
1925—Frederick L. Paxton, A History of the American Frontier.
1926—Edward Channing, A History of the U.S.

**1927**—Samuel Flagg Bemis, Pinckney's Treaty.
**1928**—Vernon Louis Parrington, Main Currents in American Thought.
**1929**—Fred A. Shannon, The Organization and Administration of the Union Army, 1861-65.
**1930**—Claude H. Van Tyne, The War of Independence.
**1931**—Bernadotte E. Schmitt, The Coming of the War, 1914.
**1932**—Gen. John J. Pershing, My Experiences in the World War.
**1933**—Frederick J. Turner, The Significance of Sections in American History.
**1934**—Herbert Agar, The People's Choice.
**1935**—Charles McLean Andrews, The Colonial Period of American History.
**1936**—Andrew C. McLaughlin, The Constitutional History of the United States.
**1937**—Van Wyck Brooks, The Flowering of New England.
**1938**—Paul Herman Buck, The Road to Reunion, 1865-1900.
**1939**—Frank Luther Mott, A History of American Magazines.
**1940**—Carl Sandburg, Abraham Lincoln: The War Years.
**1941**—Marcus Lee Hansen, The Atlantic Migration, 1607-1860.
**1942**—Margaret Leech, Reveille in Washington.
**1943**—Esther Forbes, Paul Revere and the World He Lived In.
**1944**—Merle Curti, The Growth of American Thought.
**1945**—Stephen Bonsal, Unfinished Business.
**1946**—Arthur M. Schlesinger Jr., The Age of Jackson.
**1947**—James Phinney Baxter 3d, Scientists Against Time.
**1948**—Bernard De Voto, Across the Wide Missouri.
**1949**—Roy F. Nichols, The Disruption of American Democracy.
**1950**—O. W. Larkin, Art and Life in America.
**1951**—R. Carlyle Buley, The Old Northwest: Pioneer Period 1815-1840.
**1952**—Oscar Handlin, The Uprooted.
**1953**—George Dangerfield, The Era of Good Feelings.
**1954**—Bruce Catton, A Stillness at Appomattox.
**1955**—Paul Horgan, Great River: The Rio Grande in North American History.
**1956**—Richard Hofstadter, The Age of Reform.
**1957**—George F. Kennan, Russia Leaves the War.
**1958**—Bray Hammond, Banks and Politics in America—From the Revolution to the Civil War.
**1959**—Leonard D. White and Jean Schneider, The Republican Era; 1869-1901.
**1960**—Margaret Leech, In the Days of McKinley.
**1961**—Herbert Feis, Between War and Peace: The Potsdam Conference.
**1962**—Lawrence H. Gibson, The Triumphant Empire: Thunderclouds Gather in the West.
**1963**—Constance McLaughlin Green, Washington: Village and Capital, 1800-1878.
**1964**—Sumner Chilton Powell, Puritan Village: The Formation of A New England Town.
**1965**—Irwin Unger, The Greenback Era.
**1966**—Perry Miller, Life of the Mind in America.
**1967**—William H. Goetzmann, Exploration and Empire: the Explorer and Scientist in the Winning of the American West.
**1968**—Bernard Bailyn, The Ideological Origins of the American Revolution.
**1969**—Leonard W. Levy, Origin of the Fifth Amendment.
**1970**—Dean Acheson, Present at the Creation: My Years in the State Department.
**1971**—James McGregor Burns, Roosevelt: The Soldier of Freedom.
**1972**—Carl N. Degler, Neither Black Nor White.
**1973**—Michael Kammen, People of Paradox: An Inquiry Concerning the Origins of American Civilization.
**1974**—Daniel J. Boorstin, The Americans: The Democratic Experience.
**1975**—Dumas Malone, Jefferson and His Time.
**1976**—Paul Horgan, Lamy of Santa Fe.
**1977**—David M. Potter, The Impending Crisis.
**1978**—Alfred D. Chandler Jr., The Visible Hand: The Managerial Revolution in American Business.
**1979**—Don E. Fehrenbacher, The Dred Scott Case: Its Significance in American Law and Politics.
**1980**—Leon F. Litwack, Been in the Storm So Long.
**1981**—Lawrence A. Cremin, American Education: The National Experience, 1783-1876.
**1982**—C. Vann Woodward, ed., Mary Chestnut's Civil War.
**1983**—Rhys L. Issac, The Transformation of Virginia, 1740-1790.
**1985**—Thomas K. McCraw, Prophets of Regulation.
**1986**—Walter A. McDougall, . . . The Heavens and the Earth.
**1987**—Bernard Bailyn, Voyagers to the West.
**1988**—Robert V. Bruce, The Launching of Modern American Science 1846-1876.
**1989**—Taylor Branch, Parting the Waters: America in the King Years, 1954-63; and James M. McPherson, Battle Cry of Freedom: The Civil War Era.
**1990**—Stanley Karnow, In Our Image: America's Empire in the Philippines.
**1991**—Laurel Thatcher Ulrich, A Midwife's Tale: The Life of Martha Ballard, based on her diary, 1785-1812.
**1992**—Mark E. Neely Jr., The Fate of Liberty: Abraham Lincoln and Civil Liberties.
**1993**—Gordon S. Wood, The Radicalism of the American Revolution.

## Biography or Autobiography

For a distinguished biography or autobiography by an American author.
**1917**—Laura E. Richards and Maude Howe Elliott, assisted by Florence Howe Hall, Julia Ward Howe.
**1918**—William Cabell Bruce, Benjamin Franklin, Self-Revealed.
**1919**—Henry Adams, The Education of Henry Adams.
**1920**—Albert J. Beveridge, The Life of John Marshall.
**1921**—Edward Bok, The Americanization of Edward Bok.
**1922**—Hamlin Garland, A Daughter of the Middle Border.
**1923**—Burton J. Hendrick, The Life and Letters of Walter H. Page.
**1924**—Michael Pupin, From Immigrant to Inventor.
**1925**—M. A. DeWolfe Howe, Barrett Wendell and His Letters.
**1926**—Harvey Cushing, Life of Sir William Osler.
**1927**—Emory Holloway, Whitman: An Interpretation in Narrative.
**1928**—Charles Edward Russell, The American Orchestra and Theodore Thomas.
**1929**—Burton J. Hendrick, The Training of an American: The Earlier Life and Letters of Walter H. Page.
**1930**—Marquis James, The Raven (Sam Houston).
**1931**—Henry James, Charles W. Eliot.
**1932**—Henry F. Pringle, Theodore Roosevelt.
**1933**—Allan Nevins, Grover Cleveland.
**1934**—Tyler Dennett, John Hay.
**1935**—Douglas Southall Freeman, R. E. Lee.
**1936**—Ralph Barton Perry, The Thought and Character of William James.
**1937**—Allan Nevins, Hamilton Fish: The Inner History of the Grant Administration.
**1938**—Divided between Odell Shepard, Pedlar's Progress; Marquis James, Andrew Jackson.
**1939**—Carl Van Doren, Benjamin Franklin.
**1940**—Ray Stannard Baker, Woodrow Wilson, Life and Letters.
**1941**—Ola Elizabeth Winslow, Jonathan Edwards.
**1942**—Forrest Wilson, Crusader in Crinoline.
**1943**—Samuel Eliot Morison, Admiral of the Ocean Sea (Columbus).
**1944**—Carleton Mabee, The American Leonardo: The Life of Samuel F. B. Morse.
**1945**—Russell Blaine Nye, George Bancroft; Brahmin Rebel.
**1946**—Linny Marsh Wolfe, Son of the Wilderness.
**1947**—William Allen White, The Autobiography of William Allen White.
**1948**—Margaret Clapp, Forgotten First Citizen: John Bigelow.
**1949**—Robert E. Sherwood, Roosevelt and Hopkins.
**1950**—Samuel Flag Bemis, John Quincy Adams and the Foundations of American Foreign Policy.
**1951**—Margaret Louise Coit, John C. Calhoun: American Portrait.
**1952**—Merlo J. Pusey, Charles Evans Hughes.
**1953**—David J. Mays, Edmund Pendleton, 1721-1803.
**1954**—Charles A. Lindbergh, The Spirit of St. Louis.
**1955**—William S. White, The Taft Story.
**1956**—Talbot F. Hamlin, Benjamin Henry Latrobe.
**1957**—John F. Kennedy, Profiles in Courage.
**1958**—Douglas Southall Freeman (decd. 1953), George Washington, Vols. I-VI; John Alexander Carroll and Mary Wells Ashworth, Vol. VII.
**1959**—Arthur Walworth, Woodrow Wilson: American Prophet.
**1960**—Samuel Eliot Morison, John Paul Jones.
**1961**—David Donald, Charles Sumner and the Coming of the Civil War.
**1963**—Leon Edel, Henry James: Vol. II, The Conquest of London, 1870-1881; Vol. III, The Middle Years, 1881-1895.
**1964**—Walter Jackson Bate, John Keats.
**1965**—Ernest Samuels, Henry Adams.
**1966**—Arthur M. Schlesinger Jr., A Thousand Days.
**1967**—Justin Kaplan, Mr. Clemens and Mark Twain.
**1968**—George F. Kennan, Memoirs (1925-1950).
**1969**—B. L. Reid, The Man from New York: John Quinn and his Friends.
**1970**—T. Harry Williams, Huey Long.
**1971**—Lawrence Thompson, Robert Frost: The Years of Triumph, 1915-1938.
**1972**—Joseph P. Lash, Eleanor and Franklin.
**1973**—W. A. Swanberg, Luce and His Empire.
**1974**—Louis Sheaffer, O'Neill, Son and Artist.
**1975**—Robert A. Caro, The Power Broker: Robert Moses and the Fall of New York.
**1976**—R.W.B. Lewis, Edith Wharton: A Biography.

1977—John E. Mack, A Prince of Our Disorder: The Life of T.E. Lawrence.
1978—Walter Jackson Bate, Samuel Johnson.
1979—Leonard Baker, Days of Sorrow and Pain: Leo Baeck and the Berlin Jews.
1980—Edmund Morris, The Rise of Theodore Roosevelt.
1981—Robert K. Massie, Peter the Great: His Life and World.
1982—William S. McFeely, Grant: A Biography.
1983—Russell Baker, Growing Up.
1984—Louis R. Harlan, Booker T. Washington.
1985—Kenneth Silverman, The Life and Times of Cotton Mather.
1986—Elizabeth Frank, Louise Bogan: A Portrait.
1987—David J. Garrow, Bearing the Cross: Martin Luther King Jr. and the Southern Christian Leadership Conference.
1988—David Herbert Donald, Look Homeward: A Life of Thomas Wolfe.
1989—Richard Ellmann, Oscar Wilde.
1990—Sebastian de Grazia, Machiavelli in Hell.
1991—Steven Naifeh, and Gregory White Smith, Jackson Pollock: An American Saga.
1992—Lewis B. Puller Jr., Fortunate Son: The Healing of a Vietnam Vet.
1993—David McCullough, Truman.

## American Poetry

Before this prize was established in 1922, awards were made from gifts provided by the Poetry Society: 1918—Love Songs, by Sara Teasdale. 1919—Old Road to Paradise, by Margaret Widemer; Corn Huskers, by Carl Sandburg.
1922—Edwin Arlington Robinson, Collected Poems.
1923—Edna St. Vincent Millay, The Ballad of the Harp-Weaver; A Few Figs from Thistles; Eight Sonnets in American Poetry, 1922; A Miscellany.
1924—Robert Frost, New Hampshire: A Poem with Notes and Grace Notes.
1925—Edwin Arlington Robinson, The Man Who Died Twice.
1926—Amy Lowell, What's O'Clock.
1927—Leonora Speyer, Fiddler's Farewell.
1928—Edwin Arlington Robinson, Tristram.
1929—Stephen Vincent Benet, John Brown's Body.
1930—Conrad Aiken, Selected Poems.
1931—Robert Frost, Collected Poems.
1932—George Dillon, The Flowering Stone.
1933—Archibald MacLeish, Conquistador.
1934—Robert Hillyer, Collected Verse.
1935—Audrey Wurdemann, Bright Ambush.
1936—Robert P. Tristram Coffin, Strange Holiness.
1937—Robert Frost, A Further Range.
1938—Marya Zaturenska, Cold Morning Sky.
1939—John Gould Fletcher, Selected Poems.
1940—Mark Van Doren, Collected Poems.
1941—Leonard Bacon, Sunderland Capture.
1942—William Rose Benet, The Dust Which Is God.
1943—Robert Frost, A Witness Tree.
1944—Stephen Vincent Benet, Western Star.
1945—Karl Shapiro, V-Letter and Other Poems.
1947—Robert Lowell, Lord Weary's Castle.
1948—W. H. Auden, The Age of Anxiety.
1949—Peter Viereck, Terror and Decorum.
1950—Gwendolyn Brooks, Annie Allen.
1951—Carl Sandburg, Complete Poems.
1952—Marianne Moore, Collected Poems.
1953—Archibald MacLeish, Collected Poems.
1954—Theodore Roethke, The Waking.
1955—Wallace Stevens, Collected Poems.
1956—Elizabeth Bishop, Poems, North and South.
1957—Richard Wilbur, Things of This World.
1958—Robert Penn Warren, Promises: Poems 1954-1956.
1959—Stanley Kunitz, Selected Poems 1928-1958.
1960—W. D. Snodgrass, Heart's Needle.
1961—Phyllis McGinley, Times Three: Selected Verse from Three Decades.
1962—Alan Dugan, Poems.
1963—William Carlos Williams, Pictures From Breughel.

1964—Louis Simpson, At the End of the Open Road.
1965—John Berryman, 77 Dream Songs.
1966—Richard Eberhart, Selected Poems.
1967—Anne Sexton, Live or Die.
1968—Anthony Hecht, The Hard Hours.
1969—George Oppen, Of Being Numerous.
1970—Richard Howard, Untitled Subjects.
1971—William S. Merwin, The Carrier of Ladders.
1972—James Wright, Collected Poems.
1973—Maxine Winokur Kumin, Up Country.
1975—Gary Snyder, Turtle Island.
1976—John Ashbery, Self-Portrait in a Convex Mirror.
1977—James Merrill, Divine Comedies.
1978—Howard Nemerov, Collected Poems.
1979—Robert Penn Warren, Now and Then: Poems 1976-1978.
1980—Donald Justice, Selected Poems.
1981—James Schuyler, The Morning of the Poem.
1982—Sylvia Plath, The Collected Poems.
1983—Galway Kinnell, Selected Poems.
1984—Mary Oliver, American Primitive.
1985—Carolyn Kizer, Yin.
1986—Henry Taylor, The Flying Change.
1987—Rita Dove, Thomas and Beulah.
1988—William Meredith, Partial Accounts: New and Selected Poems.
1989—Richard Wilbur, New and Collected Poems.
1990—Charles Simic, The World Doesn't End.
1991—Mona Van Duyn, Near Changes.
1992—James Tate, Selected Poems.
1993—Louise Glück, The Wild Iris.

## General Non-Fiction

1962—Theodore H. White, The Making of the President 1960.
1963—Barbara W. Tuchman, The Guns of August.
1964—Richard Hofstadter, Anti-Intellectualism in American Life.
1965—Howard Mumford Jones, O Strange New World.
1966—Edwin Way Teale, Wandering Through Winter.
1967—David Brion Davis, The Problem of Slavery in Western Culture.
1968—Will and Ariel Durant, Rousseau and Revolution.
1969—Norman Mailer, The Armies of the Night; Rene Jules Dubos, So Human an Animal: How We Are Shaped by Surroundings and Events.
1970—Eric H. Erikson, Gandhi's Truth.
1971—John Toland, The Rising Sun.
1972—Barbara W. Tuchman, Stilwell and the American Experience in China, 1911-1945.
1973—Frances FitzGerald, Fire in the Lake: The Vietnamese and the Americans in Vietnam; Robert Coles, Children of Crisis, Volumes II & III.
1974—Ernest Becker, The Denial of Death.
1975—Annie Dillard, Pilgrim at Tinker Creek.
1976—Robert N. Butler, Why Survive? Being Old in America.
1977—William W. Warner, Beautiful Swimmers.
1978—Carl Sagan, The Dragons of Eden.
1979—Edward O. Wilson, On Human Nature.
1980—Douglas R. Hofstadter, Gödel, Escher, Bach: An Eternal Golden Braid.
1981—Carl E. Schorske, Fin-de-Siecle Vienna: Politics and Culture.
1982—Tracy Kidder, The Soul of a New Machine.
1983—Susan Sheehan, Is There No Place on Earth for Me?
1984—Paul Starr, Social Transformation of American Medicine.
1985—Studs Terkel, The Good War.
1986—Joseph Lelyveld, Move Your Shadow; J. Anthony Lukas, Common Ground.
1987—David K. Shipler, Arab and Jew.
1988—Richard Rhodes, The Making of the Atomic Bomb.
1989—Neil Sheehan, A Bright Shining Lie: John Paul Vann and America in Vietnam.
1990—Dale Maharidge and Michael Williamson, And Their Children After Them.
1991—Bert Holldobler and Edward O. Wilson, The Ants.
1992—Daniel Yergin, The Prize: The Epic Quest for Oil.
1993—Garry Wills, Lincoln at Gettysburg.

## Music

For composition by an American (before 1977, by a composer resident in the U.S.), in the larger forms of chamber, orchestra, or choral music or for an operatic work including ballet. A special posthumous award was granted in 1976 to Scott Joplin.
1943—William Schuman, Secular Cantata No. 2, A Free Song.
1944—Howard Hanson, Symphony No. 4, Op. 34.
1945—Aaron Copland, Appalachian Spring.
1946—Leo Sowerby, The Canticle of the Sun.
1947—Charles E. Ives, Symphony No. 3.
1948—Walter Piston, Symphony No. 3.
1949—Virgil Thomson, Louisiana Story.

1950—Gian-Carlo Menotti, The Consul.
1951—Douglas Moore, Giants in the Earth.
1952—Gail Kubik, Symphony Concertante.
1954—Quincy Porter, Concerto for Two Pianos and Orchestra.
1955—Gian-Carlo Menotti, The Saint of Bleecker Street.
1956—Ernest Toch, Symphony No. 3.
1957—Norman Dello Joio, Meditations on Ecclesiastes.
1958—Samuel Barber, Vanessa.
1959—John La Montaine, Concerto for Piano and Orchestra.
1960—Elliott Carter, Second String Quartet.
1961—Walter Piston, Symphony No. 7.

1962—Robert Ward, The Crucible.
1963—Samuel Barber, Piano Concerto No. 1.
1966—Leslie Bassett, Variations for Orchestra.
1967—Leon Kirchner, Quartet No. 3.
1968—George Crumb, Echoes of Time and The River.
1969—Karel Husa, String Quartet No. 3.
1970—Charles W. Wuorinen, Time's Encomium.
1971—Mario Davidovsky, Synchronisms No. 6.
1972—Jacob Druckman, Windows.
1973—Elliott Carter, String Quartet No. 3.
1974—Donald Martino, Notturno. (Special citation) Roger Sessions.
1975—Dominick Argento, From the Diary of Virginia Woolf.
1976—Ned Rorem, Air Music.
1977—Richard Wernick, Visions of Terror and Wonder.
1978—Michael Colgrass, Deja Vu for Percussion and Orchestra.
1979—Joseph Schwantner, Aftertones of Infinity.

1980—David Del Tredici, In Memory of a Summer Day.
1982—Roger Sessions, Concerto For Orchestra. (Special Citation) Milton Babbitt.
1983—Ellen T. Zwilich, Three Movements for Orchestra.
1984—Bernard Rands, Canti del Sole.
1985—Stephen Albert, Symphony, RiverRun.
1986—George Perle, Wind Quintet IV.
1987—John Harbison, The Flight Into Egypt.
1988—William Bolcom, 12 New Etudes for Piano.
1989—Roger Reynolds, Whispers Out of Time.
1990—Mel Powell, Duplicates: A Concerto For Two Pianos and Orchestra.
1991—Shulamit Ran, Symphony.
1992—Wayne Peterson, The Face of the Night, The Heart of the Dark.
1993—Christopher Rouse, Trombone Concerto.

# Special Awards

Awarded in 1992 or 1993

## Books

**Academy of American Poets Awards:** Fellowship for Distinguished Poetic Achievement, $20,000: Adrienne Rich; Lamont Poetry Selection, $1,000 and purchase of 2,000 copies of book: Kathryn Stripling Byer, *Wildwood Flower*; Lavan Younger Poet Awards, $1,000 each: Cyrus Cassells, Richard Lyons, Rosanna Warren.

**Curtis Benjamin Award for Creative Publishing,** by Assn. of American Publishers: Jason Epstein, Random House.

**Bollingen Prize in Poetry,** by Yale Library, for lifetime achievement, $10,000: Mark Strand.

**Caldecott Medal,** by American Library Assn., for most distinguished American picture book: Emily Arnold McCully, *Mirette on the High Wire*.

**Christopher Awards,** by The Christophers, for expression of highest values of human spirit, bronze medallion each: Joseph Iron Eye Dudley, *Choteau Creek: A Sioux Reminiscence*; Marian Wright Edelman, *The Measure of Our Success: A Letter to My Children and Yours*; Eric Silver, *The Book of the Just: The Unsung Heroes Who Rescued Jews from Hitler*; Robert Ellsberg, ed., *Fritz Eichenberg: Works of Mercy*; Judy Barron and Sean Barron, *There's a Boy in Here*; Katie Kelly, *A Year in Saigon*.

**Golden Kite Awards,** by Society of Children's Book Writers and Illustrators, statuette each: Mary E. Lyons, *Letters from a Slave Girl*; nonfiction: Jim Murphy, *The Long Road to Gettysburg*; illustration: Patricia Polacco, *Chicken Sunday*.

**International Fiction Prize,** by Irish Times and Aer Lingus, for work of fiction published in Ireland, U.K., or U.S., $45,000: Norman Rush, *Mating*.

**Ruth Lilly Poetry Prize,** by Modern Poetry Assn. and American National Council for the Arts, for lifetime achievement, $75,000: Charles Wright.

**Lincoln Prize,** by Lincoln Soldiers Institute at Gettysburg College, for lifetime contribution to Civil War studies, $40,000 and bronze bust of Lincoln: Kenneth M. Stampp; best book on Civil War pub. 1992, $10,000: Albert Castel, *Decision in the West*.

**National Book Awards,** by National Book Foundation, $10,000 each: nonfiction: Paul Monette, *Becoming a Man*; poetry: Mary Oliver, *New and Selected Poems*; fiction: Cormac McCarthy, *All the Pretty Horses*; Medal for Distinguished Contribution to American Letters: James Laughlin, *New Directions*.

**National Book Critics Circle Awards:** fiction: Cormac McCarthy, *All the Pretty Horses*; nonfiction: Norman Maclean, *Young Men and Fire*; criticism: Garry Wills, *Lincoln at Gettysburg*; biography/autobiography: Carol Brightman, *Writing Dangerously: Mary McCarthy and Her World*; poetry: Hayden Carruth, *Collected Poems 1946-1991*.

**Newbery Award,** by American Library Assn., for most distinguished contribution to American literature for children: Cynthia Ryland, *Missing May*.

**Francis Parkman Prize,** by Society of American Historians, for scholarship combined with literary excellence, $1,000: David McCullough, *Truman*; James Fenimore Cooper Prize, for historical fiction, $1,000: Noah Gordon, *Shaman*; Allan Nevins Prize, for best-written dissertation in American history, $1,000: Amy J. Kinsel, "From These Honored Dead: Gettysburg in American Culture, 1863-1938."

**PEN/Faulkner Award for Fiction,** $15,000: E. Annie Proulx, *Postcards*.

**Edgar Allan Poe Awards,** by Mystery Writers of America, bust of Poe each: Margaret Maron, *Bootlegger's Daughter*; grand master, for lifetime achievement: Donald E. Westlake; reader of the year: President Bill Clinton.

**Rhea Award for the Short Story,** by Dungannon Foundation, for lifetime achievement, $25,000: Grace Paley.

**Whiting Writers' Awards,** by Whiting Foundation, for achievement and promise alike, $30,000 each: Roger Fanning, Eva Hoffman, R. S. Jones, J. S. Marcus, James Mead, Suzan Lori-Parks, Katha Pollitt, Keith Reddin, Jose Rivera, Damien Wilkins.

## Journalism

**Helen B. Bernstein Award,** by New York Public Library, $15,000: Samuel G. Freedman, *Upon This Rock: The Miracles of a Black Church*.

**National Journalism Awards,** by Scripps Howard Foundation, for print journalism, bronze plaques: Charles E. Scripps Award, for newspaper's service to literacy, $2,500: *Anderson* (S.C.) *Independent-Mail*; Pyle Award, for human interest writing, $2,500: Bill Harden, *Washington Post*; Stone Award, for editorial writing, $2,000: Robert Friedman, *St. Petersburg Times*; Meeman Award, for environmental reporting, $2,000 each: *Orlando* (Fla.) *Sentinel* and *National Law Journal*, New York, N.Y.; Howard Award, for public service reporting, $2,500 each: *San Francisco Examiner* and *Albuquerque* (N.M.) *Tribune*; E. W. Scripps Award, for service to First Amendment, $2,500: David Lawrence Jr., *Miami Herald*.

**National Magazine Awards,** by American Society of Magazine Editors and Columbia Univ. Graduate School of Journalism: general excellence, circulation over 1 million: *Newsweek*; under 1 million: *The Atlantic Monthly, American Photo, Lingua Franca*; single-topic issue: *Newsweek*, "How He Won: The Untold Story of Bill Clinton's Triumph"; feature writing: *The New Yorker*, "Whose Art Is It?" Jane Kramer; fiction: *The New Yorker*, "A Wilderness Station," Alice Munro; "Parachute Silk," Emily Carter; "Career Move," Martin Amis; design: *Harper's Bazaar*; photography: *Harper's Bazaar*; reporting: *IEEE Spectrum*, "Seeking Nuclear Safeguards"; personal service: *Good Housekeeping* and *Philadelphia*; public interest: *The Family Therapy Networker*; essays and criticism; *The American Lawyer*, "Maybe the Jury Was Right."

**George Polk Awards,** by Long Island Univ., for excellence in journalism: national: Gregory Vistica, *San Diego Un-*

*ion-Tribune*; local: *Los Angeles Times*; social commentary: Henry Louis Gates, op-ed article, *New York Times*; career: Herbert Mitgang, *New York Times*, and Roy Gutman, *Newsday*; health: Seth Rosenfeld, *San Francisco Examiner*; legal: Marianne Lavelle, Marcia Coyle, Claudia MacLachlan, *National Law Journal*; environmental: John-Thor Dahlburg, *Los Angeles Times*; magazine: Lawrence Weschler, *New Yorker*; photography: Carlos Guerrero, *El Nuevo Herald*.

**Reuben Awards,** by National Cartoonists Society: cartoonist of the year: Cathy Guisewite, "Cathy"; editorial cartoon: Jim Morin; animation: Eric Goldberg; comic book: Todd McFarlane; newspaper comic strip: Wiley Miller; sports cartoon: Eddie Germano; gag cartoon: Arnie Levin; newspaper panel: Don Addis; advertising illustration: Daryl Cagle; greeting cards: Sandra Boynton; magazine and book illustration: Burne Hogarth.

**Science in Society Print Journalism Awards,** by Natl. Assn. of Science Writers. $1,000 each and certificate: newspapers: Jon Van, *Chicago Tribune*; magazines: Nancy Pappas, *Consumer Reports*; commendation: Rochelle Green, *Consumer Reports.*

## Movie, TV, Radio, and Theater

**Astaire Awards,** for achievement in dance in Broadway theater, by Theater Development Fund: performance: Chita Rivera, *Kiss of the Spider Woman*; choreography: Wayne Cilento, *Tommy.*

**Susan Smith Blackburn Awards,** for female playwright, $5,000: Marlane Meyer, *Moe's Lucky Seven,* commissioned by South Coast Repertory Co., Costa Mesa, Cal.; 2d prize, $1,000: Jane Anderson, *Hotel Oubliette,* premiere at Williamstown Theater Festival, Mass.

**Christopher Awards,** by The Christophers: movies: *Enchanted April, Howards End, Lorenzo's Oil, Sarafina!*; TV specials: *Against Her Will, The Broken Cord, Father/Son, Miles from Nowhere, Jonathan: The Boy Nobody Wanted, Sr. Thea: Her Own Story, A Town Torn Apart.*

**Directors Guild of America:** movie director: Clint Eastwood, *Unforgiven*; D. W. Griffith Award, for lifetime achievement: Sidney Lumet; TV directors: comedy series: Tom Cherones, *Seinfeld,* "The Contest"; nighttime drama series: Rob Thompson, *Northern Exposure,* "Cicely"; daytime dramatic show: Helaine Head, *Wonderworks,* "You Must Remember This"; musical-variety show: Bobby Quinn, *The Tonight Show*; documentary: Joseph Berlinger and Bruce Sinofsky, *Brother's Keeper*; daytime serial: Susan Strickler, *Another World*; drama special: Ron Lagomarsino, *Picket Fences,* pilot episode; commercial: Leslie Dektor, Philips Electronics; Career Achievement Award: Harry Coyle, sports direction.

**Drama Desk Awards,** by New York theater critics writing for non-New York publications: play: Tony Kushner, *Angels in America*; musical: *Kiss of the Spider Woman*; actor: Ron Leibman, *Angels in America*; actress: Jane Alexander, *The Sisters Rosensweig*; director: George C. Wolfe, *Angels in America*; musical actor: Brent Carver, *Kiss of the Spider Woman*; musical actress: Chita Rivera, *Kiss of the Spider Woman*; musical director: Des McAnuff, *Tommy*; music: John Kander, *Kiss of the Spider Woman.*

**Alfred I. Dupont-Columbia Univ. Awards,** for broadcast journalism: gold baton: National Public Radio, for coverage of Los Angeles riots, for series including *Morning Edition, All Things Considered,* and *American Folklife,* and for reporting of Senate hearings on nomination of Clarence Thomas to Supreme Court.

**Emmy Awards,** by Academy of Television Arts and Sciences, for primetime programs, 1992-93: Dramatic series: *Picket Fences,* CBS; actor: Tom Skerritt, *Picket Fences,* CBS; actress: Kathy Baker, *Picket Fences,* CBS; supporting actor: Chad Lowe, *Life Goes On,* ABC; supporting actress: Mary Alice, *I'll Fly Away,* NBC; writing: Tom Fontana, *Homicide: Life on the Street,* NBC; directing: Barry Levinson, *Homicide: Life on the Street,* NBC. Comedy series: *Seinfeld,* NBC; actor: Ted Danson, *Cheers,* NBC; actress: Roseanne Arnold, *Roseanne,* ABC; supporting actor: Michael Richards, *Seinfeld,* NBC; supporting actress: Laurie Metcalf, *Roseanne,* ABC; writing: Larry David, *Seinfeld,* NBC; directing: Betty Thomas, *Dream On,* HBO. Variety, music, or comedy series: *Saturday Night Live,* NBC; performance: Dana Carvey, *Saturday Night Live's Presidential Bash,* NBC; writing: *The Ben Stiller Show,* Fox; directing: Walter C. Miller, *The 1992 Tony Awards,* CBS. Variety, music, or comedy special: *Bob Hope: The First 90 Years,* NBC. Made-for-TV movie (tie): *Barbarians at the Gate,* HBO, and *Stalin,* HBO. Miniseries: *Mystery!: Prime Suspect 2,* PBS; actor: Robert Morse, *Tru,* PBS; actress: Holly Hunter, *The Positively True Adventures of the Alleged Texas Cheerleader-Murdering Mom,* HBO; supporting actor: Beau Bridges, *The Positively True Adventures of the Alleged Texas Cheerleader-Murdering Mom,* HBO; supporting actress: Mary Tyler Moore, *Stolen Babies,* Lifetime; writing: Jane Anderson, *The Positively True Adventures of the Alleged Texas Cheerleader-Murdering Mom,* HBO; directing: James Sadwith, *Sinatra,* CBS.

**National Society of Film Critics:** film: *Unforgiven*; actor: Stephen Rea, *The Crying Game*; actress: Emma Thompson, *Howards End*; supporting actor: Gene Hackman, *Unforgiven*; supporting actress: Judy Davis, *Husbands and Wives*; screenplay: David Webb Peoples, *Unforgiven*; foreign film: *Raise the Red Lantern*; cinematography: *Raise the Red Lantern*; documentary: *American Dream,* Barbara Kopple; experimental: *Another Girl, Another Planet,* Michael Almereyda.

**New York Drama Critics Circle,** $1,000: play: Tony Kishner, *Angels in America*; foreign: Frank McGuiness, *Someone Who'll Watch Over Me*; musical: *Kiss of the Spider Woman.*

**Tony (Antoinette Perry) Awards:** play: Tony Kushner, *Angels in America*; musical: *Kiss of the Spider Woman*; revival: *Anna Christie*; actor: Ron Leibman, *Angels in America*; actress: Madeline Kahn, *The Sisters Rosensweig*; actor, musical: Brent Carver, *Kiss of the Spider Woman*; actress, musical: Chita Rivera, *Kiss of the Spider Woman*; featured actor: Stephen Spinella, *Angeles in America*; featured actress: Debra Monk, *Redwood Curtain*; featured actor, musical: Anthony Crivello, *Kiss of the Spider Woman*; featured actress, musical: Andrea Martin, *My Favorite Year*; director: George C. Wolfe, *Angels in America*; director, musical: Des McAnuff, *Tommy*; book, musical: Terrence McNally, *Kiss of the Spider Woman*; original musical score: John Kander and Fred Ebb, *Kiss of the Spider Woman,* and Pete Townshend, *Tommy*; scenic design: John Arnone, *Tommy*; costume design: Forence Klotz, *Kiss of the Spider Woman*; lighting design: Chris Parry, *Tommy*; choreography: Wayne Cilento, *Tommy*; special award: *Oklahoma,* in recognition of 50th anniversary; regional theater; La Jolla Playhouse, Calif.

## Miscellaneous

**American Institute of Architects Gold Medal:** Kevin Roche.

**Breakthrough Awards,** by Women and Media, for influencing change in gender stereotypes: Blanche Wisen Cook, for her biography *Eleanor Roosevelt*; AWRT Foundation and Capital Cities/ABC, for public service campaign; Barbara Reynolds, *USA Today* columnist; Jones Intercable, for funding Women in Cable; CNN.

**Charles Frankel Prizes,** by Natl. Endowment for the Humanities, for those who have increased public awareness of the humanities, $5,000 each: Eudora Welty, Shelby Foote, Allan Bloom, Richard Rodriguez, Harold K. Skramstad Jr.

**Gavel Award,** by American Bar Assn., for lifetime achievement: Fred Friendly, for PBS series on legal and social issues.

**John F. Kennedy Center for the Performing Arts Awards,** for contribution to U.S. cultural life: Lionel Hampton, Ginger Rogers, Mstislav Rostropovich, Paul Taylor, and Paul Newman and Joanne Woodward.

**McGraw-Hill Prize in Education,** for distinguished contribution to the advancement of education, $25,000 each: Shirley A. Hill, pres. of Natl. Council of Teachers of Mathematics; Thomas W. Payzant, superintendent of San Diego City Schools; Edward Zigler, co-founder of Head Start.

**National Inventors Hall of Fame,** inductees: John Ericsson, William P. Lear, John T. Parsons, Baruch S. Blumberg, Irving Millman.

**National Medal of Arts,** by White House, for outstanding contributions to cultural life in the U.S.: Marilyn Horne, Allan Houser, James Earl Jones, Minnie Pearl, Robert Saudek, Earl Scruggs, Robert Shaw, Billy Taylor, Robert Venturi, Denise Scott Brown, Robert Wise, AT&T Foundation, Lila Wallace-Reader's Digest Fund.

**Rock-and-Roll Hall of Fame,** inductees: Ruth Brown, Cream, Creedence Clearwater Revival, the Doors, Etta James, Frankie Lymon and the Teen-Agers, Van Morrison, Sly and the Family Stone; pre-rock: Dinah Washington; business: Milt Gabler, Dick Clark.

**Samuel H. Scripps American Dance Festival Award,** $25,000: Talley Beatty.

**Templeton Prize for Progress in Religion,** by Templeton Foundation, about $1 million: Charles W. Colson.

**Van Cliburn International Piano Competition:** gold medal, silver cup, $15,000: Simone Pedroni of Novara, Italy.

**Westinghouse Talent Search:** 1st prize, $40,000 scholarship: Elizabeth Michele Pine, Illinois Math & Science Academy, Aurora, Ill.

## The Spingarn Medal

The Spingarn Medal has been awarded annually since 1914 by the National Association for the Advancement of Colored People for the highest achievement by a black American.

| | | | | | | |
|---|---|---|---|---|---|---|
| 1946 | Dr. Percy L. Julian | 1961 | Robert C. Weaver | 1977 | Andrew Young |
| 1947 | Channing H. Tobias | 1962 | Medgar Wiley Evers | 1978 | Mrs. Rosa L. Parks |
| 1948 | Ralph J. Bunche | 1963 | Roy Wilkins | 1979 | Dr. Rayford W. Logan |
| 1949 | Charles Hamilton Houston | 1964 | Leontyne Price | 1980 | Coleman Young |
| 1950 | Mabel Keaton Staupers | 1965 | John H. Johnson | 1981 | Dr. Benjamin Elijah Mays |
| 1951 | Harry T. Moore | 1966 | Edward W. Brooke | 1982 | Lena Horne |
| 1952 | Paul R. Williams | 1967 | Sammy Davis Jr. | 1983 | Thomas Bradley |
| 1953 | Theodore K. Lawless | 1968 | Clarence M. Mitchell Jr. | 1984 | Bill Cosby |
| 1954 | Carl Murphy | 1969 | Jacob Lawrence | 1985 | Dr. Benjamin L. Hooks |
| 1955 | Jack Roosevelt Robinson | 1970 | Leon Howard Sullivan | 1986 | Percy E. Sutton |
| 1956 | Martin Luther King Jr. | 1971 | Gordon Parks | 1987 | Frederick Douglass Patterson |
| 1957 | Mrs. Daisy Bates and the Little Rock Nine | 1972 | Wilson C. Riles | 1988 | Jesse Jackson |
| 1958 | Edward Kennedy (Duke) Ellington | 1973 | Damon Keith | 1989 | L. Douglas Wilder |
| | | 1974 | Henry (Hank) Aaron | 1990 | Gen. Colin L. Powell |
| 1959 | Langston Hughes | 1975 | Alvin Ailey | 1991 | Barbara Jordan |
| 1960 | Kenneth B. Clark | 1976 | Alex Haley | 1992 | Dorothy I. Height |

## Miss America Winners

| | | | |
|---|---|---|---|
| 1921 | Margaret Gorman, Washington, D.C. | 1963 | Jacquelyn Mayer, Sandusky, Ohio |
| 1922-23 | Mary Campbell, Columbus, Ohio | 1964 | Donna Axum, El Dorado, Arkansas |
| 1924 | Ruth Malcolmson, Philadelphia, Pennsylvania | 1965 | Vonda Kay Van Dyke, Phoenix, Arizona |
| 1925 | Fay Lamphier, Oakland, California | 1966 | Deborah Irene Bryant, Overland Park, Kansas |
| 1926 | Norma Smallwood, Tulsa, Oklahoma | 1967 | Jane Anne Jayroe, Laverne, Oklahoma |
| 1927 | Lois Delaner, Joliet, Illinois | 1968 | Debra Dene Barnes, Moran, Kansas |
| 1933 | Marion Bergeron, West Haven, Connecticut | 1969 | Judith Anne Ford, Belvidere, Illinois |
| 1935 | Henrietta Leaver, Pittsburgh, Pennsylvania | 1970 | Pamela Anne Eldred, Birmingham, Michigan |
| 1936 | Rose Coyle, Philadelphia, Pennsylvania | 1971 | Phyllis Ann George, Denton, Texas |
| 1937 | Bette Cooper, Bertrand Island, New Jersey | 1972 | Laurie Lea Schaefer, Columbus, Ohio |
| 1938 | Marilyn Meseke, Marion, Ohio | 1973 | Terry Anne Meeuwsen, DePere, Wisconsin |
| 1939 | Patricia Donnelly, Detroit, Michigan | 1974 | Rebecca Ann King, Denver, Colorado |
| 1940 | Frances Marie Burke, Philadelphia, Pennsylvania | 1975 | Shirley Cothran, Fort Worth, Texas |
| 1941 | Rosemary LaPlanche, Los Angeles, California | 1976 | Tawney Elaine Godin, Yonkers, N.Y. |
| 1942 | Jo-Caroll Dennison, Tyler, Texas | 1977 | Dorothy Kathleen Benham, Edina, Minnesota |
| 1943 | Jean Bartel, Los Angeles, California | 1978 | Susan Perkins, Columbus, Ohio |
| 1944 | Venus Ramey, Washington, D.C. | 1979 | Kylene Barker, Galax, Virginia |
| 1945 | Bess Myerson, New York City, N.Y. | 1980 | Cheryl Prewitt, Ackerman, Mississippi |
| 1946 | Marilyn Buferd, Los Angeles, California | 1981 | Susan Powell, Elk City, Oklahoma |
| 1947 | Barbara Walker, Memphis, Tennessee | 1982 | Elizabeth Ward, Russellville, Arkansas |
| 1948 | BeBe Shopp, Hopkins, Minnesota | 1983 | Debra Maffett, Anaheim, California |
| 1949 | Jacque Mercer, Litchfield, Arizona | 1984 | Vanessa Williams, Milwood, New York* |
| | | | Suzette Charles, Mays Landing, New Jersey |
| 1951 | Yolande Betbeze, Mobile, Alabama | |
| 1952 | Coleen Kay Hutchins, Salt Lake City, Utah | 1985 | Sharlene Wells, Salt Lake City, Utah |
| 1953 | Neva Jane Langley, Macon, Georgia | 1986 | Susan Akin, Meridian, Mississippi |
| 1954 | Evelyn Margaret Ay, Ephrata, Pennsylvania | 1987 | Kellye Cash, Memphis, Tennessee |
| 1955 | Lee Meriwether, San Francisco, California | 1988 | Kaye Lani Rae Rafko, Monroe, Michigan |
| 1956 | Sharon Ritchie, Denver, Colorado | 1989 | Gretchen Carlson, Anoka, Minnesota |
| 1957 | Marian McKnight, Manning, South Carolina | 1990 | Debbye Turner, Columbia, Missouri |
| 1958 | Marilyn Van Derbur, Denver, Colorado | 1991 | Marjorie Vincent, Oak Park, Illinois |
| 1959 | Mary Ann Mobley, Brandon, Mississippi | 1992 | Carolyn Suzanne Sapp, Honolulu, Hawaii |
| 1960 | Lynda Lee Mead, Natchez, Mississippi | 1993 | Leanza Cornett, Jacksonville, Florida |
| 1961 | Nancy Fleming, Montague, Michigan | 1994 | Kimberly Aiken, Columbia, South Carolina |
| 1962 | Maria Fletcher, Asheville, North Carolina | |

* Resigned July 23, 1984.

## Motion Picture Academy Awards (Oscars)

**1927-28**

Actor: Emil Jannings, *The Way of All Flesh.*
Actress: Janet Gaynor, *Seventh Heaven.*

Director: Frank Borzage, *Seventh Heaven;* Lewis Milestone, *Two Arabian Knights.*
Picture: *Wings,* Paramount.

**1928-29**
Actor: Warner Baxter, *In Old Arizona.*
Actress: Mary Pickford, *Coquette.*
Director: Frank Lloyd, *The Divine Lady.*
Picture: *Broadway Melody,* MGM.

**1929-30**
Actor: George Arliss, *Disraeli.*
Actress: Norma Shearer, *The Divorcee.*
Director: Lewis Milestone, *All Quiet on the Western Front.*
Picture: *All Quiet on the Western Front,* Univ.

**1930-31**
Actor: Lionel Barrymore, *Free Soul.*
Actress: Marie Dressler, *Min and Bill.*
Director: Norman Taurog, *Skippy.*
Picture: *Cimarron,* RKO.

**1931-32**
Actor: Fredric March, *Dr. Jekyll and Mr. Hyde;* Wallace Beery, *The Champ* (tie).
Actress: Helen Hayes, *Sin of Madelon Claudet.*
Director: Frank Borzage, *Bad Girl.*
Picture: *Grand Hotel,* MGM.
Special: Walt Disney, *Mickey Mouse.*

**1932-33**
Actor: Charles Laughton, *Private Life of Henry VIII.*
Actress: Katharine Hepburn, *Morning Glory.*
Director: Frank Lloyd, *Cavalcade.*
Picture: *Cavalcade,* Fox.

**1934**
Actor: Clark Gable, *It Happened One Night.*
Actress: Claudette Colbert, *It Happened One Night.*
Director: Frank Capra, *It Happened One Night.*
Picture: *It Happened One Night,* Columbia.

**1935**
Actor: Victor McLaglen, *The Informer.*
Actress: Bette Davis, *Dangerous.*
Director: John Ford, *The Informer.*
Picture: *Mutiny on the Bounty,* MGM.

**1936**
Actor: Paul Muni, *Story of Louis Pasteur.*
Actress: Luise Rainer, *The Great Ziegfeld.*
Sup. Actor: Walter Brennan, *Come and Get It.*
Sup. Actress: Gale Sondergaard, *Anthony Adverse.*
Director: Frank Capra, *Mr. Deeds Goes to Town.*
Picture: *The Great Ziegfeld,* MGM.

**1937**
Actor: Spencer Tracy, *Captains Courageous.*
Actress: Luise Rainer, *The Good Earth.*
Sup. Actor: Joseph Schildkraut, *Life of Emile Zola.*
Sup. Actress: Alice Brady, *In Old Chicago.*
Director: Leo McCarey, *The Awful Truth.*
Picture: *Life of Emile Zola,* Warner.

**1938**
Actor: Spencer Tracy, *Boys Town.*
Actress: Bette Davis, *Jezebel.*
Sup. Actor: Walter Brennan, *Kentucky.*
Sup. Actress: Fay Bainter, *Jezebel.*
Director: Frank Capra, *You Can't Take It With You.*
Picture: *You Can't Take It With You,* Columbia.

**1939**
Actor: Robert Donat, *Goodbye Mr. Chips.*
Actress: Vivien Leigh, *Gone With the Wind.*
Sup. Actor: Thomas Mitchell, *Stage Coach.*
Sup. Actress: Hattie McDaniel, *Gone With the Wind.*
Director: Victor Fleming, *Gone With the Wind.*
Picture: *Gone With the Wind,* Selznick International.

**1940**
Actor: James Stewart, *The Philadelphia Story.*
Actress: Ginger Rogers, *Kitty Foyle.*
Sup. Actor: Walter Brennan, *The Westerner.*
Sup. Actress: Jane Darwell, *The Grapes of Wrath.*
Director: John Ford, *The Grapes of Wrath.*
Picture: *Rebecca,* Selznick International.

**1941**
Actor: Gary Cooper, *Sergeant York.*
Actress: Joan Fontaine, *Suspicion.*
Sup. Actor: Donald Crisp, *How Green Was My Valley.*
Sup. Actress: Mary Astor, *The Great Lie.*
Director: John Ford, *How Green Was My Valley.*
Picture: *How Green Was My Valley,* 20th Cent.-Fox.

**1942**
Actor: James Cagney, *Yankee Doodle Dandy.*
Actress: Greer Garson, *Mrs. Miniver.*
Sup. Actor: Van Heflin, *Johnny Eager.*
Sup. Actress: Teresa Wright, *Mrs. Miniver.*
Director: William Wyler, *Mrs. Miniver.*
Picture: *Mrs. Miniver,* MGM.

**1943**
Actor: Paul Lukas, *Watch on the Rhine.*
Actress: Jennifer Jones, *The Song of Bernadette.*

Sup. Actor: Charles Coburn, *The More the Merrier.*
Sup. Actress: Katina Paxinou, *For Whom the Bell Tolls.*
Director: Michael Curtiz, *Casablanca.*
Picture: *Casablanca,* Warner.

**1944**
Actor: Bing Crosby, *Going My Way.*
Actress: Ingrid Bergman, *Gaslight.*
Sup. Actor: Barry Fitzgerald, *Going My Way.*
Sup. Actress: Ethel Barrymore, *None But the Lonely Heart.*
Director: Leo McCarey, *Going My Way.*
Picture: *Going My Way,* Paramount.

**1945**
Actor: Ray Milland, *The Lost Weekend.*
Actress: Joan Crawford, *Mildred Pierce.*
Sup. Actor: James Dunn, *A Tree Grows in Brooklyn.*
Sup. Actress: Anne Revere, *National Velvet.*
Director: Billy Wilder, *The Lost Weekend.*
Picture: *The Lost Weekend,* Paramount.

**1946**
Actor: Fredric March, *Best Years of Our Lives.*
Actress: Olivia de Havilland, *To Each His Own.*
Sup. Actor: Harold Russell, *The Best Years of Our Lives.*
Sup. Actress: Anne Baxter, *The Razor's Edge.*
Director: William Wyler, *The Best Years of Our Lives.*
Picture: *The Best Years of Our Lives,* Goldwyn, RKO.

**1947**
Actor: Ronald Colman, *A Double Life.*
Actress: Loretta Young, *The Farmer's Daughter.*
Sup. Actor: Edmund Gwenn, *Miracle on 34th Street.*
Sup. Actress: Celeste Holm, *Gentleman's Agreement.*
Director: Elia Kazan, *Gentleman's Agreement.*
Picture: *Gentleman's Agreement,* 20th Cent.-Fox.

**1948**
Actor: Laurence Olivier, *Hamlet.*
Actress: Jane Wyman, *Johnny Belinda.*
Sup. Actor: Walter Huston, *Treasure of Sierra Madre.*
Sup. Actress: Claire Trevor, *Key Largo.*
Director: John Huston, *Treasure of Sierra Madre.*
Picture: *Hamlet,* Two Cities Film, Universal International.

**1949**
Actor: Broderick Crawford, *All the King's Men.*
Actress: Olivia de Havilland, *The Heiress.*
Sup. Actor: Dean Jagger, *Twelve O'Clock High.*
Sup. Actress: Mercedes McCambridge, *All the King's Men.*
Director: Joseph L. Mankiewicz, *Letter to Three Wives.*
Picture: *All the King's Men,* Columbia.

**1950**
Actor: Jose Ferrer, *Cyrano de Bergerac.*
Actress: Judy Holliday, *Born Yesterday.*
Sup. Actor: George Sanders, *All About Eve.*
Sup. Actress: Josephine Hull, *Harvey.*
Director: Joseph L. Mankiewicz, *All About Eve.*
Picture: *All About Eve,* 20th Century-Fox.

**1951**
Actor: Humphrey Bogart, *The African Queen.*
Actress: Vivien Leigh, *A Streetcar Named Desire.*
Sup. Actor: Karl Malden, *A Streetcar Named Desire.*
Sup. Actress: Kim Hunter, *A Streetcar Named Desire.*
Director: George Stevens, *A Place in the Sun.*
Picture: *An American in Paris,* MGM.

**1952**
Actor: Gary Cooper, *High Noon.*
Actress: Shirley Booth, *Come Back, Little Sheba.*
Sup. Actor: Anthony Quinn, *Viva Zapata!*
Sup. Actress: Gloria Grahame, *The Bad and the Beautiful.*
Director: John Ford, *The Quiet Man.*
Picture: *Greatest Show on Earth,* C.B. DeMille, Paramount.

**1953**
Actor: William Holden, *Stalag 17.*
Actress: Audrey Hepburn, *Roman Holiday.*
Sup. Actor: Frank Sinatra, *From Here to Eternity.*
Sup. Actress: Donna Reed, *From Here to Eternity.*
Director: Fred Zinnemann, *From Here to Eternity.*
Picture: *From Here to Eternity,* Columbia.

**1954**
Actor: Marlon Brando, *On the Waterfront.*
Actress: Grace Kelly, *The Country Girl.*
Sup. Actor: Edmond O'Brien, *The Barefoot Contessa.*
Sup. Actress: Eva Marie Saint, *On the Waterfront.*
Director: Elia Kazan, *On the Waterfront.*
Picture: *On the Waterfront,* Horizon-American, Colum.

**1955**
Actor: Ernest Borgnine, *Marty.*
Actress: Anna Magnani, *The Rose Tattoo.*
Sup. Actor: Jack Lemmon, *Mister Roberts.*
Sup. Actress: Jo Van Fleet, *East of Eden.*
Director: Delbert Mann, *Marty.*
Picture: *Marty,* Hecht and Lancaster's Steven Prods., U.A.

**1956**
Actor: Yul Brynner, *The King and I.*
Actress: Ingrid Bergman, *Anastasia.*
Sup. Actor: Anthony Quinn, *Lust for Life.*
Sup. Actress: Dorothy Malone, *Written on the Wind.*
Director: George Stevens, *Giant.*
Picture: *Around the World in 80 Days,* Michael Todd, U.A.
**1957**
Actor: Alec Guinness, *The Bridge on the River Kwai.*
Actress: Joanne Woodward, *The Three Faces of Eve.*
Sup. Actor: Red Buttons, *Sayonara.*
Sup. Actress: Miyoshi Umeki, *Sayonara.*
Director: David Lean, *The Bridge on the River Kwai.*
Picture: *The Bridge on the River Kwai,* Columbia.
**1958**
Actor: David Niven, *Separate Tables.*
Actress: Susan Hayward, *I Want to Live.*
Sup. Actor: Burl Ives, *The Big Country.*
Sup. Actress: Wendy Hiller, *Separate Tables.*
Director: Vincente Minnelli, *Gigi.*
Picture: *Gigi,* Arthur Freed Production, MGM.
**1959**
Actor: Charlton Heston, *Ben-Hur.*
Actress: Simone Signoret, *Room at the Top.*
Sup. Actor: Hugh Griffith, *Ben-Hur.*
Sup. Actress: Shelley Winters, *Diary of Anne Frank.*
Director: William Wyler, *Ben-Hur.*
Picture: *Ben-Hur,* MGM.
**1960**
Actor: Burt Lancaster, *Elmer Gantry.*
Actress: Elizabeth Taylor, *Butterfield 8.*
Sup. Actor: Peter Ustinov, *Spartacus.*
Sup. Actress: Shirley Jones, *Elmer Gantry.*
Director: Billy Wilder, *The Apartment.*
Picture: *The Apartment,* Mirisch Co., U.A.
**1961**
Actor: Maximilian Schell, *Judgment at Nuremberg.*
Actress: Sophia Loren, *Two Women.*
Sup. Actor: George Chakiris, *West Side Story.*
Sup. Actress: Rita Moreno, *West Side Story.*
Director: Jerome Robbins, Robert Wise, *West Side Story.*
Picture: *West Side Story,* United Artists.
**1962**
Actor: Gregory Peck, *To Kill a Mockingbird.*
Actress: Anne Bancroft, *The Miracle Worker.*
Sup. Actor: Ed Begley, *Sweet Bird of Youth.*
Sup. Actress: Patty Duke, *The Miracle Worker.*
Director: David Lean, *Lawrence of Arabia.*
Picture: *Lawrence of Arabia,* Columbia.
**1963**
Actor: Sidney Poitier, *Lilies of the Field.*
Actress: Patricia Neal, *Hud.*
Sup. Actor: Melvyn Douglas, *Hud.*
Sup. Actress: Margaret Rutherford, *The V.I.P.s.*
Director: Tony Richardson, *Tom Jones.*
Picture: *Tom Jones,* Woodfall Prod., UA-Lopert Pictures.
**1964**
Actor: Rex Harrison, *My Fair Lady.*
Actress: Julie Andrews, *Mary Poppins.*
Sup. Actor: Peter Ustinov, *Topkapi.*
Sup. Actress: Lila Kedrova, *Zorba the Greek.*
Director: George Cukor, *My Fair Lady.*
Picture: *My Fair Lady,* Warner Bros.
**1965**
Actor: Lee Marvin, *Cat Ballou.*
Actress: Julie Christie, *Darling.*
Sup. Actor: Martin Balsam, *A Thousand Clowns.*
Sup. Actress: Shelley Winters, *A Patch of Blue.*
Director: Robert Wise, *The Sound of Music.*
Picture: *The Sound of Music,* 20th Century-Fox.
**1966**
Actor: Paul Scofield, *A Man for All Seasons.*
Actress: Elizabeth Taylor, *Who's Afraid of Virginia Woolf?*
Sup. Actor: Walter Matthau, *The Fortune Cookie.*
Sup. Actress: Sandy Dennis, *Who's Afraid of Virginia Woolf?*
Director: Fred Zinnemann, *A Man for All Seasons.*
Picture: *A Man for All Seasons,* Columbia.
**1967**
Actor: Rod Steiger, *In the Heat of the Night.*
Actress: Katharine Hepburn, *Guess Who's Coming to Dinner.*
Sup. Actor: George Kennedy, *Cool Hand Luke.*
Sup. Actress: Estelle Parsons, *Bonnie and Clyde.*
Director: Mike Nichols, *The Graduate.*
Picture: *In the Heat of the Night.*
**1968**
Actor: Cliff Robertson, *Charly.*
Actress: Katharine Hepburn, *The Lion in Winter;* Barbra
Streisand, *Funny Girl* (tie).
Sup. Actor: Jack Albertson, *The Subject Was Roses.*

Sup. Actress: Ruth Gordon, *Rosemary's Baby.*
Director: Sir Carol Reed, *Oliver!*
Picture: *Oliver!*
**1969**
Actor: John Wayne, *True Grit.*
Actress: Maggie Smith, *The Prime of Miss Jean Brodie.*
Sup. Actor: Gig Young, *They Shoot Horses, Don't They?*
Sup. Actress: Goldie Hawn, *Cactus Flower.*
Director: John Schlesinger, *Midnight Cowboy.*
Picture: *Midnight Cowboy.*
**1970**
Actor: George C. Scott, *Patton* (refused).
Actress: Glenda Jackson, *Women in Love.*
Sup. Actor: John Mills, *Ryan's Daughter.*
Sup. Actress: Helen Hayes, *Airport.*
Director: Franklin Schaffner, *Patton.*
Picture: *Patton.*
**1971**
Actor: Gene Hackman, *The French Connection.*
Actress: Jane Fonda, *Klute.*
Sup. Actor: Ben Johnson, *The Last Picture Show.*
Sup. Actress: Cloris Leachman, *The Last Picture Show.*
Director: William Friedkin, *The French Connection.*
Picture: *The French Connection.*
**1972**
Actor: Marlon Brando, *The Godfather* (refused).
Actress: Liza Minnelli, *Cabaret.*
Sup. Actor: Joel Grey, *Cabaret.*
Sup. Actress: Eileen Heckart, *Butterflies are Free.*
Director: Bob Fosse, *Cabaret.*
Picture: *The Godfather.*
**1973**
Actor: Jack Lemmon, *Save the Tiger.*
Actress: Glenda Jackson, *A Touch of Class.*
Sup. Actor: John Houseman, *The Paper Chase.*
Sup. Actress: Tatum O'Neal, *Paper Moon.*
Director: George Roy Hill, *The Sting.*
Picture: *The Sting.*
**1974**
Actor: Art Carney, *Harry and Tonto.*
Actress: Ellen Burstyn, *Alice Doesn't Live Here Anymore.*
Sup. Actor: Robert DeNiro, *The Godfather, Part II.*
Sup. Actress: Ingrid Bergman, *Murder on the Orient Express.*
Director: Francis Ford Coppola, *The Godfather, Part II.*
Picture: *The Godfather, Part II.*
**1975**
Actor: Jack Nicholson, *One Flew Over the Cuckoo's Nest.*
Actress: Louise Fletcher, *One Flew Over the Cuckoo's Nest.*
Sup. Actor: George Burns, *The Sunshine Boys.*
Sup. Actress: Lee Grant, *Shampoo.*
Director: Milos Forman, *One Flew Over the Cuckoo's Nest.*
Picture: *One Flew Over the Cuckoo's Nest.*
**1976**
Actor: Peter Finch, *Network.*
Actress: Faye Dunaway, *Network.*
Sup. Actor: Jason Robards, *All the President's Men.*
Sup. Actress: Beatrice Straight, *Network.*
Director: John G. Avildsen, *Rocky.*
Picture: *Rocky.*
**1977**
Actor: Richard Dreyfuss, *The Goodbye Girl.*
Actress: Diane Keaton, *Annie Hall.*
Sup. Actor: Jason Robards, *Julia.*
Sup. Actress: Vanessa Redgrave, *Julia.*
Director: Woody Allen, *Annie Hall.*
Picture: *Annie Hall.*
**1978**
Actor: Jon Voight, *Coming Home.*
Actress: Jane Fonda, *Coming Home.*
Sup. Actor: Christopher Walken, *The Deer Hunter.*
Sup. Actress: Maggie Smith, *California Suite.*
Director: Michael Cimino, *The Deer Hunter.*
Picture: *The Deer Hunter.*
**1979**
Actor: Dustin Hoffman, *Kramer vs. Kramer.*
Actress: Sally Field, *Norma Rae.*
Sup. Actor: Melvyn Douglas, *Being There.*
Sup. Actress: Meryl Streep, *Kramer vs. Kramer.*
Director: Robert Benton, *Kramer vs. Kramer.*
Picture: *Kramer vs. Kramer.*
**1980**
Actor: Robert DeNiro, *Raging Bull.*
Actress: Sissy Spacek, *Coal Miner's Daughter.*
Sup. Actor: Timothy Hutton, *Ordinary People.*
Sup. Actress: Mary Steenburgen, *Melvin & Howard.*
Director: Robert Redford, *Ordinary People.*
Picture: *Ordinary People.*
**1981**
Actor: Henry Fonda, *On Golden Pond.*

Actress: Katharine Hepburn, *On Golden Pond.*
Sup. Actor: John Gielgud, *Arthur.*
Sup. Actress: Maureen Stapleton, *Reds.*
Director: Warren Beatty, *Reds.*
Picture: *Chariots of Fire.*

**1982**
Actor: Ben Kingsley, *Gandhi.*
Actress: Meryl Streep, *Sophie's Choice.*
Sup. Actor: Louis Gossett, Jr., *An Officer and a Gentleman.*
Sup. Actress: Jessica Lange, *Tootsie.*
Director: Richard Attenborough, *Gandhi.*
Picture: *Gandhi.*

**1983**
Actor: Robert Duvall, *Tender Mercies.*
Actress: Shirley MacLaine, *Terms of Endearment.*
Supporting Actor: Jack Nicholson, *Terms of Endearment.*
Supporting Actress: Linda Hunt, *The Year of Living Dangerously.*
Director: James L. Brooks, *Terms of Endearment.*
Picture: *Terms of Endearment.*

**1984**
Actor: F. Murray Abraham, *Amadeus.*
Actress: Sally Field, *Places in the Heart.*
Supporting Actor: Haing S. Ngor, *The Killing Fields.*
Supporting Actress: Peggy Ashcroft, *A Passage to India.*
Director: Milos Forman, *Amadeus.*
Picture: *Amadeus.*

**1985**
Actor: William Hurt, *Kiss of the Spider Woman.*
Actress: Geraldine Page, *The Trip to Bountiful.*
Supporting Actor: Don Ameche, *Cocoon.*
Supporting Actress: Anjelica Huston, *Prizzi's Honor.*
Director: Sydney Pollack, *Out of Africa.*
Picture: *Out of Africa.*

**1986**
Actor: Paul Newman, *The Color of Money.*
Actress: Marlee Matlin, *Children of a Lesser God.*
Supporting Actor: Michael Caine, *Hannah and Her Sisters.*
Supporting Actress: Dianne Wiest, *Hannah and Her Sisters.*
Director: Oliver Stone, *Platoon.*
Picture: *Platoon.*

**1987**
Actor: Michael Douglas, *Wall Street.*
Actress: Cher, *Moonstruck.*
Supporting Actor: Sean Connery, *The Untouchables.*
Supporting Actress: Olympia Dukakis, *Moonstruck.*
Director: Bernardo Bertolucci, *The Last Emperor.*
Picture: *The Last Emperor.*

**1988**
Actor: Dustin Hoffman, *Rain Man.*
Actress: Jodie Foster, *The Accused.*
Supporting Actor: Kevin Kline, *A Fish Called Wanda.*
Supporting Actress: Geena Davis, *The Accidental Tourist.*
Director: Barry Levinson, *Rain Man.*
Picture: *Rain Man.*

**1989**
Actor: Daniel Day-Lewis, *My Left Foot.*
Actress: Jessica Tandy, *Driving Miss Daisy.*
Supporting Actor: Denzel Washington, *Glory.*
Supporting Actress: Brenda Fricker, *My Left Foot.*
Director: Oliver Stone, *Born on the Fourth of July.*
Picture: *Driving Miss Daisy.*

**1990**
Actor: Jeremy Irons, *Reversal of Fortune.*
Actress: Kathy Bates, *Misery.*
Supporting Actor: Joe Pesci, *Goodfellas.*
Supporting Actress: Whoopi Goldberg, *Ghost.*
Director: Kevin Costner, *Dances With Wolves.*
Picture: *Dances With Wolves.*

**1991**
Actor: Anthony Hopkins, *The Silence of the Lambs.*
Actress: Jodie Foster, *The Silence of the Lambs.*
Supporting Actor: Jack Palance, *City Slickers.*
Supporting Actress: Mercedes Ruehl, *The Fisher King.*
Director: Jonathan Demme, *The Silence of the Lambs.*
Picture: *The Silence of the Lambs.*

**1992**
Picture: *Unforgiven.*
Actor: Al Pacino, *Scent of a Woman.*
Actress: Emma Thompson, *Howards End.*
Supporting Actor: Gene Hackman, *Unforgiven.*
Supporting Actress: Marisa Tomei, *My Cousin Vinny.*
Director: Clint Eastwood, *Unforgiven.*
Foreign-Language Film: *Indochine,* France
Original Screenplay: Neil Jordan, *The Crying Game.*
Adapted Screenplay: Ruth Prawer Jhabvala, *Howards End.*
Cinematography: Philippe Rousselot, *A River Runs Through It.*
Editing: Joel Cox, *Unforgiven.*
Original Score: Alan Menken, *Aladdin.*
Original Song: "Whole New World," from *Aladdin,* Alan Menken, Tim Rice.
Art Direction: Luciana Arrighi, Ian Whittaker, *Howards End.*
Costume Design: Eiko Ishioka, *Bram Stoker's Dracula.*
Makeup: Greg Cannom, Michele Burke, Matthew W. Mungle, *Bram Stoker's Dracula.*
Visual Effects: Ken Ralston, Doug Chiang, Doug Smythe, Tom Woodruff Jr., *Death Becomes Her.*
Sound: Chris Jenkins, Doug Hemphill, Mark Smith, Simon Kaye, *The Last of the Mohicans.*
Documentary Feature: *The Panama Deception.*
Documentary Short Subject: *Educating Peter.*
Short Film, Live: *Omnibus.*
Short Film, Animated: *Mona Lisa Descending a Staircase.*
Honorary Award: Federico Fellini.
Jean Hersholt Humanitarian Awards: Audrey Hepburn, Elizabeth Taylor.
Academy Award of Merit: Chadwell O'Connor.
Gordon E. Sawyer Award: Erich Kaestner.

# Grammy Awards

Source: National Academy of Recording Arts & Sciences

**1958**
Record: Domenico Modugno, *Nel Blu Dipinto Di Blu (Volare).*
Album: Henry Mancini, *The Music from Peter Gunn.*

**1959**
Record: Bobby Darin, *Mack the Knife.*
Album: Frank Sinatra, *Come Dance With Me.*

**1960**
Record: Percy Faith, *Theme From A Summer Place.*
Album: Bob Newhart, *Button Down Mind.*

**1961**
Record: Henry Mancini, *Moon River.*
Album: Judy Garland, *Judy At Carnegie Hall.*

**1962**
Record: Tony Bennett, *I Left My Heart in San Francisco.*
Album: Vaughn Meader, *The First Family.*

**1963**
Record: Henry Mancini, *The Days of Wine and Roses.*
Album: *The Barbra Streisand Album.*

**1964**
Record: Stan Getz and Astrud Gilberto, *The Girl From Ipanema.*
Album: *Getz/Gilberto.*

**1965**
Record: Herb Alpert, *A Taste Of Honey.*
Album: Frank Sinatra, *September of My Years.*

**1966**
Record: Frank Sinatra, *Strangers in the Night.*
Album: Frank Sinatra, *A Man and His Music.*

**1967**
Record: 5th Dimension, *Up, Up and Away.*
Album: The Beatles, *Sgt. Pepper's Lonely Hearts Club Band.*

**1968**
Record: Simon & Garfunkel, *Mrs. Robinson.*
Album: Glen Campbell, *By the Time I Get to Phoenix.*

**1969**
Record: 5th Dimension, *Aquarius/Let the Sunshine In.*
Album: *Blood, Sweat and Tears.*

**1970**
Record: Simon & Garfunkel, *Bridge Over Troubled Water.*
Album: *Bridge Over Troubled Water.*

**1971**
Record: Carole King, *It's Too Late.*
Album: Carole King, *Tapestry.*

**1972**
Record: Roberta Flack, *The First Time Ever I Saw Your Face.*
Album: *The Concert For Bangla Desh.*

**1973**
Record: Roberta Flack, *Killing Me Softly with His Song.*
Album: Stevie Wonder, *Innervisions.*

**1974**
Record: Olivia Newton-John, *I Honestly Love You.*
Album: Stevie Wonder, *Fulfillingness' First Finale.*

**1975**
Record: Captain & Tennille, *Love Will Keep Us Together.*
Album: Paul Simon, *Still Crazy After All These Years.*

**1976**
Record: George Benson, *This Masquerade.*
Album: Stevie Wonder, *Songs in the Key of Life.*

**1977**
Record: Eagles, *Hotel California.*
Album: Fleetwood Mac, *Rumours.*

**1978**
Record: Billy Joel, *Just the Way You Are.*
Album: Bee Gees, *Saturday Night Fever.*

**1979**
Record: The Doobie Brothers, *What a Fool Believes.*
Album: Billy Joel, *52nd Street.*

**1980**
Record: Christopher Cross, *Sailing.*
Album: Christopher Cross, *Christopher Cross.*

**1981**
Record: Kim Carnes, *Bette Davis Eyes.*
Album: John Lennon, Yoko Ono, *Double Fantasy.*

**1982**
Record: Toto, *Rosanna.*
Album: Toto, *Toto IV.*

**1983**
Record: Michael Jackson, *Beat It.*
Album: Michael Jackson, *Thriller.*

**1984**
Record: Tina Turner, *What's Love Got to Do With It.*
Album: Lionel Richie, *Can't Slow Down.*

**1985**
Record: USA for Africa, *We Are the World.*
Album: Phil Collins, *No Jacket Required.*

**1986**
Record: Steve Winwood, *Higher Love.*
Album: Paul Simon, *Graceland.*

**1987**
Record: Paul Simon, *Graceland.*
Album: U2, *The Joshua Tree.*

**1988**
Record: Bobby McFerrin, *Don't Worry, Be Happy.*
Album: George Michael, *Faith.*

**1989**
Record: Bette Midler, *Wind Beneath My Wings.*
Album: Bonnie Raitt, *Nick of Time.*

**1990**
Record: Phil Collins, *Another Day in Paradise.*
Album: Quincy Jones, *Back on the Block.*

**1991**
Record: Natalie Cole, with Nat "King" Cole, *Unforgettable.*
Album: Natalie Cole, with Nat "King" Cole, *Unforgettable.*

**1992**
Record: Eric Clapton, *Tears in Heaven.*
Album: Eric Clapton, *Unplugged.*
Song: *Tears in Heaven.*
New Artist: Arrested Development.
Female Pop Vocalist: K. D. Laing, *Constant Craving.*
Male Pop Vocalist: Eric Clapton, *Tears in Heaven.*
Duo or Group Pop Vocal: Celine Dion and Peabo Bryson, *Beauty and the Beast.*
Traditional Pop Vocalist: Tony Bennett, *Perfectly Frank.*
Pop-Musical Performance: *Beauty and the Beast,* Nuremberg Symphony Orchestra.
Female Rock Vocalist: Melissa Etheridge, *Ain't It Heavy.*
Male Rock Vocalist: Eric Clapton, *Unplugged.*
Rock Duo or Group: U2, *Achtung Baby.*
Hard Rock: Red Hot Chili Peppers, *Give It Away.*
Metal: Nine-Inch Nails, *Wish.*
Rock Instrumental Performance: Stevie Ray Vaughan and Double Trouble, *Little Wing.*
Rock Song: Eric Clapton and Jim Gordon, *Layla.*

## Newbery Medal Books

The Newbery Medal is awarded annually by the Association for Library Service to Children, a division of the American Library Association, to the author of the most distinguished contribution to American literature for children.

| Year Awarded | Book, Author |
|---|---|
| 1922 | *The Story of Mankind,* Hendrik Willem van Loon |
| 1923 | *The Voyages of Dr. Dolittle,* Hugh Lofting |
| 1924 | *The Dark Frigate,* Charles Boardman Hawes |
| 1925 | *Tales from Silver Lands,* Charles Joseph Finger |
| 1926 | *Shen of the Sea,* Arthur Bowie Chrisman |
| 1927 | *Smoky, the Cowhorse,* Will James |
| 1928 | *Gay-Neck,* Dhan Gopal Mukerji |
| 1929 | *The Trumpeter of Krakow,* Eric P. Kelly |
| 1930 | *Hitty, Her First Hundred Years,* Rachel Field |
| 1931 | *The Cat Who Went to Heaven,* Elizabeth Coatsworth |
| 1932 | *Waterless Mountain,* Laura Adams Armer |
| 1933 | *Young Fu of the Upper Yangtze,* Elizabeth Foreman Lewis |
| 1934 | *Invincible Louisa,* Cornelia Lynde Meigs |
| 1935 | *Dobry,* Monica Shannon |
| 1936 | *Caddie Woodlawn,* Carol Ryrie Brink |
| 1937 | *Roller Skates,* Ruth Sawyer |
| 1938 | *The White Stag,* Kate Seredy |
| 1939 | *Thimble Summer,* Elizabeth Enright |
| 1940 | *Daniel Boone,* James Daugherty |
| 1941 | *Call It Courage,* Armstrong Sperry |
| 1942 | *The Matchlock Gun,* Walter D. Edmonds |
| 1943 | *Adam of the Road,* Elizabeth Janet Gray |
| 1944 | *Johnny Tremain,* Esther Forbes |
| 1945 | *Rabbit Hill,* Robert Lawson |
| 1946 | *Strawberry Girl,* Lois Lenski |
| 1947 | *Miss Hickory,* Carolyn S. Bailey |
| 1948 | *Twenty-One Balloons,* William Pène Du Bois |
| 1949 | *King of the Wind,* Marguerite Henry |
| 1950 | *The Door in the Wall,* Marguerite de Angeli |
| 1951 | *Amos Fortune, Free Man,* Elizabeth Yates |
| 1952 | *Ginger Pye,* Eleanor Estes |
| 1953 | *Secret of the Andes,* Ann Nolan Clark |
| 1954 | *... And Now Miguel,* Joseph Krumgold |
| 1955 | *The Wheel on the School,* Meindert DeJong |
| 1956 | *Carry On, Mr. Bowditch,* Jean Lee Latham |
| 1957 | *Miracles on Maple Hill,* Virginia Sorensen |
| 1958 | *Rifles for Watie,* Harold Keith |

| Year Awarded | Book, Author |
|---|---|
| 1959 | *The Witch of Blackbird Pond,* Elizabeth George Speare |
| 1960 | *Onion John,* Joseph Krumgold |
| 1961 | *Island of the Blue Dolphins,* Scott O'Dell |
| 1962 | *The Bronze Bow,* Elizabeth George Speare |
| 1963 | *A Wrinkle in Time,* Madeleine L'Engle |
| 1964 | *It's Like This, Cat,* Emily Cheney Neville |
| 1965 | *Shadow of a Bull,* Maja Wojciechowska |
| 1966 | *I, Juan de Pareja,* Elizabeth Borton de Trevino |
| 1967 | *Up a Road Slowly,* Irene Hunt |
| 1968 | *From the Mixed-Up Files of Mrs. Basil E. Frankweiler,* E. L. Konigsburg |
| 1969 | *The High King,* Lloyd Alexander |
| 1970 | *Sounder,* William H. Armstrong |
| 1971 | *The Summer of the Swans,* Betsy Byars |
| 1972 | *Mrs. Frisby and the Rats of NIMH,* Robert C. O'Brien |
| 1973 | *Julie of the Wolves,* Jean George |
| 1974 | *The Slave Dancer,* Paula Fox |
| 1975 | *M. C. Higgins the Great,* Virginia Hamilton |
| 1976 | *Grey King,* Susan Cooper |
| 1977 | *Roll of Thunder, Hear My Cry,* Mildred D. Taylor |
| 1978 | *Bridge to Terabithia,* Katherine Paterson |
| 1979 | *The Westing Game,* Ellen Raskin |
| 1980 | *A Gathering of Days,* Joan Blos |
| 1981 | *Jacob Have I Loved,* Katherine Paterson |
| 1982 | *A Visit to William Blake's Inn: Poems for Innocent and Experienced Travelers,* Nancy Willard |
| 1983 | *Dicey's Song,* Cynthia Voigt |
| 1984 | *Dear Mr. Henshaw,* Beverly Cleary |
| 1985 | *The Hero and the Crown,* Robin McKinley |
| 1986 | *Sarah, Plain and Tall,* Patricia MacLachlan |
| 1987 | *The Whipping Boy,* Sid Fleischman |
| 1988 | *Lincoln: A Photobiography,* Russell Freedman |
| 1989 | *Joyful Noise: Poems for Two Voices,* Paul Fleischman |
| 1990 | *Number the Stars,* Lois Lowry |
| 1991 | *Maniac Magee,* Jerry Spinelli |
| 1992 | *Shiloh,* Phyllis Reynolds Naylor |
| 1993 | *Missing May,* Cynthia Ryland |

# NOTED PERSONALITIES

## Widely Known Americans of the Present

Statesmen, journalists, authors of nonfiction, and other prominent persons not listed in other categories; as of mid-1993.

| Name (Birthplace) | Birthdate |
|---|---|
| Ailes, Roger (Knoxville, Tenn.) | 7/3/40 |
| Albright, Madeleine (Prague, Czech.) | 5/15/37 |
| Angelou, Maya (St. Louis, Mo.) | 4/4/28 |
| Arledge, Roone (Forest Hills, N.Y.) | 7/8/31 |
| Anderson, Jack (Long Beach, Cal.) | 10/19/22 |
| Annenberg, Walter H. (Milwaukee, Wis.) | 1908 |
| Armstrong, Neil (Wapakoneta, Oh.) | 8/5/30 |
| Ash, Mary Kay (Hot Wells, Tex.) | — |
| Aspin, Les (Milwaukee, Wis.) | 7/21/38 |
| Babbitt, Bruce (Los Angeles, Cal.) | 6/27/38 |
| Baker, James A. (Houston, Tex.) | 4/28/30 |
| Baker, Russell (Loudoun Co., Va.) | 8/14/25 |
| Barry, Dave (Armonk, N.Y.) | 7/3/47 |
| Barthelmy, Sidney K. (New Orleans, La.) | 3/17/42 |
| Bennett, William J. (Salem, Oh.) | 5/4/44 |
| Bentsen, Lloyd (Mission, Tex.) | 2/11/21 |
| Biden, Joseph R. Jr. (Scranton, Pa.) | 11/20/42 |
| Blackmun, Harry (Nashville, Ill.) | 11/12/08 |
| Blass, Bill (Ft. Wayne, Ind.) | 6/22/22 |
| Bloom, Harold (New York, N.Y.) | 7/11/30 |
| Bombeck, Erma (Dayton, Oh.) | 2/21/27 |
| Boorstin, Daniel (Atlanta, Ga.) | 10/1/14 |
| Boxer, Barbara (Brooklyn, N.Y.) | 11/11/40 |
| Bradley, Ben (Boston, Mass.) | 8/26/21 |
| Bradley, Bill (Crystal City, Mo.) | 7/28/43 |
| Bradley, Ed (Philadelphia, Pa.) | 6/22/41 |
| Bradley, Thomas (Calvert, Tex.) | 12/29/17 |
| Braun, Carol Moseley (Chicago, Ill.) | 8/16/47 |
| Brennan, William J. (Newark, N.J.) | 4/25/06 |
| Breslin, Jimmy (Jamaica, N.Y.) | 10/17/30 |
| Brinkley, Christie (Monroe, Mich.) | 2/2/53 |
| Brinkley, David (Wilmington, N.C.) | 7/10/20 |
| Broder, David (Chicago Heights, Ill.) | 9/11/29 |
| Brody, Jane (Brooklyn, N.Y.) | 5/19/41 |
| Brokaw, Tom (Webster, S. Dak.) | 2/6/40 |
| Brothers, Joyce (New York, N.Y.) | 9/20/28 |
| Brown, Helen Gurley (Green Forest, Ark.) | 2/18/22 |
| Brown, Jerry (San Francisco, Cal.) | 4/7/38 |
| Brown, Ron (Washington, D.C.) | 8/1/41 |
| Buchanan, Pat (Washington, D.C.) | 11/2/38 |
| Buchwald, Art (Mt. Vernon, N.Y.) | 10/20/25 |
| Buckley, William F. (New York, N.Y.) | 11/24/25 |
| Buffet, Warren (Omaha, Neb.) | 8/30/30 |
| Bumpers, Dale (Charleston, Ark.) | 8/12/25 |
| Buscaglia, Leo (Los Angeles, Cal.) | 3/31/24 |
| Bush, Barbara (Rye, N.Y.) | 6/8/25 |
| Byrd, Robert (N. Wilkesboro, N.C.) | 11/20/17 |
| Canby, Vincent (Chicago, Ill.) | 7/27/24 |
| Carter, Jimmy (Plains, Ga.) | 10/1/24 |
| Carter, Rosalynn (Plains, Ga.) | 8/18/27 |
| Chancellor, John (Chicago, Ill.) | 7/14/27 |
| Child, Julia (Pasadena, Cal.) | 8/15/12 |
| Chisholm, Shirley (Brooklyn, N.Y.) | 11/30/24 |
| Christopher, Warren (Scranton, Pa.) | 10/27/25 |
| Chung, Connie (Washington, D.C.) | 8/20/46 |
| Claiborne, Craig (Sunflower, Miss.) | 9/4/20 |
| Claiborne, Liz (Brussels, Belg.) | 3/31/29 |
| Clinton, Bill (Hope, Ark.) | 8/19/46 |
| Clinton, Chelsea (Little Rock, Ark.) | 2/27/80 |
| Clinton, Hillary Rodham (Chicago, Ill.) | 10/26/47 |
| Collins, Martha (Shelby Cty, Ky.) | 12/7/36 |
| Commager, Henry Steele (Pittsburgh, Pa.) | 10/25/02 |
| Cooney, Joan Ganz (Phoenix, Ariz.) | 10/30/29 |
| Cosell, Howard (Winston-Salem, N.C.) | 3/25/20 |
| Couric, Katie (Washington, D.C.) | 1/7/57 |
| Crawford, Cindy (DeKalb, Ill.) | — |
| Crist, Judith (New York, N.Y.) | 2/20/66 |
| Cronkite, Walter (St. Joseph, Mo.) | 5/22/22 |
| Cuomo, Mario (Queens, N.Y.) | 11/4/16 |
| Daley, Richard M. (Chicago, Ill.) | 6/15/32 |
| D'Amato, Alfonse M. (Brooklyn, N.Y.) | 4/24/42 |
| Deford, Frank (Baltimore, Md.) | 8/1/37 |
| Dellums, Ronald (Oakland, Cal.) | 12/16/38 |
| Dershowitz, Alan (Brooklyn, N.Y.) | 11/24/35 |
| Dingell, John D. Jr. (Colorado Spngs., Col.) | 9/1/38 |
| Dinkins, David (Trenton, N.J.) | 7/8/26 |
| Dixon, Sharon Pratt (Washington, D.C.) | 7/10/27 |
| Dodd, Christopher (Willimantic, Conn.) | 1/31/44 |
| Dole, Elizabeth (Salisbury, N.C.) | 5/27/44 |
| Dole, Robert (Russell, Kan.) | 7/29/36 |
| Domenici, Pete (Albuquerque, N.M.) | 7/22/23 |
| Donaldson, Sam (El Paso, Tex.) | 5/7/32 |
|  | 3/11/34 |

| Name (Birthplace) | Birthdate |
|---|---|
| Drew, Elizabeth (Cincinnati, Oh.) | 11/16/35 |
| Dukakis, Michael S. (Boston, Mass.) | 11/3/33 |
| Edelman, Marian Wright (Bennetsville, S.C.) | 6/6/39 |
| Eisner, Michael (New York, N.Y.) | 3/7/42 |
| Ephron, Nora (New York, N.Y.) | 5/19/41 |
| Evangelista, Linda (St. Catherine's, Canada) | 5/10/65 |
| Falwell, Jerry (Lynchburg, Va.) | 8/11/33 |
| Feinstein, Dianne (San Francisco, Cal.) | 6/22/33 |
| Ferraro, Geraldine (Newburgh, N.Y.) | 8/26/35 |
| Florio, James J. (New York, N.Y.) | 8/29/37 |
| Foley, Thomas S. (Spokane, Wash.) | 3/6/29 |
| Foote, Shelby (Greenville, Miss.) | 11/17/16 |
| Ford, Betty (Chicago, Ill.) | 4/8/18 |
| Ford, Gerald R. (Omaha, Neb.) | 7/14/13 |
| Frank, Barney (Bayonne, N.J.) | 3/31/40 |
| Frankel, Max (Gera, Germany) | 4/3/30 |
| Friedan, Betty (Peoria, Ill.) | 2/4/21 |
| Friedman, Milton (Brooklyn, N.Y.) | 7/31/12 |
| Galbraith, John Kenneth (Ontario, Can.) | 10/15/08 |
| Gates, William (Seattle, Wash.) | 10/28/55 |
| Gephardt, Richard (St. Louis, Mo.) | 1/31/41 |
| Gergen, David R. (Durham, N.C.) | 5/9/42 |
| Gibson, Charles (Evanston, Ill.) | 3/9/43 |
| Gingrich, Newt (Harrisburg, Pa.) | 6/17/43 |
| Ginsberg, Allen (Paterson, N.J.) | 6/3/21 |
| Ginsburg, Ruth Bader (Brooklyn, N.Y.) | 3/15/33 |
| Glenn, John (Cambridge, Oh.) | 7/18/21 |
| Goldwater, Barry M. (Phoenix, Ariz.) | 1/1/09 |
| Goodman, Ellen (Newton, Mass.) | 4/11/41 |
| Gore, Al (Washington, D.C.) | 3/31/48 |
| Gore, Tipper (Washington, D.C.) | 8/19/48 |
| Gottlieb, Robert A. (New York) | 4/9/31 |
| Gould, Stephen Jay (New York, N.Y.) | 9/10/41 |
| Graham, Billy (Charlotte, N.C.) | 11/7/18 |
| Graham, Donald (Baltimore, Md.) | 4/22/45 |
| Graham, Katharine (New York, N.Y.) | 6/16/17 |
| Gramm, Phil (Ft. Bennington, Ga.) | 7/8/42 |
| Gray, William H. 3d (Baton Rouge, La.) | 8/20/41 |
| Greene, Bob (Columbus, Oh.) | 5/10/47 |
| Greenfield, Meg (Seattle, Wash.) | 12/27/30 |
| Greenspan, Alan (New York, N.Y.) | 3/6/26 |
| Gumbel, Bryant (New Orleans, La.) | 9/29/48 |
| Halberstam, David (New York, N.Y.) | 4/10/34 |
| Harkin, Tom (Cumming, Ia.) | 11/19/39 |
| Harvey, Paul (Tulsa, Okla.) | 9/4/18 |
| Hatfield, Mark O. (Dallas, Ore.) | 7/12/22 |
| Heflin, Howell (Poulan, Ga.) | 6/19/21 |
| Hefner, Hugh (Chicago, Ill.) | 4/9/26 |
| Helms, Jesse (Monroe, N.C.) | 10/18/21 |
| Helmsley, Leona (New York, N.Y.) | c.1920 |
| Heloise (Waco, Tex.) | 4/15/51 |
| Hollings, Ernest (Charleston, S.C.) | 1/1/22 |
| Iacocca, Lee A. (Allentown, Pa.) | 10/15/24 |
| Iman (Somalia, Ethiopia) | 7/25/55 |
| Inouye, Daniel K. (Honolulu, Ha.) | 9/7/24 |
| Jackson, Jesse (Greenville, S.C.) | 10/8/41 |
| Jennings, Peter (Toronto, Ont.) | 8/29/38 |
| Johnson, Lady Bird (Karnack, Tex.) | 12/22/12 |
| Jordan, Barbara (Houston, Tex.) | 2/21/36 |
| Kael, Pauline (Petaluma, Calif.) | 6/19/19 |
| Karan, Donna (Forest Hills, N.Y.) | 10/2/48 |
| Kassebaum, Nancy (Topeka, Kan.) | 7/29/32 |
| Keillor, Garrison (Anoka, Minn.) | 8/7/42 |
| Kemp, Jack (Los Angeles, Cal.) | 7/13/35 |
| Kennedy, Anthony (Sacramento, Cal.) | 7/23/36 |
| Kennedy, Edward M. (Brookline, Mass.) | 2/22/32 |
| Kennedy, Rose (Boston, Mass.) | 7/22/90 |
| Kerr, Walter (Evanston, Ill.) | 7/8/13 |
| King, Coretta Scott (Marion, Ala.) | 4/27/27 |
| King, Don (Cleveland, Oh.) | 12/6/32 |
| King, Larry (Brooklyn, N.Y.) | 11/19/34 |
| Kinsley, Michael (Detroit, Mich.) | 3/9/51 |
| Kirkland, Lane (Camden, S.C.) | 3/12/22 |
| Kirkpatrick, Jeane (Duncan, Okla.) | 11/19/26 |
| Kissinger, Henry (Fuerth, Germany) | 5/27/23 |
| Klein, Calvin (New York, N.Y.) | 11/19/42 |
| Koch, Edward I. (New York, N.Y.) | 12/12/24 |
| Koop, C. Everett (Brooklyn, N.Y.) | 10/14/16 |
| Koppel, Ted (Lancashire, Eng.) | 2/8/40 |
| Kryzyzewski, Mike (Chicago, Ill.) | 2/13/47 |
| Kuhn, Maggie (Buffalo, N.Y.) | 1905 |
| Kunstler, William (New York, N.Y.) | 7/7/19 |

| Name (Birthplace) | Birthdate |
|---|---|
| Kuralt, Charles (Wilmington, N.C.) | 9/10/34 |
| Landers, Ann (Sioux City, Ia.) | 7/4/18 |
| Lauder, Estee (New York, N.Y.) | 9/1/08 |
| Lauren, Ralph (Bronx, N.Y.) | 10/14/39 |
| Leahy, Patrick (Montpelier, Vt.) | 3/31/40 |
| Lear, Frances (Hudson, N.Y.) | 7/14/23 |
| Lear, Norman (New Haven, Conn.) | 7/27/22 |
| Lehrer, Jim (Wichita, Kan.) | 5/19/34 |
| Lewis, Anthony (New York, N.Y.) | 3/27/27 |
| Limbaugh, Rush (Cape Girardeau, Mo.) | 1/12/41 |
| Lindbergh, Anne Morrow (Englewood, N.J.) | 1906 |
| Lorenzo, Frank (New York, N.Y.) | 5/19/40 |
| Lott, Trent (Grenada, Miss.) | 10/9/41 |
| Lugar, Richard G. (Indianapolis, Ind.) | 4/4/32 |
| Lukas, J. Anthony (New York, N.Y.) | 4/25/33 |
| Lunden, Joan (Sacramento, Calif.) | 9/19/50 |
| MacNeil, Robert (Montreal, Que.) | 1/19/31 |
| Manchester, William (Attleboro, Mass.) | 4/1/22 |
| Martin, Lynn (Evanston, Ill.) | 12/26/39 |
| Maslin, Janet (New York, N.Y.) | 8/12/49 |
| McClendon, Sarah (Tyler, Tex.) | 7/8/10 |
| McGovern, George (Avon, S.D.) | 7/19/22 |
| McNamara, Robert (San Francisco, Cal.) | 6/9/16 |
| Metzenbaum, Howard (Cleveland, Oh.) | 6/4/17 |
| Michel, Robert H. (Peoria, Ill.) | 3/2/23 |
| Mikulski, Barbara (Baltimore, Md.) | 7/20/36 |
| Mitchell, George (Waterville, Me.) | 8/20/33 |
| Mondale, Walter (Ceylon, Minn.) | 1/5/28 |
| Mosbacher, Robert (Mt. Vernon, N.Y.) | 3/11/27 |
| Moyers, Bill (Hugo, Okla.) | 6/5/34 |
| Moynihan, Daniel P. (Tulsa, Okla.) | 3/16/27 |
| Mudd, Roger (Washington, D.C.) | 2/9/28 |
| Murray, Patty (Seattle, Wash.) | 10/11/50 |
| Nader, Ralph (Winsted, Conn.) | 2/27/34 |
| Nidetch, Jean (Brooklyn, N.Y.) | 10/12/23 |
| Nixon, Richard (Yorba Linda, Cal.) | 1/9/13 |
| North, Oliver (San Antonio, Tex.) | 10/7/43 |
| Norton, Eleanor Holmes (Washington, D.C.) | 6/13/37 |
| Novak, Robert (Joliet, Ill.) | 2/26/31 |
| Novello, Antonia (Fajardo, P.R.) | 8/23/44 |
| Nunn, Sam (Perry, Ga.) | 9/8/38 |
| O'Connor, Cardinal John (Phila., Pa.) | 1/15/20 |
| O'Connor, Sandra Day (nr. Duncan, Ariz.) | 3/26/30 |
| Onassis, Jacqueline (Southampton, N.Y.) | 7/28/29 |
| O'Neill, Thomas P. (Cambridge, Mass.) | 12/9/12 |
| Osgood, Charles (New York, N.Y.) | 1/8/33 |
| Packwood, Bob (Portland, Ore.) | 9/11/32 |
| Paglia, Camille (Endicott, N.Y.) | — |
| Panetta, Leon F. (Monterey, Cal.) | 6/28/38 |
| Pauley, Jane (Indianapolis, Ind.) | 10/31/50 |
| Pauling, Linus (Portland, Ore.) | 2/28/01 |
| Perot, H. Ross (Texarkana, Tex.) | 6/27/30 |
| Phillips, Kevin (New York, N.Y.) | 11/30/40 |
| Pickens, T. Boone (Holdenville, Okla.) | 5/22/28 |
| Pickering, Thomas (Orange, N.J.) | 11/5/31 |
| Plimpton, George (New York, N.Y.) | 3/18/27 |
| Podhoretz, Norman (New York, N.Y.) | 1/16/30 |
| Poussaint, Alvin F. (New York, N.Y.) | 5/15/34 |
| Powell, Colin (New York, N.Y.) | 4/5/37 |
| Quayle, Dan (Indianapolis, Ind.) | 2/4/47 |
| Quinn, Jane Bryant (Niagara Falls, N.Y.) | 2/5/39 |
| Rangel, Charles (New York, N.Y.) | 6/11/30 |
| Rather, Dan (Wharton, Tex.) | 10/31/31 |
| Reagan, Nancy (New York, N.Y.) | 7/6/23 |
| Reagan, Ronald (Tampico, Ill.) | 2/6/11 |
| Rehnquist, William (Milwaukee, Wis.) | 10/1/24 |
| Reich, Robert B. (Scranton, Pa.) | 6/24/46 |
| Reno, Janet (Miami, Fla.) | 7/21/38 |
| Rich, Frank (Washington, D.C.) | 6/2/49 |
| Richards, Ann (Waco, Tex.) | 9/3/33 |
| Ride, Sally K. (Encino, Calif.) | 1952 |
| Roberts, Oral (nr. Ada, Okla.) | 1/24/18 |
| Robertson, Pat (Lexington, Va.) | 3/22/30 |
| Rockefeller, David (New York, N.Y.) | 6/12/15 |
| Rockefeller, John D. 4th "Jay" (New York, N.Y.) | 6/18/37 |
| Rockefeller, Laurance S. (New York, N.Y.) | 5/26/10 |

| Name (Birthplace) | Birthdate |
|---|---|
| Rooney, Andy (Albany, N.Y.) | 1/14/19 |
| Rostenkowski, Dan (Chicago, Ill.) | 1/2/28 |
| Rukeyser, Louis (New York, N.Y.) | 1/30/33 |
| Safer, Morley (Toronto, Ontario) | 11/8/31 |
| Safire, William (New York, N.Y.) | 12/17/29 |
| Sagan, Carl (New York, N.Y.) | 11/9/34 |
| Salk, Jonas (New York, N.Y.) | 10/28/14 |
| Sawyer, Diane (Glasgow, Ky.) | 12/22/45 |
| Scalia, Antonin (Trenton, N.J.) | 3/11/36 |
| Schlesinger, Arthur Jr. (Columbus, Oh.) | 10/15/17 |
| Schroeder, Patricia (Portland, Ore.) | 7/30/40 |
| Schuller, Robert (Alton, Ia.) | 9/16/26 |
| Schwarzkopf, H. Norman (Trenton, N.J.) | 8/22/34 |
| Scott, Willard (Alexandria, Va.) | 3/7/34 |
| Scowcroft, Brent (Ogden, Ut.) | 3/19/25 |
| Seaborg, Glenn T. (Ishpeming, Mich.) | 4/19/12 |
| Shalala, Donna E. (Cleveland, Oh.) | 2/14/41 |
| Shanker, Albert (New York, N.Y.) | 9/14/28 |
| Shaw, Bernard (Chicago, Ill.) | 1940 |
| Shriver, Maria (Chicago, Ill.) | 11/6/55 |
| Shultz, George P. (New York, N.Y.) | 12/13/20 |
| Silver, Joan Micklin (Omaha, Neb.) | 5/25/35 |
| Silverstein, Shel (Chicago, Ill.) | 1932 |
| Simmons, Richard (New Orleans, La.) | 7/12/48 |
| Simon, Paul (Eugene, Ore.) | 11/29/28 |
| Simpson, Alan K. (Cody, Wyo.) | 9/2/31 |
| Skinner, Samuel (Chicago, Ill.) | 6/10/38 |
| Smith, Hedrick (Kilmacolm, Scotland) | 7/9/33 |
| Smith, Liz (Ft. Worth, Tex.) | 2/2/23 |
| Souter, David H. (Melrose, Mass.) | 9/17/39 |
| Specter, J. Arlen (Wichita, Kans.) | 2/12/30 |
| Spock, Benjamin (New Haven, Conn.) | 5/2/03 |
| Stahl, Lesley (Lynn, Mass.) | 12/16/41 |
| Steinbrenner, George (Rocky River, Oh.) | 7/4/30 |
| Steinem, Gloria (Toledo, Oh.) | 3/25/34 |
| Stephanopolous, George (Fall River, Mass.) | 2/10/61 |
| Stern, David J. (New York, N.Y.) | 9/22/42 |
| Stevens, John Paul (Chicago, Ill.) | 4/20/20 |
| Sulzberger, Arthur Ochs (New York, N.Y.) | 2/5/26 |
| Sununu, John H. (Havana, Cuba) | 7/2/39 |
| Tagliabue, Paul (Jersey City, N.J.) | 11/24/40 |
| Tartikoff, Brandon (Long Island, N.Y.) | 1949 |
| Terkel, Studs (New York, N.Y.) | 5/16/12 |
| Thomas, Clarence (Savannah, Ga.) | 6/23/48 |
| Thurmond, J. Strom (Edgefield, S.C.) | 12/5/02 |
| Tiegs, Cheryl (Minnesota) | 9/27/47 |
| Tinker, Grant (Stamford, Conn.) | 1/11/26 |
| Tisch, Laurence (New York, N.Y.) | 3/15/23 |
| Toland, John (LaCrosse, Wis.) | 6/29/12 |
| Trillin, Calvin (Kansas City, Mo.) | 12/5/35 |
| Truman, Margaret (Independence, Mo.) | 2/17/24 |
| Trump, Donald (New York, N.Y.) | 1946 |
| Turner, Ted (Cincinnati, Oh.) | 1938 |
| Udall, Morris K. (St. Johns, Ariz.) | 6/15/22 |
| Ueberroth, Peter (Chicago, Ill.) | 9/2/37 |
| Valenti, Jack (Houston, Tex.) | 9/5/21 |
| Van Buren, Abigail (Sioux City, Ia.) | 7/4/18 |
| Wallace, George (Clio, Ala.) | 8/25/19 |
| Wallace, Mike (Brookline, Mass.) | 5/9/18 |
| Walters, Barbara (Boston, Mass.) | 9/25/31 |
| Wattleton, Faye (St. Louis, Mo.) | 7/8/43 |
| Weicker, Lowell (Paris, France) | 5/16/31 |
| Wenner, Jann (New York, N.Y.) | 1/7/46 |
| Westheimer, Ruth (Germany) | 1928 |
| White, Bill (Lakewood, Fla.) | 1/28/34 |
| White, Byron (Ft. Collins, Col.) | 6/8/17 |
| Wicker, Tom (Hamlet, N.C.) | 6/18/26 |
| Wiesel, Elie (Sighet, Transyl.) | 9/30/28 |
| Wilder, L. Douglas (Richmond, Va.) | 1/17/31 |
| Will, George (Champaign, Ill.) | 1941 |
| Wilson, Pete (Lake Forest, Ill.) | 8/23/33 |
| Yamaguchi, Kristi (Hayward, Cal.) | 7/12/71 |
| Yard, Molly (Shanghai, China) | c.1910 |
| Young, Andrew (New Orleans, La.) | 3/12/32 |
| Young, Coleman (Tuscaloosa, Ala.) | 5/24/18 |
| Zahn, Paula (Omaha, Neb.) | 2/24/56 |

## Noted Black Americans

Names of black athletes and entertainers are not included here as they are listed elsewhere in The World Almanac.

**The Rev. Dr. Ralph David Abernathy,** 1926-1990, organizer, 1957, and president, 1968, of the Southern Christian Leadership Conference.

**Maya Angelou,** b. 1928, writer, read her poem "On the Pulse of Morning" at Pres. Bill Clinton's inauguration.

**Crispus Attucks,** c. 1723-1770, agitator who led group that precipitated the "Boston Massacre," Mar. 5, 1770.

**James Baldwin,** 1924-1987, author, playwright; *The Fire Next Time, Blues for Mister Charlie, Just Above My Head.*

**Benjamin Banneker,** 1731-1806, inventor, astronomer, mathematician, and gazetteer; served on commission that surveyed and laid out Washington, D. C.

**Imamu Amiri Baraka,** b. LeRoi Jones, 1934, poet, playwright.

**James P. Beckwourth,** 1798-c. 1867, western fur-trader, scout, after whom Beckwourth Pass in northern California is named.

**Dr. Mary McCleod Bethune,** 1875-1955, adviser to presidents Roosevelt, Truman; division administrator, Natl. Youth Administration, 1935; founder, pres. Bethune-Cookman College.

**Henry Blair,** 19th century, obtained patents (believed among first issued to a black) for a corn-planter, 1834, and for a cotton-planter, 1836.

**Guion S. Bluford Jr.,** b. 1942, astronaut, first black Amer. to go into space, 1983.

**Julian Bond,** b. 1940, civil rights leader first elected to the Georgia state legislature, 1965; helped found Student Nonviolent Coordinating Committee.

**Edward Bouchet,** 1852-1918, first black to earn a Ph.D., Yale, 1876, at a U.S. university; first black elected to Phi Beta Kappa.

**Thomas Bradley,** b. 1917, mayor of Los Angeles, 1973-1993.

**Andrew F. Brimmer,** b. 1926, first black member, 1966, Federal Reserve Board.

**Edward W. Brooke,** b. 1919, attorney general, 1962, of Massachusetts; first black elected to U. S. Senate, 1967, since 19th century Reconstruction.

**Gwendolyn Brooks,** b. 1917, poet, novelist; first black to win a Pulitzer Prize, 1950, for *Annie Allen.*

**Sterling A. Brown,** 1901-1989, poet, literature professor; helped establish Afro-American literary criticism.

**William Wells Brown,** 1815-1884, novelist, dramatist; first American black to publish a novel.

**Dr. Ralph Bunche,** 1904-1971, first black to win the Nobel Peace Prize, 1950; undersecretary of the UN, 1950.

**Sherian Grace Cadoria,** b. 1940, brigadier general; highest ranking black woman in U.S. armed forces as of 1990.

**Alexa Canady,** b. 1950, first black woman neurosurgeon in U.S.

**George E. Carruthers,** b. 1940, physicist developed the Apollo 16 lunar surface ultraviolet camera/spectograph.

**George Washington Carver,** 1861-1943, botanist, chemurgist, and educator; his extensive experiments in soil building and plant diseases revolutionized the economy of the South.

**Charles Waddell Chestnutt,** 1858-1932, author known primarily for his short stories, including *The Conjure Woman.*

**Shirley Chisholm,** b. 1924, first black woman elected to House of Representatives, Brooklyn, N. Y., 1968.

**Bishop Philip R. Cousin,** b. 1933, Pres., Natl. Council of Churches of Christ in the USA, 1985-.

**Countee Cullen,** 1903-1946, poet, played a prominent role in the "Harlem Renaissance" of the 1920s; "Heritage," *The Black Christ.*

**Lt. Gen. Benjamin O. Davis Jr.** b. 1912, West Point, 1936, first black Air Force general, 1954.

**Brig. Gen. Benjamin O. Davis Sr.,** 1877-1970, first black general, 1940, in U.S. Army.

**William L. Dawson,** 1886-1970, Illinois congressman, first black chairman of a major House of Representatives committee.

**David Dinkins,** b. 1927, first black mayor of New York City, 1990-.

**Sharon Pratt Dixon,** b. 1944, mayor of Washington, D.C., 1990-.

**Aaron Douglas,** 1900-1979, painter; called father of black American art.

**Frederick Douglass,** 1817-1895, author, editor, orator, diplomat; edited the abolitionist weekly, The North Star, in Rochester, N. Y.; U.S. minister and consul general to Haiti.

**St. Clair Drake,** 1911-1990, black studies pioneer, *Black Metropolis* (1945, with Horace R. Cayton); first permanent director, African and Afro-American Studies, Stanford Univ.

**Dr. Charles Richard Drew,** 1904-1950, pioneer in development of blood banks; director of American Red Cross blood donor project in World War II.

**William Edward Burghardt Du Bois,** 1868-1963, historian, sociologist; a founder of the National Association for the Advancement of Colored People (NAACP), 1909, and founder of its magazine The Crisis; author, *The Souls of Black Folk.*

**Paul Laurence Dunbar,** 1872-1906, poet, novelist; won fame with *Lyrics of Lowly Life,* 1896.

**Jean Baptiste Point du Sable,** c. 1750-1818, pioneer trader and first settler of Chicago, 1779.

**Marian Wright Edelman,** b. 1939, founder, pres. of Children's Defense Fund.

**Joycelyn Elders,** b. 1933, first black U.S. Surgeon General, confirmed 1993.

**Ralph Ellison,** b. 1914, novelist, essayist, *Invisible Man.*

**Michael Espy,** b. 1953, first black secretary of Agriculture.

**James Farmer,** b. 1920, a founder of the Congress of Racial Equality, 1942; asst. secretary, Dept. of HEW, 1969.

**Henry O. Flipper,** 1856-1940, first black to graduate, 1877, from West Point.

**Charles Fuller,** b. 1939, Pulitzer Prize-winning playwright; *A Soldier's Play.*

**Mary Hatwood Futrell,** b. 1940, president, Natl. Education Assn., 1983-.

**Marcus Garvey,** 1887-1940, founded Universal Negro Improvement Assn., 1911.

**Kenneth Gibson,** b. 1932, Newark, N.J., mayor, 1970-1986.

**Charles Gordone,** b. 1925, won 1970 Pulitzer Prize in Drama, with *No Place to Be Somebody.*

**Vice Adm. Samuel L. Gravely Jr.** b. 1922, first black admiral, 1971, served in World War II, Korea, and Vietnam; commander, Third Fleet.

**William H. Gray 3d,** b. 1941, U.S. representative from Pa., 1979—; chairman, Budget Committee, 1985-88; chairman, House Democratic Caucus, 1988-89; majority whip, 1989-.

**Ewart Guinier,** 1911-1990, trade unionist, first chairman of Harvard Univ.'s Department of Afro-American Studies.

**Alex Haley,** 1921-1992, Pulitzer Prize-winning author; *Roots, The Autobiography of Malcolm X.*

**Jupiter Hammon,** c. 1720-1800, poet; the first black American to have his works published, 1761.

**Lorraine Hansberry,** 1930-1965, playwright; won New York Drama Critics Circle Award, 1959, with *Raisin in the Sun.*

**Barbara Harris,** b. 1931, first woman Episcopal bishop.

**Patricia Roberts Harris,** 1924-1985, U. S. ambassador to Luxembourg, 1965-67; secretary, Dept. of HUD, 1977-1979, Dept. of HHS, 1979-1981.

**William H. Hastie,** 1904-1976 first black federal judge, appointed 1937; governor of Virgin Islands, 1946-49; judge, U.S. Circuit Court of Appeals, 1949.

**Matthew A. Henson,** 1866-1955, member of Peary's 1909 expedition to the North Pole; placed U.S. flag at the Pole.

**Chester Himes,** 1909-1984, novelist, *Cotton Comes to Harlem.*

**Dr. William A. Hinton,** 1883-1959, developed the Hinton and Davies-Hinton tests for detection of syphilis; first black professor, 1949, at Harvard Medical School.

**Benjamin L. Hooks,** b. 1925, first black member, 1972-1979, Federal Communications Comm.; exec. dir., NAACP, 1977—.

**Nathan I. Huggins,** 1927-1989, historian, scholar; Harvard professor from 1980, director of that university's Institute for Afro-American Research from 1981.

**Langston Hughes,** 1902-1967, poet; story, song lyric author, a major influence in the "Harlem Renaissance" of the 1920s; *The Weary Blues, Montage of a Dream Deferred.*

**Charlayne Hunter-Gault,** b. 1942, first black woman admitted to Univ. of Ga., 1961; ran *N.Y. Times* Harlem Bureau, 1968-1977; broadcast journalist, 1978—.

**Nora Zeale Hurston,** 1903-1960, novelist, folklorist; *Their Eyes Were Watching God; Mules and Men.*

**Rev. Jesse Jackson,** b. 1941, national director, Operation Bread Basket; campaigned for Democratic presidential nomination, 1984, 1988; pres., founder, Rainbow Coalition; "shadow senator" for District of Columbia, 1991-.

**Maynard Jackson,** b. 1938, mayor of Atlanta, 1973-1981; 1989-93.

**Gen. Daniel James Jr.** 1920-1978, first black 4-star general, 1975; Commander, North American Air Defense Command.

**Mae C. Jemison, M.D.,** b. 1956, astronaut, first black woman launched into space, 1992.

**Pvt. Henry Johnson,** 1897-1929, the first American decorated by France in World War I with the Croix de Guerre.

**James Weldon Johnson,** 1871-1938, poet, lyricist, novelist; first black admitted to Florida bar; U.S. consul in Venezuela and Nicaragua.

**John H. Johnson,** b. 1918, publisher, editor of Ebony, Jet, Ebony Jr. magazines, from 1942.

**Barbara Jordan,** b. 1936, former congresswoman from Texas; member, House Judiciary Committee.

**Vernon E. Jordan,** b. 1935, executive director, National Urban League, 1972.

**Ernest Everett Just,** 1883-1941, marine biologist, studied egg development; author, *Biology of Cell Surfaces,* 1941.

**Leontine T.C. Kelly,** b. 1920, United Methodist bishop; first black woman bishop of a major American denomination, 1984.

**The Rev. Dr. Martin Luther King Jr.,** 1929-1968, led 382-day Montgomery, Ala., boycott that brought 1956 U.S. Supreme Court decision holding segregation on buses unconstitutional; founder, president, Southern Christian Leadership Conference, 1957; won Nobel Peace Prize, 1964.

**Lewis H. Latimer,** 1848-1928, associate of Edison; supervised installation of first electric street lighting in N.Y.C.

**Mickey Leland,** 1944-1989, U.S. representative from Texas, 1978 until death; chairman of Congressional Black Caucus, House Select Committee on Hunger.

**Malcolm X,** 1925-1965, Black Muslim leader and black nationalist whose ideas and oratory contributed to the black pride and black power movements in the 1960s.

**Thurgood Marshall,** 1908-1993, first black U.S. solicitor general, 1965; first black justice of the U.S. Supreme Court, 1967-1991; as a lawyer led the legal battery that won the Supreme Court decision declaring racial segregation of public schools unconstitutional, 1954.

**Jan Matzeliger,** 1852-1889, invented lasting machine, patented 1883, which revolutionized the shoe industry.

**Benjamin Mays,** 1895-1984, educator, civil rights leader; headed Morehouse College, 1940-1967.

**Wade H. McCree Jr.,** 1920-1987, solicitor general of the U.S., 1977-1981.

**Donald E. McHenry,** b. 1936, U.S. ambassador to the United Nations, 1979-1981.

**Ronald McNair,** 1950-1986, physicist, astronaut; killed in *Challenger* explosion.

**Dorie Miller,** 1919-1943, Navy hero of Pearl Harbor attack; awarded the Navy Cross.

**Ernest N. Morial,** b. 1929, elected first black mayor of New Orleans, 1977.

**Toni Morrison,** b. 1931, novelist; *Song of Solomon, Sula, Tar Baby;* won 1988 Pulitzer Prize for *Beloved.*

**Willard Motley,** 1912-1965, novelist; *Knock on Any Door.*

**Elijah Muhammad,** 1897-1975, founded Black Muslims, 1931.

**Pedro Alonzo Nino,** navigator of the Nina, one of Columbus' 3 ships on his first voyage of discovery to the New World, 1492.

**Rosa Parks,** b. 1913, Montgomery Ala. citizen arrested for refusing to move to the back of the bus, Dec. 1, 1955, bringing a 382-day bus boycott led by Martin Luther King Jr.

**Frederick D. Patterson,** 1901-1988, founder of United Negro College Fund, 1944; Tuskegee Institute's third pres., 1935-1953.

**Harold R. Perry,** 1916-1991, first black American made a Roman Catholic bishop in the 20th century, 1966; first black clergyman to deliver the opening prayer in Congress, 1964.

**Adam Clayton Powell,** 1908-1972, early civil rights leader, congressman, 1945-1969; chairman, House Committee on Education and Labor, 1960-1967.

**Colin Powell,** b. 1937, first black Natl. Security Advisor, 1987-88; first black chairman of Joint Chiefs of Staff, 1989-.

**Joseph H. Rainey,** 1832-1887, first black elected to House of Representatives, 1869, from South Carolina.

**A. Philip Randolph,** 1889-1979, organized the Brotherhood of Sleeping Car Porters, 1925; organizer of 1941 and 1963 March on Washington movements; vice president, AFL-CIO.

**Charles Rangel,** b. 1930, congressman from N.Y.C. from 1970; member, Ways and Means Committee; chairman, Select Committee on Narcotics Abuse & Control.

**Hiram R. Revels,** 1822-1901, first black U.S. senator, elected in Mississippi, served 1870-1871.

**Lloyd Richards,** b. 1922(?), first black to direct a Broadway play, 1959; dean, Yale Univ. School of Drama & artistic director of Yale Repertory Theatre, 1979-1991.

**Wilson C. Riles,** b. 1917, elected, 1970, California State Superintendent of Public Instruction.

**Norbert Rillieux,** 1806-1894; invented a vacuum pan evaporator, 1846, revolutionizing the sugar-refining industry.

**Paul Robeson,** 1898-1976, actor and concert singer, graduated 1st in class at Rutgers, 1918, Phi Beta Kappa; grad. Columbia Univ. law school, 1923; associated with communist causes.

**Max Robinson,** 1939-1988, TV journalist, first black to anchor network news, 1978.

**Carl T. Rowan,** b. 1925, prize-winning journalist; director of the U.S. information Agency, 1964, the first black to sit on the National Security Council; U. S. ambassador to Finland, 1963.

**John B. Russwurm,** 1799-1851, with **Samuel E. Cornish,** 1793-1858, founded, 1827, the nation's first black newspaper, *Freedom's Journal,* in N.Y.C.

**Bayard Rustin,** 1910-1987, organizer of the 1963 March on Washington; executive director, A. Philip Randolph Institute.

**Peter Salem,** at the Battle of Bunker Hill, June 17, 1775, shot and killed British commander Maj. John Pitcairn.

**Ntozake Shange,** b. 1948, writer, *For Colored Girls Who Have Considered Suicide/When the Rainbow is Enuf.*

**Bishop Stephen Spottswood,** 1897-1974, board chairman of NAACP, 1961-1974.

**The Rev. Leon H. Sullivan,** b. 1922, economic development planner, first black on General Motors Bd. of Directors.

**Willard Townsend,** 1895-1957, organized the United Transport Service Employees, 1935 (redcaps, etc.); vice pres. AFL-CIO.

**Sojourner Truth,** 1797-1883, born Isabella Baumfree; preacher, abolitionist; raised funds for Union in Civil War; worked for black educational opportunities.

**Harriet Tubman,** 1823-1913, Underground Railroad conductor served as nurse and spy for Union Army in the Civil War.

**Nat Turner,** 1800-1831, led the most significant of over 200 slave revolts in U.S., in Southampton, Va.; hanged.

**Alice Walker,** b. 1944, novelist, essayist, *The Color Purple.*

**Booker T. Washington,** 1856-1915, founder, 1881, and first president of Tuskegee Institute; author, *Up From Slavery.*

**Harold Washington,** 1922-1987, first black mayor of Chicago, from 1983 until death.

**Dr. Robert C. Weaver,** b. 1907, first black member of the U.S. Cabinet, secretary, Dept. of HUD, 1966.

**Ida B. Wells (Barnett),** 1862-1931, journalist who waged anti-lynching crusade.

**Clifton R. Wharton Jr.,** b. 1926, first black pres. of major U.S. univ.; chancellor, nation's largest univ. system, 8 yrs.; chairman & CEO, country's largest pension fund, 1987—.

**Phillis Wheatley,** c. 1753-1784, poet; 2d American woman and first black woman to have her works published, 1770.

**Bill White,** b. 1934, first black baseball league president; named Natl. League head, 1989.

**Walter White,** 1893-1955, exec. secretary, NAACP, 1931-1955.

**L. Douglas Wilder,** b. 1931, first black elected governor, became Virginia chief executive in 1989.

**Roy Wilkins,** 1901-1981, exec. director, NAACP, 1955-1977.

**Dr. Daniel Hale Williams,** 1858-1931, performed one of first 2 open-heart operations, 1893; founded Provident, Chicago's first Negro hospital; first black elected a fellow of the American College of Surgeons.

**August Wilson,** b. 1945, playwright, won 1987 Pulitzer Prize for *Fences,* 1990 Pulitzer for *The Piano Lesson.*

**Granville T. Woods,** 1856-1910, invented the third-rail system now used in subways, a complex railway telegraph device that helped reduce train accidents, and an automatic air brake.

**Dr. Carter G. Woodson,** 1875-1950, historian; founded Assn. for the Study of Negro Life and History, 1915, and Journal of Negro History, 1916.

**Richard Wright,** 1908-1960, novelist; *Native Son, Black Boy.*

**Frank Yerby,** 1916-1991, first best-selling American black novelist; *The Foxes of Harrow, Vixen.*

**Andrew Young,** b. 1932, civil rights leader, congressman from Georgia, U.S. ambassador to the United Nations, 1977-79; mayor of Atlanta, 1982-89.

**Whitney M. Young Jr.,** 1921-1971, exec. director, 1961, National Urban League; author, lecturer, newspaper columnist.

About 5,000 blacks served in the Continental Army during the **American Revolution,** mostly in integrated units, some in all-black combat units. Some 200,000 blacks served in the Union Army during the **Civil War;** 38,000 gave their lives; 22 won the Medal of Honor, the nation's highest award. Of 367,000 blacks in the armed forces during **World War I,** 100,000 served in France. More than 1,000,000 blacks served in the armed forces during **World War II;** all-black fighter and bomber AAF units and infantry divisions gave distinguished service. In 1954 the policy of all-black units was finally abolished. Of 274,937 blacks who served in the armed forces during the **Vietnam War** (1965-1974), 5,681 were killed in combat. During the **Persian Gulf War** (1990-1991), 104,000 blacks served in the Kuwaiti theater—20 percent of U.S. soldiers, compared with 8.7% during World War II and 9.8% in Vietnam.

As of Jan. 1992, there were 338 black mayors, 2 black governors, 358 state representatives, and 26 U.S. representatives. There were then 7,552 blacks holding elected office in the U.S. and Virgin Islands, an increase of 1.0% over the previous year, according to a survey by the Joint Center for Political Studies, Washington, D.C. The number of black women elected to local, county, state, and congressional offices rose to 2,121, up by 68, or 3.3%, from the Jan. 1991 figure. From 1989 to Jan. 1992, male black elected officials increased by 19, while female black elected officials increased by 307. In Nov. 1992, Carol Moseley Braun of Illinois became the first black woman elected to the U.S. Senate.

## Notable Living American Fiction Writers and Playwrights

| Name (Birthplace) | Birthdate | Name (Birthplace) | Birthdate |
|---|---|---|---|
| Adams, Alice (Fredericksburg, Va.) | 8/14/26 | Berger, Thomas (Cincinnati, Oh.) | 7/20/24 |
| Albee, Edward (Washington, D.C.) | 3/12/28 | Blume, Judy (Elizabeth, N.J.) | 2/12/38 |
| Auchincloss, Louis (Lawrence, N.Y.) | 9/27/17 | Bradbury, Ray (Waukegan, Ill.) | 8/22/20 |
| | | Brooks, Gwendolyn (Topeka, Kan.) | 6/7/17 |
| Barth, John (Cambridge, Md.) | 5/27/30 | | |
| Beattie, Ann (Washington, D.C.) | 9/7/47 | Calisher, Hortense (New York, N.Y.) | 12/20/11 |
| Bellow, Saul (Quebec, Canada) | 7/10/15 | Clancy, Tom (Baltimore, Md.) | 1947 |
| Benchley, Peter (New York, N.Y.) | 5/8/40 | Clark, Mary Higgins (New York, N.Y.) | 12/24/31 |

| Name (Birthplace) | Birthdate |
|---|---|
| Clavell, James (England) | 10/10/24 |
| Cleary, Beverly (McMinnville, Ore.) | 1916 |
| Connell, Evan S. (Kansas City, Mo.) | 8/17/24 |
| Conroy, Pat (Atlanta, Ga.) | 10/26/45 |
| Crews, Harry (Alma, Ga.) | 6/6/35 |
| Crichton, Michael (Chicago, Ill.) | 10/23/42 |
| Dailey, Janet (Storm Lake, Ia.) | 5/21/44 |
| De Vries, Peter (Chicago, Ill.) | 2/27/10 |
| Didion, Joan (Sacramento, Cal.) | 12/5/34 |
| Doctorow, E. L. (New York, N.Y.) | 1/6/31 |
| Dunne, John Gregory (Hartford, Conn.) | 5/25/32 |
| Elkin, Stanley (New York, N.Y.) | 5/11/30 |
| Ellison, Ralph (Oklahoma City, Okla.) | 3/1/14 |
| Fast, Howard (New York, N.Y.) | 11/11/14 |
| Fox, Paula (New York, N.Y.) | 4/22/23 |
| French, Marilyn (New York, N.Y.) | 11/21/29 |
| Fuller, Charles (Philadelphia, Pa.) | 3/5/39 |
| Gaddis, William (New York, N.Y.) | 1922 |
| Gilroy, Frank (New York, N.Y.) | 10/13/25 |
| Godwin, Gail (Birmingham, Ala.) | 6/18/37 |
| Goldman, William (Chicago, Ill.) | 8/12/31 |
| Gordon, Mary (Long Island, N.Y.) | 12/8/49 |
| Grau, Shirley Ann (New Orleans, La.) | 7/8/29 |
| Grisham, John (Jonesboro, Ark.) | 2/8/55 |
| Guare, John (New York, N.Y.) | 2/5/38 |
| Hailey, Arthur (Luton, England) | 4/5/20 |
| Haley, Alex (Ithaca, N.Y.) | 8/11/21 |
| Hawkes, John (Stamford, Conn.) | 8/17/25 |
| Heller, Joseph (Brooklyn, N.Y.) | 5/1/23 |
| Helprin, Mark (New York, N.Y.) | 6/28/47 |
| Hersey, John (Tientsin, China) | 6/17/14 |
| Hinton, S.E. (Tulsa, Okla.) | 1948 |
| Irving, John (Exeter, N.H.) | 3/2/42 |
| Jong, Erica (New York, N.Y.) | 3/26/42 |
| Kennedy, William (Albany, N.Y.) | 1/16/28 |
| Kerr, Jean (Scranton, Pa.) | 7/10/23 |
| King, Stephen (Portland, Me.) | 9/21/47 |
| Kingston, Maxine Hong (Stockton, Cal.) | 10/27/40 |
| Knowles, John (Fairmont, W. Va.) | 9/16/26 |
| Krantz, Judith (New York, N.Y.) | 1/9/28 |
| LeGuin, Ursula (Berkeley, Cal.) | 10/21/29 |
| L'Engle, Madeleine (New York, N.Y.) | 11/29/18 |
| Leonard, Elmore (New Orleans, La.) | 10/11/25 |
| Levin, Ira (New York, N.Y.) | 8/27/29 |
| Ludlum, Robert (New York, N.Y.) | 5/25/27 |
| Lurie, Alison (Chicago, Ill.) | 9/3/26 |
| Mailer, Norman (Long Branch, N.J.) | 1/31/23 |
| Mamet, David (Chicago, Ill.) | 11/30/47 |

| Name (Birthplace) | Birthdate |
|---|---|
| McGuane, Thomas (Wyandotte, Mich.) | 12/11/39 |
| McMurtry, Larry (Wichita Falls, Tex.) | 6/3/36 |
| Michener, James A. (New York, N.Y.) | 2/3/07 |
| Miller, Arthur (New York, N.Y.) | 10/17/15 |
| Morris, Wright (Central City, Neb.) | 1/6/10 |
| Morrison, Toni (Lorain, Oh.) | 2/18/31 |
| Oates, Joyce Carol (Lockport, N.Y.) | 6/16/38 |
| Ozick, Cynthia (New York, N.Y.) | 4/17/28 |
| Paley, Grace (New York, N.Y.) | 12/11/22 |
| Piercy, Marge (Detroit, Mich.) | 3/31/36 |
| Potok, Chaim (New York, N.Y.) | 2/17/29 |
| Price, Reynolds (Macon, N.C.) | 2/1/33 |
| Puzo, Mario (New York, N.Y.) | 10/15/20 |
| Pynchon, Thomas (Glen Cove, N.Y.) | 5/8/37 |
| Rabe, David (Dubuque, Ia.) | 3/10/40 |
| Reed, Ishmael (Chattanooga, Tenn.) | 2/22/38 |
| Rice, Anne (New Orleans, La.) | 10/14/41 |
| Roth, Henry (Austria-Hungary) | 2/8/06 |
| Roth, Philip (Newark, N.J.) | 3/19/33 |
| Salinger, J. D. (New York, N.Y.) | 1/1/19 |
| Sanders, Lawrence (New York, N.Y.) | 1920 |
| Sendak, Maurice (New York, N.Y.) | 6/10/28 |
| Shepard, Sam (Ft. Sheridan, Ill.) | 11/5/43 |
| Simon, Neil (New York, N.Y.) | 7/4/27 |
| Spillane, Mickey (Brooklyn, N.Y.) | 3/9/18 |
| Stegner, Wallace (Lake Mills, Ia.) | 2/18/09 |
| Stern, Richard (New York, N.Y.) | 2/25/28 |
| Stone, Robert (Brooklyn, N.Y.) | 8/21/37 |
| Styron, William (Newport News, Va.) | 6/11/25 |
| Taylor, Peter (Trenton, Tenn.) | 1/8/17 |
| Theroux, Paul (Medford, Mass.) | 4/10/41 |
| Turow, Scott F. (Chicago, Ill.) | 4/12/49 |
| Tyler, Anne (Minneapolis, Minn.) | 10/25/41 |
| Updike, John (Shillington, Pa.) | 3/18/32 |
| Uris, Leon (Baltimore, Md.) | 8/3/24 |
| Vidal, Gore (West Point, N.Y.) | 10/3/25 |
| Vonnegut, Kurt Jr. (Indianapolis, Ind.) | 11/11/22 |
| Walker, Alice (Eatonton, Ga.) | 2/9/44 |
| Wambaugh, Joseph (East Pittsburgh, Pa.) | 1/22/37 |
| Wasserstein, Wendy (New York, N.Y.) | |
| Welty, Eudora (Jackson, Miss.) | 4/13/09 |
| Wideman, John Edgar (Pittsburgh, Pa.) | 6/14/41 |
| Wilson, August (Pittsburgh, Pa.) | 4/27/45 |
| Wilson, Lanford (Lebanon, Mo.) | 4/13/37 |
| Wolfe, Tom (Richmond, Va.) | 3/2/31 |
| Wolff, Tobias (Birmingham, Ala.) | 6/19/45 |
| Wouk, Herman (New York, N.Y.) | 5/27/15 |

## American Architects and Some of Their Achievements

**Max Abramovitz,** b. 1908, Avery Fisher Hall, Lincoln Center, N.Y.C.

**Henry Bacon,** 1866-1924, Lincoln Memorial.

**Pietro Belluschi,** b. 1899, Juilliard School of Music, Lincoln Center, N.Y.C.

**Marcel Breuer,** 1902-1981, Whitney Museum of American Art, N.Y.C. (with Hamilton Smith).

**Charles Bulfinch,** 1763-1844, State House, Boston; Capitol, Wash. D.C., (part).

**Gordon Bunshaft,** 1909-1990, Lever House, Park Ave, N.Y.C.; Hirshhorn Museum, Wash., D.C.

**Daniel H. Burnham,** 1846-1912, Union Station, Wash. D.C.; Flatiron, N.Y.C.

**Irwin Chanin,** 1892-1988, New York City theaters, skyscrapers.

**Ralph Adams Cram,** 1863-1942, Cathedral of St. John the Divine, N.Y.C.; U.S. Military Academy (part).

**R. Buckminster Fuller,** 1895-1983, U.S. Pavilion, Expo 67, Montreal (geodesic domes).

**Cass Gilbert,** 1859-1934, Custom House, Woolworth Bldg., N.Y.C.; Supreme Court bldg., Wash., D.C.

**Bertram G. Goodhue,** 1869-1924, Capitol, Lincoln, Neb.; St. Thomas, St. Bartholomew, N.Y.C.

**Walter Gropius,** 1883-1969, Pan Am Building, N.Y.C. (with Pietro Belluschi).

**Peter Harrison,** 1716-1775, Touro Synagogue, Redwood Library, Newport, R.I.

**Wallace K. Harrison,** 1895-1981, Metropolitan Opera House, Lincoln Center, N.Y.C.

**Thomas Hastings,** 1860-1929, Public Library, Frick Mansion, N.Y.C.

**James Hoban,** 1762-1831, The White House.

**Raymond Hood,** 1881-1934, Rockefeller Center, N.Y.C. (part); Daily News, N.Y.C.; Tribune, Chicago.

**Richard M. Hunt,** 1827-1895, Metropolitan Museum, N.Y.C. (part); Natl. Observatory, Wash., D.C.

**William Le Baron Jenney,** 1832-1907, Home Insurance, Chicago (demolished 1931).

**Philip C. Johnson,** b. 1906, N.Y. State Theater, Lincoln Center, N.Y.C.

**Albert Kahn,** 1869-1942, Athletic Club Bldg., General Motors Bldg., Detroit.

**Louis Kahn,** 1901-1974, Salk Laboratory, La Jolla, Cal.; Yale Art Gallery.

**Christopher Grant LaFarge,** 1862-1938, Roman Catholic Chapel, West Point.

**Benjamin H. Latrobe,** 1764-1820, U.S. Capitol (part).

**William Lescaze,** 1896-1969, Philadelphia Savings Fund Society; Borg-Warner Bldg., Chicago.

**Bernard R. Maybeck,** 1862-1957, Hearst Hall, Chick House, Univ. of Cal., First Church of Christ Scientist, Berkeley.

**Charles F. McKim,** 1847-1909, Public Library, Boston, Columbia Univ., N.Y.C. (part).

**Charles M. McKim,** b. 1920, KUHT-TV Transmitter Building, Houston; Lutheran Church of the Redeemer, Houston.

**Ludwig Mies van der Rohe,** 1886-1969, Seagram Building, N.Y.C. (with Philip C. Johnson); National Gallery, Berlin.

**Robert Mills,** 1781-1855, Washington Monument.

**Richard J. Neutra,** 1892-1970, Mathematics Park, Princeton; Orange Co. Courthouse, Santa Ana, Cal.

**Gyo Obata,** b. 1923, Natl. Air & Space Mus., Smithsonian Institution; Dallas-Ft. Worth Airport.

**Frederick L. Olmsted,** 1822-1903, Central Park, N.Y.C.; Fairmount Park, Philadelphia.

**I(eoh) M(ing) Pei,** b. 1917, National Center for Atmospheric Research, Boulder, Col.; East Wing, Natl. Gallery of Art, Wash., D.C.; Pyramid, The Louvre, Paris.

**William Pereira,** 1909-1985, Cape Canaveral; Transamerica Bldg., San Francisco.
**John Russell Pope,** 1874-1937, National Gallery.
**John Portman,** b. 1924, Peachtree Center, Atlanta.
**George Browne Post,** 1837-1913, New York Stock Exchange, Wisconsin state capitol.
**James Renwick Jr.,** 1818-1895, Grace Church, St. Patrick's Cathedral, N.Y.C.; Smithsonian, Corcoran Galleries, Wash., D.C.
**Henry H. Richardson,** 1838-1886, Trinity Church, Boston.
**Kevin Roche,** b. 1922, Oakland Cal. Museum; Fine Arts Center, U. of Mass.
**James Gamble Rogers,** 1867-1947, Columbia-Presbyterian Medical Center, N.Y.C.; Northwestern Univ., Chicago.
**John Wellborn Root,** 1887-1963, Palmolive Building, Chicago; Hotel Statler, Washington; Hotel Tamanaco, Caracas.
**Paul Rudolph,** b. 1918, Jewitt Art Center, Wellesley College; Art & Architecture Bldg., Yale.
**Charles M. Russell,** 1866-1926, Western life.
**Eero Saarinen,** 1910-1961, Gateway to the West Arch, St. Louis; Trans World Flight Center, N.Y.C.

**Louis Skidmore,** 1897-1962, AEC town site, Oak Ridge, Tenn.; Terrace Plaza Hotel, Cincinnati.
**Clarence S. Stein,** 1882-1975, Temple Emanu-El, N.Y.C.
**Edward Durell Stone,** 1902-1978, U.S. Embassy, New Delhi, India; (H. Hartford) Gallery of Modern Art, N.Y.C.
**Louis H. Sullivan,** 1856-1924, Auditorium, Chicago.
**Richard Upjohn,** 1802-1878, Trinity Church, N.Y.C.
**Ralph T. Walker,** 1889-1973, N.Y. Telephone Hdqrs., N.Y.C.; IBM Research Lab., Poughkeepsie, N.Y.
**Roland A. Wank,** 1898-1970, Cincinnati Union Terminal; head architect TVA, 1933-44.
**Stanford White,** 1853-1906, Washington Arch; first Madison Square Garden, N.Y.C.
**Frank Lloyd Wright,** 1867 (or 1869)-1959, Imperial Hotel, Tokyo; Guggenheim Museum, N.Y.C.; Unity Church, Oak Park, Ill; Robie House, Chicago; Taliesin, Wis.
**William Wurster,** 1895-1973, Ghirardelli Sq., San Francisco; Cowell College, U. Cal., Berkeley.
**Minoru Yamasaki,** 1912-1986, World Trade Center, N.Y.C.

## Noted American Cartoonists

**Charles Addams,** 1912-1988, macabre cartoons.
**Brad Anderson,** b. 1924, Marmaduke.
**Peter Arno,** 1904-1968, *New Yorker* urban characterizations.
**Tex Avery,** 1908-1980, **Friz Freleng,** b. 1905?, **Chuck Jones,** b. 1912, animators of Bugs Bunny, Porky Pig, Daffy Duck.
**George Baker,** 1915-1975, The Sad Sack.
**C. C. Beck,** 1910-1989, Captain Marvel.
**Jim Berry,** b. 1932, Berry's World.
**Herb Block (Herblock),** b. 1909, leading political cartoonist.
**George Booth,** b. 1926, *New Yorker* cartoonist.
**Berke Breathed,** b. 1957, Bloom County.
**Clare Briggs,** 1875-1930, Mr. & Mrs.
**Dik Browne,** 1917-1989, Hi & Lois, Hagar the Horrible.
**Marjorie Buell,** 1904-1993, Little Lulu.
**Ernie Bushmiller,** 1905-1982, Nancy.
**Milton Caniff,** 1907-1988, Terry & the Pirates; Steve Canyon.
**Al Capp,** 1909-1979, Li'l Abner.
**Roz Chast,** b. 1954, *New Yorker* "bonfire of the banalities" cartoons.
**Paul Conrad,** 1924, political cartoonist.
**Roy Crane,** 1901-1977, Captain Easy; Buz Sawyer.
**Robert Crumb,** b. 1943, "Underground" cartoonist.
**Jay N. Darling (Ding),** 1876-1962, political cartoonist.
**Jack Davis,** b. 1926, *Mad* magazine.
**Jim Davis,** b. 1945, Garfield.
**Billy DeBeck,** 1890-1942, Barney Google.
**Rudolph Dirks,** 1877-1968, The Katzenjammer Kids.
**Walt Disney,** 1901-1966, producer of animated cartoons; created Mickey Mouse and Donald Duck.
**Steve Ditko,** b. 1927, Spider-Man.
**Mort Drucker,** b. 1929, *Mad* magazine.
**Jules Feiffer,** b. 1929, satirical *Village Voice* cartoonist.
**Bud Fisher,** 1884-1954, Mutt & Jeff.
**Ham Fisher,** 1900-1955, Joe Palooka.
**James Montgomery Flagg,** 1877-1960, illustrator; created the famous Uncle Sam recruiting poster during WWI.
**Max Fleischer,** 1883-1972, creator of Betty Boop, Popeye cartoons.
**Hal Foster,** 1892-1982, Tarzan; Prince Valiant.
**Fontaine Fox,** 1884-1964, Toonerville Folks.
**Rube Goldberg,** 1883-1970, Boob McNutt.
**Chester Gould,** 1900-1985, Dick Tracy.
**Harold Gray,** 1894-1968, Little Orphan Annie.
**Matt Groening,** b. 1954, Life is Hell, The Simpsons.
**Cathy Guisewite,** b. 1950, Cathy.
**Bill Hanna,** b. 1910, & **Joe Barbera,** b. 1911, animators of Tom & Jerry, Huckleberry Hound, Yogi Bear, Flintstones.
**Johnny Hart,** b. 1931, BC, Wizard of Id.
**Jimmy Hatlo,** 1898-1963, Little Iodine.
**John Held Jr.,** 1889-1958, "Jazz Age" cartoonist.
**George Herriman,** 1881-1944, Krazy Kat.
**Harry Hershfield,** 1885-1974, Abie the Agent.
**Al Hirschfeld,** b. 1903, *N.Y. Times* theater caricaturist.
**Burne Hogarth,** b. 1911, Tarzan.
**Helen Hokinson,** 1900-1949, satirized clubwomen.
**Nicole Hollander,** b. 1939, Sylvia.
**Lynn Johnston,** b. 1947, For Better Or For Worse.
**Bob Kane,** b. 1916, Batman.
**Bil Keane,** b. 1922, The Family Circus.

**Walt Kelly,** 1913-1973, Pogo.
**Hank Ketcham,** b. 1920, Dennis the Menace.
**Ted Key,** b. 1912, Hazel.
**Frank King,** 1883-1969, Gasoline Alley.
**Jack Kirby,** b. 1917, Fantastic Four.
**Rollin Kirby,** 1875-1952, political cartoonist.
**B(ernard) Kliban,** 1935-1991, cat books.
**Edward Koren,** b. 1935, *New Yorker* woolly characters.
**Harvey Kurtzman,** 1921-1993, *Mad* magazine.
**Walter Lantz,** b. 1900, Woody Woodpecker.
**Gary Larson,** b. 1950, The Far Side.
**Mell Lazarus,** b. 1929, Momma, Miss Peach.
**Stan Lee,** b. 1922, Marvel Comics.
**David Levine,** b. 1926, *N.Y. Review of Books* caricatures.
**Doug Marlette,** b. 1949, editorial cartoonist; Kudzu.
**Don Martin,** b. 1931, *Mad* magazine.
**Bill Mauldin,** b. 1921, depicted squalid life of the G.I. in WWII.
**Jeff MacNelly,** b. 1947, political cartoonist, and strip Shoe.
**Winsor McCay,** 1872-1934, Little Nemo.
**John T. McCutcheon,** 1870-1949, midwestern rural life.
**George McManus,** 1884-1954, Bringing Up Father.
**Dale Messick,** b. 1906, Brenda Starr.
**Norman Mingo,** 1896-1980, Alfred E. Neuman.
**Bob Montana,** 1920-1975, Archie.
**Dick Moores,** 1909-1986, Gasoline Alley.
**Willard Mullin,** 1902-1978, sports cartoonist; created Dodgers "Bum" and Mets "Kid".
**Russell Myers,** b. 1938, Broom Hilda.
**Thomas Nast,** 1840-1902, political cartoonist; created the Democratic donkey and Republican elephant.
**Pat Oliphant,** b. 1935, political cartoonist.
**Frederick Burr Opper,** 1857-1937, Happy Hooligan.
**Richard Outcault,** 1863-1928, Yellow Kid; Buster Brown.
**Mike Peters,** b. 1943, editorial cartoons; Mother Goose & Grimm.
**George Price,** b. 1901, *New Yorker* lower-class life.
**Alex Raymond,** 1909-1956, Flash Gordon; Jungle Jim.
**Art Sansom,** 1920-1991, The Born Loser.
**Charles Schulz,** b. 1922, Peanuts.
**Elzie C. Segar,** 1894-1938, Popeye.
**Jerry Siegel,** b. 1914, & **Joe Shuster,** b. 1914, Superman.
**Sydney Smith,** 1887-1935, The Gumps.
**Otto Soglow,** 1900-1975, Little King; Canyon Kiddies.
**Art Spiegelman,** b. 1948, Raw; Maus.
**William Steig,** b. 1907, *New Yorker* cartoonist.
**James Swinnerton,** 1875-1974, Little Jimmy.
**Paul Terry,** 1887-1971, animator of Mighty Mouse.
**Bob Thaves,** b. 1924, Frank and Ernest.
**James Thurber,** 1894-1961, *New Yorker* cartoonist.
**Garry Trudeau,** b. 1948, Doonesbury.
**Mort Walker,** b. 1923, Beetle Bailey.
**Bill Watterson,** b. 1958, Calvin and Hobbes.
**Russ Westover,** 1887-1966, Tillie the Toiler.
**Frank Willard,** 1893-1958, Moon Mullins.
**J. R. Williams,** 1888-1957, The Willets Family; Out Our Way.
**Gahan Wilson,** b. 1930, cartoonist of the macabre.
**Tom Wilson,** b. 1931, Ziggy.
**Art Young,** 1866-1943, political radical and satirist.
**Chic Young,** 1901-1973, Blondie.

## Noted Political Leaders of the Past

(U.S. presidents and vice presidents, Supreme Court justices, signers of Declaration of Independence, listed elsewhere.)

**Abu Bakr,** 573-634, Mohammedan leader, first caliph, chosen successor to Mohammed.

**Dean Acheson,** 1893-1971, (U.S.) secretary of state, chief architect of cold war foreign policy.

**Samuel Adams,** 1722-1803, (U.S.) patriot, Boston Tea Party firebrand.

**Konrad Adenauer,** 1876-1967, (G.) West German chancellor.

**Emilio Aguinaldo,** 1869-1964, (Philip.) revolutionary, fought against Spain and the U.S.

**Akbar,** 1542-1605, greatest Mogul emperor of India.

**Salvador Allende Gossens,** 1908-1973, (Chil.) president, advocate of democratic socialism.

**Herbert H. Asquith,** 1852-1928, (Br.) Liberal prime minister, instituted an advanced program of social reform.

**Atahualpa,** ?-1533, Inca (ruling chief) of Peru.

**Kemal Atatürk,** 1881-1938, (Turk.) founded modern Turkey.

**Clement Attlee,** 1883-1967, (Br.) Labour party leader, prime minister, enacted national health, nationalized many industries.

**Stephen F. Austin,** 1793-1836, (U.S.) led Texas colonization.

**Mikhail Bakunin,** 1814-1876, (R.) revolutionary, leading exponent of anarchism.

**Arthur J. Balfour,** 1848-1930, (Br.) as foreign secretary under Lloyd George issued Balfour Declaration expressing official British approval of Zionism.

**Bernard M. Baruch,** 1870-1965, (U.S.) financier, gvt. adviser.

**Fulgencio Batista y Zaldívar,** 1901-1973, (Cub.) ruler overthrown by Castro.

**Lord Beaverbrook,** 1879-1964, (Br.) financier, statesman, newspaper owner.

**Menachem Begin,** 1914-1992, (Isr.) Israeli prime minister, won 1978 Nobel Peace Prize.

**Eduard Benes,** 1884-1948, (Czech.) president during interwar and post-WW II eras.

**David Ben-Gurion,** 1886-1973, (Isr.) first premier of Israel.

**Thomas Hart Benton,** 1782-1858, (U.S.) Missouri senator, championed agrarian interests and westward expansion.

**Lavrenti Beria,** 1899-1953, (USSR) Communist leader prominent in political purges under Stalin.

**Aneurin Bevan,** 1897-1960, (Br.) Labour party leader.

**Ernest Bevin,** 1881-1951, (Br.) Labour party leader, foreign minister, helped lay foundation for NATO.

**Otto von Bismarck,** 1815-1898, (G.) statesman known as the Iron Chancellor, uniter of Germany, 1870.

**James G. Blaine,** 1830-1893, (U.S.) Republican politician, diplomat, influential in launching Pan-American movement.

**Léon Blum,** 1872-1950, (F.) socialist leader, writer, headed first Popular Front government.

**Simón Bolívar,** 1783-1830, (Venez.) South American revolutionary who liberated much of the continent from Spanish rule.

**William E. Borah,** 1865-1940, (U.S.) isolationist senator, instrumental in blocking U.S. membership in League of Nations and the World Court.

**Cesare Borgia,** 1476-1507, (It.) soldier, politician, an outstanding figure of the Italian Renaissance.

**Leonid Brezhnev,** 1906-1982, (USSR) leader of the Soviet Union, 1964-82.

**Aristide Briand,** 1862-1932, (F.) foreign minister, chief architect of Locarno Pact and anti-war Kellogg-Briand Pact.

**William Jennings Bryan,** 1860-1925, (U.S.) Democratic, populist leader, orator, 3 times lost race for presidency.

**Nikolai Bukharin,** 1888-1938, (USSR) communist leader.

**William C. Bullitt,** 1891-1967, (U.S.) diplomat, first ambassador to USSR, ambassador to France.

**Ralph Bunche,** 1904-1971, (U.S.) a founder and key diplomat of United Nations for more than 20 years.

**John C. Calhoun,** 1782-1850, (U.S.) political leader, champion of states' rights and a symbol of the Old South.

**Robert Castlereagh,** 1769-1822, (Br.) foreign secy, guided Grand Alliance against Napoleon.

**Camillo Benso Cavour,** 1810-1861, (It.) statesman, largely responsible for uniting Italy under the House of Savoy.

**Nicolae Ceausescu,** 1918-1989, Rumanian Communist leader, head of state from 1967-1989.

**Austen Chamberlain,** 1863-1937, (Br.) Conservative party leader, largely responsible for Locarno Pact of 1925.

**Neville Chamberlain,** 1869-1940, (Br.) Conservative prime minister whose appeasement of Hitler led to Munich Pact.

**Salmon P. Chase,** 1808-1873, (U.S.) public official, abolitionist, jurist, 6th Supreme Court chief justice.

**Chiang Kai-shek,** 1887-1975, (Chin.) Nationalist Chinese president whose govt. was driven from mainland to Taiwan.

**Chou En-lai,** 1898-1976, (Chin.) diplomat, prime minister, a leading figure of the Chinese Communist party.

**Winston Churchill,** 1874-1965, (Br.) prime minister, soldier, author, guided Britain through WW II.

**Galeazzo Ciano,** 1903-1944, (It.) fascist foreign minister, helped create Rome-Berlin Axis, executed by Mussolini.

**Henry Clay,** 1777-1852, (U.S.) "The Great Compromiser," one of most influential pre-Civil War political leaders.

**Georges Clemenceau,** 1841-1929, (F.) twice premier, Wilson's chief antagonist at Paris Peace Conference after WW I.

**DeWitt Clinton,** 1769-1828, (U.S.) political leader, responsible for promoting idea of the Erie Canal.

**Robert Clive,** 1725-1774, (Br.) first administrator of Bengal, laid foundation for British Empire in India.

**Jean Baptiste Colbert,** 1619-1683, (F.) statesman, influential under Louis XIV, created the French navy.

**Oliver Cromwell,** 1599-1658, (Br.) Lord Protector of England, led parliamentary forces during Civil War.

**Curzon of Kedleston,** 1859-1925, (Br.) viceroy of India, foreign secretary, major force in dealing with post-WW I problems in Europe and Far East.

**Édouard Daladier,** 1884-1970, (F.) radical socialist politician, arrested by Vichy, interned by Germans until liberation in 1945.

**Georges Danton,** 1759-1794, (F.) a leading figure in the French Revolution.

**Jefferson Davis,** 1808-1889, (U.S.) president of the Confederate States of America.

**Charles G. Dawes,** 1865-1951, (U.S.) statesman, banker, advanced Dawes Plan to stabilize post-WW I German finances.

**Alcide De Gasperi,** 1881-1954, (It.) premier, founder of the Christian Democratic party.

**Charles DeGaulle,** 1890-1970, (F.) general, statesman, and first president of the Fifth Republic.

**Eamon De Valera,** 1882-1975, (Ir.-U.S.) statesman, led fight for Irish independence.

**Thomas E. Dewey,** 1902-1971, (U.S.) New York governor, twice loser in try for presidency.

**Ngo Dinh Diem,** 1901-1963, (Viet.) South Vietnamese president, assassinated in government take-over.

**Everett M. Dirksen,** 1896-1969, (U.S.) Senate Republican minority leader, orator.

**Benjamin Disraeli,** 1804-1881, (Br.) prime minister, considered founder of modern Conservative party.

**Engelbert Dollfuss,** 1892-1934, (Aus.) chancellor, assassinated by Austrian Nazis.

**Andrea Doria,** 1466-1560, (It.) Genoese admiral, statesman, called "Father of Peace" and "Liberator of Genoa."

**Stephen A. Douglas,** 1813-1861, (U.S.) Democratic leader, orator, opposed Lincoln for the presidency.

**Alexander Dubcek,** 1921-1992, (Czech.) statesman whose attempted liberalization was crushed, 1968.

**John Foster Dulles,** 1888-1959, (U.S.) secretary of state under Eisenhower, cold war policy maker.

**Friedrich Ebert,** 1871-1925, (G.) Social Democratic movement leader, instrumental in bringing about Weimar constitution.

**Sir Anthony Eden,** 1897-1977, (Br.) foreign secretary, prime minister during Suez invasion of 1956.

**Ludwig Erhard,** 1897-1977, (G.) economist, West German chancellor, led nation's economic rise after WW II.

**Hamilton Fish,** 1808-1893, (U.S.) secretary of state, successfully mediated disputes with Great Britain, Latin America.

**James V. Forrestal,** 1892-1949, (U.S.) secretary of navy, first secretary of defense.

**Francisco Franco,** 1892-1975, (Sp.) leader of rebel forces during Spanish Civil War and dictator of Spain.

**Benjamin Franklin,** 1706-1790, (U.S.) printer, publisher, author, inventor, scientist, diplomat.

**Louis de Frontenac,** 1620-1698, (F.) governor of New France (Canada); encouraged explorations, fought Iroquois.

**Hugh Gaitskell,** 1906-1963, (Br.) Labour party leader, major force in reversing its stand for unilateral disarmament.

**Albert Gallatin,** 1761-1849, (U.S.) secretary of treasury who was instrumental in negotiating end of War of 1812.

**Léon Gambetta,** 1838-1882, (F.) statesman, politician, one of the founders of the Third Republic.

**Indira Gandhi,** 1917-1984, (Ind.) succeeded father, Jawaharlal Nehru, as prime minister, assassinated.

**Mohandas K. Gandhi,** 1869-1948, (Ind.) political leader, ascetic, led nationalist movement against British rule.

**Giuseppe Garibaldi,** 1807-1882, (It.) patriot, soldier, a leading figure in the Risorgimento, the Italian unification movement.

**Genghis Khan,** c. 1167-1227, Mongol conqueror, ruler of vast Asian empire.

**William E. Gladstone,** 1809-1898, (Br.) prime minister 4 times, dominant force of Liberal party from 1868 to 1894.

**Paul Joseph Goebbels,** 1897-1945, (G.) Nazi propagandist, master of mass psychology.

**Klement Gottwald,** 1896-1953, (Czech.) communist leader ushered communism into his country.

**Che (Ernesto) Guevara,** 1928-1967, (Arg.) guerilla leader, prominent in Cuban revolution, killed in Bolivia.

**Haile Selassie,** 1891-1975, (Eth.) emperor, maintained monarchy through invasion, occupation, internal resistance.

**Alexander Hamilton,** 1755-1804, (U.S.) first treasury secretary, champion of strong central government.

**Dag Hammarskjold,** 1905-1961, (Swed.) statesman, UN secretary general.

**John Hancock,** 1737-1793, (U.S.) revolutionary leader, first signer of Declaration of Independence.

**John Hay,** 1838-1905, (U.S.) secretary of state, primarily associated with Open Door Policy toward China.

**Patrick Henry,** 1736-1799, (U.S.) major revolutionary figure, remarkable orator.

**Édouard Herriot,** 1872-1957, (F.) Radical Socialist leader, twice premier, president of National Assembly.

**Theodor Herzl,** 1860-1904, (Aus.) founder of modern Zionism.

**Heinrich Himmler,** 1900-1945, (G.) chief of Nazi SS and Gestapo, primarily responsible for the Holocaust.

**Paul von Hindenburg,** 1847-1934, (G.) field marshal, president.

**Hirohito,** 1902-1989; emperor of Japan from 1926.

**Adolf Hitler,** 1889-1945, (G.) dictator, founder of National Socialism; wrote *Mein Kampf,* strategy for world domination.

**Ho Chi Minh,** 1890-1969, (Viet.) North Vietnamese president, Vietnamese Communist leader, national hero.

**Harry L. Hopkins,** 1890-1946, (U.S.) New Deal administrator, closest adviser to FDR during WW II.

**Edward M. House,** 1858-1938, (U.S.) diplomat, confidential adviser to Woodrow Wilson.

**Samuel Houston,** 1793-1863, (U.S.) leader of struggle to win control of Texas from Mexico.

**Cordell Hull,** 1871-1955, (U.S.) secretary of state, initiated reciprocal trade to lower tariffs, helped organize UN.

**Hubert H. Humphrey,** 1911-1978, (U.S.) Minnesota Democrat, senator, vice president, spent 32 years in public service.

**Ibn Saud,** c. 1888-1953, (S. Arab.) founder of Saudi Arabia and its first king.

**Jacob Javits,** 1904-1986 (U.S.) U.S. senator from New York for 24 years.

**Jinnah, Muhammed Ali,** 1876-1948, (Pak.) founder, first governor-general of Pakistan.

**Benito Juarez,** 1806-1872, (Mex.) rallied countrymen against foreign threats, sought to create democratic, federal republic.

**Kamehameha I,** c. 1758-1819, (Haw.) founder, first monarch of unified Hawaii.

**Frank B. Kellogg,** 1856-1937, (U.S.) secretary of state, negotiated Kellogg-Briand Pact to outlaw war.

**Robert F. Kennedy,** 1925-1968, (U.S.) attorney general, senator, assassinated while seeking presidential nomination.

**Aleksandr Kerensky,** 1881-1970, (R.) revolutionary, served as premier after Feb. 1917 revolution until Bolshevik overthrow.

**Ruhollah Khomeini,** 1900-1989, (Iran), religious leader with Islamic title "ayatollah," directed overthrow of shah, 1979, became source of political authority in succeeding governments.

**Nikita Khrushchev,** 1894-1971, (USSR) premier, first secretary of Communist party, initiated de-Stalinization.

**Lajos Kossuth,** 1802-1894, (Hung.) principal figure in 1848 Hungarian revolution.

**Pyotr Kropotkin,** 1842-1921, (R.) anarchist, championed the peasants but opposed Bolshevism.

**Kublai Khan,** c. 1215-1294, Mongol emperor, founder of Yüan dynasty in China.

**Béla Kun,** 1886-c.1939, (Hung.) communist, member of 3d International, tried to foment worldwide revolution.

**Robert M. LaFollette,** 1855-1925, (U.S.) Wisconsin public official, leader of progressive movement.

**Pierre Laval,** 1883-1945, (F.) politician, Vichy foreign minister, executed for treason.

**Andrew Bonar Law,** 1858-1923, (Br.) Conservative party politician, led opposition to Irish home rule.

**Vladimir Ilyich Lenin (Ulyanov),** 1870-1924, (USSR) revolutionary, founder of Bolshevism, Soviet leader 1917-1924.

**Ferdinand de Lesseps,** 1805-1894, (F.) diplomat, engineer, conceived idea of Suez Canal.

**Rene Levesque,** 1922-1987 (Can.) Premier of Quebec, 1976-85; led unsuccessful fight to separate from Canada.

**Maxim Litvinov,** 1876-1951, (USSR) revolutionary, commissar of foreign affairs, favored cooperation with Western powers.

**Liu Shao-ch'i,** c.1898-1974, (Chin.) communist leader, fell from grace during "cultural revolution."

**David Lloyd George,** 1863-1945, (Br.) Liberal party prime minister, laid foundations for modern welfare state.

**Henry Cabot Lodge,** 1850-1924, (U.S.) Republican senator, led opposition to participation in League of Nations.

**Huey P. Long,** 1893-1935, (U.S.) Louisiana political demagogue, governor, assassinated.

**Rosa Luxemburg,** 1871-1919, (G.) revolutionary, leader of the German Social Democratic party and Spartacus party.

**J. Ramsay MacDonald,** 1866-1937, (Br.) first Labour party prime minister of Great Britain.

**Harold Macmillan,** 1895-1987 (Br.) prime minister of Great Britain, 1957-63.

**Joseph R. McCarthy,** 1908-1957, (U.S.) senator notorious for his witch hunt for communists in the government.

**Makarios III,** 1913-1977, (Cypr.) Greek Orthodox archbishop, first president of Cyprus.

**Malcolm X (Malcolm Little),** 1925-1965, (U.S.) black separatist leader, assassinated.

**Mao Tse-tung,** 1893-1976, (Chin.) chief Chinese Marxist theorist, soldier, led Chinese revolution establishing his nation as an important communist state.

**Jean Paul Marat,** 1743-1793, (F.) revolutionary, politician, identified with radical Jacobins, assassinated.

**José Marti,** 1853-1895, (Cub.) patriot, poet, leader of Cuban struggle for independence.

**Jan Masaryk,** 1886-1948, (Czech.) foreign minister, died by mysterious suicide following communist coup.

**Thomas G. Masaryk,** 1850-1937, (Czech.) statesman, philosopher, first president of Czechoslovak Republic.

**Jules Mazarin,** 1602-1661, (F.) cardinal, statesman, prime minister under Louis XIII and queen regent Anne of Austria.

**Giussepe Mazzini,** 1805-1872, (It.) reformer dedicated to the Risorgimento, 19th-century movement for the political and social renewal of Italy.

**Tom Mboya,** 1930-1969, (Kenyan) political leader, instrumental in securing independence for his country.

**Cosimo I de' Medici,** 1519-1574, (It.) Duke of Florence, grand duke of Tuscany.

**Lorenzo de' Medici,** the Magnificent, 1449-1492, (It.) merchant prince, a towering figure in Italian Renaissance.

**Catherine de Medicis,** 1519-1589, (F.) queen consort of Henry II, influential in Catholic-Huguenot wars.

**Golda Meir,** 1898-1979, (Isr.) prime minister, 1969-74.

**Klemens W.N.L. Metternich,** 1773-1859, (Aus.) statesman, arbiter of post-Napoleonic Europe.

**Anastas Mikoyan,** 1895-1978, (USSR) prominent Soviet leader from 1917; president 1964-65.

**Guy Mollet,** 1905-1975, (F.) social politician, resistance leader.

**Henry Morgenthau Jr.,** 1891-1967, (U.S.) secretary of treasury, raised funds to finance New Deal and U.S. WW II activities.

**Gouverneur Morris,** 1752-1816, (U.S.) statesman, diplomat, financial expert who helped plan decimal coinage system.

**Wayne Morse,** 1900-1974, (U.S.) senator, long-time critic of Vietnam War.

**Muhammad Ali,** 1769?-1849, (Egypt), pasha, founder of dynasty that encouraged emergence of modern Egyptian state.

**Benito Mussolini,** 1883-1945, (It.) dictator and leader of the Italian fascist state.

**Imre Nagy,** c. 1895-1958, (Hung.) communist premier, assassinated after Soviets crushed 1956 uprising.

**Gamal Abdel Nasser,** 1918-1970, (Egypt.) leader of Arab unification, second Egyptian president.

**Jawaharlal Nehru,** 1889-1964, (Ind.) prime minister, guided India through its early years of independence.

**Kwame Nkrumah,** 1909-1972, (Ghan.) dictatorial prime minister, deposed in 1966.

**Frederick North,** 1732-1792, (Br.) prime minister, his inept policies led to loss of American colonies.

**Daniel O'Connell,** 1775-1847, (Ir.) political leader, known as The Liberator.

**Omar,** c.581-644, Mohammedan leader, 2d caliph, led Islam to become an imperial power.

**Ignace Paderewski,** 1860-1941, (Pol.) statesman, pianist, composer, briefly prime minister, an ardent patriot.

**Viscount Palmerston,** 1784-1865, (Br.) Whig-Liberal prime minister, foreign minister, embodied British nationalism.

**George Papandreou,** 1888-1968, (Gk.) Republican politician, served three times as prime minister.

**Franz von Papen,** 1879-1969, (G.) politician, played major role in overthrow of Weimar Republic and rise of Hitler.

**Charles Stewart Parnell,** 1846-1891, (Ir.) nationalist leader, "uncrowned king of Ireland."

**Lester Pearson,** 1897-1972, (Can.) diplomat, Liberal party leader, prime minister.

**Robert Peel,** 1788-1850, (Br.) reformist prime minister, founder of Conservative party.

**Juan Perón,** 1895-1974, (Arg.) president, dictator.

**Joseph Pilsudski,** 1867-1935, (Pol.) statesman, instrumental in re-establishing Polish state in the 20th century.

**Charles Pinckney,** 1757-1824, (U.S.) founding father, his Pinckney plan was largely incorporated into constitution.

**William Pitt, the Elder,** 1708-1778, (Br.) statesman, called the "Great Commoner," transformed Britain into imperial power.

**William Pitt, the Younger,** 1759-1806, (Br.) prime minister during French Revolutionary wars.

**Georgi Plekhanov,** 1857-1918, (R.) revolutionary, social philosopher, called "father of Russian Marxism."

**Raymond Poincaré,** 1860-1934, (F.) 9th president of the Republic, advocated harsh punishment of Germany after WW I.

**Georges Pompidou,** 1911-1974, (F.) Gaullist political leader, president from 1969 to 1974.

**Grigori Potemkin,** 1739-1791, (R.) field marshal, favorite of Catherine II.

**Edmund Randolph,** 1753-1813, (U.S.) attorney, prominent in drafting, ratification of constitution.

**John Randolph,** 1773-1833, (U.S.) southern planter, strong advocate of states' rights.

**Jeannette Rankin,** 1880-1973, (U.S.) pacifist, first woman member of U.S. Congress.

**Walter Rathenau,** 1867-1922, (G.) industrialist, social theorist, statesman.

**Sam Rayburn,** 1882-1961, (U.S.) Democratic leader, representative for 47 years, House speaker for 17.

**Paul Reynaud,** 1878-1966, (F.) statesman, premier in 1940 at the time of France's defeat by Germany.

**Syngman Rhee,** 1875-1965, (Kor.) first president of the Republic of Korea.

**Cecil Rhodes,** 1853-1902, (Br.) imperialist, industrial magnate, established Rhodes scholarships in his will.

**Cardinal de Richelieu,** 1585-1642, (F.) statesman, known as "red eminence," chief minister to Louis XIII.

**Maximilien Robespierre,** 1758-1794, (F.) leading figure of French Revolution, responsible for much of Reign of Terror.

**Nelson Rockefeller,** 1908-1979, (U.S.) Republican gov. of N.Y., 1959-73; U.S. vice president, 1974-77.

**Eleanor Roosevelt,** 1884-1962, (U.S.) humanitarian, United Nations diplomat.

**Elihu Root,** 1845-1937, (U.S.) lawyer, statesman, diplomat, leading Republican supporter of the League of Nations.

**John Russell,** 1792-1878, (Br.) Liberal prime minister during the Irish potato famine.

**Anwar el-Sadat,** 1918-1981, (Egypt) president, 1970-1981, promoted peace with Israel; assassinated.

**Antônio de O. Salazar,** 1899-1970, (Port.) statesman, long-time dictator.

**José de San Martín,** 1778-1850, South American revolutionary, protector of Peru.

**Eisaku Sato,** 1901-1975, (Jap.) prime minister, presided over Japan's post-WW II emergence as major world power.

**Philipp Scheidemann,** 1865-1939, (G.) Social Democratic leader, first chancellor of the German republic.

**Robert Schuman,** 1886-1963, (F.) statesman, founded European Coal and Steel Community.

**Carl Schurz,** 1829-1906, (U.S.) German-American political leader, journalist, orator, dedicated reformer.

**Kurt Schuschnigg,** 1897-1977, (Aus.) chancellor, unsuccessful in stopping his country's annexation by Germany.

**William H. Seward,** 1801-1872, (U.S.) anti-slavery activist, as Lincoln's secretary of state purchased Alaska.

**Carlo Sforza,** 1872-1952, (It.) foreign minister, anti-fascist.

**Sitting Bull,** c. 1831-1890, (U.S.) Sioux leader in Battle of Little Bighorn over George A. Custer, 1876; fostered Ghost Dance religion.

**Alfred E. Smith,** 1873-1944, (U.S.) New York Democratic governor, first Roman Catholic to run for presidency.

**Jan C. Smuts,** 1870-1950, (S.Af.) statesman, philosopher, soldier, prime minister.

**Paul Henri Spaak,** 1899-1972, (Belg.) statesman, socialist leader.

**Joseph Stalin,** 1879-1953, (USSR) Soviet dictator, 1924-53.

**Edwin M. Stanton,** 1814-1869, (U.S.) Lincoln's secretary of war during the Civil War.

**Edward R. Stettinius Jr.,** 1900-1949, (U.S.) industrialist, secretary of state who coordinated aid to WW II allies.

**Adlai E. Stevenson,** 1900-1965, (U.S.) Democratic leader, diplomat, Illinois governor, presidential candidate.

**Henry L. Stimson,** 1867-1950, (U.S.) statesman, served in 5 administrations, influenced foreign policy in 1930s and 1940s.

**Gustav Stresemann,** 1878-1929, (G.) chancellor, foreign minister, dedicated to regaining friendship for post-WW I Germany.

**Sukarno,** 1901-1970, (Indon.) dictatorial first president of the Indonesian republic.

**Sun Yat-sen,** 1866-1925, (Chin.) revolutionary, leader of Kuomintang, regarded as the father of modern China.

**Robert A. Taft,** 1889-1953, (U.S.) conservative Senate leader, called "Mr. Republican."

**Charles de Talleyrand,** 1754-1838, (F.) statesman, diplomat, the major force of the Congress of Vienna of 1814-15.

**U Thant,** 1909-1974 (Bur.) statesman, UN secretary-general.

**Norman M. Thomas,** 1884-1968, (U.S.) social reformer, 6 times unsuccessful Socialist party presidential candidate.

**Josip Broz Tito,** 1892-1980, (Yug.) president of Yugoslavia from 1953, World War II guerrilla chief, postwar rival of Stalin, leader of 3d world movement.

**Palmiro Togliatti,** 1893-1964, (It.) major leader of Italian Communist party.

**Hideki Tojo,** 1885-1948, (Jap.) statesman, soldier, prime minister during most of WW II.

**François Toussaint L'Ouverture,** c. 1744-1803, (Hait.) patriot, martyr, thwarted French colonial aims.

**Leon Trotsky,** 1879-1940, (USSR) revolutionary, founded Red Army, expelled from party in conflict with Stalin.

**Rafael L. Trujillo Molina,** 1891-1961, (Dom.) absolute dictator, assassinated.

**Moise K. Tshombe,** 1919-1969, (Cong.) politician, president of secessionist Katanga, premier of Republic of Congo (Zaire).

**William M. Tweed,** 1823-1878, (U.S.) politician, absolute leader of Tammany Hall, NYC's Democratic political machine.

**Walter Ulbricht,** 1893-1973, (G.) communist leader of German Democratic Republic.

**Arthur H. Vandenberg,** 1884-1951, (U.S.) senator, proponent of anti-communist bipartisan foreign policy after WW II.

**Eleutherios Venizelos,** 1864-1936, (Gk.) most prominent Greek statesman in early 20th century; expanded territory.

**Hendrik F. Verwoerd,** 1901-1966, (S.Af.) prime minister, rigorously applied apartheid policy despite protest.

**Robert Walpole,** 1676-1745, (Br.) statesman, generally considered Britain's first prime minister.

**Daniel Webster,** 1782-1852, (U.S.) orator, politician, advocate of business interests during Jacksonian agrarianism.

**Chaim Weizmann,** 1874-1952, Zionist leader, scientist, first Israeli president.

**Wendell L. Willkie,** 1892-1944, (U.S.) Republican who tried to unseat FDR when he ran for his 3d term.

**Emiliano Zapata,** c. 1879-1919, (Mex.) revolutionary, major influence on modern Mexico.

## Notable Military and Naval Leaders of the Past

**Creighton Abrams,** 1914-1974, (U.S.) commanded forces in Vietnam, 1968-72.

**Harold Alexander,** 1891-1969, (Br.) led Allied invasion of Italy, WW2, 1943.

**Ethan Allen,** 1738-1789, (U.S.) headed Green Mountain Boys; captured Ft. Ticonderoga, 1775, Amer. Revolutionary War.

**Edmund Allenby,** 1861-1936, (Br.) in Boer War, WW1; led Egyptian expeditionary force, 1917-18.

**Benedict Arnold,** 1741-1801, (U.S.) victorious at Saratoga; tried to betray West Point to British, Amer. Revolutionary War.

**Henry "Hap" Arnold,** 1886-1950, (U.S.) commanded Army Air Force in WW2.

**John Barry,** 1745-1803, (U.S.) won numerous sea battles during Amer. Revolutionary War.

**Pierre Beauregard,** 1818-1893, (U.S.) Confederate general ordered bombardment of Ft. Sumter that began the Civil War.

**Gebhard v. Blücher,** 1742-1819, (G.) helped defeat Napoleon at Waterloo.

**Napoleon Bonaparte,** 1769-1821, (F.) defeated Russia and Austria at Austerlitz, 1805; invaded Russia, 1812; defeated at Waterloo, 1815.

**Edward Braddock,** 1695-1755, (Br.) commanded forces in French and Indian War.

**Omar N. Bradley,** 1893-1981, (U.S.) headed U.S. ground troops in Normandy invasion, WW2, 1944.

**John Burgoyne,** 1722-1792, (Br.) defeated at Saratoga, Amer. Revolutionary War.

**Claire Chennault,** 1890-1958, (U.S.) headed Flying Tigers in WW2.

**Mark Clark,** 1896-1984, (U.S.) led forces in WW2 and Korean War.

**Karl v. Clausewitz,** 1780-1831, (G.) wrote books on military theory.

**Lucius D. Clay,** 1897-1978, (U.S.) led Berlin airlift, 1948-49.

**Henry Clinton,** 1738-1795, (Br.) commander of forces in American Revolutionary War, 1778-81.

**Cochise,** c. 1815-1874, (Native Amer.) Chief of Chiricahua band of Apache Indians in Arizona.

**Charles Cornwallis,** 1738-1805, (Br.) victorious at Brandywine, 1777; surrendered at Yorktown, Amer. Revolutionary War.

**Crazy Horse,** 1849-1877, (U.S.) Sioux war chief victorious at Little Big Horn.

**George A. Custer,** 1839-1876, (U.S.) defeated and killed at Little Big Horn.

**Moshe Dayan,** 1915-1981, (Isr.) directed campaigns in the 1967, 1973 Arab-Israeli wars.

**Stephen Decatur,** 1779-1820, (U.S.) naval hero of Barbary wars, War of 1812.

**Anton Denikin,** 1872-1947, (R.) led White forces in Russian civil war.

**George Dewey,** 1837-1917, (U.S.) destroyed Spanish fleet at Manila, 1898, Spanish-American War.

**Hugh C. Dowding,** 1883-1970, (Br.) headed RAF, WW2, 1936-40.

**Jubal Early,** 1816-1894, (U.S.) Confederate general led raid on Washington, Civil War, 1864.

**Dwight D. Eisenhower,** 1890-1969, (U.S.) commanded Allied forces in Europe, WW2.

**David Farragut,** 1801-1870, (U.S.) Union admiral captured New Orleans, Mobile Bay, Civil War.

**Ferdinand Foch,** 1851-1929, (F.) headed victorious Allied armies, WW1, 1918.

**Nathan Bedford Forrest**, 1821-1877, (U.S.) Confederate general led cavalry raids against Union supply lines, Civil War.

**Frederick the Great**, 1712-1786, (G.) led Prussia in The Seven Years War.

**Horatio Gates**, 1728-1806, (U.S.) commanded army at Saratoga, Amer. Revolutionary War.

**Geronimo**, 1829-1909 (Native Amer.) leader of Chiricahua band of Apache Indians.

**Charles G. Gordon**, 1833-1885, (Br.) led forces in China, Crimean War; killed at Khartoum.

**Ulysses S. Grant**, 1822-1885, (U.S.) headed Union army, Civil War, 1864-65; forced Lee's surrender, 1865.

**Nathanael Greene**, 1742-1786, (U.S.) defeated British in Southern campaign, 1780-81.

**Heinz Guderian**, 1888-1953, (G.) tank theorist, led panzer forces in Poland, France, Russia, WW2.

**Douglas Haig**, 1861-1928, (Br.) led British armies in France, WW1, 1915-18.

**William F. Halsey**, 1882-1959, (U.S.) defeated Japanese fleet at Leyte Gulf, WW2, 1944.

**Sir Arthur Travers Harris**, 1895-1984, (Br.) led Britain's WW2 bomber command.

**Richard Howe**, 1726-1799, (Br.) commanded navy in Amer. Revolutionary War, 1776-78; June 1 victory against French, 1794.

**William Howe**, 1729-1814, (Br.) commanded forces in American Revolutionary War, 1776-78.

**Isaac Hull**, 1773-1843, (U.S.) sunk British frigate *Guerriere*, War of 1812.

**Thomas (Stonewall) Jackson**, 1824-1863, (U.S.) Confederate general led Shenandoah Valley campaign, Civil War.

**Joseph Joffre**, 1852-1931, (F.) headed Allied armies, won Battle of the Marne, WW1, 1914.

**John Paul Jones**, 1747-1792, (U.S.) commanded *Bonhomme Richard* in victory over Serapis, Amer. Revolutionary War, 1779.

**Stephen Kearny**, 1794-1848, (U.S.) headed Army of the West in Mexican War.

**Ernest J. King**, 1878-1956, (U.S.) chief naval strategist in WW2.

**Horatio H. Kitchener**, 1850-1916, (Br.) led forces in Boer War; victorious at Khartoum; organized army in WW1.

**Lavrenti Kornilov**, 1870-1918, (R.) Commander-in-Chief, 1917; led counter-revolutionary march on Petrograd.

**Thaddeus Kosciusko**, 1746-1817, (P.) aided American cause in Amer. Revolutionary War.

**Mikhail Kutuzov**, 1745-1813, (R.) fought French at Borodino, Napoleonic Wars, 1812; abandoned Moscow; forced French retreat.

**Marquis de Lafayette**, 1757-1834, (F.) aided American cause in Amer. Revolutionary War.

**T(homas) E. Lawrence (of Arabia)**, 1888-1935, (Br.) organized revolt of Arabs against Turks in WW1.

**Henry (Light-Horse Harry) Lee**, 1756-1818, (U.S.) cavalry officer in Amer. Revolutionary War.

**Robert E. Lee**, 1807-1870, (U.S.) Confederate general defeated at Gettysburg, Civil War; surrendered to Grant, 1865.

**Lyman Lemnitzer**, 1899-1988, (U.S.) WWII hero, later general, chairman of Joint Chiefs of Staff.

**James Longstreet**, 1821-1904, (U.S.) aided Lee at Gettysburg, Civil War.

**Douglas MacArthur**, 1880-1964, (U.S.) commanded forces in SW Pacific in WW2; headed occupation forces in Japan, 1945-51; UN commander in Korean War.

**Francis Marion**, 1733-1795, (U.S.) led guerrilla actions in S.C. during Amer. Revolutionary War.

**Duke of Marlborough**, 1650-1722, (Br.) led forces against Louis XIV in War of the Spanish Succession.

**George C. Marshall**, 1880-1959, (U.S.) chief of staff in WW2; authored Marshall Plan.

**George B. McClellan**, 1826-1885, (U.S.) Union general, commanded Army of the Potomac, Civil War, 1861-62.

**George Meade**, 1815-1872, (U.S.) commanded Union forces at Gettysburg, Civil War.

**Billy Mitchell**, 1879-1936, (U.S.) WW1 air-power advocate; court-martialed for insubordination, later vindicated.

**Helmuth v. Moltke**, 1800-1891; (G.) victorious in Austro-Prussian, Franco-Prussian wars.

**Louis de Montcalm**, 1712-1759, (F.) headed troops in Canada, French and Indian War; defeated at Quebec, 1759.

**Bernard Law Montgomery**, 1887-1976, (Br.) stopped German offensive at Alamein, WW2, 1942; helped plan Normandy invasion.

**Daniel Morgan**, 1736-1802, (U.S.) victorious at Cowpens, 1781, Amer. Revolutionary War.

**Louis Mountbatten**, 1900-1979, (Br.) Supreme Allied Commander of SE Asia, WW2, 1943-46.

**Joachim Murat**, 1767-1815, (F.) leader of cavalry at Marengo, 1800; Austerlitz, 1805; and Jena, 1806, Napoleonic Wars.

**Horatio Nelson**, 1758-1805, (Br.) naval commander destroyed French fleet at Trafalgar.

**Michel Ney**, 1769-1815, (F.) commanded forces in Switzerland, Austria, Russia, Napoleonic Wars; defeated at Waterloo.

**Chester Nimitz**, 1885-1966, (U.S.) commander of naval forces in Pacific in WW2.

**George S. Patton**, 1885-1945, (U.S.) led assault on Sicily, 1943, 3d Army invasion of German-occupied Europe, WW2.

**Oliver Perry**, 1785-1819, (U.S.) won Battle of Lake Erie in War of 1812.

**John Pershing**, 1860-1948, (U.S.) commanded Mexican border campaign, 1916; American expeditionary forces in WW1.

**Henri Philippe Pétain**, 1856-1951, (F.) defended Verdun, 1916; headed Vichy government in WW2.

**George E. Pickett**, 1825-1875, (U.S.) Confederate general famed for "charge" at Gettysburg, Civil War.

**Hyman Rickover**, 1900-1986 (U.S.) father of the nuclear navy.

**Erwin Rommel**, 1891-1944, (G.) headed Afrika Korps, WW2.

**Karl v. Rundstedt**, 1875-1953, (G.) supreme commander in West, WW2, 1943-45.

**Aleksandr Samsonov**, 1859-1914, (R.) led invasion of E. Prussia, WW1, defeated at Tannenberg, 1914.

**Winfield Scott**, 1786-1866, (U.S.) hero of War of 1812; headed forces in Mexican war, took Mexico City.

**Philip Sheridan**, 1831-1888, (U.S.) Union cavalry officer, headed Army of the Shenandoah, Civil War, 1864-65.

**William T. Sherman**, 1820-1891, (U.S.) Union general, sacked Atlanta during "march to the sea," Civil War, 1864.

**Carl Spaatz**, 1891-1974, (U.S.) directed strategic bombing against Germany, later Japan, in WW2.

**Raymond Spruance**, 1886-1969, (U.S.) victorious at Midway Island, WW2, 1942.

**Joseph W. Stilwell**, 1883-1946, (U.S.) headed forces in the China, Burma, India theater in WW2.

**J.E.B. Stuart**, 1833-1864, (U.S.) Confederate cavalry commander, Civil War.

**George H. Thomas**, 1816-1870, (U.S.) saved Union army at Chattanooga, 1863; victorious at Nashville, 1864, Civil War.

**Semyon Timoshenko**, 1895-1970, (USSR) defended Moscow, Stalingrad, WW2; led winter offensive, 1942-43.

**Alfred v. Tirpitz**, 1849-1930, (G.) responsible for submarine blockade in WW1.

**Jonathan M. Wainwright**, 1883-1953, (U.S.) forced to surrender on Corregidor, WW2, 1942.

**George Washington**, 1732-1799, (U.S.) led Continental army, Amer. Revolutionary War, 1775-83.

**Archibald Wavell**, 1883-1950, (Br.) commanded forces in N. and E. Africa, and SE Asia in WW2.

**Anthony Wayne**, 1745-1796, (U.S.) captured Stony Point, 1779, Amer. Revolutionary War; defeated Indians at Fallen Timbers, 1794.

**Duke of Wellington**, 1769-1852, (Br.) defeated Napoleon at Waterloo.

**James Wolfe**, 1727-1759, (Br.) captured Quebec from French, French and Indian War, 1759.

**Georgi Zhukov**, 1895-1974, (USSR) defended Moscow, 1941, led assault on Berlin, WW2.

## Poets Laureate of England

There is no authentic record of the origin of the office of Poet Laureate of England. According to Warton, there was a Versificator Regis, or King's Poet, in the reign of Henry III (1216-1272), and he was paid 100 shillings a year. Geoffrey Chaucer (1340-1400) assumed the title of Poet Laureate, and in 1389 got a royal grant of a yearly allowance of wine. In the reign of Edward IV (1461-1483), John Kay held the post. Under Henry VII (1485-1509), Andrew Bernard was the Poet Laureate, and was succeeded under Henry VIII (1509-1547) by John Skelton. Next came Edmund Spenser, who died in 1599; then Samuel Daniel, appointed 1599, and then Ben Jonson, 1619. Sir William D'Avenant was appointed in 1637. He was a godson of William Shakespeare.

Others were John Dryden, 1670; Thomas Shadwell, 1688; Nahum Tate, 1692; Nicholas Rowe, 1715; the Rev. Laurence Eusden, 1718; Colley Cibber, 1730; William Whitehead, 1757, on the refusal of Gray; Rev. Thomas Warton, 1785, on the refusal of Mason; Henry J. Pye, 1790; Robert Southey, 1813, on the refusal of Sir Walter Scott; William Wordsworth, 1843; Alfred, Lord Tennyson, 1850; Alfred Austin, 1896; Robert Bridges, 1913; John Masefield, 1930; Cecil Day Lewis, 1967; Sir John Betjeman, 1972; Ted Hughes, 1984.

## U.S. Poet Laureate

Robert Penn Warren, the poet, novelist, and essayist, was named the country's first official Poet Laureate on Feb. 26, 1986. The only writer to have won the Pulitzer Prize for fiction and poetry (twice), Warren was chosen by Daniel J. Boorstin, the Librarian of Congress. The appointment began in September, 1986. Other appointments, all beginning in September, are: 1987, Richard Wilbur; 1988, Howard Nemerov; 1990, Mark Strand; 1991, Joseph Brodsky; 1992, Mona Van Duyn, the first female poet laureate; 1993, Rita Dove, the first black poet laureate.

## Noted Writers of the Past

**George Ade,** 1866-1944, (U.S.) humorist. *Fables in Slang.*

**Conrad Aiken,** 1889-1973, (U.S.) poet, critic. *Ushant.*

**Louisa May Aicott,** 1832-1888, (U.S.) novelist. *Little Women.*

**Sholom Aleichem,** 1859-1916, (R.) Yiddish writer. *Tevye's Daughter, Adventures of Mottel, The Old Country.*

**Vicente Aleixandre,** 1898-1984, (Sp.) poet. *La destrucción o el amor, Dialogolos del conocimiento.*

**Horatio Alger,** 1832-1899, (U.S.) "rags-to-riches" books.

**Hans Christian Andersen,** 1805-1875, (Den.) author of fairy tales. *The Princess and the Pea, The Ugly Duckling.*

**Maxwell Anderson,** 1888-1959, (U.S.) playwright. *What Price Glory?, High Tor, Winterset, Key Largo.*

**Sherwood Anderson,** 1876-1941, (U.S.) short-story writer, "Death in the Woods"; *Winesburg, Ohio* (collection).

**Matthew Arnold,** 1822-1888, (Br.) poet, critic. "Thyrsis," "Dover Beach", "The Gypsy Scholar"; "Culture and Anarchy."

**Jane Austen,** 1775-1817, (Br.) novelist. *Pride and Prejudice, Sense and Sensibility, Emma, Mansfield Park, Persuasion.*

**Isaac Babel,** 1894-1941, (R.) short-story writer, playwright. *Odessa Tales, Red Cavalry.*

**Honoré de Balzac,** 1799-1850, (Fr.) novelist. *Le Père Goriot, Cousine Bette, Eugénie Grandet, The Human Comedy.*

**James M. Barrie,** 1860-1937, (Br.) playwright, novelist. *Peter Pan, Dear Brutus, What Every Woman Knows.*

**Charles Baudelaire,** 1821-1867, (Fr.) symbolist poet. *Les Fleurs du Mal.*

**L. Frank Baum,** 1856-1919, (U.S.) writer. Wizard of Oz series of children's books.

**Simone de Beauvoir,** 1908-1986, (Fr.) novelist, essayist. *The Second Sex, Memoirs of a Dutiful Daughter.*

**Samuel Beckett,** 1906-1989, (Ir.) novelist, playwright, in French and English. *Waiting for Godot, Endgame* (plays); *Murphy, Watt, Molloy* (novels).

**Brendan Behan,** 1923-1964, (Ir.) playwright. *The Quare Fellow, The Hostage, Borstal Boy.*

**Robert Benchley,** 1889-1945, (U.S.) humorist. *From Bed to Worse, My Ten Years in a Quandary.*

**Stephen Vincent Benét,** 1898-1943, (U.S.) poet, novelist. *John Brown's Body.*

**John Berryman,** 1914-1972, (U.S.) poet. *Homage to Mistress Bradstreet.*

**Ambrose Bierce,** 1842-1914, (U.S.) short-story writer, journalist. *In the Midst of Life, The Devil's Dictionary.*

**William Blake,** 1757-1827, (Br.) poet, artist. *Songs of Innocence, Songs of Experience, The Marriage of Heaven and Hell.*

**Giovanni Boccaccio,** 1313-1375, (It.) poet, storyteller. *Decameron, Filostrato.*

**Jorge Luis Borges,** 1900-1986, (Arg.) short-story writer, poet, essayist, *Labyrinths.*

**James Boswell,** 1740-1795, (Sc.) biographer. *The Life of Samuel Johnson, A Journal of a Tour of the Hebrides.*

**Anne Bradstreet,** c. 1612-1672, (U.S.) poet. *The Tenth Muse Lately Sprung Up in America.*

**Bertolt Brecht,** 1898-1956, (G.) dramatist, poet. *The Threepenny Opera, Mother Courage and Her Children.*

**Charlotte Brontë,** 1816-1855, (Br.) novelist. *Jane Eyre.*

**Emily Brontë,** 1818-1848, (Br.) novelist. *Wuthering Heights.*

**Elizabeth Barrett Browning,** 1806-1861, (Br.) poet. *Sonnets from the Portuguese, Aurora Leigh.*

**Robert Browning,** 1812-1889, (Br.) poet. "My Last Duchess," "Fra Lippo Lippi"; *The Ring and the Book.*

**Pearl Buck,** 1892-1973, (U.S.) novelist. *The Good Earth.*

**Mikhail Bulgakov,** 1891-1940, (R.) novelist, playwright. *The Heart of a Dog, The Master and Margarita.*

**John Bunyan,** 1628-1688, (Br.) writer. *Pilgrim's Progress.*

**Robert Burns,** 1759-1796, (Sc.) poet. "Flow Gently, Sweet Afton," "My Heart's in the Highlands," "Auld Lang Syne."

**Edgar Rice Burroughs,** 1875-1950, (U.S.) novelist. *Tarzan of the Apes.*

**George Gordon Lord Byron,** 1788-1824, (Br.) poet. *Don Juan, Childe Harold, Manfred, Cain.*

**Italo Calvino,** 1923-1985 (It.) novelist, short story writer. *If on a Winter's Night a Traveler . . .*

**Albert Camus,** 1913-1960, (F.) novelist. *The Plague, The Stranger, Caligula, The Fall.*

**Karel Capek,** 1890-1938, (Czech.) playwright, novelist, essayist. *R.U.R. (Rossum's Universal Robots).*

**Lewis Carroll,** 1832-1898, (Br.) writer, mathematician. *Alice's Adventures in Wonderland, Through the Looking Glass.*

**Giacomo Casanova,** 1725-1798, (It.) adventurer, memoirist.

**Willa Cather,** 1876-1947, (U.S.) novelist, essayist. *O Pioneers!, My Antonia, Death Comes for the Archbishop.*

**Miguel de Cervantes Saavedra,** 1547-1616, (Sp.) novelist, dramatist, poet. *Don Quixote de la Mancha.*

**Raymond Chandler,** 1888-1959, (U.S.) writer of detective fiction. Philip Marlowe series.

**Geoffrey Chaucer,** c. 1340-1400, (Br.) poet. *The Canterbury Tales, Troilus and Criseyde.*

**John Cheever,** 1912-1982, (U.S.) short story writer, novelist. *The Wapshot Scandal,* "The Country Husband."

**Anton Chekhov,** 1860-1904, (R.) short-story writer, dramatist. *Uncle Vanya, The Cherry Orchard, The Three Sisters.*

**G.K. Chesterton,** 1874-1936, (Br.) critic, novelist. Father Brown series of mysteries.

**Kate Chopin,** 1851-1904, (U.S.) novelist, short-story writer. *The Awakening.*

**Agatha Christie,** 1891-1976, (Br.) mystery writer. *And Then There Were None, Murder on the Orient Express.*

**Jean Cocteau,** 1889-1963, (F.) writer, visual artist, filmmaker. *The Beauty and the Beast, Enfants Terribles.*

**Samuel Taylor Coleridge,** 1772-1834, (Br.) poet, critic. "Kubla Khan," "The Rime of the Ancient Mariner," "Christabel."

**(Sidonie) Colette,** 1873-1954, (F.) novelist. *Claudine, Gigi.*

**Joseph Conrad,** 1857-1924, (Br.) novelist. *Lord Jim, Heart of Darkness, The Nigger of the Narcissus, Nostromo.*

**James Fenimore Cooper,** 1789-1851, (U.S.) novelist. *Leather-Stocking Tales.*

**Pierre Corneille,** 1606-1684, (F.) dramatist. *Medeè, Le Cid, Horace, Cinna, Polyeucte.*

**Hart Crane,** 1899-1932, (U.S.) poet. "The Bridge."

**Stephen Crane,** 1871-1900, (U.S.) novelist, short-story writer. *The Red Badge of Courage,* "The Open Boat."

**e.e. cummings,** 1894-1962, (U.S.) poet. *Tulips and Chimneys.*

**Roald Dahl,** (Br.) 1916-1990, (U.S.) writer. *Charlie and the Chocolate Factory.*

**Gabriele D'Annunzio,** 1863-1938, (It.) poet, novelist, dramatist. *The Child of Pleasure, The Intruder, The Victim.*

**Dante Alighieri,** 1265-1321, (It.) poet. *The Divine Comedy.*

**Daniel Defoe,** 1660-1731, (Br.) writer. *Robinson Crusoe, Moll Flanders, Journal of the Plague Year.*

**Charles Dickens,** 1812-1870, (Br.) novelist. *David Copperfield, Oliver Twist, Great Expectations, The Pickwick Papers.*

**Emily Dickinson,** 1830-1886, (U.S.) poet.

**Isak Dinesen** (Karen Blixen), 1885-1962, (Dan.) author. *Out of Africa, Seven Gothic Tales, Winter's Tales.*

**John Donne,** 1573-1631, (Br.) poet. *Songs and Sonnets.*

**John Dos Passos,** 1896-1970, (U.S.) novelist. *U.S.A.*

**Fyodor Dostoyevsky,** 1821-1881, (R.) novelist. *Crime and Punishment, The Brothers Karamazov, The Possessed.*

**Arthur Conan Doyle,** 1859-1930, (Br.) novelist, created Sherlock Holmes mystery series.

**Theodore Dreiser,** 1871-1945, (U.S.) novelist. *An American Tragedy, Sister Carrie.*

**John Dryden,** 1631-1700, (Br.) poet, dramatist, critic. *All for Love, Mac Flecknoe, Absalom and Achitopel.*

**Alexandre Dumas,** 1802-1870, (F.) novelist, dramatist. *The Three Musketeers, The Count of Monte Cristo.*

**Alexandre Dumas** (fils), 1824-1895, (F.) dramatist, novelist. *La Dame aux camélias, Le Demi-Monde.*

**Ilya G. Ehrenburg,** 1891-1967, (R.) writer. *The Thaw.*

**George Eliot (Mary Ann Evans or Marian Evans),** 1819-1880, (Br.) novelist. *Adam Bede, Silas Marner, Middlemarch, The Mill on the Floss, Daniel Deronda.*

**T.S. Eliot,** 1888-1965, (Br.) poet, critic. *The Waste Land,* "The Love Song of J. Alfred Prufrock," *Four Quartets.*

**Ralph Waldo Emerson,** 1803-1882, (U.S.) poet, essayist. "Brahma," "Nature," "The Over-Soul," "Self-Reliance."

**James T. Farrell,** 1904-1979, (U.S.) novelist. *Studs Lonigan.*

**William Faulkner,** 1897-1962, (U.S.) novelist. *Sanctuary, Light in August, The Sound and the Fury, Absalom, Absalom!*

**Henry Fielding,** 1707-1754, (Br.) novelist. *Tom Jones.*

**F. Scott Fitzgerald,** 1896-1940, (U.S.) short-story writer, novelist. *The Great Gatsby, Tender is the Night.*

**Gustave Flaubert,** 1821-1880, (F.) novelist. *Madame Bovary.*

**C.S. Forester,** 1899-1966, (Br.) novelist. *Horatio Hornblower* series.

**E.M. Forster,** 1879-1970, (Br.) novelist. *A Passage to India.*

**Anatole France,** 1844-1924. (F.) writer. *Penguin Island, My Friend's Book, Le Crime de Sylvestre Bonnard.*

**Robert Frost,** 1874-1963, (U.S.) poet. "Birches," "Fire and Ice," "Stopping by Woods on a Snowy Evening."

**John Galsworthy,** 1867-1933, (Br.) novelist, dramatist. *The Forsyte Saga, A Modern Comedy.*

**Erle Stanley Gardner,** 1889-1970, (U.S.) novelist. *Perry Mason* series of mysteries.

**Jean Genet,** 1911-1986, (Fr.) playwright, novelist. *The Blacks, The Maids, The Balcony.*

**André Gide,** 1869-1951, (F.) writer, *The Immoralist, The Pastoral Symphony, Strait is the Gate.*

**Jean Giraudoux,** 1882-1944, (F.) novelist, dramatist. *Electra, The Madwoman of Chaillot, Ondine, Tiger at the Gate.*

**Johann W. von Goethe,** 1749-1832, (G.) poet, dramatist, novelist. *Faust, The Sorrows of Young Werther.*

**Nikolai Gogol,** 1809-1852, (R.) short-story writer, dramatist, novelist. *Dead Souls, The Inspector General.*

**Oliver Goldsmith,** 1730?-1774, (Br.-Ir.) writer. *The Vicar of Wakefield, She Stoops to Conquer.*

**Maxim Gorky,** 1868-1936, (R.) writer. *The Lower Depths.*

**Robert Graves,** 1895-1985, (Br.) poet, classical scholar, novelist. *I, Claudius; The White Goddess.*

**Thomas Gray,** 1716-1771, (Br.) poet. "Elegy Written in a Country Churchyard," "The Progress of Poesy."

**Graham Greene,** 1904-1991, (Br.) novelist. *The Power and the Glory, The Heart of the Matter, The Ministry of Fear.*

**Zane Grey,** 1875-1939, (U.S.) writer of western stories.

**Jakob Grimm,** 1785-1863, (G.) philologist, folklorist. *German Methodology, Grimm's Fairy Tales.*

**Wilhelm Grimm,** 1786-1859, (G.) philologist, folklorist. *Grimm's Fairy Tales.*

**Dashiell Hammett,** 1894-1961, (U.S.) writer of detective fiction, created Sam Spade.

**Knute Hamsun,** 1859-1952 (Nor.) novelist. *Hunger.*

**Thomas Hardy,** 1840-1928, (Br.) novelist, poet. *The Return of the Native, Tess of the D'Urbervilles, Jude the Obscure.*

**Joel Chandler Harris,** 1848-1908, (U.S.) short-story writer. *Uncle Remus* series.

**Moss Hart,** 1904-1961, (U.S.) playwright. *Once in a Lifetime, You Can't Take It With You, The Man Who Came to Dinner.*

**Bret Harte,** 1836-1902, (U.S.) short-story writer, poet. *The Luck of Roaring Camp.*

**Jaroslav Hasek,** 1883-1923, (Czech.) writer. *The Good Soldier Schweik.*

**Nathaniel Hawthorne,** 1804-1864, (U.S.) novelist, short story writer. *The Scarlet Letter,* "The Artist of the Beautiful."

**Heinrich Heine,** 1797-1856, (G.) poet. *Book of Songs.*

**Lillian Hellman,** 1905-1984, (U.S.) playwright, author of memoirs, "The Little Foxes," *An Unfinished Woman, Pentimento.*

**Ernest Hemingway,** 1899-1961, (U.S.) novelist, short-story writer. *A Farewell to Arms, For Whom the Bell Tolls.*

**O. Henry** (W.S. Porter), 1862-1910, (U.S.) short-story writer. "The Gift of the Magi."

**Hermann Hesse,** 1877-1962, (G.) novelist, poet. *Death and the Lover, Steppenwolf, Siddhartha.*

**Oliver Wendell Holmes,** 1809-1894, (U.S.) poet, novelist. *The Autocrat of the Breakfast-Table.*

**Alfred E. Housman,** 1859-1936, (Br.) poet. *A Shropshire Lad.*

**William Dean Howells,** 1837-1920, (U.S.) novelist, critic. *The Rise of Silas Lapham.*

**Langston Hughes,** 1902-1967, (U.S.) poet, playwright. *The Weary Blues, One-Way Ticket, Shakespeare in Harlem.*

**Victor Hugo,** 1802-1885, (F.) poet, dramatist, novelist. *Notre Dame de Paris, Les Misérables.*

**Nora Zeale Hurston,** 1903-1960, novelist, folklorist. *Their Eyes Were Watching God, Mules and Men.*

**Aldous Huxley** 1894-1963, (Br.) writer. *Brave New World.*

**Henrik Ibsen,** 1828-1906, (Nor.) dramatist, poet. *A Doll's House, Ghosts, The Wild Duck, Hedda Gabler.*

**Washington Irving,** 1783-1859, (U.S.) writer. "Rip Van Winkle," "The Legend of Sleepy Hollow."

**Shirley Jackson,** 1919-1965, (U.S.) writer. "The Lottery."

**Henry James,** 1843-1916, (U.S.) novelist, short-story writer, critic. *The Portrait of a Lady, The American, Daisy Miller.*

**Robinson Jeffers,** 1887-1962, (U.S.) poet, dramatist. *Tamar and Other Poems, Medea.*

**Samuel Johnson,** 1709-1784, (Br.) author, scholar, critic. *Dictionary of the English Language.*

**Ben Jonson,** 1572-1637, (Br.) dramatist, poet. *Volpone.*

**James Joyce,** 1882-1941, (Ir.) writer. *Ulysses, Dubliners, A Portrait of the Artist as a Young Man, Finnegans Wake.*

**Franz Kafka,** 1883-1924, (G.) novelist, short-story writer. *The Trial, Amerika, The Castle, The Metamorphosis.*

**George S. Kaufman,** 1889-1961, (U.S.) playwright. *The Man Who Came to Dinner, You Can't Take It With You, Stage Door.*

**Nikos Kazantzakis,** 1883?-1957, (Gk.) novelist. *Zorba the Greek, A Greek Passion.*

**John Keats,** 1795-1821, (Br.) poet. "Ode on a Grecian Urn," "Ode to a Nightingale," "La Belle Dame Sans Merci."

**Joyce Kilmer,** 1886-1918, (U.S.) poet, "Trees."

**Rudyard Kipling,** 1865-1936, (Br.) author, poet. "The White Man's Burden," "Gunga Din," *The Jungle Book.*

**Jean de la Fontaine,** 1621-1695, (F.) poet. *Fables choisies.*

**Pär Lagerkvist,** 1891-1974, (Swed.) poet, dramatist, novelist. *Barabbas, The Sybil.*

**Selma Lagerlöf,** 1858-1940, (Swed.) novelist. *Jerusalem, The Ring of the Lowenskolds.*

**Alphonse de Lamartine,** 1790-1869, (F.) poet, novelist, statesman. *Méditations poétiques.*

**Charles Lamb,** 1775-1834, (Br.) essayist. *Specimens of English Dramatic Poets, Essays of Elia.*

**Giuseppe di Lampedusa,** 1896-1957, (It.) novelist. *The Leopard.*

**Ring Lardner,** 1885-1933, (U.S.) short story writer, humorist. *You Know Me, Al.*

**D. H. Lawrence,** 1885-1930, (Br.) novelist. *Sons and Lovers, Women in Love, Lady Chatterley's Lover.*

**Mikhail Lermontov,** 1814-1841, (R.) novelist, poet. "Demon," *Hero of Our Time.*

**Alain-René Lesage,** 1668-1747, (F.) novelist. *Gil Blas de Santillane.*

**Gotthold Lessing,** 1729-1781, (G.) dramatist, philosopher, critic. *Miss Sara Sampson, Minna von Barnhelm.*

**Sinclair Lewis,** 1885-1951, (U.S.) novelist. *Babbitt, Arrowsmith, Dodsworth, Main Street.*

**Vachel Lindsay,** 1879-1931, (U.S.) poet. *General William Booth Enters into Heaven, The Congo.*

**Hugh Lofting,** 1886-1947, (Br.) writer. *Dr. Doolittle* series of children's books.

**Jack London,** 1876-1916, (U.S.) novelist, journalist. *Call of the Wild, The Sea-Wolf.*

**Henry Wadsworth Longfellow,** 1807-1882, (U.S.) poet. *Evangeline, The Song of Hiawatha.*

**Amy Lowell,** 1874-1925, (U.S.) poet, critic. "Lilacs."

**James Russell Lowell,** 1819-1891, (U.S.) poet, editor. *Poems, The Biglow Papers.*

**Robert Lowell,** 1917-1977, (U.S.) poet. "Lord Weary's Castle," "For the Union Dead."

**Niccolò Machiavelli,** 1469-1527, (It.) writer, statesman. *The Prince, Discourses on Livy.*

**Bernard Malamud,** 1914-1986, (U.S.) short story writer, novelist. "The Magic Barrel," *The Assistant, The Fixer.*

**Stéphane Mallarmé,** 1842-1898, (F.) poet. *The Afternoon of a Faun.*

**Thomas Malory,** ?-1471, (Br.) writer. *Morte d'Arthur.*

**Andre Malraux,** 1901-1976, (F.) novelist. *Man's Fate.*

**Osip Mandelstam,** 1891-1938, (R.) poet. *Stone, Tristia.*

**Thomas Mann,** 1875-1955, (G.) novelist, essayist. *Buddenbrooks, Death in Venice, The Magic Mountain.*

**Katherine Mansfield,** 1888-1923, (Br.) short story writer. "Bliss," "The Garden Party."

**Christopher Marlowe,** 1564-1593, (Br.) dramatist, poet. *Tamburlaine the Great, Dr. Faustus, The Jew of Malta.*

**John Masefield,** 1878-1967, (Br.) poet. "Sea Fever," "Cargoes," *Salt Water Ballads.*

**Edgar Lee Masters,** 1869-1950, (U.S.) poet, biographer. *Spoon River Anthology.*

**W. Somerset Maugham,** 1874-1965, (Br.) author. *Of Human Bondage, The Razor's Edge, The Moon and Sixpence.*

**Guy de Maupassant,** 1850-1893, (F.) novelist, short-story writer. "A Life," "Bel-Ami," "The Necklace."

**François Mauriac,** 1885-1970, (F.) novelist, dramatist. *Viper's Tangle, The Kiss to the Leper.*

**Vladimir Mayakovsky,** 1893-1930, (R.) poet, dramatist. *The Cloud in Trousers.*

**Mary McCarthy,** 1912-1989, (U.S.) critic, novelist. *Memories of a Catholic Girlhood.*

**Carson McCullers,** 1917-1967, (U.S.) novelist. *The Heart is a Lonely Hunter, Member of the Wedding.*

**Herman Melville,** 1819-1891, (U.S.) novelist. *Moby Dick, Typee, Billy Budd, Omoo.*

**H.L. Mencken,** 1880-1956, (U.S.) author, critic, editor. *Prejudices, The American Language.*

**George Meredith,** 1828-1909, (Br.) novelist, poet. *The Ordeal of Richard Feverel, The Egoist.*

**Prosper Mérimée,** 1803-1870, (F.) author. *Carmen.*

**Edna St. Vincent Millay,** 1892-1950, (U.S.) poet. *The Harp Weaver and Other Poems, A Few Figs from Thistles.*

**A.A. Milne,** 1882-1956, (Br.) author. *Winnie-the-Pooh.*

**John Milton,** 1608-1674, (Br.) poet. *Paradise Lost.*

**Mishima Yukio** (Hiraoka Kimitake), 1925-1970, (Jap.) writer. *Confessions of a Mask.*

**Gabriela Mistral,** 1889-1957, (Chil.) poet. *Sonnets of Death, Desolación, Tala, Lagar.*

**Margaret Mitchell,** 1900-1949, (U.S.) novelist. *Gone With the Wind.*

**Jean Baptiste Molière,** 1622-1673, (F.) dramatist. *Le Tartuffe, Le Misanthrope, Le Bourgeois Gentilhomme.*

**Ferenc Molnár,** 1878-1952, (Hung.) dramatist, novelist. *Liliom, The Guardsman, The Swan.*

**Michel de Montaigne,** 1533-1592, (F.) essayist. *Essais.*

**Eugenio Montale,** 1896-1981, (It.) poet.

**Clement C. Moore,** 1779-1863, (U.S.) poet, educator. "A Visit from Saint Nicholas."

**Marianne Moore,** 1887-1972, (U.S.) poet. *O to Be a Dragon.*

**Thomas More,** 1478-1535, (Br.) writer. *Utopia.*

**H.H. Munro** (Saki), 1870-1916, (Br.) writer. *Reginald, The Chronicles of Clovis, Beasts and Super-Beasts.*

**Murasaki (Shikibu), Lady,** c. 978-1031?, (Jap.) novelist. *The Tale of Genji.*

**Alfred de Musset,** 1810-1857, (F.) poet, dramatist. *Confession d'un enfant du siècle.*

**Vladimir Nabokov,** 1899-1977, (Rus.-U.S.) novelist. *Lolita.*

**Ogden Nash,** 1902-1971, (U.S.) poet. *Hard Lines, I'm a Stranger Here Myself, The Private Dining Room.*

**Pablo Neruda,** 1904-1973, (Chil.) poet. *Twenty Love Poems and One Song of Despair, Toward the Splendid City.*

**Sean O'Casey,** 1884-1964, (Ir.) dramatist. *Juno and the Paycock, The Plough and the Stars.*

**Flannery O'Connor,** 1925-1964, (U.S.) novelist, short story writer. *Wise Blood,* "A Good Man Is Hard to Find."

**Clifford Odets,** 1906-1963, (U.S.) playwright. *Waiting for Lefty, Awake and Sing, Golden Boy, The Country Girl.*

**John O'Hara,** 1905-1970, (U.S.) novelist, short-story writer. *From the Terrace, Appointment in Samarra, Pal Joey.*

**Omar Khayyam,** c. 1028-1122, (Per.) poet. *Rubaiyat.*

**Eugene O'Neill,** 1888-1953, (U.S.) playwright. *Emperor Jones, Anna Christie, Long Day's Journey into Night.*

**George Orwell,** 1903-1950, (Br.) novelist, essayist. *Animal Farm, Nineteen Eighty-Four.*

**Thomas (Tom) Paine,** 1737-1809, (U.S.) writer, political theorist. *Common Sense.*

**Dorothy Parker,** 1893-1967, (U.S.) poet, short-story writer. *Enough Rope, Laments for the Living.*

**Boris Pasternak,** 1890-1960, (R.) poet, novelist. *Doctor Zhivago, My Sister, Life.*

**Samuel Pepys,** 1633-1703, (Br.) public official, diarist.

**S. J. Perelman,** 1904-1979, (U.S.) humorist. *The Road to Miltown, Under the Spreading Atrophy.*

**Francesco Petrarca,** 1304-1374, (It.) poet. *Africa, Trionfi, Canzoniere, On Solitude.*

**Luigi Pirandello,** 1867-1936, (It.) novelist, dramatist. *Six Characters in Search of an Author.*

**Edgar Allan Poe,** 1809-1849, (U.S.) poet, short-story writer, critic. "Annabel Lee," "The Raven," "The Purloined Letter."

**Alexander Pope,** 1688-1744, (Br.) poet. *The Rape of the Lock, An Essay on Man.*

**Katherine Anne Porter,** 1890-1980, (U.S.) novelist, short story writer. *Ship of Fools.*

**Ezra Pound,** 1885-1972, (U.S.) poet. *Cantos.*

**Marcel Proust,** 1871-1922, (F.) novelist. *A la recherche du temps perdu (Remembrance of Things Past).*

**Aleksandr Pushkin,** 1799-1837, (R.) poet, prose writer. *Boris Godunov, Eugene Onegin, The Bronze Horseman.*

**François Rabelais,** 1495-1553, (F.) writer. *Gargantua, Pantagruel.*

**Jean Racine,** 1639-1699, (F.) dramatist. *Andromaque, Phèdre, Bérénice, Britannicus.*

**Ayn Rand,** 1905-1982 (Rus.-U.S.) novelist, philosopher. *The Fountainhead, Atlas Shrugged.*

**Erich Maria Remarque,** 1898-1970, (Ger.-U.S.) novelist. *All Quiet on the Western Front.*

**Samuel Richardson,** 1689-1761, (Br.) novelist. *Clarissa Harlowe, Pamela; or, Virtue Rewarded.*

**Rainer Maria Rilke,** 1875-1926, (G.) poet. *Life and Songs, Duino Elegies, Poems from the Book of Hours.*

**Arthur Rimbaud,** 1854-1891, (F.) poet. *A Season in Hell.*

**Edwin Arlington Robinson,** 1869-1935, (U.S.) poet. "Richard Cory," "Miniver Cheevy."

**Theodore Roethke,** 1908-1963, (U.S.) poet. *Open House, The Waking, The Far Field.*

**Romain Rolland,** 1866-1944, (F.) novelist, biographer. *Jean-Christophe.*

**Pierre de Ronsard,** 1524-1585, (F.) poet. *Sonnets pour Hélène, La Franciade.*

**Edmond Rostand,** 1868-1918, (F.) poet, dramatist. *Cyrano de Bergerac.*

**Damon Runyon,** 1880-1946, (U.S.) short-story writer, journalist. *Guys and Dolls, Blue Plate Special.*

**John Ruskin,** 1819-1900, (Br.) critic, social theorist. *Modern Painters, The Seven Lamps of Architecture.*

**Antoine de Saint-Exupery,** 1900-1944, (F.) writer. *Wind, Sand and Stars, Le Petit Prince.*

**George Sand (Amandine Aurore Dupine),** 1804-1876, (F.) novelist. *Consuelo, The Haunted Pool, The Master Bell-Ringer.*

**Carl Sandburg,** 1878-1967, (U.S.) poet. *The People, Yes; Chicago Poems, Smoke and Steel, Harvest Poems.*

**George Santayana,** 1863-1952, (U.S.) poet, essayist, philosopher. *The Sense of Beauty, The Realms of Being.*

**William Saroyan,** 1908-1981, (U.S.) playwright, novelist. *The Time of Your Life, The Human Comedy.*

**Jean-Paul Sartre,** 1905-1980, (Fr.) philosopher, novelist, playwright. *Nausea, No Exit, Being and Nothingness.*

**Friedrich von Schiller,** 1759-1805, (G.) dramatist, poet, historian. *Don Carlos, Maria Stuart, Wilhelm Tell.*

**Sir Walter Scott,** 1771-1832, (Sc.) novelist, poet. *Ivanhoe.*

**Jaroslav Seifert,** 1902-1986, (Cz.) poet.

**Dr. Seuss (Theodor Seuss Geisel),** 1904-1991, (U.S.) children's book author & illustrator. *The Cat in the Hat.*

**William Shakespeare,** 1564-1616, (Br.) dramatist, poet. *Romeo and Juliet, Hamlet, King Lear, Julius Caesar, The Merchant of Venice, Othello, Macbeth, The Tempest;* sonnets.

**George Bernard Shaw,** 1856-1950, (Ir.-Br.) playwright, critic. *St. Joan, Pygmalion, Major Barbara, Man and Superman.*

**Mary Wollstonecraft Shelley,** 1797-1851, (Br.) novelist. *Frankenstein.*

**Percy Bysshe Shelley,** 1792-1822, (Br.) poet. *Prometheus Unbound, Adonais,* "Ode to the West Wind," "To a Skylark."

**Richard B. Sheridan,** 1751-1816, (Br.) dramatist. *The Rivals, School for Scandal.*

**Mikhail Sholokhov,** 1906-1984 (U.S.S.R.) writer. *And Quiet Flows the Don.*

**Upton Sinclair,** 1878-1968, (U.S.) novelist. *The Jungle.*

**Isaac Bashevis Singer,** 1904-1991, (Pol.-U.S.) novelist, short-story writer, in Yiddish. *The Magician of Lublin.*

**Edmund Spenser,** 1552-1599, (Br.) poet. *The Faerie Queen.*

**Christina Stead,** 1903-1983 (Austral.) novelist, short-story writer. *The Man Who Loved Children.*

**Richard Steele,** 1672-1729, (Br.) essayist, playwright, began the Tatler and Spectator. *The Conscious Lovers.*

**Lincoln Steffens,** 1866-1936, (U.S.) editor, writer. *The Shame of the Cities.*

**Gertrude Stein,** 1874-1946, (U.S.) writer. *Three Lives.*

**John Steinbeck,** 1902-1968, (U.S.) novelist. *Grapes of Wrath, Of Mice and Men, Winter of Our Discontent.*

**Stendhal (Marie Henri Beyle),** 1783-1842, (F.) novelist. *The Red and the Black, The Charterhouse of Parma.*

**Laurence Sterne,** 1713-1768, (Br.) novelist. *Tristram Shandy.*

**Wallace Stevens,** 1879-1955, (U.S.) poet. *Harmonium, The Man With the Blue Guitar, Notes toward a Supreme Fiction.*

**Robert Louis Stevenson,** 1850-1894, (Br.) novelist, poet, essayist. *Treasure Island, A Child's Garden of Verses.*

**Rex Stout,** 1886-1975, (U.S.) novelist, created Nero Wolfe.

**Harriet Beecher Stowe,** 1811-1896, (U.S.) novelist. *Uncle Tom's Cabin.*

**Lytton Strachey,** 1880-1932, (Br.) biographer, critic. *Eminent Victorians, Queen Victoria, Elizabeth and Essex.*

**August Strindberg,** 1849-1912, (Swed.) dramatist, novelist. *The Father, Miss Julie, The Creditors.*

**Jonathan Swift,** 1667-1745, (Br.) writer. *Gulliver's Travels.*

**Algernon C. Swinburne,** 1837-1909, (Br.) poet, critic. *Atalanta.*

**John M. Synge,** 1871-1909, (Ir.) poet, dramatist. *Riders to the Sea, The Playboy of the Western World.*

**Rabindranath Tagore,** 1861-1941, (Ind.), author, poet. *Sadhana, The Realization of Life, Gitanjali.*

**Booth Tarkington,** 1869-1946, (U.S.) novelist. *Seventeen, Alice Adams, Penrod.*

**Sara Teasdale,** 1884-1933, (U.S.) poet. *Helen of Troy and Other Poems, Rivers to the Sea, Flame and Shadow.*

**Alfred Lord Tennyson,** 1809-1892, (Br.) poet. *Idylls of the King, In Memoriam,* "The Charge of the Light Brigade."

**William Makepeace Thackeray,** 1811-1863, (Br.) novelist. *Vanity Fair, Henry Esmond, Pendennis.*

**Dylan Thomas,** 1914-1953, (Welsh) poet. *Under Milk Wood, A Child's Christmas in Wales.*

**Henry David Thoreau,** 1817-1862, (U.S.) transcendentalist thinker, writer. *Walden.*

**James Thurber,** 1894-1961, (U.S.) humorist, cartoonist. "The Secret Life of Walter Mitty," *My Life and Hard Times.*

**J.R.R. Tolkien,** 1892-1973, (Br.) writer. *Lord of the Rings.*

**Leo Tolstoy,** 1828-1910, (R.) novelist, short-story writer. *War and Peace, Anna Karenina,* "The Death of Ivan Ilyich."

**Anthony Trollope,** 1815-1882, (Br.) novelist. *The Warden, Barchester Towers, The Palliser novels.*

**Ivan Turgenev,** 1818-1883, (R.) novelist, short-story writer. *Fathers and Sons, First Love, A Month in the Country.*

**Mark Twain (Samuel Clemens),** 1835-1910, (U.S.) novelist, humorist. *The Adventures of Huckleberry Finn, Tom Sawyer.*

**Sigrid Undset,** 1881-1949, (Nor.) novelist, poet. *Kristin Lavransdatter.*

**Paul Valéry,** 1871-1945, (F.) poet, critic. *La Jeune Parque, The Graveyard by the Sea.*

**Jules Verne,** 1828-1905, (F.) novelist. *Twenty Thousand Leagues Under the Sea.*

**François Villon,** 1431-1463?, (F.) poet. *Le petit et le Grand Testament.*

**Evelyn Waugh,** 1903-1966, (Br.) novelist. *The Loved One.*

**H.G. Wells,** 1866-1946, (Br.) novelist. *The Time Machine, The Invisible Man, The War of the Worlds.*

**Rebecca West,** 1893-1983 (Br.) critic. *Black Lamb and Grey Falcon.*

**Edith Wharton,** 1862-1937, (U.S.) novelist. *The Age of Innocence, The House of Mirth, Ethan Frome.*

**E.B. White,** 1899-1985 (U.S.), essayist, novelist. *Here is New York, Charlotte's Web, Stuart Little.*

**T.H. White,** 1906-1964, (Br.) author. *The Once and Future King, A Book of Beasts.*

**Walt Whitman,** 1819-1892, (U.S.) poet. *Leaves of Grass.*

**John Greenleaf Whittier,** 1807-1892, (U.S.) poet, journalist. *Snow-bound.*

**Oscar Wilde,** 1854-1900, (Ir.) playwright, story-writer. *The Picture of Dorian Gray, The Importance of Being Earnest.*

**Laura Ingalls Wilder,** 1867-1957, (U.S.) novelist. *Little House on the Prairie* series of children's books.

**Thornton Wilder,** 1897-1975, (U.S.) playwright. *Our Town, The Skin of Our Teeth, The Matchmaker.*

**Tennessee Williams,** 1912-1983 (U.S.) playwright. *A Streetcar Named Desire, Cat on a Hot Tin Roof, The Glass Menagerie.*

**William Carlos Williams,** 1883-1963, (U.S.) poet. *Tempers, Al Que Quiere!, Paterson.*

**Edmund Wilson,** 1895-1972, (U.S.) critic, novelist. *Axel's Castle, To the Finland Station.*

**P.G. Wodehouse,** 1881-1975, (U.S.) humorist. The "Jeeves" novels, *Anything Goes.*

**Thomas Wolfe,** 1900-1938, (U.S.) novelist. *Look Homeward, Angel, You Can't Go Home Again, Of Time and the River.*

**Virginia Woolf,** 1882-1941, (Br.) novelist, essayist. *Mrs. Dalloway, To the Lighthouse, The Waves, A Room of One's Own.*

**William Wordsworth,** 1770-1850, (Br.) poet. "Tintern Abbey," "Ode: Intimations of Immortality," *The Prelude.*

**William Butler Yeats,** 1865-1939, (Ir.) poet, playwright. *The Wild Swans at Coole, The Tower, Last Poems.*

**Émile Zola,** 1840-1902, (F.) novelist. *Nana, The Dram Shop.*

## Noted Artists and Sculptors of the Past

Artists are painters unless otherwise indicated.

**Washington Allston,** 1779-1843, (U.S.) landscapist. *Belshazzar's Feast.*

**Albrecht Altdorfer,** 1480-1538, (Ger.) landscapist. *Battle of Alexander.*

**Andrea del Sarto,** 1486-1530, frescoes. *Madonna of the Harpies.*

**Fra Angelico,** c. 1400-1455, (It.) Renaissance muralist. *Madonna of the Linen Drapers' Guild.*

**Alexsandr Archipenko,** 1887-1964, (U.S.) sculptor. *Boxing Match, Medranos.*

**John James Audubon,** 1785-1851, (U.S.) *Birds of America.*

**Hans Baldung Grien,** 1484-1545, (Ger.) *Todentanz.*

**Ernst Barlach,** 1870-1938, (Ger.) Expressionist sculptor. *Man Drawing a Sword.*

**Frederic-Auguste Bartholdi,** 1834-1904, (Fr.) *Liberty Enlightening the World, Lion of Belfort.*

**Fra Bartolommeo,** 1472-1517, (It.) *Vision of St. Bernard.*

**Aubrey Beardsley,** 1872-1898, (Br.) illustrator. *Salome, Lysistrata.*

**Max Beckmann,** 1884-1950, (Ger.) Expressionist. *The Descent from the Cross.*

**Gentile Bellini,** 1426-1507, (It.) Renaissance. *Procession in St. Mark's Square.*

**Giovanni Bellini,** 1428-1516, (It.) *St. Francis in Ecstasy.*

**Jacopo Bellini,** 1400-1470, (It.) *Crucifixion.*

**George Wesley Bellows,** 1882-1925, (U.S.) sports artist. *Stag at Sharkey's.*

**Thomas Hart Benton,** 1889-1975, (U.S.) American regionalist. *Threshing Wheat, Arts of the West.*

**Gianlorenzo Bernini,** 1598-1680, (It.) Baroque sculpture. *The Assumption.*

**Albert Bierstadt,** 1830-1902, (U.S.) landscapist. *The Rocky Mountains, Mount Corcoran.*

**George Caleb Bingham,** 1811-1879, (U.S.) *Fur Traders Descending the Missouri.*

**William Blake,** 1752-1827, (Br.) engraver. *Book of Job, Songs of Innocence, Songs of Experience.*

**Rosa Bonheur,** 1822-1899, (Fr.) *The Horse Fair.*

**Pierre Bonnard,** 1867-1947, (Fr.) Intimist. *The Breakfast Room.*

**Gutzon Borglum,** 1871-1941, (U.S.) sculptor. *Mt. Rushmore Memorial.*

**Hieronymus Bosch,** 1450-1516, (Flem.) religious allegories. *The Crowning with Thorns.*

**Sandro Botticelli,** 1444-1510, (It.) Renaissance. *Birth of Venus.*

**Constantin Brancusi,** 1876-1957, (Rum.) Nonobjective sculptor. *Flying Turtle, The Kiss.*

**Georges Braque,** 1882-1963, (Fr.) Cubist. *Violin and Palette.*

**Pieter Bruegel the Elder,** c. 1525-1569, (Flem.) *The Peasant Dance.*

**Pieter Bruegel the Younger,** 1564-1638, (Flem.) *Village Fair, The Crucifixion.*

**Edward Burne-Jones,** 1833-1898, (Br.) Pre-Raphaelite artist-craftsman. *The Mirror of Venus.*

**Alexander Calder,** 1898-1976, (U.S.) sculptor. *Lobster Trap and Fish Tail.*

**Michelangelo Merisi da Caravaggio,** 1573-1610, (It.) Baroque. *The Supper at Emmaus.*

**Emily Carr,** 1871-1945, (Can.) landscapist. *Blunden Harbour, Big Raven.*

**Carlo Carra,** 1881-1966, (It.) Metaphysical school. *Lot's Daughters.*

**Mary Cassatt,** 1845-1926, (U.S.) Impressionist. *Woman Bathing.*

**George Catlin,** 1796-1872, (U.S.) American Indian life. *Gallery of Indians.*

**Benvenuto Cellini,** 1500-1571, (It.) Mannerist sculptor, goldsmith. *Perseus.*

**Paul Cezanne,** 1839-1906, (Fr.) *Card Players, Mont-Sainte-Victoire with Large Pine Trees.*

**Marc Chagall,** 1887-1985, (Rus.) Jewish life and folklore. *I and the Village.*

**Jean Simeon Chardin,** 1699-1779, (Fr.) still lifes. *The Kiss, The Grace.*

**Frederic Church,** 1826-1900, (U.S.) Hudson River school. *Niagara, Andes of Ecuador.*

**Giovanni Cimabue,** 1240-1302, (It.) Byzantine mosaicist. *Madonna Enthroned with St. Francis.*

**Claude Lorrain,** 1600-1682, (Fr.) ideal-landscapist. *The Enchanted Castle.*

**Thomas Cole,** 1801-1848, (U.S.) Hudson River school. *The Ox-Bow.*

**John Constable,** 1776-1837, (Br.) landscapist. *Salisbury Cathedral from the Bishop's Grounds.*

**John Singleton Copley,** 1738-1815, (U.S.) portraitist. *Samuel Adams, Watson and the Shark.*

**Lovis Corinth,** 1858-1925, (Ger.) Expressionist. *Apocalypse.*

**Jean-Baptiste-Camille Corot,** 1796-1875, (Fr.) landscapist. *Souvenir de Mortefontaine, Pastorale.*

**Correggio,** 1494-1534, (It.) Renaissance muralist. *Mystic Marriages of St. Catherine.*

**Gustave Courbet,** 1819-1877, (Fr.) Realist. *The Artist's Studio.*

**Lucas Cranach the Elder,** 1472-1553, (Ger.) Protestant Reformation portraitist. *Luther.*

**Nathaniel Currier,** 1813-1888, **and James M. Ives,** 1824-1895, (both U.S.) lithographers. *A Midnight Race on the Mississippi.*

**John Steuart Curry,** 1897-1946, (U.S.) Americana, murals. *Baptism in Kansas.*

**Salvador Dali,** 1904-1989, (Sp.) Surrealist. *Persistence of Memory.*

**Honore Daumier,** 1808-1879, (Fr.) caricaturist. *The Third-Class Carriage.*

**Jacques-Louis David,** 1748-1825, (Fr.) Neoclassicist. *The Oath of the Horatii.*

**Arthur Davies,** 1862-1928, (U.S.) Romantic landscapist. *Unicorns.*

**Edgar Degas,** 1834-1917, (Fr.) *The Ballet Class.*

**Eugene Delacroix,** 1789-1863, (Fr.) Romantic. *Massacre at Chios.*

**Paul Delaroche,** 1797-1856, (Fr.) historical themes. *Children of Edward IV.*

**Luca Della Robbia,** 1400-1482, (It.) Renaissance terracotta artist. *Cantoria (singing gallery), Florence cathedral.*

**Donatello,** 1386-1466, (It.) Renaissance sculptor. *David, Gattamelata.*

**Jean Dubuffet,** 1902-1985, (Fr.) painter, sculptor, printmaker. *Group of Four Trees.*

**Marcel Duchamp,** 1887-1968, (Fr.) *Nude Descending a Staircase.*

**Raoul Dufy,** 1877-1953, (Fr.) Fauvist. *Chateau and Horses.*

**Asher Brown Durand,** 1796-1886, (U.S.) Hudson River school. Kindred Spirits.

**Albrecht Durer,** 1471-1528, (Ger.) Renaissance engraver, woodcuts. St. Jerome in His Study, Melancholia I, Apocalypse.

**Anthony van Dyck,** 1599-1641, (Flem.) Baroque portraitist. Portrait of Charles I Hunting.

**Thomas Eakins,** 1844-1916, (U.S.) Realist. The Gross Clinic.

**Jacob Epstein,** 1880-1959, (Br.) religious and allegorical sculptor. Genesis, Ecce Homo.

**Jan van Eyck,** 1380-1441, (Flem.) naturalistic panels. Adoration of the Lamb.

**Anselm Feuerbach,** 1829-1880, (Ger.) Romantic Classicism. Judgement of Paris, Iphigenia.

**John Bernard Flannagan,** 1895-1942, (U.S.) animal sculptor. Triumph of the Egg.

**Jean-Honore Fragonard,** 1732-1806, (Fr.) Rococo. The Swing.

**Daniel Chester French,** 1850-1931, (U.S.) The Minute Man of Concord; seated Lincoln, Lincoln Memorial, Washington, D.C.

**Caspar David Friedrich,** 1774-1840, (Ger.) Romantic landscapes. Man and Woman Gazing at the Moon.

**Thomas Gainsborough,** 1727-1788, (Br.) portraitist. The Blue Boy.

**Paul Gauguin,** 1848-1903, (Fr.) Post-impressionist. The Tahitians.

**Lorenzo Ghiberti,** 1378-1455, (It.) Renaissance sculptor. Gates of Paradise baptistry doors, Florence.

**Alberto Giacometti,** 1901-1966, (It.) attenuated sculptures of solitary figures. Man Pointing.

**Giorgione,** c. 1477-1510, (It.) Renaissance. The Tempest.

**Giotto di Bondone,** 1267-1337, (It.) Renaissance. Presentation of Christ in the Temple.

**Francois Girardon,** 1628-1715, (Fr.) Baroque sculptor of classical themes. Apollo Tended by the Nymphs.

**Vincent van Gogh,** 1853-1890, (Dutch) The Starry Night, L'Arlesienne.

**Arshile Gorky,** 1905-1948, (U.S.) Surrealist. The Liver Is the Cock's Comb.

**Francisco de Goya y Lucientes,** 1746-1828, (Sp.) The Naked Maja, The Disasters of War (etchings).

**El Greco,** 1541-1614, View of Toledo.

**Horatio Greenough,** 1805-1852, (U.S.) Neo-classical sculptor. George Washington.

**Matthias Grünewald,** 1480-1528, (Ger.) mystical religious themes. The Resurrection.

**Frans Hals,** c. 1580-1666, (Dutch) portraitist. Laughing Cavalier, Gypsy Girl.

**Childe Hassam,** 1859-1935, (U.S.) Impressionist. Southwest Wind.

**Edward Hicks,** 1780-1849, (U.S.) folk painter. The Peaceable Kingdom.

**Hans Hofmann,** 1880-1966, (U.S.) early Abstract Expressionist. Spring. The Gate.

**William Hogarth,** 1697-1764, (Br.) caricaturist. The Rake's Progress.

**Katsushika Hokusai,** 1760-1849, (Jap.) printmaker. Crabs.

**Hans Holbein the Elder,** 1460-1524, (Ger.) late Gothic. Presentation of Christ in the Temple.

**Hans Holbein the Younger,** 1497-1543, (Ger.) portraitist. Henry VIII.

**Winslow Homer,** 1836-1910, (U.S.) marine themes. Marine Coast, High Cliff.

**Edward Hopper,** 1882-1967, (U.S.) realistic urban scenes. Sunlight in a Cafeteria.

**Jean-Auguste-Dominique Ingres,** 1780-1867, (Fr.) Classicist. Valpincon Bather.

**George Inness,** 1825-1894, (U.S.) luminous landscapist. Delaware Water Gap.

**Vasily Kandinsky,** 1866-1944, (Rus.) Abstractionist. Capricious Forms.

**Paul Klee,** 1879-1940, (Swiss) Abstractionist. Twittering Machine.

**Oscar Kokoschka,** 1886-1980, (Aus.) Expressionist. View of Prague.

**Kathe Kollwitz,** 1867-1945, (Ger.) printmaker, social justice themes. The Peasant War.

**Gaston Lachaise,** 1882-1935, (U.S.) figurative sculptor. Standing Woman.

**John La Farge,** 1835-1910, (U.S.) muralist. Red and White Peonies.

**Fernand Leger,** 1881-1955, (Fr.) machine art. The Cyclists.

**Leonardo da Vinci,** 1452-1519, (It.) Mona Lisa, Last Supper, The Annunciation.

**Emanuel Leutze,** 1816-1868, (U.S.) historical themes. Washington Crossing the Delaware.

**Jacques Lipchitz,** 1891-1973, (Fr.) Cubist sculptor. Harpist.

**Filippino Lippi,** 1457-1504, (It.) Renaissance. The Vision of St. Bernard.

**Fra Filippo Lippi,** 1406-1469, (It.) Renaissance. Coronation of the Virgin.

**Morris Louis,** 1912-1962, (U.S.) Abstract Expressionist. Signa, Stripes.

**Aristide Maillol,** 1861-1944, (Fr.) sculptor. The Mediterranean.

**Edouard Manet,** 1832-1883, (Fr.) forerunner of Impressionism. Luncheon on the Grass, Olympia.

**Andrea Mantegna,** 1431-1506, (It.) Renaissance frescoes. Triumph of Caesar.

**Franz Marc,** 1880-1916, (Ger.) Expressionist. Blue Horses.

**John Marin,** 1870-1953, (U.S.) expressionist seascapes. Maine Island.

**Reginald Marsh,** 1898-1954, (U.S.) satirical artist. Tattoo and Haircut.

**Masaccio,** 1401-1428, (It.) Renaissance. The Tribute Money.

**Henri Matisse,** 1869-1954, (Fr.) Fauvist. Woman with the Hat.

**Michelangelo Buonarroti,** 1475-1564, (It.) Pieta, David, Moses, The Last Judgment, Sistine Ceiling.

**Jean-Francois Millet,** 1814-1875, (Fr.) painter of peasant subjects. The Gleaners, The Man with a Hoe.

**Joan Miró,** 1893-1983, (Sp.) Exuberant colors, playful images. Catalan landscape, Dutch Interior.

**Amedeo Modigliani,** 1884-1920, (It.) Reclining Nude.

**Piet Mondrian,** 1872-1944, (Dutch) Abstractionist. Composition.

**Claude Monet,** 1840-1926, (Fr.) Impressionist. The Bridge at Argenteuil, Haystacks.

**Henry Moore,** 1898-1986, (Br.) sculptor of large-scale, abstract works. Reclining Figure (several).

**Gustave Moreau,** 1826-1898, (Fr.) Symbolist. The Apparition, Dance of Salome.

**James Wilson Morrice,** 1865-1924, (Can.) landscapist. The Ferry, Quebec, Venice, Looking Over the Lagoon.

**Grandma Moses,** 1860-1961, (U.S.) folk painter. Out for the Christmas Trees.

**Edvard Munch,** 1863-1944, (Nor.) Expressionist. The Cry.

**Bartolome Murillo,** 1618-1682, (Sp.) Baroque religious artist. Vision of St. Anthony. The Two Trinities.

**Barnett Newman,** 1905-1970, (U.S.) Abstract Expressionist. Stations of the Cross.

**Isamu Noguchi,** 1904-1988, (U.S.) trad. Japanese art, modern techniques.

**Georgia O'Keeffe,** 1887-1986, (U.S.) Southwest motifs. Cow's Skull.

**Jose Clemente Orozco,** 1883-1949, (Mex.) frescoes. House of Tears.

**Charles Willson Peale,** 1741-1827, (U.S.) American Revolutionary portraitist. Washington, Franklin, Jefferson, John Adams.

**Rembrandt Peale,** 1778-1860, (U.S.) portraitist. Thomas Jefferson.

**Pietro Perugino,** 1446-1523, (It.) Renaissance. Delivery of the Keys to St. Peter.

**Pablo Picasso,** 1881-1973, (Sp.) Guernica, Dove, Head of a Woman.

**Piero della Francesca,** c. 1415-1492, (It.) Renaissance. Duke of Urbino, Flagellation of Christ.

**Camille Pissarro,** 1830-1903, (Fr.) Impressionist. Morning Sunlight.

**Jackson Pollock,** 1912-1956, (U.S.) Abstract Expressionist. Autumn Rhythm.

**Nicolas Poussin,** 1594-1665, (Fr.) Baroque pictorial classicism. St. John on Patmos.

**Maurice B. Prendergast,** c. 1860-1924, (U.S.) Post-impressionist water colorist. Umbrellas in the Rain.

**Pierre-Paul Prud'hon,** 1758-1823, (Fr.) Romanticist. Crime pursued by Vengeance and Justice.

**Pierre Cecile Puvis de Chavannes,** 1824-1898, (Fr.) muralist. The Poor Fisherman.

**Raphael Sanzio,** 1483-1520, (It.) Renaissance. Disputa, School of Athens, Sistine Madonna.

**Man Ray,** 1890-1976, (U.S.) Dadaist. Observing Time, The Lovers.

**Odilon Redon,** 1840-1916, (Fr.) Symbolist lithographer. In the Dream.

**Rembrandt van Rijn,** 1606-1669, (Dutch) The Bridal Couple, The Night Watch.

**Frederic Remington,** 1861-1909, (U.S.) painter, sculptor, portrayer of the American West. Bronco Buster.

**Pierre-Auguste Renoir,** 1841-1919, (Fr.) Impressionist. The Luncheon of the Boating Party.

**Joshua Reynolds,** 1723-1792, (Br.) portraitist. Mrs. Siddons as the Tragic Muse.

**Diego Rivera,** 1886-1957, (Mex.) frescoes. The Fecund Earth.

**Norman Rockwell,** 1894-1978, (U.S.) illustrator. Saturday Evening Post covers.

**Auguste Rodin,** 1840-1917, (Fr.) sculptor. The Thinker, The Burghers of Calais.

**Mark Rothko**, 1903-1970, (U.S.) Abstract Expressionist. Light, Earth and Blue.

**Georges Rouault**, 1871-1958, (Fr.) Expressionist. The Old King.

**Henri Rousseau**, 1844-1910, (Fr.) primitive exotic themes. The Snake Charmer.

**Theodore Rousseau**, 1812-1867, (Swiss-Fr.) landscapist. Under the Birches, Evening.

**Peter Paul Rubens**, 1577-1640, (Flem.) Baroque. Mystic Marriage of St. Catherine.

**Jacob van Ruisdael**, c. 1628-1682, (Dutch) landscapist. Jewish Cemetery.

**Salomon van Ruysdael**, c. 1600-1670, (Dutch) landscapist. River with Ferry-Boat.

**Albert Pinkham Ryder**, 1847-1917, (U.S.) seascapes and allegories. Toilers of the Sea.

**Augustus Saint-Gaudens**, 1848-1907, (U.S.) memorial statues. Farragut, Mrs. Henry Adams (Grief).

**Andrea Sansovino**, 1460-1529, (It.) Renaissance sculptor. Baptism of Christ.

**Jacopo Sansovino**, 1486-1570, (It.) Renaissance sculptor. St. John the Baptist.

**John Singer Sargent**, 1856-1925, (U.S.) Edwardian society portraitist. The Wyndham Sisters, Madam X.

**Georges Seurat**, 1859-1891, (Fr.) Pointillist. Sunday Afternoon on the Island of Grande Jatte.

**Gino Severini**, 1883-1966, (It.) Futurist and Cubist. Dynamic Hieroglyph of the Bal Tabarin.

**Ben Shahn**, 1898-1969, (U.S.) social and political themes. Sacco and Vanzetti series, Seurat's Lunch, Handball.

**Charles Sheeler**, 1883-1965, (U.S.) Abstractionist. Upper Deck.

**David Alfaro Siqueiros**, 1896-1974, (Mex.) political muralist. March of Humanity.

**John F. Sloan**, 1871-1951, (U.S.) depictions of New York City. Wake of the Ferry.

**David Smith**, 1906-1965, (U.S.) welded metal sculpture. Hudson River Landscape, Zig, Cubi series.

**Gilbert Stuart**, 1755-1828, (U.S.) portraitist. George Washington.

**Thomas Sully**, 1783-1872, (U.S.) portraitist. Col. Thomas Handasyd Perkins, The Passage of the Delaware.

**Yves Tanguy**, 1900-1955, (Fr.) Surrealist. Rose of the Four Winds.

**Giovanni Battista Tiepolo**, 1696-1770, (It.) Rococo frescoes. The Crucifixion.

**Jacopo Tintoretto**, 1518-1594, (It.) Mannerist. The Last Supper.

**Titian**, c. 1485-1576, (It.) Renaissance. Venus and the Lute Player, The Bacchanal.

**Henri de Toulouse-Lautrec**, 1864-1901, (Fr.) At the Moulin Rouge.

**John Trumbull**, 1756-1843, (U.S.) historical themes. The Declaration of Independence.

**J(oseph) M(allord) W(illiam) Turner**, 1775-1851, (Br.) Romantic landscapist. Snow Storm.

**Paolo Uccello**, 1397-1475, (It.) Gothic-Renaissance. The Rout of San Romano.

**Maurice Utrillo**, 1883-1955, (Fr.) Impressionist. Sacre-Coeur de Montmartre.

**John Vanderlyn**, 1775-1852, (U.S.) Neo-classicist. Ariadne Asleep on the Island of Naxos.

**Diego Velazquez**, 1599-1660, (Sp.) Baroque. Las Meninas, Portrait of Juan de Pareja.

**Jan Vermeer**, 1632-1675, (Dutch) interior genre subjects. Young Woman with a Water Jug.

**Paolo Veronese**, 1528-1588, (It.) devotional themes, vastly peopled canvases. The Temptation of St. Anthony.

**Andrea del Verrocchio**, 1435-1488, (It.) Florentine sculptor. Colleoni.

**Maurice de Vlaminck**, 1876-1958, (Fr.) Fauvist landscapist. The Storm.

**Andy Warhol**, 1928-1987 (U.S.) Pop Art. Campbell's Soup Cans.

**Antoine Watteau**, 1684-1721, (Fr.) Rococo painter of "scenes of gallantry". The Embarkation for Cythera.

**George Frederic Watts**, 1817-1904, (Br.) painter and sculptor of grandiose allegorical themes. Hope, Physical Energy.

**Benjamin West**, 1738-1820, (U.S.) realistic historical themes. Death of General Wolfe.

**James Abbott McNeill Whistler**, 1834-1903, (U.S.) Arrangement in Grey and Black, No. 1: The Artist's Mother.

**Archibald M. Willard**, 1836-1918, (U.S.) The Spirit of '76.

**Grant Wood**, 1891-1942, (U.S.) Midwestern regionalist. American Gothic, Daughters of Revolution.

**Ossip Zadkine**, 1890-1967, (Rus.) School of Paris sculptor. The Destroyed City, Musicians, Christ.

## Noted Philosophers and Religionists of the Past

**Lyman Abbott**, 1835-1922, (U.S.) clergyman, reformer; advocate of Christian Socialism.

**Pierre Abelard**, 1079-1142, (F.) philosopher, theologian, and teacher; used dialectic method to support Christian dogma.

**Felix Adler**, 1851-1933, (U.S.) German-born founder of the Ethical Culture Society.

**Aristotle**, 384-322 B.C., (Gr.) philosopher, emphasized direct observation of nature.

**St. Augustine**, 354-430, Latin bishop considered the founder of formalized Christian theology.

**Averroes**, 1126-1198, (Sp.) Islamic philosopher.

**Roger Bacon**, c.1214-1294, (Br.) philosopher and scientist.

**Bahaullah (Mirza Husayn Ali)**, 1817-1892, (Pers.) founder of Bahai faith.

**Karl Barth**, 1886-1968, (Sw.) theologian, a leading force in 20th-century Protestantism.

**St. Benedict**, c.480-547, (It.) founded the Benedictines.

**Jeremy Bentham**, 1748-1832, (Br.) philosopher, reformer, founder of Utilitarianism.

**Henri Bergson**, 1859-1941, (F.) philosopher of evolution.

**George Berkeley**, 1685-1753, (Ir.) philosopher, churchman.

**John Biddle**, 1615-1662, (Br.) founder of English Unitarianism.

**Jakob Boehme**, 1575-1624, (G.) theosophist and mystic.

**William Brewster**, 1567-1644, (Br.) headed Pilgrims, signed Mayflower Compact.

**Emil Brunner**, 1889-1966, (Sw.) Protestant theologian.

**Giordano Bruno**, 1548-1600, (It.) philosopher, first to state the cosmic theory.

**Martin Buber**, 1878-1965, (G.) Jewish philosopher, theologian, wrote I and Thou.

**Buddha (Siddhartha Gautama)**, c.563-c.483 BC, (Ind.) philosopher, founded Buddhism.

**John Calvin**, 1509-1564, (F.) theologian, a key figure in the Protestant Reformation.

**Rudolph Carnap**, 1891-1970, (U.S.) German-born philosopher, a founder of logical positivism.

**William Ellery Channing**, 1780-1842, (U.S.) clergyman, early spokesman for Unitarianism.

**Auguste Comte**, 1798-1857, (F.) philosopher, the founder of positivism.

**Confucius**, 551-479 BC, (Chin.) founder of Confucianism.

**John Cotton**, 1584-1652, (Br.) Puritan theologian.

**Thomas Cranmer**, 1489-1556, (Br.) churchman, wrote much of Book of Common Prayer; promoter of English Reformation.

**René Descartes**, 1596-1650, (F.) philosopher, mathematician, "father of modern philosophy."

**John Dewey**, 1859-1952, (U.S.) philosopher, educator; helped inaugurate the progressive education movement.

**Denis Diderot**, 1713-1784, (F.) philosopher, creator of first modern encyclopedia.

**Mary Baker Eddy**, 1821-1910, (U.S.) founder of Christian Science, wrote Science and Health.

**Jonathan Edwards**, 1703-1758, (U.S.) preacher, theologian.

**(Desiderius) Erasmus**, c.1466-1536, (Du.) Renaissance humanist, wrote On the Freedom of the Will.

**Johann Fichte**, 1762-1814, (G.) philosopher, the first of the Transcendental Idealists.

**George Fox**, 1624-1691, (Br.) founder of Society of Friends.

**St. Francis of Assisi**, 1182-1226, (It.) founded Franciscans.

**al Ghazali**, 1058-1111, Islamic philosopher.

**Georg W. Hegel**, 1770-1831, (G.) Idealist philosopher.

**Martin Heidegger**, 1889-1976, (G.) existentialist philosopher, affected fields ranging from physics to literary criticism.

**Johann G. Herder**, 1744-1803, (G.) philosopher, cultural historian; a founder of German Romanticism.

**David Hume**, 1711-1776, (Sc.) philosopher, historian.

**Jan Hus**, 1369-1415, (Czech.) religious reformer.

**Edmund Husserl**, 1859-1938, (G.) philosopher, founded the Phenomenological movement.

**Thomas Huxley**, 1825-1895, (Br.) philosopher, educator.

**Ignatius of Loyola**, 1491-1556, (Sp.) founder of the Jesuits.

**William Inge**, 1860-1954, (Br.) theologian, explored the mystic aspects of Christianity.

**William James**, 1842-1910, (U.S.) philosopher, psychologist; advanced theory of the pragmatic nature of truth.

**Karl Jaspers**, 1883-1969, (G.) existentialist philosopher.

**Immanuel Kant**, 1724-1804, (G.) metaphysician, preeminent founder of modern critical philosophy; Critique of Pure Reason.

**Soren Kierkegaard**, 1813-1855, (Den.) philosopher, considered the father of Existentialism.

**John Knox**, 1505-1572, (Sc.) leader of the Protestant Reformation in Scotland.

**Lao-Tzu**, 604-531 BC, (Chin.) philosopher, considered the founder of the Taoist religion.

**Gottfried von Leibniz**, 1646-1716, (G.) philosopher, mathematician, influenced German Enlightenment.

**Martin Luther**, 1483-1546, (G.) leader of the Protestant Reformation, founded Lutheran church.

**Maimonides**, 1135-1204, (Sp.) Jewish philosopher.

**Jacques Maritain**, 1882-1973, (F.) Neo-Thomist philosopher.

**Cotton Mather**, 1663-1728, (U.S.) defender of orthodox Puritanism; founded Yale, 1701.

**Philipp Melanchthon**, 1497-1560, (G.) theologian, humanist; an important voice in the Reformation.

**Thomas Merton**, 1915-1968, (U.S.) Trappist monk, spiritual writer; *The Seven Storey Mountain*.

**John Stuart Mill**, 1806-1873, (Br.) philosopher, economist; *Essay on Liberty*.

**Mohammed**, c.570-632, Arab prophet of the religion of Islam.

**Dwight Moody**, 1837-1899, (U.S.) evangelist.

**George E. Moore**, 1873-1958, (Br.) ethical theorist.

**Elijah Muhammad**, 1897-1975, (U.S.) leader of the Black Muslim sect.

**Heinrich Muhlenberg**, 1711-1787, (G.) organized the Lutheran Church in America.

**John H. Newman**, 1801-1890, (Br.) Roman Catholic cardinal, led Oxford Movement; *Apologia pro Vita Sua*.

**Reinhold Niebuhr**, 1892-1971, (U.S.) Protestant theologian, social and political critic.

**Friedrich Nietzsche**, 1844-1900, (G.) moral philosopher; *The Birth of Tragedy, Thus Spake Zarathustra*.

**Blaise Pascal**, 1623-1662, (F.) philosopher, mathematician.

**St. Patrick**, c.389-c.461, brought Christianity to Ireland.

**St. Paul**, ?-c.67, a founder of Christianity; his epistles are first Christian theological writing.

**Charles S. Peirce**, 1839-1914, (U.S.) philosopher, logician; originated concept of Pragmatism, 1878.

**Plato**, 427?-347? B.C., (Gr.) philosopher, argued for independent reality of ideas; *Republic*.

**Josiah Royce** 1855-1916, (U.S.) Idealist philosopher.

**Charles T. Russell**, 1852-1916, (U.S.) founder of Jehovah's Witnesses.

**Fredrich von Schelling**, 1775-1854, (G.) philosopher of romantic movement.

**Friedrich Schleiermacher**, 1768-1834, (G.) theologian, a founder of modern Protestant theology.

**Arthur Schopenhauer**, 1788-1860, (G.) philosopher.

**Joseph Smith**, 1805-1844, (U.S.) founded Latter Day Saints (Mormon) movement, 1830.

**Socrates**, 469-399 B.C., (Gr.) philosopher, refined dialectic method.

**Herbert Spencer**, 1820-1903, (Br.) philosopher of evolution.

**Baruch Spinoza**, 1632-1677, (Du.) rationalist philosopher.

**Billy Sunday**, 1862-1935, (U.S.) evangelist.

**Daisetz Teitaro Suzuki**, 1870-1966, (Jap.) Buddhist scholar.

**Emanuel Swedenborg**, 1688-1772, (Swed.) philosopher, mystic.

**Thomas à Becket**, 1118-1170, (Br.) archbishop of Canterbury, opposed Henry II.

**Thomas à Kempis**, c.1380-1471, (G.) theologian probably wrote *Imitation of Christ*.

**Thomas Aquinas**, 1225-1274, (It.) Roman Catholic saint, founder of system declared official Catholic philosophy; *Summa Theologica*.

**Paul Tillich**, 1886-1965, (U.S.) German-born philosopher and theologian; brought depth psychology to Protestantism.

**John Wesley**, 1703-1791, (Br.) theologian, evangelist; founded Methodism.

**Alfred North Whitehead**, 1861-1947, (Br.) philosopher, mathematician; *Principia Mathematica* (with Bertrand Russell).

**William of Occam**, c.1285-c.1349 (Br.) medieval scholastic philosopher.

**Roger Williams**, c.1603-1683, (U.S.) clergyman, championed religious freedom and separation of church and state.

**Ludwig Wittgenstein**, 1889-1951, (Aus.) philosopher, influenced language philosophy.

**John Wycliffe**, 1320-1384, (Br.) theologian, reformer.

**Brigham Young**, 1801-1877, (U.S.) Mormon leader after Smith's assassination, colonized Utah.

**Huldrych Zwingli**, 1484-1531, (Sw.) theologian, led Swiss Protestant Reformation.

## Noted Social Reformers and Educators of the Past

**Jane Addams**, 1860-1935, (U.S.) co-founder of Hull House; won Nobel Peace Prize, 1931.

**Susan B. Anthony**, 1820-1906, (U.S.) a leader in temperance, anti-slavery, and women's suffrage movements.

**Henry Barnard**, 1811-1900, (U.S.) public school reformer.

**Thomas Barnardo**, 1845-1905, (Br.) social reformer, pioneered in the care of destitute children.

**Clara Barton**, 1821-1912, (U.S.) organizer of the American Red Cross.

**Henry Ward Beecher**, 1813-1887, (U.S.) clergyman, abolitionist.

**Sarah G. Blanding**, 1899-1985, (U.S.), head of Vassar College, 1946-64.

**Amelia Bloomer**, 1818-1894, (U.S.) social reformer, women's rights advocate.

**William Booth**, 1829-1912, (Br.) founded the Salvation Army.

**John Brown**, 1800-1859, (U.S.) abolitionist who led murder of 5 pro-slavery men, was hanged.

**Nicholas Murray Butler**, 1862-1947, (U.S.) educator headed Columbia Univ., 1902-45; won Nobel Peace Prize, 1931.

**Frances X. (Mother) Cabrini**, 1850-1917, (U.S.) Italian-born nun founded charitable institutions; first American canonized.

**Carrie Chapman Catt**, 1859-1947, (U.S.) suffragette, helped win passage of the 19th amendment.

**Clarence Darrow**, 1857-1938, (U.S.) lawyer, defender of "underdog," opponent of capital punishment.

**Dorothy Day**, 1897-1980, (U.S.) founder of Catholic Worker Movement.

**Eugene V. Debs**, 1855-1926, (U.S.) labor leader, led Pullman strike, 1894; 4-time Socialist presidential candidate.

**Melvil Dewey**, 1851-1931, (U.S.) devised decimal system of library-book classification.

**Dorothea Dix**, 1802-1887, (U.S.) crusader for humane care of mentally ill.

**Frederick Douglass**, 1817-1895, (U.S.) abolitionist.

**W.E.B. DuBois**, 1868-1963, (U.S.) Negro-rights leader, educator, and writer.

**William Lloyd Garrison**, 1805-1879, (U.S.) abolitionist, reformer.

**Giovanni Gentile**, 1875-1944, (It.) philosopher, educator; reformed Italian educational system.

**Emma Goldman**, 1869-1940, (Rus.-U.S.) published anarchist *Mother Earth*, birth control advocate.

**Samuel Gompers**, 1850-1924, (U.S.) labor leader; a founder and president of AFL.

**William Green**, 1873-1952, (U.S.) president of AFL, 1924-52.

**Michael Harrington**, 1928-1989, (U.S.) revealed poverty in affluent U.S. in *The Other America*, 1963.

**Sidney Hillman**, 1887-1946, (U.S.) labor leader, helped organize CIO.

**John Holt**, 1924-1985, (U.S.) educator and author, *How Children Fail*.

**Samuel G. Howe**, 1801-1876, (U.S.) social reformer, changed public attitudes toward the handicapped.

**Helen Keller**, 1880-1968, (U.S.) crusader for better treatment for the handicapped.

**Martin Luther King Jr.**, 1929-1968, (U.S.) civil rights leader; won Nobel Peace Prize, 1964.

**John L. Lewis**, 1880-1969, (U.S.) labor leader, headed United Mine Workers, 1920-60.

**Horace Mann**, 1796-1859, (U.S.) pioneered modern public school system.

**William H. McGuffey**, 1800-1873, (U.S.) author of *Reader*, the mainstay of 19th century U.S. public education.

**Alexander Meiklejohn**, 1872-1964, (U.S.) British-born educator, championed academic freedom and experimental curricula.

**Karl Menninger**, 1893-1991, (U.S.) with brother William made Menninger Clinic, and Menninger Foundation in Topeka, Kans., the center of U.S. psychiatry.

**Lucretia Mott**, 1793-1880, (U.S.) reformer, pioneer feminist.

**Philip Murray**, 1886-1952, (U.S.) Scotch-born labor leader.

**Florence Nightingale**, 1820-1910, (Br.) founder of modern nursing.

**Emmeline Pankhurst**, 1858-1928, (Br.) woman suffragist.

**Elizabeth P. Peabody**, 1804-1894, (U.S.) education pioneer, founded 1st kindergarten in U.S., 1860.

**Walter Reuther**, 1907-1970, (U.S.) labor leader, headed UAW.

**Jacob Riis**, 1849-1914, (U.S.) crusader for urban reforms.

**Margaret Sanger**, 1883-1966, (U.S.) social reformer, pioneered the birth control movement.

**Elizabeth Seton**, 1774-1821, (U.S.) established parochial school education in U.S.

**Earl of Shaftesbury (A.A. Cooper)**, 1801-1885, (Br.) social reformer.

**Elizabeth Cady Stanton**, 1815-1902, (U.S.) women's suffrage pioneer.

**Lucy Stone**, 1818-1893, (U.S.) feminist, abolitionist.

**Harriet Tubman**, c.1820-1913, (U.S.) abolitionist, ran Underground Railroad.

**Booker T. Washington**, 1856-1915, (U.S.) educator, reformer; championed vocational training for blacks.

**Walter F. White**, 1893-1955, (U.S.) headed NAACP, 1931-55.

**William Wilberforce**, 1759-1833, (Br.) social reformer, prominent in struggle to abolish the slave trade.

**Emma Hart Willard,** 1787-1870, (U.S.) pioneered higher education for women.

**Frances E. Willard,** 1839-1898, (U.S.) temperance, woman's rights leader.

**Mary Wollstonecraft,** 1759-1797 (Br.) wrote *Vindication of the Rights of Women.*

**Whitney M. Young Jr.,** 1921-1971, (U.S.) civil rights leader, headed National Urban League, 1961-71.

## Noted Historians, Economists, and Social Scientists of the Past

**Brooks Adams,** 1848-1927, (U.S.) historian, political theoretician; *The Law of Civilization and Decay.*

**Henry Adams,** 1838-1911, (U.S.) historian; *History of the United States of America, The Education of Henry Adams.*

**Francis Bacon,** 1561-1626, (Br.) philosopher, essayist, and statesman; applied scientific induction to philosophy.

**George Bancroft,** 1800-1891, (U.S.) historian, wrote 10-volume *History of the United States.*

**Charles A. Beard,** 1874-1948, (U.S.) historian; *The Economic Basis of Politics;* helped found New School for Social Research.

**Bede (the Venerable),** c.673-735, (Br.) scholar historian whose writings virtually comprise the learning of his time.

**Ruth Benedict,** 1887-1948, (U.S.) anthropologist, studied Indian tribes of the Southwest.

**Bruno Bettelheim,** 1903-1990, (Aust.-U.S.) psychoanalyst specializing in autistic children; *The Uses of Enchantment.*

**Louis Blanc,** 1811-1882, (F.) Socialist leader and historian whose ideas were a link between utopian and Marxist socialism.

**Leonard Bloomfield,** 1887-1949, (U.S.) linguist. *Language.*

**Franz Boas,** 1858-1942, (U.S.) German-born anthropologist, studied American Indians.

**Van Wyck Brooks,** 1886-1963, (U.S.) historian, critic of New England culture, esp. literature.

**Edmund Burke,** 1729-1797, (Ir.) British parliamentarian and political philosopher; influenced many Federalists.

**Joseph Campbell,** 1904-1987, (U.S.) wrote books on mythology, folklore.

**Thomas Carlyle,** 1795-1881, (Sc.) historian, critic; *Sartor Resartus, Past and Present, The French Revolution.*

**Edward Channing,** 1856-1931, (U.S.) historian, wrote 6-volume *A History of the United States.*

**John R. Commons,** 1862-1945, (U.S.) economist, labor historian; *Legal Foundations of Capitalism.*

**Benedetto Croce,** 1866-1952, (It.) philosopher, statesman, and historian; *Philosophy of the Spirit.*

**Bernard A. De Voto,** 1897-1955, (U.S.) historian; wrote trilogy on American West; edited Mark Twain manuscripts.

**Ariel Durant,** 1898-1981, (U.S.) historian, collaborated with husband on 11-volume *The Story of Civilization.*

**Will Durant,** 1885-1981, (U.S.) historian. *The Story of Civilization, The Story of Philosophy.*

**Emile Durkheim,** 1858-1917, (F.) a founder of modern sociology; *The Rules of Sociological Method.*

**Friedrich Engels,** 1820-1895, (G.) political writer, with Marx wrote the *Communist Manifesto.*

**Irving Fisher,** 1867-1947, (U.S.) economist, contributed to the development of modern monetary theory.

**John Fiske,** 1842-1901, (U.S.) historian and lecturer, popularized Darwinian theory of evolution.

**Charles Fourier,** 1772-1837, (F.) utopian socialist.

**Henry George,** 1839-1897, (U.S.) economist, reformer, led single-tax movement.

**Edward Gibbon,** 1737-1794, (Br.) historian, wrote *The History of the Decline and Fall of the Roman Empire.*

**Francesco Guicciardini,** 1483-1540, (It.) historian, wrote *Storia d'Italia,* principal historical work of the 16th-century.

**Thomas Hobbes,** 1588-1679, (Br.) political philosopher; *Leviathan.*

**Richard Hofstadter,** 1916-1970, (U.S.) historian; *The Age of Reform.*

**John Maynard Keynes,** 1883-1946, (Br.) economist, principal advocate of deficit spending.

**Alfred L. Kroeber,** 1876-1960, (U.S.) cultural anthropologist, studied Indians of North and South America.

**James L. Laughlin,** 1850-1933, (U.S.) economist, helped establish Federal Reserve System.

**Lucien Lévy-Bruhl,** 1857-1939, (F.) philosopher, studied the psychology of primitive societies; *Primitive Mentality.*

**Kurt Lewin,** 1890-1947, (U.S.) German-born psychologist, studied human motivation and group dynamics.

**John Locke,** 1632-1704, (Br.) philosopher; *Essay Concerning Human Understanding.*

**Konrad Lorenz,** 1904-1989, (Aus.) ethologist, pioneer in study of animal behavior.

**Thomas B. Macaulay,** 1800-1859, (Br.) historian, statesman.

**Bronislaw Malinowski,** 1884-1942, (Pol.) considered the father of social anthropology.

**Thomas R. Malthus,** 1766-1834, (Br.) economist, famed for *Essay on the Principle of Population.*

**Karl Mannheim,** 1893-1947, (Hung.) sociologist, historian; *Ideology and Utopia.*

**Karl Marx,** 1818-1883, (G.) political philosopher, proponent of modern communism; *Communist Manifesto, Das Kapital.*

**Giuseppe Mazzini,** 1805-1872, (It.) political philosopher.

**George H. Mead,** 1863-1931, (U.S.) philosopher, social psychologist.

**Margaret Mead,** 1901-1978, (U.S.) cultural anthropologist, popularized field; *Coming of Age in Samoa.*

**James Mill,** 1773-1836, (Sc.) philosopher, historian, economist; a proponent of Utilitarianism.

**John Stuart Mill,** 1806-1873, (Br.) philosopher, political economist; *Essay on Liberty.*

**Perry G. Miller,** 1905-1963, (U.S.) historian, interpreted 17th-century New England.

**Theodor Mommsen,** 1817-1903, (G.) historian; *The History of Rome.*

**Charles-Louis Montesquieu,** 1689-1755, (F.) social philosopher; *The Spirit of Laws.*

**Samuel Eliot Morison,** 1887-1976, (U.S.) historian, chronicled voyages of early explorers.

**Lewis Mumford,** 1895-1990, (U.S.) sociologist, critic, *The Culture of Cities.*

**Gunnar Myrdal,** 1898-1987 (Swe.) economist, social scientist.

**Allan Nevins,** 1890-1971, (U.S.) historian, biographer; *The Ordeal of the Union.*

**Jose Ortega y Gasset,** 1883-1955, (Sp.) philosopher, advocated control by elite; *The Revolt of the Masses.*

**Robert Owen,** 1771-1858, (Br.) political philosopher, reformer; pioneer in cooperative movement.

**Vilfredo Pareto,** 1848-1923, (It.) economist, sociologist.

**Francis Parkman,** 1823-1893, (U.S.) historian; *France and England in North America, 1851-92.*

**Marco Polo,** c.1254-1324, (It.) narrated an account of his travels to China.

**William Prescott,** 1796-1859, (U.S.) early American historian; *The Conquest of Peru.*

**Pierre Joseph Proudhon,** 1809-1865, (F.) social theorist, the father of anarchism; *The Philosophy of Property.*

**Francois Quesnay,** 1694-1774, (F.) economic theorist, demonstrated circular flow of economic activity through society.

**David Ricardo,** 1772-1823, (Br.) economic theorist, advocated free international trade.

**James H. Robinson,** 1863-1936, (U.S.) historian, educator.

**Carl Rogers,** 1902-1987, (U.S.) psychotherapist, author.

**Jean-Jacques Rousseau,** 1712-1778, (F.) social philosopher, the father of romantic sensibility; *Confessions.*

**Edward Sapir,** 1884-1939 (Ger.-U.S.) anthropologist, studied ethnology and linguistics of some U.S. Indian groups.

**Ferdinand de Saussure,** 1857-1913, (Swiss) a founder of modern linguistics.

**Hjalmar Schacht,** 1877-1970, (G.) economist; Reichsbank president.

**Joseph Schumpeter,** 1883-1950, (U.S.) Czech.-born economist, championed big business, capitalism.

**Albert Schweitzer,** 1875-1965, (Alsatian) social philosopher, theologian, medical missionary.

**George Simmel,** 1858-1918, (G.) sociologist, helped establish German sociology.

**B.F. Skinner,** 1904-1989, (U.S.) psychologist, championed behaviorism.

**Adam Smith,** 1723-1790, (Br.) economist, advocated laissez-faire economy and free trade.

**Jared Sparks,** 1789-1866, (U.S.) historian, educator, editor; *The Library of American Biography.*

**Oswald Spengler,** 1880-1936, (G.) philosopher and historian; *The Decline of the West.*

**William G. Sumner,** 1840-1910, (U.S.) social scientist, economist; championed laissez-faire economy, Social Darwinism.

**Hippolyte Taine,** 1828-1893, (F.) historian, basis of naturalistic school; *The Origins of Contemporary France.*

**Frank W. Taussig,** 1859-1940, (U.S.) economist, educator.

**A(lan) J(ohn) P(ercivale) Taylor,** 1906-1989, (Br.) historian, *The Origins of the Second World War.*

**Nikolaas Tinbergen,** 1907-1988, (Dutch-Br.) ethologist, pioneer in study of animal behavior.

**Alexis de Tocqueville,** 1805-1859, (F.) political scientist, historian; *Democracy in America.*

**Francis E. Townsend,** 1867-1960, (U.S.) led old-age pension movement, 1933.

**Arnold Toynbee,** 1889-1975, (Br.) historian; *A Study of History.*

**Heinrich von Treitschke,** 1834-1896, (G.) historian, political writer; *A History of Germany in the 19th Century.*

**George Trevelyan,** 1838-1928, (Br.) historian, statesman; favored "literary" over "scientific" history; *History of England.*

**Barbara Tuchman**, 1912-1989, (U.S.) author of popular history books, *The Guns of August, The March of Folly.*

**Frederick J. Turner**, 1861-1932, (U.S.) historian, educator; *The Frontier in American History.*

**Thorstein B. Veblen**, 1857-1929, (U.S.) economist, social philosopher; *The Theory of the Leisure Class.*

**Giovanni Vico**, 1668-1744, (It.) historian, philosopher; regarded by many as first modern historian. *New Science.*

**Voltaire (F.M. Arouet)**, 1694-1778, (F.) philosopher, historian, writer of "philosophical romances," *Candide.*

**Izaak Walton**, 1593-1683, (Br.) wrote biographies, political-philosophical study of fishing, *The Compleat Angler.*

**Sidney J.**, 1859-1947, and wife **Beatrice**, 1858-1943, **Webb** (Br.) leading figures in Fabian Society and British Labour Party.

**Walter P. Webb**, 1888-1963, (U.S.) historian of the West.

**Max Weber**, 1864-1920, (G.) sociologist. *The Protestant Ethic and the Spirit of Capitalism.*

# Noted Scientists of the Past

**Howard H. Aiken**, 1900-1973, (U.S.) mathematician, credited with designing forerunner of digital computer.

**Albertus Magnus**, 1193-1280, (G.) theologian, philosopher, established medieval Christian study of natural science.

**Andre-Marie Ampère**, 1775-1836, (F.) scientist known for contributions to electrodynamics.

**Amedeo Avogadro**, 1776-1856, (It.) chemist, physicist, advanced important theories on properties of gases.

**John Bardeen**, 1908-1991, (U.S.) co-inventor of the transistor that led to modern electronics.

**A.C. Becquerel**, 1788-1878, (F.) physicist, pioneer in electrochemical science.

**A.H. Becquerel**, 1852-1908, (F.) physicist, discovered radioactivity in uranium.

**Alexander Graham Bell**, 1847-1922, (U.S.) inventor, first to patent and commercially exploit the telephone, 1876.

**Daniel Bernoulli**, 1700-1782, (Swiss) mathematician, advanced kinetic theory of gases and fluids.

**Jöns Jakob Berzelius**, 1779-1848, (Swed.) chemist, developed modern chemical symbols and formulas.

**Henry Bessemer**, 1813-1898, (Br.) engineer, invented Bessemer steel-making process.

**Louis Blériot**, 1872-1936, (F.) engineer, pioneer aviator, invented and constructed monoplanes.

**Niels Bohr**, 1885-1962, (Dan.) physicist, leading figure in the development of quantum theory.

**Max Born**, 1882-1970, (G.) physicist known for research in quantum mechanics.

**Satyendranath Bose**, 1894-1974, (In.) physicist, chemist, mathematician known for Bose statistics, forerunner of modern quantum theory.

**Walter Brattain**, 1902-1987, (U.S.) inventor, worked on invention of transistor.

**Louis de Broglie**, 1893-1987, (F.) physicist, best known for wave theory.

**Robert Bunsen**, 1811-1899, (G.) chemist, invented Bunsen burner.

**Luther Burbank**, 1849-1926, (U.S.) plant breeder whose work developed plant breeding into a modern science.

**Vannevar Bush**, 1890-1974, (U.S.) electrical engineer, developed differential analyzer, first electronic analogue computer.

**Alexis Carrel**, 1873-1944, (F.) surgeon, biologist, developed methods of suturing blood vessels and transplanting organs.

**George Washington Carver**, 1860?-1943, (U.S.) agricultural chemist at Tuskegee Institute, discovered hundreds of uses for peanut, sweet potato, soybean.

**Henry Cavendish**, 1731-1810, (Br.) chemist, physicist, discovered hydrogen.

**James Chadwick**, 1891-1974, (Br.) physicist, discovered the neutron.

**Jean M. Charcot**, 1825-1893, (F.) neurologist known for work on hysteria, hypnotism, sclerosis.

**Albert Claude**, 1899-1983, (Belg.) a founder of modern cell biology.

**John D. Cockcroft**, 1897-1967, (Br.) nuclear physicist, constructed first atomic particle accelerator with E.T.S. Walton.

**Nicholas Copernicus**, 1473-1543, (Pol.) astronomer who first described solar system, with earth as one of planets revolving around sun.

**William Crookes**, 1832-1919, (Br.) physicist, chemist, discovered thallium, invented a cathode-ray tube, radiometer.

**Marie Curie**, 1867-1934, (Pol.-F.) physical chemist known for work on radium and its compounds.

**Pierre Curie**, 1859-1906, (F.) physical chemist known for work with his wife on radioactivity.

**Gottlieb Daimler**, 1834-1900, (G.) engineer, inventor, pioneer automobile manufacturer.

**John Dalton**, 1766-1844, (Br.) chemist, physicist, formulated atomic theory, made first table of atomic weights.

**Charles Darwin**, 1809-1882, (Br.) naturalist, established theory of organic evolution; *Origin of Species.*

**Humphry Davy**, 1778-1829, (Br.) chemist, research in electrochemistry led to isolation of potassium, sodium, calcium, barium, boron, magnesium, and strontium.

**Lee De Forest**, 1873-1961, (U.S.) inventor, pioneer in development of wireless telegraphy, sound pictures, television.

**Max Delbruck**, 1907-1981, (U.S.) pioneer in modern molecular genetics.

**Rudolf Diesel**, 1858-1913, (G.) mechanical engineer, patented Diesel engine.

**Thomas Dooley**, 1927-1961, (U.S.) "jungle doctor," noted for efforts to supply medical aid to underdeveloped countries.

**Christian Doppler**, 1803-1853, (Aus.) physicist, demonstrated Doppler effect (change in energy wavelengths caused by motion).

**Thomas A. Edison**, 1847-1931, (U.S.) inventor, held over 1,000 patents, including incandescent electric lamp, phonograph.

**Paul Ehrlich**, 1854-1915, (G.) bacteriologist, pioneer in modern immunology and bacteriology.

**Albert Einstein**, 1879-1955, (Ger.-U.S.) theoretical physicist, known for formulation of relativity theory.

**John F. Enders**, 1897-1985, (U.S.) virologist who helped discover vaccines against polio, measles, and mumps.

**Leonhard Euler**, 1707-1783, (Swiss) mathematician, physicist, authored first calculus book.

**Gabriel Fahrenheit**, 1686-1736, (G.) physicist, introduced Fahrenheit scale for thermometers.

**Michael Faraday**, 1791-1867, (Br.) chemist, physicist, known for work in field of electricity.

**Pierre de Fermat**, 1601-1665, (F.) mathematician, discovered analytic geometry, founded modern theory of numbers and calculus of probabilities.

**Enrico Fermi**, 1901-1954, (It.) physicist, one of chief architects of the nuclear age.

**Galileo Ferraris**, 1847-1897, (It.) physicist, electrical engineer, discovered principle of rotary magnetic field.

**Richard Feynman**, 1918-1988, (U.S.) a leading theoretical physicist of the postwar generation.

**Camille Flammarion**, 1842-1925, (F.) astronomer, popularized study of astronomy.

**Alexander Fleming**, 1881-1955, (Scot.) bacteriologist, discovered penicillin.

**Jean B.J. Fourier**, 1768-1830, (F.) mathematician, discovered theorem governing periodic oscillation.

**James Franck**, 1882-1964, (G.) physicist, proved value of quantum theory.

**Sigmund Freud**, 1856-1939, (Aus.) psychiatrist, founder of psychoanalysis.

**Galileo Galilei**, 1564-1642, (It.) astronomer, physicist, a founder of the experimental method.

**Luigi Galvani**, 1737-1798, (It.) physician, physicist, known as founder of galvanism.

**Carl Friedrich Gauss**, 1777-1855, (G.) mathematician, astronomer, physicist, made important contributions to almost every field of physical science, founded a number of new fields.

**Joseph Gay-Lussac**, 1778-1850, (F.) chemist, physicist, investigated behavior of gases, discovered law of combining volumes.

**Josiah W. Gibbs**, 1839-1903, (U.S.) theoretical physicist, chemist, founded chemical thermodynamics.

**Robert H. Goddard**, 1882-1945 (U.S.) physicist, father of modern rocketry.

**George W. Goethals**, 1858-1928, (U.S.) army engineer, built the Panama Canal.

**William C. Gorgas**, 1854-1920, (U.S.) sanitarian, U.S. army surgeon-general, his work to prevent yellow fever, malaria helped insure construction of Panama Canal.

**Ernest Haeckel**, 1834-1919, (G.) zoologist, evolutionist, a strong proponent of Darwin.

**Otto Hahn**, 1879-1968, (G.) chemist, worked on atomic fission.

**J.B.S. Haldane**, 1892-1964, (Sc.) scientist, known for work as geneticist and application of mathematics to science.

**James Hall**, 1761-1832, (Br.) geologist, chemist, founded experimental geology, geochemistry.

**Edmund Halley**, 1656-1742, (Br.) astronomer, calculated the orbits of many planets.

**William Harvey**, 1578-1657, (Br.) physician, anatomist, discovered circulation of the blood.

**Hermann v. Helmholtz**, 1821-1894, (G.) physicist, anatomist, physiologist, made fundamental contributions to physiology, optics, electrodynamics, mathematics, meteorology.

**William Herschel**, 1738-1822, (Br.) astronomer, discovered Uranus.

**Heinrich Hertz**, 1857-1894, (G.) physicist, his discoveries led to wireless telegraphy.

**David Hilbert,** 1862-1943, (G.) mathematician, formulated first satisfactory set of axioms for modern Euclidean geometry.

**Edwin P. Hubble,** 1889-1953, (U.S.) astronomer, produced first observational evidence of expanding universe.

**Alexander v. Humboldt,** 1769-1859, (G.) explorer, naturalist, propagator of earth sciences, originated ecology, geophysics.

**Julian Huxley,** 1887-1975, (Br.) biologist, a gifted exponent and philosopher of science.

**Edward Jenner,** 1749-1823, (Br.) physician, discovered vaccination.

**William Jenner,** 1815-1898, (Br.) physician, pathological anatomist.

**Frederic Joliot-Curie,** 1900-1958, (F.) physicist, with his wife continued work of Curies on radioactivity.

**Irene Joliot-Curie,** 1897-1956, (F.) physicist, continued work of Curies in radioactivity.

**James P. Joule,** 1818-1889, (Br.) physicist, determined relationship between heat and mechanical energy (conservation of energy).

**Carl Jung,** 1875-1961, (Sw.) psychiatrist, founder of analytical psychology.

**Wm. Thomson Kelvin,** 1824-1907, (Br.) mathematician, physicist, known for work on heat and electricity.

**Sister Elizabeth Kenny,** 1886-1952, (Austral.) nurse, developed method of treatment for polio.

**Johannes Kepler,** 1571-1630, (G.) astronomer, discovered important laws of planetary motion.

**Joseph Lagrange,** 1736-1813, (F.) geometer, astronomer, worked in all fields of analysis, and number theory, and analytical and celestial mechanics.

**Jean B. Lamarck,** 1744-1829, (F.) naturalist, forerunner of Darwin in evolutionary theory.

**Edwin Land,** 1910-1991, (U.S.) invented Polaroid camera.

**Irving Langmuir,** 1881-1957, (U.S.) physical chemist, his studies of molecular films on solid and liquid surfaces opened new fields in colloid research and biochemistry.

**Pierre S. Laplace,** 1749-1827, (F.) astronomer, physicist, put forth nebular hypothesis of origin of solar system.

**Antoine Lavoisier,** 1743-1794, (F.) chemist, founder of modern chemistry.

**Ernest O. Lawrence,** 1901-1958, (U.S.) physicist, invented the cyclotron.

**Louis Leakey,** 1903-1972, (Br.) anthropologist, discovered important fossils, remains of early hominids.

**Anton van Leeuwenhoek,** 1632-1723, (Du.) microscopist, father of microbiology.

**Gottfried Wilhelm Leibniz,** 1646-1716, (G.) mathematician, developed theories of differential and integral calculus.

**Justus von Liebig,** 1803-1873, (G.) chemist, established quantitative organic chemical analysis.

**Joseph Lister,** 1827-1912, (Br.) pioneer of antiseptic surgery.

**Percival Lowell,** 1855-1916, (U.S.) astronomer, predicted the existence of Pluto.

**Louis** (1864-1984) and **Auguste Lumière,** 1862-1954, (Fr.) invented cinematograph, first mechanism to project moving pictures on screen.

**Guglielmo Marconi,** 1874-1937, (It.) physicist, known for his development of wireless telegraphy.

**James Clerk Maxwell,** 1831-1879, (Sc.) physicist, known especially for his work in electricity and magnetism.

**Maria Goeppert Mayer,** 1906-1972, (G.-U.S.) physicist, independently developed theory of structure of atomic nuclei.

**Lise Meitner,** 1878-1968, (Aus.) physicist whose work contributed to the development of the atomic bomb.

**Gregor J. Mendel,** 1822-1884, (Aus.) botanist, known for his experimental work on heredity.

**Franz Mesmer,** 1734-1815, (G.) physician, developed theory of animal magnetism.

**Albert A. Michelson,** 1852-1931, (U.S.) physicist, established speed of light as a fundamental constant.

**Robert A. Millikan,** 1868-1953, (U.S.) physicist, noted for study of elementary electronic charge and photoelectric effect.

**Thomas Hunt Morgan,** 1866-1945, (U.S.) geneticist, embryologist, established chromosome theory of heredity.

**Isaac Newton,** 1642-1727, (Br.) natural philosopher, mathematician, discovered law of gravitation, laws of motion.

**Robert N. Noyce,** 1927-1989, (U.S.) inventor of the microchip, which revolutionized the electronics industry.

**J. Robert Oppenheimer,** 1904-1967, (U.S.) physicist, director of Los Alamos during development of the atomic bomb.

**Wilhelm Ostwald,** 1853-1932, (G.) physical chemist, philosopher, chief founder of physical chemistry.

**Robert Morris Page,** 1903-1992, (U.S.) physicist, research director of U.S. Naval Research Laboratory, a leading figure in development of radar technology.

**Louis Pasteur,** 1822-1895, (F.) chemist, originated process of pasteurization.

**Max Planck,** 1858-1947, (G.) physicist, originated and developed quantum theory.

**Henri Poincaré,** 1854-1912, (F.) mathematician, physicist, influenced cosmology, relativity, and topology.

**Joseph Priestley,** 1733-1804, (Br.) chemist, one of the discoverers of oxygen.

**Rabi, Isidor Isaac,** 1899-1988 (U.S.) physicist, pioneered atom exploration.

**Walter S. Reed,** 1851-1902, (U.S.) army pathologist, bacteriologist, proved mosquitos transmit yellow fever.

**Bernhard Riemann,** 1826-1866, (G.) mathematician, contributed to development of calculus, complex variable theory, and mathematical physics.

**Wilhelm Roentgen,** 1845-1923, (G.) physicist, discovered X-rays.

**Bertrand Russell,** 1872-1970, (Br.) logician, philosopher, one of the founders of modern logic, wrote *Principia Mathematica.*

**Ernest Rutherford,** 1871-1937, (Br.) physicist, discovered the atomic nucleus.

**Albert B. Sabin,** 1906-1993, (Rus.-U.S.) In 1954, developed oral polio vaccine, which was licensed in 1961.

**Giovanni Schiaparelli,** 1835-1910, (It.) astronomer, hypothesized canals on the surface of Mars.

**Arigelo Secchi,** 1818-1878, (It.) astronomer, pioneer in classifying stars by their spectra.

**Harlow Shapley,** 1885-1972, (U.S.) astronomer, noted for his studies of the galaxy.

**Charles P. Steinmetz,** 1865-1923, (G.-U.S.) electrical engineer, developed basic ideas on alternating current systems.

**Leo Szilard,** 1898-1964, (Hung.-U.S.) physicist, helped create first sustained nuclear reaction.

**Nikola Tesla,** 1856-1943, (Croatia-U.S.) electrical engineer, contributed to most developments in electronics.

**Rudolf Virchow,** 1821-1902, (G.) pathologist, a founder of cellular pathology.

**Alessandro Volta,** 1745-1827, (It.) physicist, pioneer in electricity.

**Werner von Braun,** 1912-1977 (G-U.S.) pioneered development of rockets for warfare and space exploration.

**Alfred Russell Wallace,** 1823-1913, (Br.) naturalist, proposed concept of evolution similar to Darwin.

**August v. Wasserman,** 1866-1925, (G.) bacteriologist, discovered reaction used as test for syphilis.

**James E. Watt,** 1736-1819, (Sc.) mechanical engineer, inventor, invented modern steam condensing engine.

**Alfred L. Wegener,** 1880-1930, (G.) meteorologist, geophysicist, postulated theory of continental drift.

**Norbert Wiener,** 1894-1964, (U.S.) mathematician, founder of the science of cybernetics.

**Sewall Wright,** 1889-1988 (U.S.) evolutionary theorist.

**Ferdinand v. Zeppelin,** 1838-1917 (G.) soldier, aeronaut, airship designer.

## Noted Business Leaders, Industrialists, and Philanthropists of the Past

**Elizabeth Arden (F.N. Graham),** 1884-1966, (U.S.) Canadian-born founder of cosmetics empire.

**Philip D. Armour,** 1832-1901, (U.S.) industrialist, streamlined meat packing.

**John Jacob Astor,** 1763-1848, (U.S.) German-born fur trader, banker, real estate magnate; at death, richest in U.S.

**Francis W. Ayer,** 1848-1923, (U.S.) ad industry pioneer.

**August Belmont,** 1816-1890, (U.S.) German-born financier.

**James B. (Diamond Jim) Brady,** 1856-1917, (U.S.) financier, philanthropist, legendary bon vivant.

**Adolphus Busch,** 1839-1913, (U.S.) German-born businessman, established brewery empire.

**Asa Candler,** 1851-1929, (U.S.) founded Coca-Cola Co.

**Andrew Carnegie,** 1835-1919, (U.S.) Scots-born industrialist, founded U.S. Steel; financed over 2,800 libraries.

**Tom Carvel,** 1908-1989, (Gr.-U.S.) founded ice cream chain.

**William Colgate,** 1783-1857, (U.S.) British-born businessman, philanthropist; founded soap-making empire.

**Jay Cooke,** 1821-1905, (U.S.) financier, sold $1 billion in Union bonds during Civil War.

**Peter Cooper,** 1791-1883, (U.S.) industrialist, inventor, philanthropist.

**Ezra Cornell,** 1807-1874, (U.S.) businessman, philanthropist; headed Western Union, established univ.

**Erastus Corning,** 1794-1872, (U.S.) financier, headed N.Y. Central.

**Charles Crocker,** 1822-1888, (U.S.) railroad builder, financier.

**Samuel Cunard,** 1787-1865, (Can.) pioneered trans-Atlantic steam navigation.

**Marcus Daly,** 1841-1900, (U.S.) Irish-born copper magnate.

**George T. Delacorte,** 1893-1991, (U.S.) publisher; Central Park donations included Alice in Wonderland statue.

**Walt Disney,** 1901-1966, (U.S.) pioneer in cinema animation, built entertainment empire.

**Herbert H. Dow,** 1866-1930, (U.S.) Canadian-born founder of chemical co.

**James Duke,** 1856-1925, (U.S.) founded American Tobacco, Duke Univ.

**Eleuthere I. du Pont,** 1771-1834, (U.S.) French-born gunpowder manufacturer; founded one of world's largest business empires.

**Thomas C. Durant,** 1820-1885, (U.S.) railroad official, financier.

**William C. Durant,** 1861-1947, (U.S.) industrialist, formed General Motors.

**George Eastman,** 1854-1932, (U.S.) inventor, manufacturer of photographic equipment.

**Marshall Field,** 1834-1906, (U.S.) merchant, founded Chicago's largest department store.

**Harvey Firestone,** 1868-1938, (U.S.) industrialist, founded tire co.

**Henry M. Flagler,** 1830-1913, (U.S.) financier, helped form Standard Oil; developed Florida as resort state.

**Malcolm Forbes,** 1919-1990, (U.S.) *Forbes* magazine publisher.

**Henry Ford,** 1863-1947, (U.S.) auto maker, developed first popular low-priced car.

**Henry Ford 2d,** 1917-1987, (U.S.) headed auto company founded by grandfather.

**Henry C. Frick,** 1849-1919, (U.S.) industrialist, helped organize U.S. Steel.

**Jakob Fugger (Jakob the Rich),** 1459-1525, (G.) headed leading banking house, trading concern, in 16th-century Europe.

**Alfred C. Fuller,** 1885-1973, (U.S.) Canadian-born businessman, founded brush co.

**Elbert H. Gary,** 1846-1927, (U.S.) U.S. Steel head, 1903-27.

**Jean Paul Getty,** 1892-1976, (U.S.) founded oil empire.

**Amadeo P. Giannini,** 1870-1949, (U.S.) founded Bank of America.

**Stephen Girard,** 1750-1831, (U.S.) French-born financier, philanthropist; richest man in U.S. at his death.

**Jay Gould,** 1836-1892, (U.S.) railroad magnate, financier, speculator.

**Hetty Green,** 1834-1916, (U.S.) financier, the "witch of Wall St."; richest woman in U.S. in her day.

**William Gregg,** 1800-1867, (U.S.) launched textile industry in the South.

**Meyer Guggenheim,** 1828-1905, (U.S.) Swiss-born merchant, philanthropist; built merchandising, mining empires.

**Armand Hammer,** 1898-1990, (U.S.) headed Occidental Petroleum; promoted U.S.-Soviet ties.

**Edward H. Harriman,** 1848-1909, (U.S.) railroad financier, administrator; headed Union Pacific.

**William Randolph Hearst,** 1863-1951, (U.S.) a dominant figure in American journalism; built vast publishing empire.

**Henry J. Heinz,** 1844-1919, (U.S.) founded food empire.

**James J. Hill,** 1838-1916, (U.S.) Canadian-born railroad magnate, financier; founded Great Northern Railway.

**Conrad N. Hilton,** 1888-1979, (U.S.) intl. hotel chain founder.

**Howard Hughes,** 1905-1976, (U.S.) industrialist, financier, movie maker.

**H.L. Hunt,** 1889-1974, (U.S.) oil magnate.

**Collis P. Huntington,** 1821-1900, (U.S.) railroad magnate.

**Henry E. Huntington,** 1850-1927, (U.S.) railroad builder, philanthropist.

**Walter L. Jacobs,** 1898-1985, (U.S.) founder of the first rental car agency, which later became Hertz.

**Howard Johnson,** 1896-1972, (U.S.) founded restaurants.

**Henry J. Kaiser,** 1882-1967, (U.S.) industrialist, built empire in steel, aluminum.

**Minor C. Keith,** 1848-1929, (U.S.) railroad magnate; founded United Fruit Co.

**Will K. Kellogg,** 1860-1951, (U.S.) businessman, philanthropist, founded breakfast food co.

**Richard King,** 1825-1885, (U.S.) cattleman, founded half-million acre King Ranch in Texas.

**William S. Knudsen,** 1879-1948, (U.S.) Danish-born auto industry executive.

**Samuel H. Kress,** 1863-1955, (U.S.) businessman, art collector, philanthropist; founded "dime store" chain.

**Ray A. Kroc,** 1902-1984, (U.S.) builder of McDonald's fast food empire; owner, San Diego Padres baseball team.

**Alfred Krupp,** 1812-1887, (G.) armaments magnate.

**Albert Lasker,** 1880-1952, (U.S.) businessman, philanthropist.

**Thomas Lipton,** 1850-1931, (Scot.) merchant, built tea empire.

**James McGill,** 1744-1813, (Can.) Scots-born fur trader, founded univ.

**Andrew W. Mellon,** 1855-1937, (U.S.) financier, industrialist; benefactor of National Gallery of Art.

**Charles E. Merrill,** 1885-1956, (U.S.) financier, developed firm of Merrill Lynch.

**John Pierpont Morgan,** 1837-1913, (U.S.) most powerful figure in finance and industry at the turn-of-the-century.

**Malcolm Muir,** 1885-1979, (U.S.) created *Business Week* magazine; headed *Newsweek,* 1937-61.

**Samuel Newhouse,** 1895-1979, (U.S.) publishing and broadcasting magnate, built communications empire.

**Aristotle Onassis,** 1900-1975, (Gr.) shipping magnate.

**William S. Paley,** 1901-1989, (U.S.) built CBS communications empire.

**George Peabody,** 1795-1869, (U.S.) merchant, financier, philanthropist.

**James C. Penney,** 1875-1971, (U.S.) businessman, developed department store chain.

**William C. Procter,** 1862-1934, (U.S.) headed soap co.

**John D. Rockefeller,** 1839-1937, (U.S.) industrialist, established Standard Oil; became world's wealthiest person.

**John D. Rockefeller Jr.,** 1874-1960, (U.S.) philanthropist, established foundation; provided land for United Nations.

**Meyer A. Rothschild,** 1743-1812, (G.) founded international banking house.

**Thomas Fortune Ryan,** 1851-1928, (U.S.) financier, dominated N.Y. City public transport; a founder of Amer. Tobacco.

**Russell Sage,** 1816-1906, (U.S.) financier.

**David Sarnoff,** 1891-1971, (U.S.) broadcasting pioneer, established first radio network, NBC.

**Richard W. Sears,** 1863-1914, (U.S.) founded mail-order co.

**(Ernst) Werner von Siemens,** 1816-1892, (G.) industrialist, inventor.

**Alfred P. Sloan,** 1875-1966, (U.S.) industrialist, philanthropist; headed General Motors.

**A. Leland Stanford,** 1824-1893, (U.S.) railroad official, philanthropist; founded univ.

**Nathan Strauss,** 1848-1931, (U.S.) German-born merchant, philanthropist; headed Macy's.

**Levi Strauss,** c.1829-1902, (U.S.) pants manufacturer.

**Clement Studebaker,** 1831-1901, (U.S.) wagon, carriage manufacturer.

**Gustavus Swift,** 1839-1903, (U.S.) pioneer meat-packer; promoted refrigerated railroad cars.

**Gerard Swope,** 1872-1957, (U.S.) industrialist, economist; headed General Electric.

**James Walter Thompson,** 1847-1928, (U.S.) ad executive.

**Theodore N. Vail,** 1845-1920, (U.S.) organized Bell Telephone system, headed ATT.

**Cornelius Vanderbilt,** 1794-1877, (U.S.) financier, established steamship, railroad empires.

**Henry Villard,** 1835-1900, (U.S.) German-born railroad executive, financier.

**Charles R. Walgreen,** 1873-1939, (U.S.) founded drugstore chain.

**DeWitt Wallace,** 1890-1981, (U.S.) and **Lila Wallace,** 1890-1984, (U.S.) co-founders of *Reader's Digest* magazine, philanthropists.

**Sam Walton,** 1918-1992, (U.S.) founder of Wal-Mart stores.

**John Wanamaker,** 1838-1922, (U.S.) pioneered department-store merchandising.

**Aaron Montgomery Ward,** 1843-1913, (U.S.) established first mail-order firm.

**Thomas J. Watson,** 1874-1956, (U.S.) headed IBM, 1924-49.

**John Hay Whitney,** 1905-1982, (U.S.) publisher, sportsman, philanthropist.

**Charles E. Wilson,** 1890-1961, (U.S.) auto industry executive; public official.

**Frank W. Woolworth,** 1852-1919, (U.S.) created 5 & 10 chain.

**William Wrigley Jr.,** 1861-1932, (U.S.) founded chewing gum company.

## Composers of the Western World

**Carl Philipp Emanuel Bach,** 1714-1788, (G.) Prussian and Wurtembergian Sonatas.

**Johann Christian Bach,** 1735-1782, (G.) Concertos; sonatas.

**Johann Sebastian Bach,** 1685-1750, (G.) St. Matthew Passion, The Well-Tempered Clavichord.

**Samuel Barber,** 1910-1981, (U.S.) Adagio for Strings, Vanessa.

**Bela Bartok,** 1881-1945, (Hung.) Concerto for Orchestra, The Miraculous Mandarin.

**Ludwig Van Beethoven,** 1770-1827, (G.) Concertos (Emperor); sonatas (Moonlight, Pastorale, Pathetique); symphonies (Eroica).

**Vincenzo Bellini,** 1801-1835, (It.) La Sonnambula, Norma, I Puritani.

**Alban Berg,** 1885-1935, (Aus.) Wozzeck, Lulu.

Hector Berlioz, 1803-1869, (F.) Damnation of Faust, Symphonie Fantastique, Requiem.

Leonard Bernstein, 1918-1990, (U.S.) Jeremiah Symphony, Chichester Psalms, Mass.

Georges Bizet, 1838-1875, (F.) Carmen, Pearl Fishers.

Ernest Bloch, 1880-1959, (Swiss-U.S.) Schelomo, Voice in the Wilderness, Sacred Service.

Luigi Boccherini, 1743-1805, (It.) Cello Concerto in B Flat, Symphony in C.

Alexander Borodin, 1833-1887, (R.) Prince Igor, In the Steppes of Central Asia.

Johannes Brahms, 1833-1897, (G.) Liebeslieder Waltzes, Rhapsody in E Flat Major, Opus 119 for Piano, Academic Festival Overture; symphonies; quartets.

Benjamin Britten, 1913-1976, (Br.) Peter Grimes, Turn of the Screw, Ceremony of Carols, War Requiem.

Anton Bruckner, 1824-1896, (Aus.) Symphonies (Romantic), Intermezzo for String Quintet.

Ferruccio Busoni, 1866-1924, (It.) Doctor Faust, Comedy Overture.

Dietrich Buxtehude, 1637-1707, (D.) Cantatas, trio sonatas.

William Byrd, 1543-1623, (Br.) Masses, sacred songs.

(Alexis-) Emmanuel Chabrier, 1841-1894, (Fr.) Le Roi Malgre Lui, Espana.

Gustave Charpentier, 1860-1956, (F.) Louise.

Frederic Chopin, 1810-1849, (P.) Polonaises, mazurkas, waltzes, etudes, nocturnes. Polonaise No. 6 in A Flat Major (Heroic); sonatas.

Aaron Copland, 1900-1990, (U.S.) Appalachian Spring.

(Achille-) Claude Debussy, 1862-1918, (F.) Pelleas et Melisande, La Mer, Prelude to the Afternoon of a Faun.

C.P. Leo Delibes, 1836-1891, (F.) Lakme, Coppelia, Sylvia.

Norman Dello Joio, b. 1913, (U.S.), Triumph of St. Joan, Psalm of David.

Gaetano Donizetti, 1797-1848, (It.) Elixir of Love, Lucia Di Lammermoor, Daughter of the Regiment.

Paul Dukas, 1865-1935, (Fr.) Sorcerer's Apprentice.

Antonin Dvorak, 1841-1904, (C.) Symphony in E Minor (From the New World).

Edward Elgar, 1857-1934, (Br.) Pomp and Circumstance.

Manuel de Falla, 1876-1946, (Sp.) La Vide Breve, El Amor Brujo.

Gabriel Faure, 1845-1924, (Fr.) Requiem, Ballade.

Friedrich von Flotow, 1812-1883, (G.) Martha.

Cesar Franck, 1822-1890, (Belg.) D Minor Symphony.

George Gershwin, 1898-1937, (U.S.) Rhapsody in Blue, American in Paris, Porgy and Bess.

Umberto Giordano, 1867-1948, (It.) Andrea Chenier.

Alexander K. Glazunoff, 1865-1936, (R.) Symphonies, Stenka Razin.

Mikhail Glinka, 1804-1857, (R.) Ruslan and Ludmilla.

Christoph W. Gluck, 1714-1787, (G.) Alceste, Iphigenie en Tauride.

Charles Gounod, 1818-1893, (F.) Faust, Romeo and Juliet.

Edvard Grieg, 1843-1907, (Nor.) Peer Gynt Suite, Concerto in A Minor.

George Frederick Handel, 1685-1759, (G., Br.) Messiah, Xerxes, Berenice.

Howard Hanson, 1896-1981, (U.S.) Symphonies No. 1 (Nordic) and 2 (Romantic).

Roy Harris, 1898-1979, (U.S.) Symphonies, Amer. Portraits.

Joseph Haydn, 1732-1809, (Aus.) Symphonies (Clock); oratorios; chamber music.

Paul Hindemith, 1895-1963, (U.S.) Mathis Der Maler.

Gustav Holst, 1874-1934, (Br.) The Planets.

Arthur Honegger, 1892-1955, (Swiss) Judith, Le Roi David, Pacific 231.

Alan Hovhaness, b. 1911, (U.S.) Symphonies, Magnificat.

Engelbert Humperdinck, 1854-1921, (G.) Hansel and Gretel.

Charles Ives, 1874-1954, (U.S.) Third Symphony.

Aram Khachaturian, 1903-1978, (Armen.) Gayane (ballet), symphonies.

Zoltan Kodaly, 1882-1967, (Hung.) Hary Janos, Psalmus Hungaricus.

Fritz Kreisler, 1875-1962, (Aus.) Caprice Viennois, Tambourin Chinois.

Rodolphe Kreutzer, 1766-1831, (F.) 40 etudes for violin.

Edouard V.A. Lalo, 1823-1892, (F.) Symphonie Espagnole.

Ruggiero Leoncavallo, 1857-1919, (It.) Pagliacci.

Franz Liszt, 1811-1886, (Hung.) 20 Hungarian rhapsodies, symphonic poems.

Edward MacDowell, 1861-1908, (U.S.) To a Wild Rose.

Gustav Mahler, 1860-1911, (Aus.) Lied von der Erde.

Pietro Mascagni, 1863-1945, (It.) Cavalleria Rusticana.

Jules Massenet, 1842-1912, (F.) Manon, Le Cid, Thais.

Felix Mendelssohn, 1809-1847, (G.) Midsummer Night's Dream, Songs Without Words.

Gian-Carlo Menotti, b. 1911, (It.-U.S.) The Medium, The Consul, Amahl and the Night Visitors.

Giacomo Meyerbeer, 1791-1864, (G.) Robert le Diable, Les Huguenots.

Claudio Monteverdi, 1567-1643, (It.) Opera; masses; madrigals.

Modest Moussorgsky, 1835-1881, (R.) Boris Godunov, Pictures at an Exhibition.

Wolfgang Amadeus Mozart, 1756-1791, (Aus.) Magic Flute, Marriage of Figaro; concertos; symphonies; etc.

Jacques Offenbach, 1819-1880, (F.) Tales of Hoffmann.

Carl Orff, 1895-1982, (G.) Carmina Burana.

Ignace Paderewski, 1860-1941, (P.) Minuet in G.

Niccolo Paganini, 1782-1840, (It.) Violinist, many bravura variations for violin.

Giovanni P. da Palestrina, c. 1525-1594, (It.) Masses; madrigals.

Amilcare Ponchielli, 1834-1886, (It.) La Gioconda.

Francis Poulenc, 1899-1963, (F.) Dialogues des Carmelites.

Serge Prokofiev, 1891-1953, (R.) Love for Three Oranges, Lt. Kije, Peter and the Wolf.

Giacomo Puccini, 1858-1924, (It.) La Boheme, Manon Lescaut, Tosca, Madame Butterfly.

Sergei Rachmaninov, 1873-1943, (R.) 24 preludes, 4 concerti, 4 symphonies. Prelude in C Sharp Minor.

Maurice Ravel, 1875-1937, (F.) Bolero, Daphnis et Chloe, Rapsodie Espagnole.

Nikolai Rimsky-Korsakov, 1844-1908, (R.) Golden Cockerel, Capriccio Espagnol, Scheherazade, Russian Easter Overture.

Gioacchino Rossini, 1792-1868, (It.) Barber of Seville, Semiramide, William Tell.

Chas. Camille Saint-Saens, 1835-1921, (F.) Samson and Delilah, Danse Macabre.

Alessandro Scarlatti, 1660-1725, (It.) Cantatas; concertos.

Domenico Scarlatti, 1685-1757, (It.) Harpsichord sonatas.

Arnold Schoenberg, 1874-1951, (Aus.) Pelleas and Melisande, Transfigured Night, De Profundis.

Franz Schubert, 1797-1828, (A.) Lieder; symphonies (Unfinished); overtures (Rosamunde).

William Schuman, b. 1910, (U.S.) Credendum, New England Triptych.

Robert Schumann, 1810-1856, (G.) Symphonies, songs.

Aleksandr Scriabin, 1872-1915, (R.) Prometheus.

Dimitri Shostakovich, 1906-1975, (R.) Symphonies, Lady Macbeth of Mzensk, The Nose.

Jean Sibelius, 1865-1957, (Finn.) Finlandia, Karelia.

Bedrich Smetana, 1824-1884, (Cz.) The Bartered Bride.

Karlheinz Stockhausen, b. 1928, (G.) Kontrapunkte, Kontakte.

Richard Strauss, 1864-1949, (G.) Salome, Elektra, Der Rosenkavalier, Thus Spake Zarathustra.

Igor F. Stravinsky, 1882-1971, (R.-U.S.) Oedipus Rex, Le Sacre du Printemps, Petrushka.

Peter I. Tchaikovsky, 1840-1893, (R.) Nutcracker Suite, Swan Lake, Eugene Onegin.

Ambroise Thomas, 1811-1896, (F.) Mignon.

Virgil Thomson, 1896-1989, (U.S.) Opera, ballet; Four Saints in Three Acts.

Ralph Vaughan Williams, 1872-1958, (Br.) Job, London Symphony, Symphony No. 7 (Antartica).

Giuseppe Verdi, 1813-1901, (It.) Aida, Rigoletto, Don Carlo, Il Trovatore, La Traviata, Falstaff, Macbeth.

Heitor Villa-Lobos, 1887-1959, (Brazil) Choros.

Antonio Vivaldi, 1678-1741, (It.) Concerti, The Four Seasons.

Richard Wagner, 1813-1883, (G.) Rienzi, Tannhauser, Lohengrin, Tristan and Isolde.

Carl Maria von Weber, 1786-1826, (G.) Der Freischutz.

## Composers of Operettas, Musicals, and Popular Music

Richard Adler, b. 1921, (U.S.) *Pajama Game; Damn Yankees.*

Milton Ager, 1893-1979, (U.S.) *I Wonder What's Become of Sally; Hard Hearted Hannah; Ain't She Sweet?*

Leroy Anderson, 1908-1975, (U.S.) *Syncopated Clock.*

Paul Anka, b. 1941, (Can.) *My Way; She's a Lady; Tonight Show* theme.

Harold Arlen, 1905-1986, (U.S.) *Stormy Weather; Over the Rainbow; Blues in the Night; That Old Black Magic.*

Burt Bacharach, b. 1928, (U.S.) *Raindrops Keep Fallin' on My Head; Walk on By; What the World Needs Now is Love.*

Ernest Ball, 1878-1927, (U.S.) *Mother Machree; When Irish Eyes Are Smiling.*

Irving Berlin, 1888-1989 (U.S.) *This is the Army; Annie Get Your Gun; Call Me Madam; God Bless America; White Christmas.*

Leonard Bernstein, 1918-1990, (U.S.) *On the Town; Wonderful Town; Candide; West Side Story.*

**Eubie Blake,** 1883-1983, (U.S.) *Shuffle Along; I'm Just Wild about Harry.*

**Jerry Bock,** b. 1928, (U.S.) *Mr. Wonderful; Fiorello; Fiddler on the Roof; The Rothschilds.*

**Carrie Jacobs Bond,** 1862-1946, (U.S.) *I Love You Truly.*

**Nacio Herb Brown,** 1896-1964, (U.S.) *Singing in the Rain; You Were Meant for Me; All I Do Is Dream of You.*

**Hoagy Carmichael,** 1899-1981, (U.S.) *Stardust; Georgia on My Mind; Old Buttermilk Sky.*

**George M. Cohan,** 1878-1942, (U.S.) *Give My Regards to Broadway; You're A Grand Old Flag; Over There.*

**Cy Coleman,** b. 1929, (U.S.) *Sweet Charity; Witchcraft.*

**Noel Coward,** 1899-1973 (Br.) *Bitter Sweet; Mad Dogs and Englishmen; Mad About the Boy.*

**Neil Diamond,** b. 1941, (U.S.) *I'm a Believer; Sweet Caroline.*

**Walter Donaldson,** 1893-1947, (U.S.) *My Buddy; Carolina in the Morning; You're Driving Me Crazy; Makin' Whoopee.*

**Vernon Duke,** 1903-1969, (U.S.) *April in Paris.*

**Bob Dylan,** b. 1941, (U.S.) *Blowin' in the Wind.*

**Gus Edwards,** 1879-1945, (U.S.) *School Days; By the Light of the Silvery Moon; In My Merry Oldsmobile.*

**Sherman Edwards,** 1919-1981, (U.S.) *See You in September; Wonderful! Wonderful!*

**Duke Ellington,** 1899-1974, (U.S.) *Sophisticated Lady; Satin Doll; It Don't Mean a Thing; Solitude.*

**Sammy Fain,** 1902-1989, (U.S.) *I'll Be Seeing You; Love Is a Many-Splendored Thing.*

**Fred Fisher,** 1875-1942, (U.S.) *Peg O' My Heart; Chicago.*

**Stephen Collins Foster,** 1826-1864, (U.S.) *My Old Kentucky Home; Old Folks At Home.*

**Rudolf Friml,** 1879-1972, (naturalized U.S.) *The Firefly; Rose Marie; Vagabond King; Bird of Paradise.*

**John Gay,** 1685-1732, (Br.) *The Beggar's Opera.*

**George Gershwin,** 1898-1937, (U.S.) *Someone to Watch Over Me; I've Got a Crush on You; Embraceable You.*

**Ferde Grofe,** 1892-1972, (U.S.) *Grand Canyon Suite.*

**Marvin Hamlisch,** b. 1944, (U.S.) *The Way We Were, Nobody Does It Better, A Chorus Line.*

**W. C. Handy,** 1873-1958, (U.S.) *St. Louis Blues.*

**Ray Henderson,** 1896-1970, (U.S.) *George White's Scandals; That Old Gang of Mine; Five Foot Two, Eyes of Blue.*

**Victor Herbert,** 1859-1924, (Ir.-U.S.) *Mlle. Modiste; Babes in Toyland; The Red Mill; Naughty Marietta; Sweethearts.*

**Jerry Herman,** b. 1932, (U.S.) *Hello Dolly; Mame.*

**Brian Holland,** b. 1941, **Lamont Dozier,** b. 1941, **Eddie Holland,** b. 1939, (all U.S.) *Heat Wave; Stop! In the Name of Love; Baby, I Need Your Loving.*

**Scott Joplin,** 1868-1917, (U.S.) *Treemonisha*

**John Kander,** b. 1927, (U.S.) *Cabaret; Chicago; Funny Lady.*

**Jerome Kern,** 1885-1945, (U.S.) *Sally; Sunny; Show Boat.*

**Carole King,** b. 1942, (U.S.) *Will You Love Me Tomorrow?; Natural Woman; One Fine Day; Up on the Roof.*

**Burton Lane,** b. 1912, (U.S.) *Finian's Rainbow.*

**Franz Lehar,** 1870-1948, (Hung.) *Merry Widow.*

**Jerry Leiber,** & **Mike Stoller,** both b. 1933, (both U.S.) *Hound Dog; Searchin'; Yakety Yak; Love Me Tender.*

**Mitch Leigh,** b. 1928, (U.S.) *Man of La Mancha.*

**John Lennon,** 1940-1980, & **Paul McCartney,** b. 1942, (both Br.) *I Want to Hold Your Hand; She Loves You; Hard Day's Night; Can't Buy Me Love; And I Love Her.*

**Frank Loesser,** 1910-1969, (U.S.) *Guys and Dolls; Where's Charley?; The Most Happy Fella; How to Succeed . . . .*

**Frederick Loewe,** 1901-1988, (Aust.-U.S.) *The Day Before Spring; Brigadoon; Paint Your Wagon; My Fair Lady; Camelot.*

**Henry Mancini,** b. 1924, (U.S.) *Moon River; Days of Wine and Roses; Pink Panther Theme.*

**Barry Mann,** b. 1939, & **Cynthia Weil,** b. 1937, (both U.S.) *You've Lost That Loving Feeling, Saturday Night at the Movies.*

**Jimmy McHugh,** 1894-1969 (U.S.) *Don't Blame Me; I'm in the Mood for Love; I Feel a Song Coming On.*

**Alan Menken,** b. 1950, (U.S.) *Little Shop of Horrors.*

**Joseph Meyer,** 1894-1987, (U.S.) *If You Knew Susie; California, Here I Come; Crazy Rhythm.*

**Chauncey Olcott,** 1860-1932, (U.S.) *Mother Machree.*

**Jerome "Doc" Pomus,** 1925-1991, (U.S.) *Save the Last Dance for Me, A Teenager in Love.*

**Cole Porter,** 1893-1964, (U.S.) *Anything Goes; Kiss Me Kate; Can Can; Silk Stockings.*

**Smokey Robinson,** b. 1940, (U.S.) *Shop Around; My Guy; My Girl; Get Ready.*

**Richard Rodgers,** 1902-1979, (U.S.) *Connecticut Yankee; Oklahoma!; Carousel; South Pacific; The King and I; The Sound of Music.*

**Sigmund Romberg,** 1887-1951, (Hung.) *Maytime; The Student Prince; Desert Song; Blossom Time.*

**Harold Rome,** b. 1908, (U.S.) *Pins and Needles; Call Me Mister; Wish You Were Here; Fanny; Destry Rides Again.*

**Vincent Rose,** b. 1880-1944, (U.S.) *Avalon; Whispering; Blueberry Hill.*

**Harry Ruby,** 1895-1974, (U.S.) *Three Little Words; Who's Sorry Now?*

**Arthur Schwartz,** 1900-1984, (U.S.) *The Band Wagon; Dancing in the Dark; By Myself; That's Entertainment.*

**Neil Sedaka,** b. 1939, (U.S.) *Breaking Up Is Hard to Do.*

**Paul Simon,** b. 1942, (U.S.) *Sounds of Silence; I Am a Rock; Mrs. Robinson; Bridge Over Troubled Waters.*

**Stephen Sondheim,** b. 1930, (U.S.) *A Little Night Music; Company; Sweeney Todd; Sunday in the Park with George.*

**John Philip Sousa,** 1854-1932, (U.S.) *El Capitan; Stars and Stripes Forever.*

**Oskar Straus,** 1870-1954, (Aus.) *Chocolate Soldier.*

**Johann Strauss,** 1825-1899, (Aus.) *Gypsy Baron; Die Fledermaus;* waltzes: *Blue Danube, Artist's Life.*

**Charles Strouse,** b. 1928, (U.S.) *Bye Bye, Birdie; Annie.*

**Jule Styne,** b. 1905, (b.-Br.-U.S.) *Gentlemen Prefer Blondes; Bells Are Ringing; Gypsy; Funny Girl.*

**Arthur S. Sullivan,** 1842-1900, (Br.) *H.M.S. Pinafore, Pirates of Penzance; The Mikado.*

**Deems Taylor,** 1885-1966, (U.S.) *Peter Ibbetson.*

**Egbert van Alstyne,** 1882-1951, (U.S.) *In the Shade of the Old Apple Tree; Memories; Pretty Baby.*

**Jimmy Van Heusen,** 1913-1990, (U.S.) *Moonlight Becomes You; Swinging on a Star; All the Way; Love and Marriage.*

**Albert von Tilzer,** 1878-1956, (U.S.) *I'll Be With You in Apple Blossom Time; Take Me Out to the Ball Game.*

**Harry von Tilzer,** 1872-1946, (U.S.) *Only a Bird in a Gilded Cage; On a Sunday Afternoon.*

**Fats Waller,** 1904-1943, (U.S.) *Honeysuckle Rose; Ain't Misbehavin'.*

**Harry Warren,** 1893-1981, (U.S.) *You're My Everything; We're in the Money; I Only Have Eyes for You.*

**Jimmy Webb,** b. 1946, (U.S.) *Up, Up and Away; By the Time I Get to Phoenix; Didn't We?; Wichita Lineman.*

**Andrew Lloyd Webber,** b. 1948, (Br.) *Jesus Christ Superstar, Evita, Cats, The Phantom of the Opera.*

**Kurt Weill,** 1900-1950, (G.-U.S.) *Threepenny Opera; Lady in the Dark; Knickerbocker Holiday; One Touch of Venus.*

**Percy Wenrich,** 1887-1952, (U.S.) *When You Wore a Tulip; Moonlight Bay; Put On Your Old Gray Bonnet.*

**Richard A. Whiting,** 1891-1938, (U.S.) *Till We Meet Again; Sleepytime Gal; Beyond the Blue Horizon; My Ideal.*

**John Williams,** b. 1932, (U.S.) *Jaws, E.T., Star Wars* series, *Raiders of the Lost Ark* series.

**Meredith Willson,** 1902-1984, (U.S.) *The Music Man.*

**Stevie Wonder,** b. 1950, (U.S.) *You Are the Sunshine of My Life; Signed, Sealed, Delivered, I'm Yours.*

**Vincent Youmans,** 1898-1946, (U.S.) *Two Little Girls in Blue; Wildflower; No, No, Nanette; Hit the Deck; Rainbow; Smiles.*

## Lyricists

**Howard Ashman,** 1950-1991, (U.S.) *Little Shop of Horrors, The Little Mermaid.*

**Johnny Burke,** 1908-1984, (U.S.) *What's New?; Misty; Imagination; Polka Dots and Moonbeams.*

**Sammy Cahn,** 1913-1993, (U.S.) *High Hopes; Love and Marriage; The Second Time Around; It's Magic.*

**Betty Comden,** b. 1919 (U.S.) and **Adolph Green,** b. 1915 (U.S.) *The Party's Over; Just in Time; New York, New York.*

**Hal David,** b. 1921 (U.S.) *What the World Needs Now Is Love; Close to You.*

**Buddy De Sylva,** 1895-1950, (U.S.) *When Day is Done; Look for the Silver Lining; April Showers.*

**Howard Dietz,** 1896-1983, (U.S.) *Dancing in the Dark; You and the Night and the Music; That's Entertainment.*

**Al Dubin,** 1891-1945, (U.S.) *Tiptoe Through the Tulips; Anniversary Waltz; Lullaby of Broadway.*

**Fred Ebb,** b. 1936 (U.S.) *Cabaret, Zorba, Woman of the Year.*

**Dorothy Fields,** 1905-1974, (U.S.) *On the Sunny Side of the Street; Don't Blame Me; The Way You Look Tonight.*

**Ira Gershwin,** 1896-1983, (U.S.) *The Man I Love; Fascinating Rhythm; S'Wonderful; Embraceable You.*

**William S. Gilbert,** 1836-1911, (Br.) *The Mikado; H.M.S. Pinafore, Pirates of Penzance.*

**Gerry Goffin,** b. 1939, (U.S.) *Will You Love Me Tomorrow, Take Good Care of My Baby, Up on the Roof, One Fine Day.*

**Mack Gordon,** 1905-1959, (Pol.-U.S.) *You'll Never Know; The More I See You; Chattanooga Choo-Choo.*

**Oscar Hammerstein II,** 1895-1960, (U.S.) *Ol' Man River; Oklahoma; Carousel.*

**E. Y. (Yip) Harburg,** 1898-1981, (U.S.) *Brother, Can You Spare a Dime; April in Paris; Over the Rainbow.*

**Lorenz Hart,** 1895-1943, (U.S.) *Isn't It Romantic; Blue Moon; Lover; Manhattan; My Funny Valentine; Mountain Greenery.*

**DuBose Heyward**, 1885-1940, (U.S.) Summertime; A Woman Is A Sometime Thing.

**Gus Kahn**, 1886-1941, (U.S.) Memories; Ain't We Got Fun.

**Alan J. Lerner**, 1918-1986, (U.S.) Brigadoon; My Fair Lady; Camelot; Gigi.; On a Clear Day You Can See Forever.

**Johnny Mercer**, 1909-1976, (U.S.) Blues in the Night; Come Rain or Come Shine; Laura; That Old Black Magic.

**Bob Merrill**, b. 1921, (U.S.) People; Don't Rain on My Parade.

**Jack Norworth**, 1879-1959, (U.S.) Take Me Out to the Ball Game; Shine On Harvest Moon.

**Mitchell Parish**, 1901-1993, (U.S.) Stairway to the Stars; Stardust.

**Andy Razaf**, 1895-1973, (U.S.) Honeysuckle Rose, Ain't Misbehavin', S'posin'.

**Leo Robin**, 1900-1984, (U.S.) Thanks for the Memory; Hooray for Love; Diamonds are a Girl's Best Friend.

**Paul Francis Webster**, 1907-1984, (U.S.) I Got It Bad and That Ain't Good, Secret Love, The Shadow of Your Smile, Love Is a Many-Splendored Thing.

**Jack Yellen**, 1892-1991, (U.S.) Down by the O-Hi-O; Ain't She Sweet; Happy Days Are Here Again.

## Noted Jazz Artists

Jazz has been called America's only completely unique contribution to Western culture. The following individuals have made major contributions in this field:

**Julian "Cannonball" Adderley**, 1928-1975: alto sax.

**Louis "Satchmo" Armstrong**, 1900-1971: trumpet, singer; originated the "scat" vocal.

**Mildred Bailey**, 1907-1951: blues singer.

**Chet Baker**, 1929-1988: trumpet.

**Count Basie**, 1904-1984: orchestra leader, piano.

**Sidney Bechet**, 1897-1959: early innovator, soprano sax.

**Bix Beiderbecke**, 1903-1931: cornet, piano, composer.

**Bunny Berigan**, 1909-1942: trumpet, singer.

**Barney Bigard**, 1906-1980: clarinet.

**Art Blakey**, 1919-1990: drums, leader.

**Jimmy Blanton**, 1921-1942: bass.

**Charles "Buddy" Bolden**, 1868-1931: cornet; formed the first jazz band in the 1890s.

**Big Bill Broonzy**, 1893-1958: blues singer, guitar.

**Clifford Brown**, 1930-1956: trumpet.

**Ray Brown**, b. 1926: bass.

**Dave Brubeck**, b. 1920: piano, combo leader.

**Don Byas**, 1912-1972: tenor sax.

**Harry Carney**, 1910-1974: baritone sax.

**Benny Carter**, b. 1907: alto sax, trumpet, clarinet.

**Ron Carter**, b. 1937: bass, cello.

**Sidney Catlett**, 1910-1951: drums.

**Charlie Christian**, 1919-1942: guitar.

**Kenny Clarke**, 1914-1985: pioneer of modern drums.

**Buck Clayton**, b. 1911: trumpet, arranger.

**Al Cohn**, 1925-1988: tenor sax, composer.

**Cozy Cole**, 1909-1981: drums.

**Ornette Coleman**, b. 1930: saxophone; unorthodox style.

**John Coltrane**, 1926-1967: tenor sax innovator.

**Eddie Condon**, 1904-1973: guitar, band leader; promoter of Dixieland.

**Chick Corea**, b. 1941: pianist, composer.

**Tadd Dameron**, 1917-1965: piano, composer.

**Eddie "Lockjaw" Davis**, 1921-1986: tenor sax.

**Miles Davis**, 1926-1991: trumpet; pioneer of cool jazz.

**Wild Bill Davison**, 1906-1989: cornet, leader; prominent in early Chicago jazz.

**Buddy De Franco**, b. 1933: clarinet.

**Paul Desmond**, 1924-1977: alto sax.

**Vic Dickenson**, 1906-1984: trombone, composer.

**Warren "Baby" Dodds**, 1898-1959: Dixieland drummer.

**Johnny Dodds**, 1892-1940: clarinet.

**Eric Dolphy**, 1928-1964: alto sax, composer.

**Jimmy Dorsey**, 1904-1957: clarinet, alto sax; band leader.

**Tommy Dorsey**, 1905-1956: trombone; band leader.

**Roy Eldridge**, 1911-1989: trumpet, drums, singer.

**Duke Ellington**, 1899-1974: piano, band leader, composer.

**Bill Evans**, 1929-1980: piano.

**Gil Evans**, 1912-1988: composer, arranger, piano.

**Ella Fitzgerald**, b. 1918: singer.

**"Red" Garland**, 1923-1984: piano.

**Erroll Garner**, 1921-1977: piano, composer, "Misty."

**Stan Getz**, 1927-1991: tenor sax.

**Dizzy Gillespie**, 1917-1993: trumpet, composer; bop developer.

**Benny Goodman**, 1909-1986: clarinet, band and combo leader.

**Dexter Gordon**, 1923-1990: tenor sax; bop-derived style.

**Stephane Grappelli**, b. 1908: violin.

**Bobby Hackett**, 1915-1976: trumpet, cornet.

**Lionel Hampton**, b. 1913: vibes, drums, piano, combo leader.

**Herbie Hancock**, b. 1940: piano, composer.

**W. C. Handy**, 1873-1958: composer, "St. Louis Blues."

**Coleman Hawkins**, 1904-1969: tenor sax; 1939 recording of "Body and Soul" a classic.

**Roy Haynes**, b. 1926: drums.

**Fletcher Henderson**, 1898-1952: orchestra leader, arranger; pioneered jazz and dance bands of the 30s.

**Woody Herman**, 1913-87: clarinet, alto sax, band leader.

**Jay C. Higginbotham**, 1906-1973: trombone.

**Earl "Fatha" Hines**, 1905-1983: piano, songwriter.

**Johnny Hodges**, 1906-1970: alto sax.

**Billie Holiday**, 1915-1959: blues singer, "Strange Fruit."

**Sam "Lightnin' " Hopkins**, 1912-1982: blues singer, guitar.

**Mahalia Jackson**, 1911-1972: gospel singer.

**Milt Jackson**, b. 1923: vibes, piano, guitar.

**Illinois Jacquet**, b. 1922: tenor sax.

**Keith Jarrett**, b. 1945: technically phenomenal pianist.

**Blind Lemon Jefferson**, 1897-1930: blues singer, guitar.

**Bunk Johnson**, 1879-1949: cornet, trumpet.

**James P. Johnson**, 1891-1955: piano, composer.

**J. J. Johnson**, b. 1924: trombone, composer.

**Elvin Jones**, b. 1927: drums.

**Jo Jones**, 1911-1985: drums.

**Philly Joe Jones**, 1923-1985: drums.

**Quincy Jones**, b. 1933: arranger.

**Thad Jones**, 1923-1986: trumpet, cornet.

**Scott Joplin**, 1868-1917: composer; "Maple Leaf Rag."

**Stan Kenton**, 1912-1979: orchestra leader, composer, piano.

**Barney Kessel**, b. 1923: guitar.

**Lee Konitz**, b. 1927: alto sax.

**Gene Krupa**, 1909-1973: drums, band and combo leader.

**Scott LaFaro**, 1936-1961: bass.

**Huddie Ledbetter (Leadbelly)**, 1888-1949: blues singer, guitar.

**John Lewis**, b. 1920: composer, piano, combo leader.

**Mel Lewis**, 1929-1990: drummer, orchestra leader.

**Jimmie Lunceford**, 1902-1947: band leader, sax.

**Herbie Mann**, b. 1930: flute.

**Wynton Marsalis**, b. 1961: trumpet.

**Jimmy McPartland**, b. 1907: trumpet.

**Marian McPartland**, b. 1920: piano.

**Glenn Miller**, 1904-1944: trombone, dance band leader.

**Charles Mingus**, 1922-1979: bass, composer, combo leader.

**Thelonious Monk**, 1920-1982: piano, composer, combo leader; a developer of bop.

**Wes Montgomery**, 1925-1968: guitar.

**"Jelly Roll" Morton**, 1885-1941: composer, piano, singer.

**Bennie Moten**, 1894-1935: piano; an early organizer of large jazz orchestras.

**Gerry Mulligan**, b. 1927: baritone sax, arranger, leader.

**Turk Murphy**, 1915-1987: trombone, band leader.

**Theodore "Fats" Navarro**, 1923-1950: trumpet.

**Red Nichols**, 1905-1965: cornet, combo leader.

**Red Norvo**, b. 1908: vibes, band leader.

**Anita O'Day**, b. 1919: singer.

**King Oliver**, 1885-1938: cornet, band leader; teacher of Louis Armstrong.

**Sy Oliver**, 1910-1988: Swing Era arranger, composer, conductor.

**Kid Ory**, 1886-1973: trombone, "Muskrat Ramble".

**Charlie "Bird" Parker**, 1920-1955: alto sax, composer; rated by many as the greatest jazz improviser.

**Art Pepper**, 1925-1982: alto sax.

**Oscar Peterson**, b. 1925: piano, composer, combo leader.

**Oscar Pettiford**, 1922-1960: a leading bassist in the bop era.

**Bud Powell**, 1924-1966: piano; modern jazz pioneer.

**Tito Puente**, b. 1923: band leader.

**Sun Ra**, 1915?-1993: big band leader, pianist, composer.

**Gertrude "Ma" Rainey**, 1886-1939: blues singer.

**Don Redman**, 1900-1964: composer, arranger; pioneer in the evolution of the large orchestra.

**Django Reinhardt**, 1910-1953: guitar; Belgian gypsy, first European to influence American jazz.

**Buddy Rich**, 1917-1987: drums, band leader.

**Max Roach**, b. 1925: drums.

**Sonny Rollins**, b. 1929: tenor sax.

**Frank Rosolino**, 1926-1978: trombone.

**Jimmy Rushing**, 1903-1972: blues singer.

**George Russell**, b. 1923: composer, piano.

**Pee Wee Russell**, 1906-1969: clarinet.

**Artie Shaw**, b. 1910: clarinet, combo leader.

**George Shearing**, b. 1919: piano, composer.

**Horace Silver**, b. 1928: piano, combo leader.

**Zoot Sims**, 1925-1985: tenor, alto sax; clarinet.

**Zutty Singleton**, 1898-1975: Dixieland drummer.
**Bessie Smith**, 1894-1937: blues singer.
**Clarence "Pinetop" Smith**, 1904-1929: piano; singer; pioneer of boogie woogie.
**Willie "The Lion" Smith**, 1897-1973: stride style pianist.
**Muggsy Spanier**, 1906-1967: cornet, band leader.
**Billy Strayhorn**, 1915-67: composer, piano.
**Sonny Stitt**, 1924-1982: alto, tenor sax.
**Art Tatum**, 1910-1956: piano; technical virtuoso.
**Billy Taylor**, b. 1921: piano, composer.
**Cecil Taylor**, b. 1933: piano, composer.
**Jack Teagarden**, 1905-1964: trombone, singer.
**Mel Torme**, b. 1925: singer.
**Dave Tough**, 1908-1948: drums.
**Lennie Tristano**, 1919-1978: piano, composer.
**Joe Turner**, 1911-1985: blues singer.
**McCoy Tyner**, b. 1938: piano, composer.
**Sarah Vaughan**, 1924-1990: singer.

**Joe Venuti**, 1904-1978: first great jazz violinist.
**Thomas "Fats" Waller**, 1904-1943: piano, singer, composer. "Ain't Misbehavin' ".
**Dinah Washington**, 1924-1963: singer.
**Chick Webb**, 1902-1939: band leader, drums.
**Ben Webster**, 1909-1973: tenor sax.
**Paul Whiteman**, 1890-1967: orchestra leader; a major figure in the introduction of jazz to a large audience.
**Charles "Cootie" Williams**, 1908-1985: trumpet, band leader.
**Mary Lou Williams**, 1914-1981: piano, composer.
**Teddy Wilson**, 1912-1986: piano, composer.
**Kai Winding**, 1922-1983: trombone, composer.
**Jimmy Yancey**, 1894-1951: piano.
**Lester "Pres" Young**, 1909-1959: tenor sax, composer; a bop pioneer.

## Rock & Roll Notables

For more than a quarter of a century, rock & roll has been an important force in American popular culture. The following individuals or groups have made a significant impact. Next to each is an associated single record or record album.

**Paula Abdul:** "Forever Your Girl"
**Aerosmith:** "Sweet Emotion"
**The Allman Brothers Band:** "Ramblin' Man"
**The Animals:** "House of the Rising Sun"
**Paul Anka:** "Lonely Boy"
**The Association:** "Cherish"
**Frankie Avalon:** "Venus"

**The Band:** "The Weight"
**The Beach Boys:** "Good Vibrations"
**The Beatles:** *Sergeant Pepper's Lonely-Hearts Club Band*
**The Bee Gees:** "Stayin' Alive"
**Pat Benatar:** "Hit Me With Your Best Shot"
**Chuck Berry:** "Johnny B. Goode"
**The Big Bopper:** "Chantilly Lace"
**Black Sabbath:** "Paranoid"
**Blind Faith:** "Can't Find My Way Home"
**Blondie:** "Heart of Glass"
**Blood, Sweat and Tears:** "Spinning Wheel"
**Bon Jovi:** *Slippery When Wet*
**Gary "U.S." Bonds:** "Quarter to Three"
**Booker T. and the MGs:** "Green Onions"
**Earl Bostic:** "Flamingo"
**David Bowie:** "Let's Dance"
**James Brown:** "Papa's Got a Brand New Bag"
**Jackson Browne:** "Doctor My Eyes"
**Buffalo Springfield:** "For What It's Worth"
**The Byrds:** "Turn! Turn! Turn!"

**Canned Heat:** "Going Up the Country"
**The Cars:** "Shake It Up"
**Tracy Chapman:** "Fast Car"
**Ray Charles:** "Georgia on My Mind"
**Chubby Checker:** "The Twist"
**Chicago:** "Saturday in the Park"
**Eric Clapton:** "Layla"
**The Coasters:** "Yakety Yak"
**Eddie Cochran:** "Summertime Blues"
**Phil Collins:** "Another Day in Paradise"
**Sam Cooke:** "You Send Me"
**Alice Cooper:** "School's Out"
**Elvis Costello:** "Alison"
**Cream:** "Sunshine of Your Love"
**Credence Clearwater Revival:** "Proud Mary"
**Crosby, Stills, Nash and Young:** "Suite: Judy Blue Eyes"
**The Crystals:** "Da Doo Ron Ron"

**DJ Jazzy Jeff & the Fresh Prince:** "Summertime"
**Danny and the Juniors:** "At the Hop"
**Bobby Darin:** "Splish Splash"
**Spencer Davis Group:** "Gimme Some Lovin' "
**Bo Diddley:** "Who Do You Love?"
**Dion and the Belmonts:** "A Teenager in Love"
**Dire Straits:** *Brothers in Arms*
**Fats Domino:** "Blueberry Hill"
**The Doobie Brothers:** "What a Fool Believes"
**The Doors:** "Light My Fire"
**The Drifters:** "Save the Last Dance for Me"
**Bob Dylan:** "Like a Rolling Stone"

**The Eagles:** "Hotel California"
**Earth, Wind and Fire:** "Shining Star"
**Emerson, Lake and Palmer:** "From the Beginning"
**The Eurythmics:** "Sweet Dreams (Are Made of This)"
**Everly Brothers:** "Wake Up Little Susie"

**The Five Satins:** "In the Still of the Night"

**Fleetwood Mac:** *Rumours*
**The Four Seasons:** "Sherry"
**The Four Tops:** "I Can't Help Myself"
**Aretha Franklin:** "Respect"

**Marvin Gaye:** "I Heard It through the Grapevine"
**Grand Funk Railroad:** "We're an American Band"
**The Grateful Dead:** "Truckin' "
**Guns 'N Roses:** *Appetite for Destruction*

**Bill Haley and the Comets:** "Rock Around the Clock"
**M.C. Hammer:** "U Can't Touch This"
**Jimi Hendrix:** *Are You Experienced?*
**Buddy Holly and the Crickets:** "That'll Be the Day"
**Whitney Houston:** "The Greatest Love"

**The Isley Brothers:** "It's Your Thing"

**The Jackson 5/The Jacksons:** "ABC"
**Janet Jackson:** *Rhythm Nation*
**Michael Jackson:** *Thriller*
**Tommy James & The Shondells:** "Crimson and Clover"
**Jay and the Americans:** "This Magic Moment"
**The Jefferson Airplane/Jefferson Starship:** "White Rabbit"
**Jethro Tull:** *Aqualung*
**Joan Jett:** "I Love Rock n' Roll"
**Billy Joel:** "Piano Man"
**Elton John:** "Sad Songs"
**Janis Joplin:** "Me and Bobby McGee"

**Chaka Khan:** "I Feel for You"
**B.B. King:** "The Thrill Is Gone"
**Carole King:** *Tapestry*
**The Kinks:** "You Really Got Me"
**Kiss:** "Rock' n' Roll All Night"
**Gladys Knight and the Pips:** "Midnight Train to Georgia"

**L.L. Cool J:** "Mama Said Knock You Out"
**Led Zeppelin:** "Stairway to Heaven"
**Brenda Lee:** "I'm Sorry"
**Jerry Lee Lewis:** "Whole Lotta Shakin' Going On"
**Little Anthony and the Imperials:** "Tears on My Pillow"
**Little Richard:** "Tutti Frutti"
**Lovin Spoonful:** "Do You Believe in Magic?"
**Frankie Lymon:** "Why Do Fools Fall in Love?"
**Lynyrd Skynyrd:** "Freebird"

**Madonna:** "Material Girl"
**The Mamas and the Papas:** "Monday, Monday"
**Bob Marley:** "Jamming"
**Martha and the Vandellas:** "Dancin' in the Streets"
**The Marvelettes:** "Please Mr. Postman"
**Clyde McPhatter:** "Money Honey"
**John Mellencamp:** "Hurt So Good"
**George Michael:** *Faith*
**Joni Mitchell:** "Big Yellow Taxi"
**The Monkees:** "I'm a Believer"
**Moody Blues:** "Nights in White Satin"

**Rick Nelson:** "Hello Mary Lou"

**Roy Orbison:** "Oh Pretty Woman"

**Carl Perkins:** "Blue Suede Shoes"
**Tom Petty and the Heartbreakers:** "Refugee"
**Pink Floyd:** *The Wall*
**Poco:** *Deliverin'*
**The Police:** "Every Breath You Take"

**Iggy Pop:** "Lust for Life"
**Elvis Presley:** "Love Me Tender"
**The Pretenders:** *Learning to Crawl*
**Lloyd Price:** "Stagger Lee"
**Prince:** "Purple Rain"
**Procul Harum:** "A Whiter Shade of Pale"
**Public Enemy:** "Fight the Power"

**Queen:** "Bohemian Rhapsody"

**R.E.M.:** "Losing My Religion"
**The Rascals:** "Good Lovin' "
**Otis Redding:** "The Dock of the Bay"
**Lou Reed:** "Walk on the Wild Side"
**Righteous Brothers:** "You've Lost that Lovin' Feeling"
**Johnny Rivers:** "Poor Side of Town"
**Smokey Robinson and the Miracles:** "Ooh Baby Baby"
**The Rolling Stones:** "Satisfaction"
**The Ronettes:** "Be My Baby"
**Linda Ronstadt:** "You're No Good"
**Run D.M.C.:** "Raisin' Hell"

**Sam and Dave:** "Soul Man"
**Santana:** "Black Magic Woman"
**Neil Sedaka:** "Breaking Up is Hard to Do"
**Del Shannon:** "Runaway"
**The Shirelles:** "Soldier Boy"
**Simon and Garfunkel:** "Bridge Over Troubled Water"
**Carly Simon:** "You're So Vain"
**Sly and the Family Stone:** "Everyday People"
**Patti Smith:** "Because the Night"
**Southside Johnny and the Asbury Jukes:** *This Time*

**Dusty Springfield:** "You Don't Have to Say You Love Me"
**Bruce Springsteen:** "Born in the U.S.A."
**Steely Dan:** "Rikki Don't Lose That Number"
**Steppenwolf:** "Born to Be Wild"
**Rod Stewart:** "Maggie Mae"
**Sting:** "If You Love Somebody, Set Them Free"
**Donna Summer:** "She Works Hard for the Money"
**The Supremes:** "Stop! In the Name of Love"

**Talking Heads:** "Once in a Lifetime"
**James Taylor:** "You've Got a Friend"
**The Temptations:** "My Girl"
**Three Dog Night:** "Joy to the World"
**Traffic:** "Feelin' Alright"
**Big Joe Turner:** "Shake, Rattle & Roll"
**Tina Turner:** "What's Love Got to Do with It?"

**U2:** *Joshua Tree*

**Van Halen:** "Jump"

**Dionne Warwick:** "I'll Never Fall in Love Again"
**Muddy Waters:** "Rollin' Stone"
**Mary Wells:** "My Guy"
**The Who:** "My Generation"
**Jackie Wilson:** "That's Why"
**Stevie Wonder:** "You Are the Sunshine of My Life"

**The Yardbirds:** "For Your Love"
**Yes:** "Yours Is No Disgrace"

**Frank Zappa/Mothers of Invention:** *Sheik Yerbouti*

# Entertainment Personalities — Where and When Born

Actors, Actresses, Dancers, Musicians, Producers, Directors, Radio-TV Performers, Singers
(As of mid-1993)

| Name | Birthplace | Born | Name | Birthplace | Born |
|---|---|---|---|---|---|
| Abbado, Claudio | Milan, Italy | 6/26/33 | Andress, Ursula | Bern, Switzerland | 3/19/36 |
| Abbott, George | Forestville, N.Y. | 6/25/87 | Andrews, Anthony | London, England | 1/12/48 |
| Abdul, Paula | San Fernando, Cal. | 6/19/62 | Andrews, Julie | Walton, England | 10/1/35 |
| Abraham, F. Murray | Pittsburgh, Pa. | 10/24/39 | Andrews, Maxene | Minneapolis, Minn. | 1/3/18 |
| Adams, Bryan | Kingston, Ont. | 11/5/59 | Andrews, Patty | Minneapolis, Minn. | 2/16/20 |
| Adams, Don | New York, N.Y. | 4/19/26 | Anka, Paul | Ottawa, Ont. | 7/30/41 |
| Adams, Edie | Kingston, Pa. | 4/16/29 | Ann-Margret | Stockholm, Sweden | 4/28/41 |
| Adams, Joey | New York, N.Y. | 1/6/11 | Anton, Susan | Oak Glen, Cal. | 10/12/50 |
| Adams, Mason | New York, N.Y. | 2/26/19 | Applegate, Christina | Los Angeles, Cal. | 11/25/72 |
| Adjani, Isabelle | W. Germany | 6/27/55 | Archer, Anne | Los Angeles, Cal. | 8/25/50 |
| Agutter, Jenny | London, England | 12/20/52 | Arkin, Alan | New York, N.Y. | 3/26/34 |
| Aiello, Danny | New York, N.Y. | 6/20/33 | Arnaz, Desi Jr. | Los Angeles, Cal. | 1/19/53 |
| Aimee, Anouk | Paris, France | 4/27/32 | Arnaz, Lucie | Hollywood, Cal. | 7/17/51 |
| Akins, Claude | Nelson, Ga. | 5/25/18 | Arness, James | Minneapolis, Minn. | 5/26/23 |
| Albanese, Licia | Bari, Italy | 7/22/13 | Arnold, Eddy | Henderson, Tenn. | 5/15/18 |
| Alberghetti, Anna Maria | Pesaro, Italy | 5/15/36 | Arnold, Roseanne | Salt Lake City, Ut. | 11/3/52 |
| Albert, Eddie | Rock Island, Ill. | 4/22/08 | Arquette, Rosanna | New York, N.Y. | 8/10/59 |
| Albert, Marv | New York, N.Y. | 6/12/43 | Arroyo, Martina | New York, N.Y. | 2/2/37 |
| Alda, Alan | New York, N.Y. | 1/28/36 | Arthur, Beatrice | New York, N.Y. | 5/13/26 |
| Alexander, Jane | Boston, Mass. | 10/28/39 | Ashley, Elizabeth | Ocala, Fla. | 8/30/41 |
| Alexander, Jason | Newark, N.J. | 9/23/59 | Asner, Ed. | Kansas City, Mo. | 11/15/29 |
| Allen, Debbie | Houston, Tex. | 1/16/50 | Assante, Armand | New York, N.Y. | 10/4/49 |
| Allen, Joan | Rochelle, Ill. | 8/20/56 | Astin, John | Baltimore, Md. | 3/30/30 |
| Allen, Karen | Carrollton, Ill. | 10/5/51 | Atherton, William | New Haven, Conn. | 7/30/47 |
| Allen, Mel. | Birmingham, Ala. | 2/14/13 | Atkins, Chet | Luttrell, Tenn. | 6/20/24 |
| Allen, Nancy | New York, N.Y. | 6/24/49 | Attenborough, Richard | Cambridge, England | 8/29/23 |
| Allen, Steve | New York, N.Y. | 12/26/21 | Auberjonois, Rene. | New York, N.Y. | 6/1/40 |
| Allen, Tim. | Denver, Col. | 6/13/– | Aumont, Jean-Pierre | Paris, France | 1/5/09 |
| Allen, Woody | Brooklyn, N.Y. | 12/1/35 | Austin, Patti | New York, N.Y. | 8/10/48 |
| Alley, Kirstie | Wichita, Kan. | 1/12/55 | Autry, Alan | Shreveport, La. | 7/31/52 |
| Allman, Gregg | Nashville, Tenn. | 12/7/47 | Autry, Gene | Tioga, Tex. | 9/29/07 |
| Allyson, June. | New York, N.Y. | 10/7/17 | Avalon, Frankie | Philadelphia, Pa. | 9/18/39 |
| Alonso, Maria Conchita | Cuba | 1957 | Ax, Emmanuel | Lvov, USSR | 6/8/49 |
| Alpert, Herb | Los Angeles, Cal. | 3/31/35 | Axton, Hoyt | Duncan, Okla. | 3/25/38 |
| Altman, Robert | Kansas City, Mo. | 2/20/25 | Aykroyd, Dan | Ottawa, Ont. | 7/1/52 |
| Ameche, Don | Kenosha, Wis. | 5/31/08 | Ayres, Lew | Minneapolis, Minn. | 12/28/08 |
| Ames, Ed. | Boston, Mass. | 7/9/27 | Aznavour, Charles | Paris, France | 5/22/24 |
| Ames, Leon | Portland, Ind. | 1/20/03 | | | |
| Amos, John | Newark, N.J. | 12/27/42 | Bacall, Lauren | New York, N.Y. | 9/16/24 |
| Amsterdam, Morey | Chicago, Ill. | 12/14/14 | Bacon, Kevin | Philadelphia, Pa. | 7/8/58 |
| Anderson, Harry. | Newport, R.I. | 10/14/49 | Baez, Joan | Staten Island, N.Y. | 1/9/41 |
| Anderson, Ian | Dunfermline, Scotland | 8/10/47 | Bain, Conrad | Lethbridge, Alta. | 2/4/23 |
| Anderson, Kevin | Illinois | 1/13/60 | Baio, Scott | Brooklyn, N.Y. | 9/22/61 |
| Anderson, Loni | St. Paul, Minn. | 8/5/46 | Baker, Anita | Toledo, Oh. | 1/26/58 |
| Anderson, Lynn | Grand Forks, N.D. | 9/26/47 | Baker, Carroll | Johnstown, Pa. | 5/28/31 |
| Anderson, Melissa Sue | Berkeley, Cal. | 9/26/62 | Baker, Joe Don | Groesbeck, Tex. | 2/12/36 |
| Anderson, Richard | Long Branch, N.J. | 8/8/26 | Bakula, Scott. | St. Louis, Mo. | 10/9/– |
| Anderson, Richard Dean | Minneapolis, Minn. | 1/23/50 | Baldwin, Alec | Massapequa, N.Y. | 4/3/58 |
| Andersson, Bibi | Stockholm, Sweden | 11/11/35 | Baldwin, William | Massapequa, N.Y. | 1963 |
| | | | Ballard, Kaye | Cleveland, Oh. | 11/20/26 |

| Name | Birthplace | Born |
|---|---|---|
| Balsam, Martin | New York, N.Y. | 11/4/19 |
| Bancroft, Anne | New York, N.Y. | 9/17/31 |
| Banks, Jonathan | Washington, D.C. | 1/31/47 |
| Bannon, Jack | Los Angeles, Cal. | 6/14/40 |
| Bardot, Brigitte | Paris, France | 9/28/34 |
| Barker, Bob | Darrington, Wash. | 12/12/23 |
| Barkin, Ellen | New York, N.Y. | 4/16/55 |
| Barrault, Jean-Louis | Vesinet, France | 9/8/10 |
| Barrie, Barbara | Chicago, Ill. | 5/23/31 |
| Barry, Gene | New York, N.Y. | 6/14/19 |
| Barty, Billy | Millsboro, Pa. | 10/25/24 |
| Barrymore, Drew | Los Angeles, Cal. | 2/22/75 |
| Baryshnikov, Mikhail | Riga, Latvia | 1/28/48 |
| Basinger, Kim | Athens, Ga. | 12/8/53 |
| Bassey, Shirley | Cardiff, Wales | 1/8/37 |
| Bateman, Jason | Rye, N.Y. | 1/14/69 |
| Bateman, Justine | Rye, N.Y. | 2/19/66 |
| Bates, Alan | Allestree, England | 2/17/34 |
| Bates, Kathy | Memphis, Tenn. | 6/28/48 |
| Battle, Kathleen | Portsmouth, Oh. | 8/13/48 |
| Baxter, Meredith | Los Angeles, Cal. | 6/21/47 |
| Beal, John | Joplin, Mo. | 8/13/09 |
| Beasley, Allyce | New York, N.Y. | 7/6/54 |
| Beatty, Ned | Louisville, Ky. | 7/6/37 |
| Beatty, Warren | Richmond, Va. | 3/30/37 |
| Beck, John | Chicago, Ill. | 1/28/43 |
| Bedelia, Bonnie | New York, N.Y. | 3/25/48 |
| Beery, Noah Jr. | New York, N.Y. | 8/10/13 |
| Begley, Ed Jr. | Los Angeles, Cal. | 9/16/49 |
| Belafonte, Harry | New York, N.Y. | 3/1/27 |
| Bel Geddes, Barbara | New York, N.Y. | 10/31/22 |
| Belmondo, Jean-Paul | Neuilly-sur-Seine, France | 4/9/33 |
| Belushi, Jim | Chicago, Ill. | 6/15/54 |
| Benatar, Pat | Brooklyn, N.Y. | 1/10/53 |
| Benedict, Dirk | Helena, Mont. | 3/1/45 |
| Bening, Annette | Topeka, Kan. | 1958 |
| Benjamin, Richard | New York, N.Y. | 5/22/38 |
| Bennett, Tony | New York, N.Y. | 8/3/26 |
| Benson, George | Pittsburgh, Pa. | 3/22/43 |
| Benson, Robby | Dallas, Tex. | 1/21/55 |
| Beradino, John | Los Angeles, Cal. | 5/1/17 |
| Berenger, Tom | Chicago, Ill. | 5/31/50 |
| Bergen, Candice | Beverly Hills, Cal. | 5/9/46 |
| Bergen, Polly | Knoxville, Tenn. | 7/14/30 |
| Bergerac, Jacques | Biarritz, France | 5/26/27 |
| Bergman, Ingmar | Uppsala, Sweden | 7/14/18 |
| Berle, Milton | New York, N.Y. | 7/12/08 |
| Berlinger, Warren | Brooklyn, N.Y. | 8/31/37 |
| Berman, Lazar | Leningrad, USSR | 2/26/30 |
| Berman, Shelley | Chicago, Ill. | 2/3/26 |
| Bernard, Crystal | Dallas, Tex. | 9/30/64 |
| Bernhard, Sandra | Flint, Mich. | 6/6/55 |
| Bernsen, Corbin | No. Hollywood, Cal. | 9/7/55 |
| Berry, Chuck | St. Louis, Mo. | 10/18/26 |
| Berry, Halle | Cleveland, Oh. | 1969 |
| Berry, Ken | Moline, Ill. | 11/3/33 |
| Bertinelli, Valerie | Wilmington, Del. | 4/23/60 |
| Bialik, Mayim | San Diego, Cal. | 12/12/75 |
| Bikel, Theodore | Vienna, Austria | 5/2/24 |
| Birney, David | Washington, D.C. | 4/23/39 |
| Bishop, Joey | Bronx, N.Y. | 2/3/18 |
| Bisoglio, Val | New York, N.Y. | 5/7/26 |
| Bisset, Jacqueline | Weybridge, England | 9/13/44 |
| Bixby, Bill | San Francisco, Cal. | 1/22/34 |
| Black, Clint | Katy, Tex. | 1962 |
| Black, Karen | Park Ridge, Ill. | 7/1/42 |
| Blackstone Jr., Harry | Three Rivers, Mich. | 6/30/34 |
| Blades, Ruben | Panama City, Panama | 7/16/48 |
| Blaine, Vivian | Newark, N.J. | 11/21/21 |
| Blair, Linda | St. Louis, Mo. | 1/22/59 |
| Blake, Robert | Nutley, N.J. | 9/18/33 |
| Bledsoe, Tempestt | Chicago, Ill. | 8/1/73 |
| Bloom, Claire | London, England | 2/15/31 |
| Blyth, Ann | Mt. Kisco, N.Y. | 8/16/28 |
| Bochco, Steven | New York, N.Y. | 12/16/43 |
| Bogarde, Dirk | London, England | 3/28/20 |
| Bogosian, Eric | Boston, Mass. | 4/24/53 |
| Bogdanovich, Peter | Kingston, N.Y. | 7/30/39 |
| Bolton, Michael | New Haven, Conn. | — |
| Bonham-Carter, Helena | London, England | 5/26/66 |
| Bon Jovi, Jon | Sayreville, N.J. | 3/2/62 |
| Bono, Sonny | Detroit, Mich. | 2/16/35 |
| Booke, Sorrell | Buffalo, N.Y. | 1/4/30 |
| Boone, Debby | Hackensack, N.J. | 9/22/56 |
| Boone, Pat | Jacksonville, Fla. | 6/1/34 |
| Borge, Victor | Copenhagen, Denmark | 1/3/09 |
| Borgnine, Ernest | Hamden, Conn. | 1/24/17 |
| Bosco, Philip | Jersey City, N.J. | 9/26/30 |
| Bosley, Tom | Chicago, Ill. | 10/1/27 |
| Bostwick, Barry | San Mateo, Cal. | 2/24/46 |
| Bottoms, Timothy | Santa Barbara, Cal. | 8/30/51 |
| Bowie, David | London, England | 1/8/47 |
| Boxleitner, Bruce | Elgin, Ill. | 5/12/50 |
| Boy George | London, England | 6/14/61 |
| Boyle, Peter | Philadelphia, Pa. | 10/18/33 |
| Bracco, Lorraine | New York, N.Y. | 1955 |
| Bracken, Eddie | New York, N.Y. | 2/7/20 |
| Branagh, Kenneth | Belfast, No. Ireland | 12/10/60 |
| Brando, Marlon | Omaha, Neb. | 4/3/24 |
| Brazzi, Rossano | Bologna, Italy | 9/18/16 |
| Brennan, Eileen | Los Angeles, Cal. | 9/3/35 |
| Brenner, David | Philadelphia, Pa. | 2/4/45 |
| Brewer, Teresa | Toledo, Oh. | 5/7/31 |
| Bridges, Beau | Hollywood, Cal. | 12/9/41 |
| Bridges, Jeff | Los Angeles, Cal. | 12/4/49 |
| Bridges, Lloyd | San Leandro, Cal. | 1/15/13 |
| Brimley, Wilford | Salt Lake City, Ut. | 9/27/34 |
| Broderick, Matthew | New York, N.Y. | 3/21/62 |
| Brolin, James | Los Angeles, Cal. | 7/18/40 |
| Bronson, Charles | Ehrenfeld, Pa. | 11/3/22 |
| Brooks, Albert | Beverly Hills, Cal. | 7/22/47 |
| Brooks, Avery | Evansville, Ind. | 10/2/48 |
| Brooks, Garth | Tulsa, Okla. | 2/2/62 |
| Brooks, Mel | New York, N.Y. | 6/28/26 |
| Brosnan, Pierce | Co. Meath, Ireland | 5/15/53 |
| Brown, Blair | Washington, D.C. | 1948 |
| Brown, Bryan | Sydney, Australia. | 1947 |
| Brown, James | Pulaski, Tenn. | 6/17/28 |
| Brown, Jim | St. Simons Island, Ga. | 2/17/36 |
| Brown, Les | Reinerton, Pa. | 3/14/12 |
| Brown, Ray | Pittsburgh, Pa. | 10/13/26 |
| Browne, Roscoe Lee | Woodbury, N.J. | 5/2/25 |
| Buckley, Betty | Ft. Worth, Tex. | 7/3/47 |
| Bujold, Genevieve | Montreal, Que. | 7/1/42 |
| Bumbry, Grace | St. Louis, Mo. | 1/4/37 |
| Burghoff, Gary | Bristol, Conn. | 5/24/40 |
| Burke, Delta | Orlando, Fla. | 7/30/56 |
| Burnett, Carol | San Antonio, Tex. | 4/26/33 |
| Burns, George | New York, N.Y. | 1/20/96 |
| Burr, Raymond | New Westminster, B.C. | 5/21/17 |
| Burrows, Darren E. | Winfield, Kan. | 9/12/66 |
| Burstyn, Ellen | Detroit, Mich. | 12/7/32 |
| Burton, LeVar | Landstuhl, W. Germany | 2/16/57 |
| Busey, Gary | Goose Creek, Tex. | 6/29/44 |
| Busfield, Timothy | Lansing, Mich. | 6/12/57 |
| Butkus, Dick | Chicago, Ill. | 12/9/42 |
| Buttons, Red | New York, N.Y. | 2/5/19 |
| Buzzi, Ruth | Westerly, R.I. | 7/24/36 |
| Byrne, David | Dumbarton, Scotland. | 5/14/52 |
| Caan, James | New York, N.Y. | 3/26/39 |
| Caballe, Montserrat | Barcelona, Spain | 4/12/33 |
| Caesar, Sid | Yonkers, N.Y. | 9/8/22 |
| Cage, Nicolas | Long Beach, Cal. | 1/7/64 |
| Caine, Michael | London, England | 3/14/33 |
| Caldwell, Sarah | Maryville, Mo. | 3/6/24 |
| Caldwell, Zoe | Melbourne, Australia | 9/14/33 |
| Calhoun, Rory | Los Angeles, Cal. | 8/8/23 |
| Calloway, Cab | Rochester, N.Y. | 12/25/07 |
| Cameron, Kirk | Panorama City, Cal. | 10/12/70 |
| Camp, Hamilton | London, England | 10/30/34 |
| Campanella, Joseph | New York, N.Y. | 11/21/27 |
| Campbell, Glen | Billstown, Ark. | 4/22/36 |
| Candy, John | Toronto, Ont. | 10/31/50 |
| Cannell, Stephen J. | Los Angeles, Cal. | 2/5/42 |
| Cannon, Dyan | Tacoma, Wash. | 1/4/37 |
| Cantrell, Lana | Sydney, Australia. | 8/7/43 |
| Cara, Irene | New York, N.Y. | 3/18/59 |
| Carey, Macdonald | Sioux City, Ia. | 3/15/13 |
| Carey, Mariah | Huntington, N.Y. | 1970 |
| Cariou, Len | Winnipeg, Canada | 9/30/39 |
| Carlin, George | New York, N.Y. | 5/12/37 |
| Carlisle, Kitty | New Orleans, La. | 9/3/15 |
| Carmen, Eric | Cleveland, Oh. | 8/11/49 |
| Carmichael, Ian | Hull, England | 6/18/20 |
| Carney, Art | Mt. Vernon, N.Y. | 11/4/18 |
| Caron, Leslie | Boulogne, France | 7/1/31 |
| Carr, Vikki | El Paso, Tex. | 7/19/41 |
| Carradine, David | Hollywood, Cal. | 10/8/36 |
| Carradine, Keith | San Mateo, Cal. | 8/8/49 |
| Carreras, Jose | Barcelona, Spain | 12/5/47 |
| Carroll, Diahann | Bronx, N.Y. | 7/17/35 |
| Carroll, Pat | Shreveport, La. | 5/5/27 |
| Carson, Johnny | Corning, Ia. | 10/23/25 |
| Carter, Dixie | McLemoresville, Tenn. | 5/25/39 |
| Carter, Jack | New York, N.Y. | 6/24/23 |
| Carter, June | Maces Spring, Va. | 6/23/29 |

| Name | Birthplace | Born |
|---|---|---|
| Carter, Lynda | Phoenix, Ariz. | 7/24/51 |
| Carter, Nell. | Birmingham, Ala. | 9/13/48 |
| Carvey, Dana | Missoula, Mont. | 6/6/55 |
| Casadesus, Gaby | Marseilles, France | 8/9/01 |
| Cash, Johnny | Kingsland, Ark. | 2/26/32 |
| Cash, Rosanne | Memphis, Tenn. | 5/24/55 |
| Cass, Peggy | Boston, Mass. | 5/21/24 |
| Cassidy, David | New York, N.Y. | 4/12/50 |
| Cavett, Dick | Gibbon, Neb. | 11/19/36 |
| Chamberlain, Richard. | Beverly Hills, Cal. | 3/31/35 |
| Channing, Carol | Seattle, Wash. | 1/31/23 |
| Channing, Stockard. | New York, N.Y. | 2/13/44 |
| Chaplin, Geraldine. | Santa Monica, Cal. | 7/31/44 |
| Chapman, Tracy. | Cleveland, Oh. | 1964 |
| Charisse, Cyd | Amarillo, Tex. | 3/8/21 |
| Charles, Ray | Albany, Ga. | 9/23/30 |
| Charo | Murcia, Spain | 1/15/51 |
| Chase, Chevy | New York, N.Y. | 10/8/43 |
| Checker, Chubby | Philadelphia, Pa. | 10/3/41 |
| Cher | El Centro, Cal. | 5/20/46 |
| Chiklis, Michael | Lowell, Mass. | 8/30/63 |
| Chong, Rae Dawn | California | 1962 |
| Chong, Thomas | Edmonton, Alta. | 5/24/38 |
| Christie, Julie. | Assam, India | 4/14/40 |
| Christopher, William. | Evanston, Ill. | 10/20/32 |
| Clapton, Eric | Surrey, England. | 3/30/45 |
| Clark, Dane | New York, N.Y. | 2/18/13 |
| Clark, Dick | Mt. Vernon, N.Y. | 11/30/29 |
| Clark, Petula | Ewell, Surrey, England. | 11/15/32 |
| Clark, Roy | Meherrin, Va. | 4/15/33 |
| Clark, Susan | Sarnia, Ont. | 3/8/40 |
| Clary, Robert | Paris, France | 3/1/26 |
| Clayburgh, Jill | New York, N.Y. | 4/30/44 |
| Cleese, John. | England | 10/27/39 |
| Cliburn, Van | Shreveport, La. | 7/12/34 |
| Clooney, Rosemary | Maysville, Ky. | 5/23/28 |
| Close, Glenn | Greenwich, Conn. | 3/19/47 |
| Coburn, James | Laurel, Neb. | 8/31/28 |
| Coca, Imogene | Philadelphia, Pa. | 11/18/08 |
| Colbert, Claudette. | Paris, France | 9/13/03 |
| Cole, Gary | Park Ridge, Ill. | 9/20/57 |
| Cole, Natalie. | Los Angeles, Cal. | 2/6/50 |
| Cole, Olivia. | Memphis, Tenn. | 11/26/42 |
| Coleman, Dabney | Austin, Tex. | 1/3/32 |
| Coleman, Gary | Zion, Ill. | 2/8/68 |
| Collins, Joan | London, England | 5/23/33 |
| Collins, Judy | Seattle, Wash. | 5/1/39 |
| Collins, Pauline | Exmouth, England | 9/3/40 |
| Collins, Phil. | London, England | 1/30/51 |
| Comden, Betty. | Brooklyn, N.Y. | 5/3/19 |
| Como, Perry | Canonsburg, Pa. | 5/18/12 |
| Conner, Nadine | Compton, Cal. | 2/20/13 |
| Connery, Sean. | Edinburgh, Scotland | 8/25/30 |
| Connick Jr., Harry. | New Orleans, La. | 9/11/67 |
| Conniff, Ray | Attleboro, Mass. | 11/6/16 |
| Connors, Mike | Fresno, Cal. | 8/15/25 |
| Conrad, Robert | Chicago, Ill. | 3/1/35 |
| Conrad, William | Louisville, Ky. | 9/27/20 |
| Constantine, Michael | Reading, Pa. | 5/22/27 |
| Conti, Tom | Paisley, Scotland | 11/22/41 |
| Conway, Tim. | Willoughby, Oh. | 12/15/33 |
| Cook, Barbara | Atlanta, Ga. | 10/25/27 |
| Cook, Peter | Torquay, England. | 11/17/37 |
| Cooke, Alistair | Manchester, England. | 11/20/08 |
| Coolidge, Rita | Nashville, Tenn. | 5/1/45 |
| Cooper, Alice | Detroit, Mich. | 2/4/48 |
| Cooper, Jackie | Los Angeles, Cal. | 9/15/21 |
| Copperfield, David. | Metuchen, N.J. | 9/16/56 |
| Coppola, Francis | Detroit, Mich. | 4/7/39 |
| Corbin, Barry. | Lamesa, Tex. | 10/16/40 |
| Corby, Ellen | Racine, Wis. | 6/3/13 |
| Cord, Alex | New York, N.Y. | 8/3/31 |
| Corea, Chick. | Chelsea, Mass. | 6/12/41 |
| Corelli, Franco | Ancona, Italy | 4/8/23 |
| Corey, Jeff | New York, N.Y. | 8/10/14 |
| Cosby, Bill | Philadelphia, Pa. | 7/12/37 |
| Costas, Bob | New York, N.Y. | 3/22/52 |
| Costello, Elvis | London, England | 8/25/54 |
| Costner, Kevin | Compton, Cal. | 1/18/55 |
| Cotten, Joseph | Petersburg, Va. | 5/15/05 |
| Cougar, John | Seymour, Ind. | 10/7/51 |
| Courtenay, Tom | Hull, England | 2/25/37 |
| Cox, Ronny | Cloudcroft, N.M. | 8/23/38 |
| Craddock, Crash | Greensboro, N.C. | 6/16/40 |
| Crain, Jeanne | Barstow, Cal. | 5/25/25 |
| Crawford, Michael. | Salisbury, England | 1/19/42 |
| Crenna, Richard | Los Angeles, Cal. | 11/30/26 |
| Crespin, Regine | Marseilles, France | 2/23/26 |

| Name | Birthplace | Born |
|---|---|---|
| Cronyn, Hume | London, Ont. | 7/18/11 |
| Crosby, David | Los Angeles, Cal. | 8/14/41 |
| Cross, Ben | London, England | 12/16/47 |
| Crouse, Lindsay | New York, N.Y. | 5/12/48 |
| Crowell, Rodney. | Houston, Tex. | 8/17/50 |
| Cruise, Tom | Syracuse, N.Y. | 7/3/62 |
| Crystal, Billy | Long Beach, N.Y. | 3/14/47 |
| Culkin, Macaulay | New York, N.Y. | 8/26/80 |
| Cullum, John. | Knoxville, Tenn. | 3/2/30 |
| Culp, Robert | Oakland, Cal. | 8/16/30 |
| Cummings, Constance | Seattle, Wash. | 5/15/10 |
| Curry, Tim | Cheshire, England | 4/19/46 |
| Curtin, Jane | Cambridge, Mass. | 9/6/47 |
| Curtis, Jamie Lee | Los Angeles, Cal. | 11/22/58 |
| Curtis, Keene | Salt Lake City, Ut. | 2/15/23 |
| Curtis, Tony | New York, N.Y. | 6/3/25 |
| Cusack, Cyril. | Durban, S. Africa | 11/26/10 |
| Cusack, Joan | Evanston, Ill. | 10/11/62 |
| Cusack, John | Evanston, Ill. | 6/28/66 |
| Cushing, Peter. | Surrey, England. | 5/26/13 |
| Cyrus, Billy Ray | Flatwoods, Ky. | 1961 |
| Dafoe, Willem | Appleton, Wis. | 7/22/55 |
| Dahl, Arlene | Minneapolis, Minn. | 8/11/28 |
| Dale, Jim | Rothwell, England | 8/15/35 |
| Dalton, Abby | Las Vegas, Nev. | 8/15/32 |
| Dalton, Timothy | Wales | 3/21/44 |
| Daltrey, Roger | London, England | 3/1/44 |
| Daly, Timothy | Suffern, N.J. | 3/1/58 |
| Daly, Tyne | Madison, Wis. | 2/21/47 |
| Damone, Vic | Brooklyn, N.Y. | 6/12/28 |
| D'Angelo, Beverly | Columbus, Oh. | 11/15/54 |
| Dangerfield, Rodney | Babylon, N.Y. | 11/22/22 |
| Daniels, Charlie | Wilmington, N.C. | 10/28/36 |
| Daniels, Jeff | Georgia | 2/19/55 |
| Daniels, William | Brooklyn, N.Y. | 3/31/27 |
| Danner, Blythe | Philadelphia, Pa. | 2/3/44 |
| Danson, Ted | San Diego, Cal. | 12/29/47 |
| Danza, Tony | New York, N.Y. | 4/21/50 |
| Darby, Kim | Hollywood, Cal. | 7/8/48 |
| D'Arby, Terence Trent | New York, N.Y. | 3/15/62 |
| Davidson, John | Pittsburgh, Pa. | 12/13/41 |
| Davis, Ann B. | Schenectady, N.Y. | 5/5/26 |
| Davis, Clifton | Chicago, Ill. | 10/4/45 |
| Davis, Geena | Wareham, Mass. | 1/21/57 |
| Davis, Judy | Perth, Australia | 1956 |
| Davis, Mac | Lubbock, Tex. | 1/21/42 |
| Davis, Ossie | Cogdell, Ga. | 12/18/17 |
| Dawber, Pam | Farmington Hills, Mich. | 10/18/51 |
| Dawson, Richard | Hampshire, England | 11/20/32 |
| Day, Doris | Cincinnati, Oh. | 4/3/24 |
| Day-Lewis, Daniel | London, England | 4/29/57 |
| Dean, Jimmy | Plainview, Tex. | 8/10/28 |
| De Camp, Rosemary | Prescott, Ariz. | 11/14/10 |
| DeCarlo, Yvonne | Vancouver, B.C. | 9/1/22 |
| Dee, Frances | Los Angeles, Cal. | 11/26/07 |
| Dee, Ruby | Cleveland, Oh. | 10/27/23 |
| Dee, Sandra | Bayonne, N.J. | 4/23/42 |
| Defore, Don | Cedar Rapids, Ia. | 8/25/17 |
| DeHaven, Gloria | Los Angeles, Cal. | 7/23/25 |
| De Havilland, Olivia | Tokyo, Japan | 7/1/16 |
| Delany, Dana | New York, N.Y. | 3/13/57 |
| Della Chiesa, Vivienne | Chicago, Ill. | 10/9/20 |
| Delon, Alain | Sceaux, France. | 11/8/35 |
| DeLuise, Dom | Brooklyn, N.Y. | 8/1/33 |
| De Mille, Agnes | New York, N.Y. | 9/18/05 |
| Demme, Jonathan | Rockville Centre, N.Y. | 2/22/44 |
| De Mornay, Rebecca | Santa Rosa, Cal. | 11/29/61 |
| Deneuve, Catherine | Paris, France | 10/22/43 |
| De Niro, Robert | New York, N.Y. | 8/17/43 |
| Dennehy, Brian | Bridgeport, Conn. | 7/9/38 |
| Denver, Bob | New Rochelle, N.Y. | 1/9/35 |
| Denver, John. | Roswell, N.M. | 12/31/43 |
| DePalma, Brian | Newark, N.J. | 9/11/40 |
| Depardieu, Gerard | Chateauroux, France. | 12/27/48 |
| Depp, Johnny | Owensboro, Ky. | 6/9/63 |
| Derek, Bo | Long Beach, Cal. | 11/20/56 |
| Derek, John | Hollywood, Cal. | 8/12/26 |
| Dern, Bruce | Chicago, Ill. | 6/4/36 |
| Dern, Laura | Santa Monica, Cal. | 2/1/67 |
| Devane, William | Albany, N.Y. | 9/5/37 |
| DeVito, Danny | Neptune, N.J. | 11/17/44 |
| DeWitt, Joyce | Wheeling, W.Va. | 4/23/49 |
| Dey, Susan. | Pekin, Ill. | 12/10/52 |
| Diamond, Neil | Brooklyn, N.Y. | 1/24/41 |
| Dickinson, Angie | Kulm, N.D. | 9/30/31 |
| Diddley, Bo. | McComb, Miss. | 12/20/28 |
| Diller, Phyllis | Lima, Oh. | 7/17/17 |
| Dillman, Bradford | San Francisco, Cal. | 4/14/30 |

| Name | Birthplace | Born |
|---|---|---|
| Dillon, Matt | New Rochelle, N.Y. | 2/18/64 |
| Dobson, Kevin | New York, N.Y. | 3/18/44 |
| Domingo, Placido | Madrid, Spain | 1/21/41 |
| Domino, Fats | New Orleans, La. | 2/26/28 |
| Donahue, Phil | Cleveland, Oh. | 12/21/35 |
| Donahue, Troy | New York, N.Y. | 1/27/36 |
| Dotrice, Roy | Guernsey, England | 5/26/23 |
| Douglas, Kirk | Amsterdam, N.Y. | 12/9/18 |
| Douglas, Michael | New Brunswick, N.J. | 9/25/44 |
| Down, Leslie-Ann | London, England | 3/17/54 |
| Downey, Robert Jr. | New York, N.Y. | 4/4/65 |
| Downs, Hugh | Akron, Oh. | 2/14/21 |
| Drake, Larry | Tulsa, Okla. | 2/21/- |
| Drew, Ellen | Kansas City, Mo. | 11/23/15 |
| Dryer, Fred | Hawthorne, Cal. | 7/6/46 |
| Dreyfuss, Richard | Brooklyn, N.Y. | 10/29/47 |
| Dru, Joanne | Logan, W.Va. | 1/31/23 |
| Duffy, Julia | Minneapolis, Minn. | 6/27/51 |
| Duffy, Patrick | Townsend, Mont. | 3/17/49 |
| Dufour, Val | New Orleans, La. | 2/5/27 |
| Dukakis, Olympia | Lowell, Mass. | 6/20/31 |
| Duke, Patty | New York, N.Y. | 12/14/46 |
| Dukes, David | San Francisco, Cal. | 6/6/45 |
| Dullea, Keir | Cleveland, Oh. | 5/30/36 |
| Dunaway, Faye | Bascom, Fla. | 1/14/41 |
| Duncan, Sandy | Henderson, Tex. | 2/20/46 |
| Dunham, Katherine | Joliet, Ill. | 6/22/10 |
| Dunne, Griffin | New York, N.Y. | 6/8/55 |
| Durbin, Deanna | Winnipeg, Man. | 12/4/21 |
| Durning, Charles | Highland Falls, N.Y. | 2/28/23 |
| Dussault, Nancy | Pensacola, Fla. | 6/30/36 |
| Dutton, Charles S. | Baltimore, Md. | 1/30/51 |
| Duvall, Robert | San Diego, Cal. | 1/5/31 |
| Duvall, Shelley | Houston, Tex. | 7/7/49 |
| Dylan, Bob | Duluth, Minn. | 5/24/41 |
| Dysart, Richard | Augusta, Me. | 3/30/29 |
| Dzundza, George | Rosenheim, Germany | 7/19/45 |
| Easton, Sheena | Bellshill, Scotland. | 4/27/59 |
| Eastwood, Clint | San Francisco, Cal. | 5/31/30 |
| Ebert, Roger | Urbana, Ill. | 6/18/42 |
| Ebsen, Buddy | Belleville, Ill. | 4/2/08 |
| Edelman, Herb | Brooklyn, N.Y. | 11/5/33 |
| Eden, Barbara | Tucson, Ariz. | 8/23/34 |
| Edwards, Anthony | Santa Barbara, Cal. | 1/19/62 |
| Edwards, Blake | Tulsa, Okla. | 7/26/22 |
| Edwards, Ralph | Merino, Col. | 6/13/13 |
| Eichhorn, Lisa | Reading, Pa. | 2/4/52 |
| Eikenberry, Jill | New Haven, Conn. | 1/21/47 |
| Ekberg, Anita | Malmo, Sweden | 9/29/31 |
| Ekland, Britt | Stockholm, Sweden | 10/6/42 |
| Elam, Jack | Miami, Ariz. | 11/13/16 |
| Elizondo, Hector | New York, N.Y. | 12/22/36 |
| Elliott, Bob | Boston, Mass. | 3/26/23 |
| Elliott, Sam | Sacramento, Cal. | 8/9/44 |
| Englund, Robert | Hollywood, Cal. | 6/6/48 |
| Elvira (Cassandra Peterson) | Manhattan, Kan. | 9/17/51 |
| Estefan, Gloria | Havana, Cuba. | 9/1/58 |
| Estevez, Emilio | New York, N.Y. | 5/12/62 |
| Estrada, Erik | New York, N.Y. | 3/16/49 |
| Evans, Dale | Uvalde, Tex. | 10/31/12 |
| Evans, Linda | Hartford, Conn. | 11/18/42 |
| Evans, Robert | New York, N.Y. | 6/29/30 |
| Everett, Chad | South Bend, Ind. | 6/11/36 |
| Everly, Don | Brownie, Ky. | 2/1/37 |
| Everly, Phil | Chicago, Ill. | 1/19/38 |
| Evigan, Greg | S. Amboy, N.J. | 10/14/53 |
| Ewell, Tom | Owensboro, Ky. | 4/29/09 |
| Fabares, Shelley | Santa Monica, Cal. | 1/19/42 |
| Fabian (Forte) | Philadelphia, Pa. | 2/6/43 |
| Fabray, Nanette | San Diego, Cal. | 10/27/20 |
| Fairbanks, Douglas Jr. | New York, N.Y. | 12/9/09 |
| Fairchild, Morgan | Dallas, Tex. | 2/3/50 |
| Falana, Lola | Philadelphia, Pa. | 9/11/46 |
| Falk, Peter | New York, N.Y. | 9/16/27 |
| Farentino, James | Brooklyn, N.Y. | 2/24/38 |
| Fargo, Donna | Mt. Airy, N.C. | 11/10/45 |
| Farr, Jamie | Toledo, Oh. | 7/1/34 |
| Farrell, Eileen | Willimantic, Conn. | 2/13/20 |
| Farrell, Mike | St. Paul, Minn. | 2/6/39 |
| Farrow, Mia | Los Angeles, Cal. | 2/9/45 |
| Faustino, David | California | 3/3/74 |
| Fawcett, Farrah | Corpus Christi, Tex. | 2/2/47 |
| Faye, Alice | New York, N.Y. | 5/5/12 |
| Feinstein, Michael | Columbus, Oh. | 9/7/56 |
| Feld, Fritz | Berlin, Germany | 10/15/00 |
| Feldon, Barbara | Pittsburgh, Pa. | 3/12/41 |
| Feliciano, Jose | Lares, Puerto Rico | 9/10/45 |

| Name | Birthplace | Born |
|---|---|---|
| Fell, Norman | Philadelphia, Pa. | 3/24/24 |
| Fellini, Federico | Rimini, Italy | 1/20/20 |
| Fenn, Sherilyn | Detroit, Mich. | 1965 |
| Ferrell, Conchata | Charleston, W. Va. | 3/28/43 |
| Ferrer, Mel | Elberon, N.J. | 8/25/17 |
| Fiedler, John | Platville, Wis. | 2/3/25 |
| Field, Sally | Pasadena, Cal. | 11/6/46 |
| Finney, Albert | Salford, England | 5/9/36 |
| Firkusny, Rudolf | Napajedla, Czechoslovakia | 2/11/12 |
| Firth, Peter | Yorkshire, England | 10/27/53 |
| Fischer-Dieskau, Dietrich | Berlin, Germany | 5/28/25 |
| Fishburne, Larry | Augusta, Ga. | 7/30/61 |
| Fisher, Carrie | Beverly Hills, Cal. | 10/21/56 |
| Fisher, Eddie | Philadelphia, Pa. | 8/10/28 |
| Fitzgerald, Ella | Newport News, Va. | 4/25/18 |
| Fitzgerald, Geraldine | Dublin, Ireland. | 11/24/13 |
| Flack, Roberta | Black Mountain, N.C. | 2/10/39 |
| Flanagan, Fionnula | Dublin, Ireland. | 12/10/41 |
| Flanders, Ed | Minneapolis, Minn. | 12/29/34 |
| Fleming, Rhonda | Hollywood, Cal. | 8/10/23 |
| Fletcher, Louise | Birmingham, Ala. | 7/22/34 |
| Foch, Nina | Leyden, Netherlands | 4/20/24 |
| Fogelberg, Dan | Peoria, Ill. | 8/13/51 |
| Fonda, Bridget | Los Angeles, Cal. | 1964 |
| Fonda, Jane | New York, N.Y. | 12/21/37 |
| Fonda, Peter | New York, N.Y. | 2/23/39 |
| Fontaine, Joan | Tokyo, Japan | 10/22/17 |
| Ford, Faith | Alexandria, La. | 9/14/- |
| Ford, Glenn | Quebec, Canada | 5/1/16 |
| Ford, Harrison | Chicago, Ill. | 7/13/42 |
| Forrest, Steve | Huntsville, Tex. | 9/29/24 |
| Forsythe, John | Penns Grove, N.J. | 1/29/18 |
| Foster, Jodie | New York, N.Y. | 11/19/62 |
| Fox, James | London, England | 5/19/39 |
| Fox, Michael J. | Edmonton, Alta. | 6/9/61 |
| Foxworth, Robert | Houston, Tex. | 11/1/41 |
| Frampton, Peter | Kent, England. | 4/22/50 |
| Franciosa, Anthony | New York, N.Y. | 10/25/28 |
| Francis, Anne | Ossining, N.Y. | 9/16/30 |
| Francis, Arlene | Boston, Mass. | 10/20/08 |
| Francis, Connie | Newark, N.J. | 12/12/38 |
| Frankenheimer, John | Malba, N.Y. | 2/19/30 |
| Franklin, Aretha | Memphis, Tenn. | 3/25/42 |
| Franklin, Bonnie | Santa Monica, Cal. | 1/6/44 |
| Franklin, Joe | New York, N.Y. | 1929 |
| Frann, Mary | St. Louis, Mo. | 2/27/43 |
| Franz, Dennis | Maywood, Ill. | 10/28/44 |
| Freeman Jr., Al | San Antonio, Tex. | 3/21/34 |
| Freeman, Morgan | Memphis, Tenn. | 6/1/37 |
| Friedkin, William | Chicago, Ill. | 8/29/39 |
| Frost, David | Tenterden, England | 4/7/39 |
| Funicello, Annette | Utica, N.Y. | 10/22/42 |
| Funt, Allen | New York, N.Y. | 9/16/14 |
| Gabor, Eva | Hungary | 1921 |
| Gabor, Zsa Zsa | Hungary | 2/6/17 |
| Gabriel, John | Niagara Falls, N.Y. | 5/25/31 |
| Gabriel, Peter | London, England | 2/13/50 |
| Gail, Max | Detroit, Mich. | 4/5/43 |
| Galway, James | Belfast, Ireland | 12/8/39 |
| Garagiola, Joe | St. Louis, Mo. | 2/12/26 |
| Garcia, Andy | Havana, Cuba. | 4/12/56 |
| Garfunkel, Art | New York, N.Y. | 11/5/41 |
| Garland, Beverly | Santa Cruz, Cal. | 10/17/26 |
| Garner, James | Norman, Okla. | 4/7/28 |
| Garr, Teri | Lakewood, Oh. | 12/11/45 |
| Garrett, Betty | St. Joseph, Mo. | 5/23/19 |
| Garson, Greer | Co. Down, N. Ireland. | 9/29/08 |
| Gatlin, Larry | Seminole, Tex. | 5/2/48 |
| Gayle, Crystal | Paintsville, Ky. | 1/9/51 |
| Gaynor, Mitzi | Chicago, Ill. | 9/4/30 |
| Gazzara, Ben | New York, N.Y. | 8/28/30 |
| Gedda, Nicolai | Stockholm, Sweden | 7/11/25 |
| Gere, Richard | Philadelphia, Pa. | 8/31/49 |
| Getty, Estelle | New York, N.Y. | 7/25/24 |
| Ghostley, Alice | Eve, Mo. | 8/14/26 |
| Giannini, Giancarlo | Spezia, Italy | 8/1/42 |
| Gibbs, Marla | Chicago, Ill. | 6/14/31 |
| Gibson, Debbie | New York, N.Y. | 8/31/70 |
| Gibson, Henry | Germantown, Pa. | 9/21/35 |
| Gibson, Mel | Peekskill, N.Y. | 1/3/56 |
| Gielgud, John | London, England | 4/14/04 |
| Gifford, Frank | Santa Monica, Cal. | 8/16/30 |
| Gilbert, Melissa | Los Angeles, Cal. | 5/8/64 |
| Gilberto, Astrud | Salvador, Brazil. | 3/30/40 |
| Gillette, Anita | Baltimore, Md. | 8/16/38 |
| Gilley, Mickey | Natchez, Miss. | 3/9/36 |
| Ginty, Robert | New York, N.Y. | 11/14/48 |

| Name | Birthplace | Born |
|------|-----------|------|
| Givens, Robin | New York, N.Y. | 11/27/64 |
| Glaser, Paul Michael | Cambridge, Mass. | 3/25/42 |
| Glenn, Scott | Pittsburgh, Pa. | 1/26/42 |
| Gless, Sharon | Los Angeles, Cal. | 5/31/43 |
| Glover, Danny | San Francisco, Cal. | 7/22/47 |
| Godard, Jean Luc | Paris, France | 12/3/30 |
| Godunov, Alexander | Sakhalin Is., USSR | 11/28/49 |
| Goldberg, Whoopi | New York, N.Y. | 11/13/50 |
| Goldblum, Jeff | Pittsburgh, Pa. | 10/22/52 |
| Goldsboro, Bobby | Marianna, Fla. | 1/18/42 |
| Goldthwait, Bob | Syracuse, N.Y. | 1962 |
| Goodman, John | St. Louis, Mo. | 6/20/53 |
| Gordon, Gale | New York, N.Y. | 2/2/06 |
| Gorme, Eydie | Bronx, N.Y. | 8/16/32 |
| Gorshin, Frank | Pittsburgh, Pa. | 4/5/34 |
| Gossett Jr., Louis | Brooklyn, N.Y. | 5/27/36 |
| Gould, Elliott | Brooklyn, N.Y. | 8/29/38 |
| Gould, Harold | Schenectady, N.Y. | 12/10/23 |
| Gould, Morton | Richmond Hill, N.Y. | 12/10/13 |
| Goulet, Robert | Lawrence, Mass. | 11/26/33 |
| Gowdy, Curt | Green River, Wyo. | 7/31/19 |
| Graham, Virginia | Chicago, Ill. | 7/4/12 |
| Grammer, Kelsey | Virgin Islands | 2/20/- |
| Granger, Farley | San Jose, Cal. | 7/1/25 |
| Granger, Stewart | London, England | 5/6/13 |
| Grant, Amy | Augusta, Ga. | 12/25/60 |
| Grant, Lee | New York, N.Y. | 10/31/29 |
| Graves, Peter | Minneapolis, Minn. | 3/18/26 |
| Gray, Linda | Santa Monica, Cal. | 9/12/40 |
| Grayson, Kathryn | Winston-Salem, N.C. | 2/9/22 |
| Greco, Jose | Abruzzi, Italy | 12/23/18 |
| Green, Adolph | New York, N.Y. | 12/2/15 |
| Green, Al | Forest City, Ark. | 4/13/46 |
| Greene, Michele | Las Vegas, Nev. | 2/3/- |
| Greene, Shecky | Chicago, Ill. | 4/8/26 |
| Gregory, Cynthia | Los Angeles, Cal. | 7/8/46 |
| Gregory, Dick | St. Louis, Mo. | 10/12/32 |
| Gregory, James | Bronx, N.Y. | 12/23/11 |
| Grey, Jennifer | New York, N.Y. | 3/22/60 |
| Grey, Joel | Cleveland, Oh. | 4/11/32 |
| Grier, David Alan | Detroit, Mich. | 6/30/55 |
| Griffin, Merv | San Mateo, Cal. | 7/6/25 |
| Griffith, Andy | Mount Airy, N.C. | 6/1/26 |
| Griffith, Melanie | New York, N.Y. | 8/9/57 |
| Grimes, Tammy | Lynn, Mass. | 1/30/34 |
| Grizzard, George | Roanoke Rapids, N.C. | 4/1/28 |
| Grodin, Charles | Pittsburgh, Pa. | 4/21/35 |
| Groh, David | New York, N.Y. | 5/21/41 |
| Grosbard, Ulu | Antwerp, Belgium | 1/19/29 |
| Gross, Michael | Chicago, Ill. | 6/21/47 |
| Guardino, Harry | New York, N.Y. | 12/23/25 |
| Guillaume, Robert | St. Louis, Mo. | 11/30/37 |
| Guinness, Alec | London, England | 4/2/14 |
| Gumbel, Greg | New Orleans, La. | 5/3/46 |
| Guthrie, Arlo | New York, N.Y. | 7/10/47 |
| Guttenberg, Steve | New York, N.Y. | 8/24/58 |
| Guy, Jasmine | Boston, Mass. | 3/10/64 |
| Hackett, Buddy | Brooklyn, N.Y. | 8/31/24 |
| Hackman, Gene | San Bernardino, Cal. | 1/30/30 |
| Hagen, Uta | Gottingen, Germany | 6/12/19 |
| Haggard, Merle | Bakersfield, Cal. | 4/6/37 |
| Hagman, Larry | Weatherford, Tex. | 9/21/31 |
| Haid, Charles | San Francisco, Cal. | 6/2/44 |
| Hale, Barbara | DeKalb, Ill. | 4/18/22 |
| Hall, Arsenio | Cleveland, Oh. | 2/12/55 |
| Hall, Daryl | Pottstown, Pa. | 10/11/48 |
| Hall, Deidre | Milwaukee, Wis. | 10/31/48 |
| Hall, Huntz | New York, N.Y. | 8/15/19 |
| Hall, Monty | Winnipeg, Man. | 8/25/25 |
| Hall, Tom T. | Olive Hill, Ky. | 5/25/36 |
| Hamel, Veronica | Philadelphia, Pa. | 11/20/43 |
| Hamill, Mark | Oakland, Cal. | 9/25/51 |
| Hamilton, George | Memphis, Tenn. | 8/12/39 |
| Hamilton, Linda | Salisbury, Md. | 9/26/56 |
| Hamlin, Harry | Pasadena, Cal. | 10/30/51 |
| Hammer | Oakland, Cal. | 1962 |
| Hampton, Lionel | Birmingham, Ala. | 4/12/13 |
| Hancock, Herbie | Chicago, Ill. | 4/12/40 |
| Hanks, Tom | Oakland, Cal. | 7/9/56 |
| Hannah, Daryl | Chicago, Ill. | 1961 |
| Hardison, Kadeem | New York, N.Y. | 7/24/- |
| Harewood, Dorian | Dayton, Oh. | 8/6/51 |
| Harmon, Mark | Burbank, Cal. | 9/2/51 |
| Harper, Jessica | Chicago, Ill. | 10/10/49 |
| Harper, Tess | Mammoth Springs, Ark. | 8/15/50 |
| Harper, Valerie | Suffern, N.Y. | 8/22/40 |
| Harrelson, Woody | Midland, Tex. | 7/23/61 |
| Harrington, Pat | New York, N.Y. | 8/13/29 |

| Name | Birthplace | Born |
|------|-----------|------|
| Harris, Barbara | Evanston, Ill. | 7/25/35 |
| Harris, Ed | Englewood, N.J. | 11/28/50 |
| Harris, Emmylou | Birmingham, Ala. | 4/2/47 |
| Harris, Julie | Grosse Pte. Park, Mich. | 12/2/25 |
| Harris, Neil Patrick | Albuquerque, N.M. | 6/15/73 |
| Harris, Phil | Linton, Ind. | 6/24/04 |
| Harris, Richard | Co. Limerick, Ireland | 10/1/33 |
| Harris, Rosemary | Ashby, England | 9/19/30 |
| Harrison, George | Liverpool, England | 2/25/43 |
| Harrison, Gregory | Avalon, Cal. | 5/31/50 |
| Harry, Deborah | Miami, Fla. | 7/1/45 |
| Hart, Mary | Madison, S.D. | 11/8/51 |
| Hartley, Mariette | New York, N.Y. | 6/21/40 |
| Hartman, David | Pawtucket, R.I. | 5/19/35 |
| Hartman, Lisa | Houston, Tex. | 6/1/56 |
| Hartman, Phil | Ontario, Canada | 9/24/48 |
| Hasselhoff, David | Baltimore, Md. | 7/17/52 |
| Hasso, Signe | Stockholm, Sweden | 8/15/10 |
| Hauer, Rutger | Netherlands | 1/23/44 |
| Haver, June | Rock Island, Ill. | 6/10/26 |
| Havoc, June | Seattle, Wash. | 11/8/16 |
| Hawn, Goldie | Washington, D.C. | 11/21/45 |
| Hayden, Melissa | Toronto, Ont. | 4/25/23 |
| Hayes, Isaac | Covington, Tenn. | 8/20/42 |
| Hays, Robert | Bethesda, Md. | 7/24/47 |
| Heard, John | Washington, D.C. | 3/7/45 |
| Hearn, George | Memphis, Tenn. | 1935 |
| Heckart, Eileen | Columbus, Oh. | 3/29/19 |
| Helmond, Katherine | Galveston, Tex. | 7/5/34 |
| Hemingway, Margaux | Portland, Ore. | 2/19/55 |
| Hemingway, Mariel | Mill Valley, Cal. | 11/21/61 |
| Hemmings, David | Guildford, England | 11/18/41 |
| Hemsley, Sherman | Philadelphia, Pa. | 2/1/38 |
| Henderson, Florence | Dale, Ind. | 2/14/34 |
| Henderson, Skitch | Halstad, Minn. | 1/27/18 |
| Henley, Don | Gilmer, Tex. | 7/22/47 |
| Henner, Marilu | Chicago, Ill. | 4/6/52 |
| Henning, Doug | Ft. Garry, Man. | 5/3/47 |
| Hepburn, Katharine | Hartford, Conn. | 5/12/07 |
| Herman, Pee-wee | Peekskill, N.Y. | 8/27/52 |
| Herrmann, Edward | Washington, D.C. | 7/21/43 |
| Hershey, Barbara | Los Angeles, Cal. | 2/5/48 |
| Hesseman, Howard | Lebanon, Ore. | 2/27/40 |
| Heston, Charlton | Evanston, Ill. | 10/4/24 |
| Hewett, Christopher | Sussex, England | 4/5/- |
| Hildegarde | Adell, Wis. | 2/1/06 |
| Hill, Arthur | Melfort, Sask. | 8/1/22 |
| Hill, Steven | Seattle, Wash. | 2/24/22 |
| Hill, George Roy | Minneapolis, Minn. | 12/20/22 |
| Hiller, Wendy | Stockport, England | 8/15/12 |
| Hillerman, John | Denison, Tex. | 12/30/32 |
| Hines, Gregory | New York, N.Y. | 2/14/46 |
| Hines, Jerome | Hollywood, Cal. | 11/8/21 |
| Hingle, Pat | Miami, Fla. | 7/19/24 |
| Hirsch, Judd | New York, N.Y. | 3/15/35 |
| Hirt, Al | New Orleans, La. | 11/7/22 |
| Ho, Don | Kakaako, Oahu, Ha. | 8/13/30 |
| Hoffman, Dustin | Los Angeles, Cal. | 8/8/37 |
| Hogan, Paul | New South Wales, Australia | 10/8/39 |
| Holbrook, Hal | Cleveland, Oh. | 2/17/25 |
| Holder, Geoffrey | Trinidad | 8/1/30 |
| Holliman, Earl | Delhi, La. | 9/11/28 |
| Holm, Celeste | New York, N.Y. | 4/29/19 |
| Hooks, Jan | Decatur, Ga. | 4/23/57 |
| Hooks, Robert | Washington, D.C. | 4/18/37 |
| Hope, Bob | London, England | 5/29/03 |
| Hopkins, Anthony | Wales | 12/31/37 |
| Hopkins, Telma | Louisville, Ky. | 10/28/48 |
| Hopper, Dennis | Dodge City, Kan. | 5/17/36 |
| Horne, Lena | Brooklyn, N.Y. | 6/30/17 |
| Horne, Marilyn | Bradford, Pa. | 1/16/34 |
| Horsley, Lee | Muleshoe, Tex. | 5/15/55 |
| Hoskins, Bob | Suffolk, England | 10/26/42 |
| Houston, Whitney | E. Orange, N.J. | 8/9/63 |
| Howard, Ken | El Centro, Cal. | 3/28/44 |
| Howard, Ron | Duncan, Okla. | 3/1/53 |
| Howell, C. Thomas | Los Angeles, Cal. | 12/7/66 |
| Howes, Sally Ann | London, England | 7/20/30 |
| Hughes, Barnard | Bedford Hills, N.Y. | 7/16/15 |
| Hulce, Tom | Whitewater, Wis. | 12/6/53 |
| Humperdinck, Engelbert | Madras, India | 5/3/36 |
| Hunt, Helen | Los Angeles, Cal. | 6/15/63 |
| Hunt, Linda | Morristown, N.J. | 4/2/45 |
| Hunter, Holly | Conyers, Ga. | 3/20/58 |
| Hunter, Kim | Detroit, Mich. | 11/12/22 |
| Hunter, Ross | Cleveland, Oh. | 5/6/21 |
| Hunter, Tab | New York, N.Y. | 7/11/31 |

| Name | Birthplace | Born |
|------|-----------|------|
| Hurt, John | Chesterfield, England | 1/22/40 |
| Hurt, Mary Beth | Marshalltown, Ia. | 9/26/46 |
| Hurt, William | Washington, D.C. | 3/20/50 |
| Hussey, Ruth | Providence, R.I. | 10/30/14 |
| Huston, Anjelica | Ireland | 7/8/51 |
| Hutton, Betty | Battle Creek, Mich. | 2/26/21 |
| Hutton, Timothy | Malibu, Cal. | 8/16/60 |
| Hyman, Earle | Rocky Mount, N.C. | 10/11/26 |
| Ian, Janis | New York, N.Y. | 4/7/51 |
| Idol, Billy | London, England | 11/30/55 |
| Iglesias, Julio | Madrid, Spain | 9/23/43 |
| Ingram, James | Akron, Oh. | 2/16/56 |
| Irons, Jeremy | Cowes, England | 9/19/48 |
| Irving, Amy | Palo Alto, Cal. | 9/10/53 |
| Irving, George S. | Springfield, Mass. | 11/1/22 |
| Ives, Burl | Hunt Township, Ill. | 6/14/09 |
| Ivey, Judith | El Paso, Tex. | 9/4/51 |
| Ivory, James | Berkeley, Cal. | 6/7/28 |
| Jackee | Winston-Salem, N.C. | 8/14/57 |
| Jackson, Anne | Allegheny, Pa. | 9/3/25 |
| Jackson, Glenda | Liverpool, England | 5/9/36 |
| Jackson, Janet | Gary, Ind. | 5/16/66 |
| Jackson, Jermaine | Gary, Ind. | 12/11/54 |
| Jackson, La Toya | Gary, Ind. | 5/29/56 |
| Jackson, Kate | Birmingham, Ala. | 10/29/48 |
| Jackson, Michael | Gary, Ind. | 8/29/58 |
| Jacobi, Derek | London, England | 10/22/38 |
| Jaeckel, Richard | Long Beach, N.Y. | 10/10/26 |
| Jagger, Mick | Dartford, England | 7/26/43 |
| James, Dennis | Jersey City, N.J. | 8/24/17 |
| Janis, Conrad | New York, N.Y. | 2/11/28 |
| Jarreau, Al | Milwaukee, Wis | 3/12/40 |
| Jeffreys, Anne | Goldsboro, N.C. | 1/26/23 |
| Jennings, Waylon | Littlefield, Tex. | 6/15/37 |
| Jeter, Michael | Lawrenceburg, Tenn. | 8/20/52 |
| Jett, Joan | Philadelphia, Pa. | 9/22/60 |
| Jewison, Norman | Toronto, Ont. | 7/21/26 |
| Jillian, Ann | Cambridge, Mass. | 1/29/50 |
| Joel, Billy | Bronx, N.Y. | 5/9/49 |
| John, Elton | Middlesex, England. | 3/25/47 |
| Johns, Glynis | Durban, S. Africa | 10/5/23 |
| Johnson, Anne-Marie | Los Angeles, Cal. | 7/18/- |
| Johnson, Arte | Benton Harbor, Mich. | 1/20/29 |
| Johnson, Ben | Foraker, Okla. | 6/13/18 |
| Johnson, Don | Flatt Creek, Mo. | 12/15/49 |
| Johnson, Van | Newport, R.I. | 8/25/16 |
| Jones, Charlie | Ft. Smith, Ark. | 11/9/30 |
| Jones, Dean | Morgan City, Ala. | 1/25/35 |
| Jones, George | Saratoga, Tex. | 9/12/31 |
| Jones, Grace | Spanishtown, Jamaica | 5/19/52 |
| Jones, Grandpa | Niagara, Ky. | 10/20/13 |
| Jones, Henry | Philadelphia, Pa. | 8/1/12 |
| Jones, Jack | Hollywood, Cal. | 1/14/38 |
| Jones, James Earl | Tate Co., Miss. | 1/17/31 |
| Jones, Jennifer | Tulsa, Okla. | 3/2/19 |
| Jones, Shirley | Smithton, Pa. | 3/31/34 |
| Jones, Tom | Pontypridd, Wales | 6/7/40 |
| Jones, Tommy Lee | San Saba, Tex. | 9/15/46 |
| Jordan, Richard | New York, N.Y. | 7/19/38 |
| Jourdan, Louis | Marseilles, France | 6/19/19 |
| Judd, Naomi | Ashland, Ky. | 1/11/46 |
| Judd, Wynonna | Ashland, Ky. | 5/3/64 |
| Julia, Raul | San Juan, P.R. | 3/9/40 |
| Jump, Gordon | Dayton, Oh. | 4/1/32 |
| Kahn, Madeline | Boston, Mass. | 9/29/42 |
| Kanaly, Steve | Burbank, Cal. | 3/14/46 |
| Kane, Carol | Cleveland, Oh. | 6/18/52 |
| Karlen, John | New York, N.Y. | 5/28/33 |
| Karras, Alex | Gary, Ind. | 7/15/35 |
| Kasem, Casey | Detroit, Mich. | 1933 |
| Kavner, Julie | Los Angeles, Cal. | 9/7/51 |
| Kazan, Elia | Istanbul, Turkey | 9/7/09 |
| Kazan, Lainie | New York, N.Y. | 5/15/42 |
| Keach, Stacy | Savannah, Ga. | 6/2/41 |
| Keaton, Diane | Santa Ana, Cal. | 1/5/46 |
| Keaton, Michael | Pittsburgh, Pa. | 9/9/51 |
| Keel, Howard | Gillespie, Ill. | 4/13/17 |
| Keeshan, Bob | Lynbrook, N.Y. | 6/27/27 |
| Keitel, Harvey | Brooklyn, N.Y. | — |
| Keith, Brian | Bayonne, N.J. | 11/14/21 |
| Keith, David | Knoxville, Tenn. | 5/8/54 |
| Kellerman, Sally | Long Beach, Cal. | 6/2/37 |
| Kelley, DeForest | Atlanta, Ga. | 1/20/20 |
| Kelly, Gene | Pittsburgh, Pa. | 8/23/12 |
| Kennedy, George | New York, N.Y. | 2/18/25 |
| Kennedy, Jayne | Washington, D.C. | 11/27/51 |
| Kent, Allegra | Los Angeles, Cal. | 8/11/37 |
| Kercheval, Ken | Wolcottville, Ind. | 7/15/35 |
| Kerns, Joanna | San Francisco, Cal. | 2/12/53 |
| Kerr, Deborah | Helensburgh, Scotland. | 9/30/21 |
| Khan, Chaka | Great Lakes, Ill. | 3/23/53 |
| Kidder, Margot | Yellowknife, N.W.T. | 10/17/48 |
| Kidman, Nicole | Hawaii | 1977 |
| Kiley, Richard | Chicago, Ill. | 3/31/22 |
| Kilmer, Val | Los Angeles, Cal. | 12/31/59 |
| Kimbrough, Charles | St. Paul, Minn. | 5/23/- |
| King, Alan | Brooklyn, N.Y. | 12/26/27 |
| King, B. B. | Itta Bena, Miss. | 9/16/25 |
| King, Carole | Brooklyn, N.Y. | 2/9/42 |
| King, Larry | New York, N.Y. | 11/19/33 |
| King, Perry | Alliance, Oh. | 4/30/48 |
| Kingsley, Ben | Yorkshire, England | 12/31/43 |
| Kinski, Nastassia | Berlin, W. Germany. | 1/24/60 |
| Kirby, Bruno | New York, N.Y. | 1949 |
| Kirby, Durward | Covington, Ky. | 8/24/12 |
| Kirkland, Gelsey | Bethlehem, Pa. | 12/29/53 |
| Kitt, Eartha | North, S.C. | 1/26/28 |
| Klein, Robert | New York, N.Y. | 2/8/42 |
| Klemperer, Werner | Cologne, Germany. | 3/22/19 |
| Kline, Kevin | St. Louis, Mo. | 10/24/47 |
| Klugman, Jack | Philadelphia, Pa. | 4/27/22 |
| Knight, Gladys | Atlanta, Ga. | 5/28/44 |
| Knotts, Don | Morgantown, W. Va. | 7/21/24 |
| Kopell, Bernie | New York, N.Y. | 6/21/33 |
| Korman, Harvey | Chicago, Ill. | 2/15/27 |
| Kotto, Yaphet | New York, N.Y. | 11/15/37 |
| Kramer, Stanley | New York, N.Y. | 9/29/13 |
| Kristofferson, Kris | Brownsville, Tex. | 6/22/36 |
| Kubelik, Rafael | Bychori, Czechoslovakia. | 6/29/14 |
| Kubrick, Stanley | Bronx, N.Y. | 7/26/28 |
| Kurtz, Swoosie | Omaha, Neb. | 9/6/44 |
| LaBelle, Patti | Philadelphia, Pa. | 10/4/44 |
| Ladd, Cheryl | Huron, S.D. | 7/12/51 |
| Ladd, Diane | Meridian, Miss. | 11/29/32 |
| Lahti, Christine | Detroit, Mich. | 4/5/50 |
| Laine, Cleo | Middlesex, England. | 10/28/27 |
| Laine, Frankie | Chicago, Ill. | 3/30/13 |
| Lamarr, Hedy | Vienna, Austria | 11/9/13 |
| Lamas, Lorenzo | Santa Monica, Cal. | 1/20/58 |
| Lamb, Gil | Minneapolis, Minn. | 6/14/06 |
| Lamour, Dorothy | New Orleans, La. | 12/10/14 |
| Lancaster, Burt | New York, N.Y. | 11/2/13 |
| Landau, Martin | New York, N.Y. | 6/20/34 |
| Landis, John | Chicago, Ill. | 8/3/50 |
| Lane, Diane | New York, N.Y. | 1/22/63 |
| Lane, Priscilla | Indianola, Ia. | 6/12/17 |
| Lang, K.D. | Consort, Alberta | 11/2/61 |
| Lang, Stephen | New York, N.Y. | 7/11/52 |
| Lange, Hope | Redding Ridge, Conn. | 11/28/31 |
| Lange, Jessica | Cloquet, Minn. | 4/20/49 |
| Langella, Frank | Bayonne, N.J. | 1/1/40 |
| Langford, Frances | Lakeland, Fla. | 4/4/13 |
| Lansbury, Angela | London, England | 10/16/25 |
| Lansing, Robert | San Diego, Cal. | 6/5/28 |
| Laredo, Ruth | Detroit, Mich. | 11/20/37 |
| Larroquette, John | New Orleans, La. | 11/25/47 |
| Lasser, Louise | New York, N.Y. | 4/11/39 |
| Lauper, Cyndi | New York, N.Y. | 6/20/53 |
| Laurie, Piper | Detroit, Mich. | 1/22/32 |
| Lauter, Ed | Long Beach, N.Y. | 10/30/40 |
| Lavin, Linda | Portland, Me. | 10/15/37 |
| Lawrence, Carol | Melrose Park, Ill. | 9/5/34 |
| Lawrence, Steve | Brooklyn, N.Y. | 7/8/35 |
| Lawrence, Vicki | Inglewood, Cal. | 3/26/49 |
| Leach, Robin | London, England | 8/29/41 |
| Leachman, Cloris | Des Moines, Ia. | 4/4/26 |
| Lear, Norman | New Haven, Conn. | 7/27/22 |
| Learned, Michael | Washington, D.C. | 4/9/39 |
| LeBon, Simon | Bushey, England | 10/27/58 |
| Lee, Brenda | Atlanta, Ga. | 12/11/44 |
| Lee, Christopher | London, England | 5/27/22 |
| Lee, Michele | Los Angeles, Cal. | 6/24/42 |
| Lee, Peggy | Jamestown, N.D. | 5/26/20 |
| Lee, Spike | Atlanta, Ga. | 3/20/57 |
| Legrand, Michel | Paris, France | 2/24/32 |
| Leibman, Ron | New York, N.Y. | 10/11/37 |
| Leifer, Carol | E. Williston, N.Y. | 1956 |
| Leigh, Janet | Merced, Cal. | 7/6/27 |
| Leigh, Jennifer Jason | Los Angeles, Cal. | 2/5/62 |
| Leinsdorf, Erich | Vienna, Austria | 2/4/12 |
| Leisure, David | San Diego, Cal. | 11/16/- |
| Lemmon, Jack | Boston, Mass. | 2/8/25 |
| Leno, Jay | New Rochelle, N.Y. | 4/28/50 |
| Leonard, Sheldon | New York, N.Y. | 2/22/07 |

| Name | Birthplace | Born |
|------|-----------|------|
| Leontovich, Eugenie. . . | Moscow, Russia . . . . . | 3/21/00 |
| Leslie, Joan | Detroit, Mich. | 1/26/25 |
| Letterman, David | Indianapolis, Ind. | 4/12/47 |
| Levine, James | Cincinnati, Oh. | 6/23/43 |
| Levinson, Barry | Baltimore, Md. | 6/2/32 |
| Lewis, Dawnn | New York, N.Y. | 8/13/60 |
| Lewis, Huey | New York, N.Y. | 7/5/51 |
| Lewis, Jerry | Newark, N.J. | 3/16/26 |
| Lewis, Jerry Lee | Ferriday, La.. | 9/29/35 |
| Lewis, Richard | New York, N.Y. | 6/29/47 |
| Lewis, Shari | New York, N.Y. | 1/17/34 |
| Light, Judith | Trenton, N.J. | 2/9/50 |
| Lightfoot, Gordon | Orillia, Ont. | 11/17/38 |
| Linden, Hal | New York, N.Y. | 3/20/31 |
| Lindfors, Viveca | Uppsala, Sweden. | 12/29/20 |
| Linkletter, Art | Saskatchewan, Canada . | 7/17/12 |
| Linn-Baker, Mark | St. Louis, Mo. | 6/17/53 |
| Liotta, Ray | Newark, N.J. | 12/18/55 |
| Lithgow, John | Rochester, N.Y. | 10/19/45 |
| Little, Rich | Ottawa, Ont. | 11/26/38 |
| Little Richard | Macon, Ga. | 12/5/32 |
| Lloyd, Christopher. . . . | Stamford, Conn. | 10/22/38 |
| Lloyd, Emily | England | 9/29/70 |
| Locke, Sondra | Shelbyville, Tenn. | 5/28/47 |
| Lockhart, June. | New York, N.Y. | 6/25/25 |
| Locklear, Heather | Los Angeles, Cal. | 9/25/61 |
| Loggia, Robert. | New York, N.Y. | 1/3/30 |
| Loggins, Kenny | Everett, Wash. | 1/17/47 |
| Lollobrigida, Gina | Subiaco, Italy | 7/4/27 |
| Lom, Herbert. | Prague, Czechoslovakia . | 1/9/17 |
| Long, Shelley | Ft. Wayne, Ind. | 8/23/49 |
| Lord, Jack | New York, N.Y. | 12/30/22 |
| Loren, Sophia | Rome, Italy | 9/20/34 |
| Loring, Gloria | New York, N.Y. | 12/10/46 |
| Loudon, Dorothy | Boston, Mass. | 9/17/33 |
| Louis-Dreyfus, Julia . . | New York, N.Y. | 1/13/62 |
| Lovitz, Jon | Tarzana, Cal. | 7/21/57 |
| Lowe, Rob | Charlottesville, Va. | 3/17/64 |
| Loy, Myrna | Helena, Mon. | 8/2/05 |
| Lucas, George | Modesto, Cal. | 5/14/44 |
| Lucci, Susan | Scarsdale, N.Y. | 12/23/50 |
| Luckinbill, Laurence . . | Ft. Smith, Ark. | 11/21/34 |
| Ludwig, Christa | Berlin, Germany | 3/16/28 |
| Lumet, Sidney | Philadelphia, Pa. | 6/25/24 |
| Lupino, Ida | London, England | 2/4/14 |
| LuPone, Patti. | Northport, N.Y. | 4/21/49 |
| Lynch, David | Missoula, Mont. | 1/20/46 |
| Lynn, Jeffrey | Auburn, Mass.. | 2/16/09 |
| Lynn, Loretta. | Butcher Hollow, Ky. | 4/14/35 |
| | | |
| Maazel, Lorin | Paris, France | 3/6/30 |
| MacArthur, James. | Los Angeles, Cal.. | 12/8/37 |
| MacCorkindale, Simon . . | Cambridge, England . . | 2/12/52 |
| MacDowell, Andie . . | Gaffney, S.C. | 4/21/58 |
| MacGraw, Ali | Pound Ridge, N.Y. | 4/1/38 |
| Mac Lachlan, Kyle. . | Yakima, Wash. | 2/22/59 |
| MacLaine, Shirley . | Richmond, Va. | 4/24/34 |
| MacLeod, Gavin . | Mt. Kisco, N.Y. | 2/28/30 |
| MacNee, Patrick . | London, England | 2/6/22 |
| MacNeil, Cornell . | Minneapolis, Minn. | 9/24/22 |
| Macchio, Ralph . | Long Island, N.Y. | 11/4/62 |
| Macy, Bill. . . . | Revere, Mass. | 5/18/22 |
| Madden, John . | Austin, Minn.. | 4/10/36 |
| Madigan, Amy . | Chicago, Ill. | 9/11/51 |
| Madonna (Ciccone) . . | Bay City, Mich. | 8/16/58 |
| Majors, Lee . . | Wyandotte, Mich. | 4/23/40 |
| Malbin, Elaine . | New York, N.Y. | 5/24/32 |
| Malden, Karl . | Chicago, Ill. | 3/22/13 |
| Malkovich, John . | Christopher, Ill. | 12/9/53 |
| Malle, Louis . | Thumeries, France . . | 10/30/32 |
| Malone, Dorothy . | Chicago, Ill. | 1/30/25 |
| Manchester, Melissa . | Bronx, N.Y. | 2/15/51 |
| Mancini, Henry. . | Cleveland, Oh. | 4/16/24 |
| Mandel, Howie . | Toronto, Ont. | 11/29/55 |
| Mandrell, Barbara . | Houston, Tex. | 12/25/48 |
| Mangione, Chuck . | Rochester, N.Y. | 11/29/40 |
| Manilow, Barry. . | New York, N.Y. | 6/17/46 |
| Mann, Herbie . | New York, N.Y. | 4/16/30 |
| Manoff, Dinah . | New York, N.Y. | 1/25/58 |
| Mantegna, Joe . | Chicago, Ill. | 11/13/47 |
| Marceau, Marcel . | Strasbourg, France. | 3/22/23 |
| Marchand, Nancy . | Buffalo, N.Y. | 6/19/28 |
| Margolin, Janet . | New York, N.Y. | 7/25/43 |
| Marin, Cheech . | Los Angeles, Cal. | 7/13/46 |
| Markova, Alicia . | London, England | 12/1/10 |
| Marriner, Neville . | Lincoln, England | 4/15/24 |
| Marsalis, Branford . | New Orleans, La. | 8/26/60 |
| Marsalis, Wynton . | New Orleans, La. | 10/18/61 |

| Name | Birthplace | Born |
|------|-----------|------|
| Marsh, Jean | London, England . . . . | 7/1/34 |
| Marshall, E. G. . . . . . | Owatonna, Minn. | 6/18/10 |
| Marshall, Penny . . . . | New York, N.Y. | 10/15/43 |
| Marshall, Peter | Huntington, W.Va. | 3/30/27 |
| Martin, Dean . . . . . | Steubenville, Oh. | 6/17/17 |
| Martin, Dick . . . . . | Detroit, Mich. | 1/30/23 |
| Martin, Steve. . . . . | Waco, Tex. | 4/14/45 |
| Martin, Tony . . . . | San Francisco, Cal. | 12/25/13 |
| Martins, Peter . . . . | Copenhagen, Denmark . | 10/27/46 |
| Mason, Jackie . . . . | Sheboygan, Wis. | 6/9/31 |
| Mason, Marsha . . . . | St. Louis, Mo. | 4/3/42 |
| Masterson, Mary Stuart. | Los Angeles, Cal.. | 6/28/66 |
| Mastrantonio, Mary Eliz. | Lombard, Ill. | 11/17/58 |
| Mastroianni, Marcello . . | Rome, Italy | 9/28/23 |
| Masur, Kurt. . . . . | Brieg, Germany . . . . | 7/18/27 |
| Matheson, Tim. . . . | Glendale, Cal. | 12/31/47 |
| Mathis, Johnny . . . . | San Francisco, Cal. | 9/30/35 |
| Matlin, Marlee | Morton Grove, Ill. | 8/24/65 |
| Mattea, Kathy . . . . | Cross Lanes, W. Va. | — |
| Matthau, Walter . . . . | New York, N.Y. | 10/1/20 |
| Mature, Victor . . . . | Louisville, Ky. | 1/29/16 |
| May, Elaine. . . . . | Philadelphia, Pa. | 4/21/32 |
| Mayfield, Curtis . . . . | Chicago, Ill. | 6/3/42 |
| Mayo, Virginia . . . . | St. Louis, Mo. | 11/30/20 |
| Mazursky, Paul . . . . | Brooklyn, N.Y.. | 4/25/30 |
| McArdle, Andrea . . . . | Philadelphia, Pa. | 11/5/63 |
| McBride, Patricia . . . . | Teaneck, N.J.. | 8/23/42 |
| McCallum, David . . . . | Glasgow, Scotland . . . | 9/19/33 |
| McCambridge, | | |
|   Mercedes . . . . . . | Joliet, Ill. | 3/17/18 |
| McCarthy, Andrew . . . | New York, N.Y. | 1962 |
| McCarthy, Kevin . . . . | Seattle, Wash. | 2/15/14 |
| McCartney, Paul. . . . | Liverpool, England . . . | 6/18/42 |
| McCarver, Tim. . . . . | Memphis, Tenn.. | 10/16/41 |
| McClanahan, Rue . . . . | Healdton, Okla. | 2/21/36 |
| McClure, Doug. . . . . | Glendale, Cal. | 5/11/35 |
| McClurg, Edie . . . . | Kansas City, Mo. | 7/23/51 |
| McCoo, Marilyn . . . . | Jersey City, N.J. | 9/30/43 |
| McDonnell, Mary . . . . | Ithaca, N.Y. | 1953 |
| McDowall, Roddy . . . . | London, England | 9/28/28 |
| McDowell, Malcolm . . . | Leeds, England . . . . | 6/13/43 |
| McEntire, Reba . . . . | McAlester, Okla. | 3/28/54 |
| McFerrin, Bobby . . . . | New York, N.Y. | 3/11/50 |
| McGavin, Darren . . . . | Spokane, Wash. | 5/7/22 |
| McGoohan, Patrick . . . | New York, N.Y. | 3/19/28 |
| McGovern, Elizabeth . . | Evanston, Ill.. | 7/18/61 |
| McGovern, Maureen . . | Youngstown, Oh. | 7/27/49 |
| McGuire, Al . . . . . | New York, N.Y. | 9/7/31 |
| McGuire, Dorothy . . . | Omaha, Neb. | 6/14/19 |
| McKechnie, Donna . . . | Pontiac, Mich.. | 11/16/42 |
| McKee, Lonette . . . . | Detroit, Mich. | 1954 |
| McKellen, Ian . . . . | Burnley, England . . . . | 5/25/39 |
| McLerie, Allyn . . . . | Grand Mere, Que. | 12/1/26 |
| McMahon, Ed . . . . | Detroit, Mich. | 3/6/23 |
| McNichol, Kristy . . . . | Los Angeles, Cal.. | 9/11/62 |
| McQueen, Butterfly . . . | Tampa, Fla. | 1/7/11 |
| McRaney, Gerald . . . . | Collins, Miss. | 8/19/48 |
| Meadows, Audrey . . . | Wu Chang, China. | 2/8/24 |
| Meadows, Jayne . . . . | Wu Chang, China. | 9/27/20 |
| Meara, Anne . . . . | New York, N.Y. | 9/20/29 |
| Mehta, Zubin . . . . | Bombay, India. | 4/29/36 |
| Mendes, Sergio . . . . | Niteroi, Brazil | 2/11/41 |
| Menuhin, Yehudi . . . . | New York, N.Y. | 4/22/16 |
| Mercer, Marian . . . . | Akron, Oh. | 11/26/35 |
| Mercouri, Melina . . . . | Athens, Greece . . . . | 10/18/25 |
| Meredith, Burgess . . . | Cleveland, Oh. | 11/16/08 |
| Merrick, David . . . . | Hong Kong | 11/27/12 |
| Merrill, Dina . . . . | New York, N.Y.. | 12/9/25 |
| Merrill, Robert . . . . | Brooklyn, N.Y.. | 6/4/19 |
| Messina, Jim. . . . . | Maywood, Cal. | 12/5/47 |
| Metcalf, Laurie . . . . | Carbondale, Ill. | 6/16/55 |
| Meyers, Ari . . . . . | San Juan, Puerto Rico . | 4/6/69 |
| Michael, George . . . . | Watford, England . . . . | 6/26/63 |
| Michaels, Al . . . . . | New York, N.Y. | 11/12/44 |
| Midler, Bette . . . . | Paterson, N.J. | 12/1/45 |
| Milano, Alyssa . . . . | New York, N.Y. | 12/19/72 |
| Miles, Sarah . . . . | Ingatestone, England. . . | 12/31/41 |
| Miles, Vera . . . . . | near Boise City, Okla. | 8/23/29 |
| Miller, Ann . . . . . | Houston, Tex. | 4/12/19 |
| Miller, Dennis . . . . | Pittsburgh, Pa. | 11/3/53 |
| Miller, Mitch . . . . | Rochester, N.Y. | 7/4/11 |
| Miller, Penelope Ann . . | Los Angeles, Cal. | 1/13/64 |
| Mills, Donna . . . . | Chicago, Ill. | 12/11/42 |
| Mills, John . . . . . | Suffolk, England . . . . | 2/22/08 |
| Milner, Martin . . . . | Detroit, Mich. | 12/28/27 |
| Milnes, Sherrill . . . . | Downers Grove, Ill. | 1/10/35 |
| Milsap, Ronnie . . . . | Robinsville, N.C. | 1/16/44 |
| Minnelli, Liza . . . . | Los Angeles, Cal.. | 3/12/46 |

| Name | Birthplace | Born |
|------|-----------|------|
| Mitchell, Cameron | Dallastown, Pa. | 4/11/18 |
| Mitchell, James | Sacramento, Cal. | 2/29/20 |
| Mitchell, Joni | McLeod, Alta. | 11/7/43 |
| Mitchum, Robert | Bridgeport, Conn. | 8/6/17 |
| Modine, Matthew | Loma Linda, Cal. | 3/22/59 |
| Moffat, Donald | Plymouth, England | 12/26/30 |
| Moffo, Anna | Wayne, Pa. | 6/27/27 |
| Molinaro, Al | Kenosha, Wis. | 6/24/19 |
| Moll, Richard | Pasadena, Cal. | 1/13/43 |
| Montalban, Ricardo | Mexico City, Mexico | 11/25/20 |
| Montgomery, Elizabeth | Hollywood, Cal. | 4/15/33 |
| Moody, Ron | London, England | 1/8/24 |
| Moore, Clayton | Chicago, Ill. | 9/14/08 |
| Moore, Demi | Roswell, N.M. | 11/11/62 |
| Moore, Dudley | London, England | 4/19/35 |
| Moore, Garry | Baltimore, Md. | 1/31/15 |
| Moore, Mary Tyler | Brooklyn, N.Y. | 12/29/37 |
| Moore, Melba | New York, N.Y. | 10/29/45 |
| Moore, Roger | London, England | 10/14/27 |
| Moore, Terry | Los Angeles, Cal. | 1/1/29 |
| Moranis, Rick | Toronto, Ont. | 4/18/53 |
| Moreno, Rita | Humacao, P.R. | 12/11/31 |
| Morgan, Dennis | Prentice, Wis. | 12/10/10 |
| Morgan, Harry | Detroit, Mich. | 4/10/15 |
| Morgan, Henry | New York, N.Y. | 3/31/15 |
| Moriarty, Michael | Detroit, Mich. | 4/5/41 |
| Morita, Pat | Isleton, Cal. | 6/28/32 |
| Morris, Howard | New York, N.Y. | 9/4/25 |
| Morrow, Rob | New Rochelle, N.Y. | 9/21/62 |
| Morse, Robert | Newton, Mass. | 5/18/31 |
| Morton, Joe | New York, N.Y. | 10/18/47 |
| Moses, William | Los Angeles, Cal. | 11/17/59 |
| Muldaur, Diana | New York, N.Y. | 8/19/38 |
| Mulgrew, Kate | Dubuque, Ia. | 4/29/55 |
| Muhare, Edward | Ireland | 4/8/23 |
| Mull, Martin | Chicago, Ill. | 8/18/43 |
| Mulligan, Richard | New York, N.Y. | 11/13/32 |
| Munsel, Patrice | Spokane, Wash. | 5/14/25 |
| Murphy, Ben | Jonesboro, Ark. | 3/6/42 |
| Murphy, Eddie | Brooklyn, N.Y. | 4/3/61 |
| Murphy, Michael | Los Angeles, Cal. | 5/5/38 |
| Murray, Anne | Springhill, Nova Scotia | 6/20/45 |
| Murray, Bill | Evanston, Ill. | 9/21/50 |
| Murray, Don | Hollywood, Cal. | 7/31/29 |
| Musante, Tony | Bridgeport, Conn. | 6/30/36 |
| Musburger, Brent | Portland, Ore. | 5/26/39 |
| Muti, Riccardo | Naples, Italy | 7/28/41 |
| Myers, Mike | Toronto, Ont. | 1962 |
| Nabors, Jim | Sylacauga, Ala. | 6/12/33 |
| Nash, Graham | Blackpool, England | 2/2/42 |
| Natwick, Mildred | Baltimore, Md. | 6/19/08 |
| Naughton, James | Middletown, Conn. | 7/6/46 |
| Neal, Patricia | Packard, Ky. | 1/20/26 |
| Nealon, Kevin | Bridgeport, Conn. | 11/18/53 |
| Neeson, Liam | N. Ireland | 6/7/52 |
| Neill, Sam | New Zealand | 1948 |
| Nelligan, Kate | London, Ontario. | 3/16/51 |
| Nelson, Craig T. | Spokane, Wash. | 4/4/46 |
| Nelson, Ed | New Orleans, La. | 12/21/28 |
| Nelson, Harriet (Hilliard) | Des Moines, Ia. | 7/18/14 |
| Nelson, Judd | Portland, Me. | 11/28/59 |
| Nelson, Tracy | Santa Monica, Cal. | 10/25/63 |
| Nelson, Willie | Abbott, Tex. | 4/30/33 |
| Nero, Peter | New York, N.Y. | 5/22/34 |
| Neuwirth, Bebe | Newark, N.J. | 12/31/- |
| New Kids On The Block | | |
|     Knight, Jonathan | Worcester, Mass. | 11/29/68 |
|     Knight, Jordan | Worcester, Mass. | 5/17/70 |
|     McIntyre, Joe | Needham, Mass. | 12/31/72 |
|     Wahlberg, Donnie | Boston, Mass. | 8/17/69 |
|     Wood, Danny | Boston, Mass. | 5/14/69 |
| Newhart, Bob | Oak Park, Ill. | 9/29/29 |
| Newley, Anthony | Hackney, England | 9/24/31 |
| Newman, Paul | Cleveland, Oh. | 1/26/25 |
| Newman, Randy | Los Angeles, Cal. | 11/28/43 |
| Newton, Wayne | Norfolk, Va. | 4/3/42 |
| Newton-John, Olivia | Cambridge, England | 9/26/47 |
| Nicholas, Denise | Detroit, Mich. | 7/12/44 |
| Nicholas, Fayard | Philadelphia, Pa. | 10/20/14 |
| Nicholas, Harold | Philadelphia, Pa. | 3/27/24 |
| Nichols, Mike | Berlin, Germany | 11/6/31 |
| Nicholson, Jack | Neptune, N.J. | 4/28/37 |
| Nicks, Stevie | Phoenix, Ariz. | 5/26/48 |
| Nielsen, Leslie | Regina, Sask. | 2/11/26 |
| Nilsson, Birgit | Karup, Sweden | 5/17/18 |
| Nimoy, Leonard | Boston, Mass. | 3/26/31 |
| Nolte, Nick | Omaha, Neb. | 2/8/40 |
| Norman, Jessye | Augusta, Ga. | 9/15/45 |
| Norris, Chuck | Ryan, Okla. | 3/10/40 |
| North, Sheree | Los Angeles, Cal. | 1/17/33 |
| Noth, Christopher | Madison, Wis. | 11/13/- |
| Novak, Kim | Chicago, Ill. | 2/13/33 |
| Oates, John | New York, N.Y. | 4/7/48 |
| O'Brian, Hugh | Rochester, N.Y. | 4/19/25 |
| O'Brien, Conan | Brookline, Mass. | 1963 |
| O'Brien, Margaret | San Diego, Cal. | 1/15/37 |
| Ocean, Billy | Trinidad | 1/21/50 |
| O'Connell, Helen | Lima, Oh. | 5/23/21 |
| O'Connor, Carroll | New York, N.Y. | 8/2/24 |
| O'Connor, Donald | Chicago, Ill. | 8/28/25 |
| O'Connor, Sinead | Dublin, Ireland. | 12/8/67 |
| Odetta | Birmingham, Ala. | 12/31/30 |
| O'Donnell, Chris | Winnetka, Ill. | 1970 |
| O'Hara, Maureen | Dublin, Ireland. | 8/17/20 |
| O'Herlihy, Dan | Wexford, Ireland | 5/1/19 |
| Oldman, Gary | London, England | 3/21/58 |
| Olin, Ken | Chicago, Ill. | 7/30/54 |
| Olin, Lena | Sweden | 3/22/55 |
| Olmos, Edward James | E. Los Angeles, Cal. | 2/24/47 |
| Olsen, Merlin | Logan, Ut. | 9/15/40 |
| O'Neal, Patrick | Ocala, Fla. | 9/26/27 |
| O'Neal, Ryan | Los Angeles, Cal. | 4/20/41 |
| O'Neal, Tatum | Los Angeles, Cal. | 11/5/63 |
| O'Neill, Ed | Youngstown, Oh. | 1946 |
| Ontkean, Michael | Vancouver, B.C. | 1/24/46 |
| Orbach, Jerry | New York, N.Y. | 10/20/35 |
| Orlando, Tony | New York, N.Y. | 4/3/44 |
| Osbourne, Ozzy | Birmingham, England. | 12/3/46 |
| O'Shea, Milo | Dublin, Ireland. | 6/2/26 |
| Oslin, K.T. | Crossit, Ark. | 1942 |
| Osmond, Donny | Ogden, Ut. | 12/9/57 |
| Osmond, Marie | Ogden, Ut. | 10/13/59 |
| O'Sullivan, Maureen | Boyle, Ireland | 5/17/11 |
| O'Toole, Annette | Houston, Tex. | 4/1/53 |
| O'Toole, Peter | Connemara, Ireland | 8/2/32 |
| Owens, Buck | Sherman, Tex. | 8/12/29 |
| Oz, Frank | Herford, England | 5/25/44 |
| Ozawa, Seiji | Shenyang, China | 9/1/35 |
| Paar, Jack | Canton, Oh. | 5/1/18 |
| Pacino, Al | New York, N.Y. | 4/25/40 |
| Packer, Billy | Wellsville, N.Y. | 2/25/40 |
| Page, Patti | Claremore, Okla. | 11/8/27 |
| Paige, Janis | Tacoma, Wash. | 9/16/22 |
| Palance, Jack | Lattimer, Pa. | 2/18/20 |
| Palin, Michael | England | 5/5/43 |
| Palmer, Betsy | East Chicago, Ind. | 11/1/29 |
| Papas, Irene | Greece. | 3/9/26 |
| Parker, Alan | London, England | 2/14/44 |
| Parker, Eleanor | Cedarville, Oh. | 6/26/22 |
| Parker, Fess | Ft. Worth, Tex. | 8/16/25 |
| Parker, Jameson | Baltimore, Md. | 11/18/47 |
| Parker, Jean | Deer Lodge, Mon. | 8/11/12 |
| Parker, Sarah Jessica | Nelsonville, Oh. | 3/25/65 |
| Parsons, Estelle | Lynn, Mass. | 11/20/27 |
| Parton, Dolly | Sevierville, Tenn. | 1/19/46 |
| Patinkin, Mandy | Chicago, Ill. | 11/30/52 |
| Pavarotti, Luciano | Modena, Italy | 10/12/35 |
| Paycheck, Johnny | Greenfield, Oh. | 5/31/41 |
| Pearl, Minnie | Centerville, Tenn. | 10/25/12 |
| Peck, Gregory | La Jolla, Cal. | 4/5/16 |
| Pendergrass, Teddy | Philadelphia, Pa. | 3/26/50 |
| Penn, Arthur | Philadelphia, Pa. | 9/27/22 |
| Penn, Sean | Burbank, Cal. | 8/17/60 |
| Penny, Joe | London, England | 9/14/56 |
| Peppard, George | Detroit, Mich. | 10/1/28 |
| Perkins, Elizabeth | New York, N.Y. | 11/18/60 |
| Perlman, Itzhak | Tel Aviv, Israel | 8/31/45 |
| Perlman, Rhea | Brooklyn, N.Y. | 3/31/48 |
| Perlman, Ron | New York, N.Y. | 4/13/50 |
| Perrine, Valerie | Galveston, Tex. | 9/3/43 |
| Perry, Luke | Fredericktown, Oh. | 10/11/- |
| Persoff, Nehemiah | Jerusalem, Palestine | 8/14/20 |
| Pesci, Joe | Newark, N.J. | 2/9/43 |
| Peters, Bernadette | New York, N.Y. | 2/28/48 |
| Peters, Brock | New York, N.Y. | 7/2/27 |
| Peters, Roberta | New York, N.Y. | 5/4/30 |
| Petty, Tom | Gainesville, Fla. | 10/20/53 |
| Pfeiffer, Michelle | Santa Ana, Cal. | 4/29/57 |
| Phillips, Lou Diamond | Philippines. | 2/17/62 |
| Phillips, Michelle | Long Beach, Cal. | 6/4/44 |
| Phoenix, River | Madras, Ore. | 8/23/70 |
| Pickett, Cindy | Norman, Okla. | 4/18/47 |
| Pinchot, Bronson | New York, N.Y. | 5/20/59 |
| Piscopo, Joe | Passaic, N.J. | 6/17/51 |
| Pitt, Brad | Missouri | 12/18/65 |
| Pleasence, Donald | Worksop, England | 10/5/19 |

| Name | Birthplace | Born |
|------|-----------|------|
| Pleshette, Suzanne | New York, N.Y. | 1/31/37 |
| Plowright, Joan | Brigg, England | 10/28/29 |
| Plummer, Amanda | New York, N.Y. | 3/23/57 |
| Plummer, Christopher. | Toronto, Ont. | 12/13/27 |
| Poitier, Sidney | Miami, Fla. | 2/20/27 |
| Polanski, Roman | Paris, France | 8/18/33 |
| Pollack, Sydney | Lafayette, Ind. | 7/1/34 |
| Ponti, Carlo | Milan, Italy | 12/11/13 |
| Post, Markie | Palo Alto, Cal. | 11/4/50 |
| Poston, Tom | Columbus, Oh. | 10/17/27 |
| Potts, Annie | Nashville, Tenn. | 10/28/52 |
| Povich, Maury | Washington, D.C. | 1/17/39 |
| Powell, Jane | Portland, Ore. | 4/1/28 |
| Powers, Stefanie | Hollywood, Cal. | 11/2/42 |
| Prentiss, Paula | San Antonio, Tex. | 3/4/39 |
| Presley, Priscilla | New York, N.Y. | 5/24/46 |
| Preston, Billy | Houston, Tex. | 9/9/46 |
| Previn, Andre | Berlin, Germany | 4/6/29 |
| Price, Leontyne | Laurel, Miss. | 2/10/27 |
| Price, Ray | Perryville, Tex. | 1/12/26 |
| Price, Vincent | St. Louis, Mo. | 5/27/11 |
| Pride, Charlie | Sledge, Miss. | 3/18/39 |
| Priestley, Jason | Vancouver, B.C. | 8/28/69 |
| Prince | Minneapolis, Minn. | 6/7/58 |
| Principal, Victoria | Japan | — |
| Prosky, Robert. | Philadelphia, Pa. | 12/13/30 |
| Pryce, Jonathan | Wales | 6/1/47 |
| Pryor, Richard | Peoria, Ill. | 12/1/40 |
| Pulliam, Keshia Knight | Newark, N.J. | 4/9/79 |
| Pyle, Denver | Bethune, Col. | 5/11/20 |
| Quaid, Dennis | Houston, Tex. | 4/9/54 |
| Quaid, Randy | Houston, Tex. | 10/1/50 |
| Quinn, Aidan | Chicago, Ill. | 3/8/59 |
| Quinn, Anthony | Chihuahua, Mexico | 4/21/15 |
| Quinn, Martha | Albany, N.Y. | 5/11/59 |
| Rabb, Ellis | Memphis, Tenn. | 6/20/30 |
| Rabbitt, Eddie | Brooklyn, N.Y. | 11/27/41 |
| Rachins, Alan | Cambridge, Mass. | 10/10/47 |
| Rae, Charlotte | Milwaukee, Wis. | 4/22/26 |
| Rainer, Luise | Vienna, Austria | 1/12/09 |
| Raitt, Bonnie | Burbank, Cal. | 11/8/49 |
| Ralston, Esther | Bar Harbor, Me. | 9/17/02 |
| Ramey, Samuel | Colby, Kan. | 3/28/42 |
| Rampal, Jean-Pierre | Marseilles, France | 1/7/22 |
| Randall, Tony | Tulsa, Okla. | 2/26/20 |
| Randolph, John | New York, N.Y. | 6/1/15 |
| Randolph, Joyce. | Detroit, Mich. | 10/21/25 |
| Raphael, Sally Jessy | Easton, Pa. | 2/25/43 |
| Rashad, Phylicia | Houston, Tex. | 6/17/48 |
| Ratzenberger, John | Bridgeport, Conn. | 4/6/47 |
| Rawls, Lou | Chicago, Ill. | 12/1/36 |
| Raye, Martha | Butte, Mon. | 8/27/16 |
| Raymond, Gene | New York, N.Y. | 8/13/08 |
| Reddy, Helen | Melbourne, Australia | 10/25/41 |
| Redford, Robert | Santa Monica, Cal. | 8/18/37 |
| Redgrave, Lynn | London, England | 3/8/43 |
| Redgrave, Vanessa | London, England | 1/30/37 |
| Reed, Jerry | Atlanta, Ga. | 3/20/37 |
| Reed, Oliver | London, England | 2/13/38 |
| Reed, Rex | Ft. Worth, Tex. | 10/2/38 |
| Reed, Shanna | Kansas City, Kan. | 10/30/- |
| Reese, Della | Detroit, Mich. | 7/6/31 |
| Reeve, Christopher | New York, N.Y. | 9/25/52 |
| Reeves, Keanu | Beirut, Lebanon | 9/2/64 |
| Regalbuto, Joe | New York, N.Y. | 8/24/- |
| Reid, Tim | Norfolk, Va. | 12/19/44 |
| Reilly, Charles Nelson | New York, N.Y. | 1/13/31 |
| Reiner, Carl | Bronx, N.Y. | 3/20/22 |
| Reiner, Rob | Bronx, N.Y. | 3/6/45 |
| Reinhold, Judge | Wilmington, Del. | 5/21/56 |
| Reinking, Ann | Seattle, Wash. | 11/10/50 |
| Reiser, Paul | New York, N.Y. | 3/30/57 |
| Resnik, Regina | New York, N.Y. | 8/30/24 |
| Reynolds, Burt. | Waycross, Ga. | 2/11/36 |
| Reynolds, Debbie | El Paso, Tex. | 4/1/32 |
| Rhue, Madlyn | Washington, D.C. | 10/3/34 |
| Rich, Charlie | Forest City, Ark. | 12/14/32 |
| Richards, Keith | Kent, England | 12/18/43 |
| Richards, Michael | Los Angeles, Cal. | — |
| Richardson, Miranda | Lancashire, England | 1958 |
| Richardson, Natasha | London, England | 5/11/63 |
| Richie, Lionel | Tuskegee, Ala. | 6/20/50 |
| Rickles, Don | New York, N.Y. | 5/8/26 |
| Rickman, Alan | London, England | 1946 |
| Riegert, Peter | New York, N.Y. | 4/11/47 |
| Rigg, Diana. | Doncaster, England | 7/20/38 |
| Ringwald, Molly | Rosewood, Cal. | 2/14/68 |
| Ritter, John. | Burbank, Cal. | 9/17/48 |

| Name | Birthplace | Born |
|------|-----------|------|
| Rivera, Chita | Washington, D.C. | 1/23/33 |
| Rivera, Geraldo | New York, N.Y. | 7/4/43 |
| Rivers, Joan | Brooklyn, N.Y. | 6/8/37 |
| Robards, Jason Jr. | Chicago, Ill. | 7/26/22 |
| Robbins, Jerome | New York, N.Y. | 10/11/18 |
| Robbins, Tim | W. Covina, Cal. | 10/16/58 |
| Roberts, Doris | St. Louis, Mo. | 11/4/29 |
| Roberts, Eric | Biloxi, Miss. | 4/18/56 |
| Roberts, Julia | Smyrna, Ga. | 10/25/67 |
| Roberts, Pernell | Waycross, Ga. | 5/18/30 |
| Roberts, Tony | New York, N.Y. | 10/22/39 |
| Robertson, Cliff | La Jolla, Cal. | 9/9/25 |
| Robertson, Dale | Harrah, Okla. | 7/14/23 |
| Robinson, Charles | Houston, Tex. | 11/9/- |
| Robinson, Smokey | Detroit, Mich. | 2/19/40 |
| Roche, Eugene | Boston, Mass. | 9/22/28 |
| Rodgers, Jimmy | Camas, Wash. | 9/18/33 |
| Rodrigues, Percy | Montreal, Que. | 6/13/24 |
| Rodriquez, Johnny | Sabinal, Tex. | 12/10/51 |
| Rogers, Fred | Latrobe, Pa. | 3/20/28 |
| Rogers, Ginger | Independence, Mo. | 7/16/11 |
| Rogers, Kenny | Houston, Tex. | 8/21/38 |
| Rogers, Mimi | Coral Gables, Fla. | 1/27/56 |
| Rogers, Roy | Cincinnati, Oh. | 11/5/12 |
| Roland, Gilbert. | Juarez, Mexico | 12/11/05 |
| Rolle, Esther | Pompano Beach, Fla. | 11/8/33 |
| Rollins, Howard | Baltimore, Md. | 10/17/50 |
| Romero, Cesar | New York, N.Y. | 2/15/07 |
| Ronstadt, Linda | Tucson, Ariz. | 7/15/46 |
| Rooney, Mickey | Brooklyn, N.Y. | 9/23/20 |
| Rose Marie | New York, N.Y. | 8/15/25 |
| Ross, Diana | Detroit, Mich. | 3/26/44 |
| Ross, Katharine | Hollywood, Cal. | 1/29/42 |
| Ross, Marion. | Albert Lea, Minn. | 10/25/28 |
| Rossellini, Isabella. | Rome, Italy | 6/18/52 |
| Rostropovich, Mstislav | Baku, USSR. | 3/12/27 |
| Roth, David Lee | Bloomington, Ind. | 10/10/55 |
| Rourke, Mickey | Miami, Fla. | 1953 |
| Rowlands, Gena. | Cambria, Wis. | 6/19/34 |
| Ruehl, Mercedes | New York, N.Y. | — |
| Rush, Barbara | Denver, Col. | 1/4/30 |
| Russell, Jane | Bemidji, Minn. | 6/21/21 |
| Russell, Ken | Southampton, England. | 7/3/27 |
| Russell, Kurt | Springfield, Mass. | 3/17/51 |
| Russell, Mark | Buffalo, N.Y. | 8/23/32 |
| Russell, Nipsey | Atlanta, Ga. | 10/13/24 |
| Russell, Theresa | San Diego, Cal. | 3/20/57 |
| Rutherford, Ann | Toronto, Ont. | 11/2/20 |
| Ruttan, Susan | Oregon City, Ore. | 9/16/50 |
| Ryan, Meg | Fairfield, Conn. | 11/19/63 |
| Ryan, Peggy | Long Beach, Cal. | 8/28/24 |
| Ryan, Roz | Detroit, Mich. | 7/7/51 |
| Rydell, Bobby | Philadelphia, Pa. | 4/26/42 |
| Ryder, Winona | Winona, Minn. | 10/29/71 |
| Saget, Bob. | Philadelphia, Pa. | 5/17/56 |
| Sahl, Mort | Montreal, Que. | 5/11/27 |
| Saint, Eva Marie | Newark, N.J. | 7/4/24 |
| St. James, Susan | Los Angeles, Cal. | 8/14/46 |
| St. John, Jill | Los Angeles, Cal. | 8/19/40 |
| Sajak, Pat | Chicago, Ill. | 10/26/47 |
| Saks, Gene | New York, N.Y. | 11/8/21 |
| Sales, Soupy | Franklinton, N.C. | 1/8/26 |
| Samms, Emma | London, England | 8/28/60 |
| Sanderson, William | Memphis, Tenn. | 1/10/48 |
| Sandy, Gary | Dayton, Oh. | 12/25/45 |
| Sanford, Isabel | New York, N.Y. | 8/29/17 |
| Sarandon, Susan | New York, N.Y. | 10/4/46 |
| Sarnoff, Dorothy | New York, N.Y. | 5/25/17 |
| Savage, Fred | Highland Park, Ill. | 7/9/76 |
| Savalas, Telly | Garden City, N.Y. | 1/21/24 |
| Saxon, John | Brooklyn, N.Y. | 8/5/35 |
| Sayles, John | Schenectady, N.Y. | 9/28/50 |
| Scaggs, Boz | Dallas, Tex. | 6/8/44 |
| Schallert, William | Los Angeles, Cal. | 7/6/22 |
| Scheider, Roy | Orange, N.J. | 11/10/32 |
| Schell, Maria | Vienna, Austria | 1/15/26 |
| Schell, Maximilian | Vienna, Austria | 12/8/30 |
| Schenkel, Chris | Bippus, Ind. | 8/21/23 |
| Schnabel, Stefan | Berlin, Germany | 2/2/12 |
| Schneider, John | Mt. Kisco, N.Y. | 4/8/54 |
| Schroder, Rick. | Staten Island, N.Y. | 4/3/70 |
| Schwarzenegger, Arnold | Graz, Austria | 7/30/47 |
| Schwarzkopf, Elisabeth | Jarotschin, Poland | 12/9/15 |
| Sciorra, Annabella. | New York, N.Y. | 1964 |
| Scofield, Paul | Hurst, Pierpont, England. | 1/21/22 |
| Scolari, Peter | New Rochelle, Ill. | 9/12/54 |
| Scorsese, Martin | New York, N.Y. | 11/17/42 |

| Name | Birthplace | Born | Name | Birthplace | Born |
|------|-----------|------|------|-----------|------|
| Scott, George C. | Wise, Va. | 10/18/27 | Stamos, John | Cypress, Cal. | 8/19/63 |
| Scott, Lizabeth. | Scranton, Pa. | 9/29/22 | Stamp, Terence | Stepney, England. | 7/22/39 |
| Scott, Martha | Jamesport, Mo. | 9/22/14 | Stander, Lionel | New York, N.Y. | 1/11/08 |
| Scotto, Renata. | Savona, Italy | 2/24/35 | Stang, Arnold | New York, N.Y. | 9/28/25 |
| Scully, Vin | New York, N.Y. | 11/29/27 | Stanley, Kim | Tularosa, N.M. | 2/11/25 |
| Seagal, Steven | Lansing, Mich. | 4/10/51 | Stanton, Harry Dean | Kentucky | 7/14/26 |
| Sedaka, Neil | New York, N.Y. | 3/13/39 | Stapleton, Jean | New York, N.Y. | 1/19/23 |
| Seeger, Pete. | New York, N.Y. | 5/3/19 | Stapleton, Maureen | Troy, N.Y. | 6/21/25 |
| Segal, George | Great Neck, N.Y. | 2/13/34 | Starr, Ringo | Liverpool, England | 7/7/40 |
| Segal, Vivienne | Philadelphia, Pa. | 4/19/97 | Steenburgen, Mary | Newport, Ariz. | 2/8/53 |
| Seidelman, Susan. | Philadelphia, Pa. | 12/11/52 | Steiger, Rod | W. Hampton, N.Y. | 4/14/25 |
| Seinfeld, Jerry | New York, N.Y. | 1954 | Stephens, James | Mt. Kisco, N.Y. | 5/18/51 |
| Sellecca, Connie | New York, N.Y. | 5/25/55 | Stern, Daniel | Stamford, Conn. | 5/28/57 |
| Selleck, Tom. | Detroit, Mich. | 1/29/45 | Stern, Howard | New York, N.Y. | 1/12/54 |
| Severinsen, Doc. | Arlington, Ore. | 7/7/27 | Stern, Isaac | Kreminiecz, Russia | 7/21/20 |
| Seymour, Jane | Middlesex, England. | 2/15/51 | Sternhagen, Frances | Washington, D.C. | 1/13/30 |
| Shackelford, Ted | Oklahoma City, Okla. | 6/23/46 | Stevens, Andrew | Memphis, Tenn. | 6/10/55 |
| Shaffer, Paul. | Thunder Bay, Ont. | 11/28/49 | Stevens, Cat. | London, England | 7/21/48 |
| Shandling, Garry | Tucson, Ariz. | 11/29/49 | Stevens, Connie | Brooklyn, N.Y. | 8/8/38 |
| Shankar, Ravi | India | 4/7/20 | Stevens, Rise | New York, N.Y. | 6/11/13 |
| Sharif, Omar. | Alexandria, Egypt. | 4/10/32 | Stevens, Stella | Yazoo City, Miss. | 10/1/36 |
| Shatner, William | Montreal, Que. | 3/22/31 | Stevenson, McLean. | Normal, Ill. | 11/14/29 |
| Shea, John. | N. Conway, N.H. | 4/14/49 | Stevenson, Parker | Philadelphia, Pa. | 6/4/52 |
| Shearer, Moira. | Scotland | 1/17/26 | Stewart, James | Indiana, Pa. | 5/20/08 |
| Sheedy, Ally | New York, N.Y. | 6/12/62 | Stewart, Patrick | Mirfield, England | 7/13/40 |
| Sheen, Charlie. | New York, N.Y. | 9/3/65 | Stewart, Rod | London, England | 1/10/45 |
| Sheen, Martin | Dayton, Oh. | 8/3/40 | Stickney, Dorothy | Dickinson, N.D. | 6/21/00 |
| Shelley, Carole | London, England | 8/16/39 | Stiers, David Ogden. | Peoria, Ill. | 10/31/42 |
| Shepard, Sam | Ft. Sheridan, Ill. | 11/5/43 | Stiller, Jerry | New York, N.Y. | 6/8/29 |
| Shepherd, Cybill. | Memphis, Tenn. | 2/18/49 | Stills, Stephen | Dallas, Tex. | 1/3/45 |
| Shields, Brooke | New York, N.Y. | 5/31/65 | Sting (G. Sumner). | Newcastle, England | 10/2/51 |
| Shire, Talia. | New York, N.Y. | 4/25/46 | Stockwell, Dean | Hollywood, Cal. | 3/5/36 |
| Shore, Dinah. | Winchester, Tenn. | 3/1/17 | Stoltz, Eric | American Samoa | 1961 |
| Short, Bobby. | Danville, Ill. | 9/15/24 | Stone, Oliver. | New York, N.Y. | 9/15/46 |
| Short, Martin | Hamilton, Ont. | 3/26/50 | Stone, Sharon | Meadville, Pa. | 1958 |
| Shull, Richard B. | Evanston, Ill. | 2/24/29 | Stookey, Paul | Baltimore, Md. | 12/30/37 |
| Sidney, Sylvia | New York, N.Y. | 8/8/10 | Storch, Larry | New York, N.Y. | 1/8/23 |
| Siepi, Cesare | Milan, Italy. | 2/10/23 | Storm, Gale | Bloomington, Tex. | 4/5/22 |
| Sikking, James B. | Los Angeles, Cal. | 3/5/34 | Stowe, Madeleine | Los Angeles, Cal. | 8/18/58 |
| Sills, Beverly | Brooklyn, N.Y. | 5/25/29 | Straight, Beatrice | Old Westbury, N.Y. | 8/2/18 |
| Silver, Ron | New York, N.Y. | 7/2/46 | Strait, George | Pearsall, Tex. | 5/1/52 |
| Simmons, Gene | Haifa, Israel | 8/25/49 | Strasser, Robin | New York, N.Y. | 5/7/45 |
| Simmons, Jean | London, England | 1/31/29 | Stratas, Teresa | Toronto, Ont. | 5/26/38 |
| Simmons, Richard. | New Orleans, La. | 7/12/48 | Strauss, Peter | New York, N.Y. | 2/20/47 |
| Simon, Carly | New York, N.Y. | 6/25/45 | Streep, Meryl | Summit, N.J. | 6/22/49 |
| Simon, Paul | Newark, N.J. | 10/13/41 | Streisand, Barbra | Brooklyn, N.Y. | 4/24/42 |
| Simone, Nina. | Tyron, N.C. | 2/21/33 | Stritch, Elaine | Detroit, Mich. | 2/2/26 |
| Sinatra, Frank | Hoboken, N.J. | 12/12/15 | Struthers, Sally | Portland, Ore. | 7/28/48 |
| Sinbad | Benton Harbor, Mich. | 11/10/- | Stuarti, Enzo | Rome, Italy | 3/3/25 |
| Sinclair, Madge | Kingston, Jamaica | 4/28/38 | Sullivan, Barry | New York, N.Y. | 8/29/12 |
| Siskel, Gene | Chicago, Ill. | 1/26/46 | Sullivan, Susan | New York, N.Y. | 11/18/44 |
| Skelton, Red (Richard) | Vincennes, Ind. | 7/18/13 | Sumac, Yma | Ichocan, Peru | 9/10/27 |
| Skerritt, Tom. | Detroit, Mich. | 8/25/33 | Summer, Donna | Boston, Mass. | 12/31/48 |
| Slater, Christian | New York, N.Y. | 8/19/69 | Sutherland, Donald | St. John, New Brunswick | 7/17/34 |
| Slater, Helen. | Massapequa, N.Y. | 12/14/63 | Sutherland, Joan | Sydney, Australia. | 11/7/26 |
| Slezak, Erika. | Hollywood, Cal. | 8/5/46 | Sutherland, Kiefer. | London, England | 12/20/66 |
| Slick, Grace | Chicago, Ill. | 10/30/39 | Swayze, Patrick | Houston, Tex. | 8/18/54 |
| Smirnoff, Yakov | Odessa, USSR | 1/24/51 | Swit, Loretta | Passaic, N.J. | 11/4/37 |
| Smith, Allison | New York, N.Y. | 12/9/69 | | | |
| Smith, Buffalo Bob | Buffalo, N.Y. | 11/27/17 | Mr. T (Lawrence Tero) | Chicago, Ill. | 5/21/52 |
| Smith, Jaclyn | Houston, Tex. | 10/26/47 | Tallchief, Maria | Fairfax, Okla. | 1/24/25 |
| Smith, Keely | Norfolk, Va. | 3/9/35 | Tandy, Jessica. | London, England | 6/7/09 |
| Smith, Maggie | Ilford, England. | 12/28/34 | Tarkenton, Fran | Richmond, Va. | 2/3/40 |
| Smith, Will | Philadelphia, Pa. | 9/25/69 | Taylor, Elizabeth. | London, England | 2/27/32 |
| Smits, Jimmy | New York, N.Y. | 7/9/55 | Taylor, James | Boston, Mass. | 3/12/48 |
| Smothers, Dick | New York, N.Y. | 11/20/39 | Taylor, Rip | Washington, D.C. | 1/13/30 |
| Smothers, Tom | New York, N.Y. | 2/2/37 | Taylor, Rod | Sydney, Australia. | 1/11/29 |
| Snipes, Wesley | Orlando, Fla. | 7/31/63 | Te Kanawa, Kiri | Gisborne, New Zealand | 3/6/44 |
| Snow, Hank | Nova Scotia, Canada | 5/9/14 | Tebaldi, Renata | Pesaro, Italy. | 2/1/22 |
| Solti, Georg | Budapest, Hungary. | 10/21/12 | Temple, Shirley | Santa Monica, Cal. | 4/23/28 |
| Somers, Suzanne | San Bruno, Cal. | 10/16/46 | Tennant, Victoria | London, England | 9/30/50 |
| Sommer, Elke | Berlin, Germany | 11/5/41 | Tennille, Toni. | Montgomery, Ala. | 5/8/43 |
| Sorvino, Paul. | New York, N.Y. | 1939 | Tharp, Twyla. | Portland, Ind. | 7/1/41 |
| Sothern, Ann. | Valley City, N.D. | 1/22/09 | Thicke, Alan | Kirkland Lake, Ont. | 3/1/47 |
| Soul, David. | Chicago, Ill. | 8/28/43 | Thomas, Jay | New Orleans, La. | 7/12/48 |
| Spacek, Sissy | Quitman, Tex. | 12/25/49 | Thomas, Marlo. | Detroit, Mich. | 11/21/43 |
| Spacey, Kevin | S. Orange, N.J. | 7/26/59 | Thomas, Philip Michael | Columbus, Oh. | 5/26/49 |
| Spader, James | Boston, Mass. | 2/7/60 | Thomas, Richard | New York, N.Y. | 6/13/51 |
| Spelling, Aaron | Dallas, Tex. | 4/22/28 | Thompson, Emma. | London, England | 4/15/59 |
| Spencer, John | New Jersey | 1946 | Thompson, Jack. | Sydney, Australia. | 8/31/40 |
| Spielberg, Steven | Cincinnati, Oh. | 12/18/47 | Thompson, Lea | Rochester, Minn. | 5/31/61 |
| Springfield, Dusty | London, England | 4/16/39 | Thompson, Sada | Des Moines, Ia. | 9/27/29 |
| Springfield, Rick | Sydney, Australia. | 8/23/49 | Thulin, Ingrid | Sweden | 1/27/29 |
| Springsteen, Bruce | Freehold, N.J. | 9/23/49 | Tiegs, Cheryl. | Minnesota | 9/27/47 |
| Stack, Robert | Los Angeles, Cal. | 1/13/19 | Tiffany | Norwalk, Cal. | 10/2/71 |
| Stafford, Jo | Coalinga, Cal. | 11/12/18 | Tillis, Mel | Tampa, Fla. | 8/8/32 |
| Stahl, Richard | Detroit, Mich. | 1/4/32 | Tiny Tim | New York, N.Y. | 4/12/23 |
| Stallone, Sylvester | New York, N.Y. | 7/6/46 | Todd, Richard | Dublin, Ireland. | 6/11/19 |

| Name | Birthplace | Born |
|------|-----------|------|
| Tomei, Marisa | New York, N.Y. | 12/4/64 |
| Tomlin, Lily | Detroit, Mich. | 9/1/39 |
| Tomlinson, David | Scotland | 5/7/17 |
| Torme, Mel | Chicago, Ill. | 9/13/25 |
| Torn, Rip | Temple, Tex. | 2/6/31 |
| Townsend, Robert | Chicago, Ill. | 2/6/57 |
| Travanti, Daniel J. | Kenosha, Wis. | 3/7/40 |
| Travers, Mary | Louisville, Ky. | 11/9/36 |
| Travis, Nancy | New York, N.Y. | 9/21/61 |
| Travis, Randy | Marshville, N.C. | 5/4/59 |
| Travolta, John | Englewood, N.J. | 2/18/54 |
| Trebek, Alex | Sudbury, Ont. | 7/22/40 |
| Trevor, Claire | New York, N.Y. | 3/8/09 |
| Troyanos, Tatiana | New York, N.Y. | 9/12/38 |
| Tucker, Michael | Baltimore, Md. | 2/6/44 |
| Tucker, Tanya | Seminole, Tex. | 10/10/58 |
| Tune, Tommy | Wichita Falls, Tex. | 2/28/39 |
| Turner, Janine | Lincoln, Neb. | 12/6/62 |
| Turner, Kathleen | Springfield, Mo. | 6/19/54 |
| Turner, Lana | Wallace, Ida. | 2/8/20 |
| Turner, Tina | Nutbush, Tenn. | 11/26/38 |
| Turturro, John | New York, N.Y. | 2/28/57 |
| Twiggy (Leslie Hornby) | London, England | 9/19/46 |
| Tyson, Cicely | New York, N.Y. | 12/19/33 |
| Uecker, Bob | Milwaukee, Wis. | 1/26/35 |
| Uggams, Leslie | New York, N.Y. | 5/25/43 |
| Ullman, Tracey | Slough, England | 12/30/59 |
| Ullmann, Liv | Tokyo, Japan | 12/16/38 |
| Underwood, Blair | Tacoma, Wash. | 8/25/64 |
| Urich, Robert | Toronto, Oh. | 12/19/46 |
| Ustinov, Peter | London, England | 4/16/21 |
| Vaccaro, Brenda | Brooklyn, N.Y. | 11/18/39 |
| Vale, Jerry | New York, N.Y. | 7/8/31 |
| Valente, Caterina | Paris, France | 1/14/31 |
| Valli, Frankie | Newark, N.J. | 5/3/37 |
| Van Ark, Joan | New York, N.Y. | 6/16/43 |
| Vandross, Luther | New York, N.Y. | 4/20/51 |
| Van Dyke, Dick | West Plains, Mo. | 12/13/25 |
| Van Dyke, Jerry | Danville, Ill. | 7/27/31 |
| Van Fleet, Jo | Oakland, Cal. | 12/30/22 |
| Van Halen, Eddie | Nijmegan, Netherlands | 1/26/57 |
| Van Pallandt, Nina | Copenhagen, Denmark | 7/15/32 |
| Van Patten, Dick | New York, N.Y. | 12/9/28 |
| Van Peebles, Mario | Mexico | 1/15/57 |
| Vaughn, Robert | New York, N.Y. | 11/22/32 |
| Venuta, Benay | San Francisco, Cal. | 1/27/11 |
| Verdon, Gwen | Los Angeles, Cal. | 1/13/25 |
| Vereen, Ben | Miami, Fla. | 10/10/46 |
| Verrett, Shirley | New Orleans, La. | 5/31/31 |
| Vickers, Jon | Prince Albert, Sask. | 10/26/26 |
| Vigoda, Abe | New York, N.Y. | 2/24/21 |
| Vincent, Jan-Michael | Denver, Col. | 7/15/44 |
| Vinson, Helen | Beaumont, Tex. | 9/17/07 |
| Vinton, Bobby | Canonsburg, Pa. | 4/16/35 |
| Vitale, Dick | E. Rutherford, N.J. | 6/9/40 |
| Voight, Jon | Yonkers, N.Y. | 12/29/38 |
| Von Stade, Frederica | Somerville, N.J. | 6/1/45 |
| Von Sydow, Max | Lund, Sweden. | 4/10/29 |
| Wagner, Lindsay | Los Angeles, Cal. | 6/22/49 |
| Wagner, Robert | Detroit, Mich. | 2/10/30 |
| Wagoner, Porter | West Plains, Mo. | 8/12/27 |
| Wahl, Ken | Chicago, Ill. | 2/14/56 |
| Wain, Bea | Bronx, N.Y. | 4/30/17 |
| Waite, Ralph | White Plains, N.Y. | 6/22/29 |
| Walden, Robert | New York, N.Y. | 9/25/43 |
| Walken, Christopher | New York, N.Y. | 3/31/43 |
| Wallach, Eli | Brooklyn, N.Y. | 12/7/15 |
| Walston, Ray | Laurel, Miss. | 11/2/24 |
| Walter, Jessica | New York, N.Y. | 1/31/44 |
| Wanamaker, Sam | Chicago, Ill. | 6/14/19 |
| Ward, Fred | San Diego, Cal. | 1943 |
| Ward, Simon | London, England | 10/19/41 |
| Warden, Jack | Newark, N.J. | 9/18/20 |
| Warfield, William | W. Helena, Ark. | 1/22/20 |
| Warner, Malcolm-Jamal | Jersey City, N.J. | 8/18/70 |
| Warren, Lesley Ann | New York, N.Y. | 8/16/46 |
| Warrick, Ruth | St. Joseph, Mo. | 6/29/16 |
| Warwick, Dionne | E. Orange, N.J. | 12/12/41 |
| Washington, Denzel | Mt. Vernon, N.Y. | 12/28/54 |
| Waterston, Sam | Cambridge, Mass. | 11/15/40 |
| Watkins, Carlene | Hartford, Conn. | 6/4/52 |
| Watts, Andre | Nuremberg, Germany | 6/20/46 |
| Wayans, Damon | New York, N.Y. | 1960 |
| Wayans, Keenan Ivory | New York, N.Y. | 6/8/58 |
| Wayne, David | Traverse City, Mich. | 1/30/14 |
| Waxman, Al | Toronto, Ont. | 3/2/35 |
| Weaver, Dennis | Joplin, Mo. | 6/4/24 |
| Weaver, Fritz | Pittsburgh, Pa. | 1/19/26 |
| Weaver, Sigourney | New York, N.Y. | 10/8/49 |
| Weir, Peter | Sydney, Australia. | 8/8/44 |
| Weitz, Bruce | Norwalk, Conn. | 5/27/43 |
| Welch, Raquel | Chicago, Ill. | 9/5/40 |
| Weld, Tuesday | New York, N.Y. | 8/27/43 |
| Wells, Kitty | Nashville, Tenn. | 8/30/19 |
| Wendt, George | Chicago, Ill. | 10/17/48 |
| Weston, Jack | Cleveland, Oh. | 8/21/24 |
| Wheaton, Wil | Burbank, Cal. | 7/29/72 |
| Whitaker, Forest | Longview, Tex. | 7/15/61 |
| White, Barry | Galveston, Tex. | 9/12/44 |
| White, Betty | Oak Park, Ill. | 1/17/22 |
| White, Jesse | Buffalo, N.Y. | 1/3/19 |
| White, Vanna | N. Myrtle Beach, S.C. | 2/18/57 |
| Whiting, Margaret | Detroit, Mich. | 7/22/24 |
| Whitmore, James | White Plains, N.Y. | 10/1/21 |
| Widmark, Richard | Sunrise, Minn. | 12/26/14 |
| Wiest, Dianne | Kansas City, Mo. | 3/28/48 |
| Wilder, Billy | Vienna, Austria | 6/22/06 |
| Wilder, Gene | Milwaukee, Wis. | 6/11/35 |
| Williams, Andy | Wall Lake, Ia. | 12/3/30 |
| Williams, Billy Dee | New York, N.Y. | 4/6/37 |
| Williams, Cindy | Van Nuys, Cal. | 8/22/47 |
| Williams, Esther | Los Angeles, Cal. | 8/8/23 |
| Williams, Hal | Columbus, Oh. | 12/14/38 |
| Williams Jr., Hank | Shreveport, La. | 5/26/49 |
| Williams, Joe | Cordele, Ga. | 12/12/18 |
| Williams, JoBeth | Houston, Tex. | 1953 |
| Williams, Paul | Omaha, Neb. | 9/19/40 |
| Williams, Robin | Chicago, Ill. | 7/21/52 |
| Williams, Treat | Rowayton, Conn. | 12/1/51 |
| Williams, Vanessa | New York, N.Y. | 3/18/63 |
| Williamson, Nicol | Hamilton, Scotland | 9/14/38 |
| Willis, Bruce | W. Germany | 3/19/55 |
| Wilson, Demond | Valdosta, Ga. | 10/13/46 |
| Wilson, Elizabeth | Grand Rapids, Mich. | 4/4/25 |
| Wilson, Flip | Jersey City, N.J. | 12/8/33 |
| Wilson, Nancy | Chillicothe, Oh. | 2/20/37 |
| Windom, William | New York, N.Y. | 9/28/23 |
| Winfield, Paul | Los Angeles, Cal. | 5/22/41 |
| Winfrey, Oprah | Kosciusko, Miss. | 1/29/54 |
| Winger, Debra | Cleveland, Oh. | 5/16/55 |
| Winkler, Henry | New York, N.Y. | 10/30/45 |
| Winningham, Mare | Phoenix, Ariz. | 5/6/59 |
| Winters, Jonathan | Dayton, Oh. | 11/11/25 |
| Winters, Shelley | St. Louis, Mo. | 8/18/22 |
| Winwood, Steve | Birmingham, England. | 5/12/48 |
| Wiseman, Joseph | Montreal, Que. | 5/15/18 |
| Withers, Jane | Atlanta, Ga. | 4/12/26 |
| Wonder, Stevie | Saginaw, Mich. | 5/13/50 |
| Woodard, Alfre | Tulsa, Okla. | 11/2/53 |
| Woods, James | Vernal, N.J. | 4/18/47 |
| Woodward, Edward | Croyden, England | 6/1/30 |
| Woodward, Joanne | Thomasville, Ga. | 2/27/30 |
| Woolery, Chuck | Ashland, Ky. | 3/16/- |
| Worth, Irene | Nebraska | 6/23/16 |
| Wray, Fay | Alberta, Canada | 9/10/07 |
| Wright, Martha | Seattle, Wash. | 3/23/26 |
| Wright, Max | Detroit, Mich. | 8/2/- |
| Wright, Steven | New York, N.Y. | 12/6/55 |
| Wright, Teresa | New York, N.Y. | 10/27/18 |
| Wyatt, Jane | Campgaw, N.J. | 8/10/11 |
| Wyman, Jane | St. Joseph, Mo. | 1/4/14 |
| Wynette, Tammy | Red Bay, Ala. | 5/5/42 |
| Yarborough, Glenn | Milwaukee, Wis. | 1/12/30 |
| Yarrow, Peter | New York, N.Y. | 5/31/38 |
| York, Michael | Fulmer, England | 3/27/42 |
| York, Susannah | London, England | 1/9/42 |
| Young, Alan | Northumberland, England | 11/19/19 |
| Young, Burt | New York, N.Y. | 4/30/40 |
| Young, Loretta | Salt Lake City, Ut. | 1/6/13 |
| Young, Neil | Toronto, Ont. | 11/12/45 |
| Young, Robert | Chicago, Ill. | 2/22/07 |
| Young, Sean | Louisville, Ky. | 11/20/59 |
| Youngman, Henny | Liverpool, England | 1/12/06 |
| Zappa, Frank | Baltimore, Md. | 12/21/40 |
| Zeffirelli, Franco | Florence, Italy. | 2/12/23 |
| Zerbe, Anthony | Long Beach, Cal. | 5/20/36 |
| Zimbalist, Efrem Jr. | New York, N.Y. | 11/30/23 |
| Zukerman, Pinchas | Tel Aviv, Israel | 7/16/48 |

# Entertainment Personalities of the Past

(as of mid-1993)

| Born | Died | Name |
|------|------|------|
| 1895 | 1974 | Abbott, Bud |
| 1903 | 1992 | Acuff, Roy |
| 1872 | 1953 | Adams, Maude |
| 1855 | 1926 | Adler, Jacob P. |
| 1903 | 1984 | Adler, Luther |
| 1898 | 1933 | Adoree, Renee |
| 1902 | 1986 | Aherne, Brian |
| 1931 | 1989 | Ailey, Alvin |
| 1909 | 1964 | Albertson, Frank |
| 1907 | 1981 | Albertson, Jack |
| 1894 | 1956 | Allen, Fred |
| 1906 | 1964 | Allen, Gracie |
| 1883 | 1950 | Allgood, Sara |
| 1902 | 1993 | Anderson, Marian |
| 1909 | 1992 | Andrews, Dana |
| 1913 | 1967 | Andrews, Laverne |
| 1887 | 1933 | Arbuckle, Fatty (Roscoe) |
| 1908 | 1990 | Arden, Eve |
| 1900 | 1976 | Arlen, Richard |
| 1868 | 1946 | Arliss, George |
| 1888 | 1945 | Armetta, Henry |
| 1900 | 1971 | Armstrong, Louis |
| 1917 | 1986 | Arnaz, Desi |
| 1890 | 1956 | Arnold, Edward |
| 1905 | 1974 | Arquette, Cliff |
| 1900 | 1991 | Arthur, Jean |
| 1899 | 1987 | Astaire, Fred |
| 1906 | 1987 | Astor, Mary |
| 1885 | 1946 | Atwill, Lionel |
| 1905 | 1967 | Auer, Mischa |
| 1900 | 1972 | Austin, Gene |
| 1913 | 1989 | Backus, Jim |
| 1918 | 1990 | Bailey, Pearl |
| 1892 | 1968 | Bainter, Fay |
| 1906 | 1975 | Baker, Josephine |
| 1904 | 1983 | Balanchine, George |
| 1911 | 1989 | Ball, Lucille |
| 1882 | 1956 | Bancroft, George |
| 1902 | 1968 | Bankhead, Tallulah |
| 1890 | 1952 | Banks, Leslie |
| 1890 | 1955 | Bara, Theda |
| 1810 | 1891 | Barnum, Phineas T. |
| 1879 | 1959 | Barrymore, Ethel |
| 1882 | 1942 | Barrymore, John |
| 1878 | 1954 | Barrymore, Lionel |
| 1848 | 1905 | Barrymore, Maurice |
| 1897 | 1963 | Barthelmess, Richard |
| 1914 | 1984 | Basehart, Richard |
| 1904 | 1984 | Basie, Count |
| 1923 | 1985 | Baxter, Anne |
| 1889 | 1951 | Baxter, Warner |
| 1904 | 1965 | Beatty, Clyde |
| 1902 | 1962 | Beavers, Louise |
| 1884 | 1946 | Beery, Noah |
| 1889 | 1949 | Beery, Wallace |
| 1901 | 1970 | Begley, Ed |
| 1904 | 1991 | Bellamy, Ralph |
| 1949 | 1982 | Belushi, John |
| 1906 | 1968 | Benaderet, Bea |
| 1906 | 1964 | Bendix, William |
| 1904 | 1965 | Bennett, Constance |
| 1910 | 1990 | Bennett, Joan |
| 1943 | 1987 | Bennett, Michael |
| 1894 | 1974 | Benny, Jack |
| 1924 | 1970 | Benzell, Mimi |
| 1899 | 1966 | Berg, Gertrude |
| 1903 | 1978 | Bergen, Edgar |
| 1915 | 1982 | Bergman, Ingrid |
| 1895 | 1976 | Berkeley, Busby |
| 1923 | 1986 | Bernardi, Herschel |
| 1844 | 1923 | Bernhardt, Sarah |
| 1893 | 1943 | Bernie, Ben |
| 1889 | 1967 | Bickford, Charles |
| 1911 | 1960 | Bjoerling, Jussi |
| 1895 | 1973 | Blackmer, Sidney |
| 1908 | 1989 | Blanc, Mel |
| 1928 | 1972 | Blocker, Dan |
| 1909 | 1979 | Blondell, Joan |
| 1888 | 1959 | Blore, Eric |
| 1901 | 1975 | Blue, Ben |
| 1899 | 1957 | Bogart, Humphrey |
| 1880 | 1965 | Boland, Mary |
| 1895 | 1969 | Boles, John |

| Born | Died | Name |
|------|------|------|
| 1904 | 1987 | Bolger, Ray |
| 1903 | 1960 | Bond, Ward |
| 1892 | 1981 | Bondi, Beulah |
| 1917 | 1981 | Boone, Richard |
| 1833 | 1893 | Booth, Edwin |
| 1796 | 1852 | Booth, Junius Brutus |
| 1907 | 1992 | Booth, Shirley |
| 1905 | 1965 | Bow, Clara |
| 1874 | 1946 | Bowes, Maj. Edward |
| 1928 | 1977 | Boyd, Stephen |
| 1898 | 1972 | Boyd, William |
| 1899 | 1978 | Boyer, Charles |
| 1893 | 1939 | Brady, Alice |
| 1894 | 1974 | Brennan, Walter |
| 1904 | 1979 | Brent, George |
| 1891 | 1951 | Brice, Fanny |
| 1891 | 1959 | Broderick, Helen |
| 1892 | 1973 | Brown, Joe E. |
| 1926 | 1966 | Bruce, Lenny |
| 1895 | 1953 | Bruce, Nigel |
| 1910 | 1982 | Bruce, Virginia |
| 1915 | 1985 | Brynner, Yul |
| 1903 | 1979 | Buchanan, Edgar |
| 1938 | 1982 | Buono, Victor |
| 1885 | 1970 | Burke, Billie |
| 1911 | 1967 | Burnette, Smiley |
| 1925 | 1984 | Burton, Richard |
| 1897 | 1946 | Busch, Mae |
| 1883 | 1966 | Bushman, Francis X. |
| 1896 | 1946 | Butterworth, Charles |
| 1893 | 1971 | Byington, Spring |
| 1904 | 1972 | Cabot, Bruce |
| 1918 | 1977 | Cabot, Sebastian |
| 1899 | 1986 | Cagney, James |
| 1895 | 1956 | Calhern, Louis |
| 1923 | 1977 | Callas, Maria |
| 1933 | 1976 | Cambridge, Godfrey |
| 1865 | 1940 | Campbell, Mrs. Patrick |
| 1892 | 1964 | Cantor, Eddie |
| 1897 | 1991 | Capra, Frank |
| 1878 | 1947 | Carey, Harry |
| 1950 | 1983 | Carpenter, Karen |
| 1906 | 1988 | Carradine, John |
| 1880 | 1961 | Carrillo, Leo |
| 1892 | 1972 | Carroll, Leo G. |
| 1905 | 1965 | Carroll, Nancy |
| 1910 | 1963 | Carson, Jack |
| 1873 | 1921 | Caruso, Enrico |
| 1876 | 1973 | Casals, Pablo |
| 1929 | 1989 | Cassavetes, John |
| 1893 | 1969 | Castle, Irene |
| 1887 | 1918 | Castle, Vernon |
| 1873 | 1938 | Chaliapin, Feodor |
| 1919 | 1980 | Champion, Gower |
| 1918 | 1961 | Chandler, Jeff |
| 1883 | 1930 | Chaney, Lon |
| 1905 | 1973 | Chaney Jr., Lon |
| 1942 | 1981 | Chapin, Harry |
| 1889 | 1977 | Chaplin, Charles |
| 1893 | 1961 | Chatterton, Ruth |
| 1888 | 1972 | Chevalier, Maurice |
| 1888 | 1960 | Clark, Bobby |
| 1914 | 1968 | Clark, Fred |
| 1920 | 1966 | Clift, Montgomery |
| 1932 | 1963 | Cline, Patsy |
| 1892 | 1967 | Clyde, Andy |
| 1911 | 1976 | Cobb, Lee J. |
| 1877 | 1961 | Coburn, Charles |
| 1878 | 1942 | Cohan, George M. |
| 1902 | 1986 | Cohen, Myron |
| 1919 | 1965 | Cole, Nat (King) |
| 1890 | 1965 | Collins, Ray |
| 1891 | 1958 | Colman, Ronald |
| 1908 | 1934 | Columbo, Russ |
| 1917 | 1982 | Conried, Hans |
| 1911 | 1975 | Conte, Richard |
| 1914 | 1984 | Coogan, Jackie |
| 1935 | 1964 | Cooke, Sam |
| 1901 | 1961 | Cooper, Gary |
| 1888 | 1971 | Cooper, Gladys |
| 1896 | 1973 | Cooper, Melville |
| 1914 | 1968 | Corey, Wendell |
| 1893 | 1974 | Cornell, Katherine |

| Born | Died | Name |
|------|------|------|
| 1890 | 1972 | Correll, Charles (Andy) |
| 1905 | 1979 | Costello, Dolores |
| 1906 | 1959 | Costello, Lou |
| 1899 | 1973 | Coward, Noel |
| 1924 | 1973 | Cox, Wally |
| 1908 | 1983 | Crabbe, Buster |
| 1928 | 1978 | Crane, Bob |
| 1911 | 1986 | Crawford, Broderick |
| 1908 | 1977 | Crawford, Joan |
| 1880 | 1942 | Crews, Laura Hope |
| 1880 | 1974 | Crisp, Donald |
| 1942 | 1973 | Croce, Jim |
| 1903 | 1977 | Crosby, Bing |
| 1910 | 1986 | Crothers, Scatman |
| 1908 | 1990 | Cummings, Robert |
| 1878 | 1968 | Currie, Finlay |
| 1914 | 1978 | Dailey, Dan |
| 1923 | 1965 | Dandridge, Dorothy |
| 1894 | 1963 | Daniell, Henry |
| 1901 | 1971 | Daniels, Bebe |
| 1936 | 1973 | Darin, Bobby |
| 1921 | 1965 | Darnell, Linda |
| 1879 | 1967 | Darwell, Jane |
| 1909 | 1986 | Da Silva, Howard |
| 1866 | 1949 | Davenport, Harry |
| 1908 | 1989 | Davis, Bette |
| 1907 | 1961 | Davis, Joan |
| 1925 | 1990 | Davis Jr., Sammy |
| 1931 | 1955 | Dean, James |
| 1905 | 1968 | Dekker, Albert |
| 1905 | 1983 | Del Rio, Dolores |
| 1892 | 1983 | Demarest, William |
| 1881 | 1959 | DeMille, Cecil B. |
| 1891 | 1967 | Denny, Reginald |
| 1901 | 1974 | DeSica, Vittorio |
| 1905 | 1977 | Devine, Andy |
| 1924 | 1991 | Dewhurst, Colleen |
| 1942 | 1972 | De Wilde, Brandon |
| 1907 | 1974 | De Wolfe, Billy |
| 1920 | 1985 | Diamond, Selma |
| 1901 | 1992 | Dietrich, Marlene |
| 1879 | 1947 | Digges, Dudley |
| 1901 | 1966 | Disney, Walt |
| 1894 | 1949 | Dix, Richard |
| 1905 | 1958 | Donat, Robert |
| 1889 | 1972 | Donlevy, Brian |
| 1901 | 1981 | Douglas, Melvyn |
| 1907 | 1959 | Douglas, Paul |
| 1889 | 1956 | Draper, Ruth |
| 1881 | 1965 | Dresser, Louise |
| 1869 | 1934 | Dressler, Marie |
| 1820 | 1897 | Drew, Mrs. John |
| 1909 | 1951 | Duchin, Eddy |
| 1890 | 1974 | Dumbrille, Douglass |
| 1889 | 1965 | Dumont, Margaret |
| 1878 | 1927 | Duncan, Isadora |
| 1905 | 1967 | Dunn, James |
| 1898 | 1990 | Dunne, Irene |
| 1893 | 1980 | Durante, Jimmy |
| 1907 | 1968 | Duryea, Dan |
| 1858 | 1924 | Duse, Eleanora |
| 1894 | 1929 | Eagels, Jeanne |
| 1914 | 1993 | Eckstine, Billy |
| 1901 | 1967 | Eddy, Nelson |
| 1897 | 1971 | Edwards, Cliff |
| 1879 | 1945 | Edwards, Gus |
| 1899 | 1974 | Ellington, Duke |
| 1941 | 1974 | Elliot, Cass |
| 1891 | 1967 | Elman, Mischa |
| 1881 | 1951 | Errol, Leon |
| 1888 | 1976 | Evans, Edith |
| 1901 | 1989 | Evans, Maurice |
| 1883 | 1939 | Fairbanks, Douglas |
| 1914 | 1970 | Farmer, Frances |
| 1870 | 1929 | Farnum, Dustin |
| 1876 | 1953 | Farnum, William |
| 1882 | 1967 | Farrar, Geraldine |
| 1904 | 1971 | Farrell, Glenda |
| 1897 | 1961 | Fay, Frank |
| 1895 | 1962 | Fazenda, Louise |
| 1933 | 1982 | Feldman, Marty |
| 1912 | 1992 | Ferrer, Jose |

| Born | Died | Name | Born | Died | Name | Born | Died | Name |
|------|------|------|------|------|------|------|------|------|
| 1920 | 1980 | Medford, Kay | 1892 | 1957 | Pinza, Ezio | 1879 | 1953 | Stone, Lewis |
| 1880 | 1946 | Meek, Donald | 1898 | 1963 | Pitts, Zasu | 1904 | 1980 | Stone, Milburn |
| 1861 | 1931 | Melba, Nellie | 1904 | 1976 | Pons, Lily | 1898 | 1959 | Sturges, Preston |
| 1890 | 1973 | Melchior, Lauritz | 1897 | 1981 | Ponselle, Rosa | 1911 | 1960 | Sullavan, Margaret |
| 1890 | 1963 | Menjou, Adolphe | 1904 | 1963 | Powell, Dick | 1902 | 1974 | Sullivan, Ed |
| 1902 | 1966 | Menken, Helen | 1912 | 1982 | Powell, Eleanor | 1903 | 1956 | Sullivan, Francis L. |
| 1908 | 1984 | Merman, Ethel | 1892 | 1984 | Powell, William | 1892 | 1946 | Summerville, Slim |
| 1905 | 1986 | Milland, Ray | 1913 | 1958 | Power, Tyrone | 1899 | 1983 | Swanson, Gloria |
| 1904 | 1944 | Miller, Glenn | 1905 | 1986 | Preminger, Otto | 1904 | 1969 | Swarthout, Gladys |
| 1898 | 1936 | Miller, Marilyn | 1935 | 1977 | Presley, Elvis | | | |
| 1903 | 1955 | Minnevitch, Borrah | 1918 | 1987 | Preston, Robert | 1893 | 1957 | Talmadge, Norma |
| 1913 | 1955 | Miranda, Carmen | 1911 | 1978 | Prima, Louis | 1899 | 1972 | Tamiroff, Akim |
| 1892 | 1962 | Mitchell, Thomas | 1954 | 1977 | Prinze, Freddie | 1878 | 1947 | Tanguay, Eva |
| 1880 | 1940 | Mix, Tom | | | | 1885 | 1966 | Taylor, Deems |
| 1926 | 1962 | Monroe, Marilyn | 1946 | 1989 | Radner, Gilda | 1899 | 1958 | Taylor, Estelle |
| 1911 | 1973 | Monroe, Vaughn | 1895 | 1980 | Raft, George | 1887 | 1946 | Taylor, Laurette |
| 1917 | 1951 | Montez, Maria | 1890 | 1967 | Rains, Claude | 1911 | 1969 | Taylor, Robert |
| 1904 | 1981 | Montgomery, Robert | 1892 | 1967 | Rathbone, Basil | 1847 | 1928 | Terry, Ellen |
| 1901 | 1947 | Moore, Grace | 1897 | 1960 | Ratoff, Gregory | 1899 | 1936 | Thalberg, Irving |
| 1876 | 1962 | Moore, Victor | 1941 | 1967 | Redding, Otis | 1912 | 1991 | Thomas, Danny |
| 1906 | 1974 | Moorehead, Agnes | 1908 | 1985 | Redgrave, Michael | 1882 | 1976 | Thorndike, Sybil |
| 1890 | 1949 | Morgan, Frank | 1921 | 1986 | Reed, Donna | 1896 | 1960 | Tibbett, Lawrence |
| 1900 | 1941 | Morgan, Helen | 1932 | 1992 | Reed, Robert | 1920 | 1991 | Tierney, Gene |
| 1901 | 1970 | Morris, Chester | 1914 | 1959 | Reeves, George | 1909 | 1958 | Todd, Michael |
| 1914 | 1959 | Morris, Wayne | 1873 | 1943 | Reinhardt, Max | 1903 | 1968 | Tone, Franchot |
| 1943 | 1971 | Morrison, Jim | 1935 | 1991 | Remick, Lee | 1867 | 1957 | Toscanini, Arturo |
| 1932 | 1982 | Morrow, Vic | 1909 | 1971 | Rennie, Michael | 1898 | 1968 | Tracy, Lee |
| 1915 | 1977 | Mostel, Zero | 1902 | 1983 | Richardson, Ralph | 1900 | 1967 | Tracy, Spencer |
| 1897 | 1969 | Mowbray, Alan | 1921 | 1985 | Riddle, Nelson | 1903 | 1972 | Traubel, Helen |
| 1895 | 1967 | Muni, Paul | 1898 | 1977 | Ritchard, Cyril | 1894 | 1975 | Treacher, Arthur |
| 1915 | 1970 | Munshin, Jules | 1907 | 1974 | Ritter, Tex | 1853 | 1917 | Tree, Herbert Beerbohm |
| 1924 | 1971 | Murphy, Audie | 1905 | 1969 | Ritter, Thelma | 1890 | 1973 | Truex, Ernest |
| 1902 | 1992 | Murphy, George | 1901 | 1965 | Ritz, Al | 1932 | 1984 | Truffaut, Francois |
| 1885 | 1965 | Murray, Mae | 1906 | 1986 | Ritz, Harry | 1919 | 1986 | Tucker, Forrest |
| | | | 1903 | 1985 | Ritz, Jimmy | 1915 | 1975 | Tucker, Richard |
| 1896 | 1970 | Nagel, Conrad | 1925 | 1982 | Robbins, Marty | 1884 | 1966 | Tucker, Sophie |
| 1900 | 1973 | Naish, J. Carroll | 1898 | 1976 | Robeson, Paul | 1874 | 1940 | Turpin, Ben |
| 1898 | 1961 | Naldi, Nita | 1878 | 1949 | Robinson, Bill | 1908 | 1959 | Twelvetrees, Helen |
| 1906 | 1975 | Nelson, Ozzie | 1893 | 1973 | Robinson, Edward G. | 1933 | 1993 | Twitty, Conway |
| 1940 | 1985 | Nelson, Rick | 1905 | 1977 | Rochester (E. Anderson) | | | |
| 1885 | 1967 | Nesbit, Evelyn | 1897 | 1933 | Rodgers, Jimmie | 1895 | 1926 | Valentino, Rudolph |
| 1909 | 1983 | Niven, David | 1879 | 1935 | Rogers, Will | 1901 | 1986 | Vallee, Rudy |
| 1890 | 1950 | Nijinsky, Vaslav | 1880 | 1962 | Rooney, Pat | 1911 | 1979 | Vance, Vivian |
| 1893 | 1974 | Nilsson, Anna Q. | 1899 | 1966 | Rose, Billy | 1924 | 1990 | Vaughan, Sarah |
| 1902 | 1985 | Nolan, Lloyd | 1922 | 1987 | Rowan, Dan | 1893 | 1943 | Veidt, Conrad |
| 1894 | 1930 | Normand, Mabel | 1887 | 1982 | Rubinstein, Artur | 1926 | 1981 | Vera-Ellen |
| 1899 | 1968 | Novarro, Ramon | 1886 | 1970 | Ruggles, Charles | 1885 | 1957 | Von Stroheim, Erich |
| 1938 | 1993 | Nureyev, Rudolf | 1924 | 1961 | Russell, Gail | 1906 | 1981 | Von Zell, Harry |
| | | | 1861 | 1922 | Russell, Lillian | | | |
| 1903 | 1978 | Oakie, Jack | 1911 | 1976 | Russell, Rosalind | 1922 | 1992 | Walker, Nancy |
| 1860 | 1926 | Oakley, Annie | 1892 | 1972 | Rutherford, Margaret | 1914 | 1951 | Walker, Robert |
| 1928 | 1982 | Oates, Warren | 1903 | 1973 | Ryan, Irene | 1887 | 1980 | Walsh, Raoul |
| 1911 | 1979 | Oberon, Merle | 1909 | 1973 | Ryan, Robert | 1876 | 1962 | Walter, Bruno |
| 1915 | 1985 | O'Brien, Edmond | | | | 1858 | 1958 | Warner, H. B. |
| 1899 | 1983 | O'Brien, Pat | 1877 | 1968 | St. Denis, Ruth | 1924 | 1963 | Washington, Dinah |
| 1908 | 1981 | O'Connell, Arthur | 1884 | 1955 | Sakall, S.Z. | 1900 | 1977 | Waters, Ethel |
| 1880 | 1959 | O'Connor, Una | 1885 | 1936 | Sale (Chic), Charles | 1907 | 1979 | Wayne, John |
| 1908 | 1968 | O'Keefe, Dennis | 1906 | 1972 | Sanders, George | 1891 | 1966 | Webb, Clifton |
| 1880 | 1938 | Oland, Warner | 1895 | 1964 | Schildkraut, Joseph | 1920 | 1982 | Webb, Jack |
| 1860 | 1932 | Olcott, Chauncey | 1889 | 1965 | Schipa, Tito | 1903 | 1992 | Welk, Lawrence |
| 1883 | 1942 | Oliver, Edna May | 1882 | 1951 | Schnabel, Artur | 1915 | 1985 | Welles, Orson |
| 1907 | 1989 | Olivier, Laurence | 1920 | 1981 | Scott, Hazel | 1896 | 1975 | Wellman, William |
| 1892 | 1963 | Olsen, Ole | 1898 | 1987 | Scott, Randolph | 1892 | 1980 | West, Mae |
| 1849 | 1920 | O'Neill, James | 1914 | 1965 | Scott, Zachary | 1895 | 1968 | Wheeler, Bert |
| 1936 | 1988 | Orbison, Roy | 1843 | 1896 | Scott-Siddons, Mrs. | 1889 | 1938 | White, Pearl |
| 1899 | 1985 | Ormandy, Eugene | 1938 | 1979 | Seberg, Jean | 1891 | 1967 | Whiteman, Paul |
| 1876 | 1949 | Ouspenskaya, Maria | 1892 | 1974 | Seeley, Blossom | 1865 | 1948 | Whitty, May |
| 1887 | 1972 | Owen, Reginald | 1893 | 1987 | Segovia, Andres | 1912 | 1979 | Wilding, Michael |
| | | | 1925 | 1980 | Sellers, Peter | 1877 | 1922 | Williams, Bert |
| 1860 | 1941 | Paderewski, Ignace | 1902 | 1965 | Selznick, David O. | 1923 | 1953 | Williams, Hank |
| 1924 | 1987 | Page, Geraldine | 1884 | 1960 | Sennett, Mack | 1905 | 1975 | Wills, Bob |
| 1889 | 1954 | Pallette, Eugene | 1927 | 1978 | Shaw, Robert | 1903 | 1978 | Wills, Chill |
| 1914 | 1986 | Palmer, Lilli | 1891 | 1972 | Shawn, Ted | 1917 | 1972 | Wilson, Marie |
| 1894 | 1958 | Pangborn, Franklin | 1868 | 1949 | Shean, Al | 1884 | 1969 | Winninger, Charles |
| 1914 | 1992 | Parks, Bert | 1902 | 1983 | Shearer, Norma | 1904 | 1959 | Withers, Grant |
| 1914 | 1975 | Parks, Larry | 1915 | 1967 | Sheridan, Ann | 1907 | 1961 | Wong, Anna May |
| 1881 | 1940 | Pasternack, Josef A. | 1875 | 1953 | Shubert, Lee | 1938 | 1981 | Wood, Natalie |
| 1837 | 1908 | Pastor, Tony | 1921 | 1985 | Signoret, Simone | 1892 | 1978 | Wood, Peggy |
| 1843 | 1919 | Patti, Adelina | 1912 | 1985 | Silvers, Phil | 1888 | 1963 | Woolley, Monty |
| 1840 | 1889 | Patti, Carlotta | 1900 | 1976 | Sim, Alastair | 1902 | 1981 | Wyler, William |
| 1885 | 1931 | Pavlova, Anna | 1858 | 1942 | Skinner, Otis | 1886 | 1966 | Wynn, Ed |
| 1912 | 1989 | Payne, John | 1863 | 1948 | Smith, C. Aubrey | 1916 | 1986 | Wynn, Keenan |
| 1904 | 1984 | Peerce, Jan | 1907 | 1986 | Smith, Kate | | | |
| 1899 | 1967 | Pendleton, Nat | 1854 | 1932 | Sousa, John Philip | 1890 | 1960 | Young, Clara Kimball |
| 1905 | 1941 | Penner, Joe | 1884 | 1957 | Sparks, Ned | 1913 | 1978 | Young, Gig |
| 1932 | 1992 | Perkins, Anthony | 1907 | 1990 | Stanwyck, Barbara | 1887 | 1953 | Young, Roland |
| 1915 | 1963 | Piaf, Edith | 1934 | 1970 | Stevens, Inger | | | |
| 1893 | 1979 | Pickford, Mary | 1882 | 1977 | Stokowski, Leopold | 1902 | 1979 | Zanuck, Darryl F. |
| 1897 | 1984 | Pidgeon, Walter | | | | 1869 | 1932 | Ziegfeld, Florenz |
| | | | | | | 1873 | 1976 | Zukor, Adolph |

## Original Names of Selected Entertainers

**Edie Adams:** Elizabeth Edith Enke
**Eddie Albert:** Edward Albert Heimberger
**Alan Alda:** Alphonso D'Abruzzo
**Jane Alexander:** Jane Quigley
**Fred Allen:** John Sullivan
**Woody Allen:** Allen Konigsberg
**Julie Andrews:** Julia Wells
**Eve Arden:** Eunice Quedens
**Beatrice Arthur:** Bernice Frankel
**Jean Arthur:** Gladys Greene
**Fred Astaire:** Frederick Austerlitz
**Alan Autry:** Carlos Brown
**Lauren Bacall:** Betty Joan Perske
**Anne Bancroft:** Anna Maria Italiano
**Brigitte Bardot:** Camille Javal
**Gene Barry:** Eugene Klass
**Orson Bean:** Dallas Burrows
**Bonnie Bedelia:** Bonnie Culkin
**Pat Benatar:** Patricia Andrejewski
**Robbie Benson:** Robert Segal
**Tony Bennett:** Anthony Benedetto
**Busby Berkeley:** William Berkeley Enos
**Jack Benny:** Benjamin Kubelsky
**Joey Bishop:** Joseph Gottlieb
**Robert Blake:** Michael Gubitosi
**Victor Borge:** Borge Rosenbaum
**David Bowie:** David Robert Jones
**Boy George:** George Alan O'Dowd
**Fanny Brice:** Fanny Borach
**Charles Bronson:** Charles Buchinski
**Albert Brooks:** Albert Einstein
**Mel Brooks:** Melvin Kaminsky
**George Burns:** Nathan Birnbaum
**Ellen Burstyn:** Edna Gilhooley
**Richard Burton:** Richard Jenkins
**Red Buttons:** Aaron Chwatt
**Nicolas Cage:** Nicholas Coppola
**Michael Caine:** Maurice Micklewhite
**Maria Callas:** Maria Kalogeropoulos
**Vikki Carr:** Florencia Casillas
**Diahann Carroll:** Carol Diahann Johnson
**Cyd Charisse:** Tula Finklea
**Ray Charles:** Ray Charles Robinson
**Cher:** Cherilyn Sarkisian
**Patsy Cline:** Virginia Patterson Hensley
**Lee J. Cobb:** Leo Jacoby
**Claudette Colbert:** Lily Chauchoin
**Michael Connors:** Kreker Ohanian
**Robert Conrad:** Conrad Robert Falk
**Alice Cooper:** Vincent Furnier
**David Copperfield:** David Kotkin
**Howard Cosell:** Howard Cohen
**Elvis Costello:** Declan Patrick McManus
**Lou Costello:** Louis Cristillo
**Joan Crawford:** Lucille Le Sueur
**Michael Crawford:** Michael Dumbell-Smith
**Tom Cruise:** Thomas Mapother
**Tony Curtis:** Bernard Schwartz
**Vic Damone:** Vito Farinola
**Rodney Dangerfield:** Jacob Cohen
**Bobby Darin:** Walden Robert Cassotto
**Doris Day:** Doris von Kappelhoff
**Yvonne De Carlo:** Peggy Middleton
**Sandra Dee:** Alexandra Zuck
**John Denver:** Henry John Deutschendorf Jr.
**Bo Derek:** Cathleen Collins
**John Derek:** Derek Harris
**Danny DeVito:** Daniel Michaeli
**Susan Dey:** Susan Smith
**Angie Dickinson:** Angeline Brown
**Bo Diddley:** Elias Bates
**Phyllis Diller:** Phyllis Driver
**Diana Dors:** Diana Fluck
**Kirk Douglas:** Issur Danielovitch
**Melvyn Douglas:** Melvyn Hesselberg
**Bob Dylan:** Robert Zimmerman
**Sheena Easton:** Sheena Shirley Orr
**Barbara Eden:** Barbara Huffman
**Ron Ely:** Ronald Pierce
**Chad Everett:** Raymond Cramton
**Tom Ewell:** S. Yewell Tompkins
**Douglas Fairbanks:** Douglas Ullman
**Morgan Fairchild:** Patsy McClenny
**Alice Faye:** Ann Leppert
**Stepin Fetchit:** Lincoln Perry
**Sally Field:** Sally Mahoney

**W.C. Fields:** William Claude Dukenfield
**Peter Finch:** William Mitchell
**Barry Fitzgerald:** William Joseph Shields
**Joan Fontaine:** Joan de Havilland
**John Ford:** Sean O'Fearna
**John Forsythe:** John Freund
**Redd Foxx :** John Sanford
**Anthony Franciosa:** Anthony Papaleo
**Arlene Francis:** Arlene Kazanjian
**Connie Francis:** Concetta Franconero
**Greta Garbo:** Greta Gustafsson
**Vincent Gardenia:** Vincent Scognamiglio
**John Garfield:** Julius Garfinkle
**Judy Garland:** Frances Gumm
**James Garner:** James Bumgarner
**Crystal Gayle:** Brenda Gayle Webb
**Paulette Goddard:** Marion Levy
**Whoopi Goldberg:** Caryn Johnson
**Eydie Gorme:** Edith Gormezano
**Stewart Granger:** James Stewart
**Cary Grant:** Archibald Leach
**Lee Grant:** Lyova Rosenthal
**Joel Grey:** Joe Katz
**Robert Guillaume:** Robert Williams
**Buddy Hackett:** Leonard Hacker
**Hammer:** Stanley Kirk Burrell
**Jean Harlow:** Harlean Carpentier
**Rex Harrison:** Reginald Carey
**Laurence Harvey:** Larushka Skikne
**Helen Hayes:** Helen Brown
**Susan Hayward:** Edythe Marriner
**Rita Hayworth:** Margarita Cansino
**Pee-Wee Herman:** Paul Rubenfeld
**Barbara Hershey:** Barbara Herzstine
**William Holden:** William Beedle
**Judy Holliday:** Judith Tuvim
**Harry Houdini:** Ehrich Weiss
**Leslie Howard:** Leslie Stainer
**Moe Howard:** Moses Horowitz
**Rock Hudson:** Roy Scherer Jr. (later Fitzgerald)
**Engelbert Humperdinck:** Arnold Dorsey
**Kim Hunter:** Janet Cole
**Mary Beth Hurt:** Mary Supinger
**Betty Hutton:** Betty Thornberg
**David Janssen:** David Meyer
**Elton John:** Reginald Dwight
**Don Johnson:** Donald Wayne
**Jennifer Jones:** Phyllis Isley
**Tom Jones:** Thomas Woodward
**Louis Jourdan:** Louis Gendre
**Boris Karloff:** William Henry Pratt
**Danny Kaye:** David Kaminsky
**Diane Keaton:** Diane Hall
**Michael Keaton:** Michael Douglas
**Howard Keel:** Harold Leek
**Chaka Khan:** Yvette Stevens
**Carole King:** Carole Klein
**Larry King:** Larry Zeigler
**Ben Kingsley:** Krishna Banji
**Nastassja Kinski:** Nastassja Naksyznyski
**Ted Knight:** Tadeus Wladyslaw Konopka
**Cheryl Ladd:** Cheryl Stoppelmoor
**Veronica Lake:** Constance Ockleman
**Dorothy Lamour:** Mary Kaumeyer
**Michael Landon:** Eugene Orowitz
**Mario Lanza:** Alfredo Cocozza
**Stan Laurel:** Arthur Jefferson
**Steve Lawrence:** Sidney Leibowitz
**Brenda Lee:** Brenda Mae Tarpley
**Bruce Lee:** Lee Yuen Kam
**Gypsy Rose Lee:** Rose Louise Hovick
**Michelle Lee:** Michelle Dusiak
**Peggy Lee:** Norma Egstrom
**Janet Leigh:** Jeanette Morrison
**Vivien Leigh:** Vivien Hartley
**Huey Lewis:** Hugh Cregg
**Jerry Lewis:** Joseph Levitch
**Hal Linden:** Harold Lipshitz
**Carole Lombard:** Jane Peters
**Jack Lord:** John Joseph Ryan
**Sophia Loren:** Sophia Scicoloni
**Peter Lorre:** Laszio Lowenstein
**Myrna Loy:** Myrna Williams
**Bela Lugosi:** Bela Ferenc Blasko
**Moms Mabley:** Loretta Mary Aitken
**Shirley MacLaine:** Shirley Beaty

**Madonna:** Madonna Louise Ciccone
**Lee Majors:** Harvey Lee Yeary 2d
**Karl Malden:** Malden Sekulovich
**Jayne Mansfield:** Vera Jane Palmer
**Fredric March:** Frederick Bickel
**Peter Marshall:** Pierre LaCock
**Dean Martin:** Dino Crocetti
**Ethel Merman:** Ethel Zimmerman
**George Michael:** Georgios Panayiotou
**Ray Milland:** Reginald Truscott-Jones
**Ann Miller:** Lucille Collier
**Joni Mitchell:** Roberta Joan Anderson
**Marilyn Monroe:** Norma Jean Mortenson, (later) Baker
**Yves Montand:** Ivo Levi
**Ron Moody:** Ronald Moodnick
**Demi Moore:** Demi Guynes
**Garry Moore:** Thomas Garrison Morfit
**Rita Moreno:** Rosita Alverio
**Harry Morgan:** Harry Bratsburg
**Paul Muni:** Muni Weisenfreund
**Mike Nichols:** Michael Igor Peschowsky
**Chuck Norris:** Carlos Ray
**Sheree North:** Dawn Bethel
**Hugh O'Brian:** Hugh Krampke
**Maureen O'Hara:** Maureen Fitzsimmons
**Patti Page:** Clara Ann Fowler
**Jack Palance:** Walter Palanuik
**Bert Parks:** Bert Jacobson
**Minnie Pearl:** Sarah Ophelia Cannon
**Bernadette Peters:** Bernadette Lazzaro
**Edith Piaf:** Edith Gassion
**Slim Pickens:** Louis Lindley
**Mary Pickford:** Gladys Smith
**Stephanie Powers:** Stefania Federkiewicz
**Paula Prentiss:** Paula Ragusa
**Robert Preston:** Robert Preston Meservey
**Prince:** Prince Rogers Nelson
**Tony Randall:** Leonard Rosenberg
**Martha Raye:** Margaret O'Reed
**Donna Reed:** Donna Belle Mullenger
**Della Reese:** Delloreese Patricia Early
**Joan Rivers:** Joan Sandra Molinsky
**Edward G. Robinson:** Emmanuel Goldenberg
**Ginger Rogers:** Virginia McMath

**Roy Rogers:** Leonard Slye
**Mickey Rooney:** Joe Yule Jr.
**Lillian Russell:** Helen Leonard
**Theresa Russell:** Theresa Paup
**Winona Ryder:** Winona Horowitz
**Susan St. James:** Susan Miller
**Soupy Sales:** Milton Hines
**Susan Sarandon:** Susan Tomaling
**Randolph Scott:** George Randolph Crane
**Jane Seymour:** Joyce Frankenberg
**Omar Sharif:** Michael Shalhoub
**Martin Sheen:** Ramon Estevez
**Beverly Sills:** Belle Silverman
**Talia Shire:** Talia Coppola
**Phil Silvers:** Philip Silversmith
**Suzanne Somers:** Suzanne Mahoney
**Ann Sothern:** Harriette Lake
**Robert Stack:** Robert Modini
**Barbara Stanwyck:** Ruby Stevens
**Jean Stapleton:** Jeanne Murray
**Ringo Starr:** Richard Starkey
**Connie Stevens:** Concetta Ingolia
**Sting:** Gordon Sumner
**Donna Summer:** La Donna Gaines
**Rip Taylor:** Charles Elmer Jr.
**Robert Taylor:** Spangler Arlington Brugh
**Danny Thomas:** Muzyad Yakhoob, later Amos Jacobs
**Randy Travis:** Randy Traywick
**Sophie Tucker:** Sophia Kalish
**Tina Turner:** Annie Mae Bullock
**Conway Twitty:** Harold Lloyd Jenkins
**Rudolph Valentino:** Rudolpho D'Antonguolla
**Frankie Valli:** Frank Castelluccio
**David Wayne:** Wayne McMeekan
**John Wayne:** Marion Morrison
**Clifton Webb:** Webb Parmalee Hollenbeck
**Raquel Welch:** Raquel Tejada
**Gene Wilder:** Jerome Silberman
**Shelley Winters:** Shirley Schrift
**Stevie Wonder:** Stevland Morris
**Natalie Wood:** Natasha Gurdin
**Jane Wyman:** Sarah Jane Fulks
**Gig Young:** Byron Barr

## Selected International Figures of the Present

(Excluding heads of state, entertainers, and athletes; for heads of state, see individual nations)

| Name (Birthplace) | Birthdate | Name (Birthplace) | Birthdate |
|---|---|---|---|
| Chinua Achebe (Ogidi, Nigeria) | 11/16/30 | Nadine Gordimer (Springs, South Africa) | 11/2/23 |
| Jorge Amado (Bahia, Brazil) | 8/1/12 | Germaine Greer (Melbourne, Australia) | 1/29/39 |
| Martin Amis (Oxford, England) | 8/25/49 | Stephen Hawking (Oxford, England) | 1/8/42 |
| Yasir Arafat (Jerusalem, Palestine) | 1929 | Michael Heseltine (Swansea, Wales) | 3/21/33 |
| Moshe Arens (Kaunas, Lithuania) | 12/27/25 | Morihiro Hosokawa (Kumamoto, Japan) | 1/14/38 |
| Oscar Arias Sanchez (Heredia, Costa Rica) | 9/13/41 | Ted Hughes (Mytholmroyd, England) | 8/17/30 |
| Hanan Ashrawi (Ramallah, Palestine) | 1946 | P.D. James (Oxford, England) | 8/3/20 |
| Margaret Atwood (Ottawa, Ontario) | 11/18/39 | Milan Kundera (Brno, Czechoslovakia) | 4/1/29 |
| Benazir Bhutto (Karachi, Pakistan) | 6/21/53 | John le Carré (Poole, England) | 10/19/31 |
| Boutros Boutros-Ghali (Cairo, Egypt) | 11/14/22 | Doris Lessing (Kermanshah, Persia) | 10/22/19 |
| British Royal Family |  | Naguib Mahfouz (Cairo, Egypt) | 12/11/11 |
|     Queen Elizabeth II (London, England) | 4/21/26 | Nelson Mandela (Transkei, South Africa) | 1918 |
|     Prince Philip (Corfu, Greece) | 6/1/21 | Winnie Mandela (Transkei, South Africa) | 1934 |
|     Prince Charles (London, England) | 11/14/48 | Crown Princess Masako (Tokyo, Japan) | 12/9/63 |
|     Princess Diana (Sandringham, England) | 7/1/61 | Czesław Milosz (Sateiniai, Lithuania) | 6/3/11 |
|     Prince William (London, England) | 6/21/82 | Monaco Royal Family |  |
|     Prince Henry (London, England) | 9/15/84 |     Prince Ranier III (Monaco) | 5/31/23 |
|     Princess Anne (London, England) | 8/15/50 |     Prince Albert (Monte Carlo, Monaco) | 3/14/58 |
|     Prince Andrew (London, England) | 2/19/60 |     Princess Caroline (Monte Carlo, Monaco) | 1/23/57 |
|     Sarah Ferguson (London, England) | 10/15/59 |     Princess Stephanie (Monaco-Ville, Monaco) | 2/1/65 |
|     Princess Beatrice (London, England) | 8/8/88 | Alice Munro (Wingham, Ontario) | 7/10/31 |
|     Princess Eugenie (London, England) | 3/23/90 | Iris Murdoch (Dublin, Ireland) | 7/15/19 |
|     Prince Edward (London, England) | 3/1/64 | Rupert Murdoch (Melbourne, Australia) | 3/11/31 |
|     Princess Margaret (Glamis, Scotland) | 8/21/30 | Crown Price Naruhito (Tokyo, Japan) | 2/23/60 |
| Tina Brown (Maidenhead, England) | 11/21/53 | Edna O'Brien (Tuamgraney, Ireland) | 12/15/31 |
| Gro Harlem Bruntland (Oslo, Norway) | 4/2/39 | Amoz Oz (Jerusalem, Palestine) | 5/4/39 |
| Kim Campbell (Port Alberni, British Columbia) | 3/10/47 | Andreas Papandreou (Chios, Greece) | 2/5/19 |
| Elias Canetti (Ruschuk, Bulgaria) | 7/25/05 | Octavio Paz (Mexico City, Mexico) | 3/31/14 |
| Camilo Jose Cela (Ira Flavia, Spain) | 5/11/16 | Shimon Perez (Wolozyn, Poland) | 8/16/23 |
| Dalai Lama: Tenzin Gyatso (Kokonor, Tibet) | 6/6/35 | Yitzak Rabin (Jerusalem, Palestine) | 3/1/22 |
| Robertson Davies (Thamesville, Ontario) | 8/28/13 | Mordecai Richler (Montreal, Quebec) | 1/27/31 |
| Jacques Derrida (El Biar, Algeria) | 7/15/30 | Mary Robinson (Ballina, Ireland) | 5/21/44 |
| Takako Doi (Hyogo, Japan) | 11/30/28 | Salman Rushdie (Bombay, India) | 6/19/47 |
| Margaret Drabble (Sheffield, England) | 6/5/39 | Yitzak Shamir (Kuzinoy, Poland) | 11/3/14 |
| Valery Giscard d'Estaing (Koblenz, Germany) | 2/2/26 | Eduard Shevardnadze (Mamati, USSR) | 1/25/28 |
| Carlos Fuentes (Mexico City, Mexico) | 11/11/28 | Wole Soyinka (Abeokuta, Nigeria) | 7/13/34 |
| Athol Fugard (Kanroo, South Africa) | 1932 | Muriel Spark (Edinburgh, Scotland) | 2/1/18 |
| Gabriel Garcia Marquez (Aracata, Colombia) | 3/6/28 | Hanna Suchocka (Pleszewa, Poland) | 4/3/46 |
| Mikhail Gorbachev (Privalnaye, Stavropol, USSR) | 3/21/31 | Mother Teresa (Skopje, Macedonia) | 8/27/10 |
| Raisa Gorbachev (Rubtsovsk, USSR) | 1934 | Margaret Thatcher (Grantham, England) | 10/13/25 |

# UNITED STATES POPULATION

## A Typical American as Seen Through the Eyes
## of the Census Bureau

by
Dr. Harry A. Scarr
Deputy Director, Bureau of the Census
U.S. Department of Commerce

I am often asked to describe a typical American: What do we do? Where do we live? How much money do we make? Based upon Census Bureau data, I see typical America as a patchwork of cultures, lifestyles, and economic groups.

### Who We Are

Typical America contains many racial and ethnic groups. More than 23 million of us (9.3 percent) are of Hispanic origin, and 8 million of us (3.2 percent) identify ourselves as Asians or Pacific Islanders. Blacks number over 31 million, or 12.4 percent of the population, and the American Indian/Eskimo/Aleut populations make up about 2 million (0.8 percent). Nearly 190 million people (75.2 percent) consider themselves to be non-Hispanic white.

According to the 1990 Census, nearly 20 million of us were not born in America but call it home. In 1992, about 33 percent of our population growth came from net immigration.

This means America speaks many languages: over 31.8 million of us speak a language other than English at home; over half of this number speaks Spanish.

We are also aging: our median age has risen from 30.0 years in 1980 to 33.1 in 1991 (the median for blacks is 28.1, and the median for whites is 34.1). Nearly 26 percent of us are under 18 years of age, and over 12.6 percent are 65 and older.

Women outnumber men in America by 6.2 million; 51 percent of the total population is female.

There are 95.7 million households in our nation; 70 percent of them contain families. Of all households, 55 percent are maintained by married couples, but only 26 percent of all households with children under 18 include a married couple. About one-fourth of all households contain a person living alone.

### What We Do

About 67 percent of Americans 16 years and over are in the labor force: almost 76 percent of men and nearly 58 percent of women. Over 8 million working-age Americans are prevented from working because of a disability.

Our top three occupation groups are administrative support, including clerical; professional specialty; and executive, administrative, and managerial. There are 19.6 million employed persons working in the retail sales industry.

Of the over 115 million employed workers, 73 percent drive to work alone and 13 percent are in carpools. About 76 percent of us work in the county in which we live, and our commuting time averages about 22 minutes.

Workers are well represented among mothers: almost 58 percent of mothers with children under 6, and 75.9 percent of mothers with children 6 to 17 are in the labor force.

The number of women-owned businesses (sole proprietorship, partnership, or subchapter S companies) increased by a dramatic 57 percent in the late 1980s. Minority-owned firms also dramatically increased in number: Asian-Pacific Islander by 89 percent, Hispanic by 81 percent, American Indian/Eskimo/Aleut by 58 percent, and black by 38 percent.

Most state and local government employees are in education-related activities: two-fifths of the 4.5 million state employees and over one-half of the 10.9 million local government workers.

Personal and business services grew 13 times faster than the population in the late 1980s.

### Where We Live

Typical America, or at least half of it (55.6 percent), lives in the South and West regions of the country. Between 1980 and 1990, the West grew by 22.3 percent, and the South grew by 13.4 percent. This dramatic growth rate caused a shift of 19 seats in the House of Representatives. Eight states gained seats: California (+7), Florida (+4), Texas (+3), and Arizona, Georgia, North Carolina, Virginia, and Washington (+1 each). Thirteen states lost seats: New York (−3); Illinois, Michigan, Ohio, and Pennsylvania (−2 each); and Iowa, Kansas, Kentucky, Louisiana, Massachusetts, Montana, New Jersey, and West Virginia (−1 each).

Since 1990, the U.S. population has been increasing by about 3 million persons a year. Our five most populous states are California (30.9 million), New York (18.1 million), Texas (17.7 million), Florida (13.5 million), and Pennsylvania (12 million). The five states at the other end of the spectrum are Delaware (689,000), North Dakota (636,000), Alaska (587,000), Vermont (570,000), and Wyoming (466,000).

Most of us—79.5 percent—live in metropolitan areas, and over half of us (53.7) live in one of the 41 metropolitan areas with populations of at least 1 million.

Our five largest metropolitan areas are scattered across the map: New York/Northern New Jersey/Long Island (19.4 million), Los Angeles/Riverside/Orange County (14.8 million), Chicago/Gary/Kenosha Counties (8.3 million), Washington/Baltimore (6.8 million), and San Francisco/Oakland/San Jose (6.3 million). Although the New York area remains in first position, the Los Angeles area is growing at a much faster rate (2 versus 0.2 percent since 1990).

Within those metro areas are some big cities. Our five largest cities are New York (7.3 million), Los Angeles (3.5 million), Chicago (2.8 million), Houston (1.6 million), and Philadelphia (1.6 million).

Our five largest counties are Los Angeles, CA (9.0 million), Cook, IL (5.1 million), Harris, TX (2.9 million), San Diego, CA (2.5 million), and Orange, CA (2.4 million).

### How We Live

Typical Americans live in a household with others. The average number of people living in a household in the United States was 2.62 in 1992.

We have a total of about 105 million housing units nationwide; nearly 93 million of them are occupied. The vast majority of housing units have public water and sewer service, and our top two house heating fuel sources are utility gas (51 million units) and electricity (27 million units). About 3 million units lack complete plumbing facilities, and 4 million lack complete kitchen facilities.

Almost two thirds (64 percent) of us are homeowners. Of the 60 million owner units, nearly 35 million have mortgages. The median monthly costs for all owner units is $455. The median for mortgage units is $761, while the median for non-mortgage units is $222. The median value of owner homes is $80,000.

If you live in one of the 33 million renter-occupied housing units, your housing costs are $462 per month.

### Quality of Life

Education: America has a higher proportion of high school graduates than at any other time in U.S. history: more than 79 percent of all Americans age 25 and over. About 27 percent of these graduates have gone on to earn a bachelor's degree or higher.

Educational attainment has a direct impact on many aspects of life, but most directly on earnings. Average annual earnings for persons without a high school diploma are $14,078; with a diploma, $19,567; with a bachelor's degree, $32,728; with a doctorate, $53,705; and with a professional degree, $65,648. We spend an average of $4,700 annually per student in our public elementary and secondary schools.

Assets: Home ownership accounts for over 40 percent of Americans' net worth. Interest-earning assets account for almost 20 percent. About 20 percent of America's households hold about 44 percent of our nation's net worth.

Pensions: Two-thirds of the work force is covered by a pension of some type. Most of us (92 percent) are covered by Social Security. Nearly all government employees (92 percent) are covered by pensions, while only 36 percent of agricultural and personal service workers are covered by employer-sponsored pensions.

Health insurance: Nearly 86 percent of us have health insurance. Those most likely to be insured are the elderly, the employed, and those with at least a high school diploma.

Child care: Families with working mothers and preschool children spend about 8 percent of their combined income on child care for their children. Most of the care for preschoolers takes place in a home environment, such as with relatives or neighbors (67 percent); about 23 percent of child care for preschoolers is in organized facilities, such as nursery schools and day care centers; 9 percent are cared for by the mother while she works; and 1 percent are involved in a school-based activity.

Child support: Of the 5.7 million women awarded child support, 5.0 million were supposed to receive payments in 1989. Of the women due payments, about half received the full amount they were due. The average amount of child support received in 1989 was $2,995. The aggregate amount of child support received in 1989 was $11.2 billion, 69 percent of $16.3 billion due.

Assistance: About 4 percent of our adult population needs assistance with everyday activities. This need increases to 45 percent for persons 85 and over. Most caregivers are female relatives.

Voting: The 1992 presidential election was decided by 61.3 percent of our voting-age population. That was better than the 57 percent who determined the outcome of the 1988 presidential election. Voter registration increased for the 1992 election; about 68 percent of us who are old enough to vote registered to do so in 1992, up slightly from 67 percent in 1988.

Federal Aid: In fiscal year 1992, the federal government dispensed nearly $2 trillion to state and local governments and U.S. territories. California received $140 billion of these funds. On a per capita basis, Alaska received the most, with spending of over $6,800 per person.

Funds were divided this way: $612 billion in payments to individuals, such as Social Security; $162 billion in salaries to military and civilian employees; $200 billion in contracts; $178 billion in grants to state and local governments, for example: Medicaid, Aid to Families With Dependent Children, and highway construction; and $40 billion in other programs, including research grants and agricultural subsidies.

Lotteries: Thirty-two states operate lotteries, which produced $8.8 billion in net revenue in fiscal year 1991. During the same time, state general expenditures amounted to $554.6 billion. State expenditures for highways were up 6.3 percent in 1991 to $47 billion. Expenditures for hospitals rose 8.1 percent to $24.5 billion in 1991.

## Estimated Population of American Colonies: 1630-1780

Source: Bureau of the Census (thousands)

| Colony | 1780 | 1770 | 1750 | 1740 | 1720 | 1700 | 1690 | 1670 | 1650 | 1630 |
|---|---|---|---|---|---|---|---|---|---|---|
| Total . . . . . . . | 2,780.4 | 2,148.1 | 1,170.8 | 905.6 | 466.2 | 250.9 | 210.4 | 111.9 | 50.4 | 4.6 |
| Maine (counties)[1] . . | 49.1 | 31.3 | . . . | . . . | . . . | . . . | . . . | . . . | 1.0 | 0.4 |
| New Hampshire[2] . . | 87.8 | 62.4 | 27.5 | 23.3 | 9.4 | 5.0 | 4.2 | 1.8 | 1.3 | 0.5 |
| Vermont[3]. . . . . . | 47.6 | 10.0 | . . . | . . . | . . . | . . . | . . . | . . . | . . . | . . . |
| Plymouth and Massachusetts[1,2,4] | 268.6 | 235.3 | 188.0 | 151.6 | 91.0 | 55.9 | 56.9 | 35.3 | 15.6 | 0.9 |
| Rhode Island[2] . . . . | 52.9 | 58.2 | 33.2 | 25.3 | 11.7 | 5.9 | 4.2 | 2.2 | 0.8 | . . . |
| Connecticut[2]. . . . . | 206.7 | 183.9 | 111.3 | 89.6 | 58.8 | 26.0 | 21.6 | 12.6 | 4.1 | . . . |
| New York[2]. . . . . | 210.5 | 162.9 | 76.7 | 63.7 | 36.9 | 19.1 | 13.9 | 5.8 | 4.1 | 0.4 |
| New Jersey[2]. . . . . | 139.6 | 117.4 | 71.4 | 51.4 | 29.8 | 14.0 | 8.0 | 1.0 | . . . | . . . |
| Pennsylvania[2] . . . . | 327.3 | 240.1 | 119.7 | 85.6 | 31.0 | 18.0 | 11.4 | . . . | . . . | . . . |
| Delaware[2]. . . . . . | 45.4 | 35.5 | 28.7 | 19.9 | 5.4 | 2.5 | 1.5 | 0.7 | 0.2 | . . . |
| Maryland[2]. . . . . . | 245.5 | 202.6 | 141.1 | 116.1 | 66.1 | 29.6 | 24.0 | 13.2 | 4.5 | . . . |
| Virginia[2] . . . . . . | 538.0 | 447.0 | 231.0 | 180.4 | 87.8 | 58.6 | 53.0 | 35.3 | 18.7 | 2.5 |
| North Carolina[2] . . . | 270.1 | 197.2 | 73.0 | 51.8 | 21.3 | 10.7 | 7.6 | 3.8 | . . . | . . . |
| South Carolina[2]. . . | 180.0 | 124.2 | 64.0 | 45.0 | 17.0 | 5.7 | 3.9 | 0.2 | . . . | . . . |
| Georgia[2]. . . . . . | 56.1 | 23.4 | 5.2 | 2.0 | . . . | . . . | . . . | . . . | . . . | . . . |
| Kentucky[5]. . . . . . | 45.0 | 15.7 | . . . | . . . | . . . | . . . | . . . | . . . | . . . | . . . |
| Tennessee[6] . . . . . | 10.0 | 1.0 | . . . | . . . | . . . | . . . | . . . | . . . | . . . | . . . |

(1) For 1660-1750, Maine counties included with Massachusetts. Maine was a part of Massachusetts until it became a separate state in 1820. (2) One of the original 13 states. (3) Admitted to statehood in 1791. (4) Plymouth became a part of the Province of Massachusetts in 1691. (5) Admitted to statehood in 1792. (6) Admitted to statehood in 1796.

## U.S. Population by Official

(Members of the Armed Forces overseas or

| State | 1790[1] | 1800[1] | 1810[1] | 1820 | 1830 | 1840 | 1850 | 1860 | 1870 | 1880 | 1890 |
|---|---|---|---|---|---|---|---|---|---|---|---|
| Ala. . . | ........ | 1 | 9 | 127,901 | 309,527 | 590,756 | 771,623 | 964,201 | 996,992 | 1,262,505 | 1,513,401 |
| Alas. . | ........ | ........ | ........ | ........ | ........ | ........ | ........ | ........ | ........ | 33,426 | 32,052 |
| Ariz. . | ........ | ........ | ........ | ........ | ........ | ........ | ........ | ........ | 9,658 | 40,440 | 88,243 |
| Ark. . . | ........ | ........ | 1 | 14,273 | 30,388 | 97,574 | 209,897 | 435,450 | 484,471 | 802,525 | 1,128,211 |
| Cal. . . | ........ | ........ | ........ | ........ | ........ | ........ | 92,597 | 379,994 | 560,247 | 864,694 | 1,213,398 |
| Col. . . | ........ | ........ | ........ | ........ | ........ | ........ | ........ | 34,277 | 39,864 | 194,327 | 413,249 |
| Conn. . | 238 | 251 | 262 | 275,248 | 297,675 | 309,978 | 370,792 | 460,147 | 537,454 | 622,700 | 746,258 |
| Del. . . | 59 | 64 | 73 | 72,749 | 76,748 | 78,085 | 91,532 | 112,216 | 125,015 | 146,608 | 168,493 |
| D.C. . . | ........ | 8 | 16 | 23,336 | 30,261 | 33,745 | 51,687 | 75,080 | 131,700 | 177,624 | 230,392 |
| Fla. . . | ........ | ........ | ........ | ........ | 34,730 | 54,477 | 87,445 | 140,424 | 187,748 | 269,493 | 391,422 |
| Ga. . . | 83 | 163 | 252 | 340,989 | 516,823 | 691,392 | 906,185 | 1,057,286 | 1,184,109 | 1,542,180 | 1,837,353 |
| Ha. . . | ........ | ........ | ........ | ........ | ........ | ........ | ........ | ........ | ........ | ........ | ........ |
| Ida. . . | ........ | ........ | ........ | ........ | ........ | ........ | ........ | ........ | 14,999 | 32,610 | 88,548 |
| Ill. . . | ........ | ........ | 12 | 55,211 | 157,445 | 476,183 | 851,470 | 1,711,951 | 2,539,891 | 3,077,871 | 3,826,352 |
| Ind. . . | ........ | 6 | 25 | 147,178 | 343,031 | 685,866 | 988,416 | 1,350,428 | 1,680,637 | 1,978,301 | 2,192,404 |
| Ia. . . . | ........ | ........ | ........ | ........ | ........ | 43,112 | 192,214 | 674,913 | 1,194,020 | 1,624,615 | 1,912,297 |
| Kan. . . | ........ | ........ | ........ | ........ | ........ | ........ | ........ | 107,206 | 364,399 | 996,096 | 1,428,108 |
| Ky. . . . | 74 | 221 | 407 | 564,317 | 687,917 | 779,828 | 982,405 | 1,155,684 | 1,321,011 | 1,648,690 | 1,858,635 |
| La. . . . | ........ | ........ | 77 | 153,407 | 215,739 | 352,411 | 517,762 | 708,002 | 726,915 | 939,946 | 1,118,588 |
| Me. . . | 97 | 152 | 229 | 298,335 | 399,455 | 501,793 | 583,169 | 628,279 | 626,915 | 648,936 | 661,086 |
| Md. . . | 320 | 342 | 381 | 407,350 | 447,040 | 470,019 | 583,034 | 687,049 | 780,894 | 934,943 | 1,042,390 |
| Mass. . | 379 | 423 | 472 | 523,287 | 610,408 | 737,699 | 994,514 | 1,231,066 | 1,457,351 | 1,783,085 | 2,238,947 |
| Mich. . | ........ | ........ | 5 | 8,896 | 31,639 | 212,267 | 397,654 | 749,113 | 1,184,059 | 1,636,937 | 2,093,890 |
| Minn. . | ........ | ........ | ........ | ........ | ........ | ........ | 6,077 | 172,023 | 439,706 | 780,773 | 1,310,283 |
| Miss. . | ........ | 8 | 31 | 75,448 | 136,621 | 375,651 | 606,526 | 791,305 | 827,922 | 1,131,597 | 1,289,600 |
| Mo. . . | ........ | ........ | 20 | 66,586 | 140,455 | 383,702 | 682,044 | 1,182,012 | 1,721,295 | 2,168,380 | 2,679,185 |
| Mon.. . | ........ | ........ | ........ | ........ | ........ | ........ | ........ | ........ | 20,595 | 39,159 | 142,924 |
| Neb.. . | ........ | ........ | ........ | ........ | ........ | ........ | ........ | 28,841 | 122,993 | 452,402 | 1,062,656 |
| Nev.. . | ........ | ........ | ........ | ........ | ........ | ........ | ........ | 6,857 | 42,491 | 62,266 | 47,355 |
| N.H. . | 142 | 184 | 214 | 244,161 | 269,328 | 284,574 | 317,976 | 326,073 | 318,300 | 346,991 | 376,530 |
| N.J. . . | 184 | 211 | 246 | 277,575 | 320,823 | 373,306 | 489,555 | 672,035 | 906,096 | 1,131,116 | 1,444,933 |
| N.M.. . | ........ | ........ | ........ | ........ | ........ | ........ | 61,547 | 93,516 | 91,874 | 119,565 | 160,282 |
| N.Y. . . | 340 | 589 | 959 | 1,372,812 | 1,918,608 | 2,428,921 | 3,097,394 | 3,880,735 | 4,382,759 | 5,082,871 | 6,003,174 |
| N.C.. . | 394 | 478 | 556 | 638,829 | 737,987 | 753,419 | 869,039 | 992,622 | 1,071,361 | 1,399,750 | 1,617,949 |
| N.D. . . | ........ | ........ | ........ | ........ | ........ | ........ | ........ | ........ | 2,405[2] | 36,909 | 190,983 |
| Oh. . . | ........ | 45 | 231 | 581,434 | 937,903 | 1,519,467 | 1,980,329 | 2,339,511 | 2,665,260 | 3,198,062 | 3,672,329 |
| Okla. . | ........ | ........ | ........ | ........ | ........ | ........ | ........ | ........ | ........ | ........ | 258,657 |
| Ore. . . | ........ | ........ | ........ | ........ | ........ | ........ | 12,093 | 52,465 | 90,923 | 174,768 | 317,704 |
| Pa. . . | 434 | 602 | 810 | 1,049,458 | 1,348,233 | 1,724,033 | 2,311,786 | 2,906,215 | 3,521,951 | 4,282,891 | 5,258,113 |
| R.I. . . | 69 | 69 | 77 | 83,059 | 97,199 | 108,830 | 147,545 | 174,620 | 217,353 | 276,531 | 345,506 |
| S.C.. . | 249 | 346 | 415 | 502,741 | 581,185 | 594,398 | 668,507 | 703,708 | 705,606 | 995,577 | 1,151,149 |
| S.D.. . | ........ | ........ | ........ | ........ | ........ | ........ | ........ | 4,837[2] | 11,776[2] | 98,268 | 348,600 |
| Tenn. . | 36 | 106 | 262 | 422,823 | 681,904 | 829,210 | 1,002,717 | 1,109,801 | 1,258,520 | 1,542,359 | 1,767,518 |
| Tex.. . | ........ | ........ | ........ | ........ | ........ | ........ | 212,592 | 604,215 | 818,579 | 1,591,749 | 2,235,527 |
| Ut.. . . | ........ | ........ | ........ | ........ | ........ | ........ | 11,380 | 40,273 | 86,786 | 143,963 | 210,779 |
| Vt. . . . | 85 | 154 | 218 | 235,981 | 280,652 | 291,948 | 314,120 | 315,098 | 330,551 | 332,286 | 332,422 |
| Va. . . | 692 | 808 | 878 | 938,261 | 1,044,054 | 1,025,227 | 1,119,348 | 1,219,630 | 1,225,163 | 1,512,565 | 1,655,980 |
| Wash.. | ........ | ........ | ........ | ........ | ........ | ........ | 1,201 | 11,594 | 23,955 | 75,116 | 357,232 |
| W. Va.. | 56 | 79 | 105 | 136,808 | 176,924 | 224,537 | 302,313 | 376,688 | 442,014 | 618,457 | 762,794 |
| Wis. . . | ........ | ........ | ........ | ........ | ........ | 30,945 | 305,391 | 775,881 | 1,054,670 | 1,315,497 | 1,693,330 |
| Wy. . . | ........ | ........ | ........ | ........ | ........ | ........ | ........ | ........ | 9,118 | 20,789 | 62,555 |
| U.S.. . | 3,929 | 5,308 | 7,240 | 9,638,453 | 12,860,702 | 17,063,353[3] | 23,191,876 | 31,443,321[3] | 38,558,371 | 50,189,209 | 62,979,766 |

Note: Where possible, population shown is that of 1990 area of state.
(1) Totals for 1790, 1800, and 1810 are in thousands. (2) 1860 figure is for Dakota Territory; 1870 figures are for parts of Dakota Territory. (3) U.S. total includes persons (5,318 in 1830 and 6,100 in 1840) on public ships in the service of the United States not credited to any region, division, or state.

## Congressional Apportionment

| | 1990 | 1980 | | 1990 | 1980 | | 1990 | 1980 | | 1990 | 1980 | | 1990 | 1980 |
|---|---|---|---|---|---|---|---|---|---|---|---|---|---|---|
| AL .. | 7 | 7 | ID. . . | 2 | 2 | MN. . | 8 | 8 | ND . . | 1 | 1 | UT . . | 3 | 3 |
| AK .. | 1 | 1 | IL. . . | 20 | 22 | MS . . | 5 | 5 | OH. . | 19 | 21 | VT . . | 1 | 1 |
| AZ .. | 6 | 5 | IN. . . | 10 | 10 | MO. . | 9 | 9 | OK .. | 6 | 6 | VA . . | 11 | 10 |
| AR .. | 4 | 4 | IA. . . | 5 | 6 | MT . . | 1 | 2 | OR . . | 5 | 5 | WA.. | 9 | 8 |
| CA .. | 52 | 45 | KS . . | 4 | 5 | NE . . | 3 | 3 | PA . . | 21 | 23 | WV.. | 3 | 4 |
| CO .. | 6 | 6 | KY . . | 6 | 7 | NV . . | 2 | 2 | RI . . | 2 | 2 | WI . . | 9 | 9 |
| CT .. | 6 | 6 | LA . . | 7 | 8 | NH . . | 2 | 2 | SC . . | 6 | 6 | WY.. | 1 | 1 |
| DE . . | 1 | 1 | ME . . | 2 | 2 | NJ . . | 13 | 14 | SD . . | 1 | 1 | | | |
| FL . . | 23 | 19 | MD. . | 8 | 8 | NM. . | 3 | 3 | TN . . | 9 | 9 | Totals | 435 | 435 |
| GA . . | 11 | 10 | MA.. | 10 | 11 | NY . . | 31 | 34 | TX . . | 30 | 27 | | | |
| HI . . | 2 | 2 | MI. . . | 16 | 18 | NC . . | 12 | 11 | | | | | | |

The primary reason the Constitution provided for a census of the population every 10 years was to give a basis for apportionment of representatives among the states. This apportionment largely determines the number of electoral votes allotted to each state.

The number of representatives of each state in Congress is determined by the state's population, but each state is entitled to one representative regardless of population. A Congressional apportionment has been made after each decennial census except that of 1920.

Under provisions of a law that became effective Nov. 15, 1941, apportionment of representatives is made by the method of equal proportions. In the application of this method, the apportionment is made so that the average population per representative has the least possible variation between one state and any other. The first House of Representatives, in 1789, had 65 members, as provided by the Constitution. As the population grew, the number of representatives was increased, but the total membership has been fixed at 435 since the apportionment based on the 1910 census.

## Census from 1790 to 1990

other U.S. nationals overseas are not included.)

| 1900 | 1910 | 1920 | 1930 | 1940 | 1950 | 1960 | 1970 | 1980 | 1990 |
|---|---|---|---|---|---|---|---|---|---|
| 1,828,697 | 2,138,093 | 2,348,174 | 2,646,248 | 2,832,961 | 3,061,743 | 3,266,740 | 3,444,354 | 3,894,025 | 4,040,587 |
| 63,592 | 64,356 | 55,036 | 59,278 | 72,524 | 128,643 | 226,167 | 302,583 | 401,851 | 550,043 |
| 122,931 | 204,354 | 334,162 | 435,573 | 499,261 | 749,587 | 1,302,161 | 1,775,399 | 2,716,546 | 3,665,228 |
| 1,311,564 | 1,574,449 | 1,752,204 | 1,854,482 | 1,949,387 | 1,909,511 | 1,786,272 | 1,923,322 | 2,286,357 | 2,350,725 |
| 1,485,053 | 2,377,549 | 3,426,861 | 5,677,251 | 6,907,387 | 10,586,223 | 15,717,204 | 19,971,069 | 23,667,764 | 29,760,021 |
| 539,700 | 799,024 | 939,629 | 1,035,791 | 1,123,296 | 1,325,089 | 1,753,947 | 2,209,596 | 2,889,735 | 3,294,394 |
| 908,420 | 1,114,756 | 1,380,631 | 1,606,903 | 1,709,242 | 2,007,280 | 2,535,234 | 3,032,217 | 3,107,564 | 3,287,116 |
| 184,735 | 202,322 | 223,003 | 238,380 | 266,505 | 318,085 | 446,292 | 548,104 | 594,338 | 666,168 |
| 278,718 | 331,069 | 437,571 | 486,869 | 663,091 | 802,178 | 763,956 | 756,668 | 638,432 | 606,900 |
| 528,542 | 752,619 | 968,470 | 1,468,211 | 1,897,414 | 2,771,305 | 4,951,560 | 6,791,418 | 9,746,961 | 12,937,926 |
| 2,216,331 | 2,609,121 | 2,895,832 | 2,908,506 | 3,123,723 | 3,444,578 | 3,943,116 | 4,587,930 | 5,462,982 | 6,478,216 |
| 154,001 | 191,874 | 255,881 | 368,300 | 422,770 | 499,794 | 632,772 | 769,913 | 964,691 | 1,108,229 |
| 161,772 | 325,594 | 431,866 | 445,032 | 524,873 | 588,637 | 667,191 | 713,015 | 944,127 | 1,006,749 |
| 4,821,550 | 5,638,591 | 6,485,280 | 7,630,654 | 7,897,241 | 8,712,176 | 10,081,158 | 11,110,285 | 11,427,409 | 11,430,602 |
| 2,516,462 | 2,700,876 | 2,930,390 | 3,238,503 | 3,427,796 | 3,934,224 | 4,662,498 | 5,195,392 | 5,490,214 | 5,544,159 |
| 2,231,853 | 2,224,771 | 2,404,021 | 2,470,939 | 2,538,268 | 2,621,073 | 2,757,537 | 2,825,368 | 2,913,808 | 2,776,755 |
| 1,470,495 | 1,690,949 | 1,769,257 | 1,880,999 | 1,801,028 | 1,905,299 | 2,178,611 | 2,249,071 | 2,364,236 | 2,477,574 |
| 2,147,174 | 2,289,905 | 2,416,630 | 2,614,589 | 2,845,627 | 2,944,806 | 3,038,156 | 3,220,711 | 3,660,324 | 3,685,296 |
| 1,381,625 | 1,656,388 | 1,798,509 | 2,101,593 | 2,363,880 | 2,683,516 | 3,257,022 | 3,644,637 | 4,206,116 | 4,219,973 |
| 694,466 | 742,371 | 768,014 | 797,423 | 847,226 | 913,774 | 969,265 | 993,722 | 1,125,043 | 1,227,928 |
| 1,188,044 | 1,295,346 | 1,449,661 | 1,631,526 | 1,821,244 | 2,343,001 | 3,100,689 | 3,923,897 | 4,216,933 | 4,781,468 |
| 2,805,346 | 3,366,416 | 3,852,356 | 4,249,614 | 4,316,721 | 4,690,514 | 5,148,578 | 5,689,170 | 5,737,093 | 6,016,425 |
| 2,420,982 | 2,810,173 | 3,668,412 | 4,842,325 | 5,256,106 | 6,371,766 | 7,823,194 | 8,881,826 | 9,262,044 | 9,295,297 |
| 1,751,394 | 2,075,708 | 2,387,125 | 2,563,953 | 2,792,300 | 2,982,483 | 3,413,864 | 3,806,103 | 4,075,970 | 4,375,099 |
| 1,551,270 | 1,797,114 | 1,790,618 | 2,009,821 | 2,183,796 | 2,178,914 | 2,178,141 | 2,216,994 | 2,520,770 | 2,573,216 |
| 3,106,665 | 3,293,335 | 3,404,055 | 3,629,367 | 3,784,664 | 3,954,653 | 4,319,813 | 4,677,623 | 4,916,766 | 5,117,073 |
| 243,329 | 376,053 | 548,889 | 537,606 | 559,456 | 591,024 | 674,767 | 694,409 | 786,690 | 799,065 |
| 1,066,300 | 1,192,214 | 1,296,372 | 1,377,963 | 1,315,834 | 1,325,510 | 1,411,330 | 1,485,333 | 1,569,825 | 1,578,385 |
| 42,335 | 81,875 | 77,407 | 91,058 | 110,247 | 160,083 | 285,278 | 488,738 | 800,508 | 1,201,833 |
| 411,588 | 430,572 | 443,083 | 465,293 | 491,524 | 533,242 | 606,921 | 737,681 | 920,610 | 1,109,252 |
| 1,883,669 | 2,537,167 | 3,155,900 | 4,041,334 | 4,160,165 | 4,835,329 | 6,066,782 | 7,171,112 | 7,365,011 | 7,730,188 |
| 195,310 | 327,301 | 360,350 | 423,317 | 531,818 | 681,187 | 951,023 | 1,017,055 | 1,303,302 | 1,515,069 |
| 7,268,894 | 9,113,614 | 10,385,227 | 12,588,066 | 13,479,142 | 14,830,192 | 16,782,304 | 18,241,391 | 17,558,165 | 17,990,455 |
| 1,893,810 | 2,206,287 | 2,559,123 | 3,170,276 | 3,571,623 | 4,061,929 | 4,556,155 | 5,084,411 | 5,880,095 | 6,628,637 |
| 319,146 | 577,056 | 646,872 | 680,845 | 641,935 | 619,636 | 632,446 | 617,792 | 652,717 | 638,800 |
| 4,157,545 | 4,767,121 | 5,759,394 | 6,646,697 | 6,907,612 | 7,946,627 | 9,706,397 | 10,657,423 | 10,797,603 | 10,847,115 |
| 790,391 | 1,657,155 | 2,028,283 | 2,396,040 | 2,336,434 | 2,233,351 | 2,328,284 | 2,559,463 | 3,025,487 | 3,145,585 |
| 413,536 | 672,765 | 783,389 | 953,786 | 1,089,684 | 1,521,341 | 1,768,687 | 2,091,533 | 2,633,156 | 2,842,321 |
| 6,302,115 | 7,665,111 | 8,720,017 | 9,631,350 | 9,900,180 | 10,498,012 | 11,319,366 | 11,800,766 | 11,864,720 | 11,881,643 |
| 428,556 | 542,610 | 604,397 | 687,497 | 713,346 | 791,896 | 859,488 | 949,723 | 947,154 | 1,003,464 |
| 1,340,316 | 1,515,400 | 1,683,724 | 1,738,765 | 1,899,804 | 2,117,027 | 2,382,594 | 2,590,713 | 3,120,729 | 3,486,703 |
| 401,570 | 583,888 | 636,547 | 692,849 | 642,961 | 652,740 | 680,514 | 666,257 | 690,768 | 696,004 |
| 2,020,616 | 2,184,789 | 2,337,885 | 2,616,556 | 2,915,841 | 3,291,718 | 3,567,089 | 3,926,018 | 4,591,023 | 4,877,185 |
| 3,048,710 | 3,896,542 | 4,663,228 | 5,824,715 | 6,414,824 | 7,711,194 | 9,579,677 | 11,198,655 | 14,225,513 | 16,986,510 |
| 276,749 | 373,351 | 449,396 | 507,847 | 550,310 | 688,862 | 890,627 | 1,059,273 | 1,461,037 | 1,722,850 |
| 343,641 | 355,956 | 352,428 | 359,611 | 359,231 | 377,747 | 389,881 | 444,732 | 511,456 | 562,758 |
| 1,854,184 | 2,061,612 | 2,309,187 | 2,421,851 | 2,677,773 | 3,318,680 | 3,966,949 | 4,651,448 | 5,346,797 | 6,187,358 |
| 518,103 | 1,141,990 | 1,356,621 | 1,563,396 | 1,736,191 | 2,378,963 | 2,853,214 | 3,413,244 | 4,132,353 | 4,866,692 |
| 958,800 | 1,221,119 | 1,463,701 | 1,729,205 | 1,901,974 | 2,005,552 | 1,860,421 | 1,744,237 | 1,950,186 | 1,793,477 |
| 2,069,042 | 2,333,860 | 2,632,067 | 2,939,006 | 3,137,587 | 3,434,575 | 3,951,777 | 4,417,821 | 4,705,642 | 4,891,769 |
| 92,531 | 145,965 | 194,402 | 225,565 | 250,742 | 290,529 | 330,066 | 332,416 | 469,557 | 453,588 |

76,212,168   92,228,496 106,021,537 123,202,624 132,164,569 151,325,798   179,323,175 203,302,031 226,542,203 248,709,873

## U.S. Center of Population, 1790-1990

Center of Population is that point which may be considered as center of population gravity of the U.S. or that point upon which the U.S. would balance if it were a rigid plane without weight and the population distributed thereon with each individual being assumed to have equal weight and to exert an influence on a central point proportional to his or her distance from that point. The 1990 center is 818.6 miles from the 1790 center of population, and 39.5 miles southwest of the 1980 center.

| Year | | N. Lat. | | | W.Long. | | | Approximate location |
|---|---|---|---|---|---|---|---|---|
| | | ° | ′ | ″ | ° | ′ | ″ | |
| 1790 | | 39 | 16 | 30 | 76 | 11 | 12 | 23 miles east of Baltimore, Md. |
| 1800 | | 39 | 16 | 6 | 76 | 56 | 30 | 18 miles west of Baltimore, Md. |
| 1810 | | 39 | 11 | 30 | 77 | 37 | 12 | 40 miles northwest of Washington, D.C. (in Va.) |
| 1820 | | 39 | 5 | 42 | 78 | 33 | 0 | 16 miles east of Moorefield, W. Va.[1] |
| 1830 | | 38 | 57 | 54 | 79 | 16 | 54 | 19 miles west-southwest of Moorefield, W. Va.[1] |
| 1840 | | 39 | 2 | 0 | 80 | 18 | 0 | 16 miles south of Clarksburg, W. Va.[1] |
| 1850 | | 38 | 59 | 0 | 81 | 19 | 0 | 23 miles southeast of Parkersburg, W. Va.[1] |
| 1860 | | 39 | 0 | 24 | 82 | 48 | 48 | 20 miles south by east of Chillicothe, Oh. |
| 1870 | | 39 | 12 | 0 | 83 | 35 | 42 | 48 miles east by north of Cincinnati, Oh. |
| 1880 | | 39 | 4 | 8 | 84 | 39 | 40 | 8 miles west by south of Cincinnati, Oh. (in Ky.) |
| 1890 | | 39 | 11 | 56 | 85 | 32 | 53 | 20 miles east of Columbus, Ind. |
| 1900 | | 39 | 9 | 36 | 85 | 48 | 54 | 6 miles southeast of Columbus, Ind. |
| 1910 | | 39 | 10 | 12 | 86 | 32 | 20 | In the city of Bloomington, Ind. |
| 1920 | | 39 | 10 | 21 | 86 | 43 | 15 | 8 miles south-southeast of Spencer, Owen County, Ind. |
| 1930 | | 39 | 3 | 45 | 87 | 8 | 6 | 3 miles northeast of Linton, Greene County, Ind. |
| 1940 | | 38 | 56 | 54 | 87 | 22 | 35 | 2 miles southeast by east of Carlisle, Haddon township, Sullivan Co., Ind. |
| 1950 (Inc. Alaska & Hawaii) | | 38 | 48 | 15 | 88 | 22 | 8 | 3 miles northeast of Louisville, Clay County, Ill. |
| 1960 | | 38 | 35 | 58 | 89 | 12 | 35 | 6 1/2 miles northwest of Centralia, Clinton Co., Ill. |
| 1970 | | 38 | 27 | 47 | 89 | 42 | 22 | 5 miles east southeast of Mascoutah, St. Clair County, Ill. |
| 1980 | | 38 | 8 | 13 | 90 | 34 | 26 | 1/4 mile west of De Soto, Jefferson Co., Mo. |
| 1990 | | 37 | 52 | 20 | 91 | 12 | 55 | 9.7 miles northwest of Steelville, Mo. |

(1) West Virginia was set off from Virginia Dec. 31, 1862, and admitted as a state June 20, 1863.

# Race and Hispanic Origin for the United States: 1990 and 1980

Source: Bureau of the Census

| | 1990 Census | | 1980 Census | | Percent change 1980-1990 |
|---|---|---|---|---|---|
| | Number | Percent | Number | Percent | |
| **Race** | | | | | |
| All persons . . . . . . . . . . . . . . . . . . . . . . . . | 248,709,873 | 100.0 | 226,545,805 | 100.0 | 9.8 |
| White . . . . . . . . . . . . . . . . . . . . . . . . . . . . . | 199,686,070 | 80.3 | 188,371,622 | 83.1 | 6.0 |
| Black. . . . . . . . . . . . . . . . . . . . . . . . . . . . . . | 29,986,060 | 12.1 | 26,495,025 | 11.7 | 13.2 |
| American Indian, Eskimo, or Aleut . . . . . . . . . . . . . . . | 1,959,234 | 0.8 | 1,420,400 | 0.6 | 37.9 |
| American Indian . . . . . . . . . . . . . . . . . . . . | 1,878,285 | 0.8 | 1,364,033 | 0.6 | 37.7 |
| Eskimo . . . . . . . . . . . . . . . . . . . . . . . . . . | 57,152 | 0.0 | 42,162 | 0.0 | 35.6 |
| Aleut . . . . . . . . . . . . . . . . . . . . . . . . . . . | 23,797 | 0.0 | 14,205 | 0.0 | 67.5 |
| Asian or Pacific Islander . . . . . . . . . . . . . . . . . . . | 7,273,662 | 2.9 | 3,500,439[1] | 1.5 | 107.8 |
| Chinese . . . . . . . . . . . . . . . . . . . . . . . . . | 1,645,472 | 0.7 | 806,040 | 0.4 | 104.1 |
| Filipino . . . . . . . . . . . . . . . . . . . . . . . . . | 1,406,770 | 0.6 | 774,652 | 0.3 | 81.6 |
| Japanese . . . . . . . . . . . . . . . . . . . . . . . . | 847,562 | 0.3 | 700,974 | 0.3 | 20.9 |
| Asian Indian. . . . . . . . . . . . . . . . . . . . . . . | 815,447 | 0.3 | 361,531 | 0.2 | 125.6 |
| Korean. . . . . . . . . . . . . . . . . . . . . . . . . . | 798,849 | 0.3 | 354,593 | 0.2 | 125.3 |
| Vietnamese . . . . . . . . . . . . . . . . . . . . . . . | 614,547 | 0.2 | 261,729 | 0.1 | 134.8 |
| Hawaiian . . . . . . . . . . . . . . . . . . . . . . . . | 211,014 | 0.1 | 166,814 | 0.1 | 26.5 |
| Samoan . . . . . . . . . . . . . . . . . . . . . . . . . | 62,964 | 0.0 | 41,948 | 0.0 | 50.1 |
| Guamanian . . . . . . . . . . . . . . . . . . . . . . . | 49,345 | 0.0 | 32,158 | 0.0 | 53.4 |
| Other Asian or Pacific Islander . . . . . . . . . . . . | 821,692 | 0.3 | (NA) | (NA) | (NA) |
| Other race . . . . . . . . . . . . . . . . . . . . . . . . . . | 9,804,847 | 3.9 | 6,758,319 | 3.0 | 45.1 |
| **Hispanic Origin** | | | | | |
| Hispanic origin[2] . . . . . . . . . . . . . . . . . . . . . . . | 22,354,059 | 9.0 | 14,608,673 | 6.4 | 53.0 |
| Mexican . . . . . . . . . . . . . . . . . . . . . . . . . | 13,495,938 | 5.4 | 8,740,439 | 3.9 | 54.4 |
| Puerto Rican . . . . . . . . . . . . . . . . . . . . . . . | 2,727,754 | 1.1 | 2,013,945 | 0.9 | 35.4 |
| Cuban . . . . . . . . . . . . . . . . . . . . . . . . . . | 1,043,932 | 0.4 | 803,226 | 0.4 | 30.0 |
| Other Hispanic. . . . . . . . . . . . . . . . . . . . . . | 5,086,435 | 2.0 | 3,051,063 | 1.3 | 66.7 |
| Not of Hispanic origin . . . . . . . . . . . . . . . . . . . . . | 226,355,814 | 91.0 | 211,937,132 | 93.6 | 6.8 |

(NA) Not Available from 1980 100-percent tabulations. (1) The 1980 numbers for Asians or Pacific Islanders shown in this table are not entirely comparable with 1990 counts. The 1980 count of 3,500,439 Asians or Pacific Islanders based on 100-percent tabulations includes only the nine specific Asian or Pacific Islander groups listed separately in the 1980 race item. The 1980 total Asian or Pacific Islander population of 3,726,440 from sample tabulations is comparable to the 1990 count; these figures include groups not listed separately in the race item on the 1980 census form. (2) Persons of Hispanic origin may be of any race.

## Definitions of Race and Hispanic Origin Groups

Source: Bureau of the Census

**Race**

    The concept of race as used by the Census Bureau reflects self-identification. It does not denote any clear-cut scientific definition of biological stock. The data for race represent self-classification by people according to the race with which they most closely identify.

    Persons identified their race by classifying themselves in one of the categories listed, i.e., White, Black, American Indian, Eskimo, Aleut, Chinese, Filipino, Japanese, Asian Indian, Korean, Vietnamese, Hawaiian, Samoan, Guamanian, Other API, or Other race. In cases where persons did not identify with any of the given race categories they were directed to identify as "Other API" ("API" means Asian or Pacific Islander) or "Other race" and write in the name of their race in the space provided. Thus, data for the Asian or Pacific Islander groups not listed on the census questionnaire but contained in Census Bureau tables—Cambodian, Hmong, Laotian, Thai, Bangladeshi, Burmese, Indonesian, Malayan, Okinawan, Pakistani, Sri Lankan, Tongan, Tahitian, Northern Mariana Islander, Palauan, and Fijian—were tabulated from write-in responses.

    The "Other race" category includes persons not included in the race categories described above. Persons reporting in the "Other race" category and providing write-in entries such as a Spanish/Hispanic origin group (i.e., Mexican, Cuban, Puerto Rican) are included here.

**Spanish/Hispanic origin**

    Persons of Spanish/Hispanic origin or descent are those who classify themselves in one of the specific Hispanic origin categories listed on the census questionnaire—for example, Mexican, Puerto Rican, or Cuban—as well as those who indicated that they were of other Spanish/Hispanic origin. Persons reporting "Other Spanish/Hispanic" are those whose origins are from other Spanish-speaking countries of the Caribbean, Central or South America, or from Spain, or persons identifying themselves generally as Spanish, Spanish-American, Hispano, Hispanic, Latino, etc.

    Spanish origin and race are distinct; thus, persons of Spanish/Hispanic origin may be of any race.

## The Census

    On April 1, 1990, the Bureau of the Census began to take the 21st decennial census of the United States. The Census Bureau took the first census in 1790, when it counted 3.9 million people, and has conducted a census every 10 years over the past 200 years, as mandated by the U.S. Constitution, Article 1, Section 2. The primary purpose of the census was, and is, to provide population counts needed to apportion seats in the U.S. House of Representatives, and to subsequently determine state legislative district boundaries. In addition, the findings of the 1990 census are critical to many other federal, state, and local programs, including federal programs that determine compliances with the Voting Rights Act and amendments; allocate funds from federal grant programs; identify areas needing bilingual education; assess the need for equal employment opportunity programs; allocate funds and

analyze programs for American Indians and Alaska Natives; identify areas needing energy assistance; develop programs to reduce unemployment; identify areas needing programs to stimulate economic growth; establish fair lending practices; assess the need for developing or expanding low-income housing programs; and identify areas requiring child assistance programs. For state and local government programs, the census results help develop social services programs, including programs for the elderly and handicapped; assess transportation systems and improve commuting patterns; identify areas for low-cost housing programs; establish occupational and vocational education programs; plan school district boundaries and school construction programs; and assess the need for state housing bonds for below-market interest rates on mortgages.

## U.S. Population by Age, Sex and Household, 1990

Source: Bureau of the Census; 1990 Census

| | | | |
|---|---|---|---|
| Total population . . . . . . . . . . . . . . . | 248,709,873 | **Households by Type** | |
| **Sex** | | Total households. . . . . . . . . . . . | 91,947,410 |
| Male . . . . . . . . . . . . . . . . . . . . . . | 121,239,418 | Family households (families) . . . . . . . . . . . . | 64,517,947 |
| Female. . . . . . . . . . . . . . . . . . . . . | 127,470,455 | Married-couple families. . . . . . . . . . . . . . | 50,708,322 |
| **Age** | | Percent of total households . . . . . . | 55.1 |
| Under 5 years. . . . . . . . . . . . . . . . . | 18,354,443 | Other family, male householder . . . . . . . . . | 3,143,582 |
| 5 to 17 years . . . . . . . . . . . . . . . . . | 45,249,989 | Other family, female householder . . . . . . . . | 10,666,043 |
| 18 to 20 years. . . . . . . . . . . . . . . . . | 11,726,868 | Nonfamily households . . . . . . . . . . . . . . . | 27,429,463 |
| 21 to 24 years. . . . . . . . . . . . . . . . . | 15,010,898 | Percent of total households . . . . . . . . . | 29.8 |
| 25 to 44 years. . . . . . . . . . . . . . . . . | 80,754,835 | Householder living alone . . . . . . . . . . . . | 22,580,420 |
| 45 to 54 years. . . . . . . . . . . . . . . . . | 25,223,086 | Householder 65 years and over . . . . . . . | 8,824,845 |
| 55 to 59 years. . . . . . . . . . . . . . . . . | 10,531,756 | Persons living in households . . . . . . . . . . . . | 242,012,129 |
| 60 to 64 years. . . . . . . . . . . . . . . . . | 10,616,167 | Persons per household . . . . . . . . . . . . . . | 2.63 |
| 65 to 74 years. . . . . . . . . . . . . . . . . | 18,106,558 | | |
| 75 to 84 years. . . . . . . . . . . . . . . . . | 10,055,108 | | |
| 85 years and over. . . . . . . . . . . . . . . | 3,080,165 | | |
| Median age . . . . . . . . . . . . . . . . . | 32.9 | | |
| Under 18 years. . . . . . . . . . . . . . . . . | 63,604,432 | **Group Quarters** | |
| Percent of total population . . . . . . . . | 25.6 | Persons living in group quarters . . . . . . . . . . | 6,697,744 |
| 65 years and over. . . . . . . . . . . . . . . | 31,241,831 | Institutionalized persons . . . . . . . . . . . . . | 3,334,018 |
| Percent of total population . . . . . . . . | 12.6 | Other persons in group quarters. . . . . . . . . | 3,363,726 |

## Projections of Total Population by Race: 1994 to 2050

Source: Bureau of the Census; based upon 1990 Census

| | Total Population (1,000) | | | | By Race (middle series) Number (1,000) | | | | Percent distribution | | | |
|---|---|---|---|---|---|---|---|---|---|---|---|---|
| Year | Lowest series | Middle series | Highest series | Zero migration | White | Black | American Indian[1] | Asian/ Pacific Islander | White | Black | American Indian[1] | Asian/ Pacific Islander |
| 1994 . . | 258,932 | 260,202 | 261,399 | 257,484 | 215,948 | 32,662 | 2,215 | 9,377 | 82.9 | 12.6 | 0.9 | 3.6 |
| 1995 . . | 260,715 | 262,754 | 264,685 | 259,078 | 217,511 | 33,147 | 2,247 | 9,849 | 82.8 | 12.6 | 0.9 | 3.7 |
| 2000 . . | 268,108 | 274,815 | 281,306 | 265,984 | 224,594 | 35,525 | 2,409 | 12,287 | 81.7 | 12.9 | 0.9 | 4.5 |
| 2005 . . | 273,605 | 286,324 | 298,773 | 271,807 | 230,993 | 37,907 | 2,583 | 14,840 | 80.7 | 13.2 | 0.9 | 5.2 |
| 2010 . . | 278,078 | 298,109 | 317,895 | 277,497 | 237,412 | 40,429 | 2,772 | 17,496 | 79.6 | 13.6 | 0.9 | 5.9 |
| 2015 . . | 282,045 | 310,370 | 338,580 | 283,320 | 244,073 | 43,074 | 2,971 | 20,252 | 78.6 | 13.9 | 1.0 | 6.5 |
| 2020 . . | 285,200 | 322,602 | 360,123 | 288,752 | 250,587 | 45,743 | 3,175 | 23,096 | 77.7 | 14.2 | 1.0 | 7.2 |
| 2030 . . | 286,710 | 344,951 | 405,130 | 296,313 | 261,318 | 51,031 | 3,610 | 28,993 | 75.8 | 14.8 | 1.0 | 8.4 |
| 2040 . . | 282,286 | 364,349 | 453,687 | 299,606 | 268,778 | 56,445 | 4,099 | 35,027 | 73.8 | 15.5 | 1.1 | 9.6 |
| 2050 . . | 275,647 | 382,674 | 506,740 | 301,010 | 274,761 | 62,181 | 4,641 | 41,091 | 71.8 | 16.2 | 1.2 | 10.7 |

For the series shown, different assumptions were made regarding fertility rates (lifetime births per woman), life expectancy, and immigration in the coming decades. Yearly net immigration was assumed to be 350,000 for the lowest series; 880,000 for the middle series; and 1,370,000 for the highest series. Immigration is not a factor in the zero migration series. All figures shown are for July 1st of the given year.
[1] American Indian refers to American Indian, Eskimo, and Aleut.

## U.S. Asian and Pacific Islander Population, Social and Economic Characteristics: 1991

Source: Bureau of the Census
(Figures are estimates from March 1, 1991, Sample Survey)

| Characteristics | Total (in thousands)[1] | Percent Distribution[1] |
|---|---|---|
| Total persons . . . . . . | 7,023 | 100.0 |
| Under 5 years old . . . . . . | 606 | 8.6 |
| 5 to 14 years old . . . . . . . | 1,170 | 16.7 |
| 15 to 44 years old . . . . . . | 3,494 | 49.8 |
| 45 to 64 years old . . . . . . | 1,240 | 17.6 |
| 65 years old and over . . . . . | 514 | 7.3 |
| **YEARS OF SCHOOL COMPLETED** | | |
| **Characteristics** | | |
| Persons 25 years old and over . . . . . . . | 4,158 | 100.0 |
| Elementary: 0 to 8 years . . . | 515 | 12.4 |
| High School: 1 to 3 years . . . | 243 | 5.8 |
| 4 years . . . . . . . . . . . . | 1,186 | 28.5 |
| College: 1 to 3 years . . . . . | 591 | 14.2 |
| 4 years or more . . . . . | 1,623 | 39.0 |
| **LABOR FORCE STATUS** | | |
| **Characteristics** | | |
| Civilians 16 years old and over . . . . . . | 5,121 | 100.0 |
| Civilian labor force . . . . . . . | 3,261 | 63.7 |
| Employed . . . . . . . . | 3,054 | 59.6 |
| Unemployed . . . . . . . . | 207 | 4.0 |
| Unemployment rate[2] . . . | 6.3 | (NA) |
| Not in labor force . . . . . . . | 1,860 | 36.3 |

| Characteristics | Total (in thousands)[1] | Percent Distribution[1] |
|---|---|---|
| **FAMILY TYPE AND INCOME IN 1990** | | |
| **Characteristics** | | |
| Total families . . . . . . | 1,536 | 100.0 |
| Married couple . . . . . . . . | 1,230 | 80.1 |
| Female householder, no spouse present . . . . . . | 194 | 12.7 |
| Male householder, no spouse present . . . . . . | 112 | 7.3 |
| Less than $5,000 . . . . . . . . | 60 | 3.9 |
| $5,000 to $9,999 . . . . . . . . | 70 | 4.6 |
| $10,000 to $14,999 . . . . . . . | 88 | 5.7 |
| $15,000 to $24,999 . . . . . . . | 193 | 12.5 |
| $25,000 to $34,999 . . . . . . . | 197 | 12.8 |
| $35,000 to $49,999 . . . . . . . | 303 | 19.7 |
| $50,000 and over . . . . . . . | 626 | 40.7 |
| Median income ($) . . . . . . . | 42,245[3] | (NA) |
| **POVERTY** | | |
| **Characteristics** | | |
| Families below poverty level . . | 169 | 11.0 |
| Persons below poverty level . | 858 | 12.2 |
| **HOUSING TENURE** | | |
| **Characteristics** | | |
| Total occupied units . . | 1,958 | 100.0 |
| Owner-occupied . . . . . . . . | 995 | 50.8 |
| Renter-occupied . . . . . . . . | 947 | 48.4 |
| No cash rent . . . . . . . . . | 15 | 0.8 |

(NA) = not applicable. [1] Due to rounding, figures may not equal totals. [2] Total unemployment as percent of civilian labor force. [3] Number not in thousands.

## Population by State: 1990

Source: Bureau of the Census

| State | 1990 population | Percent change 1980-90 | Minority population 1990 | Minority percent change 1980-90 | State | 1990 population | Percent change 1980-90 | Minority population 1990 | Minority percent change 1980-90 |
|---|---|---|---|---|---|---|---|---|---|
| U.S. . . . . . | 248,709,873 | 9.8% | 60,581,577 | 30.9% | CO. . . . . . | 3,294,394 | 14.0 | 635,449 | 27.2 |
| CA. . . . . . | 29,760,021 | 25.7 | 12,730,895 | 61.1 | CT. . . . . . | 3,287,116 | 5.8 | 532,932 | 43.2 |
| NY. . . . . . | 17,990,455 | 2.5 | 5,530,266 | 25.9 | OK. . . . . . | 3,145,585 | 4.0 | 597,997 | 31.6 |
| TX. . . . . . | 16,986,510 | 19.4 | 6,694,830 | 37.2 | OR. . . . . . | 2,842,321 | 7.9 | 262,589 | 48.3 |
| FL. . . . . . | 12,937,926 | 32.7 | 3,462,600 | 52.3 | IA . . . . . . | 2,776,755 | -4.7 | 112,915 | 24.8 |
| PA. . . . . . | 11,881,643 | 0.1 | 1,459,585 | 13.3 | MS. . . . . . | 2,573,216 | 2.1 | 949,018 | 3.5 |
| IL. . . . . . | 11,430,602 | 0.0 | 2,880,394 | 14.5 | KS. . . . . . | 2,477,574 | 4.8 | 287,050 | 27.5 |
| OH. . . . . . | 10,847,115 | 0.5 | 1,402,493 | 10.4 | AR. . . . . . | 2,350,725 | 2.8 | 417,643 | 2.7 |
| MI . . . . . . | 9,295,297 | 0.4 | 1,645,346 | 11.4 | WV. . . . . . | 1,793,477 | -8.0 | 74,581 | -13.3 |
| NJ . . . . . . | 7,730,188 | 5.0 | 2,011,222 | 30.7 | UT. . . . . . | 1,722,850 | 17.9 | 151,596 | 37.1 |
| NC. . . . . . | 6,628,637 | 12.7 | 1,657,510 | 14.1 | NE. . . . . . | 1,578,385 | 0.5 | 118,290 | 25.2 |
| GA. . . . . . | 6,478,216 | 18.6 | 1,934,791 | 24.9 | NM. . . . . . | 1,515,069 | 16.3 | 750,905 | 21.7 |
| VA. . . . . . | 6,187,358 | 15.7 | 1,485,708 | 27.3 | ME. . . . . . | 1,227,928 | 9.2 | 24,571 | 30.7 |
| MA. . . . . . | 6,016,425 | 4.9 | 736,133 | 66.2 | NV. . . . . . | 1,201,833 | 50.1 | 255,476 | 90.5 |
| IN . . . . . . | 5,544,159 | 1.0 | 578,917 | 7.9 | NH. . . . . . | 1,109,252 | 20.5 | 29,768 | 97.1 |
| MO . . . . . . | 5,117,073 | 4.1 | 668,608 | 10.5 | HI . . . . . . | 1,108,229 | 14.9 | 760,585 | 14.4 |
| WI . . . . . . | 4,891,769 | 4.0 | 427,092 | 42.3 | ID . . . . . . | 1,006,749 | 6.7 | 78,088 | 35.2 |
| TN . . . . . . | 4,877,185 | 6.2 | 849,554 | 9.2 | RI . . . . . . | 1,003,464 | 5.9 | 107,355 | 71.8 |
| WA. . . . . . | 4,866,692 | 17.8 | 645,070 | 58.8 | MT. . . . . . | 799,065 | 1.6 | 65,187 | 24.7 |
| MD. . . . . . | 4,781,468 | 13.4 | 1,455,359 | 32.2 | SD. . . . . . | 696,004 | 0.8 | 61,216 | 14.9 |
| MN. . . . . . | 4,375,099 | 7.3 | 273,833 | 71.7 | DE. . . . . . | 666,168 | 12.1 | 138,076 | 24.2 |
| LA . . . . . . | 4,219,973 | 0.3 | 1,443,951 | 5.8 | ND. . . . . . | 638,800 | -2.1 | 37,208 | 26.1 |
| AL . . . . . . | 4,040,587 | 3.8 | 1,080,420 | 4.1 | DC. . . . . . | 606,900 | -4.9 | 440,769 | -7.0 |
| KY . . . . . . | 3,685,296 | 0.7 | 307,274 | 1.7 | VT. . . . . . | 562,758 | 10.0 | 10,574 | 39.4 |
| AZ . . . . . . | 3,665,228 | 34.8 | 1,039,043 | 50.2 | AK. . . . . . | 550,043 | 36.9 | 143,321 | 47.4 |
| SC. . . . . . | 3,486,703 | 11.7 | 1,096,647 | 10.8 | WY. . . . . . | 453,588 | -3.4 | 40,877 | 8.7 |

*Note: "Minority" includes blacks, Asians, other races, and Hispanics.

## Density of Population by State

Source: Bureau of the Census

(Per square mile, land area only)

| State | 1920 | 1960 | 1980 | 1990 | State | 1920 | 1960 | 1980 | 1990 | State | 1920 | 1960 | 1980 | 1990 |
|---|---|---|---|---|---|---|---|---|---|---|---|---|---|---|
| AL . . | 45.8 | 64.2 | 76.6 | 79.6 | LA . . | 39.6 | 72.2 | 94.5 | 96.9 | OH . . | 141.4 | 236.6 | 263.3 | 264.9 |
| AK*. . | 0.1 | 0.4 | 0.7 | 1.0 | ME . . | 25.7 | 31.3 | 36.3 | 39.8 | OK . . | 29.2 | 33.8 | 44.1 | 45.8 |
| AZ . . | 2.9 | 11.5 | 23.9 | 32.3 | MD . . | 145.8 | 313.5 | 428.7 | 489.2 | OR . . | 8.2 | 18.4 | 27.4 | 29.6 |
| AR . . | 33.4 | 34.2 | 43.9 | 45.1 | MA . . | 479.2 | 657.3 | 733.3 | 767.6 | PA . . | 194.5 | 251.4 | 264.3 | 265.1 |
| CA . . | 22.0 | 100.4 | 151.4 | 190.8 | MI . . | 63.8 | 137.7 | 162.6 | 163.6 | RI . . | 566.4 | 819.3 | 897.8 | 960.3 |
| CO . . | 9.1 | 16.9 | 27.9 | 31.8 | MN . . | 29.5 | 43.1 | 51.2 | 55.0 | SC . . | 55.2 | 78.7 | 103.4 | 115.8 |
| CT . . | 286.4 | 520.6 | 637.8 | 678.4 | MS . . | 38.6 | 46.0 | 53.4 | 54.9 | SD . . | 8.3 | 9.0 | 9.1 | 9.2 |
| DE . . | 113.5 | 225.2 | 307.6 | 340.8 | MO . . | 49.5 | 62.6 | 71.3 | 74.3 | TN . . | 56.1 | 86.2 | 111.6 | 118.3 |
| DC . . | 7,292.9 | 12,523.9 | 10,132.3 | 9,882.8 | MT . . | 3.8 | 4.6 | 5.4 | 5.5 | TX . . | 17.8 | 36.4 | 54.3 | 64.9 |
| FL . . | 17.7 | 91.5 | 180.0 | 239.6 | NE . . | 16.9 | 18.4 | 20.5 | 20.5 | UT . . | 5.5 | 10.8 | 17.8 | 21.0 |
| GA . . | 49.3 | 67.8 | 94.1 | 111.9 | NV . . | .7 | 2.6 | 7.3 | 10.9 | VT . . | 38.6 | 42.0 | 55.2 | 60.8 |
| HI* . . | 39.9 | 98.5 | 150.1 | 172.5 | NH . . | 49.1 | 67.2 | 102.4 | 123.7 | VA . . | 57.4 | 99.6 | 134.7 | 156.3 |
| ID . . | 5.2 | 8.1 | 11.5 | 12.2 | NJ . . | 420.0 | 805.5 | 986.2 | 1,042.0 | WA . . | 20.3 | 42.8 | 62.1 | 73.1 |
| IL . . | 115.7 | 180.4 | 205.3 | 205.6 | NM . . | 2.9 | 7.8 | 10.7 | 12.5 | WV . . | 60.9 | 77.2 | 80.8 | 74.5 |
| IN . . | 81.3 | 128.8 | 152.8 | 154.6 | NY . . | 217.9 | 350.6 | 370.6 | 381.0 | WI . . | 47.6 | 72.6 | 86.5 | 90.1 |
| IA . . | 43.2 | 49.2 | 52.1 | 49.7 | NC . . | 52.5 | 93.2 | 120.4 | 136.1 | WY . . | 2.0 | 3.4 | 4.9 | 4.7 |
| KS . . | 21.6 | 26.6 | 28.9 | 30.3 | ND . . | 9.2 | 9.1 | 9.4 | 9.3 | U.S. . . | *29.9 | 50.6 | 64.0 | 70.3 |
| KY . . | 60.1 | 76.2 | 92.3 | 92.8 | | | | | | | | | | |

* For purposes of comparison, Alaska and Hawaii included in above tabulation for 1920, even though not states then.

## Counties with 1990 Population over 1 Million

Source: Bureau of the Census

| County | April 1, 1990 census | April 1, 1980 census | Percent change, 1980-90 | County | April 1, 1990 census | April 1, 1980 census | Percent change, 1980-90 |
|---|---|---|---|---|---|---|---|
| Los Angeles, CA . . . . . | 8,863,052 | 7,477,238 | 18.5 | San Bernardino, CA . . . | 1,418,380 | 895,016 | 58.5 |
| Cook, IL . . . . . . . . . . | 5,105,067 | 5,253,628 | -2.8 | Cuyahoga, OH . . . . . . . | 1,412,140 | 1,498,400 | -5.8 |
| Harris, TX . . . . . . . . . | 2,818,199 | 2,409,547 | 17.0 | Middlesex, MA . . . . . . . | 1,398,468 | 1,367,034 | 2.3 |
| San Diego, CA . . . . . . | 2,498,016 | 1,861,846 | 34.2 | Allegheny, PA . . . . . . . | 1,336,449 | 1,450,195 | -7.8 |
| Orange, CA . . . . . . . | 2,410,668 | 1,932,921 | 24.7 | Suffolk, NY . . . . . . . . . | 1,321,768 | 1,284,231 | 2.9 |
| Kings, NY . . . . . . . . . | 2,300,664 | 2,231,028 | 3.1 | Nassau, NY . . . . . . . . . | 1,287,444 | 1,321,582 | -2.6 |
| Maricopa, AZ . . . . . . . | 2,122,101 | 1,509,175 | 40.6 | Alameda, CA . . . . . . . . | 1,279,702 | 1,105,379 | 15.8 |
| Wayne, Mi . . . . . . . . | 2,111,687 | 2,337,843 | -9.7 | Broward, FL. . . . . . . . . | 1,255,518 | 1,018,257 | 23.3 |
| Queens, NY . . . . . . . | 1,951,598 | 1,891,325 | 3.2 | Bronx, NY . . . . . . . . . | 1,203,789 | 1,168,972 | 3.0 |
| Dade, FL. . . . . . . . . | 1,937,194 | 1,625,509 | 19.2 | Bexar, TX . . . . . . . . . | 1,185,394 | 988,971 | 19.9 |
| Dallas, TX . . . . . . . . | 1,852,810 | 1,556,419 | 19.0 | Riverside, CA . . . . . . . | 1,170,413 | 663,199 | 76.5 |
| Philadelphia, PA. . . . . | 1,585,577 | 1,688,210 | -6.1 | Tarrant, TX . . . . . . . . | 1,170,103 | 860,880 | 35.9 |
| King, WA. . . . . . . . . | 1,507,305 | 1,269,898 | 18.7 | Oakland, MI . . . . . . . . | 1,083,592 | 1,011,793 | 7.1 |
| Santa Clara, CA . . . . . | 1,497,577 | 1,295,071 | 15.6 | Sacramento, CA . . . . . . | 1,041,219 | 783,381 | 32.9 |
| New York, NY . . . . . . . | 1,487,536 | 1,428,285 | 4.1 | Hennepin, MN . . . . . . . | 1,032,431 | 941,411 | 9.7 |

Los Angeles County, the nation's largest, also had the largest numeric increase, 1.4 million, followed by San Diego and Maricopa (Phoenix) each with over 600,000, and San Bernardino and Riverside each with more than 500,000. New York City encompasses 5 counties, 4 of which exceed a million population. The largest is Kings (Brooklyn), with 2.3 million, followed by Queens, New York (Manhattan), and Bronx. For the first time since 1950, the population of all five counties increased.

## 1990 Population of U.S. Counties, Under Age 18

Source: Bureau of the Census

**Counties with the highest share of residents under age 18, among counties of 10,000 or more; 1990 Census**

The national average for counties' population under age 18 is 26 percent. Thirty-one percent of the nation's 64 million children are members of minorities, who, on average, have more children than do non-Hispanic whites. However, Utah, with only 8.8 percent minority population, has 11 of the 25 counties with the highest share of children. Sixty-nine percent of Utah residents belong to the Church of Jesus Christ of Latter Day Saints, and the birthrate for Mormon women was 2.5 births per woman in 1987, compared with 1.9 nationwide.

| Rank/County, State | Percent under 18 | Rank/County, State | Percent under 18 | Rank/County, State | Percent under 18 |
|---|---|---|---|---|---|
| 1. San Juan, UT | 43.3 | 18. Rolette, ND | 38.2 | 35. Washington, UT | 36.2 |
| 2. Emery, UT | 43.0 | 19. Lincoln, WY | 38.1 | 36. Tooele, UT | 36.2 |
| 3. Duchesne, UT | 43.0 | 20. Sanpete, UT | 38.0 | 37. Holmes, OH | 35.8 |
| 4. Millard, UT | 42.9 | 21. Maverick, TX | 38.0 | 38. Humphreys, MS | 35.8 |
| 5. Apache, AZ | 41.7 | 22. Fremont, ID | 37.9 | 39. Zavala, TX | 35.7 |
| 6. Uintah, UT | 41.4 | 23. Utah, UT | 37.7 | 40. Campbell, WY | 35.7 |
| 7. Box Elder, UT | 40.6 | 24. Glacier, MT | 37.1 | 41. Iron, UT | 35.5 |
| 8. Jefferson, ID | 40.4 | 25. Webb, TX | 36.7 | 42. Deaf Smith, TX | 35.3 |
| 9. Davis, UT | 40.2 | 26. Big Horn, MT | 36.7 | 43. Matanuska-Susitna Borough, AK | 35.3 |
| 10. Uinta, WY | 39.8 | 27. Hidalgo, TX | 36.6 | 44. Cameron, TX | 35.3 |
| 11. Wasatch, UT | 39.5 | 28. Cassia, ID | 36.6 | 45. Roosevelt, MT | 35.2 |
| 12. Starr, TX | 39.4 | 29. Willacy, TX | 36.6 | 46. Bonneville, ID | 35.2 |
| 13. Sevier, UT | 39.3 | 30. Cache, UT | 36.5 | 47. Lagrange, IN | 35.1 |
| 14. Bethel Census Area, AK | 39.0 | 31. Rosebud, MT | 36.5 | 48. Minidoka, ID | 35.1 |
| 15. McKinley, NM | 38.8 | 32. Gaines, TX | 36.4 | 49. Holmes, MS | 35.0 |
| 16. Bingham, ID | 38.6 | 33. San Juan, NM | 36.4 | 50. Frio, TX | 34.8 |
| 17. Navajo, AZ | 38.4 | 34. Dimmit, TX | 36.3 | | |

**Counties with the lowest share of residents under age 18, among counties of 10,000 or more; 1990 Census**

Of the 25 counties with the lowest share of children, 3 are adult resort/vacation areas: Williamsburg, Llano, and Pitkin (Aspen); 8 of the counties are popular Florida retirement places, as is Watauga; 4 (New York, San Francisco, Alexandria, and Arlington) are urban areas that contain high concentrations of affluent single residents; and the other 9 are predominantly rural counties dominated by large colleges or universities.

| Rank/County, State | Percent under 18 | Rank/County, State | Percent under 18 | Rank/County, State | Percent under 18 |
|---|---|---|---|---|---|
| 1. Williamsburg (city), VA | 9.2 | 18. Pasco, FL | 17.9 | 35. Hampshire, MA | 19.3 |
| 2. Radford (city), VA | 12.7 | 19. Montgomery, VA | 17.9 | 36. Washington, DC | 19.3 |
| 3. Arlington, VA | 15.1 | 20. Charlottesville (city), VA | 18.0 | 37. Suffolk, MA | 19.3 |
| 4. Alexandria (city), VA | 15.4 | 21. Centre, PA | 18.3 | 38. Polk, NC | 19.4 |
| 5. Charlotte, FL | 15.6 | 22. McDonough, IL | 18.4 | 39. Tompkins, NY | 19.4 |
| 6. Harrisonburg (city), VA | 15.6 | 23. Monroe, IN | 18.4 | 40. Indian River, FL | 19.4 |
| 7. Sarasota, FL | 15.7 | 24. Hernando, FL | 18.4 | 41. Baxter, AR | 19.4 |
| 8. San Francisco, CA | 16.1 | 25. Fredericksburg (city), VA | 18.6 | 42. Calloway, KY | 19.5 |
| 9. Llano, TX | 16.4 | 26. Highlands, FL | 18.7 | 43. Lee, FL | 19.6 |
| 10. New York, NY | 16.6 | 27. Amador, CA | 18.8 | 44. Palm Beach, FL | 19.6 |
| 11. Pitkin, CO | 16.8 | 28. Orange, NC | 18.9 | 45. Salem (city), VA | 19.7 |
| 12. Watauga, NC | 17.1 | 29. Jackson, IL | 19.0 | 46. Volusia, FL | 19.7 |
| 13. Monroe, FL | 17.4 | 30. Walker, TX | 19.0 | 47. West Feliciana Parish, LA | 19.7 |
| 14. Martin, FL | 17.6 | 31. Flagler, FL | 19.1 | 48. Story, IA | 19.8 |
| 15. Citrus, FL | 17.6 | 32. Marin, CA | 19.1 | 49. Johnson, IL | 19.8 |
| 16. Whitman, WA | 17.8 | 33. Fairfax (city), VA | 19.2 | 50. Macon, NC | 19.8 |
| 17. Pinellas, FL | 17.8 | 34. Manatee, FL | 19.2 | | |

## The 50 Most Racially Diverse Counties in the U.S.

Source: Bureau of the Census

Using 1990 census results, counties were ranked according to the proportions of non-Hispanic whites, non-Hispanic blacks, Hispanics, and non-Hispanic other races. Those areas with proportions nearest to being equal were considered to be among the most diverse.

Fourteen of the 50 most diverse counties have populations of 1 million or more, and 33 are in metropolitan areas. Four of New York City's five boroughs, as well as the counties that contain San Francisco, Los Angeles, Chicago, Houston, San Diego, Miami, Dallas, Philadelphia, San Jose, San Bernardino, and Oakland are on the list.

Of the 60 counties with populations more than 99.5 percent non-Hispanic white in 1990, 12 are in Nebraska, 12 are in North Dakota, 7 are in Kentucky, and 6 are in South Dakota.

| Rank/County | State | Rank/County | State | Rank/County | State |
|---|---|---|---|---|---|
| 1. Queens | New York | 18. Fresno | California | 35. Socorro | New Mexico |
| 2. San Francisco | California | 19. San Joaquin | California | 36. Aleutians West Census Area | Alaska |
| 3. Los Angeles | California | 20. Santa Clara | California | 37. Passaic | New Jersey |
| 4. Kings | New York | 21. San Mateo | California | 38. Pinal | Arizona |
| 5. Alameda | California | 22. Cook | Illinois | 39. Alexandria (city) | Virginia |
| 6. New York | New York | 23. Merced | California | 40. Waller | Texas |
| 7. Bronx | New York | 24. Hoke | North Carolina | 41. Caldwell | Texas |
| 8. Hudson | New Jersey | 25. Chattahoochee | Georgia | 42. San Diego | California |
| 9. Fort Bend | Texas | 26. Kings | California | 43. Liberty | Georgia |
| 10. Cibola | New Mexico | 27. Dallas | Texas | 44. Prince George's | Maryland |
| 11. Harris | Texas | 28. Suffolk | Massachusetts | 45. Wharton | Texas |
| 12. Robeson | North Carolina | 29. Hendry | Florida | 46. Philadelphia | Pennsylvania |
| 13. Solano | California | 30. Matagorda | Texas | 47. Bell | Texas |
| 14. Essex | New Jersey | 31. Graham | Arizona | 48. Otero | New Mexico |
| 15. Dade | Florida | 32. Denver | Colorado | 49. Union | New Jersey |
| 16. Sandoval | New Mexico | 33. San Juan | New Mexico | 50. Coconino | Arizona |
| 17. Monterey | California | 34. San Bernardino | California | | |

## Coastal Counties of the U.S.
Source: Bureau of the Census

According to the Census Bureau, 135 million people, or 54 percent of all Americans, lived in the 672 counties adjacent to the Atlantic and Pacific Oceans, the Gulf of Mexico, and the Great Lakes in 1991. Since 1960, the U.S. coastal population has increased by almost 41 million. This 43 percent increase is slightly faster than the U.S. growth rate of 40.6 percent. It also is much higher than the 38 percent growth rate of the interior U.S.

The most rapid coastal growth since 1960 has occurred along the Pacific and Gulf coasts. In 1991 more than 33.9

million people lived in Pacific coastal counties, while nearly 15.6 million people lived in counties along the Gulf of Mexico. The Pacific and Gulf coast areas showed an increase in population of 89.3 percent and 85.8 percent, respectively. The population of the Atlantic coast increased by a third since 1960. In 1991 an estimated 59.5 million people resided along the Atlantic coast. The fourth major coastal region rims the five Great Lakes. With 26.1 million people in 1991, its population has remained relatively stable since 1960, showing only a 10.3 percent increase.

## Geographical Mobility Rates, By Type of Movement: 1950-1991
(In thousands)
Source: Bureau of the Census

About 17 percent of Americans changed residence between March 1990 and March 1991. Rates of moving are down from the 1950s and 1960s when 20 percent or more of the population moved every year.

Metropolitan areas have shown modest net in-migration from nonmetropolitan areas since the 1980s. Suburbs gained 6.0 million persons from central cities and nonmetropolitan areas between 1990 and 1991 while losing 3.4 million out-migrants. Central cities gained 3.2 million from in-migration but lost 5.7 million movers.

| Mobility period | Total, 1 year old and over | Total movers | Residing in the U.S. at beginning of the period | | | | | | Residing outside the U.S. at beginning of the period |
|---|---|---|---|---|---|---|---|---|---|
| | | | | Different house, same county | Different county | | | | |
| | | | Total | | Total | Same State | Different State | Different region | |
| Number | | | | | | | | | |
| 1990-91 . . . . | 244,884 | 41,539 | 40,154 | 25,151 | 15,003 | 7,881 | 7,122 | 3,384 | 1,385 |
| 1985-86 . . . . | 232,998 | 43,237 | 42,037 | 26,401 | 15,636 | 8,665 | 6,971 | 3,778 | 1,200 |
| 1980-81 . . . . | 221,641 | 38,200 | 36,887 | 23,097 | 13,789 | 7,614 | 6,175 | 3,363 | 1,313 |
| 1975-76 . . . . | 208,069 | 36,793 | 35,645 | 22,399 | 13,246 | 7,106 | 6,140 | 3,279 | 1,148 |
| 1970-71 . . . . | 201,506 | 37,705 | 36,161 | 23,018 | 13,143 | 6,197 | 6,946 | 3,936 | 1,544 |
| 1965-66 . . . . | 190,242 | 37,586 | 36,703 | 24,165 | 12,538 | 6,275 | 6,263 | 3,348 | 883 |
| 1960-61 . . . . | 177,354 | 36,533 | 35,535 | 24,289 | 11,246 | 5,493 | 5,753 | 3,097 | 998 |
| 1955-56 . . . . | 161,497 | 34,040 | 33,098 | 22,186 | 10,912 | 5,859 | 5,053 | (NA) | 942 |
| 1950-51 . . . . | 148,400 | 31,464 | 31,158 | 20,694 | 10,464 | 5,276 | 5,188 | (NA) | 306 |
| Percent | | | | | | | | | |
| 1990-91 . . . . | 100.0 | 17.0 | 16.4 | 10.3 | 6.1 | 3.2 | 2.9 | 1.4 | 0.6 |
| 1985-86 . . . . | 100.0 | 18.6 | 18.0 | 11.3 | 6.7 | 3.7 | 3.0 | 1.6 | 0.5 |
| 1980-81 . . . . | 100.0 | 17.2 | 16.6 | 10.4 | 6.2 | 3.4 | 2.8 | 1.5 | 0.6 |
| 1975-76 . . . . | 100.0 | 17.7 | 17.1 | 10.8 | 6.4 | 3.4 | 3.0 | 1.6 | 0.6 |
| 1970-71 . . . . | 100.0 | 18.7 | 17.9 | 11.4 | 6.5 | 3.1 | 3.4 | 2.0 | 0.8 |
| 1965-66 . . . . | 100.0 | 19.8 | 19.3 | 12.7 | 6.6 | 3.3 | 3.3 | 1.8 | 0.5 |
| 1960-61 . . . . | 100.0 | 20.6 | 20.0 | 13.7 | 6.3 | 3.1 | 3.2 | 1.7 | 0.6 |
| 1955-56 . . . . | 100.0 | 21.1 | 20.5 | 13.7 | 6.8 | 3.6 | 3.1 | (NA) | 0.6 |
| 1950-51 . . . . | 100.0 | 21.2 | 21.0 | 13.9 | 7.1 | 3.6 | 3.5 | (NA) | 0.2 |

(NA) = Not available.

## The 50 Fastest-Growing Metropolitan Areas
Source: Bureau of the Census

| | 1990 population | Percent change 1980-1990 | | 1990 population | Percent change 1980-1990 | | 1990 population | Percent change 1980-1990 |
|---|---|---|---|---|---|---|---|---|
| 1. Punta Gorda, FL | 110,975 | 89.8 | 17. Sarasota-Bradenton, FL . . | 489,483 | 39.6 | 37. Colorado Springs, CO . . | 397,014 | 28.3 |
| 2. Naples, FL . . | 152,099 | 76.9 | 18. Modesto, CA . . | 370,522 | 39.3 | 38. Tampa-St. Petersburg-Clearwater, FL . . . | 2,067,959 | 28.2 |
| 3. Fort Pierce-Port Saint Lucie, FL . . . | 251,071 | 66.1 | 19. Stockton-Lodi, CA . . . . . | 480,628 | 38.4 | | | |
| | | | 20. McAllen-Edinburg-Mission, TX . . | 383,545 | 35.4 | 39. Redding, CA . . | 147,036 | 27.2 |
| 4. Fort Myers-Cape Coral, FL . . | 335,113 | 63.3 | 21. Bakersfield, CA . | 543,477 | 34.8 | 40. Visalia-Tulare-Porterville, CA | 311,921 | 26.9 |
| 5. Las Vegas, NV-AZ . . . . | 852,737 | 61.5 | 22. Sacramento-Yolo, CA . . . . | 1,481,102 | 34.7 | 41. Chico-Paradise, CA . . . . . . . | 182,120 | 26.6 |
| 6. Ocala, FL . . . . | 194,833 | 59.1 | 23. San Diego, CA . | 2,498,016 | 34.2 | | | |
| 7. Orlando, FL . . . | 1,224,852 | 52.2 | 24. Laredo, TX . . . | 133,239 | 34.2 | 42. Los Angeles-Riverside-Orange County, CA CMSA[1] . . . . . | 14,531,529 | 26.4 |
| 8. West Palm Beach-Boca Raton, FL . . . | 863,518 | 49.7 | 25. Jacksonville, NC | 149,838 | 32.9 | | | |
| | | | 26. Merced, CA . . . | 178,403 | 32.6 | 43. Lakeland-Winter Haven, FL . . . | 405,382 | 26.0 |
| 9. Daytona Beach, FL . . . . . . . | 399,413 | 48.1 | 27. Dallas-Fort Worth, TX CMSA[1] . . . . . | 4,037,282 | 32.5 | 44. Santa Fe, NM . . | 117,043 | 25.7 |
| 10. Melbourne-Titusville-Palm Bay, FL . . . . . . . | 398,978 | 46.2 | 28. Atlanta, GA . . . | 2,233,229 | 32.5 | 45. Jacksonville, FL . . . . . . . | 906,727 | 25.5 |
| | | | 29. Reno, NV . . . . | 254,667 | 31.5 | 46. Tucson, AZ . . . | 666,880 | 25.5 |
| 11. Austin-San Marcos, TX . . | 846,227 | 44.6 | 30. Fresno, CA . . . | 755,580 | 30.8 | 47. Fort Collins-Loveland, CO . | 186,136 | 24.8 |
| 12. Myrtle Beach, SC . . . . . . | 144,053 | 42.0 | 31. Fort Walton Beach, FL . . . | 143,776 | 30.8 | 48. Brownsville-Harlingen-San Benito, TX . . . | 260,120 | 24.0 |
| 13. Las Cruces, NM | 135,510 | 40.7 | 32. Barnstable-Yarmouth, MA . . | 134,954 | 30.8 | | | |
| 14. Yuma, AZ . . . . | 106,895 | 40.3 | 33. Bryan-College Station, TX . . | 121,862 | 30.2 | 49. Santa Barbara-Santa Maria-Lompoc, CA . . | 369,608 | 23.7 |
| 15. Phoenix-Mesa, AZ . . . . . . . | 2,238,480 | 39.9 | 34. Panama City, FL | 126,994 | 29.9 | | | |
| 16. San Luis Obispo-Atascadero-Paso Robles, CA . . . . . . . | 217,162 | 39.7 | 35. Anchorage, AK . | 226,338 | 29.8 | 50. El Paso, TX . . . | 591,610 | 23.3 |
| | | | 36. Raleigh-Durham-Chapel Hill, NC | 855,545 | 28.7 | | | |

[1] CMSA = Consolidated Metropolitan Statistical Area.

# Metropolitan Statistical Areas

Source: Bureau of the Census
(MSAs over 400,000 listed by 1990 population)

Metropolitan areas are defined for federal statistical use by the Office of Management and Budget (OMB), with technical assistance from the Bureau of the Census. Most individual metropolitan areas are designated as Metropolitan Statistical Areas (MSAs). Metropolitan areas over 1 million may under specified circumstances be subdivided into component Primary Metropolitan Statistical Areas (PMSAs), in which case the area as a whole is designated a Consolidated Metropolitan Statistical Area (CMSA).

Effective December 31, 1992, the OMB designated 253 MSAs, 62 PMSAs, and 19 CMSAs for the U.S. and Puerto Rico based on standards published in the *Federal Register* on March 30, 1990, and used in the 1990 Census. The revised definition and the results of the 1990 Census established 9 new MSAs, 16 new PMSAs, and 2 additional CMSAs. A new definition, which went into effect June 30, 1993, made some minor additional adjustments.

| MSA | Population | | Percent change 1980 to 1990 |
|---|---|---|---|
| | 1990 census | 1980 census | |
| New York-Northern New Jersey-Long Island, NY-NJ-CT-PA CMSA | 19,342,013 | 18,713,425 | 3.4 |
| Los Angeles-Riverside-Orange County, CA CMSA | 14,531,529 | 11,497,548 | 26.4 |
| Chicago-Gary-Kenosha, IL-IN-WI CMSA | 8,239,820 | 8,114,844 | 1.5 |
| Washington-Baltimore, DC-MD-VA-WV CMSA | 6,727,050 | 5,790,555 | 16.2 |
| San Francisco-Oakland-San Jose, CA CMSA | 6,253,311 | 5,367,900 | 16.5 |
| Philadelphia-Wilmington-Atlantic City, PA-NJ-DE-MD CMSA | 5,892,937 | 5,649,031 | 4.3 |
| Boston-Brockton-Nashua, MA-NH-ME-CT CMSA | 5,455,403 | 5,121,673 | 6.5 |
| Detroit-Ann Arbor-Flint, MI CMSA | 5,187,171 | 5,293,161 | -2.0 |
| Dallas-Fort Worth, TX CMSA | 4,037,282 | 3,046,136 | 32.5 |
| Houston-Galveston-Brazoria, TX CMSA | 3,731,131 | 3,118,480 | 19.6 |
| Miami-Fort Lauderdale, FL CMSA | 3,192,582 | 2,643,766 | 20.8 |
| Seattle-Tacoma-Bremerton, WA CMSA | 2,970,328 | 2,408,749 | 23.3 |
| Atlanta, GA | 2,959,950 | 2,233,229 | 32.5 |
| Cleveland-Akron, OH CMSA | 2,859,644 | 2,938,277 | -2.7 |
| Minneapolis-St. Paul, MN-WI | 2,538,834 | 2,198,190 | 15.5 |
| San Diego, CA | 2,498,016 | 1,861,846 | 34.2 |
| St. Louis, MO-IL | 2,492,525 | 2,414,061 | 3.3 |
| Pittsburgh, PA | 2,394,811 | 2,571,223 | -6.9 |
| Phoenix-Mesa, AZ | 2,238,480 | 1,600,093 | 39.9 |
| Tampa-St. Petersburg-Clearwater, FL | 2,067,959 | 1,613,600 | 28.2 |
| Denver-Boulder-Greeley, CO CMSA | 1,980,140 | 1,741,899 | 13.7 |
| Cincinnati-Hamilton, OH-KY-IN CMSA | 1,817,571 | 1,726,430 | 5.3 |
| Portland-Salem, OR-WA CMSA | 1,793,476 | 1,583,518 | 13.3 |
| Milwaukee-Racine, WI CMSA | 1,607,183 | 1,570,152 | 2.4 |
| Kansas City, MO-KS | 1,582,875 | 1,449,380 | 9.2 |
| Sacramento-Yolo, CA CMSA | 1,481,102 | 1,099,814 | 34.7 |
| Norfolk-Virginia Beach-Newport News, VA-NC | 1,443,244 | 1,200,998 | 20.2 |
| Indianapolis, IN | 1,380,491 | 1,305,911 | 5.7 |
| Columbus, OH | 1,345,450 | 1,214,291 | 10.8 |
| San Antonio, TX | 1,324,749 | 1,088,881 | 21.7 |
| New Orleans, LA | 1,285,270 | 1,304,212 | -1.5 |
| Orlando, FL | 1,224,852 | 804,774 | 52.2 |
| Buffalo-Niagara Falls, NY | 1,189,288 | 1,242,826 | -4.3 |
| Charlotte-Gastonia-Rock Hill, NC-SC | 1,162,093 | 971,447 | 19.6 |
| Hartford, CT | 1,157,585 | 1,080,710 | 7.1 |
| Providence-Fall River-Warwick, RI-MA | 1,134,350 | 1,076,557 | 5.4 |
| Salt Lake City-Ogden, UT | 1,072,227 | 910,222 | 17.8 |
| Rochester, NY | 1,062,470 | 1,030,630 | 3.1 |
| Greensboro-Winston-Salem-High Point, NC | 1,050,304 | 950,763 | 10.5 |
| Memphis, TN-AR-MS | 1,007,306 | 938,777 | 7.3 |
| Nashville, TN | 985,026 | 850,505 | 15.8 |
| Oklahoma City, OK | 958,839 | 860,969 | 11.4 |
| Dayton-Springfield, OH | 951,270 | 942,083 | 1.0 |
| Louisville, KY-IN | 948,829 | 953,520 | -0.5 |
| Grand Rapids-Muskegon-Holland, MI | 937,891 | 840,824 | 11.5 |
| Jacksonville, FL | 906,727 | 722,252 | 25.5 |
| Richmond-Petersburg, VA | 865,640 | 761,311 | 13.7 |
| West Palm Beach-Boca Raton, FL | 863,518 | 576,758 | 49.7 |
| Albany-Schenectady-Troy, NY | 861,424 | 824,729 | 4.4 |
| Raleigh-Durham-Chapel Hill, NC | 855,545 | 664,788 | 28.7 |
| Las Vegas, NV-AZ | 852,737 | 528,000 | 61.5 |
| Austin-San Marcos, TX | 846,227 | 585,051 | 44.6 |
| Birmingham, AL | 840,140 | 815,333 | 3.0 |
| Honolulu, HI | 836,231 | 762,565 | 9.7 |
| Greenville-Spartanburg-Anderson, SC | 830,563 | 744,428 | 11.6 |
| Fresno, CA | 755,580 | 577,737 | 30.8 |
| Syracuse, NY | 742,177 | 722,865 | 2.7 |
| Tulsa, OK | 708,954 | 657,173 | 7.9 |
| Tucson, AZ | 666,880 | 531,443 | 25.5 |
| Omaha, NE-IA | 639,580 | 605,419 | 5.6 |
| Scranton-Wilkes-Barre-Hazleton, PA | 638,466 | 659,387 | -3.2 |
| Toledo, OH | 614,128 | 616,864 | -0.4 |
| Youngstown-Warren, OH | 600,895 | 644,922 | -6.8 |
| Allentown-Bethlehem-Easton, PA | 595,081 | 551,052 | 8.0 |
| El Paso, TX | 591,610 | 479,899 | 23.3 |
| Albuquerque, NM | 589,131 | 485,429 | 21.4 |
| Harrisburg-Lebanon-Carlisle, PA | 587,986 | 556,242 | 5.7 |
| Springfield, MA | 587,884 | 569,777 | 3.2 |
| Knoxville, TN | 585,960 | 546,488 | 7.2 |
| Bakersfield, CA | 543,477 | 403,089 | 34.8 |
| Little Rock-North Little Rock, AK | 513,117 | 474,463 | 8.1 |
| Charleston-North Charleston, SC | 506,875 | 430,346 | 17.8 |
| Sarasota-Bradenton, FL | 489,483 | 350,696 | 39.6 |
| Wichita, KS | 485,270 | 442,401 | 9.7 |
| Stockton-Lodi, CA | 480,628 | 347,342 | 38.4 |
| Mobile, AL | 476,923 | 443,536 | 7.5 |
| Baton Rouge, LA | 470,050 | 444,083 | 5.8 |
| Fort Wayne, IN | 456,281 | 444,772 | 2.6 |
| Columbia, SC | 453,331 | 409,953 | 10.6 |
| Johnson City-Kingsport-Bristol, TN-VA | 436,047 | 433,638 | 0.6 |
| Lansing-East Lansing, MI | 432,674 | 419,750 | 3.1 |
| Kalamazoo-Battle Creek, MI | 429,453 | 420,771 | 2.1 |
| Lancaster, PA | 422,822 | 362,346 | 16.7 |
| Lexington, KY | 405,936 | 370,900 | 9.4 |
| Lakeland-Winter Haven, FL | 405,382 | 321,652 | 26.0 |

Final 1990 census figures showed that the nation had 40 metropolitan areas of at least 1 million population, including 5 that reached that size since 1980. **The 40 areas had 128.2 million people, or 51.5 percent of the U.S. population.** The 1950 census showed only 14 metropolitan areas of 1 million people, and their combined population of about 45 million amounted to less than 30 percent of the national total.

The census showed that the U.S. population living in all metropolitan areas totaled 197,466,567, an increase of just over 20.8 million (11.8 percent) since 1980. The same areas grew by 10.6 percent in the 1970s. The population living outside metropolitan areas totaled 51,243,306, an increase of 2.1 million (3.9 percent). **The metropolitan population in 1990 constituted 79.4 percent of the U.S. total** compared with 76.2 percent in 1980. More than 90 percent of the nation's growth in the 1980s took place in metropolitan areas.

## Population of U.S. Cities

Source: Bureau of the Census (100 most populous cities ranked by April 1990 census; revised April 1993)

| Rank | City | 1990 | 1980 | 1970 | 1960 | 1950 | 1900 | 1850 |
|---|---|---|---|---|---|---|---|---|
| 1 | New York, NY | 7,322,564 | 7,071,639 | 7,895,563 | 7,781,984 | 7,891,957 | 3,437,202 | 696,115 |
| 2 | Los Angeles, CA | 3,485,398 | 2,966,850 | 2,811,801 | 2,479,015 | 1,970,358 | 102,479 | 1,610 |
| 3 | Chicago, IL | 2,783,726 | 3,005,072 | 3,369,357 | 3,550,404 | 3,620,962 | 1,698,575 | 29,963 |
| 4 | Houston, TX | 1,630,553 | 1,595,138 | 1,233,535 | 938,219 | 596,163 | 44,633 | 2,396 |
| 5 | Philadelphia, PA | 1,585,577 | 1,688,210 | 1,949,996 | 2,002,512 | 2,071,605 | 1,293,697 | 121,376 |
| 6 | San Diego, CA | 1,110,549 | 875,538 | 697,471 | 573,224 | 334,387 | 17,700 | ... |
| 7 | Detroit, MI | 1,027,974 | 1,203,368 | 1,514,063 | 1,670,144 | 1,849,568 | 285,704 | 21,019 |
| 8 | Dallas, TX | 1,007,618 | 904,078 | 844,401 | 679,684 | 434,462 | 42,638 | ... |
| 9 | Phoenix, AZ | 983,395 | 789,704 | 584,303 | 439,170 | 106,818 | 5,544 | ... |
| 10 | San Antonio, TX | 935,933 | 785,880 | 654,153 | 587,718 | 408,442 | 53,321 | 3,488 |
| 11 | San Jose, CA | 782,248 | 629,442 | 459,913 | 204,196 | 95,280 | 21,500 | ... |
| 12 | Indianapolis, IN | 741,952 | 700,807 | 736,856 | 476,258 | 427,173 | 169,164 | 8,091 |
| 13 | Baltimore, MD | 736,014 | 786,741 | 905,787 | 939,024 | 949,708 | 508,957 | 169,054 |
| 14 | San Francisco, CA | 723,959 | 678,974 | 715,674 | 740,316 | 775,357 | 342,782 | 34,776 |
| 15 | Jacksonville, FL | 672,971 | 540,920 | 504,265 | 201,030 | 204,517 | 28,429 | 1,045 |
| 16 | Columbus, OH | 632,945 | 564,871 | 540,025 | 471,316 | 375,901 | 125,560 | 17,882 |
| 17 | Milwaukee, WI | 628,088 | 636,212 | 717,372 | 741,324 | 637,392 | 285,315 | 20,061 |
| 18 | Memphis, TN | 610,337 | 646,170 | 623,988 | 497,524 | 396,000 | 102,320 | 8,841 |
| 19 | Washington, DC | 606,900 | 638,432 | 756,668 | 763,956 | 802,178 | 278,718 | 40,001 |
| 20 | Boston, MA | 574,283 | 562,994 | 641,071 | 697,197 | 801,444 | 560,892 | 136,881 |
| 21 | Seattle, WA | 516,259 | 493,846 | 530,831 | 557,087 | 467,591 | 80,671 | ... |
| 22 | El Paso, TX | 515,342 | 425,259 | 322,261 | 276,687 | 130,485 | 15,906 | ... |
| 23 | Nashville-Davidson, TN | 510,784 | 455,651 | 426,029 | 170,874 | 174,307 | 80,865 | 10,165 |
| 24 | Cleveland, OH | 505,616 | 573,822 | 750,879 | 876,050 | 914,808 | 381,768 | 17,034 |
| 25 | New Orleans, LA | 496,938 | 557,927 | 593,471 | 627,525 | 570,445 | 287,104 | 116,375 |
| 26 | Denver, CO | 467,610 | 492,694 | 514,678 | 493,887 | 415,786 | 133,859 | ... |
| 27 | Austin, TX | 465,622 | 345,496 | 253,539 | 186,545 | 132,459 | 22,258 | 629 |
| 28 | Fort Worth, TX | 447,619 | 385,164 | 393,455 | 356,268 | 278,778 | 26,688 | ... |
| 29 | Oklahoma City, OK | 444,719 | 403,213 | 368,164 | 324,253 | 243,504 | 10,037 | ... |
| 30 | Portland, OR | 438,802 | 366,383 | 379,967 | 372,676 | 373,628 | 90,426 | ... |
| 31 | Kansas City, MO | 434,829 | 448,159 | 507,330 | 475,539 | 456,622 | 163,752 | ... |
| 32 | Long Beach, CA | 429,321 | 361,334 | 358,879 | 344,168 | 250,767 | 2,252 | ... |
| 33 | Tucson, AZ | 405,371 | 330,537 | 262,933 | 212,892 | 45,454 | 7,531 | ... |
| 34 | St. Louis, MO | 396,685 | 452,801 | 622,236 | 750,026 | 856,796 | 575,238 | 77,860 |
| 35 | Charlotte, NC | 395,934 | 314,447 | 241,420 | 201,564 | 134,042 | 18,091 | 1,065 |
| 36 | Atlanta, GA | 394,017 | 425,022 | 495,039 | 487,455 | 331,314 | 89,872 | 2,572 |
| 37 | Virginia Beach, VA | 393,089 | 262,199 | 172,106 | 8,091 | 5,390 | ... | ... |
| 38 | Albuquerque, NM | 384,619 | 331,767 | 244,501 | 201,189 | 96,815 | 6,238 | ... |
| 39 | Oakland, CA | 372,242 | 339,337 | 361,561 | 367,548 | 384,575 | 66,960 | ... |
| 40 | Pittsburgh, PA | 369,879 | 423,960 | 520,089 | 604,332 | 676,806 | 321,616 | 46,601 |
| 41 | Sacramento, CA | 369,365 | 275,741 | 257,105 | 191,667 | 137,572 | 29,282 | 6,820 |
| 42 | Minneapolis, MN | 368,383 | 370,951 | 434,400 | 482,872 | 521,718 | 202,718 | ... |
| 43 | Tulsa, OK | 367,302 | 360,919 | 330,350 | 261,685 | 182,740 | 1,390 | ... |
| 44 | Honolulu, HI | 365,272 | 365,048 | 324,871 | 294,194 | 248,034 | 39,306 | ... |
| 45 | Cincinnati, OH | 364,114 | 385,410 | 453,514 | 502,550 | 503,998 | 325,902 | 115,435 |
| 46 | Miami, FL | 358,648 | 346,865 | 334,859 | 291,688 | 249,276 | 1,681 | ... |
| 47 | Fresno, CA | 354,091 | 218,202 | 165,655 | 133,929 | 91,669 | 12,470 | ... |
| 48 | Omaha, NE | 335,719 | 314,255 | 346,929 | 301,598 | 251,117 | 102,555 | ... |
| 49 | Toledo, OH | 332,943 | 354,635 | 383,062 | 318,003 | 303,616 | 131,822 | 3,829 |
| 50 | Buffalo, NY | 328,175 | 357,870 | 462,768 | 532,759 | 580,132 | 352,387 | 42,261 |
| 51 | Wichita, KS | 304,017 | 279,272 | 276,554 | 254,698 | 168,279 | 24,671 | ... |
| 52 | Santa Ana, CA | 293,827 | 203,713 | 155,710 | 100,350 | 45,533 | 4,933 | ... |
| 53 | Mesa, AZ | 288,104 | 152,453 | 63,049 | 33,772 | 16,790 | 722 | ... |
| 54 | Colorado Springs, CO | 281,140 | 215,150 | 135,517 | 70,194 | 45,472 | 21,085 | ... |
| 55 | Tampa, FL | 280,015 | 271,523 | 277,714 | 274,970 | 124,681 | 15,839 | ... |
| 56 | Newark, NJ | 275,221 | 329,248 | 381,930 | 405,220 | 438,776 | 246,070 | 38,894 |
| 57 | St. Paul, MN | 272,235 | 270,230 | 309,866 | 313,411 | 311,349 | 163,065 | 1,112 |
| 58 | Louisville, KY | 269,555 | 298,694 | 361,706 | 390,639 | 369,129 | 204,731 | 43,194 |
| 59 | Anaheim, CA | 266,406 | 219,311 | 166,408 | 104,184 | 14,556 | 1,456 | ... |
| 60 | Birmingham, AL | 265,965 | 288,297 | 300,910 | 340,887 | 326,037 | 38,415 | ... |
| 61 | Arlington, TX | 261,721 | 160,113 | 90,229 | 44,775 | 7,692 | 1,079 | ... |
| 62 | Norfolk, VA | 261,250 | 266,979 | 307,951 | 304,869 | 213,513 | 46,624 | 14,326 |
| 63 | Las Vegas, NV | 258,204 | 164,674 | 125,787 | 64,405 | 24,624 | ... | ... |
| 64 | Corpus Christi, TX | 257,453 | 231,999 | 204,525 | 167,690 | 108,287 | 4,703 | ... |
| 65 | St. Petersburg, FL | 240,318 | 238,647 | 216,159 | 181,298 | 96,738 | 1,575 | ... |
| 66 | Rochester, NY | 230,356 | 241,741 | 295,011 | 318,611 | 332,488 | 162,608 | 36,403 |
| 67 | Jersey City, NJ | 228,537 | 223,532 | 260,350 | 276,101 | 299,017 | 206,433 | 6,856 |
| 68 | Riverside, CA | 226,546 | 170,876 | 140,089 | 84,332 | 46,764 | 7,973 | ... |
| 69 | Anchorage, AK | 226,338 | 174,431 | 48,081 | 44,237 | 11,254 | ... | ... |
| 70 | Lexington-Fayette, KY | 225,366 | 204,165 | 108,137 | 62,810 | 55,534 | 26,369 | 8,159 |
| 71 | Akron, OH | 223,019 | 237,590 | 275,425 | 290,351 | 274,605 | 42,728 | 3,266 |
| 72 | Aurora, CO | 222,103 | 158,588 | 74,974 | 48,548 | 11,421 | 202 | ... |
| 73 | Baton Rouge, LA | 219,531 | 220,394 | 165,921 | 152,419 | 125,629 | 11,269 | 3,905 |
| 74 | Raleigh, NC | 212,050 | 150,255 | 122,830 | 93,931 | 65,679 | 13,643 | 4,518 |
| 75 | Stockton, CA | 210,943 | 149,779 | 109,963 | 86,321 | 70,853 | 17,506 | ... |
| 76 | Richmond, VA | 202,798 | 219,214 | 249,332 | 219,958 | 230,310 | 85,050 | 27,570 |
| 77 | Shreveport, LA | 198,525 | 205,820 | 182,064 | 164,372 | 127,206 | 16,013 | 1,728 |
| 78 | Jackson, MS | 196,637 | 202,895 | 153,968 | 144,422 | 98,271 | 7,816 | 1,881 |
| 79 | Mobile, AL | 196,278 | 200,452 | 190,026 | 194,856 | 129,009 | 38,469 | 20,515 |
| 80 | Des Moines, IA | 193,189 | 191,003 | 201,404 | 208,982 | 177,965 | 62,139 | ... |
| 81 | Lincoln, NE | 191,972 | 171,932 | 149,518 | 128,521 | 98,884 | 40,169 | ... |
| 82 | Madison, WI | 191,262 | 170,616 | 171,809 | 126,706 | 96,056 | 19,164 | 1,525 |
| 83 | Grand Rapids, MI | 189,126 | 181,843 | 197,649 | 177,313 | 176,515 | 87,565 | 2,686 |
| 84 | Yonkers, NY | 188,082 | 195,351 | 204,297 | 190,634 | 152,798 | 47,931 | ... |

| Rank | City | 1990 | 1980 | 1970 | 1960 | 1950 | 1900 | 1850 |
|---|---|---|---|---|---|---|---|---|
| 85 | Hialeah, FL | 188,008 | 145,254 | 102,452 | 66,972 | 19,676 | ... | ... |
| 86 | Montgomery, AL | 187,543 | 177,857 | 133,386 | 134,393 | 106,525 | 30,346 | 8,728 |
| 87 | Lubbock, TX | 186,206 | 173,979 | 149,101 | 126,691 | 71,747 | ... | ... |
| 88 | Greensboro, NC | 183,894 | 170,279 | 144,076 | 119,574 | 74,389 | 10,035 | ... |
| 89 | Dayton, OH | 182,005 | 193,549 | 243,023 | 262,332 | 243,872 | 85,333 | 10,977 |
| 90 | Huntington Beach, CA | 181,519 | 170,505 | 115,960 | 11,492 | 5,237 | ... | ... |
| 91 | Garland, TX | 180,650 | 138,857 | 81,437 | 38,501 | 10,571 | 819 | ... |
| 92 | Glendale, CA | 180,038 | 139,060 | 133,000 | 119,000 | 96,000 | ... | ... |
| 93 | Columbus, GA | 179,278 | 169,441 | 155,028 | 116,779 | 79,611 | 17,614 | 9,621 |
| 94 | Spokane, WA | 177,165 | 171,300 | 170,516 | 181,608 | 161,721 | 36,848 | ... |
| 95 | Tacoma, WA | 176,664 | 158,501 | 154,407 | 147,979 | 143,673 | 37,714 | ... |
| 96 | Little Rock, AR | 175,727 | 158,461 | 132,483 | 107,813 | 102,213 | 38,307 | 2,167 |
| 97 | Bakersfield, CA | 174,820 | 105,611 | ... | 56,848 | ... | ... | ... |
| 98 | Fremont, CA | 173,339 | 131,945 | 100,869 | 43,790 | ... | ... | ... |
| 99 | Fort Wayne, IN | 173,072 | 172,196 | 178,269 | 161,776 | 133,607 | 45,115 | 4,282 |
| 100 | Newport News, VA | 171,439 | 144,903 | 138,000 | 114,000 | 42,000 | ... | ... |

## Cities with Largest Percentage Loss in Population, 1980-1990

Source: Bureau of the Census; 1990 Census

| | City | 1990 | 1980 | Change | | City | 1990 | 1980 | Change |
|---|---|---|---|---|---|---|---|---|---|
| 1. | Gary, IN | 116,646 | 151,968 | −23.2% | 16. | Birmingham, AL | 265,965 | 288,297 | −7.7 |
| 2. | Newark | 275,221 | 329,248 | −16.4 | 17. | Richmond | 202,798 | 219,214 | −7.5 |
| 3. | Detroit | 1,027,974 | 1,203,368 | −14.6 | 18. | Chicago | 2,783,726 | 3,005,072 | −7.4 |
| 4. | Pittsburgh | 369,879 | 423,960 | −12.8 | 19. | Atlanta | 394,017 | 425,022 | −7.3 |
| 5. | St. Louis | 396,685 | 452,801 | −12.4 | 20. | Kansas City, KS | 149,800 | 161,148 | −7.0 |
| 6. | Cleveland | 505,616 | 573,822 | −11.9 | 21. | Baltimore | 736,014 | 786,741 | −6.4 |
| 7. | Flint, MI | 140,761 | 159,611 | −11.8 | 22. | Akron, OH | 223,019 | 237,590 | −6.1 |
| 8. | New Orleans | 496,938 | 557,927 | −10.9 | 23. | Toledo, OH | 332,943 | 354,635 | −6.1 |
| 9. | Warren, MI | 144,864 | 161,134 | −10.1 | 24. | Philadelphia | 1,585,577 | 1,688,210 | −6.1 |
| 10. | Chattanooga, TN | 152,494 | 169,514 | −10.0 | 25. | Dayton, OH | 182,055 | 193,549 | −5.9 |
| 11. | Louisville, KY | 269,555 | 298,694 | −9.8 | 26. | Knoxville, TN | 165,039 | 175,045 | −5.7 |
| 12. | Peoria, IL | 113,504 | 124,160 | −8.9 | 27. | Memphis | 610,337 | 646,170 | −5.5 |
| 13. | Erie, PA | 108,718 | 119,123 | −8.7 | 28. | Cincinnati | 364,114 | 385,410 | −5.5 |
| 14. | Buffalo | 328,175 | 357,870 | −8.3 | 29. | Denver | 467,610 | 492,694 | −5.1 |
| 15. | Macon, GA | 107,365 | 116,896 | −8.2 | 30. | Washington, DC | 606,900 | 638,432 | −4.9 |

## Fastest Growing Cities, 1980-1990

Source: Bureau of the Census; cities of more than 100,000 with the largest percentage increases in population from 1980 to 1990 Census

| | City | Suburb of ... | 1990 | 1980 | % Change |
|---|---|---|---|---|---|
| 1. | Moreno Valley, CA | Riverside | 118,779 | 28,309 | 319.6 |
| 2. | Mesa, AZ | Phoenix | 288,104 | 152,404 | 89.0 |
| 3. | Rancho Cucamonga, CA | Los Angeles | 101,409 | 55,250 | 83.5 |
| 4. | Plano, TX | Dallas | 128,885 | 72,331 | 78.2 |
| 5. | Irvine, CA | Los Angeles | 110,330 | 62,134 | 77.6 |
| 6. | Escondido, CA | San Diego | 108,635 | 64,355 | 68.8 |
| 7. | Oceanside, CA | — | 128,154 | 76,698 | 67.1 |
| 8. | Santa Clarita, CA | Los Angeles | 110,690 | 66,730 | 65.9 |
| 9. | Bakersfield, CA | — | 174,820 | 105,611 | 65.5 |
| 10. | Arlington, TX | Fort Worth | 261,721 | 160,113 | 63.5 |
| 11. | Fresno, CA | — | 354,091 | 217,491 | 62.8 |
| 12. | Chula Vista, CA | San Diego | 135,163 | 83,927 | 61.0 |
| 13. | Las Vegas, NV | — | 258,204 | 164,674 | 56.8 |
| 14. | Modesto, CA | — | 164,746 | 106,963 | 54.0 |
| 15. | Tallahassee, FL | — | 124,773 | 81,548 | 53.0 |
| 16. | Glendale, AZ | Phoenix | 147,864 | 97,172 | 52.2 |
| 17. | Mesquite, TX | Dallas | 101,484 | 67,053 | 51.3 |
| 18. | Ontario, CA | Los Angeles | 133,179 | 88,820 | 49.9 |
| 19. | Virginia Beach, VA | Norfolk | 393,089 | 262,199 | 49.9 |
| 20. | Scottsdale, AZ | Phoenix | 130,075 | 88,622 | 46.5 |
| 21. | Santa Ana, CA | Los Angeles | 293,827 | 204,023 | 44.0 |
| 22. | Stockton, CA | — | 210,943 | 148,283 | 42.3 |
| 23. | Pomona, CA | Los Angeles | 131,723 | 92,742 | 42.0 |
| 24. | Raleigh, NC | — | 212,050 | 150,255 | 41.1 |
| 25. | Irving, TX | Dallas | 155,037 | 109,943 | 41.0 |
| 26. | Aurora, CO | Denver | 222,103 | 158,588 | 40.1 |
| 27. | San Bernardino, CA | — | 164,164 | 118,794 | 38.2 |
| 28. | Santa Rosa, CA | San Francisco | 113,313 | 82,658 | 37.1 |
| 29. | Overland Park, KS | Kansas City | 111,790 | 81,784 | 36.7 |
| 30. | Vallejo, CA | San Francisco | 109,199 | 80,303 | 36.0 |
| 31. | Thousand Oaks, CA | Los Angeles | 104,381 | 77,072 | 35.4 |
| 32. | Salinas, CA | — | 108,777 | 80,479 | 35.2 |
| 33. | Durham, NC | — | 136,612 | 101,149 | 35.1 |
| 34. | Austin, TX | — | 465,622 | 345,890 | 34.6 |
| 35. | Laredo, TX | — | 122,899 | 91,449 | 34.4 |
| 36. | Sacramento, CA | — | 369,365 | 275,741 | 34.0 |
| 37. | El Monte, CA | Los Angeles | 106,162 | 79,494 | 33.6 |
| 38. | Reno, NV | — | 133,850 | 100,756 | 32.8 |
| 39. | Riverside, CA | — | 226,546 | 170,591 | 32.8 |
| 40. | Chesapeake, VA | Norfolk | 151,982 | 114,486 | 32.8 |
| 41. | Tempe, AZ | Phoenix | 141,993 | 106,919 | 32.8 |
| 42. | Oxnard, CA | Los Angeles | 142,560 | 108,195 | 31.8 |
| 43. | Fremont, CA | San Jose/Oakland | 173,339 | 131,945 | 31.4 |
| 44. | Colorado Springs, CO | — | 281,140 | 215,105 | 30.7 |
| 45. | Garland, TX | Dallas | 180,650 | 138,857 | 30.1 |

## Immigration by Country of Last Residence: 1820-1992

Source: U.S. Immigration and Naturalization Service
(In thousands; for fiscal years ending in year shown)

| Country | Total | | | | | | | | Percent | | | |
|---|---|---|---|---|---|---|---|---|---|---|---|---|
| | 1820-1992 | 1961-1970 | 1971-1980 | 1981-1990 | 1988[10] | 1989[11] | 1991[14] | 1992[14] | 1820-1992 | 1961-1970 | 1971-1980 | 1981-1990 |
| All countries* . . | 59,795 | 3,321.7 | 4,493.3 | 7,338.0 | 643.0 | 1,090.9 | 1,827.2 | 974.0 | 100.0 | 100.0 | 100.0 | 100.0 |
| Europe . . . . . . . | 37,401 | 1,123.5 | 800.4 | 761.5 | 71.8 | 94.3 | 146.7 | 153.3 | 62.5 | 33.8 | 17.8 | 10.4 |
| Austria[1] . . . . . . . | 1,836 | 20.6 | 9.5 | 18.9 | 2.5 | 2.8 | 3.5 | 2.9 | 3.1 | 0.6 | 0.2 | 0.3 |
| Belgium . . . . . . | 212 | 9.2 | 5.3 | 6.6 | 0.7 | 0.7 | 0.9 | 1.0 | 0.4 | 0.3 | 0.1 | 0.1 |
| Czechoslovakia . . | 147 | 3.3 | 6.0 | 5.4 | 0.7 | 0.5 | 0.6 | 0.9 | 0.2 | 0.1 | 0.1 | 0.1 |
| Denmark . . . . . . | 372 | 9.2 | 4.4 | 2.8 | 0.6 | 0.6 | 0.6 | 0.8 | 0.6 | 0.3 | 0.1 | 0.1 |
| France . . . . . . | 797 | 45.2 | 25.1 | 92.1 | 3.6 | 4.1 | 4.0 | 4.5 | 1.3 | 1.4 | 0.6 | 1.3 |
| Germany[1] . . . . . . | 7,107 | 190.8 | 74.4 | 159.0 | 9.7 | 10.4 | 10.9 | 12.9 | 11.9 | 5.7 | 1.7 | 2.2 |
| Greece . . . . . . | 709 | 86.0 | 92.4 | 31.9 | 4.7 | 4.6 | 2.9 | 2.2 | 1.2 | 2.6 | 2.1 | 0.4 |
| Hungary[1] . . . . . . | 1,670 | 5.4 | 6.6 | 5.9 | 0.7 | 0.7 | 0.9 | 1.0 | 2.8 | 0.2 | 0.1 | 0.1 |
| Ireland. . . . . . . | 4,742 | 33.0 | 11.5 | 67.2 | 5.1 | 7.0 | 4.6 | 12.0 | 7.9 | 1.0 | 0.3 | 0.9 |
| Italy . . . . . . . . . | 5,415 | 214.1 | 129.4 | 12.3 | 5.3 | 11.1 | 30.3 | 12.0 | 9.1 | 6.4 | 2.9 | 0.2 |
| Netherlands . . . . | 378 | 30.6 | 10.5 | 4.2 | 1.2 | 1.2 | 1.3 | 1.7 | 0.6 | 0.9 | 0.2 | 0.1 |
| Norway[9] . . . . . . | 803 | 15.5 | 3.9 | 83.2 | 0.4 | 0.6 | 0.6 | 0.8 | 1.3 | 0.5 | 0.1 | 1.1 |
| Poland[1] . . . . . . . | 648 | 53.5 | 37.2 | 40.3 | 7.3 | 13.3 | 17.1 | 24.5 | 1.1 | 1.6 | 0.8 | 0.5 |
| Portugal. . . . . . . | 509 | 76.1 | 101.7 | 20.5 | 3.3 | 3.9 | 4.6 | 2.8 | 0.9 | 2.3 | 2.3 | 0.3 |
| Spain . . . . . . . . | 290 | 44.7 | 39.1 | 11.1 | 2.0 | 2.2 | 2.7 | 2.0 | 0.5 | 1.3 | 0.9 | 0.2 |
| Sweden[9] . . . . . . | 1,288 | 17.1 | 6.5 | 8.0 | 1.2 | 1.2 | 1.2 | 1.5 | 2.2 | 0.5 | 0.1 | 0.1 |
| Switzerland. . . . . | 361 | 18.5 | 8.2 | 57.6 | 0.9 | 1.1 | 1.0 | 1.3 | 0.6 | 0.6 | 0.2 | 0.8 |
| USSR[1,3,15] . . . | 3,512 | 2.5 | 39.0 | 18.7 | 1.4 | 4.6 | 31.6 | 37.4 | 5.9 | 0.1 | 0.9 | 0.3 |
| United Kingdom[2] . . . | 5,158 | 213.8 | 137.4 | 159.2 | 14.7 | 17.0 | 16.8 | 21.9 | 8.6 | 6.4 | 3.1 | 2.2 |
| Yugoslavia[16] . . . | 142 | 20.4 | 30.5 | 37.3 | 2.0 | 2.5 | 2.8 | 2.7 | 0.2 | 0.6 | 0.7 | 0.5 |
| Other Europe. . . . | 190 | 9.1 | 18.9 | 7.7 | 0.8 | 0.7 | 1.2 | 6.5 | 0.3 | 0.2 | 0.2 | 0.0 |
| Asia . . . . . . . . . | 6,706 | 427.6 | 1,588.2 | 2,738.1 | 254.7 | 296.4 | 342.2 | 344.8 | 11.2 | 12.9 | 35.2 | 37.3 |
| China[4]. . . . | 968 | 34.8 | 124.3 | 298.9 | 34.3 | 39.3 | 24.0 | 29.6 | 1.6 | 1.0 | 2.8 | 4.1 |
| Hong Kong[4] . . . | 335 | 75.0 | 113.5 | 98.2 | 11.8 | 15.2 | 15.9 | 16.8 | 0.6 | 2.3 | 2.5 | 1.3 |
| India. . . . . . . . . | 533 | 27.2 | 164.1 | 250.7 | 25.3 | 28.6 | 42.7 | 34.8 | 0.9 | 0.8 | 3.7 | 3.4 |
| Iran[4] . . . . . . . . | 194 | 10.3 | 45.1 | 116.0 | 9.8 | 13.0 | 9.9 | 7.0 | 0.3 | 0.3 | 1.0 | 1.6 |
| Israel[4]. . . . . . . | 149 | 29.6 | 37.7 | 44.2 | 4.4 | 5.5 | 5.1 | 5.9 | 0.2 | 0.9 | 0.8 | 0.6 |
| Japan[4] . . . . . . | 480 | 40.0 | 49.8 | 47.0 | 5.1 | 5.4 | 5.6 | 11.7 | 0.8 | 1.2 | 1.1 | 0.6 |
| Korea[4] . . . . . . | 687 | 34.5 | 267.6 | 333.8 | 34.2 | 33.0 | 25.4 | 18.7 | 1.1 | 1.0 | 6.0 | 4.5 |
| Philippines[5] . . . . . | 1,159 | 98.4 | 355.0 | 548.7 | 61.0 | 66.1 | 68.8 | 63.5 | 1.9 | 3.0 | 7.9 | 7.5 |
| Turkey . . . . . . . | 419 | 10.1 | 13.4 | 23.4 | 2.2 | 2.5 | 3.5 | 3.2 | 0.7 | 0.3 | 0.3 | 0.3 |
| Vietnam[6] . . . . . . | 504 | 4.3 | 172.8 | 281.0 | 12.8 | 13.3 | 14.8 | 31.2 | 0.8 | 1.1 | 3.8 | 3.8 |
| Other Asia . . . . . | 1,279 | 36.5 | 176.1 | 631.4 | 53.7 | 74.5 | 126.4 | 122.4 | 2.1 | 1.1 | 3.8 | 8.6 |
| America. . . . . . . . | 14,810 | 1,716.4 | 1,982.5 | 3,615.6 | 294.9 | 672.6 | 1,297.6 | 445.2 | 24.8 | 51.7 | 44.3 | 49.3 |
| Argentina[7] . . . . . | 139 | 49.7 | 29.9 | 27.3 | 2.6 | 3.8 | 4.2 | 4.1 | 0.2 | 1.5 | 0.7 | 0.4 |
| Canada[7] . . . . . . | 4,338 | 413.3 | 169.9 | 158.0 | 15.8 | 18.3 | 19.9 | 21.5 | 7.3 | 12.4 | 3.8 | 2.2 |
| Colombia . . . . . . | 328 | 72.0 | 77.3 | 122.9 | 10.2 | 14.9 | 19.3 | 12.9 | 0.5 | 2.2 | 1.7 | 1.7 |
| Cuba[8] . . . . . . . . | 769 | 208.5 | 264.9 | 144.6 | 16.6 | 9.5 | 9.5 | 10.9 | 1.3 | 6.3 | 5.9 | 2.0 |
| Dominican Rep.[7] . . | 594 | 93.3 | 148.1 | 252.0 | 27.2 | 26.7 | 42.4 | 41.9 | 1.0 | 2.8 | 3.3 | 3.4 |
| Ecuador[7] . . . . . . | 173 | 36.8 | 50.1 | 56.2 | 4.7 | 7.6 | 10.0 | 7.3 | 0.3 | 1.1 | 1.1 | 0.8 |
| El Salvador[7] . . . . | 348 | 15.0 | 34.4 | 213.5 | 12.0 | 57.6 | 46.9 | 26.1 | 0.6 | 0.5 | 0.8 | 2.9 |
| Haiti[8] . . . . . . . | 293 | 34.5 | 56.3 | 138.4 | 34.8 | 13.3 | 47.0 | 10.8 | 0.5 | 1.0 | 1.3 | 1.9 |
| Jamaica[12]. . . . . . | 470 | 74.9 | 137.6 | 208.1 | 20.4 | 23.6 | 23.0 | 18.3 | 0.8 | 2.3 | 3.1 | 2.8 |
| Mexico[7] . . . . . . . | 5,051 | 453.9 | 640.3 | 1,655.7 | 95.2 | 405.6 | 947.9 | 214.1 | 8.4 | 13.7 | 14.3 | 22.6 |
| Other America . . . | 2,308 | 264.4 | 373.8 | 639.3 | 55.3 | 91.6 | 128.4 | 77.3 | 3.9 | 7.9 | 8.3 | 8.7 |
| Africa . . . . . . . . | 393 | 29.0 | 80.8 | 176.8 | 17.1 | 22.5 | 33.5 | 24.7 | 0.7 | 0.9 | 1.8 | 2.4 |
| Oceania[13]. . . . . . | 218 | 25.1 | 41.2 | 45.2 | 4.3 | 5.0 | 7.1 | 6.0 | 0.4 | 0.8 | 0.9 | 0.6 |
| Unknown or Not Reported. . . . . | 269 | 0.1 | — | 1.0 | 0.1 | 0.1 | 0.2 | 0.2 | 4.5 | — | — | — |

* Figures may not add to total due to rounding. Figures include immigrants as well as nonimmigrants and refugees already in the U.S. who subsequently changed their status to immigrants. Nonimmigrants are nonresident aliens admitted to the U.S. for a temporary period. (1) 1938-1945, Austria included with Germany; 1899-1919, Poland included with Austria-Hungary, Germany, and USSR. 1820-1917 includes area occupied by the former Soviet Union. (2) Beginning 1952, includes data for United Kingdom not specified, formerly included with "Other Europe". (3) Europe and Asia. (4) Prior to 1951, included with "Other Asia". (5) Prior to 1951, Philippines included with "Other Asia." (6) Prior to 1953, data for Vietnam not available. (7) Prior to 1951, included with "Other America". (8) Prior to 1951, included with "West Indies". (9) Norway and Sweden were combined from 1820-1868. (10) First full year with Immigration Reform and Control Act of 1986 in effect. (11) Data include 478,814 previously illegal aliens who were granted permanent resident status under section 245A of the Immigration Reform and Control Act of 1986 (IRCA). These aliens are not new residents of the United States. (12) Data for Jamaica not collected until 1953. (13) Includes Australia and New Zealand. (14) Includes IRCA aliens. (15) Figures for 1991 and 1992 include Lithuania, Latvia, Estonia, and other former Soviet republics. (16) 1992 figures include Bosnia and Herzegovina, Croatia, Macedonia, Slovenia, and the Republic of Yugoslavia.

## Immigrants Admitted for Top 10 Metropolitan Areas of Intended Residence: 1992

Source: Immigration and Naturalization Service

| Metropolitan statistical area of intended residence | Total | | Metropolitan statistical area of intended residence | Total | |
|---|---|---|---|---|---|
| | Number | Percent | | Number | Percent |
| Total . . . . . . . . . . . . . . | 973,977 | 100.0 | 6. Washington, DC-MD-VA . . . . | 27,387 | 2.8 |
| 1. Los Angeles-Long Beach, CA . | 129,266 | 13.3 | 7. Houston, TX . . . . . . . . . . . | 27,067 | 2.8 |
| 2. New York, NY . . . . . . . . | 127,875 | 13.1 | 8. San Jose, CA . . . . . . . . . . | 23,537 | 2.4 |
| 3. Chicago, IL . . . . . . . . . . | 37,236 | 3.8 | 9. San Francisco, CA . . . . . . . . | 21,276 | 2.2 |
| 4. Anaheim-Santa Ana, CA . . . . | 34,417 | 3.5 | 10. San Diego, CA . . . . . . . . . . | 20,936 | 2.1 |
| 5. Miami-Hialeah, FL . . . . . . . . | 31,627 | 3.2 | | | |

## Poverty Rate

Source: Bureau of the Census

The poverty rate is the proportion of the population whose income falls below the government's official poverty level, which is adjusted each year to take account of inflation. The national poverty rate of 14.2 percent in 1991 was lower than the recent peak of 15.2 percent reached in 1983, but remained well above the levels reached in any year from 1969 through 1980. Nationwide, children living in poverty increased 22 percent in the 1980s. Children remain overrepresented among the poor, with a poverty rate of 21.8 percent. As a group the elderly are slightly underrepresented. Poverty rates for children under 18 years and persons 18 to 44 years increased between 1990 and 1991.

## Poverty by Family Status, Sex, and Race, 1978 to 1991

Source: Bureau of the Census; in thousands

|  | 1991 No.[1] | 1991 %[2] | 1990 No.[1] | 1990 %[2] | 1986 No.[1] | 1986 %[2] | 1978 No.[1] | 1978 %[2] |
|---|---|---|---|---|---|---|---|---|
| Total poor . . . . . . . . . . . . . . . | 35,708 | 14.2 | 33,585 | 13.5 | 32,370 | 13.6 | 24,497 | 11.4 |
| In families . . . . . . . . . . . . . . | 27,143 | 12.8 | 25,232 | 12.0 | 24,754 | 12.0 | 19,062 | 10.0 |
| Head of household . . . . . . . . . | 7,712 | 11.5 | 7,098 | 10.7 | 7,023 | 10.9 | 5,280 | 9.1 |
| Related children . . . . . . . . . . | 13,658 | 21.1 | 12,715 | 19.9 | 12,257 | 19.8 | 9,722 | 15.7 |
| Unrelated individuals . . . . . . . . | 7,773 | 21.1 | 7,446 | 20.7 | 6,846 | 21.6 | 5,435 | 22.1 |
| In families with a female household-er, no husband present . . . . | 13,824 | 39.7 | 12,578 | 37.2 | 11,944 | 38.3 | 9,269 | 35.6 |
| Head of household . . . . . . . . . | 4,161 | 35.6 | 3,768 | 33.4 | 3,613 | 34.6 | 2,654 | 31.4 |
| Related children . . . . . . . . . . | 8,065 | 55.5 | 7,363 | 53.4 | 6,943 | 54.4 | 5,687 | 50.6 |
| Unrelated female individuals . . . . | 4,762 | 24.5 | 4,589 | 24.0 | 4,311 | 25.1 | 3,611 | 26.0 |
| All other . . . . . . . . . . . . . . . | 13,319 | 7.5 | 12,654 | 7.1 | 12,811 | 7.3 | 9,793 | 5.9 |
| Head of household . . . . . . . . . | 3,551 | 5.6 | 3,330 | 6.0 | 3,410 | 6.3 | 2,626 | 5.3 |
| Related children . . . . . . . . . . | 5,593 | 9.9 | 5,352 | 10.7 | 5,313 | 10.8 | 4,035 | 7.9 |
| Unrelated male individuals . . . . . | 3,012 | 17.3 | 2,857 | 16.9 | 2,536 | 17.5 | 1,824 | 17.1 |
| Total white poor . . . . . . . . . . . | 23,747 | 11.3 | 22,326 | 10.7 | 22,183 | 11.0 | 16,259 | 8.7 |
| In families . . . . . . . . . . . . . . | 17,268 | 9.7 | 15,916 | 9.0 | 16,393 | 9.4 | 12,050 | 7.3 |
| Head of household . . . . . . . . . | 5,022 | 8.8 | 4,622 | 8.1 | 4,811 | 8.6 | 3,523 | 6.9 |
| Female . . . . . . . . . . . . . . | 2,192 | 28.4 | 2,010 | 26.8 | 2,041 | 28.2 | 1,391 | 23.5 |
| Related children . . . . . . . . . | 8,321 | 16.1 | 7,696 | 15.1 | 7,714 | 15.3 | 5,674 | 11.0 |
| Unrelated individuals . . . . . . . . | 5,872 | 18.8 | 5,739 | 18.6 | 5,198 | 19.2 | 4,209 | 19.8 |
| Total black poor . . . . . . . . . . . | 10,242 | 32.7 | 9,837 | 31.9 | 8,983 | 31.1 | 7,625 | 30.6 |
| In families . . . . . . . . . . . . . . | 8,504 | 32.0 | 8,160 | 31.0 | 7,401 | 29.7 | 6,493 | 29.5 |
| Head of household . . . . . . . . . | 2,343 | 30.4 | 2,193 | 24.3 | 1,987 | 28.0 | 1,622 | 27.5 |
| Female . . . . . . . . . . . . . . | 1,834 | 51.2 | 1,648 | 48.1 | 1,488 | 50.1 | 1,208 | 50.6 |
| Related children . . . . . . . . . | 4,637 | 45.6 | 4,412 | 44.2 | 4,039 | 42.7 | 3,781 | 41.2 |
| Unrelated individuals . . . . . . . . | 1,590 | 35.3 | 1,491 | 35.1 | 1,431 | 38.5 | 1,132 | 38.6 |

[1] Beginning in 1980, total includes members of unrelated subfamilies not shown separately. For earlier years, unrelated subfamily members are included in the "in family" category. [2] Percent of total population in that general category who fell below poverty level. For example, of all black female heads of households in 1978, 50.6% were poor.

## Poverty Level by Family Size, 1990 and 1991

Source: Bureau of the Census

|  | 1990 | 1991 |  | 1990 | 1991 |
|---|---|---|---|---|---|
| 1 person . . . . . . . . . . . . . . | $ 6,652 | $ 6,932 | 3 persons . . . . . . . . . . . . . | $ 10,419 | $10,860 |
| Under 65 years . . . . . . . . | 6,800 | 7,086 | 4 persons . . . . . . . . . . . . . | 13,359 | 13,924 |
| 65 years and over . . . . . . . | 6,268 | 6,532 | 5 persons . . . . . . . . . . . . . | 15,792 | 16,456 |
| 2 persons . . . . . . . . . . . . . | 8,509 | 8,865 | 6 persons . . . . . . . . . . . . . | 17,839 | 18,587 |
| Householder under 65 years . | 8,794 | 9,165 | 7 persons . . . . . . . . . . . . . | 20,241 | 21,058 |
| Householder 65 years and over . . . . . . . . . . . . | 7,905 | 8,241 | 8 persons . . . . . . . . . . . . . | 22,582 | 23,605 |
|  |  |  | 9 persons or more . . . . . . . . | 26,848 | 27,942 |

## Persons Below Poverty Level, 1960-1991

Source: Bureau of the Census

|  | Number Below Poverty Level (mil.) | | | | Percent Below Poverty Level | | | | Avg. income cutoffs for nonfarm family of 4 |
|---|---|---|---|---|---|---|---|---|---|
| Year | All races[1] | White | Black | Hispanic origin[2] | All races[1] | White | Black | Hispanic origin[2] | at poverty level[3] |
| 1960 | 39.9 | 28.3 | NA | NA | 22.2 | 17.8 | NA | NA | $3,022 |
| 1965 | 33.2 | 22.5 | NA | NA | 17.3 | 13.3 | NA | NA | 3,223 |
| 1970 | 25.4 | 17.5 | 7.5 | NA | 12.6 | 9.9 | 33.5 | NA | 3,968 |
| 1975 | 25.9 | 17.8 | 7.5 | 3.0 | 12.3 | 9.7 | 31.3 | 26.9 | 5,500 |
| 1980[4] | 29.3 | 19.7 | 8.6 | 3.5 | 13.0 | 10.2 | 32.5 | 25.7 | 8,414 |
| 1986[4] | 32.4 | 22.2 | 9.0 | 5.1 | 13.6 | 11.0 | 31.1 | 27.3 | 11,203 |
| 1989 | 31.5 | 20.8 | 9.3 | 5.4 | 12.8 | 10.0 | 30.7 | 26.2 | 12,674 |
| 1990 | 33.6 | 22.3 | 9.8 | 6.0 | 13.5 | 10.7 | 31.9 | 28.1 | 13,359 |
| 1991 | 35.7 | 23.7 | 10.2 | 6.3 | 14.2 | 11.3 | 32.7 | 28.7 | 13,924 |

NA = Not Available. [1] Includes other races not shown separately. [2] Persons of Hispanic origin may be of any race. [3] Beginning in 1981, income cutoffs for nonfarm families are applied to both farm and nonfarm families. [4] Data based on revised poverty definition.

## Income Distribution by Population Fifths

Source: Bureau of the Census

| Families, 1991 Race | Upper limit of each fifth[1] | | | | | Percent distribution of total income | | | | | |
|---|---|---|---|---|---|---|---|---|---|---|---|
|  | Lowest | Second | Third | Fourth | Top 5%[2] | Lowest fifth | Second fifth | Third fifth | Fourth fifth | Highest fifth | Top 5% |
| Total . . . . . . . . . . . | $17,000 | $29,111 | $43,000 | $62,991 | $102,824 | 4.5 | 10.7 | 16.6 | 24.1 | 44.2 | 17.1 |
| White . . . . . . . . . . | 18,922 | 31,000 | 44,874 | 64,950 | 106,119 | 5.0 | 11.0 | 16.7 | 23.8 | 43.4 | 16.8 |
| Black . . . . . . . . . . | 7,780 | 16,000 | 27,530 | 43,900 | 72,800 | 3.2 | 8.4 | 15.7 | 25.4 | 47.4 | 17.3 |

[1] The highest fifth does not have an upper limit. [2] Lower limit for top 5%.

## Aid to Families with Dependent Children

Source: Admin. for Children and Families, Office of Family Assistance, U.S. Dept. of Health and Human Services

| FY 1992 State | Total Assistance Payments[1] | Average Monthly Caseload | Average Monthly Recipients | Average Monthly Children | Average Payment per Family | Average Payment per Person |
|---|---|---|---|---|---|---|
| Alabama | $85,459 | 50,631 | 141,941 | 100,722 | $140.66 | $50.17 |
| Alaska | 96,389 | 10,808 | 31,919 | 20,243 | 743.22 | 251.65 |
| Arizona | 243,261 | 63,598 | 180,501 | 125,908 | 318.75 | 112.31 |
| Arkansas | 60,549 | 26,769 | 73,112 | 53,422 | 188.49 | 67.18 |
| California | 5,865,131 | 806,086 | 2,306,509 | 1,601,785 | 606.34 | 211.91 |
| Colorado | 162,497 | 42,081 | 122,379 | 81,504 | 321.79 | 110.65 |
| Connecticut | 376,890 | 55,500 | 156,989 | 105,087 | 565.91 | 200.06 |
| Delaware | 37,341 | 10,661 | 26,450 | 17,925 | 291.88 | 117.65 |
| Dist. of Columbia | 102,849 | 22,566 | 59,997 | 42,171 | 379.80 | 142.85 |
| Florida | 738,540 | 221,205 | 601,172 | 416,910 | 278.23 | 102.38 |
| Georgia | 421,812 | 135,972 | 388,022 | 268,271 | 258.52 | 90.59 |
| Guam | 7,834 | 1,283 | 4,574 | 3,249 | 508.94 | 142.74 |
| Hawaii | 125,495 | 16,350 | 50,424 | 33,686 | 632.67 | 207.40 |
| Idaho | 24,013 | 7,335 | 19,708 | 13,258 | 272.81 | 101.54 |
| Illinois | 898,275 | 228,625 | 687,572 | 471,798 | 327.42 | 108.87 |
| Indiana | 218,662 | 69,134 | 199,264 | 133,042 | 263.57 | 91.45 |
| Iowa | 164,283 | 37,081 | 102,540 | 66,981 | 369.20 | 133.51 |
| Kansas | 119,209 | 28,741 | 84,639 | 56,677 | 345.64 | 117.37 |
| Kentucky | 213,634 | 83,133 | 229,444 | 147,082 | 214.17 | 77.60 |
| Louisiana | 186,427 | 92,900 | 273,747 | 195,487 | 168.30 | 56.75 |
| Maine | 118,316 | 23,920 | 68,108 | 42,344 | 412.20 | 144.77 |
| Maryland | 333,195 | 79,807 | 220,837 | 148,841 | 347.92 | 125.73 |
| Massachusetts | 751,170 | 111,448 | 309,786 | 208,026 | 561.68 | 202.07 |
| Michigan | 1,160,829 | 225,609 | 674,235 | 440,943 | 428.78 | 143.47 |
| Minnesota | 388,592 | 63,656 | 191,797 | 123,073 | 508.71 | 168.84 |
| Mississippi | 88,721 | 60,810 | 177,325 | 127,717 | 121.58 | 41.69 |
| Missouri | 281,769 | 85,176 | 230,690 | 164,336 | 275.67 | 93.66 |
| Montana | 45,658 | 10,909 | 32,154 | 20,659 | 348.77 | 118.33 |
| Nebraska | 65,389 | 16,551 | 48,187 | 32,623 | 329.24 | 113.08 |
| Nevada | 41,020 | 11,867 | 32,198 | 22,347 | 288.06 | 106.17 |
| New Hampshire | 54,474 | 10,500 | 28,273 | 17,915 | 432.33 | 160.56 |
| New Jersey | 511,893 | 125,847 | 352,710 | 240,970 | 338.95 | 120.94 |
| New Mexico | 105,473 | 28,764 | 87,806 | 56,926 | 305.57 | 100.10 |
| New York | 2,587,058 | 397,172 | 1,116,986 | 742,555 | 542.81 | 193.01 |
| North Carolina | 336,577 | 121,427 | 313,479 | 209,535 | 230.99 | 89.47 |
| North Dakota | 27,513 | 6,394 | 18,258 | 11,853 | 358.60 | 125.58 |
| Ohio | 983,959 | 264,271 | 749,076 | 489,028 | 310.27 | 109.46 |
| Oklahoma | 169,652 | 46,837 | 134,865 | 91,998 | 301.85 | 104.83 |
| Oregon | 200,252 | 41,460 | 116,072 | 76,249 | 402.50 | 143.77 |
| Pennsylvania | 924,821 | 200,699 | 593,928 | 396,569 | 384.00 | 129.76 |
| Puerto Rico | 77,338 | 61,375 | 194,389 | 132,321 | 105.01 | 33.15 |
| Rhode Island | 128,776 | 21,289 | 59,396 | 38,919 | 504.09 | 180.67 |
| South Carolina | 119,225 | 49,710 | 139,553 | 99,573 | 199.87 | 71.19 |
| South Dakota | 25,255 | 7,223 | 20,368 | 14,351 | 291.38 | 103.33 |
| Tennessee | 206,251 | 95,179 | 266,125 | 179,520 | 180.58 | 64.58 |
| Texas | 517,857 | 265,819 | 757,948 | 528,338 | 162.35 | 56.94 |
| Utah | 75,567 | 17,882 | 51,829 | 34,482 | 352.07 | 121.47 |
| Vermont | 67,207 | 10,047 | 28,987 | 17,697 | 557.44 | 193.21 |
| Virgin Islands | 3,503 | 1,053 | 3,767 | 2,801 | 277.21 | 77.49 |
| Virginia | 224,816 | 70,677 | 188,442 | 129,000 | 265.07 | 99.42 |
| Washington | 569,517 | 96,407 | 273,466 | 175,910 | 492.28 | 173.55 |
| West Virginia | 120,655 | 40,469 | 118,609 | 73,353 | 248.45 | 84.77 |
| Wisconsin | 453,707 | 81,680 | 243,857 | 139,896 | 426.89 | 155.05 |
| Wyoming | 27,159 | 6,625 | 18,935 | 12,604 | 341.63 | 119.53 |
| U.S. Total | $21,941,692 | 4,768,495 | 13,625,342 | 9,200,516 | $383.45 | $134.20 |

(1) Numbers are in thousands. Total assistance payments include AFDC-Basic, AFDC-Unemployed Parent, Title IV-A Payments under JOBS, Home Repair, and payments to Indian tribes.

## Some Notable Cities, Population Under 5,000

Unless otherwise noted all population figures are from the Bureau of the Census. The number of annual visitors is from local sources, such as chambers of commerce or convention and visitors bureaus.

| ZIP Code | Place | 1990 Pop. | Attraction | Estimated Visitors Annually |
|---|---|---|---|---|
| 52203 | Amana, IA | 1,700[1] | historic communal village | 1,500,000 |
| 04609 | Bar Harbor, ME | 4,443 | summer resort; borders Acadia National Park and other recreational areas | 4,000,000 |
| 65616 | Branson, MO | 3,706 | country music center; 32 indoor theaters, 3 theme parks, and 3 outdoor amphitheaters | 5,000,000 |
| 93921* | Carmel-by-the-Sea, CA | 4,239 | artist community and resort | 1,500,000 |
| 98611 | Castle Rock, WA | 2,067 | Mount St. Helens National Volcanic Monument | 1,500,000 |
| 37738 | Gatlinburg, TN | 3,417 | Tourist office for the Great Smoky Mountains | 9,000,000[2] |
| 57751 | Keystone, SD | 232 | gateway to Mount Rushmore National Memorial | 2,500,000 |
| 87571 | Taos, NM | 4,065 | Indian pueblo; skiing and outdoor recreation; artists' and writers' colony | 2,500,000 |
| 89440 | Virginia City, NV | 788 | former mining town | 1,500,000 |
| 54758 | West Yellowstone, MT | 913 | West entrance to Yellowstone National Park | 2,000,000 |

* More than one ZIP code for this area. [1] Estimated population. [2] Figure for entire national park.

# U.S. Places of 5,000 or More Population—With ZIP and Area Codes

Source: Bureau of the Census. 1990 Census; updated as of April 1993

This listing presents the official 1990 Census counts. They show the official urban population of the United States. "Urban population" is defined as all persons living in (a) places of 5,000 inhabitants or more incorporated as cities, villages, boroughs (except Alaska), and towns (except in New England, New York, New Jersey, Pennsylvania, and Wisconsin), but excluding those persons living in the rural portions of extended cities; (b) unincorporated places of 5,000 inhabitants or more; and (c) other territory, incorporated or unincorporated, included in urbanized areas.

The non-urban portion of an extended city contains one or more areas at least 5 square miles in extent and with a population density of less than 100 persons per square mile. The area or areas constitute at least 25 percent of the legal city's land area of a total of 25 square miles or more.

In New England, New York, New Jersey, Pennsylvania, and Wisconsin, minor civil divisions called "towns" often include rural areas and one or more urban areas. Only the urban areas of these "towns" are included here, except in the case of New England where entire town populations, which may include some rural population, are shown; these towns are indicated by italics. Boroughs in Alaska may contain one or more urban areas which are included here. Population in Hawaii is counted by county subdivisions.

(u) means place is unincorporated.

*The ZIP Code of each place appears before the name of that place, if it is obtainable. Telephone Area Code appears in parentheses after the name of the state or, if a state has more than one number, after the name of the place. Please be aware some cities have more than one area code.*

CAUTION—Where an asterisk (*) appears before the ZIP Code, ask your local postmaster for the correct ZIP Code for a specific address within the place listed.

## Alabama (205)

| ZIP code | Place | 1990 | 1980 |
|---|---|---|---|
| 35007 | Alabaster. . . . . . . . . . . . . . | 14,738 | 7,079 |
| 35950 | Albertville . . . . . . . . . . . | 14,507 | 12,039 |
| 35010 | Alexander City. . . . . . . . . | 14,917 | 13,807 |
| 36420 | Andalusia . . . . . . . . . . . | 9,269 | 10,415 |
| 36201 | Anniston . . . . . . . . . . . . | 26,634 | 29,135 |
| 35016 | Arab . . . . . . . . . . . . . | 6,321 | 6,053 |
| 35611 | Athens . . . . . . . . . . . . | 16,901 | 14,558 |
| 36502 | Atmore . . . . . . . . . . . . | 8,046 | 8,789 |
| 35954 | Attalla . . . . . . . . . . . . | 6,859 | 7,737 |
| 36830 | Auburn . . . . . . . . . . . | 33,830 | 28,471 |
| 36507 | Bay Minette . . . . . . . . | 7,168 | 7,455 |
| 35020 | Bessemer . . . . . . . . . . | 33,497 | 31,729 |
| *35203 | Birmingham . . . . . . . . | 265,985 | 288,297 |
| 35957 | Boaz . . . . . . . . . . . . | 6,928 | 7,151 |
| 36426 | Brewton . . . . . . . . . . | 5,885 | 6,680 |
| 35215 | Center Point(u) . . . . . . . | 22,658 | 23,317 |
| 36611 | Chickasaw. . . . . . . . . . | 6,649 | 7,402 |
| 35045 | Clanton. . . . . . . . . . . | 7,669 | 5,832 |
| 35055 | Cullman . . . . . . . . . . | 13,367 | 13,084 |
| 36362 | Daleville . . . . . . . . . . | 5,117 | 4,250 |
| 36526 | Daphne . . . . . . . . . . . | 11,291 | 3,406 |
| 35601 | Decatur. . . . . . . . . . . | 48,778 | 42,002 |
| 36732 | Demopolis . . . . . . . . . | 7,512 | 7,678 |
| 36301 | Dothan . . . . . . . . . . . | 53,721 | 48,750 |
| 36330 | Enterprise . . . . . . . . . | 20,119 | 18,033 |
| 36027 | Eufaula . . . . . . . . . . . | 13,220 | 12,097 |
| 35064 | Fairfield. . . . . . . . . . | 12,200 | 13,242 |
| 36532 | Fairhope . . . . . . . . . . | 8,490 | 7,286 |
| 35630 | Florence . . . . . . . . . . | 36,426 | 37,029 |
| 35214 | Forestdale(u) . . . . . . . . | 10,395 | 10,814 |
| 35967 | Fort Payne. . . . . . . . . | 11,838 | 11,485 |
| 36360 | Fort Rucker(u). . . . . . . | 7,593 | 8,932 |
| 35068 | Fultondale . . . . . . . . . | 6,400 | 6,217 |
| *35901 | Gadsden . . . . . . . . . . | 42,523 | 47,565 |
| 35071 | Gardendale . . . . . . . . | 9,251 | 8,005 |
| 36037 | Greenville . . . . . . . . . | 7,492 | 7,807 |
| 35976 | Guntersville . . . . . . . . | 7,038 | 7,041 |
| 35570 | Hamilton . . . . . . . . . | 5,787 | 5,093 |
| 35640 | Hartselle . . . . . . . . . . | 10,867 | 8,858 |
| 35209 | Homewood . . . . . . . . . | 23,644 | 21,412 |
| 35226 | Hoover . . . . . . . . . . . | 39,785 | 18,996 |
| 35020 | Hueytown . . . . . . . . . | 15,280 | 13,452 |
| *35804 | Huntsville . . . . . . . . . | 159,880 | 142,513 |
| 35210 | Irondale . . . . . . . . . . | 9,454 | 6,510 |
| 36545 | Jackson . . . . . . . . . . | 5,819 | 6,073 |
| 36265 | Jacksonville . . . . . . . . | 10,283 | 9,735 |
| 35501 | Jasper . . . . . . . . . . . | 13,553 | 11,894 |
| 36863 | Lanett . . . . . . . . . . . | 8,985 | 8,922 |
| 35094 | Leeds. . . . . . . . . . . . | 10,009 | 8,638 |
| 35758 | Madison . . . . . . . . . . | 14,792 | 4,057 |
| 35228 | Midfield. . . . . . . . . . | 5,559 | 6,182 |
| 36054 | Millbrook . . . . . . . . . | 6,046 | 3,101 |
| *36601 | Mobile . . . . . . . . . . . | 196,278 | 200,452 |
| 36460 | Monroeville . . . . . . . . | 6,993 | 5,674 |
| *36104 | Montgomery . . . . . . . . | 187,543 | 177,857 |
| 35223 | Mountain Brook . . . . . . | 19,810 | 19,718 |
| 35660 | Muscle Shoals. . . . . . . | 9,611 | 8,911 |
| 35476 | Northport. . . . . . . . . | 17,297 | 14,291 |
| 36801 | Opelika. . . . . . . . . . | 22,122 | 21,896 |
| 36467 | Opp. . . . . . . . . . . . | 6,985 | 7,204 |
| 36203 | Oxford . . . . . . . . . . | 9,603 | 8,939 |
| 36360 | Ozark. . . . . . . . . . . | 13,030 | 13,188 |
| 35124 | Pelham . . . . . . . . . . . | 9,421 | 6,759 |
| 35125 | Pell City . . . . . . . . . . | 7,945 | 6,616 |

| ZIP code | Place | 1990 | 1980 |
|---|---|---|---|
| 36867 | Phenix City. . . . . . . . . . | 25,311 | 26,928 |
| 36272 | Piedmont. . . . . . . . . . . | 5,347 | 5,544 |
| 35126 | Pinson-Clay-Chalkville(u) . . . . | 10,987 | .... |
| 35127 | Pleasant Grove . . . . . . . | 8,458 | 7,102 |
| 36067 | Prattville . . . . . . . . . . | 19,816 | 18,647 |
| 36610 | Prichard . . . . . . . . . . | 34,320 | 39,541 |
| 35901 | Rainbow City . . . . . . . . | 7,667 | 6,299 |
| 36274 | Roanoke . . . . . . . . . . | 6,362 | 5,809 |
| 35653 | Russellville. . . . . . . . . | 7,812 | 8,195 |
| 36201 | Saks(u). . . . . . . . . . . | 11,138 | 11,118 |
| 36571 | Saraland . . . . . . . . . . | 11,760 | 9,833 |
| 36572 | Satsuma . . . . . . . . . . | 5,194 | 3,822 |
| 35768 | Scottsboro . . . . . . . . . | 13,786 | 14,758 |
| 36701 | Selma . . . . . . . . . . . | 23,755 | 26,684 |
| 35660 | Sheffield . . . . . . . . . . | 10,380 | 11,903 |
| 35901 | Southside . . . . . . . . . | 5,580 | 5,141 |
| 35150 | Sylacauga . . . . . . . . . | 12,520 | 12,708 |
| 35160 | Talladega . . . . . . . . . | 18,175 | 19,128 |
| 36045 | Tallassee. . . . . . . . . . | 5,112 | 4,763 |
| 35217 | Tarrant City. . . . . . . . | 8,046 | 8,148 |
| 36582 | Theodore(u) . . . . . . . . | 6,509 | 6,392 |
| 36619 | Tillman's Corner(u) . . . . . . | 17,988 | 15,941 |
| 36081 | Troy. . . . . . . . . . . . | 13,051 | 13,124 |
| 35173 | Trussville. . . . . . . . . . | 8,283 | 3,507 |
| 35401 | Tuscaloosa . . . . . . . . . | 77,759 | 75,211 |
| 35674 | Tuscumbia . . . . . . . . . | 8,413 | 9,137 |
| 36083 | Tuskegee . . . . . . . . . | 12,257 | 13,327 |
| 36858 | Valley. . . . . . . . . . . | 8,215 | 8,946 |
| 35216 | Vestavia Hills . . . . . . . | 19,554 | 15,722 |

### Alaska (907)

| ZIP code | Place | 1990 | 1980 |
|---|---|---|---|
| *99502 | Anchorage . . . . . . . . . . | 226,338 | 174,431 |
| 99708 | College. . . . . . . . . . . | 11,249 | 4,043 |
| 99702 | Eielson AFB(u) . . . . . . . | 5,251 | 5,232 |
| *99701 | Fairbanks . . . . . . . . . | 30,843 | 22,645 |
| 99801 | Juneau . . . . . . . . . . | 26,751 | 19,528 |
| 99611 | Kenai. . . . . . . . . . . | 6,327 | 4,324 |
| 99901 | Ketchikan . . . . . . . . . | 8,263 | 7,198 |
| 99615 | Kodiak . . . . . . . . . . | 6,365 | 4,756 |
| 99639 | Ninilchik(u) . . . . . . . . | 10,523 | 341 |
| 99835 | Sitka . . . . . . . . . . . | 8,588 | 7,803 |

### Arizona (602)

| ZIP code | Place | 1990 | 1980 |
|---|---|---|---|
| 85220 | Apache Junction . . . . . . | 18,092 | 9,935 |
| 85323 | Avondale. . . . . . . . . . | 16,169 | 8,168 |
| 85603 | Bisbee . . . . . . . . . . | 6,288 | 7,154 |
| 85326 | Buckeye . . . . . . . . . . | 5,038 | 3,434 |
| 86430 | Bullhead City . . . . . . . | 21,951 | 10,719 |
| 86322 | Camp Verde . . . . . . . . | 6,243 | 3,824 |
| 85222 | Casa Grande . . . . . . . . | 19,076 | 14,971 |
| *85224 | Chandler . . . . . . . . . | 89,862 | 29,673 |
| 86503 | Chinle(u) . . . . . . . . . | 5,059 | 2,815 |
| 85228 | Coolidge . . . . . . . . . | 6,934 | 6,851 |
| 86326 | Cottonwood . . . . . . . . | 5,918 | 4,550 |
| ..... | Cottonwood-Verde Village(u) . . . | 7,037 | .... |
| 85607 | Douglas . . . . . . . . . . | 13,137 | 13,058 |

| ZIP code | Place | 1990 | 1980 |
|---|---|---|---|
| 85335 | El Mirage. . . . . . . . . . . . . . | 5,001 | 4,307 |
| 85231 | Eloy. . . . . . | 7,211 | 6,240 |
| *85001 | Flagstaff . . . . . . . . . . . | 45,857 | 34,743 |
| 85232 | Florence . . . . . . . . . . . | 7,510 | 3,391 |
| 85726 | Flowing Wells . . . . . . . . | 14,013 | .... |
| ..... | Fortuna Foothills(u) . . . . . . | 7,737 | .... |
| 85268 | Fountain Hills . . . . . . . . | 10,030 | 2,771 |
| 85234 | Gilbert . . . . . . . . . . . | 29,122 | 5,717 |
| *85301 | Glendale . . . . . . . . . | 147,864 | 97,172 |
| 85501 | Globe. . . . . . . . . . . | 6,062 | 6,886 |
| 85323 | Goodyear . . . . . . . . . | 6,258 | 2,747 |
| 85614 | Green Valley(u) . . . . . | 13,231 | 7,999 |
| 85283 | Guadalupe . . . . . . . . | 5,458 | 4,506 |
| 86401 | Kingman . . . . . . . . . | 12,722 | 9,257 |
| 86403 | Lake Havasu City . . . . | 24,363 | 15,909 |
| *85201 | Mesa . . . . . . . . . . . | 288,104 | 152,404 |
| 86440 | Mohave Valley(u) . . . . . | 6,962 | .... |
| ..... | New Kingman-Butler(u). . . . | 11,627 | .... |
| 85621 | Nogales . . . . . . . . . | 19,489 | 15,683 |
| 85737 | Oro Valley . . . . . . . . | 6,670 | 1,489 |
| 86040 | Page . . . . . . . . . . . | 6,598 | 4,907 |
| 85253 | Paradise Valley . . . . . | 11,773 | 11,085 |
| 85541 | Payson . . . . . . . . . | 8,377 | 5,068 |
| 85345 | Peoria . . . . . . . . . | 50,675 | 12,171 |
| *85026 | Phoenix. . . . . . . . . | 983,392 | 789,704 |
| 86301 | Prescott . . . . . . . . | 26,592 | 19,865 |
| 86314 | Prescott Valley . . . . . | 8,904 | 2,284 |
| 85546 | Safford . . . . . . . . | 7,359 | 7,010 |
| *85251 | Scottsdale . . . . . . . | 130,075 | 88,622 |
| 86336 | Sedona . . . . . . . . | 7,720 | 5,319 |
| 85901 | Show Low . . . . . . . | 5,020 | 4,298 |
| *85635 | Sierra Vista . . . . . . | 32,983 | 24,937 |
| 85635 | Sierra Vista Southeast(u) | 9,237 | .... |
| 85350 | Somerton . . . . . . . | 5,282 | 3,969 |
| 85713 | South Tucson . . . . . | 5,171 | 6,554 |
| *85351 | Sun City(u). . . . . . . | 38,126 | 40,505 |
| 85375 | Sun City West(u) . . . . | 15,997 | 3,772 |
| 85248 | Sun Lakes(u) . . . . . . | 6,578 | .... |
| 85374 | Surprise . . . . . . . . | 7,122 | 3,723 |
| *85282 | Tempe . . . . . . . . . | 141,993 | 106,919 |
| 86045 | Tuba City(u) . . . . . . | 7,323 | 5,045 |
| *85726 | Tucson . . . . . . . . | 405,371 | 330,537 |
| 86047 | Winslow . . . . . . . . | 9,279 | 7,921 |
| *85364 | Yuma . . . . . . . . . | 54,923 | 42,481 |

## Arkansas (501)

| ZIP code | Place | 1990 | 1980 |
|---|---|---|---|
| 71923 | Arkadelphia . . . . . . . . | 10,014 | 10,005 |
| 71822 | Ashdown . . . . . . . . . | 5,150 | 4,218 |
| 72501 | Batesville. . . . . . . . . | 9,187 | 8,447 |
| 72714 | Bella Vista(u) . . . . . . . | 9,083 | 2,589 |
| 72015 | Benton . . . . . . . . . | 18,177 | 17,717 |
| 72712 | Bentonville . . . . . . . . | 11,257 | 8,756 |
| 72315 | Blytheville . . . . . . . . | 22,533 | 23,844 |
| 72022 | Bryant . . . . . . . . . | 5,269 | 2,682 |
| 72023 | Cabot. . . . . . . . . . | 8,319 | 4,806 |
| 71701 | Camden . . . . . . . . | 14,701 | 15,356 |
| 72830 | Clarksville . . . . . . . | 5,833 | 5,237 |
| 72032 | Conway . . . . . . . . | 26,481 | 20,375 |
| 71635 | Crossett . . . . . . . . | 6,282 | 6,706 |
| 71639 | Dumas . . . . . . . . . | 5,520 | 6,091 |
| 71730 | El Dorado . . . . . . . | 23,146 | 25,270 |
| 72701 | Fayetteville . . . . . . . | 42,247 | 36,608 |
| 72335 | Forrest City . . . . . . | 13,364 | 13,803 |
| 72901 | Fort Smith . . . . . . . | 72,798 | 71,626 |
| 72601 | Harrison . . . . . . . . | 9,936 | 9,567 |
| 72543 | Heber Springs . . . . . | 5,628 | 4,589 |
| 72342 | Helena . . . . . . . . . | 7,491 | 9,598 |
| 71801 | Hope . . . . . . . . . | 9,768 | 10,290 |
| 71901 | Hot Springs . . . . . . | 32,462 | 35,781 |
| 71909 | Hot Springs Village(u) | 6,361 | 2,083 |
| 72076 | Jacksonville . . . . . . | 29,101 | 27,589 |
| 72401 | Jonesboro . . . . . . . | 46,535 | 31,530 |
| *72201 | Little Rock . . . . . . . | 175,727 | 159,151 |
| 71753 | Magnolia . . . . . . . . | 11,151 | 11,909 |
| 72104 | Malvern . . . . . . . . | 9,236 | 10,163 |
| 72360 | Marianna . . . . . . . . | 6,033 | 6,220 |
| 72113 | Maumelle . . . . . . . | 6,714 | 1,368 |
| 71953 | Mena . . . . . . . . . | 5,475 | 5,154 |
| 71655 | Monticello . . . . . . . | 8,119 | 8,259 |
| 72110 | Morrilton . . . . . . . . | 6,551 | 7,355 |
| 72653 | Mountain Home . . . . | 9,027 | 8,066 |
| 72112 | Newport . . . . . . . . | 7,459 | 8,339 |
| *72114 | North Little Rock . . . . | 61,829 | 64,388 |
| 72370 | Osceola . . . . . . . . | 8,930 | 8,881 |
| 72450 | Paragould . . . . . . . | 18,540 | 15,248 |
| 71601 | Pine Bluff. . . . . . . . | 57,140 | 56,636 |
| 72455 | Pocahontas . . . . . . | 6,151 | 5,995 |
| 72756 | Rogers . . . . . . . . | 24,692 | 17,429 |
| 72801 | Russellville . . . . . . | 21,260 | 14,518 |
| 72143 | Searcy . . . . . . . . | 15,180 | 13,612 |
| 72116 | Sherwood . . . . . . . | 18,878 | 10,423 |
| 72761 | Siloam Springs . . . . | 8,151 | 7,940 |
| 72764 | Springdale . . . . . . . | 29,945 | 23,458 |
| 72160 | Stuttgart . . . . . . . . | 10,420 | 10,941 |
| 75502 | Texarkana . . . . . . . | 22,631 | 21,459 |
| 72472 | Trumann . . . . . . . . | 6,346 | 6,395 |

| ZIP code | Place | 1990 | 1980 |
|---|---|---|---|
| 72956 | Van Buren . . . . . . . . . . . | 14,979 | 12,020 |
| 71671 | Warren . . . . . . . . . . . | 6,455 | 7,646 |
| 72390 | West Helena. . . . . . . . . | 10,137 | 11,367 |
| 72301 | West Memphis . . . . . . | 28,259 | 28,138 |
| 72396 | Wynne . . . . . . . . . . | 8,817 | 7,927 |

## California

| ZIP code | Place | | 1990 | 1980 |
|---|---|---|---|---|
| 94501 | Adelanto . . . . . . . . . . . | | 8,521 | 2,164 |
| 91301 | Agoura Hills . . . . . . . | (818) | 20,390 | 11,399 |
| 94501 | Alameda. . . . . . . . . | (510) | 73,979 | 63,852 |
| 94507 | Alamo(u). . . . . . . . . | (510) | 12,277 | 8,505 |
| 94706 | Albany . . . . . . . . . | (510) | 16,327 | 15,130 |
| *91802 | Alhambra . . . . . . . . | (818) | 82,106 | 64,767 |
| 92656 | Aliso Viejo(u) . . . . . . | | 7,612 | .... |
| 90249 | Alondra Park(u). . . . . | (310) | 12,215 | 12,096 |
| 91901 | Alpine(u) . . . . . . . . | (619) | 9,695 | 5,368 |
| 91001 | Altadena(u) . . . . . . . | (818) | 42,658 | 40,510 |
| 95945 | Alta Sierra(u) . . . . . . | | 5,709 | 2,168 |
| 94590 | American Canyon(u) . . | (707) | 7,706 | 5,712 |
| *92803 | Anaheim . . . . . . . . | (714) | 266,406 | 219,494 |
| 96007 | Anderson . . . . . . . . | (916) | 8,299 | 7,381 |
| 94509 | Antioch. . . . . . . . . | (510) | 62,195 | 42,683 |
| 92307 | Apple Valley. . . . . . . | (619) | 46,079 | 16,748 |
| 95003 | Aptos(u) . . . . . . . . | (408) | 9,061 | 7,039 |
| 91006 | Arcadia. . . . . . . . . | (818) | 48,284 | 45,993 |
| 95521 | Arcata. . . . . . . . . | (707) | 15,197 | 12,849 |
| 95825 | Arden-Arcade(u) . . . . | (916) | 92,040 | 87,570 |
| 93420 | Arroyo Grande . . . . . | (805) | 14,432 | 11,290 |
| 90701 | Artesia . . . . . . . . . | (310) | 15,464 | 14,301 |
| 93203 | Arvin. . . . . . . . . . | (805) | 9,286 | 6,863 |
| 94577 | Ashland(u). . . . . . . | (510) | 16,590 | 13,893 |
| 93422 | Atascadero . . . . . . . | (805) | 23,138 | 16,232 |
| 94025 | Atherton . . . . . . . . | (415) | 7,163 | 7,797 |
| 95301 | Atwater. . . . . . . . . | (209) | 22,282 | 17,530 |
| 95603 | Auburn. . . . . . . . . | (916) | 10,592 | 7,540 |
| 92505 | August(u) . . . . . . . | (714) | 6,376 | 5,445 |
| 93204 | Avenal . . . . . . . . . | | 9,770 | 4,137 |
| 91746 | Avocado Heights(u). . . | (818) | 14,232 | 11,721 |
| 91702 | Azusa . . . . . . . . . | (818) | 41,333 | 29,380 |
| *93302 | Bakersfield. . . . . . . | (805) | 174,820 | 105,611 |
| 91706 | Baldwin Park . . . . . . | (818) | 69,330 | 50,554 |
| 92220 | Banning . . . . . . . . | (714) | 20,572 | 14,020 |
| 92311 | Barstow . . . . . . . . | (619) | 21,472 | 17,690 |
| 93402 | Baywood-Los Osos(u) . | (805) | 14,377 | 10,933 |
| 95903 | Beale AFB East(u) . . . | (916) | 6,912 | 6,329 |
| 92223 | Beaumont . . . . . . . | (714) | 9,685 | 6,818 |
| 90201 | Bell. . . . . . . . . . | (213) | 34,365 | 25,450 |
| 90706 | Bellflower . . . . . . . | (310) | 61,815 | 53,441 |
| 90201 | Bell Gardens . . . . . . | (213) | 42,355 | 34,117 |
| 94002 | Belmont . . . . . . . . | (415) | 24,127 | 24,505 |
| 94510 | Benicia . . . . . . . . | (707) | 24,437 | 15,376 |
| 95005 | Ben Lomond(u) . . . . . | (408) | 7,884 | 7,238 |
| *94704 | Berkeley . . . . . . . . | (510) | 102,724 | 103,328 |
| *90213 | Beverly Hills . . . . . . | (310) | 31,971 | 32,646 |
| 92314 | Big Bear Lake . . . . . | (714) | 5,351 | 4,896 |
| 94506 | Black Hawk(u). . . . . . | | 6,199 | .... |
| 92316 | Bloomington(u) . . . . . | (714) | 15,116 | 12,781 |
| 92225 | Blythe . . . . . . . . . | (619) | 8,448 | 6,805 |
| ..... | Bonadella Ranchos-Madera Ranchos(u) . . . . . | | 5,705 | 3,272 |
| 91902 | Bonita(u) . . . . . . . . | (619) | 12,542 | 6,257 |
| 92021 | Bostonia(u). . . . . . . | | 13,670 | .... |
| 95006 | Boulder Creek(u) . . . . | (408) | 6,725 | 5,662 |
| 95416 | Boyes Hot Springs(u). . | | 5,973 | 4,177 |
| 92227 | Brawley . . . . . . . . | (619) | 18,923 | 14,946 |
| 92621 | Brea . . . . . . . . . | (714) | 32,873 | 27,913 |
| 94513 | Brentwood. . . . . . . | (510) | 7,563 | 4,434 |
| *90620 | Buena Park . . . . . . . | (714) | 68,784 | 64,165 |
| *91505 | Burbank . . . . . . . . | (818) | 93,643 | 84,625 |
| 94010 | Burlingame . . . . . . . | (415) | 26,666 | 26,173 |
| 92231 | Calexico . . . . . . . . | (619) | 18,633 | 14,412 |
| 93505 | California City . . . . . | | 5,955 | 2,743 |
| 93010 | Camarillo . . . . . . . | (805) | 52,297 | 37,797 |
| 93428 | Cambria . . . . . . . . | | 5,382 | 3,061 |
| 95682 | Cameron Park(u) . . . . | (916) | 11,897 | 5,607 |
| 95008 | Campbell. . . . . . . . | (408) | 36,048 | 26,843 |
| 92055 | Camp Pendleton North(u) . . | (714) | 10,373 | 2,065 |
| 92055 | Camp Pendleton South(u) . . | (714) | 11,299 | 7,952 |
| 92380 | Canyon Lake(u) . . . . . | | 7,938 | 2,039 |
| 95010 | Capitola . . . . . . . . | (408) | 10,171 | 9,095 |
| *92008 | Carlsbad . . . . . . . . | (619) | 63,126 | 35,490 |
| 95608 | Carmichael(u). . . . . . | (916) | 48,702 | 43,108 |
| 93013 | Carpinteria. . . . . . . | (805) | 13,747 | 10,835 |
| 90744 | Carson . . . . . . . . | (310) | 83,995 | 81,221 |
| 92077 | Casa de Oro-Mt. Helix(u) . | (619) | 30,727 | 19,651 |
| 94546 | Castro Valley(u). . . . . | (510) | 48,619 | 44,011 |
| 95012 | Castroville . . . . . . . | (408) | 5,272 | 4,396 |
| 92235 | Cathedral City . . . . . | (619) | 30,085 | 11,096 |
| 95307 | Ceres . . . . . . . . . | (209) | 26,413 | 13,281 |
| 90701 | Cerritos . . . . . . . . | (310) | 53,244 | 53,020 |
| 91724 | Charter Oak(u) . . . . . | (818) | 8,858 | 6,840 |
| 94541 | Cherryland(u). . . . . . | (415) | 11,088 | 9,425 |
| 92223 | Cherry Valley(u) . . . . | (714) | 5,945 | 5,012 |
| 95926 | Chico . . . . . . . . . | (916) | 40,079 | 26,716 |
| 91710 | Chino . . . . . . . . . | (714) | 59,682 | 40,165 |
| 91709 | Chino Hills . . . . . . . | | 27,608 | .... |

| ZIP code | Place | | 1990 | 1980 | ZIP code | Place | | 1990 | 1980 |
|---|---|---|---|---|---|---|---|---|---|
| 93610 | Chowchilla | (209) | 5,930 | 5,122 | *91209 | Glendale | (818) | 180,038 | 139,060 |
| *91910 | Chula Vista | (619) | 135,163 | 83,927 | 91740 | Glendora | (818) | 47,832 | 38,500 |
| 95610 | Citrus(u) | (916) | 9,481 | 12,450 | 93561 | Golden Hills(u) | | 5,423 | |
| *95610 | Citrus Heights(u) | (916) | 107,439 | 85,911 | 92324 | Grand Terrace | (714) | 10,946 | 8,498 |
| 91711 | Claremont | (714) | 32,539 | 31,028 | 95945 | Grass Valley | (916) | 9,048 | 6,697 |
| 94517 | Clayton | | 7,317 | 4,325 | 93308 | Greenacres(u) | (805) | 7,379 | 5,381 |
| 95422 | Clearlake | | 11,804 | 8,343 | 93927 | Greenfield | (805) | 7,464 | 4,181 |
| 93612 | Clovis | (209) | 50,323 | 33,021 | 94533 | Grover City | (805) | 11,602 | 8,827 |
| 92236 | Coachella | (619) | 16,896 | 9,129 | 93434 | Guadalupe | | 5,479 | 3,629 |
| 93210 | Coalinga | (209) | 8,212 | 6,593 | 91745 | Hacienda Heights(u) | (818) | 52,354 | 49,422 |
| 92324 | Colton | (714) | 40,273 | 21,310 | 94019 | Half Moon Bay | (415) | 8,886 | 7,282 |
| 90022 | Commerce | (310) | 12,135 | 10,509 | 93230 | Hanford | (209) | 30,897 | 20,958 |
| *90220 | Compton | (310) | 90,454 | 81,350 | 90716 | Hawaiian Gardens | (213) | 13,639 | 10,548 |
| *94520 | Concord | (510) | 111,308 | 103,763 | 90250 | Hawthorne | (310) | 71,349 | 56,437 |
| 93212 | Corcoran | (209) | 13,360 | 6,454 | *94544 | Hayward | (510) | 111,343 | 93,585 |
| 96021 | Corning | (916) | 5,870 | 4,745 | 95448 | Healdsburg | (707) | 9,469 | 7,217 |
| 91720 | Corona | (714) | 76,095 | 37,791 | 92343 | Hemet | (714) | 36,094 | 22,537 |
| 92118 | Coronado | (619) | 26,540 | 18,790 | 94547 | Hercules | (415) | 16,829 | 5,963 |
| 94925 | Corte Madera | (415) | 8,272 | 8,074 | 90254 | Hermosa Beach | (310) | 18,219 | 18,070 |
| *92626 | Costa Mesa | (714) | 96,357 | 82,562 | 92345 | Hesperia | (619) | 50,418 | 20,612 |
| 94927 | Cotati | (707) | 5,714 | 3,346 | 92346 | Highland | (714) | 34,439 | 21,720 |
| 94556 | Country Club(u) | (209) | 9,325 | 9,585 | 94010 | Hillsborough | (415) | 10,667 | 10,372 |
| *91722 | Covina | (818) | 43,207 | 32,746 | 95023 | Hollister | (408) | 19,212 | 11,488 |
| 92325 | Crestline(u) | (714) | 8,594 | 6,715 | 91720 | Home Gardens(u) | (714) | 7,780 | 5,783 |
| 90201 | Cudahy | (213) | 22,817 | 18,275 | *92647 | Huntington Beach | (714) | 181,519 | 170,505 |
| *90230 | Culver City | (310) | 38,793 | 38,139 | 90255 | Huntington Park | (213) | 56,065 | 45,932 |
| 95014 | Cupertino | (408) | 39,967 | 34,297 | 91932 | Imperial Beach | (619) | 26,512 | 22,689 |
| 90630 | Cypress | (714) | 42,655 | 40,738 | 92201 | Indio | (619) | 36,850 | 21,611 |
| *94017 | Daly City | (415) | 92,311 | 78,519 | *90306 | Inglewood | (310) | 109,602 | 94,162 |
| 92629 | Dana Point | (714) | 31,896 | 21,271 | | Interlaken(u) | | 6,404 | |
| *94526 | Danville | (510) | 31,306 | 26,143 | 95640 | Ione | | 6,516 | 2,207 |
| 95616 | Davis | (916) | 46,322 | 36,640 | *92711 | Irvine | (714) | 110,330 | 62,134 |
| 90250 | Del Aire(u) | (310) | 8,040 | 8,487 | 93117 | Isla Vista(u) | (805) | 20,395 | |
| 93215 | Delano | (805) | 22,762 | 16,491 | 94904 | Kentfield(u) | (415) | 6,030 | |
| | Del Monte Forest(u) | | 5,069 | | 93630 | Kerman | (209) | 5,448 | 4,002 |
| 92240 | Desert Hot Springs | (619) | 11,668 | 5,941 | 93930 | King City | (408) | 7,634 | 5,495 |
| 91765 | Diamond Bar | (714) | 53,672 | 30,736 | 93631 | Kingsburg | (209) | 7,245 | 5,115 |
| 93618 | Dinuba | (209) | 12,743 | 9,907 | 91011 | La Canada-Flintridge | (818) | 19,378 | 20,153 |
| 94514 | Discovery Bay(u) | | 5,351 | 1,326 | 91214 | La Crescenta-Montrose(u) | (818) | 16,968 | 16,531 |
| 95620 | Dixon | (916) | 10,417 | 7,541 | 90045 | Ladera Heights(u) | (310) | 6,316 | 6,647 |
| *90241 | Downey | (310) | 91,4444 | 82,602 | 94549 | Lafayette | (510) | 23,366 | 20,837 |
| 91010 | Duarte | (818) | 20,688 | 16,766 | | Laguna(u) | | 9,828 | |
| 94568 | Dublin | (510) | 23,229 | 13,496 | *92651 | Laguna Beach | (714) | 23,170 | 17,858 |
| 93219 | Earlimart(u) | (805) | 5,881 | 4,578 | 92653 | Laguna Hills(u) | (714) | 46,731 | 33,600 |
| 90220 | East Compton(u) | (310) | 7,967 | 6,435 | 92677 | Laguna Niguel | (714) | 44,400 | 12,237 |
| | East Foothills(u) | | 14,898 | | 90631 | La Habra | (310) | 51,266 | 45,232 |
| 92343 | East Hemet(u) | (714) | 17,611 | 14,712 | | La Habra Heights(u) | (310) | 6,226 | 4,786 |
| 90638 | East La Mirada(u) | (310) | 9,367 | 9,688 | 92352 | Lake Arrowhead(u) | (714) | 6,539 | 6,272 |
| 90022 | East Los Angeles(u) | (310) | 126,379 | 110,017 | 92330 | Lake Elsinore | (714) | 18,316 | 5,982 |
| 94303 | East Palo Alto | (415) | 23,451 | 18,106 | 92530 | Lakeland Village(u) | | 5,159 | 2,796 |
| 91117 | East Pasadena(u) | | 5,910 | | 93535 | Lake Los Angeles(u) | | 7,977 | |
| 93257 | East Porterville(u) | (209) | 5,790 | 5,218 | 92040 | Lakeside(u) | (619) | 39,412 | 23,921 |
| | East San Gabriel(u) | | 12,736 | | *90714 | Lakewood | (310) | 73,553 | 74,511 |
| 93523 | Edwards AFB(u) | (805) | 7,423 | 8,554 | 91941 | La Mesa | (619) | 52,931 | 50,308 |
| *92020 | El Cajon | (619) | 88,693 | 73,892 | 90638 | La Mirada | (714) | 40,452 | 40,986 |
| 92243 | El Centro | (619) | 31,405 | 23,996 | 93241 | Lamont(u) | (805) | 11,517 | 9,616 |
| 94530 | El Cerrito | (510) | 22,869 | 22,731 | 93534 | Lancaster | (805) | 97,291 | 48,027 |
| 95630 | El Dorado Hills(u) | | 6,395 | | 90624 | La Palma | (714) | 15,392 | 15,399 |
| 95624 | Elk Grove(u) | (916) | 17,483 | 10,959 | 91747 | La Puente | (818) | 36,955 | 30,882 |
| *91734 | El Monte | (818) | 106,162 | 79,494 | 92253 | La Quinta | | 11,215 | 4,027 |
| 93446 | El Paso de Robles | (310) | 18,583 | 9,163 | | La Riviera(u) | (916) | 10,986 | 10,906 |
| 93030 | El Rio(u) | (805) | 6,419 | 5,674 | 95403 | Larkfield-Wikiup(u) | | 6,779 | |
| 90245 | El Segundo | (310) | 15,223 | 13,752 | 94499 | Larkspur | (415) | 11,068 | 11,064 |
| 94803 | El Sobrante(u) | (510) | 9,852 | 10,535 | 95330 | Lathrop | | 6,841 | 4,112 |
| 92630 | El Toro | (714) | 62,685 | 38,153 | 91750 | La Verne | (714) | 30,861 | 23,508 |
| 92709 | El Toro Station(u) | (714) | 6,869 | 7,632 | 90260 | Lawndale | (310) | 27,331 | 23,460 |
| 94608 | Emeryville | (510) | 5,740 | 3,714 | 91945 | Lemon Grove | (619) | 23,984 | 20,780 |
| 92024 | Encinitas | (619) | 55,386 | 36,550 | 93245 | Lemoore | (209) | 13,622 | 6,832 |
| *92025 | Escondido | (619) | 108,635 | 64,355 | 90304 | Lennox(u) | (310) | 22,757 | 18,445 |
| 95501 | Eureka | (707) | 27,025 | 24,153 | 95207 | Lincoln Village(u) | (916) | 7,248 | 4,132 |
| 93221 | Exeter | (209) | 7,276 | 5,606 | 95901 | Linda(u) | (916) | 13,033 | 10,225 |
| 94930 | Fairfax | (415) | 6,931 | 7,391 | 93247 | Lindsay | (209) | 8,338 | 6,936 |
| 94533 | Fairfield | (707) | 78,650 | 58,099 | 95062 | Live Oak(u) | (916) | 15,212 | 11,482 |
| 95628 | Fair Oaks(u) | (916) | 26,867 | 22,602 | 94550 | Livermore | (510) | 56,741 | 48,349 |
| 95238 | Fairview(u) | | 9,045 | | 95334 | Livingston | (209) | 7,317 | 5,326 |
| 92028 | Fallbrook(u) | (619) | 22,095 | 14,041 | *95240 | Lodi | (209) | 51,874 | 35,221 |
| 93223 | Farmersville | (209) | 6,235 | 5,544 | 92354 | Loma Linda | (714) | 18,470 | 10,694 |
| 95018 | Felton | (408) | 5,350 | 4,564 | 90717 | Lomita | (213) | 19,382 | 18,807 |
| 93015 | Fillmore | (805) | 11,992 | 9,602 | 93436 | Lompoc | (805) | 37,649 | 26,267 |
| 90001 | Florence-Graham(u) | (213) | 57,147 | 48,662 | *90801 | Long Beach | (310) | 429,321 | 361,498 |
| 95828 | Florin(u) | (916) | 24,330 | 16,523 | 95650 | Loomis | | 5,705 | 3,663 |
| 95630 | Folsom | (916) | 29,802 | 11,003 | 90720 | Los Alamitos | (310) | 11,788 | 11,529 |
| *92335 | Fontana | (714) | 87,535 | 36,804 | 94022 | Los Altos | (415) | 26,599 | 25,769 |
| 95841 | Foothill Farms(u) | (916) | 17,135 | 13,700 | 94022 | Los Altos Hills | (415) | 7,514 | 7,421 |
| 95437 | Fort Bragg | (707) | 6,078 | 5,019 | *90052 | Los Angeles | (213) | 3,485,398 | 2,968,528 |
| 95540 | Fortuna | (707) | 8,788 | 7,591 | 95030 | Los Banos | (209) | 14,519 | 10,341 |
| 94404 | Foster City | (415) | 28,176 | 23,287 | 95030 | Los Gatos | (408) | 27,357 | 26,906 |
| 92708 | Fountain Valley | (714) | 53,691 | 55,080 | 91709 | Los Serranos(u) | | 7,099 | |
| 95019 | Freedom(u) | (408) | 8,361 | 6,416 | 94903 | Lucas Valley-Marinwood(u) | (415) | 5,982 | 6,409 |
| *94536 | Fremont | (510) | 173,339 | 131,945 | 90262 | Lynwood | (310) | 61,945 | 48,289 |
| 93706 | Fresno | (209) | 354,091 | 217,491 | 93250 | Mc Farland | (805) | 7,005 | 5,151 |
| *92631 | Fullerton | (714) | 114,144 | 102,246 | 95521 | McKinleyville(u) | (707) | 10,749 | 7,772 |
| 95632 | Galt | (209) | 8,889 | 5,514 | 93637 | Madera | (209) | 29,282 | 21,732 |
| *90247 | Gardena | (310) | 49,841 | 45,165 | | Madera Acres(u) | | 5,245 | 2,173 |
| 95205 | Garden Acres(u) | (213) | 8,547 | 7,361 | 95954 | Magalia(u) | | 8,987 | |
| *92640 | Garden Grove | (714) | 143,965 | 123,307 | 90266 | Manhattan Beach | (310) | 32,063 | 31,542 |
| 92392 | George AFB(u) | (619) | 5,085 | 7,061 | 95336 | Manteca | (209) | 40,773 | 24,925 |
| 95020 | Gilroy | (408) | 31,487 | 21,641 | 92518 | March AFB(u) | (714) | 5,523 | 3,607 |
| 92509 | Glen Avon(u) | (714) | 12,663 | 8,444 | 93933 | Marina | (408) | 26,512 | 20,647 |

| ZIP code | Place | | 1990 | 1980 |
|---|---|---|---|---|
| 90292 | Marina Del Rey(u) | (310) | 7,431 | 8,065 |
| 94553 | Martinez | (510) | 31,808 | 22,582 |
| 95901 | Marysville | (916) | 12,324 | 9,898 |
| 90270 | Maywood | (213) | 27,850 | 21,810 |
| 93640 | Mendota | (209) | 6,821 | 5,038 |
| 94025 | Menlo Park | (415) | 28,403 | 26,438 |
| 92359 | Mentone(u) | (714) | 5,675 | .... |
| *95340 | Merced | (209) | 56,216 | 36,423 |
| 94030 | Millbrae | (415) | 20,414 | 20,058 |
| 94941 | Mill Valley | (415) | 13,038 | 12,967 |
| 95035 | Milpitas | (408) | 50,686 | 37,820 |
| 91752 | Mira Loma(u) | (714) | 15,786 | 8,707 |
| 93641 | Mira Monte(u) | ... | 7,744 | .... |
| 92675 | Mission Viejo | (714) | 72,820 | 48,503 |
| *95350 | Modesto | (209) | 164,746 | 106,963 |
| 91016 | Monrovia | (818) | 35,761 | 30,531 |
| 91763 | Montclair | (714) | 28,434 | 22,628 |
| 90640 | Montebello | (213) | 59,564 | 52,929 |
| 93940 | Monterey | (408) | 31,954 | 27,558 |
| 91754 | Monterey Park | (818) | 60,738 | 54,338 |
| 93020 | Moorpark | (805) | 25,494 | 7,798 |
| 94556 | Moraga Town | (510) | 15,987 | 15,014 |
| *92303 | Moreno Valley | (714) | 118,779 | 28,139 |
| 95037 | Morgan Hill | (408) | 23,928 | 17,060 |
| 93442 | Morro Bay | (805) | 9,664 | 9,064 |
| *94042 | Mountain View | (415) | 67,365 | 58,655 |
| 92405 | Muscoy(u) | (714) | 7,541 | 6,188 |
| 94558 | Napa | (707) | 61,842 | 50,879 |
| 91950 | National City | (619) | 54,249 | 48,772 |
| 92363 | Needles | (619) | 5,191 | 4,120 |
| 94560 | Newark | (510) | 37,861 | 32,126 |
| *92660 | Newport Beach | (714) | 66,643 | 62,556 |
| 93444 | Nipomo(u) | (805) | 7,109 | 5,247 |
| 91760 | Norco | (714) | 23,302 | 19,732 |
| 95603 | North Auburn(u) | (916) | 10,301 | 7,619 |
| 94025 | North Fair Oaks(u) | (415) | 13,912 | 10,308 |
| 95660 | North Highlands(u) | (916) | 42,105 | 37,825 |
| 90650 | Norwalk | (310) | 94,279 | 84,901 |
| 94947 | Novato | (415) | 47,585 | 43,916 |
| 95361 | Oakdale | (209) | 11,978 | 8,474 |
| *94615 | Oakland | (510) | 372,242 | 339,337 |
| 94561 | Oakley(u) | ... | 18,374 | 2,816 |
| 93445 | Oceano(u) | ... | 6,169 | 4,478 |
| *92054 | Oceanside | (619) | 128,154 | 76,698 |
| 93308 | Oildale(u) | (805) | 26,553 | 23,382 |
| 93023 | Ojai | (805) | 7,613 | 6,816 |
| 95961 | Olivehurst(u) | (916) | 9,738 | 8,929 |
| *91761 | Ontario | (714) | 133,179 | 88,820 |
| 95060 | Opal Cliffs(u) | (408) | 5,940 | 5,041 |
| *92667 | Orange | (714) | 110,658 | 91,450 |
| 93646 | Orange Cove | (209) | 5,604 | 4,026 |
| 95662 | Orangevale(u) | (916) | 26,266 | 20,585 |
| 94563 | Orinda | (510) | 16,642 | 17,030 |
| 95963 | Orland | (916) | 5,052 | 4,031 |
| 93647 | Orosi(u) | ... | 5,486 | 4,076 |
| 95965 | Oroville | (916) | 11,960 | 8,683 |
| | Oroville East(u) | ... | 8,462 | .... |
| *93030 | Oxnard | (805) | 142,560 | 108,195 |
| 94044 | Pacifica | (415) | 37,670 | 36,866 |
| 93950 | Pacific Grove | (408) | 16,117 | 15,755 |
| 95968 | Palermo(u) | ... | 5,260 | 2,572 |
| 93550 | Palmdale | (805) | 68,842 | 12,277 |
| 92260 | Palm Desert | (619) | 23,252 | 11,801 |
| | Palm Desert Country(u) | ... | 5,626 | .... |
| 92262 | Palm Springs | (619) | 40,144 | 32,359 |
| *94302 | Palo Alto | (415) | 55,900 | 55,225 |
| 90274 | Palos Verdes Estates | (310) | 13,512 | 14,376 |
| 95669 | Paradise | (916) | 25,401 | 22,571 |
| 90723 | Paramount | (310) | 47,669 | 36,407 |
| 95823 | Parkway-So. Sacramento(u) | (916) | 31,903 | 26,815 |
| 93648 | Parlier | (209) | 7,938 | 2,902 |
| *91100 | Pasadena | (818) | 131,591 | 118,072 |
| 95363 | Patterson | (209) | 8,626 | 3,908 |
| 92509 | Pedley(u) | ... | 8,869 | .... |
| 92370 | Perris | (714) | 21,460 | 6,827 |
| 94952 | Petaluma | (707) | 43,184 | 33,834 |
| 90660 | Pico Rivera | (310) | 59,177 | 53,387 |
| 94611 | Piedmont | (510) | 10,602 | 10,498 |
| 94564 | Pinole | (510) | 17,460 | 14,253 |
| 93449 | Pismo Beach | (805) | 7,669 | 5,364 |
| 94565 | Pittsburg | (510) | 47,607 | 33,465 |
| 92670 | Placentia | (714) | 41,259 | 35,041 |
| 95667 | Placerville | (916) | 8,355 | 6,739 |
| 94523 | Pleasant Hill | (510) | 31,583 | 25,547 |
| *94566 | Pleasanton | (510) | 50,570 | 35,160 |
| *91766 | Pomona | (714) | 131,723 | 92,742 |
| 93257 | Porterville | (209) | 29,521 | 19707 |
| 93041 | Port Hueneme | (805) | 20,322 | 17,803 |
| 92064 | Poway | (619) | 43,516 | 33,439 |
| 93907 | Prunedale(u) | ... | 7,393 | .... |
| 93534 | Quartz Hill(u) | (805) | 9,626 | 7,421 |
| 92065 | Ramona(u) | (619) | 13,040 | 8,173 |
| 95670 | Rancho Cordova(u) | (916) | 48,731 | 42,881 |
| 91730 | Rancho Cucamonga | (714) | 101,409 | 55,250 |
| 92270 | Rancho Mirage | (619) | 9,778 | 6,281 |
| 90274 | Rancho Palos Verdes | (310) | 41,659 | 36,577 |
| | Rancho San Diego(u) | ... | 6,977 | .... |
| 92688 | Rancho Santa Margarita(u) | ... | 11,390 | .... |
| 96080 | Red Bluff | (916) | 12,363 | 9,490 |
| *96049 | Redding | (916) | 66,462 | 42,103 |
| 92373 | Redlands | (714) | 60,394 | 43,619 |
| *90277 | Redondo Beach | (310) | 60,167 | 57,102 |
| *94064 | Redwood City | (415) | 66,072 | 54,951 |
| 92376 | Rialto | (714) | 72,395 | 37,862 |
| *94802 | Richmond | (510) | 87,619 | 74,676 |
| 93555 | Ridgecrest | (619) | 28,295 | 15,929 |
| 95003 | Rio Del Mar(u) | (408) | 8,919 | 7,067 |
| 95673 | Rio Linda(u) | (916) | 9,481 | 7,359 |
| 95366 | Ripon | (209) | 7,455 | 3,509 |
| 95367 | Riverbank | (209) | 8,591 | 5,695 |
| *92502 | Riverside | (714) | 226,546 | 170,591 |
| 95677 | Rocklin | (916) | 18,806 | 7,344 |
| 94572 | Rodeo(u) | (415) | 7,589 | 8,286 |
| 94928 | Rohnert Park | (707) | 36,326 | 22,965 |
| 90274 | Rolling Hills Estates | (310) | 7,789 | 7,701 |
| 93560 | Rosamond(u) | (805) | 7,430 | 2,869 |
| 95401 | Roseland(u) | (707) | 8,779 | 7,915 |
| 91770 | Rosemead | (818) | 51,638 | 42,604 |
| 95826 | Rosemont(u) | (916) | 22,851 | 18,888 |
| 95678 | Roseville | (916) | 44,685 | 24,347 |
| 90720 | Rossmoor(u) | (310) | 9,893 | 10,457 |
| 91745 | Rowland Heights(u) | (818) | 42,647 | 28,252 |
| 92509 | Rubidoux(u) | (714) | 24,367 | 16,763 |
| *95813 | Sacramento | (916) | 369,365 | 275,741 |
| 93901 | Salinas | (408) | 108,777 | 80,479 |
| 94960 | San Anselmo | (415) | 11,735 | 12,067 |
| *92403 | San Bernardino | (714) | 164,164 | 118,794 |
| 94066 | San Bruno | (415) | 38,961 | 35,417 |
| *93001 | San Buenaventura (Ventura) | (805) | 92,557 | 73,774 |
| 94070 | San Carlos | (415) | 26,167 | 24,710 |
| 92672 | San Clemente | (714) | 41,100 | 27,325 |
| *92109 | San Diego | (619) | 1,110,554 | 875,538 |
| .... | San Diego Country Estates(u) | ... | 6,874 | .... |
| 91773 | San Dimas | (714) | 32,402 | 24,014 |
| *91340 | San Fernando | (818) | 22,580 | 17,731 |
| *94101 | San Francisco | (415) | 723,959 | 678,974 |
| 91776 | San Gabriel | (818) | 37,120 | 30,072 |
| 93657 | Sanger | (209) | 16,839 | 12,542 |
| 92383 | San Jacinto | (714) | 16,210 | 7,098 |
| *95101 | San Jose | (408) | 782,248 | 629,400 |
| 92375 | San Juan Capistrano | (714) | 26,183 | 18,959 |
| *94577 | San Leandro | (510) | 68,223 | 63,952 |
| 94580 | San Lorenzo(u) | (510) | 19,987 | 20,545 |
| 93401 | San Luis Obispo | (805) | 41,958 | 34,252 |
| 92069 | San Marcos | (619) | 38,974 | 17,479 |
| 91108 | San Marino | (818) | 12,959 | 13,307 |
| *94402 | San Mateo | (415) | 85,619 | 77,640 |
| 94806 | San Pablo | (510) | 25,158 | 19,750 |
| *94901 | San Rafael | (415) | 48,410 | 44,700 |
| 94583 | San Ramon | (510) | 35,303 | 20,511 |
| *92711 | Santa Ana | (714) | 293,827 | 204,023 |
| *93102 | Santa Barbara | (805) | 85,571 | 74,414 |
| *95050 | Santa Clara | (408) | 93,613 | 87,700 |
| *91380 | Santa Clarita | (805) | 110,690 | 66,730 |
| 95060 | Santa Cruz | (408) | 49,711 | 41,483 |
| 95670 | Santa Fe Springs | (310) | 15,520 | 14,520 |
| 93454 | Santa Maria | (805) | 61,552 | 39,685 |
| *90406 | Santa Monica | (310) | 86,905 | 88,314 |
| 93060 | Santa Paula | (805) | 25,062 | 20,658 |
| *95402 | Santa Rosa | (707) | 113,313 | 82,658 |
| 92071 | Santee | (619) | 52,902 | 40,298 |
| 95070 | Saratoga | (408) | 28,061 | 29,261 |
| 94965 | Sausalito | (415) | 7,152 | 7,338 |
| 95066 | Scotts Valley | (408) | 8,667 | 6,891 |
| 90740 | Seal Beach | (310) | 25,098 | 25,975 |
| 93955 | Seaside | (408) | 38,826 | 36,567 |
| 95472 | Sebastopol | (707) | 7,004 | 5,595 |
| 93662 | Selma | (209) | 14,757 | 10,942 |
| 93263 | Shafter | (805) | 8,409 | 7,010 |
| 91024 | Sierra Madre | (818) | 10,762 | 10,837 |
| 90806 | Signal Hill | (310) | 8,371 | 5,734 |
| *93065 | Simi Valley | (805) | 100,218 | 77,500 |
| 92075 | Solana Beach | (619) | 12,968 | 12,250 |
| 93960 | Soledad | (408) | 7,161 | 5,928 |
| 95476 | Sonoma | (707) | 8,168 | 6,054 |
| 95073 | Soquel(u) | (408) | 9,188 | 6,212 |
| 91733 | South El Monte | (213) | 20,850 | 16,623 |
| 90280 | South Gate | (213) | 86,284 | 66,784 |
| 95705 | South Lake Tahoe | (916) | 21,586 | 20,681 |
| 95965 | South Oroville(u) | (916) | 7,463 | 7,240 |
| 91030 | South Pasadena | (818) | 23,936 | 22,681 |
| 94080 | South San Francisco | (415) | 54,312 | 49,393 |
| 91770 | South San Gabriel(u) | (213) | 7,700 | 5,421 |
| 91744 | South San Jose Hills(u) | (408) | 17,814 | 16,049 |
| 90605 | South Whittier(u) | (310) | 49,514 | 43,815 |
| 95991 | South Yuba City(u) | (916) | 8,816 | 7,530 |
| *91979 | Spring Valley(u) | (619) | 55,331 | 40,191 |
| 94305 | Stanford(u) | (415) | 18,097 | 11,045 |
| 95680 | Stanton | (714) | 30,491 | 23,723 |
| *95204 | Stockton | (209) | 210,943 | 148,283 |
| 94585 | Suisun City | (707) | 22,704 | 11,087 |
| 92381 | Sun City(u) | (714) | 14,930 | 8,460 |
| *94086 | Sunnyvale | (408) | 117,324 | 106,618 |
| 96130 | Susanville | (916) | 7,279 | 6,520 |
| 93268 | Taft | (805) | 5,902 | 5,316 |
| 94941 | Tamalpais-Homestead Valley(u) | (415) | 9,601 | 8,511 |

| ZIP code | Place | | 1990 | 1980 |
|---|---|---|---|---|
| 93561 | Tehachapi | (805) | 6,182 | 4,126 |
| *92391 | Temecula | (909) | 27,099 | 4,289 |
| 91780 | Temple City | (818) | 31,153 | 28,972 |
| 95965 | Thermalito(u) | | 5,646 | 4,961 |
| *91360 | Thousand Oaks | (805) | 104,381 | 77,072 |
| 94920 | Tiburon | (415) | 7,532 | 6,685 |
| *90510 | Torrance | (310) | 133,107 | 129,881 |
| 95396 | Tracy | (209) | 33,558 | 18,428 |
| 93274 | Tulare | (209) | 33,249 | 22,530 |
| 95380 | Turlock | (209) | 42,224 | 26,287 |
| 92680 | Tustin | (714) | 50,689 | 32,248 |
| 92705 | Tustin Foothills(u) | | 24,358 | 26,174 |
| 92277 | Twentynine Palms | (619) | 11,821 | 8,802 |
| 92278 | Twentynine Palms Base(u) | (619) | 10,606 | 7,079 |
| | Twin Lakes(u) | | 5,379 | 4,502 |
| 95482 | Ukiah | (707) | 14,632 | 12,035 |
| 94587 | Union City | (510) | 53,762 | 39,406 |
| 91786 | Upland | (714) | 63,374 | 47,647 |
| *95688 | Vacaville | (707) | 71,476 | 43,367 |
| 91744 | Valinda(u) | (818) | 18,735 | 18,700 |
| *94590 | Vallejo | (707) | 109,199 | 80,303 |
| 92343 | Valle Vista(u) | (714) | 8,751 | 5,474 |
| 93437 | Vandenberg AFB(u) | (805) | 9,846 | 5,839 |
| 93436 | Vandenberg Village(u) | (805) | 5,971 | 5,839 |
| 92392 | Victorville | (619) | 40,674 | 14,220 |
| 90043 | View Park-Windsor Hills(u) | (310) | 11,769 | 12,101 |
| 92667 | Villa Park | (714) | 6,299 | 7,137 |
| | Vincent(u) | | 13,711 | |
| 93277 | Visalia | (209) | 75,659 | 49,729 |
| 92083 | Vista | (619) | 71,865 | 35,834 |
| *91789 | Walnut | (714) | 29,105 | 12,478 |
| *94596 | Walnut Creek | (510) | 60,569 | 54,033 |
| 90255 | Walnut Park(u) | (310) | 14,722 | 11,811 |
| 93280 | Wasco | (805) | 12,412 | 9,613 |
| 95076 | Watsonville | (408) | 31,099 | 23,662 |
| 90044 | West Athens(u) | (310) | 8,859 | 8,531 |
| 90502 | West Carson(u) | (213) | 20,143 | 17,997 |
| 90247 | West Compton(u) | (310) | 5,451 | 5,907 |
| *91793 | West Covina | (818) | 96,086 | 80,292 |
| 90069 | West Hollywood | (310) | 36,118 | 35,754 |
| 91359 | Westlake Village | | 7,455 | 6,130 |
| 92683 | Westminster | (714) | 78,293 | 71,133 |
| 90047 | Westmont(u) | (213) | 31,044 | 27,916 |
| 94565 | West Pittsburg(u) | (510) | 17,453 | 8,773 |
| 91746 | West Puente Valley(u) | (818) | 20,254 | 20,445 |
| 95691 | West Sacramento | (916) | 28,898 | 24,482 |
| *90606 | West Whittier-Los Nietos(u) | (310) | 24,164 | 21,001 |
| *90605 | Whittier | (310) | 77,671 | 68,558 |
| 92395 | Wildomar(u) | | 10,411 | |
| 95429 | Willits | (707) | 5,027 | 4,008 |
| 90222 | Willowbrook(u) | (213) | 32,772 | 30,845 |
| 95988 | Willows | (916) | 5,988 | 4,777 |
| 95492 | Windsor(u) | | 13,371 | |
| 95388 | Winton(u) | | 7,559 | 4,995 |
| 92502 | Woodcrest(u) | | 7,796 | |
| 93286 | Woodlake | (209) | 5,678 | 4,343 |
| 95695 | Woodland | (916) | 40,230 | 30,235 |
| 94062 | Woodside | (415) | 5,034 | 5,291 |
| 92686 | Yorba Linda | (714) | 52,422 | 28,254 |
| 96097 | Yreka City | (916) | 6,948 | 5,916 |
| 95991 | Yuba City | (916) | 27,437 | 18,736 |
| 92399 | Yucaipa(u) | (714) | 32,824 | 27,654 |
| 92284 | Yucca Valley(u) | (619) | 13,701 | 8,294 |

## Colorado

| | | | | |
|---|---|---|---|---|
| 80840 | Air Force Academy | (719) | 9,062 | 8,655 |
| 81101 | Alamosa | (719) | 7,579 | 6,830 |
| 80401 | Applewood(u) | (303) | 11,069 | 12,040 |
| *80001 | Arvada | (303) | 89,218 | 84,576 |
| 81611 | Aspen | (303) | 5,049 | 3,678 |
| *80010 | Aurora | (303) | 222,103 | 158,588 |
| | Black Forest(u) | (719) | 8,143 | 3,372 |
| *80302 | Boulder | (303) | 83,295 | 76,685 |
| 80601 | Brighton | (303) | 14,203 | 12,773 |
| 80020 | Broomfield | (303) | 24,638 | 20,730 |
| 81212 | Canon City | (719) | 12,687 | 13,037 |
| 80104 | Castle Rock | (303) | 8,710 | 3,921 |
| | Castlewood(u) | (303) | 24,392 | 16,413 |
| 80110 | Cherry Hills Village | (303) | 5,245 | 5,127 |
| 81220 | Cimarron Hills | (719) | 11,160 | 6,597 |
| 81520 | Clifton | (303) | 12,671 | 5,223 |
| *80901 | Colorado Springs | (719) | 281,140 | 215,105 |
| 80120 | Columbine | (303) | 23,969 | 23,523 |
| 80022 | Commerce City | (303) | 16,466 | 16,234 |
| 81321 | Cortez | (303) | 7,284 | 7,095 |
| 81625 | Craig | (303) | 8,091 | 8,133 |
| *80817 | Denver | (303) | 467,610 | 492,686 |
| 80022 | Derby(u) | (303) | 6,043 | 8,578 |
| 81301 | Durango | (303) | 12,439 | 11,649 |
| *80110 | Englewood | (303) | 29,396 | 30,021 |
| 80620 | Evans | (303) | 5,877 | 5,063 |
| 80439 | Evergreen | (303) | 7,582 | 6,376 |
| 80221 | Federal Heights | (303) | 9,342 | 7,838 |
| 80913 | Fort Carson(u) | (719) | 11,309 | 13,219 |
| *80521 | Fort Collins | (303) | 87,491 | 65,092 |
| 80621 | Fort Lupton | (303) | 5,159 | 4,251 |

| ZIP code | Place | | 1990 | 1980 |
|---|---|---|---|---|
| 80701 | Fort Morgan | (303) | 9,068 | 8,768 |
| 80817 | Fountain | (719) | 10,175 | 8,324 |
| 81504 | Fruitvale(u) | | 5,222 | .... |
| 81522 | Gateway(u) | (303) | 7,510 | |
| 81601 | Glenwood Springs | (303) | 6,561 | 4,637 |
| 80401 | Golden | (303) | 13,127 | 12,237 |
| 81501 | Grand Junction | (303) | 29,255 | 27,956 |
| *80631 | Greeley | (303) | 60,454 | 53,006 |
| 80110 | Greenwood Village | (303) | 7,589 | 5,729 |
| 80501 | Gunbarrel(u) | (303) | 9,388 | 5,172 |
| 80126 | Highlands Ranch(u) | | 10,181 | .... |
| | Ken Caryl | (303) | 24,391 | 10,661 |
| 80026 | Lafayette | (303) | 14,708 | 8,985 |
| 81050 | La Junta | (719) | 7,678 | 8,338 |
| 80215 | Lakewood | (303) | 126,475 | 113,808 |
| 81052 | Lamar | (719) | 8,343 | 7,713 |
| *80120 | Littleton | (303) | 33,711 | 28,631 |
| 80501 | Longmont | (303) | 51,529 | 42,942 |
| 80027 | Louisville | (303) | 12,363 | 5,593 |
| *80537 | Loveland | (303) | 37,357 | 30,215 |
| 81401 | Montrose | (303) | 8,854 | 8,722 |
| 80233 | Northglenn | (303) | 27,195 | 29,847 |
| 80649 | Orchard Mesa(u) | | 5,977 | 4,876 |
| 80134 | Parker | (303) | 5,450 | 290 |
| *81001 | Pueblo | (719) | 98,640 | 101,686 |
| | Redlands(u) | | 9,355 | .... |
| 80911 | Security-Widefield(u) | (719) | 23,822 | 18,768 |
| 80221 | Sherrelwood(u) | (303) | 16,636 | 17,629 |
| 80122 | Southglenn(u) | (303) | 43,087 | 37,787 |
| 80477 | Steamboat Springs | (303) | 6,695 | 5,098 |
| 80751 | Sterling | (303) | 10,362 | 11,385 |
| 80906 | Stratmoor(u) | (719) | 5,854 | 5,519 |
| 80229 | Thornton | (303) | 55,031 | 42,054 |
| 81082 | Trinidad | (719) | 8,580 | 9,663 |
| 80229 | Welby(u) | (303) | 10,218 | 9,668 |
| *80030 | Westminster | (303) | 74,619 | 50,211 |
| 80221 | Westminster East(u) | (303) | 5,197 | 6,002 |
| 80033 | Wheat Ridge | (303) | 29,419 | 30,293 |
| 80550 | Windsor | (303) | 5,062 | 4,277 |

## Connecticut (203)

*See Note on Page 373*

| | | | | |
|---|---|---|---|---|
| 06401 | Ansonia | | 18,403 | 19,039 |
| 06001 | Avon | | 13,937 | 11,201 |
| 06403 | Beacon Falls | | 5,083 | .... |
| 06037 | Berlin | | 16,787 | 15,121 |
| 06801 | Bethel | | 17,541 | 16,004 |
| 06002 | Bloomfield | | 19,483 | 18,608 |
| 06405 | Branford | | 27,603 | 23,363 |
| *06602 | Bridgeport | | 141,686 | 142,546 |
| 06010 | Bristol | | 60,640 | 57,370 |
| 06804 | Brookfield | | 14,113 | 12,872 |
| 06234 | Brooklyn | | 6,681 | 5,691 |
| 06013 | Burlington | | 7,026 | 5,660 |
| 06019 | Canton | | 8,268 | 7,635 |
| 06040 | Central Manchester(u) | | 30,934 | 21,103 |
| 06410 | Cheshire | | 25,684 | 21,788 |
| 06413 | Clinton | | 12,767 | 11,195 |
| 06415 | Colchester | | 10,980 | 7,761 |
| 06340 | Conning Towers-Nautilus Park(u) | | 10,013 | 9,665 |
| 06238 | Coventry | | 10,063 | 8,895 |
| 06416 | Cromwell | | 12,286 | 10,265 |
| 06810 | Danbury | | 65,585 | 60,470 |
| 06820 | Darien | | 18,130 | 18,892 |
| 06418 | Derby | | 12,199 | 12,346 |
| 06422 | Durham | | 5,732 | 5,143 |
| 06423 | East Haddam | | 6,676 | 5,621 |
| 06424 | East Hampton | | 10,428 | 8,572 |
| 06108 | East Hartford | | 50,452 | 52,563 |
| 06512 | East Haven | | 26,144 | 25,028 |
| 06333 | East Lyme | | 13,870 | 11,399 |
| 06016 | East Windsor | | 10,081 | 8,925 |
| 06425 | Easton | | 6,303 | 5,962 |
| 06029 | Ellington | | 11,197 | 9,711 |
| 06082 | Enfield | | 45,532 | 42,695 |
| 06426 | Essex | | 5,904 | 5,078 |
| 06430 | Fairfield | | 53,418 | 54,849 |
| 06032 | Farmington | | 20,608 | 16,407 |
| 06033 | Glastonbury Center | | 27,901 | 24,327 |
| 06035 | Granby | | 9,369 | 7,956 |
| 06830 | Greenwich | | 58,441 | 59,578 |
| 06351 | Griswold | | 10,384 | 8,967 |
| 06340 | Groton | | 45,144 | 41,062 |
| 06340 | Groton Borough | | 9,837 | 10,086 |
| 06437 | Guilford | | 19,848 | 17,375 |
| 06438 | Haddam | | 6,769 | 6,383 |
| 06514 | Hamden | | 52,434 | 51,071 |
| *06101 | Hartford | | 139,739 | 136,392 |
| 06791 | Harwinton | | 5,228 | .... |
| 06082 | Hazardville(u) | | 5,179 | 5,436 |
| 06248 | Hebron | | 7,079 | 5,453 |
| 06037 | Kensington(u) | | 8,306 | 7,502 |
| 06239 | Killingly | | 15,889 | 14,519 |
| 06249 | Lebanon | | 6,041 | |
| 06339 | Ledyard | | 14,913 | 13,735 |
| 06759 | Litchfield | | 8,365 | 7,365 |

| ZIP code | Place | 1990 | 1980 |
|---|---|---|---|
| 06443 | Madison | 14,031 | 9,768 |
| 06040 | Manchester | 49,761 | 51,618 |
| 06250 | Mansfield | 20,634 | 19,994 |
| 06447 | Marlborough | 5,535 | ..... |
| 06450 | Meriden | 59,479 | 57,118 |
| 06762 | Middlebury | 6,145 | 5,995 |
| 06457 | Middletown | 42,762 | 39,040 |
| 06460 | Milford | 48,938 | 48,168 |
| 06468 | Monroe | 16,896 | 14,010 |
| 06353 | Montville | 16,673 | 16,455 |
| 06770 | Naugatuck | 30,625 | 26,456 |
| *06050 | New Britain | 75,491 | 73,840 |
| 06840 | New Canaan | 17,864 | 17,931 |
| 06810 | New Fairfield | 12,911 | 11,260 |
| 06057 | New Hartford | 5,769 | ..... |
| *06510 | New Haven | 130,474 | 126,089 |
| 06111 | Newington | 29,208 | 28,841 |
| 06320 | New London | 28,540 | 28,842 |
| 06776 | New Milford | 23,629 | 19,420 |
| 06470 | Newtown | 20,779 | 19,107 |
| 06471 | North Branford | 12,996 | 11,554 |
| 06473 | North Haven | 22,249 | 22,080 |
| 06856 | Norwalk | 78,331 | 77,767 |
| 06360 | Norwich | 37,391 | 38,074 |
| 06779 | Oakville(u) | 8,741 | 8,737 |
| 06371 | Old Lyme | 6,535 | 6,159 |
| 06475 | Old Saybrook | 9,552 | 9,287 |
| 06477 | Orange | 12,830 | 13,237 |
| 06483 | Oxford | 8,685 | ..... |
| 02891 | Pawcatuck(u) | 5,289 | 5,216 |
| 06374 | Plainfield | 14,363 | 17,392 |
| 06062 | Plainville | 16,401 | 16,733 |
| 06782 | Plymouth | 11,832 | 10,732 |
| 06480 | Portland | 8,418 | 8,383 |
| 06360 | Preston | 5,006 | ..... |
| 06712 | Prospect | 7,775 | 6,807 |
| 06260 | Putnam | 6,835 | 6,855 |
| ..... | Putnam | 9,031 | 8,580 |
| 06875 | Redding | 7,927 | 7,272 |
| 06877 | Ridgefield Center(u) | 6,363 | 6,066 |
| 06877 | Ridgefield | 20,919 | 20,120 |
| 06067 | Rocky Hill | 16,554 | 14,559 |
| 06483 | Seymour | 14,288 | 13,434 |
| 06484 | Shelton | 35,418 | 31,314 |
| 06082 | Sherwood Manor(u) | 6,357 | 6,303 |
| 06070 | Simsbury | 22,023 | 21,161 |
| 06071 | Somers | 9,108 | ..... |
| 06488 | Southbury | 15,818 | 14,156 |
| 06489 | Southington | 38,518 | 36,879 |
| 06074 | South Windsor | 22,090 | 17,198 |
| 06082 | Southwood Acres(u) | 8,963 | 9,779 |
| 06075 | Stafford | 11,091 | 9,268 |
| *06904 | Stamford | 108,056 | 102,466 |
| 06378 | Stonington | 16,919 | 6,220 |
| 06268 | Storrs(u) | 12,198 | 11,394 |
| 06497 | Stratford | 49,389 | 50,541 |
| 06078 | Suffield | 11,427 | 9,294 |
| 06786 | Terryville(u) | 5,426 | 5,234 |
| 06787 | Thomaston | 6,947 | 6,272 |
| 06277 | Thompson | 8,668 | 8,141 |
| 06082 | Thompsonville(u) | 8,458 | ..... |
| 06084 | Tolland | 11,001 | 9,694 |
| 06790 | Torrington | 33,687 | 30,987 |
| 06611 | Trumbull | 32,016 | 32,989 |
| 06066 | Vernon | 29,841 | 27,974 |
| 06492 | Wallingford | 40,822 | 37,274 |
| *06701 | Waterbury | 108,961 | 103,266 |
| 06385 | Waterford | 17,930 | 17,843 |
| 06795 | Watertown | 20,456 | 19,489 |
| 06107 | West Hartford | 60,110 | 61,301 |
| 06516 | West Haven | 54,021 | 53,184 |
| 06498 | Westbrook | 5,414 | 5,216 |
| 06883 | Weston | 8,648 | 8,284 |
| 06880 | Westport | 24,410 | 24,407 |
| 06109 | Wethersfield | 25,651 | 25,651 |
| 06226 | Willimantic | 14,746 | 14,652 |
| 06279 | Willington | 5,979 | ..... |
| 06897 | Wilton | 15,989 | 15,351 |
| 06094 | Winchester | 11,524 | 10,841 |
| 06280 | Windham | 22,039 | 21,062 |
| 06095 | Windsor | 27,817 | 25,204 |
| 06096 | Windsor Locks | 12,358 | 12,190 |
| 06098 | Winsted | 8,254 | 8,092 |
| 06716 | Wolcott | 13,700 | 13,008 |
| 06525 | Woodbridge | 7,924 | 7,761 |
| 06798 | Woodbury | 8,131 | 6,942 |
| 06281 | Woodstock | 6,008 | 5,117 |

### Delaware (302)

| ZIP code | Place | 1990 | 1980 |
|---|---|---|---|
| 19713 | Brookside(u) | 15,307 | 15,255 |
| 19703 | Claymont(u) | 9,800 | 10,022 |
| 19901 | Dover | 27,630 | 23,507 |
| 19802 | Edgemoor(u) | 5,853 | 7,397 |
| 19805 | Elsmere | 5,935 | 6,493 |
| 19963 | Milford | 6,032 | 5,366 |
| *19711 | Newark | 26,463 | 25,247 |

| ZIP code | Place | 1990 | 1980 |
|---|---|---|---|
| 19800 | Pike Creek(u) | 10,163 | ..... |
| 19973 | Seaford | 5,689 | 5,256 |
| 19977 | Smyrna | 5,231 | 4,750 |
| 19804 | Stanton(u) | 5,028 | 5,495 |
| 19803 | Talleyville(u) | 6,346 | 6,880 |
| *19899 | Wilmington | 71,529 | 70,195 |
| 19720 | Wilmington Manor | 8,568 | 9,233 |

### District of Columbia (202)

| ZIP code | Place | 1990 | 1980 |
|---|---|---|---|
| *20013 | Washington | 606,900 | 638,432 |

### Florida

| ZIP code | Place | | 1990 | 1980 |
|---|---|---|---|---|
| *32701 | Altamonte Springs | (407) | 35,167 | 21,105 |
| ..... | Andover(u) | | 6,251 | ..... |
| 33572 | Apollo Beach(u) | | 6,025 | 4,014 |
| 32703 | Apopka | (407) | 13,611 | 6,019 |
| 33821 | Arcadia | (813) | 6,488 | 6,002 |
| 32233 | Atlantic Beach | (904) | 11,636 | 7,847 |
| 33823 | Auburndale | (813) | 8,858 | 6,501 |
| ..... | Aventura(u) | (305) | 14,914 | 9,698 |
| 33825 | Avon Park | (813) | 8,078 | 8,026 |
| 32807 | Azalea Park(u) | (407) | 8,926 | 8,301 |
| 33830 | Bartow | (813) | 14,716 | 14,780 |
| ..... | Bay Hill(u) | | 5,346 | ..... |
| 34667 | Bayonet Point(u) | (813) | 21,860 | 16,455 |
| 33505 | Bayshore Gardens(u) | (813) | 17,062 | 14,945 |
| 33589 | Beacon Square(u) | (813) | 6,265 | 6,513 |
| ..... | Bee Ridge | | 6,406 | 3,313 |
| 32073 | Bellair-Meadowbrook Terrace(u) | (813) | 15,606 | 12,144 |
| 33430 | Belle Glade | (407) | 16,177 | 16,535 |
| ..... | Belle Isle | | 5,272 | 2,848 |
| 32506 | Belleview | (904) | 19,386 | 15,439 |
| 32665 | Beverly Hills(u) | (904) | 6,163 | 5,024 |
| ..... | Bloomingdale(u) | | 13,912 | ..... |
| ..... | Boca Del Mar(u) | | 17,754 | ..... |
| *33487 | Boca Raton | (407) | 61,486 | 49,447 |
| 33959 | Bonita Springs(u) | (813) | 13,600 | 5,435 |
| 33435 | Boynton Beach | (407) | 46,284 | 35,624 |
| *34206 | Bradenton | (813) | 43,769 | 30,228 |
| 33511 | Brandon(u) | (813) | 57,985 | 41,826 |
| 32525 | Brent(u) | (904) | 21,624 | 21,872 |
| 33317 | Broadview Park(u) | (305) | 6,109 | 6,022 |
| 33313 | Broadview-Pompano Park(u) | (305) | 5,230 | 5,256 |
| *34601 | Brooksville | (904) | 7,589 | 5,582 |
| 33311 | Browardale(u) | (305) | 6,257 | 7,571 |
| 33142 | Brownsville(u) | (813) | 15,607 | 18,058 |
| 34743 | Buena Ventura Lakes(u) | | 14,148 | ..... |
| 32401 | Callaway | (904) | 12,253 | 7,154 |
| 32920 | Cape Canaveral | (407) | 8,014 | 5,733 |
| 33904 | Cape Coral | (813) | 74,991 | 32,103 |
| 33055 | Carol City(u) | (305) | 53,331 | 47,349 |
| 33688 | Carrollwood(u) | (813) | 7,195 | ..... |
| ..... | Carrollwood Village(u) | | 15,051 | ..... |
| 32707 | Casselberry | (407) | 18,911 | 15,037 |
| 33401 | Century Village(u) | (305) | 8,363 | 10,619 |
| *34615 | Clearwater City | (813) | 98,784 | 85,170 |
| 32711 | Clermont | (904) | 6,910 | 5,461 |
| 33440 | Clewiston | (813) | 6,085 | 5,219 |
| 32922 | Cocoa | (407) | 17,722 | 16,096 |
| 32931 | Cocoa Beach | (407) | 12,123 | 10,926 |
| 32922 | Cocoa West(u) | (407) | 6,160 | 6,432 |
| 33066 | Coconut Creek | (305) | 27,484 | 6,288 |
| 33064 | Collier Manor-Cresthaven(u) | (305) | 7,322 | 7,045 |
| 33801 | Combee Settlement(u) | (813) | 5,463 | 5,400 |
| 32809 | Conway(u) | (407) | 13,159 | 24,027 |
| 33314 | Cooper City | (305) | 21,335 | 10,140 |
| 33134 | Coral Gables | (305) | 40,091 | 43,241 |
| 33065 | Coral Springs | (305) | 79,443 | 37,349 |
| ..... | Coral Terrace(u) | (305) | 23,255 | 22,702 |
| 32536 | Crestview | (904) | 9,886 | 7,617 |
| 33803 | Crystal Lake(u) | (813) | 5,300 | 6,827 |
| 33157 | Cutler(u) | (305) | 16,201 | 15,593 |
| 33157 | Cutler Ridge(u) | (305) | 21,268 | 20,886 |
| 33880 | Cypress Gardens(u) | (813) | 9,188 | 8,043 |
| ..... | Cypress Lake(u) | (813) | 10,491 | 8,721 |
| 33525 | Dade City | (904) | 5,633 | 4,923 |
| 33004 | Dania | (305) | 13,183 | 11,796 |
| 33314 | Davie | (305) | 47,835 | 20,515 |
| *32015 | Daytona Beach | (904) | 61,991 | 54,176 |
| 32713 | De Bary | (407) | 7,176 | 4,980 |
| 33441 | Deerfield Beach | (305) | 46,997 | 39,193 |
| 32433 | DeFuniak Springs | (904) | 5,200 | 5,563 |
| 32720 | De Land | (904) | 16,622 | 15,354 |
| *33444 | Delray Beach | (407) | 47,181 | 34,329 |
| 33617 | Del Rio(u) | (813) | 8,248 | 7,409 |
| 32725 | Deltona(u) | (407) | 50,828 | 15,710 |
| 32541 | Destin | (904) | 8,090 | 3,913 |
| ..... | Doctor Phillips(u) | | 7,963 | ..... |
| *34698 | Dunedin | (813) | 33,997 | 30,203 |
| 33610 | East Lake-Orient Park(u) | (813) | 6,171 | 5,612 |
| 33940 | East Naples(u) | (813) | 22,951 | 12,127 |
| 32032 | Edgewater | (904) | 15,351 | 6,726 |
| 32542 | Eglin AFB(u) | (904) | 8,347 | 7,574 |

| ZIP code | Place | | 1990 | 1980 |
|---|---|---|---|---|
| 33614 | Egypt Lake(u) | (813) | 14,580 | 11,932 |
| 34680 | Elfers(u) | (813) | 12,356 | 11,396 |
| *34223 | Englewood(u) | (813) | 15,025 | 10,229 |
| 32504 | Ensley(u) | (904) | 16,362 | 14,422 |
| 32726 | Eustis | (904) | 12,867 | 9,453 |
| 32804 | Fairview Shores(u) | (305) | 13,192 | 10,174 |
| 32034 | Fernandina Beach | (904) | 8,765 | 7,224 |
| 32730 | Fern Park(u) | (407) | 8,294 | 8,890 |
| 32504 | Ferry Pass(u) | (904) | 26,301 | 16,910 |
| 33030 | Florida City | (305) | 5,978 | 6,174 |
| ..... | Florida Ridge | | 12,218 | 4,988 |
| 32751 | Forest City(u) | (407) | 10,638 | 6,819 |
| ..... | Forest Island Park(u) | | 5,988 | |
| *33319 | Fort Lauderdale | (305) | 149,238 | 153,279 |
| *33901 | Fort Myers | (813) | 45,206 | 36,638 |
| 33931 | Fort Myers Beach(u) | (813) | 9,284 | 5,753 |
| ..... | Fort Myers Shores(u) | | 5,460 | 4,426 |
| *34950 | Fort Pierce | (407) | 36,830 | 33,802 |
| 33452 | Fort Pierce North(u) | (407) | 5,833 | 5,929 |
| ..... | Fort Pierce South(u) | (407) | 5,320 | 3,324 |
| 32548 | Fort Walton Beach | (904) | 21,407 | 20,829 |
| ..... | Fruit Cove(u) | | 5,904 | 3,906 |
| ..... | Fruitville(u) | (813) | 9,808 | 3,070 |
| *32601 | Gainesville | (904) | 85,075 | 81,371 |
| 33801 | Gibsonia(u) | (813) | 5,168 | 5,011 |
| 33534 | Gibsonton(u) | (813) | 7,706 | .... |
| 32960 | Gifford(u) | (407) | 6,278 | 6,240 |
| ..... | Gladeview(u) | (305) | 15,637 | 18,919 |
| 33143 | Glenvar Heights(u) | (305) | 14,823 | 13,216 |
| 33999 | Golden Gate(u) | (813) | 14,148 | 4,327 |
| 33055 | Golden Glades(u) | (305) | 25,474 | 23,154 |
| 32733 | Goldenrod(u) | (407) | 12,362 | 13,681 |
| 32560 | Gonzalez(u) | (904) | 7,669 | 6,084 |
| 33170 | Goulds(u) | (305) | 7,284 | 7,078 |
| ..... | Greater Northdale(u) | | 16,318 | .... |
| 33463 | Greenacres City | (407) | 18,683 | 8,870 |
| 32561 | Gulf Breeze | (904) | 5,530 | 5,478 |
| 33581 | Gulf Gate Estates(u) | (813) | 11,622 | 9,248 |
| 33707 | Gulfport | (813) | 11,709 | 11,180 |
| 33844 | Haines City | (813) | 11,683 | 10,799 |
| 33009 | Hallandale | (305) | 30,997 | 36,460 |
| ..... | Hammocks(u) | | 10,897 | .... |
| ..... | Hamptons at Boca Raton(u) | | 11,686 | .... |
| *33010 | Hialeah | (305) | 188,008 | 145,254 |
| 33016 | Hialeah Gardens | | 7,727 | 2,700 |
| ..... | Highpoint(u) | | 13,818 | .... |
| 33455 | Hobe Sound(u) | (407) | 11,507 | 6,822 |
| 34690 | Holiday(u) | (813) | 19,360 | 18,392 |
| 32017 | Holly Hill | (904) | 11,141 | 9,953 |
| *33022 | Hollywood | (305) | 121,720 | 121,323 |
| 33030 | Homestead | (305) | 26,694 | 20,668 |
| 33030 | Homestead AFB | (305) | 5,153 | 7,594 |
| 32646 | Homosassa Springs(u) | (904) | 6,271 | 1,426 |
| 34667 | Hudson(u) | (813) | 7,344 | 5,799 |
| 33934 | Immokalee(u) | (813) | 14,120 | 11,038 |
| 32937 | Indian Harbour Beach | (407) | 6,933 | 5,967 |
| 32650 | Inverness | (904) | 5,797 | 4,095 |
| 33880 | Inwood(u) | (813) | 6,824 | 6,668 |
| ..... | Iona(u) | | 9,565 | .... |
| 33162 | Ives Estates(u) | (305) | 13,531 | 12,623 |
| 32250 | Jacksonville Beach | (904) | 17,839 | 15,462 |
| *32201 | Jacksonville | (904) | 635,230 | 540,920 |
| ..... | Jan Phyl Village(u) | | 5,308 | 2,785 |
| 33568 | Jasmine Estates(u) | (813) | 17,136 | 11,995 |
| *34957 | Jensen Beach(u) | (407) | 9,884 | 6,639 |
| 33458 | Jupiter | (407) | 24,907 | 9,868 |
| 33183 | Kendale Lakes(u) | (305) | 48,524 | 32,769 |
| 33156 | Kendall(u) | (305) | 87,271 | 73,758 |
| ..... | Kendall Lakes West | | 6,038 | .... |
| 33149 | Key Biscayne(u) | (305) | 8,854 | 6,313 |
| 33037 | Key Largo(u) | (305) | 11,336 | 7,447 |
| 33040 | Key West | (305) | 24,832 | 24,382 |
| ..... | Kings Point(u) | (305) | 12,422 | 8,724 |
| 32741 | Kissimmee | (407) | 30,050 | 15,487 |
| 32159 | Lady Lake | | 8,071 | 1,193 |
| 32055 | Lake City | (904) | 9,626 | 9,257 |
| *33802 | Lakeland | (813) | 70,576 | 47,406 |
| 33801 | Lakeland Highlands(u) | (813) | 9,972 | 10,426 |
| ..... | Lake Lorraine(u) | (904) | 6,779 | 5,427 |
| 33054 | Lake Lucerne(u) | (305) | 9,478 | 9,762 |
| 33612 | Lake Magdalene(u) | (813) | 15,973 | 13,331 |
| 32746 | Lake Mary | (407) | 5,929 | 2,853 |
| 33403 | Lake Park | (407) | 6,704 | 6,909 |
| ..... | Lakes by the Bay(u) | | 5,615 | .... |
| ..... | Lakeside(u) | (904) | 29,137 | 10,534 |
| 33853 | Lake Wales | (813) | 9,670 | 8,466 |
| ..... | Lakewood Park(u) | | 7,211 | 3,411 |
| 33460 | Lake Worth | (407) | 28,564 | 27,048 |
| 34639 | Land O' Lakes(u) | | 7,892 | 4,515 |
| 33460 | Lantana | | 8,392 | 8,048 |
| *34640 | Largo | (813) | 65,910 | 57,958 |
| 33313 | Lauderdale Lakes | (305) | 27,341 | 25,426 |
| 33313 | Lauderhill | (305) | 49,708 | 37,271 |
| 34272 | Laurel(u) | (813) | 8,245 | 6,368 |
| 33717 | Lealman(u) | (813) | 21,748 | 19,873 |
| 32748 | Leesburg | (904) | 14,903 | 13,191 |
| *33936 | Lehigh Acres(u) | (813) | 13,611 | 9,604 |
| 33033 | Leisure City(u) | (305) | 19,379 | 17,905 |
| 33064 | Lighthouse Point | (305) | 10,378 | 11,488 |

| ZIP code | Place | | 1990 | 1980 |
|---|---|---|---|---|
| ..... | Lindgren Acres(u) | (305) | 22,290 | 11,986 |
| 32060 | Live Oak | (904) | 6,332 | 6,732 |
| 32810 | Lockhart(u) | (407) | 11,636 | 10,569 |
| 34228 | Longboat Key | (813) | 5,937 | 4,843 |
| *32750 | Longwood | (407) | 13,316 | 10,029 |
| 33549 | Lutz(u) | (813) | 10,552 | 5,555 |
| 32444 | Lynn Haven | (904) | 9,298 | 6,239 |
| ..... | McGregor(u) | | 6,504 | .... |
| 32751 | Maitland | (407) | 8,932 | 8,763 |
| 33550 | Mango(u) | (813) | 8,700 | 6,493 |
| 33050 | Marathon(u) | (305) | 8,857 | 7,568 |
| 33937 | Marco(u) | | 9,493 | 4,679 |
| 33063 | Margate | (305) | 42,985 | 35,900 |
| 32446 | Marianna | (904) | 6,292 | 7,006 |
| *32901 | Melbourne | (407) | 60,034 | 46,536 |
| 33314 | Melrose Park(u) | (904) | 6,477 | 5,662 |
| 33561 | Memphis(u) | (813) | 6,760 | 5,501 |
| 32952 | Merritt Island(u) | (407) | 32,886 | 30,708 |
| *33152 | Miami | (305) | 358,648 | 346,681 |
| 33139 | Miami Beach | (305) | 92,639 | 96,298 |
| 33023 | Miami Gardens —Utopia-Carver(u) | (305) | 7,448 | 9025 |
| 33014 | Miami Lakes(u) | (305) | 12,750 | 9,809 |
| 33153 | Miami Shores | (305) | 10,084 | 9,244 |
| 33166 | Miami Springs | (305) | 13,268 | 12,350 |
| ..... | Micco(u) | | 8,757 | .... |
| 32068 | Middleburg(u) | | 6,223 | 3,585 |
| 32570 | Milton | (904) | 7,216 | 7,206 |
| 32754 | Mims(u) | (407) | 9,412 | 7,583 |
| 33023 | Miramar | (305) | 40,663 | 32,813 |
| 32757 | Mount Dora | (904) | 7,316 | 5,883 |
| 32506 | Myrtle Grove(u) | (904) | 17,402 | 14,238 |
| *33962 | Naples | (813) | 19,505 | 17,581 |
| 33940 | Naples Park(u) | (813) | 8,002 | 5,436 |
| 33032 | Naranja(u) | (305) | 5,790 | 10,381 |
| 33860 | Neptune Beach | (904) | 6,816 | 5,248 |
| *34652 | New Port Richey | (813) | 14,044 | 11,196 |
| 33552 | New Port Richey East(u) | (813) | 9,683 | 6,147 |
| 32169 | New Smyrna Beach | (904) | 16,549 | 13,557 |
| 32578 | Niceville | (904) | 10,509 | 8,543 |
| 33169 | Norland(u) | (305) | 22,109 | 19,471 |
| 33308 | North Andrews Gardens(u) | (305) | 9,002 | 8,967 |
| 33141 | North Bay Village | | 5,383 | 4,920 |
| 33903 | North Fort Myers(u) | (813) | 30,027 | 22,808 |
| 33068 | North Lauderdale | (305) | 26,473 | 18,479 |
| 33161 | North Miami | (305) | 50,001 | 42,566 |
| 33160 | North Miami Beach | (305) | 35,361 | 36,553 |
| 33940 | North Naples(u) | (813) | 13,422 | 7,950 |
| 33408 | North Palm Beach | (407) | 11,284 | 11,344 |
| 33596 | North Port | (813) | 11,973 | 6,205 |
| ..... | North Sarasota(u) | | 6,702 | 4,997 |
| 33860 | Oak Ridge(u) | (813) | 15,388 | 15,477 |
| 33307 | Oakland Park | (305) | 26,326 | 22,944 |
| 32670 | Ocala | (904) | 42,045 | 37,170 |
| 32548 | Ocean City(u) | (904) | 5,422 | 5,582 |
| 32761 | Ocoee | (407) | 12,778 | 7,803 |
| 33163 | Ojus(u) | (305) | 15,519 | 17,344 |
| 34677 | Oldsmar | | 8,361 | 2,608 |
| 33165 | Olympia Heights(u) | (305) | 37,792 | 33,112 |
| 33054 | Opa-Locka | (305) | 15,283 | 14,460 |
| 33054 | Opa-Locka North(u) | (305) | 6,568 | 5,721 |
| 32774 | Orange City | | 5,347 | 2,795 |
| 32073 | Orange Park | (904) | 9,488 | 8,766 |
| *32820 | Orlando | (407) | 164,674 | 128,291 |
| 32811 | Orlovista(u) | (407) | 5,990 | 6,474 |
| 32176 | Ormond Beach | (904) | 29,721 | 21,438 |
| 32074 | Ormond By-The-Sea(u) | (904) | 8,157 | 7,665 |
| 32765 | Oviedo | (407) | 11,114 | 3,074 |
| 32570 | Pace(u) | (904) | 6,277 | 5,006 |
| ..... | Page Park-Pine Manor(u) | | 5,116 | 5,006 |
| 33476 | Pahokee | (407) | 6,822 | 6,346 |
| 32077 | Palatka | (904) | 10,444 | 10,175 |
| 32905 | Palm Bay | (407) | 62,543 | 18,560 |
| 33480 | Palm Beach | (407) | 9,814 | 9,729 |
| 33403 | Palm Beach Gardens | (407) | 22,990 | 14,407 |
| 32135 | Palm Coast(u) | | 14,287 | 2,837 |
| 34221 | Palmetto | (813) | 9,268 | 8,637 |
| 33157 | Palmetto Estates(u) | (305) | 12,293 | 11,116 |
| *34683 | Palm Harbor(u) | (813) | 50,256 | 5,215 |
| 33619 | Palm River-Clair Mel(u) | (813) | 13,691 | 14,447 |
| 33460 | Palm Springs | (407) | 9,763 | 8,166 |
| 33012 | Palm Springs North(u) | (407) | 5,300 | 5,838 |
| ..... | Palm Valley | | 9,960 | .... |
| 32401 | Panama City | (904) | 34,396 | 33,346 |
| 33023 | Pembroke Pines | (305) | 65,566 | 35,776 |
| *32502 | Pensacola | (904) | 58,198 | 57,619 |
| 33157 | Perrine(u) | (305) | 15,576 | 16,129 |
| 32347 | Perry | (904) | 7,151 | 8,254 |
| 32809 | Pine Castle(u) | (407) | 8,276 | 9,992 |
| 32808 | Pine Hills(u) | (407) | 35,322 | 35,771 |
| ..... | Pine Island Ridge | | 5,244 | .... |
| *34665 | Pinellas Park | (813) | 43,571 | 32,811 |
| 33168 | Pinewood(u) | (305) | 15,518 | 16,252 |
| *33317 | Plantation | (305) | 66,692 | 48,653 |
| 33566 | Plant City | (813) | 22,754 | 17,064 |
| *33067 | Pompano Beach | (305) | 72,411 | 52,618 |
| 33064 | Pompano Beach Highlands(u) | (305) | 17,915 | 16,154 |
| 33950 | Port Charlotte(u) | (813) | 41,535 | 25,770 |
| 32019 | Port Orange | (904) | 35,307 | 18,756 |

| ZIP code | Place | | 1990 | 1980 |
|---|---|---|---|---|
| 32927 | Port St. John(u) | | 8,933 | 1,837 |
| 34952 | Port St. Lucie | (407) | 55,866 | 14,690 |
| 34992 | Port Salerno(u) | | 7,786 | 4,511 |
| 33032 | Princeton(u) | (305) | 7,073 | .... |
| *33950 | Punta Gorda | (813) | 10,637 | 6,797 |
| 32351 | Quincy | (904) | 7,452 | 8,591 |
| 33156 | Richmond Heights(u) | (305) | 8,583 | 8,577 |
| 33312 | Riverland (u) | (305) | 5,376 | 5,919 |
| 33569 | Riverview(u) | | 6,478 | .... |
| 33404 | Riviera Beach | (407) | 27,644 | 26,489 |
| 32955 | Rockledge | (407) | 16,023 | 11,877 |
| ..... | Royal Palm Beach | (407) | 15,532 | 3,423 |
| 33570 | Ruskin(u) | (813) | 6,046 | 5,117 |
| 34695 | Safety Harbor | (813) | 15,120 | 6,461 |
| 32084 | Saint Augustine | (904) | 11,692 | 11,985 |
| 34769 | Saint Cloud | (407) | 12,652 | 7,840 |
| *33702 | Saint Petersburg | (813) | 240,318 | 238,647 |
| 33706 | Saint Petersburg Beach | (813) | 9,200 | 9,354 |
| ..... | San Carlos Park(u) | | 11,785 | 3,590 |
| 33432 | Sandalfoot Cove(u) | (305) | 14,214 | 5,299 |
| 32771 | Sanford | (407) | 32,387 | 23,176 |
| 33957 | Sanibel | | 5,468 | 3,363 |
| *34236 | Sarasota | (813) | 50,897 | 48,868 |
| 33577 | Sarasota Springs(u) | (813) | 16,088 | 13,860 |
| 32937 | Satellite Beach | (407) | 9,889 | 9,163 |
| ..... | Scott Lake(u) | (305) | 14,588 | 14,154 |
| 32958 | Sebastian | (407) | 10,248 | 2,831 |
| *33870 | Sebring | (813) | 8,641 | 8,736 |
| 33584 | Seffner(u) | | 5,371 | .... |
| 34642 | Seminole | (813) | 9,251 | 4,856 |
| 33578 | Siesta Key(u) | (813) | 7,772 | 7,010 |
| 32688 | Silver Springs Shores(u) | | 6,421 | 3,983 |
| 32809 | Sky Lake(u) | (407) | 6,202 | 6,692 |
| 32703 | South Apopka(u) | (407) | 6,360 | 5,687 |
| 33505 | South Bradenton(u) | (813) | 20,398 | 14,297 |
| 32021 | South Daytona | (904) | 12,488 | 11,252 |
| 33579 | Southgate(u) | (813) | 7,324 | 7,322 |
| ..... | South Gate Ridge(u) | | 5,924 | 4,259 |
| 33143 | South Miami | (305) | 10,404 | 10,895 |
| 33157 | South Miami Heights(u) | (305) | 30,030 | 23,559 |
| ..... | South Pasadena | | 5,644 | 4,188 |
| 32937 | South Patrick Shores(u) | (407) | 10,249 | 9,816 |
| ..... | South Sarasota(u) | | 5,298 | 4,267 |
| 33595 | South Venice(u) | (813) | 11,951 | 6,075 |
| 32401 | Springfield | (904) | 8,715 | 7,220 |
| 34606 | Spring Hill(u) | (904) | 31,117 | 6,468 |
| 32091 | Starke | (904) | 5,226 | 5,306 |
| *34994 | Stuart | (407) | 11,936 | 9,467 |
| 33573 | Sun City Center(u) | (813) | 8,326 | 5,605 |
| 33160 | Sunny Isles(u) | (305) | 11,772 | 12,564 |
| 33304 | Sunrise | (305) | 64,407 | 39,681 |
| 33139 | Sunset(u) | (305) | 15,810 | 13,531 |
| 33144 | Sweetwater | (305) | 13,909 | 8,067 |
| *32303 | Tallahassee | (904) | 124,773 | 81,548 |
| 33313 | Tamarac | (305) | 44,822 | 29,376 |
| 33144 | Tamiami(u) | (305) | 33,845 | 17,607 |
| *33625 | Tampa | (813) | 280,015 | 271,577 |
| *34689 | Tarpon Springs | (813) | 17,874 | 13,251 |
| 32778 | Tavares | (904) | 7,383 | 4,398 |
| 33617 | Temple Terrace | (813) | 16,444 | 11,097 |
| 32780 | Titusville | (407) | 39,394 | 31,910 |
| 32505 | Town 'n' Country(u) | (813) | 60,946 | 37,834 |
| 33706 | Treasure Island | (813) | 7,266 | 6,316 |
| 32807 | Union Park(u) | (407) | 6,890 | 19,175 |
| 33620 | University West(u) | (904) | 23,760 | 24,514 |
| ..... | Upper Grand Lagoon(u) | | 7,855 | 3,314 |
| 32580 | Valparaiso | (904) | 6,316 | 6,142 |
| *34285 | Venice | (813) | 17,052 | 12,153 |
| 33595 | Venice Gardens(u) | (813) | 7,701 | 6,568 |
| 32960 | Vero Beach | (407) | 17,350 | 16,176 |
| 32960 | Vero Beach South(u) | (407) | 16,973 | 12,636 |
| ..... | Villages of Oriole(u) | | 5,698 | 8,724 |
| 33901 | Villas(u) | (813) | 9,898 | 8,724 |
| 32507 | Warrington(u) | (904) | 16,040 | 15,792 |
| 33314 | Washington Park(u) | (305) | 6,930 | 7,240 |
| 32703 | Wekiva Springs(u) | (407) | 23,026 | 13,386 |
| ..... | Wellington(u) | | 20,670 | 4,622 |
| 33155 | Westchester(u) | (305) | 29,883 | 29,272 |
| ..... | Westgate-Belvedere Homes(u) | | 6,880 | .... |
| 33138 | West Little River(u) | (305) | 33,575 | 32,492 |
| 32901 | West Melbourne | (407) | 8,399 | 5,078 |
| 33144 | West Miami | (305) | 5,727 | 6,076 |
| *33404 | West Palm Beach | (407) | 67,764 | 63,305 |
| ..... | West Park(u) | | 10,347 | .... |
| 32505 | West Pensacola(u) | (904) | 22,107 | 24,371 |
| 33168 | Westview(u) | (305) | 9,668 | 9,102 |
| 33165 | Westwood Lakes(u) | (305) | 11,522 | 11,478 |
| ..... | Whiskey Creek(u) | | 5,061 | .... |
| 33305 | Wilton Manors | (305) | 11,804 | 12,742 |
| 33803 | Winston(u) | (813) | 9,118 | 9,315 |
| *32787 | Winter Garden | (407) | 9,863 | 6,789 |
| 33880 | Winter Haven | (813) | 24,725 | 21,119 |
| *32789 | Winter Park | (407) | 22,623 | 22,339 |
| 32708 | Winter Springs | (407) | 22,151 | 10,475 |
| 32548 | Wright(u) | (904) | 18,945 | 13,011 |
| 32097 | Yulee(u) | | 6,915 | .... |
| 33599 | Zephyrhills | (813) | 8,220 | 5,742 |

# Georgia

| ZIP code | Place | | 1990 | 1980 |
|---|---|---|---|---|
| 31620 | Adel | (912) | 5,093 | 5,592 |
| *31701 | Albany | (912) | 78,804 | 74,425 |
| 30201 | Alpharetta | | 13,002 | 3,128 |
| 31709 | Americus | (912) | 16,512 | 16,120 |
| *30601 | Athens | (706) | 45,734 | 42,549 |
| *30304 | Atlanta | (404) | 393,929 | 425,022 |
| *30901 | Augusta | (706) | 44,639 | 47,532 |
| 31717 | Bainbridge | (912) | 10,803 | 10,553 |
| 30032 | Belvedere Park(u) | (404) | 18,089 | 17,766 |
| 31723 | Blakely | (912) | 5,595 | 5,880 |
| 31520 | Brunswick | (912) | 16,433 | 17,605 |
| 30518 | Buford | (404) | 8,771 | 6,578 |
| 31728 | Cairo | (912) | 9,035 | 8,777 |
| 30701 | Calhoun | (706) | 7,135 | 5,563 |
| 31730 | Camilla | (912) | 5,124 | 5,414 |
| 30032 | Candler-McAfee(u) | (404) | 29,491 | 27,306 |
| 30117 | Carrollton | (404) | 16,029 | 14,078 |
| 30120 | Cartersville | (404) | 12,037 | 9,247 |
| 30125 | Cedartown | (404) | 7,978 | 8,619 |
| 30341 | Chamblee | (404) | 7,668 | 7,137 |
| 30021 | Clarkston | (404) | 5,385 | 4,539 |
| 30337 | College Park | (404) | 20,645 | 24,632 |
| *31902 | Columbus | (706) | 178,681 | 169,441 |
| 30027 | Conley(u) | (404) | 5,528 | 6,033 |
| 30207 | Conyers | (404) | 7,380 | 6,567 |
| 31015 | Cordele | (912) | 10,836 | 11,184 |
| ..... | Country Club Estates(u) | | 7,500 | .... |
| 30209 | Covington | (404) | 10,056 | 10,586 |
| 30720 | Dalton | (706) | 22,213 | 20,581 |
| 31742 | Dawson | (912) | 5,295 | 5,699 |
| *30030 | Decatur | (404) | 17,304 | 18,404 |
| 31520 | Dock Junction(u) | (912) | 7,094 | 6,189 |
| 30340 | Doraville | (404) | 7,626 | 7,414 |
| 31533 | Douglas | (912) | 10,464 | 10,980 |
| 30134 | Douglasville | (404) | 11,635 | 7,641 |
| 30333 | Druid Hills(u) | (404) | 12,174 | 12,700 |
| 31021 | Dublin | (912) | 16,312 | 16,083 |
| 30136 | Duluth | | 9,029 | 2,956 |
| 30338 | Dunwoody(u) | (404) | 26,302 | 17,768 |
| 31023 | Eastman | (912) | 5,241 | 5,330 |
| 30344 | East Point | (404) | 34,595 | 37,486 |
| 30635 | Elberton | (706) | 5,682 | 5,686 |
| 30809 | Evans(u) | (404) | 13,713 | .... |
| 30060 | Fair Oaks(u) | (404) | 6,996 | 8,486 |
| 30535 | Fairview(u) | (404) | 6,444 | 6,558 |
| 30214 | Fayetteville | | 5,827 | 2,715 |
| 31750 | Fitzgerald | (912) | 8,810 | 10,187 |
| 30050 | Forest Park | (404) | 16,958 | 18,782 |
| 31905 | Fort Benning South(u) | (404) | 14,617 | 15,074 |
| 30905 | Fort Gordon(u) | (404) | 9,140 | 14,069 |
| 30741 | Fort Oglethorpe | (404) | 5,880 | 5,443 |
| 31313 | Fort Stewart(u) | (912) | 13,774 | 15,031 |
| 31030 | Fort Valley | (912) | 8,198 | 9,000 |
| ..... | Gaines School(u) | | 11,354 | .... |
| 30501 | Gainesville | (404) | 17,885 | 15,280 |
| 31408 | Garden City | (912) | 7,410 | 6,895 |
| 31754 | Georgetown | (912) | 5,554 | 2,785 |
| 30316 | Gresham Park(u) | (404) | 9,000 | 6,232 |
| 30223 | Griffin | (404) | 21,347 | 20,728 |
| 30354 | Hapeville | (404) | 5,483 | 6,166 |
| 31313 | Hinesville | (912) | 21,596 | 11,309 |
| 31545 | Jesup | (912) | 8,958 | 9,418 |
| 30144 | Kennesaw | (404) | 8,936 | 5,095 |
| 31547 | Kingsland | (912) | 5,474 | .... |
| 30728 | La Fayette | (706) | 6,313 | 6,517 |
| 30240 | La Grange | (706) | 25,574 | 24,204 |
| ..... | Lakeview(u) | | 5,237 | 5,403 |
| 30245 | Lawrenceville | (404) | 17,251 | 8,928 |
| 30247 | Lilburn | | 9,301 | 3,765 |
| 30057 | Lithia Springs(u) | (404) | 11,403 | 9,145 |
| 30059 | Mableton(u) | (404) | 25,725 | 25,111 |
| *31201 | Macon | (912) | 107,365 | 116,896 |
| 30060 | Marietta | (404) | 44,129 | 30,821 |
| 30907 | Martinez(u) | (404) | 33,731 | 16,472 |
| 31061 | Milledgeville | (912) | 17,727 | 12,176 |
| 30655 | Monroe | (404) | 9,759 | 8,854 |
| 30260 | Morrow | | 5,168 | 3,791 |
| 31768 | Moultrie | (912) | 14,865 | 15,105 |
| 30075 | Mountain Park(u) | (404) | 11,025 | 9,425 |
| 30263 | Newnan | (404) | 12,497 | 11,449 |
| 30091 | Norcross | (404) | 5,947 | 3,363 |
| 30319 | North Atlanta(u) | (404) | 27,812 | 30,521 |
| 30033 | North Decatur(u) | (404) | 13,936 | 11,830 |
| 30033 | North Druid Hills(u) | (404) | 14,170 | 12,438 |
| 30032 | Panthersville(u) | (404) | 9,874 | 11,366 |
| 30269 | Peachtree City | (404) | 19,027 | 6,429 |
| 31069 | Perry | (912) | 9,452 | 9,453 |
| 30073 | Powder Springs | (404) | 6,862 | 3,381 |
| 31643 | Quitman | (912) | 5,292 | 5,188 |
| 30074 | Redan(u) | | 24,376 | .... |
| *30274 | Riverdale | (404) | 9,455 | 7,121 |
| 30161 | Rome | (706) | 30,326 | 28,915 |
| 30075 | Roswell | (404) | 47,923 | 23,337 |
| 31558 | Saint Marys | | 8,204 | 3,596 |
| 31522 | Saint Simons Island(u) | (912) | 12,026 | 6,566 |
| 31082 | Sandersville | (912) | 6,290 | 6,137 |

| ZIP code | Place | | 1990 | 1980 |
|---|---|---|---|---|
| 30328 | Sandy Springs(u) | (404) | 67,842 | 46,877 |
| *31401 | Savannah | (912) | 137,812 | 141,654 |
| 30079 | Scottdale(u) | (404) | 8,636 | 8,770 |
| 30080 | Smyrna | (404) | 30,981 | 20,312 |
| 30278 | Snellville | (404) | 12,084 | 8,514 |
| 30901 | South Augusta(u) | (404) | 55,998 | 51,072 |
| 30458 | Statesboro | (912) | 15,854 | 14,866 |
| 30086 | Stone Mountain | | 6,494 | 4,867 |
| 30747 | Summerville | (706) | 5,025 | 4,878 |
| 30401 | Swainsboro | (912) | 7,361 | 7,602 |
| 31791 | Sylvester | (912) | 6,023 | 5,860 |
| 30286 | Thomaston | (706) | 9,127 | 9,682 |
| 31792 | Thomasville | (912) | 17,554 | 18,463 |
| 30824 | Thomson | (706) | 6,862 | 7,001 |
| 31794 | Tifton | (912) | 14,215 | 13,749 |
| 30577 | Toccoa | (706) | 8,530 | 8,869 |
| 30084 | Tucker(u) | (404) | 25,781 | 25,399 |
| 30291 | Union City | (404) | 8,887 | 4,780 |
| 31601 | Valdosta | (912) | 40,038 | 37,596 |
| 30474 | Vidalia | (912) | 11,118 | 10,393 |
| 30180 | Villa Rica | | 6,542 | 3,420 |
| ...... | Vinings(u) | | 7,417 | .... |
| 31093 | Warner Robins | (912) | 43,861 | 39,893 |
| 31501 | Waycross | (912) | 16,410 | 19,371 |
| 30830 | Waynesboro | (706) | 5,669 | 5,760 |
| 30901 | West Augusta(u) | (404) | 27,637 | 24,242 |
| 31410 | Wilmington Island(u) | (912) | 11,230 | 7,546 |
| 30680 | Winder | (404) | 7,373 | 6,705 |

## Hawaii (808)

*See Note on Page 373*

| ZIP code | Place | 1990 | 1980 |
|---|---|---|---|
| 96706 | Aiea | 8,906 | 32,879 |
| ...... | Aliamanu | 8,835 | .... |
| 96706 | Ewa | 14,315 | 14,369 |
| ...... | Halawa | 13,408 | .... |
| ...... | Heeia | 5,010 | 5,432 |
| ...... | Hickman | 6,553 | 4,425 |
| 96720 | Hilo | 37,808 | 35,269 |
| *96815 | Honolulu | 365,272 | 365,048 |
| 96732 | Kahului | 16,889 | 12,978 |
| 96734 | Kailua | 9,126 | 4,751 |
| 96863 | Kailua | 36,818 | 35,812 |
| 96744 | Kaneohe | 35,448 | 29,919 |
| ...... | Kaneohe Station | 11,662 | .... |
| 96746 | Kapaa | 8,149 | 4,467 |
| 96753 | Kihei | 11,107 | 5,644 |
| 96761 | Lahaina | 9,073 | 6,095 |
| 96762 | Laie | 5,577 | 4,643 |
| 96766 | Lihue | 5,536 | 4,000 |
| ...... | Maili | 6,059 | 5,026 |
| ...... | Makaha | 7,990 | 6,582 |
| ...... | Makailo | 9,828 | 7,691 |
| 96768 | Makawao-Paia | 5,405 | 2,900 |
| 96789 | Mililani Town | 29,359 | 21,365 |
| 96792 | Nanakuli | 9,575 | 8,185 |
| 96782 | Pearl City | 30,993 | 42,575 |
| 96788 | Pukalani | 5,879 | 3,950 |
| ...... | Schofield Barracks | 19,597 | .... |
| ...... | Village Park | 7,407 | 18,851 |
| 96786 | Wahiawa | 17,386 | 16,911 |
| 96792 | Waianae | 8,758 | 7,941 |
| 96793 | Wailuku | 10,688 | 10,260 |
| ...... | Waimalu | 29,967 | .... |
| 96796 | Waimea | 5,972 | 1,179 |
| 96797 | Waipahu | 31,435 | 29,139 |
| ...... | Waipio | 11,812 | .... |
| ...... | Waipio Acre | 5,304 | 4,091 |

## Idaho (208)

| ZIP code | Place | 1990 | 1980 |
|---|---|---|---|
| 83401 | Ammon | 5,002 | 4,669 |
| 83221 | Blackfoot | 9,646 | 10,065 |
| *83708 | Boise City | 125,551 | 102,249 |
| 83318 | Burley | 8,702 | 8,761 |
| 83605 | Caldwell | 18,400 | 17,699 |
| 83201 | Chubbuck | 7,794 | 7,052 |
| 83814 | Coeur D'Alene | 24,563 | 19,913 |
| 83714 | Garden City | 6,369 | 4,571 |
| *83401 | Idaho Falls | 43,929 | 39,739 |
| 83338 | Jerome | 6,529 | 6,891 |
| 83501 | Lewiston | 28,082 | 27,986 |
| 83642 | Meridian | 9,596 | 6,658 |
| 83843 | Moscow | 18,519 | 16,513 |
| 83647 | Mountain Home | 7,913 | 7,540 |
| 83648 | Mountain Home AFB(u) | 5,936 | 6,403 |
| *83651 | Nampa | 28,365 | 25,112 |
| 83661 | Payette | 5,667 | 5,448 |
| *83201 | Pocatello | 46,111 | 46,340 |
| 83854 | Post Falls | 7,349 | 5,736 |
| 83440 | Rexburg | 14,302 | 11,559 |
| 83350 | Rupert | 5,455 | 5,476 |
| 83809 | Sandpoint | 5,203 | 4,460 |
| 83301 | Twin Falls | 27,591 | 26,209 |

## Illinois

| ZIP code | Place | | 1990 | 1980 |
|---|---|---|---|---|
| 60101 | Addison | (708) | 32,053 | 29,826 |
| 60102 | Algonquin | (708) | 11,693 | 5,834 |
| 60658 | Alsip | (708) | 18,227 | 17,134 |
| 62002 | Alton | (618) | 33,064 | 34,171 |
| 60002 | Antioch | (708) | 6,105 | 4,419 |
| *60004 | Arlington Heights | (708) | 75,462 | 66,116 |
| *60507 | Aurora | (708) | 99,556 | 81,293 |
| 60010 | Barrington | (708) | 9,538 | 9,029 |
| 60103 | Bartlett | (708) | 19,373 | 13,254 |
| 61607 | Bartonville | (309) | 5,643 | 6,137 |
| 60510 | Batavia | (708) | 17,076 | 12,574 |
| ...... | Beach Park | (708) | 9,513 | 8,468 |
| 62618 | Beardstown | (217) | 5,270 | 6,338 |
| *62220 | Belleville | (618) | 42,806 | 41,580 |
| 60104 | Bellwood | (708) | 20,241 | 19,811 |
| 61008 | Belvidere | (815) | 15,962 | 15,176 |
| 60106 | Bensenville | (708) | 17,767 | 16,106 |
| 62812 | Benton | (618) | 7,216 | 7,778 |
| 60162 | Berkeley | (708) | 5,137 | 5,467 |
| 60402 | Berwyn | (708) | 45,426 | 46,849 |
| 62010 | Bethalto | (618) | 9,507 | 8,630 |
| 60108 | Bloomingdale | (708) | 16,614 | 12,656 |
| 61701 | Bloomington | (309) | 51,889 | 44,189 |
| 60406 | Blue Island | (708) | 21,203 | 21,855 |
| 60439 | Bolingbrook | (708) | 40,843 | 37,261 |
| 60538 | Boulder Hill(u) | (708) | 8,894 | 9,333 |
| 60914 | Bourbonnais | (815) | 13,927 | 13,280 |
| 60915 | Bradley | (815) | 10,910 | 11,015 |
| 60455 | Bridgeview | (708) | 14,402 | 14,155 |
| 60153 | Broadview | (708) | 8,538 | 8,618 |
| 60513 | Brookfield | (708) | 18,876 | 19,395 |
| 60089 | Buffalo Grove | (708) | 36,398 | 22,230 |
| 60459 | Burbank | (708) | 27,600 | 28,462 |
| 60521 | Burr Ridge | (708) | 7,669 | 3,838 |
| 62206 | Cahokia | (618) | 17,550 | 18,904 |
| 60409 | Calumet City | (708) | 37,840 | 39,697 |
| 60643 | Calumet Park | (708) | 8,418 | 8,788 |
| 61520 | Canton | (309) | 13,959 | 14,626 |
| 62901 | Carbondale | (618) | 27,033 | 26,414 |
| 62626 | Carlinville | (217) | 5,416 | 5,439 |
| 62821 | Carmi | (618) | 5,626 | 6,107 |
| 60187 | Carol Stream | (708) | 31,759 | 15,472 |
| 60110 | Carpentersville | (708) | 23,049 | 23,272 |
| 60013 | Cary | (708) | 10,043 | 6,640 |
| 62801 | Centralia | (618) | 14,274 | 15,126 |
| 62206 | Centreville | (618) | 7,489 | 9,747 |
| 61820 | Champaign | (217) | 63,502 | 58,267 |
| 61920 | Charleston | (217) | 20,398 | 19,355 |
| 62629 | Chatham | (217) | 6,074 | 5,597 |
| 62233 | Chester | (618) | 8,204 | 8,401 |
| *60607 | Chicago | (312) | 2,783,726 | 3,005,072 |
| 60411 | Chicago Heights | (708) | 32,966 | 37,026 |
| 60415 | Chicago Ridge | (708) | 13,643 | 13,473 |
| 61523 | Chillicothe | (309) | 5,959 | 6,176 |
| 60650 | Cicero | (708) | 67,436 | 61,232 |
| 60514 | Clarendon Hills | (708) | 6,994 | 6,870 |
| 61727 | Clinton | (217) | 7,437 | 8,014 |
| 62234 | Collinsville | (618) | 22,424 | 19,475 |
| 62236 | Columbia | (618) | 5,524 | 4,269 |
| 60477 | Country Club Hills | (708) | 15,431 | 14,676 |
| 60525 | Countryside | (708) | 5,961 | 6,242 |
| 60435 | Crest Hill | (815) | 10,996 | 9,252 |
| 60445 | Crestwood | (708) | 10,823 | 10,852 |
| 60417 | Crete | (708) | 6,773 | 5,417 |
| 61611 | Creve Coeur | (309) | 5,938 | 6,851 |
| 60014 | Crystal Lake | (815) | 24,696 | 18,590 |
| 61832 | Danville | (217) | 33,828 | 38,985 |
| 60559 | Darien | (708) | 18,193 | 14,956 |
| *62521 | Decatur | (217) | 83,900 | 93,939 |
| 60015 | Deerfield | (708) | 17,327 | 17,432 |
| 60115 | De Kalb | (815) | 35,076 | 33,157 |
| *60016 | Des Plaines | (708) | 53,414 | 53,568 |
| 61021 | Dixon | (815) | 15,134 | 15,710 |
| 60419 | Dolton | (708) | 23,956 | 24,766 |
| 60515 | Downers Grove | (708) | 46,845 | 42,259 |
| 62832 | Du Quoin | (618) | 6,697 | 6,594 |
| 62024 | East Alton | (618) | 7,063 | 7,096 |
| 61244 | East Moline | (309) | 20,147 | 20,907 |
| 61611 | East Peoria | (309) | 21,378 | 22,385 |
| *62201 | East St. Louis | (618) | 40,944 | 55,200 |
| 62025 | Edwardsville | (618) | 14,579 | 12,480 |
| 62401 | Effingham | (217) | 11,851 | 11,270 |
| 60120 | Elgin | (708) | 77,010 | 63,668 |
| 60007 | Elk Grove Village | (708) | 33,429 | 28,679 |
| 60126 | Elmhurst | (708) | 42,029 | 44,276 |
| 60635 | Elmwood Park | (708) | 23,206 | 24,016 |
| *60204 | Evanston | (708) | 73,233 | 73,706 |
| 60642 | Evergreen Park | (708) | 20,874 | 22,260 |
| 62837 | Fairfield | (618) | 5,439 | 5,944 |
| 62208 | Fairview Heights | (618) | 14,351 | 12,111 |
| 62839 | Flora | (618) | 5,093 | 5,379 |
| 60422 | Flossmoor | (708) | 8,651 | 8,423 |
| 60130 | Forest Park | (708) | 14,918 | 15,177 |
| 60020 | Fox Lake | (708) | 7,478 | 6,831 |
| 60423 | Frankfort | | 7,180 | 4,357 |
| ...... | Frankfort Square(u) | | 6,227 | .... |

| ZIP code | Place | | 1990 | 1980 |
|---|---|---|---|---|
| 60131 | Franklin Park | (708) | 18,485 | 17,507 |
| 61032 | Freeport | (815) | 25,840 | 26,266 |
| 60030 | Gages Lake(u) | (708) | 8,349 | 3,814 |
| 61401 | Galesburg | (309) | 33,530 | 35,305 |
| 61254 | Geneseo | (309) | 5,990 | 6,373 |
| 60134 | Geneva | (708) | 12,617 | 9,881 |
| 62034 | Glen Carbon | (618) | 7,731 | 5,197 |
| 60022 | Glencoe | (708) | 8,499 | 9,200 |
| 60137 | Glendale Heights | (708) | 27,973 | 23,251 |
| 60137 | Glen Ellyn | (708) | 24,944 | 23,691 |
| 60025 | Glenview | (708) | 37,093 | 32,060 |
| 60425 | Glenwood | (708) | 9,289 | 10,538 |
| 62002 | Godfrey(u) | (618) | 5,436 | |
| ..... | Goodings Grove(u) | ... | 14,054 | |
| 62040 | Granite City | (618) | 32,769 | 36,815 |
| 60030 | Grays Lake | (708) | 7,388 | 5,260 |
| 62246 | Greenville | (618) | 5,108 | |
| 60031 | Gurnee | (708) | 13,701 | 7,179 |
| 60103 | Hanover Park | (708) | 32,895 | 28,719 |
| 62946 | Harrisburg | (618) | 9,318 | 10,410 |
| 60033 | Harvard | (815) | 5,975 | 5,126 |
| 60426 | Harvey | (708) | 29,771 | 35,810 |
| 60656 | Harwood Heights | (312) | 7,680 | 8,228 |
| 60429 | Hazel Crest | (708) | 13,334 | 13,973 |
| 62948 | Herrin | (618) | 10,857 | 10,708 |
| 60457 | Hickory Hills | (708) | 13,021 | 13,778 |
| 62249 | Highland | (618) | 7,525 | 7,122 |
| 60035 | Highland Park | (708) | 30,575 | 30,599 |
| 60040 | Highwood | (708) | 5,331 | 5,455 |
| 60162 | Hillside | (708) | 7,672 | 8,279 |
| 60521 | Hinsdale | (708) | 16,029 | 16,726 |
| 60172 | Hoffman Estates | (708) | 46,363 | 37,272 |
| 60430 | Homewood | (708) | 19,278 | 19,724 |
| 60942 | Hoopeston | (217) | 5,871 | 6,411 |
| 60067 | Inverness | (708) | 6,503 | 4,046 |
| 60143 | Itasca | (708) | 6,947 | 7,129 |
| 62650 | Jacksonville | (217) | 19,327 | 20,284 |
| 62052 | Jerseyville | (618) | 7,382 | 7,506 |
| *60431 | Joliet | (815) | 76,628 | 77,956 |
| 60458 | Justice | (708) | 11,137 | 10,552 |
| 60901 | Kankakee | (815) | 27,531 | 29,633 |
| 61443 | Kewanee | (309) | 12,969 | 14,508 |
| 60525 | La Grange | (708) | 15,362 | 15,693 |
| 60525 | La Grange Park | (708) | 12,861 | 13,359 |
| 60044 | Lake Bluff | (708) | 5,486 | 4,434 |
| 60045 | Lake Forest | (708) | 17,836 | 15,245 |
| 60102 | Lake in the Hills | (708) | 5,866 | 5,651 |
| 60047 | Lake Zurich | (708) | 14,927 | 8,225 |
| 60438 | Lansing | (708) | 28,089 | 29,039 |
| 61301 | La Salle | (815) | 9,717 | 10,347 |
| 60439 | Lemont | (708) | 7,348 | 5,640 |
| 60048 | Libertyville | (708) | 19,174 | 16,520 |
| 62656 | Lincoln | (217) | 15,418 | 16,327 |
| 60645 | Lincolnwood | (708) | 11,365 | 11,921 |
| 60046 | Lindenhurst | (708) | 8,038 | 6,220 |
| 60532 | Lisle | (708) | 19,512 | 13,638 |
| 62056 | Litchfield | (217) | 6,883 | 7,204 |
| 60441 | Lockport | (815) | 9,401 | 9,192 |
| 60148 | Lombard | (708) | 39,408 | 36,879 |
| 61111 | Loves Park | (815) | 15,462 | 13,192 |
| 60411 | Lynwood | (708) | 6,535 | 4,195 |
| 60534 | Lyons | (708) | 9,828 | 9,925 |
| 60050 | McHenry | (815) | 16,177 | 10,737 |
| 61111 | Machesney Park | (815) | 19,033 | 19,514 |
| 61455 | Macomb | (309) | 19,952 | 19,863 |
| 62959 | Marion | (618) | 14,545 | 14,031 |
| 60426 | Markham | (708) | 13,136 | 15,172 |
| 62258 | Mascoutah | (618) | 5,511 | 4,962 |
| 60443 | Matteson | (708) | 11,378 | 10,223 |
| 61938 | Mattoon | (217) | 18,441 | 19,293 |
| 60153 | Maywood | (708) | 27,139 | 27,998 |
| *60160 | Melrose Park | (708) | 20,859 | 20,735 |
| 61342 | Mendota | (815) | 7,018 | 7,134 |
| 62960 | Metropolis | (618) | 6,734 | 7,171 |
| 60445 | Midlothian | (708) | 14,372 | 14,274 |
| 61264 | Milan | (309) | 5,753 | 6,371 |
| 60448 | Mokena | (708) | 6,128 | 4,578 |
| 61265 | Moline | (309) | 43,127 | 46,407 |
| 61462 | Monmouth | (309) | 9,489 | 10,706 |
| 60450 | Morris | (815) | 10,270 | 8,833 |
| 61550 | Morton | (309) | 13,799 | 14,178 |
| 60053 | Morton Grove | (708) | 22,373 | 23,747 |
| 62863 | Mount Carmel | (618) | 8,287 | 8,908 |
| 60056 | Mount Prospect | (708) | 53,168 | 52,634 |
| 62864 | Mount Vernon | (618) | 17,080 | 17,193 |
| 60060 | Mundelein | (708) | 21,215 | 17,053 |
| 62966 | Murphysboro | (618) | 9,176 | 9,866 |
| 60540 | Naperville | (708) | 85,351 | 42,601 |
| 60451 | New Lenox | (815) | 9,618 | 5,792 |
| 60648 | Niles | (708) | 28,375 | 30,363 |
| 61761 | Normal | (309) | 40,023 | 35,672 |
| 60542 | North Aurora | (708) | 5,940 | 5,205 |
| 60062 | Northbrook | (708) | 32,308 | 30,778 |
| 60064 | North Chicago | (708) | 34,978 | 38,774 |
| 60164 | Northlake | (708) | 12,505 | 12,166 |
| 60546 | North Riverside | (708) | 6,180 | 6,764 |
| 60521 | Oak Brook | (708) | 9,087 | 6,676 |

| ZIP code | Place | | 1990 | 1980 |
|---|---|---|---|---|
| 60452 | Oak Forest | (708) | 26,203 | 25,040 |
| *60454 | Oak Lawn | (708) | 56,182 | 60,590 |
| *60301 | Oak Park | (708) | 53,648 | 54,887 |
| 62269 | O'Fallon | (618) | 16,073 | 12,173 |
| 62450 | Olney | (618) | 8,664 | 9,026 |
| 60477 | Orland Hills | ... | 5,510 | 2,784 |
| 60462 | Orland Park | (708) | 35,720 | 23,045 |
| 61350 | Ottawa | (815) | 17,541 | 18,166 |
| 60067 | Palatine | (708) | 39,655 | 32,176 |
| 60463 | Palos Heights | (708) | 11,478 | 11,096 |
| 60465 | Palos Hills | (708) | 17,803 | 16,654 |
| 62557 | Pana | (217) | 5,796 | 6,040 |
| 61944 | Paris | (217) | 9,016 | 9,885 |
| 60466 | Park Forest | (708) | 24,656 | 26,222 |
| 60068 | Park Ridge | (708) | 36,175 | 38,704 |
| 61554 | Pekin | (309) | 32,254 | 33,967 |
| *61601 | Peoria | (309) | 113,504 | 124,160 |
| 61614 | Peoria Heights | (309) | 6,930 | 7,453 |
| 61354 | Peru | (815) | 9,302 | 10,886 |
| 60545 | Plano | (708) | 5,104 | 4,875 |
| 61764 | Pontiac | (815) | 11,428 | 11,227 |
| 61356 | Princeton | (815) | 7,197 | 7,342 |
| 60070 | Prospect Heights | (708) | 15,239 | 11,823 |
| 62301 | Quincy | (217) | 39,681 | 42,554 |
| 61866 | Rantoul | (217) | 17,212 | 20,161 |
| 60471 | Richton Park | (708) | 10,523 | 9,403 |
| 60627 | Riverdale | (708) | 13,671 | 13,233 |
| 60305 | River Forest | (708) | 11,669 | 12,392 |
| 60171 | River Grove | (708) | 9,961 | 10,368 |
| 60546 | Riverside | (708) | 8,774 | 9,236 |
| 60472 | Robbins | (708) | 7,498 | 8,853 |
| 62454 | Robinson | (618) | 6,740 | 7,285 |
| 61068 | Rochelle | (815) | 8,769 | 8,982 |
| 61071 | Rock Falls | (815) | 9,654 | 10,633 |
| *61125 | Rockford | (815) | 139,943 | 139,712 |
| 61201 | Rock Island | (309) | 40,630 | 46,821 |
| 60008 | Rolling Meadows | (708) | 22,591 | 20,167 |
| 60441 | Romeoville | (815) | 14,101 | 15,519 |
| 60172 | Roselle | (708) | 20,819 | 17,034 |
| 60073 | Round Lake Beach | (708) | 16,434 | 12,921 |
| 60174 | Saint Charles | (708) | 22,502 | 17,492 |
| 62881 | Salem | (618) | 7,470 | 7,813 |
| 60548 | Sandwich | (815) | 5,607 | 5,356 |
| 60411 | Sauk Village | (708) | 9,926 | 10,906 |
| 60172 | Schaumburg | (708) | 68,586 | 53,355 |
| 60176 | Schiller Park | (708) | 11,189 | 11,458 |
| 62225 | Scott AFB(u) | (618) | 7,245 | 8,648 |
| 60436 | Shorewood | (815) | 6,264 | 4,714 |
| 61282 | Silvis | (309) | 6,926 | 7,130 |
| 60076 | Skokie | (708) | 59,432 | 60,278 |
| 60177 | South Elgin | (708) | 7,474 | 5,970 |
| 60473 | South Holland | (708) | 22,105 | 24,977 |
| *62703 | Springfield | (217) | 105,227 | 100,054 |
| 61362 | Spring Valley | (815) | 5,246 | 5,822 |
| 60475 | Steger | (708) | 8,584 | 9,269 |
| 61081 | Sterling | (815) | 15,142 | 16,281 |
| 60402 | Stickney | (708) | 5,678 | 5,893 |
| 60103 | Streamwood | (708) | 31,197 | 23,456 |
| 61364 | Streator | (815) | 14,121 | 14,795 |
| 60501 | Summit | (708) | 9,971 | 10,110 |
| 62221 | Swansea | (618) | 8,201 | 5,529 |
| 60178 | Sycamore | (815) | 9,708 | 9,219 |
| 62568 | Taylorville | (217) | 11,133 | 11,386 |
| 60477 | Tinley Park | (708) | 37,121 | 26,178 |
| 62294 | Troy | (618) | 6,046 | 3,772 |
| 60466 | University Park | (708) | 6,204 | 6,245 |
| 61801 | Urbana | (217) | 36,344 | 35,978 |
| 62471 | Vandalia | (618) | 6,114 | 5,338 |
| 60061 | Vernon Hills | (708) | 15,319 | 9,827 |
| 60181 | Villa Park | (708) | 22,253 | 23,155 |
| 60555 | Warrenville | (708) | 11,390 | 7,519 |
| 61571 | Washington | (309) | 10,099 | 10,364 |
| 62204 | Washington Park | (618) | 7,431 | 8,223 |
| 62298 | Waterloo | (618) | 5,072 | 4,646 |
| 60970 | Watseka | (815) | 5,424 | 5,543 |
| 60084 | Wauconda | (708) | 6,294 | 5,688 |
| 60085 | Waukegan | (708) | 69,392 | 67,653 |
| 60153 | Westchester | (708) | 17,301 | 17,730 |
| 60185 | West Chicago | (708) | 14,796 | 12,550 |
| 60558 | Western Springs | (708) | 11,956 | 12,876 |
| 62896 | West Frankfort | (618) | 8,526 | 9,437 |
| 60559 | Westmont | (708) | 21,228 | 17,353 |
| 61604 | West Peoria(u) | (309) | 5,314 | 5,219 |
| 60187 | Wheaton | (708) | 51,464 | 43,043 |
| 60090 | Wheeling | (708) | 29,911 | 23,266 |
| 60514 | Willowbrook | (708) | 8,701 | 4,953 |
| 60091 | Wilmette | (708) | 26,694 | 28,221 |
| 60190 | Winfield | (708) | 7,096 | 4,422 |
| 60093 | Winnetka | (708) | 12,210 | 12,772 |
| 60096 | Winthrop Harbor | (708) | 6,240 | 5,427 |
| 60097 | Wonder Lake(u) | (815) | 6,664 | 5,917 |
| 60191 | Wood Dale | (708) | 12,425 | 11,251 |
| 60515 | Woodridge | (708) | 26,256 | 21,763 |
| 62095 | Wood River | (618) | 11,490 | 12,446 |
| 60098 | Woodstock | (815) | 14,353 | 11,725 |
| 60482 | Worth | (708) | 11,208 | 11,592 |
| 60099 | Zion | (708) | 19,775 | 17,865 |

## Indiana

| ZIP code | Place | | 1990 | 1980 |
|---|---|---|---|---|
| 46001 | Alexandria | (317) | 5,709 | 6,028 |
| 46011 | Anderson | (317) | 59,459 | 64,695 |
| 46703 | Angola | (219) | 5,851 | 5,486 |
| 46706 | Auburn | (219) | 9,386 | 8,122 |
| 47421 | Bedford | (812) | 13,817 | 14,410 |
| 46107 | Beech Grove | (317) | 13,383 | 13,196 |
| 47401 | Bloomington | (812) | 60,633 | 52,663 |
| 46714 | Bluffton | (219) | 9,104 | 8,705 |
| 47601 | Boonville | (812) | 6,686 | 6,300 |
| 47834 | Brazil | (812) | 7,640 | 7,852 |
| 46112 | Brownsburg | (317) | 7,628 | 6,242 |
| 46032 | Carmel | (317) | 25,380 | 18,272 |
| 46303 | Cedar Lake | (219) | 8,885 | 8,754 |
| 47111 | Charlestown | (812) | 5,889 | 5,596 |
| 46304 | Chesterton | (219) | 9,118 | 8,531 |
| 47130 | Clarksville | (812) | 19,838 | 15,164 |
| 47842 | Clinton | (317) | 5,040 | 5,267 |
| 46725 | Columbia City | (219) | 5,700 | 5,091 |
| 47201 | Columbus | (812) | 31,802 | 30,614 |
| 47331 | Connersville | (317) | 15,550 | 17,023 |
| 47933 | Crawfordsville | (317) | 13,584 | 13,325 |
| 46307 | Crown Point | (219) | 17,728 | 16,455 |
| 46733 | Decatur | (219) | 8,642 | 8,649 |
| 46514 | Dunlap(u) | (219) | 5,705 | 5,397 |
| 46311 | Dyer | (219) | 10,923 | 9,555 |
| 46312 | East Chicago | (219) | 33,892 | 39,786 |
| 46514 | Elkhart | (219) | 43,627 | 41,305 |
| 46036 | Elwood | (317) | 9,494 | 10,867 |
| *47708 | Evansville | (812) | 126,272 | 130,496 |
| 46038 | Fishers | | 7,508 | 2,008 |
| *46802 | Fort Wayne | (219) | 172,971 | 172,391 |
| 46041 | Frankfort | (317) | 14,754 | 15,168 |
| 46131 | Franklin | (317) | 12,932 | 11,563 |
| 46738 | Garrett | (219) | 5,349 | 4,751 |
| *46401 | Gary | (219) | 116,646 | 151,968 |
| 46933 | Gas City | (317) | 6,296 | 6,370 |
| 46526 | Goshen | (219) | 23,794 | 19,665 |
| 46530 | Granger(u) | | 20,241 | |
| 46135 | Greencastle | (317) | 8,984 | 8,403 |
| 46140 | Greenfield | (317) | 11,657 | 11,288 |
| 47240 | Greensburg | (812) | 9,286 | 9,254 |
| 46142 | Greenwood | (317) | 26,507 | 19,327 |
| 46319 | Griffith | (219) | 17,914 | 17,026 |
| *46320 | Hammond | (219) | 84,236 | 93,714 |
| 47348 | Hartford City | (317) | 6,960 | 7,622 |
| 46322 | Highland | (219) | 23,696 | 25,935 |
| 46342 | Hobart | (219) | 21,822 | 22,987 |
| 47542 | Huntingburg | (812) | 5,236 | 5,376 |
| 46750 | Huntington | (219) | 16,389 | 16,202 |
| *46206 | Indianapolis | (317) | 731,327 | 700,807 |
| 47546 | Jasper | (812) | 10,030 | 9,097 |
| 47130 | Jeffersonville | (812) | 21,968 | 21,220 |
| 46755 | Kendallville | (219) | 7,773 | 7,299 |
| 46901 | Kokomo | (317) | 44,996 | 47,808 |
| *47901 | Lafayette | (317) | 43,758 | 43,011 |
| ..... | Lakes of the Four Seasons(u) | | 6,556 | ---- |
| 46405 | Lake Station | (219) | 13,899 | 15,087 |
| 46350 | La Porte | (219) | 21,507 | 21,796 |
| 46226 | Lawrence | (317) | 26,779 | 25,591 |
| 46052 | Lebanon | (317) | 12,059 | 11,456 |
| 47441 | Linton | (812) | 5,814 | 6,315 |
| 46947 | Logansport | (219) | 16,865 | 17,731 |
| 46356 | Lowell | (219) | 6,430 | 5,827 |
| 47250 | Madison | (812) | 12,006 | 12,472 |
| 46952 | Marion | (317) | 32,607 | 35,874 |
| 46151 | Martinsville | (317) | 11,677 | 11,311 |
| 46410 | Merrillville | (219) | 27,257 | 27,677 |
| 46360 | Michigan City | (219) | 33,822 | 36,850 |
| 46544 | Mishawaka | (219) | 42,635 | 40,201 |
| 47960 | Monticello | (219) | 5,237 | 5,162 |
| 46158 | Mooresville | (317) | 5,541 | 5,349 |
| 47620 | Mount Vernon | (812) | 7,217 | 7,656 |
| *47302 | Muncie | (317) | 71,170 | 77,216 |
| 46321 | Munster | (219) | 19,949 | 20,671 |
| 46550 | Nappanee | | 5,474 | 4,694 |
| 47150 | New Albany | (812) | 36,322 | 37,103 |
| 47362 | New Castle | (317) | 17,753 | 20,056 |
| 46774 | New Haven | (219) | 9,320 | 6,714 |
| 46060 | Noblesville | (317) | 17,655 | 12,253 |
| 46962 | North Manchester | (219) | 6,383 | 5,998 |
| 47265 | North Vernon | (812) | 5,129 | 5,768 |
| 47130 | Oak Park(u) | (812) | 5,630 | 5,871 |
| 46970 | Peru | (317) | 12,843 | 13,764 |
| 46168 | Plainfield | (317) | 10,433 | 9,191 |
| 46563 | Plymouth | (219) | 8,291 | 7,693 |
| 46368 | Portage | (219) | 29,062 | 27,409 |
| 47371 | Portland | (219) | 6,483 | 7,074 |
| 47670 | Princeton | (812) | 8,127 | 8,976 |
| 47978 | Rensselaer | (219) | 5,045 | 4,944 |
| 47374 | Richmond | (317) | 38,705 | 41,349 |
| 46975 | Rochester | (219) | 5,969 | 5,050 |
| 46173 | Rushville | (317) | 5,533 | 6,113 |
| 47167 | Salem | (812) | 5,619 | 5,290 |
| 46375 | Schererville | (219) | 20,155 | 13,209 |
| 47170 | Scottsburg | (812) | 5,334 | 5,068 |
| 47172 | Sellersburg | (812) | 5,914 | 3,211 |

| ZIP code | Place | | 1990 | 1980 |
|---|---|---|---|---|
| 47274 | Seymour | (812) | 15,579 | 15,050 |
| 46176 | Shelbyville | (317) | 15,347 | 14,989 |
| *46624 | South Bend | (219) | 105,511 | 109,727 |
| 46383 | South Haven(u) | (219) | 6,112 | 6,679 |
| 46224 | Speedway | (317) | 13,092 | 12,641 |
| 47586 | Tell City | (812) | 8,088 | 8,704 |
| *47808 | Terre Haute | (812) | 57,483 | 61,125 |
| 46383 | Valparaiso | (219) | 24,414 | 22,247 |
| 47591 | Vincennes | (812) | 19,867 | 20,857 |
| 46992 | Wabash | (219) | 12,127 | 12,985 |
| 46580 | Warsaw | (219) | 10,968 | 10,647 |
| 47501 | Washington | (812) | 10,864 | 11,325 |
| 47906 | West Lafayette | (317) | 26,144 | 21,247 |
| 46391 | Westville | | 5,255 | 2,887 |
| 46394 | Whiting | (219) | 5,155 | 5,630 |
| 47394 | Winchester | (317) | 5,095 | 5,659 |
| 46077 | Zionsville | | 5,281 | 3,948 |

## Iowa

| ZIP code | Place | | 1990 | 1980 |
|---|---|---|---|---|
| 50511 | Algona | (515) | 6,015 | 6,289 |
| 50009 | Altoona | (515) | 7,242 | 5,764 |
| 50010 | Ames | (515) | 47,198 | 45,775 |
| 52205 | Anamosa | (319) | 5,100 | 4,958 |
| 50021 | Ankeny | (515) | 18,482 | 15,429 |
| 50022 | Atlantic | (712) | 7,432 | 7,789 |
| 52722 | Bettendorf | (319) | 28,139 | 27,381 |
| 50036 | Boone | (515) | 12,392 | 12,602 |
| 52601 | Burlington | (319) | 27,208 | 29,529 |
| 51401 | Carroll | (712) | 9,579 | 9,705 |
| 50613 | Cedar Falls | (319) | 34,298 | 36,322 |
| *52401 | Cedar Rapids | (319) | 108,780 | 110,243 |
| 52544 | Centerville | (515) | 5,936 | 6,558 |
| 50616 | Charles City | (515) | 7,878 | 8,778 |
| 51012 | Cherokee | (712) | 6,026 | 7,004 |
| 51632 | Clarinda | (712) | 5,104 | 5,458 |
| 50428 | Clear Lake City | (515) | 8,183 | 7,458 |
| 52732 | Clinton | (319) | 29,201 | 32,828 |
| 50053 | Clive | (515) | 7,462 | 6,064 |
| 52240 | Coralville | (319) | 10,347 | 7,687 |
| 51501 | Council Bluffs | (712) | 54,315 | 56,449 |
| 50801 | Creston | (515) | 7,911 | 8,429 |
| *52802 | Davenport | (319) | 95,333 | 103,264 |
| 52101 | Decorah | (319) | 8,063 | 7,991 |
| 51442 | Denison | (712) | 6,604 | 6,675 |
| *50318 | Des Moines | (515) | 193,189 | 191,003 |
| 52001 | Dubuque | (319) | 57,546 | 62,374 |
| 51334 | Estherville | (712) | 6,720 | 7,518 |
| 52556 | Fairfield | (515) | 9,768 | 9,428 |
| 50501 | Fort Dodge | (515) | 25,894 | 29,423 |
| 52627 | Fort Madison | (319) | 11,618 | 13,520 |
| 50112 | Grinnell | (515) | 8,902 | 8,868 |
| 51537 | Harlan | (712) | 5,148 | 5,357 |
| 50644 | Independence | (319) | 5,972 | 6,392 |
| 50125 | Indianola | (515) | 11,340 | 10,843 |
| 52240 | Iowa City | (319) | 59,735 | 50,508 |
| 50126 | Iowa Falls | (515) | 5,435 | 6,174 |
| 52632 | Keokuk | (319) | 12,451 | 13,536 |
| 50138 | Knoxville | (515) | 8,232 | 8,143 |
| 51031 | Le Mars | (712) | 8,454 | 8,276 |
| 52057 | Manchester | (319) | 5,137 | 4,942 |
| 52060 | Maquoketa | (319) | 6,129 | 6,313 |
| 52302 | Marion | (319) | 20,374 | 19,474 |
| 50158 | Marshalltown | (515) | 25,178 | 26,938 |
| 50401 | Mason City | (515) | 29,040 | 30,144 |
| 52641 | Mount Pleasant | (319) | 8,027 | 7,322 |
| 52761 | Muscatine | (319) | 22,881 | 23,467 |
| 50201 | Nevada | (515) | 6,009 | 5,912 |
| 50208 | Newton | (515) | 14,799 | 15,292 |
| 50211 | Norwalk | | 5,726 | 2,676 |
| 50662 | Oelwein | (319) | 6,493 | 7,564 |
| 52577 | Oskaloosa | (515) | 10,600 | 10,989 |
| 52501 | Ottumwa | (515) | 24,488 | 27,381 |
| 50219 | Pella | (515) | 9,270 | 8,349 |
| 50220 | Perry | (515) | 6,652 | 7,053 |
| 51566 | Red Oak | (712) | 6,264 | 6,810 |
| 51601 | Shenandoah | (712) | 5,572 | 6,274 |
| 51250 | Sioux Center | (712) | 5,074 | 4,588 |
| *51101 | Sioux City | (712) | 80,505 | 82,003 |
| 51301 | Spencer | (712) | 11,066 | 11,726 |
| 50588 | Storm Lake | (712) | 8,769 | 8,814 |
| 50322 | Urbandale | (515) | 23,500 | 17,869 |
| 52349 | Vinton | (319) | 5,103 | 5,040 |
| *52353 | Washington | (319) | 7,074 | 6,584 |
| *50701 | Waterloo | (319) | 66,467 | 75,985 |
| 50677 | Waverly | (319) | 8,539 | 8,444 |
| 50595 | Webster City | (515) | 7,894 | 8,572 |
| 50265 | West Des Moines | (515) | 31,702 | 21,894 |
| 50311 | Windsor Heights | (515) | 5,190 | 5,474 |

## Kansas

| ZIP code | Place | | 1990 | 1980 |
|---|---|---|---|---|
| 67410 | Abilene | (913) | 6,242 | 6,572 |
| 67005 | Arkansas City | (316) | 12,762 | 13,201 |
| 66002 | Atchison | (913) | 10,656 | 11,407 |
| 67010 | Augusta | (316) | 7,848 | 6,968 |

| ZIP code | Place | | 1990 | 1980 |
|---|---|---|---|---|
| 66012 | Bonner Springs | (913) | 6,413 | 6,266 |
| 66720 | Chanute | (316) | 9,488 | 10,506 |
| 67337 | Coffeyville | (316) | 12,917 | 15,185 |
| 67701 | Colby | (913) | 5,510 | 5,544 |
| 67037 | Derby | (316) | 14,699 | 9,786 |
| 67801 | Dodge City | (316) | 21,129 | 18,001 |
| 67042 | El Dorado | (316) | 11,495 | 11,551 |
| 66801 | Emporia | (316) | 25,512 | 25,287 |
| 66442 | Fort Riley North(u) | (913) | 12,848 | 16,086 |
| 66701 | Fort Scott | (316) | 8,362 | 8,893 |
| 67846 | Garden City | (316) | 24,097 | 18,256 |
| 67530 | Great Bend | (316) | 15,427 | 16,608 |
| 67601 | Hays | (913) | 17,807 | 16,301 |
| 67060 | Haysville | (316) | 8,364 | 8,006 |
| 67501 | Hutchinson | (316) | 39,308 | 40,284 |
| 67301 | Independence | (316) | 10,030 | 10,598 |
| 66749 | Iola | (316) | 6,351 | 6,938 |
| 66441 | Junction City | (913) | 20,642 | 19,305 |
| *66110 | Kansas City | (913) | 149,800 | 161,148 |
| 66043 | Lansing | (913) | 7,120 | 5,307 |
| 66044 | Lawrence | (913) | 65,608 | 52,738 |
| 66048 | Leavenworth | (913) | 38,495 | 33,656 |
| 66206 | Leawood | (913) | 19,693 | 13,360 |
| 66215 | Lenexa | (913) | 34,110 | 18,639 |
| 67901 | Liberal | (316) | 16,573 | 14,911 |
| 67460 | McPherson | (316) | 12,422 | 11,753 |
| 66502 | Manhattan | (913) | 37,737 | 32,644 |
| 66203 | Merriam | (913) | 11,819 | 10,794 |
| 66222 | Mission | (913) | 9,504 | 8,643 |
| 67114 | Newton | (316) | 16,700 | 16,332 |
| 66061 | Olathe | (913) | 63,402 | 37,258 |
| 66067 | Ottawa | (913) | 10,667 | 11,016 |
| 66204 | Overland Park | (913) | 111,790 | 81,784 |
| ..... | Park City | | 5,054 | 4,056 |
| 67357 | Parsons | (316) | 11,919 | 12,898 |
| 66762 | Pittsburg | (316) | 17,789 | 18,770 |
| 66208 | Prairie Village | (913) | 23,186 | 24,657 |
| 67124 | Pratt | (316) | 6,687 | 6,885 |
| 66203 | Roeland Park | (913) | 7,706 | 7,962 |
| 67401 | Salina | (913) | 42,299 | 41,843 |
| *66203 | Shawnee | (913) | 37,962 | 29,653 |
| *66603 | Topeka | (913) | 119,883 | 118,690 |
| 67880 | Ulysses | (316) | 5,474 | 4,653 |
| 67152 | Wellington | (316) | 8,517 | 8,212 |
| *67202 | Wichita | (316) | 304,017 | 279,838 |
| 67156 | Winfield | (316) | 11,931 | 10,736 |

## Kentucky

| ZIP code | Place | | 1990 | 1980 |
|---|---|---|---|---|
| 41001 | Alexandria | | 5,592 | 4,735 |
| 41101 | Ashland | (606) | 23,622 | 27,064 |
| 40004 | Bardstown | (502) | 6,712 | 6,155 |
| 41073 | Bellevue | (606) | 6,997 | 7,678 |
| 40403 | Berea | (606) | 9,129 | 8,226 |
| 42101 | Bowling Green | (502) | 40,688 | 40,450 |
| 40218 | Buechel(u) | (502) | 7,081 | 6,912 |
| 41005 | Burlington(u) | | 6,070 | .... |
| 42718 | Campbellsville | (502) | 9,592 | 8,715 |
| 40701 | Corbin | (606) | 7,644 | 8,075 |
| *41011 | Covington | (606) | 43,264 | 49,585 |
| 41031 | Cynthiana | (606) | 6,497 | 5,881 |
| 40422 | Danville | (606) | 12,449 | 12,942 |
| 41074 | Dayton | (606) | 6,576 | 6,979 |
| ..... | Douglass Hills | (502) | 5,431 | 4,384 |
| 41017 | Edgewood | (606) | 8,143 | 7,243 |
| 42701 | Elizabethtown | (502) | 18,167 | 15,380 |
| 41018 | Elsmere | (606) | 6,847 | 7,203 |
| 41018 | Erlanger | (606) | 15,979 | 14,466 |
| 40118 | Fairdale(u) | (502) | 6,563 | 7,315 |
| 40291 | Fern Creek(u) | (502) | 16,406 | 16,866 |
| 41139 | Flatwoods | (606) | 7,799 | 8,354 |
| 41042 | Florence | (606) | 18,586 | 15,586 |
| 42223 | Fort Campbell North(u) | (502) | 18,861 | 17,211 |
| 40121 | Fort Knox(u) | (502) | 21,495 | 31,055 |
| 41017 | Fort Mitchell | (606) | 7,438 | 7,294 |
| 41075 | Fort Thomas | (606) | 16,032 | 16,012 |
| 41011 | Fort Wright | | 6,570 | 4,481 |
| 40601 | Frankfort | (502) | 26,535 | 25,973 |
| 42134 | Franklin | (502) | 7,607 | 7,738 |
| 40324 | Georgetown | (502) | 11,414 | 10,972 |
| 42141 | Glasgow | (502) | 12,351 | 12,958 |
| 40330 | Harrodsburg | (606) | 7,335 | 7,265 |
| 41701 | Hazard | (606) | 5,416 | 5,371 |
| 42420 | Henderson | (502) | 25,945 | 24,834 |
| 40228 | Highview(u) | (502) | 14,814 | 13,286 |
| 40229 | Hillview | (502) | 6,119 | 5,196 |
| 42240 | Hopkinsville | (502) | 29,818 | 27,318 |
| 41051 | Independence | (606) | 10,444 | 7,998 |
| 40299 | Jeffersontown | (502) | 23,223 | 15,795 |
| 40342 | Lawrenceburg | (502) | 5,911 | 5,167 |
| 40033 | Lebanon | (502) | 5,695 | 6,590 |
| *40511 | Lexington-Fayette | (606) | 225,366 | 204,165 |
| 40741 | London | (606) | 5,757 | 4,002 |
| *40201 | Louisville | (502) | 269,555 | 298,694 |
| ..... | Lyndon | | 8,037 | 1,553 |
| 42431 | Madisonville | (502) | 16,203 | 16,979 |

| ZIP code | Place | | 1990 | 1980 |
|---|---|---|---|---|
| 42066 | Mayfield | (502) | 9,935 | 10,705 |
| 41056 | Maysville | (606) | 7,169 | 7,983 |
| 40965 | Middlesboro | (606) | 11,328 | 12,251 |
| 40243 | Middletown | ... | 5,016 | 4,262 |
| 42633 | Monticello | (606) | 5,357 | 5,677 |
| 40351 | Morehead | (606) | 8,357 | 7,789 |
| 40353 | Mount Sterling | (606) | 5,362 | 5,820 |
| 40047 | Mount Washington | (502) | 5,256 | 3,997 |
| 42071 | Murray | (502) | 14,442 | 14,248 |
| 40218 | Newburg(u) | (502) | 21,647 | 24,612 |
| *41071 | Newport | (606) | 18,871 | 21,587 |
| 40356 | Nicholasville | (606) | 13,603 | 10,400 |
| 40219 | Okolona(u) | (502) | 18,902 | 20,039 |
| 42301 | Owensboro | (502) | 53,579 | 54,450 |
| 42001 | Paducah | (502) | 27,256 | 29,315 |
| 40361 | Paris | (606) | 8,730 | 7,935 |
| 41501 | Pikeville | (606) | 6,324 | 4,756 |
| 40258 | Pleasure Ridge Park(u) | (502) | 25,131 | 27,332 |
| 42445 | Princeton | (502) | 6,940 | 7,073 |
| 40160 | Radcliff | (502) | 19,778 | 14,656 |
| 40475 | Richmond | (606) | 21,183 | 21,705 |
| 42276 | Russellville | (502) | 7,454 | 7,520 |
| ..... | Saint Dennis(u) | | 10,326 | .... |
| 40207 | Saint Matthews | (502) | 15,691 | 13,519 |
| 40065 | Shelbyville | (502) | 6,155 | 5,329 |
| 40216 | Shively | (502) | 15,535 | 16,645 |
| 42501 | Somerset | (606) | 10,735 | 10,649 |
| ..... | Taylor Mill | | 5,530 | 4,509 |
| 40272 | Valley Station(u) | (502) | 22,840 | 24,474 |
| 40383 | Versailles | (606) | 7,269 | 6,427 |
| ..... | Villa Hills | (606) | 7,370 | 4,384 |
| 41101 | Westwoods(u) | (606) | 5,300 | 5,973 |
| 40769 | Williamsburg | (606) | 5,493 | 5,560 |
| 40391 | Winchester | (606) | 15,799 | 15,216 |

## Louisiana

| ZIP code | Place | | 1990 | 1980 |
|---|---|---|---|---|
| 70510 | Abbeville | (318) | 11,187 | 12,391 |
| 71301 | Alexandria | (318) | 49,087 | 51,648 |
| 70032 | Arabi(u) | (504) | 8,787 | 10,248 |
| 70094 | Avondale(u) | (504) | 5,813 | 6,699 |
| 70714 | Baker | (504) | 13,087 | 12,865 |
| 71220 | Bastrop | (318) | 13,916 | 15,527 |
| *70821 | Baton Rouge | (504) | 219,531 | 220,394 |
| 70360 | Bayou Cane(u) | (504) | 15,876 | 15,723 |
| 70037 | Belle Chasse(u) | (504) | 8,512 | 5,412 |
| 70427 | Bogalusa | (504) | 14,280 | 16,976 |
| 71010 | Bossier City | (318) | 52,721 | 50,817 |
| 70517 | Breaux Bridge | (318) | 6,694 | 5,922 |
| 70094 | Bridge(u) | | 8,327 | .... |
| 70811 | Brownfields(u) | (504) | 5,229 | .... |
| 71291 | Brownsville-Bawcomville(u) | (318) | 7,397 | 7,252 |
| 71322 | Bunkie | (318) | 5,044 | 5,364 |
| 70520 | Carencro | | 5,429 | 3,712 |
| 70043 | Chalmette(u) | (504) | 31,860 | 33,847 |
| 71291 | Claiborne(u) | (318) | 8,300 | 6,278 |
| 70433 | Covington | (504) | 7,691 | 7,892 |
| 70526 | Crowley | (318) | 13,983 | 16,036 |
| 70345 | Cut Off(u) | (504) | 5,325 | 5,049 |
| 70726 | Denham Springs | (504) | 8,381 | 8,563 |
| 70634 | De Ridder | (318) | 9,868 | 10,337 |
| 70047 | Destrehan | (504) | 8,031 | 2,382 |
| 70346 | Donaldsonville | (504) | 7,949 | 7,901 |
| 70072 | Estelle(u) | (504) | 14,091 | 12,724 |
| 70535 | Eunice | (318) | 11,162 | 12,479 |
| 71459 | Fort Polk South | (318) | 10,911 | 12,498 |
| 70538 | Franklin | (318) | 9,004 | 9,584 |
| 70820 | Gardere | | 7,209 | .... |
| 70737 | Gonzales | (504) | 7,208 | 7,287 |
| 71245 | Grambling | | 5,512 | 4,226 |
| 70053 | Gretna | (504) | 17,208 | 20,615 |
| 70401 | Hammond | (504) | 15,871 | 15,226 |
| 70123 | Harahan | (504) | 9,927 | 11,384 |
| 70058 | Harvey(u) | (504) | 21,222 | 22,709 |
| 70360 | Houma | (504) | 30,495 | 32,602 |
| 70544 | Jeanerette | (318) | 6,205 | 6,511 |
| 70121 | Jefferson(u) | (504) | 14,521 | 15,550 |
| 70546 | Jennings | (318) | 11,305 | 12,401 |
| 70062 | Kenner | (504) | 72,033 | 66,382 |
| 70445 | Lacombe(u) | (504) | 6,523 | 5,146 |
| 70501 | Lafayette | (318) | 94,440 | 80,584 |
| 70601 | Lake Charles | (318) | 70,580 | 75,226 |
| 71254 | Lake Providence | (318) | 5,380 | 6,361 |
| 70068 | La Place(u) | (504) | 24,194 | 16,112 |
| 70373 | Larose(u) | (504) | 5,772 | 5,234 |
| 71446 | Leesville | (318) | 7,638 | 9,054 |
| 70448 | Mandeville | (504) | 7,474 | 6,076 |
| 71052 | Mansfield | (318) | 5,389 | 6,485 |
| 71351 | Marksville | (318) | 5,526 | 5,113 |
| 70072 | Marrero(u) | (504) | 36,671 | 36,548 |
| 70075 | Meraux(u) | (504) | 8,849 | .... |
| 70812 | Merrydale(u) | | 10,395 | .... |
| *70004 | Metairie(u) | (504) | 149,428 | 164,160 |
| 71055 | Minden | (318) | 13,661 | 15,084 |
| 71201 | Monroe | (318) | 54,909 | 57,597 |
| 70380 | Morgan City | (504) | 14,531 | 16,114 |
| 70601 | Moss Bluff(u) | (318) | 8,039 | 7,004 |

| ZIP code | Place | | 1990 | 1980 |
|---|---|---|---|---|
| 71457 | Natchitoches | (318) | 16,609 | 16,664 |
| 70560 | New Iberia | (318) | 31,828 | 32,766 |
| *70113 | New Orleans | (504) | 496,938 | 557,927 |
| 70760 | New Roads | | 5,303 | 3,924 |
| 71463 | Oakdale | (318) | 6,837 | 7,155 |
| 70810 | Oak Hills Place | | 5,479 | .... |
| 70570 | Opelousas | (318) | 19,091 | 18,903 |
| 70392 | Patterson | (504) | 5,166 | 4,693 |
| 71360 | Pineville | (318) | 12,251 | 12,034 |
| 70764 | Plaquemine | (504) | 7,101 | 7,521 |
| 70454 | Ponchatoula | (504) | 5,425 | 5,469 |
| 70767 | Port Allen | (504) | 6,277 | 6,114 |
| 70601 | Prien(u) | (318) | 6,448 | 6,224 |
| 70394 | Raceland(u) | (504) | 5,564 | 6,302 |
| 70578 | Rayne | (318) | 8,502 | 9,066 |
| .... | Red Chute(u) | | 5,431 | .... |
| 70084 | Reserve(u) | (504) | 8,847 | 7,288 |
| 70123 | River Ridge(u) | (504) | 14,800 | 17,146 |
| 71270 | Ruston | (318) | 20,071 | 20,585 |
| 70582 | Saint Martinville | (318) | 7,226 | 7,965 |
| 70087 | Saint Rose(u) | (504) | 6,259 | .... |
| 70817 | Shenandoah(u) | | 13,429 | .... |
| *71102 | Shreveport | (318) | 198,525 | 206,989 |
| 70458 | Slidell | (504) | 24,124 | 26,718 |
| 71075 | Springhill | (318) | 5,668 | 6,516 |
| 70663 | Sulphur | (318) | 20,125 | 19,709 |
| 71282 | Tallulah | (318) | 8,526 | 11,341 |
| 70056 | Terrytown(u) | (504) | 23,787 | 23,548 |
| 70301 | Thibodaux | (504) | 14,125 | 15,810 |
| 70053 | Timberlane(u) | (504) | 12,614 | 11,579 |
| 70809 | Village Saint George(u) | | 6,242 | .... |
| 70586 | Ville Platte | (318) | 9,037 | 9,201 |
| 70092 | Violet(u) | (504) | 8,574 | 11,678 |
| 70094 | Waggaman(u) | (504) | 9,405 | 9,004 |
| 70669 | Westlake | (318) | 5,007 | 5,246 |
| 71291 | West Monroe | (318) | 14,096 | 14,993 |
| 70094 | Westwego | (504) | 11,218 | 12,663 |
| 71483 | Winnfield | (318) | 6,138 | 7,311 |
| 71295 | Winnsboro | (318) | 5,755 | 5,921 |
| 70791 | Zachary | (504) | 9,036 | 7,297 |

## Maine (207)

See Note on Page 373

| ZIP code | Place | 1990 | 1980 |
|---|---|---|---|
| 04210 | Auburn | 24,309 | 23,128 |
| 04330 | Augusta | 21,325 | 21,819 |
| 04401 | Bangor | 33,181 | 31,643 |
| 04530 | Bath | 9,799 | 10,246 |
| 04915 | Belfast | 6,355 | 6,243 |
| 03901 | Berwick | 5,995 | .... |
| 04005 | Biddeford | 20,710 | 19,638 |
| 04412 | Brewer | 9,021 | 9,017 |
| 04011 | Brunswick Center(u) | 14,683 | 10,990 |
| 04011 | Brunswick | 20,906 | 17,366 |
| 04093 | Buxton | 6,494 | 5,775 |
| 04843 | Camden | 5,060 | .... |
| 04107 | Cape Elizabeth | 8,854 | 7,838 |
| 04736 | Caribou | 9,415 | 9,916 |
| 04021 | Cumberland | 5,836 | 5,284 |
| 03903 | Eliot | 5,329 | .... |
| 04605 | Ellsworth | 5,975 | 5,179 |
| 04937 | Fairfield | 6,718 | 6,113 |
| 04105 | Falmouth | 7,610 | 6,853 |
| 04938 | Farmington | 7,436 | 6,730 |
| 04032 | Freeport | 6,905 | 5,863 |
| 04345 | Gardiner | 6,746 | 6,485 |
| 04038 | Gorham | 11,856 | 10,101 |
| 04039 | Gray | 5,904 | .... |
| 04444 | Hampden | 5,974 | 5,250 |
| .... | Harpswell | 5,012 | .... |
| 04730 | Houlton Center(u) | 5,627 | 5,730 |
| 04730 | Houlton | 6,613 | 6,766 |
| 04239 | Jay | 5,080 | 5,080 |
| 04043 | Kennebunk | 8,004 | 6,621 |
| 03904 | Kittery Center(u) | 5,151 | 5,465 |
| 03904 | Kittery | 9,372 | 9,314 |
| 04240 | Lewiston | 39,757 | 40,481 |
| 04750 | Limestone | 9,922 | 8,719 |
| 04457 | Lincoln | 5,587 | 5,066 |
| 04250 | Lisbon | 9,457 | 8,769 |
| 04750 | Loring(u) | 5,494 | 6,572 |
| 04462 | Millinocket Center(u) | 6,922 | 7,567 |
| 04462 | Millinocket | 7,567 | 7,742 |
| 04963 | Oakland | 5,595 | 5,162 |
| 04064 | Old Orchard Beach Ctr.(u) | 7,789 | 6,023 |
| 04064 | Old Orchard Beach | 7,789 | 6,291 |
| 04468 | Old Town | 8,317 | 8,422 |
| 04473 | Orono Center(u) | 9,789 | 9,891 |
| 04473 | Orono | 10,573 | 10,578 |
| *04101 | Portland | 64,358 | 61,572 |
| 04769 | Presque Isle | 10,550 | 11,172 |
| 04841 | Rockland | 7,972 | 7,919 |
| 04276 | Rumford Compact(u) | 5,419 | 6,256 |
| 04276 | Rumford | 7,078 | 8,240 |
| 04072 | Saco | 15,181 | 12,921 |
| 04073 | Sanford Center(u) | 10,296 | 10,268 |
| 04073 | Sanford | 20,463 | 18,020 |

| ZIP code | Place | | 1990 | 1980 |
|---|---|---|---|---|
| 04074 | Scarborough | | 12,518 | 11,347 |
| 04976 | Skowhegan Center(u) | | 6,990 | 6,517 |
| 04976 | Skowhegan | | 8,725 | 8,098 |
| 03908 | South Berwick | | 5,877 | .... |
| 04106 | South Portland | | 23,163 | 22,712 |
| 04084 | Standish | | 7,678 | 5,946 |
| 04086 | Topsham | | 8,746 | 6,147 |
| 04901 | Waterville | | 17,173 | 17,779 |
| 04090 | Wells | | 7,778 | 8,211 |
| 04092 | Westbrook | | 16,121 | 14,976 |
| 04082 | Windham | | 13,020 | 11,282 |
| 04901 | Winslow Center(u) | | 5,436 | 5,903 |
| 04901 | Winslow | | 7,997 | 8,057 |
| 04364 | Winthrop | | 5,986 | 5,889 |
| 04096 | Yarmouth | | 7,862 | 6,585 |
| 03909 | York | | 9,818 | 8,465 |

## Maryland

| ZIP code | Place | | 1990 | 1980 |
|---|---|---|---|---|
| 21001 | Aberdeen | (410) | 13,087 | 11,533 |
| 21005 | Aberdeen Proving Ground(u) | | 5,267 | 5,722 |
| 20783 | Adelphi(u) | (301) | 13,524 | 12,530 |
| 20331 | Andrews AFB(u) | (410) | 10,228 | 10,064 |
| *21401 | Annapolis | (410) | 33,195 | 31,740 |
| 21227 | Arbutus(u) | (410) | 19,750 | 20,163 |
| 21012 | Arnold(u) | (410) | 20,261 | 12,285 |
| 20906 | Aspen Hill(u) | (301) | 45,494 | 47,455 |
| .... | Ballenger Creek | | 5,546 | 2,659 |
| *21233 | Baltimore | (410) | 736,014 | 786,741 |
| 21014 | Bel Air | (410) | 8,942 | 7,814 |
| 21050 | Bel Air North(u) | (410) | 14,880 | 5,043 |
| 21014 | Bel Air South(u) | (410) | 26,421 | 8,461 |
| 20705 | Beltsville(u) | (301) | 14,476 | 12,760 |
| *20815 | Bethesda(u) | (301) | 62,936 | 62,736 |
| 20710 | Bladensburg | (301) | 8,064 | 7,691 |
| *20715 | Bowie | (301) | 37,642 | 33,695 |
| .... | Bowleys Quarters(u) | | 5,595 | .... |
| 21225 | Brooklyn Park(u) | (410) | 10,987 | 11,508 |
| 20866 | Burtonsville(u) | | 5,853 | 2,046 |
| 20818 | Cabin John-Brookmont(u) | | 5,341 | 5,135 |
| 20619 | California(u) | (410) | 7,626 | 5,770 |
| .... | Calverton(u) | (301) | 12,046 | .... |
| 21613 | Cambridge | (410) | 11,514 | 11,703 |
| 20748 | Camp Springs(u) | (301) | 16,392 | 16,118 |
| 21401 | Cape St. Clair(u) | (410) | 7,878 | 6,022 |
| 21234 | Carney(u) | (410) | 25,578 | 21,488 |
| 21228 | Catonsville(u) | (410) | 35,233 | 33,208 |
| .... | Chesapeake Ranch Estates(u) | | 5,423 | .... |
| 20785 | Cheverly | (301) | 6,023 | 5,751 |
| 20815 | Chevy Chase(u) | (301) | 8,559 | 12,232 |
| 20783 | Chillum(u) | (301) | 31,309 | 32,775 |
| 20735 | Clinton(u) | (301) | 19,987 | 16,438 |
| 20904 | Cloverly(u) | (301) | 7,904 | 5,153 |
| 21030 | Cockeysville(u) | (410) | 18,668 | 17,013 |
| 20904 | Colesville(u) | (301) | 18,819 | 14,359 |
| 20740 | College Park | (301) | 23,714 | 23,614 |
| *21044 | Columbia(u) | (301) | 75,883 | 52,518 |
| 20743 | Coral Hills(u) | (410) | 11,032 | 11,602 |
| 21114 | Crofton(u) | (410) | 12,781 | 12,009 |
| 21502 | Cumberland | (301) | 23,712 | 25,933 |
| 20872 | Damascus(u) | (301) | 9,817 | 4,129 |
| 20747 | District Heights | (301) | 6,711 | 6,799 |
| 21222 | Dundalk(u) | (410) | 65,800 | 71,293 |
| 21601 | Easton | (410) | 9,372 | 7,536 |
| 20737 | East Riverdale(u) | (301) | 14,187 | 14,117 |
| 21219 | Edgemere(u) | (410) | 9,226 | 9,078 |
| 21040 | Edgewood(u) | (410) | 23,903 | 19,455 |
| 21784 | Eldersburg(u) | | 9,720 | 4,959 |
| .... | Elkridge(u) | | 12,953 | .... |
| 21921 | Elkton | (410) | 9,073 | 6,468 |
| 21043 | Ellicott City(u) | (410) | 41,396 | 21,784 |
| 21221 | Essex(u) | (410) | 40,872 | 39,614 |
| 20904 | Fairland(u) | (301) | 19,828 | 5,154 |
| 21047 | Fallston(u) | (410) | 5,730 | 5,572 |
| 21061 | Ferndale(u) | (410) | 16,355 | 14,314 |
| 20747 | Forestville(u) | (301) | 16,731 | 16,401 |
| 20755 | Fort Meade(u) | (301) | 12,509 | 14,083 |
| 20744 | Fort Washington(u) | | 24,032 | .... |
| 21701 | Frederick | (301) | 40,186 | 28,086 |
| .... | Friendly(u) | (301) | 9,028 | 8,848 |
| 21532 | Frostburg | (301) | 8,069 | 7,715 |
| *20877 | Gaithersburg | (301) | 39,676 | 26,424 |
| 21055 | Garrison(u) | | 5,045 | .... |
| 20874 | Germantown(u) | (301) | 41,145 | 9,721 |
| 20706 | Glenarden | | 5,025 | 4,993 |
| 21061 | Glen Burnie(u) | (410) | 37,305 | 37,263 |
| 20769 | Glen Dale(u) | (301) | 9,689 | 5,106 |
| 20772 | Greater Upper Marlboro | | 11,528 | .... |
| 20770 | Greenbelt | (301) | 20,561 | 17,332 |
| 21122 | Green Haven(u) | (410) | 14,416 | 6,577 |
| .... | Green Valley(u) | | 9,424 | 4,504 |
| 21740 | Hagerstown | (301) | 35,445 | 34,132 |
| 21740 | Halfway(u) | (301) | 8,873 | 8,659 |
| 21078 | Havre De Grace | (410) | 8,952 | 8,763 |
| 20903 | Hillandale(u) | | 10,318 | 9,686 |
| 20748 | Hillcrest Heights(u) | (301) | 17,136 | 17,021 |
| *20780 | Hyattsville | (301) | 13,864 | 12,709 |

| ZIP code | Place | | 1990 | 1980 |
|---|---|---|---|---|
| 20794 | Jessup(u) | | 6,537 | 4,288 |
| 21085 | Joppatowne(u) | (410) | 11,084 | 11,348 |
| 20785 | Kentland(u) | (301) | 7,967 | 8,596 |
| 20772 | Kettering(u) | | 9,901 | 6,972 |
| 21122 | Lake Shore(u) | (410) | 13,269 | 10,181 |
| 20785 | Landover(u) | (301) | 5,052 | 5,374 |
| 20787 | Langley Park(u) | (301) | 17,474 | 14,038 |
| 20706 | Lanham-Seabrook(u) | (301) | 16,792 | 15,814 |
| 21227 | Lansdowne-Baltimore Highlands(u) | | 15,509 | 16,759 |
| 20646 | La Plata | (301) | 5,841 | 2,484 |
| 20772 | Largo(u) | (301) | 9,475 | 5,557 |
| *20707 | Laurel | (301) | 19,550 | 12,103 |
| 20653 | Lexington Pk.(u). | (410) | 9,943 | 10,361 |
| 21090 | Linthicum(u) | (410) | 7,547 | 7,457 |
| 21207 | Lochearn(u) | (410) | 25,240 | 26,908 |
| 21037 | Londontowne(u) | (410) | 6,992 | 6,052 |
| | Long Meadow(u) | | 5,594 | 1,203 |
| 21093 | Lutherville-Timonium(u). | | 16,442 | 17,854 |
| 20748 | Marlow Heights(u) | (301) | 5,885 | 5,824 |
| | Marlton | | 5,523 | |
| 20707 | Maryland City(u) | | 6,813 | 6,949 |
| | Mays Chapel(u) | | 10,132 | 5,213 |
| 21220 | Middle River(u) | (410) | 24,616 | 26,756 |
| | Milford Mill(u) | | 22,547 | 20,354 |
| 20717 | Mitchellville | | 12,593 | |
| 20879 | Montgomery Village(u). | (301) | 32,315 | 18,725 |
| 20822 | Mount Rainier | (301) | 7,954 | 7,361 |
| 21402 | Naval Academy(u) | (410) | 5,420 | 5,367 |
| 20784 | New Carrollton | (301) | 12,002 | 12,632 |
| 20815 | North Bethesda(u) | (301) | 29,656 | 22,671 |
| 20895 | North Kensington(u) | (301) | 8,607 | 9,039 |
| 20707 | North Laurel(u) | (301) | 15,008 | 6,093 |
| | North Potomac(u). | (301) | 18,456 | |
| 21842 | Ocean City | (410) | 5,146 | 4,946 |
| 21113 | Odenton(u) | (410) | 12,833 | 13,270 |
| 20832 | Olney(u) | (301) | 23,019 | 13,026 |
| 21206 | Overlea(u). | (410) | 12,137 | 12,965 |
| 21117 | Owings Mills(u) | (410) | 9,474 | 9,526 |
| 20745 | Oxon Hill-Glassmanor(u). | (301) | 35,794 | 36,267 |
| 20785 | Palmer Park(u) | (301) | 7,019 | 7,986 |
| 21234 | Parkville | (410) | 31,617 | 35,159 |
| 21401 | Parole | | 10,054 | 3,377 |
| 21122 | Pasadena(u) | (410) | 10,012 | 7,439 |
| 21128 | Perry Hall(u) | (410) | 22,723 | 13,455 |
| 21208 | Pikesville(u) | (410) | 24,815 | 22,555 |
| 20854 | Potomac(u) | (301) | 45,634 | 40,402 |
| 21227 | Pumphrey(u) | | 5,483 | 5,666 |
| 21133 | Randallstown(u). | (301) | 26,277 | 25,927 |
| | Redland(u) | (301) | 16,145 | 10,759 |
| 21136 | Reisterstown(u) | (410) | 19,314 | 19,385 |
| 20737 | Riverdale | | 5,191 | 4,761 |
| 21122 | Riviera Beach(u) | (410) | 11,376 | 6,812 |
| *20850 | Rockville(u) | (301) | 44,830 | 43,811 |
| | Rosaryville(u) | | 8,976 | |
| 21237 | Rosedale(u) | (410) | 18,703 | 19,956 |
| | Rossmoor(u) | | 6,182 | 8,646 |
| 21221 | Rossville(u) | | 9,492 | 8,646 |
| 20601 | Saint Charles(u). | (301) | 28,717 | 13,921 |
| 21801 | Salisbury. | (410) | 20,592 | 16,429 |
| 20763 | Savage-Guilford(u) | | 9,669 | 2,928 |
| 20743 | Seat Pleasant | (301) | 5,359 | 5,217 |
| 21144 | Severn(u) | (410) | 24,499 | 20,147 |
| 21146 | Severna Park(u) | (410) | 25,879 | 21,253 |
| *20907 | Silver Spring(u) | (301) | 76,046 | 72,893 |
| 21061 | South Gate(u) | (410) | 27,564 | 24,185 |
| 20895 | South Kensington(u) | (301) | 8,777 | 9,344 |
| 20707 | South Laurel(u) | | 18,591 | 18,034 |
| 20746 | Suitland-Silver Hills(u) | (301) | 35,111 | 32,164 |
| 20912 | Takoma Park | (301) | 16,724 | 16,231 |
| 20748 | Temple Hills(u) | (301) | 6,865 | 6,630 |
| 21204 | Towson(u) | (410) | 49,445 | 51,083 |
| 20601 | Waldorf(u) | (301) | 15,058 | 9,782 |
| 20743 | Walker Mill(u) | (301) | 10,920 | 10,651 |
| 21157 | Westminster | (410) | 13,060 | 8,808 |
| 20902 | Wheaton Glenmont(u) | (301) | 53,720 | 48,598 |
| 21162 | White Marsh(u) | | 8,183 | |
| 20903 | White Oak(u) | (301) | 18,671 | 13,700 |
| 21207 | Woodlawn(u) | (410) | 32,907 | |
| 21207 | Woodlawn(u) | | 5,329 | 5,306 |

## Massachusetts

*See Note on Page 373*

| ZIP code | Place | | 1990 | 1980 |
|---|---|---|---|---|
| 02351 | Abington | (617) | 13,817 | 13,887 |
| 01720 | Acton | (508) | 17,872 | 17,544 |
| 02743 | Acushnet | (508) | 9,554 | 8,704 |
| 01220 | Adams Center(u) | (413) | 6,356 | 6,857 |
| 01220 | Adams. | (413) | 9,445 | 10,381 |
| 01001 | Agawam. | (413) | 27,323 | 26,271 |
| 01913 | Amesbury Center(u) | (508) | 12,109 | 12,236 |
| 01913 | Amesbury. | (508) | 14,997 | 13,971 |
| 01002 | Amherst Center. | (413) | 17,824 | 17,773 |
| 01002 | Amherst. | (413) | 35,228 | 33,229 |
| 01810 | Andover | (508) | 8,242 | 8,445 |
| 01810 | Andover. | (508) | 29,151 | 26,370 |
| 02174 | Arlington. | (617) | 44,630 | 44,630 |
| 01430 | Ashburnham. | (508) | 5,433 | |

| ZIP code | Place | | 1990 | 1980 |
|---|---|---|---|---|
| 01721 | Ashland | (508) | 12,066 | 9,165 |
| 01331 | Athol Center(u) | (508) | 8,732 | 8,708 |
| 01331 | Athol. | (508) | 11,451 | 10,634 |
| 02703 | Attleboro. | (508) | 38,383 | 34,196 |
| 01501 | Auburn. | (508) | 15,005 | 14,845 |
| *01432 | Ayer. | (508) | 6,871 | 6,993 |
| 02630 | Barnstable. | (508) | 40,949 | 30,898 |
| 01730 | Bedford. | (617) | 12,996 | 13,067 |
| 01007 | Belchertown. | (413) | 10,579 | 8,339 |
| 02019 | Bellingham. | (508) | 14,877 | 14,300 |
| 02178 | Belmont. | (617) | 24,720 | 24,720 |
| 01915 | Beverly. | (508) | 38,195 | 37,655 |
| 01821 | Billerica. | (508) | 37,609 | 36,727 |
| 01504 | Blackstone. | (508) | 8,023 | 6,570 |
| *02109 | Boston. | (617) | 574,283 | 562,994 |
| 02532 | Bourne. | (508) | 16,064 | 13,874 |
| 01921 | Boxford. | (508) | 6,266 | 5,374 |
| 02184 | Braintree. | (617) | 33,836 | 36,337 |
| 02631 | Brewster. | (508) | 8,440 | 5,226 |
| 02324 | Bridgewater. | (508) | 21,249 | 7,242 |
| *02403 | Brockton. | (508) | 92,788 | 95,172 |
| 02146 | Brookline. | (617) | 54,718 | 55,062 |
| 01803 | Burlington. | (617) | 23,302 | 23,486 |
| *02138 | Cambridge. | (617) | 95,802 | 95,322 |
| 02021 | Canton. | (617) | 18,530 | 18,182 |
| 02330 | Carver. | (508) | 10,590 | 6,988 |
| 02632 | Centerville. | (508) | 9,190 | 3,640 |
| 01507 | Charlton. | (508) | 9,576 | 6,719 |
| 02633 | Chatham. | (508) | 6,579 | 6,071 |
| 01824 | Chelmsford. | (508) | 32,383 | 32,388 |
| 02150 | Chelsea. | (617) | 28,710 | 25,431 |
| *01021 | Chicopee. | (413) | 56,632 | 55,112 |
| 01510 | Clinton. | (508) | 13,222 | 7,943 |
| 01778 | Cochituate(u). | (508) | 6,046 | 6,126 |
| 02025 | Cohasset. | (617) | 7,075 | 7,174 |
| 01742 | Concord. | (508) | 17,076 | 16,293 |
| 01226 | Dalton. | (413) | 7,155 | 6,797 |
| 01923 | Danvers. | (508) | 24,174 | 24,174 |
| 02714 | Dartmouth. | (508) | 27,244 | 23,966 |
| 02026 | Dedham. | (617) | 23,782 | 25,298 |
| 01342 | Deerfield. | (413) | 5,018 | |
| 02638 | Dennis. | (508) | 13,864 | 12,360 |
| 02715 | Dighton. | (508) | 5,631 | 5,352 |
| | Douglas. | (508) | 5,438 | |
| 01826 | Dracut. | (508) | 25,594 | 21,249 |
| 01570 | Dudley. | (508) | 9,540 | 8,717 |
| 02332 | Duxbury. | (617) | 13,895 | 11,807 |
| 02333 | East Bridgewater. | (508) | 11,104 | 9,945 |
| 02536 | East Falmouth(u). | (508) | 5,577 | 5,141 |
| 01027 | Easthampton. | (413) | 15,537 | 15,580 |
| 01028 | East Longmeadow. | (413) | 13,367 | 12,905 |
| 02334 | Easton. | (508) | 19,807 | 16,623 |
| 02149 | Everett. | (617) | 35,701 | 37,195 |
| 02719 | Fairhaven. | (508) | 16,132 | 15,759 |
| *02722 | Fall River. | (508) | 92,703 | 92,574 |
| 02540 | Falmouth. | (508) | 27,960 | 41,194 |
| 01420 | Fitchburg. | (508) | 41,194 | 39,580 |
| 01433 | Fort Devens(u). | (508) | 8,973 | 9,546 |
| 02035 | Foxborough. | (508) | 14,637 | 5,706 |
| 01701 | Framingham. | (508) | 64,994 | 65,113 |
| 02038 | Franklin Center(u). | (508) | 9,965 | 9,296 |
| 02038 | Franklin. | (508) | 22,095 | 18,217 |
| 02702 | Freetown. | (508) | 8,522 | 7,058 |
| 01440 | Gardner. | (508) | 20,125 | 17,900 |
| 01833 | Georgetown. | (508) | 6,384 | 5,687 |
| 01930 | Gloucester. | (508) | 28,716 | 27,768 |
| 01519 | Grafton. | (508) | 13,035 | 11,238 |
| 01033 | Granby. | (413) | 5,565 | 5,380 |
| 01230 | Great Barrington. | (413) | 7,725 | 7,405 |
| 01301 | Greenfield Center(u). | (413) | 14,016 | 14,198 |
| 01302 | Greenfield. | (413) | 18,666 | 18,436 |
| 01450 | Groton. | (508) | 7,511 | 6,154 |
| 01834 | Groveland. | (508) | 5,214 | 5,040 |
| 02338 | Halifax. | (617) | 6,526 | 5,513 |
| 01936 | Hamilton. | (508) | 7,280 | 6,960 |
| 02339 | Hanover. | (617) | 11,912 | 11,358 |
| 02341 | Hanson. | (617) | 9,028 | 8,508 |
| 01451 | Harvard. | (508) | 12,329 | 12,170 |
| 02645 | Harwich. | (508) | 10,275 | 8,971 |
| 01830 | Haverhill. | (508) | 51,418 | 46,865 |
| 02043 | Hingham. | (617) | 19,821 | 18,845 |
| 02343 | Holbrook. | (617) | 11,041 | 11,041 |
| 01520 | Holden. | (508) | 14,628 | 13,336 |
| 01746 | Holliston. | (508) | 12,926 | 12,622 |
| 01040 | Holyoke. | (413) | 43,704 | 44,678 |
| 01747 | Hopedale. | (508) | 5,666 | |
| 01748 | Hopkinton. | (508) | 9,191 | 7,114 |
| 01749 | Hudson Center(u). | (508) | 14,267 | 14,156 |
| 01749 | Hudson. | (508) | 17,233 | 14,267 |
| 02045 | Hull. | (617) | 10,466 | 10,466 |
| 02601 | Hyannis(u). | (508) | 14,120 | 9,118 |
| 01938 | Ipswich. | (508) | *11,873 | 11,158 |
| 02364 | Kingston. | (617) | 9,045 | 7,362 |
| 02346 | Lakeville. | (508) | 7,785 | 5,931 |
| 01523 | Lancaster. | (508) | 6,661 | 6,334 |
| *01842 | Lawrence. | (508) | 70,207 | 63,175 |
| 01238 | Lee. | (413) | 5,849 | 6,247 |
| 01524 | Leicester. | (508) | 10,191 | 9,446 |
| 01240 | Lenox. | (413) | 5,069 | 6,523 |

| ZIP code | Place | 1990 | 1980 |
|---|---|---|---|
| 01453 | Leominster. . . . . . . . . . . (508) | 38,145 | 34,508 |
| 02173 | Lexington . . . . . . . . . . (617) | 28,974 | 29,479 |
| 01773 | Lincoln . . . . . . . . . . . (617) | 7,666 | 7,098 |
| 01460 | Littleton . . . . . . . . . . (508) | 7,051 | 6,970 |
| 01106 | Longmeadow . . . . . . . (413) | 15,467 | 15,467 |
| *01853 | Lowell . . . . . . . . . . . . (508) | 103,439 | 92,418 |
| 01056 | Ludlow . . . . . . . . . . . (413) | 18,820 | 18,150 |
| 01462 | Lunenburg . . . . . . . . . (508) | 9,117 | 8,405 |
| *01901 | Lynn . . . . . . . . . . . . . (617) | 81,245 | 78,471 |
| 01940 | Lynnfield . . . . . . . . . . (617) | 11,274 | 11,267 |
| 02148 | Malden . . . . . . . . . . . (617) | 53,884 | 53,386 |
| 01944 | Manchester . . . . . . . . (508) | 5,286 | 5,424 |
| 02048 | Mansfield . . . . . . . . . . (508) | 16,568 | 7,170 |
| 01945 | Marblehead . . . . . . . . (617) | 19,971 | 19,971 |
| 01752 | Marlborough . . . . . . . . (508) | 31,813 | 30,617 |
| 02050 | Marshfield . . . . . . . . . (617) | 21,531 | 20,916 |
| 02648 | Marstons Mills(u) . . . . . | 8,017 | .... |
| 02649 | Mashpee . . . . . . . . . . (508) | 7,884 | .... |
| 02739 | Mattapoisett . . . . . . . . (508) | 5,850 | 5,597 |
| 01754 | Maynard . . . . . . . . . . (508) | 10,325 | 10,325 |
| 02052 | Medfield . . . . . . . . . . (508) | 10,531 | 5,985 |
| 02155 | Medford . . . . . . . . . . (617) | 57,407 | 58,076 |
| 02053 | Medway . . . . . . . . . . (508) | 9,931 | 8,447 |
| 02176 | Melrose . . . . . . . . . . (617) | 28,150 | 30,055 |
| 01860 | Merrimac. . . . . . . . . . (508) | 5,166 | .... |
| 01844 | Methuen . . . . . . . . . . (508) | 39,990 | 36,701 |
| 02346 | Middleborough Center(u) . . (617) | 6,837 | 7,012 |
| 02346 | Middleborough . . . . . . . (617) | 17,867 | 16,404 |
| 01757 | Milford Center(u) . . . . . (508) | 23,339 | 21,730 |
| 01757 | Milford . . . . . . . . . . . (508) | 25,355 | 23,390 |
| 01527 | Millbury . . . . . . . . . . (508) | 12,228 | 11,808 |
| 02054 | Millis . . . . . . . . . . . . (508) | 7,613 | 6,908 |
| 02186 | Milton . . . . . . . . . . . (617) | 25,725 | 25,860 |
| 01057 | Monson . . . . . . . . . . (413) | 7,776 | 7,315 |
| 01351 | Montague . . . . . . . . . (508) | 8,316 | 8,011 |
| 02554 | Nantucket . . . . . . . . . (508) | 6,012 | 5,087 |
| 01760 | Natick . . . . . . . . . . . (508) | 30,510 | 29,461 |
| 02192 | Needham . . . . . . . . . . (617) | 27,557 | 27,901 |
| *02741 | New Bedford . . . . . . . . (508) | 99,922 | 98,478 |
| 01951 | Newbury . . . . . . . . . . (508) | 5,623 | .... |
| 01950 | Newburyport . . . . . . . . (508) | 16,317 | 15,900 |
| 02158 | Newton . . . . . . . . . . . (617) | 82,585 | 83,622 |
| 02056 | Norfolk . . . . . . . . . . . (508) | 9,270 | 6,363 |
| 01247 | North Adams . . . . . . . . (413) | 16,797 | 18,063 |
| 01002 | North Amherst(u) . . . . . (413) | 6,239 | 5,616 |
| 01060 | Northampton . . . . . . . . (413) | 29,289 | 29,286 |
| 01845 | North Andover . . . . . . . (508) | 22,792 | 20,129 |
| *02760 | North Attleborough . . . . (508) | 25,038 | 16,178 |
| 01532 | Northborough . . . . . . . (508) | 11,929 | 5,761 |
| 01534 | Northbridge . . . . . . . . (508) | 13,371 | 12,246 |
| 01864 | North Reading . . . . . . . (508) | 12,002 | 11,455 |
| 02766 | Norton . . . . . . . . . . . (508) | 14,265 | 12,690 |
| 02061 | Norwell . . . . . . . . . . . (617) | 9,279 | 9,182 |
| 02062 | Norwood . . . . . . . . . . (617) | 28,700 | 29,711 |
| 01364 | Orange . . . . . . . . . . . (508) | 7,312 | 6,844 |
| 02653 | Orleans . . . . . . . . . . (508) | 5,838 | 5,306 |
| 01540 | Oxford Center(u) . . . . . (508) | 5,969 | 6,369 |
| 01540 | Oxford . . . . . . . . . . . (508) | 12,588 | 11,680 |
| 01069 | Palmer . . . . . . . . . . . (413) | 12,054 | 11,389 |
| 01960 | Peabody . . . . . . . . . . (508) | 47,264 | 45,976 |
| 02359 | Pembroke . . . . . . . . . (617) | 14,544 | 13,487 |
| 01463 | Pepperell . . . . . . . . . (508) | 10,098 | 8,061 |
| 01866 | Pinehurst(u) . . . . . . . . (508) | 6,614 | 6,588 |
| 01201 | Pittsfield . . . . . . . . . . (413) | 48,622 | 51,974 |
| 02762 | Plainville . . . . . . . . . . (508) | 6,871 | 5,857 |
| *02360 | Plymouth Center(u). . . . . (508) | 7,258 | 7,232 |
| 02360 | Plymouth. . . . . . . . . . (508) | 45,608 | 35,913 |
| 02169 | Quincy . . . . . . . . . . . (617) | 84,985 | 84,743 |
| 02368 | Randolph . . . . . . . . . . (617) | 30,093 | 28,218 |
| 02767 | Raynham . . . . . . . . . . (508) | 9,867 | 9,085 |
| 01867 | Reading . . . . . . . . . . (617) | 22,539 | 22,678 |
| 02769 | Rehoboth . . . . . . . . . . (508) | 8,656 | 7,570 |
| 02151 | Revere . . . . . . . . . . . (617) | 42,786 | 42,423 |
| 02370 | Rockland . . . . . . . . . . (617) | 16,123 | 15,695 |
| 01966 | Rockport . . . . . . . . . . (508) | 7,482 | 5,448 |
| 01970 | Salem . . . . . . . . . . . (508) | 38,091 | 38,276 |
| 01950 | Salisbury . . . . . . . . . . (508) | 6,882 | 5,973 |
| 02563 | Sandwich . . . . . . . . . (508) | 15,489 | 8,727 |
| 01906 | Saugus . . . . . . . . . . . (617) | 25,549 | 25,549 |
| 02066 | Scituate . . . . . . . . . . (617) | 16,786 | 5,180 |
| 02771 | Seekonk . . . . . . . . . . (508) | 13,046 | 12,269 |
| 02067 | Sharon . . . . . . . . . . . (617) | 15,517 | 5,893 |
| 01464 | Shirley . . . . . . . . . . . (508) | 6,118 | 5,124 |
| 01545 | Shrewsbury . . . . . . . . (508) | 24,146 | 22,674 |
| 02725 | Somerset . . . . . . . . . . (508) | 17,655 | 18,813 |
| 02143 | Somerville(u) . . . . . . . (617) | 76,210 | 77,372 |
| 01002 | South Amherst . . . . . . . (413) | 5,053 | 4,861 |
| 01772 | Southborough . . . . . . . (508) | 6,628 | 6,193 |
| 01550 | Southbridge Center(u) . . (508) | 12,882 | 14,261 |
| 01550 | Southbridge . . . . . . . . (508) | 17,816 | 13,631 |
| 01075 | South Hadley . . . . . . . . (413) | 16,685 | 16,399 |
| 01077 | Southwick . . . . . . . . . (413) | 7,667 | 7,382 |
| 02664 | South Yarmouth(u) . . . . (508) | 10,358 | 7,525 |
| 01562 | Spencer Center(u) . . . . (508) | 6,306 | 6,350 |
| 01562 | Spencer . . . . . . . . . . (508) | 11,645 | 10,774 |
| *01101 | Springfield. . . . . . . . . (413) | 156,983 | 152,319 |
| 01564 | Sterling . . . . . . . . . . . (508) | 6,481 | 5,440 |
| 02180 | Stoneham . . . . . . . . . (617) | 22,203 | 21,424 |
| 02072 | Stoughton . . . . . . . . . (617) | 26,777 | 26,710 |

| ZIP code | Place | 1990 | 1980 |
|---|---|---|---|
| 01775 | Stow . . . . . . . . . . . . . (508) | 5,328 | 5,144 |
| 01566 | Sturbridge . . . . . . . . . (508) | 7,775 | 5,976 |
| 01776 | Sudbury . . . . . . . . . . (508) | 14,358 | 14,027 |
| 01527 | Sutton . . . . . . . . . . . (508) | 6,824 | 5,855 |
| 01907 | Swampscott . . . . . . . . (617) | 13,650 | 13,837 |
| 02777 | Swansea . . . . . . . . . . (508) | 15,411 | 15,461 |
| 02780 | Taunton . . . . . . . . . . (508) | 49,832 | 45,001 |
| 01468 | Templeton . . . . . . . . . (508) | 6,438 | 6,070 |
| 01876 | Tewksbury . . . . . . . . . (508) | 27,266 | 24,635 |
| 01983 | Topsfield . . . . . . . . . . (508) | 5,754 | 5,709 |
| 01469 | Townsend . . . . . . . . . (508) | 8,496 | 7,201 |
| 01879 | Tyngsborough . . . . . . . (508) | 8,642 | 5,683 |
| 01569 | Uxbridge . . . . . . . . . . (508) | 10,415 | 8,374 |
| 01880 | Wakefield . . . . . . . . . . (617) | 24,825 | 24,895 |
| 02081 | Walpole . . . . . . . . . . . (508) | 20,212 | 5,495 |
| 02154 | Waltham . . . . . . . . . . (617) | 57,878 | 58,200 |
| 01082 | Ware Center(u) . . . . . . (413) | 6,533 | 6,806 |
| 01082 | Ware. . . . . . . . . . . . . (413) | 9,808 | 8,953 |
| 02571 | Wareham . . . . . . . . . . (508) | 19,232 | 18,457 |
| 02172 | Watertown . . . . . . . . . (617) | 33,284 | 34,384 |
| 01778 | Wayland . . . . . . . . . . (508) | 11,874 | 12,170 |
| 01570 | Webster Center(u) . . . . (508) | 11,849 | 11,175 |
| 01570 | Webster . . . . . . . . . . (508) | 16,196 | 14,480 |
| 02181 | Wellesley . . . . . . . . . . (617) | 26,615 | 27,209 |
| 01581 | Westborough . . . . . . . . (508) | 14,133 | 13,619 |
| 01583 | West Boylston. . . . . . . . (508) | 6,611 | 6,204 |
| 02379 | West Bridgewater. . . . . . (508) | 6,389 | 6,359 |
| 01742 | West Concord(u) . . . . . . (508) | 5,761 | 5,331 |
| 01085 | Westfield . . . . . . . . . . (413) | 38,372 | 36,465 |
| 01886 | Westford . . . . . . . . . . (508) | 16,392 | 13,434 |
| 01473 | Westminster . . . . . . . . (508) | 6,191 | 5,139 |
| 02193 | Weston . . . . . . . . . . . (617) | 10,200 | 11,169 |
| 02790 | Westport . . . . . . . . . . (508) | 13,852 | 13,763 |
| 01089 | West Springfield . . . . . . (413) | 27,537 | 27,042 |
| 02090 | Westwood . . . . . . . . . (617) | 12,557 | 13,212 |
| 02673 | West Yarmouth . . . . . . . (508) | 5,409 | 3,852 |
| 02188 | Weymouth . . . . . . . . . (617) | 54,063 | 55,601 |
| 01588 | Whitinsville(u) . . . . . . . (508) | 5,639 | 5,379 |
| 02382 | Whitman . . . . . . . . . . (617) | 13,240 | 13,534 |
| 01095 | Wilbraham . . . . . . . . . (413) | 12,635 | 12,053 |
| 01267 | Williamstown . . . . . . . . (413) | 8,220 | 8,741 |
| 01887 | Wilmington. . . . . . . . . (508) | 17,654 | 17,471 |
| 01475 | Winchendon . . . . . . . . (508) | 8,805 | 7,019 |
| 01890 | Winchester. . . . . . . . . (617) | 20,267 | 20,701 |
| 02152 | Winthrop . . . . . . . . . . (617) | 18,127 | 19,294 |
| 01801 | Woburn. . . . . . . . . . . (617) | 35,943 | 36,626 |
| *01613 | Worcester . . . . . . . . . (508) | 169,759 | 161,799 |
| 02093 | Wrentham . . . . . . . . . (508) | 9,006 | 7,580 |
| 02675 | Yarmouth . . . . . . . . . . (508) | 21,174 | 18,449 |

## Michigan

| | | | |
|---|---|---|---|
| 49221 | Adrian . . . . . . . . . . . . (517) | 22,097 | 21,276 |
| 49224 | Albion . . . . . . . . . . . . (517) | 10,066 | 11,059 |
| 49401 | Allendale(u) . . . . . . . . | 6,950 | .... |
| 48101 | Allen Park . . . . . . . . . (313) | 31,092 | 34,196 |
| 48801 | Alma . . . . . . . . . . . . (517) | 9,034 | 9,652 |
| 49707 | Alpena . . . . . . . . . . . (517) | 11,354 | 12,214 |
| *48106 | Ann Arbor . . . . . . . . . (313) | 109,608 | 107,969 |
| 48057 | Auburn Hills . . . . . . . . (313) | 17,076 | 15,388 |
| 49016 | Battle Creek. . . . . . . . . (616) | 53,516 | 35,724 |
| 48706 | Bay City . . . . . . . . . . (517) | 38,936 | 41,593 |
| 48505 | Beecher(u) . . . . . . . . . (313) | 14,465 | 17,178 |
| 48809 | Belding . . . . . . . . . . . (616) | 5,969 | 5,634 |
| 49022 | Benton Harbor . . . . . . . (616) | 12,818 | 14,707 |
| 49022 | Benton Heights(u). . . . . . (616) | 5,465 | 6,787 |
| 48072 | Berkley . . . . . . . . . . . (313) | 16,960 | 18,637 |
| 48009 | Beverly Hills . . . . . . . . (313) | 10,610 | 11,598 |
| 49307 | Big Rapids . . . . . . . . . (616) | 12,603 | 14,361 |
| *48012 | Birmingham . . . . . . . . (313) | 19,997 | 21,689 |
| 48013 | Bloomfield(u) . . . . . . . . (313) | 42,137 | 42,876 |
| 48722 | Bridgeport(u) . . . . . . . . (517) | 8,569 | .... |
| 48116 | Brighton . . . . . . . . . . (313) | 5,686 | 4,268 |
| 48601 | Buena Vista . . . . . . . . | 8,196 | .... |
| *48502 | Burton . . . . . . . . . . . (313) | 27,437 | 29,976 |
| 49601 | Cadillac . . . . . . . . . . (616) | 10,104 | 10,199 |
| 48187 | Canton(u) . . . . . . . . . (313) | 57,047 | .... |
| 48724 | Carrollton(u). . . . . . . . . (517) | 6,521 | 7,482 |
| 48015 | Center Line . . . . . . . . . (313) | 9,026 | 9,293 |
| 48813 | Charlotte. . . . . . . . . . (517) | 8,083 | 8,251 |
| 48017 | Clawson . . . . . . . . . . (313) | 13,874 | 15,103 |
| 48043 | Clinton(u) . . . . . . . . . (313) | 85,866 | 72,400 |
| 49036 | Coldwater . . . . . . . . . (517) | 9,607 | 9,461 |
| 49321 | Comstock Park(u) . . . . . (616) | 6,530 | 5,506 |
| 49508 | Cutlerville(u). . . . . . . . . (616) | 11,228 | 8,256 |
| 48423 | Davison . . . . . . . . . . (313) | 5,693 | 6,087 |
| *48120 | Dearborn. . . . . . . . . . (313) | 89,286 | 90,660 |
| 48127 | Dearborn Heights. . . . . . (313) | 60,838 | 67,706 |
| *48233 | Detroit. . . . . . . . . . . (313) | 1,027,974 | 1,203,368 |
| 49047 | Dowagiac . . . . . . . . . (616) | 6,418 | 6,307 |
| 49506 | East Grand Rapids . . . . . (616) | 10,807 | 10,914 |
| 48823 | East Lansing. . . . . . . . . (517) | 50,677 | 51,392 |
| 48021 | Eastpointe . . . . . . . . . (313) | 35,283 | 38,280 |
| 49001 | Eastwood(u). . . . . . . . . (616) | 6,340 | 7,186 |
| 48229 | Ecorse . . . . . . . . . . . (313) | 12,180 | 14,447 |
| 49829 | Escanaba . . . . . . . . . (906) | 13,659 | 14,355 |
| 49022 | Fair Plain(u). . . . . . . . . (616) | 8,051 | 8,289 |

| ZIP code | Place | | 1990 | 1980 |
|---|---|---|---|---|
| 48024 | Farmington | (313) | 10,170 | 11,022 |
| 48024 | Farmington Hills. | (313) | 74,614 | 58,056 |
| 48430 | Fenton. | (313) | 8,434 | 8,098 |
| 48220 | Ferndale. | (313) | 25,084 | 26,227 |
| 48134 | Flat Rock | (313) | 7,290 | 6,853 |
| *48502 | Flint. | (313) | 140,761 | 159,611 |
| 48433 | Flushing | (313) | 8,542 | 8,624 |
| 49506 | Forest Hills. | | 16,690 | |
| 48026 | Fraser. | (313) | 13,899 | 14,560 |
| 48135 | Garden City. | (313) | 31,846 | 35,640 |
| 48439 | Grand Blanc. | (313) | 7,760 | 6,848 |
| 49417 | Grand Haven. | (616) | 11,951 | 11,763 |
| 48837 | Grand Ledge. | (517) | 7,562 | 6,920 |
| *49501 | Grand Rapids. | (616) | 189,126 | 181,843 |
| 49418 | Grandville. | (616) | 15,624 | 12,412 |
| 48838 | Greenville. | (616) | 8,101 | 8,019 |
| 48138 | Grosse Ile(u). | (313) | 9,781 | 9,320 |
| 48236 | Grosse Pointe. | (313) | 5,681 | 5,901 |
| 48236 | Grosse Pointe Farms. | (313) | 10,092 | 10,551 |
| 48236 | Grosse Pointe Park. | (313) | 12,857 | 13,562 |
| 48236 | Grosse Pointe Woods | (313) | 17,715 | 18,886 |
| 48212 | Hamtramck. | (313) | 18,372 | 21,300 |
| 48225 | Harper Woods. | (313) | 14,903 | 16,361 |
| 48625 | Harrison(u). | (517) | 24,685 | 23,649 |
| 48840 | Haslett(u). | (517) | 10,230 | 7,025 |
| 49058 | Hastings. | (616) | 6,549 | 6,418 |
| 48030 | Hazel Park. | (313) | 20,051 | 20,914 |
| 48203 | Highland Park. | (313) | 20,121 | 27,909 |
| 49242 | Hillsdale. | (517) | 8,175 | 7,432 |
| 49423 | Holland. | (616) | 30,745 | 26,281 |
| 48442 | Holly. | (313) | 5,595 | 4,874 |
| 48842 | Holt(u). | (517) | 11,744 | 10,097 |
| 49931 | Houghton. | (906) | 7,498 | 7,512 |
| 48843 | Howell. | (517) | 8,147 | 6,976 |
| 49426 | Hudsonville | | 6,170 | 4,844 |
| 48070 | Huntington Woods | (313) | 6,419 | 6,937 |
| 48141 | Inkster. | (313) | 30,772 | 35,190 |
| 48846 | Ionia. | (616) | 5,990 | 5,920 |
| 49801 | Iron Mountain. | (906) | 8,525 | 8,341 |
| 49938 | Ironwood. | (906) | 6,849 | 7,741 |
| 49849 | Ishpeming | (906) | 7,200 | 7,538 |
| *49201 | Jackson. | (517) | 37,425 | 39,739 |
| 49428 | Jenison(u). | (616) | 17,882 | 16,330 |
| *49001 | Kalamazoo. | (616) | 80,277 | 79,722 |
| 49508 | Kentwood | (616) | 37,826 | 30,438 |
| 49801 | Kingsford. | (906) | 5,480 | 5,290 |
| 49843 | K.I. Sawyer(u). | (906) | 6,577 | 7,345 |
| 48144 | Lambertville(u). | (313) | 7,860 | 6,341 |
| *48924 | Lansing. | (517) | 127,321 | 130,414 |
| 48446 | Lapeer. | (313) | 7,759 | 6,198 |
| 48146 | Lincoln Park. | (313) | 41,832 | 45,105 |
| *48150 | Livonia. | (313) | 100,850 | 104,814 |
| 49431 | Ludington | (616) | 8,507 | 8,937 |
| 48071 | Madison Heights | (313) | 32,196 | 35,375 |
| 49660 | Manistee. | (616) | 6,734 | 7,665 |
| 49855 | Marquette. | (906) | 21,977 | 23,288 |
| 49068 | Marshall. | (616) | 6,941 | 7,201 |
| 48040 | Marysville. | (313) | 8,515 | 7,345 |
| 48854 | Mason. | (517) | 6,768 | 6,019 |
| 48122 | Melvindale. | (313) | 11,216 | 12,322 |
| 49858 | Menominee. | (906) | 9,398 | 10,099 |
| 48640 | Midland. | (517) | 38,053 | 37,269 |
| 48042 | Milford. | (313) | 5,500 | 5,041 |
| 48161 | Monroe. | (313) | 22,902 | 23,531 |
| 48043 | Mount Clemens. | (313) | 18,405 | 18,991 |
| 48858 | Mount Pleasant. | (517) | 23,299 | 23,746 |
| *49440 | Muskegon. | (616) | 39,809 | 40,823 |
| 49444 | Muskegon Heights | (616) | 13,176 | 14,611 |
| 48047 | New Baltimore. | (313) | 5,798 | 5,439 |
| 49120 | Niles. | (616) | 12,458 | 13,115 |
| | Northview(u). | | 13,712 | 11,662 |
| 48167 | Northville. | (313) | 6,226 | 5,698 |
| 49441 | Norton Shores. | (616) | 21,755 | 22,025 |
| 48050 | Novi. | (313) | 32,998 | 22,525 |
| 48237 | Oak Park. | (313) | 30,468 | 31,537 |
| 48864 | Okemos(u). | (517) | 20,216 | 8,882 |
| 48867 | Owosso. | (517) | 16,322 | 16,455 |
| 49770 | Petoskey. | (616) | 6,056 | 6,097 |
| 48170 | Plymouth. | (313) | 9,560 | 9,986 |
| 48170 | Plymouth Township(u) . | (313) | 23,646 | |
| *48053 | Pontiac. | (313) | 71,136 | 76,715 |
| 49081 | Portage. | (616) | 41,042 | 38,157 |
| 48060 | Port Huron. | (313) | 33,694 | 33,981 |
| 48239 | Redford(u). | (313) | 54,387 | 58,441 |
| 48218 | River Rouge. | (313) | 11,314 | 12,912 |
| 48192 | Riverview. | (313) | 13,894 | 14,569 |
| 48063 | Rochester. | (313) | 7,130 | 7,203 |
| 48307 | Rochester Hills. | | 61,766 | 40,704 |
| 48174 | Romulus. | (313) | 22,897 | 24,857 |
| 48066 | Roseville. | (313) | 51,412 | 54,311 |
| *48068 | Royal Oak. | (313) | 65,410 | 70,893 |
| *48605 | Saginaw. | (517) | 69,512 | 77,508 |
| 48604 | Saginaw Township North. | (517) | 23,018 | |
| 48603 | Saginaw Township South. | (517) | 13,987 | |
| 48079 | Saint Clair. | (313) | 5,116 | 4,780 |
| *48082 | Saint Clair Shores. | (313) | 68,107 | 76,210 |
| 48879 | Saint Johns. | (517) | 7,392 | 7,376 |
| 49085 | Saint Joseph. | (616) | 9,214 | 9,622 |
| 48176 | Saline. | (313) | 6,660 | 6,483 |

| ZIP code | Place | | 1990 | 1980 |
|---|---|---|---|---|
| 49783 | Sault Sainte Marie | (906) | 14,689 | 14,448 |
| 49455 | Shelby. | | 48,655 | |
| 48609 | Shields. | | 6,634 | |
| *48075 | Southfield. | (313) | 75,727 | 75,568 |
| 48198 | Southgate. | (313) | 30,771 | 32,058 |
| 49090 | South Haven. | (616) | 5,563 | 5,943 |
| 48178 | South Lyon. | (313) | 6,479 | 5,214 |
| 48161 | South Monroe(u) . | | 5,266 | 4,232 |
| 49015 | Springfield. | (616) | 5,582 | 5,917 |
| *48078 | Sterling Heights. | (313) | 117,810 | 108,999 |
| 49091 | Sturgis. | (616) | 10,130 | 9,468 |
| 48180 | Taylor. | (313) | 70,811 | 77,568 |
| 49286 | Tecumseh. | (517) | 7,462 | 7,320 |
| 48182 | Temperance. | (313) | 6,542 | |
| 49093 | Three Rivers. | (616) | 7,464 | 7,015 |
| 49684 | Traverse City. | (616) | 15,155 | 15,516 |
| 48183 | Trenton. | (313) | 20,586 | 22,762 |
| 48084 | Troy. | (313) | 72,884 | 67,102 |
| 48087 | Utica. | (313) | 5,081 | 5,282 |
| 49504 | Walker. | (616) | 17,279 | 15,088 |
| 48088 | Walled Lake. | | 6,278 | 4,748 |
| *48089 | Warren. | (313) | 144,864 | 161,134 |
| 48095 | Waterford(u). | (313) | 66,692 | 64,250 |
| 48917 | Waverly. | | 15,614 | |
| 48184 | Wayne. | (313) | 19,899 | 21,159 |
| 48033 | West Bloomfield(u). | (313) | 54,843 | 41,962 |
| 48185 | Westland. | (313) | 84,724 | 84,603 |
| 49007 | Westwood(u). | (616) | 8,957 | 8,519 |
| 48096 | Wixom. | (313) | 8,550 | 6,705 |
| 48183 | Woodhaven. | (313) | 11,631 | 10,902 |
| 48753 | Wurtsmith AFB(u). | (517) | 5,080 | 5,166 |
| *48192 | Wyandotte. | (313) | 30,938 | 34,006 |
| 49509 | Wyoming. | (616) | 63,891 | 59,616 |
| 48197 | Ypsilanti. | (313) | 24,846 | 24,031 |
| 49464 | Zeeland. | (616) | 5,417 | 4,764 |

## Minnesota

| ZIP code | Place | | 1990 | 1980 |
|---|---|---|---|---|
| 56007 | Albert Lea. | (507) | 18,310 | 19,200 |
| 56308 | Alexandria. | (612) | 8,029 | 7,608 |
| 55303 | Andover. | (612) | 15,216 | 9,387 |
| 55303 | Anoka. | (612) | 17,192 | 15,634 |
| 55124 | Apple Valley. | (612) | 34,598 | 21,818 |
| 55112 | Arden Hills. | (612) | 9,199 | 8,012 |
| 55912 | Austin. | (507) | 21,926 | 23,020 |
| 56601 | Bemidji. | (218) | 11,165 | 10,949 |
| 55433 | Blaine. | (612) | 38,975 | 28,558 |
| 55420 | Bloomington. | (612) | 86,335 | 81,831 |
| 56401 | Brainerd. | (218) | 12,353 | 11,489 |
| 55429 | Brooklyn Center. | (612) | 28,887 | 31,230 |
| 55429 | Brooklyn Park. | (612) | 56,381 | 43,332 |
| 55313 | Buffalo. | (612) | 6,856 | 4,560 |
| 55337 | Burnsville. | (612) | 51,288 | 35,674 |
| 55008 | Cambridge. | | 5,094 | 3,287 |
| 55316 | Champlin. | (612) | 16,849 | 9,006 |
| 55317 | Chanhassen. | (612) | 11,732 | 6,359 |
| 55318 | Chaska. | (612) | 11,339 | 8,346 |
| 55719 | Chisholm. | (218) | 5,290 | 5,930 |
| 55720 | Cloquet. | (218) | 10,885 | 11,142 |
| 55421 | Columbia Heights. | (612) | 18,910 | 20,029 |
| 55433 | Coon Rapids. | (612) | 52,978 | 35,826 |
| | Corcoran. | (612) | 5,199 | 4,252 |
| 55016 | Cottage Grove. | (612) | 22,935 | 18,994 |
| 56716 | Crookston. | (218) | 8,119 | 8,628 |
| 55428 | Crystal. | (612) | 23,788 | 25,543 |
| 56501 | Detroit Lakes. | (218) | 6,635 | 7,106 |
| *55806 | Duluth. | (218) | 85,493 | 92,811 |
| 55121 | Eagan. | (612) | 47,409 | 20,700 |
| 55005 | East Bethel. | (612) | 8,050 | 6,626 |
| 56721 | East Grand Forks. | (218) | 8,658 | 8,537 |
| *55343 | Eden Prairie. | (612) | 39,311 | 16,263 |
| 55435 | Edina. | (612) | 46,075 | 46,073 |
| 55330 | Elk River. | (612) | 11,143 | 6,785 |
| 56031 | Fairmont. | (612) | 11,265 | 11,506 |
| 55113 | Falcon Heights. | (612) | 5,380 | 5,291 |
| 55021 | Faribault. | (507) | 17,085 | 16,241 |
| 55024 | Farmington. | (612) | 5,940 | 4,370 |
| 56537 | Fergus Falls. | (218) | 12,362 | 12,519 |
| 55025 | Forest Lake. | (612) | 5,833 | 4,596 |
| 55432 | Fridley. | (612) | 28,335 | 30,228 |
| 55416 | Golden Valley. | (612) | 20,971 | 22,775 |
| 55744 | Grand Rapids. | (218) | 7,976 | 7,934 |
| *55303 | Ham Lake. | (612) | 8,924 | 7,832 |
| 55033 | Hastings. | (612) | 15,478 | 12,827 |
| 55811 | Hermantown. | (218) | 6,761 | 6,759 |
| 55746 | Hibbing. | (218) | 18,046 | 21,193 |
| 55343 | Hopkins. | (612) | 16,529 | 15,336 |
| 55350 | Hutchinson. | (612) | 11,459 | 9,244 |
| 56649 | International Falls. | (218) | 8,301 | 5,611 |
| 55075 | Inver Grove Heights. | (612) | 22,477 | 17,171 |
| 55042 | Lake Elmo. | (612) | 5,900 | 5,296 |
| 55044 | Lakeville. | (612) | 24,854 | 14,790 |
| | Lino Lakes. | (612) | 8,807 | 4,966 |
| 55355 | Litchfield. | (612) | 6,041 | 5,904 |
| 55110 | Little Canada. | (612) | 8,971 | 7,102 |
| 56345 | Little Falls. | (612) | 7,371 | 7,250 |
| 55115 | Mahtomedi. | (612) | 5,633 | 3,851 |

| ZIP code | Place | | 1990 | 1980 |
|---|---|---|---|---|
| 56001 | Mankato | (507) | 31,405 | 28,646 |
| 55369 | Maple Grove | (612) | 38,736 | 20,525 |
| 55109 | Maplewood | (612) | 30,954 | 26,990 |
| 56258 | Marshall | (507) | 12,023 | 11,161 |
| 55118 | Mendota Heights | (612) | 9,388 | 7,288 |
| *55401 | Minneapolis | (612) | 368,383 | 370,951 |
| 55343 | Minnetonka | (612) | 48,370 | 38,683 |
| 56265 | Montevideo | (612) | 5,499 | 5,845 |
| 55362 | Monticello | (612) | 5,045 | .... |
| 56560 | Moorhead | (218) | 32,295 | 29,998 |
| 56267 | Morris | (612) | 5,613 | 5,367 |
| 55364 | Mound | (612) | 9,634 | 9,280 |
| 55112 | Mounds View | (612) | 12,541 | 12,593 |
| 55112 | New Brighton | (612) | 22,207 | 23,269 |
| 54428 | New Hope | (612) | 21,853 | 23,087 |
| 56073 | New Ulm | (507) | 13,132 | 13,755 |
| 55057 | Northfield | (507) | 14,684 | 12,562 |
| 56001 | North Mankato | (507) | 10,662 | 9,145 |
| 55109 | North Saint Paul | (612) | 12,376 | 11,921 |
| 55119 | Oakdale | (612) | 18,377 | 12,123 |
| 55323 | Orono | (612) | 7,285 | 6,845 |
| 55060 | Owatonna | (507) | 19,386 | 18,632 |
| 55427 | Plymouth | (612) | 50,889 | 31,615 |
| 55372 | Prior Lake | (612) | 11,482 | 7,284 |
| 55303 | Ramsey | (612) | 12,408 | 10,093 |
| 55066 | Red Wing | (612) | 15,134 | 13,736 |
| 55423 | Richfield | (612) | 35,710 | 37,851 |
| 55112 | Robbinsdale | (612) | 14,396 | 14,422 |
| 55901 | Rochester | (507) | 70,729 | 57,906 |
| 55068 | Rosemount | (612) | 8,622 | 5,083 |
| 55113 | Roseville | (612) | 33,485 | 35,820 |
| 55418 | Saint Anthony | (612) | 7,727 | 7,981 |
| 56301 | Saint Cloud | (612) | 48,812 | 42,566 |
| 55426 | Saint Louis Park | (612) | 43,787 | 42,931 |
| *55101 | Saint Paul | (612) | 272,235 | 270,230 |
| 56082 | Saint Peter | (507) | 9,481 | 9,056 |
| 56377 | Sartell | (612) | 5,409 | 3,427 |
| 56379 | Sauk Rapids | (612) | 7,825 | 5,793 |
| 56337 | Savage | (612) | 9,906 | 3,954 |
| 55379 | Shakopee | (612) | 11,739 | 9,941 |
| 55126 | Shoreview | (612) | 24,587 | 17,300 |
| 55331 | Shorewood | (612) | 5,917 | 4,646 |
| 55075 | South Saint Paul | (612) | 20,197 | 21,235 |
| 55432 | Spring Lake Park | (612) | 6,532 | 6,477 |
| 55082 | Stillwater | (612) | 13,882 | 12,290 |
| 56701 | Thief River Falls | (218) | 8,010 | 9,105 |
| 55110 | Vadnais Heights | (612) | 11,041 | 5,111 |
| 55792 | Virginia | (218) | 9,410 | 11,056 |
| 56387 | Waite Park | ... | 5,020 | 3,496 |
| 56093 | Waseca | (507) | 8,385 | 8,219 |
| 55118 | West Saint Paul | (612) | 19,248 | 18,527 |
| 55110 | White Bear Lake | (612) | 24,622 | 22,538 |
| 56201 | Willmar | (612) | 17,531 | 15,895 |
| 55987 | Winona | (507) | 25,435 | 25,075 |
| 55119 | Woodbury | (612) | 20,075 | 10,297 |
| 56187 | Worthington | (507) | 9,977 | 10,243 |

## Mississippi (601)

| ZIP code | Place | 1990 | 1980 |
|---|---|---|---|
| 39730 | Aberdeen | 6,837 | 7,184 |
| 38821 | Amory | 7,093 | 7,307 |
| 38606 | Batesville | 6,403 | 5,162 |
| 39520 | Bay Saint Louis | 8,063 | 7,850 |
| *39530 | Biloxi | 46,319 | 49,311 |
| 38829 | Booneville | 7,955 | 6,199 |
| 39042 | Brandon | 11,077 | 9,626 |
| 39601 | Brookhaven | 10,243 | 10,800 |
| 39046 | Canton | 10,062 | 11,116 |
| 38614 | Clarksdale | 19,717 | 21,137 |
| 38732 | Cleveland | 15,384 | 14,524 |
| 39056 | Clinton | 21,847 | 14,660 |
| 39429 | Columbia | 6,815 | 7,733 |
| 39701 | Columbus | 23,799 | 27,503 |
| 38834 | Corinth | 11,820 | 13,178 |
| 39059 | Crystal Springs | 5,643 | 4,902 |
| 39532 | D'Iberville | 6,566 | 6,236 |
| 39074 | Forest | 5,060 | 5,229 |
| 39553 | Gautier | 10,088 | 10,392 |
| 38701 | Greenville | 45,226 | 40,613 |
| 38930 | Greenwood | 18,906 | 20,115 |
| 38901 | Grenada | 10,864 | 11,508 |
| ..... | Gulf Hills(u) | 5,004 | 4,512 |
| 39501 | Gulfport | 40,775 | 39,676 |
| 39401 | Hattiesburg | 41,882 | 40,829 |
| 38635 | Holly Springs | 7,261 | 7,285 |
| 38637 | Horn Lake | 9,069 | 4,326 |
| 38751 | Indianola | 11,809 | 8,050 |
| *39205 | Jackson | 196,637 | 202,895 |
| 39090 | Kosciusko | 6,986 | 7,415 |
| 39440 | Laurel | 18,827 | 21,897 |
| 38756 | Leland | 6,366 | 6,667 |
| 39560 | Long Beach | 15,804 | 14,199 |
| 39339 | Louisville | 7,165 | 7,323 |
| 39648 | McComb | 11,797 | 12,331 |
| 39110 | Madison | 7,471 | 2,241 |
| 39301 | Meridian | 41,036 | 46,577 |
| 39563 | Moss Point | 17,837 | 18,998 |

| ZIP code | Place | 1990 | 1980 |
|---|---|---|---|
| 39120 | Natchez | 19,460 | 22,209 |
| 38652 | New Albany | 6,775 | 7,072 |
| 39564 | Ocean Springs | 14,658 | 14,504 |
| 39567 | Orange Grove(u) | 15,676 | 13,476 |
| 38655 | Oxford | 10,026 | 9,882 |
| 39567 | Pascagoula | 25,899 | 29,318 |
| 39571 | Pass Christian | 5,557 | 5,014 |
| 39208 | Pearl | 19,588 | 18,602 |
| 39465 | Petal | 7,883 | 8,476 |
| 39350 | Philadelphia | 6,758 | 6,434 |
| 39466 | Picayune | 10,633 | 10,361 |
| 39157 | Ridgeland | 11,714 | 5,461 |
| 38663 | Ripley | 5,371 | 4,271 |
| ..... | Saint Martin(u) | 6,349 | .... |
| 38671 | Southaven | 17,949 | 16,441 |
| 39759 | Starkville | 18,458 | 16,139 |
| 38801 | Tupelo | 30,685 | 23,905 |
| 39180 | Vicksburg | 20,908 | 25,434 |
| 39576 | Waveland | 5,369 | 4,186 |
| 39367 | Waynesboro | 5,143 | 5,349 |
| ..... | West Hattiesburg(u) | 5,450 | .... |
| 39773 | West Point | 8,489 | 8,811 |
| 38967 | Winona | 5,705 | 6,177 |
| 39194 | Yazoo City | 12,427 | 12,092 |

## Missouri

| ZIP code | Place | | 1990 | 1980 |
|---|---|---|---|---|
| 63123 | Affton(u) | (314) | 21,106 | 23,181 |
| 63010 | Arnold | (314) | 18,828 | 19,141 |
| 65605 | Aurora | (417) | 6,459 | 6,437 |
| 63011 | Ballwin | (314) | 21,406 | 12,656 |
| 63137 | Bellefontaine Neighbors | (314) | 10,918 | 12,082 |
| 64012 | Belton | (816) | 18,145 | 12,708 |
| 63134 | Berkeley | (314) | 12,250 | 15,922 |
| 63031 | Black Jack | (314) | 6,131 | 5,293 |
| 64015 | Blue Springs | (816) | 40,103 | 25,936 |
| 65613 | Bolivar | (417) | 6,845 | 5,919 |
| 65233 | Boonville | (816) | 7,095 | 6,959 |
| 63114 | Breckenridge Hills | (314) | 5,181 | 5,666 |
| 63144 | Brentwood | (314) | 8,150 | 8,209 |
| 63044 | Bridgeton | (314) | 17,732 | 18,445 |
| 63701 | Cape Girardeau | (314) | 34,475 | 34,361 |
| 64836 | Carthage | (417) | 10,747 | 11,104 |
| 63830 | Caruthersville | (314) | 7,389 | 7,958 |
| 63834 | Charleston | (314) | 5,085 | 5,230 |
| 63005 | Chesterfield | (314) | 38,630 | 28,384 |
| 64601 | Chillicothe | (816) | 8,799 | 9,089 |
| 63105 | Clayton | (314) | 13,926 | 14,306 |
| 64735 | Clinton | (816) | 8,703 | 8,366 |
| 65201 | Columbia | (314) | 69,133 | 62,061 |
| 63128 | Concord(u) | (314) | 19,859 | 20,896 |
| 63126 | Crestwood | (314) | 11,229 | 12,815 |
| 63141 | Creve Coeur | (314) | 12,289 | 11,743 |
| 63136 | Dellwood | (314) | 5,245 | 6,200 |
| 63020 | De Soto | (314) | 5,993 | 5,993 |
| 63131 | Des Peres | (314) | 8,388 | 7,953 |
| 63841 | Dexter | (314) | 7,506 | 7,043 |
| 63011 | Ellisville | (314) | 7,183 | 6,233 |
| 64024 | Excelsior Springs | (816) | 10,373 | 10,424 |
| 63640 | Farmington | (314) | 11,596 | 8,270 |
| 63135 | Ferguson | (314) | 22,290 | 24,549 |
| 63028 | Festus | (314) | 8,105 | 7,574 |
| *63033 | Florissant | (314) | 51,038 | 55,721 |
| 65473 | Fort Leonard Wood(u) | (314) | 15,863 | 21,262 |
| 65251 | Fulton | (314) | 10,033 | 11,046 |
| 64118 | Gladstone | (816) | 26,243 | 24,990 |
| 65254 | Glasgow Village(u) | (314) | 5,199 | .... |
| 63122 | Glendale | (314) | 5,945 | 6,035 |
| 64030 | Grandview | (816) | 24,973 | 24,561 |
| 63401 | Hannibal | (314) | 18,004 | 18,811 |
| 64701 | Harrisonville | (816) | 7,683 | 6,372 |
| *63042 | Hazelwood | (314) | 15,512 | 13,098 |
| *64051 | Independence | (816) | 112,301 | 111,797 |
| 63755 | Jackson | (314) | 9,256 | 7,827 |
| 65101 | Jefferson City | (314) | 35,517 | 33,619 |
| 63136 | Jennings | (314) | 15,841 | 16,934 |
| 64801 | Joplin | (417) | 40,866 | 39,126 |
| *64108 | Kansas City | (816) | 434,829 | 448,028 |
| 63857 | Kennett | (314) | 10,941 | 10,145 |
| 63501 | Kirksville | (816) | 17,152 | 17,167 |
| 63122 | Kirkwood | (314) | 27,291 | 27,739 |
| 63124 | Ladue | (314) | 8,795 | 9,369 |
| 63367 | Lake Saint Louis | (314) | 7,536 | 3,843 |
| 65536 | Lebanon | (417) | 9,983 | 9,507 |
| 64063 | Lee's Summit | (816) | 46,418 | 28,741 |
| 63125 | Lemay(u) | (314) | 18,005 | 35,424 |
| 64068 | Liberty | (816) | 20,459 | 16,251 |
| 63552 | Macon | (816) | 5,571 | 5,680 |
| 63863 | Malden | (314) | 5,123 | 6,096 |
| 63011 | Manchester | (314) | 6,537 | 6,351 |
| 63143 | Maplewood | (314) | 9,962 | 10,960 |
| 65340 | Marshall | (816) | 12,711 | 12,781 |
| 63043 | Maryland Heights(u) | (314) | 25,440 | 26,413 |
| 64668 | Maryville | (816) | 10,663 | 9,558 |
| ..... | Mehlville(u) | | 27,557 | .... |
| 65265 | Mexico | (314) | 11,290 | 12,276 |
| 65270 | Moberly | (816) | 12,839 | 13,418 |

| ZIP code | Place | | 1990 | 1980 |
|---|---|---|---|---|
| 65708 | Monett............ | (417) | 6,529 | 6,148 |
| 63026 | Murphy(u)......... | (314) | 9,342 | 8,121 |
| 64850 | Neosho........... | (417) | 9,254 | 9,493 |
| 64772 | Nevada........... | (417) | 8,597 | 9,044 |
| 63121 | Normandy......... | (314) | 5,063 | 5,174 |
| 63121 | Northwoods........ | (314) | 5,106 | 5,831 |
| ..... | Oakville(u)........ | .... | 31,750 | .... |
| 63366 | O'Fallon.......... | (314) | 17,427 | 8,677 |
| 63132 | Olivette.......... | (314) | 7,573 | 7,952 |
| 63114 | Overland.......... | (314) | 17,987 | 19,620 |
| 63775 | Perryville......... | (314) | 6,933 | 7,343 |
| 63120 | Pine Lawn......... | (314) | 5,083 | 6,570 |
| 63901 | Poplar Bluff....... | (314) | 16,841 | 17,139 |
| 64083 | Raymore.......... | (816) | 5,592 | 3,154 |
| 64133 | Raytown.......... | (816) | 30,601 | 31,831 |
| 65738 | Republic.......... | | 6,290 | 4,485 |
| 64085 | Richmond......... | (816) | 5,738 | 5,499 |
| 63117 | Richmond Heights...... | (314) | 10,448 | 11,516 |
| 63124 | Rock Hill......... | (314) | 5,217 | 5,702 |
| 65401 | Rolla............ | (314) | 14,090 | 13,303 |
| 63074 | Saint Ann......... | (314) | 14,449 | 15,523 |
| 63301 | Saint Charles...... | (314) | 50,634 | 37,379 |
| 63114 | Saint John........ | (314) | 7,475 | 7,854 |
| *64501 | Saint Joseph....... | (816) | 71,852 | 76,691 |
| *63155 | Saint Louis........ | (314) | 396,685 | 452,801 |
| 63376 | Saint Peters....... | (314) | 40,660 | 15,700 |
| 63126 | Sappington(u)....... | (314) | 10,917 | 11,388 |
| 65301 | Sedalia.......... | (816) | 19,800 | 20,927 |
| 63119 | Shrewsbury........ | (314) | 6,416 | 5,077 |
| 63801 | Sikeston......... | (314) | 17,641 | 17,431 |
| 63138 | Spanish Lake(u)..... | (314) | 20,322 | 20,632 |
| *65801 | Springfield........ | (417) | 140,494 | 133,116 |
| 63080 | Sullivan.......... | (314) | 5,661 | 5,461 |
| ..... | Town and Country...... | | 9,503 | 3,187 |
| 64683 | Trenton.......... | (816) | 6,129 | 6,811 |
| 63084 | Union............ | (314) | 5,776 | 5,506 |
| 63130 | University City...... | (314) | 40,087 | 42,690 |
| 64093 | Warrensburg....... | (816) | 15,244 | 13,807 |
| 63090 | Washington........ | (314) | 10,704 | 9,251 |
| 64870 | Webb City......... | (417) | 7,449 | 7,309 |
| 63119 | Webster Groves..... | (314) | 22,992 | 23,097 |
| 63385 | Wentzville........ | (314) | 5,088 | 3,193 |
| 65775 | West Plains........ | (417) | 8,913 | 7,741 |

### Montana (406)

| | | | | |
|---|---|---|---|---|
| 59711 | Anaconda-Deer Lodge County .. | | 10,356 | 12,518 |
| *59101 | Billings.......... | | 81,125 | 66,818 |
| 59715 | Bozeman.......... | | 22,660 | 21,645 |
| 59701 | Butte-Silver Bow..... | | 33,336 | 37,205 |
| *59401 | Great Falls........ | | 55,125 | 56,884 |
| 59501 | Havre........... | | 10,201 | 10,891 |
| 59601 | Helena........... | | 24,609 | 23,938 |
| ..... | Helena Valley West Central(u) .. | | 6,327 | .... |
| 59901 | Kalispell......... | | 11,917 | 10,689 |
| 59044 | Laurel........... | | 5,686 | 5,481 |
| 59457 | Lewistown........ | | 6,097 | 7,104 |
| 59047 | Livingston........ | | 6,701 | 6,994 |
| 59402 | Malmstrom AFB(u)..... | | 5,938 | 6,675 |
| 59301 | Miles City........ | | 8,461 | 9,602 |
| *59801 | Missoula......... | | 42,918 | 33,351 |
| 59801 | Orchard Homes(u)..... | | 10,317 | 10,837 |
| 59270 | Sidney........... | | 5,217 | 5,726 |

### Nebraska

| | | | | |
|---|---|---|---|---|
| 69301 | Alliance.......... | (308) | 9,765 | 9,920 |
| 68310 | Beatrice.......... | (402) | 12,352 | 12,891 |
| 68005 | Bellevue.......... | (402) | 30,982 | 21,813 |
| 68008 | Blair............ | (402) | 6,860 | 6,418 |
| 69337 | Chadron.......... | (308) | 5,588 | 5,933 |
| ..... | Chalco(u)......... | | 7,337 | .... |
| 68601 | Columbus......... | (402) | 19,480 | 17,328 |
| 68025 | Fremont.......... | (402) | 23,680 | 23,979 |
| 69341 | Gering........... | (308) | 7,946 | 7,760 |
| 68801 | Grand Island....... | (308) | 39,487 | 33,180 |
| 68901 | Hastings......... | (402) | 22,837 | 23,045 |
| 68949 | Holdrege......... | (308) | 5,671 | 5,624 |
| 68847 | Kearney.......... | (308) | 24,396 | 21,158 |
| 68128 | La Vista......... | (402) | 9,840 | 9,588 |
| 68850 | Lexington......... | (308) | 6,600 | 7,040 |
| *68501 | Lincoln.......... | (402) | 191,972 | 171,932 |
| 69001 | McCook.......... | (308) | 8,112 | 8,404 |
| 68410 | Nebraska City...... | (402) | 6,547 | 7,127 |
| 68701 | Norfolk.......... | (402) | 21,476 | 19,449 |
| 69101 | North Platte....... | (308) | 22,605 | 24,509 |
| 68113 | Offutt AFB West(u)..... | (402) | 10,883 | 8,787 |
| 69153 | Ogallala......... | (308) | 5,095 | 5,638 |
| *68108 | Omaha........... | (402) | 335,719 | 313,939 |
| 68046 | Papillion......... | (402) | 10,378 | 6,399 |
| 68048 | Plattsmouth....... | (402) | 6,415 | 6,295 |
| 68127 | Ralston.......... | (402) | 6,236 | 5,143 |
| 69361 | Scottsbluff........ | (308) | 13,711 | 14,156 |
| 68434 | Seward........... | (402) | 5,641 | 5,713 |
| 69162 | Sidney........... | (308) | 5,959 | 6,010 |
| 68776 | South Sioux City...... | (402) | 9,677 | 9,339 |

| ZIP code | Place | | 1990 | 1980 |
|---|---|---|---|---|
| 68787 | Wayne........... | (402) | 5,142 | 5,240 |
| 68467 | York............ | (402) | 7,940 | 7,723 |

### Nevada (702)

| | | | | |
|---|---|---|---|---|
| 89005 | Boulder City....... | | 12,567 | 9,590 |
| *89701 | Carson City........ | | 40,443 | 32,022 |
| 89112 | East Las Vegas(u)...... | | 11,087 | 6,449 |
| 89801 | Elko............ | | 14,836 | 8,758 |
| ..... | Enterprise(u)....... | | 6,412 | .... |
| 89406 | Fallon........... | | 6,430 | 4,262 |
| 89408 | Fernley(u)......... | | 5,164 | .... |
| 89410 | Gardnerville Ranchos(u)...... | | 7,455 | 3,542 |
| 89015 | Henderson........ | | 64,948 | 24,363 |
| 89450 | Incline Village-Crystal Bay(u) ... | | 7,119 | 6,225 |
| *89114 | Las Vegas........ | | 258,204 | 164,674 |
| 89110 | Nellis AFB(u)....... | | 8,377 | 7,476 |
| *89030 | North Las Vegas..... | | 47,849 | 42,739 |
| 89041 | Pahrump(u)........ | | 7,424 | 84,818 |
| 89109 | Paradise(u)........ | | 124,682 | 84,818 |
| *89501 | Reno............ | | 133,850 | 100,756 |
| *89431 | Sparks........... | | 53,367 | 40,780 |
| ..... | Spring Creek(u)...... | | 5,866 | 4,155 |
| ..... | Spring Valley(u)...... | | 51,726 | .... |
| 89110 | Sunrise Manor(u)..... | | 95,362 | 44,155 |
| 89431 | Sun Valley(u)....... | | 11,391 | 8,822 |
| 89101 | Winchester(u)....... | | 23,365 | 19,728 |
| 89445 | Winnemucca....... | | 6,102 | 4,140 |

### New Hampshire (603)

*See Note on Page 373*

| | | | | |
|---|---|---|---|---|
| 03031 | Amherst.......... | | 9,068 | .... |
| 03811 | Atkinson......... | | 5,188 | .... |
| 03825 | Barrington........ | | 6,164 | .... |
| 03102 | Bedford.......... | | 12,563 | 9,481 |
| 03220 | Belmont.......... | | 5,796 | .... |
| 03570 | Berlin........... | | 11,824 | 13,084 |
| 03304 | Bow............ | | 5,500 | .... |
| 03743 | Claremont........ | | 13,902 | 14,557 |
| 03301 | Concord.......... | | 36,006 | 30,400 |
| 03818 | Conway.......... | | 7,940 | 7,158 |
| 03038 | Derry Compact(u)..... | | 20,446 | 12,248 |
| 03038 | Derry............ | | 29,603 | 18,875 |
| 03820 | Dover........... | | 25,042 | 22,377 |
| 03824 | Durham Compact(u)..... | | 9,236 | 8,448 |
| 03824 | Durham.......... | | 11,818 | 10,652 |
| 03042 | Epping........... | | 5,162 | .... |
| 03833 | Exeter Compact(u)..... | | 9,556 | 8,947 |
| 03833 | Exeter........... | | 12,481 | 11,024 |
| 03835 | Farmington........ | | 5,739 | .... |
| 03235 | Franklin.......... | | 8,304 | 7,901 |
| 03246 | Gilford........... | | 5,867 | .... |
| 03045 | Goffstown......... | | 14,621 | 11,315 |
| 03841 | Hampstead........ | | 6,732 | .... |
| 03842 | Hampton Compact(u)..... | | 7,989 | 6,779 |
| 03842 | Hampton.......... | | 12,278 | 10,493 |
| 03755 | Hanover Compact(u)..... | | 6,538 | 6,861 |
| 03756 | Hanover.......... | | 9,212 | 9,119 |
| 03049 | Hollis........... | | 5,705 | .... |
| 03106 | Hooksett.......... | | 8,767 | 7,303 |
| 03051 | Hudson.......... | | 19,530 | 7,626 |
| 03452 | Jaffrey.......... | | 5,361 | .... |
| 03431 | Keene........... | | 22,430 | 21,449 |
| 03848 | Kingston......... | | 5,591 | .... |
| 03246 | Laconia.......... | | 15,743 | 15,575 |
| 03766 | Lebanon.......... | | 12,183 | 11,134 |
| ..... | Litchfield......... | | 5,516 | .... |
| 03561 | Littleton.......... | | 5,827 | 5,558 |
| 03053 | Londonderry Compact(u)..... | | 10,114 | .... |
| 03053 | Londonderry........ | | 19,781 | 10,114 |
| *03101 | Manchester........ | | 99,332 | 90,936 |
| 03054 | Merrimack......... | | 22,156 | 15,406 |
| 03055 | Milford Compact(u)..... | | 8,015 | .... |
| 03055 | Milford.......... | | 11,795 | 8,015 |
| *03060 | Nashua.......... | | 79,662 | 67,865 |
| 03857 | Newmarket........ | | 7,157 | .... |
| 03773 | Newport.......... | | 6,110 | 6,229 |
| 03076 | Pelham.......... | | 9,408 | 8,090 |
| 03275 | Pembroke......... | | 6,561 | .... |
| 03458 | Peterborough...... | | 5,239 | .... |
| 03865 | Plaistow......... | | 7,316 | 5,609 |
| 03264 | Plymouth......... | | 5,811 | .... |
| 03801 | Portsmouth........ | | 25,925 | 26,254 |
| 03077 | Raymond.......... | | 8,713 | 5,453 |
| 03867 | Rochester......... | | 26,630 | 21,560 |
| 03079 | Salem........... | | 25,746 | 24,124 |
| 03874 | Seabrook......... | | 6,503 | 5,917 |
| 03878 | Somersworth....... | | 11,249 | 10,350 |
| 03275 | Suncook(u)........ | | 5,214 | 4,698 |
| ..... | Swanzey.......... | | 6,236 | .... |
| 03281 | Weare........... | | 6,193 | .... |
| 03087 | Windham.......... | | 9,000 | 5,664 |

## New Jersey

| ZIP code | Place | | 1990 | 1980 |
|---|---|---|---|---|
| 08201 | Absecon | (609) | 7,298 | 6,859 |
| 07401 | Allendale | (201) | 5,900 | 5,901 |
| 07712 | Asbury Park | (908) | 16,799 | 17,015 |
| *08401 | Atlantic City | (609) | 37,986 | 40,199 |
| 08106 | Audubon | (609) | 9,205 | 9,533 |
| 07001 | Avenel(u) | (908) | 15,504 | .... |
| 08007 | Barrington | (609) | 6,792 | 7,418 |
| 07002 | Bayonne | (201) | 61,464 | 65,047 |
| 08722 | Beachwood | (908) | 9,324 | 7,687 |
| 07109 | Belleville(u) | (201) | 34,213 | 35,367 |
| 08031 | Bellmawr | (609) | 12,603 | 13,721 |
| 07719 | Belmar | (908) | 5,877 | 6,771 |
| 07621 | Bergenfield | (201) | 24,458 | 25,568 |
| 07922 | Berkeley Heights Twp.(u) | (908) | 11,980 | 12,549 |
| 08009 | Berlin | (609) | 5,672 | 5,786 |
| 07924 | Bernardsville | (908) | 6,597 | 6,715 |
| 08012 | Blackwood(u) | (609) | 5,120 | 5,219 |
| 07003 | Bloomfield(u) | (201) | 45,061 | 47,792 |
| 07403 | Bloomingdale | (201) | 7,530 | 7,867 |
| 07603 | Bogota | (201) | 7,824 | 8,344 |
| 07005 | Boonton | (201) | 8,343 | 8,620 |
| 08805 | Bound Brook | (908) | 9,487 | 9,710 |
| 08723 | Brick Twp.(u) | (201) | 66,473 | 53,629 |
| 08302 | Bridgeton | (609) | 18,942 | 18,795 |
| 08807 | Bridgewater Twp. | (908) | 32,509 | .... |
| 08203 | Brigantine | (609) | 11,354 | 8,318 |
| 08015 | Browns Mills(u) | (609) | 11,429 | 10,568 |
| 07828 | Budd Lake(u) | (908) | 7,272 | 6,523 |
| 08016 | Burlington | (609) | 9,835 | 10,246 |
| 07405 | Butler | (201) | 7,392 | 7,616 |
| 07006 | Caldwell(u) | (201) | 7,549 | 7,624 |
| *08101 | Camden | (609) | 87,492 | 84,910 |
| 07072 | Carlstadt | (201) | 5,510 | 6,166 |
| 08069 | Carney's Point(u) | (609) | 7,686 | 7,574 |
| 07008 | Carteret | (908) | 19,025 | 20,598 |
| 07009 | Cedar Grove Twp.(u) | (201) | 12,053 | 12,600 |
| 07928 | Chatham | (201) | 8,007 | 8,537 |
| *08002 | Cherry Hill Twp.(u) | (609) | 69,319 | 68,785 |
| 08077 | Cinnaminson Twp.(u) | (609) | 14,583 | 16,072 |
| 07066 | Clark Twp.(u) | (908) | 14,629 | 16,699 |
| 08312 | Clayton | (609) | 6,155 | 6,013 |
| 08021 | Clementon | (609) | 5,601 | 5,764 |
| 07010 | Cliffside Park | (201) | 20,393 | 21,464 |
| *07015 | Clifton | (201) | 71,984 | 74,388 |
| 07624 | Closter | (201) | 8,094 | 8,164 |
| 08108 | Collingswood | (609) | 15,289 | 15,838 |
| 07067 | Colonia(u) | (908) | 18,238 | .... |
| 07016 | Cranford Twp. | (908) | 22,624 | 24,573 |
| 07626 | Cresskill | (201) | 7,558 | 7,609 |
| ..... | Crestwood Village(u) | (201) | 8,030 | 7,965 |
| 07801 | Dover | (201) | 15,115 | 14,681 |
| 07628 | Dumont | (201) | 17,187 | 18,334 |
| 08812 | Dunellen | (908) | 6,528 | 6,593 |
| 08816 | East Brunswick Twp. | (908) | 43,548 | 37,711 |
| 07936 | East Hanover | (201) | 9,926 | 9,319 |
| *07019 | East Orange | (201) | 73,552 | 77,878 |
| 07073 | East Rutherford | (201) | 7,902 | 7,849 |
| 07724 | Eatontown | (908) | 13,800 | 12,703 |
| 07020 | Edgewater Borough | (201) | 5,001 | 4,628 |
| 08010 | Edgewater Park | (609) | 8,388 | 9,273 |
| 08817 | Edison Twp.(u) | (908) | 88,680 | 70,193 |
| *07201 | Elizabeth | (908) | 110,002 | 106,201 |
| 07407 | Elmwood Park | (201) | 17,623 | 18,377 |
| 07630 | Emerson | (201) | 6,930 | 7,793 |
| *07631 | Englewood | (201) | 24,850 | 23,701 |
| 07632 | Englewood Cliffs | (201) | 5,634 | 5,698 |
| 08618 | Ewing Twp. | (609) | 34,185 | 34,842 |
| 07006 | Fairfield | (201) | 7,615 | 7,987 |
| 07701 | Fair Haven | (908) | 5,270 | 5,679 |
| 07410 | Fair Lawn | (201) | 30,548 | 32,229 |
| 07022 | Fairview | (201) | 10,733 | 10,519 |
| 07023 | Fanwood | (908) | 7,115 | 7,767 |
| 07518 | Florence-Roebling(u) | (609) | 8,564 | 7,677 |
| 07932 | Florham Park | (201) | 8,521 | 9,359 |
| 08863 | Fords(u) | (201) | 14,392 | .... |
| 08640 | Fort Dix(u) | (609) | 10,205 | 14,297 |
| 07024 | Fort Lee | (201) | 31,997 | 32,449 |
| 07417 | Franklin Lakes | (201) | 9,873 | 8,769 |
| ..... | Franklin Twp. | (201) | 42,780 | .... |
| 07728 | Freehold | (908) | 10,742 | 10,020 |
| 07026 | Garfield | (201) | 26,727 | 26,803 |
| 08753 | Gilford Park(u) | (908) | 8,668 | 6,528 |
| 08028 | Glassboro | (609) | 15,614 | 14,574 |
| 08029 | Glendora(u) | (609) | 5,201 | 5,632 |
| 07028 | Glen Ridge(u) | (201) | 7,076 | 7,855 |
| 07452 | Glen Rock | (201) | 10,883 | 11,497 |
| 08030 | Gloucester City | (609) | 12,649 | 13,121 |
| 07093 | Guttenberg | (201) | 8,268 | 7,340 |
| *07602 | Hackensack | (201) | 37,049 | 36,039 |
| 07840 | Hackettstown | (908) | 8,120 | 8,850 |
| 08033 | Haddonfield | (609) | 11,633 | 12,337 |
| 08035 | Haddon Heights | (609) | 7,860 | 8,361 |
| 07508 | Haledon | (201) | 6,951 | 6,607 |
| *08609 | Hamilton Twp.(u) | (609) | 86,553 | 82,811 |
| 08037 | Hammonton | (609) | 12,208 | 12,298 |
| 07981 | Hanover Twp.(u) | (201) | 11,538 | 11,846 |
| 07029 | Harrison | (201) | 13,425 | 12,242 |
| 07604 | Hasbrouck Heights | (201) | 11,488 | 12,166 |
| 07506 | Hawthorne | (201) | 17,084 | 18,200 |
| 07730 | Hazlet Twp.(u) | (908) | 21,976 | 23,013 |
| 08904 | Highland Park | (201) | 13,279 | 13,396 |
| 08520 | Hightstown | (609) | 5,126 | 4 581 |
| 07642 | Hillsdale | (201) | 9,750 | 10,495 |
| 07205 | Hillside Twp.(u) | (908) | 21,044 | 21,440 |
| 07030 | Hoboken | (201) | 33,397 | 42,460 |
| 08753 | Holiday City-Berkeley(u) | (908) | 14,293 | 9,019 |
| ..... | Holiday City South(u) | (908) | 5,452 | .... |
| 07843 | Hopatcong | (201) | 15,586 | 15,531 |
| *08560 | Hopewell Twp. (Mercer)(u) | (609) | 10,893 | 11,590 |
| 07111 | Irvington(u) | (201) | 59,774 | 61,473 |
| 08830 | Iselin(u) | (908) | 16,141 | .... |
| *08527 | Jackson Twp.(u) | (908) | 33,283 | 25,644 |
| 08831 | Jamesburg | (609) | 5,294 | 4,114 |
| *07303 | Jersey City | (201) | 228,517 | 223,532 |
| 07734 | Keansburg | (908) | 11,069 | 10,613 |
| 07032 | Kearny | (201) | 34,874 | 35,735 |
| 08824 | Kendall Park(u) | (908) | 7,127 | 7,419 |
| 07033 | Kenilworth | (908) | 7,574 | 8,221 |
| 07735 | Keyport | (908) | 7,586 | 7,413 |
| 07405 | Kinnelon | (201) | 8,470 | 7,770 |
| 07871 | Lake Mohawk(u) | (201) | 8,930 | 8,498 |
| 08701 | Lakewood(u) | (908) | 26,095 | 22,863 |
| 08879 | Laurence Harbor(u) | (908) | 6,361 | 6,737 |
| 08648 | Lawrenceville(u) | (201) | 6,446 | .... |
| ..... | Leisure Village West–Pine Lake Park(u) | | 10,139 | .... |
| 07605 | Leonia | (201) | 8,365 | 8,027 |
| 07035 | Lincoln Park | (201) | 10,978 | 8,806 |
| 07738 | Lincroft(u) | (201) | 6,193 | .... |
| 07036 | Linden | (908) | 36,701 | 37,836 |
| 08021 | Lindenwold | (609) | 18,734 | 18,196 |
| 08221 | Linwood | (609) | 6,866 | 6,144 |
| 07424 | Little Falls Twp.(u) | (201) | 11,294 | 11,496 |
| 07643 | Little Ferry | (201) | 9,989 | 9,399 |
| 07739 | Little Silver | (908) | 5,721 | 5,548 |
| 07039 | Livingston Twp.(u) | (201) | 26,609 | 28,040 |
| 07644 | Lodi | (201) | 22,355 | 23,956 |
| 07740 | Long Branch | (908) | 28,658 | 29,819 |
| *07946 | Long Hill Twp.(u) | (908) | 7,826 | 7,275 |
| 07071 | Lyndhurst Twp.(u) | (201) | 18,262 | 20,326 |
| 08641 | McGuire AFB(u) | (609) | 7,580 | 7,853 |
| 07940 | Madison | (201) | 15,850 | 15,357 |
| 08859 | Madison Park(u) | (201) | 7,490 | 7,447 |
| *07430 | Mahwah Twp.(u) | (201) | 17,905 | 12,137 |
| 08736 | Manasquan | (908) | 5,369 | 5,354 |
| 08835 | Manville | (908) | 10,567 | 11,278 |
| 08052 | Maple Shade Twp.(u) | (609) | 19,211 | 20,525 |
| 07040 | Maplewood Twp.(u) | (201) | 21,756 | 22,950 |
| 08402 | Margate City | (609) | 8,431 | 9,179 |
| 07746 | Marlboro Twp.(u) | (908) | 27,974 | 17,560 |
| 08053 | Marlton(u) | (609) | 10,228 | 9,411 |
| 07747 | Matawan | (908) | 9,239 | 8,837 |
| 07607 | Maywood | (201) | 9,536 | 9,895 |
| 08619 | Mercerville-Hamilton Sq.(u) | (609) | 26,873 | 25,446 |
| 08840 | Metuchen | (908) | 12,804 | 13,762 |
| 08846 | Middlesex | (908) | 13,055 | 13,480 |
| 07748 | Middletown | (908) | 68,183 | 61,615 |
| 07432 | Midland Park | (201) | 7,047 | 7,381 |
| 07041 | Millburn Twp.(u) | (201) | 18,630 | 19,543 |
| 08850 | Milltown | (908) | 6,968 | 7,136 |
| 08332 | Millville | (609) | 25,992 | 24,815 |
| 08094 | Monroe Twp. (Gloucester)(u) | (609) | 26,703 | 21,639 |
| *07042 | Montclair(u) | (201) | 37,729 | 38,321 |
| 07645 | Montvale | (201) | 6,946 | 7,318 |
| 07045 | Montville Twp.(u) | (201) | 15,600 | 14,290 |
| 08057 | Moorestown-Lenola(u) | (609) | 13,242 | 13,695 |
| 07950 | Morris Plains | (201) | 5,219 | 5,305 |
| 07960 | Morristown | (201) | 16,189 | 16,614 |
| 07092 | Mountainside | (908) | 6,657 | 7,118 |
| 08060 | Mount Holly Twp.(u) | (609) | 10,639 | 10,818 |
| 08087 | Mystic Island(u) | (609) | 7,400 | 4,929 |
| *07753 | Neptune Twp.(u) | (908) | 28,148 | 28,366 |
| *07102 | Newark | (201) | 275,221 | 329,248 |
| *08901 | New Brunswick | (908) | 41,711 | 41,442 |
| 07646 | New Milford | (201) | 15,990 | 16,876 |
| 07974 | New Providence | (201) | 11,439 | 12,426 |
| 07860 | Newton | (201) | 7,521 | 7,748 |
| 07032 | North Arlington | (201) | 13,790 | 16,587 |
| 07047 | North Bergen Twp.(u) | (201) | 48,414 | 47,019 |
| 08902 | North Brunswick Twp.(u) | (908) | 31,287 | 22,220 |
| 07006 | North Caldwell(u) | (201) | 6,706 | 5,832 |
| 08225 | Northfield | (609) | 7,305 | 7,795 |
| 07508 | North Haledon | (201) | 7,987 | 8,177 |
| 07060 | North Plainfield | (908) | 18,820 | 19,108 |
| 08260 | North Wildwood | | 5,017 | 4,714 |
| 07110 | Nutley | (201) | 27,099 | 28,998 |
| 07436 | Oakland | (201) | 11,997 | 13,443 |
| *08758 | Ocean Twp.(u) | (908) | 5,416 | 23,570 |
| ..... | Ocean Acres(u) | | 5,587 | 4,850 |
| 08226 | Ocean City | (609) | 15,512 | 13,949 |
| 07757 | Oceanport | (908) | 6,146 | 5,888 |
| 08857 | Old Bridge(u) | (908) | 22,151 | 21,815 |
| 08857 | Old Bridge Twp.(u) | (908) | 56,475 | 51,515 |
| 07649 | Oradell | (201) | 8,024 | 8,658 |
| *07050 | Orange(u) | (201) | 29,925 | 31,136 |

| ZIP code | Place | | 1990 | 1980 |
|---|---|---|---|---|
| 07650 | Palisades Park | (201) | 14,536 | 13,732 |
| 08065 | Palmyra | (609) | 7,056 | 7,085 |
| 07652 | Paramus | (201) | 25,004 | 26,474 |
| 07656 | Park Ridge | (201) | 8,102 | 8,515 |
| 07054 | Parsippany-Troy Hills(u) | (201) | 48,478 | 49,868 |
| *07055 | Passaic | (201) | 58,041 | 52,463 |
| *07510 | Paterson | (201) | 140,891 | 137,970 |
| 08066 | Paulsboro | (609) | 6,577 | 6,944 |
| 08110 | Pennsauken Twp.(u) | (609) | 34,733 | 33,775 |
| 08069 | Penns Grove | (609) | 5,228 | 5,760 |
| 08070 | Pennsville Center(u) | (609) | 12,218 | 12,467 |
| 07440 | Pequannock Twp. | (201) | 12,844 | 13,776 |
| *08861 | Perth Amboy | (908) | 41,967 | 38,951 |
| 08865 | Phillipsburg | (908) | 15,757 | 16,647 |
| 08021 | Pine Hill | (609) | 9,854 | 8,684 |
| *08854 | Piscataway Twp.(u) | (908) | 47,089 | 42,223 |
| 08071 | Pitman | (609) | 9,365 | 9,7447 |
| *07061 | Plainfield | (908) | 46,577 | 45,555 |
| 08232 | Pleasantville | (609) | 16,027 | 13,435 |
| 08742 | Point Pleasant | (908) | 18,177 | 17,747 |
| 08742 | Point Pleasant Beach | (908) | 5,112 | 5,415 |
| 07442 | Pompton Lakes | (201) | 10,539 | 10,660 |
| 08540 | Princeton | (609) | 12,016 | 12,035 |
| 07508 | Prospect Park | (201) | 5,053 | 5,142 |
| *07065 | Rahway | (908) | 25,325 | 26,723 |
| 08057 | Ramblewood(u) | (609) | 6,181 | 6,475 |
| 07446 | Ramsey | (201) | 13,228 | 12,899 |
| 07869 | Randolph Twp.(u) | (201) | 19,974 | 17,828 |
| 08869 | Raritan | (908) | 5,798 | 6,128 |
| 07701 | Red Bank | (908) | 10,636 | 12,031 |
| 07657 | Ridgefield | (201) | 9,996 | 10,294 |
| 07660 | Ridgefield Park | (201) | 12,454 | 12,738 |
| *07451 | Ridgewood | (201) | 24,152 | 25,208 |
| 07456 | Ringwood | (201) | 12,623 | 12,625 |
| 07661 | River Edge | (201) | 10,603 | 11,111 |
| 08075 | Riverside Twp.(u) | (609) | 7,974 | 7,941 |
| 07675 | River Vale(u) | (201) | 9,410 | 9,489 |
| 07726 | Robertsville(u) | (908) | 9,841 | 8,461 |
| 07662 | Rochelle Park Twp. | (201) | 5,587 | 5,603 |
| 07866 | Rockaway | (201) | 6,243 | 6,852 |
| 07203 | Roselle | (908) | 20,314 | 20,641 |
| 07204 | Roselle Park | (201) | 12,805 | 13,377 |
| 07760 | Rumson | (908) | 6,701 | 7,623 |
| 08078 | Runnemede | (609) | 9,042 | 9,461 |
| *07070 | Rutherford | (201) | 17,790 | 19,068 |
| 07662 | Saddle Brook Twp.(u) | (201) | 13,296 | 14,084 |
| 08079 | Salem | (609) | 6,883 | 6,959 |
| 08872 | Sayreville | (908) | 34,998 | 29,969 |
| 07076 | Scotch Plains Twp.(u) | (908) | 21,160 | 20,774 |
| 07094 | Secaucus | (201) | 14,061 | 13,719 |
| 08753 | Silverton | (908) | 9,175 | 7,236 |
| 08083 | Somerdale | (609) | 5,440 | 5,900 |
| 08873 | Somerset(u) | (908) | 22,070 | 21,731 |
| 08244 | Somers Point | (609) | 11,216 | 10,330 |
| 08876 | Somerville | (908) | 11,632 | 11,973 |
| 08879 | South Amboy | (908) | 7,851 | 8,322 |
| 07079 | South Orange Twp.(u) | (201) | 16,390 | 15,864 |
| 07080 | South Plainfield | (908) | 20,489 | 20,521 |
| 08882 | South River | (908) | 13,692 | 14,361 |
| 07871 | Sparta Twp.(u) | (201) | 15,157 | 7,333 |
| 08884 | Spotswood | (908) | 7,983 | 7,840 |
| 07081 | Springfield Twp.(u) | (201) | 13,420 | 13,955 |
| 07762 | Spring Lake Heights | (908) | 5,341 | 5,424 |
| 08084 | Stratford | (609) | 7,614 | 8,005 |
| 07747 | Strathmore(u) | (201) | 7,060 | .... |
| 07876 | Succasunna-Kenvil(u) | (201) | 11,781 | 10,931 |
| 07901 | Summit | (908) | 19,757 | 21,071 |
| 07666 | Teaneck Twp.(u) | (201) | 37,825 | 39,007 |
| 07670 | Tenafly | (201) | 13,326 | 13,552 |
| 07724 | Tinton Falls | (908) | 12,361 | 7,740 |
| *08753 | Toms River(u) | (908) | 7,524 | 7,465 |
| 07512 | Totowa | (201) | 10,177 | 11,448 |
| *08608 | Trenton | (609) | 88,675 | 92,124 |
| 08520 | Twin Rivers(u) | (609) | 7,715 | 7,742 |
| 07083 | Union Twp.(u) | (908) | 50,024 | 50,184 |
| 07735 | Union Beach | (908) | 6,156 | 6,354 |
| 07087 | Union City | (201) | 58,012 | 55,593 |
| 07458 | Upper Saddle River | (201) | 7,198 | 7,958 |
| 08406 | Ventnor City | (609) | 11,005 | 11,704 |
| 07044 | Verona(u) | (201) | 13,597 | 14,166 |
| 08251 | Villas(u) | (609) | 8,136 | 5,909 |
| 08360 | Vineland | (609) | 54,780 | 53,753 |
| 07463 | Waldwick | (201) | 9,757 | 10,802 |
| 07057 | Wallington | (201) | 10,828 | 10,741 |
| 07465 | Wanaque | (201) | 9,711 | 10,025 |
| 07882 | Washington | (908) | 6,474 | 6,429 |
| 07675 | Washington Twp. (Bergen)(u) | (201) | 9,245 | 9,550 |
| 07060 | Watchung | (908) | 5,110 | 5,290 |
| 07470 | Wayne Twp.(u) | (201) | 47,025 | 46,474 |
| 07087 | Weehawken Twp.(u) | (201) | 12,385 | 13,168 |
| 07006 | West Caldwell(u) | (201) | 10,422 | 11,407 |
| *07091 | Westfield | (908) | 28,870 | 30,447 |
| 07728 | West Freehold(u) | (908) | 11,166 | 9,929 |
| 07764 | West Long Branch | (908) | 7,690 | 7,380 |
| 07480 | West Milford Twp.(u) | (201) | 25,430 | 22,750 |
| 07093 | West New York | (201) | 38,125 | 39,194 |
| 07052 | West Orange | (201) | 39,103 | 39,510 |
| 07424 | West Paterson | (201) | 10,982 | 11,293 |
| 07675 | Westwood | (201) | 10,446 | 10,714 |

| ZIP code | Place | | 1990 | 1980 |
|---|---|---|---|---|
| 07885 | Wharton | (201) | 5,405 | 5,485 |
| 08610 | White Horse(u) | (609) | 9,397 | 10,098 |
| 07886 | White Meadow Lake(u) | (201) | 8,002 | 8,429 |
| 08094 | Williamstown | (609) | 10,891 | 5,768 |
| 08046 | Willingboro Twp.(u) | (609) | 36,291 | 39,912 |
| 08095 | Winslow Twp.(u) | (609) | 30,087 | 20,034 |
| 07095 | Woodbridge Twp.(u) | (908) | 93,086 | 90,074 |
| 08096 | Woodbury | (609) | 10,904 | 10,353 |
| 07675 | Woodcliff Lake | (201) | 5,303 | 5,644 |
| 07075 | Wood-Ridge | (201) | 7,506 | 7,929 |
| 07481 | Wyckoff Twp.(u) | (201) | 15,372 | 15,500 |
| 08620 | Yardville-Grovesville(u) | (609) | 9,248 | 9,414 |
| ..... | Yorketown(u) | (609) | 6,313 | 5,330 |

### New Mexico (505)

| ZIP code | Place | 1990 | 1980 |
|---|---|---|---|
| 88310 | Alamogordo | 27,596 | 24,024 |
| *87101 | Albuquerque | 384,619 | 332,920 |
| 88021 | Anthony(u) | 5,160 | .... |
| 88210 | Artesia | 10,610 | 10,385 |
| 87410 | Aztec | 5,480 | 5,512 |
| 87002 | Belen | 6,547 | 5,617 |
| 87001 | Bernalillo | 5,960 | 2,988 |
| 87413 | Bloomfield | 5,214 | 4,881 |
| 88220 | Carlsbad | 24,952 | 25,496 |
| 88101 | Clovis | 30,954 | 31,194 |
| 87048 | Corrales | 5,453 | 2,791 |
| 88030 | Deming | 10,970 | 9,964 |
| 87532 | Espanola | 8,389 | 6,803 |
| 87401 | Farmington | 33,997 | 31,222 |
| 87301 | Gallup | 19,157 | 18,167 |
| 87020 | Grants | 8,626 | 11,439 |
| 88240 | Hobbs | 29,121 | 29,153 |
| 88330 | Holloman AFB(u) | 5,891 | 7,245 |
| *88001 | Las Cruces | 62,360 | 45,086 |
| 87701 | Las Vegas | 14,753 | 14,322 |
| 87544 | Los Alamos(u) | 11,455 | 11,039 |
| 87031 | Los Lunas | 6,013 | 3,525 |
| 88260 | Lovington | 9,322 | 9,727 |
| 87107 | North Valley(u) | 12,507 | 5,096 |
| 87114 | Paradise Hills(u) | 5,513 | 5,096 |
| 88130 | Portales | 10,690 | 9,940 |
| 87740 | Raton | 7,372 | 8,225 |
| 87124 | Rio Rancho | 32,512 | 9,985 |
| 88201 | Roswell | 44,260 | 39,676 |
| 87115 | Sandia(u) | 6,742 | 5,288 |
| *87501 | Santa Fe | 56,537 | 49,160 |
| 87420 | Shiprock | 7,687 | 7,237 |
| 88061 | Silver City | 10,683 | 9,887 |
| 87801 | Socorro | 8,159 | 7,173 |
| 87105 | South Valley(u) | 35,701 | 38,916 |
| 88063 | Sunland Park | 8,179 | 4,313 |
| 87901 | Truth or Consequences | 6,221 | 5,219 |
| 88401 | Tucumcari | 6,827 | 6,765 |
| 87544 | White Rock(u) | 6,192 | 6,560 |
| 87327 | Zuni Pueblo(u) | 5,857 | 5,551 |

### New York

| ZIP code | Place | | 1990 | 1980 |
|---|---|---|---|---|
| 10901 | Airmont(u) | | 7,835 | .... |
| *12207 | Albany | (518) | 100,031 | 101,727 |
| 11507 | Albertson(u) | (516) | 5,166 | 5,561 |
| 14411 | Albion | (716) | 5,863 | 4,897 |
| 11701 | Amityville | (516) | 9,286 | 9,076 |
| 12010 | Amsterdam | (518) | 20,714 | 21,872 |
| 12603 | Arlington | (914) | 11,948 | 11,305 |
| 13021 | Auburn | (315) | 31,258 | 32,548 |
| *11702 | Babylon | (516) | 12,249 | 12,388 |
| 11510 | Baldwin(u) | (516) | 22,719 | 31,630 |
| 11510 | Baldwin Harbor(u) | | 7,899 | .... |
| 13027 | Baldwinsville | (315) | 6,591 | 6,446 |
| 12020 | Ballston Spa | (518) | 5,194 | .... |
| 14020 | Batavia | (716) | 16,310 | 16,703 |
| 14810 | Bath | (607) | 5,801 | 6,042 |
| 11705 | Bayport(u) | (516) | 7,702 | 9,282 |
| 11706 | Bay Shore(u) | (516) | 21,279 | 10,784 |
| 11709 | Bayville | (516) | 7,193 | 7,034 |
| ..... | Baywood(u) | | 7,351 | .... |
| 12508 | Beacon | (914) | 13,243 | 12,937 |
| 11710 | Bellmore(u) | (516) | 16,438 | 18,106 |
| 11714 | Bethpage(u) | (516) | 15,761 | 16,840 |
| *13902 | Binghamton | (607) | 53,008 | 55,860 |
| 11716 | Bohemia(u) | (516) | 9,556 | 9,308 |
| 11717 | Brentwood(u) | (516) | 45,218 | 44,321 |
| 10510 | Briarcliff Manor | (914) | 7,070 | 7,115 |
| 14610 | Brighton(u) | (716) | 34,455 | 35,776 |
| 14420 | Brockport | (716) | 8,749 | 9,776 |
| 10708 | Bronxville | (914) | 6,028 | 6,267 |
| *14240 | Buffalo | (716) | 328,175 | 357,870 |
| 14424 | Canandaigua | (716) | 10,725 | 10,419 |
| 13617 | Canton | (315) | 6,379 | 7,055 |
| 11514 | Carle Place(u) | (516) | 5,107 | 5,470 |
| 11516 | Cedarhurst | (516) | 5,716 | 6,162 |
| 11720 | Centereach(u) | (516) | 26,720 | 30,136 |
| 11934 | Center Moriches(u) | (516) | 5,987 | 5,703 |
| 11721 | Centerport(u) | (516) | 5,333 | 6,576 |

| ZIP code | Place | Area code | 1990 | 1980 |
|---|---|---|---|---|
| 11722 | Central Islip(u) | (516) | 26,028 | 19,734 |
| 14225 | Cheektowaga(u) | (716) | 84,387 | 92,145 |
| 10977 | Chestnut Ridge | | 7,517 | 8,217 |
| 12043 | Cobleskill | (518) | 5,268 | 5,272 |
| 12047 | Cohoes | (518) | 16,825 | 18,144 |
| 12205 | Colonie | (518) | 8,019 | 8,869 |
| 11725 | Commack(u) | (516) | 36,124 | 34,719 |
| 10920 | Congers(u) | (914) | 8,003 | 7,123 |
| 11726 | Copiague(u) | (516) | 20,769 | 20,132 |
| 11727 | Coram(u) | (516) | 30,111 | 24,752 |
| 14830 | Corning | (607) | 11,938 | 12,953 |
| 13045 | Cortland | (607) | 19,801 | 20,138 |
| 10520 | Croton-on-Hudson | (914) | 7,018 | 6,889 |
| 14437 | Dansville | (716) | 5,002 | 4,979 |
| 11729 | Deer Park(u) | (516) | 28,840 | 30,394 |
| 12054 | Delmar(u) | (518) | 8,360 | 8,423 |
| 14043 | Depew | (716) | 17,673 | 19,819 |
| 13214 | DeWitt(u) | (315) | 8,244 | 9,024 |
| 11746 | Dix Hills(u) | (516) | 25,849 | 26,693 |
| 10522 | Dobbs Ferry | (914) | 9,940 | 10,053 |
| 14048 | Dunkirk | (716) | 13,989 | 15,310 |
| 14052 | East Aurora | (716) | 6,647 | 6,803 |
| 10709 | Eastchester(u) | (914) | 18,537 | 20,305 |
| 12302 | East Glenville(u) | (518) | 6,518 | 6,537 |
| 11576 | East Hills | (516) | 6,746 | 7,160 |
| 11730 | East Islip(u) | (516) | 14,325 | 13,852 |
| 11758 | East Massapequa(u) | (516) | 19,550 | 13,987 |
| 11554 | East Meadow(u) | (516) | 36,909 | 39,317 |
| 11731 | East Northport(u) | (516) | 20,411 | 20,187 |
| 11772 | East Patchogue(u) | (516) | 20,195 | 18,139 |
| 14445 | East Rochester | (516) | 6,932 | 7,596 |
| 11518 | East Rockaway | (516) | 10,152 | 10,917 |
| 11786 | East Shoreham | | 5,461 | ---- |
| *14901 | Elmira | (607) | 33,724 | 35,327 |
| 11003 | Elmont(u) | (516) | 28,612 | 27,592 |
| 11731 | Elmwood(u) | (516) | 10,916 | 11,847 |
| 13760 | Endicott | (607) | 13,531 | 14,457 |
| 13760 | Endwell(u) | (607) | 12,602 | 13,745 |
| 13219 | Fairmount(u) | (315) | 12,266 | 13,415 |
| 14450 | Fairport | (716) | 5,943 | 5,970 |
| 11735 | Farmingdale | (516) | 8,022 | 7,946 |
| 11738 | Farmingville(u) | (516) | 14,842 | 13,398 |
| *11001 | Floral Park | (516) | 15,947 | 16,805 |
| 13603 | Fort Drum(u) | | 11,578 | ---- |
| 11768 | Fort Salonga(u) | (516) | 9,176 | 9,550 |
| 11010 | Franklin Square(u) | (516) | 28,205 | 29,051 |
| 14063 | Fredonia | (716) | 10,436 | 11,126 |
| 11520 | Freeport | (516) | 39,894 | 38,272 |
| 13069 | Fulton | (315) | 12,929 | 13,312 |
| 11530 | Garden City | (516) | 21,675 | 22,927 |
| 11040 | Garden City Park(u) | (516) | 7,437 | 7,712 |
| 14624 | Gates-North Gates(u) | (716) | 14,995 | 15,244 |
| 14454 | Geneseo | (716) | 7,187 | 6,746 |
| 14456 | Geneva | (315) | 14,143 | 15,133 |
| 11542 | Glen Cove | (516) | 24,149 | 24,618 |
| 12801 | Glens Falls | (518) | 15,023 | 15,897 |
| 12801 | Glens Falls North(u) | (518) | 7,978 | 6,956 |
| 12078 | Gloversville | (518) | 16,656 | 17,836 |
| 10924 | Goshen | (914) | 5,255 | 4,874 |
| *11022 | Great Neck | (516) | 8,745 | 9,168 |
| 11020 | Great Neck Plaza | (516) | 5,897 | 5,604 |
| 14616 | Greece(u) | (716) | 15,632 | 16,177 |
| 11740 | Greenlawn(u) | (516) | 13,208 | 13,869 |
| 12083 | Greenville(u) | (716) | 9,528 | 8,706 |
| 14075 | Hamburg | (716) | 10,442 | 10,582 |
| 11946 | Hampton Bays(u) | (516) | 7,893 | 7,256 |
| 10528 | Harrison | (914) | 23,308 | 23,046 |
| 10530 | Hartsdale(u) | (914) | 9,587 | 10,216 |
| 10706 | Hastings-on-Hudson | (914) | 8,000 | 8,573 |
| 11787 | Hauppauge(u) | (516) | 19,750 | 20,960 |
| 10927 | Haverstraw | (914) | 9,438 | 8,800 |
| *11551 | Hempstead | (516) | 47,051 | 40,404 |
| 13350 | Herkimer | (315) | 7,945 | 8,383 |
| 11557 | Hewlett(u) | (516) | 6,620 | 6,986 |
| *11802 | Hicksville(u) | (516) | 40,174 | 43,245 |
| 10977 | Hillcrest(u) | (914) | 6,447 | 5,733 |
| 14468 | Hilton | | 5,216 | 4,151 |
| 11741 | Holbrook(u) | (516) | 25,273 | 24,382 |
| 11742 | Holtsville(u) | (516) | 14,972 | 13,515 |
| 14843 | Hornell | (607) | 9,877 | 10,234 |
| 14845 | Horseheads | (607) | 6,802 | 7,348 |
| 12534 | Hudson | (518) | 8,034 | 7,986 |
| 12839 | Hudson Falls | (518) | 7,651 | 7,419 |
| 11743 | Huntington(u) | (516) | 18,243 | 21,727 |
| 11746 | Huntington Station(u) | (516) | 28,247 | 28,769 |
| 13357 | Ilion | (315) | 8,888 | 9,450 |
| 11696 | Inwood(u) | (516) | 7,767 | 8,228 |
| 14617 | Irondequoit(u) | (716) | 52,322 | 57,648 |
| 10533 | Irvington | (914) | 6,348 | 5,774 |
| 11751 | Islip(u) | (516) | 18,924 | 13,438 |
| 11752 | Islip Terrace(u) | (516) | 5,530 | 5,588 |
| 14850 | Ithaca | (607) | 29,541 | 28,732 |
| 14701 | Jamestown | (716) | 34,681 | 35,775 |
| 10535 | Jefferson Valley-Yorktown(u) | (914) | 14,118 | 13,380 |
| 11753 | Jericho(u) | (516) | 13,141 | 12,739 |
| 13790 | Johnson City | (607) | 16,578 | 17,126 |
| 12095 | Johnstown | (518) | 9,058 | 9,360 |
| 14217 | Kenmore | (716) | 17,180 | 18,474 |
| 11754 | Kings Park(u) | (516) | 17,773 | 16,131 |
| 12401 | Kingston | (914) | 23,095 | 24,481 |
| ..... | Kiryas Joel | | 7,437 | 2,088 |
| 14218 | Lackawanna | (716) | 20,585 | 22,701 |
| 10512 | Lake Carmel(u) | (914) | 8,489 | 7,295 |
| 11755 | Lake Grove | (516) | 9,612 | 9,692 |
| 11779 | Lake Ronkonkoma(u) | (516) | 18,997 | 38,336 |
| 11552 | Lakeview(u) | (516) | 5,476 | 5,276 |
| 14086 | Lancaster | (716) | 11,940 | 13,056 |
| 10538 | Larchmont | (914) | 6,181 | 6,308 |
| 12110 | Latham(u) | (518) | 10,131 | 11,182 |
| 11559 | Lawrence | (516) | 6,513 | 6,175 |
| 11756 | Levittown(u) | (516) | 53,286 | 57,045 |
| 11757 | Lindenhurst | (516) | 26,879 | 26,919 |
| 13365 | Little Falls | (315) | 5,829 | 6,156 |
| 14094 | Lockport | (716) | 24,426 | 24,844 |
| 11561 | Long Beach | (516) | 33,510 | 34,073 |
| 12211 | Loudonville(u) | (518) | 10,822 | 11,480 |
| 11563 | Lynbrook | (516) | 19,208 | 20,424 |
| 10541 | Mahopac(u) | (914) | 7,755 | 7,681 |
| 12953 | Malone | (518) | 6,777 | 7,668 |
| 11565 | Malverne | (516) | 9,054 | 9,262 |
| 10543 | Mamaroneck | (914) | 17,325 | 17,616 |
| 11030 | Manhasset(u) | (516) | 7,718 | 8,485 |
| 11050 | Manorhaven | (516) | 5,672 | 5,384 |
| 11949 | Manorville(u) | (516) | 6,198 | ---- |
| 11758 | Massapequa(u) | (516) | 22,018 | 24,454 |
| 11762 | Massapequa Park | (516) | 18,044 | 19,779 |
| 13662 | Massena | (315) | 11,716 | 12,851 |
| 11950 | Mastic(u) | (516) | 13,778 | 10,413 |
| 11951 | Mastic Beach(u) | (516) | 10,293 | 8,318 |
| 13211 | Mattydale(u) | (315) | 6,418 | 7,511 |
| 12118 | Mechanicville | (518) | 5,249 | 5,500 |
| 11763 | Medford(u) | (516) | 21,274 | 20,418 |
| 14103 | Medina | (716) | 6,686 | 6,362 |
| 11746 | Melville(u) | (516) | 12,586 | 8,139 |
| 11566 | Merrick(u) | (516) | 23,042 | 24,478 |
| 11953 | Middle Island(u) | (516) | 7,848 | 5,703 |
| 10940 | Middletown | (914) | 24,160 | 21,454 |
| 11764 | Miller Place(u) | (516) | 9,315 | 7,877 |
| 11501 | Mineola | (516) | 19,005 | 20,757 |
| 10950 | Monroe | (914) | 6,672 | 5,996 |
| 10952 | Monsey(u) | (914) | 13,986 | 12,380 |
| 12701 | Monticello | (914) | 6,597 | 6,306 |
| 10970 | Mount Ivy(u) | | 6,013 | ---- |
| 10549 | Mount Kisco | (914) | 9,108 | 8,025 |
| 11766 | Mount Sinai(u) | (516) | 8,023 | 6,591 |
| *10551 | Mount Vernon | (914) | 67,153 | 66,713 |
| 12590 | Myers Corner(u) | (914) | 5,599 | 5,180 |
| 10954 | Nanuet(u) | (914) | 14,065 | 12,578 |
| 11767 | Nesconset(u) | (516) | 10,712 | 10,706 |
| 14513 | Newark | (315) | 9,849 | 10,017 |
| 12550 | Newburgh | (914) | 26,454 | 23,438 |
| 11590 | New Cassel(u) | (516) | 10,257 | 9,635 |
| 10956 | New City(u) | (914) | 33,673 | 35,859 |
| 11040 | New Hyde Park | (516) | 9,728 | 9,801 |
| 12561 | New Paltz | (914) | 5,470 | 4,938 |
| *10802 | New Rochelle | (914) | 67,265 | 70,794 |
| *12550 | New Windsor Center(u) | (914) | 8,898 | 7,812 |
| *10001 | New York | (212) | 7,322,564 | 7,071,639 |
| *14302 | Niagara Falls | (716) | 61,840 | 71,384 |
| 11701 | North Amityville(u) | (516) | 13,849 | 13,140 |
| 11703 | North Babylon(u) | (516) | 18,081 | 19,019 |
| 11706 | North Bay Shore(u) | (516) | 12,799 | 35,020 |
| 11710 | North Bellmore(u) | (516) | 19,707 | 20,630 |
| 11713 | North Bellport(u) | (516) | 8,182 | 7,432 |
| 11757 | North Lindenhurst(u) | (516) | 10,563 | 11,511 |
| 11758 | North Massapequa(u) | (516) | 19,365 | 21,385 |
| 11566 | North Merrick(u) | (516) | 12,113 | 12,848 |
| 11040 | North New Hyde Park(u) | (516) | 14,359 | 15,114 |
| 11772 | North Patchogue(u) | (516) | 7,374 | 7,126 |
| 11768 | Northport | (516) | 7,572 | 7,651 |
| 13212 | North Syracuse | (315) | 7,363 | 7,970 |
| 10591 | North Tarrytown(u) | (914) | 8,152 | 7,994 |
| 14120 | North Tonawanda | (716) | 34,989 | 35,760 |
| 11580 | North Valley Stream(u) | (516) | 14,574 | 14,530 |
| 11793 | North Wantagh(u) | (516) | 12,276 | 12,677 |
| 13815 | Norwich | (607) | 7,613 | 8,082 |
| 10960 | Nyack | (914) | 6,558 | 6,428 |
| 11769 | Oakdale(u) | (516) | 7,875 | 8,090 |
| 11572 | Oceanside(u) | (516) | 32,423 | 33,639 |
| 13669 | Ogdensburg | (315) | 13,521 | 12,375 |
| 11804 | Old Bethpage(u) | (516) | 5,610 | 6,215 |
| 14760 | Olean | (716) | 16,946 | 18,207 |
| 13421 | Oneida | (315) | 10,850 | 10,810 |
| 13820 | Oneonta | (607) | 13,954 | 14,933 |
| 12550 | Orange Lake(u) | (914) | 5,196 | 5,120 |
| 10562 | Ossining | (914) | 22,582 | 20,196 |
| 13126 | Oswego | (315) | 19,195 | 19,793 |
| 11771 | Oyster Bay(u) | (516) | 6,687 | 6,497 |
| 11772 | Patchogue | (516) | 11,060 | 11,291 |
| 10965 | Pearl River(u) | (914) | 15,314 | 15,893 |
| 10566 | Peekskill | (914) | 19,536 | 18,236 |
| 10803 | Pelham | (914) | 6,413 | 6,848 |
| 10803 | Pelham Manor | (914) | 5,443 | 6,130 |
| 14527 | Penn Yan | (315) | 5,257 | 5,242 |
| 11714 | Plainedge(u) | (516) | 8,739 | 9,629 |
| 11803 | Plainview(u) | (516) | 26,207 | 28,037 |
| 12901 | Plattsburgh | (518) | 21,255 | 21,057 |
| 12903 | Plattsburgh AFB(u) | (518) | 5,483 | 5,905 |

| ZIP code | Place | | 1990 | 1980 |
|---|---|---|---|---|
| 10570 | Pleasantville. | (914) | 6,592 | 6,749 |
| 10573 | Port Chester. | (914) | 24,728 | 23,565 |
| 11777 | Port Jefferson. | (516) | 7,455 | 6,731 |
| 11776 | Port Jefferson Station(u). | (516) | 7,232 | 17,009 |
| 12771 | Port Jervis. | (914) | 9,060 | 8,699 |
| 11050 | Port Washington(u). | (516) | 15,387 | 14,521 |
| 13676 | Potsdam. | (315) | 10,251 | 10,635 |
| *12601 | Poughkeepsie. | (914) | 28,844 | 29,757 |
| 12144 | Rensselaer. | (518) | 8,255 | 9,047 |
| 11961 | Ridge(u). | (516) | 11,734 | 8,977 |
| 11901 | Riverhead(u). | (516) | 8,814 | 6,339 |
| *14603 | Rochester. | (716) | 230,356 | 241,741 |
| *11570 | Rockville Centre. | (516) | 24,727 | 25,412 |
| 11778 | Rocky Point(u). | (516) | 8,596 | 7,012 |
| 12205 | Roessleville(u). | (518) | 10,753 | 11,685 |
| 13440 | Rome. | (315) | 44,350 | 43,826 |
| 11779 | Ronkonkoma. | (516) | 20,391 | |
| 11575 | Roosevelt(u). | (516) | 15,030 | 14,109 |
| 11577 | Roslyn Heights(u). | (516) | 6,405 | 6,546 |
| 12303 | Rotterdam(u). | (518) | 21,228 | 22,933 |
| 10580 | Rye. | (914) | 14,936 | 15,083 |
| 10573 | Rye Brook. | | 7,765 | 7,996 |
| 11780 | Saint James(u). | (516) | 12,703 | 12,122 |
| 14779 | Salamanca. | (716) | 6,566 | 6,890 |
| 13454 | Salisbury(u). | | 12,226 | |
| 12983 | Saranac Lake. | (518) | 5,377 | 5,578 |
| 12866 | Saratoga Springs. | (518) | 25,001 | 23,906 |
| 11782 | Sayville(u). | (516) | 16,550 | 12,013 |
| 10583 | Scarsdale. | (914) | 16,987 | 17,650 |
| *12301 | Schenectady. | (518) | 65,566 | 67,972 |
| 10940 | Scotchtown(u). | (914) | 8,765 | 7,352 |
| 12302 | Scotia. | (518) | 7,359 | 7,280 |
| 11579 | Sea Cliff. | (516) | 5,054 | 5,364 |
| 11783 | Seaford(u). | (516) | 15,597 | 16,117 |
| 11507 | Searingtown(u). | | 5,020 | |
| 11784 | Selden(u). | (516) | 20,608 | 17,259 |
| 13148 | Seneca Falls. | (315) | 7,370 | 7,466 |
| 11733 | Setauket-East Setauket(u). | (516) | 13,634 | 10,176 |
| 11967 | Shirley(u). | (516) | 22,936 | 18,072 |
| 11787 | Smithtown(u). | (516) | 25,638 | 30,906 |
| 13209 | Solvay. | (315) | 6,717 | 7,140 |
| 11789 | Sound Beach(u). | (516) | 9,102 | 8,071 |
| 11735 | South Farmingdale(u). | (516) | 15,377 | 16,439 |
| 14850 | South Hill(u). | (607) | 5,423 | |
| 11746 | South Huntington(u). | (516) | 9,624 | 14,854 |
| 14094 | South Lockport(u). | | 7,112 | 3,366 |
| 11971 | Southold(u). | | 5,192 | 4,770 |
| 14904 | Southport(u). | (607) | 7,753 | 8,329 |
| 11581 | South Valley Stream(u). | (516) | 5,328 | 5,462 |
| 10977 | Spring Valley. | (914) | 21,802 | 20,537 |
| 11790 | Stony Brook(u). | (516) | 13,726 | 16,155 |
| 10980 | Stony Point(u). | (315) | 10,587 | 8,686 |
| 10901 | Suffern. | (914) | 11,055 | 10,794 |
| 11791 | Syosset(u). | (516) | 18,967 | 9,818 |
| *13201 | Syracuse. | (315) | 163,860 | 170,105 |
| 10983 | Tappan(u). | (914) | 6,867 | 8,267 |
| 10591 | Tarrytown. | (914) | 10,739 | 10,648 |
| 11776 | Terryville(u). | | 10,275 | |
| 10984 | Thiells. | | 5,204 | |
| 10594 | Thornwood(u). | (914) | 7,025 | 7,197 |
| 14150 | Tonawanda. | (716) | 17,284 | 18,693 |
| 14151 | Tonawanda(u). | (716) | 65,284 | 72,795 |
| *12180 | Troy. | (518) | 54,269 | 56,638 |
| 10707 | Tuckahoe. | (914) | 6,302 | 6,076 |
| 11553 | Uniondale(u). | (516) | 20,328 | 20,016 |
| *13503 | Utica. | (315) | 68,637 | 75,632 |
| 10989 | Valley Cottage(u). | (914) | 9,007 | 8,214 |
| *11580 | Valley Stream. | (516) | 33,946 | 35,769 |
| 11792 | Wading River. | | 5,317 | |
| 12586 | Walden. | (914) | 5,836 | 5,659 |
| 11793 | Wantagh(u). | (516) | 18,567 | 19,817 |
| 10990 | Warwick. | | 5,984 | 4,320 |
| 13165 | Waterloo. | (315) | 5,116 | 5,303 |
| 13601 | Watertown. | (315) | 29,429 | 27,861 |
| 12189 | Watervliet. | (518) | 11,061 | 11,354 |
| 14580 | Webster. | (716) | 5,464 | 5,499 |
| 14895 | Wellsville. | (716) | 5,241 | 5,769 |
| 11704 | West Babylon(u). | (516) | 42,410 | 41,699 |
| 11590 | Westbury. | (516) | 13,060 | 13,871 |
| 14905 | West Elmira(u). | (607) | 5,218 | 5,485 |
| 12801 | West Glens Falls(u). | (518) | 5,964 | 5,331 |
| 10993 | West Haverstraw. | (914) | 9,183 | 9,181 |
| 11552 | West Hempstead(u). | (516) | 17,689 | 18,536 |
| 11743 | West Hills(u). | (516) | 5,849 | 6,071 |
| 11795 | West Islip(u). | (516) | 28,419 | 29,533 |
| 12203 | Westmere(u). | (518) | 6,750 | 6,881 |
| 10996 | West Point(u). | (914) | 8,024 | 8,105 |
| 14224 | West Seneca(u). | (716) | 47,866 | 51,210 |
| 13219 | Westvale(u). | (315) | 5,952 | 6,169 |
| 11798 | Wheatley Heights(u). | | 5,027 | |
| 10602 | White Plains. | (914) | 48,718 | 46,999 |
| 14221 | Williamsville. | (716) | 5,583 | 6,017 |
| 11596 | Williston Park. | (516) | 7,516 | 8,216 |
| 11797 | Woodbury(u). | (516) | 8,008 | 7,043 |
| 11598 | Woodmere(u). | (516) | 15,578 | 17,205 |
| 11798 | Wyandach(u). | (516) | 8,950 | 13,215 |
| *10701 | Yonkers. | (914) | 188,082 | 195,351 |
| 10598 | Yorktown Heights(u). | (914) | 7,690 | 7,696 |

## North Carolina

| ZIP code | Place | | 1990 | 1980 |
|---|---|---|---|---|
| 28001 | Albemarle. | (704) | 14,940 | 15,110 |
| 27263 | Archdale. | (919) | 6,975 | 5,326 |
| 27203 | Asheboro. | (919) | 16,362 | 15,252 |
| *28801 | Asheville. | (704) | 61,855 | 54,022 |
| 28012 | Belmont. | (704) | 8,434 | 4,607 |
| 28711 | Black Mountain. | | 5,533 | 4,083 |
| 28607 | Boone. | (704) | 12,949 | 10,191 |
| 28712 | Brevard. | (704) | 5,388 | 5,323 |
| 27215 | Burlington. | (919) | 39,498 | 37,266 |
| 28542 | Camp Le Jeune(u). | (919) | 36,716 | 30,764 |
| 27510 | Carrboro. | (919) | 12,134 | 7,336 |
| 27511 | Cary. | (919) | 43,457 | 21,763 |
| 27514 | Chapel Hill. | (919) | 38,711 | 32,421 |
| *28202 | Charlotte. | (704) | 395,934 | 315,474 |
| 27012 | Clemmons(u). | (919) | 6,020 | 4,842 |
| 28328 | Clinton. | (919) | 8,385 | 7,552 |
| 28025 | Concord. | (704) | 27,347 | 16,942 |
| 28613 | Conover. | (704) | 5,465 | 4,245 |
| 28334 | Dunn. | (919) | 8,556 | 8,962 |
| *27701 | Durham. | (919) | 136,612 | 101,149 |
| 27288 | Eden. | (919) | 15,238 | 15,672 |
| 27932 | Edenton. | (919) | 5,268 | 5,357 |
| 27909 | Elizabeth City. | (919) | 14,292 | 14,004 |
| *28302 | Fayetteville. | (919) | 75,850 | 59,507 |
| 28043 | Forest City. | (704) | 7,475 | 7,688 |
| 28307 | Fort Bragg(u). | (919) | 34,744 | 37,834 |
| 27529 | Garner. | (919) | 14,716 | 10,073 |
| 28052 | Gastonia. | (704) | 54,725 | 47,218 |
| 27530 | Goldsboro. | (919) | 40,709 | 31,871 |
| 27253 | Graham. | (919) | 10,368 | 8,674 |
| *27420 | Greensboro. | (919) | 183,894 | 155,642 |
| 27834 | Greenville. | (919) | 46,305 | 35,740 |
| ..... | Half Moon(u). | | 6,306 | 3,592 |
| 28345 | Hamlet. | (919) | 6,324 | 4,720 |
| 28532 | Havelock. | (919) | 20,300 | 17,718 |
| 27536 | Henderson. | (919) | 15,655 | 13,522 |
| 28739 | Hendersonville. | | 7,284 | 6,862 |
| 28601 | Hickory. | (704) | 28,301 | 20,757 |
| *27260 | High Point. | (919) | 69,424 | 63,479 |
| 28348 | Hope Mills. | (919) | 8,272 | 5,412 |
| 28540 | Jacksonville. | (919) | 30,001 | 18,237 |
| 28081 | Kannapolis. | (704) | 29,696 | 30,303 |
| 27284 | Kernersville. | (919) | 10,836 | 5,875 |
| 28086 | Kings Mountain. | (704) | 8,763 | 9,080 |
| 28501 | Kinston. | (919) | 25,295 | 25,234 |
| 28352 | Laurinburg. | (919) | 11,643 | 11,480 |
| 28645 | Lenoir. | (704) | 14,192 | 13,748 |
| 27292 | Lexington. | (704) | 16,581 | 15,711 |
| 28092 | Lincolnton. | (704) | 6,955 | 4,879 |
| 28358 | Lumberton. | (919) | 18,733 | 18,241 |
| ..... | Masonboro(u). | | 7,010 | 3,881 |
| 28105 | Matthews. | (704) | 13,651 | 1,648 |
| 28212 | Mint Hill. | (704) | 11,615 | 7,915 |
| 28110 | Monroe. | (704) | 16,385 | 12,639 |
| 28115 | Mooresville. | (704) | 9,317 | 8,575 |
| 28557 | Morehead. | (919) | 6,046 | 4,359 |
| 28655 | Morganton. | (704) | 15,085 | 13,763 |
| 27030 | Mount Airy. | (919) | 7,156 | 6,862 |
| 28120 | Mount Holly. | (704) | 7,710 | 4,530 |
| 28560 | New Bern. | (919) | 17,363 | 14,557 |
| 27604 | New Hope (Wake)(u). | (704) | 5,694 | 6,745 |
| 28540 | New River Station(u). | (919) | 9,732 | 5,401 |
| 28658 | Newton. | (704) | 9,304 | 7,624 |
| 27565 | Oxford. | (919) | 7,965 | 7,709 |
| 28374 | Pinehurst. | (919) | 5,091 | 1,746 |
| 28399 | Piney Green-White Oak(u). | (919) | 8,999 | 6,058 |
| *27611 | Raleigh. | (919) | 212,050 | 150,255 |
| 27320 | Reidsville. | (919) | 12,183 | 12,492 |
| 27870 | Roanoke Rapids. | (919) | 15,722 | 14,702 |
| 28379 | Rockingham. | (919) | 9,399 | 8,300 |
| 27801 | Rocky Mount. | (919) | 49,438 | 41,526 |
| 27573 | Roxboro. | (919) | 7,332 | 7,532 |
| 28601 | Saint Stephens(u). | (704) | 8,734 | 10,797 |
| 28144 | Salisbury. | (704) | 23,621 | 22,677 |
| 27330 | Sanford. | (919) | 14,755 | 14,773 |
| ..... | Seagate(u). | | 5,444 | 3,422 |
| 28150 | Shelby. | (704) | 14,669 | 15,310 |
| ..... | Smith Creek(u). | | 7,461 | |
| 27577 | Smithfield. | (919) | 7,540 | 7,288 |
| 28387 | Southern Pines. | (919) | 9,213 | 8,620 |
| ..... | South Gastonia. | | 5,487 | 4,767 |
| 28390 | Spring Lake. | (919) | 7,524 | 6,273 |
| 28677 | Statesville. | (704) | 17,567 | 18,622 |
| 27886 | Tarboro. | (919) | 11,037 | 8,741 |
| 27360 | Thomasville. | (919) | 15,915 | 14,144 |
| 27370 | Trinity(u). | (919) | 5,469 | 6,887 |
| 27587 | Wake Forest. | (919) | 5,832 | 3,780 |
| 27889 | Washington. | (919) | 9,160 | 8,418 |
| 28786 | Waynesville. | (704) | 6,758 | 6,765 |
| 28472 | Whiteville. | (919) | 5,078 | 5,565 |
| 27892 | Williamston. | (919) | 5,503 | 6,159 |
| 28401 | Wilmington. | (919) | 55,530 | 44,000 |
| 27893 | Wilson. | (919) | 36,930 | 34,424 |
| *27102 | Winston-Salem. | (919) | 143,485 | 131,885 |

## North Dakota (701)

| ZIP code | Place | | 1990 | 1980 |
|---|---|---|---|---|
| 58501 | Bismarck | | 49,272 | 44,485 |
| 58301 | Devils Lake | | 7,782 | 7,442 |
| 58601 | Dickinson | | 16,097 | 15,924 |
| 58102 | Fargo | | 74,084 | 61,383 |
| 58201 | Grand Forks | | 49,417 | 43,765 |
| 58201 | Grand Forks AFB(u) | | 9,343 | 9,390 |
| 58401 | Jamestown | | 15,571 | 16,280 |
| 58554 | Mandan | | 15,177 | 15,513 |
| 58701 | Minot | | 34,544 | 32,843 |
| 58701 | Minot AFB(u) | | 9,095 | 9,880 |
| 58072 | Valley City | | 7,163 | 7,774 |
| 58075 | Wahpeton | | 8,751 | 9,064 |
| 58078 | West Fargo | | 12,287 | 10,099 |
| 58801 | Williston | | 13,136 | 13,336 |

## Ohio

| ZIP code | Place | | 1990 | 1980 |
|---|---|---|---|---|
| 45810 | Ada | (419) | 5,428 | 5,669 |
| *44309 | Akron | (216) | 223,019 | 237,177 |
| 44601 | Alliance | (216) | 23,376 | 24,315 |
| 44001 | Amherst | (216) | 10,332 | 10,638 |
| 44805 | Ashland | (419) | 20,079 | 20,326 |
| 44004 | Ashtabula | (216) | 21,633 | 23,449 |
| 45701 | Athens | (614) | 21,265 | 19,743 |
| 44202 | Aurora | (216) | 9,192 | 8,177 |
| 44515 | Austintown(u) | (216) | 32,371 | 33,636 |
| 44011 | Avon | (216) | 7,337 | 7,241 |
| 44012 | Avon Lake | (216) | 15,066 | 13,222 |
| 44203 | Barberton | (216) | 27,623 | 29,751 |
| 44140 | Bay Village | (216) | 17,000 | 17,846 |
| 44122 | Beachwood | (216) | 10,644 | 9,983 |
| 45385 | Beavercreek | (513) | 33,626 | 31,589 |
| 44146 | Bedford | (216) | 14,822 | 15,056 |
| 44146 | Bedford Heights | (216) | 12,131 | 13,214 |
| 43906 | Bellaire | (614) | 6,028 | 8,241 |
| 45305 | Bellbrook | (513) | 6,511 | 5,174 |
| 43311 | Bellefontaine | (513) | 12,126 | 11,888 |
| 44811 | Bellevue | (419) | 8,157 | 8,187 |
| 45714 | Belpre | (614) | 6,796 | 7,193 |
| 44017 | Berea | (216) | 19,051 | 19,567 |
| 43209 | Bexley | (614) | 13,088 | 13,405 |
| 43004 | Blacklick Estates(u) | (614) | 10,080 | 11,223 |
| 45242 | Blue Ash | (513) | 11,923 | 9,510 |
| 44512 | Boardman(u) | (216) | 38,596 | 39,161 |
| 43402 | Bowling Green | (419) | 28,176 | 25,728 |
| 44141 | Brecksville | (216) | 11,818 | 10,132 |
| 45211 | Bridgetown North | (513) | 11,748 | 11,460 |
| 44141 | Broadview Heights | (216) | 12,219 | 10,920 |
| 44144 | Brooklyn | (216) | 11,706 | 12,342 |
| 44142 | Brook Park | (216) | 22,865 | 26,195 |
| 44212 | Brunswick | (216) | 28,218 | 28,104 |
| 43506 | Bryan | (419) | 8,348 | 7,879 |
| 44820 | Bucyrus | (419) | 13,496 | 13,433 |
| 43725 | Cambridge | (614) | 11,748 | 13,573 |
| 44405 | Campbell | (216) | 10,038 | 11,619 |
| 44406 | Canfield | (216) | 5,409 | 5,535 |
| *44711 | Canton | (216) | 84,161 | 93,077 |
| 45822 | Celina | (419) | 9,923 | 9,137 |
| 45459 | Centerville | (513) | 21,082 | 18,886 |
| 45211 | Cheviot | (513) | 9,616 | 9,888 |
| 45601 | Chillicothe | (614) | 21,923 | 23,420 |
| *45234 | Cincinnati | (513) | 364,114 | 385,409 |
| 43113 | Circleville | (614) | 11,666 | 11,700 |
| *44101 | Cleveland | (216) | 505,616 | 573,822 |
| 44118 | Cleveland Heights | (216) | 54,052 | 56,438 |
| 43410 | Clyde | (419) | 5,776 | 5,489 |
| *43235 | Columbus | (614) | 632,945 | 565,021 |
| 44030 | Conneaut | (216) | 13,241 | 13,835 |
| 44410 | Cortland | (216) | 5,652 | 5,011 |
| 43812 | Coshocton | (614) | 12,193 | 13,405 |
| 45238 | Covedale(u) | (513) | 6,669 | 5,830 |
| *44222 | Cuyahoga Falls | (216) | 48,950 | 50,526 |
| *45401 | Dayton | (513) | 182,005 | 193,536 |
| 45236 | Deer Park | (513) | 6,181 | 6,745 |
| 43512 | Defiance | (419) | 16,787 | 16,810 |
| 43015 | Delaware | (614) | 19,966 | 18,780 |
| 45833 | Delphos | (419) | 7,093 | 7,314 |
| 45247 | Dent(u) | | 6,416 | |
| 44622 | Dover | (216) | 11,329 | 11,782 |
| 45427 | Drexel(u) | | 5,143 | |
| | Dry Run(u) | | 5,389 | |
| 43017 | Dublin | (614) | 16,366 | 3,855 |
| 44112 | East Cleveland | (216) | 33,096 | 36,957 |
| 44094 | Eastlake | (216) | 21,161 | 22,104 |
| 43920 | East Liverpool | (216) | 13,654 | 16,687 |
| 44413 | East Palestine | (216) | 5,168 | 5,306 |
| 45320 | Eaton | (513) | 7,396 | 6,839 |
| 44004 | Edgewood(u) | | 5,189 | 3,099 |
| *44035 | Elyria | (216) | 56,746 | 57,538 |
| 45322 | Englewood | (513) | 11,402 | 11,329 |
| 44117 | Euclid | (216) | 54,875 | 59,999 |
| 45324 | Fairborn | (513) | 31,300 | 29,702 |
| 45014 | Fairfield | (513) | 39,709 | 30,777 |
| 44313 | Fairlawn | (216) | 5,779 | 6,100 |

| ZIP code | Place | | 1990 | 1980 |
|---|---|---|---|---|
| 44126 | Fairview Park | (216) | 18,028 | 19,311 |
| 45840 | Findlay | (419) | 35,703 | 35,594 |
| 45224 | Finneytown(u) | | 13,096 | |
| 45405 | Forest Park | (513) | 18,621 | 18,566 |
| 45230 | Forestville(u) | | 9,185 | |
| 45426 | Fort McKinley(u) | (513) | 9,740 | 10,161 |
| 44830 | Fostoria | (419) | 14,971 | 15,743 |
| 45005 | Franklin | (513) | 11,026 | 10,711 |
| 43420 | Fremont | (419) | 17,619 | 17,834 |
| 43230 | Gahanna | (614) | 23,898 | 18,001 |
| 44833 | Galion | (419) | 11,859 | 12,391 |
| 44125 | Garfield Heights | (216) | 31,739 | 34,938 |
| 44041 | Geneva | (216) | 6,597 | 6,655 |
| 44420 | Girard | (216) | 11,304 | 12,517 |
| 43212 | Grandview Heights | (614) | 7,010 | 7,420 |
| 45123 | Greenfield | (513) | 5,172 | 5,150 |
| 45331 | Greenville | (513) | 12,863 | 12,999 |
| 45239 | Groesbeck(u) | (513) | 6,684 | 9,594 |
| 43123 | Grove City | (614) | 19,661 | 16,816 |
| *45012 | Hamilton | (513) | 61,436 | 63,189 |
| 45030 | Harrison | (513) | 7,520 | 5,855 |
| 43055 | Heath | (614) | 7,231 | 6,969 |
| 44124 | Highland Heights | (216) | 6,249 | 5,739 |
| 43026 | Hilliard | (614) | 11,794 | 8,131 |
| 45133 | Hillsboro | (513) | 6,235 | 6,356 |
| 44425 | Howland(u) | (216) | 6,732 | 7,441 |
| 44425 | Hubbard | (216) | 8,248 | 9,245 |
| 45424 | Huber Heights | (513) | 38,696 | 35,480 |
| 45081 | Huber Ridge(u) | (614) | 5,255 | 5,835 |
| 44236 | Hudson | (216) | 5,159 | 4,615 |
| 44131 | Independence | (216) | 6,500 | 6,607 |
| 45638 | Ironton | (614) | 12,751 | 14,290 |
| 45640 | Jackson | (614) | 6,167 | 6,675 |
| 44240 | Kent | (216) | 28,835 | 26,164 |
| 43326 | Kenton | (419) | 8,356 | 8,605 |
| 45236 | Kenwood(u) | (513) | 7,469 | 9,928 |
| 45429 | Kettering | (513) | 60,569 | 61,186 |
| 44094 | Kirtland | (216) | 5,881 | 5,969 |
| 44107 | Lakewood | (216) | 59,718 | 61,963 |
| 43130 | Lancaster | (614) | 34,507 | 34,953 |
| 45039 | Landen(u) | | 9,263 | 2,870 |
| 45036 | Lebanon | (513) | 10,461 | 9,636 |
| *45804 | Lima | (419) | 45,553 | 47,827 |
| 43228 | Lincoln Village(u) | (614) | 9,958 | 10,548 |
| 43138 | Logan | (614) | 6,725 | 6,557 |
| 43140 | London | (614) | 7,807 | 6,958 |
| *44052 | Lorain | (216) | 71,245 | 75,416 |
| 44641 | Louisville | (216) | 8,087 | 7,996 |
| 45140 | Loveland | (513) | 10,122 | 9,106 |
| 44124 | Lyndhurst | (216) | 15,982 | 18,092 |
| 44056 | Macedonia | (216) | 7,509 | 6,571 |
| | Mack South(u) | | 5,767 | |
| 45243 | Madeira | (513) | 9,141 | 9,341 |
| *44901 | Mansfield | (419) | 50,627 | 53,927 |
| 44137 | Maple Heights | (216) | 27,089 | 29,735 |
| 45750 | Marietta | (614) | 15,026 | 16,467 |
| 43302 | Marion | (614) | 34,075 | 37,040 |
| 43935 | Martins Ferry | (614) | 8,003 | 9,331 |
| 43040 | Marysville | (513) | 9,656 | 7,414 |
| 45040 | Mason | (513) | 11,450 | 8,692 |
| 44646 | Massillon | (216) | 30,969 | 30,557 |
| 43537 | Maumee | (419) | 15,561 | 15,747 |
| 44124 | Mayfield Heights | (216) | 19,847 | 21,550 |
| 44256 | Medina | (216) | 19,231 | 15,268 |
| 44060 | Mentor | (216) | 47,491 | 42,065 |
| 44060 | Mentor-on-the-Lake | (216) | 8,271 | 7,919 |
| 45342 | Miamisburg | (513) | 17,834 | 15,304 |
| 44130 | Middleburg Heights | (216) | 14,702 | 16,218 |
| 45042 | Middletown | (513) | 46,022 | 43,719 |
| 45150 | Milford | (513) | 5,660 | 5,679 |
| 45242 | Montgomery | (513) | 9,733 | 10,084 |
| 45439 | Moraine | (513) | 5,989 | 5,325 |
| 45231 | Mount Healthy | (513) | 7,580 | 7,562 |
| 43050 | Mount Vernon | (614) | 14,550 | 14,323 |
| 44262 | Munroe Falls | (216) | 5,359 | 4,731 |
| 43545 | Napoleon | (419) | 8,884 | 8,614 |
| 43055 | Newark | (614) | 44,396 | 41,200 |
| 45344 | New Carlisle | (513) | 6,049 | 6,498 |
| 43764 | New Lexington | (614) | 5,117 | 5,179 |
| 44663 | New Philadelphia | (216) | 15,698 | 16,883 |
| 44446 | Niles | (216) | 21,128 | 23,088 |
| 45239 | Northbrook(u) | (513) | 11,471 | 8,357 |
| 44720 | North Canton | (216) | 14,748 | 14,228 |
| 45239 | North College Hill | (513) | 11,002 | 11,114 |
| | Northgate | | 7,864 | |
| 44057 | North Madison(u) | (216) | 8,699 | 8,741 |
| 44070 | North Olmsted | (216) | 34,204 | 36,486 |
| 45502 | Northridge(u) | (513) | 5,939 | 5,559 |
| 45414 | Northridge(u) (Montgomery) | (513) | 9,448 | 9,720 |
| 44039 | North Ridgeville | (216) | 21,564 | 21,522 |
| 44133 | North Royalton | (216) | 23,197 | 17,671 |
| | Northview(u) | (419) | 10,337 | 9,973 |
| 43619 | Northwood | (419) | 5,506 | 5,495 |
| 44203 | Norton | (216) | 11,477 | 12,242 |
| 44857 | Norwalk | (419) | 14,731 | 14,358 |
| 45212 | Norwood | (513) | 23,674 | 26,342 |
| 45873 | Oakwood | (419) | 8,957 | 9,372 |
| 44074 | Oberlin | (216) | 8,191 | 8,660 |

| ZIP code | Place | | 1990 | 1980 |
|---|---|---|---|---|
| 44138 | Olmsted Falls | (216) | 6,741 | 5,868 |
| 43616 | Oregon | (419) | 18,334 | 18,675 |
| 44667 | Orrville | (216) | 7,712 | 7,511 |
| 45431 | Overlook-Page Manor(u) | (513) | 13,242 | 14,825 |
| 45056 | Oxford | (513) | 18,937 | 17,655 |
| 44077 | Painesville | (216) | 15,769 | 16,391 |
| 44129 | Parma | (216) | 87,876 | 92,548 |
| 44130 | Parma Heights | (216) | 21,448 | 23,112 |
| 44124 | Pepper Pike | (216) | 6,185 | 6,177 |
| 44646 | Perry Heights(u) | (216) | 9,055 | 9,206 |
| 43551 | Perrysburg | (419) | 12,551 | 10,215 |
| 43147 | Pickerington | | 5,668 | 3,917 |
| 45356 | Piqua | (513) | 20,612 | 20,480 |
| 44319 | Portage Lakes(u) | (216) | 13,373 | 11,310 |
| 43452 | Port Clinton | (419) | 7,106 | 7,223 |
| 45662 | Portsmouth | (614) | 22,676 | 25,943 |
| 44266 | Ravenna | (216) | 12,069 | 11,987 |
| 45215 | Reading | (513) | 12,038 | 12,843 |
| 43068 | Reynoldsburg | (614) | 25,748 | 20,661 |
| 44143 | Richmond Heights | (216) | 9,611 | 10,095 |
| 44270 | Rittman | (216) | 6,147 | 6,063 |
| 44116 | Rocky River | (216) | 20,410 | 21,084 |
| 43460 | Rossford | (419) | 5,861 | 5,978 |
| 45217 | Saint Bernard | (513) | 5,344 | 5,396 |
| 43950 | Saint Clairsville | (614) | 5,136 | 5,452 |
| 45885 | Saint Marys | (419) | 8,441 | 8,414 |
| 44460 | Salem | (216) | 12,233 | 12,869 |
| 44870 | Sandusky | (419) | 29,764 | 31,360 |
| 44870 | Sandusky South(u) | (419) | 6,336 | 6,548 |
| 44131 | Seven Hills | (216) | 12,339 | 13,650 |
| 44120 | Shaker Heights | (216) | 30,867 | 32,487 |
| 45241 | Sharonville | (513) | 13,121 | 10,108 |
| 44054 | Sheffield Lake | (216) | 9,825 | 10,484 |
| 44875 | Shelby | (419) | 9,610 | 9,703 |
| 44878 | Shiloh | (419) | 11,607 | 11,735 |
| 45365 | Sidney | (513) | 18,710 | 17,657 |
| 45236 | Silverton | (513) | 5,859 | 6,172 |
| 44139 | Solon | (216) | 18,548 | 14,341 |
| 44121 | South Euclid | (216) | 23,866 | 25,713 |
| 45066 | Springboro | (513) | 6,574 | 4,962 |
| 45246 | Springdale | (513) | 10,621 | 10,111 |
| *45501 | Springfield | (513) | 70,487 | 72,563 |
| 43952 | Steubenville | (614) | 22,125 | 26,400 |
| 44224 | Stow | (216) | 27,998 | 25,303 |
| 44240 | Streetsboro | (216) | 9,932 | 9,055 |
| 44136 | Strongsville | (216) | 35,308 | 28,577 |
| 44471 | Struthers | (216) | 12,284 | 13,624 |
| 43560 | Sylvania | (419) | 17,489 | 15,527 |
| 44278 | Tallmadge | (216) | 14,870 | 15,269 |
| 45243 | The Village of Indian Hill | (513) | 5,383 | 5,521 |
| 44883 | Tiffin | (419) | 18,604 | 19,549 |
| 45371 | Tipp City | (513) | 6,027 | 5,595 |
| *43601 | Toledo | (419) | 332,943 | 354,635 |
| 43964 | Toronto | (614) | 6,127 | 6,934 |
| 45067 | Trenton | (513) | 6,189 | 6,401 |
| 45426 | Trotwood | (513) | 8,816 | 7,802 |
| 45373 | Troy | (513) | 19,478 | 19,086 |
| 44087 | Twinsburg | (216) | 9,606 | 7,632 |
| 44683 | Uhrichsville | (614) | 5,604 | 6,130 |
| 45322 | Union | (513) | 5,531 | 5,219 |
| 44118 | University Heights | (216) | 14,787 | 15,401 |
| 43221 | Upper Arlington | (614) | 34,128 | 35,648 |
| 43351 | Upper Sandusky | (419) | 5,906 | 5,967 |
| 43078 | Urbana | (513) | 11,353 | 10,762 |
| 45377 | Vandalia | (513) | 13,872 | 13,161 |
| 45891 | Van Wert | (419) | 10,922 | 11,035 |
| 44089 | Vermilion | (216) | 11,127 | 11,012 |
| 44281 | Wadsworth | (216) | 15,718 | 15,166 |
| 45895 | Wapakoneta | (419) | 9,214 | 8,402 |
| *44481 | Warren | (216) | 50,793 | 56,629 |
| 44122 | Warrensville Heights | (216) | 15,745 | 16,565 |
| 43160 | Washington C.H. | (614) | 13,080 | 12,682 |
| 43567 | Wauseon | (419) | 6,322 | 6,173 |
| 45692 | Wellston | (614) | 6,049 | 6,016 |
| 45449 | West Carrollton | (513) | 14,403 | 13,148 |
| 43081 | Westerville | (614) | 30,269 | 23,414 |
| 44145 | Westlake | (216) | 27,018 | 19,483 |
| 45694 | Wheelersburg(u) | | 5,113 | 4,796 |
| 43213 | Whitehall | | 20,572 | 21,299 |
| 45239 | White Oak(u) | (614) | 12,430 | 9,563 |
| 44092 | Wickliffe | (216) | 14,558 | 16,790 |
| 44890 | Willard | (419) | 6,210 | 5,720 |
| 44094 | Willoughby | (216) | 20,510 | 19,329 |
| 44094 | Willoughby Hills | (216) | 8,427 | 8,612 |
| 45177 | Wilmington | (216) | 15,269 | 17,834 |
| 45459 | Woodbourne-Hyde Park(u) | (513) | 11,199 | 10,431 |
| 44691 | Wooster | (513) | 7,837 | 8,826 |
| 43085 | Worthington | (216) | 22,427 | 19,289 |
| 45433 | Wright-Patterson AFB(u) | (614) | 14,869 | 14,666 |
| 45215 | Wyoming | (513) | 8,579 | ____ |
| 45385 | Xenia | (513) | 8,128 | 8,282 |
| *44501 | Youngstown | (513) | 24,836 | 24,653 |
| 43701 | Zanesville | (216) | 95,732 | 115,511 |
| | | (614) | 26,778 | 28,655 |

## Oklahoma

| ZIP code | Place | | 1990 | 1980 |
|---|---|---|---|---|
| 74820 | Ada | (405) | 15,820 | 15,902 |
| 73521 | Altus | (405) | 21,910 | 23,101 |
| 73717 | Alva | (405) | 5,495 | 6,416 |
| 73005 | Anadarko | (405) | 6,586 | 6,378 |
| 73401 | Ardmore | (405) | 23,079 | 23,689 |
| 74003 | Bartlesville | (918) | 34,256 | 34,568 |
| 73008 | Bethany | (405) | 20,075 | 22,038 |
| 74008 | Bixby | (918) | 9,502 | 6,969 |
| 74631 | Blackwell | (405) | 7,538 | 8,400 |
| 74012 | Broken Arrow | (918) | 58,043 | 35,761 |
| 73018 | Chickasha | (405) | 14,988 | 15,828 |
| 73020 | Choctaw | (405) | 8,545 | 7,520 |
| 74017 | Claremore | (918) | 13,280 | 12,085 |
| 73601 | Clinton | (405) | 9,298 | 8,796 |
| 74429 | Coweta | (918) | 6,159 | 4,554 |
| 74023 | Cushing | (918) | 7,218 | 7,720 |
| 73115 | Del City | (405) | 23,928 | 28,523 |
| 73533 | Duncan | (405) | 21,732 | 22,517 |
| 74701 | Durant | (405) | 12,831 | 11,972 |
| 73034 | Edmond | (405) | 52,315 | 34,637 |
| 73644 | Elk City | (405) | 10,428 | 9,579 |
| 73036 | El Reno | (405) | 15,414 | 15,486 |
| 73701 | Enid | (405) | 45,309 | 50,363 |
| 73503 | Fort Sill(u) | (405) | 12,107 | 15,924 |
| 73542 | Frederick | (405) | 5,221 | 6,153 |
| 74033 | Glenpool | (918) | 6,688 | 2,706 |
| 73044 | Guthrie | (405) | 10,518 | 10,312 |
| 73942 | Guymon | (405) | 7,803 | 8,492 |
| 74437 | Henryetta | (918) | 5,872 | 6,432 |
| 74743 | Hugo | (405) | 5,978 | 7,172 |
| 74745 | Idabel | (405) | 6,957 | 7,622 |
| 74037 | Jenks | (918) | 7,493 | 5,876 |
| 73501 | Lawton | (405) | 80,561 | 80,054 |
| 74501 | McAlester | (918) | 16,370 | 17,255 |
| 74354 | Miami | (918) | 13,142 | 14,237 |
| 73110 | Midwest City | (405) | 52,267 | 49,559 |
| 73060 | Moore | (405) | 40,318 | 35,063 |
| 74401 | Muskogee | (918) | 37,708 | 40,011 |
| 73064 | Mustang | (405) | 10,434 | 7,496 |
| 73069 | Norman | (405) | 80,071 | 68,020 |
| *73125 | Oklahoma City | (405) | 444,719 | 404,014 |
| 74447 | Okmulgee | (918) | 13,441 | 16,263 |
| 74055 | Owasso | (918) | 11,151 | 6,149 |
| 73075 | Pauls Valley | (405) | 6,150 | 5,664 |
| 74601 | Ponca City | (405) | 26,359 | 26,238 |
| 74953 | Poteau | (918) | 7,210 | 7,089 |
| 74361 | Pryor Creek | (918) | 8,327 | 8,483 |
| 74955 | Sallisaw | (918) | 7,122 | 6,403 |
| 74063 | Sand Springs | (918) | 15,346 | 13,121 |
| 74066 | Sapulpa | (918) | 18,074 | 15,853 |
| 74868 | Seminole | (405) | 7,071 | 8,590 |
| 74801 | Shawnee | (405) | 26,017 | 26,506 |
| 74074 | Stillwater | (405) | 36,676 | 38,268 |
| 74873 | Tahlequah | (918) | 10,398 | 9,708 |
| 73120 | Tecumseh | (405) | 5,570 | 5,123 |
| *74101 | The Village | (405) | 10,353 | 11,114 |
| 74301 | Tulsa | (918) | 367,302 | 360,919 |
| 74467 | Vinita | (918) | 5,804 | 6,740 |
| 73132 | Wagoner | (918) | 6,894 | 6,191 |
| 73096 | Warr Acres | (405) | 9,288 | 9,940 |
| 73801 | Weatherford | (405) | 10,124 | 9,640 |
| 73099 | Woodward | (405) | 12,340 | 13,781 |
| | Yukon | (405) | 20,935 | 17,112 |

## Oregon (503)

| ZIP code | Place | | 1990 | 1980 |
|---|---|---|---|---|
| 97321 | Albany | | 29,540 | 26,511 |
| 97005 | Aloha(u) | | 34,284 | 28,353 |
| 97601 | Altamont(u) | | 18,591 | 19,805 |
| 97520 | Ashland | | 16,252 | 14,943 |
| 97103 | Astoria | | 10,069 | 9,998 |
| 97814 | Baker | | 9,140 | 9,471 |
| 97005 | Beaverton | | 53,307 | 31,962 |
| 97701 | Bend | | 20,447 | 17,263 |
| 97013 | Canby | | 8,990 | 7,659 |
| 97225 | Cedar Hills(u) | | 9,294 | 9,619 |
| 97291 | Cedar Mill(u) | | 9,697 | 22,118 |
| 97502 | Central Point | | 7,512 | 6,357 |
| 97058 | City of The Dalles | | 11,021 | 10,820 |
| 97420 | Coos Bay | | 15,076 | 14,424 |
| 97113 | Cornelius | | 6,148 | 4,462 |
| 97330 | Corvallis | | 44,757 | 40,960 |
| 97424 | Cottage Grove | | 7,403 | 7,148 |
| 97338 | Dallas | | 9,422 | 8,530 |
| *97401 | Eugene | | 112,773 | 105,664 |
| 97439 | Florence | | 5,171 | 4,411 |
| 97116 | Forest Grove | | 13,559 | 11,499 |
| 97301 | Four Corners(u) | | 12,156 | 11,331 |
| 97223 | Garden Home-Whitford(u) | | 6,652 | 6,926 |
| 97027 | Gladstone | | 10,152 | 9,500 |
| 97526 | Grants Pass | | 17,503 | 15,032 |
| 97030 | Gresham | | 68,249 | 33,005 |
| 97303 | Hayesville(u) | | 14,318 | 9,213 |
| 97230 | Hazelwood(u) | | 11,480 | 25,541 |
| 97838 | Hermiston | | 10,047 | 9,408 |
| 97123 | Hillsboro | | 37,598 | 27,664 |

| ZIP code | Place | 1990 | 1980 |
|---|---|---|---|
|  | Jennings Lodge(u) | 6,530 |  |
| 97303 | Keizer | 21,884 | 19,785 |
| 97601 | Klamath Falls | 17,737 | 16,661 |
| 97850 | La Grande | 11,766 | 11,354 |
| 97034 | Lake Oswego | 30,576 | 22,527 |
| 97355 | Lebanon | 10,950 | 10,413 |
| 97367 | Lincoln City | 5,908 | 5,469 |
| 97128 | McMinnville | 17,894 | 14,080 |
| 97501 | Medford | 47,021 | 39,746 |
| 97862 | Milton-Freewater | 5,533 | 5,086 |
| 97222 | Milwaukie | 18,670 | 17,931 |
| 97361 | Monmouth | 6,288 | 5,594 |
| 97132 | Newberg | 13,086 | 10,394 |
| 97365 | Newport | 8,437 | 7,519 |
| 97459 | North Bend | 9,614 | 9,779 |
|  | North Springfield(u) | 5,451 | 6,140 |
| 97268 | Oak Grove(u) | 12,576 | 11,640 |
|  | Oak Hills | 6,450 |  |
|  | Oatfield | 15,348 |  |
| 97914 | Ontario | 9,394 | 8,814 |
| 97045 | Oregon City | 14,698 | 14,673 |
| 97801 | Pendleton | 15,142 | 14,521 |
| *97208 | Portland | 438,802 | 368,148 |
| 97236 | Powellhurst(u) | 28,756 | 20,132 |
| 97754 | Prineville | 5,355 | 5,276 |
| 97225 | Raleigh Hills(u) | 6,066 | 6,517 |
| 97756 | Redmond | 7,165 | 6,452 |
| 97404 | River Road(u) | 9,443 | 10,370 |
|  | Rockcreek | 8,282 |  |
| 97470 | Roseburg | 17,069 | 16,644 |
| 97470 | Roseburg North(u) | 6,831 |  |
| 97051 | Saint Helens | 7,535 | 7,064 |
| *97301 | Salem | 107,793 | 89,091 |
| 97401 | Santa Clara(u) | 12,834 | 14,288 |
| 97138 | Seaside | 5,359 | 5,193 |
| 97381 | Silverton | 5,635 | 5,168 |
| 97477 | Springfield | 44,664 | 41,621 |
| 97383 | Stayton | 5,011 | 4,396 |
| 97479 | Sutherlin | 5,020 | 4,560 |
| 97396 | Sweet Home | 6,850 | 6,921 |
| 97223 | Tigard | 29,435 | 14,799 |
| 97060 | Troutdale | 7,852 | 5,908 |
| 97062 | Tualatin | 14,664 | 7,483 |
|  | West Haven-Sylvan | 6,009 |  |
| 97068 | West Linn | 16,389 | 11,358 |
| 97225 | West Slope(u) | 7,959 | 5,364 |
| 97501 | White City(u) | 5,891 | 5,445 |
| 97070 | Wilsonville | 7,106 | 2,920 |
| 97071 | Woodburn | 13,404 | 11,196 |

## Pennsylvania

*The 610 area code takes effect January 8, 1994. Until then, the area code for places that will use 610 is 215. Communities with area codes marked with a dagger (†) will be split between area codes 215 and 610; consult local operators.*

| ZIP code | Place | Area code | 1990 | 1980 |
|---|---|---|---|---|
| 15001 | Aliquippa | (412) | 13,374 | 17,094 |
| *18101 | Allentown | (610) | 105,301 | 103,758 |
| *16603 | Altoona | (814) | 51,881 | 57,078 |
| 19002 | Ambler | (215)† | 6,609 | 6,628 |
| 15003 | Ambridge | (412) | 8,133 | 9,575 |
| 18403 | Archbald | (717) | 6,291 | 6,295 |
| 19003 | Ardmore(u) | (610) | 12,646 |  |
| 15068 | Arnold | (412) | 6,113 | 6,853 |
| 19407 | Audubon(u) |  |  |  |
| 15202 | Avalon | (412) | 5,784 | 6,240 |
| 15005 | Baden | (412) | 5,074 | 5,318 |
| 15234 | Baldwin | (412) | 21,923 | 24,714 |
| 18013 | Bangor | (610) | 5,383 | 5,006 |
| 15009 | Beaver | (412) | 5,028 | 5,441 |
| 15010 | Beaver Falls | (814) | 10,687 | 12,525 |
| 16823 | Bellefonte | (814) | 6,358 | 6,300 |
| 15202 | Bellevue | (412) | 9,126 | 10,128 |
| 18603 | Berwick | (717) | 10,976 | 11,850 |
| 15102 | Bethel Park | (412) | 33,823 | 34,755 |
| *18016 | Bethlehem | (610) | 71,427 | 70,419 |
| 18447 | Blakely | (717) | 7,222 | 7,438 |
| 17815 | Bloomsburg | (717) | 12,439 | 11,717 |
| 19422 | Blue Bell(u) |  | 6,091 |  |
| 19061 | Boothwyn(u) |  | 5,069 |  |
| 16701 | Bradford | (814) | 9,625 | 11,211 |
| 15227 | Brentwood | (412) | 10,823 | 11,859 |
| 15017 | Bridgeville | (412) | 5,445 | 6,154 |
| 15007 | Bristol | (215) | 10,405 | 10,867 |
| 19015 | Brookhaven | (610) | 8,567 | 7,912 |
| 15008 | Broomall(u) | (610) | 10,930 |  |
| 16001 | Butler | (412) | 15,714 | 17,026 |
| 15419 | California | (412) | 5,748 | 5,703 |
| 17011 | Camp Hill | (717) | 7,831 | 8,422 |
| 15317 | Canonsburg | (412) | 9,200 | 10,459 |
| 18407 | Carbondale | (717) | 10,664 | 11,255 |
| 17013 | Carlisle | (717) | 18,419 | 18,314 |
| 15106 | Carnegie | (412) | 9,278 | 10,099 |
| 15108 | Carnot-Moon(u) | (412) | 10,187 | 11,102 |
| 15234 | Castle Shannon | (412) | 9,135 | 10,164 |
| 18032 | Catasauqua | (610) | 6,662 | 6,711 |

| ZIP code | Place | Area code | 1990 | 1980 |
|---|---|---|---|---|
| 17201 | Chambersburg | (717) | 16,647 | 16,174 |
| 15022 | Charleroi | (412) | 5,014 | 5,717 |
| *19013 | Chester | (610) | 41,856 | 45,794 |
| 19013 | Chester Twp(u) | (610) | 5,399 | 5,687 |
| 15025 | Clairton | (412) | 9,656 | 12,188 |
| 16214 | Clarion | (814) | 6,457 | 6,198 |
| 18411 | Clarks Summit | (717) | 5,433 | 5,272 |
| 16830 | Clearfield | (814) | 6,633 | 7,580 |
| 19018 | Clifton Heights | (610) | 7,111 | 7,320 |
| 19320 | Coatesville | (610) | 11,038 | 10,698 |
| 19023 | Collingdale | (610) | 9,175 | 9,539 |
|  | Colonial Park(u) |  | 13,777 |  |
| 17512 | Columbia | (717) | 10,701 | 10,466 |
| 15425 | Connellsville | (412) | 9,229 | 10,319 |
| 19428 | Conshohocken | (215)† | 8,064 | 8,591 |
| 15108 | Coraopolis | (412) | 6,747 | 7,308 |
| 16407 | Corry | (814) | 7,216 | 7,149 |
| 15205 | Crafton | (412) | 7,188 | 7,623 |
| 19020 | Croydon(u) | (215) | 9,967 |  |
| 17821 | Danville | (717) | 5,165 | 5,239 |
| 19023 | Darby | (610) | 11,140 | 11,513 |
| 19036 | Darby Twp(u) | (610) | 10,955 | 12,264 |
| 19333 | Devon-Berwyn(u) | (717) | 5,019 | 5,246 |
| 18519 | Dickson City | (610) | 6,276 | 6,699 |
| 15033 | Donora | (412) | 5,928 | 7,524 |
| 15216 | Dormont | (412) | 9,772 | 11,275 |
| 19335 | Downingtown | (610) | 7,749 | 7,650 |
| 18901 | Doylestown | (215) | 8,575 | 8,717 |
| 19026 | Drexel Hill(u) | (610) | 29,744 |  |
| 15801 | Du Bois | (814) | 8,286 | 9,290 |
| 18512 | Dunmore | (717) | 15,403 | 16,781 |
| 15110 | Duquesne | (412) | 8,525 | 10,094 |
| 19401 | East Norriton(u) | (215)† | 13,324 | 12,711 |
| 18042 | Easton | (610) | 26,276 | 26,027 |
| 18301 | East Stroudsburg | (717) | 8,781 | 8,039 |
| 17405 | East York(u) | (717) | 8,487 |  |
| 15005 | Economy | (412) | 9,305 | 9,538 |
| 16412 | Edinboro | (814) | 7,736 | 6,324 |
| 18704 | Edwardsville | (717) | 5,399 | 5,729 |
| 17022 | Elizabethtown | (717) | 9,952 | 8,233 |
| 16117 | Ellwood City | (412) | 8,894 | 9,998 |
| 18049 | Emmaus | (610) | 11,157 | 11,001 |
| 17025 | Enola(u) | (717) | 5,961 |  |
| 17522 | Ephrata | (717) | 12,133 | 11,095 |
| *16501 | Erie | (814) | 108,718 | 119,123 |
| 18643 | Exeter | (717) | 5,691 | 5,493 |
| 19030 | Fairless Hills(u) | (215) | 9,026 |  |
| 16121 | Farrell | (412) | 6,835 | 8,645 |
| 19047 | Feasterville-Trevose(u) | (215) | 6,696 |  |
|  | Fernway(u) |  | 9,072 | 3,843 |
| 19032 | Folcroft | (610) | 7,506 | 8,231 |
| 15221 | Forest Hills | (412) | 8,173 | 8,198 |
| 18704 | Forty Fort | (717) | 5,049 | 5,590 |
| 15238 | Fox Chapel | (412) | 5,319 | 5,049 |
| 16323 | Franklin | (814) | 7,329 | 8,146 |
| 15143 | Franklin Park | (412) | 10,109 | 6,135 |
| 18052 | Fullerton(u) | (610) | 13,127 | 8,055 |
| 17325 | Gettysburg | (717) | 7,025 | 7,194 |
| 15045 | Glassport | (412) | 5,582 | 6,242 |
| 15036 | Glenolden | (610) | 7,260 | 7,633 |
|  | Glenside(u) | (215) | 8,704 |  |
| 15601 | Greensburg | (412) | 16,318 | 17,558 |
| 16125 | Greenville | (412) | 6,734 | 7,730 |
| 16127 | Grove City | (412) | 8,240 | 8,162 |
|  | Hampton Township(u) |  | 15,568 |  |
| 17331 | Hanover | (717) | 14,399 | 14,890 |
| 19438 | Harleysville(u) | (215)† | 7,405 | 3,673 |
| *17105 | Harrisburg | (717) | 52,376 | 53,264 |
| 15636 | Harrison Township(u) |  | 11,763 |  |
| 19040 | Hatboro | (215) | 7,382 | 7,579 |
| 18201 | Hazleton | (717) | 24,730 | 27,318 |
| 18055 | Hellertown | (610) | 5,662 | 6,025 |
| 16148 | Hermitage | (412) | 15,260 | 16,365 |
| 17033 | Hershey(u) | (717) | 11,860 | 13,249 |
| 16648 | Hollidaysburg | (814) | 5,624 | 5,892 |
| 16001 | Homeacre-Lyndora(u) | (412) | 7,511 | 8,333 |
| 19044 | Horsham(u) | (215) | 15,051 | 9,900 |
| 16652 | Huntingdon | (814) | 6,843 | 7,042 |
| 15701 | Indiana | (412) | 15,174 | 16,051 |
| 15644 | Jeannette | (412) | 11,221 | 13,106 |
| 15344 | Jefferson | (412) | 9,533 | 8,643 |
| 18229 | Jim Thorpe | (717) | 5,048 | 5,263 |
| *15901 | Johnstown | (814) | 28,134 | 35,496 |
| 15108 | Kennedy Twp(u) | (412) | 7,152 | 7,159 |
| 19348 | Kennett Square | (610) | 5,218 | 4,715 |
| 19406 | King of Prussia(u) | (215)† | 18,406 |  |
| 18704 | Kingston | (717) | 14,507 | 15,681 |
| 16201 | Kittanning | (412) | 5,120 | 5,432 |
| 19443 | Kulpsville(u) | (215) | 5,183 |  |
| *17604 | Lancaster | (717) | 55,551 | 54,725 |
| 19446 | Lansdale | (215) | 16,362 | 16,526 |
| 19050 | Lansdowne | (610) | 11,712 | 11,891 |
| 15650 | Latrobe | (412) | 9,265 | 10,799 |
| 17540 | Leacock-Leola-Bareville(u) | (717) | 5,685 |  |
| 17042 | Lebanon | (717) | 24,800 | 25,711 |
| 18235 | Lehighton | (610) | 5,914 | 5,826 |
| 19053 | Levittown(u) | (215) | 55,362 |  |
| 17837 | Lewisburg | (717) | 5,785 | 5,407 |
| 17044 | Lewistown | (717) | 9,341 | 9,830 |

| ZIP code | Place | | 1990 | 1980 |
|---|---|---|---|---|
| 17112 | Linglestown(u) | | 5,862 | .... |
| 19353 | Lionville-Marchwood(u) | (610) | 6,468 | .... |
| 17543 | Lititz | (717) | 8,280 | 7,590 |
| 17745 | Lock Haven | (717) | 9,230 | 9,617 |
| .... | Lower Allen(u) | | 6,329 | .... |
| 15068 | Lower Burrell | (412) | 12,251 | 13,200 |
| 15237 | McCandless Twp(u) | (412) | 28,781 | 26,250 |
| *15134 | McKeesport | (412) | 26,016 | 31,012 |
| 15136 | McKees Rocks | (412) | 7,691 | 8,742 |
| 17948 | Mahanoy City | (717) | 5,209 | 6,167 |
| 17545 | Manheim | (717) | 5,011 | 5,015 |
| 19002 | Maple Glen(u) | | 5,881 | .... |
| 16335 | Meadville | (814) | 14,318 | 15,544 |
| 17055 | Mechanicsburg | (717) | 9,452 | 9,487 |
| *19063 | Media | (610) | 5,957 | 6,119 |
| 17057 | Middletown (Dauphin) | (717) | 9,254 | 10,122 |
| 18017 | Middletown (Northampton)(u) | (610) | 6,866 | 5,801 |
| 17551 | Millersville | (717) | 8,099 | 7,668 |
| 17847 | Milton | (717) | 6,746 | 6,730 |
| 15061 | Monaca | (412) | 6,739 | 7,661 |
| 15062 | Monessen | (412) | 9,901 | 11,928 |
| 18936 | Montgomeryville(u) | (215) | 9,114 | .... |
| 18507 | Moosic | (717) | 5,397 | 6,068 |
| 19067 | Morrisville | (215) | 9,765 | 9,845 |
| 17851 | Mount Carmel | (717) | 7,196 | 8,190 |
| 17552 | Mount Joy | (717) | 6,398 | 5,680 |
| 15228 | Mount Lebanon(u) | (412) | 33,362 | 34,414 |
| 15120 | Munhall | (412) | 13,158 | 14,535 |
| 15146 | Municipality of Monroeville | (412) | 29,169 | 30,977 |
| 15668 | Municipality of Murrysville | (412) | 17,240 | 16,036 |
| 18634 | Nanticoke | (717) | 12,267 | 13,044 |
| 18064 | Nazareth | (610) | 5,713 | 5,443 |
| .... | Nether Providence Twp(u) | (610) | 13,229 | 12,730 |
| 15066 | New Brighton | (412) | 6,854 | 7,364 |
| *16101 | New Castle | (412) | 28,334 | 33,621 |
| 17070 | New Cumberland | (717) | 7,665 | 8,051 |
| 15068 | New Kensington | (412) | 15,894 | 17,660 |
| *19401 | Norristown | (610) | 30,754 | 34,684 |
| 18067 | Northampton | (610) | 8,717 | 8,240 |
| 15104 | North Braddock | (412) | 7,036 | 8,711 |
| 15137 | North Versailles(u) | (412) | 12,302 | 13,294 |
| 16421 | Northwest Harborcreek(u) | (814) | 6,662 | 7,485 |
| 19074 | Norwood | (610) | 6,162 | 6,647 |
| 15139 | Oakmont | (412) | 6,961 | 7,039 |
| .... | O'Hara(u) | | 9,096 | .... |
| 16301 | Oil City | (814) | 11,949 | 13,881 |
| 18518 | Old Forge | (717) | 8,834 | 9,304 |
| 18447 | Olyphant | (717) | 5,222 | 5,204 |
| 19075 | Oreland(u) | | 5,695 | .... |
| 18071 | Palmerton | (610) | 5,394 | 5,455 |
| 17078 | Palmyra | (717) | 6,910 | 7,228 |
| 19301 | Paoli(u) | (610) | 5,603 | 5,277 |
| .... | Park Forest Village(u) | | 6,703 | .... |
| 17331 | Parkville(u) | (717) | 6,014 | 5,009 |
| 15235 | Penn Hills(u) | (717) | 51,430 | 57,632 |
| .... | Penn Wynne(u) | | 5,807 | .... |
| 18944 | Perkasie | (215) | 7,787 | 5,241 |
| *19104 | Philadelphia | (215) | 1,585,577 | 1,688,210 |
| 19460 | Phoenixville | (610) | 15,066 | 14,165 |
| *15219 | Pittsburgh | (412) | 369,879 | 423,959 |
| *18640 | Pittston | (717) | 9,389 | 9,9303 |
| 15236 | Pleasant Hills | (412) | 8,884 | 9,604 |
| 15239 | Plum | (412) | 25,609 | 25,309 |
| 18651 | Plymouth | (717) | 7,134 | 7,605 |
| 19462 | Plymouth Meeting(u) | (215)† | 6,241 | .... |
| 19464 | Pottstown | (610) | 21,831 | 22,729 |
| 17901 | Pottsville | (717) | 16,603 | 18,195 |
| .... | Progress(u) | | 9,654 | .... |
| 19076 | Prospect Park | (610) | 6,764, | 6,593 |
| 15767 | Punxsutawney | (814) | 6,782 | 7,479 |
| 18951 | Quakertown | (215) | 8,982 | 8,867 |
| 19087 | Radnor Twp(u) | (610) | 28,705 | 27,676 |
| *19603 | Reading | (610) | 78,380 | 78,686 |
| 17356 | Red Lion | (717) | 6,130 | 5,824 |
| 18954 | Richboro(u) | (215) | 5,332 | 5,141 |
| 19078 | Ridley Park | (610) | 7,592 | 7,889 |
| 15949 | Robinson(u) | | 10,830 | .... |
| 15237 | Ross Twp(u) | (412) | 33,482 | 35,102 |
| 15857 | Saint Marys | (814) | 5,511 | 6,417 |
| 19464 | Sanatoga(u) | | 5,534 | 3,723 |
| 18840 | Sayre | (717) | 5,791 | 6,951 |
| 17972 | Schuylkill Haven | (717) | 5,610 | 5,977 |
| 15683 | Scottdale | (412) | 5,184 | 5,833 |
| 15106 | Scott Twp(u) | (412) | 17,118 | 20,413 |
| *18503 | Scranton | (717) | 81,805 | 88,117 |
| 17870 | Selinsgrove | (717) | 5,384 | 5,227 |
| 15116 | Shaler Twp(u) | (412) | 30,533 | 33,694 |
| 17872 | Shamokin | (717) | 9,184 | 10,357 |
| 16146 | Sharon | (412) | 17,533 | 19,057 |
| 19079 | Sharon Hill | (610) | 5,771 | 6,221 |
| 17976 | Shenandoah | (717) | 6,221 | 7,589 |
| 19607 | Shillington | (610) | 5,062 | 5,601 |
| 17404 | Shiloh(u) | (717) | 8,245 | 5,315 |
| 17257 | Shippensburg | (717) | 5,331 | 5,261 |
| 15501 | Somerset | (814) | 6,454 | 6,474 |
| 18964 | Souderton | (215) | 5,957 | 6,657 |
| .... | South Park(u) | | 14,292 | .... |
| 17701 | South Williamsport | (717) | 6,496 | 6,581 |

| ZIP code | Place | | 1990 | 1980 |
|---|---|---|---|---|
| 19064 | Springfield(u) | (717) | 24,160 | 25,326 |
| 16801 | State College | (814) | 38,981 | 36,130 |
| 17113 | Steelton | (717) | 5,152 | 6,484 |
| 15136 | Stowe Twp(u) | (412) | 7,681 | 9,202 |
| 18360 | Stroudsburg | (717) | 5,312 | 5,148 |
| 16323 | Sugar Creek | (717) | 5,532 | 5,954 |
| 17801 | Sunbury | (717) | 11,591 | 12,292 |
| 19081 | Swarthmore | (610) | 6,157 | 5,950 |
| 15218 | Swissvale | (412) | 10,637 | 11,345 |
| 18704 | Swoyersville | (717) | 5,630 | 5,795 |
| 18252 | Tamaqua | (717) | 7,943 | 8,843 |
| 15084 | Tarentum | (412) | 5,674 | 6,419 |
| 18517 | Taylor | (717) | 6,941 | 7,246 |
| 16354 | Titusville | (814) | 6,434 | 6,884 |
| 19401 | Trooper(u) | (610) | 5,137 | 7,370 |
| 15145 | Turtle Creek | (412) | 6,556 | 6,959 |
| 16686 | Tyrone | (814) | 5,743 | 6,346 |
| 17401 | Uniontown | (412) | 12,034 | 14,510 |
| 19063 | Upper Providence Twp(u) | (610) | 9,727 | 9,477 |
| 15241 | Upper Saint Clair(u) | (412) | 19,692 | 19,023 |
| 15690 | Vandergrift | (412) | 5,904 | 6,823 |
| .... | Village Green-Green Ridge(u) | | 9,026 | .... |
| 16365 | Warren | (814) | 11,122 | 12,146 |
| 15301 | Washington | (412) | 15,864 | 18,363 |
| 17268 | Waynesboro | (717) | 9,578 | 9,726 |
| .... | Weigelstown(u) | (717) | 8,665 | 5,213 |
| *19380 | West Chester | (610) | 18,041 | 17,435 |
| 19380 | West Goshen(u) | (610) | 8,948 | 7,998 |
| 15122 | West Mifflin | (412) | 23,644 | 26,322 |
| 15905 | Westmont | (814) | 5,789 | 6,113 |
| 19401 | West Norriton(u) | (610) | 15,209 | 14,034 |
| 18643 | West Pittston | (717) | 5,590 | 5,980 |
| 15229 | West View | (412) | 7,734 | 7,648 |
| 18052 | Whitehall | (610) | 14,451 | 15,143 |
| 15131 | White Oak | (717) | 8,761 | 9,480 |
| *18701 | Wilkes-Barre | (717) | 47,523 | 51,551 |
| 15221 | Wilkinsburg | (412) | 21,080 | 23,669 |
| 15145 | Wilkins Twp(u) | (412) | 7,487 | 8,472 |
| 17701 | Williamsport | (717) | 31,933 | 33,401 |
| 19090 | Willow Grove(u) | (610) | 16,325 | .... |
| 17584 | Willow Street(u) | | 5,817 | .... |
| 15025 | Wilson | (412) | 7,830 | 7,564 |
| 19094 | Woodlyn(u) | (610) | 10,151 | .... |
| 19118 | Wyndmoor(u) | (215) | 5,682 | .... |
| 19610 | Wyomissing | (610) | 7,332 | 6,551 |
| 19050 | Yeadon | (610) | 11,980 | 11,727 |
| *17405 | York | (717) | 42,192 | 44,619 |

## Rhode Island (401)

*See Note on Page 373*

| ZIP code | Place | 1990 | 1980 |
|---|---|---|---|
| 02806 | Barrington(u) | 15,849 | 16,174 |
| 02809 | Bristol(u) | 21,625 | 20,128 |
| 02830 | Burrillville | 16,230 | 13,164 |
| 02863 | Central Falls | 17,637 | 16,995 |
| 02813 | Charlestown | 6,478 | .... |
| 02816 | Coventry | 31,083 | 27,065 |
| 02910 | Cranston | 76,060 | 71,992 |
| 02864 | Cumberland | 29,038 | 27,069 |
| 02864 | Cumberland Hill(u) | 6,379 | 5,421 |
| 02818 | East Greenwich | 11,865 | 10,211 |
| 02914 | East Providence | 50,380 | 50,980 |
| 02822 | Exeter | 5,461 | .... |
| 02814 | Glocester | 9,227 | 7,550 |
| 02828 | Greenville(u) | 8,303 | 7,576 |
| 02833 | Hopkinton | 6,873 | 6,406 |
| 02919 | Johnston | 26,542 | 24,907 |
| 02881 | Kingston(u) | 6,504 | 5,479 |
| 02865 | Lincoln | 18,045 | 16,949 |
| 02840 | Middletown | 19,460 | 17,216 |
| 02882 | Narragansett | 14,985 | 12,088 |
| 02840 | Newport | 28,227 | 29,259 |
| 02843 | Newport East(u) | 11,080 | 11,030 |
| 02852 | North Kingstown | 23,786 | 21,938 |
| 02908 | North Providence(u) | 32,090 | 29,188 |
| 02876 | North Smithfield | 10,497 | 9,972 |
| 02859 | Pascoag(u) | 5,011 | 3,807 |
| *02860 | Pawtucket | 72,644 | 71,204 |
| 02871 | Portsmouth | 16,857 | 14,257 |
| *02904 | Providence | 160,728 | 156,804 |
| .... | Richmond | 5,351 | .... |
| 02857 | Scituate | 9,796 | 8,405 |
| 02917 | Smithfield | 19,163 | 16,886 |
| 02879 | South Kingstown | 24,631 | 20,414 |
| 02878 | Tiverton(u) | 14,312 | 13,526 |
| 02864 | Valley Falls(u) | 11,175 | 10,892 |
| *02880 | Wakefield-Peacedale(u) | 7,134 | 6,474 |
| 02885 | Warren | 11,385 | 10,640 |
| *02887 | Warwick | 85,427 | 87,123 |
| 02891 | Westerly | 21,605 | 18,580 |
| 02891 | Westerly Center(u) | 16,477 | 14,093 |
| 02893 | West Warwick(u) | 29,268 | 27,026 |
| 02895 | Woonsocket | 43,877 | 45,914 |

## South Carolina (803)

| ZIP code | Place | 1990 | 1980 |
|---|---|---|---|
| 29620 | Abbeville | 5,778 | 5,833 |
| 29801 | Aiken | 20,386 | 14,978 |
| 29621 | Anderson | 26,385 | 27,546 |
| 29812 | Barnwell | 5,255 | 5,572 |
| 29902 | Beaufort | 9,576 | 8,634 |
| 29841 | Belvedere(u) | 6,133 | 6,859 |
| 29512 | Bennettsville | 10,095 | 8,774 |
| 29611 | Berea(u) | 13,535 | 13,164 |
| .... | Brookdale(u) | 5,339 | 6,123 |
| 29902 | Burton(u) | 6,917 | 3,619 |
| 29020 | Camden | 6,696 | 7,462 |
| 29033 | Cayce | 10,807 | 11,701 |
| *29401 | Charleston | 80,467 | 69,779 |
| 29520 | Cheraw | 5,553 | 5,654 |
| 29706 | Chester | 7,158 | 6,820 |
| 29631 | Clemson | 11,145 | 8,118 |
| 29325 | Clinton | 9,603 | 8,596 |
| *29201 | Columbia | 103,477 | 101,229 |
| 29526 | Conway | 9,819 | 10,240 |
| 29532 | Darlington | 7,310 | 7,989 |
| 29204 | Dentsville(u) | 11,839 | 13,579 |
| 29536 | Dillon | 6,829 | 7,060 |
| 29640 | Easley | 15,179 | 14,264 |
| 29501 | Florence | 29,913 | 29,842 |
| 29206 | Forest Acres | 7,181 | 6,062 |
| 29340 | Gaffney | 13,149 | 13,453 |
| 29605 | Gantt(u) | 13,891 | 13,719 |
| .... | Garden City(u) | 6,305 | .... |
| 29440 | Georgetown | 9,517 | 10,144 |
| 29445 | Goose Creek | 24,692 | 17,811 |
| *29602 | Greenville | 58,256 | 58,242 |
| 29646 | Greenwood | 20,807 | 21,613 |
| 29651 | Greer | 10,322 | 10,525 |
| 29410 | Hanahan | 13,176 | 13,224 |
| 29550 | Hartsville | 8,372 | 7,631 |
| 29928 | Hilton Head Island | 23,694 | 11,239 |
| 29621 | Homeland Park(u) | 6,569 | 6,720 |
| 29063 | Irmo | 11,277 | 3,957 |
| 29456 | Ladson(u) | 13,540 | 13,246 |
| 29560 | Lake City | 7,153 | 6,731 |
| 29720 | Lancaster | 8,914 | 9,703 |
| 29360 | Laurens | 9,694 | 10,587 |
| 29571 | Marion | 7,658 | 7,700 |
| 29662 | Mauldin | 11,662 | 8,143 |
| 29430 | Moncks Corner | 5,599 | 4,179 |
| 29464 | Mount Pleasant | 30,108 | 14,464 |
| 29574 | Mullins | 5,910 | 6,068 |
| 29577 | Myrtle Beach | 24,848 | 18,446 |
| 29108 | Newberry | 10,543 | 9,866 |
| 29841 | North Augusta | 15,684 | 13,593 |
| 29406 | North Charleston | 70,218 | 62,479 |
| 29582 | North Myrtle Beach | 8,731 | 3,960 |
| 29565 | Oak Grove(u) | 7,173 | 7,092 |
| 29115 | Orangeburg | 13,772 | 14,933 |
| .... | Parker(u) | 11,072 | .... |
| 29905 | Parris Island(u) | 7,172 | 7,752 |
| .... | Red Bank(u) | 5,950 | .... |
| .... | Red Hill(u) | 6,112 | .... |
| 29730 | Rock Hill | 41,610 | 35,327 |
| 29210 | Saint Andrews(u) | 25,692 | 20,245 |
| 29609 | Sans Souci(u) | 7,612 | 8,393 |
| 29678 | Seneca | 7,726 | 7,436 |
| .... | Seven Oaks(u) | 15,722 | 16,604 |
| 29681 | Simpsonville | 11,744 | 9,037 |
| 29577 | Socastee(u) | 10,426 | 1,082 |
| *29301 | Spartanburg | 43,479 | 43,826 |
| 29483 | Summerville | 22,519 | 6,492 |
| 29150 | Sumter | 42,299 | 24,921 |
| 29687 | Taylors(u) | 19,619 | 15,801 |
| 29379 | Union | 9,840 | 10,523 |
| 29607 | Wade Hampton(u) | 20,014 | 20,180 |
| 29488 | Walterboro | 5,595 | 6,209 |
| 29611 | Welcome(u) | 6,560 | 6,922 |
| 29169 | West Columbia | 10,944 | 10,409 |
| 29206 | Woodfield(u) | 8,862 | 9,588 |
| 29745 | York | 6,709 | 6,412 |

## South Dakota (605)

| ZIP code | Place | 1990 | 1980 |
|---|---|---|---|
| 57401 | Aberdeen | 24,995 | 25,851 |
| 57006 | Brookings | 16,270 | 14,951 |
| 57706 | Ellsworth AFB(u) | 7,017 | 4,766 |
| 57350 | Huron | 12,448 | 13,000 |
| 57042 | Madison | 6,257 | 6,210 |
| 57301 | Mitchell | 13,798 | 13,916 |
| 57501 | Pierre | 12,906 | 11,973 |
| 57701 | Rapid City | 54,523 | 46,492 |
| .... | Rapid Valley(u) | 5,968 | 3,265 |
| *57101 | Sioux Falls | 100,836 | 81,343 |
| 57783 | Spearfish | 6,966 | 5,251 |
| 57785 | Sturgis | 5,330 | 5,184 |
| 57069 | Vermillion | 10,034 | 10,136 |
| 57201 | Watertown | 17,632 | 15,649 |
| 57078 | Yankton | 12,703 | 12,011 |

## Tennessee

| ZIP code | Place | | 1990 | 1980 |
|---|---|---|---|---|
| 37701 | Alcoa | (615) | 6,400 | 6,870 |
| 37303 | Athens | (615) | 12,054 | 12,080 |
| 38134 | Bartlett | (901) | 26,989 | 17,170 |
| 37660 | Bloomingdale(u) | (615) | 10,953 | 12,088 |
| 38008 | Bolivar | (901) | 5,969 | 6,597 |
| 37027 | Brentwood | (615) | 16,392 | 9,431 |
| 37620 | Bristol | (615) | 23,421 | 23,986 |
| 38012 | Brownsville | (901) | 10,017 | 9,307 |
| *37401 | Chattanooga | (615) | 152,494 | 169,514 |
| 37040 | Clarksville | (615) | 75,542 | 54,777 |
| 37311 | Cleveland | (615) | 30,354 | 26,415 |
| 37716 | Clinton | (615) | 8,972 | 5,245 |
| 37315 | Collegedale | (615) | 5,048 | 4,607 |
| 38017 | Collierville | (901) | 14,427 | 7,839 |
| 37663 | Colonial Heights(u) | (615) | 6,716 | 6,744 |
| 38401 | Columbia | (615) | 28,583 | 26,571 |
| 38501 | Cookeville | (615) | 21,744 | 20,535 |
| 38019 | Covington | (901) | 7,487 | 6,065 |
| 38555 | Crossville | (615) | 6,930 | 6,394 |
| 37321 | Dayton | (615) | 5,671 | 5,233 |
| 37055 | Dickson | (615) | 8,783 | 7,040 |
| 38024 | Dyersburg | (901) | 16,317 | 15,856 |
| 37801 | Eagleton Village(u) | (615) | 5,169 | 5,331 |
| 37411 | East Brainerd(u) | | 11,594 | .... |
| 37412 | East Ridge | (615) | 21,101 | 21,236 |
| 37643 | Elizabethton | (615) | 11,931 | 12,431 |
| 37650 | Erwin | (615) | 5,015 | 4,739 |
| 37922 | Farragut | (615) | 12,802 | 5,992 |
| 37334 | Fayetteville | (615) | 7,158 | 7,559 |
| 37064 | Franklin | (615) | 20,098 | 12,407 |
| 37066 | Gallatin | (615) | 18,794 | 17,191 |
| 38138 | Germantown | (901) | 32,893 | 21,467 |
| 37072 | Goodlettsville | (615) | 11,219 | 8,327 |
| 37743 | Greeneville | (615) | 13,532 | 14,097 |
| 37215 | Green Hills(u) | | 6,763 | .... |
| 37918 | Halls(u) | (901) | 6,450 | 10,363 |
| 37748 | Harriman | (615) | 7,119 | 8,303 |
| 37341 | Harrison(u) | (615) | 7,191 | 6,206 |
| 37075 | Hendersonville | (615) | 32,188 | 26,561 |
| 38343 | Humboldt | (901) | 9,651 | 10,209 |
| 38301 | Jackson | (901) | 49,115 | 49,258 |
| 37760 | Jefferson City | (615) | 5,522 | 5,612 |
| 37601 | Johnson City | (615) | 49,479 | 39,753 |
| *37662 | Kingsport | (615) | 36,365 | 32,027 |
| *37901 | Knoxville | (615) | 165,039 | 175,045 |
| 37766 | La Follette | (615) | 7,192 | 8,198 |
| 37086 | LaVergne | (615) | 7,499 | 5,495 |
| 38464 | Lawrenceburg | (615) | 10,397 | 10,184 |
| 37087 | Lebanon | (615) | 15,208 | 11,872 |
| 37771 | Lenoir City | (615) | 6,147 | 5,180 |
| 37091 | Lewisburg | (615) | 9,879 | 8,760 |
| 38351 | Lexington | (901) | 5,810 | 5,934 |
| 38201 | McKenzie | (901) | 5,168 | 5,405 |
| 37110 | McMinnville | (615) | 11,194 | 10,683 |
| 37355 | Manchester | (615) | 7,709 | 7,250 |
| 38237 | Martin | (901) | 8,588 | 8,898 |
| 37801 | Maryville | (615) | 19,208 | 17,480 |
| *38101 | Memphis | (901) | 610,337 | 646,174 |
| 37343 | Middle Valley(u) | (615) | 12,255 | 11,420 |
| 38358 | Milan | (901) | 7,512 | 8,083 |
| 38053 | Millington | (901) | 17,866 | 20,236 |
| 37814 | Morristown | (615) | 21,385 | 19,570 |
| 37122 | Mount Juliet | (615) | 5,389 | 2,879 |
| 37130 | Murfreesboro | (615) | 44,922 | 32,845 |
| *37202 | Nashville-Davidson | (615) | 488,374 | 455,651 |
| 37821 | Newport | (615) | 7,123 | 7,580 |
| 37830 | Oak Ridge | (615) | 27,310 | 27,662 |
| 38242 | Paris | (901) | 9,332 | 10,728 |
| 37148 | Portland | (615) | 5,165 | 4,030 |
| 37849 | Powell(u) | (615) | 7,534 | 7,220 |
| 38478 | Pulaski | (615) | 7,916 | 7,184 |
| 37415 | Red Bank | (615) | 12,320 | 13,129 |
| 38063 | Ripley | (901) | 6,188 | 6,366 |
| 37854 | Rockwood | (615) | 5,348 | 5,687 |
| 38372 | Savannah | (901) | 6,547 | 6,992 |
| 37862 | Sevierville | (615) | 7,178 | 4,556 |
| 37865 | Seymour(u) | | 7,026 | .... |
| 37160 | Shelbyville | (615) | 14,049 | 13,530 |
| 37377 | Signal Mountain | (615) | 7,034 | 5,818 |
| 37167 | Smyrna | (615) | 13,647 | 8,839 |
| 37379 | Soddy-Daisy | (615) | 8,240 | 8,388 |
| .... | South Cleveland(u) | | 5,372 | 4,360 |
| 37172 | Springfield | (615) | 11,227 | 10,814 |
| 37874 | Sweetwater | (615) | 5,066 | 4,725 |
| 37388 | Tullahoma | (615) | 16,761 | 15,800 |
| 38261 | Union City | (901) | 10,513 | 10,436 |
| 37398 | Winchester | (615) | 6,305 | 5,821 |

## Texas

| ZIP code | Place | | 1990 | 1980 |
|---|---|---|---|---|
| *79604 | Abilene | (915) | 106,707 | 98,315 |
| 75001 | Addison | (214) | 8,783 | 5,553 |
| 78516 | Alamo | (210) | 8,210 | 5,831 |
| 78209 | Alamo Heights | (210) | 6,502 | 6,252 |

| ZIP code | Place | | 1990 | 1980 |
|---|---|---|---|---|
| 77039 | Aldine(u) | (713) | 11,133 | 12,623 |
| 78332 | Alice | (512) | 19,788 | 20,961 |
| 75002 | Allen | (214) | 9,198 | 8,314 |
| 79830 | Alpine | (915) | 5,637 | 5,465 |
| 77511 | Alvin | (713) | 19,220 | 16,515 |
| *79105 | Amarillo | (806) | 157,571 | 149,230 |
| 78750 | Anderson Mill(u) | | 9,468 | .... |
| 79714 | Andrews | (915) | 10,678 | 11,061 |
| 77515 | Angleton | (409) | 17,140 | 13,929 |
| 78336 | Aransas Pass | (512) | 7,180 | 7,173 |
| *76010 | Arlington | (817) | 261,721 | 160,113 |
| 75751 | Athens | (903) | 10,982 | 10,197 |
| 75551 | Atlanta | (214) | 6,118 | 6,272 |
| *78710 | Austin | (512) | 465,622 | 345,890 |
| 76020 | Azle | (817) | 8,868 | 5,822 |
| 75149 | Balch Springs | (214) | 17,406 | 13,746 |
| 77414 | Bay City | (409) | 18,170 | 17,837 |
| 77520 | Baytown | (713) | 63,850 | 56,923 |
| *77704 | Beaumont | (409) | 114,323 | 118,102 |
| 76021 | Bedford | (817) | 43,762 | 20,821 |
| 78102 | Beeville | (512) | 13,547 | 14,574 |
| 77401 | Bellaire | (713) | 13,842 | 14,950 |
| 76704 | Bellmead | (817) | 8,336 | 7,569 |
| 76513 | Belton | (817) | 12,476 | 10,660 |
| 76126 | Benbrook | (817) | 19,564 | 13,579 |
| 79720 | Big Spring | (915) | 23,093 | 24,804 |
| 75418 | Bonham | (903) | 6,686 | 7,338 |
| 79007 | Borger | (806) | 15,675 | 15,837 |
| 76825 | Brady | (915) | 5,946 | 5,969 |
| 76024 | Breckenridge | (817) | 5,665 | 6,921 |
| 77833 | Brenham | (409) | 11,952 | 10,966 |
| 77611 | Bridge City | (409) | 8,034 | 7,667 |
| 79316 | Brownfield | (806) | 9,560 | 10,387 |
| 78520 | Brownsville | (210) | 98,962 | 84,997 |
| 76801 | Brownwood | (915) | 18,387 | 19,396 |
| 78717 | Brushy Creek(u) | | 5,833 | .... |
| 77801 | Bryan | (409) | 55,002 | 44,337 |
| 76354 | Burkburnett | (817) | 10,145 | 10,668 |
| 76028 | Burleson | (817) | 16,113 | 11,734 |
| 76520 | Cameron | (817) | 5,635 | 5,721 |
| 79015 | Canyon | (806) | 11,365 | 10,724 |
| 78133 | Canyon Lake(u) | | 9,975 | .... |
| 78834 | Carrizo Springs | (210) | 5,745 | 6,886 |
| 75006 | Carrollton | (214) | 82,169 | 40,595 |
| 75633 | Carthage | (903) | 6,496 | 6,447 |
| 75104 | Cedar Hill | (214) | 19,976 | 6,849 |
| 78613 | Cedar Park | | 5,161 | 3,474 |
| 77530 | Channelview(u) | (713) | 25,564 | 17,471 |
| 79201 | Childress | (817) | 5,055 | 5,817 |
| 76031 | Cleburne | (817) | 22,205 | 19,218 |
| 77327 | Cleveland | (713) | 7,124 | 5,977 |
| 77015 | Clover Leaf(u) | (713) | 18,230 | 17,317 |
| 77531 | Clute | (409) | 9,467 | 9,577 |
| 76834 | Coleman | (915) | 5,410 | 5,960 |
| 77840 | College Station | (409) | 52,456 | 37,272 |
| 76034 | Colleyville | (817) | 12,724 | 6,700 |
| 75428 | Commerce | (903) | 6,825 | 8,136 |
| 77301 | Conroe | (409) | 27,610 | 18,034 |
| 78109 | Converse | (512) | 8,887 | 5,150 |
| 75019 | Coppell | | 16,881 | 3,826 |
| 76522 | Copperas Cove | (817) | 24,079 | 19,469 |
| *78408 | Corpus Christi | (512) | 257,453 | 232,134 |
| 75110 | Corsicana | (903) | 22,911 | 21,712 |
| 75835 | Crockett | (409) | 7,024 | 7,405 |
| 76036 | Crowley | (817) | 6,974 | 5,852 |
| 78839 | Crystal City | (512) | 8,263 | 8,334 |
| 77954 | Cuero | (512) | 6,700 | 7,124 |
| 79022 | Dalhart | (806) | 6,246 | 6,854 |
| *75260 | Dallas | (214) | 1,007,618 | 904,599 |
| 77535 | Dayton | (409) | 5,151 | 4,908 |
| 77536 | Deer Park | (713) | 27,658 | 22,648 |
| 78840 | Del Rio | (210) | 30,705 | 30,034 |
| 75020 | Denison | (903) | 21,505 | 23,884 |
| 76201 | Denton | (817) | 66,270 | 48,063 |
| 79323 | Denver City | | 5,145 | 4,704 |
| 75115 | De Soto | (214) | 30,544 | 15,538 |
| 77539 | Dickinson | (713) | 9,497 | 7,505 |
| 78537 | Donna | (210) | 12,652 | 9,952 |
| 79029 | Dumas | (806) | 12,871 | 12,194 |
| 75116 | Duncanville | (214) | 35,008 | 27,781 |
| 76135 | Eagle Mountain(u) | | 5,847 | .... |
| 78852 | Eagle Pass | (210) | 20,651 | 21,407 |
| 78539 | Edinburg | (210) | 29,885 | 24,075 |
| 77957 | Edna | (512) | 5,343 | 5,650 |
| 77437 | El Campo | (409) | 10,511 | 10,462 |
| *79910 | El Paso | (915) | 515,342 | 425,259 |
| 78543 | Elsa | (210) | 5,242 | 5,061 |
| 75119 | Ennis | (214) | 13,883 | 12,110 |
| 76039 | Euless | (817) | 38,149 | 24,002 |
| 76140 | Everman | (817) | 5,672 | 5,387 |
| 79838 | Fabens(u) | | 5,599 | 4,285 |
| 78355 | Falfurrias | (512) | 5,788 | 6,103 |
| 75234 | Farmers Branch | (214) | 24,250 | 24,863 |
| ..... | First Colony(u) | | 18,327 | .... |
| 78114 | Floresville | | 5,247 | 4,381 |
| 75028 | Flower Mound | | 15,527 | 4,402 |
| 76119 | Forest Hill | (817) | 11,482 | 11,684 |
| 79906 | Fort Bliss(u) | (915) | 13,915 | 12,687 |
| 76544 | Fort Hood(u) | (817) | 35,580 | 31,250 |

| ZIP code | Place | | 1990 | 1980 |
|---|---|---|---|---|
| 79735 | Fort Stockton | (915) | 8,524 | 8,688 |
| *76101 | Fort Worth | (817) | 447,619 | 385,164 |
| 78624 | Fredericksburg | (210) | 6,934 | 6,412 |
| 77541 | Freeport | (409) | 11,389 | 13,444 |
| 77546 | Friendswood | (713) | 22,814 | 10,719 |
| 75034 | Frisco | | 6,141 | 3,499 |
| 76240 | Gainesville | (817) | 14,256 | 14,081 |
| 77547 | Galena Park | (713) | 10,033 | 9,879 |
| 77550 | Galveston | (409) | 59,067 | 61,902 |
| *75040 | Garland | (214) | 180,650 | 138,857 |
| 76528 | Gatesville | (817) | 11,492 | 6,078 |
| 78626 | Georgetown | (512) | 14,842 | 9,468 |
| 75647 | Gladewater | (903) | 6,027 | 6,548 |
| 78629 | Gonzales | (210) | 6,527 | 7,152 |
| 76046 | Graham | (817) | 8,986 | 9,170 |
| *75050 | Grand Prairie | (214) | 99,616 | 71,462 |
| 76051 | Grapevine | (817) | 29,202 | 11,801 |
| 75401 | Greenville | (903) | 23,071 | 22,161 |
| 77619 | Groves | (409) | 16,744 | 17,090 |
| 76117 | Haltom City | (817) | 32,856 | 29,014 |
| 76541 | Harker Heights | (817) | 12,841 | 7,345 |
| 78550 | Harlingen | (210) | 48,735 | 43,543 |
| 77859 | Hearne | (409) | 5,132 | 5,418 |
| 75652 | Henderson | (903) | 11,139 | 11,473 |
| 79045 | Hereford | (806) | 14,745 | 15,853 |
| 76643 | Hewitt | (817) | 8,983 | 5,247 |
| 75205 | Highland Park | (214) | 8,739 | 8,909 |
| 77562 | Highlands(u) | (713) | 6,632 | 6,467 |
| 75067 | Highland Village | | 7,027 | 3,246 |
| 76645 | Hillsboro | (817) | 7,072 | 7,397 |
| 77563 | Hitchcock | (409) | 5,868 | 6,103 |
| 78861 | Hondo | (210) | 6,018 | 6,057 |
| *77013 | Houston | (713) | 1,630,864 | 1,595,138 |
| 77338 | Humble | (713) | 12,060 | 6,729 |
| 77340 | Huntsville | (409) | 27,925 | 23,936 |
| 76053 | Hurst | (817) | 33,574 | 31,420 |
| 78362 | Ingleside | (512) | 5,696 | 5,436 |
| 76351 | Iowa Park | (817) | 6,072 | 6,184 |
| *75061 | Irving | (214) | 155,037 | 109,943 |
| 77029 | Jacinto City | (713) | 9,343 | 8,953 |
| 75766 | Jacksonville | (214) | 12,765 | 12,264 |
| 75951 | Jasper | (409) | 7,160 | 6,959 |
| 78729 | Jollyville | | 15,206 | .... |
| 77450 | Katy | (713) | 8,005 | 5,660 |
| 75142 | Kaufman | (214) | 5,238 | 4,658 |
| 76248 | Keller | (817) | 13,683 | 4,156 |
| 79745 | Kermit | (915) | 6,875 | 8,015 |
| 78028 | Kerrville | (210) | 17,384 | 15,276 |
| 75662 | Kilgore | (903) | 11,066 | 11,331 |
| 76541 | Killeen | (817) | 63,535 | 46,296 |
| 78363 | Kingsville | (512) | 25,276 | 28,808 |
| 77325 | Kingwood | (713) | 37,397 | 16,261 |
| 78219 | Kirby | (210) | 8,326 | 6,435 |
| 78236 | Lackland AFB(u) | (210) | 9,352 | 14,459 |
| 77566 | Lake Jackson | (409) | 22,776 | 19,102 |
| 77568 | La Marque | (409) | 14,120 | 15,372 |
| 79631 | Lamesa | (806) | 10,809 | 11,790 |
| 76550 | Lampasas | (512) | 6,382 | 6,165 |
| 75146 | Lancaster | (214) | 22,117 | 14,807 |
| 77571 | La Porte | (713) | 27,910 | 14,062 |
| 78040 | Laredo | (210) | 122,899 | 91,449 |
| 77573 | League City | (713) | 30,159 | 16,578 |
| 78238 | Leon Valley | (210) | 9,581 | 9,088 |
| 79336 | Levelland | (806) | 13,986 | 13,809 |
| 75067 | Lewisville | (214) | 46,521 | 24,273 |
| 77575 | Liberty | (713) | 7,690 | 7,945 |
| 79339 | Littlefield | (806) | 6,489 | 7,409 |
| 78233 | Live Oak | (210) | 10,023 | 8,183 |
| 77351 | Livingston | (409) | 5,019 | 4,928 |
| 78644 | Lockhart | (512) | 9,205 | 7,953 |
| 75601 | Longview | (903) | 70,311 | 62,762 |
| *79408 | Lubbock | (806) | 186,206 | 174,361 |
| 75901 | Lufkin | (409) | 30,206 | 28,562 |
| 77656 | Lumberton | | 6,640 | 2,480 |
| 78501 | McAllen | (210) | 84,021 | 66,281 |
| 75069 | McKinney | (214) | 21,283 | 16,256 |
| 77063 | Mansfield | (817) | 15,607 | 8,102 |
| 76661 | Marlin | (817) | 6,386 | 7,099 |
| 75670 | Marshall | (903) | 23,682 | 24,921 |
| 78368 | Mathis | (512) | 5,423 | 5,667 |
| 78570 | Mercedes | (210) | 12,694 | 11,851 |
| 75149 | Mesquite | (214) | 101,484 | 67,053 |
| 76667 | Mexia | (817) | 6,933 | 7,094 |
| 79701 | Midland | (915) | 89,443 | 70,525 |
| 76065 | Midlothian | (214) | 5,141 | 3,219 |
| 76067 | Mineral Wells | (817) | 14,870 | 14,468 |
| 78572 | Mission | (210) | 28,653 | 22,653 |
| | Mission Bend(u) | | 24,945 | .... |
| 77459 | Missouri City | (713) | 36,176 | 24,423 |
| 79756 | Monahans | (915) | 8,101 | 8,397 |
| 75455 | Mount Pleasant | (903) | 12,291 | 11,003 |
| 75961 | Nacogdoches | (409) | 30,872 | 27,149 |
| 77868 | Navasota | (409) | 6,296 | 5,971 |
| 77627 | Nederland | (409) | 16,192 | 16,855 |
| 75570 | New Boston | | 5,057 | 4,628 |
| 78130 | New Braunfels | (210) | 27,334 | 22,402 |
| 76118 | North Richland Hills | (817) | 45,895 | 30,592 |
| *79760 | Odessa | (915) | 89,699 | 90,027 |
| 77630 | Orange | (409) | 19,381 | 23,628 |

| ZIP code | Place | | 1990 | 1980 |
|---|---|---|---|---|
| 75801 | Palestine | (903) | 18,042 | 15,948 |
| 79065 | Pampa | (806) | 19,959 | 21,396 |
| 75460 | Paris | (903) | 24,799 | 25,498 |
| *77501 | Pasadena | (713) | 119,608 | 112,560 |
| 77581 | Pearland | (713) | 18,697 | 13,248 |
| 78061 | Pearsall | (210) | 6,924 | 7,383 |
| | | | 9,502 | |
| 78721 | Pecan Grove(u) | | 12,069 | 12,855 |
| 79772 | Pecos | (915) | 7,619 | 7,991 |
| 79070 | Perryton | (806) | 32,921 | 21,381 |
| 78577 | Pharr | (210) | 21,700 | 22,187 |
| 79072 | Plainview | (806) | 127,885 | 72,331 |
| *75075 | Plano | (214) | 7,678 | 6,346 |
| 78064 | Pleasanton | (210) | 58,551 | 61,251 |
| 77640 | Port Arthur | (409) | 12,224 | 12,023 |
| 78374 | Portland | (512) | 10,886 | 10,911 |
| 77979 | Port Lavaca | (512) | 12,908 | 13,944 |
| 77651 | Port Neches | (409) | 8,880 | 9,493 |
| 78580 | Raymondville | (210) | 7,658 | |
| 76028 | Rendon(u) | | 74,840 | 72,496 |
| *75080 | Richardson | (214) | 7,978 | 7,977 |
| 76118 | Richland Hills | (817) | 9,801 | 9,692 |
| 77469 | Richmond | (713) | 9,891 | 8,930 |
| 78582 | Rio Grande City(u) | (210) | 6,580 | 6,890 |
| 77019 | River Oaks | (817) | 7,111 | 6,074 |
| 76701 | Robinson | (817) | 12,849 | 12,100 |
| 78380 | Robstown | (512) | 5,235 | 5,611 |
| 76567 | Rockdale | (512) | 10,486 | 5,939 |
| 75087 | Rockwall | (214) | 8,059 | 3,384 |
| 78584 | Roma | | 20,183 | 17,840 |
| 77471 | Rosenberg | (713) | 30,923 | 12,740 |
| 78664 | Round Rock | (512) | 23,260 | 7,522 |
| 75088 | Rowlett | (214) | 5,346 | 1,640 |
| 75048 | Sachse | | 8,551 | 5,736 |
| 76179 | Saginaw | (817) | 84,474 | 73,240 |
| 76901 | San Angelo | (915) | 935,933 | 785,940 |
| *78284 | San Antonio | (210) | 20,125 | 17,988 |
| 78586 | San Benito | (210) | 10,815 | 7,608 |
| 78589 | San Juan | (210) | 28,743 | 23,420 |
| 78666 | San Marcos | (512) | 8,429 | 6,172 |
| 77550 | Santa Fe | (713) | 10,597 | 7,262 |
| 78154 | Schertz | (210) | 6,685 | 4,670 |
| 77586 | Seabrook | (713) | 8,969 | 7,304 |
| 75159 | Seagoville | (214) | 18,853 | 17,854 |
| 78155 | Seguin | (210) | 6,342 | 6,080 |
| 79360 | Seminole | (915) | 31,601 | 30,413 |
| 75090 | Sherman | (903) | 6,368 | 7,684 |
| 77566 | Silsbee | (409) | 5,549 | 6,044 |
| 78387 | Sinton | (512) | 6,078 | 6,804 |
| 79364 | Slaton | (806) | 12,195 | 12,705 |
| 79549 | Snyder | (915) | 22,995 | 12,341 |
| 79910 | Socorro | | 14,207 | 13,293 |
| 77587 | South Houston | (713) | 7,065 | 2,808 |
| 76051 | Southlake | | 33,111 | |
| 77373 | Spring(u) | (713) | 8,397 | 4,755 |
| 77777 | Stafford | (713) | 13,502 | 11,881 |
| 76401 | Stephenville | (817) | 24,528 | 8,826 |
| 77478 | Sugar Land | (713) | 14,062 | 12,804 |
| 75482 | Sulphur Springs | (903) | 11,967 | 12,242 |
| 79556 | Sweetwater | (915) | 11,472 | 10,619 |
| 76574 | Taylor | (512) | 46,109 | 42,354 |
| 76501 | Temple | (817) | 12,490 | 13,269 |
| 75160 | Terrell | (214) | 31,656 | 31,271 |
| 75501 | Texarkana | (903) | 40,822 | 41,201 |
| 77590 | Texas City | (409) | 22,113 | 11,586 |
| 75056 | The Colony | (214) | 29,205 | 8,443 |
| 77380 | The Woodlands(u) | (713) | 6,370 | 3,996 |
| 77337 | Tomball | (713) | 6,166 | |
| | Town West(u) | | 75,450 | 70,508 |
| 75701 | Tyler | (903) | 13,057 | 10,720 |
| 78148 | Universal City | (512) | 22,259 | 22,254 |
| 76308 | University Park | (214) | 14,729 | 14,178 |
| 78801 | Uvalde | (210) | 12,001 | 12,695 |
| 76384 | Vernon | (817) | 55,076 | 50,695 |
| 77901 | Victoria | (512) | 10,935 | 11,834 |
| 77662 | Vidor | (409) | 103,590 | 101,261 |
| *76701 | Waco | (817) | 20,009 | 10,284 |
| 76148 | Watauga | (817) | 18,168 | 14,624 |
| 75165 | Waxahachie | (214) | 14,804 | 12,049 |
| 76086 | Weatherford | (817) | 7,094 | |
| 78728 | Wells Branch(u) | | 21,877 | 19,331 |
| 78596 | Weslaco | (210) | 16,568 | |
| 79764 | West Odessa(u) | | 12,920 | 12,010 |
| 77005 | West University Place | (713) | 9,011 | 9,033 |
| 77488 | Wharton | (409) | 5,136 | 4,415 |
| 75693 | White Oak | | 15,472 | 13,508 |
| 76108 | White Settlement | (817) | 96,259 | 94,201 |
| *76307 | Wichita Falls | (817) | 5,331 | 5,332 |
| 78239 | Windcrest | (210) | 8,695 | 7,091 |
| 76710 | Woodway | (817) | 8,716 | 3,152 |
| 75098 | Wylie | | 5,611 | 6,148 |
| 77995 | Yoakum | (512) | 7,119 | 3,831 |
| 78076 | Zapata(u) | (512) | | |

## Utah (801)

| ZIP code | Place | | 1990 | 1980 |
|---|---|---|---|---|
| 84003 | American Fork | | 15,722 | 12,564 |
| *84010 | Bountiful | | 36,659 | 32,877 |

| ZIP code | Place | | 1990 | 1980 |
|---|---|---|---|---|
| 84302 | Brigham City | | 15,644 | 15,596 |
| 84109 | Canyon Rim(u) | | 10,527 | |
| 84720 | Cedar City | | 13,443 | 10,972 |
| 84014 | Centerville | | 11,500 | 8,069 |
| 84015 | Clearfield | | 21,435 | 17,982 |
| 84015 | Clinton | | 7,945 | 5,777 |
| 84121 | Cottonwood Heights(u) | | 28,766 | 22,665 |
| | Cottonwood West(u) | | 17,476 | |
| 84020 | Draper | | 7,143 | 5,521 |
| 84109 | East Millcreek(u) | | 21,184 | 24,150 |
| 84025 | Farmington | | 9,049 | 4,691 |
| 84004 | Highland | | 5,007 | 2,435 |
| 84117 | Holladay-Cottonwood(u) | | 14,095 | 22,189 |
| 84037 | Kaysville | | 13,961 | 9,811 |
| 84118 | Kearns(u) | | 28,374 | 21,353 |
| *84041 | Layton | | 41,784 | 22,862 |
| 84043 | Lehi | | 8,475 | 6,848 |
| | Little Cottonwood Creek Valley(u) | | 5,042 | |
| 84321 | Logan | | 32,771 | 26,844 |
| 84044 | Magna(u) | | 17,829 | 13,138 |
| 84047 | Midvale | | 11,886 | 10,146 |
| 84109 | Millcreek(u) | | 32,230 | |
| 84117 | Mount Olympus(u) | | 7,413 | 6,068 |
| 84107 | Murray | | 31,274 | 25,750 |
| 84404 | North Ogden | | 11,593 | 9,309 |
| 84054 | North Salt Lake | | 6,454 | 5,548 |
| *84401 | Ogden | | 63,943 | 64,407 |
| | Oquirrh(u) | | 7,593 | |
| *84057 | Orem | | 67,561 | 52,399 |
| 84651 | Payson | | 9,510 | 8,246 |
| 84062 | Pleasant Grove | | 13,476 | 10,833 |
| 84501 | Price | | 8,712 | 9,086 |
| *84601 | Provo | | 86,835 | 74,111 |
| 84701 | Richfield | | 5,593 | 5,482 |
| 84403 | Riverdale | | 6,419 | 6,031 |
| 84065 | Riverton | | 11,261 | 7,032 |
| 84067 | Roy | | 24,595 | 19,694 |
| 84770 | Saint George | | 28,572 | 11,350 |
| *84101 | Salt Lake City | | 159,928 | 163,034 |
| *84070 | Sandy | | 75,240 | 52,210 |
| 84335 | Smithfield | | 5,566 | 4,993 |
| 84065 | South Jordan | | 12,215 | 7,492 |
| 84403 | South Ogden | | 12,105 | 11,366 |
| 84115 | South Salt Lake | | 10,129 | 10,413 |
| 84660 | Spanish Fork | | 11,272 | 9,825 |
| 84663 | Springville | | 13,950 | 12,101 |
| 84015 | Sunset | | 5,128 | 5,733 |
| 84107 | Taylorsville-Bennion(u) | | 52,351 | 17,448 |
| 84074 | Tooele | | 13,887 | 14,335 |
| 84047 | Union(u) | | 13,684 | 9,665 |
| 84078 | Vernal | | 6,640 | 6,600 |
| 84403 | Washington Terrace | | 8,189 | 8,212 |
| *84084 | West Jordan | | 42,915 | 27,325 |
| *84119 | West Valley City | | 86,969 | 72,509 |
| 84070 | White City(u) | | 6,506 | 7,180 |
| 84087 | Woods Cross | | 5,384 | 4,263 |

## Vermont (802)

*See Note on Page 373*

| ZIP code | Place | | 1990 | 1980 |
|---|---|---|---|---|
| 05641 | Barre | | 9,482 | 9,824 |
| 05641 | *Barre* | | 7,411 | 6,509 |
| 05201 | Bennington | | 16,451 | 15,815 |
| 05201 | Bennington(u) | | 9,532 | 9,349 |
| 05301 | Brattleboro Center(u) | | 8,612 | 8,596 |
| 05301 | *Brattleboro* | | 12,241 | 11,886 |
| 05401 | Burlington | | 39,127 | 37,712 |
| 05446 | *Colchester* | | 14,731 | 12,629 |
| 05451 | Essex | | 16,498 | 14,392 |
| 05452 | Essex Junction | | 8,398 | 7,033 |
| 05047 | Hartford | | 9,404 | |
| 05849 | Lyndon | | 5,371 | |
| 05753 | *Middlebury(u)* | | 8,034 | 6,007 |
| 05468 | Milton | | 8,404 | |
| 05602 | Montpelier | | 8,247 | 8,241 |
| 05663 | Northfield | | 5,610 | |
| | Rockingham | | 5,484 | |
| 05701 | Rutland | | 18,230 | 18,436 |
| 05478 | Saint Albans | | 7,339 | 7,308 |
| 05819 | *Saint Johnsbury(u)* | | 7,608 | 6,424 |
| 05482 | Shelburne | | 5,871 | |
| 05401 | *South Burlington* | | 12,809 | 10,679 |
| 05156 | Springfield | | 9,579 | 10,190 |
| 05488 | Swanton | | 5,636 | |
| 05404 | Winooski | | 6,649 | 6,318 |

## Virginia

| ZIP code | Place | | 1990 | 1980 |
|---|---|---|---|---|
| 24210 | Abingdon | (703) | 7,003 | 4,318 |
| *22313 | Alexandria | (703) | 111,182 | 103,217 |
| 22003 | Annandale(u) | (703) | 50,975 | 49,524 |
| | Aquia Harbour(u) | (703) | 6,308 | 2,870 |
| *22210 | Arlington(u) | (703) | 170,936 | 152,599 |
| 23005 | Ashland | (804) | 5,864 | 4,640 |
| 22041 | Bailey's Crossroads(u) | (703) | 19,507 | 12,564 |

| ZIP code | Place | | 1990 | 1980 |
|---|---|---|---|---|
| 24523 | Bedford | (703) | 6,073 | 5,991 |
| 22307 | Belle Haven(u) | (804) | 6,427 | 6,520 |
| 23234 | Bellwood(u) | (804) | 6,178 | 6,439 |
| 23234 | Bensley(u) | (804) | 5,093 | 5,299 |
| 24060 | Blacksburg | (703) | 34,590 | 30,638 |
| 24605 | Bluefield | (703) | 5,363 | 5,946 |
| 23235 | Bon Air(u) | (804) | 16,413 | 16,224 |
| 24201 | Bristol | (703) | 18,426 | 19,042 |
| 24416 | Buena Vista | (703) | 6,406 | 6,717 |
| ..... | Bull Run(u) | | 5,525 | .... |
| 22015 | Burke(u) | (703) | 57,734 | 33,835 |
| 24018 | Cave Spring(u) | (703) | 24,053 | 21,682 |
| 22020 | Centreville(u) | (703) | 26,585 | 7,473 |
| 22021 | Chantilly(u) | (703) | 29,337 | 12,259 |
| *22906 | Charlottesville | (804) | 40,475 | 39,916 |
| *23320 | Chesapeake | (804) | 151,982 | 114,486 |
| 23831 | Chester(u) | (804) | 14,986 | 11,728 |
| 24073 | Christiansburg | (703) | 15,004 | 10,345 |
| 24078 | Collinsville(u) | (703) | 7,280 | 7,517 |
| 23834 | Colonial Heights | (804) | 16,064 | 16,509 |
| ..... | Commonwealth(u) | | 5,538 | 3,505 |
| ..... | Countryside(u) | | 8,349 | .... |
| 24426 | Covington | (703) | 6,991 | 9,063 |
| 22701 | Culpeper | (703) | 8,581 | 6,621 |
| 22191 | Dale City(u) | (703) | 47,170 | 33,127 |
| 24541 | Danville | (804) | 53,056 | 45,642 |
| 23228 | Dumbarton(u) | (804) | 8,526 | 8,149 |
| 22027 | Dunn Loring(u) | (703) | 6,509 | 6,077 |
| 23222 | East Highland Park(u) | (804) | 11,850 | 11,797 |
| 23847 | Emporia | (804) | 5,479 | 4,840 |
| 23803 | Ettrick(u) | (804) | 5,290 | 4,890 |
| 22030 | Fairfax | (703) | 19,622 | 19,390 |
| *22046 | Falls Church | (703) | 9,578 | 9,515 |
| 23901 | Farmville | (804) | 6,046 | 6,067 |
| 24551 | Forest(u) | (804) | 5,624 | .... |
| 22060 | Fort Belvoir(u) | (703) | 8,590 | 7,726 |
| 22308 | Fort Hunt(u) | (703) | 12,989 | 14,294 |
| 23801 | Fort Lee(u) | (804) | 6,895 | 9,784 |
| 22310 | Franconia(u) | (703) | 19,882 | 8,476 |
| 23851 | Franklin | (804) | 7,864 | 7,308 |
| 22401 | Fredericksburg | (703) | 19,027 | 15,322 |
| 22630 | Front Royal | (703) | 11,880 | 11,126 |
| 24333 | Galax | (703) | 6,670 | 6,524 |
| 23060 | Glen Allen(u) | (804) | 9,010 | 6,202 |
| 23062 | Gloucester Point(u) | (804) | 8,509 | 5,841 |
| 22066 | Great Falls(u) | | 6,945 | 2,419 |
| 22306 | Groveton(u) | (703) | 19,997 | 18,860 |
| *23660 | Hampton | (804) | 133,811 | 122,617 |
| 22801 | Harrisonburg | (703) | 30,707 | 19,671 |
| *22070 | Herndon | (703) | 16,139 | 11,449 |
| 23075 | Highland Springs(u) | (804) | 13,823 | 12,146 |
| 24019 | Hollins(u) | (703) | 13,305 | 12,295 |
| 23860 | Hopewell | (804) | 23,101 | 23,397 |
| 22303 | Huntington(u) | (703) | 7,489 | 5,813 |
| 22306 | Hybla Valley(u) | (703) | 15,491 | 15,533 |
| 22043 | Idylwood(u) | (703) | 14,710 | 11,982 |
| 22042 | Jefferson(u) | (804) | 25,782 | 24,342 |
| 22041 | Lake Barcroft(u) | (703) | 8,686 | 8,725 |
| 22191 | Lake Ridge(u) | (703) | 23,862 | 11,072 |
| 23228 | Lakeside(u) | (804) | 12,081 | 12,289 |
| 23060 | Laurel(u) | (804) | 13,011 | 10,569 |
| 22075 | Leesburg | (703) | 16,202 | 8,357 |
| 22450 | Lexington | (703) | 6,959 | 7,292 |
| 22312 | Lincolnia(u) | (703) | 13,041 | 10,350 |
| 22079 | Lorton(u) | (703) | 15,385 | 5,813 |
| *24505 | Lynchburg | (804) | 66,049 | 66,743 |
| 22101 | McLean(u) | (703) | 38,168 | 35,664 |
| 24572 | Madison Heights(u) | (804) | 11,700 | 14,146 |
| 22110 | Manassas | (703) | 27,957 | 15,438 |
| 22110 | Manassas Park | (703) | 6,734 | 6,524 |
| 22030 | Mantua(u) | (703) | 6,804 | 6,523 |
| 24354 | Marion | (703) | 6,630 | 7,287 |
| 24112 | Martinsville | (703) | 16,162 | 18,149 |
| 23111 | Mechanicsville(u) | (804) | 22,027 | 9,269 |
| 22116 | Merrifield(u) | (703) | 8,399 | 7,525 |
| ..... | Montclair(u) | | 11,399 | .... |
| 23230 | Montrose(u) | (804) | 6,405 | 5,349 |
| 22121 | Mount Vernon(u) | (703) | 27,485 | 24,058 |
| 22122 | Newington(u) | (703) | 17,965 | 8,313 |
| *23607 | Newport News | (804) | 171,439 | 144,903 |
| *23501 | Norfolk | (804) | 261,250 | 266,979 |
| 22151 | North Springfield(u) | (703) | 8,996 | 9,538 |
| 22124 | Oakton(u) | (703) | 24,610 | 19,150 |
| 23803 | Petersburg | (804) | 37,027 | 41,055 |
| 22043 | Pimmit Hills(u) | (703) | 6,019 | 6,658 |
| 23662 | Poquoson | (804) | 11,005 | 8,726 |
| *23705 | Portsmouth | (804) | 103,910 | 104,577 |
| 24301 | Pulaski | (703) | 9,985 | 10,1069 |
| 22134 | Quantico Station(u) | (703) | 7,425 | 7,121 |
| 24141 | Radford | (703) | 15,940 | 13,225 |
| 22090 | Reston(u) | (703) | 48,556 | 36,407 |
| *23232 | Richmond | (804) | 202,798 | 219,214 |
| *24001 | Roanoke | (703) | 96,509 | 100,220 |
| 22310 | Rose Hill(u) | (703) | 12,675 | 11,926 |
| 24153 | Salem | (703) | 23,756 | 23,958 |
| 22044 | Seven Corners(u) | (703) | 72,80 | 6,058 |
| 24592 | South Boston | (804) | 6,997 | 7,093 |
| *22150 | Springfield | (703) | 23,706 | 21,435 |
| 24401 | Staunton | (703) | 24,461 | 21,857 |

| ZIP cod | Place | | 1990 | 1980 |
|---|---|---|---|---|
| 221.. | Sterling(u) | (703) | 20,512 | 16,080 |
| 24477 | Stuarts Draft(u) | | 5,087 | 1,776 |
| 23162 | Studley(u) | | 7,321 | 4,674 |
| 23434 | Suffolk | (804) | 52,143 | 47,621 |
| 22770 | Sugarland Run(u) | (703) | 9,357 | 6,258 |
| 24502 | Timberlake(u) | (804) | 10,314 | 9,697 |
| 23229 | Tuckahoe(u) | (804) | 42,629 | 39,868 |
| 22101 | Tysons Corner(u) | (703) | 13,124 | 10,065 |
| ..... | University Heights(u) | | 6,900 | 6,736 |
| 22180 | Vienna | (703) | 14,852 | 15,469 |
| 24179 | Vinton | (703) | 7,643 | 8,027 |
| *23458 | Virginia Beach | (804) | 393,089 | 262,199 |
| 22980 | Waynesboro | (703) | 18,549 | 15,329 |
| 22110 | West Gate(u) | (703) | 6,565 | 7,119 |
| 22152 | West Springfield(u) | (703) | 28,126 | 25,012 |
| 23185 | Williamsburg | (804) | 11,530 | 9,870 |
| 22601 | Winchester | (703) | 21,947 | 20,217 |
| 24592 | Wolf Trap(u) | (804) | 13,133 | 9,875 |
| 22191 | Woodbridge(u) | (703) | 26,401 | 24,004 |
| 24382 | Wytheville | (703) | 8,036 | 7,135 |
| ..... | Yorkshire(u) | | 5,699 | 4,940 |

## Washington

| ZIP cod | Place | | 1990 | 1980 |
|---|---|---|---|---|
| 98520 | Aberdeen | (206) | 16,565 | 18,739 |
| 98036 | Alderwood Manor(u) | (206) | 22,945 | 16,524 |
| 98221 | Anacortes | (206) | 11,451 | 9,013 |
| 98335 | Artondale(u) | | 7,141 | .... |
| 98002 | Auburn | (206) | 33,650 | 26,417. |
| *98009 | Bellevue | (206) | 86,872 | 73,903 |
| 98225 | Bellingham | (206) | 52,179 | 45,794 |
| 98390 | Bonney Lake | (206) | 7,494 | 5,328 |
| 98011 | Bothell | (206) | 12,345 | 7,943 |
| 98310 | Bremerton | (206) | 38,142 | 36,208 |
| 98036 | Brier | (206) | 5,633 | 2,915 |
| 98178 | Bryn Mawr-Skyway(u) | (206) | 12,514 | 11,754 |
| 98166 | Burien(u) | (206) | 25,089 | 23,189 |
| 98607 | Camas | (206) | 6,442 | 5,681 |
| 98055 | Cascade-Fairwood(u) | (206) | 30,107 | 16,939 |
| 98684 | Cascade Park East(u) | | 6,996 | .... |
| 98684 | Cascade Park West(u) | | 6,656 | .... |
| 98531 | Centralia | (206) | 12,101 | 11,555 |
| 98532 | Chehalis | (206) | 6,527 | 6,100 |
| 99004 | Cheney | (509) | 7,723 | 7,630 |
| 99403 | Clarkston | (509) | 6,753 | 6,903 |
| 99324 | College Place | (509) | 6,308 | 5,771 |
| ..... | Country Homes(u) | | 5,126 | .... |
| 98042 | Covington-Sawyer-Wilderness(u) | | 24,321 | .... |
| 98198 | Des Moines | (206) | 17,283 | 7,378 |
| 99213 | Dishman(u) | (509) | 9,671 | 10,169 |
| ..... | East Hill-Meridian(u) | | 42,696 | .... |
| 98366 | East Port Orchard(u) | | 9,409 | 4,631 |
| 98056 | East Renton Highlands(u) | (206) | 13,218 | 12,033 |
| 98801 | East Wenatchee Bench(u) | (509) | 12,539 | 11,410 |
| ..... | Edgewood-North Hill(u) | | 9,120 | .... |
| 98020 | Edmonds | (206) | 30,743 | 27,679 |
| 98387 | Elk Plain(u) | | 12,197 | .... |
| 98926 | Ellensburg | (509) | 12,360 | 11,752 |
| ..... | Ellsworth North(u) | | 5,796 | .... |
| 98022 | Enumclaw | (206) | 7,227 | 5,427 |
| 98823 | Ephrata | (509) | 5,349 | 5,359 |
| 99210 | Esperance(u) | (509) | 11,236 | 11,120 |
| *98201 | Everett | (206) | 69,961 | 54,413 |
| ..... | Evergreen(u) | | 11,249 | .... |
| 98055 | Fairwood(u) | (206) | 5,807 | 5,337 |
| *98003 | Federal Way | (206) | 67,554 | .... |
| 98248 | Ferndale | (206) | 5,398 | 3,855 |
| 98466 | Fircrest | (206) | 5,258 | 5,477 |
| 98597 | Five Corners(u) | | 6,776 | .... |
| 98433 | Fort Lewis(u) | (206) | 22,224 | 23,761 |
| 98930 | Grandview | (509) | 7,169 | 5,615 |
| ..... | Harbour Pointe(u) | | 9,107 | .... |
| 98660 | Hazel Dell North(u) | (206) | 6,924 | 15,386 |
| 98665 | Hazel Dell South(u) | (206) | 5,796 | .... |
| 98550 | Hoquiam | (206) | 8,972 | 9,719 |
| 98011 | Inglewood-Finn Hill(u) | (206) | 29,132 | 12,467 |
| 98027 | Issaquah | (206) | 7,786 | 5,536 |
| 98626 | Kelso | (206) | 11,767 | 11,129 |
| 98028 | Kenmore(u) | (206) | 8,917 | 7,281 |
| 99336 | Kennewick | (509) | 42,148 | 34,397 |
| 98031 | Kent | (206) | 37,960 | 22,961 |
| 98033 | Kingsgate(u) | (206) | 14,259 | 12,652 |
| 98033 | Kirkland | (206) | 40,059 | 18,785 |
| 98503 | Lacey | (206) | 19,279 | 13,940 |
| 98155 | Lake Forest North(u) | (206) | 8,002 | 7,995 |
| ..... | Lakeland North(u) | (206) | 14,402 | 11,451 |
| ..... | Lakeland South(u) | (206) | 9,027 | 5,225 |
| 98036 | Lake Serene-North Lynnwood(u) | (206) | 14,290 | 54,533 |
| ..... | Lake Shore(u) | | 6,268 | .... |
| ..... | Lakewood(u) | (206) | 58,412 | .... |
| 98259 | Longview | (206) | 31,499 | 31,052 |
| 98632 | Lynden | (206) | 5,709 | 4,022 |
| 98264 | Lynnwood | (206) | 28,637 | 22,641 |
| 98036 | Martha Lake(u) | (206) | 10,155 | 7,022 |
| 98270 | Marysville | (206) | 10,328 | 5,080 |
| 98040 | Mercer Island | (206) | 20,816 | 21,522 |
| ..... | Midland(u) | | 5,587 | .... |

| ZIP code | Place | | 1990 | 1980 |
|---|---|---|---|---|
| 98012 | Mill Creek | | 7,180 | 1,803 |
| ...... | Minnehaha(u) | | 9,661 | .... |
| 98837 | Moses Lake | (509) | 11,235 | 10,629 |
| 98043 | Mountlake Terrace | (206) | 19,320 | 16,534 |
| 98273 | Mount Vernon | (206) | 17,647 | 13,009 |
| 98275 | Mukilteo | (206) | 7,007 | 1,426 |
| 98006 | Newport Hills(u) | (206) | 14,736 | 12,245 |
| 98166 | Normandy Park | (206) | 6,709 | 4,268 |
| 98155 | North City-Ridgecrest(u) | (206) | 13,832 | 13,551 |
| ...... | North Creek-Canyon Park(u) | | 23,236 | 13,551 |
| ...... | North Hill(u) | | 5,706 | 10,170 |
| 98270 | North Marysville(u) | (206) | 18,711 | 15,159 |
| 98277 | Oak Harbor | (206) | 17,176 | 12,271 |
| *98501 | Olympia | (206) | 33,729 | 27,447 |
| 99214 | Opportunity(u) | (509) | 22,326 | 21,241 |
| 98662 | Orchards North(u) | (206) | 6,479 | 8,828 |
| 98662 | Orchards South(u) | (206) | 12,956 | .... |
| 99027 | Otis Orchards-East Farms(u) | | 5,811 | 4,597 |
| ...... | Paine Field-Lake Stickney(u) | | 18,670 | .... |
| 98444 | Parkland(u) | (206) | 20,882 | 23,355 |
| 98366 | Parkwood(u) | | 6,853 | 4,599 |
| 99301 | Pasco | (509) | 20,337 | 18,428 |
| 98027 | Pine Lake(u) | | 13,940 | .... |
| 98362 | Port Angeles | (206) | 17,710 | 17,311 |
| 98368 | Port Townsend | (206) | 7,001 | 6,067 |
| 98390 | Prairie Ridge(u) | | 8,278 | .... |
| 99163 | Pullman | (509) | 23,478 | 23,579 |
| 98371 | Puyallup | (206) | 23,878 | 18,251 |
| 98052 | Redmond | (206) | 35,800 | 23,318 |
| 98055 | Renton | (206) | 41,688 | 31,031 |
| 99352 | Richland | (509) | 32,315 | 33,578 |
| 98160 | Richmond Beach-Innis Arden | (206) | 7,242 | 6,700 |
| 98113 | Richmond Highlands(u) | (206) | 26,037 | 24,463 |
| 98188 | Riverton-Boulevard Park(u) | (206) | 15,337 | 14,182 |
| ...... | Sahalee(u) | | 13,951 | .... |
| 98686 | Salmon Creek(u) | | 11,989 | .... |
| *98188 | SeaTac | (206) | 22,694 | .... |
| *98109 | Seattle | (206) | 516,259 | 493,846 |
| 98284 | Sedro Woolley | (206) | 6,333 | 6,110 |
| 98942 | Selah | (509) | 5,113 | 4,500 |
| 98584 | Shelton | (206) | 7,241 | 7,629 |
| 98155 | Sheridan Beach(u) | (206) | 6,516 | 6,873 |
| 98315 | Silverdale(u) | | 7,660 | .... |
| 98201 | Silver Lake-Fircrest(u) | (206) | 24,474 | 10,299 |
| 98290 | Snohomish | (206) | 6,499 | 5,294 |
| 98373 | South Hill(u) | | 12,963 | .... |
| 98387 | Spanaway(u) | (206) | 15,001 | 8,868 |
| *99210 | Spokane | (509) | 177,165 | 171,300 |
| 98388 | Steilacoom | (206) | 5,728 | 4,886 |
| 98371 | Summit(u) | | 6,312 | .... |
| 98390 | Sumner | (206) | 6,459 | 4,936 |
| 98944 | Sunnyside | (509) | 11,238 | 9,225 |
| *98402 | Tacoma | (206) | 176,664 | 158,501 |
| 98501 | Tanglewilde-Thompson Place(u) | | 6,061 | 5,910 |
| 98948 | Toppenish | (509) | 7,419 | 6,517 |
| 98188 | Tukwila | (206) | 11,874 | 3,578 |
| 98502 | Tumwater | (206) | 9,976 | 6,705 |
| 98406 | University Place(u) | (206) | 27,701 | 20,381 |
| *98660 | Vancouver | (206) | 46,380 | 42,834 |
| 98662 | Vancouver Mall(u) | (206) | 6,938 | .... |
| 99037 | Veradale(u) | (509) | 7,836 | 7,256 |
| 99362 | Walla Walla | (509) | 26,482 | 25,618 |
| ...... | Waller(u) | | 6,415 | .... |
| 98801 | Wenatchee | (509) | 21,756 | 17,257 |
| ...... | West Lake Sammamish(u) | | 6,087 | .... |
| 98258 | West Lake Stevens(u) | (206) | 12,453 | .... |
| 99301 | West Pasco(u) | (509) | 7,312 | 6,210 |
| 98181 | West Valley(u) | | 6,594 | .... |
| 98166 | White Center-Shorewood(u) | (206) | 20,531 | 19,362 |
| 98072 | Woodinville(u) | | 23,654 | .... |
| 98032 | Woodmont Beach(u) | | 7,493 | .... |
| *98901 | Yakima | (509) | 54,843 | 49,826 |

## West Virginia (304)

| ZIP code | Place | 1990 | 1980 |
|---|---|---|---|
| 25801 | Beckley | 18,296 | 20,492 |
| 24701 | Bluefield | 12,756 | 16,060 |
| 26330 | Bridgeport | 6,739 | 6,604 |
| 26201 | Buckhannon | 5,909 | 6,820 |
| *25301 | Charleston | 57,287 | 63,968 |
| 26301 | Clarksburg | 18,059 | 22,371 |
| 25301 | Cross Lanes(u) | 10,878 | .... |
| 25064 | Dunbar | 8,697 | 9,285 |
| 26241 | Elkins | 7,420 | 8,536 |
| 26554 | Fairmont | 20,210 | 23,863 |
| 26354 | Grafton | 5,524 | 6,845 |
| *25701 | Huntington | 54,844 | 63,684 |
| 26726 | Keyser | 5,870 | 6,569 |
| 25401 | Martinsburg | 14,073 | 13,063 |
| 26505 | Morgantown | 25,879 | 27,605 |
| 26041 | Moundsville | 10,753 | 12,419 |
| 26155 | New Martinsville | 6,705 | 7,109 |
| 25143 | Nitro | 6,851 | 8,074 |
| 25901 | Oak Hill | 6,812 | 7,120 |
| 26101 | Parkersburg | 33,862 | 39,946 |
| ...... | Pea Ridge(u) | 6,535 | .... |
| 24740 | Princeton | 7,043 | 7,538 |
| 25177 | Saint Albans | 11,194 | 12,402 |
| 25303 | South Charleston | 13,645 | 15,968 |
| 25569 | Teays Valley(u) | 8,436 | .... |
| 26105 | Vienna | 10,862 | 11,618 |
| 26062 | Weirton | 22,124 | 25,371 |
| 26003 | Wheeling | 34,882 | 43,070 |

# Wisconsin

| ZIP code | Place | | 1990 | 1980 |
|---|---|---|---|---|
| 54301 | Allouez | (414) | 14,431 | 14,882 |
| 54720 | Altoona | | 5,889 | 4,393 |
| 54409 | Antigo | (715) | 8,275 | 8,653 |
| 54911 | Appleton | (414) | 65,695 | 58,913 |
| 54806 | Ashland | (715) | 8,695 | 9,115 |
| 54304 | Ashwaubenon | (414) | 16,376 | 14,486 |
| 53913 | Baraboo | (608) | 9,203 | 8,081 |
| 53916 | Beaver Dam | (414) | 14,196 | 14,149 |
| ...... | Bellevue Town(u) | | 7,541 | .... |
| 53511 | Beloit | (608) | 35,571 | 35,207 |
| 54923 | Berlin | (414) | 5,377 | 5,478 |
| 53005 | Brookfield | (414) | 35,184 | 34,035 |
| 53209 | Brown Deer | (414) | 12,236 | 12,921 |
| 53105 | Burlington | (414) | 8,855 | 8,385 |
| 53012 | Cedarburg | (414) | 10,086 | 9,005 |
| 54729 | Chippewa Falls | (715) | 12,727 | 12,270 |
| 53110 | Cudahy | (414) | 18,659 | 19,547 |
| 53018 | Delafield | | 5,347 | 4,083 |
| 53115 | Delavan | (414) | 6,073 | 5,684 |
| 54115 | De Pere | (414) | 16,569 | 14,892 |
| 54701 | Eau Claire | (715) | 56,806 | 51,509 |
| 53121 | Elkhorn | (414) | 5,337 | 4,605 |
| 53122 | Elm Grove | (414) | 6,261 | 6,735 |
| 53714 | Fitchburg | (608) | 15,648 | 11,965 |
| 54935 | Fond Du Lac | (414) | 37,757 | 35,863 |
| 53538 | Fort Atkinson | (414) | 10,213 | 9,785 |
| 53217 | Fox Point | (414) | 7,238 | 7,649 |
| 53132 | Franklin | (414) | 21,855 | 16,871 |
| 53022 | Germantown | (414) | 13,658 | 10,729 |
| 53209 | Glendale | (414) | 14,088 | 13,882 |
| 53024 | Grafton | (414) | 9,340 | 8,381 |
| *54305 | Green Bay | (414) | 96,466 | 87,899 |
| 53129 | Greendale | (414) | 15,128 | 16,928 |
| 53220 | Greenfield | (414) | 33,403 | 31,353 |
| 53130 | Hales Corners | (414) | 7,623 | 7,110 |
| 53027 | Hartford | (414) | 8,188 | 7,159 |
| 53029 | Hartland | (414) | 6,906 | 5,559 |
| 54303 | Howard | (414) | 9,874 | 8,240 |
| 54016 | Hudson | (715) | 6,378 | 5,434 |
| 53545 | Janesville | (608) | 52,210 | 51,071 |
| 53549 | Jefferson | (414) | 6,078 | 5,647 |
| 54130 | Kaukauna | (414) | 11,982 | 11,310 |
| 53140 | Kenosha | (414) | 80,426 | 77,685 |
| 53136 | Kimberly | (414) | 5,406 | 5,881 |
| 54601 | La Crosse | (608) | 51,120 | 48,347 |
| 53147 | Lake Geneva | (414) | 5,979 | 5,612 |
| 54140 | Little Chute | (414) | 9,207 | 7,907 |
| 53558 | McFarland | (608) | 5,232 | 3,783 |
| *53701 | Madison | (608) | 190,766 | 170,616 |
| 54220 | Manitowoc | (414) | 32,520 | 32,547 |
| 54143 | Marinette | (715) | 11,843 | 11,965 |
| 54449 | Marshfield | (715) | 19,291 | 18,290 |
| 54952 | Menasha | (414) | 14,711 | 14,728 |
| 53051 | Menomonee Falls | (414) | 26,840 | 27,845 |
| 54751 | Menomonie | (715) | 13,547 | 12,769 |
| 53092 | Mequon | (414) | 18,885 | 16,193 |
| 54452 | Merrill | (715) | 9,860 | 9,578 |
| 53562 | Middleton | (608) | 13,785 | 11,851 |
| *53203 | Milwaukee | (414) | 628,088 | 636,297 |
| 53716 | Monona | (608) | 8,637 | 8,809 |
| 53566 | Monroe | (608) | 10,241 | 10,027 |
| 53150 | Muskego | (414) | 16,813 | 15,277 |
| 54956 | Neenah | (414) | 23,219 | 22,432 |
| 53151 | New Berlin | (414) | 33,592 | 30,529 |
| 54961 | New London | (414) | 6,658 | 6,210 |
| 54017 | New Richmond | (715) | 5,106 | 4,306 |
| 53154 | Oak Creek | (414) | 19,513 | 16,932 |
| 53066 | Oconomowoc | (414) | 10,993 | 9,909 |
| 54650 | Onalaska | (608) | 11,414 | 9,249 |
| 54901 | Oshkosh | (414) | 55,006 | 49,620 |
| ...... | Pewaukee | | 5,287 | .... |
| 53072 | Pewaukee | (608) | 9,862 | 9,580 |
| 53818 | Platteville | (608) | 12,037 | 12,176 |
| 53158 | Pleasant Prairie | (715) | 8,176 | 5,310 |
| 54467 | Plover | (414) | 6,769 | 6,027 |
| 53073 | Plymouth | (608) | 8,640 | 7,896 |
| 53901 | Portage | (414) | 9,338 | 8,612 |
| 53074 | Port Washington | (608) | 5,657 | 5,859 |
| 53821 | Prairie du Chien | (414) | 84,298 | 85,725 |
| *53401 | Racine | (608) | 5,834 | 5,038 |
| 53959 | Reedsburg | (715) | 7,427 | 7,873 |
| 54501 | Rhinelander | (715) | 7,998 | 7,691 |
| 54868 | Rice Lake | (608) | 5,018 | 4,997 |
| 53581 | Richland Center | (414) | 7,241 | 7,111 |
| 54971 | Ripon | (414) | 10,610 | 9,019 |
| 54022 | River Falls | (414) | 9,245 | 10,095 |
| 53207 | Saint Francis | (715) | 7,598 | 7,013 |
| 54166 | Shawano | (414) | 49,587 | 48,085 |
| 53081 | Sheboygan | (414) | | |

| ZIP code | Place | | 1990 | 1980 |
|---|---|---|---|---|
| 53085 | Sheboygan Falls | (414) | 5,823 | 5,253 |
| 53211 | Shorewood | (414) | 14,116 | 14,327 |
| 53172 | South Milwaukee | (414) | 20,958 | 21,069 |
| 54656 | Sparta | (608) | 7,788 | 6,934 |
| 54481 | Stevens Point | (715) | 23,006 | 22,970 |
| 53589 | Stoughton | (608) | 8,786 | 7,589 |
| 54235 | Sturgeon Bay | (414) | 9,176 | 8,847 |
| 53590 | Sun Prairie | (608) | 15,333 | 12,931 |
| 54880 | Superior | (715) | 27,134 | 29,571 |
| 53089 | Sussex | | 5,039 | 3,482 |
| 54660 | Tomah | (608) | 7,570 | 7,204 |
| 54241 | Two Rivers | (414) | 13,030 | 13,354 |
| 53593 | Verona | | 5,374 | 3,336 |
| 53094 | Watertown | (414) | 19,142 | 18,113 |
| 53186 | Waukesha | (414) | 56,958 | 50,365 |
| 53597 | Waunakee | | 5,897 | 3,866 |
| 53963 | Waupun | (414) | 8,844 | 8,132 |
| 54401 | Wausau | (715) | 37,060 | 32,426 |
| 53213 | Wauwatosa | (414) | 49,366 | 51,308* |
| 53214 | West Allis | (414) | 63,221 | 63,982 |
| 53095 | West Bend | (414) | 23,470 | 21,484 |
| 54476 | Weston(u) | (715) | 9,714 | 8,775 |
| 53217 | Whitefish Bay | (414) | 14,272 | 14,930 |

| ZIP code | Place | | 1990 | 1980 |
|---|---|---|---|---|
| 53190 | Whitewater | (414) | 12,636 | 11,520 |
| 54494 | Wisconsin Rapids | (715) | 18,245 | 17,995 |

## Wyoming (307)

| | Place | 1990 | 1980 |
|---|---|---|---|
| *82601 | Casper | 46,765 | 51,016 |
| *82001 | Cheyenne | 50,008 | 47,283 |
| 82414 | Cody | 7,897 | 6,599 |
| 82633 | Douglas | 5,076 | 6,030 |
| 82930 | Evanston | 10,904 | 6,265 |
| 82716 | Gillette | 17,545 | 12,134 |
| 82935 | Green River | 12,711 | 12,807 |
| 82520 | Lander | 7,023 | 7,867 |
| 82070 | Laramie | 26,687 | 24,410 |
| 82435 | Powell | 5,292 | 5,310 |
| 82301 | Rawlins | 9,380 | 11,547 |
| 82501 | Riverton | 9,202 | 9,562 |
| 82901 | Rock Springs | 19,050 | 19,458 |
| 82801 | Sheridan | 13,904 | 15,146 |
| 82240 | Torrington | 5,651 | 5,441 |
| 82401 | Worland | 5,742 | 6,391 |

# Census and Areas of Counties and States

Source: Bureau of the Census
With names of county seats or court houses

Population figures listed below are final counts in the 1990 census, conducted on Apr. 1, 1990; updated as of Apr. 1993.

## Alabama

(67 counties, 50,767 sq. mi. land; pop. 4,040,587)

| County | Pop. | County Seat or court house | Land area sq. mi. |
|---|---|---|---|
| Autauga | 34,222 | Prattville | 596 |
| Baldwin | 98,280 | Bay Minette | 1,596 |
| Barbour | 25,417 | Clayton | 885 |
| Bibb | 16,576 | Centreville | 622 |
| Blount | 39,248 | Oneonta | 645 |
| Bullock | 11,042 | Union Springs | 625 |
| Butler | 21,892 | Greenville | 776 |
| Calhoun | 116,032 | Anniston | 608 |
| Chambers | 36,876 | Lafayette | 597 |
| Cherokee | 19,543 | Centre | 553 |
| Chilton | 32,458 | Clanton | 694 |
| Choctaw | 16,018 | Butler | 913 |
| Clarke | 27,240 | Grove Hill | 1,238 |
| Clay | 13,252 | Ashland | 605 |
| Cleburne | 12,730 | Heflin | 560 |
| Coffee | 40,240 | Elba | 679 |
| Colbert | 51,666 | Tuscumbia | 594 |
| Conecuh | 14,054 | Evergreen | 850 |
| Coosa | 11,063 | Rockford | 652 |
| Covington | 36,478 | Andalusia | 1,034 |
| Crenshaw | 13,635 | Luverne | 609 |
| Cullman | 67,613 | Cullman | 738 |
| Dale | 49,633 | Ozark | 561 |
| Dallas | 48,130 | Selma | 980 |
| De Kalb | 54,651 | Fort Payne | 777 |
| Elmore | 49,210 | Wetumpka | 621 |
| Escambia | 35,518 | Brewton | 947 |
| Etowah | 99,840 | Gadsden | 534 |
| Fayette | 17,962 | Fayette | 627 |
| Franklin | 27,814 | Russellville | 635 |
| Geneva | 23,647 | Geneva | 576 |
| Greene | 10,153 | Eutaw | 645 |
| Hale | 15,498 | Greensboro | 643 |
| Henry | 15,374 | Abbeville | 561 |
| Houston | 81,331 | Dothan | 580 |
| Jackson | 47,796 | Scottsboro | 1,078 |
| Jefferson | 651,520 | Birmingham | 1,112 |
| Lamar | 15,715 | Vernon | 604 |
| Lauderdale | 79,661 | Florence | 669 |
| Lawrence | 31,513 | Moulton | 693 |
| Lee | 87,146 | Opelika | 608 |
| Limestone | 46,005 | Athens | 568 |
| Lowndes | 12,658 | Hayneville | 718 |
| Macon | 24,928 | Tuskegee | 610 |
| Madison | 238,912 | Huntsville | 804 |
| Marengo | 23,084 | Linden | 977 |
| Marion | 29,830 | Hamilton | 741 |
| Marshall | 70,832 | Guntersville | 567 |
| Mobile | 378,643 | Mobile | 1,233 |
| Monroe | 23,968 | Monroeville | 1,025 |
| Montgomery | 209,085 | Montgomery | 789 |
| Morgan | 100,043 | Decatur | 599 |
| Perry | 12,759 | Marion | 719 |
| Pickens | 20,699 | Carrollton | 881 |
| Pike | 27,595 | Troy | 671 |

| County | Pop. | County Seat or court house | Land area sq. mi. |
|---|---|---|---|
| Randolph | 19,881 | Wedowee | 581 |
| Russell | 46,860 | Phenix City | 641 |
| Saint Clair | 49,811 | Ashville & Pell City | 633 |
| Shelby | 99,363 | Columbiana | 794 |
| Sumter | 16,174 | Livingston | 904 |
| Talladega | 74,109 | Talladega | 739 |
| Tallapoosa | 38,826 | Dadeville | 718 |
| Tuscaloosa | 150,522 | Tuscaloosa | 1,325 |
| Walker | 67,670 | Jasper | 794 |
| Washington | 16,694 | Chatom | 1,080 |
| Wilcox | 13,568 | Camden | 888 |
| Winston | 22,053 | Double Springs | 614 |

## Alaska

(25 divisions, 570,833 sq. mi. land; pop. 550,043)

| Census Division | Pop. | Land area sq. mi. |
|---|---|---|
| Aleutian East Borough | 2,464 | 6,985 |
| Aleutians West Census Area | 9,478 | 4,402 |
| Anchorage Borough | 226,338 | 1,732 |
| Bethel Census Area | 13,656 | 36,104 |
| Bristol Bay Borough | 1,410 | 531 |
| Dillingham Census Area | 4,012 | 46,042 |
| Fairbanks North Star Borough | 77,720 | 7,404 |
| Haines Borough | 2,117 | 2,374 |
| Juneau Borough | 26,751 | 2,626 |
| Kenai Peninsula Borough | 40,802 | 16,056 |
| Ketchikan Gateway Borough | 13,828 | 1,242 |
| Kodiak Island Borough | 13,309 | 4,796 |
| Lake and Peninsula Borough | 1,668 | |
| Matanuska-Susitna Borough | 39,683 | 24,502 |
| Nome Census Area | 8,288 | 23,871 |
| North Slope Borough | 5,979 | 90,955 |
| Northwest Arctic Borough | 6,113 | |
| Prince of Wales-Outer Ketchikan Census Area | 6,278 | 7,660 |
| Sitka Borough | 8,588 | 2,938 |
| Skagway-Yakutat-Angoon Census Area | 4,385 | 13,239 |
| Southeast Fairbanks Census Area | 5,913 | 24,169 |
| Valdez-Cordova Census Area | 9,952 | 39,229 |
| Wade Hampton Census Area | 5,791 | 17,816 |
| Wrangell-Petersburg Census Area | 7,042 | 6,167 |
| Yukon-Koyukuk Census Area | 8,478 | 159,099 |

## Arizona

(15 counties, 113,508 sq. mi. land; pop. 3,665,228)

| County | Pop. | County Seat or court house | Land area sq. mi. |
|---|---|---|---|
| Apache | 61,591 | Saint Johns | 11,211 |
| Cochise | 97,624 | Bisbee | 6,218 |

| County | Pop. | County Seat or court house | Land area sq. mi. |
|---|---|---|---|
| Coconino | 96,591 | Flagstaff | 18,608 |
| Gila | 40,216 | Globe | 4,752 |
| Graham | 26,554 | Safford | 4,630 |
| Greenlee | 8,008 | Clifton | 1,837 |
| La Paz | 13,844 | Parker | 4,430 |
| Maricopa | 2,122,101 | Phoenix | 9,127 |
| Mohave | 93,497 | Kingman | 13,285 |
| Navajo | 77,674 | Holbrook | 9,955 |
| Pima | 666,957 | Tucson | 9,187 |
| Pinal | 116,379 | Florence | 5,343 |
| Santa Cruz | 29,676 | Nogales | 1,238 |
| Yavapai | 107,714 | Prescott | 8,123 |
| Yuma | 106,895 | Yuma | 5,564 |

## Arkansas

(75 counties, 52,078 sq. mi. land; pop. 2,350,725)

| County | Pop. | County Seat or court house | Land area sq. mi. |
|---|---|---|---|
| Arkansas | 21,653 | DeWitt & Stuttgart | 1,033 |
| Ashley | 24,319 | Hamburg | 939 |
| Baxter | 31,186 | Mountain Home | 586 |
| Benton | 97,499 | Bentonville | 876 |
| Boone | 28,297 | Harrison | 601 |
| Bradley | 11,793 | Warren | 654 |
| Calhoun | 5,826 | Hampton | 632 |
| Carroll | 18,654 | Berryville & Eureka Sp. | 642 |
| Chicot | 15,713 | Lake Village | 690 |
| Clark | 21,437 | Arkadelphia | 882 |
| Clay | 18,107 | Corning & Piggott | 641 |
| Cleburne | 19,411 | Heber Springs | 591 |
| Cleveland | 7,781 | Rison | 598 |
| Columbia | 25,691 | Magnolia | 766 |
| Conway | 19,151 | Morrilton | 566 |
| Craighead | 68,956 | Jonesboro & Lake City | 713 |
| Crawford | 42,493 | Van Buren | 604 |
| Crittenden | 49,939 | Marion | 636 |
| Cross | 19,225 | Wynne | 622 |
| Dallas | 9,614 | Fordyce | 668 |
| Desha | 16,798 | Arkansas City | 819 |
| Drew | 17,369 | Monticello | 835 |
| Faulkner | 60,006 | Conway | 664 |
| Franklin | 14,897 | Charleston & Ozark | 919 |
| Fulton | 10,037 | Salem | 620 |
| Garland | 73,397 | Hot Springs | 734 |
| Grant | 13,948 | Sheridan | 633 |
| Greene | 31,804 | Paragould | 579 |
| Hempstead | 21,621 | Hope | 741 |
| Hot Spring | 26,115 | Malvern | 622 |
| Howard | 13,569 | Nashville | 595 |
| Independence | 31,192 | Batesville | 771 |
| Izard | 11,364 | Melbourne | 584 |
| Jackson | 18,944 | Newport | 641 |
| Jefferson | 85,487 | Pine Bluff | 913 |
| Johnson | 18,221 | Clarksville | 682 |
| Lafayette | 9,643 | Lewisville | 545 |
| Lawrence | 17,455 | Walnut Ridge | 592 |
| Lee | 13,053 | Marianna | 619 |
| Lincoln | 13,690 | Star City | 572 |
| Little River | 13,966 | Ashdown | 564 |
| Logan | 20,557 | Booneville & Paris | 731 |
| Lonoke | 39,268 | Lonoke | 802 |
| Madison | 11,618 | Huntsville | 837 |
| Marion | 12,001 | Yellville | 640 |
| Miller | 38,467 | Texarkana | 637 |
| Mississippi | 57,525 | Blytheville & Osceola | 919 |
| Monroe | 11,333 | Clarendon | 621 |
| Montgomery | 7,841 | Mount Ida | 800 |
| Nevada | 10,101 | Prescott | 620 |
| Newton | 7,666 | Jasper | 823 |
| Ouachita | 30,574 | Camden | 739 |
| Perry | 7,969 | Perryville | 560 |
| Phillips | 28,836 | Helena | 727 |
| Pike | 10,086 | Murfreesboro | 613 |
| Poinsett | 24,664 | Harrisburg | 763 |
| Polk | 17,347 | Mena | 862 |
| Pope | 45,883 | Russellville | 830 |
| Prairie | 9,518 | Des Arc & De Valls Bluff | 675 |
| Pulaski | 349,569 | Little Rock | 807 |
| Randolph | 16,558 | Pocahontas | 656 |
| Saint Francis | 28,497 | Forrest City | 642 |
| Saline | 64,183 | Benton | 730 |
| Scott | 10,205 | Waldron | 898 |
| Searcy | 7,841 | Marshall | 668 |
| Sebastian | 99,590 | Fort Smith & Greenwood | 546 |
| Sevier | 13,637 | De Queen | 581 |
| Sharp | 14,109 | Ash Flat | 606 |
| Stone | 9,775 | Mountain View | 609 |
| Union | 46,719 | El Dorado | 1,055 |
| Van Buren | 14,008 | Clinton | 724 |
| Washington | 113,409 | Fayetteville | 956 |
| White | 54,676 | Searcy | 1,042 |
| Woodruff | 9,520 | Augusta | 594 |
| Yell | 17,759 | Danville & Dardanelle | 948 |

## California

(58 counties, 156,299 sq. mi. land; pop. 29,760,021)

| County | Pop. | County Seat or court house | Land area sq. mi. |
|---|---|---|---|
| Alameda | 1,276,702 | Oakland | 736 |
| Alpine | 1,113 | Markleeville | 738 |
| Amador | 30,039 | Jackson | 589 |
| Butte | 182,120 | Oroville | 1,646 |
| Calaveras | 31,998 | San Andreas | 1,021 |
| Colusa | 16,275 | Colusa | 1,152 |
| Contra Costa | 803,732 | Martinez | 730 |
| Del Norte | 23,460 | Crescent City | 1,007 |
| El Dorado | 125,995 | Placerville | 1,715 |
| Fresno | 667,490 | Fresno | 5,978 |
| Glenn | 24,798 | Willows | 1,319 |
| Humboldt | 119,118 | Eureka | 3,579 |
| Imperial | 109,303 | El Centro | 4,173 |
| Inyo | 18,281 | Independence | 10,223 |
| Kern | 543,981 | Bakersfield | 8,130 |
| Kings | 101,469 | Hanford | 1,392 |
| Lake | 50,631 | Lakeport | 1,262 |
| Lassen | 27,598 | Susanville | 4,553 |
| Los Angeles | 8,863,052 | Los Angeles | 4,070 |
| Madera | 88,090 | Madera | 2,145 |
| Marin | 230,096 | San Rafael | 523 |
| Mariposa | 14,302 | Mariposa | 1,456 |
| Mendocino | 80,345 | Ukiah | 3,512 |
| Merced | 178,403 | Merced | 1,944 |
| Modoc | 9,678 | Alturas | 4,064 |
| Mono | 9,956 | Bridgeport | 3,018 |
| Monterey | 355,660 | Salinas | 3,303 |
| Napa | 110,765 | Napa | 744 |
| Nevada | 78,510 | Nevada City | 960 |
| Orange | 2,410,668 | Santa Ana | 798 |
| Placer | 172,796 | Auburn | 1,416 |
| Plumas | 19,739 | Quincy | 2,573 |
| Riverside | 1,170,413 | Riverside | 7,214 |
| Sacramento | 1,041,219 | Sacramento | 971 |
| San Benito | 36,697 | Hollister | 1,388 |
| San Bernardino | 1,418,380 | San Bernardino | 20,064 |
| San Diego | 2,498,016 | San Diego | 4,212 |
| San Francisco | 723,959 | San Francisco | 46 |
| San Joaquin | 480,628 | Stockton | 1,415 |
| San Luis Obispo | 217,162 | San Luis Obispo | 3,308 |
| San Mateo | 649,623 | Redwood City | 447 |
| Santa Barbara | 369,608 | Santa Barbara | 2,748 |
| Santa Clara | 1,497,577 | San Jose | 1,293 |
| Santa Cruz | 229,734 | Santa Cruz | 446 |
| Shasta | 147,036 | Redding | 3,786 |
| Sierra | 3,318 | Downieville | 959 |
| Siskiyou | 43,531 | Yreka | 6,281 |
| Solano | 339,471 | Fairfield | 834 |
| Sonoma | 388,222 | Santa Rosa | 1,604 |
| Stanislaus | 370,522 | Modesto | 1,506 |
| Sutter | 64,415 | Yuba City | 602 |
| Tehama | 49,625 | Red Bluff | 2,953 |
| Trinity | 13,063 | Weaverville | 3,190 |
| Tulare | 311,921 | Visalia | 4,808 |
| Tuolumne | 48,456 | Sonora | 2,234 |
| Ventura | 669,016 | Ventura | 1,862 |
| Yolo | 141,210 | Woodland | 1,014 |
| Yuba | 58,228 | Marysville | 640 |

## Colorado

(63 counties, 103,595 sq. mi. land; pop. 3,294,394)

| County | Pop. | County Seat or court house | Land area sq. mi. |
|---|---|---|---|
| Adams | 265,038 | Brighton | 1,235 |
| Alamosa | 13,617 | Alamosa | 719 |
| Arapahoe | 391,511 | Littleton | 800 |
| Archuleta | 5,345 | Pagosa Springs | 1,353 |
| Baca | 4,556 | Springfield | 2,554 |
| Bent | 5,048 | Las Animas | 1,517 |
| Boulder | 225,339 | Boulder | 742 |
| Chaffee | 12,684 | Salida | 1,008 |
| Cheyenne | 2,397 | Cheyenne Wells | 1,783 |
| Clear Creek | 7,619 | Georgetown | 396 |
| Conejos | 7,453 | Conejos | 1,284 |
| Costilla | 3,190 | San Luis | 1,227 |
| Crowley | 3,946 | Ordway | 790 |
| Custer | 1,926 | Westcliffe | 740 |
| Delta | 20,980 | Delta | 1,141 |
| Denver | 467,610 | Denver | 111 |
| Dolores | 1,504 | Dove Creek | 1,064 |
| Douglas | 60,391 | Castle Rock | 841 |
| Eagle | 21,928 | Eagle | 1,690 |
| Elbert | 9,646 | Kiowa | 1,851 |
| El Paso | 397,014 | Colorado Springs | 2,129 |
| Fremont | 32,273 | Canon City | 1,538 |
| Garfield | 29,974 | Glenwood Springs | 2,952 |
| Gilpin | 3,070 | Central City | 149 |
| Grand | 7,966 | Hot Sulphur Springs | 1,854 |
| Gunnison | 10,273 | Gunnison | 3,238 |
| Hinsdale | 467 | Lake City | 1,115 |

| County | Pop. | County Seat or court house | Land area sq. mi. |
|---|---|---|---|
| Huerfano | 6,009 | Walsenburg | 1,584 |
| Jackson | 1,605 | Walden | 1,614 |
| Jefferson | 438,430 | Golden | 768 |
| Kiowa | 1,688 | Eads | 1,758 |
| Kit Carson | 7,140 | Burlington | 2,160 |
| Lake | 6,007 | Leadville | 379 |
| La Plata | 32,284 | Durango | 1,692 |
| Larimer | 186,136 | Fort Collins | 2,604 |
| Las Animas | 13,765 | Trinidad | 4,771 |
| Lincoln | 4,529 | Hugo | 2,586 |
| Logan | 17,567 | Sterling | 1,818 |
| Mesa | 93,145 | Grand Junction | 3,309 |
| Mineral | 558 | Creede | 877 |
| Moffat | 11,357 | Craig | 4,732 |
| Montezuma | 18,672 | Cortez | 2,038 |
| Montrose | 24,423 | Montrose | 2,240 |
| Morgan | 21,939 | Fort Morgan | 1,276 |
| Otero | 20,185 | La Junta | 1,247 |
| Ouray | 2,295 | Ouray | 542 |
| Park | 7,174 | Fairplay | 2,192 |
| Phillips | 4,189 | Holyoke | 688 |
| Pitkin | 12,661 | Aspen | 968 |
| Prowers | 13,347 | Lamar | 1,629 |
| Pueblo | 123,051 | Pueblo | 2,377 |
| Rio Blanco | 5,972 | Meeker | 3,222 |
| Rio Grande | 10,770 | Del Norte | 913 |
| Routt | 14,088 | Steamboat Springs | 2,367 |
| Saguache | 4,619 | Saguache | 3,167 |
| San Juan | 745 | Silverton | 388 |
| San Miguel | 3,653 | Telluride | 1,287 |
| Sedgwick | 2,690 | Julesburg | 540 |
| Summit | 12,881 | Breckenridge | 607 |
| Teller | 12,468 | Cripple Creek | 559 |
| Washington | 4,812 | Akron | 2,520 |
| Weld | 131,821 | Greeley | 3,990 |
| Yuma | 8,954 | Wray | 2,365 |

## Connecticut

(8 counties, 4,872 sq. mi. land; pop. 3,287,116)

| County | Pop. | County Seat | Land area |
|---|---|---|---|
| Fairfield | 827,645 | Bridgeport | 632 |
| Hartford | 852,783 | Hartford | 739 |
| Litchfield | 174,092 | Litchfield | 921 |
| Middlesex | 143,196 | Middletown | 373 |
| New Haven | 804,219 | New Haven | 610 |
| New London | 254,957 | Norwich | 669 |
| Tolland | 128,699 | Rockville | 412 |
| Windham | 102,525 | Putnam | 515 |

## Delaware

(3 counties, 1,932 sq. mi. land; pop. 666,168)

| County | Pop. | County Seat | Land area |
|---|---|---|---|
| Kent | 110,993 | Dover | 595 |
| New Castle | 441,946 | Wilmington | 396 |
| Sussex | 113,229 | Georgetown | 942 |

## District of Columbia

(63 sq. mi. land; pop. 606,900)

## Florida

(67 counties, 54,153 sq. mi. land; pop. 12,937,926)

| County | Pop. | County Seat | Land area |
|---|---|---|---|
| Alachua | 181,596 | Gainesville | 901 |
| Baker | 18,486 | Macclenny | 585 |
| Bay | 126,994 | Panama City | 758 |
| Bradford | 22,515 | Starke | 293 |
| Brevard | 398,978 | Titusville | 995 |
| Broward | 1,255,518 | Fort Lauderdale | 1,211 |
| Calhoun | 11,011 | Blountstown | 568 |
| Charlotte | 110,975 | Punta Gorda | 690 |
| Citrus | 93,513 | Inverness | 629 |
| Clay | 105,986 | Green Cove Springs | 592 |
| Collier | 152,099 | Naples | 1,994 |
| Columbia | 42,613 | Lake City | 796 |
| Dade | 1,937,194 | Miami | 1,955 |
| De Soto | 23,865 | Arcadia | 636 |
| Dixie | 10,585 | Cross City | 701 |
| Duval | 672,971 | Jacksonville | 776 |
| Escambia | 262,798 | Pensacola | 660 |
| Flagler | 28,701 | Bunnell | 491 |
| Franklin | 8,967 | Apalachicola | 545 |
| Gadsden | 41,116 | Quincy | 518 |
| Gilchrist | 9,667 | Trenton | 354 |
| Glades | 7,591 | Moore Haven | 763 |
| Gulf | 11,504 | Port Saint Joe | 559 |

| County | Pop. | County Seat or court house | Land area sq. mi. |
|---|---|---|---|
| Hamilton | 10,930 | Jasper | 517 |
| Hardee | 19,499 | Wauchula | 637 |
| Hendry | 25,773 | La Belle | 1,163 |
| Hernando | 101,115 | Brooksville | 477 |
| Highlands | 68,432 | Sebring | 1,029 |
| Hillsborough | 834,054 | Tampa | 1,053 |
| Holmes | 15,778 | Bonifay | 488 |
| Indian River | 90,208 | Vero Beach | 497 |
| Jackson | 41,375 | Marianna | 942 |
| Jefferson | 11,296 | Monticello | 609 |
| Lafayette | 5,578 | Mayo | 545 |
| Lake | 152,104 | Tavares | 954 |
| Lee | 335,113 | Fort Myers | 803 |
| Leon | 192,493 | Tallahassee | 676 |
| Levy | 25,912 | Bronson | 1,100 |
| Liberty | 5,569 | Bristol | 837 |
| Madison | 16,569 | Madison | 710 |
| Manatee | 211,707 | Bradenton | 747 |
| Marion | 194,835 | Ocala | 1,610 |
| Martin | 100,900 | Stuart | 555 |
| Monroe | 78,024 | Key West | 1,034 |
| Nassau | 43,941 | Fernandina Beach | 649 |
| Okaloosa | 143,777 | Crestview | 936 |
| Okeechobee | 29,627 | Okeechobee | 770 |
| Orange | 677,491 | Orlando | 910 |
| Osceola | 107,728 | Kissimmee | 1,350 |
| Palm Beach | 863,503 | West Palm Beach | 1,993 |
| Pasco | 281,131 | New Port Richey | 738 |
| Pinellas | 851,659 | Clearwater | 280 |
| Polk | 405,382 | Bartow | 1,823 |
| Putnam | 65,070 | Palatka | 733 |
| Saint Johns | 83,829 | Saint Augustine | 617 |
| Saint Lucie | 150,171 | Fort Pierce | 581 |
| Santa Rosa | 81,608 | Milton | 1,024 |
| Sarasota | 277,776 | Sarasota | 573 |
| Seminole | 287,521 | Sanford | 298 |
| Sumter | 31,577 | Bushnell | 561 |
| Suwannee | 26,780 | Live Oak | 690 |
| Taylor | 17,111 | Perry | 1,058 |
| Union | 10,252 | Lake Butler | 246 |
| Volusia | 370,737 | De Land | 1,113 |
| Wakulla | 14,759 | Crawfordville | 601 |
| Walton | 27,759 | De Funiak Springs | 1,066 |
| Washington | 16,919 | Chipley | 590 |

## Georgia

(159 counties, 58,056 sq. mi. land; pop. 6,478,216)

| County | Pop. | County Seat | Land area |
|---|---|---|---|
| Appling | 15,744 | Baxley | 510 |
| Atkinson | 6,213 | Pearson | 344 |
| Bacon | 9,566 | Alma | 286 |
| Baker | 3,615 | Newton | 347 |
| Baldwin | 39,530 | Milledgeville | 257 |
| Banks | 10,308 | Homer | 234 |
| Barrow | 29,721 | Winder | 163 |
| Bartow | 55,915 | Cartersville | 456 |
| Ben Hill | 16,245 | Fitzgerald | 254 |
| Berrien | 14,153 | Nashville | 456 |
| Bibb | 150,137 | Macon | 253 |
| Bleckley | 10,430 | Cochran | 219 |
| Brantley | 11,077 | Nahunta | 445 |
| Brooks | 15,398 | Quitman | 491 |
| Bryan | 15,438 | Pembroke | 441 |
| Bulloch | 43,125 | Statesboro | 678 |
| Burke | 20,579 | Waynesboro | 833 |
| Butts | 15,326 | Jackson | 187 |
| Calhoun | 5,013 | Morgan | 284 |
| Camden | 30,167 | Woodbine | 649 |
| Candler | 7,744 | Metter | 248 |
| Carroll | 71,422 | Carrollton | 501 |
| Catoosa | 42,464 | Ringgold | 162 |
| Charlton | 8,496 | Folkston | 780 |
| Chatham | 216,774 | Savannah | 443 |
| Chattahoochee | 16,934 | Cusseta | 250 |
| Chattooga | 22,242 | Summerville | 313 |
| Cherokee | 90,204 | Canton | 424 |
| Clarke | 87,594 | Athens | 122 |
| Clay | 3,364 | Fort Gaines | 196 |
| Clayton | 182,052 | Jonesboro | 148 |
| Clinch | 6,160 | Homerville | 821 |
| Cobb | 447,745 | Marietta | 343 |
| Coffee | 29,592 | Douglas | 602 |
| Colquitt | 36,645 | Moultrie | 557 |
| Columbia | 66,031 | Appling | 290 |
| Cook | 13,456 | Adel | 233 |
| Coweta | 53,853 | Newnan | 444 |
| Crawford | 8,991 | Knoxville | 328 |
| Crisp | 20,011 | Cordele | 275 |
| Dade | 13,147 | Trenton | 176 |
| Dawson | 9,429 | Dawsonville | 210 |
| Decatur | 25,517 | Bainbridge | 586 |
| De Kalb | 546,171 | Decatur | 270 |
| Dodge | 17,607 | Eastman | 504 |
| Dooly | 9,901 | Vienna | 397 |

| County | Pop. | County Seat or court house | Land area sq. mi. |
|---|---|---|---|
| Dougherty | 96,321 | Albany | 330 |
| Douglas | 71,120 | Douglasville | 203 |
| Early | 11,854 | Blakely | 516 |
| Echols | 2,334 | Statenville | 421 |
| Effingham | 25,687 | Springfield | 482 |
| Elbert | 18,949 | Elberton | 367 |
| Emanuel | 20,546 | Swainsboro | 688 |
| Evans | 8,724 | Claxton | 186 |
| Fannin | 15,992 | Blue Ridge | 384 |
| Fayette | 62,415 | Fayetteville | 199 |
| Floyd | 81,251 | Rome | 519 |
| Forsyth | 44,083 | Cumming | 226 |
| Franklin | 16,650 | Carnesville | 264 |
| Fulton | 648,779 | Atlanta | 534 |
| Gilmer | 13,368 | Ellijay | 427 |
| Glascock | 2,357 | Gibson | 144 |
| Glynn | 62,496 | Brunswick | 412 |
| Gordon | 35,067 | Calhoun | 355 |
| Grady | 20,279 | Cairo | 459 |
| Greene | 11,793 | Greensboro | 389 |
| Gwinnett | 352,910 | Lawrenceville | 435 |
| Habersham | 27,622 | Clarkesville | 278 |
| Hall | 95,434 | Gainesville | 379 |
| Hancock | 8,908 | Sparta | 470 |
| Haralson | 21,966 | Buchanan | 283 |
| Harris | 17,788 | Hamilton | 464 |
| Hart | 19,712 | Hartwell | 230 |
| Heard | 8,628 | Franklin | 292 |
| Henry | 58,741 | McDonough | 321 |
| Houston | 89,208 | Perry | 380 |
| Irwin | 8,649 | Ocilla | 362 |
| Jackson | 30,005 | Jefferson | 342 |
| Jasper | 8,453 | Monticello | 371 |
| Jeff Davis | 12,032 | Hazlehurst | 335 |
| Jefferson | 17,408 | Louisville | 529 |
| Jenkins | 8,247 | Millen | 353 |
| Johnson | 8,329 | Wrightsville | 306 |
| Jones | 20,739 | Gray | 394 |
| Lamar | 13,038 | Barnesville | 186 |
| Lanier | 5,531 | Lakeland | 194 |
| Laurens | 39,988 | Dublin | 816 |
| Lee | 16,250 | Leesburg | 358 |
| Liberty | 52,745 | Hinesville | 517 |
| Lincoln | 7,442 | Lincolnton | 196 |
| Long | 6,202 | Ludowici | 402 |
| Lowndes | 75,981 | Valdosta | 507 |
| Lumpkin | 14,573 | Dahlonega | 287 |
| McDuffie | 20,119 | Thomson | 256 |
| McIntosh | 8,634 | Darien | 425 |
| Macon | 13,114 | Oglethorpe | 404 |
| Madison | 21,050 | Danielsville | 285 |
| Marion | 5,590 | Buena Vista | 366 |
| Meriwether | 22,411 | Greenville | 506 |
| Miller | 6,280 | Colquitt | 284 |
| Mitchell | 20,275 | Camilla | 512 |
| Monroe | 17,113 | Forsyth | 397 |
| Montgomery | 7,379 | Mount Vernon | 244 |
| Morgan | 12,883 | Madison | 349 |
| Murray | 26,147 | Chatsworth | 345 |
| Muscogee | 179,278 | Columbus | 218 |
| Newton | 41,808 | Covington | 277 |
| Oconee | 17,618 | Watkinsville | 186 |
| Oglethorpe | 9,763 | Lexington | 442 |
| Paulding | 41,611 | Dallas | 312 |
| Peach | 21,189 | Fort Valley | 152 |
| Pickens | 14,432 | Jasper | 232 |
| Pierce | 13,328 | Blackshear | 344 |
| Pike | 10,224 | Zebulon | 219 |
| Polk | 33,815 | Cedartown | 311 |
| Pulaski | 8,108 | Hawkinsville | 249 |
| Putnam | 14,137 | Eatonton | 344 |
| Quitman | 2,209 | Georgetown | 146 |
| Rabun | 11,648 | Clayton | 370 |
| Randolph | 8,023 | Cuthbert | 431 |
| Richmond | 189,719 | Augusta | 326 |
| Rockdale | 54,091 | Conyers | 132 |
| Schley | 3,588 | Ellaville | 169 |
| Screven | 13,842 | Sylvania | 655 |
| Seminole | 9,010 | Donalsonville | 225 |
| Spalding | 54,457 | Griffin | 199 |
| Stephens | 23,251 | Toccoa | 177 |
| Stewart | 5,654 | Lumpkin | 452 |
| Sumter | 30,228 | Americus | 489 |
| Talbot | 6,524 | Talbotton | 395 |
| Taliaferro | 1,915 | Crawfordville | 196 |
| Tattnall | 17,722 | Reidsville | 484 |
| Taylor | 7,642 | Butler | 382 |
| Telfair | 11,000 | McRae | 444 |
| Terrell | 10,653 | Dawson | 337 |
| Thomas | 38,943 | Thomasville | 551 |
| Tift | 34,998 | Tifton | 268 |
| Toombs | 24,072 | Lyons | 371 |
| Towns | 6,754 | Hiawassee | 165 |
| Treutlen | 5,994 | Soperton | 202 |
| Troup | 55,532 | La Grange | 414 |
| Turner | 8,703 | Ashburn | 289 |
| Twiggs | 9,806 | Jeffersonville | 362 |
| Union | 11,993 | Blairsville | 320 |

| County | Pop. | County Seat or court house | Land area sq. mi. |
|---|---|---|---|
| Upson | 26,300 | Thomaston | 326 |
| Walker | 58,340 | La Fayette | 446 |
| Walton | 38,586 | Monroe | 330 |
| Ware | 35,471 | Waycross | 907 |
| Warren | 6,078 | Warrenton | 286 |
| Washington | 19,112 | Sandersville | 684 |
| Wayne | 22,356 | Jesup | 647 |
| Webster | 2,263 | Preston | 210 |
| Wheeler | 4,903 | Alamo | 299 |
| White | 13,006 | Cleveland | 242 |
| Whitfield | 72,462 | Dalton | 291 |
| Wilcox | 7,008 | Abbeville | 382 |
| Wilkes | 10,597 | Washington | 470 |
| Wilkinson | 10,228 | Irwinton | 451 |
| Worth | 19,744 | Sylvester | 575 |

## Hawaii

(4 counties, 6,645 sq. mi. land; pop. 1,108,229)

| County | Pop. | County Seat or court house | Land area sq. mi. |
|---|---|---|---|
| Hawaii | 120,317 | Hilo | 4,034 |
| Honolulu | 836,231 | Honolulu | 596 |
| Kauai | 51,177 | Lihue | 620 |
| Maui | 100,374 | Wailuku | 1,175 |

## Idaho

(44 counties, 82,412 sq. mi. land; pop. 1,006,749)

| County | Pop. | County Seat or court house | Land area sq. mi. |
|---|---|---|---|
| Ada | 205,775 | Boise | 1,052 |
| Adams | 3,254 | Council | 1,362 |
| Bannock | 66,026 | Pocatello | 1,112 |
| Bear Lake | 6,084 | Paris | 990 |
| Benewah | 7,937 | Saint Maries | 784 |
| Bingham | 37,583 | Blackfoot | 2,096 |
| Blaine | 13,552 | Hailey | 2,634 |
| Boise | 3,509 | Idaho City | 1,901 |
| Bonner | 26,622 | Sandpoint | 1,726 |
| Bonneville | 72,207 | Idaho Falls | 1,840 |
| Boundary | 8,332 | Bonners Ferry | 1,268 |
| Butte | 2,918 | Arco | 2,236 |
| Camas | 727 | Fairfield | 1,071 |
| Canyon | 90,076 | Caldwell | 584 |
| Caribou | 6,963 | Soda Springs | 1,763 |
| Cassia | 19,532 | Burley | 2,560 |
| Clark | 762 | Dubois | 1,763 |
| Clearwater | 8,505 | Orofino | 2,460 |
| Custer | 4,133 | Challis | 4,927 |
| Elmore | 21,205 | Mountain Home | 3,071 |
| Franklin | 9,232 | Preston | 664 |
| Fremont | 10,937 | Saint Anthony | 1,852 |
| Gem | 11,844 | Emmett | 558 |
| Gooding | 11,633 | Gooding | 728 |
| Idaho | 13,768 | Grangeville | 8,497 |
| Jefferson | 16,543 | Rigby | 1,093 |
| Jerome | 15,138 | Jerome | 601 |
| Kootenai | 69,795 | Coeur d'Alene | 1,240 |
| Latah | 30,617 | Moscow | 1,077 |
| Lemhi | 6,899 | Salmon | 4,564 |
| Lewis | 3,516 | Nezperce | 478 |
| Lincoln | 3,308 | Shoshone | 1,205 |
| Madison | 23,674 | Rexberg | 468 |
| Minidoka | 19,361 | Rupert | 757 |
| Nez Perce | 33,754 | Lewiston | 845 |
| Oneida | 3,492 | Malad City | 1,200 |
| Owyhee | 8,392 | Murphy | 7,643 |
| Payette | 16,434 | Payette | 405 |
| Power | 7,086 | American Falls | 1,403 |
| Shoshone | 13,931 | Wallace | 2,641 |
| Teton | 3,439 | Driggs | 448 |
| Twin Falls | 53,580 | Twin Falls | 1,944 |
| Valley | 6,109 | Cascade | 3,670 |
| Washington | 8,550 | Weiser | 1,454 |

## Illinois

(102 counties, 55,646 sq. mi. land; pop. 11,430,602)

| County | Pop. | County Seat or court house | Land area sq. mi. |
|---|---|---|---|
| Adams | 66,090 | Quincy | 862 |
| Alexander | 10,626 | Cairo | 229 |
| Bond | 14,991 | Greenville | 378 |
| Boone | 30,806 | Belvidere | 283 |
| Brown | 5,836 | Mount Sterling | 306 |
| Bureau | 35,688 | Princeton | 866 |
| Calhoun | 5,322 | Hardin | 247 |
| Carroll | 16,805 | Mount Carroll | 456 |
| Cass | 13,437 | Virginia | 371 |
| Champaign | 173,025 | Urbana | 1,000 |
| Christian | 34,418 | Taylorville | 709 |
| Clark | 15,921 | Marshall | 505 |
| Clay | 14,460 | Louisville | 464 |

| County | Pop. | County Seat or court house | Land area sq. mi. |
|---|---|---|---|
| Clinton | 33,944 | Carlyle | 434 |
| Coles | 51,644 | Charleston | 506 |
| Cook | 5,105,067 | Chicago | 954 |
| Crawford | 19,464 | Robinson | 443 |
| Cumberland | 10,670 | Toledo | 347 |
| DeKalb | 77,932 | Sycamore | 636 |
| De Witt | 16,516 | Clinton | 399 |
| Douglas | 19,464 | Tuscola | 420 |
| Du Page | 781,666 | Wheaton | 337 |
| Edgar | 19,595 | Paris | 628 |
| Edwards | 7,440 | Albion | 225 |
| Effingham | 31,704 | Effingham | 481 |
| Fayette | 20,893 | Vandalia | 703 |
| Ford | 14,275 | Paxton | 488 |
| Franklin | 40,319 | Benton | 434 |
| Fulton | 38,080 | Lewiston | 877 |
| Gallatin | 6,909 | Shawneetown | 328 |
| Greene | 15,317 | Carrollton | 543 |
| Grundy | 32,337 | Morris | 432 |
| Hamilton | 8,499 | McLeansboro | 435 |
| Hancock | 21,373 | Carthage | 797 |
| Hardin | 5,189 | Elizabethtown | 183 |
| Henderson | 8,096 | Oquawka | 376 |
| Henry | 51,159 | Cambridge | 826 |
| Iroquois | 30,787 | Watseka | 1,122 |
| Jackson | 61,067 | Murphysboro | 605 |
| Jasper | 10,609 | Newton | 495 |
| Jefferson | 37,020 | Mount Vernon | 573 |
| Jersey | 20,539 | Jerseyville | 376 |
| Jo Daviess | 21,821 | Galena | 606 |
| Johnson | 11,347 | Vienna | 345 |
| Kane | 317,471 | Geneva | 520 |
| Kankakee | 96,255 | Kankakee | 678 |
| Kendall | 39,413 | Yorkville | 320 |
| Knox | 56,393 | Galesburg | 728 |
| Lake | 516,418 | Waukegan | 457 |
| La Salle | 106,913 | Ottawa | 1,150 |
| Lawrence | 15,972 | Lawrenceville | 374 |
| Lee | 34,392 | Dixon | 728 |
| Livingston | 39,301 | Pontiac | 1,043 |
| Logan | 30,798 | Lincoln | 622 |
| McDonough | 35,244 | Macomb | 582 |
| McHenry | 183,241 | Woodstock | 610 |
| McLean | 129,180 | Bloomington | 1,173 |
| Macon | 117,206 | Decatur | 578 |
| Macoupin | 47,679 | Carlinville | 872 |
| Madison | 249,238 | Edwardsville | 733 |
| Marion | 41,561 | Salem | 579 |
| Marshall | 12,846 | Lacon | 391 |
| Mason | 16,269 | Havana | 541 |
| Massac | 14,752 | Metropolis | 245 |
| Menard | 11,164 | Petersburg | 312 |
| Mercer | 17,290 | Aledo | 556 |
| Monroe | 22,422 | Waterloo | 382 |
| Montgomery | 30,728 | Hillsboro | 705 |
| Morgan | 36,397 | Jacksonville | 561 |
| Moultrie | 13,930 | Sullivan | 326 |
| Ogle | 45,957 | Oregon | 758 |
| Peoria | 182,827 | Peoria | 623 |
| Perry | 21,412 | Pinckneyville | 439 |
| Piatt | 15,548 | Monticello | 437 |
| Pike | 17,577 | Pittsfield | 828 |
| Pope | 4,373 | Golconda | 381 |
| Pulaski | 7,523 | Mound City | 204 |
| Putnam | 5,730 | Hennepin | 160 |
| Randolph | 34,583 | Chester | 594 |
| Richland | 16,545 | Olney | 364 |
| Rock Island | 148,723 | Rock Island | 424 |
| Saint Clair | 262,852 | Belleville | 673 |
| Saline | 26,551 | Harrisburg | 383 |
| Sangamon | 178,386 | Springfield | 879 |
| Schuyler | 7,498 | Rushville | 434 |
| Scott | 5,644 | Winchester | 251 |
| Shelby | 22,261 | Shelbyville | 752 |
| Stark | 6,534 | Toulon | 291 |
| Stephenson | 48,052 | Freeport | 568 |
| Tazewell | 123,692 | Pekin | 652 |
| Union | 17,619 | Jonesboro | 416 |
| Vermilion | 88,257 | Danville | 899 |
| Wabash | 13,111 | Mount Carmel | 222 |
| Warren | 19,181 | Monmouth | 541 |
| Washington | 14,965 | Nashville | 564 |
| Wayne | 17,241 | Fairfield | 715 |
| White | 16,522 | Carmi | 502 |
| Whiteside | 60,186 | Morrison | 687 |
| Will | 357,313 | Joliet | 847 |
| Williamson | 57,733 | Marion | 429 |
| Winnebago | 252,913 | Rockford | 519 |
| Woodford | 32,653 | Eureka | 528 |

## Indiana

(92 counties, 35,870 sq. mi. land; pop. 5,544,159)

| County | Pop. | County Seat or court house | Land area sq. mi. |
|---|---|---|---|
| Adams | 31,095 | Decatur | 339 |
| Allen | 300,836 | Fort Wayne | 657 |
| Bartholomew | 63,657 | Columbus | 407 |
| Benton | 9,441 | Fowler | 406 |
| Blackford | 14,067 | Hartford City | 165 |
| Boone | 38,147 | Lebanon | 423 |
| Brown | 14,080 | Nashville | 312 |
| Carroll | 18,809 | Delphi | 372 |
| Cass | 38,413 | Logansport | 413 |
| Clark | 87,774 | Jeffersonville | 375 |
| Clay | 24,705 | Brazil | 358 |
| Clinton | 30,974 | Frankfort | 405 |
| Crawford | 9,914 | English | 306 |
| Daviess | 27,533 | Washington | 431 |
| Dearborn | 38,835 | Lawrenceburg | 305 |
| Decatur | 23,645 | Greensburg | 373 |
| DeKalb | 35,324 | Auburn | 363 |
| Delaware | 119,659 | Muncie | 393 |
| Dubois | 36,616 | Jasper | 430 |
| Elkhart | 156,198 | Goshen | 464 |
| Fayette | 26,015 | Connersville | 215 |
| Floyd | 64,404 | New Albany | 148 |
| Fountain | 17,808 | Covington | 396 |
| Franklin | 19,580 | Brookville | 386 |
| Fulton | 18,840 | Rochester | 369 |
| Gibson | 31,913 | Princeton | 489 |
| Grant | 74,169 | Marion | 414 |
| Greene | 30,410 | Bloomfield | 542 |
| Hamilton | 108,936 | Noblesville | 398 |
| Hancock | 45,527 | Greenfield | 306 |
| Harrison | 29,890 | Corydon | 485 |
| Hendricks | 75,717 | Danville | 408 |
| Henry | 48,139 | New Castle | 393 |
| Howard | 80,827 | Kokomo | 293 |
| Huntington | 35,427 | Huntington | 383 |
| Jackson | 37,730 | Brownstown | 509 |
| Jasper | 24,960 | Rensselaer | 560 |
| Jay | 21,512 | Portland | 384 |
| Jefferson | 29,797 | Madison | 361 |
| Jennings | 23,661 | Vernon | 377 |
| Johnson | 88,109 | Franklin | 320 |
| Knox | 39,884 | Vincennes | 516 |
| Kosciusko | 65,294 | Warsaw | 538 |
| Lagrange | 29,477 | Lagrange | 380 |
| Lake | 475,594 | Crown Point | 497 |
| La Porte | 107,066 | La Porte | 598 |
| Lawrence | 42,836 | Bedford | 449 |
| Madison | 130,669 | Anderson | 452 |
| Marion | 797,159 | Indianapolis | 396 |
| Marshall | 42,182 | Plymouth | 444 |
| Martin | 10,369 | Shoals | 336 |
| Miami | 36,897 | Peru | 376 |
| Monroe | 108,978 | Bloomington | 394 |
| Montgomery | 34,436 | Crawfordsville | 505 |
| Morgan | 55,920 | Martinsville | 407 |
| Newton | 13,551 | Kentland | 402 |
| Noble | 37,877 | Albion | 411 |
| Ohio | 5,315 | Rising Sun | 87 |
| Orange | 18,409 | Paoli | 400 |
| Owen | 17,281 | Spencer | 385 |
| Parke | 15,410 | Rockville | 445 |
| Perry | 19,107 | Cannelton | 381 |
| Pike | 12,509 | Petersburg | 336 |
| Porter | 128,932 | Valparaiso | 418 |
| Posey | 25,968 | Mount Vernon | 409 |
| Pulaski | 12,643 | Winamac | 434 |
| Putnam | 30,315 | Greencastle | 480 |
| Randolph | 27,148 | Winchester | 453 |
| Ripley | 24,616 | Versailles | 446 |
| Rush | 18,129 | Rushville | 408 |
| Saint Joseph | 247,052 | South Bend | 457 |
| Scott | 20,991 | Scottsburg | 190 |
| Shelby | 40,307 | Shelbyville | 413 |
| Spencer | 19,490 | Rockport | 399 |
| Starke | 22,747 | Knox | 309 |
| Steuben | 27,446 | Angola | 309 |
| Sullivan | 18,993 | Sullivan | 447 |
| Switzerland | 7,738 | Vevay | 221 |
| Tippecanoe | 130,598 | Lafayette | 500 |
| Tipton | 16,119 | Tipton | 260 |
| Union | 6,976 | Liberty | 162 |
| Vanderburgh | 165,058 | Evansville | 235 |
| Vermillion | 16,773 | Newport | 257 |
| Vigo | 106,107 | Terre Haute | 403 |
| Wabash | 35,069 | Wabash | 413 |
| Warren | 8,176 | Williamsport | 365 |
| Warrick | 44,920 | Boonville | 384 |
| Washington | 23,717 | Salem | 515 |
| Wayne | 71,951 | Richmond | 404 |
| Wells | 25,948 | Bluffton | 370 |
| White | 23,265 | Monticello | 505 |
| Whitley | 27,651 | Columbia City | 336 |

## Iowa

(99 counties; 55,965 sq. mi. land; pop. 2,776,755)

| County | Pop. | County Seat or court house | Land area sq. mi. |
|---|---|---|---|
| Adair | 8,409 | Greenfield | 570 |
| Adams | 4,866 | Corning | 426 |
| Allamakee | 13,855 | Waukon | 660 |
| Appanoose | 13,743 | Centerville | 515 |
| Audubon | 7,334 | Audubon | 444 |
| Benton | 22,429 | Vinton | 718 |
| Black Hawk | 123,798 | Waterloo | 573 |
| Boone | 25,186 | Boone | 574 |
| Bremer | 22,813 | Waverly | 439 |
| Buchanan | 20,844 | Independence | 573 |
| Buena Vista | 19,965 | Storm Lake | 580 |
| Butler | 15,731 | Allison | 582 |
| Calhoun | 11,508 | Rockwell City | 573 |
| Carroll | 21,423 | Carroll | 570 |
| Cass | 15,128 | Atlantic | 565 |
| Cedar | 17,444 | Tipton | 582 |
| Cerro Gordo | 46,733 | Mason City | 575 |
| Cherokee | 14,098 | Cherokee | 577 |
| Chickasaw | 13,295 | New Hampton | 505 |
| Clarke | 8,287 | Osceola | 431 |
| Clay | 17,585 | Spencer | 573 |
| Clayton | 19,054 | Elkader | 795 |
| Clinton | 51,040 | Clinton | 710 |
| Crawford | 16,775 | Denison | 714 |
| Dallas | 29,755 | Adel | 591 |
| Davis | 8,312 | Bloomfield | 505 |
| Decatur | 8,338 | Leon | 535 |
| Delaware | 18,035 | Manchester | 579 |
| Des Moines | 42,614 | Burlington | 429 |
| Dickinson | 14,909 | Spirit Lake | 404 |
| Dubuque | 86,403 | Dubuque | 616 |
| Emmet | 11,569 | Estherville | 402 |
| Fayette | 21,843 | West Union | 731 |
| Floyd | 17,058 | Charles City | 501 |
| Franklin | 11,364 | Hampton | 583 |
| Fremont | 8,226 | Sidney | 517 |
| Greene | 10,045 | Jefferson | 572 |
| Grundy | 12,029 | Grundy Center | 501 |
| Guthrie | 10,935 | Guthrie Center | 594 |
| Hamilton | 16,071 | Webster City | 577 |
| Hancock | 12,638 | Garner | 573 |
| Hardin | 19,094 | Eldora | 569 |
| Harrison | 14,730 | Logan | 701 |
| Henry | 19,226 | Mount Pleasant | 436 |
| Howard | 9,809 | Cresco | 473 |
| Humboldt | 10,756 | Dakota City | 436 |
| Ida | 8,365 | Ida Grove | 432 |
| Iowa | 14,630 | Marengo | 588 |
| Jackson | 19,950 | Maquoketa | 650 |
| Jasper | 34,795 | Newton | 732 |
| Jefferson | 16,310 | Fairfield | 440 |
| Johnson | 96,119 | Iowa City | 623 |
| Jones | 19,444 | Anamosa | 576 |
| Keokuk | 11,624 | Sigourney | 580 |
| Kossuth | 18,591 | Algona | 976 |
| Lee | 38,687 | Fort Madison and Keokuk | 540 |
| Linn | 168,767 | Cedar Rapids | 724 |
| Louisa | 11,592 | Wapello | 417 |
| Lucas | 9,070 | Chariton | 435 |
| Lyon | 11,952 | Rock Rapids | 588 |
| Madison | 12,483 | Winterset | 563 |
| Mahaska | 21,532 | Oskaloosa | 572 |
| Marion | 30,001 | Knoxville | 575 |
| Marshall | 38,276 | Marshalltown | 573 |
| Mills | 13,202 | Glenwood | 441 |
| Mitchell | 10,928 | Osage | 470 |
| Monona | 10,034 | Onawa | 699 |
| Monroe | 8,114 | Albia | 434 |
| Montgomery | 12,076 | Red Oak | 424 |
| Muscatine | 39,907 | Muscatine | 449 |
| O'Brien | 15,444 | Primghar | 574 |
| Osceola | 7,267 | Sibley | 399 |
| Page | 16,870 | Clarinda | 535 |
| Palo Alto | 10,669 | Emmetsburg | 568 |
| Plymouth | 23,388 | Le Mars | 864 |
| Pocahontas | 9,525 | Pocahontas | 578 |
| Polk | 327,140 | Des Moines | 592 |
| Pottawattamie | 82,628 | Council Bluffs | 959 |
| Poweshiek | 19,033 | Montezuma | 586 |
| Ringgold | 5,420 | Mount Ayr | 536 |
| Sac | 12,324 | Sac City | 578 |
| Scott | 150,973 | Davenport | 469 |
| Shelby | 13,230 | Harlan | 591 |
| Sioux | 29,903 | Orange City | 769 |
| Story | 74,252 | Nevada | 574 |
| Tama | 17,419 | Toledo | 722 |
| Taylor | 7,114 | Bedford | 537 |
| Union | 12,750 | Creston | 427 |
| Van Buren | 7,676 | Keosauqua | 489 |
| Wapello | 35,696 | Ottumwa | 436 |
| Warren | 36,033 | Indianola | 573 |
| Washington | 19,612 | Washington | 571 |
| Wayne | 7,067 | Corydon | 527 |
| Webster | 40,342 | Fort Dodge | 718 |
| Winnebago | 12,122 | Forest City | 402 |
| Winneshiek | 20,847 | Decorah | 690 |
| Woodbury | 98,276 | Sioux City | 877 |
| Worth | 7,991 | Northwood | 402 |
| Wright | 14,269 | Clarion | 582 |

## Kansas

(105 counties, 81,782 sq. mi. land; pop. 2,477,574)

| County | Pop. | County Seat or court house | Land area sq. mi. |
|---|---|---|---|
| Allen | 14,638 | Iola | 505 |
| Anderson | 7,803 | Garnett | 584 |
| Atchison | 16,932 | Atchison | 431 |
| Barber | 5,874 | Medicine Lodge | 1,136 |
| Barton | 29,382 | Great Bend | 895 |
| Bourbon | 14,966 | Fort Scott | 638 |
| Brown | 11,128 | Hiawatha | 572 |
| Butler | 50,580 | El Dorado | 1,443 |
| Chase | 3,021 | Cottonwood Falls | 777 |
| Chautauqua | 4,407 | Sedan | 644 |
| Cherokee | 21,374 | Columbus | 590 |
| Cheyenne | 3,243 | Saint Francis | 1,021 |
| Clark | 2,418 | Ashland | 975 |
| Clay | 9,158 | Clay Center | 632 |
| Cloud | 11,023 | Concordia | 718 |
| Coffey | 8,404 | Burlington | 615 |
| Comanche | 2,313 | Coldwater | 789 |
| Cowley | 36,915 | Winfield | 1,128 |
| Crawford | 35,582 | Girard | 595 |
| Decatur | 4,021 | Oberlin | 894 |
| Dickinson | 18,958 | Abilene | 852 |
| Doniphan | 8,134 | Troy | 388 |
| Douglas | 81,798 | Lawrence | 461 |
| Edwards | 3,787 | Kinsley | 620 |
| Elk | 3,327 | Howard | 650 |
| Ellis | 26,004 | Hays | 900 |
| Ellsworth | 6,586 | Ellsworth | 717 |
| Finney | 33,070 | Garden City | 1,302 |
| Ford | 27,463 | Dodge City | 1,099 |
| Franklin | 21,994 | Ottawa | 577 |
| Geary | 30,453 | Junction City | 377 |
| Gove | 3,231 | Gove | 1,072 |
| Graham | 3,543 | Hill City | 898 |
| Grant | 7,159 | Ulysses | 575 |
| Gray | 5,396 | Cimarron | 868 |
| Greeley | 1,774 | Tribune | 778 |
| Greenwood | 7,847 | Eureka | 1,135 |
| Hamilton | 2,388 | Syracuse | 998 |
| Harper | 7,124 | Anthony | 802 |
| Harvey | 31,028 | Newton | 540 |
| Haskell | 3,886 | Sublette | 578 |
| Hodgeman | 2,177 | Jetmore | 860 |
| Jackson | 11,525 | Holton | 658 |
| Jefferson | 15,905 | Oskaloosa | 535 |
| Jewell | 4,251 | Mankato | 910 |
| Johnson | 355,021 | Olathe | 478 |
| Kearny | 4,027 | Lakin | 868 |
| Kingman | 8,292 | Kingman | 865 |
| Kiowa | 3,660 | Greensburg | 723 |
| Labette | 23,693 | Oswego | 653 |
| Lane | 2,375 | Dighton | 717 |
| Leavenworth | 64,371 | Leavenworth | 463 |
| Lincoln | 3,653 | Lincoln | 720 |
| Linn | 8,254 | Mound City | 601 |
| Logan | 3,081 | Oakley | 1,073 |
| Lyon | 34,732 | Emporia | 844 |
| McPherson | 27,268 | McPherson | 900 |
| Marion | 12,888 | Marion | 944 |
| Marshall | 11,705 | Marysville | 878 |
| Meade | 4,247 | Meade | 979 |
| Miami | 23,466 | Paola | 590 |
| Mitchell | 7,203 | Beloit | 717 |
| Montgomery | 38,816 | Independence | 646 |
| Morris | 6,198 | Council Grove | 693 |
| Morton | 3,480 | Elkhart | 731 |
| Nemaha | 10,446 | Seneca | 719 |
| Neosho | 17,035 | Erie | 576 |
| Ness | 4,033 | Ness City | 1,074 |
| Norton | 5,947 | Norton | 873 |
| Osage | 15,248 | Lyndon | 695 |
| Osborne | 4,867 | Osborne | 882 |
| Ottawa | 5,634 | Minneapolis | 721 |
| Pawnee | 7,555 | Larned | 755 |
| Phillips | 6,590 | Phillipsburg | 887 |
| Pottawatomie | 16,128 | Westmoreland | 828 |
| Pratt | 9,702 | Pratt | 735 |
| Rawlins | 3,404 | Atwood | 1,069 |
| Reno | 62,389 | Hutchinson | 1,259 |
| Republic | 6,482 | Belleville | 719 |
| Rice | 10,610 | Lyons | 728 |
| Riley | 67,139 | Manhattan | 593 |
| Rooks | 6,039 | Stockton | 888 |
| Rush | 3,842 | LaCrosse | 718 |
| Russell | 7,835 | Russell | 869 |

| County | Pop. | County Seat or court house | Land area sq. mi. |
|---|---|---|---|
| Saline | 49,301 | Salina | 721 |
| Scott | 5,289 | Scott City | 718 |
| Sedgwick | 403,662 | Wichita | 1,007 |
| Seward | 18,743 | Liberal | 640 |
| Shawnee | 160,976 | Topeka | 549 |
| Sheridan | 3,043 | Hoxie | 896 |
| Sherman | 6,926 | Goodland | 1,057 |
| Smith | 5,078 | Smith Center | 897 |
| Stafford | 5,365 | Saint John | 788 |
| Stanton | 2,333 | Johnson | 681 |
| Stevens | 5,048 | Hugoton | 727 |
| Sumner | 25,841 | Wellington | 1,183 |
| Thomas | 8,258 | Colby | 1,075 |
| Trego | 3,694 | WaKeeney | 890 |
| Wabaunsee | 6,603 | Alma | 797 |
| Wallace | 1,821 | Sharon Springs | 914 |
| Washington | 7,073 | Washington | 898 |
| Wichita | 2,758 | Leoti | 719 |
| Wilson | 10,289 | Fredonia | 575 |
| Woodson | 4,116 | Yates Center | 498 |
| Wyandotte | 162,026 | Kansas City | 149 |

## Kentucky

(120 counties, 39,732 sq. mi. land; pop. 3,685,296)

| County | Pop. | County Seat or court house | Land area sq. mi. |
|---|---|---|---|
| Adair | 15,360 | Columbia | 407 |
| Allen | 14,628 | Scottsville | 346 |
| Anderson | 14,571 | Lawrenceburg | 203 |
| Ballard | 7,902 | Wickliffe | 251 |
| Barren | 34,001 | Glasgow | 491 |
| Bath | 9,692 | Owingsville | 279 |
| Bell | 31,506 | Pineville | 361 |
| Boone | 57,589 | Burlington | 246 |
| Bourbon | 19,236 | Paris | 291 |
| Boyd | 51,150 | Catlettsburg | 160 |
| Boyle | 25,641 | Danville | 182 |
| Bracken | 7,766 | Brooksville | 203 |
| Breathitt | 15,703 | Jackson | 495 |
| Breckinridge | 16,312 | Hardinsburg | 572 |
| Bullitt | 47,567 | Shepherdsville | 299 |
| Butler | 11,245 | Morgantown | 428 |
| Caldwell | 13,232 | Princeton | 347 |
| Calloway | 30,735 | Murray | 386 |
| Campbell | 83,866 | Newport | 152 |
| Carlisle | 5,238 | Bardwell | 193 |
| Carroll | 9,292 | Carrollton | 130 |
| Carter | 24,340 | Grayson | 411 |
| Casey | 14,211 | Liberty | 446 |
| Christian | 68,941 | Hopkinsville | 721 |
| Clark | 29,496 | Winchester | 254 |
| Clay | 21,746 | Manchester | 471 |
| Clinton | 9,135 | Albany | 198 |
| Crittenden | 9,196 | Marion | 362 |
| Cumberland | 6,784 | Burkesville | 306 |
| Daviess | 87,189 | Owensboro | 462 |
| Edmonson | 10,357 | Brownsville | 303 |
| Elliott | 6,455 | Sandy Hook | 234 |
| Estill | 14,614 | Irvine | 254 |
| Fayette | 225,366 | Lexington | 286 |
| Fleming | 12,292 | Flemingsburg | 351 |
| Floyd | 43,586 | Prestonsburg | 394 |
| Franklin | 44,143 | Frankfort | 211 |
| Fulton | 8,271 | Hickman | 209 |
| Gallatin | 5,393 | Warsaw | 99 |
| Garrard | 11,579 | Lancaster | 231 |
| Grant | 15,737 | Williamstown | 260 |
| Graves | 33,550 | Mayfield | 556 |
| Grayson | 21,050 | Leitchfield | 504 |
| Green | 10,371 | Greensburg | 289 |
| Greenup | 36,742 | Greenup | 346 |
| Hancock | 7,864 | Hawesville | 189 |
| Hardin | 89,240 | Elizabethtown | 628 |
| Harlan | 36,574 | Harlan | 467 |
| Harrison | 16,248 | Cynthiana | 310 |
| Hart | 14,890 | Munfordville | 416 |
| Henderson | 43,044 | Henderson | 440 |
| Henry | 12,823 | New Castle | 289 |
| Hickman | 5,566 | Clinton | 245 |
| Hopkins | 46,126 | Madisonville | 551 |
| Jackson | 11,955 | McKee | 346 |
| Jefferson | 665,123 | Louisville | 385 |
| Jessamine | 30,508 | Nicholasville | 173 |
| Johnson | 23,248 | Paintsville | 262 |
| Kenton | 142,031 | Covington | 163 |
| Knott | 17,906 | Hindman | 352 |
| Knox | 29,676 | Barbourville | 388 |
| Larue | 11,679 | Hodgenville | 263 |
| Laurel | 43,438 | London | 436 |
| Lawrence | 13,998 | Louisa | 419 |
| Lee | 7,422 | Beattyville | 210 |
| Leslie | 13,642 | Hyden | 404 |
| Letcher | 27,000 | Whitesburg | 339 |
| Lewis | 13,029 | Vanceburg | 485 |
| Lincoln | 20,045 | Stanford | 337 |

| County | Pop. | County Seat or court house | Land area sq. mi. |
|---|---|---|---|
| Livingston | 9,062 | Smithland | 316 |
| Logan | 24,416 | Russellville | 556 |
| Lyon | 6,624 | Eddyville | 216 |
| McCracken | 62,879 | Paducah | 251 |
| McCreary | 15,603 | Whitley City | 428 |
| McLean | 9,628 | Calhoun | 254 |
| Madison | 57,508 | Richmond | 441 |
| Magoffin | 13,077 | Salyersville | 310 |
| Marion | 16,499 | Lebanon | 347 |
| Marshall | 27,205 | Benton | 305 |
| Martin | 12,526 | Inez | 231 |
| Mason | 16,666 | Maysville | 241 |
| Meade | 24,170 | Brandenburg | 309 |
| Menifee | 5,092 | Frenchburg | 204 |
| Mercer | 19,148 | Harrodsburg | 251 |
| Metcalfe | 8,963 | Edmonton | 291 |
| Monroe | 11,401 | Tompkinsville | 331 |
| Montgomery | 19,561 | Mount Sterling | 199 |
| Morgan | 11,648 | West Liberty | 381 |
| Muhlenberg | 31,318 | Greenville | 475 |
| Nelson | 29,710 | Bardstown | 423 |
| Nicholas | 6,725 | Carlisle | 197 |
| Ohio | 21,105 | Hartford | 594 |
| Oldham | 33,263 | La Grange | 189 |
| Owen | 9,035 | Owenton | 352 |
| Owsley | 5,036 | Booneville | 198 |
| Pendleton | 12,036 | Falmouth | 280 |
| Perry | 30,283 | Hazard | 342 |
| Pike | 72,583 | Pikeville | 788 |
| Powell | 11,686 | Stanton | 180 |
| Pulaski | 49,489 | Somerset | 662 |
| Robertson | 2,124 | Mount Olivet | 100 |
| Rockcastle | 14,803 | Mount Vernon | 318 |
| Rowan | 20,353 | Morehead | 281 |
| Russell | 14,716 | Jamestown | 254 |
| Scott | 23,867 | Georgetown | 285 |
| Shelby | 24,824 | Shelbyville | 384 |
| Simpson | 15,145 | Franklin | 236 |
| Spencer | 6,801 | Taylorsville | 186 |
| Taylor | 21,146 | Campbellsville | 270 |
| Todd | 10,940 | Elkton | 376 |
| Trigg | 10,361 | Cadiz | 443 |
| Trimble | 6,090 | Bedford | 149 |
| Union | 16,557 | Morganfield | 345 |
| Warren | 77,720 | Bowling Green | 545 |
| Washington | 10,441 | Springfield | 301 |
| Wayne | 17,468 | Monticello | 459 |
| Webster | 13,955 | Dixon | 335 |
| Whitley | 33,326 | Williamsburg | 440 |
| Wolfe | 6,503 | Campton | 223 |
| Woodford | 19,955 | Versailles | 191 |

## Louisiana

(64 parishes, 44,521 sq. mi. land; pop. 4,219,973)

| County | Pop. | County Seat or court house | Land area sq. mi. |
|---|---|---|---|
| Acadia | 55,882 | Crowley | 657 |
| Allen | 21,226 | Oberlin | 765 |
| Ascension | 58,214 | Donaldsonville | 296 |
| Assumption | 22,753 | Napoleonville | 342 |
| Avoyelles | 39,159 | Marksville | 846 |
| Beauregard | 30,083 | De Ridder | 1,163 |
| Bienville | 15,979 | Arcadia | 816 |
| Bossier | 86,088 | Benton | 845 |
| Caddo | 248,253 | Shreveport | 894 |
| Calcasieu | 168,134 | Lake Charles | 1,082 |
| Caldwell | 9,806 | Columbia | 541 |
| Cameron | 9,260 | Cameron | 1,417 |
| Catahoula | 11,065 | Harrisonburg | 732 |
| Claiborne | 17,405 | Homer | 765 |
| Concordia | 20,828 | Vidalia | 717 |
| De Soto | 25,346 | Mansfield | 880 |
| East Baton Rouge | 380,105 | Baton Rouge | 458 |
| East Carroll | 9,709 | Lake Providence | 426 |
| East Feliciana | 19,211 | Clinton | 455 |
| Evangeline | 33,274 | Ville Platte | 667 |
| Franklin | 22,387 | Winnsboro | 635 |
| Grant | 17,526 | Colfax | 653 |
| Iberia | 68,297 | New Iberia | 589 |
| Iberville | 31,049 | Plaquemine | 638 |
| Jackson | 15,705 | Jonesboro | 579 |
| Jefferson | 448,306 | Gretna | 348 |
| Jefferson Davis | 30,722 | Jennings | 655 |
| Lafayette | 164,762 | Lafayette | 270 |
| Lafourche | 85,860 | Thibodaux | 1,141 |
| La Salle | 13,662 | Jena | 638 |
| Lincoln | 41,745 | Ruston | 472 |
| Livingston | 70,523 | Livingston | 661 |
| Madison | 12,463 | Tallulah | 631 |
| Morehouse | 31,938 | Bastrop | 807 |
| Natchitoches | 36,689 | Natchitoches | 1,264 |
| Orleans | 496,938 | New Orleans | 199 |
| Ouachita | 142,191 | Monroe | 627 |
| Plaquemines | 25,575 | Pointe a la Hache | 1,035 |
| Pointe Coupee | 22,540 | New Roads | 566 |

| County | Pop. | County Seat or court house | Land area sq. mi. |
|---|---|---|---|
| Rapides | 131,556 | Alexandria | 1,341 |
| Red River | 9,387 | Coushatta | 394 |
| Richland | 20,629 | Rayville | 563 |
| Sabine | 22,646 | Many | 855 |
| Saint Bernard | 66,631 | Chalmette | 486 |
| Saint Charles | 42,437 | Hahnville | 286 |
| Saint Helena | 9,874 | Greensburg | 409 |
| Saint James | 20,879 | Convent | 248 |
| Saint John The Baptist | 39,996 | Edgard | 213 |
| Saint Landry | 80,312 | Opelousas | 936 |
| Saint Martin | 44,097 | Saint Martinville | 749 |
| Saint Mary | 58,086 | Franklin | 613 |
| Saint Tammany | 144,500 | Covington | 873 |
| Tangipahoa | 85,709 | Amite | 783 |
| Tensas | 7,103 | Saint Joseph | 623 |
| Terrebonne | 96,982 | Houma | 1,367 |
| Union | 20,796 | Farmerville | 884 |
| Vermilion | 50,055 | Abbeville | 1,205 |
| Vernon | 61,961 | Leesville | 1,332 |
| Washington | 43,185 | Franklinton | 676 |
| Webster | 41,989 | Minden | 602 |
| West Baton Rouge | 19,419 | Port Allen | 194 |
| West Carroll | 12,093 | Oak Grove | 360 |
| West Feliciana | 12,915 | Saint Francisville | 406 |
| Winn | 16,269 | Winnfield | 953 |

## Maine

(16 counties; 30,995 sq. mi. land; pop. 1,227,928)

| County | Pop. | County Seat or court house | Land area sq. mi. |
|---|---|---|---|
| Androscoggin | 105,259 | Auburn | 477 |
| Aroostook | 86,936 | Houlton | 6,721 |
| Cumberland | 243,135 | Portland | 876 |
| Franklin | 29,008 | Farmington | 1,699 |
| Hancock | 46,948 | Ellsworth | 1,537 |
| Kennebec | 115,904 | Augusta | 876 |
| Knox | 36,310 | Rockland | 370 |
| Lincoln | 30,357 | Wiscasset | 458 |
| Oxford | 52,602 | South Paris | 2,053 |
| Penobscot | 146,601 | Bangor | 3,430 |
| Piscataquis | 18,653 | Dover-Foxcroft | 3,986 |
| Sagadahoc | 33,535 | Bath | 257 |
| Somerset | 49,767 | Skowhegan | 3,930 |
| Waldo | 33,018 | Belfast | 730 |
| Washington | 35,308 | Machias | 2,586 |
| York | 164,587 | Alfred | 1,008 |

## Maryland

(23 cos., 1 ind. city, 9,837 sq. mi. land; pop. 4,781,468)

| County | Pop. | County Seat or court house | Land area sq. mi. |
|---|---|---|---|
| Allegany | 74,946 | Cumberland | 421 |
| Anne Arundel | 427,239 | Annapolis | 418 |
| Baltimore | 692,134 | Towson | 598 |
| Calvert | 51,372 | Prince Frederick | 213 |
| Caroline | 27,035 | Denton | 321 |
| Carroll | 123,372 | Westminster | 452 |
| Cecil | 71,347 | Elkton | 360 |
| Charles | 101,154 | La Plata | 452 |
| Dorchester | 30,236 | Cambridge | 593 |
| Frederick | 150,208 | Frederick | 663 |
| Garrett | 28,138 | Oakland | 657 |
| Harford | 182,132 | Bel Air | 448 |
| Howard | 187,328 | Ellicott City | 251 |
| Kent | 17,842 | Chestertown | 278 |
| Montgomery | 757,027 | Rockville | 495 |
| Prince Georges | 729,268 | Upper Marlboro | 487 |
| Queen Annes | 33,953 | Centreville | 372 |
| Saint Mary's | 75,974 | Leonardtown | 373 |
| Somerset | 23,440 | Princess Anne | 338 |
| Talbot | 30,549 | Easton | 259 |
| Washington | 121,393 | Hagerstown | 455 |
| Wicomico | 74,339 | Salisbury | 379 |
| Worcester | 35,028 | Snow Hill | 475 |
| independent City | | | |
| Baltimore | 736,014 | | 80 |

## Massachusetts

(14 counties; 7,824 sq. mi. land; pop. 6,016,425)

| County | Pop. | County Seat or court house | Land area sq. mi. |
|---|---|---|---|
| Barnstable | 186,605 | Barnstable | 400 |
| Berkshire | 139,352 | Pittsfield | 929 |
| Bristol | 11,639 | Taunton | 557 |
| Dukes | 670,080 | Edgartown | 102 |
| Essex | 70,092 | Salem | 495 |
| Franklin | 456,310 | Greenfield | 702 |
| Hampden | 146,568 | Springfield | 618 |
| Hampshire | 1,398,468 | Northampton | 528 |
| Middlesex | 6,012 | East Cambridge | 822 |
| Nantucket | | Nantucket | 47 |

| County | Pop. | County Seat or court house | Land area sq. mi. |
|---|---|---|---|
| Norfolk | 616,087 | Dedham | 400 |
| Plymouth | 435,276 | Plymouth | 655 |
| Suffolk | 663,906 | Boston | 57 |
| Worcester | 709,705 | Worcester | 1,513 |

## Michigan

(83 counties; 56,954 sq. mi. land; pop. 9,295,297)

| County | Pop. | County Seat or court house | Land area sq. mi. |
|---|---|---|---|
| Alcona | 10,145 | Harrisville | 679 |
| Alger | 8,972 | Munising | 912 |
| Allegan | 90,509 | Allegan | 832 |
| Alpena | 30,605 | Alpena | 567 |
| Antrim | 18,185 | Bellaire | 480 |
| Arenac | 14,906 | Standish | 367 |
| Baraga | 7,954 | L'Anse | 901 |
| Barry | 50,057 | Hastings | 560 |
| Bay | 111,723 | Bay City | 447 |
| Benzie | 12,200 | Beulah | 322 |
| Berrien | 161,378 | Saint Joseph | 576 |
| Branch | 41,502 | Coldwater | 508 |
| Calhoun | 135,982 | Marshall | 712 |
| Cass | 49,477 | Cassopolis | 496 |
| Charlevoix | 21,468 | Charlevoix | 421 |
| Cheboygan | 21,398 | Cheboygan | 720 |
| Chippewa | 34,604 | Sault Sainte Marie | 1,590 |
| Clare | 24,952 | Harrison | 570 |
| Clinton | 57,883 | Saint Johns | 573 |
| Crawford | 12,260 | Grayling | 559 |
| Delta | 37,780 | Escanaba | 1,173 |
| Dickinson | 26,831 | Iron Mountain | 770 |
| Eaton | 92,879 | Charlotte | 579 |
| Emmet | 25,040 | Petoskey | 468 |
| Genesee | 430,459 | Flint | 642 |
| Gladwin | 21,896 | Gladwin | 505 |
| Gogebic | 18,052 | Bessemer | 1,105 |
| Grand Traverse | 64,273 | Traverse City | 466 |
| Gratiot | 38,982 | Ithaca | 570 |
| Hillsdale | 43,431 | Hillsdale | 603 |
| Houghton | 35,446 | Houghton | 1,014 |
| Huron | 34,951 | Bad Axe | 830 |
| Ingham | 281,912 | Mason | 560 |
| Ionia | 57,024 | Ionia | 577 |
| Iosco | 30,209 | Tawas City | 546 |
| Iron | 13,175 | Crystal Falls | 1,163 |
| Isabella | 54,624 | Mount Pleasant | 577 |
| Jackson | 149,756 | Jackson | 705 |
| Kalamazoo | 223,411 | Kalamazoo | 562 |
| Kalkaska | 13,497 | Kalkaska | 563 |
| Kent | 500,631 | Grand Rapids | 862 |
| Keweenaw | 1,701 | Eagle River | 543 |
| Lake | 8,583 | Baldwin | 568 |
| Lapeer | 74,768 | Lapeer | 658 |
| Leelanau | 16,527 | Leland | 341 |
| Lenawee | 91,476 | Adrian | 753 |
| Livingston | 115,645 | Howell | 574 |
| Luce | 5,763 | Newberry | 904 |
| Mackinac | 10,674 | Saint Ignace | 1,025 |
| Macomb | 717,400 | Mount Clemens | 482 |
| Manistee | 21,265 | Manistee | 543 |
| Marquette | 70,887 | Marquette | 1,821 |
| Mason | 25,537 | Ludington | 494 |
| Mecosta | 37,308 | Big Rapids | 560 |
| Menominee | 24,920 | Menominee | 1,045 |
| Midland | 75,651 | Midland | 528 |
| Missaukee | 12,147 | Lake City | 565 |
| Monroe | 133,600 | Monroe | 557 |
| Montcalm | 53,059 | Stanton | 713 |
| Montmorency | 8,936 | Atlanta | 550 |
| Muskegon | 158,983 | Muskegon | 507 |
| Newaygo | 38,206 | White Cloud | 847 |
| Oakland | 1,083,592 | Pontiac | 875 |
| Oceana | 22,455 | Hart | 541 |
| Ogemaw | 18,681 | West Branch | 570 |
| Ontonagon | 8,854 | Ontonagon | 1,311 |
| Osceola | 20,146 | Reed City | 569 |
| Oscoda | 7,842 | Mio | 568 |
| Otsego | 17,957 | Gaylord | 516 |
| Ottawa | 187,768 | Grand Haven | 567 |
| Presque Isle | 13,743 | Rogers City | 656 |
| Roscommon | 19,776 | Roscommon | 528 |
| Saginaw | 211,946 | Saginaw | 815 |
| Saint Clair | 145,607 | Port Huron | 734 |
| Saint Joseph | 58,913 | Centreville | 503 |
| Sanilac | 39,928 | Sandusky | 964 |
| Schoolcraft | 8,302 | Manistique | 1,173 |
| Shiawassee | 69,770 | Corunna | 540 |
| Tuscola | 55,498 | Caro | 812 |
| Van Buren | 70,060 | Paw Paw | 611 |
| Washtenaw | 282,937 | Ann Arbor | 710 |
| Wayne | 2,111,687 | Detroit | 615 |
| Wexford | 26,360 | Cadillac | 566 |

## Minnesota

(87 counties; 79,548 sq. mi. land; pop., 4,375,099)

| County | Pop. | County Seat or court house | Land area sq. mi. |
|---|---|---|---|
| Aitkin | 12,425 | Aitkin | 1,834 |
| Anoka | 243,641 | Anoka | 430 |
| Becker | 27,881 | Detroit Lakes | 1,312 |
| Beltrami | 34,384 | Bemidji | 2,507 |
| Benton | 30,185 | Foley | 408 |
| Big Stone | 6,285 | Ortonville | 497 |
| Blue Earth | 54,044 | Mankato | 749 |
| Brown | 26,984 | New Ulm | 610 |
| Carlton | 29,259 | Carlton | 864 |
| Carver | 47,915 | Chaska | 351 |
| Cass | 21,791 | Walker | 2,033 |
| Chippewa | 13,228 | Montevideo | 584 |
| Chisago | 30,521 | Center City | 417 |
| Clay | 50,422 | Moorhead | 1,049 |
| Clearwater | 8,309 | Bagley | 999 |
| Cook | 3,868 | Grand Marais | 1,412 |
| Cottonwood | 12,694 | Windom | 640 |
| Crow Wing | 44,249 | Brainerd | 1,008 |
| Dakota | 275,189 | Hastings | 574 |
| Dodge | 15,731 | Mantorville | 439 |
| Douglas | 28,674 | Alexandria | 643 |
| Faribault | 16,937 | Blue Earth | 714 |
| Fillmore | 20,777 | Preston | 862 |
| Freeborn | 33,060 | Albert Lea | 705 |
| Goodhue | 40,690 | Red Wing | 763 |
| Grant | 6,246 | Elbow Lake | 547 |
| Hennepin | 1,032,431 | Minneapolis | 541 |
| Houston | 18,497 | Caledonia | 564 |
| Hubbard | 14,939 | Park Rapids | 936 |
| Isanti | 25,921 | Cambridge | 440 |
| Itasca | 40,863 | Grand Rapids | 2,661 |
| Jackson | 11,677 | Jackson | 699 |
| Kanabec | 12,802 | Mora | 527 |
| Kandiyohi | 38,761 | Willmar | 784 |
| Kittson | 5,767 | Hallock | 1,104 |
| Koochiching | 16,299 | International Falls | 3,108 |
| Lac qui Parle | 8,924 | Madison | 772 |
| Lake | 10,415 | Two Harbors | 2,053 |
| Lake of the Woods | 4,076 | Baudette | 1,296 |
| Le Sueur | 23,239 | Le Center | 446 |
| Lincoln | 6,890 | Ivanhoe | 538 |
| Lyon | 24,789 | Marshall | 714 |
| McLeod | 32,030 | Glencoe | 489 |
| Mahnomen | 5,044 | Mahnomen | 559 |
| Marshall | 10,993 | Warren | 1,760 |
| Martin | 22,914 | Fairmont | 706 |
| Meeker | 20,846 | Litchfield | 624 |
| Mille Lacs | 18,670 | Milaca | 578 |
| Morrison | 29,604 | Little Falls | 1,124 |
| Mower | 37,385 | Austin | 711 |
| Murray | 9,660 | Slayton | 702 |
| Nicollet | 28,076 | Saint Peter | 440 |
| Nobles | 20,098 | Worthington | 714 |
| Norman | 7,975 | Ada | 877 |
| Olmsted | 106,470 | Rochester | 655 |
| Otter Tail | 50,714 | Fergus Falls | 1,973 |
| Pennington | 13,306 | Thief River Falls | 618 |
| Pine | 21,264 | Pine City | 1,421 |
| Pipestone | 10,491 | Pipestone | 466 |
| Polk | 32,589 | Crookston | 1,982 |
| Pope | 10,745 | Glenwood | 668 |
| Ramsey | 485,765 | Saint Paul | 154 |
| Red Lake | 4,525 | Red Lake Falls | 433 |
| Redwood | 17,254 | Redwood Falls | 882 |
| Renville | 17,673 | Olivia | 984 |
| Rice | 49,183 | Faribault | 501 |
| Rock | 9,806 | Luverne | 483 |
| Roseau | 15,026 | Roseau | 1,677 |
| Saint Louis | 198,213 | Duluth | 6,125 |
| Scott | 57,846 | Shakopee | 357 |
| Sherburne | 41,945 | Elk River | 435 |
| Sibley | 14,366 | Gaylord | 593 |
| Stearns | 119,324 | Saint Cloud | 1,338 |
| Steele | 30,729 | Owatonna | 431 |
| Stevens | 10,634 | Morris | 560 |
| Swift | 10,724 | Benson | 743 |
| Todd | 23,363 | Long Prairie | 941 |
| Traverse | 4,463 | Wheaton | 575 |
| Wabasha | 19,744 | Wabasha | 537 |
| Wadena | 13,154 | Wadena | 538 |
| Waseca | 18,079 | Waseca | 422 |
| Washington | 145,858 | Stillwater | 390 |
| Watonwan | 11,682 | Saint James | 435 |
| Wilkin | 7,516 | Breckenridge | 751 |
| Winona | 47,828 | Winona | 630 |
| Wright | 68,710 | Buffalo | 672 |
| Yellow Medicine | 11,684 | Granite Falls | 758 |

## Mississippi

(82 counties, 47,233 sq. mi. land; pop. 2,573,216)

| County | Pop. | County Seat or court house | Land area sq. mi. |
|---|---|---|---|
| Adams | 35,356 | Natchez | 456 |
| Alcorn | 31,722 | Corinth | 401 |
| Amite | 13,328 | Liberty | 732 |
| Attala | 18,481 | Kosciusko | 737 |
| Benton | 8,046 | Ashland | 407 |
| Bolivar | 41,875 | Cleveland & Rosedale | 892 |
| Calhoun | 14,908 | Pittsboro | 573 |
| Carroll | 9,237 | Carrollton & Vaiden | 634 |
| Chickasaw | 18,085 | Houston & Okolona | 503 |
| Choctaw | 9,071 | Ackerman | 420 |
| Claiborne | 11,370 | Port Gibson | 494 |
| Clarke | 17,313 | Quitman | 692 |
| Clay | 21,120 | West Point | 415 |
| Coahoma | 31,665 | Clarksdale | 559 |
| Copiah | 27,592 | Hazlehurst | 779 |
| Covington | 16,527 | Collins | 416 |
| De Soto | 67,910 | Hernando | 483 |
| Forrest | 68,314 | Hattiesburg | 469 |
| Franklin | 8,377 | Meadville | 566 |
| George | 16,673 | Lucedale | 483 |
| Greene | 10,220 | Leakesville | 718 |
| Grenada | 21,555 | Grenada | 421 |
| Hancock | 31,760 | Bay Saint Louis | 478 |
| Harrison | 165,365 | Gulfport | 581 |
| Hinds | 254,441 | Jackson & Raymond | 875 |
| Holmes | 21,604 | Lexington | 759 |
| Humphreys | 12,134 | Belzoni | 430 |
| Issaquena | 1,909 | Mayersville | 406 |
| Itawamba | 20,017 | Fulton | 541 |
| Jackson | 115,243 | Pascagoula | 731 |
| Jasper | 17,114 | Bay Springs & Paulding | 678 |
| Jefferson | 8,653 | Fayette | 523 |
| Jefferson Davis | 14,051 | Prentiss | 409 |
| Jones | 62,031 | Ellisville & Laurel | 695 |
| Kemper | 10,356 | De Kalb | 766 |
| Lafayette | 31,826 | Oxford | 669 |
| Lamar | 30,424 | Purvis | 499 |
| Lauderdale | 75,555 | Meridian | 705 |
| Lawrence | 12,458 | Monticello | 435 |
| Leake | 18,436 | Carthage | 584 |
| Lee | 65,579 | Tupelo | 451 |
| Leflore | 37,341 | Greenwood | 605 |
| Lincoln | 30,278 | Brookhaven | 586 |
| Lowndes | 59,308 | Columbus | 517 |
| Madison | 53,794 | Canton | 717 |
| Marion | 25,544 | Columbia | 548 |
| Marshall | 30,361 | Holly Springs | 709 |
| Monroe | 36,582 | Aberdeen | 772 |
| Montgomery | 12,388 | Winona | 408 |
| Neshoba | 24,800 | Philadelphia | 571 |
| Newton | 20,291 | Decatur | 580 |
| Noxubee | 12,604 | Macon | 698 |
| Oktibbeha | 38,375 | Starkville | 459 |
| Panola | 29,996 | Batesville & Sardis | 695 |
| Pearl River | 38,714 | Poplarville | 819 |
| Perry | 10,865 | New Augusta | 651 |
| Pike | 36,882 | Magnolia | 410 |
| Pontotoc | 22,237 | Pontotoc | 499 |
| Prentiss | 23,278 | Booneville | 417 |
| Quitman | 10,490 | Marks | 406 |
| Rankin | 87,161 | Brandon | 782 |
| Scott | 24,137 | Forest | 610 |
| Sharkey | 7,066 | Rolling Fork | 435 |
| Simpson | 23,953 | Mendenhall | 591 |
| Smith | 14,798 | Raleigh | 635 |
| Stone | 10,750 | Wiggins | 446 |
| Sunflower | 35,129 | Indianola | 707 |
| Tallahatchie | 15,210 | Charleston & Sumner | 651 |
| Tate | 21,432 | Senatobia | 406 |
| Tippah | 19,523 | Ripley | 458 |
| Tishomingo | 17,683 | Iuka | 434 |
| Tunica | 8,164 | Tunica | 460 |
| Union | 22,085 | New Albany | 417 |
| Walthall | 14,352 | Tylertown | 404 |
| Warren | 47,880 | Vicksburg | 597 |
| Washington | 67,935 | Greenville | 733 |
| Wayne | 19,517 | Waynesboro | 813 |
| Webster | 10,222 | Walthall | 424 |
| Wilkinson | 9,678 | Woodville | 678 |
| Winston | 19,433 | Louisville | 610 |
| Yalobusha | 12,033 | Coffeeville & Water Valley | 478 |
| Yazoo | 25,506 | Yazoo City | 933 |

## Missouri

(114 cos., 1 ind. city, 68,945 sq. mi. land; pop. 5,117,073)

| County | Pop. | County Seat or court house | Land area sq. mi. |
|---|---|---|---|
| Adair | 24,577 | Kirksville | 567 |
| Andrew | 14,632 | Savannah | 435 |
| Atchison | 7,457 | Rockport | 542 |
| Audrain | 23,599 | Mexico | 697 |
| Barry | 27,547 | Cassville | 773 |

| County | Pop. | County Seat or court house | Land area sq. mi. |
|---|---|---|---|
| Barton | 11,312 | Lamar | 596 |
| Bates | 15,025 | Butler | 849 |
| Benton | 13,859 | Warsaw | 729 |
| Bollinger | 10,619 | Marble Hill | 621 |
| Boone | 112,379 | Columbia | 687 |
| Buchanan | 83,083 | Saint Joseph | 409 |
| Butler | 38,765 | Poplar Bluff | 698 |
| Caldwell | 8,380 | Kingston | 430 |
| Callaway | 32,809 | Fulton | 842 |
| Camden | 27,495 | Camdenton | 641 |
| Cape Girardeau | 61,633 | Jackson | 577 |
| Carroll | 10,748 | Carrollton | 695 |
| Carter | 5,515 | Van Buren | 509 |
| Cass | 63,808 | Harrisonville | 701 |
| Cedar | 12,093 | Stockton | 470 |
| Chariton | 9,202 | Keytesville | 758 |
| Christian | 32,644 | Ozark | 564 |
| Clark | 7,547 | Kahoka | 507 |
| Clay | 153,411 | Liberty | 403 |
| Clinton | 16,595 | Plattsburg | 423 |
| Cole | 63,579 | Jefferson City | 392 |
| Cooper | 14,835 | Boonville | 567 |
| Crawford | 19,173 | Steelville | 744 |
| Dade | 7,449 | Greenfield | 491 |
| Dallas | 12,646 | Buffalo | 543 |
| Daviess | 7,865 | Gallatin | 568 |
| De Kalb | 9,967 | Maysville | 425 |
| Dent | 13,702 | Salem | 755 |
| Douglas | 11,876 | Ava | 814 |
| Dunklin | 33,112 | Kennett | 547 |
| Franklin | 80,603 | Union | 922 |
| Gasconade | 14,006 | Hermann | 521 |
| Gentry | 6,854 | Albany | 493 |
| Greene | 207,949 | Springfield | 677 |
| Grundy | 10,536 | Trenton | 437 |
| Harrison | 8,469 | Bethany | 725 |
| Henry | 20,044 | Clinton | 729 |
| Hickory | 7,335 | Hermitage | 379 |
| Holt | 6,034 | Oregon | 457 |
| Howard | 9,631 | Fayette | 465 |
| Howell | 31,447 | West Plains | 928 |
| Iron | 10,726 | Ironton | 552 |
| Jackson | 633,234 | Kansas City | 611 |
| Jasper | 90,465 | Carthage | 641 |
| Jefferson | 171,380 | Hillsboro | 661 |
| Johnson | 42,514 | Warrensburg | 834 |
| Knox | 4,482 | Edina | 507 |
| Laclede | 27,158 | Lebanon | 768 |
| Lafayette | 31,107 | Lexington | 632 |
| Lawrence | 30,236 | Mount Vernon | 613 |
| Lewis | 10,233 | Monticello | 509 |
| Lincoln | 28,892 | Troy | 627 |
| Linn | 13,885 | Linneus | 620 |
| Livingston | 14,592 | Chillicothe | 537 |
| McDonald | 16,938 | Pineville | 540 |
| Macon | 15,345 | Macon | 797 |
| Madison | 11,127 | Fredericktown | 497 |
| Maries | 7,976 | Vienna | 528 |
| Marion | 27,682 | Palmyra | 438 |
| Mercer | 3,723 | Princeton | 454 |
| Miller | 20,700 | Tuscumbia | 593 |
| Mississippi | 14,442 | Charleston | 410 |
| Moniteau | 12,298 | California | 417 |
| Monroe | 9,104 | Paris | 670 |
| Montgomery | 11,355 | Montgomery City | 540 |
| Morgan | 15,574 | Versailles | 594 |
| New Madrid | 20,928 | New Madrid | 658 |
| Newton | 44,445 | Neosho | 627 |
| Nodaway | 21,709 | Maryville | 875 |
| Oregon | 9,470 | Alton | 792 |
| Osage | 12,018 | Linn | 606 |
| Ozark | 8,598 | Gainesville | 731 |
| Pemiscot | 21,921 | Caruthersville | 517 |
| Perry | 16,648 | Perryville | 473 |
| Pettis | 35,437 | Sedalia | 686 |
| Phelps | 35,248 | Rolla | 674 |
| Pike | 15,969 | Bowling Green | 673 |
| Platte | 57,867 | Platte City | 421 |
| Polk | 21,826 | Bolivar | 636 |
| Pulaski | 41,307 | Waynesville | 550 |
| Putnam | 5,079 | Unionville | 520 |
| Ralls | 8,476 | New London | 482 |
| Randolph | 24,370 | Huntsville | 477 |
| Ray | 21,968 | Richmond | 568 |
| Reynolds | 6,661 | Centerville | 809 |
| Ripley | 12,303 | Doniphan | 631 |
| Saint Charles | 212,751 | Saint Charles | 558 |
| Saint Clair | 8,457 | Osceola | 699 |
| Saint Francis | 48,904 | Farmington | 451 |
| Saint Louis | 993,528 | Clayton | 506 |
| Sainte Genevieve | 16,037 | Sainte Genevieve | 504 |
| Saline | 23,523 | Marshall | 755 |
| Schuyler | 4,236 | Lancaster | 309 |
| Scotland | 4,822 | Memphis | 438 |
| Scott | 39,376 | Benton | 423 |
| Shannon | 7,613 | Eminence | 1,004 |
| Shelby | 6,942 | Shelbyville | 501 |
| Stoddard | 28,895 | Bloomfield | 815 |

| County | Pop. | County Seat or court house | Land area sq. mi. |
|---|---|---|---|
| Stone | 19,078 | Galena | 451 |
| Sullivan | 6,326 | Milan | 651 |
| Taney | 25,561 | Forsyth | 608 |
| Texas | 21,476 | Houston | 1,180 |
| Vernon | 19,041 | Nevada | 837 |
| Warren | 19,534 | Warrenton | 429 |
| Washington | 20,380 | Potosi | 762 |
| Wayne | 11,543 | Greenville | 762 |
| Webster | 23,753 | Marshfield | 594 |
| Worth | 2,440 | Grant City | 266 |
| Wright | 16,758 | Hartville | 682 |
| Independent City Saint Louis | 396,685 | | 61 |

## Montana

(56 counties, 145,556 sq. mi. land; pop., 799,065)

| County | Pop. | County Seat or court house | Land area sq. mi. |
|---|---|---|---|
| Beaverhead | 8,424 | Dillon | 5,542 |
| Big Horn | 11,337 | Hardin | 4,995 |
| Blaine | 6,728 | Chinook | 4,226 |
| Broadwater | 3,318 | Townsend | 1,191 |
| Carbon | 8,080 | Red Lodge | 2,048 |
| Carter | 1,503 | Ekalaka | 3,340 |
| Cascade | 77,691 | Great Falls | 2,698 |
| Chouteau | 5,452 | Fort Benton | 3,973 |
| Custer | 11,697 | Miles City | 3,783 |
| Daniels | 2,266 | Scobey | 1,426 |
| Dawson | 9,505 | Glendive | 2,373 |
| Deer Lodge | 10,356 | Anaconda | 737 |
| Fallon | 3,103 | Baker | 1,620 |
| Fergus | 12,083 | Lewistown | 4,339 |
| Flathead | 59,218 | Kalispell | 5,099 |
| Gallatin | 50,463 | Bozeman | 2,507 |
| Garfield | 1,589 | Jordan | 4,668 |
| Glacier | 12,121 | Cut Bank | 2,995 |
| Golden Valley | 912 | Ryegate | 1,175 |
| Granite | 2,548 | Philipsburg | 1,728 |
| Hill | 17,654 | Havre | 2,896 |
| Jefferson | 7,939 | Boulder | 1,657 |
| Judith Basin | 2,282 | Stanford | 1,870 |
| Lake | 21,041 | Polson | 1,494 |
| Lewis & Clark | 47,495 | Helena | 3,461 |
| Liberty | 2,295 | Chester | 1,430 |
| Lincoln | 17,481 | Libby | 3,613 |
| McCone | 2,276 | Circle | 2,643 |
| Madison | 5,989 | Virginia City | 3,587 |
| Meagher | 1,819 | White Sulphur Springs | 2,392 |
| Mineral | 3,315 | Superior | 1,220 |
| Missoula | 78,687 | Missoula | 2,598 |
| Musselshell | 4,106 | Roundup | 1,867 |
| Park | 14,484 | Livingston | 2,656 |
| Petroleum | 519 | Winnett | 1,654 |
| Phillips | 5,163 | Malta | 5,140 |
| Pondera | 6,433 | Conrad | 1,625 |
| Powder River | 2,090 | Broadus | 3,297 |
| Powell | 6,620 | Deer Lodge | 2,326 |
| Prairie | 1,383 | Terry | 1,737 |
| Ravalli | 25,010 | Hamilton | 2,394 |
| Richland | 10,716 | Sidney | 2,084 |
| Roosevelt | 10,999 | Wolf Point | 2,356 |
| Rosebud | 10,505 | Forsyth | 5,012 |
| Sanders | 8,669 | Thompson Falls | 2,762 |
| Sheridan | 4,732 | Plentywood | 1,677 |
| Silver Bow | 33,941 | Butte | 718 |
| Stillwater | 6,536 | Columbus | 1,795 |
| Sweet Grass | 3,154 | Big Timber | 1,855 |
| Teton | 6,271 | Choteau | 2,273 |
| Toole | 5,046 | Shelby | 1,911 |
| Treasure | 874 | Hysham | 979 |
| Valley | 8,239 | Glasgow | 4,921 |
| Wheatland | 2,246 | Harlowton | 1,423 |
| Wibaux | 1,191 | Wibaux | 869 |
| Yellowstone | 113,419 | Billings | 2,635 |

## Nebraska

(93 counties, 76,644 sq. mi. land; pop., 1,578,385)

| County | Pop. | County Seat or court house | Land area sq. mi. |
|---|---|---|---|
| Adams | 29,625 | Hastings | 564 |
| Antelope | 7,965 | Neligh | 859 |
| Arthur | 462 | Arthur | 711 |
| Banner | 852 | Harrisburg | 747 |
| Blaine | 675 | Brewster | 714 |
| Boone | 6,667 | Albion | 687 |
| Box Butte | 13,130 | Alliance | 1,077 |
| Boyd | 2,835 | Butte | 532 |
| Brown | 3,657 | Ainsworth | 1,214 |
| Buffalo | 37,447 | Kearney | 945 |
| Burt | 7,868 | Tekamah | 486 |
| Butler | 8,601 | David City | 584 |
| Cass | 21,318 | Plattsmouth | 557 |
| Cedar | 10,131 | Hartington | 740 |

| County | Pop. | County Seat or court house | Land area sq. mi. |
|---|---|---|---|
| Chase | 4,381 | Imperial | 894 |
| Cherry | 6,307 | Valentine | 5,961 |
| Cheyenne | 9,494 | Sidney | 1,196 |
| Clay | 7,123 | Clay Center | 574 |
| Colfax | 9,139 | Schuyler | 410 |
| Cuming | 10,117 | West Point | 575 |
| Custer | 12,270 | Broken Bow | 2,571 |
| Dakota | 16,742 | Dakota City | 258 |
| Dawes | 9,021 | Chadron | 1,397 |
| Dawson | 19,940 | Lexington | 982 |
| Deuel | 2,237 | Chappell | 437 |
| Dixon | 6,143 | Ponca | 474 |
| Dodge | 34,500 | Fremont | 534 |
| Douglas | 416,444 | Omaha | 333 |
| Dundy | 2,582 | Benkelman | 920 |
| Fillmore | 7,103 | Geneva | 576 |
| Franklin | 3,938 | Franklin | 576 |
| Frontier | 3,101 | Stockville | 976 |
| Furnas | 5,553 | Beaver City | 721 |
| Gage | 22,794 | Beatrice | 858 |
| Garden | 2,460 | Oshkosh | 1,680 |
| Garfield | 2,141 | Burwell | 570 |
| Gosper | 1,928 | Elwood | 461 |
| Grant | 769 | Hyannis | 775 |
| Greeley | 3,006 | Greeley | 570 |
| Hall | 48,925 | Grand Island | 537 |
| Hamilton | 8,862 | Aurora | 543 |
| Harlan | 3,810 | Alma | 555 |
| Hayes | 1,222 | Hayes Center | 713 |
| Hitchcock | 3,750 | Trenton | 709 |
| Holt | 12,599 | O'Neill | 2,406 |
| Hooker | 793 | Mullen | 721 |
| Howard | 6,057 | Saint Paul | 564 |
| Jefferson | 8,759 | Fairbury | 575 |
| Johnson | 4,673 | Tecumseh | 377 |
| Kearney | 6,629 | Minden | 519 |
| Keith | 8,584 | Ogallala | 1,039 |
| Keya Paha | 1,029 | Springview | 769 |
| Kimball | 4,108 | Kimball | 952 |
| Knox | 9,564 | Center | 1,105 |
| Lancaster | 213,641 | Lincoln | 839 |
| Lincoln | 32,508 | North Platte | 2,525 |
| Logan | 878 | Stapleton | 571 |
| Loup | 683 | Taylor | 574 |
| McPherson | 546 | Tryon | 859 |
| Madison | 32,655 | Madison | 575 |
| Merrick | 8,049 | Central City | 478 |
| Morrill | 5,423 | Bridgeport | 1,405 |
| Nance | 4,275 | Fullerton | 439 |
| Nemaha | 7,980 | Auburn | 409 |
| Nuckolls | 5,786 | Nelson | 576 |
| Otoe | 14,252 | Nebraska City | 615 |
| Pawnee | 3,317 | Pawnee City | 433 |
| Perkins | 3,367 | Grant | 885 |
| Phelps | 9,715 | Holdrege | 540 |
| Pierce | 7,827 | Pierce | 575 |
| Platte | 29,820 | Columbus | 669 |
| Polk | 5,668 | Osceola | 437 |
| Red Willow | 11,705 | McCook | 718 |
| Richardson | 9,937 | Falls City | 553 |
| Rock | 2,019 | Bassett | 1,003 |
| Saline | 12,715 | Wilber | 575 |
| Sarpy | 102,583 | Papillion | 238 |
| Saunders | 18,285 | Wahoo | 753 |
| Scotts Bluff | 36,025 | Gering | 725 |
| Seward | 15,450 | Seward | 575 |
| Sheridan | 6,750 | Rushville | 2,453 |
| Sherman | 3,718 | Loup City | 564 |
| Sioux | 1,549 | Harrison | 2,070 |
| Stanton | 6,244 | Stanton | 431 |
| Thayer | 6,635 | Hebron | 575 |
| Thomas | 851 | Thedford | 713 |
| Thurston | 6,936 | Pender | 391 |
| Valley | 5,169 | Ord | 567 |
| Washington | 16,607 | Blair | 386 |
| Wayne | 9,364 | Wayne | 443 |
| Webster | 4,279 | Red Cloud | 575 |
| Wheeler | 948 | Bartlett | 575 |
| York | 14,428 | York | 576 |

## Nevada

(16 cos., 1 ind. city, 109,894 sq. mi. land; pop., 1,201,833)

| County | Pop. | County Seat or court house | Land area sq. mi. |
|---|---|---|---|
| Churchill | 17,938 | Fallon | 4,913 |
| Clark | 741,368 | Las Vegas | 8,084 |
| Douglas | 27,637 | Minden | 751 |
| Elko | 33,463 | Elko | 17,181 |
| Esmeralda | 1,344 | Goldfield | 3,570 |
| Eureka | 1,547 | Eureka | 4,182 |
| Humboldt | 12,844 | Winnemucca | 9,704 |
| Lander | 6,266 | Battle Mountain | 5,621 |
| Lincoln | 3,775 | Pioche | 10,650 |
| Lyon | 20,001 | Yerington | 2,024 |
| Mineral | 6,475 | Hawthorne | 3,837 |
| Nye | 17,781 | Tonopah | 18,064 |
| Pershing | 4,336 | Lovelock | 6,031 |
| Storey | 2,526 | Virginia City | 262 |
| Washoe | 254,667 | Reno | 6,608 |
| White Pine | 9,264 | Ely | 8,905 |
| Independent City | | | |
| Carson City | 40,443 | Carson City | 153 |

## New Hampshire

(10 counties, 8,993 sq. mi. land; pop., 1,109,252)

| County | Pop. | County Seat or court house | Land area sq. mi. |
|---|---|---|---|
| Belknap | 49,216 | Laconia | 404 |
| Carroll | 35,410 | Ossipee | 933 |
| Cheshire | 70,121 | Keene | 711 |
| Coos | 34,693 | Lancaster | 1,804 |
| Grafton | 74,929 | Woodsville | 1,719 |
| Hillsborough | 335,838 | Nashua | 876 |
| Merrimack | 120,240 | Concord | 936 |
| Rockingham | 245,845 | Exeter | 699 |
| Strafford | 104,233 | Dover | 370 |
| Sullivan | 38,592 | Newport | 540 |

## New Jersey

(21 counties, 7,468 sq. mi. land; pop., 7,730,188)

| County | Pop. | County Seat or court house | Land area sq. mi. |
|---|---|---|---|
| Atlantic | 224,327 | Mays Landing | 568 |
| Bergen | 825,380 | Hackensack | 237 |
| Burlington | 395,066 | Mount Holly | 808 |
| Camden | 502,824 | Camden | 223 |
| Cape May | 95,089 | Cape May Court House | 263 |
| Cumberland | 138,053 | Bridgeton | 498 |
| Essex | 778,964 | Newark | 127 |
| Gloucester | 230,082 | Woodbury | 327 |
| Hudson | 553,099 | Jersey City | 46 |
| Hunterdon | 107,802 | Flemington | 426 |
| Mercer | 325,824 | Trenton | 227 |
| Middlesex | 671,811 | New Brunswick | 316 |
| Monmouth | 553,093 | Freehold | 472 |
| Morris | 421,361 | Morristown | 470 |
| Ocean | 433,203 | Toms River | 641 |
| Passaic | 453,060 | Paterson | 187 |
| Salem | 65,294 | Salem | 338 |
| Somerset | 240,245 | Somerville | 305 |
| Sussex | 130,943 | Newton | 526 |
| Union | 493,819 | Elizabeth | 103 |
| Warren | 91,607 | Belvidere | 359 |

## New Mexico

(33 counties, 121,336 sq. mi. land; pop., 1,515,069)

| County | Pop. | County Seat or court house | Land area sq. mi. |
|---|---|---|---|
| Bernalillo | 480,577 | Albuquerque | 1,169 |
| Catron | 2,563 | Reserve | 6,929 |
| Chaves | 57,849 | Roswell | 6,066 |
| Cibola | 23,794 | Grants | 4,468 |
| Colfax | 12,925 | Raton | 3,762 |
| Curry | 42,207 | Clovis | 1,408 |
| De Baca | 2,252 | Fort Sumner | 2,323 |
| Dona Ana | 135,510 | Las Cruces | 3,819 |
| Eddy | 48,605 | Carlsbad | 4,184 |
| Grant | 27,676 | Silver City | 3,969 |
| Guadalupe | 4,156 | Santa Rosa | 3,032 |
| Harding | 987 | Mosquero | 2,122 |
| Hidalgo | 5,958 | Lordsburg | 3,445 |
| Lea | 55,765 | Lovington | 4,390 |
| Lincoln | 12,219 | Carrizozo | 4,832 |
| Los Alamos | 18,115 | Los Alamos | 109 |
| Luna | 18,110 | Deming | 2,965 |
| McKinley | 60,686 | Gallup | 5,442 |
| Mora | 4,264 | Mora | 1,930 |
| Otero | 51,928 | Alamogordo | 6,626 |
| Quay | 10,823 | Tucumcari | 2,874 |
| Rio Arriba | 34,365 | Tierra Amarilla | 5,856 |
| Roosevelt | 16,702 | Portales | 2,453 |
| Sandoval | 63,319 | Bernalillo | 3,707 |
| San Juan | 91,605 | Aztec | 5,522 |
| San Miguel | 25,743 | Las Vegas | 4,709 |
| Santa Fe | 98,928 | Santa Fe | 1,905 |
| Sierra | 9,912 | Truth or Consequences | 4,178 |
| Socorro | 14,764 | Socorro | 6,625 |
| Taos | 23,118 | Taos | 2,204 |
| Torrance | 10,285 | Estancia | 3,335 |
| Union | 4,124 | Clayton | 3,830 |
| Valencia | 45,235 | Los Lunas | 1,068 |

## New York

(62 counties, 47,377 sq. mi. land; pop., 17,990,455)

| County | Pop. | County Seat or court house | Land area sq. mi. |
|---|---|---|---|
| Albany | 292,793 | Albany | 524 |
| Allegany | 50,470 | Belmont | 1,031 |
| Bronx | 1,203,789 | Bronx | 42 |
| Broome | 212,160 | Binghamton | 707 |
| Cattaraugus | 84,234 | Little Valley | 1,310 |
| Cayuga | 82,313 | Auburn | 693 |
| Chautauqua | 141,895 | Mayville | 1,062 |
| Chemung | 95,195 | Elmira | 408 |
| Chenango | 51,768 | Norwich | 894 |
| Clinton | 85,969 | Plattsburgh | 1,039 |
| Columbia | 62,982 | Hudson | 636 |
| Cortland | 48,963 | Cortland | 500 |
| Delaware | 47,225 | Delhi | 1,446 |
| Dutchess | 259,462 | Poughkeepsie | 802 |
| Erie | 968,584 | Buffalo | 1,045 |
| Essex | 37,152 | Elizabethtown | 1,797 |
| Franklin | 46,540 | Malone | 1,632 |
| Fulton | 54,191 | Johnstown | 496 |
| Genesee | 60,060 | Batavia | 494 |
| Greene | 44,739 | Catskill | 648 |
| Hamilton | 5,279 | Lake Pleasant | 1,721 |
| Herkimer | 65,809 | Herkimer | 1,412 |
| Jefferson | 110,943 | Watertown | 1,272 |
| Kings | 2,300,664 | Brooklyn | 71 |
| Lewis | 26,796 | Lowville | 1,276 |
| Livingston | 62,372 | Geneseo | 632 |
| Madison | 69,166 | Wampsville | 656 |
| Monroe | 713,968 | Rochester | 659 |
| Montgomery | 51,981 | Fonda | 405 |
| Nassau | 1,287,444 | Mineola | 287 |
| New York | 1,487,536 | New York | 28 |
| Niagara | 220,756 | Lockport | 523 |
| Oneida | 250,836 | Utica | 1,213 |
| Onondaga | 468,973 | Syracuse | 780 |
| Ontario | 95,101 | Canandaigua | 644 |
| Orange | 307,647 | Goshen | 816 |
| Orleans | 41,846 | Albion | 391 |
| Oswego | 121,785 | Oswego | 953 |
| Otsego | 60,517 | Cooperstown | 1,003 |
| Putnam | 83,941 | Carmel | 232 |
| Queens | 1,951,598 | Jamaica | 109 |
| Rensselaer | 154,429 | Troy | 654 |
| Richmond | 378,977 | Saint George | 59 |
| Rockland | 265,475 | New City | 174 |
| Saint Lawrence | 111,974 | Canton | 2,686 |
| Saratoga | 181,276 | Ballston Spa | 812 |
| Schenectady | 149,285 | Schenectady | 206 |
| Schoharie | 31,859 | Schoharie | 622 |
| Schuyler | 18,662 | Watkins Glen | 329 |
| Seneca | 33,683 | Ovid & Waterloo | 325 |
| Steuben | 99,088 | Bath | 1,393 |
| Suffolk | 1,321,768 | Riverhead | 911 |
| Sullivan | 69,277 | Monticello | 970 |
| Tioga | 52,337 | Owego | 519 |
| Tompkins | 94,097 | Ithaca | 476 |
| Ulster | 165,304 | Kingston | 1,127 |
| Warren | 59,209 | Queensbury | 870 |
| Washington | 59,330 | Hudson Falls | 836 |
| Wayne | 89,123 | Lyons | 604 |
| Westchester | 874,866 | White Plains | 433 |
| Wyoming | 42,507 | Warsaw | 593 |
| Yates | 22,810 | Penn Yan | 338 |

## North Carolina

(100 counties, 48,843 sq. mi. land; pop., 6,628,637)

| County | Pop. | County Seat or court house | Land area sq. mi. |
|---|---|---|---|
| Alamance | 108,213 | Graham | 433 |
| Alexander | 27,544 | Taylorsville | 259 |
| Alleghany | 9,590 | Sparta | 235 |
| Anson | 23,474 | Wadesboro | 533 |
| Ashe | 22,209 | Jefferson | 426 |
| Avery | 14,867 | Newland | 247 |
| Beaufort | 42,283 | Washington | 826 |
| Bertie | 20,388 | Windsor | 701 |
| Bladen | 28,663 | Elizabethtown | 879 |
| Brunswick | 50,985 | Bolivia | 860 |
| Buncombe | 174,819 | Asheville | 659 |
| Burke | 75,744 | Morganton | 504 |
| Cabarrus | 98,935 | Concord | 364 |
| Caldwell | 70,709 | Lenoir | 471 |
| Camden | 5,904 | Camden | 240 |
| Carteret | 52,556 | Beaufort | 526 |
| Caswell | 20,693 | Yanceyville | 428 |
| Catawba | 118,412 | Newton | 396 |
| Chatham | 38,759 | Pittsboro | 708 |
| Cherokee | 20,170 | Murphy | 452 |
| Chowan | 13,506 | Edenton | 182 |
| Clay | 7,155 | Hayesville | 214 |
| Cleveland | 84,714 | Shelby | 468 |
| Columbus | 49,587 | Whiteville | 938 |
| Craven | 81,613 | New Bern | 701 |
| Cumberland | 274,566 | Fayetteville | 657 |
| Currituck | 13,736 | Currituck | 256 |
| Dare | 22,746 | Manteo | 391 |
| Davidson | 126,677 | Lexington | 548 |
| Davie | 27,859 | Mocksville | 267 |
| Duplin | 39,995 | Kenansville | 819 |
| Durham | 181,854 | Durham | 298 |
| Edgecombe | 56,692 | Tarboro | 506 |
| Forsyth | 265,878 | Winston-Salem | 412 |
| Franklin | 36,414 | Louisburg | 494 |
| Gaston | 175,093 | Gastonia | 357 |
| Gates | 9,305 | Gatesville | 338 |
| Graham | 7,196 | Robbinsville | 289 |
| Granville | 38,341 | Oxford | 534 |
| Greene | 15,384 | Snow Hill | 266 |
| Guilford | 347,420 | Greensboro | 651 |
| Halifax | 55,516 | Halifax | 724 |
| Harnett | 67,833 | Lillington | 601 |
| Haywood | 46,942 | Waynesville | 555 |
| Henderson | 69,285 | Hendersonville | 374 |
| Hertford | 22,523 | Winton | 356 |
| Hoke | 22,856 | Raeford | 391 |
| Hyde | 5,411 | Swan Quarter | 624 |
| Iredell | 92,935 | Statesville | 574 |
| Jackson | 26,846 | Sylva | 491 |
| Johnston | 81,306 | Smithfield | 795 |
| Jones | 9,414 | Trenton | 470 |
| Lee | 41,370 | Sanford | 259 |
| Lenoir | 57,274 | Kinston | 402 |
| Lincoln | 50,319 | Lincolnton | 298 |
| McDowell | 35,681 | Marion | 437 |
| Macon | 23,499 | Franklin | 517 |
| Madison | 16,953 | Marshall | 451 |
| Martin | 25,078 | Williamston | 461 |
| Mecklenburg | 511,481 | Charlotte | 528 |
| Mitchell | 14,433 | Bakersville | 222 |
| Montgomery | 23,352 | Troy | 490 |
| Moore | 59,000 | Carthage | 701 |
| Nash | 76,677 | Nashville | 540 |
| New Hanover | 120,284 | Wilmington | 185 |
| Northampton | 20,798 | Jackson | 538 |
| Onslow | 149,838 | Jacksonville | 763 |
| Orange | 93,851 | Hillsborough | 400 |
| Pamlico | 11,368 | Bayboro | 341 |
| Pasquotank | 31,298 | Elizabeth City | 228 |
| Pender | 28,885 | Burgaw | 875 |
| Perquimans | 10,447 | Hertford | 246 |
| Person | 30,180 | Roxboro | 398 |
| Pitt | 108,480 | Greenville | 657 |
| Polk | 14,416 | Columbus | 238 |
| Randolph | 106,546 | Asheboro | 789 |
| Richmond | 44,518 | Rockingham | 477 |
| Robeson | 105,170 | Lumberton | 949 |
| Rockingham | 86,064 | Wentworth | 569 |
| Rowan | 110,605 | Salisbury | 519 |
| Rutherford | 56,918 | Rutherfordton | 568 |
| Sampson | 47,297 | Clinton | 947 |
| Scotland | 33,763 | Laurinburg | 319 |
| Stanly | 51,765 | Albemarle | 396 |
| Stokes | 37,223 | Danbury | 452 |
| Surry | 61,704 | Dobson | 539 |
| Swain | 11,268 | Bryson City | 526 |
| Transylvania | 25,520 | Brevard | 378 |
| Tyrrell | 3,856 | Columbia | 407 |
| Union | 84,210 | Monroe | 639 |
| Vance | 38,892 | Henderson | 249 |
| Wake | 426,301 | Raleigh | 854 |
| Warren | 17,265 | Warrenton | 427 |
| Washington | 13,997 | Plymouth | 332 |
| Watauga | 36,952 | Boone | 314 |
| Wayne | 104,666 | Goldsboro | 554 |
| Wilkes | 59,393 | Wilkesboro | 752 |
| Wilson | 66,061 | Wilson | 374 |
| Yadkin | 30,488 | Yadkinville | 336 |
| Yancey | 15,419 | Burnsville | 314 |

## North Dakota

(53 counties, 69,300 sq. mi. land; pop., 638,800)

| County | Pop. | County Seat or court house | Land area sq. mi. |
|---|---|---|---|
| Adams | 3,174 | Hettinger | 988 |
| Barnes | 12,545 | Valley City | 1,498 |
| Benson | 7,198 | Minnewaukan | 1,412 |
| Billings | 1,108 | Medora | 1,152 |
| Bottineau | 8,011 | Bottineau | 1,668 |
| Bowman | 3,596 | Bowman | 1,162 |
| Burke | 3,002 | Bowbells | 1,118 |
| Burleigh | 60,131 | Bismarck | 1,618 |
| Cass | 102,874 | Fargo | 1,767 |
| Cavalier | 6,064 | Langdon | 1,507 |
| Dickey | 6,107 | Ellendale | 1,139 |
| Divide | 2,899 | Crosby | 1,288 |
| Dunn | 4,005 | Manning | 1,993 |

| County | Pop. | County Seat or court house | Land area sq. mi. | County | Pop. | County Seat or court house | Land area sq. mi. |
|---|---|---|---|---|---|---|---|
| Eddy | 2,951 | New Rockford | 634 | Marion | 64,274 | Marion | 403 |
| Emmons | 4,830 | Linton | 1,499 | Medina | 122,354 | Medina | 422 |
| Foster | 3,983 | Carrington | 640 | Meigs | 22,987 | Pomeroy | 432 |
| Golden Valley | 2,108 | Beach | 1,003 | Mercer | 39,443 | Celina | 457 |
| Grand Forks | 70,683 | Grand Forks | 1,440 | Miami | 93,182 | Troy | 410 |
| Grant | 3,549 | Carson | 1,660 | Monroe | 15,497 | Woodsfield | 457 |
| Griggs | 3,303 | Cooperstown | 708 | Montgomery | 573,809 | Dayton | 458 |
| Hettinger | 3,445 | Mott | 1,133 | Morgan | 14,194 | McConnelsville | 420 |
| Kidder | 3,332 | Steele | 1,362 | Morrow | 27,749 | Mount Gilead | 406 |
| La Moure | 5,383 | La Moure | 1,150 | Muskingum | 82,068 | Zanesville | 654 |
| Logan | 2,847 | Napoleon | 1,000 | Noble | 11,336 | Caldwell | 399 |
| McHenry | 6,528 | Towner | 1,897 | Ottawa | 40,029 | Port Clinton | 253 |
| McIntosh | 4,021 | Ashley | 984 | Paulding | 20,488 | Paulding | 419 |
| McKenzie | 6,383 | Watford City | 2,754 | Perry | 31,557 | New Lexington | 412 |
| McLean | 10,457 | Washburn | 2,065 | Pickaway | 48,244 | Circleville | 503 |
| Mercer | 9,808 | Stanton | 1,044 | Pike | 24,249 | Waverly | 443 |
| Morton | 23,700 | Mandan | 1,921 | Portage | 142,585 | Ravenna | 493 |
| Mountrail | 7,021 | Stanley | 1,837 | Preble | 40,113 | Eaton | 426 |
| Nelson | 4,410 | Lakota | 991 | Putnam | 33,819 | Ottawa | 484 |
| Oliver | 2,381 | Center | 723 | Richland | 126,137 | Mansfield | 497 |
| Pembina | 9,238 | Cavalier | 1,120 | Ross | 69,330 | Chillicothe | 692 |
| Pierce | 5,052 | Rugby | 1,037 | Sandusky | 61,963 | Fremont | 409 |
| Ramsey | 12,681 | Devils Lake | 1,241 | Scioto | 80,327 | Portsmouth | 613 |
| Ransom | 5,921 | Lisbon | 862 | Seneca | 59,733 | Tiffin | 553 |
| Renville | 3,160 | Mohall | 874 | Shelby | 44,915 | Sidney | 409 |
| Richland | 18,148 | Wahpeton | 1,436 | Stark | 367,585 | Canton | 574 |
| Rolette | 12,772 | Rolla | 914 | Summit | 514,990 | Akron | 412 |
| Sargent | 4,549 | Forman | 857 | Trumbull | 227,813 | Warren | 612 |
| Sheridan | 2,148 | McClusky | 989 | Tuscarawas | 84,090 | New Philadelphia | 570 |
| Sioux | 3,761 | Fort Yates | 1,099 | Union | 31,969 | Marysville | 437 |
| Slope | 907 | Amidon | 1,219 | Van Wert | 30,464 | Van Wert | 410 |
| Stark | 22,832 | Dickinson | 1,338 | Vinton | 11,098 | McArthur | 414 |
| Steele | 2,420 | Finley | 713 | Warren | 113,927 | Lebanon | 403 |
| Stutsman | 22,241 | Jamestown | 2,263 | Washington | 62,254 | Marietta | 640 |
| Towner | 3,627 | Cando | 1,035 | Wayne | 101,461 | Wooster | 557 |
| Traill | 8,752 | Hillsboro | 861 | Williams | 36,956 | Bryan | 422 |
| Walsh | 13,840 | Grafton | 1,290 | Wood | 113,269 | Bowling Green | 619 |
| Ward | 57,921 | Minot | 2,041 | Wyandot | 22,254 | Upper Sandusky | 406 |
| Wells | 5,864 | Fessenden | 1,288 | | | | |
| Williams | 21,129 | Williston | 2,074 | | | | |

## Ohio

(88 counties, 41,004 sq. mi. land; pop., 10,847,115)

## Oklahoma

(77 counties, 68,655 sq. mi. land; pop., 3,145,585)

| County | Pop. | County Seat or court house | Land area sq. mi. | County | Pop. | County Seat or court house | Land area sq. mi. |
|---|---|---|---|---|---|---|---|
| Adams | 25,371 | West Union | 586 | Adair | 18,421 | Stilwell | 577 |
| Allen | 109,755 | Lima | 405 | Alfalfa | 6,416 | Cherokee | 864 |
| Ashland | 47,507 | Ashland | 424 | Atoka | 12,778 | Atoka | 980 |
| Ashtabula | 99,821 | Jefferson | 703 | Beaver | 6,023 | Beaver | 1,808 |
| Athens | 59,549 | Athens | 508 | Beckham | 18,812 | Sayre | 904 |
| Auglaize | 44,585 | Wapakoneta | 398 | Blaine | 11,470 | Watonga | 920 |
| Belmont | 71,074 | Saint Clairsville | 537 | Bryan | 32,089 | Durant | 902 |
| Brown | 34,966 | Georgetown | 493 | Caddo | 29,550 | Anadarko | 1,286 |
| Butler | 291,479 | Hamilton | 470 | Canadian | 74,409 | El Reno | 901 |
| Carroll | 26,521 | Carrollton | 393 | Carter | 42,919 | Ardmore | 828 |
| Champaign | 36,019 | Urbana | 429 | Cherokee | 34,049 | Tahlequah | 748 |
| Clark | 147,548 | Springfield | 398 | Choctaw | 15,302 | Hugo | 762 |
| Clermont | 150,167 | Batavia | 456 | Cimarron | 3,301 | Boise City | 1,842 |
| Clinton | 35,417 | Wilmington | 410 | Cleveland | 174,253 | Norman | 529 |
| Columbiana | 108,276 | Lisbon | 534 | Coal | 5,780 | Coalgate | 520 |
| Coshocton | 35,427 | Coshocton | 566 | Comanche | 111,486 | Lawton | 1,076 |
| Crawford | 47,870 | Bucyrus | 403 | Cotton | 6,651 | Walters | 656 |
| Cuyahoga | 1,412,140 | Cleveland | 459 | Craig | 14,104 | Vinita | 763 |
| Darke | 53,619 | Greenville | 600 | Creek | 60,915 | Sapulpa | 930 |
| Defiance | 39,350 | Defiance | 414 | Custer | 26,897 | Arapaho | 981 |
| Delaware | 66,929 | Delaware | 443 | Delaware | 28,070 | Jay | 720 |
| Erie | 76,779 | Sandusky | 264 | Dewey | 5,551 | Taloga | 1,007 |
| Fairfield | 103,461 | Lancaster | 506 | Ellis | 4,497 | Arnett | 1,232 |
| Fayette | 27,466 | Washington Court House | 405 | Garfield | 56,735 | Enid | 1,060 |
| Franklin | 961,437 | Columbus | 543 | Garvin | 26,605 | Pauls Valley | 813 |
| Fulton | 38,498 | Wauseon | 407 | Grady | 41,747 | Chickasha | 1,106 |
| Gallia | 30,954 | Gallipolis | 471 | Grant | 5,689 | Medford | 1,004 |
| Geauga | 81,129 | Chardon | 408 | Greer | 6,559 | Mangum | 638 |
| Greene | 136,731 | Xenia | 416 | Harmon | 3,793 | Hollis | 537 |
| Guernsey | 39,024 | Cambridge | 522 | Harper | 4,063 | Buffalo | 1,039 |
| Hamilton | 866,228 | Cincinnati | 412 | Haskell | 10,940 | Stigler | 570 |
| Hancock | 65,536 | Findlay | 532 | Hughes | 13,014 | Holdenville | 806 |
| Hardin | 31,111 | Kenton | 471 | Jackson | 28,764 | Altus | 817 |
| Harrison | 16,085 | Cadiz | 400 | Jefferson | 7,010 | Waurika | 769 |
| Henry | 29,108 | Napoleon | 415 | Johnston | 10,032 | Tishomingo | 639 |
| Highland | 35,728 | Hillsboro | 553 | Kay | 48,056 | Newkirk | 921 |
| Hocking | 25,533 | Logan | 423 | Kingfisher | 13,212 | Kingfisher | 906 |
| Holmes | 32,849 | Millersburg | 424 | Kiowa | 11,347 | Hobart | 1,019 |
| Huron | 56,240 | Norwalk | 494 | Latimer | 10,333 | Wilburton | 728 |
| Jackson | 30,230 | Jackson | 420 | Le Flore | 43,270 | Poteau | 1,585 |
| Jefferson | 80,298 | Steubenville | 410 | Lincoln | 29,216 | Chandler | 964 |
| Knox | 47,473 | Mount Vernon | 529 | Logan | 29,011 | Guthrie | 748 |
| Lake | 215,499 | Painesville | 231 | Love | 8,157 | Marietta | 519 |
| Lawrence | 61,834 | Ironton | 457 | McClain | 22,795 | Purcell | 582 |
| Licking | 128,300 | Newark | 686 | McCurtain | 33,433 | Idabel | 1,826 |
| Logan | 42,310 | Bellefontaine | 458 | McIntosh | 16,779 | Eufaula | 599 |
| Lorain | 271,126 | Elyria | 495 | Major | 8,055 | Fairview | 958 |
| Lucas | 462,361 | Toledo | 341 | Marshall | 10,829 | Madill | 372 |
| Madison | 37,068 | London | 467 | Mayes | 33,366 | Pryor | 644 |
| Mahoning | 264,806 | Youngstown | 417 | Murray | 12,042 | Sulphur | 420 |
| | | | | Muskogee | 68,078 | Muskogee | 815 |
| | | | | Noble | 11,045 | Perry | 736 |

| County | Pop. | County Seat or court house | Land area sq. mi. |
|---|---|---|---|
| Nowata | 9,992 | Nowata | 540 |
| Okfuskee | 11,551 | Okemah | 628 |
| Oklahoma | 599,611 | Oklahoma City | 708 |
| Okmulgee | 36,490 | Okmulgee | 698 |
| Osage | 41,645 | Pawhuska | 2,265 |
| Ottawa | 30,561 | Miami | 465 |
| Pawnee | 15,575 | Pawnee | 551 |
| Payne | 61,507 | Stillwater | 691 |
| Pittsburg | 40,581 | McAlester | 1,251 |
| Pontotoc | 34,119 | Ada | 717 |
| Pottawatomie | 58,760 | Shawnee | 783 |
| Pushmataha | 10,997 | Antlers | 1,417 |
| Roger Mills | 4,147 | Cheyenne | 1,146 |
| Rogers | 55,170 | Claremore | 683 |
| Seminole | 25,412 | Wewoka | 639 |
| Sequoyah | 33,828 | Sallisaw | 678 |
| Stephens | 42,299 | Duncan | 884 |
| Texas | 16,419 | Guymon | 2,040 |
| Tillman | 10,384 | Frederick | 904 |
| Tulsa | 503,341 | Tulsa | 572 |
| Wagoner | 47,883 | Wagoner | 559 |
| Washington | 48,066 | Bartlesville | 423 |
| Washita | 11,441 | Cordell | 1,006 |
| Woods | 9,103 | Alva | 1,291 |
| Woodward | 18,976 | Woodward | 1,242 |

## Oregon

(36 counties, 96,184 sq. mi. land; pop., 2,842,321)

| County | Pop. | County Seat or court house | Land area sq. mi. |
|---|---|---|---|
| Baker | 15,317 | Baker City | 3,089 |
| Benton | 70,811 | Corvallis | 679 |
| Clackamas | 278,850 | Oregon City | 1,870 |
| Clatsop | 33,301 | Astoria | 873 |
| Columbia | 37,557 | Saint Helens | 687 |
| Coos | 60,273 | Coquille | 1,629 |
| Crook | 14,111 | Prineville | 2,991 |
| Curry | 19,327 | Gold Beach | 1,648 |
| Deschutes | 74,976 | Bend | 3,055 |
| Douglas | 94,649 | Roseburg | 5,071 |
| Gilliam | 1,717 | Condon | 1,223 |
| Grant | 7,853 | Canyon City | 4,525 |
| Harney | 7,060 | Burns | 10,228 |
| Hood River | 16,903 | Hood River | 533 |
| Jackson | 146,387 | Medford | 2,801 |
| Jefferson | 13,676 | Madras | 1,791 |
| Josephine | 62,649 | Grants Pass | 1,640 |
| Klamath | 57,702 | Klamath Falls | 6,135 |
| Lake | 7,186 | Lakeview | 8,359 |
| Lane | 282,912 | Eugene | 4,620 |
| Lincoln | 38,889 | Newport | 992 |
| Linn | 91,227 | Albany | 2,296 |
| Malheur | 26,038 | Vale | 9,926 |
| Marion | 228,483 | Salem | 1,194 |
| Morrow | 7,625 | Heppner | 2,094 |
| Multnomah | 583,887 | Portland | 465 |
| Polk | 49,541 | Dallas | 741 |
| Sherman | 1,918 | Moro | 831 |
| Tillamook | 21,570 | Tillamook | 1,125 |
| Umatilla | 59,249 | Pendleton | 3,218 |
| Union | 23,598 | La Grande | 2,038 |
| Wallowa | 6,911 | Enterprise | 3,150 |
| Wasco | 21,683 | The Dalles | 2,396 |
| Washington | 311,554 | Hillsboro | 727 |
| Wheeler | 1,396 | Fossil | 1,713 |
| Yamhill | 65,551 | McMinnville | 718 |

## Pennsylvania

(67 counties, 44,888 sq. mi. land; pop., 11,881,643)

| County | Pop. | County Seat or court house | Land area sq. mi. |
|---|---|---|---|
| Adams | 78,274 | Gettysburg | 521 |
| Allegheny | 1,336,449 | Pittsburgh | 727 |
| Armstrong | 73,478 | Kittanning | 646 |
| Beaver | 186,093 | Beaver | 436 |
| Bedford | 47,919 | Bedford | 1,017 |
| Berks | 336,523 | Reading | 861 |
| Blair | 130,542 | Hollidaysburg | 527 |
| Bradford | 60,967 | Towanda | 1,152 |
| Bucks | 541,174 | Doylestown | 610 |
| Butler | 152,013 | Butler | 789 |
| Cambria | 163,029 | Ebensburg | 691 |
| Cameron | 5,913 | Emporium | 398 |
| Carbon | 56,973 | Jim Thorpe | 384 |
| Centre | 124,812 | Bellefonte | 1,106 |
| Chester | 376,396 | West Chester | 758 |
| Clarion | 41,699 | Clarion | 607 |
| Clearfield | 78,097 | Clearfield | 1,149 |
| Clinton | 37,182 | Lock Haven | 891 |
| Columbia | 63,202 | Bloomsburg | 486 |
| Crawford | 86,169 | Meadville | 1,011 |
| Cumberland | 195,257 | Carlisle | 547 |
| Dauphin | 237,813 | Harrisburg | 528 |

| County | Pop. | County Seat or court house | Land area sq. mi. |
|---|---|---|---|
| Delaware | 547,651 | Media | 184 |
| Elk | 34,878 | Ridgway | 830 |
| Erie | 275,572 | Erie | 804 |
| Fayette | 145,351 | Uniontown | 794 |
| Forest | 4,802 | Tionesta | 428 |
| Franklin | 121,082 | Chambersburg | 774 |
| Fulton | 13,837 | McConnellsburg | 438 |
| Greene | 39,550 | Waynesburg | 577 |
| Huntingdon | 44,164 | Huntingdon | 877 |
| Indiana | 89,994 | Indiana | 829 |
| Jefferson | 46,083 | Brookville | 657 |
| Juniata | 20,625 | Mifflintown | 392 |
| Lackawanna | 219,097 | Scranton | 461 |
| Lancaster | 422,822 | Lancaster | 952 |
| Lawrence | 96,246 | New Castle | 363 |
| Lebanon | 113,744 | Lebanon | 363 |
| Lehigh | 291,130 | Allentown | 348 |
| Luzerne | 328,149 | Wilkes-Barre | 891 |
| Lycoming | 118,710 | Williamsport | 1,237 |
| McKean | 47,131 | Smethport | 979 |
| Mercer | 121,003 | Mercer | 672 |
| Mifflin | 46,197 | Lewistown | 413 |
| Monroe | 95,582 | Stroudsburg | 609 |
| Montgomery | 678,111 | Norristown | 486 |
| Montour | 17,735 | Danville | 131 |
| Northampton | 247,105 | Easton | 376 |
| Northumberland | 96,771 | Sunbury | 461 |
| Perry | 41,172 | New Bloomfield | 557 |
| Philadelphia | 1,585,577 | Philadelphia | 136 |
| Pike | 27,966 | Milford | 550 |
| Potter | 16,717 | Coudersport | 1,081 |
| Schuylkill | 152,585 | Pottsville | 782 |
| Snyder | 36,680 | Middleburg | 329 |
| Somerset | 78,218 | Somerset | 1,073 |
| Sullivan | 6,104 | Laporte | 451 |
| Susquehanna | 40,380 | Montrose | 826 |
| Tioga | 41,126 | Wellsboro | 1,131 |
| Union | 36,176 | Lewisburg | 317 |
| Venango | 59,381 | Franklin | 679 |
| Warren | 45,049 | Warren | 885 |
| Washington | 204,584 | Washington | 958 |
| Wayne | 39,944 | Honesdale | 731 |
| Westmoreland | 370,321 | Greensburg | 1,033 |
| Wyoming | 28,076 | Tunkhannock | 399 |
| York | 339,574 | York | 906 |

## Rhode Island

(5 counties, 1,055 sq. mi. land; pop., 1,003,464)

| County | Pop. | County Seat or court house | Land area sq. mi. |
|---|---|---|---|
| Bristol | 48,859 | Bristol | 26 |
| Kent | 161,135 | East Greenwich | 172 |
| Newport | 87,194 | Newport | 107 |
| Providence | 596,270 | Providence | 416 |
| Washington | 110,006 | West Kingston | 333 |

## South Carolina

(46 counties, 30,203 sq. mi. land; pop., 3,486,703)

| County | Pop. | County Seat or court house | Land area sq. mi. |
|---|---|---|---|
| Abbeville | 23,862 | Abbeville | 508 |
| Aiken | 120,991 | Aiken | 1,092 |
| Allendale | 11,722 | Allendale | 413 |
| Anderson | 145,177 | Anderson | 718 |
| Bamberg | 16,902 | Bamberg | 395 |
| Barnwell | 20,293 | Barnwell | 558 |
| Beaufort | 86,425 | Beaufort | 579 |
| Berkeley | 128,776 | Moncks Corner | 1,108 |
| Calhoun | 12,753 | Saint Matthews | 380 |
| Charleston | 295,041 | Charleston | 938 |
| Cherokee | 44,506 | Gaffney | 396 |
| Chester | 32,170 | Chester | 580 |
| Chesterfield | 38,575 | Chesterfield | 802 |
| Clarendon | 28,450 | Manning | 602 |
| Colleton | 34,377 | Walterboro | 1,052 |
| Darlington | 61,851 | Darlington | 563 |
| Dillon | 29,114 | Dillon | 406 |
| Dorchester | 83,060 | Saint George | 575 |
| Edgefield | 18,360 | Edgefield | 490 |
| Fairfield | 22,295 | Winnsboro | 685 |
| Florence | 114,344 | Florence | 804 |
| Georgetown | 46,302 | Georgetown | 822 |
| Greenville | 320,167 | Greenville | 795 |
| Greenwood | 59,567 | Greenwood | 451 |
| Hampton | 18,191 | Hampton | 561 |
| Horry | 144,053 | Conway | 1,143 |
| Jasper | 15,487 | Ridgeland | 655 |
| Kershaw | 43,599 | Camden | 723 |
| Lancaster | 54,516 | Lancaster | 552 |
| Laurens | 58,092 | Laurens | 712 |
| Lee | 18,437 | Bishopville | 411 |
| Lexington | 167,611 | Lexington | 707 |
| McCormick | 8,868 | McCormick | 350 |

| County | Pop. | County Seat or court house | Land area sq. mi. |
|---|---|---|---|
| Marion | 33,899 | Marion | 493 |
| Marlboro | 29,716 | Bennettsville | 483 |
| Newberry | 33,172 | Newberry | 634 |
| Oconee | 57,494 | Walhalla | 629 |
| Orangeburg | 84,803 | Orangeburg | 1,111 |
| Pickens | 93,896 | Pickens | 499 |
| Richland | 286,321 | Columbia | 762 |
| Saluda | 16,357 | Saluda | 456 |
| Spartanburg | 226,793 | Spartanburg | 814 |
| Sumter | 102,637 | Sumter | 665 |
| Union | 30,337 | Union | 515 |
| Williamsburg | 36,815 | Kingstree | 934 |
| York | 131,497 | York | 685 |

## South Dakota

(67 counties, 75,952 sq. mi. land; pop., 696,004)

| County | Pop. | County Seat or court house | Land area sq. mi. |
|---|---|---|---|
| Aurora | 3,135 | Plankinton | 707 |
| Beadle | 18,253 | Huron | 1,259 |
| Bennett | 3,206 | Martin | 1,182 |
| Bon Homme | 7,089 | Tyndall | 552 |
| Brookings | 25,207 | Brookings | 795 |
| Brown | 35,580 | Aberdeen | 1,722 |
| Brule | 5,485 | Chamberlain | 815 |
| Buffalo | 1,759 | Gannvalley | 475 |
| Butte | 7,914 | Belle Fourche | 2,251 |
| Campbell | 1,965 | Mound City | 732 |
| Charles Mix | 9,131 | Lake Andes | 1,090 |
| Clark | 4,403 | Clark | 953 |
| Clay | 13,186 | Vermillion | 409 |
| Codington | 22,698 | Watertown | 694 |
| Corson | 4,195 | McIntosh | 2,467 |
| Custer | 6,179 | Custer | 1,559 |
| Davison | 17,503 | Mitchell | 436 |
| Day | 6,978 | Webster | 1,022 |
| Deuel | 4,522 | Clear Lake | 631 |
| Dewey | 5,523 | Timber Lake | 2,310 |
| Douglas | 3,746 | Armour | 434 |
| Edmunds | 4,356 | Ipswich | 1,149 |
| Fall River | 7,353 | Hot Springs | 4,742 |
| Faulk | 2,744 | Faulkton | 1,004 |
| Grant | 8,372 | Milbank | 681 |
| Gregory | 5,359 | Burke | 1,013 |
| Haakon | 2,624 | Philip | 1,822 |
| Hamlin | 4,974 | Hayti | 512 |
| Hand | 4,272 | Miller | 1,437 |
| Hanson | 2,994 | Alexandria | 433 |
| Harding | 1,669 | Buffalo | 2,678 |
| Hughes | 14,817 | Pierre | 757 |
| Hutchinson | 8,262 | Olivet | 816 |
| Hyde | 1,696 | Highmore | 860 |
| Jackson | 2,811 | Kadoka | 1,872 |
| Jerauld | 2,425 | Wessington Springs | 530 |
| Jones | 1,324 | Murdo | 971 |
| Kingsbury | 5,925 | De Smet | 824 |
| Lake | 10,550 | Madison | 560 |
| Lawrence | 20,655 | Deadwood | 800 |
| Lincoln | 15,427 | Canton | 578 |
| Lyman | 3,638 | Kennebec | 1,679 |
| McCook | 5,688 | Salem | 576 |
| McPherson | 3,228 | Leola | 1,148 |
| Marshall | 4,844 | Britton | 848 |
| Meade | 21,878 | Sturgis | 3,481 |
| Mellette | 2,137 | White River | 1,311 |
| Miner | 3,272 | Howard | 570 |
| Minnehaha | 123,809 | Sioux Falls | 810 |
| Moody | 6,507 | Flandreau | 520 |
| Pennington | 81,343 | Rapid City | 2,783 |
| Perkins | 3,932 | Bison | 2,884 |
| Potter | 3,190 | Gettysburg | 869 |
| Roberts | 9,914 | Sisseton | 1,102 |
| Sanborn | 2,833 | Woonsocket | 569 |
| Shannon | 9,902 | (Attached to Fall River) | 2,094 |
| Spink | 7,981 | Redfield | 1,505 |
| Stanley | 2,453 | Fort Pierre | 1,431 |
| Sully | 1,589 | Onida | 972 |
| Todd | 8,352 | (Attached to Tripp) | 1,388 |
| Tripp | 6,924 | Winner | 1,618 |
| Turner | 8,576 | Parker | 617 |
| Union | 10,189 | Elk Point | 453 |
| Walworth | 6,087 | Selby | 707 |
| Yankton | 19,252 | Yankton | 518 |
| Ziebach | 2,220 | Dupree | 1,969 |

## Tennessee

(95 counties, 41,155 sq. mi. land; pop., 4,877,185)

| County | Pop. | County Seat or court house | Land area sq. mi. |
|---|---|---|---|
| Anderson | 68,250 | Clinton | 339 |
| Bedford | 30,411 | Shelbyville | 475 |
| Benton | 14,524 | Camden | 392 |
| Bledsoe | 9,669 | Pikeville | 407 |
| Blount | 85,969 | Maryville | 558 |
| Bradley | 73,712 | Cleveland | 327 |
| Campbell | 35,079 | Jacksboro | 479 |
| Cannon | 10,467 | Woodbury | 266 |
| Carroll | 27,514 | Huntingdon | 600 |
| Carter | 51,505 | Elizabethton | 341 |
| Cheatham | 27,140 | Ashland City | 304 |
| Chester | 12,819 | Henderson | 289 |
| Claiborne | 26,137 | Tazewell | 432 |
| Clay | 7,238 | Celina | 227 |
| Cocke | 29,141 | Newport | 432 |
| Coffee | 40,339 | Manchester | 428 |
| Crockett | 13,378 | Alamo | 266 |
| Cumberland | 34,736 | Crossville | 682 |
| Davidson | 510,784 | Nashville | 501 |
| Decatur | 10,472 | Decaturville | 330 |
| De Kalb | 14,360 | Smithville | 291 |
| Dickson | 35,061 | Charlotte | 491 |
| Dyer | 34,854 | Dyersburg | 520 |
| Fayette | 25,559 | Somerville | 705 |
| Fentress | 14,669 | Jamestown | 498 |
| Franklin | 34,725 | Winchester | 543 |
| Gibson | 46,315 | Trenton | 602 |
| Giles | 25,741 | Pulaski | 610 |
| Grainger | 17,095 | Rutledge | 273 |
| Greene | 55,853 | Greeneville | 619 |
| Grundy | 13,362 | Altamont | 361 |
| Hamblen | 50,480 | Morristown | 156 |
| Hamilton | 285,536 | Chattanooga | 539 |
| Hancock | 6,739 | Sneedville | 223 |
| Hardeman | 23,377 | Bolivar | 670 |
| Hardin | 22,633 | Savannah | 578 |
| Hawkins | 44,565 | Rogersville | 486 |
| Haywood | 19,437 | Brownsville | 534 |
| Henderson | 21,844 | Lexington | 520 |
| Henry | 27,888 | Paris | 560 |
| Hickman | 16,754 | Centerville | 610 |
| Houston | 7,018 | Erin | 200 |
| Humphreys | 15,813 | Waverly | 528 |
| Jackson | 9,297 | Gainesboro | 308 |
| Jefferson | 33,016 | Dandridge | 265 |
| Johnson | 13,766 | Mountain City | 297 |
| Knox | 335,749 | Knoxville | 506 |
| Lake | 7,129 | Tiptonville | 169 |
| Lauderdale | 23,491 | Ripley | 474 |
| Lawrence | 35,303 | Lawrenceburg | 617 |
| Lewis | 9,247 | Hohenwald | 282 |
| Lincoln | 28,157 | Fayetteville | 571 |
| Loudon | 31,255 | Loudon | 235 |
| McMinn | 42,383 | Athens | 429 |
| McNairy | 22,422 | Selmer | 562 |
| Macon | 15,906 | Lafayette | 307 |
| Madison | 77,982 | Jackson | 558 |
| Marion | 24,860 | Jasper | 512 |
| Marshall | 21,539 | Lewisburg | 376 |
| Maury | 54,812 | Columbia | 616 |
| Meigs | 8,033 | Decatur | 189 |
| Monroe | 30,541 | Madisonville | 648 |
| Montgomery | 100,498 | Clarksville | 539 |
| Moore | 4,721 | Lynchburg | 129 |
| Morgan | 17,300 | Wartburg | 523 |
| Obion | 31,717 | Union City | 550 |
| Overton | 17,636 | Livingston | 433 |
| Perry | 6,612 | Linden | 412 |
| Pickett | 4,548 | Byrdstown | 159 |
| Polk | 13,643 | Benton | 438 |
| Putnam | 51,373 | Cookeville | 399 |
| Rhea | 24,344 | Dayton | 309 |
| Roane | 47,227 | Kingston | 357 |
| Robertson | 41,492 | Springfield | 476 |
| Rutherford | 118,570 | Murfreesboro | 606 |
| Scott | 18,358 | Huntsville | 528 |
| Sequatchie | 8,863 | Dunlap | 266 |
| Sevier | 51,043 | Sevierville | 590 |
| Shelby | 826,330 | Memphis | 772 |
| Smith | 14,143 | Carthage | 313 |
| Stewart | 9,479 | Dover | 454 |
| Sullivan | 143,596 | Blountville | 415 |
| Sumner | 103,281 | Gallatin | 529 |
| Tipton | 37,568 | Covington | 454 |
| Trousdale | 5,920 | Hartsville | 114 |
| Unicoi | 16,549 | Erwin | 186 |
| Union | 13,694 | Maynardville | 218 |
| Van Buren | 4,846 | Spencer | 273 |
| Warren | 32,992 | McMinnville | 431 |
| Washington | 92,315 | Jonesboro | 326 |
| Wayne | 13,935 | Waynesboro | 734 |
| Weakley | 31,972 | Dresden | 581 |
| White | 20,090 | Sparta | 373 |
| Williamson | 81,021 | Franklin | 584 |
| Wilson | 67,675 | Lebanon | 570 |

## Texas

(254 counties, 262,017 sq. mi. land; pop., 16,986,510)

| County | Pop. | County Seat or court house | Land area sq. mi. |
|---|---|---|---|
| Anderson | 48,024 | Palestine | 1,077 |
| Andrews | 14,338 | Andrews | 1,501 |
| Angelina | 69,884 | Lufkin | 807 |
| Aransas | 17,892 | Rockport | 280 |
| Archer | 7,973 | Archer City | 907 |
| Armstrong | 2,021 | Claude | 909 |
| Atascosa | 30,533 | Jourdanton | 1,218 |
| Austin | 19,832 | Bellville | 656 |
| Bailey | 7,064 | Muleshoe | 826 |
| Bandera | 10,562 | Bandera | 793 |
| Bastrop | 38,263 | Bastrop | 895 |
| Baylor | 4,385 | Seymour | 862 |
| Bee | 25,135 | Beeville | 880 |
| Bell | 191,088 | Belton | 1,055 |
| Bexar | 1,185,394 | San Antonio | 1,248 |
| Blanco | 5,972 | Johnson City | 714 |
| Borden | 799 | Gail | 900 |
| Bosque | 15,125 | Meridian | 988 |
| Bowie | 81,665 | Boston | 891 |
| Brazoria | 191,707 | Angleton | 1,407 |
| Brazos | 121,862 | Bryan | 589 |
| Brewster | 8,681 | Alpine | 6,169 |
| Briscoe | 1,971 | Silverton | 887 |
| Brooks | 8,204 | Falfurrias | 942 |
| Brown | 34,371 | Brownwood | 936 |
| Burleson | 13,625 | Caldwell | 669 |
| Burnet | 22,677 | Burnet | 994 |
| Caldwell | 26,392 | Lockhart | 546 |
| Calhoun | 19,053 | Port Lavaca | 540 |
| Callahan | 11,859 | Baird | 899 |
| Cameron | 260,120 | Brownsville | 906 |
| Camp | 9,904 | Pittsburg | 203 |
| Carson | 6,576 | Panhandle | 924 |
| Cass | 29,982 | Linden | 937 |
| Castro | 9,070 | Dimmitt | 899 |
| Chambers | 20,088 | Anahuac | 616 |
| Cherokee | 41,049 | Rusk | 1,052 |
| Childress | 5,953 | Childress | 707 |
| Clay | 10,024 | Henrietta | 1,086 |
| Cochran | 4,377 | Morton | 775 |
| Coke | 3,424 | Robert Lee | 908 |
| Coleman | 9,710 | Coleman | 1,277 |
| Collin | 264,036 | McKinney | 851 |
| Collingsworth | 3,573 | Wellington | 909 |
| Colorado | 18,383 | Columbus | 965 |
| Comal | 51,832 | New Braunfels | 555 |
| Comanche | 13,381 | Comanche | 930 |
| Concho | 3,044 | Paint Rock | 992 |
| Cooke | 30,777 | Gainesville | 893 |
| Coryell | 64,213 | Gatesville | 1,057 |
| Cottle | 2,247 | Paducah | 895 |
| Crane | 4,652 | Crane | 782 |
| Crockett | 4,078 | Ozona | 2,806 |
| Crosby | 7,304 | Crosbyton | 3,815 |
| Culberson | 3,407 | Van Horn | 1,505 |
| Dallam | 5,461 | Dalhart | 1,505 |
| Dallas | 1,852,810 | Dallas | 880 |
| Dawson | 14,349 | Lamesa | 903 |
| Deaf Smith | 19,153 | Hereford | 1,497 |
| Delta | 4,857 | Cooper | 278 |
| Denton | 273,525 | Denton | 911 |
| Dewitt | 18,840 | Cuero | 910 |
| Dickens | 2,571 | Dickens | 907 |
| Dimmit | 10,433 | Carrizo Springs | 1,307 |
| Donley | 3,696 | Clarendon | 929 |
| Duval | 12,918 | San Diego | 1,795 |
| Eastland | 18,488 | Eastland | 924 |
| Ector | 118,934 | Odessa | 903 |
| Edwards | 2,266 | Rocksprings | 2,121 |
| Ellis | 85,167 | Waxahachie | 939 |
| El Paso | 591,610 | El Paso | 1,014 |
| Erath | 27,991 | Stephenville | 1,080 |
| Falls | 17,712 | Marlin | 770 |
| Fannin | 24,804 | Bonham | 895 |
| Fayette | 20,095 | La Grange | 950 |
| Fisher | 4,842 | Roby | 897 |
| Floyd | 8,497 | Floydada | 992 |
| Foard | 1,794 | Crowell | 703 |
| Fort Bend | 225,421 | Richmond | 876 |
| Franklin | 7,802 | Mount Vernon | 294 |
| Freestone | 15,818 | Fairfield | 888 |
| Frio | 13,472 | Pearsall | 1,133 |
| Gaines | 14,123 | Seminole | 1,504 |
| Galveston | 217,396 | Galveston | 399 |
| Garza | 5,143 | Post | 895 |
| Gillespie | 17,204 | Fredericksburg | 1,061 |
| Glasscock | 1,447 | Garden City | 900 |
| Goliad | 5,980 | Goliad | 859 |
| Gonzales | 17,205 | Gonzales | 1,068 |
| Gray | 23,967 | Pampa | 921 |
| Grayson | 95,021 | Sherman | 934 |
| Gregg | 104,948 | Longview | 273 |
| Grimes | 18,828 | Anderson | 799 |

| County | Pop. | County Seat or court house | Land area sq. mi. |
|---|---|---|---|
| Guadalupe | 64,873 | Seguin | 713 |
| Hale | 34,671 | Plainview | 1,005 |
| Hall | 3,905 | Memphis | 877 |
| Hamilton | 7,733 | Hamilton | 836 |
| Hansford | 5,848 | Spearman | 921 |
| Hardeman | 5,283 | Quanah | 688 |
| Hardin | 41,320 | Kountze | 898 |
| Harris | 2,818,199 | Houston | 1,734 |
| Harrison | 57,483 | Marshall | 908 |
| Hartley | 3,634 | Channing | 1,462 |
| Haskell | 6,820 | Haskell | 901 |
| Hays | 65,614 | San Marcos | 678 |
| Hemphill | 3,720 | Canadian | 903 |
| Henderson | 58,543 | Athens | 888 |
| Hidalgo | 383,545 | Edinburg | 1,569 |
| Hill | 27,146 | Hillsboro | 968 |
| Hockley | 24,199 | Levelland | 908 |
| Hood | 28,981 | Granbury | 425 |
| Hopkins | 28,833 | Sulphur Springs | 789 |
| Houston | 21,375 | Crockett | 1,234 |
| Howard | 32,343 | Big Spring | 901 |
| Hudspeth | 2,915 | Sierra Blanca | 4,567 |
| Hunt | 64,343 | Greenville | 840 |
| Hutchinson | 25,689 | Stinnett | 872 |
| Irion | 1,629 | Mertzon | 1,052 |
| Jack | 6,981 | Jacksboro | 920 |
| Jackson | 13,039 | Edna | 844 |
| Jasper | 31,102 | Jasper | 921 |
| Jeff Davis | 1,946 | Fort Davis | 2,257 |
| Jefferson | 239,389 | Beaumont | 937 |
| Jim Hogg | 5,109 | Hebbronville | 1,136 |
| Jim Wells | 37,679 | Alice | 867 |
| Johnson | 97,165 | Cleburne | 730 |
| Jones | 16,490 | Anson | 931 |
| Karnes | 12,455 | Karnes City | 753 |
| Kaufman | 52,220 | Kaufman | 788 |
| Kendall | 14,589 | Boerne | 663 |
| Kenedy | 460 | Sarita | 1,389 |
| Kent | 1,010 | Jayton | 878 |
| Kerr | 36,304 | Kerrville | 1,107 |
| Kimble | 4,122 | Junction | 1,250 |
| King | 354 | Guthrie | 914 |
| Kinney | 3,119 | Brackettville | 1,359 |
| Kleberg | 30,274 | Kingsville | 853 |
| Knox | 4,837 | Benjamin | 845 |
| Lamar | 43,949 | Paris | 919 |
| Lamb | 15,072 | Littlefield | 1,013 |
| Lampasas | 13,521 | Lampasas | 714 |
| La Salle | 5,254 | Cotulla | 1,517 |
| Lavaca | 18,690 | Hallettsville | 971 |
| Lee | 12,854 | Giddings | 631 |
| Leon | 12,665 | Centerville | 1,079 |
| Liberty | 52,726 | Liberty | 1,174 |
| Limestone | 20,946 | Groesbeck | 930 |
| Lipscomb | 3,143 | Lipscomb | 933 |
| Live Oak | 9,556 | George West | 1,057 |
| Llano | 11,631 | Llano | 939 |
| Loving | 107 | Mentone | 670 |
| Lubbock | 222,636 | Lubbock | 900 |
| Lynn | 6,758 | Tahoka | 888 |
| McCulloch | 8,778 | Brady | 1,071 |
| McLennan | 189,123 | Waco | 1,031 |
| McMullen | 817 | Tilden | 1,163 |
| Madison | 10,931 | Madisonville | 472 |
| Marion | 9,984 | Jefferson | 385 |
| Martin | 4,956 | Stanton | 914 |
| Mason | 3,423 | Mason | 934 |
| Matagorda | 36,928 | Bay City | 1,127 |
| Maverick | 36,378 | Eagle Pass | 1,287 |
| Medina | 27,312 | Hondo | 1,331 |
| Menard | 2,252 | Menard | 902 |
| Midland | 106,611 | Midland | 1,019 |
| Milam | 22,946 | Cameron | 1,019 |
| Mills | 4,531 | Goldthwaite | 748 |
| Mitchell | 8,016 | Colorado City | 912 |
| Montague | 17,274 | Montague | 928 |
| Montgomery | 182,201 | Conroe | 1,047 |
| Moore | 17,865 | Dumas | 905 |
| Morris | 13,200 | Daingerfield | 256 |
| Motley | 1,532 | Matador | 959 |
| Nacogdoches | 54,753 | Nacogdoches | 939 |
| Navarro | 39,926 | Corsicana | 1,068 |
| Newton | 13,569 | Newton | 935 |
| Nolan | 16,594 | Sweetwater | 915 |
| Nueces | 291,145 | Corpus Christi | 847 |
| Ochiltree | 9,128 | Perryton | 919 |
| Oldham | 2,278 | Vega | 1,485 |
| Orange | 80,509 | Orange | 362 |
| Palo Pinto | 25,055 | Palo Pinto | 949 |
| Panola | 22,035 | Carthage | 812 |
| Parker | 64,785 | Weatherford | 902 |
| Parmer | 9,863 | Farwell | 885 |
| Pecos | 14,675 | Fort Stockton | 4,777 |
| Polk | 30,687 | Livingston | 1,061 |
| Potter | 97,841 | Amarillo | 902 |
| Presidio | 6,637 | Marfa | 3,857 |
| Rains | 6,715 | Emory | 243 |
| Randall | 89,673 | Canyon | 917 |

| County | Pop. | County Seat or court house | Land area sq. mi. |
|---|---|---|---|
| Reagan | 4,514 | Big Lake | 1,173 |
| Real | 2,412 | Leakey | 697 |
| Red River | 14,317 | Clarksville | 1,054 |
| Reeves | 15,852 | Pecos | 2,626 |
| Refugio | 7,976 | Refugio | 771 |
| Roberts | 1,025 | Miami | 915 |
| Robertson | 15,511 | Franklin | 864 |
| Rockwall | 25,604 | Rockwall | 128 |
| Runnels | 11,294 | Ballinger | 1,056 |
| Rusk | 43,735 | Henderson | 932 |
| Sabine | 9,586 | Hemphill | 486 |
| San Augustine | 7,999 | San Augustine | 524 |
| San Jacinto | 16,372 | Coldspring | 572 |
| San Patricio | 58,749 | Sinton | 693 |
| San Saba | 5,401 | San Saba | 1,136 |
| Schleicher | 2,990 | Eldorado | 1,309 |
| Scurry | 18,634 | Snyder | 900 |
| Shackelford | 3,316 | Albany | 915 |
| Shelby | 22,034 | Center | 791 |
| Sherman | 2,858 | Stratford | 923 |
| Smith | 151,309 | Tyler | 932 |
| Somervell | 5,360 | Glen Rose | 188 |
| Starr | 40,518 | Rio Grande City | 1,226 |
| Stephens | 9,010 | Breckenridge | 894 |
| Sterling | 1,438 | Sterling City | 923 |
| Stonewall | 2,013 | Aspermont | 925 |
| Sutton | 4,135 | Sonora | 1,455 |
| Swisher | 8,133 | Tulia | 902 |
| Tarrant | 1,170,103 | Fort Worth | 868 |
| Taylor | 119,655 | Abilene | 917 |
| Terrell | 1,410 | Sanderson | 2,357 |
| Terry | 13,218 | Brownfield | 887 |
| Throckmorton | 1,880 | Throckmorton | 912 |
| Titus | 24,009 | Mount Pleasant | 412 |
| Tom Green | 98,458 | San Angelo | 1,515 |
| Travis | 576,407 | Austin | 989 |
| Trinity | 11,445 | Groveton | 692 |
| Tyler | 16,646 | Woodville | 922 |
| Upshur | 31,370 | Gilmer | 587 |
| Upton | 4,447 | Rankin | 1,243 |
| Uvalde | 23,340 | Uvalde | 1,564 |
| Val Verde | 38,721 | Del Rio | 3,150 |
| Van Zandt | 37,944 | Canton | 855 |
| Victoria | 74,361 | Victoria | 887 |
| Walker | 50,917 | Huntsville | 786 |
| Waller | 23,389 | Hempstead | 514 |
| Ward | 13,115 | Monahans | 836 |
| Washington | 26,154 | Brenham | 610 |
| Webb | 133,239 | Laredo | 3,362 |
| Wharton | 39,955 | Wharton | 1,086 |
| Wheeler | 5,879 | Wheeler | 904 |
| Wichita | 122,378 | Wichita Falls | 606 |
| Wilbarger | 15,121 | Vernon | 947 |
| Willacy | 17,705 | Raymondville | 589 |
| Williamson | 139,551 | Georgetown | 1,137 |
| Wilson | 22,650 | Floresville | 807 |
| Winkler | 8,626 | Kermit | 840 |
| Wise | 34,679 | Decatur | 902 |
| Wood | 29,380 | Quitman | 689 |
| Yoakum | 8,786 | Plains | 800 |
| Young | 18,126 | Graham | 919 |
| Zapata | 9,279 | Zapata | 999 |
| Zavala | 12,162 | Crystal City | 1,298 |

## Utah

(29 counties, 82,168 sq. mi. land; pop. 1,722,850)

| County | Pop. | County Seat or court house | Land area sq. mi. |
|---|---|---|---|
| Beaver | 4,765 | Beaver | 2,590 |
| Box Elder | 36,485 | Brigham City | 5,724 |
| Cache | 70,183 | Logan | 1,165 |
| Carbon | 20,228 | Price | 1,479 |
| Daggett | 690 | Manila | 698 |
| Davis | 187,941 | Farmington | 305 |
| Duchesne | 12,645 | Duchesne | 3,238 |
| Emery | 10,332 | Castle Dale | 4,452 |
| Garfield | 3,980 | Panguitch | 5,175 |
| Grand | 6,620 | Moab | 3,682 |
| Iron | 20,789 | Parowan | 3,299 |
| Juab | 5,817 | Nephi | 3,392 |
| Kane | 5,169 | Kanab | 3,992 |
| Millard | 11,333 | Fillmore | 6,590 |
| Morgan | 5,528 | Morgan | 609 |
| Piute | 1,277 | Junction | 758 |
| Rich | 1,725 | Randolph | 1,029 |
| Salt Lake | 725,956 | Salt Lake City | 737 |
| San Juan | 12,621 | Monticello | 7,821 |
| Sanpete | 16,259 | Manti | 1,588 |
| Sevier | 15,431 | Richfield | 1,910 |
| Summit | 15,518 | Coalville | 1,871 |
| Tooele | 26,601 | Tooele | 6,946 |
| Uintah | 22,211 | Vernal | 4,477 |
| Utah | 263,590 | Provo | 1,998 |
| Wasatch | 10,089 | Heber City | 1,181 |
| Washington | 48,560 | Saint George | 2,427 |
| Wayne | 2,177 | Loa | 2,461 |
| Weber | 158,330 | Ogden | 576 |

## Vermont

(14 counties, 9,273 sq. mi. land; pop. 562,758)

| County | Pop. | County Seat or court house | Land area sq. mi. |
|---|---|---|---|
| Addison | 32,953 | Middlebury | 773 |
| Bennington | 35,845 | Bennington | 676 |
| Caledonia | 27,846 | Saint Johnsbury | 651 |
| Chittenden | 131,761 | Burlington | 540 |
| Essex | 6,405 | Guildhall | 666 |
| Franklin | 39,980 | Saint Albans | 649 |
| Grand Isle | 5,318 | North Hero | 89 |
| Lamoille | 19,735 | Hyde Park | 461 |
| Orange | 26,149 | Chelsea | 690 |
| Orleans | 24,053 | Newport | 697 |
| Rutland | 62,142 | Rutland | 932 |
| Washington | 54,928 | Montpelier | 690 |
| Windham | 41,588 | Newfane | 786 |
| Windsor | 54,055 | Woodstock | 972 |

## Virginia

(95 cos., 41 ind. cities, 39,704 sq. mi. land; pop. 6,216,568)

| County | Pop. | County Seat or court house | Land area sq. mi. |
|---|---|---|---|
| Accomack | 31,703 | Accomac | 476 |
| Albemarle | 68,172 | Charlottesville | 740 |
| Alleghany | 13,176 | Covington | 444 |
| Amelia | 8,787 | Amelia Court House | 366 |
| Amherst | 28,578 | Amherst | 470 |
| Appomattox | 12,298 | Appomattox | 345 |
| Arlington | 170,886 | Arlington | 26 |
| Augusta | 54,677 | Staunton | 968 |
| Bath | 4,799 | Warm Springs | 540 |
| Bedford | 45,656 | Bedford | 771 |
| Bland | 6,514 | Bland | 369 |
| Botetourt | 24,992 | Fincastle | 549 |
| Brunswick | 15,987 | Lawrenceville | 579 |
| Buchanan | 31,333 | Grundy | 508 |
| Buckingham | 12,873 | Buckingham | 582 |
| Campbell | 47,572 | Rustburg | 511 |
| Caroline | 19,217 | Bowling Green | 549 |
| Carroll | 26,594 | Hillsville | 494 |
| Charles City | 6,282 | Charles City | 208 |
| Charlotte | 11,688 | Charlotte Court House | 471 |
| Chesterfield | 209,564 | Chesterfield | 446 |
| Clarke | 12,101 | Berryville | 174 |
| Craig | 4,372 | New Castle | 336 |
| Culpeper | 27,791 | Culpeper | 389 |
| Cumberland | 7,825 | Cumberland | 292 |
| Dickenson | 17,620 | Clintwood | 335 |
| Dinwiddie | 22,319 | Dinwiddie | 502 |
| Essex | 8,689 | Tappahannock | 264 |
| Fairfax | 818,584 | Fairfax | 399 |
| Fauquier | 48,860 | Warrenton | 660 |
| Floyd | 11,965 | Floyd | 383 |
| Fluvanna | 12,429 | Palmyra | 282 |
| Franklin | 39,549 | Rocky Mount | 721 |
| Frederick | 45,723 | Winchester | 432 |
| Giles | 16,366 | Pearisburg | 369 |
| Gloucester | 30,131 | Gloucester | 257 |
| Goochland | 14,163 | Goochland | 289 |
| Grayson | 16,278 | Independence | 494 |
| Greene | 10,297 | Stanardsville | 153 |
| Greensville | 8,630 | Emporia | 301 |
| Halifax | 29,033 | Halifax | 806 |
| Hanover | 63,306 | Hanover | 436 |
| Henrico | 217,849 | Henrico | 244 |
| Henry | 56,942 | Martinsville | 385 |
| Highland | 2,635 | Monterey | 416 |
| Isle of Wight | 25,053 | Isle of Wight | 319 |
| James City | 34,970 | Williamsburg | 144 |
| King and Queen | 6,289 | King and Queen Court House | 327 |
| King George | 13,527 | King George | 183 |
| King William | 10,913 | King William | 286 |
| Lancaster | 10,896 | Lancaster | 153 |
| Lee | 24,496 | Jonesville | 438 |
| Loudoun | 86,129 | Leesburg | 517 |
| Louisa | 20,325 | Louisa | 514 |
| Lunenburg | 11,419 | Lunenburg | 443 |
| Madison | 11,949 | Madison | 327 |
| Mathews | 8,348 | Mathews | 87 |
| Mecklenburg | 29,241 | Boydton | 675 |
| Middlesex | 8,653 | Saluda | 138 |
| Montgomery | 73,913 | Christiansburg | 395 |
| Nelson | 12,778 | Lovingston | 471 |
| New Kent | 10,445 | New Kent | 210 |
| Northampton | 13,061 | Eastville | 209 |
| Northumberland | 10,524 | Heathsville | 223 |
| Nottoway | 14,993 | Nottoway | 308 |
| Orange | 21,421 | Orange | 355 |

| County | Pop. | County Seat or court house | Land area sq. mi. |
|---|---|---|---|
| Page | 21,690 | Luray | 310 |
| Patrick | 17,473 | Stuart | 467 |
| Pittsylvania | 55,672 | Chatham | 985 |
| Powhatan | 15,328 | Powhatan | 272 |
| Prince Edward | 17,320 | Farmville | 357 |
| Prince George | 27,394 | Prince George | 276 |
| Prince William | 215,677 | Manassas | 345 |
| Pulaski | 34,496 | Pulaski | 335 |
| Rappahannock | 6,622 | Washington | 267 |
| Richmond | 7,273 | Warsaw | 203 |
| Roanoke | 79,332 | Salem | 248 |
| Rockbridge | 18,350 | Lexington | 604 |
| Rockingham | 57,482 | Harrisonburg | 865 |
| Russell | 28,667 | Lebanon | 483 |
| Scott | 23,204 | Gate City | 539 |
| Shenandoah | 31,636 | Woodstock | 507 |
| Smyth | 32,370 | Marion | 435 |
| Southampton | 17,550 | Courtland | 599 |
| Spotsylvania | 57,403 | Spotsylvania | 409 |
| Stafford | 61,236 | Stafford | 277 |
| Surry | 6,145 | Surry | 306 |
| Sussex | 10,248 | Sussex | 496 |
| Tazewell | 45,960 | Tazewell | 522 |
| Warren | 26,142 | Front Royal | 219 |
| Washington | 45,887 | Abingdon | 578 |
| Westmoreland | 15,480 | Montross | 250 |
| Wise | 39,573 | Wise | 405 |
| Wythe | 25,471 | Wytheville | 460 |
| York | 42,434 | Yorktown | 122 |
| **Independent cities** | | | |
| Alexandria | 111,183 | | 16 |
| Bedford | 6,073 | | 7 |
| Bristol | 18,426 | | 12 |
| Buena Vista | 6,406 | | 7 |
| Charlottesville | 40,341 | | 10 |
| Chesapeake | 151,976 | | 353 |
| Clifton Forge | 4,679 | | 3 |
| Colonial Heights | 16,064 | | 8 |
| Covington | 6,991 | | 5 |
| Danville | 53,056 | | 44 |
| Emporia | 5,306 | | 7 |
| Fairfax | 19,622 | | 6 |
| Falls Church | 9,578 | | 2 |
| Franklin | 7,864 | | 8 |
| Fredericksburg | 19,027 | | 10 |
| Galax | 6,670 | | 8 |
| Hampton | 133,793 | | 57 |
| Harrisonburg | 30,707 | | 17 |
| Hopewell | 23,101 | | 11 |
| Lexington | 6,959 | | 2 |
| Lynchburg | 66,049 | | 50 |
| Manassas | 27,957 | | 11 |
| Manassas Park | 6,734 | | 3 |
| Martinsville | 16,162 | | 11 |
| Newport News | 170,045 | | 69 |
| Norfolk | 261,229 | | 66 |
| Norton | 4,247 | | 7 |
| Petersburg | 38,386 | | 23 |
| Poquoson | 11,005 | | 10 |
| Portsmouth | 103,907 | | 30 |
| Radford | 15,940 | | 9 |
| Richmond | 203,056 | | 63 |
| Roanoke | 96,397 | | 43 |
| Salem | 23,756 | | 14 |
| South Boston | 6,997 | | 5 |
| Staunton | 24,461 | | 20 |
| Suffolk | 52,141 | | 430 |
| Virginia Beach | 393,069 | | 310 |
| Waynesboro | 18,549 | | 14 |
| Williamsburg | 11,530 | | 9 |
| Winchester | 21,947 | | 9 |

## Washington

(39 counties, 66,511 sq. mi. land; pop., 4,866,692)

| County | Pop. | County Seat or court house | Land area sq. mi. |
|---|---|---|---|
| Adams | 13,603 | Ritzville | 1,921 |
| Asotin | 17,605 | Asotin | 635 |
| Benton | 112,560 | Prosser | 1,715 |
| Chelan | 52,250 | Wenatchee | 2,916 |
| Clallam | 56,210 | Port Angeles | 1,753 |
| Clark | 238,053 | Vancouver | 627 |
| Columbia | 4,024 | Dayton | 865 |
| Cowlitz | 82,119 | Kelso | 1,140 |
| Douglas | 26,205 | Waterville | 1,817 |
| Ferry | 6,295 | Republic | 2,200 |
| Franklin | 37,473 | Pasco | 1,243 |
| Garfield | 2,248 | Pomeroy | 706 |
| Grant | 54,798 | Ephrata | 2,660 |
| Grays Harbor | 64,175 | Montesano | 1,918 |
| Island | 60,195 | Coupeville | 212 |
| Jefferson | 20,406 | Port Townsend | 1,805 |
| King | 1,507,305 | Seattle | 2,128 |
| Kitsap | 189,731 | Port Orchard | 393 |
| Kittitas | 26,725 | Ellensburg | 2,308 |
| Klickitat | 16,616 | Goldendale | 1,880 |
| Lewis | 59,358 | Chehalis | 2,409 |
| Lincoln | 8,864 | Davenport | 2,310 |
| Mason | 38,341 | Shelton | 961 |
| Okanogan | 33,350 | Okanogan | 5,281 |
| Pacific | 18,882 | South Bend | 908 |
| Pend Oreille | 8,915 | Newport | 1,400 |
| Pierce | 586,203 | Tacoma | 1,675 |
| San Juan | 10,035 | Friday Harbor | 179 |
| Skagit | 79,545 | Mount Vernon | 1,735 |
| Skamania | 8,289 | Stevenson | 1,672 |
| Snohomish | 465,642 | Everett | 2,098 |
| Spokane | 361,333 | Spokane | 1,762 |
| Stevens | 30,948 | Colville | 2,470 |
| Thurston | 161,238 | Olympia | 727 |
| Wahkiakum | 3,327 | Cathlamet | 261 |
| Walla Walla | 48,439 | Walla Walla | 1,261 |
| Whatcom | 127,780 | Bellingham | 2,125 |
| Whitman | 38,775 | Colfax | 2,151 |
| Yakima | 188,823 | Yakima | 4,287 |

## West Virginia

(55 counties, 24,119 sq. mi. land; pop., 1,793,477)

| County | Pop. | County Seat or court house | Land area sq. mi. |
|---|---|---|---|
| Barbour | 15,699 | Philippi | 343 |
| Berkeley | 59,253 | Martinsburg | 321 |
| Boone | 25,870 | Madison | 503 |
| Braxton | 12,998 | Sutton | 513 |
| Brooke | 26,992 | Wellsburg | 90 |
| Cabell | 96,827 | Huntington | 282 |
| Calhoun | 7,885 | Grantsville | 280 |
| Clay | 9,983 | Clay | 346 |
| Doddridge | 6,994 | West Union | 321 |
| Fayette | 47,952 | Fayetteville | 667 |
| Gilmer | 7,669 | Glenville | 340 |
| Grant | 10,428 | Petersburg | 480 |
| Greenbrier | 34,693 | Lewisburg | 1,025 |
| Hampshire | 16,498 | Romney | 644 |
| Hancock | 35,233 | New Cumberland | 84 |
| Hardy | 10,977 | Moorefield | 585 |
| Harrison | 69,371 | Clarksburg | 417 |
| Jackson | 25,938 | Ripley | 464 |
| Jefferson | 35,926 | Charles Town | 209 |
| Kanawha | 207,619 | Charleston | 901 |
| Lewis | 17,223 | Weston | 389 |
| Lincoln | 21,382 | Hamlin | 439 |
| Logan | 43,032 | Logan | 456 |
| McDowell | 35,233 | Welch | 535 |
| Marion | 57,249 | Fairmont | 312 |
| Marshall | 37,356 | Moundsville | 305 |
| Mason | 25,178 | Point Pleasant | 433 |
| Mercer | 64,980 | Princeton | 420 |
| Mineral | 26,697 | Keyser | 329 |
| Mingo | 33,739 | Williamson | 424 |
| Monongalia | 75,509 | Morgantown | 363 |
| Monroe | 12,406 | Union | 473 |
| Morgan | 12,128 | Berkeley Springs | 230 |
| Nicholas | 26,775 | Summersville | 650 |
| Ohio | 50,871 | Wheeling | 106 |
| Pendleton | 8,054 | Franklin | 698 |
| Pleasants | 7,546 | St. Marys | 131 |
| Pocahontas | 9,008 | Marlinton | 942 |
| Preston | 29,037 | Kingwood | 651 |
| Putnam | 42,835 | Winfield | 346 |
| Raleigh | 76,819 | Beckley | 608 |
| Randolph | 27,803 | Elkins | 1,040 |
| Ritchie | 10,233 | Harrisville | 454 |
| Roane | 15,120 | Spencer | 484 |
| Summers | 14,204 | Hinton | 353 |
| Taylor | 15,144 | Grafton | 174 |
| Tucker | 7,728 | Parsons | 421 |
| Tyler | 9,796 | Middlebourne | 258 |
| Upshur | 22,867 | Buckhannon | 355 |
| Wayne | 41,636 | Wayne | 508 |
| Webster | 10,729 | Webster Springs | 556 |
| Wetzel | 19,258 | New Martinsville | 359 |
| Wirt | 5,192 | Elizabeth | 235 |
| Wood | 86,915 | Parkersburg | 367 |
| Wyoming | 28,990 | Pineville | 502 |

## Wisconsin

(72 counties, 54,426 sq. mi. land; pop., 4,891,769)

| County | Pop. | County Seat or court house | Land area sq. mi. |
|---|---|---|---|
| Adams | 15,682 | Friendship | 648 |
| Ashland | 16,307 | Ashland | 1,048 |
| Barron | 40,750 | Barron | 865 |
| Bayfield | 14,008 | Washburn | 1,462 |
| Brown | 194,594 | Green Bay | 524 |
| Buffalo | 13,584 | Alma | 699 |
| Burnett | 13,084 | Meenon | 818 |
| Calumet | 34,291 | Chilton | 326 |

| County | Pop. | County Seat or court house | Land area sq. mi. |
|---|---|---|---|
| Chippewa | 52,360 | Chippewa Falls | 1,017 |
| Clark | 31,647 | Neillsville | 1,218 |
| Columbia | 45,088 | Portage | 771 |
| Crawford | 15,940 | Prairie du Chien | 566 |
| Dane | 367,085 | Madison | 1,205 |
| Dodge | 76,559 | Juneau | 887 |
| Door | 25,690 | Sturgeon Bay | 492 |
| Douglas | 41,758 | Superior | 1,305 |
| Dunn | 35,909 | Menomonie | 853 |
| Eau Claire | 85,183 | Eau Claire | 638 |
| Florence | 4,590 | Florence | 486 |
| Fond du Lac | 90,083 | Fond du Lac | 725 |
| Forest | 8,776 | Crandon | 1,011 |
| Grant | 49,266 | Lancaster | 1,144 |
| Green | 30,339 | Monroe | 583 |
| Green Lake | 18,651 | Green Lake | 357 |
| Iowa | 20,150 | Dodgeville | 760 |
| Iron | 6,153 | Hurley | 751 |
| Jackson | 16,588 | Black River Falls | 998 |
| Jefferson | 67,783 | Jefferson | 562 |
| Juneau | 21,650 | Mauston | 774 |
| Kenosha | 128,181 | Kenosha | 273 |
| Kewaunee | 18,878 | Kewaunee | 343 |
| La Crosse | 97,904 | La Crosse | 457 |
| Lafayette | 16,074 | Darlington | 634 |
| Langlade | 19,505 | Antigo | 873 |
| Lincoln | 26,993 | Merrill | 886 |
| Manitowoc | 80,421 | Manitowoc | 594 |
| Marathon | 115,400 | Wausau | 1,559 |
| Marinette | 40,548 | Marinette | 1,395 |
| Marquette | 12,321 | Montello | 455 |
| Menominee | 3,890 | Keshena | 359 |
| Milwaukee | 959,275 | Milwaukee | 241 |
| Monroe | 36,633 | Sparta | 904 |
| Oconto | 30,226 | Oconto | 1,002 |
| Oneida | 31,679 | Rhinelander | 1,130 |
| Outagamie | 140,510 | Appleton | 642 |
| Ozaukee | 72,831 | Port Washington | 235 |
| Pepin | 7,107 | Durand | 231 |
| Pierce | 32,765 | Ellsworth | 576 |
| Polk | 34,773 | Balsam Lake | 919 |
| Portage | 61,405 | Stevens Point | 810 |
| Price | 15,600 | Phillips | 1,256 |
| Racine | 175,034 | Racine | 334 |
| Richland | 17,521 | Richland Center | 585 |
| Rock | 139,510 | Janesville | 724 |
| Rusk | 15,079 | Ladysmith | 913 |
| Saint Croix | 50,251 | Hudson | 723 |

| County | Pop. | County Seat or court house | Land area sq. mi. |
|---|---|---|---|
| Sauk | 46,975 | Baraboo | 838 |
| Sawyer | 14,181 | Hayward | 1,255 |
| Shawano | 37,157 | Shawano | 897 |
| Sheboygan | 103,877 | Sheboygan | 515 |
| Taylor | 18,901 | Medford | 975 |
| Trempealeau | 25,263 | Whitehall | 736 |
| Vernon | 25,617 | Viroqua | 808 |
| Vilas | 17,707 | Eagle River | 867 |
| Walworth | 75,000 | Elkhorn | 556 |
| Washburn | 13,772 | Shell Lake | 815 |
| Washington | 95,328 | West Bend | 431 |
| Waukesha | 304,715 | Waukesha | 554 |
| Waupaca | 46,104 | Waupaca | 754 |
| Waushara | 19,385 | Wautoma | 628 |
| Winnebago | 140,320 | Oshkosh | 449 |
| Wood | 73,605 | Wisconsin Rapids | 801 |

## Wyoming

(23 counties, 96,989 sq. mi. land; pop., 453,588)

| County | Pop. | County Seat or court house | Land area sq. mi. |
|---|---|---|---|
| Albany | 30,797 | Laramie | 4,268 |
| Big Horn | 10,525 | Basin | 3,139 |
| Campbell | 29,370 | Gillette | 4,796 |
| Carbon | 16,659 | Rawlins | 7,877 |
| Converse | 11,128 | Douglas | 4,271 |
| Crook | 5,294 | Sundance | 2,855 |
| Fremont | 33,662 | Lander | 9,181 |
| Goshen | 12,373 | Torrington | 2,186 |
| Hot Springs | 4,809 | Thermopolis | 2,005 |
| Johnson | 6,145 | Buffalo | 4,166 |
| Laramie | 73,142 | Cheyenne | 2,684 |
| Lincoln | 12,625 | Kemmerer | 4,070 |
| Natrona | 61,226 | Casper | 5,347 |
| Niobrara | 2,499 | Lusk | 2,684 |
| Park | 23,178 | Cody | 6,936 |
| Platte | 8,145 | Wheatland | 2,023 |
| Sheridan | 23,562 | Sheridan | 2,532 |
| Sublette | 4,843 | Pinedale | 4,872 |
| Sweetwater | 38,823 | Green River | 10,352 |
| Teton | 11,173 | Jackson | 4,011 |
| Uinta | 18,705 | Evanston | 2,085 |
| Washakie | 8,388 | Worland | 2,243 |
| Weston | 6,518 | Newcastle | 2,402 |

## Population of Outlying Areas

Source: Bureau of the Census
(Final counts from the census conducted on Apr. 1, 1990.)

### Commonwealth of Puerto Rico

| Zip code | Municipios | Pop. | Land area sq. mi. |
|---|---|---|---|
| 00601 | Adjuntas | 19,451 | 67 |
| 00602 | Aguada | 35,911 | 31 |
| *00603 | Aguadilla | 59,335 | 37 |
| 00703 | Aguas Buenas | 25,424 | 31 |
| 00705 | Aibonito | 24,971 | 31 |
| 00610 | Anasco | 25,234 | 39 |
| *00612 | Arecibo | 93,385 | 126 |
| 00714 | Arroyo | 18,910 | 15 |
| 00617 | Barceloneta | 20,947 | 23 |
| *00794 | Barranquitas | 25,605 | 34 |
| *00979 | Bayamon | 220,262 | 44 |
| 00623 | Cabo Rojo | 38,521 | 70 |
| 00725 | Caguas | 133,447 | 59 |
| 00627 | Camuy | 28,917 | 46 |
| 00729 | Canovanas | 36,816 | 33 |
| *00979 | Carolina | 177,806 | 45 |
| 00962 | Catano | 34,587 | 5 |
| 00736 | Cayey | 46,553 | 52 |
| 00735 | Ceiba | 17,145 | 29 |
| 00638 | Cidles | 18,084 | 57 |
| 00739 | Cidra | 35,601 | 36 |
| 00769 | Coamo | 33,837 | 78 |
| 00782 | Comerio | 20,265 | 28 |
| 00783 | Corozal | 33,095 | 43 |
| 00775 | Culebra | 1,542 | 12 |
| 00646 | Dorado | 30,759 | 23 |
| 00738 | Fajardo | 36,882 | 30 |

| Zip code | Municipios | Pop. | Land area sq. mi. |
|---|---|---|---|
| 00650 | Florida | 8,689 | 10 |
| 00653 | Guanica | 19,984 | 37 |
| 00784 | Guayama | 41,588 | 65 |
| 00656 | Guayanilla | 21,581 | 42 |
| *00965 | Guaynabo | 92,886 | 27 |
| 00778 | Gurabo | 28,737 | 28 |
| 00659 | Hatillo | 32,703 | 42 |
| 00660 | Hormigueros | 15,212 | 11 |
| 00791 | Humacao | 55,203 | 45 |
| 00662 | Isabela | 39,147 | 55 |
| 00664 | Jayuya | 15,527 | 45 |
| 00795 | Juana Diaz | 45,198 | 60 |
| 00777 | Juncos | 30,612 | 27 |
| 00667 | Lajas | 23,271 | 60 |
| 00669 | Lares | 29,015 | 62 |
| 00670 | Las Marias | 9,306 | 46 |
| 00771 | Las Piedras | 27,896 | 34 |
| 00772 | Loiza | 29,307 | 19 |
| 00773 | Luquillo | 18,100 | 26 |
| 00674 | Manati | 38,692 | 45 |
| 00606 | Maricao | 6,206 | 37 |
| 00707 | Maunabo | 12,347 | 21 |
| 00680 | Mayaguez | 100,371 | 78 |
| 00676 | Moca | 32,926 | 50 |
| 00687 | Morovis | 25,288 | 39 |
| 00718 | Naguabo | 22,620 | 52 |

| Zip code | Municipios | Pop. | Land area sq. mi. |
|---|---|---|---|
| 00719 | Naranjito | 27,914 | 27 |
| 00720 | Orocovis | 21,158 | 64 |
| 00723 | Patillas | 19,633 | 47 |
| 00624 | Penuelas | 22,515 | 45 |
| *00731 | Ponce | 187,749 | 116 |
| 00678 | Quebradillas | 21,425 | 23 |
| 00677 | Rincon | 12,213 | 14 |
| 00745 | Rio Grande | 45,648 | 61 |
| 00637 | Sabana Grande | 22,843 | 36 |
| 00751 | Salinas | 28,335 | 69 |
| 00683 | San German | 34,962 | 55 |
| *00936 | San Juan | 437,745 | 48 |
| 00754 | San Lorenzo | 35,163 | 53 |
| 00685 | San Sebastian | 38,799 | 70 |
| 00757 | Santa Isabel | 19,318 | 34 |
| *00953 | Toa Alta | 44,101 | 27 |
| *00949 | Toa Baja | 89,454 | 23 |
| *00976 | Trujillo Alto | 61,120 | 21 |
| 00641 | Utuado | 34,980 | 114 |
| 00692 | Vega Alta | 34,559 | 28 |
| 00693 | Vega Baja | 55,997 | 46 |
| 00765 | Vieques | 8,602 | 51 |
| 00766 | Villalba | 23,559 | 36 |
| 00767 | Yabucoa | 36,483 | 55 |
| 00698 | Yauco | 42,058 | 68 |
| | Total | 3,522,037 | 3,427 |

### Commonwealth of the Northern Mariannas

| Zip code | Municipality | Pop. | Land area sq. mi. |
|---|---|---|---|
| 96950 | Northern Islands | 36 | 60 |
| 96951 | Rota | 2,295 | 33 |

| Zip code | Municipality | Pop. | Land area sq. mi. |
|---|---|---|---|
| 96950 | Saipan | 38,896 | 45 |
| 96952 | Tinian | 2,118 | 42 |

| | Pop. | Land area sq. mi. |
|---|---|---|
| Total | 43,345 | 180[1] |

## U.S. External Territories

| Zip code | Area | Pop. | Land area sq. mi. |
|---|---|---|---|
| | **American Samoa** | | |
| 96799 | American Samoa | 46,773 | 77 |
| | **Guam** | | |
| 96910 | Agana | 1,139 | 1 |
| ..... | Agana Hts. | 3,646 | 1 |
| 96915 | Agat | 4,960 | 10 |
| ..... | Asan | 2,070 | 6 |
| 96913 | Barrigada | 8,846 | 9 |
| ..... | Chalan-Pago-Ordot | 4,451 | 6 |
| 96912 | Dededo | 31,728 | 30 |

| Zip code | Area | Pop. | Land area sq. mi. |
|---|---|---|---|
| 96916 | Inarajan | 2,469 | 19 |
| ..... | Mangilao | 10,483 | 10 |
| 96916 | Merizo | 1,742 | 6 |
| ..... | Mongmong-Toto-Maite | 5,845 | 2 |
| ..... | Piti | 1,827 | 7 |
| 96915 | Santa Rita | 11,857 | 17 |
| ..... | Sinajana | 2,658 | 1 |
| ..... | Talofofo | 2,310 | 17 |
| 96911 | Tamuning | 16,673 | 6 |
| 96918 | Umatac | 897 | 6 |
| 96921 | Yigo | 14,213 | 35 |
| 96914 | Yona | 5,338 | 20 |
| | Total | 133,152 | 210 [1] |

| Zip code | Area | Pop. | Land area sq. mi. |
|---|---|---|---|
| | **Virgin Islands** | | |
| ..... | Saint Croix | 50,139 | 83 |
| ..... | Saint John | 3,504 | 20 |
| ..... | Saint Thomas | 48,166 | 31 |
| 00801 | Charlotte Amalie. | 12,331 | |
| 00820 | Christiansted | 2,555 | |
| 00840 | Frederiksted | 1,064 | |
| | Total | 101,809 | 134 |
| | **Trust Territory** | | |
| 96940 | Palau (Belau) | 15,122 | 192 |

[1]Figures may not add due to independent rounding.

## U.S. Area and Population: 1790 to 1990

Source: Bureau of the Census

| Census date | Area (square miles) | | | Population | | Increase over preceding census | |
|---|---|---|---|---|---|---|---|
| | Gross | Land | Water | Number | Per sq. mile of land | Number | % |
| 1990 (Apr. 1) | 3,787,425 | 3,536,342 | 251,083 [1] | 248,709,873 | 70.3 | 22,164,068 | 9.8 |
| 1980 (Apr. 1) | 3,618,770 | 3,539,289 | 79,481 | 226,542,203 | 64.0 | 23,240,172 | 11.4 |
| 1970 (Apr. 1) | 3,618,770 | 3,536,855 | 81,915 | 203,302,031 | 57.5 | 23,978,856 | 13.4 |
| 1960 (Apr. 1) | 3,618,770 | 3,540,911 | 77,859 | 179,323,175 | 50.6 | 27,997,377 | 18.5 |
| 1950 (Apr. 1) | 3,618,770 | 3,552,206 | 66,564 | 151,325,798 | 42.6 | 19,161,229 | 14.5 |
| 1940 (Apr. 1) | 3,618,770 | 3,554,608 | 64,162 | 132,164,569 | 37.2 | 8,961,945 | 7.3 |
| 1930 (Apr. 1) | 3,618,770 | 3,551,608 | 67,162 | 123,202,624 | 34.7 | 17,181,087 | 16.2 |
| 1920 (Jan. 1) | 3,618,770 | 3,546,931 | 71,839 | 106,021,537 | 29.9 | 13,793,041 | 15.0 |
| 1910 (Apr. 15) [2] | 3,618,770 | 3,547,045 | 71,725 | 92,228,496 | 26.0 | 16,016,328 | 21.0 |
| 1900 (June 1) | 3,618,770 | 3,547,314 | 71,456 | 76,212,168 | 21.5 | 13,232,402 | 21.0 |
| 1890 (June 1) | 3,612,299 | 3,540,705 | 71,594 | 62,979,766 | 17.8 | 12,790,557 | 25.5 |
| 1880 (June 1) | 3,612,299 | 3,540,705 | 71,594 | 50,189,209 | 14.2 | 11,630,838 | 30.2 |
| 1870 (June 1) | 3,612,299 | 3,540,705 | 71,594 | 38,558,371 | 10.9 | 7,115,050 | 22.6 |
| 1860 (June 1) | 3,021,295 | 2,969,640 | 51,655 | 31,443,321 | 10.6 | 8,251,445 | 35.6 |
| 1850 (June 1) | 2,991,655 | 2,940,042 | 51,613 | 23,191,876 | 7.9 | 6,122,423 | 35.9 |
| 1840 (June 1) | 1,792,552 | 1,749,462 | 43,090 | 17,069,453 | 9.8 | 4,203,433 | 32.7 |
| 1830 (June 1) | 1,792,552 | 1,749,462 | 43,090 | 12,866,020 | 7.4 | 3,227,567 | 33.5 |
| 1820 (June 1) | 1,792,552 | 1,749,462 | 43,090 | 9,638,453 | 5.5 | 2,398,572 | 33.1 |
| 1810 (Aug. 6) | 1,722,685 | 1,681,828 | 40,857 | 7,239,881 | 4.3 | 1,931,398 | 36.4 |
| 1800 (Aug. 4) | 891,364 | 864,746 | 26,618 | 5,308,483 | 6.1 | 1,379,269 | 35.1 |
| 1790 (Aug. 2) | 891,364 | 864,746 | 26,618 | 3,929,214 | 4.5 | | |

(1) Comprises inland, coastal, Great Lakes, and territorial water. Data for prior years cover inland water only.
NOTE: Percent changes are computed on basis of change in population since preceding census date, and period covered therefore is not always exactly 10 years.
Population density figures given for various years represent the area within the boundaries of the United States which was under the jurisdiction on date in question, including in some cases considerable areas not organized or settled and not covered by the census. In 1870, for example, Alaska was not covered by the census.
Revised figure of 39,818,449 for the 1870 population includes adjustments for undernumeration in the Southern states. On the basis of the revised figure, the population increased by 8,375,128, or 26.6 percent between 1860 and 1870, and by 10,370,760, or 26.1 percent between 1870 and 1880.

## Resident Population by Sex, Race, Residence, and Median Age: 1790 to 1990

Source: Bureau of the Census (in thousands, except as indicated)

| Date | Sex | | Race | | | | Residence | | Median Age (years) | | |
|---|---|---|---|---|---|---|---|---|---|---|---|
| | Male | Female | White | Black Number | Black Percent | Other | Urban | Rural | All races | White | Black |
| **Conterminous U.S.** [1] | | | | | | | | | | | |
| 1790 (Aug. 2) | NA | NA | 3,172 | 757 | 19.3 | NA | 202 | 3,728 | NA | NA | NA |
| 1810 (Aug. 6) | NA | NA | 5,862 | 1,378 | 19.0 | NA | 525 | 6,714 | 16.7 | 16.0 | NA |
| 1820 (Aug. 7) | 4,897 | 4,742 | 7,867 | 1,772 | 18.4 | NA | 693 | 8,945 | 16.7 | 16.5 | 17.2 |
| 1840 (June 1) | 8,689 | 8,381 | 14,196 | 2,874 | 16.8 | 79 | 1,845 | 15,224 | 17.8 | 17.9 | 17.3 |
| 1860 (June 1) | 16,085 | 15,358 | 26,923 | 4,442 | 14.1 | 89 | 6,217 | 25,227 | 19.4 | 19.7 | 17.7 |
| 1870 (June 1) | 19,494 | 19,065 | 33,589 | 4,880 | 12.7 | 89 | 9,902 | 28,656 | 20.2 | 20.4 | 18.5 |
| 1880 (June 1) | 25,519 | 24,637 | 43,403 | 6,581 | 13.1 | 172 | 14,130 | 36,026 | 20.9 | 21.4 | 18.0 |
| 1890 (June 1) | 32,237 | 30,711 | 55,101 | 7,489 | 11.9 | 358 | 22,106 | 40,841 | 22.0 | 22.5 | 17.8 |
| 1900 (June 1) | 38,816 | 37,178 | 66,809 | 8,834 | 11.6 | 351 | 30,160 | 45,835 | 22.9 | 23.4 | 19.4 |
| 1920 (Jan. 1) | 53,900 | 51,810 | 94,821 | 10,463 | 9.9 | 427 | 54,158 | 51,553 | 25.3 | 25.6 | 22.3 |
| 1930 (Apr. 1) | 62,137 | 60,638 | 110,287 | 11,891 | 9.7 | 597 | 68,955 | 53,820 | 26.4 | 26.9 | 22.3 |
| 1940 (Apr. 1) | 66,062 | 65,608 | 118,215 | 12,866 | 9.8 | 589 | 74,424 | 57,246 | 29.0 | 29.5 | 25.3 |
| **United States** | | | | | | | | | | | |
| 1950 (Apr. 1) | 75,187 | 76,139 | 135,150 | 15,045 | 9.9 | 1,131 | 96,847 | 54,479 | 30.2 | 30.7 | 26.2 |
| 1960 (Apr. 1) | 88,331 | 90,992 | 158,832 | 18,872 | 10.5 | 1,620 | 125,269 | 54,054 | 29.5 | 30.3 | 23.5 |
| 1970 (Apr. 1) [2] | 98,926 | 104,309 | 178,098 | 22,581 | 11.1 | 2,557 | 149,325 | 53,887 | 28.0 | 28.9 | 22.4 |
| 1980 (Apr. 1) [3] | 110,053 | 116,493 | 194,713 | 26,683 | 11.8 | 5,150 | 167,051 | 59,495 | 30.0 | 30.9 | 24.9 |
| 1983 (July 1) | 113,119 | 120,365 | 199,849 | 28,056 | 12.0 | 6,379 | NA | NA | 30.8 | 31.7 | 25.9 |
| 1984 (July 1) | 115,022 | 121,455 | 201,290 | 28,457 | 12.0 | 6,730 | NA | NA | 31.1 | 32.0 | 26.3 |
| 1985 (July 1, est) | 116,160 | 122,576 | 202,769 | 28,870 | 12.1 | 7,097 | NA | NA | 31.4 | 32.3 | 26.6 |
| 1990 (Apr. 1) | 121,239 | 127,470 | 199,686 | 29,986 | 12.1 | 9,805 | 187,053 | 61,656 | 32.9 | 34.4 | 28.1 |

(NA) Not available. (1) Excludes Alaska and Hawaii. (2) The revised 1970 resident population count is 203,302,031, which incorporates changes due to errors found after tabulations were completed. The race and sex data shown here reflect the official 1970 census count while the residence data come from the tabulated count. (3) The race data shown for April 1, 1980 have been modified.

# UNITED STATES FACTS
## Superlative U.S. Statistics
Source: U.S. Geological Survey; U.S. Bureau of the Census; World Almanac Research

| | | |
|---|---|---|
| Area for 50 states and D. of C. | Total | 3,618,770 sq. mi. |
| | Land 3,539,289 sq. mi.—Water 79,481 sq. mi. | |
| Largest state. | Alaska | 591,004 sq. mi. |
| Smallest state | Rhode Island | 1,212 sq. mi. |
| Largest county (excludes Alaska) | San Bernardino County, California | 20,064 sq. mi. |
| Smallest county | Kalawo, Hawaii | 14 sq. mi. |
| Northernmost city | Barrow, Alaska | 71°17'N. |
| Northernmost point | Point Barrow, Alaska | 71°23'N. |
| Southernmost city | Hilo, Hawaii | 19°43'N. |
| Southernmost settlement | Naalehu, Hawaii | 19°03'N. |
| Southernmost point | Ka Lae (South Cape), Island of Hawaii | 18°55'N. (155°41'W.) |
| Easternmost city | Eastport, Maine | 66°59'02"W. |
| *Easternmost settlement | Amchitka I., Alaska | 179°15'E. |
| *Easternmost point | Semisopochnoi I., Alaska | 179°52'E. |
| Westernmost city | Atka, Alaska | 174°20'W. |
| Westernmost settlement | Adak Station, Alaska | 176°39'W. |
| Westernmost point | Amatignak I., Alaska | 179°06'W. |
| Highest settlement | Climax, Colorado | 11,560 ft. |
| Lowest settlement | Calipatria, California | −185 ft. |
| Highest point on Atlantic coast. | Cadillac Mountain, Mount Desert I., Maine | 1,530 ft. |
| Oldest national park | Yellowstone National Park (1872), Wyoming, Montana, Idaho | 3,468 sq. mi. |
| Largest national park | Wrangell-St. Elias, Alaska | 13,018 sq. mi. |
| Largest national monument | Death Valley, California, Nevada | 3,231 sq. mi. |
| Highest waterfall | Yosemite Falls—Total in three sections | 2,425 ft. |
| | Upper Yosemite Fall | 1,430 ft. |
| | Cascades in middle section | 675 ft. |
| | Lower Yosemite Fall | 320 ft. |
| Longest river. | Mississippi-Missouri | 3,710 mi. |
| Highest mountain | Mount McKinley, Alaska | 20,320 ft. |
| Lowest point | Death Valley, California | −282 ft. |
| Deepest lake | Crater Lake, Oregon | 1,932 ft. |
| Rainiest spot. | Mt. Waialeale, Hawaii | Annual aver. rainfall 460 inches |
| Largest gorge | Grand Canyon, Colorado River, Arizona | 277 miles long, 600 ft. to 18 miles wide, 1 mile deep |
| Deepest gorge. | Hell's Canyon, Snake River, Idaho-Oregon | 7,900 ft. |
| Strongest surface wind | Mount Washington, New Hampshire recorded 1934 | 231 mph |
| Biggest dam | New Cornelia Tailings, Ten Mile Wash, Arizona | 274,026,000 cu. yds. material used |
| Tallest building. | Sears Tower, Chicago, Illinois | 1,454 ft. |
| Largest building | Boeing 747 Manufacturing Plant, Everett, Washington | 205,600,000 cu. ft.; covers 47 acres. |
| Tallest structure | TV tower, Blanchard, North Dakota | 2,063 ft. |
| Longest bridge span | Verrazano-Narrows, New York | 4,260 ft. |
| Highest bridge | Royal Gorge, Colorado | 1,053 ft. above water |
| Deepest well | Gas well, Washita County, Oklahoma | 31,441 ft. |

## The 48 Contiguous States

| | | |
|---|---|---|
| Area for 48 states | Total | 3,021,295 sq. mi. |
| | Land 2,962,031 sq. mi.—Water 59,264 sq. mi. | |
| Largest state. | Texas | 266,807 sq. mi |
| Northernmost city | Bellingham, Washington | 48°46'N. |
| Northernmost settlement | Angle Inlet, Minnesota | 49°21'N. |
| Northernmost point | Northwest Angle, Minnesota | 49°23'N. |
| Southernmost city | Key West, Florida | 24°33'N. |
| Southernmost mainland city | Florida City, Florida | 25°27'N. |
| Southernmost point | Key West, Florida | 24°33'N. |
| Easternmost settlement | Lubec, Maine | 66°58'49"W. |
| Easternmost point. | West Quoddy Head, Maine | 66°57'W. |
| Westernmost town | La Push, Washington | 124°38'W. |
| Westernmost point | Cape Alava, Washington | 124°44'W. |
| Highest mountain | Mount Whitney, California | 14,494 ft. |

*Alaska's Aleutian Islands extend into the eastern hemisphere and therefore technically contain the easternmost point and settlement in the United States.

## Geodetic Datum of North America

In July 1986, the National Oceanic and Atmospheric Administration's National Geodetic Survey (NGS) completed the readjustment and redefinition of the North American Datum. This new datum is known as the North American Datum of 1983. Rapid advances in economic growth and scientific exploration in the United States after World War II resulted in an increasing need for accurate coordinate information. To facilitate the use of satellite surveying and navigation systems, the new datum was redefined using the Geodetic Reference System 1980 as the reference ellipsoid because this model more closely approximates the true size and shape of the Earth. The readjustment of the datum resulted in position changes of as much as 330 feet in the Continental United States and as much as 1/4 mile in Hawaii, the Aleutian Islands, Puerto Rico, and the Virgin Islands.

## Statistical Information about the U.S.

In the *Statistical Abstract of the United States* the Bureau of the Census, U.S. Dept. of Commerce, annually publishes a summary of social, political, and economic information. A book of almost 1,000 pages, it presents comprehensive data on population, housing, health, education, employment, income, prices, business, banking, energy, science, defense, trade, government finance, foreign country comparison, and other subjects. Special features include data from the 1990 Census, sections on State Rankings and Metropolitan Statistical Areas and a new section on computer technology in the office. The book is prepared under the direction of Glenn W. King, Chief, Statistical Compendia Staff, Bureau of the Census. Information concerning these and other publications may be obtained from the Supt. of Documents, Government Printing Office, Wash., D.C. 20402, or from the U.S. Bureau of the Census, Data User Services Division, Wash., D.C. 20233.

## Highest and Lowest Altitudes in the U.S. and Territories

Source: U.S. Geological Survey (Minus sign means below sea level; elevations are in feet.)

| State | Highest Point Name | County | Elev. | Lowest Point Name | County | Elev. |
|---|---|---|---|---|---|---|
| Alabama | Cheaha Mountain | Cleburne | 2,405 | Gulf of Mexico | | Sea level |
| Alaska | Mount McKinley | | 20,320 | Pacific Ocean | | Sea level |
| Arizona | Humphreys Peak | Coconino | 12,633 | Colorado R. | Yuma | 70 |
| Arkansas | Magazine Mountain | Logan | 2,753 | Ouachita R. | Ashley-Union | 55 |
| California | Mount Whitney | Inyo-Tulare | 14,494 | Death Valley | Inyo | −282 |
| Colorado | Mount Elbert | Lake | 14,433 | Arkansas R. | Prowers | 3,350 |
| Connecticut | Mount Frissell | Litchfield | 2,380 | L.I. Sound | | Sea level |
| Delaware | On Ebright Road | New Castle | 442 | Atlantic Ocean | | Sea level |
| Dist. of Col. | Tenleytown | N. W. part | 410 | Potomac R. | | 1 |
| Florida | Sec. 30, T 6N, R 20W | Walton | 345 | Atlantic Ocean | | Sea level |
| Georgia | Brasstown Bald | Towns-Union | 4,784 | Atlantic Ocean | | Sea level |
| Guam | Mount Lamlam | Agat District | 1,332 | Pacific Ocean | | Sea level |
| Hawaii | Mauna Kea | Hawaii | 13,796 | Pacific Ocean | | Sea level |
| Idaho | Borah Peak | Custer | 12,662 | Snake R. | Nez Perce | 710 |
| Illinois | Charles Mound | Jo Daviess | 1,235 | Mississippi R. | Alexander | 279 |
| Indiana | Franklin Township | Wayne | 1,257 | Ohio R. | Posey | 320 |
| Iowa | Sec. 29, T 100N, R 41W. | Osceola | 1,670 | Mississippi R. | Lee | 480 |
| Kansas | Mount Sunflower | Wallace | 4,039 | Verdigris R. | Montgomery | 679 |
| Kentucky | Black Mountain | Harlan | 4,139 | Mississippi R. | Fulton | 257 |
| Louisiana | Driskill Mountain | Bienville | 535 | New Orleans | Orleans | −8 |
| Maine | Mount Katahdin | Piscataquis | 5,267 | Atlantic Ocean | | Sea level |
| Maryland | Backbone Mountain | Garrett | 3,360 | Atlantic Ocean | | Sea level |
| Massachusetts | Mount Greylock | Berkshire | 3,487 | Atlantic Ocean | | Sea level |
| Michigan | Mount Arvon | Baraga | 1,979 | Lake Erie | Monroe | 571 |
| Minnesota | Eagle Mountain | Cook | 2,301 | Lake Superior | | 600 |
| Mississippi | Woodall Mountain | Tishomingo | 806 | Gulf of Mexico | | Sea level |
| Missouri | Taum Sauk Mt. | Iron | 1,772 | St. Francis R. | Dunklin | 230 |
| Montana | Granite Peak | Park | 12,799 | Kootenai R. | Lincoln | 1,800 |
| Nebraska | Johnson Township | Kimball | 5,426 | Missouri R. | Richardson | 840 |
| Nevada | Boundary Peak | Esmeralda | 13,140 | Mount Manchester | Clark | 479 |
| New Hamp. | Mt. Washington | Coos | 6,288 | Atlantic Ocean | Rockingham | Sea level |
| New Jersey | High Point | Sussex | 1,803 | Atlantic Ocean | | Sea level |
| New Mexico | Wheeler Peak | Taos | 13,161 | Red Bluff Res. | Eddy | 2,842 |
| New York | Mount Marcy | Essex | 5,344 | Atlantic Ocean | | Sea level |
| North Carolina | Mount Mitchell | Yancey | 6,684 | Atlantic Ocean | | Sea level |
| North Dakota | White Butte | Slope | 3,506 | Red R. | Pembina | 750 |
| Ohio | Campbell Hill | Logan | 1,549 | Ohio R. | Hamilton | 455 |
| Oklahoma | Black Mesa | Cimarron | 4,973 | Little R. | McCurtain | 289 |
| Oregon | Mount Hood | Clackamas-Hood R. | 11,239 | Pacific Ocean | | Sea level |
| Pennsylvania | Mt. Davis | Somerset | 3,213 | Delaware R. | Delaware | Sea level |
| Puerto Rico | Cerro de Punta | Ponce District | 4,390 | Atlantic Ocean | | Sea level |
| Rhode Island | Jerimoth Hill | Providence | 812 | Atlantic Ocean | | Sea level |
| Samoa | Lata Mountain | Tau Island | 3,160 | Pacific Ocean | | Sea level |
| South Carolina | Sassafras Mountain | Pickens | 3,560 | Atlantic Ocean | | Sea level |
| South Dakota | Harney Peak | Pennington | 7,242 | Big Stone Lake | Roberts | 966 |
| Tennessee | Clingmans Dome | Sevier | 6,643 | Mississippi R. | Shelby | 178 |
| Texas | Guadalupe Peak | Culberson | 8,749 | Gulf of Mexico | | Sea level |
| Utah | Kings Peak | Duchesne | 13,528 | Beaverdam Wash. | Washington | 2,000 |
| Vermont | Mount Mansfield | Lamoille | 4,393 | Lake Champlain | | 95 |
| Virginia | Mount Rogers | Grayson-Smyth | 5,729 | Atlantic Ocean | | Sea level |
| Virgin Islands | Crown Mountain | St. Thomas Island | 1,556 | Atlantic Ocean | | Sea level |
| Washington | Mount Rainier | Pierce | 14,410 | Pacific Ocean | | Sea level |
| West Virginia | Spruce Knob | Pendleton | 4,861 | Potomac R. | Jefferson | 240 |
| Wisconsin | Timms Hill | Price | 1,951 | Lake Michigan | | 579 |
| Wyoming | Gannett Peak | Fremont | 13,804 | B. Fourche R. | Crook | 3,099 |

## U.S. Coastline by States

Source: NOAA, U.S. Dept. of Commerce
(statute miles)

| State | Coastline[1] | Shoreline[2] | State | Coastline[1] | Shoreline[2] |
|---|---|---|---|---|---|
| **Atlantic coast** | **2,069** | **28,673** | **Gulf coast** | **1,631** | **17,141** |
| Connecticut | 0 | 618 | Alabama | 53 | 607 |
| Delaware | 28 | 381 | Florida | 770 | 5,095 |
| Florida | 580 | 3,331 | Louisiana | 397 | 7,721 |
| Georgia | 100 | 2,344 | Mississippi | 44 | 359 |
| Maine | 228 | 3,478 | Texas | 367 | 3,359 |
| Maryland | 31 | 3,190 | | | |
| Massachusetts | 192 | 1,519 | **Pacific coast** | **7,623** | **40,298** |
| New Hampshire | 13 | 131 | Alaska | 5,580 | 31,383 |
| New Jersey | 130 | 1,792 | California | 840 | 3,427 |
| New York | 127 | 1,850 | Hawaii | 750 | 1,052 |
| North Carolina | 301 | 3,375 | Oregon | 296 | 1,410 |
| Pennsylvania | 0 | 89 | Washington | 157 | 3,026 |
| Rhode Island | 40 | 384 | | | |
| South Carolina | 187 | 2,876 | **Arctic coast, Alaska** | **1,060** | **2,521** |
| Virginia | 112 | 3,315 | **United States** | **12,383** | **88,633** |

(1) Figures are lengths of general outline of seacoast. Measurements were made with a unit measure of 30 minutes of latitude on charts as near the scale of 1:1,200,000 as possible. Coastline of sounds and bays is included to a point where they narrow to width of unit measure, and includes the distance across at such point. (2) Figures obtained in 1939-40 with a recording instrument on the largest-scale charts and maps then available. Shoreline of outer coast, offshore islands, sounds, bays, rivers, and creeks is included to the head of tidewater or to a point where tidal waters narrow to a width of 100 feet.

## States: Settled, Capitals, Entry into Union, Area, Rank

The original 13 states—The 13 colonies that seceded from Great Britain and fought the War of Independence (American Revolution) became the 13 original states. They were: Delaware, Pennsylvania, New Jersey, Georgia, Connecticut, Massachusetts, Maryland, South Carolina, New Hampshire, Virginia, New York, North Carolina, and Rhode Island. The order for the original 13 states is the order in which they ratified the Constitution.

| State | Settled* | Capital | Entered Union Date | Order | Extent in miles Long (approx. mean) | Wide | Area in square miles Land | Inland Water | Total | Rank in area |
|---|---|---|---|---|---|---|---|---|---|---|
| Ala. . . | 1702 . . | Montgomery . . | Dec. 14, 1819 | 22 | 330 | 190 | 50,767 | 938 | 51,705 | 29 |
| Alas. . | 1784 . . | Juneau . . . . . | Jan. 3, 1959 | 49 | (a)1,480 | 810 | 570,833 | 20,171 | 591,004 | 1 |
| Ariz. . . | 1776 . . | Phoenix. . . . . | Feb. 14, 1912 | 48 | 400 | 310 | 113,508 | 492 | 114,000 | 6 |
| Ark. . . | 1686 . . | Little Rock . . . | June 15, 1836 | 25 | 260 | 240 | 52,078 | 1,109 | 53,187 | 27 |
| Cal. . . | 1769 . . | Sacramento . . | Sept. 9, 1850 | 31 | 770 | 250 | 156,299 | 2,407 | 158,706 | 3 |
| Col. . . | 1858 . . | Denver . . . . . | Aug. 1, 1876 | 38 | 380 | 280 | 103,595 | 496 | 104,091 | 8 |
| Conn. . | 1634 . . | Hartford . . . . | Jan. 9, 1788 | 5 | 110 | 70 | 4,872 | 147 | 5,018 | 48 |
| Del. . . | 1638 . . | Dover . . . . . . | Dec. 7, 1787 | 1 | 100 | 30 | 1,932 | 112 | 2,045 | 49 |
| D.C. . . | . . . . . | Washington. . . | . . . . | . . | . . . | . . . | 63 | 6 | 69 | 51 |
| Fla. . . | 1565 . . | Tallahassee . . | Mar. 3, 1845 | 27 | 500 | 160 | 54,153 | 4,511 | 58,664 | 22 |
| Ga. . . | 1733 . . | Atlanta . . . . . | Jan. 2, 1788 | 4 | 300 | 230 | 58,056 | 854 | 58,910 | 21 |
| Ha. . . | 1820 . . | Honolulu . . . . | Aug. 21, 1959 | 50 | . . . | . . . | 6,425 | 46 | 6,471 | 47 |
| Ida. . . | 1842 . . | Boise . . . . . . | July 3, 1890 | 43 | 570 | 300 | 82,412 | 1,153 | 83,564 | 13 |
| Ill. . . . | 1720 . . | Springfield . . . | Dec. 3, 1818 | 21 | 390 | 210 | 55,645 | 700 | 56,345 | 24 |
| Ind. . . | 1733 . . | Indianapolis. . . | Dec. 11, 1816 | 19 | 270 | 140 | 35,932 | 253 | 36,185 | 38 |
| Ia. . . . | 1788 . . | Des Moines . . | Dec. 28, 1846 | 29 | 310 | 200 | 55,965 | 310 | 56,275 | 25 |
| Kan. . . | 1727 . . | Topeka . . . . . | Jan. 29, 1861 | 34 | 400 | 210 | 81,778 | 499 | 82,277 | 14 |
| Ky. . . . | 1774 . . | Frankfort . . . . | June 1, 1792 | 15 | 380 | 140 | 39,669 | 740 | 40,410 | 37 |
| La. . . . | 1699 . . | Baton Rouge. . | Apr. 30, 1812 | 18 | 380 | 130 | 44,521 | 3,230 | 47,752 | 31 |
| Me. . . . | 1624 . . | Augusta. . . . . | Mar. 15, 1820 | 23 | 320 | 190 | 30,995 | 2,270 | 33,265 | 39 |
| Md. . . | 1634 . . | Annapolis. . . . | Apr. 28, 1788 | 7 | 250 | 90 | 9,837 | 623 | 10,460 | 42 |
| Mass. . | 1620 . . | Boston . . . . . | Feb. 6, 1788 | 6 | 190 | 50 | 7,824 | 460 | 8,284 | 45 |
| Mich. . | 1668 . . | Lansing . . . . . | Jan. 26, 1837 | 26 | 490 | 240 | 56,954 | 1,573 | 58,527 | 23 |
| Minn. . | 1805 . . | St. Paul . . . . | May 11, 1858 | 32 | 400 | 250 | 79,548 | 4,854 | 84,402 | 12 |
| Miss. . | 1699 . . | Jackson. . . . . | Dec. 10, 1817 | 20 | 340 | 170 | 47,233 | 457 | 47,689 | 32 |
| Mo. . . | 1735 . . | Jefferson City . | Aug. 10, 1821 | 24 | 300 | 240 | 68,945 | 752 | 69,697 | 19 |
| Mon. . | 1809 . . | Helena . . . . . | Nov. 8, 1889 | 41 | 630 | 280 | 145,388 | 1,658 | 147,046 | 4 |
| Neb. . . | 1823 . . | Lincoln . . . . . | Mar. 1, 1867 | 37 | 430 | 210 | 76,644 | 711 | 77,355 | 15 |
| Nev. . . | 1849 . . | Carson City . . | Oct. 31, 1864 | 36 | 490 | 320 | 109,894 | 667 | 110,561 | 7 |
| N.H. . . | 1623 . . | Concord . . . . | June 21, 1788 | 9 | 190 | 70 | 8,993 | 286 | 9,279 | 44 |
| N.J. . . | 1660 . . | Trenton . . . . . | Dec. 18, 1787 | 3 | 150 | 70 | 7,468 | 319 | 7,787 | 46 |
| N.M. . . | 1610 . . | Santa Fe . . . . | Jan. 6, 1912 | 47 | 370 | 343 | 121,335 | 258 | 121,593 | 5 |
| N.Y. . . | 1614 . . | Albany . . . . . | July 26, 1788 | 11 | 330 | 283 | 47,377 | 1,731 | 49,108 | 30 |
| N.C. . . | 1660 . . | Raleigh . . . . . | Nov. 21, 1789 | 12 | 500 | 150 | 48,843 | 3,826 | 52,669 | 28 |
| N.D. . . | 1812 . . | Bismarck . . . . | Nov. 2, 1889 | 39 | 340 | 211 | 69,300 | 1,403 | 70,702 | 17 |
| Oh. . . | 1788 . . | Columbus . . . | Mar. 1, 1803 | 17 | 220 | 220 | 41,004 | 325 | 41,330 | 35 |
| Okla. . | 1889 . . | Oklahoma City. | Nov. 16, 1907 | 46 | 400 | 220 | 68,655 | 1,301 | 69,956 | 18 |
| Ore. . . | 1811 . . | Salem . . . . . | Feb. 14, 1859 | 33 | 360 | 261 | 96,184 | 889 | 97,073 | 10 |
| Pa. . . . | 1682 . . | Harrisburg . . . | Dec. 12, 1787 | 2 | 283 | 160 | 44,888 | 420 | 45,308 | 33 |
| R.I. . . . | 1636 . . | Providence . . . | May 29, 1790 | 13 | 40 | 30 | 1,055 | 158 | 1,212 | 50 |
| S.C. . . | 1670 . . | Columbia . . . . | May 23, 1788 | 8 | 260 | 200 | 30,203 | 909 | 31,113 | 40 |
| S.D. . . | 1859 . . | Pierre . . . . . . | Nov. 2, 1889 | 40 | 380 | 210 | 75,952 | 1,164 | 77,116 | 16 |
| Tenn. . | 1769 . . | Nashville . . . . | June 1, 1796 | 16 | 440 | 120 | 41,155 | 989 | 42,144 | 34 |
| Tex. . . | 1682 . . | Austin . . . . . | Dec. 29, 1845 | 28 | 790 | 660 | 262,017 | 4,790 | 266,807 | 2 |
| Ut. . . . | 1847 . . | Salt Lake City . | Jan. 4, 1896 | 45 | 350 | 270 | 82,073 | 2,826 | 84,899 | 11 |
| Vt. . . . | 1724 . . | Montpelier . . . | Mar. 4, 1791 | 14 | 160 | 80 | 9,273 | 341 | 9,614 | 43 |
| Va. . . . | 1607 . . | Richmond . . . . | June 25, 1788 | 10 | 430 | 200 | 39,704 | 1,063 | 40,767 | 36 |
| Wash. . | 1811 . . | Olympia . . . . | Nov. 11, 1889 | 42 | 360 | 240 | 66,511 | 1,627 | 68,139 | 20 |
| W.Va. . | 1727 . . | Charleston . . . | June 20, 1863 | 35 | 240 | 130 | 24,119 | 112 | 24,232 | 41 |
| Wis. . . | 1766 . . | Madison . . . . | May 29, 1848 | 30 | 310 | 260 | 54,426 | 1,727 | 56,153 | 26 |
| Wy. . . | 1834 . . | Cheyenne . . . | July 10, 1890 | 44 | 360 | 280 | 96,989 | 820 | 97,809 | 9 |

* First European permanent settlement. (a) Aleutian Islands and Alexander Archipelago are not considered in these lengths.

## The Continental Divide

The Continental Divide: watershed, created by mountain ranges or table-lands of the Rocky Mountains, from which the drainage is easterly or westerly; the easterly flowing waters reaching the Atlantic Ocean chiefly through the Gulf of Mexico, and the westerly flowing waters reaching the Pacific Ocean through the Columbia River, or through the Colorado River, which flows into the Gulf of California.

The location and route of the Continental Divide across the United States may briefly be described as follows:

Beginning at point of crossing the United States-Mexican boundary, near long. 108°45'W., the Divide, in a northerly direction, crosses New Mexico along the western edge of the Rio Grande drainage basin, entering Colorado near long. 106°41'W.

Thence by a very irregular route northerly across Colorado along the western summits of the Rio Grande and of the Arkansas, the South Platte, and the North Platte River basins, and across Rocky Mountain National Park, entering Wyoming near long. 106°52'W.

Thence in a northwesterly direction, forming the western rims of the North Platte, Big Horn, and Yellowstone River basins, crossing the southwestern portion of Yellowstone National Park.

Thence in a westerly and then a northerly direction forming the common boundary of Idaho and Montana, to a point on said boundary near long. 114°00'W.

Thence northeasterly and northwesterly through Montana and the Glacier National Park, entering Canada near long. 114°04'W.

## Chronological List of Territories

Source: National Archives and Records Service

| Name of territory | Date of Organic Act | | | Organic Act effective | | | Admission as state | | | Yrs. terr. |
|---|---|---|---|---|---|---|---|---|---|---|
| Northwest Territory(a) | July | 13, | 1787 | No fixed date. | | | Mar. | 1, | 1803(b) | 16 |
| Territory southwest of River Ohio | May | 26, | 1790 | No fixed date. | | | June | 1, | 1796(c) | 6 |
| Mississippi | Apr. | 7, | 1798 | When president acted. | | | Dec. | 10, | 1817 | 19 |
| Indiana | May | 7, | 1800 | July 4, 1800 | | | Dec. | 11, | 1816 | 16 |
| Orleans | Mar. | 26, | 1804 | Oct. 1, 1804 | | | Apr. | 30, | 1812(d) | 7 |
| Michigan | Jan. | 11, | 1805 | June 30, 1805 | | | Jan. | 26, | 1837 | 31 |
| Louisiana-Missouri(e) | Mar. | 3, | 1805 | July 4, 1805 | | | Aug. | 10, | 1821 | 16 |
| Illinois | Feb. | 3, | 1809 | Mar. 1, 1809 | | | Dec. | 3, | 1818 | 9 |
| Alabama | Mar. | 3, | 1817 | When Miss. became a state | | | Dec. | 14, | 1819 | 2 |
| Arkansas | Mar. | 2, | 1819 | July 4, 1819 | | | June | 15, | 1836 | 17 |
| Florida | Mar. | 30, | 1822 | No fixed date | | | Mar. | 3, | 1845 | 23 |
| Wisconsin | Apr. | 20, | 1836 | July 3, 1836 | | | May | 29, | 1848 | 12 |
| Iowa | June | 12, | 1838 | July 3, 1838 | | | Dec. | 28, | 1846 | 7 |
| Oregon | Aug. | 14, | 1848 | Date of act | | | Feb. | 14, | 1859 | 10 |
| Minnesota | Mar. | 3, | 1849 | Date of act | | | May | 11, | 1858 | 9 |
| New Mexico | Sept. | 9, | 1850 | On president's proclamation | | | Jan. | 6, | 1912 | 61 |
| Utah | Sept. | 9, | 1850 | Date of act | | | Jan. | 4, | 1896 | 44 |
| Washington | Mar. | 2, | 1853 | Date of act | | | Nov. | 11, | 1889 | 36 |
| Nebraska | May | 30, | 1854 | Date of act | | | Mar. | 1, | 1867 | 12 |
| Kansas | May | 30, | 1854 | Date of act | | | Jan. | 29, | 1861 | 6 |
| Colorado | Feb. | 28, | 1861 | Date of act | | | Aug. | 1, | 1876 | 15 |
| Nevada | Mar. | 2, | 1861 | Date of act | | | Oct. | 31, | 1864 | 3 |
| Dakota | Mar. | 2, | 1861 | Date of act | | | Nov. | 2, | 1889 | 28 |
| Arizona | Feb. | 24, | 1863 | Date of act | | | Feb. | 14, | 1912 | 49 |
| Idaho | Mar. | 3, | 1863 | Date of act | | | July | 3, | 1890 | 27 |
| Montana | May | 26, | 1864 | Date of act | | | Nov. | 8, | 1889 | 25 |
| Wyoming | July | 25, | 1868 | When officers were qualified | | | July | 10, | 1890 | 22 |
| Alaska(f) | May | 17, | 1884 | No fixed date | | | Jan. | 3, | 1959 | 75 |
| Oklahoma | May | 2, | 1890 | Date of act | | | Nov. | 16, | 1907 | 17 |
| Hawaii | Apr. | 30, | 1900 | June 14, 1900 | | | Aug. | 21, | 1959 | 59 |

(a) Included Ohio, Indiana, Illinois, Michigan, Wisconsin, eastern Minnesota; (b) as the state of Ohio; (c) as the state of Tennessee; (d) as the state of Louisiana; (e) organic act for Missouri Territory of June 4, 1812, became effective Dec. 7, 1812; (f) Although the May 17, 1884 act actually constituted Alaska as a district, it was often referred to as a territory, and unofficially administered as such. The Territory of Alaska was legally and formally organized by an act of Aug. 24, 1912.

## Geographic Centers, U.S. and Each State

Source: U.S. Geological Survey

**United States, including Alaska and Hawaii** — South Dakota; Butte County, W of Castle Rock, Approx. lat. 44°58'N. long. 103°46'W.

**Contiguous U. S. (48 states)** — Near Lebanon, Smith Co., Kansas, lat. 39°50'N. long. 98°35'W.

**North American continent** — The geographic center is in Pierce County, North Dakota, 6 miles W of Balta, latitude 48°10', longitude 100°10'W.

### State—county, locality

Alabama—Chilton, 12 miles SW of Clanton.
Alaska—lat. 63°50'N. long. 152°W. Approx. 60 mi. NW of Mt. McKinley.
Arizona—Yavapai, 55 miles ESE of Prescott.
Arkansas—Pulaski, 12 miles NW of Little Rock.
California—Madera, 38 miles E of Madera.
Colorado—Park, 30 miles NW of Pikes Peak.
Connecticut—Hartford, at East Berlin.
Delaware—Kent, 11 miles S of Dover.
District of Columbia—Near 4th and L Sts., NW.
Florida—Hernando, 12 miles NNW of Brooksville.
Georgia—Twiggs, 18 miles SE of Macon.
Hawaii—Hawaii, 20°15'N, 156°20'W, off Maui Island.
Idaho—Custer, at Custer, 40 miles NE of Challis.
Illinois—Logan, 28 miles NE of Springfield.
Indiana—Boone, 14 miles NNW of Indianapolis.
Iowa—Story, 5 miles NE of Ames.
Kansas—Barton, 15 miles NE of Great Bend.
Kentucky—Marion, 3 miles NNW of Lebanon.
Louisiana—Avoyelles, 3 miles SE of Marksville.
Maine—Piscataquis, 18 miles north of Dover.

Maryland—Prince Georges, 4.5 miles NW of Davidsonville.
Massachusetts—Worcester, north part of city.
Michigan—Wexford, 5 miles NNW of Cadillac.
Minnesota—Crow Wing, 10 miles SW of Brainerd.
Mississippi—Leake, 9 miles WNW of Carthage.
Missouri—Miller, 20 miles SW of Jefferson City.
Montana—Fergus, 11 miles west of Lewistown.
Nebraska—Custer, 10 miles NW of Broken Bow.
Nevada—Lander, 26 miles SE of Austin.
New Hampshire—Belknap, 3 miles E of Ashland.
New Jersey—Mercer, 5 miles SE of Trenton.
New Mexico—Torrance, 12 miles SSW of Willard.
New York—Madison, 12 miles S of Oneida and 26 miles SW of Utica.
North Carolina—Chatham, 10 miles NW of Sanford.
North Dakota—Sheridan, 5 miles SW of McClusky.
Ohio—Delaware, 25 miles NNE of Columbus.
Oklahoma—Oklahoma, 8 miles N of Oklahoma City.
Oregon—Crook, 25 miles SSE of Prineville.
Pennsylvania—Centre, 2.5 miles SW of Bellefonte.
Rhode Island—Kent, 1 mile SSW of Crompton.
South Carolina—Richland, 13 miles SE of Columbia.
South Dakota—Hughes, 8 miles NE of Pierre.
Tennessee—Rutherford, 5 mi. NE of Murfreesboro.
Texas—McCulloch, 15 miles NE of Brady.
Utah—Sanpete, 3 miles N of Manti.
Vermont—Washington, 3 miles E of Roxbury.
Virginia—Buckingham, 5 miles SW of Buckingham.
Washington—Chelan, 10 mi. WSW of Wenatchee.
West Virginia—Braxton, 4 miles E of Sutton.
Wisconsin—Wood, 9 miles SW of Marshfield.
Wyoming—Fremont, 58 miles ENE of Lander.

There is no generally accepted definition of geographic center, and no satisfactory method for determining it. The geographic center of an area may be defined as the center of gravity of the surface, or that point on which the surface of the area would balance if it were a plane of uniform thickness.

No marked or monumented point has been established by any government agency as the geographic center of either the 50 states, the contiguous United States, or the North American continent. A monument was erected in Lebanon, Kan., contiguous U.S. center, by a group of citizens. A cairn in Rugby, N.D. marks the center of the North American continent.

## International Boundary Lines of the U.S.

The length of the northern boundary of the contiguous U.S. — the U.S.-Canadian border, excluding Alaska — is 3,987 miles according to the U.S. Geological Survey, Dept. of the Interior. The length of the Alaskan-Canadian border is 1,538 miles. The length of the U.S.-Mexican border, from the Gulf of Mexico to the Pacific Ocean, is approximately 1,933 miles (1963 boundary agreement).

# Origin of the Names of U.S. States

Source: State officials, the Smithsonian Institution, and the Topographic Division, U.S. Geological Survey.

**Alabama**—Indian for tribal town, later a tribe (Alabamas or Alibamons) of the Creek confederacy.

**Alaska**—Russian version of Aleutian (Eskimo) word, alakshak, for "peninsula," "great lands," or "land that is not an island."

**Arizona**—Spanish version of Pima Indian word for "little spring place," or Aztec arizuma, meaning "silver-bearing."

**Arkansas**—French variant of Quapaw, a Siouan people meaning "downstream people."

**California**—Bestowed by the Spanish conquistadors (possibly by Cortez). It was the name of an imaginary island, an earthly paradise, in "Las Serges de Esplandian," a Spanish romance written by Montalvo in 1510. Baja California (Lower California, in Mexico) was first visited by Spanish in 1533. The present U.S. state was called Alta (Upper) California.

**Colorado**—Spanish, red, first applied to Colorado River.

**Connecticut**—From Mohican and other Algonquin words meaning "long river place."

**Delaware**—Named for Lord De La Warr, early governor of Virginia; first applied to river, then to Indian tribe (Lenni-Lenape), and the state.

**District of Columbia**—For Columbus, 1791.

**Florida**—Named by Ponce de Leon on Pascua Florida, "Flowery Easter," on Easter Sunday, 1513.

**Georgia**—For King George II of England by James Oglethorpe, colonial administrator, 1732.

**Hawaii**—Possibly derived from native word for homeland, Hawaiki or Owhyhee.

**Idaho**—A coined name with an invented Indian meaning: "gem of the mountains;" originally suggested for the Pike's Peak mining territory (Colorado), then applied to the new mining territory of the Pacific Northwest. Another theory suggests Idaho may be a Kiowa Apache term for the Comanche.

**Illinois**—French for Illini or land of Illini, Algonquin word meaning men or warriors.

**Indiana**—Means "land of the Indians."

**Iowa**—Indian word variously translated as "one who puts to sleep" or "beautiful land."

**Kansas**—Sioux word for "south wind people."

**Kentucky**—Indian word variously translated as "dark and bloody ground," "meadow land" and "land of tomorrow."

**Louisiana**—Part of territory called Louisiana by Sieur de La Salle for French King Louis XIV.

**Maine**—From Maine, ancient French province. Also: descriptive, referring to the mainland as distinct from the many coastal islands.

**Maryland**—For Queen Henrietta Maria, wife of Charles I of England.

**Massachusetts**—From Indian tribe named after "large hill place" identified by Capt. John Smith as being near Milton, Mass.

**Michigan**—From Chippewa words mici gama meaning "great water," after the lake of the same name.

**Minnesota**—From Dakota Sioux word meaning "cloudy water" or "sky-tinted water" of the Minnesota River.

**Mississippi**—Probably Chippewa; mici zibi, "great river" or "gathering-in of all the waters." Also: Algonquin word, "Messipi."

**Missouri**—An Algonquin Indian term meaning "river of the big canoes."

**Montana**—Latin or Spanish for "mountainous."

**Nebraska**—From Omaha or Otos Indian word meaning "broad water" or "flat river," describing the Platte River.

**Nevada**—Spanish, meaning snow-clad.

**New Hampshire**—Named 1629 by Capt. John Mason of Plymouth Council for his home county in England.

**New Jersey**—The Duke of York, 1664, gave a patent to John Berkeley and Sir George Carteret to be called Nova Caesaria, or New Jersey, after England's Isle of Jersey.

**New Mexico**—Spaniards in Mexico applied term to land north and west of Rio Grande in the 16th century.

**New York**—For Duke of York and Albany who received patent to New Netherland from his brother Charles II and sent an expedition to capture it, 1664.

**North Carolina**—In 1619 Charles I gave a large patent to Sir Robert Heath to be called Province of Carolana, from Carolus, Latin name for Charles. A new patent was granted by Charles II to Earl of Clarendon and others. Divided into North and South Carolina, 1710.

**North Dakota**—Dakota is Sioux for friend or ally.

**Ohio**—Iroquois word for "fine or good river."

**Oklahoma**—Choctaw coined word meaning red man, proposed by Rev. Allen Wright, Choctaw-speaking Indian.

**Oregon**—Origin unknown. One theory holds that the name may have been derived from that of the Wisconsin River shown on a 1715 French map as "Ouaricon-sint."

**Pennsylvania**—William Penn, the Quaker, who was made full proprietor by King Charles II in 1681, suggested Sylvania, or woodland, for his tract. The king's government owed Penn's father, Admiral William Penn, £16,000, and the land was granted as partial settlement. Charles II added the Penn to Sylvania, against the desires of the modest proprietor, in honor of the admiral.

**Puerto Rico**—Spanish for Rich Port.

**Rhode Island**—Exact origin is unknown. One theory notes that Giovanni de Verrazano recorded an island about the size of Rhodes in the Mediterranean in 1524, but others believe the state was named Roode Eylandt by Adriaen Block, Dutch explorer, because of its red clay.

**South Carolina**—See North Carolina.

**South Dakota**—See North Dakota.

**Tennessee**—Tanasi was the name of Cherokee villages on the Little Tennessee River. From 1784 to 1788 this was the State of Franklin, or Frankland.

**Texas**—Variant of word used by Caddo and other Indians meaning friends or allies, and applied to them by the Spanish in eastern Texas. Also written texias, tejas, teysas.

**Utah**—From a Navajo word meaning upper, or higher up, as applied to a Shoshone tribe called Ute. Spanish form is Yutta, English Uta or Utah. Proposed name Deseret, "land of honeybees," from Book of Mormon, was rejected by Congress.

**Vermont**—From French words vert (green) and mont (mountain). The Green Mountains were said to have been named by Samuel de Champlain. When the state was formed, 1777, Dr. Thomas Young suggested combining vert and mont into Vermont.

**Virginia**—Named by Sir Walter Raleigh, who fitted out the expedition of 1584, in honor of Queen Elizabeth, the Virgin Queen of England.

**Washington**—Named after George Washington. When the bill creating the Territory of Columbia was introduced in the 32d Congress, the name was changed to Washington because of the existence of the District of Columbia.

**West Virginia**—So named when western counties of Virginia refused to secede from the United States, 1863.

**Wisconsin**—An Indian name, spelled Ouisconsin and Mesconsing by early chroniclers. Believed to mean "grassy place" in Chippewa. Congress made it Wisconsin.

**Wyoming**—The word was taken from Wyoming Valley, Pa., which was the site of an Indian massacre and became widely known by Campbell's poem, "Gertrude of Wyoming." In Algonquin it means "large prairie place."

## Territorial Sea of the U.S.

According to a December 27, 1988 proclamation by Pres. Ronald Reagan: "The territorial sea of the United States henceforth extends to 12 nautical miles from the baselines of the United States determined in accordance with international law. In accordance with international law, as reflected in the applicable provisions of the 1982 United Nations Convention on the Law of the Sea, within the territorial sea of the United States, the ships of all countries enjoy the right of innocent passage and the ships and aircraft of all countries enjoy the right of transit passage through international straits."

## Accession of Territory by the U.S.

Source: Bureau of the Census. U.S. Dept. of Commerce

| | Acquisition date | Total Area Sq. mi. | | Acquisition date | Total Area Sq. mi. | | Acquisition date | Total Area Sq. mi. |
|---|---|---|---|---|---|---|---|---|
| Total U.S. . . . . | (x) | 3,623,434 | Gadsden Purchase | 1853 | 29,640 | Virgin Islands of | | |
| United States. . . . . | (x) | 3,618,770 | Alaska . . . . . . | 1867 | 591,004 | the U.S. . . . . . . | 1917 | 151 |
| Territory in 1790[1] . | (x) | 891,364 | Hawaii . . . . . . | 1898 | 6,471 | Pacific Islands, | | |
| Louisiana Purchase | 1803 | 831,321 | Other areas: | | | Trust Territory | | |
| Purchase of Florida | 1819 | 69,866 | Puerto Rico . . . . | [2]1898 | 3,492 | of the (Palau)[5] . . . | 1947 | 217 |
| Texas. . . . . . . | 1845 | 384,958 | Guam. . . . . . . . | [3]1898 | 217 | No. Mariana Islands[5] | 1947 | 181 |
| Oregon. . . . . . . | 1846 | 283,439 | American Samoa . | [4]1899 | 84 | All other[6] . . . . . . | (x) | 14 |
| Mexican Cession . | 1848 | 530,706 | | | | | | |

(x) Not applicable. (1) Includes that part of drainage basin of Red River of the North, south of 49th parallel, sometimes considered part of Louisiana Purchase. (2) Ceded by Spain in 1898, ratified in 1899, and became Commonwealth of Puerto Rico by Act of Congress on July 25, 1952. (3) Acquired 1898; ratified 1899. (4) Acquired 1899; ratified 1900. (5) The Trust Territory formerly included the Marshall Islands and Micronesia, both officially recognized as independent nations in 1991, and the Northern Mariana Islands, which became a U.S. commonwealth in 1986. (6) Comprises the following islands with gross areas as indicated, in sq. mi.: Midway (2), Wake (3), Palmyra (4), Navassa (2), Baker, Howland, and Jarvis (combined area, 3), Johnston Atoll (combined area, less than .5), and Kingman Reef (less than .5). Excludes Canton and Enderbury Islands (combined area 27 sq. mi.), which are considered to be under the jurisdiction of Kiribati since 1979, and Swan Islands (1 sq. mi.), which were returned to Honduras in 1972.

## Public Lands of the U. S.

Source: Bureau of Land Management. U.S. Dept. of the Interior

### Disposition of Public Lands 1781 to 1992

| Disposition by methods not elsewhere | Acres | Granted to states for: | Acres |
|---|---|---|---|
| classified[1] . . . . . . . . . . . . . . | 303,500,000 | Support of common schools . . . . . . . | 77,630,000 |
| Granted or sold to homesteaders . . . . . | 287,500,000 | Reclamation of swampland . . . . . . . . | 64,920,000 |
| Granted to railroad corporations . . . . | 94,400,000 | Construction of railroads . . . . . . . . | 37,130,000 |
| Granted to veterans as military bounties. . | 61,000,000 | Support of misc. institutions[6] . . . . . . | 21,700,000 |
| Confirmed as private land claims[2] . . . . | 34,000,000 | Purposes not elsewhere classified[7] . . . | 117,600,000 |
| Sold under timber and stone law[3] . . . . . | 13,900,000 | Canals and rivers . . . . . . . . . . . | 6,100,000 |
| Granted or sold under timber culture law[4] . | 10,900,000 | Construction of wagon roads . . . . . . | 3,400,000 |
| Sold under desert land law[5] . . . . . . . . | 10,700,000 | **Total granted to states** . . . . . | **328,480,000** |

(1) Chiefly public, private, and preemption sales, but includes mineral entries, scrip locations, sales of townsites and townlots. (2) The Government has confirmed title to lands claimed under valid grants made by foreign governments prior to the acquisition of the public domain by the United States. (3) The law provided for the sale of lands valuable for timber or stone and unfit for cultivation. (4) The law provided for the granting of public lands to settlers on condition that they plant and cultivate trees on the lands granted. (5) The law provided for the sale of arid agricultural public lands to settlers who irrigate them and bring them under cultivation. (6) Universities, hospitals, asylums, etc. (7) For construction of various public improvements (individual items not specified in the granting act) reclamation of desert lands, construction of water reservoirs, etc.

### Public Lands Administered by Federal Agencies

| Agency (Acres, Sept. 30, 1992) | Public domain | Acquired | Total |
|---|---|---|---|
| Forest Service . . . . . . . . . . . . . | 161,038,854.3 | 28,341,223.5 | 189,380,077.8 |
| Bureau of Land Management. . . . . . . . . . . | 269,710,529 | 2,318,889 | 272,029,418 |
| Bureau of Reclamation . . . . . . . . . . . | 3,533,817.5 | 1,969,275.9 | 5,503,093.4 |
| Fish and Wildlife Service . . . . . . . . . . | 81,321,344 | 10,097,347 | 91,318,691 |
| National Park Service . . . . . . . . . . . | 64,325,741.0 | 8,517,114.8 | 72,842,855.8 |
| Bureau of Indian Affairs . . . . . . . . . . . | 2,554,358.7 | 193,079.6 | 2,747,438.3 |
| Tennessee Valley Authority. . . . . . . . . . . | 0 | 1,040,231.3 | 1,040,231.3 |
| Corps of Engineers . . . . . . . . . . . | 604,971.2 | 4,869,200.0 | 5,474,171.2 |
| U.S. Army. . . . . . . . . . . . . . . | 3,187,901.0 | 6,495,173.0 | 9,683,074.0 |
| U.S. Navy. . . . . . . . . . . . . . . | 618,005.6 | 1,743,750.2 | 2,361,755.8 |
| U.S. Air Force . . . . . . . . . . . . . | 6,858,510.0 | 1,255,022.0 | 8,113,532.0 |
| Department of Energy. . . . . . . . . . . | 1,465,862.4 | 700,478.8 | 2,166,341.2 |
| **Total, all agencies (incl. those not shown) . .** | **660,976,655.8** | **63,089,515.1** | **724,066,170.9** |

## National Recreation Areas Administered by Forest Service

| | | | Acreage | | | | Acreage |
|---|---|---|---|---|---|---|---|
| Allegheny . . . . . . . . . . . . . . | Pa. . . . . | 1984 | 23,063 | Pine Ridge . . . . . . . . . . . . . | Neb. . . . . | 1986 | 6,600 |
| Arapaho . . . . . . . . . . . . . . . | Col. . . . . | 1978 | 34,928 | Rattlesnake. . . . . . . . . . . . . . | Mon. . . . . | 1980 | 61,000 |
| Flaming Gorge . . . . . . . . . . . . | Ut.-Wyo. . . . | 1968 | 201,114 | Sawtooth . . . . . . . . . . . . . . | Ida. . . . . | 1972 | 756,019 |
| Grand Island . . . . . . . . . . . . | Mich. . . . | 1990 | 12,957 | Smith River . . . . . . . . . . . . . | Col. . . . . | 1990 | 331,229 |
| Hells Canyon . . . . . . . . . . . . . | Ida.-Ore. . . | 1975 | 541,336 | Spruce Knob-Seneca Rocks . . . | W. Va. . . . | 1965 | 100,000 |
| Mount Baker . . . . . . . . . . . . | Wash. . . . | 1984 | 8,473 | Whiskeytown Shasta-Trinity . . . | Cal. . . . . | 1965 | 203,587 |
| Mount Rogers . . . . . . . . . . . . | Va. . . . . | 1966 | 154,816 | White Rocks . . . . . . . . . . . . . | Vt. . . . . | 1984 | 36,400 |
| Oregon Dunes . . . . . . . . . . . . | Ore. . . . . | 1972 | 31,566 | Winding Stair Mtn. . . . . . . . . . | Okl. . . . . | 1988 | 26,445 |

## National Parks, Other Areas Administered by National Park Service

Figures given are date area initially protected by Congress or presidential proclamation, date given current designation, and gross area in acres 12/31/92.

### National Parks

**Acadia,** Me. (1916/1929) 41,888. Includes Mount Desert Island, half of Isle au Haut, Schoodic Point on mainland. Highest elevation on Eastern seaboard.

**Arches,** Ut. (1929/1971) 73,379. Contains giant red sandstone arches and other products of erosion.

**Badlands,** S.D. (1929/1978) 242,756; eroded prairie, bison, bighorn and antelope. Contains animal fossils of 40 million years ago.

**Big Bend,** Tex. (1935/1944) 801,163. Rio Grande, Chisos Mts.

**Biscayne,** Fla. (1968/1980) 173,467. Aquatic park encompasses chain of islands south of Miami.

**Bryce Canyon,** Ut. (1923/1928) 35,835. Spectacularly colorful and unusual display of erosion effects.

**Canyonlands,** Ut. (1964) 337,570. At junction of Colorado and Green rivers, extensive evidence of prehistoric Indians.

**Capitol Reef,** Ut. (1937/1971) 241,904. A 60-mile uplift of sandstone cliffs dissected by high-walled gorges.

**Carlsbad Caverns,** N.M. (1923/1930) 46,775. Largest known caverns; not yet fully explored.

**Channel Islands,** Cal. (1938/1980) 249,354. Sea lion breeding place, nesting sea birds, unique plants.

**Crater Lake,** Ore. (1902) 183,224. Extraordinary blue lake in crater of extinct volcano encircled by lava walls 500 to 2,000 feet high.

**Denali,** Alas. (1917/1980) 4,716,726. Name changed from Mt. McKinley NP. Contains highest mountain in U.S.; wildlife.

**Dry Tortugas,** Fla. (1935/1992) 64,700. Formerly Ft. Jefferson National Monument.

**Everglades,** Fla. (1934) 1,506,499. Largest remaining subtropical wilderness in continental U.S.

**Gates of the Arctic,** Alas. (1978/1980) 7,523,888. Vast wilderness in north central region.

**Glacier,** Mon. (1910) 1,013,572. Superb Rocky Mt. scenery, numerous glaciers and glacial lakes. Part of Waterton-Glacier Intl. Peace Park established by U.S. and Canada in 1932.

**Glacier Bay,** Alas. (1925/1980) 3,225,284. Great tidewater glaciers that move down mountain sides and break up into the sea; much wildlife.

**Grand Canyon,** Ariz. (1908/1919) 1,218,375. Most spectacular part of Colorado River's greatest canyon.

**Grand Teton,** Wy. (1929) 309,994. Most impressive part of the Teton Mountains, winter feeding ground of largest American elk herd.

**Great Basin,** Nev. (1922/1986) 77,100. Wide basins and high mountain ranges.

**Great Smoky Mountains,** N.C.-Tenn. (1926/1934) 520,269. Largest eastern mountain range, magnificent forests.

**Guadalupe Mountains,** Tex. (1966/1972) 86,416. Extensive Permian limestone fossil reef; tremendous earth fault.

**Haleakala,** Ha. (1916/1960) 28,655. Dormant volcano on Maui with large colorful craters.

**Hawaii Volcanoes,** Ha. (1916/1961) 229,177. Contains Kilauea and Mauna Loa, active volcanoes.

**Hopewell Culture,** Oh. (1923/1992) 270. Formerly Mound City Group National Monument.

**Hot Springs,** Ark. (1832/1921) 5,839. Government supervised bath houses use waters of 45 of the 47 natural hot springs.

**Isle Royale,** Mich. (1931) 571,790. Largest island in Lake Superior, noted for its wilderness area and wildlife.

**Katmai,** Alas. (1918/1980) 3,716,000. Valley of Ten Thousand Smokes, scene of 1912 volcanic eruption.

**Kenai Fjords,** Alas. (1978/1980) 669,541. Abundant mountain goats, marine mammals, birdlife; the Harding Icefield, one of the major icecaps in U.S.

**Kings Canyon,** Cal. (1890/1940) 461,901. Mountain wilderness, dominated by Kings River Canyons and High Sierra; contains giant sequoias.

**Kobuk Valley,** Alas. (1978/1980) 1,750,421. Broad river is core of native culture.

**Lake Clark,** Alas. (1978/1980) 2,636,839. Across Cook Inlet from Anchorage. A scenic wilderness rich in fish and wildlife.

**Lassen Volcanic,** Cal. (1907/1916) 106,372. Contains Lassen Peak, recently active volcano, and other volcanic phenomena.

**Mammoth Cave,** Ky. (1926/1941) 52,419. 144 miles of surveyed underground passages, beautiful natural formations, river 300 feet below surface.

**Mesa Verde,** Col. (1906) 52,122. Most notable and best preserved prehistoric cliff dwellings in the United States.

**Mount Rainier,** Wash. (1899) 235,612. Greatest single-peak glacial system in the lower 48 states.

**North Cascades,** Wash. (1968) 504,781. Spectacular mountainous region with many glaciers, lakes.

**Olympic,** Wash. (1909/1938) 922,654. Mountain wilderness containing finest remnant of Pacific Northwest rain forest, active glaciers, Pacific shoreline, rare elk.

**Petrified Forest,** Ariz. (1906/1962) 93,533. Extensive petrified wood and Indian artifacts. Contains part of Painted Desert.

**Redwood,** Cal. (1968) 110,132. Forty miles of Pacific coastline, groves of ancient redwoods and world's tallest trees.

**Rocky Mountain,** Col. (1915) 265,198. On the continental divide, includes 107 named peaks over 11,000 feet.

**Samoa,** American Samoa (1988) 9,000. Features the only paleotropical rain forest.

**Sequoia,** Cal. (1890) 402,482. Groves of giant sequoias, highest mountain in contiguous United States — Mount Whitney (14,494 feet). World's largest tree.

**Shenandoah,** Va. (1926/1935) 195,039. Portion of the Blue Ridge Mountains; overlooks Shenandoah Valley; Skyline Drive.

**Theodore Roosevelt,** N.D. (1947/1978) 70,447. Contains part of T.R.'s ranch and scenic badlands.

**Virgin Islands,** V.I. (1956) 14,689. Covers 75% of St. John Island, lush growth, lovely beaches, Indian relics, evidence of colonial Danes.

**Voyageurs,** Minn. (1971/1975) 218,035. Abundant lakes, forests, wildlife, canoeing, boating.

**Wind Cave,** S.D. (1903) 28,295. Limestone caverns in Black Hills. Extensive wildlife includes a herd of bison.

**Wrangell-St. Elias,** Alas. (1978/1980) 8,331,604. Largest area in park system, most peaks over 16,000 feet, abundant wildlife; day's drive east of Anchorage.

**Yellowstone,** Ida., Mon., Wy., (1872) 2,219,791. Oldest national park. World's greatest geyser area has about 3,000 geysers and hot springs; spectacular falls and impressive canyons of the Yellowstone River; grizzly bear, moose, and bison.

**Yosemite,** Cal. (1890) 761,170. Yosemite Valley, the nation's highest waterfall, 3 groves of sequoias, and mountainous.

**Zion,** Ut. (1909/1919) 146,598. Unusual shapes and landscapes have resulted from erosion and faulting; Zion Canyon, with sheer walls ranging up to 2,500 feet, is readily accessible.

### National Historical Parks

**Appomattox Court House,** Va. (1930/1954) 1,325. Where Lee surrendered to Grant.

**Boston,** Mass. (1974) 41. Includes Faneuil Hall, Old North Church, Bunker Hill, Paul Revere House.

**Chaco Culture,** N.M. (1907/1980) 33,974. Ruins of pueblos built by prehistoric Indians.

**Chesapeake and Ohio Canal,** Md.-W.Va.-D.C. (1961/1971) 20,781. 184 mile historic canal; D.C. to Cumberland, Md.

**Colonial,** Va. (1930/1936) 9,327. Includes most of Jamestown Island, site of first successful English colony; Yorktown, site of Cornwallis' surrender to George Washington; and the Colonial Parkway.

**Cumberland Gap,** Ky.-Tenn.-Va. (1940) 20,274. Mountain pass of the Wilderness Road which carried the first great migration of pioneers into America's interior.

**George Rogers Clark,** Vincennes, Ind. (1966) 26. Commemorates American defeat of British in west during Revolution.

**Dayton Aviation,** Oh. (1992). Commemorates the area's aviation heritage.

**Harpers Ferry,** Md., W. Va. (1944/1963) 2,239. At the confluence of the Shenandoah and Potomac rivers, the site of John Brown's 1859 raid on the Army arsenal.

**Independence,** Pa. (1948/1956) 45. Contains several properties in Philadelphia associated with the Revolutionary War and the founding of the U.S. Includes Independence Hall.

**Jean Laffite** (and preserve), La. (1939/1978) 20,020. Includes Chalmette, site of 1815 Battle of New Orleans; French Quarter.

**Kalaupapa,** Ha. (1980) 10,779. Molokai's former leper colony site and other historic areas.

**Kaloko-Honokohau,** Ha. (1978) 1,161. Culture center has 234 historic features and grave of first king, Kamehameha.

**Keweenaw,** Mich. (1992). Site of first significant Copper Mine in U.S.

**Klondike Gold Rush,** Alas.-Wash. (1976) 13,191. Alaskan Trails in 1898 Gold Rush. Museum in Seattle.

**Lowell,** Mass. (1978) 137. Seven mills, canal, 19th C. structures, park to show planned city of Industrial Revolution.

**Lyndon B. Johnson,** Tex. (1969/1980) 1,571. President's birthplace, boyhood home, ranch.

**Marsh-Billings,** Vt. (1992) 550. Boyhood home of George Perkins March.

**Minute Man,** Mass. (1959) 750. Where the colonial Minute Men battled the British, April 19, 1775. Also contains Nathaniel Hawthorne's home.

**Morristown,** N.J. (1933) 1,671. Sites of important military encampments during the Revolutionary War; Washington's headquarters 1777, 1779-80.

**Natchez,** Miss. (1988) 80. Mansions, townhouses, and villas concerning history of Natchez, Miss.

**Nez Perce,** Ida. (1965) 2,109. Illustrates the history and culture of the Nez Perce Indian country. 20 separate sites.

**Pecos,** N.M. (1965/1990) 6,547. Ruins of ancient 15th century Pueblo of Pecos, archeological sites, and 2 associated Spanish colonial missions from the 17th and 18th centuries.

**Pu'uhonua o Honaunau,** Ha. (1955/1978) 182. Until 1819, a sanctuary for Hawaiians vanquished in battle, and those guilty of crimes or breaking taboos.

**Salt River Bay,** St. Croix, V.I. (1922). The only site known where, 500 years ago, members of a Columbus party landed on what is now territory of the U.S.

**San Antonio Missions,** Tex. (1978/1983) 493. Four of finest Spanish missions in U.S., 18th C. irrigation system.

**San Francisco Maritime** (1988) 50. Artifacts, photographs, and historic vessels related to the development of the Pacific Coast.

**San Juan Island,** Wash. (1966) 1,752. Commemorates peaceful relations of the U.S., Canada and Great Britain since the 1872 boundary disputes.

**Saratoga,** N.Y. (1938) 3,393. Scene of a major battle which became a turning point in the War of Independence.

**Sitka,** Alas. (1910/1972) 107. Scene of last major resistance of the Tlingit Indians to the Russians, 1804.

**Tumacacori,** Ariz. (1908/1990) 17. Historic Spanish Catholic mission building stands near the site first visited by Jesuit Father Kino in 1691.

**Valley Forge,** Pa. (1976) 3,468. Continental Army campsite in 1777-78 winter.

**War in the Pacific,** Guam (1978) 1,960. Scenic park memorial for WWII combatants in Pacific.

**Women's Rights,** N.Y. (1980) 6. Seneca Falls site where Susan B. Anthony, Elizabeth Cady Stanton began rights movement in 1848.

**Zuni-Cibola,** N. Mex. (1988) 800. Historical, archeological, and cultural site associated with the Zuni Tribe over its 1700-year cultural continuum.

## National Battlefields

**Antietam,** Md. (1890/1978) 3,244. Battle ended first Confederate invasion of North, Sept. 17, 1862.

**Big Hole,** Mon. (1910/1963) 656. Site of major battle with Nez Perce Indians.

**Cowpens,** S.C. (1929/1972) 842. Revolutionary War battlefield.

**Fort Donelson,** Tenn. (1928/1985) 536. Site of first major Union victory.

**Fort Necessity,** Pa. (1931/1961) 903. First battle of French and Indian War.

**Monocacy,** Md. (1934/1976) 1,647. Civil War battle in defense of Wash., D.C., July 9, 1864.

**Moores Creek,** N.C. (1926/1980) 87. 1776 battle between Patriots and Loyalists commemorated here.

**Petersburg,** Va. (1926/1962) 2,735. Scene of 10-month Union campaign 1864-65.

**Stones River,** Tenn. (1927/1960) 403. Civil War battle leading to Sherman's "March to the Sea."

**Tupelo,** Miss. (1929/1961) 1. Crucial battle over Sherman's supply line.

**Wilson's Creek,** Mo. (1960/1970) 1,750. Civil War battle for control of Missouri.

## National Battlefield Parks

**Kennesaw Mountain,** Ga. (1917/1935) 2,885. Two major battles of Atlanta campaign in Civil War.

**Manassas,** Va. (1940) 5,072. Two battles of Bull Run in Civil War, 1861 and 1862.

**Richmond,** Va. (1936) 769. Site of battles defending Confederate capital.

## National Battlefield Site

**Brices Cross Roads,** Miss. (1929) 1. Civil War battlefield.

## National Military Parks

**Chickamauga and Chattanooga,** Ga.-Tenn. (1890) 8,106. Four Civil War battlefields.

**Fredericksburg and Spotsylvania County,** Va. (1927) 7,688. Sites of several major Civil War battles and campaigns.

**Gettysburg,** Pa. (1895) 3,942. Site of decisive Confederate defeat in North. Gettysburg Address.

**Guilford Courthouse,** N.C. (1917) 220. Revolutionary War battle site.

**Horseshoe Bend,** Ala. (1956) 2,040. On Tallapoosa River, where Gen. Andrew Jackson broke the power of the Creek Indian Confederacy.

**Kings Mountain,** S.C. (1931) 3,945. Revolutionary War battle.

**Pea Ridge,** Ark. (1956) 4,300. Civil War battle.

**Shiloh,** Tenn. (1894) 3,838. Major Civil War battle; site includes some well-preserved Indian burial mounds.

**Vicksburg,** Miss. (1899) 1,620. Union victory gave North control of the Mississippi and split the Confederacy in two.

## National Memorials

**Arkansas Post,** Ark. (1960) 389. First permanent French settlement in the lower Mississippi River valley.

**Arlington House,** the Robert E. Lee Memorial, Va. (1925/1972) 28. Lee's home overlooking the Potomac.

**Chamizal,** El Paso, Tex. (1966/1974) 55. Commemorates 1963 settlement of 99-year border dispute with Mexico.

**Coronado,** Ariz. (1941/1952) 4,750. Commemorates first European exploration of the Southwest.

**DeSoto,** Fla. (1948) 27. Commemorates 16th-century Spanish explorations.

**Federal Hall,** N.Y. (1939/1955) 0.45. First seat of U.S. government under the Constitution.

**Fort Caroline,** Fla. (1950) 138. On St. Johns River, overlooks site of second attempt by French Huguenots to colonize North America.

**Fort Clatsop,** Ore. (1958) 125. Lewis and Clark encampment 1805-06.

**General Grant,** N.Y. (1958) 0.76. Tombs of Pres. and wife.

**Hamilton Grange,** N.Y. (1962) 0.11. Home of Alexander Hamilton.

**John F. Kennedy Center for the Performing Arts,** D.C. (1958/1964) 18.

**Johnstown Flood,** Pa. (1964) 164. Commemorates tragic flood of 1889.

**Lincoln Boyhood,** Ind. (1962) 200. Lincoln grew up here.

**Lincoln Memorial,** D.C. (1911) 110.

**Lyndon B. Johnson Grove on the Potomac,** D.C. (1973) 17.

**Mount Rushmore,** S.D. (1925) 1,278. World famous sculpture of 4 presidents.

**Perry's Victory and International Peace Memorial,** Put-in-Bay, Oh. (1936/1978) 25. The world's most massive Doric column, constructed 1912-15, to inculcate the lessons of international peace by arbitration and disarmament.

**Roger Williams,** R.I. (1965) 5. Memorial to founder of Rhode Island.

**Thaddeus Kosciuszko,** Pa. (1972) 0.02. Memorial to Polish hero of American Revolution.

**Theodore Roosevelt Island,** D.C. (1932) 89.

**Thomas Jefferson Memorial,** D.C. (1934) 18.

**USS Arizona,** Ha. (1980). 00. Memorializes American losses at Pearl Harbor.

**Vietnam Veterans,** D.C. (1980) 2. Black granite wall inscribed with names of killed in action and missing in the Vietnam War.

**Washington Monument,** D.C. (1848) 106.

**Wright Brothers,** N.C. (1927/1953) 431. Site of first powered flight.

## National Historic Sites

**Abraham Lincoln Birthplace,** Hodgenville, Ky. (1916/1959) 117.

**Adams,** Quincy, Mass. (1946/1952) 10. Home of Presidents John Adams, John Quincy Adams, and celebrated descendants.

**Allegheny Portage Railroad,** Pa. (1964) 1,247. Part of the Pennsylvania Canal system.

**Andersonville,** Andersonville, Ga. (1970) 495. Noted Civil War prison.

**Andrew Johnson,** Greeneville, Tenn. (1935/1963) 17. Home of the President.

**Bent's Old Fort,** Col. (1960) 800. Old West fur-trading post.

**Boston African American** (1980) Pre-Civil War black history structures.

**Brown v. Board of Education,** Kan. (1992). Commemorates the landmark 1954 U.S. Supreme Court Decision.

**Carl Sandburg Home,** N.C. (1968/1972) 264. Poet's home.

**Charles Pinckney,** S.C. (1988) 25.

**Christiansted,** St. Croix; V.I. (1952/1961) 27. Commemorates Danish colony.

**Clara Barton,** Md. (1974) 9. Home of founder of American Red Cross.

**Edgar Allan Poe,** Pa. (1978/1980) 1. Poet's home.

**Edison,** West Orange, N.J. (1955/1962) 21. Home and laboratory.

**Eisenhower,** Gettysburg, Pa. (1967/1969) 690. Home of 34th president.

**Eleanor Roosevelt,** Hyde Park, N.Y. (1977) 181. Personal retreat.

**Eugene O'Neill,** Danville, Cal. (1976) 13. Playwright's home.

**Ford's Theatre,** Washington, D.C. (1866/1970) 0.29. Includes theater, now restored, where Lincoln was assassinated, house where he died, and Lincoln Museum.

**Fort Bowie,** Ariz. (1964/1972) 1,000. Focal point of operations against Geronimo and the Apaches.

**Fort Davis,** Tex. (1961/1963) 460. Frontier outpost battled Comanches and Apaches.

**Fort Laramie,** Wy. (1938/1960) 833. Military post on Oregon Trail.

**Fort Larned,** Kan. (1964/1966) 718. Military post on Santa Fe Trail.

**Fort Point,** San Francisco, Cal. (1970) 29. Largest West Coast fortification.

**Fort Raleigh,** N.C. (1941) 157. First English settlement.

**Fort Scott,** Kan. (1965/1978) 17. Commemorates U.S. frontier of 1840-50.

**Fort Smith,** Ark. (1961) 75. Active post from 1817 to 1890.

**Fort Union Trading Post,** Mon., N.D. (1966) 442. Principal fur-trading post on upper Missouri, 1829-1867.

**Fort Vancouver,** Wash. (1948/1961) 209. Hdqts. for Hudson's Bay Company in 1825. Early military and political seat.

**Frederick Douglass Home,** D.C. (1962/1988) 9. Home of nation's leading black spokesman.

**Frederick Law Olmsted,** Mass. (1979) 2. Home of famous park planner (1822-1903).

**Friendship Hill,** Pa. (1978) 675. Home of Albert Gallatin, Jefferson's Sec'y of Treasury. Not open to public.

**Golden Spike,** Utah (1957) 2,735. Commemorates completion of first transcontinental railroad in 1869.

**Grant-Kohrs Ranch,** Mon. (1972) 1,498. Ranch house and part of 19th-century ranch.

**Hampton,** Md. (1948) 62. 18th-century Georgian mansion.

**Harry S. Truman,** Mo. (1983). 0.78. Home of Pres. Truman after 1919.

**Herbert Hoover,** West Branch, Ia. (1965) 187. Birthplace and boyhood home of 31st president.

**Home of Franklin D. Roosevelt,** Hyde Park, N.Y. (1944) 290. Birthplace, home and "Summer White House".

**Hopewell Furnace,** Pa. (1938/1985) 848. 19th-century iron making village.

**Hubbell Trading Post,** Ariz. (1965) 160. Indian trading post.

**James A. Garfield,** Mentor, Oh. (1980) 8. President's home.

**Jefferson National Expansion Memorial,** St. Louis, Mo. (1935/1969) 191. Commemorates westward expansion.

**Jimmy Carter,** Ga. (1987) 70. Birthplace and home of 39th president.

**John Fitzgerald Kennedy,** Brookline, Mass. (1967) 0.09. Birthplace and childhood home of the President.

**John Muir,** Martinez, Cal. (1964) 340. Home of early conservationist and writer.

**Knife River Indian Villages,** N.D. (1974) 1,293. Remnants of 5 Hidatsa villages.

**Lincoln Home,** Springfield, Ill. (1971) 12. Lincoln's residence when he was elected President, 1860.

**Longfellow,** Cambridge, Mass. (1972) 2. Longfellow's home, 1837-82, and Washington's hq. during Boston Siege, 1775-76.

**Maggie L. Walker,** Va. (1978) 1. Richmond home of black leader and 1903 founder of bank.

**Manzanar,** Lone Pine, Cal. (1992) 640. Commemorates Manzanar War Relocation Ctr., a Japanese-American internment camp during WWII.

**Martin Luther King, Jr.,** Atlanta, Ga. (1980) 23. Birthplace, grave.

**Martin Van Buren,** N.Y. (1974) 40. Lindenwald, home of 8th president, near Kinderhook.

**Mary McLeod Bethune Council House,** D.C. (1991). Museum dedicated to the lives and achievements of black American women.

**Ninety Six,** S.C. (1976) 989. Colonial trading village.

**Palo Alto Battlefield,** Tex. (1978) 50. One of 2 Mexican War battles fought in U.S.

**Pennsylvania Avenue,** D.C. (1965) NA. Includes area between Capitol and White House, Ford's Theatre.

**Puukohola Heiau,** Ha. (1972) 80. Ruins of temple built by King Kamehameha.

**Sagamore Hill,** Oyster Bay, N.Y. (1962) 83. Home of President Theodore Roosevelt from 1885 until his death in 1919.

**Saint-Gaudens,** Cornish, N.H. (1964/1977) 148. Home, studio and gardens of American sculptor Augustus Saint-Gaudens.

**Saint Paul's Church,** N.Y. (1943/1978) 6. 18th-century site of John Peter Zenger's "freedom of press" trial.

**Salem Maritime,** Mass. (1938) 9. Only port never seized from the patriots by the British. Major fishing and whaling port.

**San Juan,** P.R. (1949) 75. 16th-century Spanish fortifications.

**Saugus Iron Works,** Mass. (1968) 9. Reconstructed 17th-century colonial ironworks.

**Springfield Armory,** Mass. (1974) 55. Small arms manufacturing center for nearly 200 years.

**Steamtown,** Pa. (1986) 44. Railyard, roadhouse and repair shops of former Delaware, Lackawanna and Western Railroad.

**Theodore Roosevelt Birthplace,** N.Y., N.Y. (1962) 0.11.

**Theodore Roosevelt Inaugural,** Buffalo, N.Y. (1966) 1. Wilcox House where he took oath of office, 1901.

**Thomas Stone,** Md. (1978) 328. Home of signer of Declaration, built in 1771. Not open to public.

**Tuskegee Institute,** Ala. (1974) 68. College founded by Booker T. Washington in 1881 for blacks.

**Ulysses S. Grant,** St. Louis Co., Mo. (1989) 10. Home of Grant during pre-Civil War years.

**Vanderbilt Mansion,** Hyde Park, N.Y. (1940) 212. Mansion of 19th-century financier.

**Weir Farm,** Witon, Conn. (1990) 62. Home and studios of American Impressionist painter J. Alden Weir.

**Whitman Mission,** Wash. (1936/1963) 98. Site where Dr. and Mrs. Marcus Whitman ministered to the Indians until slain by them in 1847.

**William Howard Taft,** Cincinnati, Oh. (1969) 3. Birthplace and early home of the 27th president.

## National Monuments

| Name | State | Year | Acreage |
|---|---|---|---|
| Agate Fossil Beds | Neb. | 1965 | 3,055 |
| Alibates Flint Quarries | N.M.-Tex. | 1965 | 1,371 |
| Aniakchak | Alas. | 1978 | 17 |
| Aztec Ruins | N.M. | 1923 | 319 |
| Bandelier | N.M. | 1916 | 32,737 |
| Black Canyon of the Gunnison | Col. | 1933 | 20,766 |
| Booker T. Washington | Va. | 1956 | 224 |
| Buck Island Reef | V.I. | 1961 | 880 |
| Cabrillo | Cal. | 1913 | 137 |
| Canyon de Chelly | Ariz. | 1931 | 83,840 |
| Cape Krusenstern | Alas. | 1978 | 659,807 |
| Capulin Volcano | N.M. | 1916 | 793 |
| Casa Grande Ruins | Ariz. | 1892 | 473 |
| Castillo de San Marcos | Fla. | 1924 | 20 |
| Castle Clinton | N.Y. | 1946 | 1 |
| Cedar Breaks | Ut. | 1933 | 6,155 |
| Chiricahua | Ariz. | 1924 | 11,985 |
| Colorado | Col. | 1911 | 20,454 |
| Congaree Swamp | S.C. | 1976 | 22,200 |
| Craters of the Moon | Ida. | 1924 | 53,545 |
| Death Valley | Cal.-Nev. | 1933 | 2,067,628 |
| Devils Postpile | Cal. | 1911 | 798 |
| Devils Tower | Wy. | 1906 | 1,347 |
| Dinosaur | Col.-Ut. | 1915 | 210,844 |
| Effigy Mounds | Ia. | 1949 | 1,481 |
| El Malpais | N.M. | 1987 | 114,335 |
| El Morro | N.M. | 1906 | 1,279 |
| Florissant Fossil Beds** | Col. | 1969 | 5,998 |
| Fort Frederica | Ga. | 1936 | 216 |
| Fort Matanzas | Fla. | 1924 | 228 |
| Fort McHenry National Monument and Historic Shrine | Md. | 1925 | 43 |
| Fort Pulaski | Ga. | 1924 | 5,623 |
| Fort Stanwix | N.Y. | 1935 | 16 |
| Fort Sumter | S.C. | 1948 | 194 |
| Fort Union | N.M. | 1954 | 721 |
| Fossil Butte | Wy. | 1972 | 8,198 |
| G. Washington Birthplace | Va. | 1930 | 533 |
| George Washington Carver | Mo. | 1943 | 210 |
| Gila Cliff Dwellings | N.M. | 1907 | 533 |
| Grand Portage | Minn. | 1951 | 710 |
| Great Sand Dunes | Col. | 1932 | 38,662 |
| Hagerman Fossil Beds | Ida. | 1988 | 4,280 |
| Hohokam Pima* | Ariz. | 1972 | 1,690 |
| Homestead Nat'l. Monument of America | Neb. | 1936 | 195 |
| Hovenweep | Col.-Ut. | 1923 | 785 |
| Jewel Cave | S.D. | 1908 | 1,274 |
| John Day Fossil Beds | Ore. | 1974 | 14,014 |
| Joshua Tree | Cal. | 1936 | 559,955 |
| Lava Beds | Cal. | 1925 | 46,560 |
| Little Big Horn Battlefield | Mon. | 1879 | 765 |
| Montezuma Castle | Ariz. | 1906 | 858 |
| Muir Woods | Cal. | 1908 | 554 |
| Natural Bridges | Ut. | 1908 | 7,636 |
| Navajo | Ariz. | 1909 | 360 |
| Ocmulgee | Ga. | 1934 | 683 |
| Oregon Caves | Ore. | 1909 | 488 |
| Organ Pipe Cactus | Ariz. | 1937 | 330,689 |
| Petroglyph | N.M. | 1990 | 5,207 |
| Pinnacles | Cal. | 1908 | 16,265 |
| Pipe Spring | Ariz. | 1923 | 40 |

| Name | State | Year | Acreage |
|------|-------|------|---------|
| Pipestone | Minn. | 1937 | 282 |
| Poverty Point | La. | 1988 | 911 |
| Rainbow Bridge | Ut. | 1910 | 160 |
| Russell Cave | Ala. | 1961 | 310 |
| Saguaro | Ariz. | 1933 | 83,574 |
| Salinas | N.M. | 1909 | 1,077 |
| Scotts Bluff | Neb. | 1919 | 2,997 |
| Statue of Liberty | N.J.-N.Y. | 1924 | 58 |
| Sunset Crater | Ariz. | 1930 | 3,040 |
| Timpanogos Cave | Ut. | 1922 | 250 |
| Tonto | Ariz. | 1907 | 1,120 |
| Tuzigoot | Ariz. | 1939 | 801 |
| Walnut Canyon | Ariz. | 1915 | 2,249 |
| White Sands | N.M. | 1933 | 143,733 |
| Wupatki | Ariz. | 1924 | 35,253 |
| Yucca House* | Col. | 1919 | 10 |

## National Preserves

| Name | State | Year | Acreage |
|------|-------|------|---------|
| Aniakchak | Alas. | 1978 | 465,603 |
| Bering Land Bridge | Alas. | 1978 | 2,784,960 |
| Big Cypress | Fla. | 1974 | 716,000 |
| Big Thicket | Tex. | 1974 | 85,736 |
| Denali | Alas. | 1917 | 1,311,365 |
| Gates of the Arctic | Alas. | 1978 | 948,629 |
| Glacier Bay | Alas. | 1925 | 57,884 |
| Katmai | Alas. | 1918 | 374,000 |
| Lake Clark | Alas. | 1978 | 1,407,293 |
| Little River Canyon | Ala. | 1992 | NA |
| Noatak | Alas. | 1978 | 6,574,481 |
| Timucuan Ecological & Historic Preserve | Fla. | 1988 | 46,000 |
| Wrangell-St. Elias | Alas. | 1978 | 4,856,721 |
| Yukon-Charley Rivers | Alas. | 1978 | 2,523,509 |

## National Seashores

| Name | State | Year | Acreage |
|------|-------|------|---------|
| Assateague Island | Md.-Va. | 1965 | 39,631 |
| Canaveral | Fla. | 1975 | 57,662 |
| Cape Cod | Mass. | 1961 | 43,558 |
| Cape Hatteras | N.C. | 1937 | 30,319 |
| Cape Lookout** | N.C. | 1966 | 28,243 |
| Cumberland Island | Ga. | 1972 | 36,415 |
| Fire Island | N.Y. | 1964 | 19,579 |
| Gulf Islands | Fla.-Miss. | 1971 | 135,618 |
| Padre Island | Tex. | 1962 | 130,434 |
| Point Reyes | Cal. | 1962 | 71,050 |

## National Parkways

| Name | State | Year | Acreage |
|------|-------|------|---------|
| Blue Ridge | Va.-N.C. | 1936 | 86,941 |
| George Washington Memorial | Va.-Md. | 1930 | 7,159 |
| John D. Rockefeller Jr. Mem. | Wy. | 1972 | 23,777 |
| Natchez Trace | Ala.-Miss.-Tenn. | 1938 | 51,742 |

## National Lakeshores

| Name | State | Year | Acreage |
|------|-------|------|---------|
| Apostle Islands | Wis. | 1970 | 69,372 |
| Indiana Dunes | Ind. | 1966 | 13,845 |
| Pictured Rocks | Mich. | 1966 | 72,903 |
| Sleeping Bear Dunes | Mich. | 1970 | 71,188 |

## National Reserve

| Name | State | Year | Acreage |
|------|-------|------|---------|
| City of Rocks | Ida. | 1988 | 14,407 |

| Name | State | Year | Acreage |
|------|-------|------|---------|
| Ebeys Landing | Wash. | 1992 | 8,000 |

## National Rivers

| Name | State | Year | Acreage |
|------|-------|------|---------|
| Big South Fork Natl. R. and Recreation | Tenn.-Ky. | 1976 | 122,960 |
| Buffalo | Ark. | 1972 | 94,219 |
| New River Gorge | W.Va. | 1978 | 62,144 |
| Ozark | Mo. | 1964 | 80,791 |
| Mississippi Natl. R. and Recreation | Minn. | 1988 | 50,000 |
| Niobrara/Missouri | Neb.-S.D. | 1991 | 76 |

## National Wild and Scenic Rivers

| Name | State | Year | Acreage |
|------|-------|------|---------|
| Alagnak Wild | Alas. | 1980 | 24,038 |
| Bluestone | W.Va. | 1988 | N.A. |
| Delaware | N.Y.-N.J.-Pa. | 1978 | 1,973 |
| Great Egg Harbor | N.J. | 1992 | NA |
| Obed Wild | Tenn. | 1976 | 5,075 |
| Rio Grande | Tex. | 1978 | 9,600 |
| Saint Croix | Minn.-Wis. | 1968 | 67,379 |
| Upper Delaware | N.Y.-N.J. | 1978 | 75,000 |

## Parks (no other classification)

| Name | State | Year | Acreage |
|------|-------|------|---------|
| Catoctin Mountain | Md. | 1954 | 5,770 |
| Constitution Gardens | D.C. | 1978 | 52 |
| Fort Washington | Md. | 1930 | 341 |
| Greenbelt | Md. | 1950 | 1,176 |
| National Capital | D.C. | 1992 | 6,524 |
| Piscataway | Md. | 1961 | 4,263 |
| Prince William Forest | Va. | 1948 | 18,572 |
| Rock Creek | D.C. | 1890 | 1,754 |
| White House | D.C. | 1992 | 18 |
| Wolf Trap Farm Park for the Performing Arts | Va. | 1966 | 130 |

## National Recreation Areas

| Name | State | Year | Acreage |
|------|-------|------|---------|
| Amistad | Tex. | 1965 | 57,292 |
| Bighorn Canyon | Mon.-Wy. | 1966 | 120,296 |
| Chattahoochee R. | Ga. | 1978 | 9,257 |
| Chickasaw | Okla. | 1902 | 9,522 |
| Coulee Dam | Wash. | 1946 | 100,390 |
| Curecanti | Col. | 1965 | 42,114 |
| Cuyahoga Valley | Oh. | 1974 | 32,525 |
| Delaware Water Gap | N.J.-Pa. | 1965 | 66,652 |
| Gateway | N.Y.-N.J. | 1972 | 26,311 |
| Gauley R. | W.Va. | 1988 | 10,300 |
| Glen Canyon | Ariz.-Ut. | 1958 | 1,236,880 |
| Golden Gate | Cal. | 1972 | 73,122 |
| Lake Chelan | Wash. | 1968 | 61,883 |
| Lake Mead | Ariz.-Nev. | 1936 | 1,495,666 |
| Lake Meredith | Tex. | 1965 | 44,978 |
| Ross Lake | Wash. | 1968 | 117,575 |
| Santa Monica Mts. | Cal. | 1978 | 150,050 |
| Whiskeytown | Cal. | 1965 | 42,503 |

## National Mall

| Name | State | Year | Acreage |
|------|-------|------|---------|
| | D.C. | 1933 | 146 |

## National Scenic Trails

| Name | State | Year | Acreage |
|------|-------|------|---------|
| Appalachian | Me. to Ga. | 1968 | 161,382 |
| Natchez Trace | Ala.-Miss.-Tenn. | 1983 | 10,995 |
| Potomac Heritage | Md.-D.C.-Va.-Pa. | 1983 | *** |

## International Historic Sites

| Name | State | Year | Acreage |
|------|-------|------|---------|
| Saint Croix Island | Me. | 1949 | 35 |

* Not open to the public. ** No federal facilities. *** Undetermined.

## National Park Service Recreation Visits in 1991

Source: National Park Service

| Park | Recreation Visits | Park | Recreation Visits |
|------|-------------------|------|-------------------|
| Blue Ridge Parkway | 16,414,294 | Gateway Natl. Recreation Area | 6,643,921 |
| Golden Gate Natl. Recreation Area | 14,650,213 | Natchez Trace Parkway | 5,832,697 |
| Lake Mead Natl. Recreation Area | 8,445,016 | Cape Cod Natl. Seashore | 5,442,379 |
| Great Smoky Mountains Natl. Park | 8,654,459 | George Washington Memorial Parkway | 5,004,736 |

Attendance at all areas administered by the National Park Service in 1991 was 267,419,196 recreation visits.

## Federal Indian Reservations and Trust Lands[1]

Source: Bureau of Indian Affairs, U.S. Dept. of the Interior (data as of 1990)

The total American Indian population according to the 1990 Census is 1,878,285.

| State | No of Reser. | Tribally-owned acreage[2] | Individually-owned acreage[2] | No. of persons[3] | Major tribes and/or nations |
|---|---|---|---|---|---|
| Alabama . . . . . | 1 | 230 | 0 | 16,504 | Poarch Creek |
| Alaska . . . . . | 1[4] | 86,773 | 1,265,432 | 85,698 | Aleut, Eskimo, Athapascan,[5] Haida, Tlingit, Tsimpshian |
| Arkansas . . . . . | 1 | 0 | 2.78 | — | unknown |
| Arizona. . . . . . | 23 | 19,775,959 | 311,579 | 203,527 | Navajo, Apache, Papago, Hopi, Yavapai, Pima |
| California. . . . . | 96 | 520,049 | 66,769 | 242,164 | Hoopa, Paiute, Yurok, Karok, Cherokee |
| Colorado . . . . . | 2 | 764,120 | 2,805 | 27,776 | Ute |
| Connecticut . . . | 1 | 1,638 | 0 | 6,654 | Mashantucket Pequot |
| Florida . . . . . . | 4 | 153,874 | 0 | 36,335 | Seminole, Miccosukee, Cherokee |
| Idaho . . . . . . . | 4 | 609,622 | 327,301 | 13,780 | Shoshone, Bannock, Nez Perce |
| Iowa . . . . . . . | 1 | 3,550 | 0 | 7,349 | Sac and Fox |
| Kansas . . . . . | 4 | 7,219 | 23,763 | 21,965 | Potawatomi, Kickapoo, Iowa |
| Louisiana. . . . . | 3 | 415 | 0 | 18,541 | Chitimacha, Coushatta, Tunica-Biloxi |
| Maine. . . . . . | 3 | 191,511 | 0 | 5,998 | Passamaquoddy, Penobscot, Maliseet |
| Massachusetts . . | 1 | 157 | 0 | — | Wampanoag |
| Michigan . . . . . | 8 | 14,411 | 9,276 | 55,638 | Chippewa, Potawatomi, Ottawa, Cherokee |
| Minnesota . . . . | 14 | 779,138 | 50,338 | 49,909 | Chippewa, Sioux |
| Mississippi . . . . | 1 | 20,486 | 0 | 8,825 | Choctaw |
| Missouri . . . . . | 1 | 0 | 374.37 | — | Cherokee |
| Montana . . . . . | 7 | 2,663,385 | 2,911,450 | 47,679 | Blackfeet, Crow, Sioux, Assiniboine, Cheyenne |
| Nebraska. . . . . | 3 | 23,792 | 43,208 | 12,410 | Omaha, Winnebago, Santee Sioux |
| Nevada. . . . . . | 19 | 1,147,088 | 78,529 | 19,637 | Paiute, Shoshone, Washoe |
| New Mexico . . . | 25 | 7,252,326 | 630,293 | 134,355 | Zuni, Apache, Navajo |
| New York . . . . | 8 | 118,199 | 0 | 62,651 | Seneca, Mohawk, Onondaga, Oneida |
| North Carolina . | 1 | 56,509 | 0 | 80,155 | Cherokee, Lumbee |
| North Dakota . . | 3 | 214,006 | 627,289 | 25,917 | Sioux, Chippewa, Mandan, Arikara, Hidatsa |
| Oklahoma . . . . | 1[6] | 96,839 | 1,000,165 | 252,420 | Cherokee, Creek, Choctaw, Chickasaw, Osage, Cheyenne, Arapahoe, Kiowa, Comanche |
| Oregon . . . . . | 7 | 660,367 | 135,053 | 38,496 | Warm Springs, Wasco, Paiute, Umatilla, Siletz |
| Rhode Island. . . | 1 | 1,800 | 0 | 4,071 | Narragansett |
| South Dakota . . | 9 | 2,399,531 | 2,121,188 | 50,573 | Sioux |
| Texas . . . . . . . | 3 | 4,726 | 0 | 65,877 | Alabama-Coushatta, Tiwa, Kickapoo |
| Utah . . . . . . . | 4 | 2,286,448 | 32,838 | 24,283 | Ute, Goshute, Southern Paiute, Navajo |
| Washington . . . | 27 | 2,250,731 | 467,785 | 81,483 | Yakima, Lummi, Quinault, Sioux |
| Wisconsin . . . | 11 | 338,097 | 80,345 | 39,387 | Chippewa, Oneida, Winnebago |
| Wyoming. . . . . | 1 | 1,958,095 | 101,537 | 9,479 | Shoshone, Arapahoe |

(1) As of 1988 the federal government recognized and acknowledged that it had a special relationship with, and a trust responsibility for, 307 federally recognized Indian entities in the continental U.S., plus some 200 tribal entities in Alaska. The term "Indian entities" encompasses Indian tribes, bands, villages, groups, pueblos, Eskimos, and Aleuts, eligible for federal services and classified in the following 3 categories: (a) Officially approved Indian organizations pursuant to federal statutory authority (Indian Reorganization Act; Oklahoma Indian Welfare Act and Alaska Native Act.) (b) Officially approved Indian organizations outside of specified federal statutory authority. (c) Traditional Indian organizations recognized without formal federal approval of organizational structure. Some reservation boundaries transcend state boundaries (e.g., Navajo which is in Arizona, New Mexico, and Utah). For statistical convenience under "Number of Reservations," such reservations are counted in the state where population is predominant and/or tribal headquarters is located. (2) The acreages refer only to Indian lands which are either owned by the tribes or individual Indians, and held in trust by the U.S. government. Many of these parcels are located off reservations. Not all lands within reservation boundaries are necessarily trust lands. Many parcels are privately-owned by tribes, individual Indians, and non-Indians. Also, some internal lands are the property of various governmental agencies. (3) Total Indian population in each state with reservation/trust area, including those persons living outside of the BIA Service area. (4) Alaskan Indian Affairs are carried out under the Alaska Native Claims Settlement Act (Dec. 18, 1971). The Act provided for the establishment of regional and village corporations to conduct business for profit and non-profit purposes. There are 13 such regional corporations, each one with organized village corporations. The Annette Island Reservation remains the only federally recognized reservation in Alaska in the sense of specific reservation boundaries, trust lands, etc. (5) Aleuts and Eskimos are racially and linguistically related. Athapascans are related to the Navajo and Apache Indians. (6) Indian land status in Oklahoma is unique and there are no reservations except for Osage in the sense that the term is used elsewhere in the U.S. Likewise, many of the Oklahoma tribes are unique in their high degree of assimilation to the white culture.

## American Indian Population: States Without Federal Reservations and Trust Lands

Source: Bureau of the Census, U.S. Dept. of Commerce, 1990 Census

| State | No. of Persons | State | No. of Persons | State | No. of Persons |
|---|---|---|---|---|---|
| Arkansas . . . . . . . . . . | 12,773 | Kentucky . . . . . . . . . . | 5,769 | Pennsylvania . . . . . . . . | 14,733 |
| Delaware . . . . . . . . . | 2,019 | Maryland . . . . . . . . . | 12,972 | South Carolina . . . . . . . | 8,246 |
| District of Columbia . . . | 1,466 | Massachusetts . . . . . . . | 12,241 | Tennessee . . . . . . . . . | 10,039 |
| Georgia . . . . . . . . . . | 13,348 | Missouri . . . . . . . . . . | 19,835 | Vermont . . . . . . . . . . | 1,696 |
| Hawaii . . . . . . . . . . | 5,099 | New Hampshire . . . . . . . | 2,134 | Virginia . . . . . . . . . . | 15,282 |
| Illinois . . . . . . . . . . | 21,836 | New Jersey . . . . . . . . . | 14,970 | West Virginia . . . . . . . | 2,458 |
| Indiana . . . . . . . . . . | 12,972 | Ohio . . . . . . . . . . . | 20,358 | | |

# UNITED STATES HISTORY

**1492**

Christopher Columbus and crew sighted land Oct. 12 in the present-day Bahamas.

**1497**

John Cabot explored northeast coast to Delaware.

**1513**

Juan Ponce de León explored Florida coast.

**1524**

Giovanni da Verrazano led French expedition along coast from Carolina north to Nova Scotia; entered New York harbor.

**1539**

Hernando de Soto landed in Florida May 28; crossed Mississippi River, 1541.

**1540**

Francisco Vásquez de Coronado explored Southwest north of Rio Grande. Hernando de Alarcón reached Colorado River, Don Garcia Lopez de Cardenas reached Grand Canyon. Others explored California coast.

**1565**

St. Augustine, Fla. founded by Pedro Menéndez. Razed by Francis Drake 1586.

**1579**

Francis Drake entered San Francisco Bay and claimed region for Britain.

**1607**

Capt. John Smith and 105 cavaliers in 3 ships landed on Virginia coast, started first permanent English settlement in New World at Jamestown in May.

**1609**

Henry Hudson, English explorer of Northwest Passage, employed by Dutch, sailed into New York harbor in Sept., and up Hudson to Albany. The same year, Samuel de Champlain explored Lake Champlain just to the north.

Spaniards settled Santa Fe, N.M.

**1619**

House of Burgesses, first representative assembly in New World, elected July 30 at Jamestown, Va.

First black laborers — indentured servants — in English N. American colonies, landed by Dutch at Jamestown in Aug. Chattel slavery legally recognized, 1650.

**1620**

Plymouth Pilgrims, Puritan separatists from Church of England, some living in Holland, left Plymouth, England Sept. 16 on Mayflower. Original destination Virginia, they reached Cape Cod Nov. 19, explored coast; 103 passengers landed Dec. 26 at Plymouth. Mayflower Compact was agreement to form a government and abide by its laws. Half of colony died during harsh winter.

**1624**

Dutch colonies started in Albany and in New York area, where New Netherland was established in May.

**1626**

Peter Minuit bought Manhattan for Dutch from Man-a-hat-a Indians during summer for goods valued at $24; named island New Amsterdam.

**1630**

Settlement of Boston established by Mass. colonists led by John Winthrop.

**1634**

Maryland founded as Catholic colony with religious tolerance.

**1636**

Roger Williams founded Providence, R.I., June, as a democratically ruled colony with separation of church and state. Charter was granted, 1644.

Harvard College founded Oct. 28, now oldest in U.S.; Grammar school, compulsory education established at Boston.

**1654**

First Jews arrived in New Amsterdam.

**1660**

British Parliament passed Navigation Act, regulating colonial commerce to suit English needs.

**1664**

Three hundred British troops Sept. 8 seized New Netherland from Dutch, who yield peacefully. Charles II granted province of New Netherland and city of New Amsterdam to brother, Duke of York; both renamed New York. The Dutch recaptured the colony Aug. 9, 1673, but ceded it to Britain Nov. 10, 1674.

**1676**

Nathaniel Bacon led planters against autocratic British Gov. Berkeley, burned Jamestown, Va. Bacon died, 23 followers executed.

Bloody Indian war in New England ended Aug. 12, King Philip, Wampanoag chief, and many Narragansett Indians killed.

**1682**

Robert Cavelier, Sieur de La Salle, claimed lower Mississippi River country for France, called it Louisiana Apr. 9. Had French outposts built in Illinois and Texas, 1684. Killed during mutiny Mar. 19, 1687.

**1683**

William Penn signed treaty with Delaware Indians and made payment for Pennsylvania lands.

**1692**

Witchcraft delusion at Salem, Mass.; 20 executed by special court.

**1696**

Capt. William Kidd, who was born in Scotland and settled in America, was hired by British to fight pirates and take booty, but himself became a pirate. Arrested and sent to England, he was hanged 1701.

**1699**

French settlements made in Mississippi, Louisiana.

**1704**

Indians attacked Deerfield, Mass. Feb. 28-29, killed 40, carried off 100.

*Boston News Letter,* first regular newspaper, started by John Campbell, postmaster. (*Publick Occurences* was suppressed after one issue 1690.)

**1709**

British-Colonial troops captured French fort, Port Royal, Nova Scotia, in Queen Anne's War 1701-13. France yielded Nova Scotia by treaty 1713.

**1712**

Slaves revolted in New York Apr. 6. Six committed suicide, 21 were executed. Second rising, 1741; 13 slaves hanged, 13 burned, 71 deported.

**1716**

First theater in colonies opened in Williamsburg, Va.

**1732**

Benjamin Franklin published first *Poor Richard's Almanac;* published annually to 1757.

**1735**

Freedom of the press recognized in New York by acquittal of John Peter Zenger, editor of *Weekly Journal,* on charge of libeling British Gov. Cosby by criticizing his conduct in office.

**1740-41**

Capt. Vitus Bering, Dane employed by Russians, reached Alaska.

**1744**

King George's War pitted British and colonials vs. French. Colonials captured Louisburg, Cape Breton Is. June 17, 1745. Returned to France 1748 by Treaty of Aix-la-Chapelle.

**1752**

Benjamin Franklin, flying kite in thunderstorm, proved lightning is electricity June 15; invented lightning rod.

**1754**

French and Indian War (in Europe called 7 Years War, started 1756) began when French occupied Ft. Duquesne (Pittsburgh). British moved Acadian French from Nova Scotia to Louisiana Oct. 8, 1755. British captured Québec Sept. 18, 1759 in battles in which French Gen. Montcalm and British Gen. Wolfe were killed. Peace signed Feb. 10, 1763.

French lost Canada and American Midwest. British tightened colonial administration in North America.

**1764**

**Sugar Act** placed duties on lumber, foodstuffs, molasses and rum in colonies, to pay French and Indian War debts.

**1765**

**Stamp Act** required revenue stamps to help defray cost of royal troops. Nine colonies, led by New York and Massachusetts at Stamp Act Congress in New York **Oct. 7-25, 1765**, adopted Declaration of Rights opposing taxation, without representation in Parliament and trial without jury by admiralty courts. Stamp Act **repealed Mar. 17, 1766.**

**1767**

**Townshend Acts** levied taxes on glass, painter's lead, paper, and tea. In 1770 all duties except on tea were repealed.

**1770**

British troops fired **Mar. 5** into Boston mob, killed 5 including **Crispus Attucks**, a black man, reportedly leader of group; later called **Boston Massacre.**

**1773**

**East India Co. tea ships** turned back at Boston, New York, Philadelphia in **May.** Cargo ship burned at Annapolis **Oct. 14,** cargo thrown overboard at **Boston Tea Party Dec. 16,** to protest the Tea Act.

**1774**

**"Intolerable Acts"** of Parliament curtailed Massachusetts self-rule; barred use of Boston harbor till tea was paid for.

**First Continental Congress** held in Philadelphia **Sept. 5-Oct. 26;** protested British measures, called for civil disobedience.

**Rhode Island** abolished slavery.

**1775**

**Patrick Henry** addressed Virginia convention, **Mar. 23** said "Give me liberty or give me death."

**Paul Revere** and William Dawes on night of **Apr. 18** rode to alert patriots that British were on way to Concord to destroy arms. At Lexington, Mass. **Apr. 19** Minutemen lost 8. On return from Concord British took 273 casualties.

Col. **Ethan Allen** (joined by Col. Benedict Arnold) captured **Ft. Ticonderoga, N.Y. May 10;** also Crown Point. Colonials headed for **Bunker Hill,** fortified Breed's Hill, Charlestown, Mass., repulsed British under Gen. William Howe twice before retreating **June 17;** British casualties 1,000; called Battle of Bunker Hill. Continental Congress **June 15** named **George Washington** commander-in-chief.

**1776**

**France** and **Spain** each agreed **May 2** to provide one million livres in arms to Americans.

In Continental Congress **June 7,** Richard Henry Lee (Va.) moved "that these united colonies are and of right ought to be free and independent states." Resolution adopted **July 2. Declaration of Independence** approved **July 4.**

Col. Moultrie's batteries at Charleston, S.C. repulsed British sea attack **June 28.**

Washington, with 10,000 men, lost **Battle of Long Island Aug. 27,** evacuated New York.

**Nathan Hale** executed as spy by British **Sept. 22.**

Brig. Gen. Arnold's **Lake Champlain** fleet was defeated at Valcour **Oct. 11,** but British returned to Canada. Howe failed to destroy Washington's army at **White Plains Oct. 28.** Hessians captured Ft. Washington, Manhattan, and 3,000 men **Nov. 16;** Ft. Lee, N.J. **Nov. 18.**

Washington in Pennsylvania, recrossed **Delaware River Dec. 25-26,** defeated 1,400 Hessians at Trenton, N.J. **Dec. 26.**

**1777**

Washington defeated Lord Cornwallis at **Princeton Jan. 3.** Continental Congress adopted Stars and Stripes. *See Flag article.*

Maj. Gen. John Burgoyne with 8,000 from Canada captured **Ft. Ticonderoga July 6.** Americans beat back Burgoyne at Bemis Heights **Oct. 7** and cut off British escape route. Burgoyne surrendered 5,000 men at **Saratoga N.Y. Oct. 17.**

**Marquis de Lafayette,** aged 20, made major general.

**Articles of Confederation** and Perpetual Union adopted by Continental Congress **Nov. 15**

**France** recognized independence of 13 colonies **Dec. 17.**

**1778**

**France** signed treaty of aid with U.S. **Feb. 6.** Sent fleet; British evacuated Philadelphia in consequence **June 18.**

**1779**

**John Paul Jones** on the *Bonhomme Richard* defeated *Serapis* in British North Sea waters **Sept. 23.**

**1780**

**Charleston, S.C.** fell to the British **May 12,** but a British force was defeated near **Kings Mountain, N.C. Oct. 7** by militiamen.

**Benedict Arnold** found to be a traitor **Sept. 23.** Arnold escaped, made brigadier general in British army.

**1781**

**Bank of North America** incorporated in Philadelphia **May 26.**

**Cornwallis,** sapped by patriot victories, retired to **Yorktown, Va. Adm.** De Grasse landed 3,000 French and stopped British fleet in Hampton Roads. Washington and Rochambeau joined forces, arrived near Williamsburg **Sept. 26.** When siege of Cornwallis began **Oct. 6,** British had 6,000, Americans 8,846, French 7,800. **Cornwallis surrendered Oct. 19.**

**1782**

**New British cabinet** agreed in **March** to recognize U.S. independence. Preliminary agreement signed in Paris **Nov. 30.**

**1783**

**Massachusetts Supreme Court outlawed slavery** in that state, noting the words in the state Bill of Rights "all men are born free and equal."

Britain, U.S. signed **peace treaty Sept. 3** (Congress ratified it **Jan. 14, 1784**).

**Washington** ordered army disbanded **Nov. 3,** bade farewell to his officers at Fraunces Tavern, N.Y. City **Dec. 4.**

**Noah Webster** published *American Spelling Book,* great bestseller.

**1784**

**Jefferson's** proposal to **ban slavery** in new territory after 1802 is narrowly defeated **Mar. 1.**

First successful daily newspaper, **Pennsylvania Packet & General Advertiser,** published **Sept. 21.**

**1786**

Delegates from 5 states at **Annapolis, Md. Sept. 11-14** asked Congress to call convention in Philadelphia to write practical constitution for the 13 states.

**1787**

**Shays's Rebellion,** of debt-ridden farmers in Massachusetts, failed **Jan. 25.**

**Northwest Ordinance** adopted **July 13** by Continental Congress. Determined government of Northwest Territory north of Ohio River, west of New York; 60,000 inhabitants could get statehood. Guaranteed freedom of religion, support for schools, no slavery.

**Constitutional convention** opened at Philadelphia **May 25** with George Washington presiding. Constitution adopted by delegates **Sept. 17;** ratification by 9th state, New Hampshire, **June 21, 1788,** meant adoption; declared in effect **Mar. 4, 1789.**

**1789**

**George Washington** chosen president by all electors voting (73 eligible, 69 voting, 4 absent); John Adams, vice president, 34 votes. **Feb. 4.** First Congress met at Federal Hall, N.Y. City; regular sessions began **Apr. 6.** Washington inaugurated there **Apr. 30.** Supreme Court created by Federal Judiciary Act **Sept. 24.** Congress submitted Bill of Rights to states **Sept. 25.**

**1790**

Congress passed **Census Act Mar. 1; Naturalization Act** (2-year residency) **Mar. 26.**

Congress met in Phila. **Dec. 6,** new temporary Capital.

## 1791
Bill of Rights went into effect **Dec. 15.**

## 1792
Coinage Act established U.S. Mint in Philadelphia **Apr. 2.**

Gen. "Mad" Anthony Wayne made commander in Ohio-Indiana area, trained "American Legion"; established string of forts. Routed Indians at Fallen Timbers on Maumee River Aug. 20, 1794, checked British at Fort Miami, Ohio.

White House cornerstone laid **Oct. 13.**

## 1793
Eli Whitney invented **cotton gin**, reviving southern slavery.

## 1794
**Whiskey Rebellion**, west Pennsylvania farmers protesting liquor tax of 1791, was suppressed by 15,000 militiamen **Sept. 1794.** Alexander Hamilton used incident to establish authority of the new federal government in enforcing its laws.

## 1795
U.S. bought peace from **Algerian pirates** by paying $1 mln. ransom for 115 seamen **Sept. 5,** followed by annual tributes.

Gen. Wayne signed peace with Indians at Fort Greenville.

Univ. of North Carolina became first operating state university.

## 1796
**Washington's Farewell Address** as president delivered **Sept. 19.** Gave strong warnings against permanent alliances with foreign powers, big public debt, large military establishment and devices of "small, artful, enterprising minority" to control or change government.

## 1797
U.S. **frigate United States** launched at Philadelphia **July 10;** Constellation at Baltimore **Sept. 7;** Constitution (Old Ironsides) at Boston **Sept. 20.**

## 1798
**Alien & Sedition Acts** passed by Federalists; intended to silence political opposition **June-July.**

**War with France** threatened over French raids on U.S. shipping and rejection of U.S. diplomats. Congress voided all treaties with France, ordered Navy to capture French armed ships. Navy (45 ships) and 365 privateers captured 84 French ships. USS Constellation took French warship Insurgente 1799. Napoleon stopped French raids after becoming First Consul.

## 1800
Federal gvt. moves from Philadelphia to **Washington, D.C.**

## 1801
**Tripoli declared war June 10** against U.S., which refused added tribute to commerce-raiding Arab corsairs. Land and naval campaigns forced Tripoli to negotiate **peace June 4, 1805.**

## 1803
Supreme Court, in **Marbury v. Madison** case, for the first time overturned a U.S. law **Feb. 24.**

Napoleon, who had recovered Louisiana from Spain by secret treaty, sold all of **Louisiana,** stretching to Canadian border, to U.S., for $11,250,000 in bonds, plus $3,750,000 indemnities to American citizens with claims against France. U.S. took title **Dec. 20.** Purchases doubled U.S. area.

## 1804
**Lewis and Clark** expedition ordered by Pres. Jefferson to explore what is now northwest U.S. Started from St. Louis **May 14;** ended **Sept. 23, 1806.** Sacagawea, an Indian woman, served as guide.

Vice Pres. **Aaron Burr,** after long political rivalry, **shot** Alexander Hamilton in a duel **July 11** in Weehawken, N.J.; Hamilton died the next day.

## 1807
**Robert Fulton** made first practical steamboat trip; left N.Y. City **Aug. 17,** reached Albany, 150 mi., in 32 hrs.

**Embargo Act** bans all trade with foreign countries, forbids ships to set sail for foreign ports **Dec. 22.**

## 1808
**Slave importation** outlawed. Some 250,000 slaves were illegally imported 1808-1860.

## 1811
**William Henry Harrison,** governor of Indiana, defeated Indians under the Prophet, in battle of Tippecanoe **Nov. 7.**

**Cumberland Road** begun at Cumberland, Md.; became important route to West.

## 1812
**War of 1812** had 3 main causes: Britain seized U.S. ships trading with France; Britain seized 4,000 naturalized U.S. sailors by 1810; Britain armed Indians who raided western border. U.S. stopped trade with Europe 1807 and 1809. Trade with Britain only was stopped, 1810.

Unaware that Britain had raised the blockade against France 2 days before, **Congress declared war June 18** by a small majority. The West favored war, New England opposed it. The British were handicapped by war with France.

**U.S. naval victories in 1812** included: USS Essex captured Alert **Aug. 13;** USS Constitution destroyed Guerriere **Aug. 19;** USS Wasp took Frolic **Oct. 18;** USS United States defeated Macedonian off Azores **Oct. 25;** Constitution beat Java **Dec. 29.** British captured Detroit **Aug. 16.**

## 1813
**Oliver H. Perry** defeated British fleet at Battle of Lake Erie, **Sept. 10.** U.S. victory at Battle of the Thames, Ont., **Oct. 5,** broke Indian allies of Britain, and made Detroit frontier safe for U.S. But Americans failed in Canadian invasion attempts. York (Toronto) and Buffalo were burned.

## 1814
**British** landed in Maryland in August, defeated U.S. force **Aug. 24, burned Capitol** and White House. Maryland militia stopped British advance **Sept. 12.** Bombardment of Ft. McHenry, Baltimore, for 25 hours, **Sept. 13-14,** by British fleet failed; Francis Scott Key wrote words to **Star Spangled Banner.**

U.S. won naval Battle of Lake Champlain **Sept. 11.** Peace treaty signed at Ghent **Dec. 24.**

## 1815
Some 5,300 British, unaware of peace treaty, attacked U.S. entrenchments near **New Orleans, Jan. 8.** British had over 2,000 casualties, Americans lost 71.

U.S. flotilla finally ended piracy by Algiers, Tunis, Tripoli by **Aug. 6.**

## 1816
Second Bank of the U.S. chartered.

## 1817
**Rush-Bagot treaty** signed **Apr. 28-29;** limited U.S., British armaments on the Great Lakes.

## 1819
Spain cedes **Florida** to U.S. **Feb. 22.**

**American steamship Savannah** made first part steam-powered, part sail-powered crossing of Atlantic, Savannah, Ga. to Liverpool, Eng., 29 days.

## 1820
First organized **immigration of blacks to Africa** from U.S. began with 86 free blacks sailing Feb. to Sierra Leone, Brit. Colony.

Henry Clay's **Missouri Compromise** bill passed by Congress **March 3.** Slavery was allowed in Missouri, but not elsewhere west of the Mississippi River north of 36° 30' latitude (the southern line of Missouri). Repealed 1854.

## 1821
**Emma Willard** founded Troy Female Seminary, first U.S. women's college.

## 1823
**Monroe Doctrine** enunciated **Dec. 2,** opposing European intervention in the Americas.

## 1824
**Pawtucket, R.I. weavers strike** in first such action by women.

## 1825
**Erie Canal opened;** first boat left Buffalo **Oct. 26,** reached N.Y. City **Nov. 4.** Canal cost $7 million but cut travel time

one-third, shipping costs nine-tenths; opened Great Lakes area, made N.Y. City chief Atlantic port.

John Stevens, of Hoboken, N.J., built and operated first experimental **steam locomotive** in U.S.

**1828**

South Carolina **Dec. 19** declared the right of state **nullification** of federal laws, opposing the "Tariff of Abominations."

**Noah Webster** published his *American Dictionary of the English Language*.

**Baltimore & Ohio**, 1st U.S. passenger RR, was begun **July 4**.

**1830**

**Mormon church** organized by Joseph Smith in Fayette, N.Y. **Apr. 6**.

**1831**

William Lloyd Garrison began abolitionist newspaper *The Liberator* **Jan. 1**.

**Nat Turner**, black slave in Virginia, led local slave rebellion, killed 57 whites in **Aug**. Troops called in, 100 slaves killed, Turner captured, tried, and hanged.

**1832**

**Black Hawk War** (Ill.-Wis.) **Apr.-Sept**. pushed Sauk and Fox Indians west across Mississippi.

South Carolina convention passed **Ordinance of Nullification** in **Nov**. against permanent tariff, threatening to withdraw from the Union. Congress **Feb. 1833** passed a compromise tariff act, whereupon South Carolina repealed its act.

**1833**

**Oberlin College**, first in U.S. to adopt coeducation; refused to bar students on account of race, **1835**.

**1835**

**Seminole Indians** in Florida under Osceola began attacks **Nov. 1**, protesting forced removal. The unpopular 8-year war ended **Aug. 14, 1842**; Indians were sent to Oklahoma. War cost the U.S. 1,500 soldiers.

**Texas proclaimed** right to secede from Mexico; Sam Houston put in command of Texas army, **Nov. 2-4**.

**Gold** discovered on Cherokee land in Georgia. Indians forced to cede lands **Dec. 20** and to cross Mississippi.

**1836**

**Texans besieged in Alamo** in San Antonio by Mexicans under Santa Anna **Feb. 23-Mar. 6**; entire garrison killed. Texas independence declared, **Mar. 2**. At San Jacinto **Apr. 21** Sam Houston and Texans defeated Mexicans.

Marcus Whitman, H.H. Spaulding and wives reached Fort Walla Walla on Columbia River, Oregon. **First white women to cross plains**.

**1838**

Cherokee Indians made "**Trail of Tears**," removed from Georgia to Oklahoma starting **Oct**.

**1841**

First emigrant **wagon train for California**, 47 persons, left Independence, Mo. **May 1**, reached Cal. **Nov. 4**.

**Brook Farm** commune set up by New England Transcendentalist intellectuals. Lasts to **1846**.

**1842**

**Webster-Ashburton Treaty** signed **Aug. 9**, fixing the U.S.-Canada border in Maine and Minnesota.

First use of **anesthetic** (sulphuric ether gas).

Settlement of Oregon begins via **Oregon Trail**.

**1843**

More than 1,000 settlers left Independence, Mo. for Oregon **May 22**, arrived **Oct**.

**1844**

First message over first **telegraph line** sent **May 24** by inventor Samuel F.B. Morse from Washington to Baltimore: "What hath God wrought!"

**1845**

**Texas** Congress voted for annexation to U.S. **July 4**. U.S. Congress admits Texas to Union **Dec. 29**.

**1846**

**Mexican War**, Pres. James K. Polk ordered Gen. Zachary Taylor to seize disputed Texan land settled by Mexicans.

After border clash, U.S. declared war **May 13**; Mexico **May 23**. Northern Whigs opposed war, southerners backed it.

Bear flag of Republic of California raised by American settlers at Sonoma **June 14**.

About 12,000 U.S. troops took Vera Cruz **Mar. 27, 1847**, Mexico City **Sept. 14, 1847**. By treaty, **Feb. 1848**, Mexico ceded claims to Texas, California, Arizona, New Mexico, Nevada, Utah, part of Colorado. U.S. assumed $3 million American claims and paid Mexico $15 million.

Treaty with Great Britain **June 15** set **boundary in Oregon** territory at 49th parallel (extension of existing line). Expansionists had used slogan "54° 40' or fight."

**Mormons**, after violent clashes with settlers over polygamy, left Nauvoo, Ill. for West under Brigham Young, settled **July 1847** at Salt Lake City, Utah.

Elias Howe invented **sewing machine**.

**1847**

First **adhesive U.S. postage stamps** on sale **July 1**; Benjamin Franklin 5¢, Washington 10¢.

**Ralph Waldo Emerson** published first book of poems; Henry Wadsworth Longfellow published *Evangeline*.

**1848**

**Gold** discovered **Jan. 24** in California; 80,000 prospectors emigrate in **1849**.

Lucretia Mott and Elizabeth Cady Stanton lead **Seneca Falls**, N.Y. **Women's Rights Convention July 19-20**.

**1850**

Sen. Henry Clay's **Compromise of 1850** admitted California as 31st state **Sept. 9**, slavery forbidden; made Utah and New Mexico territories without decision on slavery; made Fugitive Slave Law more harsh; ended District of Columbia slave trade.

**1851**

Herman Melville's *Moby Dick*, Nathaniel Hawthorne's *House of the Seven Gables* published.

**1852**

*Uncle Tom's Cabin*, by Harriet Beecher Stowe, published.

**1853**

**Commodore Matthew C. Perry**, U.S.N., received by Lord of Toda, Japan **July 14**; negotiated treaty to open Japan to U.S. ships.

**1854**

**Republican party** formed at Ripon, Wis. **Feb. 28**. Opposed Kansas-Nebraska Act (became law **May 30**), which left issue of slavery to vote of settlers.

**Henry David Thoreau** published *Walden*.

**1855**

Walt Whitman published *Leaves of Grass*.

First railroad train crossed Mississippi on the river's first bridge, Rock Island, Ill.-Davenport, Ia. **Apr. 21**.

**1856**

Republican party's first nominee for president, **John C. Fremont**, defeated. Abraham Lincoln made 50 speeches for him.

**Lawrence, Kan**. sacked **May 21** by pro-slavery group; abolitionist John Brown led anti-slavery men against Missourians at Osawatomie, Kan. **Aug. 30**

**1857**

**Dred Scott decision** by U.S. Supreme Court **Mar. 6** held, 6-3, that a slave did not become free when taken into a free state, Congress could not bar slavery from a territory, and blacks could not be citizens.

**1858**

First **Atlantic cable** completed by Cyrus W. Field **Aug. 5**; cable failed **Sept. 1**.

**Lincoln-Douglas debates** in Illinois **Aug. 21-Oct. 15**.

**1859**

First commercially productive **oil well**, drilled near Titusville, Pa., by Edwin L. Drake **Aug. 27**.

Abolitionist **John Brown** with 21 men seized U.S. Armory at Harpers Ferry (then Va.) **Oct. 16**. U.S. Marines captured raiders, killing several. Brown was hanged for treason by Virginia **Dec. 2**.

## 1860

Approximately 20,000 New England shoe workers strike Feb. 22 and win higher wages.

Abraham Lincoln, Republican, elected president in 4-way race.

First Pony Express between Sacramento, Cal. and St. Joseph, Mo. started Apr. 3; service ended Oct. 24, 1861 when first transcontinental telegraph line was completed.

## 1861

Seven southern states set up Confederate States of America Feb. 8, with Jefferson Davis as president, captured Federal arsenals and forts. Civil War began as Confederates fired on Ft. Sumter in Charleston, S.C. Apr. 12; they captured it Apr. 14.

President Lincoln called for 75,000 volunteers Apr. 15. By May, 11 states had seceded. Lincoln blockaded southern ports Apr. 19, cutting off vital exports, aid.

Confederates repelled Union forces at first Battle of Bull Run July 21.

First transcontinental telegraph was put in operation.

## 1862

Homestead Act was approved May 20; it granted free family farms to settlers.

Land Grant Act approved July 7, providing for public land sale to benefit agricultural education; eventually led to establishment of state university systems.

Union forces were victorious in western campaigns, took New Orleans. Battles in East were inconclusive.

## 1863

Lincoln issued Emancipation Proclamation Jan. 1, freeing "all slaves in areas still in rebellion."

The entire Mississippi River was in Union hands by July 4. Union forces won a major victory at Gettysburg, Pa. July 1-July 4. Lincoln read his Gettysburg Address Nov. 19.

In draft riots in N.Y. City about 1,000 were killed or wounded; some blacks were hanged by mobs July 13-16. Rioters protested provision allowing money payment in place of service. Such payments were ended 1864.

## 1864

Gen. Sherman marched through Georgia, taking Atlanta Sept. 1, Savannah Dec. 22.

Sand Creek massacre of Cheyenne and Arapaho Indians Nov. 29. Cavalry attacked Indians who were awaiting surrender terms.

## 1865

Robert E. Lee surrendered 27,800 Confederate troops to Grant at Appomattox Court House, Va. Apr. 9. J.E. Johnston surrendered 31,200 to Sherman at Durham Station, N.C. Apr. 18. Last rebel troops surrendered May 26.

President Lincoln was shot Apr. 14 by John Wilkes Booth in Ford's Theater, Washington; died the following morning. Booth was reported dead Apr. 26. Four co-conspirators were hanged July 7.

Thirteenth Amendment, abolishing slavery, took effect Dec. 18.

## 1866

Ku Klux Klan formed secretly in South to terrorize blacks who voted. Disbanded 1869-71. A second Klan was organized 1915.

Congress took control of southern Reconstruction, backed freedmen's rights.

## 1867

Alaska sold to U.S. by Russia for $7.2 million Mar. 30 through efforts of Sec. of State William H. Seward.

Horatio Alger published first book, Ragged Dick.

The Grange was organized Dec. 4, to protect farmer interests.

## 1868

The World Almanac, a publication of the New York World, appeared for the first time.

Pres. Andrew Johnson tried to remove Edwin M. Stanton, secretary of war; was impeached by House Feb. 24 for violation of Tenure of Office Act; acquitted by Senate March-May. Stanton resigned.

## 1869

Financial "Black Friday" in New York Sept. 24; caused by attempt to "corner" gold.

Transcontinental railroad completed; golden spike driven at Promontory, Utah May 10 marking the junction of Central Pacific and Union Pacific.

Knights of Labor formed in Philadelphia. By 1886, it had 700,000 members nationally.

Woman suffrage law passed in Territory of Wyoming Dec. 10.

## 1871

Great fire destroyed Chicago Oct. 8-11; loss est. at $196 million.

## 1872

Amnesty Act restored civil rights to citizens of the South May 22 except for 500 Confederate leaders.

Congress founded first national park — Yellowstone in Wyoming.

## 1873

First U.S. postal card issued May 1.

Banks failed, panic began in Sept. Depression lasted 5 years.

"Boss" William Tweed of N.Y. City convicted of stealing public funds. He died in jail in 1878.

Bellevue Hospital in N.Y. City started the first school of nursing.

## 1875

Congress passed Civil Rights Act Mar. 1 giving equal rights to blacks in public accommodations and jury duty. Act invalidated in 1883 by Supreme Court.

First Kentucky Derby held May 17 at Churchill Downs, Louisville, Ky.

## 1876

Samuel J. Tilden, Democrat, received majority of popular votes for president over Rutherford B. Hayes, Republican, but 22 electoral votes were in dispute; issue left to Congress. Hayes given presidency in Feb., 1877 after Republicans agree to end Reconstruction of South.

Col. George A. Custer and 264 soldiers of the 7th Cavalry killed June 25 in "last stand," Battle of the Little Big Horn, Mont., in Sioux Indian War.

Mark Twain published Tom Sawyer.

## 1877

Molly Maguires, Irish terrorist society in Scranton, Pa. mining areas, broken up by hanging of 11 leaders for murders of mine officials and police.

Pres. Hayes sent troops in violent national railroad strike.

## 1878

First commercial telephone exchange opened, New Haven, Conn. Jan. 28.

Thomas A. Edison founded Edison Electric Light Co. Oct. 15.

## 1879

F.W. Woolworth opened his first five-and-ten store in Utica, N.Y. Feb. 22.

Henry George published Progress & Poverty, advocating single tax on land.

## 1881

Pres. James A. Garfield shot in Washington, D.C. July 2; died Sept. 19.

Booker T. Washington founded Tuskegee Institute for blacks.

Helen Hunt Jackson published A Century of Dishonor about mistreatment of Indians.

## 1883

Pendleton Act, passed Jan. 16, reformed federal civil service.

Brooklyn Bridge opened May 24.

## 1886

Haymarket riot and bombing, evening of May 4, followed bitter labor battles for 8-hour day in Chicago; 7 police and 4 workers died, 66 wounded. Eight anarchists found guilty. Gov. John P. Altgeld denounced trial as unfair.

Geronimo, Apache Indian, finally surrendered Sept. 4.

The Statue of Liberty was dedicated Oct. 28.

American Federation of Labor (AFL) formed **Dec. 8** by 25 craft unions.

**1888**

Great blizzard in eastern U.S. **Mar. 11-14; 400** deaths.

**1889**

U.S. declared Oklahoma open to white settlement **Apr. 22**; within 24 hours **claims for 2 mln. acres** were staked by 50,000 settlers.

**Johnstown, Pa.** flood **May 31**; 2,200 lives lost.

**1890**

First execution by **electrocution**: William Kemmler **Aug. 6** at Auburn Prison, Auburn, N.Y., for murder.

Battle of **Wounded Knee, S.D. Dec. 29**, the last major conflict between Indians and U.S. troops. About 200 Indian men, women, and children, and 29 soldiers were killed.

**Sherman Antitrust Act** begins federal effort to curb monopolies.

**Jacob Riis** published *How the Other Half Lives*, about city slums.

**1891**

**Forest Reserve Act Mar. 3** let Pres. close public forest land to settlement for establishment of national parks.

**1892**

**Homestead, Pa.**, strike at Carnegie steel mills; 7 guards and 11 strikers and spectators shot to death **July 6**; setback for unions. **Ellis Island** opened as N.Y. immigration depot.

**1893**

Financial panic began, led to 4-year depression.

**1894**

Thomas A. **Edison's kinetoscope** (motion pictures) (invented **1887**) given first public showing **Apr. 14.**

**Jacob S. Coxey** led 500 unemployed from the Midwest into Washington, D.C. **Apr. 30.** Coxey was arrested for trespassing on Capitol grounds.

**1896**

**William Jennings Bryan** delivered "Cross of Gold" speech **July 7**; wins Democratic Party nomination.

Supreme Court, in **Plessy v. Ferguson**, approved racial segregation under the "separate but equal" doctrine.

**1898**

U.S. **battleship Maine** blown up **Feb. 15** at Havana, 260 killed.

U.S. **blockaded Cuba Apr. 22** in aid of independence forces. U.S. declared war on Spain, **Apr. 24**, destroyed Spanish fleet in Philippines **May 1**, took Guam **June 20**.

**Puerto Rico** taken by U.S. **July 25-Aug. 12.** Spain agreed **Dec. 10** to cede Philippines, Puerto Rico, and Guam, and approved independence for Cuba.

U.S. annexed independent republic of **Hawaii.**

**1899**

**Filipino insurgents**, unable to get recognition of independence from U.S., started guerrilla war **Feb. 4.** Crushed with capture **May 23, 1901** of leader, Emilio Aguinaldo.

U.S. declared **Open Door Policy** to make China an open international market and to preserve its integrity as a nation.

**John Dewey** published *School and Society*, backing progressive education.

**1900**

**Carry Nation**, Kansas anti-saloon agitator, began raiding with hatchet.

U.S. helped suppress **"Boxers"** in Peking.

**International Ladies' Garment Workers Union** was founded in NYC in **Nov.**

**1901**

**Texas** had its first significant **oil strike**, near Beaumont **Jan. 10.**

Pres. **William McKinley was shot Sept. 6** by an anarchist, Leon Czolgosz; died **Sept. 14.**

**1903**

Treaty between U.S. and Colombia to have U.S. dig **Panama Canal** signed **Jan. 22**, rejected by Colombia. Panama declared independence with U.S. support **Nov. 3**; recognized by Pres. Theodore Roosevelt **Nov. 6.** U.S., Panama signed canal treaty **Nov. 18.**

Wisconsin set first **direct primary** voting system **May 23.**

First **automobile trip** across U.S. from San Francisco to New York **May 23-Aug. 1.**

First successful flight in heavier-than-air mechanically propelled airplane by **Orville Wright Dec. 17** near Kitty Hawk, N.C., 120 ft. in 12 seconds. Fourth flight same day by **Wilbur Wright**, 852 ft. in 59 seconds. Improved plane patented **May 22, 1906.**

**Jack London** published *Call of the Wild.*

*Great Train Robbery*, pioneering film, produced.

**1904**

**Ida Tarbell** published muckraking *History of Standard Oil.*

**1905**

First **Rotary Club** founded in Chicago **Dec.**

**1906**

**San Francisco earthquake** and fire **Apr. 18-19** left 503 dead, $350 million damages.

**Pure Food and Drug Act** and Meat Inspection Act both passed **June 30.**

**1907**

**Financial panic** and depression started **Mar. 13.**

First round-world cruise of U.S. **"Great White Fleet"**; 16 battleships, 12,000 men.

**1908**

**Henry Ford** introduced **Model T** car, priced at **$850 Oct. 1.**

**1909**

Adm. **Robert E. Peary** reached **North Pole Apr. 6** on 6th attempt, accompanied by Matthew Henson, a black man, and 4 Eskimos.

**National Conference on the Negro** convened **May 30**, leading to founding of the National Association for the Advancement of Colored People.

**1910**

**Boy Scouts** of America founded **Feb. 8.**

**1911**

Supreme Court dissolved **Standard Oil Co. May 15.**

Building holding NYC's **Triangle Shirtwaist Co.** sweatshop caught fire **Mar. 25**; 146 died, mostly young women; some trapped and killed, others jumped to their deaths.

First **transcontinental airplane flight** (with numerous stops) by C.P. Rodgers, New York to Pasadena, **Sept. 17-Nov. 5**; time in air 82 hrs., 4 min.

**1912**

**Amer. Girl Guides** founded **Mar. 12**; name changed in 1913 to Girl Scouts.

U.S. sent marines **Aug. 14** to Nicaragua, which was in default of loans to U.S. and Europe.

**1913**

**N.Y. Armory Show** brought modern art to U.S. **Feb. 17.**

**U.S. blockaded Mexico** in support of revolutionaries.

**Charles Beard** published his *Economic Interpretation of the Constitution.*

**Federal Reserve System** was authorized **Dec. 23**, in a major reform of U.S. banking and finance.

**1914**

Ford Motor Co. raised basic wage rates from $2.40 for 9-hr. day to $5 for 8-hr. day **Jan. 5.**

When U.S. sailors were arrested at Tampico **Apr. 9**, Atlantic fleet was sent to Veracruz, occupied city.

Pres. Wilson proclaimed **U.S. neutrality** in the European war **Aug. 4.**

**Panama Canal** was officially opened **Aug. 15.**

The **Clayton Antitrust Act** was passed **Oct. 15**, strengthening federal anti-monopoly powers.

**1915**

First **telephone talk**, New York to San Francisco, **Jan. 25** by Alexander Graham Bell and Thomas A. Watson.

British ship **Lusitania** sunk **May 7** by German submarine; 128 American passengers lost (Germany had warned passengers in advance). As a result of U.S. campaign, Germany issued apology and promise of payments **Oct. 5.** Pres. Wilson asked for a military fund increase **Dec. 7.**

U.S. troops landed in **Haiti July 28.** Haiti became a virtual U.S. protectorate under **Sept. 16** treaty.

### 1916

Gen. John J. **Pershing entered Mexico** to pursue Francisco (Pancho) Villa, who had raided U.S. border areas. Forces withdrawn Feb. 5, 1917.

**Rural Credits** Act passed July 17, followed by Warehouse Act Aug. 11; both provided financial aid to farmers.

**Bomb exploded** during San Francisco Preparedness Day parade July 22, killed 10. Thomas J. Mooney, labor organizer, and Warren K. Billings, shoe worker, were convicted; both pardoned in 1939.

U.S. bought **Virgin Islands** from Denmark **Aug. 4.**

**Jeannette Rankin,** 1st U.S. Congresswoman (R-Montana) elected.

U.S. established military government in the **Dominican Republic Nov. 29.**

Trade and loans to **European Allies** soared during the year.

John Dewey published *Democracy and Education.*

Carl Sandburg published *Chicago Poems.*

### 1917

Germany, suffering from British blockade, declared almost unrestricted **submarine warfare Jan. 31.** U.S. cut diplomatic ties with Germany Feb. 3, and formally declared war Apr. 6.

**Conscription law** was passed May 18. First U.S. troops arrived in Europe June 26.

The 18th **(Prohibition)** Amendment to the Constitution was submitted to the states by Congress Dec. 18. On Jan. 16, 1919, the 36th state (Nevada) ratified it. Franklin D. Roosevelt, as 1932 presidential candidate, endorsed repeal; 21st Amendment repealed 18th; ratification completed **Dec. 5, 1933.**

### 1918

Pres. Wilson set out his **14 Points** as basis for peace **Jan. 8.**

Over one million **American troops** were in Europe by July. War ended Nov. 11.

**Influenza** epidemic killed an estimated 20 million worldwide, 548,000 in U.S.

### 1919

**First transatlantic flight,** by U.S. Navy seaplane, left Rockaway, N.Y. May 8, stopped at Newfoundland, Azores, Lisbon May 27.

**Boston police strike Sept. 9;** National Guard breaks strike.

Sherwood Anderson published *Winesburg, Ohio.*

About 250 alien **radicals** were deported **Dec. 22.**

### 1920

In national **Red Scare,** some 2,700 Communists, anarchists, and other radicals were arrested **Jan.-May.**

Senate refused Mar. 19 to ratify the **League of Nations** Covenant.

**Nicola Sacco,** 29, shoe factory employee and radical agitator, and Bartolomeo Vanzetti, 32, fish peddler and anarchist, accused of killing 2 men in Mass. payroll holdup **Apr. 15.** Found guilty 1921. A 6-year worldwide campaign for release on grounds of want of conclusive evidence and prejudice failed. Both were executed **Aug. 23, 1927.** Vindicated July 19, 1977 by proclamation of Mass. Gov. Dukakis.

First regular licensed **radio** broadcasting begun **Aug. 20.**

**19th Amendment** ratified **Aug. 26,** giving women right to vote.

**League of Women Voters** founded.

**Wall St.,** N.Y. City, bomb explosion killed 30, injured 100, did $2 million damage **Sept. 16.**

**Sinclair Lewis's** *Main Street,* **F. Scott Fitzgerald's** *This Side of Paradise* published.

### 1921

Congress sharply curbed **immigration,** set national quota system **May 19.**

Joint Congressional resolution declaring **peace** with Germany, Austria, and Hungary signed July 2 by Pres. Harding; treaties were signed in Aug.

**Limitation of Armaments** Conference met in Washington Nov. 12 to Feb. 6, 1922. Major powers agreed to curtail naval construction, outlaw poison gas, restrict submarine attacks on merchant vessels, respect integrity of China.

**Ku Klux Klan** began revival with violence against blacks in North, South, and Midwest.

### 1922

Violence during **coal-mine strike** at Herrin, Ill., **June 22-23** cost 36 lives, 21 of them non-union miners.

**Reader's Digest** founded.

### 1923

First **sound-on-film motion picture,** "Phonofilm" was shown by Lee de Forest at Rivoli Theater, N.Y. City, beginning in April.

### 1924

Law approved by Congress June 15 making all **Indians** citizens.

**Nellie Tayloe Ross** elected governor of Wyoming Nov. 9 after death of her husband Oct. 2; installed **Jan. 5, 1925,** first woman governor. Miriam (Ma) Ferguson was elected governor of Texas Nov. 9; installed Jan. 20, 1925.

George Gershwin wrote *Rhapsody in Blue.*

### 1925

**John T. Scopes** found guilty of having taught evolution in Dayton, Tenn. high school, fined $100 and costs July 24.

### 1926

Dr. Robert H. Goddard demonstrated practicality of **rockets** Mar. 16 at Auburn, Mass. with first liquid fuel rocket; rocket traveled 184 ft. in 2.5 secs.

Congress established **Army Air Corps** July 2.

**Air Commerce Act** passed Nov. 2, providing federal aid for airlines and airports.

### 1927

About 1,000 marines landed in **China Mar. 5** to protect property in civil war.

Capt. **Charles A. Lindbergh** left Roosevelt Field, N.Y. May 20 alone in plane Spirit of St. Louis on first New York-Paris nonstop flight. Reached Le Bourget airfield May 21, 3,610 miles in 33 ½ hours.

*The Jazz Singer,* with Al Jolson, demonstrated part-talking pictures in N.Y. City Oct. 6.

*Show Boat* opened in New York Dec. 27.

O. E. Rolvaag published *Giants in the Earth.*

### 1928

Herbert **Hoover** elected president against **Alfred E. Smith,** the Catholic governor of New York.

**Amelia Earhart** became first woman to fly the Atlantic June 17.

### 1929

**"St. Valentine's Day massacre"** in Chicago Feb. 14; gangsters killed 7 rivals.

Farm price stability aided by **Agricultural Marketing Act,** passed June 15.

Albert B. Fall, former sec. of the interior, was convicted of accepting a bribe of $100,000 in the leasing of the **Elk Hills** (Teapot Dome) naval oil reserve; sentenced Nov. 1 to $100,000 fine and year in prison.

**Stock Market crash Oct. 29** marked end of postwar prosperity as stock prices plummeted. Stock losses for 1929-31 estimated at $50 billion; worst American **depression** began.

Thomas Wolfe published *Look Homeward, Angel.* William Faulkner published *The Sound and the Fury.*

### 1930

**London Naval Reduction Treaty** signed by U.S., Britain, Italy, France, and Japan Apr. 22; in effect Jan. 1, 1931; expired Dec. 31, 1936.

**Hawley-Smoot Tariff** signed; rate hikes slash world trade.

### 1931

**Empire State Building** opened in N.Y. City May 1.

**Al Capone** was convicted of tax evasion Oct. 17.

**Pearl Buck** published *The Good Earth.*

### 1932

**Reconstruction Finance Corp.** established Jan. 22 to stimulate banking and business. Unemployment at 12 million.

**Charles Lindbergh Jr. kidnaped** Mar. 1, found dead May 12.

Bonus March on Washington May 29 by World War I veterans demanding Congress pay their bonus in full.

## 1933

FDR named Frances Perkins U.S. Secy of Labor; 1st woman in U.S. Cabinet.

All banks in the U.S. were ordered closed by Pres. Roosevelt Mar. 6.

In the "100 days" special session, Mar. 9—June 16, Congress passed New Deal social and economic measures.

Gold standard dropped by U.S.; announced by Pres. Roosevelt Apr. 19, ratified by Congress June 5.

Prohibition ended in the U.S. as 36th state ratified 21st Amendment Dec. 5.

U.S. foreswore armed intervention in Western Hemisphere nations Dec. 26.

## 1934

U.S. troops pull out of Haiti Aug. 6.

## 1935

Comedian Will Rogers and aviator Wiley Post killed Aug. 15 in Alaska plane crash.

Social Security Act passed by Congress Aug. 14.

Huey Long, Senator from Louisiana and national political leader, was assassinated Sept. 8.

*Porgy and Bess*, George Gershwin opera on American theme, opened Oct. 10 in N.Y. City.

Committee for Industrial Organization (CIO) formed to expand industrial unionism Nov. 9.

## 1936

Boulder Dam completed.

Margaret Mitchell published *Gone With the Wind*.

## 1937

Joe Louis knocked out James J. Braddock, became world heavyweight champ June 22.

Amelia Earhart, aviator, and co-pilot Fred Noonan lost July 2 near Howland Is. in the Pacific.

Pres. Roosevelt asked for 6 additional Supreme Court justices; "packing" plan defeated.

Auto, steel labor unions won first big contracts.

## 1938

Naval Expansion Act passed May 17.

National minimum wage enacted June 25.

Orson Welles radio dramatization of *War of the Worlds* caused nationwide scare Oct. 30.

## 1939

Pres. Roosevelt asked defense budget hike Jan. 5, 12.

N.Y. World's Fair opened Apr. 30, closed Oct. 31; reopened May 11, 1940, and finally closed Oct. 21.

Einstein alerts FDR to A-bomb opportunity in Aug. 2 letter.

U.S. declares its neutrality in European war Sept. 5.

Roosevelt proclaimed a limited national emergency Sept. 8, an unlimited emergency May 27, 1941. Both ended by Pres. Truman Apr. 28, 1952.

John Steinbeck published *Grapes of Wrath*.

## 1940

U.S. okayed sale of surplus war material to Britain June 3; announced transfer of 50 overaged destroyers Sept. 3.

First peacetime draft approved Sept. 14.

Richard Wright published *Native Son*.

## 1941

The Four Freedoms termed essential by Pres. Roosevelt in speech to Congress Jan. 6: freedom of speech and religion, freedom from want and fear.

Lend-Lease Act signed Mar. 11, providing $7 billion in military credits for Britain. Lend-Lease for USSR approved in Nov.

U.S. occupied Iceland July 7.

The Atlantic Charter, 8-point declaration of principles, issued by Roosevelt and Winston Churchill Aug. 14.

Japan attacked Pearl Harbor, Hawaii, 7:55 a.m. Hawaiian time, Dec. 7, 19 ships sunk or damaged, 2,300 dead. U.S. declared war on Japan Dec. 8, on Germany and Italy Dec. 11 after those countries declared war.

## 1942

Federal government forcibly moved 110,000 Japanese-Americans (including 75,000 U.S. citizens) from West Coast to detention camps. Exclusion lasted 3 years.

Battle of Midway June 4-7 was Japan's first major defeat.

Marines landed on Guadalcanal Aug. 7; last Japanese not expelled until Feb. 9, 1943.

U.S., Britain invaded North Africa Nov. 8.

First nuclear chain reaction (fission of uranium isotope U-235) produced at Univ. of Chicago, under physicists Arthur Compton, Enrico Fermi, others Dec. 2.

## 1943

All war contractors barred from racial discrimination May 27.

Pres. Roosevelt signed June 10 the pay-as-you-go income tax bill. Starting July 1 wage and salary earners were subject to a paycheck withholding tax.

Race riot in Detroit June 21; 34 dead, 700 injured. Riot in Harlem section of N.Y. City; 6 killed.

U.S. troops invaded Italy Sept. 9.

Marines advanced in Gilbert Is. in Nov.

## 1944

U.S., Allied forces invaded Europe at Normandy June 6.

G.I. Bill of Rights signed June 22, providing veterans benefits.

U.S. forces landed on Leyte, Philippines Oct. 20.

## 1945

Yalta Conference met in the Crimea, USSR, Feb. 3-11. Roosevelt, Churchill, and Stalin agreed Russia would enter war against Japan.

Marines landed on Iwo Jima Feb. 19; U.S. forces invaded Okinawa Apr. 1.

Pres. Roosevelt, 63, died of cerebral hemorrhage in Warm Springs, Ga. Apr. 12; V.P. Harry S. Truman became pres.

Germany surrendered May 7.

First atomic bomb, produced at Los Alamos, N.M., exploded at Alamogordo, N.M. July 16. Bomb dropped on Hiroshima Aug. 6, on Nagasaki Aug. 9. Japan surrendered Aug. 15.

U.S. forces entered Korea south of 38th parallel to displace Japanese Sept. 8.

Gen. Douglas MacArthur took over supervision of Japan Sept. 9.

## 1946

Strike by 400,000 mine workers began Apr. 1; other industries followed.

Philippines given independence by U.S. July 4.

## 1947

Truman Doctrine: Pres. Truman asked Congress to aid Greece and Turkey to combat Communist terrorism Mar. 12. Approved May 15.

United Nations Security Council voted unanimously Apr. 2 to place under U.S. trusteeship the Pacific islands formerly mandated to Japan.

Jackie Robinson on Brooklyn Dodgers Apr. 11, broke the color barrier in major league baseball.

Taft-Hartley Labor Act curbing strikes was vetoed by Truman June 20; Congress overrode the veto.

Proposals later known as the Marshall Plan, under which the U.S. would extend aid to European countries, were made by Sec. of State George C. Marshall June 5. Congress authorized some $12 billion in next 4 years.

## 1948

USSR began a land blockade of Berlin's Allied sectors Apr. 1. This blockade and Western counter-blockade were lifted Sept. 30, 1949, after British and U.S. planes had lifted 2,343,315 tons of food and coal into the city.

Organization of American States founded Apr. 30.

Alger Hiss, former State Dept. official, indicted Dec. 15 for perjury, after denying he had passed secret documents to Whittaker Chambers for transmission to a communist spy ring. His second trial ended in conviction Jan. 21, 1950, and a sentence of 5 years in prison.

Kinsey Report on Sexuality in the Human Male published.

## 1949

U.S. troops withdrawn from **Korea June 29.**

North Atlantic Treaty Organization (NATO) established **Aug. 24** by U.S., Canada, and 10 West European nations, agreeing that an armed attack against one or more of them would be considered an attack against all.

Mrs. I. Toguri D'Aquino (**Tokyo Rose** of Japanese wartime broadcasts) was sentenced **Oct. 7** to 10 years in prison for treason. Paroled **1956**, pardoned **1977.**

Eleven leaders of U.S. **Communist party** convicted **Oct. 14**, after 9-month trial in N.Y. City, of advocating violent overthrow of U.S. government. Ten defendants sentenced to 5 years in prison each and the 11th to 3 years. Supreme Court upheld the convictions **June 4, 1951.**

## 1950

U.S. **Jan. 14** recalled all consular officials from **China** after the latter seized the American consulate general in Peking.

Masked bandits robbed **Brink's Inc.**, Boston express office, **Jan. 17** of $2.8 million, of which $1.2 million was in cash. Case solved **1956**, 8 sentenced to life.

Pres. Truman authorized production of **H-bomb Jan. 31.**

United Nations asked for troops to restore Korea peace **June 25.**

Truman ordered Air Force and Navy to Korea **June 27** after North Korea invaded South. Truman approved ground forces, air strikes against North **June 30.**

U.S. sent 35 military advisers to **South Vietnam June 27**, and agreed to provide military and economic aid to anti-Communist government.

Army seized all railroads **Aug. 27** on Truman's order to prevent a general strike; roads returned to owners in 1952.

**U.S. forces landed at Inchon Sept. 15**; UN force took Pyongyang **Oct. 20**, reached China border **Nov. 20**, China sent troops across border **Nov. 26.**

Two members of a **Puerto Rican nationalist** movement tried to kill Pres. Truman **Nov. 1**. (see Assassinations)

U.S. **Dec. 8** banned shipments to **Communist China** and to Asiatic ports trading with it.

## 1951

Sen. **Estes Kefauver** led Senate investigation into organized crime. Preliminary report **Feb. 28** said gambling take was over $20 billion a year.

**Julius Rosenberg**, his wife, Ethel, and Morton Sobell, all U.S. citizens, were found guilty **Mar. 29** of conspiracy to commit wartime espionage. Rosenbergs sentenced to death, Sobell to 30 years. Rosenbergs **executed June 19, 1953.** Sobell released Jan. 14, 1969.

Gen. **Douglas MacArthur** was removed from his Korea command **Apr. 11** for unauthorized policy statements.

Korea cease-fire talks began in July; lasted 2 years. **Fighting ended July 27, 1953.**

**Tariff concessions** by the U.S. to the Soviet Union, Communist China, and all communist-dominated lands were suspended **Aug. 1.**

The U.S., **Australia**, and **New Zealand** signed a mutual security pact **Sept. 1.**

**Transcontinental television** inaugurated **Sept. 4** with Pres. Truman's address at the Japanese Peace Treaty Conference in San Francisco.

**Japanese Peace Treaty** signed in San Francisco **Sept. 8** by U.S., Japan, and 47 other nations.

J.D. Salinger published *Catcher in the Rye.*

## 1952

U.S. **seizure of nation's steel mills** was ordered by Pres. Truman **Apr. 8** to avert a strike. Ruled illegal by Supreme Court **June 2.**

**Peace contract** between West Germany, U.S., and Great Britain, and France was signed **May 26.**

The last racial and ethnic barriers to naturalization were removed, **June 26-27**, with the passage of the **Immigration and Naturalization Act of 1952.**

First **hydrogen device** explosion **Nov. 1** at Eniwetok Atoll in Pacific.

## 1953

Pres. Eisenhower announced **May 8** that U.S. had given France $60 million for **Indochina War.** More aid was announced in Sept. In **1954** it was reported that three fourths of the war's costs were met by U.S.

## 1954

**Nautilus**, first atomic-powered submarine, was launched at Groton, Conn. **Jan. 21.**

Five members of Congress were wounded in the House **Mar. 1** by 4 **Puerto Rican independence supporters** who fired at random from a spectators' gallery.

Sen. **Joseph McCarthy** led televised hearings **Apr. 22-June 17** into alleged Communist influence in the Army.

**Racial segregation** in public schools was unanimously ruled unconstitutional by the Supreme Court **May 17**, as a violation of the 14th Amendment clause guaranteeing equal protection of the laws.

Southeast Asia Treaty Organization (**SEATO**) formed by collective defense pact signed in Manila **Sept. 8** by the U.S., Britain, France, Australia, New Zealand, Philippines, Pakistan, and Thailand.

Condemnation of **Sen. Joseph R. McCarthy** (R., Wis.) voted by Senate, 67-22 **Dec. 2** for contempt of a Senate elections subcommittee, for abuse of its members, and for insults to the Senate during his Army investigation hearings.

## 1955

U.S. agreed **Feb. 12** to help train **South Vietnamese** army.

Supreme Court ordered **"all deliberate speed"** in integration of public schools **May 31.**

A **summit meeting** of leaders of U.S., Britain, France, and USSR took place **July 18-23** in Geneva, Switzerland.

**Rosa Parks** refused **Dec. 1** to give her seat to a white man on a bus in Montgomery, Ala. Bus segregation ordinance declared unconstitutional by a federal court following boycott and NAACP protest.

Merger of America's 2 largest labor organizations was effected **Dec. 5** under the name American Federation of Labor and Congress of Industrial Organizations. The merged **AFL-CIO** had a membership estimated at 15 million.

## 1956

**Massive resistance** to Supreme Court desegregation rulings was called for **Mar. 12** by 101 Southern congressmen.

**Federal-Aid Highway Act** signed **June 29**, inaugurating interstate highway system.

First transatlantic **telephone cable** went into operation **Sept. 25.**

## 1957

Congress approved first **civil rights bill** for blacks since Reconstruction **Apr. 29**, to protect voting rights.

National Guardsmen, called out by Arkansas Gov. Orval Faubus **Sept. 4**, barred 9 black students from entering previously all-white Central High School in **Little Rock.** Faubus complied **Sept. 21** with a federal court order to remove the National Guardsmen. The blacks entered school **Sept. 23** but were ordered to withdraw by local authorities because of fear of mob violence. Pres. Eisenhower sent federal troops **Sept. 24** to enforce the court's order.

Jack Kerouac published *On the Road.*

## 1958

First U.S. earth satellite to go into orbit, **Explorer I**, launched by Army **Jan. 31** at Cape Canaveral, Fla.; discovered Van Allen radiation belt.

Five thousand U.S. Marines sent to **Lebanon** to protect elected government from threatened overthrow **July-Oct.**

First domestic **jet airline** passenger service in U.S. opened by National Airlines **Dec. 10** between N.Y. and Miami.

## 1959

**Alaska** admitted as 49th state **Jan. 3**; **Hawaii** admitted **Aug. 21.**

St. Lawrence Seaway opened **Apr. 25.**

The **George Washington**, first U.S. ballistic-missile submarine, launched at Groton, Conn. **June 9.**

N.S. Savannah, world's first atomic-powered merchant ship, launched **July 21** at Camden, N.J.

Soviet Premier **Khrushchev** paid unprecedented visit to U.S. **Sept. 15-27**, made transcontinental tour.

### 1960

**Sit-ins** began **Feb. 1** when 4 black college students in Greensboro, N.C. refused to move from a Woolworth lunch counter when denied service. By **Sept. 1961** more than 70,000 students, whites and blacks, had participated in sit-ins.

U.S. launched first **weather satellite**, Tiros I, **Apr. 1**.

Congress approved a strong **voting rights act Apr. 21**.

A **U-2 reconnaisance plane** of the U.S. was shot down in the Soviet Union **May 1**. The incident led to cancellation of an imminent Paris summit conference.

Mobs attacked U.S. embassy in **Panama Sept. 17** in dispute over flying of U.S. and Panamanian flags.

U.S. announced **Dec. 15** it backed rightist group in **Laos**, which took power the next day.

### 1961

The U.S. severed diplomatic and consular relations with **Cuba Jan. 3**, after disputes over nationalizations of U.S. firms, U.S. military presence at Guantanamo base, etc.

Invasion of Cuba's **"Bay of Pigs" Apr. 17** by Cuban exiles trained, armed, and directed by the U.S., attempting to overthrow the regime of Premier Fidel Castro, failed.

**Commander Alan B. Shepard Jr.** was rocketed from Cape Canaveral, Fla., 116.5 mi. above the earth in a Mercury capsule **May 5** in the first U.S. manned sub-orbital space flight.

### 1962

**Lt. Col. John H. Glenn Jr.** became the first American in orbit **Feb. 20** when he circled the earth 3 times in the Mercury capsule **Friendship 7**.

Pres. Kennedy said **Feb. 14** U.S. military advisers in Vietnam would fire if fired upon.

Supreme Court **Mar. 26** backed **one-man one-vote** apportionment of seats in state legislatures.

First U.S. **communications satellite** launched in **July**.

**James Meredith** became first black student at Univ. of Mississippi **Oct. 1** after 3,000 troops put down riots.

A Soviet **offensive missile buildup** in Cuba was revealed **Oct. 22** by Pres. Kennedy, who ordered a naval and air quarantine on shipment of offensive military equipment to the island. Kennedy and Soviet Premier Khrushchev reached agreement **Oct. 28** on a formula to end the crisis. Kennedy announced **Nov. 2** that Soviet missile bases in Cuba were being dismantled.

**Rachel Carson's** *Silent Spring* launched environmentalist movement.

### 1963

Supreme Court ruled **Mar. 18** that all **criminal defendants** must have counsel and that illegally acquired evidence was not admissible in state as well as federal courts.

Supreme Court ruled, 8-1, **June 17** that laws requiring **recitation of the Lord's Prayer** or Bible verses in public schools were unconstitutional.

A limited **nuclear test-ban treaty** was agreed upon **July 25** by the U.S., Soviet Union and Britain, barring all nuclear tests except underground.

Washington demonstration by 200,000 persons **Aug. 28** in support of **black demands** for equal rights. Highlight was speech in which Dr. Martin Luther King said: "I have a dream that this nation will rise up and live out the true meaning of its creed, 'We hold these truths to be self-evident: that all men are created equal.' "

South Vietnam Pres. **Ngo Dinh Diem assassinated Nov. 2**; U.S. had earlier withdrawn support.

Pres. **John F. Kennedy was shot** and fatally wounded by an assassin **Nov. 22** as he rode in a motorcade through downtown Dallas, Tex. Vice Pres. Lyndon B. Johnson was inaugurated president shortly after in Dallas. Lee Harvey Oswald was arrested and charged with the murder. Oswald was shot and fatally wounded **Nov. 24** by Jack Ruby, 52, a Dallas nightclub owner, who was convicted of murder **Mar. 14, 1964** and sentenced to death. Ruby died of natural causes **Jan. 3, 1967** while awaiting retrial.

U.S. troops in **Vietnam** totalled over 15,000 by year-end; aid to South Vietnam was over $500 million in **1963**.

### 1964

**Panama** suspended relations with U.S. **Jan. 9** after riots. U.S. offered **Dec. 18** to negotiate a new canal treaty.

Supreme Court ordered **Feb. 17** that **congressional districts** have equal populations.

U.S. reported **May 27** it was sending military planes to **Laos**.

Omnibus **civil rights bill** passed **June 29** banning discrimination in voting, jobs, public accommodations, etc.

Three **civil rights workers** were reported missing in Mississippi **June 22**; found buried **Aug. 4**. Twenty-one white men were arrested. On **Oct. 20, 1967**, an all-white federal jury convicted 7 of conspiracy in the slayings.

U.S. Congress **Aug. 7** passed **Tonkin Resolution**, authorizing presidential action in Vietnam, after North Vietnam boats reportedly attacked 2 U.S. destroyers **Aug. 2**.

Congress approved **War on Poverty** bill **Aug. 11**.

The **Warren Commission** released **Sept. 27** a report concluding that Lee Harvey Oswald was solely responsible for the Kennedy assassination.

### 1965

Pres. Johnson in **Feb.** ordered continuous **bombing** of North Vietnam below 20th parallel.

Some 14,000 U.S. troops sent to **Dominican Republic** during civil war **Apr. 28**. All troops withdrawn by next year.

New **Voting Rights Act** signed **Aug. 6**.

Los Angeles riot by blacks living in **Watts** area resulted in death of 34 persons and property damage est. at $200 million **Aug. 11-16**.

**Water Quality Act** passed **Sept. 21** to meet pollution, shortage problems.

National origins quota system of **immigration** abolished **Oct. 3**.

**Electric power failure** blacked out most of northeastern U.S., parts of 2 Canadian provinces the night of **Nov. 9-10**.

U.S. forces in S. Vietnam reached 184,300 by year-end.

### 1966

U.S. forces began firing into **Cambodia May 1**.

**Bombing of Hanoi** area of North Vietnam by U.S. planes began **June 29**. By **Dec. 31**, 385,300 U.S. troops were stationed in South Vietnam, plus 60,000 offshore and 33,000 in Thailand.

**Medicare**, government program to pay part of the medical expenses of citizens over 65, began **July 1**.

**Edward Brooke** (R, Mass.) elected **Nov. 8** as first black U.S. senator in 85 years.

### 1967

Black representative **Adam Clayton Powell** (D, N.Y.) was denied **Mar. 1** his seat in Congress because of charges he misused gvt. funds. Reelected in 1968, he was seated, but fined $25,000 and stripped of his 22 years' seniority.

Pres. Johnson and Soviet Premier Aleksei Kosygin met **June 23 and 25** at Glassboro State College in N.J.; agreed not to let any crisis push them into war.

Riots by blacks in **Newark, N.J. July 12-17** killed 26, injured 1,500; over 1,000 arrested. In Detroit, Mich., **July 23-30** at least 40 died; 2,000 injured, 5,000 left homeless by rioting, looting, burning in city's black ghetto. Quelled by 4,700 federal paratroopers and 8,000 National Guardsmen.

**Thurgood Marshall** sworn in **Oct. 2** as first black U.S. Supreme Court Justice. Carl B. Stokes (D, Cleveland) and Richard G. Hatcher (D, Gary, Ind.) were elected first black mayors of major U.S. cities **Nov. 7**.

By **December** 475,000 U.S. troops were in **South Vietnam**, all North Vietnam was subject to bombing. Protests against the war mounted in U.S. during year.

### 1968

**USS Pueblo** and 83-man crew seized in Sea of Japan **Jan. 23** by North Koreans; 82 men released **Dec. 22**.

**"Tet offensive"**: Communist troops attacked Saigon, 30 province capitals **Jan. 30**, suffer heavy casualties.

Pres. Johnson curbed bombing of North Vietnam Mar. 31. Peace talks began in Paris May 10. All bombing of North halted Oct. 31.

Martin Luther King Jr., 39, assassinated Apr. 4 in Memphis, Tenn. James Earl Ray, an escaped convict, pleaded guilty to the slaying, was sentenced to 99 years.

Sen. Robert F. Kennedy (D, N.Y.), 42, shot June 5 in Hotel Ambassador, Los Angeles, after celebrating presidential primary victories. Died June 6. Sirhan Bishara Sirhan, Jordanian, convicted of murder.

Rep. Shirley Chisholm (D., N.Y.) became the first black woman elected to Congress.

### 1969

Expanded four-party Vietnam peace talks began Jan. 18. U.S. force peaked at 543,400 in April. Withdrawal started July 8. Pres. Nixon set Vietnamization policy Nov. 3.

U.S. astronaut Neil A. Armstrong, 38, commander of the Apollo 11 mission, became the first man to set foot on the moon July 20. Air Force Col. Edwin E. Aldrin Jr. accompanied Armstrong.

Anti-Vietnam War demonstrations reached peak in U.S.; some 250,000 marched in Washington, D.C. Nov. 15.

Massacre of hundreds of civilians at Mylai, South Vietnam in 1968 incident was reported Nov. 16.

### 1970

United Mine Workers official Joseph A. Yablonski, his wife, and their daughter were found shot Jan. 5 in their Clarksville, Pa. home. UMW chief W. A. (Tony) Boyle was later convicted of the killing.

A federal jury Feb. 18 found the "Chicago 7" innocent of conspiring to incite riots during the 1968 Democratic National Convention. However, 5 were convicted of crossing state lines with intent to incite riots.

Millions of Americans participated in anti-pollution demonstrations Apr. 22 to mark the first Earth Day.

U.S. and South Vietnamese forces crossed Cambodian borders Apr. 30 to get at enemy bases. Four students were killed May 4 at Kent St. Univ. in Ohio by National Guardsmen during a protest against the war.

Two women generals, the first in U.S. history, were named by Pres. Nixon May 15.

A postal reform measure was signed Aug. 12, creating an independent U.S. Postal Service, thus relinquishing governmental control of the U.S. mails after almost 2 centuries.

### 1971

Charles Manson, 36, and 3 of his followers were found guilty Jan. 26 of first-degree murder in the 1969 slaying of actress Sharon Tate and 6 others.

U.S. air and artillery forces aided a 44-day incursion by South Vietnam forces into Laos starting Feb. 8.

A Constitutional Amendment lowering the voting age to 18 in all elections was approved in the Senate by a vote of 94-0 Mar. 10. The proposed 26th Amendment got House approval by a 400-19 vote Mar. 23. Thirty-eighth state ratified June 30.

A court-martial jury Mar. 29, convicted Lt. William L. Calley Jr. of premeditated murder of 22 South Vietnamese at Mylai on Mar. 16, 1968. He was sentenced to life imprisonment Mar. 31. Sentence was reduced to 20 years Aug. 20.

Publication of classified Pentagon papers on the U.S. involvement in Vietnam was begun June 13 by the New York Times. In a 6-3 vote, the U.S. Supreme Court June 30 upheld the right of the Times and the Washington Post to publish the documents under the protection of the First Amendment.

U.S. bombers struck massively in North Vietnam for 5 days starting Dec. 26, in retaliation for alleged violations of agreements reached prior to the 1968 bombing halt. U.S. forces at year-end were down to 140,000.

### 1972

Pres. Nixon arrived in Peking Feb. 21 for an 8-day visit to China, which he called a "journey for peace." The unprecedented visit ended with a joint communique pledging that both powers would work for "a normalization of relations."

By a vote of 84 to 8, the Senate approved Mar. 22 a Constitutional Amendment banning discrimination against women because of their sex and sent the measure to the states for ratification.

North Vietnamese forces launched the biggest attacks in 4 years across the demilitarized zone Mar. 30. The U.S. responded Apr. 15 by resumption of bombing of Hanoi and Haiphong after a 4-year lull.

Nixon announced May 8 the mining of North Vietnam ports. Last U.S. combat troops left Aug. 11.

Alabama Gov. George C. Wallace, campaigning for the presidency at a Laurel, Md. shopping center May 15, was shot and seriously wounded. Arthur H. Bremer, 21, was sentenced to 63 years for shooting Wallace and 3 bystanders.

In the first visit of a U.S. president to Moscow, Nixon arrived May 22 for a week of summit talks with Kremlin leaders that culminated in a landmark strategic arms pact.

Five men were arrested June 17 for breaking into the offices of the Democratic National Committee in the Watergate office complex in Washington, D.C.

The White House announced July 8 that the U.S. would sell to the USSR at least $750 million of American wheat, corn, and other grains over a period of 3 years.

Full-scale bombing of North Vietnam resumed after Paris peace negotiations reached an impasse Dec. 18.

### 1973

Five of seven defendants in the Watergate break-in trial pleaded guilty Jan. 11 and 15, and the other 2 were convicted Jan. 30.

In Roe v. Wade, the Supreme Court ruled 7-2, Jan. 22, that a state may not prevent a woman from having an abortion during the first 3 months of pregnancy, and could regulate but not prohibit abortion during the second trimester; decision in effect overturned anti-abortion laws in 46 states.

Four-party Vietnam peace pacts were signed in Paris Jan. 27, and North Vietnam released some 590 U.S. prisoners by Apr. 1. Last U.S. troops left Mar. 29.

The end of the military draft was announced Jan. 27.

China and the U.S. agreed Feb. 22 to set up permanent liaison offices in each other's country.

Top Nixon aides H.R. Haldeman, John D. Ehrlichman, and John W. Dean, and Attorney General Richard Kleindienst resigned Apr. 30 amid charges of White House efforts to obstruct justice in the Watergate case.

The Senate Armed Services Committee July 16 began a probe into allegations that the U.S. Air Force had made 3,500 secret B-52 raids into Cambodia in 1969 and 1970.

John Dean, former Nixon counsel, told Senate hearings June 25 that Nixon, his staff and campaign aides, and the Justice Department all had conspired to cover up Watergate facts. Nixon refused July 23 to release tapes of relevant White House conversations. Some tapes were turned over to the court Nov. 26.

The U.S. officially ceased bombing in Cambodia at midnight Aug. 14 in accord with a June Congressional action.

Vice Pres. Spiro T. Agnew Oct. 10 resigned and pleaded "nolo contendere" (no contest) to charges of tax evasion on payments made to him by Maryland contractors when he was governor of that state. Gerald Rudolph Ford Oct. 12 became first appointed vice president under the 25th Amendment; sworn in Dec. 6.

A total ban on oil exports to the U.S. was imposed by Arab oil-producing nations Oct. 19-21 after the outbreak of an Arab-Israeli war. The ban was lifted Mar. 18, 1974.

Atty. Gen. Elliot Richardson resigned, and his deputy William D. Ruckelshaus and Watergate Special Prosecutor Archibald Cox were fired by Pres. Nixon Oct. 20 when Cox threatened to secure a judicial ruling that Nixon was violating a court order to turn tapes over to Watergate case Judge John Sirica.

Leon Jaworski, conservative Texas Democrat, was named Nov. 1 by the Nixon administration to be special prosecutor to succeed Archibald Cox.

Congress overrode **Nov. 7** Nixon's veto of the **war powers** bill, which curbed the president's power to commit armed forces to hostilities abroad without Congressional approval.

### 1974

**Impeachment** hearings were opened **May 9** against Nixon by the House Judiciary Committee.

John D. Ehrlichman and 3 **White House "plumbers"** were found guilty **July 12** of conspiring to violate the civil rights of Dr. Lewis Fielding, formerly psychiatrist to Pentagon Papers leaker Daniel Ellsberg, by breaking into his Beverly Hills, Cal. office.

The U.S. Supreme Court ruled, 8-0, **July 24** that Nixon had to turn over **64 tapes** of White House conversations sought by Watergate Special Prosecutor Leon Jaworski.

The House Judiciary Committee, in televised hearings **July 24-30**, recommended 3 **articles of impeachment** against Nixon. The first, voted 27-11 **July 27**, charged Nixon with taking part in a criminal conspiracy to obstruct justice in the Watergate cover-up. The second, voted 28-10 **July 29**, charged he "repeatedly" failed to carry out his constitutional oath in a series of alleged abuses of power. The third, voted 21-17 **July 30**, accused him of unconstitutional defiance of committee subpoenas. The House of Representatives voted without debate **Aug. 20**, by 412-3, to accept the committee report, which included the recommended impeachment articles.

Nixon resigned **Aug. 9**. His support began eroding **Aug. 5** when he released 3 tapes, admitting he originated plans to have the FBI stop its probe of the Watergate break-in for political as well as national security reasons. **Vice President Gerald R. Ford** was sworn in as the 38th U.S. president on **Aug. 9**.

An **unconditional pardon** to ex-Pres. Nixon for all federal crimes that he "committed or may have committed" while president was issued by Pres. Gerald Ford **Sept. 8**.

### 1975

Found guilty of **Watergate** cover-up charges **Jan. 1** were ex-Atty. Gen. John N. Mitchell, ex-presidential advisers H.R. Haldeman and John D. Ehrlichman.

U.S. civilians were evacuated from **Saigon Apr. 29** as communist forces completed takeover of South Vietnam.

U.S. merchant ship **Mayaguez** and crew of 39 seized by Cambodian forces in Gulf of Siam **May 12**. In rescue operation, U.S. Marines attacked Tang Is., planes bombed air base; Cambodia surrendered ship and crew.

Congress voted $405 million for South **Vietnam refugees May 16**; 140,000 were flown to the U.S.

Illegal **CIA operations**, including records on 300,000 persons and groups, and infiltration of agents into black, antiwar and political movements, were described by a "blue-ribbon" panel headed by Vice Pres. Rockefeller **June 10**.

FBI agents captured **Patricia (Patty) Hearst**, kidnapped **Feb. 4, 1974**, in San Francisco **Sept. 18** with others. She was indicted for bank robbery; a San Francisco jury convicted her **Mar. 20, 1976**.

### 1976

**Payments abroad** of $22 million in bribes by Lockheed Aircraft Corp. to sell its planes were revealed **Feb. 4** by a Senate subcommittee. Lockheed admitted payments in Japan, Turkey, Italy, and Holland.

The U.S. celebrated its **Bicentennial July 4**, marking the 200th anniversary of its independence with festivals, parades, and N.Y. City's Operation Sail, a gathering of tall ships from around the world viewed by 6 million persons.

A mystery ailment **"legionnaire's disease"** killed 29 persons who attended an American Legion convention **July 21-24** in Philadelphia. The cause was found to be a bacterium, it was reported **June 18, 1977**.

The **Viking II** set down on **Mars'** Utopia Plains **Sept. 3**, following the successful landing by Viking I **July 20**.

### 1977

Pres. Jimmy Carter **Jan. 21** pardoned most Vietnam War draft evaders, who numbered some 10,000.

Convicted murderer **Gary Gilmore** was executed by a Utah firing squad **Jan. 17**, in the first exercise of capital punishment anywhere in the U.S. since **1967**. Gilmore had opposed all attempts to delay the execution.

Carter signed an act **Aug. 4** creating a new Cabinet-level **Energy Department**.

### 1978

U.S. Senate voted **Apr. 18** to turn over the **Panama Canal** to Panama on Dec. 31, 1999; **Mar. 16** vote had given approval to a treaty guaranteeing the area's neutrality after the year 2000.

The U.S. Supreme Court **June 28** voted 5-4 not to allow a firm quota system in affirmative action plans; the Court did uphold programs that were more "flexible" in nature.

The **House Select Committee on Assassinations** opened hearings **Sept. 6** into assassinations of Pres. Kennedy and Martin Luther King Jr.; the committee recessed **Dec. 30** after concluding conspiracies likely in both cases, but with no further hard evidence for further prosecutions.

Congress passed the **Humphrey-Hawkins "full employment" Bill Oct. 15**, which set national goal of reducing unemployment to 4% by 1983, while reducing inflation to 3% in same period; Pres. Carter signed bill, **Oct. 27**.

### 1979

A major accident occurred, **Mar. 28**, at a nuclear reactor on **Three Mile Island** near Middletown, Pa.

The federal government announced, **Nov. 1**, a $1.5 billion loan-guarantee plan to aid the nation's 3d largest automaker, **Chrysler Corp.**, which had reported a loss of $460.6 million for the 3d quarter of 1979.

Some 90 people, including 63 Americans, were taken hostage, **Nov. 4**, at the **American embassy** in Teheran, Iran, by militant student followers of Ayatollah Khomeini who demanded the return of former Shah Mohammad Reza Pahlavi, who was undergoing medical treatment in New York City.

### 1980

Pres. Carter announced, **Jan. 4**, punitive measures against the USSR, including an embargo on the sale of grain and high technology, in retaliation for the Soviet invasion of Afghanistan. At Carter's request, the **U.S. Olympic Committee** voted, **Apr. 12**, not to attend the Moscow Summer Olympics.

Eight Americans were killed and 5 wounded, **Apr. 24**, in an ill-fated attempt to **rescue the hostages** held by Iranian **militants** at the U.S. Embassy in Teheran.

In Washington, **Mt. St. Helens** erupted, **May 18**, in a violent blast estimated to be 500 times as powerful as the Hiroshima atomic bomb. The blast, followed by others on **May 25** and **June 12**, left about 60 dead, and economic losses estimated at nearly $3 billion.

In a sweeping victory, **Nov. 4**, Ronald Wilson Reagan was elected 40th President of the United States, defeating incumbent Jimmy Carter. The stunning GOP victory extended to the U.S. Congress where Republicans gained control of the Senate and wrested 33 House seats from the Democrats.

Former Beatle **John Lennon** was shot and killed, **Dec. 8**, outside his apartment building in New York City.

### 1981

Minutes after the **inauguration** of Pres. Ronald Reagan, **Jan. 20**, the **52 Americans** who had been held **hostage in Iran** for 444 days were flown to freedom following an agreement in which the U.S. agreed to return to Iran $8 billion in frozen assets.

**President Reagan** was **shot in the chest** by a would-be assassin, **Mar. 30**, in Washington, D.C., as he walked to his limousine following an address.

The world's first reusable spacecraft, the **Space Shuttle Columbia**, was sent into space, **Apr. 12**, and completed its successful mission 2 days later.

Both houses of Congress passed, **July 29**, President Reagan's **tax-cut legislation**. The largest tax cut in the nation's history was expected to reduce taxes by $37.6 bln. in fiscal 1982, and to save taxpayers $750 bln. over the next 5 years.

Federal air traffic controllers, Aug. 3, began an illegal nationwide strike after their union rejected the government's final offer for a new contract. Most of the 13,000 striking controllers defied the back-to-work order, and were dismissed by President Reagan Aug. 5.

In a 99-0 vote, the Senate confirmed, Sept. 21, the appointment of Sandra Day O'Connor as an associate justice of the U.S. Supreme Court. She was the first woman appointed to that body.

President Reagan ordered sanctions against the new Polish military government, Dec. 23, in response to the imposition of martial law in that country.

### 1982

The 13-year-old lawsuit against AT&T by the Justice Dept. was settled Jan. 8. AT&T agreed to give up the 22 Bell System companies but in return was allowed to expand into previously prohibited areas inc. data processing, telephone and computer equipment sales, and computer communication devices.

On Mar. 2, the Senate voted 57-37 for a bill that virtually eliminated busing for the purposes of racial integration.

On June 12, in N.Y.'s Central Park, hundreds of thousands demonstrated against nuclear arms.

The Equal Rights Amendment was defeated after a 10-year struggle for ratification.

The elections on Nov. 2 resulted in gains for the Democrats—the margin in the new House was 269-166. In the Senate elections, Democrats won 20 out of 33 seats, but were still the minority, 54-46.

The highest unemployment rate since 1940, 10.4%, was reported on Nov. 5. The rate for Nov. reached 10.8%, with over 11 million unemployed.

Lech Walesa, former leader of Solidarity, the Polish labor union, was freed Nov. 13, after 11 months of internment following the imposition of martial law and the outlawing of Solidarity. Pres. Reagan lifted the U.S. embargo on sales of oil and gas equipment to the Soviet Union.

The Space Shuttle Columbia completed its first operational flight Nov. 16.

A retired dentist, Dr. Barney B. Clark, 61, became the first recipient of a permanent artificial heart during a 7½ hour operation in Salt Lake City Dec. 2. The heart was designed by Dr. Robert Jarvik, also on the surgical team.

### 1983

On Apr. 20, Pres. Reagan signed a compromise, bipartisan bill designed to rescue the Social Security System from bankruptcy.

In an 8-1 decision, the U.S. Supreme Court held, May 24, that the Internal Revenue Service could deny tax exemptions to private schools that practiced racial discrimination.

Sally Ride became the first American woman to travel in space, June 18, when the space shuttle Challenger was launched from Cape Canaveral, Fla.

On Oct. 23, 241 U.S. Marines and sailors, members of the multinational peacekeeping force in Lebanon, were killed when a TNT-laden suicide terrorist blew up Marine headquarters at Beirut Intl. Airport. Almost simultaneously, a second truck bomb blew up a French paratroop barracks two miles away, killing more than 40.

U.S. Marines and Rangers and a small force from 6 Caribbean nations invaded the island of Grenada on Oct. 25, in response to a request from the Organization of Eastern Caribbean States. After a few days, Grenadian militia and Cuban "construction workers" were overcome, hundreds of U.S. citizens evacuated safely, and the Marxist regime deposed. The U.S. Congress applied the War Powers Resolution, requiring U.S. troops to leave Grenada by Dec. 24.

### 1984

In his State of the Union address, Jan. 25, Pres. Reagan called for budget cuts of $100 billion over 3 years, but opposed increased taxes.

On Feb. 26, as the position of Pres. Amin Gemayel of Lebanon deteriorated and his army crumbled, Pres. Reagan removed U.S. Marines from Beirut and placed them on U.S. ships offshore.

The space shuttle Challenger was launched on its 4th trip into space, Feb. 3. On Feb. 7, Navy Capt. Bruce McCandless, followed by Army Lt. Colonel Robert Stewart, became the first humans to fly free of a spacecraft.

During March, the U.S. Senate rejected 2 Constitutional amendments that would have permitted prayer in the public schools.

The Central Intelligence Agency (CIA) acknowledged in April that it had participated in the mining of Nicaraguan harbors. This touched off a controversy in Congress, and the Senate, Apr. 10, adopted a nonbinding resolution condemning U.S. participation in the mining.

From Apr. 26 to May 1, Pres. Reagan visited China for the first time, holding discussions with Chinese leaders.

On May 7, American Vietnam war veterans reached an out-of-court settlement with 7 chemical companies in their class-action suit regarding the herbicide Agent Orange.

A federal judge in Salt Lake City held, May 10, that the U.S. government had been negligent in its above-ground testing of nuclear weapons in Nevada from 1951 to 1962.

On June 6, former vice president Walter Mondale won the Democratic presidental nomination. In a historic move, July 12, Mondale chose a woman, Rep. Geraldine Ferraro (N.Y.) as candidate for vice president.

Pres. Reagan, Aug. 11, signed a law prohibiting public high schools from barring students who wished to assemble for religious or political activities outside of school hours.

Ronald Reagan was reelected U.S. President Nov. 6 in the greatest Republican landslide in history, carrying 49 states against Walter F. Mondale.

### 1985

The controversial MX missile survived critical votes in the Senate and House. The Senate, Mar. 19 and 21, voted to authorize the missiles and to appropriate $1.5 million for the construction of 21 missiles. The House gave its endorsement Mar. 26 and 28.

E.F. Hutton, one of the nation's largest brokerage companies, pleaded guilty, May 2, to 2,000 federal charges related to the manipulation of its checking accounts. The company agreed to pay $2 million in fines and to pay back up to $8 million to banks it had defrauded.

"Live Aid," a 17-hour rock concert broadcast July 13 on radio and TV from London and Phila. to 152 countries, raised $70 million for the starving peoples of Africa.

On Oct. 7, 5 hijackers seized an Italian cruise ship, the Achille Lauro, in the open sea as it approached Port Said, Egypt. Some 400 persons were aboard, including about 340 crew. The hijackers, members of the Palestine Liberation Front, a faction broken from the PLO, demanded the release of 50 Palestinians held by Israel.

In November, for the first time in 6 years, the leaders of the U.S. and the Soviet Union met at a summit conference. In Geneva, Switzerland, Pres. Reagan and Mikhail Gorbachev, the general secretary of the Soviet Communist Party, talked privately for 5 hours, Nov. 19 and 20.

### 1986

On Jan. 20, for the 1st time, the U.S. officially observed Martin Luther King Day.

Moments after liftoff, Jan. 28, the space shuttle Challenger exploded, killing 6 astronauts and Christa McAuliffe, a New Hampshire teacher. Subsequent investigations found that NASA had abandoned "good judgment and common sense" regarding safety problems that caused the explosion.

U.S. warplanes struck targets in Tripoli and Benghazi, Libya, Apr. 14—retaliation against the Libyan bombing of a W. Berlin disco that killed 2, injured 200, Apr. 5. On Jan. 7, Pres. Reagan had said that the U.S. had aborted 26 "terrorist missions" in 1985. In an executive order, he banned trade with and travel to Libya, ordering Americans out. A 2nd executive order, Jan. 8, had frozen all Libyan government assets in the U.S. and U.S. bank branches abroad.

U.S. officials said, June 12, that AIDS cases and deaths would increase tenfold in the next 5 years. At that time, the government had recorded 21,517 cases, 11,713 deaths. An anti-viral drug, azidothymidine (AZT) was found to improve the health of some AIDS patient, but was not a cure.

With mounting abuse of illegal drugs in the U.S., specifically cocaine as "crack," Congress passed anti-drug laws and the U.S. joined Bolivia in raids against cocaine processing hideouts.

The U.S., via Congress's Sept. override of Pres. Reagan's veto, joined other nations in imposing economic sanctions on So. Africa, pressuring the Botha gvt. to end apartheid.

The U.S. Senate confirmed, Sept. 17, Pres. Reagan's nomination of William Rehnquist as chief justice, Antonin Scalia as associate justice of the Supreme Court.

Congress passed, in late Sept., the comprehensive Tax Reform Law. In effect in 1987, it simplified the system, drastically changing tax brackets, deductions, and more.

The U.S. and USSR reached tentative agreement on a world-wide ban of medium-range missiles, Sept. 18.

One day before the 1986 Congressional elections, it was reported that the U.S. had sent spare parts and ammunition to Iran. Over the next months it was revealed that additional arms sales had been made to Iran, and profits diverted to a fund for Nicaraguan contras.

In the Congressional races, Nov. 4, Democrats won a 55-45 Senate majority, after 6 yrs. of a Republican majority, and enlarged their House majority by 5, to 258-177.

The most scandalous year in Wall Street history ended with Ivan Boesky's agreeing, Nov. 14, to plead guilty to an unspecified criminal count, pay a $100 million fine, and return profits; he was barred for life from trading securities.

### 1987

Pres. Reagan produced the nation's first trillion-dollar budget, Jan. 5.

The stock market continued its phenomenal rise. The Dow closed at 2002.25, Jan. 8, its first finish above 2000. The Dow advanced for 13 consecutive trading days, another record, Jan. 20; the average soared 51.60 points, Jan. 22, a one-day record. At month's end, the cumulative advance was more than 250 points, yet another record.

The Tower Commission Report, Feb. 27, found Pres. Reagan confused and uninformed in Iran-contra dealings, and further faulted White House Chief of Staff Donald Regan; former Natl. Security Adviser Robert McFarlane; his successor Adm. John Poindexter; and CIA Director William Casey.

An Iraqi warplane missile killed 37 sailors on the frigate U.S.S. Stark in the Persian Gulf, May 17. Iraq called it an accident. The Stark's officers were found negligent, June 14. The U.S. escorted Kuwaiti oil tankers to the Gulf, reflagging them for the U.S.

Public hearings by the Senate and House committees investigating the Iran-contra affair went on from May-Aug. Former CIA Director Casey died, May 6, 5 months after brain surgery; Lt. Col. Oliver North, a media sensation, said he had believed all his activities authorized by his superiors; Poindexter said his own purpose had been "to provide some future deniability for the president . . ."; Shultz said Casey, McFarlane, and Poindexter had lied to him and deceived Pres. Reagan. Pres. Reagan, Aug. 12, said he had been "stubborn in pursuit of a policy that went astray," but again denied knowing of the funds' diversion to the contras.

Wall Street crashed, Oct. 19, the Dow plummeting a record 508 points—22.6 percent—after a record high of 2722.42, Aug. 25; a 200-point drop by Oct., called a correction by most; and drops of 91.55, Oct. 6; 95.46, Oct. 14; and 108.36, Oct. 16.

Pres. Reagan and Soviet leader Gorbachev met in Wash., Dec. 8, and signed an unprecedented agreement calling for the dismantling of all 1,752 U.S. and 859 Soviet missiles with a 300-3,400-mile range. The leaders agreed to meet in Moscow in 1988.

### 1988

Federal grand juries in Miami and Tampa returned indictments, Feb. 4, against Gen. Manuel Noriega, the effective ruler of Panama, charging that he had protected and otherwise assisted the Medellin drug cartel. Attempts by the U.S. to oust Noriega plunged Panama into political and economic turmoil.

Nearly 1.4 million illegal aliens met the May 4 deadline for applying for amnesty under a U.S. Immigration and Naturalization Service policy. An estimated 50+ percent of applications were in Calif.; nationwide, about 71 percent of the aliens had entered the U.S. from Mexico.

Much of the U.S. suffered the worst drought in more than 50 years. By June 23, half of the nation's agricultural counties had been designated disaster areas.

A missile, fired from the U.S. Navy warship *Vincennes*, in the Persian Gulf, struck and destroyed a commercial Iranian airliner, July 3, killing all 290 persons on the plane. Navy personnel had mistaken the airliner for an Iranian F-14 jet fighter.

Fire destroyed about 4 million acres of forest land throughout the west, including Alaska, during the late summer. Property damage was also considerable.

Failures at nuclear-power plants posed problems across the U.S., according to congressional testimony, starting Sept. 30. Problems cited including aging equipment, poor management and training, and lax safety standards.

George Bush, vice president under Ronald Reagan, was elected 41st U.S. president, Nov. 8. Bush defeated the Democratic nominee, Gov. Michael Dukakis (Mass.), by 54 to 46 percent of the popular vote, and 426 electoral votes to Dukakis's 112. Sen. Dan Quayle (Ind.) was the successful vice presidential nominee; Sen. Lloyd Bentsen (Tex.) was the Democratic nominee for v.p. Democrats continued to control both houses of Congress.

Drexel Burnham Lambert agreed, Dec. 21, to plead guilty to 6 violations of federal law, including insider trading, stock manipulation, and falsified records; and to pay penalties of $650 million, by far the largest such settlement.

### 1989

The Labor Dept. reported, Jan. 6, that unemployment was 5.3%, a 14-year low, at the end of 1988. For the whole year, the economy grew 3.8%, the most in 4 years.

The largest oil spill in U.S. history occurred after the *Exxon Valdez* struck Bligh Reef in Alaska's Prince William Sound, Mar. 24. Exxon Corp. announced, Mar. 25, that it accepted full financial responsibility for the spill, initially estimated at 240,000 barrels, then announced that the spill could not be contained; as of Mar. 29, it extended 45 miles.

Former Natl. Security Council staff member Oliver North became the first person, May 4, convicted in a jury trial in connection with the Iran-contra scandal. The jury acquitted North on 9 charges, found him guilty of 3: aiding and abetting the obstruction of Congress; altering, destroying, removing, or concealing NSC documents; receiving as an illegal gratuity a $13,800 security system for his home. North received, July 6, a 3-year suspended prison sentence, 2 years' probation, a $150,000 fine, and an order to perform 1,200 hours of community service.

House speaker Jim Wright (D. Tex.), who faced 69 ethical charges, announced his resignation as speaker and from the House, May 31. Rep. Tony Coelho (D. Calif.), also under scrutiny, announced his resignation as majority whip and from the House.

The U.S. Supreme Court announced, July 3, its 5-4 decision to put new restraints on a woman's right to have an abortion, although it did not overturn Roe v. Wade.

Jack Kemp, secy. of Housing and Urban Development, acknowledged, July 11, that an estimated $2 billion had been lost due to fraud and mismanagement during the tenure of his predecessor Samuel Pierce.

Legislation passed by Congress to rescue the savings and loan industry was signed into law, Aug. 9, by Pres. George Bush. The bill provided $166 billion over 10 years to close or merge insolvent S&Ls. The total cost was put at $400 billion over 30 years, most to be paid by taxpayers.

**Army Gen. Colin Powell** was nominated by Pres. Bush, **Aug. 10**, to serve as **chairman of the Joint Chiefs of Staff**; he became the first black to hold the post.

Minutes before the start of the 3d game of the 1989 World Series between the San Francisco Giants and the Oakland Athletics, **Oct. 17, an earthquake struck the San Francisco Bay area**, causing at least 59 deaths and massive property damage.

**Democrats** won most of the **top offices** at stake and **black candidates scored major breakthroughs**, in off-year elections, **Nov. 7**. Lt. Gov. L. Douglas Wilder, a Democrat, was elected governor of Virginia, the nation's first black governor since Reconstruction; Manhattan Borough Pres. David Dinkins, also a Democrat, became the first black elected mayor of New York City.

**Pennsylvania** became the first state, **Nov. 18, to restrict abortions**, after the U.S. Supreme Court gave states the right to do so in July.

**Pres. Bush** signed into law, **Nov. 19, an increase in the minimum wage**. Currently $3.35, the wage would rise to $4.25 an hour by 1991, with a training wage of $3.35 for 16- to 19-year-olds in their first 3 months on a job.

**U.S. troops invaded Panama, Dec. 20,** overthrowing the government of Manuel Noriega, who eluded capture, took refuge in the Vatican mission, then surrendered to the U.S. Jan. 3, 1990.

### 1990

The **Dow Jones Industrial average** pushed to an **all-time high** on Wall Street, **July 16 and 17**, finishing at 2,999.75 and averaging above 3,000.

**Pres. Bush** signed a bill that would bar **discrimination against people with physical or mental disabilities, July 26.**

**Justice William Brennan** announced, **July 20**, his immediate resignation from the U.S. Supreme Court, due to illness; Pres. Bush nominated **Judge David Souter** of the U.S. Court of Appeals for the First Circuit in Boston, **July 23**, and the Senate voted to endorse him, **Sept. 27.**

**Operation Desert Shield** forces left for **Saudi Arabia, Aug. 7,** to defend that country following the **invasion** of its neighbor **Kuwait by Iraq.**

**Pres. Bush vetoed, Oct. 22, a civil rights bill** that sought in effect to reverse 6 recent Supreme Court decisions that civil rights organizations contended had weakened anti-discrimination laws on hiring and promoting.

The Democratic Party made small gains in the Senate and House in **elections, Nov. 6.** Democrats gained one seat in the Senate, for a 56-44 margin over Republicans, and gained 8 seats in the House for a 267-167 margin. One independent was elected in Vermont. About 96 percent of incumbents seeking re-election were successful; only 15 lost. In gubernatorial elections, 14 statehouses changed parties, Democrats emerging with a 28-19 margin, compared with 29-21 before the election. Independents won in Alaska and Connecticut, and a runoff would be required in Arizona.

**Pres. Bush** signed, **Nov. 15,** a bill designed to **reduce budget deficits** by nearly $500 billion over 5 years. The top tax rate would rise from 28 to 31 percent and exemptions for upper-income Americans would be phased out; gas, cigarette, liquor taxes would increase; a luxury tax would be imposed on some planes, cars, boats, furs, and jewelry.

**Pres. Bush** signed, **Nov. 15,** the **1990 Clean Air Act,** a comprehensive updating of the original Clean Air Act of 1970.

In **Dec.** unemployment reached a 3-year high of 6.1 percent. In the 2nd half of the year, more than 1 million payroll jobs were lost. Consumer prices rose 6.1 percent during the year, the highest annual rate since 1981.

### 1991

The **U.S. and its allies defeated Iraq** in Jan. and Feb. **1991** and liberated Kuwait, which Iraq had overrun in Aug. 1990. After Iraq's invasion, for nearly 6 months, diplomats of many nations had sought to persuade Pres. Saddam Hussein to pull his occupying forces out of the oil-rich sheikhdom. Finally, in **Jan.,** the allies launched an **attack on Iraq from the air** that sharply reduced his offensive and defensive military capacity. In a **ground war in Feb.** that lasted just 100 hours, the U.S.-led attackers killed or captured many thousands of Iraqi soldiers and sent the rest into retreat before Pres. George Bush ordered a cease-fire.

The **unemployment rate** in March stood at **6.7 percent,** the highest since late 1986. However, the **Dow Jones Industrial Average** finished above 3000 for the first time, **Apr. 17,** closing at 3004.46.

**Justice Thurgood Marshall,** the first black ever to serve on the U.S. Supreme Court, announced, **June 27,** that he would retire when a successor was approved.

**Unemployment** edged up to **7.0 percent in June,** but the **Gross National Product,** the broadest measure of the economy, had **risen 0.4 percent** at an annual rate during the **2nd quarter of 1991,** and the chief economic advisor to the U.S. Pres. said, "The recession appears to have ended."

**Pres. Bush** approved, **July 10,** the recommendations of the **Defense Base Closure and Realignment Commission,** which had proposed that 34 domestic military installations be closed and 48 other realigned, due to the federal budget crunch and the end of the cold war.

**Chemical Banking Corp.** and **Manufacturers Hanover Corp.** announced, **July 15,** a merger agreement. The merger partners, both based in New York, would have combined assets of $135.46 billion.

**BankAmerica and Security Pacific Corp.** announced, **Aug. 12,** that they would merge. The agreement, if approved, would involve a $4.47 billion stock swap.

The **case against Oliver North was "terminated,"** with all charges dropped, **Sept. 16.** In 1989, North, a leading figure in the Iran-contra affair, had been convicted of obstructing a congressional investigation, destroying documents, and accepting an illegal gratuity. In 1990, a federal appeals court had overturned one conviction and sent the others back to the federal district court.

The General Accounting Office revealed that in a recent 12-month period, **8,331 checks** had been written against **insufficient funds** in a bank that operated at the Capitol with only House members for depositors. On **Oct. 3,** House Speaker Tom Foley said the bank would be closed at the end of 1991 and that the House Ethics Committee would investigate.

The **U.S. Senate approved the nomination of Clarence Thomas** to serve as an **associate justice of the Supreme Court,** after investigating an allegation of sexual harassment that had been leveled against him. Thomas and his accuser, Anita Hill, a law professor at the Univ. of Oklahoma, testified before the Senate Judiciary Committee, **Oct. 11,** while a huge TV audience watched. The Senate confirmed Thomas, 52-48.

Both major parties could claim **significant victories** in the **Nov. 5 elections.** The victory of Democrat Harris Wofford over former governor and U.S. attorney general Richard Thornburgh for the U.S. Senate Seat in Pennsylvania was seen as a signal of public concern about the state of the economy. Mississippi's incumbent governor, Democrat Ray Mabus, lost to Kirk Fordice, who would become the first Republican governor of the state since Reconstruction.

A compromise bill providing for **additional benefits for unemployed workers** was signed by Pres. George Bush, **Nov. 15.** The bill would give all unemployed workers from 6 to 20 additional weeks of benefits.

**Pres. George Bush** signed, **Nov. 21,** a **job-discrimination** bill requiring that hiring and promotion be related to job performance. Those claiming discrimination could sue for damages, not just back pay and lost benefits.

**Charles Keating** was **convicted of 17 counts of securities fraud, Dec. 4.** The prosecution asserted that as chairman of the Lincoln Savings & Loan Assn. in Cal., Keating had induced some 17,000 investors to buy $250 million in bonds that were not insured.

## 1992

In the annual State of the Union address, Jan. 28, Pres. George Bush announced proposals to reduce nuclear arsenals and to deal with the U.S. economic recession. Calling for a $50 billion reduction in the defense budget over the next 5 years, he endorsed cancellation of the Midgetman ICBM program and proposed to cap the number of MX intercontinental ballistic missiles and B-2 stealth bombers. To speed economic growth, Bush said he had instructed federal departments and agencies to impose a 3-month moratorium on new government regulations and had told the IRS to reduce the amount withheld from employees' paychecks.

Pres. Bush submitted to Congress, Jan. 29, a budget for the 1993 fiscal year, with a projected deficit of $351.9 billion. The estimated budget deficit for 1992 was a record $399.4 billion.

R.H. Macy & Co., owner of 251 retail stores in the U.S., including in New York City "the world's largest department store," filed for bankruptcy, Jan. 27. Trans World Airlines, Jan. 31, became the latest major U.S. carrier to file for bankruptcy.

The "Big 3" U.S. auto makers announced huge losses in Feb. Chrysler reported, Feb. 6, a loss of $795 million in 1991, and Ford Motor Co. said, Feb. 13, that it had lost $2.26 billion in 1991, its greatest loss ever in one year. On Feb. 24, General Motors announced a loss of $4.45 billion in 1991, at the time the greatest in history for any U.S. company. General Motors named 12 plants that it planned to close over 3 years. However, the Dow Jones Industrial Average closed, Feb. 24, at 3283.32, an all-time high, which analysts attributed to investors' belief in an imminent economic recovery.

Rioting, looting, and arson swept South-Central Los Angeles in late April and early May after a jury that included no blacks acquitted 4 policemen on all but one count in the beating of a black man, Rodney King. Protests in Atlanta, Las Vegas, San Francisco, Miami, and Seattle also turned violent. The attack on King had been videotaped and shown on TV newcasts across the country. The death toll in the L.A. violence after the acquittals was put at 52, mostly homicides; some 600 buildings were set aflame; and damage was said to run as high as $1 billion. Army, Marine, and Natl. Guard units helped restore order. The White House announced, May 4, that $700 million in federal funds would be made available to help riot victims and to rebuild damaged areas and businesses.

More than 300 members and former members of the U.S. House of Representatives were identified as having written overdraft checks at the House bank. On Apr. 1, the House Ethics Committee released the names of the 22 "worst abusers." On Apr. 3, Senate and House leaders ended free medical care and medicine for members of Congress. The House voted, Apr. 9, to give control of nonlegislative House matters to a professional manager, and the position of inspector general, or auditor, was created.

A 27th Amendment became part of the U.S. Constitution in May. Proposed by James Madison, it had been approved by Congress in 1798 and submitted to the states for ratification. It read: "No law, varying the compensation for the services of the senators and representatives shall take effect, until an election of representatives shall have intervened." Approval of three-fourths of the states, 38 at the present time, was required for an amendment to become part of the Constitution. On May 7, the Michigan legislature became the 38th to approve it.

Gov. Bill Clinton (Ark.) won primaries, June 2, in Calif., Ohio, N.J., and 3 other states, capturing enough delegates to guarantee the Democratic presidential nomination. Pres. George Bush, June 2, swept 6 primaries. Texas billionaire H. Ross Perot, mounting an independent campaign for president, was not on any ballot June 2, but according to exit polls he would run well against Bush and Clinton.

A proposed amendment to the U.S. Constitution that would have required a balanced budget in the federal government was defeated in the House, June 11. Under the amendment, expenditures could not exceed receipts in any year unless the U.S. was at war or three-fifths of the membership of both houses of Congress voted to override the balanced requirement in any year.

More than 1.1 million votes were cast in an election to choose a portrait of Elvis Presley for a U.S. postage stamp. On June 4, the U.S. Postal Service announced that voters preferred, 3-1, a portrait of the younger Elvis.

The Democratic Party nominated Gov. Bill Clinton (Ark.) as its candidate for president, July 15, and Sen. Al Gore Jr. (Tenn.) as its candidate for vice president, July 16, in New York City. Texas independent H. Ross Perot announced, July 16, that he would not seek the presidency both because the Democratic Party had "revitalized itself" and because his candidacy would cause the election to be thrown into the House for resolution, which would disrupt the country.

The Labor Dept. reported, July 1, that the nation's unemployment rate stood at 7.8 in June, the highest level since March 1984. The Senate and House, July 2, approved a bill that would extend benefits to long-term unemployed persons during recessions, and Pres. Bush signed it, July 3.

The Republican Party renominated Pres. George Bush and Vice Pres. Dan Quayle at the convention in Houston, Tex. in early August, while a Gallup Poll reported, Aug. 4, that Bush's public-approval rating had fallen to 29 percent, a new low.

Pres. Bush and Gov. Bill Clinton, the Republican and Democratic candidates for president, participated in 3 TV debates in Oct. They were joined by independent candidate H. Ross Perot who, on Oct. 1, 33 days before the election, had re-declared his candidacy, after having removed himself from consideration in July.

Congress for the first time overrode a veto by Pres. Bush, after nearly 4 years and 35 attempts. On Oct. 3, Bush vetoed a bill that reversed portions of a law that prohibited local governments from regulating cable-TV fees. The legislation required that the Federal Communications Commission establish a "reasonable" price for basic cable services. On Oct. 5, the Senate, 74-25, and the House, 308-114, voted to override by more than the two-thirds majority required.

Gov. Bill Clinton of Arkansas was elected 42nd president of the U.S. on Nov. 3, and his running mate on the Democratic ticket, Sen. Al Gore Jr. of Tennessee, was elected vice president. They carried 32 states and the District of Columbia, winning 370 electoral votes. Republican presidential candidate, Pres. George Bush, and his running mate, Vice Pres. Dan Quayle, won 18 states and 188 electoral votes. In the nationwide popular vote, the official tally gave Clinton 44,908,254 (43 percent), Bush 39,102,343 (38 percent), and independent candidate H. Ross Perot 19,741,065 (19 percent). The Democrats retained control of both houses of Congress, emerging with a 57-42 margin in the Senate, and after a Nov. 24 runoff, 57-43. In the House, the Republicans gained 10 seats, but the Democrats still held a 258-176 majority, with 1 independent. There would be 110 new House members, the biggest turnover since 1948, and the new House would include record numbers of women (47), blacks (38), and Hispanics (17). The new Senate also would have a record number of women (6); two women Democrats won Senate elections in Calif., and Carol Moseley Braun of Illinois became the first black woman to serve in the Senate. The Democrats also picked up 2 governorships, for a 30-18 margin over the Republicans.

IBM said, Dec. 15, it would cut 25,000 jobs in 1993, after cutting 40,000 in 1992 through voluntary retirements. Once the industry's leader, the company projected a $5.25 billion net loss for the 4th quarter.

A U.N.-sanctioned military force, led by American troops, arrived in Somalia beginning Dec. 9 to ensure the delivery of food to starving people in the war-torn nation by "all necessary means."

# Declaration of Independence

The Declaration of Independence was adopted by the Continental Congress in Philadelphia, on July 4, 1776. John Hancock was president of the Congress and Charles Thomson was secretary. A copy of the Declaration, engrossed on parchment, was signed by members of Congress on and after Aug. 2, 1776. On Jan. 18, 1777, Congress ordered that "an authenticated copy, with the names of the members of Congress subscribing the same, be sent to each of the United States, and that they be desired to have the same put upon record." Authenticated copies were printed in broadside form in Baltimore, where the Continental Congress was then in session. The following text is that of the original printed by John Dunlap at Philadelphia for the Continental Congress.

## IN CONGRESS, July 4, 1776.

## A DECLARATION

### By the REPRESENTATIVES of the

## UNITED STATES OF AMERICA,

### In GENERAL CONGRESS assembled

When in the Course of human Events, it becomes necessary for one People to dissolve the Political Bands which have connected them with another, and to assume among the Powers of the Earth, the separate and equal Station to which the Laws of Nature and of Nature's God entitle them, a decent Respect to the Opinions of Mankind requires that they should declare the causes which impel them to the Separation.

We hold these Truths to be self-evident, that all Men are created equal, that they are endowed by their Creator with certain unalienable Rights, that among these are Life, Liberty, and the Pursuit of Happiness—That to secure these Rights, Governments are instituted among Men, deriving their just Powers from the Consent of the Governed, that whenever any Form of Government becomes destructive of these Ends, it is the Right of the People to alter or to abolish it, and to institute new Government, laying its Foundation on such Principles, and organizing its Powers in such Form, as to them shall seem most likely to effect their Safety and Happiness. Prudence, indeed, will dictate that Governments long established should not be changed for light and transient Causes; and accordingly all Experience hath shewn, that Mankind are more disposed to suffer, while Evils are sufferable, than to right themselves by abolishing the Forms to which they are accustomed. But when a long Train of Abuses and Usurpations, pursuing invariably the same Object, evinces a Design to reduce them under absolute Despotism, it is their Right, it is their Duty, to throw off such Government, and to provide new Guards for their future Security. Such has been the patient Sufferance of these Colonies; and such is now the Necessity which constrains them to alter their former Systems of Government. The History of the present King of Great-Britain is a History of repeated Injuries and Usurpations, all having in direct Object the Establishment of an absolute Tyranny over these States. To prove this, let Facts be submitted to a candid World.

He has refused his Assent to Laws, the most wholesome and necessary for the public Good.

He has forbidden his Governors to pass Laws of immediate and pressing Importance, unless suspended in their Operation till his Assent should be obtained; and when so suspended, he has utterly neglected to attend to them.

He has refused to pass other Laws for the Accommodation of large Districts of People, unless those People would relinquish the Right of Representation in the Legislature, a Right inestimable to them, and formidable to Tyrants only.

He has called together Legislative Bodies at Places unusual, uncomfortable, and distant from the Depository of their Public Records, for the sole Purpose of fatiguing them into Compliance with his Measures.

He has dissolved Representative Houses repeatedly, for opposing with manly Firmness his Invasions on the Rights of the People.

He has refused for a long Time, after such Dissolutions, to cause others to be elected; whereby the Legislative Powers, incapable of Annihilation, have returned to the People at large for their exercise; the State remaining in the mean time exposed to all the Dangers of Invasion from without, and Convulsions within.

He has endeavoured to prevent the Population of these States; for that Purpose obstructing the Laws for Naturalization of Foreigners; refusing to pass others to encourage their Migrations hither, and raising the Conditions of new Appropriations of Lands.

He has obstructed the Administration of Justice, by refusing his Assent to Laws for establishing Judiciary Powers.

He has made Judges dependent on his Will alone, for the Tenure of their Offices, and the Amount and payment of their Salaries.

He has erected a Multitude of new Offices, and sent hither Swarms of Officers to harrass our People, and eat out their Substance.

He has kept among us, in Times of Peace, Standing Armies, without the consent of our Legislatures.

He has affected to render the Military independent of, and superior to the Civil Power.

He has combined with others to subject us to a Jurisdiction foreign to our Constitution, and unacknowledged by our Laws; giving his Assent to their Acts of pretended Legislation:

For quartering large Bodies of Armed Troops among us:

For protecting them, by a mock Trial, from Punishment for any Murders which they should commit on the Inhabitants of these States:

For cutting off our Trade with all Parts of the World:

For imposing Taxes on us without our Consent:

For depriving us, in many Cases, of the Benefits of Trial by Jury:

For transporting us beyond Seas to be tried for pretended Offences:

For abolishing the free System of English Laws in a neighbouring Province, establishing therein an arbitrary Government, and enlarging its Boundaries, so as to render it at once an Example and fit Instrument for introducing the same absolute Rule into these Colonies:

For taking away our Charters, abolishing our most valuable Laws, and altering fundamentally the Forms of our Governments:

For suspending our own Legislatures, and declaring themselves invested with Power to legislate for us in all Cases whatsoever.

He has abdicated Government here, by declaring us out of his Protection and waging War against us.

He has plundered our Seas, ravaged our Coasts, burnt our towns, and destroyed the Lives of our People.

He is, at this Time, transporting large Armies of foreign Mercenaries to complete the works of Death, Desolation, and Tyranny, already begun with circumstances of Cruelty and Perfidy, scarcely paralleled in the most barbarous Ages, and totally unworthy the Head of a civilized Nation.

He has constrained our fellow Citizens taken Captive on the high Seas to bear Arms against their Country, to become the Executioners of their Friends and Brethren, or to fall themselves by their Hands.

He has excited domestic Insurrections amongst us, and has endeavoured to bring on the Inhabitants of our Frontiers, the merciless Indian Savages, whose known Rule of Warfare, is an undistinguished Destruction, of all Ages, Sexes and Conditions.

In every stage of these Oppressions we have Petitioned for Redress in the most humble Terms: Our repeated Petitions have been answered only by repeated Injury. A Prince, whose Character is thus marked by every act which may define a Tyrant, is unfit to be the Ruler of a free People.

Nor have we been wanting in Attentions to our British Brethren. We have warned them from Time to Time of Attempts by their Legislature to extend an unwarrantable Jurisdiction over us. We have reminded them of the Circumstances of our Emigration and Settlement here. We have appealed to their native Justice and Magnanimity, and we have conjured them by the Ties of our common Kindred to disavow these Usurpations, which, would inevitably interrupt our Connections and Correspondence. They too have been deaf to the Voice of Justice and of Consanguinity. We must, therefore, acquiesce in the Necessity, which denounces our Separation, and hold them, as we hold the rest of Mankind, Enemies in War, in Peace, Friends.

We, therefore, the Representatives of the UNITED STATES OF AMERICA, in General Congress, Assembled, appealing to the Supreme Judge of the World for the Rectitude of our Intentions, do, in the Name, and by Authority of the good People of these Colonies, solemnly Publish and Declare, That these United Colonies are, and of Right ought to be, Free and Independent States; that they are absolved from all Allegiance to the British Crown, and that all political Connection between them and the State of Great-Britain, is and ought to be totally dissolved; and that as Free and Independent States, they have full Power to levy War, conclude Peace, contract Alliances, establish Commerce, and to do all other Acts and Things which Independent States may of right do. And for the support of this declaration, with a firm Reliance on the Protection of divine Providence, we mutually pledge to each other our lives, our Fortunes, and our sacred Honor.

**JOHN HANCOCK, President**

Attest.
**CHARLES THOMSON, Secretary.**

## Signers of the Declaration of Independence

| Delegate (state) | Vocation | Birthplace | Born | Died |
|---|---|---|---|---|
| Adams, John (Mass.) | Lawyer | Braintree (Quincy), Mass. | Oct. 30, 1735 | July 4, 1826 |
| Adams, Samuel (Mass.) | Political leader | Boston, Mass. | Sept. 27, 1722 | Oct. 2, 1803 |
| Bartlett, Josiah (N.H.) | Physician, judge. | Amesbury, Mass. | Nov. 21, 1729 | May 19, 1795 |
| Braxton, Carter (Va.) | Farmer | Newington Plantation, Va. | Sept. 10, 1736 | Oct. 10, 1797 |
| Carroll, Chas. of Carrollton (Md.) | Lawyer | Annapolis, Md. | Sept. 19, 1737 | Nov. 14, 1832 |
| Chase, Samuel (Md.) | Judge | Princess Anne, Md. | Apr. 17, 1741 | June 19, 1811 |
| Clark, Abraham (N.J.) | Surveyor | Roselle, N.J. | Feb. 15, 1726 | Sept. 15, 1794 |
| Clymer, George (Pa.) | Merchant | Philadelphia, Pa. | Mar. 16, 1739 | Jan. 23, 1813 |
| Ellery, William (R.I.) | Lawyer | Newport, R.I. | Dec. 22, 1727 | Feb. 15, 1820 |
| Floyd, William (N.Y.) | Soldier | Brookhaven, N.Y. | Dec. 17, 1734 | Aug. 4, 1821 |
| Franklin, Benjamin (Pa.) | Printer, publisher | Boston, Mass. | Jan. 17, 1706 | Apr. 17, 1790 |
| Gerry, Elbridge (Mass.) | Merchant | Marblehead, Mass. | July 17, 1744 | Nov. 23, 1814 |
| Gwinnett, Button (Ga.) | Merchant | Down Hatherly, England. | c. 1735 | May 19, 1777 |
| Hall, Lyman (Ga.) | Physician | Wallingford, Conn. | Apr. 12, 1724 | Oct. 19, 1790 |
| Hancock, John (Mass.) | Merchant | Braintree (Quincy), Mass. | Jan. 12, 1737 | Oct. 8, 1793 |
| Harrison, Benjamin (Va.) | Farmer | Berkeley, Va. | Apr. 5, 1726 | Apr. 24, 1791 |
| Hart, John (N.J.) | Farmer | Stonington, Conn. | c. 1711 | May 11, 1779 |
| Hewes, Joseph (N.C.) | Merchant | Princeton, N.J. | Jan. 23, 1730 | Nov. 10, 1779 |
| Heyward, Thos. Jr. (S.C.) | Lawyer, farmer | St. Luke's Parish, S.C. | July 28, 1746 | Mar. 6, 1809 |
| Hooper, William (N.C.) | Lawyer | Boston, Mass. | June 28, 1742 | Oct. 14, 1790 |
| Hopkins, Stephen (R.I.) | Judge, educator | Providence, R.I. | Mar. 7, 1707 | July 13, 1785 |
| Hopkinson, Francis (N.J.) | Judge, author | Philadelphia, Pa. | Sept. 21, 1737 | May 9, 1791 |
| Huntington, Samuel (Conn.) | Judge | Windham County, Conn. | July 3, 1731 | Jan. 5, 1796 |
| Jefferson, Thomas (Va.) | Lawyer | Shadwell, Va. | Apr. 13, 1743 | July 4, 1826 |
| Lee, Francis Lightfoot (Va.) | Farmer | Westmoreland County, Va. | Oct. 14, 1734 | Jan. 11, 1797 |
| Lee, Richard Henry (Va.) | Farmer | Westmoreland County, Va. | Jan. 20, 1732 | June 19, 1794 |
| Lewis, Francis (N.Y.) | Merchant | Llandaff, Wales | Mar., 1713 | Dec. 31, 1802 |
| Livingston, Philip (N.Y.) | Merchant | Albany, N.Y. | Jan. 15, 1716 | June 12, 1778 |
| Lynch, Thomas Jr. (S.C.) | Farmer | Winyah, S.C. | Aug. 5, 1749 | (at sea) 1779 |
| McKean, Thomas (Del.) | Lawyer | New London, Pa. | Mar. 19, 1734 | June 24, 1817 |
| Middleton, Arthur (S.C.) | Farmer | Charleston, S.C. | June 26, 1742 | Jan. 1, 1787 |
| Morris, Lewis (N.Y.) | Farmer | Morrisania (Bronx County), N.Y. | Apr. 8, 1726 | Jan. 22, 1798 |
| Morris, Robert (Pa.) | Merchant | Liverpool, England | Jan. 20, 1734 | May 9, 1806 |
| Morton, John (Pa.) | Judge | Ridley, Pa. | 1724 | Apr., 1777 |
| Nelson, Thos. Jr. (Va.) | Farmer | Yorktown, Va. | Dec. 26, 1738 | Jan. 4, 1789 |
| Paca, William (Md.) | Judge | Abingdon, Md. | Oct. 31, 1740 | Oct. 23, 1799 |
| Paine, Robert Treat (Mass.) | Judge | Boston, Mass. | Mar. 11, 1731 | May 12, 1814 |
| Penn, John (N.C.) | Lawyer | Near Port Royal, Va. | May 17, 1741 | Sept. 14, 1788 |
| Read, George (Del.) | Judge | Near North East, Md. | Sept. 18, 1733 | Sept. 21, 1798 |
| Rodney, Caesar (Del.) | Judge | Dover, Del. | Oct. 7, 1728 | June 29, 1784 |
| Ross, George (Pa.) | Judge | New Castle, Del. | May 10, 1730 | July 14, 1779 |
| Rush, Benjamin (Pa.) | Physician | Byberry, Pa. (Philadelphia). | Dec. 24, 1745 | Apr. 19, 1813 |
| Rutledge, Edward (S.C.) | Lawyer | Charleston, S.C. | Nov. 23, 1749 | Jan. 23, 1800 |
| Sherman, Roger (Conn.) | Lawyer | Newton, Mass. | Apr. 19, 1721 | July 23, 1793 |
| Smith, James (Pa.) | Lawyer | Dublin, Ireland | c. 1719 | July 11, 1806 |
| Stockton, Richard (N.J.) | Lawyer | Near Princeton, N.J. | Oct. 1, 1730 | Feb. 28, 1781 |
| Stone, Thomas (Md.) | Lawyer | Charles County, Md. | 1743 | Oct. 5, 1787 |
| Taylor, George (Pa.) | Ironmaster | Ireland | 1716 | Feb. 23, 1781 |
| Thornton, Matthew (N.H.) | Physician | Ireland | 1714 | June 24, 1803 |
| Walton, George (Ga.) | Judge | Prince Edward County, Va. | 1741 | Feb. 2, 1804 |
| Whipple, William (N.H.) | Merchant, judge. | Kittery, Me. | Jan. 14, 1730 | Nov. 28, 1785 |
| Williams, William (Conn.) | Merchant | Lebanon, Conn. | Apr. 23, 1731 | Aug. 2, 1811 |
| Wilson, James (Pa.) | Judge | Carskerdo, Scotland. | Sept. 14, 1742 | Aug. 28, 1798 |
| Witherspoon, John (N.J.) | Clergyman, educator | Gifford, Scotland | Feb. 5, 1723 | Nov. 15, 1794 |
| Wolcott, Oliver (Conn.) | Judge | Windsor, Conn. | Dec. 1, 1726 | Dec. 1, 1797 |
| Wythe, George (Va.) | Lawyer | Elizabeth City Co. (Hampton), Va. | 1726 | June 8, 1806 |

# Constitution of the United States
## The Original 7 Articles

### PREAMBLE

We, the people of the United States, in order to form a more perfect Union, establish justice, insure domestic tranquility, provide for the common defense, promote the general welfare, and secure the blessings of liberty to ourselves and our posterity do ordain and establish this Constitution for the United States of America.

### ARTICLE I.

#### Section 1—Legislative powers; in whom vested:

All legislative powers herein granted shall be vested in a Congress of the United States, which shall consist of a Senate and House of Representatives.

#### Section 2—House of Representatives, how and by whom chosen. Qualifications of a Representative. Representatives and direct taxes, how apportioned. Enumeration. Vacancies to be filled. Power of choosing officers, and of impeachment.

1. The House of Representatives shall be composed of members chosen every second year by the people of the several States, and the electors in each State shall have the qualifications requisite for electors of the most numerous branch of the State Legislature.

2. No person shall be a Representative who shall not have attained to the age of twenty-five years, and been seven years a citizen of the United States, and who shall not, when elected, be an inhabitant of that State in which he shall be chosen.

3. *(Representatives and direct taxes shall be apportioned among the several States which may be included within this Union, according to their respective numbers, which shall be determined by adding to the whole number of free persons, including those bound to service for a term of years, and excluding Indians not taxed, three-fifths of all other persons.) (The previous sentence was superseded by Amendment XIV, section 2.)* The actual enumeration shall be made within three years after the first meeting of the Congress of the United States, and within every subsequent term of ten years, in such manner as they shall by law direct. The number of Representatives shall not exceed one for every thirty thousand, but each State shall have at least one Representative; and until such enumeration shall be made, the State of New Hampshire shall be entitled to choose three, Massachusetts eight, Rhode Island and Providence Plantations one, Connecticut five, New York six, New Jersey four, Pennsylvania eight, Delaware one, Maryland six, Virginia ten, North Carolina five, South Carolina five, and Georgia three.

4. When vacancies happen in the representation from any State, the Executive Authority thereof shall issue writs of election to fill such vacancies.

5. The House of Representatives shall choose their Speaker and other officers; and shall have the sole power of impeachment.

#### Section 3—Senators, how and by whom chosen. How classified. Qualifications of a Senator. President of the Senate, his right to vote. President pro tem., and other officers of the Senate, how chosen. Power to try impeachments. When President is tried, Chief Justice to preside. Sentence.

1. The Senate of the United States shall be composed of two Senators from each State, *(chosen by the Legislature thereof). (The preceding five words were superseded by Amendment XVII, section 1.)* for six years; and each Senator shall have one vote.

2. Immediately after they shall be assembled in consequence of the first election, they shall be divided as equally as may be into three classes. The seats of the Senators of the first class shall be vacated at the expiration of the second year, of the second class at the expiration of the fourth year, and of the third class at the expiration of the sixth year, so that one-third may be chosen every second year; *(and if vacancies happen by resignation, or otherwise, during the recess of the Legislature of any State, the Executive thereof may make temporary appointments until the next meeting of the Legislature, which shall then fill such vacancies.) (The words*

*in parentheses were superseded by Amendment XVII, section 2.)*

3. No person shall be a Senator who shall not have attained to the age of thirty years, and been nine years a citizen of the United States, and who shall not, when elected, be an inhabitant of that State for which he shall be chosen.

4. The Vice President of the United States shall be President of the Senate, but shall have no vote, unless they be equally divided.

5. The Senate shall choose their other officers, and also a President pro tempore, in the absence of the Vice President, or when he shall exercise the office of President of the United States.

6. The Senate shall have the sole power to try all impeachments. When sitting for that purpose, they shall be on oath or affirmation. When the President of the United States is tried, the Chief Justice shall preside: and no person shall be convicted without the concurrence of two-thirds of the members present.

7. Judgment in cases of impeachment shall not extend further than to removal from office, and disqualification to hold and enjoy any office of honor, trust or profit under the United States: but the party convicted shall nevertheless be liable and subject to indictment, trial, judgment and punishment, according to law.

#### Section 4—Times, etc., of holding elections, how prescribed. One session each year.

1. The times, places and manner of holding elections for Senators and Representatives, shall be prescribed in each State by the Legislature thereof; but the Congress may at any time by law make or alter such regulations, except as to the places of choosing Senators.

2. The Congress shall assemble at least once in every year, and such meeting shall *(be on the first Monday in December.) (The words in parentheses were superseded by Amendment XX, section 2).* unless they shall by law appoint a different day.

#### Section 5—Membership, quorum, adjournments, rules. Power to punish or expel. Journal. Time of adjournments, how limited, etc.

1. Each House shall be the judge of the elections, returns and qualifications of its own members, and a majority of each shall constitute a quorum to do business; but a smaller number may adjourn from day to day, and may be authorized to compel the attendance of absent members, in such manner, and under such penalties as each House may provide.

2. Each House may determine the rules of its proceedings, punish its members for disorderly behavior, and, with the concurrence of two-thirds, expel a member.

3. Each House shall keep a journal of its proceedings, and from time to time publish the same, excepting such parts as may in their judgment require secrecy; and the yeas and nays of the members of either House on any question shall, at the desire of one-fifth of those present, be entered on the journal.

4. Neither House, during the session of Congress, shall, without the consent of the other, adjourn for more than three days, nor to any other place than that in which the two Houses shall be sitting.

#### Section 6—Compensation, privileges, disqualifications in certain cases.

1. The Senators and Representatives shall receive a compensation for their services, to be ascertained by law, and paid out of the Treasury of the United States. They shall in all cases, except treason, felony and breach of the peace, be privileged from arrest during their attendance at the session of their respective Houses, and in going to and returning from the same; and for any speech or debate in either House, they shall not be questioned in any other place.

2. No Senator or Representative shall, during the time for which he was elected, be appointed to any civil office under the authority of the United States, which shall have been created, or the emoluments whereof shall have been increased during such time; and no person holding any office under the United States, shall be a member of either House

during his continuance in office.

### Section 7—House to originate all revenue bills. Veto. Bill may be passed by two-thirds of each House, notwithstanding, etc. Bill, not returned in ten days, to become a law. Provisions as to orders, concurrent resolutions, etc.

1. All bills for raising revenue shall originate in the House of Representatives; but the Senate may propose or concur with amendments as on other bills.

2. Every bill which shall have passed the House of Representatives and the Senate, shall, before it becomes a law, be presented to the President of the United States; if he approves he shall sign it, but if not he shall return it, with his objections to that House in which it shall have originated, who shall enter the objections at large on their journal, and proceed to reconsider it. If after such reconsideration two-thirds of that House shall agree to pass the bill, it shall be sent, together with the objections, to the other House, by which it shall likewise be reconsidered, and if approved by two-thirds of that House, it shall become a law. But in all such cases the votes of both Houses shall be determined by yeas and nays, and the names of the persons voting for and against the bill shall be entered on the journal of each House respectively. If any bill shall not be returned by the President within ten days (Sundays excepted) after it shall have been presented to him, the same shall be a law, in like manner as if he had signed it, unless the Congress by their adjournment prevent its return, in which case it shall not be a law.

3. Every order, resolution, or vote to which the concurrence of the Senate and House of Representatives may be necessary (except on a question of adjournment) shall be presented to the President of the United States; and before the same shall take effect, shall be approved by him, or being disapproved by him, shall be repassed by two-thirds of the Senate and House of Representatives, according to the rules and limitations prescribed in the case of a bill.

### Section 8—Powers of Congress.

The Congress shall have power

1. To lay and collect taxes, duties, imposts and excises, to pay the debts and provide for the common defense and general welfare of the United States; but all duties, imposts and excises shall be uniform throughout the United States;

2. To borrow money on the credit of the United States;

3. To regulate commerce with foreign nations, and among the several States, and with the Indian tribes;

4. To establish a uniform rule of naturalization, and uniform laws on the subject of bankruptcies throughout the United States;

5. To coin money, regulate the value thereof, and of foreign coin, and fix the standard of weights and measures;

6. To provide for the punishment of counterfeiting the securities and current coin of the United States;

7. To establish post-offices and post-roads;

8. To promote the progress of science and useful arts, by securing for limited times to authors and inventors the exclusive right to their respective writings and discoveries;

9. To constitute tribunals inferior to the Supreme Court;

10. To define and punish piracies and felonies committed on the high seas, and offenses against the law of nations;

11. To declare war, grant letters of marque and reprisal, and make rules concerning captures on land and water;

12. To raise and support armies, but no appropriation of money to that use shall be for a longer term than two years;

13. To provide and maintain a navy;

14. To make rules for the government and regulation of the land and naval forces;

15. To provide for calling forth the militia to execute the laws of the Union, suppress insurrections and repel invasions;

16. To provide for organizing, arming, and disciplining the militia, and for governing such part of them as may be employed in the service of the United States, reserving to the States respectively, the appointment of the officers, and the authority of training the militia according to the discipline prescribed by Congress;

17. To exercise exclusive legislation in all cases whatsoever, over such district (not exceeding ten miles square) as

may, by cession of particular States, and the acceptance of Congress, become the seat of the Government of the United States, and to exercise like authority over all places purchased by the consent of the Legislature of the State in which the same shall be, for the erection of forts, magazines, arsenals, dockyards, and other needful buildings;—And

18. To make all laws which shall be necessary and proper for carrying into execution the foregoing powers, and all other powers vested by this Constitution in the Government of the United States, or in any department or officer thereof.

### Section 9—Provision as to migration or importation of certain persons. Habeas corpus, bills of attainder, etc. Taxes, how apportioned. No export duty. No commercial preference. Money, how drawn from Treasury, etc. No titular nobility. Officers not to receive presents, etc.

1. The migration or importation of such persons as any of the States now existing shall think proper to admit, shall not be prohibited by the Congress prior to the year one thousand eight hundred and eight, but a tax or duty may be imposed on such importation, not exceeding ten dollars for each person.

2. The privilege of the writ of habeas corpus shall not be suspended, unless when in cases of rebellion or invasion the public safety may require it.

3. No bill of attainder or ex post facto law shall be passed.

4. No capitation, or other direct, tax shall be laid, unless in proportion to the census or enumeration herein before directed to be taken. *(Modified by Amendment XVI.)*

5. No tax or duty shall be laid on articles exported from any State.

6. No preference shall be given by any regulation of commerce or revenue to the ports of one State over those of another: nor shall vessels bound to, or from, one State, be obliged to enter, clear, or pay duties in another.

7. No money shall be drawn from the Treasury, but in consequence of appropriations made by law; and a regular statement and account of the receipts and expenditures of all public money shall be published from time to time.

8. No title of nobility shall be granted by the United States: and no person holding any office of profit or trust under them, shall, without the consent of the Congress, accept of any present, emolument, office, or title, of any kind whatever, from any king, prince, or foreign state.

### Section 10—States prohibited from the exercise of certain powers.

1. No State shall enter into any treaty, alliance, or confederation; grant letters of marque and reprisal; coin money; emit bills of credit; make anything but gold and silver coin a tender in payment of debts; pass any bill of attainder, ex post facto law, or law impairing the obligation of contracts, or grant any title of nobility.

2. No State shall, without the consent of the Congress, lay any imposts or duties on imports or exports, except what may be absolutely necessary for executing its inspection laws: and the net produce of all duties and imposts, laid by any State on imports or exports, shall be for the use of the Treasury of the United States; and all such laws shall be subject to the revision and control of the Congress.

3. No State shall, without the consent of Congress, lay any duty of tonnage, keep troops, or ships of war in time of peace, enter into any agreement or compact with another State, or with a foreign power, or engage in war, unless actually invaded, or in such imminent danger as will not admit of delay.

## ARTICLE II.

### Section 1—President: his term of office. Electors of President; number and how appointed. Electors to vote on same day. Qualification of President. On whom his duties devolve in case of his removal, death, etc. President's compensation. His oath of office.

1. The Executive power shall be vested in a President of the United States of America. He shall hold his office during the term of four years, and together with the Vice President, chosen for the same term, be elected as follows

2. Each State shall appoint, in such manner as the Legis-

lature thereof may direct, a number of electors, equal to the whole number of Senators and Representatives to which the State may be entitled in the Congress: but no Senator or Representative, or person holding an office of trust or profit under the United States, shall be appointed an elector.

*(The electors shall meet in their respective States, and vote by ballot for two persons, of whom one at least shall not be an inhabitant of the same State with themselves. And they shall make a list of all the persons voted for, and of the number of votes for each; which list they shall sign and certify, and transmit sealed to the seat of the Government of the United States, directed to the President of the Senate. The President of the Senate shall, in the presence of the Senate and House of Representatives, open all the certificates, and the votes shall then be counted. The person having the greatest number of votes shall be the President, if such number be a majority of the whole number of electors appointed; and if there be more than one who have such majority, and have an equal number of votes, then the House of Representatives shall immediately choose by ballot one of them for President; and if no person have a majority, then from the five highest on the list the said House shall in like manner choose the President. But in choosing the President, the votes shall be taken by States, the representation from each State having one vote; a quorum for this purpose shall consist of a member or members from two-thirds of the States, and a majority of all the States shall be necessary to a choice. In every case, after the choice of the President, the person having the greatest number of votes of the electors shall be the Vice President. But if there should remain two or more who have equal votes, the Senate shall choose from them by ballot the Vice President.)*

*(This clause was superseded by Amendment XII.)*

3. The Congress may determine the time of choosing the electors, and the day on which they shall give their votes; which day shall be the same throughout the United States.

4. No person except a natural born citizen, or a citizen of the United States, at the time of the adoption of this Constitution, shall be eligible to the office of President; neither shall any person be eligible to that office who shall not have attained to the age of thirty-five years, and been fourteen years a resident within the United States.

*(For qualification of the Vice President, see Amendment XII.)*

5. In case of the removal of the President from office, or of his death, resignation, or inability to discharge the powers and duties of the said office, the same shall devolve on the Vice President, and the Congress may by law provide for the case of removal, death, resignation or inability, both of the President and Vice President, declaring what officer shall then act as President, and such officer shall act accordingly, until the disability be removed, or a President shall be elected.

*(This clause has been modified by Amendments XX and XXV.)*

6. The President shall, at stated times, receive for his services, a compensation, which shall neither be increased nor diminished during the period for which he shall have been elected, and he shall not receive within that period any other emolument from the United States, or any of them.

7. Before he enter on the execution of his office, he shall take the following oath or affirmation:

"I do solemnly swear (or affirm) that I will faithfully execute the office of President of the United States, and will to the best of my ability, preserve, protect and defend the Constitution of the United States."

**Section 2—President to be Commander-in-Chief. He may require opinions of cabinet officers, etc., may pardon. Treaty-making power. Nomination of certain officers. When President may fill vacancies.**

1. The President shall be Commander-in-Chief of the Army and Navy of the United States, and of the militia of the several States, when called into the actual service of the United States; he may require the opinion, in writing, of the principal officer in each of the executive departments, upon any subject relating to the duties of their respective offices, and he shall have power to grant reprieves and pardons for offenses against the United States, except in cases of impeachment.

2. He shall have power, by and with the advice and con-

sent of the Senate, to make treaties, provided two-thirds of the Senators present concur; and he shall nominate, and by and with the advice and consent of the Senate, shall appoint ambassadors, other public ministers and consuls, judges of the Supreme Court, and all other officers of the United States, whose appointments are not herein otherwise provided for, and which shall be established by law: but the Congress may by law vest the appointment of such inferior officers, as they think proper, in the President alone, in the courts of law, or in the heads of departments.

3. The President shall have power to fill up all vacancies that may happen during the recess of the Senate, by granting commissions, which shall expire at the end of their next session.

**Section 3—President shall communicate to Congress. He may convene and adjourn Congress, in case of disagreement, etc. Shall receive ambassadors, execute laws, and commission officers.**

He shall from time to time give to the Congress information of the state of the Union, and recommend to their consideration such measures as he shall judge necessary and expedient; he may, on extraordinary occasions, convene both Houses, or either of them, and in case of disagreement between them, with respect to the time of adjournment, he may adjourn them to such time as he shall think proper; he shall receive ambassadors and other public ministers; he shall take care that the laws be faithfully executed, and shall commission all the officers of the United States.

**Section 4—All civil offices forfeited for certain crimes.**

The President, Vice President, and all civil officers of the United States, shall be removed from office on impeachment for, and conviction of, treason, bribery, or other high crimes and misdemeanors.

## ARTICLE III.

### Section 1—Judicial powers, Tenure. Compensation.

The judicial power of the United States, shall be vested in one Supreme Court, and in such inferior courts as the Congress may from time to time ordain and establish. The judges, both of the Supreme and inferior courts, shall hold their offices during good behavior, and shall at stated times, receive for their services, a compensation, which shall not be diminished during their continuance in office.

**Section 2—Judicial power; to what cases it extends. Original jurisdiction of Supreme Court; appellate jurisdiction. Trial by jury, etc. Trial, where.**

1. The judicial power shall extend to all cases, in law and equity, arising under this Constitution, the laws of the United States, and treaties made, or which shall be made, under their authority; to all cases affecting ambassadors, other public ministers and consuls; to all cases of admiralty and maritime jurisdiction; to controversies to which the United States shall be a party; to controversies between two or more States; between a State and citizens of another State; between citizens of different States, between citizens of the same State claiming lands under grants of different States, and between a State, or the citizens thereof, and foreign states, citizens or subjects.

*(This section is modified by Amendment XI.)*

2. In all cases affecting ambassadors, other public ministers and consuls, and those in which a State shall be party, the Supreme Court shall have original jurisdiction. In all the other cases before mentioned, the Supreme Court shall have appellate jurisdiction, both as to law and fact, with such exceptions, and under such regulations as the Congress shall make.

3. The trial of all crimes, except in cases of impeachment, shall be by jury; and such trial shall be held in the State where the said crimes shall have been committed; but when not committed within any State, the trial shall be at such place or places as the Congress may by law have directed.

**Section 3—Treason Defined, Proof of, Punishment of.**

1. Treason against the United States, shall consist only in levying war against them, or in adhering to their enemies,

giving them aid and comfort. No person shall be convicted of treason unless on the testimony of two witnesses to the same overt act, or on confession in open court.

2. The Congress shall have power to declare the punishment of treason, but no attainder of treason shall work corruption of blood, or forfeiture except during the life of the person attainted.

## ARTICLE IV.

### Section 1—Each State to give credit to the public acts, etc., of every other State.

Full faith and credit shall be given in each State to the public acts, records, and judicial proceedings of every other State. And the Congress may by general laws prescribe the manner in which such acts, records and proceedings shall be proved, and the effect thereof.

### Section 2—Privileges of citizens of each State. Fugitives from justice to be delivered up. Persons held to service having escaped, to be delivered up.

1. The citizens of each State shall be entitled to all privileges and immunities of citizens in the several States.

2. A person charged in any State with treason, felony, or other crime, who shall flee from justice, and be found in another State, shall on demand of the Executive authority of the State from which he fled, be delivered up, to be removed to the State having jurisdiction of the crime.

*(3. No person held to service or labor in one State, under the laws thereof, escaping into another, shall in consequence of any law or regulation therein, be discharged from such service or labor, but shall be delivered up on claim of the party to whom such service or labor may be due.) (This clause was superseded by Amendment XIII.)*

### Section 3—Admission of new States. Power of Congress over territory and other property.

1. New States may be admitted by the Congress into this Union; but no new State shall be formed or erected within the jurisdiction of any other State; nor any State be formed by the junction of two or more States, or parts of States, without the consent of the Legislatures of the States concerned as well as of the Congress.

2. The Congress shall have power to dispose of and make all needful rules and regulations respecting the territory or other property belonging to the United States; and nothing in this Constitution shall be so construed as to prejudice any claims of the United States, or of any particular State.

### Section 4—Republican form of government guaranteed. Each state to be protected.

The United States shall guarantee to every State in this Union a Republican form of government, and shall protect each of them against invasion; and on application of the Legislature, or of the Executive (when the Legislature cannot be convened) against domestic violence.

## ARTICLE V.

### Constitution; how amended; proviso.

The Congress, whenever two-thirds of both Houses shall deem it necessary, shall propose amendments to this Constitution, or, on the application of the Legislatures of two-thirds of the several States, shall call a convention for proposing amendments, which, in either case, shall be valid to all intents and purposes, as part of this Constitution, when ratified by the Legislatures of three-fourths of the several States, or by conventions in three-fourths thereof, as the one

or the other mode of ratification may be proposed by the Congress; provided that no amendment which may be made prior to the year one thousand eight hundred and eight shall in any manner affect the first and fourth clauses in the Ninth Section of the First Article; and that no State, without its consent, shall be deprived of its equal suffrage in the Senate.

## ARTICLE VI.

### Certain debts, etc., declared valid. Supremacy of Constitution, treaties, and laws of the United States. Oath to support Constitution, by whom taken. No religious test.

1. All debts contracted and engagements entered into, before the adoption of this Constitution, shall be as valid against the United States under this Constitution, as under the Confederation.

2. This Constitution, and the laws of the United States which shall be made in pursuance thereof; and all treaties made, or which shall be made, under the authority of the United States, shall be the supreme law of the land; and the judges in every State shall be bound thereby, any thing in the Constitution or laws of any State to the contrary notwithstanding.

3. The Senators and Representatives before mentioned, and the members of the several State Legislatures, and all executive and judicial officers, both of the United States and of the several States, shall be bound by oath or affirmation, to support this Constitution; but no religious test shall ever be required as a qualification to any office or public trust under the United States.

## ARTICLE VII.

### What ratification shall establish Constitution.

The ratification of the Conventions of nine States, shall be sufficient for the establishment of this Constitution between the States so ratifying the same.

Done in convention by the unanimous consent of the States present the Seventeenth day of September in the year of our Lord one thousand seven hundred and eighty seven, and of the independence of the United States of America the Twelfth. In witness whereof we have hereunto subscribed our names.

George Washington, President and deputy from Virginia.

New Hampshire—John Langdon, Nicholas Gilman.

Massachusetts—Nathaniel Gorham, Rufus King.

Connecticut—Wm. Saml. Johnson, Roger Sherman.

New York—Alexander Hamilton.

New Jersey—Wil: Livingston, David Brearley, Wm. Paterson, Jona: Dayton.

Pennsylvania—B. Franklin, Thomas Mifflin, Robt. Morris, Geo. Clymer, Thos. FitzSimons, Jared Ingersoll, James Wilson, Gouv. Morris.

Delaware—Geo: Read, Gunning Bedford Jun., John Dickinson, Richard Bassett, Jaco: Broom.

Maryland—James McHenry, Daniel of Saint Thomas Jenifer, Danl. Carroll.

Virginia—John Blair, James Madison Jr.

North Carolina—Wm. Blount, Rich'd. Dobbs Spaight, Hugh Williamson.

South Carolina—J. Rutledge, Charles Cotesworth Pinckney, Charles Pinckney, Pierce Butler.

Georgia—William Few, Abr. Baldwin.

Attest: William Jackson, Secretary.

## Ten Original Amendments: The Bill of Rights
### In force Dec. 15, 1791

*(The First Congress, at its first session in the City of New York, Sept. 25, 1789, submitted to the states 12 amendments to clarify certain individual and state rights not named in the Constitution. They are generally called the Bill of Rights.*

*(Influential in framing these amendments was the Declaration of Rights of Virginia, written by George Mason (1725-1792) in 1776. Mason, a Virginia delegate to the Constitutional Convention, did not sign the Constitution and opposed its ratification on the ground that it did not sufficiently oppose slavery or safeguard individual rights.*

*(In the preamble to the resolution offering the proposed amendments, Congress said: "The conventions of a number of the States having at the time of their adopting the Constitution, expressed a desire, in order to prevent misconstruction or abuse of its powers, that further declaratory and restrictive clauses should be added, and as extending the ground of public confidence in the government will best insure the beneficent ends of its institution, be it resolved," etc.*

*(Ten of these amendments now commonly known as one to 10 inclusive, but originally 3 to 12 inclusive, were ratified by the states as follows: New Jersey, Nov. 20, 1789; Maryland, Dec. 19, 1789; North Carolina, Dec. 22, 1789; South Carolina, Jan. 19, 1790; New Hampshire, Jan. 25, 1790; Delaware, Jan. 28, 1790; New York, Feb. 27, 1790; Pennsylvania, Mar. 10, 1790; Rhode*

*Island, June 7, 1790; Vermont, Nov. 3, 1791; Virginia, Dec. 15, 1791; Massachusetts, Mar. 2, 1939; Georgia, Mar. 18, 1939; Connecticut, Apr. 19, 1939. These original 10 ratified amendments follow as Amendments I to X inclusive.*

*(Of the two original proposed amendments that were not ratified promptly by the necessary number of states, the first related to apportionment of Representatives; the second, relating to compensation of members of Congress, was ratified in 1992 and became Amendment 27.)*

## AMENDMENT I.
### Religious establishment prohibited. Freedom of speech, of the press, and right to petition.

Congress shall make no law respecting an establishment of religion, or prohibiting the free exercise thereof; or abridging the freedom of speech, or of the press; or the right of the people peaceably to assemble, and to petition the Government for a redress of grievances.

## AMENDMENT II.
### Right to keep and bear arms.

A well-regulated militia, being necessary to the security of a free State, the right of the people to keep and bear arms, shall not be infringed.

## AMENDMENT III.
### Conditions for quarters for soldiers.

No soldier shall, in time of peace be quartered in any house, without the consent of the owner, nor in time of war, but in a manner to be prescribed by law.

## AMENDMENT IV.
### Right of search and seizure regulated.

The right of the people to be secure in their persons, houses, papers, and effects, against unreasonable searches and seizures, shall not be violated, and no warrants shall issue, but upon probable cause, supported by oath or affirmation, and particularly describing the place to be searched, and the persons or things to be seized.

## AMENDMENT V.
### Provisions concerning prosecution. Trial and punishment—private property not to be taken for public use without compensation.

No person shall be held to answer for a capital, or otherwise infamous crime, unless on a presentment or indictment of a Grand Jury, except in cases arising in the land or naval forces, or in the militia, when in actual service in time of war or public danger; nor shall any person be subject for the same offense to be twice put in jeopardy of life or limb; nor

shall be compelled in any criminal case to be a witness against himself, nor be deprived of life, liberty, or property, without due process of law; nor shall private property be taken for public use without just compensation.

## AMENDMENT VI.
### Right to speedy trial, witnesses, etc.

In all criminal prosecutions, the accused shall enjoy the right to a speedy and public trial, by an impartial jury of the State and district wherein the crime shall have been committed, which district shall have been previously ascertained by law, and to be informed of the nature and cause of the accusation; to be confronted with the witnesses against him; to have compulsory process for obtaining witnesses in his favor, and to have the assistance of counsel for his defense.

## AMENDMENT VII.
### Right of trial by jury.

In suits at common law, where the value in controversy shall exceed twenty dollars, the right of trial by jury shall be preserved, and no fact tried by a jury shall be otherwise reexamined in any court of the United States, than according to the rules of the common law.

## AMENDMENT VIII.
### Excessive bail or fines and cruel punishment prohibited.

Excessive bail shall not be required, nor excessive fines imposed, nor cruel and unusual punishments inflicted.

## AMENDMENT IX.
### Rule of construction of Constitution.

The enumeration in the Constitution, of certain rights, shall not be construed to deny or disparage others retained by the people.

## AMENDMENT X.
### Rights of States under Constitution.

The powers not delegated to the United States by the Constitution, nor prohibited by it to the States, are reserved to the States respectively, or to the people.

# Amendments Since the Bill of Rights

## AMENDMENT XI.
### Judicial powers construed.

The judicial power of the United States shall not be construed to extend to any suit in law or equity, commenced or prosecuted against one of the United States by citizens of another State, or by citizens or subjects of any foreign state.

*(This amendment was proposed to the Legislatures of the several States by the Third Congress on March 4, 1794, and was declared to have been ratified in a message from the President to Congress, dated Jan. 8, 1798.*

*(It was on Jan. 5, 1798, that Secretary of State Pickering received from 12 of the States authenticated ratifications, and informed President John Adams of that fact.*

*(As a result of later research in the Department of State, it is now established that Amendment XI became part of the Constitution on Feb. 7, 1795, for on that date it had been ratified by 12 States as follows:*

*(1. New York, Mar. 27, 1794. 2. Rhode Island, Mar. 31, 1794. 3. Connecticut, May 8, 1794. 4. New Hampshire, June 16, 1794. 5. Massachusetts, June 26, 1794. 6. Vermont, between Oct. 9, 1794, and Nov. 9, 1794. 7. Virginia, Nov. 18, 1794. 8. Georgia, Nov. 29, 1794. 9. Kentucky, Dec. 7, 1794. 10. Maryland, Dec. 26, 1794. 11. Delaware, Jan. 23, 1795. 12. North Carolina, Feb. 7, 1795.*

*(On June 1, 1796, more than a year after Amendment XI had become a part of the Constitution—but before anyone was officially aware of this—Tennessee had been admitted as a State; but not until Oct. 16, 1797, was a certified copy of the resolution of Congress proposing the amendment sent to the Governor of Tennessee, John Sevier, by Secretary of State Pickering, whose office was then at Trenton, New Jersey, because*

*of the epidemic of yellow fever at Philadelphia; it seems, however, that the Legislature of Tennessee took no action on Amendment XI, owing doubtless to the fact that public announcement of its adoption was made soon thereafter.*

*(Besides the necessary 12 States, one other, South Carolina, ratified Amendment XI, but this action was not taken until Dec. 4, 1797; the two remaining States, New Jersey and Pennsylvania, failed to ratify.)*

## AMENDMENT XII.
### Manner of choosing President and Vice-President.

*(Proposed by Congress Dec. 9, 1803; ratification completed June 15, 1804.)*

The Electors shall meet in their respective States and vote by ballot for President and Vice-President, one of whom, at least, shall not be an inhabitant of the same State with themselves; they shall name in their ballots the person voted for as President, and in distinct ballots the person voted for as Vice-President, and they shall make distinct lists of all persons voted for as President, and of all persons voted for as Vice-President, and of the number of votes for each, which lists they shall sign and certify, and transmit sealed to the seat of the Government of the United States, directed to the President of the Senate; the President of the Senate shall, in the presence of the Senate and House of Representatives, open all the certificates and the votes shall then be counted;—The person having the greatest number of votes for President, shall be the President, if such number be a majority of the whole number of Electors appointed; and if no person have such majority, then from the persons having the highest numbers not exceeding three on the list of those voted for as President, the House of Representatives shall choose immediately, by ballot, the President. But in choosing the President, the votes shall be taken by States, the representation from each State having one vote; a quorum for this purpose shall consist of a member or members from two-thirds of the States, and a majority of all the States shall be necessary to a choice. *(And if the House of Representatives shall not choose a President whenever the right of choice shall devolve upon them, before the fourth day of March next following, then the Vice-President shall act as President, as in the case of the death or other constitutional disability of the President.) (The words in parentheses were superseded by Amendment XX, section 3.)* The person having the greatest number of votes as Vice-President, shall be the Vice-President, if such number be a majority of the whole number of Electors appointed, and if no person have a majority, then from the two highest numbers on the list, the Senate shall choose the Vice-President; a quorum for the purpose shall consist of two-thirds of the whole number of Senators, and a majority of the whole number shall be necessary to a choice. But no person constitutionally ineligible to the office of President shall be eligible to that of Vice-President of the United States.

## THE RECONSTRUCTION AMENDMENTS

*(Amendments XIII, XIV, and XV are commonly known as the Reconstruction Amendments, inasmuch as they followed the Civil War, and were drafted by Republicans who were bent on imposing their own policy of reconstruction on the South. Post-bellum legislatures there—Mississippi, South Carolina, Georgia, for example—had set up laws which, it was charged, were contrived to perpetuate Negro slavery under other names.)*

### AMENDMENT XIII.
#### Slavery abolished.

*(Proposed by Congress Jan. 31, 1865; ratification completed Dec. 18, 1865. The amendment, when first proposed by a resolution in Congress, was passed by the Senate, 38 to 6, on Apr. 8, 1864, but was defeated in the House, 95 to 66 on June 15, 1864. On reconsideration by the House, on Jan. 31, 1865, the resolution passed, 119 to 56. It was approved by President Lincoln on Feb. 1, 1865, although the Supreme Court had decided in 1798 that the President has nothing to do with the proposing of amendments to the Constitution, or their adoption.)*

1. Neither slavery nor involuntary servitude, except as a punishment for crime whereof the party shall have been duly convicted, shall exist within the United States or any place subject to their jurisdiction.

2. Congress shall have power to enforce this article by appropriate legislation.

### AMENDMENT XIV.
#### Citizenship rights not to be abridged.

*(The following amendment was proposed to the Legislatures of the several states by the 39th Congress, June 13, 1866, and was declared to have been ratified in a proclamation by the Secretary of State, July 28, 1868.*

*(The 14th amendment was adopted only by virtue of ratification subsequent to earlier rejections. Newly constituted legislatures in both North Carolina and South Carolina (respectively July 4 and 9, 1868), ratified the proposed amendment, although earlier legislatures had rejected the proposal. The Secretary of State issued a proclamation, which, though doubtful as to the effect of attempted withdrawals by Ohio and New Jersey, entertained no doubt as to the validity of the ratification by North and South Carolina. The following day (July 21, 1868), Congress passed a resolution which declared the 14th Amendment to be a part of the Constitution and directed the Secretary of State so to promulgate it. The Secretary waited, however, until the newly constituted Legislature of Georgia had ratified the amendment, subsequent to an earlier rejection, before the promulgation of the ratification of the new amendment.)*

1. All persons born or naturalized in the United States, and subject to the jurisdiction thereof, are citizens of the United States and of the State wherein they reside. No State shall make or enforce any law which shall abridge the privileges or immunities of citizens of the United States; nor shall any State deprive any person of life, liberty, or property, without due process of law; nor deny to any person within its jurisdiction the equal protection of the laws.

2. Representatives shall be apportioned among the several States according to their respective numbers, counting the whole number of persons in each State, excluding Indians not taxed. But when the right to vote at any election for the choice of Electors for President and Vice-President of the United States, Representatives in Congress, the executive and judicial officers of a State, or the members of the Legislature thereof, is denied to any of the male inhabitants of such State, being twenty-one years of age, and, citizens of the United States, or in any way abridged, except for participation in rebellion, or other crime, the basis of representation therein shall be reduced in the proportion which the number of such male citizens shall bear to the whole number of male citizens twenty-one years of age in such State.

3. No person shall be a Senator or Representative in Congress, or Elector of President and Vice-President, or hold any office, civil or military, under the United States, or under any State, who, having previously taken an oath, as a member of Congress, or as an officer of the United States, or as a member of any State Legislature, or as an executive or judicial officer of any State, to support the Constitution of the United States, shall have engaged in insurrection or rebellion against the same, or given aid or comfort to the enemies thereof. But Congress may by a vote of two-thirds of each House, remove such disability.

4. The validity of the public debt of the United States, authorized by law, including debts incurred for payment of pensions and bounties for services in suppressing insurrection or rebellion, shall not be questioned. But neither the United States nor any State shall assume or pay any debt or obligation incurred in aid of insurrection or rebellion against the United States, or any claim for the loss or emancipation of any slave; but all such debts, obligations and claims, shall be held illegal and void.

5. The Congress shall have power to enforce, by appropriate legislation, the provisions of this article.

### AMENDMENT XV.
#### Race no bar to voting rights.

*(The following amendment was proposed to the legislatures of the several States by the 40th Congress, Feb. 26, 1869, and was declared to have been ratified in a proclamation by the Secretary of State, Mar. 30, 1870.)*

1. The right of citizens of the United States to vote shall not be denied or abridged by the United States or by any State on account of race, color, or previous condition of servitude.

2. The Congress shall have power to enforce this article by appropriate legislation.

### AMENDMENT XVI.
#### Income taxes authorized.

*(Proposed by Congress July 12, 1909; ratification declared by the Secretary of State Feb. 25, 1913.)*

The Congress shall have power to lay and collect taxes on incomes, from whatever source derived, without apportionment among the several States, and without regard to any census or enumeration.

### AMENDMENT XVII.
#### United States Senators to be elected by direct popular vote.

*(Proposed by Congress May 13, 1912; ratification declared by the Secretary of State May 31, 1913.)*

1. The Senate of the United States shall be composed of two Senators from each State, elected by the people thereof, for six years; and each Senator shall have one vote. The electors in each State shall have the qualifications requisite for electors of the most numerous branch of the State Legislatures.

2. When vacancies happen in the representation of any State in the Senate, the executive authority of such State shall issue writs of election to fill such vacancies: Provided, That the Legislature of any State may empower the Executive thereof to make temporary appointments until the peo-

ple fill the vacancies by election as the Legislature may direct.

3. This amendment shall not be so construed as to affect the election or term of any Senator chosen before it becomes valid as part of the Constitution.

## AMENDMENT XVIII.

### Liquor prohibition amendment.

*(Proposed by Congress Dec. 18, 1917; ratification completed Jan. 16, 1919. Repealed by Amendment XXI, effective Dec. 5, 1933.)*

(1. After one year from the ratification of this article the manufacture, sale, or transportation of intoxicating liquors within, the importation thereof into, or the exportation thereof from the United States and all territory subject to the jurisdiction thereof for beverage purposes is hereby prohibited.

(2. The Congress and the several States shall have concurrent power to enforce this article by appropriate legislation.

(3. This article shall be inoperative unless it shall have been ratified as an amendment to the Constitution by the Legislatures of the several States, as provided in the Constitution, within seven years from the date of the submission hereof to the States by the Congress.)

*(The total vote in the Senates of the various States was 1,310 for, 237 against—84.6% dry. In the lower houses of the States the vote was 3,782 for, 1,035 against—78.5% dry.*

*(The amendment ultimately was adopted by all the States except Connecticut and Rhode Island.)*

## AMENDMENT XIX.

### Giving nationwide suffrage to women.

*(Proposed by Congress June 4, 1919; ratification certified by Secretary of State Aug. 26, 1920.)*

1. The right of citizens of the United States to vote shall not be denied or abridged by the United States or by any State on account of sex.

2. Congress shall have power to enforce this Article by appropriate legislation.

## AMENDMENT XX.

### Terms of President and Vice President to begin on Jan. 20; those of Senators, Representatives, Jan. 3.

*(Proposed by Congress Mar. 2, 1932; ratification completed Jan. 23, 1933.)*

1. The terms of the President and Vice President shall end at noon on the 20th day of January, and the terms of Senators and Representatives at noon on the 3rd day of January, of the years in which such terms would have ended if this article had not been ratified; and the terms of their successors shall then begin.

2. The Congress shall assemble at least once in every year, and such meeting shall begin at noon on the 3rd day of January, unless they shall by law appoint a different day.

3. If, at the time fixed for the beginning of the term of the President, the President elect shall have died, the Vice President elect shall become President. If a President shall not have been chosen before the time fixed for the beginning of his term, or if the President elect shall have failed to qualify, then the Vice President elect shall act as President until a President shall have qualified; and the Congress may by law provide for the case wherein neither a President elect nor a Vice President elect shall have qualified, declaring who shall then act as President, or the manner in which one who is to act shall be selected, and such person shall act accordingly until a President or Vice President shall have qualified.

4. The Congress may by law provide for the case of the death of any of the persons from whom the House of Representatives may choose a President whenever the right of choice shall have devolved upon them, and for the case of the death of any of the persons from whom the Senate may choose a Vice President whenever the right of choice shall have devolved upon them.

5. Sections 1 and 2 shall take effect on the 15th day of October following the ratification of this article (Oct., 1933).

6. This article shall be inoperative unless it shall have been ratified as an amendment to the Constitution by the Legislatures of three-fourths of the several States within seven years from the date of its submission.

## AMENDMENT XXI.

### Repeal of Amendment XVIII.

*(Proposed by Congress Feb. 20, 1933; ratification completed Dec. 5, 1933.)*

1. The eighteenth article of amendment to the Constitution of the United States is hereby repealed.

2. The transportation or importation into any State, Territory, or Possession of the United States for delivery or use therein of intoxicating liquors, in violation of the laws thereof, is hereby prohibited.

3. This article shall be inoperative unless it shall have been ratified as an amendment to the Constitution by conventions in the several States, as provided in the Constitution, within seven years from the date of the submission hereof to the States by the Congress.

## AMENDMENT XXII.

### Limiting Presidential terms of office.

*(Proposed by Congress Mar. 24, 1947; ratification completed Feb. 27, 1951.)*

1. No person shall be elected to the office of the President more than twice, and no person who has held the office of President, or acted as President, for more than two years of a term to which some other person was elected President shall be elected to the office of the President more than once. But this Article shall not apply to any person holding the office of President when this Article was proposed by the Congress, and shall not prevent any person who may be holding the office of President, or acting as President, during the term within which this Article becomes operative from holding the office of President or acting as President during the remainder of such term.

2. This article shall be inoperative unless it shall have been ratified as an amendment to the Constitution by the Legislatures of three-fourths of the several States within seven years from the date of its submission to the States by the Congress.

## AMENDMENT XXIII.

### Presidential vote for District of Columbia.

*(Proposed by Congress June 16, 1960; ratification completed Mar. 29, 1961.)*

1. The District constituting the seat of Government of the United States shall appoint in such manner as the Congress may direct:

A number of electors of President and Vice President equal to the whole number of Senators and Representatives in Congress to which the District would be entitled if it were a State, but in no event more than the least populous State; they shall be in addition to those appointed by the States, but they shall be considered, for the purposes of the election of President and Vice President, to be electors appointed by a State; and they shall meet in the District and perform such duties as provided by the twelfth article of amendment.

2. The Congress shall have power to enforce this article by appropriate legislation.

## AMENDMENT XXIV.

### Barring poll tax in federal elections.

*(Proposed by Congress Aug. 27, 1962; ratification completed Jan. 23, 1964.)*

1. The right of citizens of the United States to vote in any primary or other election for President or Vice President, for electors for President or Vice President, or for Senator or Representative in Congress, shall not be denied or abridged by the United States or any State by reason of failure to pay any poll tax or other tax.

2. The Congress shall have power to enforce this article by appropriate legislation.

## AMENDMENT XXV.
### Presidential disability and succession.

*(Proposed by Congress July 6, 1965; ratification completed Feb. 10, 1967.)*

1. In case of the removal of the President from office or of his death or resignation, the Vice President shall become President.

2. Whenever there is a vacancy in the office of the Vice President, the President shall nominate a Vice President who shall take office upon confirmation by a majority vote of both houses of Congress.

3. Whenever the President transmits to the President pro tempore of the Senate and the Speaker of the House of Representatives his written declaration that he is unable to discharge the powers and duties of his office, and until he transmits to them a written declaration to the contrary, such powers and duties shall be discharged by the Vice President as Acting President.

4. Whenever the Vice President and a majority of either the principal officers of the executive departments or of such other body as Congress may by law provide, transmit to the President pro tempore of the Senate and the Speaker of the House of Representatives their written declaration that the President is unable to discharge the powers and duties of his office, the Vice President shall immediately assume the powers and duties of the office as Acting President.

Thereafter, when the President transmits to the President pro tempore of the Senate and the Speaker of the House of Representatives his written declaration that no inability exists, he shall resume the powers and duties of his office unless the Vice President and a majority of either the principal officers of the executive department or of such other body as Congress may by law provide, transmit within four days to the President pro tempore of the Senate and the Speaker of the House of Representatives their written declaration that the President is unable to discharge the powers and duties of his office. Thereupon Congress shall decide the issue, assembling within forty-eight hours for that purpose if not in session. If the Congress, within twenty-one days after receipt of the latter written declaration, or, if Congress is not in session, within twenty-one days after Congress is required to assemble, determines by two-thirds vote of both houses that the President is unable to discharge the powers and duties of his office, the Vice President shall continue to discharge the same as Acting President; otherwise, the President shall resume the powers and duties of his office.

## AMENDMENT XXVI.
### Lowering voting age to 18 years.

*(Proposed by Congress Mar. 23, 1971; ratification completed July 1, 1971.)*

1. The right of citizens of the United States, who are 18 years of age or older, to vote shall not be denied or abridged by the United States or any state on account of age.

2. The Congress shall have the power to enforce this article by appropriate legislation.

## AMENDMENT XXVII.
### Congressional pay.

*(Proposed by Congress Sept. 25, 1789; ratification completed May 7, 1992.)*

No law, varying the compensation for the services of the Senators and Representatives, shall take effect, until an election of Representatives shall have intervened.

# Origin of the Constitution

The War of Independence was conducted by delegates from the original 13 states, called the Congress of the United States of America and generally known as the Continental Congress. In 1777 the Congress submitted to the legislatures of the states the Articles of Confederation and Perpetual Union, which were ratified by New Hampshire, Massachusetts, Rhode Island, Connecticut, New York, New Jersey, Pennsylvania, Delaware, Virginia, North Carolina, South Carolina, and Georgia, and finally, in 1781, by Maryland.

The first article of the instrument read: "The stile of this confederacy shall be the United States of America." This did not signify a sovereign nation, because the states delegated only those powers they could not handle individually, such as power to wage war, establish a uniform currency, make treaties with foreign nations and contract debts for general expenses (such as paying the army). Taxes for the payment of such debts were levied by the individual states. The president under the Articles signed himself "President of the United States in Congress assembled," but here the United States were considered in the plural, a cooperating group. Canada was invited to join the union on equal terms but did not act.

When the war was won it became evident that a stronger federal union was needed to protect the mutual interests of the states. The Congress left the initiative to the legislatures. Virginia in Jan. 1786 appointed commissioners to meet with representatives of other states, with the result that delegates from Virginia, Delaware, New York, New Jersey, and Pennsylvania met at Annapolis. Alexander Hamilton prepared for their call by asking delegates from all states to meet in Philadelphia in May 1787 "to render the Constitution of the Federal government adequate to the exigencies of the union." Congress endorsed the plan Feb. 21, 1787. Delegates were appointed by all states except Rhode Island.

The convention met May 14, 1787. George Washington was chosen president (presiding officer). The states certified 65 delegates, but 10 did not attend. The work was done by 55, not all of whom were present at all sessions. Of the 55 attending delegates, 16 failed to sign, and 39 actually signed Sept. 17, 1787, some with reservations. Some historians have said 74 delegates (9 more than the 65 actually certified) were named and 19 failed to attend. These 9 additional persons refused the appointment, were never delegates and never counted as absentees. Washington sent the Constitution to Congress with a covering letter and that body, Sept. 28, 1787, ordered it sent to the legislatures, "in order to be submitted to a convention of delegates chosen in each state by the people thereof."

The Constitution was ratified by votes of state conventions as follows: Delaware, Dec. 7, 1787, unanimous; Pennsylvania, Dec. 12, 1787, 43 to 23; New Jersey, Dec. 18, 1787, unanimous; Georgia, Jan 2, 1788, unanimous; Connecticut, Jan. 9, 1788, 128 to 40; Massachusetts, Feb. 6, 1788, 187 to 168; Maryland, Apr. 28, 1788, 63 to 11; South Carolina, May 23, 1788, 149 to 73; New Hampshire, June 21, 1788, 57 to 46; Virginia, June 25, 1788, 89 to 79; New York, July 26, 1788, 30 to 27. Nine states were needed to establish the operation of the Constitution "between the states so ratifying the same" and New Hampshire was the 9th state. The government did not declare the Constitution in effect until the first Wednesday in Mar. 1789, which was Mar. 4. After that North Carolina ratified it Nov. 21, 1789, 194 to 77; and Rhode Island, May 29, 1790, 34 to 32. Vermont in convention ratified it Jan. 10, 1791, and by act of Congress approved Feb. 18, 1791, was admitted into the Union as the 14th state, Mar. 4, 1791.

There have been calls to hold a second constitutional convention. The Constitution stipulates that a convention must be held when 34 states pass bills to hold a convention.

## Selected Landmark Decisions of the U.S. Supreme Court

**1803: Marbury v. Madison.** The Court ruled that Congress exceeded its power in the Judiciary Act of 1789; thus, the Court established its power to review acts of Congress and declare invalid those it found in conflict with the Constitution.

**1819: McCulloch v. Maryland.** The Court ruled that Congress had the authority to charter a national bank, under the Constitution's granting of the power to enact all laws "necessary and proper" to exact the responsibilities of government. The Court also held that the national bank was immune to state taxation.

**1819: Trustees of Dartmouth College v. Woodward.** The Court ruled that a state could not arbitrarily alter the terms of a college's contract. (In later years the Court widened the implications by using the same principle to limit the states' ability to interfere with business contracts.)

**1857: Dred Scott v. Sanford.** The Court declared unconstitutional the already-repealed Missouri Compromise of 1820 because it deprived a person of his property—a slave—without due process of law. The Court also ruled that slaves were not citizens of any state nor of the U.S. (The latter part of the decision was overturned by ratification of the 14th Amendment in 1868.)

**1896: Plessy v. Ferguson.** The Court ruled that a state law requiring federal railroad trains to provide separate but equal facilities for black and white passengers neither infringed upon federal authority to regulate interstate commerce nor violated the 13th and 14th Amendments. (The "separate but equal" doctrine remained effective until the 1954 Brown v. Board of Education decision.)

**1904: Northern Securities Co. v. U.S.** The Court ruled that a holding company formed solely to eliminate competition between two railroad lines was a combination in restraint of trade, thus a violation of the federal antitrust act.

**1908: Muller v. Oregon.** The Court ruled to uphold a state law limiting the maximum working hours of women. (Instead of presenting legal arguments, Louis D. Brandeis, counsel for the state, brought forth evidence from social workers, physicians, and factory inspectors that the number of hours women worked affected their health and morals.)

**1911: Standard Oil Co. of New Jersey et al. v. U.S.** The Court ruled that the Standard Oil Trust must be dissolved because of its unreasonable restraint of trade, not because of its size.

**1919: Schenck v. U.S.** In its first decision regarding the extent of protection afforded by the First Amendment, the Court sustained the Espionage Act of 1917, maintaining that freedom of speech and press could be constrained if "the words used are in such circumstances and are of such a nature as to create a clear and present danger. . ."

**1925: Gitlow v. New York.** The Court ruled that the First Amendment prohibition against government abridgement of the freedom of speech applied to the states as well as to the federal government. The decision was the first of a number of rulings holding that the 14th Amendment extended the guarantees of the Bill of Rights to state action.

**1935: Schechter Poultry Corp. v. U.S.** The Court ruled that Congress exceeded its authority to delegate legislative powers and to regulate interstate commerce when it enacted the National Industrial Recovery Act, which afforded the U.S. president too much discretionary power.

**1951: Dennis et al. v. U.S.** The Court upheld convictions under the Smith Act of 1940 for speaking about communist theory that advocated the forcible overthrow of the government. (In the 1957 Yates v. U.S. decision, the Court moderated this ruling by allowing such advocacy in the abstract, if not connected to action to achieve the goal.)

**1954: Brown v. Board of Education of Topeka.** The Court ruled that separate public schools for black and white students were inherently unequal, thus state-sanctioned segregation in public schools violated the equal protection guar-

antee of the 14th Amendment. And in **Bolling v. Sharpe** the Court ruled that the congressionally-mandated segregated public school system in the District of Columbia violated the Fifth Amendment's due process guarantee of personal liberty. (The Brown ruling also led to the abolition of state-sponsored segregation in other public facilities.)

**1957: Roth v. U.S., Alberts v. California.** The Court ruled that obscene material was not protected by the First Amendment guarantees of freedom of speech and press, defining obscene as "utterly without redeeming social value" and appealing to "prurient interests" in the view of the average person. (This definition, the first offered by the Court, was modified in several subsequent decisions, and the "average person" standard was replaced by the "local community" standard in the 1973 Miller v. California case.)

**1961: Mapp v. Ohio.** The Court ruled that evidence obtained in violation of the 4th Amendment guarantee against unreasonable search and seizure must be excluded from use at state as well as federal trials.

**1962: Engel v. Vitale.** The Court ruled that public school officials could not require pupils to recite a state-composed prayer at the start of each school day, even if the prayer was non-denominational and pupils who so desired could be excused from reciting it, because such official state sanction of religious utterances was an unconstitutional attempt to establish religion.

**1962: Baker v. Carr.** The Court held that the constitutional challenges to the unequal distribution of voters among legislative districts could be resolved by federal courts, rejecting the doctrine set out in Colegrove v. Green in 1946 that such apportionment challenges were "political questions."

**1963: Gideon v. Wainwright.** The Court ruled that the due process clause of the 14th Amendment extended to state as well as federal defendants, thus all persons charged with serious crimes must be provided with an attorney, and states were required to appoint counsel for defendants unable to pay their own attorneys' fees.

**1964: New York Times Co. v. Sullivan.** The Court ruled that the First Amendment guarantee of freedom of the press protected the press from libel suits for defamatory reports on public officials unless the officials proved that the reports were made from actual malice. The Court defined malice as "with knowledge that (the defamatory statement) was false or with reckless disregard of whether it was false or not."

**1965: Griswold v. Conn.** The Court ruled that a state unconstitutionally interfered with personal privacy in the marriage relationship when it prohibited anyone, including married couples, from using contraceptives.

**1966: Miranda v. Arizona.** The Court ruled that the guarantee of due process required that before any questioning of suspects in police custody, the suspects must be informed of their right to remain silent, that anything they say may be used against them, and that they have the right to counsel.

**1973: Roe v. Wade, Doe v. Bolton.** The Court ruled that the right to privacy inherent in the 14th Amendment's due process guarantee of personal liberty protected a woman's decision whether or not to bear a child, and was impermissibly abridged by state laws that made abortion a crime. During the first trimester of pregnancy, the Court maintained, the decision to have an abortion should be left entirely to a woman and her physician.

**1974: U.S. v. Nixon.** The Court ruled that neither the separation of powers nor the need to preserve the confidentiality of presidential communications could alone justify an absolute executive privilege of immunity from judicial demands for evidence to be used in a criminal trial.

**1976: Gregg v. Georgia, Profitt v. Fla., Jurek v. Texas.** The Court held that death, as a punishment for persons convicted of first degree murder, was not in and of itself cruel and unusual punishment in violation of the 8th Amendment.

The Court also ruled that the Amendment required the sentencing judge and jury to consider the individual character of the offender and the circumstances of the particular crime before deciding whether or not to impose the death sentence. In the associated Woodson v. N.C., Roberts v. LA., the Court ruled that states could not make death the mandatory penalty for first-degree murder, since that would fail to meet the constitutional requirement for the consideration of the individual offender and offense.

**1978: Regents of Univ. of Calif. v. Bakke.** The Court ruled that a special admissions program for a state medical school under which a set number of places were set aside for minority group members, with white applicants denied the opportunity to compete for those seats, violated Title XIV of the 1964 Civil Rights Act, which forbids the exclusion of anyone, because of race, from participation in a federally-funded program. The Court also ruled that admissions programs that considered race as one of a complex of factors involved in the decision to admit or reject an applicant were not unconstitutional.

**1979: United Steelworkers of America v. Weber, Kaiser Aluminum v. Weber, U.S. v. Weber.** The Court ruled that Title VII of the 1964 Civil Rights Act, which forbids racial discrimination in employment, did not forbid employers to adopt voluntarily race-conscious affirmative action programs to encourage minority participation in areas in which they traditionally were underrepresented.

**1986: Bowers v. Hardwick.** The Court refused to extend the right of privacy inherent in the Constitution to homosexual activity, upholding a Georgia law that made sodomy a crime. (Although the Georgia law covered heterosexual sodomy as well as homosexual sodomy, enforcement in Georgia and most other states had been confined to homosexual activity.)

**1990: Cruzan v. Missouri.** The Court ruled that a person had the right to refuse life-sustaining medical treatment. However, the Court also ruled that such treatment could not be withheld from comatose patients unless there was "clear and convincing evidence" that the person would not have wanted to live under those conditions.

## Patrick Henry's Speech to the Virginia Convention

The following is an excerpt from Patrick Henry's speech to the Virginia Convention on Mar. 23, 1775:

Gentlemen may cry, peace, peace—but there is no peace. The war is actually begun! The next gale that sweeps from the north will bring to our ears the clash of resounding arms! Our brethren are already in the field! Why stand we here idle? What is it that gentlemen wish? What would they have? Is life so dear, or peace so sweet, as to be purchased at the price of chains and slavery? Forbid it, Almighty God! I know not what course others may take; but as for me, give me liberty, or give me death!

## *Common Sense*

The following is an excerpt from Thomas Paine's *Common Sense.* Paine adopted the doctrine of separation from Britain after the battles of Lexington and Concord, and published his pamphlet in Jan. 1776.

The cause of America is in great measure the cause of all mankind. Many circumstances hath, and will arise, which are not local, but universal, and through which principles of all Lovers of Mankind are affected, and in the Event of which, their Affections are interested. The laying a Country desolate with Fire and Sword, declaring war against natural rights of all Mankind, and extirpating the Defenders thereof from the Face of the Earth, is the Concern of every Man to whom Nature hath given the Power of feeling; ... It is repugnant to reason, to the universal order of things, to all examples from former ages, to suppose, that this continent can longer remain subject to any external power ...

The last cord is now broken, the people of England are presenting addresses against us. There are injuries which nature cannot forgive; she would cease to be nature if she did

...

O ye that love mankind! Ye that dare oppose, not only the tyranny, but the tyrant, stand forth! Every spot of the old world is overrun with oppression. Freedom hath been hunted round the globe. Asia, and Africa, have long expelled her—Europe regards her like a stranger, and England hath given her warning to depart. O! Receive the fugitive, and prepare in time an asylum for mankind.

## Law on Succession to the Presidency

If by reason of death, resignation, removal from office, inability, or failure to qualify there is neither a president nor vice president to discharge the powers and duties of the office of president, then the speaker of the House of Representatives shall upon his resignation as speaker and as representative, act as president. The same rule shall apply in the case of the death, resignation, removal from office, or inability of an individual acting as president.

If at the time when a speaker is to begin the discharge of the powers and duties of the office of president there is no speaker, or the speaker fails to qualify as acting president, then the president pro tempore of the Senate, upon his resignation as president pro tempore and as senator, shall act as president.

An individual acting as president shall continue to act until the expiration of the then current presidential term, except that (1) if his discharge of the powers and duties of the office is founded in whole or in part in the failure of both the president-elect and the vice president-elect to qualify, then he shall act only until a president or vice president qualifies, and (2) if his discharge of the powers and duties of the office is founded in whole or in part on the inability of the president or vice president, then he shall act only until the removal of the disability of one of such individuals.

If, by reason of death, resignation, removal from office, or failure to qualify, there is no president pro tempore to act as president, then the officer of the United States who is highest on the following list, and who is not under any disability to discharge the powers and duties of president shall act as president; the secretaries of state, treasury, defense, attorney general; secretaries of interior, agriculture, commerce, labor, health and human services, housing and urban development, transportation, energy, education.

*(Legislation approved July 18, 1947; amended Sept. 9, 1965, Oct. 15, 1966, Aug. 4, 1977, and Sept. 27, 1979. (See also Constitutional Amendment XXV.)*

## Presidential Oath of Office

The Constitution (Article II) directs that the President shall take the following oath or affirmation: "I do solemnly swear (affirm) that I will faithfully execute the office of President of the United States, and will, to the best of my ability, preserve, protect, and defend the Constitution of the United States." (Custom decrees the use of the words "So help me God" at the end of the oath when taken by the President-elect, his/her left hand on the Bible for the duration of the oath, with his/her right hand slightly raised.)

## How the Declaration of Independence Was Adopted

On June 7, 1776, Richard Henry Lee, who had issued the first call for a congress of the colonies, introduced in the Continental Congress at Philadelphia a resolution declaring "that these United Colonies are, and of right ought to be, free and independent states, that they are absolved from all allegiance to the British Crown, and that all political connection between them and the state of Great Britain is, and ought to be, totally dissolved."

The resolution, seconded by John Adams on behalf of the Massachusetts delegation, came up again June 10 when a committee of 5, headed by Thomas Jefferson, was appointed to express the purpose of the resolution in a declaration of independence. The others on the committee were John Adams, Benjamin Franklin, Robert R. Livingston, and Roger Sherman.

Drafting the Declaration was assigned to Jefferson, who worked on a portable desk of his own construction in a room at Market and 7th Sts. The committee reported the result June 28, 1776. The members of the Congress suggested a number of changes, which Jefferson called "deplorable." They didn't approve Jefferson's arraignment of the British people and King George III for encouraging and fostering the slave trade, which Jefferson called "an execrable commerce." They made 86 changes, eliminating 480 words and leaving 1,337. In the final form capitalization was erratic. Jefferson had written that men were endowed with "inalienable" rights; in the final copy it came out as "unalienable" and has been thus ever since.

The Lee-Adams resolution of independence was adopted by 12 yeas July 2 — the actual date of the act of independence. The Declaration, which explains the act, was adopted July 4, in the evening.

After the Declaration was adopted, July 4, 1776, it was turned over to John Dunlap, printer, to be printed on broadsides. The original copy was lost and one of his broadsides was attached to a page in the journal of the Congress. It was read aloud July 8 in Philadelphia, Easton, Pa., and Trenton, N.J. On July 9 at 6 p.m. it was read by order of Gen. George Washington to the troops assembled on the Common in New York City (City Hall Park).

The Continental Congress of July 19, 1776, adopted the following resolution:

"Resolved, That the Declaration passed on the 4th, be fairly engrossed on parchment with the title and stile of 'The Unanimous Declaration of the thirteen United States of America' and that the same, when engrossed, be signed by every member of Congress."

Not all delegates who signed the engrossed Declaration were present on July 4. Robert Morris (Pa.), William Williams (Conn.) and Samuel Chase (Md.) signed on Aug. 2, Oliver Wolcott (Conn.), George Wythe (Va.), Richard Henry Lee (Va.) and Elbridge Gerry (Mass.) signed in August and September, Matthew Thornton (N. H.) joined the Congress Nov. 4 and signed later. Thomas McKean (Del.) rejoined Washington's army before signing and said later that he signed in 1781.

Charles Carroll of Carrollton was appointed a delegate by Maryland on July 4, 1776, presented his credentials July 18, and signed the engrossed Declaration Aug. 2. Born Sept. 19, 1737, he was 95 years old and the last surviving signer when he died Nov. 14, 1832.

Two Pennsylvania delegates who did not support the Declaration on July 4 were replaced.

The 4 New York delegates did not have authority from their state to vote on July 4. On July 9 the New York state convention authorized its delegates to approve the Declaration and the Congress was so notified on July 15, 1776. The 4 signed the Declaration on Aug. 2.

The original engrossed Declaration is preserved in the National Archives Building in Washington.

## The Continental Congress: Meetings, Presidents

| Meeting places | Dates of meetings | Congress presidents | Date elected |
|---|---|---|---|
| Philadelphia | Sept. 5 to Oct. 26, 1774 | Peyton Randolph, Va. (1) . . . . . . . . . | Sept. 5, 1774 |
| " | " | Henry Middleton, S.C. . . . . . . . . . . | Oct. 22, 1774 |
| Philadelphia | May 10, 1775 to Dec. 12, 1776 | Peyton Randolph, Va. . . . . . . . . . . | May 10, 1775 |
| " | " | John Hancock, Mass. . . . . . . . . . . | May 24, 1775 |
| Baltimore | Dec. 20, 1776 to Mar. 4, 1777 | " | |
| Philadelphia | Mar. 5 to Sept. 18, 1777 | " | |
| Lancaster, Pa. | Sept. 27, 1777 (one day) | " | |
| York, Pa. | Sept. 30, 1777 to June 27, 1778 | Henry Laurens, S.C. . . . . . . . . . . . | Nov. 1, 1777(4) |
| Philadelphia | July 2, 1778 to June 21, 1783 | John Jay, N.Y. . . . . . . . . . . . . . . | Dec. 10, 1778 |
| " | " | Samuel Huntington, Conn. . . . . . . . | Sept. 28, 1779 |
| " | " | Thomas McKean, Del. . . . . . . . . . . | July 10, 1781 |
| " | " | John Hanson, Md. (2) . . . . . . . . . . | Nov. 5, 1781 |
| " | " | Elias Boudinot, N.J. . . . . . . . . . . . | Nov. 4, 1782 |
| Princeton, N.J. | June 30 to Nov. 4, 1783 | Thomas Mifflin, Pa. . . . . . . . . . . . | Nov. 3, 1783 |
| Annapolis, Md. | Nov. 26, 1783 to June 3, 1784 | | |
| Trenton, N.J. | Nov. 1 to Dec. 24, 1784 | Richard Henry Lee, Va. . . . . . . . . . | Nov. 30, 1784 |
| New York City | Jan. 11 to Nov. 4, 1785 | | |
| " | Nov. 7, 1785 to Nov. 3, 1786 | John Hancock, Mass. (3) . . . . . . . . | Nov. 23, 1785 |
| " | " | Nathaniel Gorham, Mass. . . . . . . . . | June 6, 1786 |
| " | Nov. 6, 1786 to Oct. 30, 1787 | Arthur St. Clair, Pa. . . . . . . . . . . . | Feb. 2, 1787 |
| " | Nov. 5, 1787 to Oct. 21, 1788 | Cyrus Griffin, Va. . . . . . . . . . . . . | Jan. 22, 1788 |
| " | Nov. 3, 1788 to Mar. 2, 1789 | | |

(1) Resigned Oct. 22, 1774. (2) Titled "President of the United States in Congress Assembled," John Hanson is considered by some to be the first U.S. President as he was the first to serve under the Articles of Confederation. He was, however, little more than presiding officer of the Congress, which retained full executive power. He could be considered the head of government, but not head of state. (3) Resigned May 29, 1786, without serving, because of illness. (4) Articles of Confederation agreed upon, Nov. 15, 1777; last ratification from Maryland, Mar. 1, 1781.

## Origin of the United States National Motto

*In God We Trust,* designated as the U. S. National Motto by Congress in 1956, originated during the Civil War as an inscription for U. S. coins, although it was used by Francis Scott Key in a slightly different form when he wrote The Star Spangled Banner in 1814. On Nov. 13, 1861, when Union morale had been shaken by battlefield defeats, the Rev. M. R. Watkinson, of Ridleyville, Pa., wrote to Secy. of the Treasury Salmon P. Chase. "From my heart I have felt our national shame in disowning God as not the least of our present national disasters," the minister wrote, suggesting "recognition of the Almighty God in some form on our coins." Secy. Chase ordered designs prepared with the inscription *In God We Trust* and backed coinage legislation that authorized use of this slogan. It first appeared on some U. S. coins in 1864, disappeared and reappeared on various coins until 1955, when Congress ordered it placed on all paper money and all coins.

# The Great Seal of the U.S.

On July 4, 1776, the Continental Congress appointed a committee consisting of Benjamin Franklin, John Adams and Thomas Jefferson "to bring in a device for a seal of the United States of America." After many delays, a verbal description of a design by William Barton was finally approved by Congress on June 20, 1782. The seal shows an American bald eagle with a ribbon in its mouth bearing the device *E pluribus unum* (One out of many). In its talons are the arrows of war and an olive branch of peace. On the reverse side it shows an unfinished pyramid with an eye (the eye of Providence) above it.

# The American's Creed

**William Tyler Page, Clerk of the U.S. House of Representatives, wrote "The American's Creed" in 1917.**
**It was accepted by the House on behalf of the American people on April 3, 1918.**

"I believe in the United States of America as a government of the people, by the people, for the people; whose just powers are derived from the consent of the governed; a democracy in a republic; a sovereign Nation of many sovereign States; a perfect union, one and inseparable; established upon those principles of freedom, equality, justice, and humanity for which American patriots sacrificed their lives and fortunes.

"I therefore believe it is my duty to my country to love it, to support its Constitution, to obey its laws, to respect its flag, and to defend it against all enemies."

# The Flag of the U.S.—The Stars and Stripes

The 50-star flag of the United States was raised for the first time officially at 12:01 a.m. on July 4, 1960, at Fort McHenry National Monument in Baltimore, Md. The 50th star had been added for Hawaii; a year earlier the 49th, for Alaska. Before that, no star had been added since 1912, when N.M. and Ariz. were admitted to the Union.

The true history of the Stars and Stripes has become so cluttered by a volume of myth and tradition that the facts are difficult, and in some cases impossible, to establish. For example, it is not certain who designed the Stars and Stripes, who made the first such flag, or even whether it ever flew in any sea fight or land battle of the American Revolution.

One thing all agree on is that the Stars and Stripes originated as the result of a resolution offered by the Marine Committee of the Second Continental Congress at Philadelphia and adopted June 14, 1777. It read:

*Resolved: that the flag of the United States be thirteen stripes, alternate red and white; that the union be thirteen stars, white in a blue field, representing a new constellation.*

Congress gave no hint as to the designer of the flag, no instructions as to the arrangement of the stars, and no information on its appropriate uses. Historians have been unable to find the original flag law.

The resolution establishing the flag was not even published until Sept. 2, 1777. Despite repeated requests, Washington did not get the flags until 1783, after the Revolutionary War was over. And there is no certainty that they were the Stars and Stripes.

## Early Flags

Although it was never officially adopted by the Continental Congress, many historians consider the first flag of the U.S. to have been the Grand Union (sometimes called Great Union) flag. This was a modification of the British Meteor flag, which had the red cross of St. George and the white cross of St. Andrew combined in the blue canton. For the Grand Union flag, 6 horizontal stripes were imposed on the red field, dividing it into 13 alternate red and white stripes. On Jan. 1, 1776, when the Continental Army came into formal existence, this flag was unfurled on Prospect Hill, Somerville, Mass. Washington wrote that "we hoisted the Union Flag in compliment to the United Colonies."

One of several flags about which controversy has raged for years is at Easton, Pa. Containing the devices of the national flag in reversed order, this has been in the public library at Easton for over 150 years. Some contend that this flag was actually the first Stars and Stripes, first displayed on July 8, 1776. This flag has 13 red and white stripes in the canton, 13 white stars centered in a blue field.

A flag was hastily improvised from garments by the defenders of Fort Schuyler at Rome, N.Y., Aug. 3-22, 1777. Historians believe it was the Grand Union Flag.

The Sons of Liberty had a flag of 9 red and white stripes, to signify 9 colonies, when they met in New York in 1765 to oppose the Stamp Tax. By 1775, the flag had grown to 13 red and white stripes, with a rattlesnake on it.

At Concord, Apr. 19, 1775, the minute men from Bedford, Mass., are said to have carried a flag having a silver arm with sword on a red field.

At Cambridge, Mass., the Sons of Liberty used a plain red flag with a green pine tree on it.

In June 1775, Washington went from Philadelphia to Boston to take command of the army, escorted to New York by the Philadelphia Light Horse Troop. It carried a yellow flag which had an elaborate coat of arms — the shield charged with 13 knots, the motto "For These We Strive" — and a canton of 13 blue and silver stripes.

In Feb., 1776, Col. Christopher Gadsden, member of the Continental Congress, gave the S. Carolina Provincial Congress a flag "such as is to be used by the commander-in-chief of the American Navy." It had a yellow field, with a rattlesnake about to strike and the words "Don't Tread on Me."

At the battle of Bennington, Aug. 16, 1777, patriots used a flag of 7 white and 6 red stripes with a blue canton extending down 9 stripes and showing an arch of 11 white stars over the figure 76 and a star in each of the upper corners. The stars are seven-pointed. This flag is preserved in the Historical Museum at Bennington, Vt.

At the Battle of Cowpens, Jan. 17, 1781, the 3d Maryland Regt. is said to have carried a flag of 13 red and white stripes, with a blue canton containing 12 stars in a circle around one star.

**Who Designed the Flag?** No one knows for certain. Francis Hopkinson, designer of a naval flag, declared he also had designed the flag and in 1781 asked Congress to reimburse him for his services. Congress did not do so. Dumas Malone of Columbia Univ. wrote: "This talented man ... designed the American flag."

**Who Called the Flag Old Glory?** — The flag is said to have been named Old Glory by William Driver, a sea captain of Salem, Mass. One legend has it that when he raised the flag on his brig, the Charles Doggett, in 1824, he said: "I name thee Old Glory." But his daughter, who presented the flag to the Smithsonian Institution, said he named it at his 21st birthday celebration Mar. 17, 1824, when his mother presented the homemade flag to him.

**The Betsy Ross Legend** — The widely publicized legend that Mrs. Betsy Ross made the first Stars and Stripes in June 1776, at the request of a committee composed of George Washington, Robert Morris, and George Ross, an uncle, was first made public in 1870, by a grandson of Mrs. Ross. Historians have been unable to find a historical record of such a meeting or committee.

## Adding New Stars

The flag of 1777 was used until 1795. Then, on the admission of Vermont and Kentucky to the Union, Congress passed and Pres. Washington signed an act that after May 1, 1795, the flag should have 15 stripes, alternate red and white, and 15 white stars on a blue field in the union.

When new states were admitted it became evident that the flag would become burdened with stripes. Congress thereupon ordered that after July 4, 1818, the flag should have 13 stripes, symbolizing the 13 original states; that the union have 20 stars, and that whenever a new state was admitted a new star should be added on the July 4 following admission. No law designates the permanent arrangement of the stars. However, since 1912 when a new state has been admitted, the new design has been announced by executive order. No star is specifically identified with any state.

## Code of Etiquette for Display and Use of the U.S. Flag

Although the Stars and Stripes originated in 1777, it was not until 146 years later that there was a serious attempt to establish a uniform code of etiquette for the U.S. flag. The War Department issued Feb. 15, 1923, a circular on the rules of flag usage. These were adopted almost in their entirety June 14, 1923, by a conference of 68 patriotic organizations in Washington. Finally, on June 22, 1942, a joint resolution of Congress, amended by Public Law 94-344 July 7, 1976, codified "existing rules and customs pertaining to the display and use of the flag . . ."

**When to Display the Flag**—The flag should be displayed on all days, especially on legal holidays and other special occasions, on official buildings when in use, in or near polling places on election days, and in or near schools when in session. Citizens may fly the flag at any time they wish. It is customary to display the flag only from sunrise to sunset on buildings and on stationary flagstaffs in the open. However, it may be displayed at night on special occasions, preferably lighted. In Washington, the flag now flies over the White House both day and night. It flies over the Senate wing of the Capitol when the Senate is in session and over the House wing when that body is in session. It flies day and night over the east and west fronts of the Capitol, without floodlights at night but receiving light from the illuminated Capitol Dome. It flies 24 hours a day at several other places, including the Fort McHenry Nat'l Monument in Baltimore, where it inspired Francis Scott Key to write The Star Spangled Banner. The flag also flies 24 hours a day, properly illuminated, at U.S. Customs ports of entry.

**How to Fly the Flag**—The flag should be hoisted briskly and lowered ceremoniously, and should never be allowed to touch the ground or the floor. When hung over a sidewalk from a rope extending from a building to a pole, the union should be away from the building. When hung over the center of a street it should have the union to the north in an east-west street and to the east in a north-south street. No other flag may be flown above or, if on the same level, to the right of the U.S. flag, except that at the United Nations Headquarters the UN flag may be placed above flags of all member nations and other national flags may be flown with equal prominence or honor with the flag of the U.S. At services by Navy chaplains at sea, the church pennant may be flown above the flag.

When two flags are placed against a wall with crossed staffs, the U.S. flag should be at right—its own right, and its staff should be in front of the staff of the other flag; when a number of flags are grouped and displayed from staffs, it should be at the center and highest point of the group.

**Church and Platform Use**—In an auditorium, the flag may be displayed flat, above and behind the speaker. When displayed from a staff in a church or public auditorium, the flag should hold the position of superior prominence, in advance of the audience, and in the position of honor at the clergyman's or speaker's right as he faces the audience. Any other flag so displayed should be placed on the left of the clergyman or speaker or to the right of the audience.

When the flag is displayed horizontally or vertically against a wall, the stars should be uppermost and at the observer's left.

**How to Dispose of Worn Flags**—The flag, when it is in such condition that it is no longer a fitting emblem for display, should be destroyed in a dignified way, preferably by burning.

**When to Salute the Flag**—All persons present should face the flag, stand at attention and salute on the following occasions: (1) When the flag is passing in a parade or in a review, (2) During the ceremony of hoisting or lowering, (3) When the National Anthem is played, and (4) During the Pledge of Allegiance. Those present in uniform should render the military salute. Those not in uniform should place the right hand over the heart. A man wearing a hat should remove it with his right hand and hold it to his left shoulder during the salute.

On Memorial Day, the flag should fly at half-staff until noon, then be raised to the peak.

As provided by Presidential proclamation the flag should fly at half-staff for 30 days from the day of death of a president or former president; for 10 days from the day of death of a vice president, chief justice or retired chief justice of the U.S., or speaker of the House of Representatives; from day of death until burial of an associate justice of the Supreme Court, cabinet member, former vice president, or Senate president pro tempore, majority or minority Senate leader, or majority or minority House leader; for a U.S. senator, representative, territorial delegate, or the resident commissioner of Puerto Rico, on day of death and the following day within the metropolitan area of the District of Columbia and from day of death until burial within the decedent's state, congressional district, territory or commonwealth; and for the death of the governor of a state, territory, or possession of the U.S., from day of death until burial within that state, territory, or possession.

When used to cover a casket, the flag should be placed so that the union is at the head and over the left shoulder. It should not be lowered into the grave nor touch the ground.

**Prohibited Uses of the Flag**—The flag should not be dipped to any person or thing. (An exception—customarily, ships salute by dipping their colors.) It should never be displayed with the union down save as a distress signal. It should never be carried flat or horizontally, but always aloft and free.

It should not be displayed on a float, motor car or boat except from a staff.

It should never be used as a covering for a ceiling, nor have placed upon it any word, design, or drawing. It should never be used as a receptacle for carrying anything. It should not be used to cover a statue or a monument.

The flag should never be used for advertising purposes, nor be embroidered on such articles as cushions or hankerchiefs, printed or otherwise impressed on boxes or anything that is designed for temporary use and discard; or used as a costume or athletic uniform. Advertising signs should not be fastened to its staff or halyard.

The flag should never be used as drapery of any sort, never festooned, drawn back, nor up, in folds, but always allowed to fall free. Bunting of blue, white and red always arranged with the blue above and the white in the middle, should be used for covering a speaker's desk, draping the front of a platform, and for decoration in general.

An Act of Congress approved Feb. 8, 1917, provided certain penalties for the desecration, mutilation or improper use of the flag within the District of Columbia. A 1968 federal law provided penalties of up to a year's imprisonment or a $1,000 fine or both, for publicly burning or otherwise desecrating any flag of the United States. In addition, many states have laws against flag desecration. In 1989, the Supreme Court ruled that no laws could prohibit political protesters from burning the flag. The decision had the effect of declaring unconstitutional the flag desecration laws of 48 states, as well as a similar Federal statute, in cases of peaceful political expression.

The Supreme Court, June 1990, declared that a new Federal law making it a crime to burn or deface the American flag violates the free-speech guarantee of the First Amendment. The 5-4 decision led to renewed calls in Congress for a constitutional amendment to make it possible to prosecute flag burning.

## Pledge of Allegiance to the Flag

*I pledge allegiance to the flag of the United States of America and to the republic for which it stands, one nation under God, indivisible, with liberty and justice for all.*

This, the current official version of the Pledge of Allegiance, has developed from the original pledge, which was first published in the Sept. 8, 1892, issue of the Youth's Companion, a weekly magazine then published in Boston. The original pledge contained the phrase "my flag," which was changed more than 30 years later to "flag of the United States of America." An act of Congress in 1954 added the words "under God."

The authorship of the pledge had been in dispute for many years. The Youth's Companion stated in 1917 that the original draft was written by James B. Upham, an executive of the magazine who died in 1910. A leaflet circulated by the magazine later named Upham as the originator of the draft "afterwards condensed and perfected by him and his associates of the Companion force."

Francis Bellamy, a former member of the Youth's Companion editorial staff, publicly claimed authorship of the pledge in 1923. The United States Flag Assn., acting on the advice of a committee named to study the controversy, upheld in 1939 the claim of Bellamy, who had died 8 years earlier. The Library of Congress issued in 1957 a report attributing the authorship to Bellamy.

## The National Anthem — The Star-Spangled Banner

The Star-Spangled Banner was ordered played by the military and naval services by President Woodrow Wilson in 1916. It was designated the National Anthem by Act of Congress, Mar. 3, 1931. It was written by Francis Scott Key, of Georgetown, D. C., during the bombardment of Fort McHenry, Baltimore, Md., Sept. 13-14, 1814. Key was a lawyer, a graduate of St. John's College, Annapolis, and a volunteer in a light artillery company. When a friend, Dr. Beanes, a physician of Upper Marlborough, Md., was taken aboard Admiral Cockburn's British squadron for interfering with ground troops, Key and J. S. Skinner, carrying a note from President Madison, went to the fleet under a flag of truce on a cartel ship to ask Beanes' release. Admiral Cockburn consented, but as the fleet was about to sail up the Patapsco to bombard Fort McHenry he detained them, first on H. M. S. Surprise, and then on a supply ship.

Key witnessed the bombardment from his own vessel. It began at 7 a.m., Sept. 13, 1814, and lasted, with intermissions, for 25 hours. The British fired over 1,500 shells, each weighing as much as 220 lbs. They were unable to approach closely because the Americans had sunk 22 vessels in the channel. Only four Americans were killed and 24 wounded. A British bomb-ship was disabled.

During the bombardment Key wrote a stanza on the back of an envelope. Next day at Indian Queen Inn, Baltimore, he wrote out the poem and gave it to his brother-in-law, Judge J. H. Nicholson. Nicholson suggested the tune, Anacreon in Heaven, and had the poem printed on broadsides, of which two survive. On Sept. 20 it appeared in the "Baltimore American." Later Key made 3 copies; one is in the Library of Congress and one in the Pennsylvania Historical Society.

The copy that Key wrote in his hotel Sept. 14, 1814, remained in the Nicholson family for 93 years. In 1907 it was sold to Henry Walters of Baltimore. In 1934 it was bought at auction in New York from the Walters estate by the Walters Art Gallery, Baltimore, for $26,400. The Walters Gallery in 1953 sold the manuscript to the Maryland Historical Society for the same price.

The flag that Key saw during the bombardment is preserved in the Smithsonian Institution, Washington. It is 30 by 42 ft., and has 15 alternate red and white stripes and 15 stars, for the original 13 states plus Kentucky and Vermont. It was made by Mary Young Pickersgill. The Baltimore Flag House, a museum, occupies her premises, which were restored in 1953.

### The Star-Spangled Banner

I

Oh, say can you see by the dawn's early light
  What so proudly we hailed at the twilight's last gleaming?
Whose broad stripes and bright stars thru the perilous fight,
  O'er the ramparts we watched were so gallantly streaming?
And the rocket's red glare, the bombs bursting in air,
  Gave proof through the night that our flag was still there.
Oh, say does that star-spangled banner yet wave
  O'er the land of the free and the home of the brave?

II

On the shore, dimly seen through the mists of the deep,
  Where the foe's haughty host in dread silence reposes,
What is that which the breeze, o'er the towering steep,
  As it fitfully blows, half conceals, half discloses?
Now it catches the gleam of the morning's first beam,
  In full glory reflected now shines in the stream:
'Tis the star-spangled banner! Oh long may it wave
  O'er the land of the free and the home of the brave!

III

And where is that band who so vauntingly swore
  That the havoc of war and the battle's confusion,
A home and a country should leave us no more!
  Their blood has washed out their foul footsteps' pollution.
No refuge could save the hireling and slave
  From the terror of flight, or the gloom of the grave:
And the star-spangled banner in triumph doth wave
  O'er the land of the free and the home of the brave!

IV

Oh! thus be it ever, when freemen shall stand
  Between their loved home and the war's desolation!
Blest with victory and peace, may the heav'n rescued land
  Praise the Power that hath made and preserved us a nation.
Then conquer we must, when our cause it is just,
  And this be our motto: "In God is our trust."
And the star-spangled banner in triumph shall wave
  O'er the land of the free and the home of the brave!

## America
## (My Country 'Tis of Thee)

First sung in public on July 4, 1831, at a service in the Park Street Church, Boston, the words were written by Rev. Samuel Francis Smith, a Baptist clergyman, who set them to a melody he found in a German songbook, unaware that it was the tune for the British anthem, "God Save the King/Queen."

My country, 'tis of thee,
Sweet land of liberty, Of thee I sing.
Land where my fathers died!
Land of the Pilgrims' pride!
From ev'ry mountainside,
Let freedom ring!

My native country, thee,
Land of the noble free,
Thy name I love.
I love thy rocks and rills,
Thy woods and templed hills;
My heart with rapture thrills
Like that above.

Let music swell the breeze,
And ring from all the trees
Sweet freedom's song.
Let mortal tongues awake;
Let all that breathe partake;
Let rocks their silence break,
The sound prolong.

Our fathers' God, to Thee,
Author of liberty,
To Thee we sing.
Long may our land be bright
With freedom's holy light;
Protect us by Thy might,
Great God, our King!

# America, the Beautiful

Composed by Katherine Lee Bates, a Massachusetts educator and author, in 1893. It was inspired by the view Bates experienced atop Pike's Peak. Its final form was established in 1911 and is set to the music of Samuel A. Ward's "Materna."

O beautiful for spacious skies,
For amber waves of grain,
For purple mountain majesties
Above the fruited plain.
America! America!
God shed His grace on thee,
And crown thy good with brotherhood
From sea to shining sea.
O beautiful for pilgrim feet
Whose stern impassion'd stress
A thorough-fare for freedom beat
Across the wilderness.
America! America!
God mend thine ev'ry flaw,
Confirm thy soul in self control,
Thy liberty in law.

O beautiful for heroes prov'd
In liberating strife,
Who more than self their country lov'd
And mercy more than life.
America! America!
May God thy gold refine
Till all success be nobleness,
And ev'ry gain divine.
O beautiful for patriot dream
That sees beyond the years,
Thine alabaster cities gleam,
Undimmed by human tears.
America! America!
God shed His grace on thee,
And crown thy good with brotherhood
From sea to shining sea.

# The Liberty Bell: Its History and Significance

The Liberty Bell, in Independence Hall, Philadelphia, is an object of great reverence to Americans because of its association with the historic events of the War of Independence.

The original Province bell, ordered to commemorate the 50th anniversary of the Commonwealth of Pennsylvania, was cast by Thomas Lister, Whitechapel, London, and reached Philadelphia in Aug. 1752. It bore an inscription from Leviticus XXV, 10: "Proclaim liberty throughout all the land unto all the inhabitants thereof."

The bell was cracked by a stroke of its clapper in Sept. 1752 while it hung on a truss in the State House yard for testing. Pass & Stow, Philadelphia founders, recast the bell, adding 1 1/2 ounces of copper to a pound of the original metal to reduce brittleness. It was found that the bell contained too much copper, injuring its tone, so Pass & Stow recast it again, this time successfully.

In June 1753 the bell was hung in the wooden steeple of the State House, erected on top of the brick tower. In use while the Continental Congress was in session in the State House, it rang out in defiance of British tax and trade restrictions, and proclaimed the Boston Tea Party and the first public reading of the Declaration of Independence.

On Sept. 18, 1777, when the British Army was about to occupy Philadelphia, the bell was moved in a baggage train of the American Army to Allentown, Pa. where it was hidden in the Zion Reformed Church until June 27, 1778. It was moved back to Philadelphia after the British left.

In July 1781 the wooden steeple became insecure and had to be taken down. The bell was lowered into the brick section of the tower. Because of its association with the War of Independence it was not recast but remained mute in this location until 1846, the year of the Mexican War, when it was placed on exhibition in the Declaration Chamber of Independence Hall.

In 1876, when many thousands of Americans visited Philadelphia for the Centennial Exposition, it was placed in its old walnut frame in the tower hallway. In 1877 it was hung from the ceiling of the tower by a chain of 13 links. It was returned again to the Declaration Chamber and in 1896 taken back to the tower hall, where it occupied a glass case. In 1915 the case was removed so that the public might touch it. On Jan. 1, 1976, just after midnight to mark the opening of the Bicentennial Year, the bell was moved to a new glass and steel pavilion behind Independence Hall for easier viewing by the larger number of visitors expected during the year.

The measurements of the bell follow: circumference around the lip, 12 ft.; circumference around the crown, 7 ft. 6 in.; lip to the crown, 3 ft.; height over the crown, 2 ft. 3 in.; thickness at lip, 3 in.; thickness at crown, 1 1/4 in.; weight, 2080 lbs.; length of clapper, 3 ft. 2 in.; cost, £60 14s 5d.

The specific source of the crack in the bell is unknown.

# Statue of Liberty National Monument

Since 1886, the Statue of Liberty Enlightening the World has stood as a symbol of freedom in New York harbor. It also commemorates French-American friendship for it was given by the people of France, designed by Frederic Auguste Bartholdi (1834-1904). A $2.5 million building housing the American Museum of Immigration was opened by Pres. Nixon Sept. 26, 1972, at the base of the statue. It houses a permanent exhibition of photos, posters, and artifacts tracing the history of American immigration. The Monument is administered by the National Park Service.

Nearby Ellis Island, gateway to America for more than 12 million immigrants between 1892 and 1954, was proclaimed part of the National Monument in 1965 by Pres. Johnson.

Edouard de Laboulaye, French historian and admirer of American political institutions, suggested that the French present a monument to the United States, the latter to provide pedestal and site. Bartholdi visualized a colossal statue at the entrance of New York harbor, welcoming the peoples of the world with the torch of liberty.

On Washington's birthday, Feb. 22, 1877, Congress approved the use of a site on Bedloe's Island suggested by Bartholdi. This island of 12 acres had been owned in the 17th century by a Walloon named Isaac Bedloe. It was called Bedloe's until Aug. 3, 1956, when Pres. Eisenhower approved a resolution of Congress changing the name to Liberty Island.

The statue was finished May 21, 1884, and formally presented to U.S. Minister Morton July 4, 1884, by Ferdinand de Lesseps, head of the Franco-American Union, promoter of the Panama Canal, and builder of the Suez Canal.

On Aug. 5, 1884, the Americans laid the cornerstone for the pedestal. This was to be built on the foundations of Fort Wood, which had been erected by the Government in 1811. The American committee had raised $125,000, but this was found to be inadequate. Joseph Pulitzer, owner of the New York World, appealed on Mar. 16, 1885, for general donations. By Aug. 11, 1885, he had raised $100,000.

The statue arrived dismantled, in 214 packing cases, from Rouen, France, in June, 1885. The last rivet of the statue was driven Oct. 28, 1886, when Pres. Grover Cleveland dedicated the monument.

The statue weighs 450,000 lbs. or 225 tons. The copper sheeting weighs 200,000 lbs. There are 167 steps from the land level to the top of the pedestal, 168 steps inside the statue to the head, and 54 rungs on the ladder leading to the arm that holds the torch.

Two years of restoration work was completed before the statue's centennial celebration on July 4, 1986. Among other repairs, the multi-million dollar project included replacing the 1,600 wrought iron bands that hold its copper skin to its frame, replacing its torch, and installing an elevator.

A four-day extravaganza of concerts, tall ships, ethnic festivals, and fireworks celebrated the 100th anniversary. The festivities included Chief Justice Warren E. Burger's swearing-in of 5,000 new citizens on Ellis Island, while 20,000 others across the country were simultaneously sworn in through a satellite telecast.

The ceremonies were followed by others on Oct. 28, 1986, the statue's 100th birthday.

### Emma Lazarus' Famous Poem

A poem by Emma Lazarus is graven on a tablet within the pedestal on which the statue stands.

#### The New Colossus

*Not like the brazen giant of Greek fame,*
*With conquering limbs astride from land to land;*
*Here at our sea-washed, sunset gates shall stand*

*A mighty woman with a torch, whose flame*
*Is the imprisoned lightning, and her name*
*Mother of Exiles. From her beacon-hand*
*Glows world-wide welcome; her mild eyes command*
*The air-bridged harbor that twin cities frame.*
*"Keep ancient lands, your storied pomp!" cries she*
*With silent lips. "Give me your tired, your poor,*
*Your huddled masses yearning to breathe free,*
*The wretched refuse of your teeming shore.*
*Send these, the homeless, tempest-tost to me,*
*I lift my lamp beside the golden door!"*

| Dimensions of the Statue | Ft. | In. |
|---|---|---|
| Height from base to torch (45.3 meters) . . . . . | 151 | 1 |
| Foundation of pedestal to torch (91.5 meters). . . | 305 | 1 |
| Heel to top of head . . . . . . . . . . . . . . . . | 111 | 1 |
| Length of hand . . . . . . . . . . . . . . . . . . | 16 | 5 |
| Index finger . . . . . . . . . . . . . . . . . . . | 8 | 0 |
| Circumference at second joint. . . . . . . . . . | 3 | 6 |
| Size of finger nail . . . . . . . . . . . . . 13x10 in. | | |
| Head from chin to cranium. . . . . . . . . . . . | 17 | 3 |
| Head thickness from ear to ear . . . . . . . . . . | 10 | 0 |
| Distance across the eye . . . . . . . . . . . . . | 2 | 6 |
| Length of nose . . . . . . . . . . . . . . . . . . | 4 | 6 |
| Right arm, length . . . . . . . . . . . . . . . . | 42 | 0 |
| Right arm, greatest thickness . . . . . . . . . . | 12 | 0 |
| Thickness of waist . . . . . . . . . . . . . . . . | 35 | 0 |
| Width of mouth . . . . . . . . . . . . . . . . . | 3 | 0 |
| Tablet, length . . . . . . . . . . . . . . . . . . | 23 | 7 |
| Tablet, width. . . . . . . . . . . . . . . . . . . | 13 | 7 |
| Tablet, thickness . . . . . . . . . . . . . . . . | 2 | 0 |

## Lincoln's Address at Gettysburg, 1863

Fourscore and seven years ago our fathers brought forth on this continent a new nation, conceived in liberty and dedicated to the proposition that all men are created equal.

Now we are engaged in a great civil war, testing whether that nation or any nation so conceived and so dedicated can long endure. We are met on a great battle field of that war. We have come to dedicate a portion of that field, as a final resting-place for those who here gave their lives that that nation might live. It is altogether fitting and proper that we should do this.

But, in a larger sense, we can not dedicate — we can not consecrate — we can not hallow — this ground. The brave men, living and dead, who struggled here, have consecrated it, far above our poor power to add or detract. The world will little note, nor long remember, what we say here, but it can never forget what they did here. It is for us the living, rather, to be dedicated here to the unfinished work which they who fought here have thus far so nobly advanced. It is rather for us to be here dedicated to the great task remaining before us — that from these honored dead we take increased devotion to that cause for which they gave the last full measure of devotion — that we here highly resolve that these dead shall not have died in vain — that this nation, under God, shall have a new birth of freedom — and that government of the people, by the people, for the people, shall not perish from the earth.

## Confederate States and Secession

The American Civil War, 1861-65, grew out of sectional disputes over the continued existence of slavery in the South and the contention of Southern legislators that the states retained many sovereign rights, including the right to secede from the Union.

The war was not fought by state against state but by one federal regime against another, the Confederate government in Richmond assuming control over the economic, political, and military life of the South, under protest from Georgia and South Carolina.

South Carolina voted an ordinance of secession from the Union, repealing its 1788 ratification of the U.S. Constitution on Dec. 20, 1860, to take effect Dec. 24. Other states seceded in 1861. Their votes in conventions were:

Mississippi, Jan. 9, 84-15; Florida, Jan. 10, 62-7; Alabama, Jan. 11, 61-39; Georgia, Jan. 19, 208-89; Louisiana, Jan. 26, 113-17; Texas, Feb. 1, 166-7, ratified by popular vote Feb. 23 (for 34,794, against 11,325); Virginia, Apr. 17, 88-55, ratified by popular vote May 23 (for 128,884; against

32,134); Arkansas, May 6, 69-1; Tennessee, May 7, ratified by popular vote June 8 (for 104,019, against 47,238); North Carolina, May 21.

Missouri Unionists stopped secession in conventions Feb. 28 and Mar. 9. The legislature condemned secession Mar. 7. Under the protection of Confederate troops, secessionist members of the legislature adopted a resolution of secession at Neosho, Oct. 31. The Confederate Congress seated the secessionists' representatives.

Kentucky did not secede and its government remained Unionist. In a part occupied by Confederate troops, Kentuckians approved secession and the Confederate Congress admitted their representatives.

The Maryland legislature voted against secession Apr. 27, 53-13. Delaware did not secede. Western Virginia held conventions at Wheeling, named a pro-Union governor June 11, 1861; admitted to Union as West Virginia June 20, 1863; its constitution provided for gradual abolition of slavery.

## Confederate Government

Forty-two delegates from South Carolina, Georgia, Alabama, Mississippi, Louisiana, and Florida met in convention at Montgomery, Ala., Feb. 4, 1861. They adopted a provisional constitution of the Confederate States of America, and elected Jefferson Davis (Miss.) provisional president, and Alexander H. Stephens (Ga.) provisional vice president.

A permanent constitution was adopted Mar. 11; it abolished the African slave trade. The Congress moved to Richmond, Va. July 20. Davis was elected president in October,

and was inaugurated Feb. 22, 1862.

The Congress adopted a flag, consisting of a red field with a white stripe, and a blue jack with a circle of white stars. Later the more popular flag was the red field with blue diagonal cross bars that held 13 white stars. The stars represented the 11 states actually in the Confederacy plus Kentucky and Missouri.

*(See also Civil War, U.S., in Index)*

# The Mayflower Compact

The threat of James I to "harry them out of the land" sent a little band of religious dissenters from England to Holland in 1608. They were known as "Separatists" because they wished to cut all ties with the Established Church. In 1620, some of them, known now as the Pilgrims, joined with a larger group in England to set sail on the *Mayflower* for the New World. A joint stock company financed their venture.

In November, they sighted Cape Cod and decided to land an exploring party at Plymouth Harbor. However, a rebellious group picked up at Southampton and London troubled the Pilgrim leaders, and to control their actions forty-one of the Pilgrims drew up the "Mayflower Compact," which was signed before going ashore. The voluntary agreement to govern themselves was America's first written constitution.

In the name of God, Amen. We, whose names are underwritten, the Loyal Subjects of our dread Sovereign Lord, King *James*, by the Grace of God, of *Great Britain, France and Ireland,* King, *Defender of the Faith,* etc.

Having undertaken for the Glory of God, and Advancement of the Christian Faith, and the Honour of our King and Country, a voyage to plant the first colony in the northern Parts of *Virginia;* do by these Presents, solemnly and mutually in the Presence of God and one of another, convenant and combine ouselves together into a civil Body Politick, for our better Ordering and Preservation, and Further-ance of the Ends aforesaid; And by Virtue hereof to enact, constitute, and frame, such just and equal Laws, Ordinances, Acts, Constitutions and Offices, from time to time, as shall be thought most meet and convenient for the General good of the Colony; unto which we promise all due Submission and Obedience.

In Witness whereof we have hereunto subscribed our names at *Cape Cod* the eleventh of *November,* in the Reign of our Sovereign Lord, King *James* of *England, France* and *Ireland,* the eighteenth, and of *Scotland* the fifty-fourth. *Anno Domini, 1620.*

# Forms of Address for Persons of Rank and Public Office

In these examples John Smith is used as a representative American name. The salutation Dear Sir or Dear Madam is always permissible when addressing a person not known to the writer. Female equivalents should be substituted where appropriate.

### President of the United States

**Address:** The President, The White House, Washington, DC 20500. Also, The President and Mrs. ——.
**Salutation:** Dear Sir or Mr. President or Dear Mr. President. More intimately: My dear Mr. President. Also: Dear Mr. President and Mrs. ——.
The vice president takes the same forms.

### Cabinet Officers

**Address:** Mr. John Smith, Secretary of State, Washington, D.C. Or The Hon. John Smith. Similar addresses for other members of the cabinet. Also: Secretary and Mrs. John Smith.
**Salutation:** Dear Sir, or Dear Mr. Secretary. Also: Dear Mr. and Mrs. Smith.

### The Bench

**Address:** The Hon. John Smith, Chief Justice of the United States. The Hon. John Smith, Associate Justice of the Supreme Court of the United States. The Hon. John Smith, Associate Judge, U.S. District Court.
**Salutation:** Dear Sir, or Dear Mr. Chief Justice. Dear Mr. Justice. Dear Judge Smith.

### Members of Congress

**Address:** The Hon. John Smith, United States Senate, Washington, DC 20510, or Sen. John Smith, etc. Also The Hon. John Smith, House of Representatives, Washington, DC 20515, or Rep. John Smith, etc.
**Salutation:** Dear Mr. Senator or Dear Mr. Smith; for Representative, Dear Mr. Smith.

### Officers of Armed Forces

**Address:** Careful attention should be given to the precise rank, thus: General of the Army John Smith, Fleet Admiral John Smith. The rules for Air Force are same as Army.
**Salutation:** Dear Sir, or Dear General. All general officers, whatever rank, are entitled to be addressed as generals. Likewise a lieutenant colonel is addressed as colonel and first and second lieutenants are addressed as lieutenant.
Warrant officers and flight officers are addressed as Mister. Chaplains are addressed as Chaplain. A Catholic chaplain may be addressed as Father. Students of the U.S. Military Academy and Air Force Academy are addressed as Cadet, students of the U.S. Naval Academy are addressed as Midshipman/woman. Noncommissioned officers are addressed by their titles.

### Ambassador, Governor, Mayor

**Address:** The Hon. John Smith, followed by his or her title. They can be addressed either at their embassy, or at the Department of State, Washington, D.C. An ambassador from a foreign nation may be addressed as His or Her Excellency. An American is not to be so addressed.
**Salutation:** Dear Mr. or Madam Ambassador. An ambassador from a foreign nation may be called Your Excellency.
Governors and mayors are often addressed as The Hon. Jane Smith, Governor of ——, or The Hon. John Smith, Mayor of ——; also Governor John Smith, State House, Albany, N.Y., or Mayor Jane Smith, City Hall, Erie, Pa.

### The Clergy

**Address:** His Holiness, the Pope, or His Holiness Pope (name), State of Vatican City, Italy.
**Salutation:** Your Holiness or Most Holy Father.
Also: His Eminence, John, Cardinal Smith; salutation: Your Eminence. An archbishop or a bishop is addressed The Most Reverend, and the salutation is Your Excellency. A monsignor who is a papal chamberlain is The Very Reverend Monsignor and the salutation is Dear Sir or Very Reverend Monsignor; a monsignor who is a domestic prelate is The Right Reverend Monsignor and salutation is Right Reverend Monsignor. A priest is addressed Reverend John Smith. A brother of an order is addressed Brother ——. A sister takes the same form.
A bishop of the Episcopal Church is The Right Reverend John Smith; salutation is Right Reverend Sir, or Dear Bishop Smith. If a clergyman is a doctor of divinity, he is addressed: The Reverend John Smith, D.D., and the salutation is Reverend Sir, or Dear Dr. Smith. When a clergyman does not have the degree the salutation is Dear Mr. Smith, or Dear Father Smith.
A bishop of the Methodist Church is addressed Bishop John Smith with titles following.

### Royalty and Nobility

An emperor is to be addressed in a letter as Sir, or Your Imperial Majesty.
A king or queen is addressed as His Majesty (Name), King of (Name), or Her Majesty (Name), Queen of (Name), Salutation: Sir, or Madam, or May it please Your Majesty.
Princes and princesses and other persons of royal blood are addressed as His (or Her) Royal Highness, and saluted with Mav it please Your Royal Highness.
A duke or marquis is My Lord Duke (or Marquis), a duke is His (or Your) Grace.

# BIOGRAPHIES OF U.S. PRESIDENTS

## George Washington (1789-1797)

George Washington, first president, was born Feb. 22, 1732 (Feb. 11, 1731, old style), the son of Augustine Washington and Mary Ball, at Wakefield on Pope's Creek, Westmoreland Co., Va. His early childhood was spent on a farm, near Fredericksburg. His father died when George was 11. He studied mathematics and surveying and when 16 went to live with his half brother Lawrence, who built and named Mount Vernon. George surveyed the lands of William Fairfax in the Shenandoah Valley, keeping a diary. He accompanied Lawrence to Barbados, West Indies, contracted small pox, and was deeply scarred. Lawrence died in 1752 and George acquired his property by inheritance. He valued land and when he died owned 70,000 acres in Virginia and 40,000 acres in what is now West Virginia.

Washington's military service began in 1753 when Gov. Dinwiddie of Virginia sent him on missions deep into Ohio country. He clashed with the French and had to surrender Fort Necessity July 3, 1754. He was an aide to Braddock and at his side when the army was ambushed and defeated on a march to Ft. Duquesne, July 9, 1755. He helped take Fort Duquesne from the French in 1758.

After his marriage to Martha Dandridge Custis, a widow, in 1759, Washington managed his family estate at Mount Vernon. Although not at first for independence, he opposed British exactions and took charge of the Virginia troops before war broke out. He was made commander-in-chief by the Continental Congress June 15, 1775.

The successful issue of a war filled with hardships was due to his leadership. He was resourceful, a stern disciplinarian, and the one strong, dependable force for unity. He favored a federal government and became chairman of the Constitutional Convention of 1787. He helped get the Constitution ratified and was unanimously elected president by the electoral college and inaugurated, Apr. 30, 1789, on the balcony of New York's Federal Hall.

He was reelected 1792, but refused to consider a 3d term and retired to Mount Vernon. He suffered acute laryngitis after a ride in snow and rain around his estate, was bled profusely, and died Dec. 14, 1799.

## John Adams (1797-1801)

John Adams, 2d president, Federalist, was born in Braintree (Quincy), Mass., Oct. 30, 1735 (Oct. 19, o. s.), the son of John Adams, a farmer, and Susanna Boylston. He was a great-grandson of Henry Adams who came from England in 1636. He graduated from Harvard, 1755, taught school, studied law. In 1765 he argued against taxation without representation before the royal governor. In 1770 he defended in court the British soldiers who fired on civilians in the "Boston Massacre." He was a delegate to the first Continental Congress, and signed the Declaration of Independence. He was a commissioner to France, 1778, with Benjamin Franklin and Arthur Lee; won recognition of the U.S. by The Hague, 1782; was first American minister to England, 1785-1788, and was elected vice president, 1788 and 1792.

In 1796 Adams was chosen president by the electors. Intense antagonism to America by France caused agitation for war, led by Alexander Hamilton. Adams, breaking with Hamilton, opposed war.

To fight alien influence and muzzle criticism Adams supported the Alien and Sedition laws of 1798, which led to his defeat for reelection. He died July 4, 1826, on the same day as Jefferson (the 50th anniversary of the Declaration of Independence).

## Thomas Jefferson (1801-1809)

Thomas Jefferson, 3d president, was born Apr. 13, 1743 (Apr. 2, o. s.), at Shadwell, Va., the son of Peter Jefferson, a civil engineer of Welsh descent who raised tobacco, and Jane Randolph. His father died when he was 14, leaving him 2,750 acres and his slaves. Jefferson attended the College of William and Mary, 1760-1762, read classics in Greek and Latin and played the violin. In 1769 he was elected to the House of Burgesses. In 1770 he began building Monticello, near Charlottesville. He was a member of the Virginia Committee of Correspondence and the Continental Congress. Named a member of the committee to draw up a Declaration of Independence, he wrote the basic draft. He was a member of the Virginia House of Delegates, 1776-79, elected governor to succeed Patrick Henry, 1779, reelected 1780, resigned June 1781, amid charges of ineffectual military preparation. During his term he wrote the statute on religious freedom. In the Continental Congress, 1783, he drew up an ordinance for the Northwest Territory forbidding slavery after 1800; its terms were put into the Ordinance of 1787. He was sent to Paris with Benjamin Franklin and John Adams to negotiate commercial treaties, 1784; made minister to France, 1785.

Washington appointed him secretary of state, 1789. Jefferson's strong faith in the consent of the governed, as opposed to executive control favored by Hamilton, secretary of the treasury, often led to conflict: Dec. 31, 1793, he resigned. He was the Democrat Republican candidate for president in 1796; beaten by John Adams, he became vice president. In 1800, Jefferson and Aaron Burr received equal electoral college votes for president. The House of Representatives elected Jefferson. Major events of his administration were the Louisiana Purchase, 1803, and the Lewis and Clark Expedition. He established the Univ. of Virginia and designed its buildings. He died July 4, 1826, on the same day as John Adams.

## James Madison (1809-1817)

James Madison, 4th president, Democrat Republican, was born Mar. 16, 1751 (Mar. 5, 1750, o. s.) at Port Conway, King George Co., Va., eldest son of James Madison and Eleanor Rose Conway. Madison was graduated from Princeton, 1771; studied theology, 1772; sat in the Virginia Constitutional Convention, 1776. He was a member of the Continental Congress. He was chief recorder at the Constitutional Convention in 1787, and supported ratification in the Federalist Papers, written with Alexander Hamilton and John Jay. He was elected to the House of Representatives in 1789, helped frame the Bill of Rights and fought the Alien and Sedition Acts. He became Jefferson's secretary of state, 1801.

Elected president in 1808, Madison was a "strict constructionist," opposed to the free interpretation of the Constitution by the Federalists. He was reelected in 1812 by the votes of the agrarian South and recently admitted western states. Caught between British and French maritime restrictions, the U.S. drifted into war, declared June 18, 1812. The war ended in a stalemate. He retired in 1817 to his estate at Montpelier. There he edited his famous papers on the Constitutional Convention. He became rector of the Univ. of Virginia, 1826. He died June 28, 1836.

## James Monroe (1817-1825)

James Monroe, 5th president, Democrat Republican, was born Apr. 28, 1758, in Westmoreland Co., Va., the son of Spence Monroe and Eliza Jones, who were of Scottish and Welsh descent, respectively. He attended the College of William and Mary, fought in the 3d Virginia Regiment at White Plains, Brandywine, Monmouth, and was wounded at Trenton. He studied law with Thomas Jefferson, 1780, was a member of the Virginia House of Delegates and of Congress, 1783-86. He opposed ratification of the Constitution because it lacked a bill of rights; was U.S. senator, 1790; minister to France, 1794-96; governor of Virginia, 1799-1802, and 1811. Jefferson sent him to France as minister, 1803. He helped Robert Livingston negotiate the Louisiana Purchase, 1803. He ran against Madison for president in 1808. He was elected to the Virginia Assembly, 1810-1811; was secretary of state under Madison, 1811-1817.

In 1816 Monroe was elected president; in 1820 reelected with all but one electoral college vote. Monroe's administration became the "Era of Good Feeling." He obtained Florida from Spain; settled boundaries with Canada, and eliminated border forts. He supported the anti-slavery position that led to the Missouri Compromise. His most significant contribution was the "Monroe Doctrine," which became a cornerstone of U.S. foreign policy. Monroe retired to Oak Hill, Va. Financial problems forced him to sell his property. He moved to New York City to live with a daughter. He died there July 4, 1831.

## John Quincy Adams (1825-1829)

John Quincy Adams, 6th president, independent Federalist, later Democratic Republican, was born July 11, 1767, at Braintree (Quincy), Mass., the son of John and Abigail Adams. His father was the 2d president. He was educated in Paris, Leyden, and Harvard, graduating in 1787. He served as American minister in various European capitals, and helped draft the War of 1812 peace treaty. He was U.S. Senator, 1803-08. President Monroe made him secretary of state, 1817, and he negotiated the cession of the Floridas from Spain, supported exclusion of slavery in the Missouri Compromise, and helped formulate the Monroe Doctrine. In 1824 he was elected president by the House after he failed to win an electoral college majority. His expansion of executive powers was strongly opposed and he was beaten in 1828 by Jackson. In 1831 he entered Congress and served 17 years with distinction. He opposed slavery, the annexation of Texas, and the Mexican War. He helped establish the Smithsonian Institution. He had a stroke in the House and died in the Speaker's Room, Feb. 23, 1848.

## Andrew Jackson (1829-1837)

Andrew Jackson, 7th president, was a Jeffersonian-Republican, later a Democrat. He was born in the Waxhaws district, New Lancaster Co., S.C., Mar. 15, 1767, the posthumous son of Andrew Jackson and Elizabeth Hutchinson, who were Irish immigrants. At 13, he joined the militia in the Revolution and was captured.

He read law in Salisbury, N.C., moved to Nashville, Tenn., speculated in land, married, and practiced law. In 1796 he helped draft the constitution of Tennessee and for a year occupied its one seat in Congress. He was in the Senate in 1797, and again in 1823. He defeated the Creek Indians at Horseshoe Bend, Ala., 1814. With 6,000 backwoods fighters he defeated Pakenham's 12,000 British troops at the Chalmette, outside New Orleans, Jan. 8, 1815. In 1818 he briefly invaded Spanish Florida to quell Seminoles and outlaws who harassed frontier settlements. In 1824 he ran for president against John Quincy Adams and had the most popular and electoral votes but not a majority; the election was decided by the House, which chose Adams. In 1828 he defeated Adams, carrying the West and South. He was a noisy debater and a duelist and introduced rotation in office called the "spoils system." Suspicious of privilege, he ruined the Bank of the United States by depositing federal funds with state banks. Though "Let the people rule" was his slogan, he at times supported strict constructionist policies against the expansionist West. He killed the congressional caucus for nominating presidential candidates and substituted the national convention, 1832. When South Carolina refused to collect imports under his protective tariff he ordered army and naval forces to Charleston. Jackson recognized the Republic of Texas, 1836. He died at the Hermitage, June 8, 1845.

## Martin Van Buren (1837-1841)

Martin Van Buren, 8th president, Democrat, was born Dec. 5, 1782, at Kinderhook, N.Y., the son of Abraham Van Buren, a Dutch farmer, and Mary Hoes. He was surrogate of Columbia County, N.Y., state senator and attorney general. He was U.S. senator 1821, reelected, 1827, elected governor of New York, 1828. He helped swing eastern support to Jackson in 1828 and was his secretary of state 1829-31. In 1832 he was elected vice president. He was a consummate politician, known as "the little magician," and influenced Jackson's policies. In 1836 he defeated William Henry Harrison for president and took office as the Panic of 1837 initiated a 5-year nationwide depression. He inaugurated the independent treasury system. His refusal to spend land revenues led to his defeat by Harrison in 1840. He lost the Democratic nomination in 1844 to Polk. In 1848 he ran for president on the Free Soil ticket and lost. He died July 24, 1862, at Kinderhook.

## William Henry Harrison (1841)

William Henry Harrison, 9th president, Whig, who served only 31 days, was born in Berkeley, Charles City Co., Va., Feb. 9, 1773, the 3d son of Benjamin Harrison, signer of the Declaration of Independence. He attended Hampden Sydney College. He was secretary of the Northwest Territory, 1798; its delegate in Congress, 1799; first governor of Indiana Territory, 1800; and superintendent of Indian affairs. With 900 men he routed Tecumseh's Indians at Tippecanoe, Nov. 7, 1811. A major general, he defeated British and Indians at Battle of the Thames, Oct. 5, 1813. He served in Congress, 1816-19; Senate, 1825-28. In 1840, he was elected president with a "log cabin and hard cider" slogan. He caught pneumonia during the inauguration and died Apr. 4, 1841.

## John Tyler (1841-1845)

John Tyler, 10th president, independent Whig, was born Mar. 29, 1790, in Greenway, Charles City Co., Va., son of John Tyler and Mary Armistead. His father was governor of Virginia, 1808-11. Tyler was graduated from William and Mary, 1807; member of the House of Delegates, 1811; in congress, 1816-21; in Virginia legislature, 1823-25; governor of Virginia, 1825-26; U.S. senator, 1827-36. In 1840 he was elected vice president and, on Harrison's death, succeeded him. He favored pre-emption, allowing settlers to get government land; rejected a national bank bill and thus alienated most Whig supporters; refused to honor the spoils system. He signed the resolution annexing Texas, Mar. 1, 1845. He accepted renomination, 1844, but withdrew before election. In 1861, he chaired an unsuccessful Washington conference called to avert civil war. After its failure he supported secession, sat in the provisional Confederate Congress, became a member of the Confederate House, but died in Richmond, Jan. 18, 1862, before it met.

## James Knox Polk (1845-1849)

James Knox Polk, 11th president, Democrat, was born in Mecklenburg Co., N.C., Nov. 2, 1795, the son of Samuel Polk, farmer and surveyor of Scotch-Irish descent, and Jane Knox. He graduated from the Univ. of North Carolina, 1818; member of the Tennessee state legislature, 1823-25. He served in Congress 1825-39 and as speaker 1835-39. He was governor of Tennessee 1839-41, but was defeated 1841 and 1843. In 1844, when both Clay and Van Buren announced opposition to annexing Texas, the Democrats made Polk the first dark horse nominee because he demanded control of all Oregon and annexation of Texas. Polk re-established the independent treasury system originated by Van Buren. His expansionist policy was opposed by Clay, Webster, Calhoun; he sent troops under Zachary Taylor to the Mexican border and, when Mexicans attacked, declared war existed. The Mexican war ended with the annexation of California and much of the Southwest as part of America's "manifest destiny." He compromised on the Oregon boundary ("54-40 or fight!") by accepting the 49th parallel and giving Vancouver to the British. Polk died in Nashville, June 15, 1849.

## Zachary Taylor (1849-1850)

Zachary Taylor, 12th president, Whig, who served only 16 months, was born Nov. 24, 1784, in Orange Co., Va., the son of Richard Taylor, later collector of the port of Louisville, Ky., and Sarah Strother. Taylor was commissioned first lieutenant, 1808; fought in the War of 1812; the Black Hawk War, 1832; and the second Seminole War, 1837. He was called Old Rough and Ready. He settled on a plantation near Baton Rouge, La. In 1845 Polk sent him with an army to the Rio Grande. When the Mexicans attacked him, Polk declared war. Taylor was successful at Palo Alto and Resaca de la Palma, 1846; occupied Monterrey. Polk made him major general but sent many of his troops to Gen. Winfield Scott. Outnumbered 4-1, he defeated Santa Anna at Buena Vista, 1847. A national hero, he received the Whig nomination in 1848, and was elected president. He resumed the spoils system and though once a slave-holder worked to have California admitted as a free state. He died in office July 9, 1850.

## Millard Fillmore (1850-1853)

Millard Fillmore, 13th president, Whig, was born Jan. 7, 1800, in Cayuga Co., N.Y., the son of Nathaniel Fillmore and Phoebe Millard. He taught school and studied law; admitted to the bar, 1823. He was a member of the state assembly, 1829-32; in Congress, 1833-35 and again 1837-43. He opposed the entrance of Texas as slave territory and voted for a protective tariff. In 1844 he was defeated for governor of New York. In 1848 he was elected vice president and succeeded as president July 10, 1850, after Taylor's death. Fillmore favored the Compromise of 1850 and signed the Fugitive Slave Law. His policies pleased neither expansionists nor slave-holders and he was not renominated in 1852. In 1856 he was nominated by the American (Know-Nothing) party and accepted by the Whigs, but defeated by Buchanan. He died in Buffalo, Mar. 8, 1874.

## Franklin Pierce (1853-1857)

Franklin Pierce, 14th president, Democrat, was born in Hillsboro, N. H., Nov. 23, 1804, the son of Benjamin Pierce, veteran of the Revolution and governor of New Hampshire, 1827. He graduated from Bowdoin, 1824. A lawyer, he served in the state legislature 1829-33; in Congress, supporting Jackson, 1833-37; U.S. senator, 1837-42. He enlisted in the Mexican War, became brigadier general under Gen. Winfield Scott. In 1852 Pierce was nominated on the 49th ballot over Lewis Cass, Stephen A. Douglas, and James Buchanan, and defeated Gen. Scott, Whig. Though against slavery, Pierce was influenced by pro-slavery Southerners. He approved the Kansas-Nebraska Act, leaving slavery to popular vote ("squatter sovereignty"), 1854. He signed a reciprocity treaty with Canada and approved the Gadsden Purchase from Mexico, 1853. Denied renomination by the Democrats, he spent most of his remaining years in Concord, N.H., where he died Oct. 8, 1869.

## James Buchanan (1857-1861)

James Buchanan, 15th president, Federalist, later Democrat, was born of Scottish descent near Mercersburg, Pa., Apr. 23, 1791, the son of James Buchanan, merchant, and Elizabeth Speer. He graduated from Dickinson, 1809; was a volunteer in the War of 1812; member, Pennsylvania legislature, 1814-16, Congress, 1820-31; Jackson's minister to Russia, 1831-33; U.S. senator 1834-45. As Polk's secretary of state, 1845-49, he ended the Oregon dispute with Britain, supported the Mexican War and annexation of Texas. As minister to Britain, 1853, he signed the Ostend Manifesto. Nominated by Democrats, he was elected, 1856, over John C. Fremont (Republican) and Millard Fillmore (American Know-Nothing and Whig tickets). On slavery he favored popular sovereignty and choice by state constitutions; he accepted the pro-slavery Dred Scott decision as binding. He denied the right of states to secede. A strict constructionist, he desired to keep peace and found no authority for using force. He died at Wheatland, near Lancaster, Pa., June 1, 1868.

## Abraham Lincoln (1861-1865)

Abraham Lincoln, 16th president, Republican, was born Feb. 12, 1809, in a log cabin on a farm then in Hardin Co., Ky., now in Larue. He was the son of Thomas Lincoln, a carpenter, and Nancy Hanks.

The Lincolns moved to Spencer Co., Ind., near Gentryville, when Abe was 7. When his mother died, his father married Mrs. Sarah Bush Johnston, 1819; she had a favorable influence on Abe. In 1830 the family moved to Macon Co., Ill. Lincoln lost election to the Illinois General Assembly, 1832, but later won 4 times, beginning in 1834. He enlisted in the militia for the Black Hawk War, 1832. In New Salem he ran a store, surveyed land, and was postmaster.

In 1837 Lincoln was admitted to the bar and became partner in a Springfield, Ill., law office. He was elected to Congress, 1847-49. He opposed the Mexican War. He supported Zachary Taylor, 1848. He opposed the Kansas-Nebraska Act and extension of slavery, 1854. He failed in his bid for the Senate, 1855. He supported John C. Fremont, 1856.

In 1858 Lincoln had Republican support in the Illinois legislature for the Senate but was defeated by Stephen A. Douglas, Dem., who had sponsored the Kansas-Nebraska Act.

Lincoln was nominated for president by the Republican party on an anti-slavery platform, 1860. He ran against Douglas, a northern Democrat; John C. Breckinridge, southern pro-slavery Democrat; John Bell,

Constitutional Union party. When he won the election, South Carolina seceded from the Union Dec. 20, 1860, followed in 1861 by 10 Southern states.

The Civil War erupted when Fort Sumter was attacked Apr. 12, 1861. On Sept. 22, 1862, 5 days after the battle of Antietam, he announced that slaves in territory then in rebellion would be free Jan. 1, 1863, date of the Emancipation Proclamation. His speeches, including his Gettysburg and Inaugural addresses, are remembered for their eloquence.

Lincoln was reelected, 1864, over Gen. George B. McClellan, Democrat. Lee surrendered Apr. 9, 1865. On Apr. 14, Lincoln was shot by actor John Wilkes Booth in Ford's Theatre, Washington. He died the next day.

### Andrew Johnson (1865-1869)

Andrew Johnson, 17th president, Democrat, was born in Raleigh, N.C., Dec. 29, 1808, the son of Jacob Johnson, porter at an inn and church sexton, and Mary McDonough. He was apprenticed to a tailor but ran away and eventually settled in Greeneville, Tenn. He became an alderman, 1828; mayor, 1830; state representative and senator, 1835-43; member of Congress, 1843-53; governor of Tennessee, 1853-57; U.S. senator, 1857-62. He supported John C. Breckinridge against Lincoln in 1860. He had held slaves, but opposed secession and tried to prevent his home state, Tennessee, from seceding. In Mar. 1862, Lincoln appointed him military governor of occupied Tennessee. In 1864 he was nominated for vice president with Lincoln on the National Union ticket to win Democratic support. He succeeded Lincoln as president Apr. 15, 1865. In a controversy with Congress over the president's power over the South, he proclaimed, May 26, 1865, an amnesty to all Confederates except certain leaders if they would ratify the 13th Amendment abolishing slavery. States doing so added anti-Negro provisions that enraged Congress, which restored military control over the South. When Johnson removed Edwin M. Stanton, secretary of war, without notifying the Senate, thus repudiating the Tenure of Office Act, the House impeached him for this and other reasons. He was tried by the Senate, and acquitted by only one vote, May 26, 1868. He returned to the Senate in 1875. Johnson died July 31, 1875.

### Ulysses Simpson Grant (1869-1877)

Ulysses S. Grant, 18th president, Republican, was born at Point Pleasant, Oh., Apr. 27, 1822, son of Jesse R. Grant, a tanner, and Hannah Simpson. The next year the family moved to Georgetown, Oh. Grant was named Hiram Ulysses, but on entering West Point, 1839, his name was entered as Ulysses Simpson and he adopted it. He was graduated in 1843; served under Gens. Taylor and Scott in the Mexican War; resigned, 1854; worked in St. Louis until 1860, then went to Galena, Ill. With the start of the Civil War, he was named colonel of the 21st Illinois Vols., 1861, then brigadier general; took Forts Henry and Donelson; fought at Shiloh, took Vicksburg. After his victory at Chattanooga, Lincoln placed him in command of the Union Armies. He accepted Lee's surrender at Appomattox, Apr., 1865. President Johnson appointed Grant secretary of war when he suspended Stanton, but Grant was not confirmed. He was nominated for president by the Republicans in 1868 and elected over Horatio Seymour, Democrat. The 15th Amendment, amnesty bill, and civil service reform were events of his administration. The Liberal Republicans and Democrats opposed him with Horace Greeley, 1872, but he was reelected. An attempt by the Stalwarts (Old Guard) to nominate him in 1880 failed. In 1884 the

collapse of Grant & Ward, investment house, left him penniless. He wrote his personal memoirs while ill with cancer and completed them 4 days before his death at Mt. McGregor, N.Y., July 23, 1885. The book realized over $450,000.

### Rutherford Birchard Hayes (1877-1881)

Rutherford B. Hayes, 19th president, Republican, was born in Delaware, Oh., Oct. 4, 1822, the posthumous son of Rutherford Hayes, a farmer, and Sophia Birchard. He was raised by his uncle Sardis Birchard. He graduated from Kenyon College, 1842, and Harvard Law School, 1845. He practiced law in Lower Sandusky, Oh., now Fremont; was city solicitor of Cincinnati, 1858-61. In the Civil War, he was major of the 23d Ohio Vols., was wounded several times, and rose to the rank of brevet major general, 1864. He served in Congress 1864-67, supporting Reconstruction and Johnson's impeachment. He was elected governor of Ohio, 1867 and 1869; beaten in the race for Congress, 1872; reelected governor, 1875. In 1876 he was nominated for president and believed he had lost the election to Samuel J. Tilden, Democrat. But a few Southern states submitted 2 different sets of electoral votes and the result was in dispute. An electoral commission, appointed by Congress, 8 Republicans and 7 Democrats, awarded all disputed votes to Hayes allowing him to become president by one electoral vote. Hayes, keeping a promise to southerners, withdrew troops from areas still occupied in the South, ending the era of Reconstruction. He proceeded to reform the civil service, alienating political spoilsmen. He advocated repeal of the Tenure of Office Act. He supported sound money and specie payments. Hayes died in Fremont, Oh., Jan. 17, 1893.

### James Abram Garfield (1881)

James A. Garfield, 20th president, Republican, was born Nov. 19, 1831, in Orange, Cuyahoga Co., Oh., the son of Abram Garfield and Eliza Ballou. His father died in 1833. He worked as a canal bargeman, farmer, and carpenter; attended Western Reserve Eclectic, later Hiram College, and was graduated from Williams in 1856. He taught at Hiram, and later became principal. He was in the Ohio senate in 1859. Anti-slavery and anti-secession, he volunteered for the war, became colonel of the 42d Ohio Infantry and brigadier in 1862. He fought at Shiloh, was chief of staff for Rosecrans and was made major general for gallantry at Chickamauga. He entered Congress as a radical Republican in 1863; supported specie payment as against paper money (greenbacks). On the electoral commission in 1877 he voted for Hayes against Tilden on strict party lines. He was senator-elect in 1880 when he became the Republican nominee for president. He was chosen as a compromise over Gen. Grant, James G. Blaine, and John Sherman. This alienated the Grant following but Garfield was elected. On July 2, 1881, Garfield was shot by mentally disturbed office-seeker, Charles J. Guiteau, while entering a railroad station in Washington. He died Sept. 19, 1881, at Elberon, N.J.

### Chester Alan Arthur (1881-1885)

Chester A. Arthur, 21st president, Republican, was born at Fairfield, Vt., Oct. 5, 1830, the son of the Rev. William Arthur, from County Antrim, Ireland, and Malvina Stone. He graduated from Union College, 1848, taught school at Pownall, Vt., studied law in New York. In 1853 he argued in a fugitive slave case that slaves transported through N.Y. State were thereby freed. He was made collector of the Port of New York, 1871. President Hayes, reforming the civil service, forced Arthur to resign, 1879. This made the

New York machine stalwarts enemies of Hayes. Arthur and the stalwarts tried to nominate Grant for a 3d term in 1880. When Garfield was nominated, Arthur received 2d place in the interests of harmony. When Garfield died, Arthur became president. He supported civil service reform and the tariff of 1883. He was defeated for renomination by James G. Blaine. He died in New York City Nov. 18, 1886.

## Grover Cleveland (1885-1889) (1893-1897)

*(According to a ruling of the State Dept., Grover Cleveland is both the 22d and the 24th president, because his 2 terms were not consecutive. By individuals, he is only the 22d.)*

Grover Cleveland, 22d and 24th president, Democrat, was born in Caldwell, N.J. Mar. 18, 1837, the son of Richard F. Cleveland, a Presbyterian minister, and Ann Neale. He was named Stephen Grover, but dropped the Stephen. He clerked in Clinton and Buffalo, N.Y.; taught at the N.Y. City Institution for the Blind; was admitted to the bar in Buffalo, 1859; became assistant district attorney, 1863; sheriff, 1871; mayor, 1881; governor of New York, 1882. He was an independent, honest administrator who hated corruption. He was nominated for president over Tammany Hall opposition, 1884, and defeated Republican James G. Blaine. He enlarged the civil service, vetoed many pension raids on the Treasury. In 1888 he was defeated by Benjamin Harrison, although his popular vote was larger. Reelected over Harrison in 1892, he faced a money crisis brought about by lowering of the gold reserve, circulation of paper and exorbitant silver purchases under the Sherman Act; obtained a repeal of the latter and a reduced tariff. A severe depression and labor troubles racked his administration but he refused to interfere in business matters and rejected Jacob Coxey's demand for unemployment relief. He broke the Pullman strike, 1894. In 1896, the Democrats repudiated his administration and chose silverite William Jennings Bryan as their candidate. Cleveland died in Princeton, N.J., June 24, 1908.

## Benjamin Harrison (1889-1893)

Benjamin Harrison, 23d president, Republican, was born at North Bend, Oh., Aug. 20, 1833. His great-grandfather, Benjamin Harrison, was a signer of the Declaration of Independence; his grandfather, William Henry Harrison, was 9th President; his father, John Scott Harrison, was a member of Congress. His mother was Elizabeth F. Irwin. He attended school on his father's farm; graduated from Miami Univ. at Oxford, Oh., 1852; admitted to the bar, 1853, and practiced in Indianapolis. In the Civil War, he rose to the rank of brevet brigadier general, fought at Kennesaw Mountain, Peachtree Creek, Nashville, and in the Atlanta campaign. He failed to be elected governor of Indiana, 1876; but became senator, 1881. In 1888 he defeated Cleveland for president despite having fewer popular votes. He expanded the pension list, signed the McKinley high tariff bill, the Sherman Antitrust Act, and the Sherman Silver Purchase Act. During his administration, 6 states were admitted to the union. He was defeated for reelection, 1892. He represented Venezuela in a boundary arbitration with Great Britain in Paris, 1899. He died in Indianapolis, Mar. 13, 1901.

## William McKinley (1897-1901)

William McKinley, 25th president, Republican, was born in Niles, Oh., Jan. 29, 1843, the son of William McKinley, an ironmaker, and Nancy Allison. McKinley attended school in Poland, Oh., and Allegheny College, Meadville, Pa., and enlisted for the Civil War at 18 in the 23d Ohio, in which Rutherford B. Hayes was a major. He rose to captain and in 1865 was made brevet major. He studied law in the Albany, N.Y., law school; opened an office in Canton, Oh., in 1867, and campaigned for Grant and Hayes. He served in the House of Representatives, 1877-83, 1885-91, and led the fight for passage of the McKinley Tariff, 1890. Defeated for reelection on the tariff issue in 1890, he was governor of Ohio, 1892-96. He had support for president in the convention that nominated Benjamin Harrison in 1892. In 1896 he was elected president on a protective tariff, sound money (gold standard) platform over William Jennings Bryan, Democratic proponent of free silver. McKinley was reluctant to intervene in Cuba but the loss of the battleship Maine at Havana crystallized opinion. He demanded Spain's withdrawal from Cuba; Spain made some concessions but Congress announced state of war as of Apr. 21. He was reelected in the 1900 campaign, defeating Bryan's anti-imperialist arguments with the promise of a "full dinner pail." McKinley was respected for his conciliatory nature, but conservative on business issues. On Sept. 6, 1901, while welcoming citizens at the Pan-American Exposition, Buffalo, N.Y., he was shot by Leon Czolgosz, an anarchist. He died Sept. 14.

## Theodore Roosevelt (1901-1909)

Theodore Roosevelt, 26th president, Republican, was born in N.Y. City, Oct. 27, 1858, the son of Theodore Roosevelt, a glass importer, and Martha Bulloch. He was a 5th cousin of Franklin D. Roosevelt and an uncle of Eleanor Roosevelt. Roosevelt graduated from Harvard, 1880; attended Columbia Law School briefly; sat in the N.Y. State Assembly, 1882-84; ranched in North Dakota, 1884-86; failed election as mayor of N.Y. City, 1886; member of U.S. Civil Service Commission, 1889; president, N.Y. Police Board, 1895, supporting the merit system; assistant secretary of the Navy under McKinley, 1897-98. In the war with Spain, he organized the 1st U.S. Volunteer Cavalry (Rough Riders) as lieutenant colonel; led the charge up Kettle Hill at San Juan. Elected New York governor, 1898-1900, he fought the spoils system and achieved taxation of corporation franchises. Nominated for vice president, 1900, he became nation's youngest president when McKinley died. He was reelected in 1904. As president he fought corruption of politics by big business; dissolved Northern Securities Co. and others for violating anti-trust laws; intervened in coal strike on behalf of the public, 1902; obtained Elkins Law forbidding rebates to favored corporations, 1903; Hepburn Law regulating railroad rates, 1906; Pure Food and Drugs Act, 1906, Reclamation Act and employers' liability laws. He organized conservation, mediated the peace between Japan and Russia, 1905; won the Nobel Peace Prize. He was the first to use the Hague Court of International Arbitration. By recognizing the new Republic of Panama he made Panama Canal possible.

In 1908 he obtained the nomination of William H. Taft, who was elected. Feeling that Taft had abandoned his policies, Roosevelt unsuccessfully sought the nomination in 1912. He bolted the party and ran on the Progressive "Bull Moose" ticket against Taft and Woodrow Wilson, splitting the Republicans and insuring Wilson's election. He was shot during the campaign but recovered. In 1916 he supported Charles E. Hughes, Republican. A strong friend of Britain, he fought American isolation in World War I. He wrote some 40 books on many topics; his *Winning of the West* is best known. He died Jan. 6, 1919, at Sagamore Hill, Oyster Bay, N.Y.

## William Howard Taft (1909-1913)

William Howard Taft, 27th president, Republican, was born in Cincinnati, Oh., Sept. 15, 1857, the son of Alphonso Taft and Louisa Maria Torrey. His father was secretary of war and attorney general in Grant's cabinet; minister to Austria and Russia under Arthur. Taft was graduated from Yale, 1878; Cincinnati Law School, 1880; became law reporter for Cincinnati newspapers; was assistant prosecuting attorney, 1881-83; assistant county solicitor, 1885; judge, superior court, 1887; U.S. solicitor-general, 1890; federal circuit judge, 1892. In 1900 he became head of the U.S. Philippines Commission and was first civil governor of the Philippines, 1901-04; secretary of war, 1904; provisional governor of Cuba, 1906. He was groomed for president by Roosevelt and elected over Bryan, 1908. His administration dissolved Standard Oil and tobacco trusts; instituted Dept. of Labor; drafted direct election of senators and income tax amendments. His tariff and conservation policies angered progressives; though renominated he was opposed by Roosevelt; the result was Democrat Woodrow Wilson's election. Taft, with some reservations, supported the League of Nations. He was professor of constitutional law, Yale, 1913-21; chief justice of the U.S. Supreme Court, 1921-30; illness forced him to resign. He died in Washington, Mar. 8, 1930.

## Woodrow Wilson (1913-1921)

Woodrow Wilson, 28th president, Democrat, was born at Staunton, Va., Dec. 28, 1856, as Thomas Woodrow Wilson, son of a Presbyterian minister, the Rev. Joseph Ruggles Wilson and Janet (Jessie) Woodrow. In his youth Wilson lived in Augusta, Ga., Columbia, S.C., and Wilmington, N.C. He attended Davidson College, 1873-74; was graduated from Princeton, A.B., 1879; A.M., 1882; read law at the Univ. of Virginia, 1881; practiced law, Atlanta, 1882-83; Ph.D., Johns Hopkins, 1886. He taught at Bryn Mawr, 1885-88; at Wesleyan, 1888-90; was professor of jurisprudence and political economy at Princeton, 1890-1910; president of Princeton, 1902-1910; governor of New Jersey, 1911-13. In 1912 he was nominated for president with the aid of William Jennings Bryan, who sought to block James "Champ" Clark and Tammany Hall. Wilson won the election because the Republican vote for Taft was split by the Progressives under Roosevelt.

Wilson protected American interests in revolutionary Mexico and fought for American rights on the high seas. His sharp warnings to Germany led to the resignation of his secretary of state, Bryan, a pacifist. In 1916 he was reelected by a slim margin with the slogan, "He kept us out of war." Wilson's attempts to mediate in the war failed. After 4 American ships had been sunk by the Germans, he secured a declaration of war against Germany on Apr. 6, 1917.

Wilson proposed peace Jan. 8, 1918, on the basis of his "Fourteen Points," a state paper with worldwide influence. His doctrine of self-determination continues to play a major role in territorial disputes. The Germans accepted his terms and an armistice, Nov. 11.

Wilson went to Paris to help negotiate the peace treaty, the crux of which he considered the League of Nations. The Senate demanded reservations that would not make the U.S. subordinate to the votes of other nations in case of war. Wilson refused to consider any reservations and toured the country to get support. He suffered a stroke, Oct., 1919. An invalid for months, he clung to his executive powers while his wife and doctor sought to shield him from affairs which would tire him.

He was awarded the 1919 Nobel Peace Prize, but the treaty embodying the League of Nations was rejected by the Senate, 1920. He died in Washington, Feb. 3, 1924.

## Warren Gamaliel Harding (1921-1923)

Warren Gamaliel Harding, 29th president, Republican, was born near Corsica, now Blooming Grove, Oh., Nov. 2, 1865, the son of Dr. George Tyron Harding, a physician, and Phoebe Elizabeth Dickerson. He attended Ohio Central College. He was state senator, 1900-04; lieutenant governor, 1904-06; defeated for governor, 1910; chosen U.S. senator, 1915. He supported Taft, opposed federal control of food and fuel; voted for anti-strike legislation, woman's suffrage, and the Volstead prohibition enforcement act over President Wilson's veto; and opposed the League of Nations. In 1920 he was nominated for president and defeated James M. Cox in the election. The Republicans capitalized on war weariness and fear that Wilson's League of Nations would curtail U.S. sovereignty. Harding stressed a return to "normalcy"; worked for tariff revision and repeal of excess profits law and high income taxes. Two Harding appointees, Albert B. Fall (interior) and Harry Daugherty (attorney general), became involved in the Teapot Dome scandal that embittered Harding's last days. He called the International Conference on Limitation of Armaments, 1921-22. Returning from a trip to Alaska he became ill and died in San Francisco, Aug. 2, 1923.

## Calvin Coolidge (1923-1929)

Calvin Coolidge, 30th president, Republican, was born in Plymouth, Vt., July 4, 1872, the son of John Calvin Coolidge, a storekeeper, and Victoria J. Moor, and named John Calvin Coolidge. Coolidge graduated from Amherst in 1895. He entered Republican state politics and served as mayor of Northampton, Mass., state senator, lieutenant governor, and, in 1919, governor. In Sept., 1919, Coolidge attained national prominence by calling out the state guard in the Boston police strike. He declared: "There is no right to strike against the public safety by anybody, anywhere, anytime." This brought his name before the Republican convention of 1920, where he was nominated for vice president. He succeeded to the presidency on Harding's death. He opposed the League of Nations; approved the World Court; vetoed the soldiers' bonus bill, which was passed over his veto. In 1924 he was elected by a huge majority. He reduced the national debt by $2 billion in 3 years. He twice vetoed the Mc-Nary-Haugen farm bill, which would have provided relief to financially hard-pressed farmers. With Republicans eager to renominate him he announced, Aug. 2, 1927: "I do not choose to run for president in 1928." He died in Northampton, Jan. 5, 1933.

## Herbert Clark Hoover (1929-1933)

Herbert C. Hoover, 31st president, Republican, was born at West Branch, Ia., Aug. 10, 1874, son of Jesse Clark Hoover, a blacksmith, and Hulda Randall Minthorn. Hoover grew up in Indian Territory (now Oklahoma) and Oregon; won his A.B. in engineering at Stanford, 1891. He worked briefly with U.S. Geological Survey and western mines; then was a mining engineer in Australia, Asia, Europe, Africa, U.S. While chief engineer, imperial mines, China, he directed food relief for victims of Boxer Rebellion, 1900. He directed American Relief Committee, London, 1914-15; U.S. Comm. for Relief in Belgium, 1915-1919; was U.S. Food Administrator, 1917-1919; American Relief Administrator, 1918-1923, feeding children in defeated nations; Russian Relief, 1918-1923. He was secy. of commerce, 1921-28. He was elected president over Alfred E. Smith, 1928. In 1929 the stock market crashed and the economy collapsed. During the depression, Hoover inaugurated government assistance programs but opposed direct federal aid to the unemployed. He was defeated in the 1932 election by Franklin D. Roosevelt. President Truman made him coordinator of European Food Program, 1947, chairman of the Commission for Reorganization of the Executive Branch, 1947-49. He died in N.Y. City, Oct. 20, 1964.

## Franklin Delano Roosevelt (1933-1945)

Franklin D. Roosevelt, 32d president, Democrat, was born near Hyde Park, N.Y., Jan. 30, 1882, the son of James Roosevelt and Sara Delano. He graduated from Harvard, 1904; attended Columbia Law School; was admitted to the bar. He went to the N.Y. Senate, 1910 and 1913. In 1913 President Wilson made him assistant secretary of the navy.

Roosevelt ran for vice president, 1920, with James Cox and was defeated. From 1920 to 1928 he was a N.Y. lawyer and vice president of Fidelity & Deposit Co. In Aug., 1921, polio paralyzed his legs. He learned to walk with leg braces and a cane.

Roosevelt was elected governor of New York, 1928 and 1930. In 1932, W. G. McAdoo, pledged to John N. Garner, threw his votes to Roosevelt, who was nominated for president. The depression and the promise to repeal prohibition ensured his election. He asked emergency powers, proclaimed the New Deal, and put into effect a vast number of administrative changes. Foremost was the use of public funds for relief and public works, resulting in deficit financing. He greatly expanded the federal government's regulation of business and by an excess profits tax and progressive income taxes produced a redistribution of earnings on an unprecedented scale. The Wagner Act gave labor many advantages in organizing and collective bargaining. He was the last president inaugurated on Mar. 4 (1933) and the first inaugurated on Jan. 20 (1937).

Roosevelt was the first president to use radio for "fireside chats." When the Supreme Court nullified some New Deal laws, he sought power to "pack" the court with additional justices, but Congress refused to give him the authority. He was the first president to break the "no 3d term" tradition (1940) and was elected to a 4th term, 1944, despite failing health. He was openly hostile to fascist governments before World War II and launched a lend-lease program on behalf of the Allies. He wrote the principles of fair dealing into the Atlantic Charter, Aug. 14, 1941 (with Winston Churchill), and urged the Four Freedoms (freedom of speech, of worship, from want, from fear) Jan. 6, 1941. When Japan attacked Pearl Harbor, Dec. 7, 1941, the U.S. entered the war. He conferred with allied heads of state at Casablanca, Jan., 1943; Quebec, Aug., 1943; Teheran, Nov.-Dec., 1943; Cairo, Dec., 1943; Yalta, Feb., 1945. He died at Warm Springs, Ga., Apr. 12, 1945.

## Harry S. Truman (1945-1953)

Harry S. Truman, 33d president, Democrat, was born at Lamar, Mo., May 8, 1884, the son of John Anderson Truman and Martha Ellen Young. A family disagreement on whether his middle name was Shippe or Solomon, after names of 2 grandfathers, resulted in his using only the middle initial S. He attended public schools in Independence, Mo., worked for the Kansas City Star, 1901, and as railroad timekeeper, and helper in Kansas City banks up to 1905. He ran his family's farm, 1906-17. He was commissioned a first lieutenant and took part in the Vosges, Meuse-Argonne, and St. Mihiel actions in World War I. After the war he ran a

haberdashery, became judge of Jackson Co. Court, 1922-24; attended Kansas City School of Law, 1923-25.

Truman was elected U.S. senator in 1934; reelected 1940. In 1944 with Roosevelt's backing he was nominated for vice president and elected. On Roosevelt's death Truman became president. In 1948 he was elected president.

Truman authorized the first uses of the atomic bomb (Hiroshima and Nagasaki, Aug. 6 and 9, 1945), bringing World War II to a rapid end. He was responsible for creating NATO, the Marshall Plan, and what came to be called the Truman Doctrine (to aid nations such as Greece and Turkey, threatened by communist takeover). He broke a Soviet blockade of West Berlin with a massive airlift, 1948-49. When communist North Korea invaded South Korea, June, 1950, he won UN approval for a "police action" and sent in forces under Gen. Douglas MacArthur. When MacArthur opposed his policy of limited objectives, Truman removed him from command.

Truman was responsible for higher minimum-wage, increased social-security, and aid-for-housing laws. Truman died Dec. 26, 1972, in Kansas City, Mo.

## Dwight David Eisenhower (1953-1961)

Dwight D. Eisenhower, 34th president, Republican, was born Oct. 14, 1890, at Denison, Tex., the son of David Jacob Eisenhower and Ida Elizabeth Stover. The next year, the family moved to Abilene, Kan. He graduated from West Point, 1915. He was on the American military mission to the Philippines, 1935-39 and during 4 of those years on the staff of Gen. Douglas MacArthur. He was made commander of Allied forces landing in North Africa, 1942, full general, 1943. He became supreme Allied commander in Europe, 1943, and as such led the Normandy invasion June 6, 1944. He was given the rank of general of the army Dec. 20, 1944, made permanent in 1946. On May 7, 1945, he received the surrender of the Germans at Rheims. He returned to the U.S. to serve as chief of staff, 1945-1948. In 1948, Eisenhower published *Crusade in Europe*, his war memoirs, which quickly became a best seller. From 1948 to 1953, he was president of Columbia Univ., but took leave of absence in 1950, to command NATO forces.

Eisenhower resigned from the army and was nominated for president by the Republicans, 1952. He defeated Adlai E. Stevenson in the election. He again defeated Stevenson, 1956. He called himself a moderate, favored "free market system" vs. government price and wage controls; kept goverment out of labor disputes; reorganized defense establishment; promoted missile programs. He continued foreign aid; sped end of Korean fighting; endorsed Taiwan and SE Asia defense treaties; backed UN in condemning Anglo-French raid on Egypt; advocated "open skies" policy of mutual inspection to USSR. He sent U.S. troops into Little Rock, Ark., Sept., 1957, during the segregation crisis and ordered Marines into Lebanon July-Aug., 1958.

During his retirement at his farm near Gettysburg, Pa., Eisenhower took up the role of elder statesman, counseling his 3 successors in the White House. He died Mar. 28, 1969, in Washington.

## John Fitzgerald Kennedy (1961-1963)

John F. Kennedy, 35th president, Democrat, was born May 29, 1917, in Brookline, Mass., the son of Joseph P. Kennedy, financier, who later became ambassador to Great Britain, and Rose Fitzgerald. He entered Harvard, attended the London School of

Economics briefly in 1935, received a B.S., from Harvard, 1940. He served in the Navy, 1941-1945, commanded a PT boat in the Solomons and won the Navy and Marine Corps Medal. He wrote *Profiles in Courage*, which won a Pulitzer prize. He served as representative in Congress, 1947-1953; was elected to the Senate in 1952, reelected 1958. He nearly won the vice presidential nomination in 1956.

In 1960, Kennedy won the Democratic nomination for president and defeated Richard M. Nixon, Republican. He was the first Roman Catholic president.

In Apr. 1961, Kennedy's new administration suffered a severe setback when an invasion force of anti-Castro Cubans, trained and directed by the U.S. Central Intelligence Agency, failed to establish a beachhead at the Bay of Pigs in Cuba.

Kennedy's most important act was his successful demand Oct. 22, 1962, that the Soviet Union dismantle its missile bases in Cuba. He established a quarantine of arms shipments to Cuba and continued surveillance by air. He defied Soviet attempts to force the Allies out of Berlin. He made the steel industry rescind a price rise. He backed civil rights, a mental health program, arbitration of railroad disputes, and expanded medical care for the aged. Astronaut flights and satellite orbiting were greatly developed during his administration.

On Nov. 22, 1963, Kennedy was assassinated in Dallas, Tex.

### Lyndon Baines Johnson (1963-1969)

Lyndon B. Johnson, 36th president, Democrat, was born near Stonewall, Tex., Aug. 27, 1908, son of Sam Ealy Johnson and Rebekah Baines. He graduated from Southwest Texas State Teachers College, 1930, attended Georgetown Univ. Law School, Washington, 1935. He taught public speaking in Houston, 1930-32; served as secretary to Rep. R. M. Kleberg, 1932-35. In 1937 Johnson won a contest to fill the vacancy caused by the death of a representative and in 1938 was elected to the full term, after which he returned for 4 terms. He was elected U.S. senator in 1948 and reelected in 1954. He became Democratic leader, 1953. Johnson had strong support for the Democratic presidential nomination at the 1960 convention, where the nominee, John F. Kennedy, asked him to run for vice president. His campaigning helped overcome religious bias against Kennedy in the South.

Johnson became president when Kennedy was assassinated. Johnson worked hard for welfare legislation, signed civil rights, anti-poverty, and tax reduction laws. He was elected to a full term, 1964. The war in Vietnam overshadowed other developments during his administration, such as the "Great Society" social programs.

In face of increasing division in the nation and his own party over his handling of the war, Johnson announced that he would not seek another term, Mar. 31, 1968.

Retiring to his ranch near Johnson City, Tex., Johnson wrote his memoirs and oversaw the construction of the Lyndon Baines Johnson Library. He died Jan. 22, 1973.

### Richard Milhous Nixon (1969-1974)

Richard M. Nixon, 37th president, Republican, was the only president to resign without completing an elected term. He was born in Yorba Linda, Cal., Jan. 9, 1913, the son of Francis Anthony Nixon and Hannah Milhous. Nixon graduated from Whittier College, 1934; Duke Univ. Law School, 1937. After practicing law in Whittier and serving briefly in the Office of Price Administration in 1942, he entered the navy, and served in the South Pacific.

Nixon was elected to the House of Representatives in 1946 and 1948. He achieved prominence as the House Un-American Activities Committee member who forced the showdown that resulted in the Alger Hiss perjury conviction. In 1950 Nixon was elected to the Senate.

He was elected vice president in the Eisenhower landslides of 1952 and 1956. With Eisenhower's endorsement, Nixon won the Republican nomination in 1960. He was defeated by Democrat John F. Kennedy, returned to Cal. and was defeated in his race for governor, 1962.

In 1968, he won the presidential nomination and went on to defeat Democrat Hubert H. Humphrey.

Nixon was the first U.S. president to visit China and Russia (1972). He and his foreign affairs advisor, Henry A. Kissinger, achieved a detente with China. Nixon appointed 4 Supreme Court justices, including the chief justice, thus altering the court's balance in favor of a more conservative view.

Reelected 1972, Nixon secured a cease-fire agreement in Vietnam and completed the withdrawal of U.S. troops.

Nixon's 2d term was cut short by a series of scandals beginning with the burglary of Democratic party national headquarters in the Watergate office complex on June 17, 1972. On July 16, 1973, a White House aide, under questioning by a Senate committee, revealed that most of Nixon's office conversations and phone calls had been recorded. Nixon claimed executive privilege to keep the tapes secret and the courts and Congress sought the tapes for criminal proceedings against former White House aides and for a House inquiry into possible impeachment.

On July 24, 1974, the Supreme Court ruled that Nixon's claim of executive privilege must fall before the special prosecutor's subpoenas of tapes relevant to criminal trial proceedings. That same day, the House Judiciary Committee opened debate on impeachment. On July 30, the committee recommended House adoption of 3 articles of impeachment charging Nixon with obstruction of justice, abuse of power, and contempt of Congress.

On Aug. 5, Nixon released transcripts of conversations held 6 days after the Watergate break-in showing that Nixon had known of, approved, and directed Watergate cover-up activities. Nixon resigned from office Aug. 9.

### Gerald Rudolph Ford (1974-1977)

Gerald R. Ford, 38th president, Republican, was born July 14, 1913, in Omaha, Neb., son of Leslie King and Dorothy Gardner, and was named Leslie Jr. When he was 2, his parents were divorced and his mother moved with the boy to Grand Rapids, Mich. There she met and married Gerald R. Ford, who formally adopted the boy and gave him his own name.

He graduated from the Univ. of Michigan, 1935, and Yale Law School, 1941.

He began practicing law in Grand Rapids, but in 1942 joined the navy and served in the Pacific, leaving the service in 1946 as a lieutenant commander.

He entered congress in 1949 and spent 25 years in the House, 8 of them as Republican leader.

On Oct. 12, 1973, after Vice President Spiro T. Agnew resigned, Ford was nominated by President Nixon to replace him. It was the first use of the procedures set out in the 25th Amendment.

When Nixon resigned Aug. 9, 1974, Ford became president, the first to serve without being chosen in a national election. On Sept. 8 he pardoned Nixon for any federal crimes he might have committed as president. Ford vetoed 48 bills in his first 21 months in office, saying most would prove too costly. He visited China. In 1976, he was defeated in the election by Democrat Jimmy Carter.

## Jimmy (James Earl) Carter (1977-1981)

Jimmy (James Earl) Carter, 39th president, Democrat, was the first president from the Deep South since before the Civil War. He was born Oct. 1, 1924, at Plains, Ga., where his parents, James and Lillian Gordy Carter, had a farm and several businesses.

He attended Georgia Tech, and graduated from the U.S. Naval Academy. He entered the Navy's nuclear submarine program as an aide to Adm. Hyman Rickover, and studied nuclear physics at Union College.

His father died in 1953 and Carter left the Navy to take over the family businesses — peanut-raising, warehousing, and cotton-ginning. He was elected to the Georgia state senate, was defeated for governor, 1966, but elected in 1970.

Carter won the Democratic nomination and defeated President Gerald R. Ford in the election of 1976. He played a major role in the peace negotiations between Israel and Egypt. In Nov. 1979, Iranian student militants attacked the U.S. embassy in Teheran and held members of the embassy staff hostage.

Carter was widely criticized for the poor state of the economy and high inflation. He was also viewed as weak in his handling of foreign policy. He reacted to the Soviet invasion of Afghanistan by imposing a grain embargo and boycotting the Moscow Olympic games. His failure to obtain the release of the remaining 52 hostages held in Iran plagued Carter to the end of his term. He was defeated by Ronald Reagan in the 1980 election. Carter finally succeeded in obtaining the release of the hostages on Inauguration Day, as the new president was taking the oath of office.

## Ronald Wilson Reagan (1981-1989)

Ronald Wilson Reagan, 40th president, Republican, was born Feb. 6, 1911, in Tampico, Ill., the son of John Edward Reagan and Nellie Wilson. Reagan graduated from Eureka (Ill.) College in 1932. Following his graduation, he worked as a sports announcer in Des Moines, Ia.

Reagan began a successful career as a film actor in 1937, and starred in numerous movies, and later television, until the 1960s. He was a captain in the Army Air Force during World War II.

He served as president of the Screen Actors Guild from 1947 to 1952, and in 1959.

Once a liberal Democrat, Reagan became active in Republican politics during the 1964 presidential campaign of Barry Goldwater. He was elected governor of California in 1966, and reelected in 1970.

In 1980, he gained the Republican nomination and won a landslide victory over Jimmy Carter. He was easily reelected in 1984. Reagan, at 73, was the oldest man ever elected president.

Reagan successfully forged a bipartisan coalition in Congress which led to enactment of an economic program which included the largest budget and tax cuts in U.S. history, and a Social Security reform bill designed to insure the long-term solvency of the system. In 1986, he signed into law a revolutionary tax-reform bill. He was shot in an assassination attempt in 1981, and had major surgery in 1985 and 1987.

In 1983, Reagan sent a task force to lead the invasion of Grenada, and joined 3 European nations in maintaining a peacekeeping force in Beirut, Lebanon.

His opposition to international terrorism led to the U.S. bombing of Libyan military installations in 1986. He strongly supported El Salvador, the Nicaraguan contras, and other anti-communist governments and forces throughout the world. Aid was sent to the rebels fighting Soviet troops in Afghanistan. When the Iran/Iraq war threatened freedom of the seas, U.S. Navy ships were sent to the Persian Gulf.

Reagan held summit meetings with Soviet leader Mikhail Gorbachev in 1985 in Geneva, 1986 in Iceland, 1987 in Washington, D.C., where an historic treaty eliminating short and medium-range missiles from Europe was signed, and 1988 in Moscow where Reagan criticized the Soviet record on human rights, and met with Soviet dissidents.

Reagan faced a major crisis in 1986-1987, when it was revealed that the U.S. had sold weapons to Iran in exchange for the release of U.S. hostages being held in Lebanon and that subsequently some of the money was diverted to the Nicaraguan contras (Congress had barred aid to the contras). The scandal led to the resignation of leading White House aides.

As Reagan left office, the nation was experiencing its 6th consecutive year of economic prosperity. Along with the strong economy, the nation enjoyed low unemployment, energy costs, and inflation. Reagan, however, was unable to control the high budget deficits which plagued him throughout his administration.

## George Herbert Walker Bush (1989-1993)

George Herbert Walker Bush, 41st president, Republican, was born June 12, 1924, in Milton, Mass., the son of Prescott Bush, U.S. senator from Connecticut, and Dorothy Walker. He served as a U.S. Navy pilot in World War II, earning the Distinguished Flying Cross and three Air Medals for service in the Pacific. After graduating from Yale Univ. (1948), he settled in Texas where, in 1953, he helped found an oil company.

After losing a bid for a U.S. Senate seat in Texas, 1964, he was elected to the House of Representatives in 1966 and 1968. He lost a 2d U.S. Senate race in 1970. He served as U.S. ambassador to the United Nations, 1971-73, headed the U.S. Liaison Office in Beijing, 1974-75, and was director of the Central Intelligence Agency, 1976-77.

Following an unsuccessful bid for the 1980 Republican presidential nomination, Bush was chosen by Ronald Reagan as his vice presidential running mate. He served as U.S. vice president, 1981-89.

In 1988, he gained the Republican presidential nomination and defeated Democrat Michael Dukakis in the election. Calling on Americans "to make kinder the face of the nation and gentler the face of the world," Bush took office faced with the ongoing U.S. budget and trade deficits as well as the rescue of insolvent U.S. savings and loan institutions.

Bush made no major changes from Reagan's policies during his presidency. He annually faced a severe budget deficit, struggled with military cutbacks in light of reduced "cold war" tensions, and vetoed congressional actions favorable to freedom of choice on abortion, a minimum-wage law, and an anti-discrimination bill that didn't reflect his own views.

Bush supported Soviet reforms and Eastern Europe democratization. He was criticized, however, for not supporting strongly enough the independence effort of the Baltic republics, for keeping U.S. policy tied for too long to Mikhail Gorbachev as the Soviet leader lost power and his nation broke apart, and for his soft reaction to the Chinese government's violent repression of a pro-democracy movement.

In Dec. 1989, Bush sent military forces to Panama which overthrew the government and captured military strongman Gen. Manuel Noriega.

Bush reacted to Iraq's Aug. 1990 invasion of Kuwait by sending U.S. forces to the Persian Gulf area and assembling a U.N.-backed coalition including NATO and Arab League members. A U.S.-led international force launched air and missile attacks on Iraq, Jan. 1991, after a U.N. deadline for withdrawal from Kuwait had passed. In Feb., Allied forces retook Kuwait after a 4-day ground assault. The quick victory gave Bush one of the highest presidential approval ratings in history. His popularity plummeted by the end of 1991 as the economy struggled through a prolonged recession, and he was perceived as being indifferent to the nation's domestic problems. He was defeated by Bill Clinton in the 1992 election.

### Bill (William Jefferson) Clinton (1993-  )

Bill Clinton was born William Jefferson Blythe 3rd on Aug. 19, 1946 in Hope, Ark., the son of William and Virginia Blythe. Blythe, a traveling salesman, died in an auto accident before his son was born. His mother married Roger Clinton and several years later, at age 16, Bill Blythe changed his name to Bill Clinton.

Clinton attended Georgetown Univ., Oxford Univ. in England as a Rhodes scholar, and Yale Law School.

Clinton worked on George McGovern's 1972 presidential campaign and for the House Judiciary Committee in 1973. He taught at the Univ. of Arkansas, 1974-76. He was elected Arkansas State Attorney General in 1976.

In 1978, he was elected the nation's youngest governor, but was defeated for reelection in 1980. He successfully ran for governor again in 1982, 1984, 1986, and 1990. He married Hillary Rodham in 1975. She became a successful lawyer and a social activist. They had a daughter, Chelsea, in 1980.

Despite personal attacks on his character, he won the majority of the 1992 presidential primaries while moving the Democratic Party toward the center, trying to appeal to middle-class suburbanites who had deserted the party during the Reagan era. He defeated Pres. George Bush in the presidential election.

In August 1993, Clinton narrowly won congressional passage of some $500 billion in taxes and spending cuts to reduce the federal budget deficits. He also made a strong commitment to health-care reform. At an April 1993 summit meeting with Boris Yeltsin, he unveiled a $1.62-billion package of aid to Russia.

## Wives and Children of the Presidents

Listed in order of presidential administrations.

| Name (Born–died, married) | State | Sons/ daughters | Name (Born–died, married) | State | Sons/ daughters |
|---|---|---|---|---|---|
| Martha Dandridge Custis Washington (1732-1802, 1759) | Va. | None | Caroline Lavinia Scott Harrison (1832-1892, 1853) | Oh. | 1/1 |
| Abigail Smith Adams (1744-1818, 1764). | Mass. | 3/2 | Mary Scott Lord Dimmick Harrison (1858-1948, 1896) | Pa. | .../1 |
| Martha Wayles Skelton Jefferson (1748-1782, 1772) | Va. | 1/5 | Ida Saxton McKinley (1847-1907, 1871). | Oh. | .../2 |
| Dorothea "Dolley" Payne Todd Madison (1768-1849, 1794) | N.C. | None | Alice Hathaway Lee Roosevelt (1861-1884, 1880) | Mass. | .../1 |
| Elizabeth Kortright Monroe (1768-1830, 1786) | N.Y. | .../2 (A) | Edith Kermit Carow Roosevelt (1861-1948, 1886) | Conn. | 4/1 |
| Louisa Catherine Johnson Adams (1775-1852, 1797) | Md.(B) | 3/1 | Helen Herron Taft (1861-1943, 1886) | Oh. | 2/1 |
| Rachel Donelson Robards Jackson (1767-1828, 1791) | Va. | None | Ellen Louise Axson Wilson (1860-1914, 1885) | Ga. | .../3 |
| Hannah Hoes Van Buren (1783-1819, 1807) | N.Y. | 4/... | Edith Bolling Galt Wilson (1872-1961, 1915) | Va. | None |
| Anna Symmes Harrison (1775-1864, 1795) | N.J. | 6/4 | Florence Kling De Wolfe Harding (1860-1924, 1891) | Oh. | None |
| Letitia Christian Tyler (1790-1842, 1813) | Va. | 3/5 | Grace Anna Goodhue Coolidge (1879-1957, 1905) | Vt. | 2/... |
| Julia Gardiner Tyler (1820-1889, 1844) | N.Y. | 5/2 | Lou Henry Hoover (1875-1944, 1899) | Ia. | 2/... |
| Sarah Childress Polk (1803-1891, 1824) | Tenn. | None | Anna Eleanor Roosevelt Roosevelt (1884-1962, 1905) | N.Y. | 4/1 (A) |
| Margaret Smith Taylor (1788-1852, 1810) | Md. | 1/5 | Bess Wallace Truman (1885-1982, 1919) | Mo. | .../1 |
| Abigail Powers Fillmore (1798-1853, 1826) | N.Y. | 1/1 | Mamie Geneva Doud Eisenhower (1896-1979, 1916) | Ia. | 1/...(A) |
| Caroline Carmichael McIntosh Fillmore (1813-1881, 1858) | N.J. | None | Jacqueline Lee Bouvier Kennedy (b. 1929, 1953) | N.Y. | 1/1 (A) |
| Jane Means Appleton Pierce (1806-1863, 1834) | N.H. | 3/... | Claudia "Lady Bird" Alta Taylor Johnson (b. 1912, 1934). | Tex. | .../2 |
| Mary Todd Lincoln (1818-1882, 1842) | Ky. | 4/... | Thelma Catherine Patricia Ryan Nixon (1912-1993, 1940) | Nev. | .../2 |
| Eliza McCardle Johnson (1810-1876, 1827) | Tenn. | 3/2 | Elizabeth Bloomer Warren Ford (b. 1918, 1948) | Ill. | 3/1 |
| Julia Dent Grant (1826-1902, 1848) | Mo. | 3/1 | Rosalynn Smith Carter (b. 1927, 1946) | Ga. | 3/1 |
| Lucy Ware Webb Hayes (1831-1889, 1852) | Oh. | 7/1 | Anne Frances "Nancy" Robbins Davis Reagan (b. 1921, 1952) | N.Y. | 1/1 (C) |
| Lucretia Rudolph Garfield (1832-1918, 1858) | Oh. | 4/1 | Barbara Pierce Bush (b. 1925, 1945). | N.Y. | 4/2 |
| Ellen Lewis Herndon Arthur (1837-1880, 1859) | Va. | 2/1 | Hillary Rodham Clinton (b. 1947, 1975) | Ill. | .../1 |
| Frances Folsom Cleveland (1864-1947, 1886) | N.Y. | 2/3 | | | |

James Buchanan, 15th president, was unmarried. (A) plus one infant, deceased. (B) Born London, father a Md. citizen. (C) President Reagan married and divorced Jane Wyman. They had a son and a daughter.

## First Lady: Hillary Rodham Clinton

The first lady was born in Chicago, Ill. in 1947, the daughter of Hugh and Dorothy Rodham. She graduated from Wellesley College and Yale Law School. She married Bill Clinton in 1975. Their daughter, Chelsea, was born in 1980.

She has been active in the areas of children's rights and education reform. From 1979 to 1992, she was a partner in a Little Rock law firm and, in 1988 and 1991, was voted one of the "100 Most Influential Lawyers in America" by the National Law Journal.

President Clinton named her as head of a commission, Jan.-May 1993, to devise a plan for reforming the U.S. health-care system.

## Burial Places of the Presidents

| | | | |
|---|---|---|---|
| Washington . . . | Mt. Vernon, Va. | Fillmore . . . . . | Buffalo, N.Y. |
| J. Adams. . . . . | Quincy, Mass. | Pierce . . . . . . | Concord, N.H. |
| Jefferson . . . . | Charlottesville, Va. | Buchanan . . . . | Lancaster, Pa. |
| Madison . . . . . | Montpelier Station, Va. | Lincoln. . . . . . | Springfield, Ill. |
| Monroe . . . . . | Richmond, Va. | A. Johnson . . . . | Greeneville, Tenn. |
| J.Q. Adams . . . | Quincy, Mass. | Grant. . . . . . . | New York City |
| Jackson . . . . . | Nashville, Tenn. | Hayes . . . . . . | Fremont, Oh. |
| Van Buren. . . . | Kinderhook, N.Y. | Garfield . . . . . | Cleveland, Oh. |
| W.H. Harrison. . | North Bend, Oh. | Arthur . . . . . . | Albany, N.Y. |
| Tyler . . . . . . . | Richmond, Va. | Cleveland . . . | Princeton, N.J. |
| Polk . . . . . . . | Nashville, Tenn. | B. Harrison. . . | Indianapolis, Ind. |
| Taylor . . . . . . | Louisville, Ky. | McKinley. . . . . | Canton, Oh. |

| | |
|---|---|
| T. Roosevelt. . . | Oyster Bay, N.Y. |
| Taft. . . . . . . . | Arlington Nat'l. Cem'y. |
| Wilson . . . . . . | Washington Cathedral |
| Harding . . . . . | Marion, Oh. |
| Coolidge . . . . . | Plymouth, Vt. |
| Hoover. . . . . . | West Branch, Ia. |
| F.D. Roosevelt . | Hyde Park, N.Y. |
| Truman . . . . . | Independence, Mo. |
| Eisenhower . . . | Abilene, Kan. |
| Kennedy. . . . . | Arlington Nat'l. Cem'y. |
| L.B. Johnson . . | Stonewall, Tex. |

## National Political Convention Sites: 1856-1992[1]

| Year | Democrats | Republicans | Year | Democrats | Republicans | Year | Democrats | Republicans |
|---|---|---|---|---|---|---|---|---|
| 1856 | Cincinnati | Philadelphia | 1904 | St. Louis | Chicago | 1952 | Chicago | Chicago |
| 1860 | Charleston, S.C. | Chicago | 1908 | Denver | Chicago | 1956 | Chicago | San Francisco |
| 1864 | Chicago | Baltimore | 1912 | Baltimore | Chicago | 1960 | Los Angeles | Chicago |
| 1868 | New York City | Chicago | 1916 | St. Louis | Chicago | 1964 | Atlantic City | San Francisco |
| 1872 | Baltimore | Philadelphia | 1920 | San Francisco | Chicago | 1968 | Chicago | Miami Beach |
| 1876 | St. Louis | Cincinnati | 1924 | New York City | Cleveland | 1972 | Miami Beach | Miami Beach |
| 1880 | Cincinnati | Chicago | 1928 | Houston | Kansas City | 1976 | New York City | Kansas City, Mo. |
| 1884 | Chicago | Chicago | 1932 | Chicago | Chicago | 1980 | New York City | Detroit |
| 1888 | St. Louis | Chicago | 1936 | Philadelphia | Cleveland | 1984 | San Francisco | Dallas |
| 1892 | Chicago | Minneapolis | 1940 | Chicago | Philadelphia | 1988 | Atlanta | New Orleans |
| 1896 | Chicago | St. Louis | 1944 | Chicago | Chicago | 1992 | New York City | Houston |
| 1900 | Kansas City, Mo. | Philadelphia | 1948 | Philadelphia | Philadelphia | | | |

(1) The first Democratic National Convention was held in 1832. All conventions prior to 1856 were held in Baltimore. The first Republican National Convention was held in 1856. Chicago has hosted more conventions than any other city (24).

## Librarians of Congress

| Librarian | Served | Appointed by President | Librarian | Served | Appointed by President |
|---|---|---|---|---|---|
| John J. Beckley | 1802-1807 | Jefferson | Herbert Putnam | 1899-1939 | McKinley |
| Patrick Magruder | 1807-1815 | Jefferson | Archibald MacLeish | 1939-1944 | F. Roosevelt |
| George Watterston | 1815-1829 | Madison | Luther H. Evans | 1945-1953 | Truman |
| John Silva Meehan | 1829-1861 | Jackson | L. Quincy Mumford | 1954-1974 | Eisenhower |
| John G. Stephenson | 1861-1864 | Lincoln | Daniel J. Boorstin | 1975-1987 | Ford |
| Ainsworth Rand Spofford | 1864-1897 | Lincoln | James H. Billington | 1987- | Reagan |
| John Russell Young | 1897-1899 | McKinley | | | |

## Federal Bureau of Investigation

The Federal Bureau of Investigation (FBI) is the principal investigative arm of the U.S. Department of Justice, and is located at 10th Street and Pennsylvania Avenue, Northwest, Washington, D.C. 20535. It investigates all violations of Federal law except those specifically assigned to some other agency by legislative action. The FBI's jurisdiction includes a wide range of responsibilities in the criminal, civil, and security fields. Priority has been assigned to five areas—counterterrorism, foreign counterintelligence, organized crime/drugs, white-collar crime, and violent crime. On Jan. 28, 1982, the Attorney General assigned concurrent jurisdiction for the enforcement of the Controlled Substances Act to the FBI and the Drug Enforcement Administration (DEA).

The FBI also offers cooperative services to duly authorized law enforcement agencies; these services include fingerprint identification, laboratory examination, police training, and the National Crime Information Center.

The FBI has 56 field offices in the principal cities of the country. (Consult telephone directories for locations and phone numbers.)

An applicant for the position of Special Agent of the FBI must be a citizen of the U.S., at least 23 and under 37 years old, and a graduate of an accredited law school or of an accredited college or university. Special agents may be appointed under five entry programs: law, accounting, engineering/science, language, and diversified. Other degree titles may also qualify for the Special Agent position. Please consult your local FBI field office applicant coordinator. Those appointed to the Special Agent position must complete an initial training period of 16 weeks at the FBI Academy, Quantico, Va.

AFGHANISTAN

ALBANIA

ALGERIA

ANDORRA

ANGOLA

ANTIGUA AND BARBUDA

ARGENTINA

ARMENIA

AUSTRALIA

AUSTRIA

AZERBAIJAN

THE BAHAMAS

BAHRAIN

BANGLADESH

BARBADOS

BELARUS

BELGIUM

BELIZE

BENIN

BHUTAN

BOLIVIA

BOSNIA AND HERZEGOVINA

BOTSWANA

BRAZIL

BRUNEI DARUSSALAM

BULGARIA

BURKINA FASO

BURUNDI

CAMBODIA

CAMEROON

CANADA

CAPE VERDE

CENTRAL AFRICAN REPUBLIC

CHAD

CHILE

CHINA

COLOMBIA

COMOROS

CONGO

COSTA RICA

COTE D'IVOIRE

CROATIA

CUBA

CYPRUS

CZECH REPUBLIC

DENMARK

DJIBOUTI

DOMINICA

DOMINICAN REPUBLIC

ECUADOR

EGYPT

EL SALVADOR

EQUATORIAL GUINEA

ERITREA

ESTONIA

482

ETHIOPIA

FIJI

FINLAND

FRANCE

GABON

THE GAMBIA

GEORGIA

GERMANY

GHANA

GREECE

GRENADA

GUATEMALA

GUINEA

GUINEA-BISSAU

GUYANA

HAITI

HONDURAS

HUNGARY

ICELAND

INDIA

INDONESIA

IRAN

IRAQ

IRELAND

ISRAEL

ITALY

JAMAICA

JAPAN

JORDAN

KAZAKHSTAN

KENYA

KIRIBATI

NORTH KOREA

SOUTH KOREA

KUWAIT

KYRGYZSTAN

LAOS

LATVIA

LEBANON

LESOTHO

LIBERIA

LIBYA

LIECHTENSTEIN

LITHUANIA

LUXEMBOURG

MACEDONIA

MADAGASCAR

MALAWI

MALAYSIA

MALDIVES

MALI

MALTA

MARSHALL ISLANDS

MAURITANIA

MAURITIUS

MEXICO

MICRONESIA, FEDERATED STATES OF

MOLDOVA

MONACO

MONGOLIA

MOROCCO

MOZAMBIQUE

MYANMAR (BURMA)

NAMIBIA

NAURU

NEPAL

NETHERLANDS

NEW ZEALAND

NICARAGUA

NIGER

NIGERIA

NORWAY

OMAN

PAKISTAN

PANAMA

PAPUA NEW GUINEA

PARAGUAY

PERU

PHILIPPINES

POLAND

PORTUGAL

QATAR

ROMANIA

RUSSIA

RWANDA

ST. KITTS AND NEVIS

ST. LUCIA

ST. VINCENT AND THE GRENADINES

SAN MARINO

SAO TOME AND PRINCIPE

SAUDI ARABIA

SENEGAL

SEYCHELLES

SIERRA LEONE

SINGAPORE

SLOVAKIA

SLOVENIA

SOLOMON ISLANDS

SOMALIA

SOUTH AFRICA

SPAIN

SRI LANKA

SUDAN

SURINAME

SWAZILAND

SWEDEN

SWITZERLAND

SYRIA

TAIWAN

TAJIKISTAN

| | | | | |
|---|---|---|---|---|
| TANZANIA | THAILAND | TOGO | TONGA | TRINIDAD AND TOBAGO |
| TUNISIA | TURKEY | TURKMENISTAN | TUVALU | UGANDA |
| UKRAINE | UNITED ARAB EMIRATES | UNITED KINGDOM | UNITED STATES | URUGUAY |
| UZBEKISTAN | VANUATU | VATICAN CITY | VENEZUELA | VIETNAM |
| WESTERN SAMOA | YEMEN | YUGOSLAVIA | ZAIRE | ZAMBIA |

ZIMBABWE

## INTERNATIONAL TIME ZONES

The world is divided into 24 time zones, each 15° longitude wide. The longitudinal meridian passing through Greenwich, England, is the starting point, and is called the *prime meridian*. The 12th zone is divided by the 180th meridian (International Date Line). When the line is crossed going west, the date is advanced one day; when crossed going east, the date becomes a day earlier.

© The World Almanac and Book of Facts, 1994

# NORTH AMERICA

RUSSIA

ARCTIC OCEAN

Cape Morris Jesup
Nord

Cape Columbia
Alert
Ellesmere

Greenland
(Kalaallit Nunaat)
(Denmark)

ICELAND

Bering Sea
Chukchi Sea

St. Lawrence I.
Bering Strait
SEWARD PENINSULA
Nome
Barrow
Point Barrow

Queen Elizabeth Islands
Island

Qaanaaq
(Thule)

Nunivak I.
Bethel
Alaska
Mt. McKinley 20,320
Highest point in North America
ALASKA RANGE
Fairbanks
Fort McPherson
Inuvik
Dawson

Melville I.
Banks I.
Sachs Harbour
Devon I.
Resolute
Pond Inlet

Baffin Bay

Tasiilaq

Mt. Katmai 6,716
Kodiak I.
Anchorage
Seward
Valdez

Victoria I.
Cambridge Bay
Baffin
Island
Pangnirtung

Nuuk
(Godthab)

Cape Farewell

Gulf of Alaska
Mt. Logan 19,850
YUKON PLATEAU
Carmacks
Whitehorse

Great Bear Lake

Arctic Circle

Iqaluit

Davis Strait

Labrador Sea

Juneau
Sitka
Alexander Archipelago
Ketchikan
Prince Rupert
Queen Charlotte Islands
Kitimat

Watson Lake
Fort Simpson
Hay River
Fort Nelson

Yellowknife
Great Slave Lake
Fort Smith
Uranium City
Arviat

CANADA

Rankin Inlet

Southampton I.

Hudson Strait

UNGAVA PENINSULA
Povungnituk

Hebron

Labrador City
St. Anthony

Happy Valley
Goose Bay
Schefferville

Prince George
Mt. Waddington 13,175
Port Hardy
Vancouver I.
Vancouver
Victoria
Seattle
Mt. Rainier 14,410
Portland
Eugene

Mt. Robson 12,972
Jasper
Grande Prairie
Dawson Creek
Peace River
Fort McMurray
La Loche
Williams Lake
Kamloops
Edmonton
Calgary
Lethbridge

Lake Athabasca
La Ronge
Flin Flon
Prince Albert
Saskatoon
Regina
Brandon

Churchill

York Factory
Thompson

Hudson Bay

James Bay
Moosonee

LABRADOR

Sept-Iles
Chicoutimi
Chibougamau

Newfoundland
St. John's
Corner Brook
Cape Breton I.
Sydney
NOVA SCOTIA
Gander

Spokane
Missoula
Great Falls
Williston

Winnipeg

Thunder Bay
Timmins
Val-d'Or
Sudbury

Quebec
Montreal
Ottawa

Fredericton
Bangor
Portland
Cape Sable
Halifax

Portland
Boise
Butte
Billings
Bismarck
Fargo
Duluth

Lake Superior

Green Bay

Lake Huron

Lake Ontario
Toronto
Rochester
Buffalo

CANADIAN SHIELD

St. Lawrence

Eureka
Reno
Pocatello
Great Salt Lake
Salt Lake City
Casper
Cheyenne
Rapid City
Sioux Falls

Minneapolis
Des Moines

Lake Michigan
Milwaukee
Chicago

Detroit
Cleveland
Pittsburgh

Lake Erie

New York City
Philadelphia
Boston

San Francisco
San Jose
Fresno

GREAT BASIN
Mt. Whitney 14,494

Denver
COLORADO PLATEAU
Mt. Elbert 14,433

Omaha
Kansas City

UNITED STATES

Columbus
Indianapolis
Louisville
Ohio

Washington, D.C.
Richmond

Santa Barbara
Point Conception
Los Angeles
San Diego
Tijuana

Death Valley
Lowest point in North America
Las Vegas

Wichita
St. Louis
Nashville
Mt. Mitchell 6,684

Raleigh
Charlotte
Cape Hatteras

ATLANTIC OCEAN

PACIFIC OCEAN

Mexicali
Nogales
Hermosillo

Phoenix
Tucson
Ciudad Juarez
El Paso

Albuquerque
Amarillo
Lubbock

Oklahoma City

Little Rock
Red
Dallas

Memphis
Atlanta

Birmingham

Charleston
Savannah
Jacksonville

Austin

San Antonio
Nuevo Laredo
Brownsville
Matamoros
Monterrey

Houston
New Orleans

Jackson
Mobile

COASTAL PLAIN

Tampa
St. Petersburg
Miami

Freeport
Nassau
THE BAHAMAS

Tropic of Cancer

Ciudad Obregon
Cerro Mohinora 13,097
La Paz
Durango
Mazatlan

Chihuahua

Gulf of Mexico

Cape Sable
Havana

CUBA

Pico Duarte 10,416
DOMINICAN REPUBLIC
HAITI
Port-au-Prince
Santo Domingo

False Cape

Aguascalientes
Cape Corrientes
Guadalajara
Colima

Tampico

MEXICO
Leon
Mexico City
Puebla
Citlaltepec 18,700
Veracruz
Oaxaca

Bay of Campeche
Merida
Campeche
YUCATAN PENINSULA
Cancun

Greater
JAMAICA
Kingston

Antilles

Caribbean Sea

Acapulco

Villahermosa
Tuxtla Gutierrez
Belmopan
BELIZE
GUATEMALA
Tajumulco 13,845
Guatemala
EL SALVADOR
San Salvador

HONDURAS
Tegucigalpa
NICARAGUA
Managua
Lake Nicaragua

San Jose
COSTA RICA
ISTHMUS OF PANAMA
Panama Canal
PANAMA
Panama

SOUTH AMERICA

## NORTH AMERICA

### Elevation

| Meters | Feet |
|---|---|
| 4,000 | 13,120 |
| 2,000 | 6,560 |
| 500 | 1,640 |
| 200 | 656 |
| 0 | 0 |
| Below Sea Level | Below Sea Level |

0    250    500    750    1000 Miles

0  250 500  1000  1200 Kilometers

© The World Almanac and Book of Facts, 1994

**ALASKA....See page 485**

90° 85° 80° 75° 70° 65° 60°

**CANADIAN SHIELD**

James Bay

Waskaganish

Moosonee

**CANADA**

Sept-Iles
Port-Cartier

Chibougamau

Matagami

Mistassini

Alma

Chicoutimi

Riviere-du-Loup

Baie-Comeau

Gaspe

Anticosti I.

**Gulf of St. Lawrence**

Channel-Port aux Basques

Cape Breton I.

Sydney

Canso

Hearst

Geraldton

Kapuskasing

Iroquois Falls

Timmins

Kirkland Lake

Rouyn-Noranda
Val-d'Or

**Quebec**

Shawinigan
Trois-Rivieres

Matane
Causapscal
Dalhousie
Rimouski
Edmundston

Newcastle

Grand Falls

Bathurst

**Prince Edward I.**

Charlottetown

Lake Nipigon

Atikokan
**Thunder Bay**

Nipigon

Marathon

Wawa

Chapleau

New Liskeard

Mont-Laurier

Caribou

Houlton

Mt. Katahdin 5,267

St. Georges

Moncton

Fredericton

Saint John

New Glasgow
Amherst
Truro

**NOVA SCOTIA**

Superior

Houghton

Marquette

Iron Mountain

Cheboygan

**Sault Ste. Marie**

Sault Ste. Marie

Elliot Lake

Sudbury

North Bay

Deep River

Pembroke

Parry Sound

**Montreal**

Cornwall

Hull
**Ottawa**

Burlington

Mt. Washington 6,268

Sherbrooke

Bangor

**Maine**

Calais

Digby
Yarmouth

Dartmouth
**Halifax**

Shelburne

Cape Sable

Bay of Fundy

**Wisconsin**

Eau Claire

Green Bay

Appleton

La Crosse

**Madison**

**Milwaukee**

Wausau

**Michigan**

Traverse City

Alpena

Owen Sound

Saginaw

**Grand Rapids**

Flint

Lansing

Sarnia

London

Bracebridge

**Toronto**

Oshawa

Kingston

Peterborough

Barrie

Kitchener

Hamilton

Niagara Falls

**Buffalo**

Montpelier

Vt. N.H.

Rutland

Concord

**Boston**

Manchester

Portsmouth

Portland

Augusta

Bar Harbor

**ADIRONDACK MTS.**

**New York**

Syracuse

**Rochester**

Albany

**Springfield**

Mass.

Hartford

R.I. Providence

New Bedford

Cape Cod

Long Island Sound

Long I.

Cedar Rapids

**Chicago**

Davenport

Rock Island

Peoria

Champaign

**Detroit**

Windsor

Kalamazoo

South Bend

Gary

Fort Wayne

Toledo

Akron

**Cleveland**

Youngstown

Erie

Pa.

Altoona

**Pittsburgh**

Binghamton

Scranton

Allentown

Trenton

**Philadelphia**

**New York City**

N.J.

Newark

New Haven

Conn.

**ATLANTIC OCEAN**

**Indiana**

Muncie

**Ohio**

Dayton

Mansfield

Wheeling

Harrisburg

**Columbus**

Parkersburg

Del.

Dover

Wilmington

**Baltimore**

Annapolis

**Washington D.C.**

Md.

Salisbury

Chesapeake Bay

**Springfield**

Bloomington

**Indianapolis**

**Cincinnati**

Spruce Knob 4,861

W. Va.

Charleston

Huntington

Frankfort

Lexington

**Richmond**

Newport News

Norfolk

**Illinois**

Hannibal

Columbia

Jefferson City

Rolla

**St. Louis**

**Louisville**

Evansville

**Kentucky**

Owensboro

Bowling Green

Paducah

Johnson City

**Virginia**

Roanoke

Greensboro

**Raleigh**

Cape Hatteras

Cape Girardeau

Poplar Bluff

Jonesboro

**Nashville**

Jackson

**Tennessee**

Knoxville

Chattanooga

Asheville

Mt. Mitchell 6,684

Winston-Salem

**North Carolina**

New Bern

**APPALACHIAN MOUNTAINS**

Little Rock

Pine Bluff

**Memphis**

Tupelo

Columbus

Huntsville

Athens

Gadsden

**Birmingham**

Tuscaloosa

Greensboro

Fayetteville

**Charlotte**

Greenville

**Columbia**

Florence

Wilmington

**South Carolina**

**ATLANTIC COASTAL PLAIN**

Monroe

Greenville

**Mississippi**

Meridian

Montgomery

Columbus

**Atlanta**

Augusta

Macon

**Georgia**

Albany

**La.**

Natchez

Hattiesburg

**Jackson**

Dothan

**Alabama**

Brunswick

**Savannah**

Valdosta

Baton Rouge

Biloxi

Pensacola

**Mobile**

Panama City

**Tallahassee**

**Jacksonville**

St. Augustine

**New Orleans**

Morgan City

Lafayette

Gainesville

Daytona Beach

Orlando

Cape Canaveral

Melbourne

**Gulf of Mexico**

Tampa

St. Petersburg

Sarasota

**Florida**

Lake Okeechobee

West Palm Beach

Fort Myers

**Fort Lauderdale**

**Miami**

Cape Sable

Key West

Florida Keys

Straits of Florida

**BAHAMAS**

**UNITED STATES, CANADA, MEXICO**

**Elevation**

| Meters | | Feet |
|---|---|---|
| 2,000 | | 6,560 |
| 1,000 | | 3,280 |
| 500 | | 1,640 |
| 200 | | 656 |
| 0 | | 0 |
| Below Sea Level | | Below Sea Level |

**CUBA**

**DOMINICAN REPUBLIC**

**HAITI**

**Merida**

Cancun

Cozumel I.

Campeche

**YUCATAN PENINSULA**

**JAMAICA**

0    250    500 Miles

0    250    500    750 Kilometers

© The World Almanac and Book of Facts, 1994

# EUROPE

### Elevation

| Meters | Feet |
|--------|------|
| 4,000 | 13,120 |
| 2,000 | 6,560 |
| 500 | 1,640 |
| 200 | 656 |
| 0 | 0 |
| Below Sea Level | Below Sea Level |

Greenland
(Den.)

Arctic Circle

ATLANTIC OCEAN

Norwegian Sea

North Cape

Hammerfest

Tromso

Murmansk

Ivalo

LAPLAND

Bodo

Kiruna

Arkhangelsk

Rovaniemi

Belomorsk

Lulea

Oulu

Keflavik
Reykjavik
Akureyri
ICELAND
Hekla
4,892

NORWAY

Trondheim

Umea

FINLAND

Lake Onega

Alesund

Ostersund

Kuopio

Petrozavodsk

Faeroe Is.
(Den.)

SWEDEN

Vaasa

Lake Ladoga

Tampere

Shetland Is.
(U.K.)

Bergen

Glittertind
8,113

Gavle

Aland Is.
(Fin.)

Turku

Helsinki

St. Petersburg

Orkney Is.

Oslo

Uppsala

Stockholm

Novgorod

Hebrides

Stavanger

Skien

Linkoping

Gotland
(Swe.)

Riga

LATVIA

RUSSIA

Inverness

Kristiansand

Jonkoping

Daugavpils

Smolensk

Aberdeen

Glasgow

Dundee
Edinburgh

North Sea

Alborg

Goteborg

Helsingborg

LITHUANIA

Vitsyebsk

Klaipeda

Belfast

Newcastle

Jutland

Arhus

Malmo

Kaunas

Vilnius

Minsk

Mahilyow

IRELAND

UNITED KINGDOM

Copenhagen

Odense

Bornholm
(Den.)

Gdansk

Kaliningrad

BELARUS

Bryansk

Dublin

Liverpool

Leeds

Sheffield

DENMARK

Hamburg

Rostock

Szczecin

POLAND

Bialystok

Homyel

Limerick

Manchester

NETHERLANDS

Bremen

Berlin

Poznan

Warsaw

Brest

Cork

Birmingham

Cardiff

London

Amsterdam

Hannover

Magdeburg

Lodz

Lublin

Kiev

Land's End

Bristol

Hague

Rotterdam

Essen

Cologne

Leipzig

Dresden

Wroclaw

Katowice

Kracow

Lviv

UKRAINE

Plymouth

Portsmouth

Antwerp

BELGIUM

Bonn

GERMANY

Prague

Ostrava

SLOVAKIA

Kosice

Vynnytsya

English Channel

Le Havre

Brussels

Luxembourg

Frankfurt

Nurnberg

CZECH REP.

Brno

CARPATHIAN MOUNTAINS

Channel Is.
(U.K.)

Brest

Rouen

LUX.

Mannheim

Iasi

MOLDOVA

Nantes

Paris

Orleans

Strasbourg

Stuttgart

Munich

Linz

Vienna

Bratislava

Miskolc

Debrecen

Chisinau

Odesa

Loire

Dijon

Basel

Zurich

Salzburg

AUSTRIA

Budapest

Cluj-Napoca

ROMANIA

FRANCE

Limoges

Geneva

Bern

SWITZ.

LIECH.

Graz

HUNGARY

Pecs

Timisoara

Brasov

Bordeaux

Lyon

Grenoble

Mt. Blanc
15,771

Matterhorn 14,690

Milan

SLOVE.

Ljubljana

Zagreb

Belgrade

Bucharest

Constanta

Bay of Biscay

La Coruna

Gijon

Bilbao

San Sebastian

Toulouse

Nice

Turin

Verona

Venice

CROATIA

BOS. & HERZ.

SERBIA

Ruse

Varna

Black Sea

Vigo

Valladolid

Pico de Aneto
11,168

PYRENEES

Marseille

MONACO

Genoa

Florence

SAN MARINO

Split

Sarajevo

YUGO.

Danube

Burgas

BULGARIA

Oporto

Coimbra

IBERIAN

ANDORRA

Corsica
(Fr.)

Elba

Dubrovnik

MONT.

Skopje

Sofia

Plovdiv

PORTUGAL

Lisbon

Madrid

Zaragoza

Barcelona

APENNINES

Ajaccio

Rome

ITALY

Tirana

MACE.

Thessaloniki

TURKEY

Cape St. Vincent

SPAIN

PENINSULA

Cordoba

Valencia

Palma

Balearic Is.
(Sp.)

Sardinia
(It.)

Naples

Vesuvius
4,202

Bari

ALBANIA

Vlore

Olympus
9,570

Larisa

Volos

Cadiz

Seville

Granada

Alicante

Cagliari

Corfu

GREECE

Athens

Gibraltar
(U.K.)

Malaga

Tyrrhenian Sea

Palermo

Messina

Ionian Sea

Patras

Rhodes

Strait of Gibraltar

Tagus

Ebro

Mediterranean Sea

Etna
11,053

Catania

Sicily

MALTA

Peloponnesus

Iraklion

AFRICA

Crete

| 0 | 250 | 500 Miles |
| 0 | 250 | 500 | 750 Kilometers |

© The World Almanac and Book of Facts, 1994

## RUSSIA, UKRAINE & CENTRAL ASIA

**PACIFIC OCEAN**

*Bering Sea*

Provideniya

Anadyr

*Chukchi Sea*

*Bering Strait*

KAMCHATKA PENINSULA

Shiveluch 10,771
Kluchevskaya 15,584
Karymsky 4,869

Petropavlovsk-Kamchatsky

*Sea of Okhotsk*

Palana

*Shelikhov Gulf*

Okhotsk

Susuman

Magadan

Wrangel I.

*East Siberian Sea*

Chersky

Zyryanka

*Kolyma*

KOLYMA MOUNTAINS

Indigirka

Verkhoyansk

Yakutsk

*Lena*

Vilyuysk

Aldan

Berkakit

Tynda

Svobodny

Komsomolsk

Khabarovsk

Blagoveshchensk

Okha

Sakhalin

*Tatar Strait*

Yuzhno-Sakhalinsk

Tiatia 6,013

Kuril Islands

Alaid 7,662

*Sea of Japan*

Ussuriysk

Vladivostok

SOUTH ASIA

S T A N O V O Y   R A N G E

YABLONOVYY RANGE

Chita

Ulan-Ude

*Lake Baykal*

Bratsk

Ust-Kut

Lensk

*Lena*

Tiksi

VERKHOYANSK R.A.

*Laptev Sea*

New Siberian Islands

Nordvik

*Lower Tunguska*

Tura

CENTRAL SIBERIAN PLATEAU

Norilsk

Dikson

Severnaya Zemlya

*Kara Sea*

Novaya Zemlya

*Barents Sea*

Franz Josef Land

**ARCTIC OCEAN**

Vorkuta

Inta

Ukhta

Pechora

Salekhard

*Ob*

Novyy Urengoy

Surgut

Nizhnevartovsk

*Yenisey*

Tara

Tobolsk

Tomsk

Kolpashevo

Achinsk

Kansk

Krasnoyarsk

Lesosibirsk

Tashtagol

SAYAN MTS.

Irkutsk

Tulun

Tayshet

Angara

Kemerovo

Novokuznetsk

Barnaul

Semey

Oskemen

Ayaguz

Novosibirsk

Omsk

Pavlodar

Qaraghandy

KAZAKH UPLAND

Ayaguz

Alma-Ata

Pobedy Pk. 24,406

Bishkek

KYRGYZSTAN

Communism Pk. 23,405

Andijan

Namangan

Angren

Tashkent

Dushanbe

TAJIKISTAN

PAMIRS

Samarqand

Shymkent

Taldy-Kurgan

Zhezqazghan

Aqmola

Qyzylorda

*Syr Darya*

*Aral Sea*

Balqash

*Lake Balkhash*

Zhambyl

Turkistan

KAZAKHSTAN

Oral

Oqtyabrsk

Atyrau

Aqtau

Ozinki

U R A L   M O U N T A I N S

Mt. Narodnaya 6,217

Serov

Nizhniy Tagil

Yekaterinburg

Tyumen

Kurgan

Petropavl

Chelyabinsk

Magnitogorsk

Orsk

Ufa

Orenburg

Samara

Tolyatti

Izhevsk

Perm

Berezniki

Kotlas

Syktyvkar

Kirov

*Kama*

Kazan

Nizhniy Novgorod

Cheboksary

*Volga*

Penza

Saratov

*Ural*

Atyrau

Astrakhan

*Caspian Sea*

KARA KUM DESERT

Krasnovodsk

TURKMENISTAN

Ashgabat

Nukus

Urgench

Bukhoro

*Amu Darya*

KYZYL KUM DESERT

UZBEKISTAN

Chardzhou

Qarshi

RUSSIA

WEST SIBERIAN PLAIN

Nizhnevartovsk

EUROPEAN PLAIN

NORTH EUROPEAN PLAIN

Murmansk

Arkhangelsk

KOLA PENINSULA

*Severnaya Dvina*

Belomorsk

*Lake Onega*

*Lake Ladoga*

Petrozavodsk

St. Petersburg

Cherepovets

Vologda

Tver

Yaroslavl

Ivanovo

Ryazan

Moscow

Tula

Lipetsk

Voronezh

Tambov

Volgograd

Rostov

Krasnodar

Stavropol

Sochi

Grozny

CAUCASUS MTS.

Highest point in Europe: Mt. Elbrus 18,510

GEORGIA

Tbilisi

ARMENIA

Yerevan

Sakhi

AZERBAIJAN

Baku

Makhachkala

Batumi

*Black Sea*

CRIMEA PENINSULA

Sevastopol

Simferopol

Mariupol

Donetsk

Luhansk

UKRAINE

Kharkiv

Dnipropetrovsk

Zaporizhzhya

Kryvyy Rih

Berdyansk

Odesa

Kiev

Vinnytsya

Lviv

EUROPE

Bryansk

Kursk

Smolensk

Novgorod

*Dnieper*

*Don*

Balta

Rostov

MILES

KILOMETERS

### Elevation

| Meters | Feet |
|--------|------|
| 4,000 | 13,120 |
| 2,000 | 6,560 |
| 500 | 1,640 |
| 200 | 656 |
| 0 | 0 |
| Below Sea Level | Below Sea Level |

0  250  500  750 Miles
0  250  500  750  1,000 Kilometers

*Arctic Circle*

492

Istanbul
Izmir • Bursa
Ankara
Samsun
Konya
Adana
TURKEY
Trabzon
Nicosia
CYPRUS
Mersin
Erzurum
Latakia
Beirut
Aleppo
Diyarbakir
Mt. Ararat 16,804
Lake Van
ISRAEL • LEBANON
Tel Aviv-
Yafo
Damascus
Mosul
Tabriz
Lake
Urmia
West Bank
SYRIA
SYRIAN
Amman
DESERT
Arbil
Rasht
Jerusalem
JORDAN
Karkuke
Lowest point in
Asia • Tabuk
IRAQ
Baghdad
Mt. Damavand 18,606
Teheran
Gorgan
Al Hillah
Qom
DASHT-E
KAVIR
Mashhad
Hail
Buraydah
Basra
Abadan
IRAN
Yazd
Birjand
DASHT-E LUT
Mazar-e
Sharif
Medina
Kuwait
Esfahan
KUWAIT
Shiraz
Kerman
Herat
AFGHANISTAN
Kabul
Peshawar
Jidda
Mecca
At Taif
Riyadh
Ad Dammam
BAHRAIN
Al Hufuf
Farah
Qandahar
SAUDI
ARABIA
QATAR • Doha
Zahedan
Quetta
Rawalpindi
Faisalabad
Abha
Abu Dhabi
UNITED
ARAB
EMIRATES
Bandar Abbas
OMAN
Dubai
PAKISTAN
Multan
Lahore
RUB AL KHALI
Gulf of Oman
Turbat
Sukkur
Muscat
Sur
Karachi
THAR
DESERT
Sanaa
Al Hudaydah
OMAN
Ras al Hadd
Tropic of Cancer
Hydetabad
YEMEN
Salalah
Aden
Al Mukalla
Arabian
Sea

NORTHERN ASIA

Yining
Urumqi
Pobedy Peak 24,406
Kashi
TAKLIMAKAN
DESERT
Shache
K2 28,250
KUNLUN MOUNTA
PLATEAU OF TIBET
Srinagar
Chandigarh
HIMALAY
Delhi
New
Delhi
NEPAL
Jaipur
Pokhara
Mt. Everest 29
Xigaze
Agra
Lucknow
Kathmandu
Jodhpur
Kanpur
Darjeeling
Allahabad
Varanasi
Patna
Ahmedabad
Indore
Bhopal
Jabalpur
Asansol
Khulna
Calcutta
Rajkot
Nagpur
Ranchi
Surat
DECCAN
Raipur
Cuttack
PLATEAU
Bombay
Poona
INDIA
Sholapur
Hyderabad
Vishakhapatnam
Panaji
Hubli
Vijayawada
Bangalore
Madras
Mysore
Coimbatore
Cochin
Madurai
Trivandrum
Trincomalee
Cape Comorin
SRI LANKA
Colombo
Galle
Male
MALDIVES

Bay of
Bengal

Socotra
(Yemen)

AFRICA
Gulf of Aden

Equator

SOUTH ASIA

Elevation

| Meters | Feet |
|--------|------|
| 4,000 | 13,120 |
| 2,000 | 6,560 |
| 500 | 1,640 |
| 200 | 656 |
| 0 | 0 |
| Below Sea Level | Below Sea Level |

INDIAN    OCEAN

Chagos
Archipelago
(U.K.)

0      250    500    750    1,000 Miles
0  250  500  1,000  1,250 Kilometers

© The World Almanac and Book of Facts, 1994

# AFRICA

**Elevation**

| Meters | Feet |
|---|---|
| 4,000 | 13,120 |
| 2,000 | 6,560 |
| 500 | 1,640 |
| 200 | 656 |
| 0 | 0 |
| Below Sea Level | Below Sea Level |

0 250 500 750 Miles
0 250 500 750 1,000 Kilometers

© The World Almanac and Book of Facts, 1994

496

# AUSTRALIA & THE PACIFIC

**Elevation**

| Meters | Feet |
|--------|------|
| 2,000 | 6,560 |
| 1,000 | 3,280 |
| 200 | 656 |
| 0 | 0 |
| Below Sea Level | Below Sea Level |

Marquesas Islands

French Polynesia (Fr.)

Tuamotu Archipelago

Papeete Tahiti

Society Islands

Austral Islands

Tropic of Capricorn

Kiritimati (Christmas)

Line Islands

Jarvis I. (U.S.)

Palmyra Atoll (U.S.)

Cook Islands (N.Z.)

Avarua

PACIFIC OCEAN

Howland I. (U.S.)
Baker I. (U.S.)

KIRIBATI Enderbury

Canton I. Phoenix Islands

Tokelau (N.Z.)

Niue (N.Z.)

American Samoa (U.S.)
Pago Pago

W. SAMOA
Apia

TONGA
Nuku'alofa

Wallis and Futuna (Fr.)

Wake I. (U.S.)

MARSHALL ISLANDS

Bikini Atoll
Ratak Chain
Ralik Chain
Kwajalein Atoll
Enewetak Atoll

Majuro

Tarawa
Gilbert Islands
Banaba

NAURU
Yaren

TUVALU
Funafuti

Santa Cruz Is.

FIJI
Vanua Levu
Viti Levu
Suva

Vila
Espiritu Santo

VANUATU

Malakula

New Caledonia (Fr.)
Noumea
Loyalty Is.

Kermadec Is. (N.Z.)

Norfolk I. (Aust.)

Chatham Is. (N.Z.)

Pohnpei

Yap Is.

Truk Is.

Caroline Islands

FEDERATED STATES OF MICRONESIA

Palau (U.S.)

Northern Mariana Islands (U.S.)

Guam (U.S.)
Saipan

PAPUA NEW GUINEA

Admiralty Is.
Bismarck Arch.
New Ireland
New Britain
Rabaul
Bougainville

New Guinea
Mt. Wilhelm 14,793

Madang
Lae
Port Moresby

SOLOMON ISLANDS
Solomon Is.
Guadalcanal
Honiara

Coral Sea

Great Barrier Reef

Auckland
Hamilton
Tauranga
North Island
New Plymouth
Gisborne
Napier

NEW ZEALAND
Nelson
Wellington
Christchurch
South Island
Mt. Cook 12,349 Highest Point

Dunedin
Invercargill
Stewart I.

Tasman Sea

Brisbane
Southport
Bundaberg
Rockhampton
Mackay
Townsville
Cairns

GREAT DIVIDING RANGE

Newcastle
Sydney
Wollongong
Canberra
Mt. Kosciusko 7,310 Highest Point in Australia

Toowoomba
Tamworth
Orange
Charleville
Longreach

GREAT ARTESIAN BASIN

Melbourne
Geelong
Ballarat
Bendigo
Wagga Wagga
Albury

Hobart
Launceston
Tasmania

Bass Strait

Cape York

Weipa

Gulf of Carpentaria

Arafura Sea

Jayapura
Sorong
Ambon
Banda Sea
Celebes
Ujung Pandang
Banjarmasin
Borneo
Manado

INDONESIA

Timor
Timor Sea

Melville I.
Darwin
Katherine

SIMPSON DESERT

GIBSON DESERT
Alice Springs
Ayers Rock 2,844

AUSTRALIA

GREAT SANDY DESERT

GREAT VICTORIA DESERT

NULLARBOR PLAIN

Lake Eyre
Lowest Point in Australia

Cooper Creek

Broken Hill
Port Augusta
Port Lincoln
Whyalla
Kangaroo I.
Adelaide

Mount Isa

Coober Pedy

Woomera

Murray

Great Australian Bight

INDIAN OCEAN

Cape Leveque
Broome
Port Hedland
North West Cape
Dampier
Newman

Carnarvon
Geraldton

Perth
Kalgoorlie
Bunbury
Esperance
Albany
Cape Leeuwin

PHILIPPINES
Manila
Luzon
Mindanao

Philippine Sea

BRUNEI
MALAYSIA

Merauke

Equator

Philippine Sea

Philippines

The World Almanac and Book of Facts, 1994

| 0 | 400 | 800 | 1,200 Miles |
| 0 | 400 | 800 | 1,200 | 1,600 Kilometers |

# WORLD HISTORY

## Prehistory: Our Ancestors Take Over

*Homo sapiens.* The precise origins of *Homo sapiens*, the species to which all humans belong, are subject to broad speculation based on a small number of fossils, genetic and anatomical studies, and the geological record. But most scientists agree that we evolved from ape-like primate ancestors in a process that began millions of years ago.

Current theories trace the first hominid (human-like primate) to Africa, where 2 lines of hominids appeared 5 to 4 million years ago. One was *Australopithecus*, a social animal, who lived from perhaps 4 to 3 million years ago, and then apparently became extinct.

The 2nd was a human line, *Homo habilis*, a large-brained specimen that walked upright and had a dextrous hand. *Homo habilis* appeared some 2.5 million years ago, lived in semi-permanent camps and had a food-gathering and sharing economy.

*Homo erectus*, our nearest ancestor, appeared in Africa perhaps 1.75 million years ago, and began spreading into Asia and Europe soon after. It had a fairly large brain and a skeletal structure similar to ours. *Homo erectus* learned to control fire, and probably had primitive language skills. The final brain development to *Homo sapiens* and then to our sub-species *Homo sapiens sapiens* occurred between 500,000 and 50,000 years ago, either in one place — probably Africa — or virtually simultaneously and independently in different places in Africa, Europe, and Asia. There is no question that all modern races are members of the same sub-species, *Homo sapiens sapiens.*

The spread of mankind into the remaining habitable continents probably took place near the end of the last ice age: to the Americas across a land bridge from Asia, and to Australia across the Timor Straits.

**Earliest cultures.** A variety of cultural modes — in tool-making, diet, shelter, and possibly social arrangements and spiritual expression, arose as early mankind adapted to different geographic and climatic zones.

Three basic tool-making traditions are recognized by archeologists as arising and often coexisting from one million years ago to the near past: the *chopper tradition*, found largely in E. Asia, with crude chopping tools and simple flake tools; the *flake tradition*, found in Africa and W. Europe, with a variety of small cutting and flaking tools; and the *biface tradition*, found in all of Africa, W. and S. Europe, and S. Asia, producing pointed hand axes chipped on both faces. Later biface sites yield more refined axes and a variety of other tools, weapons, and ornaments using bone, antler, and wood as well as stone.

Only sketchy evidence remains for the different stages in man's increasing control over the environment. Traces of 400,000-year-old covered wood shelters have been found at Nice, France. Scraping tools at Neanderthal sites (200,000-30,000 BC in Europe, N. Africa, the Middle East and Central Asia) suggest the treatment of skins for clothing. Sites from all parts of the world show seasonal migration patterns and exploitation of a wide range of plant and animal food sources.

Painting and decoration, for which there is evidence at the Nice site, flourished along with stone and ivory sculpture after 30,000 years ago; 60 caves in France and 30 in Spain show remarkable examples of wall painting. Other examples have been found in Africa. Proto-religious rites are suggested by these works, and by evidence of ritual cannibalism by Peking Man, 500,000 BC, and of ritual burial with medicinal plants and flowers by Neanderthals at Shanidar in Iraq.

**The Neolithic Revolution.** Sometime after 10,000 BC, among widely separated human communities, a series of dramatic technological and social changes occurred that are summed up as the Neolithic Revolution. The cultivation of previously wild plants encouraged the growth of permanent settlements. Animals were domesticated as a work force and food source. The manufacture of pottery and cloth began. These techniques permitted a huge increase in world population and in human control over the earth.

No region can safely claim priority as the "inventor" of these techniques. Dispersed sites in Cen. and S. America, S.E. Europe, and the Middle East show roughly contemporaneous (10-8,000 BC) evidence of one or another "neolithic" trait. Dates near 6-3,000 BC have been given for E. and S. Asian, W. European, and sub-Saharan African neolithic remains. The variety of crops — field grains, rice, maize, and roots, and the varying mix of other traits suggest that the revolution occurred independently in all these regions.

## History Begins: 4000 - 1000 BC

**Near Eastern cradle.** If history began with writing, the first chapter opened in Mesopotamia, the Tigris-Euphrates river valley. Clay tablets with pictographs were used by the Sumerians to keep records after 4000 BC. A **cuneiform** (wedge shaped) script evolved by 3000 BC as a full syllabic alphabet. Neighboring peoples adapted the script to their own language.

**Sumerian** life centered, from 4000 BC, on large cities (Eridu, Ur, Uruk, Nippur, Kish, Lagash) organized around temples and priestly bureaucracies, with the surrounding plains watered by vast irrigation works and worked with traction plows. Sailboats, wheeled vehicles, potters wheels, and kilns were used. Copper was smelted and tempered in Sumeria from c4000 BC and bronze was produced not long after. Ores, as well as precious stones and metals were obtained through long-distance ship and caravan trade. Iron was used from c2000 BC. Improved ironworking, developed partly by the Hittites, became widespread by 1200 BC.

Sumerian political primacy passed among cities and their kingly dynasties. Semitic-speaking peoples, with cultures derived from the Sumerian, founded a succession of dynasties that ruled in Mesopotamia and neighboring areas for most of 1800 years; among them the **Akkadians** (first under Sargon c2350 BC), and the **Amorites** (whose laws, codified by **Hammurabi**, c1792-1750 BC, have Biblical parallels), and the Assyrians, with interludes of rule by the Hittites, Kassites, and Mitanni, all possibly Indo-Europeans. The political and cultural center of gravity shifted northwest with each successive empire.

Mesopotamian learning, maintained by scribes and preserved by successive rulers in vast libraries, was not abstract or theoretical. Algebraic and geometric problems could be solved on a practical basis in construction, commerce, or administration. Systematic lists of astronomical phenomena, plants, animals and stones were kept; medical texts listed ailments and their herbal cures.

The Sumerians worshipped anthropomorphic gods representing natural forces — Anu, god of heaven; Enlil (Ea), god of water. Epic poetry related these and other gods in a hierarchy. Sacrifices were made at ziggurats — huge stepped temples. Gods were thought to control all events, which could be foretold using oracular materials. This religious pattern persisted into the first millenium BC.

The Syria-Palestine area, site of some of the earliest urban remains (Jericho, 7000 BC), and of the recently uncovered **Ebla** civilization (fl. 2500 BC), experienced Egyptian cultural and political influence along with Mesopotamian. The **Phoenician** coast was an active commercial center. A phonetic alphabet was invented here before 1600 BC. It became the ancestor of all European, Middle Eastern, Indian, S.E.

2500 BC

Asian, Ethiopian, and Korean alphabets.

Regional commerce and diplomacy were aided by the use of Akkadian as a *lingua franca*, later replaced by Aramaic.

**Egypt.** Agricultural villages along the Nile were united by 3300 BC into two kingdoms, Upper and Lower Egypt, unified under the Pharaoh Menes c3100 BC; control over Nubia to the south was asserted beginning 2600 BC. A national bureaucracy supervised construction of canals and monuments (pyramids starting 2700 BC). Brilliant First Dynasty achievements in architecture, sculpture, and painting set the standards and forms for all subsequent Egyptian civilization and are still admired. **Hieroglyphic writing** appeared by 3400 BC, recording a sophisticated literature including romantic and philosophical modes after 2300 BC.

An ordered hierarchy of gods, including totemistic animal elements, was served by a powerful priesthood in Memphis. The pharaoh was identified with the falcon god Horus. Later trends were the belief in an afterlife, and the quasi-monotheistic reforms of Akhenaton (c1379-1362 BC).

After a period of dominance by Semitic Hyksos from Asia (c1700-1550 BC), the New Kingdom established an empire in Syria. Egypt became increasingly embroiled in Asiatic wars and diplomacy. Eventually it was conquered by Persia in 525 BC, and it faded away as an independent culture.

**India.** An urban civilization with a so-far-undeciphered writing system stretched across the Indus Valley and along the Arabian Sea c3000-1500 BC. Major sites as Harappa and **Mohenjo-Daro** in Pakistan, well-planned geometric cities with underground sewers and vast granaries. The entire region (600,000 sq. mi.) may have been ruled as a single state. Bronze was used, and arts and crafts were highly developed. Religious life apparently took the form of fertility cults.

Indus civilization was probably in decline when it was destroyed by **Aryan invaders** from the northwest, speaking an Indo-European language from which all the languages of Pakistan, north India and Bangladesh descend. Led by a warrior aristocracy whose legendary deeds are recorded in the **Rig Veda**, the Aryans spread east and south, bringing their pantheon of sky gods, elaborate priestly (Brahmin) ritual, and the beginnings of the caste system; local customs and beliefs were assimilated by the conquerors.

**Europe.** On Crete, the bronze-age **Minoan civilization** emerged c2500 BC. A prosperous economy and richly decorative art (e.g. at Knossos palace) was supported by seaborne commerce. Mycenae and other cities in Greece and Asia Minor (e.g. **Troy**) preserved elements of the culture to c1100 BC. Cretan Linear A script, c2000-1700 BC, is undeciphered; Linear B, c1300-1200 BC, records a Greek dialect.

Possible connection between Minoan-Mycenaean monumental stonework and the great megalithic monuments and tombs of W. Europe, Iberia, and Malta (c4000-1500 BC) is unclear.

**China.** Proto-Chinese neolithic cultures had long covered northern and southeastern China when the first large political state was organized in the north by the **Shang dynasty** c1500 BC. Shang kings called themselves Sons of Heaven, and presided over a cult of human and animal sacrifice to ancestors and nature gods. The Chou dynasty, starting c1100 BC, expanded the area of the Son of Heaven's dominion, but feudal states exercised most temporal power.

A writing system with 2,000 different characters was already in use under the Shang, with **pictographs** later supplemented by phonetic characters. The system, with modifications, is still in use, despite changes in spoken Chinese.

Technical advances allowed urban specialists to create fine ceramic and jade products, and bronze casting after 1500 BC was the most advanced in the world.

Bronze artifacts have recently been discovered in northern Thailand dating to 3600 BC, hundreds of years before similar Middle Eastern finds.

**Americas.** Olmecs settled on the Gulf coast of Mexico, 1500 BC, and soon developed the first civilization in the Western Hemisphere. Temple cities and huge stone sculpture date to 1200 BC. A rudimentary calendar and writing system existed. Olmec religion, centering on a jaguar god, and art forms influenced all later Meso-American cultures.

Neolithic ceremonial centers were built on the Peruvian desert coast, c2000 BC.

# Classical Era of Old World Civilizations

**Greece.** After a period of decline during the Dorian Greek invasions (1200-1000 BC), Greece and the Aegean area developed a unique civilization. Drawing upon Mycenaean traditions, Mesopotamian learning (weights and measures, lunisolar calendar, astronomy, musical scales), the Phoenician alphabet (modified for Greek), and Egyptian art, the revived **Greek city-states** saw a rich elaboration of intellectual life. Long-range commerce was aided by metal coinage (introduced by the Lydians in Asia Minor before 700 BC); colonies were founded around the Mediterranean and Black Sea shores (Cumae in Italy 760 BC, Massalia in France c600 BC).

Philosophy, starting with Ionian speculation on the nature of matter and the universe (Thales c634-546), and including mathematical speculation (Pythagoras c580-c500), culminated in Athens in the rationalist idealism of **Plato** (c428-347) and **Socrates** (c470-399); the latter was executed for alleged impiety. **Aristotle** (384-322) united all fields of study in his system. The arts were highly valued. Architecture culminated in the **Parthenon** in Athens (438, sculpture by Phidias); poetry and drama (Aeschylus 525-456) thrived. Male beauty and strength, a chief artistic theme, were enhanced at the gymnasium and celebrated at the national games at Olympia.

Ruled by local tyrants or oligarchies, the Greeks were never politically united, but managed to resist inclusion in the Persian Empire (Darius defeated at Marathon 490 BC, Xerxes at Salamis, Plataea 479 BC). Local warfare was common; the **Peloponnesian Wars**, 431-404 BC, ended in Sparta's victory over Athens. Greek political power waned, but classical Greek cultural forms spread thoughout the ancient world from the Atlantic to India.

**Hebrews.** Nomadic Hebrew tribes entered Canaan before 1200 BC, settling among other Semitic peoples speaking the same language. They brought from the desert a **monotheistic faith** said to have been revealed to Abraham in Canaan c1800 BC and to Moses at Mt. Sinai c1250 BC, after the Hebrews' escape from bondage in Egypt. David (ruled 1000-961 BC) and Solomon (ruled 961-922 BC) united the Hebrews in a kingdom that briefly dominated the area. Phoenicians to the north established colonies

(continued on p. 500)

1000 BC

*The following appear as vertical timeline labels in the left margin (top to bottom):*

Ebla civilization
Bronze-age Minoan civilization emerges on Crete
Egyptian literature begins
Peruvian neolithic ceremonial centers
Phonetic alphabet invented before 1600
1750 — Hammurabi
Aryans invade India
Chinese Shang dynasty
Mt. Sinai revelations to Moses
Mexican Olmec civilization established

# Paleontology: The History of Life

All dates are approximate, and are subject to change based on new fossil finds or new dating techniques; but the sequence of events is generally accepted. Dates are in years before the present.

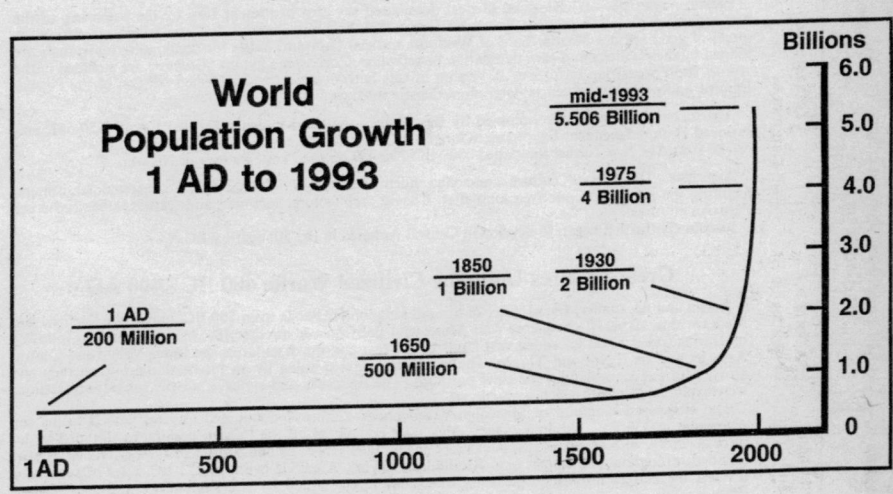

1000 BC

800

600

400 BC

*Chavin dynasty begins in Peru*

*Hebrew kingdom divided*

*Chou dynasty begins in China*

*Carthage established*

*Nubia begins rule of Egypt*

*Metal coins in Asia Minor*

*Isaiah d.*

*Zoroaster b.*

*Pythagoras b.*

*Indian Buddhism, Jainism begin*

*Confucius b.*

*Siddarta b.*

*Aeschylus b.*

*Socrates b.*

*Plato b.*

*Parthenon*

*Peloponnesian Wars*

around the E. and W. Mediterranean (**Carthage** c814 BC) and sailed into the Atlantic.

A temple in Jerusalem became the national religious center, with sacrifices performed by a hereditary priesthood. Polytheistic influences, especially of the fertility cult of Baal, were opposed by **prophets** (Elijah, Amos, Isaiah).

Divided into **two kingdoms** after Solomon, the Hebrews were unable to resist the revived Assyrian empire, which conquered Israel, the northern kingdom in 722 BC. Judah, the southern kingdom, was conquered in 586 BC by the Babylonians under Nebuchadnezzar II. But with the fixing of most of the Biblical canon by the mid-fourth century BC, and the emergence of rabbis, arbiters of law and custom, Judaism successfully survived the loss of Hebrew autonomy. A Jewish kingdom was revived under the Hasmoneans (168-42 BC).

**China.** During the **Eastern Chou** dynasty (770-256 BC), Chinese culture spread east to the sea and south to the Yangtze. Large feudal states on the periphery of the empire contended for pre-eminence, but continued to recognize the Son of Heaven (king), who retained a purely ritual role enriched with courtly music and dance. In the Age of Warring States (403-221 BC), when the first sections of the **Great Wall** were built, the Ch'in state in the West gained supremacy, and finally united all of China.

Iron tools entered China c500 BC, and casting techniques were advanced, aiding agriculture. Peasants owned their land, and owed civil and military service to nobles. Cities grew in number and size, though barter remained the chief trade medium.

Intellectual ferment among noble scribes and officials produced the Classical Age of Chinese literature and philosophy. **Confucius** (551-479 BC) urged a restoration of a supposedly harmonious social order of the past through proper conduct in accordance with one's station and through filial and ceremonial piety. The *Analects*, attributed to him, are revered throughout East Asia. Mencius (d. 289 BC) added the view that the Mandate of Heaven can be removed from an unjust dynasty. The Legalists sought to curb the supposed natural wickedness of people through new institutions and harsh laws; they aided the Ch'in rise to power. The Naturalists emphasized the balance of opposites — yin, yang — in the world. Taoists sought mystical knowledge through meditation and disengagement.

**India.** The political and cultural center of India shifted from the Indus to the Ganges River Valley. Buddhism, Jainism, and mystical revisions of orthodox Vedism all developed around 500-300 BC. The *Upanishads*, last part of the *Veda*, urged escape from the illusory physical world. Vedism remained the preserve of the priestly Brahmin caste. In contrast, **Buddhism**, founded by Siddarta Gautama (c563-c483 BC), appealed to merchants in the growing urban centers, and took hold at first (and most lastingly) on the geographic fringes of Indian civilization. The classic Indian epics were composed in this era: The *Ramayana* perhaps around 300 BC, the *Mahabharata* over a period starting 400 BC.

Northern India was divided into a large number of monarchies and aristocratic republics, probably derived from tribal groupings, when the Magadha kingdom was formed in Bihar c542 BC. It soon became the dominant power. The **Maurya dynasty**, founded by Chandragupta c321 BC, expanded the kingdom, uniting most of N. India in a centralized bureaucratic empire. The third Mauryan king, **Asoka** (ruled c274-236) conquered most of the subcontinent: he converted to Buddhism, and inscribed its tenets on pillars throughout India. He downplayed the caste system and tried to end expensive sacrificial rites.

Before its final decline in India, Buddhism developed the popular worship of heavenly Bodhisatvas (enlightened beings), and produced a refined architecture (stupa—shrine—at Sanchi 100 AD) and sculpture (Gandhara reliefs 1-400 AD).

**Persia.** Aryan peoples (Persians, Medes) dominated the area of present Iran by the beginning of the first millenium BC. The prophet **Zoroaster** (born c628 BC) introduced a dualistic religion in which forces of good (Ahura Mazda, Lord of Wisdom) and evil (Ahiram) battle for dominance; individuals are judged by their actions and earn damnation or salvation. Zoroaster's hymns (*Gathas*) are included in the *Avesta*, the Zoroastrian scriptures. A version of this faith became the established religion of the Persian Empire, and probably influenced later monotheistic religions.

**Africa.** Nubia, periodically occupied by Egypt since the third millenium BC, ruled Egypt c750-661, and survived as an independent Egyptianized kingdom (**Kush**; capital Meroe) for 1,000 years. The Iron Age Nok culture flourished c500 BC-200 AD on the Benue Plateau of Nigeria.

**Americas.** The Chavin culture controlled north Peru from 900-200 BC. Its ceremonial centers, featuring the jaguar god, survived long after. Chavin architecture, ceramics, and textiles influenced other Peruvian cultures.

**Mayan civilization** began to develop in Central America in the 5th century BC.

## Great Empires Unite the Civilized World: 400 BC - 400 AD

**Persia and Alexander.** Cyrus, ruler of a small kingdom in Persia from 559 BC, united the Persians and Medes within 10 years, conquered Asia Minor and Babylonia in another 10. His son Cambyses followed by Darius (ruled 522-486) added vast lands to the east and north as far as the Indus Valley and Central Asia, as well as Egypt and Thrace. The whole empire was ruled by an international bureaucracy and army, with Persians holding the chief positions. The resources and styles of all the subject civilizations were exploited to create a rich syncretic art.

The Hellenized kingdom of Macedon, which under Phillip II dominated Greece, passed to his son Alexander in 336 BC. Within 13 years, Alexander conquered all the Persian dominions. Imbued by his tutor Aristotle with Greek ideals, Alexander encouraged Greek colonization, and Greek-style cities were founded throughout the empire (e.g. Alexandria, Egypt). After his death in 323 BC, wars of succession divided the empire into three parts — **Macedon**, Egypt (ruled by the **Ptolemies**), and the **Seleucid** Empire.

In the ensuing 300 years (the **Hellenistic Era**), a cosmopolitan Greek-oriented culture permeated the ancient world from W. Europe to the borders of India, absorbing native elites everywhere.

Hellenistic philosophy stressed the private individual's search for happiness. The Cynics followed Diogenes (c372-287), who stressed satisfaction of animal needs and contempt for social convention. Zeno (c335-c263) and the Stoics exalted reason, identified it with virtue, and counseled an ascetic disregard for misfortune. The Epicureans tried to build lives of moderate pleasure without political or emotional

*(continued on p. 502)*

# The Seven Wonders of the World

These ancient works of art and architecture were considered awe-inspiring in splendor and/or size by the Greek and Roman world of the Alexandrian epoch and later. Classical writers disagreed as to which works made up the list of Wonders, but the following were usually included:

**The Pyramids of Egypt:** The only surviving Wonder, these monumental structures of masonry located on the west bank of the Nile River above Cairo were built from 3000 to 1800 B.C. as royal tombs. Three—Khufu, Khafra, and Menkaura—were often grouped as the first Wonder of the World. The largest, **The Great Pyramid of Khufu,** or Cheops, is a solid mass of limestone blocks covering 13 acres. It is estimated to contain 2.3 million blocks of stone, the stones themselves averaging 2½ tons and some weighing 30 tons. Its construction reputedly took 100,000 laborers 20 years.

**The Hanging Gardens of Babylon:** These gardens were laid out on a brick terrace about 400 feet square and 75 feet above the ground. To irrigate the trees, shrubs, and flowers, screws were turned to lift water from the Euphrates River. The gardens were probably built by King Nebuchadnezzar II around 600 B.C. **The Walls of Babylon,** long, thick, and made of colorfully glazed brick, were considered by some to be among the Seven Wonders.

**The Statue of Zeus (Jupiter) at Olympia:** This statue of the king of the gods showed him seated on a throne. His flesh was made of ivory, his robe and ornaments of gold. Reputedly 40 feet high, the statue was made by Phidias and was placed in the great temple of Zeus in the sacred grove of Olympia around 457 B.C.

**The Colossus of Rhodes:** A bronze statue of the sun god Helios, the Colossus was worked on for 12 years in the early 200's B.C. by the sculptor Chares. It was probably 120 feet high. A symbol of the city of Rhodes at its height, the statue stood on a promontory overlooking the harbor.

**The Temple of Artemis (Diana) at Ephesus:** This largest and most complex temple of ancient times was built around 550 B.C. and was made of marble except for its tile-covered wooden roof. It was begun in honor of a non-Hellenic goddess who later became identified with the Greek goddess of the same name. Ephesus was one of the greatest of the Ionian cities.

**The Mausoleum at Halicarnassus:** The source of our word "mausoleum," this marble tomb was built in what is now southeastern Turkey by Artemisia for her husband Mausolus, an official of the Persian Empire who died in 353 B.C. About 135 feet high, it was adorned with the works of 4 sculptors.

**The Pharos (Lighthouse) of Alexandria:** This sculpture was designed around 270 B.C., during the reign of King Ptolemy II, by the Greek architect Sostratos. Estimates of its height range from 200 to 600 feet.

Africa 1914

- [∴] British
- [▓] French
- [☐] German
- [▨] Belgian
- [∴] Italian
- [▒] Portuguese
- [▥] Spanish
- [▨] Independent

Timeline labels (left margin, top to bottom):

400 BC — Alexander becomes king; Aristotle b.; Mahabharata begun; Chinese Age of Warring States; Euclid's geometry

200 BC — Great Wall of China begun; 1st Roman slave revolt; Hannibal invades Italy; Punic Wars end; Julius Caesar b.; Hellenistic Era; Antony, Cleopatra defeated

1 AD — Julian calendar; Jesus d.; Mayan civilization begins in Guatemala; Roman Empire; Nero's persecution

200 AD

involvement. Hellenistic arts imitated life realistically, especially in sculpture and literature (comedies of Menander, 342-292).

The sciences thrived, especially at Alexandria, where the Ptolemies financed a great library and museum. Fields of study included mathematics (**Euclid's** geometry, c300 BC; Menelaus' non-Euclidean geometry, c100 AD); astronomy (heliocentric theory of Aristarchus, 310-230 BC; Julian calendar 45 BC; Ptolemy's *Almagest*, c150 AD); geography (world map of Eratosthenes, 276-194 BC); hydraulics (**Archimedes**, 287-212 BC); medicine (Galen, 130-200 AD); and chemistry. Inventors refined uses for siphons, valves, gears, springs, screws, levers, cams, and pulleys.

A restored Persian empire under the **Parthians** (N. Iranian tribesmen) controlled the eastern Hellenistic world 250 BC-229 AD. The Parthians and the succeeding Sassanian dynasty (229-651) fought with Rome periodically. The **Sassanians** revived Zoroastrianism as a state religion, and patronized a nationalistic artistic and scholarly renaissance.

**Rome.** The city of Rome was founded, according to legend, by Romulus in 753 BC. Through military expansion and colonization, and by granting citizenship to conquered tribes, the city annexed all of Italy south of the Po in the 100-year period before 268 BC. The Latin and other Italic tribes were annexed first, followed by the Etruscans (a civilized people north of Rome) and the Greek colonies in the south. With a large standing army and reserve forces of several hundred thousand, Rome was able to defeat Carthage in the 3 **Punic Wars**, 264-241, 218-201, 149-146 (despite the invasion of Italy by Hannibal, 218), thus gaining Sicily and territory in Spain and North Africa.

New provinces were added in the East, as Rome exploited local disputes to conquer Greece and Asia Minor in the 2d century BC, and Egypt in the first (after the defeat and suicide of **Antony and Cleopatra**, 30 BC). All the Mediterranean civilized world up to the disputed Parthian border was now Roman, and remained so for 500 years. Less civilized regions were added to the Empire: Gaul (conquered by Julius Caesar, 56-49 BC), Britain (43 AD) and Dacia NE of the Danube (117 AD).

The original aristocratic republican government, with democratic features added in the fifth and fourth centuries BC, deteriorated under the pressures of empire and class conflict (**Gracchus** brothers, social reformers, murdered 133, 121; slave revolts 135, 73). After a series of civil wars (Marius vs. Sulla 88-82, Caesar vs. Pompey 49-45, triumvirate vs. Caesar's assassins 44-43, Antony vs. Octavian 32-30), the empire came under the rule of a deified monarch (first emperor, **Augustus**, 27 BC-14 AD). Provincials (nearly all granted citizenship by Caracalla, 212 AD) came to dominate the army and civil service. Traditional Roman law, systematized and interpreted by independent jurists, and local self-rule in provincial cities were supplanted by a vast tax-collecting bureaucracy in the 3d and 4th centuries. The legal rights of women, children, and slaves were strengthened.

Roman innovations in **civil engineering** included water mills, windmills, and rotary mills, and the use of cement that hardened under water. Monumental architecture (baths, theaters, apartment houses) relied on the arch and the dome. The network of roads (some still standing) stretched 53,000 miles, passing through mountain tunnels as long as 3.5 miles. Aqueducts brought water to cities, underground sewers removed waste.

Roman art and literature were derivative of Greek models. Innovations were made in sculpture (naturalistic busts and equestrian statues), decorative wall painting (as at Pompeii), satire (Juvenal, 60-127), history (Tacitus, 56-120), prose romance (Petronius, d. 66 AD). Violence and torture dominated mass public amusements, which were supported by the state.

**India.** The Gupta monarchs reunited N. India c320 AD. Their peaceful and prosperous reign saw a revival of Hindu religious thought and Brahmin power. The old Vedic traditions were combined with devotion to a plethora of indigenous deities (who were seen as manifestations of Vedic gods). Caste lines were reinforced, and Buddhism gradually disappeared. The art (often erotic), architecture, and literature of the period, patronized by the Gupta court, are considered to be among India's finest achievements (Kalidasa, poet and dramatist, fl. c400). Mathematical innovations included the use of zero and decimal numbers. Invasions by White Huns from the NW destroyed the empire c550.

Rich cultures also developed in S. India in this era. Emotional Tamil religious poetry aided the Hindu revival. The Pallava kingdom controlled much of S. India c350-880, and helped spread Indian civilization to S.E. Asia.

**China.** The Ch'in ruler Shih Huang Ti (ruled 221-210 BC), known as the First Emperor, centralized political authority in China, standardized the written language, laws, weights, measures, and coinage, and conducted a census, but tried to destroy most philosophical texts. The **Han dynasty** (206 BC-220 AD) instituted the Mandarin bureaucracy, which lasted for 2,000 years. Local officials were selected by examination in the Confucian classics and trained at the imperial university and at provincial schools. The invention of **paper** facilitated this bureaucratic system. Agriculture was promoted, but the peasants bore most of the tax burden. Irrigation was improved; water clocks and sundials were used; astronomy and mathematics thrived; landscape painting was perfected.

With the expansion south and west (to nearly the present borders of today's China), trade was opened with India, S.E. Asia, and the Middle East, over sea and caravan routes. Indian missionaries brought Mahayana Buddhism to China by the first century AD, and spawned a variety of sects. Taoism was revived, and merged with popular superstitions. Taoist and Buddhist monasteries and convents multiplied in the turbulent centuries after the collapse of the Han dynasty.

## Monotheism Emerges: 1-750 AD

**Christianity.** Religions indigenous to particular Middle Eastern nations became international in the first 3 centuries of the Roman Empire. Roman citizens worshipped Isis of Egypt, **Mithras** of Persia, **Demeter** of Greece, and the great mother **Cybele** of Phrygia. Their cults centered on mysteries (secret ceremonies) and the promise of an afterlife, symbolized by the death and rebirth of the god. Judaism, which had begun as the national cult of Judea, also spread by emigration and conversion. It was the only ancient religion west of India to survive.

Christians, who emerged as a distinct sect in the second half of the 1st century AD, revered **Jesus**, a Jewish preacher killed by the Romans at the request of Jewish authorities in Jerusalem c30 AD. They considered him the Savior (Messiah, or Christ) who rose from the dead and could grant eternal life to the faithful, despite their sinfulness. They believed he was an incarnation of the one god worshipped by the Jews, and that he would return soon to pass final judgment on the world. The missionary activities of such early leaders as **Paul of Tarsus** spread the faith, at first mostly among Jews or among quasi-Jews attracted by the Pauline rejection of such difficult Jewish laws as circumcision. Intermittent persecution, as in Rome under **Nero** in 64 AD, on grounds of suspected disloyalty, failed to disrupt the Christian communities. Each congregation, generally urban and of plebeian character, was tightly organized under a leader (bishop), elders (presbyters or priests), and assistants (deacons). Stories about Jesus (the Gospels) and the early church (Acts) were written down in the late first and early 2d centuries, and circulated along with letters of Paul. An authoritative canon of these writings was not fixed until the 4th century.

A school for priests was established at Alexandria in the second century. Its teachers (**Origen** c182-251) helped define Christian doctrine and promote the faith in Greek-style philosophical works. Pagan Neoplatonism was given Christian coloration in the works of Church Fathers such as Augustine (354-430). Christian hermits, often drawn from the lower classes, began to associate in monasteries, first in Egypt (St. Pachomius c290-345), then in other eastern lands, then in the West (**St. Benedict's rule,** 529). Popular devotion to saints, especially Mary, mother of Jesus, spread.

Under **Constantine** (ruled 306-337), Christianity became in effect the established religion of the Empire. Pagan temples were expropriated, state funds were used to build huge churches and support the hierarchy, and laws were adjusted in accordance with Christian notions. Pagan worship was banned by the end of the fourth century, and severe restrictions were placed on Judaism.

The newly established church was rocked by doctrinal disputes, often exacerbated by regional rivalries both within and outside the Empire. Chief heresies (as defined by church councils backed by imperial authority) were **Arianism,** which denied the divinity of Jesus; **Donatism,** which rejected the convergence of church and state and denied the validity of sacraments performed by sinful clergy; and the **Monophysite** position denying the dual nature of Christ.

**Judaism.** First century Judaism embraced several sects, including: the **Sadducees,** mostly drawn from the Temple priesthood, who were culturally Hellenized; the **Pharisees,** who upheld the full range of traditional customs and practices as of equal weight to literal scriptural law, and elaborated synagogue worship; and the **Essenes,** an ascetic, millenarian sect. Messianic fervor led to repeated, unsuccessful rebellions against Rome (66-70, 135). As a result, the Temple was destroyed, and the population decimated.

To avoid the dissolution of the faith, a program of codification of law was begun at the academy of Yavneh. The work continued for some 500 years in Palestine and Babylonia, ending in the final redaction of the **Talmud** (c600), a huge collection of legal and moral debates, rulings, liturgy, Biblical exegesis, and legendary materials.

**Islam.** The earliest Arab civilization emerged by the end of the 2d millenium BC in the watered highlands of Yemen. Seaborne and caravan trade in frankincense and myrrh connected the area with the Nile and Fertile Crescent. The Minaean, Sabean (Sheba), and Himyarite states successively held sway. By Mohammed's time (7th century AD), the region was a province of Sassanian Persia. In the North, the **Nabataean kingdom** at Petra and the kingdom of Palmyra were first Aramaicized and then Romanized, and finally absorbed like neighboring Judea into the Roman Empire. Nomads shared the central region with a few trading towns and oases. Wars between tribes and raids on settled communities were common, and were celebrated in a poetic tradition that by the 6th century helped establish a classic literary Arabic.

In 611 **Mohammed,** a 40-year-old Arab of Mecca, announced a revelation from the one true God, calling on him to repudiate pagan idolatry. Drawing on elements of Judaism and Christianity, and eventually incorporating some Arab pagan traditions (such as reverence for the black stone at the kaaba shrine in Mecca), Mohammed's teachings, recorded in the **Koran,** forged a new religion, Islam (submission to Allah). Opposed by the leaders of Mecca, Mohammed made a *hejira* (migration) to Medina to the north in 622, the beginning of the Moslem lunar calendar. He and his followers defeated the Meccans in 624 in the first *jihad* (holy war), and by his death (632), nearly all the Arabian peninsula accepted his religious and secular leadership.

Under the first two **caliphs** (successors), Abu Bakr (632-34) and Omar (634-44), Moslem rule was confirmed over Arabia. Raiding parties into Byzantine and Persian border areas developed into campaigns of conquest against the two empires, which had been weakened by wars and by disaffection among subject peoples (including Coptic and Syriac Christians opposed to the Byzantine orthodox church). Syria, Palestine, Egypt, Iraq, and Persia all fell to the inspired Arab armies. The Arabs at first remained a distinct minority, using non-Moslems in the new administrative system, and tolerating Christians, Jews, and Zoroastrians as self-governing "Peoples of the Book," whose taxes supported the empire.

Disputes over the succession, and puritan reaction to the wealth and refinement that empire brought to the ruling strata, led to the growth of schismatic movements. The followers of Mohammed's son-in-law Ali (assassinated 661) and his descendants became the founders of the more mystical **Shi'ite** sect, still the largest non-orthodox Moslem sect. The **Karijites,** puritanical, militant, and egalitarian, persist as a minor sect to the present.

Under the **Omayyad** caliphs (661-750), the boundaries of Islam were extended across N. Africa and into Spain. Arab armies in the West were stopped at Tours in 732 by the Frank **Charles Martel.** Asia Minor, the Indus Valley, and Transoxiana were conquered in the East. The vast majority of the subject population gradually converted to Islam, encouraged by tax and career privileges. The Arab language supplanted the local tongues in the central and western areas, but Arab soldiers and rulers in the East eventually became assimilated to the indigenous languages.

## New Peoples Enter History: 400-900

**Barbarian invasions.** Germanic tribes infiltrated S and E from their Baltic homeland during the 1st millenium BC, reaching S. Germany by 100 BC and the Black Sea by 214 AD. Organized into large federated tribes under elected kings, most resisted Roman domination and raided the empire in time of civil war (Goths took Dacia 214, raided Thrace 251-269). German troops and commanders came to dominate the Roman armies by the end of the 4th century. **Huns,** invaders from Asia, entered Europe 372, driving more Germans into the western empire. Emperor Valens allowed Visigoths to cross

200 AD

African Axum kingdom expands

1st Christian monastery

Constantinople founded

Augustine b.

Japan united

350

Ghana begins rule

Gupta Empire in India

Huns in Europe

W. Roman Empire ends

Patrick converts Ireland

500

Justinian code
Benedict founds monastery

Clovis unites Franks

Sui dynasty begins

Mohammed's life

Tang dynasty
Talmud
completed

650 AD

650

Greek replaces Latin in Byzantium

Slav-Turk Bulgarian Empire begins

Chinese poet Li Po b.

Nara period begins, Japan

750

Baghdad founded

Charlemagne rules

Viking explorations, raids

850

Arab-Moslem golden age

Vietnam independent

950

the Danube 376. Huns under Attila (d. 453) raided Gaul, Italy, Balkans. The western empire, weakened by overtaxation and social stagnation, was overrun in the 5th century. Gaul was effectively lost 406-7, Spain 409, Britain 410, Africa 429-39. Rome was sacked 410 by Visigoths under Alaric, 455 by Vandals. The last western emperor, Romulus Augustulus, was deposed 476 by the Germanic chief Odoacer.

**Celts.** Celtic cultures, which in pre-Roman times covered most of W. Europe, were confined almost entirely to the British Isles after the Germanic invasions. **St. Patrick** completed the conversion of Ireland (c457-92). A strong monastic tradition took hold. Irish monastic missionaries in Scotland, England, and the continent (Columba c521-597; Columban c543-615) helped restore Christianity after the Germanic invasions. The monasteries became renowned centers of classic and Christian learning, and presided over the recording of a Christianized Celtic mythology, elaborated by secular writers and bards. An intricate decorative art style developed, especially in book illumination (Lindisfarne Gospels, c700, Book of Kells, 8th century).

**Successor states.** The Visigoth kingdom in Spain (from 419) and much of France (to 507) saw a continuation of much Roman administration, language, and law (Breviary of Alaric 506), until its destruction by the Moslems, 711. The Vandal kingdom in Africa, from 429, was conquered by the Byzantines, 533. Italy was ruled in succession by an Ostrogothic kingdom under Byzantine suzerainty 489-554, direct Byzantine government, and the German Lombards (568-774). The latter divided the peninsula with the Byzantines and the papacy under the dynamic reformer Pope Gregory the Great (590-604) and his successors.

King **Clovis** (ruled 481-511) united the Franks on both sides of the Rhine, and after his conversion to orthodox Christianity, defeated the Arian Burgundians (after 500) and Visigoths (507) with the support of the native clergy and the papacy. Under the **Merovingian** kings a feudal system emerged: power was fragmented among hierarchies of military landowners. Social stratification, which in late Roman times had acquired legal, hereditary sanction, was reinforced. The Carolingians (747-987) expanded the kingdom and restored central power. **Charlemagne** (ruled 768-814) conquered nearly all the Germanic lands, including Lombard Italy, and was crowned Emperor by Pope Leo III in Rome in 800. A centuries-long decline in commerce and the arts was reversed under Charlemagne's patronage. He welcomed Jews to his kingdom, which became a center of Jewish learning (Rashi 1040-1105). He sponsored the "Carolingian Renaissance" of learning under the Anglo-Latin scholar Alcuin (c732-804), who reformed church liturgy.

**Byzantine Empire.** Under Diocletian (ruled 284-305) the empire had been divided into 2 parts to facilitate administration and defense. Constantine founded **Constantinople**, 330, (at old Byzantium) as a fully Christian city. Commerce and taxation financed a sumptuous, orientalized court, a class of hereditary bureaucratic families, and magnificent urban construction (Hagia Sophia, 532-37). The city's fortifications and naval innovations (Greek fire) repelled assaults by Goths, Huns, Slavs, Bulgars, Avars, Arabs, and Scandinavians. Greek replaced Latin as the official language by c700. Byzantine art, a solemn, sacral, and stylized variation of late classical styles (mosaics at S. Vitale, Ravenna, 526-48) was a starting point for medieval art in E. and W. Europe.

**Justinian** (ruled 527-65) reconquered parts of Spain, N. Africa, and Italy, codified Roman law (*codex Justinianus*, 529, was medieval Europe's chief legal text), closed the Platonic Academy at Athens and ordered all pagans to convert. Lombards in Italy, Arabs in Africa retook most of his conquests. The Isaurian dynasty from Anatolia (from 717) and the Macedonian dynasty (867-1054) restored military and commercial power. The Iconoclast controversy (726-843) over the permissibility of images, helped alienate the Eastern Church from the papacy.

**Arab Empire. Baghdad**, founded 762, became the seat of the **Abbasid** Caliphate (founded 750), while Ummayads continued to rule in Spain. A brilliant cosmopolitan civilization emerged, inaugurating an Arab-Moslem golden age. Arab lyric poetry revived; Greek, Syriac, Persian, and Sanskrit books were translated into Arabic, often by Syriac Christians and Jews, whose theology and Talmudic law, respectively, influenced Islam. The arts and music flourished at the court of **Harun al-Rashid** (786-809), celebrated in *The Arabian Nights*. The sciences, medicine, and mathematics were pursued at Baghdad, Cordova, and Cairo (founded 969). Science and Aristotelian philosophy culminated in the systems of Avicenna (980-1037), Averroes (1126-98), and Maimonides (1135-1204), a Jew; all influenced later Christian scholarship and theology. The Islamic ban on images encouraged a sinuous, geometric decorative tradition, applied to architecture and illumination. A gradual loss of Arab control in Persia (from 874) led to the capture of Baghdad by Persians, 945. By the next century, Spain and N. Africa were ruled by Berbers, while Turks prevailed in Asia Minor and the Levant. The loss of political power by the caliphs allowed for the growth of non-orthodox trends, especially the mystical **Sufi** tradition (theologian Ghazali, 1058-1111).

**Africa.** Immigrants from Saba in S. Arabia helped set up the **Axum** kingdom in Ethiopia in the 2d century (their language, Ge'ez, is preserved by the Ethiopian Church). In the 4th century, when the kingdom became Christianized, it defeated Kushite Meroe and expanded into Yemen. Axum was the center of a vast ivory trade; it controlled the Red Sea coast until c1100. Arab conquest in Egypt cut Axum's political and economic ties with Byzantium.

The Iron Age entered W. Africa by the end of the 1st millenium BC. **Ghana**, the first known sub-Saharan state, ruled in the upper Senegal-Niger region c400-1240, controlling the trade of gold from mines in the S to trans-Sahara caravan routes to the N. The **Bantu** peoples, probably of W. African origin, began to spread E and S perhaps 2000 years ago, displacing the Pygmies and Bushmen of central and southern Africa over a 1,500-year period.

**Japan.** The advanced Neolithic Yayoi period, when irrigation, rice farming, and iron and bronze casting techniques were introduced from China or Korea, persisted to c400 AD. The myriad Japanese states were then united by the **Yamato** clan, under an emperor who acted as the chief priest of the animistic **Shinto** cult. Japanese political and military intervention in Korea by the 6th century quickened a Chinese cultural invasion, bringing Buddhism, the Chinese language (which long remained a literary and governmental medium), Chinese ideographs and Buddhist styles in painting, sculpture, literature, and architecture (7th c. Horyu-ji temple at Nara). The Taika Reforms, 646, tried to centralize Japan according to Chinese bureaucratic and Buddhist philosophical values, but failed to curb traditional Japanese decentralization. A nativist reaction against the Buddhist **Nara period** (710-94) ushered in the

**Heian period** (794-1185) centered at the new capital, Kyoto. Japanese elegance and simplicity modified Chinese styles in architecture, scroll painting, and literature; the writing system was also simplified. The courtly novel *Tale of Genji* (1010-20) testifies to the enhanced role of women.

**Southeast Asia.** The historic peoples of southeast Asia began arriving some 2500 years ago from China and Tibet, displacing scattered aborigines. Their agriculture relied on rice and tubers (yams), which they may have introduced to Africa. Indian cultural influences were strongest; literacy and Hindu and Buddhist ideas followed the southern India-China trade route. From the southern tip of Indochina, the kingdom of **Funan** (1st-7th centuries) traded as far west as Persia. It was absorbed by Chenla, itself conquered by the **Khmer** Empire (600-1300). The Khmers, under Hindu god-kings (Suryavarman II, 1113-c1150), built the monumental Angkor Wat temple center for the royal phallic cult. The **Nam-Viet** kingdom in Annam, dominated by China and Chinese culture for 1,000 years, emerged in the 10th century, growing at the expense of the Khmers, who also lost ground in the NW to the new, highly-organized **Thai** kingdom. On Sumatra, the **Srivijaya** Empire at Palembang controlled vital sea lanes (7th to 10th centuries). A Buddhist dynasty, the Sailendras, ruled central **Java** (8th-9th centuries), building at Borobudur one of the largest stupas in the world.

**China.** The short-lived Sui dynasty (581-618) ushered in a period of commercial, artistic, and scientific achievement in China, continuing under the **T'ang** dynasty (618-906). Such inventions as the magnetic compass, gunpowder, the abacus, and printing were introduced or perfected. Medical innovations included cataract surgery. The state, from the cosmopolitan capital, Ch'ang-an, supervised foreign trade, which exchanged Chinese silks, porcelains, and art works for spices, ivory, etc., over Central Asian caravan routes and sea routes reaching Africa. A golden age of poetry bequeathed tens of thousands of works to later generations (Tu Fu 712-70, Li Po 701-62). Landscape painting flourished. Commercial and industrial expansion continued under the **Northern Sung** dynasty (960-1126), facilitated by paper money and credit notes. But commerce never achieved respectability; government monopolies expropriated successful merchants. The population, long stable at 50 million, doubled in 200 years with the introduction of early-ripening rice and the double harvest. In art, native Chinese styles were revived.

**Americas.** A Native American empire stretched from the Valley of Mexico to Guatemala, 300-600, centering on the huge city **Teotihuacan** (founded 100 BC). To the S, in Guatemala, a high **Mayan** civilization developed, 150-900, around hundreds of rural ceremonial centers. The Mayans improved on Olmec writing and the calendar, and pursued astronomy and mathematics (using the idea of zero). In S. America, a widespread pre-Inca culture grew from **Tiahuanaco** near Lake Titicaca (Gateway of the Sun, c700).

## Christian Europe Regroups and Expands: 900-1300

**Scandinavians.** Pagan Danish and Norse (**Viking**) adventurers, traders, and pirates raided the coasts of the British Isles (Dublin founded c831), France, and even the Mediterranean for over 200 years beginning in the late 8th century. Inland settlement in the W was limited to Great Britain (King Canute, 994-1035) and **Normandy**, settled under Rollo, 911, as a fief of France. Other Vikings reached Iceland (874), Greenland (c986), and N. America (Leif Eriksson c1000). Norse traders (**Varangians**) developed Russian river commerce from the 8th-11th centuries, and helped set up a state at Kiev in the late 9th century. Conversion to Christianity occurred during the 10th century, reaching Sweden 100 years later. Eleventh century Norman bands conquered S. Italy and Sicily. Duke **William of Normandy** conquered England, 1066, bringing continental feudalism and the French language, essential elements in later English civilization.

**East Europe.** Slavs inhabited areas of E. Central Europe in prehistoric times, and reached most of their present limits by c850. The first Slavic states were in the Balkans (Slav-Turk **Bulgarian** Empire, 680-1018) and Moravia (628). Missions of St. Cyril (whose Greek-based Cyrillic alphabet is still used by S. and E. Slavs) converted Moravia, 863. The Eastern Slavs, part-civilized under the overlordship of the Turkish-Jewish **Khazar** trading empire (7th-10th centuries), gravitated toward Constantinople by the 9th century. The **Kievan** state adopted Eastern Christianity under Prince Vladimir, 989. King Boleslav I (992-1025) began **Poland's** long history of eastern conquest. The Magyars (**Hungarians**), in present-day Hungary since 896, accepted Latin Christianity, 1001.

**Germany.** The German kingdom that emerged after the breakup of Charlemagne's Empire remained a confederation of largely autonomous states. The Saxon Otto I, king from 936, established the **Holy Roman Empire** of Germany and Italy in alliance with Pope John XII, who crowned him emperor, 962; he defeated the Magyars, 955. Imperial power was greatest under the **Hohenstaufens** (1138-1254), despite the growing opposition of the papacy, which ruled central Italy, and the Lombard League cities. **Frederick II** (1194-1250) improved administration, patronized the arts; after his death German influence was removed from Italy.

**Christian Spain.** From its northern mountain redoubts, Christian rule slowly migrated south through the 11th century, when Moslem unity collapsed. After the capture of **Toledo** (1085), the kingdoms of Portugal, Castile, and Aragon undertook repeated crusades of reconquest, finally completed in 1492. Elements of Islamic civilization persisted in recaptured areas, influencing all W. Europe.

**Crusades.** Pope Urban II called, 1095, for a crusade to restore Asia Minor to Byzantium and conquer the Holy Land from the Turks. Some 10 crusades (to 1291) succeeded only in founding 4 temporary Frankish states in the Levant. The 4th crusade sacked **Constantinople**, 1204. In Rhineland (1096), England (1290), France (1306), Jews were massacred or expelled, and wars were launched against Christian heretics (**Albigensian** crusade in France, 1229). Trade in eastern luxuries expanded, led by the Venetian naval empire.

**Economy.** The agricultural base of European life benefitted from improvements in **plow** design c1000, and by draining of lowlands and clearing of forests, leading to a rural population increase. Towns grew in N. Italy, Flanders, and N. Germany (**Hanseatic League**). Improvements in **loom** design permitted factory textile production. **Guilds** dominated urban trades from the 12th century. Banking (centered in Italy, 12th-15th century) facilitated long-distance trade.

**The Church.** The split between the Eastern and Western churches was formalized in 1054. W. and

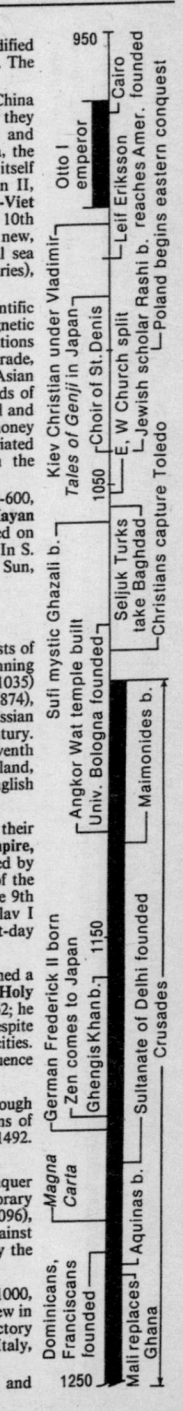

950 — Otto I emperor
— Cairo founded
— Kiev Christian under Vladimir
— Leif Eriksson reaches Amer.
— Tales of Genji in Japan
— Choir of St. Denis
— E. W Church split
— Jewish scholar Rashi b.
— Poland begins eastern conquest
1050 — Seljuk Turks take Baghdad
— Christians capture Toledo
— Sufi mystic Ghazali b.
— Angkor Wat temple built
— Univ. Bologna founded
— Maimonides b.
1150 — German Frederick II born
— Zen comes to Japan
— Ghengis Khan b.
— Sultanate of Delhi founded
— Crusades
— Magna Carta
— Aquinas b.
— Dominicans, Franciscans founded
— Mali replaces Ghana
1250

Central Europe was divided into 500 bishoprics under one united hierarchy, but conflicts between secular and church authorities were frequent (German **Investiture Controversy**, 1075-1122). Clerical power was first strengthened through the international monastic reform begun at Cluny, 910. Popular religious enthusiasm often expressed itself in heretical movements (Waldensians from 1173), but was channelled by the **Dominican** (1215) and **Franciscan** (1223) friars into the religious mainstream.

**Arts.** **Romanesque** architecture (11th-12th centuries) expanded on late Roman models, using the rounded arch and massed stone to support enlarged basilicas. Painting and sculpture followed Byzantine models. The literature of **chivalry** was exemplified by the epic (Chanson de Roland, c1100) and by courtly love poems of the troubadours of Provence and minnesingers of Germany. **Gothic architecture** emerged in France (choir of St. Denis, c1040) and spread as French cultural influence predominated in Europe. Rib vaulting and pointed arches were used to combine soaring heights with delicacy, and freed walls for display of stained glass. Exteriors were covered with painted relief sculpture and elaborate architectural detail.

**Learning.** Law, medicine, and philosophy were advanced at independent **universities** (Bologna, late 11th century), originally corporations of students and masters. Twelfth century translations of Greek classics, especially Aristotle, encouraged an analytic approach. Scholastic philosophy, from Anselm (1033-1109) to Aquinas (1225-74) attempted to reconcile reason and revelation.

## Apogee of Central Asian Power; Islam Grows: 1250-1500

**Turks.** Turkic peoples, of Central Asian ancestry, were a military threat to the Byzantine and Persian Empires from the 6th century. After several waves of invasions, during which most of the Turks adopted Islam, the **Seljuk Turks** took Baghdad, 1055. They ruled Persia, Iraq, and, after 1071, Asia Minor, where massive numbers of Turks settled. The empire was divided in the 12th century into smaller states ruled by Seljuks, Kurds (**Saladin** c1137-93), and Mamelukes (a military caste of former Turk, Kurd, and Circassian slaves), which governed Egypt and the Middle East until the Ottoman era (c1290-1922).

Osman I (ruled c1290-1326) and succeeding sultans united Anatolian Turkish warriors in a militaristic state that waged holy war against Byzantine and Balkan Christians. Most of the Balkans had been subdued, and Anatolia united, when **Constantinople fell**, 1453. By the mid-16th century, Hungary, the Middle East, and North Africa had been conquered. The Turkish advance was stopped at Vienna, 1529, and at the naval battle of Lepanto, 1571, by Spain, Venice, and the papacy.

**The Ottoman state** was governed in accordance with orthodox Moslem law. Greek, Armenian, and Jewish communities were segregated, and ruled by religious leaders responsible for taxation; they dominated trade. State offices and most army ranks were filled by slaves through a system of child conscription among Christians.

**India.** Mahmud of Ghazni (971-1030) led repeated Turkish raids into N. India. Turkish power was consolidated in 1206 with the start of the **Sultanate at Delhi**. Centralization of state power under the early Delhi sultans went far beyond traditional Indian practice. Moslem rule of most of the subcontinent lasted until the British conquest some 600 years later.

**Mongols.** Genghis Khan (c1162-1227) first united the feuding Mongol tribes, and built their armies into an effective offensive force around a core of highly mobile cavalry. He and his immediate successors created the largest land empire in history; by 1279 it stretched from the east coast of Asia to the Danube, from the Siberian steppes to the Arabian Sea. East-West trade and contacts were facilitated (Marco Polo c1254-1324). The western Mongols were Islamized by 1295; successor states soon lost their Mongol character by assimilation. They were briefly reunited under the Turk Tamerlane (1336-1405).

Kublai Khan ruled China from his new capital Peking (founded 1264). Naval campaigns against Japan (1274, 1281) and Java (1293) were defeated, the latter by the Hindu-Buddhist maritime kingdom of Majapahit. The Yuan dynasty made use of Mongols and other foreigners (including Europeans) in official posts, and tolerated the return of Nestorian Christianity (suppressed 841-45) and the spread of Islam in the South and West. A native reaction expelled the Mongols, 1367-68.

**Russia.** The Kievan state in Russia, weakened by the decline of Byzantium and the rise of the Catholic Polish-Lithuanian state, was overrun by the Mongols, 1238-40. Only the northern trading republic of Novgorod remained independent. The grand dukes of Moscow emerged as leaders of a coalition of princes that eventually defeated the Mongols, by 1481. With the fall of Constantinople, the **Tsars** (Caesars) at Moscow (from Ivan III, ruled 1462-1505) set up an independent Russian Orthodox Church. Commerce failed to revive. The isolated Russian state remained agrarian, with the peasant class falling into serfdom.

**Persia.** A revival of Persian literature, using the Arab alphabet and literary forms, began in the 10th century (epic of Firdausi, 935-1020). An art revival, influenced by Chinese styles, began in the 12th. Persian cultural and political forms, and often the Persian language, were used for centuries by Turkish and Mongol elites from the Balkans to India. Persian mystics from Rumi (1207-73) to Jami (1414-92) promoted Sufism in their poetry.

**Africa.** Two militant Islamic Berber dynasties emerged from the Sahara to carve out empires from the Sahel to central Spain — the Almoravids, c1050-1140, and the fanatical Almohads, c1125-1269. The Ghanaian empire was replaced in the upper Niger by Mali, c1230-c1340, whose Moslem rulers imported Egyptians to help make Timbuktu a center of commerce (in gold, leather, slaves) and learning. The Songhay empire (to 1590) replaced Mali. To the S, forest kingdoms produced refined art works (Ife terra cotta, Benin bronzes). Other Moslem states in Nigeria (Hausas) and Chad originated in the 11th century, and continued in some form until the 19th century European conquest. Less developed Bantu kingdoms existed across central Africa.

Some 40 Moslem Arab-Persian trading colonies and city-states were established all along the E. African coast from the 10th century (Kilwa, Mogadishu). The interchange with Bantu peoples produced the Swahili language and culture. Gold, palm oil, and slaves were brought from the interior, stimulating the growth of the Monamatapa kingdom of the Zambezi (15th century). The Christian Ethiopian empire (from 13th century) continued the traditions of Axum.

**Southeast Asia.** Islam was introduced into Malaya and the Indonesian islands by Arab, Persian, and

Indian traders. Coastal Moslem cities and states (starting before 1300), enriched by trade, soon dominated the interior. Chief among these was the **Malacca** state, on the Malay peninsula, c1400-1511.

## Arts and Statecraft Thrive in Europe: 1350-1600

**Italian Renaissance & humanism.** Distinctive Italian achievements in the arts in the late Middle Ages (Dante, 1265-1321, Giotto, 1276-1337) led to the vigorous new styles of the Renaissance (14th-16th centuries). Patronized by the rulers of the quarreling petty states of Italy (Medicis in Florence and the papacy, c1400-1737), the plastic arts perfected realistic techniques, including **perspective** (Masaccio, 1401-28, Leonardo 1452-1519). Classical motifs were used in architecture and increased talent and expense were put into secular buildings. The Florentine dialect was refined as a national literary language (Petrarch, 1304-74). Greek refugees from the E strengthened the respect of humanist scholars for the classic sources (Bruni 1370-1444). Soon an international movement aided by the spread of **printing** (Gutenberg c1400-1468), **humanism** was optimistic about the power of human reason (Erasmus of Rotterdam, 1466-1536, Thomas More's *Utopia*, 1516) and valued individual effort in the arts and in politics (Machiavelli, 1469-1527).

**France.** The French monarchy, strengthened in its repeated struggles with powerful nobles (Burgundy, Flanders, Aquitaine) by alliances with the growing commercial towns, consolidated bureaucratic control under Philip IV (ruled 1285-1314) and extended French influence into Germany and Italy (popes at Avignon, France, 1309-1417). The **Hundred Years War**, 1337-1453, ended English dynastic claims in France (battles of Crécy, 1346, Poitiers, 1356; Joan of Arc executed, 1431). A French Renaissance, dating from royal invasions of Italy, 1494, 1499, was encouraged at the court of Francis I (ruled 1515-47), who centralized taxation and law. French vernacular literature consciously asserted its independence (La Pleiade, 1549).

**England.** The evolution of England's unique political institutions began with the Magna Carta, 1215, by which King John guaranteed the privileges of nobles and church against the monarchy and assured jury trial. After the Wars of the Roses (1455-85), the **Tudor dynasty** reasserted royal prerogatives (Henry VIII, ruled 1509-47), but the trend toward independent departments and ministerial government also continued. English trade (wool exports from c1340) was protected by the nation's growing maritime power (**Spanish Armada** destroyed, 1588).

English replaced French and Latin in the late 14th century in law and literature (Chaucer, 1340-1400) and English translation of the Bible began (Wycliffe, 1380s). Elizabeth I (ruled 1558-1603) presided over a confident flowering of poetry (Spenser, 1552-99), drama (Shakespeare, 1564-1616), and music.

**German Empire.** From among a welter of minor feudal states, church lands, and independent cities, the Hapsburgs assembled a far-flung territorial domain, based in Austria from 1276. The family held the title Holy Roman Emperor from 1452 to the Empire's dissolution in 1806, but failed to centralize its domains, leaving Germany disunited for centuries. Resistance to Turkish expansion brought Hungary under Austrian control from the 16th century. The Netherlands, Luxembourg, and Burgundy were added in 1477, curbing French expansion.

The Flemish painting tradition of naturalism, technical proficiency, and bourgeois subject matter began in the 15th century (Jan Van Eyck, 1366-1440), the earliest northern manifestation of the Renaissance. Dürer (1471-1528) typified the merging of late Gothic and Italian trends in 16th century German art. Imposing civic architecture flourished in the prosperous commercial cities.

**Spain.** Despite the unification of Castile and Aragon in 1479, the 2 countries retained separate governments, and the nobility, especially in Aragon and Catalonia, retained many privileges. Spanish lands in Italy (Naples, Sicily) and the Netherlands entangled the country in European wars through the mid-17th century, while explorers, traders, and conquerors built up a Spanish empire in the Americas and the Philippines.

From the late 15th century, a **golden age** of literature and art produced works of social satire (plays of Lope de Vega, 1562-1635; Cervantes, 1547-1616), as well as spiritual intensity (El Greco, 1541-1614; Velazquez, 1599-1660).

**Black Death.** The bubonic plague reached Europe from the E in 1348, killing as much as half the population by 1350. Labor scarcity forced a rise in wages and brought greater freedom to the peasantry, making possible **peasant uprisings** (Jacquerie in France, 1358, Wat Tyler's rebellion in England, 1381). In the *ciompi* revolt, 1378, Florentine wage earners demanded a say in economic and political power.

**Explorations.** Organized European maritime exploration began, seeking to evade the Venice-Ottoman monopoly of eastern trade and to promote Christianity. Expeditions from Portugal beginning 1418 explored the west coast of Africa, until Vasco da Gama rounded the Cape of Good Hope in 1497 and reached India. A Portuguese trading empire was consolidated by the seizure of Goa, 1510, and Malacca, 1551. Japan was reached in 1542. Spanish voyages (**Columbus**, 1492-1504) uncovered a new world, which Spain hastened to subdue. Navigation schools in Spain and Portugal, the development of large sailing ships (carracks), and the invention of the rifle, c1475, aided European penetration.

**Mughals and Safavids.** East of the Ottoman empire, two Moslem dynasties ruled unchallenged in the 16th and 17th centuries. The Mughal empire in India, founded by Persianized Turkish invaders from the NW under Babur, dates from their 1526 conquest of Delhi. The dynasty ruled most of India for over 200 years, surviving nominally until 1857. **Akbar** (ruled 1556-1605) consolidated administration at his glorious court, where Urdu (Persian-influenced Hindi) developed. Trade relations with Europe increased. Under Shah Jahan (1629-58), a secularized art fusing Hindu and Moslem elements flourished in miniature painting and in architecture (**Taj Mahal**). Sikhism, founded c1519, combined elements of both faiths. Suppression of Hindus and Shi'ite Moslems in S India in the late 17th century weakened the empire.

Fanatical devotion to the Shi'ite sect characterized the Safavids of Persia, 1502-1736, and led to hostilities with the Sunni Ottomans for over a century. The prosperity and strength of the empire are evidenced by the mosques at its capital, **Isfahan**. The dynasty enhanced Iranian national consciousness.

**China.** The Ming emperors, 1368-1644, the last native dynasty in China, wielded unprecedented personal power, while the Confucian bureaucracy began to suffer from inertia. European trade (Portuguese

1500

Brazil discovered

Calvin b.

Vesalius b.

Watch invented

St. Theresa of Avila b.

Persian Safavids rule

Luther's 95 Theses

Cortes conquers Aztecs

Mughal empire starts

So. Ger. peasants rise

Pizarro conquers Incas

Jesuits founded

Council of Trent

1550

Dutch republic founded

Velazquez b.

Japan persecutes Christians

Civil War in France

Descartes b.

1600

monopoly through **Macao** from 1557) was strictly controlled. Jesuit scholars and scientists (Matteo Ricci 1552-1610) introduced some Western science; their writings familiarized the West with China. Chinese technological inventiveness declined from this era, but the arts thrived, especially painting and ceramics.

**Japan.** After the decline of the first hereditary shogunate (chief generalship) at **Kamakura** (1185-1333), fragmentation of power accelerated, as did the consequent social mobility. Under Kamakura and the Ashikaga shogunate, 1338-1573, the daimyos (lords) and samurai (warriors) grew more powerful and promoted a martial ideology. Japanese pirates and traders plied the China coast. Popular Buddhist movements included the nationalist Nichiren sect (from c1250) and **Zen** (brought from China, 1191), which stressed meditation and a disciplined esthetic (tea ceremony, landscape gardening, judo, Noh drama).

# Reformed Europe Expands Overseas: 1500-1700

**Reformation begun.** Theological debate and protests against real and perceived clerical corruption existed in the medieval Christian world, expressed by such dissenters as Wycliffe (c1320-84) and his followers, the Lollards, in England, and Huss (burned as a heretic, 1415) in Bohemia.

**Luther** (1483-1546) preached that only faith could lead to salvation, without the mediation of clergy or good works. He attacked the authority of the Pope, rejected priestly celibacy, and recommended individual study of the Bible (which he translated, c1525). His 95 Theses (1517) led to his excommunication (1521). **Calvin** (1509-64) said God's elect were predestined for salvation; good conduct and success were signs of election. Calvin in Geneva and Knox (1505-72) in Scotland erected theocratic states.

**Henry VIII** asserted English national authority and secular power by breaking away from the Catholic church, 1534. Monastic property was confiscated, and some Protestant doctrines given official sanction.

**Religious wars.** A century and a half of religious wars began with a South German peasant uprising, 1524, repressed with Luther's support. Radical sects—democratic, pacifist, millenarian—arose (Anabaptists ruled Muenster, 1534-35), and were suppressed violently. Civil war in France from 1562 between Huguenots (Protestant nobles and merchants) and Catholics ended with the 1598 Edict of Nantes tolerating Protestants (revoked 1685). Hapsburg attempts to restore Catholicism in Germany were resisted in 25 years of fighting; the 1555 Peace of Augsburg guarantee of religious independence to local princes and cities was confirmed only after the **Thirty Years War**, 1618-48, when much of Germany was devastated by local and foreign armies (Sweden, France).

A Catholic Reformation, or **counter-reformation**, met the Protestant challenge, clearly defining an official theology at the Council of Trent, 1545-63. The **Jesuit** order, founded 1534 by Loyola (1491-1556), helped reconvert large areas of Poland, Hungary, and S. Germany and sent missionaries to the New World, India, and China, while the Inquisition helped suppress heresy in Catholic countries. A revival of piety appeared in the devotional literature (Theresa of Avila, 1515-82) and the grandiose Baroque art (Bernini, 1598-1680) of Roman Catholic countries.

**Scientific Revolution.** The late nominalist thinkers (Ockham, c1300-49) of Paris and Oxford challenged Aristotelian orthodoxy, allowing for a freer scientific approach. But metaphysical values, such as the Neoplatonic faith in an orderly, mathematical cosmos, still motivated and directed subsequent inquiry. **Copernicus** (1473-1543) promoted the heliocentric theory, which was confirmed when Kepler (1571-1630) discovered the mathematical laws describing the orbits of the planets. The Christian-Aristotelian belief that heavens and earth were fundamentally different collapsed when **Galileo** (1564-1642) discovered moving sunspots, irregular moon topography, and moons around Jupiter. He and **Newton** (1642-1727) developed a mechanics that unified cosmic and earthly phenomena. To meet the needs of the new physics, Newton and Leibnitz (1646-1716) invented calculus, Descartes (1596-1650) invented analytic geometry.

An explosion of observational science included the discovery of blood circulation (Harvey, 1578-1657) and microscopic life (Leeuwenhoek, 1632-1723), and advances in anatomy (Vesalius, 1514-64, dissected corpses) and chemistry (Boyle, 1627-91). Scientific research institutes were founded: Florence, 1657, London (**Royal Society**), 1660, Paris, 1666. Inventions proliferated (Savery's steam engine, 1696).

**Arts.** Mannerist trends of the high Renaissance (**Michelangelo**, 1475-1564) exploited virtuosity, grace, novelty, and exotic subjects and poses. The notion of artistic genius was promoted, in contrast to the anonymous medieval artisan. Private connoisseurs entered the art market. These trends were elaborated in the 17th century **Baroque** era, on a grander scale. Dynamic movement in painting and sculpture was emphasized by sharp lighting effects, use of rich materials (colored marble, gilt), realistic details. Curved facades, broken lines, rich, deep-cut detail, and ceiling decoration characterized Baroque architecture, especially in Germany. Monarchs, princes, and prelates, usually Catholic, used Baroque art to enhance and embellish their authority, as in royal portraits by Velazquez (1599-1660) and Van Dyck (1599-1641).

National styles emerged. In France, a taste for rectilinear order and serenity (Poussin, 1594-1665), linked to the new rational philosophy, was expressed in classical forms. The influence of **classical values** in French literature (tragedies of Racine, 1639-99) gave rise to the "battle of the Ancients and Moderns." New forms included the essay (Montaigne, 1533-92) and novel (*Princesse de Cleves*, La Fayette, 1678).

Dutch painting of the 17th century was unique in its wide social distribution. The Flemish tradition of undemonstrative realism reached its peak in **Rembrandt** (1606-69) and **Vermeer** (1632-75).

**Economy.** European economic expansion was stimulated by the new trade with the East, New World gold and silver, and a doubling of population (50 mln. in 1450, 100 mln. in 1600). New business and financial techniques were developed and refined, such as joint-stock companies, insurance, and letters of credit and exchange. The Bank of Amsterdam, 1609, and the Bank of England, 1694, broke the old monopoly of private banking families. The rise of a business mentality was typified by the spread of clock towers in cities in the 14th century. By the mid-15th century, portable clocks were available; the first watch was invented in 1502.

By 1650, most governments had adopted the **mercantile system**, in which they sought to amass metallic wealth by protecting their merchants' foreign and colonial trade monopolies. The rise in prices and the new coin-based economy undermined the craft guild and feudal manorial systems. Expanding industries, such as clothweaving and mining, benefitted from technical advances. Coal replaced disappearing wood as the chief fuel; it was used to fuel new 16th century blast furnaces making cast iron.

Timeline (left margin):

1600 —
Jamestown founded
French settle Canada
Tokugawa Ieyasu shogun
Bank of Amsterdam
Kepler d.
Plymouth founded
Thirty Years War
Galileo d.
Van Dyck d.
Manchus rule 1640
English Revolution
Charles I killed
Royal Soc. founded
Fronde
Mazarin d.
Bernini d.
Rembrandt d.
Spinoza d.
*Princesse de Cleves*
1680 —

**New World.** The **Aztecs** united much of the Meso-American culture area in a militarist empire by 1519, from their capital, Tenochtitlán (pop. 300,000), which was the center of a cult requiring enormous levels of ritual human sacrifice. Most of the civilized areas of S. America were ruled by the centralized **Inca Empire** (1476-1534), stretching 2,000 miles from Ecuador to N.W. Argentina. Lavish and sophisticated traditions in pottery, weaving, sculpture, and architecture were maintained in both regions.

These empires, beset by revolts, fell in 2 short campaigns to gold-seeking Spanish forces based in the Antilles and Panama. **Cortes** took Mexico, 1519-21; **Pizarro** Peru, 1531-35. From these centers, land and sea expeditions claimed most of N. and S. America for Spain. The Indian high cultures did not survive the impact of Christian missionaries and the new upper class of whites and mestizos. In turn, New World silver, and such Indian products as potatoes, tobacco, corn, peanuts, chocolate, and rubber exercised a major economic influence on Europe. While the Spanish administration intermittently concerned itself with the welfare of Indians, the population remained impoverished at most levels, despite the growth of a distinct South American civilization. European diseases reduced the native population.

**Brazil**, which the Portuguese reached in 1500 and settled after 1530, and the Caribbean colonies of several European nations developed a plantation economy where sugarcane, tobacco, cotton, coffee, rice, indigo, and lumber were grown commercially by slaves. From the early 16th to the late 19th centuries, some 10 million Africans were transported to **slavery** in the New World.

**Netherlands.** The urban, Calvinist northern provinces of the Netherlands rebelled against Hapsburg Spain, 1568, and founded an oligarchic mercantile republic. Their strategic control of the Baltic grain market enabled them to exploit Mediterranean food shortages. Religious refugees — French and Belgian Protestants, Iberian Jews — added to the cosmopolitan commercial talent pool. After Spain absorbed Portugal in 1580, the Dutch seized Portuguese possessions and created a vast, though generally short-lived commercial empire in Brazil, the Antilles, Africa, India, Ceylon, Malacca, Indonesia, and Taiwan, and challenged or supplanted Portuguese traders in China and Japan. Revolution in 1640 restored Portuguese independence.

**England.** Anglicanism became firmly established under Elizabeth I after a brief Catholic interlude under "Bloody Mary," 1553-58. But religious and political conflicts led to a rebellion by Parliament, 1642. Roundheads (Puritans) defeated Cavaliers (Royalists); Charles I was beheaded, 1649. The new **Commonwealth** was ruled as a military dictatorship by Cromwell, who also brutally crushed an Irish rebellion, 1649-51. Conflicts within the Puritan camp (democratic Levelers defeated 1649) aided the Stuart restoration, 1660, but Parliament was permanently strengthened and the peaceful **"Glorious Revolution"**, 1688, advanced political and religious liberties (writings of Locke, 1632-1704). British privateers (Drake, 1540-96) challenged Spanish control of the New World, and penetrated Asian trade routes (Madras taken, 1639). N. American colonies (Jamestown, 1607, Plymouth, 1620) provided an outlet for religious dissenters.

**France.** Emerging from the religious civil wars in 1628, France regained military and commercial great power status under the ministries of **Richelieu** (1624-42), **Mazarin** (1643-61), and **Colbert** (1662-83). Under Louis XIV (ruled 1643-1715) royal absolutism triumphed over nobles and local *parlements* (defeat of Fronde, 1648-53). Permanent colonies were founded in Canada (1608), the Caribbean (1626), and India (1674).

**Sweden.** Sweden seceded from the Scandinavian Union in 1523. The thinly-populated agrarian state (with copper, iron, and timber exports) was united by the Vasa kings, whose conquests by the mid-17th century made Sweden the dominant Baltic power. The empire collapsed in the Great Northern War (1700-21).

**Poland.** After the union with Lithuania in 1447, Poland ruled vast territories from the Baltic to the Black Sea, resisting German and Turkish incursions. Catholic nobles failed to gain the loyalty of the Orthodox Christian peasantry in the East; commerce and trades were practiced by German and Jewish immigrants. The bloody 1648-49 cossack uprising began the kingdom's dismemberment.

**China.** A new dynasty, the **Manchus**, invaded from the NE, seized power in 1644, and expanded Chinese control to its greatest extent in Central and Southeast Asia. Trade and diplomatic contact with Europe grew, carefully controlled by China. New crops (sweet potato, maize, peanut) allowed an economic and population growth (300 million pop. in 1800). Traditional arts and literature were pursued with increased sophistication (*Dream of the Red Chamber*, novel, mid-18th century).

**Japan.** Tokugawa Ieyasu, shogun from 1603, finally unified and pacified feudal Japan. Hereditary daimyos and samurai monopolized government office and the professions. An urban merchant class grew, literacy spread, and a cultural renaissance occurred (haiku of Basho, 1644-94). Fear of European domination led to persecution of Christian converts from 1597, and stringent isolation from outside contact from 1640.

## Philosophy, Industry, and Revolution: 1700-1800

**Science and Reason.** Faith in human reason and science as the source of truth and a means to improve the physical and social environment, espoused since the Renaissance (Francis Bacon, 1561-1626), was bolstered by scientific discoveries in spite of theological opposition (Galileo's forced retraction, 1633). Descartes applied the logical method of mathematics to discover "self-evident" scientific and philosophical truths, while Newton emphasized induction from experimental observation.

The challenge of reason to traditional religious and political values and institutions began with Spinoza (1632-77), who interpreted the Bible historically and called for political and intellectual freedom.

French philosophes assumed leadership of the **"Enlightenment"** in the 18th century. Montesquieu (1689-1755) used British history to support his notions of limited government. Voltaire's (1694-1778) diaries and novels of exotic travel illustrated the intellectual trends toward secular ethics and relativism. Rousseau's (1712-1778) radical concepts of the **social contract** and of the inherent goodness of the common man gave impetus to anti-monarchical republicanism. The *Encyclopedia*, 1751-72, edited by Diderot and d'Alembert, designed as a monument to reason, was largely devoted to practical technology.

In England, ideals of political and religious liberty were connected with empiricist philosophy and science in the followers of Locke. But the extreme **empiricism** of Hume (1711-76) and Berkeley

(right margin timeline, top to bottom)

1680

Savery's steam engine

Glorious Revolution

Bank of England

Edict of Nantes revoked

Racine d.

St. Petersburg founded

Locke d.

Great Northern War

Newcomen engine

Spectator

Louis XIV d.

1715

Newton d.

Maria Theresa rule

Frederick II,

Voltaire's *Lettres philosophiques*

Watteau d.

Vico d.

Hume's *Human Understanding*

Montesquieu's *Spirit of Laws*

Poor Richard's Almanack

1750

Timeline (left margin, top to bottom):
1750 — Rosseau's Social Contract — Spinning jenny — Brit. rules Bengal — Encyclopedia — Watt's engine — Edinburgh plan — Kant's Critique of Pure Reason — American Revolution — Austria serfs free — 1775 — Bastille stormed — Divisions of Poland — Fr. Repub. declared — Adam Smith d. — Burke d. — China pop. at 300 mln. — China bans opium — 1800

(1685-1753) posed limits to the identification of reason with absolute truth, as did the evolutionary approach to law and politics of Burke (1729-97) and the utilitarianism of Bentham (1748-1832). Adam Smith (1723-90) and other **physiocrats** called for a rationalization of economic activity by removing artificial barriers to a supposedly natural free exchange of goods.

Despite the political disunity and backwardness of most of Germany, German writers participated in the new philosophical trends popularized by Wolff (1679-1754). **Kant's (1724-1804) idealism,** unifying an empirical epistemology with *a priori* moral and logical concepts, directed German thought away from skepticism. Italian contributions included work on electricity by Galvani (1737-98) and Volta (1745-1827), the pioneer **historiography of Vico** (1668-1744), and writings on penal reform by Beccaria (1738-94). The American Franklin (1706-90) was celebrated in Europe for his varied achievements.

The growth of the **press** (*Spectator*, 1711-14) and the wide distribution of realistic but sentimental **novels** attested to the increase of a large bourgeois public.

**Arts.** Rococo art, characterized by extravagant decorative effects, asymmetries copied from organic models, and artificial pastoral subjects, was favored by the continental aristocracy for most of the century (Watteau, 1684-1721), and had musical analogies in the ornamentalized polyphony of late Baroque. The Neoclassical art after 1750, associated with the new scientific archeology, was more streamlined, and infused with the supposed moral and geometric rectitude of the Roman Republic (David, 1748-1825). In England, **town** planning on a grand scale began.

**Industrial Revolution in England.** Agricultural improvements, such as the sowing drill (1701) and livestock breeding, were implemented on the large fields provided by enclosure of common lands by private owners. Profits from agriculture and from colonial and foreign trade (1800 volume, £ 54 million) were channelled through hundreds of banks and the **Stock Exchange** (founded 1773) into new industrial processes.

The Newcomen steam pump (1712) aided coal mining. Coal fueled the new efficient steam engines patented by Watt in 1769, and coke-smelting produced cheap, sturdy iron for machinery by the 1730s. The **flying shuttle** (1733) and **spinning jenny** (1764) were used in the large new cotton textile factories, where women and children were much of the work force. Goods were transported cheaply over **canals** (2,000 miles built 1760-1800).

**American Revolution.** The British colonies in N. America attracted a mass immigration of religious dissenters and poor people throughout the 17th and 18th centuries, coming from all parts of the British Isles, Germany, the Netherlands, and other countries. The population reached 3 million whites and blacks by the 1770s. The small native population was decimated by European diseases and wars with and between the various colonies. British attempts to control colonial trade, and to tax the colonists to pay for the costs of colonial administration and defense clashed with traditions of local self government, and eventually provoked the colonies to rebellion. (*See American Revolution in Index.*)

**Central and East Europe.** The monarchs of the three states that dominated eastern Europe — Austria, Prussia, and Russia — accepted the advice and legitimation of philosophers in creating more modern, centralized institutions in their kingdoms, enlarged by the division of Poland (1772-95).

Under **Frederick II** (ruled 1740-86) Prussia, with its efficient modern army, doubled in size. State monopolies and tariff protection fostered industry, and some legal reforms were introduced. Austria's heterogeneous realms were legally unified under **Maria Theresa** (ruled 1740-80) and **Joseph II** (1780-90). Reforms in education, law, and religion were enacted, and the Austrian serfs were freed (1781). With its defeat in the Seven Years' War in 1763, Austria lost Silesia and ceased its active role in Germany, but was compensated by expansion in the E and S (Hungary, Slavonia, 1699, Galicia, 1772).

Russia, whose borders continued to expand in all directions, adopted some Western bureaucratic and economic policies under **Peter I** (ruled 1682-1725) and **Catherine II** (ruled 1762-96). Trade and cultural contacts with the West multiplied from the new Baltic Sea capital, **St. Petersburg** (founded 1703).

**French Revolution.** The growing French middle class lacked political power, and resented aristocratic tax privileges, especially in light of liberal political ideals popularized by the American Revolution. Peasants lacked adequate land and were burdened with feudal obligations to nobles. Wars with Britain drained the treasury, finally forcing the king to call the **Estates-General** in 1789 (first time since 1614), in an atmosphere of food riots (poor crop in 1788).

Aristocratic resistance to absolutism was soon overshadowed by the reformist Third Estate (middle class), which proclaimed itself the **National Constituent Assembly** June 17 and took the "Tennis Court oath" on June 20 to secure a constitution. The storming of the **Bastille** July 14 by Parisian artisans was followed by looting and seizure of aristocratic property throughout France. Assembly reforms included abolition of class and regional privileges, a Declaration of Rights, suffrage by taxpayers (75% of males), and the **Civil Constitution of the Clergy** providing for election and loyalty oaths for priests. A republic was declared Sept. 22, 1792, in spite of royalist pressure from Austria and Prussia, which had declared war in April (joined by Britain the next year). Louis XVI was beheaded Jan. 21, 1793, Queen Marie Antoinette was beheaded Oct. 16, 1793.

Royalist uprisings in La Vendée and military reverses led to a **reign of terror** in which tens of thousands of opponents of the Revolution and criminals were executed. Radical reforms in the **Convention** period (Sept. 1793-Oct. 1795) included the abolition of colonial slavery, economic measures to aid the poor, support of public education, and a short-lived de-Christianization.

Division among radicals (execution of Hebert, March 1794, Danton, April, and Robespierre, July) aided the ascendance of a moderate **Directory,** which consolidated military victories. **Napoleon Bonaparte** (1769-1821), a popular young general, exploited political divisions and participated in a coup Nov. 9, 1799, making himself first consul (dictator).

**India.** Sikh and Hindu rebels (Rajputs, Marathas) and Afghans destroyed the power of the Mughals during the 18th century. After France's defeat in the Seven Years War, 1763, Britain was the chief European trade power in India. Its control of inland **Bengal** and **Bihar** was recognized by the Mughal shah in 1765, who granted the **British East India Co.** (under Clive, 1727-74) the right to collect land revenue there. Despite objections from Parliament (1784 India Act) the company's involvement in local wars and politics led to repeated acquisitions of new territory. The company exported Indian textiles, sugar, and indigo.

# Change Gathers Steam: 1800-1840

**French ideals and empire spread.** Inspired by the ideals of the French Revolution, and supported by the expanding French armies, new republican regimes arose near France: the **Batavian Republic** in the Netherlands (1795-1806), the **Helvetic Republic** in Switzerland (1798-1803), the **Cisalpine Republic** in N. Italy (1797-1805), the **Ligurian Republic** in Genoa (1797-1805), and the **Parthenopean Republic** in S. Italy (1799). A Roman Republic existed briefly in 1798 after Pope Pius VI was arrested by French troops. In Italy and Germany, new nationalist sentiments were stimulated both in imitation of and reaction to France (anti-French and anti-Jacobin peasant uprisings in Italy, 1796-9).

From 1804, when Napoleon declared himself emperor, to 1812, a succession of military victories (Austerlitz, 1805, Jena, 1806) extended his control over most of Europe, through puppet states (**Confederation of the Rhine** united W. German states for the first time and **Grand Duchy of Warsaw** revived Polish national hopes), expansion of the empire, and alliances.

Among the lasting reforms initiated under Napoleon's absolutist reign were: establishment of the Bank of France, centralization of tax collection, codification of law along Roman models (*Code Napoleon*), and reform and extension of secondary and university education. In an 1801 concordat, the papacy recognized the effective autonomy of the French Catholic Church. Some 400,000 French soldiers were killed in the Napoleonic Wars, along with 600,000 foreign troops.

**Last gasp of old regime.** France's coastal blockade of Europe (**Continental System**) failed to neutralize Britain. The disastrous 1812 invasion of Russia exposed Napoleon's overextension. After an 1814 exile at Elba, Napoleon's armies were defeated at **Waterloo**, 1815, by British and Prussian troops.

At the **Congress of Vienna**, the monarchs and princes of Europe redrew their boundaries, to the advantage of Prussia (in Saxony and the Ruhr), Austria (in Illyria and Venetia), and Russia (in Poland and Finland). British conquest of Dutch and French colonies (S. Africa, Ceylon, Mauritius) was recognized, and France, under the restored Bourbons, retained its expanded 1792 borders. The settlement brought 50 years of international peace to Europe.

But the Congress was unable to check the advance of liberal ideals and of nationalism among the smaller European nations. The 1825 **Decembrist** uprising by liberal officers in Russia was easily suppressed. But an independence movement in Greece, stirred by commercial prosperity and a cultural revival, succeeded in expelling Ottoman rule by 1831, with the aid of Britain, France, and Russia.

A constitutional monarchy was secured in France by an **1830 revolution;** Louis Philippe became king. The revolutionary contagion spread to **Belgium,** which gained its independence from the Dutch monarchy, 1830; to **Poland,** whose rebellion was defeated by Russia, 1830-31; and to Germany.

**Romanticism.** A new style in intellectual and artistic life began to replace Neo-classicism and Rococo after the mid-18th century. By the early 19th, this style, Romanticism, had prevailed in the European world.

**Rousseau** had begun the reaction against excessive rationalism and skepticism; in education (*Emile*, 1762) he stressed subjective spontaneity over regularized instruction. In Germany, Lessing (1729-81) and Herder (1744-1803) favorably compared the German folk song to classical forms, and began a cult of Shakespeare, whose passion and "natural" wisdom was a model for the Romantic *Sturm und Drang* (storm and stress) movement. Goethe's *Sorrows of Young Werther* (1774) set the model for the tragic, passionate genius.

A new interest in **Gothic architecture** in England after 1760 (Walpole, 1717-97) spread through Europe, associated with an aesthetic Christian and mystic revival (Blake, 1757-1827). Celtic, Norse, and German mythology and folk tales were revived or imitated (Macpherson's Ossian translation, 1762, Grimm's *Fairy Tales,* 1812-22). The medieval revival (Scott's *Ivanhoe,* 1819) led to a new interest in history, stressing national differences and organic growth (Carlyle, 1795-1881; Michelet, 1798-1874), corresponding to theories of natural evolution (Lamarck's *Philosophie zoologique,* 1809, Lyell's *Geology,* 1830-33).

Revolution and war fed an obsession with freedom and conflict, expressed by poets (**Byron,** 1788-1824, **Hugo,** 1802-85) and philosophers (**Hegel,** 1770-1831).

Wild gardens replaced the formal French variety, and painters favored rural, stormy, and mountainous landscapes (**Turner,** 1775-1851; **Constable,** 1776-1837). Clothing became freer, with wigs, hoops, and ruffles discarded. Originality and genius were expected in the life as well as the work of inspired artists (Murger's *Scenes from Bohemian Life,* 1847-49). Exotic locales and themes (as in "Gothic" horror stories) were used in art and literature (Delacroix, 1798-1863, **Poe,** 1809-49).

Music exhibited the new dramatic style and a breakdown of classical forms (Beethoven, 1770-1827). The use of folk melodies and modes aided the growth of distinct national traditions (Glinka in Russia, 1804-57).

**Latin America.** Haiti, under the former slave **Toussaint L'Ouverture,** was the first Latin American independent state, 1800. All the mainland Spanish colonies won their independence 1810-24, under such leaders as Bolivar (1783-1830). Brazil became an independent empire under the Portuguese prince regent, 1822. A new class of military officers divided power with large landholders and the church.

**United States.** Heavy immigration and exploitation of ample natural resources fueled rapid economic growth. The spread of the franchise, public education, and antislavery sentiment were signs of a widespread democratic ethic.

**China.** Failure to keep pace with Western arms technology exposed China to greater European influence, and hampered efforts to bar imports of opium, which had damaged Chinese society and drained wealth overseas. In the **Opium War,** 1839-42, Britain forced China to expand trade opportunities and to cede Hong Kong

1800
Haiti indep. — Hugo b.
Dix b.
Mill b.
Lamarck's *Philosophie Zoologique*
Congress of Vienna — Napoleon emperor
1815
Scott's *Ivanhoe*
Brazil indep. — S. Amer. colonies win indep.
Byron d. — Grimm's *Fairy Tales*
Decembrist uprising
Greek indep. movement
1830
Blake d. — Volta d.
indep. Beethoven d.
Belgian-indep.
1st Eng. reform bill
1st Brit. Factory Act.
Brit. Emp. slavery banned
Brook Farm, Mass.
Opium War
Telegraph perfected by Morse
1845

# Triumph of Progress: 1840-80

**Idea of Progress.** As a result of the cumulative scientific, economic, and political changes of the preceding eras, the idea took hold among literate people in the West that continuing growth and improvement was the usual state of human and natural life.

Darwin's statement of the **theory of evolution** and survival of the fittest (*Origin of Species*, 1859), defended by intellectuals and scientists against theological objections, was taken as confirmation that progress was the natural direction of life. The controversy helped define popular ideas of the dedicated scientist and ever-expanding human knowledge of and control over the world (Foucault's demonstration of earth's rotation, 1851, Pasteur's germ theory, 1861).

Liberals following Ricardo (1772-1823) in their faith that unrestrained competition would bring continuous economic expansion sought to adjust political life to the new social realities, and believed that unregulated competition of ideas would yield truth (Mill, 1806-73). In England, successive reform bills (1832, 1867, 1884) gave representation to the new industrial towns, and extended the franchise to the middle and lower classes and to Catholics, Dissenters, and Jews. On both sides of the Atlantic, reformists tried to improve conditions for the mentally ill (Dix, 1802-87), women (Anthony, 1820-1906), and prisoners. Slavery was barred in the British Empire, 1833; the United States, 1865; and Brazil, 1888.

Socialist theories based on ideas of human perfectibility or historical progress were widely disseminated. Utopian socialists like Saint-Simon (1760-1825) envisaged an orderly, just society directed by a technocratic elite. A model factory town, New Lanark, Scotland, was set up by utopian Robert Owen (1771-1858), and utopian communal experiments were tried in the U.S. (Brook Farm, Mass., 1841-7). Bakunin's (1814-76) anarchism represented the opposite utopian extreme of total freedom. Marx (1818-83) posited the inevitable triumph of socialism in the industrial countries through a historical process of class conflict.

**Spread of industry.** The technical processes and managerial innovations of the English industrial revolution spread to Europe (especially Germany) and the U.S., causing an explosion of industrial production, demand for raw materials, and competition for markets. Inventors, both trained and self-educated, provided the means for larger-scale production (Bessemer steel, 1856, sewing machine, 1846). Many inventions were shown at the 1851 London Great Exhibition at the Crystal Palace, the theme of which was universal prosperity.

Local specialization and long-distance trade were aided by a revolution in transportation and communication. Railroads were first introduced in the 1820s in England and the U.S. Over 150,000 miles of track had been laid worldwide by 1880, with another 100,000 miles laid in the next decade. Steamships were improved (*Savannah* crossed Atlantic, 1819). The telegraph, perfected by 1844 (Morse), connected the Old and New Worlds by cable in 1866, and quickened the pace of international commerce and politics. The first commercial telephone exchange went into operation in the U.S. in 1878.

The new class of industrial workers, uprooted from their rural homes, lacked job security, and suffered from dangerous overcrowded conditions at work and at home. Many responded by organizing trade unions (legalized in England, 1824; France, 1884). The U.S. Knights of Labor had 700,000 members by 1886. The First International, 1864-76, tried to unite workers internationally around a Marxist program. The quasi-Socialist Paris Commune uprising, 1871, was violently suppressed. Factory Acts to reduce child labor and regulate conditions were passed (1833-50 in England). Social security measures were introduced by the Bismarck regime in Germany, 1883-89.

**Revolutions of 1848.** Among the causes of the continent-wide revolutions were an international collapse of credit and resulting unemployment, bad harvests in 1845-7, and a cholera epidemic. The new urban proletarian and expanding bourgeoisie demanded a greater political role. Republics were proclaimed in France, Rome, and Venice. Nationalist feelings reached fever pitch in the Hapsburg empire, as Hungary declared independence under Kossuth, a Slav Congress demanded equality, and Piedmont tried to drive Austria from Lombardy. A national liberal assembly at Frankfurt called for German unification.

But riots fueled bourgeois fears of socialism (Marx and Engels' 1848 *Communist Manifesto*) and peasants remained conservative. The old establishment — The Papacy, the Hapsburgs (using Croats and Romanians against Hungary), the Russian army — was able to rout the revolutionaries by 1849. The French Republic succumbed to a renewed monarchy by 1852 (Emperor Napoleon III).

**Great nations unified.** Using the "blood and iron" tactics of Bismarck from 1862, Prussia controlled N. Germany by 1867 (war with Denmark, 1864, Austria, 1866). After defeating France in 1870 (annexation of Alsace-Lorraine), it won the allegiance of S. German states. A new **German Empire** was proclaimed, 1871. **Italy**, inspired by Mazzini (1805-72) and Garibaldi (1807-82), was unified by the reformed Piedmont kingdom through uprisings, plebiscites, and war.

The U.S., its area expanded after the 1846-47 Mexican War, defeated a secession attempt by slave states, 1861-65. The Canadian provinces were united in an autonomous **Dominion of Canada**, 1867. Control in **India** was removed from the East India Co. and centralized under British administration after the 1857-58 Sepoy rebellion, laying the groundwork for the modern Indian State. Queen Victoria was named Empress of India, 1876.

**Europe dominates Asia.** The Ottoman Empire began to collapse in the face of Balkan nationalisms and European imperial incursions in N. Africa (Suez Canal, 1869). The Turks had lost control of most of both regions by 1882. Russia completed its expansion south by 1884 (despite the temporary setback of the Crimean War with Turkey, Britain, and France, 1853-56) taking Turkestan, all the Caucasus, and Chinese areas in the East and sponsoring Balkan Slavs against the Turks. A succession of reformist and reactionary regimes presided over a slow modernization (serfs freed, 1861). Persian independence suffered as Russia and British India competed for influence.

China was forced to sign a series of unequal treaties with European powers and Japan. Overpopulation and an inefficient dynasty brought misery and caused rebellions (Taiping, Moslems) leaving tens of millions dead. Japan was forced by the U.S. (Commodore Perry's visits, 1853-54) and Europe to end its isolation. The Meiji restoration, 1868, gave power to a Westernizing oligarchy. Intensified empire-building gave Burma to Britain, 1824-86, and Indochina to France, 1862-95. Christian missionary activity followed imperial and trade expansion in Asia.

**Respectability.** The fine arts were expected to reflect and encourage the progress of morals and manners among the different classes. "Victorian" prudery, exaggerated delicacy, and familial piety were heralded by **Bowdler's** expurgated edition of Shakespeare (1818). Government-supported mass education inculcated a work ethic as a means to escape poverty (Horatio Alger, 1832-99).

The official **Beaux Arts** school in Paris set an international style of imposing public buildings (Paris Opera, 1861-74, Vienna Opera, 1861-69) and uplifting statues (Bartholdi's *Statue of Liberty*, 1885). Realist painting, influenced by photography (Daguerre, 1837), appealed to a new mass audience with social or historical narrative (Wilkie, 1785-1841, Poynter, 1836-1919) or with serious religious, moral, or social messages (pre-Raphaelites, Millet's *Angelus*, 1858) often drawn from ordinary life. The **Impressionists** (Pissarro, 1830-1903, Renoir, 1841-1919) rejected the central role of serious subject matter in favor of a colorful and sensual depiction of a moment, but their sunny, placid depictions of bourgeois scenes kept them within the respectable consensus.

Realistic **novelists** presented the full panorama of social classes and personalities, but retained sentimentality and moral judgment (Dickens, 1812-70, Eliot, 1819-80, Tolstoy, 1828-1910, Balzac, 1799-1850).

## Veneer of Stability: 1880-1900

Livingst... ...The vast African interior, visited by European explorers (Barth, 1821-65, coastal bases afte... ...Moslem kingdoms (Fulani), ...ed by the European powers in rapid, comp...tive thrusts from their ...political and international strategic r...sons. W. African alike subdued. Only Christian Ethiopia (def... ...1896), and Bantu military confedera...s (Zulu) were (W. Africa) and Britain ("Cape to Cairo," Boer War, 1899-1902) ...and Liberia resisted successfully. France ideology of "the white man's burden" (Kipling, *Barrack Room Ballads*, 1892) or of a "civilizing mission" were the major beneficiaries. (France) justified the conquests. (See map on page 501.)

West European foreign capital investment soared to nearly $40 billion by 1914, but most was in E. Europe (France, Germany), the Americas (Britain) and the Europeans' colonies. The foundation of the modern interdependent world economy was laid, with cartels dominating raw material trade.

**An industrious world.** Industrial and technological proficiency characterized the 2 new great powers — Germany and the U.S. Coal and iron deposits enabled Germany to reach second or third place status in iron, steel, and shipbuilding by the 1900s. German electrical and chemical industries were world leaders. The U.S. post-civil war boom (interrupted by "panics," 1884, 1893, 1896) was shaped by massive immigration from S. and E. Europe from 1880, government subsidy of railroads, and huge private monopolies (Standard Oil, 1870, U.S. Steel, 1901). The **Spanish-American War**, 1898 (Philippine rebellion, 1899-1901), and the Open Door policy in China (1899) made the U.S. a world power.

England led in **urbanization** (72% by 1890), with **London** the world capital of finance, insurance, and shipping. Sewer systems (Paris, 1850s), electric subways (London, 1890), parks, and bargain department stores helped improve living standards for most of the urban population of the industrial world.

**Asians assimilate.** Asian reaction to European economic, military, and religious incursions took the form of imitation of Western techniques and adoption of Western ideas of progress and freedom. The Chinese "self-strengthening" movement of the 1860s and 70s included rail, port, and arsenal improvements and metal and textile mills. Reformers like **K'ang Yu-wei** (1858-1927) won liberalizing reforms in 1898, right after the European and Japanese "scramble for concessions."

A universal education system in Japan and importation of foreign industrial, scientific, and military experts aided Japan's unprecedented rapid modernization after 1868, under the authoritarian Meiji regime. Japan's victory in the **Sino-Japanese War**, 1894-95, put Formosa and Korea in its power.

In India, the British alliance with the remaining princely states masked reform sentiment among the Westernized urban elite; higher education had been conducted largely in English for 50 years. The **Indian National Congress**, founded in 1885, demanded a larger government role for Indians.

**"Fin-de-siecle" sophistication.** **Naturalist** writers pushed realism to its extreme limits, adopting a quasi-scientific attitude and writing about formerly taboo subjects like sex, crime, extreme poverty, and corruption (Flaubert, 1821-80, Zola, 1840-1902, Hardy, 1840-1928). Unseen or repressed psychological motivations were explored in the clinical and theoretical works of **Freud** (1856-1939) and in the fiction of Dostoevsky (1821-81), James (1843-1916), Schnitzler (1862-1931) and others.

A contempt for bourgeois life or a desire to shock a complacent audience was shared by the French **symbolist** poets (Verlaine, 1844-96, Rimbaud, 1854-91), neo-pagan English writers (Swinburne, 1837-1909), continental dramatists (Ibsen, 1828-1906) and satirists (Wilde, 1854-1900). **Nietzsche** (1844-1900) was influential in his elitism and pessimism.

Post-impressionist art neglected long-cherished conventions of representation (Cezanne, 1839-1906) and showed a willingness to learn from primitive and non-European art (Gauguin, 1848-1903, Japanese prints).

**Racism.** Gobineau (1816-82) gave a pseudo-biological foundation to modern racist theories, which spread in the latter 19th century along with **Social Darwinism**, the belief that societies are and should be organized as a struggle for survival of the fittest. The Medieval period was interpreted as an era of natural Germanic rule (Chamberlain, 1855-1927) and notions of superiority were associated with German national aspirations (Treitschke, 1834-96). **Anti-Semitism**, with a new racist rationale, became a significant political force in Germany (Anti-Semitic Petition, 1880), Austria (Lueger, 1844-1910), and France (Dreyfus case, 1894-1906).

## Last Respite: 1900-1909

**Alliances.** While the peace of Europe (and its dependencies) continued to hold (1907 Hague Conference extended the rules of war and international arbitration procedures), imperial rivalries, protectionist trade practices (in Germany and France), and the escalating arms race (British *Dreadnought* battleship launched, Germany widens Kiel canal, 1906) exacerbated minor disputes (German-French Moroccan "crises", 1905, 1911).

1880

Dostoyevsky d.

Marx d.

Indian Natl. Cong.

Brazil bans slavery

1885

Europe conquers Africa

Kipling's *Barrack Room Ballads*

Rimbaud d.

radio

Sino-Jap. War

1895

Span.-Am. War

Russ. Soc. Dem. Party

Boxer rebellion

Dreyfus case

Gorky's *Lower Depths*

Wilde d.

Ford Motor Co.

Panama Canal

Australia united

1904

Security was sought through alliances: **Triple Alliance** (Germany, Austria-Hungary, Italy) renewed 1902, 1907; Anglo-Japanese Alliance, 1902; Franco-Russian Alliance, 1899; **Entente Cordiale** (Britain, France), 1904; Anglo-Russian Treaty, 1907; German-Ottoman friendship.

**Ottomans decline.** The inefficient, corrupt Ottoman government was unable to resist further loss of territory. Nearly all European lands were lost in 1912 to Serbia, Greece, Montenegro, and Bulgaria. Italy took Libya and the Dodecanese islands the same year, and Britain took Kuwait, 1899, and the Sinai, 1906. The **Young Turk** revolution in 1908 forced the sultan to restore a constitution, and introduced some social reform, industrialization, and secularization.

**British Empire.** British trade and cultural influence remained dominant in the empire, but constitutional reforms presaged its eventual dissolution: the colonies of Australia were united in 1901 under a self-governing commonwealth. New Zealand acquired dominion status in 1907. The old Boer republics joined Cape Colony and Natal in the self-governing Union of South Africa in 1910.

The 1909 Indian Councils Act enhanced the role of elected province legislatures in India. The M(co) League, founded 1906, sought separate communal representation.

**East Asia.** Japan exploited its growing industrial power to expand its empire. nfucian exam system war against Russia (naval battle of Tsushima, 1905) assured Japan's domina.              and Manchuria (took Port Ar our 1905).

In China, central authority began to crumble (empress died     at-sen (1866-1925) fomented periodic ended 1905, moder  ation of the army, building of r"                 equate and secret societies of reformers and  tionalists, inspired by the W        uprisings i   e south.

**Siam**, whose independence had been guaranteed by Britain and France in 1896, was split into spheres of influence by those countries in 1907.

**Russia.** The population of the Russian Empire approached 150 million in 1900. Reforms in education, law, and local institutions (*zemstvos*), and an industrial boom starting in the 1880s (oil, railroads) created the beginnings of a modern state, despite the autocratic tsarist regime. Liberals (1903 Union of Liberation), Socialists (Social Democrats founded 1898, Bolsheviks split off 1903), and populists (Social Revolutionaries founded 1901) were periodically repressed, and national minorities persecuted (anti-Jewish pogroms, 1903, 1905-6).

An industrial crisis after 1900 and harvest failures aggravated poverty among urban workers, and the 1904-05 defeat by Japan (which checked Russia's Asian expansion) sparked the revolution of 1905-06. A **Duma** (parliament) was created, and an agricultural reform (under Stolypin, prime minister 1906-11) created a large class of landowning peasants (kulaks).

**The world shrinks.** Developments in transportation and communication and mass population movements helped create an awareness of an interdependent world. Early **automobiles** (Daimler, Benz, 1885) were experimental, or designed as luxuries. Assembly-line mass production (Ford Motor Co., 1903) made the invention practicable, and by 1910 nearly 500,000 motor vehicles were registered in the U.S. alone. **Heavier-than-air flights** began in 1903 in the U.S. (Wright brothers), preceded by glider, balloon, and model plane advances in several countries. Trade was advanced by improvements in ship design (gyrocompass, 1907), speed (Lusitania crossed Atlantic in 5 days, 1907), and reach (Panama Canal begun, 1904).

The first transatlantic radio telegraphic transmission occurred in 1901, 6 years after Marconi discovered radio. Radio transmission of human speech began in 1900. Telegraphic transmission of photos was achieved in 1904, lending immediacy to news reports. **Phonographs**, popularized by Caruso's recordings (starting 1902), made for quick international spread of musical styles (ragtime). **Motion pictures**, perfected in the 1890s (Dickson, Lumière brothers), became a popular and artistic medium after 1900; newsreels appeared in 1909.

**Emigration** from crowded European centers soared in the decade: 9 million migrated to the U.S., and millions more went to Siberia, Canada, Argentina, Australia, South Africa, and Algeria. Some 70 million Europeans emigrated in the century before 1914. Several million Chinese, Indians, and Japanese migrated to Southeast Asia, where their urban skills often enabled them to take a predominant economic role.

**Social reform.** The social and economic problems of the poor were kept in the public eye by realist fiction writers (Dreiser's *Sister Carrie*, 1900; Gorky's *Lower Depths*, 1902; Sinclair's *Jungle*, 1906), journalists (U.S. **muckrakers** — Steffens, Tarbell) and artists (Ashcan school). Frequent labor strikes and occasional assassinations by anarchists or radicals (Austrian Empress, 1898; King Umberto I of Italy, 1900; U.S. Pres. McKinley, 1901; Russian Interior Minister Plehve, 1904; Portugal's King Carlos, 1908) added to social tension and fear of revolution.

But democratic reformism prevailed. In Germany, Bernstein's (1850-1932) **revisionist Marxism**, downgrading revolution, was accepted by the powerful Social Democrats and trade unions. The British Fabian Society (the Webbs, Shaw) and the Labour Party (founded 1906) worked for reforms such as social security and union rights (1906), while women's suffragists grew more militant. U.S. **progressives** fought big business (Pure Food and Drug Act, 1906). In France, the 10-hour work day (1904) and separation of church and state (1905) were reform victories, as was universal suffrage in Austria (1907).

**Arts.** An unprecedented period of experimentation, centered in France, produced several new **painting** styles: fauvism exploited bold color areas (Matisse, *Woman with Hat*, 1905); expressionism reflected powerful inner emotions (the Brücke group, 1905); cubism combined several views of an object on one flat surface (Picasso's *Demoiselles*, 1906-07); futurism tried to depict speed and motion (Italian Futurist Manifesto, 1910). **Architects** explored new uses of steel structures, with facades either neo-classical (Adler and Sullivan in U.S.); curvilinear Art Nouveau (Gaudi's Casa Mila, 1905-10); or functionally streamlined (Wright's Robie House, 1909).

**Music and Dance** shared the experimental spirit. Ruth St. Denis (1877-1968) and Isadora Duncan (1878-1927) pioneered modern dance, while Diaghilev in Paris revitalized classic ballet from 1909. Composers explored atonal music (Debussy, 1862-1918) and dissonance (Schönberg, 1874-1951), or revolutionized classical forms (Stravinsky, 1882-1971), often showing jazz or folk music influences.

---

Timeline (left margin, top to bottom):

- 1904
- Russo-Jap. War
- Pure Food & Drug Act
- Rev. in Russia
- Labour Party
- Ibsen d.
- Dreadnought launched
- Hague Conf.
- Young Turks rev.
- Robie House
- Futurist Manifesto
- Japan annexes Korea
- Mex. rev. starts
- Portugal rev. starts
- 1910
- 2d Morocco crisis
- Diaz Mex. rule ends
- Chinese repub.
- Ottomans lose Europe
- Maugham's "Of Human Bondage"
- Theory of Relativity
- World War I
- 1916

# War and Revolution: 1910-1919

**War threatens.** Germany under Wilhelm II sought a political and imperial role consonant with its industrial strength, challenging Britain's world supremacy and threatening France, still resenting the loss of Alsace-Lorraine. Austria wanted to curb an expanded Serbia (after 1912) and the threat it posed to its own Slav lands. Russia feared Austrian and German political and economic aims in the Balkans and Turkey. An accelerated arms race resulted: the German standing army rose to over 2 million men by 1914. Russia and France had over a million each, Austria and the British Empire nearly a million each. Dozens of enormous battleships were built by the powers after 1906.

The **assassination of Austrian Archduke Franz Ferdinand** by a Serbian, June 28, 1914, was the pretext for war. The system of alliances made the conflict Europe-wide; Germany's invasion of Belgium to outflank France forced Britain to enter the war. Patriotic fervor was nearly unanimous among all classes in most countries.

**World War I.** German forces were stopped in France in one month. The rival armies dug **trench networks**. Artillery and improved machine guns prevented either side from any lasting advance despite repeated assaults (600,000 dead at **Verdun**, Feb.-July 1916). Poison gas, used by Germany in 1915, proved ineffective. Over one million U.S. troops tipped the balance after mid-1917, forcing Germany to sue for peace.

In the East, the Russian armies were thrown back (battle of **Tannenberg**, Aug. 20, 1914) and the war grew unpopular. An allied attempt to relieve Russia through Turkey failed (**Gallipoli** 1915). The new Bolshevik regime signed the capitulatory Brest-Litovsk peace in March, 1918. Italy entered the war on the allied side, May 1915, but was pushed back by Oct. 1917. A renewed offensive with Allied aid in Oct.-Nov. 1918 forced Austria to surrender.

The British Navy successfully blockaded Germany, which responded with submarine U-boat attacks; **unrestricted submarine warfare** against neutrals after Jan. 1917 helped bring the U.S. into the war. Other battlefields included Palestine and Mesopotamia, both of which Britain wrested from the Turks in 1917, and the African and Pacific colonies of Germany, most of which fell to Britain, France, Australia, Japan, and South Africa.

From 1916, the civilian populations and economies of both sides were mobilized to an unprecedented degree. Hardships intensified among fighting nations in 1917 (French mutiny crushed in May). More than 10 million soldiers died in the war.

**Settlement.** At the **Versailles conference** (Jan.-June 1919) and in subsequent negotiations and local wars (Russian-Polish War 1920), the map of Europe was redrawn with a nod to U.S. Pres. Wilson's principle of self-determination. Austria and Hungary were separated and much of their land was given to Yugoslavia (formerly Serbia), Romania, Italy, and the newly independent Poland and Czechoslovakia. Germany lost territory in the West, North, and East, while Finland and the Baltic states were detached from Russia. Turkey lost nearly all its Arab lands to British-sponsored Arab states or to direct French and British rule.

A huge **reparations** burden and partial demilitarization were imposed on Germany. Wilson obtained approval for a League of Nations, but the U.S. Senate refused to allow the U.S. to join.

**Russian revolution.** Military defeats and high casualties caused a contagious lack of confidence in Tsar Nicholas, who was forced to abdicate, Mar. 1917. A liberal provisional government failed to end the war, and massive desertions, riots, and fighting between factions followed. A moderate socialist government under Kerensky was overthrown in a violent **coup by the Bolsheviks** in Petrograd under Lenin, who disbanded the elected Constituent Assembly, Nov. 1917.

The Bolsheviks brutally suppressed all opposition and ended the war with Germany, Mar. 1918. **Civil war** broke out in the summer between the Red Army, including the Bolsheviks and their supporters, and monarchists, anarchists, nationalities (Ukrainians, Georgians, Poles) and others. Small U.S., British, French and Japanese units also opposed the Bolsheviks, 1918-19 (Japan in Vladivostok to 1922). The civil war, anarchy, and pogroms devastated the country until the 1920 Red Army victory. The wartime total monopoly of political, economic, and police power by the Communist Party leadership was retained.

**Other European revolutions.** An unpopular monarchy in **Portugal** was overthrown in 1910. The new republic took severe anti-clerical measures, 1911.

After a century of Home Rule agitation, during which **Ireland** was devastated by famine (one million dead, 1846-47) and emigration, republican militants staged an unsuccessful uprising in Dublin, Easter 1916. The execution of the leaders and mass arrests by the British won popular support for the rebels. The Irish Free State, comprising all but the 6 northern counties, achieved dominion status in 1922.

In the aftermath of the world war, radical revolutions were attempted in Germany (**Spartacist** uprising Jan. 1919), Hungary (Kun regime 1919), and elsewhere. All were suppressed or failed for lack of support.

**Chinese revolution.** The Manchu Dynasty was overthrown and a republic proclaimed, Oct. 1911. First president Sun Yat-sen resigned in favor of strongman Yuan Shih-k'ai. Sun organized the parliamentarian **Kuomintang** party.

Students launched protests May 4, 1919 against League of Nations concessions in China to Japan. Nationalist, liberal, and socialist ideas and political groups spread. The **Communist Party** was founded 1921. A communist regime took power in Mongolia with Soviet support in 1921.

**India restive.** Indian objections to British rule erupted in nationalist riots as well as in the non-violent tactics of Gandhi (1869-1948). Nearly 400 unarmed demonstrators were shot at **Amritsar**, Apr. 1919. Britain approved limited self-rule that year.

**Mexican revolution.** Under the long Diaz dictatorship (1876-1911) the economy advanced, but Indian and mestizo lands were confiscated, and concessions to foreigners (mostly U.S.) damaged the middle class. A **revolution in 1910** led to civil wars and U.S. intervention (1914, 1916-17). Land reform and a more democratic constitution (1917) were achieved.

1916

World War I
— China May 4 protest
— Russian Civil War
Dada movement
— Amritsar riots
— Bolshevik coup

U.S. prohibition

— Iraq,
— Transjordan
— Rathenau killed
Russia's
NEP
1922

U.S. women's vote
— Reza Khan in Persia
— Ulysses

— Lenin d.
Irish Free State
Fasc. March on Rome
Eng. Labour govt.

Kafka's *Trial*

— Portugal coup

Kellogg-Briand Pact
— *Threepenny Opera*

1928

## The Aftermath of War: 1920-29

Left margin timeline (vertical labels, top to bottom):

- 1928
- Stock market crash
- Smoot-Hawley Tariff
- India salt march
- Alfonso leaves Spain
- Japan seizes Manchuria
- Gandhi's fast
- Hitler dictator
- International Style
- 1933
- FDR in office
- Hitler takes Rhineland
- Nuremberg Laws
- Long March in China
- Fr. Popular Front
- Italy takes Ethiopia
- Japan invades China
- Civil War in Spain
- 1938

**U.S.** Easy credit, technological ingenuity, and war-related industrial decline in Europe caused a long economic boom, in which ownership of the new products — autos, phones, radios — became democratized. Prosperity, an increase in women workers, women's suffrage (1920) and drastic change in fashion (flappers, mannish bob for women, clean-shaven men), created a wide perception of social change, despite prohibition of alcoholic beverages (1919-33). Union membership and strikes increased. Fear of radicals led to Palmer raids (1919-20) and Sacco/Vanzetti case (1921-27).

**Europe sorts itself out.** Germany's liberal **Weimar constitution** (1919) could not guarantee a stable government in the face of rightist violence (Rathenau assassinated 1922) and Communist refusal to cooperate with Socialists. Reparations and allied occupation of the Rhineland caused staggering inflation which destroyed middle class savings, but economic expansion resumed after mid-decade, aided by U.S. loans. A sophisticated, innovative culture developed in architecture and design (Bauhaus, 1919-28), film (Lang, *M*, 1931), painting (Grosz), music (Weill, *Threepenny Opera*, 1928), theater (Brecht, *A Man's a Man*, 1926), criticism (Benjamin), philosophy (Jung), and fashion. This culture was considered decadent and socially disruptive by rightists.

**England** elected its first labor governments (Jan. 1924, June 1929). A 10-day general strike in support of coal miners failed, May 1926. In **Italy**, strikes, political chaos and violence by small Fascist bands culminated in the Oct. 1922 Fascist March on Rome, which established Mussolini's dictatorship. Strikes were outlawed (1926), and Italian influence was pressed in the Balkans (Albania a protectorate 1926). A conservative dictatorship was also established in **Portugal** in a 1926 military coup.

**Czechoslovakia**, the only stable democracy to emerge from the war in Central or East Europe, faced opposition from Germans (in the Sudetenland), Ruthenians, and some Slovaks. As the industrial heartland of the old Hapsburg empire, it remained fairly prosperous. With French backing, it formed the Little Entente with Yugoslavia (1920) and **Romania** (1921) to block Austrian or Hungarian irredentism. **Hungary** remained dominated by the landholding classes and expansionist feeling. Croats and Slovenes in **Yugoslavia** demanded a federal state until King Alexander proclaimed a dictatorship (1929). **Poland** faced nationality problems as well (Germans, Ukrainians, Jews); Pilsudski ruled as dictator from 1926. The **Baltic** states were threatened by traditionally dominant ethnic Germans and by Soviet-supported communists.

An economic collapse and famine in **Russia**, 1921-22, claimed 5 million lives. The New Economic Policy (1921) allowed land ownership by peasants and some private commerce and industry. Stalin was absolute ruler within 4 years of Lenin's 1924 death. He inaugurated a brutal collectivization program 1929-32, and used foreign communist parties for Soviet state advantage.

**Internationalism.** Revulsion against World War I led to pacifist agitation, the Kellogg-Briand Pact renouncing aggressive war (1928), and **naval disarmament** pacts (Washington, 1922, London, 1930). But the League of Nations was able to arbitrate only minor disputes (Greece-Bulgaria, 1925).

**Middle East.** Mustafa Kemal (Ataturk) led **Turkish** nationalists in resisting Italian, French, and Greek military advances, 1919-23. The sultanate was abolished 1922, and elaborate reforms passed, including secularization of law and adoption of the Latin alphabet. Ethnic conflict led to persecution of **Armenians** (over 1 million dead in 1915, 1 million expelled), Greeks (forced Greek-Turk population exchange, 1923), and Kurds (1925 uprising).

With evacuation of the Turks from **Arab** lands, the puritanical Wahabi dynasty of eastern Arabia conquered present Saudi Arabia, 1919-25. British, French, and Arab dynastic and nationalist maneuvering resulted in the creation of two more Arab monarchies in 1921: Iraq and Transjordan (both under British control), and two French mandates: Syria and Lebanon. Jewish immigration into British-mandated **Palestine**, inspired by the Zionist movement, was resisted by Arabs, at times violently (1921, 1929 massacres).

Reza Khan ruled **Persia** after his 1921 coup (shah from 1925), centralized control, and created the trappings of a modern state.

**China.** The Kuomintang under **Chiang Kai-shek** (1887-1975) subdued the warlords by 1928. The Communists were brutally suppressed after their alliance with the Kuomintang was broken in 1927. Relative peace thereafter allowed for industrial and financial improvements, with some Russian, British, and U.S. cooperation.

**Arts.** Nearly all bounds of subject matter, style, and attitude were broken in the arts of the period. Abstract art first took inspiration from natural forms or narrative themes (Kandinsky from 1911), then worked free of any representational aims (Malevich's suprematism, 1915-19, Mondrian's geometric style from 1917). The **Dada** movement from 1916 mocked artistic pretension with absurd collages and constructions (Arp, Tzara, from 1916). Paradox, illusion, and psychological taboos were exploited by surrealists by the 1920s (Dali, Magritte). Architectural schools celebrated industrial values, whether vigorous abstract constructivism (Tatlin, *Monument to 3rd International*, 1919) or the machined, streamlined **Bauhaus** style, which was extended to many design fields (Helvetica type face).

Prose writers explored revolutionary narrative modes related to dreams (Kafka's *Trial*, 1925), internal monologue (Joyce's *Ulysses*, 1922), and word play (Stein's *Making of Americans*, 1925). Poets and novelists wrote of modern alienation (Eliot's *Waste Land*, 1922) and aimlessness (Lost Generation).

**Sciences.** Scientific specialization prevailed by the 20th century. Advances in knowledge and technological aptitude increased with the geometric increase in the number of practitioners. Physicists challenged common-sense views of causality, observation, and a mechanistic universe, putting science further beyond popular grasp (Einstein's general theory of relativity, 1915; Bohr's quantum mechanics, 1913; Heisenberg's uncertainty principle, 1927).

## Rise of the Totalitarians: 1930-39

**Depression.** A worldwide financial panic and economic depression began with the Oct. 1929 U.S. stock market crash and the May 1931 failure of the Austrian Credit-Anstalt. A credit crunch caused international bankruptcies and **unemployment**: 12 million jobless by 1932 in the U.S., 5.6 million in Germany, 2.7 million in England. Governments responded with **tariff restrictions** (Smoot-Hawley Act, 1930; Ottawa Imperial Conference, 1932), which dried up world trade. Government public works programs were vitiated by deflationary budget balancing.

**Germany.** Years of agitation by violent extremists were brought to a head by the Depression. Nazi leader **Hitler** was named chancellor by Pres. Hindenburg Jan. 1933, and given dictatorial power by the Reichstag in Mar. Opposition parties were disbanded, strikes banned, and all aspects of economic, cultural, and religious life brought under central government and Nazi party control and manipulated by sophisticated propaganda. Severe persecution of Jews began (Nuremberg Laws Sept. 1935). Many Jews, political opponents and others were sent to concentration camps (Dachau, 1933) where thousands died or were killed. Public works, renewed conscription (1935), arms production, and a 4-year plan (1936) all but ended unemployment.

Hitler's expansionism started with reincorporation of the Saar (1935), occupation of the **Rhineland** (Mar. 1936), and annexation of Austria (Mar. 1938). At **Munich**, Sept. 1938, an indecisive Britain and France sanctioned German dismemberment of Czechoslovakia.

**Russia.** Urbanization and education advanced. Rapid industrialization was achieved through successive **5-year-plans** starting 1928, using severe labor discipline and mass forced labor. Industry was financed by a decline in living standards and exploitation of agriculture, which was almost totally collectivized by the early 1930s (*kolkhoz*, collective farm; *sovkhoz*, state farm, often in newly-worked lands). Successive **purges** increased the role of professionals and management at the expense of workers. Millions perished in a series of man-made disasters: elimination of kulaks (peasant land-owners), 1929-34; severe famine, 1932-33; party purges (Great Purge, 1936-38); suppression of nationalities; and poor conditions in labor camps.

**Spain.** An industrial revolution during World War I created an urban proletariat, which was attracted to socialism and anarchism; Catalan nationalists challenged central authority. The 5 years after King Alfonso left Spain, Apr. 1931, were dominated by tension between intermittent leftist and anti-clerical governments and clericals, monarchists and other rightists. Anarchist and communist rebellions were crushed, but a July, 1936, extreme right rebellion led by Gen. Francisco Franco and aided by Nazi Germany and Fascist Italy succeeded, after a 3-year **civil war** (over 1 million dead in battles and atrocities). The war polarized international public opinion.

**Italy.** Despite propaganda for the ideal of the Corporate State, few domestic reforms were attempted. An entente with Hungary and Austria, Mar. 1934, a pact with Germany and Japan, Nov. 1937, and intervention by 50-75,000 troops in Spain, 1936-39, sealed Italy's identification with the fascist bloc (anti-Semitic laws after Mar. 1938). Ethiopia was conquered, 1935-37, and **Albania** annexed, Jan. 1939, in conscious imitation of ancient Rome.

**East Europe.** Repressive regimes fought for power against an active opposition (liberals, socialists, communists, peasants, Nazis). Minority groups and Jews were restricted within national boundaries that did not coincide with ethnic population patterns. In the destruction of Czechoslovakia, **Hungary** occupied southern Slovakia (Nov. 1938) and Ruthenia (Mar. 1939), and a pro-Nazi regime took power in the rest of Slovakia. Other boundary disputes (e.g. Poland-Lithuania, Yugoslavia-Bulgaria, Romania-Hungary) doomed attempts to build joint fronts against Germany or Russia. Economic depression was severe.

**East Asia.** After a period of liberalism in **Japan,** nativist militarists dominated the government with peasant support. Manchuria was seized, Sept. 1931-Feb. 1932, and a puppet state set up (Manchukuo). Adjacent Jehol (Inner Mongolia) was occupied in 1933. China proper was invaded July 1937; large areas were conquered by Oct. 1938.

In **China** Communist forces left Kuomintang-besieged strongholds in the South in a Long March (1934-35) to the North. The Kuomintang-Communist civil war was suspended Jan. 1937 in the face of threatening Japan.

**The democracies.** The Roosevelt Administration, in office Mar. 1933, embarked on an extensive program of social reform and economic stimulation, including protection for labor unions (heavy industries organized), social security, public works, wages and hours laws, assistance to farmers. Isolationist sentiment (1937 Neutrality Act) prevented U.S. intervention in Europe, but military expenditures were increased in 1939.

French political instability and polarization prevented resolution of economic and international security questions. The **Popular Front** government under Blum (June 1936-Apr. 1938) passed social reforms (40-hour week) and raised arms spending. National coalition governments ruled Britain from Aug. 1931, brought some economic recovery, but failed to define a consistent foreign policy until Chamberlain's government (from May 1937), which practiced deliberate **appeasement** of Germany and Italy.

**India.** Twenty years of agitation for autonomy and then for independence (Gandhi's **salt march**, 1930) achieved some constitutional reform (extended provincial powers, 1935) despite Moslem-Hindu strife. Social issues assumed prominence with peasant uprisings (1921), strikes (1928), Gandhi's efforts for untouchables (1932 "fast unto death"), and social and agrarian reform by the provinces after 1937.

**Arts.** The streamlined, geometric design motifs of Art Deco (from 1925) prevailed through the 1930s. Abstract art flourished (Moore sculptures from 1931) alongside a new realism related to social and political concerns (**Socialist Realism** the official Soviet style from 1934; Mexican muralists Rivera, 1886-1957, and Orozco, 1883-1949), which was also expressed in fiction and poetry (Steinbeck's *Grapes of Wrath*, 1939; Sandburg's *The People, Yes*, 1936). Modern architecture (*International Style*, 1932) was unchallenged in its use of man-made materials (concrete, glass), lack of decoration, and monumentality (Rockefeller Center, 1929-40). U.S.-made films captured a world-wide audience with their larger-than-life fantasies (*Gone with the Wind*, 1939).

# War, Hot and Cold: 1940-49

**War in Europe.** The Nazi-Soviet non-aggression pact (Aug. '39) freed Germany to attack Poland (Sept.). Britain and France, who had guaranteed Polish independence, declared war on Germany. Russia seized East Poland (Sept.), attacked Finland (Nov.), and took the Baltic states (July '40). Mobile German forces staged **"blitzkrieg"** attacks Apr.-June '40, conquering neutral Denmark, Norway, and the Low Countries and defeating France; 350,000 British and French troops were evacuated at Dunkirk (May). The Battle of Britain, June-Dec. '40, denied Germany air superiority. German-Italian campaigns won the Balkans by Apr. '41. Three million Axis troops **invaded Russia** June '41, marching through Ukraine to the Caucasus, and through White Russia and the Baltic republics to Moscow and Leningrad.

Russian winter counterthrusts, '41-'42 and '42-'43, stopped the German advance (Stalingrad Sept. '42-Feb. '43). With British and U.S. Lend-Lease aid and sustaining great casualties, the Russians drove the Axis from all E. Europe and the Balkans in the next 2 years. Invasions of N. Africa (Nov. '42), Italy (Sept. '43), and Normandy (June '44) brought U.S., British, Free French and allied troops to Germany by spring '45. Germany surrendered May 7, 1945.

**War in Asia-Pacific.** Japan occupied Indochina Sept. '40, dominated Thailand Dec. '41, attacked Hawaii, the Philippines, Hong Kong, Malaya Dec. 7, 1941. Indonesia was attacked Jan. '42, Burma conquered Mar. '42. Battle of Midway (June '42) turned back the Japanese advance. "Island-hopping" battles (Guadalcanal Aug. '42-Jan. '43, Leyte Gulf Oct. '44, Iwo Jima Feb.-Mar. '45, Okinawa Apr. '45) and massive bombing raids on Japan from June '44 wore out Japanese defenses. Two U.S. atom bombs, dropped Aug. 6 and 9, forced Japan to surrender Aug. 14, 1945.

**Atrocities.** The war brought 20th-century cruelty to its peak. Nazi murder camps (Auschwitz) systematically killed 6 million Jews. Gypsies, political opponents, sick and retarded people, and others deemed undesirable were murdered by the Nazis, as were vast numbers of Slavs, especially leaders.

**Civilian deaths.** German bombs killed 70,000 English civilians. Some 100,000 Chinese civilians were killed by Japanese forces in the capture of Nanking. Severe retaliation by the Soviet army, E. European partisans, Free French and others took a heavy toll. U.S. and British bombing of Germany killed hundreds of thousands, as did U.S. bombing of Japan (80-200,000 at Hiroshima alone). Some 45 million people lost their lives in the war.

**Settlement.** The United Nations charter was signed in San Francisco June 26, 1945 by 50 nations. The International Tribunal at Nuremberg convicted 22 German leaders for war crimes Sept. '46, 23 Japanese leaders were convicted Nov. '48. Postwar border changes included large gains in territory for the USSR, losses for Germany, a shift westward in Polish borders, and minor losses for Italy. Communist regimes, supported by Soviet troops, took power in most of E. Europe, including Soviet-occupied Germany (GDR proclaimed Oct. '49). Japan lost all overseas lands.

**Recovery.** Basic political and social changes were imposed on Japan and W. Germany by the western allies (Japan constitution Nov. '46, W. German basic law May '49). U.S. Marshall Plan aid ($12 billion '47-'51) spurred W. European economic recovery after a period of severe inflation and strikes in Europe and the U.S. The British Labour Party introduced a national health service and nationalized basic industries in 1946.

**Cold War.** Western fears of further Soviet advances (Cominform formed Oct. '47, Czechoslovakia coup, Feb. '48, Berlin blockade Apr.'48-Sept. '49) led to formation of NATO. Civil War in Greece and Soviet pressure on Turkey led to U.S. aid under the Truman Doctrine (Mar. '47). Other anti-communist security pacts were the Org. of American States (Apr. '48) and Southeast Asia Treaty Org. (Sept. '54). A new wave of Soviet purges and repression intensified in the last years of Stalin's rule, extending to E. Europe (Slansky trial in Czechoslovakia, 1951). Only Yugoslavia resisted Soviet control (expelled by Cominform, June '48; U.S. aid, June '49).

**China, Korea.** Communist forces emerged from World War II strengthened by the Soviet takeover of industrial Manchuria. In 4 years of fighting, the Kuomintang was driven from the mainland; the People's Republic was proclaimed Oct. 1, 1949. Korea was divided by Russian and U.S. occupation forces. Separate republics were proclaimed in the 2 zones Aug.-Sept. '48.

**India.** India and Pakistan became independent dominions Aug. 15, 1947. Millions of Hindu and Moslem refugees were created by the partition; riots, 1946-47, took hundreds of thousands of lives; Gandhi himself was assassinated Jan. '48. Burma became completely independent Jan. '48; Ceylon took dominion status in Feb.

**Middle East.** The UN approved partition of Palestine into Jewish and Arab states. Israel was proclaimed May 14, 1948. Arabs rejected partition, but failed to defeat Israel in war, May '48-July '49. Immigration from Europe and the Middle East swelled Israel's Jewish population. British and French forces left Lebanon and Syria, 1946. Transjordan occupied most of Arab Palestine.

**Southeast Asia.** Communists and others fought against restoration of French rule in Indochina from 1946; a non-communist government was recognized by France Mar. '49, but fighting continued. Both Indonesia and the Philippines became independent, the former in 1949 after 4 years of war with Netherlands, the latter in 1946. Philippine economic and military ties with the U.S. remained strong; a communist-led peasant rising was checked in '48.

**Arts.** New York became the center of the world art market; abstract expressionism was the chief mode (Pollock from '43, de Kooning from '47). Literature and philosophy explored existentialism (Camus's *Stranger*, 1942, Sartre's *Being and Nothingness*, 1943). Non-western attempts to revive or create regional styles (Senghor's Negritude, Mishima's novels) only confirmed the emergence of a universal culture. Radio and phonograph records spread American popular music (swing, bebop) around the world.

# The American Decade: 1950-59

**Polite decolonization.** The peaceful decline of European political and military power in Asia and Africa accelerated in the 1950s. Nearly all of N. Africa was freed by 1956, but France fought a bitter war to retain Algeria, with its large European minority, until 1962. **Ghana**, independent 1957, led a parade of new black African nations (over 2 dozen by 1962), which altered the political character of the UN. Ethnic disputes often exploded in the new nations after decolonization (UN troops in Cyprus 1964; **Nigeria** civil war 1967-70). Leaders of the new states, mostly sharing socialist ideologies, tried to create an Afro-Asian bloc (Bandung Conf. 1955), but Western economic influence and U.S. political ties remained strong (Baghdad Pact, 1955).

**Trade.** World trade volume soared, in an atmosphere of monetary stability assured by international accords (**Bretton Woods** 1944). In Europe, economic integration advanced (**European Economic Community** 1957, European Free Trade Association 1960). Comecon (1949) coordinated the economies of Soviet-bloc countries.

**U.S.** Economic growth produced an abundance of consumer goods (9.3 million motor vehicles sold, 1955). Suburban housing tracts changed life patterns for middle and working classes (Levittown 1946-51). **Eisenhower's** landslide election victories (1952, 1956) reflected consensus politics. Censure of McCarthy (Dec. '54) curbed the political abuse of anti-communism. A system of alliances and military bases bolstered U.S. influence on all continents. Trade and payments surpluses were balanced by overseas investments and foreign aid ($50 billion, 1950-59).

**USSR.** In the "thaw" after Stalin's death in 1953, relations with the West improved (evacuation of Vienna, Geneva summit conf., both 1955). Repression of scientific and cultural life eased, and many prisoners were freed or rehabilitated culminating in de-**Stalinization** (1956). Khrushchev's leadership aimed at consumer growth, but farm production lagged, despite the virgin lands program (from 1954). The 1956 Hungarian revolution, the 1960 U-2 spy plane episode, and other incidents renewed East-West tension and domestic curbs.

**East Europe.** Resentment of Russian domination and Stalinist repression combined with nationalist, economic and religious factors to produce periodic violence. East Berlin workers rioted in 1953, Polish workers rioted in Poznan, June 1956, and a broad-based revolution broke out in Hungary, Oct. 1956. All were suppressed by Soviet force or threats (at least 7,000 dead in Hungary). But Poland was allowed to restore private ownership of farms, and a degree of personal and economic freedom returned to Hungary. Yugoslavia experimented with worker self-management and a market economy.

**Korea.** The 1945 division of Korea left industry in the North, which was organized into a militant regime and armed by Russia. The South was politically disunited. Over 60,000 North Korean troops invaded the South June 25, 1950. The U.S., backed by the UN Security Council, sent troops. UN troops reached the Chinese border in Nov. Some 200,000 Chinese troops crossed the Yalu River and drove back UN forces. Cease-fire in July 1951 found the opposing forces near the original 38th parallel border. After 2 years of sporadic fighting, an armistice was signed July 27, 1953. U.S. troops remained in the South, and U.S. economic and military aid continued. The war stimulated rapid economic recovery in Japan.

**China.** Starting in 1952, industry, agriculture, and social institutions were forcibly collectivized. As many as several million people were executed as Kuomintang supporters or as class and political enemies. The Great Leap Forward, 1958-60, unsuccessfully tried to force the pace of development by substituting labor for investment.

**Indochina.** Ho's forces, aided by Russia and the new Chinese Communist government, fought French and pro-French Vietnamese forces to a standstill, and captured the strategic Dienbienphu camp in May, 1954. The Geneva Agreements divided Vietnam in half pending elections (never held), and recognized Laos and Cambodia as independent. The U.S. aided the anti-Communist Republic of Vietnam in the South.

**Middle East.** Arab revolutions placed leftist, militantly nationalist regimes in power in Egypt (1952) and Iraq (1958). But Arab unity attempts failed (United Arab Republic joined Egypt, Syria, Yemen 1958-61). Arab refusal to recognize Israel (Arab League economic blockade began Sept. 1951) led to a permanent state of war, with repeated incidents (Gaza, 1955). Israel occupied Sinai, Britain and France took the Suez Canal, Oct. 1956, but were replaced by the UN Emergency Force. The Mossadegh government in Iran nationalized the British-owned oil industry May 1951, but was overthrown in a U.S.-aided coup Aug. 1953.

**Latin America.** Argentinian Dictator Juan Peron, in office 1946, enforced land reform, some nationalization, welfare state measures, and curbs on the Roman Catholic Church, but crushed opposition. A Sept. 1955 coup deposed Peron. The 1952 revolution in Bolivia brought land reform, nationalization of tin mines, and improvement in the status of Indians, who nevertheless remained poor. The Batista regime in Cuba was overthrown, Jan. 1959, by Fidel Castro, who imposed a communist dictatorship, aligned Cuba with Russia, improved education and health care. A U.S.-backed anti-Castro invasion (Bay of Pigs, Apr. 1961) was crushed. Self-government advanced in the British Caribbean.

**Technology.** Large outlays on research and development in the U.S. and USSR focused on military applications (H-bomb in U.S. 1952, USSR 1953, Britain 1957, intercontinental missiles late 1950s). Soviet launching of the Sputnik satellite, Oct. 1957, spurred increases in U.S. science education funds (National Defense Education Act).

**Literature and letters.** Alienation from social and literary conventions reached an extreme in the theater of the absurd (Beckett's *Waiting for Godot* 1952), the "new novel" (Robbe-Grillet's *Voyeur* 1955), and avant-garde film (Antonioni's *L'Avventura* 1960). U.S. Beatniks (Kerouac's *On the Road* 1957) and others rejected the supposed conformism of Americans (Riesman's *Lonely Crowd* 1950).

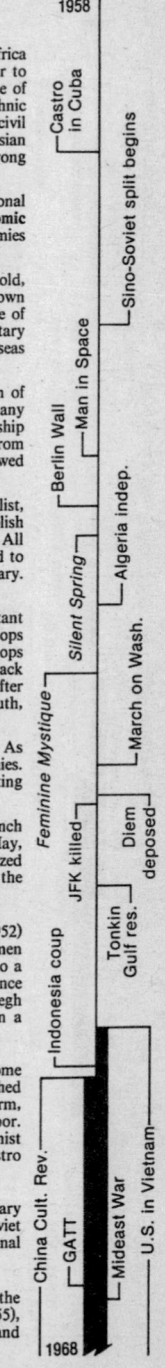

1958

Castro in Cuba

Sino-Soviet split begins

Berlin Wall

Man in Space

Algeria indep.

Silent Spring

March on Wash.

Feminine Mystique

JFK killed

Diem deposed

Tonkin Gulf res.

Indonesia coup

China Cult. Rev.

GATT

Mideast War

U.S. in Vietnam

1968

# Rising Expectations: 1960-69

**Economic boom.** The longest sustained economic boom on record spanned almost the entire decade in the capitalist world; the closely-watched GNP figure doubled in the U.S. 1960-70, fueled by Vietnam War-related budget deficits. The **General Agreement on Tariffs and Trade**, 1967, stimulated West European prosperity, which spread to peripheral areas (Spain, Italy, E. Germany). Japan became a top economic power ($20 billion exports 1970). Foreign investment aided the industrialization of Brazil. Soviet 1965 economic reform attempts (decentralization, material incentives) were limited, but growth continued.

**Reform and radicalization.** Pres. John F. Kennedy, inaugurated 1961, emphasized youthful idealism, vigor; he was assassinated Nov. 22, 1963. A series of political and social reform movements took root in the U.S., later spreading to other countries with the help of ubiquitous U.S. film and television programs and heavy overseas travel (2.2 million U.S. passports issued 1970). Blacks agitated peaceably and with partial success against segregation and poverty (1963 March on Washington, 1964 **Civil Rights Act**); but some urban ghettos erupted in extensive riots (Watts, 1965; Detroit, 1967; King assassination, Apr. 4, 1968). New concern for the poor (Harrington's *Other America*, 1963) led to Pres. Johnson's **"Great Society"** programs (Medicare, Water Quality Act, Higher Education Act, all 1965). Concern with the environment surged (Carson's *Silent Spring*, 1962). **Feminism** revived as a cultural and political movement (Friedan's *Feminine Mystique*, 1963, National Organization for Women founded 1966) and a movement for homosexual rights emerged (Stonewall riot, in NYC, 1969). Pope John XXIII called Vatican II, 1962-65, which liberalized Roman Catholic liturgy.

Opposition to U.S. involvement in Vietnam, especially among university students (**Moratorium** protest Nov. '69), turned violent (Weatherman Chicago riots Oct. '69). New Left and Marxist theories became popular, and membership in radical groups swelled (Students for a Democratic Society, Black Panthers). Maoist groups, especially in Europe, called for total transformation of society. In France, students sparked a nationwide strike affecting 10 million workers May-June '68, but an electoral reaction barred revolutionary change.

**Arts and styles.** The boundary between fine and popular arts was blurred by Pop Art (Warhol) and rock musicals (Hair, 1968). Informality and exaggeration prevailed in fashion (beards, miniskirts). A non-political "counterculture" developed, rejecting traditional bourgeois life goals and personal habits, and use of marijuana and hallucinogens spread (Woodstock festival Aug. '69). Indian influence was felt in music (Beatles), religion (Ram Dass), and fashion.

**Science.** Achievements in space (men on moon July '69) and electronics (lasers, integrated circuits) encouraged a faith in scientific solutions to problems in agriculture ("green revolution"), medicine (heart transplants 1967) and other areas. The harmful effects of science, it was believed, could be controlled (1963 nuclear weapon test ban treaty, 1968 non-proliferation treaty).

**China.** Mao's revolutionary militance caused disputes with Russia under "revisionist" Khrushchev, starting 1960. The two powers exchanged fire in 1969 border disputes. China used force to capture areas disputed with India 1962. The "Great Proletarian Cultural Revolution" tried to impose a utopian egalitarian program in China and spread revolution abroad; political struggle, often violent, convulsed China 1965-68.

**Indochina.** Communist-led guerrillas aided by N. Vietnam fought from 1960 against the S. Vietnam government of Ngo Dinh Diem (killed 1963). The U.S. military role increased after the 1964 Tonkin Gulf incident. U.S. forces peaked at 543,400, Apr. '69. Massive numbers of N. Viet troops also fought. Laotian and Cambodian neutrality were threatened by communist insurgencies, with N. Vietnamese aid, and U.S. intrigues.

**Third World.** A bloc of authoritarian leftist regimes among the newly independent nations emerged in political opposition to the U.S.-led Western alliance, and came to dominate the conference of nonaligned nations (Belgrade 1961, Cairo 1964, Lusaka 1970). Soviet political ties and military bases were established in Cuba, Egypt, Algeria, Guinea, and other countries, whose leaders were regarded as revolutionary heros by opposition groups in pro-Western or colonial countries. Some leaders were ousted in coups by pro-Western groups—Zaire's Lumumba (killed 1961), Ghana's Nkrumah (exiled 1966), and Indonesia's Sukarno (effectively ousted 1965 after a Communist coup failed).

**Middle East.** Arab-Israeli tension erupted into a brief war June 1967. Israel emerged as a major regional power. Military shipments before and after the war brought much of the Arab world into the Soviet political sphere. Most Arab states broke U.S. diplomatic ties, while Communist countries cut their ties to Israel. Intra-Arab disputes continued: Egypt and Saudi Arabia supported rival factions in a bloody Yemen civil war 1962-70; Lebanese troops fought Palestinian commandos 1969.

**East Europe.** To stop the large-scale exodus of citizens, E. German authorities built a fortified wall across Berlin Aug. '61. Soviet sway in the Balkans was weakened by Albania's support of China (USSR broke ties Dec. '61) and Romania's assertion of industrial and foreign policy autonomy 1964. Liberalization in Czechoslovakia, spring 1968, was crushed by troops of 5 Warsaw Pact countries. West German treaties with Russia and Poland, 1970, facilitated the transfer of German technology and confirmed post-war boundaries.

# Disillusionment: 1970-79

**U.S.: Caution and neoconservatism.** A relatively sluggish economy, energy and resource shortages (natural gas crunch 1975, gasoline shortage 1979) and environmental problems contributed to a **"limits of growth"** philosophy. Suspicion of science and technology killed or delayed major projects (supersonic transport dropped 1971, DNA recombination curbed 1976, Seabrook A-plant protests 1977-78) and was fed by the Three Mile Island nuclear reactor accident Mar. '79.

Mistrust of big government weakened support for government reform plans among liberals. School busing and racial quotas were opposed (Bakke decision June '78); the Equal Rights Amendment for women languished; civil rights for homosexuals were opposed (Dade County referendum June '77).

Completion of communist forces' takeover of S. Vietnam (evacuation of U.S. civilians Apr. '75), revelations of Central Intelligence Agency misdeeds (Rockefeller Commission report June '75), and **Watergate** scandals (Nixon quit Aug. '74) reduced faith in U.S. moral and material capacity to influence world affairs. Revelations of Soviet crimes (Solzhenitsyn's *Gulag Archipelago* from 1974) and Russian intervention in Africa aided a revival of anti-Communist sentiment.

---

Timeline (left margin):

1968

Sino-Soviet fighting
First Earth Day
Pentagon Papers published
Woodstock festival
Men on moon
Roe v. Wade abortion ruling
U.S. SST barred
Bangladesh indep.
Nixon in Peking
Israel-Arab 6-Day War
Worldwide recession
Nixon resigns
Indochina War ends
1 mln. die in Cambodia
Franco d.
Mao d.
U.S. hostages taken in Iran
Khomeini govt. in Iran
Egypt-Israel treaty
3 Mile Island
USSR invades Afghanistan
18% inflation rate in U.S.

1980

**Economy sluggish.** The 1960s boom faltered in the 1970s; a severe recession in the U.S. and Europe 1974-75 followed a huge oil price hike Dec. '73. Monetary instability (U.S. cut ties to gold Aug. '71), the decline of the dollar, and **protectionist** moves by industrial countries (1977-78) threatened trade. Business investment and spending for research declined. Severe inflation plagued many countries (25% in Britain 1975; 18% in U.S. 1979).

**China picks up pieces.** After the 1976 deaths of Mao and Zhou, a power struggle for the leadership succession was won by pragmatists. A nationwide purge of orthodox Maoists was carried out and the "Gang of Four" led by Mao's widow Chiang Ching was arrested.

The new leaders freed over 100,000 political prisoners, and reduced public adulation of Mao. Political and trade ties were expanded with Japan, Europe, and U.S. in the late 1970's, as relations worsened with Russia, Cuba, and Vietnam (4-week invasion by China 1979). Ideological guidelines in industry, science, education, and the armed forces, which the ruling faction said had caused chaos and decline, were reversed (bonuses to workers Dec. '77; exams for college entrance Oct. '77). Severe restrictions on cultural expression were eased (Beethoven ban lifted Mar. '77).

**Europe.** European unity moves (EEC-EFTA trade accord 1972) faltered as economic problems appeared (Britain floated pound 1972; France floated franc 1974). Germany and Switzerland curbed guest workers from S. Europe. Greece and Turkey quarreled over Cyprus (Turks intervened 1974), Aegean oil rights.

All non-Communist Europe was under democratic rule after free elections were held in **Spain** June '76, 7 months after the death of Franco. The conservative, colonialist regime in **Portugal** was overthrown Apr. '74. In **Greece**, the 7-year-old military dictatorship yielded power in 1974. Northern Europe, though ruled mostly by Socialists (**Swedish** Socialists unseated 1976, after 44 years in power), turned conservative. The **British** Labour government imposed wage curbs 1975, and suspended nationalization schemes. Terrorism in **Germany** (1972 Munich Olympics killings) led to laws curbing some civil liberties. French "new philosophers" rejected leftist ideologies and the shaky Socialist-Communist coalition lost a 1978 election bid.

**Religion back in politics.** The improvement in Moslem countries' political fortunes by the 1950s (with the exception of Central Asia under Soviet and Chinese rule) and the growth of Arab oil wealth, was followed by a resurgence of traditional piety. **Libyan** dictator Qaddafy mixed strict Islamic laws with socialism in his militant ideology, called for an eventual Moslem return to Spain and Sicily. The illegal Moslem Brotherhood in **Egypt** was accused of violence, while extreme Moslem groups bombed theaters, 1977, to protest secular values.

In **Turkey**, the National Salvation Party was the first Islamic group to share power (1974) since secularization in the 1920s. Religious authorities, such as Ayatollah Ruhollah Khomeini, led the **Iranian** revolution and religiously motivated Moslems took part in the insurrection in Saudi Arabia that briefly seized the Grand Mosque in Mecca 1979. Moslem puritan opposition to **Pakistan** Pres. Bhutto helped lead to his overthrow July '77. However, Moslem solidarity could not prevent Pakistan's eastern province (**Bangladesh**) from declaring independence, Dec. '71, after a bloody civil war.

Moslem and Hindu resentment against coerced sterilization in **India** helped defeat the Gandhi government, which was replaced Mar. '77 by a coalition including religious Hindu parties and led by devout Hindu Desai. Moslems in the southern **Philippines**, aided by Libya, conducted a long rebellion against central rule from 1973.

Evangelical Protestant groups grew in numbers and prosperity in the U.S. A revival of interest in Orthodox Christianity occurred among **Russian** intellectuals (Solzhenitsyn). The secularist **Israeli** Labor party, after decades of rule, was ousted in 1977 by conservatives led by Begin, an observant Jew; religious militants founded settlements on the disputed West Bank, part of Biblically-promised Israel. U.S. Reform Judaism revived many previously discarded traditional practices.

The Buddhist Soka Gakkai movement launched the Komeito party in Japan 1964, which became a major opposition party in 1972 and 1976 elections.

Old-fashioned religious wars raged intermittently in **N. Ireland** (Catholic vs. Protestant 1969- ) and **Lebanon** (Christian vs. Moslem 1975- ) while religious militancy complicated the Israel-Arab dispute (1973 Israel-Arab war). In spite of a **1979 peace treaty between Egypt and Israel** which looked forward to a resolution of the Palestinian issue, increased religious militancy on the West Bank made a resolution unlikely.

**Latin America.** Repressive conservative regimes strengthened their hold on most of the continent, with the violent coup against the elected Allende government in **Chile**, Sept. '73, the 1976 military coup in **Argentina**, and coups against reformist regimes in **Bolivia**, 1971 and 1979, and **Peru**, 1976. In Central America, increasing liberal and leftist militancy led to the ouster of the Somoza regime of Nicaragua in 1979 and civil conflict in El Salvador.

**Indochina.** Communist victory in Vietnam, Cambodia, and Laos by May '75 did not bring peace. Attempts at radical social reorganization left over one million dead in Cambodia 1975-78 and caused hundreds of thousands of ethnic Chinese and others to flee Vietnam ("boat people" 1979). The Vietnamese invasion of Cambodia swelled the refugee population and contributed to widespread starvation in that devastated country.

**Russian expansion.** Soviet influence, checked in some countries (troops ousted by Egypt 1972) was projected further afield, often with the use of Cuban troops (Angola 1975-89, Ethiopia 1977-88) and aided by a growing navy, merchant fleet, and international banking ability. Detente with the West — 1972 Berlin pact, 1972 strategic arms pact (**SALT**) — gave way to a more antagonistic relationship in the late 1970s, exacerbated by the Soviet invasion of Afghanistan 1979.

**Africa.** The last remaining European colonies were granted independence (**Spanish Sahara** 1976, **Djibouti** 1977) and, after 10 years of civil war and many negotiation sessions, a black government took over **Zimbabwe** (Rhodesia) 1979; white domination remained in **S. Africa.** Great power involvement in local wars (Russia in **Angola, Ethiopia;** France in **Chad, Zaire, Mauritania**) and the use of tens of thousands of Cuban troops was denounced by some African leaders as neocolonialism. Ethnic or tribal clashes made Africa the chief world locus of sustained warfare in the late 1970s.

**Arts.** Traditional modes in painting, architecture, and music, pursued in relative obscurity for much of the 20th century, returned to popular and critical attention in the 1970s. The pictorial emphasis in neorealist and photorealist painting, the return of many architects to detail, decoration, and traditional natural materials, and the concern with ordered structure in musical composition were, ironically, novel experiences for artistic consumers after the exhaustion of experimental possibilities. However, these more conservative styles coexisted with modernist works in an atmosphere of variety and tolerance.

1980

Iran-Iraq War begins

Solidarity founded

ERA defeated

Israel invades Lebanon — U.S. hostages held in Iran

U.S. Congress O.K.'s tax cut

U.S.-led boycott of Moscow Olympics

S. Africa gives voice to Coloureds, Asians

U.S. invades Grenada

Gorbachev made USSR Gen-Secy

U.S. mines Nicaragua ports

Reagan landslide re-election

Achille Lauro terrorism

Challenger explodes

150 mln. Africans near famine

U.S. Tax Reform Law

U.S. stock market crash

Nicaragua cease-fire

U.S. bombs Libya

Iran-contra scandal

USSR withdraws from Afghanistan

Iran-Iraq cease-fire

"evolutionary change" S. Africa

Poland free election

Tiananmen Sq. protests crushed

Berlin Wall opens

Eastern Europe Marxist economies fall

1990

## Revitalization of Capitalism, Demand for Democracy: 1980-89

**USSR, Eastern Europe.** A troublesome 1980-85 for the USSR was followed by 5 years of astonishing change: the surrender of the Communist monopoly, remaking of the Soviet state, and disintegration of the Soviet empire. After deaths of Brezhnev 1982, Andropov 1984, Chernenko 1985; harsh treatment of dissent; restriction of emigration; invasion of Afghanistan Dec.'79; Gen. Secy. Mikhail Gorbachev (1985-1991) promoted **glasnost, perestroika**, economic and social reform (Jan.'87), supported by Communist Party (July '88); signed **INF treaty** (Dec.'87). Gorbachev pledged to cut the military budget (1988); military withdrawal from Afghanistan was completed Feb.'89; democratization was not hindered in Poland, Hungary; the Soviet people chose part of the new Congress from competing candidates Mar.'89. At decade's end, Gorbachev was widely considered responsible for the **1989 ending of the Cold War.**

**Poland. Solidarity,** the labor union founded 1980 by Lech Walesa, outlawed 1982, was legalized 1988, after years of unrest. Poland's first free election since the Communist takeover brought Solidarity victory (June '89); Tadeusz Mazowiecki, a Walesa advisor, became Prime Minister in a government with the Communists (Aug.'89).

In the fall of 1989 the failure of Marxist economies in Hungary, E. Germany, Czechoslovakia, Bulgaria, and Romania brought the fall of the Communist monopoly, the demand for democracy. The Berlin Wall was opened Nov.'89.

**U.S. "The Reagan Years"** (1981-88) brought the **longest economic boom** in U.S. history via budget and tax cuts, deregulation, "junk bond" financing, leveraged buyouts, mergers and takeovers; a **strong anti-Communist stance**, via increased defense spending, aid to anti-communists in Central America, invasion of Cuba-threatened Grenada, championing of MX missile system and "Star Wars." Four Reagan-Gorbachev summits, 1985-88, climaxed in INF treaty 1987. Financial scandals mounted (E.F. Hutton 1985, Ivan Boesky 1986), the stock market crashed Oct.'87, the trade imbalance grew (esp. with Japan), the budget deficit soared ($3.2 trillion 1988); homelessness, drug abuse (esp. "crack") grew. The Iran-contra affair (North TV testimony July'87) was the low point, but V.P. Bush was elected pres. 1988.

**Middle East.** This area remained militarily unstable, with sharp divisions on economic, political, racial, and religious lines. In Iran, the revolution (1979-80) and violent political upheavals after, brought strong anti-U.S. stance. A dispute with Iraq over the Shatt al-Arab waterway became warfare Sept.'80-July'88, with millions killed.

**Libya's** support for international terrorism caused the U.S. to close the diplomatic mission (May'81), embargo oil (Mar.'82); U.S. accused Muammar al-Qaddafy of aiding terrorists in Dec.'85 Rome, Vienna airport attacks, retaliated by bombing Libya Apr.'86.

**Israel** affirmed all Jerusalem as its capital (July'80); destroyed an Iraqi atomic reactor 1981; invaded Lebanon 1982, bringing the PLO to agree to withdraw. A **Palestinian uprising**, inc. women, children hurling rocks, bottles at troops, began Dec.'87 in Israeli-occupied Gaza, spread to the West Bank; troops responded with force, killing 300 by 1988's end, with 6,000 more in detention camps.

Israeli withdrawal from **Lebanon** began Feb.'85, ended June'85, as Lebanon continued torn with military and political conflict between rival factions. Premier Karami was assassinated June'87. Artillery duels between Christian East Beirut and Moslem West Beirut, Mar.-Apr.'89, left 200 dead, 700 wounded. At decade's end, violence still dominated.

**Central America.** In Nicaragua, the leftist Sandinista National Liberation Front, in power after the 1979 civil war, faced problems due to Nicaragua's military aid to leftist guerrillas in El Salvador, U.S. backing of anti-government contras. The U.S. CIA admitted directing the mining of Nicaraguan ports 1984; U.S. sent aid, humanitarian 1985, military 1986. Profits from secret arms sales to Iran were found diverted to contras 1987. Cease-fire talks between Sandinista government and contras came in 1988, elections in Feb.'90.

In El Salvador, a military coup (Oct.'79) failed to halt extreme right-wing violence and left-wing activity. Archbishop Oscar Romero was assassinated Mar.'80; Jan.-June some 4,000 civilians reportedly were killed. In 1984, newly-elected Pres. Duarte decreased rights abuses. Leftist guerrillas continued their offensive 1989.

**Africa.** 1980-85 marked the rapid decline of the economies of virtually all Africa's 61 countries, due to accelerating desertification, the world economic recession, heavy indebtedness to overseas creditors, rapid population growth, political instability. Some 60 million Africans, almost one-fifth of the population, faced prolonged hunger 1981; much of Africa had one of the worst droughts ever 1983, and by year's end **150 million faced near-famine.** "Live Aid" marathon rock concert (July'85), U.S. and Western nations sent aid Sept.'85. Economic hardship fueled political unrest, coups. Wars in Ethiopia, Sudan, military strife in 6 other nations continued through 1989. AIDS took a heavy toll.

**South Africa.** Anti-apartheid sentiment gathered **force**, demonstrations and violent police response grew. South African white voters approved (Nov.'83) the first constitution to give "Coloureds," Asians a voice, while still excluding blacks—70% of the population. The U.S. imposed economic sanctions Aug.'85, 11 Western nations followed in Sept. **P.W. Botha**, '80s president, was succeeded by **F.W. de Klerk**, Sept.'89, on a platform of "evolutionary" change via negotiation with the black population.

**China.** From 1980 through mid-1989 the Communist Party, under Chairman Deng Xiaoping, pursued **far-reaching changes** in political and economic institutions, expanding commercial and technical ties to the industrialized world, increasing the role of market forces in stimulating urban economic development. But Apr.'89 brought the demand for more changes: students camped out in Tiananmen Sq., Beijing; some 100,000 students and workers marched, at least 20 other cities saw protests. Martial law was imposed; army troops crushed protests in Tiananmen Sq., June 3-4 with death toll estimates 500-7,000, up to 10,000 injured, up to 10,000 dissidents arrested, 31 tried and executed. The conciliatory Communist Party chief was ousted; the Politburo adopted reforms against official corruption (July).

**Japan.** Relations with other nations, esp. U.S., 1980-89, were dominated by **trade imbalances favoring Japan**. In 1985 the U.S. trade deficit with Japan was $49.7 billion, one-third of the total U.S. trade deficit. After Japan was found to sell semiconductors, computer memory chips below cost (Apr.'86), the U.S. was assured a "fair share" of the market, but charged Japan with failing to live up to the agreement Mar.'87. The **Omnibus Trade Bill**, Aug.'88, provided for retaliation; Pres. Bush called Japan's practices "unjustifiable," the law gave Japan 18 months to stop or face trade restrictions.

**European Community.** With the addition of Greece, Portugal, and Spain, the EC became a **common market of over 300 million people**, the West's largest trading entity. **Margaret Thatcher** became the first British prime minister in this century to win 3 consecutive terms 1987. France elected its first socialist president, **Francois Mitterand** 1981, re-elected 1988. Italy elected its first socialist premier, **Bettino Craxi** 1983.

**International Terrorism.** With the 1979 overthrow of the Shah of Iran, terrorism became a prominent political tactic that increased through the '80s, but with fewer high profile attacks after 1985. Iranian militants held 52 Americans hostage in Iran for 444 days, 1979-81; a TNT-laden suicide terrorist blew up U.S. Marine headquarters in Beirut, killing 241 Americans, while a truck bomb blew up a French paratroop barracks, killing 58, 1984; the *Achille Lauro* was hijacked, an American passenger killed, and the U.S. subsequently intercepted the Egyptian plane flying the terrorists to safety 1985. Incidents rose to 700 in 1985, 1,000+ in 1988. The Pentagon reported 52 terrorist groups Jan.'89.

**Assassinations** included Egypt's Pres. **Anwar al-Sadat** 1981; India's Prime Minister **Indira Gandhi** 1984; Lebanese Premier **Rashid Karami** 1987; Pakistan's Pres. **Mohammed Zia ul-Haq** 1988.

# HISTORICAL FIGURES

## Ancient Greeks and Latins

### Greeks

Aeschines, orator, 389-314BC.
Aeschylus, dramatist, 525-456BC.
Aesop, fableist, c620-c560BC.
Alcibiades, politician, 450-404BC.
Anacreon, poet, c582-c485BC.
Anaxagoras, philosopher, c500-428BC.
Anaximander, philosopher, 611-546BC.
Antiphon, speechwriter, c480-411BC.
Apollonius, mathematician, c265-170BC.
Archimedes, math. c287-212BC.
Aristophanes, dramatist, c448-380BC.
Aristotle, philosopher, 384-322BC.
Athenaeus, scholar, fl.c200.
Callicrates, architect, fl.5th cent.BC.
Callimachus, poet, c305-240BC.
Cratinus, comic dramatist, 520-421BC.
Democritus, philosopher, c460-370BC.
Demosthenes, orator, 384-322BC.
Diodorus, historian, fl.20BC.
Diogenes, philosopher, c372-c287BC.

Dionysius, historian, d.c7BC.
Empedocles, philosopher, c490-430BC.
Epicharmus, dramatist, c530-440BC.
Epictetus, philosopher, c55-c135.
Epicurus, philosopher, 341-270BC.
Eratosthenes, scientist, c276-194BC.
Euclid, mathematician, fl.c300BC.
Euripides, dramatist, c484-406BC.
Galen, physician, c129-199.
Heraclitus, philosopher, c535-c475BC.
Herodotus, historian, c484-420BC.
Hesiod, poet, 8th cent. BC.
Hippocrates, physician, c460-377BC.
Homer, poet, believed lived c850BC.
Isocrates, orator, 436-338BC.
Menander, dramatist, 342-292BC.
Phidias, sculptor, c500-435BC.
Pindar, poet, c518-c438BC.
Plato, philosopher, c428-c347BC.
Plutarch, biographer, c46-120.

Polybius, historian, c200-c118BC.
Praxiteles, sculptor, 400-330BC.
Pythagoras, phil., math., c580-c500BC.
Sappho, poet, c610-c580BC.
Simonides, poet, 556-c468BC.
Socrates, philosopher, c470-399BC.
Solon, statesman, 640-560BC.
Sophocles, dramatist, c496-406BC.
Strabo, geographer, c63BC-AD24.
Thales, philosopher, c634-c546BC.
Themistocles, politician, c524-c460BC.
Theocritus, poet, c310-250BC.
Theophrastus, phil. c372-c287BC.
Thucydides, historian, fl.5th cent.BC.
Timon, philosopher, c320-c230BC.
Xenophon, historian, c434-c355BC.
Zeno, philosopher, c495-c430BC.

### Latins

Ammianus, historian, c330-395.
Apuleius, satirist, c124-c170.
Boethius, scholar, c480-524
Caesar, Julius, general, 100-44BC.
Catilina, politician, c108-62BC.
Cato(Elder), statesman, 234-149BC.
Catullus, poet, c84-54BC.
Cicero, orator, 106-43BC.
Claudian, poet, c370-c404.
Ennius, poet, 239-170BC.
Gellius, author, c130-c165.
Horace, poet, 65-8BC.

Juvenal, satirist, c60-c127.
Livy, historian, 59BC-AD17.
Lucan, poet, 39-65.
Lucilius, poet, c180-c102BC.
Lucretius, poet, c99-c55BC.
Martial, epigrammatist, c38-c103.
Nepos, historian, c100-c25BC.
Ovid, poet, 43BC-AD17.
Persius, satirist, 34-62.
Plautus, dramatist, c254-c184BC.
Pliny, scholar, 23-79.
Pliny(Younger), author, 62-113.

Quintilian, rhetorician, c35-c97.
Sallust, historian, 86-34BC.
Seneca, philosopher, 4BC-AD65.
Silius, poet, c25-101.
Statius, poet, c45-c96.
Suetonius, biographer, c69-c122.
Tacitus, historian, c56-c120.
Terence, dramatist, 185-c159BC.
Tibullus, poet, c55-c19BC.
Virgil, poet, 70-19BC.
Vitruvius, architect, fl.1st cent.BC.

## Rulers of England and Great Britain

| Name | England | Began | Died | Age | Rgd |
|---|---|---|---|---|---|
| | **Saxons and Danes** | | | | |
| Egbert | King of Wessex, won allegiance of all English | 829 | 839 | — | 10 |
| Ethelwulf | Son, King of Wessex, Sussex, Kent, Essex | 839 | 858 | — | 19 |
| Ethelbald | Son of Ethelwulf, displaced father in Wessex | 858 | 860 | — | 2 |
| Ethelbert | 2d son of Ethelwulf, united Kent and Wessex | 860 | 866 | — | 6 |
| Ethelred I | 3d son, King of Wessex, fought Danes | 866 | 871 | — | 5 |
| Alfred | The Great, 4th son, defeated Danes, fortified London | 871 | 899 | 52 | 28 |
| Edward | The Elder, Alfred's son, united English, claimed Scotland | 899 | 924 | 55 | 25 |
| Athelstan | The Glorious, Edward's son, King of Mercia, Wessex | 924 | 940 | 45 | 16 |
| Edmund I | 3d son of Edward, King of Wessex, Mercia | 940 | 946 | 25 | 6 |
| Edred | 4th son of Edward | 946 | 955 | 32 | 9 |
| Edwy | The Fair, eldest son of Edmund, King of Wessex | 955 | 959 | 18 | 3 |
| Edgar | The Peaceful, 2d son of Edmund, ruled all English | 959 | 975 | 32 | 17 |
| Edward | The Martyr, eldest son of Edgar, murdered by stepmother | 975 | 978 | 17 | 4 |
| Ethelred II | The Unready, 2d son of Edgar, married Emma of Normandy | 978 | 1016 | 48 | 37 |
| Edmund II | Ironside, son of Ethelred II, King of London | 1016 | 1016 | 27 | 0 |
| Canute | The Dane, gave Wessex to Edmund, married Emma | 1016 | 1035 | 40 | 19 |
| Harold I | Harefoot, natural son of Canute | 1035 | 1040 | — | 5 |
| Hardecanute | Son of Canute by Emma, Danish King | 1040 | 1042 | 24 | 2 |
| Edward | The Confessor, son of Ethelred II (Canonized 1161) | 1042 | 1066 | 62 | 24 |
| Harold II | Edward's brother-in-law, last Saxon King | 1066 | 1066 | 44 | 0 |
| | **House of Normandy** | | | | |
| William I | The Conqueror, defeated Harold at Hastings | 1066 | 1087 | 60 | 21 |
| William II | Rufus, 3d son of William I, killed by arrow | 1087 | 1100 | 43 | 13 |
| Henry I | Beauclerc, youngest son of William I | 1100 | 1135 | 67 | 35 |
| | **House of Blois** | | | | |
| Stephen | Son of Adela, daughter of William I, and Count of Blois | 1135 | 1154 | 50 | 19 |
| | **House of Plantagenet** | | | | |
| Henry II | Son of Geoffrey Plantagenet (Angevin) by Matilda, dau. of Henry I | 1154 | 1189 | 56 | 35 |
| Richard I | Coeur de Lion, son of Henry II, crusader | 1189 | 1199 | 42 | 10 |
| John | Lackland, son of Henry II, signed Magna Carta, 1215 | 1199 | 1216 | 50 | 17 |
| Henry III | Son of John, acceded at 9, under regency until 1227 | 1216 | 1272 | 65 | 56 |
| Edward I | Longshanks, son of Henry III | 1272 | 1307 | 68 | 35 |
| Edward II | Son of Edward I, deposed by Parliament, 1327 | 1307 | 1327 | 43 | 20 |
| Edward III | Of Windsor, son of Edward II | 1327 | 1377 | 65 | 50 |
| Richard II | Grandson of Edw. III, minor until 1389, deposed 1399 | 1377 | 1400 | 33 | 22 |
| | **House of Lancaster** | | | | |
| Henry IV | Son of John of Gaunt, Duke of Lancaster, son of Edw. III | 1399 | 1413 | 47 | 13 |
| Henry V | Son of Henry IV, victor of Agincourt | 1413 | 1422 | 34 | 9 |
| Henry VI | Son of Henry V, deposed 1461, died in Tower | 1422 | 1471 | 49 | 39 |

| Name | | Began | Died | Age | Rgd |
|---|---|---|---|---|---|
| **House of York** | | | | | |
| Edward IV | Great-great-grandson of Edward III, son of Duke of York | 1461 | 1483 | 41 | 22 |
| Edward V | Son of Edward IV, murdered in Tower of London | 1483 | 1483 | 13 | 0 |
| Richard III | Crookback, bro. of Edward IV, fell at Bosworth Field | 1483 | 1485 | 35 | 2 |
| **House of Tudor** | | | | | |
| Henry VII | Son of Edmund Tudor, Earl of Richmond, whose father had married the widow of Henry V; descended from Edward III through his mother, Margaret Beaufort via John of Gaunt. By marriage with dau. of Edward IV he united Lancaster and York | 1485 | 1509 | 53 | 24 |
| Henry VIII | Son of Henry VII by Elizabeth, dau. of Edward IV. | 1509 | 1547 | 56 | 38 |
| Edward VI | Son of Henry VIII, by Jane Seymour, his 3d queen. Ruled under regents. Was forced to name Lady Jane Grey his successor. Council of State proclaimed her queen July 10, 1553. Mary Tudor won Council, was proclaimed queen July 19, 1553. Mary had Lady Jane Grey beheaded for treason, Feb., 1554 | 1547 | 1553 | 16 | 6 |
| Mary I | Daughter of Henry VIII, by Catherine of Aragon | 1553 | 1558 | 43 | 5 |
| Elizabeth I | Daughter of Henry VIII, by Anne Boleyn | 1558 | 1603 | 69 | 44 |

## Great Britain
### House of Stuart

| Name | | Began | Died | Age | Rgd |
|---|---|---|---|---|---|
| James I | James VI of Scotland, son of Mary, Queen of Scots. *First to call himself King of Great Britain. This became official with the Act of Union, 1707* | 1603 | 1625 | 59 | 22 |
| Charles I | Only surviving son of James I; beheaded Jan. 30, 1649 | 1625 | 1649 | 48 | 24 |

### Commonwealth, 1649-1660
#### Council of State, 1649; Protectorate, 1653

| Name | | Began | Died | Age | Rgd |
|---|---|---|---|---|---|
| The Cromwells | Oliver Cromwell, Lord Protector | 1653 | 1658 | 59 | — |
| | Richard Cromwell, son, Lord Protector, resigned May 25, 1659 | 1658 | 1712 | 86 | — |

### House of Stuart (Restored)

| Name | | Began | Died | Age | Rgd |
|---|---|---|---|---|---|
| Charles II | Eldest son of Charles I, died without issue | 1660 | 1685 | 55 | 25 |
| James II | 2d son of Charles I. Deposed 1688. Interregnum Dec. 11, 1688, to Feb. 13, 1689 | 1685 | 1701 | 68 | 3 |
| William III | Son of William, Prince of Orange, by Mary, dau. of Charles I | 1689 | 1702 | 51 | 13 |
| and Mary II | Eldest daughter of James II and wife of William III | | 1694 | 33 | 6 |
| Anne | 2d daughter of James II | 1702 | 1714 | 49 | 12 |

### House of Hanover

| Name | | Began | Died | Age | Rgd |
|---|---|---|---|---|---|
| George I | Son of Elector of Hanover, by Sophia, grand-dau. of James I | 1714 | 1727 | 67 | 13 |
| George II | Only son of George I, married Caroline of Brandenburg | 1727 | 1760 | 77 | 33 |
| George III | Grandson of George II, married Charlotte of Mecklenburg | 1760 | 1820 | 81 | 59 |
| George IV | Eldest son of George III, Prince Regent, from Feb., 1811 | 1820 | 1830 | 67 | 10 |
| William IV | 3d son of George III, married Adelaide of Saxe-Meiningen | 1830 | 1837 | 71 | 7 |
| Victoria | Dau. of Edward, 4th son of George III; married (1840) Prince Albert of Saxe-Coburg and Gotha, who became Prince Consort | 1837 | 1901 | 81 | 63 |

### House of Saxe-Coburg and Gotha

| Name | | Began | Died | Age | Rgd |
|---|---|---|---|---|---|
| Edward VII | Eldest son of Victoria, married Alexandra, Princess of Denmark | 1901 | 1910 | 68 | 9 |

### House of Windsor
#### *Name Adopted July 17, 1917*

| Name | | Began | Died | Age | Rgd |
|---|---|---|---|---|---|
| George V | 2d son of Edward VII, married Princess Mary of Teck | 1910 | 1936 | 70 | 25 |
| Edward VIII | Eldest son of George V; acceded Jan. 20, 1936, abdicated Dec. 11 | 1936 | 1972 | 77 | 1 |
| George VI | 2d son of George V; married Lady Elizabeth Bowes-Lyon | 1936 | 1952 | 56 | 15 |
| Elizabeth II | Elder daughter of George VI, acceded Feb. 6, 1952 | 1952 | — | — | — |

## Rulers of Scotland

Kenneth I MacAlpin was the first Scot to rule both Scots and Picts, 846 AD.

Duncan I was the first general ruler, 1034. Macbeth seized the kingdom 1040, was slain by Duncan's son, Malcolm III MacDuncan (Canmore), 1057.

Malcolm married Margaret, Saxon princess who had fled from the Normans. Queen Margaret introduced English language and English monastic customs. She was canonized, 1250. Her son Edgar, 1097, moved the court to Edinburgh. His brothers Alexander I and David I succeeded. Malcolm IV, the Maiden, 1153, grandson of David I, was followed by his brother, William the Lion, 1165, whose son was Alexander II, 1214. The latter's son, Alexander III, 1249, defeated the Norse and regained the Hebrides. When he died, 1286, his granddaughter, Margaret, child of Eric of Norway and grandniece of Edward I of England, known as the Maid of Norway, was chosen ruler, but died 1290, aged 8.

John Baliol, 1292-1296. (Interregnum, 10 years).

Robert Bruce (The Bruce), 1306-1329, victor at Bannockburn, 1314.

David II, only son of Robert Bruce, ruled 1329-1371.

Robert II, 1371-1390, grandson of Robert Bruce, son of Walter, the Steward of Scotland, was called The Steward, first of the so-called Stuart line.

Robert III, son of Robert II, 1390-1406.

James I, son of Robert III, 1406-1437.

James II, son of James I, 1437-1460.

James III, eldest son of James II, 1460-1488.

James IV, eldest son of James III, 1488-1513.

James V, eldest son of James IV, 1513-1542.

Mary, daughter of James V, born 1542, became queen when one week old; was crowned 1543. Married, 1558, Francis, son of Henry II of France, who became king 1559, died 1560. Mary ruled Scots 1561 until abdication, 1567. She also married (2) Henry Stewart, Lord Darnley, and (3) James, Earl of Bothwell. Imprisoned by Elizabeth I, Mary was beheaded 1587.

James VI, 1566-1625, son of Mary and Lord Darnley, became King of England on death of Elizabeth in 1603. Although the thrones were thus united, the legislative union of Scotland and England was not effected until the Act of Union, May 1, 1707.

## Prime Ministers of Great Britain

(W = Whig; T = Tory; Cl = Coalition; P = Peelite; L = Liberal; C = Conservative; La = Labour)

| | | | | | | | |
|---|---|---|---|---|---|---|---|
| Sir Robert Walpole (W) | 1721-1742 | Viscount Goderich (T) | 1827-1828 | Herbert H. Asquith | 1915-1916 |
| Earl of Wilmington (W) | 1742-1743 | Duke of Wellington (T) | 1828-1830 | David Lloyd George (Cl) | 1916-1922 |
| Henry Pelham (W) | 1743-1754 | Earl Grey (W) | 1830-1834 | Andrew Bonar Law (C) | 1922-1923 |
| Duke of Newcastle (W) | 1754-1756 | Viscount Melbourne (W) | 1834 | Stanley Baldwin (C) | 1923-1924 |
| Duke of Devonshire (W) | 1756-1757 | Sir Robert Peel (T) | 1834-1835 | James Ramsay MacDonald | |
| Duke of Newcastle (W) | 1757-1762 | Viscount Melbourne (W) | 1835-1841 | (La) | 1924 |
| Earl of Bute (T) | 1762-1763 | Sir Robert Peel (T) | 1841-1846 | Stanley Baldwin (C) | 1924-1929 |
| George Grenville (W) | 1763-1765 | Lord John Russell (later | | James Ramsay MacDonald | |
| Marquess of Rockingham | | Earl) (W) | 1846-1852 | (La) | 1929-1931 |
| (W) | 1765-1766 | Earl of Derby (T) | 1852 | James Ramsay MacDonald | |
| William Pitt the Elder | | Earl of Aberdeen (P) | 1852-1855 | (Cl) | 1931-1935 |
| (Earl of Chatham) (W) | 1766-1768 | Viscount Palmerston (L) | 1855-1858 | Stanley Baldwin (Cl) | 1935-1937 |
| Duke of Grafton (W) | 1768-1770 | Earl of Derby (C) | 1858-1859 | Neville Chamberlain (Cl) | 1937-1940 |
| Frederick North (Lord | | Viscount Palmerston (L) | 1859-1865 | Winston Churchill (Cl) | 1940-1945 |
| North) (T) | 1770-1782 | Earl Russell (L) | 1865-1866 | Winston Churchill (C) | 1945 |
| Marquess of Rockingham | | Earl of Derby (C) | 1866-1868 | Clement Attlee (La) | 1945-1951 |
| (W) | 1782 | Benjamin Disraeli (C) | 1868 | Sir Winston Churchill (C) | 1951-1955 |
| Earl of Shelburne (W) | 1782-1783 | William E. Gladstone (L) | 1868-1874 | Sir Anthony Eden (C) | 1955-1957 |
| Duke of Portland (Cl) | 1783 | Benjamin Disraeli (C) | 1874-1880 | Harold Macmillan (C) | 1957-1963 |
| William Pitt the Younger | | William E. Gladstone (L) | 1880-1885 | Sir Alec Douglas-Home | |
| (T) | 1783-1801 | Marquess of Salisbury (C) | 1885-1886 | (C) | 1963-1964 |
| Henry Addington (T) | 1801-1804 | William E. Gladstone (L) | 1886 | Harold Wilson (La) | 1964-1970 |
| William Pitt the Younger | | Marquess of Salisbury (C) | 1886-1892 | Edward Heath (C) | 1970-1974 |
| (T) | 1804-1806 | William E. Gladstone (L) | 1892-1894 | Harold Wilson (La) | 1974-1976 |
| William Wyndham Grenville, | | Earl of Rosebery (L) | 1894-1895 | James Callaghan (La) | 1976-1979 |
| Baron Grenville (W) | 1806-1807 | Marquess of Salisbury (C) | 1895-1902 | Margaret Thatcher (C) | 1979-1990 |
| Duke of Portland (T) | 1807-1809 | Arthur J. Balfour (C) | 1902-1905 | John Major (C) | 1990- |
| Spencer Perceval (T) | 1809-1812 | Sir Henry | | | |
| Earl of Liverpool (T) | 1812-1827 | Campbell-Bannerman (L) | 1905-1908 | | |
| George Canning (T) | 1827 | Herbert H. Asquith (L) | 1908-1915 | | |

## Historical Periods of Japan

| | | | | | | |
|---|---|---|---|---|---|
| Yamato | c.300-592 | Conquest of Yamato plain c. 300 A.D. | Ashikaga | 1338-1573 | Ashikaga Takauji becomes shogun, 1338. |
| Asuka | 592-710 | Accession of Empress Suiko, 592. | Muromachi | 1392-1573 | Unification of Southern and Northern Courts, 1392. |
| Nara | 710-794 | Completion of Heijo (Nara), 710; capital moves to Naga-oka, 784. | Sengoku | 1467-1600 | Beginning of the Onin war, 1467. |
| Heian | 794-1192 | Completion of Heian (Kyoto), 794. | Momoyama | 1573-1603 | Oda Nobunaga enters Kyoto, 1568; Nobunaga deposes last Ashikaga shogun, 1573; Tokugawa Ieyasu victor at Sekigahara, 1600. |
| Fujiwara | 858-1160 | Fujiwara-no-Yoshifusa becomes regent, 858. | | | |
| Taira | 1160-1185 | Taira-no-Kiyomori assumes control, 1160; Minamoto-no-Yoritomo victor over Taira, 1185. | Edo | 1603-1867 | Ieyasu becomes shogun, 1603. |
| | | | Meiji | 1868-1912 | Enthronement of Emperor Mutsuhito (Meiji), 1867; Meiji Restoration and Charter Oath, 1868. |
| Kamakura | 1192-1333 | Yoritomo becomes shogun, 1192. | | | |
| Namboku | 1334-1392 | Restoration of Emperor Godaigo, 1334; Southern Court established by Godaigo at Yoshino, 1336. | Taisho | 1912-1926 | Accession of Emperor Yoshihito, 1912. |
| | | | Showa | 1926-1989 | Accession of Emperor Hirohito, 1926. |
| | | | Heisei | 1989- | Accession of Emperor Akihito, 1989. |

## Rulers of France: Kings, Queens, Presidents

### Caesar to Charlemagne

Julius Caesar subdued the Gauls, native tribes of Gaul (France) 57 to 52 BC. The Romans ruled 500 years. The Franks, a Teutonic tribe, reached the Somme from the East ca. 250 AD. By the 5th century the Merovingian Franks ousted the Romans. In 451 AD, with the help of Visigoths, Burgundians and others, they defeated Attila and the Huns at Chalons-sur-Marne.

Childeric I became leader of the Merovingians 458 AD. His son Clovis I (Chlodwig, Ludwig, Louis), crowned 481, founded the dynasty. After defeating the Alemanni (Germans) 496, he was baptized a Christian and made Paris his capital. His line ruled until Childeric III was deposed, 751.

The West Merovingians were called Neustrians, the eastern Austrasians. Pepin of Herstal (687-714) major domus, or head of

the palace, of Austrasia, took over Neustria as dux (leader) of the Franks. Pepin's son, Charles, called Martel (the Hammer) defeated the Saracens at Tours-Poitiers, 732; was succeeded by his son, Pepin the Short, 741, who deposed Childeric III and ruled as king until 768.

His son, Charlemagne, or Charles the Great (742-814) became king of the Franks, 768, with his brother Carloman, who died 771. He ruled France, Germany, parts of Italy, Spain, Austria, and enforced Christianity. Crowned Emperor of the Romans by Pope Leo III in St. Peter's, Rome, Dec. 25, 800 AD. Succeeded by son, Louis I the Pious, 814. At death, 840, Louis left empire to sons, Lothair (Roman emperor); Pepin I (king of Aquitaine); Louis II (of Germany); Charles the Bald (France). They quarreled and by the peace of Verdun, 843, divided the empire.

(continued)

**AD Name, year of accession**

### The Carolingians

843   Charles I (the Bald), Roman Emperor, 875
877   Louis II (the Stammerer), son
879   Louis III (died 882) and Carloman, brothers
885   Charles II (the Fat), Roman Emperor, 881
888   Eudes (Odo) elected by nobles
898   Charles III (the Simple), son of Louis II, defeated by
922   Robert, brother of Eudes, killed in war
923   Rudolph (Raoul) Duke of Burgundy
936   Louis IV, son of Charles III
954   Lothair, son, aged 13, defeated by Capet
986   Louis V (the Sluggard), left no heirs

### The Capets

987   Hugh Capet, son of Hugh the Great
996   Robert II (the Wise), his son
1031   Henry I, his son
1060   Philip I (the Fair), son
1108   Louis VI (the Fat), son
1137   Louis VII (the Younger), son
1180   Philip II (Augustus), son, crowned at Reims
1223   Louis VIII (the Lion), son
1226   Louis IX, son, crusader; Louis IX (1214-1270) reigned 44 years, arbitrated disputes with English King Henry III; led crusades, 1248 (captured in Egypt 1250) and 1270, when he died of plague in Tunis. Canonized 1297 as St. Louis.
1270   Philip III (the Hardy), son
1285   Philip IV (the Fair), son, king at 17
1314   Louis X (the Headstrong), son. His posthumous son, John I, lived only 7 days
1316   Philip V (the Tall), brother of Louis X
1322   Charles IV (the Fair), brother of Louis X

### House of Valois

1328   Philip VI (of Valois), grandson of Philip III
1350   John II (the Good), his son, retired to England
1364   Charles V (the Wise), son
1380   Charles VI (the Beloved), son
1422   Charles VII (the Victorious), son. In 1429 Joan of Arc (Jeanne d'Arc) promised Charles to oust the English, who occupied northern France. Joan won at Orleans and Patay and had Charles crowned at Reims July 17, 1429. Joan was captured May 24, 1430, and executed May 30, 1431, at Rouen for heresy. Charles ordered her rehabilitation, effected 1455.
1461   Louis XI (the Cruel), son, civil reformer
1483   Charles VIII (the Affable), son
1498   Louis XII, great-grandson of Charles V
1515   Francis I, of Angouleme, nephew, son-in-law. Francis I (1494-1547) reigned 32 years, fought 4 big wars, was patron of the arts, aided Cellini, del Sarto, Leonardo da Vinci, Rabelais, embellished Fontainebleau.
1547   Henry II, son, killed at a joust in a tournament. He was the husband of Catherine de Medicis (1519-1589) and the lover of Diane de Poitiers (1499-1566). Catherine was born in Florence, daughter of Lorenzo de Medicis. By her marriage to Henry II she became the mother of Francis II, Charles IX, Henry III and Queen Margaret (Reine Margot) wife of Henry IV. She persuaded Charles IX to order the massacre of Huguenots on the Feast of St. Bartholomew, Aug. 24, 1572, the day her daughter was married to Henry of Navarre.
1559   Francis II, son. In 1548, Mary, Queen of Scots since infancy, was betrothed when 6 to Francis, aged 4. They were married 1558. Francis died 1560, aged 16; Mary ruled Scotland, abdicated 1567.
1560   Charles IX, brother
1574   Henry III, brother, assassinated

### House of Bourbon

1589   Henry IV, of Navarre, assassinated. Henry IV made enemies when he gave tolerance to Protestants by Edict of Nantes, 1598. He was grandson of Queen Margaret of Navarre, literary patron. He married Margaret of Valois, daughter of Henry II and Catherine de Medicis; was divorced; in 1600 married Marie de Medicis, who became Regent of France, 1610-17 for her son, Louis XIII, but was exiled by Richelieu, 1631.

1610   Louis XIII (the Just), son. Louis XIII (1601-1643) married Anne of Austria. His ministers were Cardinals Richelieu and Mazarin.
1643   Louis XIV (The Grand Monarch), son. Louis XIV was king 72 years. He exhausted a prosperous country in wars for thrones and territory. By revoking the Edict of Nantes (1685) he caused the emigration of the Huguenots. He said: "I am the state."
1715   Louis XV, great-grandson. Louis XV married a Polish princess; lost Canada to the English. His favorites, Mme. Pompadour and Mme. Du Barry, influenced policies. Noted for saying "After me, the deluge".
1774   Louis XVI, grandson; married Marie Antoinette, daughter of Empress Maria Therese of Austria. King and queen beheaded by Revolution, 1793. Their son, called Louis XVII, died in prison, never ruled.

### First Republic

1792   National Convention of the French Revolution
1795   Directory, under Barras and others
1799   Consulate, Napoleon Bonaparte, first consul. Elected consul for life, 1802.

### First Empire

1804   Napoleon I, emperor. Josephine (de Beauharnais) empress, 1804-09; Marie Louise, empress, 1810-1814. Her son, Francois (1811-1832), titular King of Rome, later Duke de Reichstadt and "Napoleon II," never ruled. Napoleon abdicated 1814, died 1821.

### Bourbons Restored

1814   Louis XVIII king; brother of Louis XVI.
1824   Charles X, brother; reactionary; deposed by the July Revolution, 1830.

### House of Orleans

1830   Louis-Philippe, the "citizen king."

### Second Republic

1848   Louis Napoleon Bonaparte, president, nephew of Napoleon I. He became:

### Second Empire

1852   Napoleon III, emperor; Eugenie (de Montijo) empress. Lost Franco-Prussian war, deposed 1870. Son, Prince Imperial (1856-79), died in Zulu War. Eugenie died 1920.

### Third Republic—Presidents

1871   Thiers, Louis Adolphe (1797-1877)
1873   MacMahon, Marshal Patrice M. de (1808-1893)
1879   Grevy, Paul J. (1807-1891)
1887   Sadi-Carnot, M. (1837-1894), assassinated
1894   Casimir-Perier, Jean P. P. (1847-1907)
1895   Faure, Francois Felix (1841-1899)
1899   Loubet, Emile (1838-1929)
1906   Fallieres, C. Armand (1841-1931)
1913   Poincare, Raymond (1860-1934)
1920   Deschanel, Paul (1856-1922)
1920   Millerand, Alexandre (1859-1943)
1924   Doumergue, Gaston (1863-1937)
1931   Doumer, Paul (1857-1932), assassinated
1932   Lebrun, Albert (1871-1950), resigned 1940
1940   Vichy govt. under German armistice: Henri Philippe Petain (1856-1951) Chief of State, 1940-1944. Provisional govt. after liberation: Charles de Gaulle (1890-1970) Oct. 1944-Jan. 21, 1946; Felix Gouin (1884-1977) Jan. 23, 1946; Georges Bidault (1899-1983) June 24, 1946.

### Fourth Republic—Presidents

1947   Auriol, Vincent (1884-1966)
1954   Coty, Rene (1882-1962)

### Fifth Republic—Presidents

1959   de Gaulle, Charles Andre J. M. (1890-1970)
1969   Pompidou, Georges (1911-1974)
1974   Giscard d'Estaing, Valery (1926-   )
1981   Mitterrand, Francois (1916-   )

## Rulers of Middle Europe; Rise and Fall of Dynasties

### Carolingian Dynasty

Charles the Great, or Charlemagne, ruled France, Italy, and Middle Europe; established Ostmark (later Austria); crowned Roman emperor by pope in Rome, 800 AD; died 814.

Louis I (Ludwig) the Pious, son; crowned by Charlemagne 814, d. 840.

Louis II, the German, son; succeeded to East Francia (Germany) 843-876.

Charles the Fat, son; inherited East Francia and West Francia (France) 876, reunited empire, crowned emperor by pope, 881, deposed 887.

Arnulf, nephew, 887-899. Partition of empire.

Louis the Child, 899-911, last direct descendant of Charlemagne.

Conrad I, duke of Franconia, first elected German king, 911-918, founded House of Franconia.

## Saxon Dynasty; First Reich

Henry I, the Fowler, duke of Saxony, 919-936.

Otto I, the Great, 936-973, son; crowned Holy Roman Emperor by pope, 962.

Otto II, 973-983, son; failed to oust Greeks and Arabs from Sicily.

Otto III, 983-1002, son; crowned emperor at 16.

Henry II, the Saint, duke of Bavaria, 1002-1024, great-grandson of Otto the Great.

## House of Franconia

Conrad II, 1024-1039, elected king of Germany.

Henry III, the Black, 1039-1056, son; deposed 3 popes; annexed Burgundy.

Henry IV, 1056-1106, son; regency by his mother, Agnes of Poitou. Banned by Pope Gregory VII, he did penance at Canossa.

Henry V, 1106-1125, son; last of Salic House.

Lothair, duke of Saxony, 1125-1137. Crowned emperor in Rome, 1134.

## House of Hohenstaufen

Conrad III, duke of Swabia, 1138-1152. In 2d Crusade.

Frederick I, Barbarossa, 1152-1190; Conrad's nephew.

Henry VI, 1190-1196, took lower Italy from Normans. Son became king of Sicily.

Philip of Swabia, 1197-1208, brother.

Otto IV, of House of Welf, 1198-1215; deposed.

Frederick II, 1215-1250, son of Henry VI; king of Sicily; crowned king of Jerusalem; in 5th Crusade.

Conrad IV, 1250-1254, son; lost lower Italy to Charles of Anjou.

Conradin (1252-1268) son, king of Jerusalem and Sicily, beheaded. Last Hohenstaufen.

Interregnum, 1254-1273, Rise of the Electors.

## Transition

Rudolph I of Hapsburg, 1273-1291, defeated King Ottocar II of Bohemia. Bequeathed duchy of Austria to eldest son, Albert.

Adolph of Nassau, 1292-1298, killed in war with Albert of Austria.

Albert I, king of Germany, 1298-1308, son of Rudolph.

Henry VII, of Luxemburg, 1308-1313, crowned emperor in Rome. Seized Bohemia, 1310.

Louis IV of Bavaria (Wittelsbach), 1314-1347. Also elected was Frederick of Austria, 1314-1330 (Hapsburg). Abolition of papal sanction for election of Holy Roman Emperor.

Charles IV, of Luxemburg, 1347-1378, grandson of Henry VII, German emperor and king of Bohemia, Lombardy, Burgundy; took Mark of Brandenburg.

Wenceslaus, 1378-1400, deposed.

Rupert, Duke of Palatine, 1400-1410.

Sigismund, 1411-1437.

## Hungary

Stephen I, house of Arpad, 997-1038. Crowned king 1000; converted Magyars; canonized 1083. After several centuries of feuds Charles Robert of Anjou became Charles I, 1308-1342.

Louis I, the Great, son, 1342-1382; joint ruler of Poland with Casimir III, 1370. Defeated Turks.

Mary, daughter, 1382-1395, ruled with husband. Sigismund of Luxemburg, 1387-1437, also king of Bohemia. As bro. of Wenceslaus he succeeded Rupert as Holy Roman Emperor, 1410.

Albert, 1438-1439, son-in-law of Sigismund; also Roman emperor as Albert II. *(see under Hapsburg.)*

Ulaszlo I of Poland, 1440-1444.

Ladislaus V, posthumous son of Albert II, 1444-1457. John Hunyadi (Hunyadi Janos), governor (1446-1452), fought Turks, Czechs; died 1456.

Matthias I (Corvinus), son of Hunyadi, 1458-1490. Shared rule of Bohemia, captured Vienna, 1485, annexed Austria, Styria, Carinthia.

Ulaszlo II (king of Bohemia), 1490-1516.

Louis II, son, aged 10, 1516-1526. Wars with Suleiman, Turk. In 1527 Hungary was split between Ferdinand I, Archduke of

Austria, bro.-in-law of Louis II, and John Zapolya of Transylvania. After Turkish invasion, 1547, Hungary was split between Ferdinand, Prince John Sigismund (Transylvania) and the Turks.

## House of Hapsburg

Albert V of Austria, Hapsburg, crowned king of Hungary, Jan. 1436, Roman emperor, March, 1438, as Albert II; died 1439.

Frederick III, cousin, 1440-1493. Fought Turks.

Maximilian I, son, 1493-1519. Assumed title of Holy Roman Emperor (German), 1493.

Charles V, grandson, 1519-1556. King of Spain with mother co-regent; crowned Roman emperor at Aix, 1520. Confronted Luther at Worms; attempted church reform and religious conciliation; abdicated 1556.

Ferdinand I, king of Bohemia, 1526, of Hungary, 1527; disputed. German king, 1531. Crowned Roman emperor on abdication of brother Charles V, 1556.

Maximilian II, son, 1564-1576.

Rudolph II, son, 1576-1612.

Matthias, brother, 1612-1619, king of Bohemia and Hungary.

Ferdinand II of Styria, king of Bohemia, 1617, of Hungary, 1618, Roman emperor, 1619. Bohemian Protestants deposed him, elected Frederick V of Palatine, starting Thirty Years War.

Ferdinand III, son, king of Hungary, 1625, Bohemia, 1627, Roman emperor, 1637. Peace of Westphalia, 1648, ended war. Leopold I, 1658-1705; Joseph I, 1705-1711; Charles VI, 1711-1740.

Maria Theresa, daughter, 1740-1780, Archduchess of Austria, queen of Hungary; ousted pretender, Charles VII, crowned 1742; in 1745 obtained election of her husband Francis I as Roman emperor and co-regent (d. 1765). Fought Seven Years' War with Frederick II (the Great) of Prussia. Mother of Marie Antoinette, Queen of France.

Joseph II, son, 1765-1790, Roman emperor, reformer; powers restricted by Empress Maria Theresa until her death, 1780. First partition of Poland. Leopold II, 1790-1792.

Francis II, son, 1792-1835. Fought Napoleon. Proclaimed first hereditary emperor of Austria, 1804. Forced to abdicate as Roman emperor, 1806; last use of title. Ferdinand I, son, 1835-1848, abdicated during revolution.

## Austro-Hungarian Monarchy

Francis Joseph I, nephew, 1848-1916, emperor of Austria, king of Hungary. Dual monarchy of Austria-Hungary formed, 1867. After assassination of heir, Archduke Francis Ferdinand, June 28, 1914, Austrian diplomacy precipitated World War I.

Charles I, grand-nephew, 1916-1918, last emperor of Austria and king of Hungary. Abdicated Nov. 11-13, 1918, died 1922.

## Rulers of Prussia

Nucleus of Prussia was the Mark of Brandenburg. First margrave was Albert the Bear (Albrecht), 1134-1170. First Hohenzollern margrave was Frederick, burgrave of Nuremberg, 1417-1440.

Frederick William, 1640-1688, the Great Elector. Son, Frederick III, 1688-1713, was crowned King Frederick of Prussia, 1701.

Frederick William I, son, 1713-1740.

Frederick II, the Great, son, 1740-1786, annexed Silesia, part of Austria.

Frederick William II, nephew, 1786-1797.

Frederick William III, son, 1797-1840. Napoleonic wars.

Frederick William IV, son, 1840-1861. Uprising of 1848 and first parliament and constitution.

## Second and Third Reich

William I, 1861-1888, brother. Annexation of Schleswig and Hanover; Franco-Prussian war, 1870-71, proclamation of German Reich, Jan. 18, 1871, at Versailles; William, German emperor (Deutscher Kaiser), Bismarck, chancellor.

Frederick III, son, 1888.

William II, son, 1888-1918. Led Germany in World War I, abdicated as German emperor and king of Prussia, Nov. 9, 1918. Died in exile in Netherlands June 4, 1941. Minor rulers of Bavaria, Saxony, Wurttemberg also abdicated.

Germany proclaimed republic at Weimar, July 1, 1919. Presidents: Frederick Ebert, 1919-1925, Paul von Hindenburg-Beneckendorff, 1925, reelected 1932, d. Aug. 2, 1934. Adolf Hitler, chancellor, chosen successor as Leader-Chancellor (Fuehrer-Reichskanzler) of Third Reich. Annexed Austria, March, 1938. Precipitated World War II, 1939-1945. Suicide April 30, 1945.

# Rulers of Poland

## House of Piasts

Miesko I, 962?-992; Poland Christianized 966. Expansion under 3 Boleslavs: I, 992-1025, son, crowned king 1024; II,

1058-1079, great-grandson, exiled after killing bishop Stanislav who became chief patron saint of Poland; III, 1106-1138, nephew, divided Poland among 4 sons, eldest suzerain.

*(continued)*

1138-1306, feudal division. 1226 founding in Prussia of military order Teutonic Knights. 1226 invasion by Tartars/Mongols.

Vladislav I, 1306-1333, reunited most Polish territories, crowned king 1320. Casimir III the Great, 1333-1370, son, developed economic, cultural life, foreign policy.

## House of Anjou

Louis I, 1370-1382, nephew/identical with Louis I of Hungary.

Jadwiga, 1384-1399, daughter, married 1386 Jagiello, Grand Duke of Lituania.

## House of Jagelloneans

Vladislav II, 1386-1434, Christianized Lituania, founded personal union between Poland & Lituania. Defeated 1410 Teutonic Knights at Grunwald.

Vladislav III, 1434-1444, son, simultaneously king of Hungary. Fought Turks, killed 1444 in battle of Varna.

Casimir IV, 1446-1492, brother, competed with Hapsburgs, put son Vladislav on throne of Bohemia, later also of Hungary.

Sigismund I, 1506-1548, brother, patronized science & arts, his & son's reign "Golden Age."

Sigismund II, 1548-1572, son, established 1569 real union of Poland and Lituania (lasted until 1795).

## Elective kings

Polish nobles proclaimed 1572 Poland a Republic headed by king to be elected by whole nobility.

Stephen Batory, 1576-1586, duke of Transylvania, married Ann, sister of Sigismund II August. Fought Russians.

Sigismund II Vasa, 1587-1632, nephew of Sigismund II. 1592-1598 also king of Sweden. His generals fought Russians, Turks.

Vladislav II Vasa, 1632-1648, son. Fought Russians.

John II Casimir Vasa, 1648-1668, brother. Fought Cossacks, Swedes, Russians, Turks, Tartars (the "Deluge"). Abdicated 1668.

John III Sobieski, 1674-1696. Won Vienna from besieging Turks, 1683.

Stanislav II, 1764-1795, last king. Encouraged reforms; 1791 1st modern Constitution in Europe. 1772, 1793, 1795 Poland partitioned among Russia, Prussia, Austria. Unsuccessful insurrection against foreign invasion 1794 under Kosciuszko, Amer-Polish gen.

## 1795-1918 Poland under foreign rule

1807-1815 Grand Duchy of Warsaw created by Napoleon I, Frederick August of Saxony grand duke.

1815 Congress of Vienna proclaimed part of Poland "Kingdom" in personal union with Russia.

Polish uprisings: 1830 against Russia, 1846, 1848 against Austria, 1863 against Russia—all repressed.

## 1918-1939 Second Republic

1918-1922 Head of State Jozef Pilsudski. Presidents: Gabriel Narutowicz 1922, assassinated. Stanislav Wojciechowski 1922-1926, had to abdicate after Pilsudski's coup d'état. Ignacy Moscicki, 1926-1939, ruled with Pilsudski as (until 1935) virtual dictator.

## 1939-1945 Poland under foreign occupation

Nazi aggression Sept. 1939. Polish govt.-in-exile, first in France, then in England. Vladislav Raczkiewicz pres., Gen. Vladislav Sikorski, then Stanislav Mikolajczyk, prime ministers. Polish Committee of Natl. Liberation proclaimed at Lublin July 1944, transformed into govt. Jan. 1, 1945.

# Rulers of Denmark, Sweden, Norway

## Denmark

Earliest rulers invaded Britain; King Canute, who ruled in London 1016-1035, was most famous. The Valdemars furnished kings until the 15th century. In 1282 the Danes won the first national assembly, Danehof, from King Erik V.

Most redoubtable medieval character was Margaret, daughter of Valdemar IV, born 1353, married at 10 to King Haakon VI of Norway. In 1376 she had her first infant son Olaf made king of Denmark. After his death, 1387, she was regent of Denmark and Norway. In 1388 Sweden accepted her as sovereign. In 1389 she made her grand-nephew, Duke Erik of Pomerania, titular king of Denmark, Sweden, and Norway, with herself as regent. In 1397 she effected the Union of Kalmar of the three kingdoms and had Erik VII crowned. In 1439 the three kingdoms deposed him and elected, 1440, Christopher of Bavaria king (Christopher III). On his death, 1448, the union broke up.

Succeeding rulers were unable to enforce their claims as rulers of Sweden until 1520, when Christian II conquered Sweden. He was thrown out 1522, and in 1523 Gustavus Vasa united Sweden. Denmark continued to dominate Norway until the Napoleonic wars, when Frederick VI, 1808-1839, joined the Napoleonic cause after Britain had destroyed the Danish fleet, 1807. In 1814 he was forced to cede Norway to Sweden and Helgoland to Britain, receiving Lauenburg. Successors Christian VIII, 1839; Frederick VII, 1848; Christian IX, 1863; Frederick VIII, 1906; Christian X, 1912; Frederick IX, 1947; Margrethe II, 1972.

## Sweden

Early kings ruled at Uppsala, but did not dominate the country. Sverker, c1130-c1156, united the Swedes and Goths. In 1435 Sweden obtained the Riksdag, or parliament. After the Union of Kalmar, 1397, the Danes either ruled or harried the country until Christian II of Denmark conquered it anew, 1520. This led to a rising under Gustavus Vasa, who ruled Sweden 1523-1560, and established an independent kingdom. Charles IX, 1599-1611, crowned 1604, conquered Moscow. Gustavus II Adolphus, 1611-1632, was called the Lion of the North. Later rulers: Christina, 1632; Charles X, Gustavus 1654; Charles XI, 1660; Charles XII (invader of Russia and Poland, defeated at Poltava, June 28, 1709), 1697; Ulrika Eleanora, sister, elected queen 1718; Frederick I (of Hesse), her husband, 1720; Adolphus Frederick, 1751; Gustavus III, 1771; Gustavus IV Adolphus, 1792; Charles XIII, 1809. (Union with Norway began 1814.) Charles XIV John, 1818. He was Jean Bernadotte, Napoleon's Prince of Ponte Corvo, elected 1810 to succeed Charles XIII. He founded the present dynasty: Oscar I, 1844; Charles XV, 1859; Oscar II, 1872; Gustavus V, 1907; Gustav VI Adolf, 1950; Carl XVI Gustaf, 1973.

## Norway

Overcoming many rivals, Harald Haarfager, 872-930, conquered Norway, Orkneys, and Shetlands; Olaf I, great-grandson, 995-1000, brought Christianity into Norway, Iceland, and Greenland. In 1035 Magnus the Good also became king of Denmark. Haakon V, 1299-1319, had married his daughter to Erik of Sweden. Their son, Magnus, became ruler of Norway and Sweden at 6. His son, Haakon VI, married Margaret of Denmark; their son Olaf IV became king of Norway and Denmark, followed by Margaret's regency and the Union of Kalmar, 1397.

In 1450 Norway became subservient to Denmark. Christian IV, 1588-1648, founded Christiania, now Oslo. After Napoleonic wars, when Denmark ceded Norway to Sweden, a strong nationalist movement forced recognition of Norway as an independent kingdom united with Sweden under the Swedish kings, 1814-1905. In 1905 the union was dissolved and Prince Carl of Denmark became Haakon VII. He died Sept. 21, 1957; succeeded by son, Olav V. Olav V died January 17, 1991; succeeded by son, Harald V.

## Rulers of the Netherlands and Belgium

### The Netherlands (Holland)

William Frederick, Prince of Orange, led a revolt against French rule, 1813, and was crowned King of the Netherlands, 1815. Belgium seceded Oct. 4, 1830, after a revolt. The secession was ratified by the two kingdoms by treaty Apr. 19, 1839.

Succession: William II, son, 1840; William III, son, 1849; Wilhelmina, daughter of William III and his 2d wife Princess Emma of Waldeck, 1890; Wilhelmina abdicated, Sept. 4, 1948, in favor of daughter, Juliana. Juliana abdicated Apr. 30, 1980, in favor of daughter, Beatrix.

### Belgium

A national congress elected Prince Leopold of Saxe-Coburg King; he took the throne July 21, 1831, as Leopold I. Succession: Leopold II, son 1865; Albert I, nephew of Leopold II, 1909; Leopold III, son of Albert, 1934; Prince Charles, Regent 1944; Leopold returned 1950, yielded powers to son Baudouin, Prince Royal, Aug. 6, 1950, abdicated July 16, 1951. Baudouin I took throne July 17, 1951; died July 31, 1993; succeeded by brother, Albert II.

*For political history prior to 1830 see articles on the Netherlands and Belgium.*

## Roman Rulers

From Romulus to the end of the Empire in the West. Rulers of the Roman Empire in the East sat in Constantinople and for a brief period in Nicaea, until the capture of Constantinople by the Turks in 1453, when Byzantium was succeeded by the Ottoman Empire.

| BC | Name | AD | Name | AD | Name |
|---|---|---|---|---|---|
| | **The Kingdom** | 98 | Trajanus | 324 | Constantinus I (the Great) |
| 753 | Romulus (Quirinus) | 117 | Hadrianus | 337 | Constantinus II, Constans I, |
| 716 | Numa Pompilius | 138 | Antoninus Pius | | Constantius II |
| 673 | Tullus Hostilius | 161 | Marcus Aurelius and Lucius Verus | 340 | Constantius II and Constans I |
| 640 | Ancus Marcius | 169 | Marcus Aurelius (alone) | 350 | Constantius II |
| 616 | L. Tarquinius Priscus | 180 | Commodus | 361 | Julianus II (the Apostate) |
| 578 | Servius Tullius | 193 | Pertinax; Julianus I | 363 | Jovianus |
| 534 | L. Tarquinius Superbus | 193 | Septimius Severus | | **West (Rome) and East** |
| | **The Republic** | 211 | Caracalla and Geta | | **(Constantinople)** |
| 509 | Consulate established | 212 | Caracalla (alone) | 364 | Valentinianus I (West) and Valens |
| 509 | Quaestorship instituted | 217 | Macrinus | | (East) |
| 498 | Dictatorship introduced | 218 | Elagabalus (Heliogabalus) | 367 | Valentinianus I with |
| 494 | Plebeian Tribunate created | 222 | Alexander Severus | | Gratianus (West) and Valens (East) |
| 494 | Plebeian Aedileship created | 235 | Maximinus I (the Thracian) | 375 | Gratianus with Valentinianus |
| 444 | Consular Tribunate organized | 238 | Gordianus I and Gordianus II; | | II (West) and Valens (East) |
| 435 | Censorship instituted | | Pupienus and Balbinus | 378 | Gratianus with Valentinianus II |
| 366 | Praetorship established | 238 | Gordianus III | | (West) Theodosius I (East) |
| 366 | Curule Aedileship created | 244 | Philippus (the Arabian) | 383 | Valentinianus II (West) and |
| 362 | Military Tribunate elected | 249 | Decius | | Theodosius I (East) |
| 326 | Proconsulate introduced | 251 | Gallus and Volusianus | 394 | Theodosius I (the Great) |
| 311 | Naval Duumvirate elected | 253 | Aemilianus | 395 | Honorius (West) and Arcadius |
| 217 | Dictatorship of Fabius Maximus | 253 | Valerianus and Gallienus | | (East) |
| 133 | Tribunate of Tiberius Gracchus | 258 | Gallienus (alone) | 408 | Honorius (West) and Theodosius II |
| 123 | Tribunate of Gaius Gracchus | 268 | Claudius Gothicus | | (East) |
| 82 | Dictatorship of Sulla | 270 | Quintillus | 423 | Valentinianus III (West) and |
| 60 | First Triumvirate formed | 270 | Aurelianus | | Theodosius II (East) |
| | (Caesar, Pompeius, Crassus) | 275 | Tacitus | 450 | Valentinianus III (West) |
| 46 | Dictatorship of Caesar | 276 | Florianus | | and Marcianus (East) |
| 43 | Second Triumvirate formed | 276 | Probus | 455 | Maximus (West), Avitus |
| | (Octavianus, Antonius, Lepidus) | 282 | Carus | | (West); Marcianus (East) |
| | **The Empire** | 283 | Carinus and Numerianus | 456 | Avitus (West), Marcianus (East) |
| 27 | Augustus (Gaius Julius | 284 | Diocletianus | 457 | Majorianus (West), Leo I (East) |
| | Caesar Octavianus) | 286 | Diocletianus and Maximianus | 461 | Severus II (West), Leo I (East) |
| **AD** | | 305 | Galerius and Constantius I | 467 | Anthemius (West), Leo I (East) |
| 14 | Tiberius I | 306 | Galerius, Maximinus II, Severus I | 472 | Olybrius (West), Leo I (East) |
| 37 | Gaius Caesar (Caligula) | 307 | Galerius, Maximinus | 473 | Glycerius (West), Leo I (East) |
| 41 | Claudius I | | II, Constantinus I, Licinius, | 474 | Julius Nepos (West), Leo II (East) |
| 54 | Nero | | Maxentius | 475 | Romulus Augustulus (West) and |
| 68 | Galba | 311 | Maximinus II, Constantinus I, | | Zeno (East) |
| 69 | Galba; Otho, Vitellius | | Licinius, Maxentius | 476 | End of Empire in West; Odovacar, |
| 69 | Vespasianus | 314 | Maximinus II, Constantinus I, | | King, drops title of Emperor; |
| 79 | Titus | | Licinius | | murdered by King Theodoric of |
| 81 | Domitianus | 314 | Constantinus I and Licinius | | Ostrogoths 493 AD |
| 96 | Nerva | | | | |

## Rulers of Modern Italy

After the fall of Napoleon in 1814, the Congress of Vienna, 1815, restored Italy as a political patchwork, comprising the Kingdom of Naples and Sicily, the Papal States, and smaller units. Piedmont and Genoa were awarded to Sardinia, ruled by King Victor Emmanuel I of Savoy.

United Italy emerged under the leadership of Camillo, Count di Cavour (1810-1861), Sardinian prime minister. Agitation was led by Giuseppe Mazzini (1805-1872) and Giuseppe Garibaldi (1807-1882), soldier, Victor Emmanuel I abdicated 1821. After a brief regency for a brother, Charles Albert was King 1831-1849, abdicating when defeated by the Austrians at Novara. Succeeded by Victor Emmanuel II, 1849-1861.

In 1859 France forced Austria to cede Lombardy to Sardinia, which gave rights to Savoy and Nice to France. In 1860 Garibaldi led 1,000 volunteers in a spectacular campaign, took Sicily and expelled the King of Naples. In 1860 the House of Savoy annexed Tuscany, Parma, Modena, Romagna, the Two Sicilies, the Marches, and Umbria. Victor Emmanuel assumed the title of King of Italy at Turin Mar. 17, 1861. In 1866 he allied with Prussia in the Austro-Prussian War, with Prussia's victory received Venetia. On Sept. 20, 1870, his troops under Gen. Raffaele Cadorna entered Rome and took over the Papal States, ending the temporal power of the Roman Catholic Church.

Succession: Umberto I, 1878, assassinated 1900; Victor Emmanuel III, 1900, abdicated 1946, died 1947; Umberto II, 1946, ruled a month. In 1921 Benito Mussolini (1883-1945) formed the Fascist party and became prime minister Oct. 31, 1922. He entered World War II as an ally of Hitler. He was deposed July 25, 1943.

At a plebiscite June 2, 1946, Italy voted for a republic; Premier Alcide de Gasperi became chief of state June 13, 1946. On June 28, 1946, the Constituent Assembly elected Enrico de Nicola, Liberal, provisional president. Successive presidents: Luigi Einaudi, elected May 11, 1948; Giovanni Gronchi, Apr. 29, 1955; Antonio Segni, May 6, 1962; Giuseppe Saragat, Dec. 28, 1964; Giovanni Leone, Dec. 29, 1971; Alessandro Pertini, July 9, 1978; Francesco Cossiga, July 9, 1985; Oscar Luigi Scalfaro, May 25, 1992.

## Rulers of Spain

From 8th to 11th centuries Spain was dominated by the Moors (Arabs and Berbers). The Christian reconquest established small kingdoms (Asturias, Aragon, Castile, Catalonia, Leon, Navarre, and Valencia). In 1474 Isabella, b. 1451, became Queen of Castile & Leon. Her husband, Ferdinand, b. 1452, inherited Aragon 1479, with Catalonia, Valencia, and the Balearic Islands, became Ferdinand V of Castile. By Isabella's request Pope Sixtus IV established the Inquisition, 1478. Last Moorish kingdom, Granada, fell 1492. Columbus opened New World of colonies, 1492. Isabella died 1504, succeeded by her daughter, Juana "the Mad," but Ferdinand ruled until his death 1516.

Charles I, b. 1500, son of Juana and grandson of Ferdinand and Isabella, and of Maximilian I of Hapsburg; succeeded later as Holy Roman Emperor, Charles V, 1520; abdicated 1556. Philip II, son, 1556-1598, inherited only Spanish throne; conquered Portugal, fought Turks, persecuted non-Catholics, sent Armada against England. Was married to Mary I of England, 1554-1558. Succession: Philip III, 1598-1621; Philip IV, 1621-1665; Charles II, 1665-1700, left Spain to Philip of Anjou, grandson of Louis XIV, who as Philip V, 1700-1746, founded Bourbon dynasty; Ferdinand VI, 1746-1759; Charles III, 1759-1788; Charles IV, 1788-1808, abdicated.

Napoleon now dominated politics and made his brother Joseph King of Spain 1808, but the Spanish ousted him in 1813. Ferdinand VII, 1808, 1814-1833, lost American colonies; succeeded by daughter Isabella II, aged 3, with wife Maria Christina of Naples regent until 1843. Isabella deposed by revolution 1868. Elected king by the Cortes, Amadeo of Savoy, 1870; abdicated 1873. First republic, 1873-74. Alphonso XII, son of Isabella, 1875-85. His posthumous son was Alphonso XIII, with his mother, Queen Maria Christina regent; Spanish-American war, Spain lost Cuba, gave up Puerto Rico, Philippines, Sulu Is., Marianas. Alphonso took throne 1902, aged 16, married British Princess Victoria Eugenia of Battenberg. The dictatorship of Primo de Rivera, 1923-30, precipitated the revolution of 1931. Alphonso agreed to leave without formal abdication. The monarchy was abolished and the second republic established, with socialist backing. Presidents were Niceto Alcala Zamora, to 1936, when Manuel Azaña was chosen.

In July, 1936, the army in Morocco revolted against the government and General Francisco Franco led the troops into Spain. The revolution succeeded by Feb., 1939, when Azaña resigned. Franco became chief of state, with provisions that if he was incapacitated the Regency Council by two-thirds vote may propose a king to the Cortes, which must have a two-thirds majority to elect him.

Alphonso XIII died in Rome Feb. 28, 1941, aged 54. His property and citizenship had been restored.

A succession law restoring the monarchy was approved in a 1947 referendum. Prince Juan Carlos, son of the pretender to the throne, was designated by Franco and the Cortes in 1969 as the future king and chief of state. Upon Franco's death, Nov. 20, 1975, Juan Carlos was proclaimed king, Nov. 22, 1975.

## Leaders in the South American Wars of Liberation

Simon Bolivar (1783-1830), Jose Francisco de San Martin (1778-1850), and Francisco Antonio Gabriel Miranda (1750-1816), are among the heroes of the early 19th century struggles of South American nations to free themselves from Spain. All three, and their contemporaries, operated in periods of factional strife, during which soldiers and civilians suffered.

Miranda, a Venezuelan, who had served with the French in the American Revolution and commanded parts of the French Revolutionary armies in the Netherlands, attempted to start a revolt in Venezuela in 1806 and failed. In 1810, with British and American backing, he returned and was briefly a dictator, until the British withdrew their support. In 1812 he was overcome by the royalists in Venezuela and taken prisoner, dying in a Spanish prison in 1816.

San Martin was born in Argentina and during 1789-1811 served in campaigns of the Spanish armies in Europe and Africa. He first joined the independence movement in Argentina in 1812 and in 1817 invaded Chile with 4,000 men over the mountain passes. Here he and Gen. Bernardo O'Higgins (1778-1842) defeated the Spaniards at Chacabuco, 1817, and O'Higgins was named Liberator and became first director of Chile, 1817-23. In 1821 San Martin occupied Lima and Callao, Peru, and became protector of Peru.

Bolivar, the greatest leader of South American liberation from Spain, was born in Venezuela, the son of an aristocratic family. He first served under Miranda in 1812 and in 1813 captured Caracas, where he was named Liberator. Forced out next year by civil strife, he led a campaign that captured Bogota in 1814. In 1817 he was again in control of Venezuela and was named dictator. He organized Nueva Granada with the help of General Francisco de Paula Santander (1792-1840). By joining Nueva Granada, Venezuela, and the present terrain of Panama and Ecuador, the republic of Colombia was formed with Bolivar president. After numerous setbacks he decisively defeated the Spaniards in the second battle of Carabobo, Venezuela, June 24, 1821.

In May, 1822, Gen. Antonio Jose de Sucre, Bolivar's lieutenant, took Quito. Bolivar went to Guayaquil to confer with San Martin, who resigned as protector of Peru and withdrew from politics. With a new army of Colombians and Peruvians Bolivar defeated the Spaniards in a battle at Junin in 1824 and cleared Peru.

De Sucre organized Charcas (Upper Peru) as Republica Bolivar (now Bolivia) and acted as president in place of Bolivar, who wrote its constitution. De Sucre defeated the Spanish faction of Peru at Ayacucho, Dec. 19, 1824.

Continued civil strife finally caused the Colombian federation to break apart. Santander turned against Bolivar, but the latter defeated him and banished him. In 1828 Bolivar gave up the presidency he had held precariously for 14 years. He became ill from tuberculosis and died Dec. 17, 1830. He is buried in the national pantheon in Caracas.

## Rulers of Prerevolutionary Russia; Leaders of the USSR

First ruler to consolidate Slavic tribes was Rurik, leader of the Russians who established himself at Novgorod, 862 AD. He and his immediate successors had Scandinavian affiliations. They moved to Kiev after 972 AD and ruled as Dukes of Kiev. In 988 Vladimir was converted and adopted the Byzantine Greek Orthodox service, later modified by Slav influences. Important as organizer and lawgiver was Yaroslav, 1019-1054, whose daughters married kings of Norway, Hungary, and France. His grandson, Vladimir II (Monomakh), 1113-1125, was progenitor of several rulers, but in 1169 Andrew Bogolubski overthrew Kiev and began the line known as Grand Dukes of Vladimir.

Of the Grand Dukes of Vladimir, Alexander Nevsky, 1246-1263, had a son, Daniel, first to be called Duke of Muscovy (Moscow) who ruled 1294-1303. His successors became Grand Dukes of Muscovy. After Dmitri III Donskoi defeated the Tartars in 1380, they also became Grand Dukes of all Russia. Independence of the Tartars and considerable territorial expansion were achieved under Ivan III, 1462-1505.

Tsars of Muscovy—Ivan III was referred to in church ritual as Tsar. He married Sofia, niece of the last Byzantine emperor. His successor, Basil III, died in 1533 when Basil's son Ivan was only 3. He became Ivan IV, "the Terrible"; crowned 1547 as Tsar of all the Russias, ruled till 1584. Under the weak rule of his son, Feodor I, 1584-1598, Boris Godunov had control. The dynasty died, and after years of tribal strife and intervention by Polish and Swedish armies, the Russians united under 17-year-old Michael Romanov, distantly related to the first wife of Ivan IV. He ruled 1613-1645 and established the Romanov line. Fourth ruler after Michael was Peter I.

Tsars, or Emperors of Russia (Romanovs)—Peter I, 1682-1725, known as Peter the Great, took title of Emperor in 1721. His successors and dates of accession were: Catherine, his widow, 1725; Peter II, his grandson, 1727; Anne, Duchess of Courland, 1730, daughter of Peter the Great's brother, Tsar Ivan V; Ivan VI, 1740, great-grandson of Ivan V, child, kept in prison and murdered 1764; Elizabeth, daughter of Peter I, 1741; Peter III, grandson of Peter I, 1761, deposed 1762 for his consort, Catherine II, former princess of Anhalt Zerbst (Germany) who is known as Catherine the Great; Paul I, her son, 1796, killed 1801; Alexander I, son of Paul, 1801, defeated Napoleon; Nicholas I, his brother, 1825; Alexander II, son of Nicholas, 1855, assassinated 1881 by terrorists; Alexander III, son, 1881.

Nicholas II, son, 1894-1917, last Tsar of Russia, was forced to abdicate by the Revolution that followed losses to Germany in WWI. The Tsar, the Empress, the Tsesarevich (Crown Prince) and the Tsar's 4 daughters were murdered by the Bolsheviks in Ekaterinburg, July 16, 1918.

Provisional Government—Prince Georgi Lvov and Alexander Kerensky, premiers, 1917.

### Union of Soviet Socialist Republics

Bolshevik Revolution, Nov. 7, 1917, displaced Kerensky; council of People's Commissars formed, Lenin (Vladimir Ilyich Ulyanov), premier. Lenin died Jan. 21, 1924. Aleksei Rykov (executed 1938) and V. M. Molotov held the office, but actual ruler was Joseph Stalin (Joseph Vissarionovich Djugashvili), general secretary of the Central Committee of the Communist Party. Stalin became president of the Council of Ministers (premier) May 7, 1941, died Mar. 5, 1953. Succeeded by Georgi M. Malenkov, as head of the Council and premier and Nikita S. Khrushchev, first secretary of the Central Committee. Malenkov resigned Feb. 8, 1955, became deputy premier, was dropped July 3, 1957. Marshal Nikolai A. Bulganin became premier Feb. 8, 1955; was demoted and Khrushchev became premier Mar. 27, 1958. Khrushchev was ousted Oct. 14-15, 1964, replaced by Leonid I. Brezhnev as first secretary of the party and by Aleksei N. Kosygin as premier. On June 16, 1977, Brezhnev took office as president. Brezhnev died Nov. 10, 1982; 2 days later the Central Committee unanimously elected former KGB head Yuri V. Andropov president. Andropov died Feb. 9, 1984; on Feb. 13, Konstantin U. Chernenko was chosen by Central Committee as its general secretary. Chernenko died Mar. 10, 1985. On Mar. 11, he was succeeded as general secretary by Mikhail Gorbachev, who replaced Andrei Gromyko as president on Oct. 1, 1988. Gorbachev resigned Dec. 25, 1991, and the Soviet Union officially disbanded the next day. A loose Commonwealth of Independent States, made up of 11 of the 15 former Soviet constituent republics, was created.

## Governments of China

(Until 221 BC and frequently thereafter, China was not a unified state. Where dynastic dates overlap, the rulers or events referred to appeared in different areas of China.)

| | | |
|---|---|---|
| Hsia | c1994BC | c1523BC |
| Shang | c1523 | c1028 |
| Western Chou | c1027 | 770 |
| Eastern Chou | 770 | 256 |
| Warring States | 403 | 222 |
| Ch'in (first unified empire) | 221 | 206 |
| Han | 202BC | 220AD |
| Western Han (expanded Chinese state beyond the Yellow and Yangtze River valleys) | 202BC | 9AD |
| Hsin (Wang Mang, usurper) | 9AD | 23AD |
| Eastern Han (expanded Chinese state into Indo-China and Turkestan) | 25 | 220 |
| Three Kingdoms (Wei, Shu, Wu) | 220 | 265 |
| Chin (western) | 265 | 317 |
| (eastern) | 317 | 420 |
| Northern Dynasties (followed several short-lived governments by Turks, Mongols, etc.) | 386 | 581 |
| Southern Dynasties (capital: Nanking) | 420 | 589 |
| Sui (reunified China) | 581 | 618 |
| Tang (a golden age of Chinese culture; capital: Sian) | 618 | 906 |
| Five Dynasties (Yellow River basin) | 902 | 960 |
| Ten Kingdoms (southern China) | 907 | 979 |
| Liao (Khitan Mongols; capital: Peking) | 947 | 1125 |
| Sung | 960 | 1279 |
| Northern Sung (reunified central and southern China) | 960 | 1126 |
| Western Hsai (non-Chinese rulers in northwest) | 990 | 1227 |
| Chin (Tartars; drove Sung out of central China) | 1115 | 1234 |
| Yuan (Mongols; Kublai Khan made Peking his capital in 1267) | 1271 | 1368 |
| Ming (China reunified under Chinese rule; capital: Nanking, then Peking in 1420) | 1368 | 1644 |
| Ch'ing (Manchus, descendents of Tartars) | 1644 | 1911 |
| Republic (disunity; provincial rulers, warlords) | 1912 | 1949 |
| People's Republic of China | 1949 | |

## Leaders Since 1949

| | |
|---|---|
| Mao Zedong | Chairman, Central People's Administrative Council, Communist Party (CPC), 1949-1976 |
| Zhou Enlai | Premier, foreign minister, 1949-1976 |
| Deng Xiaoping | Vice Premier, 1949-1976; 1977-1987 |
| Liu Shaoqi | President, 1959-1969 |
| Hua Guofeng | Premier, 1976-1980; CPC Chairman, 1976-1981 |
| Zhao Ziyang | Premier, 1980-88; CPC Chairman, 1987-89 |
| Hu Yaobang | CPC Chairman, 1981-1987 |
| Li Xiannian | President, 1983-1988 |
| Yong Shang-Kun | President, 1988-1993 |
| Li Peng | Premier, 1988- |
| Jiang Zemin | CPC Chairman, 1989- ; President, 1993- |

## Chronological List of Popes

Source: Annuario Pontificio. Table lists year of accession of each Pope.

The Roman Catholic Church names the Apostle Peter as founder of the Church in Rome. He arrived there c. 42, was martyred there c. 67, and raised to sainthood.

**The Pope's temporal title is:** Sovereign of the State of Vatican City.

**The Pope's spiritual titles are:** Bishop of Rome, Vicar of Jesus Christ, Successor of St. Peter, Prince of the Apostles, Supreme Pontiff of the Universal Church, Patriarch of the West, Primate of Italy, Archbishop and Metropolitan of the Roman Province.

**Anti-Popes** are in *Italics*. Anti-Popes were illegitimate claimants of or pretenders to the papal throne.

| Year | Pope | Year | Pope | Year | Pope | Year | Pope |
|---|---|---|---|---|---|---|---|
| See above | St. Peter | | or Adeodatus | 983 | John XIV | 1316 | John XXII |
| 67 | St. Linus | 619 | Boniface V | 985 | John XV | *1328* | *Nicholas V* |
| 76 | St. Anacletus | 625 | Honorius I | 996 | Gregory V | 1334 | Benedict XII |
| | or Cletus | 640 | Severinus | *997* | *John XVI* | 1342 | Clement VI |
| 88 | St. Clement I | 642 | Theodore I | 999 | Sylvester II | 1352 | Innocent VI |
| 97 | St. Evaristus | 649 | St. Martin I, Martyr | 1003 | John XVII | 1362 | Bl. Urban V |
| 105 | St. Alexander I | 654 | St. Eugene I | 1004 | John XVIII | 1370 | Gregory XI |
| 115 | St. Sixtus I | 657 | St. Vitalian | 1009 | Sergius IV | 1378 | Urban VI |
| 125 | St. Telesphorus | 672 | Adeodatus II | 1012 | Benedict VIII | *1378* | *Clement VII* |
| 136 | St. Hyginus | 676 | Donus | *1012* | *Gregory* | 1389 | Boniface IX |
| 140 | St. Pius I | 678 | St. Agatho | 1024 | John XIX | *1394* | *Benedict XIII* |
| 155 | St. Anicetus | 682 | St. Leo II | 1032 | Benedict IX | 1404 | Innocent VII |
| 166 | St. Soter | 684 | St. Benedict II | 1045 | Sylvester III | 1406 | Gregory XII |
| 175 | St. Eleutherius | 685 | John V | 1045 | Benedict IX | *1409* | *Alexander V* |
| 189 | St. Victor I | 686 | Conon | 1045 | Gregory VI | *1410* | *John XXIII* |
| 199 | St. Zephyrinus | *687* | *Theodore* | 1046 | Clement II | 1417 | Martin V |
| 217 | St. Callistus I | *687* | *Paschal* | 1047 | Benedict IX | 1431 | Eugene IV |
| *217* | *St. Hippolytus* | 687 | St. Sergius I | 1048 | Damasus II | *1439* | *Felix V* |
| 222 | St. Urban I | 701 | John VI | 1049 | St. Leo IX | 1447 | Nicholas V |
| 230 | St. Pontian | 705 | John VII | 1055 | Victor II | 1455 | Callistus III |
| 235 | St. Anterus | 708 | Sisinnius | 1057 | Stephen IX (X) | 1458 | Pius II |
| 236 | St. Fabian | 708 | Constantine | *1058* | *Benedict X* | 1464 | Paul II |
| 251 | St. Cornelius | 715 | St. Gregory II | 1059 | Nicholas II | 1471 | Sixtus IV |
| *251* | *Novatian* | 731 | St. Gregory III | 1061 | Alexander II | 1484 | Innocent VIII |
| 253 | St. Lucius I | 741 | St. Zachary | *1061* | *Honorius II* | 1492 | Alexander VI |
| 254 | St. Stephen I | 752 | Stephen II (III) | 1073 | St. Gregory VII | 1503 | Pius III |
| 257 | St. Sixtus II | 757 | St. Paul I | *1080* | *Clement III* | 1503 | Julius II |
| 259 | St. Dionysius | *767* | *Constantine* | 1086 | Bl. Victor III | 1513 | Leo X |
| 269 | St. Felix I | *768* | *Philip* | 1088 | Bl. Urban II | 1522 | Adrian VI |
| 275 | St. Eutychian | 768 | Stephen III (IV) | 1099 | Paschal II | 1523 | Clement VII |
| 283 | St. Caius | 772 | Adrian I | *1100* | *Theodoric* | 1534 | Paul III |
| 296 | St. Marcellinus | 795 | St. Leo III | *1102* | *Albert* | 1550 | Julius III |
| 308 | St. Marcellus I | 816 | Stephen IV (V) | *1105* | *Sylvester IV* | 1555 | Marcellus II |
| 309 | St. Eusebius | 817 | St. Paschal I | 1118 | Gelasius II | 1555 | Paul IV |
| 311 | St. Melchiades | 824 | Eugene II | *1118* | *Gregory VIII* | 1559 | Pius IV |
| 314 | St. Sylvester I | 827 | Valentine | 1119 | Callistus II | 1566 | St. Pius V |
| 336 | St. Marcus | 827 | Gregory IV | 1124 | Honorius II | 1572 | Gregory XIII |
| 337 | St. Julius I | *844* | *John* | *1124* | *Celestine II* | 1585 | Sixtus V |
| 352 | Liberius | 844 | Sergius II | 1130 | Innocent II | 1590 | Urban VII |
| *355* | *Felix II* | 847 | St. Leo IV | *1130* | *Anacletus II* | 1590 | Gregory XIV |
| 366 | St. Damasus I | 855 | Benedict III | *1138* | *Victor IV* | 1591 | Innocent IX |
| *366* | *Ursinus* | *855* | *Anastasius* | 1143 | Celestine II | 1592 | Clement VIII |
| 384 | St. Siricius | 858 | St. Nicholas I | 1144 | Lucius II | 1605 | Leo XI |
| 399 | St. Anastasius I | 867 | Adrian II | 1145 | Bl. Eugene III | 1605 | Paul V |
| 401 | St. Innocent I | 872 | John VIII | 1153 | Anastasius IV | 1621 | Gregory XV |
| 417 | St. Zosimus | 882 | Marinus I | 1154 | Adrian IV | 1623 | Urban VIII |
| 418 | St. Boniface I | 884 | St. Adrian III | 1159 | Alexander III | 1644 | Innocent X |
| *418* | *Eulalius* | 885 | Stephen V (VI) | *1159* | *Victor IV* | 1655 | Alexander VII |
| 422 | St. Celestine I | 891 | Formosus | 1164 | Paschal III | 1667 | Clement IX |
| 432 | St. Sixtus III | 896 | Boniface VI | 1168 | Callistus III | 1670 | Clement X |
| 440 | St. Leo I | 896 | Stephen VI (VII) | *1179* | *Innocent III* | 1676 | Bl. Innocent XI |
| 461 | St. Hilary | 897 | Romanus | 1181 | Lucius III | 1689 | Alexander VIII |
| 468 | St. Simplicius | 897 | Theodore II | 1185 | Urban III | 1691 | Innocent XII |
| 483 | St. Felix III (II) | 898 | John IX | 1187 | Gregory VIII | 1700 | Clement XI |
| 492 | St. Gelasius I | 900 | Benedict IV | 1187 | Clement III | 1721 | Innocent XIII |
| 496 | Anastasius II | 903 | Leo V | 1191 | Celestine III | 1724 | Benedict XIII |
| 498 | St. Symmachus | *903* | *Christopher* | 1198 | Innocent III | 1730 | Clement XII |
| *498* | *Lawrence* | 904 | Sergius III | 1216 | Honorius III | 1740 | Benedict XIV |
| | *(501-505)* | 911 | Anastasius III | 1227 | Gregory IX | 1758 | Clement XIII |
| 514 | St. Hormisdas | 913 | Landus | 1241 | Celestine IV | 1769 | Clement XIV |
| 523 | St. John I, Martyr | 914 | John X | 1243 | Innocent IV | 1775 | Pius VI |
| 526 | St. Felix IV (III) | 928 | Leo VI | 1254 | Alexander IV | 1800 | Pius VII |
| 530 | Boniface II | 928 | Stephen VII | 1261 | Urban IV | 1823 | Leo XII |
| *530* | *Dioscorus* | | (VIII) | 1265 | Clement IV | 1829 | Pius VIII |
| 533 | John II | 931 | John XI | 1271 | Bl. Gregory X | 1831 | Gregory XVI |
| 535 | St. Agapitus I | 936 | Leo VII | 1276 | Bl. Innocent V | 1846 | Pius IX |
| 536 | St. Silverius, Martyr | 939 | Stephen VIII | 1276 | Adrian V | 1878 | Leo XIII |
| 537 | Vigilius | | (IX) | 1276 | John XXI | 1903 | St. Pius X |
| 556 | Pelagius I | 942 | Marinus II | 1277 | Nicholas III | 1914 | Benedict XV |
| 561 | John III | 946 | Agapitus II | 1281 | Martin IV | 1922 | Pius XI |
| 575 | Benedict I | 955 | John XII | 1285 | Honorius IV | 1939 | Pius XII |
| 579 | Pelagius II | 963 | Leo VIII | 1288 | Nicholas IV | 1958 | John XXIII |
| 590 | St. Gregory I | 964 | Benedict V | 1294 | St. Celestine V | 1963 | Paul VI |
| 604 | Sabinian | 965 | John XIII | 1294 | Boniface VIII | 1978 | John Paul I |
| 607 | Boniface III | 973 | Benedict VI | 1303 | Bl. Benedict XI | 1978 | John Paul II |
| 608 | St. Boniface IV | *974* | *Boniface VII* | 1305 | Clement V | | |
| 615 | St. Deusdedit | 974 | Benedict VII | | | | |

# WORLD EXPLORATION AND GEOGRAPHY

## Early Explorers of the Western Hemisphere

The first people to discover the New World or Western Hemisphere are believed to have walked across a "land bridge" from Siberia to Alaska, an isthmus since broken by the Bering Strait. From Alaska, these ancestors of the Indians spread through North, Central, and South America. Anthropologists have placed these crossings at between 18,000 and 14,000 B.C., but evidence found in 1967 near Puebla, Mex., indicates people may have reached there as early as 35,000-40,000 years ago.

At first, these people were hunters using flint weapons and tools. In Mexico, about 7000-6000 B.C., they founded farming cultures, developing corn, squash, etc. Eventually, they created complex civilizations — Olmec, Toltec, Aztec, and Maya and, in South America, Inca. Carbon-14 tests show humans lived about 8000 B.C. near what are now Front Royal, Va., Kanawha, W.Va., and Dutchess Quarry, N.Y. The Hopewell Culture, based on farming, flourished about 1000 B.C.; remains of it are seen today in large mounds in Ohio and other states.

Norsemen (Norwegian Vikings sailing out of Iceland and Greenland) are credited by most scholars with being the first Europeans to discover America, with at least 5 voyages around 1000 A.D. to areas they called Helluland, Markland, Vinland—possibly Labrador, Nova Scotia or Newfoundland, and New England.

Christopher Columbus, the most famous explorer, was born Cristoforo Colombo in or near Genoa, Italy, probably in 1451, but made his voyages of exploration for the Spanish rulers Ferdinand and Isabella. Dates of his voyages, places he reached, and other information follow:

**1492—First voyage.** Left Palos, Spain, Aug. 3 with 88 men (est.). His fleet consisted of 3 vessels—the *Nina*, the *Pinta*, and the *Santa Maria.* Landed San Salvador, (Guanahani or Watling Is., Bahamas) Oct. 12. Also Cuba, Hispaniola (Haiti-Dominican Republic); built Fort La Navidad on latter.

**1493—Second voyage, first part,** Sept. 25, with 17 ships, 1,500 men. Dominica (Lesser Antilles) Nov. 3; Guadeloupe, Montserrat, Antigua, San Martin, Santa Cruz, Puerto Rico, Virgin Islands. Settled Isabela on Hispaniola. **Second part** (Columbus having remained in Western Hemisphere), Jamaica, Isle of Pines, La Mona Is.

**1498—Third voyage.** Left Spain, May 30, 1498, 6 ships. Landed Trinidad. Saw South American continent, Aug. 1, 1498, but called it Isla Sancta (Holy Island). Entered Gulf of Paria and landed, first time on continental soil. At mouth of Orinoco, Aug. 14, he decided this was the mainland.

**1502—Fourth voyage,** 4 caravels, 150 men. St. Lucia, Guanaja off Honduras; Cape Gracias a Dios, Honduras; San Juan River, Costa Rica; Almirante, Portobelo, and Laguna de Chiriqui, Panama.

| Year | Explorer | Nationality and employer | Area reached or explored |
|---|---|---|---|
| 1497 | John Cabot | Italian-English | Newfoundland or Nova Scotia |
| 1498 | John and Sebastian Cabot | Italian-English | Labrador to Hatteras |
| 1499 | Alonso de Ojeda | Spanish | South American coast, Venezuela |
| 1500, Feb. | Vicente y Pinzon | Spanish | South American coast, Amazon River |
| 1500, Apr. | Pedro Alvarez Cabral | Portuguese | Brazil (for Portugal) |
| 1500-02 | Gaspar Corte-Real | Portuguese | Labrador |
| 1501 | Rodrigo de Bastidas | Spanish | Central America |
| 1513 | Vasco Nunez de Balboa | Spanish | Pacific Ocean |
| 1513 | Juan Ponce de Leon | Spanish | Florida |
| 1515 | Juan de Solis | Spanish | Rio de la Plata |
| 1519 | Alonso de Pineda | Spanish | Mouth of Mississippi River |
| 1519 | Hernando Cortes | Spanish | Mexico |
| 1520 | Ferdinand Magellan | Portuguese-Spanish | Straits of Magellan, Tierra del Fuego |
| 1524 | Giovanni da Verrazano | Italian-French | Atlantic coast-New York harbor |
| 1532 | Francisco Pizarro | Spanish | Peru |
| 1534 | Jacques Cartier | French | Canada, Gulf of St. Lawrence |
| 1536 | Pedro de Mendoza | Spanish | Buenos Aires |
| 1536 | A.N. Cabeza de Vaca | Spanish | Texas coast and interior |
| 1539 | Francisco de Ulloa | Spanish | California coast |
| 1539-41 | Hernando de Soto | Spanish | Mississippi River near Memphis |
| 1539 | Marcos de Niza | Italian-Spanish | Southwest (now U.S.) |
| 1540 | Francisco V. de Coronado | Spanish | Southwest (now U.S.) |
| 1540 | Hernando Alarcon | Spanish | Colorado River |
| 1540 | Garcia de L. Cardenas | Spanish | Grand Canyon of the Colorado |
| 1541 | Francisco de Orellana | Spanish | Amazon River |
| 1542 | Juan Rodriguez Cabrillo | Portuguese-Spanish | San Diego harbor |
| 1565 | Pedro Menendez de Aviles | Spanish | St. Augustine |
| 1576 | Martin Frobisher | English | Frobisher's Bay, Canada |
| 1577-80 | Francis Drake | English | California coast |
| 1582 | Antonio de Espejo | Spanish | Southwest (named New Mexico) |
| 1584 | Amadas & Barlow (for Raleigh) | English | Virginia |
| 1585-87 | Sir Walter Raleigh's men | English | Roanoke Is., N.C. |
| 1595 | Sir Walter Raleigh | English | Orinoco River |
| 1603-09 | Samuel de Champlain | French | Canadian interior, Lake Champlain |
| 1607 | Capt. John Smith | English | Atlantic coast |
| 1609-10 | Henry Hudson | English-Dutch | Hudson River, Hudson Bay |
| 1634 | Jean Nicolet | French | Lake Michigan; Wisconsin |
| 1673 | Jacques Marquette, Louis Jolliet | French | Mississippi S to Arkansas |
| 1682 | Sieur de La Salle | French | Mississippi S to Gulf of Mexico |
| 1789 | Alexander Mackenzie | Canadian | Canadian Northwest |

## Arctic Exploration

### Early Explorers

**1587** — John Davis (England). Davis Strait to Sanderson's Hope, 72° 12' N.

**1596** — Willem Barents and Jacob van Heemskerck (Holland). Discovered Bear Island, touched northwest tip of Spitsbergen, 79° 49' N, rounded Novaya Zemlya, wintered at Ice Haven.

**1607** — Henry Hudson (England). North along Greenland's east coast to Cape Hold-with-Hope, 73° 30', then north of Spitsbergen to 80° 23'. Returning he discovered Hudson's Touches (Jan Mayen).

**1616** — William Baffin and Robert Bylot (England). Baffin Bay to Smith Sound.

**1728** — Vitus Bering (Russia). Proved Asia and America were separated by sailing through strait.

**1733-40** — Great Northern Expedition (Russia). Surveyed Siberian Arctic coast.

**1741** — Vitus Bering (Russia). Sighted Alaska from sea, named Mount St. Elias. His lieutenant, Chirikof, discovered coast.

**1771** — Samuel Hearne (Hudson's Bay Co.). Overland from Prince of Wales Fort (Churchill) on Hudson Bay to mouth of Coppermine River.

**1778** — James Cook (Britain). Through Bering Strait to Icy Cape, Alaska, and North Cape, Siberia.

**1789** — Alexander Mackenzie (North West Co., Britain). Montreal to mouth of Mackenzie River.

**1806** — William Scoresby (Britain). N. of Spitsbergen to 81° 30'.

**1820-3** — Ferdinand von Wrangel (Russia). Completed a survey of Siberian Arctic coast. His exploration joined that of James Cook at North Cape, confirming separation of the continents.

**1845** — Sir John Franklin (Britain) was one of many to seek the Northwest Passage—an ocean route connecting the Atlantic and Pacific via the Arctic. His 2 ships (the *Erebus* and *Terror*) were last seen entering Lancaster Sound July, 26.

**1881** — The steamer *Jeanette* on an expedition led by Lt. Cmdr. George W. DeLong was trapped in ice and crushed, June 1881. DeLong and 11 crewmen died; 12 others survived.

**1888** — Fridtjof Nansen (Norway) crossed Greenland's icecap, 1893-96 — Nansen in Fram drifted from New Siberian Is. to Spitsbergen; tried polar dash in 1895, reached Franz Josef Land.

**1897** — Salomon A. Andree (Sweden) and 2 others started in balloon from Danes, Is., Spitsbergen, July 11, to drift across pole to America, and disappeared. Over 33 years later, Aug. 6, 1930, their frozen bodies were found on White Is., 82° 57' N 29° 52' E.

**1903-06** — Roald Amundsen (Norway) first sailed Northwest Passage.

### Discovery of North Pole

Robert E. Peary explored Greenland's coast, 1891-92, tried for North Pole, 1893. In 1900 he reached northern limit of Greenland and 83° 50' N; in 1902 he reached 84° 06' N; in 1906 he went from Ellesmere Is. to 87° 06' N. He sailed in the *Roosevelt*, July, 1908, to winter off Cape Sheridan, Grant Land. The dash for the North Pole began Mar. 1 from Cape Columbia, Ellesmere Land. Peary reached the pole, 90° N, Apr. 6, 1909.

Peary had several supporting groups carrying supplies until the last group turned back at 87° 47' N. Peary, Matthew Henson, and 4 Eskimos proceeded with dog teams and sleds. They crossed the pole several times, finally built an igloo at 90°, remained 36 hours. Started south, Apr. 7 at 4 p.m., for Cape Columbia. The Eskimos were Coqueeh, Ootah, Eginwah, and Seegloo.

**1914** — Donald MacMillan (U.S.). Northwest, 200 miles, from Axel Heiberg Island to seek Peary's Crocker Land.

**1915-17** — Vihjalmur Stefansson (Canada) discovered Borden, Brock, Meighen, and Lougheed Islands.

**1918-20** — Roald Amundsen sailed Northeast Passage.

**1925** — Amundsen and Lincoln Ellsworth (U.S.) reached 87° 44' N in attempt to fly to North Pole from Spitsbergen.

**1926** — Richard E. Byrd and Floyd Bennett (U.S.) first over North Pole by air, May 9.

**1926** — Amundsen, Ellsworth, and Umberto Nobile (Italy) flew from Spitsbergen over North Pole May 12, to Teller, Alaska, in dirigible *Norge*.

**1928** — Nobile crossed North Pole in airship, May 24, crashed, May 25. Amundsen lost while trying to effect rescue by plane.

### North Pole Exploration Records

On Aug. 3, 1958, the *Nautilus*, under Comdr. William R. Anderson, became the first ship to cross the North Pole beneath the Arctic ice.

The nuclear-powered U.S. submarine *Seadragon*, Comdr. George P. Steele 2d, made the first east-west underwater transit through the Northwest Passage during August, 1960. It sailed from Portsmouth N.H., headed between Greenland and Labrador through Baffin Bay, then west through Lancaster Sound and McClure Strait to the Beaufort Sea. Traveling submerged for the most part, the submarine made 850 miles from Baffin Bay to the Beaufort Sea in 6 days.

On Aug. 16, 1977, the Soviet nuclear icebreaker *Arktika* reached the North Pole and became the first surface ship to break through the Arctic ice pack to the top of the world.

On April 30, 1978, Naomi Uemura, a Japanese explorer, became the first man to reach the North Pole alone by dog sled. During the 54-day, 600-mile trek over the frozen Arctic, Uemura survived attacks by a marauding polar bear.

In April, 1982, Sir Ranulph Fiennes and Charles Burton, British explorers, reached the North Pole and became the first to circle the earth from pole to pole. They had reached the South Pole 16 months earlier. The 52,000-mile trek took 3 years, involved 23 people, and cost an estimated $18 million. The expedition was also the first to travel down the Scott Glacier and the first to journey up the Yukon and through the Northwest Passage in a single season.

On May 2, 1986, 6 American and Canadian explorers reached the North Pole assisted only by dogs. They became the first to reach the Pole without mechanical assistance since Robert E. Peary planted a flag there in 1909. The explorers, Americans Will Steger, Paul Schurke, Anne Bancroft, and Geoff Carroll, and Canadians Brent Boddy and Richard Weber completed the 500-mile journey in 56 days.

# Antarctic Exploration

### Early History

Antarctica has been approached since 1773-75, when Capt. James Cook (Britain) reached 71° 10' S. Many sea and landmarks bear names of early explorers. Bellingshausen (Russia) discovered Peter I and Alexander I Islands, 1819-21. Nathaniel Palmer (U.S.) discovered Palmer Peninsula, 60° W, 1820, without realizing that this was a continent. James Weddell (Britain) found Weddell Sea, 74° 15' S, 1823.

First to announce existence of the continent of Antarctica was Charles Wilkes (U.S.), who followed the coast for 1,500 mi., 1840. Adelie Coast, 140° E, was found by Dumont d'Urville (France), 1840. Ross Ice Shelf was found by James Clark Ross (Britain), 1841-42.

**1895** — Leonard Kristensen (Norway) landed a party on the coast of Victoria Land. They were the first ashore on the main continental mass. C.E. Borchgrevink, a member of that

party, returned in 1899 with a British expedition, first to winter on Antarctica.

**1902-04** — Robert F. Scott (Britain) discovered Edward VII Peninsula. He reached 82° 17' S, 146° 33' E from McMurdo Sound.

**1908-09** — Ernest Shackleton (Britain) introduced the use of Manchurian ponies in Antarctic sledging. He reached 88° 23' S, discovering a route on to the plateau by way of the Beardmore Glacier and pioneering the way to the pole.

### Discovery of South Pole

**1911** — Roald Amundsen (Norway) with 4 men and dog teams reached the pole, Dec. 14.

**1912** — Capt. Scott reached the pole from Ross Island, Jan. 18, with 4 companions. They found Amundsen's tent. None of Scott's party survived. They were found, Nov. 12.

**1928** — First man to use an airplane over Antarctica was Hubert Wilkins (Britain).

**1929** — Richard E. Byrd (U.S.) established Little America on Bay of Whales. On 1,600-mi. airplane flight begun, Nov. 28, he crossed South Pole, Nov. 29 with 3 others.

**1934-35** — Byrd led 2d expedition to Little America, explored 450,000 sq. mi., wintered alone at weather station, 80° 08' S.

**1934-37** — John Rymill led British Graham Land expedition; discovered that Palmer Peninsula is part of Antarctic mainland.

**1935** — Lincoln Ellsworth (U.S.) flew south along Palmer Peninsula's east coast, then crossed continent to Little America, making 4 landings on unprepared terrain in bad weather.

**1939-41** — U.S. Antarctic Service built West Base on Ross Ice Shelf under Paul Siple, and East Base on Palmer Peninsula under Richard Black. U.S. Navy plane flights discovered about 150,000 sq. miles of new land.

**1940** — Byrd charted most of coast between Ross Sea and Palmer Peninsula.

**1946-47** — U.S. Navy undertook Operation High-jump under Byrd. Expedition included 13 ships and 4,000 men. Airplanes photomapped coastline and penetrated beyond pole.

**1946-48** — Ronne Antarctic Research Expedition. Comdr. Finn Ronne, USNR, determined the Antarctic to be only one continent with no strait between Weddell Sea and Ross Sea; discovered 250,000 sq. miles of land by flights to 79° S Lat., and made 14,000 aerial photographs over 450,000 sq. miles of land. Mrs. Ronne and Mrs. H. Darlington were the first women to winter on Antarctica.

**1955-57** — U.S. Navy's Operation Deep Freeze led by Adm. Byrd. Supporting U.S. scientific efforts for the International Geophysical Year, the operation was commanded by Rear Adm. George Dufek. It established 5 coastal stations fronting the Indian, Pacific, and Atlantic oceans and also 3 interior stations; explored more than 1,000,000 sq. miles in Wilkes Land.

**1957-58** — During the International Geophysical year, July 1957, through Dec. 1958, scientists from 12 countries conducted ambitious programs of Antarctic research. A network of some 60 stations on the continent and sub-Arctic islands studied oceanography, glaciology, meteorology, seismology, geomagnetism, the ionosphere, cosmic rays, aurora, and airglow.

Dr. V.E. Fuchs led a 12-man Trans-Antarctic Expedition on the first land crossing of Antarctica. Starting from the Weddell Sea, they reached Scott Station, Mar. 2, 1958, after traveling 2,158 miles in 98 days.

**1958** — A group of 5 U.S. scientists led by Edward C. Thiel, seismologist, moving by tractor from Ellsworth Station on Weddell Sea, identified a huge mountain range, 5,000 ft. above the ice sheet and 9,000 ft. above sea level. The range, originally seen by a Navy plane, was named the Dufek Massif, for Rear Adm. George Dufek.

**1959** — Twelve nations — Argentina, Australia, Belgium, Chile, France, Japan, New Zealand, Norway, South Africa, the Soviet Union, the United Kingdom, and the U.S. — signed a treaty suspending any territorial claims for 30 years and reserving the continent for research.

**1961-62** — Scientists discovered a trough, the Bentley Trench, running from Ross Ice Shelf, Pacific, into Marie Byrd Land, around the end of the Ellsworth Mtns., toward the Weddell Sea.

**1962** — First nuclear power plant began operation at McMurdo Sound.

**1963** — On Feb. 22 a U.S. plane made the longest nonstop flight ever made in the S. Pole area, covering 3,600 miles in 10 hours. The flight was from McMurdo Station south past the geographical S. Pole to Shackleton Mtns., southeast to the "Area of Inaccessibility" and back to McMurdo Station.

**1964** — A British survey team was landed by helicopter on Cook Island, the first recorded visit since its discovery in 1775.

**1964** — New Zealanders completed one of the last and most important surveys when they mapped the mountain area from Cape Adare west some 400 miles to Pennell Glacier.

**1989** — Two Americans, Victoria Murden and Shirley Metz, became the first women to reach the South Pole overland when they arrived with 9 others on Jan. 17, 1989. The 51-day trek on skis covered 740 miles.

## Volcanoes

Source: Global Volcanism Network, Smithsonian Institution

More than 75 percent of the world's 850 active volcanoes lie within the "Ring of Fire," a zone running along the west coast of the Americas from Chile to Alaska and down the east coast of Asia from Siberia to New Zealand. Twenty per cent of these volcanoes are located in Indonesia. Other prominent groupings are located in Japan, the Aleutian Islands, and Central America. Almost all active regions are found at the boundaries of the large moving plates which comprise the earth's surface. The "Ring of Fire" marks the boundary between the plates underlying the Pacific Ocean and those underlying the surrounding continents. Other active regions, such as the Mediterranean Sea and Iceland, are located on plate boundaries.

### Major Historical Eruptions

Approximately 7,000 years ago, Mazama, a 9,900-feet-high volcano in southern Oregon, erupted violently, ejecting ash and lava. The ash spread over the entire northwestern United States and as far away as Saskatchewan, Canada. During the eruption, the top of the mountain collapsed, leaving a caldera 6 miles across and about a half mile deep, which filled with rain water to form what is now called Crater Lake.

In 79 A.D., Vesuvio, or Vesuvius, a 4,190 feet volcano overlooking Naples Bay became active after several centuries of quiescence. On Aug. 24 of that year, a heated mud and ash flow swept down the mountain engulfing the cities of Pompeii, Herculaneum, and Stabiae with debris over 60 feet deep. About 10 percent of the population of the 3 towns was killed.

The largest eruptions in recent centuries have been in Indonesia. In 1883, an eruption similar to the Mazama eruption occurred on the island of Krakatau. On August 27, the 2,640-feet-high peak of the volcano collapsed to 1,000 feet below sea level, leaving only a small portion of the island standing above the sea. Ash from the eruption colored sunsets around the world for 2 years. A tsunami ("tidal wave") generated by the collapse killed 36,000 people in nearby Java and Sumatra and eventually reached England. A similar, but even more powerful, eruption had taken place 68 years earlier at Tambora volcano on the Indonesian island of Sumbawa.

### Notable Active Volcanoes

| Name, latest activity | Location | Height (feet) | Name, latest activity | Location | Height (feet) |
|---|---|---|---|---|---|
| | | | Erta-Ale (1992) | Ethiopia | 1,650 |
| **Africa** | | | | | |
| | | | **Antarctica** | | |
| Cameroon (1982) | Cameroon | 13,354 | Erebus (1991) | Ross Island | 12,450 |
| Nyirangongo (1977) | Zaire | 11,400 | Deception Island (1970) | South Shetland | |
| Nyamuragira (1991) | Zaire | 10,028 | | Islands | 1,890 |
| Karthala (1977) | Comoro Is. | 8,000 | | | |
| Piton de la Fournaise (1991) | Reunion Is. | 5,981 | | | *(continued )* |

| Name, latest activity | Location | Height (feet) |
|---|---|---|
| **Asia-Oceania** | | |
| Kliuchevskol (1991) | Russia | 15,584 |
| Kerinci (1987) | Sumatra | 12,467 |
| Semeru (1991) | Java | 12,060 |
| Slamet (1988) | Java | 11,247 |
| Raung (1991) | Java | 10,932 |
| On-Take (1991) | Japan | 10,049 |
| Mayon (1993) | Philippines | 9,991 |
| Merapi (1993) | Java | 9,551 |
| Marapi (1988) | Sumatra | 9,485 |
| Ruapehu (1992) | New Zealand | 9,175 |
| Asama (1991) | Japan | 8,300 |
| Niigata Yakeyama (1989) | Japan | 8,111 |
| Canlaon (1991) | Philippines | 8,070 |
| Alaid (1972) | Kuril Is. | 7,662 |
| Ulawun (1992) | New Britain | 7,532 |
| Ngaurhoe (1975) | New Zealand | 7,515 |
| Chokai (1974) | Japan | 7,300 |
| Galunggung (1982) | Java | 7,113 |
| Azuma (1978) | Japan | 6,700 |
| Pinatubo (1992) | Philippines | 5,770 |
| Sangeang Api (1988) | Indonesia | 6,351 |
| Nasu (1977) | Japan | 6,210 |
| Tiatia (1973) | Kuril Islands | 6,013 |
| Manam (1992) | Papua New Guinea | 6,000 |
| Soputan (1989) | Indonesia | 5,994 |
| Siau (1976) | Indonesia | 5,853 |
| Kelud (1990) | Java | 5,679 |
| Kirisima (1982) | Japan | 5,577 |
| Bagana (1992) | Papua New Guinea | 6,558 |
| Akita Komaga take (1970) | Japan | 5,449 |
| Gamkonora (1981) | Indonesia | 5,364 |
| Aso (1993) | Japan | 5,223 |
| Lokon-Empung (1991) | Indonesia | 5,187 |
| Bulusan (1988) | Philippines | 5,115 |
| Sarycheva (1976) | Kuril Islands | 4,960 |
| Karkar (1981) | Papua New Guinea | 4,920 |
| Lopevi (1982) | Vanuatu | 4,755 |
| Unzen (1993) | Japan | 4,462 |
| Ambrym (1991) | Vanuatu | 4,376 |
| Awu (1992) | Indonesia | 4,350 |
| Sakurajima (1993) | Japan | 3,668 |
| Langila (1992) | New Britain | 3,586 |
| Suwanosezima (1991) | Japan | 2,640 |
| Oshima (1990) | Japan | 2,550 |
| Usu (1978) | Japan | 2,400 |
| Pagan (1990) | Mariana Is. | 1,870 |
| White Island (1993) | New Zealand | 1,075 |
| Taal (1988) | Philippines | 984 |
| **Central America—Caribbean** | | |
| Acatenango (1972) | Guatemala | 12,992 |
| Fuego (1991) | Guatemala | 12,582 |
| Tacana (1988) | Guatemala | 12,400 |
| Santiaguito (Santa Maria) (1991) | Guatemala | 12,362 |
| Irazu (1992) | Costa Rica | 11,260 |
| Turrialba (1992) | Costa Rica | 10,650 |
| Poas (1992) | Costa Rica | 8,930 |
| Pacaya (1991) | Guatemala | 8,346 |
| San Miguel (1986) | El Salvador | 6,994 |

| Name, latest activity | Location | Height (feet) |
|---|---|---|
| Rincon de la Vieja (1993) | Costa Rica | 6,234 |
| El Viejo (San Cristobal) (1991) | Nicaragua | 5,840 |
| Ometepe (Concepcion) (1986) | Nicaragua | 5,106 |
| Arenal (1993) | Costa Rica | 5,092 |
| Momotombo (1982) | Nicaragua | 4,199 |
| Soufriere (1979) | St. Vincent | 4,048 |
| Telica (1987) | Nicaragua | 3,409 |
| **South America** | | |
| Guallatiri (1987) | Chile | 19,882 |
| Lascar (1991) | Chile | 19,652 |
| Cotopaxi (1975) | Ecuador | 19,347 |
| Tupungatito (1986) | Chile | 18,504 |
| Ruiz (1992) | Colombia | 17,716 |
| Sangay (1988) | Ecuador | 17,159 |
| Guagua Pichincha (1988) | Ecuador | 15,696 |
| Purace (1977) | Colombia | 15,601 |
| Galeras (1993) | Colombia | 13,996 |
| Llaima (1990) | Chile | 10,239 |
| Villarrica (1992) | Chile | 9,318 |
| Hudson (1991) | Chile | 8,580 |
| Alcedo (1970) | Galapagos Is. | 3,599 |
| **Mid-Pacific** | | |
| Mauna Loa (1987) | Hawaii | 13,680 |
| Kilauea (1993) | Hawaii | 4,077 |
| **Mid-Atlantic Ridge** | | |
| Beerenberg (1985) | Jan Mayen Is. | 7,470 |
| Hekla (1991) | Iceland | 4,892 |
| Leirhnukur (1975) | Iceland | 2,145 |
| Krafla (1984) | Iceland | 2,145 |
| **Europe** | | |
| Etna (1993) | Italy | 11,053 |
| Stromboli (1993) | Italy | 3,038 |
| **North America** | | |
| Colima (1991) | Mexico | 14,003 |
| Redoubt (1991) | Alaska | 10,197 |
| Iliamna (1978) | Alaska | 10,016 |
| Shishaldin (1987) | Aleutian Is. | 9,387 |
| Mt. St. Helens (1991) | Washington | 8,300+ |
| Pavlof (1988) | Aleutian Is. | 8,261 |
| Veniaminof (1987) | Alaska | 8,225 |
| El Chichon (1983) | Mexico | 7,300 |
| Katmai (1974) | Alaska | 6,715 |
| Makushin (1987) | Alaska | 6,680 |
| Great Sitkin (1974) | Aleutian Is. | 5,710 |
| Cleveland (1987) | Aleutian Is. | 5,675 |
| Gareloi (1982) | Aleutian Is. | 5,334 |
| Korovin (1987) | Aleutian Is. | 4,852 |
| Akutan (1992) | Aleutian Is. | 4,275 |
| Kiska (1990) | Aleutian Is. | 4,275 |
| Augustine (1988) | Alaska | 3,999 |
| Okmok (1988) | Aleutian Is. | 3,519 |
| Seguam (1977) | Alaska | 3,458 |

## Notable Volcanic Eruptions

| Date | Volcano | Deaths | Date | Volcano | Deaths |
|---|---|---|---|---|---|
| 79 A.D. | Mt. Vesuvius, Italy | 16,000 | May 8, 1902 | Mt. Pelée, Martinique | 30,000 |
| 1169 | Mt. Etna, Sicily | 15,000 | 1911 | Mt. Taal, Philippines | 1,400 |
| 1631 | Mt. Vesuvius, Italy | 4,000 | 1919 | Mt. Kelud, Java | 5,000 |
| 1669 | Mt. Etna, Sicily | 20,000 | Jan. 18-21, 1951 | Mt. Lamington, New Guinea | 3,000 |
| 1772 | Mt. Papandayan, Java | 3,000 | Apr. 26, 1966 | Mt. Kelud, Java | 1,000 |
| 1792 | Mt. Unzen-Dake, Japan | 10,400 | May 18, 1980 | Mt. St. Helens, U.S. | 60 |
| 1815 | Tamboro, Java | 12,000 | Nov. 13, 1985 | Nevado del Ruiz, Colombia | 22,940 |
| Aug. 26-28, 1883 | Krakatau, Indonesia | 35,000 | Aug. 24, 1986 | NW Cameroon | 1,700+ |
| Apr. 8, 1902 | Santa Maria, Guatemala | 1,000 | | | |

## Mountains

### Height of Mount Everest

Mt. Everest was considered to be 29,002 ft. tall when Edmund Hillary and Tenzing Norgay scaled it in 1953. This triangulation figure had been accepted since 1850. In 1954 the Surveyor General of the Republic of India set the height at 29,028 ft., plus or minus 10 ft. because of snow. The National Geographic Society accepts the new figure, but many mountaineering groups still use 29,002 ft.

In 1987, new calculations based on satellite measurements indicate that the Himalayan peak K-2 rose 29,064 feet above sea level and that Mt. Everest is 800 feet higher. The National Geographic Society has not accepted the revised figure.

## United States, Canada, Mexico

| Name | Place | Height (feet) | Name | Place | Height (feet) | Name | Place | Height (feet) |
|---|---|---|---|---|---|---|---|---|
| McKinley | Alaska | 20,320 | Alverstone | Alas-Yukon | 14,565 | Princeton | Col | 14,197 |
| Logan | Yukon | 19,850 | Browne Tower | Alaska | 14,530 | Crestone Needle | Col | 14,197 |
| Citlaltepec (Orizaba) | Mexico | 18,700 | Whitney | Cal | 14,494 | Yale | Col | 14,196 |
| St. Elias | Alas-Yukon | 18,008 | Elbert | Col | 14,433 | Bross | Col | 14,172 |
| Popocatepetl | Mexico | 17,887 | Massive | Col | 14,421 | Kit Carson | Col | 14,165 |
| Foraker | Alaska | 17,400 | Harvard | Col | 14,420 | Wrangell | Alaska | 14,163 |
| Iztaccihuatl | Mexico | 17,343 | Rainier | Wash | 14,410 | Shasta | Cal | 14,162 |
| Lucania | Yukon | 17,147 | Williamson | Cal | 14,375 | Sill | Cal | 14,162 |
| King | Yukon | 16,971 | Blanca Peak | Col | 14,345 | El Diente | Col | 14,159 |
| Steele | Yukon | 16,644 | La Plata | Col | 14,336 | Maroon | Col | 14,156 |
| Bona | Alaska | 16,550 | Uncompahgre | Col | 14,309 | Tabeguache | Col | 14,155 |
| Blackburn | Alaska | 16,390 | Crestone | Col | 14,294 | Oxford | Col | 14,153 |
| Kennedy | Alaska | 16,286 | Lincoln | Col | 14,286 | Sneffels | Col | 14,150 |
| Sanford | Alaska | 16,237 | Grays Peak | Col | 14,270 | Point Success | Wash | 14,150 |
| South Buttress | Alaska | 15,885 | Antero | Col | 14,269 | Democrat | Col | 14,148 |
| Wood | Yukon | 15,885 | Torreys | Col | 14,267 | Capitol | Col | 14,130 |
| Vancouver | Alas-Yukon | 15,700 | Castle | Col | 14,265 | Liberty Cap | Wash | 14,112 |
| Churchill | Alaska | 15,638 | Quandary | Col | 14,265 | Pikes Peak | Col | 14,110 |
| Fairweather | Alas-Yukon | 15,300 | Evans | Col | 14,264 | Snowmass | Col | 14,092 |
| Zinantecatl (Toluca) | Mexico | 15,016 | Longs Peak | Col | 14,256 | Windom | Col | 14,087 |
| Hubbard | Alas-Yukon | 15,015 | McArthur | Yukon | 14,253 | Russell | Cal | 14,086 |
| Bear | Alaska | 14,831 | Wilson | Col | 14,246 | Eolus | Col | 14,084 |
| Walsh | Yukon | 14,780 | White | Cal | 14,246 | Columbia | Col | 14,073 |
| East Buttress | Alaska | 14,730 | North Palisade | Cal | 14,242 | Augusta | Alas-Yukon | 14,070 |
| Matlalcueyetl | Mexico | 14,636 | Shavano | Col | 14,229 | Missouri | Col | 14,067 |
| Hunter | Alaska | 14,573 | Belford | Col | 14,197 | Humboldt | Col | 14,064 |

## South America

| Peak, country | Height (feet) | Peak, country | Height (feet) | Peak, country | Height (feet) |
|---|---|---|---|---|---|
| Aconcagua, Argentina | 22,834 | Laudo, Argentina | 20,997 | Polleras, Argentina | 20,456 |
| Ojos del Salado, Arg.-Chile | 22,572 | Ancohuma, Bolivia | 20,958 | Pular, Chile | 20,423 |
| Bonete, Argentina | 22,546 | Ausangate, Peru | 20,945 | Chani, Argentina | 20,341 |
| Tupungato, Argentina-Chile | 22,310 | Toro, Argentina-Chile | 20,932 | Aucanquilcha, Chile | 20,295 |
| Pissis, Argentina | 22,241 | Illampu, Bolivia | 20,873 | Juncal, Argentina-Chile | 20,276 |
| Mercedario, Argentina | 22,211 | Tres Cruces, Argentina-Chile | 20,853 | Negro, Argentina | 20,184 |
| Huascaran, Peru | 22,205 | Huandoy, Peru | 20,852 | Quela, Argentina | 20,128 |
| Llullaillaco, Argentina-Chile | 22,057 | Parinacota, Bolivia-Chile | 20,768 | Condoriri, Bolivia | 20,095 |
| El Libertador, Argentina | 22,047 | Tortolas, Argentina-Chile | 20,745 | Palermo, Argentina | 20,079 |
| Cachi, Argentina | 22,047 | Ampato, Peru | 20,702 | Solimana, Peru | 20,068 |
| Yerupaja, Peru | 21,709 | Condor, Argentina | 20,669 | San Juan, Argentina-Chile | 20,049 |
| Galan, Argentina | 21,654 | Salcantay, Peru | 20,574 | Sierra Nevada, Arg.-Chile | 20,023 |
| El Muerto, Argentina-Chile | 21,457 | Chimborazo, Ecuador | 20,561 | Antofalla, Argentina | 20,013 |
| Sajama, Bolivia | 21,391 | Huancarhuas, Peru | 20,531 | Marmolejo, Argentina-Chile | 20,013 |
| Nacimiento, Argentina | 21,302 | Famatina, Argentina | 20,505 | Chachani, Peru | 19,931 |
| Illimani, Bolivia | 21,201 | Pumasillo, Peru | 20,492 | Licancabur, Argentina-Chile | 19,425 |
| Coropuna, Peru | 21,083 | Solo, Argentina | 20,492 | | |

The highest point in the West Indies is in the Dominican Republic, Pico Duarte (10,417 ft.)

## Africa, Southeast Asia, Australia, New Zealand

| Peak, country/island | Height (feet) | Peak, country/island | Height (feet) | Peak, country/island | Height (feet) |
|---|---|---|---|---|---|
| Kilimanjaro, Tanzania | 19,340 | Wilhelm, New Guinea | 14,793 | Kinabalu, Malaysia | 13,455 |
| Kenya, Kenya | 17,058 | Karisimbi, Zaire-Rwanda | 14,787 | Cameroon, Cameroon | 13,353 |
| Margherita Pk., Uganda-Zaire | 16,763 | Elgon, Kenya-Uganda | 14,178 | Kerinci, Sumatra | 12,467 |
| Jaja, New Guinea | 16,500 | Batu, Ethiopia | 14,131 | Cook, New Zealand | 12,349 |
| Trikora, New Guinea | 15,585 | Guna, Ethiopia | 13,881 | Teide, Canary Islands | 12,198 |
| Mandala, New Guinea | 15,420 | Gughe, Ethiopia | 13,780 | Semeru, Java | 12,060 |
| Ras Dashan, Ethiopia | 15,158 | Toubkal, Morocco | 13,661 | Kosciusko, Australia | 7,310 |
| Meru, Tanzania | 14,979 | | | | |

## Europe

| Peak, country | Height (feet) | Peak, country | Height (feet) | Peak, country | Height (feet) |
|---|---|---|---|---|---|
| **Alps** | | Nadelhorn, Switz. | 14,196 | Dent D'Herens, Switz. | 13,686 |
| | | Grand Combin, Switz. | 14,154 | Breithorn, It., Switz. | 13,665 |
| Mont Blanc, Fr.-It. | 15,771 | Lenzpitze, Switz. | 14,088 | Bishorn, Switz. | 13,645 |
| Monte Rosa (highest peak of group), Switz. | 15,203 | Finsteraarhorn, Switz. | 14,022 | Jungfrau, Switz. | 13,642 |
| | | Castor, Switz. | 13,865 | Ecrins, Fr. | 13,461 |
| Dom, Switz. | 14,911 | Zinalrothorn, Switz. | 13,849 | Monch, Switz. | 13,448 |
| Liskamm, It., Switz. | 14,852 | Hohberghorn, Switz. | 13,842 | Pollux, Switz. | 13,422 |
| Weisshorn, Switz. | 14,780 | Alphubel, Switz. | 13,799 | Schreckhorn, Switz. | 13,379 |
| Taschhorn, Switz. | 14,733 | Rimpfischhorn, Switz. | 13,776 | Ober Gabelhorn, Switz. | 13,330 |
| Matterhorn, It., Switz. | 14,690 | Aletschorn, Switz. | 13,763 | Gran Paradiso, It. | 13,323 |
| Dent Blanche, Switz. | 14,293 | Strahlhorn, Switz. | 13,747 | | *(continued)* |

| Peak, country | Height (feet) | Peak, country | Height (feet) | Peak, country | Height (feet) |
|---|---|---|---|---|---|
| Bernina, It., Switz. | 13,284 | Schalihorn, Switz. | 13,040 | Estats, Sp. | 10,304 |
| Fiescherhorn, Switz. | 13,283 | Scerscen, Switz. | 13,028 | Montcalm, Sp. | 10,105 |
| Grunhorn, Switz. | 13,266 | Eiger, Switz. | 13,025 | | |
| Lauteraarhorn, Switz. | 13,261 | Jagerhorn, Switz. | 13,024 | | |
| Durrenhorn, Switz. | 13,238 | Rottalhorn, Switz. | 13,022 | **Caucasus (Europe-Asia)** | |
| Allalinhorn, Switz. | 13,213 | | | El'brus, Russia | 18,510 |
| Weissmies, Switz. | 13,199 | **Pyrenees** | | Shkara, Russia | 17,064 |
| Lagginhorn, Switz. | 13,156 | | | Dykh Tau, Russia | 17,054 |
| Zupo, Switz. | 13,120 | Aneto, Sp. | 11,168 | Kashtan Tau, Russia | 16,877 |
| Fletschhorn, Switz. | 13,110 | Posets, Sp. | 11,073 | Dzhangi Tau, Russia | 16,565 |
| Adlerhorn, Switz. | 13,081 | Perdido, Sp. | 11,007 | Kazbek, Russia | 16,558 |
| Gletscherhorn, Switz. | 13,068 | Vignemale, Fr.-Sp. | 10,820 | | |
| | | Long, Sp. | 10,479 | | |

## Asia

| Peak | Country | Height (feet) | Peak | Country | Height (feet) | Peak | Country | Height (feet) |
|---|---|---|---|---|---|---|---|---|
| Everest | Nepal-Tibet. | 29,028 | Kungur. | Sinkiang. | 25,325 | Badrinath | India. | 23,420 |
| K2 (Godwin Austen) | Kashmir. | 28,250 | Tirich Mir | Pakistan. | 25,230 | Nunkun | Kashmir. | 23,410 |
| Kanchenjunga | India-Nepal. | 28,208 | Makalu II. | Nepal-Tibet. | 25,120 | Lenin Peak | Tajikistan. | 23,405 |
| Lhotse I (Everest) | Nepal-Tibet. | 27,923 | Minya Konka | China. | 24,900 | Pyramid | India-Nepal. | 23,400 |
| Makalu I | Nepal-Tibet. | 27,824 | Kula Gangri | Bhutan-Tibet | 24,784 | Api | Nepal. | 23,399 |
| Lhotse II (Everest) | Nepal-Tibet. | 27,560 | Changtzu (Everest) | Nepal-Tibet. | 24,780 | Pauhunri. | India-Tibet. | 23,385 |
| Dhaulagiri | Nepal. | 26,810 | Muz Tagh Ata. | Sinkiang. | 24,757 | Trisul. | Nepal. | 23,360 |
| Manaslu I | Nepal. | 26,760 | Skyang Kangri | Kashmir. | 24,750 | Kangto. | India-Tibet. | 23,260 |
| Cho Oyu. | Nepal-Tibet. | 26,750 | Communism Peak | Tajikistan. | 24,590 | Nyenchhen Thanglha | Tibet. | 23,255 |
| Nanga Parbat. | Kashmir. | 26,660 | Jongsang Peak | India-Nepal. | 24,472 | Trisuli | India. | 23,210 |
| Annapurna I. | Nepal. | 26,504 | Pobedy Peak | Sinkiang-Kyrgyzstan. | 24,406 | Pumori. | Nepal-Tibet. | 23,190 |
| Gasherbrum | Kashmir. | 26,470 | Sia Kangri | Kashmir. | 24,350 | Dunagiri | India. | 23,184 |
| Broad | Kashmir. | 26,400 | Haramosh Peak | Pakistan. | 24,270 | Lombo Kangra | Tibet. | 23,165 |
| Gosainthan | Tibet. | 26,287 | Istoro Nal | Pakistan. | 24,240 | Saipal | Nepal. | 23,100 |
| Annapurna II | Nepal. | 26,041 | Tent Peak | India-Nepal. | 24,165 | Macha Pucchare | Nepal. | 22,958 |
| Gyachung Kang | Nepal-Tibet. | 25,910 | Chomo Lhari | Bhutan-Tibet | 24,040 | Numbar | Nepal. | 22,817 |
| Disteghil Sar | Kashmir. | 25,868 | Chamlang | Nepal. | 24,012 | Kanjiroba | Nepal. | 22,580 |
| Himalchuli | Nepal. | 25,801 | Kabru | India-Nepal. | 24,002 | Ama Dablam | Nepal. | 22,350 |
| Nuptse (Everest) | Nepal-Tibet. | 25,726 | Alung Gangri | Tibet. | 24,000 | Cho Polu | Nepal. | 22,093 |
| Masherbrum | Kashmir. | 25,660 | Baltoro Kangri | Kashmir. | 23,990 | Lingtren | Nepal-Tibet. | 21,972 |
| Nanda Devi | India. | 25,645 | Mussu Shan. | Sinkiang. | 23,890 | Khumbutse | Nepal-Tibet. | 21,785 |
| Rakaposhi. | Kashmir. | 25,550 | Mana | India. | 23,860 | Hlako Gangri | Tibet. | 21,266 |
| Kamet | India-Tibet. | 25,447 | Baruntse. | Nepal. | 23,688 | Mt. Grosvenor | China. | 21,190 |
| Namcha Barwa. | Tibet. | 25,445 | Nepal Peak | India-Nepal. | 23,500 | Thagchhab Gangri | Tibet. | 20,970 |
| Gurla Mandhata | Tibet. | 25,355 | Amne Machin. | China. | 23,490 | Damavand | Iran. | 18,606 |
| Ulugh Muz Tagh | Sinkiang-Tibet. | 25,340 | Gauri Sankar | Nepal-Tibet. | 23,440 | Ararat | Turkey. | 16,804 |

## Antarctica

| Peak | Height (feet) | Peak | Height (feet) | Peak | Height (feet) | Peak | Height (feet) |
|---|---|---|---|---|---|---|---|
| Vinson Massif | 16,864 | Andrew Jackson | 13,750 | Shear | 13,100 | Campbell | 12,434 |
| Tyree. | 16,290 | Sidley | 13,720 | Odishaw | 13,008 | Don Pedro Christophersen | 12,355 |
| Shinn. | 15,750 | Ostenso | 13,710 | Donaldson | 12,894 | Lysaght | 12,326 |
| Gardner | 15,375 | Minto | 13,668 | Ray. | 12,808 | Huggins | 12,247 |
| Epperly | 15,100 | Miller. | 13,650 | Sellery | 12,779 | Sabine | 12,200 |
| Kirkpatrick. | 14,855 | Long Gables. | 13,620 | Waterman | 12,730 | Astor | 12,175 |
| Elizabeth. | 14,698 | Dickerson | 13,517 | Anne | 12,703 | Mohl | 12,172 |
| Markham | 14,290 | Giovinetto | 13,412 | Press. | 12,566 | Frankes | 12,064 |
| Bell. | 14,117 | Wade. | 13,400 | Falla | 12,549 | Jones | 12,040 |
| Mackellar | 14,098 | Fisher | 13,386 | Rucker | 12,520 | Gjelsvik | 12,008 |
| Anderson | 13,957 | Fridtjof Nansen | 13,350 | Goldthwait | 12,510 | Coman | 12,000 |
| Bentley. | 13,934 | Wexler | 13,202 | Morris | 12,500 | | |
| Kaplan. | 13,878 | Lister | 13,200 | Erebus | 12,450 | | |

## Some Notable U.S. Mountains

| Name | Place | Height (feet) | Name | Place | Height (feet) | Name | Place | Height (feet) |
|---|---|---|---|---|---|---|---|---|
| Gannett Peak | Wyo. | 13,804 | Adams | Wash. | 12,307 | Clingmans Dome | N.C.-Tenn. | 6,643 |
| Grand Teton | Wyo. | 13,766 | San Gorgonio | Cal. | 11,502 | Washington | N.H. | 6,288 |
| Kings | Utah | 13,528 | Hood | Ore. | 11,235 | Rogers | Va. | 5,927 |
| Cloud | Wyo. | 13,175 | Lassen | Cal. | 10,457 | Marcy | N.Y. | 5,344 |
| Boundary | Nevada | 13,140 | Granite | Cal. | 10,321 | Katahdin | Maine | 5,268 |
| Wheeler | N.M. | 13,065 | Guadalupe | Texas | 8,751 | Spruce Knob | W. Va. | 4,862 |
| Granite | Montana | 12,799 | Olympus | Wash. | 7,965 | Mansfield | Vt. | 4,393 |
| Borah | Idaho | 12,662 | Harney | S.D. | 7,242 | Black Mountain | Ky. | 4,145 |
| Humphreys | Ariz. | 12,633 | Mitchell | N.C. | 6,684 | | | |

## Ocean Areas and Average Depths

Four major bodies of water are recognized by geographers and mapmakers: the Pacific, Atlantic, Indian, and Arctic oceans. The Atlantic and Pacific oceans are considered divided at the equator into the No. and So. Atlantic; the No. and So. Pacific. The Arctic Ocean is the name for waters north of the continental land masses in the region of the Arctic Circle.

| | Sq. miles | Avg. depth (feet) | | Sq. miles | Avg. depth (feet) |
|---|---|---|---|---|---|
| Pacific Ocean | 64,186,300 | 12,925 | Hudson Bay | 281,900 | 305 |
| Atlantic Ocean | 33,420,000 | 11,730 | East China Sea | 256,600 | 620 |
| Indian Ocean | 28,350,500 | 12,598 | Andaman Sea | 218,100 | 3,667 |
| Arctic Ocean | 5,105,700 | 3,407 | Black Sea | 196,100 | 3,906 |
| South China Sea | 1,148,500 | 4,802 | Red Sea | 174,900 | 1,764 |
| Caribbean Sea | 971,400 | 8,448 | North Sea | 164,900 | 308 |
| Mediterranean Sea | 969,100 | 4,926 | Baltic Sea | 147,500 | 180 |
| Bering Sea | 873,000 | 4,893 | Yellow Sea | 113,500 | 121 |
| Gulf of Mexico | 582,100 | 5,297 | Persian Gulf | 88,800 | 328 |
| Sea of Okhotsk | 537,500 | 3,192 | Gulf of California | 59,100 | 2,375 |
| Sea of Japan | 391,100 | 5,468 | | | |

## Principal Ocean Depths

Source: Defense Mapping Agency Hydrographic/Topographic Center, U.S. Dept. of Defense

| Name of area | Location | Depth Meters | Depth Fathoms | Feet |
|---|---|---|---|---|
| **Pacific Ocean** | | | | |
| Mariana Trench | 11°22'N | 142°36'E | 10,924 | 5,973 | 35,840 |
| Tonga Trench | 23°16'S | 174°44'W | 10,800 | 5,906 | 35,433 |
| Philippine Trench | 10°38'N | 126°36'E | 10,057 | 5,499 | 32,995 |
| Kermadec Trench | 31°53'S | 177°21'W | 10,047 | 5,494 | 32,963 |
| Bonin Trench | 24°30'N | 143°24'E | 9,994 | 5,331 | 32,788 |
| Kuril Trench | 44°15'N | 150°34'E | 9,750 | 5,331 | 31,988 |
| Izu Trench | 31°05'N | 142°10'E | 9,695 | 5,301 | 31,808 |
| New Britain Trench | 06°19'S | 153°45'E | 8,940 | 4,888 | 29,331 |
| Yap Trench | 08°33'N | 138°02'E | 8,527 | 4,663 | 27,976 |
| Japan Trench | 36°08'N | 142°43'E | 8,412 | 4,600 | 27,599 |
| Peru-Chile Trench | 23°18'S | 71°14'W | 8,064 | 4,409 | 26,457 |
| Palau Trench | 07°52'N | 134°56'E | 8,054 | 4,404 | 26,424 |
| Aleutian Trench | 50°51'N | 177°11'E | 7,679 | 4,199 | 25,194 |
| New Hebrides Trench | 20°36'S | 168°37'E | 7,570 | 4,139 | 24,836 |
| North Ryukyu Trench | 24°00'N | 126°48'E | 7,181 | 3,927 | 23,560 |
| Mid. America Trench | 14°02'N | 93°39'W | 6,662 | 3,643 | 21,857 |
| **Atlantic Ocean** | | | | |
| Puerto Rico Trench | 19°55'N | 65°27'W | 8,605 | 4,705 | 28,232 |
| So. Sandwich Trench | 55°42'S | 25°56'E | 8,325 | 4,552 | 27,313 |
| Romanche Gap | 0°13'S | 18°26'W | 7,728 | 4,226 | 25,354 |
| Cayman Trench | 19°12'N | 80°00'W | 7,535 | 4,120 | 24,721 |
| Brazil Basin | 09°10'S | 23°02'W | 6,119 | 3,346 | 20,076 |
| **Indian Ocean** | | | | |
| Java Trench | 10°19'S | 109°58'E | 7,125 | 3,896 | 23,376 |
| Ob' Trench | 09°45'S | 67°18'E | 6,874 | 3,759 | 22,553 |
| Diamantina Trench | 35°50'S | 105°14'E | 6,602 | 3,610 | 21,660 |
| Vema Trench | 09°08'S | 67°15'E | 6,402 | 3,501 | 21,004 |
| Agulhas Basin | 45°20'S | 26°50'E | 6,195 | 3,387 | 20,325 |
| **Arctic Ocean** | | | | |
| Eurasia Basin | 82°23'N | 19°31'E | 5,450 | 2,980 | 17,881 |
| **Mediterranean Sea** | | | | |
| Ionian Basin | 36°32'N | 21°06'E | 5,150 | 2,816 | 16,896 |

Note: Deeper depths have been reported in some of the above areas. However, they are not official unless confirmed by research vessels.

## Principal World Rivers

Source: Geological Survey, U.S. Dept. of the Interior

| River | Outflow | Length (Miles) | River | Outflow | Length (Miles) | River | Outflow | Length (Miles) |
|---|---|---|---|---|---|---|---|---|
| Albany | James Bay | 610 | Chang Jiang | E. China Sea | 3,964 | Dvina, North | White Sea | 824 |
| Amazon | Atlantic Ocean | 4,000 | Churchill, Man. | Hudson Bay | 1,000 | Dvina, West | Gulf of Riga | 634 |
| Amu | Aral Sea | 1,578 | Churchill, Que. | Atlantic Ocean | 532 | Ebro | Mediterranean | 565 |
| Amur | Tatar Strait | 2,744 | Colorado | Gulf of Calif. | 1,450 | Elbe | North Sea | 724 |
| Angara | Yenisey River | 1,151 | Columbia | Pacific Ocean | 1,243 | Euphrates | Shatt al-Arab. | 1,700 |
| Arkansas | Mississippi | 1,459 | Congo | Atlantic Ocean | 2,718 | Fraser | Str. of Georgia | 850 |
| Back | Arctic Ocean | 605 | Danube | Black Sea | 1,776 | Gambia | Atlantic Ocean | 700 |
| Brahmaputra | Bay of Bengal | 1,800 | Dnieper | Black Sea | 1,420 | Ganges | Bay of Bengal | 1,560 |
| Bug, Southern | Dnieper River | 532 | Dniester | Black Sea | 877 | Garonne | Bay of Biscay | 357 |
| Bug, Western | Wisla River | 481 | Don | Sea of Azov | 1,224 | Huang | Yellow Sea | 3,395 |
| Canadian | Arkansas River | 906 | Drava | Danube River | 447 | Indus | Arabian Sea | 1,800 |

| River | Outflow | Length (Miles) |
|---|---|---|
| Irrawaddy | Bay of Bengal | 1,337 |
| Japura | Amazon River | 1,750 |
| Jordan | Dead Sea | 200 |
| Kootenay | Columbia River | 485 |
| Lena | Laptev Sea | 2,734 |
| Loire | Bay of Biscay | 634 |
| Mackenzie | Arctic Ocean | 2,635 |
| Madeira | Amazon River | 2,013 |
| Magdalena | Caribbean Sea | 956 |
| Marne | Seine River | 326 |
| Mekong | S. China Sea | 2,600 |
| Meuse | North Sea | 580 |
| Mississippi | Gulf of Mexico | 2,340 |
| Missouri | Mississippi | 2,315 |
| Murray-Darling | Indian Ocean | 2,310 |
| Negro | Amazon | 1,400 |
| Nelson | Hudson Bay | 410 |
| Niger | Gulf of Guinea | 2,590 |
| Nile | Mediterranean | 4,160 |
| Ob-Irtysh | Gulf of Ob | 3,362 |
| Oder | Baltic Sea | 567 |
| Ohio | Mississippi | 981 |

| River | Outflow | Length (Miles) |
|---|---|---|
| Orange | Atlantic Ocean | 1,300 |
| Orinoco | Atantic Ocean | 1,600 |
| Ottawa | St. Lawrence R. | 790 |
| Paraguay | Parana River | 1,584 |
| Parana | Rio de la Plata | 2,485 |
| Peace | Slave River | 1,210 |
| Pilcomayo | Paraguay River | 1,000 |
| Po | Adriatic Sea | 405 |
| Purus | Amazon River | 2,100 |
| Red | Mississippi | 1,290 |
| Red River of N. | Lake Winnipeg | 545 |
| Rhine | North Sea | 820 |
| Rhone | Gulf of Lions | 505 |
| Rio de la Plata | Atlantic Ocean | 150 |
| Rio Grande | Gulf of Mexico | 1,900 |
| Rio Roosevelt | Aripuana | 400 |
| Saguenay | St. Lawrence R. | 434 |
| St. John | Bay of Fundy | 418 |
| St. Lawrence | Gulf of St. Law. | 800 |
| Salween | Andaman Sea | 1,500 |
| Sao Francisco | Atlantic Ocean | 1,988 |
| Saskatchewan | Lake Winnipeg | 1,205 |

| River | Outflow | Length (Miles) |
|---|---|---|
| Seine | English Chan. | 496 |
| Shannon | Atlantic Ocean | 230 |
| Snake | Columbia River | 1,038 |
| Songhua | Amur River | 1,150 |
| Syr | Aral Sea | 1,370 |
| Tajo, Tagus | Atlantic Ocean | 626 |
| Tennessee | Ohio River | 652 |
| Thames | North Sea | 236 |
| Tiber | Tyrrhenian Sea | 252 |
| Tigris | Shatt al-Arab. | 1,180 |
| Tisza | Danube River | 600 |
| Tocantins | Para River | 1,677 |
| Ural | Caspian Sea | 1,575 |
| Uruguay | Rio de la Plata | 1,000 |
| Volga | Caspian Sea | 2,290 |
| Weser | North Sea | 454 |
| Wisla | Bay of Danzig | 675 |
| Xi | S. China Sea | 1,200 |
| Yellow (See Huang) | | |
| Yenisey | Kara Sea | 2,543 |
| Yukon | Bering Sea | 1,979 |
| Zambezi | Indian Ocean | 1,700 |

## Major Rivers in North America

Source: Geological Survey, U.S. Dept. of the Interior

| River | Source or Upper Limit of Length | Outflow | Miles |
|---|---|---|---|
| Alabama | Gilmer County, Ga. | Mobile River | 729 |
| Albany | Lake St. Joseph, Ontario | James Bay | 610 |
| Allegheny | Potter County, Pa. | Ohio River | 325 |
| Altamaha-Ocmulgee | Junction of Yellow and South Rivers, Newton County, Ga. | Atlantic Ocean | 392 |
| Apalachicola-Chattahoochee | Towns County, Ga. | Gulf of Mexico | 524 |
| Arkansas | Lake County, Col. | Mississippi River | 1,459 |
| Assiniboine | Eastern Saskatchewan | Red River | 450 |
| Attawapiskat | Attawapiskat, Ontario | James Bay | 465 |
| Back (N.W.T.) | Contwoyto Lake | Chantrey Inlet | 605 |
| Big Black (Miss.) | Webster County, Miss. | Mississippi River | 330 |
| Brazos | Junction of Salt and Double Mountain Forks, Stonewall County, Tex. | Gulf of Mexico | 923 |
| Canadian | Las Animas County, Col. | Arkansas River | 906 |
| Cedar (Iowa) | Dodge County, Minn. | Iowa River | 329 |
| Cheyenne | Junction of Antelope Creek and Dry Fork, Converse County, Wyo. | Missouri River | 290 |
| Churchill | Methy Lake, Saskatchewan | Hudson Bay | 1,000 |
| Cimarron | Colfax County, N.M. | Arkansas River | 600 |
| Colorado (Ariz.) | Rocky Mountain National Park, Col. (90 miles in Mexico) | Gulf of Cal. | 1,450 |
| Colorado (Texas) | West Texas | Matagorda Bay | 862 |
| Columbia | Columbia Lake, British Columbia | Pacific Ocean, bet. Ore. and Wash. | 1,243 |
| Columbia, Upper | Columbia Lake, British Columbia | To mouth of Snake River | 890 |
| Connecticut | Third Connecticut Lake, N.H. | L.I. Sound, Conn. | 407 |
| Coppermine (N.W.T.) | Lac de Gras | Coronation Gulf (Arctic Ocean) | 525 |
| Cumberland | Letcher County, Ky. | Ohio River | 720 |
| Delaware | Schoharie County, N.Y. | Liston Point, Delaware Bay | 390 |
| Fraser | Near Mount Robson (on Continental Divide) | Strait of Georgia | 850 |
| Gila | Catron County, N.M. | Colorado River | 649 |
| Green (Ut.-Wyo.) | Junction of Wells and Trail Creeks, Sublette County, Wyo. | Colorado River | 730 |
| Hamilton (Lab.) | Lake Ashuanipi | Atlantic Ocean | 532 |
| Hudson | Henderson Lake, Essex County, N.Y. | Upper N.Y. Bay | 306 |
| Illinois | St. Joseph County, Ind. | Mississippi River | 420 |
| James (N.D.-S.D.) | Wells County, N.D. | Missouri River | 710 |
| James (Va.) | Junction of Jackson and Cowpasture Rivers, Botetourt County, Va. | Hampton Roads | 340 |
| Kanawha-New | Junction of North and South Forks of New River, N.C. | Ohio River | 352 |
| Kentucky | Junction of North and Middle Forks, Lee County, Ky. | Ohio River | 259 |
| Klamath | Lake Ewauna, Klamath Falls, Ore. | Pacific Ocean | 250 |
| Koyukuk | Endicott Mountains, Alaska | Yukon River | 470 |
| Kuskokwim | Alaska Range | Kuskokwim Bay | 724 |
| Liard | Southern Yukon, Alaska | Mackenzie River | 693 |
| Little Missouri | Crook County, Wyo. | Missouri River | 560 |
| Mackenzie | Great Slave Lake, N.W.T. | Arctic Ocean | 2,635 |
| Milk | Junction of North and South Forks, Alberta | Missouri River | 625 |
| Minnesota | Big Stone Lake, Minn. | Mississippi River | 332 |
| Mississippi | Lake Itasca, Minn. | Mouth of Southwest Pass | 2,340 |
| Mississippi, Upper | Lake Itasca, Minn. | To mouth of Missouri River | 1,171 |
| Mississippi-Missouri-Red Rock | Source of Red Rock, Beaverhead Co., Mon. | Mouth of Southwest Pass | 3,710 |
| Missouri | Junction of Jefferson, Madison, and Gallatin rivers, Madison County, Mon. | Mississippi River | 2,315 |
| Missouri-Red Rock | Source of Red Rock, Beaverhead Co., Mon. | Mississippi River | 2,540 |
| Mobile-Alabama-Coosa | Gilmer County, Ga. | Mobile Bay | 774 |
| Nelson (Manitoba) | Lake Winnipeg | Hudson Bay | 410 |

| River | Source or Upper Limit of Length | Outflow | Miles |
|---|---|---|---|
| Neosho | Morris County, Kan. | Arkansas River, Okla. | 460 |
| Niobrara | Niobrara County, Wyo. | Missouri River, Neb. | 431 |
| North Canadian | Union County, N.M. | Canadian River, Okla. | 800 |
| North Platte | Junction of Grizzly and Little Grizzly creeks, Jackson County, Col. | Platte River, Neb. | 618 |
| Ohio | Junction of Allegheny and Monongahela rivers, Pittsburgh, Pa. | Mississippi River | 981 |
| Ohio-Allegheny | Potter County, Pa. | Mississippi River | 1,310 |
| Osage | East-central Kansas | Missouri River | 500 |
| Ottawa | Lake Capimitchigama | St. Lawrence River | 790 |
| Ouachita | Polk County, Ark. | Red River | 605 |
| Peace | Stikine Mountains, B.C. | Slave River | 1,210 |
| Pearl | Neshoba County, Miss. | Gulf of Mexico | 411 |
| Pecos | Mora County, N.M. | Rio Grande | 926 |
| Pee Dee-Yadkin | Watauga County, N.C. | Winyah Bay | 435 |
| Pend Oreille-Clark Fork | Near Butte, Mon. | Columbia River | 531 |
| Platte | Junction of North and South Platte Rivers, Neb. | Missouri River | 310 |
| Porcupine | Ogilvie Mountains, Alaska | Yukon River, Alaska | 569 |
| Potomac | Garrett County, Md. | Chesapeake Bay | 383 |
| Powder | Junction of South and Middle Forks, Wyo. | Yellowstone River | 375 |
| Red (Okla.-Tex.-La.) | Curry County, N.M. | Mississippi River | 1,290 |
| Red River of the North | Junction of Otter Tail and Bois de Sioux Rivers, Wilkin County, Minn. | Lake Winnipeg | 545 |
| Republican | Junction of North Fork and Arikaree River, Neb. | Kansas River | 445 |
| Rio Grande | San Juan County, Col. | Gulf of Mexico | 1,900 |
| Roanoke | Junction of North and South Forks, Montgomery County, Va. | Albemarle Sound | 380 |
| Rock (Ill.-Wis.) | Dodge County, Wis. | Mississippi River | 300 |
| Sabine | Junction of South and Caddo Forks, Hunt County, Tex. | Sabine Lake | 380 |
| Sacramento | Siskiyou County, Cal. | Suisun Bay | 377 |
| St. Francis | Iron County, Mo. | Mississippi River | 425 |
| St. Lawrence | Lake Ontario | Gulf of St. Lawrence (Atlantic Ocean) | 800 |
| Salmon (Idaho) | Custer County, Ida. | Snake River | 420 |
| San Joaquin | Junction of South and Middle Forks, Madera County, Cal. | Suisun Bay | 350 |
| San Juan | Silver Lake, Archuleta County, Col. | Colorado River | 360 |
| Santee-Wateree-Catawba | McDowell County, N.C. | Atlantic Ocean | 538 |
| Saskatchewan, North | Rocky Mountains | Saskatchewan R. | 800 |
| Saskatchewan, South | Rocky Mountains | Saskatchewan R. | 865 |
| Savannah | Junction of Seneca and Tugaloo rivers, Anderson County, S.C. | Atlantic Ocean, Ga.-S.C. | 314 |
| Severn (Ontario) | Sandy Lake | Hudson Bay | 610 |
| Smoky Hill | Cheyenne County, Col. | Kansas River, Kan. | 540 |
| Snake | Teton County, Wyo. | Columbia River, Wash. | 1,038 |
| South Platte | Junction of South and Middle Forks, Park County, Col. | Platte River | 424 |
| Susitna | Alaska Range | Cook Inlet | 313 |
| Susquehanna | Otsego Lake, Otsego County, N.Y. | Chesapeake Bay | 444 |
| Tallahatchie | Tippah County, Miss. | Yazoo River | 301 |
| Tanana | Wrangell Mountains, Alaska | Yukon River | 659 |
| Tennessee | Junction of French Broad and Holston Rivers | Ohio River | 652 |
| Tennessee-French Broad | Transylvania County, N.C. | Ohio River | 883 |
| Tombigbee | Prentiss County, Miss. | Mobile River | 525 |
| Trinity | North of Dallas, Tex. | Galveston Bay | 360 |
| Wabash | Darke County, Oh. | Ohio River | 512 |
| Washita | Hemphill County, Tex. | Red River, Okla. | 500 |
| White (Ark.-Mo.) | Madison County, Ark. | Mississippi River | 722 |
| Willamette | Douglas County, Ore. | Columbia River | 309 |
| Wind-Bighorn | Junction of Wind and Little Wind Rivers, Fremont Co., Wyo. (Source of Wind R. is Togwotee Pass, Teton Co., Wyo.) | Yellowstone River | 336 |
| Wisconsin | Lac Vieux Desert, Vilas County, Wis. | Mississippi River | 430 |
| Yellowstone | Park County, Wyo. | Missouri River | 692 |
| Yukon | Coast Mountains of British Columbia | Bering Sea | 1,979 |

## Lakes of the World

Source: Geological Survey, U.S. Dept. of the Interior

A lake is a body of water surrounded by land. Although some lakes are called seas (such as the Caspian Sea and the Aral Sea), they are lakes by definition.

| Name | Continent | Area (sq. mi.) | Length (miles) | Depth (feet) | Elevation (feet) |
|---|---|---|---|---|---|
| Caspian Sea | Asia-Europe | 143,244 | 760 | 3,363 | −92 |
| Superior | North America | 31,700 | 350 | 1,330 | 600 |
| Victoria | Africa | 26,828 | 250 | 270 | 3,720 |
| Aral Sea | Asia | 24,904(A) | 280 | 220 | 174 |
| Huron | North America | 23,000 | 206 | 750 | 579 |
| Michigan | North America | 22,300 | 307 | 923 | 579 |
| Tanganyika | Africa | 12,700 | 420 | 4,823 | 2,534 |
| Baykal | Asia | 12,162 | 395 | 5,315 | 1,493 |
| Great Bear | North America | 12,096 | 192 | 1,463 | 512 |
| Nyasa | Africa | 11,150 | 360 | 2,280 | 1,550 |

(continued)

| Name | Continent | Area (sq. mi.) | Length (miles) | Depth (feet) | Elevation (feet) |
|---|---|---|---|---|---|
| Great Slave | North America | 11,031 | 298 | 2,015 | 513 |
| Erie | North America | 9,910 | 241 | 210 | 570 |
| Winnipeg | North America | 9,417 | 266 | 60 | 713 |
| Ontario | North America | 7,550 | 193 | 802 | 245 |
| Balkhash | Asia | 7,115 | 376 | 85 | 1,115 |
| Ladoga | Europe | 6,835 | 124 | 738 | 13 |
| Chad | Africa | 6,300 | 175 | 24 | 787 |
| Maracaibo | South America | 5,217 | 133 | 115 | Sea level |
| Onega | Europe | 3,710 | 145 | 328 | 108 |
| Eyre | Australia | 3,600 | 90 | 4 | −52 |
| Volta | Africa | 3,276 | 250 | .... | .... |
| Titicaca | South America | 3,200 | 122 | 922 | 12,500 |
| Nicaragua | North America | 3,100 | 102 | 230 | 102 |
| Athabasca | North America | 3,064 | 208 | 407 | 700 |
| Reindeer | North America | 2,568 | 143 | 720 | 1,106 |
| Rudolf | Africa | 2,473 | 154 | 240 | 1,230 |
| Issyk Kul | Asia | 2,355 | 115 | 2,303 | 5,279 |
| Torrens | Australia | 2,230 | 130 | .... | 92 |
| Vanern | Europe | 2,156 | 91 | 328 | 144 |
| Nettilling | North America | 2,140 | 67 | .... | 95 |
| Winnipegosis | North America | 2,075 | 141 | 38 | 830 |
| Albert | Africa | 2,075 | 100 | 168 | 2,030 |
| Kariba | Africa | 2,050 | 175 | 390 | 1,590 |
| Nipigon | North America | 1,872 | 72 | 540 | 1,050 |
| Gairdner | Australia | 1,840 | 90 | .... | 112 |
| Urmia | Asia | 1,815 | 90 | 49 | 4,180 |
| Manitoba | North America | 1,799 | 140 | 12 | 813 |

(A) Probably less because of the diversion of feeder rivers.

# The Great Lakes

Source: National Ocean Service. U.S. Dept. of Commerce

The Great Lakes form the largest body of fresh water in the world and with their connecting waterways are the largest inland water transportation unit. Draining the great North Central basin of the U.S., they enable shipping to reach the Atlantic via their outlet, the St. Lawrence R., and also the Gulf of Mexico via the Illinois Waterway, from Lake Michigan to the Mississippi R. A third outlet connects with the Hudson R. and thence the Atlantic via the N. Y. State Barge Canal System. Traffic on the Illinois Waterway and the N.Y. State Barge Canal System is limited to recreational boating and small shipping vessels.

Only one of the lakes, Lake Michigan, is wholly in the United States; the others are shared with Canada. Ships move from the shores of Lake Superior to Whitefish Bay at the east end of the lake, thence through the Soo (Sault Ste. Marie) locks, through the St. Mary's River and into Lake Huron. To reach Gary, and Port of Indiana and South Chicago, Ill., ships move west from Lake Huron to Lake Michigan through the Straits of Mackinac.

Lake Superior is 600 feet above mean water level at Point-au-Pere, Quebec, on the International Great Lakes Datum (1955). From Duluth, Minn., to the eastern end of Lake Ontario is 1,156 mi.

| | Superior | Michigan | Huron | Erie | Ontario |
|---|---|---|---|---|---|
| Length in miles | 350 | 307 | 206 | 241 | 193 |
| Breadth in miles | 160 | 118 | 183 | 57 | 53 |
| Deepest soundings in feet | 1,330 | 923 | 750 | 210 | 802 |
| Volume of water in cubic miles | 2,900 | 1,180 | 850 | 116 | 393 |
| Area (sq. miles) water surface—U.S. | 20,600 | 22,300 | 9,100 | 4,980 | 3,560 |
| Canada | 11,100 | ..... | 13,900 | 4,930 | 3,990 |
| Area (sq. miles) entire drainage basin—U.S. | 16,900 | 45,600 | 16,200 | 18,000 | 15,200 |
| Canada | 32,400 | ..... | 35,500 | 4,720 | 12,100 |
| **Total Area (sq. miles) U.S. and Canada** | **81,000** | **67,900** | **74,700** | **32,630** | **34,850** |
| Mean surface above mean water level at Point-au-Pere, Quebec, aver. level in feet (1900-1988) | 600.61 | 578.34 | 578.34 | 570.53 | 244.74 |
| Latitude, North | 46° 25′ | 41° 37′ | 43° 00′ | 41° 23′ | 43° 11′ |
| | 49° 00′ | 46° 06′ | 46° 17′ | 42° 52′ | 44° 15′ |
| Longitude, West | 84° 22′ | 84° 45′ | 79° 43′ | 78° 51′ | 76° 03′ |
| | 92° 06′ | 88° 02′ | 84° 45′ | 83° 29′ | 79° 53′ |
| National boundary line in miles | 282.8 | None | 260.8 | 251.5 | 174.6 |
| United States shore line (mainland only) miles | 863 | 1,400 | 580 | 431 | 300 |

# Highest and Lowest Continental Altitudes

Source: National Geographic Society

| Continent | Highest point | Elevation (feet) | Lowest point | Elevation (feet) below sea level |
|---|---|---|---|---|
| Asia | Mount Everest, Nepal-Tibet | 29,028 | Dead Sea, Israel-Jordan | 1,312 |
| South America | Mount Aconcagua, Argentina | 22,834 | Valdes Peninsula, Argentina | 131 |
| North America | Mount McKinley, Alaska | 20,320 | Death Valley, California | 282 |
| Africa | Kilimanjaro, Tanzania | 19,340 | Lake Assal, Djibouti | 512 |
| Europe | Mount El'brus, Russia | 18,510 | Caspian Sea, Russia, Azerbaijan | 92 |
| Antarctica | Vinson Massif | 16,864 | Unknown | ..... |
| Australia | Mount Kosciusko, New South Wales | 7,310 | Lake Eyre, South Australia | 52 |

# Famous Waterfalls

Source: National Geographic Society

The earth has thousands of waterfalls, some of considerable magnitude. Their importance is determined not only by height but volume of flow, steadiness of flow, crest width, whether the water drops sheerly or over a sloping surface, and in one leap or a succession of leaps. A series of low falls flowing over a considerable distance is known as a cascade.

Estimated mean annual flow, in cubic feet per second, of major waterfalls are: Niagara, 212,200; Paulo Afonso, 100,000; Urubupunga, 97,000; Iguazu, 61,000; Patos-Maribondo, 53,000; Victoria, 35,400; and Kaieteur, 23,400.

Height = total drop in feet in one or more leaps. † = falls of more than one leap; * = falls that diminish greatly seasonally; ** = falls that reduce to a trickle or are dry for part of each year. If river names not shown, they are same as the falls. R. = river; L. = lake; (C) = cascade type.

| Name and location | Elevation (Feet) |
|---|---|
| **Africa** | |
| **Angola** | |
| Ruacana, Cuene R. | 406 |
| **Ethiopia** | |
| Fincha | 508 |
| **Lesotho** | |
| *Maletsunyane | 630 |
| **Zimbabwe-Zambia** | |
| *Victoria, Zambezi R. | 343 |
| **South Africa** | |
| *Augrabies, Orange R. | 480 |
| † Tugela | 2,014 |
| **Tanzania-Zambia** | |
| *Kalambo | 726 |
| **Asia** | |
| India—*Cauvery | 330 |
| *Jog (Gersoppa), Sharavathi R. | 830 |
| **Japan** | |
| *Kegon, Daiya R. | 330 |
| **Australasia** | |
| **Australia** | |
| New South Wales | |
| Wentworth | 614 |
| Wollomombi | 1,100 |
| Queensland | |
| Tully | 885 |
| † Wallaman, Stony Cr. | 1,137 |
| New Zealand | |
| Helena | 890 |
| † Sutherland, Arthur R. | 1,904 |
| **Europe** | |
| Austria—† Gastein. | 492 |
| † Krimml | 1,312 |
| France—*Gavarnie | 1,385 |
| **Great Britain—Scotland** | |
| Glomach | 370 |

| Name and location | Elevation (Feet) |
|---|---|
| Wales | |
| Rhaiadr | 240 |
| Italy—Frua, Toce R. (C.) | 470 |
| **Norway** | |
| Mardalsfossen (Northern) | 1,535 |
| † Mardalsfossen (Southern) | 2,149 |
| † **Skjeggedal, Nybuai R. | 1,378 |
| **Skykje | 984 |
| Vetti, Morka-Koldedola R. | 900 |
| **Sweden** | |
| † Handol | 427 |
| **Switzerland** | |
| Giessbach (C) | 984 |
| † Reichenbach | 656 |
| † Simmen | 459 |
| Staubbach | 984 |
| † Trummelbach | 1,312 |
| **North America** | |
| **Canada** | |
| Alberta | |
| Panther, Nigel Cr. | 600 |
| British Columbia | |
| † Della | 1,443 |
| † Takakkaw, Daly Glacier | 1,200 |
| Quebec | |
| Montmorency | 274 |
| **Canada—United States** | |
| Niagara: American | 182 |
| Horseshoe | 173 |
| **United States** | |
| California | |
| *Feather, Fall R. | 640 |
| Yosemite National Park | |
| *Bridalveil | 620 |
| *Illilouette | 370 |
| *Nevada, Merced R. | 594 |
| **Ribbon | 1,612 |
| **Silver Strand, Meadow Br. | 1,170 |
| *Vernal, Merced R. | 317 |
| † **Yosemite | 2,425 |
| Colorado | |
| † Seven, South Cheyenne Cr. | 300 |
| Hawaii | |
| Akaka, Kolekole Str. | 442 |
| Idaho | |
| **Shoshone, Snake R. | 212 |

| Name and location | Elevation (Feet) |
|---|---|
| Kentucky | |
| Cumberland | 68 |
| Maryland | |
| *Great, Potomac R. (C) | 71 |
| Minnesota | |
| **Minnehaha | 53 |
| New Jersey | |
| Passaic | 70 |
| New York | |
| *Taughannock | 215 |
| Oregon | |
| † Multnomah | 620 |
| Tennessee | |
| Fall Creek | 256 |
| Washington | |
| Mt. Rainier Natl. Park | |
| Sluiskin, Paradise R. | 300 |
| **Snoqualmie | 268 |
| Wisconsin | |
| *Big Manitou, Black R. (C) | 165 |
| Wyoming | |
| Yellowstone Natl. Pk. Tower. | 132 |
| *Yellowstone (upper) | 109 |
| *Yellowstone (lower) | 308 |
| **Mexico** | |
| El Salto | 218 |
| **South America** | |
| **Argentina-Brazil** | |
| Iguazu | 230 |
| **Brazil** | |
| Glass | 1,325 |
| Patos-Maribondo, Grande R. | 115 |
| Paulo Afonso, Sao Francisco R. | 275 |
| **Colombia** | |
| Catarata de Candelas, | |
| Cusiana R. | 984 |
| *Tequendama, Bogota R. | 427 |
| **Ecuador** | |
| *Agoyan, Pastaza R. | 200 |
| **Guyana** | |
| Kaieteur, Potaro R. | 741 |
| Great, Kamarang R. | 1,600 |
| † Marina, Ipobe R. | 500 |
| **Venezuela—** | |
| † *Angel | 3,212 |
| Cuquenan | 2,000 |

# Notable Deserts of the World

**Arabian (Eastern)**, 70,000 sq. mi. in Egypt between the Nile river and Red Sea, extending southward into Sudan.

**Atacama**, 600 mi. long area rich in nitrate and copper deposits in N. Chile.

**Chihuahuan**, 140,000 sq. mi. in Tex., N.M., Ariz., and Mexico.

**Death Valley**, 3,300 sq. mi. in E. Cal. and SW Nev. Contains lowest point below sea level (282 ft.) in Western Hemisphere.

**Gibson**, 120,000 sq. mi. in the interior of W. Australia.

**Gobi**, 500,000 sq. mi. in Mongolia and China.

**Great Sandy**, 150,000 sq. mi. in W. Australia.

**Great Victoria**, 150,000 sq. mi. in W. and S. Australia.

**Kalahari**, 225,000 sq. mi. in southern Africa.

**Kara-Kum**, 120,000 sq. mi. in Turkmenistan.

**Kyzyl Kum**, 100,000 sq. mi. in Kazakhstan & Uzbekistan.

**Libyan**, 450,000 sq. mi. in the Sahara extending from Lybia through SW Egypt into Sudan.

**Lut (Dasht-e Lut)**, 20,000 sq. mi. in E. Iran.

**Mojave**, 15,000 sq. mi. in S. Cal.

**Namib**, long narrow area extending 800 miles along SW coast of Africa.

**Nubian**, 100,000 sq. mi. in the Sahara in NE Sudan.

**Painted Desert**, section of high plateau in N. Ariz. extending 150 mi.

**Rub al Khali (Empty Quarter)**, 250,000 sq. mi. in the south Arabian Peninsula.

**Sahara**, 3,500,000 sq. mi. in N. Africa extending westward to the Atlantic. Largest desert in the world.

**Sonoran**, 70,000 sq. mi. in SW Ariz. and SE Cal. extending into Mexico.

**Syrian**, 100,000 sq. mi. arid wasteland extending over much of N. Saudi Arabia, E. Jordan, S. Syria, and W. Iraq.

**Taklimakan**, 140,000 sq. mi. in Sinkiang Province, China.

**Thar (Great Indian)**, 100,000 sq. mi. arid area extending 400 mi. along India-Pakistan border.

## Important Islands and Their Areas

Figure in parentheses shows rank among the world's 10 largest islands; some islands have not been surveyed accurately; in such cases estimated areas are shown.

### Location-Ownership
#### Area in square miles

### Arctic Ocean

#### Canadian

| | |
|---|---|
| Axel Heiberg | 15,779 |
| Baffin (5) | 183,810 |
| Banks | 27,038 |
| Bathurst | 7,609 |
| Devon | 20,861 |
| Ellesmere (9) | 82,119 |
| Melville | 16,369 |
| Prince of Wales | 12,830 |
| Somerset | 9,370 |
| Southampton | 15,700 |
| Victoria (10) | 81,930 |

#### Norwegian

| | |
|---|---|
| Svalbard | 23,940 |
| Nordaustlandet | 5,410 |
| Spitsbergen | 15,060 |

#### Russian

| | |
|---|---|
| Franz Josef Land | 8,000 |
| Novaya Zemlya (two is.) | 31,730 |
| Wrangel | 2,800 |

### Atlantic Ocean

| | |
|---|---|
| Anticosti, Canada | 3,043 |
| Ascension, UK | 34 |
| Azores, Portugal | 888 |
| Faial | 67 |
| Sao Miguel | 291 |
| Bahamas | 5,386 |
| Bermuda Is., UK | 20 |
| Bioko Is. | |
| Equatorial Guinea | 785 |
| Block, Rhode Island | 10 |
| Canary Is., Spain | 2,808 |
| Fuerteventura | 668 |
| Gran Canaria | 592 |
| Tenerife | 795 |
| Cape Breton, Canada | 3,970 |
| Cape Verde Is. | 1,557 |
| Faeroe Is., Denmark | 540 |
| Falkland Is., UK | 4,700 |
| Fernando de Noronha Archipelago, Brazil | 7 |
| Greenland, Denmark (1) | 840,000 |
| Iceland | 39,769 |
| Long Island, N.Y. | 1,396 |
| Madeira Is., Portugal | 307 |
| Marajo, Brazil | 15,444 |
| Martha's Vineyard, Mass. | 108 |
| Mount Desert, Me. | 108 |
| Nantucket, Mass. | 57 |
| Newfoundland, Canada | 42,030 |
| Prince Edward, Canada | 2,184 |
| St. Helena, UK | 47 |
| South Georgia, UK | 1,450 |
| Tierra del Fuego, Chile and Argentina | 18,800 |
| Tristan da Cunha, UK | 40 |

#### British Isles

| | |
|---|---|
| Great Britain, mainland (8) | 84,200 |
| Channel Islands | 75 |
| Guernsey | 24 |
| Jersey | 45 |
| Sark | 2 |
| Hebrides | 2,744 |
| Ireland | 32,599 |
| Irish Republic | 27,136 |
| Northern Ireland | 5,463 |
| Man | 227 |

| | |
|---|---|
| Orkney Is. | 390 |
| Scilly Is. | 6 |
| Shetland Is. | 567 |
| Skye | 670 |
| Wight | 147 |

### Baltic Sea

| | |
|---|---|
| Aland Is., Finland | 581 |
| Bornholm, Denmark | 227 |
| Gotland, Sweden | 1,159 |

### Caribbean Sea

| | |
|---|---|
| Antigua | 108 |
| Aruba, Netherlands | 75 |
| Barbados | 166 |
| Cuba | 44,218 |
| Isle of Youth | 1,182 |
| Curacao, Netherlands | 171 |
| Dominica | 290 |
| Guadeloupe, France | 687 |
| Hispaniola, Haiti and Dominican Republic | 29,371 |
| Jamaica | 4,244 |
| Martinique, France | 425 |
| Puerto Rico, U.S. | 3,435 |
| Tobago | 116 |
| Trinidad | 1,864 |
| Virgin Is., UK | 59 |
| Virgin Is., U.S. | 132 |

### Indian Ocean

| | |
|---|---|
| Andaman Is., India | 2,500 |
| Madagascar (4) | 226,658 |
| Mauritius | 720 |
| Pemba, Tanzania | 380 |
| Reunion, France | 969 |
| Seychelles | 171 |
| Sri Lanka | 25,332 |
| Zanzibar, Tanzania | 640 |

#### Persian Gulf

| | |
|---|---|
| Bahrain | 255 |

### Mediterranean Sea

| | |
|---|---|
| Balearic Is., Spain | 1,936 |
| Corfu, Greece | 229 |
| Corsica, France | 3,369 |
| Crete, Greece | 3,189 |
| Cyprus | 3,572 |
| Elba, Italy | 86 |
| Euboea, Greece | 1,411 |
| Malta | 95 |
| Rhodes, Greece | 540 |
| Sardinia, Italy | 9,262 |
| Sicily, Italy | 9,822 |

### Pacific Ocean

| | |
|---|---|
| Aleutian Is., U.S. | 6,821 |
| Adak | 289 |
| Amchitka | 121 |
| Attu | 388 |
| Kanaga | 135 |
| Kiska | 110 |
| Tanaga | 209 |
| Umnak | 675 |
| Unalaska | 1,064 |
| Unimak | 1,600 |
| Canton, Kiribati* | |
| Caroline, Kiribati* | 4 |
| Christmas, Kiribati* | 94 |
| Clipperton, France | 2 |

| | |
|---|---|
| Diomede, Big, Russia | 11 |
| Diomede, Little, U.S. | 2 |
| Easter, Chile | 69 |
| Fiji | 7,056 |
| Vanua Levu | 2,242 |
| Viti Levu | 4,109 |
| Funafuti, Tuvalu* | 2 |
| Galapagos Is., Ecuador | 3,043 |
| Guadalcanal | 2,180 |
| Guam | 209 |
| Hainan, China | 13,000 |
| Hawaiian Is., U.S. | 6,450 |
| Hawaii | 4,037 |
| Oahu | 593 |
| Hong Kong | 29 |
| Japan | 145,809 |
| Hokkaido | 30,144 |
| Honshu (7) | 87,805 |
| Iwo Jima | 8 |
| Kyushu | 14,114 |
| Okinawa | 459 |
| Shikoku | 7,049 |
| Kodiak, U.S. | 3,670 |
| Marquesas Is., France | 492 |
| Marshall Is. | 70 |
| Bikini* | 2 |
| Nauru | 8 |
| New Caledonia, France | 6,530 |
| New Guinea (2) | 306,000 |
| New Zealand | 103,883 |
| Chatham | 372 |
| North | 44,035 |
| South | 58,305 |
| Stewart | 674 |
| Northern Mariana Is. | 184 |
| Philippines | 115,831 |
| Leyte | 2,787 |
| Luzon | 40,880 |
| Mindanao | 36,775 |
| Mindoro | 3,790 |
| Negros | 4,907 |
| Palawan | 4,554 |
| Panay | 4,446 |
| Samar | 5,050 |
| Quemoy | 56 |
| Sakhalin, Russia | 29,500 |
| Samoa Is. | 1,177 |
| American Samoa | 77 |
| Tutuila | 52 |
| Samoa (Western) | 1,133 |
| Savaii | 670 |
| Upolu | 429 |
| Santa Catalina, U.S. | 72 |
| Tahiti, France | 402 |
| Taiwan | 13,823 |
| Tasmania, Australia | 26,178 |
| Tonga Is. | 270 |
| Vancouver, Canada | 12,079 |
| Vanuatu | 5,700 |

### East Indies

| | |
|---|---|
| Bali, Indonesia | 2,171 |
| Borneo, Indonesia-Malaysia, Brunei (3) | 280,100 |
| Celebes, Indonesia | 69,000 |
| Java, Indonesia | 48,900 |
| Madura, Indonesia | 2,113 |
| Moluccas, Indonesia | 32,307 |
| New Britain, Papua New Guinea | 14,093 |
| New Ireland, Papua New Guinea | 3,707 |
| Sumatra, Indonesia (6) | 165,000 |
| Timor | 13,094 |

* **Atolls:** Bikini (lagoon area, 230 sq. mi., land area 2 sq. mi.); Canton (lagoon 20 sq. mi., land 4 sq. mi.), Kiribati; Christmas (lagoon 140 sq. mi., land 94 sq. mi.), Kiribati; Funafuti (lagoon 84 sq. mi., land 2 sq. mi.), Tuvalu. **Australia,** often called an island, is a continent.

**Islands in minor waters:** Manhattan (22 sq mi.), Staten (59 sq. mi.), and Governors (173 acres), all in New York Harbor, U.S.; Isle Royale (209 sq. mi.), Lake Superior, U.S.; Manitoulin (1,068 sq. mi.), Lake Huron, Canada; Pinang (110 sq. mi.), Strait of Malacca, Malaysia; Singapore (239 sq. mi.), Singapore Strait, Singapore.

# DISASTERS

## Some Notable Shipwrecks Since 1850

(Figures indicate estimated lives lost; as of mid-1993)

**1854, Mar.—City of Glasgow;** British steamer missing in North Atlantic; 480.

**1854, Sept. 27—Arctic;** U.S. (Collins Line) steamer sunk in collision with French steamer Vesta near Cape Race; 285-351.

**1856, Jan. 23—Pacific;** U.S. (Collins Line) steamer missing in North Atlantic; 186-286.

**1858, Sept. 23—Austria;** German steamer destroyed by fire in North Atlantic; 471.

**1863, Apr. 27—Anglo-Saxon;** British steamer wrecked at Cape Race; 238.

**1865, Apr. 27—Sultana;** a Mississippi River steamer blew up near Memphis, Tenn; 1,450.

**1869, Oct. 27—Stonewall;** steamer burned on Mississippi River below Cairo, Ill.; 200.

**1870, Jan. 25—City of Boston;** British (Inman Line) steamer vanished between New York and Liverpool; 177.

**1870, Oct. 19—Cambria;** British steamer wrecked off northern Ireland; 196.

**1872, Nov. 7—Mary Celeste;** U.S. half-brig sailed from New York for Genoa; found abandoned in Atlantic 4 weeks later in mystery of sea; crew never heard from; loss of life unknown.

**1873, Jan. 22—Northfleet;** British steamer foundered off Dungeness, England; 300.

**1873, Apr. 1—Atlantic;** British (White Star) steamer wrecked off Nova Scotia; 585.

**1873, Nov. 23—Ville du Havre;** French steamer, sunk after collision with British sailing ship Loch Earn; 226.

**1875, May 7—Schiller;** German steamer wrecked off Scilly Isles; 312.

**1875, Nov. 4—Pacific;** U.S. steamer sunk after collision off Cape Flattery; 236.

**1878, Sept. 3—Princess Alice;** British steamer sank after collision in Thames River; 700.

**1878, Dec. 18—Byzantin;** French steamer sank after Dardanelles collision; 210.

**1881, May 24—Victoria;** steamer capsized in Thames River, Canada; 200.

**1883, Jan. 19—Cimbria;** German steamer sunk in collision with British steamer Sultan in North Sea; 389.

**1887, Nov. 15—Wah Yeung;** British steamer burned at sea; 400.

**1890, Feb. 17—Duburg;** British steamer wrecked, China Sea; 400.

**1890, Sept. 19—Ertogrul;** Turkish frigate foundered off Japan; 540.

**1891, Mar. 17—Utopia;** British steamer sank in collision with British ironclad Anson off Gibraltar; 562.

**1895, Jan. 30—Elbe;** German steamer sank in collision with British steamer Craithie in North Sea; 332.

**1895, Mar. 11—Reina Regenta;** Spanish cruiser foundered near Gibraltar; 400.

**1898, Feb. 15—Maine;** U.S. battleship blown up in Havana Harbor; 260.

**1898, July 4—La Bourgogne;** French steamer sunk in collision with British sailing ship Cromartyshire off Nova Scotia; 549.

**1898, Nov. 26—Portland;** U.S. steamer wrecked off Cape Cod; 157.

**1904, June 15—General Slocum;** excursion steamer burned in East River, New York City; 1,030.

**1904, June 28—Norge;** Danish steamer wrecked on Rockall Island, Scotland; 620.

**1906, Aug. 4—Sirio;** Italian steamer wrecked off Cape Palos, Spain; 350.

**1908, Mar. 23—Matsu Maru;** Japanese steamer sank in collision near Hakodate, Japan; 300.

**1909, Aug. 1—Waratah;** British steamer, Sydney to London, vanished; 300.

**1910, Feb. 9—General Chanzy;** French steamer wrecked off Minorca, Spain; 200.

**1911, Sept. 25—Liberté;** French battleship exploded at Toulon; 285.

**1912, Mar. 5—Principe de Asturias;** Spanish steamer wrecked off Spain; 500.

**1912, Apr. 14-15—Titanic;** British (White Star) steamer hit iceberg in North Atlantic; 1,503.

**1912, Sept. 28—Kichemaru;** Japanese steamer sank off Japanese coast; 1,000.

**1914, May 29—Empress of Ireland;** British (Canadian Pacific) steamer sunk in collision with Norwegian collier in St. Lawrence River; 1,014.

**1915, May 7—Lusitania;** British (Cunard Line) steamer torpedoed and sunk by German submarine off Ireland; 1,198.

**1915, July 24—Eastland;** excursion steamer capsized in Chicago River; 812.

**1916, Feb. 26—Provence;** French cruiser sank in Mediterranean; 3,100.

**1916, Mar. 3—Principe de Asturias;** Spanish steamer wrecked near Santos, Brazil; 558.

**1916, Aug. 29—Hsin Yu;** Chinese steamer sank off Chinese coast; 1,000.

**1917, Dec. 6—Mont Blanc, Imo;** French ammunition ship and Belgian steamer collided in Halifax Harbor; 1,600.

**1918, Apr. 25—Kiang-Kwan** Chinese steamer sank in collision off Hankow; 500.

**1918, July 12—Kawachi;** Japanese battleship blew up in Tokayama Bay; 500.

**1918, Oct. 25—Princess Sophia;** Canadian steamer sank off Alaskan coast; 398.

**1919, Jan. 17—Chaonia;** French steamer lost in Straits of Messina, Italy; 460.

**1919, Sept. 9—Valbanera;** Spanish steamer lost off Florida coast; 500.

**1921, Mar. 18—Hong Kong;** steamer wrecked in South China Sea; 1,000.

**1922, Aug. 26—Niitaka;** Japanese cruiser sank in storm off Kamchatka, USSR; 300.

**1927, Oct. 25—Principessa Mafalda;** Italian steamer blew up, sank off Porto Seguro, Brazil; 314.

**1928, Nov. 12—Vestris;** British steamer sank in gale off Virginia; 113.

**1934, Sept. 8—Morro Castle;** U.S. steamer, Havana to New York, burned off Asbury Park, N.J.; 134.

**1939, May 23—Squalus;** U.S. submarine sank off Portsmouth, N.H.; 26.

**1939, June 1—Thetis;** British submarine, sank in Liverpool Bay; 99.

**1942, Feb. 18—Truxtun and Pollux;** U.S. destroyer and cargo ship ran aground, sank off Newfoundland; 204.

**1942, Oct. 2—Curacao;** British cruiser sank after collision with liner Queen Mary; 338.

**1944, Dec. 17-18—3** U.S. Third Fleet destroyers sank during typhoon in Philippine Sea; 790.

**1947, Jan. 19—Himera;** Greek steamer hit a mine off Athens; 392.

**1947, Apr. 16—Grandcamp;** French freighter exploded in Texas City, Tex., Harbor, starting fires; 510.

**1948, Nov.—Chinese** army evacuation ship exploded and sunk off S. Manchuria; 6,000.

**1948, Dec. 3—Kiangya;** Chinese refugee ship wrecked in explosion S. of Shanghai; 1,100+.

**1949, Sept. 17—Noronic;** Canadian Great Lakes Cruiser burned at Toronto dock; 130.

**1952, Apr. 26—Hobson and Wasp;** U.S. destroyer and aircraft carrier collided in Atlantic; 176.

**1953, Jan. 31—Princess Victoria;** British ferry sank in storm off northern Irish coast; 134.

**1954, Sept. 26—Toya Maru;** Japanese ferry sank in Tsugaru Strait, Japan; 1,172.

**1956, July 26—Andrea Doria and Stockholm;** Italian liner and Swedish liner collided off Nantucket; 51.

**1957, July 14—Eshghabad;** Soviet ship ran aground in Caspian Sea; 270.

**1961, July 8—Save;** Portuguese ship ran aground off Mozambique; 259.

**1962, Apr. 8—Dara;** British liner exploded and sunk in Persian Gulf; 236.

**1963, Apr. 10—Thresher;** U.S. Navy atomic submarine sank in North Atlantic; 129.

**1964, Feb. 10—Voyager, Melbourne;** Australian destroyer sank after collision with Australian aircraft carrier Melbourne off New South Wales; 82.

**1965, Nov. 13—Yarmouth Castle;** Panamanian registered cruise ship burned and sank off Nassau; 90.

**1967, July 29—Forrestal;** U.S. aircraft carrier caught fire off N. Vietnam; 134.

**1968, Jan. 25—Dakar;** Israeli submarine vanished in Mediterranean Sea; 69.

**1968, Jan. 27—Minerve;** French submarine vanished in Mediterranean; 52.

**1968, late May—Scorpion;** U.S. nuclear submarine sank in Atlantic near Azores; 99 (located Oct. 31).

**1969, June 2—Evans;** U.S. destroyer cut in half by Australian carrier Melbourne, S. China Sea; 74.

**1970, Mar. 4—Eurydice;** French submarine sank in Mediterranean near Toulon; 57.

**1970, Dec. 15—Namyong-Ho;** South Korean ferry sank in Korea Strait; 308.

**1974, May 1—** Motor launch capsized off Bangladesh; 250.

**1974, Sept. 26**— Soviet destroyer burned and sank in Black Sea; 200+.

**1976, Oct. 20**—**George Prince and Frosta;** ferryboat and Norwegian tanker collided on Mississippi R. at Luling, La.; 77.

**1976, Dec. 25**—**Patria;** Egyptian liner caught fire and sank in the Red Sea; c. 100.

**1977, Jan. 11**—**Grand Zenith;** Panamanian-registered tanker sank off Cape Cod, Mass.; 38.

**1979, Aug. 14**—23 yachts competing in Fastnet yacht race sunk or abandoned during storm in S. Irish Sea; 18.

**1981, Jan. 27**—**Tamponas II;** Indonesian passenger ship caught fire and sank in Java Sea; 580.

**1981, May 26**—**Nimitz;** U.S. Marine combat jet crashed on deck of U.S. aircraft carrier; 14.

**1983, Feb. 12**—**Marine Electric;** coal freighter sank during storm off Chincoteague, Va.; 33.

**1983, May 25**—**10th of Ramadan;** Nile steamer caught fire and sank in L. Nassar; 357.

**1986, Aug. 31**—Soviet passenger ship **Admiral Nakhimov** and Soviet freighter **Pyotr Vasev** collided in Black Sea; 398.

**1987, Mar. 6**—British ferry capsized off Zeebrugge, Belgium; 188.

**1987, Dec. 20**—Philippine ferry **Dona Paz** and oil tanker **Victor** collided in Tablas Strait; 3,000+.

**1988, Aug. 6**—Indian ferry capsized on Ganges R.; 400+.

**1989, Apr. 7**—Soviet submarine sank off Norway; 42.

**1989, Apr. 19**—**USS Iowa;** U.S. battleship; explosion in gun turret; 47.

**1989, Aug. 20**—British barge **Bowbelle** struck British pleasure cruiser **Marchioness** on Thames R. in central London; 56.

**1989, Sept. 10**—Romanian pleasure boat and Bulgarian barge collided on Danube R.; 161.

**1991, Apr. 10**—Auto ferry and oil tanker collided outside Livorno Harbor, Italy; 140.

**1991, Dec. 14**—**Salem Express;** ferry rammed coral reef nr. Safaga, Egypt; 462.

**1993, Feb. 17**—**Neptune;** ferry capsized off Port-au-Prince, Haiti; 500+.

# Some Notable Aircraft Disasters Since 1937

| Date | | Aircraft | Site of accident | Deaths |
|------|---|----------|------------------|--------|
| 1937 | May 6 | German zeppelin Hindenburg | Burned at mooring, Lakehurst, N.J. | 36 |
| 1944 | Aug. 23 | U.S. Air Force B-24 | Hit school, Freckelton, England | 76[1] |
| 1945 | July 28 | U.S. Army B-25 | Hit Empire State bldg., N.Y.C. | 14[1] |
| 1947 | May 30 | Eastern Air Lines DC-4 | Crashed near Port Deposit, Md. | 53 |
| 1952 | Dec. 20 | U.S. Air Force C-124 | Fell, burned, Moses Lake, Wash. | 87 |
| 1953 | Mar. 3 | Canadian Pacific Comet Jet | Karachi, Pakistan | 11[2] |
| 1953 | June 18 | U.S. Air Force C-124 | Crashed, burned near Tokyo | 129 |
| 1955 | Nov. 1 | United Air Lines DC-6B | Exploded, crashed near Longmont, Col. | 44[3] |
| 1956 | June 20 | Venezuelan Super-Constellation | Crashed in Atlantic off Asbury Park, N.J. | 74 |
| 1956 | June 30 | TWA Super-Const., United DC-7 | Collided over Grand Canyon, Arizona | 128 |
| 1960 | Dec. 16 | United DC-8 jet, TWA Super-Const. | Collided over N.Y. City | 134[4] |
| 1962 | Mar. 16 | Flying Tiger Super-Const. | Vanished in Western Pacific | 107 |
| 1962 | June 3 | Air France Boeing 707 jet | Crashed on takeoff from Paris | 130 |
| 1962 | June 22 | Air France Boeing 707 jet | Crashed in storm, Guadeloupe, W.I. | 113 |
| 1963 | June 3 | Chartered Northw. Airlines DC-7 | Crashed in Pacific off British Columbia | 101 |
| 1963 | Nov. 29 | Trans-Canada Airlines DC-8F | Crashed after takeoff from Montreal | 118 |
| 1965 | May 20 | Pakistani Boeing 720-B | Crashed at Cairo, Egypt, airport | 121 |
| 1966 | Jan. 24 | Air India Boeing 707 jetliner | Crashed on Mont Blanc, France-Italy | 117 |
| 1966 | Feb. 4 | All-Nippon Boeing 727 | Plunged into Tokyo Bay | 133 |
| 1966 | Mar. 5 | BOAC Boeing 707 jetliner | Crashed on Mount Fuji, Japan | 124 |
| 1966 | Dec. 24 | U.S. military-chartered CL-44 | Crashed into village in So. Vietnam | 129[1] |
| 1967 | Apr. 20 | Swiss Britannia turboprop | Crashed at Nicosia, Cyprus | 126 |
| 1967 | July 19 | Piedmont Boeing 727, Cessna 310 | Collided in air, Hendersonville, N.C. | 82 |
| 1968 | Apr. 20 | S. African Airways Boeing 707 | Crashed on takeoff, Windhoek, SW Africa | 122 |
| 1968 | May 3 | Braniff International Electra | Crashed in storm near Dawson, Tex. | 85 |
| 1969 | Mar. 16 | Venezuelan DC-9 | Crashed after takeoff from Maracaibo, Venezuela | 155[5] |
| 1969 | Dec. 8 | Olympia Airways DC-6B | Crashed near Athens in storm | 93 |
| 1970 | Feb. 15 | Dominican DC-9 | Crashed into sea off Santo Domingo | 102 |
| 1970 | July 3 | British chartered jetliner | Crashed near Barcelona, Spain | 112 |
| 1970 | July 5 | Air Canada DC-8 | Crashed near Toronto International Airport | 108 |
| 1970 | Aug. 9 | Peruvian turbojet | Crashed after takeoff from Cuzco, Peru | 101[1] |
| 1970 | Nov. 14 | Southern Airways DC-9 | Crashed in mountains near Huntington, W. Va. | 75[6] |
| 1971 | July 30 | All-Nippon Boeing 727 and Japanese Air Force F-86 | Collided over Morioka, Japan | 162[7] |
| 1971 | Sept. 4 | Alaska Airlines Boeing 727 | Crashed into mountain near Juneau, Alaska | 111 |
| 1972 | Aug. 14 | E. German Ilyushin-62 | Crashed on take-off East Berlin | 156 |
| 1972 | Oct. 13 | Aeroflot Ilyushin-62 | E. German airline crashed near Moscow | 176 |
| 1972 | Dec. 3 | Chartered Spanish airliner | Crashed on take-off, Canary Islands | 155 |
| 1972 | Dec. 29 | Eastern Airlines Lockheed Tristar | Crashed on approach to Miami Int'l. Airport | 101 |
| 1973 | Jan. 22 | Chartered Boeing 707 | Burst into flames during landing, Kano Airport, Nigeria | 176 |
| 1973 | Feb. 21 | Libyan jetliner | Shot down by Israeli fighter planes over Sinai | 108 |
| 1973 | Apr. 10 | British Vanguard turboprop | Crashed during snowstorm at Basel, Switzerland | 104 |
| 1973 | June 3 | Soviet Supersonic TU-144 | Crashed near Goussainville, France | 14[8] |
| 1973 | July 11 | Brazilian Boeing 707 | Crashed on approach to Orly Airport, Paris | 122 |
| 1973 | July 31 | Delta Airlines jetliner | Crashed, landing in fog at Logan Airport, Boston | 89 |
| 1973 | Dec. 23 | French Caravelle jet | Crashed in Morocco | 106 |
| 1974 | Mar. 3 | Turkish DC-10 jet | Crashed at Ermenonville near Paris | 346 |
| 1974 | Apr. 23 | Pan American 707 jet | Crashed in Bali, Indonesia | 107 |
| 1974 | Dec. 1 | TWA-727 | Crashed in storm, Upperville, Va. | 92 |
| 1974 | Dec. 4 | Dutch-chartered DC-8 | Crashed in storm near Colombo, Sri Lanka | 191 |
| 1975 | Apr. 4 | Air Force Galaxy C-5B | Crashed near Saigon, So. Vietnam, after takeoff with load of orphans | 172 |
| 1975 | June 24 | Eastern Airlines 727 jet | Crashed in storm, JFK Airport, N.Y. City | 113 |
| 1975 | Aug. 3 | Chartered 707 | Hit mountainside, Agadir, Morocco | 188 |
| 1976 | Sept. 10 | British Airways Trident, Yugoslav DC-9 | Collided near Zagreb, Yugoslavia | 176 |
| 1976 | Sept. 19 | Turkish 727 | Hit mountain, southern Turkey | 155 |
| 1976 | Oct. 13 | Bolivian 707 cargo jet | Crashed in Santa Cruz, Bolivia | 100[9] |
| 1977 | Jan. 13 | Aeroflot TU-104 | Exploded and crashed at Alma-Ata, Central Asia | 90 |
| 1977 | Mar. 27 | KLM 747, Pan American 747 | Collided on runway, Tenerife, Canary Islands | 582 |
| 1977 | Nov. 19 | TAP Boeing 727 | Crashed on Madeira | 130 |
| 1977 | Dec. 4 | Malaysian Boeing 737 | Hijacked, then exploded in mid-air over Straits of Johore | 100 |
| 1977 | Dec. 13 | U.S. DC-3 | Crashed after takeoff at Evansville, Ind. | 29[10] |
| 1978 | Jan. 1 | Air India 747 | Exploded, crashed into sea off Bombay | 213 |
| 1978 | Sept. 25 | Boeing 727, Cessna 172 | Collided in air, San Diego, Cal. | 150 |

| Date | | Aircraft | Site of accident | Deaths |
|---|---|---|---|---|
| 1978 | Nov. 15 | Chartered DC-8 | Crashed near Colombo, Sri Lanka | 183 |
| 1979 | May 25 | American Airlines DC-10 | Crashed after takeoff at O'Hare Intl. Airport, Chicago | 275[11] |
| 1979 | Aug. 17 | Two Soviet Aeroflot jetliners | Collided over Ukraine | 173 |
| 1979 | Oct. 31 | Western Airlines DC-10 | Mexico City Airport | 74 |
| 1979 | Nov. 26 | Pakistani Boeing 707 | Crashed near Jidda, Saudi Arabia | 156 |
| 1979 | Nov. 28 | New Zealand DC-10 | Crashed into mountain in Antarctica | 257 |
| 1980 | Mar. 14 | Polish Ilyushin 62 | Crashed making emergency landing, Warsaw | 87[12] |
| 1980 | Aug. 19 | Saudi Arabian Tristar | Burned after emergency landing, Riyadh | 301 |
| 1981 | Dec. 1 | Yugoslavian DC-9 | Crashed into mountain in Corsica | 174 |
| 1982 | Jan. 13 | Air Florida Boeing 737 | Crashed into Potomac River after takeoff | 78 |
| 1982 | July 9 | Pan-Am Boeing 727 | Crashed after takeoff at Kenner, La. | 153[13] |
| 1982 | Sept. 11 | U.S. Army CH-47 Chinook helicopter | Crashed during air show in Mannheim, W. Germany | 46 |
| 1983 | Sept. 1 | S. Korean Boeing 747 | Shot down after violating Soviet airspace | 269 |
| 1983 | Nov. 27 | Colombian Boeing 747 | Crashed near Barajas Airport, Madrid | 183 |
| 1985 | Feb. 19 | Spanish Boeing 727 | Crashed into Mt. Oiz, Spain | 148 |
| 1985 | June 23 | Air-India Boeing 747 | Crashed into Atlantic Ocean S. of Ireland | 329 |
| 1985 | Aug. 2 | Delta Air Lines jumbo jet | Crashed at Dallas-Ft. Worth Intl. Airport | 133 |
| 1985 | Aug. 12 | Japan Air Lines Boeing 747 | Crashed into Mt. Ogura, Japan | 520[14] |
| 1985 | Dec. 12 | Arrow Air DC 8 | Crashed after takeoff in Gander, Newfoundland | 256[15] |
| 1986 | Mar. 31 | Mexican Boeing 727 | Crashed NW of Mexico City | 166 |
| 1986 | Aug. 31 | Aeromexico DC-9 | Collided with Piper PA-28 over Cerritos, Cal. | 82[16] |
| 1987 | May 9 | Ilyushin 62M | Crashed after takeoff in Warsaw, Poland | 183 |
| 1987 | Aug. 16 | Northwest Airlines MD-82 | Crashed after takeoff in Romulus, Mich. | 156 |
| 1988 | July 3 | Iranian A300 Airbus | Shot down by U.S. Navy warship *Vincennes* over Persian Gulf | 290 |
| 1988 | Dec. 21 | Pan Am Boeing 747 | Exploded and crashed in Lockerbie, Scotland | 270[17] |
| 1989 | Feb. 8 | Boeing 707 | Crashed into mountain in Azores Islands off Portugal | 144 |
| 1989 | June 7 | Suriname DC-8 | Crashed near Paramaribo Airport, Suriname | 168 |
| 1989 | July 19 | United Airlines DC-10 | Crashed while landing with a disabled hydraulic system, Sioux City, Ia. | 111 |
| 1989 | Sept. 19 | French DC-10 | Exploded in air over Niger | 171 |
| 1991 | May 26 | Austrian Boeing 767-300 | Exploded over rural Thailand | 223 |
| 1991 | July 11 | Nigerian DC-8 | Crashed while landing at Jidda, Saudi Arabia | 261 |

(1) Including those on the ground and in buildings. (2) First fatal crash of commercial jet plane. (3) Caused by bomb planted by John G. Graham in insurance plot to kill his mother, a passenger. (4) Including all 128 aboard the planes and 6 on ground. (5) Killed 84 on plane and 71 on ground. (6) Including 43 Marshall U. football players and coaches. (7) Airliner-fighter crash, pilot of fighter parachuted to safety, was arrested for negligence. (8) First supersonic plane crash killed 6 crewmen and 8 on the ground; there were no passengers. (9) Crew of 3 killed; 97, mostly children, killed on ground. (10) Including U. of Evansville basketball team. (11) Highest death toll in U.S. aviation history. (12) Including 22 members of U.S. boxing team. (13) Including 8 on ground. (14) Worst single-plane disaster. (15) Incl. 248 members of U.S. 101st Airborne Division. (16) Incl. 15 on the ground. (17) Incl. 11 on the ground.

## Notable Railroad Disasters

| Date | | Location | Deaths | Date | | Location | Deaths |
|---|---|---|---|---|---|---|---|
| 1876 | Dec. 29 | Ashtabula, Oh. | 92 | 1926 | Sept. 5 | Waco, Col. | 30 |
| 1880 | Aug. 11 | Mays Landing, N. J. | 40 | 1928 | Aug. 24 | I.R.T. subway, Times Sq., N. Y. | 18 |
| 1887 | Aug. 10 | Chatsworth, Ill. | 81 | 1937 | July 16 | Nr. Patna, India | 107 |
| 1888 | Oct. 10 | Mud Run, Pa. | 55 | 1938 | June 19 | Saugus, Mont. | 47 |
| 1891 | June 14 | Nr. Basel, Switzerland | 100 | 1939 | Aug. 12 | Harney, Nev. | 24 |
| 1896 | July 30 | Atlantic City, N. J. | 60 | 1939 | Dec. 22 | Nr. Magdeburg, Germany | 132 |
| 1903 | Dec. 23 | Laurel Run, Pa. | 53 | 1939 | Dec. 22 | Nr. Friedrichshafen, Germany | 99 |
| 1904 | Aug. 7 | Eden, Col. | 96 | 1940 | Apr. 19 | Little Falls, N. Y. | 31 |
| 1904 | Sept. 24 | New Market Tenn. | 56 | 1940 | July 31 | Cuyahoga Falls, Oh. | 43 |
| 1906 | Mar. 16 | Florence, Col. | 35 | 1943 | Aug. 29 | Wayland, N. Y. | 27 |
| 1906 | Oct. 28 | Atlantic City, N. J. | 40 | 1943 | Sept. 6 | Frankford Junction, Philadelphia, Pa. | 79 |
| 1906 | Dec. 30 | Washington, D. C. | 53 | 1943 | Dec. 16 | Between Rennert and Buie, N. C. | 72 |
| 1907 | Jan. 2 | Volland, Kan. | 33 | 1944 | Jan. 16 | Leon Province, Spain | 500 |
| 1907 | Jan. 19 | Fowler, Ind. | 29 | 1944 | Mar. 2 | Salerno, Italy | 521 |
| 1907 | Feb. 16 | New York, N.Y. | 22 | 1944 | July 6 | High Bluff, Tenn. | 35 |
| 1907 | Feb. 23 | Colton, Cal. | 26 | 1944 | Aug. 4 | Near Stockton, Ga. | 47 |
| 1907 | May 11 | Lompoc, Cal. | 36 | 1944 | Sept. 14 | Dewey, Ind. | 29 |
| 1907 | July 20 | Salem, Mich. | 33 | 1944 | Dec. 31 | Bagley, Utah | 50 |
| 1910 | Mar. 1 | Wellington, Wash. | 96 | 1945 | Aug. 9 | Michigan, N. D. | 34 |
| 1910 | Mar. 21 | Green Mountain, Ia. | 55 | 1946 | Mar. 20 | Aracaju, Mexico | 185 |
| 1911 | Aug. 25 | Manchester, N. Y. | 29 | 1946 | Apr. 25 | Naperville, Ill. | 45 |
| 1912 | July 4 | East Corning, N. Y. | 39 | 1947 | Feb. 18 | Gallitzin, Pa. | 24 |
| 1912 | July 5 | Ligonier, Pa. | 23 | 1949 | Oct. 22 | Nr. Dwor, Poland | 200+ |
| 1914 | Aug. 5 | Tipton Ford, Mo. | 43 | 1950 | Feb. 17 | Rockville Centre, N. Y. | 31 |
| 1914 | Sept. 15 | Lebanon, Mo. | 28 | 1950 | Sept. 11 | Coshocton, Oh. | 33 |
| 1915 | May 22 | Nr. Gretna, Scotland | 227 | 1950 | Nov. 22 | Richmond Hill, N. Y. | 79 |
| 1916 | Mar. 29 | Amherst, Oh. | 27 | 1951 | Feb. 6 | Woodbridge, N. J. | 84 |
| 1917 | Sept. 28 | Kellyville, Okla. | 23 | 1951 | Nov. 12 | Wyuta, Wyo. | 17 |
| 1917 | Dec. 12 | Modane, France | 543[1] | 1951 | Nov. 25 | Woodstock, Ala. | 17 |
| 1917 | Dec. 20 | Shepherdsville, Ky. | 46 | 1952 | Mar. 4 | Nr. Rio de Janeiro, Brazil | 119 |
| 1918 | June 22 | Ivanhoe, Ind. | 68 | 1952 | July 9 | Rzepin, Poland | 160 |
| 1918 | July 9 | Nashville, Tenn. | 101 | 1952 | Oct. 8 | Harrow, England | 112 |
| 1918 | Nov. 1 | Brooklyn, N. Y. | 97 | 1953 | Mar. 27 | Conneaut, Oh. | 21 |
| 1919 | Jan. 12 | South Byron, N. Y. | 22 | 1955 | Apr. 3 | Guadalajara, Mexico | 300 |
| 1919 | July 1 | Dunkirk, N. Y. | 12 | 1956 | Jan. 22 | Los Angeles, Cal. | 30 |
| 1919 | Dec. 20 | Onawa, Maine | 23 | 1956 | Feb. 28 | Swampscott, Mass. | 13 |
| 1921 | Feb. 27 | Porter, Ind. | 37 | 1956 | Sept. 5 | Springer, N. M. | 20 |
| 1921 | Dec. 5 | Woodmont, Pa. | 27 | 1957 | June 11 | Vroman, Col. | 12 |
| 1922 | Aug. 5 | Sulphur Spring, Mo. | 34 | 1957 | Sept. 1 | Kendal, Jamaica | 178 |
| 1922 | Dec. 13 | Humble, Tex. | 22 | 1957 | Sept. 29 | Montgomery, W. Pakistan | 250 |
| 1923 | Sept. 27 | Lockett, Wy. | 31 | 1957 | Dec. 4 | London, England | 90 |
| 1925 | June 16 | Hackettstown, N. J. | 50 | 1958 | May 8 | Rio de Janeiro, Brazil | 128 |
| 1925 | Oct. 27 | Victoria, Miss. | 21 | 1958 | Sept. 15 | Elizabethport, N. J. | 48 |

| Date | | Location | Deaths |
|------|--|----------|--------|
| 1960 | Mar. 14 | Bakersfield, Cal. | 14 |
| 1960 | Nov. 14 | Pardubice, Czech. | 110 |
| 1962 | Jan. 8 | Woerden, Netherlands | 91 |
| 1962 | May 3 | Tokyo, Japan | 163 |
| 1962 | July 28 | Steelton, Pa. | 19 |
| 1964 | July 26 | Oporto, Portugal | 94 |
| 1966 | Dec. 28 | Everett, Mass. | 13 |
| 1970 | Feb. 1 | Buenos Aires, Argentina | 236 |
| 1971 | June 10 | Salem, Ill. | 11 |
| 1972 | June 16 | Vierzy, France | 107 |
| 1972 | July 21 | Seville, Spain | 76 |
| 1972 | Oct. 6 | Saltillo, Mexico | 208 |
| 1972 | Oct. 30 | Chicago, Ill. | 45 |
| 1974 | Aug. 30 | Zagreb, Yugoslavia | 153 |
| 1977 | Jan. 18 | Granville, Australia | 82 |
| 1977 | Feb. 4 | Chicago, Ill., elevated train | 11 |
| 1981 | June 6 | Bihar, India | 500+ |
| 1982 | Jan. 27 | El Asnam, Algeria | 130 |
| 1982 | July 11 | Tepic, Mexico | 120 |
| 1983 | Feb. 19 | Empalme, Mexico | 100 |
| 1987 | Jan. 4 | Essex, Md. | 16 |
| 1988 | Dec. 12 | London, England | 115 |
| 1989 | Jan. 15 | Maizdi Khan, Bangladesh | 110+ |
| 1990 | Jan. 4 | Sindh Province, Pakistan | 210+ |
| 1991 | May 14 | Shigaraki, Japan | 42 |
| 1991 | July 31 | Camden, S.C. | 7 |
| 1991 | Aug. 28 | N.Y. City subway | 5 |
| 1993 | Jan. 18 | Gary, Ind. | 7 |

(1) World's worst train wreck; passenger train derailed.

## Principal U.S. Mine Disasters Since 1900

Source: Bureau of Mines. U.S. Interior Department

Note: Prior to 1968, only disasters with losses of 60 or more lives are listed; since 1968, all disasters in which 5 or more people were killed are listed. Only fatalities to mining company employees are included. All bituminous-coal mines unless otherwise noted.

| Date | | Location | Deaths |
|------|--|----------|--------|
| 1900 | May 1 | Scofield, Ut. | 200 |
| 1902 | May 19 | Coal Creek, Tenn. | 184 |
| 1902 | July 10 | Johnstown, Pa. | 112 |
| 1903 | June 30 | Hanna, Wy. | 169 |
| 1904 | Jan. 25 | Cheswick, Pa. | 179 |
| 1905 | Feb. 20 | Virginia City, Ala. | 112 |
| 1907 | Jan. 29 | Stuart W. Va. | 84 |
| 1907 | Dec. 6 | Monongah, W. Va. | 361 |
| 1907 | Dec. 19 | Jacobs Creek, Pa. | 239 |
| 1908 | Nov. 28 | Marianna, Pa. | 154 |
| 1909 | Jan. 12 | Switchback, W. Va. | 67 |
| 1909 | Nov. 13 | Cherry, Ill. | 259 |
| 1910 | Jan. 31 | Primero, Col. | 75 |
| 1910 | May 5 | Palos, Ala. | 90 |
| 1910 | Nov. 8 | Delagua, Col. | 79 |
| 1911[1] | Apr. 7 | Throop, Pa. | 72 |
| 1911 | Apr. 8 | Littleton, Ala. | 128 |
| 1911 | Dec. 9 | Briceville, Tenn. | 84 |
| 1912 | Mar. 20 | McCurtain, Okla. | 73 |
| 1912 | Mar. 26 | Jed, W. Va. | 83 |
| 1913 | Apr. 23 | Finleyville, Pa. | 96 |
| 1913 | Oct. 22 | Dawson, N.M. | 263 |
| 1914 | Apr. 28 | Eccles, W. Va. | 181 |
| 1915 | Mar. 2 | Layland, W. Va. | 112 |
| 1917 | Apr. 27 | Hastings, Col. | 121 |
| 1917[2] | June 8 | Butte, Mon. | 163 |
| 1917 | Aug. 4 | Clay, Ky. | 62 |
| 1919[1] | June 5 | Wilkes-Barre, Pa. | 92 |
| 1922 | Nov. 6 | Spangler, Pa. | 77 |
| 1922 | Nov. 22 | Dolomite, Ala. | 90 |
| 1923 | Feb. 8 | Dawson, N.M. | 120 |
| 1923 | Aug. 14 | Kemmerer, Wy. | 99 |
| 1924 | Mar. 8 | Castle Gate, Ut. | 171 |
| 1924 | Apr. 28 | Benwood, W. Va. | 119 |
| 1926 | Jan. 13 | Wilburton, Okla. | 91 |
| 1926[2] | Nov. 3 | Ishpeming, Mich. | 51 |
| 1927 | Apr. 30 | Everettville, W. Va. | 97 |
| 1928 | May 19 | Mather, Pa. | 195 |
| 1929 | Dec. 17 | McAlester, Okla. | 61 |
| 1930 | Nov. 5 | Millfield, Oh. | 79 |
| 1940 | Jan. 10 | Bartley, W. Va. | 91 |
| 1940 | Mar. 16 | St. Clairsville, Oh. | 72 |
| 1940 | July 15 | Portage, Pa. | 63 |
| 1943 | Feb. 27 | Washoe, Mon. | 74 |
| 1944 | July 5 | Belmont, Oh. | 66 |
| 1947 | Mar. 25 | Centralia, Ill. | 111 |
| 1951 | Dec. 21 | West Frankfort, Ill. | 119 |
| 1968[3] | Mar. 6 | Calumet, La. | 21 |
| 1968 | Nov. 20 | Farmington, W. Va. | 78 |
| 1970 | Dec. 30 | Hyden, Ky. | 38 |
| 1972[2] | May 2 | Kellogg, Ida. | 91 |
| 1976 | Mar. 9, 11 | Oven Fork, Ky. | 26 |
| 1977 | Mar. 1 | Tower City, Pa. | 9 |
| 1981 | Apr. 15 | Redstone, Col. | 15 |
| 1981 | Dec. 7 | Topmost, Ky. | 8 |
| 1981 | Dec. 8 | nr. Chattanooga, Tenn. | 13 |
| 1982 | Jan. 20 | Floyd County, Ky. | 7 |
| 1983 | June 21 | McClure, Va | 7 |
| 1984 | Dec. 19 | Huntington, Ut. | 27 |
| 1989 | Sept. 13 | Wheatcroft, Ky. | 10 |
| 1992 | Dec. 7 | Norton, Va. | 8 |

(1) Anthracite mine. (2) Metal mine. (3) Nonmetal mine.
World's worst mine disaster killed 1,549 workers in Honkeiko Colliery in Manchuria Apr. 25, 1942.

## Some Notable Tornadoes In U.S. Since 1925

| Date | | Location | Deaths |
|------|--|----------|--------|
| 1925 | Mar. 18 | Mo., Ill. Ind. | 689 |
| 1927 | Apr. 12 | Rock Springs, Tex. | 74 |
| 1927 | May 9 | Arkansas, Poplar Bluff, Mo. | 92 |
| 1927 | Sept. 29 | St. Louis, Mo. | 90 |
| 1930 | May 6 | Hill, Navarro, Ellis Co., Tex. | 41 |
| 1932 | Mar. 21 | Ala. (series of tornadoes) | 268 |
| 1936 | Apr. 5 | Miss., Ga. | 455 |
| 1936 | Apr. 6 | Gainesville, Ga. | 203 |
| 1938 | Sept. 29 | Charleston, S.C. | 32 |
| 1942 | Mar. 16 | Central to NE Miss. | 75 |
| 1942 | Apr. 27 | Rogers & Mayes Co., Okla. | 52 |
| 1944 | June 23 | Oh., Pa., W. Va., Md. | 150 |
| 1945 | Apr. 12 | Okla.-Ark. | 102 |
| 1947 | Apr. 9 | Tex., Okla. & Kan. | 169 |
| 1948 | Mar. 19 | Bunker Hill & Gillespie, Ill. | 33 |
| 1949 | Jan. 3 | La. & Ark. | 58 |
| 1952 | Mar. 21 | Ark., Mo., Tenn. (series) | 208 |
| 1953 | May 11 | Waco, Tex. | 114 |
| 1953 | June 8 | Mich., Oh. | 142 |
| 1953 | June 9 | Worcester and vicinity, Mass. | 90 |
| 1953 | Dec. 5 | Vicksburg, Miss. | 38 |
| 1955 | May 25 | Kan., Mo., Okla., Tex. | 115 |
| 1957 | May 20 | Kan., Mo. | 48 |
| 1958 | June 4 | Northwestern Wisconsin | 30 |
| 1959 | Feb. 10 | St. Louis, Mo. | 21 |
| 1960 | May 5, 6 | SE Oklahoma, Arkansas | 30 |
| 1965 | Apr. 11 | Ind., Ill., Oh., Mich., Wis. | 271 |
| 1966 | Mar. 3 | Jackson, Miss. | 57 |
| 1966 | Mar. 3 | Mississippi, Alabama | 61 |
| 1967 | Apr. 21 | Ill., Mich. | 33 |
| 1968 | May 15 | Midwest | 71 |
| 1969 | Jan. 23 | Mississippi | 32 |
| 1971 | Feb. 21 | Mississippi delta | 110 |
| 1973 | May 26-27 | South, Midwest (series) | 47 |
| 1974 | Apr. 3-4 | Ala., Ga., Tenn., Ky., Oh. | 350 |
| 1977 | Apr. 4 | Ala., Miss., Ga. | 22 |
| 1979 | Apr. 10 | Tex., Okla. | 60 |
| 1980 | June 3 | Grand Island, Neb. (series) | 4 |
| 1982 | Mar. 2-4 | South, Midwest (series) | 17 |
| 1982 | May 29 | So. Ill. | 10 |
| 1983 | May 18-22 | Tex. | 12 |
| 1984 | Mar. 28 | N. Carolina; S. Carolina | 67 |
| 1984 | Apr. 21-22 | Mississippi | 15 |
| 1984 | Apr. 26 | Series Okla to Minn. | 17 |
| 1985 | May 31 | N.Y., Pa., Oh., Ont. (series) | 90 |
| 1987 | May 22 | Saragosa, Tex. | 29 |
| 1989 | Nov. 15 | Huntsville, Ala. | 18 |
| 1989 | Nov. 16 | Newburgh, N.Y. | 13 |
| 1990 | June 2-3 | Midwest, Great Lakes | 13 |
| 1990 | Aug. 28 | N. Ill. | 25 |
| 1991 | Apr. 26 | Kan., Okla. | 23 |
| 1992 | Nov. 21-23 | South, Midwest | 25 |
| 1993 | Aug. 6 | Petersburg, Va. | 4 |

## Hurricanes, Typhoons, Blizzards, Other Storms

Names of hurricanes and typhoons in italics—H.—hurricane; T.—typhoon

| Date | Location | Deaths | Date | Location | Deaths |
|---|---|---|---|---|---|
| 1888 Mar. 11-14 | Blizzard, Eastern U.S. | 400 | 1967 Dec. 12-20 | Blizzard, Southwest, U.S. | 51 |
| 1900 Aug.-Sept. | H., Galveston, Tex. | 6,000 | 1968 Nov. 18-28 | T. Nina, Philippines | 63 |
| 1906 Sept. 21 | H., La., Miss. | 350 | 1969 Aug. 17-18 | H. Camille, Miss., La. | 256 |
| 1906 Sept. 18 | Typhoon, Hong Kong | 10,000 | 1970 July 30– | | |
| 1926 Sept. 11-22 | H., Fla., Ala. | 243 |   Aug. 5 | H. Celia, Cuba, Fla., Tex. | 31 |
| 1926 Oct. 20 | H., Cuba | 600 | 1970 Aug. 20-21 | H. Dorothy, Martinique | 42 |
| 1928 Sept. 6-20 | H., So. Fla. | 1,836 | 1970 Sept. 15 | T. Georgia, Philippines | 300 |
| 1930 Sept. 3 | H., Dominican Rep. | 2,000 | 1970 Oct. 14 | T. Sening, Philippines | 583 |
| 1938 Sept. 21 | H., Long Island N.Y., New England | 600 | 1970 Oct. 15 | T. Titang, Philippines | 526 |
| 1940 Nov. 11-12 | Blizzard, U.S. NE, Midwest | 144 | 1970 Nov. 13 | Cyclone, Bangladesh | 300,000 |
| 1942 Oct. 15-16 | H., Bengal, India | 40,000 | 1971 Aug. 1 | T. Rose, Hong Kong. | 130 |
| 1944 Sept. 9-16 | H., N.C. to New Eng. | 46 | 1972 June 19-29 | H. Agnes, Fla. to N.Y. | 118 |
| 1952 Oct. 22 | Typhoon, Philippines | 440 | 1972 Dec. 3 | T. Theresa, Philippines | 169 |
| 1954 Aug. 30 | H. Carol, Northeast U.S. | 68 | 1973 June-Aug. | Monsoon rains in India | 1,217 |
| 1954 Oct. 5-18 | H. Hazel, Eastern, U.S., Haiti. | 347 | 1974 June 11 | Storm Dinah, Luzon Is., Philip. | 71 |
| 1955 Aug. 12-13 | H. Connie, Carolinas, Va., Md. | 43 | 1974 July 11 | T. Gilda, Japan, S. Korea | 108 |
| 1955 Aug. 7-21 | H. Diane, Eastern U.S. | 400 | 1974 Sept. 19-20 | T. Fifi, Honduras | 2,000 |
| 1955 Sept. 19 | H. Hilda, Mexico | 200 | 1974 Dec. 25 | Cyclone leveled Darwin, Aus. | 50 |
| 1955 Sept. 22-28 | H. Janet, Caribbean | 500 | 1975 Sept. 13-27 | H. Eloise, Caribbean, NE U.S. | 71 |
| 1956 Feb. 1-29 | Blizzard, Western Europe. | 1,000 | 1976 May 20 | T. Olga, floods, Philippines | 215 |
| 1957 June 25-30 | H. Audrey, Tex. to Ala. | 390 | 1977 July 25, 31 | T. Thelma, T. Vera, Taiwan. | 39 |
| 1958 Feb. 15-16 | Blizzard, NE U.S. | 171 | 1978 Oct. 27 | T. Rita, Philippines. | c. 400 |
| 1959 Sept. 17-19 | T. Sarah, Japan, S. Korea | 2,000 | 1979 Aug. 30– | | |
| 1959 Sept. 26-27 | T. Vera, Honshu, Japan. | 4,466 |   Sept. 7 | H. David, Caribbean, East. U.S. | 1,100 |
| 1960 Sept. 4-12 | H. Donna, Caribbean, E. U.S. | 148 | 1980 Aug. 4-11 | H. Allen, Caribbean, Texas. | 272 |
| 1961 Sept. 11-14 | H. Carla, Tex. | 46 | 1981 Nov. 25 | T. Irma, Luzon Is., Philippines. | 176 |
| 1961 Oct. 31 | H. Hattie, Br. Honduras | 400 | 1983 June | Monsoon rains in India | 900 |
| 1963 May 28-29 | Windstorm, Bangladesh. | 22,000 | 1983 Aug. 18 | H. Alicia, southern Texas | 17 |
| 1963 Oct. 4-8 | H. Flora, Caribbean | 6,000 | 1984 Sept. 2 | T. Ike, southern Philippines | 1,363 |
| 1964 Oct. 4-7 | H. Hilda, La., Miss., Ga. | 38 | 1985 May 25 | Cyclone, Bangladesh | 10,000 |
| 1964 June 30 | T. Winnie, N. Philippines | 107 | 1985 Oct. 26– | | |
| 1964 Sept. 5 | T. Ruby, Hong Kong and China | 735 |   Nov. 6 | H. Juan, SE U.S. | 97 |
| 1965 May 11-12 | Windstorm, Bangladesh. | 17,000 | 1987 Nov. 25 | T. Nina, Philippines | 650 |
| 1965 June 1-2 | Windstorm, Bangladesh. | 30,000 | 1988 Sept. 10-17 | H. Gilbert, Caribbean, G. of Mexico | 260 |
| 1965 Sept. 7-12 | H. Betsy, Fla., Miss., La. | 74 | 1989 Sept. 16-22 | H. Hugo, Caribbean, SE U.S. | 504 |
| 1965 Dec. 15 | Windstorm, Bangladesh. | 10,000 | 1990 May 6-11 | Cyclones, SE India | 450 |
| 1966 June 4-10 | H. Alma, Honduras, SE U.S. | 51 | 1991 Apr. 30 | Cyclone, Bangladesh | 70,000 |
| 1966 Sept. 24-30 | H. Inez, Carib., Fla., Mex. | 293 | 1992 Aug. 24-26 | H. Andrew, S. Fla., La. | 14 |
| 1967 July 9 | T. Billie, SW Japan | 347 | 1993 Mar. 13-14 | Blizzard, Eastern U.S. | 200 |
| 1967 Sept. 5-23 | H. Beulah, Carib., Mex., Tex. | 54 | | | |

## Floods, Tidal Waves

| Date | | Location | Deaths | Date | | Location | Deaths |
|---|---|---|---|---|---|---|---|
| 1228 | .... | Holland | 100,000 | 1969 | Oct. 1-8 | Tunisia | 500 |
| 1642 | .... | China | 300,000 | 1970 | May 20 | Central Romania. | 160 |
| 1887 | .... | Huang He River, China | 900,000 | 1970 | July 22 | Himalayas, India. | 500 |
| 1889 | May 31 | Johnstown, Pa. | 2,200 | 1971 | Feb. 26 | Rio de Janeiro, Brazil | 130 |
| 1900 | Sept. 8 | Galveston, Tex. | 5,000 | 1972 | Feb. 26 | Buffalo Creek, W. Va. | 118 |
| 1903 | June 15 | Heppner, Ore. | 325 | 1972 | June 9 | Rapid City, S.D. | 236 |
| 1911 | .... | Chang Jiang River, China. | 100,000 | 1972 | Aug. 7 | Luzon Is., Philippines | 454 |
| 1913 | Mar. 25-27 | Ohio, Indiana. | 732 | 1973 | Aug. 19-31 | Pakistan | 1,500 |
| 1915 | Aug. 17 | Galveston, Tex. | 275 | 1974 | Mar. 29 | Tubaro, Brazil | 1,000 |
| 1928 | Mar. 13 | Collapse of St. Francis Dam, Saugus, Cal. | 450 | 1974 | Aug. 12 | Monty-Iofo, Bangladesh | 2,500 |
| 1928 | Sept. 13 | Lake Okeechobee, Fla. | 2,000 | 1976 | June 5 | Teton Dam collapse, Ida. | 11 |
| 1931 | Aug. | Huang He River, China | 3,700,000 | 1976 | July 31 | Big Thompson Canyon, Col. | 139 |
| 1937 | Jan. 22 | Ohio, Miss. Valleys | 250 | 1976 | Nov. 17 | East Java, Indonesia | 136 |
| 1939 | .... | Northern China. | 200,000 | 1977 | July 19-20 | Johnstown, Pa. | 68 |
| 1946 | Apr. 1 | Hawaii, Alaska | 159 | 1978 | June-Sept. | Northern India | 1,200 |
| 1947 | .... | Honshu Island, Japan | 1,900 | 1979 | Jan.-Feb. | Brazil | 204 |
| 1951 | Aug. | Manchuria | 1,800 | 1979 | July 17 | Lomblem Is., Indonesia | 539 |
| 1953 | Jan. 31 | Western Europe | 2,000 | 1979 | Aug. 11 | Morvi, India | 5,000-15,000 |
| 1954 | Aug. 17 | Farahzad, Iran | 2,000 | 1980 | Feb. 13-22 | So. Cal., Ariz. | 26 |
| 1955 | Oct. 7-12 | India, Pakistan | 1,700 | 1981 | Apr. | Northern China. | 550 |
| 1959 | Nov. 1 | Western Mexico | 2,000 | 1981 | July | Sichuan, Hubei Prov., China | 1,300 |
| 1959 | Dec. 2 | Frejus, France | 412 | 1982 | Jan. 23 | Nr. Lima, Peru | 600 |
| 1960 | Oct. 10 | Bangladesh. | 6,000 | 1982 | May 12 | Guangdong, China. | 430 |
| 1960 | Oct. 31 | Bangladesh. | 4,000 | 1982 | June 6 | So. Conn. | 12 |
| 1962 | Feb. 17 | German North Sea coast | 343 | 1982 | Sept. 17-21 | El Salvador, Guatemala. | 1,300+ |
| 1962 | Sept. 27 | Barcelona, Spain | 445 | 1982 | Dec. 2-9 | Ill., Mo., Ark. | 22 |
| 1963 | Oct. 9 | Dam collapse, Vaiont, Italy | 1,800 | 1983 | Feb.-Mar. | Cal. coast. | 13 |
| 1966 | Nov. 3-4 | Florence, Venice, Italy. | 113 | 1983 | Apr. 6-12 | Ala., La., Miss., Tenn. | 15 |
| 1967 | Jan. 18-24 | Eastern Brazil | 894 | 1984 | May 27 | Tulsa, Okla. | 13 |
| 1967 | Mar. 19 | Rio de Janeiro, Brazil | 436 | 1984 | Aug-Sept. | S. Korea | 200+ |
| 1967 | Nov. 26 | Lisbon, Portugal | 464 | 1985 | July 19 | Northern Italy, dam burst | 361 |
| 1968 | Aug. 7-14 | Gujarat State, India | 1,000 | 1987 | Aug.-Sept. | Northern Bangladesh | 1,000+ |
| 1968 | Oct. 7 | Northeastern India. | 780 | 1988 | Sept. | Northern India | 1,000+ |
| 1969 | Jan. 18-26 | So. Cal. | 100 | 1990 | June 14 | Shadyside, Oh. | 23 |
| 1969 | Mar. 17 | Mundau Valley, Alagoas, Brazil | 218 | 1991 | Dec. 18-26 | Texas | 18 |
| 1969 | Aug. 20-22 | Western Virginia | 189 | 1992 | Feb. 9-15 | So. Cal. | 13 |
| 1969 | Sept. 15 | South Korea | 250 | 1992 | Apr. 13 | Downtown Chicago | 0 |
| | | | | 1993 | July-Aug. | Midwest. | 50+ |

# Fires

| Date | | Location | Deaths |
|---|---|---|---|
| 1835 | Dec. 16 | New York City, 500 bldgs. destroyed | — |
| 1845 | May | Canton, China, theater | 1,670 |
| 1871 | Oct. 8 | Chicago, $196 million loss | 250 |
| 1871 | Oct. 8 | Peshtigo, Wis., forest fire | 1,182 |
| 1872 | Nov. 9 | Boston, 800 bldgs. destroyed | — |
| 1876 | Dec. 5 | Brooklyn (N.Y.), theater | 295 |
| 1877 | June 20 | St. John, N. B., Canada | 100 |
| 1881 | Dec. 8 | Ring Theater, Vienna | 850 |
| 1887 | May 25 | Opera Comique, Paris | 200 |
| 1887 | Sept. 4 | Exeter, England, theater | 200 |
| 1894 | Sept. 1 | Minn., forest fire | 413 |
| 1897 | May 4 | Paris, charity bazaar | 150 |
| 1900 | June 30 | Hoboken, N. J., docks | 326 |
| 1902 | Sept. 20 | Birmingham, Ala., church | 115 |
| 1903 | Dec. 30 | Iroquois Theater, Chicago | 602 |
| 1908 | Jan. 13 | Rhoads Theater, Boyertown, Pa. | 170 |
| 1908 | Mar. 4 | Collinwood, Oh., school | 176 |
| 1911 | Mar. 25 | Triangle factory, N. Y. City | 145 |
| 1913 | Oct. 14 | Mid Glamorgan, Wales, colliery | 439 |
| 1918 | Apr. 13 | Norman Okla., state hospital | 38 |
| 1918 | Oct. 12 | Cloquet, Minn., forest fire | 400 |
| 1919 | June 20 | Mayaguez Theater, San Juan. | 150 |
| 1923 | May 17 | Camden, S. C., school | 76 |
| 1924 | Dec. 24 | Hobart, Okla., school | 35 |
| 1929 | May 15 | Cleveland, Oh., clinic | 125 |
| 1930 | Apr. 21 | Columbus, Oh., penitentiary | 320 |
| 1931 | July 24 | Pittsburgh, Pa., home for aged | 48 |
| 1934 | Dec. 11 | Hotel Kerns, Lansing, Mich. | 34 |
| 1938 | May 16 | Atlanta, Ga., Terminal Hotel. | 35 |
| 1940 | Apr. 23 | Natchez, Miss., dance hall. | 198 |
| 1942 | Nov. 28 | Cocoanut Grove, Boston | 491 |
| 1942 | | St. John's, Newfoundland, hostel. | 100 |
| 1943 | Sept. 7 | Gulf Hotel, Houston | 55 |
| 1944 | July 6 | Ringling Circus, Hartford. | 168 |
| 1946 | June 5 | LaSalle Hotel, Chicago | 61 |
| 1946 | Dec. 7 | Winecoff Hotel, Atlanta | 119 |
| 1946 | Dec. 12 | New York, ice plant, tenement. | 37 |
| 1949 | Apr. 5 | Effingham, Ill., hospital | 77 |
| 1950 | Jan. 7 | Davenport, Ia., Mercy Hospital | 41 |
| 1953 | Mar. 29 | Largo, Fla., nursing home | 35 |
| 1953 | Apr. 16 | Chicago, metalworking plant | 35 |
| 1957 | Feb. 17 | Warrenton, Mo., home for aged. | 72 |
| 1958 | Mar. 19 | New York City, loft building | 24 |
| 1958 | Dec. 1 | Chicago, parochial school | 95 |
| 1958 | Dec. 16 | Bogota, Colombia, store. | 83 |
| 1959 | June 23 | Stalheim, Norway, resort hotel | 34 |
| 1960 | Mar. 12 | Pusan, Korea, chemical plant. | 68 |
| 1960 | July 14 | Guatemala City, mental hospital | 225 |
| 1960 | Nov. 13 | Amude, Syria, movie theater | 152 |
| 1961 | Jan. 6 | Thomas Hotel, San Francisco. | 20 |
| 1961 | Dec. 8 | Hartford, Conn., hospital. | 16 |
| 1961 | Dec. 17 | Niteroi, Brazil, circus | 323 |
| 1963 | May 4 | Diourbel, Senegal, theater. | 64 |
| 1963 | Nov. 18 | Surfside Hotel, Atlantic City, N.J. | 25 |
| 1963 | Nov. 23 | Fitchville, Oh., rest home | 63 |
| 1963 | Dec. 29 | Roosevelt Hotel, Jacksonville, Fla. | 22 |
| 1964 | May 8 | Manila, apartment bldg. | 30 |
| 1964 | Dec. 18 | Fountaintown, Ind., nursing home. | 20 |
| 1965 | Mar. 1 | LaSalle, Canada, apartment | 28 |
| 1966 | Mar. 1 | Numata, Japan, 2 ski resorts | 31 |
| 1966 | Aug. 13 | Melbourne, Australia, hotel | 29 |
| 1966 | Sept. 12 | Anchorage, Alaska, hotel | 14 |
| 1966 | Oct. 17 | N. Y. City bldg. (firemen) | 12 |

| Date | | Location | Deaths |
|---|---|---|---|
| 1966 | Dec. 7 | Erzurum, Turkey, barracks | 68 |
| 1967 | Feb. 7 | Montgomery, Ala., restaurant | 25 |
| 1967 | May 22 | Brussels, Belgium, store | 322 |
| 1967 | July 16 | Jay, Fla., state prison | 37 |
| 1968 | Feb. 26 | Shrewsbury, England, hospital | 22 |
| 1968 | May 11 | Vijayawada, India, wedding hall. | 58 |
| 1968 | Nov. 18 | Glasgow, Scotland, factory | 24 |
| 1969 | Jan. 26 | Victoria Hotel, Dunnville, Ont. | 13 |
| 1969 | Dec. 2 | Notre Dame, Can., nursing home. | 54 |
| 1970 | Jan. 9 | Marietta, Oh., nursing home. | 27 |
| 1970 | Mar. 20 | Seattle, Wash., hotel | 19 |
| 1970 | Nov. 1 | Grenoble, France, dance hall | 145 |
| 1970 | Dec. 20 | Tucson, Arizona, hotel | 28 |
| 1971 | Mar. 6 | Burghoezli, Switzerland, psychiatric clinic | 28 |
| 1971 | Apr. 20 | Hotel, Bangkok, Thailand | 24 |
| 1971 | Oct. 19 | Honesdale, Pa., nursing home | 15 |
| 1971 | Dec. 25 | Hotel, Seoul, So. Korea | 162 |
| 1972 | May 13 | Osaka, Japan, nightclub | 116 |
| 1972 | July 5 | Sherborne, England, hospital | 30 |
| 1973 | Feb. 6 | Paris, France, school. | 21 |
| 1973 | Nov. 6 | Fukui, Japan, train | 28 |
| 1973 | Nov. 29 | Kumamoto, Japan, department store | 107 |
| 1973 | Dec. 2 | Seoul, Korea, theater | 50 |
| 1974 | Feb. 1 | Sao Paulo, Brazil, bank building | 189 |
| 1974 | June 30 | Port Chester, N. Y., discotheque | 24 |
| 1974 | Nov. 3 | Seoul, So. Korea, hotel discotheque | 88 |
| 1975 | Dec. 12 | Mina, Saudi Arabia, tent city. | 138 |
| 1976 | Oct. 24 | Bronx, N.Y., social club | 25 |
| 1977 | Feb. 25 | Moscow, Rossiya hotel | 45 |
| 1977 | May 28 | Southgate, Ky., nightclub | 164 |
| 1977 | June 9 | Abidjan, Ivory Coast, nightclub | 41 |
| 1977 | June 26 | Columbia, Tenn., jail | 42 |
| 1977 | Nov. 14 | Manila, Philippines, hotel. | 47 |
| 1978 | Jan. 28 | Kansas City, Coates House Hotel | 16 |
| 1979 | July 14 | Saragossa, Spain, hotel | 80 |
| 1979 | Dec. 31 | Chapais, Quebec, social club | 42 |
| 1980 | May 20 | Kingston, Jamaica, nursing home. | 157 |
| 1980 | Nov. 21 | MGM Grand Hotel, Las Vegas | 84 |
| 1980 | Dec. 4 | Stouffer Inn, Harrison, N.Y. | 26 |
| 1981 | Jan. 9 | Keansburg, N.J., boarding home | 30 |
| 1981 | Feb. 10 | Las Vegas Hilton | 8 |
| 1981 | Feb. 14 | Dublin, Ireland, discotheque. | 44 |
| 1982 | Sept. 4 | Los Angeles, apartment house | 24 |
| 1982 | Nov. 8 | Biloxi, Miss., county jail | 29 |
| 1983 | Feb. 13 | Turin, Italy, movie theater | 64 |
| 1983 | Dec. 17 | Madrid, Spain, discotheque | 83 |
| 1984 | May 11 | Great Adventure Amusement Park, N.J. | 8 |
| 1985 | Apr. 21 | Tabaco, Philippines, movie theater | 44 |
| 1985 | Apr. 26 | Buenos Aires, Argentina hospital | 79 |
| 1985 | May 11 | Bradford, England, soccer stadium. | 53 |
| 1986 | Dec. 31 | Puerto Rico, Dupont Plaza Hotel | 96 |
| 1987 | May 6– June 2 | Northern China forest fire | 193 |
| 1987 | Nov. 17 | London, England, subway | 30 |
| 1990 | Mar. 25 | N.Y. City social club | 87 |
| 1991 | Sept. 3 | Hamlet, N.C. chicken-processing plant | 25 |
| 1991 | Oct. 20-21 | Oakland, Berkeley, Cal. wildfire | 24 |
| 1992 | Nov. 20 | Windsor Castle, England | 0 |
| 1993 | Apr. 19 | Waco, Tex., cult compound | 72 |

# Explosions

| Date | | Location | Deaths |
|---|---|---|---|
| 1910 | Oct. 1 | Los Angeles Times Bldg. | 21 |
| 1913 | Mar. 7 | Dynamite, Baltimore harbor | 55 |
| 1915 | Sept. 27 | Gasoline tank car, Ardmore, Okla. | 47 |
| 1917 | Apr. 10 | Munitions plant, Eddystone, Pa. | 133 |
| 1917 | Dec. 6 | Halifax Harbor, Canada | 1,654 |
| 1918 | May 18 | Chemical plant, Oakdale, Pa. | 193 |
| 1918 | July 2 | Explosives, Split Rock, N.Y. | 50 |
| 1918 | Oct. 4 | Shell plant, Morgan Station, N.J. | 64 |
| 1919 | May 22 | Food plant, Cedar Rapids, Ia. | 44 |
| 1920 | Sept. 16 | Wall Street, New York, bomb | 30 |
| 1924 | Jan. 3 | Food plant, Pekin, Ill. | 42 |
| 1928 | April 13 | Dance hall, West Plains, Mo. | 40 |
| 1937 | Mar. 18 | New London, Tex., school | 413 |
| 1940 | Sept. 12 | Hercules Powder, Kenvil, N.J. | 55 |
| 1942 | June 5 | Ordnance plant, Elwood, Ill. | 49 |
| 1944 | Apr. 14 | Bombay, India, harbor | 700 |

| Date | | Location | Deaths |
|---|---|---|---|
| 1944 | July 17 | Port Chicago, Cal., pier. | 322 |
| 1944 | Oct. 21 | Liquid gas tank, Cleveland | 135 |
| 1947 | Apr. 16 | Texas City, Tex., pier | 561 |
| 1948 | July 28 | Farben works, Ludwigshafen, Ger. | 184 |
| 1950 | May 19 | Munitions barges, S. Amboy, N. J. | 30 |
| 1956 | Aug. 7 | Dynamite trucks, Cali, Colombia | 1,100 |
| 1958 | Apr. 18 | Sunken munitions ship, Okinawa | 40 |
| 1958 | May 22 | Nike missiles, Leonardo, N.J. | 10 |
| 1959 | Apr. 10 | World War II bomb, Philippines | 38 |
| 1959 | June 28 | Rail tank cars, Meldrin, Ga. | 25 |
| 1959 | Aug. 7 | Dynamite truck, Roseburg, Ore. | 13 |
| 1959 | Nov. 2 | Jamuri Bazar, India, explosives | 46 |
| 1959 | Dec. 13 | Dortmund, Ger., 2 apt. bldgs. | 26 |
| 1960 | Mar. 4 | Belgian munitions ship, Havana | 100 |
| 1960 | Oct. 25 | Gas, Windsor, Ont., store | 11 |
| 1962 | Jan. 16 | Gas pipeline, Edson, Alberta, Canada. | 8 |

| Date | | Location | Deaths |
|---|---|---|---|
| 1962 | Oct. 3 | Telephone Co. office, N. Y. City . . . | 23 |
| 1963 | Jan. 2 | Packing plant, Terre Haute, Ind. . . . | 16 |
| 1963 | Mar. 9 | Dynamite plant, S. Africa. . . . . . . | 45 |
| 1963 | Aug. 13 | Explosives dump, Gauhiti, India . . . | 32 |
| 1963 | Oct. 31 | State Fair Coliseum, Indianapolis . . | 73 |
| 1964 | July 23 | Bone, Algeria, harbor munitions . . . | 100 |
| 1965 | Mar. 4 | Gas pipeline, Natchitoches, La. . . . | 17 |
| 1965 | Aug. 9 | Missile silo, Searcy, Ark. . . . . . . . | 53 |
| 1965 | Oct. 21 | Bridge, Tila Bund, Pakistan . . . . . . | 80 |
| 1965 | Oct. 30 | Cartagena, Colombia. . . . . . . . . | 48 |
| 1965 | Nov. 24 | Armory, Keokuk, Ia. . . . . . . . . . | 20 |
| 1966 | Oct. 13 | Chemical plant, La Salle, Que. . . . | 11 |
| 1967 | Feb. 17 | Chemical plant, Hawthorne, N.J. . . | 11 |
| 1967 | Dec. 25 | Apartment bldg., Moscow . . . . . . | 20 |
| 1968 | Apr. 6 | Sports store, Richmond, Ind. . . . . | 43 |
| 1970 | Apr. 8 | Subway construction, Osaka, Japan | 73 |
| 1971 | June 24 | Tunnel, Sylmar, Cal. . . . . . . . . . | 17 |
| 1971 | June 28 | School, fireworks, Pueblo, Mex. . . . | 13 |
| 1971 | Oct. 21 | Shopping center, Glasgow, Scot. . . | 20 |
| 1973 | Feb. 10 | Liquified gas tank, Staten Is., N.Y. . . | 40 |
| 1975 | Dec. 27 | Chasnala, India, mine. . . . . . . . . | 431 |
| 1976 | Apr. 13 | Lapua, Finland, munitions works . . | 40 |
| 1977 | Nov. 11 | Freight train, Iri, S. Korea. . . . . . . | 57 |

| Date | | Location | Deaths |
|---|---|---|---|
| 1977 | Dec. 22 | Grain elevator, Westwego, La. . . . | 35 |
| 1978 | Feb. 24 | Derailed tank car, Waverly, Tenn.. . | 12 |
| 1978 | July 11 | Propylene tank truck, Spanish coastal campsite . . . . . . . . . . . | 150 |
| 1980 | Oct. 23 | School, Ortuella, Spain. . . . . . . . | 64 |
| 1981 | Feb. 13 | Sewer system, Louisville, Ky. . . . . | 0 |
| 1982 | Apr. 7 | Tanker truck, tunnel, Oakland, Cal. . | 7 |
| 1982 | Apr. 25 | Antiques exhibition, Todi, Italy . . . . | 33 |
| 1982 | Nov. 2 | Salang Tunnel, Afghanistan. . 1,000-3,000 |  |
| 1984 | Feb. 25 | Oil pipeline, Cubatao, Brazil . . . . . | 508 |
| 1984 | June 21 | Naval supply depot, Severomorsk, USSR. . . . . . . . . . . . . . | 200+ |
| 1984 | Nov. 19 | Gas storage area, NE Mexico City . | 334 |
| 1984 | Dec. 5 | Coal mine, Taipei, Taiwan . . . . . . | 94 |
| 1985 | June 25 | Fireworks factory, Hallett, Okla. . . . | 21 |
| 1988 | July 6 | Oil rig, North Sea . . . . . . . . . . . | 167 |
| 1989 | June 3 | Gas pipeline, between Ufa, Asha, USSR . . . . . . . . . . . . . . | 650+ |
| 1992 | Mar. 3 | Coal mine, Kozlu, Turkey . . . . . . | 270+ |
| 1992 | Apr. 22 | Guadalajara, Mexico sewer . . . . . | 190 |
| 1992 | May 9 | Coal mine, Plymouth, Nova Scotia . | 26 |
| 1993 | Feb. 26 | World Trade Center, N.Y. City. . . . | 6 |

## Notable Nuclear Accidents

**Oct. 7, 1957** — A fire in the Windscale plutonium production reactor north of Liverpool, England spread radioactive material throughout the countryside. In 1983, the British government said that 39 people probably died of cancer as a result.

**1957** — A chemical explosion in Kasli, USSR, in tanks containing nuclear waste, spread radioactive material and forced a major evacuation.

**Jan. 3, 1961** — An experimental reactor at a federal installation near Idaho Falls, Id. killed three workers—the only deaths in U.S. reactor operations. The plant had high radiation levels but damage was contained.

**Oct. 5, 1966** — A sodium cooling system malfunction caused a partial core meltdown at the Enrico Fermi demonstration breeder reactor near Detroit, Mich. Radiation was contained.

**Jan. 21, 1969** — A coolant malfunction from an experimental underground reactor at Lucens Vad, Switzerland resulted in the release of a large amount of radiation into a cavern, which was then sealed.

**Mar. 22, 1975** — A technician checking for air leaks with a lighted candle caused a $100 million fire at the Brown's Ferry reactor in Decatur, Ala. The fire burned out electrical controls, lowering the cooling water to dangerous levels.

**Mar. 28, 1979** — The worst commercial nuclear accident in the U.S. occurred as equipment failures and human mistakes led to a loss of coolant and partial core meltdown at the Three Mile Island reactor in Middletown, Pa.

**Feb. 11, 1981** — Eight workers were contaminated when over 100,000 gallons of radioactive coolant leaked into the containment building of the TVA's Sequoyah 1 plant in Tennessee.

**Apr. 25, 1981** — Some 100 workers were exposed to radioactive material during repairs of a nuclear plant at Tsuruga, Japan.

**Jan. 6, 1986** — A cylinder of nuclear material burst after being improperly heated at a Kerr-McGee plant at Gore, Okla. One worker died and 100 were hospitalized.

**Apr. 26, 1986** — In the worst accident in the history of the nuclear power industry, fires and explosions resulting from an unauthorized experiment at the Chernobyl nuclear power plant near Kiev in the Soviet Union left at least 31 people dead in the immediate aftermath of the disaster and spread significant quantities of radioactive material over much of Europe. An estimated 135,000 people were evacuated from areas around Chernobyl, some of which were rendered uninhabitable for years. As a result of the radiation released into the atmosphere, tens of thousands of excess cancer deaths (as well as increased rates of birth defects) were expected in succeeding decades.

## Record Oil Spills

As a rule, the number of tons can be multiplied by 7 to estimate the number of barrels spilled; the exact number of barrels in a ton varies with the type of oil. Each barrel contains 42 gallons.

| Name, place | Date | Cause | Tons |
|---|---|---|---|
| Ixtoc I oil well, southern Gulf of Mexico . . . . . . . . . . . . . . . . . . | June 3, 1979 . . . . . | Blowout . . . . . . . . . | 600,000 |
| Nowruz oil field, Persian Gulf. . . . . . . . . . . . . . . . . . . . . . . . | Feb., 1983 . . . . . . . | Blowout . . . . . . . . . | 600,000 (est.) |
| Atlantic Empress & Aegean Captain, off Trinidad & Tobago . . . | July 19, 1979. . . . . | Collision . . . . . . . . . | 300,000 |
| Castillo de Beliver, off Cape Town, South Africa. . . . . . . . . . . | Aug. 6, 1983 . . . . . | Fire. . . . . . . . . . . . . | 250,000 |
| Amoco Cadiz, near Portsall, France. . . . . . . . . . . . . . . . . . . | March 16, 1978 . . . . | Grounding . . . . . . . . | 223,000 |
| Torrey Canyon, off Land's End, England . . . . . . . . . . . . . . . . | March 18, 1967 . . . . | Grounding . . . . . . . . | 119,000 |
| Sea Star, Gulf of Oman . . . . . . . . . . . . . . . . . . . . . . . . . . . | Dec. 19, 1972 . . . . . | Collision . . . . . . . . . | 115,000 |
| Urquiola, La Coruna, Spain . . . . . . . . . . . . . . . . . . . . . . . . . | May 12, 1976. . . . . . | Grounding . . . . . . . . | 100,000 |
| Hawaiian Patriot, northern Pacific . . . . . . . . . . . . . . . . . . . . | Feb. 25, 1977. . . . . | Fire. . . . . . . . . . . . . | 99,000 |
| Othello, Tralhavet Bay, Sweden . . . . . . . . . . . . . . . . . . . . . | March 20, 1970 . . . . | Collision . . . . . . 60,000-100,000 | |

### Other Notable Oil Spills

| Name, place | Date | Cause | Gallons |
|---|---|---|---|
| Persian Gulf . . . . . . . . . . . . . . . . . . . . . . . . . . . . . . . . . . | Jan. 23, 1991 (began) | Spillage by Iraq . . . . | 130,000,000* |
| Braer, off Shetland Islands . . . . . . . . . . . . . . . . . . . . . . . . . | Jan. 5, 1993 . . . . . . | Grounding . . . . . . . . | 26,000,000 |
| Aegean Sea, off northern Spain . . . . . . . . . . . . . . . . . . . . . | Dec. 3, 1992 . . . . . . | Unknown . . . . . . . . . | 21,500,000 |
| World Glory, off South Africa. . . . . . . . . . . . . . . . . . . . . . . . | June 13, 1968 . . . . . | Hull failure. . . . . . . . | 13,524,000 |
| Burmah Agate, Galveston Bay, Tex.. . . . . . . . . . . . . . . . . . . | Nov. 1, 1979 . . . . . . | Collision . . . . . . . . . | 10,700,000 |
| Exxon Valdez, Prince William Sound, Alas.. . . . . . . . . . . . . . | Mar. 24, 1989 . . . . . | Grounding . . . . . . . . | 10,080,000 |
| Keo, off Massachusetts. . . . . . . . . . . . . . . . . . . . . . . . . . . | Nov. 5, 1969 . . . . . . | Hull failure. . . . . . . . | 8,820,000 |
| Storage tank, Sewaren, N.J.. . . . . . . . . . . . . . . . . . . . . . . . | Nov. 4, 1969 . . . . . . | Tank rupture. . . . . . . | 8,400,000 |

(continued)

## Other Notable Oil Spills *(continued)*

| Name, place | Date | Cause | Gallons |
|---|---|---|---|
| Ekofisk oil field, North Sea | Apr. 22, 1977 | Well blowout | 8,200,000 |
| Argo Merchant, Nantucket, Mass. | Dec. 15, 1976 | Grounding | 7,700,000 |
| Pipeline, West Delta, La. | Oct. 15, 1967 | Dragging anchor | 6,720,000 |
| Tanker off Japan. | Nov. 30, 1971 | Ship broke in half | 6,258,000 |
| Storage tank, Monongahela River | Jan. 2, 1988 | Tank rupture | 3,800,000 |

\* Estimated by Saudi Arabia. Some estimates are as low as 25,000,000 gallons.

# Major Earthquakes

Magnitude of earthquakes (Mag.), distinct from deaths or damage caused, is measured on the Richter scale, on which each higher number represents a tenfold increase in energy measured in ground motion. Adopted in 1935, the scale has been applied in the following table to earthquakes as far back as reliable seismograms are available.

| Date | Location | Deaths | Mag. | Date | Location | Deaths | Mag. |
|---|---|---|---|---|---|---|---|
| 526 May 20 | Syria, Antioch | 250,000 | N.A. | 1966 Aug. 19 | Eastern Turkey | 2,520 | 6.9 |
| 856 .... | Greece, Corinth | 45,000 | " | 1968 Aug. 31 | Northeastern Iran | 12,000 | 7.4 |
| 1057 .... | China, Chihli | 25,000 | " | 1970 Jan. 5 | Yunnan Province, China | 10,000 | 7.7 |
| 1268 .... | Asia Minor, Cilicia | 60,000 | " | 1970 Mar. 28 | Western Turkey | 1,086 | 7.4 |
| 1290 Sept. 27 | China, Chihli | 100,000 | " | 1970 May 31 | Northern Peru | 66,794 | 7.7 |
| 1293 May 20 | Japan, Kamakura | 30,000 | " | 1971 Feb. 9 | San Fernando Valley, Cal. | 65 | 6.6 |
| 1531 Jan. 26 | Portugal, Lisbon | 30,000 | " | 1972 Apr. 10 | Southern Iran | 5,057 | 6.9 |
| 1556 Jan. 24 | China, Shaanxi | 830,000 | " | 1972 Dec. 23 | Nicaragua | 5,000 | 6.2 |
| 1667 Nov. | Caucasia, Shemaka | 80,000 | " | 1974 Dec. 28 | Pakistan (9 towns) | 5,200 | 6.3 |
| 1693 Jan. 11 | Italy, Catania | 60,000 | " | 1975 Sept. 6 | Turkey (Lice, etc.) | 2,312 | 6.8 |
| 1730 Dec. 30 | Japan, Hokkaido | 137,000 | " | 1976 Feb. 4 | Guatemala | 22,778 | 7.5 |
| 1737 Oct. 11 | India, Calcutta | 300,000 | " | 1976 May 6 | Northeast Italy | 946 | 6.5 |
| 1755 June 7 | Northern Persia | 40,000 | " | 1976 June 26 | New Guinea, Irian Jaya | 443 | 7.1 |
| 1755 Nov. 1 | Portugal, Lisbon | 60,000 | 8.75* | 1976 July 28 | China, Tangshan | 242,000 | 8.2 |
| 1783 Feb. 4 | Italy, Calabria | 30,000 | N.A. | 1976 Aug. 17 | Philippines, Mindanao | 8,000 | 7.8 |
| 1797 Feb. 4 | Ecuador, Quito | 41,000 | " | 1976 Nov. 24 | E. Turkey | 4,000 | 7.9 |
| 1811-12 | New Madrid, Mo. (series) | — | 8.7* | 1977 Mar. 4 | Romania | 1,541 | 7.5 |
| 1822 Sept. 5 | Asia Minor, Aleppo | 22,000 | N.A. | 1977 Aug. 19 | Indonesia | 200 | 8.0 |
| 1828 Dec. 28 | Japan, Echigo | 30,000 | " | 1977 Nov. 23 | Northwestern Argentina | 100 | 8.2 |
| 1868 Aug. 13-15 | Peru and Ecuador | 40,000 | " | 1978 June 12 | Japan, Sendai | 21 | 7.5 |
| 1875 May 16 | Venezuela, Colombia | 16,000 | " | 1978 Sept. 16 | Northeast Iran | 25,000 | 7.7 |
| 1886 Aug. 31 | Charleston, S.C. | 60 | 6.6 | 1979 Sept. 12 | Indonesia | 100 | 8.1 |
| 1896 June 15 | Japan, sea wave | 27,120 | N.A. | 1979 Dec. 12 | Colombia, Ecuador | 800 | 7.9 |
| 1906 Apr. 18-19 | San Francisco, Cal. | 503 | 8.3 | 1980 Oct. 10 | Northwestern Algeria | 4,500 | 7.3 |
| 1906 Aug. 16 | Chile, Valparaiso | 20,000 | 8.6 | 1980 Nov. 23 | Southern Italy | 4,800 | 7.2 |
| 1908 Dec. 28 | Italy, Messina | 83,000 | 7.5 | 1982 Dec. 13 | North Yemen | 2,800 | 6.0 |
| 1915 Jan. 13 | Italy, Avezzano | 29,980 | 7.5 | 1983 Mar. 31 | Southern Colombia | 250 | 5.5 |
| 1920 Dec. 16 | China, Gansu | 100,000 | 8.6 | 1983 May 26 | N. Honshu, Japan | 81 | 7.7 |
| 1923 Sept. 1 | Japan, Yokohama | 200,000 | 8.3 | 1983 Oct. 30 | Eastern Turkey | 1,300 | 7.1 |
| 1927 May 22 | China, Nan-Shan | 200,000 | 8.3 | 1985 Mar. 3 | Chile | 146 | 7.8 |
| 1932 Dec. 26 | China, Gansu | 70,000 | 7.6 | 1985 Sept. 19, 21 | Mexico City | 4,200+ | 8.1 |
| 1933 Mar. 2 | Japan | 2,990 | 8.9 | 1987 Mar. 5-6 | NE Ecuador | 4,000+ | 7.3 |
| 1933 Mar. 10 | Long Beach, Cal. | 115 | 6.2 | 1988 Aug. 20 | India/Nepal border | 1,000+ | 6.5 |
| 1934 Jan. 15 | India, Bihar-Nepal | 10,700 | 8.4 | 1988 Nov. 6 | China/Burma border | 1,000 | 7.3 |
| 1935 May 31 | India, Quetta | 50,000 | 7.5 | 1988 Dec. 7 | NW Armenia | 55,000+ | 6.8 |
| 1939 Jan. 24 | Chile, Chillan | 28,000 | 8.3 | 1989 Oct. 17 | San Francisco Bay area | 62 | 6.9 |
| 1939 Dec. 26 | Turkey, Erzincan | 30,000 | 7.9 | 1990 May 30 | N. Peru | 115 | 6.3 |
| 1946 Dec. 21 | Japan, Honshu | 2,000 | 8.4 | 1990 May 30 | Romania | 8 | 6.5 |
| 1948 June 28 | Japan, Fukui | 5,131 | 7.3 | 1990 June 21 | NW Iran | 40,000+ | 7.7 |
| 1949 Aug. 5 | Ecuador, Pelileo | 6,000 | 6.8 | 1990 July 16 | Luzon, Philippines | 1,621 | 7.7 |
| 1950 Aug. 15 | India, Assam | 1,530 | 8.7 | 1991 Feb. 1 | Pakistan, Afghanistan border | 1,200 | 6.8 |
| 1953 Mar. 18 | NW Turkey | 1,200 | 7.2 | 1992 Mar. 13, 15 | E. Turkey | 4,000 | 6.2/6.0 |
| 1956 June 10-17 | N. Afghanistan | 2,000 | 7.7 | 1992 June 28 | S. Cal. | 1 | 7.5/6.6 |
| 1957 July 2 | Northern Iran | 2,500 | 7.4 | 1992 Oct. 12 | Cairo, Egypt | 450 | 5.9 |
| 1957 Dec. 13 | Western Iran | 2,000 | 7.1 | 1992 Dec. 12 | Flores, Indonesia | 2,500 | 7.5 |
| 1960 Feb. 29 | Morocco, Agadir | 12,000 | 5.8 | 1993 July 12 | off Hokkaido, Japan | 200+ | 7.8 |
| 1960 May 21-30 | Southern Chile | 5,000 | 8.3 | | | | |
| 1962 Sept. 1 | Northwestern Iran | 12,230 | 7.1 | | | | |
| 1963 July 26 | Yugoslavia, Skopje | 1,100 | 6.0 | | | | |
| 1964 Mar. 27 | Alaska | 131 | 8.4 | | | | |

(*) estimated from earthquake intensity. (N.A.) not available.

# Some Recent Earthquakes

Source: Global Volcanism Network, Smithsonian Institution

| Date | Location | Magnitude | Date | Location | Magnitude |
|---|---|---|---|---|---|
| Aug. 8, 1993 | Agana, Guam | 8.0 | Oct. 12 | Cairo, Egypt | 5.9 |
| July 12 | off Hokkaido, Japan | 7.8 | Sept. 11 | SE Zaire | 6.8 |
| Mar. 26 | S. Greece | 5.1 | Sept. 2 | off Nicaragua | 7.2 |
| Mar. 12 | Fiji | 6.5 | Aug. 19 | Kyrgyzstan | 7.5 |
| Mar. 6 | Solomon Islands | 6.5 | Aug. 7 | Gulf of Alaska | 6.5 |
| Mar. 6 | Fiji | 6.5 | June 28 | S. California | 7.5/6.6 |
| Mar. 6 | Santa Cruz Islands | 7.1 | May 25 | Cabo Cruz, Cuba | 7.0 |
| Jan. 15 | Kushiro, Japan | 7.0 | May 15 | Kyrgyzstan | 6.2 |
| Dec. 20, 1992 | Banda Sea, Indonesia | 7.0 | Apr. 25 | N. California | 7.0 |
| Dec. 12 | Flores, Indonesia | 7.5 | Apr. 13 | SE Netherlands | 5.0 |
| Nov. 8 | Fiji | 6.5 | Mar. 13 | Turkey | 6.2 |
| Oct. 23 | Papua New Guinea | 6.7 | Feb. 27 | E. New Guinea | 6.7 |
| Oct. 17 | Murindo, Colombia | 7.2 | Feb. 13 | Vanuatu | 6.8 |

# Historic Assassinations Since 1865

**1865**—Apr. 14. U. S. Pres. Abraham Lincoln, shot by John Wilkes Booth in Washington, D. C.; died Apr. 15.

**1881**—Mar. 13. Alexander II, of Russia—July 2. U. S. Pres. James A. Garfield, shot by Charles J. Guiteau, Washington D.C.; died Sept. 19.

**1900**—July 29. Umberto I, king of Italy.

**1901**—Sept. 6. U. S. Pres. William McKinley in Buffalo, N. Y., died Sept. 14. Leon Czolgosz executed for the crime Oct. 29.

**1913**—Feb. 23. Mexican Pres. Francisco I. Madero and Vice Pres. Jose Pino Suarez.—Mar. 18. George, king of Greece.

**1914**—June 28. Archduke Francis Ferdinand of Austria-Hungary and his wife in Sarajevo, Bosnia (later part of Yugoslavia), by Gavrilo Princip.

**1916**—Dec. 30. Grigori Rasputin, politically powerful Russian monk.

**1918**—July 12. Grand Duke Michael of Russia, at Perm.—July 16. Nicholas II, abdicated as czar of Russia; his wife, the Czarina Alexandra; their son, Czarevitch Alexis; their daughters, Grand Duchesses Olga, Tatiana, Marie, Anastasia; and 4 members of their household were executed by Bolsheviks at Ekaterinburg.

**1920**—May 20. Mexican Pres. Gen. Venustiano Carranza in Tlaxcalantongo.

**1922**—Aug. 22. Michael Collins, Irish revolutionary.—Dec. 16. Polish President Gabriel Narutowicz in Warsaw by an anarchist.

**1923**—July 20. Gen. Francisco "Pancho" Villa, ex-rebel leader, in Parral, Mexico.

**1928**—July 17. Gen. Alvaro Obregon, president-elect of Mexico, in San Angel, Mexico.

**1933**—Feb. 15. In Miami, Fla., Joseph Zangara, anarchist, shot at Pres.-elect Franklin D. Roosevelt, but a woman seized his arm, and the bullet fatally wounded Mayor Anton J. Cermak, of Chicago, who died Mar. 6. Zangara was electrocuted on Mar. 20, 1933.

**1934**—July 25. In Vienna, Austrian Chancellor Engelbert Dollfuss by Nazis.

**1935**—Sept. 8. U. S. Sen. Huey P. Long, shot in Baton Rouge, La., by Dr. Carl Austin Weiss, who was slain by Long's bodyguards; Long died Sept. 10.

**1940**—Aug. 20. Leon Trotsky (Lev Bronstein), 63, exiled Russian war minister, near Mexico City. Killer identified as Ramon Mercador del Rio, a Spaniard, served 20 years in Mexican prison.

**1948**—Jan. 30. Mohandas K. Gandhi, 78, shot in New Delhi, India, by Nathuram Vinayak Godse.—Sept. 17. Count Folke Bernadotte, UN mediator for Palestine, ambushed in Jerusalem.

**1951**—July 20. King Abdullah ibn Hussein of Jordan.—Oct. 16. Prime Min. Liaquat Ali Khan of Pakistan shot in Rawalpindi.

**1956**—Sept. 21. Pres. Anastasio Somoza of Nicaragua, in Leon; died Sept. 29.

**1957**—July 26. Pres. Carlos Castillo Armas of Guatemala, in Guatemala City by one of his own guards.

**1958**—July 14. King Faisal of Iraq; his uncle, Crown Prince Abdullah; and July 15, Premier Nuri as-Said, by rebels in Baghdad.

**1959**—Sept. 25. Prime Minister Solomon Bandaranaike of Ceylon, by Buddhist monk in Colombo.

**1961**—Jan. 17. Ex-Premier Patrice Lumumba of the Congo, in Katanga Province—May 30. Dominican dictator Rafael Leonidas Trujillo Molina shot to death by assassins near Ciudad Trujillo.

**1963**—June 12. Medgar W. Evers, NAACP's Mississippi field secretary, in Jackson, Miss.—Nov. 2. Pres. Ngo Dinh Diem of the Republic of Vietnam and his brother, Ngo Dinh Nhu, in a military coup.—Nov. 22. U. S. Pres. John F. Kennedy fatally shot in Dallas, Tex.; accused Lee Harvey Oswald murdered by Jack Ruby while awaiting trial.

**1965**—Jan. 21. Iranian premier Hassan Ali Mansour fatally wounded by assassin in Teheran; 4 executed.—Feb. 21. Malcolm X, black nationalist, fatally shot in N. Y. City.

**1966**—Sept. 6. Prime Minister Hendrik F. Verwoerd of South Africa stabbed to death in parliament at Capetown.

**1968**—Apr. 4. Rev. Dr. Martin Luther King Jr. fatally shot in Memphis, Tenn. by James Earl Ray.—June 5. Sen. Robert F. Kennedy (D-N. Y.) fatally shot in Los Angeles; Sirhan Sirhan, resident alien, convicted of murder.

**1971**—Nov. 28. Prime Minister Wasfi Tal of Jordan, in Cairo, by Palestinian guerrillas.

**1973**—Mar. 2. U. S. Ambassador Cleo A. Noel Jr., U. S. Charge d'Affaires George C. Moore and Belgian Charge d'Affaires Guy Eid killed by Palestinian guerrillas in Khartoum, Sudan.

**1974**—Aug. 19. U. S. Ambassador to Cyprus, Rodger P. Davies, killed by sniper's bullet in Nicosia.

**1975**—Feb. 11. Pres. Richard Ratsimandrava, of Madagascar, shot in Tananarive.—Mar. 25. King Faisal of Saudi Arabia shot by nephew Prince Musad Abdel Aziz, in royal palace, Riyadh.—Aug. 15. Bangladesh Pres. Sheik Mujibur Rahman killed in coup.

**1976**—Feb. 13. Nigerian head of state, Gen. Murtala Ramat Mohammed, slain by self-styled "young revolutionaries."

**1977**—Mar. 16. Kamal Jumblat, Lebanese Druse chieftain, was shot near Beirut.—Mar. 18. Congo Pres. Marien Ngouabi shot in Brazzaville.

**1978**—July 9. Former Iraqi Premier Abdul Razak Al-Naif shot in London.

**1979**—Feb. 14. U.S. Ambassador Adolph Dubs shot and killed by Afghan Moslem extremists in Kabul.—Aug. 27. Lord Mountbatten, WW2 hero, and 2 others were killed when a bomb exploded on his fishing boat off the coast of Co. Sligo, Ire. The IRA claimed responsibility. —Oct. 26. So. Korean President Park Chung Hee and 6 bodyguards fatally shot by Kim Jae Kyu, head of Korean CIA, and 5 aides in Seoul.

**1980**—Apr. 12. Liberian President William R. Tolbert slain in military coup.—Sept. 17. Former Nicaraguan President Anastasio Somoza Debayle shot in Paraguay.

**1981**—Oct. 6. Egyptian President Anwar al-Sadat fatally shot by a band of commandos while reviewing a military parade in Cairo.

**1982**—Sept. 14. Lebanese President-elect Bashir Gemayel killed by bomb in east Beirut.

**1983**—Aug. 21. Philippine opposition political leader Benigno Aquino Jr. fatally shot by a gunman at Manila International Airport.

**1984**—Oct. 31. Indian Prime Minister Indira Gandhi shot and killed by 2 of her bodyguards, who were members of the minority Sikh sect, in New Delhi.

**1986**—Feb. 28. Swedish Premier Olaf Palme shot and killed by a gunman in Stockholm.

**1988**—June 1. Lebanese Premier Rashid Karami killed when a bomb exploded aboard a helicopter in which he was traveling. —Apr. 16. PLO military chief Khalil Wazir (Abu Jihad) was gunned down by Israeli commandos in Tunisia.

**1989**—Aug. 18. Colombian Liberal Party presidential candidate Luis Carlos Galan was killed by Medellín cartel drug traffickers at a campaign rally in Bogotá.—Nov. 22. Lebanese President Rene Moawad was killed when a bomb exploded next to his motorcade.

**1990**—Mar. 22. Colombian Patriotic Union presidential candidate Bernando Jamamillo Ossa was shot by a gunman at an airport in Bogotá.

**1991**—May 21. Rajiv Gandhi, former prime minister of India, was killed when a bomb exploded during an election rally in Madras.

**1992**—June 29. Mohammed Boudiaf, president of Algeria, was shot by a gunman in Annaba.

**1993**—May 1. Ranasinghe Premadasa, president of Sri Lanka, killed by bomb in Colombo.—Apr. 10. Chris Hani, S. African communist leader, shot by gunman in Boksburg.

## Assassination Attempts

1910—Aug. 6. N. Y. City Mayor William J. Gaynor shot and seriously wounded by discharged city employee.

1912—Oct. 14. Former U. S. President Theodore Roosevelt shot and seriously wounded by demented man in Milwaukee, Wis.

1950—Nov. 1. In an attempt to assassinate President Truman, 2 members of a Puerto Rican nationalist movement—Griselio Torresola and Oscar Collazo—tried to shoot their way into Blair House. Torresola was killed, and a guard, Pvt. Leslie Coffelt was fatally shot. Collazo was convicted Mar. 7, 1951, for the murder of Coffelt.

1970—Nov. 27. Pope Paul VI unharmed by knife-wielding assailant who attempted to attack him in Manila airport.

1972—May 15. Alabama Gov. George Wallace shot in Laurel, Md. by Arthur Bremer; seriously crippled.

1972—Dec. 7. Mrs. Ferdinand E. Marcos, wife of the Philippine president, was stabbed and seriously injured in Pasay City, Philippines.

1975—Sept. 5. Pres. Gerald R. Ford was unharmed when a Secret Service agent grabbed a pistol aimed at him by Lynette (Squeaky) Fromme, a Charles Manson follower, in Sacramento.

1975—Sept. 22. Pres. Ford escaped unharmed when Sara Jane Moore, a political activist, fired a revolver at him.

1980—May 29. Civil rights leader Vernon E. Jordan Jr. shot and wounded in Ft. Wayne, Ind.

1981—Jan. 16. Irish political activist Bernadette Devlin McAliskey and her husband were shot and seriously wounded by 3 members of a Protestant paramilitary group in Co. Tyrone, Ire.

1981—Mar. 30. Pres. Ronald Reagan, Press Secy. James Brady, Secret Service agent Timothy J. McCarthy, and Washington, D.C. policeman Thomas Delahanty were shot and seriously wounded by John W. Hinckley Jr. in Washington, D.C.

1981—May 13. Pope John Paul II and 2 bystanders were shot and wounded by Mehmet Ali Agca, an escaped Turkish murderer, in St. Peter's Square, Rome.

1982—May 12. Pope John Paul II was unharmed when a man with a knife was overpowered by guards, in Fatima, Portugal.

1982—June 3. Israel's ambassador to Britain Shlomo Argov was shot and seriously wounded by Arab terrorists in London.

1986—Sept. 7. Chilean President Gen. Augusto Pinochet Ugarte escaped unharmed when his motorcade was attacked by rebels using rockets, bazookas, grenades, and rifles.

## Notable Kidnappings in the U.S.

Edward A. Cudahy Jr., 16, in Omaha, Neb., Dec. 18, 1900. Returned Dec. 20 after $25,000 paid. Pat Crowe confessed.

Robert Franks, 13, in Chicago, May 22, 1924, by 2 youths, Richard Loeb and Nathan Leopold, who killed boy. Demand for $10,000 ignored. Loeb died in prison, Leopold paroled 1958.

Charles A. Lindbergh Jr., 20 mos. old, in Hopewell, N.J., Mar. 1, 1932; found dead May 12. Ransom of $50,000 was paid to man identified as Bruno Richard Hauptmann, 35, paroled German convict who entered U.S. illegally. Hauptmann was convicted after spectacular trial at Flemington, and electrocuted in Trenton, N.J. prison, Apr. 3, 1936.

William A. Hamm Jr., 39, in St. Paul, June 15, 1933. $100,000 paid. Alvin Karpis given life, paroled in 1969.

Charles F. Urschel, in Oklahoma City, July 22, 1933. Released July 31 after $200,000 paid. George (Machine Gun) Kelly and 5 others given life.

Brooke L. Hart, 22, in San Jose, Cal. Thomas Thurmond and John Holmes arrested after demanding $40,000 ransom. When Hart's body was found in San Francisco Bay, Nov. 26, 1933, a mob attacked the jail at San Jose and lynched the 2 kidnappers.

George Weyerhaeuser, 9, in Tacoma, Wash., May 24, 1935. Returned home June 1 after $200,000 paid. Kidnappers given 20 to 60 years.

Charles Mattson, 10, in Tacoma, Wash., Dec. 27, 1936. Found dead Jan. 11, 1937. Kidnapper asked $28,000, failed to contact.

Arthur Fried, in White Plains, N.Y., Dec. 4, 1937. Body not found. Two kidnappers executed.

Robert C. Greenlease, 6, taken from Kansas City, Mo. school Sept. 28, 1953, and held for $600,000. Body found Oct. 7. Bonnie Brown Heady and Carl A. Hall pleaded guilty and were executed.

Peter Weinberger, 32 days old, Westbury, N.Y., July 4, 1956, for $2,000 ransom, not paid. Child found dead. Angelo John LaMarca, 31, convicted, executed.

Lee Crary, in Everett, Wash., Sept. 22, 1957; $10,000 ransom, not paid. He escaped after 3 days, led police to George E. Collins, who was convicted.

Frank Sinatra Jr., 19, from hotel room in Lake Tahoe, Cal., Dec. 8, 1963. Released Dec. 11 after his father paid $240,000 ransom. Three men sentenced to prison.

Barbara Jane Mackle, 20, abducted Dec. 17, 1968, from Atlanta, Ga., motel, was found unharmed 3 days later, buried in a coffin-like wooden box 18 inches underground, after her father had paid $500,000 ransom; Gary Steven Krist sentenced to life, Ruth Eisenmann-Schier to 7 years.

Mrs. Roy Fuchs, 35, and 3 children held hostage 2 hours, May 14, 1969, in Long Island, N. Y., released after her husband, a bank manager, paid kidnappers $129,000 in bank funds; 4 men arrested, ransom recovered.

Virginia Piper, 49, abducted July 27, 1972, from her home in suburban Minneapolis; found unharmed near Duluth 2 days later after her husband paid $1 million ransom.

Patricia (Patty) Hearst, 19, taken from her Berkeley, Cal., apartment Feb. 4, 1974. Symbionese Liberation Army demanded her father, Randolph A. Hearst, publisher, give millions to poor. She was identified by FBI as taking part in a San Francisco bank holdup, Apr. 15. FBI, Sept. 18, 1975, captured her and others in San Francisco; they were indicted on various charges. Patricia Hearst convicted of bank robbery, Mar. 20, 1976. She was released from prison under executive clemency, Feb. 1, 1979. In 1978, William and Emily Harris were sentenced to 10 years to life for the Hearst kidnapping. Both were paroled in 1983.

J. Reginald Murphy, 40, an editor of *Atlanta* (Ga.) *Constitution*, kidnapped Feb. 20, 1974; freed Feb. 22 after payment of $700,000 ransom by the newspaper. Police arrested William A. H. Williams, a contractor; most of the money was recovered.

E. B. Reville, Hepzibah, Ga., banker, and wife, Jean, kidnapped Sept. 30, 1974. Ransom of $30,000 paid. He was found alive; Jean Reville was found dead Oct. 2.

Jack Teich, Kings Point, N.Y., steel executive, seized Nov. 12, 1974; released Nov. 19 after payment of $750,000.

Sidney J. Reso, oil co. executive, seized Apr. 29, 1992; died May 3; Arthur D. Seale and wife, Irene, arrested June 19. Arthur Seale pleaded guilty and was sentenced to life in prison; Irene Seale was sentenced to a 20-year prison term.

Katie Beers, 9, Long Island, N.Y., disappeared Dec. 28, 1992, found unharmed Jan. 13, 1993, in an underground bunker in the home of a family friend. John Esposito indicted Jan. 19, 1993.

# ASSOCIATIONS AND SOCIETIES

Source: World Almanac questionnaire

Arranged according to key words in titles. Founding year of organization in parentheses; last figure after ZIP code indicates membership.

**AFS Intercultural Programs** (1917), 313 E. 43rd Street, N.Y., NY 10017; 22,000.

**ASM International** (1913), 9639 Kinsman Rd., Materials Park, OH 44073-0002; 48,625.

**ASTM** (1898), 1916 Race St., Philadelphia, PA 19103.

**Aaron Burr Assn.** (1946), 4520 King Edward Ct., Annandle, VA 22003; 600.

**Abortion Federation, Natl.** (1977), 1436 U St. NW, Suite 103, Washington, DC 20009; 300 organizations.

**Accountants, Amer. Institute of Certified Public** (1887), 1211 Ave. of the Americas, N.Y., NY 10036; 305,465.

**Accountants, Natl. Assn. of** (1919), 10 Paragon Dr., Box 433, Montvale, NJ 07645-1760; 85,000.

**Accountants for Cooperatives, Natl. Soc. of** (1936), 6320 Augusta Dr., Ste. 800, Springfield, VA 22150; 2,000.

**Acoustical Society of America** (1929), 500 Sunnyside Blvd., Woodbury, NY 11797; 7,000.

**Actors' Equity Assn.** (1913), 165 W. 46 St., N.Y., NY 10036.

**Actuaries, Society of** (1949), 475 N. Martingale Rd., Suite 800, Schaumburg, IL 60173-2226; 13,830.

**Advertisers, Assn. of Natl.** (1910), 155 E. 44th St., N.Y., NY 10017; 245 cos.

**Advertising Agencies, Amer. Assn. of** (1917), 666 Third Ave., N.Y., NY 10017; 700 agencies.

**Aeronautic Assn., Natl.** (1905), 1815 N. Fort Myer Dr., Ste. 700, Arlington, VA 22209.

**Aerospace Industries Assn. of America** (1919), 1250 Eye St. NW, Wash., DC 20005; 55 cos.

**Aerospace Medical Assn.** (1929), 320 S. Henry St., Alexandria, VA 22314-3579; 4,500.

**Afro-American Life and History, Assn. for the Study of** (1915), 1401 14th St. NW, Wash., DC 20005; 1,800.

**Aging Assn., Amer.** (1970), 600 South 42nd St., Omaha, NE 68198-4635; 400.

**Agricultural Chemicals Assn., Natl.** (1933), 1155 15th St. NW, Wash., DC 20005; 80 cos.

**Agricultural Economics Assn., Amer.** (1910), 80 Heady Hall, Iowa State Univ., Ames, IA 50011; 4,500.

**Agricultural History Society** (1919), Room 928, 1301 New York Ave. NW, Wash., DC 20250; 1,400.

**Agronomy, Amer. Society of** (1907), 677 S. Segoe Rd., Madison, WI 53711; 12,747.

**Aircraft Assn., Experimental** (1953), EAA Aviation Center, Oshkosh, WI 54903-3086; 130,000.

**Aircraft Owners and Pilots Assn.** (1939), 421 Aviation Way, Frederick, MD 2l701; 300,000.

**Air Force Assn.** (1946), 1501 Lee Hwy., Arlington, VA 22209.

**Air Force Gunners Assn.** (1986), 3644 Elk Grove Ct., Land O'Lakes, FL 34639; 1,407.

**Air Line Pilots Assn.** (1931), 1625 Massachusetts Ave. NW, Wash., DC 20036; 41,000.

**Airmen, Assn. of Independent** (1989), 1625 Massachusetts Ave. NW, Washington, DC 20036; 3,000.

**Air Transport Assn. of America** (1936), 1709 New York Ave. NW, Wash., DC 20006; 19 airlines.

**Air & Waste Management Assn.** (1907), P.O. Box 2861, Pittsburgh, PA 15230; 14,057.

**Al-Anon Family Groups** (1950), P.O. Box 862, Midtown Sta., N.Y., NY 10018; 24,918.

**Alcohol Problems, Amer. Council on** (1895), 3426 Bridgeland Dr., Bridgeton, MO 63044; 37 state affiliates.

**Alcoholics Anonymous** (1935), P.O. Box 459, Grand Central Station, N.Y., NY 10163.

**Alcoholism and Drug Dependence, Natl. Council on** (1944), 12 W. 21st St., N.Y., NY 10010; 200 affiliates.

**Allergy and Immunology, Amer. Academy of** (1943), 611 E. Wells St., Milwaukee, WI 53202; 4,800.

**Alpine Club, Amer.** (1902), 113 E. 90th St., N.Y., NY 10028.

**Alzheimer's Assn.** (1980), 919 Michigan Ave., Chicago, IL 60611.

**Amer. Indian Affairs, Assn. on** (1922), 245 Fifth Ave., Ste. 1801, N.Y., NY, 10016-8728; 50,000.

**American Legion, The** (1919), 700 N. Pennsylvania St., Indianapolis, IN 46204; 3.1 mln. **American Legion Auxiliary** (1919), 777 N. Meridian St., Indianapolis, IN 46204; 1 mln.

**Amer. Veterans (AMVETS)** (1947); **AMVETS Auxiliary** (1946), 4647 Forbes Blvd., Lanham, MD 20706-9961; 200,000.

**Americares Foundation** (1982), 161 Cherry St., New Canaan, CT 06840.

**Amideast** (Amer. Mideast Educational & Training Services) (1951), 1100 17th St. NW, Ste. 300, Wash., DC 20036-4601.

**Amnesty Intl. USA** (1961), 322 Eighth Ave., N.Y., NY 10001.

**Amputation Foundation, Natl.** (1919), 12-45 150th St., Whitestone, NY 11357; 2,500.

**Anachronism, Society for Creative** (1966), P.O. Box 360743, Milpitas, CA 95036-0743; 23,000.

**Animal Protection Institute of America** (1968), 2831 Fruitridge Rd., Sacramento, CA 95822; 150,000.

**Animal Welfare Institute** (1951), P.O. Box 3650, Wash., DC 20007; 8,500.

**Animals, Amer. Society for Prevention of Cruelty to (ASPCA)** (1866), 424 E. 92d St., N.Y., NY 10128; 350,000.

**Animals, People for the Ethical Treatment of** (1980), P.O. Box 42516, Wash., DC 20015; 350,000.

**Anthropological Assn., Amer.** (1902), 1703 New Hampshire Ave. NW, Wash., DC 20009; 11,000.

**Antiquarian Society, Amer.** (1812), 185 Salisbury St., Worcester, MA 01609-1634; 552.

**Anti-Vivisection Society, New England** (1895), 333 Washington St., Boston, MA 02108-5100; 10,000.

**Appalachian Mountain Club** (1876), 5 Joy St., Boston, MA 02108; 54,952.

**Appalachian Trail Conference** (1925), Washington & Jackson Sts., Harpers Ferry, WV 25425; 23,000.

**Appraisers, Amer. Society of** (1936), 535 Herndon Pwky., #150, Herndon, VA 22070; 6,500.

**Arab Americans, Natl. Assn. of** (1972), 2033 M St. NW, Wash., DC 20036.

**Arbitration Assn., Amer.** (1926), 140 W. 51st St., N.Y., NY 10020-1203; 6,523.

**Arc, The** (1950), 500 E. Border St., Ste. 300, Arlington, TX 76010; 140,000.

**Archaeological Institute of America** (1879), 675 Commonwealth Ave., Boston, MA 02215; 11,500.

**Archaeology, Institute of Nautical** (1976), P.O. Drawer HG, College Station, TX 77841-5137; 1,100.

**Archery Assn., Natl.** (1879), One Olympic Plaza, Colorado Springs, CO 80909; 3,800.

**Architects, Amer. Institute of** (1857), 1735 New York Ave. NW, Wash., DC 20006; 51,000.

**Architectural Historians, Society of** (1940), 1232 Pine Street, Phila., PA 19107-5944; 3,500.

**Armed Forces Communications and Electronics Assn.** (1946), 4400 Fair Lakes Ct., Fairfax, VA 22033; 40,000.

**Army, Assn. of the United States** (1950), 2425 Wilson Blvd., Arlington, VA 22201-3385; 113,500.

**Arthritis Foundation** (1948), 1314 Spring St. NW, Atlanta, GA 30309; 500,000.

**Arts, Amer. Council for the** (1960), 1285 Avenue of the Americas, N.Y., NY 10019; 1,725.

**Arts, Amer. Federation of** (1909), 41 E. 65th St., N.Y., NY 10021.

**Arts and Letters, Natl. Society of** (1944), 655 15th St. NW, Washington, DC 20005; 1,600.

**Arts & Sciences, Amer. Academy of** (1780), Norton's Woods, 136 Irving St., Cambridge, MA 02138; 4,000.

**Association Executives, American Society of** (1920), 1575 Eye St. NW, Wash., DC 20005; 18,000.

**Association Publications, Society of Natl.** (1963), 3299 K St. NW, Suite 700, Wash., DC 20007; 210 publications.

**Astrologers, Amer. Federation of** (1938), 6535 S. Rural Rd., Tempe, AZ 85283; 4,500.

**Astronautical Society, Amer.** (1954), 6352 Rolling Mill Pl., Suite 102, Springfield, VA 22152; 1,550.

**Astronomical Society, Amer.** (1899), 2000 Florida Ave., NW, Suite 300, Wash., DC 20009; 5,700.

**Ataxia Foundation, Natl.** (1957), 600 Twelve Oaks Cntr., 15500 Wayzata Blvd., Wayzata MN 55391; 1,400.

**Atheists, Amer.** (1963), P.O. Box 140195, Austin, TX 78714.

**Athletic Assn., Natl. Jr. College** (1939), P.O. Box 7305, Colorado Springs, CO 80933-7305; 530.

**Athletic Associations, Natl. Federation of State H. S.** (1920), 11724 Plaza Circle, Box 20626, Kansas City, MO 64195.

**Athletic Union of the U.S., Amateur** (1888), 3400 W. 86th St., Indianapolis, IN 46268; 230,000+.

**Auctioneers Assn., Natl.** (1949), 8880 Ballentine, Overland Park, KS 66214; 5,487.

**Audubon Society, Natl.** (1905), 950 Third Ave., N.Y., NY 10022; 1 mln.

**Authors Guild, Inc., The** (1921), 330 W. 42nd St., New York, NY 10036; 14,000.

**Authors League of America** (1912), 234 W. 44th St., N.Y., NY 10036; 15,000.

**Autism Society of America,** (1965), 7910 Woodmont Ave., Ste. 650, Bethesda, MD 20814; 11,500.

**Autograph Collectors Club, Universal** (1965), P.O. Box 6181, Wash., DC 20044-6181; 2,447.

**Automobile Assn., Amer.** (1902), 1000 AAA Dr., Heathrow, FL 32746: 34 mln.

**Automobile Club, Natl.** (1924), One Market Plaza, San Francisco, CA 94105; 316,000.

**Automobile Club of America, Antique** (1935), 501 W. Governor Rd., Hershey, PA 17033; 53,000.

**Automobile Dealers Assn., Natl.** (1917), 8400 Westpark Dr., McLean, VA 22102; 19,000.

**Automobile License Plate Collectors' Assn.** (1954), P.O. Box 77, Horner, W. VA 26372; 2,750.

**Automotive Hall of Fame** (1939), 3225 Cook Rd., P. O. Box 1727, Midland, MI 48641-1727; 2,500

**Badminton Assn., U.S.** (1936), 920 O Street, Lincoln, NE 68508-3624.

**Baker Street Irregulars** (1934), 34 Pierson Ave., Norwood, NJ 07648; 275.

**Bald-Headed Men of America** (1973), 102 Bald Drive, Morehead City, N.C. 28557; 26,000.

**Ball Players of Amer., Assn. of Professional** (1924), 12062 Valley View St., #211, Garden Grove, CA 92645; 58,000.

**Band & Choral Directors Hall of Fame, Natl.** (1985), 519 N. Halifax Ave., Daytona Beach, FL 32118.

**Bankers Assn., Amer.** (1875), 1120 Connecticut Ave. NW, Wash., DC 20036.

**Bankers Assn. of America, Independent** (1930), One Thomas Circle NW, Suite 950, Wash. DC 20005; 6,400 banks.

**Bar Assn., Federal** (1920), 1815 H St. NW, Wash., DC 20006; 14,300.

**Barbershop Quartet Singing in Amer., Soc. for Preservation & Encouragement of** (1938), 6315 Third Ave., Kenosha, WI 53140-5199; 35,000.

**Baseball Congress, Amer. Amateur** (1935), 118-19 Redfield Plaza, Marshall, MI 49068; 10,625 teams.

**Baseball Congress, Natl.** (1931), P.O. Box 1420, Wichita, KS 67201.

**Baseball Research, Society for Amer.** (1971), P.O. Box 93183, Cleveland, OH 44101; 6,226.

**Basketball Assn., Natl.** (1946), 645 Fifth Ave., N.Y., NY 10022.

**Battleship Assn., Amer.** (1964), P.O. Box 711247, San Diego, CA 92171; 1,300.

**Beer Can Collectors of America** (1970), 747 Merus Ct., Fenton, MO 63026-2092; 4,100.

**Beta Gamma Sigma** (1913), 11701 Borman Dr., Ste. 320, St. Louis, MO 63146-4194; 295,000.

**Beta Sigma Phi** (1931), 1800 W. 91st Place, Kansas City, MO 64114; 250,000.

**Bible Society, Amer.** (1816), 1865 Broadway, N.Y., NY 10023; 188,500.

**Biblical Literature, Society of** (1880), 1549 Clairmont Rd., Ste. 204, Decatur, GA 30033-4635; 5,500.

**Bibliographical Society of America** (1904), P.O. Box 397, Grand Central Sta., N.Y., NY 10163; 1,257.

**Big Brothers/Big Sisters of America** (1902), 230 No. 13th St., Philadelphia, PA 19107; 494 agencies.

**Biochemistry and Molecular Biology, Amer. Society for** (1906), 9650 Rockville Pike, Bethesda, MD 20814-3996; 9,000.

**Biological Sciences, American Institute of** (1947), 730 11th St. NW, Washington, DC 20001-4521; 14,000.

**Bison Assn., Amer.** (1976), P.O. Box 16660, Denver, CO 80216.

**Black History Honors & Awards, Contemporary &** (1990), 6514 Georgia Road, Birmingham, AL 35212; 250.

**Blind, Amer. Council of the** (1961), 1155 15th St. NW, Washington, DC 20005; 40,000.

**Blind, Natl. Federation of** (1940), 1800 Johnson St., Baltimore, MD 21230; 30,000+.

**Blindness, Natl. Society to Prevent** (1908), 500 E. Remington Rd., Schaumburg, IL 60173; 26 affiliates.

**Blue Angels Assn.** (1982), 4600 Twin Oaks Dr., Apt. 702, Pensacola, FL 32506; 250.

**Blue Cross and Blue Shield Assn.** (1946), 676 St. Clair, Chicago, IL 60611; 74 plans.

**Blueberry Council, No. Amer.** (1965), P.O. Box 166, Marmora, NJ 08223.

**B'nai B'rith Intl.** (1853), 1640 Rhode Island Ave. NW, Wash., DC 20036; 500,000.

**Boat Club, Chris Craft Antique** (1973), 217 S. Adams St., Tallahassee, FL 32301; 2,000.

**Boat Owners Assn. of the U.S.** (1966), 880 S. Pickett St., Alexandria, VA 22304; 350,000.

**Bodybuilders Assn., Amer.** (1981), 6991 Simson St., Oakland, CA 94605-2226; 854.

**Bookplate Collectors and Designers, Amer. Soc. of** (1922), 605 N. Stoneman Ave. #F, Alhambra, CA 91801; 200.

**Booksellers Assn., Amer.** (1900), 122 E. 42d St., N.Y., NY 10168; 8,500+.

**Bottle Collectors, Federation of Historical** (1969), 4098 Faxon Ave., Memphis, TN 38122; 600.

**Bowling Congress, Amer.** (1895), 5301 S. 76th St., Greendale, WI 53129; 2.7 mln.

**Boys' Clubs of America** (1906), 771 First Ave., N.Y., NY 10017; 1.2 mln.

**Boy Scouts of America** (1910), 1325 Walnut Hill Lane, Irving, TX 75015-2079; 3.8 mln.

**Bridge, Tunnel and Turnpike Assn., Intl.** (1932), 2120 L St. NW, Suite 305, Wash., DC 20037; 250 organizations.

**Brith Sholom, Natl.** (1905), 3939 Conshohocken Ave., Philadelphia, PA 19131; 4,500.

**Broadcasters, Natl. Assn. of** (1922), 1771 N St. NW, Wash., DC 20036.

**Burroughs Bibliophiles, The** (1960), 454 Elaine Dr., Pittsburgh, PA 15236-2417; 462.

**Business Bureaus, Council of Better** (1970), 4200 Wilson Blvd., Arlington, VA 22203; 180 bureaus.

**Business Clubs, Natl. Assn. of Amer.** (1922), 3315 No. Main St., High Point, NC 27262; 6,727.

**Business Communicators, Intl. Assn. of** (1970), One Hallidie Pl., Suite 600, San Francisco, CA 94102.

**Business Education Assn., Natl.** (1946), 1906 Association Dr., Reston, VA 22091; 18,000.

**Button Society, Natl.** (1938), 2733 Juno Pl., Akron, OH 44313-4137; 3,560.

**Byron Society, The** (1971 England, 1973 in U.S.), 259 New Jersey Ave., Collingswood, NJ 08108; 300.

**CLU & CHFC, Amer. Soc. of** (1928), 270 S. Bryn Mawr Ave., Bryn Mawr, PA 19010; 32,000.

**CPCU, The Society of** (1944), 720 Providence Rd., Malvern, PA 19355-0709; 24,000.

**Camp Fire Boys & Girls** (1910), 4601 Madison Ave., Kansas City, MO 64112; 600,000.

**Campers & Hikers Assn., Inc.** (1954), 4804 Transit Rd., Bldg. 2, Depew, NY 14043; 21,000 families.

**Camping Assn., Amer.** (1910), 5000 State Rd. 67 N., Martinsville, IN 46131; 5,231.

**Cancer Society, Amer.** (1913), 90 Park Ave., N.Y., NY 10017.

**Carillonneurs in North America, Guild of** (1936), 3718 Settle Rd., Cincinnati, OH 45227; 507.

**Carnegie Hero Fund Commission** (1904), 2307 Oliver Bldg., Pittsburgh, PA 15222; 21 members.

**Cartoonists Society, Natl.** (1946), 157 W. 57th St., Suite 904, N.Y., NY 10019; 500.

**Cat Fanciers' Assn.** (1906), 1805 Atlantic Ave., Manasquan, NJ 08736-1005.

**Catholic Bishops, Natl. Conference of/U.S. Cath. Conference** (1966), 1312 Massachusetts Ave. NW, Wash., DC 20005.

**Catholic Church Extension Society of the U.S.A.** (1905), 35 E. Wacker Dr., #400, Chicago, IL 60601; 220,000.

**Catholic Daughters of the Americas** (1903), 10 W. 71st St., N.Y., NY 10023; 140,000.

**Catholic Educational Assn., Natl.** (1904), 1077-30th St. NW, Suite 100, Wash, DC 20007; 18,353.

**Catholic Historical Soc., Amer.** (1884), 263 S. Fourth St., P.O. Box 84, Philadelphia, PA 19106-3819; 900.

**Catholic Library Assn.** (1921), 461 W. Lancaster Ave., Haverford, PA 19041; 1,518.

**Catholic Rural Life Conference, Natl.** (1923), 4625 Beaver Ave., Des Moines, IA 50310-2199; 1,900.

**Catholic War Veterans of the U.S.A.** (1935), 419 North Lee Street, Alexandria, VA 22314; 30,000.

**Cemetery Assn., Amer.** (1889), 5201 Leesburg Pike, Falls Church, VA 22041; 1,600.

**Ceramic Society, Amer.** (1898), 735 Ceramic Pl., Westerville, OH 43081; 13,000.

**Cerebral Palsy Assns., United** (1949), 7 Penn Plaza, N.Y., NY 10001; 180 affiliates.

**Chamber Music Players, Amateur** (1948), 545 Eighth Ave., N.Y., NY 10018.

**Chamber of Commerce of the U.S.A.** (1912), 1615 H St. NW, Wash., DC 20062; 185,000.

**Chaplain's Intl. Assn.** (1960), Adjutant General Office, 5045 N. Robberson, Springfield, MO 65803; 963.

**Checker Federation, Amer.** (1948), 3475 Belmont Ave., Baton Rouge, LA 70808; 1,000.

**Chemical Manufacturers Assn.** (1872), 2501 M St. NW, Wash., DC 20037; 171 companies.

**Chemical Society, Amer.** (1876), 1155 16th St. NW, Wash., DC 20036; 135,000.

**Chemists, Amer. Assn. of Cereal** (1915), 3340 Pilot Knob Rd., St. Paul, MN 55121; 3,891.

**Chemists, Amer. Society of Brewing** (1934), 3340 Pilot Knob Rd., St. Paul MN 55121; 730.

**Chess Federation, U.S.** (1939), 186 Rt. 9W, New Windsor, NY 12553; 69,000.

Chess League of Amer., Correspondence (1897), P.O. Box 3481, Barrington, IL 60011-3481; 900.

Child Welfare League of America (1920), 440 First St. NW, Wash., DC 20001-2085; 670 agencies.

Childhood Education, Intl. Assn. for (1892), 11501 Georgia Ave., Suite 315, Wheaton, MD 20902; 11,000.

Children, Natl. Center for Missing and Exploited (1984), 2101 Wilson Blvd., Arlington, VA 22201.

Children of the Amer. Revolution, Natl. Society of the (1895), 1776 D St. NW, Wash., DC 20006.

Children's Aid Society (1853), 105 E. 22d St., N.Y., NY 10010; 1,207.

Children's Book Council (1945), 568 Broadway, Suite 404, N.Y., NY 10012; 65 publishing houses.

Chiropractic Assn., Amer. (1930), 1916 Wilson Blvd., Arlington, VA 22201; 20,000.

Christian Endeavor, Intl. (1881), 1221 E. Broad St., P.O. Box 1110, Columbus, OH 43216.

Christian Laity Counseling Board (1970), 5901 Plainfield Dr., Charlotte, NC 28215; 38 mln.

Christians and Jews, Natl. Conference of (1927), 71 Fifth Ave., Suite 1100 N.Y., NY 10003.

Church Federation, Ecumenical (1982), 13014-270 N. Dalemabry, Tampa, FL 33618-2808.

Churches, U.S. Conference for the World Council of (1948), 475 Riverside Dr., N.Y., NY 10115; 317 denominations.

Church Women United (1941), 475 Riverside Dr., Rm. 812, N.Y., NY 10115.

Cincinnati, Society of the (1783), 2118 Massachusetts Ave. NW, Wash., DC 20008; 3,300.

Circulation Managers Assn., Intl. (1889), 11600 Sunrise Valley Dr., Reston, VA 22091; 1,705.

Cities, Natl. League of (1924), 1301 Pennsylvania Ave. NW, Wash., DC 20004; 1,450 cities.

City/County Management Assn., Intl. (1914), 777 North Capitol St. NE, Ste. 500, Wash., DC 20002; 8,000.

Civil Air Patrol (1941), HQ CAP-USAF, Maxwell AFB, AL 36112-5572; 63,000.

Civil Engineers, Amer. Society of (1852), 345 E. 47th St., N.Y., NY 10017; 104,000.

Civil Liberties Union, Amer. (1920), 132 W. 43rd St., N.Y. NY 10036; 250,000.

Civic League, Natl. (1894), 55 West 44th St., N.Y., NY 10036; 3,000.

Civitan Internatl. (1920), One Civitan Pl., Birmingham, AL 35213-1983; 50,000.

Classical League, Amer. (1919), Hall, Miami Univ., Oxford, OH 45056; 3,604.

Clinical Pathologists, Amer. Society of (1922), 2100 W. Harrison St., Chicago, IL 60612; 58,757.

Coal Association, Natl. (1917), 1130 17th St. NW, Wash., DC 20036; 150 corporate members.

Coast Guard Combat Veterans Assn. (1985), 6858 Lafayette Rd., Medina, OH 44256; 1,366.

Co-Dependents Anonymous (1986), P.O. Box 33577, Phoenix, AZ 85067-3577.

College Board, The (1900), 45 Columbus Ave., N.Y., NY 10023; 2,900 institutions.

College Music Society (1958), 202 W. Spruce St., Missoula, MT 59802; 4,000.

College Placement Council (1956), 62 Highland Ave., Bethlehem, PA 18017; 2,966.

Colleges, Amer. Assn. of Community and Jr. (1921), One Dupont Circle NW, Suite 410, Wash., DC 20036.

Colleges, Assn. of Amer. (1915), 1818 R St. NW, Wash., DC 20009; 635 institutions.

Colleges and Universities, Assn. of Intl. (1973), I301 S. Noland Rd., Independence, MO 64055; 10,572.

Collegiate Athletic Assn., Natl. (1906), 6201 College Blvd., Overland Park, KS 66211-2422; 828 inst.

Collegiate Schools of Business, Amer. Assembly of (1916), 605 Old Ballas Rd., St. Louis, MO 63141-7077.

Colonial Dames XVII Century, Natl. Society (1915), 1300 New Hampshire Ave. NW, Wash., DC 20036-1595; 13,750.

Colonial Wars, General Society of (1892), 840 Woodbine Ave., Glendale, WA 45246; 4,300.

Commerce, U.S. Junior Chamber of (1920), 4 W. 21st St., Tulsa, OK 74114-1116; 225,000.

Commercial Collectors Assn., Amer. (1970), 4040 W. 70th St., Minneapolis, MN 55435; 3,225.

Commercial Law League of America (1895), 175 W. Jackson, #1541, Chicago, IL 60604; 5,100.

Commercial Travelers of America, Order of United (1888), 632 N. Park St., Columbus, OH 43215; 186,000.

Common Cause (1970), 2030 M St. NW, Wash., DC 20036.

Communication, Intl. Training In (1938), 2519 Woodland Dr., Anaheim, CA 92801; 18,000.

Communities, Federation of Egalitarian (1976), E. Wind, Rt. 3, Box 6B2, Tecumseh, MO 65760; 250+.

Community Cultural Center Assoc., Amer. (1978), 19 Foothills Dr., Pompton Plains, NJ 07444.

Composers/USA, Natl. Assn. of (1932), P.O. Box 49652, Barrington Sta., Los Angeles, CA 90049; 600.

Composers, Authors & Publishers, Amer. Society of (ASCAP) (1914), One Lincoln Plaza, N.Y., NY 10023; 24,000.

Computer Professionals, Inst. for Certification of (1973), 2200 E. Devon Ave., Ste. 268, Des Plaines, IL 60018-4503; 47,000.

Computing Machinery, Assn. for (1947), 1515 Broadway, N.Y., NY 10036; 55,000.

Concrete Institute, Amer. (1904), 22400 W. Seven Mile Rd., Detroit, MI 48219-1849.

Conscientious Objectors, Central Committee for (1948), 2208 South St., Phila., PA 19146.

Conservation Engineers, Assn. of (1961), Alabama Dept. of Conservation, 64 N. Union St., Montgomery, AL 36130; 225.

Constantian Society, The (1970), 123 Orr Rd., Pittsburgh, PA 15241; 550.

Construction Industry Manufacturers Assn. (1911), 111 E. Wisconsin Ave., Milwaukee, WI 53202; 150 companies.

Construction Specifications Institute (1948), 601 Madison St., Alexandria, VA 22314-1791; 19,200.

Consulting Organizations, Council of (1989), 521 5th Ave., N.Y., NY 10175.

Consumer Credit Assn., Intl. (1912), 243 N. Lindbergh, St. Louis, MO 63141; 20,000.

Consumer Federation of America (1968), 1424 16th St. NW, #604, Wash., DC 20036; 240 organizations.

Consumer interests, Amer. Council on (1953), 240 Stanley Hall, Univ. of Missouri, Columbia, MO 65211; 1,500.

Consumer Protection Institute (1970), 5901 Plainfield Dr., Charlotte, NC 28215.

Consumers Union of the U.S. (1936), 101 Truman Ave., Yonkers, NY 10703; 405,990.

Contract Bridge League, Amer. (1937), 2990 Airways Blvd., Memphis, TN 38116-3847; 200,000+.

Contract Management Assn., Natl. (1959), 6728 Old McLean Village Dr., McLean, VA 22101; 20,176.

Contractors of Amer., General (1919), 1957 E St. NW, Wash., DC 20006; 32,000.

Cooperative Business Assn., Natl. (1916), 1401 New York Ave. NW, #1100, Wash., DC 20005; 450.

Cooperative League of the U.S.A. (1916), 1401 New York Ave. NW, Suite 1100, Wash., DC 20005; 285 co-ops.

Correctional Assn., Amer. (1870), 8025 Laurel Lakes Court, Laurel, MD 20707; 20,000+.

Correctional Officers, Intl. Assn. of (1977), 8600 Glenarden Pky,Glenarden, MD 20706-1599.

Cosmetology Assn., Natl. (1921), 3510 Olive St., St. Louis, MO 63103; 47,000.

Cotton Council of America, Natl. (1938), 1918 North Parkway, Memphis, TN 38112; 297 delegates.

Counseling and Development, Amer. Assn. for (1952), 5999 Stevenson Ave., Alexandria, VA 22304; 58,065.

Country Music Assn. (1958), One Music Circle S., Nashville, TN 37203; 6,588.

Creative Children and Adults, Natl. Assn. for (1974), 8080 Springvalley Dr., Cincinnati, OH 45236-1395; 1,500.

Credit Assn., International (1912), 243 N. Lindberg, St. Louis, MO 63141; 10,000.

Credit Union Natl. Assn. (1934), 5710 Mineral Point Rd., Madison, WI 53705; 52 state credit union leagues.

Crime and Delinquency, Natl. Council on (1907), 685 Market St., Suite 620, San Francisco, CA 94105; 500.

Criminology, Amer. Society of (1941), 1314 Kinnear Rd., Ste. 212, Columbus, OH 43212.

Crop Science Society of America (1955), 677 S. Segoe Rd., Madison, WI 53711; 5,345.

Cryogenic Soc. of Amer. (1964), 1033 South Blvd., #13, Oak Park, IL 60302.

Customs Brokers & Forwarders Assn. of Am., Natl. (1897), One World Trade Center, Ste. 1153, N.Y., NY 10048.

Cystic Fibrosis Foundation (1955), 6931 Arlington Rd., Bethesda, MD 20814; 60,000.

Dairy Council, Natl. (1915), 6300 N. River Rd., Rosemont, IL 60018.

Dairy and Food Industries Supply Assn. (1917), 6245 Executive Blvd., Rockville, MD 20852; 800 companies.

Dairy Goat Assn., American (1904), 209 W. Main St., Spindale, NC 28160; 13,000.

Danish Brotherhood in America (1882), 3717 Harney St., Omaha, NE 68131; 8,600.

Daughters of the American Revolution, Natl. Society, (1890), 1776 D St. NW, Wash., DC 20006-5392; 200,000.

Daughters of the British Empire in the U.S.A. (1909), 14611 NE 50th Pl., F-4, Bellevue, WA 98007; 5,206.

Daughters of the Confederacy, United (1894), 328 N. Blvd., Richmond, VA 23220-4057; 24,000.

Daughters of the Republic of Texas (1891), 510 E. Anderson Ln., Austin, TX 78752; 6,400.

Daughters of Union Veterans of the Civil War (1885), 503 S. Walnut St., Springfield, IL 62704; 4,100+.

Deaf, Alexander Graham Bell Assn. for the (1890), 3417 Volta Pl. NW, Washington, DC 20007.

Deaf, Natl. Assn. of the (1880), 814 Thayer Ave., Silver Spring, MD 20910.

Death and Dying, Natl. Council on (1990), 250 W. 50th St., N.Y., NY 10019; 120,000.

Defense Preparedness Assn., Amer. (1919), 2101 Wilson Blvd., Ste. 400, Arlington, VA 22201-3061; 29,000.

Delta Kappa Gamma Society Intl. (1929), 416 W. 12th St., Austin, TX 78701; 165,000.

Deltiologists of America (1960), P.O. Box 8, Norwood, PA 19074; 800+.

Democratic Natl. Committee, (1792), 430 S. Capitol St. SE, Wash., DC 20003.

DeMolay, Intl. Supreme Council, Order of (1919), 10200 N. Executive Hills Blvd., Kansas City, MO 64153-1367; 30,000.

Dental Assn., Amer. (1859), 211 E. Chicago Ave., Chicago, IL 60611; 148,542.

Descendants of the Colonial Clergy, Society of the (1933), 30 Leewood Rd., Wellesley, MA 02181; 1,400.

Descendants of the Signers of the Declaration of Independence (1907), 9th & Chestnut Sts., Phila., PA 19105; 873.

Descendants of Washington's Army at Valley Forge, Society of (1976), P.O. Box 915, Valley Forge, PA 19482-0915.

Desert Protective Council (1954), P.O. Box 2312, Valley Center, CA 92082; 305.

Diabetes Assn., Amer. (1940), 1660 Duke St., Alexandria, VA 22314; 259,000.

Dialect Society, Amer. (1889), c/o Allan Metcalf, English Dept., MacMurray College, Jacksonville, IL 62650; 600.

Direct Marketing Assn. (1917), 6 E. 43d St., N.Y., NY 10017.

Directors Guild of America (1936), 7920 Sunset Blvd., Los Angeles, CA 90046; 9,700.

Disabled Amer. Veterans (1923), 3725 Alexandria Pike, Cold Spring, KY 41076; 1.2 mln.

Disabled Collectors' Correspondence Club (1991), 457 Washington Blvd., Fremont, CA 94539.

Dogs Intl., Therapy (1980), 260 Fox Chase Rd., Chester, NJ 07930; 2,500+.

Dogs on Stamp Study Unit (1979), 3208 Hana Rd., Edison, NJ 08817-2552; 400.

Dozenal Society of America (1944), Math Dept., Nassau Community College, Garden City, NY 11530; 144.

Dracula Society, Count (1962), 334 W. 54th St., Los Angeles, CA 90037; 500.

Drug, Chemical and Allied Trades Assn. (1890), 2 Roosevelt Ave., Syosset, NY 11791; 2,018.

Ducks Unlimited (1937), One Waterfowl Way, Memphis, TN 38120; 500,000+.

Dutch Settlers Soc. of Albany (1924), RD#2 Box 313, Altamont, NY 12009-9531; 250.

Eagles, Fraternal Order of (1898), 12660 West Capitol Dr., Brookfield, WI 53055; 1.1 mln.

Easter Seal Society, Natl. (1919), 70 E. Lake St., Chicago, IL 60601.

Eastern Star, General Grand Chapter, Order of the (1876), 1618 New Hampshire Ave. NW, Wash., DC 20009; 1.7 mln.

Economic Assn., Amer. (1885), 2014 Broadway, Ste. 305, Nashville, TN 37203; 27,316.

Edsel Club, Intl. (1969), P.O. Box 371, Sully, IA 50251; 1,011.

Education, Amer. Council on (1918), One Dupont Circle NW, #800, Wash., DC 20036; 1,600 institutions.

Education, Amer. Soc. for Engineering (1893), 11 Dupont Circle NW, Suite 200, Washington, DC 20036; 10,000+.

Education, Council for Advancement & Support of (1974), 11 Dupont Circle NW, Wash., DC 20036; 2,950 schools.

Education, Council for Basic (1956), 725 15th St. NW, Wash., DC 20005; 10,000.

Education, Institute of Intl. (1919), 809 United Nations Plaza, N.Y., NY 10017; 700 U.S. colleges, univ.

Education, Natl. Assn. for Family and Community (1936), 5963 Jefferson St., Burlington, KY 41005-9596; 341,651.

Education Assn., Natl. (1857), 1201 16th St. NW, Wash., DC 20036; 2 mln.

Education of Young Children, Natl. Assn. for the (1926), 1509 16th St. NW, Washington, DC 20036; 82,000.

Educational Exchange, Council on Intl. (1947), 205 E. 42d St., N.Y., NY 10017; 240 organizations.

Educational Research Assn., Amer. (1916), 1230 17th St. NW, Wash., DC 20036; 17,000.

8th Air Force Historical Society (1975), P.O. Box 7215, St. Paul, MN 55107; 17,000.

82nd Airborne Division Assn., Inc. (1944), NFCS, P.O. Box 9308, Fayetteville, NC 28311-7694; 22,000.

88th Infantry Division Assn., Inc. (1948), P.O. Box 925, Havertown, PA 19083; 5,152.

Electrical and Electronics Engineers, Institute of (1884), 345 E. 47th St., N.Y., NY 10017; 300,000.

Electrical Manufacturers Assn., Natl. (1926), 2101 L St. NW, Wash., DC 20037; 560 companies.

Electrochemical Society (1902), 10 S. Main St., Pennington, NJ 08534-2896; 6,300.

Electronic Circuits, The Institute for Interconnecting & Packaging (1957), 7380 N. Lincoln, Lincolnwood, IL 60646-1705; 1900 cos.

Electronic Industries Assn. (1924), 2001 Pennsylvania Ave., Wash., DC 20006-1813; 1,058 companies.

Electronics Technicians, Intl. Society of Certified (1970), 2708 W. Berry, Ft. Worth, TX 76109; 2,000.

Electroplaters' and Surface Finishers' Society, Amer. (1909), 12644 Research Pkwy, Orlando, FL 32826; 8,500.

Elks of the U.S.A., Benevolent and Protective Order of (1868), 2750 N. Lakeview Ave., Chicago, IL 60614; 1.5 mln.

Elvis Burning Love Fan Club (1983). 1904 Williamsburg Dr., Streamwood, IL 60107.

Elvis Presley Fan Club of Ceylon (1964), 113/1, Pirivena Rd., Mt. Lavania, Sri Lanka; 2,000.

Energy Research Institute, Clean (1974), 1251 Memorial Dr., 219 MacArthur Engineering Bldg., Coral Gables, FL, 33146.

Engineering, Natl. Academy of (1964), 2101 Constitution Ave. NW, Wash., DC 20418; 1,700.

Engineering, Soc. for the Advancement of Material & Process (1944), P.O. Box 2459, Covina, CA 91722; 10,000.

Engineering Society of N. America, Illuminating (1906), 345 E. 47th St., N.Y., NY 10017; 10,000.

Engineers, Amer. Inst. of Chemical (1908), 345 E. 47th St., N.Y., N.Y. 10017; 53,622.

Engineers, Amer. Institute of Mining, Metallurgical and Petroleum (1871), 345 E. 47th St., N.Y., NY 10017.

Engineers, Amer. Soc. of Agricultural (1907), 2950 Niles Rd., St. Joseph, MI 49085-9659; 8,000.

Engineers, Amer. Soc. of Civil (1852), 345 E. 47th St., N.Y., NY 10017; 111,112.

Engineers, American Soc. of Mechanical (1881), 345 E. 47th St., N.Y., NY 10017; 120,000.

Engineers, Amer. Soc. of Naval (1888), 1452 Duke St., Alexandria, VA 22314; 7,500.

Engineers, Amer. Soc. of Safety (1911), 1800 E. Oakton St., Des Plains, IL 60018-2187; 28,000.

Engineers, Assn. of Energy (1977), 4025 Pleasantdale Rd., Suite 420, Atlanta, GA 30340; 8,500.

Engineers, Inst. of Industrial (1948), 25 Technology Park, Atlanta, GA 30092; 43,000.

Engineers, Inst. of Transportation (1930), Suite 410, 525 School St. NW, Wash., DC 20024, 7,700.

Engineers, Natl. Society of Professional (1934), 1420 King St., Alexandria, VA 22314; 75,000.

Engineers, Soc. of Fire Protection (1950), One Liberty Sq., Boston, MA 02109; 4,026.

Engineers, Soc. of Logistics (1966), 8100 Professional Pl., Ste. 211, New Carrollton, MD 20785; 8,500.

Engineers, Soc. of Manufacturing (1932), One SME Drive, P.O. Box 930, Dearborn, MI 48121; 80,000.

Engineers, Society of Mining (1871), 8307 Shaffer Pkwy., Littleton, CO 80127; 23,058.

Engineers, Society of Plastics (1942), 14 Fairfield Dr., Brookfield Ctr., CT 06805; 25,000.

English, U.S. (1983), 818 Connecticut Ave. NW, Ste. 200, Washington, DC 20006; 250,000.

English Assn., College (1939), English Dept., Nazareth College of Rochester, Rochester, NY 14618; 1,250.

Entomological Society of America (1897), 9301 Annapolis Rd., Lanham, MD 20706-3115; 8,665.

Environmental Health Assn., Natl. (1937), 720 S. Colorado Blvd., Suite 970, Denver, CO 80222; 5,000.

Environmental Information Assn. (1983), 1777 NE Expressway, Ste. 150, Atlanta, GA 30329; 3,000.

Epigraphic Society, Inc., The (1974), 6625 Bamburgh Dr., San Diego, CA 92117; 800.

Esperanto League for North America (1952), P.O. Box 1129, El Cerrito, CA 94530; 1,000.

Evangelism Crusades, Intl. (1959), 14617 Victory Blvd., Van Nuys, CA 91411; 1,500.

Exchange Club, Natl. (1911), 3050 Central Ave., Toledo, OH 43606-1700.

Fairs & Expositions, Intl. Assn. of (1919), P.O. Box 985, Springfield, MO 65801; 2,400.

Family Relations, Natl. Council on (1938), 3989 Central Ave. NE, Suite 550, Minneapolis, MN 55421; 3,800.

**Family Service America** (1911), 11700 W. Lake Park Dr., Park Pl, Milwaukee, WI 53224; 300 agencies.

**Farm Bureau Federation, Amer.** (1919), 225 Touhy Ave., Park Ridge, IL 60068; 4 mln.

**Farmers Union, Natl.** (1902), Denver, CO 80251; 250,000.

**Farmers' Educational and Co-Operative Union of America** (1902), 10065 E. Harvard Ave., Denver, CO 80231; 250,000.

**Fat Acceptance, Natl. Assn. to Advance (NAAFA)** (1969), P.O. Box 188620, Sacramento, CA 95818; 3,500.

**Federal Employees, Natl. Assn. of Retired** (1921), 1533 New Hampshire Ave. NW, Washington, DC 20036-1279.

**Federal Employees, Natl. Fed. of** (1917), 1016 16th St. NW, Wash., DC 20036.

**Feminists for Life of America** (1972), 811 E. 47th St., Kansas City, MO 64110; 5,000.

**Financial Analysts Federation** (1945), #5 Boar's Head Lane, Charlottesville, VA 22903; 22,700.

**Financial Executives Institute** (1931), 10 Madison Ave., P.O. Box 1938, Morristown, NJ 07962-1938; 14,000.

**Financiers, Intl. Soc. of** (1979), P.O. Box 18508, Asheville, NC 28814; 275.

**Fire Chiefs, Intl. Assn. of** (1873), 4025 Fair Ridge Dr., Fairfax, VA 22033-2868.

**Fire Protection Assn., Natl.** (1896), Batterymarch Park, Quincy MA 02269; 38,000.

**First Amendment Studies, Institute for** (1984), P.O. Box 589, Great Barrington, MA 01230; 27,000.

**Fish Assn., Intl. Game** (1939), 1301 E. Atlantic Blvd., Pompano Beach, FL 33060; 20,000.

**Fisheries Soc., American** (1870), 5410 Grosvenor Lane, Ste. 110, Bethesda, MD 20814; 8,500.

**Fishes, Soc. for the Protection of Old** (1967), School of Fisheries, WH-10 Univ. of Washington, Seattle, WA 98195; 275.

**Fishing Tackle Manufacturers Assn., Amer.** (1933), 1250 Grove Ave., Barrington, IL 60010; 500 cos.

**Flag Research Center, The** (1962), Box 580, Winchester, MA 01890; 1,300.

**Flight Attendants, Assn. of** (1973), 1625 Massachusetts Ave. NW, Wash., DC 20036; 28,000.

**Fly Fishers, Fed. of** (1965), Box 1088, 200 Yellowstone Ave., W. Yellowstone, MT 59758; 10,000.

**Flying Disc Fed., World** (1985), Gnejsvägen 24, 85240; Sundsvall, Sweden; 15,000.

**Food Brokers Assn., Natl.** (1904), 1010 Massachusetts Ave. NW, Wash., DC 20001; 1,800 companies.

**Food Institute, Amer. Frozen** (1942), 1764 Old Meadow Ln., Suite 350, McLean, VA 22102; 550 firms.

**Footwear Industries Assn., Amer.** (1871), 3700 Market St., Philadelphia, PA 19104; 180.

**Foreign Student Affairs, Natl. Assn. for** (1948), 1860 19th St. NW, Wash., DC 20009; 5,500.

**Foreign Study, Amer. Institute for** (1964), 102 Greenwich Ave., Greenwich, CT 06830; 300,000.

**Foreign Trade Council, Inc., Natl.** (1914), 1625 K St. NW, Washington, DC 20006; 500 companies.

**Forensic Sciences, Amer. Academy of** (1948), 410 N. 21st St., Ste. 203, Colorado Springs, CO 80904; 3,435.

**Forest & Paper Assn., Amer.** (1993), 1250 Connecticut Ave. NW, 2nd Floor, Washington, DC 20036.

**Forest Council** (1932), 1250 Connecticut Ave. NW, Suite 320, Washington, DC 20036.

**Forest History Society** (1946), 701 Vickers Ave., Durham, NC 27701; 2,000.

**Forest Products Research Society** (1947), 2801 Marshall Ct., Madison, WI 53705; 3,000.

**Foresters, Society of Amer.** (1900), 5400 Grosvenor La., Bethesda, MD 20814; 18,324.

**Forestry Assn., Amer.** (1875), 1516 P St. NW, Wash., DC 20005; 112,000.

**Forests, Amer.** (1875), 1516 P St. NW, Wash., DC 20005; 115,000.

**Fortean Organization, Intl.** (1966), P.O. Box 367, Arlington, VA 22210-0367; 850.

**Founders and Patriots of Amer., The Order of the** (1896), 3813 Acapulco Ct., Irving, TX 75062; 1,250.

**Foundrymen's Society, Amer.** (1896), 505 State St., Des Plaines, IL 60016-8399; 13,389.

**4-H Clubs** (1901-1905), Extension Service, U.S. Dept of Agriculture, Wash., DC 20250; 5.8 mln.

**Frederick A. Cook Soc., The** (1957), Sullivan County Historical Museum, P.O. Box 247, Hurleyville, NY 12747-0247; 200.

**Freedom of Information Center** (1958), 20 Walter Williams Hall, Univ. of Missouri, Columbia, MO 65211.

**Freedoms Foundation at Valley Forge** (1949), Valley Forge, PA 19481; 4,800.

**French Institute/Alliance Francaise** (1971), 22 E. 60th St., N.Y., NY 10022-1077; 8,500.

**Friendship and Good Will, Intl. Soc. of** (1978), 211 W. 4th Ave., P.O. Box 2637, Gastonia, NC 28053-2637; 4,239.

**Funeral and Memorial Societies, Continental Assn. of** (1963), 2001 S. St. NW, Suite 530, Washington, DC 20009.

**Future Farmers of Amer. Org., Natl.** (1928), 5632 Mt. Vernon Memorial Hwy., Alexandria, VA 22309-0160; 401,574.

**Gamblers Anonymous** (1957), P.O. Box 17173, Los Angeles, CA 90017.

**Garden Club of Amer.** (1913), 598 Madison Ave., N.Y., NY 10022; 15,000.

**Garden Clubs, Natl. Council of State** (1929), 4401 Magnolia Ave., St. Louis, MO 63110; 308,623.

**Garden Clubs of America, Men's** (1932), 5560 Merle Hay Rd., Johnston, IA 50131; 9,500.

**Gas Appliance Manufacturers Assn.** (1935), 1901 N. Moore St., Arlington, VA 22209; 210 companies.

**Gas Assn., Amer.** (1918), 1515 Wilson Blvd., Arlington, VA 22209; 229 companies; 3,000 individuals.

**Gay and Lesbian Task Force, Natl.** (1973), 1734 14th St. NW, Washington, DC 20009; 20,000.

**Genealogical Society, Natl.** (1903), 4527 17th St. N., Arlington, VA 22207; 12,000.

**Genetic Assn., Amer.** (1903), P.O. Box 39, Buckeystown, MD 21717; 800.

**Geographers, Assn. of Amer.** (1904), 1710 16th St. NW, Wash., DC 20009-3198; 6,600.

**Geographic Education, Natl. Council for** (1915), 16A Leonard Hall, IUPA, Indiana, PA 15705; 3,700.

**Geographic Society, Natl.** (1888), 1145 17th St. NW, Wash., DC 20036; 9.7 mln.

**Geographical Society, Amer.** (1851), 156 Fifth Ave., Suite 600, N.Y., NY 10010-7002; 1,900.

**Geological Society of America** (1888), 3300 Penrose Pl., P.O. Box 9140, Boulder, CO 80301; 17,000.

**Geologists, Amer. Assn. of Petroleum** (1917), 1444 So. Boulder, Tulsa, OK 74119; 33,050.

**Geophysicists, Society of Exploration** (1930), P.O. Box 702740, Tulsa, OK 74170; 14,500.

**Geriatrics Society, Amer.** (1942), 770 Lexington Ave., Suite 300, N.Y., NY 10021; 6,686.

**Gideons Intl.** (1899), 2900 Lebanon Rd., Nashville, TN 37214; 104,000.

**Gifted Children, Natl. Assn. for** (1957), 1155 15th St. NW, Ste. 1002, Wash., DC 20005; 6,500.

**Girls Clubs of America** (1945), 30 E. 33d St., N.Y., NY 10016; 250,000+.

**Girl Scouts of the U.S.A.** (1912), 830 Third Ave., N.Y., NY 10022; 3.2 mln.

**Glenn Miller Birthplace Soc.** (1976), P.O. Box 61, Clarinda, IA 51632; 1,200.

**Gold Star Mothers, Amer.** (1928), 2128 Leroy Pl. NW, Wash., DC 20008; 3,000.

**Golf Association, U.S.** (1894), Box 708, Far Hills, NJ 07931.

**Gospel Music Assn.** (1964), 7 Music Circle N., Nashville, TN 37203; 2,900.

**Government Finance Officers Assn.** (1906), 180 N. Michigan Ave., Suite 800, Chicago, IL 60601; 12,500.

**Graduate Schools in the U.S., Council of** (1961), One Dupont Circle NW, Wash., DC 20036; 402 institutions.

**Grandmothers Clubs of America, Natl. Federation of** (1934), 203 N. Wabash Ave., Chicago, IL 60601; 10,000.

**Grange, Natl.** (1867), 1616 H St. NW, Wash., DC 20006.

**Graphic Arts, Amer. Institute of** (1914), 1059 Third Ave., N.Y., NY 10021; 6,000.

**Gray Panthers** (1970), 1424 16th St. NW, Suite 602, Wash., DC 20036; 45,000.

**Green Mountain Club, The** (1910), RR1, Box 650, Waterbury Ctr., VT 05677; 5,200.

**Grocers, Natl. Assn. of** (1893), 1825 Samuel Morse Dr., Reston, VA 22090.

**Grocery Manufacturers of America** (1908), 1010 Wisconsin Ave., Suite 800, Wash., DC 20007; 140 companies.

**Guide Dog Foundation for the Blind** (1946), 371 E. Jericho Tpke., Smithtown, NY 11787-2976.

**Gyro Intl.** (1912), 1096 Mentor Ave., Painesville, OH 44077.

**HIAS (Hebrew Immigrant Aid Society)** (1880), 333 7th Ave., 17th Floor, N.Y., NY 10001-5004.

**Hadassah, the Women's Zionist Organization of America** (1912), 50 W. 58th St., N.Y., NY 10019; 385,000.

**Hairdressers and Cosmetologists Assn., Natl.** (1921), 3510 Olive St., St. Louis, MO 63103; 50,406.

**Handball Assn., U.S.** (1951), 930 N. Benton Ave., Tucson, AZ 85711; 8,300.

**Handicapped, Federation of the** (1935), 211 W. 14th St., N.Y., NY 10011; 650.

**Handicapped, Natl. Assn. of the Physically** (1958), Bethesda Scarlet Oaks, #117, 440 Lafayette Ave., Cincinnati, OH 45220-1000; 700.

**Handicapped Sports, Natl.** (1967), 451 Hungerford Dr., Ste. 100, Rockville, MD 20850; 20,000.

**Health Council, Natl.** (1920), 1730 M St. NW, Ste. 500, Washington, DC 20036.

**Health Info. Management Assoc., American** (1928), 919 N. Michigan Ave., #1400, Chicago, IL 60611-1683; 34,000.

**Health, Physical Education, Recreation and Dance, Amer. Alliance for** (1885), 1900 Association Dr., Reston, VA 22091.

**Health Professions, Assn. of Schools of Allied** (1967), 1101 Connecticut Ave. NW, Ste. 700, Wash., DC 20036-4387.

**Hearing Society, Intl.** (1951), 20361 Middlebelt Rd., Livonia, MI 48152; 2,800.

**Hearing and Speech Action, Natl. Assn. for** (1910), 10801 Rockville Pike, Rockville, MD 20852.

**Heart Assn., Amer.** (1924), 7320 Greenville Ave., Dallas TX 75231; 200,000.

**Hearts, Mended** (1951), 7320 Greenville Ave., Dallas TX 75231; 20,000.

**Heating, Refrigerating & Air Conditioning Engineers, Amer. Soc. of** (1894), 1791 Tullie Circle NE, Atlanta, GA 30329.

**Helicopter Assn. Intl.** (1948), 1619 Duke St., Alexandria, VA 22314; 1,800.

**Helicopter Society, Amer.** (1943), 217 N. Washington St., Alexandria VA 22314; 6,500.

**Hemispheric Affairs, Council on** (1975), 724 9th St. NW, Wash., DC 20001; 2,800.

**Highpointers Club** (1987), Box 327, Mtn. Home, AR 72653; 691.

**High School Assns., Natl. Federation of State** (1920), P.O. Box 20626, Kansas City, MO 64195.

**High Twelve Internatl.** (1921), 11155-B2 South Towne Square, St. Louis, MO 63123-7823; 24,000.

**Hiking Society, Amer.** (1977), P.O. Box 20160, Wash., DC 20041-2160; 4,500.

**Historians, Organization of Amer.** (1907), 112 N. Bryan St., Bloomington, IN 47408; 12,000.

**Historical Assn., Amer.** (1884), 400 A St. SE, Wash., DC 20003; 15,200.

**Historic Preservation, Natl. Trust for** (1949), 1785 Massachusetts Ave. NW, Wash., DC 20036; 250,000.

**Hockey, U.S.A.** (1937), 2997 Broadmoor Valley Rd., Colorado Springs, CO 80906; 250,000.

**Home Builders, Natl. Assn. of** (1942), 1201 15th St. NW, Wash., DC 20005; 157,000.

**Home Economics Assn., Amer.** (1909), 1555 King St., Alexandria, VA 22314; 20,000.

**Homemakers of America, Future** (1945), 1910 Association Dr., Reston, VA 22091; 281,000+.

**Honor Society, Natl.** (1921), 1904 Association Dr., Reston, VA 22091; 22,000.

**Horatio Alger Soc.** (1961), 4907 Allison Dr., Lansing, MI 48910; 300.

**Horse Council, American** (1969), 1700 K St. NW, #300, Washington, DC 20006; 2,500.

**Horse Protection Assn., Amer.** (1966), 1000 29th St. NW, Suite T-100, Wash., DC 20007; 5,000.

**Horse Shows Assn., Amer.** (1917), 220 E. 42 St., N.Y., NY 10017-5806; 56,500+.

**Hospital Association, Amer.** (1899), 840 N. Lake Shore Dr., Chicago, IL 60611; 40,000.

**Hospital Marketing and Public Relations, Amer. Society for** (1964), 840 N. Lake Shore Dr., Chicago, IL 60611; 3,167.

**Hot Rod Assn., Natl.** (1951), 2035 Financial Way, Glendora, CA 91740; 74,524.

**Hotel & Motel Assn., Amer.** (1910), 1201 New York Ave., NW, Washington, DC 20005-3917.

**Humanism, Council for Democratic and Secular** (1980), Box 664, Buffalo, NY 14228; 20,000.

**Human Resource Management, Society for** (1948), 606 N. Washington St., Alexandria, VA 22314; 45,000.

**Humane Society of the U.S.** (1954), 2100 L St. NW, Wash., DC 20037; 650,000.

**Hydrogen Energy, Intl. Assn. for** (1975), P.O. Box 248266, Coral Gables, FL 33124; 2,500.

**Hygiene Assn., Amer. Industrial** (1939), P.O. Box 8390, 345 White Pond Dr., Akron, OH 44320.

**Idaho, U.S.S. (BB-42) Assn.** (1957), P.O. Box 711247, San Diego, CA 92171; 925.

**Identification, Intl. Assn. for** (1916), P.O. Box 2423, Alameda, CA 94501; 3,300.

**Illustrators, Society of** (1901), 128 E. 63 St., N.Y., NY 10021; 901.

**Impotence Inst. of Amer.** (1983), 2020 Pennsylvania Ave. NW, Ste. 292, Washington, DC 20006.

**Industrial Designers Society of America** (1965), 1142-E Walker Rd., Great Falls, VA 22066; 2,200.

**Industrial Engineers, Amer. Institute of** (1948), 25 Technology Park, Norcross, GA 30092; 40,000.

**Industrial Health Foundation** (1935), 34 Penn Circle West, Pittsburgh, PA 15206; 170 companies.

**Industrial Security, Amer. Soc. for** (1955), 1655 N. Ft. Myer Dr., Suite 1200, Arlington, VA 22209; 25,000.

**Information and Image Management, Assn. for** (1943), 1100 Wayne Ave., Ste. 1100, Silver Springs, MD 20910; 10,000.

**Information Industry Assn.** (1968), 555 New Jersey Ave. NW, Suite 800, Wash., DC 20001; 500 companies.

**Inner Network, The** (1991), 300 Darby Hill Rd., RD #1, Delanson, NY 12053; 450.

**Insurance Assn., Amer.** (1964), 1130 Connecticut Ave. NW, Suite 1000, Wash., DC 20036; 250+ companies.

**Insurance Society, Inc., Intl.** (1957), Box 870223, Tuscaloosa, AL 35487-0223; 1,200.

**Intellectual Property Owners** (1972), 1255 23rd St. NW, Washington, DC 20037; 300.

**Intelligence Officers, Assn. of Former** (1975), 6723 Whittier Ave., Suite 303A, McLean, VA 22101; 3,300.

**Intercollegiate Athletics, Natl. Assn. of** (1940), 1221 Baltimore Ave., Kansas City, MO 64105; 412 schools.

**Interior Designers, Amer. Society of** (1931), 608 Mass. Ave. NE, Washington, DC 20002; 33,000.

**International Interculture Programs, AFS** (1947), 313 E. 43rd St., N.Y., NY 10017; 100,000.

**Inventors, Amer. Assn. of** (1891), 2020 Pennsylvania Ave. NW, Wash., DC 20006; 5,727.

**Investment Clubs, Natl. Assn. of** (1951), 1515 E. Eleven Mile Rd., Royal Oak, MI 44067; 140,000.

**Investors Corp., Natl. Assn. of** (1951), 1515 E. Eleven Mile Rd., Royal Oak, MI 48067; 181,161.

**Irish-American Cultural Inst.** (1962), 2115 Summit Ave., #5026, Univ. of St. Thomas, St. Paul, MN 55105; 5,000.

**Iron Castings Society** (1897), 455 State St., Des Plaines, IL 60016; 200 firms.

**Iron and Steel Engineers, Assn. of** (1907), Three Gateway Center, Suite 2350, Pittsburgh, PA 15222; 10,000.

**Iron and Steel Institute, Amer.** (1855), 1101 17th St. NW, Ste. 1300, Wash., DC 20036; 1,100.

**Italian Historical Society of America** (1949), 111 Columbia Heights, Bklyn., NY 11201.

**Izaak Walton League of America, The** (1922), 1401 Wilson Blvd., Level B, Arlington, VA 22209; 54,000.

**Jamestowne Society** (1936), P.O. Box 14523, Richmond, VA 23221; 3,000.

**Jane Austen Society of N. Amer.** (1979), 207 Pinecroft Dr., Raleigh, NC 27609; 2,800.

**Japanese Amer. Citizens League** (1929), 1765 Sutter St., San Francisco, CA 94115; 24,000.

**Jewish Book Council** (1943), 15 E. 26th St., N.Y., NY 10010.

**Jewish Committee, Amer.** (1906), 165 E. 56th St., N.Y., NY 10022; 50,000.

**Jewish Community Centers Assn.** (1917), 15 E. 26th St., N.Y., NY 10010.

**Jewish Congress, Amer.** (1918), 15 E. 84th St., N.Y., NY 10028; 50,000.

**Jewish Federations, Council of** (1932), 730 Broadway, N.Y., NY 10003; 200 agencies.

**Jewish Historical Society, Amer.** (1892), 2 Thornton Rd., Waltham, MA 02154; 1,500.

**Jewish War Veterans of the U.S.A.** (1896), 1811 R St. NW, Wash., DC 20009; 150,000.

**Jewish Women, Natl. Council of** (1893), 53 W. 23rd St., N.Y., NY 10010; 100,000.

**Job's Daughters, Internatl. Order of** (1920), 233 W. 6th St., Papillion, NE 68046; 24,000.

**Jockey Club** (1894), 380 Madison Ave., N.Y., NY 10017; 90.

**John Birch Society** (1958), P.O. Box 8040, Appleton, WI 54913.

**Joseph Diseases Foundation, Intl.** (1977), P.O. Box 2550, Livermore, CA 94550; 800.

**Journalists, Society of Professional** (1909), P.O. Box 77, Greencastle, IN 46135; 16,000.

**Journalists and Authors, Amer. Society of** (1948), 1501 Broadway, Suite 1907, N.Y., NY 10036; 850.

**Judaism, Amer. Council for** (1943), P.O. Box 9009, Alexandria, VA 22304.

**Judicature Society, Amer.** (1913), 25 E. Washington, Chicago, IL 60602; 20,000.

**Juggler's Assn., Intl.** (1947), P.O. Box 218, Montague, MA 01351; 3,300.

**Junior Achievement** (1919), 550 Summer St., Stamford, CT 06901; 300,000.

**Junior Auxiliaries, Natl. Assn. of** (1941), 845 S. Main, Greenville, MS 38701; 10,500.

**Junior Leagues, Assn. of** (1921), 660 First Ave., N.Y., NY 10016; 190,000.

**Kennel Club, Amer.** (1884), 51 Madison Ave., N.Y., NY 10010; 500+ clubs.

**Kidney Fund, Amer.** (1971), 6110 Executive Blvd., #1010, Rockville, MD 20852.

**Kiwanis Intl.** (1915), 3636 Woodview Trace, Indianapolis, IN 46268-3196; 329,000.

**Knights of Columbus** (1882), One Columbus Plaza, New Haven, CT 06507; 1.4 mln.

**Knights of Pythias** (1864), 2785 E. Desert Inn Rd., #150, Las Vegas, NV 89121; 96,000.

**Knights Templar U.S.A., Grand Encampment** (1816), 5097 N. Elston, Ste. 101, Chicago, IL 60630.

**Krishna Consciousness, Intl. Soc. for (ISKON)** (1966) 3764 Watseka Ave., Los Angeles, CA 92109; 1 mln.

**LCI National Assn., U.S.S.** (1991), 134 Lancaster Ave., Columbia, PA 17512; 1,500.

**La Leche League Intl.** (1956), 9616 Minneapolis Ave., P.O. Box 1209, Franklin Park, IL 60131; 48,000.

**Lambs, The** (1874), 3 W. 51st St., N.Y., NY 10019; 202.

**Landscape Architects, Amer. Society of** (1899), 4401 Connecticut Ave., NW, Wash., DC 20008-2302; 10,000.

**Law, Amer. Society of International** (1906), 2223 Massachusetts Ave. NW, Washington, DC 20008; 4,300.

**Law Enforcement Officers Assn., Amer.** (1966), 1000 Connecticut Ave. NW, Suite 9, Wash., DC 20036; 50,000.

**Law Libraries, Amer. Assn. of** (1906), 53 W. Jackson Blvd., Chicago, IL 60604; 4,630.

**Learned Societies, Amer. Council of** (1919), 228 E. 45th St., N.Y., NY 10017; 45 societies.

**Lefthanders Intl.** (1975), P.O. Box 8249, Topeka, KS 66608.

**Legal Administrators, Assn. of** (1971), 175 E. Hawthorn Pkwy. #325, Vernon Hills, IL 60061-1428; 8,000.

**Legion of Valor of the U.S.A.** (1890), 92 Oak Leaf Lane, Chapel Hill, NC 27516; 780.

**Leif Ericson Society** (1962), Box 301, Chicago, IL 60690-0301; 1,250.

**Leprosy Missions, Amer.** (1906), One Alm Way, Greenville, SC 29601.

**Leukemia Society of America** (1949), 733 Third Ave., N.Y., NY 10017; 57 chapters.

**Lewis and Clark Trail Heritage Foundation, Inc.** (1969), P.O. Box 3434, Great Falls, MT 59403; 1,493.

**Lewis Carroll Society of N. America** (1974), 617 Rockford Rd., Silver Spring, MD 20902; 400.

**Libertarian Natl. Committee** (1971), 1528 Pennsylvania Ave. SE, Washington, DC 20003-3116.

**Liberty Lobby** (1955), 300 Independence Ave. SE, Wash., DC 20003; 16,000.

**Libraries Assn., Special** (1909), 1700 18th St., NW, Wash., DC 20009; 13,800.

**Library Assn., Amer.** (1876), 50 E. Huron St., Chicago, IL 60611; 50,000.

**Library Assn., Am. Theological** (1947), 820 Church St., Ste. 300, Evanston, IL 60201; 188 libraries.

**Library Assn., Medical** (1861), 6 N. Michigan Ave., Suite 300, Chicago, IL 60602; 5,000+.

**Life, Americans United for** (1971), 343 S. Dearborn St., Ste. 1804, Chicago, IL 60604.

**Life Insurance, Amer. Council of** (1976), 1001 Pennsylvania Ave., NW, Wash., DC 20004; 616 firms.

**Life Underwriters, Amer. Soc. of Certified** (1929), 270 Bryn Mawr Ave., Byrn Mawr, PA 19010; 28,000.

**Life Underwriters, Natl. Assn. of** (1890), 1922 F St. NW, Wash., DC 20006; 135,000.

**Lions Clubs, Intl. Assn. of** (1917), 300 22d St., Oak Brook, IL 60521-8842; 1,363,000.

**Liquid Crystal Soc., Intl.** (1990), Liquid Crystal Institute, Kent State Univ., Kent, OH 44242-0001; 700.

**Litchfield Institute, The** (1984), 2121 W. Oakland Park Blvd., #333,Ft. Lauderdale, FL 33311-1507; 51.

**Literacy Volunteers of America** (1962), 5795 Widewaters Parkway, Syracuse, NY 13214.

**Little League Baseball** (1939), Route #15, S. Williamsport, PA 17701; 17,816 charters.

**Little People of America** (1957), P.O. Box 9897, Washington, DC 20016; 2,000.

**London Club** (1975), 214 N. 2100 Road, Lecompton, KS 66050; 100+.

**Lung Assn., Amer.** (1904), 1740 Broadway, N.Y., NY 10019.

**Lutheran Education Assn.** (1942), 7400 Augusta St., River Forest, IL 60305; 3,800.

**Magazine Photographers, Am. Soc. of** (1944), 419 Park Ave. South, N.Y., NY 10016; 5,000+.

**Magazine Publishers of America** (1919), 575 Lexington Ave., N.Y., NY 10022; 200 publishers.

**Magicians, Intl. Brotherhood of** (1926). P.O. Box 192090, Saint Louis, MO 63119-9998; 13,500.

**Magicians, Society of Amer.** (1902), 1333 Cory St., Yellow Springs, OH 45387; 5,500.

**Management Assn., Amer.** (1923), 135 W. 50th St., N.Y., NY 10020; 70,000.

**Management Consultants, Institute of** (1968), 521 5th Ave., 35th Floor, N.Y., NY 10175-3598; 2,201.

**Manufacturers, Natl. Assn. of** (1897), 1331 Penna. Ave. NW, Ste. 1500N, Wash., DC 20004-1703; 12,500 companies.

**Manufacturers' Agents Natl. Assn.** (1947), 23016 Mill Creek Rd., P.O. Box 3467, Laguna Hills, CA 92654; 10,000.

**March of Dimes Birth Defects Foundation** (1938), 1275 Mamaroneck Ave., White Plains, NY 10605; 2 mln.+.

**Marine Corps League** (1923), P.O. Box 3070, Merrifield, VA 22116-3070; 38,000.

**Marine Manufacturers Assn., Natl.** (1904), 401 N. Michigan Ave., Chicago, IL 60611; 1,650 companies.

**Marketing Assn., Amer.** (1934), 250 S. Wacker Dr., Chicago, IL 60606; 49,122.

**Masonic Relief Assn. of U.S. and Canada** (1880), 3827 Canal St., New Orleans, LA 70119.

**Masons, Ancient and Accepted Scottish Rite, Southern Jurisdiction, Supreme Council 33°** (1801), 1733 16th St. NW, Wash., DC 20009; 528,837.

**Masons, Supreme Council 33°, Ancient and Accepted Scottish Rite, Northern Masonic Jurisdiction** (1813), 33 Marrett Rd., Lexington, MA 02173; 385,870.

**Masons, Royal Arch, General Grand Chapter** (1797), P.O. Box 489, 111 S. 4th St., Danville, KY 40423-0489; 245,000.

**Mathematical Society, Amer.** (1888), 201 Charles St., Providence, RI 02904; 30,000.

**Mathematical Statistics, Institute of** (1935), 3401 Investment Blvd., Ste. 7, Hayward, CA 94545; 4,000.

**Mathematics, Society for Industrial and Applied** (1952), 3600 University City Science Ctr., Phila., PA 19104-2688; 8,100.

**Mayflower Descendants, General Society of** (1897), 4 Winslow St., P.O. Box 3297, Plymouth, MA 02361; 23,500.

**Mayors, U.S. Conference of** (1932), 1620 Eye St. NW, Wash., DC 20006.

**Mechanics, Amer. Academy of** (1969), Dept. of Civil Engineering, Northwestern Univ., Evanston, IL 60201; 1,200.

**Medical Assn., Amer.** (1847), 535 N. Dearborn St., Chicago, IL 60610; 290,000.

**Medical Assn., Natl.** (1895), 1012 Tenth St. NW, Wash., DC 20001; 14,000.

**Medical Record Assn., Amer.** (1928), 919 N. Michigan Ave., Chicago, IL 60611; 31,000.

**Medieval Academy of America** (1926), 1430 Massachusetts Ave., Cambridge, MA 02138; 3,936.

**Men, Natl. Coalition of Free** (1977), P.O. Box 129, Manhasset, NY 11030; 2,000.

**Mensa, Amer.** (1960), 2626 E. 14th St., Brooklyn, NY 11235.

**Mental Health Assn., Natl.** (1909), 1021 Prince St., Alexandria, VA 22314; 1 mln.

**Mental Health Program Directors, Natl. Assn. of State** (1959), 66 Canal Ctr. Plaza, Ste. 302, Alexandria, VA 22314; 55.

**Mentally Ill, Natl. Alliance for the** (1979), 2101 Wilson Blvd., Suite 302, Arlington, VA 22201; 80,000.

**Merchant Marine Library Assn., Amer.** (1921), One World Trade Center, Suite 2161, N.Y., NY 10048.

**Merchant Marine Veterans of WWII, U.S.** (1945), P.O. Box 629, San Pedro, CA 90733; 7,090.

**Merchants Assn., Natl. Retail** (1911), 100 W. 31st St., N.Y., NY 10001; 45,000.

**Merrill's Marauders Assn.** (1946), 11244 N. 33rd St., Phoenix, AZ 85028-2723; 1,695.

**Metallurgy Institute, Amer. Powder** (1959), 105 College Rd. East, Princeton, NJ 08540; 2,800.

**Metal Powder Industries Federation** (1943), 105 College Rd. East, Princeton, NJ 08540; 230 cos.

**Metals, Amer. Society for (ASM Internatl.)** (1913), Metals Park, OH 44073; 53,000.

**Meteorological Society, Amer.** (1919), 45 Beacon St., Boston, MA 02108; 10,200.

**Metric Assn., U.S.** (1966), 10245 Andasol Ave., Northridge, CA 91325; 1,400.

**Microbiology, Amer. Society for** (1899), 1325 Massachusetts Ave. NW, Wash, DC 20005; 37,000.

**Military Order of the Loyal Legion of the U.S.A.** (1865), 1805 Pine St., Phila., PA 19103; 900.

**Military Order of the Purple Heart of the USA** (1932), 5413-B Backlick Rd., Springfield, VA 22151; 30,000.

**Military Order of the World Wars** (1919), 435 N. Lee St., Alexandria, VA 22314; 14,000.

**Military Service, Veterans of Underage** (1991), 3444 Walker Dr., Ellicott City, MD 21042; 532.

**Miniatures, Friends of** (1988), Dollhouse Museum of the Southwest, 2208 Routh St., Dallas, TX 75201; 274.

**Mining, Metallurgy and Exploration, Inc., Society for** (1871), 8307 Shaffer Pkwy., Littleton, CO 80127; 20,279.

**Ministerial Assn., Amer.** (1929), 2210 Wilshire Blvd., Suite 582, Santa Monica, CA 90403; 3,000.

**Model Railroad Assn., Natl.** (1935), 4121 Cromwell Rd., Chattanooga, TN 37421; 25,000.

**Modern Language Assn. of America** (1883), 10 Astor Pl., N.Y., NY 10003; 32,000.

**Modern Language Teachers Assns., Natl. Federation of** (1916), Gannon Univ., Erie, PA 16541; 7,200.

**Moose Intl., Inc.** (1988), Mooseheart, IL 60539; 1.8 mln.

**Mothers, American** (1935), 301 Park Ave., N.Y., NY 10022; 3,000.

**Mothers of Twins Clubs, Natl. Organization of** (1960), P.O. Box 23188, Albuquerque, NM 87192-1188; 14,000.

**Motion Picture Arts & Sciences, Academy of** (1927), 8949 Wilshire Blvd., Beverly Hills, CA 90211; 5,300.

**Motion Picture, Natl. Board of Review of** (1909), P.O. Box 589, Lenox Hill Sta., N.Y., NY 10021.

**Motion Picture & Television Engineers, Society of** (1916), 595 West Hartsdale Ave., White Plains, NY 10607; 9,500.

**Motor Fire Apparatus in Amer., Soc. for the Preservation & Appreciation of Antique** (1958), P.O. Box 2005, Syracuse, NY 13220-2005; 3,000.

**Motor Vehicle Manufacturers Assn.** (1903), 7430 2nd Ave., Suite 300, Detroit, MI 48202; 7 companies.

**Motorcyclist Assn., American** (1924), 33 Collegeview Rd., Westerville, OH 43081-6114.

**Multiple Sclerosis Society, Natl.** (1946), 733 Third Ave., N.Y., NY 10017; 400,000.

**Muscular Dystrophy Assn.** (1950), 3300 E. Sunrise Dr., Tucson, AZ 85718.

**Museums, Amer. Assn. of** (1906), 1225 Eye St. NW, Ste. 200, Wash., DC 20005; 12,000.

**Music Center, Amer.** (1939), 30 W. 26th St., N.Y., NY 10010.

**Music Council, Natl.** (1940), 40 W. 37th St., N.Y., NY 10018; 50 organizations.

**Music Educators Natl. Conference** (1907), 1902 Association Dr., Reston, VA 22090; 60,000.

**Music Scholarship Assn., Amer.** (1956), 1826 Carew Tower, Cincinnati, OH 45202; 15,000.

**Music Teachers Natl. Assn.** (1876), 617 Vine St., Suite 1432, Cincinnati, OH 45202-2439; 25,000.

**Musicological Society, Amer.** (1934), 201 S. 34th St., Phila., PA 19104; 3,500.

**Muzzle Loading Rifle Assn., Natl.** (1933), P.O. Box 67, Friendship, IN 47021; 26,000.

**Myasthenia Gravis Foundation, The** (1952), 53 W. Jackson Blvd., Ste. 660, Chicago, IL 60604; 30,000.

**NAACP (Natl. Assn. for the Advancement of Colored People)** (1909), 4805 Mt. Hope Drive, Baltimore, MD 21215.

**Na'amat USA** (1925), 200 Madison Ave., N.Y., NY 10016.

**Narcolepsy and Cataplexy Foundation of Amer.** (1975), 1410 York Ave., Suite 2D, N.Y. NY 10021; 3,991.

**Narcotics Anonymous** (1953), P.O. Box 9999, Van Nuys, CA 91409; 1 million.

**National Guard Assn. of the U.S.** (1878), One Massachusetts Ave. NW, Wash., DC 20001; 54,000.

**Nature Conservancy** (1951), 1815 N. Lynn St., Arlington, VA 22209; 692,000.

**Naturist Society, The** (1980), P.O. Box 132, Oshkosh, WI 54902; 20,000.

**Naval Architects & Marine Engineers, The Society of** (1893), 601 Pavonia Ave., Ste. 400, Jersey City, NJ 07306.

**Naval Institute, U.S.** (1873), 118 Maryland Ave., Annapolis, MD 21402; 100,000.

**Naval Reserve Assn.** (1954), 1619 King St., Alexandria, VA 22314; 24,500.

**Navigation, Institute of** (1945), 1026 16th St. NW, Suite 104, Wash., DC 20036; 3,200.

**Navy League of the U.S.** (1902); 2300 Wilson Blvd., Arlington, VA 22201; 73,000.

**Needlework Guild of America** (1885), 1007-B Street Rd., Southampton, PA 18966; 100,000.

**Negro College Fund, United** (1944), 500 E. 62d St., N.Y., NY 10021; 42 institutions.

**Neurofibromatosis Foundation, Natl.** (1978), 141 Fifth Ave., Suite 7-S, N.Y., NY 10010; 7,000.

**New Age Walkers** (1982), 3301 Bellaire Dr., Altadena, CA 91001; 4,700.

**Newspaper Assn. of Amer.** (1992), NAA, The Newspaper Center, 11600 Sunrise Valley Dr., Reston, VA 22091.

**Newspaper Editors, Amer. Society of** (1922), P.O. Box 17004, Washington, DC 20041.

**Newspaper Marketing Assn., Intl.** (1930), 11600 Sunrise Valley Dr., Reston, VA 22091; 1,300+.

**Newswomen's Club of N.Y.** (1922), 15 Gramercy Park S., N.Y., NY 10003; 200.

**Nikola Tesla Walkers** (1982), 10799 Sherman Grove Ave., #18, Sunland, CA 91040; 4,800.

**Ninety-Nines (Intl. Organization of Women Pilots)** (1929), P.O. Box 59965, Will Rogers Airport, Oklahoma City, OK 73159.

**Nobel Committee, Amer.** (1942), 1 Morningside Dr. N., Westport, CT 06880.

**Non-Commissioned Officers Assn.** (1960), 10635 IH 35 North, San Antonio, TX 78233; 160,000.

**Northern Cross Society** (1986), Route One, Big Springs, KS 66050; 50.

**Notaries, Amer. Society of** (1965), 918 16th St. NW, Wash., DC 20006; 21,499.

**Nuclear Society, Amer.** (1954), 555 N. Kensington Ave., La Grange Park, IL 60525; 16,777.

**Numismatic Assn., Amer.** (1891), 818 N. Cascade Ave., Colorado Springs, CO 80903-3279; 29,000.

**Numismatic Society, Amer.** (1858), Broadway at 155th St., N.Y., NY 10032; 2,369.

**Nurses' Assn., Amer.** (1896), 2420 Pershing Rd., Kansas City, MO 64108.

**Nursing, Natl. League for** (1952), 350 Hudson St., N.Y., NY 10014; 18,000.

**Nutrition, Amer. Institute of** (1928), 9650 Rockville Pike, Bethesda, MD 20814; 3,000.

**ORT Federation, Amer. (Org. for Rehabilitation through Training)** (1924), 817 Broadway, N.Y., NY 10019; 20,000.

**Odd Fellows, Independent Order of** (1819), 422 N. Trade St., Winston-Salem, NC 27101-2830; 453,612.

**Old Crows, Assn. of** (1964), 1000 N. Payne St., Alexandria, VA 22314-1696; 25,000.

**Olympic Committee, U.S.** (1921), 1750 E. Boulder St., Colorado Springs, CO 80909; 70 organizations.

**Opthalmology, Amer. Academy of** (1979), 655 Beach St., San Francisco, CA 94109; 16,250.

**Optical Society of America** (1916), 2010 Massachusetts Ave. NW, Wash., DC 20036; 12,200.

**Optimist Intl.** (1919), 4494 Lindell Blvd., St. Louis, MO 63108.

**Optometric Assn., Amer.** (1898), 243 N. Lindbergh Blvd., St. Louis, MO 63141; 28,000.

**Organists, Amer. Guild of** (1896), 475 Riverside Dr., Suite 1260, N.Y., NY 10115; 20,200.

**Oriental Society, Amer.** (1842), 329 Sterling Memorial Library, Yale Sta., New Haven, CT 06520; 1,440.

**Ornithologists' Union, Amer.** (1883), c/o National Museum of Natural History, Smithsonian, Wash., DC 20560; 5,000.

**Osteopathic Assn., Amer.** (1887), 212 E. Ohio St., Chicago, IL 60611; 23,292.

**Ostomy Assn., United** (1963), 36 Executive Park, Suite 120, Irving, CA 92714, 41,009.

**Outlaw and Lawman History, Natl. Organization for** (1974), 615-C N. 8th St., Killeen, TX 76541; 559.

**Overeaters Anonymous** (1960), World Service Office, 383 Van Ness Ave., #1601, Torrance, CA 90501; 152,000.

**PTA (Natl. Congress of Parents and Teachers), Natl.** (1897), 700 N. Rush St., Chicago, IL 60611; 6.8 mln.

**Paper Industry, Technical Assn. of the Pulp and** (1915), 15 Technology Pkwy. S., Norcross, GA 30092; 33,000.

**Parametric Analysts, Intl. Soc. of** (1979), P.O. Box 1056, Germantown, MD 20878; 600.

**Parents Without Partners** (1957), 8807 Colesville Rd., Silver Spring, MD 20910; 100,000.

**Parkinson's Disease Foundation** (1957), 650-170 W. 168th St., N.Y., NY 10032.

**Parliamentarians, Natl. Assn. of** (1930), 6601 Winchester, Kansas City, MO 64133-4600; 4,400.

**Parliamentary Law, Intl. Organization of Professionals in** (1975), 3611 Victoria Ave., Los Angeles, CA 90016; 250.

**Pasta Assn., Natl.** (1904), 2101 Wilson Blvd., Suite 920, Arlington, VA 22201.

**Pathologists, Amer. Assn. of** (1976), 9650 Rockville Pike, Bethesda, MD 20814; 2,000.

**Pathology, Amer. Soc. for Investigative** (1900), 9650 Rockville Pike, Bethesda, MD 20814-3993; 2,200.

**Patton Historical Soc., George S. Jr.** (1970), 3116 Thorn St., San Diego, CA 92104-4618.

**Pearl Harbor History Associates** (1983), P.O. Box 205, Sperryville, VA 22740-0205; 500.

**PEN Amer. Center** (1922), 568 Broadway, N.Y., NY 10012.

**PEN Women, Natl. League of Amer.** (1897), 1300 17th St. NW, Wash., DC 20036-1973; 5,000.

**Pen Friends, Intl.** (1967), Box 65, Brooklyn, NY 11229; 300,000.

**Pension Actuaries, Amer. Society of** (1966), 4350 N. Fairfax Dr., Ste. 820, Arlington, VA 22203; 3,000.

**P.E.O. (Philanthropic Educational Organization) Sisterhood** (1869), 3700 Grand Ave., Des Moines, IA 50312; 242,000.

**Personnel Administration, Amer. Society for** (1948), 606 N. Washington St., Alexandria, VA 22314; 40,000.

**Petroleum Equipment Inst.** (1951), 3739 E. 31st St., Tulsa, OK 74135; 1,200 member companies.

**Petroleum Institute, Amer.** (1919), 1220 L St. NW, Wash., DC 20005; 250 corporations.

**Pharmaceutical Assn., Amer.** (1852), 2215 Constitution Ave. NW, Wash., DC 20037; 40,000.

**Phi Delta Kappa** (1906), 8th & Union, Box 789, Bloomington, IN 47401-0789; 132,000.

**Philatelic Pages & Panels, Amer. Soc. for** (1984), 4116 Kilmer Ave., Allentown, PA 18104; 950.

**Philatelic Society, Amer.** (1886), 100 Oakwood Ave., P.O. Box 8000, State College, PA 16803; 57,000.

**Philological Assn., Amer.** (1869), Dept. of Classics, Fordham Univ., Bronx, NY 10458; 2,500.

**Philosophical Assn., Amer.** (1900), Univ. of Delaware, Newark, DE 19716; 8,500.

**Philosophical Enquiry, Intl. Soc. For** (1974), 277 Washington Blvd., Hudson, NY 12534-1322; 530.

**Philosophical Society, Amer.** (1743), 104 S. 5th St., Phila., PA 19106; 690.

**Photogrammetry and Remote Sensing, Amer. Society of** (1934), 5410 Grosvenor Ln., Ste. 210, Bethesda, MD 20814.

**Photographers of America, Professional** (1880), 1090 Executive Way, Des Plaines, IL 60018; 15,000.

**Photographic Society of Amer.** (1934), 3000 United Founders Blvd. #103, Oklahoma City, OK 73112.

**Physical Therapy Assn., Amer.** (1921), 1111 N. Fairfax St., Alexandria, VA 22314; 56,000.

**Physicians, Amer. Academy of Family** (1947), 8880 Ward Pkwy., Kansas City, MO 64114; 72,000.

**Physics, Amer. Inst. of** (1931), 335 E. 45th St., N.Y., NY 10017-3483.

**Physiological Society, Amer.** (1887), 9650 Rockville Pike, Bethesda, MD 20814; 7,000.

**Pilgrim Society** (1820), 75 Court St., Plymouth, MA 02360-3891; 600.

**Pilot Intl.** (1921), P.O. Box 4844, 244 College St., Macon, GA 31213-0599; 19,000.

**Planetary Society** (1980), 65 N. Catalina Ave., Pasadena, CA 91106; 100,000.

**Planned Parenthood Federation of America** (1916), 810 Seventh Ave., N.Y., NY 10019; 187 affiliates.

**Plastic Modelers Society, Intl.** (1963), P.O. Box 6138, Warner Robins, GA 31095-6138; 3,750.

**Plastics Industry, Society of** (1937), 1275 K St. NW, Suite 400, Washington, DC 20005; 2,200 cos.

**Platform Assn., Intl.** (1831), Box 250, Winnetka, IL 60093.

**Poetry Day Committee, Natl.** (1947), 1110 N. Venetian Dr., Miami, FL 33139-1019; 17,500.

**Poetry Society of America** (1910), 15 Gramercy Park, N.Y., NY 10003; 1,700.

**Poets, Academy of Amer.** (1934), 584 Broadway, N.Y., NY 10024; 2,220.

**Police, Internatl. Assn. of Chiefs of** (1893), 1110 N. Glebe Rd., Suite 200, Arlington, VA 22201; 13,500.

**Polish Army Veterans Assn. of America** (1921), 155 Noble St., Brooklyn, NY 11222; 3,500.

**Polish Cultural Society of America** (1940), P.O. Box 31, Wall Street, N.Y., NY 10005; 104,001.

**Political Items Collectors, Amer.** (1945), P.O. Box 340339, San Antonio, TX 78234; 3,100.

**Political Science, Academy of** (1880), 475 Riverside Dr., Suite 1274, N.Y., NY 10115-0012; 8,500.

**Political Science Assn., Amer.** (1903), 1527 New Hampshire Ave. NW, Wash., DC 20036; 12,152.

**Political & Social Science, Amer. Academy of** (1889), 3937 Chestnut St., Phila., PA 19104; 4,000.

**Pollution Control, Internatl. Assn. for** (1970), 444 N. Capital St. NW, Wash. DC 20001.

**Polo Assn., U.S.** (1890), 4059 Iron Works Pike, Lexington, KY, 40511; 3,000.

**Population Assn. of America** (1931), 1722 N. St. NW, Washington, DC 20036; 2,600.

**Portuguese-American Federation, Inc.** (1965), Linden Pl., 500 Hope St., Bristol, RI 02809; 250.

**Portuguese Continental Union of the U.S.A.** (1925), 899 Boylston St., Boston, MA 02115.

**Postmasters of the U.S., Natl. Assn. of** (1898), 8 Herbert St., Arlington, VA 22305; 43,000.

**Postmasters of the U.S., Natl. League of** (1904), 1023 N. Royal St., Alexandria, VA 22314; 21,874.

**Poultry Science Assn.** (1921), 309 W. Clark St., Champaign, IL 61820.

**Power Boat Assn., Amer.** (1903), 17640 E. Nine Mile Rd., P.O. Box 377, E. Detroit, MI 48021.

**Precancel Collectors, Natl. Assn. of** (1950), 5121 Park Blvd., Wildwood, NJ 08260-0121; 7,600.

**Press, Associated** (1848), 50 Rockefeller Plaza, N.Y., NY 10020; 1,558 newspapers & 6,000 broadcast stations.

**Press Club, Natl.** (1908), 529 14th St. NW, Wash., DC 20045.

**Press Intl., United** (1907), 1400 I St. NW, Wash. DC 20005.

**Press and Radio Club** (1948), P.O. Box 70023, Montgomery, AL 36107; 741.

**Printing Industries of America** (1887), 100 Dangerfield Rd., Alexandria, VA 22314; 14,000.

**Prisoners of War, Amer. Ex-** (1942), 3201 E. Pioneer Pkwy., #40, Arlington, TX 76010-5396; 32,000.

**Procrastinators Club of America** (1956), Box 712, Bryn Athyn, PA 19009; 10,000.

**Production and Inventory Control Soc., American,** 500 W. Annandale Rd., Falls Church, VA 22046-4274; 65,000.

**Psychiatric Assn., Amer.** (1844), 1400 K St. NW, Wash., DC 20005; 37,380.

**Psychical Research, Amer. Society for** (1907), 5 W. 73d St., N.Y., NY 10023; 2,000.

**Psychoanalytic Assn., Amer.** (1911), 309 E. 49th St., N.Y., NY 10017; 3,000.

**Psychological Assn., Amer.** (1892), 750 1st St. NE, Washington, DC 20002-4242; 119,000.

**Psychological Assn. for Psychoanalysis, Natl.** (1948), 150 W. 13th St., N.Y., NY 10011-7891; 353.

**Psychological Minorities, Society for the Aid of** (1953), 42-25 Hampton St., Elmhurst, NY 11373; 530.

**Psoriasis Foundation, Natl** (1968), 6443 SW Beaverton Hwy., #210, Portland, OR 97221; 14,000.

**Public Administration, Amer. Soc. for** (1939), 1120 G St. NW, Wash, DC 20005; 14,800.

**Public Health Assn., World Fed. of** (1967), 1015 15th St. NW, Wash., DC 20005; 48 natl. assn.

**Public Relations Soc. of Amer.** (1947), 33 Irving Pl., N.Y., NY 10003-2376; 15,462.

**Publishers, Assn. of Amer.** (1970), 220 E. 23rd St., N.Y., NY 10010; 230 cos.

**Puppeteers of Amer.** (1937), 5 Cricklewood Path, Pasadena, CA 91107; 2,200.

**Puzzle Buffs Intl.** (1978), 1772 State Road, Cuyahoga Falls, OH 44223; 39,000.

**Quality Control, Amer. Society for** (1946), 611 E. Wisconsin Ave., Milwaukee, WI 53201-3005, 90,000.

**Rabbis, Central Conference of Amer.** (1889), 192 Lexington Ave., N.Y., NY 10016; 1,540.

**Racial Equality, Congress of (CORE)** (1942), 1457 Flatbush Ave., Brooklyn, NY 11210; 100,000.

**Radio, Natl. Assn. of Business and Educational** (1965), 1501 Duke St., Alexandria, VA 22314; 3,000.

**Radio Union, Intl. Amateur** (1925), P.O. Box AAA, Newington, CT 06111; 126 societies.

**Radio and TV Society, Intl.** (1939), 420 Lexington Ave., Ste. 1714, N.Y., NY 10170; 1,600.

**Radio Relay League, Amer.** (1914), 225 Main St., Newington, CT 06111; 160,000.

**Railway Historical Society, Natl.** (1935), P.O. Box 58153, Phila., PA 19102-8153; 19,000+.

**Railway Progress Institute** (1908), 700 N. Fairfax St., Suite 601, Alexandria, VA 22314-2098; 104 companies.

**Range Management, Society for** (1948), 1839 York Street, Denver, CO 80206; 5,400.

**Reading Assn., Intl.** (1956), P.O. Box 8139, 800 Barksdale Rd., Newark, DE 19714-8139; 93,000.

**Real Estate Institute, Intl.** (1975), 8383 E. Evans Rd., Scottsdale, AZ 85260-3614; 4,500.

**Rebekah Assemblies, Intl. Assn. of** (1916), 422 N. Trade, Winston-Salem, NC 27101; 182,158.

**Reconciliation, Fellowship of** (1915), 523 N. Broadway, Nyack, NY 10960; 10,000.

**Records Managers & Administrators, Assn. of** (1975), 4200 Somerset Dr., Suite 215, Prairie Village, KS 66208; 11,000.

**Recreation and Park Assn., Natl.** (1965), 2775 S. Quincy St., Ste. 300, Arlington, VA 22206-2204; 22,000+.

**Recycling Coalition, Natl.,** 1101 30th St. NW, Ste. 305, Wash., DC 20007.

**Red Cross, American** (1881), 17th & D Sts. NW, Wash., DC 20006; 1.9 mln. volunteers.

**Red Men, Improved Order of** (1765), 4521 Speight Ave., Waco, TX, 76711-1708; 29,000.

**Redwoods League, Save-the-** (1918), 114 Sansome St., Rm. 605, San Francisco, CA 94104; 45,000.

**Rehabilitation Assn., Natl.** (1925), 1910 Association Dr., Ste. 205, Reston, VA 22091.

**Religion, Amer. Academy of** (1909), 501 Hall of Languages, Syracuse Univ., Syracuse, NY 13244-1170; 5,600.

**Religion Foundation, Freedom from** (1978), P.O. Box 750, Madison, WI 53701; 3,100.

**Renaissance Society of America** (1954), 24 W. 12th St., N.Y., NY 10011; 2,411.

**Republican National Committee** (1856), 310 1st Street SE, Washington, DC 20003-1801.

**Reserve Officers Assn. of the U.S.** (1922), One Constitution Ave., NE, Wash., DC 20002; 123,000.

**Restaurant Assn., Natl.** (1919), 1200 17th St. NW, Wash., DC 20036; 20,000.

**Retail Federation, Natl.** (1918), 100 West 31st St., N.Y., NY 10001; 50,000.

**Retired Credit Union People, Natl. Assn. for** (1978), P.O. Box 391, 5910 Mineral Pt. Rd., Madison, WI 53705; 81,180.

**Retired Federal Employees, Natl. Assn. of** (1921), 1533 New Hampshire Ave. NW, Wash., DC 20036; 500,000.

**Retired Officers Assn.** (1929), 201 N. Washington St., Alexandria, VA 22314-2529; 380,000.

**Retired Persons, Amer. Assn. of** (1958), 1909 K St. NW, Wash., DC 20049; 32 mln.

**Retired Teachers Assn., Natl.** (1947), 1909 K St. NW, Wash., DC 20049; 540,000.

**Revolver Assn., U.S.** (1900), 96 W. Union St., Ashland, MA 01721; 1,400.

**Reye's Syndrome Foundation, Natl.** (1974), 426 N. Lewis, Bryan, OH 43506; 5,000+.

**Richard III Society** (1969), P.O. Box 13787, New Orleans, LA 70185; 700.

**Rifle Assn., Natl.** (1871), 1600 Rhode Island Ave. NW, Wash., DC 20036; 3.17 mln.

**Road & Transportation Builders' Assn., Amer.** (1902), 501 School St. SW, Wash., DC 20024-2713; 3,600.

**Rocky Horror Picture Show Preservation Soc. of Terra** (1993), One Caddo Ct., Kenner, LA 70065-3920.

**Rodeo Cowboys Assn., Professional** (1936), 101 Pro Rodeo Dr., Colorado Springs, CO 80919; 8,983.

**Roller Skating, U.S. Amateur Confederation of** (1937), 4730 South St., P.O. Box 6579, Lincoln, NE 68506; 21,000.

**Rose Society, Amer.** (1892), 8877 Jefferson Paige Rd., Shreveport, LA 71119; 38,000.

**Rotary Intl.** (1905), 1560 Sherman Ave., Evanston, IL 60201.

**Running and Fitness Assn., Amer.** (1968), 9310 Old Georgetown Rd., Bethesda, MD 20814; 18,000.

**Ruritan Natl.** (1928), Ruritan Natl. Rd., Dublin, VA 24084.

**Safety and Fairness Everywhere, Natl. Assn. Taunting** (1980), P.O. Box 5743WA, Montecito, CA 93150; 12,000.

**Safety Council, Natl.** (1913), 444 N. Michigan Ave., Chicago, IL 60611; 12,500.

**Sailors, Tin Can** (1976), P.O. Box 100, Somerset, MA 02726; 17,000.

**Sailors Assn., Destroyer-Escort** (1975), 352 W. Story Rd., Ocoee, FL 34761, 12,000.

**St. Andrew, The Brotherhood of** (1883), 1109 Merchant St., P.O. Box 632, Ambridge, PA 15003; 5,000.

**St. Paul, Natl. Guild of** (1937), 601 Hill 'n Dale, Lexington, KY 40503; 13,652.

**Salespersons, Natl. Assn. of Professional** (1970), P.O. Box 76461, Atlanta, GA 30358; 35,000.

**Salt Institute** (1914), 700 N. Fairfax St., Ste. 600, Alexandria, VA, 22314-2040; 23 companies.

**Sane Nuclear Policy, Committee for a** (1957), 711 G St. SE, Wash., DC 20003; 130,000.

**Savings Institutions, Natl. Council of** (1983), 1101 15th St. NW, Wash., DC 20005; 550 members.

**School Administrators, Amer. Assn. of** (1865), 1801 N. Moore St., Arlington, VA 22209; 18,000.

**School Boards Assn., Natl.** (1940), 1680 Duke St., Alexandria, VA 22314.

**School Counselor Assn., Amer.** (1953), 5999 Stevenson Ave., Alexandria, VA 22304; 13,000.

**Schools of Art, Natl. Assn. of** (also: **School of Art and Design, School of Dance, Music, and Theater**) (1944), 11250 Roger Bacon Dr., Reston, VA 22090; 161.

**Schools & Colleges, Amer. Council on** (1927), 13014 Dale Mabry Hwy., Ste. 270-B, Tampa, FL 33180-2808; 400+.

**Science, Amer. Assn. for the Advancement of** (1848), 1333 H St. NW, Wash., DC 20005; 135,000.

**Science Fiction Society, World** (1939), P.O. Box 1270, Kendall Sq. Sta., Cambridge, MA 02142; 5,000.

**Science Service** (1921), 1719 N St. NW, Wash., DC 20036.

**Science Teachers Assn., Natl.** (1985), 1742 Connecticut Ave. NW, Wash., DC 20009; 49,000.

**Science Writers, Natl. Assn. of** (1934), P.O. Box 294, Greenlawn, NY 11740; 1,650.

**Sciences, Natl. Academy of** (1863), 2101 Constitution Ave. NW, Wash., DC 20418; 1,936.

**Scrabble Assn., Natl.** (1978), Box 700, Greenport, NY 11944; 10,000.

**Screen Actors Guild** (1933), 7065 Hollywood Blvd., Hollywood, CA 90028; 78,000.

**Screen Printing Assn. Intl.** (1948), 10015 Main St., Fairfax, VA 22031.

**Sculpture Soc., Natl.** (1893), 1177 Ave. of the Americas, N.Y., NY 10036; 3,600.

**2d Air Division Assn.** (1947), 1 Jeffrey's Neck Rd., Ipswich, MA 01938; 7,852.

**Secondary School Principals, Natl. Assn. of** (1916), 1904 Association Dr., Reston, VA 22091; 42,000.

**Secretaries Intl., Professional** (1942), P.O. Box 20404, Kansas City, MO 64195-0404; 40,000.

**Secretaries, Natl. Assn. of Legal** (1920), 2250 E 73, Ste. 550, Tulsa, OK 74136-6864; 16,000.

**Securities Industry Assn.** (1972), 120 Broadway, N.Y., NY 10271; 600 firms.

**Separation of Church & State, Americans United for** (1947), 8120 Fenton St., Silver Spring, MD 20910; 50,000.

**Sertoma Internatl.** (1912), 1912 E. Meyer Blvd., Kansas City, MO 64132; 29,000.

**Sex Information & Education Council of the U.S. (SIECUS)** (1964), 130 W. 42 St., Ste. 2500, N.Y., NY 10036; 2,000+.

**Sharkhunters Intl.** (1983), P.O. Box 1539, Hernanado, FL 32642; 2,700.

**Shipbuilders Council of America** (1921), 1110 Vermont Ave. NW, Wash., DC 20005; 50 organizations.

**Ships-in-Bottles Assn. of Amer.** (1983), P.O. Box 180550, Coronado, CA 92178; 400.

**Shore & Beach Preservation Assn., Amer.** (1926), P.O. Box 279, Middletown, CA 95461; 900.

**Shrine, Ancient Arabic Order of the Nobles of the Mystic** (1872), 2900 Rocky Pt. Dr., Tampa, FL 33607; 799,000.

**Sierra Club** (1892), 730 Polk St., San Francisco, CA 94109.

**Skeet Shooting Assn., Natl.** (1946), P.O. Box 680007, San Antonio, TX 78268; 15,800.

**Ski Assn., U.S.** (1904), P.O. Box 100, Park City, UT 84060.

**Small Business, Amer. Federation of** (1938), 18200 Sherman St., Lansing, IL 60438-3104.

**Small Business United, Natl.** (1986), 1155 15th St. NW, Suite 710, Wash., DC 20005; 65,000.

**Smoking & Health, Natl. Clearinghouse for** (1965), Center for Disease Control, 1600 Clifton Road NE, Atlanta, GA 30333.

**Soccer Federation, U.S.** (1913), 1801-1811 S. Prairie Ave., Chicago, IL 60616; 2 mln.

**Social Sciences, Natl. Institute of** (1865), 444 Madison Ave., Ste. 2901, N.Y., NY 10022; 300.

**Social Work Education, Council on** (1952), 1600 Duke Street, Alexandria, VA 22314; 2,500.

**Social Workers, Natl. Assn. of** (1955), 750 First St. NE, Ste. 700, Washington, DC 20002-4241; 138,000.

**Sociological Assn., Amer.** (1905), 1722 N St. NW, Wash., DC 20036; 13,000.

**Softball Association, Amateur** (1933), 2801 N.E. 50th St., Oklahoma City, OK 73111; 4.5 mln.

**Soft Drink Assn., Natl.** (1921), 1101 16th St. NW, Wash., DC 20036; 1,000.

**Soil & Water Conservation Society of America** (1945), 7515 N.E. Ankeny Rd., Ankeny, IA 50021-9764; 11,000.

**Soil Science Society of America** (1936), 677 S. Segoe Rd., Madison, WI 53711; 6,018.

**Soldier's, Sailor's and Airmen's Club** (1919), 283 Lexington Ave., N.Y., NY 10016.

**Songwriters Guild of America, The** (1931), 276 Fifth Ave., Ste. 306, N.Y., NY 10001; 3,500.

**Sons of the Amer. Legion** (1932), Box 1055, Indianapolis, IN 46206; 147,893.

**Sons of the American Revolution, Natl. Society of** (1889), 1000 S. 4th, Louisville, KY 40203; 27,000.

**Sons of Confederate Veterans** (1896), Southern Station, Box 5164, Hattiesburg, MS 39406-5164; 13,000.

**Sons of the Desert** (1965), P.O. Box 8341, Universal City, CA 91608; 10,000.

**Sons of Italy in America, Order** (1905), 219 E. St., NE, Wash. DC 20002; 500,000.

**Sons of Norway** (1895), 1455 W. Lake St., Minneapolis, MN 55408; 76,030.

**Sons of Poland, Assn. of the** (1903), 591 Summit Ave., Rm. 702, Jersey City, NJ 07306; 10,000.

**Sons of the Republic of Texas, The** (1922), 5942 Abrams Rd., #222, Dallas, TX 75231; 2,400.

**Sons of St. Patrick, Society of the Friendly** (1784), 80 Wall St., N.Y., NY 10005; 1,500.

**Sons of Sherman's March to the Sea** (1966), 1725 Farmers Ave., Tempe, AZ 85281-6533; 705.

**Sons of Union Veterans of the Civil War** (1881), 411 Bartlett St., Lansing, MI 48915; 2,700.

**Soroptimist Intl. of the Americas** (1921), 1616 Walnut St., Phila., PA 19103; 50,000.

**Southern Christian Leadership Conference** (1957), 334 Auburn Ave. NE, Atlanta, GA 30303; 1 mln.

**Space Education Assoc., U.S.** (1973), P.O. Box 249, Rheems, PA 17570-0249; 1,500.

**Special Olympics Intl.** (1968), 1350 New York Ave. NW, Ste. 500, Washington, DC 20005.

**Speech Communication Assn.** (1914), 5105 Backlick Rd., Annandale, VA 22003; 6,800.

**Speech-Language-Hearing Assn., Amer.** (1925), 10801 Rockville Pike, Rockville, MD 20852.

**Speedskating Union of the U.S., Amateur** (1927), 1033 Shady Lane, Glen Ellyn, IL 60137; 3,000.

**Speleological Society, Natl.** (1941), 2813 Cave Ave., Huntsville, AL 35810; 11,000.

**Spiritual Awareness, Assn. for** (1984), P.O. Box 41, Clifton Hill, MO 65244; 1,500.

**Sports Car Club of America** (1944), 9033 E. Eastern Pl., Englewood, CO 80112; 50,000+.

**Sports Club, Indoor** (1930), 1145 Highland St., Napoleon, OH 43545; 950.

**Sportscasters Assn., Amer.** (1980), 5 Beekman St., N.Y., NY 10038; 500+.

**State Governments, Council of** (1933), P.O. Box 11910, Lexington, KY 40517; 50 states, 4 territories.

**State & Local History, Amer. Assn. for** (1940), 530 Church St., Ste. 600, Nashville, TN 37219; 5,600.

**Statistical Assn., Amer.** (1839), 1429 Duke St., Alexandria, VA 22314-3402; 15,000.

**Steamship Historical Society of America** (1935), 300 Ray Dr., Ste. 4, Providence, RI 02906; 3,500.

**Steel Construction, Amer. Institute of** (1921), 1 E. Wacker Dr., Ste. 3100, Chicago, IL 60601-2001; 2,770.

**Stock Car Auto Racing, Natl. Assn. for (NASCAR)** (1947), P.O. Box 2875, Daytona Beach, FL 32120-2875; 45,000.

**Stock Exchange, Amer.** (1911), 86 Trinity Pl., N.Y., NY 10006; 871.

**Stock Exchange, N.Y.** (1792), 11 Wall St., N.Y., NY 10005.

**Stock Exchange, Phila.** (1790), 1900 Market St., Phila., PA 19103; 505.

**Student Councils, Natl. Assn. of** (1931), 1904 Association Dr., Reston, VA 22091; 9,000 schools.

**Stuttering Project, Natl.** (1977), 2151 Irving St., Ste. 208, San Francisco, CA 94122-1609; 4,000.

**Sudden Infant Death Syndrome Alliance, Natl.** (1987), 10500 Little Patuxent Pkwy., Ste. 420, Columbia, MD 21044.

**Sugar Brokers Assn., Natl.** (1903), 1 World Trade Center, N.Y., NY 10047; 100.

**Sunbathing Assn., Amer.** (1931), 1703 N. Main St., Kissimmee, FL 34744; 40,000.

**Surfing Committee, U.S.** (1960), Box 545921, Surfhouse, Surfside, FL 33154-5492; 5,876,182.

**Surgeons, Amer. College of** (1913), 55 E. Erie St., Chicago IL 60611-2797; 52,127.

**Surgeons of the U.S., Assn. of Military** (1891), 9320 Old Georgetown Rd., Bethesda, MD 20814; 14,500.

**Surveying & Mapping, Amer. Congress on** (1941), 5410 Grosvenor Ln., Bethesda, MD 20814-2122; 9,500.

**Symphony Orchestra League, Amer.** (1942), 777 14th St. NW, Ste. 500, Wash., DC 20005; 860 orchestras.

**Systems Management, Assn. for** (1947), 1433 West Bagley Rd., Berea, OH 44017; 8,000.

**Table Tennis Assn., U.S.** (1933), One Olympic Plaza, Colorado Springs, CO 80909; 7,000.

**Tailhook Assn., The** (1957), P.O. Box 40, Bonita, CA 91908.

**Tax Accountants, Natl. Assn. of Enrolled Federal** (1960), P.O. Box 59-009, Chicago, IL 60659-0009; 450.

**Tax Administrators, Federation of** (1937), 444 N. Capitol St. NW, Wash., DC 20001.

**Tax Assn., Natl.–Tax Institute of America** (1907), 5310 E. Main St., Suite 104, Columbus, OH 43213; 3,570.

**Tax Foundation, Inc.** (1937), 1250 H St. NW, Ste. 750, Washington, DC 20005.

**Taxpayers Union, Natl.** (1969), 325 Pennsylvania Ave. SE, Wash., DC 20003; 200,000.

**Tea Assn. of the U.S.A.** (1899), 230 Park Ave., N.Y., NY 10169; 140.

**Teachers of English, Natl. Council of** (1911), 1111 Kenyon Rd., Urbana, IL 61801; 125,000.

**Teachers of English to Speakers of Other Languages** (1969), 1600 Cameron St., Suite 300, Alexandria, VA 22314.

**Teachers of French, Amer. Assn. of** (1927), 57 E. Armory Ave., Champaign, IL 61820; 11,000.

**Teachers of Mathematics, Natl. Council of** (1920), 1906 Association Dr., Reston, VA 22091; 91,740.

**Teachers of Singing, Natl. Assn. of** (1944), 2800 Univ. Blvd. N, J.U. Sta., Jacksonville, FL 32211; 5,000.

**Teachers of Spanish & Portuguese, Amer. Assn. of** (1917), P.O. Box 6349, 218 Lee Hall, MSU., MS 39762-6349.

**Technicians Assn., Market** (1973), 71 Broadway, 2nd Fl., N.Y., NY 10006; 600.

**Telephone Pioneers of Amer.** (1911), 930 15th St., 12th Fl., Denver, CO 80202; 820,000.

**Television Arts & Sciences, Natl. Academy of** (1947), 111 W. 57th St., Suite 1020, N.Y., NY 10019; 12,000.

**Television Bureau of Advertising** (1954), 477 Madison Ave., N.Y., NY 10022.

**Television & Radio Artists, Amer. Federation of** (1937), 1350 Ave. of the Americas, N.Y., NY 10019; 66,000.

**Telluride Assn.** (1911), 217 West Ave., Ithaca, NY 14850.

**Tennis Assn., U.S.** (1881), 1212 Ave. of Americas, N.Y., NY 10036.

**Terraplane Club, Hudson-Essex** (1959), 100 E. Cross St., Ypsilanti, MI 48198; 3,200.

**Tesla Memorial Soc., Inc.** (1979), 453 Martin Rd., Buffalo, NY 14218; 1,900.

**Testing & Materials, Amer. Society for** (1898), 1916 Race St., Phila., PA 19103; 32,000.

**Textile Manufacturers Institute, Amer.** (1949), 1801 K St. NW, Suite 900, Wash., DC 20006.

**Theodore Roosevelt Assn.** (1919), P.O. Box 719, Oyster Bay, NY 11771; 2,200.

**Theological Schools in the U.S. and Canada, Assn. of** (1918), 10 Summit Park Dr., Pittsburgh, PA 15275-1103.

**Theosophical Society in America, The** (1886), 1926 N. Main St., Wheaton, IL 60189-0270; 5,000.

**Thoreau Society** (1941), 156 Belknap St., Concord, MA 01742; 1,500.

**Thoroughbred Racing Assns.** (1942), 420 Fair Hill Dr., Ste. 1, Elkton, MD 21921; 53 racing associations.

**Titanic Historical Society** (1963), P.O. Box 51053, Indian Orchard, MA 01151-0053; 5,100.

**Toastmasters Intl.** (1924), 23182 Arroyo Vista, Rancho Santa Margarita, CA 92688.

**Topical Assn., Amer.** (1949), P.O. Box 630, Johnstown, PA 15907; 7,000.

**Toy Manufacturers of America** (1916), 200 Fifth Ave., N.Y., NY 10010; 240.

**Track & Field, USA** (1979), P.O. Box 120, Indianapolis, IN 46206; 100,000+.

**Transit Assn., Amer. Public** (1974), 1201 New York Ave. NW, Wash., DC 20005; 11,000 organizations.

**Translators Assn., Amer.** (1960), 1735 Jefferson Davis Hwy., #903, Arlington, VA 22202-3413; 4,850.

**Trapshooting Assn., Amateur** (1923), 601 W. National Rd., Vandalia, OH 45377; 100,000+.

**Travel Agents, Amer. Society of** (1936), 1101 King St., Alexandria, VA 22314; 20,000.

**Travelers Protective Assn. of America** (1890), 3755 Lindell Blvd., St. Louis, MO 63108; 161,866.

**Trilateral Commission, The** (1973), 345 E. 46th St., N.Y., NY 10017; 311.

**Truck Historical Soc., Amer.** (1971), 300 Office Park Dr., Ste. 120, Birmingham, AL 35223; 15,000+.

**Trucking Assn., Amer.** (1933), 2200 Mill Rd., Alexandria, VA 22314-4677; 4,000 cos.

**True Sisters, United Order** (1846), 212 Fifth Ave., N.Y., NY 10010; 10,000.

**T.S. Eliot Soc.** (1980), 5007 Waterman Blvd., St. Louis. MO 63108; 200.

**Tuberous Sclerosis Assn. of Amer.** (1970), P.O. Box 44, Rockland, MA 02370; 2,500.

**UFOs, Natl. Investigation Committee on** (1967), 14617 Victory Blvd., Suite 4, Van Nuys, CA 91411.

**UNICEF, U.S. Committee for** (1947), 333 E. 38th St., N.Y., NY 10016.

**USO (United Service Organizations)** (1941), 601 Indiana Ave., NW, Wash., DC 20004.

**Underwriters, Amer. Soc. of Chartered Life** (1927), 270 Bryn Mawr Ave., Bryn Mawr, PA 19010; 30,000.

**Underwriters, Soc. of Chartered Property and Casualty** (1944), Kahler Hall, 720 Providence Rd., Malvern, PA 19355.

**United Nations Assn. of the U.S.A.** (1923, as League of Nations Assn.), 485 Fifth Ave., N.Y., NY 10017; 29,000.

**United Way of America** (1918), 801 N. Fairfax St., Alexandria, VA 22309; 1,200.

**Universities, Assn. of Amer.** (1914), One Dupont Circle, Suite 730, Wash., DC 20036; 59 institutions.

**Universities & Colleges, Assn. of Governing Bds. of** (1921), One Dupont Circle NW, Suite 400, Wash., DC 20036.

**University Continuing Education Assn., Natl.** (1915), One Dupont Circle, Ste. 615, Wash., DC 20036; 2,000.

**University Extension Assn., Natl.** (1915), One Dupont Circle NW, Suite 400, Wash., DC 20036; 1,100.

**University Foundation, Intl.** (1973), 1301 S. Noland Rd., Independence, MO 64055; 67,780.

**University Professors, Amer. Assn. of** (1915), 1012 14th St. NW, Suite 500, Wash., DC 20005; 41,000.

**University Women, Amer. Assn. of** (1881), 1111 16th St. NW, Wash., DC 20036.

**Urban Coalition, Natl.** (1967), 1120 G St. NW, Suite 900, Wash., DC 20005; 42 affiliates.

**Urban League, Natl.** (1910), 500 E. 62d St., N.Y., NY 10020.

**Useless Skills, Institute of Totally** (1987), Box 181, Temple, NH 03084; 424.

**Utility Commissioners, Natl. Assn. of Regulatory** (1889), 1102 Interstate Commerce Commission Bldg., 12th & Constitution Ave. NW, Wash., DC 20044-0684.

**Vampire Research Center** (1972), P.O. Box 252, Elmhurst, NY 11373; 650.

**Variety Clubs Intl.** (1928), 1560 Bdway., N.Y., NY 10036.

**VASA Order of America** (1896), 65 Bryant Rd., Cranston, R.I. 02910; 30,000.

**Ventriloquists, No. American Assn. of** (1944), Box 420, Littleton, CO 80160; 1,475.

**Veterans Assn., Blinded** (1958), 477 H St. NW, Wash., DC 20001; 7,500.

**Veterans of Foreign Wars of the U.S.** (1899) **& Ladies Auxiliary** (1914), 406 W. 34th St., Kansas City, MO 64111.

**Veterans of the Vietnam War** (1980), 760 Jumper Rd., Wilkes-Barre, PA 18702-8033; 30,000.

**Veterans of World War I** (1958), 941 N. Capitol St. NE, Room 1201-C, Wash., DC 20002-4234; 52,000.

**Veterans of WWII, U.S. Submarine** (1955), 6523 San Joaquin St., Sacramento, CA 95820; 8,000.

**Veterinary Medical Assn., Amer.** (1863), 1931 N. Meacham Rd., Schaumburg, IL 60173; 53,512.

**Victorian Society in America** (1965), 219 S. Sixth St., Phila., PA 19106; 2,300.

**Violet Soc. of Amer., African** (1946), P.O. Box 3609, Beaumont, TX 77704; 15,000.

**Virgil Fox Society, The** (1977), 88 Chestnut St., Brooklyn, NY 11208; 450+.

**Volleyball Assn., U.S.** (1928), 3595 E. Fountain Blvd., Ste. I-2, Colorado Springs, CO 80910-1740; 78,911.

**Walking Society, American** (1980), Viana House, Box 1315, Beverly Hills, CA 90213.

**War Mothers, Amer.** (1917), 2615 Woodley Pl. NW, Wash., DC 20008; 2,000.

**Warrant and Warrant Officers' Assn., Chief, U.S. Coast Guard** (1929), c/o Fort McNair Yacht Basin, 200 V Street, SW, Wash., DC 20024; 3,346.

**Watch & Clock Collectors, Natl. Assn. of** (1943), 514 Poplar St., Columbia, PA 17512; 35,000.

**Watercolor Soc., American** (1867), 47 Fifth Ave., N.Y., NY 10003; 506.

**Water Environment Federation** (1928), 601 Wythe St., Alexandria, VA 22314; 40,000.

**Water Pollution Control Admin., Assn. of State and Interstate** (1961), 750 First St. NE, Ste. 910, Wash., DC 20001.

**Water Pollution Control Federation** (1928), 601 Wythe St., Alexandria, VA 22314-1994; 32,000.

**Water Resources Assn., Amer.** (1964), 5410 Grosvenor Ln., Suite 220, Bethesda, MD 20814-2192; 4,000.

**Water Ski Assn., Amer.** (1939), 799 Overlook Dr. SE, Winter Haven, FL 33884.

**Water Assn., Natl. Ground** (1948), 6375 Riverside Drive, Dublin, OH 43017; 24,000.

**Water Works Assn., Amer.** (1881), 6666 W. Quincy Ave., Denver, CO 80235; 52,000.

**Welding Society, Amer.** (1919), 550 NW LeJeune Rd., Miami, FL 33126; 41,000.

**Wheelchair Athletic Assn., Natl.** (1956), 3595 E. Fountain Blvd., Suite L-1, Colorado Springs, CO 80918; 1,500.

**Widows, Society of Military** (1968), 5535 Hemstead Way, Springfield, VA 22151; 2,000.

**Wilderness Society** (1935), 900 17th St. NW, Wash., DC 20006; 350,000.

**Wildflower Research Center, Natl.** (1982), 2600 FM 973 N., Austin, TX 78725-4201; 16,000.

**Wildlife, Defenders of** (1947), 1244 19th St. NW, Wash., DC 20036; 80,000.

**Wildlife Federation, Natl.** (1936), 1400 16th St. NW, Wash., DC 20036-2266; 5.8 mln.

**Wildlife Fund, World** (1961), 1250 24th St. NW, Wash., DC 20037; 1.2 mln.

**Wildlife Management Institute** (1911), 1101 14th St., Suite 725, NW, Wash., DC 20005.

**William Penn Assn.** (1886), 709 Brighton Rd., Pittsburgh, PA 15233; 90,000.

**Wireless Pioneers, Society of** (1968), P.O. Box 86, Geyserville, CA 85441; 5,200.

**Wizard of Oz Club, Intl.** (1957), Box 95, Kinderhook, IL 62345; 3,000.

**Women, Natl. Assn. of Bank** (1920), 500 No. Michigan Ave., Suite 1400, Chicago, IL 60611; 30,000.

**Women, Natl. Organization for (NOW)** (1966), 1000 16th St. NW, Ste. 700, Wash., DC 20036; 250,000.

**Women Artists, Natl. Assn. of** (1889), 41 Union Sq., N.Y., NY 10003; 725.

**Women Engineers, Society of** (1950), 345 E. 47th St., N.Y., NY 10017; 16,000.

**Women for America, Concerned** (1979), 370 L'Enfant Promenade SW, #800, Washington, DC 20024; 600,000.

**Women in Communications** (1908), 2101 Wilson Blvd., Ste. 417, Arlington, VA 22201; 11,000.

**Women in Radio and TV, Inc.** (1951), 1101 Connecticut Ave. NW, #700, Washington, DC 20036; 2,500.

**Women Intl., Financial** (1921), 500 N. Michigan Ave., Ste. 1400, Chicago, IL 60611; 35,000.

**Women Strike for Peace** (1961), 110 Maryland Ave. NE, Ste. 302, Washington, DC 20002; 10,000.

**Women of the U.S., Natl. Council of** (1888), 777 U.N. Plaza, N.Y., NY 10017; 500.

**Women Voters of the U.S., League of** (1920), 1730 M St. NW, Wash., DC 20036; 120,000.

**Women World War Veterans** (1919), 237 Madison Ave., N.Y., NY 10016; 35,000.

**Women's Army Corps Veterans Assn.** (1947), Hwy. 21, Anniston, AL 36206; 3,500.

**Women's Association, American Business** (1949), 9100 Ward Parkway, P.O. Box 8728, Kansas City, MO 64114.

**Women's Christian Temperance Union, Natl.** (1874), 1730 Chicago Ave., Evanston, IL 60201; 40,000.

**Women's Clubs, General Federation of** (1890), 1734 N St. NW, Wash. DC, 20036-2990; 350,000 U.S.

**Women's Clubs, Natl. Federation of Business & Professional** (1919), 2012 Massachusetts Ave. NW, Wash., DC 20036.

**Women's Intl. League for Peace & Freedom** (1915), 1213 Race St., Phila., PA 19107; 50,000.

**Women's Legal Defense Fund** (1971), 1875 Connecticut Ave. NW, Suite 710, Washington, DC 20009; 2,500.

**Women's Overseas Service League** (1921), P.O. Box 39058, Friendship Station, Washington, DC 20016; 1,164.

**Woodmen of America, Modern** (1883), 1701 1st Ave., Rock Island, IL 61201; 704,833.

**Woodmen of the World Life Insurance Soc.** (1890), 1700 Farnam St., Omaha, NE 68102; 980,000.

**Workmen's Circle** (1900), 45 E. 33d St., N.Y., NY 10016.

**World Federalist Assn.** (1975), 418 7th St. SE, Washington, DC 20003; 10,000.

**World Future Society** (1966), 7910 Woodmont Ave., Ste. 450, Bethesda, MD 20814; 30,000.

**World Learning Inc.** (1932), Kipling Rd., P.O. Box 676, Brattleboro, VT 05302-0676; 60,000.

**World Peace, Intl Assn. of Educators for** (1969), P.O. Box 3282, Mastin Lake Sta., Huntsville, AL 35810-0282; 21,500.

**World's Fair Collectors Soc.** (1968), P.O. Box 20806, Sarasota, FL 34276-3806; 540.

**Writers Guild of America, West** (1933), 8955 Beverly Blvd., W. Hollywood, CA 90048; 7,500+.

**Yachting Assn., Southern California** (1921), 1086 Peninsula St., Ventura, CA 93001; 20,000 families.

**Young America's Foundation** (1971), 110 Elden St., Herndon, VA 22070.

**Young Men's Christian Assns. of the U.S.A.** (1851), 101 N. Wacker Dr., Chicago, IL 60606; 13 mln.

**YM-YMHAs of Greater New York, Associated** (1957), 130 E. 59th St., N.Y., NY 10020; 55,100.

**Young Women's Christian Assn. of the U.S.A.** (1906), 726 Broadway, N.Y., NY 10003; 1.6 mln.

**Youth Hostels, American** (1934), P.O. Box 37613, Wash., DC 20013-7613; 200,000.

**Zero Population Growth** (1968), 1400 16th St. NW, Suite 320, Wash., DC 20036; 50,000.

**Zionist Organization of America** (1897), 4 E. 34th St., N.Y., NY 10016; 110,000.

**Zoological Parks & Aquariums, Amer. Assn. of** (1924), 7970-D Old Georgetown Rd., Bethesda, MD 20814-2493; 6,300.

**Zoologists, Amer. Society of** (1902), 401 N. Michigan Ave., Chicago, IL 60611; 3,500.

# POSTAL INFORMATION

## U.S. Postal Service

The Postal Reorganization Act, creating a government-owned postal service under the executive branch and replacing the old Post Office Department, was signed into law by President Richard Nixon on Aug. 12, 1970. The service officially came into being on July 1, 1971.

The U.S. Postal Service is governed by an 11-person Board of Governors. Nine members are appointed to 9-year terms by the president with Senate approval. These 9, in turn, choose a postmaster general. The board and the postmaster general choose the 11th member, who serves as deputy postmaster general. An independent Postal Rate Commission of 5 members, appointed by the president, recommends postal rates to the Board of Governors for their approval.

As of Sept. 30, 1992, there were 39,595 post offices, stations, and branches throughout the U.S. and possessions.

## U.S. Domestic Rates

Postal rates and fees shown below were implemented on Feb. 3, 1991. Domestic rates apply to the U.S., its territories and possessions, and APOs and FPOs.

### First Class

Letters written, and matter sealed against inspection, 29¢ for 1st oz. or fraction, 23¢ for each additional oz. or fraction. U.S. Postal Service cards, single 19¢, double 38¢; private postcards, same.

First class includes written matter, namely letters, postal cards, postcards (private mailing cards) and all other matter wholly or partly in writing, whether sealed or unsealed, except manuscripts for books, periodical articles and music, manuscript copy accompanying proofsheets or corrected proofsheets of the same and the writing authorized by law on matter of other classes. Also matter sealed or closed against inspection, bills and statements of accounts.

### Express Mail

Express Mail Service is available for any mailable article up to 70 pounds, and guarantees delivery between major U.S. cities or your money back. Articles received by the acceptance time authorized by the postmaster at a postal facility offering Express Mail will be delivered by 3 p.m. the next day to some locations or will be delivered by noon the next day to other destinations. Or, if you prefer, your shipment can be picked up as early as 10 a.m. the next business day. Second day service is available to locations not on the Next Day Delivery Network. Rates include insurance, Shipment Receipt, and Record of Delivery at the destination post office.

Consult Postmaster for other Express Mail Services and rates. (The Postal Service will refund, upon application to originating office, the postage for any Express Mail shipments not meeting the service standard except for those delayed by strike or work stoppage, delay or cancellation of flights, or governmental action beyond the control of the Postal Service.)

### Third Class

Third class (limit up to but not including 16 ounces): Mailable matter not in 1st and 2d classes.

Single mailing: Publications, small parcels, printed matter, booklets and catalogs, 29¢ the first ounce, 52¢ for over 1 to 2 ozs., 75¢ for over 2 to 3 ozs., 98¢ for over 3 to 4 ozs., $1.21 for over 4 to 6 ozs., $1.33 for over 6 to 8 ozs., $1.44 for over 8 to 10 ozs., $1.56 for over 10 to 12 ozs., $1.67 for over 12 to 14 ozs., $1.79 for over 14 but less than 16 ozs.

Bulk mailing: At least 200 pieces or 50 pounds of such items as solicitations, newsletters, advertising materials, books and cassettes, each item of which individually weighs less than one pound. Minimum rate per piece: Basic presort, $0.198 for pieces weighing 3.3067 ounces or less; for pieces weighing more than 3.3067 ounces, the rate is $0.109 per piece + $0.600 per pound. Contact your post office for the discounts offered for presorted, destination entry and automation compatible mail.

Separate rates for some nonprofit organizations. Bulk mailing fee, $75 per calendar year. Apply to postmaster for permit. One-time fee for permit imprint, $75.

### Parcel Post—Fourth Class

Fourth class or parcel post (16 ounces and over): merchandise, printed matter, etc., may be sealed, subject to inspection.

### Priority Mail Flat Rate

First class mail of more than 11 ounces can be sent "Priority Mail" service. The most expeditious handling and transportation available will be used for fastest delivery.

The pickup service for Priority Mail costs $4.50 for each stop by the Postal Service. There is also a $2.90 flat Priority Mail rate for matter sent in the Special Postal Service-provided envelope.

### Forwarding Addresses

The mailer, in order to obtain a forwarding address, must endorse the envelope or cover "Address Correction Requested." The destination post office then will determine whether a forwarding address has been left on file and provide it for a fee of 35¢ per manual correction and 20¢ per automated correction.

## Priority Mail

Packages weighing up to 70 pounds and not exceeding 108 inches in length and girth combined, including written and other material of the first class, whether sealed or unsealed, fractions of a pound being charged as a full pound.

Rates according to zone apply between the U.S. and Puerto Rico and Virgin Islands. The mileage between the specific geographic locations of 3-digit ZIP codes determines the zone number to be used. The mileage range represented by the zone number is: Zone 1—up to 50 miles; 2—51 to 150 miles; 3—151 to 300 miles; 4—301 to 600 miles; 5—601 to 1,000 miles; 6—1,001 to 1,400 miles; 7—1,401 to 1,800 miles; 8—over 1,800 miles.

Parcels weighing less than 15 pounds, measuring over 84 inches but not exceeding 108 inches in length and girth combined are chargeable with a minimum rate equal to that for a 15 pound parcel for the zone to which addressed.

| Zones | To 2 lbs | 3 lbs | 4 lbs | 5 lbs* |
|---|---|---|---|---|
| 1, 2, 3, 4, 5, 6, 7, 8 | $2.90 | $4.10 | $4.65 | $5.45 |

*Consult postmaster for rates for parcels over 5 lbs.

## Special Handling

Third and fourth class parcels will be handled and delivered as expeditiously as practicable (but not special delivery) upon payment, in addition to the regular postage: up to 10 lbs., $1.80; over 10 lbs., $2.50. Such parcels must be endorsed, Special Handling.

## Special Delivery

First class mail up to 2 lbs., $7.65; over 2 lbs. and up to 10 lbs., $7.95; over 10 lbs., $8.55. All other classes up to 2 lbs., $8.05; over 2 and up to 10 lbs., $8.65; over 10 lbs., $9.30.

## Bound Printed Matter Rates
### (Single Piece Zone Rate)
Fourth-Class Mail: Single-Piece Bound Printed Matter

| Weight lbs. | Local | 1&2 | 3 | 4 | Rate Zones 5 | 6 | 7 | 8 |
|---|---|---|---|---|---|---|---|---|
| 1.5 | $0.93 | $1.27 | $1.30 | $1.36 | $1.45 | $1.54 | $1.65 | $1.75 |
| 2 | 0.94 | 1.30 | 1.34 | 1.42 | 1.53 | 1.66 | 1.81 | 1.93 |
| 2.5 | 0.96 | 1.33 | 1.38 | 1.48 | 1.62 | 1.78 | 1.97 | 2.12 |
| 3 | 0.98 | 1.35 | 1.42 | 1.54 | 1.71 | 1.90 | 2.12 | 2.31 |
| 3.5 | 0.99 | 1.38 | 1.46 | 1.60 | 1.80 | 2.02 | 2.28 | 2.50 |
| 4 | 1.01 | 1.41 | 1.50 | 1.66 | 1.89 | 2.14 | 2.44 | 2.69 |
| 4.5 | 1.02 | 1.44 | 1.54 | 1.72 | 1.98 | 2.26 | 2.59 | 2.88 |
| 5 | 1.04 | 1.47 | 1.58 | 1.78 | 2.07 | 2.38 | 2.75 | 3.07 |
| 6 | 1.07 | 1.53 | 1.66 | 1.89 | 2.24 | 2.61 | 3.06 | 3.44 |
| 7 | 1.10 | 1.59 | 1.74 | 2.01 | 2.42 | 2.85 | 3.38 | 3.82 |
| 8 | 1.14 | 1.64 | 1.82 | 2.13 | 2.60 | 3.09 | 3.69 | 4.20 |
| 9 | 1.17 | 1.70 | 1.90 | 2.25 | 2.77 | 3.33 | 4.01 | 4.57 |
| 10 | 1.20 | 1.76 | 1.98 | 2.37 | 2.95 | 3.57 | 4.32 | 4.95 |

(Includes both catalogs and similar bound printed matter.)

(Bound printed matter must weigh at least 1 pound and not more than 10 pounds. Bound printed matter includes catalogs, directories and books not eligible for special fourth-class rates.)

## Domestic Mail Special Services

**Registry** — Only matter prepaid with postage at First-class postage rates may be registered. Stamps or meter stamps must be attached. The face of the article must be at least 5″ long, 3½″ high. The mailer is required to declare the value of mail presented for registration.

### Registered Mail

| Value | Insured | Uninsured |
|---|---|---|
| $0.00 to $100 . . . . | $4.50 | $4.40 |
| $100.01 to $500 . . . | 4.85 | 4.70 |
| $500.01 to $1,000 . . | 5.25 | 5.05 |
| $1,000.01 to $2,000 . | 5.70 | 5.40 |
| $2,000.01 to $3,000 . | 6.15 | 5.75 |
| $3,000.01 to $4,000 . | 6.60 | 6.10 |
| $4,000.01 to $5,000 . | 7.05 | 6.45 |
| $5,000.01 to $6,000 . | 7.50 | 6.80 |
| $6,000.01 to $7,000 . | 7.95 | 7.15 |
| $7,000.01 to $8,000 . | 8.40 | 7.50 |
| $8,000.01 to $9,000 . | 8.85 | 7.85 |
| $9,000.01 to $10,000 | 9.30 | 8.20 |

Consult postmaster for registry rates above $10,000.

**C.O.D.:** Unregistered — is applicable to first-, third-, fourth-class, and express mail matter. Such mail must be based on bona fide orders or be in conformity with agreements between senders and addressees. **Registered** — for details consult postmaster.

**Insurance** — is applicable to third and fourth class matter. Matter for sale addressed to prospective purchasers who have not ordered it or authorized its sending will not be insured.

### Insured Mail

| | |
|---|---|
| $0.01 to $50 . . . . . . . . . . . . . . . . . . . . . . . . | $0.75 |
| 50.01 to $100. . . . . . . . . . . . . . . . . . . . . . . | 1.60 |
| 100.01 to $150. . . . . . . . . . . . . . . . . . . . . . | 2.40 |
| 150.01 to $200. . . . . . . . . . . . . . . . . . . . . . | 2.40 |
| 200.01 to $300. . . . . . . . . . . . . . . . . . . . . . | 3.50 |
| 300.01 to $400. . . . . . . . . . . . . . . . . . . . . . | 4.60 |
| 400.01 to $500. . . . . . . . . . . . . . . . . . . . . . | 5.40 |
| 500.01 to $600. . . . . . . . . . . . . . . . . . . . . . | 6.20 |

Liability for insured mail is limited to $600.

**Certified mail** — service is available for any matter having no intrinsic value on which 1st class or air mail postage is paid. Receipt is furnished at time of mailing and evidence of delivery obtained. The fee is $1.00 in addition to postage. Return receipt, restricted delivery, and special delivery are available upon payment of additional fees. No indemnity.

## Special Fourth Class Rate
### (limit 70 lbs.)

First pound or fraction, $1.05 (59¢ if 500 pieces or more of special rate matter are presorted to 5 digit ZIP code or 88¢ if 500 pieces or more are presorted to Bulk Mail Cntrs.); each additional pound or fraction through 7 pounds, 43¢; each additional pound, 25¢. Only the following specific articles: Books of at least 8 printed pages consisting wholly of reading matter or scholarly bibliography, or reading matter with incidental blank spaces for notations and containing no advertising matter other than incidental announcements of books; 16-millimeter or narrower width films in final form and catalogs of such films of 24 pages or more (at least 22 of which are printed) except films and film catalogs sent to or from commercial theaters; printed music in bound or sheet form; printed objective test materials; sound recordings, playscripts and manuscripts for books, periodicals, and music; printed educational reference charts; loose-leaf pages and binders thereof consisting of medical information for distribution to doctors, hospitals, medical schools, and medical students; computer-readable media containing prerecorded information and guides for use with such media. Package must be marked "Special 4th Class Rate" stating item contained.

## Library Rate (limit 70 lbs.)

First pound 65¢, each additional pound through 7 pounds, 24¢; each additional pound, 12¢. Books when loaned or exchanged between and sent to or from schools, colleges, public libraries, and certain non-profit organizations; books, printed music, bound academic theses, periodicals, sound recordings, other library materials, museum materials (specimens, collections), scientific or mathematical kits, instruments or other devices; also catalogs, guides or scripts for some of these materials. Must be marked "Library Rate".

Also qualifying for library rate are: Books mailed from publishers or distributors to schools, libraries, colleges or universities or to bookstores owned, operated and controlled by schools, colleges or universities.

## Parcel Post Rate Schedule
(Inter BMC/ASF Zip Codes Only, Machinable Parcels, No Discount, No Surcharge)

| Weight up to but not exceeding—(pounds) | 1 and 2 | 3 | 4 | Zones 5 | 6 | 7 | 8 |
|---|---|---|---|---|---|---|---|
| 2. . . . . . . . . . . . . | $2.19 | $2.32 | $2.46 | $2.74 | $2.85 | $2.85 | $2.85 |
| 3. . . . . . . . . . . . . | 2.29 | 2.49 | 2.70 | 3.12 | 3.54 | 4.00 | 4.05 |
| 4. . . . . . . . . . . . . | 2.39 | 2.65 | 2.94 | 3.50 | 4.06 | 4.35 | 4.60 |
| 5. . . . . . . . . . . . . | 2.49 | 2.81 | 3.17 | 3.88 | 4.58 | 5.20 | 5.40 |
| 6. . . . . . . . . . . . . | 2.59 | 2.98 | 3.41 | 4.26 | 5.10 | 6.33 | 8.55 |
| 7. . . . . . . . . . . . . | 2.68 | 3.14 | 3.65 | 4.64 | 5.62 | 7.06 | 9.60 |
| 8. . . . . . . . . . . . . | 2.78 | 3.31 | 3.89 | 5.02 | 6.14 | 7.78 | 10.65 |
| 9. . . . . . . . . . . . . | 2.88 | 3.47 | 4.12 | 5.40 | 6.67 | 8.51 | 11.70 |
| 10. . . . . . . . . . . . . | 2.98 | 3.63 | 4.36 | 5.78 | 7.19 | 9.24 | 12.75 |
| 11. . . . . . . . . . . . . | 3.08 | 3.80 | 4.60 | 6.16 | 7.71 | 9.97 | 13.75 |

| Weight up to but not exceeding—(pounds) | Zones | | | | | | | |
|---|---|---|---|---|---|---|---|---|
| | 1 and 2 | 3 | 4 | 5 | 6 | 7 | 8 |
| 12. | 3.18 | 3.96 | 4.83 | 6.54 | 8.23 | 10.69 | 14.80 |
| 13. | 3.25 | 4.08 | 4.99 | 6.79 | 8.57 | 11.17 | 15.85 |
| 14. | 3.32 | 4.19 | 5.16 | 7.04 | 8.92 | 11.65 | 16.90 |
| 15. | 3.38 | 4.28 | 5.27 | 7.23 | 9.17 | 11.99 | 17.95 |
| 16. | 3.43 | 4.36 | 5.39 | 7.40 | 9.40 | 12.31 | 19.00 |
| 17. | 3.48 | 4.44 | 5.49 | 7.56 | 9.62 | 12.61 | 19.91 |
| 18. | 3.53 | 4.51 | 5.60 | 7.72 | 9.83 | 12.90 | 20.38 |
| 19. | 3.58 | 4.59 | 5.69 | 7.87 | 10.03 | 13.17 | 20.83 |
| 20. | 3.63 | 4.65 | 5.79 | 8.01 | 10.22 | 13.43 | 21.26 |
| 21. | 3.68 | 4.72 | 5.88 | 8.15 | 10.40 | 13.68 | 21.66 |
| 22. | 3.72 | 4.79 | 5.97 | 8.28 | 10.57 | 13.91 | 22.05 |
| 23. | 3.77 | 4.85 | 6.05 | 8.40 | 10.74 | 14.14 | 22.43 |
| 24. | 3.81 | 4.91 | 6.13 | 8.52 | 10.90 | 14.36 | 22.78 |
| 25. | 3.85 | 4.97 | 6.21 | 8.64 | 11.05 | 14.57 | 23.13 |

### Postal Union Mail Special Services

**Registration** — available to practically all countries. Fee $4.40. The maximum indemnity payable — generally only in case of complete loss (of both contents and wrapper) — is $32.35. To Canada only the fee is $4.50 providing indemnity for loss up to $100, $4.85 for loss up to $500, and $5.25 for loss up to $1,000.

**Return receipt** — showing to whom and date delivered, $1.00.

**Special delivery** — Available to most countries. Consult post office. Fees for International Special Delivery same for air or surface: for letters, letter packages and postcards not over 2 pounds, $7.65. If over 2 pounds, $7.95, for printed matter, matter for the blind, or small packets, $8.05 if not over 2 pounds; if over 2 pounds, $8.65.

**Marking** — an article intended for special delivery service must have affixed to the cover near the name of the country of destination "EXPRES" (special delivery) label, obtainable at the post office, or it may be marked on the cover boldly in red "EXPRES" (special delivery).

**Special handling** — entitles AO surface packages to priority handling between mailing point and U.S. point of dispatch. Fees: $1.80 for packages to 10 pounds, and $2.50 for packages over 10 pounds.

**Airmail** — there is daily air service to practically all countries.

**Prepayment of replies from other countries** — a mailer who wishes to prepay a reply by letter from another country may do so by sending his correspondent one or more international reply coupons, which may be purchased at United States post offices. One coupon should be accepted in any country in exchange for stamps to prepay a surface letter of the first unit of weight to the U.S.

**Additional international special services: Insurance:** Available to many countries for loss of or damage to items paid at parcel post rate. Consult postmaster for indemnity limits for individual countries.

| Limit of Indemnity Not Over | Fees | |
|---|---|---|
| | Canada | All Other Countries |
| $50 | $0.75 | $1.60 |
| 100 | 1.60 | 2.40 |
| 200 | 2.40 | 3.50 |
| 300 | 3.50 | 4.60 |
| 400 | 4.60 | 5.40 |
| 500 | 5.40 | 6.20 |
| 600 | 6.20 | 6.60 |
| 700 | | 6.90 |
| 800 | | 7.20 |
| 900 | | 7.50 |
| 1,000 | | 7.80 |
| 1,100 | | 8.10 |
| 1,200 | | 8.40 |

**Restricted Delivery:** Available to many countries for registered mail, limits who may receive an item. Fee: $2.50.

## Post Office-Authorized 2-Letter State Abbreviations

The abbreviations below are approved by the U.S. Postal Service for use in addresses only. They do not replace the traditional abbreviations in other contexts. The official list follows, including the District of Columbia, Guam, Puerto Rico, the Canal Zone, and the Virgin Islands (all capital letters are used):

| | | | | | | | |
|---|---|---|---|---|---|---|---|
| Alabama | AL | Hawaii | HI | Mississippi | MS | Pennsylvania | PA |
| Alaska | AK | Idaho | ID | Missouri | MO | Puerto Rico | PR |
| American Samoa | AS | Illinois | IL | Montana | MT | Rhode Island | RI |
| Arizona | AZ | Indiana | IN | Nebraska | NE | South Carolina | SC |
| Arkansas | AR | Iowa | IA | Nevada | NV | South Dakota | SD |
| California | CA | Kansas | KS | New Hampshire | NH | Tennessee | TN |
| Colorado | CO | Kentucky | KY | New Jersey | NJ | Texas | TX |
| Connecticut | CT | Louisiana | LA | New Mexico | NM | Utah | UT |
| Delaware | DE | Maine | ME | New York | NY | Vermont | VT |
| Dist. of Col. | DC | Marshall Islands | MH | North Carolina | NC | Virginia | VA |
| Federated States of Micronesia | FM | Maryland | MD | North Dakota | ND | Virgin Islands | VI |
| | | Massachusetts | MA | Northern Mariana Is. | MP | Washington | WA |
| Florida | FL | Michigan | MI | Ohio | OH | West Virginia | WV |
| Georgia | GA | Minnesota | MN | Oklahoma | OK | Wisconsin | WI |
| Guam | GU | | | Oregon | OR | Wyoming | WY |

Also approved for use in addressing mail are the following abbreviations:

| | | | | | | | |
|---|---|---|---|---|---|---|---|
| Alley | Aly | Court | Ct | Gardens | Gdns | Road | Rd |
| Arcade | Arc | Courts | Cts | Grove | Grv | Rural | R |
| Avenue | Ave | Crescent | Cres | Heights | Hts | Square | Sq |
| Boulevard | Blvd | Drive | Dr | Highway | Hwy | Street | St |
| Branch | Br | Expressway | Expy | Lane | Ln | Terrace | Ter |
| Bypass | Byp | Extended | Ext | Manor | Mnr | Trail | Trl |
| Causeway | Cswy | Extension | Ext | Place | Pl | Turnpike | Tpke |
| Center | Ctr | Freeway | Fwy | Plaza | Plz | Viaduct | Via |
| Circle | Cir | | | Point | Pt | Vista | Vis |

# International Air Mail

**Aerogrammes** — 45¢ each to all countries.
**Air mail postcards** (single) - 40¢ to all countries except Canada and Mexico (30¢ each)
**International letters and letter packages: airmail to Canada and Mexico** (there are no surface rates to these countries)—weight not over 0.5 ozs., 40¢ to Canada, 35¢ to Mexico; not over 1.0 ozs., 40¢ to Canada, 45¢ to Mexico; not over 2 ozs., 63¢ to Canada, 65¢ to Mexico; not over 3 ozs., 86¢ to Canada, 90¢ to Mexico.

## Air Mail, Letter and Letter Package Rates, Countries Other Than Canada and Mexico

| Weight not over | Rate | Weight not over | Rate | Weight not over | Rate | Weight not over | Rate |
|---|---|---|---|---|---|---|---|
| 0.5 ozs. | $ 0.50 | 12.5 ozs. | $ 9.92 | 24.5 ozs. | $19.28 | 41 ozs. | $28.64 |
| 1.0 | 0.95 | 13.0 | 10.31 | 25.0 | 19.67 | 42 | 29.03 |
| 1.5 | 1.34 | 13.5 | 10.70 | 25.5 | 20.06 | 43 | 29.42 |
| 2.0 | 1.73 | 14.0 | 11.09 | 26.0 | 20.45 | 44 | 29.81 |
| 2.5 | 2.12 | 14.5 | 11.48 | 26.5 | 20.84 | 45 | 30.20 |
| 3.0 | 2.51 | 15.0 | 11.87 | 27.0 | 21.23 | 46 | 30.59 |
| 3.5 | 2.90 | 15.5 | 12.26 | 27.5 | 21.62 | 47 | 30.98 |
| 4.0 | 3.29 | 16.0 | 12.65 | 28.0 | 22.01 | 48 | 31.37 |
| 4.5 | 3.68 | 16.5 | 13.04 | 28.5 | 22.40 | 49 | 31.76 |
| 5.0 | 4.07 | 17.0 | 13.43 | 29.0 | 22.79 | 50 | 32.15 |
| 5.5 | 4.46 | 17.5 | 13.82 | 29.5 | 23.18 | 51 | 32.54 |
| 6.0 | 4.85 | 18.0 | 14.21 | 30.0 | 23.57 | 52 | 32.93 |
| 6.5 | 5.24 | 18.5 | 14.60 | 30.5 | 23.96 | 53 | 33.32 |
| 7.0 | 5.63 | 19.0 | 14.99 | 31.0 | 24.35 | 54 | 33.71 |
| 7.5 | 6.02 | 19.5 | 15.38 | 31.5 | 24.74 | 55 | 34.10 |
| 8.0 | 6.41 | 20.0 | 15.77 | 32.0 | 25.13 | 56 | 34.49 |
| 8.5 | 6.80 | 20.5 | 16.16 | 33 | 25.52 | 57 | 34.88 |
| 9.0 | 7.19 | 21.0 | 16.55 | 34 | 25.91 | 58 | 35.27 |
| 9.5 | 7.58 | 21.5 | 16.94 | 35 | 26.30 | 59 | 35.66 |
| 10.0 | 7.97 | 22.0 | 17.33 | 36 | 26.69 | 60 | 36.05 |
| 10.5 | 8.36 | 22.5 | 17.72 | 37 | 27.08 | 61 | 36.44 |
| 11.0 | 8.75 | 23.0 | 18.11 | 38 | 27.47 | 62 | 36.83 |
| 11.5 | 9.14 | 23.5 | 18.50 | 39 | 27.86 | 63 | 37.22 |
| 12.0 | 9.53 | 24.0 | 18.89 | 40 | 28.25 | 64 | 37.61 |

**Weight limit: 64 oz. (4 lbs.)**

## Air Mail, Parcel Post Rates

| Weight steps | Air Parcel post rate groups | | | | |
|---|---|---|---|---|---|
| | A | B | C | D | E |
| First pound . . . . . . . . . . . . . . . . . . . | $6.00 | $7.75 | $9.25 | $10.70 | $12.30 |
| Each additional pound or fraction up to 5 pounds. . . . | 3.00 | 4.25 | 5.00 | 6.00 | 7.00 |
| Each additional pound or fraction over 5 pounds . . . . | 2.00 | 3.00 | 4.00 | 5.00 | 6.00 |

**Air Parcel Post Rate Groups** (For further information, consult your local post office.)

| Country | Rate group | Maximum weight limit | Country | Rate group | Maximum weight limit |
|---|---|---|---|---|---|
| Afghanistan. . . . . . . . . . | D. . . . . . . . | 44 | Burkina Faso . . . . . . . . . | D. . . . . . . | 44 |
| Albania . . . . . . . . . . . . . | C. . . . . . . . | 44 | Burma. . . . . . . . . . . . . . . | D. . . . . . . . | 22 |
| Algeria . . . . . . . . . . . . . | D. . . . . . . . | 44 | Burundi . . . . . . . . . . . . | E. . . . . . . . . | 44 |
| Andorra . . . . . . . . . . . . | B. . . . . . . . | 44 | Cambodia. . . . . . . . . . . | No Parcel Post Service. | |
| Angola . . . . . . . . . . . . . | E. . . . . . . . | 22 | Cameroon . . . . . . . . . . | D. . . . . . . . | 44 |
| Anguilla . . . . . . . . . . . . | A. . . . . . . . | 22 | Canada . . . . . . . . . . . . . | Separate Rate | 66 |
| Antigua & Barbuda. . . . . . | A. . . . . . . . | 22 | | Group. | |
| Argentina. . . . . . . . . . . | D. . . . . . . . | 44 | Cape Verde. . . . . . . . . . | D. . . . . . . . | 22 |
| Armenia. . . . . . . . . . . . | E. . . . . . . . | 22 | Cayman Islands . . . . . . . | A. . . . . . . . | 44 |
| Aruba . . . . . . . . . . . . . . | A. . . . . . . . | 44 | Central African Rep. . . . . . | E. . . . . . . . | 44 |
| Ascension. . . . . . . . . . . | No Air Service . | | Chad . . . . . . . . . . . . . . | D. . . . . . . . | 44 |
| Australia . . . . . . . . . . . | D. . . . . . . . | 44 | Chile. . . . . . . . . . . . . . . | D. . . . . . . . | 44 |
| Austria . . . . . . . . . . . . . | B. . . . . . . . | 44 | China (Peoples | | |
| Azerbaijan . . . . . . . . . . | E. . . . . . . . | 22 | Republic of) . . . . . . . . . | D. . . . . . . . | 44 |
| Azores . . . . . . . . . . . . . | C. . . . . . . . | 44 | Colombia . . . . . . . . . . . | B. . . . . . . . | 44 |
| Bahamas . . . . . . . . . . . | A. . . . . . . . | 22 | Comoros . . . . . . . . . . . | E. . . . . . . . | 44 |
| Bahrain . . . . . . . . . . . . | D. . . . . . . . | 22 | Congo . . . . . . . . . . . . . | D. . . . . . . . | 44 |
| Bangladesh . . . . . . . . . | E. . . . . . . . | 22 | Corsica . . . . . . . . . . . . | E. . . . . . . . | 44 |
| Barbados . . . . . . . . . . . | B. . . . . . . . | 44 | Costa Rica . . . . . . . . . . | A. . . . . . . . | 44 |
| Belarus . . . . . . . . . . . . | E. . . . . . . . | 22 | Cote d'Ivoire (Ivory Coast). | D. . . . . . . . | 44 |
| Belgium . . . . . . . . . . . . | D. . . . . . . . | 44 | Croatia . . . . . . . . . . . . | C. . . . . . . . | 44 |
| Belize . . . . . . . . . . . . . | A. . . . . . . . | 44 | Cuba . . . . . . . . . . . . . . | No Parcel Post Service. | |
| Benin . . . . . . . . . . . . . . | C. . . . . . . . | 44 | Cyprus . . . . . . . . . . . . | C. . . . . . . . | 44 |
| Bermuda . . . . . . . . . . . | A. . . . . . . . | 44 | Czech Republic . . . . . . . | C. . . . . . . . | 33 |
| Bhutan . . . . . . . . . . . . . | E. . . . . . . . | 44 | Denmark . . . . . . . . . . . | C. . . . . . . . | 66 |
| Bolivia . . . . . . . . . . . . . | B. . . . . . . . | 44 | Djibouti . . . . . . . . . . . . | D. . . . . . . . | 44 |
| Bosnia and Herzegovina . . . | C. . . . . . . . | 33 | Dominica . . . . . . . . . . . | A. . . . . . . . | 22 |
| Botswana . . . . . . . . . . . | E. . . . . . . . | 22 | Dominican Rep. . . . . . . . | A. . . . . . . . | 44 |
| Brazil . . . . . . . . . . . . . . | E. . . . . . . . | 44 | East Timor . . . . . . . . . . | No Parcel Post Service. | |
| British Virgin Islands . . . . . | A. . . . . . . . | 44 | Ecuador. . . . . . . . . . . . | C. . . . . . . . | 44 |
| Brunei . . . . . . . . . . . . . | D. . . . . . . . | 22 | Egypt . . . . . . . . . . . . . . | D. . . . . . . . | 44 |
| Bulgaria . . . . . . . . . . . . | D. . . . . . . . | 44 | El Salvador . . . . . . . . . . | B. . . . . . . . | 44 |

| Country | Rate group | Maximum weight limit | Country | Rate group | Maximum weight limit |
|---|---|---|---|---|---|
| Equatorial Guinea | D | 44 | Nepal | D | 44 |
| Estonia | E | 22 | Netherlands | C | 44 |
| Ethiopia | D | 44 | Netherlands Antilles | A | 44 |
| Falkland Islands | D | 44 | New Caledonia | D | 44 |
| Faeroe Islands | C | 44 | New Zealand | D | 44 |
| Fiji | B | 44 | Nicaragua | B | 44 |
| Finland | D | 44 | Niger | D | 44 |
| France | E | 44 | Nigeria | C | 22 |
| French Guiana | C | 44 | Norway | D | 44 |
| French Polynesia | D | 44 | Oman | D | 22 |
| Gabon | D | 44 | Pakistan | D | 22 |
| Gambia | B | 22 | Panama | A | 44 |
| Georgia, Republic of | E | 22 | Papua New Guinea | D | 44 |
| Germany | C | 44 | Paraguay | D | 44 |
| Ghana | D | 22 | Peru | B | 44 |
| Gibraltar | C | 44 | Philippines | D | 44 |
| Great Britain and Northern Ireland | C | 50 | Pitcairn Islands | B | 22 |
| Greece | C | 44 | Poland | B | 33 |
| Greenland | D | 44 | Portugal | C | 22 |
| Grenada | A | 44 | Qatar | C | 44 |
| Guadeloupe | A | 44 | Reunion | E | 44 |
| Guatemala | A | 44 | Romania | C | 44 |
| Guinea | B | 44 | Russia | E | 22 |
| Guinea-Bissau | B | 22 | Rwanda | D | 44 |
| Guyana | B | 44 | Saint Christopher & Nevis | A | 44 |
| Haiti | A | 44 | Saint Helena | C | 44 |
| Honduras | B | 44 | Saint Lucia | A | 44 |
| Hong Kong | C | 44 | Saint Pierre & Miquelon | A | 44 |
| Hungary | C | 44 | Saint Vincent & the Grenadines | A | 22 |
| Iceland | C | 44 | San Marino | C | 44 |
| India | D | 44 | Sao Tome & Principe | D | 44 |
| Indonesia | E | 44 | Saudi Arabia | D | 22 |
| Iran | D | 44 | Senegal | D | 44 |
| Iraq | D | 44 | Seychelles | D | 22 |
| Ireland (Eire) | C | 50 | Sierra Leone | D | 44 |
| Israel | C | 33 | Singapore | D | 44 |
| Italy (incl. San Marino) | C | 44 | Slovakia | E | 22 |
| Jamaica | A | 22 | Slovenia | C | 44 |
| Japan | E | 44 | Solomon Islands | D | 44 |
| Jordan | C | 44 | Somalia | D | 44 |
| Kazakhstan | E | 22 | South Africa | C | 44 |
| Kenya | D | 44 | Spain | C | 44 |
| Kiribati | B | 44 | Sri Lanka | D | 44 |
| Korea, Democratic People's Rep. of (North) | No Parcel Post Service. | | Sudan | D | 44 |
| Korea, Republic of (South) | C | 44 | Suriname | B | 44 |
| Kuwait | C | 44 | Swaziland | D | 44 |
| Kyrgyzstan | E | 22 | Sweden | D | 44 |
| Laos | E | 44 | Switzerland | B | 44 |
| Latvia | E | 44 | Syria | C | 44 |
| Lebanon | C | 11 | Taiwan | C | 44 |
| Lesotho | E | 44 | Tajikistan | E | 22 |
| Liberia | C | 22 | Tanzania | E | 22 |
| Libya | D | 44 | Thailand | D | 44 |
| Liechtenstein | B | 44 | Togo | D | 44 |
| Lithuania | E | 22 | Tonga | B | 22 |
| Luxembourg | B | 44 | Trinidad & Tobago | B | 22 |
| Macao | C | 44 | Tristan da Cunha | E | 22 |
| Macedonia | C | 33 | Tunisia | C | 44 |
| Madagascar | E | 44 | Turkey | C | 44 |
| Madeira Islands | B | 44 | Turkmenistan | E | 22 |
| Malawi | D | 22 | Turks and Caicos Islands | A | 44 |
| Malaysia | D | 22 | Tuvalu | B | 44 |
| Maldives | D | 22 | Uganda | D | 22 |
| Mali | C | 44 | Ukraine | E | 22 |
| Malta | C | 22 | United Arab Emirates | D | 44 |
| Martinique | A | 44 | Uruguay | E | 44 |
| Mauritania | D | 44 | Uzbekistan | E | 22 |
| Mauritius | E | 22 | Vanuatu | B | 44 |
| Mexico | A | 44 | Vatican City State | C | 44 |
| Moldova | E | 22 | Venezuela | B | 44 |
| Monaco | E | 44 | Vietnam | No Parcel Post Service. | |
| Mongolia | No Parcel Post Service. | | Wallis & Futuna Islands | D | 44 |
| Montserrat | A | 44 | Western Samoa | B | 22 |
| Morocco | C | 44 | Yemen | E | 44 |
| Mozambique | E | 22 | Yugoslavia | C | 33 |
| Namibia | D | 44 | Zaire | E | 33 |
| Nauru | C | 44 | Zambia | E | 44 |
| | | | Zimbabwe | E | 44 |

## International Post Cards, Surface Rates

Canada and Mexico: 30¢. All other countries: 35¢. Maximum size permitted, 6 × 4¼ inches; minimum size, 5½ × 3½ inches.

# LANGUAGE

Sources for this section: *The World Almanac Guide to Good Word Usage; The Columbia Encyclopedia; Webster's Third New International Dictionary; The Oxford English Dictionary, 2nd ed.; The Associated Press Stylebook and Libel Manual; The Encyclopedia Americana.*

## Neologisms

("New" words; from the Second Edition of the *Oxford English Dictionary*, Oxford Univ. Press, 1989.)

**arcade game:** a (mechanical or electronic) game of a type orig. popularized in amusement arcades.

**assertiveness training:** a technique by which diffident persons are trained to behave (more) assuredly.

**astroturfed:** carpeted with artificial turf.

**birth parent:** a natural (as opposed to an adoptive) parent.

**build-down:** a systematic reduction of nuclear armaments, by destroying two or more for each new one deployed.

**bulimarexic:** suffering from or characteristic of bulimia nervosa; one who suffers from bulimia nervosa.

**camp-on:** a facility of some telephone systems by which the caller of an engaged number can arrange for the system to ring it automatically as soon as it becomes free (in some cases ringing the caller also if he or she has replaced the receiver).

**car-phone:** a radio-telephone designed for use in a motor vehicle.

**CD-ROM** (compact disk-read only memory): a compact disk with data that can be viewed but not altered.

**crack:** a potent, crystalline form of cocaine usually smoked for its stimulating effect.

**debit card:** a card issued by an organization, giving the holder access to an account, via an appropriate computer terminal, esp. in order to authorize the transfer of funds to the account of another party when making a purchase, etc., without incurring revolving finance charges for credit.

**designer drug:** a drug synthesized to mimic a legally restricted or prohibited drug without itself being subject to restriction.

**E-mail:** colloq. shortening of electronic mail.

**fast tracker:** a high-flyer; an ambitious or thrusting person.

**foodie:** also foody. One who is particular about food, a gourmet.

**gender gap:** the difference in (esp. political) attitudes between men and women.

**hate mail:** letters (often anonymous) in which the senders express their hostility toward the recipient.

**HIV** (human immunodeficiency virus): either of 2 retroviruses (HIV-1, HIV-2) that cause AIDS.

**microwavable:** of food and food containers: suitable for cooking or heating in a microwave oven.

**NIMBY, nimby** (not in my backyard): a slogan expressing objection to the siting of something considered unpleasant, such as nuclear waste, in one's own locality.

**passive smoking:** the inhalation of smoke involuntarily from the tobacco being smoked by others, considered as a health risk.

**right to die:** the alleged right of a brain-damaged or otherwise incurably ill person to the termination of life-sustaining treatment.

**street credibility:** popularity with, or accessibility to, ordinary people, esp. those involved in urban street culture; the appearance or fact of being "street-wise," hence (apparent) familiarity with contemporary trends, fashions, social issues.

**yuppiedom:** the condition or fact of being a yuppie; the domain of yuppies; yuppies as a class.

## Eponyms (words named for people)

**Bloody Mary**—a vodka and tomato juice drink; after the nickname of Mary I, Queen of England, 1553-58, notorious for her persecution of Protestants.

**Bloomers**—full, loose trousers gathered at the knee; after Mrs. Amelia Bloomer, an American social reformer who advocated such clothing, 1851.

**Bobbies**—in Great Britain, police officers; after Sir Robert Peel, the statesman who organized the London police force, 1850.

**Bowdlerize**—to delete written matter considered indelicate; after Thomas Bowdler, British editor of an expurgated Shakespeare, 1825.

**Boycott**—to combine against in a policy of nonintercourse for economic or political reasons; after Charles C. Boycott, an English land agent in County Mayo, Ireland, ostracized in 1880 for refusing to reduce rents.

**Braille**—a system of writing for the blind; after Louis Braille, the French teacher of the blind who invented it, 1852.

**Cesarean**—surgical removal of a child from the uterus through an abdominal incision; after Julius Caesar, born c. 102 B.C. in this manner, according to legend.

**Casanova**—a man who is a promiscuous and unscrupulous lover; after Giovanni Casanova, an Italian adventurer, 1725-98.

**Chauvinist**—excessively patriotic; after Nicolas Chauvin, a legendary French soldier devoted to Napoleon.

**Derby**—a stiff felt hat with a dome-shaped crown and rather narrow rolled brim; after Edward Stanley, 12th Earl of Derby, who in 1780 founded the Derby horse race at Epsom Downs, England, to which these hats are worn.

**Gerrymander**—to divide an election district in an unnatural way, to favor one political party; after Elbridge Gerry, and the salamander, for the salamander-like shape of a Mass. election district created, 1812, during Gerry's governorship.

**Guillotine**—a machine for beheading; after Joseph Guillotine, a French physician who proposed its use in 1789 as more humane than hanging.

**Leotard**—a close-fitting garment for the torso, worn by dancers, acrobats, and the like; after Julius Leotard, a 19th-century French aerial gymnast.

**Silhouette**—an outline image; from Etienne de Silhouette, the French finance minister, 1757, who advocated economies that included buying such paper portraits instead of painted miniatures.

## Foreign Words and Phrases

(L = Latin; F = French; Y = Yiddish; R = Russian; G = Greek; I = Italian; S = Spanish)

**ad hoc** (L; ad HOK): for the particular end or purpose at hand

**ad infinitum** (L; ad in-fi-NITE-um): endless

**ad nauseam** (L; ad NAWZ-ee-um): to a sickening degree

**apropos** (L; ap-ruh-POH): to the point; appropriate

**bête noire** (F; BET NWAHR): a thing or person viewed with particular dislike

**bon appétit** (F; BOH nap-uh-teet): good appetite

**bona fide** (L; BOH nuh-feyed): genuine

**carte blanche** (F; kahrt BLANNSH): full discretionary power

**cause célèbre** (F; kawz suh-LEB-ruh): a notorious incident

**c'est la vie** (F; se lah VEE): that's life

**chutzpah** (Y; KHOOT-spuh): amazing nerve bordering on arrogance

**coup de grâce** (F; kooh duh GRAHS): the final blow

**coup d'état** (F; kooh duh tah): forceful overthrow of a government

**crème de la crème** (F; KREM duh luh KREM): the best of the best

**cum laude/magna cum laude/summa cum laude** (L; KUHM loud-ay; MAHN-ya . . .; SOO-ma . . .): with praise or honor; with great praise or honor; with the highest praise or honor

**de facto** (L; di FAK-toh): in fact; generally agreed to without a formal decision

**déjà vu** (F; DAY-zhah VOOH): the sensation that something happening has happened before

**de jure** (L; dee JOOR-ee, day YOOR-ay): determined by law, as opposed to de facto

**de rigueur** (F; duh ree-GUR): necessary according to convention

**détente** (F; day-TAHNT): an easing or relaxation of strained relations

**éminence grise** (F; ay-meh-NAHNN-suh GREEZ): one who wields power behind the scenes

**enfant terrible** (F; ahnn-FAHNN te-REE-bluh): one whose unconventional behavior causes embarrassment

**en masse** (F; ahn MAHS): in a large body

**ergo** (L; ER-goh): therefore

**esprit de corps** (F; es-PREE duh KAWR): group spirit; feeling of camaraderie

**eureka** (G; YOOR-EE-kuh): I have found it

**ex post facto** (L; eks pohst FAK-toh): an explanation or regulation concocted after the event

**fait accompli** (F; fayt uh-kom-PLEE): an accomplished fact

**faux pas** (F; fowe PAH): a social blunder

**hoi polloi** (G; hoy puh-LOY): the masses

**in loco parentis** (L; in LOH-koh puh-REN-tis): in place of a parent

**in memoriam** (L; in muh-MAWR-ee-uhm): in memory of

**in situ** (L; in SEYE-tyooh): in the original arrangement

**in toto** (L; in TOH-toh): totally

**je ne sais quoi** (F; zhuh nuh say KWAH): I don't know what; the little something that eludes description

**joie de vivre** (F; zhwah duh VEEV-ruh): joy of living, love of life

**mea culpa** (L; MAY-uh CUL-puh): my fault

**modus operandi** (L; MOH-duhs op-uh-RAN-dee): method of operation

**noblesse oblige** (F; noh-BLES uh-BLEEZH): the obligation of nobility to help the less fortunate

**non compos mentis** (L; non KOM-puhs MEN-tis): out of control of the mind; insane

**nouveau riche** (F; nooh-voh REESH): pejorative for recent rich who spend money conspicuously

**perestroika** (R; PAIR-es TROY-kuh): restructuring

**persona non grata** (L; per-SOH-nah non GRAH-tah): unacceptable person

**post-mortem** (L; pohst-MORE-tuhm): after death; autopsy; analysis after event

**prima donna** (I; pree-muh DAH-nuh): temperamental person

**pro tempore** (L; proh TEM-puh-ree): for the time being

**que sera sera** (S; keh sair-ah sair-AH): what will be, will be

**quid pro quo** (L; kwid proh KWOH): something given or received for something else

**raison d'être** (F; RAY-zohnn DET-ruh): reason for being

**shlemiel** (Y; shleh-MEEL): an unlucky bungling person

**savoir-faire** (F; sav-wahr-FAIR): dexterity in social and practical affairs

**semper fidelis** (L; SEM-puhr fee-DAY-lis): always faithful

**status quo** (L; STAY-tus QWOH): existing order of things

**tour de force** (L; TOOR duh FAWRS): feat accomplished through great skill

**terra firma** (L; TER-uh FUR-muh): solid ground

**verbatim** (L; ver-BAY-tuhm): word for word

**vis-à-vis** (F; vee-ZUH-VEE): compared with

## Figures of Speech

**hyperbaton**—any intentional deviation from normal word order

"Whom God wishes to destroy, he first makes mad." **Euripides**

"Arms and the man I sing." **Virgil**

**enallage**—an effective grammatical error

"We was robbed!" Joe Jacobs, professional prize fight manager

"Curioser and curioser" **Lewis Carroll's** *Alice's Adventures in Wonderland*

**antihimeria**—a type of enallage that substitutes one part of speech for another

"Lord Angelo dukes it well." **Shakespeare's** *Measure for Measure*

"I am going in search of the great perhaps." **Rabelais**

**catechresis**—the substitution of one word with a seemingly inappropriate one

"The Cold War" **Bernard Baruch**

"And that White Sustenance—Despair" **Emily Dickinson**

**periphrasis**—a roundabout means of expression

"To meet the demands of nature" **Sallust**

"From pro's and con's they fell to a warmer way of disputing." **Cervantes**

**antithesis**—saying something two different ways, specifically by denying its contrary and asserting it

"A man should be mourned at his birth, not at his death." **Montesquieu**

"The greatest crimes are caused by surfeit, not by want." **Aristotle**

**epanorthosis**—a statement followed by a correction
"Religion is a disease, but it is a noble disease." **Heraclitus**
"God, make me pure, but not yet." **Saint Augustine**

**polyptoton**—repetition of the same word or root with different grammatical forms or functions
"Who shall stand guard to the guards themselves?" **Juvenal**
"Love is an irresistible desire to be irresistibly desired." **Robert Frost**

**isolcolon**—repetition of the same grammatical forms in different words
"I speak Spanish to God, Italian to women, French to men, and German to my horse." **Charles V**
"The louder he talked of his honor, the faster we counted our spoons." **Ralph Waldo Emerson**

**epizeuxis**—the immediate repetition of a word or phrase
"O dark, dark, dark, amid the blaze of noon." **John Milton**
"Then kill, kill, kill, kill, kill, kill." **Shakespeare's** *King Lear*

**diacope**—repetition of a word with another word interposing
"Tomorrow, and tomorrow, and tomorrow . . ." **Shakespeare's** *Macbeth*
"A horse! a horse! my kingdom for a horse!" **Shakespeare's** *Richard III*

**anaphora**—repetition of the first word or words from one sentence to another
"Blessed are the poor in spirit: for theirs is the kingdom of heaven. Blessed are they that mourn: for they shall be comforted. Blessed are the meek: for they shall inherit the earth." **Matthew 5:3**
"We shall fight in France, we shall fight on the seas and oceans, we shall fight with growing confidence and growing strength in the air, we shall defend our island, whatever the cost may be, we shall fight on the beaches, we shall fight on the landing grounds, we shall fight in the fields and in the streets, we shall fight in the hills; we shall never surrender." **Winston Churchill**

**epistrophe**—repetition of the last word or words from one sentence to another
"When I was a child, I spake as a child, I understood as a child, I thought as a child: but when I became a man, I put away childish things." **1 Cor. 13:11**
"Selfishness is not living as one wishes to live. It is asking others to live as one wishes to live." **Thomas Macaulay**

**epanepsis**—ending a sentence or clause with the same word or phrase with which it began
"Nothing can be created out of nothing." **Lucretius**
"Common sense is not so common." **Voltaire**

**palindrome**—repetition in which the sentence reads the same forward or backward
"Able was I ere I saw Elba." attributed to **Napoleon**
"Madam, I'm Adam." attributed to the first man addressing the first woman

## Common Abbreviations

Usage of periods after abbreviations varies, but recently the tendency has been toward omission. Definitions preceding those in parentheses are in Latin.

A.A. = Alcoholics Anonymous
A.A.A. = American Automobile Association
AC = alternating current
A.D. = anno Domini (in the year of the Lord)
A.M. = ante meridiem (before noon)
A.F.L. = American Federation of Labor
AIDS = acquired immunodeficiency syndrome
A.M.A. = American Medical Association
anon. = anonymous
ASAP = as soon as possible
ASCAP = American Society of Composers, Authors, and Publishers
B.A. = Bachelor of Arts
bbl. = barrel(s)
B.C. = before Christ
B.C.E. = before the Christian era
B.S. = Bachelor of Science
B.T.U. = British thermal unit
bu. = bushel
C = centigrade, Celsius
c = copyright
c. (or ca.) = circa (about)
C.I.A. = Central Intelligence Agency
C.E.O. = chief executive officer
C.I.O. = Congress of Industrial Organizations
cm = centimeter
C.O.D. = cash (or collect) on delivery
C.P.A. = Certified Public Accountant
CPR = cardio-pulmonary resuscitation
D.A. = District Attorney
D.A.R. = Daughters of the American Revolution
DC = direct current
D.D. = Doctor of Divinity
D.D.S. = Doctor of Dental Surgery
DNA = deoxyribonucleic acid
DOA = dead on arrival
ed. = edited, edition, editor
e.g. = exempli gratia (for example)
esp. = especially
et al. = et alii (and others)
etc. = et cetera (and so forth)

F = Fahrenheit
F.B.I. = Federal Bureau of Investigation
f.o.b. = freight on board
ft. = foot
FYI = for your information
gal. = gallon
g.n.p. = gross national product
G.O.P. = Grand Old Party (Republican)
h. = hour
Hon. = the Honorable
H.R.H. = His (Her) Royal Highness
ht. = height
i.e. = id est (that is)
in. = inch
I.Q. = Intelligence Quotient
I.R.A. = Irish Republican Army
I.R.S. = Internal Revenue Service
J.D. = Juris Doctor (Doctor of Laws)
J.P. = Justice of the Peace
J.S.D. = Doctor of the Science of Law
K = 1,000
k. = karat
kg = kilogram
km = kilometer
kW = kilowatt
kWh = kilowatt-hour
l = liter
lb. = libra (pound)
LL.B. = Bachelor of Laws
m = meter
M.A. = Master of Arts
M.D. = Medicinae Doctor (Doctor of Medicine)
mfg. = manufacturing
mi. = mile
MIA = missing in action
min. = minute
ml = milliliter

mm = millimeter
mph = miles per hour
M.S. = Master of Science
MS = manuscript
MSG = monosodium glutamate
Msgr. = Monsignor
NCO = Noncommissioned Officer
No. = numero (number)
op. = opus (work)
oz. = ounce
p. = page
Ph.D. = Doctor of philosophy
P.M. = post meridiem (afternoon)
POW = prisoner of war
P.S. = post scriptum (postscript)
pt. = pint(s), part, point
qt. = quart(s)
REM = rapid eye movement
Rev. = Reverend
R.F.D. = rural free delivery
R.I.P. = Requiescat in pace (May he rest in peace)
R.N. = Registered Nurse
ROTC = Reserve Officers' Training Corps
rpm = revolutions per minute
RR = railroad
R.S.V.P. = Répondez, s'il vous plait (Please answer)
S.A.S.E. = self-addressed stamped envelope
sec. = second
S.P.C.A. = Society for the Prevention of Cruelty to Animals
St. = saint, street
T. = ton
T.N.T. = trinitrotoluene
UFO = unidentified flying object
UHF = ultra high frequency
U.S.S. = United States Ship
v. (or vs.) = versus (against)
VHF = very high frequency
W = watt
yd. = yard

# Latin and Greek Prefixes and Suffixes

**Latin prefix/English meaning**
a, abs/from
alti, alto/high
ambi/both
ante/before
aqui/water
arbori/tree
audio/hearing
avi/bird
brevi/short
centi/hundred
cerebro/brain
circum/around
ferri, ferro/iron
fissi/split
igni/fire
inter/between
juxta/close
lacto/milk
luni/moon
magni/great
mal/bad
multi/many
naso/nose
nati/birth
oculo/eye
oleo/oil
omni/all
ovi, ovo/egg
plano/flat
post/after

pre/before
pro/for
pulmo/lung
re/again
recti/straight
retro/backward
somni/sleep
stelli/star
sub/under
super/above
terri/land
trans/through
ultra/beyond
uni/one
**Latin suffix/**
**English meaning**
cide, cidal/kill
fid/split
fuge, fugal/flee from
grade/walking
pennale/wing
vorous/eating
**Greek prefix/**
**English meaning**
a/not
anti/against
astro/star
auto/self
biblio/book
bio/life
cardio/heart

chloro/green
chrono/time
cosmo/universe
ex/outside
geo/earth
geronto/old age
gluc/sweet
grapho/writing
helio/sun
hemi/half
hetero/different
homeo/similar
homo/same
hydro/water
hyper/above
kinesi/movement
litho/stone
logo/word
macro/large
mega/great
meso/middle
meta/beyond
micro/small
mono/one
necro/dead body
neo/new
ornitho/bird
osteo/bone
pan/all
para/close
phono/sound

photo/light
poly/many
proto/first
pseudo/false
psycho/mind, spirit
pyro/fire
rhino/nose
theo/god
thermo/heat
toxico/poison
zoo/living
**Greek suffix/**
**English meaning**
algia/pain
archy/government
gamy/marriage
gnomy/knowledge
iasis/disease
itis/inflammation
lepsy/seizure
logy/science of
machy/battle
meter/measure
oid/like
oma/tumor
phobe/fear
scope/observation
sect/cutting
soma/body
sophy/wisdom

# Commonly Confused English Words

**adverse:** unfavorable
**averse:** opposed

**affect:** to influence
**effect:** to cause

**aggravate:** to make worse
**annoy:** to irritate

**allusion:** an indirect reference
**illusion:** an unreal impression

**anxious:** apprehensive
**eager:** avid

**complement:** to make complete;
something that completes
**compliment:** to praise; praise

**capital:** the seat of government
**capitol:** the building in which a
legislative body meets

**discreet:** prudent
**discrete:** separate

**disinterested:** impartial
**uninterested:** without interest

**emigrate:** to leave for another place
of residence

**immigrate:** to come to another
place of residence

**elicit:** to draw or bring out
**illicit:** illegal

**denote:** to mean
**connote:** to suggest beyond the
explicit meaning

**farther:** more distant in space
**further:** an extension of time or
degree

**historic:** an important occurrence
**historical:** any occurrence in the
past

**imply:** to relay information but not
explicitly
**infer:** to understand information
that is not relayed explicitly

**imminent:** ready to take place
**eminent:** standing out

**incredible:** unbelievable
**incredulous:** skeptical

**include:** used when the items
following are part of a whole

**comprise:** used when the items
following are all of a whole

**ingenious:** clever
**ingenuous:** innocent

**insidious:** intended to trick
**invidious:** detrimental to reputation

**literally:** actually
**figuratively:** metaphorically

**oral:** spoken, as opposed to written
**verbal:** referring to skill with
language, as opposed to other skills

**prevaricate:** to lie
**procrastinate:** to put off

**pestilence:** a contagious or
infectious epidemic disease
**petulance:** rudeness

**prostrate:** stretched out flat, face
down
**prostate:** of or relating to the
prostate gland

**qualitative:** relating to quality
**quantitative:** relating to number

# National Spelling Bee Champions

The Scripps Howard National Spelling Bee, conducted by Scripps Howard Newspapers and other leading newspapers since 1939, was instituted by the Louisville (Ky.) Courier-Journal in 1925. Children under 16 years of age and not beyond the eighth grade are eligible to compete for cash prizes at the finals, which are held annually in Washington, D.C. The 1993 winners are: first prize, **Geoff Hooper**, Arlington, Tenn.; second prize, **David Urban**, Amarillo, Tex.; third prize, **Yuni Kim**, Pottsville, Pa.

## Winning Words

These were the last words given in each of the years 1965-1993 at the Scripps Howard National Spelling Bee. They were all correctly spelled, thereby determining the national champion.

| | | | |
|---|---|---|---|
| 1965 — eczema | 1973 — vouchsafe | 1980 — elucubrate | 1987 — staphylococci |
| 1966 — ratoon | 1974 — hydrophyte | 1981 — sarcophagus | 1988 — elegiacal |
| 1967 — chihuahua | 1975 — incisor | 1982 — psoriasis | 1989 — spoliator |
| 1968 — abalone | 1976 — narcolepsy | 1983 — purim | 1990 — fibranne |
| 1969 — interlocutory | 1977 — cambist | 1984 — luge | 1991 — antipyretic |
| 1970 — croissant | 1978 — deification | 1985 — milieu | 1992 — lyceum |
| 1971 — shalloon | 1979 — maculature | 1986 — odontalgia | 1993 — kamikaze |
| 1972 — macerate | | | |

## Commonly Misspelled English Words

| | | | |
|---|---|---|---|
| accidentally | convenience | government | miniature |
| accommodate | deceive | grammar | mysterious |
| acquainted | describe | humorous | necessary |
| all right | description | hurrying | opportunity |
| already | desirable | incidentally | optimistic |
| amateur | despair | independent | performance |
| appearance | desperate | inoculate | permanent |
| appropriate | eliminate | irresistible | rhythm |
| bureau | embarrass | laboratory | ridiculous |
| character | fascinating | lightning | similar |
| commitment | finally | maintenance | sincerely |
| conscious | foreign | marriage | transferred |
| conscientious | forty | | |

## Foreign Idioms

**English**
Naked as a jaybird
A bird in the hand is worth two in the bush.

To kill two birds with one stone

To eat crow
To eat like a pig
Don't bite off more than you can chew.

Pride goes before a fall.

To go by fits and starts
There is honor among thieves.
Once in a blue moon

**English**
Don't waste your breath!
To turn up like a bad penny

To talk to yourself
Let's get back to the subject.
To pull a long face
He laughs in your face.
By rule of thumb
To be knock-kneed
Put that in your pipe and smoke it!

It's Greek to me!

**English**
To hit the ceiling
Go fly a kite!
There's always room for one more.

To have the tables turned

**Italian**
Naked as a worm (Nudo come un verme)
Better a finch in hand than a thrush on a branch. (Meglio fringuello in man che tordo in frasca.)
To catch two pigeons with one bean (Pigliare due piccioni con una fava.)
To swallow the toad (Inghiottire il rospo)
To eat like a buffalo (Mangiare come un bufalo)
Don't take a step longer than your leg. (Non fare il passo piu lungo della gamba.)
Pride rode out on horseback and came back on foot. (La superbia andò a cavallo e tornò a piedi.)
To go by hiccups (Andare a singhiozzo)
A dog doesn't eat a dog. (Cane non mangia cane.)
Every death of a pope (Ad ogni morte di papa)

**French**
Save your saliva! (Epargne ta salive!)
To arrive like a hair in the soup. (Arriver comme un cheveu sur la soupe.)
To talk to angels (Parler aux anges)
Let's get back to our sheep. (Revenons à nos moutons.)
To make a funny nose (Faire un drôle de nez)
He laughs in your nose. (Il vous rit au nez.)
From the view of the nose (A vue de nez)
To have your legs in an X (Avoir les jambes en X)
Put this in your pocket with your handkerchief on top! (Mets-le dans ta poche avec ton mouchoir dessus!)
It's Chinese! (C'est du chinois!)

**Spanish**
To scream at the sky (Poner el grito en el cielo)
Go fry asparagus (Véte a freír esparragos!)
Where six can eat, seven can eat. (Donde comen seis, comen siete.)
To go out for wool and come home shorn (Ir por lana y volver esquilado)

| | |
|---|---|
| To cut off your nose to spite your face | To throw stones at your own roof (Tirar piedras contra su propio tejado) |
| To slam the door in your face | To slam the door on your nostrils (Cerrarle la puerta en las narices) |
| Give him an inch, he'll take a mile. | Give him a hand and he takes a foot. (Le da la mano y se toma el pie.) |
| To be alive and kicking | To be alive and wagging your tail (Estar vivo y coleando) |
| You can't make a silk purse out of a sow's ear. | A monkey dressed in silk is still a monkey. (Aunque la mona se vista de seda, mona se queda.) |
| To swear a blue streak | To toss out toads and snakes (Echar sapos y culebras) |

**English**
Go jump in the lake!
You can only do one thing at a time.

He's as slow as molasses.
He repeats himself.
Where there's smoke, there's fire.

Are you in a hurry?
Drop dead!
He makes a lot of trouble for me.

Go fight City Hall.
Thanks for nothing.

**Yiddish**
Go whistle in the ocean! (Gai feifen ahfenyam!)
You can't dance at two weddings at the same time. (Me ken nit tantzen auf tsvai chassenes mit ain mol.)
He creeps like a bedbug. (Er kricht vi a vantz.)
He grinds ground flour. (Er molt gemolen mel.)
When bells ring, it's usually a holiday. (Az es klingt, iz misstomeh chogeh.)
Are you standing on one leg? (Bist ahf ain fus?)
You should lie in the earth! (Zolst ligen in drerd!)
He makes my wedding black. (Er macht mir a shvartzeh chasseneh.)
Go fight with God. (Shlog zich mit Got arum.)
Many thanks in your belly button. (A shainem dank dir im pupik.)

## Names of the Days

| English | French | Italian | Spanish | German |
|---|---|---|---|---|
| Sunday | Dimanche | domenica | domingo | Sonntag |
| Monday | Lundi | lunedì | lunes | Montag |
| Tuesday | Mardi | martedì | martes | Dienstag |
| Wednesday | Mercredi | mercoledì | miércoles | Mittwoch |
| Thursday | Jeudi | giovedì | jueves | Donnerstag |
| Friday | Vendredi | venerdì | viernes | Freitag |
| Saturday | Samedi | sabato | sábado | Samstag |

## Idioms: Their Meaning and Derivation

**dyed in the wool:** to have traits deeply ingrained; from the fact that if wool is dyed before being made into yarn, or while still raw wool, the color is more firmly fixed.

**feet of clay:** a blemish in the character of one previously held above reproach; from Daniel's interpretation of Nebuchadnezzar's dream in the Old Testament. The king dreamed of an image made of precious metals, except for feet made of clay and iron. Daniel said that the feet symbolized human vulnerability to weakness and destruction.

**hands down:** effortlessly; incontestably; from the way a jockey, sure of victory, drops his hands, loosening his grip on the reins.

**in seventh heaven:** in a state of bliss; especially in Islamic beliefs, the heaven of heavens, the home of God and the highest angels.

**kiss of death:** something that seems good but is in reality the instrument of one's downfall; from the earlier phrase "Judas kiss," betraying Jesus to the authorities.

**mad as a hatter:** crazy; from mercury's use in the making of felt hats, thus hatters often were afflicted with a violent twitching of the muscles as a result of its effects.

**red herring:** a false lead; a herring cured by smoke; from the persistent odor, hence the use, trailed over the ground, for training a dog to follow this scent over any other.

**red-letter day:** a memorable day; from the custom of using red or purple colors to mark holy days on the calendar.

**to bark up the wrong tree:** to pursue a false lead; an Americanism that comes from hunting, some say specifically nocturnal racoon hunting, in which dogs often lost track of their quarry.

**to buckle down:** to adopt an attitude of effort and determination; probably from the act of buckling on armor to prepare for battle.

**to go at it with hammer and tongs:** no holds barred; from the blacksmith who, with his tongs (long-handled pincers) took a piece of red-hot metal from the forge, laid it on the anvil, and beat it into shape with his hammer.

**to hold water:** to pass a test for soundness; from testing a pitcher by filling it with water.

**to knuckle under:** to submit to another; from the time when one knelt before a conqueror, putting the "knuckles" of one's knees (the rounded part of the bone where the joint is bent) on the ground.

**to make hay while the sun shines:** to seize the opportunity; from hay's composition of mown grass dried for fodder, with the sun as the cheapest and most available drying agent.

**to strike while the iron is hot:** to seize the opportunity; from the blacksmith's need to swing the hammer while the metal on the anvil is glowing, or he must start up the forge again and reheat the iron.

## Pen Names

Currer, Ellis, and Acton Bell (Charlotte, Emily, and Anne Bronte)
Isak Dinesen (Karen Blixen)
George Eliot (Mary Ann or Marian Evans)
O. Henry (W.S. Porter)

John le Carré (David Cornwell)
George Sand (Amandine Aurore Dupine)
Dr. Seuss (Theodor Geisel)
Stendahl (Marie Henri Beyle)
Mark Twain (Samuel Clemens)

## Designations of Some King Louis of France

Louis I (778-840): the Debonair or the Pious
Louis II (846-879): the Stammerer
Louis V (966-987): the Lazy
Louis VI (1081-1137): the Fat
Louis VII (1121-1180): the Young
Louis VIII (1187-1226): the Lion

Louis X (1289-1316): the Quarrelsome
Louis XII (1462-1515): Father of the People
Louis XIV (1638-1715): the Great or the Sun King
Louis XV (1710-1774): the Well-Beloved
Louis XVII (1785-1795?): the Lost Dauphin

## Young of Animals Have Special Names

The young of many animals, birds and fish have come to be called by special names. A young eel, for example, is an elver. Many young animals, of course, are often referred to simply as infants, babies, younglets, or younglings.

**bunny:** rabbit.
**calf:** cattle, elephant, antelope, rhino, hippo, whale, etc.
**cheeper:** grouse, partridge, quail.
**chick, chicken:** fowl.
**cockerel:** rooster.
**codling, sprag:** codfish.
**colt:** horse (male).
**cub:** lion, bear, shark, fox, etc.
**cygnet:** swan.
**duckling:** duck.
**eaglet:** eagle.
**elver:** eel.
**eyas:** hawk, others.
**fawn:** deer.

**filly:** horse (female).
**fingerling:** fish generally.
**flapper:** wild fowl.
**fledgling:** birds generally.
**foal:** horse, zebra, others.
**fry:** fish generally.
**gosling:** goose.
**heifer:** cow.
**joey:** kangaroo, others.
**kid:** goat.
**kit:** fox, beaver, rabbit, cat.
**kitten, kitty, catling:** cats, other fur-bearers.
**lamb, lambkin, cosset, hog:** sheep.
**leveret:** hare.

**nestling:** birds generally.
**owlet:** owl.
**parr, smolt, grilse:** salmon.
**piglet, shoat, farrow, suckling:** pig.
**polliwog, tadpole:** frog.
**poult:** turkey.
**pullet:** hen.
**pup:** dog, seal, sea lion, fox.
**puss, pussy:** cat.
**spike, blinker, tinker:** mackerel.
**squab:** pigeon.
**squeaker:** pigeon, others.
**whelp:** dog, tiger, beasts of prey.
**yearling:** cattle, sheep, horse, etc.

## A Collection of Animal Collectives

The English language boasts an abundance of names to describe groups of things, particularly pairs or aggregations of animals. Some of these words have fallen into comparative disuse, but many of them are still in service, helping to enrich the vocabularies of those who like their language to be precise, who tire of hearing a group referred to as "a bunch of," or who enjoy the sound of words that aren't overworked.

**bale** of turtles
**band** of gorillas
**bed** of clams, oysters
**bevy** of quail, swans
**brace** of ducks
**brood** of chicks
**cast** of hawks
**cete** of badgers
**charm** of goldfinches
**cloud** of gnats
**clowder** of cats
**clutch** of chicks
**clutter** of cats
**colony** of ants
**congregation** of plovers
**covey** of quail, partridge

**crash** of rhinoceri
**cry** of hounds
**down** of hares
**drift** of swine
**drove** of cattle, sheep
**exaltation** of larks
**flight** of birds
**flock** of sheep, geese
**gaggle** of geese
**gam** of whales
**gang** of elks
**grist** of bees
**herd** of elephants
**horde** of gnats
**husk** of hares
**kindle** or **kendle** of kittens

**knot** of toads
**leap** of leopards
**leash** of greyhounds, foxes
**litter** of pigs
**mob** of kangaroos
**murder** of crows
**muster** of peacocks
**mute** of hounds
**nest** of vipers
**nest, nide** of pheasants
**pack** of hounds, wolves
**pair** of horses
**pod** of whales, seals
**pride** of lions
**school** of fish
**sedge** or **siege** of cranes

**shoal** of fish, pilchards
**skein** of geese
**skulk** of foxes
**sleuth** of bears
**sounder** of boars, swine
**span** of mules
**spring** of teals
**swarm** of bees
**team** of ducks, horses
**tribe** or **trip** of goats
**troop** of kangaroos, monkeys
**volery** of birds
**watch** of nightingales
**wing** of plovers
**yoke** of oxen

## The Principal Languages of the World

Source: S. Culbert, NI-25, University of Washington, Seattle, WA 98195; data as of mid-1993

### Languages with over 100,000,000 speakers

| | Speakers (millions) | | | Speakers (millions) | | | Speakers (millions) | |
|---|---|---|---|---|---|---|---|---|
| | Native | Total | | Native | Total | | Native | Total |
| Mandarin | 827 | 930 | Bengali | 184 | 192 | Japanese | 125 | 126 |
| Hindi | 327 | 400 | Arabic | 182 | 214 | German | 98 | 120 |
| Spanish | 326 | 371 | Russian | 172 | 291 | French | 72 | 124 |
| English | 319 | 463 | Portuguese | 167 | 179 | Malay-Indonesian | 49 | 152 |

### Total number of speakers (native plus non-native) of languages spoken by at least one million speakers

| | | | | | | |
|---|---|---|---|---|---|---|
| Achinese (N Sumatra, Indonesia) | 3 | Bashkir (Bashkortostan, in Russia) | 1 | Bugis (Indonesia; Malaysia) | 4 |
| Afrikaans (So. Africa) | 10 | Batak Toba (Indonesia) | 4 | Bulgarian (Bulgaria) | 9 |
| Akan (or Twi-Fanti) (Ghana) | 7 | Baule (Côte d'Ivoire) | 2 | Burmese (Myanmar) | 31 |
| Albanian (Albania; Kosovo) | 5 | Beja (Kassala, Sudan; Ethiopia) | 2 | Buyi (S Guizhou, S China) | 2 |
| Amharic (Ethiopia) | 19 | Bemba (Zambia) | 2 | Byelorussian (Belarus) | 10 |
| Arabic (see above) | 214 | Bengali[1] (see above) | 192 | Cantonese (China; Hong Kong) | 65 |
| Armenian (Armenia) | 5 | Berber[2] | | Catalan (NE Spain; S France; Andorra) | 9 |
| Assamese[1] (India, Bangladesh) | 23 | Beti (Cameroon; Gabon; Eq. Guinea) | 2 | Cebuano (Bohol Sea, Philippines) | 13 |
| Aymara (Bolivia; Peru) | 2 | Bhili (India) | 3 | | |
| Azerbaijani (Azerbaijan) | 15 | Bikol (SE Luzon, Philippines) | 4 | | |
| Balinese (Bali, Indonesia) | 3 | Brahui (Pakistan; Afghan.; Iran) | 2 | *(continued)* | |
| Baluchi (Baluchistan, Pakistan) | 5 | | | | |

| | |
|---|---|
| Chagga (Kilimanjaro area, Tanzania) | 1 |
| Chiga (Ankole, Uganda) | 1 |
| Chinese[3] | |
| Chuvash (Chuvash, in Russia) | 2 |
| Czech (Czech Republic) | 12 |
| Danish (Denmark) | 5 |
| Dimli (EC Turkey) | 1 |
| Dogri (Jammu-Kashmir, CE India) | 1 |
| Dong (SC China) | 2 |
| Dutch-Flemish (Netherlands; Belg.) | 21 |
| Dyerma (SW Niger) | 2 |
| Edo (Bendel, S Nigeria) | 1 |
| Efik (incl. Ibibio) (SE Nigeria) | 6 |
| English (see above) | 463 |
| Esperanto | 2 |
| Estonian (Estonia) | 1 |
| Ewe (SE Ghana; S Togo) | 3 |
| Fang-Bulu (Dialects of Beti, q. v.) | |
| Farsi (Iranian form of Persian, q. v.) | |
| Finnish (Finland; Sweden) | 6 |
| Fon (SC Benin; S Togo) | 1 |
| French (see above) | 124 |
| Fula (or Peulh) (Cameroon; Nigeria) | 13 |
| Fulakunda (Senegambia; Guinea B.) | 2 |
| Futa Jalon (Guinea; Sierra Leone) | 3 |
| Galician (Galicia, NW Spain) | 4 |
| Galla (see Oromo) | |
| Ganda (or Luganda) (S Uganda) | 3 |
| Georgian (Georgia) | 4 |
| German (see above) | 120 |
| Gilaki (Gilan, NW Iran) | 2 |
| Gogo (Riff Valley, Tanzania) | 1 |
| Gondi (Central India) | 2 |
| Greek (Greece) | 12 |
| Guarani (Paraguay) | 4 |
| Gujarati[1] (WC India; S Pakistan) | 40 |
| Gusii (Kisii District, Nyanza, Kenya) | 2 |
| Hadiyya (Arusi, Ethiopia) | 2 |
| Hakka (or Kejia) (SE China) | 34 |
| Hani (S China) | 1 |
| Hausa (N Nigeria; Niger; Cameroon) | 37 |
| Haya (Kagera, NW Tanzania) | 1 |
| Hebrew (Israel) | 4 |
| Hindi[1,4] (see above) | 400 |
| Ho (Bihar and Orissa States, India) | |
| Hungarian (or Magyar) (Hungary) | 14 |
| iban (Indonesia; Malaysia) | 1 |
| Ibibio (see Efik) | |
| Igbo (or Ibo) (lower Niger, Nigeria) | 17 |
| Ijaw (Niger River delta, Nigeria) | 2 |
| Ilocano (NW Luzon, Philippines) | 7 |
| Indonesian (see Malay-Indonesian) | |
| Italian (Italy) | 63 |
| Japanese (see above) | 126 |
| Javanese (Java, Indonesia) | 63 |
| Kabyle (W Kabylia, N Algeria) | 3 |
| Kamba (E Kenya) | |
| Kannada[1] (S India) | 43 |
| Kanuri (Nigeria; Niger; Chad; Cam.) | |
| Karen (see Pho and Sgaw) | |
| Karo-Dairi (N Sumatra, Indonesia) | |
| Kashmiri[1] (N India; NE Pakistan) | 4 |
| Kazakh (Kazakhstan) | 8 |
| Kenuzi-Dongola (S Egypt; Sudan) | 1 |
| Khalka (see Mongolian) | |
| Khmer (Kampuchea; Vietnam; Thai.) | 8 |
| Khmer, Northern (Thailand) | 1 |
| Kikuyu (or Gekoyo) (WC Kenya) | 5 |
| Kituba (Bas-Zaire, Bandundu, Zaire) | 4 |
| Kongo (W Zaire; S Congo; NW Ang.) | 3 |
| Konkani (Maharashtra and SW India) | 4 |

| | |
|---|---|
| Korean (Korea; China; Japan) | 74 |
| Kurdish (south-west of Caspian Sea) | 11 |
| Kyrgyz (Kyrgyzstan) | 2 |
| Lao[5] (Laos) | 4 |
| Lampung (Sumatra, Indonesia) | 4 |
| Latvian (Latvia) | 1 |
| Lingala (incl. Bangala) (Zaire) | 7 |
| Lithuanian (Lithuania) | 2 |
| Luba-Lulua (or Chiluba) (Zaire) | 7 |
| Luba-Shaba (Shaba, Zaire) | 1 |
| Lubu (E Sumatra, Indonesia) | 1 |
| Luhya (W Kenya) | 1 |
| Luo (Kenya; Nyanza, Tanzania) | 4 |
| Luri (SW Iran; Iraq) | 4 |
| Lwena (E Angola; W Zambia) | 2 |
| Macedonian (Macedonia) | 4 |
| Madurese (Madura, Indonesia) | 10 |
| Magindanaon (S Philippines) | 1 |
| Makassar (S Sulawesi, Indonesia) | 2 |
| Makua (S Tanzania; N Mozambique) | 4 |
| Malagasy (Madagascar) | 12 |
| Malay-Indonesian (see above) | 152 |
| Malay, Pattani (SE Thailand) | 1 |
| Malayalam[1] (Kerala, S India) | 35 |
| Malinke-Bambara-Dyula (W Africa) | 9 |
| Mandarin (see above) | 930 |
| Marathi[1] (Maharashtra, India) | 68 |
| Mazandarani (S Mazandaran, N Iran) | 2 |
| Mbundu (Benguela, Angola) | 4 |
| Mbundu (Luanda, Angola) | 3 |
| Meithei (NE India; Bangladesh) | 1 |
| Mende (Sierra Leone) | 2 |
| Meru (Eastern Province, C Tanzania) | 1 |
| Miao (or Hmong) (S China; SE Asia) | 6 |
| Mien (China; Viet.; Laos; Thailand) | 2 |
| Min (SE China; Taiwan; Malaysia) | 50 |
| Minangkabau (W Sumatra, Indon.) | 6 |
| Moldavian (included with Romanian) | |
| Mongolian (Mongolia; NE China) | 6 |
| Mordvin (Mordova, in Russia) | 1 |
| Moré (central part of Burkina Faso) | 4 |
| Nepali (Nepal; NE India; Bhutan) | 16 |
| Ngulu (Mozambique; Malawi) | 1 |
| Nkole (Western Prov., Uganda) | 1 |
| Norwegian (Norway) | 5 |
| Nung (NE of Hanoi, Vietnam; China) | 1 |
| Nupe (Kwara, Niger States, Nigeria) | 1 |
| Nyamwezi-Sukuma (NW Tanzania) | 5 |
| Nyanja (Malawi; Zambia; Zimbabwe) | 5 |
| Oriya[1] (Central and E India) | 31 |
| Oromo (West Ethiopia; N Kenya) | 10 |
| Pampangan (NW of Manila, Philip.) | |
| Panay-Hiligaynon (Philippines) | 7 |
| Pangasinan (Lingayen G., Philip.) | 2 |
| Pashtu (Pakistan; Afghanistan; Iran) | 21 |
| Pedi (see Sotho, Northern) | |
| Persian (Iran; Afghanistan) | 34 |
| Polish (Poland) | 44 |
| Portuguese (see above) | 179 |
| Provençal (S France) | 4 |
| Punjabi[1] (Punjab, Pakistan; India) | 92 |
| Pushto (see Pashtu) (many spellings) | |
| Quechua A (Peru; Boliv.; Ec.; Arg.) | 8 |
| Rejang (SW Sumatra, Indonesia) | 1 |
| Riff (N Morocco; Algerian coast) | 1 |
| Romanian (Romania; Moldova) | 26 |
| Romany (Vlach only) (Eur.; Amer.) | 3 |

| | |
|---|---|
| Ruanda (Rwanda; Uganda; Zaire) | 8 |
| Rundi (Burundi) | 6 |
| Russian (see above) | 291 |
| Samar-Leyte (Central E Philippines) | 3 |
| Sango (Central African Republic) | 4 |
| Santali (E India; Nepal) | 5 |
| Sasak (Lombok, Alas Strait, Indon.) | 2 |
| Serbo-Croatian (NW Balkan area) | 20 |
| Sgaw (SW Myanmar) | 2 |
| Shan (Shan, E Myanmar) | 3 |
| Shilha (W Algeria; S Morocco) | 3 |
| Shona (Zimbabwe) | 2 |
| Sidamo (Sidamo, S Ethiopia) | 2 |
| Sindhi[1] (SE Pakistan; W India) | 18 |
| Sinhalese (Sri Lanka) | 13 |
| Slovak (Slovakia) | 5 |
| Slovene (Slovenia) | 2 |
| Soga (Busoga, Uganda) | 1 |
| Somali (Som.; Eth.; Ken.; Djibouti) | 6 |
| Songye (Kasai Or., NW Shaba, Zaire) | 1 |
| Soninke (Mali; countries to W S E) | 1 |
| Sotho, Northern (So. Africa) | 3 |
| Sotho, Southern (So. Afr.; Lesotho) | 4 |
| Spanish (see above) | 371 |
| Sundanese (Sunda Strait, Indonesia) | 26 |
| Swahili (Kenya; Tanz.; Zaire; Ug.) | 47 |
| Swedish (Sweden; Finland) | 9 |
| Sylhetti (Bangladesh) | 5 |
| Tagalog (Philippines) | 43 |
| Tajiki (Tajikistan; Uzbek.; Kyrgyz.) | 5 |
| Tamazight (N Morocco; W Algeria) | 3 |
| Tamil[1] (Tamil Nadu, India; Sri Lanka) | 68 |
| Tatar (Tatarstan, in Russia) | 8 |
| Tausug (Philippines; Malaysia) | 1 |
| Telugu[1] (Andhra Pradesh, SE India) | 72 |
| Temne (central Sierra Leone) | 2 |
| Thai[5] (Thailand) | 49 |
| Tho (N Vietnam; S China) | 2 |
| Thonga (Mozambique; So. Africa) | 3 |
| Tibetan (SW China; N India; Nepal) | 5 |
| Tigrinya (S Eritrea; Tigre, Ethiopia) | 4 |
| Tiv (SE Nigeria; Cameroon) | 2 |
| Tong (see Dong) | |
| Tonga (SW Zambia; NW Zimbabwe) | 2 |
| Tswana (Botswana; So. Africa) | 2 |
| Tudza (N Vietnam; S China) | 1 |
| Tulu (S India) | 2 |
| Tumbuka (N Malawi; NE Zambia) | 2 |
| Turkish (Turkey) | 58 |
| Turkmen (Turkmenistan; Afghanistan) | 3 |
| Twi-Fante (see Akan) | |
| Uighur (Xinjiang, NW China) | 8 |
| Ukrainian (Ukraine; Russia; Poland) | 46 |
| Urdu[1,4] (Pakistan; India) | 98 |
| Uzbek (Uzbekistan) | 14 |
| Vietnamese (Vietnam) | 63 |
| Wolaytta (SE Ethiopia) | 2 |
| Wolof (Senegal) | 7 |
| Wu (Shanghai region, China) | 65 |
| Xhosa (SW Cape Prov., So. Africa) | 8 |
| Yao (see Mien) | |
| Yao (Malawi; Tanzania; Mozambique) | 1 |
| Yi (S and SW China) | 7 |
| Yiddish[6] | |
| Yoruba (SW Nigeria; Zou, Benin) | 19 |
| Zande (NE Zaire; SW Sudan) | 1 |
| Zhuang (S China) | 15 |
| Zulu (N. Natal, So. Africa; Lesotho) | 8 |

(1) One of the fifteen languages of the Constitution of India. (2) See Kabyle, Riff, Shilha, and Tamazight. (3) See Mandarin, Cantonese, Wu, Min, and Hakka. The "common speech" (Putonghua) or the "national language" (Guoyu) is a standardized form of Mandarin as spoken in the area of Beijing. (4) Hindi and Urdu are essentially the same language, Hindustani. As the official language of Pakistan it is written in a modified Arabic script and called Urdu. As the official language of India it is written in the Devanagari script and called Hindi. (5) The distinctions between some Thai dialects and Lao are political rather than linguistic. (6) Yiddish is usually considered a variant of German, though it has its own standard grammar and dictionaries, has a highly developed literature, and is written in Hebrew characters.

## Non-English-Speaking Americans

Source: Bureau of the Census, U.S. Dept. of Commerce

According to data from the 1990 census, more than 31.8 million people (almost 14 percent of the U.S. population age 5 and over) spoke a language other than English in 1990, compared with 23.1 million (11 percent) in 1980, an increase of almost 38 percent over the decade. After English, Spanish was the most common language, spoken by more than half of the non-English-speaking Americans. Spanish was ten times more commonly used than the next choice, French, which was followed by German, Italian, and Chinese.

## Top 25 Languages, Other Than English, Spoken at Home by Americans

Source: Bureau of the Census, U.S. Dept. of Commerce

| Language used at home | Total speakers over 5 years old 1990 | 1980 | Percentage change* | Language used at home | Total speakers over 5 years old 1990 | 1980 | Percentage change* |
|---|---|---|---|---|---|---|---|
| 1. Spanish | 17,339,000 | 11,549,000 | 50.1% | 14. Hindi, Urdu & related | 331,000 | 130,000 | 155.1% |
| 2. French | 1,703,000 | 1,572,000 | 8.3% | 15. Russian | 242,000 | 175,000 | 38.5% |
| 3. German | 1,547,000 | 1,607,000 | -3.7% | 16. Yiddish | 213,000 | 320,000 | -33.5% |
| 4. Italian | 1,309,000 | 1,633,000 | -19.9% | 17. Thai | 206,000 | 89,000 | 131.6% |
| 5. Chinese | 1,249,000 | 632,000 | 97.7% | 18. Persian | 202,000 | 109,000 | 84.7% |
| 6. Tagalog | 843,000 | 452,000 | 86.6% | 19. French Creole | 188,000 | 25,000 | 654.1% |
| 7. Polish | 723,000 | 826,000 | -12.4% | 20. Armenian | 150,000 | 102,000 | 46.3% |
| 8. Korean | 626,000 | 276,000 | 127.2% | 21. Navajo | 149,000 | 123,000 | 20.6% |
| 9. Vietnamese | 507,000 | 203,000 | 149.5% | 22. Hungarian | 148,000 | 180,000 | -17.9% |
| 10. Portuguese | 430,000 | 361,000 | 19.0% | 23. Hebrew | 144,000 | 99,000 | 45.5% |
| 11. Japanese | 428,000 | 342,000 | 25.0% | 24. Dutch | 143,000 | 146,000 | -2.6% |
| 12. Greek | 388,000 | 410,000 | -5.4% | 25. Mon-Khmer | 127,000 | 16,000 | 676.3% |
| 13. Arabic | 355,000 | 227,000 | 57.4% | | | | |

*Calculations are from numbers before rounding.

## Language Spoken at Home by Persons 5 Years and Over, by State, 1990

| State | Population 5 years and over | Speaks only English | Total non-English | Percent non-English |
|---|---|---|---|---|
| United States | 230,445,777 | 196,600,798 | 31,844,979 | 13.8 |
| Alabama | 3,759,802 | 3,651,936 | 107,866 | 2.9 |
| Alaska | 495,425 | 435,260 | 60,165 | 12.1 |
| Arizona | 3,374,806 | 2,674,519 | 700,287 | 20.8 |
| Arkansas | 2,186,665 | 2,125,884 | 60,781 | 2.8 |
| California | 27,383,547 | 18,764,213 | 8,619,334 | 31.5 |
| Colorado | 3,042,986 | 2,722,355 | 320,631 | 10.5 |
| Connecticut | 3,060,000 | 2,593,825 | 466,175 | 15.2 |
| Delaware | 617,720 | 575,393 | 42,327 | 6.9 |
| Distr. of Columbia | 570,284 | 498,936 | 71,348 | 12.5 |
| Florida | 12,095,284 | 9,996,969 | 2,098,315 | 17.3 |
| Georgia | 5,984,188 | 5,699,642 | 284,546 | 4.8 |
| Hawaii | 1,026,209 | 771,485 | 254,724 | 24.8 |
| Idaho | 926,703 | 867,708 | 58,995 | 6.4 |
| Illinois | 10,585,838 | 9,086,726 | 1,499,112 | 14.2 |
| Indiana | 5,146,160 | 4,900,334 | 245,826 | 4.8 |
| Iowa | 2,583,526 | 2,483,135 | 100,391 | 3.9 |
| Kansas | 2,289,615 | 2,158,011 | 131,604 | 5.7 |
| Kentucky | 3,434,955 | 3,348,473 | 86,482 | 2.5 |
| Louisiana | 3,886,353 | 3,494,359 | 391,994 | 10.1 |
| Maine | 1,142,122 | 1,036,681 | 105,441 | 9.2 |
| Maryland | 4,425,285 | 4,030,234 | 395,051 | 8.9 |
| Massachusetts | 5,605,751 | 4,753,523 | 852,228 | 15.2 |
| Michigan | 8,594,737 | 8,024,930 | 569,807 | 6.6 |
| Minnesota | 4,038,861 | 3,811,700 | 227,161 | 5.6 |
| Mississippi | 2,378,805 | 2,312,289 | 66,516 | 2.8 |
| Missouri | 4,748,704 | 4,570,494 | 178,210 | 3.8 |
| Montana | 740,218 | 703,198 | 37,020 | 5.0 |
| Nebraska | 1,458,904 | 1,389,032 | 69,872 | 4.8 |
| Nevada | 1,110,450 | 964,298 | 146,152 | 13.2 |
| New Hampshire | 1,024,621 | 935,825 | 88,796 | 8.7 |
| New Jersey | 7,200,696 | 5,794,548 | 1,406,148 | 19.5 |
| New Mexico | 1,390,048 | 896,049 | 493,999 | 35.5 |
| New York | 16,743,048 | 12,834,328 | 3,908,720 | 23.3 |
| North Carolina | 6,172,301 | 5,931,435 | 240,866 | 3.9 |
| North Dakota | 590,839 | 543,942 | 46,897 | 7.9 |
| Ohio | 10,063,212 | 9,517,064 | 546,148 | 5.4 |
| Oklahoma | 2,921,755 | 2,775,957 | 145,798 | 5.0 |
| Oregon | 2,640,482 | 2,448,772 | 191,710 | 7.3 |
| Pennsylvania | 11,085,170 | 10,278,294 | 806,876 | 7.3 |
| Rhode Island | 936,423 | 776,931 | 159,492 | 17.0 |
| South Carolina | 3,231,539 | 3,118,376 | 113,163 | 3.5 |
| South Dakota | 641,226 | 599,232 | 41,994 | 6.5 |
| Tennessee | 4,544,743 | 4,413,193 | 131,550 | 2.9 |
| Texas | 15,605,822 | 11,635,518 | 3,970,304 | 25.4 |
| Utah | 1,553,351 | 1,432,947 | 120,404 | 7.8 |
| Vermont | 521,521 | 491,112 | 30,409 | 5.8 |
| Virginia | 5,746,419 | 5,327,898 | 418,521 | 7.3 |
| Washington | 4,501,879 | 4,098,706 | 403,173 | 9.0 |
| West Virginia | 1,686,932 | 1,642,729 | 44,203 | 2.6 |
| Wisconsin | 4,531,134 | 4,267,496 | 263,638 | 5.8 |
| Wyoming | 418,713 | 394,904 | 23,809 | 5.7 |

# Economic and Financial Glossary

**Acquisition:** The purchase of one company by another.

**Balanced Budget:** The federal government budget is balanced when receipts are equal to current expenditure.

**Balance of payments:** The difference between all payments made to and from foreign countries over a set period of time. A *favorable* balance exists when more payments are coming in than going out; an *unfavorable* balance, when the reverse is true. Payments include gold, the cost of merchandise and services, interest and dividend payments, money spent by travelers, and repayment of principal on loans.

**Balance of trade (trade gap):** The difference between exports and imports, both in actual funds and credit. A nation's balance of trade is *favorable* when exports exceed imports and *unfavorable* when the reverse is true.

**Bear Market:** A market in which prices are falling.

**Bearer Bond:** A bond issued in bearer form rather than being registered in the owner's name. Ownership is determined by possession.

**Bond:** A written promise or IOU by the issuer to repay a fixed amount of borrowed money on a specified date and to pay a set annual rate of interest in the meantime, usually at semi-annual intervals. Bonds are generally considered safe because the borrower (whether a company or the government) usually must make interest payments before the money is spent on anything else.

**Bull Market:** A market in which prices are on the rise.

**Capital Gain (Loss):** An increase (decrease) in the market value of an asset above (below) the price originally paid, at the time the asset is sold.

**Commercial Paper:** An extremely short-term corporate IOU, generally due in 270 days or less. Available in face amounts of $100,000, $250,000, $500,000, $1,000,000 and combinations thereof.

**Convertible Bond:** A corporate bond (see below) which may be converted into a stated number of shares of common stock. Its price tends to fluctuate along with fluctuations in the price of the stock and with changes in interest rates.

**Corporate Bond:** Evidence of debt by a corporation. The bond normally has a stated life and pays a fixed rate of interest. Considered safer than the common or preferred stock of the same company.

**Cost of living:** The cost of maintaining a standard of living measured in terms of purchased goods and services. A rise in the cost of living mirrors the rate of inflation.

**Cost-of-living benefits:** Benefits that go to those persons whose money receipts increase automatically as prices rise.

**Credit crunch (liquidity crisis):** The period when cash for lending to business and consumers is in short supply.

**Debenture:** An unsecured long-term debt obligation backed only by the general credit of the issuing corporation.

**Deficit spending:** The practice whereby a government goes into debt to finance some of its expenditures.

**Depression:** A long period of economic decline when prices are low, unemployment is high, and there are many business failures.

**Devaluation:** The official lowering of a nation's currency, decreasing its value in relation to foreign currencies.

**Discount Rate:** The rate of interest set by the Federal Reserve that member banks are charged when borrowing money through the Federal Reserve System.

**Disposable income:** Income after taxes which is available to persons for spending and saving.

**Dividend:** Payment by a corporation to its shareholders, usually in the form of cash, stock shares, or other property.

**Dow-Jones Industrial Average:** A measure of stock market prices, based on 30 leading companies on the New York Stock Exchange.

**Econometrics:** The application of mathematical and statistical methods to the study of economic and financial data.

**Economic Growth:** The steady process of increasing productive capacity of the economy, and hence of increasing national income.

**Federal Deposit Insurance Corporation (FDIC):** A government-sponsored corporation that insures accounts in national banks and other qualified institutions.

**Federal Reserve System:** The entire banking system of the U.S., incorporating 12 Federal Reserve banks (one in each of 12 Federal Reserve districts), and 24 Federal Reserve branch banks, all national banks and state-chartered commercial banks and trust companies that have been admitted to its membership. The system greatly influences the nation's monetary and credit policies.

**Full employment:** The economy is said to be at full employment when only fractional unemployment exists. That is, everyone who wishes to work at the going wage-rate for his type of labor is employed. Since it takes time to switch from one job to another, there will be at any given time a small amount of unemployment.

**Golden Parachute:** Provisions in the employment contracts of executives guaranteeing substantial severance benefits if they lose their position in a corporate takeover.

**Government Bond:** An IOU of the U.S. Treasury, considered the safest security in the investment world. They are divided into two categories, those that are not marketable and those that are. *Savings Bonds* cannot be bought and sold once the original purchase is made. These include the familiar Series EE bonds. You buy them at 50 percent of their face value and when they mature, 12 years later, they will pay you back 100 percent of face value if you cash them in. Another type, Series H, are not discounted, but issued in amounts of $500, $1,000, $5,000, and $10,000 and pay their interest in semiannual checks. Marketable bonds fall into 12 categories. *Treasury Bills* are short-term U.S. obligations, maturing in 3, 6, or 12 months. They are sold at a discount of the face value, and the minimum denomination is $10,000. *Treasury Notes* mature in up to 10 years. Denominations range from $500, $1,000 to $5,000, $10,000 and up. *Treasury Bonds* mature in 10 to 30 years. The minimum investment is $1,000.

**Greenmail:** A company buys back its own shares from a suitor for more than the going market price to avoid a hostile takeover.

**Gross Domestic Product (GDP):** The market value of all goods and services that have been bought for final use during a year. It became the official measure of the U.S. economy in 1991, and replaced the *Gross National Product (GNP)* which had been in use since 1941. The GDP covers workers and capital employed within the nation's borders. The GNP covers production by American residents, regardless of location. The switch aligned the U.S. with most other industrialized countries, making comparisons easier.

**Individual Retirement Account (IRA):** A self-funded retirement plan that allows employed individuals to contribute a maximum yearly sum toward their retirement. Interest earned in the account is tax deferred.

**Inflation:** An increase in the average level of prices.

**Insider Information:** Important facts about the condition or plans of a corporation that have not been released to the general public.

**Interest:** Money paid for the use of money. There are two kinds of interest. Simple interest is interest that is earned and paid. Compound interest is the accumulated interest that is added to the principal amount.

**Junk Bonds:** Debt securities that sell at relatively low prices, because of the low credit rating of their issuers. They pay significantly higher yields than top-grade bonds to reflect their added risk. In the 1980s, they were used to finance hostile takeovers.

**Key leading indicators:** A series of eleven indicators from different segments of the economy used by the Commerce Department to foretell what will happen in the economy in the near future.

**Leveraged Buy-Out:** An acquisition of a public company by a small group, often including the company's management, which takes the company private. Much of the purchase price is borrowed with the debt repaid from company profits or by selling company assets.

**Liquid Assets:** Assets that include cash or those items that are easily converted into cash.

**Margin Account:** A brokerage account that allows a person to trade securities on credit.

**Money supply:** The currency held by the public plus checking accounts in commercial banks and savings institutions.

**Mortgage-Backed Securities:** Created when a bank, builder or government agency gathers together a group of mortgages and then sells bonds to other institutions and the public. The investors receive their proportionate share of the interest payments on the loans as well as the principal payments. Usually, these mortgages are guaranteed by the government.

**Municipal Bond:** Issued by governmental units such as states, cities, local taxing authorities and other agencies. Interest is exempt from U.S. — and sometimes state and local — income tax. *Municipal Bond Unit Investment Trusts* allow you to invest in a portfolio of many different municipal bonds chosen by professionals. The income is exempt from federal income taxes.

**Mutual Fund:** A portfolio, or selection, of professionally bought and managed stocks in which you pool your money along with thousands of other people. A share price is based on net asset value, or the value of all the investments owned by the funds, less any debt, and divided by the total number of shares. The major advantage is less risk — it is spread out over many stocks and, if one or two do badly, the remainder may shield you from the losses. *Bond Funds* are mutual funds that deal in the bond market exclusively. *Money Market Mutual Funds* buy in the so-called "Money Market" — institutions that need to borrow large sums of money for short terms. Usually the individual investor cannot afford the denominations required in the "Money Market" (i.e. treasury bills, commercial paper, certificates of deposit), but through a money market mutual fund he can take advantage of these instruments when interest rates are high. These funds offer special checking account advantages.

**National debt:** The debt of the national government as distinguished from the debts of the political subdivisions of the nation and private business and individuals.

**National debt ceiling:** Limit set by Congress beyond which the national debt cannot rise. This limit is periodically raised by congressional vote.

**Option:** A contractual agreement between a buyer and a seller to buy or sell shares of a security. A *Call* option contract gives the right to purchase shares of a specific stock at a stated price within a given period of time. A *Put* option contract gives the buyer the right to sell shares of a specific stock at a stated price within a given period of time.

**Per capita income:** The nation's total income divided by the number of people in the nation.

**Prime interest rate:** The rate charged by banks on short-term loans to large commercial customers with the highest credit rating.

**Producer price index:** A statistical measure of the change in the price of wholesale goods. It is reported for 3 different stages of the production chain: crude, intermediate, and finished goods.

**Program Trading:** A term used for trading techniques involving large numbers and large blocks of stocks, usually used in conjunction with computer programs. Techniques include *Index Arbitrage* in which traders profit from price differences between stocks and futures contracts on stock indexes, and *Portfolio Insurance* which is the use of stock-index futures to protect stock investors from large losses when the market drops.

**Public debt:** The total of the nation's debts owed by state, local, and national government. This is considered a good measure of how much of the nation's spending is financed by borrowing rather than taxation.

**Recession:** A mild decrease in economic activity marked by a decline in real GNP, employment, and trade, usually lasting 6 months to a year, and marked by widespread decline in many sectors of the economy.

**Savings Association Insurance Fund (SAIF):** Created in 1989 to insure accounts in savings and loan associations up to $100,000.

**Seasonal adjustment:** Statistical changes made to compensate for regular fluctuations in data that are so great they tend to distort the statistics and make comparisons meaningless. For instance, seasonal adjustments are made in midwinter for a slowdown in housing construction and for the rise in farm income in the fall after the summer crops are harvested.

**Stagnation:** A period of economic slowdown in which there is little growth in GDP, capital investment, and real income.

**Stock:** *Common Stocks* are shares of ownership in a corporation; they are the most direct way to participate in the fortunes of a company. There can be wide swings in the prices of this kind of stock. *Preferred Stock* is a type of stock on which a fixed dividend must be paid before holders of common stock are issued their share of the issuing corporation's earnings. Prices are higher and yields lower than comparable bonds. However, they are attractive to corporate investors because 85 percent of preferred dividends are tax exempt to corporations. *Convertible Preferred Stock* can be converted into the common stock of the company that issued the preferred. This stock has the advantage of producing a higher yield than common stock and it also has appreciation potential. *Over-the-Counter Stock* is not traded on the major or regional exchanges, but rather through dealers from whom you buy directly. *Blue Chip* stocks are so called because they have been leading stocks for a long time. *Growth* stocks are stocks whose earnings have grown over several years.

**Stock-index Futures:** A futures contract is an agreement to buy or sell a specific amount of a commodity or financial instrument at a particular price at a set date. Futures on a stock index (such as the Standard & Poor's 500) are bets on the future price of that group of stocks.

**Supply-side economics:** The school of economic thinking which stresses the importance of the costs of production as a means of revitalizing the economy. Advocates policies that raise capital and labor output by increasing the incentives to produce.

**Takeover:** The passing of control of one company by another company or group by sale or merger. A friendly takeover occurs when the acquired company's management is agreeable to the merger; when management is opposed to the merger it is an unfriendly takeover. Takeover **arbitrage** is the purchase and/or selling of the securities of companies involved in takeover situations in order to realize a profit.

**Tender Offer:** A public offer to buy a company's stock; usually priced at a premium above the market.

**Unit Investment Trust:** A portfolio of many different corporate bonds, preferred stocks, government-backed securities or utility common stocks in which you can invest with as little as $1,000. Professional managers choose the securities, arrange for safe-keeping and collect the income. You receive your pro rata share of income every month.

**Zero Coupon Bond:** A corporate or government bond that is issued at a deep discount from the maturity value and pays no interest during the life of the bond. It is redeemable at face value.

# Esperanto

Esperanto is the most commonly spoken of the international languages, artificial languages intended to provide a universal means of communication to bridge the gap between speakers of the world's many different natural languages. International languages are based on natural languages, with simplifications of grammar and spelling. Esperanto, invented in 1887 by the Polish physician and linguist Dr. Ludwik L. Zamenhof, is derived from a combination of Latin, the Romance languages, and the Germanic languages. Its name comes from the pseudonym ("Doktoro Esperanto") used by Zamenhof in his textbook describing the language. Because of its logical structure, phonemic spelling, and regular grammar, Esperanto can generally be learned more quickly than a typical natural language. An example of Esperanto:

*Inteligenta persono lernas la lingvon Esperanto rapide kaj facile. Esperanto estas la moderna, kultura lingvo por la tuta mondo.*

# PRESIDENTIAL ELECTIONS

## Popular and Electoral Vote, 1988 and 1992

Source: News Election Service; Federal Election Commission

| States | 1992 Electoral Vote Clinton | Bush | Perot | 1992 Democrat Clinton | Republican Bush | Ind. Perot | 1988 Electoral Vote Dukakis | Bush | 1988 Democrat Dukakis | Republican Bush |
|---|---|---|---|---|---|---|---|---|---|---|
| Ala.. . | 0 | 9 | 0 | 690,080 | 804,283 | 183,109 | 0 | 9 | 549,506 | 815,576 |
| Alas.. | 0 | 3 | 0 | 78,294 | 102,000 | 73,481 | 0 | 3 | 72,584 | 119,251 |
| Ariz. . | 0 | 8 | 0 | 543,050 | 572,086 | 353,741 | 0 | 7 | 454,029 | 702,541 |
| Ark. . | 6 | 0 | 0 | 505,823 | 337,324 | 99,132 | 0 | 6 | 349,237 | 466,578 |
| Cal. . | 54 | 0 | 0 | 5,121,325 | 3,630,574 | 2,296,006 | 0 | 47 | 4,702,233 | 5,054,917 |
| Col. . | 8 | 0 | 0 | 629,681 | 562,850 | 366,010 | 0 | 8 | 621,453 | 728,177 |
| Conn. | 8 | 0 | 0 | 682,318 | 578,313 | 348,771 | 0 | 8 | 676,584 | 750,241 |
| Del. . | 3 | 0 | 0 | 126,054 | 102,313 | 59,213 | 0 | 3 | 108,647 | 139,639 |
| D.C. . | 3 | 0 | 0 | 192,619 | 20,698 | 9,681 | 3 | 0 | 159,407 | 27,590 |
| Fla.. . | 0 | 25 | 0 | 2,071,651 | 2,171,781 | 1,052,481 | 0 | 21 | 1,655,851 | 2,616,597 |
| Ga.. . | 13 | 0 | 0 | 1,008,966 | 995,252 | 309,657 | 0 | 12 | 714,792 | 1,081,331 |
| Ha.. . | 4 | 0 | 0 | 179,310 | 136,822 | 53,003 | 4 | 0 | 192,364 | 158,625 |
| Ida.. . | 0 | 4 | 0 | 137,013 | 202,645 | 130,395 | 0 | 4 | 147,272 | 253,881 |
| Ill.. . | 22 | 0 | 0 | 2,453,350 | 1,734,096 | 840,515 | 0 | 24 | 2,215,940 | 2,310,939 |
| Ind.. . | 0 | 12 | 0 | 848,420 | 989,375 | 455,934 | 0 | 12 | 860,643 | 1,297,763 |
| Ia. . . | 7 | 0 | 0 | 586,353 | 504,891 | 253,468 | 8 | 0 | 670,557 | 545,355 |
| Kan. . | 0 | 6 | 0 | 390,434 | 449,951 | 312,358 | 0 | 7 | 422,636 | 554,049 |
| Ky.. . | 8 | 0 | 0 | 665,104 | 617,178 | 203,944 | 0 | 9 | 580,368 | 734,281 |
| La.. . | 9 | 0 | 0 | 815,971 | 733,386 | 211,478 | 0 | 10 | 717,460 | 883,702 |
| Me.. . | 4 | 0 | 0 | 263,420 | 206,504 | 206,820 | 0 | 4 | 243,569 | 307,131 |
| Md.. . | 10 | 0 | 0 | 988,571 | 707,094 | 281,414 | 0 | 10 | 826,304 | 876,167 |
| Mass. | 12 | 0 | 0 | 1,318,639 | 805,039 | 630,731 | 13 | 0 | 1,401,415 | 1,194,635 |
| Mich.. | 18 | 0 | 0 | 1,871,182 | 1,554,940 | 824,813 | 0 | 20 | 1,675,783 | 1,965,486 |
| Minn.. | 10 | 0 | 0 | 1,020,997 | 747,841 | 562,506 | 10 | 0 | 1,109,471 | 962,337 |
| Miss.. | 0 | 7 | 0 | 400,258 | 487,793 | 85,626 | 0 | 7 | 363,921 | 557,890 |
| Mo.. . | 11 | 0 | 0 | 1,053,873 | 811,159 | 518,741 | 0 | 11 | 1,001,619 | 1,084,953 |
| Mon.. | 3 | 0 | 0 | 154,507 | 144,207 | 107,225 | 0 | 4 | 168,936 | 190,412 |
| Neb.. | 0 | 5 | 0 | 216,864 | 343,678 | 174,104 | 0 | 5 | 259,235 | 397,956 |
| Nev.. | 4 | 0 | 0 | 189,148 | 175,828 | 132,580 | 0 | 4 | 132,738 | 206,040 |
| N.H. . | 4 | 0 | 0 | 209,040 | 202,484 | 121,337 | 0 | 4 | 163,696 | 281,537 |
| N.J. . | 15 | 0 | 0 | 1,436,206 | 1,356,865 | 521,829 | 0 | 16 | 1,317,541 | 1,740,604 |
| N.M. . | 5 | 0 | 0 | 261,617 | 212,824 | 91,895 | 0 | 5 | 244,497 | 270,341 |
| N.Y. . | 33 | 0 | 0 | 3,444,450 | 2,346,649 | 1,090,721 | 36 | 0 | 3,347,882 | 3,081,871 |
| N.C. . | 0 | 14 | 0 | 1,114,042 | 1,134,661 | 357,864 | 0 | 13 | 890,167 | 1,237,258 |
| N.D. . | 0 | 3 | 0 | 99,168 | 136,244 | 71,084 | 0 | 3 | 127,739 | 166,559 |
| Oh.. . | 21 | 0 | 0 | 1,984,942 | 1,894,310 | 1,036,426 | 0 | 23 | 1,939,629 | 2,416,549 |
| Okla.. | 0 | 8 | 0 | 473,066 | 592,929 | 319,878 | 0 | 8 | 483,423 | 678,367 |
| Ore.. . | 7 | 0 | 0 | 621,314 | 475,757 | 354,091 | 7 | 0 | 616,206 | 560,126 |
| Pa.. . | 23 | 0 | 0 | 2,239,164 | 1,791,841 | 902,667 | 0 | 25 | 2,194,944 | 2,300,087 |
| R.I.. . | 4 | 0 | 0 | 213,299 | 131,601 | 105,045 | 4 | 0 | 225,123 | 177,761 |
| S.C. . | 0 | 8 | 0 | 479,514 | 577,507 | 138,872 | 0 | 8 | 370,554 | 606,443 |
| S.D. . | 0 | 3 | 0 | 124,888 | 136,718 | 73,295 | 0 | 3 | 145,560 | 165,415 |
| Tenn.. | 11 | 0 | 0 | 933,521 | 841,300 | 199,968 | 0 | 11 | 679,794 | 947,233 |
| Tex. . | 0 | 32 | 0 | 2,281,815 | 2,496,071 | 1,354,781 | 0 | 29 | 2,352,748 | 3,036,829 |
| Ut. . . | 0 | 5 | 0 | 183,429 | 322,632 | 203,400 | 0 | 5 | 207,352 | 428,442 |
| Vt. . . | 3 | 0 | 0 | 133,590 | 88,122 | 65,985 | 0 | 3 | 115,775 | 124,331 |
| Va.. . | 0 | 13 | 0 | 1,038,650 | 1,150,517 | 348,639 | 0 | 12 | 859,799 | 1,309,162 |
| Wash. | 11 | 0 | 0 | 993,037 | 731,234 | 541,780 | 10 | 0 | 933,516 | 903,835 |
| W.Va.. | 5 | 0 | 0 | 331,001 | 241,974 | 108,829 | 5[1] | 0 | 341,016 | 310,065 |
| Wis.. . | 11 | 0 | 0 | 1,041,066 | 930,855 | 544,479 | 11 | 0 | 1,126,794 | 1,047,499 |
| Wyo.. | 0 | 3 | 0 | 68,160 | 79,347 | 51,263 | 0 | 3 | 67,113 | 106,867 |
| **Total.** | **370** | **168** | **0** | **44,908,254** | **39,102,343** | **19,741,065** | **111[1]** | **426** | **41,805,422** | **48,881,221** |

(1) Lloyd Bentsen (D.-Tex.) received 1 electoral vote from W.Va.

## Presidential Election Returns by Counties

All 1992 results are official. Results for New England states are for selected cities or towns due to unavailability of county results. Totals are always statewide.

Source: News Election Service; Federal Election Commission

### Alabama

| County | 1992 Clinton (D) | Bush (R) | Perot (I) | 1988 Dukakis (D) | Bush (R) |
|---|---|---|---|---|---|
| Autauga | 4,819 | 8,715 | 1,916 | 3,667 | 7,828 |
| Baldwin | 12,195 | 26,270 | 7,656 | 9,271 | 25,933 |
| Barbour | 4,836 | 4,475 | 1,020 | 3,836 | 4,958 |
| Bibb | 2,900 | 3,124 | 686 | 2,244 | 2,885 |
| Blount | 5,433 | 8,882 | 1,949 | 4,485 | 8,754 |
| Bullock | 3,259 | 1,253 | 266 | 3,122 | 1,421 |
| Butler | 4,021 | 3,494 | 867 | 3,465 | 3,923 |
| Calhoun | 16,453 | 20,623 | 4,717 | 12,451 | 19,806 |
| Chambers | 5,938 | 5,682 | 1,427 | 5,103 | 7,694 |
| Cherokee | 4,222 | 2,745 | 846 | 3,176 | 2,868 |
| Chilton | 4,946 | 8,126 | 1,363 | 3,820 | 8,761 |
| Choctaw | 3,941 | 3,069 | 489 | 3,491 | 3,629 |
| Clarke | 5,023 | 5,495 | 872 | 4,217 | 5,708 |
| Clay | 2,073 | 2,859 | 652 | 1,602 | 3,496 |
| Cleburne | 2,144 | 2,425 | 630 | 1,383 | 3,071 |
| Coffee | 5,776 | 7,591 | 2,021 | 4,319 | 8,890 |
| Colbert | 12,206 | 8,073 | 2,098 | 10,397 | 7,775 |
| Conecuh | 3,155 | 2,463 | 552 | 3,022 | 3,256 |
| Coosa | 2,330 | 1,973 | 476 | 1,860 | 2,405 |
| Covington | 5,004 | 6,840 | 1,880 | 3,845 | 8,130 |
| Crenshaw | 2,404 | 2,339 | 485 | 1,836 | 2,617 |
| Cullman | 10,451 | 14,411 | 4,113 | 8,517 | 14,351 |
| Dale | 5,098 | 8,123 | 2,423 | 3,476 | 9,266 |
| Dallas | 11,053 | 7,394 | 1,110 | 9,660 | 7,630 |
| DeKalb | 8,245 | 10,519 | 2,741 | 7,333 | 11,478 |
| Elmore | 6,223 | 11,356 | 2,765 | 4,501 | 10,852 |
| Escambia | 4,809 | 5,955 | 1,616 | 4,020 | 6,807 |
| Etowah | 20,558 | 17,467 | 4,277 | 17,762 | 17,828 |
| Fayette | 3,830 | 3,604 | 1,012 | 3,186 | 4,338 |
| Franklin | 5,953 | 4,794 | 1,075 | 4,961 | 5,146 |
| Geneva | 3,622 | 4,843 | 1,323 | 2,685 | 5,703 |
| Greene | 3,865 | 805 | 194 | 3,295 | 1,048 |
| Hale | 3,481 | 2,001 | 486 | 3,187 | 2,414 |
| Henry | 2,804 | 2,970 | 667 | 2,206 | 3,613 |
| Houston | 8,857 | 17,360 | 3,492 | 7,001 | 19,989 |
| Jackson | 10,628 | 5,711 | 2,462 | 7,418 | 6,090 |
| Jefferson | 125,889 | 149,832 | 22,191 | 107,766 | 148,879 |
| Lamar | 2,849 | 3,262 | 763 | 2,274 | 3,214 |
| Lauderdale | 15,936 | 13,728 | 4,009 | 12,862 | 12,942 |
| Lawrence | 6,364 | 3,576 | 1,624 | 4,646 | 3,616 |
| Lee | 13,770 | 16,885 | 4,572 | 9,078 | 17,180 |
| Limestone | 8,087 | 9,862 | 3,584 | 5,455 | 9,086 |
| Lowndes | 3,500 | 1,328 | 284 | 3,328 | 1,405 |
| Macon | 7,253 | 1,134 | 283 | 6,351 | 1,304 |
| Madison | 38,974 | 51,444 | 16,989 | 25,800 | 53,575 |
| Marengo | 5,632 | 4,470 | 919 | 4,402 | 4,241 |
| Marion | 6,167 | 5,692 | 1,389 | 4,505 | 5,955 |
| Marshall | 10,421 | 12,249 | 3,795 | 7,357 | 12,148 |
| Mobile | 54,962 | 72,935 | 15,105 | 45,524 | 72,203 |
| Monroe | 3,872 | 4,919 | 759 | 3,509 | 5,379 |
| Montgomery | 37,342 | 40,742 | 7,647 | 28,709 | 41,131 |
| Morgan | 15,091 | 21,073 | 7,683 | 10,594 | 18,679 |
| Perry | 3,712 | 1,829 | 213 | 3,574 | 2,107 |
| Pickens | 3,783 | 3,634 | 690 | 3,107 | 3,851 |
| Pike | 4,688 | 5,423 | 1,024 | 3,813 | 5,897 |
| Randolph | 3,318 | 3,813 | 919 | 2,462 | 4,625 |
| Russell | 8,647 | 5,587 | 1,360 | 6,589 | 6,333 |
| St. Clair | 6,517 | 12,447 | 2,614 | 4,335 | 10,604 |
| Shelby | 10,317 | 32,736 | 5,022 | 7,138 | 27,052 |
| Sumter | 4,810 | 1,807 | 388 | 4,390 | 2,212 |
| Talladega | 10,695 | 12,661 | 2,629 | 8,291 | 12,973 |
| Tallapoosa | 5,703 | 8,140 | 1,562 | 4,598 | 8,502 |
| Tuscaloosa | 23,495 | 27,454 | 7,011 | 18,166 | 27,396 |
| Walker | 14,831 | 11,301 | 3,344 | 11,338 | 11,011 |
| Washington | 4,046 | 3,270 | 829 | 3,402 | 3,741 |
| Wilcox | 3,439 | 1,671 | 174 | 3,369 | 1,739 |
| Winston | 3,415 | 5,550 | 1,110 | 2,954 | 6,235 |
| Totals | 690,080 | 804,283 | 183,109 | 549,506 | 815,576 |

### Alabama Vote Since 1944

1944, Roosevelt, Dem., 198,918; Dewey, Rep., 44,540; Watson, Proh., 1,095; Thomas, Soc., 190.

1948, Thurmond, States' Rights, 171,443; Dewey, Rep., 40,930; Wallace, Prog., 1,522; Watson, Proh., 1,085.

1952, Eisenhower, Rep., 149,231; Stevenson, Dem., 275,075; Hamblen, Proh., 1,814.

1956, Stevenson, Dem., 290,844; Eisenhower, Rep. 195,694; Independent electors, 20,323.

1960, Kennedy, Dem., 324,050; Nixon, Rep., 237,981; Faubus, States' Rights, 4,367; Decker, Proh., 2,106; King, Afro-Americans, 1,485; scattering, 236.

1964, Dem. 209,848 (electors unpledged); Goldwater, Rep., 479,085; scattering, 105.

1968, Nixon, Rep., 146,923; Humphrey, Dem., 196,579; Wallace, 3d party, 691,425; Munn, Proh., 4,022.

1972, Nixon, Rep., 728,701; McGovern, Dem., 219,108 plus 37,815 Natl. Demo. Party of Alabama; Schmitz, Conservative, 11,918; Munn., Proh., 8,551.

1976, Carter, Dem., 659,170; Ford, Rep., 504,070; Maddox, Am. Ind., 9,198; Bubar, Proh., 6,669; Hall, Com., 1,954; MacBride, Libertarian, 1,481.

1980, Reagan, Rep., 654,192; Carter, Dem., 636,730; Anderson, Independent, 16,481; Rarick, Amer. Ind., 15,010; Clark, Libertarian, 13,318; Bubar, Statesman, 1,743; Hall, Com., 1,629; DeBerry, Soc. Work., 1,303; McReynolds, Socialist, 1,006; Commoner, Citizens, 517.

1984, Reagan, Rep., 872,849; Mondale, Dem., 551,899; Bergland, Libertarian, 9,504.

1988, Bush, Rep., 815,576; Dukakis, Dem., 549,506; Paul, Lib., 8,460; Fulani, Ind., 3,311.

1992, Bush, Rep., 804,283; Clinton, Dem., 690,080; Perot, Ind., 183,109; Marrou, Libertarian, 5,737; Fulani, New Alliance, 2,161.

### Alaska

| Election District | 1992 Clinton (D) | Bush (R) | Perot (I) | 1988 Dukakis (D) | Bush (R) |
|---|---|---|---|---|---|
| No. 1 | 2,055 | 2,495 | 2,120 | | |
| No. 2 | 2,565 | 2,916 | 2,137 | | |
| No. 3 | 4,064 | 2,447 | 1,424 | | |
| No. 4 | 2,688 | 2,894 | 1,561 | | |
| No. 5 | 2,095 | 1,844 | 1,684 | | |
| No. 6 | 1,546 | 2,345 | 1,748 | | |
| No. 7 | 2,088 | 2,173 | 2,244 | | |
| No. 8 | 1,509 | 2,499 | 2,325 | | |
| No. 9 | 1,540 | 2,349 | 2,368 | | |
| No. 10 | 1,947 | 3,548 | 1,899 | | |
| No. 11 | 2,009 | 2,730 | 2,081 | | |
| No. 12 | 1,831 | 2,999 | 2,039 | | |
| No. 13 | 3,001 | 2,963 | 1,907 | | |
| No. 14 | 1,423 | 3,013 | 1,599 | | |
| No. 15 | 2,389 | 1,842 | 1,591 | | |
| No. 16 | 1,814 | 1,375 | 1,320 | | |
| No. 17 | 1,749 | 2,623 | 1,958 | | |
| No. 18 | 2,483 | 3,629 | 2,134 | | |
| No. 19 | 1,931 | 2,539 | 1,840 | | |
| No. 20 | 2,383 | 2,914 | 1,823 | | |
| No. 21 | 2,386 | 2,437 | 1,693 | | |
| No. 22 | 2,253 | 3,164 | 1,713 | | |
| No. 23 | 1,139 | 2,127 | 1,217 | | |
| No. 24 | 1,876 | 3,441 | 1,930 | | |
| No. 25 | 1,513 | 3,197 | 2,122 | | |
| No. 26 | 1,439 | 2,675 | 2,419 | | |
| No. 27 | 1,625 | 2,757 | 2,401 | | |
| No. 28 | 1,522 | 2,459 | 2,825 | | |
| No. 29 | 3,216 | 2,205 | 2,026 | | |
| No. 30 | 1,860 | 2,434 | 1,912 | | |
| No. 31 | 1,969 | 2,223 | 1,992 | | |
| No. 32 | 1,150 | 2,339 | 1,724 | | |
| No. 33 | 1,712 | 3,100 | 2,278 | | |
| No. 34 | 1,455 | 3,408 | 2,201 | | |
| No. 35 | 1,572 | 2,525 | 2,139 | | |
| No. 36 | 1,748 | 2,081 | 1,322 | | |
| No. 37 | 1,822 | 1,689 | 925 | | |
| No. 38 | 1,897 | 2,011 | 850 | | |
| No. 39 | 1,797 | 1,777 | 860 | | |
| No. 40 | 1,211 | 1,786 | 1,122 | | |
| Totals | 78,294 | 102,000 | 73,481 | 72,584 | 119,251 |

### Alaska Vote Since 1968

1968, Nixon, Rep., 37,600; Humphrey, Dem., 35,411; Wallace, 3d party, 10,024.

1972, Nixon, Rep., 55,349; McGovern, Dem., 32,967; Schmitz, American, 6,903.

1976, Carter, Dem., 44,058; Ford, Rep., 71,555; MacBride, Libertarian, 6,785.

1980, Reagan, Rep., 86,112; Carter, Dem., 41,842; Clark, Libertarian, 18,479; Anderson, Ind., 11,155; Write-in, 857.

1984, Reagan, Rep., 138,377; Mondale, Dem., 62,007; Bergland, Libertarian, 6,378.

1988, Bush, Rep., 119,251; Dukakis, Dem., 72,584; Paul, Lib., 5,484; Fulani, New Alliance, 1,024.

1992, Bush, Rep., 102,000; Clinton, Dem., 78,294; Perot, Ind., 73,481; Gritz, Populist/America First, 1,379; Marrou, Libertarian, 1,378.

## Arizona

| | 1992 | | | 1988 | |
|---|---|---|---|---|---|
| County | Clinton (D) | Bush (R) | Perot (I) | Dukakis (D) | Bush (R) |
| Apache | 11,218 | 4,588 | 1,979 | 8,944 | 5,347 |
| Cochise | 12,701 | 12,202 | 7,857 | 11,812 | 15,815 |
| Coconino | 18,888 | 13,769 | 9,363 | 14,660 | 16,649 |
| Gila | 7,571 | 5,781 | 4,694 | 7,147 | 7,861 |
| Graham | 3,391 | 4,169 | 1,860 | 3,407 | 5,120 |
| Greenlee | 1,695 | 1,451 | 794 | 1,733 | 1,526 |
| La Paz | 1,808 | 1,599 | 1,488 | 1,746 | 2,562 |
| Maricopa | 285,457 | 360,049 | 221,475 | 230,952 | 442,337 |
| Mohave | 13,255 | 13,684 | 12,706 | 10,197 | 17,651 |
| Navajo | 10,882 | 7,994 | 4,787 | 9,023 | 10,393 |
| Pima | 128,569 | 97,036 | 53,925 | 113,824 | 117,899 |
| Pinal | 15,468 | 11,669 | 9,231 | 13,850 | 14,966 |
| Santa Cruz | 3,512 | 3,024 | 1,447 | 3,268 | 3,320 |
| Yavapai | 18,268 | 23,419 | 16,409 | 14,514 | 27,842 |
| Yuma | 10,367 | 11,652 | 5,726 | 8,952 | 13,253 |
| Totals | 543,050 | 572,086 | 353,741 | 454,029 | 702,541 |

### Arizona Vote Since 1944

1944, Roosevelt, Dem., 80,926; Dewey, Rep., 56,287; Watson, Proh., 421.

1948, Truman, Dem., 95,251; Dewey, Rep., 77,597; Wallace, Prog., 3,310; Watson, Proh., 786; Teichert, Soc. Labor, 121.

1952, Eisenhower, Rep., 152,042; Stevenson, Dem., 108,528.

1956, Eisenhower, Rep., 176,990; Stevenson, Dem., 112,880; Andrews, Ind. 303.

1960, Kennedy, Dem., 176,781; Nixon, Rep., 221,241; Hass, Soc. Labor, 469.

1964, Johnson, Dem., 237,753; Goldwater, Rep., 242,535; Hass, Soc. Labor, 482.

1968, Nixon, Rep., 266,721; Humphrey, Dem., 170,514; Wallace, 3d party, 46,573; McCarthy, New Party, 2,751; Halstead, Soc. Worker, 85; Cleaver, Peace and Freedom, 217; Blomen, Soc. Labor, 75.

1972, Nixon, Rep., 402,812; McGovern, Dem., 198,540; Schmitz, Amer., 21,208; Soc. Workers, 30,945. Due to ballot peculiarities in 3 counties (particularly Pima), thousands of voters cast ballots for the Socialist Workers Party and one of the major candidates. Court ordered both votes counted as official.

1976, Carter, Dem., 295,602; Ford, Rep., 418,642; McCarthy, Ind., 19,229; MacBride, Libertarian, 7,647; Camejo, Soc. Workers, 928; Anderson, Amer., 564; Maddox, Am. Ind., 85.

1980, Reagan, Rep., 529,688; Carter, Dem., 246,843; Anderson, Ind., 76,952; Clark, Libertarian, 18,784; De Berry, Soc. Workers, 1,100; Commoner, Citizens, 551; Hall, Com., 25; Griswold, Workers World, 2.

1984, Reagan, Rep., 681,416; Mondale, Dem., 333,854; Bergland, Libertarian, 10,585.

1988, Bush, Rep., 702,541; Dukakis, Dem., 454,029; Paul, Lib., 13,351; Fulani, New Alliance, 1,662.

1992, Bush, Rep., 572,086; Clinton, Dem., 543,050; Perot, Ind., 353,741; Gritz, Populist/America First, 8,141; Marrou, Libertarian, 6,759; Hagelin, Natural Law, 2,267.

## Arkansas

| | 1992 | | | 1988 | |
|---|---|---|---|---|---|
| County | Clinton (D) | Bush (R) | Perot (I) | Dukakis (D) | Bush (R) |
| Arkansas | 4,709 | 2,594 | 639 | 3,075 | 4,007 |
| Ashley | 5,876 | 2,686 | 931 | 4,466 | 4,111 |
| Baxter | 6,991 | 5,640 | 2,938 | 4,808 | 8,614 |
| Benton | 15,774 | 21,126 | 6,128 | 9,399 | 24,295 |
| Boone | 6,128 | 6,094 | 2,079 | 3,998 | 7,567 |
| Bradley | 2,954 | 1,482 | 391 | 2,167 | 2,089 |
| Calhoun | 1,389 | 1,047 | 257 | 1,024 | 1,316 |
| Carroll | 3,769 | 3,535 | 1,500 | 2,632 | 4,553 |
| Chicot | 3,504 | 1,242 | 347 | 2,426 | 1,901 |
| Clark | 5,767 | 2,403 | 714 | 4,675 | 3,389 |
| Clay | 4,848 | 1,647 | 568 | 3,442 | 2,766 |
| Cleburne | 5,090 | 3,580 | 1,263 | 3,404 | 4,932 |
| Cleveland | 1,893 | 1,127 | 337 | 1,404 | 1,462 |
| Columbia | 4,747 | 3,702 | 1,090 | 3,576 | 5,810 |
| Conway | 4,898 | 2,719 | 803 | 4,134 | 4,066 |
| Craighead | 13,931 | 9,104 | 2,274 | 9,083 | 11,887 |
| Crawford | 6,656 | 6,882 | 2,442 | 3,582 | 9,092 |
| Crittenden | 9,683 | 5,910 | 848 | 6,702 | 7,441 |
| Cross | 4,058 | 2,303 | 602 | 2,989 | 3,186 |
| Dallas | 2,107 | 1,458 | 345 | 1,990 | 1,947 |
| Desha | 3,815 | 1,279 | 392 | 2,859 | 2,334 |
| Drew | 3,748 | 1,938 | 596 | 2,578 | 2,995 |
| Faulkner | 13,000 | 9,491 | 2,437 | 7,302 | 10,678 |
| Franklin | 3,217 | 2,495 | 987 | 2,458 | 3,588 |
| Fulton | 2,827 | 1,258 | 631 | 2,018 | 1,918 |
| Garland | 18,811 | 12,886 | 3,475 | 11,406 | 19,281 |
| Grant | 3,190 | 2,272 | 702 | 2,142 | 2,717 |
| Greene | 7,541 | 3,510 | 1,213 | 5,065 | 5,161 |
| Hempstead | 5,476 | 2,387 | 1,022 | 3,841 | 3,938 |
| Hot Spring | 6,308 | 3,036 | 1,209 | 5,090 | 4,181 |
| Howard | 2,764 | 1,728 | 466 | 1,818 | 2,510 |
| Independence | 7,083 | 4,232 | 1,444 | 4,523 | 6,637 |
| Izard | 3,419 | 1,532 | 606 | 2,652 | 2,824 |
| Jackson | 4,944 | 1,864 | 673 | 4,199 | 3,049 |
| Jefferson | 21,819 | 7,525 | 2,067 | 16,664 | 12,520 |
| Johnson | 3,951 | 2,563 | 1,013 | 2,818 | 4,046 |
| Lafayette | 2,273 | 1,188 | 504 | 1,915 | 1,860 |
| Lawrence | 4,146 | 2,124 | 636 | 3,179 | 3,205 |
| Lee | 3,436 | 1,293 | 308 | 2,878 | 1,863 |
| Lincoln | 2,805 | 1,142 | 390 | 2,204 | 1,557 |
| Little River | 3,327 | 1,483 | 890 | 2,740 | 2,347 |
| Logan | 3,995 | 3,408 | 1,220 | 1,254 | 2,203 |
| Lonoke | 7,963 | 6,253 | 1,554 | 4,786 | 7,215 |
| Madison | 2,415 | 2,238 | 598 | 2,106 | 3,067 |
| Marion | 2,757 | 2,023 | 1,327 | 2,033 | 2,993 |
| Miller | 7,050 | 5,273 | 2,249 | 5,437 | 7,110 |
| Mississippi | 10,046 | 4,697 | 981 | 6,759 | 7,841 |
| Monroe | 2,578 | 1,324 | 355 | 2,052 | 1,862 |
| Montgomery | 1,904 | 1,205 | 576 | 1,362 | 1,752 |
| Nevada | 2,242 | 1,217 | 455 | 1,732 | 1,714 |
| Newton | 1,765 | 1,730 | 608 | 1,489 | 2,504 |
| Ouachita | 7,411 | 3,711 | 1,238 | 5,229 | 6,297 |
| Perry | 1,906 | 1,162 | 412 | 1,470 | 1,627 |
| Phillips | 6,456 | 2,695 | 634 | 5,580 | 3,892 |
| Pike | 2,168 | 1,577 | 472 | 1,681 | 2,105 |
| Poinsett | 5,341 | 2,425 | 761 | 3,873 | 3,644 |
| Polk | 3,162 | 2,757 | 1,225 | 2,390 | 4,099 |
| Pope | 7,704 | 8,056 | 1,989 | 4,941 | 10,084 |
| Prairie | 2,366 | 1,154 | 434 | 1,688 | 1,947 |
| Pulaski | 79,482 | 47,789 | 8,751 | 55,857 | 70,562 |
| Randolph | 3,921 | 1,766 | 578 | 2,781 | 2,560 |
| St. Francis | 6,548 | 3,289 | 766 | 4,656 | 4,298 |
| Saline | 12,671 | 10,105 | 2,751 | 8,436 | 12,353 |
| Scott | 2,228 | 1,695 | 610 | 1,707 | 2,507 |
| Searcy | 1,679 | 1,772 | 503 | 1,340 | 2,743 |
| Sebastian | 16,570 | 16,817 | 6,023 | 9,684 | 24,426 |
| Sevier | 2,558 | 1,592 | 643 | 2,037 | 2,254 |
| Sharp | 3,761 | 2,486 | 921 | 2,955 | 3,623 |
| Stone | 2,622 | 1,672 | 697 | 1,728 | 2,186 |
| Union | 8,786 | 7,305 | 1,919 | 5,931 | 10,581 |
| Van Buren | 3,819 | 2,612 | 888 | 2,607 | 3,562 |
| Washington | 22,029 | 20,292 | 5,304 | 12,557 | 23,601 |
| White | 10,494 | 8,538 | 2,366 | 6,957 | 11,094 |
| Woodruff | 2,589 | 676 | 227 | 1,924 | 1,097 |
| Yell | 4,165 | 2,506 | 940 | 2,763 | 3,535 |
| Totals | 505,823 | 337,324 | 99,132 | 349,237 | 466,578 |

### Arkansas Vote Since 1944

1944, Roosevelt, Dem., 148,965; Dewey, Rep., 63,551; Thomas, Soc. 438.

1948, Truman, Dem., 149,659; Dewey, Rep., 50,959; Thurmond, States' Rights, 40,068; Thomas, Soc., 1,037; Wallace, Prog., 751; Watson, Proh., 1.

1952, Eisenhower, Rep., 177,155; Stevenson, Dem., 226,300; Hamblen, Proh., 886; MacArthur, Christian Nationalist, 458; Hass, Soc. Labor, 1.

1956, Stevenson, Dem., 213,277; Eisenhower, Rep., 186,287; Andrews, Ind., 7,008.

1960, Kennedy, Dem., 215,049; Nixon, Rep., 184,508; Nat'l. States' Rights, 28,952.

1964, Johnson, Dem., 314,197; Goldwater, Rep., 243,264; Kasper, Nat'l States Rights, 2,965.

1968, Nixon, Rep., 189,062; Humphrey, Dem., 184,901; Wallace, 3d party, 235,627.

1972, Nixon, Rep., 445,751; McGovern, Dem., 198,899; Schmitz, Amer., 3,016.

1976, Carter, Dem., 498,604; Ford, Rep., 267,903; McCarthy, Ind., 639; Anderson, Amer., 389.

1980, Reagan, Rep., 403,164; Carter, Dem., 398,041; Anderson, Ind., 22,468; Clark, Libertarian, 8,970; Commoner, Citizens, 2,345; Bubar, Statesman, 1,350; Hall, Comm., 1,244.

1984, Reagan, Rep., 534,774; Mondale, Dem., 338,646; Bergland, Libertarian, 2,220.

1988, Bush, Rep., 466,578; Dukakis, Dem., 349,237; Duke, Chr. Pop., 5,146; Paul, Lib., 3,297.

1992, Clinton, Dem., 505,823; Bush, Rep., 337,324; Perot, Ind., 99,132; Phillips, U.S. Taxpayers, 1,437; Marrou, Libertarian, 1,261; Fulani, New Alliance, 1,022.

## California

| County | 1992 Clinton (D) | Bush (R) | Perot (I) | 1988 Dukakis (D) | Bush (R) |
|---|---|---|---|---|---|
| Alameda | 334,224 | 109,292 | 81,643 | 310,283 | 162,815 |
| Alpine | 215 | 222 | 186 | 230 | 306 |
| Amador | 5,286 | 5,477 | 4,553 | 5,197 | 6,893 |
| Butte | 32,489 | 31,608 | 20,231 | 30,406 | 40,143 |
| Calaveras | 5,989 | 6,006 | 4,848 | 5,674 | 7,640 |
| Colusa | 1,798 | 2,589 | 1,206 | 2,022 | 3,077 |
| Contra Costa | 194,960 | 112,965 | 72,518 | 169,411 | 158,652 |
| Del Norte | 3,639 | 3,083 | 2,575 | 3,587 | 3,714 |
| El Dorado | 21,012 | 25,906 | 17,503 | 19,801 | 30,021 |
| Fresno | 92,418 | 89,137 | 36,299 | 92,635 | 94,835 |
| Glenn | 2,666 | 3,812 | 2,278 | 2,894 | 4,944 |
| Humboldt | 28,854 | 18,299 | 12,340 | 29,781 | 21,460 |
| Imperial | 11,109 | 9,759 | 4,247 | 10,243 | 12,889 |
| Inyo | 2,695 | 3,689 | 1,999 | 2,653 | 5,042 |
| Kern | 60,510 | 80,762 | 36,891 | 55,083 | 90,550 |
| Kings | 9,982 | 10,673 | 4,899 | 9,142 | 12,118 |
| Lake | 10,548 | 6,678 | 5,797 | 9,828 | 9,366 |
| Lassen | 3,388 | 3,836 | 3,004 | 3,446 | 5,157 |
| Los Angeles | 1,446,529 | 799,607 | 488,624 | 1,372,352 | 1,239,716 |
| Madera | 10,863 | 13,066 | 6,156 | 10,642 | 13,255 |
| Marin | 76,158 | 30,479 | 22,986 | 69,394 | 46,855 |
| Mariposa | 3,023 | 2,982 | 2,211 | 2,998 | 3,768 |
| Mendocino | 18,344 | 7,958 | 9,753 | 17,152 | 12,979 |
| Merced | 20,133 | 17,981 | 10,914 | 20,105 | 21,717 |
| Modoc | 1,489 | 1,803 | 1,269 | 1,416 | 2,518 |
| Mono | 1,489 | 1,570 | 1,248 | 1,284 | 2,177 |
| Monterey | 54,861 | 36,461 | 24,472 | 48,998 | 50,022 |
| Napa | 24,215 | 15,662 | 13,150 | 22,283 | 23,235 |
| Nevada | 15,433 | 17,343 | 11,072 | 14,980 | 21,383 |
| Orange | 306,930 | 426,613 | 232,394 | 269,013 | 586,230 |
| Placer | 30,783 | 38,298 | 21,741 | 27,516 | 42,096 |
| Plumas | 3,742 | 3,599 | 2,551 | 4,251 | 4,603 |
| Riverside | 166,241 | 159,457 | 102,233 | 133,122 | 199,979 |
| Sacramento | 197,540 | 160,366 | 91,412 | 188,557 | 201,832 |
| San Benito | 5,354 | 4,112 | 3,182 | 4,559 | 5,578 |
| San Bernardino | 183,634 | 176,563 | 109,183 | 151,118 | 235,167 |
| San Diego | 367,397 | 352,125 | 259,249 | 333,264 | 523,143 |
| San Francisco | 233,263 | 57,352 | 29,018 | 201,887 | 72,503 |
| San Joaquin | 63,655 | 58,355 | 31,205 | 61,699 | 75,309 |
| San Luis Obispo | 40,136 | 36,384 | 27,314 | 35,667 | 46,613 |
| San Mateo | 149,232 | 75,080 | 50,465 | 141,859 | 109,261 |
| Santa Barbara | 69,215 | 57,375 | 35,105 | 63,586 | 77,524 |
| Santa Clara | 296,265 | 170,870 | 128,895 | 277,810 | 254,442 |
| Santa Cruz | 66,183 | 24,916 | 21,615 | 63,133 | 37,728 |
| Shasta | 21,605 | 28,190 | 17,990 | 21,171 | 32,402 |
| Sierra | 653 | 691 | 519 | 791 | 860 |
| Siskiyou | 8,254 | 6,660 | 5,567 | 8,365 | 9,056 |
| Solano | 64,320 | 38,883 | 27,851 | 54,344 | 50,314 |
| Sonoma | 104,334 | 47,619 | 43,859 | 91,262 | 67,725 |
| Stanislaus | 52,415 | 47,275 | 27,651 | 44,685 | 51,648 |
| Sutter | 7,883 | 12,956 | 4,881 | 6,557 | 14,100 |
| Tehama | 7,508 | 7,419 | 5,884 | 7,213 | 9,854 |
| Trinity | 1,967 | 1,886 | 2,092 | 2,518 | 3,267 |
| Tulare | 31,188 | 40,482 | 16,430 | 30,711 | 46,891 |
| Tuolumne | 9,216 | 8,525 | 6,294 | 8,717 | 10,646 |
| Ventura | 99,011 | 94,911 | 71,844 | 89,065 | 147,604 |
| Yolo | 33,297 | 17,574 | 11,073 | 30,429 | 22,358 |
| Yuba | 5,785 | 7,333 | 3,637 | 5,444 | 8,937 |
| Totals | 5,121,325 | 3,630,574 | 2,296,006 | 4,702,233 | 5,054,917 |

### California Vote Since 1944

1944, Roosevelt, Dem., 1,988,564; Dewey, Rep., 1,512,965; Watson, Proh., 14,770; Thomas, Soc., 3,923; Teichert, Soc. Labor, 327.

1948, Truman, Dem., 1,913,134; Dewey, Rep., 1,895,269; Wallace, Prog., 190,381; Watson, Proh., 16,926; Thomas, Soc., 3,459; Thurmond, States' Rights, 1,228; Teichert, Soc. Labor, 195; Dobbs, Soc. Workers, 133.

1952, Eisenhower, Rep., 2,897,310; Stevenson, Dem., 2,197,548; Hallinan, Prog., 24,106; Hamblen, Proh., 15,653; MacArthur, (Tenny Ticket), 3,326; (Kellems Ticket) 178; Hass, Soc. Labor, 273; Hoopes, Soc., 206; scattered, 3,249.

1956, Eisenhower, Rep., 3,027,668; Stevenson, Dem., 2,420,136; Holtwick, Proh., 11,119; Andrews, Constitution, 6,087; Hass, Soc. Labor, 300; Hoopes, Soc., 123; Dobbs, Soc. Workers, 96; Smith, Christian Nat'l., 8.

1960, Kennedy, Dem., 3,224,099; Nixon, Rep., 3,259,722; Decker, Proh., 21,706; Hass, Soc. Labor, 1,051.

1964, Johnson, Dem., 4,171,877; Goldwater, Rep., 2,879,108; Hass, Soc. Labor, 489; DeBerry, Soc. Worker, 378; Munn, Proh., 305; Hensley, Universal, 19.

1968, Nixon, Rep., 3,467,664; Humphrey, Dem., 3,244,318; Wallace, 3d party, 487,270; Peace and Freedom party, 27,707; McCarthy, Alternative, 20,721; Gregory, write-in,

3,230; Mitchell, Com., 260; Munn, Proh., 59; Blomen, Soc. Labor, 341; Soeters, Defense, 17.

1972, Nixon, Rep., 4,602,096; McGovern, Dem., 3,475,847; Schmitz, Amer., 232,554; Spock, Peace and Freedom, 55,167; Hall, Com., 373; Hospers, Libertarian, 980; Munn, Proh., 53; Fisher, Soc. Labor, 197; Jenness, Soc. Workers, 574; Green, Universal, 21.

1976, Carter, Dem., 3,742,284; Ford, Rep., 3,882,244; Mac-Bride, Libertarian, 56,388; Maddox, Am. Ind., 51,098; Wright, People's, 41,731; Camejo, Soc. Workers, 17,259; Hall, Com., 12,766; write-in, McCarthy, 58,412; other write-in, 4,935.

1980, Reagan, Rep. 4,524,858; Carter, Dem., 3,083,661; Anderson, Ind., 739,833; Clark, Libertarian, 148,434; Commoner, Ind. 61,063; Smith, Peace & Freedom, 18,116; Rarick, Amer. Ind., 9,856.

1984, Reagan, Rep. 5,305,410; Mondale, Dem., 3,815,947; Bergland, Libertarian, 48,400.

1988, Bush, Rep., 5,054,917; Dukakis, Dem., 4,702,233; Paul, Lib., 70,105; Fulani, Ind., 31,181.

1992, Clinton, Dem., 5,121,325; Bush, Rep., 3,630,575; Perot, Ind., 2,296,006; Marrou, Libertarian, 48,139; Daniels, Ind., 18,597; Phillips, U.S. Taxpayers, 12,711.

## Colorado

| County | 1992 Clinton (D) | Bush (R) | Perot (I) | 1988 Dukakis (D) | Bush (R) |
|---|---|---|---|---|---|
| Adams | 45,357 | 30,856 | 26,379 | 49,464 | 43,163 |
| Alamosa | 1,928 | 1,572 | 1,089 | 2,146 | 2,567 |
| Arapahoe | 66,607 | 72,221 | 44,363 | 61,113 | 95,926 |
| Archuleta | 819 | 1,242 | 741 | 795 | 1,440 |
| Baca | 726 | 1,240 | 647 | 851 | 1,670 |
| Bent | 985 | 759 | 506 | 1,088 | 1,032 |
| Boulder | 64,567 | 33,553 | 27,762 | 57,265 | 48,174 |
| Chaffee | 2,284 | 2,419 | 1,549 | 2,548 | 3,080 |
| Cheyenne | 301 | 615 | 292 | 399 | 760 |
| Clear Creek | 1,744 | 1,356 | 1,308 | 1,698 | 1,820 |
| Conejos | 1,705 | 1,160 | 578 | 1,976 | 1,445 |
| Costilla | 1,180 | 366 | 199 | 1,120 | 454 |
| Crowley | 570 | 602 | 276 | 630 | 862 |
| Custer | 343 | 651 | 368 | 310 | 753 |
| Delta | 3,424 | 4,359 | 2,627 | 3,521 | 5,449 |
| Denver | 121,961 | 55,418 | 37,298 | 127,173 | 77,753 |
| Dolores | 242 | 315 | 285 | 230 | 488 |
| Douglas | 9,991 | 18,592 | 11,329 | 6,931 | 17,035 |
| Eagle | 3,870 | 3,100 | 3,821 | 3,314 | 4,366 |
| Elbert | 1,237 | 2,205 | 1,567 | 1,566 | 2,805 |
| El Paso | 45,827 | 86,044 | 34,346 | 39,995 | 96,965 |
| Fremont | 5,356 | 5,961 | 3,709 | 5,278 | 7,623 |
| Garfield | 5,082 | 4,404 | 4,408 | 4,620 | 6,358 |
| Gilpin | 726 | 462 | 545 | 804 | 728 |
| Grand | 1,678 | 1,763 | 1,454 | 1,451 | 2,306 |
| Gunnison | 2,389 | 1,662 | 1,671 | 1,897 | 2,520 |
| Hinsdale | 151 | 188 | 136 | 111 | 295 |
| Huerfano | 1,224 | 685 | 385 | 1,876 | 1,079 |
| Jackson | 216 | 422 | 326 | 294 | 584 |
| Jefferson | 80,834 | 82,705 | 58,404 | 81,824 | 110,820 |
| Kiowa | 290 | 472 | 267 | 398 | 645 |
| Kit Carson | 925 | 1,801 | 919 | 1,196 | 2,262 |
| Lake | 1,426 | 605 | 863 | 1,516 | 969 |
| La Plata | 5,913 | 5,522 | 4,083 | 5,443 | 7,714 |
| Larimer | 38,232 | 35,995 | 24,879 | 35,703 | 45,967 |
| Las Animas | 3,847 | 1,739 | 953 | 4,075 | 2,162 |
| Lincoln | 640 | 1,079 | 581 | 874 | 1,356 |
| Logan | 2,718 | 3,420 | 2,184 | 3,382 | 4,485 |
| Mesa | 15,162 | 18,169 | 10,474 | 14,372 | 22,150 |
| Mineral | 171 | 159 | 117 | 174 | 217 |
| Moffat | 1,386 | 1,809 | 1,875 | 1,634 | 2,757 |
| Montezuma | 2,270 | 3,124 | 2,205 | 2,233 | 4,208 |
| Montrose | 3,713 | 4,847 | 3,093 | 3,748 | 6,012 |
| Morgan | 2,985 | 3,724 | 2,175 | 3,728 | 4,795 |
| Otero | 3,485 | 3,120 | 1,590 | 3,910 | 4,265 |
| Ouray | 461 | 653 | 466 | 439 | 814 |
| Park | 1,307 | 1,530 | 1,396 | 1,343 | 1,909 |
| Philips | 692 | 1,075 | 525 | 923 | 1,317 |
| Pitkin | 3,820 | 1,686 | 1,907 | 3,420 | 2,801 |
| Prowers | 1,770 | 2,371 | 1,184 | 2,207 | 2,978 |
| Pueblo | 30,261 | 16,120 | 9,841 | 32,788 | 20,119 |
| Rio Blanco | 778 | 1,231 | 794 | 803 | 1,821 |
| Rio Grande | 1,541 | 1,927 | 1,043 | 1,545 | 2,626 |
| Routt | 3,188 | 2,358 | 2,564 | 2,922 | 3,264 |
| Saguache | 1,011 | 675 | 471 | 1,033 | 945 |
| San Juan | 147 | 148 | 183 | 192 | 210 |
| San Miguel | 1,380 | 628 | 634 | 961 | 798 |
| Sedgwick | 397 | 447 | 295 | 611 | 921 |
| Summit | 3,344 | 2,256 | 2,715 | 2,595 | 2,893 |
| Teller | 1,873 | 3,050 | 1,927 | 1,656 | 3,760 |
| Washington | 660 | 1,266 | 671 | 958 | 1,707 |
| Weld | 19,265 | 20,958 | 13,571 | 20,548 | 26,497 |
| Yuma | 1,269 | 2,019 | 1,197 | 1,835 | 2,513 |
| Totals | 629,681 | 562,850 | 366,010 | 621,453 | 728,177 |

## Colorado Vote Since 1944

1944, Roosevelt, Dem., 234,331; Dewey, Rep., 268,731; Thomas, Soc., 1,977.

1948, Truman, Dem., 267,288; Dewey, Rep., 239,714; Wallace, Prog., 6,115; Thomas, Soc., 1,678; Dobbs, Soc. Workers, 228; Teichert, Soc. Labor, 214.

1952, Eisenhower, Rep., 379,782; Stevenson, Dem., 245,504; MacArthur, Constitution, 2,181; Hallinan, Prog., 1,919; Hoopes, Soc., 365; Hass, Soc. Labor, 352.

1956, Eisenhower, Rep., 394,479; Stevenson, Dem., 263,997; Hass, Soc. Lab., 3,308; Andrews, Ind., 759; Hoopes, Soc., 531.

1960, Kennedy, Dem., 330,629; Nixon, Rep., 402,242; Hass, Soc. Labor, 2,803; Dobbs, Soc. Workers, 572.

1964, Johnson, Dem., 476,024; Goldwater, Rep., 296,767; Hass, Soc. Labor, 302; DeBerry, Soc. Worker, 2,537; Munn, Proh., 1,356.

1968, Nixon, Rep., 409,345; Humphrey, Dem., 335,174; Wallace, 3d party, 60,813; Blomen, Soc. Labor, 3,016; Gregory, New-party, 1,393; Munn, Proh., 275; Halstead, Soc. Worker, 235.

1972, Nixon, Rep., 597,189; McGovern, Dem., 329,980; Fisher, Soc. Labor, 4,361; Hospers, Libertarian, 1,111; Hall, Com., 432; Jenness, Soc. Workers, 555; Munn, Proh., 467; Schmitz, Amer., 17,269; Spock, Peoples, 2,403.

1976, Carter, Dem., 460,353; Ford, Rep., 584,367; McCarthy, Ind., 26,107; MacBride, Libertarian, 5,330; Bubar, Proh., 2,882.

1980, Reagan, Rep., 652,264; Carter, Dem., 367,973; Anderson, Ind., 130,633; Clark, Libertarian, 25,744; Commoner, Citizens, 5,614; Bubar, Statesman, 1,180; Pulley, Socialist, 520; Hall, Com., 487.

1984, Reagan, Rep., 821,817; Mondale, Dem., 454,975; Bergland, Libertarian, 11,257.

1988, Bush, Rep., 728,177; Dukakis, Dem., 621,453; Paul, Lib., 15,482; Dodge, Proh., 4,604.

1992, Clinton, Dem., 629,681; Bush, Rep., 562,850; Perot, Ind., 366,010; Marrou, Libertarian, 8,669; Fulani, New Alliance, 1,608.

## Connecticut

| County | 1992 Clinton (D) | Bush (R) | Perot (I) | 1988 Dukakis (D) | Bush (R) |
|---|---|---|---|---|---|
| Bridgeport | 22,321 | 13,149 | 6,263 | 23,831 | 17,084 |
| Hartford | 26,971 | 6,180 | 3,390 | 27,295 | 8,100 |
| New Britain | 14,159 | 7,040 | 4,983 | 15,843 | 9,569 |
| New Haven | 29,774 | 8,931 | 4,130 | 31,951 | 11,616 |
| Norwalk | 16,488 | 14,743 | 6,046 | 14,518 | 18,618 |
| Stamford | 23,185 | 19,809 | 6,763 | 20,773 | 24,877 |
| Waterbury | 16,366 | 16,155 | 9,188 | 18,202 | 20,018 |
| West Hartford | 19,623 | 12,266 | 5,017 | 19,311 | 16,482 |
| Totals | 682,318 | 578,313 | 348,771 | 676,584 | 750,241 |

## Connecticut Vote Since 1944

1944, Roosevelt, Dem., 435,146; Dewey, Rep., 390,527; Thomas, Soc., 5,097; Teichert, Soc. Labor, 1,220.

1948, Truman, Dem., 423,297; Dewey, Rep., 437,754; Wallace, Prog., 13,713; Thomas, Soc., 6,964; Teichert, Soc. Labor, 1,184; Dobbs, Soc. Workers, 606.

1952, Eisenhower, Rep., 611,012; Stevenson, Dem., 481,649; Hoopes, Soc., 2,244; Hallinan, Peoples, 1,466; Hass, Soc. Labor, 535; write-in, 5.

1956, Eisenhower, Rep., 711,837; Stevenson, Dem., 405,079; scattered, 205.

1960, Kennedy, Dem., 657,055; Nixon, Rep., 565,813.

1964, Johnson, Dem., 826,269; Goldwater, Rep., 390,996; scattered, 1,313.

1968, Nixon, Rep., 556,721; Humphrey, Dem., 621,561; Wallace, 3d party, 76,650; scattered, 1,300.

1972, Nixon, Rep., 810,763; McGovern, Dem., 555,498; Schmitz, Amer., 17,239; scattered, 777.

1976, Carter, Dem., 647,895; Ford, Rep., 719,261; Maddox, George Wallace Party, 7,101; LaRouche, U.S. Labor, 1,789.

1980, Reagan, Rep., 677,210; Carter, Dem., 541,732; Anderson, Ind., 171,807; Clark, Libertarian, 8,570; Commoner, Citizens, 6,130; scattered, 836.

1984, Reagan, Rep., 890,877; Mondale, Dem., 569,597.

1988, Bush, Rep., 750,241; Dukakis, Dem., 676,584; Paul, Lib., 14,071; Fulani; New A.lliance, 2,491.

1992, Clinton, Dem., 682,318; Bush, Rep., 578,313; Perot, Ind., 348,771; Marrou, Libertarian, 5,391; Fulani, New Alliance, 1,363.

## Delaware

| County | 1992 Clinton (D) | Bush (R) | Perot (I) | 1988 Dukakis (D) | Bush (R) |
|---|---|---|---|---|---|
| Kent | 15,364 | 15,562 | 8,916 | 12,996 | 19,923 |
| New Castle | 91,516 | 66,311 | 37,581 | 79,147 | 92,587 |
| Sussex | 19,174 | 20,440 | 12,716 | 16,504 | 27,129 |
| Totals | 126,054 | 102,313 | 59,213 | 108,647 | 139,639 |

## Delaware Vote Since 1944

1944, Roosevelt, Dem., 68,166; Dewey, Rep., 56,747; Watson, Proh., 294; Thomas, Soc., 154.

1948, Truman, Dem., 67,813; Dewey, Rep., 69,688; Wallace, Prog., 1,050; Watson, Proh., 343; Thomas, Soc., 250; Teichert, Soc. Labor, 29.

1952, Eisenhower, Rep., 90,059; Stevenson, Dem., 83,315; Hass, Soc. Labor, 242; Hamblen, Proh., 234; Hallinan, Prog., 155; Hoopes, Soc., 20.

1956, Eisenhower, Rep., 98,057; Stevenson, Dem., 79,421; Oltwick, Proh., 400; Hass, Soc. Labor, 110.

1960, Kennedy, Dem., 99,590; Nixon, Rep., 96,373; Faubus, States' Rights, 354; Decker, Proh., 284; Hass, Soc. Labor, 82.

1964, Johnson, Dem., 122,704; Goldwater, Rep., 78,078; Hass, Soc. Labor, 113; Munn, Proh., 425.

1968, Nixon, Rep., 96,714; Humphrey, Dem., 89,194; Wallace, 3d party, 28,459.

1972, Nixon, Rep., 140,357; McGovern, Dem., 92,283; Schmitz, Amer., 2,638; Munn, Proh., 238.

1976, Carter, Dem., 122,596; Ford, Rep., 109,831; McCarthy, non-partisan, 2,437; Anderson, Amer., 645; LaRouche, U.S. Labor, 136; Bubar, Proh., 103; Levin, Soc. Labor, 86.

1980, Reagan, Rep., 111,252; Carter, Dem., 105,754; Anderson, Ind., 16,288; Clark, Libertarian, 1,974; Greaves, American, 400.

1984, Reagan, Rep., 152,190; Mondale, Dem., 101,656; Bergland, Libertarian, 268.

1988, Bush, Rep., 139,639; Dukakis, Dem., 108,647; Paul, Lib., 1,162; Fulani, New Alliance, 443.

1992, Clinton, Dem., 126,054; Bush, Rep., 102,313; Perot, Ind., 59,213; Fulani, New Alliance, 1,105.

## District of Columbia

| County | 1992 Clinton (D) | Bush (R) | Perot (I) | 1988 Dukakis (D) | Bush (R) |
|---|---|---|---|---|---|
| Totals | 192,619 | 20,698 | 9,681 | 159,407 | 27,590 |

## District of Columbia Vote Since 1972

1972, Nixon, Rep., 35,226; McGovern, Dem., 127,627; Reed, Soc. Workers, 316; Hall, Com., 252.

1976, Carter, Dem., 137,818; Ford, Rep., 27,873; Camejo, Soc. Workers, 545; MacBride, Libertarian, 274; Hall, Com., 219; LaRouche, U.S. Labor, 157.

1980, Reagan, Rep., 23,313; Carter, Dem., 130,231; Anderson, Ind., 16,131; Commoner, Citizens, 1,826; Clark, Libertarian, 1,104; Hall, Com., 369; De Berry, Soc. Work., 173; Griswold, Workers World, 52; write-ins, 690.

1984, Mondale, Dem., 180,408; Reagan, Rep., 29,009; Bergland, Libertarian, 279.

1988, Bush, Rep., 27,590; Dukakis, Dem., 159,407; Fulani, New Alliance, 2,901; Paul, Lib., 554.

1992, Clinton, Dem., 192,619; Bush, Rep., 20,698; Perot, Ind., 9,681; Fulani, New Alliance, 1,459; Daniels, Ind., 1,186.

## Florida

| County | 1992 Clinton (D) | Bush (R) | Perot (I) | 1988 Dukakis (D) | Bush (R) |
|---|---|---|---|---|---|
| Alachua | 37,876 | 22,806 | 15,293 | 29,375 | 30,124 |
| Baker | 1,974 | 3,417 | 1,315 | 1,353 | 3,414 |
| Bay | 12,830 | 22,820 | 9,702 | 11,582 | 31,712 |
| Bradford | 3,040 | 3,671 | 1,572 | 2,386 | 4,218 |
| Brevard | 61,070 | 84,545 | 49,491 | 42,967 | 104,721 |
| Broward | 276,309 | 164,782 | 90,923 | 218,211 | 220,196 |

| | | | | | | | | | | |
|---|---|---|---|---|---|---|---|---|---|---|
| Calhoun | 1,665 | 1,721 | 1,176 | 1,329 | 2,420 | Bacon | 1,423 | 1,301 | 604 | 780 | 1,407 |
| Charlotte | 22,904 | 24,302 | 14,711 | 15,967 | 28,879 | Baker | 864 | 391 | 210 | 707 | 629 |
| Citrus | 15,935 | 16,402 | 12,310 | 12,177 | 21,052 | Baldwin | 5,813 | 4,262 | 1,679 | 4,008 | 5,852 |
| Clay | 10,597 | 26,313 | 8,414 | 7,766 | 25,882 | Banks | 1,530 | 1,551 | 583 | 984 | 1,590 |
| Collier | 18,794 | 38,447 | 14,514 | 12,768 | 38,910 | Barrow | 3,991 | 4,328 | 1,533 | 2,442 | 4,738 |
| Columbia | 5,526 | 6,489 | 2,906 | 4,072 | 7,759 | Bartow | 6,675 | 7,742 | 2,500 | 4,884 | 8,039 |
| Dade | 254,444 | 235,149 | 53,957 | 216,847 | 270,672 | Ben Hill | 2,348 | 1,476 | 619 | 1,867 | 2,005 |
| De Soto | 2,646 | 3,070 | 1,687 | 2,181 | 4,237 | Berrien | 2,103 | 1,637 | 796 | 1,381 | 2,030 |
| Dixie | 1,855 | 1,401 | 1,094 | 1,366 | 2,027 | Bibb | 28,070 | 19,847 | 6,021 | 22,084 | 22,179 |
| Duval | 92,010 | 123,480 | 33,335 | 74,832 | 127,875 | Bleckley | 1,710 | 1,570 | 662 | 1,175 | 1,950 |
| Escambia | 32,018 | 52,775 | 19,868 | 29,934 | 64,774 | Brantley | 1,883 | 1,541 | 840 | 1,450 | 1,539 |
| Flagler | 6,692 | 6,241 | 3,387 | 4,261 | 6,494 | Brooks | 1,895 | 1,779 | 630 | 1,500 | 2,136 |
| Franklin | 1,534 | 1,660 | 1,143 | 1,263 | 1,911 | Bryan | 2,031 | 2,789 | 1,095 | 1,423 | 2,802 |
| Gadsden | 8,478 | 3,975 | 1,871 | 6,368 | 5,987 | Bulloch | 4,903 | 5,690 | 2,020 | 3,417 | 6,354 |
| Gilchrist | 1,511 | 1,395 | 1,090 | 1,137 | 1,854 | Burke | 3,647 | 2,390 | 807 | 2,861 | 2,988 |
| Glades | 1,305 | 1,185 | 878 | 1,034 | 1,546 | Butts | 2,448 | 1,768 | 619 | 1,730 | 2,184 |
| Gulf | 1,938 | 2,650 | 1,245 | 1,687 | 3,040 | Calhoun | 1,301 | 464 | 248 | 901 | 644 |
| Hamilton | 1,622 | 1,402 | 695 | 1,314 | 2,062 | Camden | 2,952 | 3,517 | 1,077 | 2,090 | 2,913 |
| Hardee | 2,017 | 2,898 | 1,498 | 1,688 | 3,636 | Candler | 1,192 | 1,014 | 541 | 877 | 1,261 |
| Hendry | 2,690 | 3,279 | 2,032 | 2,036 | 3,962 | Carroll | 8,404 | 10,750 | 3,358 | 4,706 | 10,754 |
| Hernando | 19,171 | 17,896 | 11,845 | 15,432 | 21,179 | Catoosa | 4,817 | 7,599 | 2,290 | 3,588 | 9,319 |
| Highlands | 11,234 | 14,497 | 6,592 | 8,087 | 16,713 | Charlton | 1,127 | 1,333 | 427 | 943 | 1,327 |
| Hillsborough | 115,261 | 130,611 | 63,037 | 98,969 | 150,065 | Chatham | 31,533 | 31,925 | 8,269 | 25,063 | 35,623 |
| Holmes | 1,877 | 3,196 | 1,426 | 1,639 | 4,221 | Chattahoochee | 604 | 413 | 177 | 362 | 454 |
| Indian River | 12,359 | 19,137 | 12,375 | 10,447 | 24,619 | Chattooga | 2,976 | 2,439 | 965 | 2,206 | 3,665 |
| Jackson | 5,481 | 6,720 | 2,447 | 5,002 | 8,392 | Cherokee | 8,113 | 16,054 | 4,950 | 4,378 | 14,593 |
| Jefferson | 2,270 | 1,506 | 894 | 2,055 | 2,326 | Clarke | 15,403 | 10,459 | 2,987 | 11,154 | 11,150 |
| Lafayette | 866 | 1,037 | 612 | 722 | 1,450 | Clay | 778 | 264 | 155 | 595 | 398 |
| Lake | 23,199 | 30,818 | 15,606 | 16,762 | 37,314 | Clayton | 25,890 | 23,965 | 7,942 | 14,689 | 28,225 |
| Lee | 53,656 | 73,423 | 38,446 | 40,709 | 87,247 | Clinch | 759 | 790 | 286 | 594 | 863 |
| Leon | 47,770 | 31,964 | 17,207 | 33,446 | 36,032 | Cobb | 63,960 | 103,734 | 28,747 | 39,297 | 106,621 |
| Levy | 4,330 | 3,796 | 2,784 | 3,433 | 5,250 | Coffee | 3,275 | 3,778 | 1,256 | 2,777 | 4,019 |
| Liberty | 820 | 1,126 | 617 | 709 | 1,419 | Colquitt | 3,891 | 4,680 | 1,682 | 2,998 | 5,653 |
| Madison | 2,644 | 2,006 | 1,174 | 1,950 | 2,556 | Columbia | 7,115 | 16,657 | 4,379 | 4,617 | 16,401 |
| Manatee | 33,826 | 42,708 | 23,282 | 26,618 | 51,160 | Cook | 1,731 | 1,318 | 537 | 1,226 | 1,555 |
| Marion | 30,823 | 35,438 | 20,524 | 20,679 | 41,488 | Coweta | 7,093 | 9,814 | 3,587 | 4,212 | 9,668 |
| Martin | 14,778 | 24,768 | 13,433 | 11,486 | 31,270 | Crawford | 1,648 | 974 | 549 | 1,340 | 1,235 |
| Monroe | 10,435 | 9,891 | 8,306 | 10,151 | 15,919 | Crisp | 2,610 | 2,253 | 823 | 1,690 | 2,916 |
| Nassau | 5,497 | 9,364 | 3,251 | 4,138 | 8,366 | Dade | 1,782 | 2,191 | 823 | 1,120 | 2,539 |
| Okaloosa | 12,003 | 32,755 | 16,649 | 9,726 | 40,295 | Dawson | 1,399 | 1,696 | 790 | 761 | 1,908 |
| Okeechobee | 3,418 | 3,298 | 2,645 | 3,007 | 4,733 | Decatur | 3,198 | 3,142 | 1,068 | 2,348 | 3,866 |
| Orange | 82,656 | 108,738 | 44,827 | 53,991 | 117,141 | DeKalb | 124,559 | 70,282 | 19,741 | 92,521 | 90,179 |
| Osceola | 15,009 | 19,139 | 11,021 | 9,811 | 21,350 | Dodge | 3,002 | 2,287 | 978 | 2,164 | 2,677 |
| Palm Beach | 187,840 | 140,317 | 76,223 | 144,143 | 181,408 | Dooly | 1,993 | 1,034 | 350 | 1,613 | 1,386 |
| Pasco | 53,125 | 47,721 | 34,650 | 50,369 | 63,788 | Dougherty | 15,236 | 12,455 | 3,178 | 12,579 | 15,520 |
| Pinellas | 160,217 | 158,733 | 101,150 | 152,374 | 210,971 | Douglas | 8,869 | 13,349 | 4,362 | 5,086 | 13,493 |
| Polk | 51,442 | 65,952 | 28,198 | 38,236 | 77,065 | Early | 1,970 | 1,457 | 651 | 1,359 | 1,918 |
| Putnam | 10,707 | 8,909 | 5,975 | 8,569 | 11,621 | Echols | 312 | 361 | 238 | 245 | 422 |
| St. Johns | 12,284 | 20,173 | 7,397 | 7,999 | 19,164 | Effingham | 2,690 | 3,814 | 1,443 | 1,905 | 3,933 |
| St. Lucie | 23,873 | 24,397 | 19,813 | 17,427 | 32,241 | Elbert | 3,025 | 2,372 | 757 | 2,118 | 2,796 |
| Santa Rosa | 6,526 | 17,229 | 8,735 | 5,251 | 18,948 | Emanuel | 2,951 | 2,662 | 755 | 2,387 | 3,530 |
| Sarasota | 54,536 | 66,831 | 34,281 | 42,095 | 84,585 | Evans | 1,230 | 1,244 | 480 | 1,023 | 1,707 |
| Seminole | 35,649 | 57,085 | 24,477 | 22,627 | 60,328 | Fannin | 2,902 | 3,255 | 1,028 | 2,123 | 4,271 |
| Sumter | 5,027 | 4,366 | 2,901 | 3,900 | 5,933 | Fayette | 8,430 | 17,576 | 5,598 | 4,593 | 16,443 |
| Suwannee | 3,985 | 4,571 | 2,790 | 3,126 | 5,859 | Floyd | 11,614 | 12,378 | 3,779 | 8,548 | 14,697 |
| Taylor | 2,568 | 2,693 | 1,929 | 1,762 | 4,054 | Forsyth | 4,936 | 8,652 | 3,453 | 2,347 | 7,947 |
| Union | 1,247 | 1,543 | 770 | 691 | 1,643 | Franklin | 2,505 | 2,391 | 1,014 | 1,842 | 2,615 |
| Volusia | 65,213 | 59,155 | 30,813 | 55,437 | 74,116 | Fulton | 147,459 | 85,451 | 23,578 | 120,752 | 91,785 |
| Wakulla | 2,319 | 2,586 | 1,790 | 1,605 | 3,157 | Gilmer | 2,311 | 2,661 | 879 | 1,363 | 3,353 |
| Walton | 3,886 | 5,719 | 3,886 | 3,231 | 7,481 | Glascock | 316 | 516 | 180 | 210 | 580 |
| Washington | 2,544 | 3,694 | 1,596 | 2,139 | 4,366 | Glynn | 8,581 | 11,242 | 3,053 | 6,339 | 11,126 |
| **Totals** | **2,071,651** | **2,171,781** | **1,052,481** | **1,655,851** | **2,616,597** | Gordon | 4,103 | 5,265 | 1,818 | 2,369 | 6,051 |
| | | | | | | Grady | 2,520 | 2,370 | 1,126 | 1,883 | 2,989 |
| | | | | | | Greene | 2,259 | 1,307 | 483 | 1,818 | 1,432 |
| | | | | | | Gwinnett | 44,253 | 81,822 | 23,926 | 20,948 | 66,372 |
| | | | | | | Habersham | 3,098 | 4,569 | 1,444 | 2,114 | 4,871 |
| | | | | | | Hall | 11,214 | 16,108 | 5,043 | 7,782 | 17,415 |
| | | | | | | Hancock | 2,461 | 506 | 189 | 1,947 | 621 |
| | | | | | | Haralson | 3,281 | 3,142 | 1,167 | 2,404 | 4,529 |
| | | | | | | Harris | 2,679 | 3,316 | 954 | 1,905 | 3,414 |
| | | | | | | Hart | 3,614 | 2,607 | 1,376 | 2,476 | 3,044 |
| | | | | | | Heard | 1,456 | 1,190 | 617 | 874 | 1,551 |
| | | | | | | Henry | 7,817 | 12,634 | 3,769 | 4,348 | 10,882 |
| | | | | | | Houston | 12,270 | 14,119 | 6,263 | 8,664 | 15,748 |
| | | | | | | Irwin | 1,366 | 973 | 465 | 918 | 1,226 |
| | | | | | | Jackson | 3,792 | 3,976 | 1,381 | 2,607 | 4,407 |
| | | | | | | Jasper | 1,485 | 1,153 | 373 | 1,188 | 1,474 |
| | | | | | | Jeff Davis | 2,031 | 1,947 | 958 | 1,242 | 2,050 |
| | | | | | | Jefferson | 3,220 | 2,077 | 685 | 2,346 | 2,788 |
| | | | | | | Jenkins | 1,401 | 929 | 394 | 953 | 1,288 |
| | | | | | | Johnson | 1,473 | 1,314 | 502 | 927 | 1,567 |
| | | | | | | Jones | 3,338 | 2,770 | 1,159 | 2,662 | 3,618 |
| | | | | | | Lamar | 2,065 | 1,707 | 600 | 1,416 | 2,035 |
| | | | | | | Lanier | 811 | 600 | 298 | 698 | 725 |
| | | | | | | Laurens | 6,184 | 6,146 | 1,602 | 4,879 | 6,929 |
| | | | | | | Lee | 1,811 | 3,061 | 1,024 | 995 | 2,875 |
| | | | | | | Liberty | 3,853 | 2,832 | 1,176 | 2,906 | 3,100 |
| | | | | | | Lincoln | 1,327 | 1,149 | 479 | 893 | 1,417 |
| | | | | | | Long | 874 | 719 | 355 | 681 | 858 |
| | | | | | | Lowndes | 9,019 | 10,276 | 2,864 | 6,427 | 10,655 |
| | | | | | | Lumpkin | 2,010 | 1,972 | 1,035 | 1,286 | 2,688 |
| | | | | | | McDuffie | 2,640 | 2,955 | 860 | 1,704 | 3,231 |
| | | | | | | McIntosh | 1,925 | 1,027 | 550 | 1,527 | 1,273 |
| | | | | | | Macon | 2,491 | 944 | 363 | 2,268 | 1,412 |
| | | | | | | Madison | 2,393 | 3,351 | 1,129 | 1,639 | 3,724 |
| | | | | | | Marion | 1,145 | 711 | 198 | 844 | 804 |
| | | | | | | Meriwether | 4,002 | 2,364 | 942 | 2,934 | 3,101 |
| | | | | | | Miller | 934 | 826 | 455 | 515 | 1,105 |
| | | | | | | Mitchell | 3,052 | 1,917 | 818 | 2,260 | 2,590 |
| | | | | | | Monroe | 2,774 | 2,423 | 949 | 1,970 | 2,570 |
| | | | | | | Montgomery | 1,185 | 1,009 | 416 | 903 | 1,228 |

## Florida Vote Since 1944

1944, Roosevelt, Dem., 339,377; Dewey, Rep., 143,215.

1948, Truman, Dem., 281,988; Dewey, Rep., 194,280; Thurmond, States' Rights, 89,755; Wallace, Prog., 11,620.

1952, Eisenhower, Rep., 544,036; Stevenson, Dem., 444,950; scattered, 351.

1956, Eisenhower, Rep., 643,849; Stevenson, Dem., 480,371.

1960, Kennedy, Dem., 748,700; Nixon, Rep., 795,476.

1964, Johnson, Dem., 948,540; Goldwater, Rep., 905,941.

1968, Nixon, Rep., 886,804; Humphrey, Dem., 676,794; Wallace, 3d party, 624,207.

1972, Nixon, Rep., 1,857,759; McGovern, Dem., 718,117; scattered, 7,407.

1976, Carter, Dem., 1,636,000; Ford, Rep., 1,469,531; McCarthy, Ind., 23,643; Anderson, Amer., 21,325.

1980, Reagan, Rep., 2,046,951; Carter, Dem., 1,419,475; Anderson, Ind., 189,692; Clark, Libertarian, 30,524; write-ins, 285.

1984, Reagan, Rep., 2,728,775; Mondale, Dem., 1,448,344.

1988, Bush, Rep., 2,616,597; Dukakis, Dem., 1,655,851; Paul, Lib., 19,796, Fulani, New Alliance, 6,655.

1992, Bush, Rep., 2,171,781; Clinton, Dem., 2,071,651; Perot, Ind., 1,052,481; Marrou, Libertarian, 15,068.

## Georgia

| | 1992 | | | 1988 | |
|---|---|---|---|---|---|
| **County** | **Clinton (D)** | **Bush (R)** | **Perot (I)** | **Dukakis (D)** | **Bush (R)** |
| Appling | 2,455 | 2,514 | 1,047 | 1,837 | 3,000 |
| Atkinson | 1,056 | 779 | 342 | 887 | 1,126 |

| | 1992 | | | 1988 | |
|---|---|---|---|---|---|
| | Clinton (D) | Bush (R) | Perot (I) | Dukakis (D) | Bush (R) |
| Morgan | 2,057 | 1,797 | 596 | 1,508 | 2,108 |
| Murray | 2,764 | 3,256 | 1,186 | 1,679 | 3,996 |
| Muscogee | 25,476 | 21,386 | 4,327 | 18,772 | 23,058 |
| Newton | 5,811 | 5,804 | 1,998 | 3,111 | 5,809 |
| Oconee | 2,745 | 4,125 | 1,182 | 1,990 | 4,265 |
| Oglethorpe | 1,491 | 1,590 | 620 | 1,154 | 1,951 |
| Paulding | 5,212 | 7,180 | 2,654 | 2,717 | 7,329 |
| Peach | 3,677 | 2,327 | 947 | 2,972 | 2,782 |
| Pickens | 2,359 | 2,332 | 1,037 | 1,430 | 3,021 |
| Pierce | 1,852 | 1,899 | 708 | 1,558 | 1,947 |
| Pike | 1,651 | 1,822 | 623 | 1,176 | 2,074 |
| Polk | 4,872 | 4,158 | 1,598 | 2,977 | 5,454 |
| Pulaski | 1,756 | 1,075 | 614 | 1,476 | 1,400 |
| Putnam | 2,149 | 1,756 | 775 | 1,532 | 2,111 |
| Quitman | 523 | 284 | 113 | 436 | 296 |
| Rabun | 1,878 | 1,902 | 825 | 1,301 | 2,278 |
| Randolph | 1,756 | 887 | 315 | 1,369 | 1,319 |
| Richmond | 28,910 | 24,227 | 6,290 | 20,489 | 27,566 |
| Rockdale | 7,003 | 11,945 | 3,664 | 4,330 | 12,413 |
| Schley | 601 | 511 | 180 | 439 | 635 |
| Screven | 1,940 | 1,705 | 709 | 1,461 | 2,178 |
| Seminole | 1,193 | 850 | 468 | 1,171 | 1,469 |
| Spalding | 6,392 | 7,262 | 2,044 | 4,318 | 7,730 |
| Stephens | 2,976 | 4,047 | 1,448 | 2,185 | 4,329 |
| Stewart | 1,540 | 1,186 | 175 | 1,136 | 832 |
| Sumter | 4,489 | 3,616 | 1,046 | 3,332 | 4,289 |
| Talbot | 1,768 | 671 | 238 | 1,248 | 802 |
| Taliaferro | 755 | 269 | 80 | 469 | 306 |
| Tattnall | 2,360 | 2,566 | 996 | 1,694 | 3,172 |
| Taylor | 1,508 | 1,078 | 281 | 1,134 | 1,145 |
| Telfair | 2,238 | 1,324 | 613 | 1,765 | 1,805 |
| Terrell | 1,942 | 1,143 | 384 | 1,383 | 1,517 |
| Thomas | 4,841 | 5,500 | 1,591 | 3,530 | 6,572 |
| Tift | 3,930 | 4,485 | 1,139 | 2,446 | 4,760 |
| Toombs | 2,648 | 3,609 | 1,210 | 1,152 | 4,433 |
| Towns | 1,487 | 1,674 | 537 | 942 | 1,783 |
| Treutlen | 1,116 | 898 | 318 | 726 | 970 |
| Troup | 6,412 | 8,118 | 2,488 | 4,562 | 9,484 |
| Turner | 1,669 | 935 | 370 | 1,122 | 1,312 |
| Twiggs | 2,097 | 853 | 432 | 1,730 | 1,261 |
| Union | 2,304 | 2,533 | 804 | 1,258 | 2,396 |
| Upson | 3,740 | 4,053 | 1,186 | 2,666 | 4,614 |
| Walker | 6,217 | 8,489 | 2,748 | 4,753 | 10,487 |
| Walton | 4,821 | 5,619 | 1,923 | 3,091 | 5,974 |
| Ware | 4,573 | 4,573 | 1,263 | 4,292 | 4,819 |
| Warren | 1,239 | 751 | 180 | 1,091 | 897 |
| Washington | 3,508 | 2,384 | 820 | 2,615 | 2,752 |
| Wayne | 3,052 | 3,381 | 1,107 | 2,417 | 3,340 |
| Webster | 600 | 208 | 103 | 427 | 361 |
| Wheeler | 880 | 601 | 214 | 658 | 709 |
| White | 1,756 | 2,477 | 981 | 1,028 | 2,648 |
| Whitfield | 7,335 | 12,003 | 2,866 | 4,618 | 12,761 |
| Wilcox | 1,365 | 916 | 433 | 1,079 | 1,235 |
| Wilkes | 1,955 | 1,535 | 464 | 1,549 | 1,810 |
| Wilkinson | 2,286 | 1,232 | 520 | 1,831 | 1,546 |
| Worth | 2,578 | 2,344 | 905 | 1,311 | 2,668 |
| Totals | 1,008,966 | 995,252 | 309,657 | 714,792 | 1,081,331 |

## Georgia Vote Since 1944

1944, Roosevelt, Dem., 268,187; Dewey, Rep., 56,506; Watson, Proh., 36.

1948, Truman, Dem., 254,646; Dewey, Rep., 76,691; Thurmond, States' Rights, 85,055; Wallace, Prog., 1,636; Watson, Proh., 732.

1952, Eisenhower, Rep., 198,979; Stevenson, Dem., 456,823; Liberty Party, 1.

1956, Stevenson, Dem., 444,388; Eisenhower, Rep., 222,778; Andrews, Ind., write-in, 1,754.

1960, Kennedy, Dem., 458,638; Nixon, Rep., 274,472; write-in, 239.

1964, Johnson, Dem., 522,557; Goldwater, Rep., 616,600.

1968, Nixon, Rep., 380,111; Humphrey, Dem., 334,440; Wallace, 3d party, 535,550; write-in, 162.

1972, Nixon, Rep., 881,496; McGovern, Dem., 289,529; Schmitz, Amer., 2,288; scattered.

1976, Carter, Dem., 979,409; Ford, Rep., 483,743; write-in, 4,306.

1980, Reagan, Rep., 654,168; Carter, Dem., 890,955; Anderson, Ind., 36,055; Clark, Libertarian, 15,627.

1984, Reagan, Rep., 1,068,722; Mondale, Dem., 706,628.

1988, Bush, Rep., 1,081,331; Dukakis, Dem., 714,792; Paul, Lib., 8,435; Fulani, New Alliance, 5,099.

1992, Clinton, Dem., 1,008,966; Bush, Rep., 995,252; Perot, Ind., 309,657; Marrou, Libertarian, 7,110.

## Hawaii

| | 1992 | | | 1988 | |
|---|---|---|---|---|---|
| County | Clinton (D) | Bush (R) | Perot (I) | Dukakis (D) | Bush (R) |
| Hawaii | 25,725 | 15,460 | 8,889 | 24,091 | 17,125 |
| Honolulu | 123,908 | 103,937 | 35,728 | 138,971 | 120,258 |
| Kauai | 10,715 | 6,274 | 1,756 | 11,770 | 8,298 |
| Maui | 18,962 | 11,151 | 6,630 | 17,532 | 12,944 |
| Totals | 179,310 | 136,822 | 53,003 | 192,364 | 158,625 |

## Hawaii Vote Since 1968

1968, Nixon, Rep., 91,425; Humphrey, Dem., 141,324; Wallace, 3d party, 3,469.

1972, Nixon, Rep., 168,865; McGovern, Dem., 101,409.

1976, Carter, Dem., 147,375; Ford, Rep., 140,003; MacBride, Libertarian, 3,923.

1980, Reagan, Rep., 130,112; Carter, Dem., 135,879; Anderson, Ind., 32,021; Clark, Libertarian, 3,269; Commoner, Citizens, 1,548; Hall, Com., 458.

1984, Reagan, Rep., 184,934; Mondale, Dem., 147,098; Bergland, Libertarian, 2,167.

1988, Bush, Rep., 158,625; Dukakis, Dem., 192,364; Paul, Lib., 1,999; Fulani, New Alliance, 1,003.

1992, Clinton, Dem., 179,310; Bush, Rep., 136,822; Perot, Ind., 53,003; Gritz, Populist/America First, 1,452; Marrou, Libertarian, 1,119.

## Idaho

| | 1992 | | | 1988 | |
|---|---|---|---|---|---|
| County | Clinton (D) | Bush (R) | Perot (I) | Dukakis (D) | Bush (R) |
| Ada | 31,941 | 49,000 | 28,192 | 30,525 | 54,951 |
| Adams | 457 | 754 | 695 | 643 | 1,107 |
| Bannock | 11,091 | 12,016 | 8,116 | 13,074 | 14,986 |
| Bear Lake | 562 | 1,419 | 684 | 867 | 2,084 |
| Benewah | 1,270 | 1,223 | 1,165 | 1,518 | 1,650 |
| Bingham | 3,565 | 7,333 | 4,144 | 4,346 | 10,131 |
| Blaine | 2,865 | 2,243 | 2,831 | 2,498 | 3,130 |
| Boise | 623 | 912 | 754 | 620 | 1,044 |
| Bonner | 4,995 | 3,937 | 4,645 | 5,555 | 5,721 |
| Bonneville | 7,014 | 16,557 | 10,241 | 7,032 | 22,613 |
| Boundary | 1,095 | 1,479 | 1,136 | 1,336 | 1,800 |
| Butte | 433 | 602 | 392 | 521 | 899 |
| Camas | 134 | 202 | 145 | 136 | 288 |
| Canyon | 9,095 | 19,220 | 8,974 | 10,207 | 21,426 |
| Caribou | 562 | 1,350 | 1,088 | 867 | 2,239 |
| Cassia | 1,351 | 4,052 | 1,785 | 1,833 | 5,345 |
| Clark | 95 | 195 | 119 | 133 | 281 |
| Clearwater | 1,433 | 1,152 | 1,098 | 1,861 | 1,659 |
| Custer | 564 | 829 | 729 | 616 | 1,253 |
| Elmore | 1,858 | 3,087 | 1,867 | 2,078 | 3,756 |
| Franklin | 524 | 2,115 | 890 | 806 | 2,992 |
| Fremont | 903 | 2,333 | 1,349 | 1,178 | 3,401 |
| Gem | 1,609 | 2,455 | 1,555 | 2,064 | 2,926 |
| Gooding | 1,530 | 2,178 | 1,591 | 1,872 | 2,908 |
| Idaho | 1,974 | 2,709 | 1,900 | 2,198 | 3,541 |
| Jefferson | 978 | 3,471 | 2,164 | 1,198 | 5,295 |
| Jerome | 1,739 | 2,972 | 1,768 | 1,985 | 3,830 |
| Kootenai | 11,553 | 13,065 | 11,261 | 11,621 | 15,093 |
| Latah | 7,233 | 5,353 | 3,602 | 6,544 | 6,367 |
| Lemhi | 996 | 1,540 | 1,175 | 1,157 | 2,378 |
| Lewis | 674 | 593 | 491 | 807 | 786 |
| Lincoln | 514 | 656 | 441 | 574 | 918 |
| Madison | 741 | 4,591 | 1,920 | 1,009 | 6,197 |
| Minidoka | 1,815 | 3,304 | 1,875 | 2,290 | 4,623 |
| Nez Perce | 7,069 | 5,431 | 4,363 | 7,754 | 7,027 |
| Oneida | 351 | 713 | 590 | 508 | 1,269 |
| Owyhee | 686 | 1,469 | 862 | 848 | 1,707 |
| Payette | 1,656 | 2,895 | 2,055 | 1,900 | 3,786 |
| Power | 837 | 1,352 | 697 | 1,095 | 1,838 |
| Shoshone | 3,182 | 1,441 | 1,878 | 3,379 | 2,134 |
| Teton | 472 | 762 | 608 | 531 | 982 |
| Twin Falls | 6,593 | 10,335 | 6,043 | 7,078 | 13,243 |
| Valley | 1,259 | 1,548 | 1,313 | 1,251 | 1,897 |
| Washington | 1,122 | 1,802 | 1,204 | 1,359 | 2,380 |
| Totals | 137,013 | 202,645 | 130,395 | 147,272 | 253,881 |

## Idaho Vote Since 1944

1944, Roosevelt, Dem., 107,399; Dewey, Rep., 100,137; Watson, Proh., 503; Thomas, Soc., 282.

1948, Truman, Dem., 107,370; Dewey, Rep., 101,514; Wallace, Prog., 4,972; Watson, Proh., 628; Thomas, Soc., 332.

1952, Eisenhower, Rep., 180,707; Stevenson Dem., 95,081; Hallinan, Prog., 443; write-in, 23.

1956, Eisenhower, Rep., 166,979; Stevenson, Dem., 105,868; Andrews, Ind., 126; write-in, 16.

1960, Kennedy, Dem., 138,853; Nixon, Rep., 161,597.

1964, Johnson, Dem., 148,920; Goldwater, Rep., 143,557.

1968, Nixon, Rep., 165,369; Humphrey, Dem., 89,273; Wallace, 3d party, 36,541.

1972, Nixon, Rep., 199,384; McGovern, Dem., 80,826; Schmitz, Amer., 28,869; Spock, Peoples, 903.

1976, Carter, Dem., 126,549; Ford, Rep., 204,151; Maddox, Amer., 5,935; MacBride, Libertarian, 3,558; LaRouche, U.S. Labor, 739.

1980, Reagan, Rep., 290,699; Carter, Dem., 110,192; Anderson, Ind., 27,058; Clark, Libertarian, 8,425; Rarick, Amer., 1,057.

1984, Reagan, Rep., 297,523; Mondale, Dem., 108,510; Bergland, Libertarian, 2,823.

1988, Bush, Rep., 253,881; Dukakis, Dem., 147,272; Paul, Lib., 5,313; Fulani, Ind., 2,502.

1992, Bush, Rep., 202,645; Clinton, Dem., 137,013; Perot, Ind., 130,395; Gritz, Populist/America First, 10,281; Marrou, Libertarian, 1,167.

## Illinois

| County | Clinton (D) 1992 | Bush (R) 1992 | Perot (I) 1992 | Dukakis (D) 1988 | Bush (R) 1988 |
|---|---|---|---|---|---|
| Adams | 11,748 | 13,529 | 6,157 | 13,768 | 15,831 |
| Alexander | 2,566 | 1,301 | 474 | 2,693 | 1,954 |
| Bond | 3,428 | 2,715 | 1,373 | 3,459 | 3,608 |
| Boone | 5,114 | 5,589 | 2,880 | 4,234 | 6,923 |
| Brown | 1,146 | 1,029 | 504 | 1,267 | 1,373 |
| Bureau | 7,551 | 6,836 | 3,465 | 7,354 | 8,896 |
| Calhoun | 1,519 | 745 | 532 | 1,544 | 1,238 |
| Carroll | 2,854 | 3,297 | 1,502 | 2,990 | 4,464 |
| Cass | 3,200 | 2,162 | 1,072 | 3,316 | 2,916 |
| Champaign | 35,003 | 27,096 | 13,571 | 29,733 | 33,247 |
| Christian | 9,042 | 5,087 | 3,401 | 8,295 | 7,040 |
| Clark | 3,338 | 3,175 | 1,450 | 3,275 | 4,508 |
| Clay | 2,962 | 2,471 | 1,193 | 2,761 | 3,494 |
| Clinton | 6,686 | 5,771 | 3,315 | 5,935 | 7,681 |
| Coles | 9,402 | 8,098 | 4,707 | 8,327 | 11,043 |
| Cook | 1,249,533 | 605,300 | 281,999 | 1,129,973 | 878,582 |
| Crawford | 3,964 | 3,606 | 2,062 | 3,555 | 4,951 |
| Cumberland | 2,111 | 1,860 | 1,209 | 1,904 | 2,667 |
| DeKalb | 13,744 | 12,655 | 7,680 | 11,811 | 17,182 |
| DeWitt | 3,009 | 3,164 | 1,543 | 2,660 | 3,942 |
| Douglas | 3,341 | 3,309 | 1,600 | 3,184 | 4,378 |
| DuPage | 114,564 | 178,271 | 76,839 | 94,285 | 217,907 |
| Edgar | 4,014 | 3,790 | 1,930 | 3,880 | 5,538 |
| Edwards | 1,299 | 1,601 | 634 | 1,218 | 2,212 |
| Effingham | 5,221 | 6,329 | 3,354 | 4,553 | 8,431 |
| Fayette | 4,833 | 3,508 | 1,730 | 4,632 | 5,452 |
| Ford | 2,175 | 3,046 | 1,222 | 2,026 | 4,059 |
| Franklin | 12,744 | 5,504 | 3,180 | 11,023 | 7,677 |
| Fulton | 9,725 | 5,062 | 2,874 | 9,046 | 6,999 |
| Gallatin | 2,371 | 990 | 568 | 2,455 | 1,580 |
| Greene | 3,164 | 2,391 | 1,461 | 3,020 | 3,136 |
| Grundy | 6,122 | 6,346 | 3,724 | 5,525 | 8,743 |
| Hamilton | 2,582 | 1,521 | 862 | 2,618 | 2,622 |
| Hancock | 4,213 | 3,714 | 2,091 | 4,740 | 4,568 |
| Hardin | 1,665 | 985 | 515 | 1,308 | 1,504 |
| Henderson | 2,013 | 1,310 | 715 | 2,085 | 1,726 |
| Henry | 11,077 | 8,989 | 4,231 | 11,594 | 11,358 |
| Iroquois | 4,440 | 6,948 | 3,073 | 4,221 | 9,596 |
| Jackson | 13,373 | 6,898 | 3,995 | 11,334 | 9,687 |
| Jasper | 2,284 | 1,996 | 1,160 | 2,135 | 3,024 |
| Jefferson | 8,665 | 5,497 | 3,402 | 7,729 | 7,624 |
| Jersey | 4,749 | 2,933 | 2,363 | 4,376 | 4,343 |
| JoDaviess | 4,044 | 4,249 | 2,102 | 4,141 | 4,923 |
| Johnson | 2,299 | 2,124 | 944 | 1,872 | 2,797 |
| Kane | 44,568 | 55,684 | 27,179 | 36,366 | 66,283 |
| Kankakee | 17,229 | 15,411 | 7,264 | 15,147 | 20,316 |
| Kendall | 5,423 | 8,521 | 4,394 | 4,347 | 10,653 |
| Knox | 12,524 | 8,331 | 4,357 | 12,752 | 10,842 |
| Lake | 81,693 | 99,000 | 42,384 | 64,327 | 114,115 |
| LaSalle | 23,276 | 16,078 | 10,434 | 22,271 | 22,166 |
| Lawrence | 3,270 | 2,681 | 1,498 | 3,140 | 3,655 |
| Lee | 5,530 | 6,652 | 3,191 | 4,608 | 8,903 |
| Livingston | 6,007 | 8,004 | 3,029 | 5,009 | 10,324 |
| Logan | 5,169 | 6,567 | 2,420 | 4,727 | 8,490 |
| McDonough | 5,814 | 5,297 | 2,770 | 5,247 | 7,173 |
| McHenry | 24,783 | 41,356 | 21,817 | 18,919 | 46,135 |
| McLean | 23,090 | 25,726 | 10,282 | 18,659 | 30,572 |
| Macon | 27,449 | 18,684 | 9,236 | 25,364 | 23,862 |
| Macoupin | 12,050 | 6,518 | 5,018 | 12,195 | 9,362 |
| Madison | 58,484 | 32,167 | 23,110 | 54,175 | 44,907 |
| Marion | 9,669 | 5,764 | 3,407 | 8,592 | 8,695 |
| Marshall | 2,819 | 2,491 | 1,169 | 2,742 | 3,588 |
| Mason | 3,969 | 2,473 | 1,245 | 3,406 | 3,424 |
| Massac | 3,347 | 2,754 | 892 | 3,227 | 3,507 |
| Menard | 2,264 | 2,834 | 1,179 | 2,103 | 3,560 |
| Mercer | 3,990 | 2,983 | 1,535 | 4,204 | 3,683 |
| Monroe | 4,894 | 4,807 | 2,813 | 4,529 | 6,275 |
| Montgomery | 7,424 | 4,407 | 2,956 | 7,293 | 6,388 |
| Morgan | 6,351 | 6,566 | 3,317 | 6,032 | 8,808 |
| Moultrie | 3,056 | 2,065 | 1,322 | 3,013 | 3,167 |
| Ogle | 6,512 | 9,008 | 4,455 | 5,641 | 11,644 |
| Peoria | 38,099 | 30,718 | 12,195 | 35,253 | 37,605 |
| Perry | 6,009 | 3,105 | 1,955 | 5,167 | 4,576 |
| Piatt | 3,520 | 3,076 | 1,822 | 3,099 | 4,137 |
| Pike | 4,016 | 3,342 | 1,643 | 4,614 | 3,965 |
| Pope | 1,063 | 951 | 391 | 996 | 1,202 |
| Pulaski | 1,987 | 1,169 | 379 | 1,793 | 1,666 |
| Putnam | 1,574 | 969 | 752 | 1,601 | 1,516 |
| Randolph | 8,529 | 4,899 | 3,092 | 7,844 | 7,396 |
| Richland | 3,286 | 3,053 | 1,689 | 2,863 | 4,264 |
| Rock Island | 37,412 | 23,212 | 10,416 | 40,174 | 27,412 |
| St. Clair | 57,625 | 31,951 | 17,592 | 55,465 | 41,439 |
| Saline | 7,258 | 3,667 | 2,302 | 6,676 | 5,798 |
| Sangamon | 40,052 | 39,641 | 16,861 | 37,729 | 50,175 |
| Schuyler | 1,650 | 1,512 | 815 | 1,866 | 2,178 |
| Scott | 1,057 | 1,132 | 588 | 1,243 | 1,535 |
| Shelby | 5,101 | 3,631 | 2,401 | 4,650 | 5,370 |
| Stark | 1,336 | 1,384 | 625 | 1,274 | 1,841 |
| Stephenson | 7,899 | 9,005 | 4,677 | 7,460 | 11,342 |
| Tazewell | 26,428 | 23,469 | 9,927 | 24,603 | 28,861 |
| Union | 4,681 | 3,003 | 1,373 | 4,197 | 4,244 |
| Vermilion | 18,383 | 11,703 | 8,162 | 17,918 | 16,943 |
| Wabash | 2,436 | 2,485 | 1,302 | 2,241 | 3,453 |
| Warren | 3,661 | 3,325 | 1,436 | 3,617 | 4,584 |
| Washington | 2,986 | 3,003 | 1,542 | 2,689 | 4,127 |
| Wayne | 3,332 | 3,809 | 1,702 | 3,135 | 5,481 |
| White | 4,308 | 3,057 | 1,428 | 4,144 | 4,354 |
| Whiteside | 12,329 | 10,146 | 4,589 | 11,328 | 12,978 |
| Will | 59,633 | 58,337 | 32,788 | 49,816 | 73,129 |
| Williamson | 14,361 | 9,462 | 4,779 | 12,712 | 12,274 |
| Winnebago | 48,298 | 42,221 | 21,227 | 45,280 | 55,699 |
| Woodford | 5,490 | 8,032 | 2,733 | 4,604 | 9,474 |
| Totals | 2,453,350 | 1,734,096 | 840,515 | 2,215,940 | 2,310,939 |

### Illinois Vote Since 1944

1944, Roosevelt, Dem., 2,079,479; Dewey, Rep., 1,939,314; Teichert, Soc. Labor, 9,677; Watson, Proh., 7,411; Thomas, Soc., 180.

1948, Truman, Dem., 1,994,715; Dewey, Rep., 1,961,103; Watson, Proh., 11,959; Thomas, Soc., 11,522; Teichert, Soc. Labor, 3,118.

1952, Eisenhower, Rep., 2,457,327; Stevenson, Dem., 2,013,920; Hass, Soc. Labor, 9,363; write-in, 448.

1956, Eisenhower, Rep., 2,623,327; Stevenson, Dem., 1,775,682; Hass, Soc. Labor, 8,342; write-in, 56.

1960, Kennedy, Dem., 2,377,846; Nixon, Rep., 2,368,988; Hass, Soc. Labor, 10,560; write-in, 15.

1964, Johnson, Dem., 2,796,833; Goldwater, Rep., 1,905,946; write-in, 62.

1968, Nixon, Rep., 2,174,774; Humphrey, Dem., 2,039,814; Wallace, 3d party, 390,958; Blomen, Soc. Labor, 13,878; write-in, 325.

1972, Nixon, Rep., 2,788,179; McGovern, Dem., 1,913,472; Fisher, Soc. Labor, 12,344; Schmitz, Amer., 2,471; Hall, Com., 4,541; others, 2,229.

1976, Carter, Dem., 2,271,295; Ford, Rep., 2,364,269; McCarthy, Ind., 55,939; Hall, Com., 9,250; MacBride, Libertarian, 8,057; Camejo, Soc. Workers, 3,615; Levin, Soc. Labor, 2,422; LaRouche, U.S. Labor, 2,018; write-in, 1,968.

1980, Reagan, Rep., 2,358,049; Carter, Dem., 1,981,413; Anderson, Ind., 346,754; Clark, Libertarian, 38,939; Commoner, Citizens, 10,692; Hall, Com., 9,711; Griswold, Workers World, 2,257; DeBerry, Socialist Workers, 1,302; write-ins, 604.

1984, Reagan, Rep., 2,707,103; Mondale, Dem., 2,086,499; Bergland, Libertarian, 10,086.

1988, Bush, Rep., 2,310,939; Dukakis, Dem., 2,215,940; Paul, Lib., 14,944; Fulani, Solid., 10,276.

1992, Clinton, Dem., 2,453,350; Bush, Rep., 1,734,096; Perot, Ind., 840,515; Marrou, Libertarian, 9,218; Fulani, New Alliance, 5,267; Gritz, Populist/America First, 3,577; Hagelin, Natural Law, 2,751; Warren, Socialist Workers, 1,361.

## Indiana

| County | Clinton (D) 1992 | Bush (R) 1992 | Perot (I) 1992 | Dukakis (D) 1988 | Bush (R) 1988 |
|---|---|---|---|---|---|
| Adams | 3,708 | 6,078 | 2,865 | 3,811 | 8,137 |
| Allen | 39,629 | 55,003 | 25,809 | 39,238 | 74,638 |
| Bartholomew | 8,284 | 13,146 | 5,882 | 8,804 | 17,364 |
| Benton | 1,221 | 2,030 | 1,056 | 1,349 | 2,698 |
| Blackford | 2,088 | 2,347 | 1,319 | 2,253 | 3,336 |
| Boone | 3,982 | 9,485 | 3,826 | 4,168 | 11,608 |
| Brown | 2,029 | 2,633 | 1,635 | 2,115 | 3,348 |
| Carroll | 2,561 | 3,800 | 2,173 | 2,952 | 4,981 |
| Cass | 4,757 | 7,421 | 3,944 | 5,784 | 10,970 |
| Clark | 17,460 | 13,333 | 5,653 | 14,528 | 16,544 |
| Clay | 3,306 | 4,696 | 2,134 | 3,724 | 5,852 |
| Clinton | 3,490 | 6,141 | 2,535 | 4,412 | 8,570 |
| Crawford | 2,260 | 1,903 | 819 | 2,036 | 2,532 |
| Daviess | 3,201 | 5,591 | 1,695 | 3,483 | 6,768 |
| Dearborn | 5,116 | 6,974 | 3,384 | 5,066 | 8,195 |
| Decatur | 2,774 | 5,195 | 2,299 | 2,979 | 6,245 |
| Dekalb | 4,652 | 6,682 | 3,554 | 4,657 | 9,018 |
| Delaware | 19,556 | 20,473 | 10,453 | 20,548 | 27,348 |
| Dubois | 5,878 | 6,785 | 3,195 | 5,954 | 9,995 |
| Elkhart | 14,660 | 27,920 | 9,450 | 14,236 | 33,793 |
| Fayette | 3,969 | 4,376 | 2,299 | 4,118 | 5,949 |
| Floyd | 13,166 | 11,932 | 4,421 | 11,024 | 14,291 |

| | | | | | |
|---|---|---|---|---|---|
| Fountain | 2,829 | 3,391 | 2,162 | 3,279 | 5,113 |
| Franklin | 2,456 | 3,831 | 1,858 | 2,472 | 4,777 |
| Fulton | 2,552 | 3,982 | 1,963 | 2,788 | 5,234 |
| Gibson | 6,909 | 5,172 | 2,680 | 7,031 | 7,610 |
| Grant | 9,211 | 13,806 | 5,597 | 10,799 | 18,441 |
| Greene | 5,431 | 5,410 | 2,610 | 5,979 | 7,689 |
| Hamilton | 10,215 | 34,622 | 10,365 | 8,853 | 36,654 |
| Hancock | 4,752 | 11,072 | 4,752 | 5,355 | 13,374 |
| Harrison | 5,768 | 5,403 | 2,469 | 4,933 | 6,702 |
| Hendricks | 7,071 | 18,373 | 7,519 | 7,643 | 22,090 |
| Henry | 6,794 | 8,720 | 4,416 | 7,779 | 11,280 |
| Howard | 10,288 | 15,306 | 8,575 | 11,518 | 19,971 |
| Huntington | 3,855 | 9,093 | 2,967 | 3,873 | 11,675 |
| Jackson | 5,663 | 7,246 | 3,148 | 5,550 | 9,470 |
| Jasper | 3,033 | 4,809 | 2,019 | 3,237 | 6,009 |
| Jay | 3,208 | 3,609 | 1,994 | 3,212 | 5,363 |
| Jefferson | 5,510 | 4,937 | 2,565 | 5,221 | 6,949 |
| Jennings | 3,471 | 4,392 | 2,370 | 3,667 | 5,636 |
| Johnson | 8,712 | 20,353 | 8,246 | 9,001 | 24,654 |
| Knox | 6,718 | 6,683 | 3,719 | 7,006 | 9,813 |
| Kosciusko | 5,307 | 14,179 | 5,115 | 5,321 | 17,761 |
| LaGrange | 2,093 | 3,584 | 1,736 | 2,029 | 4,495 |
| Lake | 102,778 | 53,867 | 28,635 | 105,026 | 79,929 |
| LaPorte | 17,717 | 14,962 | 9,641 | 17,585 | 20,537 |
| Lawrence | 5,557 | 7,712 | 3,452 | 5,787 | 10,742 |
| Madison | 22,276 | 23,479 | 13,100 | 24,443 | 32,596 |
| Marion | 122,234 | 141,369 | 57,878 | 128,627 | 184,519 |
| Marshall | 4,912 | 8,048 | 3,522 | 5,488 | 10,490 |
| Martin | 2,018 | 2,523 | 883 | 2,132 | 3,066 |
| Miami | 3,967 | 6,416 | 3,428 | 4,613 | 8,533 |
| Monroe | 19,712 | 16,661 | 6,943 | 15,855 | 20,756 |
| Montgomery | 3,371 | 7,602 | 3,511 | 3,623 | 10,793 |
| Morgan | 4,690 | 10,939 | 5,375 | 5,375 | 14,284 |
| Newton | 1,757 | 2,295 | 1,274 | 1,744 | 3,274 |
| Noble | 4,411 | 5,883 | 3,328 | 4,143 | 7,889 |
| Ohio | 970 | 1,009 | 527 | 1,113 | 1,412 |
| Orange | 2,948 | 3,738 | 1,296 | 2,739 | 5,245 |
| Owen | 2,207 | 2,753 | 1,563 | 2,484 | 3,837 |
| Parke | 2,429 | 2,953 | 1,696 | 2,563 | 4,458 |
| Perry | 4,829 | 2,973 | 1,560 | 4,804 | 4,720 |
| Pike | 2,960 | 2,156 | 1,238 | 3,037 | 3,294 |
| Porter | 21,022 | 22,644 | 13,096 | 19,390 | 29,790 |
| Posey | 4,632 | 4,435 | 2,357 | 4,468 | 5,987 |
| Pulaski | 1,950 | 2,712 | 1,214 | 2,213 | 3,677 |
| Putnam | 3,487 | 5,341 | 3,174 | 3,850 | 7,119 |
| Randolph | 3,870 | 4,937 | 2,939 | 3,990 | 6,856 |
| Ripley | 3,480 | 5,033 | 2,406 | 3,605 | 6,414 |
| Rush | 2,168 | 3,873 | 1,948 | 2,451 | 5,112 |
| St. Joseph | 46,203 | 38,934 | 18,828 | 48,056 | 49,481 |
| Scott | 4,085 | 2,649 | 1,092 | 3,378 | 3,455 |
| Shelby | 4,560 | 8,075 | 3,521 | 5,382 | 10,176 |
| Spencer | 4,301 | 3,789 | 1,464 | 4,061 | 4,964 |
| Starke | 3,695 | 3,100 | 1,885 | 4,104 | 4,458 |
| Steuben | 3,630 | 4,868 | 2,896 | 3,114 | 6,855 |
| Sullivan | 4,211 | 3,052 | 1,857 | 4,320 | 4,246 |
| Switzerland | 1,535 | 1,211 | 636 | 1,479 | 1,572 |
| Tippecanoe | 17,343 | 23,050 | 9,684 | 16,256 | 27,897 |
| Tipton | 2,125 | 3,906 | 1,816 | 2,485 | 5,148 |
| Union | 898 | 1,394 | 664 | 946 | 1,814 |
| Vanderburgh | 33,799 | 30,271 | 12,513 | 31,270 | 38,928 |
| Vermillion | 3,652 | 2,360 | 1,794 | 4,044 | 3,674 |
| Vigo | 18,050 | 15,834 | 8,141 | 19,192 | 21,929 |
| Wabash | 4,518 | 7,062 | 3,424 | 4,168 | 9,153 |
| Warren | 1,367 | 1,601 | 1,020 | 1,542 | 2,243 |
| Warrick | 8,612 | 8,087 | 3,862 | 7,999 | 10,504 |
| Washington | 4,092 | 4,043 | 1,846 | 3,370 | 4,908 |
| Wayne | 9,960 | 12,221 | 5,095 | 10,209 | 16,388 |
| Wells | 3,282 | 5,799 | 2,890 | 3,437 | 7,712 |
| White | 2,988 | 4,622 | 2,582 | 3,256 | 6,220 |
| Whitley | 3,569 | 5,217 | 3,195 | 3,642 | 7,679 |
| **Totals** | **848,420** | **989,375** | **455,934** | **860,643** | **1,297,763** |

## Indiana Vote Since 1944

1944, Roosevelt, Dem., 781,403; Dewey, Rep., 875,891; Watson, Proh., 12,574; Thomas, Soc., 2,223.

1948, Truman, Dem., 807,833; Dewey, Rep., 821,079; Watson, Proh., 14,711; Wallace, Prog., 9,649; Thomas, Soc., 2,179; Teichert, Soc. Labor, 763.

1952, Eisenhower, Rep., 1,136,259; Stevenson, Dem., 801,530; Hamblen, Proh., 15,335; Hallinan, Prog., 1,222; Hass, Soc. Labor, 979.

1956, Eisenhower, Rep., 1,182,811; Stevenson, Dem., 783,908; Holtwick, Proh., 6,554; Hass, Soc. Labor, 1,334.

1960, Kennedy, Dem., 952,358; Nixon, Rep., 1,175,120; Decker, Proh., 6,746; Hass, Soc. Labor, 1,136.

1964, Johnson, Dem. 1,170,848; Goldwater, Rep., 911,118; Munn, Proh., 8,266; Hass, Soc. Labor, 1,374.

1968, Nixon, Rep., 1,067,885; Humphrey, Dem., 806,659; Wallace, 3d party, 243,108; Munn, Proh., 4,616; Halstead, Soc. Worker, 1,293; Gregory, write-in, 36.

1972, Nixon, Rep., 1,405,154; McGovern, Dem., 708,568; Reed, Soc. Workers, 5,575; Fisher, Soc. Labor, 1,688; Spock, Peace & Freedom, 4,544.

1976, Carter, Dem., 1,014,714; Ford, Rep., 1,185,958; Anderson, Amer., 14,048; Camejo, Soc. Workers, 5,695; LaRouche, U.S. Labor, 1,947.

1980 Reagan, Rep., 1,255,656; Carter, Dem., 844,197; Anderson, Ind., 111,639; Clark, Libertarian, 19,627; Commoner, Citizens, 4,852; Greaves, American, 4,750; Hall, Com., 702; DeBerry, Soc., 610.

1984 Reagan, Rep., 1,377,230; Mondale, Dem., 841,481; Bergland, Libertarian, 6,741.

1988, Bush, Rep., 1,297,763; Dukakis, Dem., 860,643; Fulani, New Alliance, 10,215.

1992, Bush, Rep., 989,375; Clinton, Dem., 848,420; Perot, Ind., 455,934; Marrou, Libertarian, 7,936; Fulani, New Alliance, 2,583.

## Iowa

| | 1992 | | | 1988 | |
|---|---|---|---|---|---|
| County | Clinton (D) | Bush (R) | Perot (I) | Dukakis (D) | Bush (R) |
| Adair | 1,655 | 1,713 | 814 | 2,261 | 1,833 |
| Adams | 1,034 | 863 | 679 | 1,283 | 1,080 |
| Allamakee | 2,362 | 2,627 | 1,543 | 2,768 | 3,186 |
| Appanoose | 2,810 | 2,346 | 1,161 | 3,209 | 2,779 |
| Audubon | 1,589 | 1,373 | 887 | 1,863 | 1,478 |
| Benton | 4,467 | 3,469 | 2,454 | 5,873 | 4,011 |
| Black Hawk | 29,584 | 21,398 | 10,182 | 31,657 | 24,112 |
| Boone | 5,913 | 4,148 | 2,070 | 7,232 | 4,381 |
| Bremer | 4,774 | 4,482 | 2,338 | 4,961 | 5,079 |
| Buchanan | 4,166 | 3,313 | 2,126 | 4,778 | 3,495 |
| Buena Vista | 3,374 | 3,863 | 1,955 | 4,580 | 4,170 |
| Butler | 2,548 | 3,209 | 1,333 | 2,593 | 3,523 |
| Calhoun | 2,140 | 2,169 | 946 | 2,990 | 2,474 |
| Carroll | 3,800 | 3,439 | 2,192 | 5,437 | 3,701 |
| Cass | 2,231 | 3,176 | 1,608 | 2,934 | 3,962 |
| Cedar | 3,296 | 2,965 | 1,945 | 4,032 | 3,373 |
| Cerro Gordo | 11,415 | 8,250 | 4,498 | 12,857 | 9,358 |
| Cherokee | 2,590 | 2,768 | 1,503 | 3,574 | 3,218 |
| Chickasaw | 2,913 | 2,129 | 1,566 | 3,530 | 2,549 |
| Clarke | 1,921 | 1,417 | 899 | 2,262 | 1,631 |
| Clay | 3,346 | 3,011 | 1,964 | 4,173 | 3,641 |
| Clayton | 3,742 | 3,044 | 2,309 | 4,320 | 3,839 |
| Clinton | 11,683 | 8,746 | 4,414 | 12,549 | 10,243 |
| Crawford | 3,004 | 2,693 | 1,905 | 3,868 | 3,375 |
| Dallas | 6,554 | 5,587 | 2,665 | 7,501 | 4,858 |
| Davis | 1,962 | 1,344 | 718 | 2,246 | 1,263 |
| Decatur | 1,866 | 1,316 | 786 | 2,192 | 1,406 |
| Delaware | 3,093 | 3,195 | 2,144 | 3,947 | 3,425 |
| Des Moines | 11,309 | 6,378 | 3,386 | 11,593 | 7,652 |
| Dickinson | 3,106 | 3,196 | 1,974 | 3,342 | 3,678 |
| Dubuque | 20,539 | 14,007 | 8,208 | 23,797 | 14,530 |
| Emmet | 2,239 | 1,749 | 1,010 | 2,778 | 2,173 |
| Fayette | 4,412 | 3,879 | 2,493 | 5,304 | 4,921 |
| Floyd | 3,688 | 2,404 | 1,611 | 4,377 | 3,266 |
| Franklin | 2,049 | 2,137 | 1,045 | 2,594 | 2,320 |
| Fremont | 1,422 | 1,459 | 1,003 | 1,547 | 1,946 |
| Greene | 2,422 | 1,952 | 956 | 3,011 | 2,091 |
| Grundy | 1,895 | 3,160 | 1,069 | 2,211 | 3,433 |
| Guthrie | 2,234 | 1,962 | 1,216 | 2,910 | 2,005 |
| Hamilton | 3,262 | 3,031 | 1,348 | 4,156 | 3,277 |
| Hancock | 2,175 | 2,428 | 1,170 | 2,831 | 2,731 |
| Hardin | 3,792 | 3,590 | 1,547 | 5,088 | 3,856 |
| Harrison | 2,349 | 2,763 | 1,691 | 2,883 | 3,108 |
| Henry | 3,544 | 3,435 | 1,522 | 3,754 | 3,951 |
| Howard | 2,099 | 1,516 | 1,193 | 2,330 | 1,970 |
| Humboldt | 1,765 | 2,299 | 1,093 | 2,713 | 2,594 |
| Ida | 1,449 | 1,714 | 1,061 | 1,787 | 1,951 |
| Iowa | 2,560 | 2,656 | 1,709 | 3,338 | 3,247 |
| Jackson | 4,421 | 2,673 | 2,096 | 4,864 | 3,237 |
| Jasper | 8,120 | 6,866 | 2,972 | 8,940 | 6,703 |
| Jefferson | 2,562 | 2,541 | 1,241 | 3,594 | 3,614 |
| Johnson | 28,656 | 14,041 | 8,625 | 28,759 | 15,453 |
| Jones | 3,508 | 3,071 | 2,306 | 4,641 | 3,496 |
| Keokuk | 2,329 | 1,981 | 1,238 | 2,899 | 2,278 |
| Kossuth | 3,660 | 3,464 | 1,906 | 5,088 | 3,938 |
| Lee | 9,366 | 4,777 | 2,920 | 10,911 | 6,428 |
| Linn | 38,567 | 30,215 | 19,643 | 42,993 | 33,129 |
| Louisa | 2,091 | 1,691 | 1,044 | 2,268 | 2,060 |
| Lucas | 2,072 | 1,734 | 848 | 2,454 | 1,776 |
| Lyon | 1,331 | 3,272 | 1,068 | 1,706 | 3,517 |
| Madison | 2,525 | 2,421 | 1,168 | 3,421 | 2,410 |
| Mahaska | 3,714 | 4,953 | 1,508 | 4,451 | 4,798 |
| Marion | 5,531 | 6,062 | 1,896 | 6,922 | 5,914 |
| Marshall | 8,303 | 6,784 | 3,100 | 9,760 | 7,657 |
| Mills | 1,798 | 2,699 | 1,638 | 2,092 | 3,212 |
| Mitchell | 2,177 | 1,933 | 1,199 | 2,870 | 2,338 |
| Monona | 1,939 | 1,660 | 1,231 | 2,408 | 2,068 |
| Monroe | 1,829 | 1,323 | 612 | 2,338 | 1,313 |
| Montgomery | 1,599 | 2,404 | 1,341 | 1,898 | 3,166 |
| Muscatine | 7,089 | 6,087 | 3,583 | 7,059 | 6,904 |
| O'Brien | 2,122 | 3,869 | 1,557 | 2,768 | 4,241 |
| Osceola | 990 | 1,756 | 813 | 1,277 | 1,951 |
| Page | 1,951 | 3,670 | 1,669 | 2,185 | 4,583 |
| Palo Alto | 2,374 | 1,789 | 1,186 | 3,377 | 2,041 |
| Plymouth | 3,171 | 5,196 | 2,039 | 4,220 | 5,316 |
| Pocahontas | 1,919 | 1,743 | 942 | 2,722 | 1,871 |
| Polk | 78,585 | 63,708 | 24,155 | 84,476 | 57,854 |

| County | | | | | |
|---|---|---|---|---|---|
| Pottawattamie | 13,228 | 15,671 | 8,035 | 14,958 | 17,193 |
| Poweshiek | 4,056 | 3,245 | 1,680 | 4,876 | 3,683 |
| Ringgold | 1,341 | 967 | 551 | 1,609 | 1,110 |
| Sac | 1,896 | 2,138 | 1,157 | 2,613 | 2,411 |
| Scott | 33,765 | 28,844 | 11,423 | 34,415 | 31,025 |
| Shelby | 2,094 | 2,809 | 1,614 | 2,806 | 3,019 |
| Sioux | 2,226 | 10,637 | 1,771 | 2,923 | 10,270 |
| Story | 17,118 | 12,702 | 6,275 | 19,051 | 13,782 |
| Tama | 3,573 | 2,948 | 1,748 | 4,584 | 3,362 |
| Taylor | 1,430 | 1,200 | 910 | 1,671 | 1,647 |
| Union | 2,565 | 2,224 | 1,280 | 3,236 | 2,751 |
| Van Buren | 1,464 | 1,418 | 811 | 1,612 | 1,692 |
| Wapello | 8,670 | 4,852 | 2,513 | 10,177 | 5,350 |
| Warren | 8,612 | 7,242 | 3,217 | 9,627 | 6,424 |
| Washington | 3,384 | 3,576 | 1,994 | 3,776 | 3,741 |
| Wayne | 1,632 | 1,299 | 642 | 1,988 | 1,467 |
| Webster | 8,562 | 6,992 | 3,272 | 10,267 | 6,926 |
| Winnebago | 2,322 | 2,407 | 1,329 | 2,804 | 2,863 |
| Winneshiek | 3,791 | 3,331 | 2,416 | 4,443 | 4,194 |
| Woodbury | 17,398 | 18,148 | 7,182 | 20,153 | 18,790 |
| Worth | 2,009 | 1,382 | 1,044 | 2,440 | 1,488 |
| Wright | 2,776 | 2,708 | 1,151 | 3,353 | 2,658 |
| Totals | 586,353 | 504,891 | 253,468 | 670,557 | 545,355 |

## Iowa Vote Since 1944

1944, Roosevelt, Dem., 499,876; Dewey, Rep., 547,267; Watson, Proh., 3,752; Thomas, Soc., 1,511; Teichert, Soc. Labor, 193.

1948, Truman, Dem., 522,380; Dewey, Rep., 494,018; Wallace, Prog., 12,125; Teichert, Soc. Labor, 4,274; Watson, Proh., 3,382; Thomas, Soc., 1,829; Dobbs, Soc. Workers, 26.

1952, Eisenhower, Rep., 808,906; Stevenson, Dem., 451,513; Hallinan, Prog., 5,085; Hamblen, Proh., 2,882; Hoopes, Soc., 219; Hass, Soc. Labor, 139; scattering 29.

1956, Eisenhower, Rep., 729,187; Stevenson, Dem., 501,858; Andrews (A.C.P. of Iowa), 3,202; Hoopes, Soc., 192; Hass, Soc. Labor, 125.

1960, Kennedy, Dem., 550,565; Nixon, Rep., 722,381; Hass, Soc. Labor, 230; write-in, 634.

1964, Johnson, Dem., 733,030; Goldwater, Rep., 449,148; Hass, Soc. Labor, 182; DeBerry, Soc. Worker, 159; Munn, Proh., 1,902.

1968, Nixon, Rep., 619,106; Humphrey, Dem., 476,699; Wallace, 3d party, 66,422; Munn, Proh., 362; Halstead, Soc. Worker, 3,377; Cleaver, Peace and Freedom, 1,332; Blomen, Soc. Labor, 241.

1972, Nixon, Rep., 706,207; McGovern, Dem., 496,206; Schmitz, Amer., 22,056; Jenness, Soc. Workers, 488; Fisher, Soc. Labor, 195; Hall, Com. 272; Green, Universal, 199; scattered, 321.

1976, Carter, Dem., 619,931; Ford, Rep., 632,863; McCarthy, Ind., 20,051; Anderson, Amer., 3,040; MacBride, Libertarian, 1,452.

1980, Reagan, Rep., 676,026; Carter, Dem., 508,672; Anderson, Ind., 115,633; Clark, Libertarian, 13,123; Commoner, Citizens, 2,273; McReynolds, Socialist, 534; Hall Com., 298; DeBerry, Soc. Work., 244; Greaves, American, 189; Bubar, Statesman, 150; scattering, 519.

1984, Reagan, Rep., 703,088; Mondale, Dem., 605,620; Bergland, Libertarian, 1,844.

1988, Bush, Rep., 545,355; Dukakis, Dem., 670,557; LaRouche, Ind., 3,526; Paul, Lib., 2,494.

1992, Clinton, Dem., 586,353; Bush, Rep., 504,891; Perot, Ind., 253,468; Hagelin, Natural Law, 3,079; Gritz, Populist/America First, 1,177; Marrou, Libertarian, 1,076.

## Kansas

| County | 1992 Clinton (D) | Bush (R) | Perot (I) | 1988 Dukakis (D) | Bush (R) |
|---|---|---|---|---|---|
| Allen | 2,312 | 2,351 | 1,746 | 2,392 | 3,429 |
| Anderson | 1,178 | 1,218 | 1,282 | 1,466 | 1,781 |
| Atchison | 2,959 | 2,521 | 2,020 | 3,177 | 3,243 |
| Barber | 759 | 1,225 | 893 | 1,118 | 1,539 |
| Barton | 3,846 | 5,113 | 4,574 | 5,024 | 7,741 |
| Bourbon | 2,509 | 2,876 | 1,763 | 2,623 | 3,660 |
| Brown | 1,476 | 2,203 | 1,603 | 1,719 | 3,059 |
| Butler | 7,029 | 9,166 | 7,355 | 7,690 | 10,976 |
| Chase | 470 | 610 | 600 | 538 | 884 |
| Chautauqua | 598 | 653 | 607 | 661 | 1,247 |
| Cherokee | 4,083 | 3,599 | 2,067 | 4,069 | 4,281 |
| Cheyenne | 407 | 863 | 477 | 594 | 1,105 |
| Clark | 293 | 676 | 341 | 409 | 876 |
| Clay | 947 | 2,198 | 1,434 | 1,112 | 2,997 |
| Cloud | 1,720 | 2,131 | 1,578 | 2,022 | 3,043 |
| Coffey | 1,021 | 1,824 | 1,443 | 1,246 | 2,581 |
| Comanche | 325 | 636 | 324 | 375 | 738 |

| County | | | | | |
|---|---|---|---|---|---|
| Cowley | 5,405 | 5,422 | 4,911 | 6,186 | 7,778 |
| Crawford | 7,366 | 5,468 | 3,706 | 7,783 | 6,940 |
| Decatur | 576 | 940 | 565 | 793 | 1,291 |
| Dickinson | 2,518 | 3,851 | 2,833 | 2,870 | 5,121 |
| Doniphan | 1,177 | 1,579 | 1,200 | 1,312 | 2,162 |
| Douglas | 19,439 | 12,949 | 9,630 | 15,752 | 16,149 |
| Edwards | 567 | 769 | 584 | 792 | 993 |
| Elk | 485 | 748 | 503 | 608 | 1,075 |
| Ellis | 4,544 | 3,985 | 3,887 | 5,289 | 5,194 |
| Ellsworth | 1,010 | 1,197 | 1,020 | 1,219 | 1,711 |
| Finney | 2,612 | 5,278 | 3,011 | 3,408 | 5,381 |
| Ford | 2,635 | 4,342 | 3,341 | 3,817 | 5,685 |
| Franklin | 2,968 | 3,699 | 3,184 | 3,592 | 4,777 |
| Geary | 2,559 | 2,928 | 2,057 | 2,721 | 3,782 |
| Gove | 379 | 792 | 532 | 663 | 966 |
| Graham | 554 | 752 | 603 | 702 | 1,139 |
| Grant | 619 | 1,561 | 835 | 907 | 1,654 |
| Gray | 443 | 1,039 | 686 | 696 | 1,180 |
| Greeley | 191 | 504 | 175 | 317 | 506 |
| Greenwood | 1,262 | 1,411 | 1,167 | 1,421 | 2,217 |
| Hamilton | 386 | 716 | 271 | 517 | 801 |
| Harper | 845 | 1,371 | 1,151 | 1,235 | 1,941 |
| Harvey | 5,047 | 6,259 | 3,653 | 5,503 | 6,893 |
| Haskell | 336 | 1,023 | 462 | 427 | 964 |
| Hodgeman | 258 | 625 | 343 | 439 | 732 |
| Jackson | 1,639 | 1,970 | 1,927 | 2,261 | 2,759 |
| Jefferson | 2,538 | 2,569 | 2,642 | 2,810 | 3,605 |
| Jewell | 546 | 1,050 | 698 | 684 | 1,546 |
| Johnson | 59,573 | 85,418 | 49,136 | 55,183 | 95,591 |
| Kearny | 384 | 943 | 376 | 524 | 1,073 |
| Kingman | 1,100 | 1,680 | 1,370 | 1,420 | 2,205 |
| Kiowa | 355 | 1,057 | 475 | 485 | 1,276 |
| Labette | 4,196 | 3,368 | 2,577 | 4,433 | 5,125 |
| Lane | 265 | 674 | 356 | 450 | 768 |
| Leavenworth | 8,077 | 7,738 | 7,306 | 8,797 | 9,913 |
| Lincoln | 612 | 893 | 657 | 796 | 1,229 |
| Linn | 1,353 | 1,413 | 1,358 | 1,497 | 2,163 |
| Logan | 355 | 905 | 446 | 503 | 988 |
| Lyon | 4,811 | 5,090 | 4,717 | 5,314 | 6,820 |
| McPherson | 3,645 | 5,745 | 3,561 | 4,354 | 6,563 |
| Marion | 1,627 | 3,142 | 1,557 | 2,024 | 3,685 |
| Marshall | 2,022 | 2,030 | 1,786 | 2,560 | 3,140 |
| Meade | 430 | 1,135 | 592 | 664 | 1,322 |
| Miami | 3,835 | 3,528 | 3,701 | 4,427 | 4,807 |
| Mitchell | 938 | 1,601 | 1,098 | 1,145 | 2,257 |
| Montgomery | 5,453 | 6,848 | 3,570 | 5,429 | 9,067 |
| Morris | 957 | 1,071 | 1,071 | 1,165 | 1,682 |
| Morton | 398 | 915 | 350 | 569 | 1,074 |
| Nemaha | 1,580 | 2,220 | 1,804 | 2,261 | 2,849 |
| Neosho | 2,799 | 2,926 | 2,136 | 3,402 | 3,739 |
| Ness | 565 | 967 | 678 | 887 | 1,230 |
| Norton | 779 | 1,469 | 815 | 855 | 1,923 |
| Osage | 2,297 | 2,561 | 2,532 | 2,840 | 3,496 |
| Osborne | 779 | 1,003 | 819 | 943 | 1,541 |
| Ottawa | 764 | 1,284 | 762 | 953 | 1,836 |
| Pawnee | 1,118 | 1,357 | 1,097 | 1,474 | 1,825 |
| Phillips | 843 | 1,579 | 955 | 960 | 2,316 |
| Pottawatomie | 2,099 | 3,106 | 2,759 | 2,544 | 3,897 |
| Pratt | 1,466 | 1,779 | 1,528 | 1,651 | 2,505 |
| Rawlins | 393 | 1,023 | 517 | 612 | 1,318 |
| Reno | 9,257 | 11,377 | 7,636 | 11,545 | 12,753 |
| Republic | 939 | 1,767 | 1,084 | 1,069 | 2,346 |
| Rice | 1,555 | 2,158 | 1,543 | 2,033 | 2,503 |
| Riley | 7,933 | 8,394 | 5,387 | 7,283 | 9,507 |
| Rooks | 771 | 1,249 | 1,063 | 1,012 | 1,938 |
| Rush | 689 | 756 | 665 | 1,020 | 1,045 |
| Russell | 1,178 | 1,434 | 1,395 | 1,448 | 2,403 |
| Saline | 7,890 | 8,565 | 7,108 | 7,998 | 11,371 |
| Scott | 480 | 1,426 | 621 | 717 | 1,590 |
| Sedgwick | 62,670 | 75,577 | 47,238 | 65,618 | 86,124 |
| Seward | 1,488 | 3,477 | 1,818 | 1,655 | 4,089 |
| Shawnee | 31,972 | 29,344 | 20,653 | 33,940 | 35,489 |
| Sheridan | 347 | 739 | 546 | 600 | 901 |
| Sherman | 810 | 1,630 | 828 | 1,082 | 1,929 |
| Smith | 789 | 1,236 | 816 | 1,004 | 1,951 |
| Stafford | 777 | 1,064 | 910 | 1,121 | 1,532 |
| Stanton | 224 | 556 | 214 | 310 | 592 |
| Stevens | 390 | 1,408 | 674 | 612 | 1,642 |
| Summer | 3,564 | 4,087 | 3,887 | 4,417 | 5,394 |
| Thomas | 932 | 1,849 | 1,129 | 1,408 | 2,342 |
| Trego | 608 | 727 | 574 | 795 | 979 |
| Wabaunsee | 851 | 1,254 | 1,258 | 1,166 | 1,737 |
| Wallace | 164 | 679 | 219 | 257 | 655 |
| Washington | 893 | 1,740 | 1,054 | 1,063 | 2,269 |
| Wichita | 241 | 681 | 303 | 399 | 721 |
| Wilson | 1,331 | 1,925 | 1,365 | 1,545 | 2,743 |
| Woodson | 590 | 662 | 604 | 761 | 1,062 |
| Wyandotte | 34,397 | 12,872 | 13,620 | 38,678 | 19,097 |
| Totals | 390,434 | 449,951 | 312,358 | 422,636 | 554,049 |

## Kansas Vote Since 1944

1944, Roosevelt, Dem., 287,458; Dewey, Rep., 442,096; Watson, Proh., 2,609; Thomas, Soc., 1,613.

1948, Truman, Dem., 351,902; Dewey, Rep., 423,039; Watson, Proh., 6,468; Wallace, Prog., 4,603; Thomas, Soc., 2,807.

1952, Eisenhower, Rep., 616,302; Stevenson, Dem., 273,296; Hamblen, Proh., 6,038; Hoopes, Soc., 530.

1956, Eisenhower, Rep., 566,878; Stevenson. Dem., 296,317; Holtwick, Proh., 3,048.

1960, Kennedy, Dem., 363,213; Nixon, Rep., 561,474; Decker, Proh., 4,138.

1964, Johnson, Dem., 464,028; Goldwater, Rep., 386,579; Munn, Proh., 5,393; Hass, Soc. Labor, 1,901.

1968, Nixon, Rep., 478,674; Humphrey, Dem., 302,996; Wallace, 3d, 88,921; Munn, Proh., 2,192.

1972, Nixon, Rep., 619,812; McGovern, Dem., 270,287; Schmitz, Cons., 21,808; Munn, Proh., 4,188.

1976, Carter, Dem., 430,421; Ford, Rep., 502,752; McCarthy, Ind., 13,185; Anderson, Amer., 4,724; MacBride, Libertarian, 3,242; Maddox, Cons., 2,118; Bubar, Proh., 1,403.

1980, Reagan, Rep., 566,812; Carter, Dem., 326,150; Anderson, Ind., 68,231; Clark, Libertarian, 14,470; Shelton, American, 1,555; Hall, Com., 967; Bubar, Statesman, 821; Rarick, Conservative, 789.

1984, Reagan, Rep., 674,646; Mondale, Dem., 332,471; Bergland, Libertarian, 3,585.

1988, Bush, Rep., 554,049; Dukakis, Dem., 422,636; Paul, Ind., 12,553; Fulani, Ind., 3,806.

1992, Bush, Rep., 449,951; Clinton, Dem., 390,434; Perot, Ind., 312,358; Marrou, Libertarian, 4,314.

## Kentucky

| | 1992 | | | 1988 | |
|---|---|---|---|---|---|
| County | Clinton (D) | Bush (R) | Perot (I) | Dukakis (D) | Bush (R) |
| Adair | 2,044 | 3,740 | 617 | 1,723 | 4,346 |
| Allen | 2,040 | 2,747 | 606 | 1,573 | 3,342 |
| Anderson | 2,491 | 2,731 | 1,219 | 2,176 | 3,225 |
| Ballard | 2,268 | 1,108 | 500 | 2,162 | 1,460 |
| Barren | 5,688 | 5,467 | 1,778 | 4,799 | 6,653 |
| Bath | 2,229 | 1,259 | 694 | 2,099 | 1,614 |
| Bell | 5,745 | 4,501 | 1,193 | 5,182 | 5,759 |
| Boone | 6,514 | 12,306 | 4,676 | 5,382 | 12,667 |
| Bourbon | 2,895 | 2,707 | 1,290 | 2,793 | 3,308 |
| Boyd | 10,496 | 7,387 | 3,195 | 9,552 | 9,379 |
| Boyle | 3,894 | 4,019 | 1,335 | 3,575 | 4,746 |
| Bracken | 1,259 | 1,162 | 500 | 1,176 | 1,630 |
| Breathitt | 3,496 | 1,303 | 515 | 3,387 | 2,149 |
| Breckinridge | 3,113 | 2,941 | 945 | 2,765 | 3,841 |
| Bullitt | 7,830 | 7,745 | 3,333 | 6,005 | 8,859 |
| Butler | 1,468 | 2,729 | 596 | 1,245 | 3,278 |
| Caldwell | 3,000 | 1,966 | 670 | 2,564 | 2,952 |
| Calloway | 6,181 | 4,654 | 1,853 | 5,287 | 6,225 |
| Campbell | 10,673 | 16,382 | 5,659 | 9,553 | 19,387 |
| Carlisle | 1,363 | 844 | 309 | 1,428 | 1,104 |
| Carroll | 2,119 | 1,046 | 566 | 1,913 | 1,702 |
| Carter | 4,224 | 3,305 | 989 | 4,570 | 4,325 |
| Casey | 1,409 | 3,317 | 542 | 1,216 | 3,857 |
| Christian | 6,709 | 7,737 | 1,789 | 5,704 | 9,250 |
| Clark | 4,892 | 4,625 | 1,955 | 4,252 | 5,329 |
| Clay | 2,012 | 4,747 | 648 | 1,709 | 4,156 |
| Clinton | 1,241 | 2,830 | 348 | 899 | 3,248 |
| Crittenden | 1,740 | 1,576 | 495 | 1,443 | 2,211 |
| Cumberland | 917 | 1,866 | 268 | 753 | 2,231 |
| Daviess | 16,592 | 14,936 | 5,112 | 14,815 | 17,356 |
| Edmonson | 1,653 | 2,486 | 438 | 1,243 | 2,555 |
| Elliott | 1,796 | 444 | 273 | 1,797 | 550 |
| Estill | 1,837 | 2,453 | 736 | 1,692 | 3,077 |
| Fayette | 38,306 | 41,908 | 14,215 | 32,554 | 48,065 |
| Fleming | 2,257 | 2,045 | 815 | 2,086 | 2,409 |
| Floyd | 13,351 | 3,540 | 1,723 | 12,327 | 5,296 |
| Franklin | 9,896 | 7,591 | 3,340 | 9,271 | 9,805 |
| Fulton | 1,813 | 1,073 | 306 | 1,531 | 1,474 |
| Gallatin | 1,171 | 699 | 445 | 1,060 | 881 |
| Garrard | 1,730 | 2,359 | 697 | 1,710 | 2,681 |
| Grant | 2,097 | 2,128 | 1,149 | 1,896 | 2,835 |
| Graves | 8,001 | 5,311 | 1,943 | 7,153 | 6,274 |
| Grayson | 2,909 | 4,533 | 993 | 2,575 | 5,186 |
| Green | 1,760 | 2,709 | 500 | 1,595 | 3,139 |
| Greenup | 7,214 | 4,975 | 2,188 | 6,956 | 6,559 |
| Hancock | 1,714 | 1,261 | 551 | 1,478 | 1,733 |
| Hardin | 9,417 | 12,299 | 4,026 | 7,262 | 13,240 |
| Harlan | 6,796 | 3,970 | 1,391 | 7,341 | 5,166 |
| Harrison | 2,795 | 2,148 | 1,225 | 2,748 | 2,983 |
| Hart | 2,852 | 2,401 | 579 | 2,519 | 2,927 |
| Henderson | 8,270 | 5,125 | 2,678 | 7,648 | 6,911 |
| Henry | 2,838 | 1,640 | 720 | 2,544 | 2,286 |
| Hickman | 1,296 | 861 | 294 | 1,158 | 1,142 |
| Hopkins | 8,881 | 6,032 | 2,565 | 7,453 | 7,979 |
| Jackson | 776 | 3,398 | 341 | 678 | 3,926 |
| Jefferson | 152,728 | 116,566 | 39,822 | 127,936 | 139,711 |
| Jessamine | 3,764 | 6,474 | 2,059 | 2,955 | 7,057 |
| Johnson | 3,669 | 3,614 | 1,118 | 3,538 | 4,619 |
| Kenton | 16,344 | 27,261 | 9,336 | 14,838 | 30,738 |
| Knott | 5,500 | 1,243 | 560 | 5,185 | 1,691 |
| Knox | 3,787 | 5,011 | 972 | 2,919 | 4,903 |
| Larue | 2,190 | 2,154 | 582 | 1,822 | 2,590 |
| Laurel | 4,560 | 8,583 | 1,859 | 3,620 | 9,296 |

| County | Clinton (D) | Bush (R) | Perot (I) | Dukakis (D) | Bush (R) |
|---|---|---|---|---|---|
| Lawrence | 2,400 | 2,084 | 557 | 2,198 | 2,294 |
| Lee | 1,170 | 1,617 | 356 | 984 | 1,588 |
| Leslie | 1,591 | 2,879 | 450 | 1,105 | 3,280 |
| Letcher | 5,817 | 3,011 | 1,206 | 4,697 | 3,601 |
| Lewis | 1,713 | 2,493 | 673 | 1,568 | 3,108 |
| Lincoln | 2,532 | 2,624 | 762 | 2,677 | 3,530 |
| Livingston | 2,386 | 1,339 | 578 | 2,052 | 1,834 |
| Logan | 4,064 | 3,710 | 1,043 | 3,379 | 4,295 |
| Lyon | 1,583 | 820 | 293 | 1,337 | 1,077 |
| McCracken | 13,341 | 10,657 | 3,077 | 12,208 | 12,160 |
| McCreary | 1,934 | 3,588 | 624 | 1,644 | 3,477 |
| McLean | 2,223 | 1,355 | 529 | 2,269 | 1,829 |
| Madison | 8,005 | 8,719 | 3,038 | 6,672 | 9,958 |
| Magoffin | 3,261 | 1,992 | 440 | 2,895 | 2,158 |
| Marion | 3,403 | 2,091 | 805 | 3,152 | 2,500 |
| Marshall | 6,576 | 4,368 | 1,773 | 5,888 | 5,256 |
| Martin | 1,715 | 1,961 | 393 | 1,581 | 2,587 |
| Mason | 2,657 | 2,432 | 916 | 2,721 | 3,158 |
| Meade | 3,387 | 2,641 | 1,298 | 3,079 | 3,441 |
| Menifee | 1,311 | 557 | 254 | 1,096 | 670 |
| Mercer | 3,010 | 3,211 | 1,298 | 2,832 | 3,904 |
| Metcalfe | 1,703 | 1,683 | 409 | 1,705 | 2,179 |
| Monroe | 1,515 | 3,776 | 480 | 1,025 | 4,214 |
| Montgomery | 3,686 | 2,590 | 1,308 | 3,082 | 3,435 |
| Morgan | 2,655 | 1,239 | 498 | 2,329 | 1,452 |
| Muhlenberg | 7,901 | 3,551 | 1,624 | 6,912 | 5,369 |
| Nelson | 5,437 | 4,495 | 1,638 | 4,788 | 5,283 |
| Nicholas | 1,341 | 894 | 513 | 1,242 | 1,271 |
| Ohio | 4,022 | 3,385 | 1,423 | 3,612 | 4,910 |
| Oldham | 5,457 | 8,263 | 2,855 | 4,025 | 8,716 |
| Owen | 1,830 | 1,108 | 613 | 1,823 | 1,468 |
| Owsley | 678 | 1,437 | 209 | 345 | 1,266 |
| Pendleton | 1,740 | 1,810 | 1,086 | 1,576 | 2,487 |
| Perry | 6,619 | 4,128 | 1,308 | 5,557 | 5,154 |
| Pike | 17,358 | 8,212 | 2,444 | 16,339 | 9,976 |
| Powell | 2,323 | 1,809 | 874 | 2,113 | 2,128 |
| Pulaski | 5,465 | 11,423 | 2,449 | 4,788 | 13,482 |
| Robertson | 439 | 329 | 170 | 515 | 511 |
| Rockcastle | 1,144 | 3,287 | 446 | 1,041 | 3,880 |
| Rowan | 3,558 | 2,469 | 1,212 | 2,968 | 3,093 |
| Russell | 1,950 | 4,641 | 673 | 1,455 | 4,292 |
| Scott | 3,639 | 3,810 | 1,800 | 3,380 | 4,482 |
| Shelby | 4,398 | 4,550 | 1,451 | 3,834 | 4,998 |
| Simpson | 2,834 | 2,280 | 708 | 2,138 | 2,699 |
| Spencer | 1,383 | 1,305 | 466 | 1,121 | 1,368 |
| Taylor | 3,518 | 4,319 | 1,044 | 2,879 | 5,362 |
| Todd | 1,858 | 1,691 | 612 | 1,632 | 2,282 |
| Trigg | 2,438 | 1,820 | 573 | 1,991 | 2,427 |
| Trimble | 1,413 | 789 | 413 | 1,342 | 1,083 |
| Union | 3,325 | 1,605 | 794 | 3,316 | 2,292 |
| Warren | 11,529 | 14,748 | 3,533 | 9,684 | 16,703 |
| Washington | 2,008 | 2,098 | 542 | 1,950 | 2,445 |
| Wayne | 2,516 | 3,412 | 560 | 2,057 | 3,672 |
| Webster | 3,380 | 1,408 | 854 | 3,019 | 2,159 |
| Whitley | 4,600 | 5,998 | 1,533 | 3,794 | 7,337 |
| Wolfe | 1,674 | 697 | 297 | 1,516 | 916 |
| Woodford | 3,161 | 3,992 | 1,535 | 2,653 | 4,512 |
| Totals | 665,104 | 617,178 | 203,944 | 580,368 | 734,281 |

### Kentucky Vote Since 1944

1944, Roosevelt, Dem., 472,589; Dewey, Rep., 392,448; Watson, Proh., 2,023; Thomas, Soc., 535; Teichert, Soc. Labor, 326.

1948, Truman, Dem., 466,756; Dewey, Rep., 341,210; Thurmond, States' Rights, 10,411; Wallace, Prog., 1,567; Thomas, Soc., 1,284; Watson, Proh., 1,245; Teichert, Soc. Labor, 185.

1952, Eisenhower, Rep., 495,029; Stevenson, Dem., 495,729; Hamblen, Proh., 1,161; Hass, Soc. Labor, 893; Hallinan, Proh., 336.

1956, Eisenhower, Rep., 572,192; Stevenson, Dem., 476,453; Byrd, States' Rights, 2,657; Holtwick, Proh., 2,145; Hass, Soc. Labor, 358.

1960, Kennedy, Dem., 521,855; Nixon, Rep., 602,607.

1964, Johnson, Dem., 669,659; Goldwater, Rep., 372,977; John Kasper, Nat'l. States Rights, 3,469.

1968, Nixon, Rep., 462,411; Humphrey, Dem., 397,547; Wallace, 3d p., 193,098; Halstead, Soc. Worker, 2,843.

1972, Nixon, Rep., 676,446; McGovern, Dem., 371,159; Schmitz, Amer., 17,627; Jenness, Soc. Workers, 685; Hall, Com., 464; Spock, Peoples, 1,118.

1976, Carter, Dem., 615,717; Ford, Rep., 531,852; Anderson, Amer., 8,308; McCarthy, Ind., 6,837; Maddox, Amer. Ind., 2,328; MacBride, Libertarian, 814.

1980, Reagan, Rep., 635,274; Carter, Dem., 616,417; Anderson, Ind., 31,127; Clark, Libertarian, 5,531; McCormack, Respect For Life, 4,233; Commoner, Citizens, 1,304; Pulley, Socialist, 393; Hall, Com., 348.

1984, Reagan, Rep. 815,345; Mondale, Dem., 536,756.

1988, Bush, Rep., 734,281; Dukakis, Dem., 580,368; Duke, Pop., 4,494; Paul, Lib., 2,118.

1992, Clinton. Dem., 665,104; Bush, Rep., 617,178; Perot, Ind., 203,944; Marrou, Libertarian, 4,513.

## Louisiana

| | 1992 | | | 1988 | |
| Parish | Clinton (D) | Bush (R) | Perot (I) | Dukakis (D) | Bush (R) |
|---|---|---|---|---|---|
| Acadia | 12,276 | 9,017 | 3,145 | 11,510 | 11,319 |
| Allen | 5,626 | 3,069 | 1,245 | 5,204 | 3,674 |
| Ascension | 13,036 | 10,275 | 4,295 | 12,147 | 10,726 |
| Assumption | 5,639 | 2,928 | 1,358 | 5,610 | 4,017 |
| Avoyelles | 8,696 | 4,851 | 2,139 | 7,353 | 7,659 |
| Beauregard | 5,037 | 5,119 | 2,103 | 4,704 | 6,466 |
| Bienville | 3,899 | 2,412 | 832 | 3,705 | 3,680 |
| Bossier | 11,313 | 15,628 | 4,863 | 9,035 | 20,807 |
| Caddo | 47,733 | 42,665 | 11,830 | 39,204 | 54,498 |
| Calcasieu | 33,570 | 24,847 | 10,980 | 33,932 | 29,649 |
| Caldwell | 2,061 | 1,752 | 653 | 1,423 | 2,997 |
| Cameron | 1,985 | 1,329 | 995 | 2,257 | 1,775 |
| Catahoula | 2,570 | 1,976 | 773 | 1,916 | 2,862 |
| Claiborne | 3,263 | 2,599 | 926 | 3,158 | 3,756 |
| Concordia | 4,283 | 3,223 | 1,317 | 3,461 | 5,037 |
| DeSoto | 5,671 | 3,643 | 1,358 | 5,366 | 5,022 |
| E. Baton Rouge | 68,622 | 81,072 | 16,102 | 59,270 | 86,791 |
| East Carroll | 1,835 | 1,142 | 283 | 1,809 | 1,536 |
| East Feliciana | 4,093 | 2,813 | 932 | 3,659 | 3,527 |
| Evangeline | 8,564 | 5,147 | 2,124 | 7,693 | 7,437 |
| Franklin | 4,127 | 3,889 | 1,311 | 3,043 | 5,520 |
| Grant | 3,122 | 3,214 | 1,174 | 2,628 | 4,402 |
| Iberia | 13,040 | 11,905 | 4,337 | 12,166 | 15,438 |
| Iberville | 8,218 | 5,211 | 1,543 | 8,678 | 5,855 |
| Jackson | 3,370 | 3,072 | 882 | 2,842 | 4,251 |
| Jefferson | 64,302 | 100,493 | 21,278 | 53,035 | 110,942 |
| Jefferson Davis | 7,022 | 4,513 | 2,221 | 6,799 | 5,851 |
| Lafayette | 28,583 | 32,406 | 9,124 | 24,133 | 36,648 |
| Lafourche | 16,182 | 12,744 | 5,077 | 15,013 | 16,152 |
| LaSalle | 2,389 | 3,068 | 993 | 1,622 | 4,559 |
| Lincoln | 7,205 | 7,220 | 1,751 | 5,427 | 8,853 |
| Livingston | 11,499 | 14,808 | 4,971 | 9,659 | 15,779 |
| Madison | 2,773 | 1,702 | 469 | 2,416 | 2,334 |
| Morehouse | 6,013 | 5,364 | 1,727 | 4,496 | 7,335 |
| Natchitoches | 6,974 | 5,694 | 1,606 | 6,151 | 7,224 |
| Orleans | 133,261 | 52,019 | 10,889 | 116,851 | 64,763 |
| Ouachita | 20,835 | 27,600 | 6,612 | 15,429 | 33,858 |
| Plaquemines | 4,467 | 5,018 | 1,729 | 3,997 | 6,084 |
| Pointe Coupee | 6,512 | 3,563 | 1,157 | 6,308 | 4,333 |
| Rapides | 20,873 | 22,783 | 6,599 | 17,928 | 29,977 |
| Red River | 2,360 | 1,649 | 566 | 2,254 | 2,266 |
| Richland | 3,706 | 3,808 | 1,054 | 2,833 | 5,226 |
| Sabine | 4,173 | 3,586 | 1,219 | 3,532 | 4,767 |
| St. Bernard | 12,305 | 16,131 | 4,308 | 11,406 | 19,609 |
| St. Charles | 8,810 | 9,158 | 2,593 | 7,973 | 9,685 |
| St. Helena | 3,416 | 1,515 | 589 | 3,013 | 2,006 |
| St. James | 6,609 | 3,339 | 993 | 6,707 | 3,799 |
| St. John The Baptist | 8,977 | 6,730 | 1,922 | 8,366 | 7,464 |
| St. Landry | 20,383 | 11,882 | 4,266 | 19,091 | 15,790 |
| St. Martin | 11,252 | 5,909 | 2,573 | 10,148 | 7,541 |
| St. Mary | 10,648 | 8,792 | 3,257 | 10,364 | 11,540 |
| St. Tammany | 19,735 | 37,839 | 9,005 | 15,638 | 38,334 |
| Tangipahoa | 15,194 | 14,128 | 4,612 | 13,527 | 16,669 |
| Tensas | 1,666 | 1,153 | 353 | 1,556 | 1,645 |
| Terrebonne | 13,325 | 14,662 | 5,505 | 12,686 | 18,745 |
| Union | 4,005 | 4,434 | 1,209 | 3,210 | 5,900 |
| Vermilion | 12,324 | 7,062 | 3,127 | 12,180 | 9,224 |
| Vernon | 6,005 | 5,912 | 2,313 | 4,998 | 7,453 |
| Washington | 9,095 | 7,227 | 2,303 | 8,369 | 9,374 |
| Webster | 8,380 | 6,640 | 2,629 | 7,434 | 10,204 |
| W. Baton Rouge | 5,131 | 3,522 | 1,249 | 4,686 | 3,972 |
| West Carroll | 2,068 | 2,082 | 771 | 1,607 | 3,077 |
| West Feliciana | 2,328 | 1,501 | 516 | 2,146 | 1,854 |
| Winn | 3,537 | 2,932 | 843 | 2,699 | 4,165 |
| Totals | 815,971 | 733,386 | 211,478 | 717,460 | 883,702 |

### Louisiana Vote Since 1944

1944, Roosevelt, Dem., 281,564; Dewey, Rep., 67,750.

1948, Thurmond, States' Rights, 204,290; Truman, Dem., 136,344; Dewey, Rep., 72,657; Wallace, Prog., 3,035.

1952, Eisenhower, Rep., 306,925, Stevenson, Dem., 345,027.

1956, Eisenhower, Rep., 329,047; Stevenson, Dem., 243,977; Andrews, States' Rights, 44,520.

1960, Kennedy, Dem., 407,339; Nixon, Rep., 230,890; States' Rights (unpledged) 169,572.

1964, Johnson, Dem., 387,068; Goldwater, Rep., 509,225.

1968, Nixon, Rep., 257,535; Humphrey, Dem., 309,615; Wallace, 3d party, 530,300.

1972, Nixon, Rep., 686,852; McGovern, Dem., 298,142; Schmitz, Amer., 52,099; Jenness, Soc. Workers, 14,398.

1976, Carter, Dem., 661,365; Ford, Rep., 587,446; Maddox, Amer., 10,058; Hall, Com., 7,417; McCarthy, Ind., 6,588; MacBride, Libertarian, 3,325.

1980, Reagan, Rep., 792,853; Carter, Dem., 708,453; Anderson, Ind., 26,345; Rarick, Amer. Ind., 10,333; Clark, Libertarian, 8,240; Commoner, Citizens, 1,584; DeBerry, Soc. Work., 783.

1984, Reagan, Rep., 1,037,299; Mondale, Dem., 651,586; Bergland, Libertarian, 1,876.

1988, Bush, Rep., 883,702; Dukakis, Dem., 717,460; Duke, Pop., 18,612; Paul, Lib., 4,115.

1992, Clinton, Dem., 815,971; Bush, Rep., 733,386; Perot, Ind., 211,478; Gritz, Populist/America First, 18,545; Marrou, Libertarian, 3,155; Daniels, Ind., 1,663; Phillips, U.S. Taxpayers, 1,552; Fulani, New Alliance, 1,434; LaRouche, Ind., 1,136.

## Maine

| | 1992 | | | 1988 | |
| City | Clinton (D) | Bush (R) | Perot (I) | Dukakis (D) | Bush (R) |
|---|---|---|---|---|---|
| Auburn | 5,025 | 3,653 | 3,964 | 4,629 | 5,947 |
| Augusta | 4,657 | 3,003 | 3,002 | 4,576 | 5,182 |
| Bangor | 6,826 | 5,185 | 4,689 | 6,534 | 7,194 |
| Bath | 1,988 | 1,630 | 1,458 | 1,838 | 2,543 |
| Biddeford | 4,945 | 2,533 | 2,717 | 5,017 | 4,375 |
| Brewer | 1,788 | 1,907 | 1,625 | 1,784 | 2,908 |
| Gardiner | 1,391 | 1,054 | 1,115 | 1,395 | 1,609 |
| Lewiston | 9,265 | 4,372 | 6,180 | 9,225 | 7,265 |
| Old Town | 2,272 | 1,173 | 1,302 | 2,220 | 1,640 |
| Portland | 19,510 | 8,660 | 6,910 | 18,234 | 11,676 |
| Rockland | 1,192 | 1,081 | 1,059 | 1,198 | 1,850 |
| Saco | 4,000 | 2,769 | 2,303 | 3,169 | 3,852 |
| Sanford | 3,854 | 3,030 | 3,215 | 3,456 | 4,541 |
| South Portland | 5,933 | 3,999 | 2,734 | 5,820 | 5,744 |
| Waterville | 3,868 | 1,832 | 2,257 | 4,031 | 3,158 |
| Westbrook | 3,665 | 2,904 | 2,512 | 3,648 | 4,086 |
| Totals | 263,420 | 206,504 | 206,820 | 243,569 | 307,131 |

### Maine Vote Since 1944

1944, Roosevelt, Dem., 140,631; Dewey, Rep., 155,434; Teichert, Soc. Labor, 335.

1948, Truman, Dem., 111,916; Dewey, Rep., 150,234; Wallace, Prog., 1,884; Thomas, Soc., 547; Teichert, Soc. Labor, 206.

1952, Eisenhower, Rep., 232,353; Stevenson, Dem., 118,806; Hallinan, Prog., 332; Hass, Soc. Labor, 156; Hoopes, Soc., 138; scattered, 1.

1956, Eisenhower, Rep., 249,238; Stevenson, Dem., 102,468.

1960, Kennedy, Dem., 181,159; Nixon, Rep., 240,608.

1964, Johnson, Dem., 262,264; Goldwater, Rep., 118,701.

1968, Nixon, Rep., 169,254; Humphrey, Dem., 217,312; Wallace, 3d party, 6,370.

1972, Nixon, Rep., 256,458; McGovern, Dem., 160,584; scattered, 229.

1976, Carter, Dem., 232,279; Ford, Rep., 236,320; McCarthy, Ind., 10,874; Bubar, Proh., 3,495.

1980, Reagan, Rep., 238,522; Carter, Dem., 220,974; Anderson, Ind., 53,327; Clark, Libertarian, 5,119; Commoner, Citizens, 4,394; Hall, Com., 591; write-ins, 84.

1984, Reagan, Rep., 336,500; Mondale, Dem., 214,515.

1988, Bush, Rep., 307,131; Dukakis, Dem., 243,569; Paul, Lib., 2,700; Fulani, New Alliance, 1,405.

1992, Clinton, Dem., 263,420; Perot, Ind., 206,820; Bush, Rep., 206,504; Marrou, Libertarian, 1,681.

## Maryland

| | 1992 | | | 1988 | |
| County | Clinton (D) | Bush (R) | Perot (I) | Dukakis (D) | Bush (R) |
|---|---|---|---|---|---|
| Allegany | 11,501 | 13,862 | 5,081 | 11,844 | 17,462 |
| Anne Arundel | 68,629 | 81,467 | 35,191 | 55,440 | 98,540 |
| Baltimore | 143,498 | 126,728 | 51,757 | 121,570 | 163,881 |
| Calvert | 8,619 | 10,026 | 4,499 | 6,376 | 10,956 |
| Caroline | 2,822 | 3,856 | 1,729 | 2,440 | 4,661 |
| Carroll | 15,447 | 28,405 | 10,965 | 12,368 | 31,224 |
| Cecil | 10,232 | 10,784 | 6,115 | 7,807 | 13,224 |
| Charles | 14,498 | 17,293 | 6,501 | 11,823 | 20,828 |
| Dorchester | 3,933 | 4,934 | 2,010 | 3,709 | 6,343 |
| Frederick | 21,848 | 31,290 | 11,373 | 17,061 | 32,575 |
| Garrett | 2,856 | 5,714 | 1,987 | 2,557 | 6,665 |
| Harford | 27,164 | 36,350 | 17,002 | 19,803 | 38,493 |
| Howard | 44,763 | 38,594 | 16,182 | 34,007 | 44,153 |
| Kent | 3,093 | 3,094 | 1,411 | 2,925 | 3,761 |
| Montgomery | 199,757 | 119,705 | 41,971 | 165,187 | 154,741 |
| Prince George's | 168,691 | 62,955 | 23,355 | 133,816 | 86,545 |
| Queen Anne's | 4,668 | 6,829 | 2,958 | 3,857 | 7,803 |
| St. Mary's | 8,931 | 11,485 | 4,550 | 7,434 | 12,767 |
| Somerset | 3,210 | 3,450 | 1,230 | 2,911 | 4,222 |
| Talbot | 4,642 | 6,774 | 2,233 | 3,948 | 8,170 |
| Washington | 16,495 | 21,977 | 7,537 | 14,408 | 25,912 |
| Wicomico | 11,481 | 13,560 | 5,140 | 9,413 | 16,272 |
| Worcester | 6,040 | 7,237 | 3,256 | 4,787 | 8,430 |

| City | | | | | |
|---|---|---|---|---|---|
| Baltimore | 185,753 | 40,725 | 17,381 | 170,813 | 59,089 |
| Totals | 988,571 | 707,094 | 281,414 | 826,304 | 876,167 |

## Maryland Vote Since 1944

1944, Roosevelt, Dem., 315,490; Dewey, Rep., 292,949.

1948, Truman, Dem., 286,521; Dewey, Rep., 294,814; Wallace, Prog., 9,983; Thomas, Soc., 2,941; Thurmond, States' Rights, 2,476; Wright, write-in, 2,294.

1952, Eisenhower, Rep., 499,424; Stevenson, Dem., 395,337; Hallinan, Prog., 7,313.

1956, Eisenhower, Rep., 559,738; Stevenson, Dem., 372,613.

1960, Kennedy, Dem., 565,800; Nixon, Rep., 489,538.

1964, Johnson, Dem., 730,912; Goldwater, Rep., 385,495; write-in, 50.

1968, Nixon, Rep., 517,995; Humphrey, Dem., 538,310; Wallace, 3d party, 178,734.

1972, Nixon, Rep., 829,305; McGovern, Dem., 505,781; Schmitz, Amer., 18,726.

1976, Carter, Dem., 759,612; Ford, Rep., 672,661.

1980, Reagan, Rep., 680,606; Carter, Dem., 726,161; Anderson, Ind., 119,537; Clark, Libertarian, 14,192.

1984, Reagan, Rep., 879,918; Mondale, Dem., 787,935; Bergland, Libertarian, 5,721.

1988, Bush, Rep., 876,167; Dukakis, Dem., 826,304; Paul, Lib., 6,748; Fulani, New Alliance, 5,115.

1992, Clinton, Dem., 988,571; Bush, Rep., 707,094; Perot, Ind., 281,414; Marrou, Libertarian, 4,715; Fulani, New Alliance, 2,786.

## Massachusetts

| | 1992 | | | 1988 | |
|---|---|---|---|---|---|
| City | Clinton (D) | Bush (R) | Perot (I) | Dukakis (D) | Bush (R) |
| Boston | 114,260 | 41,868 | 25,189 | 122,349 | 62,202 |
| Brockton | 13,209 | 8,863 | 7,579 | 14,776 | 16,056 |
| Cambridge | 30,737 | 5,847 | 4,106 | 32,027 | 8,770 |
| Fall River | 18,652 | 5,456 | 6,922 | 20,184 | 8,394 |
| Framingham | 15,165 | 8,114 | 6,089 | 15,826 | 12,745 |
| Lawrence | 7,698 | 5,079 | 3,245 | 9,255 | 8,265 |
| Lowell | 14,492 | 8,467 | 8,893 | 16,391 | 13,998 |
| Lynn | 15,275 | 7,350 | 7,665 | 18,540 | 12,182 |
| New Bedford | 20,880 | 5,255 | 6,965 | 22,609 | 9,901 |
| Newton | 29,136 | 9,623 | 5,685 | 29,039 | 13,892 |
| Quincy | 18,891 | 12,306 | 9,068 | 20,911 | 18,403 |
| Somerville | 19,792 | 5,883 | 4,416 | 21,612 | 8,931 |
| Springfield | 27,302 | 12,200 | 10,361 | 30,113 | 16,244 |
| Worcester | 32,326 | 17,228 | 10,488 | 34,369 | 24,355 |
| Totals | 1,318,639 | 805,039 | 630,731 | 1,401,415 | 1,194,635 |

## Massachusetts Vote Since 1944

1944, Roosevelt, Dem., 1,035,296; Dewey, Rep., 921,350; Teichert, Soc. Labor, 2,780; Watson, Proh., 973.

1948, Truman, Dem., 1,151,788; Dewey, Rep., 909,370; Wallace, Prog., 38,157; Teichert, Soc. Labor, 5,535; Watson, Proh., 1,663.

1952, Eisenhower, Rep., 1,292,325; Stevenson, Dem., 1,083,525; Hallinan, Prog., 4,636; Hass, Soc. Labor, 1,957; Hamblen, Proh., 886; scattered, 69; blanks, 41,150.

1956, Eisenhower, Rep., 1,393,197; Stevenson, Dem., 948,190; Hass, Soc. Labor, 5,573; Holtwick, Proh., 1,205; others, 341.

1960, Kennedy, Dem., 1,487,174; Nixon, Rep., 976,750; Hass, Soc. Labor, 3,892; Decker, Proh., 1,633; others, 31; blank and void, 26,024.

1964, Johnson, Dem., 1,786,422; Goldwater, Rep., 549,727; Hass, Soc. Labor, 4,755; Munn, Proh., 3,735; scattered, 159; blank, 48,104.

1968, Nixon, Rep., 766,844; Humphrey, Dem., 1,469,218; Wallace, 3d party, 87,088; Blomen, Soc. Labor, 6,180; Munn, Proh., 2,369; scattered, 53; blanks, 25,394.

1972, Nixon, Rep., 1,112,078; McGovern, Dem., 1,332,540; Jenness, Soc. Workers, 10,600; Fisher, Soc. Labor, 129; Schmitz, Amer., 2,877; Spock, Peoples, 101; Hall, Com., 46; Hospers, Libertarian, 43; scattered, 342.

1976, Carter, Dem., 1,429,475; Ford, Rep., 1,030,276; McCarthy, Ind., 65,637; Camejo, Soc. Workers, 8,138; Anderson, Amer., 7,555; La Rouche, U.S. Labor, 4,922; MacBride, Libertarian, 135.

1980, Reagan, Rep., 1,057,631; Carter, Dem., 1,053,802; Anderson, Ind., 382,539; Clark, Libertarian, 22,038; DeBerry, Soc. Workers, 3,735; Commoner, Citizens, 2,056;

McReynolds, Socialist, 62; Bubar, Statesman, 34; Griswold, Workers World, 19; scattered, 2,382.

1984, Reagan, Rep., 1,310,936; Mondale, Dem., 1,239,606.

1988, Bush, Rep., 1,194,635; Dukakis, Dem., 1,401,415; Paul, Lib., 24,251; Fulani, New Alliance, 9,561.

1992, Clinton, Dem., 1,318,639; Bush, Rep., 805,039; Perot, Ind., 630,731; Marrou, Libertarian, 9,021; Fulani, New Alliance, 3,172; Phillips, U.S. Taxpayers, 2,218; Hagelin, Natural Law, 1,812; LaRouche, Ind., 1,027.

## Michigan

| | 1992 | | | 1988 | |
|---|---|---|---|---|---|
| County | Clinton (D) | Bush (R) | Perot (I) | Dukakis (D) | Bush (R) |
| Alcona | 2,383 | 2,247 | 1,117 | 1,918 | 2,966 |
| Alger | 2,144 | 1,471 | 941 | 2,210 | 1,830 |
| Allegan | 12,823 | 19,077 | 8,742 | 10,785 | 22,163 |
| Alpena | 6,894 | 4,878 | 3,236 | 6,341 | 6,664 |
| Antrim | 3,431 | 3,984 | 2,528 | 3,159 | 5,231 |
| Arenac | 3,244 | 2,330 | 1,608 | 3,211 | 3,064 |
| Baraga | 1,695 | 1,160 | 754 | 1,753 | 1,630 |
| Barry | 6,652 | 9,489 | 6,303 | 7,983 | 12,546 |
| Bay | 26,492 | 16,383 | 11,258 | 28,225 | 20,710 |
| Benzie | 2,715 | 2,438 | 1,657 | 2,437 | 3,240 |
| Berrien | 25,840 | 29,252 | 14,056 | 21,948 | 37,799 |
| Branch | 5,850 | 5,976 | 4,683 | 5,231 | 9,225 |
| Calhoun | 25,542 | 19,791 | 13,058 | 22,717 | 26,771 |
| Cass | 8,047 | 7,391 | 4,756 | 7,444 | 10,229 |
| Charlevoix | 4,063 | 4,017 | 3,360 | 3,875 | 5,802 |
| Cheboygan | 4,459 | 3,864 | 2,495 | 3,943 | 5,395 |
| Chippewa | 5,434 | 5,462 | 2,706 | 5,222 | 6,786 |
| Clare | 5,346 | 3,916 | 2,812 | 4,710 | 5,661 |
| Clinton | 10,116 | 12,216 | 7,877 | 9,225 | 15,497 |
| Crawford | 2,252 | 2,193 | 1,442 | 1,825 | 3,097 |
| Delta | 8,387 | 6,027 | 3,485 | 8,891 | 7,114 |
| Dickinson | 5,689 | 4,273 | 3,022 | 6,129 | 6,158 |
| Eaton | 16,752 | 18,669 | 12,208 | 15,322 | 24,193 |
| Emmet | 4,245 | 5,312 | 3,576 | 4,170 | 7,105 |
| Genesee | 105,156 | 47,834 | 46,259 | 104,880 | 70,922 |
| Gladwin | 4,457 | 3,616 | 2,649 | 4,164 | 4,746 |
| Gogebic | 4,792 | 2,838 | 1,543 | 5,151 | 3,509 |
| Grand Traverse | 11,148 | 13,629 | 9,495 | 10,098 | 17,191 |
| Gratiot | 5,678 | 6,280 | 3,866 | 5,719 | 8,447 |
| Hillsdale | 5,244 | 7,579 | 4,968 | 4,763 | 10,571 |
| Houghton | 6,558 | 5,575 | 2,945 | 6,510 | 7,098 |
| Huron | 6,023 | 6,491 | 4,064 | 5,714 | 9,419 |
| Ingham | 61,596 | 43,926 | 27,683 | 55,984 | 58,363 |
| Ionia | 8,370 | 9,135 | 6,211 | 8,160 | 12,028 |
| Iosco | 5,369 | 4,912 | 3,131 | 4,929 | 7,234 |
| Iron | 3,648 | 1,971 | 1,344 | 3,774 | 2,866 |
| Isabella | 8,784 | 7,706 | 5,434 | 7,960 | 10,362 |
| Jackson | 23,686 | 25,424 | 15,194 | 21,865 | 33,885 |
| Kalamazoo | 43,568 | 38,035 | 21,666 | 39,457 | 50,205 |
| Kalkaska | 2,297 | 2,173 | 1,915 | 2,092 | 3,369 |
| Kent | 82,305 | 115,285 | 43,707 | 73,467 | 131,910 |
| Keweenaw | 582 | 378 | 212 | 631 | 536 |
| Lake | 2,351 | 1,194 | 981 | 1,958 | 1,713 |
| Lapeer | 11,982 | 12,326 | 10,541 | 10,736 | 16,670 |
| Leelanau | 3,445 | 3,993 | 2,685 | 3,331 | 5,215 |
| Lenawee | 15,399 | 14,297 | 9,517 | 13,690 | 19,115 |
| Livingston | 17,851 | 27,539 | 15,971 | 13,749 | 31,331 |
| Luce | 972 | 958 | 660 | 864 | 1,528 |
| Mackinac | 2,293 | 2,278 | 1,379 | 2,093 | 3,127 |
| Macomb | 130,732 | 147,795 | 67,954 | 112,856 | 175,632 |
| Manistee | 5,193 | 3,491 | 2,923 | 4,765 | 5,368 |
| Marquette | 16,038 | 9,665 | 5,768 | 15,418 | 11,704 |
| Mason | 4,829 | 5,102 | 3,096 | 4,531 | 6,800 |
| Mecosta | 6,097 | 6,047 | 3,612 | 4,736 | 8,181 |
| Menominee | 4,559 | 3,995 | 2,487 | 4,918 | 5,440 |
| Midland | 13,382 | 16,149 | 8,945 | 13,452 | 19,994 |
| Missaukee | 1,893 | 2,829 | 1,306 | 1,621 | 3,566 |
| Monroe | 24,957 | 20,250 | 13,551 | 21,847 | 26,189 |
| Montcalm | 8,730 | 8,420 | 5,504 | 7,664 | 10,963 |
| Montmorency | 1,903 | 1,794 | 1,077 | 1,563 | 2,514 |
| Muskegon | 32,515 | 23,769 | 15,268 | 28,977 | 33,567 |
| Newaygo | 6,455 | 7,333 | 4,056 | 5,389 | 9,896 |
| Oakland | 214,733 | 242,160 | 94,911 | 174,745 | 283,359 |
| Oceana | 3,846 | 3,944 | 2,713 | 3,356 | 5,693 |
| Ogemaw | 4,016 | 2,936 | 2,122 | 4,012 | 4,091 |
| Ontonagon | 2,451 | 1,463 | 805 | 2,517 | 2,023 |
| Osceola | 3,529 | 3,606 | 2,199 | 2,860 | 5,218 |
| Oscoda | 1,471 | 1,583 | 755 | 1,170 | 1,972 |
| Otsego | 3,129 | 3,393 | 2,635 | 2,635 | 4,620 |
| Ottawa | 22,180 | 56,862 | 16,855 | 18,769 | 61,515 |
| Presque Isle | 3,308 | 2,398 | 1,612 | 3,025 | 3,614 |
| Roscommon | 5,243 | 4,170 | 2,551 | 4,394 | 5,866 |
| Saginaw | 43,819 | 32,103 | 20,523 | 45,616 | 42,401 |
| St. Clair | 23,385 | 24,508 | 18,523 | 20,909 | 32,336 |
| St. Joseph | 7,817 | 9,836 | 6,209 | 7,017 | 13,084 |
| Sanilac | 5,868 | 7,891 | 4,894 | 5,445 | 10,653 |
| Schoolcraft | 2,139 | 1,253 | 721 | 2,071 | 1,802 |
| Shiawassee | 12,629 | 10,930 | 8,632 | 13,056 | 15,506 |
| Tuscola | 9,138 | 8,636 | 6,765 | 9,060 | 12,093 |
| Van Buren | 12,466 | 10,357 | 7,255 | 10,648 | 14,522 |
| Washtenaw | 73,325 | 41,386 | 21,889 | 61,799 | 55,029 |
| Wayne | 508,464 | 227,002 | 102,074 | 450,222 | 291,996 |

| | | | | | |
|---|---|---|---|---|---|
| Wexford...... | 4,894 | 4,696 | 2,923 | 4,287 | 6,043 |
| Totals........ | 1,871,182 | 1,554,940 | 824,813 | 1,675,783 | 1,965,486 |

## Michigan Vote Since 1944

1944, Roosevelt, Dem., 1,106,899; Dewey, Rep., 1,084,423; Watson, Proh., 6,503; Thomas, Soc., 4,598; Smith, America First, 1,530; Teichert, Soc. Labor, 1,264.

1948, Truman, Dem., 1,003,448; Dewey, Rep., 1,038,595; Wallace, Prog., 46,515; Watson, Proh., 13,052; Thomas, Soc. 6,063; Teichert, Soc. Labor, 1,263; Dobbs, Soc. Workers, 672.

1952, Eisenhower, Rep., 1,551,529; Stevenson, Dem., 1,230,657; Hamblen, Proh., 10,331; Hallinan, Prog., 3,922; Hass, Soc. Labor, 1,495; Dobbs, Soc. Workers, 655; scattered, 3.

1956, Eisenhower, Rep., 1,713,647; Stevenson, Dem., 1,359,898; Holtwick, Proh., 6,923.

1960, Kennedy, Dem., 1,687,269; Nixon, Rep., 1,620,428; Dobbs, Soc. Workers, 4,347; Decker, Proh., 2,029; Daly, Tax Cut, 1,767; Hass, Soc. Labor, 1,718; Ind. American, 539.

1964, Johnson, Dem., 2,136,615; Goldwater, Rep., 1,060,152; DeBerry, Soc. Workers, 3,817; Hass, Soc. Labor, 1,704; Proh. (no candidate listed), 699, scattering, 145.

1968, Nixon, Rep., 1,370,665; Humphrey, Dem., 1,593,082; Wallace, 3d party, 331,968; Halstead, Soc. Worker, 4,099; Blomen, Soc. Labor, 1,762; Cleaver, New Politics, 4,585; Munn, Proh., 60; scattering, 29.

1972, Nixon, Rep., 1,961,721; McGovern, Dem., 1,459,435; Schmitz, Amer., 63,321; Fisher, Soc. Labor, 2,437; Jenness, Soc. Workers, 1,603; Hall, Com., 1,210.

1976, Carter, Dem., 1,696,714; Ford, Rep., 1,893,742; McCarthy, Ind., 47,905; MacBride, Libertarian, 5,406; Wright, People's, 3,504, Camejo, Soc. Workers, 1,804; LaRouche, U.S. Labor, 1,366; Levin, Soc. Labor, 1,148; scattering, 2,160.

1980, Reagan, Rep., 1,915,225; Carter, Dem., 1,661,532; Anderson, Ind., 275,223; Clark, Libertarian, 41,597; Commoner, Citizens, 11,930; Hall, Com., 3,262; Griswold, Workers World, 30; Greaves, American, 21; Bubar, Statesman, 9.

1984, Reagan, Rep., 2,251,571; Mondale, Dem., 1,529,638; Bergland, Libertarian, 10,055.

1988, Bush, Rep., 1,965,486; Dukakis, Dem., 1,675,783; Paul, Lib., 18,336; Fulani, Ind., 2,513.

1992, Clinton, Dem., 1,871,182; Bush, Rep., 1,554,940; Perot, Ind., 824,813; Marrou, Libertarian, 10,175; Phillips, U.S. Taxpayers, 8,263; Hagelin, Natural Law, 2,954.

## Minnesota

| | 1992 | | | 1988 | |
|---|---|---|---|---|---|
| County | Clinton (D) | Bush (R) | Perot (I) | Dukakis (D) | Bush (R) |
| Aitkin......... | 3,400 | 2,151 | 1,951 | 3,863 | 3,011 |
| Anoka........ | 54,621 | 39,458 | 35,140 | 57,953 | 46,853 |
| Becker....... | 4,958 | 5,430 | 3,238 | 5,787 | 6,738 |
| Beltrami...... | 7,210 | 5,204 | 3,473 | 7,566 | 6,652 |
| Benton....... | 5,156 | 5,053 | 4,048 | 5,861 | 6,060 |
| Big Stone.... | 1,610 | 1,052 | 740 | 2,026 | 1,469 |
| Blue Earth.... | 11,531 | 8,813 | 7,299 | 12,375 | 11,959 |
| Brown....... | 4,278 | 5,390 | 3,845 | 5,109 | 6,898 |
| Carlton...... | 7,736 | 3,922 | 3,005 | 8,790 | 4,626 |
| Carver....... | 8,349 | 10,201 | 7,942 | 8,439 | 12,560 |
| Cass......... | 4,901 | 4,276 | 2,939 | 5,127 | 5,895 |
| Chippewa..... | 2,929 | 2,143 | 1,505 | 3,238 | 3,190 |
| Chisago...... | 7,077 | 4,813 | 5,098 | 7,875 | 6,163 |
| Clay......... | 9,845 | 9,666 | 3,835 | 11,186 | 10,380 |
| Clearwater.... | 1,587 | 1,315 | 841 | 1,769 | 1,763 |
| Cook........ | 1,005 | 878 | 704 | 1,080 | 1,078 |
| Cottonwood... | 2,382 | 2,481 | 1,749 | 3,095 | 3,390 |
| Crow Wing.... | 8,896 | 9,112 | 6,367 | 9,674 | 11,017 |
| Dakota....... | 63,660 | 52,312 | 40,244 | 61,942 | 61,606 |
| Dodge....... | 2,620 | 3,049 | 2,231 | 2,925 | 3,848 |
| Douglas...... | 5,252 | 6,356 | 4,138 | 5,803 | 7,898 |
| Faribault..... | 3,339 | 3,439 | 2,322 | 3,879 | 4,846 |
| Fillmore...... | 3,977 | 3,583 | 3,011 | 4,114 | 5,004 |
| Freeborn..... | 7,759 | 5,089 | 4,878 | 8,836 | 7,226 |
| Goodhue..... | 7,916 | 7,321 | 5,790 | 9,438 | 9,455 |
| Grant........ | 1,561 | 1,201 | 885 | 1,950 | 1,693 |
| Hennepin..... | 278,648 | 179,581 | 123,659 | 292,909 | 240,209 |
| Houston...... | 3,744 | 3,853 | 2,697 | 3,936 | 4,777 |
| Hubbard..... | 3,362 | 3,227 | 1,949 | 3,306 | 4,365 |
| Isanti........ | 5,386 | 3,988 | 3,898 | 6,075 | 5,246 |
| Itasca....... | 9,621 | 5,952 | 5,147 | 10,517 | 8,358 |
| Jackson...... | 2,481 | 1,824 | 1,918 | 3,275 | 2,629 |
| Kanabec...... | 2,532 | 1,876 | 1,836 | 2,970 | 2,571 |

| | | | | | |
|---|---|---|---|---|---|
| Kandiyohi...... | 7,914 | 6,784 | 4,869 | 8,962 | 8,634 |
| Kittson....... | 1,307 | 1,098 | 558 | 1,650 | 1,381 |
| Koochiching.... | 3,474 | 1,954 | 1,993 | 3,867 | 2,842 |
| LacQuiParle.... | 2,342 | 1,435 | 1,163 | 2,805 | 2,116 |
| Lake........ | 3,415 | 1,465 | 1,437 | 3,887 | 1,838 |
| Lake O'Woods... | 794 | 762 | 629 | 798 | 984 |
| Le Sueur..... | 4,662 | 3,858 | 3,363 | 5,410 | 5,415 |
| Lincoln...... | 1,555 | 1,084 | 967 | 1,891 | 1,479 |
| Lyon........ | 4,481 | 4,591 | 3,180 | 5,657 | 5,969 |
| McLeod...... | 4,919 | 5,422 | 4,933 | 5,736 | 7,967 |
| Mahnomen.... | 1,035 | 854 | 483 | 1,277 | 1,051 |
| Marshall..... | 2,309 | 2,136 | 1,306 | 3,001 | 2,752 |
| Martin....... | 4,019 | 4,438 | 3,089 | 4,922 | 5,724 |
| Meeker...... | 3,861 | 3,497 | 3,120 | 4,544 | 4,999 |
| Mille Lacs.... | 3,648 | 2,814 | 2,615 | 4,327 | 3,862 |
| Morrison..... | 5,588 | 5,038 | 3,710 | 6,469 | 6,598 |
| Mower....... | 9,935 | 5,147 | 5,001 | 11,893 | 6,969 |
| Murray...... | 1,993 | 1,609 | 1,588 | 2,840 | 2,316 |
| Nicollet...... | 6,055 | 5,091 | 3,799 | 6,786 | 6,878 |
| Nobles....... | 3,756 | 3,548 | 2,586 | 4,953 | 4,348 |
| Norman...... | 1,784 | 1,541 | 776 | 2,149 | 1,789 |
| Olmsted...... | 19,039 | 23,404 | 13,806 | 19,423 | 27,683 |
| Otter Tail..... | 9,176 | 11,074 | 6,274 | 10,373 | 14,015 |
| Pennington.... | 2,578 | 2,155 | 1,598 | 3,105 | 2,920 |
| Pine........ | 4,929 | 2,841 | 2,952 | 5,540 | 3,857 |
| Pipestone..... | 1,773 | 1,953 | 1,429 | 2,382 | 2,760 |
| Polk........ | 5,850 | 5,817 | 3,176 | 7,523 | 7,032 |
| Pope........ | 2,619 | 1,886 | 1,390 | 3,074 | 2,627 |
| Ramsey...... | 130,932 | 68,206 | 50,757 | 143,767 | 88,736 |
| Red Lake..... | 1,020 | 691 | 472 | 1,229 | 918 |
| Redwood..... | 2,740 | 3,408 | 2,710 | 3,178 | 5,076 |
| Renville...... | 3,414 | 2,852 | 2,598 | 4,454 | 4,356 |
| Rice......... | 10,908 | 7,015 | 6,057 | 11,570 | 9,460 |
| Rock........ | 2,006 | 2,065 | 1,244 | 2,435 | 2,737 |
| Roseau...... | 2,346 | 2,785 | 2,099 | 2,630 | 3,500 |
| St. Louis..... | 61,813 | 24,579 | 21,714 | 70,344 | 31,799 |
| Scott........ | 11,225 | 10,936 | 9,881 | 11,405 | 13,050 |
| Sherburne.... | 7,843 | 7,339 | 6,534 | 7,959 | 8,360 |
| Sibley....... | 2,421 | 2,315 | 2,407 | 3,154 | 3,655 |
| Stearns...... | 21,451 | 22,502 | 14,834 | 23,798 | 27,529 |
| Steele....... | 5,152 | 5,964 | 4,542 | 5,496 | 7,981 |
| Stevens...... | 2,466 | 2,229 | 1,086 | 2,721 | 2,679 |
| Swift........ | 2,980 | 1,603 | 1,359 | 3,579 | 2,156 |
| Todd........ | 4,059 | 3,990 | 2,976 | 5,023 | 5,633 |
| Traverse..... | 1,053 | 841 | 582 | 1,399 | 1,061 |
| Wabasha..... | 3,736 | 3,397 | 3,012 | 4,442 | 4,681 |
| Wadena...... | 2,340 | 2,492 | 1,535 | 2,484 | 3,733 |
| Waseca...... | 3,146 | 3,118 | 2,621 | 3,721 | 4,471 |
| Washington... | 35,820 | 26,568 | 22,585 | 34,952 | 30,850 |
| Watonwan.... | 2,100 | 1,871 | 1,574 | 2,544 | 2,821 |
| Wilkin....... | 1,122 | 1,626 | 748 | 1,486 | 1,933 |
| Winona...... | 9,707 | 8,585 | 5,993 | 10,310 | 11,012 |
| Wright....... | 12,465 | 11,650 | 10,829 | 14,177 | 14,987 |
| Yellow Med.... | 2,593 | 1,909 | 1,645 | 3,282 | 2,925 |
| Totals........ | 1,020,997 | 747,841 | 562,506 | 1,109,471 | 962,337 |

## Minnesota Vote Since 1944

1944, Roosevelt, Dem., 589,864; Dewey, Rep., 527,416; Thomas, Soc., 5,073; Teichert, Ind. Gov't., 3,176.

1948, Truman, Dem., 692,966; Dewey, Rep., 483,617; Wallace, Prog., 27,866; Thomas, Soc., 4,646; Teichert, Soc. Labor, 2,525; Dobbs, Soc. Workers, 606.

1952, Eisenhower, Rep., 763,211; Stevenson, Dem., 608,458; Hallinan, Prog., 2,666; Hass, Soc. Labor, 2,383; Hamblen, Proh., 2,147; Dobbs, Soc. Workers, 618.

1956, Eisenhower, Rep., 719,302; Stevenson, Dem., 617,525; Hass, Soc. Labor (Ind. Gov.), 2,080; Dobbs, Soc. Workers, 1,098.

1960, Kennedy, Dem., 779,933; Nixon, Rep., 757,915; Dobbs, Soc. Workers, 3,077; Industrial Gov., 962.

1964, Johnson, Dem., 991,117; Goldwater, Rep., 559,624; DeBerry, Soc. Workers, 1,177; Hass, Industrial Gov., 2,544.

1968, Nixon, Rep., 658,643; Humphrey, Dem., 857,738; Wallace, 3d party, 68,931; scattered, 2,443; Halstead, Soc. Worker, 808; Blomen, Ind. Gov't., 285; Mitchell, Com., 415; Cleaver, Peace, 935; McCarthy, write-in, 585; scattered, 170.

1972, Nixon, Rep., 898,269; McGovern, Dem., 802,346; Schmitz, Amer., 31,407; Spock, Peoples, 2,805; Fisher, Soc. Labor, 4,261; Jenness, Soc. Workers, 940; Hall, Com., 662; scattered, 962.

1976, Carter, Dem., 1,070,440; Ford, Rep., 819,395; McCarthy, Ind., 35,490; Anderson, Amer., 13,592; Camejo, Soc. Workers, 4,149; MacBride, Libertarian, 3,529; Hall, Com., 1,092.

1980, Reagan, Rep., 873,268; Carter, Dem., 954,173; Anderson, Ind., 174,997; Clark, Libertarian, 31,593; Commoner, Citizens, 8,406; Hall, Com., 1,117; DeBerry, Soc. Workers, 711; Griswold, Workers World, 698; McReynolds, Socialist, 536; write-ins, 281.

1984, Mondale, Dem., 1,036,364; Reagan, Rep., 1,032,603; Bergland, Libertarian, 2,996.

1988, Bush., 962,337; Dukakis, Dem., 1,109,471; McCarthy, Minn. Prog., 5,403; Paul, Lib., 5,109.

1992, Clinton, Dem., 1,020,997; Bush, Rep., 747,841; Perot, Ind., 526,506; Marrou, Libertarian, 3,373; Gritz, Populist/America First, 3,363; Hagelin, Natural Law, 1,406.

## Mississippi

| County | 1992 Clinton (D) | Bush (R) | Perot (I) | 1988 Dukakis (D) | Bush (R) |
|---|---|---|---|---|---|
| Adams | 8,255 | 5,831 | 1,753 | 7,732 | 8,116 |
| Alcorn | 6,373 | 6,249 | 1,349 | 5,335 | 6,641 |
| Amite | 2,608 | 2,561 | 498 | 2,834 | 3,333 |
| Attala | 3,015 | 3,520 | 529 | 2,997 | 4,524 |
| Benton | 2,402 | 1,253 | 293 | 1,718 | 1,565 |
| Bolivar | 8,801 | 4,752 | 593 | 7,606 | 6,105 |
| Calhoun | 2,462 | 3,191 | 607 | 2,086 | 3,375 |
| Carroll | 1,182 | 1,695 | 200 | 1,560 | 2,628 |
| Chickasaw | 3,220 | 3,150 | 629 | 2,713 | 3,390 |
| Choctaw | 1,435 | 2,026 | 298 | 1,335 | 2,297 |
| Claiborne | 3,302 | 935 | 161 | 3,083 | 1,233 |
| Clarke | 2,259 | 4,207 | 450 | 2,576 | 4,522 |
| Clay | 4,620 | 3,297 | 626 | 3,849 | 3,645 |
| Coahoma | 6,409 | 4,120 | 518 | 6,139 | 4,939 |
| Copiah | 4,397 | 4,600 | 409 | 4,175 | 5,100 |
| Covington | 2,775 | 3,525 | 654 | 2,591 | 4,005 |
| DeSoto | 8,833 | 16,104 | 2,569 | 5,449 | 14,681 |
| Forrest | 8,333 | 12,432 | 1,909 | 6,953 | 14,249 |
| Franklin | 1,587 | 1,942 | 393 | 1,563 | 2,376 |
| George | 2,650 | 4,141 | 1,335 | 2,435 | 4,545 |
| Greene | 1,664 | 2,406 | 559 | 1,637 | 2,837 |
| Grenada | 4,203 | 4,721 | 609 | 3,683 | 5,352 |
| Hancock | 4,651 | 6,422 | 2,302 | 3,760 | 7,763 |
| Harrison | 15,268 | 25,049 | 6,855 | 14,439 | 32,892 |
| Hinds | 43,434 | 45,031 | 5,341 | 41,058 | 52,749 |
| Holmes | 4,092 | 1,694 | 203 | 5,350 | 2,737 |
| Humphreys | 2,696 | 1,721 | 258 | 2,644 | 2,018 |
| Issaquena | 550 | 298 | 79 | 511 | 424 |
| Itawamba | 3,635 | 4,142 | 918 | 3,143 | 4,535 |
| Jackson | 13,017 | 25,321 | 6,484 | 10,328 | 29,830 |
| Jasper | 3,059 | 2,789 | 568 | 3,184 | 3,368 |
| Jefferson | 2,796 | 562 | 156 | 2,693 | 702 |
| Jefferson Davis | 2,991 | 2,228 | 382 | 2,948 | 2,745 |
| Jones | 8,035 | 13,824 | 2,523 | 7,383 | 16,764 |
| Kemper | 2,243 | 1,830 | 278 | 2,069 | 2,128 |
| Lafayette | 5,224 | 5,251 | 861 | 3,967 | 5,841 |
| Lamar | 3,208 | 8,259 | 1,543 | 2,535 | 9,145 |
| Lauderdale | 8,489 | 17,098 | 1,659 | 7,967 | 18,302 |
| Lawrence | 2,582 | 2,689 | 765 | 2,517 | 3,682 |
| Leake | 3,333 | 3,943 | 497 | 2,787 | 4,168 |
| Lee | 7,710 | 12,231 | 2,041 | 6,604 | 13,767 |
| Leflore | 6,374 | 5,298 | 611 | 5,830 | 6,409 |
| Lincoln | 4,744 | 7,040 | 1,281 | 4,534 | 8,710 |
| Lowndes | 6,552 | 10,509 | 1,716 | 5,993 | 11,258 |
| Madison | 9,386 | 12,810 | 1,478 | 8,242 | 11,399 |
| Marion | 4,654 | 5,776 | 1,162 | 4,240 | 7,019 |
| Marshall | 7,913 | 3,847 | 689 | 6,982 | 4,668 |
| Monroe | 4,933 | 5,994 | 1,255 | 4,669 | 6,447 |
| Montgomery | 2,076 | 2,324 | 370 | 1,893 | 2,504 |
| Neshoba | 3,090 | 6,135 | 794 | 2,942 | 6,363 |
| Newton | 2,146 | 5,128 | 494 | 2,332 | 5,658 |
| Noxubee | 3,188 | 1,623 | 203 | 2,722 | 1,870 |
| Oktibbeha | 5,726 | 6,381 | 984 | 5,100 | 7,126 |
| Panola | 6,066 | 4,644 | 729 | 5,222 | 5,382 |
| Pearl River | 4,683 | 7,726 | 2,352 | 3,939 | 10,220 |
| Perry | 1,490 | 2,538 | 462 | 1,326 | 2,983 |
| Pike | 6,279 | 6,005 | 1,380 | 6,531 | 7,637 |
| Pontotoc | 2,965 | 4,595 | 777 | 2,772 | 4,939 |
| Prentiss | 3,385 | 4,317 | 781 | 3,429 | 4,348 |
| Quitman | 2,422 | 1,451 | 210 | 2,497 | 1,832 |
| Rankin | 8,155 | 24,537 | 3,454 | 6,201 | 22,937 |
| Scott | 3,349 | 5,268 | 691 | 2,939 | 5,522 |
| Sharkey | 1,526 | 1,008 | 145 | 1,609 | 1,277 |
| Simpson | 3,213 | 5,358 | 726 | 3,016 | 6,151 |
| Smith | 1,968 | 4,106 | 680 | 1,660 | 4,573 |
| Stone | 1,447 | 2,295 | 447 | 1,452 | 3,007 |
| Sunflower | 5,050 | 3,726 | 600 | 4,898 | 4,362 |
| Tallahatchie | 2,902 | 2,213 | 380 | 2,881 | 2,633 |
| Tate | 3,519 | 4,196 | 634 | 2,872 | 4,553 |
| Tippah | 3,475 | 4,444 | 802 | 2,958 | 4,593 |
| Tishomingo | 3,910 | 3,393 | 751 | 3,378 | 3,646 |
| Tunica | 1,451 | 693 | 96 | 1,510 | 896 |
| Union | 3,714 | 5,173 | 816 | 3,044 | 5,511 |
| Walthall | 2,476 | 2,728 | 711 | 2,354 | 3,103 |
| Warren | 8,175 | 10,209 | 2,146 | 7,437 | 12,507 |
| Washington | 10,588 | 7,598 | 795 | 10,222 | 10,229 |
| Wayne | 3,064 | 3,874 | 824 | 2,889 | 4,496 |
| Webster | 1,746 | 2,791 | 444 | 1,550 | 3,061 |
| Wilkinson | 3,210 | 1,399 | 307 | 2,678 | 1,528 |
| Winston | 3,953 | 4,311 | 688 | 3,851 | 5,317 |
| Yalobusha | 2,617 | 2,179 | 438 | 2,402 | 2,660 |
| Yazoo | 4,880 | 5,113 | 669 | 4,989 | 5,538 |
| Totals | 400,258 | 487,793 | 85,626 | 363,921 | 557,890 |

## Mississippi Vote Since 1944

1944, Roosevelt, Dem., 158,515; Dewey, Rep., 3,742; Reg. Dem., 9,964; Ind. Rep., 7,859.

1948, Thurmond, States' Rights, 167,538; Truman, Dem., 19,384; Dewey, Rep., 5,043; Wallace, Prog., 225.

1952, Eisenhower, Ind. vote pledged to Rep. candidate, 112,966; Stevenson, Dem., 172,566.

1956, Stevenson, Dem., 144,498; Eisenhower, Rep., 56,372; Black and Tan Grand Old Party, 4,313; total, 60,685; Byrd, Ind., 42,966.

1960, Democratic unpledged electors, 116,248; Kennedy, Dem., 108,362; Nixon, Rep., 73,561. Mississippi's victorious slate of 8 unpledged Democratic electors cast their votes for Sen. Harry F. Byrd (D-Va.).

1964, Johnson, Dem., 52,618; Goldwater, Rep., 356,528.

1968, Nixon, Rep., 88,516; Humphrey, Dem., 150,644; Wallace, 3d party, 415,349.

1972, Nixon, Rep., 505,125; McGovern, Dem., 126,782; Schmitz, Amer., 11,598; Jenness, Soc. Workers, 2,458.

1976, Carter, Dem., 381,309; Ford, Rep., 366,846; Anderson, Amer., 6,678; McCarthy, Ind., 4,074; Maddox, Ind., 4,049; Camejo, Soc. Workers, 2,805; MacBride, Libertarian, 2,609.

1980, Reagan, Rep., 441,089; Carter, Dem., 429,281; Anderson, Ind., 12,036; Clark, Libertarian, 5,465; Griswold, Workers World, 2,402; Pulley, Soc. Worker, 2,347.

1984, Reagan, Rep., 582,377; Mondale, Dem., 352,192; Bergland, Libertarian, 2,336.

1988, Bush, Rep., 557,890; Dukakis, Dem., 363,921; Duke, Ind., 4,232; Paul, Lib., 3,329.

1992, Bush, Rep., 487,793; Clinton, Dem., 400,258; Perot, Ind., 85,626; Fulani, New Alliance, 2,625; Marrou, Libertarian, 2,154; Phillips, U.S. Taxpayers, 1,652; Hagelin, Natural Law, 1,140.

## Missouri

| County | 1992 Clinton (D) | Bush (R) | Perot (I) | 1988 Dukakis (D) | Bush (R) |
|---|---|---|---|---|---|
| Adair | 4,232 | 4,141 | 2,224 | 3,571 | 5,721 |
| Andrew | 2,675 | 2,652 | 2,151 | 3,108 | 3,407 |
| Atchison | 1,208 | 1,140 | 840 | 1,468 | 1,761 |
| Audrain | 4,731 | 3,798 | 2,099 | 5,226 | 5,072 |
| Barry | 4,791 | 5,565 | 2,381 | 4,210 | 7,231 |
| Barton | 1,433 | 2,775 | 971 | 1,603 | 3,339 |
| Bates | 2,993 | 2,499 | 2,225 | 3,332 | 3,574 |
| Benton | 3,195 | 2,511 | 1,551 | 2,654 | 3,467 |
| Bollinger | 2,150 | 2,289 | 909 | 1,883 | 2,710 |
| Boone | 26,176 | 19,405 | 12,040 | 24,370 | 22,948 |
| Buchanan | 16,570 | 11,275 | 9,404 | 18,601 | 15,336 |
| Butler | 6,602 | 6,450 | 2,189 | 5,751 | 7,968 |
| Caldwell | 1,456 | 1,295 | 1,283 | 1,726 | 2,074 |
| Callaway | 5,799 | 4,880 | 3,266 | 5,209 | 6,687 |
| Camden | 5,140 | 5,554 | 3,891 | 3,930 | 7,773 |
| Cape Girardeau | 9,605 | 13,464 | 5,199 | 7,904 | 16,583 |
| Carroll | 2,100 | 1,774 | 1,495 | 2,330 | 2,811 |
| Carter | 1,169 | 1,101 | 405 | 1,087 | 1,429 |
| Cass | 10,246 | 10,349 | 9,216 | 10,092 | 12,799 |
| Cedar | 2,064 | 2,085 | 1,173 | 1,774 | 2,966 |
| Chariton | 2,141 | 1,378 | 1,067 | 2,347 | 2,193 |
| Christian | 6,242 | 7,422 | 3,422 | 4,724 | 7,670 |
| Clark | 1,815 | 1,039 | 725 | 1,925 | 1,493 |
| Clay | 30,565 | 23,798 | 20,951 | 29,620 | 30,293 |
| Clinton | 3,400 | 2,391 | 2,423 | 3,653 | 3,282 |
| Cole | 10,201 | 15,270 | 5,770 | 8,359 | 18,023 |
| Cooper | 2,709 | 2,867 | 1,735 | 2,510 | 3,737 |
| Crawford | 3,515 | 2,831 | 2,002 | 3,107 | 3,856 |
| Dade | 1,332 | 1,577 | 834 | 1,315 | 2,154 |
| Dallas | 2,533 | 2,116 | 1,392 | 2,293 | 2,898 |
| Daviess | 1,477 | 1,107 | 1,143 | 1,743 | 1,765 |
| DeKalb | 1,630 | 1,318 | 1,207 | 1,970 | 1,863 |
| Dent | 2,689 | 2,125 | 1,049 | 2,421 | 2,975 |
| Douglas | 2,126 | 2,569 | 1,081 | 1,735 | 3,225 |
| Dunklin | 6,277 | 4,024 | 1,166 | 5,281 | 5,026 |
| Franklin | 13,431 | 11,477 | 11,043 | 11,891 | 16,611 |
| Gasconade | 1,952 | 2,690 | 1,672 | 1,621 | 4,216 |
| Gentry | 1,519 | 1,272 | 921 | 1,872 | 1,554 |
| Greene | 41,137 | 46,457 | 17,770 | 35,475 | 52,211 |
| Grundy | 1,968 | 1,749 | 1,372 | 2,052 | 2,668 |
| Harrison | 1,590 | 1,563 | 1,059 | 1,776 | 2,271 |
| Henry | 4,232 | 2,681 | 2,807 | 4,135 | 4,167 |
| Hickory | 1,929 | 1,259 | 864 | 1,677 | 2,043 |
| Holt | 1,050 | 1,202 | 781 | 1,258 | 1,583 |
| Howard | 2,085 | 1,253 | 1,090 | 2,446 | 1,865 |
| Howell | 5,492 | 5,360 | 2,650 | 4,324 | 7,277 |
| Iron | 2,507 | 1,276 | 841 | 2,283 | 1,877 |
| Jackson | 145,999 | 78,611 | 66,142 | 147,964 | 107,810 |
| Jasper | 11,727 | 17,592 | 6,440 | 11,159 | 19,934 |
| Jefferson | 32,569 | 20,637 | 20,057 | 27,738 | 29,229 |

| | | | | | |
|---|---|---|---|---|---|
| Johnson | 5,546 | 5,032 | 4,578 | 5,373 | 7,512 |
| Knox | 1,010 | 724 | 523 | 1,255 | 1,212 |
| Laclede | 4,179 | 5,176 | 2,852 | 3,442 | 6,070 |
| Lafayette | 5,213 | 4,651 | 3,561 | 5,654 | 6,825 |
| Lawrence | 4,666 | 5,608 | 2,570 | 4,432 | 6,911 |
| Lewis | 2,196 | 1,461 | 892 | 2,460 | 1,803 |
| Lincoln | 5,453 | 3,718 | 3,572 | 4,605 | 5,305 |
| Linn | 2,916 | 1,967 | 1,524 | 3,150 | 3,061 |
| Livingston | 2,505 | 2,370 | 1,976 | 3,077 | 3,462 |
| McDonald | 2,281 | 3,010 | 1,551 | 2,299 | 3,812 |
| Macon | 3,194 | 2,256 | 1,697 | 3,215 | 3,406 |
| Madison | 2,501 | 1,673 | 899 | 2,167 | 2,528 |
| Maries | 1,732 | 1,356 | 915 | 1,552 | 1,919 |
| Marion | 5,156 | 4,762 | 1,841 | 5,617 | 5,034 |
| Mercer | 843 | 626 | 378 | 877 | 875 |
| Miller | 2,905 | 4,175 | 2,391 | 2,555 | 5,662 |
| Missouri | 3,226 | 1,675 | 776 | 2,814 | 2,218 |
| Moniteau | 2,018 | 2,566 | 1,499 | 1,936 | 3,502 |
| Monroe | 2,060 | 1,153 | 969 | 2,461 | 1,542 |
| Montgomery | 2,063 | 1,974 | 1,266 | 2,064 | 2,714 |
| Morgan | 2,906 | 2,819 | 2,028 | 2,604 | 3,958 |
| New Madrid | 4,883 | 2,431 | 952 | 3,812 | 3,387 |
| Newton | 5,987 | 8,804 | 3,567 | 5,798 | 10,617 |
| Nodaway | 3,723 | 3,147 | 2,484 | 4,240 | 4,103 |
| Oregon | 2,258 | 1,402 | 564 | 2,042 | 1,717 |
| Osage | 1,860 | 2,784 | 1,423 | 1,771 | 3,885 |
| Ozark | 1,581 | 1,772 | 906 | 1,329 | 2,404 |
| Pemiscot | 3,924 | 2,161 | 670 | 3,288 | 3,066 |
| Perry | 2,525 | 3,205 | 1,498 | 2,136 | 3,836 |
| Pettis | 5,314 | 6,823 | 4,278 | 5,486 | 9,648 |
| Phelps | 6,852 | 6,040 | 3,774 | 5,867 | 8,329 |
| Pike | 3,609 | 2,255 | 1,464 | 3,816 | 3,271 |
| Platte | 10,920 | 9,380 | 9,062 | 11,225 | 11,838 |
| Polk | 3,316 | 3,465 | 1,879 | 3,419 | 5,030 |
| Pulaski | 4,113 | 3,793 | 2,057 | 3,446 | 4,642 |
| Putnam | 838 | 1,143 | 522 | 803 | 1,365 |
| Ralls | 2,158 | 1,349 | 880 | 2,489 | 1,494 |
| Randolph | 4,951 | 3,025 | 2,212 | 5,291 | 4,384 |
| Ray | 4,457 | 2,563 | 2,567 | 4,879 | 3,763 |
| Reynolds | 2,014 | 776 | 532 | 1,864 | 1,162 |
| Ripley | 2,300 | 1,814 | 739 | 1,961 | 2,647 |
| St. Charles | 37,263 | 38,673 | 30,351 | 29,286 | 50,005 |
| St. Clair | 1,965 | 1,555 | 1,083 | 1,864 | 2,312 |
| St. Francois | 9,367 | 5,889 | 3,635 | 8,158 | 7,923 |
| St. Louis | 235,760 | 188,285 | 109,099 | 216,534 | 262,784 |
| Ste. Genevieve | 3,795 | 1,780 | 1,547 | 3,612 | 2,532 |
| Saline | 4,643 | 2,688 | 2,815 | 5,039 | 4,625 |
| Schuyler | 936 | 742 | 487 | 1,013 | 1,063 |
| Scotland | 1,070 | 798 | 617 | 1,117 | 1,248 |
| Scott | 7,452 | 6,265 | 2,763 | 5,914 | 8,013 |
| Shannon | 2,135 | 1,224 | 579 | 1,796 | 1,696 |
| Shelby | 1,435 | 1,169 | 786 | 1,818 | 1,586 |
| Stoddard | 5,720 | 4,608 | 1,977 | 4,701 | 5,822 |
| Stone | 3,256 | 4,035 | 1,884 | 2,889 | 5,080 |
| Sullivan | 1,510 | 1,326 | 596 | 1,562 | 1,897 |
| Taney | 4,682 | 6,081 | 2,395 | 3,888 | 7,043 |
| Texas | 4,597 | 3,470 | 1,900 | 3,887 | 4,584 |
| Vernon | 3,546 | 2,851 | 1,890 | 3,402 | 4,149 |
| Warren | 3,213 | 2,953 | 2,471 | 2,935 | 4,452 |
| Washington | 4,211 | 2,157 | 1,618 | 3,744 | 3,240 |
| Wayne | 3,073 | 2,101 | 837 | 2,456 | 2,648 |
| Webster | 4,149 | 4,361 | 2,108 | 3,890 | 5,123 |
| Worth | 599 | 483 | 328 | 732 | 677 |
| Wright | 2,814 | 3,427 | 1,425 | 2,232 | 4,151 |
| City | | | | | |
| St. Louis | 102,356 | 25,441 | 18,864 | 110,076 | 40,906 |
| Totals | 1,053,873 | 811,159 | 518,741 | 1,001,619 | 1,084,953 |

## Missouri Vote Since 1944

1944, Roosevelt, Dem., 807,357; Dewey, Rep., 761,175; Thomas, Soc., 1,750; Watson, Proh., 1,175; Teichert, Soc. Labor, 221.

1948, Truman, Dem., 917,315; Dewey, Rep., 655,039; Wallace, Prog., 3,998; Thomas, Soc., 2,222.

1952, Eisenhower, Rep., 959,429; Stevenson, Dem., 929,830; Hallinan, Prog., 987; Hamblen, Proh., 885; MacArthur, Christian Nationalist, 302; America First, 233; Hoopes, Soc., 227; Hass, Soc. Labor, 169.

1956, Stevenson, Dem., 918,273; Eisenhower, Rep., 914,299.

1960, Kennedy, Dem., 972,201; Nixon, Rep., 962,221.

1964, Johnson, Dem., 1,164,344; Goldwater, Rep., 653,535.

1968, Nixon, Rep., 811,932; Humphrey, Dem., 791,444; Wallace, 3d party, 206,126.

1972, Nixon, Rep., 1,154,058; McGovern, Dem., 698,531.

1976, Carter, Dem., 999,163; Ford, Rep., 928,808; McCarthy, Ind., 24,329.

1980, Reagan, Rep., 1,074,181; Carter, Dem., 931,182; Anderson, Ind., 77,920; Clark, Libertarian, 14,422; DeBerry, Soc. Workers, 1,515; Commoner, Citizens, 573; write-ins, 31.

1984, Reagan, Rep., 1,274,188; Mondale, Dem., 848,583.

1988, Bush, Rep., 1,084,953; Dukakis, Dem., 1,001,619; Fulani, New Alliance, 6,656; Paul, write-in, 434.

1992, Clinton, Dem., 1,053,873; Bush, Rep., 811,159; Perot, Ind., 518,741; Marrou, Libertarian, 7,497.

## Montana

| | 1992 | | | 1988 | |
|---|---|---|---|---|---|
| County | Clinton (D) | Bush (R) | Perot (I) | Dukakis (D) | Bush (R) |
| Beaverhead | 1,098 | 1,746 | 1,202 | 1,274 | 2,668 |
| Big Horn | 2,154 | 1,377 | 840 | 2,233 | 1,711 |
| Blaine | 1,355 | 971 | 699 | 1,460 | 1,402 |
| Broadwater | 491 | 830 | 505 | 592 | 1,054 |
| Carbon | 1,549 | 1,562 | 1,482 | 2,039 | 2,360 |
| Carter | 154 | 497 | 220 | 242 | 686 |
| Cascade | 14,719 | 12,494 | 9,151 | 15,718 | 15,946 |
| Chouteau | 959 | 1,380 | 870 | 1,166 | 1,980 |
| Custer | 1,968 | 2,105 | 1,505 | 2,343 | 3,007 |
| Daniels | 457 | 496 | 402 | 571 | 802 |
| Dawson | 1,785 | 1,679 | 1,370 | 2,120 | 2,658 |
| Deer Lodge | 3,174 | 832 | 1,207 | 3,185 | 1,168 |
| Fallon | 446 | 731 | 427 | 612 | 1,002 |
| Fergus | 1,615 | 2,736 | 1,934 | 2,052 | 3,948 |
| Flathead | 9,746 | 11,699 | 9,109 | 10,202 | 14,461 |
| Gallatin | 9,535 | 11,109 | 7,711 | 9,527 | 13,214 |
| Garfield | 125 | 403 | 281 | 196 | 631 |
| Glacier | 2,076 | 1,222 | 997 | 2,151 | 1,728 |
| Golden Valley | 142 | 192 | 157 | 203 | 335 |
| Granite | 358 | 556 | 386 | 511 | 789 |
| Hill | 3,618 | 2,408 | 2,017 | 4,219 | 3,467 |
| Jefferson | 1,415 | 1,541 | 1,172 | 1,746 | 2,007 |
| Judith Basin | 409 | 610 | 415 | 590 | 902 |
| Lake | 3,938 | 3,596 | 2,878 | 4,109 | 4,883 |
| Lewis & Clark | 11,117 | 9,351 | 5,560 | 11,932 | 10,946 |
| Liberty | 321 | 512 | 363 | 418 | 771 |
| Lincoln | 2,765 | 2,799 | 2,637 | 3,601 | 3,500 |
| Madison | 779 | 1,415 | 1,043 | 878 | 2,045 |
| McCone | 424 | 528 | 395 | 567 | 814 |
| Meagher | 260 | 422 | 310 | 337 | 656 |
| Mineral | 664 | 403 | 543 | 789 | 616 |
| Missoula | 20,347 | 12,898 | 9,735 | 19,178 | 15,965 |
| Musselshell | 648 | 876 | 691 | 898 | 1,280 |
| Park | 2,258 | 2,846 | 2,182 | 2,526 | 3,823 |
| Petroleum | 61 | 135 | 95 | 91 | 204 |
| Phillips | 634 | 1,026 | 949 | 905 | 1,462 |
| Pondera | 1,046 | 1,252 | 855 | 1,245 | 1,795 |
| Powder River | 258 | 547 | 340 | 395 | 815 |
| Powell | 989 | 1,058 | 872 | 1,174 | 1,574 |
| Prairie | 290 | 412 | 179 | 343 | 541 |
| Ravalli | 4,644 | 5,392 | 4,573 | 4,763 | 7,418 |
| Richland | 1,440 | 1,760 | 1,525 | 1,824 | 2,628 |
| Roosevelt | 1,827 | 1,212 | 1,089 | 2,083 | 1,957 |
| Rosebud | 1,669 | 1,130 | 1,099 | 1,869 | 1,822 |
| Sanders | 1,689 | 1,361 | 1,378 | 1,959 | 2,152 |
| Sheridan | 1,077 | 795 | 782 | 1,354 | 1,381 |
| Silver Bow | 9,960 | 3,491 | 4,570 | 11,422 | 5,043 |
| Stillwater | 1,178 | 1,390 | 1,056 | 1,407 | 1,920 |
| Sweet Grass | 395 | 880 | 507 | 462 | 1,242 |
| Teton | 1,043 | 1,364 | 969 | 1,303 | 1,876 |
| Toole | 854 | 943 | 903 | 1,070 | 1,505 |
| Treasure | 157 | 206 | 178 | 231 | 291 |
| Valley | 1,715 | 1,497 | 1,320 | 2,163 | 2,467 |
| Wheatland | 384 | 478 | 284 | 443 | 667 |
| Wibaux | 195 | 234 | 173 | 258 | 358 |
| Yellowstone | 20,163 | 22,822 | 13,133 | 21,987 | 28,069 |
| Totals | 154,507 | 144,207 | 107,225 | 168,936 | 190,412 |

## Montana Vote Since 1944

1944, Roosevelt, Dem., 112,556; Dewey, Rep., 93,163; Thomas, Soc., 1,296; Watson, Proh., 340.

1948, Truman, Dem., 119,071; Dewey, Rep., 96,770; Wallace, Prog., 7,313; Thomas, Soc., 695; Watson, Proh., 429.

1952, Eisenhower, Rep., 157,394; Stevenson, Dem., 106,213; Hallinan, Prog., 723; Hamblen, Proh., 548; Hoopes, Soc., 159.

1956, Eisenhower, Rep., 154,933; Stevenson, Dem., 116,238.

1960, Kennedy, Dem., 134,891; Nixon, Rep., 141,841; Decker, Proh., 456; Dobbs, Soc. Workers, 391.

1964, Johnson, Dem., 164,246; Goldwater, Rep., 113,032; Kasper, Nat'l States Rights, 519; Munn, Proh., 499; DeBerry, Soc. Worker, 332.

1968, Nixon, Rep., 138,835; Humphrey, Dem., 114,117; Wallace, 3d party, 20,015; Halstead, Soc. Worker, 457; Munn, Proh., 510; Caton, New Reform, 470.

1972, Nixon, Rep., 183,976; McGovern, Dem., 120,197; Schmitz, Amer., 13,430.

1976, Carter, Dem., 149,259; Ford, Rep., 173,703; Anderson, Amer., 5,772.

1980, Reagan, Rep., 206,814; Carter, Dem., 118,032; Anderson, Ind., 29,281; Clark, Libertarian, 9,825.

1984, Reagan, Rep., 232,450; Mondale, Dem., 146,742; Bergland, Libertarian, 5,185.

1988, Bush, Rep., 190,412; Dukakis, Dem., 168,936; Paul, Lib., 5,047; Fulani, New Alliance, 1,279.

1992, Clinton, Dem., 154,507; Bush, Rep., 144,207; Perot, Ind., 107,225; Gritz, Populist/America First, 3,658.

## Nebraska

| County | 1992 Clinton (D) | 1992 Bush (R) | Perot (I) | 1988 Dukakis (D) | 1988 Bush (R) |
|---|---|---|---|---|---|
| Adams | 3,445 | 6,346 | 3,273 | 4,145 | 8,063 |
| Antelope | 650 | 1,979 | 1,134 | 933 | 2,626 |
| Arthur | 18 | 148 | 97 | 58 | 210 |
| Banner | 68 | 284 | 128 | 112 | 361 |
| Blaine | 64 | 256 | 130 | 72 | 338 |
| Boone | 604 | 1,588 | 956 | 976 | 2,160 |
| Box Butte | 1,935 | 2,198 | 1,508 | 2,466 | 3,253 |
| Boyd | 353 | 744 | 468 | 480 | 967 |
| Brown | 311 | 999 | 525 | 435 | 1,335 |
| Buffalo | 3,742 | 9,708 | 4,083 | 4,700 | 9,980 |
| Burt | 1,224 | 1,667 | 1,009 | 1,458 | 2,050 |
| Butler | 1,087 | 1,881 | 1,157 | 1,715 | 2,083 |
| Cass | 2,949 | 4,314 | 2,657 | 3,674 | 4,658 |
| Cedar | 1,007 | 1,981 | 1,507 | 1,759 | 2,462 |
| Chase | 398 | 1,000 | 674 | 597 | 1,446 |
| Cherry | 563 | 1,707 | 730 | 642 | 2,240 |
| Cheyenne | 967 | 2,197 | 1,061 | 1,333 | 2,862 |
| Clay | 802 | 1,818 | 952 | 1,097 | 2,352 |
| Colfax | 1,011 | 1,915 | 1,197 | 1,542 | 2,329 |
| Cuming | 835 | 2,711 | 1,192 | 1,238 | 3,201 |
| Custer | 1,126 | 3,180 | 1,492 | 1,496 | 4,202 |
| Dakota | 2,322 | 2,771 | 1,307 | 2,941 | 2,744 |
| Dawes | 987 | 1,961 | 1,103 | 1,122 | 2,618 |
| Dawson | 1,739 | 4,710 | 2,305 | 2,184 | 5,529 |
| Deuel | 232 | 558 | 327 | 302 | 769 |
| Dixon | 830 | 1,484 | 726 | 1,166 | 1,802 |
| Dodge | 4,665 | 7,269 | 4,432 | 6,116 | 8,412 |
| Douglas | 67,003 | 93,421 | 38,641 | 76,444 | 99,806 |
| Dundy | 244 | 664 | 332 | 333 | 828 |
| Fillmore | 988 | 1,495 | 993 | 1,433 | 1,952 |
| Franklin | 477 | 967 | 527 | 768 | 1,294 |
| Frontier | 302 | 785 | 479 | 384 | 1,057 |
| Furnas | 624 | 1,365 | 804 | 791 | 1,830 |
| Gage | 3,309 | 3,995 | 2,726 | 4,008 | 5,114 |
| Garden | 212 | 697 | 385 | 366 | 986 |
| Garfield | 221 | 595 | 270 | 234 | 803 |
| Gosper | 254 | 492 | 297 | 331 | 694 |
| Grant | 75 | 247 | 124 | 89 | 301 |
| Greeley | 435 | 587 | 395 | 670 | 763 |
| Hall | 5,519 | 9,264 | 5,822 | 6,822 | 12,020 |
| Hamilton | 992 | 2,379 | 1,213 | 1,289 | 3,019 |
| Harlan | 488 | 991 | 623 | 725 | 1,403 |
| Hayes | 85 | 362 | 207 | 160 | 512 |
| Hitchcock | 359 | 824 | 540 | 480 | 1,132 |
| Holt | 835 | 3,131 | 1,714 | 1,327 | 4,081 |
| Hooker | 70 | 283 | 102 | 91 | 378 |
| Howard | 778 | 1,138 | 940 | 1,186 | 1,526 |
| Jefferson | 1,506 | 1,783 | 1,177 | 1,819 | 2,470 |
| Johnson | 822 | 885 | 642 | 1,162 | 1,182 |
| Kearney | 644 | 1,751 | 844 | 1,056 | 2,120 |
| Keith | 731 | 2,019 | 1,130 | 1,067 | 2,879 |
| Keya Paha | 105 | 368 | 158 | 145 | 446 |
| Kimball | 408 | 931 | 440 | 540 | 1,321 |
| Knox | 968 | 2,112 | 1,166 | 1,477 | 2,644 |
| Lancaster | 41,207 | 41,400 | 21,783 | 44,260 | 44,605 |
| Lincoln | 5,142 | 7,025 | 3,384 | 6,070 | 8,395 |
| Logan | 80 | 271 | 98 | 93 | 373 |
| Loup | 58 | 233 | 96 | 97 | 295 |
| McPherson | 49 | 217 | 62 | 60 | 229 |
| Madison | 2,352 | 7,851 | 3,486 | 2,779 | 9,135 |
| Merrick | 864 | 1,854 | 1,072 | 1,192 | 2,376 |
| Morrill | 577 | 1,184 | 752 | 753 | 1,554 |
| Nance | 559 | 851 | 569 | 794 | 1,185 |
| Nemaha | 1,110 | 1,696 | 1,020 | 1,457 | 2,293 |
| Nuckolls | 834 | 1,277 | 825 | 1,114 | 1,750 |
| Otoe | 2,038 | 2,960 | 1,800 | 2,616 | 3,724 |
| Pawnee | 566 | 670 | 565 | 767 | 975 |
| Perkins | 300 | 842 | 522 | 467 | 1,117 |
| Phelps | 829 | 2,748 | 1,298 | 1,047 | 3,316 |
| Pierce | 611 | 1,853 | 1,084 | 914 | 2,474 |
| Platte | 2,409 | 7,712 | 3,656 | 3,285 | 9,029 |
| Polk | 661 | 1,435 | 812 | 944 | 1,768 |
| Red Willow | 1,164 | 2,488 | 1,660 | 1,505 | 3,325 |
| Richardson | 1,513 | 2,050 | 1,356 | 1,926 | 2,702 |
| Rock | 162 | 588 | 233 | 198 | 756 |
| Saline | 2,425 | 1,740 | 1,576 | 3,119 | 2,352 |
| Sarpy | 10,720 | 20,482 | 9,270 | 10,936 | 20,179 |
| Saunders | 2,509 | 4,037 | 2,567 | 3,524 | 4,454 |
| Scotts Bluff | 4,173 | 7,213 | 3,514 | 4,454 | 8,594 |
| Seward | 2,118 | 3,044 | 1,722 | 2,682 | 3,467 |
| Sheridan | 535 | 1,698 | 751 | 612 | 2,251 |
| Sherman | 568 | 736 | 582 | 839 | 914 |
| Sioux | 148 | 445 | 206 | 194 | 568 |
| Stanton | 496 | 1,274 | 786 | 637 | 1,709 |
| Thayer | 923 | 1,387 | 1,077 | 1,322 | 1,981 |
| Thomas | 69 | 283 | 115 | 81 | 383 |
| Thurston | 865 | 898 | 487 | 1,225 | 1,105 |
| Valley | 716 | 1,173 | 693 | 873 | 1,603 |
| Washington | 2,108 | 4,035 | 2,148 | 2,552 | 4,567 |
| Wayne | 921 | 2,122 | 1,047 | 1,111 | 2,473 |
| Webster | 624 | 972 | 657 | 891 | 1,314 |
| Wheeler | 88 | 246 | 127 | 141 | 309 |
| York | 1,385 | 3,783 | 1,825 | 1,748 | 4,744 |
| Totals | 216,864 | 343,678 | 174,104 | 259,235 | 397,956 |

### Nebraska Vote Since 1944

1944, Roosevelt, Dem., 233,246; Dewey, Rep., 329,880.

1948, Truman, Dem., 224,165; Dewey, Rep., 264,774.

1952, Eisenhower, Rep., 421,603; Stevenson Dem., 188,057.

1956, Eisenhower, Rep., 378,108; Stevenson, Dem., 199,029.

1960, Kennedy, Dem., 232,542; Nixon, Rep., 380,553.

1964, Johnson, Dem., 307,307; Goldwater, Rep., 276,847.

1968, Nixon, Rep., 321,163; Humphrey, Dem., 170,784; Wallace, 3d party, 44,904.

1972, Nixon, Rep., 406,298; McGovern, Dem., 169,991; scattered 817.

1976, Carter, Dem., 233,287; Ford, Rep., 359,219; McCarthy, Ind., 9,383; Maddox, Amer. Ind., 3,378; MacBride, Libertarian, 1,476.

1980, Reagan, Rep., 419,214; Carter, Dem., 166,424; Anderson, Ind., 44,854; Clark, Libertarian, 9,041.

1984, Reagan, Rep., 459,135; Mondale, Dem., 187,475; Bergland, Libertarian, 2,075.

1988, Bush, Rep., 397,956; Dukakis, Dem., 259,235; Paul, Lib., 2,534; Fulani, New Alliance, 1,740.

1992, Bush, Rep., 343,678; Clinton, Dem., 216,864; Perot, Ind., 174,104; Marrou, Libertarian, 1,340.

## Nevada

| County | 1992 Clinton (D) | 1992 Bush (R) | Perot (I) | 1988 Dukakis (D) | 1988 Bush (R) |
|---|---|---|---|---|---|
| Churchill | 1,770 | 3,789 | 1,964 | 1,481 | 4,578 |
| Clark | 124,586 | 97,403 | 75,364 | 78,359 | 108,110 |
| Douglas | 3,928 | 6,182 | 4,814 | 3,107 | 7,074 |
| Elko | 2,782 | 5,208 | 3,628 | 2,310 | 5,722 |
| Esmeralda | 118 | 221 | 220 | 143 | 380 |
| Eureka | 129 | 330 | 214 | 151 | 413 |
| Humboldt | 810 | 1,505 | 1,149 | 1,024 | 2,378 |
| Lander | 423 | 885 | 652 | 439 | 1,214 |
| Lincoln | 511 | 890 | 394 | 466 | 1,035 |
| Lyon | 2,777 | 3,509 | 2,716 | 2,301 | 4,390 |
| Mineral | 909 | 918 | 746 | 978 | 1,480 |
| Nye | 2,561 | 2,743 | 2,501 | 1,748 | 3,619 |
| Pershing | 467 | 643 | 429 | 458 | 867 |
| Storey | 488 | 458 | 550 | 432 | 651 |
| Washoe | 39,500 | 42,636 | 30,974 | 32,902 | 52,654 |
| White Pine | 1,354 | 1,206 | 1,070 | 1,351 | 1,774 |
| City | | | | | |
| Carson City | 6,035 | 7,302 | 5,195 | 5,088 | 9,701 |
| Totals | 189,148 | 175,828 | 132,580 | 132,738 | 206,040 |

### Nevada Vote Since 1944

1944, Roosevelt, Dem., 29,623; Dewey, Rep., 24,611.

1948, Truman, Dem., 31,291; Dewey, Rep., 29,357; Wallace, Prog., 1,469.

1952, Eisenhower, Rep., 50,502; Stevenson, Dem., 31,688.

1956, Eisenhower, Rep., 56,049; Stevenson, Dem., 40,640.

1960, Kennedy, Dem., 54,880; Nixon, Rep., 52,387.

1964, Johnson, Dem., 79,339; Goldwater, Rep., 56,094.

1968, Nixon, Rep., 73,188; Humphrey, Dem., 60,598; Wallace, 3d party, 20,432.

1972, Nixon, Rep., 115,750; McGovern, Dem. 66,016.

1976, Carter Dem., 92,479; Ford, Rep., 101,273; MacBride, Libertarian, 1,519; Maddox, Amer. Ind., 1,497; scattered 5,108.

1980, Reagan, Rep., 155,017; Carter, Dem., 66,666; Anderson, Ind., 17,651; Clark, Libertarian, 4,358.

1984, Reagan, Rep., 188,770; Mondale, Dem., 91,655; Bergland, Libertarian, 2,292.

1988, Bush, Rep., 206,040; Dukakis, Dem., 132,738; Paul, Lib., 3,520; Fulani, New Alliance, 835.

1992, Clinton, Dem., 189,148; Bush, Rep., 175,828; Perot, Ind., 132,580; Gritz, Populist/America First, 2,892; Marrou, Libertarian, 1,835.

## New Hampshire

| City | 1992 Clinton (D) | 1992 Bush (R) | Perot (I) | 1988 Dukakis (D) | 1988 Bush (R) |
|---|---|---|---|---|---|
| Berlin City | 2,680 | 1,272 | 1,162 | 2,271 | 2,529 |
| Claremont | 2,650 | 1,822 | 904 | 2,254 | 2,513 |

| | | | | | |
|---|---|---|---|---|---|
| Concord........ | 8,325 | 5,651 | 2,843 | 6,698 | 7,439 |
| Dover.......... | 5,449 | 4,197 | 2,246 | 4,803 | 5,357 |
| Keene......... | 5,210 | 3,257 | 1,736 | 4,466 | 4,535 |
| Laconia........ | 2,390 | 3,033 | 1,496 | 2,111 | 3,835 |
| Manchester..... | 16,627 | 16,298 | 7,441 | 12,567 | 23,893 |
| Nashua........ | 14,777 | 12,514 | 8,306 | 12,833 | 19,369 |
| Portsmith...... | 6,132 | 3,563 | 2,088 | 5,377 | 4,827 |
| Rochester...... | 4,588 | 4,272 | 2,541 | 3,591 | 5,368 |
| Totals........ | 209,040 | 202,484 | 121,337 | 163,696 | 281,537 |

### New Hampshire Vote Since 1944

1944, Roosevelt, Dem., 119,663; Dewey, Rep., 109,916; Thomas, Soc., 46.

1948, Truman, Dem., 107,995; Dewey, Rep., 121,299; Wallace, Prog., 1,970; Thomas, Soc., 86; Teichert, Soc. Labor, 83; Thurmond, States' Rights, 7.

1952, Eisenhower, Rep., 166,287; Stevenson, Dem., 106,663.

1956, Eisenhower, Rep., 176,519; Stevenson, Dem., 90,364; Andrews, Const., 111.

1960, Kennedy, Dem., 137,772; Nixon, Rep., 157,989.

1964, Johnson, Dem., 182,065; Goldwater, Rep., 104,029.

1968, Nixon, Rep., 154,903; Humphrey, Dem., 130,589; Wallace, 3d party, 11,173; New Party, 421; Halstead, Soc. Worker, 104.

1972, Nixon, Rep., 213,724; McGovern, Dem., 116,435; Schmitz, Amer., 3,386; Jenness, Soc. Workers, 368; scattered, 142.

1976, Carter, Dem., 147,645; Ford, Rep., 185,935; McCarthy, Ind., 4,095; MacBride, Libertarian, 936; Reagan, write-in, 388; La Rouche, U.S. Labor, 186; Camejo, Soc. Workers, 161; Levin, Soc. Labor, 66; scattered, 215.

1980, Reagan, Rep., 221,705; Carter, Dem., 108,864; Anderson, Ind., 49,693; Clark, Libertarian, 2,067; Commoner, Citizens, 1,325; Hall, Com., 629; Griswold, Workers World, 76; DeBerry, Soc. Workers, 72; scattered, 68.

1984, Reagan, Rep., 267,051; Mondale, Dem., 120,377; Bergland, Libertarian, 735.

1988, Bush, Rep., 281,537; Dukakis, Dem., 163,696; Paul, Lib., 4,502; Fulani, New Alliance, 790.

1992, Clinton, Dem., 209,040; Bush, Rep., 202,484; Perot, Ind., 121,337; Marrou, Libertarian, 3,548.

### New Jersey

| | 1992 | | | 1988 | |
|---|---|---|---|---|---|
| County | Clinton (D) | Bush (R) | Perot (I) | Dukakis (D) | Bush (R) |
| Atlantic ....... | 39,633 | 34,279 | 15,890 | 34,047 | 44,748 |
| Bergen ....... | 171,104 | 178,223 | 52,082 | 160,655 | 226,885 |
| Burlington...... | 72,845 | 63,709 | 35,322 | 61,140 | 87,416 |
| Camden....... | 104,915 | 67,205 | 37,144 | 90,704 | 100,072 |
| Cape May..... | 17,324 | 21,502 | 9,798 | 15,105 | 28,738 |
| Cumberland .... | 22,220 | 19,253 | 9,901 | 21,869 | 26,024 |
| Essex ........ | 158,130 | 89,146 | 26,961 | 156,098 | 111,491 |
| Gloucester .... | 42,425 | 37,335 | 24,132 | 35,479 | 51,708 |
| Hudson ....... | 99,799 | 66,505 | 14,569 | 95,696 | 81,807 |
| Hunterdon..... | 15,423 | 25,130 | 12,736 | 13,758 | 31,907 |
| Mercer........ | 71,383 | 50,473 | 22,503 | 68,712 | 65,384 |
| Middlesex ..... | 128,824 | 108,701 | 45,055 | 117,149 | 143,361 |
| Monmouth..... | 101,750 | 117,715 | 45,445 | 91,844 | 147,320 |
| Morris ....... | 67,593 | 108,431 | 32,447 | 58,721 | 127,420 |
| Ocean........ | 75,431 | 95,984 | 41,668 | 64,474 | 124,587 |
| Passaic ...... | 70,030 | 71,147 | 21,494 | 66,254 | 88,070 |
| Salem ........ | 10,062 | 10,363 | 7,274 | 9,956 | 15,240 |
| Somerset ..... | 42,867 | 56,044 | 21,014 | 37,406 | 67,658 |
| Sussex ....... | 14,775 | 29,510 | 12,537 | 13,676 | 36,086 |
| Union ........ | 96,671 | 87,742 | 23,991 | 93,158 | 112,967 |
| Warren ....... | 13,002 | 18,468 | 9,866 | 11,640 | 21,715 |
| Totals........ | 1,436,206 | 1,356,865 | 521,829 | 1,317,541 | 1,740,604 |

### New Jersey Vote Since 1944

1944, Roosevelt, Dem., 987,874; Dewey, Rep., 961,335; Teichert, Soc. Labor, 6,939; Watson, Nat'l. Proh., 4,255; Thomas, Soc., 3,385.

1948, Truman, Dem., 895,455; Dewey, Rep., 981,124; Wallace, Prog., 42,683; Watson, Proh., 10,593; Thomas, Soc., 10,521; Dobbs, Soc. Workers, 5,825; Teichert, Soc. Labor, 3,354.

1952, Eisenhower, Rep., 1,373,613; Stevenson, Dem., 1,015,902; Hoopes, Soc., 8,593; Hass, Soc. Labor, 5,815; Hallinan, Prog., 5,589; Krajewski, Poor Man's, 4,203; Dobbs, Soc. Workers, 3,850; Hamblen, Proh., 989.

1956, Eisenhower, Rep., 1,606,942; Stevenson Dem., 850,337; Holtwick, Proh., 9,147; Hass, Soc. Labor, 6,736; Andrews, Conservative, 5,317; Dobbs, Soc. Workers, 4,004; Krajewski, American Third Party, 1,829.

1960, Kennedy, Dem., 1,385,415; Nixon, Rep., 1,363,324; Dobbs, Soc. Workers, 11,402; Lee, Conservative, 8,708; Hass, Soc. Labor, 4,262.

1964, Johnson, Dem., 1,867,671; Goldwater, Rep., 963,843; DeBerry, Soc. Workers, 8,181; Hass, Soc. Labor, 7,075.

1968, Nixon, Rep., 1,325,467; Humphrey, Dem., 1,264,206; Wallace, 3d party, 262,187; Halstead, Soc. Worker, 8,667; Gregory, Peace Freedom, 8,084; Blomen, Soc. Labor, 6,784.

1972, Nixon, Rep., 1,845,502; McGovern, Dem., 1,102,211; Schmitz, Amer., 34,378; Spock, Peoples, 5,355; Fisher, Soc. Labor, 4,544; Jenness, Soc. Workers, 2,233; Mahalchik, Amer. First, 1,743; Hall, Com., 1,263.

1976, Carter, Dem., 1,444,653; Ford, Rep., 1,509,688; McCarthy, Ind., 32,717; MacBride, Libertarian, 9,449; Maddox, Amer., 7,716; Levin, Soc. Labor, 3,686; Hall, Com., 1,662; LaRouche, U.S. Labor, 1,650; Camejo, Soc. Workers, 1,184; Wright, People's, 1,044; Bubar, Proh., 554; Zeidler, Soc., 469.

1980, Reagan, Rep., 1,546,557; Carter, Dem., 1,147,364; Anderson, Ind., 234,632; Clark, Libertarian, 20,652; Commoner, Citizens, 8,203; McCormack, Right to Life, 3,927; Lynen, Middle Class, 3,694; Hall, Com., 2,555; Pulley, Soc. Workers, 2,198; McReynolds, Soc., 1,973; Gahres, Down With Lawyers, 1,718; Griswold, Workers World, 1,288; Wendelken, Ind., 923.

1984, Reagan, Rep., 1,933,630; Mondale, Dem., 1,261,323; Bergland, Libertarian, 6,416.

1988, Bush, Rep., 1,740,604; Dukakis, Dem., 1,317,541; Lewin, Peace & Freedom, 9,953; Paul, Lib., 8,421.

1992, Clinton, Dem., 1,436,206; Bush, Rep., 1,356,865; Perot, Ind., 521,829; Marrou, Libertarian, 6,822; Fulani, New Alliance, 3,513; Phillips, U.S. Taxpayers, 2,670; LaRouche, Ind., 2,095; Warren, Socialist Workers, 2,011; Daniels, Ind., 1,996; Gritz, Populist/America First, 1,867; Hagelin, Natural Law, 1,353.

### New Mexico

| | 1992 | | | 1988 | |
|---|---|---|---|---|---|
| County | Clinton (D) | Bush (R) | Perot (I) | Dukakis (D) | Bush (R) |
| Bernalillo .... | 90,863 | 77,304 | 31,241 | 78,346 | 92,830 |
| Catron........ | 465 | 771 | 289 | 490 | 925 |
| Chaves ....... | 6,360 | 8,872 | 3,590 | 6,730 | 13,367 |
| Cibola ........ | 3,334 | 2,051 | 847 | 3,458 | 2,640 |
| Colfax........ | 2,607 | 1,730 | 871 | 2,785 | 2,256 |
| Curry ........ | 3,699 | 6,831 | 2,056 | 3,995 | 8,032 |
| De Baca ...... | 451 | 526 | 204 | 480 | 643 |
| Dona Ana ..... | 19,894 | 16,308 | 7,682 | 19,608 | 21,582 |
| Eddy......... | 7,409 | 7,313 | 3,430 | 8,544 | 9,805 |
| Grant ........ | 5,603 | 2,917 | 1,685 | 5,443 | 4,196 |
| Guadalupe .... | 1,225 | 691 | 173 | 1,243 | 861 |
| Harding....... | 268 | 312 | 98 | 291 | 377 |
| Hidalgo ...... | 995 | 871 | 442 | 901 | 1,100 |
| Lea .......... | 5,047 | 7,921 | 3,233 | 5,879 | 11,309 |
| Lincoln....... | 1,730 | 2,669 | 1,431 | 1,690 | 3,511 |
| Los Alamos.... | 3,897 | 4,320 | 2,339 | 3,275 | 6,622 |
| Luna ......... | 2,637 | 2,166 | 1,445 | 3,066 | 3,415 |
| McKinley ..... | 9,405 | 4,720 | 1,304 | 9,595 | 5,694 |
| Mora......... | 1,555 | 668 | 188 | 1,601 | 923 |
| Otero ........ | 5,377 | 7,481 | 3,257 | 5,284 | 9,984 |
| Quay......... | 1,758 | 1,759 | 755 | 1,901 | 2,454 |
| Rio Arriba .... | 7,832 | 2,680 | 984 | 7,503 | 3,024 |
| Roosevelt..... | 2,172 | 3,215 | 1,085 | 2,033 | 3,589 |
| Sandoval ..... | 10,951 | 8,491 | 3,954 | 9,332 | 9,411 |
| San Juan ..... | 11,302 | 13,415 | 5,351 | 11,094 | 16,202 |
| San Miguel .... | 6,186 | 2,183 | 965 | 6,131 | 2,763 |
| Santa Fe ..... | 27,189 | 9,684 | 5,656 | 23,581 | 12,891 |
| Sierra ........ | 1,771 | 1,562 | 1,055 | 1,595 | 2,507 |
| Socorro ...... | 2,908 | 2,186 | 918 | 2,960 | 3,114 |
| Taos......... | 7,051 | 2,260 | 1,300 | 6,271 | 2,897 |
| Torrance ..... | 1,662 | 1,667 | 810 | 1,618 | 2,252 |
| Union ........ | 519 | 975 | 355 | 638 | 1,291 |
| Valencia...... | 7,495 | 6,305 | 2,902 | 7,136 | 7,874 |
| Totals........ | 261,617 | 212,824 | 91,895 | 244,497 | 270,341 |

### New Mexico Vote Since 1944

1944, Roosevelt, Dem., 81,389; Dewey, Rep., 70,688; Watson, Proh., 148.

1948, Truman, Dem., 105,464; Dewey, Rep., 80,303; Wallace, Prog., 1,037; Watson, Proh., 127; Thomas, Soc., 83; Teichert, Soc. Labor, 49.

1952, Eisenhower, Rep., 132,170; Stevenson, Dem., 105,661; Hamblen, Proh., 297; Hallinan, Ind. Prog., 225; MacArthur, Christian National, 220; Hass, Soc. Labor, 35.

1956, Eisenhower, Rep., 146,788; Stevenson, Dem., 106,098; Holtwick, Proh., 607; Andrews, Ind., 364; Hass, Soc. Labor, 69.

1960, Kennedy, Dem., 156,027; Nixon, Rep., 153,733; Decker, Proh., 777; Hass, Soc. Labor, 570.

1964, Johnson, Dem., 194,017; Goldwater, Rep., 131,838; Hass, Soc. Labor, 1,217; Munn, Proh., 543.

1968, Nixon, Rep., 169,692; Humphrey, Dem., 130,081; Wallace, 3d party, 25,737; Chavez, 1,519; Halstead, Soc. Worker, 252.

1972, Nixon, Rep., 235,606; McGovern, Dem., 141,084; Schmitz, Amer., 8,767; Jenness, Soc. Workers, 474.

1976, Carter, Dem., 201,148; Ford, Rep., 211,419; Camejo, Soc. Workers, 2,462; MacBride, Libertarian, 1,110; Zeidler, Soc., 240; Bubar, Proh., 211.

1980, Reagan, Rep., 250,779; Carter, Dem., 167,826; Anderson, Ind., 29,459; Clark, Libertarian, 4,365; Commoner, Citizens, 2,202; Bubar, Statesman, 1,281; Pulley, Soc. Worker, 325.

1984, Reagan, Rep., 307,101; Mondale, Dem., 201,769; Bergland, Libertarian, 4,459.

1988, Bush, Rep., 270,341; Dukakis, Dem., 244,497; Paul, Lib., 3,268; Fulani, New Alliance, 2,237.

1992, Clinton, Dem., 261,617; Bush, Rep., 212,824; Perot, Ind., 91,895; Marrou, Libertarian, 1,615.

## New York

| County | 1992 Clinton (D) | Bush (R) | Perot (I) | 1988 Dukakis (D) | Bush (R) |
|---|---|---|---|---|---|
| Albany | 80,641 | 49,452 | 24,064 | 86,564 | 59,534 |
| Allegany | 4,848 | 8,976 | 4,703 | 5,614 | 11,880 |
| Bronx | 225,038 | 63,310 | 15,115 | 218,245 | 76,043 |
| Broome | 43,444 | 34,653 | 21,280 | 48,130 | 47,610 |
| Cattaraugus | 10,150 | 13,944 | 10,662 | 12,447 | 19,691 |
| Cayuga | 13,088 | 12,065 | 10,279 | 15,044 | 16,934 |
| Chautauqua | 22,645 | 21,222 | 18,455 | 25,814 | 31,642 |
| Chemung | 15,099 | 16,088 | 7,493 | 15,966 | 20,951 |
| Chenango | 8,017 | 8,114 | 5,356 | 8,021 | 11,727 |
| Clinton | 12,881 | 13,455 | 5,389 | 12,670 | 15,702 |
| Columbia | 11,368 | 11,568 | 5,829 | 11,585 | 15,111 |
| Cortland | 7,815 | 7,782 | 5,098 | 7,673 | 10,934 |
| Delaware | 7,152 | 8,829 | 4,404 | 7,463 | 11,391 |
| Dutchess | 41,655 | 46,709 | 26,320 | 38,968 | 62,165 |
| Erie | 196,233 | 129,444 | 123,358 | 238,779 | 188,796 |
| Essex | 6,717 | 8,278 | 3,784 | 6,623 | 10,350 |
| Franklin | 7,654 | 6,635 | 3,857 | 7,928 | 9,135 |
| Fulton | 8,400 | 9,137 | 5,120 | 9,012 | 11,757 |
| Genesee | 8,071 | 11,663 | 6,192 | 9,945 | 14,182 |
| Greene | 6,924 | 9,390 | 4,689 | 7,265 | 11,874 |
| Hamilton | 963 | 2,038 | 793 | 976 | 2,320 |
| Herkimer | 10,880 | 12,052 | 6,866 | 12,694 | 15,104 |
| Jefferson | 13,380 | 14,227 | 9,461 | 14,137 | 19,304 |
| Kings | 411,183 | 133,344 | 33,014 | 363,916 | 178,961 |
| Lewis | 3,676 | 4,101 | 3,164 | 4,252 | 5,787 |
| Livingston | 8,648 | 12,122 | 5,775 | 9,506 | 14,004 |
| Madison | 10,099 | 11,293 | 7,391 | 10,665 | 14,902 |
| Monroe | 141,502 | 134,021 | 63,229 | 153,650 | 155,271 |
| Montgomery | 9,509 | 8,802 | 5,020 | 11,371 | 11,128 |
| Nassau | 282,593 | 246,881 | 77,097 | 250,130 | 337,430 |
| New York | 416,142 | 84,501 | 27,689 | 385,675 | 115,927 |
| Niagara | 35,649 | 30,401 | 30,126 | 43,801 | 42,537 |
| Oneida | 40,966 | 43,806 | 22,717 | 47,665 | 55,039 |
| Onondaga | 90,645 | 77,642 | 45,175 | 94,751 | 104,080 |
| Ontario | 16,064 | 18,995 | 9,571 | 17,341 | 21,780 |
| Orange | 45,946 | 53,493 | 22,499 | 38,465 | 65,446 |
| Orleans | 4,927 | 7,468 | 4,275 | 5,913 | 9,028 |
| Oswego | 16,990 | 18,530 | 14,853 | 18,430 | 25,362 |
| Otsego | 10,471 | 10,141 | 5,841 | 11,069 | 13,021 |
| Putnam | 14,048 | 18,934 | 8,011 | 12,158 | 24,086 |
| Queens | 349,520 | 157,561 | 46,014 | 325,147 | 217,049 |
| Rensselaer | 29,793 | 28,937 | 15,198 | 33,066 | 35,412 |
| Richmond | 56,901 | 70,707 | 19,678 | 47,812 | 77,427 |
| Rockland | 56,759 | 49,608 | 15,026 | 47,634 | 63,825 |
| St. Lawrence | 18,197 | 13,901 | 9,758 | 18,921 | 20,290 |
| Saratoga | 33,011 | 36,917 | 19,091 | 31,684 | 43,498 |
| Schenectady | 32,335 | 26,258 | 14,838 | 36,483 | 33,364 |
| Schoharie | 4,997 | 5,678 | 3,327 | 5,389 | 7,008 |
| Schuyler | 2,859 | 3,226 | 2,051 | 2,900 | 4,291 |
| Seneca | 5,810 | 5,432 | 3,660 | 6,215 | 7,221 |
| Steuben | 12,043 | 19,761 | 9,378 | 12,824 | 25,359 |
| Suffolk | 220,811 | 229,467 | 112,973 | 199,215 | 311,242 |
| Sullivan | 13,717 | 11,396 | 6,336 | 11,635 | 15,713 |
| Tioga | 7,791 | 9,287 | 5,867 | 8,102 | 12,670 |
| Tompkins | 23,197 | 11,520 | 6,704 | 21,455 | 14,932 |
| Ulster | 32,886 | 29,223 | 17,952 | 30,744 | 41,173 |
| Warren | 9,820 | 12,260 | 6,401 | 8,580 | 15,860 |
| Washington | 8,429 | 10,305 | 6,143 | 8,201 | 14,103 |
| Wayne | 11,866 | 18,019 | 9,188 | 12,959 | 20,613 |
| Westchester | 184,300 | 151,990 | 39,933 | 169,860 | 197,956 |
| Wyoming | 4,045 | 7,324 | 4,837 | 5,228 | 9,451 |
| Yates | 3,242 | 4,366 | 2,354 | 3,507 | 5,488 |
| Totals | 3,444,450 | 2,346,649 | 1,090,721 | 3,347,882 | 3,081,871 |

## New York Vote Since 1944

1944, Roosevelt, Dem., 2,478,598; American Lab., 496,405; Liberal, 329,325; total, 3,304,238; Dewey, Rep., 2,987,647; Teichert, Ind. Gov't., 14,352; Thomas, Soc., 10,553.

1948, Truman, Dem., 2,557,642; Liberal, 222,562; total, 2,780,204; Dewey, Rep., 2,841,163; Wallace, Amer. Lab., 509,559; Thomas, Soc. Workers, 40,879; Teichert, Ind. Gov't., 2,729; Dobbs, Soc. Workers, 2,675.

1952, Eisenhower, Rep., 3,952,815; Stevenson, Dem., 2,687,890, Liberal, 416,711; total, 3,104,601; Hallinan, American Lab., 64,211; Hoopes, Soc., 2,664; Dobbs, Soc. Workers, 2,212; Hass, Ind. Gov't., 1,560; scattering, 178; blank and void, 87,813.

1956, Eisenhower, Rep., 4,340,340; Stevenson, Dem., 2,458,212; Liberal, 292,557; total, 2,750,769; write-in votes for Andrews, 1,027; Werdel, 492; Hass, 150; Hoopes, 82; others, 476.

1960, Kennedy, Dem., 3,423,909; Liberal, 406,176; total, 3,830,085; Nixon, Rep., 3,446,419; Dobbs, Soc. Workers, 14,319; scattering, 256; blank and void, 88,896.

1964, Johnson, Dem., 4,913,156; Goldwater, Rep., 2,243,559; Hass, Soc. Labor, 6,085; DeBerry, Soc. Workers, 3,215; scattering, 188; blank and void, 151,383.

1968, Nixon, Rep., 3,007,932; Humphrey, Dem., 3,378,470; Wallace, 3d party, 358,864; Blomen, Soc. Labor, 8,432; Halstead, Soc. Worker, 11,851; Gregory, Freedom and Peace, 24,517; blank, void, and scattering, 171,624.

1972, Nixon, Rep., 3,824,642; Conservative, 368,136; McGovern, Dem., 2,767,956; Liberal, 183,128; Reed, Soc. Workers, 7,797; Fisher, Soc. Labor, 4,530; Hall, Com., 5,641; blank, void, or scattered, 161,641.

1976, Carter, Dem., 3,389,558; Ford, Rep., 3,100,791; MacBride, Libertarian, 12,197; Hall, Com., 10,270; Camejo, Soc. Workers, 6,996; LaRouche, U.S. Labor, 5,413; blank, void, or scattered, 143,037.

1980, Reagan, Rep., 2,893,831; Carter, Dem., 2,728,372; Anderson, Lib., 467,801; Clark, Libertarian, 52,648; McCormack, Right To Life, 24,159; Commoner, Citizens, 23,186; Hall, Com., 7,414; DeBerry, Soc. Workers, 2,068; Griswold, Workers World, 1,416; scattering, 1,064.

1984, Reagan, Rep., 3,664,763; Mondale, Dem., 3,119,609; Bergland, Libertarian, 11,949.

1988, Bush, Rep., 3,081,871; Dukakis, Dem., 3,347,882; Marra, Right to Life, 20,497; Fulani, New Alliance, 15,845.

1992, Clinton, Dem., 3,444,450; Bush, Rep., 2,346,649; Perot, Ind., 1,090,721; Warren, Socialist Workers, 15,472; Marrou, Libertarian, 13,451; Fulani, New Alliance, 11,318; Hagelin, Natural Law, 4,420.

## North Carolina

| County | 1992 Clinton (D) | Bush (R) | Perot (I) | 1988 Dukakis (D) | Bush (R) |
|---|---|---|---|---|---|
| Alamance | 15,521 | 20,637 | 6,444 | 12,642 | 24,131 |
| Alexander | 4,849 | 6,764 | 2,002 | 4,148 | 7,968 |
| Alleghany | 2,271 | 1,853 | 600 | 2,087 | 2,174 |
| Anson | 5,269 | 2,334 | 921 | 4,831 | 2,782 |
| Ashe | 4,624 | 5,200 | 1,220 | 4,004 | 6,019 |
| Avery | 1,755 | 3,895 | 1,123 | 1,367 | 4,277 |
| Beaufort | 6,445 | 7,337 | 2,174 | 5,352 | 8,190 |
| Bertie | 4,382 | 1,756 | 600 | 3,762 | 2,145 |
| Bladen | 5,700 | 3,214 | 1,248 | 5,031 | 3,770 |
| Brunswick | 10,177 | 8,833 | 3,349 | 7,881 | 10,007 |
| Buncombe | 32,955 | 30,892 | 11,481 | 26,964 | 36,828 |
| Burke | 12,565 | 13,397 | 4,124 | 10,848 | 15,933 |
| Cabarrus | 13,513 | 21,281 | 6,251 | 10,686 | 22,524 |
| Caldwell | 9,033 | 12,543 | 3,965 | 7,862 | 15,176 |
| Camden | 1,153 | 1,039 | 479 | 1,081 | 1,144 |
| Carteret | 8,028 | 10,334 | 3,401 | 6,859 | 11,076 |
| Caswell | 4,725 | 2,793 | 827 | 4,189 | 3,299 |
| Catawba | 16,334 | 25,466 | 7,523 | 12,922 | 28,872 |
| Chatham | 9,520 | 6,568 | 2,425 | 7,600 | 6,999 |
| Cherokee | 3,686 | 4,021 | 1,040 | 2,567 | 4,557 |
| Chowan | 2,136 | 1,661 | 700 | 1,756 | 1,884 |
| Clay | 1,600 | 1,890 | 465 | 1,289 | 2,174 |
| Cleveland | 13,037 | 13,650 | 3,784 | 10,321 | 14,039 |
| Columbus | 11,469 | 5,462 | 1,963 | 9,172 | 6,659 |
| Craven | 9,998 | 11,575 | 3,679 | 7,313 | 12,057 |
| Cumberland | 30,291 | 27,139 | 6,792 | 23,789 | 27,057 |
| Currituck | 1,935 | 2,188 | 1,163 | 1,555 | 2,443 |
| Dare | 3,925 | 4,357 | 2,388 | 2,806 | 5,234 |

| | 1992 Clinton | Bush | Perot | 1988 Dukakis | Bush |
|---|---|---|---|---|---|
| Davidson | 16,462 | 24,869 | 8,324 | 13,215 | 28,374 |
| Davie | 3,675 | 6,796 | 1,903 | 3,166 | 7,988 |
| Duplin | 6,816 | 5,286 | 1,636 | 5,945 | 5,774 |
| Durham | 47,331 | 27,581 | 7,504 | 35,441 | 29,928 |
| Edgecombe | 11,174 | 6,275 | 2,175 | 9,044 | 6,831 |
| Forsyth | 49,006 | 52,787 | 14,262 | 39,726 | 57,688 |
| Franklin | 6,517 | 4,669 | 2,062 | 5,438 | 5,499 |
| Gaston | 19,121 | 34,714 | 7,490 | 14,582 | 34,775 |
| Gates | 2,206 | 1,158 | 466 | 2,024 | 1,451 |
| Graham | 1,551 | 1,919 | 403 | 1,313 | 2,091 |
| Granville | 6,178 | 4,538 | 1,321 | 5,280 | 4,880 |
| Greene | 2,768 | 2,180 | 780 | 2,729 | 2,498 |
| Guilford | 66,319 | 60,140 | 19,601 | 50,351 | 66,060 |
| Halifax | 9,960 | 5,769 | 2,047 | 8,726 | 7,462 |
| Harnett | 8,473 | 9,751 | 2,684 | 7,259 | 9,749 |
| Haywood | 10,385 | 7,292 | 3,303 | 9,010 | 8,957 |
| Henderson | 10,747 | 17,010 | 5,260 | 9,338 | 19,711 |
| Hertford | 4,609 | 2,208 | 846 | 4,943 | 2,977 |
| Hoke | 3,730 | 1,711 | 887 | 3,281 | 2,020 |
| Hyde | 1,206 | 740 | 340 | 1,316 | 940 |
| Iredell | 13,263 | 19,411 | 6,204 | 10,530 | 21,536 |
| Jackson | 5,753 | 4,275 | 1,516 | 4,933 | 5,166 |
| Johnston | 11,284 | 15,418 | 4,939 | 8,717 | 15,563 |
| Jones | 1,962 | 1,438 | 444 | 1,946 | 1,649 |
| Lee | 5,852 | 6,658 | 2,125 | 4,231 | 7,104 |
| Lenoir | 8,793 | 8,932 | 2,107 | 7,649 | 10,669 |
| Lincoln | 8,150 | 11,018 | 3,142 | 6,444 | 11,651 |
| McDowell | 5,309 | 6,090 | 1,881 | 4,449 | 6,526 |
| Macon | 4,624 | 4,797 | 1,829 | 3,773 | 6,026 |
| Madison | 3,980 | 3,121 | 857 | 3,033 | 3,453 |
| Martin | 4,069 | 2,958 | 981 | 3,598 | 3,149 |
| Mecklenburg | 97,065 | 99,496 | 31,283 | 71,907 | 106,236 |
| Mitchell | 1,727 | 4,405 | 877 | 1,377 | 4,620 |
| Montgomery | 4,422 | 3,543 | 1,185 | 3,995 | 4,504 |
| Moore | 9,649 | 12,448 | 4,448 | 7,642 | 14,543 |
| Nash | 10,809 | 14,446 | 4,544 | 8,740 | 15,906 |
| New Hanover | 20,291 | 24,338 | 7,401 | 15,401 | 23,807 |
| Northampton | 5,195 | 1,845 | 916 | 4,599 | 2,415 |
| Onslow | 8,045 | 11,842 | 4,387 | 7,162 | 12,253 |
| Orange | 28,595 | 13,009 | 5,535 | 22,326 | 14,503 |
| Pamlico | 2,229 | 1,929 | 809 | 2,188 | 2,297 |
| Pasquotank | 4,709 | 3,419 | 1,434 | 3,860 | 4,006 |
| Pender | 5,825 | 4,857 | 1,725 | 4,377 | 4,926 |
| Perquimans | 1,818 | 1,429 | 624 | 1,543 | 1,781 |
| Person | 4,323 | 4,460 | 1,431 | 3,777 | 4,832 |
| Pitt | 17,959 | 16,609 | 5,262 | 14,777 | 18,245 |
| Polk | 2,939 | 3,448 | 1,134 | 2,534 | 3,874 |
| Randolph | 11,274 | 20,697 | 6,870 | 8,641 | 23,881 |
| Richmond | 9,163 | 4,356 | 2,015 | 7,151 | 5,073 |
| Robeson | 19,378 | 7,777 | 3,277 | 16,988 | 9,908 |
| Rockingham | 13,880 | 12,678 | 4,671 | 11,551 | 14,591 |
| Rowan | 14,308 | 21,297 | 7,053 | 12,127 | 23,192 |
| Rutherford | 7,855 | 9,748 | 2,695 | 6,926 | 10,337 |
| Sampson | 8,698 | 8,007 | 1,852 | 8,009 | 8,524 |
| Scotland | 5,175 | 2,980 | 1,196 | 3,865 | 3,199 |
| Stanly | 7,735 | 11,030 | 2,855 | 6,627 | 11,885 |
| Stokes | 6,463 | 7,979 | 2,183 | 5,319 | 8,661 |
| Surry | 9,392 | 10,866 | 3,164 | 7,245 | 11,393 |
| Swain | 2,117 | 1,640 | 568 | 1,821 | 1,795 |
| Transylvania | 5,120 | 5,984 | 2,006 | 4,280 | 7,009 |
| Tyrrell | 928 | 553 | 189 | 785 | 637 |
| Union | 10,789 | 16,542 | 4,601 | 8,820 | 17,015 |
| Vance | 6,598 | 4,747 | 1,444 | 5,631 | 5,625 |
| Wake | 88,979 | 86,798 | 31,140 | 61,352 | 81,613 |
| Warren | 4,656 | 1,767 | 693 | 4,249 | 2,163 |
| Washington | 2,902 | 1,780 | 563 | 2,806 | 2,186 |
| Watauga | 8,262 | 7,899 | 3,007 | 6,048 | 8,662 |
| Wayne | 10,307 | 14,397 | 2,798 | 9,135 | 15,292 |
| Wilkes | 7,991 | 12,547 | 3,307 | 7,230 | 15,231 |
| Wilson | 10,105 | 10,176 | 2,630 | 8,214 | 10,997 |
| Yadkin | 3,913 | 7,311 | 1,725 | 3,195 | 7,918 |
| Yancey | 4,285 | 3,994 | 917 | 3,803 | 4,160 |
| Totals | 1,114,042 | 1,134,661 | 357,864 | 890,167 | 1,237,258 |

## North Carolina Vote Since 1944

1944, Roosevelt, Dem., 527,399; Dewey, Rep., 263,155.

1948, Truman, Dem., 459,070; Dewey, Rep., 258,572; Thurmond, States' Rights, 69,652; Wallace, Prog., 3,915.

1952, Eisenhower, Rep., 558,107; Stevenson, Dem., 652,803.

1956, Eisenhower, Rep., 575,062; Stevenson, Dem., 590,530.

1960, Kennedy, Dem., 713,136; Nixon, Rep., 655,420.

1964, Johnson, Dem., 800,139; Goldwater Rep., 624,844.

1968, Nixon, Rep., 627,192; Humphrey, Dem., 464,113; Wallace, 3d party, 496,188.

1972, Nixon, Rep., 1,054,889; McGovern, Dem., 438,705; Schmitz, Amer., 25,018.

1976, Carter, Dem., 927,365; Ford, Rep., 741,960; Anderson, Amer., 5,607; MacBride, Libertarian, 2,219; LaRouche, U.S. Labor, 755.

1980, Reagan, Rep., 915,018; Carter, Dem., 875,635; Anderson, Ind., 52,800; Clark, Libertarian, 9,677; Commoner, Citizens, 2,287; DeBerry, Soc. Workers, 416.

1984, Reagan, Rep., 1,346,481; Mondale, Dem., 824,287; Bergland, Libertarian, 3,794.

1988, Bush, Rep., 1,237,258; Dukakis, Dem., 890,167; Fulani, New Alliance, 5,682; Paul, write-in, 1,263.

1992, Bush, Rep., 1,134,661; Clinton, Dem., 1,114,042; Perot, Ind., 357,864; Marrou, Libertarian, 5,171.

# North Dakota

| County | 1992 Clinton (D) | Bush (R) | Perot (I) | 1988 Dukakis (D) | Bush (R) |
|---|---|---|---|---|---|
| Adams | 469 | 647 | 499 | 708 | 1,018 |
| Barnes | 2,124 | 2,728 | 1,568 | 2,858 | 3,631 |
| Benson | 1,126 | 874 | 610 | 1,691 | 1,316 |
| Billings | 123 | 279 | 270 | 211 | 437 |
| Bottineau | 1,266 | 1,787 | 1,036 | 1,684 | 2,530 |
| Bowman | 506 | 712 | 678 | 737 | 1,111 |
| Burke | 458 | 551 | 506 | 693 | 971 |
| Burleigh | 8,940 | 16,484 | 6,780 | 10,760 | 18,000 |
| Cass | 18,077 | 25,312 | 9,513 | 22,107 | 26,699 |
| Cavalier | 866 | 1,527 | 723 | 1,333 | 2,096 |
| Dickey | 918 | 1,514 | 616 | 1,249 | 2,064 |
| Divide | 634 | 515 | 456 | 875 | 869 |
| Dunn | 667 | 784 | 637 | 892 | 1,263 |
| Eddy | 575 | 591 | 432 | 748 | 891 |
| Emmons | 595 | 1,047 | 774 | 925 | 1,634 |
| Foster | 565 | 803 | 556 | 837 | 1,218 |
| Golden Valley | 255 | 503 | 352 | 388 | 781 |
| Grand Forks | 10,930 | 13,705 | 6,349 | 12,494 | 14,801 |
| Grant | 415 | 900 | 629 | 654 | 1,351 |
| Griggs | 647 | 773 | 330 | 846 | 1,020 |
| Hettinger | 465 | 854 | 500 | 698 | 1,395 |
| Kidder | 468 | 739 | 489 | 678 | 1,039 |
| La Moure | 797 | 1,270 | 679 | 1,223 | 1,642 |
| Logan | 383 | 703 | 390 | 540 | 1,111 |
| McHenry | 1,173 | 1,321 | 886 | 1,665 | 1,888 |
| McIntosh | 450 | 1,134 | 454 | 598 | 1,726 |
| McKenzie | 787 | 1,324 | 969 | 1,273 | 1,949 |
| McLean | 1,808 | 2,124 | 1,330 | 2,428 | 2,906 |
| Mercer | 1,323 | 2,274 | 1,378 | 1,843 | 3,013 |
| Morton | 3,594 | 5,042 | 2,787 | 4,708 | 5,588 |
| Mountrail | 1,393 | 1,017 | 861 | 1,977 | 1,443 |
| Nelson | 841 | 864 | 486 | 1,151 | 1,078 |
| Oliver | 306 | 503 | 407 | 526 | 696 |
| Pembina | 1,186 | 1,917 | 991 | 1,616 | 2,471 |
| Pierce | 761 | 1,099 | 554 | 1,008 | 1,422 |
| Ramsey | 2,008 | 2,516 | 1,507 | 2,665 | 3,103 |
| Ransom | 1,166 | 1,102 | 625 | 1,459 | 1,362 |
| Renville | 580 | 655 | 429 | 837 | 893 |
| Richland | 2,688 | 3,873 | 1,698 | 3,523 | 4,670 |
| Rolette | 2,002 | 895 | 660 | 2,426 | 1,126 |
| Sargent | 961 | 816 | 463 | 1,306 | 1,119 |
| Sheridan | 276 | 589 | 304 | 428 | 885 |
| Sioux | 463 | 264 | 24 | 701 | 325 |
| Slope | 145 | 226 | 162 | 202 | 315 |
| Stark | 3,003 | 4,491 | 3,123 | 3,678 | 6,137 |
| Steele | 598 | 503 | 267 | 895 | 690 |
| Stutsman | 3,313 | 4,039 | 2,580 | 4,214 | 5,375 |
| Towner | 748 | 600 | 402 | 970 | 946 |
| Traill | 1,638 | 2,019 | 875 | 1,940 | 2,562 |
| Walsh | 1,936 | 2,544 | 1,384 | 2,646 | 3,250 |
| Ward | 7,856 | 12,056 | 5,856 | 9,906 | 13,179 |
| Wells | 888 | 1,171 | 850 | 1,317 | 1,901 |
| Williams | 3,008 | 3,603 | 3,180 | 4,004 | 5,653 |
| Totals | 99,168 | 136,244 | 71,084 | 127,739 | 166,559 |

## North Dakota Vote Since 1944

1944, Roosevelt, Dem., 100,144; Dewey, Rep., 118,535; Thomas, Soc., 943, Watson, Proh., 549.

1948, Truman, Dem., 95,812; Dewey, Rep., 115,139; Wallace, Prog., 8,391; Thomas, Soc., 1,000, Thurmond, States' Rights, 374.

1952, Eisenhower, Rep., 191,712; Stevenson, Dem., 76,694; MacArthur, Christian Nationalist, 1,075; Hallinan, Prog., 344; Hamblen, Proh., 302.

1956, Eisenhower, Rep., 156,766; Stevenson, Dem., 96,742; Andrews, Amer., 483.

1960, Kennedy, Dem., 123,963; Nixon, Rep., 154,310; Dobbs, Soc. Workers, 158.

1964, Johnson, Dem., 149,784; Goldwater, Rep., 108,207; DeBerry, Soc. Worker, 224; Munn, Proh., 174.

1968, Nixon, Rep., 138,669; Humphrey, Dem., 94,769; Wallace, 3d party, 14,244; Halstead, Soc. Worker, 128; Munn, Prohibition, 38; Troxell, Ind., 34.

1972, Nixon, Rep., 174,109; McGovern, Dem., 100,384; Jenness, Soc. Workers, 288; Hall, Com., 87; Schmitz, Amer., 5,646.

1976, Carter, Dem., 136,078; Ford, Rep., 153,470; Anderson, Amer., 3,698; McCarthy, Ind., 2,952; Maddox, Amer. Ind., 269; MacBride, Libertarian, 256; scattering, 371.

1980, Reagan, Rep., 193,695; Carter, Dem., 79,189; Anderson, Ind., 23,640; Clark, Libertarian, 3,743; Commoner,

Libertarian, 429; McLain, Nat'l People's League, 296; Greaves, American, 235; Hall, Com., 93; DeBerry, Soc. Workers, 89; McReynolds, Soc., 82; Bubar, Statesman, 54.

1984, Reagan, Rep., 200,336; Mondale, Dem., 104,429; Bergland, Libertarian, 703.

1988, Bush, Rep., 166,559; Dukakis, Dem., 127,739; Paul, Lib., 1,315; LaRouche, Natl. Econ. Recovery, 905.

1992, Bush, Rep., 136,244; Clinton, Dem., 99,168; Perot, Ind., 71,084.

## Ohio

| County | 1992 Clinton (D) | Bush (R) | Perot (I) | 1988 Dukakis (D) | Bush (R) |
|---|---|---|---|---|---|
| Adams. . . . . . . | 3,998 | 4,722 | 1,993 | 3,740 | 5,916 |
| Allen. . . . . . . | 13,777 | 25,322 | 8,131 | 13,727 | 31,021 |
| Ashland . . . . . | 5,985 | 9,864 | 4,950 | 6,072 | 12,726 |
| Ashtabula . . . . | 18,843 | 13,254 | 10,765 | 20,536 | 17,654 |
| Athens. . . . . . | 13,423 | 7,184 | 5,074 | 10,795 | 9,314 |
| Auglaize. . . . . | 4,960 | 10,455 | 4,840 | 4,756 | 13,562 |
| Belmont. . . . . | 18,527 | 8,614 | 6,142 | 19,515 | 12,214 |
| Brown . . . . . . | 5,540 | 5,912 | 3,676 | 5,047 | 7,539 |
| Butler . . . . . . | 39,682 | 63,375 | 27,527 | 33,770 | 75,725 |
| Carroll. . . . . . | 4,731 | 4,224 | 3,434 | 4,667 | 6,179 |
| Champaign . . . | 5,201 | 7,004 | 3,992 | 4,272 | 8,995 |
| Clark. . . . . . . | 26,692 | 24,011 | 12,571 | 23,247 | 32,729 |
| Clermont . . . . | 17,558 | 32,065 | 14,279 | 15,352 | 37,417 |
| Clinton. . . . . . | 4,638 | 7,290 | 3,402 | 3,746 | 8,856 |
| Columbiana . . . | 19,765 | 15,016 | 12,611 | 21,581 | 21,175 |
| Coshocton . . . . | 6,212 | 5,705 | 4,081 | 6,020 | 8,282 |
| Crawford . . . . | 6,351 | 8,618 | 5,764 | 6,018 | 12,472 |
| Cuyahoga . . . . | 337,548 | 187,186 | 112,352 | 353,401 | 242,439 |
| Darke . . . . . . | 7,016 | 11,098 | 6,217 | 6,851 | 14,914 |
| Defiance. . . . . | 5,735 | 7,195 | 4,187 | 5,448 | 9,566 |
| Delaware . . . . | 9,263 | 18,225 | 9,244 | 7,590 | 20,693 |
| Erie . . . . . . . | 14,531 | 12,459 | 8,720 | 15,097 | 16,670 |
| Fairfield . . . . . | 14,249 | 24,125 | 12,246 | 12,504 | 29,208 |
| Fayette . . . . . | 2,976 | 4,916 | 2,162 | 2,623 | 6,186 |
| Franklin . . . . . | 176,656 | 186,324 | 79,049 | 147,585 | 226,265 |
| Fulton . . . . . . | 5,576 | 8,358 | 4,798 | 5,076 | 10,230 |
| Gallia . . . . . . | 5,350 | 5,776 | 2,549 | 4,834 | 7,399 |
| Geauga . . . . . | 11,466 | 18,200 | 10,577 | 11,874 | 22,339 |
| Greene . . . . . | 20,139 | 27,651 | 11,459 | 18,025 | 34,432 |
| Guernsey . . . . | 6,428 | 5,749 | 4,103 | 5,926 | 8,507 |
| Hamilton . . . . | 148,409 | 192,447 | 60,145 | 140,354 | 227,004 |
| Hancock . . . . . | 7,944 | 16,821 | 7,002 | 7,435 | 19,896 |
| Hardin . . . . . . | 4,364 | 5,851 | 2,867 | 4,145 | 7,291 |
| Harrison . . . . . | 3,830 | 2,289 | 1,679 | 3,881 | 3,298 |
| Henry . . . . . . | 3,933 | 6,196 | 3,178 | 3,764 | 8,618 |
| Highland . . . . | 4,866 | 7,020 | 3,315 | 4,278 | 8,776 |
| Hocking . . . . . | 3,935 | 3,761 | 2,831 | 3,706 | 5,426 |
| Holmes . . . . . | 1,969 | 5,079 | 1,945 | 2,179 | 5,064 |
| Huron . . . . . . | 7,930 | 9,480 | 6,751 | 7,794 | 12,633 |
| Jackson . . . . . | 5,016 | 5,422 | 2,389 | 4,505 | 6,671 |
| Jefferson . . . . | 20,978 | 10,764 | 6,910 | 22,095 | 14,141 |
| Knox. . . . . . . | 7,259 | 9,044 | 5,282 | 6,882 | 12,180 |
| Lake . . . . . . . | 37,682 | 40,766 | 26,878 | 39,667 | 52,963 |
| Lawrence . . . . | 12,325 | 10,044 | 4,536 | 11,628 | 12,937 |
| Licking. . . . . . | 18,898 | 26,918 | 13,806 | 16,793 | 34,540 |
| Logan . . . . . . | 4,889 | 9,364 | 4,472 | 4,484 | 11,099 |
| Lorain . . . . . . | 50,962 | 36,803 | 30,425 | 55,600 | 50,410 |
| Lucas . . . . . . | 99,989 | 63,297 | 38,108 | 99,755 | 83,788 |
| Madison . . . . . | 3,998 | 6,865 | 3,170 | 3,421 | 8,303 |
| Mahoning . . . . | 64,731 | 31,191 | 29,417 | 75,524 | 43,722 |
| Marion. . . . . . | 9,444 | 11,675 | 6,471 | 9,596 | 14,864 |
| Medina . . . . . | 18,995 | 24,090 | 17,290 | 19,505 | 29,962 |
| Meigs . . . . . . | 4,226 | 3,916 | 2,098 | 3,699 | 5,486 |
| Mercer. . . . . . | 4,883 | 8,683 | 4,913 | 4,978 | 11,162 |
| Miami . . . . . . | 12,547 | 19,741 | 10,544 | 11,138 | 24,915 |
| Monroe . . . . . | 4,235 | 1,823 | 1,505 | 4,269 | 2,557 |
| Montgomery . . . | 108,017 | 104,751 | 47,854 | 95,737 | 131,596 |
| Morgan . . . . . | 2,402 | 2,719 | 1,551 | 2,085 | 3,713 |
| Morrow . . . . . | 3,907 | 5,208 | 3,623 | 3,515 | 7,130 |
| Muskingum . . . | 11,670 | 14,168 | 8,731 | 11,691 | 19,736 |
| Noble . . . . . . | 2,201 | 2,223 | 1,429 | 2,079 | 3,155 |
| Ottawa . . . . . | 6,128 | 6,782 | 4,832 | 8,038 | 9,352 |
| Paulding . . . . | 3,293 | 3,652 | 2,510 | 3,114 | 5,381 |
| Perry. . . . . . . | 4,972 | 4,712 | 3,810 | 5,011 | 6,602 |
| Pickaway . . . . | 5,765 | 8,690 | 4,319 | 4,905 | 10,796 |
| Pike . . . . . . . | 5,057 | 4,094 | 2,192 | 5,191 | 5,611 |
| Portage . . . . . | 26,325 | 18,447 | 17,065 | 25,607 | 26,334 |
| Preble. . . . . . | 5,557 | 8,023 | 4,460 | 4,937 | 10,297 |
| Putnam . . . . . | 3,962 | 9,338 | 3,648 | 4,004 | 11,183 |
| Richland. . . . . | 19,606 | 23,532 | 13,370 | 19,617 | 30,047 |
| Ross. . . . . . . | 10,452 | 10,825 | 5,616 | 9,271 | 14,563 |
| Sandusky . . . . | 9,878 | 10,772 | 6,682 | 9,709 | 14,203 |
| Scioto . . . . . . | 14,715 | 11,931 | 6,860 | 14,442 | 16,029 |
| Seneca . . . . . | 9,280 | 9,763 | 6,967 | 9,504 | 13,704 |
| Shelby. . . . . . | 5,262 | 8,854 | 5,835 | 5,065 | 12,198 |
| Stark. . . . . . . | 70,064 | 61,863 | 42,413 | 69,639 | 87,087 |
| Summit . . . . . | 107,881 | 77,530 | 55,151 | 112,612 | 101,155 |
| Trumbull . . . . | 54,591 | 25,831 | 26,791 | 58,674 | 38,815 |
| Tuscarawas. . . . | 14,787 | 13,179 | 8,785 | 14,185 | 17,145 |
| Union . . . . . . | 3,465 | 7,818 | 3,433 | 3,130 | 8,846 |
| Van Wert . . . . | 3,822 | 7,227 | 3,102 | 3,848 | 9,410 |
| Vinton . . . . . . | 2,308 | 1,975 | 1,050 | 2,385 | 2,652 |

| County | 1992 Clinton (D) | Bush (R) | Perot (I) | 1988 Dukakis (D) | Bush (R) |
|---|---|---|---|---|---|
| Warren . . . . . . | 13,542 | 27,998 | 11,115 | 11,145 | 31,419 |
| Washington . . . . | 10,380 | 12,204 | 5,415 | 9,967 | 14,767 |
| Wayne. . . . . . | 13,953 | 18,350 | 9,482 | 13,571 | 22,320 |
| Williams . . . . . | 4,862 | 7,614 | 4,902 | 4,666 | 10,782 |
| Wood . . . . . . | 20,754 | 20,579 | 11,682 | 18,579 | 26,013 |
| Wyandot . . . . . | 3,031 | 4,411 | 2,929 | 2,936 | 6,178 |
| Totals . . . . . . . . | 1,984,942 | 1,894,310 | 1,036,426 | 1,939,629 | 2,416,549 |

## Ohio Vote Since 1944

1944, Roosevelt, Dem., 1,570,763; Dewey, Rep., 1,582,293.

1948, Truman, Dem., 1,452,791; Dewey, Rep., 1,445,684; Wallace, Prog., 37,596.

1952, Eisenhower, Rep., 2,100,391; Stevenson, Dem., 1,600,367.

1956, Eisenhower, Rep., 2,262,610; Stevenson, Dem., 1,439,655.

1960, Kennedy, Dem., 1,944,248; Nixon, Rep., 2,217,611.

1964, Johnson, Dem., 2,498,331; Goldwater, Rep., 1,470,865.

1968, Nixon, Rep., 1,791,014; Humphrey, Dem., 1,700,586; Wallace, 3d party, 467,495; Gregory, 372; Munn, Proh., 19; Blomen, Soc. Labor, 120; Halstead, Soc. Worker, 69; Mitchell, Com., 23.

1972, Nixon, Rep., 2,441,827; McGovern, Dem., 1,558,889; Fisher, Soc. Labor, 7,107; Hall, Com., 6,437; Schmitz, Amer., 80,067; Wallace, Ind., 460.

1976, Carter, Dem., 2,011,621; Ford, Rep., 2,000,505; Mc-Carthy, Ind., 58,258; Maddox, Amer. Ind., 15,529; MacBride, Libertarian, 8,961; Hall, Com., 7,817; Camejo, Soc. Workers, 4,717; LaRouche, U.S. Labor, 4,335; scattered, 130.

1980, Reagan, Rep., 2,206,545; Carter, Dem., 1,752,414; Anderson, Ind., 254,472; Clark, Libertarian, 49,033; Commoner, Citizens, 8,564; Hall, Com., 4,729; Congress, Ind. 4,029; Griswold, Workers World, 3,790; Bubar, Statesman, 27.

1984, Reagan, Rep., 2,678,559; Mondale, Dem., 1,825,440; Bergland, Libertarian, 5,886.

1988, Bush, Rep., 2,416,549; Dukakis, Dem., 1,939,629; Fulani, Ind., 12,017; Paul, Ind., 11,926.

1992, Clinton, Dem., 1,984,942; Bush, Rep., 1,894,310; Perot, Ind., 1,036,426; Marrou, Libertarian, 7,252; Fulani, New Alliance, 6,413; Gritz, Populist/America First, 4,699; Hagelin, Natural Law, 3,437; LaRouche, Ind., 2,446.

## Oklahoma

| County | 1992 Clinton (D) | Bush (R) | Perot (I) | 1988 Dukakis (D) | Bush (R) |
|---|---|---|---|---|---|
| Adair. . . . . . . | 2,645 | 2,994 | 914 | 2,624 | 3,558 |
| Alfalfa . . . . . . | 741 | 1,567 | 722 | 1,117 | 1,960 |
| Atoka . . . . . . | 2,336 | 1,561 | 1,255 | 2,565 | 1,971 |
| Beaver. . . . . . | 580 | 1,699 | 565 | 777 | 2,013 |
| Beckham . . . . | 2,947 | 2,913 | 1,929 | 3,388 | 3,463 |
| Blaine . . . . . . | 1,564 | 2,209 | 1,258 | 1,775 | 2,889 |
| Bryan . . . . . . | 6,259 | 3,452 | 3,713 | 6,849 | 4,615 |
| Caddo . . . . . . | 4,861 | 3,664 | 2,911 | 5,387 | 4,689 |
| Canadian . . . . | 7,215 | 16,756 | 8,985 | 7,453 | 17,872 |
| Carter . . . . . . | 7,171 | 5,947 | 5,188 | 7,988 | 8,430 |
| Cherokee . . . . | 6,794 | 4,977 | 3,297 | 6,483 | 5,838 |
| Choctaw. . . . . | 3,413 | 1,641 | 1,298 | 3,362 | 2,217 |
| Cimarron . . . . | 395 | 965 | 254 | 470 | 1,153 |
| Cleveland . . . . | 24,404 | 35,561 | 20,352 | 22,067 | 36,313 |
| Coal . . . . . . . | 1,448 | 714 | 618 | 1,365 | 891 |
| Comanche . . . . | 12,237 | 15,704 | 7,463 | 11,441 | 17,464 |
| Cotton . . . . . . | 1,314 | 910 | 853 | 1,482 | 1,266 |
| Craig. . . . . . . | 2,780 | 2,106 | 1,316 | 2,940 | 2,463 |
| Creek . . . . . . | 9,118 | 10,055 | 5,984 | 9,512 | 11,308 |
| Custer . . . . . . | 3,540 | 5,362 | 2,741 | 3,697 | 6,735 |
| Delaware . . . . | 4,842 | 4,840 | 2,689 | 4,889 | 5,248 |
| Dewey . . . . . . | 845 | 1,244 | 684 | 963 | 1,543 |
| Ellis . . . . . . . | 594 | 1,072 | 632 | 786 | 1,422 |
| Garfield . . . . . | 6,720 | 13,095 | 5,559 | 8,067 | 15,248 |
| Garvin . . . . . . | 4,811 | 3,983 | 3,014 | 5,438 | 5,109 |
| Grady . . . . . . | 6,177 | 6,997 | 4,528 | 6,689 | 7,994 |
| Grant . . . . . . | 864 | 1,311 | 871 | 1,249 | 1,690 |
| Greer . . . . . . | 1,162 | 964 | 640 | 1,256 | 1,225 |
| Harmon . . . . . | 783 | 496 | 326 | 890 | 611 |
| Harper. . . . . . | 486 | 1,038 | 501 | 593 | 1,281 |
| Haskell . . . . . | 3,069 | 1,461 | 995 | 2,963 | 1,822 |
| Hughes . . . . . | 2,850 | 1,522 | 1,158 | 3,259 | 2,037 |
| Jackson . . . . . | 3,273 | 3,893 | 2,227 | 3,542 | 4,423 |
| Jefferson . . . . | 1,580 | 671 | 758 | 1,767 | 1,063 |
| Johnston . . . . | 2,096 | 1,191 | 1,040 | 2,042 | 1,518 |
| Kay . . . . . . . | 6,643 | 9,115 | 6,984 | 7,751 | 12,646 |
| Kingfisher . . . . | 1,379 | 3,479 | 1,534 | 1,777 | 4,011 |
| Kiowa . . . . . . | 2,143 | 1,635 | 1,114 | 2,296 | 2,030 |
| Latimer . . . . . | 2,606 | 1,212 | 1,049 | 2,365 | 1,830 |

| | | | | |
|---|---|---|---|---|
| Le Flore | 7,843 | 5,850 | 3,021 | 6,594 | 6,964 |
| Lincoln | 3,904 | 5,315 | 3,160 | 4,225 | 6,409 |
| Logan | 4,453 | 6,071 | 3,239 | 4,603 | 6,947 |
| Love | 1,708 | 922 | 1,033 | 1,889 | 1,961 |
| McClain | 3,378 | 4,377 | 2,996 | 3,594 | 4,771 |
| McCurtain | 5,082 | 3,519 | 2,852 | 4,928 | 4,920 |
| McIntosh | 4,184 | 2,225 | 1,469 | 4,041 | 2,665 |
| Major | 731 | 2,154 | 857 | 982 | 2,638 |
| Marshall | 2,519 | 1,478 | 1,486 | 2,730 | 1,911 |
| Mayes | 6,432 | 5,445 | 3,235 | 6,691 | 6,115 |
| Murray | 2,594 | 1,536 | 1,447 | 2,697 | 2,056 |
| Muskogee | 13,619 | 8,782 | 5,454 | 13,760 | 11,147 |
| Noble | 1,333 | 2,474 | 1,449 | 1,661 | 3,015 |
| Nowata | 1,912 | 1,531 | 1,063 | 2,203 | 2,000 |
| Okfuskee | 2,141 | 1,580 | 889 | 2,209 | 1,851 |
| Oklahoma | 76,271 | 126,788 | 56,139 | 75,812 | 135,376 |
| Okmulgee | 7,767 | 4,586 | 3,013 | 8,262 | 5,674 |
| Osage | 6,894 | 5,891 | 4,477 | 7,778 | 7,162 |
| Ottawa | 6,304 | 4,141 | 2,721 | 6,658 | 5,026 |
| Pawnee | 2,612 | 2,675 | 1,656 | 2,781 | 3,324 |
| Payne | 9,886 | 13,032 | 7,852 | 10,568 | 16,027 |
| Pittsburg | 8,523 | 5,659 | 4,594 | 8,623 | 7,594 |
| Pontotoc | 6,350 | 5,206 | 3,916 | 6,484 | 6,609 |
| Pottawatomie | 8,616 | 10,350 | 6,520 | 8,873 | 12,099 |
| Pushmataha | 2,553 | 1,319 | 1,000 | 2,430 | 1,841 |
| Roger Mills | 767 | 890 | 505 | 866 | 1,132 |
| Rogers | 8,257 | 12,455 | 7,101 | 8,771 | 12,940 |
| Seminole | 4,624 | 3,253 | 2,330 | 4,911 | 4,078 |
| Sequoyah | 6,092 | 4,925 | 2,486 | 4,951 | 5,710 |
| Stephens | 7,644 | 7,085 | 5,692 | 7,833 | 9,844 |
| Texas | 1,487 | 4,059 | 1,417 | 1,717 | 4,971 |
| Tillman | 1,749 | 1,377 | 1,039 | 2,148 | 1,754 |
| Tulsa | 71,165 | 117,465 | 49,760 | 69,044 | 127,512 |
| Wagoner | 7,041 | 9,053 | 5,381 | 7,378 | 10,219 |
| Washington | 6,593 | 11,342 | 5,664 | 6,971 | 14,613 |
| Washita | 1,929 | 1,912 | 1,468 | 2,290 | 2,402 |
| Woods | 1,361 | 2,225 | 1,167 | 1,735 | 2,835 |
| Woodward | 2,063 | 4,006 | 2,411 | 2,408 | 4,996 |
| Totals | 473,066 | 592,929 | 319,878 | 483,423 | 678,367 |

| | | | | | |
|---|---|---|---|---|---|
| Polk | 9,551 | 10,082 | 5,818 | 9,626 | 10,553 |
| Sherman | 362 | 424 | 326 | 435 | 555 |
| Tillamook | 5,040 | 3,359 | 2,997 | 5,529 | 4,297 |
| Umatilla | 6,787 | 7,095 | 5,581 | 8,327 | 10,254 |
| Union | 3,990 | 4,223 | 3,305 | 4,682 | 5,061 |
| Wallowa | 1,203 | 1,630 | 1,209 | 1,425 | 1,993 |
| Wasco | 4,663 | 3,242 | 3,008 | 5,141 | 4,462 |
| Washington | 67,528 | 57,146 | 41,575 | 59,837 | 67,018 |
| Wheeler | 267 | 357 | 227 | 274 | 361 |
| Yamhill | 11,148 | 11,693 | 8,312 | 11,423 | 13,321 |
| Totals | 621,314 | 475,757 | 354,091 | 616,206 | 560,126 |

## Oklahoma Vote Since 1944

1944, Roosevelt, Dem., 401,549; Dewey, Rep., 319,424; Watson, Proh., 1,663.

1948, Truman, Dem., 452,782; Dewey, Rep., 268,817.

1952, Eisenhower, Rep., 518,045; Stevenson, Dem., 430,939.

1956, Eisenhower, Rep., 473,769; Stevenson, Dem., 385,581.

1960, Kennedy, Dem., 370,111; Nixon, Rep., 533,039.

1964, Johnson, Dem., 519,834; Goldwater, Rep. 412,665.

1968, Nixon, Rep., 449,697; Humphrey, Dem., 301,658; Wallace, 3d party, 191,731.

1972, Nixon, Rep. 759,025; McGovern, Dem., 247,147; Schmitz, Amer., 23,728.

1976, Carter, Dem., 532,442; Ford, Rep., 545,708; McCarthy, Ind., 14,101.

1980, Reagan, Rep., 695,570; Carter, Dem., 402,026; Anderson, Ind., 38,284; Clark, Libertarian, 13,828.

1984, Reagan, Rep., 861,530; Mondale, Dem., 385,080; Bergland, Libertarian, 9,066.

1988, Bush, Rep., 678,367; Dukakis, Dem., 483,423; Paul, Lib., 6,261; Fulani, New Alliance, 2,985.

1992, Bush, Rep., 592,929; Clinton, Dem., 473,066; Perot, Ind., 319,878; Marrou, Libertarian, 4,486.

## Oregon Vote Since 1944

1944, Roosevelt, Dem., 248,635; Dewey, Rep., 225,365; Thomas, Soc., 3,785; Watson, Proh., 2,362.

1948, Truman, Dem., 243,147; Dewey, Rep., 260,904; Wallace, Prog., 14,978; Thomas, Soc., 5,051.

1952, Eisenhower, Rep., 420,815; Stevenson, Dem., 270,579; Hallinan, Ind., 3,665.

1956, Eisenhower, Rep., 406,393; Stevenson, Dem., 329,204.

1960, Kennedy, Dem., 367,402; Nixon, Rep., 408,060.

1964, Johnson, Dem., 501,017; Goldwater, Rep., 282,779; write-in, 2,509.

1968, Nixon, Rep., 408,433; Humphrey, Dem., 358,866; Wallace, 3d party, 49,683; write-in, McCarthy, 1,496; N. Rockefeller, 69; others, 1,075.

1972, Nixon, Rep. 486,686; McGovern, Dem., 392,760; Schmitz, Amer., 46,211; write-in, 2,289.

1976, Carter, Dem., 490,407; Ford, Rep., 492,120; McCarthy, Ind., 40,207; write-in, 7,142.

1980, Reagan, Rep., 571,044; Carter, Dem., 456,890; Anderson, Ind., 112,389; Clark, Libertarian, 25,838; Commoner, Citizens, 13,642; scattered, 1,713.

1984, Reagan, Rep., 658,700; Mondale, Dem., 536,479.

1988, Bush, Rep., 560,126; Dukakis, Dem., 616,206; Paul, Lib., 14,811; Fulani, Ind., 6,487.

1992, Clinton, Dem., 621,314; Bush, Rep., 475,757; Perot, Ind., 354,091; Marrou, Libertarian, 4,277; Fulani, New Alliance, 3,030.

# Oregon

| | 1992 | | | 1988 | |
|---|---|---|---|---|---|
| County | Clinton (D) | Bush (R) | Perot (I) | Dukakis (D) | Bush (R) |
| Baker | 2,395 | 2,862 | 2,191 | 2,896 | 3,696 |
| Benton | 17,966 | 11,550 | 8,103 | 16,930 | 14,004 |
| Clackamas | 60,310 | 53,724 | 39,776 | 59,799 | 61,381 |
| Clatsop | 7,700 | 4,683 | 4,316 | 8,074 | 5,956 |
| Columbia | 8,298 | 5,227 | 5,670 | 8,983 | 6,424 |
| Coos | 12,072 | 9,284 | 7,989 | 13,996 | 10,153 |
| Crook | 2,508 | 2,703 | 2,024 | 2,719 | 3,049 |
| Curry | 3,841 | 3,809 | 3,310 | 4,015 | 4,761 |
| Deschutes | 15,693 | 15,655 | 12,293 | 14,264 | 16,425 |
| Douglas | 14,137 | 19,011 | 12,377 | 17,255 | 20,120 |
| Gilliam | 374 | 377 | 283 | 417 | 470 |
| Grant | 1,135 | 1,496 | 1,302 | 1,417 | 2,264 |
| Harney | 973 | 1,350 | 1,024 | 1,379 | 1,833 |
| Hood River | 3,106 | 2,453 | 2,235 | 3,275 | 3,257 |
| Jackson | 29,146 | 28,704 | 18,633 | 28,028 | 32,516 |
| Jefferson | 2,161 | 1,962 | 1,741 | 2,346 | 2,509 |
| Josephine | 11,007 | 13,003 | 8,426 | 10,646 | 15,876 |
| Klamath | 7,918 | 11,864 | 6,636 | 8,429 | 13,484 |
| Lake | 1,019 | 1,791 | 980 | 1,237 | 2,161 |
| Lane | 74,083 | 41,789 | 34,906 | 69,883 | 47,563 |
| Lincoln | 9,603 | 5,716 | 6,127 | 9,598 | 7,364 |
| Linn | 15,399 | 16,461 | 13,256 | 17,007 | 18,312 |
| Malheur | 2,539 | 5,374 | 2,654 | 2,965 | 6,285 |
| Marion | 41,137 | 42,145 | 26,156 | 41,193 | 45,292 |
| Morrow | 1,174 | 1,187 | 1,089 | 1,375 | 1,529 |
| Multnomah | 165,081 | 72,326 | 58,236 | 161,361 | 95,561 |

# Pennsylvania

| | 1992 | | | 1988 | |
|---|---|---|---|---|---|
| County | Clinton (D) | Bush (R) | Perot (I) | Dukakis (D) | Bush (R) |
| Adams | 9,576 | 13,552 | 6,313 | 8,299 | 15,059 |
| Allegheny | 324,004 | 183,035 | 103,470 | 348,814 | 231,137 |
| Armstrong | 12,995 | 9,122 | 6,166 | 13,892 | 11,509 |
| Beaver | 44,877 | 21,361 | 15,954 | 50,327 | 25,764 |
| Bedford | 5,840 | 9,216 | 3,731 | 5,754 | 11,123 |
| Berks | 46,031 | 52,939 | 31,663 | 41,040 | 70,153 |
| Blair | 14,857 | 21,447 | 8,284 | 15,568 | 25,623 |
| Bradford | 6,903 | 10,221 | 5,452 | 6,635 | 13,568 |
| Bucks | 97,902 | 94,584 | 53,931 | 82,472 | 127,563 |
| Butler | 22,303 | 23,656 | 15,013 | 22,341 | 27,777 |
| Cambria | 34,203 | 20,770 | 11,070 | 38,517 | 25,626 |
| Cameron | 824 | 1,173 | 676 | 901 | 1,731 |
| Carbon | 9,072 | 7,243 | 5,222 | 9,104 | 10,232 |
| Centre | 21,177 | 20,478 | 9,356 | 18,357 | 23,875 |
| Chester | 59,643 | 74,002 | 34,536 | 44,853 | 93,522 |
| Clarion | 5,584 | 6,477 | 3,619 | 5,616 | 8,026 |
| Clearfield | 12,247 | 11,553 | 6,989 | 12,235 | 14,296 |
| Clinton | 5,397 | 4,471 | 2,654 | 5,759 | 5,735 |
| Columbia | 8,261 | 9,742 | 5,683 | 7,767 | 12,114 |
| Crawford | 12,813 | 14,112 | 7,392 | 13,021 | 17,249 |
| Cumberland | 26,635 | 43,447 | 14,344 | 24,613 | 47,292 |
| Dauphin | 36,990 | 45,479 | 16,063 | 35,079 | 48,917 |
| Delaware | 111,210 | 108,587 | 43,728 | 96,144 | 147,656 |
| Elk | 5,016 | 4,908 | 3,885 | 5,879 | 6,737 |
| Erie | 56,381 | 39,283 | 21,510 | 53,913 | 48,306 |
| Fayette | 30,577 | 12,820 | 10,162 | 33,098 | 16,915 |
| Forest | 890 | 801 | 448 | 895 | 1,159 |
| Franklin | 13,440 | 23,387 | 6,941 | 12,368 | 27,086 |
| Fulton | 1,588 | 2,558 | 869 | 1,532 | 3,086 |
| Greene | 8,438 | 3,482 | 3,186 | 9,126 | 4,879 |
| Huntingdon | 5,153 | 7,249 | 3,273 | 4,752 | 8,800 |
| Indiana | 15,194 | 10,966 | 7,089 | 16,514 | 14,983 |
| Jefferson | 5,998 | 7,271 | 4,403 | 6,235 | 9,743 |
| Juniata | 2,601 | 3,980 | 1,819 | 2,834 | 4,881 |
| Lackawanna | 45,054 | 33,443 | 15,667 | 45,591 | 42,063 |
| Lancaster | 44,255 | 68,447 | 26,807 | 38,982 | 96,979 |
| Lawrence | 20,830 | 12,359 | 7,950 | 21,884 | 15,825 |
| Lebanon | 12,350 | 21,512 | 9,005 | 11,912 | 24,415 |
| Lehigh | 46,711 | 42,631 | 24,853 | 42,801 | 56,363 |
| Luzerne | 56,623 | 49,285 | 21,007 | 58,553 | 59,059 |
| Lycoming | 13,315 | 20,536 | 9,170 | 13,528 | 24,792 |
| McKean | 5,331 | 6,965 | 4,019 | 5,300 | 9,323 |
| Mercer | 23,264 | 16,081 | 10,277 | 24,278 | 21,301 |
| Mifflin | 4,946 | 6,300 | 3,382 | 4,790 | 8,170 |
| Monroe | 13,468 | 14,557 | 9,257 | 9,859 | 17,185 |
| Montgomery | 136,572 | 125,704 | 53,738 | 109,834 | 170,294 |
| Montour | 2,150 | 3,096 | 1,373 | 2,031 | 3,617 |
| Northampton | 42,203 | 34,429 | 20,234 | 39,264 | 42,748 |

| | | | | | |
|---|---|---|---|---|---|
| Northumberland . . | 12,814 | 15,057 | 7,782 | 14,255 | 20,207 |
| Perry. . . . . . . . | 4,086 | 7,871 | 3,334 | 3,910 | 8,545 |
| Philadelphia. . . . . | 434,904 | 133,328 | 65,455 | 449,566 | 219,053 |
| Pike . . . . . . . | 4,382 | 6,084 | 3,019 | 3,097 | 6,659 |
| Potter . . . . . . | 1,892 | 3,452 | 1,687 | 2,119 | 4,432 |
| Schuylkill . . . . . . | 23,679 | 25,780 | 13,398 | 24,797 | 32,666 |
| Snyder . . . . . . . | 2,952 | 6,934 | 2,686 | 2,658 | 9,054 |
| Somerset . . . . . . | 12,493 | 13,858 | 6,333 | 13,815 | 16,809 |
| Sullivan . . . . . . . | 1,030 | 1,340 | 731 | 1,091 | 1,808 |
| Susquehanna. . . . | 5,368 | 7,356 | 3,946 | 4,871 | 9,077 |
| Tioga . . . . . . . . | 4,868 | 7,823 | 3,804 | 4,807 | 9,471 |
| Union . . . . . . . | 3,623 | 6,362 | 2,255 | 3,163 | 7,912 |
| Venango . . . . . | 8,230 | 8,545 | 4,695 | 8,624 | 11,468 |
| Warren . . . . . . | 6,972 | 6,585 | 4,795 | 6,790 | 8,991 |
| Washington. . . . . | 46,143 | 21,977 | 16,083 | 47,527 | 28,651 |
| Wayne. . . . . . . | 4,817 | 8,184 | 3,727 | 3,775 | 9,926 |
| Westmoreland . . . | 69,817 | 47,315 | 37,036 | 76,710 | 61,472 |
| Wyoming . . . . . | 3,158 | 5,143 | 2,525 | 2,797 | 6,607 |
| York . . . . . . . . | 46,113 | 60,130 | 27,743 | 37,691 | 72,406 |
| Totals. . . . . . . . | 2,239,164 | 1,791,841 | 902,667 | 2,194,944 | 2,300,087 |

## Pennsylvania Vote Since 1944

1944, Roosevelt, Dem., 1,940,479; Dewey, Rep., 1,835,054; Thomas, Soc., 11,721; Watson, Proh., 5,750; Teichert, Ind. Gov., 1,789.

1948, Truman, Dem., 1,752,426; Dewey, Rep., 1,902,197; Wallace, Prog., 55,161; Thomas, Soc., 11,325; Watson, Proh., 10,338; Dobbs, Militant Workers, 2,133; Teichert, Ind. Gov., 1,461.

1952, Eisenhower, Rep., 2,415,789; Stevenson, Dem., 2,146,269; Hamblen, Proh., 8,771; Hallinan, Prog., 4,200; Hoopes, Soc., 2,684; Dobbs, Militant Workers, 1,502; Hass, Ind. Gov., 1,347; scattered, 155.

1956, Eisenhower, Rep., 2,585,252; Stevenson, Dem., 1,981,769; Hass, Soc. Labor, 7,447; Dobbs, Militant Workers, 2,035.

1960, Kennedy, Dem., 2,556,282; Nixon, Rep., 2,439,956; Hass, Soc. Labor, 7,185; Dobbs, Soc. Workers, 2,678; scattering, 440.

1964, Johnson, Dem., 3,130,954; Goldwater, Rep., 1,673,657; DeBerry, Soc. Workers, 10,456; Hass, Soc. Labor, 5,092; scattering, 2,531.

1968, Nixon, Rep., 2,090,017; Humphrey, Dem., 2,259,405; Wallace, 3d party, 378,582; Blomen, Soc. Labor, 4,977; Halstead, Soc. Workers, 4,862; Gregory, 7,821; others, 2,264.

1972, Nixon, Rep., 2,714,521; McGovern, Dem., 1,796,951; Schmitz, Amer., 70,593; Jenness, Soc. Workers, 4,639; Hall, Com., 2,686; others, 2,715.

1976, Carter, Dem., 2,328,677; Ford, Rep., 2,205,604; McCarthy, Ind., 50,584; Maddox, Constitution, 25,344; Camejo, Soc. Workers, 3,009; LaRouche, U.S. Labor, 2,744; Hall, Com., 1,891; others, 2,934.

1980, Reagan, Rep., 2,261,872; Carter, Dem., 1,937,540; Anderson, Ind., 292,921; Clark, Libertarian, 33,263; DeBerry, Soc. Workers, 20,291; Commoner, Consumer, 10,430; Hall, Com., 5,184.

1984, Reagan, Rep., 2,584,323; Mondale, Dem., 2,228,131; Bergland, Libertarian, 6,982.

1988, Bush, Rep., 2,300,087; Dukakis, Dem., 2,194,944; McCarthy, Consumer, 19,158; Paul, Lib., 12,051.

1992, Clinton, Dem., 2,239,164; Bush, Rep., 1,791,841; Perot, Ind., 902,667; Marrou, Libertarian, 21,477; Fulani, New Alliance, 4,661.

## Rhode Island

| | 1992 | | | 1988 | |
|---|---|---|---|---|---|
| | Clinton | Bush | Perot | Dukakis | Bush |
| City | (D) | (R) | (I) | (D) | (R) |
| Cranston . . . . . . | 18,589 | 12,450 | 8,331 | 19,711 | 17,129 |
| East Providence . . | 11,701 | 5,843 | 4,661 | 11,948 | 8,181 |
| Pawtucket. . . . . . | 14,177 | 6,322 | 6,244 | 15,985 | 9,359 |
| Providence . . . . . | 32,536 | 11,519 | 7,816 | 34,806 | 15,310 |
| Warwick . . . . . . | 20,504 | 13,348 | 10,526 | 21,662 | 18,052 |
| Totals. . . . . . . . | 213,299 | 131,601 | 105,045 | 225,123 | 177,761 |

## Rhode Island Vote Since 1944

1944, Roosevelt, Dem., 175,356; Dewey, Rep., 123,487; Watson, Proh., 433.

1948, Truman, Dem., 188,736; Dewey, Rep., 135,787; Wallace, Prog., 2,619; Thomas, Soc., 429; Teichert, Soc. Labor, 131.

1952, Eisenhower, Rep., 210,935; Stevenson, Dem., 203,293; Hallinan, Prog., 187; Hass, Soc. Labor, 83.

1956, Eisenhower, Rep., 225,819; Stevenson, Dem., 161,790.

---

1960, Kennedy, Dem., 258,032; Nixon, Rep., 147,502.

1964, Johnson, Dem., 315,463; Goldwater, Rep., 74,615.

1968, Nixon, Rep., 122,359; Humphrey, Dem., 246,518; Wallace, 3d party, 15,678; Halstead, Soc. Worker, 383.

1972, Nixon, Rep., 220,383; McGovern, Dem., 194,645; Jenness, Soc. Workers, 729.

1976, Carter, Dem., 227,636; Ford, Rep., 181,249; MacBride, Libertarian, 715; Camejo, Soc. Workers, 462; Hall, Com., 334; Levin, Soc. Labor, 188.

1980, Reagan, Rep., 154,793; Carter, Dem., 198,342; Anderson, Ind., 59,819; Clark, Libertarian, 2,458; Hall, Com., 218; McReynolds, Socialist, 170; DeBerry, Soc. Worker, 90; Griswold, Workers World, 77.

1984, Reagan, Rep., 212,080; Mondale, Dem., 197,106; Bergland, Libertarian, 277.

1988, Bush, Rep., 177,761; Dukakis, Dem., 225,123; Paul, Lib., 825; Fulani, New Alliance, 280.

1992, Clinton, Dem., 213,299; Bush, Rep., 131,601; Perot, Ind., 105,045; Fulani, New Alliance, 1,878.

## South Carolina

| | 1992 | | | 1988 | |
|---|---|---|---|---|---|
| | Clinton | Bush | Perot | Dukakis | Bush |
| County | (D) | (R) | (I) | (D) | (R) |
| Abbeville . . . . . . | 3,968 | 3,317 | 1,036 | 3,629 | 3,738 |
| Aiken . . . . . . . | 14,802 | 25,731 | 6,056 | 10,598 | 27,665 |
| Allendale . . . . . | 2,159 | 1,049 | 212 | 1,796 | 1,295 |
| Anderson . . . . . | 16,072 | 24,793 | 6,966 | 12,281 | 25,939 |
| Bamberg . . . . . . | 3,426 | 1,906 | 360 | 2,830 | 2,403 |
| Barnwell. . . . . . | 3,344 | 4,026 | 752 | 2,564 | 4,467 |
| Beaufort. . . . . . | 11,466 | 14,735 | 4,966 | 8,691 | 16,184 |
| Berkeley . . . . . | 12,533 | 18,048 | 4,632 | 9,312 | 16,779 |
| Calhoun . . . . . . | 2,770 | 2,418 | 564 | 2,175 | 2,585 |
| Charleston . . . . . | 40,095 | 47,403 | 10,354 | 32,977 | 49,149 |
| Cherokee . . . . . | 5,453 | 6,887 | 2,186 | 4,322 | 7,763 |
| Chester . . . . . . | 5,458 | 3,451 | 1,350 | 3,737 | 3,968 |
| Chesterfield. . . . | 5,691 | 4,183 | 1,315 | 4,699 | 4,999 |
| Clarendon . . . . . | 6,033 | 4,147 | 744 | 5,030 | 4,337 |
| Colleton . . . . . . | 5,455 | 4,545 | 1,245 | 4,508 | 4,962 |
| Darlington . . . . . | 9,090 | 8,912 | 1,863 | 7,625 | 9,854 |
| Dillon . . . . . . . | 4,953 | 3,575 | 831 | 3,251 | 3,793 |
| Dorchester . . . . | 9,160 | 15,004 | 3,648 | 7,371 | 14,756 |
| Edgefield . . . . . | 3,433 | 3,339 | 596 | 3,020 | 3,814 |
| Fairfield . . . . . . | 4,867 | 2,518 | 652 | 3,827 | 2,714 |
| Florence . . . . . . | 15,569 | 19,802 | 3,499 | 12,531 | 19,490 |
| Georgetown . . . . | 7,494 | 6,870 | 1,840 | 5,402 | 7,032 |
| Greenville . . . . . | 34,651 | 65,066 | 13,699 | 27,188 | 67,371 |
| Greenwood . . . . | 7,621 | 9,079 | 2,101 | 6,511 | 9,096 |
| Hampton . . . . . | 4,332 | 2,402 | 564 | 3,435 | 2,826 |
| Horry . . . . . . . | 18,896 | 23,489 | 8,472 | 13,316 | 24,843 |
| Jasper. . . . . . . | 3,453 | 1,725 | 549 | 2,894 | 2,004 |
| Kershaw. . . . . . | 6,585 | 8,499 | 2,150 | 4,494 | 8,877 |
| Lancaster. . . . . | 8,307 | 7,757 | 2,563 | 6,181 | 9,152 |
| Laurens . . . . . . | 6,638 | 8,347 | 2,157 | 5,930 | 9,731 |
| Lee . . . . . . . . | 4,454 | 2,730 | 611 | 3,423 | 2,936 |
| Lexington . . . . . | 18,312 | 41,759 | 8,652 | 11,366 | 41,467 |
| McCormick . . . . | 1,846 | 899 | 295 | 1,722 | 1,172 |
| Marion. . . . . . . | 5,843 | 3,647 | 822 | 5,008 | 4,403 |
| Marlboro . . . . . | 5,111 | 2,526 | 895 | 3,937 | 2,921 |
| Newberry . . . . . | 4,896 | 5,980 | 1,393 | 3,825 | 6,427 |
| Oconee . . . . . . | 6,617 | 10,379 | 3,405 | 4,299 | 10,184 |
| Orangeburg . . . . | 18,440 | 11,328 | 2,383 | 14,655 | 13,281 |
| Pickens . . . . . . | 8,275 | 17,008 | 4,128 | 6,103 | 17,448 |
| Richland. . . . . . | 53,648 | 43,744 | 7,918 | 36,420 | 43,841 |
| Saluda. . . . . . . | 2,393 | 2,968 | 833 | 1,984 | 3,225 |
| Spartanburg . . . . | 25,488 | 37,707 | 8,900 | 22,964 | 40,801 |
| Sumter . . . . . . | 11,852 | 12,576 | 2,062 | 9,502 | 13,161 |
| Union . . . . . . . | 4,644 | 4,647 | 1,371 | 4,420 | 6,019 |
| Williamsburg . . . | 8,077 | 5,289 | 864 | 7,343 | 5,914 |
| York . . . . . . . . | 15,844 | 21,297 | 6,419 | 11,458 | 21,657 |
| Totals. . . . . . . . | 479,514 | 577,507 | 138,872 | 370,554 | 606,443 |

## South Carolina Vote Since 1944

1944, Roosevelt, Dem., 90,601; Dewey, Rep., 4,547; Southern Democrats, 7,799; Watson, Proh., 365; Rep. Tolbert faction, 63.

1948, Thurmond, States' Rights, 102,607; Truman, Dem., 34,423; Dewey, Rep., 5,386; Wallace, Prog., 154; Thomas, Soc., 1.

1952, Eisenhower ran on two tickets. Under state law vote cast for two Eisenhower slates of electors could not be combined. Eisenhower, Ind., 158,289; Rep., 9,793; total, 168,082; Stevenson, Dem., 173,004; Hamblen, Proh., 1.

1956, Stevenson, Dem., 136,372; Byrd, Ind., 88,509; Eisenhower, Rep., 75,700; Andrews, Ind., 2.

1960, Kennedy, Dem., 198,129; Nixon, Rep., 188,558; write-in, 1.

1964, Johnson, Dem., 215,700; Goldwater, Rep., 309,048; write-ins: Nixon, 1, Wallace, 5; Powell, 1; Thurmond, 1.

1968, Nixon, Rep., 254,062; Humphrey, Dem., 197,486; Wallace, 3d party, 215,430.

1972, Nixon, Rep., 477,044; McGovern, Dem., 184,559; United Citizens, 2,265; Schmitz, Amer., 10,075; write-in, 17.

1976, Carter, Dem., 450,807; Ford, Rep., 346,149; Anderson, Amer., 2,996; Maddox, Amer. Ind., 1,950; write-in, 681.

1980, Reagan, Rep., 439,277; Carter, Dem., 428,220; Anderson, Ind., 13,868; Clark, Libertarian, 4,807; Rarick, Amer. Ind., 2,086.

1984, Reagan, Rep., 615,539; Mondale, Dem., 344,459; Bergland, Libertarian, 4,359.

1988, Bush, Rep., 606,443; Dukakis, Dem., 370,554; Paul, Lib., 4,935; Fulani, United Citizens, 4,077.

1992, Bush, Rep., 577,507; Clinton, Dem., 479,514; Perot, Ind., 138,872; Marrou, Libertarian, 2,719; Phillips, U.S. Taxpayers, 2,680; Fulani, New Alliance, 1,235.

## South Dakota

| County | 1992 Clinton (D) | Bush (R) | Perot (I) | 1988 Dukakis (D) | Bush (R) |
|---|---|---|---|---|---|
| Aurora | 680 | 594 | 435 | 987 | 856 |
| Beadle | 3,925 | 3,363 | 1,819 | 4,523 | 4,611 |
| Bennett | 413 | 556 | 221 | 579 | 663 |
| Bon Homme | 1,294 | 1,212 | 836 | 1,574 | 1,826 |
| Brookings | 4,645 | 4,698 | 2,614 | 4,860 | 5,394 |
| Brown | 7,521 | 6,665 | 3,812 | 8,673 | 8,537 |
| Brule | 1,060 | 908 | 687 | 991 | 971 |
| Buffalo | 282 | 137 | 72 | 334 | 151 |
| Butte | 973 | 1,674 | 1,039 | 1,256 | 2,291 |
| Campbell | 222 | 574 | 252 | 334 | 909 |
| Chas. Mix | 1,639 | 1,570 | 886 | 2,205 | 1,966 |
| Clark | 799 | 803 | 761 | 1,164 | 1,247 |
| Clay | 2,826 | 1,869 | 1,303 | 2,859 | 2,307 |
| Codington | 3,701 | 3,943 | 3,262 | 4,570 | 5,050 |
| Corson | 444 | 483 | 321 | 722 | 710 |
| Custer | 1,078 | 1,422 | 845 | 1,180 | 1,806 |
| Davison | 3,285 | 3,111 | 1,706 | 3,705 | 4,024 |
| Day | 1,578 | 1,161 | 973 | 2,137 | 1,616 |
| Deuel | 880 | 778 | 761 | 1,246 | 1,251 |
| Dewey | 766 | 642 | 340 | 1,007 | 765 |
| Douglas | 481 | 1,175 | 403 | 695 | 1,438 |
| Edmunds | 894 | 944 | 415 | 1,259 | 1,327 |
| Fall River | 1,416 | 1,533 | 792 | 1,380 | 2,002 |
| Faulk | 488 | 658 | 281 | 714 | 842 |
| Grant | 1,484 | 1,595 | 1,018 | 1,988 | 2,148 |
| Gregory | 879 | 1,027 | 688 | 1,138 | 1,566 |
| Haakon | 209 | 860 | 245 | 379 | 958 |
| Hamlin | 826 | 1,133 | 774 | 1,258 | 1,380 |
| Hand | 785 | 1,130 | 624 | 1,101 | 1,461 |
| Hanson | 566 | 522 | 341 | 776 | 786 |
| Harding | 139 | 515 | 225 | 259 | 633 |
| Hughes | 2,578 | 4,325 | 1,160 | 2,853 | 4,545 |
| Hutchinson | 1,211 | 2,002 | 920 | 1,594 | 2,700 |
| Hyde | 301 | 440 | 211 | 436 | 546 |
| Jackson | 351 | 627 | 184 | 450 | 671 |
| Jerauld | 600 | 518 | 346 | 751 | 777 |
| Jones | 166 | 454 | 154 | 261 | 521 |
| Kingsbury | 1,267 | 1,113 | 744 | 1,472 | 1,592 |
| Lake | 2,388 | 1,890 | 1,299 | 2,663 | 2,439 |
| Lawrence | 3,157 | 3,770 | 2,673 | 3,705 | 5,570 |
| Lincoln | 2,943 | 3,365 | 1,593 | 3,190 | 3,537 |
| Lyman | 486 | 669 | 311 | 631 | 843 |
| McCook | 1,167 | 1,177 | 617 | 1,492 | 1,501 |
| McPherson | 478 | 945 | 322 | 571 | 1,358 |
| Marshall | 1,056 | 810 | 427 | 1,372 | 1,142 |
| Meade | 2,694 | 4,724 | 2,611 | 3,212 | 5,189 |
| Mellette | 277 | 417 | 140 | 385 | 460 |
| Miner | 698 | 543 | 332 | 955 | 795 |
| Minnehaha | 27,016 | 25,081 | 11,496 | 29,135 | 26,765 |
| Moody | 1,473 | 898 | 715 | 1,715 | 1,161 |
| Pennington | 11,106 | 18,052 | 8,358 | 12,068 | 19,510 |
| Perkins | 566 | 872 | 541 | 851 | 1,326 |
| Potter | 493 | 901 | 375 | 701 | 1,175 |
| Roberts | 1,716 | 1,437 | 954 | 2,267 | 2,012 |
| Sanborn | 632 | 595 | 376 | 770 | 815 |
| Shannon | 1,267 | 225 | 137 | 1,206 | 256 |
| Spink | 1,732 | 1,527 | 839 | 2,071 | 1,969 |
| Stanley | 427 | 719 | 240 | 511 | 698 |
| Sully | 273 | 565 | 167 | 393 | 571 |
| Todd | 915 | 456 | 246 | 1,117 | 535 |
| Tripp | 1,046 | 1,459 | 848 | 1,219 | 2,113 |
| Turner | 1,507 | 1,906 | 867 | 1,780 | 2,436 |
| Union | 2,210 | 1,784 | 1,085 | 2,612 | 1,907 |
| Walworth | 829 | 1,439 | 628 | 1,094 | 1,940 |
| Yankton | 3,404 | 3,430 | 2,511 | 3,777 | 4,186 |
| Ziebach | 280 | 328 | 117 | 427 | 362 |
| Totals | 124,888 | 136,718 | 73,295 | 145,560 | 165,415 |

### South Dakota Vote Since 1944

1944, Roosevelt, Dem., 96,711; Dewey, Rep., 135,365.

---

1948, Truman, Dem., 117,653; Dewey, Rep., 129,651; Wallace, Prog., 2,801.

1952, Eisenhower, Rep., 203,857; Stevenson, Dem., 90,426.

1956, Eisenhower, Rep., 171,569; Stevenson, Dem., 122,288.

1960, Kennedy, Dem., 128,070; Nixon, Rep., 178,417.

1964, Johnson, Dem., 163,010; Goldwater, Rep., 130,108.

1968, Nixon, Rep., 149,841; Humphrey, Dem., 118,023; Wallace, 3d party, 13,400.

1972, Nixon, Rep., 166,476; McGovern, Dem., 139,945; Jenness, Soc. Workers, 994.

1976, Carter, Dem., 147,068; Ford, Rep., 151,505; MacBride, Libertarian, 1,619; Hall, Com., 318; Camejo, Soc. Workers, 168.

1980, Reagan, Rep., 198,343; Carter, Dem., 103,855; Anderson, Ind., 21,431; Clark, Libertarian, 3,824; Pulley, Soc. Workers, 250.

1984, Reagan, Rep., 200,267; Mondale, Dem., 116,113.

1988, Bush, Rep., 165,415; Dukakis, Dem., 145,560; Paul, Lib., 1,060; Fulani, New Alliance, 730.

1992, Bush, Rep., 136,718; Clinton, Dem., 124,888; Perot, Ind., 73,295.

## Tennessee

| County | 1992 Clinton (D) | Bush (R) | Perot (I) | 1988 Dukakis (D) | Bush (R) |
|---|---|---|---|---|---|
| Anderson | 13,482 | 11,838 | 3,149 | 9,589 | 15,056 |
| Bedford | 5,978 | 3,836 | 1,541 | 4,046 | 4,856 |
| Benton | 3,896 | 1,625 | 559 | 2,826 | 2,167 |
| Bledsoe | 1,884 | 1,776 | 352 | 1,274 | 1,858 |
| Blount | 14,655 | 18,415 | 4,468 | 9,602 | 20,027 |
| Bradley | 9,889 | 16,528 | 3,212 | 6,122 | 15,829 |
| Campbell | 6,756 | 4,897 | 1,240 | 4,188 | 5,197 |
| Cannon | 2,593 | 1,229 | 495 | 1,726 | 1,604 |
| Carroll | 5,741 | 4,842 | 1,139 | 4,151 | 5,635 |
| Carter | 6,502 | 10,712 | 1,898 | 4,634 | 12,036 |
| Cheatham | 4,817 | 3,496 | 1,433 | 3,067 | 4,132 |
| Chester | 2,317 | 2,834 | 439 | 1,757 | 2,781 |
| Claiborne | 4,509 | 4,065 | 860 | 2,977 | 4,071 |
| Clay | 1,922 | 1,072 | 223 | 1,183 | 1,291 |
| Cocke | 3,495 | 5,298 | 1,124 | 2,115 | 5,430 |
| Coffee | 8,534 | 6,047 | 2,420 | 5,686 | 7,837 |
| Crockett | 2,657 | 2,180 | 507 | 1,742 | 2,214 |
| Cumberland | 6,393 | 7,116 | 2,200 | 3,964 | 7,557 |
| Davidson | 106,355 | 76,567 | 20,184 | 89,270 | 98,599 |
| Decatur | 2,633 | 1,667 | 351 | 1,880 | 2,286 |
| De Kalb | 4,382 | 1,714 | 608 | 2,452 | 2,098 |
| Dickson | 7,863 | 4,450 | 1,730 | 5,129 | 5,343 |
| Dyer | 5,845 | 5,668 | 1,241 | 3,690 | 6,508 |
| Fayette | 4,211 | 3,713 | 657 | 3,292 | 3,573 |
| Fentress | 2,730 | 2,391 | 606 | 1,856 | 3,103 |
| Franklin | 7,773 | 4,507 | 1,837 | 5,442 | 5,381 |
| Gibson | 9,555 | 7,161 | 1,536 | 7,542 | 8,415 |
| Giles | 5,601 | 2,827 | 1,309 | 3,918 | 3,518 |
| Grainger | 2,242 | 2,772 | 513 | 1,423 | 2,734 |
| Greene | 7,857 | 9,912 | 2,930 | 5,077 | 11,947 |
| Grundy | 2,997 | 1,004 | 366 | 2,415 | 1,429 |
| Hamblen | 7,114 | 8,898 | 1,760 | 5,061 | 10,418 |
| Hamilton | 46,770 | 53,476 | 14,400 | 40,990 | 68,111 |
| Hancock | 1,000 | 1,274 | 151 | 737 | 1,303 |
| Hardeman | 4,832 | 3,122 | 594 | 3,526 | 3,547 |
| Hardin | 3,922 | 3,875 | 734 | 2,808 | 4,252 |
| Hawkins | 6,623 | 7,758 | 1,847 | 5,212 | 9,356 |
| Haywood | 3,511 | 2,518 | 331 | 2,923 | 2,687 |
| Henderson | 3,502 | 4,719 | 785 | 2,296 | 5,418 |
| Henry | 6,797 | 3,661 | 1,588 | 5,138 | 4,784 |
| Hickman | 4,093 | 1,820 | 795 | 2,643 | 2,246 |
| Houston | 2,012 | 648 | 280 | 1,467 | 882 |
| Humphreys | 3,875 | 1,641 | 609 | 3,037 | 2,132 |
| Jackson | 3,208 | 708 | 332 | 1,962 | 1,168 |
| Jefferson | 4,740 | 6,184 | 1,385 | 3,168 | 6,832 |
| Johnson | 1,781 | 3,170 | 574 | 1,329 | 3,715 |
| Knox | 59,702 | 66,607 | 15,669 | 41,829 | 73,092 |
| Lake | 1,449 | 680 | 151 | 935 | 806 |
| Lauderdale | 4,452 | 2,928 | 561 | 3,296 | 3,308 |
| Lawrence | 6,816 | 5,608 | 1,403 | 4,903 | 6,273 |
| Lewis | 2,491 | 1,218 | 434 | 1,419 | 1,324 |
| Lincoln | 5,063 | 3,814 | 1,371 | 3,672 | 4,288 |
| Loudon | 5,414 | 6,444 | 1,602 | 3,480 | 7,122 |
| McMinn | 6,682 | 7,453 | 1,812 | 4,568 | 8,462 |
| McNairy | 4,691 | 4,093 | 774 | 3,510 | 4,625 |
| Macon | 2,961 | 2,299 | 443 | 1,538 | 2,962 |
| Madison | 13,629 | 14,869 | 2,634 | 11,001 | 16,952 |
| Marion | 5,589 | 3,262 | 1,186 | 4,175 | 4,407 |
| Marshall | 4,491 | 2,516 | 1,050 | 2,795 | 2,975 |
| Maury | 9,997 | 7,440 | 2,821 | 6,280 | 8,397 |
| Meigs | 1,673 | 1,355 | 453 | 1,048 | 1,507 |
| Monroe | 5,384 | 6,025 | 936 | 4,000 | 6,355 |
| Montgomery | 14,507 | 13,011 | 3,753 | 9,145 | 12,599 |
| Moore | 1,151 | 661 | 337 | 731 | 786 |
| Morgan | 3,190 | 2,306 | 658 | 1,941 | 2,576 |
| Obion | 6,497 | 4,812 | 1,494 | 4,785 | 6,037 |
| Overton | 4,489 | 1,657 | 468 | 2,511 | 1,873 |

| | Clinton (D) | Bush (R) | Perot (I) | Dukakis (D) | Bush (R) |
|---|---|---|---|---|---|
| Perry | 1,889 | 708 | 317 | 1,208 | 854 |
| Pickett | 1,144 | 1,094 | 121 | 634 | 1,118 |
| Polk | 2,583 | 1,584 | 419 | 2,073 | 2,297 |
| Putnam | 10,858 | 7,998 | 2,473 | 6,606 | 9,547 |
| Rhea | 4,289 | 4,860 | 1,163 | 2,595 | 5,144 |
| Roane | 9,812 | 8,719 | 2,396 | 6,535 | 10,881 |
| Robertson | 8,498 | 5,271 | 1,978 | 5,884 | 5,714 |
| Rutherford | 21,084 | 18,877 | 7,005 | 12,245 | 20,397 |
| Scott | 2,730 | 3,011 | 643 | 1,611 | 2,562 |
| Sequatchie | 1,754 | 1,381 | 405 | 1,196 | 1,659 |
| Sevier | 6,719 | 11,714 | 2,760 | 3,643 | 11,920 |
| Shelby | 191,322 | 153,310 | 20,223 | 149,759 | 157,457 |
| Smith | 5,061 | 1,482 | 486 | 2,522 | 2,138 |
| Stewart | 2,779 | 1,046 | 487 | 1,979 | 1,302 |
| Sullivan | 20,935 | 28,801 | 6,730 | 17,396 | 32,996 |
| Sumner | 19,387 | 17,401 | 5,177 | 11,702 | 19,523 |
| Tipton | 5,652 | 6,757 | 1,279 | 3,824 | 6,052 |
| Trousdale | 1,846 | 565 | 243 | 1,193 | 969 |
| Unicoi | 2,375 | 3,344 | 709 | 1,794 | 3,664 |
| Union | 2,478 | 2,274 | 580 | 1,431 | 2,110 |
| Van Buren | 1,329 | 555 | 191 | 796 | 780 |
| Warren | 7,189 | 3,704 | 1,415 | 4,646 | 4,529 |
| Washington | 13,071 | 18,206 | 4,002 | 10,087 | 19,615 |
| Wayne | 1,868 | 2,955 | 424 | 1,516 | 3,405 |
| Weakley | 5,691 | 4,800 | 1,355 | 4,239 | 5,701 |
| White | 4,102 | 2,118 | 821 | 2,562 | 2,646 |
| Williamson | 13,053 | 22,015 | 5,026 | 7,864 | 20,847 |
| Wilson | 13,861 | 12,061 | 3,848 | 8,360 | 13,317 |
| Totals | 933,521 | 841,300 | 199,968 | 679,794 | 947,233 |

## Tennessee Vote Since 1944

1944, Roosevelt, Dem., 308,707; Dewey, Rep., 200,311; Watson, Proh., 882; Thomas, Soc., 892.

1948, Truman, Dem., 270,402; Dewey, Rep., 202,914; Thurmond, States' Rights, 73,815; Wallace, Prog., 1,864; Thomas, Soc., 1,288.

1952, Eisenhower, Rep., 446,147; Stevenson, Dem., 443,710; Hamblen, Proh., 1,432; Hallinan, Prog., 885; MacArthur, Christian Nationalist, 379.

1956, Eisenhower, Rep., 462,288; Stevenson, Dem., 456,507; Andrews, Ind., 19,820; Holtwick, Proh., 789.

1960, Kennedy, Dem., 481,453; Nixon, Rep., 556,577; Faubus, States' Rights, 11,304; Decker, Proh., 2,458.

1964, Johnson, Dem. 635,047; Goldwater, Rep., 508,965; write-in, 34.

1968, Nixon, Rep., 472,592; Humphrey, Dem., 351,233; Wallace, 3d party, 424,792.

1972, Nixon, Rep., 813,147; McGovern, Dem., 357,293; Schmitz, Amer., 30,373; write-in, 369.

1976, Carter, Dem., 825,879; Ford, Rep., 633,969; Anderson, Amer., 5,769; McCarthy, Ind., 5,004; Maddox, Am. Ind., 2,303; MacBride, Libertarian, 1,375; Hall, Com., 547; LaRouche, U.S. Labor, 512; Bubar, Proh., 442; Miller, Ind., 316; write-in, 230.

1980, Reagan, Rep., 787,761; Carter, Dem., 783,051; Anderson, Ind., 35,991; Clark, Libertarian, 7,116; Commoner, Citizens, 1,112; Bubar, Statesman, 521; McReynolds, Socialist, 519; Hall, Com., 503; DeBerry, Soc. Worker, 490; Griswold, Workers World, 400; write-ins, 152.

1984, Reagan, Rep., 990,212; Mondale, Dem., 711,714; Bergland, Libertarian, 3,072.

1988, Bush, Rep., 947,233; Dukakis, Dem., 679,794; Paul, Ind., 2,041; Duke, Ind., 1,807.

1992, Clinton, Dem., 933,521; Bush, Rep., 841,300; Perot, Ind., 199,968; Marrou, Libertarian, 1,847.

## Texas

| | 1992 | | | 1988 | |
|---|---|---|---|---|---|
| County | Clinton (D) | Bush (R) | Perot (I) | Dukakis (D) | Bush (R) |
| Anderson | 5,322 | 5,598 | 3,519 | 6,128 | 7,858 |
| Andrews | 1,081 | 2,266 | 875 | 1,122 | 3,052 |
| Angelina | 10,318 | 9,722 | 6,204 | 10,849 | 12,738 |
| Aransas | 2,246 | 2,826 | 1,676 | 2,305 | 3,858 |
| Archer | 1,284 | 1,560 | 1,106 | 1,627 | 2,010 |
| Armstrong | 278 | 561 | 187 | 314 | 720 |
| Atascosa | 3,766 | 3,806 | 2,035 | 4,657 | 4,777 |
| Austin | 2,278 | 4,015 | 1,585 | 2,593 | 4,524 |
| Bailey | 677 | 1,308 | 376 | 876 | 1,459 |
| Bandera | 1,059 | 2,674 | 1,537 | 1,251 | 3,435 |
| Bastrop | 6,252 | 4,980 | 3,240 | 8,004 | 5,991 |
| Baylor | 990 | 611 | 529 | 1,153 | 914 |
| Bee | 4,083 | 3,633 | 1,367 | 4,616 | 4,620 |
| Bell | 18,684 | 24,936 | 11,026 | 17,751 | 29,382 |
| Bexar | 172,513 | 168,816 | 72,110 | 174,036 | 193,192 |
| Blanco | 891 | 1,370 | 830 | 1,012 | 1,680 |
| Borden | 106 | 184 | 87 | 169 | 283 |
| Bosque | 2,173 | 2,300 | 1,999 | 2,670 | 3,458 |
| Bowie | 11,825 | 11,776 | 6,659 | 12,331 | 15,454 |
| Brazoria | 21,861 | 30,384 | 18,954 | 23,436 | 34,028 |
| Brazos | 14,819 | 23,943 | 10,372 | 14,885 | 29,369 |
| Brewster | 1,383 | 1,127 | 712 | 1,569 | 1,708 |
| Briscoe | 430 | 360 | 164 | 574 | 464 |
| Brooks | 2,856 | 585 | 318 | 2,859 | 608 |
| Brown | 4,264 | 5,313 | 3,034 | 4,763 | 6,810 |
| Burleson | 2,511 | 2,013 | 1,179 | 3,085 | 2,242 |
| Burnet | 3,638 | 4,272 | 2,865 | 4,343 | 5,120 |
| Caldwell | 3,794 | 2,749 | 1,776 | 4,649 | 3,553 |
| Calhoun | 2,550 | 2,640 | 1,579 | 3,314 | 3,183 |
| Callahan | 1,694 | 2,134 | 1,452 | 2,017 | 2,887 |
| Cameron | 29,435 | 20,123 | 9,286 | 30,972 | 24,263 |
| Camp | 1,938 | 1,219 | 821 | 2,121 | 1,908 |
| Carson | 825 | 1,647 | 578 | 1,034 | 2,100 |
| Cass | 5,476 | 3,999 | 2,168 | 5,941 | 5,305 |
| Castro | 1,113 | 1,307 | 485 | 1,436 | 1,604 |
| Chambers | 2,832 | 3,398 | 2,122 | 3,035 | 3,694 |
| Cherokee | 5,003 | 5,847 | 3,273 | 5,604 | 7,520 |
| Childress | 881 | 1,033 | 421 | 1,060 | 1,201 |
| Clay | 1,919 | 1,586 | 1,397 | 2,288 | 2,043 |
| Cochran | 454 | 750 | 255 | 681 | 771 |
| Coke | 580 | 640 | 393 | 674 | 863 |
| Coleman | 1,579 | 1,462 | 1,095 | 1,978 | 2,340 |
| Collin | 24,508 | 60,514 | 43,287 | 22,934 | 67,776 |
| Collingsworth | 635 | 697 | 265 | 809 | 872 |
| Colorado | 2,442 | 3,286 | 1,421 | 2,847 | 3,723 |
| Comal | 6,312 | 12,651 | 5,841 | 5,716 | 13,994 |
| Comanche | 2,296 | 1,666 | 1,281 | 2,622 | 2,120 |
| Concho | 489 | 414 | 329 | 643 | 617 |
| Cooke | 3,105 | 5,299 | 4,658 | 4,217 | 7,196 |
| Coryell | 4,157 | 6,144 | 3,974 | 4,026 | 7,461 |
| Cottle | 542 | 245 | 235 | 690 | 379 |
| Crane | 514 | 918 | 412 | 596 | 1,219 |
| Crockett | 653 | 623 | 368 | 881 | 932 |
| Crosby | 1,010 | 1,006 | 313 | 1,435 | 1,121 |
| Culberson | 424 | 251 | 171 | 557 | 417 |
| Dallam | 434 | 922 | 325 | 645 | 1,205 |
| Dallas | 231,412 | 256,007 | 170,571 | 243,198 | 347,094 |
| Dawson | 1,639 | 2,691 | 518 | 2,155 | 3,154 |
| Deaf Smith | 1,642 | 3,137 | 772 | 1,930 | 3,744 |
| Delta | 864 | 599 | 551 | 1,244 | 849 |
| Denton | 27,891 | 48,492 | 39,653 | 26,204 | 57,444 |
| DeWitt | 2,127 | 3,238 | 1,346 | 2,579 | 3,628 |
| Dickens | 536 | 373 | 250 | 696 | 435 |
| Dimmit | 3,172 | 844 | 361 | 2,735 | 900 |
| Donley | 578 | 893 | 260 | 661 | 1,043 |
| Duval | 4,006 | 698 | 326 | 4,177 | 907 |
| Eastland | 2,738 | 2,830 | 1,698 | 3,215 | 3,929 |
| Ector | 11,130 | 18,161 | 6,668 | 10,825 | 23,155 |
| Edwards | 254 | 460 | 171 | 368 | 556 |
| Ellis | 9,537 | 13,564 | 10,303 | 11,169 | 16,422 |
| El Paso | 67,715 | 47,224 | 19,738 | 62,622 | 55,573 |
| Erath | 3,531 | 3,835 | 3,046 | 4,113 | 5,427 |
| Falls | 2,761 | 1,826 | 1,185 | 2,877 | 2,344 |
| Fannin | 4,164 | 2,510 | 2,919 | 5,163 | 4,024 |
| Fayette | 2,923 | 3,789 | 2,088 | 3,390 | 4,551 |
| Fisher | 1,242 | 539 | 442 | 1,516 | 721 |
| Floyd | 947 | 1,676 | 385 | 1,391 | 1,741 |
| Foard | 435 | 207 | 152 | 513 | 306 |
| Fort Bend | 29,992 | 41,039 | 16,853 | 23,351 | 39,818 |
| Franklin | 1,338 | 1,058 | 942 | 1,453 | 1,439 |
| Freestone | 2,415 | 2,316 | 1,596 | 2,916 | 3,159 |
| Frio | 2,377 | 1,275 | 654 | 3,016 | 1,505 |
| Gaines | 1,095 | 2,138 | 696 | 1,310 | 2,265 |
| Galveston | 38,623 | 31,303 | 20,103 | 38,633 | 34,913 |
| Garza | 558 | 982 | 345 | 989 | 1,183 |
| Gillespie | 1,600 | 4,712 | 2,018 | 1,588 | 5,662 |
| Glasscock | 100 | 379 | 93 | 143 | 384 |
| Goliad | 1,069 | 1,236 | 521 | 1,358 | 1,427 |
| Gonzales | 2,006 | 2,502 | 1,018 | 2,897 | 2,983 |
| Gray | 2,426 | 6,105 | 1,810 | 2,460 | 7,259 |
| Grayson | 12,547 | 12,322 | 13,327 | 14,347 | 18,825 |
| Gregg | 12,797 | 20,542 | 8,437 | 12,486 | 26,465 |
| Grimes | 2,594 | 2,402 | 1,213 | 2,735 | 2,820 |
| Guadalupe | 6,567 | 10,818 | 5,618 | 7,111 | 13,265 |
| Hale | 2,761 | 6,098 | 1,357 | 3,502 | 6,284 |
| Hall | 819 | 631 | 263 | 1,029 | 714 |
| Hamilton | 1,100 | 1,232 | 921 | 1,355 | 1,718 |
| Hansford | 345 | 1,660 | 398 | 443 | 1,967 |
| Hardeman | 954 | 614 | 362 | 1,143 | 855 |
| Hardin | 6,753 | 5,885 | 4,129 | 8,245 | 6,897 |
| Harris | 360,171 | 406,778 | 172,922 | 342,919 | 464,217 |
| Harrison | 9,538 | 8,733 | 4,371 | 8,974 | 11,957 |
| Hartley | 406 | 1,081 | 308 | 505 | 1,229 |
| Haskell | 1,438 | 852 | 562 | 1,715 | 1,193 |
| Hays | 10,842 | 10,008 | 6,252 | 11,187 | 11,716 |
| Hemphill | 479 | 989 | 232 | 527 | 1,170 |
| Henderson | 9,105 | 8,368 | 6,746 | 9,819 | 11,005 |
| Hidalgo | 51,205 | 26,976 | 9,757 | 54,330 | 29,246 |
| Hill | 3,929 | 3,669 | 2,752 | 4,381 | 4,796 |
| Hockley | 2,301 | 4,261 | 1,291 | 2,850 | 4,368 |
| Hood | 4,359 | 5,313 | 4,457 | 4,255 | 7,400 |
| Hopkins | 4,085 | 3,398 | 3,147 | 4,984 | 5,133 |
| Houston | 3,250 | 3,067 | 1,690 | 3,846 | 3,882 |
| Howard | 3,735 | 5,129 | 1,984 | 4,445 | 6,024 |
| Hudspeth | 364 | 325 | 178 | 406 | 405 |
| Hunt | 7,452 | 9,739 | 7,387 | 8,820 | 12,331 |
| Hutchinson | 2,833 | 6,034 | 1,993 | 2,950 | 7,526 |
| Irion | 256 | 283 | 290 | 326 | 539 |
| Jack | 1,254 | 1,041 | 1,045 | 1,521 | 1,542 |
| Jackson | 1,722 | 2,451 | 976 | 2,141 | 2,954 |
| Jasper | 5,658 | 3,870 | 2,539 | 6,613 | 4,985 |

| County | | | | | |
|---|--:|--:|--:|--:|--:|
| Jeff Davis | 321 | 360 | 187 | 325 | 524 |
| Jefferson | 48,405 | 29,622 | 17,242 | 55,649 | 35,754 |
| Jim Hogg | 1,520 | 478 | 107 | 1,630 | 510 |
| Jim Wells | 7,812 | 3,311 | 1,413 | 8,495 | 4,335 |
| Johnson | 12,030 | 13,473 | 11,573 | 12,507 | 17,509 |
| Jones | 2,400 | 2,088 | 1,436 | 2,898 | 3,000 |
| Karnes | 1,897 | 1,990 | 802 | 2,529 | 2,383 |
| Kaufman | 6,498 | 6,578 | 5,913 | 7,358 | 8,466 |
| Kendall | 1,374 | 4,162 | 1,773 | 1,446 | 4,875 |
| Kenedy | 87 | 69 | 18 | 119 | 76 |
| Kent | 271 | 175 | 163 | 398 | 274 |
| Kerr | 3,707 | 8,787 | 3,790 | 3,587 | 11,207 |
| Kimble | 467 | 790 | 354 | 551 | 1,061 |
| King | 54 | 79 | 56 | 64 | 111 |
| Kinney | 598 | 634 | 299 | 669 | 771 |
| Kleberg | 5,109 | 3,897 | 1,470 | 5,367 | 4,443 |
| Knox | 854 | 521 | 438 | 1,013 | 765 |
| Lamar | 6,328 | 5,778 | 4,093 | 7,553 | 8,021 |
| Lamb | 1,737 | 2,998 | 709 | 2,230 | 3,064 |
| Lampasas | 1,508 | 2,233 | 1,432 | 1,954 | 3,000 |
| LaSalle | 1,522 | 586 | 211 | 1,651 | 693 |
| Lavaca | 2,700 | 3,362 | 1,696 | 3,531 | 4,377 |
| Lee | 1,847 | 2,108 | 1,088 | 2,527 | 2,513 |
| Leon | 2,042 | 2,212 | 1,251 | 2,316 | 2,778 |
| Liberty | 7,036 | 6,959 | 4,311 | 8,343 | 8,524 |
| Limestone | 3,188 | 2,358 | 1,505 | 3,476 | 3,257 |
| Lipscomb | 338 | 839 | 270 | 377 | 1,111 |
| Live Oak | 1,345 | 1,805 | 806 | 1,573 | 2,277 |
| Llano | 2,409 | 3,056 | 1,799 | 2,629 | 3,550 |
| Loving | 20 | 31 | 45 | 23 | 54 |
| Lubbock | 22,240 | 48,847 | 11,618 | 22,202 | 50,760 |
| Lynn | 902 | 1,233 | 291 | 1,086 | 1,279 |
| McCulloch | 1,393 | 1,108 | 986 | 1,665 | 1,618 |
| McLennan | 25,903 | 28,473 | 15,505 | 27,545 | 38,606 |
| McMullen | 78 | 274 | 89 | 94 | 302 |
| Madison | 1,553 | 1,544 | 778 | 1,835 | 1,896 |
| Marion | 2,156 | 1,245 | 882 | 2,255 | 1,857 |
| Martin | 641 | 986 | 356 | 632 | 1,017 |
| Mason | 570 | 776 | 364 | 671 | 975 |
| Matagorda | 4,759 | 5,328 | 3,045 | 5,675 | 6,787 |
| Maverick | 4,540 | 2,002 | 771 | 4,395 | 1,592 |
| Medina | 3,650 | 4,912 | 2,167 | 4,227 | 5,722 |
| Menard | 553 | 354 | 367 | 614 | 652 |
| Midland | 9,160 | 24,143 | 7,880 | 8,487 | 30,618 |
| Milam | 3,542 | 2,414 | 1,495 | 4,865 | 3,512 |
| Mills | 753 | 702 | 530 | 842 | 1,043 |
| Mitchell | 1,353 | 1,128 | 604 | 1,773 | 1,596 |
| Montague | 2,885 | 2,304 | 2,330 | 3,689 | 3,475 |
| Montgomery | 18,551 | 39,976 | 19,203 | 18,394 | 40,360 |
| Moore | 1,361 | 3,147 | 976 | 1,537 | 3,710 |
| Morris | 3,028 | 1,400 | 1,138 | 3,522 | 2,104 |
| Motley | 256 | 446 | 117 | 262 | 429 |
| Nacogdoches | 6,937 | 9,864 | 4,803 | 6,886 | 11,767 |
| Navarro | 6,006 | 4,897 | 3,800 | 6,749 | 6,445 |
| Newton | 3,249 | 1,212 | 1,032 | 3,640 | 1,659 |
| Nolan | 2,490 | 1,993 | 1,455 | 2,853 | 2,734 |
| Nueces | 46,317 | 36,781 | 17,374 | 49,209 | 46,337 |
| Ochiltree | 557 | 2,419 | 576 | 579 | 2,928 |
| Oldham | 225 | 583 | 177 | 303 | 691 |
| Orange | 15,305 | 9,793 | 7,321 | 17,834 | 11,959 |
| Palo Pinto | 3,392 | 2,852 | 3,010 | 3,930 | 4,649 |
| Panola | 3,950 | 3,473 | 1,906 | 4,123 | 4,642 |
| Parker | 7,934 | 10,321 | 9,148 | 8,517 | 14,090 |
| Parmer | 637 | 1,829 | 564 | 764 | 2,061 |
| Pecos | 1,778 | 1,836 | 895 | 1,960 | 2,483 |
| Polk | 5,942 | 5,390 | 2,884 | 5,943 | 5,831 |
| Potter | 9,527 | 13,510 | 4,655 | 9,563 | 16,400 |
| Presidio | 1,189 | 400 | 290 | 1,176 | 586 |
| Rains | 1,108 | 975 | 890 | 1,448 | 1,281 |
| Randall | 9,119 | 24,971 | 6,340 | 8,492 | 27,986 |
| Reagan | 337 | 651 | 259 | 418 | 935 |
| Real | 463 | 787 | 386 | 483 | 795 |
| Red River | 2,686 | 1,735 | 1,228 | 3,165 | 2,475 |
| Reeves | 2,569 | 1,244 | 734 | 2,812 | 1,724 |
| Refugio | 1,531 | 1,469 | 716 | 1,831 | 1,883 |
| Roberts | 126 | 391 | 99 | 135 | 441 |
| Robertson | 2,927 | 1,707 | 963 | 3,630 | 2,184 |
| Rockwall | 2,397 | 6,427 | 4,393 | 2,659 | 7,214 |
| Runnels | 1,401 | 1,653 | 1,279 | 1,720 | 2,417 |
| Rusk | 5,391 | 7,560 | 3,575 | 5,140 | 9,117 |
| Sabine | 2,288 | 1,490 | 894 | 2,053 | 1,925 |
| San Augustine | 1,737 | 1,243 | 667 | 2,118 | 1,946 |
| San Jacinto | 2,846 | 2,494 | 1,653 | 2,972 | 2,691 |
| San Patricio | 8,202 | 7,456 | 3,178 | 9,920 | 9,159 |
| San Saba | 716 | 723 | 660 | 1,145 | 1,099 |
| Schleicher | 420 | 452 | 355 | 494 | 653 |
| Scurry | 1,609 | 2,670 | 1,826 | 2,119 | 3,749 |
| Shackelford | 484 | 623 | 422 | 681 | 865 |
| Shelby | 3,986 | 3,217 | 1,487 | 4,261 | 3,999 |
| Sherman | 261 | 851 | 256 | 340 | 1,145 |
| Smith | 17,514 | 27,753 | 13,569 | 18,719 | 34,658 |
| Somervell | 782 | 872 | 903 | 983 | 1,304 |
| Starr | 7,668 | 1,209 | 345 | 6,958 | 1,218 |
| Stephens | 1,115 | 1,573 | 1,062 | 1,519 | 2,342 |
| Sterling | 127 | 322 | 182 | 188 | 464 |
| Stonewall | 561 | 242 | 322 | 724 | 421 |
| Sutton | 524 | 687 | 387 | 571 | 996 |
| Swisher | 1,413 | 989 | 541 | 1,893 | 1,271 |
| Tarrant | 156,230 | 183,387 | 129,998 | 151,310 | 242,660 |
| Taylor | 12,382 | 22,614 | 10,331 | 13,073 | 28,563 |
| Terrell | 325 | 176 | 128 | 390 | |

| County | | | | | |
|---|--:|--:|--:|--:|--:|
| Terry | 1,461 | 2,309 | 619 | 1,941 | 2,645 |
| Throckmorton | 401* | 389 | 228 | 534 | 455 |
| Titus | 3,625 | 3,024 | 2,146 | 4,357 | 4,247 |
| Tom Green | 11,437 | 14,989 | 10,244 | 12,283 | 21,463 |
| Travis | 130,546 | 88,105 | 56,158 | 127,783 | 105,915 |
| Trinity | 2,784 | 1,988 | 1,133 | 2,657 | 2,448 |
| Tyler | 3,465 | 2,357 | 1,529 | 4,198 | 3,070 |
| Upshur | 4,776 | 4,511 | 2,896 | 5,242 | 5,991 |
| Upton | 489 | 908 | 313 | 544 | 1,189 |
| Uvalde | 3,482 | 3,635 | 1,387 | 3,684 | 4,266 |
| Val Verde | 4,748 | 4,102 | 2,093 | 5,044 | 5,109 |
| Van Zandt | 5,310 | 5,810 | 5,239 | 6,153 | 7,371 |
| Victoria | 7,604 | 13,086 | 5,136 | 8,923 | 15,056 |
| Walker | 5,619 | 6,662 | 3,619 | 5,826 | 8,473 |
| Waller | 4,270 | 3,065 | 1,692 | 3,957 | 3,607 |
| Ward | 1,695 | 1,769 | 948 | 1,858 | 2,709 |
| Washington | 3,283 | 5,817 | 1,738 | 2,960 | 6,041 |
| Webb | 14,509 | 7,789 | 2,517 | 16,227 | 7,528 |
| Wharton | 4,643 | 5,503 | 2,624 | 5,935 | 6,978 |
| Wheeler | 938 | 1,458 | 367 | 1,067 | 1,703 |
| Wichita | 17,021 | 17,956 | 11,478 | 17,956 | 23,324 |
| Wilbarger | 1,924 | 1,959 | 1,453 | 2,248 | 2,669 |
| Willacy | 3,359 | 1,490 | 652 | 3,165 | 1,750 |
| Williamson | 19,437 | 26,208 | 15,415 | 19,589 | 27,322 |
| Wilson | 3,711 | 3,766 | 2,105 | 3,953 | 4,436 |
| Winkler | 942 | 1,173 | 582 | 947 | 1,656 |
| Wise | 4,478 | 4,555 | 4,485 | 5,288 | 6,064 |
| Wood | 4,084 | 4,708 | 3,494 | 4,553 | 6,216 |
| Yoakum | 595 | 1,486 | 484 | 727 | 1,762 |
| Young | 2,464 | 2,894 | 2,302 | 3,007 | 4,156 |
| Zapata | 2,052 | 866 | 326 | 2,171 | 958 |
| Zavala | 3,058 | 571 | 237 | 3,338 | 628 |
| Totals | 2,281,815 | 2,496,071 | 1,354,781 | 2,352,748 | 3,036,829 |

## Texas Vote Since 1944

1944, Roosevelt, Dem., 821,605; Dewey, Rep., 191,425; Texas Regulars, 135,439; Watson, Proh., 1,017; Thomas, Soc., 594; America First, 250.

1948, Truman, Dem., 750,700; Dewey, Rep., 282,240; Thurmond, States' Rights, 106,909; Wallace, Prog., 3,764; Watson, Proh., 2,758; Thomas, Soc., 874.

1952, Eisenhower, Rep., 1,102,878; Stevenson, Dem., 969,228; Hamblen, Proh., 1,983; MacArthur, Christian Nationalist, 833; MacArthur, Constitution, 730; Hallinan, Prog., 294.

1956, Eisenhower, Rep., 1,080,619; Stevenson, Dem., 859,958; Andrews, Ind., 14,591.

1960, Kennedy, Dem., 1,167,932; Nixon, Rep., 1,121,699; Sullivan, Constitution, 18,169; Decker, Proh., 3,870; write-in, 15.

1964, Johnson, Dem., 1,663,185; Goldwater, Rep., 958,566; Lightburn, Constitution, 5,060.

1968, Nixon, Rep., 1,227,844; Humphrey, Dem., 1,266,804; Wallace, 3d party, 584,269; write-in, 489.

1972, Nixon, Rep., 2,298,896; McGovern, Dem., 1,154,289; Schmitz, Amer., 6,039; Jenness, Soc. Workers, 8,664; others, 3,393.

1976, Carter, Dem., 2,082,319; Ford, Rep., 1,953,300; McCarthy, Ind., 20,118; Anderson, Amer., 11,442; Camejo, Soc. Workers, 1,723; write-in, 2,982.

1980, Reagan, Rep., 2,510,705; Carter, Dem., 1,881,147; Anderson, Ind., 111,613; Clark, Libertarian, 37,643; write-in, 528.

1984, Reagan, Rep., 3,433,428; Mondale, Dem., 1,949,276.

1988, Bush, Rep., 3,036,829; Dukakis, Dem., 2,352,748; Paul, Lib., 30,355; Fulani, New Alliance, 7,208.

1992, Bush, Rep., 2,496,071; Clinton, Dem., 2,281,815; Perot, Ind., 1,354,781; Marrou, Libertarian, 19,699.

## Utah

| County | 1992 | | | 1988 | |
|---|--:|--:|--:|--:|--:|
| | Clinton (D) | Bush (R) | Perot (I) | Dukakis (D) | Bush (R) |
| Beaver | 668 | 1,040 | 330 | 816 | 1,286 |
| Box Elder | 2,186 | 7,712 | 4,507 | 2,736 | 12,585 |
| Cache | 4,973 | 15,971 | 8,032 | 5,871 | 21,766 |
| Carbon | 4,480 | 2,038 | 2,002 | 5,521 | 3,019 |
| Daggett | 122 | 117 | 112 | 132 | 272 |
| Davis | 14,924 | 39,087 | 24,105 | 16,868 | 50,469 |
| Duchesne | 772 | 1,983 | 1,229 | 1,227 | 3,118 |
| Emery | 1,349 | 1,643 | 1,138 | 1,788 | 2,322 |
| Garfield | 309 | 1,235 | 355 | 370 | 1,470 |
| Grand | 1,160 | 1,100 | 991 | 1,287 | 1,486 |
| Iron | 1,537 | 5,616 | 1,693 | 1,736 | 6,038 |
| Juab | 823 | 1,237 | 616 | 974 | 1,505 |
| Kane | 295 | 1,241 | 534 | 398 | 1,788 |
| Millard | 742 | 2,496 | 1,064 | 1,124 | 3,515 |
| Morgan | 520 | 1,339 | 851 | 647 | 1,889 |
| Piute | 169 | 429 | 146 | 206 | 476 |
| Rich | 154 | 525 | 187 | 234 | 621 |

| | | | | | |
|---|---|---|---|---|---|
| Salt Lake | 100,082 | 117,247 | 91,968 | 107,453 | 163,557 |
| San Juan | 1,639 | 2,004 | 576 | 1,407 | 2,377 |
| Sanpete | 1,302 | 2,995 | 1,742 | 1,822 | 4,579 |
| Sevier | 1,039 | 3,160 | 1,671 | 1,403 | 4,747 |
| Summit | 3,013 | 3,133 | 3,060 | 2,545 | 3,881 |
| Tooele | 3,270 | 3,676 | 3,011 | 4,166 | 5,539 |
| Uintah | 1,374 | 3,505 | 2,250 | 1,799 | 5,341 |
| Utah | 14,090 | 61,398 | 24,558 | 18,533 | 68,134 |
| Wasatch | 1,042 | 1,822 | 1,234 | 1,451 | 2,487 |
| Washington | 3,364 | 11,310 | 4,623 | 3,054 | 13,306 |
| Wayne | 236 | 706 | 251 | 353 | 784 |
| Weber | 17,795 | 26,812 | 20,559 | 21,431 | 39,676 |
| Totals | 183,429 | 322,632 | 203,400 | 207,352 | 428,442 |

## Utah Vote Since 1944

1944, Roosevelt, Dem., 150,088; Dewey, Rep., 97,891; Thomas, Soc., 340.

1948, Truman, Dem., 149,151; Dewey, Rep., 124,402; Wallace, Prog., 2,679; Dobbs, Soc. Workers, 73.

1952, Eisenhower, Rep., 194,190; Stevenson, Dem., 135,364.

1956, Eisenhower, Rep., 215,631; Stevenson, Dem., 118,364.

1960, Kennedy, Dem., 169,248; Nixon, Rep., 205,361; Dobbs, Soc. Workers, 100.

1964, Johnson, Dem., 219,628; Goldwater, Rep., 181,785.

1968, Nixon, Rep., 238,728; Humphrey, Dem., 156,665; Wallace, 3d party, 26,906; Halstead, Soc. Worker, 89; Peace and Freedom, 180.

1972, Nixon, Rep., 323,643; McGovern, Dem., 126,284; Schmitz, Amer., 28,549.

1976, Carter, Dem., 182,110; Ford, Rep., 337,908; Anderson, Amer., 13,304; McCarthy, Ind., 3,907; MacBride, Libertarian, 2,438; Maddox, Am. Ind., 1,162; Camejo, Soc. Workers, 268; Hall, Com., 121.

1980, Reagan, Rep., 439,687; Carter, Dem., 124,266; Anderson, Ind., 30,284; Clark, Libertarian, 7,226; Commoner, Citizens, 1,009; Greaves, American, 965; Rarick, Amer. Ind., 522; Hall, Com., 139; DeBerry, Soc. Worker, 124.

1984, Reagan, Rep., 469,105; Mondale, Dem., 155,369; Bergland, Libertarian, 2,447.

1988, Bush, Rep., 428,442; Dukakis, Dem., 207,352; Paul, Lib., 7,473; Dennis, American, 2,158.

1992, Bush, Rep., 322,632; Perot, Ind., 203,400; Clinton, Dem., 183,429; Gritz, Populist/America First, 28,602; Marrou, Libertarian, 1,900; Hagelin, Natural Law, 1,319; LaRouche, Ind., 1,089.

## Vermont

| | 1992 | | | 1988 | |
|---|---|---|---|---|---|
| City | Clinton (D) | Bush (R) | Perot (I) | Dukakis (D) | Bush (R) |
| Barre City | 1,807 | 1,508 | 1,035 | 2,132 | 2,100 |
| Bennington | 3,646 | 2,151 | 1,536 | 3,180 | 2,748 |
| Brattleboro | 3,519 | 1,447 | 847 | 3,136 | 2,044 |
| Burlington | 12,508 | 4,462 | 3,241 | 9,748 | 6,382 |
| Montpelier | 2,490 | 1,407 | 657 | 2,351 | 2,013 |
| Rutland City | 3,888 | 2,915 | 1,722 | 3,590 | 3,631 |
| St. Albans City | 1,455 | 887 | 744 | 1,441 | 1,295 |
| St. Johnsbury | 1,249 | 1,243 | 836 | 1,188 | 1,974 |
| South Burlington | 3,730 | 2,131 | 1,359 | 3,373 | 3,136 |
| Winooski | 1,462 | 733 | 646 | 1,426 | 1,014 |
| Totals | 133,590 | 88,122 | 65,985 | 115,775 | 124,331 |

## Vermont Vote Since 1944

1944, Roosevelt, Dem., 53,820; Dewey, Rep., 71,527.

1948, Truman, Dem., 45,557; Dewey, Rep., 75,926; Wallace, Prog., 1,279; Thomas, Soc., 585.

1952, Eisenhower, Rep., 109,717; Stevenson, Dem., 43,355; Hallinan, Prog., 282; Hoopes, Soc., 185.

1956, Eisenhower, Rep., 110,390; Stevenson, Dem., 42,549; scattering, 39.

1960, Kennedy, Dem., 69,186; Nixon, Rep., 98,131.

1964, Johnson, Dem., 107,674; Goldwater, Rep., 54,868.

1968, Nixon, Rep., 85,142; Humphrey, Dem., 70,255; Wallace, 3d party, 5,104; Halstead, Soc. Worker, 295; Gregory, New Party, 579.

1972, Nixon, Rep., 117,149; McGovern, Dem., 68,174; Spock, Liberty Union, 1,010; Jenness, Soc. Workers, 296; scattered, 318.

1976, Carter, Dem., 77,798; Carter, Ind. Vermonter, 991; Ford, Rep., 100,387; McCarthy, Ind., 4,001; Camejo, Soc. Workers, 430; LaRouche, U.S. Labor, 196; scattered, 99.

1980, Reagan, Rep., 94,598; Carter, Dem., 81,891; Anderson, Ind., 31,760; Commoner, Citizens, 2,316; Clark, Lib-

ertarian, 1,900; McReynolds, Liberty Union, 136; Hall, Com. 118; DeBerry, Soc. Worker, 75; scattering, 413.

1984, Reagan, Rep., 135,865; Mondale, Dem., 95,730; Bergland, Libertarian, 1,002.

1988, Bush, Rep., 124,331; Dukakis, Dem., 115,775; Paul, Lib., 1,000; LaRouche, Ind., 275.

1992, Clinton, Dem., 133,590; Bush, Rep., 88,122; Perot, Ind., 65,985.

## Virginia

| | 1992 | | | 1988 | |
|---|---|---|---|---|---|
| County | Clinton (D) | Bush (R) | Perot (I) | Dukakis (D) | Bush (R) |
| Accomack | 4,950 | 5,666 | 2,304 | 4,443 | 6,926 |
| Albemarle | 13,886 | 13,894 | 3,855 | 10,363 | 15,117 |
| Alleghany | 2,396 | 2,294 | 926 | 2,316 | 2,555 |
| Amelia | 1,534 | 2,062 | 574 | 1,359 | 2,187 |
| Amherst | 4,101 | 5,482 | 1,268 | 3,567 | 6,507 |
| Appomattox | 1,919 | 2,830 | 801 | 1,740 | 3,205 |
| Arlington | 47,756 | 26,376 | 7,992 | 40,314 | 34,191 |
| Augusta | 5,190 | 12,896 | 3,397 | 4,170 | 13,251 |
| Bath | 855 | 1,075 | 354 | 881 | 1,273 |
| Bedford | 6,792 | 10,496 | 3,251 | 5,406 | 10,702 |
| Bland | 1,001 | 1,368 | 408 | 937 | 1,556 |
| Botetourt | 4,349 | 5,904 | 1,819 | 3,763 | 5,687 |
| Brunswick | 3,687 | 2,480 | 479 | 3,070 | 2,742 |
| Buchanan | 7,405 | 3,297 | 815 | 6,935 | 3,912 |
| Buckingham | 2,193 | 2,368 | 459 | 1,941 | 2,481 |
| Campbell | 5,999 | 10,931 | 2,553 | 4,574 | 12,713 |
| Caroline | 3,770 | 2,947 | 965 | 3,186 | 3,065 |
| Carroll | 3,790 | 5,664 | 1,388 | 3,190 | 6,377 |
| Charles City | 2,010 | 729 | 251 | 1,839 | 826 |
| Charlotte | 2,098 | 2,293 | 640 | 1,923 | 2,699 |
| Chesterfield | 28,028 | 56,626 | 16,898 | 18,723 | 58,828 |
| Clarke | 1,811 | 1,994 | 802 | 1,478 | 2,502 |
| Craig | 965 | 1,008 | 304 | 864 | 1,112 |
| Culpeper | 3,444 | 5,226 | 1,640 | 2,555 | 5,896 |
| Cumberland | 1,284 | 1,643 | 372 | 1,132 | 1,978 |
| Dickenson | 4,839 | 2,574 | 660 | 4,461 | 3,061 |
| Dinwiddie | 3,624 | 3,648 | 1,198 | 3,405 | 4,165 |
| Essex | 1,583 | 1,897 | 382 | 1,294 | 2,038 |
| Fairfax | 160,186 | 170,488 | 53,012 | 125,711 | 200,631 |
| Fauquier | 6,600 | 10,497 | 3,464 | 4,837 | 11,733 |
| Floyd | 2,026 | 2,575 | 672 | 1,727 | 2,921 |
| Fluvanna | 2,134 | 2,811 | 871 | 1,562 | 2,447 |
| Franklin | 6,590 | 6,724 | 2,232 | 5,734 | 7,391 |
| Frederick | 4,942 | 9,425 | 2,981 | 3,707 | 9,921 |
| Giles | 3,346 | 3,023 | 1,142 | 3,042 | 3,490 |
| Gloucester | 4,058 | 6,461 | 2,640 | 3,372 | 7,646 |
| Goochland | 2,589 | 3,834 | 994 | 2,209 | 3,765 |
| Grayson | 2,615 | 3,378 | 860 | 2,441 | 3,968 |
| Greene | 1,353 | 2,265 | 627 | 899 | 2,234 |
| Greensville | 2,237 | 1,335 | 360 | 2,083 | 1,610 |
| Halifax | 4,752 | 5,199 | 1,140 | 4,282 | 5,671 |
| Hanover | 8,021 | 20,336 | 5,674 | 5,985 | 20,570 |
| Henrico | 36,807 | 56,910 | 14,720 | 26,980 | 62,284 |
| Henry | 9,296 | 9,005 | 3,212 | 7,536 | 10,871 |
| Highland | 494 | 686 | 212 | 456 | 807 |
| Isle of Wight | 4,380 | 5,370 | 1,536 | 3,747 | 5,779 |
| James City | 6,536 | 8,781 | 2,675 | 4,642 | 8,945 |
| King George | 1,363 | 1,206 | 323 | 1,519 | 2,587 |
| King and Queen | 1,811 | 2,570 | 918 | 1,309 | 1,376 |
| King William | 1,822 | 2,591 | 758 | 1,561 | 2,735 |
| Lancaster | 1,812 | 2,841 | 739 | 1,551 | 3,380 |
| Lee | 5,215 | 3,504 | 1,002 | 4,906 | 4,080 |
| Loudoun | 14,462 | 19,290 | 7,391 | 10,101 | 20,448 |
| Louisa | 3,399 | 3,461 | 1,381 | 2,789 | 3,831 |
| Lunenburg | 2,082 | 2,227 | 505 | 1,870 | 2,530 |
| Madison | 1,700 | 2,341 | 653 | 1,427 | 2,501 |
| Mathews | 1,402 | 2,179 | 884 | 1,235 | 2,752 |
| Mecklenburg | 4,273 | 5,401 | 1,128 | 3,275 | 5,887 |
| Middlesex | 1,597 | 2,224 | 768 | 1,361 | 2,571 |
| Montgomery | 10,658 | 10,606 | 3,449 | 8,909 | 12,326 |
| Nelson | 2,586 | 2,159 | 748 | 2,272 | 2,502 |
| New Kent | 1,738 | 2,708 | 1,017 | 1,427 | 2,917 |
| Northampton | 2,568 | 2,088 | 844 | 2,242 | 2,562 |
| Northumberland | 1,862 | 2,667 | 729 | 1,506 | 2,984 |
| Nottoway | 2,411 | 2,610 | 606 | 2,217 | 3,161 |
| Orange | 3,348 | 4,092 | 1,425 | 2,592 | 4,319 |
| Page | 3,010 | 4,203 | 1,163 | 2,499 | 5,013 |
| Patrick | 2,465 | 3,521 | 1,026 | 2,093 | 3,990 |
| Pittsylvania | 7,675 | 11,467 | 2,296 | 6,612 | 12,229 |
| Powhatan | 1,950 | 3,832 | 1,232 | 1,467 | 4,040 |
| Prince Edward | 2,775 | 2,858 | 635 | 2,434 | 3,147 |
| Prince George | 3,087 | 4,799 | 1,459 | 2,469 | 4,982 |
| Prince William | 26,486 | 35,432 | 13,190 | 19,198 | 39,654 |
| Pulaski | 5,633 | 6,148 | 2,066 | 4,686 | 6,844 |
| Rappahannock | 1,273 | 1,410 | 487 | 1,003 | 1,657 |
| Richmond | 1,034 | 1,609 | 366 | 924 | 1,862 |
| Roanoke | 14,704 | 20,667 | 5,477 | 12,938 | 22,011 |
| Rockbridge | 2,908 | 3,228 | 1,254 | 2,412 | 3,541 |
| Rockingham | 5,407 | 13,016 | 2,839 | 4,716 | 13,241 |
| Russell | 6,480 | 3,891 | 958 | 6,222 | 4,374 |
| Scott | 3,979 | 4,515 | 957 | 3,616 | 4,986 |
| Shenandoah | 3,956 | 7,746 | 2,063 | 3,276 | 8,612 |
| Smyth | 4,924 | 6,128 | 1,618 | 3,989 | 7,446 |
| Southampton | 3,199 | 2,844 | 754 | 3,000 | 3,439 |

| | | | | | |
|---|---|---|---|---|---|
| Spotsylvania | 8,133 | 11,829 | 3,918 | 5,486 | 10,978 |
| Stafford | 7,718 | 12,528 | 4,481 | 5,380 | 12,234 |
| Surry | 1,823 | 1,046 | 364 | 1,602 | 1,246 |
| Sussex | 2,193 | 1,527 | 446 | 1,958 | 1,822 |
| Tazewell | 8,586 | 6,375 | 1,872 | 8,098 | 7,165 |
| Warren | 3,554 | 4,319 | 1,650 | 2,769 | 4,700 |
| Washington | 7,269 | 9,150 | 2,268 | 5,819 | 10,722 |
| Westmoreland | 2,758 | 2,554 | 818 | 2,311 | 2,974 |
| Wise | 7,681 | 5,144 | 1,835 | 7,017 | 6,189 |
| Wythe | 3,616 | 5,121 | 1,557 | 3,201 | 5,827 |
| York | 6,218 | 10,197 | 3,426 | 4,639 | 11,103 |
| **City** | | | | | |
| Alexandria | 30,784 | 16,700 | 4,934 | 24,358 | 20,913 |
| Bedford | 963 | 1,091 | 313 | 960 | 1,322 |
| Bristol | 2,948 | 3,616 | 851 | 2,446 | 4,407 |
| Buena Vista | 1,023 | 849 | 291 | 828 | 1,121 |
| Charlottesville | 8,685 | 4,705 | 1,397 | 7,671 | 5,817 |
| Chesapeake | 23,495 | 28,909 | 9,237 | 18,828 | 29,738 |
| Clifton Forge | 958 | 632 | 251 | 961 | 759 |
| Colonial Heights | 1,721 | 5,296 | 1,312 | 1,581 | 6,001 |
| Covington | 1,442 | 995 | 402 | 1,567 | 1,274 |
| Danville | 8,134 | 9,584 | 1,679 | 7,353 | 12,221 |
| Emporia | 1,048 | 1,094 | 157 | 977 | 1,289 |
| Fairfax | 3,884 | 4,333 | 1,439 | 3,430 | 5,576 |
| Falls Church | 2,864 | 1,912 | 599 | 2,484 | 2,470 |
| Franklin | 1,696 | 1,347 | 272 | 1,630 | 1,557 |
| Fredericksburg | 3,266 | 2,819 | 738 | 2,683 | 3,401 |
| Galax | 957 | 1,087 | 276 | 907 | 1,278 |
| Hampton | 23,395 | 19,219 | 6,581 | 19,106 | 24,034 |
| Harrisonburg | 3,414 | 4,935 | 1,162 | 2,799 | 5,376 |
| Hopewell | 2,863 | 3,818 | 1,227 | 2,566 | 4,672 |
| Lexington | 1,128 | 894 | 228 | 997 | 994 |
| Lynchburg | 9,587 | 12,518 | 2,545 | 8,279 | 15,323 |
| Manassas | 3,647 | 5,453 | 1,971 | 2,658 | 5,980 |
| Manassas Park | 567 | 792 | 356 | 434 | 993 |
| Martinsville | 3,073 | 2,690 | 748 | 2,794 | 3,360 |
| Newport News | 25,743 | 26,779 | 8,217 | 21,413 | 32,570 |
| Norfolk | 37,602 | 22,362 | 8,732 | 37,778 | 30,538 |
| Norton | 871 | 472 | 182 | 795 | 608 |
| Petersburg | 8,671 | 3,125 | 834 | 8,177 | 4,231 |
| Poquoson | 1,086 | 3,354 | 960 | 877 | 3,840 |
| Portsmouth | 20,416 | 12,575 | 4,360 | 19,698 | 16,087 |
| Radford | 2,183 | 1,996 | 582 | 1,855 | 2,481 |
| Richmond | 47,642 | 24,341 | 6,992 | 42,155 | 31,586 |
| Roanoke | 17,724 | 13,443 | 3,753 | 17,185 | 15,389 |
| Salem | 4,028 | 5,143 | 1,430 | 3,760 | 5,694 |
| South Boston | 1,051 | 1,435 | 252 | 936 | 1,694 |
| Staunton | 2,851 | 4,989 | 1,146 | 2,457 | 5,775 |
| Suffolk | 9,196 | 8,697 | 2,150 | 8,080 | 9,742 |
| Virginia Beach | 44,294 | 68,936 | 24,087 | 33,780 | 76,481 |
| Waynesboro | 2,302 | 3,758 | 961 | 2,038 | 4,672 |
| Williamsburg | 1,856 | 1,349 | 445 | 1,534 | 1,648 |
| Winchester | 2,768 | 3,833 | 1,048 | 2,300 | 4,497 |
| Totals | 1,038,650 | 1,150,517 | 348,639 | 859,799 | 1,309,162 |

## Virginia Vote Since 1944

1944, Roosevelt, Dem., 242,276; Dewey, Rep., 145,243; Watson, Proh., 459; Thomas, Soc., 417; Teichert, Soc. Labor, 90.

1948, Truman, Dem., 200,786; Dewey, Rep., 172,070; Thurmond, States' Rights, 43,393; Wallace, Prog., 2,047; Thomas, Soc., 726; Teichert, Soc. Labor, 234.

1952, Eisenhower, Rep., 349,037; Stevenson, Dem., 268,677; Hass, Soc. Labor, 1,160; Hoopes, Social Dem., 504; Hallinan, Prog., 311.

1956, Eisenhower, Rep., 386,459; Stevenson, Dem., 267,760; Andrews, States' Rights, 42,964; Hoopes, Soc. Dem., 444; Hass, Soc. Labor, 351.

1960, Kennedy, Dem., 362,327; Nixon, Rep., 404,521; Coiner, Conservative, 4,204; Hass, Soc. Labor, 397.

1964, Johnson, Dem., 558,038; Goldwater, Rep., 481,334; Hass, Soc. Labor, 2,895.

1968, Nixon, Rep., 590,319; Humphrey, Dem., 442,387; Wallace, 3d party, *320,272; Blomen, Soc. Labor, 4,671; Munn, Proh., 601; Gregory, Peace and Freedom, 1,680.

*10,561 votes for Wallace were omitted in the count.

1972, Nixon, Rep., 988,493; McGovern, Dem., 438,887; Schmitz, Amer., 19,721; Fisher, Soc. Labor, 9,918.

1976, Carter, Dem., 813,896; Ford, Rep., 836,554; Camejo, Soc. Workers, 17,802; Anderson, Amer., 16,686; LaRouche, U.S. Labor, 7,508; MacBride, Libertarian, 4,648.

1980, Reagan, Rep., 989,609; Carter, Dem., 752,174; Anderson, Ind., 95,418; Commoner, Citizens, 14,024; Clark, Libertarian, 12,821; DeBerry, Soc. Worker, 1,986.

1984, Reagan, Rep., 1,337,078; Mondale, Dem., 796,250.

1988, Bush, Rep., 1,309,162; Dukakis, Dem., 859,799; Fulani, Ind., 14,312; Paul, Lib., 8,336.

1992, Bush, Rep., 1,150,517; Clinton, Dem., 1,038,650; Perot, Ind., 348,639; LaRouche, Ind., 11,937; Marrou, Libertarian, 5,730; Fulani, New Alliance, 3,192.

# Washington

| | 1992 | | | 1988 | |
|---|---|---|---|---|---|
| | Clinton | Bush | Perot | Dukakis | Bush |
| County | (D) | (R) | (I) | (D) | (R) |
| Adams | 1,449 | 2,087 | 1,010 | 1,612 | 2,612 |
| Asotin | 3,239 | 2,425 | 1,849 | 3,422 | 2,874 |
| Benton | 16,459 | 22,883 | 12,878 | 14,817 | 28,688 |
| Chelan | 7,860 | 10,716 | 4,606 | 8,183 | 11,601 |
| Clallam | 10,820 | 9,765 | 7,775 | 11,123 | 11,200 |
| Clark | 42,648 | 36,906 | 26,163 | 40,021 | 37,285 |
| Columbia | 668 | 761 | 466 | 730 | 1,172 |
| Cowlitz | 15,052 | 10,000 | 9,246 | 16,090 | 12,009 |
| Douglas | 3,731 | 4,920 | 2,315 | 3,760 | 5,378 |
| Ferry | 963 | 773 | 762 | 972 | 972 |
| Franklin | 3,743 | 4,486 | 2,597 | 4,772 | 6,488 |
| Garfield | 473 | 620 | 222 | 593 | 714 |
| Grant | 7,278 | 9,503 | 4,898 | 7,564 | 10,859 |
| Grays Harbor | 12,599 | 6,904 | 7,460 | 14,097 | 8,860 |
| Island | 9,555 | 9,526 | 7,889 | 8,510 | 12,552 |
| Jefferson | 6,148 | 3,467 | 3,168 | 5,270 | 4,184 |
| King | 391,050 | 212,986 | 167,216 | 349,663 | 290,574 |
| Kitsap | 34,442 | 29,340 | 23,873 | 33,748 | 34,743 |
| Kittitas | 5,432 | 4,078 | 2,778 | 5,318 | 5,048 |
| Klickitat | 2,758 | 2,085 | 1,938 | 2,991 | 2,920 |
| Lewis | 7,810 | 12,316 | 6,684 | 8,629 | 14,184 |
| Lincoln | 1,653 | 2,152 | 1,098 | 1,884 | 2,689 |
| Mason | 8,076 | 5,776 | 5,577 | 7,826 | 7,426 |
| Okanogan | 5,015 | 4,265 | 3,541 | 5,630 | 5,856 |
| Pacific | 4,587 | 2,243 | 2,351 | 5,017 | 3,073 |
| Pend Oreille | 1,798 | 1,528 | 1,340 | 1,925 | 1,802 |
| Pierce | 102,243 | 77,410 | 59,523 | 96,688 | 94,167 |
| San Juan | 3,353 | 1,901 | 1,776 | 3,008 | 2,660 |
| Skagit | 15,936 | 13,388 | 10,973 | 15,159 | 16,550 |
| Skamania | 1,474 | 1,102 | 1,050 | 1,748 | 1,356 |
| Snohomish | 88,643 | 69,137 | 65,838 | 80,694 | 84,158 |
| Spokane | 69,526 | 59,984 | 38,251 | 68,520 | 68,787 |
| Stevens | 4,960 | 5,706 | 3,769 | 5,068 | 6,576 |
| Thurston | 38,293 | 25,643 | 19,551 | 33,860 | 31,980 |
| Wahkiakum | 696 | 488 | 584 | 961 | 629 |
| Walla Walla | 7,325 | 7,894 | 4,507 | 7,448 | 9,683 |
| Whatcom | 26,619 | 23,801 | 12,455 | 25,571 | 23,820 |
| Whitman | 7,637 | 6,428 | 3,220 | 7,403 | 7,680 |
| Yakima | 21,026 | 25,841 | 10,583 | 23,221 | 30,026 |
| Totals | 993,037 | 731,234 | 541,780 | 933,516 | 903,835 |

## Washington Vote Since 1944

1944, Roosevelt, Dem., 486,774; Dewey, Rep., 361,689; Thomas, Soc., 3,824; Watson, Proh., 2,396; Teichert, Soc. Labor, 1,645.

1948, Truman, Dem., 476,165; Dewey, Rep., 386,315; Wallace, Prog., 31,692; Watson, Proh., 6,117; Thomas, Soc., 3,534; Teichert, Soc. Labor, 1,133; Dobbs, Soc. Workers, 103.

1952, Eisenhower, Rep., 599,107; Stevenson, Dem., 492,845; MacArthur, Christian Nationalist, 7,290; Hallinan, Prog., 2,460; Hass, Soc. Labor, 633; Hoopes, Soc., 254; Dobbs, Soc. Workers, 119.

1956, Eisenhower, Rep., 620,430; Stevenson, Dem., 523,002; Hass, Soc. Labor, 7,457.

1960, Kennedy, Dem., 599,298; Nixon, Rep., 629,273; Hass, Soc. Labor, 10,895; Curtis, Constitution, 1,401; Dobbs, Soc. Workers, 705.

1964, Johnson, Dem., 779,699; Goldwater, Rep., 470,366; Hass, Soc. Labor, 7,772; DeBerry, Freedom Soc., 537.

1968, Nixon, Rep., 588,510; Humphrey, Dem., 616,037; Wallace, 3d party, 96,990; Blomen, Soc. Labor, 488; Cleaver, Peace and Freedom, 1,609; Halstead, Soc. Worker, 270; Mitchell, Free Ballot, 377.

1972, Nixon, Rep., 837,135; McGovern, Dem., 568,334; Schmitz, Amer., 58,906; Spock, Ind., 2,644; Fisher, Soc. Labor, 1,102; Jenness, Soc. Worker, 623; Hall, Com., 566; Hospers, Libertarian, 1,537.

1976, Carter, Dem., 717,323; Ford, Rep., 777,732; McCarthy, Ind., 36,986; Maddox, Amer. Ind., 8,585; Anderson, Amer., 5,046; MacBride, Libertarian, 5,042; Wright, People's, 1,124; Camejo, Soc. Workers, 905; LaRouche, U.S. Labor, 903; Hall, Com., 817; Levin, Soc. Labor, 713; Zeidler, Soc., 358.

1980, Reagan, Rep., 865,244; Carter, Dem., 650,193; Anderson, Ind., 185,073; Clark, Libertarian, 29,213; Commoner, Citizens, 9,403; DeBerry, Soc. Worker, 1,137; McReynolds, Socialist, 956; Hall, Com., 834; Griswold, Workers World, 341.

1984, Reagan, Rep., 1,051,670; Mondale, Dem., 798,352; Bergland, Libertarian, 8,844.

1988, Bush, Rep., 903,835; Dukakis, Dem., 933,516; Paul, Lib., 17,240; LaRouche, Ind., 4,412.

1992, Clinton, Dem., 993,037; Bush, Rep., 731,234; Perot, Ind., 541,780; Marrou, Libertarian, 7,533; Gritz, Populist/America First, 4,854; Hagelin, Natural Law, 2,456; Phillips, U.S. Taxpayers, 2,354; Fulani, New Alliance, 1,776; Daniels, Ind., 1,171.

## West Virginia

| | 1992 | | | 1988 | |
| County | Clinton (D) | Bush (R) | Perot (I) | Dukakis (D) | Bush (R) |
|---|---|---|---|---|---|
| Barbour | 3,467 | 2,322 | 1,153 | 3,221 | 3,023 |
| Berkeley | 7,159 | 9,134 | 3,645 | 6,313 | 10,761 |
| Boone | 6,576 | 2,021 | 1,037 | 6,539 | 2,786 |
| Braxton | 3,396 | 1,535 | 823 | 3,377 | 2,024 |
| Brooke | 5,693 | 2,582 | 2,103 | 6,258 | 4,006 |
| Cabell | 15,111 | 13,203 | 5,311 | 15,368 | 17,197 |
| Calhoun | 1,627 | 1,095 | 537 | 1,644 | 1,395 |
| Clay | 1,928 | 1,255 | 462 | 2,263 | 1,536 |
| Doddridge | 968 | 1,500 | 515 | 955 | 1,880 |
| Fayette | 9,574 | 3,991 | 2,002 | 11,009 | 5,143 |
| Gilmer | 1,576 | 1,085 | 484 | 1,661 | 1,387 |
| Grant | 1,011 | 2,762 | 519 | 893 | 3,215 |
| Greenbrier | 5,784 | 4,442 | 1,898 | 6,091 | 5,395 |
| Hampshire | 2,365 | 2,767 | 1,022 | 2,085 | 3,253 |
| Hancock | 7,830 | 3,897 | 3,267 | 8,338 | 5,882 |
| Hardy | 1,917 | 2,144 | 602 | 1,689 | 2,581 |
| Harrison | 15,480 | 9,687 | 5,131 | 17,005 | 13,364 |
| Jackson | 5,102 | 4,192 | 1,908 | 4,573 | 5,696 |
| Jefferson | 5,363 | 4,656 | 2,114 | 4,334 | 5,349 |
| Kanawha | 38,315 | 31,358 | 11,778 | 41,144 | 38,140 |
| Lewis | 2,931 | 2,413 | 1,197 | 3,272 | 3,602 |
| Lincoln | 4,502 | 2,637 | 787 | 5,049 | 3,457 |
| Logan | 11,095 | 3,336 | 1,835 | 11,317 | 4,244 |
| McDowell | 7,019 | 1,941 | 803 | 7,204 | 2,463 |
| Marion | 14,042 | 6,380 | 4,736 | 14,441 | 9,229 |
| Marshall | 7,298 | 4,463 | 3,402 | 7,903 | 6,793 |
| Mason | 5,331 | 3,808 | 2,045 | 5,468 | 5,332 |
| Mercer | 9,511 | 7,888 | 2,817 | 10,152 | 10,221 |
| Mineral | 3,992 | 4,837 | 1,884 | 4,059 | 6,015 |
| Mingo | 7,342 | 2,584 | 915 | 7,429 | 2,896 |
| Monongalia | 14,142 | 9,831 | 4,576 | 14,178 | 12,091 |
| Monroe | 2,418 | 2,311 | 685 | 2,427 | 2,719 |
| Morgan | 1,854 | 2,585 | 886 | 1,545 | 3,002 |
| Nicholas | 5,042 | 2,959 | 1,495 | 5,173 | 3,731 |
| Ohio | 9,522 | 7,421 | 3,632 | 10,121 | 10,341 |
| Pendleton | 1,626 | 1,589 | 362 | 1,595 | 1,901 |
| Pleasants | 1,387 | 1,248 | 731 | 1,421 | 1,761 |
| Pocahontas | 1,741 | 1,401 | 627 | 1,958 | 1,876 |
| Preston | 3,933 | 4,429 | 2,109 | 4,357 | 5,804 |
| Putnam | 6,817 | 7,653 | 2,910 | 6,540 | 8,163 |
| Raleigh | 13,171 | 8,700 | 3,247 | 14,302 | 10,395 |
| Randolph | 5,097 | 3,496 | 1,582 | 5,233 | 4,746 |
| Ritchie | 1,474 | 2,184 | 745 | 1,446 | 2,874 |
| Roane | 2,607 | 2,207 | 1,009 | 2,447 | 2,861 |
| Summers | 2,650 | 1,652 | 565 | 3,072 | 2,231 |
| Taylor | 2,843 | 2,022 | 1,242 | 2,852 | 2,816 |
| Tucker | 1,805 | 1,261 | 550 | 1,869 | 1,699 |
| Tyler | 1,587 | 1,593 | 1,013 | 1,501 | 2,365 |
| Upshur | 3,161 | 3,505 | 1,558 | 3,065 | 4,813 |
| Wayne | 8,392 | 5,729 | 2,199 | 8,621 | 7,123 |
| Webster | 2,320 | 811 | 436 | 2,185 | 1,016 |
| Wetzel | 3,753 | 2,271 | 1,550 | 3,928 | 3,381 |
| Wirt | 1,043 | 939 | 394 | 929 | 1,125 |
| Wood | 13,529 | 15,441 | 6,998 | 12,959 | 19,450 |
| Wyoming | 5,782 | 2,821 | 996 | 6,138 | 3,516 |
| Totals | 331,001 | 241,974 | 108,829 | 341,016 | 310,065 |

### West Virginia Vote Since 1944

1944, Roosevelt, Dem., 392,777; Dewey, Rep., 322,819.

1948, Truman, Dem., 429,188; Dewey, Rep., 316,251; Wallace, Prog., 3,311.

1952, Eisenhower, Rep., 419,970; Stevenson, Dem., 453,578.

1956, Eisenhower, Rep., 449,297; Stevenson, Dem., 381,534.

1960, Kennedy, Dem., 441,786; Nixon, Rep., 395,995.

1964, Johnson, Dem., 538,087; Goldwater, Rep., 253,953.

1968, Nixon, Rep., 307,555; Humphrey, Dem., 374,091; Wallace, 3d party, 72,560.

1972, Nixon, Rep., 484,964; McGovern, Dem., 277,435.

1976, Carter, Dem., 435,864; Ford, Rep., 314,726.

1980, Reagan, Rep., 334,206; Carter, Dem., 367,462; Anderson, Ind., 31,691; Clark, Libertarian, 4,356.

1984, Reagan, Rep., 405,483; Mondale, Dem., 328,125.

1988, Bush, Rep., 310,065; Dukakis, Dem., 341,016; Fulani, New Alliance, 2,230.

1992, Clinton, Dem., 331,001; Bush, Rep., 241,974; Perot, Ind., 108,829; Marrou, Libertarian, 1,873.

## Wisconsin

| | 1992 | | | 1988 | |
| County | Clinton (D) | Bush (R) | Perot (I) | Dukakis (D) | Bush (R) |
|---|---|---|---|---|---|
| Adams | 3,539 | 2,465 | 2,003 | 3,598 | 3,258 |
| Ashland | 4,213 | 2,372 | 1,746 | 4,526 | 2,926 |
| Barron | 8,063 | 6,572 | 5,479 | 8,951 | 8,527 |
| Bayfield | 3,873 | 2,393 | 1,786 | 4,323 | 3,095 |
| Brown | 37,513 | 42,352 | 22,395 | 41,788 | 43,625 |
| Buffalo | 2,996 | 2,029 | 1,889 | 3,481 | 2,783 |
| Burnet | 3,172 | 2,340 | 1,855 | 3,537 | 2,884 |
| Calumet | 5,701 | 7,541 | 5,055 | 6,481 | 8,107 |
| Chippewa | 10,487 | 8,215 | 6,408 | 11,447 | 9,757 |
| Clark | 5,540 | 4,977 | 4,284 | 6,642 | 6,296 |
| Columbia | 9,348 | 9,099 | 5,439 | 9,132 | 10,475 |
| Crawford | 3,540 | 2,390 | 1,797 | 3,608 | 3,238 |
| Dane | 114,724 | 61,957 | 31,874 | 105,414 | 69,143 |
| Dodge | 11,438 | 14,971 | 9,136 | 12,663 | 17,003 |
| Door | 4,735 | 5,468 | 3,506 | 5,425 | 6,907 |
| Douglas | 12,319 | 5,679 | 4,150 | 13,907 | 6,440 |
| Dunn | 7,965 | 5,283 | 4,809 | 9,205 | 7,273 |
| Eau Claire | 21,221 | 15,915 | 9,783 | 21,150 | 17,664 |
| Florence | 978 | 942 | 719 | 1,018 | 1,106 |
| Fond duLac | 13,757 | 19,785 | 10,660 | 15,887 | 21,985 |
| Forest | 1,904 | 1,393 | 1,062 | 2,142 | 1,845 |
| Grant | 8,914 | 7,678 | 6,405 | 9,421 | 10,049 |
| Green | 5,467 | 4,887 | 3,735 | 5,153 | 6,636 |
| Green Lake | 2,772 | 3,897 | 2,827 | 3,033 | 5,205 |
| Iowa | 4,467 | 3,288 | 2,341 | 4,268 | 4,240 |
| Iron | 1,762 | 1,273 | 835 | 2,090 | 1,599 |
| Jackson | 3,681 | 2,644 | 2,040 | 3,924 | 3,555 |
| Jefferson | 11,593 | 13,072 | 7,960 | 11,816 | 14,309 |
| Juneau | 4,177 | 4,051 | 2,670 | 3,734 | 4,869 |
| Kenosha | 27,341 | 19,854 | 14,232 | 30,089 | 21,661 |
| Kewaunee | 4,050 | 3,570 | 2,700 | 4,786 | 4,330 |
| La Crosse | 22,838 | 18,891 | 10,224 | 22,204 | 21,548 |
| La Fayette | 3,143 | 2,582 | 2,079 | 3,521 | 3,665 |
| Langlade | 3,630 | 3,890 | 2,444 | 4,254 | 4,884 |
| Lincoln | 5,297 | 4,321 | 3,605 | 5,819 | 5,257 |
| Manitowoc | 15,903 | 14,008 | 11,179 | 19,680 | 16,020 |
| Marathon | 21,482 | 20,948 | 14,600 | 24,658 | 24,482 |
| Marinette | 7,626 | 7,984 | 5,412 | 8,030 | 9,637 |
| Marquette | 2,533 | 2,322 | 1,818 | 2,463 | 3,059 |
| Menominee | 691 | 244 | 221 | 1,026 | 381 |
| Milwaukee | 235,521 | 151,314 | 76,039 | 268,287 | 168,363 |
| Monroe | 6,427 | 6,118 | 4,183 | 6,437 | 7,073 |
| Oconto | 5,898 | 5,720 | 4,405 | 6,549 | 7,084 |
| Oneida | 7,160 | 6,725 | 4,782 | 7,414 | 8,130 |
| Outagamie | 23,735 | 30,370 | 18,479 | 27,771 | 33,113 |
| Ozaukee | 11,879 | 22,805 | 8,002 | 12,661 | 22,899 |
| Pepin | 1,673 | 1,098 | 781 | 1,906 | 1,311 |
| Pierce | 7,824 | 4,844 | 4,492 | 8,659 | 6,045 |
| Polk | 7,746 | 5,446 | 4,753 | 8,981 | 6,866 |
| Portage | 15,553 | 10,914 | 7,083 | 16,317 | 12,057 |
| Price | 3,575 | 2,654 | 2,286 | 3,987 | 3,450 |
| Racine | 34,875 | 32,310 | 20,227 | 39,631 | 36,342 |
| Richland | 3,458 | 3,144 | 1,899 | 3,643 | 4,026 |
| Rock | 31,154 | 21,942 | 15,700 | 29,576 | 28,178 |
| Rusk | 3,376 | 2,430 | 2,085 | 3,888 | 3,063 |
| St. Croix | 10,281 | 8,114 | 7,125 | 11,392 | 9,960 |
| Sauk | 9,128 | 8,886 | 5,280 | 8,324 | 10,225 |
| Sawyer | 2,796 | 2,658 | 1,861 | 3,231 | 3,260 |
| Shawano | 6,062 | 7,253 | 4,540 | 6,587 | 8,362 |
| Sheboygan | 20,568 | 22,526 | 11,295 | 23,429 | 23,471 |
| Taylor | 3,305 | 3,415 | 2,590 | 3,785 | 4,254 |
| Trempealeau | 6,218 | 3,577 | 3,160 | 6,212 | 4,902 |
| Vernon | 5,673 | 4,072 | 2,890 | 5,754 | 5,226 |
| Vilas | 3,764 | 4,616 | 2,827 | 3,781 | 5,842 |
| Walworth | 11,825 | 15,727 | 9,029 | 12,203 | 18,259 |
| Washburn | 3,080 | 2,586 | 1,978 | 3,393 | 3,074 |
| Washington | 13,339 | 22,739 | 13,045 | 15,907 | 24,328 |
| Waukesha | 50,270 | 91,461 | 36,622 | 57,598 | 90,467 |
| Waupaca | 6,666 | 10,252 | 6,088 | 7,078 | 11,559 |
| Waushara | 3,402 | 4,045 | 2,829 | 3,535 | 4,953 |
| Winnebago | 27,234 | 33,709 | 16,140 | 28,508 | 35,085 |
| Wood | 13,208 | 13,843 | 8,822 | 16,074 | 16,549 |
| Totals | 1,041,066 | 930,855 | 544,479 | 1,126,794 | 1,047,499 |

### Wisconsin Vote Since 1944

1944, Roosevelt, Dem., 650,413; Dewey, Rep., 674,532; Thomas, Soc., 13,205; Teichert, Soc. Labor, 1,002.

1948, Truman, Dem., 647,310; Dewey, Rep., 590,959; Wallace, Prog., 25,282; Thomas, Soc., 12,547; Teichert, Soc. Labor, 399; Dobbs, Soc. Workers, 303.

1952, Eisenhower, Rep., 979,744; Stevenson, Dem., 622,175; Hallinan, Ind., 2,174; Dobbs, Ind., 1,350; Hoopes, Ind., 1,157; Hass, Ind., 770.

1956, Eisenhower, Rep., 954,844; Stevenson, Dem., 586,768; Andrews, Ind., 6,918; Hoopes, Soc., 754; Hass, Soc. Labor, 710; Dobbs, Soc. Workers, 564.

1960, Kennedy, Dem., 830,805; Nixon, Rep., 895,175; Dobbs, Soc. Workers, 1,792; Hass, Soc. Labor, 1,310.

1964, Johnson, Dem., 1,050,424; Goldwater, Rep., 638,495; DeBerry, Soc. Worker, 1,692; Hass, Soc. Labor, 1,204.

1968, Nixon, Rep., 809,997; Humphrey, Dem., 748,804; Wallace, 3d party, 127,835; Blomen, Soc. Labor, 1,338; Halstead, Soc. Worker, 1,222; scattered, 2,342.

1972 Nixon, Rep., 989,430; McGovern, Dem., 810,174; Schmitz, Amer., 47,525; Spock, Ind., 2,701; Fisher, Soc. Labor, 998; Hall, Com., 663; Reed, Ind., 506; scattered, 893.

1976, Carter, Dem., 1,040,232; Ford, Rep., 1,004,987; McCarthy, Ind., 34,943; Maddox, Amer. Ind., 8,552; Zeidler, Soc., 4,298; MacBride, Libertarian, 3,814; Camejo, Soc. Workers, 1,691; Wright, People's, 943; Hall, Com., 749; LaRouche, U.S. Lab., 738; Levin, Soc. Labor, 389; scattered, 2,839.

1980, Reagan, Rep., 1,088,845; Carter, Dem., 981,584; Anderson, Ind., 160,657; Clark, Libertarian, 29,135; Commoner, Citizens, 7,767; Rarick, Constitution, 1,519; McReynolds, Socialist, 808; Hall, Com., 772; Griswold, Workers World, 414; DeBerry, Soc. Workers, 383; scattering, 1,337.

1984, Reagan, Rep., 1,198,584; Mondale, Dem., 995,740; Bergland, Libertarian, 4,883.

1988, Bush, Rep., 1,047,499; Dukakis, Dem., 1,126,794; Paul, Lib., 5,157; Duke, Pop., 3,056.

1992, Clinton, Dem., 1,041,066; Bush, Rep., 930,855; Perot, Ind., 544,479; Marrou, Libertarian, 2,877; Gritz, Populist/America First, 2,311; Daniels, Ind., 1,883; Phillips, U.S. Taxpayers, 1,772; Hagelin, Natural Law, 1,070.

## Wyoming

| County | 1992 Clinton (D) | 1992 Bush (R) | 1992 Perot (I) | 1988 Dukakis (D) | 1988 Bush (R) |
|---|---|---|---|---|---|
| Albany | 5,713 | 4,176 | 2,862 | 5,486 | 5,653 |
| Big Horn | 1,216 | 2,216 | 1,236 | 1,469 | 3,258 |
| Campbell | 2,709 | 5,315 | 3,133 | 2,288 | 6,702 |
| Carbon | 2,737 | 2,320 | 1,579 | 2,555 | 3,336 |
| Converse | 1,307 | 2,159 | 1,260 | 1,301 | 2,885 |
| Crook | 568 | 1,377 | 718 | 553 | 1,939 |
| Fremont | 4,765 | 5,387 | 3,594 | 5,020 | 7,681 |
| Goshen | 1,754 | 2,395 | 1,144 | 1,875 | 3,075 |
| Hot Springs | 740 | 978 | 652 | 800 | 1,490 |
| Johnson | 656 | 1,614 | 844 | 707 | 2,081 |
| Laramie | 12,177 | 12,890 | 6,607 | 11,851 | 15,561 |
| Lincoln | 1,430 | 2,595 | 1,495 | 1,592 | 3,237 |
| Natrona | 9,817 | 9,717 | 7,647 | 9,148 | 14,005 |
| Niobrara | 298 | 635 | 355 | 354 | 825 |
| Park | 2,771 | 5,218 | 3,145 | 2,646 | 6,884 |
| Platte | 1,398 | 1,668 | 956 | 1,482 | 2,253 |
| Sheridan | 4,139 | 4,303 | 3,035 | 4,655 | 5,980 |
| Sublette | 536 | 1,168 | 828 | 576 | 1,636 |
| Sweetwater | 6,417 | 4,476 | 3,879 | 6,720 | 6,780 |
| Teton | 3,120 | 2,854 | 2,340 | 2,217 | 3,616 |
| Uinta | 2,047 | 2,701 | 2,041 | 1,922 | 3,464 |
| Washakie | 1,118 | 1,720 | 1,084 | 1,197 | 2,538 |
| Weston | 727 | 1,465 | 829 | 699 | 1,988 |
| Totals | 68,160 | 79,347 | 51,263 | 67,113 | 106,867 |

### Wyoming Vote Since 1944

1944, Roosevelt, Dem., 49,419; Dewey, Rep., 51,921.

1948, Truman, Dem., 52,354; Dewey, Rep., 47,947; Wallace, Prog., 931; Thomas, Soc., 137; Teichert, Soc. Labor, 56.

1952, Eisenhower, Rep., 81,047; Stevenson, Dem., 47,934; Hamblen, Proh., 194; Hoopes, Soc., 40; Haas, Soc. Labor, 36.

1956, Eisenhower, Rep., 74,573; Stevenson, Dem., 49,554.

1960, Kennedy, Dem., 63,331; Nixon, Rep., 77,451.

1964, Johnson, Dem., 80,718; Goldwater, Rep., 61,998.

1968, Nixon, Rep., 70,927; Humphrey, Dem., 45,173; Wallace, 3d party, 11,105.

1972, Nixon, Rep., 100,464; McGovern, Dem., 44,358; Schmitz, Amer., 748.

1976, Carter, Dem., 62,239; Ford, Rep., 92,717; McCarthy, Ind., 624; Reagan, Ind., 307; Anderson, Amer., 290; MacBride, Libertarian, 89; Brown, Ind., 47; Maddox, Amer. Ind., 30.

1980, Reagan, Rep., 110,700; Carter, Dem., 49,427; Anderson, Ind., 12,072; Clark, Libertarian, 4,514.

1984, Reagan, Rep., 133,241; Mondale, Dem., 53,370; Bergland, Libertarian, 2,357.

1988, Bush, Rep., 106,867; Dukakis, Dem., 67,113; Paul, Lib., 2,026; Fulani, New Alliance, 545.

1992, Bush, Rep., 79,347; Clinton, Dem., 68,160; Perot, Ind., 51,263.

## Electoral Votes for President

(based on 1990 Census)

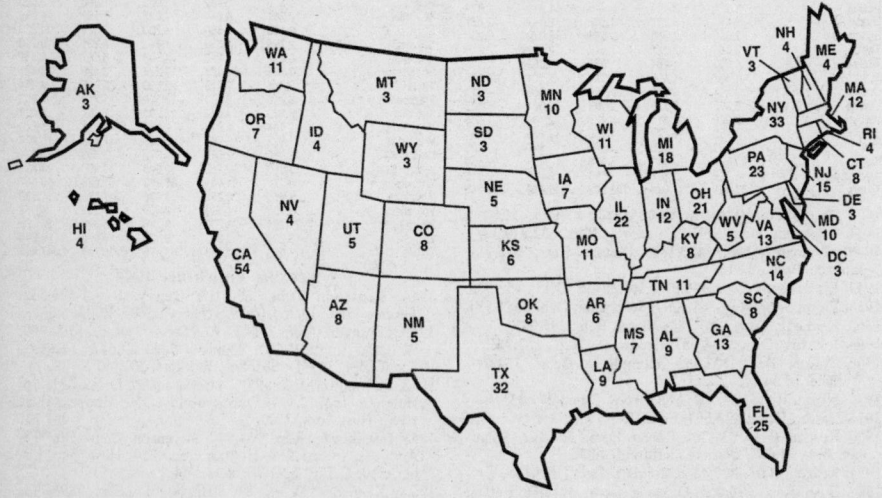

## 1992 Official Presidential General Election Results

Source: State Elections Offices; News Election Service

| Candidate (Party) | Popular Vote | Percent of Popular Vote | Candidate (Party) | Popular Vote | Percent of Popular Vote |
|---|---|---|---|---|---|
| Bill Clinton (Democrat) | 44,908,254 | 42.95 | Helen Halyard (Workers League) | 3,050 | .00 |
| George Bush (Republican) | 39,102,343 | 37.40 | John Quinn Brisben (Socialist) | 2,909 | .00 |
| Ross Perot (Independent) | 19,741,065 | 18.86 | John Yiamouyiannis (Independent) | 2,199 | .00 |
| Andre Marrou (Libertarian) | 291,612 | .28 | | | |
| James "Bo" Gritz (Populist/ America First) | 98,918 | .09 | Delbert Ehlers (Independent) | 1,149 | .00 |
| Lenora Fulani (New Alliance) | 73,248 | .07 | Jim Boren (Apathy) | 956 | .00 |
| Howard Phillips (U.S. Taxpayers) | 42,960 | .04 | Earl Dodge (Prohibition) | 935 | .00 |
| | | | Eugene Hem (Third Party) | 405 | .00 |
| John Hagelin (Natural Law) | 37,137 | .04 | Isabelle Masters (Looking Back Group) | 327 | .00 |
| Ron Daniels (Independent) | 27,396 | .03 | | | |
| Lyndon LaRouche (Independent) | 25,863 | .02 | Robert J. Smith (American) | 292 | .00 |
| | | | Gloria Estella La Riva (Workers World) | 181 | .00 |
| James Mac Warren (Socialist Workers) | 22,883 | .02 | Write-In | 177,207 | .17 |
| Drew Bradford (Independent) | 4,749 | .00 | None of the Above (Nevada) | 2,537 | .00 |
| Jack Herer (Grassroots) | 3,875 | .00 | **Total** | **104,552,736** | **100** |

Note: Party designations may vary from one state to another.

## America's Third Parties

Since 1860, there have been only 5 presidential elections in which all "third parties" together polled more than 10% of the vote. The major vote-getters in those elections were the Populists (James Baird Weaver) in 1892, the National Progressives (Theodore Roosevelt) in 1912, the La Follette Progressives in 1924, George Wallace's American Party in 1968, and independent H. Ross Perot in 1992. In 1948, the combined third parties (Henry Wallace's Progessives, Strom Thurmond's States' Rights Party or Dixiecrats, Prohibition, Socialists, and others) received only 5.75% of the vote. In most elections since 1860, fewer than one vote in 20 has been cast for a third party. The only successful third party in American history was the Republican Party in the election of Abraham Lincoln in 1860.

### Notable Third Parties

| Party | Presidential nominee | Year | Issues | Strength in |
|---|---|---|---|---|
| Anti-Masonic | William Wirt | 1832 | Against secret societies and oaths | Pa., Vt. |
| Liberty | James G. Birney | 1844 | Anti-slavery | North |
| Free Soil | Martin Van Buren | 1848 | Anti-slavery | New York, Oh. |
| American (Know Nothing) | Millard Fillmore | 1856 | Anti-immigrant | Northeast, South |
| Greenback | Peter Cooper | 1876 | For "cheap money," | |
| Greenback | James B. Weaver | 1880 | labor rights | National |
| Prohibition | John P. St. John | 1884 | Anti-liquor | National |
| Populist | James B. Weaver | 1892 | For "cheap money," end of national banks | South, West |
| Socialist | Eugene V. Debs | 1900-20 | For public ownership | National |
| Progressive (Bull Moose) | Theodore Roosevelt | 1912 | Against high tariffs | Midwest, West |
| Progressive | Robert M. La Follette | 1924 | Farmer & labor rights | Midwest, West |
| Socialist | Norman Thomas | 1928-48 | Liberal reforms | National |
| Union | William Lemke | 1936 | Anti "New Deal" | National |
| States' Rights | Strom Thurmond | 1948 | For states' rights | South |
| Progressive | Henry Wallace | 1948 | Anti-cold war | N.Y., Calif. |
| American Independent | George Wallace | 1968 | For states' rights | South |
| American | John G. Schmitz | 1972 | For "law and order" | Far West, Oh., La. |
| None (Independent) | John B. Anderson | 1980 | A 3d choice | National |
| None (Independent) | H. Ross Perot | 1992 | Federal budget deficit | National |

## Political Action Committee Contributions to Federal Candidates: 1992 Election

### Largest Contributions from Political Action Committees

Source: Federal Election Commission

| | | |
|---|---|---|
| 1. National Association of Realtors | $2,950,138 | 4. Association of Trial Lawyers — 2,336,135 |
| 2. American Medical Association | 2,936,086 | 5. National Education Association — 2,323,122 |
| 3. International Brotherhood of Teamsters | 2,442,552 | 6. United Auto Workers — 2,231,917 |

### Political Action Committees, Health Care Industry

Source: Center for Responsive Politics

Second in growth only to lawyers and lobbyists, the health care industry increased its contributions in the 1992 election by 36 percent. Listed below are PACs that contributed more than $200,000.

| Political Action Committee | Type of organization | Contribution |
|---|---|---|
| American Medical Assoc.[1] | Professional | $2,936,086 |
| American Dental Assoc.[1] | Professional | 1,420,958 |
| American Academy of Opthalmology | Professional | 801,527 |
| American Chiropractic Assoc.[1] | Professional | 641,746 |
| American Hospital Assoc.[1] | Hospitals and nursing homes | 505,888 |
| American Podiatry Assoc. | Professional | 401,000 |
| American Optometric Assoc. | Professional | 398,366 |
| American Health Care Assoc. | Hospitals and nursing homes | 382,019 |
| American College of Emergency Physicians | Professional | 330,725 |
| American Nurses Assoc. | Professional | 306,519 |
| Assoc. for the Advancement of Psychology | Professional | 273,743 |

[1]Does not include affiliated PACs.

## Major Parties' Popular and Electoral Vote for President

(F) Federalist; (D) Democrat; (R) Republican; (DR) Democratic Republican; (NR) National Republican;
(W) Whig; (P) People's; (PR) Progressive; (SR) States' Rights; (LR) Liberal Republican; Asterisk (*)—See notes.

| Year | President elected | Popular | Elec. | Losing candidate | Popular | Elec. |
|---|---|---|---|---|---|---|
| 1789 | George Washington (F) . . . . | Unknown | 69 | No opposition . . . . . . . . . . | — | — |
| 1792 | George Washington (F) . . . . | Unknown | 132 | No opposition . . . . . . . . . . | — | — |
| 1796 | John Adams (F). . . . . . . . | Unknown | 71 | Thomas Jefferson (DR) . . . . | Unknown | 68 |
| 1800* | Thomas Jefferson (DR) . . . . | Unknown | 73 | Aaron Burr (DR) . . . . . . . . | Unknown | 73 |
| 1804 | Thomas Jefferson (DR) . . . . | Unknown | 162 | Charles Pinckney (F) . . . . . | Unknown | 14 |
| 1808 | James Madison (DR). . . . . . | Unknown | 122 | Charles Pinckney (F) . . . . . | Unknown | 47 |
| 1812 | James Madison (DR). . . . . . | Unknown | 128 | DeWitt Clinton (F) . . . . . . . | Unknown | 89 |
| 1816 | James Monroe (DR) . . . . . . | Unknown | 183 | Rufus King (F) . . . . . . . . . | Unknown | 34 |
| 1820 | James Monroe (DR) . . . . . . | Unknown | 231 | John Quincy Adams (DR) . . . . | Unknown | 1 |
| 1824* | John Quincy Adams (DR) . . . | 105,321 | 84 | Andrew Jackson (DR) . . . . . . | 155,872 | 99 |
| | | | | Henry Clay (DR) . . . . . . . . | 46,587 | 37 |
| | | | | William H. Crawford (DR) . . . . | 44,282 | 41 |
| 1828 | Andrew Jackson (D) . . . . . . | 647,231 | 178 | John Quincy Adams (NR) . . . . | 509,097 | 83 |
| 1832 | Andrew Jackson (D) . . . . . . | 687,502 | 219 | Henry Clay (NR) . . . . . . . . | 530,189 | 49 |
| 1836 | Martin Van Buren (D). . . . . . | 762,678 | 170 | William H. Harrison (W) . . . . . | 548,007 | 73 |
| 1840 | William H. Harrison (W) . . . . | 1,275,017 | 234 | Martin Van Buren (D) . . . . . . | 1,128,702 | 60 |
| 1844 | James K. Polk (D). . . . . . . | 1,337,243 | 170 | Henry Clay (W). . . . . . . . . | 1,299,068 | 105 |
| 1848 | Zachary Taylor (W). . . . . . . | 1,360,101 | 163 | Lewis Cass (D) . . . . . . . . . | 1,220,544 | 127 |
| 1852 | Franklin Pierce (D) . . . . . . | 1,601,474 | 254 | Winfield Scott (W) . . . . . . . | 1,386,578 | 42 |
| 1856 | James Buchanan (D). . . . . . | 1,927,995 | 174 | John C. Fremont (R). . . . . . . | 1,391,555 | 114 |
| 1860 | Abraham Lincoln (R) . . . . . . | 1,866,352 | 180 | Stephen A. Douglas (D) . . . . . | 1,375,157 | 12 |
| | | | | John C. Breckinridge (D) . . . . | 845,763 | 72 |
| | | | | John Bell (Const. Union). . . . . | 589,581 | 39 |
| 1864 | Abraham Lincoln (R) . . . . . . | 2,216,067 | 212 | George McClellan (D) . . . . . . | 1,808,725 | 21 |
| 1868 | Ulysses S. Grant (R) . . . . . . | 3,015,071 | 214 | Horatio Seymour (D). . . . . . . | 2,709,615 | 80 |
| 1872* | Ulysses S. Grant (R) . . . . . . | 3,597,070 | 286 | Horace Greeley (D-LR) . . . . . | 2,834,079 | — |
| 1876* | Rutherford B. Hayes (R) . . . . | 4,033,950 | 185 | Samuel J. Tilden (D) . . . . . . | 4,284,757 | 184 |
| 1880 | James A. Garfield (R) . . . . . | 4,449,053 | 214 | Winfield S. Hancock (D) . . . . . | 4,442,030 | 155 |
| 1884 | Grover Cleveland (D) . . . . . | 4,911,017 | 219 | James G. Blaine (R). . . . . . . | 4,848,334 | 182 |
| 1888* | Benjamin Harrison (R) . . . . . | 5,444,337 | 233 | Grover Cleveland (D) . . . . . . | 5,540,050 | 168 |
| 1892 | Grover Cleveland (D) . . . . . | 5,554,414 | 277 | Benjamin Harrison (R). . . . . . | 5,190,802 | 145 |
| | | | | James Weaver (P). . . . . . . . | 1,027,329 | 22 |
| 1896 | William McKinley (R) . . . . . . | 7,035,638 | 271 | William J. Bryan (D-P) . . . . . . | 6,467,946 | 176 |
| 1900 | William McKinley (R) . . . . . . | 7,219,530 | 292 | William J. Bryan (D) . . . . . . . | 6,358,071 | 155 |
| 1904 | Theodore Roosevelt (R) . . . . | 7,628,834 | 336 | Alton B. Parker (D) . . . . . . . | 5,084,491 | 140 |
| 1908 | William H. Taft (R) . . . . . . | 7,679,006 | 321 | William J. Bryan (D) . . . . . . . | 6,409,106 | 162 |
| 1912 | Woodrow Wilson (D) . . . . . . | 6,286,214 | 435 | Theodore Roosevelt (PR) . . . . | 4,216,020 | 88 |
| | | | | William H. Taft (R) . . . . . . . | 3,483,922 | 8 |
| 1916 | Woodrow Wilson (D) . . . . . . | 9,129,606 | 277 | Charles E. Hughes (R). . . . . . | 8,538,221 | 254 |
| 1920 | Warren G. Harding (R) . . . . . | 16,152,200 | 404 | James M. Cox (D) . . . . . . . . | 9,147,353 | 127 |
| 1924 | Calvin Coolidge (R). . . . . . | 15,725,016 | 382 | John W. Davis (D) . . . . . . . . | 8,385,586 | 136 |
| | | | | Robert M. LaFollette (PR) . . . . | 4,822,856 | 13 |
| 1928 | Herbert Hoover (R). . . . . . . | 21,392,190 | 444 | Alfred E. Smith (D) . . . . . . . | 15,016,443 | 87 |
| 1932 | Franklin D. Roosevelt (D) . . . | 22,821,857 | 472 | Herbert Hoover (R) . . . . . . . | 15,761,841 | 59 |
| | | | | Norman Thomas (Socialist). . . | 884,781 | — |
| 1936 | Franklin D. Roosevelt (D) . . . | 27,751,597 | 523 | Alfred Landon (R) . . . . . . . . | 16,679,583 | 8 |
| 1940 | Franklin D. Roosevelt (D) . . . | 27,243,466 | 449 | Wendell Willkie (R). . . . . . . | 22,304,755 | 82 |
| 1944 | Franklin D. Roosevelt (D) . . . | 25,602,505 | 432 | Thomas E. Dewey (R) . . . . . . | 22,006,278 | 99 |
| 1948 | Harry S. Truman (D) . . . . . . | 24,105,812 | 303 | Thomas E. Dewey (R) . . . . . . | 21,970,065 | 189 |
| | | | | J. Strom Thurmond (SR) . . . . | 1,169,021 | 39 |
| | | | | Henry A. Wallace (PR) . . . . . | 1,157,172 | — |
| 1952 | Dwight D. Eisenhower (R) . . . | 33,936,252 | 442 | Adlai E. Stevenson (D) . . . . . | 27,314,992 | 89 |
| 1956* | Dwight D. Eisenhower (R) . . . | 35,585,316 | 457 | Adlai E. Stevenson (D) . . . . . | 26,031,322 | 73 |
| 1960* | John F. Kennedy (D) . . . . . . | 34,227,096 | 303 | Richard M. Nixon (R). . . . . . . | 34,108,546 | 219 |
| 1964 | Lyndon B. Johnson (D). . . . . | 43,126,506 | 486 | Barry M. Goldwater (R) . . . . . | 27,176,799 | 52 |
| 1968 | Richard M. Nixon (R). . . . . . | 31,785,480 | 301 | Hubert H. Humphrey (D) . . . . | 31,275,166 | 191 |
| | | | | George C. Wallace (3d party) . . | 9,906,473 | 46 |
| 1972* | Richard M. Nixon (R) . . . . . . | 47,165,234 | 520 | George S. McGovern (D) . . . . | 29,170,774 | 17 |
| 1976* | Jimmy Carter (D). . . . . . . . | 40,828,929 | 297 | Gerald R. Ford (R) . . . . . . . | 39,148,940 | 240 |
| 1980 | Ronald Reagan (R) . . . . . . . | 43,899,248 | 489 | Jimmy Carter (D). . . . . . . . | 35,481,435 | 49 |
| | | | | John B. Anderson (independent) | 5,719,437 | — |
| 1984 | Ronald Reagan (R). . . . . . . | 54,281,858 | 525 | Walter F. Mondale (D) . . . . . . | 37,457,215 | 13 |
| 1988* | George Bush (R) . . . . . . . . | 48,881,221 | 426 | Michael S. Dukakis (D) . . . . . | 41,805,422 | 111 |
| 1992 | Bill Clinton (D). . . . . . . . . | 44,908,254 | 370 | George Bush (R) . . . . . . . . | 39,102,343 | 168 |
| | | | | H. Ross Perot (independent) . . | 19,741,065 | — |

1800—Elected by House of Representatives because of tied electoral vote. 1824—Elected by House of Representatives. No candidate polled a majority. In 1824, the Democratic Republicans had become a loose coalition of competing political groups. By 1828, the supporters of Jackson were known as Democrats, and the J.Q. Adams and Henry Clay supporters as National Republicans. 1872—Greeley died Nov. 29, 1872. His electoral votes were split among 4 individuals. 1876—Fla., La., Ore., and S.C. election returns were disputed. Congress in joint session (Mar. 2, 1877) declared Hayes and Wheeler elected President and Vice-President. 1888—Cleveland had more votes than Harrison but the 233 electoral votes cast for Harrison against the 168 for Cleveland elected Harrison president. 1956—Democrats elected 74 electors but one from Alabama refused to vote for Stevenson. 1960—Sen. Harry F. Byrd (D-Va.) received 15 electoral votes. 1972—John Hospers of Cal. and Theodora Nathan of Ore. received one vote from an elector of Virginia. 1976—Ronald Reagan of Cal. received one vote from an elector of Washington. 1988—Sen. Lloyd Bentsen (D.-Tex.) received 1 electoral vote.

# The Electoral College

The president and the vice president of the United States are the only elective federal officials not elected by direct vote of the people. They are elected by the members of the Electoral College, an institution that has survived since the founding of the nation despite repeated attempts in Congress to alter or abolish it. In the elections of 1824, 1876, and 1888 the presidential candidate receiving the largest popular vote failed to win a majority of the electoral votes.

On presidential election day, the first Tuesday after the first Monday in November of every 4th year, each state chooses as many electors as it has senators and representatives in Congress. In 1964, for the first time, as provided by the 23d Amendment to the Constitution, the District of Columbia voted for 3 electors. Thus, with 100 senators and 435 representatives, there are 538 members of the Electoral College, with a majority of 270 electoral votes needed to elect the president and vice president.

Political parties customarily nominate their lists of electors at their respective state conventions. An elector cannot be a member of Congress or anyone holding federal office.

Some states print the names of the candidates for president and vice president at the top of the November ballot while others list only the names of the electors. In either case, the electors of the party receiving the highest vote are elected. The electors meet on the first Monday after the 2d Wednesday in December in their respective state capitals or in some other place prescribed by state legislatures. By long-established custom they vote for their party nominees, although the Constitution does not require them to do so. The only Constitutional requirement is that at least one of the persons each elector votes for shall not be an inhabitant of that elector's home state.

Certified and sealed lists of the votes of the electors in each state are mailed to the president of the U.S. Senate. He opens them in the presence of the members of the Senate and House of Representatives in a joint session held on Jan. 6 (the next day if that falls on a Sunday), and the electoral votes of all the states are then counted. If no candidate for president has a majority, the House of Representatives chooses a president from among the 3 highest candidates, with all representatives from each state combining to cast one vote for that state. If no candidate for vice president has a majority, the Senate chooses from the top 2, with the senators voting as individuals.

# Voting for President

Source: Federal Election Commission; Commission for Study of American Electorate

| Candidates | Voter Participation (% of voting-age population) | | Candidates | Voter Participation (% of voting-age population) |
|---|---|---|---|---|
| 1932 Roosevelt-Hoover | 52.4 | | 1964 Johnson-Goldwater | 61.9 |
| 1936 Roosevelt-Landon | 56.0 | | 1968 Humphrey-Nixon | 60.9 |
| 1940 Roosevelt-Willkie | 58.9 | | 1972 McGovern-Nixon | 55.2(a) |
| 1944 Roosevelt-Dewey | 56.0 | | 1976 Carter-Ford | 53.5 |
| 1948 Truman-Dewey | 51.1 | | 1980 Carter-Reagan | 54.0 |
| 1952 Stevenson-Eisenhower | 61.6 | | 1984 Mondale-Reagan | 53.1 |
| 1956 Stevenson-Eisenhower | 59.3 | | 1988 Dukakis-Bush | 50.2 |
| 1960 Kennedy-Nixon | 62.8 | | 1992 Clinton-Bush-Perot | 55.9 |

(a) The sharp drop in 1972 reflects the expansion of eligibility with the enfranchisement of 18 to 21 year olds.

# Party Nominees for President and Vice President

Asterisk (*) denotes winning ticket

| | Democratic | | Republican | |
|---|---|---|---|---|
| Year | President | Vice President | President | Vice President |
| 1844 | James K. Polk* | George M. Dallas | Henry Clay (Whig) | Theo. Frelinghuysen |
| 1848 | Lewis Cass | William Butler | Zachary Taylor* (Whig) | Millard Fillmore |
| 1852 | Franklin Pierce* | William King | Winfield Scott (Whig) | William Graham |
| 1856 | James Buchanan* | John Breckinridge | John Fremont | William Dayton |
| 1860 | John Breckinridge | Joseph Lane | Abraham Lincoln* | Hannibal Hamlin |
| 1864 | George McClellan | G.H. Pendleton | Abraham Lincoln* | Andrew Johnson |
| 1868 | Horatio Seymour | Francis Blair | Ulysses S. Grant* | Schuyler Colfax |
| 1872 | Horace Greeley | B. Gratz Brown | Ulysses S. Grant* | Henry Wilson |
| 1876 | Samuel J. Tilden | Thomas Hendricks | Rutherford B. Hayes* | William Wheeler |
| 1880 | Winfield Hancock | William English | James A. Garfield* | Chester A. Arthur |
| 1884 | Grover Cleveland* | Thomas Hendricks | James Blaine | John Logan |
| 1888 | Grover Cleveland* | A.G. Thurman | Benjamin Harrison* | Levi Morton |
| 1892 | Grover Cleveland* | Adlai Stevenson | Benjamin Harrison | Whitelaw Reid |
| 1896 | William J. Bryan | Arthur Sewall | William McKinley* | Garret Hobart |
| 1900 | William J. Bryan | Adlai Stevenson | William McKinley* | Theodore Roosevelt |
| 1904 | Alton Parker | Henry Davis | Theodore Roosevelt* | Charles Fairbanks |
| 1908 | William J. Bryan | John Kern | William H. Taft* | James Sherman |
| 1912 | Woodrow Wilson* | Thomas Marshall | William H. Taft | James Sherman[1] |
| 1916 | Woodrow Wilson* | Thomas Marshall | Charles Hughes | Charles Fairbanks |
| 1920 | James M. Cox | Franklin D. Roosevelt | Warren G. Harding* | Calvin Coolidge |
| 1924 | John W. Davis | Charles W. Bryan | Calvin Coolidge* | Charles G. Dawes |
| 1928 | Alfred E. Smith | Joseph T. Robinson | Herbert Hoover* | Charles Curtis |
| 1932 | Franklin D. Roosevelt* | John N. Garner | Herbert Hoover | Charles Curtis |
| 1936 | Franklin D. Roosevelt* | John N. Garner | Alfred M. Landon | Frank Knox |
| 1940 | Franklin D. Roosevelt* | Henry A. Wallace | Wendell L. Willkie | Charles McNary |
| 1944 | Franklin D. Roosevelt* | Harry S. Truman | Thomas E. Dewey | John W. Bricker |
| 1948 | Harry S. Truman* | Alben W. Barkley | Thomas E. Dewey | Earl Warren |
| 1952 | Adlai E. Stevenson | John J. Sparkman | Dwight D. Eisenhower* | Richard M. Nixon |
| 1956 | Adlai E. Stevenson | Estes Kefauver | Dwight D. Eisenhower* | Richard M. Nixon |
| 1960 | John F. Kennedy* | Lyndon B. Johnson | Richard M. Nixon | Henry Cabot Lodge |
| 1964 | Lyndon B. Johnson* | Hubert H. Humphrey | Barry M. Goldwater | William E. Miller |
| 1968 | Hubert H. Humphrey | Edmund S. Muskie | Richard M. Nixon* | Spiro T. Agnew |
| 1972 | George S. McGovern | R. Sargent Shriver Jr. | Richard M. Nixon* | Spiro T. Agnew |
| 1976 | Jimmy Carter* | Walter F. Mondale | Gerald R. Ford | Robert J. Dole |
| 1980 | Jimmy Carter | Walter F. Mondale | Ronald Reagan* | George Bush |
| 1984 | Walter F. Mondale | Geraldine Ferraro | Ronald Reagan* | George Bush |
| 1988 | Michael S. Dukakis | Lloyd Bentsen | George Bush* | Dan Quayle |
| 1992 | Bill Clinton* | Al Gore | George Bush | Dan Quayle |

(1) Died Oct. 30; replaced on ballot by Nicholas Butler.

## Presidents of the U.S.

| No. | Name | Politics | Born | in | Inaug. | at age | Died | at age |
|---|---|---|---|---|---|---|---|---|
| 1 | George Washington | Fed. | 1732, Feb. 22 | Va. | 1789 | 57 | 1799, Dec. 14 | 67 |
| 2 | John Adams | Fed. | 1735, Oct. 30 | Mass. | 1797 | 61 | 1826, July 4 | 90 |
| 3 | Thomas Jefferson | Dem.-Rep. | 1743, Apr. 13 | Va. | 1801 | 57 | 1826, July 4 | 83 |
| 4 | James Madison | Dem.-Rep. | 1751, Mar. 16 | Va. | 1809 | 57 | 1836, June 28 | 85 |
| 5 | James Monroe | Dem.-Rep. | 1758, Apr. 28 | Va. | 1817 | 58 | 1831, July 4 | 73 |
| 6 | John Quincy Adams | Dem.-Rep. | 1767, July 11 | Mass. | 1825 | 57 | 1848, Feb. 23 | 80 |
| 7 | Andrew Jackson | Dem. | 1767, Mar. 15 | S.C. | 1829 | 61 | 1845, June 8 | 78 |
| 8 | Martin Van Buren | Dem. | 1782, Dec. 5 | N.Y. | 1837 | 54 | 1862, July 24 | 79 |
| 9 | William Henry Harrison | Whig | 1773, Feb. 9 | Va. | 1841 | 68 | 1841, Apr. 4 | 68 |
| 10 | John Tyler | Whig | 1790, Mar. 29 | Va. | 1841 | 51 | 1862, Jan. 18 | 71 |
| 11 | James Knox Polk | Dem. | 1795, Nov. 2 | N.C. | 1845 | 49 | 1849, June 15 | 53 |
| 12 | Zachary Taylor | Whig | 1784, Nov. 24 | Va. | 1849 | 64 | 1850, July 9 | 65 |
| 13 | Millard Fillmore | Whig | 1800, Jan. 7 | N.Y. | 1850 | 50 | 1874, Mar. 8 | 74 |
| 14 | Franklin Pierce | Dem. | 1804, Nov. 23 | N.H. | 1853 | 48 | 1869, Oct. 8 | 64 |
| 15 | James Buchanan | Dem. | 1791, Apr. 23 | Pa. | 1857 | 65 | 1868, June 1 | 77 |
| 16 | Abraham Lincoln | Rep. | 1809, Feb. 12 | Ky. | 1861 | 52 | 1865, Apr. 15 | 56 |
| 17 | Andrew Johnson | (1) | 1808, Dec. 29 | N.C. | 1865 | 56 | 1875, July 31 | 66 |
| 18 | Ulysses Simpson Grant | Rep. | 1822, Apr. 27 | Oh. | 1869 | 46 | 1885, July 23 | 63 |
| 19 | Rutherford Birchard Hayes | Rep. | 1822, Oct. 4 | Oh. | 1877 | 54 | 1893, Jan. 17 | 70 |
| 20 | James Abram Garfield | Rep. | 1831, Nov. 19 | Oh. | 1881 | 49 | 1881, Sept. 19 | 49 |
| 21 | Chester Alan Arthur | Rep. | 1830, Oct. 5 | Vt. | 1881 | 50 | 1886, Nov. 18 | 56 |
| 22 | Grover Cleveland | Dem. | 1837, Mar. 18 | N.J. | 1885 | 47 | 1908, June 24 | 71 |
| 23 | Benjamin Harrison | Rep. | 1833, Aug. 20 | Oh. | 1889 | 55 | 1901, Mar. 13 | 67 |
| 24 | Grover Cleveland | Dem. | 1837, Mar. 18 | N.J. | 1893 | 55 | 1908, June 24 | 71 |
| 25 | William McKinley | Rep. | 1843, Jan. 29 | Oh. | 1897 | 54 | 1901, Sept. 14 | 58 |
| 26 | Theodore Roosevelt | Rep. | 1858, Oct. 27 | N.Y. | 1901 | 42 | 1919, Jan. 6 | 60 |
| 27 | William Howard Taft | Rep. | 1857, Sept. 15 | Oh. | 1909 | 51 | 1930, Mar. 8 | 72 |
| 28 | Woodrow Wilson | Dem. | 1856, Dec. 28 | Va. | 1913 | 56 | 1924, Feb. 3 | 67 |
| 29 | Warren Gamaliel Harding | Rep. | 1865, Nov. 2 | Oh. | 1921 | 55 | 1923, Aug. 2 | 57 |
| 30 | Calvin Coolidge | Rep. | 1872, July 4 | Vt. | 1923 | 51 | 1933, Jan. 5 | 60 |
| 31 | Herbert Clark Hoover | Rep. | 1874, Aug. 10 | Ia. | 1929 | 54 | 1964, Oct. 20 | 90 |
| 32 | Franklin Delano Roosevelt | Dem. | 1882, Jan. 30 | N.Y. | 1933 | 51 | 1945, Apr. 12 | 63 |
| 33 | Harry S. Truman | Dem. | 1884, May 8 | Mo. | 1945 | 60 | 1972, Dec. 26 | 88 |
| 34 | Dwight David Eisenhower | Rep. | 1890, Oct. 14 | Tex. | 1953 | 62 | 1969, Mar. 28 | 78 |
| 35 | John Fitzgerald Kennedy | Dem. | 1917, May 29 | Mass. | 1961 | 43 | 1963, Nov. 22 | 46 |
| 36 | Lyndon Baines Johnson | Dem. | 1908, Aug. 27 | Tex. | 1963 | 55 | 1973, Jan. 22 | 64 |
| 37 | Richard Milhous Nixon (2) | Rep. | 1913, Jan. 9 | Cal. | 1969 | 56 | | |
| 38 | Gerald Rudolph Ford | Rep. | 1913, July 14 | Nebr. | 1974 | 61 | | |
| 39 | Jimmy (James Earl) Carter | Dem. | 1924, Oct. 1 | Ga. | 1977 | 52 | | |
| 40 | Ronald Reagan | Rep. | 1911, Feb. 6 | Ill. | 1981 | 69 | | |
| 41 | George Bush | Rep. | 1924, June 12 | Mass. | 1989 | 64 | | |
| 42 | Bill Clinton | Dem. | 1946, Aug. 19 | Ark. | 1993 | 46 | | |

(1) Andrew Johnson — a Democrat, nominated vice president by Republicans and elected with Lincoln on National Union ticket. (2) Resigned Aug. 9, 1974.

## Presidents, Vice Presidents, Congresses

| | President | Service | | Vice President | Congress |
|---|---|---|---|---|---|
| 1 | George Washington | Apr. 30, 1789—Mar. 3, 1797 | 1 | John Adams | 1, 2, 3, 4 |
| 2 | John Adams | Mar. 4, 1797—Mar. 3, 1801 | 2 | Thomas Jefferson | 5, 6 |
| 3 | Thomas Jefferson | Mar. 4, 1801—Mar. 3, 1805 | 3 | Aaron Burr | 7, 8 |
| | " | Mar. 4, 1805—Mar. 3, 1809 | 4 | George Clinton | 9, 10 |
| 4 | James Madison | Mar. 4, 1809—Mar. 3, 1813 | | "(1) | 11, 12 |
| | " | Mar. 4, 1813—Mar. 3, 1817 | 5 | Elbridge Gerry (2) | 13, 14 |
| 5 | James Monroe | Mar. 4, 1817—Mar. 3, 1825 | 6 | Daniel D. Tompkins | 15, 16, 17, 18 |
| 6 | John Quincy Adams | Mar. 4, 1825—Mar. 3, 1829 | 7 | John C. Calhoun | 19, 20 |
| 7 | Andrew Jackson | Mar. 4, 1829—Mar. 3, 1833 | | "(3) | 21, 22 |
| | " | Mar. 4, 1833—Mar. 3, 1837 | 8 | Martin Van Buren | 23, 24 |
| 8 | Martin Van Buren | Mar. 4, 1837—Mar. 3, 1841 | 9 | Richard M. Johnson | 25, 26 |
| 9 | William Henry Harrison (4) | Mar. 4, 1841—Apr. 4, 1841 | 10 | John Tyler | 27 |
| 10 | John Tyler | Apr. 6, 1841—Mar. 3, 1845 | | | 27, 28 |
| 11 | James K. Polk | Mar. 4, 1845—Mar. 3, 1849 | 11 | George M. Dallas | 29, 30 |
| 12 | Zachary Taylor (4) | Mar. 5, 1849—July 9, 1850 | 12 | Millard Fillmore | 31 |
| 13 | Millard Fillmore | July 10, 1850—Mar. 3, 1853 | | | 31, 32 |
| 14 | Franklin Pierce | Mar. 4, 1853—Mar. 3, 1857 | 13 | William R. King (5) | 33, 34 |
| 15 | James Buchanan | Mar. 4, 1857—Mar. 3, 1861 | 14 | John C. Breckinridge | 35, 36 |
| 16 | Abraham Lincoln | Mar. 4, 1861—Mar. 3, 1865 | 15 | Hannibal Hamlin | 37, 38 |
| | "(4) | Mar. 4, 1865—Apr. 15, 1865 | 16 | Andrew Johnson | 39 |
| 17 | Andrew Johnson | Apr. 15, 1865—Mar. 3, 1869 | | | 39, 40 |
| 18 | Ulysses S. Grant | Mar. 4, 1869—Mar. 3, 1873 | 17 | Schuyler Colfax | 41, 42 |
| | " | Mar. 4, 1873—Mar. 3, 1877 | 18 | Henry Wilson (6) | 43, 44 |
| 19 | Rutherford B. Hayes | Mar. 4, 1877—Mar. 3, 1881 | 19 | William A. Wheeler | 45, 46 |
| 20 | James A. Garfield (4) | Mar. 4, 1881—Sept. 19, 1881 | 20 | Chester A. Arthur | 47 |
| 21 | Chester A. Arthur | Sept. 20, 1881—Mar. 3, 1885 | | | 47, 48 |
| 22 | Grover Cleveland (7) | Mar. 4, 1885—Mar. 3, 1889 | 21 | Thomas A. Hendricks (8) | 49, 50 |
| 23 | Benjamin Harrison | Mar. 4, 1889—Mar. 3, 1893 | 22 | Levi P. Morton | 51, 52 |
| 24 | Grover Cleveland (7) | Mar. 4, 1893—Mar. 3, 1897 | 23 | Adlai E. Stevenson | 53, 54 |
| 25 | William McKinley | Mar. 4, 1897—Mar. 3, 1901 | 24 | Garret A. Hobart (9) | 55, 56 |
| | "(4) | Mar. 4, 1901—Sept. 14, 1901 | 25 | Theodore Roosevelt | 57 |
| 26 | Theodore Roosevelt | Sept. 14, 1901—Mar. 3, 1905 | | | 57, 58 |
| | " | Mar. 4, 1905—Mar. 3, 1909 | 26 | Charles W. Fairbanks | 59, 60 |
| 27 | William H. Taft | Mar. 4, 1909—Mar. 3, 1913 | 27 | James S. Sherman (10) | 61, 62 |
| 28 | Woodrow Wilson | Mar. 4, 1913—Mar. 3, 1921 | 28 | Thomas R. Marshall | 63, 64, 65, 66 |

(continued)

## Presidents, Vice Presidents, Congresses (continued)

| President | Service | Vice President | Congress |
|---|---|---|---|
| 29 Warren G. Harding (4) | Mar. 4, 1921—Aug. 2, 1923 | 29 Calvin Coolidge | 67 |
| 30 Calvin Coolidge | Aug. 3, 1923—Mar. 3, 1925 | | 68 |
| " | Mar. 4, 1925—Mar. 3, 1929 | 30 Charles G. Dawes | 69, 70 |
| 31 Herbert C. Hoover | Mar. 4, 1929—Mar. 3, 1933 | 31 Charles Curtis | 71, 72 |
| 32 Franklin D. Roosevelt (16) | Mar. 4, 1933—Jan. 20, 1941 | 32 John N. Garner | 73, 74, 75, 76 |
| " | Jan. 20, 1941—Jan. 20, 1945 | 33 Henry A. Wallace | 77, 78 |
| "(4) | Jan. 20, 1945—Apr. 12, 1945 | 34 Harry S. Truman | 79 |
| 33 Harry S. Truman | Apr. 12, 1945—Jan. 20, 1949 | | 79, 80 |
| " | Jan. 20, 1949—Jan. 20, 1953 | 35 Alben W. Barkley | 81, 82 |
| 34 Dwight D. Eisenhower | Jan. 20, 1953—Jan. 20, 1961 | 36 Richard M. Nixon | 83, 84, 85, 86 |
| 35 John F. Kennedy (4) | Jan. 20, 1961—Nov. 22, 1963 | 37 Lyndon B. Johnson | 87, 88 |
| 36 Lyndon B. Johnson | Nov. 22, 1963—Jan. 20, 1965 | | 88 |
| " | Jan. 20, 1965—Jan. 20, 1969 | 38 Hubert H. Humphrey | 89, 90 |
| 37 Richard M. Nixon | Jan. 20, 1969—Jan. 20, 1973 | 39 Spiro T. Agnew (11) | 91, 92, 93 |
| "(12) | Jan. 20, 1973—Aug. 9, 1974 | 40 Gerald R. Ford (13) | 93 |
| 38 Gerald R. Ford (14) | Aug. 9, 1974—Jan. 20, 1977 | 41 Nelson A. Rockefeller (15) | 93, 94 |
| 39 Jimmy (James Earl)Carter | Jan. 20, 1977—Jan. 20, 1981 | 42 Walter F. Mondale | 95, 96 |
| 40 Ronald Reagan | Jan. 20, 1981—Jan. 20, 1989 | 43 George Bush | 97, 98, 99, 100 |
| 41 George Bush | Jan. 20, 1989—Jan. 20, 1993 | 44 Dan Quayle | 101, 102 |
| 42 Bill Clinton | Jan. 20, 1993— | 45 Al Gore | 103 |

(1) Died Apr. 20, 1812. (2) Died Nov. 23, 1814. (3) Resigned Dec. 28, 1832, to become U.S. Senator. (4) Died in office. (5) Died Apr. 18, 1853. (6) Died Nov. 22, 1875. (7) Terms not consecutive. (8) Died Nov. 25, 1885. (9) Died Nov. 21, 1899. (10) Died Oct. 30, 1912. (11) Resigned Oct. 10, 1973. (12) Resigned Aug. 9, 1974. (13) First non-elected vice president, chosen under 25th Amendment procedure. (14) First non-elected president. (15) 2d non-elected vice president. (16) First president to be inaugurated under 20th Amendment, Jan. 20, 1937.

## Vice Presidents of the U.S.

The numerals given vice presidents do not coincide with those given presidents, because some presidents had none and some had more than one.

| Name | Birthplace | Year | Home | Inaug. | Politics | Place of death | Year | Age |
|---|---|---|---|---|---|---|---|---|
| 1 John Adams | Quincy, Mass. | 1735 | Mass. | 1789 | Fed. | Quincy, Mass. | 1826 | 90 |
| 2 Thomas Jefferson | Shadwell, Va. | 1743 | Va. | 1797 | Dem.-Rep. | Monticello, Va. | 1826 | 83 |
| 3 Aaron Burr | Newark, N.J. | 1756 | N.Y. | 1801 | Dem.-Rep. | Staten Island, N.Y. | 1836 | 80 |
| 4 George Clinton | Ulster Co., N.Y. | 1739 | N.Y. | 1805 | Dem.-Rep. | Washington, D.C. | 1812 | 73 |
| 5 Elbridge Gerry | Marblehead, Mass. | 1744 | Mass. | 1813 | Dem.-Rep. | Washington, D.C. | 1814 | 70 |
| 6 Daniel D. Tompkins | Scarsdale, N.Y. | 1774 | N.Y. | 1817 | Dem.-Rep. | Staten Island, N.Y. | 1825 | 51 |
| 7 John C. Calhoun (1) | Abbeville, S.C. | 1782 | S.C. | 1825 | Dem.-Rep. | Washington, D.C. | 1850 | 68 |
| 8 Martin Van Buren | Kinderhook, N.Y. | 1782 | N.Y. | 1833 | Dem. | Kinderhook, N.Y. | 1862 | 79 |
| 9 Richard M. Johnson | Louisville, Ky. | 1780 | Ky. | 1837 | Dem. | Frankfort, Ky. | 1850 | 70 |
| 10 John Tyler | Greenway, Va. | 1790 | Va. | 1841 | Whig | Richmond, Va. | 1862 | 71 |
| 11 George M. Dallas | Philadelphia, Pa. | 1792 | Pa. | 1845 | Dem. | Philadelphia, Pa. | 1864 | 72 |
| 12 Millard Fillmore | Summerhill, N.Y. | 1800 | N.Y. | 1849 | Whig | Buffalo, N.Y. | 1874 | 74 |
| 13 William R. King | Sampson Co., N.C. | 1786 | Ala. | 1853 | Dem. | Dallas Co., Ala. | 1853 | 67 |
| 14 John C. Breckinridge | Lexington, Ky. | 1821 | Ky. | 1857 | Dem. | Lexington, Ky. | 1875 | 54 |
| 15 Hannibal Hamlin | Paris, Me. | 1809 | Me. | 1861 | Rep. | Bangor, Me. | 1891 | 81 |
| 16 Andrew Johnson | Raleigh, N.C. | 1808 | Tenn. | 1865 | (2) | Carter Co., Tenn. | 1875 | 66 |
| 17 Schuyler Colfax | New York, N.Y. | 1823 | Ind. | 1869 | Rep. | Mankato, Minn. | 1885 | 62 |
| 18 Henry Wilson | Farmington, N.H. | 1812 | Mass. | 1873 | Rep. | Washington, D.C. | 1875 | 63 |
| 19 William A. Wheeler | Malone, N.Y. | 1819 | N.Y. | 1877 | Rep. | Malone, N.Y. | 1887 | 68 |
| 20 Chester A. Arthur | Fairfield, Vt. | 1829 | N.Y. | 1881 | Rep. | New York, N.Y. | 1886 | 57 |
| 21 Thomas A. Hendricks | Muskingum Co., Oh. | 1819 | Ind. | 1885 | Dem. | Indianapolis, Ind. | 1885 | 66 |
| 22 Levi P. Morton | Shoreham, Vt. | 1824 | N.Y. | 1889 | Rep. | Rhinebeck, N.Y. | 1920 | 96 |
| 23 Adlai E. Stevenson (3) | Christian Co., Ky. | 1835 | Ill. | 1893 | Dem. | Chicago, Ill. | 1914 | 78 |
| 24 Garret A. Hobart | Long Branch, N.J. | 1844 | N.J. | 1897 | Rep. | Paterson, N.J. | 1899 | 55 |
| 25 Theodore Roosevelt | New York, N.Y. | 1858 | N.Y. | 1901 | Rep. | Oyster Bay, N.Y. | 1919 | 60 |
| 26 Charles W. Fairbanks | Unionville Centre, Oh. | 1852 | Ind. | 1905 | Rep. | Indianapolis, Ind. | 1918 | 66 |
| 27 James S. Sherman | Utica, N.Y. | 1855 | N.Y. | 1909 | Rep. | Utica, N.Y. | 1912 | 57 |
| 28 Thomas R. Marshall | N. Manchester, Ind. | 1854 | Ind. | 1913 | Dem. | Washington, D.C. | 1925 | 71 |
| 29 Calvin Coolidge | Plymouth, Vt. | 1872 | Mass. | 1921 | Rep. | Northampton, Mass. | 1933 | 60 |
| 30 Charles G. Dawes | Marietta, Oh. | 1865 | Ill. | 1925 | Rep. | Evanston, Ill. | 1951 | 85 |
| 31 Charles Curtis | Topeka, Kan. | 1860 | Kan. | 1929 | Rep. | Washington, D.C. | 1936 | 76 |
| 32 John Nance Garner | Red River Co., Tex. | 1868 | Tex. | 1933 | Dem. | Uvalde, Tex. | 1967 | 98 |
| 33 Henry Agard Wallace | Adair County, Ia. | 1888 | Iowa | 1941 | Dem. | Danbury, Conn. | 1965 | 77 |
| 34 Harry S. Truman | Lamar, Mo. | 1884 | Mo. | 1945 | Dem. | Kansas City, Mo. | 1972 | 88 |
| 35 Alben W. Barkley | Graves County, Ky. | 1877 | Ky. | 1949 | Dem. | Lexington, Va. | 1956 | 78 |
| 36 Richard M. Nixon | Yorba Linda, Cal. | 1913 | Cal. | 1953 | Rep. | | | |
| 37 Lyndon B. Johnson | Johnson City, Tex. | 1908 | Tex. | 1961 | Dem. | San Antonio, Tex. | 1973 | 64 |
| 38 Hubert H. Humphrey | Wallace, S.D. | 1911 | Minn. | 1965 | Dem. | Waverly, Minn. | 1978 | 66 |
| 39 Spiro T. Agnew (4) | Baltimore, Md. | 1918 | Md. | 1969 | Rep. | | | |
| 40 Gerald R. Ford | Omaha, Neb. | 1913 | Mich. | 1973 | Rep. | | | |
| 41 Nelson A. Rockefeller | Bar Harbor, Me. | 1908 | N.Y. | 1974 | Rep. | New York, N.Y. | 1979 | 70 |
| 42 Walter F. Mondale | Ceylon, Minn. | 1928 | Minn. | 1977 | Dem. | | | |
| 43 George Bush | Milton, Mass. | 1924 | Tex. | 1981 | Rep. | | | |
| 44 Dan Quayle | Indianapolis, Ind. | 1947 | Ind. | 1989 | Rep. | | | |
| 45 Al Gore | Washington, D.C. | 1948 | Tenn. | 1993 | Dem. | | | |

(1) John C. Calhoun resigned Dec. 28, 1832, having been elected to the Senate to fill a vacancy. (2) Andrew Johnson — a Democrat nominated by Republicans and elected with Lincoln on the National Union Ticket. (3) Adlai E. Stevenson, 23d vice president, was grandfather of Democratic candidate for president, 1952 and 1956. (4) Resigned Oct. 10, 1973.

# CONGRESS

## The One Hundred and Third Congress, First Session
### Membership as of Mid-1993, With 1992 Election Results

### The Senate

Terms are for 6 years and end Jan. 3 of the year preceding name. Annual salary, $133,600; President Pro Tempore, Majority Leader, and Minority Leader, $148,400. To be eligible for the U.S. Senate a person must be at least 30 years of age, a citizen of the United States for at least 9 years, and a resident of the state from which he or she is chosen. The Congress must meet annually on Jan. 3, unless it has, by law, appointed a different day.

The ZIP code of the Senate is 20510, the telephone number is 202-224-3121.

**Senate officials:** President Pro Tempore, Robert C. Byrd; Majority Leader, George J. Mitchell; Majority Whip, Wendell H. Ford; Minority Leader, Bob Dole; Minority Whip, Alan K. Simpson.

**Dem., 56; Rep., 44; Total, 100. *Incumbent. Bold face denotes winner.**

(Source: News Election Service; World Almanac research)

| Term ends | Senator (Party)/Service from[1] | 1992 Election |
|---|---|---|
| **Alabama** | | |
| 1999 | **Richard C. Shelby*** (D)/1987 | 1,022,698 |
| | Richard Sellers (R) | 522,015 |
| 1997 | Howell Heflin (D)/1979 | |
| **Alaska** | | |
| 1999 | **Frank H. Murkowski*** (R)/1981 | 127,163 |
| | Tony Smith (D) | 92,065 |
| 1997 | Ted Stevens (R)/12/24/68 | |
| **Arizona** | | |
| 1999 | **John McCain*** (R)/1987 | 771,395 |
| | Claire Sargent (D) | 436,321 |
| 1995 | Dennis DeConcini (D)/1977 | |
| **Arkansas** | | |
| 1999 | **Dale Bumpers*** (D)/1975 | 553,635 |
| | Mike Huckabee (R) | 366,373 |
| 1997 | David H. Pryor (D)/1979 | |
| **California** | | |
| 1999 | **Barbara Boxer** (D) | 5,173,467 |
| | Bruce Herschensohn (R) | 4,644,182 |
| 1995 | **Dianne Feinstein** (D) | 5,493,418 |
| | John Seymour* (R) /1/10/91 | 3,777,635 |
| **Colorado** | | |
| 1999 | **Ben Nighthorse Campbell** (D) | 803,725 |
| | Terry Considine (R) | 662,893 |
| 1997 | Hank Brown (R) | |
| **Connecticut** | | |
| 1999 | **Christopher J. Dodd*** (D)/1981 | 882,558 |
| | Brook Johnson (R) | 572,036 |
| 1995 | Joe Lieberman (D)/1989 | |
| **Delaware** | | |
| 1995 | William V. Roth, Jr. (R)/1/1/71 | |
| 1997 | Joseph R. Biden, Jr. (D)/1973 | |
| **Florida** | | |
| 1999 | **Bob Graham*** (D)/1987 | 3,244,299 |
| | Bill Grant (R) | 1,715,156 |
| 1995 | Connie Mack (R)/1989 | |
| **Georgia** | | |
| 1999 | **Paul Coverdell** (R)[2] | 634,208 |
| | Wyche Fowler, Jr.* (D) | 617,283 |
| 1997 | Sam Nunn (D)/1972 | |
| **Hawaii** | | |
| 1999 | **Daniel K. Inouye*** (D)/1963 | 208,266 |
| | Rick Reed (R) | 97,928 |
| 1995 | Daniel K. Akaka (D)/5/16/90 | |
| **Idaho** | | |
| 1999 | **Dirk Kempthorne** (R) | 270,468 |
| | Richard H. Stallings (D) | 208,036 |
| 1997 | Larry E. Craig (R) | |
| **Illinois** | | |
| 1999 | **Carol Moseley Braun** (D) | 2,631,229 |
| | Richard S. Williamson (R) | 2,126,833 |
| 1997 | Paul Simon (D)/1985 | |
| **Indiana** | | |
| 1999 | **Daniel R. Coats*** (R)/1989 | 1,267,972 |
| | Joseph H. Hogsett (D) | 900,148 |
| 1995 | Richard G. Lugar (R)/1977 | |
| **Iowa** | | |
| 1999 | **Charles E. Grassley*** (R)/1981 | 899,761 |
| | Jean Lloyd-Jones (D) | 351,561 |
| 1997 | Tom Harkin (D)/1985 | |
| **Kansas** | | |
| 1999 | **Bob Dole*** (R)/1969 | 706,246 |
| | Gloria O'Dell (D) | 349,525 |
| 1997 | Nancy Landon Kassebaum (R)/12/23/78 | |
| **Kentucky** | | |
| 1999 | **Wendell H. Ford*** (D)/12/28/74 | 836,888 |
| | David L. Williams (R) | 476,604 |
| 1997 | Mitch McConnell (R)/1985 | |
| **Louisiana** | | |
| 1999 | John B. Breaux* (D)/1987 | |
| 1997 | J. Bennett Johnston (D)/11/14/72 | |
| **Maine** | | |
| 1995 | George J. Mitchell (D)/5/17/80 | |
| 1997 | William S. Cohen (R)/1979 | |
| **Maryland** | | |
| 1999 | **Barbara A. Mikulski*** (D)/1987 | 1,307,610 |
| | Alan L. Keyes (R) | 533,688 |
| 1995 | Paul S. Sarbanes (D)/1977 | |
| **Massachusetts** | | |
| 1995 | Edward M. Kennedy (D)/11/7/62 | |
| 1997 | John F. Kerry (D)/1/2/85 | |
| **Michigan** | | |
| 1995 | Donald W. Riegle, Jr.* (D)/12/30/76 | |
| 1997 | Carl Levin (D)/1979 | |
| **Minnesota** | | |
| 1995 | David Durenberger (R)/11/8/78 | |
| 1997 | Paul David Wellstone (D) | |
| **Mississippi** | | |
| 1995 | Trent Lott (R)/3/3/89 | |
| 1997 | Thad Cochran (R)/12/27/78 | |
| **Missouri** | | |
| 1999 | **Christopher "Kit" Bond*** (R)/1987 | 1,221,901 |
| | Geri Rothman-Serot (D) | 1,057,967 |
| 1995 | John C. Danforth (R)/12/27/76 | |
| **Montana** | | |
| 1995 | Conrad Burns (R)/1989 | |
| 1997 | Max Baucus (D)/12/15/78 | |

| Term ends | Senator (Party)/Service from[1] | 1992 Election |
|---|---|---|
| | **Nebraska** | |
| 1995 | J. Robert Kerrey (D)/1989 | |
| 1997 | J. James Exon (D)/1979 | |
| | **Nevada** | |
| 1999 | **Harry M. Reid*** (D)/1987 | 253,150 |
| | Demar Dahl (R) | 199,413 |
| 1995 | Richard H. Bryan (D)/1989 | |
| | **New Hampshire** | |
| 1999 | **Judd Gregg** (R) | 249,591 |
| | John Rauh (D) | 234,982 |
| 1997 | Robert Smith (R) | |
| | **New Jersey** | |
| 1995 | Frank R. Lautenberg (D)/12/27/82 | |
| 1997 | Bill Bradley (D)/1979 | |
| | **New Mexico** | |
| 1995 | Jeff Bingaman (D)/1983 | |
| 1997 | Pete V. Domenici (R)/1973 | |
| | **New York** | |
| 1999 | **Alfonse M. D'Amato*** (R)/1981 | 3,167,061 |
| | Robert Abrams (D) | 3,086,213 |
| 1995 | Daniel Patrick Moynihan (D)/1977 | |
| | **North Carolina** | |
| 1999 | **Lauch Faircloth** (R) | 1,297,892 |
| | Terry Sanford* (D) 11/5/86 | 1,194,015 |
| 1997 | Jesse Helms (R)/1973 | |
| | **North Dakota** | |
| 1999 | **Byron L. Dorgan** (D)/1987 | 179,347 |
| | Steve Sydness (R) | 118,162 |
| 1995 | **Kent Conrad** (D)[3] | 103,246 |
| | Jack Dalrymple (R) | 55,194 |
| | **Ohio** | |
| 1999 | **John Glenn*** (D)/12/24/74 | 2,444,419 |
| | Michael DeWine (R) | 2,028,300 |
| 1995 | Howard M. Metzenbaum (D)/12/29/76 | |
| | **Oklahoma** | |
| 1999 | **Don Nickles*** (R)/1981 | 757,876 |
| | Steve Lewis (D) | 494,350 |
| 1997 | David L. Boren (D)/1979 | |
| | **Oregon** | |
| 1999 | **Bob Packwood*** (R)/1969 | 717,455 |
| | Les AuCoin (D) | 639,851 |
| 1997 | Mark O. Hatfield (R)/1/10/67 | |
| | **Pennsylvania** | |
| 1999 | **Arlen Specter*** (R)/1981 | 2,358,125 |
| | Lynn Yeakel (D) | 2,224,966 |

| Term ends | Senator (Party)/Service from[1] | 1992 Election |
|---|---|---|
| 1995 | Harris Wofford (D) | |
| | **Rhode Island** | |
| 1995 | John H. Chafee (R)/12/29/76 | |
| 1997 | Claiborne Pell (D)/1961 | |
| | **South Carolina** | |
| 1999 | **Ernest F. "Fritz" Hollings*** (D)/11/9/66 | 591,030 |
| | Thomas Hartnett (R) | 554,175 |
| 1997 | Strom Thurmond (R)/11/7/56 | |
| | **South Dakota** | |
| 1999 | **Thomas A. Daschle*** (D)/1987 | 217,095 |
| | Charlene Haar (R) | 108.733 |
| 1997 | Larry Pressler (R)/1979 | |
| | **Tennessee** | |
| 1995 | Jim Sasser (D)/1977 | |
| 1997 | Harlan Matthews (D)[4] | |
| | **Texas** | |
| 1995 | **Kay Bailey Hutchison**[5] (R) | 1,186,716 |
| | Bob Krueger* (D) | 576,538 |
| 1997 | Phil Gramm (R)/1985 | |
| | **Utah** | |
| 1999 | **Robert F. Bennett** (R) | 420,069 |
| | Wayne Owens (D) | 301,228 |
| 1995 | Orrin G. Hatch (R)/1977 | |
| | **Vermont** | |
| 1999 | **Patrick J. Leahy*** (D)/1975 | 154,762 |
| | James H. Douglas (R) | 123,854 |
| 1995 | James M. Jeffords (R)/1989 | |
| | **Virginia** | |
| 1995 | Charles S. Robb (D)/1989 | |
| 1997 | John W. Warner (R)/1/2/79 | |
| | **Washington** | |
| 1999 | **Patty Murray** (D) | 1,197,973 |
| | Rod Chandler (R) | 1,020,829 |
| 1995 | Slade Gorton (R)/1981 | |
| | **West Virginia** | |
| 1995 | Robert C. Byrd (D)/1959 | |
| 1997 | John D. Rockefeller IV (D)/1/15/85 | |
| | **Wisconsin** | |
| 1999 | **Russell D. Feingold** (D) | 1,290,662 |
| | Robert W. Kasten, Jr.* (R)/1981 | 1,129,599 |
| 1995 | Herbert H. Kohl (D)/1989 | |
| | **Wyoming** | |
| 1995 | Malcolm Wallop (R)/1977 | |
| 1997 | Alan K. Simpson (R)/1979 | |

(1) Jan. 3, unless otherwise noted. (2) In the Georgia Senate race, Nov. 3, 1992, incumbent Sen. Wyche Fowler, Jr. (D), received 1,108,416 votes and Paul Coverdell (R) received 1,073,282. Since neither candidate received an absolute majority, a runoff election was held Nov. 24. In the runoff, Coverdell emerged with 50.68 percent of the vote; Fowler received 49.32 percent. (3) A special election was held Dec. 4, 1992, to fill the seat left vacant by the death of Sen. Quentin Burdick (D). The winner will serve the remainder of Burdick's term. (4) Sen. Harlan Matthews (D) was appointed by Gov. Ned Ray McWherter to fill the seat vacated by Al Gore, Jr., who became vice president; in Nov. 1994, a special election will be held to fill the remaining two years of the term. (5) Incumbent Sen. Bob Krueger was appointed by Gov. Ann Richards on Jan. 20, 1993, to fill the seat vacated when Sen. Lloyd Bentsen (D) resigned to become secretary of the Treasury. On June 7, 1993, in a special election, Krueger lost to Kay Bailey Hutchison. She will serve the remainder of the term.

## The House of Representatives

Members' terms to Jan. 3, 1995. Annual salary, $133,600; Speaker of the House, $171,500; Majority Leader and Minority Leader, $148,400. To be eligible for membership, a person must be at least 25 years of age, a U.S. citizen for at least 7 years, and a resident of the state from which he or she is chosen. The ZIP code of the House is 20515; the telephone number is 202-225-3121.

**House Officials:** Speaker, Thomas S. Foley; Majority Leader, Richard A. Gephardt; Majority Whip, David E. Bonior; Minority Leader, Robert H. Michel; Minority Whip, Newt Gingrich.

D-Democrat; R-Republican; B-Libertarian; C-Conservative; I-Independent; L-Liberal; PF-Peace & Freedom.

Dem., 258; Rep., 176; Ind., 1; Total, 435. *Incumbent. Bold face denotes winner.
(Source: News Election Service; World Almanac research)

| Dist. | Representative (Party) | 1992 Election |
|---|---|---|
| | **Alabama** | |
| 1. | **H.L. "Sonny" Callahan*** (R) | **128,874** |
| | William A. Brewer (D) | 78,742 |
| 2. | **Terry Everett** (R) | **112,906** |
| | George C. Wallace, Jr. (D) | 109,335 |
| 3. | **Glen Browder*** (D) | **119,175** |
| | Don Sledge (R) | 73,800 |
| 4. | **Tom Bevill*** (D) | **157,907** |
| | Martha "Mickey" Strickland (R) | 66,934 |
| 5. | **Bud Cramer*** (D) | **160,060** |
| | Terry Smith (R) | 77,951 |
| 6. | **Spencer Bachus** (R) | **146,599** |
| | Ben Erdreich* (D) | 126,062 |
| 7. | **Earl F. Hilliard** (D) | **144,320** |
| | Kervin Jones (R) | 36,086 |
| | **Alaska At Large** | |
| | **Don Young*** (R) | **111,849** |
| | John C. Devens (D) | 102,378 |
| | **Arizona** | |
| 1. | **Sam Coppersmith** (D) | **130,715** |
| | John J. Rhodes III* (R) | 113,613 |
| 2. | **Ed Pastor*** (D) | **90,693** |
| | Don Shooter (R) | 41,257 |
| 3. | **Bob Stump*** (R) | **158,906** |
| | Roger Hartstone (D) | 88,830 |
| 4. | **John Kyl*** (R) | **156,330** |
| | Walter R. Mybeck II (D) | 70,572 |
| 5. | **Jim Kolbe*** (R) | **172,867** |
| | Jim Toevs (D) | 77,256 |
| 6. | **Karen English** (D) | **124,251** |
| | Doug Wead (R) | 97,074 |
| | **Arkansas** | |
| 1. | **Blanche Lambert** (D) | **149,558** |
| | Terry Hayes (R) | 64,618 |
| 2. | **Ray Thornton*** (D) | **154,946** |
| | Dennis Scott (R) | 53,978 |
| 3. | **Tim Hutchinson** (R) | **125,295** |
| | John VanWinkle (D) | 117,775 |
| 4. | **Jay Dickey** (R) | **113,009** |
| | W. J. "Bill" McCuen (D) | 102,918 |
| | **California** | |
| 1. | **Dan Hamburg** (D) | **119,676** |
| | Frank Riggs* (R) | 113,266 |
| 2. | **Wally Herger*** (R) | **167,247** |
| | Elliot Roy Freedman (D) | 71,780 |
| 3. | **Vic Fazio*** (D) | **122,149** |
| | H.L. "Bill" Richardson (R) | 96,092 |
| 4. | **John T. Doolittle*** (R) | **141,155** |
| | Patricia Malberg (D) | 129,489 |
| 5. | **Robert T. Matsui*** (D) | **158,250** |
| | Robert S. Dinsmore (R) | 58,698 |
| 6. | **Lynn Woolsey** (D) | **190,322** |
| | Bill Filante (R) | 98,171 |
| 7. | **George Miller*** (D) | **153,320** |
| | David Scholl (R) | 54,822 |
| 8. | **Nancy Pelosi*** (D) | **191,906** |
| | Marc Wolin (R) | 25,693 |
| 9. | **Ronald V. Dellums*** (D) | **164,265** |
| | G. William "Billy" Hunter (R) | 53,707 |
| 10. | **Bill Baker** (R) | **145,702** |
| | Wendell H. Williams (D) | 134,635 |
| 11. | **Richard W. Pombo** (R) | **94,453** |
| | Patricia Garamendi (D) | 90,539 |
| 12. | **Tom Lantos*** (D) | **157,205** |
| | Jim Tomlin (R) | 53,278 |
| 13. | **Fortney "Pete" Stark*** (D) | **123,795** |
| | Verne Teyler (R) | 64,953 |
| 14. | **Anna G. Eshoo** (D) | **146,873** |
| | Tom Huening (R) | 101,202 |
| 15. | **Norman Y. Mineta*** (D) | **168,617** |
| | Robert Wick (R) | 82,875 |
| 16. | **Don Edwards*** (D) | **96,661** |
| | Ted Bundesen (R) | 49,843 |
| 17. | **Sam Farr*** (D) | **53,675** |
| | Bill McCampbell (R) | 43,774 |
| 18. | **Gary A. Condit*** (D) | **139,704** |
| | Kim R. Almstrom (B) | 25,307 |
| 19. | **Rick Lehman*** (D) | **101,619** |
| | Tal L. Cloud (R) | 100,590 |
| 20. | **Calvin Dooley*** (D) | **72,679** |
| | Ed Hunt (R) | 39,680 |
| 21. | **William M. "Bill" Thomas*** (R) | **127,758** |
| | Deborah A. Vollmer (D) | 68,058 |
| 22. | **Michael Huffington** (R) | **131,242** |
| | Gloria Ochoa (D) | 87,328 |
| 23. | **Elton Gallegly*** (R) | **115,504** |
| | Anita Perez Ferguson (D) | 88,225 |
| 24. | **Anthony C. Beilenson*** (D) | **141,742** |
| | Tom McClintock (R) | 99,835 |
| 25. | **Howard P. "Buck" McKeon** (R) | **113,611** |
| | James H. "Gil" Gilmartin (D) | 72,233 |
| 26. | **Howard L. Berman*** (D) | **73,807** |
| | Gary Forsch (R) | 36,453 |
| 27. | **Carlos J. Moorhead*** (R) | **105,521** |
| | Doug Kahn (D) | 83,805 |
| 28. | **David Dreier*** (R) | **122,353** |
| | Al Wachtel (D) | 76,525 |
| 29. | **Henry A. Waxman*** (D) | **160,312** |
| | Mark A. Robbins (R) | 67,141 |
| 30. | **Xavier Becerra** (D) | **48,800** |
| | Morry Waksberg (R) | 20,034 |
| 31. | **Matthew G. Martinez*** (D) | **68,324** |
| | Reuben D. Franco (R) | 40,873 |
| 32. | **Julian C. Dixon*** (D) | **150,644** |
| | Bob Weber (B) | 12,384 |
| 33. | **Lucille Roybal-Allard** (D) | **32,010** |
| | Robert Guzman (R) | 15,428 |
| 34. | **Esteban E. Torres*** (D) | **91,738** |
| | J. "Jay" Hernandez (R) | 50,907 |
| 35. | **Maxine Waters*** (D) | **102,941** |
| | Nate Truman (R) | 17,417 |
| 36. | **Jane Harman** (D) | **125,751** |
| | Joan Milke Flores (R) | 109,684 |
| 37. | **Walter R. Tucker** (D) | **97,159** |
| | B. Kwaku Duren (PF) | 16,178 |
| 38. | **Steve Horn** (R) | **92,038** |
| | Evan Anderson Braude (D) | 82,108 |
| 39. | **Ed Royce** (R) | **122,472** |
| | Molly McClanahan (D) | 81,728 |
| 40. | **Jerry Lewis*** (R) | **129,563** |
| | Donald M. "Don" Rusk (D) | 63,881 |
| 41. | **Jay C. Kim** (R) | **101,753** |
| | Bob Baker (D) | 58,777 |
| 42. | **George E. Brown, Jr.*** (D) | **79,780** |
| | Dick Rutan (R) | 69,251 |
| 43. | **Ken Calvert** (R) | **88,987** |
| | Mark A. Takano (D) | 88,468 |
| 44. | **Al McCandless*** (R) | **110,333** |
| | Georgia Smith (D) | 81,693 |
| 45. | **Dana Rohrabacher*** (R) | **123,731** |
| | Patricia McCabe (D) | 88,508 |
| 46. | **Robert K.O. "Bob" Dornan*** (R) | **55,659** |
| | Robert John Banuelos (D) | 45,435 |
| 47. | **Christopher Cox*** (R) | **165,004** |
| | John F. Anwiler (D) | 76,924 |
| 48. | **Ron Packard*** (R) | **140,935** |
| | Michael Farber (D) | 67,415 |
| 49. | **Lynn Schenk** (D) | **127,280** |
| | Judy Jarvis (R) | 106,170 |
| 50. | **Bob Filner** (D) | **77,293** |
| | Tony Valencia (R) | 39,531 |

| Dist. | Representative (Party) | 1992 Election |
|---|---|---|
| 51. | Randy "Duke" Cunningham* (R) | 141,890 |
| | Bea Herbert (D) | 85,148 |
| 52. | Duncan Hunter* (R) | 112,995 |
| | Janet M. Gastil (D) | 88,076 |

### Colorado

| Dist. | Representative (Party) | 1992 Election |
|---|---|---|
| 1. | Patricia Schroeder* (D) | 156,629 |
| | Raymond Diaz Aragon (R) | 70,902 |
| 2. | David E. Skaggs* (D) | 164,790 |
| | Bryan Day (R) | 88,470 |
| 3. | Scott McInnis (R) | 143,293 |
| | Mike Callihan (D) | 114,480 |
| 4. | Wayne Allard* (R) | 139,884 |
| | Tom Redder (D) | 101,957 |
| 5. | Joel Hefley* (R) | 173,096 |
| | Charles A. Oriez (D) | 62,550 |
| 6. | Daniel Schaefer* (R) | 142,021 |
| | Tom Kolbe (D) | 91,073 |

### Connecticut

| Dist. | Representative (Party) | 1992 Election |
|---|---|---|
| 1. | Barbara Bailey Kennelly* (D) | 164,735 |
| | Philip F. Steele (R) | 75,113 |
| 2. | Samuel Gejdenson* (D) | 123,291 |
| | Edward W. Munster (R) | 119,416 |
| 3. | Rosa L. De Lauro* (D) | 162,568 |
| | Thomas Scott (R) | 84,952 |
| 4. | Christopher Shays* (R) | 147,816 |
| | Dave Schropfer (D) | 58,666 |
| 5. | Gary A. Franks* (R) | 104,891 |
| | James J. Lawlor (D) | 74,791 |
| 6. | Nancy L. Johnson* (R) | 166,967 |
| | Eugene F. Slason (D) | 60,373 |

### Delaware At Large

| | Representative (Party) | 1992 Election |
|---|---|---|
| | Michael N. Castle (R) | 153,037 |
| | S. B. Woo (D) | 117,426 |

### Florida

| Dist. | Representative (Party) | 1992 Election |
|---|---|---|
| 1. | Earl Hutto* (D) | 118,753 |
| | Terry Ketchel (R) | 100,136 |
| 2. | Pete Peterson* (D) | 167,151 |
| | Ray Wagner (R) | 60,378 |
| 3. | Corrine Brown (D) | 91,877 |
| | Don Weidner (R) | 63,070 |
| 4. | Tillie Fowler (R) | 135,772 |
| | Mattox Hair (D) | 103,484 |
| 5. | Karen L. Thurman (D) | 129,678 |
| | Tom Hogan (R) | 114,331 |
| 6. | Cliff Stearns* (R) | 144,120 |
| | Phil Denton (D) | 76,396 |
| 7. | John L. Mica (R) | 125,790 |
| | Dan Webster (D) | 96,926 |
| 8. | Bill McCollum* (R) | 141,925 |
| | Chuck Kovaleski (D) | 65,132 |
| 9. | Michael Bilirakis* (R) | 157,822 |
| | Cheryl Davis Knapp (D) | 110,023 |
| 10. | C.W. Bill Young* (R) | 149,347 |
| | Karen Moffitt (D) | 114,637 |
| 11. | Sam M. Gibbons* (D) | 100,962 |
| | Mark Sharpe (R) | 77,625 |
| 12. | Charles T. Canady (R) | 100,468 |
| | Tom Mims (D) | 92,333 |
| 13. | Dan Miller (R) | 158,836 |
| | Rand Snell (D) | 115,741 |
| 14. | Porter J. Goss* (R) | 220,324 |
| | James H. King (I) | 48,156 |
| 15. | Jim Bacchus* (D) | 132,385 |
| | Bill Tolley (R) | 128,830 |
| 16. | Tom Lewis* (R) | 157,253 |
| | John P. Comerford (D) | 101,217 |
| 17. | Carrie Meek (D) | Unopposed |
| 18. | Ileana Ros-Lehtinen* (R) | 104,715 |
| | Magda Montiel Davis (D) | 52,095 |
| 19. | Harry Johnston* (D) | 177,411 |
| | Larry Metz (R) | 103,848 |
| 20. | Peter Deutsch (D) | 130,946 |
| | Beverly Kennedy (R) | 91,573 |
| 21. | Lincoln Diaz-Balart (R) | Unopposed |
| 22. | E. Clay Shaw* (R) | 128,376 |
| | Gwen Margolis (D) | 91,605 |
| 23. | Alcee L. Hastings (D) | 84,232 |
| | Ed Fielding (R) | 44,800 |

### Georgia

| Dist. | Representative (Party) | 1992 Election |
|---|---|---|
| 1. | Jack Kingston (R) | 103,932 |
| | Barbara Christmas (D) | 75,808 |
| 2. | Sanford Bishop (D) | 95,789 |
| | Jim Dudley (R) | 54,593 |
| 3. | Mac Collins (R) | 114,107 |
| | Richard Ray* (D) | 94,271 |
| 4. | John Linder (R) | 126,495 |
| | Cathey Steinberg (D) | 123,819 |
| 5. | John Lewis* (D) | 147,445 |
| | Paul Stabler (R) | 56,960 |
| 6. | Newt Gingrich* (R) | 158,761 |
| | Tony Center (D) | 116,196 |
| 7. | George "Buddy" Darden* (D) | 111,374 |
| | Al Beverly (R) | 82,915 |
| 8. | J. Roy Rowland* (D) | 108,472 |
| | Robert F. "Bob" Cunningham (R) | 86,220 |
| 9. | Nathan Deal (D) | 113,024 |
| | Daniel Becker (R) | 77,919 |
| 10. | Don Johnson (D) | 108,426 |
| | Ralph Hudgens (R) | 93,059 |
| 11. | Cynthia McKinney (D) | 120,168 |
| | Woodrow Lovett (R) | 44,221 |

### Hawaii

| Dist. | Representative (Party) | 1992 Election |
|---|---|---|
| 1. | Neil Abercrombie* (D) | 129,332 |
| | Warner C. Kimo Sutton (R) | 41,575 |
| 2. | Patsy Takemoto Mink* (D) | 131,454 |
| | Kamuela Price (R) | 40,070 |

### Idaho

| Dist. | Representative (Party) | 1992 Election |
|---|---|---|
| 1. | Larry LaRocco* (D) | 140,985 |
| | Rachel S. Gilbert (R) | 90,983 |
| 2. | Michael D. Crapo (R) | 139,783 |
| | J.D. Williams (D) | 81,450 |

### Illinois

| Dist. | Representative (Party) | 1992 Election |
|---|---|---|
| 1. | Bobby L. Rush (D) | 209,258 |
| | Jay Walker (R) | 43,453 |
| 2. | Mel Reynolds (D) | 182,614 |
| | Ron Blackstone (R) | 31,957 |
| 3. | William O. Lipinski* (D) | 162,165 |
| | Harry C. Lepinske (R) | 93,128 |
| 4. | Luis V. Gutierrez (D) | 90,452 |
| | Hildegarde Rodriguez-Schieman (R) | 26,154 |
| 5. | Dan Rostenkowski* (D) | 132,889 |
| | Elias R. "Non-Incumbent" Zenkich (R) | 90,738 |
| 6. | Henry J. Hyde* (R) | 165,009 |
| | Barry W. Watkins (D) | 86,891 |
| 7. | Cardiss Collins* (D) | 182,811 |
| | Norman G. Boccio (R) | 35,346 |
| 8. | Philip M. Crane* (R) | 132,887 |
| | Sheila A. Smith (D) | 96,419 |
| 9. | Sidney R. Yates* (D) | 162,942 |
| | Herbert Sohn (R) | 64,760 |
| 10. | John E. Porter* (R) | 155,230 |
| | Michael J. Kennedy (D) | 85,400 |
| 11. | George E. Sangmeister* (D) | 135,387 |
| | Robert T. Herbolsheimer (R) | 107,860 |
| 12. | Jerry F. Costello* (D) | 168,762 |
| | Mike Starr (R) | 68,115 |
| 13. | Harris W. Fawell* (R) | 179,257 |
| | Dennis Michael Temple (D) | 82,985 |
| 14. | J. Dennis Hastert* (R) | 155,271 |
| | Jonathan Abram Reich (D) | 75,294 |
| 15. | Thomas W. Ewing* (R) | 142,167 |
| | Charles D. Mattis (D) | 97,190 |
| 16. | Donald Manzullo (R) | 142,388 |
| | John W. Cox, Jr.* (D) | 113,555 |
| 17. | Lane Evans* (D) | 156,233 |
| | Ken Schloemer (R) | 103,719 |
| 18. | Robert H. Michel* (R) | 156,533 |
| | Ronald C. Hawkins (D) | 114,413 |

| Dist. | Representative (Party) | 1992 Election |
|---|---|---|
| 19. | **Glenn Poshard** (D) . . . . . . . . . | **187,156** |
| | Douglas E. Lee (R) . . . . . . . . . . . | 83,526 |
| 20. | **Richard J. Durbin*** (D) . . . . . . . | **154,869** |
| | John M. Shimkus (R) . . . . . . . . . . | 119,219 |

### Indiana

| Dist. | Representative (Party) | 1992 Election |
|---|---|---|
| 1. | **Peter J. Visclosky*** (D) . . . . . . . | **147,054** |
| | David J. Vucich (R) . . . . . . . . . . . | 64,770 |
| 2. | **Philip R. Sharp*** (D) . . . . . . . . . | **130,881** |
| | William G. Frazier (R) . . . . . . . . . | 90,593 |
| 3. | **Timothy J. Roemer*** (D) . . . . . . . | **121,269** |
| | Carl H. Baxmeyer (R) . . . . . . . . . | 89,834 |
| 4. | **Jill L. Long*** (D) . . . . . . . . . . | **134,907** |
| | Charles W. "Chuck" Pierson (R) . . . | 82,468 |
| 5. | **Steve Buyer** (R) . . . . . . . . . . . | **112,492** |
| | James Jontz* (D) . . . . . . . . . . . | 107,973 |
| 6. | **Dan Burton*** (R) . . . . . . . . . . | **186,499** |
| | Natalie M. Bruner (D) . . . . . . . . . | 71,952 |
| 7. | **John T. Myers*** (R) . . . . . . . . . | **129,189** |
| | Ellen E. Wedum (D) . . . . . . . . . . | 88,005 |
| 8. | **Frank McCloskey*** (D) . . . . . . . | **125,244** |
| | Richard E. Mourdock (R) . . . . . . . | 108,054 |
| 9. | **Lee H. Hamilton*** (D) . . . . . . . . | **160,980** |
| | Michael E. Bailey (R) . . . . . . . . . | 70,057 |
| 10. | **Andrew Jacobs, Jr.*** (D) . . . . . . | **117,604** |
| | Janos Horvath (R) . . . . . . . . . . . | 64,378 |

### Iowa

| Dist. | Representative (Party) | 1992 Election |
|---|---|---|
| 1. | **James A. "Jim" Leach*** (R) . . . . . | **178,042** |
| | Jan J. Zonneveld (D) . . . . . . . . . | 81,600 |
| 2. | **Jim Nussle*** (R) . . . . . . . . . . . | **134,536** |
| | David R. Nagle (D) . . . . . . . . . . . | 131,570 |
| 3. | **Jim Ross Lightfoot*** (R) . . . . . . . | **125,931** |
| | Elaine Baxter (D) . . . . . . . . . . . | 121,063 |
| 4. | **Neal Smith*** (D) . . . . . . . . . . | **158,610** |
| | Paul Lunde (R) . . . . . . . . . . . . | 94,045 |
| 5. | **Fred Grandy*** (R) . . . . . . . . . . | **Unopposed** |

### Kansas

| Dist. | Representative (Party) | 1992 Election |
|---|---|---|
| 1. | **Pat Roberts*** (R) . . . . . . . . . . | **194,912** |
| | Duane E. West (D) . . . . . . . . . . . | 83,620 |
| 2. | **Jim Slattery*** (D) . . . . . . . . . . | **151,019** |
| | Jim Van Slyke (R) . . . . . . . . . . . | 109,801 |
| 3. | **Jan Meyers*** (R) . . . . . . . . . . | **169,929** |
| | Tom Love (D) . . . . . . . . . . . . . | 110,076 |
| 4. | **Dan Glickman*** (D) . . . . . . . . . | **143,671** |
| | Eric R. Yost (R) . . . . . . . . . . . . | 117,070 |

### Kentucky

| Dist. | Representative (Party) | 1992 Election |
|---|---|---|
| 1. | **Tom Barlow** (D) . . . . . . . . . . . | **128,524** |
| | Steve Hamrick (R) . . . . . . . . . . | 83,088 |
| 2. | **William H. Natcher*** (D) . . . . . . | **126,894** |
| | Bruce R. Bartley (R) . . . . . . . . . | 79,684 |
| 3. | **Romano L. Mazzoli*** (D) . . . . . . | **148,066** |
| | Susan B. Stokes (R) . . . . . . . . . | 132,689 |
| 4. | **Jim Bunning*** (R) . . . . . . . . . . | **139,634** |
| | Dr. Floyd G. Poore (D) . . . . . . . . | 86,890 |
| 5. | **Harold Rogers*** (R) . . . . . . . . | **115,255** |
| | John Doug Hays (D) . . . . . . . . . | 95,760 |
| 6. | **Scotty Baesler** (D) . . . . . . . . . | **135,613** |
| | Charles W. Ellinger (R) . . . . . . . | 87,816 |

### Louisiana

| Dist. | Representative (Party) | 1992 Election |
|---|---|---|
| 1. | **Bob Livingston*** (R) . . . . . . . . | **Declared Elected** |
| 2. | **William J. Jefferson*** (D) . . . . . . | **Declared Elected** |
| 3. | **Billy Tauzin*** (D) . . . . . . . . . . | **Declared Elected** |
| 4. | **Cleo Fields** (D) . . . . . . . . . . . | **143,980** |
| | Charles Jones (D) . . . . . . . . . . | 50,851 |
| 5. | **Jim McCrery** (R) . . . . . . . . . . | **153,501** |
| | Jerry Huckaby* (D) . . . . . . . . . . | 90,079 |
| 6. | **Richard Baker*** (R) . . . . . . . . . | **123,953** |
| | Clyde C. Holloway (R) . . . . . . . . | 121,225 |
| 7. | **James A. "Jimmy" Hayes*** (D) . . . | **Declared Elected** |

In Louisiana, all candidates of all parties run against each other in an open primary, unless they are unopposed incumbents in which case they are declared elected. All candidates who receive more than 50 percent of the primary vote are also declared elected and do not appear on the general election ballot.

### Maine

| Dist. | Representative (Party) | 1992 Election |
|---|---|---|
| 1. | **Thomas H. Andrews*** (D) . . . . . | **232,696** |
| | Linda Bean (R) . . . . . . . . . . . . | 125,236 |
| 2. | **Olympia J. Snowe*** (R) . . . . . . . | **153,022** |
| | Patrick K. McGowan (D) . . . . . . . | 130,824 |

### Maryland

| Dist. | Representative (Party) | 1992 Election |
|---|---|---|
| 1. | **Wayne T. Gilchrest*** (R) . . . . . . | **120,084** |
| | Thomas McMillen (D) . . . . . . . . . | 112,771 |
| 2. | **Helen Delich Bentley*** (R) . . . . . | **165,443** |
| | Michael C. Hickey, Jr. (D) . . . . . . | 88,658 |
| 3. | **Benjamin L. Cardin*** (D) . . . . . . | **163,354** |
| | William T.S. Bricker (R) . . . . . . . | 58,869 |
| 4. | **Albert R. Wynn*** (D) . . . . . . . . | **136,902** |
| | Michele Dyson (R) . . . . . . . . . . | 45,166 |
| 5. | **Steny H. Hoyer*** (D) . . . . . . . . | **118,312** |
| | Lawrence J. Hogan, Jr. (R) . . . . . | 97,982 |
| 6. | **Roscoe G. Bartlett** (R) . . . . . . . | **125,564** |
| | Thomas H. Hattery* (D) . . . . . . . | 106,224 |
| 7. | **Kweisi Mfume*** (D) . . . . . . . . . | **152,689** |
| | Kenneth Kondner (R) . . . . . . . . . | 26,304 |
| 8. | **Constance A. Morella*** (R) . . . . . | **203,377** |
| | Edward J. Heffernan (D) . . . . . . . | 77,042 |

### Massachusetts

| Dist. | Representative (Party) | 1992 Election |
|---|---|---|
| 1. | **John W. Olver*** (D) . . . . . . . . . | **135,049** |
| | Patrick Larkin (R) . . . . . . . . . . . | 113,828 |
| 2. | **Richard E. Neal*** (D) . . . . . . . . | **131,215** |
| | Anthony W. Ravosa, Jr. (R) . . . . . | 76,795 |
| 3. | **Peter I. Blute** (R) . . . . . . . . . . | **131,473** |
| | Joseph D. Early* (D) . . . . . . . . . | 115,587 |
| 4. | **Barney Frank*** (D) . . . . . . . . . | **182,633** |
| | Edward J. McCormick III (R) . . . . . | 70,665 |
| 5. | **Martin T. Meehan** (D) . . . . . . . . | **133,844** |
| | Paul W. Cronin (R) . . . . . . . . . . | 96,206 |
| 6. | **Peter G. Torkildsen** (R) . . . . . . . | **159,165** |
| | Nicholas Mavroules* (D) . . . . . . . | 130,248 |
| 7. | **Edward J. Markey*** (D) . . . . . . . | **174,837** |
| | Stephen A. Sohn (R) . . . . . . . . . | 78,262 |
| 8. | **Joseph P. Kennedy II*** (D) . . . . . | **149,903** |
| | Alice Harriet Nakash (I) . . . . . . . | 30,402 |
| 9. | **John Joseph Moakley*** (D) . . . . . | **175,550** |
| | Martin D. Conboy (R) . . . . . . . . . | 54,291 |
| 10. | **Gerry E. Studds*** (D) . . . . . . . . | **189,342** |
| | Daniel W. Daly (R) . . . . . . . . . . | 75,887 |

### Michigan

| Dist. | Representative (Party) | 1992 Election |
|---|---|---|
| 1. | **Bart Stupak** (D) . . . . . . . . . . . | **144,857** |
| | Philip E. Ruppe (R) . . . . . . . . . . | 117,056 |
| 2. | **Peter Hoekstra** (R) . . . . . . . . . | **155,577** |
| | John H. Miltner (D) . . . . . . . . . . | 86,265 |
| 3. | **Paul B. Henry**[2] (R) . . . . . . . . | **162,451** |
| | Carol S. Kooistra (D) . . . . . . . . . | 95,927 |
| 4. | **Dave Camp** (R) . . . . . . . . . . . | **157,337** |
| | Lisa A. Donaldson (D) . . . . . . . . | 87,573 |
| 5. | **James A. Barcia** (D) . . . . . . . . | **147,618** |
| | Keith Muxlow (R) . . . . . . . . . . . | 93,098 |
| 6. | **Fred Upton** (R) . . . . . . . . . . . | **144,083** |
| | Andy Davis (D) . . . . . . . . . . . . | 89,020 |
| 7. | **Nick Smith** (R) . . . . . . . . . . . | **133,972** |
| | Kenneth L. Proctor (B) . . . . . . . . | 18,751 |
| 8. | **Bob Carr** (D) . . . . . . . . . . . . | **135,517** |
| | Dick Chrysler (R) . . . . . . . . . . . | 131,906 |
| 9. | **Dale E. Kildee** (D) . . . . . . . . . | **133,956** |
| | Megan O'Neill (R) . . . . . . . . . . . | 111,798 |
| 10. | **David E. Bonior** (D) . . . . . . . . . | **138,193** |
| | Douglas Carl (R) . . . . . . . . . . . | 114,918 |
| 11. | **Joseph K. Knollenberg** (R) . . . . . | **168,940** |
| | Walter Briggs (D) . . . . . . . . . . . | 117,725 |
| 12. | **Sander Levin** (D) . . . . . . . . . . | **137,514** |
| | John Pappageorge (R) . . . . . . . . | 119,357 |
| 13. | **William D. Ford** (D) . . . . . . . . . | **127,642** |
| | R. Robert Geake (R) . . . . . . . . . | 105,169 |

| Dist. | Representative (Party) | 1992 Election |
|---|---|---|
| 14. | John Conyers, Jr. (D) | 165,496 |
| | John W. Gordon (R) | 32,036 |
| 15. | Barbara-Rose Collins* (D) | 148,908 |
| | Charles C. Vincent (R) | 31,849 |
| 16. | John D. Dingell* (D) | 156,964 |
| | Frank Beaumont (R) | 75,694 |

**Minnesota**

| Dist. | Representative (Party) | 1992 Election |
|---|---|---|
| 1. | Timothy J. "Tim" Penny* (D) | 206,369 |
| | Timothy R. Droogsma (R) | 72,367 |
| 2. | David Minge (D) | 132,156 |
| | Cal R. Ludeman (R) | 131,587 |
| 3. | Jim Ramstad* (R) | 200,240 |
| | Paul Mandell (D) | 104,606 |
| 4. | Bruce F. Vento* (D) | 159,796 |
| | Ian Maitland (R) | 101,744 |
| 5. | Martin Olav Sabo* (D) | 174,139 |
| | Stephen A. Moriarty (R) | 77,093 |
| 6. | Rod Grams (R) | 133,564 |
| | Gerry Sikorski* (D) | 100,016 |
| 7. | Collin C. Peterson* (D) | 133,886 |
| | Bernie Omann (R) | 130,396 |
| 8. | James L. Oberstar* (D) | 167,104 |
| | Phil Herwig (R) | 83,823 |

**Mississippi**

| Dist. | Representative (Party) | 1992 Election |
|---|---|---|
| 1. | Jamie L. Whitten* (D) | 121,664 |
| | Clyde E. Whitaker (R) | 82,952 |
| 2. | Bennie Thompson[3](D) | 72,561 |
| | Hayes Dent (R) | 58,995 |
| 3. | G. V. "Sonny" Montgomery* (D) | 162,864 |
| | Michael E. Williams (R) | 37,710 |
| 4. | Mike Parker* (D) | 130,927 |
| | Jack L. McMillan (R) | 43,705 |
| 5. | Gene Taylor* (D) | 120,766 |
| | Paul Harvey (R) | 67,619 |

**Missouri**

| Dist. | Representative (Party) | 1992 Election |
|---|---|---|
| 1. | William "Bill" Clay* (D) | 158,693 |
| | Arthur S. Montgomery (R) | 74,482 |
| 2. | James M. Talent (R) | 157,594 |
| | Joan Kelly Horn* (D) | 148,729 |
| 3. | Richard A. Gephardt* (D) | 174,000 |
| | Malcolm L. "Mack" Holekamp (R) | 90,006 |
| 4. | Ike Skelton* (D) | 176,977 |
| | John Carley (R) | 74,475 |
| 5. | Alan Wheat* (D) | 151,014 |
| | Edward "Gomer" Moody (R) | 93,562 |
| 6. | Patsy Ann "Pat" Danner (D) | 148,887 |
| | E. Thomas "Tom" Coleman* (R) | 119,637 |
| 7. | Melton D. "Mel" Hancock* (R) | 160,303 |
| | Thomas Patrick "Pat" Deaton (D) | 99,762 |
| 8. | Bill Emerson* (R) | 147,398 |
| | Thad Bullock (D) | 86,730 |
| 9. | Harold L. Volkmer* (D) | 124,694 |
| | Rick Hardy (R) | 118,811 |

**Montana At Large**

| Dist. | Representative (Party) | 1992 Election |
|---|---|---|
| 1. | Pat Williams* (D) | 203,711 |
| | Ron Marlenee (R) | 189,570 |

**Nebraska**

| Dist. | Representative (Party) | 1992 Election |
|---|---|---|
| 1. | Douglas K. Bereuter* (R) | 142,713 |
| | Gerry Finnegan (D) | 96,309 |
| 2. | Peter Hoagland* (D) | 119,512 |
| | Ronald L. Staskiewicz (R) | 113,828 |
| 3. | Bill Barrett* (R) | 170,857 |
| | Lowell Fisher (D) | 67,457 |

**Nevada**

| Dist. | Representative (Party) | 1992 Election |
|---|---|---|
| 1. | James H. Bilbray* (D) | 128,278 |
| | J. Coy Pettyjohn (R) | 84,217 |
| 2. | Barbara F. Vucanovich* (R) | 129,575 |
| | Pete Sferrazza (D) | 117,199 |

**New Hampshire**

| Dist. | Representative (Party) | 1992 Election |
|---|---|---|
| 1. | "Bill" Zeliff* (R) | 135,936 |
| | "Bob" Preston (D) | 108,578 |
| 2. | "Dick" Swett* (D) | 157,328 |
| | "Bill" Hatch (R) | 91,127 |

**New Jersey**

| Dist. | Representative (Party) | 1992 Election |
|---|---|---|
| 1. | Robert E. Andrews* (D) | 153,525 |
| | Lee A. Solomon (R) | 65,123 |
| 2. | William J. Hughes* (D) | 132,465 |
| | Frank A. LoBiondo (R) | 98,315 |
| 3. | Jim Saxton* (R) | 151,368 |
| | Timothy E. Ryan (D) | 94,012 |
| 4. | Christopher H. Smith* (R) | 149,095 |
| | Brian M. Hughes (D) | 84,514 |
| 5. | Marge Roukema* (R) | 196,198 |
| | Frank R. Lucas (D) | 67,579 |
| 6. | Frank Pallone, Jr.* (D) | 118,266 |
| | Joseph M. Kyrillos (R) | 100,949 |
| 7. | Bob Franks (R) | 132,174 |
| | Leonard R. Sendelsky (D) | 105,761 |
| 8. | Herbert C. Klein (D) | 96,742 |
| | Joseph L. Bubba (R) | 84,674 |
| 9. | Robert G. Torricelli* (D) | 139,188 |
| | Patrick J. Roma (R) | 88,179 |
| 10. | Donald M. Payne* (D) | 117,287 |
| | Alfred D. Palermo (R) | 30,160 |
| 11. | Dean A. Gallo* (R) | 188,165 |
| | Ona Spiridellis (D) | 68,871 |
| 12. | Dick Zimmer* (R) | 174,216 |
| | Frank C. Abate (D) | 83,035 |
| 13. | Robert Mendenez (D) | 93,670 |
| | Fred J. Theemling, Jr. (R) | 44,529 |

**New Mexico**

| Dist. | Representative (Party) | 1992 Election |
|---|---|---|
| 1. | Steven H. Schiff* (R) | 128,426 |
| | Robert J. Aragon (D) | 76,600 |
| 2. | Joe Skeen* (R) | 94,838 |
| | Dan Sosa, Jr. (D) | 73,157 |
| 3. | Bill Richardson* (D) | 122,850 |
| | F. Gregg Bemis, Jr. (R) | 54,569 |

**New York**

| Dist. | Representative (Party) | 1992 Election |
|---|---|---|
| 1. | George J. Hochbrueckner* (D) | 117,940 |
| | Edward P. Romaine (R) | 110,043 |
| 2. | Rick A. Lazio (R) | 109,386 |
| | Thomas J. Downey* (D) | 96,328 |
| 3. | Peter T. King (R) | 124,727 |
| | Steve A. Orlins (D) | 116,915 |
| 4. | David A. Levy (R) | 110,710 |
| | Philip Schiliro (D) | 100,386 |
| 5. | Gary L. Ackerman* (D) | 110,476 |
| | Allan E. Binder (R) | 94,907 |
| 6. | Floyd H. Flake* (D) | 96,972 |
| | Dianand D. Bnaowandin (R) | 22,687 |
| 7. | Thomas J. Manton* (D) | 72,280 |
| | Dennis C. Shea (R) | 54,639 |
| 8. | Jerrold L. Nadler (D) | 138,423 |
| | David L. Askren (R) | 25,592 |
| 9. | Charles E. Schumer* (D,L) | 116,545 |
| | Alice F. Gaffney (C) | 14,985 |
| 10. | Edolphus Towns* (D,L) | 97,509 |
| | Owen Augustin (C) | 4,315 |
| 11. | Major R. Owens* (D,L) | 80,028 |
| | Michael Gaffney (C) | 4,287 |
| 12. | Nydia M. Velazquez (D) | 55,926 |
| | Angel Diaz (R) | 14,976 |
| 13. | Susan Molinari* (R) | 107,903 |
| | Sal F. Albanese (D) | 73,520 |
| 14. | Carolyn B. Maloney (D) | 101,687 |
| | Bill Green* (R) | 97,232 |
| 15. | Charles B. Rangel* (D,L) | 105,011 |
| | Jose Suero (C) | 4,345 |
| 16. | José E. Serrano* (D) | 85,222 |
| | Michael Walters (R) | 7,975 |
| 17. | Eliot L. Engel* (D) | 98,068 |
| | Martin Richman (R) | 16,511 |
| 18. | Nita M. Lowey* (D) | 115,841 |
| | Joseph J. DioGuardi (R) | 92,687 |
| 19. | Hamilton Fish, Jr.* (R) | 139,610 |
| | Neil McCarthy (D) | 92,854 |

| Dist. | Representative (Party) | 1992 Election |
|---|---|---|
| 20. | **Benjamin A. Gilman\*** (R) . . . . . . . | **150,301** |
| | Jonathan L. Levine (D) . . . . . . . . | 66,826 |
| 21. | **Michael R. McNulty\*** (D) . . . . . . . | **166,371** |
| | Nancy Norman (R) . . . . . . . . . . | 91,184 |
| 22. | **Gerald B. H. Solomon\*** (R) . . . . . | **164,436** |
| | David Roberts (D) . . . . . . . . . . | 86,896 |
| 23. | **Sherwood L. Boehlert\*** (R) . . . . . | **139,774** |
| | Paula DiPerna (D) . . . . . . . . . . | 61,835 |
| 24. | **John M. McHugh** (R) . . . . . . . . | **122,257** |
| | Margaret M. Ravenscroft (D) . . . . . | 47,675 |
| 25. | **James T. Walsh\*** (R) . . . . . . . . | **135,076** |
| | Rhea Jezer (D) . . . . . . . . . . . | 107,310 |
| 26. | **Maurice D. Hinchey** (D) . . . . . . . | **119,557** |
| | Bob Moppert (R) . . . . . . . . . . | 110,738 |
| 27. | **Bill Paxon\*** (R) . . . . . . . . . . . | **156,596** |
| | W. Douglas Call (D) . . . . . . . . . | 89,906 |
| 28. | **Louise M. Slaughter\*** (D) . . . . . . | **140,908** |
| | William P. Polito (R) . . . . . . . . . | 112,273 |
| 29. | **John J. LaFalce\*** (D) . . . . . . . . | **128,230** |
| | William E. Miller, Jr. (R) . . . . . . . | 98,031 |
| 30. | **Jack Quinn** (R) . . . . . . . . . . . | **125,734** |
| | Dennis T. Gorski (D) . . . . . . . . | 111,445 |
| 31. | **Amo Houghton\*** (R) . . . . . . . . . | **150,696** |
| | Joseph P. Leahey (D) . . . . . . . . | 52,010 |

## North Carolina

| Dist. | Representative (Party) | 1992 Election |
|---|---|---|
| 1. | **Eva Clayton** (D) . . . . . . . . . . . | **116,078** |
| | Ted Tyler (R) . . . . . . . . . . . . | 54,457 |
| 2. | **I.T. "Tim" Valentine, Jr.\*** (D) . . . . | **113,693** |
| | Don Davis (R) . . . . . . . . . . . | 93,893 |
| 3. | **Martin Lancaster\*** (D) . . . . . . . | **101,739** |
| | Tommy Pollard (R) . . . . . . . . . | 80,759 |
| 4. | **David E. Price\*** (D) . . . . . . . . . | **171,299** |
| | LaVinia "Vicky" Rothrock Goudie (R) | 89,345 |
| 5. | **Stephen Neal\*** (D) . . . . . . . . . | **117,835** |
| | Richard M. Burr (R) . . . . . . . . . | 102,086 |
| 6. | **J. Howard Coble\*** (R) . . . . . . . . | **162,822** |
| | Robin Hood (D) . . . . . . . . . . . | 67,200 |
| 7. | **Charles C. "Charlie" Rose III\*** (D) . | **92,414** |
| | Robert C. Anderson (R) . . . . . . . | 66,536 |
| 8. | **W. G. "Bill" Hefner\*** (D) . . . . . . | **113,162** |
| | Coy C. Privette (R) . . . . . . . . . | 71,842 |
| 9. | **J. Alex McMillan\*** (R) . . . . . . . . | **153,650** |
| | Rory Blake (D) . . . . . . . . . . . | 74,583 |
| 10. | **T. Cass Ballenger\*** (R) . . . . . . . | **148,999** |
| | Ben Neill (D) . . . . . . . . . . . . | 79,206 |
| 11. | **Charles H. Taylor\*** (R) . . . . . . . | **130,158** |
| | John S. Stevens (D) . . . . . . . . . | 108,003 |
| 12. | **Melvin Watt\*** (D) . . . . . . . . . . | **127,262** |
| | Barbara Gore Washington (R) . . . . | 49,402 |

## North Dakota At Large

| Dist. | Representative (Party) | 1992 Election |
|---|---|---|
| | **Earl Pomeroy** (D) . . . . . . . . . . | **169,273** |
| | John T. Korsmo (R) . . . . . . . . . | 117,442 |

## Ohio

| Dist. | Representative (Party) | 1992 Election |
|---|---|---|
| 1. | **David Mann** (D) . . . . . . . . . . . | **120,190** |
| | Steve Grote (I) . . . . . . . . . . . | 101,498 |
| | Jim Berns (l). . . . . . . . . . . . . | 12,734 |
| 2. | **Rob Portman**[4](R) . . . . . . . . . . | **53,020** |
| | Lee Hornberger (D) . . . . . . . . . | 22,652 |
| 3. | **Tony P. Hall\*** (D). . . . . . . . . . . | **146,072** |
| | Peter W. Davis (R) . . . . . . . . . | 98,733 |
| 4. | **Michael G. Oxley\*** (R) . . . . . . . . | **147,346** |
| | Raymond M. Ball (D) . . . . . . . . | 92,608 |
| 5. | **Paul E. Gillmor\*** (R) . . . . . . . . | **Unopposed** |
| 6. | **Ted Strickland** (D) . . . . . . . . . . | **122,720** |
| | Bob McEwen\* (R) . . . . . . . . . . | 119,252 |
| 7. | **David L. Hobson\*** (R) . . . . . . . . | **164,195** |
| | Clifford S. Heskett (D) . . . . . . . | 66,237 |
| 8. | **John A. Boehner\*** (R) . . . . . . . . | **176,362** |
| | Fred Sennet (D) . . . . . . . . . . . | 62,033 |
| 9. | **Marcy Kaptur\*** (D) . . . . . . . . . . | **178,879** |
| | Ken D. Brown (R) . . . . . . . . . . | 53,011 |
| 10. | **Martin R. Hoke** (R) . . . . . . . . . | **136,433** |
| | Mary Rose Oakar\* (D) . . . . . . . . | 103,788 |
| 11. | **Louis Stokes\*** (D) . . . . . . . . . . | **154,718** |
| | Beryl E. Rothschild (R) . . . . . . . | 43,866 |

| Dist. | Representative (Party) | 1992 Election |
|---|---|---|
| 12. | **John R. Kasich\*** (R) . . . . . . . . . | **170,297** |
| | Bob Fitrakis (D) . . . . . . . . . . . | 68,761 |
| 13. | **Sherrod Brown\*** (D) . . . . . . . . | **134,486** |
| | Margaret R. Mueller (R) . . . . . . . | 88,889 |
| 14. | **Thomas C. Sawyer\*** (D) . . . . . . | **165,335** |
| | Robert Morgan (R) . . . . . . . . . | 78,659 |
| 15. | **Deborah Pryce** (R) . . . . . . . . . | **110,390** |
| | Richard Cordray (D) . . . . . . . . . | 94,907 |
| 16. | **Ralph Regula\*** (R) . . . . . . . . . . | **158,489** |
| | Warner D. Mendenhall (D). . . . . . | 90,224 |
| 17. | **James A. Traficant, Jr.\*** (D) . . . . . | **216,503** |
| | Salvatore Pansino (R) . . . . . . . . | 40,743 |
| 18. | **Douglas Applegate\*** (D) . . . . . . | **166,189** |
| | Bill Ress (R) . . . . . . . . . . . . . | 77,229 |
| 19. | **Eric D. Fingerhut** (D) . . . . . . . . | **138,465** |
| | Robert A. Gardner (R) . . . . . . . . | 124,606 |

## Oklahoma

| Dist. | Representative (Party) | 1992 Election |
|---|---|---|
| 1. | **James M. Inhofe\*** (R). . . . . . . . . | **119,211** |
| | John Selph (D) . . . . . . . . . . . | 106,619 |
| 2. | **Mike Synar\*** (D) . . . . . . . . . . . | **118,542** |
| | Jerry Hill (R) . . . . . . . . . . . . | 87,657 |
| 3. | **Bill K. Brewster\*** (D) . . . . . . . . | **155,934** |
| | Robert W. Stokes (R) . . . . . . . . | 51,725 |
| 4. | **Dave McCurdy\*** (D) . . . . . . . . . | **140,841** |
| | Howard Bell (R) . . . . . . . . . . . | 58,235 |
| 5. | **Ernest Jim Istook** (R) . . . . . . . . | **123,237** |
| | Laurie Williams (D) . . . . . . . . . | 107,579 |
| 6. | **Glenn English\*** (D) . . . . . . . . . | **134,734** |
| | Bob Anthony (R) . . . . . . . . . . | 64,068 |

## Oregon

| Dist. | Representative (Party) | 1992 Election |
|---|---|---|
| 1. | **Elizabeth Furse** (D) . . . . . . . . . | **152,917** |
| | Tony Meeker (R) . . . . . . . . . . | 140,986 |
| 2. | **Bob Smith\*** (R) . . . . . . . . . . . | **184,163** |
| | Denzel Ferguson (D) . . . . . . . . | 90,036 |
| 3. | **Ron Wyden\*** (D). . . . . . . . . . . | **208,028** |
| | Al Ritter (R) . . . . . . . . . . . . . | 50,235 |
| 4. | **Peter A. DeFazio\*** (D) . . . . . . . . | **199,372** |
| | Richard L. Schulz (R) . . . . . . . . | 79,733 |
| 5. | **Mike Kopetski\*** (D) . . . . . . . . . | **174,443** |
| | Jim Seagraves (R) . . . . . . . . . | 97,984 |

## Pennsylvania

| Dist. | Representative (Party) | 1992 Election |
|---|---|---|
| 1. | **Thomas M. Foglietta\*** (D) . . . . . . | **150,172** |
| | Craig Snyder (R) . . . . . . . . . . | 35,419 |
| 2. | **Lucien E. Blackwell\*** (D) . . . . . . | **164,355** |
| | Larry Hollin (R) . . . . . . . . . . . | 47,906 |
| 3. | **Robert A. Borski\*** (D). . . . . . . . | **130,828** |
| | Charles F. Dougherty (R) . . . . . . | 86,787 |
| 4. | **Ron Klink** (D). . . . . . . . . . . . | **186,684** |
| | Gordon R. Johnston (R) . . . . . . . | 48,484 |
| 5. | **William F. "Bill" Clinger, Jr.\*** (D) . . | **Unopposed** |
| 6. | **Tim Holden** (D) . . . . . . . . . . . | **108,312** |
| | John E. Jones (R) . . . . . . . . . . | 99,694 |
| 7. | **Curt Weldon\*** (R) . . . . . . . . . . | **180,648** |
| | Frank Daly (D) . . . . . . . . . . . | 91,623 |
| 8. | **Jim Greenwood** (R) . . . . . . . . . | **129,593** |
| | Peter H. Kostmayer\* (D) . . . . . . | 114,095 |
| 9. | **Bud Shuster\*** (R, D). . . . . . . . . | **Unopposed** |
| 10. | **Joseph M. McDade\*** (R,D) . . . . . . | **189,414** |
| | Albert A. Smith (B) . . . . . . . . . | 20,134 |
| 11. | **Paul E. Kanjorski\*** (D) . . . . . . . . | **138,675** |
| | Michael A. Fescina (R) . . . . . . . | 68,112 |
| 12. | **John P. Murtha\*** (D). . . . . . . . . | **Unopposed** |
| 13. | **Marjorie Margolies Mezvinsky** (D) . | **127,685** |
| | John D. Fox (R) . . . . . . . . . . . | 126,312 |
| 14. | **William J. Coyne\*** (D) . . . . . . . . | **165,633** |
| | Byron W. King (R) . . . . . . . . . | 61,311 |
| 15. | **Paul McHale** (D) . . . . . . . . . . | **111,419** |
| | Don Ritter\* (R) . . . . . . . . . . . | 99,520 |
| 16. | **Robert S. Walker\*** (R) . . . . . . . | **137,823** |
| | Robert Peters (D). . . . . . . . . . | 74,741 |
| 17. | **George W. Gekas\*** (R) . . . . . . . | **150,158** |
| | Bill Sturges (D) . . . . . . . . . . . | 65,881 |
| 18. | **Rick Santorum\*** (R) . . . . . . . . . | **154,024** |
| | Frank A. Pecora (D) . . . . . . . . . | 96,655 |
| 19. | **William F. Goodling\*** (R) . . . . . . | **98,599** |
| | Paul V. Kilker (D) . . . . . . . . . . | 74,798 |
| | Thomas M. Humbert (I) . . . . . . . | 44,290 |

| Dist. | Representative (Party) | 1992 Election |
|---|---|---|
| 20. | Austin J. Murphy* (D) | 124,898 |
| | Bill Townsend (R) | 111,591 |
| 21. | Thomas J. Ridge* (R) | 150,729 |
| | John C. Harkins (D) | 78,802 |

**Rhode Island**

| Dist. | Representative (Party) | 1992 Election |
|---|---|---|
| 1. | Ronald K. Machtley* (R) | 135,982 |
| | David R. Carlin, Jr. (D) | 48,092 |
| 2. | John F. Reed* (D) | 144,450 |
| | James W. Bell (R) | 49,998 |

**South Carolina**

| Dist. | Representative (Party) | 1992 Election |
|---|---|---|
| 1. | Arthur Ravenel, Jr.* (R) | 121,938 |
| | Bill Oberst, Jr. (D) | 59,908 |
| 2. | Floyd D. Spence* (R) | 148,667 |
| | Geb Newsome (B) | 20,816 |
| 3. | Butler Derrick* (D) | 119,119 |
| | Jim Bland (R) | 75,660 |
| 4. | Bob Inglis* (R) | 99,879 |
| | Liz J. Patterson (D) | 94,182 |
| 5. | John Spratt* (D) | 112,031 |
| | Bill Horne (R) | 70,866 |
| 6. | James R. Clyburn (D) | 120,647 |
| | John Chase (R) | 64,149 |

**South Dakota At Large**

| Dist. | Representative (Party) | 1992 Election |
|---|---|---|
| | Tim Johnson* (D) | 230,070 |
| | John Timmer (R) | 89,375 |

**Tennessee**

| Dist. | Representative (Party) | 1992 Election |
|---|---|---|
| 1. | James H. "Jimmy" Quillen* (R) | 114,797 |
| | J. Carr "Jack" Christian (D) | 47,809 |
| 2. | John J. Duncan, Jr.* (R) | 148,377 |
| | Troy Goodale (D) | 52,887 |
| 3. | Marilyn Lloyd* (D) | 105,693 |
| | Zack Wamp (R) | 102,763 |
| 4. | Jim Cooper* (D) | 98,984 |
| | Dale Johnson (R) | 50,340 |
| 5. | Bob Clement* (D) | 125,233 |
| | Tom Stone (R) | 49,417 |
| 6. | Bart Gordon* (D) | 120,177 |
| | Marsha Blackburn (R) | 86,289 |
| 7. | Don Sundquist* (R) | 125,101 |
| | David R. Davis (R) | 72,062 |
| 8. | John Tanner* (D) | Unopposed |
| 9. | Harold E. Ford* (D) | 123,276 |
| | Charles L. Black (R) | 60,606 |

**Texas**

| Dist. | Representative (Party) | 1992 Election |
|---|---|---|
| 1. | Jim Chapman* (D) | Unopposed |
| 2. | Charles Wilson* (D) | 118,625 |
| | Donna Peterson (R) | 92,176 |
| 3. | Sam Johnson* (R) | 201,569 |
| | Noel Kopala (B) | 32,570 |
| 4. | Ralph M. Hall* (D) | 128,008 |
| | David L. Bridges (R) | 83,875 |
| 5. | John Bryant* (D) | 98,567 |
| | Richard Stokley (R) | 62,419 |
| 6. | Joe Barton* (R) | 189,140 |
| | John Dietrich (D) | 73,933 |
| 7. | Bill Archer* (R) | Unopposed |
| 8. | Jack Fields* (R) | 179,349 |
| | Charles Robinson (D) | 53,473 |
| 9. | Jack Brooks* (D) | 118,690 |
| | Stev  Stockman (R) | 96,270 |
| 10. | J. J. "Jake" Pickle* (D) | 177,233 |
| | Her  ert Spiro (R) | 68,646 |
| 11. | Chet Edwards* (D) | 119,999 |
| | James W. Broyles (R) | 58,033 |
| 12. | Pete Geren* (D) | 125,492 |
| | David Hobbs (R) | 74,432 |
| 13. | Bill Sarpalius* (D) | 117,892 |
| | Beau Bolter (R) | 77,514 |
| 14. | Greg Laughlin* (D) | 135,930 |
| | Humberto J. "Bert" Garza (R) | 54,412 |
| 15. | E. "Kika" de la Garza* (D) | 86,351 |
| | Tom Haughey (R) | 56,549 |
| 16. | Norman Coleman* (D) | 66,731 |
| | Chip Taberski (R) | 61,870 |
| 17. | Charles W. Stenholm* (D) | 136,213 |
| | Jeannie Sadowski (R) | 69,958 |

| Dist. | Representative (Party) | 1992 Election |
|---|---|---|
| 18. | Craig A. Washington* (D) | 111,422 |
| | Edward Blum (R) | 56,080 |
| 19. | Larry Combest* (R) | 162,057 |
| | Terry Lee Moser (D) | 47,325 |
| 20. | Henry B. Gonzalez* (D) | Unopposed |
| 21. | Lamar Smith* (R) | 190,979 |
| | James M. Gaddy (D) | 62,827 |
| 22. | Tom DeLay* (R) | 150,221 |
| | Richard Konrad (D) | 67,812 |
| 23. | Henry Bonilla (R) | 98,259 |
| | Albert G. Bustamente* (D) | 63,797 |
| 24. | Martin Frost* (D) | 104,174 |
| | Steve Masterson (R) | 70,042 |
| 25. | Mike Andrews* (D) | 98,975 |
| | Dolly Madison McKenna (R) | 73,192 |
| 26. | Dick Armey* (R) | 150,209 |
| | John Wayne Caton (D) | 55,237 |
| 27. | Solomon P. Ortiz* (D) | 87,022 |
| | Jay Kimbrough (R) | 66,853 |
| 28. | Frank Tejeda (D) | 122,457 |
| | David C. Slatter (B) | 18,128 |
| 29. | Gene Green (D) | 64,064 |
| | Clark Kent Ervin (R) | 34,609 |
| 30. | Eddie Bernice Johnson (D) | 107,831 |
| | Lucy Cain (R) | 37,853 |

**Utah**

| Dist. | Representative (Party) | 1992 Election |
|---|---|---|
| 1. | James V. Hansen* (R) | 160,037 |
| | Ron Holt (D) | 68,712 |
| 2. | Karen Shepherd (D) | 127,738 |
| | Enid Greene (R) | 118,307 |
| 3. | Bill Orton* (D) | 135,029 |
| | Richard Harrington (R) | 84,019 |

**Vermont At Large**

| Dist. | Representative (Party) | 1992 Election |
|---|---|---|
| | Bernie Sanders* (I) | 162,724 |
| | Tim Philbin (R) | 86,901 |
| | Lewis E. Young (D) | 22,279 |

**Virginia**

| Dist. | Representative (Party) | 1992 Election |
|---|---|---|
| 1. | Herbert H. "Herb" Bateman* (R) | 133,537 |
| | Andrew H. "Andy" Fox (D) | 89,814 |
| 2. | Owen B. Pickett* (D) | 99,253 |
| | J. L. "Jim" Chapman (R) | 77,797 |
| 3. | Robert C. "Bobby" Scott (D) | 132,432 |
| | Daniel "Dan" Jenkins (R) | 35,780 |
| 4. | Norman Sisisky* (D) | 147,649 |
| | A.J. "Tony" Zevgolis (R) | 68,286 |
| 5. | L. F. Payne, Jr.* (D) | 133,031 |
| | W.A. "Bill" Hurlburt (R) | 60,030 |
| 6. | Robert W. "Bob" Goodlatte (R) | 127,309 |
| | Stephen Alan Musselwhite (D) | 84,618 |
| 7. | Thomas J. "Tom" Bliley, Jr.* (R) | 211,618 |
| | Gerald E. "Jerry" Berg (I) | 43,267 |
| 8. | James P. Moran, Jr.* (D) | 138,542 |
| | Kyle E. McSlarrow (R) | 102,717 |
| 9. | Frederick C. "Rick" Boucher* (D) | 133,284 |
| | L. Garrett "Gary" Weddle (R) | 77,985 |
| 10. | Frank R. Wolf* (R) | 144,471 |
| | Raymond E. "Ray" Vickery, Jr. (D) | 75,775 |
| 11. | Leslie L. Byrne (D) | 114,172 |
| | Henry N. Butler (R) | 103,119 |

**Washington**

| Dist. | Representative (Party) | 1992 Election |
|---|---|---|
| 1. | Maria Cantwell (D) | 148,844 |
| | Gary Nelson (R) | 113,897 |
| 2. | Al Swift* (D) | 133,207 |
| | Jack Metcalf (R) | 107,365 |
| 3. | Jolene Unsoeld* (D) | 138,043 |
| | Pat Fiske (R) | 108,583 |
| 4. | Jay Inslee (D) | 106,556 |
| | Richard "Doc" Hastings (R) | 103,028 |
| 5. | Thomas S. Foley* (D) | 135,965 |
| | John Sonneland (R) | 110,443 |
| 6. | Norman D. Dicks* (D) | 152,933 |
| | Lauri J. Phillips (R) | 66,664 |
| 7. | Jim McDermott* (D) | 222,604 |
| | Glenn C. Hampson (R) | 54,149 |

| Dist. | Representative (Party) | 1992 Election |
|---|---|---|
| 8. | **Jennifer Dunn** (R) | 155,874 |
| | George O. Tamblyn (D) | 87,611 |
| 9. | **Mike Kreidler** (D) | 110,902 |
| | Pete von Reichbauer (R) | 91,910 |
| | Brian Wilson (I) | 6,585 |
| | Timothy J. Brill (I) | 3,522 |

### West Virginia

| Dist. | Representative (Party) | 1992 Election |
|---|---|---|
| 1. | **Alan B. Mollohan*** (D) | Unopposed |
| 2. | **Bob Wise*** (D) | 143,988 |
| | Samuel A. Cravotta (R) | 59,102 |
| 3. | **Nick Joe Rahall II*** (D) | 122,279 |
| | Ben Waldman (R) | 64,012 |

### Wisconsin

| Dist. | Representative (Party) | 1992 Election |
|---|---|---|
| 1. | **Peter Barca**[5] (D) | 55,605 |
| | Mark W. Neumann (R) | 54,930 |
| 2. | **Scott L. Klug*** (R) | 183,366 |
| | Ada E. Deer (D) | 108,291 |

| Dist. | Representative (Party) | 1992 Election |
|---|---|---|
| 3. | **Steven C. Gunderson*** (R) | 146,903 |
| | Paul Sacia (D) | 108,664 |
| 4. | **Gerald D. Kleczka*** (D) | 173,482 |
| | Joseph L. Cook (R) | 84,872 |
| 5. | **Thomas M. Barrett** (D) | 162,344 |
| | Donalda Ann Hammersmith (R) | 71,085 |
| 6. | **Thomas E. Petri*** (R) | 143,875 |
| | Peggy A. Lautenschlager (D) | 128,232 |
| 7. | **David R. Obey*** (D) | 166,200 |
| | Dale R. Vannes (R) | 91,772 |
| 8. | **Toby Roth*** (R) | 191,704 |
| | Catherine L. Helms (D) | 81,792 |
| 9. | **F. James Sensenbrenner, Jr.*** (R) | 192,898 |
| | Ingrid K. Buxton (D) | 77,362 |

### Wyoming At Large

| | Representative (Party) | 1992 Election |
|---|---|---|
| | **Craig Thomas*** (R) | 113,882 |
| | John Herschler (D) | 77,418 |

## Resident Commissioner (Non-Voting)
### Puerto Rico

Carlos Romero Barceló (D)

## Non-Voting Delegates

| District of Columbia | Guam[6] | American Samoa |
|---|---|---|
| Eleanor Holmes Norton* (D) | Robert Underwood (D) | Eni F. H. Faleomavaega (D) |
| | **Virgin Islands** | |
| | Ron de Lugo* (D) | |

(1) A special election was held June 9, 1993, to fill the seat left vacant when Rep. Leon E. Panetta (D) resigned to become budget director. The winner will serve the remainder of Panetta's term. (2) A special election will be held Dec. 7, 1993, to fill the seat left vacant by the death of Rep. Paul B. Henry on July 31. (3) A special election was held Apr. 13, 1993, to fill the seat left vacant when Rep. Mike Espy (D) resigned to become secretary of agriculture. The winner will serve the remainder of Espy's term. (4) A special election was held May 4, 1993, to fill the seat left vacant when Rep. Willis D. Gradison, Jr. (R) resigned after 18 years in office to become a lobbyist. The winner will serve the remainder of Gradison's term. (5) A special election was held May 4, 1993, to fill the seat left vacant when Rep. Les Aspin (D) resigned to become secretary of defense. The winner will serve the remainder of Aspin's term. (6) A typhoon postponed elections on Guam until Nov. 7, 1992.

## Congressional Reapportionment for the 103rd Congress

Source: Bureau of the Census, U.S. Dept. of Commerce

As a result of population changes from 1980 to 1990, as reported in the 1990 Census, 8 states have more representatives in the 103rd Congress, which convened in January 1993. The states with the largest gains were California (+7), Florida (+4), and Texas (+3), while Washington, Arizona, Georgia, North Carolina, and Virginia each gained a seat. Thirteen states have fewer representatives. New York lost 3 seats, while Illinois, Michigan, Ohio, and Pennsylvania lost 2 seats each. West Virginia, Kentucky, Louisiana, Kansas, Massachusetts, New Jersey, Iowa, and Montana lost one seat.

The population shifts gave the West 8, and the South 7 additional seats. The Midwest lost 8, and the Northeast 7 seats.

## Political Divisions of the U.S. Senate and House of Representatives From 1955 (84th Cong.) to 1993 (103rd Cong.)

Source: Clerk of the House of Representatives; Secretary of the Senate

| | | Senate | | | | | House of Representatives | | | | |
|---|---|---|---|---|---|---|---|---|---|---|---|
| Congress | Years | Number of Senators | Democrats | Republicans | Other parties | Vacant | Number of Representatives | Democrats | Republicans | Other parties | Vacant |
| 84th | 1955-57 | 96 | 48 | 47 | 1 | | 435 | 232 | 203 | | |
| 85th | 1957-59 | 96 | 49 | 47 | | | 435 | 234 | 201 | | |
| 86th | 1959-61 | 98 | 64 | 34 | | | [1]436 | 283 | 153 | | |
| 87th | 1961-63 | 100 | 64 | 36 | | | [2]437 | 262 | 175 | | |
| 88th | 1963-65 | 100 | 67 | 33 | | | 435 | 258 | 176 | | 1 |
| 89th | 1965-67 | 100 | 68 | 32 | | | 435 | 295 | 140 | | |
| 90th | 1967-69 | 100 | 64 | 36 | | | 435 | 248 | 187 | | |
| 91st | 1969-71 | 100 | 58 | 42 | | | 435 | 243 | 192 | | |
| 92d | 1971-73 | 100 | 54 | 44 | 2 | | 435 | 255 | 180 | | |
| 93d | 1973-75 | 100 | 56 | 42 | 2 | | 435 | 242 | 192 | 1 | |
| 94th | 1975-77 | 100 | 61 | 37 | 2 | | 435 | 291 | 144 | | |
| 95th | 1977-79 | 100 | 61 | 38 | 1 | | 435 | 292 | 143 | | |
| 96th | 1979-81 | 100 | 58 | 41 | 1 | | 435 | 277 | 158 | | |
| 97th | 1981-83 | 100 | 46 | 53 | 1 | | 435 | 242 | 190 | | 3 |
| 98th | 1983-85 | 100 | 46 | 54 | | | 435 | 269 | 166 | | |
| 99th | 1985-87 | 100 | 47 | 53 | | | 435 | 253 | 182 | | |
| 100th | 1987-89 | 100 | 54 | 46 | | | 435 | 258 | 177 | | |
| 101st | 1989-91 | 100 | 57 | 43 | | | 435 | 262 | 173 | | |
| 102nd | 1991-93 | 100 | 57 | 43 | | | 435 | 266 | 164 | 1 | 4 |
| 103rd | 1993-95 | 100 | [3]56 | [3]44 | | | 435 | [3]258 | [3]176 | [3]1 | |

(1) Proclamation declaring Alaska a state issued Jan. 3, 1959. (2) Proclamation declaring Hawaii a state issued Aug. 21, 1959. (3) As of mid-1993.

## Congressional Bills Vetoed, 1789-1993
Source: Senate Library; June 16, 1993

| | Regular vetoes | Pocket vetoes | Total vetoes | Vetoes over-ridden | | Regular vetoes | Pocket vetoes | Total vetoes | Vetoes over-ridden |
|---|---|---|---|---|---|---|---|---|---|
| Washington | 2 | — | 2 | — | Benjamin Harrison | 19 | 25 | 44 | 1 |
| John Adams | — | — | — | — | Cleveland | 42 | 128 | 170 | 5 |
| Jefferson | — | — | — | — | McKinley | 6 | 36 | 42 | — |
| Madison | 5 | 2 | 7 | — | Theodore Roosevelt | 42 | 40 | 82 | 1 |
| Monroe | 1 | — | 1 | — | Taft | 30 | 9 | 39 | 1 |
| John Q. Adams | — | — | — | — | Wilson | 33 | 11 | 44 | 6 |
| Jackson | 5 | 7 | 12 | — | Harding | 5 | 1 | 6 | — |
| Van Buren | — | 1 | 1 | — | Coolidge | 20 | 30 | 50 | 4 |
| William Harrison | — | — | — | — | Hoover | 21 | 16 | 37 | 3 |
| Tyler | 6 | 4 | 10 | 1 | Franklin Roosevelt | 372 | 263 | 635 | 9 |
| Polk | 2 | 1 | 3 | — | Truman | 180 | 70 | 250 | 12 |
| Taylor | — | — | — | — | Eisenhower | 73 | 108 | 181 | 2 |
| Fillmore | — | — | — | — | Kennedy | 12 | 9 | 21 | — |
| Pierce | 9 | — | 9 | 5 | Lyndon Johnson | 16 | 14 | 30 | — |
| Buchanan | 4 | 3 | 7 | — | Nixon | 26 | 17 | 43 | 7 |
| Lincoln | 2 | 5 | 7 | — | Ford | 48 | 18 | 66 | 12 |
| Andrew Johnson | 21 | 8 | 29 | 15 | Carter | 13 | 18 | 31 | 2 |
| Grant | 45 | 48 | 93 | 4 | Reagan | 39 | 39 | 78 | 9 |
| Hayes | 12 | 1 | 13 | 1 | Bush[1] | 29 | 15 | 44 | 1 |
| Garfield | — | — | — | — | | | | | |
| Arthur | 4 | 8 | 12 | 1 | | | | | |
| Cleveland | 304 | 110 | 414 | 2 | Total[1] | 1,467 | 1,066 | 2,514 | 104 |

(1) Excluded from the figures are 2 additional bills, which Pres. Bush claimed to be vetoed but Congress considered enacted into law because the President failed to return them to Congress; the courts will decide the status of these bills.

## How a Bill Becomes a Law

1. A Senator or Representative introduces a bill by sending it to the clerk of the House or Senate, who assigns it a number and title. This procedure is termed the *first reading*. The clerk then refers the bill to the appropriate Senate or House committee.

2. If the committee opposes the bill, It will *table*, or kill, it. Otherwise, the committee holds hearings to listen to opinions and facts offered by members and other interested people. The committee then debates the bill and possibly offers amendments. A vote is taken, and if favorable, the bill is sent back to the clerk of the House or Senate.

3. The clerk reads the bill to the house. This is termed the *second reading*. Members may then debate the bill and suggest amendments.

4. After debate and possibly amendment, the bill is given a *third reading*, simply of the title, and put to a voice or roll-call vote.

5. If passed, the bill goes to the other house, where it may be defeated, or passed with or without amendments. If defeated, the bill dies. If passed with amendments, a conference committee made up of members of both houses works out the differences and arrives at a compromise.

6. After passage of the final version by both houses, the bill is sent to the President. If he signs it, the bill becomes a law. However, he may *veto* the bill by refusing to sign it and sending it back to the house where it originated, with his reasons for the veto.

7. The President's objections are then read and debated and a roll-call vote taken. If the bill receives less than a two-thirds vote, it is defeated. If it receives at least two-thirds, it is sent to the other house. If that house also passes it by at least a two-thirds majority, the veto is *overridden*, and the bill becomes a law.

8. If the President neither signs nor vetoes the bill within 10 days—not including Sundays—it automatically becomes a law even without his signature. However, if Congress has adjourned within those 10 days, the bill is automatically killed; this indirect rejection is termed a *pocket veto*.

## Congressional Committees

### Senate Standing Committees
(As of March 24, 1993)

**Agriculture, Nutrition, and Forestry**
Chairman: Patrick J. Leahy, Vt.
Ranking Rep.: Richard G. Lugar, Ind.

**Appropriations**
Chairman: Robert C. Byrd, W.V.
Ranking Rep.: Mark O. Hatfield, Ore.

**Armed Services**
Chairman: Sam Nunn, Ga.
Ranking Rep.: Strom Thurmond, S.C.

**Banking, Housing, and Urban Affairs**
Chairman: Donald W. Riegle, Jr., Mich.
Ranking Rep.: Alfonse M. D'Amato, N.Y.

**Budget**
Chairman: Jim Sasser, Tenn.
Ranking Rep.: Pete V. Domenici, N.M.

**Commerce, Science, and Transportation**
Chairman: Ernest F. "Fritz" Hollings, S.C.
Ranking Rep.: John C. Danforth, Mo.

**Energy and Natural Resources**
Chairman: J. Bennett Johnston, La.
Ranking Rep.: Malcolm Wallop, Wyo.

**Environment and Public Works**
Chairman: Max Baucus, Mon.
Ranking Rep.: John H. Chafee, R.I.

**Finance**
Chairman: Daniel Patrick Moynihan, N.Y.
Ranking Rep.: Bob Packwood, Ore.

**Foreign Relations**
Chairman: Claiborne Pell, R.I.
Ranking Rep.: Jesse Helms, N.C.

**Governmental Affairs**
Chairman: John Glenn, Ohio
Ranking Rep.: William V. Roth, Jr., Del.

**Judiciary**
Chairman: Joseph R. Biden, Jr., Del.
Ranking Rep.: Orrin G. Hatch, Ut.

**Labor and Human Resources**
Chairman: Edward M. Kennedy, Mass.
Ranking Rep.: Nancy Landon Kassebaum, Kan.

**Rules and Administration**
Chairman: Wendell H. Ford, Ky.
Ranking Rep.: Ted Stevens, Alas.

**Small Business**
Chairman: Dale Bumpers, Ark.
Ranking Rep.: Larry Pressler, S.D.

**Veterans' Affairs**
Chairman: John D. Rockefeller IV, W.V.
Ranking Rep.: Frank H. Murkowski, Alas.

## Senate, Other, Select, and Special Committees

(As of March 24, 1993)

**Aging**
Chairman: David H. Pryor, Ark.
Ranking Rep.: William S. Cohen, Me.
**Ethics**
Chairman: Richard H. Bryan, Nev.
V. Chairman: Mitch McConnell, Ky.
**Indian Affairs**
Chairman: Daniel K. Inouye, Ha.
Ranking Rep.: John McCain, Ariz.
**Intelligence**
Chairman: Dennis DeConcini, Ariz.
V. Chairman: John W. Warner, Va.

## Joint Committees of Congress

**Economic**
Chairman: Rep. David R. Obey, Wis.
V. Chairman: Sen. Paul S. Sarbanes, Md.
**Library**
Chairman: Rep. Charles C. "Charlie" Rose, N.C.
V. Chairman: Sen. Claiborne Pell, R.I.
**Organization of Congress**
Co-Chairman: Sen. David L. Boren, Okla.
Co-Chairman: Rep. Lee H. Hamilton, Ind.
V. Chairman: Sen. Pete V. Domenici, N.M.
V. Chairman: Rep. David Dreier, Cal.
**Printing**
Chairman: Sen. Wendell H. Ford, Ky.
V. Chairman: Rep. Charles C. "Charlie" Rose, N.C.
**Taxation**
Chairman: Rep. Dan Rostenkowski (D), Ill.
V. Chairman: Sen. Daniel Patrick Moynihan, N.Y.

## House Standing Committees

(As of April 5, 1993)

**Agriculture**
Chairman: E. "Kika" de la Garza, Tex.
Ranking Rep.: Pat Roberts, Kan.
**Appropriations**
Chairman: William H. Natcher, Ky.
Ranking Rep.: Joseph M. McDade, Pa.
**Armed Services**
Chairman: Ronald V. Dellums, Cal.
Ranking Rep.: Floyd D. Spence, S.C.
**Banking, Finance, and Urban Affairs**
Chairman: Henry B. Gonzalez, Tex.
Ranking Rep.: James A. "Jim" Leach, Ia.
**Budget**
Chairman: Martin Olav Sabo, Minn.
Ranking Rep.: John R. Kasich, Oh.

**District of Columbia**
Chairman: Fortney "Pete" Stark, Cal.
Ranking Rep.: Thomas J. "Tom" Bliley, Jr., Va.
**Education and Labor**
Chairman: William D. Ford, Mich.
Ranking Rep.: William F. Goodling, Pa.
**Energy and Commerce**
Chairman: John D. Dingell, Mich.
Ranking Rep.: Carlos J. Moorhead, Cal.
**Foreign Affairs**
Chairman: Lee H. Hamilton, Ind.
Ranking Rep.: Benjamin A. Gitman, N.Y.
**Government Operations**
Chairman: John Conyers, Jr., Mich.
Ranking Rep.: William F. "Bill" Clinger, Jr., Pa.
**House Administration**
Chairman: Charles C. "Charlie" Rose, N.C.
Ranking Rep.: William M. "Bill" Thomas, Cal.
**Judiciary**
Chairman: Jack Brooks, Tex.
Ranking Rep.: Hamilton Fish, Jr., N.Y.
**Merchant Marine and Fisheries**
Chairman: Gerry E. Studds, Mass.
Ranking Rep.: Jack Fields, Tex.
**Natural Resources**
Chairman: George Miller, Cal.
Ranking Rep.: Don Young, Alas.
**Post Office and Civil Service**
Chairman: William "Bill" Clay, Mo.
Ranking Rep.: John T. Meyers, Ind.
**Public Works and Transportation**
Chairman: Norman Y. Mineta, Cal.
Ranking Rep.: Bud Shuster, Pa.
**Rules**
Chairman: John Joseph Moakley, Mass.
Ranking Rep.: Gerald B. H. Solomon, N.Y.
**Science, Space, and Technology**
Chairman: George E. Brown, Jr., Cal.
Ranking Rep.: Robert S. Walker, Pa.
**Small Business**
Chairman: John J. LaFalce, N.Y.
Ranking Rep.: Jan Meyers, Kan.
**Standards of Official Conduct**
Chairman: Jim McDermott, Wash.
Ranking Rep.: Fred Grandy, Ia.
**Veterans' Affairs**
Chairman: G. V. (Sonny) Montgomery, Miss.
Ranking Rep.: Bob Stump, Ariz.
**Ways and Means**
Chairman: Dan Rostenkowski, Ill.
Ranking Rep.: Bill Archer, Tex.

## House Select Committees

**Intelligence**
Chairman: Dan Glickman, Kan.
Ranking Rep.: Larry Combest, Tex.

## Mayors and City Managers of Selected U.S. Cities

Reflects elections as of August 1993.

\* Asterisk before name denotes city manager. All others are mayors. For mayors, dates are those of next election; for city managers, they are dates of appointment.

D, Democrat; R, Republican; N-P, Non-Partisan; I, Independent

| City | Name | Term |
|------|------|------|
| Abilene, Tex. | Gary McCaleb, N-P | 1993, May |
| Abington, Pa. | *Albert Herrmann | 1978, May |
| Akron, Oh. | D.L. Plusquellic, D | 1995, Nov. |
| Alameda, Cal. | E. William Withrow, N-P | 1994, Nov. |
| Albany, Ga. | *Roy Lane | 1991, Mar. |
| Albany, N.Y. | Thomas M. Whalen,3d,D | 1993, Nov. |
| Albuquerque, N.M. | Louis Saavedra, D | 1993, Oct. |
| Alexandria, La. | Edward Randolph Jr., D | 1994, Nov. |
| Alexandria, Va. | *Vola Lawson | 1985, Sept. |
| Alhambra, Cal. | *Julio Fuentes | 1992, Aug. |
| Allentown, Pa. | Joseph S. Daddona, D | 1993, Nov. |
| Amarillo, Tex. | *John Ward | 1983, June |
| Ames, Ia. | *Steven L. Schainker | 1982, Oct. |
| Anaheim, Cal. | *James D. Ruth | 1990, May |
| Anchorage, Alas. | Tom Fink, R | 1994, Apr. |
| Anderson, Ind. | J. Mark Lawler, D | 1995, Nov. |
| Anderson, S.C. | *Richard Burnette | 1976, Sept. |
| Ann Arbor, Mich. | Ingrid B. Sheldon, R | 1994, Nov. |
| Appleton, Wis. | Richard De Broux, N-P | 1996, Apr. |
| Arcadia, Cal. | *Donald R. Duckworth | 1992, Sept. |
| Arlington, Mass. | *Donald R. Marquis | 1966, Sept. |
| Arlington, Tex. | *George Campbell | 1991, Feb. |
| Arlington Hts., Ill. | William Maki, N-P | 1993, Apr. |
| Arvada, Col. | *Neal G. Berlin | 1986, Feb. |
| Asheville, N.C. | *Douglas Bean | 1986, Apr. |
| Athens, Ga. | Gwen O'Looney, D | 1994, Nov. |
| Atlanta, Ga. | Maynard Jackson, D | 1993, Nov. |
| Atlantic City, N.J. | Jim Whelan, N-P | 1994, May |
| Augusta, Ga. | Charles Devaney, N-P | 1993, Nov. |
| Aurora, Col. | *John Pazour | 1990, May |
| Aurora, Ill. | David L. Pierce, N-P | 1997, Feb. |
| Austin, Tex. | Bruce Todd, N-P | 1994, May |
| Bakersfield, Cal. | *Alan Tandy | 1992, Aug. |
| Baldwin Park, Cal. | *Donald Penman | 1990, Jan. |
| Baltimore, Md. | Kurt Schmoke, D | 1995, Nov. |
| Baton Rouge, La. | Tom E. McHugh, D | 1996, Oct. |
| Battle Creek, Mich. | *Rance L. Leaders | 1988, June |
| Bayonne, N.J. | Richard Rutkowski, N-P | 1994, May |
| Baytown, Tex. | *Bobby Rountree | 1989, Oct. |
| Beaumont, Tex. | *Ray A. Riley | 1989, Feb. |

| City | Name | Term |
|---|---|---|
| Belleville, Ill. | Roger C. Cook, I. | 1997, Apr. |
| Belleville, N.J. | Marina Perna, N-P | 1994, May |
| Bellevue, Wash. | *Phillip Kushlan | 1985, Mar. |
| Bellingham, Wash. | Tim Douglas, N-P | 1995, Nov. |
| Bellflower, Cal. | *Linda C. Lowry | 1993, Apr. |
| Berkeley, Cal. | *Weldon Rucker | 1993, July |
| Bethlehem, Pa. | Kenneth Smith, R | 1993, Nov. |
| Beverly Hills, Cal. | *Mark Scott | 1990, Mar. |
| Billings, Mont. | *Mark S. Watson | 1993, Jan. |
| Biloxi, Miss.. | A.J. Holloway, R | 1997, June |
| Binghamton, N.Y. | Juanita M. Crabb, D. | 1993, Nov. |
| Birmingham, Ala. | Richard Arrington Jr., D. | 1995, Nov. |
| Bismarck, N.D. | Bill Sorensen, R | 1994, June |
| Bloomfield, N.J. | James P. Norton, R | 1995, Nov. |
| Bloomington, Ill. | Jesse Smart, R | 1997, Apr. |
| Bloomington, Ind. | Tomilea Allison, D | 1995, Sept. |
| Bloomington, Minn. | *Mark Bernhardson | 1991, July |
| Boca Raton, Fla. | Emil Danciu, N-P | 1995, Mar. |
| Boise, Ida. | H. Brent Coles, N-P | 1993, Nov. |
| Bossier City, La | *Lorenz Walker | 1989, July |
| Boston, Mass. | Thomas M. Menino, D. | 1993, Nov. |
| Boulder, Col. | *Stephen Honey. | 1991, Apr. |
| Bridgeport, Conn. | Joseph Ganim, D. | 1993, Nov. |
| Bristol, Conn. | William Stortz, D. | 1993, Nov. |
| Brockton, Mass. | Winthrop Farwell Jr., D | 1995, Nov. |
| Broken Arrow, Okla. | *John Vinson. | 1991, Aug. |
| Brooklyn Park, Minn. | *Craig R. Rapp | 1989, Nov. |
| Brownsville, Tex. | *Steve Fitzgibbons | 1987, Jan. |
| Bryan, Tex.. | *Michael Conduff | 1992, June |
| Buena Park, Cal. | *Kevin O'Rourke | 1985, Nov. |
| Buffalo, N.Y. | James D. Griffin, D | 1993, Nov. |
| Burbank, Cal. | *Bud Ovrom | 1985, June |
| Burlington, Vt. | Peter C. Brownell, R | 1995, Mar. |
| Calumet City, Ill. | Gerry P. Genova, I | 1997, Apr. |
| Camarillo, Cal.. | *J. William Little | 1988, Nov. |
| Cambridge, Mass. | *Robert Healy | 1981, July |
| Camden, N.J. | Aaron Thompson, D. | 1993, Nov. |
| Canton, Oh. | Richard Watkins, R | 1995, Nov. |
| Cape Coral, Fla. | Joseph Mazurkiewicz, R | 1993, Nov. |
| Carlsbad, Cal. | *Ray Patchett | 1987, Sept. |
| Carson, Cal. | *Jack Smith | 1988, Dec. |
| Casper, Wyo. | *Thomas Forslund | 1988, Aug. |
| Cedar Rapids, Ia. | Larry Serbousek, N-P. | 1993, Nov. |
| Champaign, Ill. | *Steven C. Carter | 1985, Feb. |
| Chandler, Ariz. | *John Pinch | 1989, Jan. |
| Charleston, S.C. | Joseph P. Riley Jr., D. | 1995, Nov. |
| Charleston, W. Va. | Kent S. Hall, R. | 1995, Apr. |
| Charlotte, N.C.. | Richard Vinroot, R | 1993, Nov. |
| Charlottesville, Va. | *Cole Hendrix | 1970, Jan. |
| Chattanooga, Tenn. | Gene Roberts, R | 1997, Apr. |
| Chesapeake, Va. | *James W. Rein. | 1987, Mar. |
| Chester, Pa. | Barbara Bohannan-Shepperd, D | 1995, Nov. |
| Cheyenne, Wyo. | Leo Pando, N-P | 1996, Nov. |
| Chicago, Ill. | Richard M. Daley, D. | 1995, Apr. |
| Chicopee, Mass. | Joseph Chessey, D. | 1993, Nov. |
| Chino, Cal. | Eunice M. Ulioa, R. | 1994, Nov. |
| Chula Vista, Cal. | Tim Nader, D. | 1994, Nov. |
| Cicero, Ill. | Betty L. Maltese, R | 1997, Apr. |
| Cincinnati, Oh. | *Gerald Newfarmer | 1990, Sept. |
| Clarksville, Tenn. | Don Trotter, N-P. | 1994, Nov. |
| Clearwater, Fla. | *Michael Wright | 1991, Mar. |
| Cleveland, Oh. | Michael White, D | 1993, Nov. |
| Cleveland Hgts., Oh. | *Robert Downey | 1985, Jan. |
| Clifton, N.J. | James Anzaldi, R | 1994, May |
| Col. Spgs., Col. | *Richard Zickefoose | 1990, May |
| Columbia, Mo. | *Raymond A. Beck | 1985, Aug. |
| Columbia, S.C. | *Miles Hadley | 1989, Dec. |
| Columbus, Ga. | Frank Martin, D | 1994, Nov. |
| Columbus, Oh. | Gregory Lashutka, R | 1995, Nov. |
| Compton, Cal. | *Howard Caldwell. | 1989, Nov. |
| Concord, Cal. | *F.A. Stewart | 1992, Nov. |
| Coon Rapids., Minn. | *Robert Svehla | 1991, June |
| Coral Gables, Fla. | *H.C. Eads Jr. | 1988, May |
| Corona, Cal. | *William Garrett | 1989, Dec. |
| Corpus Christi, Tex. | *Juan Garza | 1988, Apr. |
| Costa Mesa, Cal. | *Allan L. Roeder. | 1985, Oct. |
| Council Bluffs, Ia. | Tom Hanafan, N-P | 1993, Nov. |
| Covington, Ky. | Denny Bowman, D | 1995, Nov. |
| Cranston, R.I. | Michael Traficante, D | 1994, Nov. |
| Crystal, Minn. | *John Irving | 1963, Jan. |
| Cuyahoga Falls, Oh. | Don L. Robart, R | 1993, Nov. |
| Dallas, Tex. | *Jan Hart. | 1990, Apr. |
| Daly City, Cal. | *David R. Rowe | 1969, Sept. |
| Danbury, Conn. | Gene Eriquez, D | 1993, Nov. |
| Danville, Va. | *A. Ray Griffin Jr. | 1992, Mar. |
| Davenport, Ia. | Patrick J. Gibbs, R | 1993, Nov. |

| City | Name | Term |
|---|---|---|
| Davis, Cal. | *John Meyer. | 1990, Oct. |
| Dayton, Oh. | *Richard B. Helwig | 1984, June |
| Daytona Bch., Fla. | *Howard D. Tipton | 1978, Oct. |
| Dearborn , Mich. | Michael Guido, N-P | 1993, Nov. |
| Dearborn Hts., Mich. | Lyle Van Houton, R | 1993, Nov. |
| Decatur, Ill. | *James Bacon Jr. | 1988, Oct. |
| Delray Beach, Fla. | Thomas E. Lynch, N-P | 1994, Mar. |
| Denton, Tex. | *Larry Harrell | 1986, Feb. |
| Denver, Col. | Wellington Webb, N-P | 1995, May |
| Des Moines, Ia. | John Dorrian, D | 1993, Nov. |
| Des Plaines, Ill. | Ted Sherwood, N-P . | 1997, Apr. |
| Detroit, Mich. | Coleman A. Young, N-P | 1993, Nov. |
| Dothan, Ala. | Alfred Saliba, N-P | 1997, July |
| Downey, Cal. | *Gerald Caton . | 1989, Oct. |
| Dubuque, Ia. | *M. Van Milligen . | 1993, Jan. |
| Duluth, Minn. | Gary L. Doty, N-P | 1995, Nov. |
| Durham, N.C. | *Orville Powell Jr. | 1983, Mar. |
| E. Hartford, Conn. | Susan Kniep, R | 1993, Nov. |
| E. Lansing, Mich. | Liz Schweitzer, I | 1993, Nov. |
| E. Orange, N.J. | Cardell Cooper, D. | 1993, Nov. |
| Eau Claire, Wis. | *Eric Anderson | 1984, Jan. |
| Edison, N.J. | Thomas Paterniti, D | 1993, Nov. |
| Edmond, Okla. | *C. Max Speegle | 1986, Sept. |
| El Cajon, Cal. | Robert T. Acker . | 1982, July |
| El Monte, Cal. | Patricia Wallach, D | 1994, Apr. |
| El Paso, Tex.. | *Kenneth Beasley . | 1980, May |
| Elgin, Ill. | *Larry L. Rice . | 1989, Oct. |
| Elizabeth, N.J. | J.C. Bollwage, D. | 1996, Nov. |
| Elkhart, Ind. | James Perron, D | 1995, Nov. |
| Elyria, Oh. | Michael Keys, D. | 1995, Nov. |
| Enfield, Conn. | *A. Louis Hayward . | 1990, July |
| Enid, Okla. | *Jim Ferree . | 1990, July |
| Erie, Pa. | Joyce Savocchio, D. | 1993, Nov. |
| Escondido, Cal. | *Douglas Clark | 1989, June |
| Euclid, Oh. | David Lynch, R | 1995, Nov. |
| Eugene, Ore.. | *Michael Gleason . | 1981, Jan. |
| Evanston, Ill. | *Eric Anderson | 1991, June |
| Evansville, Ind. | Frank McDonald, D | 1995, Nov. |
| Everett, Wash. | Pete Kinch, N-P | 1993, Nov. |
| Fairfield, Cal.. | *Charles Long . | 1988, Sept. |
| Fairfield, Conn. | Jacquelyn Durrell, R | 1993, Nov. |
| Fall River, Mass. | John Mitchell, D | 1993, Nov. |
| Fargo, N.D. | Jon Lindgren, D | 1994, Apr. |
| Farmington Hills, Mich. | *William M. Costick | 1981, Jan. |
| Fayetteville, N.C. | *John P. Smith. | 1981, Jan. |
| Fitchburg, Mass. | Jeffrey Bean, D | 1993, Nov. |
| Flagstaff, Ariz. | *David Wilcox . | 1992, July |
| Flint, Mich. | Woodrow Stanley, D | 1995, Nov. |
| Florissant, Mo. | James J. Eagan, N-P | 1995, Apr. |
| Fontana, Cal. | Gary Boyles, R | 1994, Nov. |
| Ft. Collins, Col. | *Steven Burkett . | 1986, Apr. |
| Ft. Lauderdale, Fla. | *George Hanbury 2d | 1990, June |
| Ft. Smith, Ark. | Ray Baker, N-P | 1994, Oct. |
| Ft. Wayne, Ind.. | Paul Helmke, R | 1995, Nov. |
| Ft. Worth, Tex. | Kay Granger, N-P | 1995, May |
| Fountain Valley, Cal. | *Raymond H. Kromer . | 1991, Mar. |
| Fremont, Cal. | *Charles Kent McClain | 1981, May |
| Fresno, Cal. | *Michael Bierman . | 1990, Nov. |
| Fullerton, Cal. | *William C. Winter . | 1979, Oct. |
| Gadsden, Ala. | Steve Means, N-P. | 1994, Aug. |
| Gainesville, Fla. | James F. Painter, R. | 1994, Mar. |
| Galveston, Tex. | *Douglas W. Matthews | 1985, Mar. |
| Gardena, Cal. | *Kenneth Landau | 1985, Mar. |
| Garden Grove, Cal. | *George Tindall . | 1988, May |
| Garland, Tex. | *Ron Holifield . | 1992, Feb. |
| Gary, Ind. | Thomas Barnes, D | 1995, Nov. |
| Gastonia, N.C. | *Gary Hicks . | 1973, Dec. |
| Glendale, Ariz. | *Martin Vanacour . | 1985, Mar. |
| Glendale, Cal. | *David Ramsay . | 1988, May |
| Grand Forks, N.D. | Michael Polovitz, D | 1996, Apr. |
| Grand Prairie, Tex. | *Gary Gwyn . | 1991, July |
| Grand Rapids, Mich. | *Kurt Kimball. | 1987, Apr. |
| Greeley, Col. | William Morton, N-P. | 1993, Nov. |
| Green Bay, Wis. | Samuel Halloin, N-P. | 1995, Apr. |
| Greenville, S.C. | *Aubrey Watts Jr. | 1991, Dec. |
| Greenwich, Conn. | John Margenot, R, first selectman | 1993, Nov. |
| Groton, Conn. | *Ronald P. LeBlanc . | 1993, Nov. |
| Gulfport, Miss. | Ken Combs, R . | 1997, June |
| Harnden, Conn. | Lillian Clayman, D. | 1993, Nov. |
| Hamilton, Oh. | *Hal Shepherd. | 1989, Apr. |
| Hammond, Ind. | Duane W. Dadelow, R | 1995, Nov. |
| Hampton, Va. | *Robert O'Neill Jr. | 1984, Oct. |
| Harrisburg, Pa.. | Stephen Reed, D | 1993, Nov. |
| Hartford, Conn. | *Howard Stanback | 1992, May |
| Haverhill, Mass. | Theodore Pelosi, R | 1993, Nov. |
| Hawthorne, Cal. | *James Mitsch. | 1990, Dec. |
| Hayward, Cal. | *Jesús Armas | 1993, Feb. |

| City | Name | Term |
|---|---|---|
| Henderson, Nev. | Robert A. Groesbeck, N-P | 1997, June |
| Hesperia, Cal. | *D.J. Collins | 1992, July |
| Hialeah, Fla. | Julio Martinez, R. | 1993, Nov. |
| High Point, N.C. | Rebecca R. Smothers, N-P | 1995, Nov. |
| Hollywood, Fla. | *Robert S. Noe Jr. | 1991, Nov. |
| Holyoke, Mass. | William Hamilton, R | 1993, Nov. |
| Honolulu, Ha. | Frank Fasi, R | 1996, Nov. |
| Houston, Tex. | Bob Lanier, N-P | 1993, Nov. |
| Huntington, W. Va. | Jean Dean, R | 1997, June |
| Huntington Beach, Cal. | *Michael Ubervaga | 1990, Feb. |
| Huntington Park, Cal. | Raul Perez, R | 1994, Apr. |
| Huntsville, Ala. | Steve Hettinger, N-P | 1996, Aug. |
| Idaho Falls, Ida. | Thomas Campbell, N-P. | 1993, Nov. |
| Independence, Mo. | *L.C. Kaufman | 1990, Aug. |
| Indianapolis, Ind. | Steve Goldsmith, R | 1995, Nov. |
| Inglewood, Cal. | *Paul Eckles | 1975, Nov. |
| Iowa City, Ia. | *Stephen Atkins | 1986, July |
| Irving, Tex. | *Jack Huffman | 1974, Jan. |
| Irvington, N.J. | Michael Steele, D | 1994, May |
| Jackson, Miss. | Kane Ditto, D. | 1997, June |
| Jacksonville, Fla. | Ed Austin, D | 1995, Apr. |
| Janesville, Wis. | *Steven Sheiffer. | 1987, May |
| Jersey City, N.J. | Bret Schundler, R | 1997, May |
| Johnson City, Tenn. | *John G. Campbell | 1984, June |
| Joliet, Ill. | *John M. Mezera | 1987, Jan. |
| Kalamazoo, Mich. | *Marc A. Ott | 1993, Mar. |
| Kansas City, Kan. | *David Isabell | 1985, Sept. |
| Kansas City, Mo. | Emanuel Cleaver, D. | 1995, Mar. |
| Kenner, La. | *Charlotte Burnell | 1988, Jan. |
| Kenosha, Wis. | John Antaramian, D | 1996, Apr. |
| Kettering, Oh. | Richard Hartmann, R | 1993, Nov. |
| Killeen, Tex. | *Daniel Hobbs | 1990, Jan. |
| Knoxville, Tenn. | Victor Ashe, R | 1995, Nov. |
| Kokomo, Ind. | Robert Sargent, D. | 1995, May |
| LaCrosse, Wis. | Patrick Zielke, N-P | 1997, Apr. |
| La Habra, Cal. | *Lee Risner | 1970, Dec. |
| La Mesa, Cal. | *David Wear | 1990, Apr. |
| La Mirada, Cal. | *Gary K. Sloan | 1981, Apr. |
| Lafayette, Ind. | James Riehle, D. | 1995, Nov. |
| Lafayette, La. | Kenneth Bowen, D | 1996, Mar. |
| Lake Charles, La. | Willie L. Mount, D | 1997, Nov. |
| Lakeland, Fla. | *E.S. Strickland | 1986, Feb. |
| Lakewood, Cal. | *Howard L. Chambers | 1976, June |
| Lakewood, Col. | *Michael J. Rock | 1992, Dec. |
| Lakewood, Oh. | David Harbarger, R | 1995, Nov. |
| Lancaster, Pa. | Janice Stork, D | 1993, Nov. |
| Lansing, Mich. | James A. Crawford, N-P | 1993, Nov. |
| Laredo, Tex. | *Marvin Townsend | 1982, June |
| Largo, Fla. | *Stephen Bonczek | 1988, July |
| Las Cruces, N.M. | Ruben A. Smith, D. | 1995, Nov. |
| Las Vegas, Nev. | Jan Laverty Jones, D | 1994, May |
| Lauderhill, Fla. | Ilene Lieberman, D | 1996, Mar. |
| Lawrence, Kan. | *Mike Wildgen | 1990, Apr. |
| Lawrence, Mass. | Kevin Sullivan, N-P | 1993, Nov. |
| Lawton, Okla. | John T. Marley, D | 1995, Mar. |
| Lexington, Ky. | Scotty Baesler, N-P | 1993, Nov. |
| Lima, Oh. | David Berger, N-P | 1993, Nov. |
| Lincoln, Neb. | Mike Johanns, R. | 1995, May |
| Little Rock, Ark. | *Thomas Dalton | 1986, June |
| Livermore, Cal. | *Leland Horner | 1979, Aug. |
| Livonia, Mich. | Robert Bennett, N-P | 1995, Nov. |
| Lodi, Cal. | *Thomas A. Peterson | 1985, Apr. |
| Long Beach, Cal. | *James Hankla | 1987, Mar. |
| Longmont, Col. | *Geoff Dolan | 1987, Jan. |
| Longview, Tex. | *James Baugh | 1989, Oct. |
| Lorain, Oh. | Alex Olejko, D | 1995, Nov. |
| Los Angeles, Cal. | Richard Riordan, N-P | 1997, June |
| Louisville, Ky. | Jerry Abramson, D | 1993, Nov. |
| Lowell, Mass. | *James Campbell | 1987, Jan. |
| Lubbock, Tex. | *Bob Cass | 1992, Sept. |
| Lynchburg, Va. | *Charles Church | 1991, Oct. |
| Lynn, Mass. | Patrick McManus, D. | 1993, Nov. |
| Lynwood, Cal. | *Faustin Gonzales. | 1993, June |
| Macon, Ga. | Tommy Olmstead, D | 1995, Nov. |
| Madison, Wis. | Paul Soglin, D | 1995, Apr. |
| Malden, Mass. | Edwin C. Lucey, D. | 1993, Nov. |
| Manchester, Conn. | *Richard Sartor | 1989, June |
| Manchester, N.H. | Ray Wieczorek, R | 1993, Nov. |
| Mansfield, Oh. | Lydia J. Reid, D | 1995, Nov. |
| Marietta, Ga. | Joe Mack Wilson, D. | 1993, Nov. |
| McAllen, Tex. | Othal Brand, R. | 1997, Apr. |
| Medford, Mass. | Michael McGlynn, D. | 1993, Nov. |
| Medford, Ore. | *Harold Anderson | 1987, Sept. |
| Melbourne, Fla. | *Samuel Halter | 1978, July |
| Memphis, Tenn. | W.W. Herenton, D | 1996, Aug. |

| City | Name | Term |
|---|---|---|
| Mentor, Oh. | *Julian Suso | 1990, Apr. |
| Merced, Cal. | *James Marshall | 1992, Apr. |
| Meriden, Conn. | *Michael Aldi. | 1988, Mar. |
| Meridian, Miss. | John Robert Smith, R. | 1997, June |
| Mesa, Ariz. | *C.K. Luster | 1979, June |
| Mesquite, Tex. | *James Prugel. | 1987, Dec. |
| Miami, Fla. | Xavier Suarez, N-P | 1993, Nov. |
| Miami Beach, Fla. | *Roger Carlton | 1992, Apr. |
| Middletown, Oh. | *Ronald Olson. | 1992, Nov. |
| Midland, Tex. | J.D. Faircloth, R. | 1994, May |
| Midwest City, Okla. | *Charles Johnson | 1984, Nov. |
| Milford, Conn. | Frederick Lisman, R. | 1993, Nov. |
| Milpitas, Cal. | *Lawrence M. Moore | 1993, Feb. |
| Milwaukee, Wis. | John Norquist, D. | 1996, Apr. |
| Minneapolis, Minn. | Donald Fraser, D | 1993, Nov. |
| Minnetonka, Minn. | *James F. Miller. | 1980, Jan. |
| Mobile, Ala. | Michael Dow, R, I | 1997, Aug. |
| Modesto, Cal. | *J. Edward Tewes. | 1991, Mar. |
| Monroe, La. | Robert Powell, D | 1996, Mar. |
| Montclair, N.J. | *Bertrand Kendall | 1980, Sept. |
| Montebello, Cal. | William M. Molinari, D. | 1993, Nov. |
| Monterey Park, Cal. | *Mark Lewis | 1988, July |
| Montgomery, Ala. | Emory Folmar, R. | 1995, Nov. |
| Mt. Prospect, Ill. | *Michael Janonis | 1992, July |
| Mt. Vernon, N.Y. | Roland Blackwood, D. | 1995, Nov. |
| Mountain View, Cal. | *Bruce Liedstrand. | 1976, June |
| Muncie, Ind. | David M. Dominick, R. | 1995, Nov. |
| Muskogee, Okla. | *Walter Beckham | 1984, Feb. |
| Napa, Cal. | Ed Solomon, R. | 1996, June |
| Naperville, Ill. | Samuel MacCrane, N-P | 1995, Apr. |
| Nashua, N.H. | Rob Wagner, D | 1995, Nov. |
| Nashville, Tenn. | Philip Bredesen, D. | 1995, Aug. |
| National City, Cal. | George H. Waters, R | 1994, Nov. |
| New Bedford, Mass. | Rosemary Tierney, D | 1993, Nov. |
| New Britain, Conn. | Donald DeFronzo, D | 1993, Nov. |
| New Haven, Conn. | John Daniels, D | 1993, Nov. |
| New London, Conn. | *C.F. Driscoll. | 1969, May |
| New Orleans, La. | Sidney Barthelemy, D. | 1994, Mar. |
| New Rochelle, N.Y. | *C. Samuel Kissinger | 1975, Apr. |
| New York, N.Y. | David Dinkins, D | 1993, Nov. |
| Newark, N.J. | Sharpe James, D | 1994, May |
| Newport, R.I. | *Francis Edwards | 1987, Jan. |
| Newport Beach, Cal. | *Kevin Murphy | 1992, Mar. |
| Newport News, Va. | *Ed Maroney | 1987, Jan. |
| Newton, Mass. | Theodore Mann, R | 1993, Nov. |
| Niagara Falls, N.Y. | Jacob A. Palillo, R. | 1995, Nov. |
| Norfolk, Va. | *James B. Oliver Jr. | 1987, Jan. |
| Norman, Okla. | Bill Nations, N-P | 1995, Mar. |
| North Charleston, S.C. | Bobby Kinard, R. | 1995, May |
| No. Little Rock, Ark. | Patrick Hayes, D | 1996, Nov. |
| Norwalk, Cal. | *Richard Powers | 1988, July |
| Norwalk, Conn. | Frank Esposito, R. | 1993, Nov. |
| Novato, Cal. | *Rod Wood | 1992, July |
| Oak Park, Ill. | *J.N. Nielsen. | 1986, July |
| Oak Ridge, Tenn. | *Jeffrey J. Broughton. | 1986, Sept. |
| Oakland, Cal. | Elihu M. Harris, N-P | 1994, June |
| Oceanside, Cal. | *James Turner. | 1990, Aug. |
| Odessa, Tex. | *Jerry McGuire | 1992, Mar. |
| Ogden, Ut. | Glenn Mecham, N-P | 1995, Nov. |
| Oklahoma City, Okla. | *Donald D. Brown. | 1991, Feb. |
| Omaha, Neb. | P.J. Morgan, R. | 1997, May |
| Ontario, Cal. | *Roger Hughbanks, N-P | 1975, July |
| Orange, Cal. | *Ron Thompson, | 1989, Apr. |
| Orlando, Fla. | Glenda E. Hood, N-P | 1996, Sept. |
| Oshkosh, Wis. | *William Frueh. | 1976, Aug. |
| Overland Park, Kan. | *Donald Pipes | 1977, June |
| Owensboro, Ky. | *Max Rhoads | 1959, Sept. |
| Oxnard, Cal. | *Vernon Hazen | 1990, Aug. |
| Palm Springs, Cal. | *Dallas Flicek | 1990, Aug. |
| Palo Alto, Cal. | *William Zaner. | 1979, Sept. |
| Parma, Oh. | Michael Ries, D | 1995, Nov. |
| Pasadena, Cal. | *Philip Hawkey | 1990, June |
| Pasadena, Tex. | Johnny Isbell, N-P. | 1997, May |
| Passaic, N.J. | Margie Semler, N-P. | 1997, June |
| Paterson, N.J. | William Pascrell, D | 1994, May |
| Pawtucket, R.I. | Robert Metivier, D. | 1993, Nov. |
| Peabody, Mass. | Peter Torigian, D | 1993, Nov. |
| Pembroke Pines, Fla. | *Charles Dodge | 1989, Aug. |
| Pensacola, Fla. | *Rodney Kendig. | 1986, June |
| Peoria, Ill. | *Thomas Mikulecky | 1987, July |
| Philadelphia, Pa. | Edward Rendell, D | 1995, Nov. |
| Phoenix, Ariz. | *Frank Fairbanks. | 1990, Apr. |
| Pico Rivera, Cal. | *Dennis Courtemarche. | 1984, Nov. |
| Pine Bluff, Ark | Jerry Taylor, I | 1996, Nov. |
| Pittsburgh, Pa. | Sophie Masloff, D | 1993, Nov. |
| Pittsfield, Mass. | Edward Reilly, N-P | 1993, Nov. |
| Plainfield, N.J. | *Jewel Thompson-Chin. | 1990, Sept. |
| Plano, Tex. | *Thomas Muehlenbeck | 1987, Dec. |

| City | Name | Term |
|------|------|------|
| Plantation, Fla. | Frank Veletri, D | 1995, Mar. |
| Plymouth, Mass. | *Dwight Johnson | 1993, Feb. |
| Pocatello, Ida. | Peter Angstadt, N-P | 1993, Nov. |
| Pomona, Cal. | *Lloyd Wood | 1992, Aug. |
| Pompano Beach, Fla. | *Roy Stype | 1989, Oct. |
| Pontiac, Mich. | Wallace Holland, N-P | 1993, Nov. |
| Port Arthur, Tex. | *Mary Ellen Summerlin, D | 1995, May |
| Portland, Me. | *Robert Ganley | 1987, Sept. |
| Portland, Ore. | Vera Katz, D | 1996, Nov. |
| Portsmouth, Va. | *V. Wayne Orton | 1990, June |
| Poughkeepsie, N.Y. | *William J. Theysohn | 1982, Mar. |
| Providence, R.I. | Vincent Cianci Jr., R, I | 1993, Nov. |
| Provo, Ut. | Joseph Jenkins, R | 1993, Nov. |
| Pueblo, Col. | *Lewis A. Quigley | 1987, Jan. |
| Quincy, Ill. | Charles Wischolz, D | 1997, Apr. |
| Quincy, Mass. | James Sheets, D | 1993, Nov. |
| Racine, Wis. | N. Owen Davies, N-P | 1995, Apr. |
| Raleigh, N.C. | *Dempsey Benton. | 1983, Dec. |
| Rapid City, S.D. | Edward McLaughlin, N-P | 1995, Apr. |
| Reading, Pa. | Warren Haggerty Jr., D. | 1995, Nov. |
| Redding, Cal. | *Robert Christofferson | 1987, Jan. |
| Redlands, Cal. | *James Wheaton | 1991, Mar. |
| Redondo Beach, Cal. | *William Kirchhoff | 1991, Feb. |
| Redwood City, Cal. | *James M. Smith | 1982, Feb. |
| Reno, Nev. | *Clay Holstine | 1991, Feb. |
| Rialto, Cal. | *Gerald Johnson | 1988, July |
| Richardson, Tex. | *Bob Hughey | 1974, Jan. |
| Richmond, Cal. | George Livingstone, D | 1993, Nov. |
| Richmond, Va. | *Robert C. Bobb. | 1986, July |
| Riverside, Cal. | Terry Frizzel, R | 1993, Nov. |
| Roanoke, Va. | David Bowers, D | 1996, May |
| Rochester, Minn. | *Steven Kvenvold | 1979, June |
| Rochester, N.Y. | Thomas Ryan Jr., D. | 1993, Nov. |
| Rochester Hills, Mich. | Billie Ireland, R. | 1995, Nov. |
| Rock Hill, S.C. | *J. Russell Allen. | 1993, July |
| Rock Island, Ill. | *John Phillips | 1986, Nov. |
| Rockford, Ill. | Charles Box, D | 1997, Apr. |
| Rockville, Md. | Douglas M. Duncan, D | 1993, Nov. |
| Rome, N.Y. | Joseph Griffo, R | 1995, Nov. |
| Rosemead, Cal. | *Frank G. Tripepi | 1974, Oct. |
| Roseville, Mich. | Jeanne Riesterer, N-P | 1993, Nov. |
| Roswell, N.M. | *John Capps. | 1992, July |
| Royal Oak, Mich. | *William Baldridge. | 1975, Sept. |
| Sacramento, Cal. | *Walter Slipe. | 1976, Mar. |
| Saginaw, Mich. | *J. Marvin Baldwin | 1991, Apr. |
| St. Charles, Mo. | Grace M. Nichols, N-P | 1995, Apr. |
| St. Clair Shores, Mich. | *Mark Wollenweber. | 1990, Jan. |
| St. Cloud, Minn. | Charles Winkleman, N-P | 1993, Nov. |
| St. Joseph, Mo. | Glenda Kelly, N-P | 1994, Mar. |
| St. Louis, Mo. | Freeman R. Bosley Jr., D | 1997, Mar. |
| St. Louis Park, Minn. | *Charles Meyer | 1993, Apr. |
| St. Paul, Minn. | James Scheibel, N-P | 1993, Nov. |
| St. Petersburg, Fla. | *Norman Hickey | 1992, May |
| Salem, Ore. | *Gary Eide | 1988, Jan. |
| Salinas, Cal. | *David R. Mora | 1990, Sept. |
| Salt Lake City, Ut. | Deedee Corradini, D | 1995, Nov. |
| San Angelo, Tex. | *Alex Briseno | 1990, Apr. |
| San Antonio, Tex. | Nelson Wolff, N-P | 1995, Apr. |
| San Bernardino, Cal. | Tom Minor, R | 1997, Mar. |
| San Diego, Cal. | Susan Golding, R | 1996, Nov. |
| San Francisco, Cal. | Frank Jordan, D | 1995, Nov. |
| San Jose, Cal. | *Leslie White. | 1989, May |
| San Leandro, Cal. | *Richard H. Randall. | 1986, July |
| San Mateo, Cal. | *Arne Croce | 1990, Mar. |
| San Rafael, Cal. | *Pamela Nicolai. | 1985, Dec. |
| Sandy, Ut. | *Byron D. Jorgenson | 1986, May |
| Santa Ana, Cal. | *David Ream | 1986, July |
| Santa Barbara, Cal. | *Sandra Lizarraga. | 1993, Aug. |
| Santa Clara, Cal. | *Jennifer Sparacino. | 1987, Mar. |
| Santa Cruz, Cal. | *Richard Wilson | 1981, June |
| Santa Fe, N.M. | *David A. Sena | 1993, Aug. |
| Santa Maria, Cal. | George S. Hobbs, N-P | 1994, Nov. |
| Santa Monica, Cal. | *John Jalili | 1984, Dec. |
| Santa Rosa, Cal. | *Kenneth Blackman. | 1970, July |
| Sarasota, Fla. | *David Sollenberger | 1987, Mar. |
| Savannah, Ga. | *Arthur A. Mendonsa. | 1966, Jan. |
| Schaumburg, Ill. | *George Longmeyer | 1986, Oct. |
| Schenectady, N.Y. | Frank Duci, D | 1995, Nov. |
| Scottsdale, Ariz. | Herbert Drinkwater, R | 1996, Apr. |
| Scranton, Pa. | James Connors, R | 1993, Nov. |
| Seattle, Wash. | Norman Rice, D | 1993, Nov. |
| Sheboygan, Wis. | Richard Schneider, N-P | 1997, Apr. |
| Shreveport, La. | Hazel Beard, R | 1994, Nov. |
| Simi Valley, Cal. | *M.L. Koester | 1979, Sept. |
| Sioux City, Ia. | James R. Wharton, R. | 1993, Nov. |
| Sioux Falls, S.D. | Jack White, R | 1996, June |
| Skokie, Ill. | *Albert Rigoni | 1987, Jan. |
| Somerville, Mass. | Michael Capuano, D | 1993, Nov. |
| South Bend, Ind. | Joseph Kernan, D | 1995, Nov. |
| South Gate, Cal. | Mary Ann Buckles, R | 1994, Apr. |
| Southfield, Mich. | Donald F. Fracassi, R. | 1993, Nov. |
| Sparks, Nev. | *Patricia Thompson | 1983, Sept. |
| Spartanburg, S.C. | *Wayne Bowers | 1984, Sept. |
| Spokane, Wash. | *Roger Crum | 1992, Aug. |
| Springfield, Ill. | Ossie Langfelder, D | 1995, Apr. |
| Springfield, Mass | Robert Markel, D | 1993, Nov. |
| Springfield, Mo. | *Thomas Finnie | 1990, Apr. |
| Springfield, Oh. | *Matthew Kridler | 1988, Oct. |
| Stamford, Conn. | Stanley Esposito, R | 1993, Nov. |
| Sterling Hts., Mich. | *Steve Duchane | 1987, Dec. |
| Stockton, Cal. | *Dwane Milnes | 1991, Oct. |
| Stratford, Conn. | *Mark S. Barnhart. | 1992, July |
| Sunnyvaie, Cal. | *Thomas Lewcock | 1980, Apr. |
| Suffolk, Va. | *Richard Hedrick | 1991, July |
| Sunrise, Fla. | *Patrick Salerno. | 1990, Dec. |
| Syracuse, N.Y. | Thomas G. Young, D | 1993, Nov. |
| Tacoma, Wash. | *Ray Corpuz Jr. | 1990, Jan. |
| Tallahassee, Fla. | *Daniel A. Kleman. | 1974, Aug. |
| Tampa, Fla. | Sandra Freedman, N-P | 1995, Mar. |
| Taunton, Mass. | Robert Nunes, D | 1993, Nov. |
| Taylor, Mich. | Cameron Priebe, D | 1993, Nov. |
| Tempe, Ariz. | Harry E. Mitchell, D | 1994, Mar. |
| Temple, Tex. | *David Taylor | 1991, Dec. |
| Terre Haute, Ind. | P. Pete Chalos, D | 1995, Nov. |
| Thornton, Col. | *Jack Ethredge | 1985, Jan. |
| Thousand Oaks, Cal. | *Grant Brimhall | 1978, Jan. |
| Titusville, Fla. | *Norman Hickey. | 1974, June |
| Toledo, Oh. | *Thomas Hoover | 1990, Sept. |
| Topeka, Kan. | Butch Felker, R | 1997, Apr. |
| Torrance, Cal. | *Leroy J. Jackson. | 1983, Jan. |
| Trenton, N.J. | Douglas Palmer, N-P | 1994, May |
| Troy, Mich. | *Frank Gerstenecker | 1970, Feb |
| Troy, N.Y. | *Steven Dworsky | 1986, July |
| Tucson, Ariz. | George Miller, D. | 1995, Nov. |
| Tulsa, Okla. | M. Susan Savage, D | 1994, Mar. |
| Tuscaloosa, Ala. | Alvin DuPont, D | 1993, Oct. |
| Tyler, Tex. | *Ernest R. Clark. | 1991, Oct. |
| Union City, N.J. | Robert Menendez, D | 1994, May |
| Upland, Cal. | *Ray Silver | 1988, Dec. |
| Utica, N.Y. | Louis La Polla, R | 1995, Nov. |
| Vacaville, Cal. | *John P. Thompson. | 1984, Oct. |
| Vallejo, Cal. | *Edward Wohlenberg. | 1989, Apr. |
| Vancouver, Wash. | *John Fischbach. | 1990, Aug. |
| Ventura, Cal. | *John Baker | 1986, Nov. |
| Vineland, N.J. | Joseph Romano, I. | 1996, May |
| Virginia Beach, Va. | *James Spore. | 1991, Nov. |
| Visalia, Cal. | *Raymond W. Forsyth | 1992, Feb. |
| Vista, Cal. | Gloria McClellan, R | 1994, Nov. |
| Waco, Tex. | *John Harrison | 1977, Sept. |
| Walnut Creek, Cal. | *Donald Blubaugh. | 1988, Apr. |
| Waltham, Mass. | William Stanley, D. | 1995, Nov. |
| Warren, Mich. | Ronald Bonkowski, N-P | 1995, Nov. |
| Warren, Oh. | Daniel Sferra, D | 1995, Nov. |
| Warwick, R.I. | Lincoln D. Chafee, R | 1994, Nov. |
| Washington, D.C. | Sharon Dixon, D | 1994, Nov. |
| Waterbury, Conn. | Edward D. Bergin, D | 1993, Nov. |
| Waterloo, Ia. | Albert Manning Jr., R | 1993, Nov. |
| Waukegan, Ill. | William F. Durkin, D | 1997, Apr. |
| Waukesha, Wis. | Paul Vrakas, N-P | 1994, Apr. |
| Wauwatosa, Wis. | Maricolette Walsh, N-P | 1994, Apr. |
| W. Allis, Wis. | Joyce Ann Radtke, N-P | 1996, Apr. |
| W. Covina, Cal. | *Herman Fast | 1976, Aug. |
| W. Hartford, Conn. | Sandy Klebanoff, D | 1993, Nov. |
| W. Haven, Conn. | H. Richard Borer, D | 1993, Nov. |
| W. Palm Beach, Fla. | Nancy M. Graham, N-P | 1995, Mar. |
| Westland, Mich. | Robert Thomas, D. | 1993, Nov. |
| Westminster, Cal. | *Jerry Kenny. | 1989, Jan. |
| Westminster, Col. | Nancy Heil, N-P | 1993, Nov. |
| Wheaton, Ill. | C. James Carr, N-P | 1995, Apr. |
| White Plains, N.Y. | Alfred Del Vecchio, R | 1993, Nov. |
| Whittier, Cal. | *Thomas Mauk | 1980, Oct. |
| Wichita, Kan. | *Chris Cherches. | 1985, Oct. |
| Wichita Falls, Tex. | *James Berzina | 1983, June |
| Wilkes-Barre, Pa. | Lee Namey, D. | 1995, May |
| Wilmington, Del. | Jim Sills, D. | 1996, Nov. |
| Wilmington, N.C. | Mary M. Gornto | 1993, July |
| Winston-Salem, N.C. | *Bryce A. Stuart. | 1980, Nov. |
| Woodbridge, N.J. | James McGreevey, D. | 1995, Nov. |
| Woonsocket, R.I. | Francis Lanctot, N-P | 1993, Nov. |
| Worcester, Mass. | *William Mulford. | 1985, Nov. |
| Wyandotte, Mich. | James R. DeSana, D. | 1995, Apr. |
| Wyoming, Mich. | *Donald Mason | 1991, Aug. |
| Yakima, Wash. | Pat Berndt, N-P | 1993, Nov. |
| Yonkers, N.Y. | Terence Zaleski, D | 1995, Nov. |
| York, Pa. | William Althaus, R. | 1993, Nov. |
| Youngstown, Oh. | Patrick Ungaro, D | 1993, Nov. |
| Yuma, Ariz. | Robert Tippert, R | 1993, Dec. |

# STATES AND OTHER AREAS OF THE U.S.

**Sources:** Population: Commerce Dept., Bureau of the Census (July, 1992 est., inc. armed forces personnel in each state but excluding such personnel stationed overseas); area: Bureau of the Census, Geography Division; forested land: Agriculture Dept., Forest Service; lumber production: Bureau of the Census, Industry Division; mineral production: Interior Dept., Bureau of Mines; commercial fishing: Commerce Dept., Natl. Marine Fisheries Service; value of construction: McGraw-Hill Information Systems Co., F.W. Dodge Division; per capita income: Commerce Dept., Bureau of Economic Analysis; unemployment: Labor Dept., Bureau of Labor Statistics; finance: Federal Deposit Insurance Corp.; federal employees: Labor Dept., Office of Personnel Management; energy: Energy Dept., Energy Information Administration; education: Education Dept., National Education Assn. Other information from sources in individual states, usually Commerce Dept.

## Alabama

### Heart of Dixie, Camellia State

**People. Population** (1992): 4,135,543; **rank:** 22. **Pop. density:** 81.5 per sq. mi. **Racial distrib.** (1990): 73.6% White; 25.3% Black; 0.6% Hispanic. **Net change** (1990-92): 2.4%.

**Geography. Total area:** 51,705 sq. mi.; **rank:** 29. **Land area:** 50,750 sq. mi. **Acres forested land:** 21,725,000. **Location:** East South Central state extending N-S from Tenn. to the Gulf of Mexico; east of the Mississippi River. **Climate:** long, hot summers; mild winters; generally abundant rainfall. **Topography:** coastal plains inc. Prairie Black Belt give way to hills, broken terrain; highest elevation, 2,407 ft. **Capital:** Montgomery.

**Economy. Principal industries:** pulp and paper, chemicals, electronics, apparel, textiles, primary metals, lumber and wood prods., food processing, fabricated metals, automotive tires, oil and gas exploration. **Principal manufactured goods** (1991-1992): electronics, cast iron and plastic pipe, fabricated steel prods., ships, paper products, chemicals, steel, mobile homes, fabrics, poultry processing, soft drinks, furniture, tires. **Agriculture: Chief crops** (1991-92): peanuts, cotton, soybeans, cottonseed, catfish, hay, corn, wheat, potatoes, pecans, peaches, sweet potatoes. **Livestock** (1990): 1.8 mln. cattle; 400,000 hogs/pigs; 14.8 mln. poultry, 2.7 mln. foodsize catfish. **Timber/lumber** (1991): pine, hardwoods; 1.94 bln. bd. ft. **Nonfuel Minerals** (1992): $603.7 mln., mostly stone, cement, clays, lime, sand & gravel. **Commercial fishing** (1992): $35.6 mln. **Chief ports:** Mobile. **Value of construction** (1992): $3.2 bln. **Employment distribution** (1991): 20% mfg.; 35% trade; 16% serv. **Per capita income** (1992): $16,220. **Unemployment** (1992): 7.3%. **Tourism** (1991): tourists spent $3.4 bln. **Sales Tax** (1991): 4%.

**Finance. FDIC-insured commercial banks & trust companies** (1992): 219. **Deposits:** $33.6 bln. **Savings institutions** (1992): 25. **Assets:** $4.9 bln.

**Federal government. No. federal civilian employees** (Mar. 1992): 46,134. **Avg. salary:** $34,556. **Notable federal facilities:** George C. Marshall NASA Space Center, Huntsville; Gunter & Maxwell AFB, Montgomery; Ft. Rucker, Ozark; Ft. McClellan, Anniston; Natl. Fertilizer Development Center, Muscle Shoals; Navy Station & U.S. Corps of Engineers, Mobile; Redstone Arsenal, Huntsville.

**Energy. Electricity production** (1992, MWh, by source): Hydroelectric: 12.2 mln. Mineral: 44.7 mln. Nuclear: 19.7 mln.

**Education. Student-teacher ratio** (1991): 17.8. **Avg. salary, public school teachers** (1992-93): $27,490.

**State data. Motto:** We dare defend our rights. **Flower:** Camellia. **Bird:** Yellowhammer. **Tree:** Southern pine. **Song:** Alabama. **Entered union** Dec. 14, 1819; **rank,** 22d. **State fair at:** Birmingham; early Oct.

**History.** First Europeans were Spanish explorers in the early 1500s. The French made the first permanent settlement, on Mobile Bay, 1701-02; later, English settled in the northern areas. France ceded the entire region to England at the end of the French and Indian War, 1763, but Spanish Florida claimed the Mobile Bay area until U. S. troops took it, 1813. Gen. Andrew Jackson broke the power of the Creek Indians, 1814, and they were removed to Oklahoma. The Confederate States were organized Feb. 4, 1861, at Montgomery, the first capital.

**Tourist attractions.** Jefferson Davis' "first White House" of the Confederacy; Montgomery's Civil Rights Memorial; Ivy Green, Helen Keller's birthplace, Tuscumbia; statue of Vulcan, Birmingham; George Washington Carver Museum, Tuskegee Univ.; W.C. Handy Home & Museum, Florence; Alabama Space and Rocket Center, Huntsville; Alabama Shakespeare Festival, Montgomery; Moundville State Monument, Moundville; Pike Pioneer Museum, Troy; USS Alabama Memorial Park, Mobile; 28 hunting areas, 24 public lakes, 82 campgrounds, 21 state parks.

At Russell Cave National Monument, near Bridgeport: a detailed record of occupancy by humans from about 10,000 BC to 1650 AD.

**Famous Alabamians** include Hank Aaron, Tallulah Bankhead, Hugo L. Black, Paul "Bear" Bryant, George Washington Carver, Nat King Cole, William C. Handy, Bo Jackson, Helen Keller, Harper Lee, Joe Louis, Willie Mays, John Hunt Morgan, Jesse Owens, George Wallace, Booker T. Washington, Hank Williams.

**Alabama Business Council** (State Chamber of Commerce). 468 S. Perry St., P.O. Box 76, Montgomery, AL 36195.

**Toll-free travel information.** 1-800-392-8096; 1-800-ALABAMA out of state.

## Alaska

### The Last Frontier  (unofficial)

**People. Population** (1992): 586,872; **rank:** 48. **Racial distrib.** (1990): 75.5% White; 4.1% Black; 3.2% Hispanic; 15.6% Amer. Ind., Eskimo or Aleut; 3.6% Asian or Pacific Is. **Pop. density:** 1.03 per sq. mi. **Net change** (1990-92): 6.7%.

**Geography. Total area:** 591,000 sq. mi.; **rank:** 1. **Land area:** 570,373 sq. mi. **Acres forested land:** 129,045,000. **Location:** NW corner of North America, bordered on east by Canada. **Climate:** SE, SW, and central regions, moist and mild; far north extremely dry. Extended summer days, winter nights, throughout. **Topography:** includes Pacific and Arctic mountain systems, central plateau, and Arctic slope. Mt. McKinley, 20,320 ft., is the highest point in North America. **Capital:** Juneau.

**Economy. Principal industries:** oil, gas, tourism, commercial fishing, mining, forestry. **Principal manufactured goods:** fish products, lumber and pulp, furs. **Agriculture** (1991): Chief crops: barley, hay, greenhouse nursery prods., potatoes, lettuce, milk. **Livestock** (1990): 7,500 cattle; 2,500 sheep; 5,000 poultry; 37,000 reindeer. **Timber/lumber:** spruce, yellow cedar, hemlock. **Nonfuel minerals** (1992): $530.9 mln.; crushed and broken stone, gold, sand & gravel. **Commercial fishing** (1992): $1.6 bln. **Chief ports:** Anchorage, Dutch Harbor, Kodiak, Seward, Skagway, Juneau, Sitka, Valdez, Wrangell. **International airports at:** Anchorage, Fairbanks, Ketchikan, Juneau. **Value of construction** (1992): $905.3 mln. **Employment distribution** (1991): 29.7% gvt.; 21.3% serv.; 19.6% trade. **Per capita income** (1992): $21,603. **Unemployment** (1992): 9.1%. **Tourism** (1987-88): $500 mln.

**Finance. FDIC-insured commercial banks & trust companies** (1992): 8. **Deposits:** $3.5 bln. **Commercial bank deposits, per capita** (1990): $7,475. **Savings institutions** (1992): 1. **Assets:** $100 mln.

**Federal government. No. federal civilian employees** (Mar. 1992): 12,252. **Avg. salary:** $37,776.

**Energy. Electricity production** (1992, MWh, by source): Hydroelectric: 0.9 mln. Mineral: 91 mln.

**Education. Student-teacher ratio** (1991): 16.7. **Avg. salary, public school teachers** (1992-93): $46,373.

**State data. Motto:** North to the future. **Flower:** Forget-Me-Not. **Bird:** Willow ptarmigan. **Tree:** Sitka spruce. **Song:** Alaska's Flag. **Entered union** Jan. 3, 1959; rank, 49th. **State fair** at: Palmer; late Aug.–early Sept.

**History.** Vitus Bering, a Danish explorer working for Russia, was the first European to land in Alaska, 1741. Alexander Baranov, first governor of Russian America, set up headquarters at Archangel, near present Sitka, in 1799. Secretary of State William H. Seward in 1867 bought Alaska from Russia for $7.2 million, a bargain some called "Seward's Folly." In 1896 gold was discovered and the famed Gold Rush was on.

**Tourist attractions:** Portage Glacier, Mendenhall Glacier, Glacier Bay National Park, Katmai National Park & Preserve, Denali National Park, one of North America's great wildlife sanctuaries, surrounding Mt. McKinley, No. America's highest peak. Pribilof Islands fur seal rookeries, restored St. Michael's Russian Orthodox Cathedral, Sitka.

**Famous Alaskans** include Tom Bodett, Susan Butcher, Ernest Gruening, Sydney Laurence, Libby Riddles, Jefferson "Soapy" Smith.

**Tourist information.** Alaska Division of Tourism, P.O. Box 110801, Juneau, AK 99811-0801.

# Arizona

## Grand Canyon State

**People. Population** (1992): 3,832,294; **rank:** 23. **Pop. density:** 33.7 per sq. mi. **Racial distrib.** (1990): 80.8% White; 3.0% Black; 5.6% American Indian; 18.8% Hispanic. **Net change** (1990-92): 4.6%.

**Geography. Total area:** 114,000 sq. mi.; **rank:** 6. **Land area:** 113,642 sq. mi. **Acres forested land:** 19,384,000. **Location:** in the southwestern U.S. **Climate:** clear and dry in the southern regions and northern plateau; high central areas have heavy winter snows. **Topography:** Colorado plateau in the N, containing the Grand Canyon; Mexican Highlands running diagonally NW to SE; Sonoran Desert in the SW. **Capital:** Phoenix.

**Economy. Principal industries:** manufacturing, tourism, mining, agriculture. **Principal manufactured goods:** electronics, printing and publishing, foods, primary and fabricated metals, aircraft and missiles, apparel. **Agriculture: Chief crops:** cotton, lettuce, cauliflower, broccoli, sorghum, barley, corn, wheat, sugar beets, citrus fruits. **Livestock** (1992): 900,000 cattle; 100,000 hogs/pigs; 225,000 sheep; 325,000 poultry. **Timber/lumber** (1991): pine, fir, spruce; 325 mln. bd. ft. **Nonfuel Minerals** (1992): $3.1 bln.; copper, gold, molybdenum, silver. **International airports at:** Phoenix, Tucson, Yuma. **Value of construction** (1992): $5.4 bln. **Employment distribution** (1992): 27.9% services; 24.7% trade; 18.3% gvt.; 11.3% mfg. **Per capita income** (1992): $17,119. **Unemployment** (1992): 7.4%. **Tourism** (1992): tourists spent $7.2 bln. **Sales tax:** 5.0% (Maricopa, Pinal Countries, 5.5%).

**Finance. FDIC-insured commercial banks & trust companies** (1992): 41. **Deposits:** $30.4 bln. **Savings institutions** (1992): 2. **Assets:** $200 mln.

**Federal government: No. federal civilian employees** (Mar. 1992): 29,607. **Avg. salary:** $32,167. **Notable federal facilities:** Williams, Luke, Davis-Monthan AF bases; Ft. Huachuca Army Base; Yuma Proving Grounds.

**Energy. Electricity production** (1992, MWh, by source): Hydroelectric: 5.3 mln.; Mineral: 29.8; Nuclear: 18.1.

**Education. Student-teacher ratio** (1991): 19.3. **Avg. salary, public school teachers** (1992-93): $32,403.

**State data. Motto:** Ditat Deus (God enriches). **Flower:** Blossom of the Saguaro cactus. **Bird:** Cactus wren. **Tree:** Paloverde. **Song:** Arizona. **Entered union** Feb. 14, 1912; rank, 48th. **State fair** at: Phoenix; late Oct.–early Nov.

**History.** Marcos de Niza, a Franciscan, and Estevan, a black slave, explored the area, 1539. Eusebio Francisco Kino, Jesuit missionary, taught Indians Christianity and farming, 1690-1711, left a chain of missions. Spain ceded Arizona to Mexico, 1821. The U. S. took over at the end of the Mexican War, 1848. The area below the Gila River was obtained from Mexico in the Gadsden Purchase,

1854. Long Apache wars did not end until 1886, with Geronimo's surrender.

**Tourist attractions.** The Grand Canyon of the Colorado, an immense, vari-colored fissure 217 mi. long, 4 to 13 mi. wide at the brim, 4,000 to 5,500 ft. deep; the Painted Desert, extending for 30 mi. along U.S. 66; the Petrified Forest; Canyon Diablo, 225 ft. deep and 500 ft. wide; Meteor Crater, 4,150 ft. across, 570 ft. deep, made by a prehistoric meteor. Also, London Bridge at Lake Havasu City.

**Famous Arizonans** include Bruce Babbitt, Cochise, Geronimo, Barry Goldwater, Zane Grey, Carl Hayden, George W. P. Hunt, Helen Jacobs, Percival Lowell, Sandra Day O'Connor, William H. Pickering, John J. Rhodes, Morris Udall, Stewart Udall, Frank Lloyd Wright.

**Tourist information.** Phoenix & Valley of the Sun Visitor and Convention Bureau, 1-602-254-6500.

# Arkansas

## Land of Opportunity

**People. Population** (1992): 2,398,767; **rank:** 33. **Pop. density:** 46.1 per sq. mi. **Racial distrib.** (1990): 82.7% White; 15.9% Black; 0.8% Hispanic. **Net change** (1990-92): 2.0%.

**Geography. Total area:** 53,187 sq. mi.; **rank:** 27. **Land area:** 52,075 sq. mi. **Acres forested land:** 16,987,000. **Location:** in the west south-central U.S. **Climate:** long, hot summers, mild winters; generally abundant rainfall. **Topography:** eastern delta and prairie, southern lowland forests, and the northwestern highlands, which include the Ozark Plateaus. **Capital:** Little Rock.

**Economy. Principal industries:** manufacturing, agriculture, tourism, forestry. **Principal manufactured goods:** food prods., chemicals, lumber, paper, electric motors, furniture, home appliances, auto components, airplane parts, apparel, machinery, petroleum prods., steel. **Agriculture: Chief crops:** soybeans, rice, cotton, tomatoes, grapes, apples, commercial vegetables, peaches, wheat. **Livestock** (1991): 1.71 mln. cattle; 760,000 hogs/pigs; 980 mln. poultry. **Timber/lumber** (1991): oak, hickory, gum, cypress, pine; 1.7 bln. bd. ft. **Nonfuel Minerals** (1992): 287.0 mln.; bromine, abrasives, bauxite, sand & gravel. **Chief ports:** Little Rock, Pine Bluff, Osceola, Helena, Fort Smith, Van Buren, Camden, Dardanelle, North Little Rock, West Memphis, Crossett, McGehee. **Value of construction** (1992): $2.0 bln. **Employment distribution** (1992): 21.2% mfg.; 19.1% trade; 18.8% serv.; 15.0% gvt. **Per capita income** (1992): $15,439. **Unemployment** (1992): 7.2%. **Tourism** (1992): travelers spent $2.7 bln.

**Finance. FDIC-insured commercial banks & trust companies** (1992): 262. **Deposits:** $20.9 bln. **Savings institutions** (1992): 18. **Assets:** $2.8 bln.

**Federal government. No. federal civilian employees** (Mar. 1992): 12,669. **Avg. salary:** $30,448. **Notable federal facilities:** Nat'l. Center for Toxicological Research, Jefferson; Pine Bluff Arsenal, Little Rock AFB.

**Energy. Electricity production** (1992, MWh, by source): Hydroelectric: 3.5 mln.; Mineral: 16.9 mln.; Nuclear: 12.9 mln.

**Education. Student-teacher ratio** (1991): 17.0. **Avg. salary, public school teachers** (1992-93): $27,598.

**State data. Motto:** Regnat Populus (The people rule). **Flower:** Apple blossom. **Bird:** Mockingbird. **Tree:** Pine. **Song:** Arkansas. **Entered union** June 15, 1836; rank, 25th. **State fair** at: Little Rock; late Sept. –early Oct.

**History.** First European explorers were de Soto, 1541, Jolliet, 1673; La Salle, 1682. First settlement was by the French under Henri de Tonty, 1686, at Arkansas Post. In 1762 the area was ceded by France to Spain, then back again in 1800, and was part of the Louisiana Purchase by the U.S. in 1803. Arkansas seceded from the Union in 1861, only after the Civil War began, and more than 10,000 Arkansans fought on the Union side.

**Tourist attractions.** 5 natl. parks & 47 state parks, inc. Hot Springs National Park, water ranging from 95° to 147°F. Eureka Springs, resort since 1879; Blanchard Caverns, near Mountain View, are among the nation's largest;

Crater of Diamonds, near Murfreesboro, only U.S. diamond mine; Buffalo Natl. River; Mid-America Museum, Ozark Folk Center.

**Famous Arkansans** include Daisy Bates, Dee Brown, Glen Campbell, Johnny Cash, Hattie Caraway, President Bill Clinton, "Dizzy" Dean, Orval Faubus, James W. Fulbright, Douglas MacArthur, John L. McClellan, James S. McDonnel, Dick Powell, Winthrop Rockefeller, Mary Steenburgen, Edward Durell Stone, Archibald Yell.

**Chamber of Commerce.** One Spring Bldg., Little Rock, AR 72201-2486.

**Toll-free travel information.** 1-800-NATURAL.

# California

## Golden State

**People. Population** (1992): 30,866,851; **rank: 1. Pop. density:** 197.9 per sq. mi. **Racial distrib.** (1990): 69.0% White; 7.4% Black; 9.6% Asian; 25.8% Hispanic. **Net change** (1990-92): 3.7%.

**Geography. Total area** 158,706 sq. mi.; **rank: 3. Land area:** 155,973 sq. mi. **Acres forested land:** 39,381,000. **Location:** on western coast of the U.S. **Climate:** moderate temperatures and rainfall along the coast; extremes in the interior. **Topography:** long mountainous coastline; central valley; Sierra Nevada on the east; desert basins of the southern interior; rugged mountains of the north. **Capital:** Sacramento.

**Economy. Principal industries:** agriculture, manufacturing, services, trade. **Principal manufactured goods:** foods, printed material, primary and fabricated metals, machinery, electric and electronic equipment, transportation equipment, instruments. **Agriculture: Chief crops:** grapes, cotton, flowers, oranges, nursery products, hay, tomatoes, lettuce, strawberries, almonds, broccoli, walnuts, sugar beets, peaches, potatoes. **Livestock** (1992): 8.17 mln. cattle & calves; 250,000 hogs/pigs; 945,000 sheep and lambs; 27.6 mln. chickens exc. broilers. **Timber/lumber** (1991): fir, pine, redwood, oak; 4.1 bln. bd. ft. **Nonfuel Minerals:** (1992): $2.5 bln.; mostly asbestos, boron minerals, cement, diatomite, calcined gypsum, construction sand & gravel. **Commercial fishing** (1992): $136.3 mln. **Chief ports:** Long Beach, Los Angeles, San Diego, Oakland, San Francisco, Sacramento, Stockton. **International airports at:** Los Angeles, San Francisco, San Jose, San Diego. **Value of construction** (1992): $27.2 bln. **Employment distribution** (1992): 28.2% serv.; 23.3% trade; 15.6% mfg.; 17.2% gvt. **Per capita income** (1992): $21,278. **Unemployment** (1992): 7.1%. **Tourism** (1991): $48.5 bln. **Sales tax:** 7¼-8¾%.

**Finance. FDIC-insured commercial banks & trust companies** (1992): 480. **Deposits:** $287.1 bln. **Savings institutions** (1992): 104. **Assets:** $272.5 bln.

**Federal government. No. federal civilian employees** (Mar. 1992): 205,672. **Avg. salary:** $35,826. **Notable federal facilities:** Vandenberg, Beale, Travis, McClellan AF bases, San Francisco Mint.

**Energy. Electricity production** (1992, MWh, by source): Hydroelectric: 11.0 mln.; Mineral: 13.0 mln.; Nuclear: 32.8 mln.

**Education. Student-teacher ratio** (1991): 22.8. **Avg. salary, public school teachers** (1992-93): $41,400.

**State Data. Motto:** Eureka (I have found it). **Flower:** Golden poppy. **Bird:** California valley quail. **Tree:** California redwood. **Song:** I Love You, California. **Entered Union** Sept. 9, 1850; rank, 31st. **State fair** at: Sacramento; late Aug.—early Sept.

**History.** First European explorers were Cabrillo, 1542, and Drake, 1579. First settlement was the Spanish Alta California mission at San Diego, 1769, first in a string founded by Franciscan Father Junipero Serra. U. S. traders and settlers arrived in the 19th century and staged the abortive Bear Flag Revolt, 1846; the Mexican War began later in 1846 and U.S. forces occupied California; Mexico ceded the province to the U.S., 1848, the same year the Gold Rush began.

**Tourist attractions.** Scenic regions are Yosemite Valley; Lassen and Sequoia-Kings Canyon national parks;

Lake Tahoe; the Mojave and Colorado deserts; San Francisco Bay; Napa Valley; and Monterey Peninsula. Oldest living things on earth are believed to be a stand of Bristlecone pines in the Inyo National Forest, est. to be 4,600 years old. The world's tallest tree, the Howard Libbey redwood, 362 ft. with a girth of 44 ft., stands on Redwood Creek, Humboldt County.

Also, RMS Queen Mary, Spruce Goose, both Long Beach; Palomar Observatory; Disneyland; J. Paul Getty Museum, Malibu; Tournament of Roses and Rose Bowl; Universal Studios, Hollywood; Los Angeles County Art Museum; San Diego Zoo.

**Famous Californians** include Luther Burbank, John C. Fremont, Bret Harte, Wm. R. Hearst, Jack London, Aimee Semple McPherson, John Muir, Richard M. Nixon, William Saroyan, Junipero Serra, Leland Stanford, John Steinbeck, Earl Warren.

**Chamber of Commerce:** 1201 K St., Sacramento, CA 95814.

**Toll-free travel information.** 1-800-862-2543, x T100.

# Colorado

## Centennial State

**People. Population** (1992): 3,470,216; **rank: 26. Pop. density:** 33.5 per sq. mi. **Racial distrib.** (1990): 88.2% White; 4.0% Black; 12.9% Hispanic. **Net change** (1990-92): 5.3%.

**Geography. Total area:** 104,091 sq. mi.; **rank: 8. Land area:** 103,730 sq. mi. **Acres forested land:** 21,338,000. **Location:** in west central U.S. **Climate:** low relative humidity, abundant sunshine, wide daily, seasonal temperatures ranges; alpine conditions in the high mountains. **Topography:** eastern dry high plains; hilly to mountainous central plateau; western Rocky Mountains of high ranges alternating with broad valleys and deep, narrow canyons. **Capital:** Denver.

**Economy. Principal industries:** manufacturing, government, tourism, agriculture, aerospace, electronics equipment. **Principal manufactured goods:** computer equipment, instruments, foods, machinery, aerospace products. **Agriculture: Chief crops:** corn, wheat, hay, sugar beets, barley, potatoes, apples, peaches, pears, dry edible beans, sorghum, onions, oats. **Livestock** (1989): 2.8 mln. cattle; 220,000 hogs/pigs; 825,000 sheep; 4.0 mln. poultry. **Timber/lumber** (1991): oak, ponderosa pine, Douglas fir; 114 mln. bd. ft. **Nonfuel Minerals** (1992): $388.5 mln.; gold, construction sand & gravel, crushed stone. **International airports at:** Denver. **Value of construction** (1992): $5.8 bln. **Employment distribution** (1987 est.): 26.7% serv.; 20.8% trade; 17.0% gvt.; 10.0% mfg. **Per capita income** (1992): $20,124. **Unemployment** (1992): 5.9%. **Tourism** (1989): $5.6 bln. **Sales Tax:** 3%.

**Finance. FDIC-insured commercial banks & trust companies** (1992): 387. **Deposits:** $24.4 bln. **Savings Institutions** (1992): 19. **Assets:** $4.6 bln.

**Federal government. No. federal civilian employees** (Mar. 1992): 39,588. **Avg. salary:** $35,306. **Notable federal facilities:** U.S. Air Force Academy; U.S. Mint; Ft. Carson, Lowry AFB; Solar Energy Research Institute; U.S. Rail Transport. Test Center; N. Amer. Aerospace Defense Command; Consolidated Space Operations Center; U.S. Documents Center, Fitzsimons Army Medical Center, Federal Center.

**Energy. Electricity production** (1992, MWh, by source): Hydroelectric: 1.37 mln.; Mineral: 28.2 mln.

**Education. Student-teacher ratio** (1991): 17.9. **Avg. salary, public school teachers** (1992-93): $33,541.

**State data. Motto:** Nil Sine Numine (Nothing without Providence). **Flower:** Rocky Mountain columbine. **Bird:** Lark bunting. **Tree:** Colorado blue spruce. **Song:** Where the Columbines Grow. **Entered union** Aug. 1, 1876; rank 38th. **State fair** at: Pueblo; last week in Aug.

**History.** Early civilization centered around Mesa Verde 2,000 years ago. The U.S. acquired eastern Colorado in the Louisiana Purchase, 1803; Lt. Zebulon M. Pike explored the area, 1806, discovering the peak that bears his name. After the Mexican War, 1846-48, U.S. immigrants settled in the east, former Mexicans in the south.

**Tourist attractions.** 310 or more sunshine days per year; more than 1,000 peaks of 2 or more miles; Rocky Mountain National Park; Garden of the Gods; Great Sand Dunes, Dinosaur, Black Canyon of the Gunnison, and Colorado national monuments; Pikes Peak and Mt. Evans highways; Mesa Verde National Park (Ancient Anasazi Indian cliff dwellings); 35 major ski areas; the Grand Mesa tableland comprises Grand Mesa Forest, 659,584 acres, with 200 lakes stocked with trout. Mining towns of Central City, Silverton, Cripple Creek; Burlington's Old Town; Bent's Fort, outside La Junta; Georgetown Loop Historic Mining Railroad Park, Cumbres & Toltec Scenic Railroad.

**Famous Coloradans** include Frederick Bonfils, Molly Brown, William N. Byers, M. Scott Carpenter, Jack Dempsey, Mamie Eisenhower, Douglas Fairbanks, Scott Hamilton, "Baby Doe" Tabor, Lowell Thomas, Byron R. White, Paul Whiteman.

**Toll-free travel information.** 1-800-433-2656.

# Connecticut

*Constitution State, Nutmeg State*

**People. Population** (1992): 3,280,959; **rank:** 27. **Pop. density:** 677.2 per sq. mi. **Racial distrib.** (1990): 87.0% White; 8.3% Black; 6.5% Hispanic. **Net change** (1990-92): 0.2%.

**Geography. Total area:** 5,018 sq. mi.; **rank:** 48. **Land area:** 4,845 sq. mi. **Acres forested land:** 1,815,800. **Location:** New England state in the northeastern corner of the U.S. **Climate:** moderate; winters avg. slightly below freezing, warm, humid summers. **Topography:** western upland, the Berkshires, in the NW, highest elevations; narrow central lowland N-S; hilly eastern upland drained by rivers. **Capital:** Hartford.

**Economy. Principal industries:** manufacturing, retail trade, government, services, finances, insurance, real estate. **Principal manufactured goods:** aircraft engines and parts, submarines, helicopters, instruments, machinery & computer equipment, electronics & electrical equipment, medical instruments, pharmaceuticals. **Agriculture: Chief crops:** nursery stock, Christmas trees, mushrooms, vegetables, sweet corn, tobacco, apples. **Livestock** (1989): 73,000 cattle; 50,000 horses; 6,800 hogs/pigs; 8,400 sheep; 5.6 mln. poultry. **Timber/lumber** (1991): oak, birch, beech, maple; 46 mln. bd. ft. **Nonfuel Minerals** (1992): $94.9 mln.; crushed stone; construction sand & gravel. **Commercial fishing** (1992): $62.7 mln. **Chief ports:** New Haven, Bridgeport, New London. **International airports at:** Windsor Locks. **Value of construction** (1992): $2.9 bln. **Employment distribution** (1992): 19.3% mfg.; 28.3% serv. **Per capita income** (1992): $26,979. **Unemployment** (1992): 7.5%. **Tourism** (1991): out-of-state visitors spent $3.7 bln. **Sales tax:** 6.0%.

**Finance. FDIC-insured commercial banks & trust companies** (1992): 56. **Deposits:** $28.2 bln. **Savings institutions** (1992): 17. **Assets:** $8.6 bln.

**Federal Government. No. federal civilian employees** (Mar. 1992): 10,049. **Avg. salary:** $36,735. **Notable federal facilities:** U.S. Coast Guard Academy; U.S. Navy Submarine Base.

**Energy. Electricity production** (1992, MWh, by source): Hydroelectric: 0.3 mln.; Mineral: 1.2 mln.; Nuclear: 0.5 mln.

**Education. Student-teacher ratio** (1991): 14.0. **Avg. salary, public school teachers** (1992-93): $48,850.

**State data. Motto:** Qui Transtulit Sustinet (He who transplanted still sustains). **Flower:** Mountain laurel. **Bird:** American robin. **Tree:** White oak. **Song:** Yankee Doodle. **Fifth** of the 13 original states to ratify the Constitution, Jan. 9, 1788.

**History.** Adriaen Block, Dutch explorer, was the first European visitor, 1614. By 1634, settlers from Plymouth Bay started colonies along the Connecticut River and in 1637 defeated the Pequot Indians. In the Revolution, Connecticut men fought in most major campaigns and turned back British raids on Danbury and other towns, while Connecticut privateers captured British merchant ships.

**Tourist attractions.** Mark Twain House, Hartford; Yale University's Art Gallery, Peabody Museum, both in New Haven; Mystic Seaport; Mystic Marine Life Aquarium; P.T. Barnum Museum, Bridgeport; Gillette Castle, Hadlyme; U.S.S. Nautilus Memorial, Groton (1st nuclear-powered submarine).

**Famous "Nutmeggers"** include Ethan Allen, Phineas T. Barnum, Samuel Colt, Jonathan Edwards, Nathan Hale, Katharine Hepburn, Isaac Hull, J. Pierpont Morgan, Israel Putnam, Harriet Beecher Stowe, Mark Twain, Noah Webster, Eli Whitney.

**Tourist information.** State Dept. of Economic Development, 865 Brook St., Rocky Hill, CT 06067.

**Toll-free travel information.** 1-800-CT-BOUND (282-6863).

# Delaware

*First State, Diamond State*

**People. Population** (1992): 689,214; **rank:** 46. **Pop. density:** 352.5 per sq. mi. **Racial distrib.** (1990): 80.3% White; 16.9% Black; 2.4% Hispanic. **Net change** (1990-92): 3.5%.

**Geography. Total area:** 2,045 sq. mi.; **rank:** 49. **Land area:** 1,955 sq. mi. **Acres forested land:** 398,000. **Location:** occupies the Delmarva Peninsula on the Atlantic coastal plain. **Climate:** moderate. **Topography:** Piedmont plateau to the N, sloping to a near sea-level plain. **Capital:** Dover.

**Economy. Principal industries:** chemistry, agriculture, finance, poultry, shellfish, tourism, auto assembly, food processing, transportation equipment. **Principal manufactured goods:** nylon, apparel, luggage, foods, autos, processed meats and vegetables, railroad and aircraft equipment. **Agriculture: Chief crops:** soybeans, potatoes, corn, mushrooms, lima beans, green peas, barley, cucumbers, snap beans, watermelons, apples, wheat, sweet corn. **Livestock** (1992): 31,000 cattle, 39,000 hogs, 236.5 mln. broilers. **Nonfuel Minerals** (1992): $16.3 mln; construction sand & gravel, magnesium compounds. **Commercial fishing** (1992): $4.2 mln. **Chief ports:** Wilmington. **International airports at:** Philadelphia/Wilmington. **Value of construction** (1992): $782.5 mln. **Employment distribution** (1992): 80.3% non-manufacturing; 19.7% mfg. **Per capita income** (1992): $21,451. **Unemployment** (1992): 5.3%. **Tourism** (1989): travelers spent $785 mln.

**Finance.** FDIC-insured **commercial banks & trust companies** (1992): 42. **Deposits:** $36.0 bln. **Savings institutions** (1992): 3. **Assets:** $200 mln.

**Federal government.** No. federal civilian employees (Mar. 1992): 2,891. **Avg. salary:** $31,689. **Notable federal facilities:** Dover Air Force Base, Federal Wildlife Refuge, Bombay Hook.

**Energy. Electricity production** (1992, MWh, by source): Mineral: 6.0 mln.

**Education. Student-teacher ratio** (1991): 16.8. **Avg. salary, public school teachers** (1992-93): $36,217.

**State data. Motto:** Liberty and independence. **Flower:** Peach blossom. **Bird:** Blue hen chicken. **Tree:** American holly. **Song:** Our Delaware. **First** of original 13 states to ratify the Constitution, Dec. 7, 1787. **State fair** at: Harrington; end of July.

**History.** The Dutch first settled in Delaware near present Lewes, 1631, but were wiped out by Indians. Swedes settled at present Wilmington, 1638; Dutch settled anew, 1651, near New Castle and seized the Swedish settlement, 1655, only to lose all Delaware and New Netherland to the British, 1664.

**Tourist attractions.** Ft. Christina Monument, the site of founding of New Sweden; John Dickinson "Penman of the Revolution" home, Dover; Henry Francis du Pont Winterthur Museum; Hagley Museum, Wilmington; Rehoboth Beach, "nation's summer capitol," Rehoboth; Dover Downs Intl. Speedway, Dover; Old Swedes (Trinity Parish)

Church, erected 1698, is the oldest Protestant church in the U.S. still in use.

**Famous Delawareans** include Thomas F. Bayard, Henry Seidel Canby, E. I. du Pont, John P. Marquand, Howard Pyle, Caesar Rodney.

**Chamber of Commerce.** One Commerce Center, Wilmington, DE 19801.

**Toll-free travel information.** 1-800-441-8846.

## Florida

### Sunshine State

**People. Population** (1992): 13,487,621; **rank:** 4. **Pop. density:** 249.8 per sq. mi. **Racial distrib.** (1990): 83.1% White; 13.6% Black; 12.2% Hispanic. **Net change** (1990-92): 4.3%.

**Geography. Total area:** 58,664 sq. mi.; **rank:** 22. **Land area:** 53,997 sq. mi. **Acres forested land:** 16,721,000. **Location:** peninsula jutting southward 500 mi. bet. the Atlantic and the Gulf of Mexico. **Climate:** subtropical N of Bradenton-Lake Okeechobee-Vero Beach line; tropical S of line. **Topography:** land is flat or rolling; highest point is 345 ft. in the NW. **Capital:** Tallahassee.

**Economy. Principal industries:** services, trade, gvt., manufacturing, tourism. **Principal manufactured goods:** electric & electronic equip., transp. equipment; food; printing & publishing; machinery. **Agriculture: Chief crops:** citrus fruits, vegetables, potatoes, melons, strawberries, sugarcane. **Livestock** (1987): 1.97 mln. cattle; 150,000 hogs/pigs; 7,360 sheep; 13.5 mln. poultry. **Timber/lumber** (1991): pine, cypress, cedar; 570 mln. bd. ft. **Nonfuel Minerals** (1992): $1.4 bln.; mostly cement, phosphate rock, crushed stone. **Commercial fishing** (1992): $154.9 mln. **Chief ports:** Pensacola, Tampa, Miami, Port Everglades, Jacksonville, St. Petersburg, Canaveral. **International airports at:** Miami, Tampa, Jacksonville, Orlando, Ft. Lauderdale, W. Palm Beach. **Value of construction** (1992): $16.7 bln. **Per capita income** (1992): $19,397. **Unemployment** (1992): 8.2% **Tourism** (1990): out-of-state visitors spent $26.6 bln. **Sales tax:** 6%.

**Finance. FDIC-insured commercial banks & trust companies** (1992): 421. **Deposits:** $119.9 bln. **Savings institutions** (1992): 87. **Assets:** $38.2 bln.

**Federal government. No. federal civilian employees** (Mar. 1992): 64,887. **Avg. salary:** $34,250. **Notable federal facilities:** John F. Kennedy Space Center, NASA-Kennedy Space Center's Spaceport USA; Eglin Air Force Base.

**Energy. Electricity production** (1992, MWh, by source): Hydroelectric: 0.2 mln.; Mineral: 70.6 mln.; Nuclear: 27.7 mln.

**Education. Student-teacher ratio** (1991): 17.6. **Avg. salary, public school teachers** (1992-93): $31,153.

**State data. Motto:** In God we trust. **Flower:** Orange blossom. **Bird:** Mockingbird. **Tree:** Sabal palmetto palm. **Song:** Old Folks at Home. **Entered union** Mar. 3, 1845; **rank,** 27th. **State fair** at: Tampa; early to mid-Feb.

**History.** First European to see Florida was Ponce de León, 1513. France established a colony, Fort Caroline, on the St. Johns River, 1564; Spain settled St. Augustine, 1565, and Spanish troops massacred most of the French. Britain's Francis Drake burned St. Augustine, 1586. Britain held the area briefly, 1763-83, returning it to Spain. After Andrew Jackson led a U.S. invasion, 1818, Spain ceded Florida to the U.S., 1819. The Seminole War, 1835-42, resulted in removal of most Indians to Oklahoma. Florida seceded from the Union, 1861, was readmitted, 1868.

**Tourist attractions.** Miami, with a variety of luxury hotels at Miami Beach; St. Augustine, oldest city in U.S.; Walt Disney World's Magic Kingdom, EPCOT Center, and Disney-MGM Studios, near Orlando; Spaceport U.S.A.

Everglades National Park preserves the beauty of the vast Everglades swamp. Castillo de San Marcos, St. Augustine, is a national monument. Also, the Ringling Museum of Art and the Ringling Museum of the Circus, both in Sarasota; Sea World, Orlando; Cypress Gardens, Winter Haven; Busch Gardens, Tampa; Universal Studios, near Orlando.

**Famous Floridians** include Henry M. Flagler, James Weldon Johnson, MacKinlay Kantor, Henry B. Plant, Marjorie Kinnan Rawlings, Joseph W. Stilwell, Charles P. Summerall.

**Tourist information.** Florida Division of Tourism, 126 Van Buren St., Tallahassee, FL 32399-2000, 1-904-487-1462.

## Georgia

### Empire State of the South, Peach State

**People. Population** (1992): 6,751,404; **rank:** 11. **Pop. density:** 116.6 per sq. mi. **Racial distrib.** (1990): 71.0% White; 27.0% Black; 1.7% Hispanic. **Net change** (1990-92): 4.2%.

**Geography. Total area:** 58,910 sq. mi.; **rank:** 21. **Land area:** 57,919 sq. mi. **Acres forested land:** 23,907,000. **Location:** South Atlantic state. **Climate:** maritime tropical air masses dominate in summer; continental polar air masses in winter; east central area drier. **Topography:** most southerly of the Blue Ridge Mtns. cover NE and N central; central Piedmont extends to the fall line of rivers; coastal plain levels to the coast flatlands. **Capital:** Atlanta.

**Economy. Principal industries:** services, manufacturing, gvt., retail trade. **Principal manufactured goods** (1991): textiles, food, and kindred prods. **Agriculture: Chief crops** (1991): peanuts, cotton, corn, tobacco, hay soybeans. **Livestock** (1991): 8.8 mln. poultry; 1.4 mln. cattle; 1.1 hogs/pigs. **Timber/lumber** (1991): pine, hardwood; 2.5 bln. bd. ft. **Nonfuel Minerals** (1992): $1.5 bln.; mostly crushed stone. **Commercial fishing** (1992): $23.0 mln. **Chief ports:** Savannah, Brunswick. **International airports at:** Atlanta. **Value of construction** (1992): $8.1 bln. **Employment distribution** (1991): 20% services; 19% mfg.; 18% retail trade; 18% gvt. **Per capita income** (1992): $18,130. **Unemployment** (1992): 6.9%. **Tourism** (1991): tourists spent $10.4 bln. **Sales tax:** 4%.

**Finance. FDIC-insured commercial banks & trust companies** (1992): 405. **Deposits:** $54.9 bln. **Savings institutions** (1992): 43. **Assets:** $13.6 bln.

**Federal government. No. federal civilian employees** (Mar. 1992): 71,257. **Avg. salary:** $32,637. **Notable federal facilities:** Dobbins AFB; Fts. Benning, Gordon, McPherson; Fed. Law Enforcement Training Ctr., Glynco, Warner Robins AFB; Centers for Disease Control, Atlanta.

**Energy. Electricity production** (1992, MWh, by source): Hydroelectric: 3.6 mln.; Mineral: 39.7 mln.; Nuclear: 26.6 mln.

**Education. Student-teacher ratio** (1991): 18.5. **Avg. salary, public school teachers** (1992-93): $30,626.

**State data. Motto:** Wisdom, justice and moderation. **Flower:** Cherokee rose. **Bird:** Brown thrasher. **Tree:** Live oak. **Song:** Georgia On My Mind. **Fourth** of the 13 original states to ratify the Constitution, Jan. 2, 1788.

**History.** Gen. James Oglethorpe established the first settlements, 1733, for poor and religiously-persecuted Englishmen. Oglethorpe defeated a Spanish army from Florida at Bloody Marsh, 1742. In the Revolution, Georgians seized the Savannah armory, 1775, and sent the munitions to the Continental Army; they fought seesaw campaigns with Cornwallis' British troops, twice liberating Augusta and forcing final evacuation by the British from Savannah, 1782.

**Tourist attractions.** Atlanta area: State Capitol, Stone Mt. Park, Six Flags over Georgia, Kennesaw Mt. Natl. Battlefield Park, Martin Luther King Center, Underground Atlanta, Jimmy Carter Lib. & Museum. NW: Chickamauga Battlefield Park, Chattahoochee Natl. Forest. NE: alpine village of Helen; Dahlonega, site of America's first gold rush; Brasstown Bald Mt., Lake Lanier. SW: Roosevelt's Little White House, Callaway Gardens, Andersonville Natl. Historic Site. SE: Okefenokee Swamp. Coastal: Jekyll Island, St. Simons Island, Cumberland Island Natl. Seashore, historic riverfront district in Savannah, Ft. Pulaski.

**Famous Georgians** include Hank Aaron, Griffin Bell, James Bowie, Erskine Caldwell, Jimmy Carter, Ray Charles, Lucius D. Clay, Ty Cobb, John C. Fremont, Joel Chandler Harris, Martin Luther King Jr., Gladys Knight,

Sidney Lanier, Juliette Gordon Low, Margaret Mitchell, Flannery O'Connor, Jackie Robinson, Joseph Wheeler.

**Chamber of Commerce.** 235 International Blvd., Atlanta, GA 30303.

**Toll-free travel information.** 1-800-VISIT GA.

# Hawai'i

*The Aloha State*

**People. Population** (1992): 1,159,614; **rank:** 40. **Pop. density:** 180.5 per sq. mi. **Racial distrib.** (1990): 33.4% White; 2.5% Black; 61.8% Asian or Pacific Is.; 7.3% Hispanic. **Net change** (1990-92): 4.6%.

**Geography. Total area:** 6,471 sq. mi.; **rank:** 47. **Land area:** 6,423 sq. mi. **Acres forested land:** 1,748,000. **Location:** Hawaiian Islands lie in the North Pacific, 2,397 mi. SW from San Francisco. **Climate:** subtropical, with wide variations in rainfall; Waialeale, on Kaua'i, wettest spot in U.S. (annual rainfall 444 in.) **Topography:** islands are tops of a chain of submerged volcanic mountains; active volcanoes: Mauna Loa, Kilauea. **Capital:** Honolulu.

**Economy. Principal industries:** tourism, defense and other government, sugar refining, pineapple and diversified agriculture, aquaculture, fishing, motion pictures. **Principal manufactured goods:** sugar, canned pineapple, clothing, foods, printing and publishing. **Agriculture: Chief crops:** sugar, pineapples, macadamia nuts, fruits, coffee, vegetables, melons, floriculture. **Livestock** (1990): 214,000 cattle and calves; 36,000 hogs/pigs; 1.18 mln. chickens. **Nonfuel Minerals** (1992): $148.6 mln.; mostly crushed stone, sand, gravel & cement. **Commercial fishing** (1992): $70.2 mln. **Chief ports:** Honolulu, N₂wiliwili, Barbers Point, Kahului, Hilo. **International airports at:** Honolulu. **Value of construction** (1992): $2.9 bln. **Employment distribution** (1991): 25.3% trade; 29.4% serv.; 20.2% gvt. **Per capita income** (1992): $21,218. **Unemployment** (1992): 4.5%. **Tourism** (1992): visitors spent $9.6 bln. **General excise tax:** 4%. **Sales tax:** 4%.

**Finance. FDIC-insured commercial banks & trust companies:** (1992): 20. **Deposits:** $16.2 bln. **Savings institutions** (1992): 5. **Assets:** $4.7 bln.

**Federal government. No. federal civilian employees** (Mar. 1992): 21,560. **Avg. salary:** $34,445. **Notable federal facilities:** Pearl Harbor Naval Shipyard; Hickam AFB; Schofield Barracks.

**Energy. Electricity production** (1992, MWh, by source): Hydroelectric: 0.01 mln.; Mineral: 5.6 mln.

**Education. Student-teacher ratio** (1991): 18.5. **Avg. Salary, public school teachers** (1992-93): $36,470.

**State data. Motto:** The life of the land is perpetuated in righteousness. **Flower:** Yellow hibiscus. **Bird:** Hawaiian goose. **Tree:** Kukui (Candlenut). **Song:** Hawai'i Pono'i. **Entered union** Aug. 21, 1959; **rank,** 50th. **State fair at:** Honolulu; late May–mid-June.

**History.** Polynesians from islands 2,000 mi. to the south settled the Hawaiian Islands, probably between 300 A.D. and 600 A.D. First European visitor was British Capt. James Cook, 1778. Missionaries arrived, 1820, taught religion, reading and writing. King Kamehameha III and his chiefs created the first Constitution and a Legislature that set up a public school system. Sugar production began in 1835 and it became the dominant industry. In 1893, Queen Liliuokalani was deposed, followed, 1894, by a republic headed by Sanford B. Dole. Annexation by the U.S. came in 1898.

**Tourist attractions.** Hawaii Volcanoes, Haleakala National Parks; Polynesian Cultural Center, Waikiki Beach, Nu'uanu Pali, Bishop Museum, Waimea Canyon, Wailua River State Park, Honolulu Academy of Arts.

**Famous Hawaiians** include Bernice Pauahi Bishop, John A. Burns, Father Damien de Veuster, Daniel K. Inouye, Duke Kahanamoku, King Kamehameha the Great, Queen Ka'ahumanu, Queen Liliuokalani, Ellison Onizuka.

**Chamber of Commerce.** Dillingham Bldg., 735 Bishop St., Honolulu, HI 96813.

# Idaho

*Gem State*

**People. Population** (1992): 1,067,250; **rank:** 42. **Pop. density:** 12.9 per sq. mi. **Racial distrib.** (1990): 94.4% White; 0.3% Black; 5.3% Hispanic. **Net change** (1990-92): 6.0%.

**Geography. Total area:** 83,564 sq. mi.; **rank:** 13. **Land area:** 82,751 sq. mi. **Acres forested land:** 21,818,000. **Location:** northwestern Mountain state bordering on British Columbia. **Climate:** tempered by Pacific westerly winds; drier, colder, continental clime in SE; altitude an important factor. **Topography:** Snake R. plains in the S; central region of mountains, canyons, gorges (Hells Canyon, 7,900 ft., deepest in N.A.); subalpine northern region. **Capital:** Boise.

**Economy. Principal industries:** agriculture, manufacturing, tourism, lumber, mining, electronics. **Principal manufactured goods:** processed foods, lumber and wood products, chemical products, primary metals, fabricated metal products, machinery, electronic components. **Agriculture: Chief crops:** potatoes, peas, sugar beets, alfalfa seed, wheat, hops, barley, plums and prunes, mint, onions, corn, cherries, apples, hay. **Livestock** (1989): 1.66 mln. cattle; 296,000 sheep; 72,000 hogs; 1.1 mln. poultry. **Timber/lumber** (1991): yellow, white pine; Douglas fir; white spruce; 1.9 bln. bd. ft. **Nonfuel Minerals** (1992): $338.6 mln.; phosphate rock, silver, gold, sand & gravel. **Chief ports:** Lewiston. **Value of construction** (1992) $1.3 bln. **Employment distribution** (1990): 21% trade; 17% serv., 13% mfg.; 7% agric. **Per capita income** (1992): $16,067. **Unemployment** (1992): 6.5%. **Tourism** (1989): travelers spent $1.4 bln. **Sales tax:** 5%.

**Finance. FDIC-insured commercial banks & trust companies** (1992): 22. **Deposits:** $7.6 bln. **Savings institutions** (1992): 3. **Assets:** $500 mln.

**Federal government. No. federal civilian employees** (Mar. 1992): 7,856. **Avg. salary:** $33,265. **Notable federal facilities:** Ida. Nat'l. Engineering Lab, Idaho Falls; Mt. Home Air Force Base, Mt. Home.

**Energy. Electricity production** (1992, MWh, by source): Hydroelectric: 5.2 mln.

**Education. Student-teacher ratio** (1991): 19.4. **Avg. salary, public school teachers** (1992-93): $27,156.

**State data. Motto:** Esto Perpetua (It is perpetual). **Flower:** Syringa. **Bird:** Mountain bluebird. **Tree:** White pine. **Song:** Here We Have Idaho. **Entered union** July 3, 1890; **rank,** 43d. **State fair** at: Boise, late Aug.; and Blackfoot, early Sept.

**History.** Exploration of the Idaho area began with Lewis and Clark, 1805-06. Next came fur traders, setting up posts, 1809-34, and missionaries, establishing missions, 1830s-1850s. Mormons made their first permanent settlement at Franklin, 1860. Idaho's Gold Rush began that same year, and brought thousands of permanent settlers. Strangest of the Indian Wars was the 1,300-mi. trek in 1877 of Chief Joseph and the Nez Perce tribe, pursued by troops that caught them a few miles short of the Canadian border. In 1890, Idaho adopted a progressive Constitution and became a state.

**Tourist attractions.** Hells Canyon, deepest gorge in N.A.; World Center for Birds of Prey; Craters of the Moon; Sun Valley, year-round resort in the Sawtooth Mtns.; Crystal Falls Cave; Shoshone Falls; Lava Hot Springs; Lake Pend Oreille; Lake Coeur d'Alene; Sawtooth Natl. Recreation Area; River of No Return Wilderness Area.

**Famous Idahoans** include William E. Borah, Frank Church, Fred T. Dubois, Chief Joseph, Sacagawea.

**Tourist information.** Department of Commerce, 700 W. State St., Boise, ID 83720.

**Toll-free travel information.** 1-800-635-7820.

# Illinois

## The Prairie State

**People. Population** (1992): 11,631,131; **rank: 6. Pop. density:** 209.2 per sq. mi. **Racial distrib.** (1990): 78.3% White; 14.8% Black; 7.9% Hispanic. **Net change** (1990-92): 1.8%.

**Geography. Total area:** 56,345 sq. mi.; **rank:** 24. **Land area:** 55,593 sq. mi. **Acres forested land:** 4,265,000. **Location:** East North Central state; western, southern, and eastern boundaries formed by Mississippi, Ohio, and Wabash rivers, respectively. **Climate:** temperate; typically cold, snowy winters, hot summers. **Topography:** prairie and fertile plains throughout; open hills in the southern region. **Capital:** Springfield.

**Economy. Principal industries:** services, manufacturing, travel, wholesale and retail trade, finance, insurance, real estate, construction, gvt., health care, agriculture. **Principal manufactured goods:** machinery, electric and electronic equipment, primary and fabricated metals, chemical products, printing and publishing, food and kindred prods. **Agriculture: Chief crops:** corn, soybeans, wheat, oats, hay. **Livestock** (1991): 1.98 mln. cattle; 5.9 mln. hogs/pigs; 129,000 sheep; 3.31 mln. poultry. **Timber/lumber** (1991): oak, hickory, maple, cottonwood; 94 mln. bd. ft. **Nonfuel Minerals** (1992): $677.4 mln.; mostly crushed stone, cement, construction & industrial sand & gravel, lime. **Commercial fishing** (1992): $367,000. **Chief ports:** Chicago. **International airports at:** Chicago. **Value of construction** (1992): $10.6 bln. **Employment distribution** (1991): 26.0% serv.; 24.0% trade; 18.1% mfg. **Per capita income** (1992): $21,608. **Unemployment** (1992): 7.5%. **Tourism** (1991): out-of-state visitors spent $15 bln. **Sales tax:** 6.25%.

**Finance.** FDIC-insured commercial banks & trust companies (1992): 1,061. **Deposits:** $157.0 bln. **Savings institutions** (1992): 151. **Assets:** $43.2 bln.

**Federal government. No. federal civilian employees** (Mar. 1992): 54,139. **Avg. salary:** $35,198. **Notable federal facilities:** Fermi Nat'l. Accelerator Lab; Argonne Nat'l. Lab; Ft. Sheridan; Rock Island; Great Lakes, Naval Training Station, Scott AFB.

**Energy. Electricity production** (1992, MWh, by source): Hydroelectric: 0.1 mln.; Mineral: 47.5 mln.; Nuclear: 62.9 mln.

**Education. Student-teacher ratio** (1991): 16.8. **Avg. salary, public school teachers** (1992-93):$38,576.

**State data. Motto:** State sovereignty—national union. **Flower:** Native violet. **Bird:** Cardinal. **Tree:** White oak. **Song:** Illinois. **Entered union** Dec. 3, 1818; **rank,** 21st. **State fair** at: Springfield, mid-Aug.; DuQuoin, late Aug.

**History.** Fur traders were the first Europeans in Illinois, followed shortly, 1673, by Jolliet and Marquette, and 1680, La Salle, who built a fort near present Peoria. First settlements were French, at Fort St. Louis on the Illinois River, 1692, and Kaskaskia, 1700. France ceded the area to Britain, 1763; Amer. Gen. George Rogers Clark, 1778, took Kaskaskia from the British without a shot. Defeat of Indian tribes in Black Hawk War, 1832, and railroads in 1850s, inspired change.

**Tourist attractions:** Chicago museums, parks; Lincoln shrines at Springfield, New Salem, Sangamon; Cahokia Mounds, E. St. Louis; Starved Rock State Park; Crab Orchard Wildlife Refuge; Mormon settlement at Nauvoo; Fts. Kaskaskia, Chartres, Massac (parks); Shawnee Natl. Forest, Southern Illinois; Illinois State Museum, Springfield; Dickson Mounds Museum, btwn. Havana & Lewistown.

**Famous Illinoisans** include Jane Addams, Saul Bellow, Jack Benny, Ray Bradbury, Gwendolyn Brooks, William Jennings Bryan, St. Frances Xavier Cabrini, Clarence Darrow, John Deere, Stephen A. Douglas, James T. Farrell, George W. Ferris, Marshall Field, Betty Friedan, Benny Goodman, Ulysses S. Grant, Ernest Hemingway, Wild Bill Hickok, Abraham Lincoln, Vachel Lindsay, Edgar Lee Masters, Oscar Mayer, Cyrus McCormick, Ronald Reagan, Carl Sandburg, Adlai Stevenson, Frank Lloyd Wright, Philip Wrigley.

**Tourist information.** Illinois Dept. of Commerce and Community Affairs, 620 E. Adams St., Springfield, IL 62701. **Toll-free literature:** 1-800-223-0121.

# Indiana

## Hoosier State

**People. Population** (1992): 5,661,800; **rank: 14. Pop. density:** 157.8 per sq. mi. **Racial distrib.** (1990): 90.6% White; 7.8% Black; 1.8% Hispanic. **Net change** (1990-92): 2.1%.

**Geography. Total area:** 36,185 sq. mi.; **rank:** 38. **Land area:** 35,870 sq. mi. **Acres forested land:** 4,439,900. **Location:** East North Central state; Lake Michigan on northern border. **Climate:** 4 distinct seasons with a temperate climate. **Topography:** hilly southern region; fertile rolling plains of central region; flat, heavily glaciated north; dunes along Lake Michigan shore. **Capital:** Indianapolis.

**Economy. Principal industries:** manufacturing, services, agriculture, government, wholsesale and retail trade, transportation and public utilities. **Principal manufactured goods:** primary metals, transportation equipment, motor vehicles and equipment, machinery except electrical, fabricated metal, chemical and allied products. **Agriculture: Chief crops** (1987): corn, sorghum, oats, wheat, rye, soybeans, hay. **Livestock** (1987): 1.2 mln. cattle; 4.4 mln. hogs/pigs; 82,757 sheep; 28 mln. chickens. **Timber/lumber** (1991): oak, tulip, beech, sycamore; 208 mln. bd. ft. **Nonfuel Minerals** (1992): $465.2 mln.; mostly crushed stone, abrasives, cement, construction sand & gravel. **Commercial fishing** (1992): $2.55 mln. **Chief ports:** Burns Harbor, Portage; Southwind Maritime, Mt. Vernon; Clark Maritime, Jeffersonville. **International airports at:** Indianapolis. **Value of construction** (1992): $6.4 bln. **Employment distribution** (1989): 27.9% mfg.; 24.8% trade; 19.8% serv.; 12.3% gvt. **Per capita income** (1992): $18,043. **Unemployment** (1992): 6.5%. **Tourism** (1992): tourists spent $4.4 bln. **Sales tax:** 5%, with exemptions.

**Finance.** FDIC-insured commercial banks & trust companies (1992): 284. **Deposits:** $48.5 bln. **Savings institutions** (1992): 86. **Assets:** $13.9 bln.

**Federal government. No. federal civilian employees** (Mar. 1992): 26,040. **Avg. salary:** $32,697. **Notable federal facilities:** Naval Avionics Ctr.; Ft. Benjamin Harrison; Grissom AFB; Naval Surface Warfare Ctr., Crane.

**Energy. Electricity production** (1992 MWh, by source): Hydroelectric: 0.5 mln.; Mineral: 86.5 mln.

**Education. Student-teacher ratio** (1991): 17.5. **Avg. salary, public school teachers** (1992-93): $37,446.

**State data. Motto:** Crossroads of America. **Flower:** Peony. **Bird:** Cardinal. **Tree:** Tulip poplar. **Song:** On the Banks of the Wabash, Far Away. **Entered union** Dec. 11, 1816; **rank,** 19th. **State fair** at: Indianapolis; mid-Aug.

**History.** Pre-historic Indian Mound Builders of 1,000 years ago were the earliest known inhabitants. A French trading post was built, 1731-32, at Vincennes and La Salle visited the present South Bend area, 1679 and 1681. France ceded the area to Britain, 1763. During the Revolution, American Gen. George Rogers Clark captured Vincennes, 1778, and defeated British forces 1779; at war's end Britain ceded the area to the U.S. Miami Indians defeated U.S. troops twice, 1790, but were beaten, 1794, at Fallen Timbers by Gen. Anthony Wayne. At Tippecanoe, 1811, Gen. William H. Harrison defeated Tecumseh's Indian confederation.

**Tourist attractions.** Lincoln Boyhood, George Rogers Clark memorials; Wyandotte Cave; Vincennes, Tippecanoe sites; Indiana Dunes; Hoosier Nat'l. Forest; Benjamin Harrison Home; Basketball Hall of Fame, New Harmony; Indianapolis 500 race and museum.

**Famous "Hoosiers"** include Larry Bird, Ambrose Burnside, Hoagy Carmichael, Jim Davis, James Dean, Eugene V. Debs, Theodore Dreiser, Paul Dresser, Gil Hodges, David Letterman, Jane Pauley, Cole Porter, Gene Stratton Porter, Ernie Pyle, James Whitcomb Riley, Oscar Robertson, Red Skelton, Booth Tarkington, Lew Wallace, Wendell L. Willkie, Wilbur Wright.

**Chamber of Commerce.** One North Capital, Suite 200, Indianapolis, IN 46204.

**Toll-free travel information.** 1-800-289-6646.

# Iowa

*Hawkeye State*

**People. Population** (1992): 2,812,448; **rank:** 30. **Pop. density:** 50.3 per sq. mi. **Racial distrib.** (1990): 96.6% White; 1.7% Black; 1.2% Hispanic. **Net change** (1990-92): 1.3%.

**Geography. Total area:** 56,275 sq. mi.; **rank:** 25. **Land area:** 55,875 sq. mi. **Acres forested land:** 1,562,000. **Location:** West North Central state bordered by Mississippi R. on the E and Missouri R. on the W. **Climate:** humid, continental. **Topography:** Watershed from NW to SE; soil especially rich and land level in the N central counties. **Capital:** Des Moines.

**Economy. Principal industries:** agriculture, communications, construction, finance, insurance, trade, service, mfg. **Principal manufactured goods:** tires, farm machinery, electronic products, appliances, office furniture, chemicals, fertilizers, auto accessories. **Agriculture: Chief crops:** silage and grain corn, soybeans, oats, hay. **Livestock** (1992): 4.45 mln. cattle; 15.0 mln. swine; 345,000 sheep & lambs; 8.6 mln. turkeys. **Timber/lumber** (1991): red cedar; 31 mln. bd. ft. **Nonfuel Minerals** (1992): $387.7 mln.; mostly crushed stone, portland cement, construction sand & gravel. **Value of construction** (1992): 2.2 bln. **Employment distribution** (1992): 25.2% trade; 24.4% serv; 18.3% mfg.; 18.2% gvt. **Per capita income** (1992): $18,287. **Unemployment** (1992): 4.6%. **Tourism** (1992): tourists spent $2.5 bln. **Sales tax:** 5%.

**Finance. FDIC-insured commercial banks & trust companies** (1992): 553. **Deposits:** $30.8 bln. **Savings institutions** (1992): 31. **Assets:** $4.6 bln.

**Federal government. No. federal civilian employees** (Mar. 1992): 7,957. **Avg. salary:** $32,456.

**Energy. Electricity production** (1992, MWh, by source): Hydroelectric: 0.8 mln.; Mineral: 24.8 mln.; Nuclear: 3.3 mln.

**Education. Student-teacher ratio** (1991): 15.7. **Avg. salary, public school teachers** (1992-93): $30,124.

**State data. Motto:** Our liberties we prize and our rights we will maintain. **Flower:** Wild rose. **Bird:** Eastern goldfinch. **Tree:** Oak. **Rock:** Geode. **Entered union** Dec. 28, 1846; **rank,** 29th. **State fair** at: Des Moines; mid-Aug.

**History.** A thousand years ago several groups of prehistoric Indian Mound Builders dwelt on Iowa's fertile plains. Marquette and Jolliet gave France its claim to the area, 1673. It became U.S. territory through the 1803 Louisiana Purchase. Indian tribes were moved into the area from states further east, but by mid-19th century were forced to move on to Kansas. Before and during the Civil War, Iowans strongly supported Abraham Lincoln and became traditional Republicans.

**Tourist attractions.** Herbert Hoover birthplace and library, West Branch; Effigy Mounds Nat'l. Monument, Marquette, a pre-historic Indian burial site; Amana Colonies; Davenport Municipal Art Gallery's collection of Grant Wood's paintings and memorabilia; Living History Farms, Des Moines; Adventureland, Altoona; Boone & Scenic Valley Railroad, Boone; Greyhound Parks in Dubuque; Council Bluffs & Waterloo; Prairie Meadows horse racing, Altoona; riverboat cruises and casino gambling, Mississippi River; Iowa Great Lakes, Okoboji.

**Famous Iowans** include James A. Van Allen, Marquis Childs, Buffalo Bill Cody, Mamie Dowd Eisenhower, George Gallup, Susan Glaspell, James Norman Hall, Harry Hansen, Herbert Hoover, Glenn Miller, Billy Sunday, Carl Van Vechten, Henry Wallace, John Wayne, Meredith Willson, Grant Wood.

**Tourist information.** Division of Tourism, Iowa Dept. of Economic Development, 200 E. Grand Ave., Des Moines, IA 50309.

**Toll-free travel information.** 1-800-345-IOWA.

# Kansas

*Sunflower State*

**People. Population** (1992): 2,522,574; **rank:** 32. **Pop. density:** 30.8 per sq. mi. **Racial distrib.** (1990): 90.1% White; 5.8% Black; 3.8% Hispanic. **Net change** (1990-92): 1.8%.

**Geography. Total area:** 82,277 sq. mi.; **rank:** 14. **Land area:** 81,823 sq. mi. **Acres forested land:** 1,358,000. **Location:** West North Central state, with Missouri R. on E. **Climate:** temperate but continental, with great extremes bet. summer and winter. **Topography:** hilly Osage Plains in the E; central region level prairie and hills; high plains in the W. **Capital:** Topeka.

**Economy. Principal industries:** manufacturing, finance, insurance, real estate, services. **Principal manufactured goods:** transportation equip., machinery and computer equipment, food and kindred products, printing and publishing. **Agriculture: Chief crops:** wheat, sorghum, corn, hay, soybeans. **Livestock** (1992): 5.65 mln. cattle; 1.44 mln. hogs/pigs; 179,000 sheep & lambs; 1.8 mln. poultry. **Timber/lumber** (1992): oak, walnut. **Nonfuel Minerals** (1992): $368.9 mln.; cement, salt, crushed stone. **Chief ports:** Kansas City. **International airports at:** Wichita. **Value of construction** (1992): $2.5 bln. **Employment distribution** (1992): 21.9% trade; 20.6% serv.; 18.5% gvt.; 14.2% mfg. **Per capita income** (1992): $19,376. **Unemployment** (1992): 4.2%. **Tourism** (1991): out-of-state visitors spent $2.1 bln. **Sales tax:** 6.9% maximum.

**Finance. FDIC-insured commercial banks & trust companies** (1992): 528. **Deposits:** $25.9 bln. **Savings institutions** (1992): 31. **Assets:** $8.5 bln.

**Federal government. No. federal civilian employees** (Mar. 1992): 17,029. **Avg. salary:** $32,065. **Notable federal facilities:** McConnell AFB; Fts. Riley, Leavenworth.

**Energy. Electricity production** (1992, MWh, by source): Mineral: 20.5 mln.; Nuclear: 4.0 mln.

**Education. Student-teacher ratio** (1991): 15.2. **Avg. salary, public school teachers** (1992-93): $33,133.

**State data. Motto:** Ad Astra per Aspera (To the stars through difficulties). **Flower:** Native sunflower. **Bird:** Western meadowlark. **Tree:** Cottonwood. **Song:** Home on the Range. **Entered union** Jan. 29, 1861; **rank,** 34th. **State fair** at: Hutchinson; begins Friday after Labor Day.

**History.** Coronado marched through the Kansas area, 1541; French explorers came next. The U.S. took over in the Louisiana Purchase, 1803. In the pre-war North-South struggle over slavery, so much violence swept the area it was called Bleeding Kansas. Railroad construction after the war made Abilene and Dodge City terminals of large cattle drives from Texas.

**Tourist attractions.** Eisenhower Center and "Place of Meditation," Abilene; Agricultural Hall of Fame and National Ctr., Bonner Springs, displays farm equipment; Dodge City-Boot Hill & Frontier Town; Cowtown-historic frontier town, Wichita; Ft. Scott & Ft. Larned-restored 1800s cavalry forts. Kansas Cosmosphere and Space Discovery Center, Hutchinson.

**Famous Kansans** include Thomas Hart Benton, John Brown, Walter P. Chrysler, John Steuart Curry, Amelia Earhart, Dwight D. Eisenhower, Ron Evans, Wild Bill Hickok, Cyrus Holliday, William Inge, Walter Johnson, Alf Landon, Carry Nation, Gordon Parks, Jim Ryun, William Allen White.

**Tourist information.** Kansas Dept. of Commerce & Housing, Travel and Tourism Div., 700 SW 8th St., Suite 1300, Topeka, KS 66603; 1-913-296-2009.

**Toll-free travel information.** 1-800-2KANSAS.

# Kentucky

*Bluegrass State*

**People. Population** (1992): 3,754,715; **rank:** 24. **Pop. density:** 94.5 per sq. mi. **Racial Distrib.** (1990): 92.0% White; 7.1% Black; Hispanic 0.6%. **Net change** (1990-92): 1.9%.

**Geography. Total area:** 40,410 sq. mi.; **rank:** 37. **Land area:** 39,732 sq. mi. **Acres forested land:** 12,256,000. **Location:** East South Central state, bordered on N by Illinois, Indiana, Ohio; on E by West Virginia and Virginia; in S by Tennessee; on W by Missouri. **Climate:** moderate, with plentiful rainfall. **Topography:** mountainous in E; rounded hills of the Knobs in the N; Bluegrass, heart of state; wooded rocky hillsides of the Pennyroyal; Western Coal Field; the fertile Purchase the SW. **Capital:** Frankfort.

**Economy. Principal industries:** manufacturing, finance, insurance and real estate, services, retail trade. **Principal manufactured goods:** non-electrical machinery, electrical & electronic prods., apparel, transportation equip., printing and publishing. **Agriculture: Chief crops** (1991): tobacco, soybeans, corn. **Livestock** (1991): 2.5 mln. cattle; 920,000 hogs/pigs; 35,000 sheep; 2.2 mln. chickens; 1990 receipts for horse & mule sales, $490 mln. **Timber/lumber** (1991): hardwoods, pines; 553 mln. bd. ft. **Nonfuel Minerals** (1992): $412.5 mln.; mostly crushed stone. **Chief ports:** Paducah, Louisville, Covington, Owensboro, Ashland, Henderson County, Lyon County, Hickman-Fulton County. **International airports at:** Covington. **Value of construction** (1992): $3.9 bln. **Employment distribution** (1991): 25.6% trade; 21% mfg.; 21.2% serv.; 14.1% gvt. **Per capita income** (1992): $16,534. **Unemployment** (1992): 6.9%. **Tourism** (1992): tourists spent $5.7 bln. **Sales tax:** 6%.

**Finance. FDIC-insured commercial banks & trust companies** (1992): 320. **Deposits:** $34.1 bln. **Savings institutions** (1992): 56. **Assets:** $7.3 bln.

**Federal government. No. federal civilian employees** (Mar. 1992): 27,815. **Avg. salary:** $28,968. **Notable federal facilities:** U.S. Gold Bullion Depository, Fort Knox; Federal Correctional Institution, Lexington.

**Energy. Electricity production** (1992, MWh, by source): Hydroelectric: 3.9 mln.; Mineral: 61.3 mln.

**Education. Student-teacher ratio** (1991): 17.2. **Avg. salary, public school teachers** (1992-93): $31,487.

**State data. Motto:** United we stand, divided we fall. **Flower:** Goldenrod. **Bird:** Cardinal. **Tree:** Kentucky coffee tree. **Song:** My Old Kentucky Home. **Entered union** June 1, 1792; **rank,** 15th. **State fair** at: Louisville.

**History.** Kentucky was the first area west of the Alleghenies settled by American pioneers; first permanent settlement, Harrodsburg, 1774. Daniel Boone blazed the Wilderness Trail through the Cumberland Gap and founded Fort Boonesborough, 1775. Indian attacks, spurred by the British, were unceasing until, during the Revolution, Gen. George Rogers Clark captured British forts in Indiana and Illinois, 1778. In 1792, after Virginia dropped its claims to the region, Kentucky became the 15th state.

**Tourist attractions.** Kentucky Derby and accompanying festivities, Louisville; Land Between the Lakes Nat'l. Recreation Area encompassing Kentucky Lake and Lake Barkley; Mammoth Cave National Park with 330 mi. of explored passageways, 200-ft. high rooms, blind fish, and Echo River, 360 ft. below ground; Lake Cumberland in south central Kentucky; Lincoln birthplace, Hodgenville; My Old Kentucky Home, Bardstown; Cumberland Gap Natl. Historical Park, Middlesboro; Kentucky Horse Park, Lexington.

**Famous Kentuckians** include Muhammad Ali, John James Audubon, Alben Barkley, Daniel Boone, Louis D. Brandeis, John C. Breckinridge, Kit Carson, Albert B. "Happy" Chandler, Cassius Marcellus Clay, Henry Clay, Jefferson Davis, "Casey" Jones, Abraham Lincoln, Mary Todd Lincoln, Thomas Hunt Morgan, Carry Nation, Col. Harland Sanders, Diane Sawyer, Jesse Stuart, Adlai Stevenson, Zachary Taylor, Robert Penn Warren, Whitney Young, Jr.

**Chamber of Commerce.** 452 Versailles Rd., P.O. Box 817, Frankfort, KY 40602.

**Toll-free travel information.** 1-800-225-TRIP, extension 67 in U.S., Ontario & Quebec, Canada.

# Louisiana

*Pelican State*

**People. Population** (1992): 4,287,195; **rank:** 21. **Pop. density:** 98.4 per sq. mi. **Racial distrib.** (1990): 67.3% White; 30.8% Black; 2.2% Hispanic. **Net change** (1990-92): 1.6%.

**Geography. Total area:** 47,752 sq. mi.; **rank:** 31. **Land area:** 43,566 sq. mi. **Acres forested land:** 13,883,000. **Location:** West South Central state on the Gulf Coast. **Climate:** subtropical, affected by continental weather patterns. **Topography:** lowlands of marshes and Mississippi R. flood plain; Red R. Valley lowlands; upland hills in the Florida Parishes; average elevation, 100 ft. **Capital:** Baton Rouge.

**Economy. Principal industries:** wholesale and retail trade, government, manufacturing, construction, transportation, mining. **Principal manufactured goods** (1991): chemical products, foods, transportation equipment, electronic equipment, petroleum products, lumber, wood, and paper. **Agriculture: Chief crops** (1991): soybean, sugarcane, rice, corn, cotton, sweet potatoes, pecans, sorghum. **Livestock** (1991): 1.02 mln. cattle; 60,000 hogs/pigs; 16,000 sheep; 1.85 mln. poultry. **Timber/lumber** (1991): pines, hardwoods, oak; 870 mln. bd. ft. **Nonfuel Minerals** (1992): $272.2 mln., mostly salt, sand & gravel, sulfur. **Commercial fishing** (1992): $295.0 mln. **Chief ports:** New Orleans, Baton Rouge, Lake Charles, S. Louisiana Port Commission at La Place, Shreveport. **International airports at:** New Orleans. **Value of construction** (1992): $3.1 bln. **Employment distribution** (1991): 22.8% trade; 23.8% serv.; 21.2% gvt.; 11.4% mfg. **Per capita income** (1992): $15,712. **Unemployment** (1992): 8.1%. **Tourism** (1990): out-of-state visitors spent $8.1 bln. **Sales tax:** 4%.

**Finance. FDIC-insured commercial banks & trust companies** (1992): 226 **Deposits:** $33.0 bln. **Savings institutions** (1992): 40. **Assets:** $4.0 bln.

**Federal government. No. federal civilian employees** (Mar. 1992): 22,644. **Avg. salary:** $32,027. **Notable federal facilities:** Barksdale, England, Ft. Polk military bases; Strategic Petroleum Reserve, New Orleans; Michoud Assembly Plant, New Orleans; U.S. Public Service Hospital, Carville.

**Energy. Electricity production** (1992, MWh, by source): Mineral: 17.6 mln; Nuclear: 10.2 mln.

**Education. Student-teacher ratio** (1991): 16.6. **Avg. salary, public school teachers** (1992-93): $26,074.

**State data. Motto:** Union, justice and confidence. **Flower:** Magnolia. **Bird:** Eastern brown pelican. **Tree:** Cypress. **Song:** Give Me Louisiana. **Entered union** Apr. 30, 1812; **rank,** 18th. **State fair** at: Shreveport; Oct.

**History.** The area was first visited, 1530, by Cabeza de Vaca and Panfilo de Narvaez. The region was claimed for France by La Salle, 1682. First permanent settlement was by French at Biloxi, now in Mississippi, 1699. France ceded the region to Spain, 1762, took it back, 1800, and sold it to the U.S., 1803, in the Louisiana Purchase. During the Revolution, Spanish Louisiana aided the Americans. Admitted to statehood, 1812, Louisiana was the scene of the Battle of New Orleans, 1815.

Louisiana Creoles are descendants of early French and/or Spanish settlers. About 4,000 Acadians, French settlers in Nova Scotia, Canada, were forcibly transported by the British to Louisiana in 1755 (an event commemorated in Longfellow's *Evangeline*) and settled near Bayou Teche; their descendants became known as Cajuns. Another group, the Islenos, were descendants of Canary Islanders brought to Louisiana by a Spanish governor in 1770. Traces of Spanish and French survive in local dialects.

**Tourist attractions.** Mardi Gras, French Quarter, Superdome, Dixieland jazz, Aquarium of the Americas, all New Orleans; Battle of New Orleans site; Longfellow-Evangeline Memorial Park; Kent House Museum, Alexandria; Hodges Gardens, Natchitoches.

**Famous Louisianans** include Louis Armstrong, Pierre Beauregard, Judah P. Benjamin, Braxton Bragg, Grace King, Huey Long, Leonidas K. Polk, Henry Miller Shreve, Edward D. White Jr.

**Tourist Information.** State Dept. of Culture, Recreation & Tourism, P.O. Box 94291, Baton Rouge, LA 70804-9291.

**Toll-free travel information.** 1-800-33-GUMBO.

# Maine

*Pine Tree State*

**People. Population** (1992): 1,235,396; **rank:** 39. **Pop. density:** 40.0 per sq. mi. **Racial distrib.** (1990): 98.4% White; 0.4% Black; 0.6% Hispanic. **Net change** (1990-92): 0.6%.

**Geography. Total area:** 33,265 sq. mi.; **rank:** 39. **Land area:** 30,865 sq. mi. **Acres forested land:** 17,713,000. **Location:** New England state at northeastern tip of U.S. **Climate:** Southern interior and coastal, influenced by air masses from the S and W; northern clime harsher, avg. +100 in. snow in winter. **Topography:** Appalachian Mtns. extend through state; western borders have rugged terrain; long sand beaches on southern coast; northern coast mainly rocky promontories, peninsulas, fjords. **Capital:** Augusta.

**Economy. Principal industries:** manufacturing, services, trade, government, finance, insurance, real estate, construction. **Principal manufactured goods:** paper and wood products, transportation equipment. **Agriculture: Chief crops:** potatoes, apples, hay, blueberries. **Livestock** (1986): 135,000 cattle; 79,000 hogs/pigs; 17,000 sheep; 4.9 mln. poultry. **Timber/lumber** (1991): pine, spruce, fir; 847 mln. bd. ft. **Nonfuel Minerals** (1992): $52.9 mln.; construction sand & gravel, cement, crushed stone, dimension stone. **Commercial fishing** (1992): $163.3 mln. **Chief ports:** Searsport, Portland, Eastport. **International airports at:** Portland, Bangor. **Value of construction** (1992): $1.2 bln. **Employment distribution** (1991): 24.7% trade; 24.5% serv.; 18.7% mfg.; 18.7% gvt. **Per capita income** (1992): $18,226. **Unemployment** (1992): 7.1%. **Tourism** (1991): $2.75 bln. **Sales tax:** 6%.

**Finance.** FDIC-insured **commercial banks & trust companies** (1992): 21. **Deposits:** $7.4 bln. **Savings institutions** (1992): 12. **Assets:** $600 mln.

**Federal government. No. federal civilian employees** (Mar. 1992): 11,886. **Avg. salary:** $32,247. **Notable federal facilities:** Kittery Naval Shipyard; Brunswick Naval Air Station; Loring Air Force Base.

**Energy. Electricity production** (1992, MWh, by source): Hydroelectric: 1.9 mln.; Mineral: 1.9 mln.; Nuclear: 5.4 mln.

**Education. Student-teacher ratio** (1991): 14.0. **Avg. salary, public school teachers** (1992-93): $30,258.

**State data. Motto:** Dirigo (I direct). **Flower:** White pine cone and tassel. **Bird:** Chickadee. **Tree:** Eastern white pine. **Song:** State of Maine Song. **Entered union** Mar. 15, 1820; **rank,** 23d.

**History.** Maine's rocky coast was explored by the Cabots, 1498-99. French settlers arrived, 1604, at the St. Croix River; English, 1607, on the Kennebec. In 1691, Maine was made part of Massachusetts. In the Revolution, a Maine regiment fought at Bunker Hill; a British fleet destroyed Falmouth (now Portland), 1775, but the British ship Margaretta was captured near Machiasport. In 1820, Maine broke off from Massachusetts, became a separate state.

**Tourist attractions.** Acadia Nat'l. Park, Bar Harbor, on Mt. Desert Is.; Funtown, Saco; Bath Iron Works and Maine Maritime Museum; Boothbay (Harbor) Railway Museum; Portland Art Museum; Sugarloaf/USA Ski Area; Ogunquit, Portland, York.

**Famous "Down Easters"** include James G. Blaine, Cyrus H.K. Curtis, Hannibal Hamlin, Longfellow, Sir Hiram and Hudson Maxim, Edna St. Vincent Millay, Kate Douglas Wiggin, Ben Ames Williams.

**Chamber of Commerce and Industry.** 126 Sewall St., Augusta, ME 04330.

**Toll-free travel information.** 1-800-533-9595, winter only, out of state only; 1-207-623-0363 year round.

# Maryland

*Old Line State, Free State*

**People. Population** (1992): 4,908,453; **rank:** 19. **Pop. density:** 502.1 per sq. mi. **Racial distrib.** (1990): 71.0% White; 24.9% Black; 2.9% Asian; 2.6% Hispanic. **Net change** (1990-92): 2.7%.

**Geography. Total area:** 10,460 sq. mi.; **rank:** 42. **Land area:** 9,775 sq. mi. **Acres forested land:** 2,632,000. **Location:** South Atlantic state stretching from the Ocean to the Allegheny Mtns. **Climate:** continental in the west; humid subtropical in the east. **Topography:** Eastern Shore of coastal plain and Maryland Main of coastal plain, piedmont plateau, and the Blue Ridge, separated by the Chesapeake Bay. **Capital:** Annapolis.

**Economy. Principal industries:** manufacturing, services, tourism. **Principal manufactured goods:** electric and electronic equipment; food and kindred products; chemicals and allied products. **Agriculture: Chief crops** (1992): greenhouse & nursery prods, soybeans, corn. **Livestock** (1992): 315,000 cattle; 180,000 hogs/pigs; 33,000 sheep; 257.8 mln. poultry, 280.5 mln. broilers. **Timber/lumber:** hardwoods. **Nonfuel Minerals** (1992): $323.3 mln.; crushed stone, sand & gravel, portland cement. **Commercial fishing** (1992): $36.4 mln. **Chief ports:** Baltimore. **International airports at:** Baltimore-Washington Intl. **Value of construction** (1992): $5.3 bln. **Employment distribution** (1992): 30.3% serv.; 24.2% trade; 19.9% gvt. **Per capita income** (1992): $22,974. **Unemployment** (1992): 6.6%. **Tourism** (1992): tourists spent $4.6 bln. **Sales tax:** 5.0%.

**Finance.** FDIC-insured **commercial banks & trust companies** (1992): 102. **Deposits:** $44.0 bln. **Savings institutions** (1992): 83. **Assets:** $15.8 bln.

**Federal government. No. federal civilian employees** (Mar. 1992): 109,981. **Avg. salary:** $39,640. **Notable federal facilities:** U.S. Naval Academy, Annapolis; Natl. Agric. Research Cen.; Ft. George G. Meade, Aberdeen Proving Ground; Goddard Space Flight Center; Natl. Institutes of Health; Natl. Institute of Standards & Technology; Food & Drug Administration; Bureau of the Census.

**Energy. Electricity production** (1992, MWh, by source): Hydroelectric: 2.2 mln.; Mineral: 22.5 mln.; Nuclear: 1.2 mln.

**Education. Student-teacher ratio** (1991): 16.9 **Avg. salary, public school teachers** (1992-93): $39,141.

**State data. Motto:** Fatti Maschii, Parole Femine (Manly deeds, womanly words). **Flower:** Black-eyed susan. **Bird:** Baltimore oriole. **Tree:** White oak. **Song:** Maryland, My Maryland. **Seventh** of the original 13 states to ratify Constitution, Apr. 28, 1788. **State fair** at: Timonium; late Aug.-early Sept.

**History.** Capt. John Smith first explored Maryland, 1608. William Claiborne set up a trading post on Kent Is. in Chesapeake Bay, 1631. Britain granted land to Cecilius Calvert, Lord Baltimore, 1632; his brother led 200 settlers to St. Marys River, 1634. The bravery of Maryland troops in the Revolution, as at the Battle of Long Island, won the state its nickname, The Old Line State. In the War of 1812, when a British fleet tried to take Fort McHenry, Marylander Francis Scott Key, 1814, wrote The Star-Spangled Banner.

**Tourist Attractions.** Racing events include the Preakness and Maryland Million, both at Pimlico track, Baltimore, and the International at Laurel Race Course; Baltimore Orioles pro baseball at Oriole Park, Camden Yards. Also Annapolis yacht races; Ocean City beach resort; restored Ft. McHenry, Baltimore, near which Francis Scott Key wrote The Star-Spangled Banner; Antietam Battlefield, 1862, near Hagerstown; South Mountain Battlefield, 1862; Edgar Allan Poe house, Baltimore; National Aquarium, Baltimore Harborplace; The State House, Annapolis, 1772, the oldest still in use in the U.S.; Montgomery & Prince George's County, gateway to Washington, D.C.

**Famous Marylanders** include Benjamin Banneker, Francis Scott Key, H.L. Mencken, William Pinkney, Upton Sinclair, Roger B. Taney, Charles Willson Peale.

**Maryland Dept. of Economic & Employment Development.** 217 E. Redwood St., Baltimore, MD 21202; (410) 333-6970.
**Toll-free travel information.** 1-800-543-1036.

## Massachusetts

*Bay State, Old Colony*

**People. Population** (1992): 5,998,375; **rank:** 13. **Pop. density:** 765.3 per sq. mi. **Racial distrib.** (1990): 89.8% White; 5.0% Black; 2.4% Asian; 4.8% Hispanic. **Net change** (1990-92): −0.3%.

**Geography. Total area:** 8,284 sq. mi.; **rank:** 45. **Land area:** 7,838 sq. mi. **Acres forested land:** 3,097,000. **Location:** New England state along Atlantic seaboard. **Climate:** temperate, with colder and drier clime in western region. **Topography:** jagged indented coast from Rhode Island around Cape Cod; flat land yields to stony upland pastures near central region and gentle hilly country in west; except in west, land is rocky, sandy, and not fertile. **Capital:** Boston.

**Economy. Principal industries** (1990): services, trade, manufacturing. **Principal manufactured goods** (1990): electric and electronic equipment, machinery, industrial machinery and equipment, printing and publishing, fabricated metal products. **Agriculture: Chief crops:** cranberries, greenhouse, nursery, vegetables. **Livestock** (1983): 120,000 cattle; 50,000 hogs/pigs; 8,000 sheep; 125,000 horses, ponies; 3.6 mln. poultry. **Timber/lumber** (1991): white pine, oak, other hard woods; 45 mln. bd. ft. **Nonfuel Minerals** (1992): $156.9 mln.; mostly construction sand & gravel, crushed stone. **Commercial fishing** (1992): $280.6 mln. **Chief ports:** Boston, Fall River, New Bedford, Salem, Gloucester, Plymouth. **International airports at:** Boston. **Value of construction** (1992): $5.7 bln. **Employment distribution** (1990): 30.8% trade; 23.5% serv.; 17.5% mfg. **Per capita income** (1992): $24,059. **Unemployment** (1992): 8.5%. **Tourism** (1987): out-of-state visitors spent $12.9 bln. **Sales tax:** 5%.

**Finance.** FDIC-insured commercial banks & trust companies (1992): 73. **Deposits:** $67.8 bln. **Savings institutions** (1992): 22. **Assets:** $3.2 bln.

**Federal government. No. federal civilian employees** (Mar. 1992): 32,034. **Avg. salary:** $35,222. **Notable federal facilities:** Ft. Devens; Thomas P. O'Neill Jr. Federal Bldg., J.W. McCormack Bldg., John Fitzgerald Kennedy Federal Bldg., Boston; Q.M. Laboratory, Natick.

**Energy. Electricity production** (1992, MWh, by source): Hydroelectric: 0.5 mln.; Mineral: 29.3 mln.; Nuclear: 4.8 mln.

**Education. Student-teacher ratio** (1991): 15.1. **Avg. salary, public school teachers** (1992-93): $39,245.

**State data. Motto:** Ense Petit Placidam Sub Libertate Quietem (By the sword we seek peace, but peace only under liberty). **Flower:** Mayflower. **Bird:** Chickadee. **Tree:** American elm. **Song:** All Hail to Massachusetts. **Sixth** of the original 13 states to ratify Constitution, Feb. 6, 1788.

**History.** Pilgrims settled in Plymouth, 1620; the following year they gave thanks for their survival with the first Thanksgiving Day. Indian opposition reached a high point in King Philip's War, 1675-76, won by the colonists. Demonstrations against British restrictions set off the "Boston Massacre," 1770, and Boston "tea party," 1773. First bloodshed of the Revolution was at Lexington, 1775.

**Tourist attractions.** Cape Cod—Plymouth Rock, Plymouth Plantation, Mayflower II, Provincetown artists colony; Boston—Freedom Trail, Museum of Fine Arts, Children's Museum, Museum of Science, New England Aquarium, JFK Library, Boston Ballet, Boston Pops, Boston Symphony Orchestra; Berkshires—Tanglewood, Jacob's Pillow Dance Festival, Hancock Shaker Village, Berkshire Scenic Railroad; Old Sturbridge Village; Walden Pond; Naismith Memorial Basketball Hall of Fame, Springfield.

**Famous "Bay Staters"** include John Adams, John Quincy Adams, Samuel Adams, Louisa May Alcott, Horatio Alger, Susan B. Anthony, Crispus Attucks, Clara Barton, Alexander Graham Bell, Emily Dickinson, Ralph Waldo Emerson, John Hancock, Nathaniel Hawthorne, Oliver W. Holmes, Winslow Homer, Elias Howe, John Fitzgerald Kennedy, Samuel F.B. Morse, Edgar Allan Poe, Paul Revere, Henry David Thoreau, James McNeil Whistler, John Greenleaf Whittier.

**Tourist information.** Massachusetts Office of Travel & Tourism, 100 Cambridge St., 13th Floor, Boston, MA 02202.
**Toll-free travel information.** 1-800-624-MASS.

## Michigan

*Great Lakes State, Wolverine State*

**People. Population** (1992): 9,436,628; **rank:** 8. **Pop. density:** 166.1 per sq. mi. **Racial distrib.** (1990): 83.4% White; 13.9% Black; 2.2% Hispanic. **Net change** (1990-92): 1.5%.

**Geography. Total area:** 58,527 sq. mi.; **rank:** 23. **Land area:** 56,809 sq. mi. **Acres forested land:** 18,220,000. **Location:** East North Central state bordering on 4 of the 5 Great Lakes, divided into an Upper and Lower Peninsula by the Straits of Mackinac, which link lakes Michigan and Huron. **Climate:** well-defined seasons tempered by the Great Lakes. **Topography:** low rolling hills give way to northern tableland of hilly belts in Lower Peninsula; Upper Peninsula is level in the east, with swampy areas; western region is higher and more rugged. **Capital:** Lansing.

**Economy. Principal industries:** manufacturing, services, tourism, agriculture, mining. **Principal manufactured goods:** transportation equipment, machinery, fabricated metals, primary metals, food prods., rubber & plastics. **Agriculture: Chief crops:** corn, winter wheat, soybeans, dry beans, oats, hay, sugar beets, honey, asparagus, sweet corn, apples, cherries, grapes, peaches, blueberries, flowers. **Livestock** (1992): 1.2 mln. cattle; 1.3 mln. hogs/pigs; 103,000 sheep; 11.5 mln. poultry. **Timber/lumber** (1991): maple, oak, aspen; 313 mln. bd. ft. **Nonfuel Minerals** (1992): $1.4 bln.; iron ore, portland cement, crushed stone, sand & gravel. **Commercial fishing** (1992): $10.4 mln. **Chief ports:** Detroit, Saginaw River, Escanaba, Muskegon, Sault Ste. Marie, Port Huron, Marine City. **International airports at:** Detroit, Sault Ste. Marie. **Value of construction** (1992): $7.5 bln. **Employment distribution** (1992): 23% mfg.; 24% serv.; **Per capita income** (1992): $19,508. **Unemployment** (1992): 8.8%. **Tourism** (1990): travelers spent $16.5 bln. **Sales tax:** 4%.

**Finance.** FDIC-insured commercial banks & trust companies (1992): 230. **Deposits:** $78.7 bln. **Savings institutions** (1992): 34. **Assets:** $29.3 bln.

**Federal government. No. federal civilian employees** (Mar. 1992): 27,218. **Avg. salary:** $34,270. **Notable federal facilities:** Isle Royal, Sleeping Bear Dunes national parks.

**Energy. Electricity production** (1992, MWh, by source): Hydroelectric: 0.8 mln.; Mineral: 52.9 mln.; Nuclear: 29.0 mln.

**Education. Student-teacher ratio** (1991): 19.2. **Avg. salary, public school teachers** (1992-93): $43,331.

**State data. Motto:** Si Quaeris Peninsulam Amoenam Circumspice (If you seek a pleasant peninsula, look about you). **Flower:** Apple blossom. **Bird:** Robin. **Tree:** White pine. **Song:** Michigan, My Michigan. **Entered union** Jan. 26, 1837; rank, 26th. **State fair** at: Detroit, late Aug.-early Sept.; Upper Peninsula (Escanaba), mid-Aug; Michigan Festival, mid.-Aug.

**History.** French fur traders and missionaries visited the region, 1616, set up a mission at Sault Ste. Marie, 1641, and a settlement there, 1668. The whole region went to Britain, 1763. Anthony Wayne defeated their Indian allies at Fallen Timbers, Ohio, 1794. The British returned, 1812, seized Ft. Mackinac and Detroit. Oliver H. Perry's Lake Erie victory and William H. Harrison's troops, who carried the war to the Thames River in Canada, 1813, freed Michigan once more.

**Tourist attractions.** Henry Ford Museum, Greenfield Village, reconstruction of a typical 19th cent. American village, both in Dearborn; Michigan Space Ctr., Jackson; Tahquamenon *(Hiawatha)* Falls; DeZwaan windmill and

Tulip Festival, Holland; "Soo Locks," St. Marys Falls Ship Canal, Sault Ste. Marie.

**Famous Michiganians** include Ralph Bunche, Thomas A. Edison, Gerald R. Ford, Paul de Kruif, Edna Ferber, Henry Ford, Aretha Franklin, Edgar Guest, Lee Iacocca, Robert Ingersoll, Magic Johnson, Will Kellogg, Ring Lardner, Elmore Leonard, Charles Lindbergh, Joe Louis, Madonna, Pontiac, Diana Ross, Tom Selleck, Lily Tomlin, Stewart Edward White, Malcolm X.

**Chamber of Commerce:** 200 N. Washington Sq., Suite 400, Lansing, MI 48933.

**Toll-free travel information.** 1-800-543-2937.

# Minnesota

## North Star State, Gopher State

**People. Population** (1992): 4,480,034; **rank:** 20. **Pop. density:** 56.3 per sq. mi. **Racial distrib.** (1990): 94.4% White; 2.2% Black; 1.8% Asian; 1.2% Hispanic. **Net change** (1990-92): 2.4%.

**Geography. Total area:** 84,402 sq. mi.; **rank:** 12. **Land area:** 79,617 sq. mi. **Acres forested land:** 16,583,000. **Location:** West North Central state bounded on the E by Wisconsin and Lake Superior, on the N by Canada, on the W by the Dakotas, and on the S by Iowa. **Climate:** northern part of state lies in the moist Great Lakes storm belt; the western border lies at the edge of the semi-arid Great Plains. **Topography:** central hill and lake region covering approx. half the state; to the NE, rocky ridges and deep lakes; to the NW, flat plain; to the S, rolling plains and deep river valleys. **Capital:** St. Paul.

**Economy. Principal industries:** agri business, forest products, mining, manufacturing, tourism. **Principal manufactured goods:** food processing, non-electrical machinery, chemicals, paper, electric and electronic equipment, printing and publishing, instruments, fabricated metal products. **Agriculture: Chief crops:** corn, soybeans, wheat, sugar beets, sunflowers, barley. **Livestock** (1990): 2.95 mln. cattle; 4.25 mln. hogs/pigs; 285,000 sheep; 12.7 mln. poultry. **Timber/lumber** (1991): needleleaves and hardwoods; 95 mln. bd. ft. **Nonfuel Minerals** (1992): 1.4 bln.; mostly iron ore, construction sand & gravel, industrial sand and gravel, crushed stone. **Commercial fishing** (1992): $101,000. **Chief ports:** Duluth, St. Paul, Minneapolis. **International airports at:** Minneapolis-St. Paul. **Value of construction** (1992): $5.2 bln. **Employment distribution** (1990): 24.4% trade; 26.0% serv.; 18.3% mfg.; 15.8% govt. **Per capita income** (1992): $20,049. **Unemployment** (1992): 5.1%. **Tourism** (1987): out-of-state visitors spent $3.6 bln. **Sales tax:** 6½%.

**Finance.** FDIC-insured commercial banks & trust companies (1992): 608. **Deposits:** $45.0 bln. **Savings institutions** (1992): 24. **Assets:** $6.7 bln.

**Federal government. No. federal civilian employees** (Mar. 1992): 15,193. **Avg. salary:** $38,854.

**Energy. Electricity production** (1992, MWh, by source): Hydroelectric: 0.7 mln.; Mineral: 21.9 mln.; Nuclear: 11.1 mln.

**Education. Student-teacher ratio** (1991): 17.2. **Avg. salary, public school teachers** (1992-93): $35,656.

**State data. Motto:** L'Etoile du Nord (The star of the north). **Flower:** Pink and white lady's-slipper. **Bird:** Common loon. **Tree:** Red pine. **Song:** Hail! Minnesota. **Entered union** May 11, 1858; rank, 32d. **State fair at:** Saint Paul; late Aug. to early Sept.

**History.** Fur traders and missionaries from French Canada opened the region in the 17th century. Britain took the area east of the Mississippi, 1763. The U.S. took over that portion after the Revolution and in 1803 bought the western area as part of the Louisiana Purchase. The U.S. built present Ft. Snelling, 1820, bought lands from the Indians, 1837. Sioux Indians staged a bloody uprising, 1862, and were driven from the state.

**Tourist attractions.** Minnehaha Falls, Minneapolis, inspiration for Longfellow's *Hiawatha;* over 15,000 lakes; 66 state parks; 25 historical sites; Minneapolis Aquatennial; Ordway Theater, St. Paul; Guthrie Theater, Minneapolis; professional baseball, football, hockey. Voyageurs Nat'l.

Park, a water wilderness along the Canadian border; Mayo Clinic, Rochester; St. Paul Winter Carnival; North Shore (of Lake Superior).

**Famous Minnesotans** include F. Scott Fitzgerald, Cass Gilbert, Hubert Humphrey, Sister Elizabeth Kenny, Sinclair Lewis, Paul Manship, E. G. Marshall, William and Charles Mayo, Walter F. Mondale, Charles Schulz, Harold Stassen, Thorstein Veblen.

**Tourist Information.** Minnesota Office of Tourism, 375 Jackson St., 250 Skyway Level, St. Paul, MN 55101.

**Toll-free travel information.** 1-800-328-1461.

# Mississippi

## Magnolia State

**People. Population** (1992): 2,614,294; **rank:** 31. **Pop. density:** 55.7 per sq. mi. **Racial distrib.** (1990): 63.5% White; 35.6% Black; 0.6% Hispanic. **Net change** (1990-92): 1.6%.

**Geography. Total area:** 47,689 sq. mi.; **rank:** 32. **Land area:** 46,914 sq. mi. **Acres forested land:** 16,693,000. **Location:** East South Central state bordered on the W by the Mississippi R. and on the S by the Gulf of Mexico. **Climate:** semi-tropical, with abundant rainfall, long growing season, and extreme temperatures unusual. **Topography:** low, fertile delta bet. the Yazoo and Mississippi rivers; loess bluffs stretching around delta border; sandy Gulf coastal terraces followed by piney woods and prairie; rugged, high sandy hills in extreme NE followed by black prairie belt. Pontotoc Ridge, and flatwoods into the north central highlands. **Capital:** Jackson.

**Economy. Principal industries:** manufacturing, government, wholesale and retail trade. **Principal manufactured goods:** apparel, food & kindred prods., furniture, lumber and wood prods., electrical machinery, transportation equip. **Agriculture: Chief crops** (1990): cotton, catfish, rice, soybeans. **Livestock** (1991): 1.3 mln. cattle; 149,000 hogs/pigs; 456.5 mln. broilers. **Timber/lumber** (1991): pine, oak, hardwoods; 2.25 bln. bd. ft. **Nonfuel Minerals** (1992): $109.5 mln., mostly construction sand & gravel. **Commercial fishing** (1992): $31.3 mln. **Chief ports:** Pascagoula, Vicksburg, Gulfport, Natchez, Greenville. **Value of construction** (1992): $1.7 bln. **Employment distribution** (1992): 26.1% mfg.; 21.7% gvt.; 20.8% trade; 18.4% serv. **Per capita income** (1992): $14,088. **Unemployment** (1992): 8.1%. **Tourism** (1990): out-of-state visitors spent $1.68 bln. **Sales tax:** 7%.

**Finance.** FDIC-insured commercial banks & trust companies (1992): 123. **Deposits:** $19.1 bln. **Savings institutions** (1992): 21. **Assets:** $2.6 bln.

**Federal government. No. federal civilian employees** (Mar. 1992): 18,396. **Avg. salary:** $32,586. **Notable federal facilities:** Columbus, Keesler AF bases; Meridian Naval Air Station, John C. Stennis Space Center; U.S. Army Corps of Engineers Waterway Experiment Station.

**Energy. Electricity production** (1992, MWh, by source): Mineral: 9.1 mln.; Nuclear: 5.8 mln.

**Education. Student-teacher ratio** (1991): 17.9. **Avg. salary, public school teachers** (1992-93): $24,369.

**State data. Motto:** Virtute et Armis (By valor and arms). **Flower:** Magnolia. **Bird:** Mockingbird. **Tree:** Magnolia. **Song:** Go, Mississippi! **Entered union** Dec. 10, 1817; rank, 20th. **State fair at:** Jackson; Fall.

**History.** De Soto explored the area, 1540, sighted the Mississippi River, 1541. La Salle traced the river from Illinois to its mouth and claimed the entire valley for France, 1682. First settlement was the French Ft. Maurepas, near Ocean Springs, 1699. The area was ceded to Britain, 1763; American settlers followed. During the Revolution, Spain seized part of the area and refused to leave even after the U.S. acquired title at the end of the Revolution, finally moving out, 1798. Mississippi seceded 1861. Union forces captured Corinth and Vicksburg and destroyed Jackson and much of Meridian.

**Tourist attractions.** Vicksburg National Military Park and Cemetery, other Civil War sites; Natchez Trace; Indian mounds; Antebellum Home; pilgrimages in Natchez and some 25 other cities; Jubilee Jam, May, Jackson;

Mardi Gras and blessing of the shrimp fleet, June, both in Biloxi.

**Famous Mississippians** include Dana Andrews, Jimmy Buffet, Hodding Carter III, William Faulkner, Shelby Foote, John Grisham, Fannie Lou Hamer, Jim Henson, Robert Johnson, James Earl Jones, B.B. King, L.Q.C. Lamar, Willie Morris, Elvis Presley, Leontyne Price, Charlie Pride, Margaret Walker, Eudora Welty, Tennessee Williams, Oprah Winfrey, Richard Wright, Tammy Wynette.

**Dept. of Economic & Community Development.** P.O. Box 849, Jackson, MS 39205-0849.

**Toll-free travel information.** 1-800-359-3297; 1-800-647-2290 out of state.

# Missouri

## Show Me State

**People. Population** (1992): 5,192,632; **rank:** 15. **Pop. density:** 75.4 per sq. mi. **Racial distrib.** (1990): 87.7% White; 10.7% Black; 1.2% Hispanic. **Net change** (1990-92): 1.5%.

**Geography. Total area:** 69,697 sq. mi.; **rank:** 19. **Land area:** 68,898 sq. mi. **Acres forested land:** 12,523,000. **Location:** West North Central state near the geographic center of the conterminous U.S.; bordered on the E by the Mississippi R., on the NW by the Missouri R. **Climate:** continental, susceptible to cold Canadian air, moist, warm Gulf air, and drier SW air. **Topography:** Rolling hills, open, fertile plains, and well-watered prairie N of the Missouri R.; south of the river land is rough and hilly with deep, narrow valleys; alluvial plain in the SE; low elevation in the west. **Capital:** Jefferson City.

**Economy. Principal industries:** agriculture, manufacturing, aerospace, tourism. **Principal manufactured goods:** transportation equipment, food and related products, electrical and electronic equipment, chemicals. **Agriculture: Chief crops:** soybeans, corn, wheat, hay. **Livestock** (1991): 4.55 mln. cattle; 2.7 mln. hogs/pigs; 111,000 sheep; 7.6 mln. chickens and eggs, 21.5 mln. turkeys. **Timber/lumber** (1991): oak, hickory; 249 mln. bd. ft. **Nonfuel minerals** (1992): $924.6 mln., mostly lead, crushed stone, portland cement. **Chief ports:** St. Louis, Kansas City. **International airports at:** St. Louis, Kansas City. **Value of construction** (1992): $4.4 bln. **Employment distribution** (1991): 25.2% services; 24.0% trade; 18.1% mfg.; 16.2% gvt. **Per capita income** (1992): $18,835. **Unemployment** (1992): 5.7%. **Tourism** (1990): total travelers spent $5 bln. **Sales tax:** 4.225%.

**Finance. FDIC-insured commercial banks & trust companies** (1992): 532. **Deposits:** $54.4 bln. **Savings institutions** (1992): 61. **Assets:** $14.8 bln.

**Federal government: No. federal civilian employees** (Mar. 1992): 44,700. **Avg. salary:** $32,797. **Notable federal facilities:** Federal Reserve banks, St. Louis, Kansas City; Ft. Leonard Wood, Rolla; Jefferson Barracks, St. Louis; Whiteman AFB, Knob Noster.

**Energy. Electricity production** (1992 MWh, by source): Hydroelectric: 0.8 mln.; Mineral: 38.1 mln.; Nuclear: 7.7 mln.

**Education. Student-teacher ratio** (1991): 15.8. **Avg. salary, public school teachers** (1992-93): $29,410.

**State data. Motto:** Salus Populi Suprema Lex Esto (The welfare of the people shall be the supreme law). **Flower:** Hawthorn. **Bird:** Bluebird. **Tree:** Dogwood. **Song:** Missouri Waltz. **Entered union** Aug. 10, 1821; rank, 24th. **State fair** at: Sedalia; 3d week in Aug.

**History.** DeSoto visited the area, 1541. French hunters and lead miners made the first settlement, c. 1735, at Ste. Genevieve. The U.S. acquired Missouri as part of the Louisiana Purchase, 1803. The fur trade and the Santa Fe Trail provided prosperity; St. Louis became the "jump-off" point for pioneers on their way West. Pro- and anti-slavery forces battled each other there during the Civil War.

**Tourist attractions.** Mark Twain Area, Hannibal; Pony Express Museum, St. Joseph; Harry S. Truman Library, Independence; Gateway Arch, St. Louis; Silver Dollar City, Branson Worlds of Fun, Kansas City; Lake of the Ozarks, Churchill Memorial, Fulton; State Capitol, Jefferson City.

**Famous Missourians** include Josephine Baker, Thomas Hart Benton, George Caleb Bingham, Gen. Omar Bradley, Dale Carnegie, George Washington Carver, Walter Cronkite, Walt Disney, T.S. Eliot, Betty Grable, Jesse James, J. C. Penney, John J. Pershing, Joseph Pulitzer, Ginger Rogers, Bess Truman, Harry S. Truman, Mark Twain, Tennessee Williams.

**Chamber of Commerce:** 400 E. High St., P.O. Box 149, Jefferson City, MO 65101.

**Toll-free travel information.** 1-800-877-1234.

# Montana

## Treasure State

**People. Population** (1992): 823,697; **rank:** 44. **Pop. density:** 5.66 per sq. mi. **Racial distrib.** (1990): 92.7% White; 0.3% Black; 6.0% Amer. Indian; 1.5% Hispanic. **Net change** (1990-92): 3.1%.

**Geography. Total area:** 147,046 sq. mi.; **rank:** 4. **Land area:** 145,556 sq. mi. **Acres forested land:** 21,910,000. **Location:** Mountain state bounded on the E by the Dakotas, on the S by Wyoming, on the S/SW by Idaho, and on the N by Canada. **Climate:** colder, continental climate with low humidity. **Topography:** Rocky Mtns. in western third of the state; eastern two-thirds gently rolling northern Great Plains. **Capital:** Helena.

**Economy. Principal industries:** agriculture, timber, mining, tourism, oil & gas. **Principal manufactured goods:** food prods., wood & paper prods., primary metals, printing & publishing, petroleum & coal prods. **Agriculture: Chief crops:** wheat, barley, sugar beets, hay, oats. **Livestock** (1992): 2.6 mln. cattle; 225,000 hogs/pigs; 688,000 sheep; 780,000 poultry. **Timber/lumber** (1991): Douglas fir, pines, larch; 1.36 bln. bd. ft. **Nonfuel Minerals** (1992): $603.3 mln. mostly metallics. **International airports at:** Great Falls, Billings, Kalispell, Missoula. **Value of construction** (1992): $603.8 mln. **Employment distribution** (1991): 26.8% serv.; 22.6% trade; 18.4% govt.; 7.0% agric.; 5.6% mfg. **Per capita income** (1992): $16,062. **Unemployment** (1992): 6.7%. **Tourism** (1990): non-resident visitors spent $751 mln.

**Finance. FDIC-insured commercial banks & trust companies** (1992): 145. **Deposits:** $6.5 bln. **Savings institutions** (1992): 9. **Assets:** $1.3 bln.

**Federal government. No. federal civilian employees** (Mar. 1992): 8,782. **Avg. salary:** $32,759. **Notable federal facilities:** Malmstrom AFB; Ft. Peck, Hungry Horse, Libby, Yellowtail dams; numerous missile silos.

**Energy. Electricity production** (1992, MWh, by source): Hydroelectric: 6.9 mln; Mineral: 15.8 mln.

**Education. Student-teacher ratio** (1991): 15.8. **Avg. salary, public school teachers** (1992-93): $28,514.

**State data. Motto:** Oro y Plata (Gold and silver). **Flower:** Bitterroot. **Bird:** Western meadowlark. **Tree:** Ponderosa pine. **Song:** Montana. **Entered union** Nov. 8, 1889; rank, 41st. **State fair** at: Great Falls; late July to early Aug.

**History.** French explorers visited the region, 1742. The U.S. acquired the area partly through the Louisiana Purchase, 1803, and partly through the explorations of Lewis and Clark, 1805-06. Fur traders and missionaries established posts in the early 19th century. Indian uprisings reached their peak with the Battle of the Little Bighorn, 1876. Mining activity and the coming of the Northern Pacific Railway, 1883, brought population growth.

**Tourist attractions.** Glacier Natl. Park, on the Continental Divide, is a scenic and recreational wonderland, with 60 glaciers, 200 lakes, and many trout streams. Yellowstone Natl. Park has 3 of the 5 entrances in Montana, with 2,221,000 acres of scenic beauty, inc. geysers, mountains, canyons, streams, lakes, forests, waterfalls.

Also, Museum of the Plains Indian, Blackfeet Reservation near Browning; Little Bighorn Battlefield Natl. Monument & Custer Natl. Cemetery; Flathead Lake, in the NW; Lewis and Clark Caverns State Park, near Whitehall; 7 Indian reservations, covering over 5 million acres; state capitol and historical society, Helena.

Famous Montanans include Gary Cooper, Marcus Daly, Chet Huntley, Will James, Myrna Loy, Mike Mansfield, Brent Musberger, Jeannette Rankin, Charles M. Russell, Lester Thurow.

**Chamber of Commerce.** 2030 11th Ave., P.O. Box 1730, Helena, MT 59624.

**Toll-free travel information.** 1-800-541-1447.

Harold Lloyd, Wright Morris, J. Sterling Morton, John Neidhardt, George Norris, Gen. John J. Pershing, Chief Red Cloud, Mari Sandoz, Roscoe Pound, Malcolm X.

**Chamber of Commerce.** 1320 Lincoln Mall, Box 95128, Lincoln, NE 68501.

**Toll-free travel information.** 1-800-742-7595; 1-800-228-4307 out of state.

## Nebraska

### Cornhusker State

**People. Population** (1992): 1,605,603; **rank:** 36. **Pop. density:** 20.9 per sq. mi. **Racial distrib.** (1990): 93.8% White; 3.6% Black; 2.3% Hispanic. **Net change** (1990-92): 1.7%.

**Geography. Total area:** 77,355 sq. mi.; **rank:** 15. **Land area:** 76,878 sq. mi. **Acres forested land:** 722,000. **Location:** West North Central state with the Missouri R. for a NE/E border. **Climate:** continental semi-arid. **Topography:** till plains of the central lowland in the eastern third rising to the Great Plains and hill country of the north central and NW. **Capital:** Lincoln.

**Economy. Principal industries:** agriculture, food processing, manufacturing. **Principal manufactured goods:** foods, machinery, electric and electronic equipment, primary and fabricated metal products, transportation equipment, instruments & related prod. **Agriculture:** Chief **crops:** corn, sorghum, soybeans, hay, wheat, beans, oats, potatoes, sugar beets. **Livestock** (1990): 6 mln. cattle; 4.2 mln. hogs/pigs; 160,000 sheep; 6.2 mln. chickens, 2.1 mln. turkeys. **Nonfuel Minerals** (1992): $111.2 mln.; mostly portland cement, crushed stone, construction sand & gravel. **Chief ports:** Omaha, Sioux City, Brownville, Blair, Plattsmouth, Nebraska City. **Value of construction** (1992): $1.5 bln. **Employment distribution** (1990): 25.5% trade; 24.4% serv.; 19.7% gvt.; 13.8% mfg.; 8.8% agric. **Per capita income** (1992): $19,084. **Unemployment** (1992): 3.0%. **Tourism** (1991): traveler expenditures $1.7 bln. **Sales tax:** 5%, + some local sales taxes of .5-1.5%.

**Finance.** FDIC-insured commercial banks & trust companies (1992): 389. **Deposits:** $18.6 bln. **Savings institutions** (1992): 16. **Assets:** $7.1 bln.

**Federal government. No. federal civilian employees** (Mar. 1992): 9,135. **Avg. salary:** $33,058. **Notable federal facilities:** Strategic Air Command Base, Omaha.

**Energy. Electricity production** (1992, MWh, by source): Hydroelectric: 0.7 mln.; Mineral: 12.2 mln.; Nuclear: 8.8 mln.

**Education. Student-teacher ratio** (1991): 14.7. **Avg. salary, public school teachers** (1992-93): $28,718.

**State data. Motto:** Equality before the law. **Flower:** Goldenrod. **Bird:** Western meadowlark. **Tree:** Cottonwood. **Song:** Beautiful Nebraska. **Entered union** Mar. 1, 1867; **rank,** 37th. **State fair at:** Lincoln; late Aug. to mid-Sept.

**History.** Spanish and French explorers and fur traders visited the area prior to the Louisiana Purchase, 1803. Lewis and Clark passed through, 1804-06. First permanent settlement was Bellevue, near Omaha, 1823. Many Civil War veterans settled under free land terms of the 1862 Homestead Act; struggles followed between homesteaders and ranchers.

**Tourist attractions.** Architecturally unique, 400'-tall state capitol, Lincoln; Stuhr Museum of the Prairie Pioneer, Grand Island; Museum of the Fur Trade, Chadron; State Museum (Elephant Hall), Lincoln; Joslyn Art Museum, Omaha; Strategic Air Command Museum, Bellevue; Boys Town, founded by Fr. Flanagan, west of Omaha; Arbor Lodge State Park, Nebraska City; Buffalo Bill Ranch State Historical Park, North Platte; Pioneer Village, Minden; Oregon Trail landmarks, Scotts Bluff National Monument, Chimney Rock Historic Site, Ft. Robinson; Hastings Museum, McDonald Planetarium, Hastings.

**Famous Nebraskans** include Fred Astaire, Charles W. and William Jennings Bryan, Johnny Carson, Willa Cather, William F. "Buffalo Bill" Cody, Loren Eiseley, Rev. Edward J. Flanagan, Henry Fonda, Gerald R. Ford, Rollin Kirby,

## Nevada

### Sagebrush State, Battle Born State, Silver State

**People. Population** (1992): 1,327,387; **rank:** 38. **Pop. density:** 12.1 per sq. mi. **Racial distrib.** (1990): 84.3% White; 6.6% Black; 3.2% Asian; 10.4% Hispanic. **Net change** (1990-92): 10.5%.

**Geography. Total area:** 110,561 sq. mi.; **rank:** 7. **Land area:** 109,806 sq. mi. **Acres forested land:** 8,928,000. **Location:** Mountain state bordered on N by Oregon and Idaho, on E by Utah and Arizona, on SE by Arizona, and on SW/W by California. **Climate:** semi-arid and arid. **Topography:** rugged N-S mountain ranges; highest elevation, Boundary Peak, 13,140 ft.; southern area is within the Mojave Desert; lowest elevation, Colorado River at southern tip of state, 479 ft. **Capital:** Carson City.

**Economy. Principal industries:** gaming, tourism, mining, manufacturing, government, agriculture, warehousing, trucking. **Principal manufactured goods:** gaming devices, chemicals, aerospace prods.; lawn & garden irrigation equip.; seismic & machinery-monitoring devices. **Agriculture:** Chief **crops:** hay, alfalfa seed, potatoes, onions, garlic, barley, wheat. **Livestock** (1992): 480,000 cattle; 10,000 hogs/pigs; 91,000 sheep; 12,000 poultry. **Timber/lumber:** piñon, juniper, other pines. **Nonfuel Minerals** (1992): $2.4 bln.; mostly gold, construction sand & gravel. **International airports at:** Las Vegas, Reno. **Value of construction** (1992): $4.0 bln. **Employment distribution** (1992): 44.4% serv.; 20.3% trade; 13.4% gvt. **Per capita income** (1992): $20,266. **Unemployment** (1992): 6.6%. **Tourism** (1991): out-of-state travelers spent over $10 bln. **Sales tax:** 6.5-7%.

**Finance.** FDIC-insured commercial banks & trust companies (1992): 19. **Deposits:** $9.1 bln. **Savings institutions** (1992): 5. **Assets:** $3.8 bln.

**Federal government. No. federal civilian employees** (Mar. 1992): 7,272. **Avg. salary:** $34,817. **Notable federal facilities:** Nevada Test Site; Hawthorne Army Ammunition Plant, Nellis Air Force Base & Gunnery Range; Fallon Naval Air Station; Palomino Valley Wild Horse & Burro Placement Center.

**Energy. Electricity production** (1992, MWh, by source): Hydroelectric: 4.6 mln.; Mineral: 16.5 mln.

**Education. Student-teacher ratio** (1991): 18.6. **Avg. salary, public school teachers** (1992-93): $34,119.

**State data. Motto:** All for our country. **Flower:** Sagebrush. **Bird:** Mountain bluebird. **Trees:** Single-leaf piñon and bristlecone pine. **Song:** Home Means Nevada. **Entered union** Oct. 31, 1864; **rank,** 36th. **State fair at:** Reno; early Sept.

**History.** Nevada was first explored by Spaniards in 1776. Hudson's Bay Co. trappers explored the north and central region, 1825; trader Jedediah Smith crossed the state, 1826 and 1827. The area was acquired by the U.S., in 1848, at the end of the Mexican War. First settlement, Mormon Station, now Genoa, was est. 1849. In the early 20th century, Nevada adopted progressive measures such as the initiative, referendum, recall, and woman suffrage.

**Tourist attractions.** Legalized casino gambling provided the impetus for the development of resort facilities at Lake Tahoe, Reno, Las Vegas, Laughlin, and elsewhere. Ghost towns, rodeos, mountain climbing, skiing, golfing, trout fishing, water sports and hunting important. Notable are Hoover Dam, Lake Mead Natl. Recreation Area, Lake Tahoe, Great Basin Natl. Park, Valley of Fire State Park & Virginia City. Annual events inc. Helldorado Days & Rodeo, Las Vegas; Reno Rodeo; Basque Festival, Elko; Nevada Day, Carson City; Cowboy Poetry Gathering, Elko.

**Famous Nevadans** include Walter Van Tilburg Clark, Sarah Winnemucca Hopkins, Paul Laxalt, Dat So La Lee, John William Mackay, Pat McCarran, Key Pittman, William Morris Stewart.

**Tourist Information.** Commission on Tourism, Capitol Complex, Carson City, NV 89710.

**Toll-free travel information.** 1-800-638-2328.

# New Hampshire
## Granite State

**People. Population** (1992): 1,110,801; **rank:** 41. **Pop. density:** 123.8 per sq. mi. **Racial distrib.** (1990): 98.0% White; 0.6% Black; 1.0% Hispanic. **Net change** (1990-92): −0.1%.

**Geography. Total area:** 9,279 sq. mi.; **rank:** 44. **Land area:** 8,969 sq. mi. **Acres forested land:** 5,021,000. **Location:** New England state bounded on S by Massachusetts, on W by Vermont, on N/NW by Canada, on E by Maine and the Atlantic O. **Climate:** highly varied, due to its nearness to high mountains and ocean. **Topography:** low, rolling coast followed by countless hills and mountains rising out of a central plateau. **Capital:** Concord.

**Economy. Principal industries:** tourism, manufacturing, agriculture, trade, mining. **Principal manufactured goods:** machinery, electrical & electronic products, plastics, fabricated metal products. **Agriculture:** Chief crops: dairy products, nursery and greenhouse products, hay, vegetables, fruit, maple syrup & sugar prods. **Livestock** (1992): 55,000 cattle; 9,500 hogs/pigs; 9,000 sheep; 15,000 horses; 310,000 poultry. **Timber/lumber** (1991): white pine, hemlock, oak, birch; 203 mln. bd. ft. **Nonfuel Minerals** (1992): $42.4 mln.; mostly construction sand & gravel, crushed & dimension stone. **Commercial fishing** (1992): $11.5 mln. **Chief ports:** Portsmouth, Hampton, Rye. **Value of construction** (1992): $1.0 bln. **Employment distribution** (1992): 20.0% mfg.; 25.4% trade; 26.6% serv.; 14.9% gvt. **Per capita income** (1992): $22,934. **Unemployment** (1992): 7.5%. **Tourism** (1992): out-of-state visitors spent $3.3 bln.

**Finance. FDIC-insured commercial banks & trust companies** (1992): 32. **Deposits:** $6.9 bln. **Savings institutions** (1992): 9. **Assets:** $1.6 bln.

**Federal government. No. federal civilian employees** (Mar. 1992): 3,747. **Avg. salary:** $37,070.

**Energy. Electricity production** (1992, MWh, by source): Hydroelectric: 0.9 mln.; Mineral: 5.8 mln.; Nuclear: 8.5 mln.

**Education:** Student-teacher ratio (1991): 15.5. **Avg. salary, public school teachers** (1992-93): $33,931.

**State data.** Motto: Live free or die. **Flower:** Purple lilac. **Bird:** Purple finch. **Tree:** White birch. **Song:** Old New Hampshire. **Ninth** of the original 13 states to ratify the Constitution, June 21, 1788.

**History.** First explorers to visit the New Hampshire area were England's Martin Pring, 1603, and Champlain, 1605. First settlement was Odiorne's Point (now port of Rye), 1623. Indian raids were halted, 1759, by Robert Rogers' Rangers. Before the Revolution, New Hampshire men seized a British fort at Portsmouth, 1774, and drove the royal governor out, 1775. Three regiments served in the Continental Army and scores of privateers raided British shipping.

**Tourist attractions.** Mt. Washington, highest peak in Northeast, hub of network of trails; Lake Winnipesaukee; White Mt. Natl. Forest; Crawford, Franconia, Pinkham notches in White Mt. region—Franconia famous for the Old Man of the Mountain, described by Hawthorne as the Great Stone Face; the Flume, a spectacular gorge; the aerial tramway on Cannon Mt; Strawbery Banke, Portsmouth; Shaker Village, Canterbury; Saint-Gaudens, natl. historic site, Cornish; Mt. Monadnock.

**Famous New Hampshirites** include Salmon P. Chase, Ralph Adams Cram, Mary Baker Eddy, Daniel Chester French, Robert Frost, Horace Greeley, Sarah Buell Hale, Franklin Pierce, Augustus Saint-Gaudens, Daniel Webster.

**Tourist Information.** Department of Resources and Economic Development, Division of Travel & Tourism Development, P.O. Box 856, Concord, NH 03302-0856; 603-271-2666.

# New Jersey
## Garden State

**People. Population** (1992): 7,789,060; **rank:** 9. **Pop. density:** 1,049.9 per sq. mi. **Racial distrib.** (1990): 79.3% White; 13.4% Black; 3.5% Asian; 9.6% Hispanic. **Net change** (1990-92): 0.8%.

**Geography. Total area:** 7,787 sq. mi.; **rank:** 46. **Land area:** 7,419 sq. mi. **Acres forested land:** 1,985,000. **Location:** Middle Atlantic state bounded on the N and E by New York and the Atlantic O., on the S and W by Delaware and Pennsylvania. **Climate:** moderate, with marked difference bet. NW and SE extremities. **Topography:** Appalachian Valley in the NW also has highest elevation, High Pt., 1,801 ft.; Appalachian Highlands, flat-topped NE-SW mountain ranges; Piedmont Plateau, low plains broken by high ridges (Palisades) rising 400-500 ft.; Coastal Plain, covering three-fifths of state in SE, gradually rises from sea level to gentle slopes. **Capital:** Trenton.

**Economy. Principal industries:** services, trade, manufacturing. **Principal manufactured goods:** chemicals, electronic and electrical equipment, non-electrical machinery, fabricated metals. **Agriculture:** Chief crops: hay, corn, soybeans, tomatoes, blueberries, peaches, cranberries. **Livestock** (1992): 77,000 cattle; 24,000 hogs/pigs; 13,000 sheep; 2.1 mln. poultry. **Timber/lumber** (1991): pine, cedar, mixed hardwoods. **Nonfuel Minerals** (1992): $213.7 mln.; mostly crushed stone, construction sand & gravel. **Commercial fishing** (1992): $97.5 mln. **Chief ports:** Newark, Elizabeth, Hoboken, Camden. **International airports at:** Newark. **Value of construction** (1992): $5.5 bln. **Employment distribution** (1992): 28.2% serv.; 23.5% trade; 15.3% mfg.; 16.5% gvt. **Per capita income** (1992): $26,457. **Unemployment** (1992): 8.4%. **Tourism** (1992): tourists spent $17.9 bln. **Sales tax:** 6%.

**Finance. FDIC-insured commercial banks & trust companies** (1992): 117. **Deposits:** $81.2 bln. **Savings institutions** (1992): 81. **Assets:** $24.0 bln.

**Federal government. No. federal civilian employees** (Mar. 1992): 39,395. **Avg. salary:** $37,745. **Notable federal facilities:** McGuire AFB; Fort Dix; Fort Monmouth; Picatinny Arsenal; Lakewood Naval Air Station, Lakehurst Naval Air Engineering Center; Naval Air Warfare Center, Ewing.

**Energy. Electricity production** (1992, MWh, by source): Mineral: 8.4 mln.; Nuclear: 18.8 mln.

**Education.** Student-teacher ratio (1991): 13.8. **Avg. salary, public school teachers** (1992-93): $43,997.

**State Data.** Motto: Liberty and prosperity. **Flower:** Purple violet. **Bird:** Eastern goldfinch. **Tree:** Red oak. **Third** of the original 13 states to ratify the Constitution, Dec. 18, 1787. **State fair:** usually Aug.

**History.** The Lenni-Lenape (Delaware) Indians had mostly peaceful relations with European colonists who arrived after the explorers Verrazano, 1524, and Hudson, 1609. The Dutch were first; when the British took New Netherland, 1664, the area between the Delaware and Hudson Rivers was given to Lord John Berkeley and Sir George Carteret. New Jersey was the scene of nearly 100 battles, large and small, during the Revolution, including Trenton, 1776, Princeton, 1777, Monmouth, 1778.

**Tourist attractions.** 127 miles of beaches; Miss America Pageant and hotel-casinos, Atlantic City; Grover Cleveland birthplace, Caldwell; Cape May Historic District; Edison Labs, W. Orange; Great Adventure amusement park; Liberty State Park; Meadowlands Sports Complex; Pine Barrens wilderness area; Princeton University; numerous Revolutionary War historical sites; State Aquarium, Camden.

**Famous New Jerseyans** include Count Basie, Judy Blume, Aaron Burr, Grover Cleveland, James Fenimore Cooper, Stephen Crane, Thomas Edison, Albert Einstein,

Alexander Hamilton, Joyce Kilmer, Gen. George McClellan, Thomas Paine, Molly Pitcher, Paul Robeson, Philip Roth, Walter Schirra, Frank Sinatra, Bruce Springsteen, Walt Whitman, William Carlos Williams, Woodrow Wilson.

**Chamber of Commerce.** 50 W. State St., Trenton, NJ 08608.

**Toll-free travel information.** 1-800-JERSEY-7.

# New Mexico
## Land of Enchantment

**People. Population** (1992): 1,581,227; **rank:** 37. **Pop. density:** 13.0 per sq. mi. **Racial distrib.** (1990): 75.6% White; 2.0% Black; 8.9% Amer. Indian; 38.2% Hispanic. **Net change** (1990-92): 4.4%.

**Geography. Total area:** 121,593 sq. mi.; **rank:** 5. **Land area:** 121,364 sq. mi. **Acres forested land:** 18,526,000. **Location:** southwestern state bounded by Colorado on the N, Oklahoma, Texas, and Mexico on the E and S, and Arizona on the W. **Climate:** dry, with temperatures rising or falling 5° F with every 1,000 ft. elevation. **Topography:** eastern third, Great Plains; central third, Rocky Mtns. (85% of the state is over 4,000 ft. elevation); western third, high plateau. **Capital:** Santa Fe.

**Economy. Principal industries:** government, services, trade. **Principal manufactured goods:** foods, machinery, apparel, lumber, printing, transportation equipment. **Agriculture:** Chief crops: hay, onions, wheat, pecans, corn, cotton, sorghum. **Livestock** (1990): 1.34 mln. cattle; 27,000 hogs; 462,000 sheep; 1.43 mln. poultry. **Timber/lumber** (1991): Ponderosa pine, Douglas fir; 139 mln. bd. ft. **Nonfuel Minerals** (1992): $866.1 mln.; copper, potash, construction sand & gravel. **International airports at:** Albuquerque. **Value of construction** (1992): $1.4 bln. **Employment distribution** (1990): 26% serv.; 2% agric.; 10% mfg.; 26.2% gvt. **Per capita income** (1992): $15,353. **Unemployment** (1992): 6.8%. **Tourism** (1990): out-of-state visitors spent $2.2 bln. **Sales tax:** 5-6.75%.

**Finance. FDIC-insured commercial banks & trust companies** (1992): 83. **Deposits:** $10.7 bln. **Savings institutions** (1992): 13. **Assets:** $1.2 bln.

**Federal government. No. federal civilian employees** (Mar. 1992): 23,716. **Avg. salary:** $33,157. **Notable federal facilities:** Kirtland, Cannon, Holloman AF bases; Los Alamos Scientific Laboratory; White Sands Missile Range; National Solar Observatory; National Radio Astronomy Observatory.

**Energy. Electricity production** (1992, MWh, by source): Hydroelectric: 0.1 mln.; Mineral: 18.7 mln.

**Education. Student-teacher ratio** (1991): 17.6. **Avg. salary, public school teachers** (1992-93): $26,355.

**State data. Motto:** Crescit Eundo (It grows as it goes). **Flower:** Yucca. **Bird:** Roadrunner. **Tree:** Piñon. **Song:** O, Fair New Mexico; Asi Es Nuevo Mexico. **Entered union** Jan. 6, 1912; rank, 47th. **State fair** at: Albuquerque; mid-Sept.

**History.** Franciscan Marcos de Niza and a black slave Estevan explored the area, 1539, seeking gold. First settlements were at San Juan Pueblo, 1598, and Santa Fe, 1610. Settlers alternately traded and fought with the Apaches, Comanches, and Navajos. Trade on the Santa Fe Trail to Missouri started 1821. The Mexican War was declared May, 1846, Gen. Stephen Kearny took Santa Fe, August. In the 1870s, cattlemen staged the famed Lincoln County War in which Billy (the Kid) Bonney played a leading role. Pancho Villa raided Columbus, 1916.

**Tourist Attractions.** Carlsbad Caverns, a national park, has caverns on 3 levels and the largest natural cave "room" in the world, 1,500 by 300 ft., 300 ft. high; White Sands Natl. Monument, the largest gypsum deposit in the world.

Pueblo ruins from 100 AD, Chaco Canyon; Acoma, the "sky city," built atop a 357-ft. mesa; 19 Pueblo, 4 Navajo, and 2 Apache reservations. Also, ghost towns, dude ranches, skiing, hunting, and fishing.

**Famous New Mexicans** include Billy (the Kid) Bonney, Kit Carson, Peter Hurd, Archbishop Jean Baptiste Lamy, Nancy Lopez, Bill Mauldin, Georgia O'Keeffe, Kim Stanley, Al Unser, Bobby Unser, Lew Wallace.

**Tourist information.** New Mexico Dept. of Tourism, P.O. Box 20003, Santa Fe, N.M. 87503.

**Toll-free travel information.** 1-800-545-2040.

# New York
## Empire State

**People. Population** (1992): 18,119,416; **rank:** 2. **Pop. density:** 383.7 per sq. mi. **Racial distrib.** (1990): 74.4% White; 15.9% Black; 3.9% Asian; 12.3% Hispanic. **Net change** (1990-92): 0.7%.

**Geography. Total area:** 49,108 sq. mi.; **rank:** 30. **Land area:** 47,224 sq. mi. **Acres forested land:** 18,775,000. **Location:** Middle Atlantic state, bordered by the New England states, Atlantic Ocean, New Jersey and Pennsylvania, Lakes Ontario and Erie, and Canada. **Climate:** variable; the SE region moderated by the ocean. **Topography:** highest and most rugged mountains in the NE Adirondack upland; St. Lawrence-Champlain lowlands extend from Lake Ontario NE along the Canadian border; Hudson-Mohawk lowland follows the flows of the rivers N and W, 10-30 mi. wide; Atlantic coastal plain in the SE; Appalachian Highlands, covering half the state westward from the Hudson Valley, include the Catskill Mtns., Finger Lakes; plateau of Erie-Ontario lowlands. **Capital:** Albany.

**Economy. Principal industries:** manufacturing, finance, communications, tourism, transportation, services. **Principal manufactured goods:** books and periodicals, clothing and apparel, pharmaceuticals, machinery, instruments, toys and sporting goods, electronic equipment, automotive and aircraft components. **Agriculture:** Chief crops: apples, cabbage, cauliflower, celery, cherries, grapes, corn, peas, snap beans, sweet corn. **Products:** milk, cheese, maple syrup, wine. **Livestock** (1990): 1.6 mln. cattle; 103,000 hogs/pigs; 92,000 sheep; 9.8 mln. poultry. **Timber/lumber** (1991): saw log production; 380 mln. bd. ft. **Nonfuel Minerals** (1992): $715.0 mln.; mostly crushed stone, salt, cement, construction sand & gravel, zinc. **Commercial fishing** (1992): $54.0 mln. **Chief ports:** New York, Buffalo, Albany. **International airports at:** New York, Buffalo, Syracuse, Massena, Ogdensburg, Watertown, Niagara Falls, Newburgh, Sullivan county. **Value of construction** (1992): $14.2 bln. **Employment distribution** (1992): 30% serv.; 20% trade; 18% gvt.; 13% mfg. **Per capita income** (1992): $23,534. **Unemployment** (1992): 8.5%. **Tourism** (1991): tourists spent $19.0 bln. **Sales tax:** 4-8¼%.

**Finance. FDIC-insured commercial banks & trust companies** (1992): 189. **Deposits:** $480.7 bln. **Savings institutions** (1992): 68. **Assets:** $41.5 bln.

**Federal government. No. federal civilian employees** (Mar. 1992): 70,019. **Avg. salary:** $35,369. **Notable federal facilities:** West Point Military Academy; Merchant Marine Academy; Ft. Drum; Griffiss, Plattsburgh AF bases; Watervliet Arsenal.

**Energy. Electricity production** (1992, MWh, by source): Hydroelectric: 20.0 mln.; Mineral: 49.3 mln.; Nuclear: 27.2 mln.

**Education. Student-teacher ratio** (1991): 15.4. **Avg. salary, public school teachers** (1992-93): $44,600.

**State data. Motto:** Excelsior (Ever upward). **Flower:** Rose. **Bird:** Bluebird. **Tree:** Sugar maple. **Song:** I Love New York. **Eleventh** of the original 13 states to ratify the Constitution, July 26, 1788. **State fair** at: Syracuse; late Aug.-early Sept.

**History.** In 1609 Henry Hudson visited the river that bears his name and Champlain explored the lake, far upstate, that was named for him. Dutch built posts near present-day Albany and New York City in 1624; in 1626 they settled Manhattan. A British fleet seized New Netherland, 1664. Ninety-two of the 300 or more engagements of the Revolution were fought in New York, including the Battle of Bemis Heights-Saratoga, a turning point of the war.

**Tourist attractions.** New York City; Adirondack and Catskill mtns.; Finger Lakes, Great Lakes; Long Island beaches; Thousand Islands; Niagara Falls; Saratoga Springs racing and spas; Philipsburg Manor, Sunnyside, the restored home of Washington Irving, The Dutch Church of Sleepy Hollow, all in North Tarrytown; Corning Glass Center and Steuben factory, Corning; Fenimore House, National Baseball Hall of Fame and Museum, both in Cooperstown; Ft. Ticonderoga overlooking Lakes George and Champlain; Albany's Empire State Plaza; Lake Placid Olympic Village.

The Franklin D. Roosevelt National Historic Site, Hyde Park, includes the graves of Pres. and Mrs. Roosevelt, the family home since 1867, the Roosevelt Library. Sagamore Hill, Oyster Bay, the Theodore Roosevelt estate, includes his home.

**Famous New Yorkers** include Susan B. Anthony, Peter Cooper, George Eastman, Millard Fillmore, George and Ira Gershwin, Julia Ward Howe, Charles Evans Hughes, Henry and William James, Herman Melville, Franklin Delano Roosevelt, Theodore Roosevelt, Alfred E. Smith, Elizabeth Cady Stanton, Martin Van Buren, Walt Whitman.

**Tourist information.** N.Y. State Dept. of Economic Development, 1 Commerce Plaza, Albany, NY 12245.

**Toll-free travel information.** 1-800-CALLNYS from 50 states & U.S. territories; 1-518-474-4116 from other areas and Canada.

## North Carolina

*Tar Heel State, Old North State*

**People. Population** (1992): 6,842,691; **rank:** 10. **Pop. density:** 140.5 per sq. mi. **Racial distrib.** (1990): 75.6% White; 22.0% Black; 1.2% Amer. Indian; 1.2% Hispanic. **Net change** (1990-92): 3.2%.

**Geography. Total area:** 52,669 sq. mi.; **rank:** 28. **Land area:** 48,718 sq. mi. **Acres forested land:** 18,891,000. **Location:** South Atlantic state bounded by Virginia, South Carolina, Georgia, Tennessee, and the Atlantic O. **Climate:** sub-tropical in SE, medium-continental in mountain region; tempered by the Gulf Stream and the mountains in W. **Topography:** coastal plain and tidewater, two-fifths of state, extending to the fall line of the rivers; piedmont plateau, another two-fifths, 200 mi. wide of gentle to rugged hills; southern Appalachian Mtns. contains the Blue Ridge and Great Smoky mtns. **Capital:** Raleigh.

**Economy. Principal industries:** manufacturing, agriculture, tobacco, tourism. **Principal manufactured goods:** textiles, tobacco products, electrical/electronic equip., chemicals, furniture, food products, non-electrical machinery. **Agriculture: Chief crops:** tobacco, soybeans, corn, peanuts, sweet potatoes, feed grains, vegetables, fruits. **Livestock** (1991): 950,000 cattle; 3.6 mln. hogs/pigs; 19.3 mln. chickens. **Timber/lumber** (1991): yellow pine, oak, hickory, poplar, maple; 1.56 bln. bd. ft. **Nonfuel Minerals** (1992): Total $573.0 mln.; mostly clay, sand & gravel, crushed stone. **Commercial fishing** (1992): $57.5 mln. **Chief ports:** Morehead City, Wilmington. **Value of construction** (1992): $8.0 bln. **Employment distribution** (1992): 26.6% mfg.; 22.8% trade; 20.4% serv.; 16.3% gvt. **Per capita income** (1992): $17,667. **Unemployment** (1992): 5.9%. **Tourism** (1991): out-of-state visitors spent $7.0 bln. **Sales tax:** 6%.

**Finance. FDIC-insured commercial banks & trust companies** (1992): 81. **Deposits:** $59.7 bln. **Savings institutions** (1992): 60. **Assets:** $10.2 bln.

**Federal government. No. federal civilian employees** (Mar. 1992): 30,680. **Avg. salary:** $31,155. **Notable federal facilities:** Ft. Bragg; Camp LeJeune Marine Base; U.S. EPA Research and Development Labs, Cherry Point Marine Corps Air Station; Natl. Humanities Center; Natl. Inst. of Environmental Health Science; Natl. Center for Health Statistics Lab, Research Triangle Park.

**Energy. Electricity production** (1992, MWh, by source): Hydroelectric: 5.7 mln.; Mineral: 46.5 mln.; Nuclear: 21.7 mln.

**Education. Student-teacher ratio** (1991): 16.8. **Avg. salary, public school teachers** (1992-93): $29,367.

**State data. Motto:** Esse Quam Videri (To be rather than to seem). **Flower:** Dogwood. **Bird:** Cardinal. **Tree:** Pine. **Song:** The Old North State. **Twelfth** of the original 13 states to ratify the Constitution, Nov. 21, 1789. **State fair** at: Raleigh; mid-Oct.

**History.** The first English colony in America was the first of 2 established by Sir Walter Raleigh on Roanoke Is., 1585 and 1587. The first group returned to England; the second, the "Lost Colony," disappeared without trace. Permanent settlers came from Virginia, c. 1660. Roused by British repressions, the colonists drove out the royal governor, 1775; the province's congress was the first to vote for independence; ten regiments were furnished to the Continental Army. Cornwallis' forces were defeated at Kings Mountain, 1780, and forced out after Guilford Courthouse, 1781.

**Tourist attractions.** Cape Hatteras and Cape Lookout national seashores; Great Smoky Mtns. (half in Tennessee); Guilford Courthouse and Moore's Creek parks, 66 Revolutionary battle sites; Bennett Place, NW of Durham, where Gen. Joseph Johnston surrendered the last Confederate army to Gen. Wm. Sherman; Ft. Raleigh, Roanoke Is., where Virginia Dare, first child of English parents in the New World, was born Aug. 18, 1587; Wright Brothers National Memorial, Kitty Hawk; N.C. Zoo, Asheboro; N.C. Symphony, & N.C. Museum, Raleigh.

**Famous North Carolinians** include Richard J. Gatling, Billy Graham, Andy Griffith, Andrew Jackson, Andrew Johnson, Michael Jordan, Wm. Rufus King, Charles Kuralt, Dolley Madison, Edward R. Murrow, James K. Polk, Enos Slaughter, Thomas Wolfe.

**Tourist information.** Travel & Tourism Division, 430 No. Salisbury St., Raleigh, NC 27603.

**Toll-free travel information.** 1-800-VISITNC.

## North Dakota

*Peace Garden State*

**People. Population** (1992): 635,927; **rank:** 47. **Pop. density:** 9.2 per sq. mi. **Racial distrib.** (1990): 94.6% White; 0.6% Black; 4.1% Amer. Indian; 0.7% Hispanic. **Net change** (1990-1992): −0.5%.

**Geography. Total area:** 70,702 sq. mi.; **rank:** 17. **Land area:** 68,994 sq. mi. **Acres forested land:** 460,000. **Location:** West North Central state, situated exactly in the middle of North America, bounded on the N by Canada, on the E by Minnesota, on the S by South Dakota, on the W by Montana. **Climate:** continental, with a wide range of temperature and moderate rainfall. **Topography:** Central Lowland in the E comprises the flat Red River Valley and the Rolling Drift Prairie; Missouri Plateau of the Great Plains on the W. **Capital:** Bismarck.

**Economy. Principal industries:** agriculture, mining, tourism, manufacturing, telecommunications, energy. **Principal manufactured goods:** farm equipment, processed foods, fabricated metal, high-tech. electronics. **Agriculture: Chief crops:** spring wheat, durum, barley, rye, flaxseed, oats, potatoes, dried edible beans, honey, soybeans, sugar beets, sunflowers, hay. **Livestock** (1992): 1.85 mln. cattle; 290,000 hogs/pigs; 214,000 sheep; 1.5 mln. poultry. **Nonfuel Minerals** (1992): $17.7 mln.; mostly construction sand & gravel, lime. **International airports at:** Fargo, Grand Forks, Bismarck, Minot. **Value of construction** (1992): $586.9 mln. **Employment distribution** (1991): 22.8% trade; 35.2% serv.; 18.6% gvt.; 11.7% agric. **Per capita income** (1992): $16,854. **Unemployment** (1992): 4.9%. **Tourism** (1991): $790 mln. **Sales tax:** 5-6%.

**Finance. FDIC-insured commercial banks & trust companies** (1992): 146. **Deposits:** $6.8 bln. **Savings institutions** (1992): 4. **Assets:** $6.7 bln.

**Federal government. No. federal civilian employees** (Mar. 1992): 5,505. **Avg. salary:** $30,795. **Notable federal facilities:** Strategic Air Command bases at Minot, Grand Forks; Northern Prairie Wildlife Research Center; Garrison Dam; Theodore Roosevelt Natl. Park; Grand Forks Energy Research Center; Ft. Union Natl. Historic Site.

**Energy. Electricity production** (1992, MWh, by source): Hydroelectric: 1.9 mln.; Mineral: 24.3 mln.

**Education. Student-teacher ratio** (1991): 15.3. **Avg. salary, public school teachers** (1992-93): $25,211.

**State data. Motto:** Liberty and union, now and forever, one and inseparable. **Flower:** Wild prairie rose. **Bird:** Western meadowlark. **Tree:** American elm. **Song:** North Dakota Hymn. **Entered union** Nov. 2, 1889; rank, 39th. **State fair** at: Minot; 3d week in July.

**History.** Pierre La Verendrye was the first French fur trader in the area, 1738, followed later by the English. The U.S. acquired half the territory in the Louisiana Purchase, 1803. Lewis and Clark built Ft. Mandan, spent the winter of 1804-05 there. In 1818, American ownership of the other half was confirmed by agreement with Britain. First permanent settlement was at Pembina, 1812. Missouri River steamboats reached the area, 1832; the first railroad, 1873, bringing many homesteaders. The state was first to hold a presidential primary, 1912.

**Tourist attractions.** North Dakota Heritage Center, state capitol grounds; Bonanzaville, Fargo, restored pioneer town; Ft. Union Trading Post Natl. Historic Site, built 1829; Lake Sakakawea, 180 miles of fishing, boating, 1,600 miles of shoreline. Interntl. Peace Garden, 2,200-acre tract extending across the border into Manitoba; 65,000-acre Theodore Roosevelt National Park, Badlands, contains the president's Elkhorn Ranch; Ft. Abraham Lincoln State Park and Museum, S of Mandan.

**Famous North Dakotans** include Maxwell Anderson, Angie Dickinson, John Bernard Flannagan, Louis L'Amour, Peggy Lee, Eric Sevareid, Vilhjalmur Stefansson, Lawrence Welk.

**Chamber of Commerce.** P.O. Box 2639, 2000 Schafer St., Bismarck, ND 58501.

**Toll-free travel information.** 1-800-437-2077.

# Ohio

## Buckeye State

**People. Population** (1992): 11,016,385; **rank: 7. Pop. density:** 269.0 per sq. mi. **Racial distrib.** (1990): 87.8% White; 10.6% Black; 1.3% Hispanic. **Net change** (1990-92): 1.6%.

**Geography. Total area:** 41,330 sq. mi.; **rank: 35. Land area:** 40,953 sq. mi. **Acres forested land:** 7,309,000. **Location:** East North Central state bounded on the N by Michigan and Lake Erie; on the E and S by Pennsylvania, West Virginia, and Kentucky; on the W by Indiana. **Climate:** temperate but variable; weather subject to much precipitation. **Topography:** generally rolling plain; Allegheny plateau in E; Lake [Erie] plains extend southward; central plains in the W. **Capital:** Columbus.

**Economy. Principal industries:** manufacturing, trade, services. **Principal manufactured goods:** transportation equipment, machinery, primary and fabricated metal products. **Agriculture: Chief crops:** corn, hay, winter wheat, oats, soybeans. **Livestock** (1992): 1.6 mln. cattle; 1.9 mln. hogs/pigs; 24.9 mln. broilers, 5 mln. turkeys. **Timber/lumber** (1991): oak, ash, maple, walnut, beech; 295 mln. bd. ft. **Nonfuel Minerals** (1992): $679.9 mln.; mostly crushed stone, construction sand & gravel, lime, portland cement. **Commercial fishing** (1992): $2.6 mln. **Chief ports:** Toledo, Conneaut, Cleveland, Ashtabula. **International airports at:** Cleveland, Cincinnati, Columbus, Dayton. **Value of construction** (1992): $10.8 bln. **Employment distribution** (1992): 21.7% mfg.; 24.0% trade; 25.6% serv.; 15.2% gvt. **Per capita income** (1992): $18,624. **Unemployment** (1992): 7.2%. **Tourism** (1992): travelers spent $8.8 bln.

**Finance.** FDIC-insured commercial banks & trust companies (1992): 280. **Deposits:** $92.2 bln. **Savings institutions** (1992): 181. **Assets:** $36.5 bln.

**Federal government. No. federal civilian employees** (Mar. 1992): 55,426. **Avg. salary:** $35,745. **Notable federal facilities:** Wright Patterson AF base; Defense Construction Supply Center; Lewis Research Ctr.; Portsmouth Gaseous Diffusion Plant; Mound Laboratory.

**Energy. Electricity production** (1992, MWh, by source): Hydroelectric: 0.2 mln.; Mineral: 107.6 mln.; Nuclear: 13.9 mln.

**Education. Student-teacher ratio** (1991): 17.3. **Avg. salary, public school teachers** (1992-93): $34,600.

**State data. Motto:** With God, all things are possible. **Flower:** Scarlet carnation. **Bird:** Cardinal. **Tree:** Buckeye. **Song:** Beautiful Ohio. **Entered union** Mar. 1, 1803; rank, 17th. **State fair** at: Columbus; August.

**History.** LaSalle visited the Ohio area, 1669. American fur-traders arrived, beginning 1685; the French and Indians sought to drive them out. During the Revolution, Virginians defeated the Indians, 1774, but hostilities were renewed, 1777. The region became U.S. territory after the Revolution. First organized settlement was at Marietta, 1788. Indian warfare ended with Anthony Wayne's victory at Fallen Timbers, 1794. In the War of 1812, Oliver Hazard Perry's victory on Lake Erie and William Henry Harrison's invasion of Canada, 1813, ended British incursions.

**Tourist attractions.** Mound City Group National Monuments, a group of 24 prehistoric Indian burial mounds; Neil Armstrong Air and Space Museum, Wapakoneta; Air Force Museum, Dayton; Pro Football Hall of Fame, Canton; King's Island amusement park, King's Island; Cedar Point amusement park, Sandusky; birthplaces, homes, and memorials to Ohio's 8 U.S. presidents: William Henry Harrison, Grant, Garfield, Hayes, McKinley, Harding, Taft, Benjamin Harrison; Lake Erie Islands, Sandusky; Amish Region, Tuscarawas/Holmes counties; German Village, Columbus; Sea World, Aurora; Jack Nicklaus Sports Center, Mason; Bob Evans Farm, Rio Grande.

**Famous Ohioans** include Sherwood Anderson, Neil Armstrong, George Bellows, Ambrose Bierce, Clarence Darrow, Paul Laurence Dunbar, Thomas Edison, Clark Gable, John Glenn, Bob Hope, Jack Nicklaus, Jesse Owens, Eddie Rickenbacker, John D. Rockefeller Sr. and Jr., Pete Rose, Gen. Wm. Sherman, Harriet Beecher Stowe, Charles Taft, Robert A. Taft, William H. Taft, James Thurber, Orville Wright.

**Chamber of Commerce.** 35 E. Gay St., Columbus, OH 43215.

**Toll-free travel information.** 1-800-BUCKEYE.

# Oklahoma

## Sooner State

**People. Population** (1992): 3,212,198; **rank: 28. Pop. density:** 46.8 per sq. mi. **Racial distrib.** (1990): 82.1% White; 7.4% Black; 8.0% Amer. Indian; 2.7% Hispanic. **Net change** (1990-92): 2.1%.

**Geography. Total area:** 69,919 sq. mi.; **rank: 18. Land area:** 68,679 sq. mi. **Acres forested land:** 7,283,000. **Location:** West South Central state bounded on the N by Colorado and Kansas; on the E by Missouri and Arkansas; on the S and W by Texas and New Mexico. **Climate:** temperate; southern humid belt merging with colder northern continental; humid eastern and dry western zones. **Topography:** high plains predominate the W, hills and small mountains in the E; the east central region is dominated by the Arkansas R. Basin, and the Red R. Plains, in the S. **Capital:** Oklahoma City.

**Economy. Principal industries:** manufacturing, mineral and energy exploration and production, agriculture, services, printing & publishing. **Principal manufactured goods:** non-electrical machinery, fabricated metal products, petroleum. **Agriculture: Chief crops:** wheat, hay, peanuts, grain sorghum, soybeans, corn, pecans, oats, barley, rye. **Livestock** (1990): 5.2 mln. cattle; 215,000 hogs/pigs; 135,000 sheep; 4.75 mln. poultry. **Timber/lumber** (1991): pine, oaks, hickory; 219 mln. bd. ft. **Nonfuel Minerals** (1992): $284.3 mln.; mostly crushed stone, portland cement, iodine. **Chief ports:** Catoosa, Muskogee. **International airports at:** Oklahoma City, Tulsa. **Value of construction** (1992): $2.5 bln. **Employment distribution** (1990): 23.3% trade; 22.2% gvt.; 23.0% serv.; 14.0% mfg. **Per capita income** (1992): $16,198. **Unemployment** (1992): 5.7%. **Tourism** (1990): tourists spent $2.56 bln.

**Finance.** FDIC-insured commercial banks & trust companies (1992): 411. **Deposits:** $24.8 bln. **Savings institutions** (1992): 19. **Assets:** $5.5 bln.

**Federal government. No. federal civilian employees** (Mar. 1992): 35,022. **Avg. salary:** $32,253. **Notable federal facilities:** Federal Aviation Agency and Tinker AFB, both Oklahoma City; Ft. Sill, Lawton; Altus AFB, Altus; Vance AFB, Enid.

**Energy. Electricity production** (1992, MWh, by source): Hydroelectric: 2.5 mln.; Mineral: 26.1 mln.

**Education. Student-teacher ratio** (1991): 15.6. **Avg. salary, public school teachers** (1992-93): $26,051.

**State data. Motto:** Labor Omnia Vincit (Labor conquers all things). **Flower:** Mistletoe. **Bird:** Scissor-tailed flycatcher. **Tree:** Redbud. **Song:** Oklahoma! **Entered union** Nov. 16, 1907; rank, 46th. **State fair at:** Oklahoma City; last week of Sept.

**History.** Part of the Louisiana Purchase, 1803, Oklahoma was known as Indian Territory (but was not given territorial government) after it became the home of the "Five Civilized Tribes"—Cherokee, Choctaw, Chickasaw, Creek, and Seminole—1828-1846. The land was also used by Comanche, Osage, and other Plains Indians. As white settlers pressed west, land was opened for homesteading by runs and lottery, the first run taking place Apr. 22, 1889. The most famous run was to the Cherokee Outlet, 1893.

**Tourist attractions.** State park system—camping, hiking, water sports; Cherokee Heritage Center, Tahlequah; White Water Bay and Frontier City theme pks., both Oklahoma City; Will Rogers Memorial, Claremore; National Cowboy Hall of Fame and Remington Park Race Track, both Oklahoma City; restored Ft. Gibson Stockade, near Muskogee, the Army's largest outpost in Indian lands; Indian pow-wows; rodeos; fishing; hunting; Ouachita National Forest; Enterprise Square, museum devoted to American economic system; Tulsa's art deco district; Woolaroc Museum & Wildlife Preserve, Bartlesville.

**Famous Oklahomans** include Carl Albert, Johnny Bench, L. Gordon Cooper, Woody Guthrie, Gen. Patrick J. Hurley, Karl Jansky, Mickey Mantle, Carry Nation, Wiley Post, Oral Roberts, Will Rogers, Maria Tallchief, Jim Thorpe.

**Chamber of Commerce.** 4020 N. Lincoln Blvd., Oklahoma City, OK 73105.

**Tourism Dept.** P.O. Box 60789, Oklahoma City, OK 73146-0789.

**Toll-free travel information.** 1-800-652-6552.

# Oregon

### Beaver State

**People. Population** (1992): 2,977,331; **rank:** 29. **Pop. density:** 31.0 per sq. mi. **Racial distrib.** (1990): 92.8% White; 1.6% Black; 4.0% Hispanic. **Net change** (1990-92): 4.8%.

**Geography. Total area:** 97,073 sq. mi.; **rank:** 10. **Land area:** 96,003 sq. mi. **Acres forested land:** 28,057,000. **Location:** Pacific state, bounded on N by Washington; on E by Idaho; on S by Nevada and California; on W by the Pacific. **Climate:** coastal mild and humid climate; continental dryness and extreme temperatures in the interior. **Topography:** Coast Range of rugged mountains; fertile Willamette R. Valley to E and S; Cascade Mtn. Range of volcanic peaks E of the valley; plateau E of Cascades, remaining two-thirds of state. **Capital:** Salem.

**Economy. Principal industries:** forestry, agriculture, tourism, high technology, manufacturing. **Principal manufactured goods:** lumber & wood products, foods, machinery, fabricated metals, paper, printing & publishing, primary metals. **Agriculture: Chief crops:** greenhouse/ nursery prods., hay, farm forest prods., wheat, potatoes, grass seed, pears, onions. **Livestock** (1991): 1.5 mln. cattle; 80,000 hogs/pigs; 466,000 sheep; 3.0 mln. poultry. **Timber/lumber** (1991): Douglas fir, hemlock, ponderosa pine; 6.56 bln. bd. ft. **Nonfuel Minerals** (1992): $199.5 mln.; mostly portland cement, crushed stone, construction sand & gravel. **Commercial fishing** (1992): $76.2 mln. **Chief ports:** Portland, Astoria, Newport, Coos Bay. **International airports at:** Portland. **Value of construction** (1992): $2.9 bln. **Employment distribution** (1991):

25.7% trade; 23.2% serv.; 18.0% mfg.; 17.8% gvt. **Per capita income** (1992): $18,202. **Unemployment** (1992): 7.5%. **Tourism** (1991): travel expenditures, $2.97 bln.

**Finance: FDIC-insured commercial banks & trust companies** (1992): 51. **Deposits:** $20.3 bln. **Savings institutions** (1992): 8. **Assets:** $3.8 bln.

**Federal government. No. federal civilian employees** (Mar. 1992): 20,939. **Avg. salary:** $33,628. **Notable federal facilities:** Bonneville Power Administration.

**Energy. Electricity production** (1992, MWh, by source): Hydroelectric: 30.9 mln.; Mineral: 3.8 mln.

**Education. Student-teacher ratio** (1991): 18.6. **Avg. salary, public school teachers** (1992-93): $35,435.

**State data. Motto:** She flies with her own wings. **Flower:** Oregon grape. **Bird:** Western meadowlark. **Tree:** Douglas fir. **Song:** Oregon, My Oregon. **Entered union** Feb. 14, 1859; rank, 33d. **State fair at:** Salem; 11 days ending with Labor Day.

**History.** American Capt. Robert Gray sighted and sailed into the Columbia River, 1792; Lewis and Clark, traveling overland, wintered at its mouth 1805-06; fur traders followed. Settlers arrived in the Willamette Valley, 1834. In 1843 the first large wave of settlers arrived via the Oregon Trail. Early in the 20th century, the "Oregon System"—political reforms that included the initiative, referendum, recall, direct primary, and woman suffrage—was adopted.

**Tourist attractions.** John Day Fossil Beds National Monument; Columbia River Gorge; Mt. Hood & Timberline Lodge; Crater Lake National Park; Oregon Dunes National Recreation Area; Ft. Clatsop National Memorial; Oregon Caves National Monument; Oregon Museum of Science and Industry; Shakespearean Festival, Ashland; High Desert Museum, Bend. Also, skiing, fishing; Annual Albany Timber Carnival, Pendleton Round-Up, Portland Rose Festival.

**Famous Oregonians** include Ernest Bloch, Ernest Haycox, Chief Joseph, Edwin Markham, Tom McCall, Dr. John McLoughlin, Joaquin Miller, Linus Pauling, John Reed, Alberto Salazar, Mary Decker Slaney, William Simon U'Ren.

**Tourist Information:** Economic Development Department, 775 Summer St. NE, Salem, OR 97310.

**Toll-free travel information.** 1-800-543-8838; 1-800-547-7842 out of state.

# Pennsylvania

### Keystone State

**People. Population** (1992): 12,009,361; **rank:** 5. **Pop. density:** 267.9 per sq. mi. **Racial distrib.** (1990): 88.5% White; 9.2% Black; 2.0% Hispanic. **Net change** (1990-92): 1.1%.

**Geography. Total area:** 45,308 sq. mi.; **rank:** 33. **Land area:** 44,820 sq. mi. **Acres forested land:** 16,997,000. **Location:** Middle Atlantic state, bordered on the E by the Delaware R.; on the S by the Mason-Dixon Line; on the W by West Virginia and Ohio; on the N/NE by Lake Erie and New York. **Climate:** continental with wide fluctuations in seasonal temperatures. **Topography:** Allegheny Mtns. run SW to NE, with Piedmont and Coast Plain in the SE triangle; Allegheny Front a diagonal spine across the state's center; N and W rugged plateau falls to Lake Erie Lowland. **Capital:** Harrisburg.

**Economy. Principal industries:** steel, travel, health, apparel, machinery, food & agriculture. **Principal manufactured goods:** primary metals, foods, fabricated metal products, non-electrical machinery, electrical machinery. **Agriculture: Chief crops:** corn, hay, mushrooms, apples, potatoes, winter wheat, oats, vegetables, tobacco, grapes. **Livestock** (1985): 1.96 mln. cattle; 800,000 hogs/pigs; 88,000 sheep; 22.5 mln. poultry. **Timber/lumber** (1991): pine, oak, maple; 650 mln. bd. ft. **Nonfuel Minerals** (1992): $862.6 mln.; mostly crushed stone, cement, lime, construction sand & gravel. **Commercial fishing** (1992): $395,000. **Chief ports:** Philadelphia, Pittsburgh, Erie. **International airports at:** Philadelphia, Pittsburgh, Erie, Harrisburg. **Value of construction**

(1992): $10.0 bln. **Employment distribution** (1986): 24.4% serv.; 23.9% trade; 23.3% mfg.; 14.9% gvt. **Per capita income** (1992): $20,253 **Unemployment** (1992): 7.5%. **Tourism** (1985): out-of-state visitors spent $8.9 bln.

**Finance.** FDIC-insured commercial banks & trust companies (1992): 289. **Deposits:** $138.1 bln. **Savings institutions** (1992): 101. **Assets:** $24.1 bln.

**Federal government.** No. federal civilian employees (Mar. 1992): 85,792. **Avg. salary:** $31,999. **Notable federal facilities:** Army War College, Carlisle; Ships Control Ctr., Mechanicsburg; New Cumberland Army Depot; Philadelphia Navy Yard, Philadelphia.

**Energy. Electricity production** (1992, MWh, by source): Hydroelectric: 0.7 mln.; Mineral: 93.7 mln.; Nuclear: 60.5 mln.

**Education. Student-teacher ratio** (1991): 16.8. **Avg. salary, public school teachers** (1992-93): $41,580.

**State data. Motto:** Virtue, liberty and independence. **Flower:** Mountain laurel. **Bird:** Ruffed grouse. **Tree:** Hemlock. **Second** of the original 13 states to ratify the Constitution, Dec. 12, 1787. **State fair** at: Harrisburg; 2d week in Jan.

**History.** First settlers were Swedish, 1643, on Tinicum Is. In 1655 the Dutch seized the settlement but lost it to the British, 1664. The region was given by Charles II to William Penn, 1681, Philadelphia (brotherly love) was the capital of the colonies during most of the Revolution, and of the U.S., 1790-1800: Philadelphia was taken by the British, 1777; Washington's troops encamped at Valley Forge in the bitter winter of 1777-78. The Declaration of Independence, 1776, and the Constitution, 1787, were signed in Philadelphia.

**Tourist attractions.** Independence Hall & Natl. Historic Park, Franklin Institute Science Museum, Philadelphia Museum of Art, all in Philadelphia; Valley Forge Natl. Historic Park; Gettysburg Natl. Military Park; Pennsylvania Dutch Country; Hershey; Duquesne Incline, Carnegie Institute, Heinz Hall, all in Pittsburgh; year 'round outdoor sports in Pocono Mtns., Pine Creek River Gorge, Alleghenies, Laurel Highlands & Presque Isle State Park.

**Famous Pennsylvanians** include Marian Anderson, Maxwell Anderson, James Buchanan, Andrew Carnegie, Stephen Foster, Benjamin Franklin, George C. Marshall, Andrew W. Mellon, Robert E. Peary, Mary Roberts Rinehart, Betsy Ross.

**Chamber of Commerce.** 222 N. 3d St., Harrisburg, PA 17101.

**Toll-free travel information.** 1-800-VISITPA.

# Rhode Island

## Little Rhody, Ocean State

**People. Population** (1992): 1,005,091; **rank:** 43. **Pop. density:** 961.8 per sq. mi. **Racial distrib.** (1990): 91.4% White; 3.9% Black; 4.6% Hispanic. **Net change** (1990-92): 0.2%.

**Geography. Total area:** 1,212 sq. mi.; **rank:** 50. **Land area:** 1,045 sq. mi. **Acres forested land:** 399,000. **Location:** New England state. **Climate:** invigorating and changeable. **Topography:** eastern lowlands of Narragansett Basin; western uplands of flat and rolling hills. **Capital:** Providence.

**Economy. Principal industries:** manufacturing, services. **Principal manufactured goods:** costume jewelry, toys, machinery, textiles, electronics. **Agriculture: Chief crops:** nursery prods., turf, potatoes, apples. **Timber/lumber:** oak. **Nonfuel Minerals** (1992): $14.5 mln.; construction sand & gravel, crushed stone. **Commercial fishing** (1992): $85.7 mln. **Chief ports:** Providence, Quonset Point, Newport. **Value of construction** (1992): $650.6 mln. **Employment distribution** (1992): 31% services; 21.0% mfg.; 21.0% trade. **Per capita income** (1992): $20,299. **Unemployment** (1992): 8.9%. **Tourism** (1992): visitors spent $1.1 bln. **Sales tax:** 7%.

**Finance.** FDIC-insured commercial banks & trust companies (1992): 13. **Deposits:** $10.9 bln. **Savings institutions** (1992): 3. **Assets:** $1.9 bln.

**Federal government.** No. federal civilian employees (Mar. 1992): 5,891. **Avg. salary:** $35,734. **Notable federal facilities:** Naval War College; Naval Underwater Warfare Center.

**Energy. Electricity production** (1992, MWh, by source): Mineral: 0.3 mln.

**Education. Student-teacher ratio** (1991): 14.6. **Avg. salary, public school teachers** (1992-93): $37,510.

**State data. Motto:** Hope. **Flower:** Violet. **Bird:** Rhode Island red. **Tree:** Red maple. **Song:** Rhode Island. **Thirteenth** of original 13 states to ratify the Constitution, May 29, 1790.

**History.** Rhode Island is distinguished for its battle for freedom of conscience and action, begun by Roger Williams, founder of Providence, who was exiled from Massachusetts Bay Colony in 1636, and Anne Hutchinson, exiled in 1638. Rhode Island gave protection to Quakers in 1657 and to Jews from Holland in 1658.

The colonists broke the power of the Narragansett Indians in the Great Swamp Fight, 1675, the decisive battle in King Philip's War. British trade restrictions angered the colonists and they burned the British revenue cutter Gaspee, 1772. The colony declared its independence May 4, 1776. Gen. John Sullivan and Lafayette won a partial victory, 1778, but failed to oust the British.

**Tourist attractions.** Newport mansions; summer resorts and water sports; various yachting races inc. Newport to Bermuda; Touro Synagogue, Newport, 1763; first Baptist Church in America, Providence, 1638; Gilbert Stuart birthplace, Saunderstown; Narragansett Indian Fall Festival.

**Famous Rhode Islanders** include Ambrose Burnside, George M. Cohan, Nelson Eddy, Jabez Gorham, Nathanael Greene, Christopher and Oliver La Farge, Matthew C. and Oliver Hazard Perry, Gilbert Stuart.

**Chamber of Commerce.** 30 Exchange Terr., Providence, RI 02908.

**Toll-free travel information.** 1-800-556-2484.

# South Carolina

## Palmetto State

**People. Population** (1992): 3,603,227. **rank:** 25. **Pop. density:** 119.7 per sq. mi. **Racial distrib.** (1990): 69.0% White; 29.8% Black; 0.9% Hispanic. **Net change** (1990-92): 3.3%.

**Geography. Total area:** 31,113 sq. mi.; **rank:** 40. **Land area:** 30,111 sq. mi. **Acres forested land:** 12,257,000. **Location:** South Atlantic state, bordered by North Carolina on the N; Georgia on the SW and W; the Atlantic O. on the E, SE and S. **Climate:** humid sub-tropical. **Topography:** Blue Ridge province in NW has highest peaks; piedmont lies between the mountains and the fall line; coastal plain covers two-thirds of the state. **Capital:** Columbia.

**Economy. Principal industries:** tourism, agriculture, manufacturing. **Principal manufactured goods:** textiles, chemicals and allied products, machinery & fabricated metal products, apparel and related products. **Agriculture: Chief crops:** tobacco, soybeans, corn, cotton, peaches, hay. **Livestock** (1991): 575,000 cattle; 410,000 hogs/pigs; 7.13 mln. chickens, excl. broilers. **Timber/lumber** (1991): pine, oak; 1.3 bln. bd. ft. **Nonfuel Minerals** (1992): $347.3 mln.; mostly crushed stone, cement, clay. **Commercial fishing** (1992): $25.6 mln. **Chief ports:** Charleston, Georgetown, Port Royal. **International airports at:** Charleston. **Value of construction** (1992): $3.4 bln. **Employment distribution** (1992): 24.2% mfg.; 20.3% serv.; 22.6% trade; 6.6% gvt. **Per capita income** (1992): $15,989. **Unemployment** (1992): 6.2%. **Tourism** (1991): $6.4 bln. **Sales tax:** 5%.

**Finance.** FDIC-insured commercial banks & trust companies (1992): 83. **Deposits:** $19.0 bln. **Savings institutions** (1992): 39. **Assets:** $10.1 bln.

**Federal government.** No. federal civilian employees (Mar. 1992): 23,657. **Avg. Salary:** $31,494. **Notable federal facilities:** Polaris Submarine Base; Barnwell Nuclear

Power Plant; Ft. Jackson; Parris Island; Savannah River Plant.

**Energy. Electricity production** (1992, MWh, by source): Hydroelectric: 1.9 mln.; Mineral: 19.1 mln.; Nuclear: 40.3 mln.

**Education. Student-teacher ratio** (1991): 16.9. **Avg. salary, public school teachers** (1992-93): $29,151.

**State data. Motto:** Dum Spiro Spero (While I breathe, I hope). **Flower:** Yellow jessamine. **Bird:** Carolina wren. **Tree:** Palmetto. **Song:** Carolina. **Eighth** of the original 13 states to ratify the Constitution, May 23, 1788. **State fair** at: Columbia; mid-Oct.

**History.** The first English colonists settled, 1670, on the Ashley River, moved to the site of Charleston, 1680. The colonists seized the government, 1775, and the royal governor fled. The British took Charleston, 1780, but were defeated at Kings Mountain that year, and at Cowpens and Eutaw Springs, 1781. In the 1830s, South Carolinians, angered by federal protective tariffs, adopted the Nullification Doctrine, holding that a state can void an act of Congress. The state was the first to secede in 1861, and Confederate troops fired on and forced the surrender of U.S. troops at Ft. Sumter, in Charleston harbor, launching the Civil War.

**Tourist attractions.** Restored historic Charleston harbor area and Charleston gardens: Middleton Place, Magnolia, Cypress; other gardens at Brookgreen, Edisto, Glencairn; state parks; coastal islands; shore resorts such as Myrtle Beach and Hilton Head Island; fishing and quail hunting; Revolutionary War battle sites; Andrew Jackson State Park & Museum; Carl Sandburg Home, Hendersonville; Ft. Sumter National Monument, in Charleston Harbor; Charleston Museum, est. 1773, is the oldest museum in the U.S.; South Carolina State Museum, one of largest museums in South, Columbia; Riverbanks Zoo, Columbia.

**Famous South Carolinians** include Charles Bolden, James F. Byrnes, John C. Calhoun, DuBose Heyward, Ernest F. Hollings, Andrew Jackson, Jesse Jackson, James Longstreet, Francis Marion, Ronald McNair, Charles Pinckney, John Rutledge, Thomas Sumter, Strom Thurmond, John B. Watson.

**Tourist information:** Chamber of Commerce, 930 Richland St., P.O. Box 1360, Columbia, SC 29201; and So. Carolina Dept. of Parks, Recreation, & Tourism, (803) 734-0122; Greater Columbia Convention & Visitors' Bureau, 301 Gervais St., Columbia, SC 29201, (803) 254-0479.

**Toll-free travel information.** 1-800-346-3634.

# South Dakota

## Coyote State, Mount Rushmore State

**People. Population** (1992): 711,154; **rank:** 45. **Pop. density:** 9.37 per sq. mi. **Racial distrib.** (1990): 91.6% White; 0.5% Black; 7.3% Amer. Indian; 0.8% Hispanic. **Net change** (1990-92): 2.2%.

**Geography. Total area:** 77,116 sq. mi.; **rank:** 16. **Land area:** 75,898 sq. mi. **Acres forested land:** 1,690,000. **Location:** West North Central state bounded on the N by North Dakota; on the E by Minnesota and Iowa; on the S by Nebraska; on the W by Wyoming and Montana. **Climate:** characterized by extremes of temperature, persistent winds, low precipitation and humidity. **Topography:** Prairie Plains in the E; rolling hills of the Great Plains in the W; the Black Hills, rising 3,500 ft., in the SW corner. **Capital:** Pierre.

**Economy. Principal industries:** agriculture, services, manufacturing. **Principal manufactured goods** (1991): food & kindred prods., machinery, electric & electronic equipment. **Agriculture:** Chief crops (1992): corn, oats, wheat, sunflowers, soybeans, sorghum. **Livestock** (1992): 3.75 mln. cattle; 1.8 mln. hogs/pigs; 591,000 sheep. **Timber/lumber** (1991): ponderosa pine; 168 mln. bd. ft. **Nonfuel Minerals** (1992): $298.1 mln.; mostly gold, portland cement. **Value of construction** (1992): $585.6 mln. **Employment distribution** (1992): 22.3% serv.; 10.5% mfg. **Per capita income** (1992): $16,558. **Unem-**

ployment (1992): 3.1%. **Tourism** (1992): travelers' impact $979 mln. **Sales tax:** 4%.

**Finance. FDIC-insured commercial banks & trust companies** (1992): 125. **Deposits:** $11.3 bln. **Savings institutions** (1992): 9. **Assets:** $1.0 bln.

**Federal government. No. federal civilian employees** (Mar. 1992): 7,191. **Avg. salary:** $30,215. **Notable federal facilities:** Bureau of Indian Affairs, Ellsworth AFB, Corp of Engineers, Nat'l Park Service.

**Energy. Electricity production** (1992, MWh, by source): Hydroelectric: 2.8 mln.; Mineral: 2.3 mln.

**Education. Student-teacher ratio** (1991): 14.8. **Avg. salary, public school teachers** (1992-93): $24,125.

**State data. Motto:** Under God, the people rule. **Flower:** Pasqueflower. **Bird:** Ring-necked pheasant. **Tree:** Black Hills spruce. **Song:** Hail, South Dakota. **Entered union** Nov. 2, 1889; rank, 40th. **State fair** at: Huron; late Aug.-early Sept.

**History.** Les Verendryes explored the region, 1742-43. Lewis and Clark passed through the area, 1804 and 1806. First white American settlement was at Fort Pierre, 1817. Gold was discovered, 1874, on the Great Sioux Reservation; miners rushed in. The U.S. first tried to stop them, then relaxed its opposition. The "Great Dakota Boom" began 1879. A new Indian uprising came in 1890, climaxed by the massacre of Indian families at Wounded Knee.

**Tourist attractions.** Black Hills; Mt. Rushmore, with colossal likeness of the faces of U.S. Presidents Washington, Jefferson, Lincoln & T. Roosevelt carved by sculptor Gutzon Borglum; Needles Highway; Harney Peak, at 7,242 ft. the tallest peak east of the Rockies; Deadwood, an 1876 Gold Rush town; Custer State Park's buffalo and burro herds; Jewel Cave, the 4th longest cave in the world; Badlands Natl. Park's "moonscape"; "Great Lakes of So. Dakota"; Ft. Sisseton, restored 1864 army frontier post; Great Plains Zoo & Museum in Sioux Falls; Corn Palace in Mitchell; Wind Cave; Mammoth Site, ongoing excavation of prehistoric mammoths; Crazy Horse, mountain carving in progress.

**Famous South Dakotans** include Sparky Anderson, Catherine Bach, Tom Brokaw, "Calamity Jane", Mary Hart, Crazy Horse, Myron Floren, Alvin H. Hansen, Cheryl Ladd, Dr. Ernest O. Lawrence, George McGovern, Billy Mills, Allen Neuharth, Pat O'Brien, Sitting Bull.

**Tourist information.** South Dakota Tourism, 711 E. Wells Ave., Pierre, SD 57501-3369.

**Toll-free travel information.** 1-800-SDAKOTA (732-5682).

# Tennessee

## Volunteer State

**People. Population** (1992): 5,023,990; **rank:** 17. **Pop. density:** 121.9 per sq. mi. **Racial distrib.** (1990): 83.0% White; 16.0% Black; 0.7% Hispanic. **Net change** (1990-92): 3.0%.

**Geography. Total area:** 42,144 sq. mi.; **rank:** 34. **Land area:** 41,220 sq. mi. **Acres forested land:** 13,258,000. **Location:** East South Central state bounded on the N by Kentucky and Virginia; on the E by North Carolina; on the S by Georgia, Alabama, and Mississippi; on the W by Arkansas and Missouri. **Climate:** humid continental to the N; humid sub-tropical to the S. **Topography:** rugged country in the E; the Great Smoky Mtns. of the Unakas; low ridges of the Appalachian Valley; the flat Cumberland Plateau; slightly rolling terrain and knobs of the Interior Low Plateau, the largest region; Eastern Gulf Coastal Plain to the W, is laced with meandering streams; Mississippi Alluvial Plain, a narrow strip of swamp and flood plain in the extreme W. **Capital:** Nashville.

**Economy. Principal industries:** trade, services, construction; transp., commun., public utilities; finance, ins., real estate. **Principal manufactured goods:** chemicals, food, transportation equip., industrial machinery & equip., fabr. metal prods., rubber/plastic prods., paper & allied prods., printing and publishing. **Agriculture:** Chief crops (1991): tobacco, lint cotton, soybeans, corn, greenhouse/ nursery. **Livestock** (1992): 2.30 mln. cattle; 0.67 mln.

hogs/pigs; 1.72 mln. poultry. **Timber/lumber** (1991): red oak, white oak, yellow poplar, hickory; 519 mln. bd. ft. **Nonfuel Minerals** (1992): $579.9 mln.; mostly clay, sand and gravel, crushed stone. **Chief ports:** Memphis, Nashville, Chattanooga, Knoxville. **International airports at:** Memphis, Nashville. **Value of construction** (1992): $5.3 bln. **Employment distribution** (1992): 23.0% mfg.; 23.2% trade; 24% serv.; 16% gvt. **Per capita income** (1992): $17,341. **Unemployment** (1992): 6.4%. **Tourism** (1989): out-of-state visitors spent $3.3 bln. **Sales tax:** 6.0% state, up to 2.75% local.

**Finance. FDIC-insured commercial banks & trust companies** (1992): 250. **Deposit:** $41.3 bln. **Savings institutions** (1992): 38. **Assets:** $8.2 bln.

**Federal government. No. federal civilian employees** (Mar. 1992): 38,388. **Avg. salary:** $33,695. **Notable federal facilities:** Tennessee Valley Authority; Oak Ridge Nat'l. Laboratories; Arnold Engineering Development Center; Ft. Campbell Army Base; Millington Naval Station.

**Energy. Electricity production** (1992, MWh, by source): Hydroelectric: 1.1 mln.; Mineral: 47.8 mln.; Nuclear: 16.8 mln.

**Education. Student-teacher ratio** (1991): 19.4. **Avg. salary, public school teachers** (1992-93): $29,313.

**State data. Motto:** Agriculture and commerce. **Flower:** Iris. **Bird:** Mockingbird. **Tree:** Tulip poplar. **Song:** The Tennessee Waltz. **Entered union** June 1, 1796; rank, 16th. **State fair** at: Nashville; mid-Sept.

**History.** Spanish explorers first visited the area, 1541. English traders crossed the Great Smokies from the east while France's Marquette and Jolliet sailed down the Mississippi on the west, 1673. First permanent settlement was by Virginians on the Watauga River, 1769. During the Revolution, the colonists helped win the Battle of Kings Mountain, N.C., 1780, and joined other eastern campaigns. The state seceded from the Union 1861, and saw many engagements of the Civil War, but 30,000 soldiers fought for the Union.

**Tourist attractions.** Natural wonders include Reelfoot Lake, the reservoir basin of the Mississippi R. formed by the 1811 earthquake; Lookout Mountain, Chattanooga; Fall Creek Falls, 256 ft. high; Great Smoky Mountains National Park; Lost Sea, Sweetwater; Cherokee Natl. Forest.

Also, the Hermitage, 13 mi. E of Nashville, home of Andrew Jackson; the homes of presidents Polk and Andrew Johnson; American Museum of Science, Oak Ridge; the Parthenon, Nashville, a replica of the Parthenon of Athens; the Grand Old Opry, Nashville; Opryland, USA, theme park, Nashville; Graceland, home of Elvis Presley, Memphis; Alex Haley Home & Museum, Henning; Casey Jones Home & Museum, Jackson.

**Famous Tennesseans** include Roy Acuff, Davy Crockett, David Farragut, William C. Handy, Sam Houston, Cordell Hull, Grace Moore, Minnie Pearl, Dinah Shore, Alvin York.

**Tourist information.** Dept. of Tourist Development, 5th Floor, Rachel Jackson Bldg., 320 6th Ave. N., Nashville, TN 37202.

# Texas

*Lone Star State*

**People. Population** (1992): 17,655,650; **rank: 3. Pop. density:** 67.4 per sq. mi. **Racial distrib.** (1990): 75.2% White; 11.9% Black; 25.5% Hispanic. **Net change** (1990-92): 3.9%.

**Geography. Total area:** 266,807 sq. mi.; **rank: 2. Land area:** 261,914 sq. mi. **Acres forested land:** 13,656,000. **Location:** Southwestern state, bounded on the SE by the Gulf of Mexico; on the SW by Mexico, separated by the Rio Grande; surrounding states are Louisiana, Arkansas, Oklahoma, New Mexico. **Climate:** extremely varied; driest region is the Trans-Pecos; wettest is the NE. **Topography:** Gulf Coast Plain in the S and SE; North Central Plains slope upward with some hills; the Great Plains extend over the Panhandle, are broken by low mountains; the Trans-Pecos is the southern extension of the Rockies. **Capital:** Austin.

**Economy. Principal industries:** trade, services, manufacturing. **Principal manufactured goods:** machinery, transportation equipment, foods, electrical and electronic equip., chemicals and allied prods., apparel. **Agriculture: Chief crops:** cotton, grain sorghum, grains, vegetables, citrus and other fruits, pecans, peanuts. **Livestock** (1991): 13.4 mln. cattle; 500,000 hogs/pigs; 2.0 mln. sheep; 17.2 mln. poultry. **Timber/lumber** (1991): pine, cypress; 1.05 bln. bd. ft. **Nonfuel Minerals** (1992): $1.4 bln.; mostly cement, stone, sand & gravel. **Commercial fishing** (1992): $181.4 mln. **Chief ports:** Houston, Galveston, Brownsville, Beaumont, Port Arthur, Corpus Christi. **Major international airports at:** Houston, Dallas/Ft. Worth, San Antonio. **Value of construction** (1992) $16.5 bln. **Employment distribution** (1992): 24.1% trade; 25.4% serv.; 18.4% gvt.; 13.3% mfg. **Per capita income** (1992): $17,892. **Unemployment** (1992): 7.5%. **Tourism** (1992): out-of-state visitors spent $20.6 bln. **Sales tax:** 6.25%, + optional 1% local, 1% transit.

**Finance. FDIC-insured commercial banks & trust companies** (1992): 1,122. **Deposits:** $147.5 bln. **Savings institutions** (1992): 64. **Assets:** $47.5 bln.

**Federal government. No. federal civilian employees** (Mar. 1992): $123,721. **Avg. salary:** $32,236. **Notable federal facilities:** Fort Hood (Killeen); Kelly AFB and Ft. Sam Houston, both San Antonio.

**Energy. Electricity production** (1992, MWh, by source): Hydroelectric: 3.2 mln.; Mineral: 104 mln.; Nuclear: 23.6 mln.

**Education. Student-teacher ratio** (1991): 15.8. **Avg. salary, public school teachers** (1992-93): $29,935.

**State data. Motto:** Friendship. **Flower:** Bluebonnet. **Bird:** Mockingbird. **Tree:** Pecan. **Song:** Texas, Our Texas. **Entered union** Dec. 29, 1845; rank, 28th. **State fair** at: Dallas; mid-Oct.

**History.** Pineda sailed along the Texas coast, 1519; Cabeza de Vaca and Coronado visited the interior, 1541. Spaniards made the first settlement at Ysleta, near El Paso, 1682. Americans moved into the land early in the 19th century. Mexico, of which Texas was a part, won independence from Spain, 1821; Santa Anna became dictator, 1835. Texans rebelled; Santa Anna wiped out defenders of the Alamo, 1836. Sam Houston's Texans defeated Santa Anna at San Jacinto and independence was proclaimed the same year. In 1845, Texas was admitted to the Union.

**Tourist attractions.** Padre Island National Seashore; Big Bend, Guadalupe Mtns. national parks; The Alamo; Ft. Davis; Six Flags Amusement Park; Sea World and Fiesta Texas, both in San Antonio. Named for Pres. Lyndon B. Johnson are a state park, a natl. historic site marking his birthplace, boyhood home, and ranch, all near Johnson City, and a library in Austin.

**Famous Texans** include Stephen F. Austin, James Bowie, Carol Burnett, J. Frank Dobie, Dwight D. Eisenhower, Sam Houston, Howard Hughes, Lyndon B. Johnson, Mary Martin, Chester Nimitz, Katharine Ann Porter, Sam Rayburn.

**Chamber of Commerce.** 900 Congress, Suite 501, Austin, TX 78701.

**Toll-free travel information.** 1-800-888-8TEX.

# Utah

*Beehive State*

**People. Population** (1992): 1,813,116; **rank: 34. Pop. density:** 22.1 per sq. mi. **Racial distrib.** (1990): 93.8% White; 0.7% Black; 4.9% Hispanic. **Net change** (1990-92): 5.2%.

**Geography. Total area:** 84,899 sq. mi.; **rank: 11. Land area:** 82,168 sq. mi. **Acres forested land:** 16,234,000. **Location:** Middle Rocky Mountain state; its southeastern corner touches Colorado, New Mexico and Arizona, and is the only spot in the U.S. where 4 states join. **Climate:** arid; ranging from warm desert in SW to alpine in NE. **Topography:** high Colorado plateau is cut by brilliantly-colored canyons of the SE; broad, flat, desert-like Great Basin of the W; the Great Salt Lake and Bonneville Salt Flats to the NW; Middle Rockies in the NE run E-W; valleys and plateaus of the Wasatch Front. **Capital:** Salt Lake City.

**Economy. Principal industries:** services, trade, manufacturing, government, construction. **Principal manufactured goods:** guided missiles and parts, electronic components, food products, fabricated metals, steel, electrical equipment, automobile airbags. **Agriculture: Chief crops:** hay, wheat, apples, barley, alfalfa seed, corn, potatoes, cherries, onions. **Livestock:** 855,000 cattle; 34,000 hogs/pigs; 600,000 sheep; 3.8 mln. poultry. **Timber/lumber:** aspen, spruce, pine. **Nonfuel Minerals** (1992): $1.3 bln.; mostly copper, gold, magnesium. **International airports at:** Salt Lake City. **Value of construction** (1992): $2.0 bln. **Employment distribution** (1992): 25.6% serv.; 24.0% trade; 20.4% govt; 13.8% mfg. **Per capita income** (1992): $15,325. **Unemployment** (1992): 4.9%. **Tourism** (1986): travelers spent $2.0 bln. **Sales tax:** 6.25%.

**Finance. FDIC-insured commercial banks & trust companies** (1992): 55. **Deposits:** $10.5 bln. **Savings institutions** (1992): 5. **Assets:** $1.3 bln.

**Federal government. No. federal civilian employees** (Mar. 1992): 31,990. **Avg. salary:** $30,717. **Notable federal facilities:** Hill AFB; Tooele Army Depot; IRS Western Service Center.

**Energy. Electricity production** (1992, MWh, by source): Hydroelectric: 0.6 mln.; Mineral: 30.3 mln.

**Education. Student-teacher ratio** (1991): 24.9. **Avg. salary, public school teachers** (1992-93): $26,997.

**State data. Motto:** Industry. **Flower:** Sego lily. **Bird:** Seagull. **Tree:** Blue spruce. **Song:** Utah, We Love Thee. **Entered union** Jan. 4, 1896; rank, 45th. **State fair at:** Salt Lake City; Sept.

**History.** Spanish Franciscans visited the area, 1776, the first white men to do so. American fur traders followed. Permanent settlement began with the arrival of the Mormons, 1847. They made the arid land bloom and created a prosperous economy, organized the State of Deseret, 1849, and asked admission to the Union. This was not achieved until 1896, after a long period of controversy over the Mormon Church's doctrine of polygamy, which it discontinued in 1890.

**Tourist attractions.** Temple Square, Mormon Church hdqtrs., Salt Lake City; Great Salt Lake; fishing streams, lakes and reservoirs, numerous winter sports; campgrounds. Natural wonders may be seen at Zion, Canyonlands, Bryce Canyon, Arches, and Capitol Reef national parks; Dinosaur, Rainbow Bridge, Timpanogos Cave, and Natural Bridges national monuments. Also Lake Powell and Flaming Gorge reservoirs.

**Famous Utahans** include Maude Adams, Ezra Taft Benson, John Moses Browning, Mariner Eccles, Philo Farnsworth, James Fletcher, David M. Kennedy, J. Willard Marriott, Merlin Olsen, Osmond family, Ivy Baker Priest, George Romney, Brigham Young, Loretta Young.

**Tourist information.** Utah Travel Council, Council Hall, Salt Lake City, UT 84114.

# Vermont

### Green Mountain State

**People. Population** (1992): 569,784; **rank:** 49. **Pop. density:** 61.6 per sq. mi. **Racial distrib.** (1990): 98.6% White; 0.3% Black; 0.6% Asian; 0.7% Hispanic. **Net change** (1990-92): 1.3%.

**Geography. Total area:** 9,614 sq. mi.; **rank:** 43. **Land area:** 9,249 sq. mi. **Acres forested land:** 4,479,000. **Location:** northern New England state. **Climate:** temperate, with considerable temperature extremes; heavy snowfall in mountains. **Topography:** Green Mtns. N-S backbone 20-36 mi. wide; avg. altitude 1,000 ft. **Capital:** Montpelier.

**Economy. Principal industries:** manufacturing, tourism, agriculture, trade; finance, insurance, real estate, government. **Principal manufactured goods:** machine tools, furniture, scales, books, computer components, fishing rods. **Agriculture: Chief crops:** dairy products, apples, maple syrup, silage corn, hay. **Livestock** (1989): 320,000 cattle; 5,100 hogs/pigs; 20,456 sheep; 406,000

poultry. **Timber/lumber** (1991): pine, spruce, fir, hemlock; 186 mln. bd. ft. **Nonfuel Minerals** (1992): $67.9 mln.; mostly dimension stone, crushed stone, construction sand & gravel. **International airports at:** Burlington. **Value of construction** (1992): $583.6 mln. **Employment distribution** (1990): 27% serv.; 23% trade; 18% mfg. **Per capita income** (1992): $18,834. **Unemployment** (1992): 6.6%. **Tourism** (1990): visitors spent $1.25 bln. **Sales tax.** 5%.

**Finance. FDIC-insured commercial banks & trust companies** (1992): 24. **Deposits:** $5.3 bln. **Savings institutions** (1992): 4. **Assets:** $600 mln.

**Federal government. No. federal civilian employees** (Mar. 1992): 2,656. **Avg. salary:** $32,293.

**Energy. Electricity production** (1992, MWh, by source): Hydroelectric: 1.0 mln.; Mineral: 0.1 mln.; Nuclear: 3.6 mln.

**Education. Student-teacher ratio** (1991): 13.8. **Avg. salary, public school teachers** (1992-93): $34,824.

**State data. Motto:** Freedom and unity. **Flower:** Red clover. **Bird:** Hermit thrush. **Tree:** Sugar maple. **Song:** Hail, Vermont. **Entered union** Mar. 4, 1791; rank, 14th. **State fair at:** Rutland; early Sept.

**History.** Champlain explored the lake that bears his name, 1609. First American settlement was Ft. Dummer, 1724, near Brattleboro. Ethan Allen and the Green Mountain Boys captured Ft. Ticonderoga, 1775; John Stark defeated part of Burgoyne's forces near Bennington, 1777. In the War of 1812, Thomas MacDonough defeated a British fleet on Champlain off Plattsburgh, 1814.

**Tourist attractions.** Year-round outdoor sports, esp. hiking, camping and skiing; there are 24 alpine ski areas & 47 cross country areas in the state. Popular are the Shelburne Museum; Rock of Ages Tourist Center, Graniteville; Vermont Marble Exhibit, Proctor; Bennington Battle Monument; Pres. Coolidge homestead, Plymouth; Maple Grove Maple Museum, St. Johnsbury.

**Famous Vermonters** include Ethan Allen, Chester A. Arthur, Calvin Coolidge, Adm. George Dewey, John Dewey, Stephen A. Douglas, Dorothy Canfield Fisher, James Fisk.

**Tourist Information.** Vermont Dept. of Travel and Tourism, 134 State St., Montpelier, VT 05602.

# Virginia

### Old Dominion

**People. Population** (1992): 6,377,141; **rank:** 12. **Pop. density:** 161.0 per sq. mi. **Racial distrib.** (1990): 77.4% White; 18.8% Black; 2.6% Asian; 2.6% Hispanic. **Net change** (1990-92): 3.1%.

**Geography. Total area:** 40,767 sq. mi.; **rank:** 36. **Land area:** 39,598 sq. mi. **Acres forested land:** 15,968,000. **Location:** South Atlantic state bounded by the Atlantic O. on the E and surrounded by North Carolina, Tennessee, Kentucky, West Virginia, and Maryland. **Climate:** mild and equable. **Topography:** mountain and valley region in the W, including the Blue Ridge Mtns.; rolling piedmont plateau; tidewater, or coastal plain, including the eastern shore. **Capital:** Richmond.

**Economy. Principal industries:** services, trade, government, manufacturing, tourism, agriculture. **Principal manufactured goods:** textiles, transportation equipment, electric & electronic equipment, food processing, chemicals, printing. **Agriculture: Chief crops** (1991): soybeans, tobacco, peanuts, corn, far grain, tomatoes, apples, summer & sweet potatoes. **Livestock** (1991): 1.73 mln. cattle; 430,000 hogs/pigs; 157,000 sheep; 1.96 mln. broilers, 1.7 mln. turkeys. **Timber/lumber** (1991): pine and hardwoods; 1.09 bln. bd. ft. **Nonfuel Minerals** (1992): $416.0 mln.; mostly crushed stone. **Commercial fishing** (1992): $90.5 mln. **Chief ports:** Hampton Roads, Richmond, Alexandria. **International airports at:** Norfolk, Dulles, Richmond, Newport News. **Value of construction** (1992): $7.4 bln. **Employment distribution** (1991): 23.4% serv.; 20.5% trade; 18.6% govt.; 13.2% mfg. **Per capita income** (1992): $20,629. **Unemployment** (1992): 6.4%. **Tourism** (1990): domestic travelers spent $8 bln. **Sales tax:** 4.5%.

**Finance. FDIC-insured commercial banks & trust companies** (1992): 174. **Deposits:** $55.8 bln. **Savings institutions** (1992): 44. **Assets:** $15.0 bln.

**Federal government. No. federal civilian employees** (Mar. 1992): 140,954. **Avg. salary:** $37,918. **Notable federal facilities:** Pentagon; Naval Sta., Norfolk; Naval Air Sta., Norfolk, Virginia Beach; Naval Shipyard, Portsmouth; Marine Corps Base, Quantico; Langley AFB; NASA at Langley.

**Energy. Electricity production** (1992, MWh, by source): Hydroelectric: 0.5 mln.; Mineral: 25.5 mln.; Nuclear: 15.9 mln.

**Education. Student-teacher ratio** (1990): 15.7. **Avg. salary, public school teachers** (1992-93): $32,356.

**State data. Motto:** Sic Semper Tyrannis (Thus always to tyrants). **Flower:** Dogwood. **Bird:** Cardinal. **Tree:** Dogwood. **Song:** Carry Me Back to Old Virginia. **Tenth** of the original 13 states to ratify the Constitution, June 25, 1788. **State fair** at: Richmond; late Sept.-early Oct.

**History.** English settlers founded Jamestown, 1607. Virginians took over much of the government from royal Gov. Dunmore in 1775, forcing him to flee. Virginians under George Rogers Clark freed the Ohio-Indiana-Illinois area of British forces. Benedict Arnold burned Richmond and Petersburg for the British, 1781. That same year, Britain's Cornwallis was trapped at Yorktown and surrendered.

**Tourist attractions.** Colonial Williamsburg; Busch Gardens, Williamsburg; Wolf Trap Farm, near Falls Church; Arlington National Cemetery; Mt. Vernon, home of George Washington; Jamestown Festival Park; Yorktown; Jefferson's Monticello, Charlottesville; Robert E. Lee's birthplace, Stratford Hall, and grave, at Lexington; Appomattox; Shenandoah National Park; Blue Ridge Parkway; Virginia Beach; King's Dominion, near Richmond.

**Famous Virginians** include Richard E. Byrd, James B. Cabell, William Henry Harrison, Patrick Henry, Thomas Jefferson, Joseph E. Johnston, Robert E. Lee, Meriwether Lewis and William Clark, James Madison, John Marshall, George Mason, James Monroe, Edgar Allan Poe, Walter Reed, Zachary Taylor, John Tyler, Maggie Walker, Booker T. Washington, George Washington, Woodrow Wilson.

**Chamber of Commerce:** 9 South Fifth St., Richmond, VA 23219.

**Toll-free travel information.** 1-800-VISITVA.

# Washington

## Evergreen State

**People. Population** (1992): 5,135,731; **rank:** 16. **Pop. density:** 77.1 per sq. mi. **Racial distrib.** (1990): 88.5% White; 3.1% Black; 4.3% Asian; 4.4% Hispanic. **Net change** (1990-92): 5.5%.

**Geography. Total area:** 68,139 sq. mi.; **rank:** 20. **Land area:** 66,582 sq. mi. **Acres forested land:** 21,856,000. **Location:** Pacific state bordered by Canada on the N; Idaho on the E; Oregon on the S; and the Pacific O. on the W. **Climate:** mild, dominated by the Pacific O. and protected by the Rockies. **Topography:** Olympic Mtns. on NW peninsula; open land along coast to Columbia R.; flat terrain of Puget Sound Lowland; Cascade Mtns. region's high peaks to the E; Columbia Basin in central portion; highlands to the NE; mountains to the SE. **Capital:** Olympia.

**Economy. Principal industries:** aerospace, forest products, food products, tourism, primary metals, agriculture. **Principal manufactured goods:** aircraft, pulp and paper, lumber and plywood, aluminum, processed fruits and vegetables. **Agriculture:** Chief crops: hops, spearmint oil, wine grapes, wheat, raspberries, apples, asparagus, pears, cherries, peppermint oil, potatoes. **Livestock** (1986): 1.3 mln. cattle; 50,000 hogs/pigs; 59,000 sheep; 5.7 mln. poultry. **Timber/lumber** (1991): Douglas fir, hemlock, cedar, pine; 4.05 bln. bd. ft. **Nonfuel Minerals** (1992): $478.3 mln.; mostly construction sand & gravel, crushed stone, portland cement. **Commercial fishing** (1992): $104.5 mln. **Chief ports:** Seattle, Tacoma, Vancouver, Kelso-Longview. **International airports at:** Seat-

tle/Tacoma, Spokane, Boeing Field. **Value of construction** (1992): $7.5 bln. **Employment distribution** (1989): 24.4% trade; 20.7% serv.; 18.3% gvt.; 17.3% mfg. **Per capita income** (1992): $20,398. **Unemployment** (1992): 7.5%. **Tourism** (1990): $5.3 bln. **Sales tax:** 6.5%.

**Finance. FDIC-insured commercial banks & trust companies** (1992): 93. **Deposits:** $33.4 bln. **Savings institutions** (1992): 15. **Assets:** $15.6 bln.

**Federal government. No. federal civilian employees** (Mar. 1992): 50,825. **Avg. salary:** $34,620. **Notable federal facilities:** Bonneville Power Admin.; Ft. Lewis; McChord AFB; Hanford Nuclear Reservation; Bremerton Naval Shipyards.

**Energy. Electricity production** (1992, MWh, by source): Hydroelectric: 65.6 mln.; Mineral: 8.8 mln.; Nuclear: 8.1 mln.

**Education. Student-teacher ratio** (1991): 20.2. **Avg. salary, public school teachers** (1992-93): $35,870.

**State data. Motto:** Alki (By and by). **Flower:** Western rhododendron. **Bird:** Willow goldfinch. **Tree:** Western hemlock. **Song:** Washington, My Home. **Entered union** Nov. 11, 1889; **rank,** 42d. **State fairs** at: many county fairs, mostly in Aug. or Sept.

**History.** Spain's Bruno Hezeta sailed the coast, 1775. American Capt. Robert Gray sailed up the Columbia River, 1792. Canadian fur traders set up Spokane House, 1810; Americans under John Jacob Astor established a post at Fort Okanogan, 1811. Missionary Marcus Whitman settled near Walla Walla, 1836. Final agreement on the border of Washington and Canada was made with Britain, 1846, and gold was discovered in the state's northeast, 1855, bringing new settlers.

**Tourist attractions.** Mt. Rainier, Olympic, and North Cascades national parks; Mt. St. Helens; Pacific beaches; Puget Sound; wineries; Indian cultures; year-round outdoor recreation: Seattle Waterfront, Seattle Center, Space Needle, San Juan Islands, Grand Coulee Dam, Spokane's Riverfront Park.

**Famous Washingtonians** include Bing Crosby, William O. Douglas, Henry M. Jackson, Gary Larson, Mary McCarthy, Edward R. Murrow, Theodore Roethke, Marcus Whitman, Minoru Yamasaki.

**Local Chambers of Commerce.** P.O. Box 658, Olympia, WA 98507.

**Toll-free travel information.** 1-800-544-1800.

# West Virginia

## Mountain State

**People. Population** (1992): 1,812,194. **rank:** 35. **Pop. density:** 75.2 per sq. mi. **Racial distrib.** (1990): 96.2% White; 3.1% Black; 0.5% Hispanic. **Net change** (1990-92): 1.0%.

**Geography. Total area:** 24,232 sq. mi.; **rank:** 41. **Land area:** 24,087 sq. mi. **Acres forested land:** 11,942,000. **Location:** South Atlantic state bounded on the N by Ohio, Pennsylvania, Maryland; on the S and W by Virginia, Kentucky, Ohio; on the E by Maryland and Virginia. **Climate:** humid continental climate except for marine modification in the lower panhandle. **Topography:** ranging from hilly to mountainous; Allegheny Plateau in the W, covers two-thirds of the state; mountains here are the highest in the state, over 4,000 ft. **Capital:** Charleston.

**Economy. Principal industries:** manufacturing, services, mining, tourism. **Principal manufactured goods:** machinery, plastic and hardwood prods., fabricated metals, basic organic and inorganic chemicals, aluminum, steel. **Agriculture:** Chief crops: apples, peaches, hay, tobacco, corn, wheat, oats. **Chief products:** dairy prods., eggs. **Livestock** (1991): 520,000 cattle; 32,000 hogs/pigs; 76,000 sheep; 1.2 mln. chickens. **Timber/lumber** (1991): oak, yellow poplar, hickory, walnut, cherry; 399 mln. bd. ft. **Nonfuel Minerals** (1992): $123.7 mln.; mostly crushed stone. **Chief port:** Huntington. **Value of construction** (1992): $1.1 bln. **Employment distribution** (1993): 22.8% trade; 20.6% gvt.; 25.1% serv.; 4.5% mfg. **Per capita income** (1992): $15,065. **Unemployment**

(1992): 11.3%. **Tourism** (1992): travel-related expenditures were $2.6 bln. **Sales tax:** 6%.

**Finance. FDIC-insured commercial banks & trust companies** (1992): 169. **Deposits:** $15.7 bln. **Savings institutions** (1992): 11. **Assets:** $1.2 bln.

**Federal government. No. federal civilian employees** (Mar. 1992): 10,878. **Avg. salary:** $31,965. **Notable federal facilities:** National Radio Astronomy Observatory, Green Bank; Bureau of Public Debt Bldg., Parkersburg; Natl. Park, Harpers Ferry; Correctional Institution for Women, Alderson.

**Energy. Electricity production** (1992, MWh, by source): Hydroelectric: 0.5 mln.; Mineral: 61.3 mln.

**Education. Student-teacher ratio** (1991): 15.3. **Avg. salary, public school teachers** (1992-93): $30,301.

**State Data. Motto:** Montani Semper Liberi (Mountaineers are always free). **Flower:** Big rhododendron. **Bird:** Cardinal. **Tree:** Sugar maple. **Songs:** The West Virginia Hills; This Is My West Virginia; West Virginia, My Home, Sweet Home. **Entered union** June 20, 1863; rank, 35th. **State fair** at: Lewisburg (Fairlea); late Aug.

**History.** Early explorers included George Washington, 1753, and Daniel Boone. The area became part of Virginia and often objected to rule by the eastern part of the state. When Virginia seceded, 1861, the Wheeling Conventions repudiated the act and created a new state, Kanawha, subsequently changed to West Virginia. It was admitted to the Union as such, 1863.

**Tourist attractions.** Harpers Ferry National Historic Park has been restored to its condition in 1859, when John Brown seized the U.S. Armory.

Also Science and Cultural Center, Charleston; White Sulphur and Berkeley Springs mineral water spas; Monongahela Natl. Forest; state parks and forests; trout fishing; turkey, deer, and bear hunting; white water rafting, paddleboat tours, skiing; glass tours at Fenton Glass in Williamstown, Viking Glass in New Martinsville, Blenko Glass in Milton; Sternwheel Regatta, Charleston; Mountain State Forest Festival; Mountain State Arts & Crafts Fair, Ripley.

**Famous West Virginians** include Newton D. Baker, Pearl Buck, John W. Davis, Thomas "Stonewall" Jackson, Don Knotts, Dwight Whitney Morrow, Nick Nolte, Michael Owens, Cyrus Vance, Col. Charles "Chuck" Yeager.

**Tourist information.** Dept. of Commerce, State Capitol, Charleston WV 25305.

**Toll-free travel information.** 1-800-CALLW.VA.

# Wisconsin

## *Badger State*

**People. Population** (1992): 5,006,591; **rank:** 18. **Pop. density:** 92.2 per sq. mi. **Racial distrib.** (1990): 92.2% White; 5.0% Black; 1.9% Hispanic. **Net change** (1990-92): 2.4%.

**Geography. Total area:** 56,153 sq. mi.; **rank:** 26. **Land area:** 54,314 sq. mi. **Acres forested land:** 15,319,000. **Location:** East North Central state, bounded on the N by Lake Superior and Upper Michigan; on the E by Lake Michigan; on the S by Illinois; on the W by the St. Croix and Mississippi rivers. **Climate:** long, cold winters and short, warm summers tempered by the Great Lakes. **Topography:** narrow Lake Superior Lowland plain met by Northern Highland, which slopes gently to the sandy crescent Central Plain; Western Upland in the SW; 3 broad parallel limestone ridges running N-S are separated by wide and shallow lowlands in the SE. **Capital:** Madison.

**Economy. Principal industries:** services, manufacturing, trade, government, agriculture, tourism. **Principal manufactured goods:** industrial machinery, food products, fabricated metals, paper products, printing and publishing, electronic and electrical machinery. **Agriculture: Chief crops:** corn, beans, cherries, peas, hay, oats, cranberries. **Chief products:** milk, butter, cheese. **Livestock** (1991): 4.0 mln. cattle, 1.2 mln. hogs/pigs; 105,000 sheep; 4.2 mln. poultry. **Timber/lumber** (1991): maple, birch, oak, evergreens; 511 mln. bd. ft. **Nonfuel Minerals** (1992): $218.2 mln.; mostly crushed stone, construction &

industrial sand & gravel, lime. **Commercial fishing** (1992): $5.9 mln. **Chief ports:** Superior, Ashland, Milwaukee, Green Bay, Kewaunee, Pt. Washington, Manitowoc, Sheboygan, Marinette, Kenosha. **International airports at:** Milwaukee. **Value of construction** (1992): $4.9 bln. **Employment distribution** (1993): 22.3% trade; 22.7% mfg.; 24.0% serv.; 15.8% gvt. **Per capita income** (1992): $18,727. **Unemployment** (1992): 5.1%. **Tourism** (1992): out-of-state visitors spent $6.0 bln. **Sales tax:** 5%.

**Finance. FDIC-insured commercial banks & trust companies** (1992): 458. **Deposits:** $41.3 bln. **Savings institutions** (1992): 50. **Assets:** $13.9 bln.

**Federal government. No. federal civilian employees** (Mar. 1992): 12,643. **Avg. salary:** $31,804. **Notable federal facilities:** Ft. McCoy.

**Energy. Electricity production** (1992, MWh, by source): Hydroelectric: 1.8 mln.; Mineral: 29.1 mln.; Nuclear: 11.3 mln.

**Education. Student-teacher ratio** (1991): 15.7. **Avg. salary, public school teachers** (1992-93): $36,477.

**State Data. Motto:** Forward. **Flower:** Wood violet. **Bird:** Robin. **Tree:** Sugar maple. **Song:** On, Wisconsin! **Entered union** May 29, 1848; rank, 30th. **State fair** at: West Allis; mid-Aug.

**History.** Jean Nicolet was the first European to see the Wisconsin area, arriving in Green Bay, 1634; French missionaries and fur traders followed. The British took over, 1763. The U.S. won the land after the Revolution but the British were not ousted until after the War of 1812. Lead miners came next, then farmers. Railroads were started in 1851, serving growing wheat harvests and iron mines.

**Tourist attractions.** Old Wade House and Carriage Museum, Greenbush; Villa Louis, Prairie du Chien; Circus World Museum, Baraboo; Wisconsin Dells; Old World Wisconsin, Eagle; Door County peninsula; Chequamegon and Nicolet national forests; Lake Winnebago; numerous lakes for water sports, ice boating and fishing; skiing and hunting.

**Famous Wisconsinites** include Edna Ferber, King Camp Gillette, Harry Houdini, Robert La Follette, Alfred Lunt, Georgia O'Keeffe, Donald K. "Deke" Slayton, Spencer Tracy, Thorstein Veblen, Orson Welles, Thornton Wilder, Frank Lloyd Wright.

**Tourist information.** Wisconsin Dept. of Development, Division of Tourism, 123 W. Washington Ave., Madison, WI 53702.

**Toll-free travel information.** 1-800-372-2737.

# Wyoming

## *Equality State*

**People. Population** (1992): 466,185; **rank:** 50. **Pop. density:** 4.8 per sq. mi. **Racial distrib.** (1990): 94.2% White; 0.8% Black; 2.1% Amer. Indian; 5.7% Hispanic. **Net change** (1990-92): 2.8%.

**Geography. Total area:** 97,809 sq. mi.; **rank:** 9. **Land area:** 97,105 sq. mi. **Acres forested land:** 9,966,000. **Location:** Mountain state lying in the high western plateaus of the Great Plains. **Climate:** semi-desert conditions throughout; true desert in the Big Horn and Great Divide basins. **Topography:** the eastern Great Plains rise to the foothills of the Rocky Mtns.; the Continental Divide crosses the state from the NW to the SE. **Capital:** Cheyenne.

**Economy. Principal industries:** mineral extraction, tourism and recreation, agriculture. **Principal manufactured goods:** refined petroleum products, foods, wood products, stone, clay and glass products. **Agriculture: Chief crops:** wheat, beans, barley, oats, sugar beets, hay. **Livestock** (1992): 1.3 mln. cattle; 24,000 hogs/pigs; 850,000 sheep. **Timber/lumber** (1991): Ponderosa & lodgepole pine, Douglas fir, Engelmann spruce; 213 mln. bd. ft. **Nonfuel Minerals** (1992): $935.0 mln.; mostly portland cement, crushed stone. **International airports at:** Casper. **Value of construction** (1992): $467.9 mln. **Employment distribution** (1992): 23% trade; 20% services; 9% mining. **Per capita income** (1992): $17,423.

**Unemployment** (1992): 5.6%. **Tourism** (1992): out-of-state visitors spent $1.5 bln. **State sales tax:** 4%.

**Finance. FDIC-insured commercial banks & trust companies** (1992): 62. **Deposits:** $4.3 bln. **Savings institutions** (1992): 6. **Assets:** $800 mln.

**Federal government. No. federal civilian employees** (Mar. 1992): 4,878. **Avg. salary:** $32,062. **Notable federal facilities:** Warren AFB.

**Energy. Electricity production** (1992, MWh, by source): Hydroelectric: 0.4 mln.; Mineral: 36.1 mln.

**Education. Student-teacher ratio** (1991): 15.6. **Avg. salary, public school teachers** (1992-93): $30,850.

**State data. Motto:** Equal Rights. **Flower:** Indian paintbrush. **Bird:** Meadowlark. **Tree:** Cottonwood. **Song:** Wyoming. **Entered union** July 10, 1890; rank, 44th. **State fair at:** Douglas; late Aug.

**History.** Francés Francois and Louis La Verendrye were the first Europeans, 1743. John Colter, American, was first to traverse Yellowstone Park, 1807-08. Trappers and fur traders followed in the 1820s. Forts Laramie and Bridger became important stops on the pioneer trail to the West Coast. Indian wars followed massacres of army detachments in 1854 and 1866. Population grew after the Union Pacific crossed the state, 1869. Women won the vote, for the first time in the U.S., from the Territorial Legislature, 1869.

**Tourist attractions.** Yellowstone National Park, 3,472 sq. mi. in the NW corner of Wyoming and the adjoining edges of Montana and Idaho, the oldest U.S. national park, est. 1872, has some 10,000 geysers, hot springs, mud volcanoes, fossil forests, a volcanic glass (obsidian) mountain, the 1,000-ft.-deep canyon and 308-ft.-high waterfall of the Yellowstone River, and a wide variety of animals living free in their natural habitat.

Also, Grand Teton National Park, with mountains 13,000 ft. high; National Elk Refuge, covering 25,000 acres; Devils Tower, a columnar rock of igneous origin 1,280 ft. high; Fort Laramie and surrounding areas of pioneer trails; Buffalo Bill Museum, Cody; Cheyenne Frontier Days Celebration, last full week in July, the state's largest rodeo, and world's largest purse.

**Famous Wyomingites** include James Bridger, Buffalo Bill Cody, Nellie Tayloe Ross.

**Tourist information.** Travel Commission, Etchepare Circle, Cheyenne, WY 82002.

**Toll-free travel information.** 1-800-CALLWYO.

# District of Columbia

**Area:** 69 sq. mi. **Population** (1992): 588,620. **Motto:** Justitia omnibus (Justice for all). **Flower:** American beauty rose. **Tree:** Scarlet oak. **Bird:** Wood thrush. The city of Washington is coextensive with the District of Columbia.

The District of Columbia is the seat of the federal government of the United States. It lies on the west central edge of Maryland on the Potomac River, opposite Virginia. Its area was originally 100 sq. mi. taken from the sovereignty of Maryland and Virginia. Virginia's portion south of the Potomac was given back to that state in 1846.

The 23d Amendment, ratified in 1961, granted residents the right to vote for president and vice president for the first time and gave them 3 members in the Electoral College. The first such votes were cast in Nov. 1964.

Congress, which has legislative authority over the District under the Constitution, established in 1878 a government of 3 commissioners appointed by the president. The Reorganization Plan of 1967 substituted a single commissioner (also called mayor), assistant, and 9-member City Council. Funds were still appropriated by Congress; residents had no vote in local government, except to elect school board members.

In Sept. 1970, Congress approved legislation giving the District one delegate to the House of Representatives. The delegate could vote in committee but not on the House floor. The first was elected 1971.

In May 1974 voters approved a charter giving them the right to elect their own mayor and a 13-member city council; the first took office Jan. 2, 1975. The district won the right to levy its own taxes but Congress retained power to

veto council actions, and approve the city's annual budget.

Proposals for a "federal town" for the deliberations of the Continental Congress were made in 1783, 4 years before the adoption of the Constitution that gave the Confederation a national government. Rivalry between northern and southern delegates over the site appeared in the First Congress, 1789. John Adams, presiding officer of the Senate, cast the deciding vote of that body for Germantown, Pa. In 1790 Congress compromised by making Philadelphia the temporary capital for 10 years. The Virginia members of the House wanted a capital on the eastern bank of the Potomac; they were defeated by the Northerners, while the Southerners defeated the Northern attempt to have the nation assume the war debts of the 13 original states, the Assumption Bill fathered by Alexander Hamilton. Hamilton and Jefferson arranged a compromise: the Virginia men voted for the Assumption Bill, and the Northerners conceded the capital to the Potomac. President Washington chose the site in Oct. 1790 and persuaded landowners to sell their holdings to the government at £25, then about $66, an acre. The capital was named Washington.

Washington appointed Pierre Charles L'Enfant, a French engineer who had come over with Lafayette, to plan the capital on an area not over 10 mi. square. The L'Enfant plan, for streets 100 to 110 feet wide and one avenue 400 feet wide and a mile long, seemed grandiose and foolhardy, but Washington endorsed it. When L'Enfant ordered a wealthy landowner to remove his new manor house because it obstructed a vista, and demolished it when the owner refused, Washington stepped in and dismissed the architect. The official map and design of the city was completed by Benjamin Banneker, a distinguished black architect and astronomer, and Andrew Ellicott.

On Sept. 18, 1793, Pres. Washington laid the cornerstone of the north wing of the Capitol. On June 3, 1800, Pres. John Adams moved to Washington and on June 10, Philadelphia ceased to be the temporary capital. The City of Washington was incorporated in 1802; the District of Columbia was created as a municipal corporation in 1871, embracing Washington, Georgetown, and Washington County.

# Outlying U.S. Areas

# Commonwealth of Puerto Rico
### (Estado Libre Asociado de Puerto Rico)

**People. Population** (1992): 3,580,332 (and about 2.7 mln. more Puerto Ricans reside in the mainland U.S.). **Pop. density:** 1,035 per sq. mi. **Urban** (1990): 66.8%. **Racial distribution** (1990): 99.9% Hispanic. **Language:** On Jan. 28, 1993, the Gov. of Puerto Rico declared Spanish and English joint official languages.

**Geography. Total area:** 3,492 sq. mi. **Land area:** 3,427 sq. mi. **Location:** island lying between the Atlantic to the N and the Caribbean to the S; it is easternmost of the West Indies group called the Greater Antilles, of which Cuba, Hispaniola, and Jamaica are the larger islands. **Climate:** mild, with a mean temperature of 77° F. **Topography:** mountainous throughout three-fourths of its rectangular area, surrounded by a broken coastal plain; highest peak is Cerro Puntita, 4,389 ft. **Capital:** San Juan.

**Economy. Principal industries:** manufacturing. **Principal manufactured goods:** pharmaceuticals, chemicals, machinery and metals, electric machinery and equipment, food products, apparel, petroleum refining. **Agriculture: Chief crops:** coffee, plantains, pineapples, tomatoes, sugarcane, bananas, peppers, pumpkins, lettuce, tobacco, yams. **Livestock** (1990): 600,000 cattle; 206,000 pigs; 7.4 mln. poultry. **Nonfuel Minerals** (1991): $119.2 mln., mostly cement. **Commercial fishing** (1992): $6.2 mln. **Chief ports/river shipping:** San Juan, Ponce, Mayaguez. **Major airports at:** San Juan, Ponce, Mayaguez, Aguadilla. **Value of construction** (1992): $2.7

bln. **Employment distribution** (1992): 22.5% public admin., 19.8% trade, 16.8% mfg., 3.4% agric. **Per capita income** (1992): $6,360. **Unemployment** (1992): 16.7%. **Tourism** (1992): Visitors spent $1.51 bln.

**Finance. No. FDIC-insured commercial banks & trust companies** (1992): 17. **Deposits:** $18.8 bln. **No. savings institutions** (1992): 8. **Assets:** $4.1 bln.

**Federal government. No. federal civilian employees** (1992): 10,000. **Notable federal facilities:** U.S. Naval Station at Roosevelt Roads, Ceiba; U.S. Army Training Area and Ft. Allen at Salinas; Sabana SECA Communications Center (U.S. Navy); Ft. Buchanan at Guaynabo.

**Energy Production** (1992): 16,458 mln. kwh.

**Education. Student-teacher ratio** (1992): 21.0. **Avg. salary, public school teachers** (1992): $1,000 monthly.

**Misc. Data.** Motto: Joannes Est Nomen Eius (John is his name). **Flower:** Maga. **Bird:** Reinita. **Tree:** Ceiba. **National anthem:** La Borinqueña.

**History:** Puerto Rico (or Borinquen, after the original Arawak Indian name Boriquen), was visited by Columbus, on his second voyage, Nov. 19, 1493. In 1508 the Spanish arrived.

Sugarcane was introduced, 1515, and slaves were imported 3 years later. Gold mining petered out, 1570. Spaniards fought off a series of British and Dutch attacks; slavery was abolished, 1873. Under the treaty of Paris, Puerto Rico was ceded to the U.S. after the Spanish-American War, 1898. In 1952 the people voted in favor of Commonwealth status.

The Commonwealth of Puerto Rico is a self-governing part of the U.S. with a primary Hispanic culture. The current commonwealth political status of Puerto Rico gives the island's citizens virtually the same control over their internal affairs as the 50 states of the U.S. However, they do not vote in national elections, although they do vote in national primary elections.

Puerto Rico is represented in the U.S. Congress by a resident commissioner who has a voice but no vote, except in committees.

No federal income tax is collected from residents on income earned from local sources in Puerto Rico. Nevertheless, as part of the U.S. legal system, Puerto Rico is subject to the provisions of the U.S. Constitution; most federal laws apply as they do in the 50 states.

Puerto Rico's famous "Operation Bootstrap," begun in the late 1940s, succeeded in changing the island from "The Poorhouse of the Caribbean" to an area with the highest per capita income in Latin America. This pioneering program encouraged manufacturing and the development of the tourist trade by selective tax exemption, low-interest loans, and other incentives. Despite the marked success of Puerto Rico's development efforts over an extended period of time, per capita income in Puerto Rico is low in comparison to that of the U.S. Economic growth slowed in fiscal 1991 from the 2.2% of fiscal 1990.

**General tourist attractions:** Ponce Museum of Art; forts El Morro and San Cristobal; Old Walled City of San Juan; Arecibo Observatory; Cordillera Central and state parks; El Yunque Rain Forest; San Juan Cathedral; Porta Coeli Chapel and Museum of Religious Art, Interamerican Univ., San Germán; Condado Convention Center; Casa Blanca, Ponce de León family home, Puerto Rican Family Museum of 16th and 17th centuries and the Fine Arts Center in San Juan.

**Cultural facilities, festivals, etc.:** Festival Casals classical music concerts, mid-June; Puerto Rico Symphony Orchestra at Music Conservatory; Botanical Garden and Museum of Anthropology, Art, and History at the University of Puerto Rico; Institute of Puerto Rican Culture, at the Dominican Convent; and many popular festivals throughout the island.

**Famous Puerto Ricans include:** Miguel Hernández Agosto, José Celso Barbosa, Julia de Burgos, Pablo Casals, Orlando Cepeda, Roberto Clemente, Rafael Hernández Colón, José de Diego, José Feliciano, Luis A. Ferré, José Ferrer, Doña Felisa Rincón de Gautier, Commodore Diégo E. Hernández, Rafael Hernández (El Jibarito), Marta Casals Istomin, Raúl Juliá, Luis Muñoz Marín, René Marqués, Luis Palés Matos, Concha Meléndez, Rita Moreno, Adm. Horacio Rivero.

**Chamber of Commerce:** 100 Tetuán P.O. Box. S-3789, San Juan, PR 00904; Ponce & South: El Señorial Bldg., Ponce, PR 00731.

# Guam

## Where America's Day Begins

**People. Population** (1990): 133,152, a 26% increase over the 1980 figure of 105,979. **Pop. density:** 631.6 per sq. mi. **Urban** (1980): 39.5%. **Major ethnic groups** (1990): Chamorro 43%, Filipino 28.6%, stateside immigrants 20%, remainder Micronesians. Native Guamanians, ethnically called Chamorros, are basically of Indonesian stock, with a mixture of Spanish and Filipino. In addition to the offical language, they speak the native Chamorro. **Migration** (1990): About 52% of population were born elsewhere; of these, 48% in Asia, 40% in U.S.

**Geography. Total area:** 217 sq. mi. land, 30 mi. long and 4 to 8.5 mi. wide. **Location:** largest and southernmost of the Mariana Islands in the West Pacific, 3,700 mi. W of Hawaii. **Climate:** tropical, with temperatures from 70° to 90° F; avg. annual rainfall, about 70 in. **Topography:** coralline limestone plateau in the N; southern chain of low volcanic mountains sloping gently to the W, more steeply to coastal cliffs on the E; general elevation, 500 ft.; highest pt., Mt. Lamlam, 1,334 ft. **Capital:** Agana.

**Economy. Principal industries:** tourism, defense, construction, banking. **Principal manufactured goods:** textiles, foods. **Agriculture: Chief crops:** cabbages, eggplants, cucumber, long beans, tomatoes, bananas, coconuts, watermelon, yams, canteloupe, papayas, maize, sweet potatoes. **Livestock** (1984): 2,000 cattle; 14,000 hogs/pigs. **Chief ports:** Apra Harbor. **International airports at:** Tamuning. **Value of construction** (1980): $80.6 mln. **Employment distribution** (1987): 61.3% private sector; 38.7% gvt. **Per capita income** (1986): $7,116. **Median household income** (1989): $30,755; persons per household 3.97; persons per family 4.26. **Unemployment** (1990): 3.8%. **Tourism** (1990): visitors' receipts $550 mln.

**Finance. Notable industries:** insurance, real estate, finance. **No. banks:** 13; **No. savings and loan assns.:** 2.

**Federal government. No. federal employees** (1990): 7,200. **Notable federal facilities:** Anderson AFB; naval, air and port bases.

**Misc. Data. Flower:** Puti Tai Nobio (Bougainvillea). **Bird:** Toto (Fruit dove). **Tree:** Ifit (Intsiabijuga). **Song:** Stand Ye Guamanians.

**History.** Guam was probably settled by voyagers from the Indonesian-Philippine archipelago by at least the third century B.C. Pottery, rice cultivation, and megalithic technology show strong East Asian cultural influence. Centralized, village clan-based communities engaged in agriculture and offshore fishing. The est. population by the early 16th century was between 50,000 and 75,000 inhabitants. Magellan arrived in the Marianas Mar. 6, 1521. They were colonized in 1668 by Spanish missionaries who named them the Mariana Islands in honor of Maria Anna, queen of Spain. When Spain ceded Guam to the U.S., it sold the other Marianas to Germany. Japan obtained a League of Nations mandate over the German islands in 1919; in Dec. 1941 it seized Guam; the island was retaken by the U.S. in July 1944.

Guam is a self-governing organized unincorporated U.S. territory. The Organic Act of 1950 provides for a governor and a 21-member unicameral legislature, elected biennially by the residents who are American citizens.

In 1972 a U.S. law gave Guam one delegate to the U.S. House of Representatives; the delegate may vote in committee but not on the House floor.

Guam's quest to change its status to a U.S. Commonwealth began in the late 1970's. A Commission on Self-Determination, created in 1984, developed a Draft Commonwealth Act, which was submitted to Congress.

**General tourist attractions.** Tropical climate, oceanic marine environment; annual mid-Aug. Merizo Water Festival; Tarzan Falls; beaches; water sports; duty-free port shopping.

# Virgin Islands

### St. John, St. Croix, St. Thomas

**People. Population** (1990): 101,809 (50,139, St. Croix; 48,166, St. Thomas; 3,504, St. John). **Pop. density:** 748.6 per sq. mi. **Urban** (1980): 39%. **Racial distribution:** (1980) 15% White; 85% Black. **Major ethnic groups:** West Indian, French, Hispanic.

**Geography. Total area:** 151 sq. mi.; **Land area:** 134 sq. mi. **Location:** 3 larger and 50 smaller islands and cays in the S and W of the V.I. group (British V.I. colony to the N and E) which is situated 70 mi. E of Puerto Rico, located W of the Anegada Passage, a major channel connecting the Atlantic O. and the Caribbean Sea. **Climate:** subtropical; the sun tempered by gentle trade winds; humidity is low; average temperature, 78° F. **Topography:** St. Thomas is mainly a ridge of hills running E and W, and has little tillable land; St. Croix rises abruptly in the N but slopes to the S to flatlands and lagoons; St. John has steep, lofty hills and valleys with little level tillable land. **Capital:** Charlotte Amalie, St. Thomas.

**Economy. Principal industries:** tourism, rum, alumina prod., petroleum refining, watch industry, textiles, electronics. **Principal manufactured goods:** rum, textiles, pharmaceuticals, perfumes. **Gross Domestic Product** (1987): $1.246 bln. **Agriculture: Chief crops:** truck garden produce. **Minerals:** sand, gravel. **Chief ports:** Cruz Bay, St. John; Frederiksted and Christiansted, St. Croix; Charlotte Amalie, St. Thomas. **International airports on:** St. Thomas, St. Croix. **Value of construction** (1987): $167.0 mln. **Per capita income** (1989): $11,052. **Unemployment** (1992): 2.8%. **Tourism** (1988): $662.8. **No. banks** (1990): 8.

**Misc. data. Flower:** Yellow elder or yellow trumpet, local designation Ginger Thomas. **Bird:** Yellow breast. **Song:** Virgin Islands March.

**History.** The islands were visited by Columbus in 1493. Spanish forces, 1555, defeated the Caribes and claimed the territory; by 1596 the native population was annihilated. First permanent settlement in the U.S. territory, 1672, by the Danes; U.S. purchased the islands, 1917, for defense purposes.

The Virgin Islands has a republican form of government, headed by a governor and lieut. governor elected, since 1970, by popular vote for 4-year terms. There is a 15-member unicameral legislature, elected by popular vote. Residents of the V.I. have been U.S. citizens since 1927. Since 1973 they have elected a delegate to the U.S. House of Representatives, who may vote in committee but not in the House.

**General tourist attractions.** Magens Bay, St. Thomas; duty-free shopping; Virgin Islands National Park, 14,488 acres on St. John of lush growth, beaches, Indian relics, and evidence of colonial Danes.

**Tourist information.** Dept. of Economic Development & Agriculture, St. Thomas, P.O. Box 6400, St. Thomas, VI 00801; St. Croix, P.O. Box 4535, Christiansted, St. Croix 00820.

# American Samoa

**Capital:** Pago Pago, Island of Tutuila. **Total Area:** 84 sq. mi. **Population:** (1992) 50,923. **Motto:** Samoa Muamua le Atua (In Samoa, God Is First). **Song:** Amerika Samoa. **Flower:** Paogo (Ula-fala). **Plant:** Ava.

Blessed with spectacular scenery and delightful South Seas climate, American Samoa is the most southerly of all lands under U.S. sovereignty. It is an unincorporated territory consisting of 7 small islands of the Samoan group: **Tutuila, Aunu'u, Manu'a Group (Ta'u, Olosega and Ofu), Rose,** and **Swains Island.** The islands are 2,300 mi. SW of Honolulu.

A tripartite agreement between Great Britain, Germany, and the U.S. in 1899 gave the U.S. sovereignty over the eastern islands of the Samoan group; these islands became American Samoa. Local chiefs officially ceded Tutuila and Aunu'u to the U.S. in April 1900 and the Manu'a group in July 1904; Swains Island was annexed in 1925.

Samoa (Western), comprising the larger islands of the Samoan group, was a New Zealand mandate and UN Trusteeship until it became an independent nation Jan. 1, 1962 *(see Index).*

Tutuila and Aunu'u have an area of 53 sq. mi. Ta'u has an area of 17 sq. mi., and the islets of Ofu and Olosega, 5 sq. mi. with a population of a few thousand. Swains Island has nearly 2 sq. mi. and a population of about 100.

About 70% of the land is bush and mountains. Chief products and exports are fish products. Taro, breadfruit, yams, coconuts, pineapples, oranges, and bananas are also produced.

From 1900-1951, American Samoa was under the jurisdiction of the U.S. Navy. Since 1951, it has been under the Interior Dept. On Jan. 3, 1978, the first popularly elected Samoan governor and lieutenant governor were inaugurated. Previously, the governor was appointed by the Secretary of the Interior. American Samoa has a bicameral legislature and elects its own member of Congress, who can introduce legislation and vote in committee, but not in the House.

The American Samoans are of Polynesian origin. They are nationals of the U.S.; approximately 20,000 live in Hawaii, 65,000 in California and Washington.

# Minor Caribbean Island

**Navassa** lies between Jamaica and Haiti, 100 miles south of Guantanamo Bay, Cuba; it covers about 3 sq. mi., is reserved by the U.S. for a lighthouse and is uninhabited. It is administered by the U.S. Coast Guard.

# Wake, Midway, Other Islands

**Wake Island,** and its sister islands, **Wilkes** and **Peale,** lie in the Pacific Ocean on the direct route from Hawaii to Hong Kong, about 2,300 mi. W of Honolulu and 1,290 mi. E of Guam. The group is 4.5 mi. long, 1.5 mi. wide, and totals less than 3 sq. mi.

The U.S. flag was hoisted over Wake Island, July 4, 1898, formal possession taken Jan. 17, 1899; Wake has been administered by the U.S. Air Force since 1972. The population consists of about 200 persons.

The **Midway Islands,** acquired in 1867, consist of 2, **Sand** and **Eastern,** in the North Pacific 1,150 mi. NW of Honolulu, with area of about 3 sq. mi., administered by the U.S. Navy. There is no indigenous population; its population is about 450.

**Johnston Atoll,** 717 miles WSW of Honolulu, area 1 sq. mi., is operated by The Defense Nuclear Agency, and the Fish and Wildlife Service, U.S. Dept. of the Interior; its population is about 1,200. **Kingman Reef,** 920 miles S of Hawaii, is under Navy control.

**Howland, Jarvis,** and **Baker Islands,** 1,400-1,650 miles SW of Honolulu, uninhabited since World War II, are under the Interior Dept.

**Palmyra** is an atoll about 1,000 miles south of Hawaii, 2 sq. mi. Privately owned, it is under the Interior Dept.

# Islands Under Trusteeship

The Trust Territory of the Pacific Islands was established in 1947, as the only strategic trusteeship of the 11 trusteeships established by the U.N. For nearly 4 decades, the territory had a heterogeneous population of about 140,000 people scattered among more than 2,100 islands and atolls in 3 major archipelagos: the Carolines, the Marshalls, and the Marianas. The entire geographic area is sometimes referred to as "Micronesia," meaning "little islands." The area of the Trust Territory covered some 3 million sq. miles of the Pacific Ocean, slightly larger than the continental U.S. However, its islands constituted a land area of only 715.8 sq. miles—half the size of Rhode Island. It formerly consisted of 7 districts and now has 4 political jurisdictions: The Commonwealth of the Northern Mariana Islands (CNMI), the Federated

States of Micronesia (FSM), the Republic of the Marshall Islands (RMI), and Palau. As of Oct. 21, 1986, the RMI entered into free association with the U.S., as did the FSM effective Nov. 3, 1986. The CNMI became a commonwealth of the U.S., also effective Nov. 3. Only Palau remains under trusteeship.

## Commonwealth of the Northern Mariana Islands

Located in the perpetually warm climes between Guam and the Tropic of Cancer, the 14 islands of the Northern Marianas form a 300-mile-long archipelago, comprising a total land area of 179 sq. miles. The native population, 1990, is 43,345, and is concentrated on the 3 largest of the 6 inhabited islands: **Saipan,** the seat of government and commerce (38,896), **Rota** (2,295), and **Tinian** (2,118).

The people of the Northern Marianas are predominantly of Chamorro cultural extraction, although numbers of Carolinians and immigrants from other areas of E. Asia and Micronesia have also settled in the islands. Pursuant to the Covenant of 1976, which established the Northern Marianas as a commonwealth in political union with the U.S., most natives and many domiciliaries of these islands achieved U.S. citizenship on Nov. 13, 1986, when the U.S. terminated its administration of the U.N. trusteeship as it affected the Northern Marianas. From July 18, 1947, the U.S. had administered the Northern Marianas under a trusteeship agreement with the U.N. Security Council. English is among the several languages commonly spoken.

The Northern Mariana Islands has been self-governing since 1978, when both a constitution drafted and adopted by the people became effective and a bicameral legislature with offices of governor and lieutenant governor was inaugurated. Commercial activity has increased steadily in recent years. In 1990, more than 417,146 tourists visited.

## Palau

Palau (or Belau) consists of more than 200 islands in 16 states in the Caroline chain, of which 8 are permanently inhabited. The capital of Palau, Koror, lies 3,997 miles SW of Honolulu and 813 miles S of Guam. Population of Palau is 15,122 (1990), 10,501 (1990) in Koror. Average year-round temperature is 80 degrees, average annual rainfall 150 inches.

Until 1979, a High Commissioner, appointed by the U.S. President, in turn appoints a district administrator for Palau to oversee programs and administration there. In support of the islands' evolving political status, the U.S. recognized the Constitution of Palau and the establishment of the government of Palau, consistent with U.S. responsibilities in Palau as the administering authority of the U.N. Trust Territory of the Pacific Islands (TTPI).

The Assistant Secretary of the Interior for Territorial and International Affairs has been delegated U.S. authority with respect to Palau and may suspend any newly enacted national law in Palau, as well as any newly enacted state law that involves finance or the expenditure of funds, if the law is inconsistent with the trusteeship agreement or U.S. laws or regulations applicable to the TTPI. The Constitution became effective in 1980. The President and Vice President are elected by popular vote. A Council of Chiefs advises the President on matters concerning traditional law and custom. Palau has a bicameral national legislature composed of a House of Delegates and a Senate.

# Washington, Capital of the U.S.

### Arlington National Cemetery

**Arlington National Cemetery,** on the former Custis estate in Virginia, is the site of the **Tomb of the Unknowns** and the final resting place of John Fitzgerald Kennedy, president of the United States, who was buried there Nov. 25, 1963. A torch burns day and night over his grave. The remains of his brother Sen. Robert F. Kennedy (N.Y.) were interred on June 8, 1968, in an area adjacent. Many other famous Americans are also buried at Arlington, as well as 175,000 American soldiers from every major war.

### U.S. Marine Corps War Memorial (Iwo Jima)

North of the National Cemetery, approximately 350 yards, stands the bronze statue of the raising of the United States flag on Mt. Suribachi during WWII, executed by Felix de Weldon from the photograph by Joe Rosenthal, and presented to the nation by members and friends of the U.S. Marine Corps.

### Vietnam Veterans Memorial

Dedicated on November 13, 1982, it is a symbol of the nation's recognition of the men and women who served in the armed forces in the Vietnam War. On a V-shaped wall are inscribed the names of the more than 58,000 Americans who lost their lives or remain missing.

### The Capitol

The United States Capitol was originally designed by Dr. William Thornton, an amateur architect, who submitted a plan in the spring of 1793 that won him $500 and a city lot.

The south, or House, wing was completed in 1807 under the direction of Benjamin H. Latrobe.

The present Senate and House wings and the iron dome were designed and constructed by Thomas U. Walter, the 4th architect of the Capitol, between 1851 and 1863.

The present cast iron dome at its greatest exterior measures 135 ft. 5 in., and it is topped by the bronze Statue of Freedom that stands 19½ ft. and weighs 14,985 pounds. On

its base are the words "E Pluribus Unum" (Out of Many One).

The Capitol is normally open from 9 a.m. to 4:30 p.m; from June to Aug., to 10 p.m. Tours through the Capitol, including the House and Senate galleries, are conducted from 9 a.m. to 4 p.m. without charge.

### Folger Shakespeare Library

**The Folger Shakespeare Library,** on Capitol Hill, is a research institution devoted to the advancement of learning in the background of Anglo-American civilization in the 16th and 17th centuries and in most aspects of the continental Renaissance. It has the largest collection of Shakespeareana in the world, with 79 copies of the First Folio.

### Library of Congress

Established by and for Congress in 1800, the Library of Congress has extended its services over the years to other government agencies and other libraries, to scholars, and to the general public, and it now serves as the national library. It contains over 80 million items in 470 languages.

The library's exhibit halls are open to the public, from 8:30 a.m. to 9:30 p.m. Mon.-Fri.; to 6 p.m. Sat.; from 1 p.m. to 5 p.m. Sun. & holidays. Guided tours are given every hour from 9 a.m. through 4 p.m. Monday through Friday.

### Thomas Jefferson Memorial

Dedicated in 1943, **The Thomas Jefferson Memorial** stands on the south shore of the Tidal Basin in West Potomac Park. It is a circular stone structure, with Vermont marble on the exterior and Georgia white marble inside, and combines architectural elements of the dome of the Pantheon in Rome and the rotunda designed by Jefferson for the University of Virginia.

The memorial is open daily from 8 a.m. to midnight. An elevator and curb ramps for the handicapped are in service.

### Lincoln Memorial

**The Lincoln Memorial** in West Potomac Park, on the axis of the Capitol and the Washington Monument, consists of a large marble hall enclosing a heroic statue of Abraham Lincoln in meditation sitting on a large armchair. It was dedicated on Memorial Day, May 30, 1922. The Memorial was designed by Henry Bacon. The statue was made by Daniel Chester French and sculpted by the Piccirilli family. Murals and ornamentation on the bronze ceiling beams are by Jules Guerin.

The memorial is open daily from 8 a.m. to midnight. An elevator for the handicapped is in service.

### John F. Kennedy Center

John F. Kennedy Center for the Performing Arts, designated by Congress as the National Cultural Center and the official memorial in Washington to President Kennedy, opened September 8, 1971. Tours are available daily between 10:00 a.m. and 1:00 p.m.

### Mount Vernon

Mount Vernon, George Washington's estate, is on the south bank of the Potomac R., 16 miles below Washington, D.C., in northern Virginia.

The present house is an enlargement of one apparently built on the site by Augustine Washington, who lived there 1735-1738. His son Lawrence came there in 1743, when he renamed the plantation Mount Vernon in honor of Admiral Vernon, under whom he had served in the West Indies. Lawrence Washington died in 1752 and was succeeded as proprietor of Mount Vernon by his half-brother, George Washington.

### National Archives

The Declaration of Independence, the Constitution of the United States, and the Bill of Rights are on permanent display in the National Archives Exhibition Hall. They are sealed in glass-and-bronze cases. The National Archives also holds the permanently valuable federal records of the United States government.

### National Gallery of Art

The National Gallery of Art, situated on the north side of the Mall facing Constitution Avenue, was established by Joint Resolution of Congress Mar. 24, 1937, and opened Mar. 17, 1941.

Normally open daily from 10 a.m. to 5 p.m.; 11 a.m. to 6 p.m. Sunday. Summer, 10 a.m. to 9 p.m., noon to 9 p.m. on Sunday.

### The Pentagon

The Pentagon, headquarters of the Department of Defense, is one of the world's largest office buildings. Situated in Arlington, Va., it houses more than 23,000 employees in offices that occupy 3,707,745 square feet.

Tours are available Monday through Friday (excluding federal holidays), from 9:30 a.m. to 3:30 p.m.

### Smithsonian Institution

The Smithsonian Institution, established in 1846, the world's largest museum complex, is comprised of 14 museums and the National Zoo. It holds some 100 million artifacts and specimens in its trust "for the increase and diffusion of knowledge among men." Nine museums are located on the National Mall between the Washington Monument and the Capitol; 4 other museums and the zoo are elsewhere in Washington, and the Cooper-Hewitt Museum is in New York City. The National Air and Space Museum, the National Museum of Natural History, and the National Portrait Gallery are some of the more popular museums. They are open daily, except Dec. 25, from 10 a.m. to 5:30 p.m. unless otherwise noted.

### Washington Monument

The Washington Monument, dedicated in 1885, is a tapering shaft or obelisk of white marble, 555 ft., 5-1/8 inches in height and 55 ft., 1-1/2 inches square at base. Eight small windows, 2 on each side, are located at the 500-ft. level, where points of interest are indicated.

Open daily except Dec. 25, 9 a.m. to 4:30 p.m., 8 a.m. to midnight Apr.-Labor Day.

### The White House

The White House, the president's residence, stands on 18 acres on the south side of Pennsylvania Avenue, between the Treasury and the Executive Office Building.

The walls are of sandstone, quarried at Aquia Creek, Va. The exterior walls were painted, causing the building to be termed the "White House." On Aug. 24, 1814, during Madison's administration, the house was burned by the British. James Hoban rebuilt it by Oct. 1817.

The White House is normally open from 10 a.m. to 12 noon, Tues.-Sat., and from 10 a.m. to 2 p.m. in summer. Only the public rooms on the ground floor and state floor may be visited.

## Naturalization: How to Become an American Citizen

Source: Federal Statutes

A person who desires to be naturalized as a citizen of the United States may obtain the necessary application form as well as detailed information from the nearest office of the Immigration and Naturalization Service or from the clerk of a court handling naturalization cases.

An applicant must be at least 18 years old and must have been a lawful resident of the United States continuously for 5 years. For husbands and wives of U.S. citizens the period is 3 years in most instances. Special provisions apply to certain veterans of the Armed Forces.

An applicant must have been physically present in the country for at least half of the required 5 years' residence.

Every applicant for naturalization must:

(1) demonstrate an understanding of the English language, including an ability to read, write, and speak words in ordinary usage in the English language (persons physically unable to do so and persons who, on the date of their examinations, are over 50 years of age and have been lawful permanent residents of the United States for 20 years or more are exempt);

(2) have been a person of good moral character, attached to the principles of the Constitution, and well disposed to the good order and happiness of the United States for five years just before filing the petition or for whatever other period of residence is required in the particular case and continue to be such a person until admitted to citizenship; and

(3) demonstrate a knowledge and understanding of the fundamentals of the history, and the principles and form of government, of the United States.

At the preliminary hearing the applicant may be represented by a lawyer or social service agency. There is a 30-day wait. If action is favorable, there is a final hearing before a judge, who administers the following oath of allegiance:

I hereby declare, on oath, that I absolutely and entirely renounce and abjure all allegiance and fidelity to any foreign prince, potentate, state or sovereignty, to whom or which I have heretofore been a subject or citizen; that I will support and defend the Constitution and laws of the United States of America against all enemies, foreign and domestic; that I will bear true faith and allegiance to the same; that I will bear arms on behalf of the United States when required by the law; that I will perform noncombatant service in the armed forces of the United States when required by the law; that I will perform work of national importance under civilian direction when required by the law; and that I take this obligation freely without any mental reservation or purpose of evasion; so help me God.

# CITIES OF THE U.S.

Sources: Bureau of the Census: population (1990 Census, updated as of April 1993); population growth (1980-1990). Geography Division, Bureau of the Census: population density (1990); area (1990). Bureau of Labor Statistics: employment (1992 averages for city proper only). Bureau of Economic Analysis: per capita personal income (Metropolitan Statistical Area, 1991).

Based on 1990 Census, the 100 most populous cities (inc. = incorporated; est. = established).

## Akron, Ohio

**Population:** 223,019; **Pop. density:** 4,055 per sq. mi.; **Pop. growth:** −6.0%. **Area:** 55 sq. mi. **Employment:** 97,224 employed, 9.6% unemployed; **Per capita income:** $18,234; % change 1981-91: 69.1.
**History:** settled 1825; inc. as city 1865; located on Ohio-Erie Canal and is a port of entry; since 1870 the rubber capital of the U.S.
**Transportation:** 1 airport; major trucking industry; Conrail; metro transit system. **Communications:** 4 TV, 7 radio stations. **Medical facilities:** 11 hospitals; specialized children's treatment center. **Educational facilities:** 13 universities and colleges; 68 public schools. **Further information:** Akron Regional Development Board or Akron-Summit Convention and Visitors Bureau, Cascade Plaza, Akron, OH 44308.

## Albuquerque, New Mexico

**Population:** 384,619; **Pop. density:** 2,829 per sq. mi.; **Pop. growth:** 15.6%. **Area:** 136 sq. mi. **Employment:** 213,698 employed, 4.6% unemployed; **Per capita income:** $17,040; % change 1981-91: 73.7.
**History:** founded 1706 by the Spanish; inc. 1890.
**Transportation:** 1 international airport; 1 railroad; 2 bus lines. **Communications:** 8 TV, 31 radio stations. **Medical facilities:** 10 major hospitals. **Educational facilities:** 2 universities, 2 colleges. **Further information:** Convention & Visitors Bureau, 121 Tijeras Ave. NE, Albuquerque, NM 87125.

## Anaheim, California

**Population:** 266,406; **Pop. density:** 6,498 per sq. mi.; **Pop. growth:** 21.4%. **Area:** 41 sq. mi. **Employment:** 141,649 employed, 7.1% unemployed; **Per capita income:** $24,077; % change 1981-91: 65.4.
**History:** founded 1858; inc. 1876; now known as home of Disneyland (since 1955).
**Transportation:** 3 municipal airports; 4 railroads; Greyhound buses. **Communications:** 12 TV, 4 radio stations. **Medical facilities:** 6 general hospitals. **Educational facilities:** 3 colleges, 5 junior colleges; 62 elementary, 8 junior high, 8 high schools. **Further information:** Chamber of Commerce, 100 South Anaheim Blvd., Suite 300, Anaheim, CA 92805.

## Anchorage, Alaska

**Population:** 226,338; **Pop. density:** 131 per sq. mi.; **Pop. growth:** 29.8%. **Area:** 1,732 sq. mi. **Employment:** 109,090 employed, 7.3% unemployed; **Per capita income:** $24,464; % change 1981-91: 45.1.
**History:** founded 1914 as a construction camp for railroad; HQ of Alaska Defense Command, WWII; severely damaged in earthquake 1964.
**Transportation:** 1 international airport, 3 other airports. **Communications:** 6 TV, 16 radio stations. **Medical facilities:** 3 hospitals. **Educational facilities:** 2 universities, 1 community college. **Further information:** Chamber of Commerce, 441 W. 5th Ave., Ste. 300, Anchorage, AK 99501.

## Arlington, Texas

**Population:** 261,721; **Pop. density:** 3,313 per sq. mi.; **Pop. growth:** 63.5%. **Area:** 79 sq. mi. **Employment:** 150,988 employed, 6.2% unemployed; **Per capita income:** $18,714; % change 1981-91: 55.4.
**History:** settled in 1840s between Dallas & Ft. Worth; inc. 1884.
**Transportation:** Dallas/Ft. Worth airport is 20 minutes away; 11 railway lines; intercity transport system in planning stage. **Communications:** 13 TV, 53 radio stations. **Medical facilities:** 4 hospitals. **Educational facilities:** 1 university; 51 public schools. **Further information:** Chamber of Commerce, 316 W. Main St., Arlington, TX 76010.

## Atlanta, Georgia

**Population:** 393,929; **Pop. density:** 3,008 per sq. mi.; **Pop. growth:** −7.3%. **Area:** 131 sq. mi. **Employment:** 164,506 employed, 10.0% unemployed; **Per capita income:** $20,304; % change 1981-91: 81.6.
**History:** founded as "Terminus" 1837; renamed Atlanta 1845 after Atlantis; inc. 1847; played major role in Civil War and burned during Gen. Sherman's "March to the Sea."
**Transportation:** 1 international airport; 7 railroad lines, 2 systems; 2 bus terminals; rapid rail. **Communications:** 9 TV, 41 radio stations; 21 cable TV companies. **Medical facilities:** 60 hospitals; VA hospital; Natl. Centers for Disease. Control; Natl. Cancer Center. **Educational facilities:** 37 colleges, universities, seminaries, junior colleges. **Further information:** Chamber of Commerce, 235 International Blvd., Atlanta, GA 30303.

## Aurora, Colorado

**Population:** 222,103; **Pop. density:** 1,645 per sq. mi.; **Pop. growth:** 40.1%. **Area:** 135 sq. mi. **Employment:** 118,569 employed, 5.4% unemployed; **Per capita income:** $21,441; % change 1981-91: 59.4.
**History:** located 5 miles east of Denver; early growth stimulated by presence of military bases; fast-growing trade center.
**Transportation:** adjacent to new Denver Intl. Airport; 1 airport; 4 railroads; bus system. **Further information:** Aurora Economic Development Council, 15701 E. 1st Ave., Ste. 206, Aurora, CO 80011.

## Austin, Texas

**Population:** 465,622; **Pop. density:** 4,014 per sq. mi.; **Pop. growth:** 34.6%. **Area:** 116 sq. mi. **Employment:** 269,075 employed, 5.7% unemployed; **Per capita income:** $18,081; % change 1981-91: 71.1.
**History:** first permanent settlement 1835; capital of Rep. of Texas 1838; named after Stephen Austin; inc. 1840.
**Transportation:** 1 international airport; 4 railroads. **Communications:** 5 TV, 18 radio stations. **Medical facilities:** 15 hospitals. **Educational facilities:** 7 universities and colleges. **Further information:** Chamber of Commerce, P.O. Box 1967, Austin, TX 78767.

## Bakersfield, California

**Population:** 174,820; **Pop. density:** 2,033 per sq. mi.; **Pop. growth:** 65.5%. **Area:** 86 sq. mi. **Employment:** 80,470 employed, 11.2% unemployed; **Per capita income:** $15,791; % change 1981-91: 42.2.
**History:** incorporated in 1898.

**Transportation:** 1 airport; 3 railroads; Greyhound buses; local bus system. **Medical facilities:** 4 major hospitals; 9 convalescent; 2 psychiatric; 3 physical rehab. centers; 3 clinics; 2 urgent care centers. **Educational facilities:** 1 university, 1 community college; 9 vocational schools; 1 adult school; 1 college of law; 58 public schools. **Further information:** Greater Bakersfield Chamber of Commerce, 1033 Truxtun Avenue, Bakersfield, CA 93301.

## Baltimore, Maryland

**Population:** 736,014; **Pop. density:** 9,200 per sq. mi.; **Pop. growth:** −6.4%. **Area:** 80 sq. mi. **Employment:** 297,512 employed, 10.7% unemployed; **Per capita income:** $21,874; % change 1981-91: 84.5.
**History:** founded by Maryland legislature 1729; inc. 1797; bombing of its Ft. McHenry 1814 inspired Francis Scott Key to write "Star-Spangled Banner;" rebuilt after fire 1904.
**Transportation:** 1 major airport; 3 railroads; bus system; subway system; 2 underwater tunnels. **Communications:** 6 TV, 33 radio stations. **Medical facilities:** 29 hospitals; 2 major medical centers. **Educational facilities:** over 30 universities and colleges; 189 public schools. **Further information:** Greater Baltimore Committee, 111 S. Calvert St., Baltimore, MD 21202.

## Baton Rouge, Louisiana

**Population:** 219,531; **Pop. density:** 3,599 per sq. mi.; **Pop. growth:** −0.4%. **Area:** 61 sq. mi. **Employment:** 108,838 employed, 6.6% unemployed; **Per capita income:** $17,032; % change 1981-91: 56.5.
**History:** claimed by Spain at time of La. Purchase 1803; est. independence by rebellion 1810; inc. as town 1817; held by Union during most of Civil War.
**Transportation:** 1 airport, 7 airlines; 1 bus line; 3 railroad trunk lines. **Communications:** 5 TV, 19 radio stations. **Medical facilities:** 7 hospitals. **Educational facilities:** 2 universities; 96 public, 46 private schools. **Further information:** Chamber of Commerce, P.O. Box 3217, Baton Rouge, LA 70821.

## Birmingham, Alabama

**Population:** 265,965; **Pop. density:** 2,687 per sq. mi.; **Pop. growth:** −6.5%. **Area:** 99 sq. mi. **Employment:** 113,176 employed, 8.6% unemployed; **Per capita income:** $18,210; % change 1981-91: 83.5.
**History:** settled due to discovery of elements needed for steel production; inc. 1871; named after Great Britain's steel-making center.
**Transportation:** 1 airport; 4 major rail freight lines, Amtrak; 1 bus line; 75 truck line terminals; 4 interstate highways. **Communications:** 4 TV, 22 radio stations; 1 educational TV, 1 educational radio station. **Medical facilities:** Univ. of Alabama at Birmingham Medical Center; VA hospital with organ transplant program; 15 other hospitals. **Educational facilities:** 1 university, 2 colleges, 2 junior colleges. **Further information:** Chamber of Commerce, 2027 First Ave. N., Birmingham, AL 35202.

## Boston, Massachusetts

**Population:** 574,283; **Pop. density:** 12,484 per sq. mi.; **Pop. growth:** 2.0%. **Area:** 46 sq. mi. **Employment:** 271,288 employed, 7.8% unemployed; **Per capita income:** $23,480; % change 1981-91: 96.6.
**History:** settled 1630 by John Winthrop; capital of Mass. Bay Colony; figured strongly in Am. Revolution, earning distinction as the "Cradle of Liberty;" inc. 1822.
**Transportation:** 1 major airport; 2 railroads; city rail and subway system; 2 underwater tunnels; port. **Communications:** 8 TV, 17 radio stations. **Medical facilities:** 16 hospitals; 8 major medical research centers. **Educational facilities:** 11 universities and colleges. **Further information:** Greater Boston Chamber of Commerce, 1 Beacon St., 4th fl., Boston, MA 02108-3114.

## Buffalo, New York

**Population:** 328,175; **Pop. density:** 7,812 per sq. mi.; **Pop. growth:** −8.3%. **Area:** 42 sq. mi. **Employment:** 125,888 employed, 12.0% unemployed; **Per capita income:** $18,466; % change 1981-91: 72.8.
**History:** founded 1790 by the Dutch; raided twice by British during War of 1812; as western terminus for Erie Canal became a center for trade and manufacturing; inc. 1832.
**Transportation:** 1 international airport; 6 major railroads; metro rail system; water service to Great Lakes-St. Lawrence seaways system, and Atlantic seaboard. **Communications:** 8 TV, 31 radio stations. **Medical facilities:** 16 hospitals. **Educational facilities:** 2 universities, 11 colleges; 70 public and private schools. **Further information:** Greater Buffalo Partnership, 300 Main Place Tower, Buffalo, NY 14202.

## Charlotte, North Carolina

**Population:** 395,934; **Pop. density:** 2,869 per sq. mi.; **Pop. growth:** 25.5%. **Area:** 138 sq. mi. **Employment:** 218,604 employed, 5.5% unemployed; **Per capita income:** $18,757; % change 1981-91: 87.4.
**History:** settled by Scotch-Irish immigrants 1740s; inc. 1767 and named after Queen Charlotte, George III's wife; scene of first major U.S. gold discovery 1799.
**Transportation:** 1 airport; 2 major railway lines; 2 bus lines; 280 trucking firms. **Communications:** 6 TV, 20 radio stations. **Medical facilities:** 12 hospitals, 1 medical center. **Educational facilities:** 2 universities, 5 colleges. **Further information:** Chamber of Commerce, P.O. Box 32785, Charlotte, NC 28232.

## Chicago, Illinois

**Population:** 2,783,726; **Pop. density:** 12,209 per sq. mi.; **Pop. growth:** −7.4%. **Area:** 228 sq. mi. **Employment:** 1,232,521 employed, 9.2% unemployed; **Per capita income:** $22,849; % change 1981-91: 75.6.
**History:** site acquired from Indians 1795; area began settlement with opening of Erie Canal 1825; chartered as city 1837; boomed with arrival of railroads from east and canal to Mississippi R.; much of city destroyed by fire 1871; major grain & livestock market.
**Transportation:** 3 airports; major railroad system; major trucking industry. **Communications:** 9 TV, 31 radio stations. **Medical facilities:** over 123 hospitals. **Educational facilities:** 95 institutions of higher learning. **Further information:** Association of Commerce and Industry, 200 N. LaSalle St., Chicago, IL 60601.

## Cincinnati, Ohio

**Population:** 364,114; **Pop. density:** 4,667 per sq. mi.; **Pop. growth:** −5.5%. **Area:** 78 sq. mi. **Employment:** 173,843 employed, 7.6% unemployed; **Per capita income:** $19,273; % change 1981-91: 77.0.
**History:** founded 1788 and named after the Society of Cincinnati, an organization of Revolutionary War officers; chartered as village 1802; inc. as city 1819.
**Transportation:** 1 international airport; 3 railroads; 1 bus system. **Communications:** 6 TV, 27 radio stations. **Medical facilities:** 32 hospitals; Children's Hospital Medical Center; VA hospital. **Educational facilities:** 4 universities; 5 colleges, 8 technical & 2-year colleges. **Further information:** Chamber of Commerce, 300 Carew Tower, 441 Vine St., Cincinnati, OH 45202.

## Cleveland, Ohio

**Population:** 505,616; **Pop. density:** 6,400 per sq. mi.; **Pop. growth:** −11.9%. **Area:** 79 sq. mi. **Employment:** 192,253 employed, 12.5% unemployed; **Per capita income:** $19,995; % change 1981-91: 66.4.

History: surveyed in 1796; inc. as village 1814, as city 1836; annexed Ohio City 1854.

Transportation: 1 intl. airport; rail service; major port; rapid transit system. Communications: 9 TV, 26 radio stations. Medical facilities: 24 hospitals; major medical research center. Educational facilities: 9 universities and colleges; 127 public schools. Further information: Greater Cleveland Growth Assn., 200 Tower City Center, Cleveland, OH 44113.

## Colorado Springs, Colorado

**Population:** 281,140; **Pop. density:** 2,730 per sq. mi.; **Pop. growth:** 30.7%. **Area:** 103 sq. mi. **Employment:** 132,358 employed, 6.9% unemployed; **Per capita income:** $17,651; % change 1981-91: 66.3.

History: founded 1859 at the foot of Pikes Peak; inc. 1886.

Transportation: 1 municipal airport; 2 railroads; Greyhound-Trailways bus line. Communications: 5 TV, 22 radio stations. Medical facilities: 9 hospitals. Educational facilities: 3 universities, 7 colleges. Further information: Chamber of Commerce, P.O. Drawer B, Colorado Springs, CO 80901.

## Columbus, Georgia

**Population:** 178,681; **Pop. density:** 822 per sq. mi.; **Pop. growth:** 5.4%. **Area:** 218 sq. mi. **Employment:** 70,718 employed, 7.1% unemployed; **Per capita income:** $15,401; % change 1981-91: 86.9.

History: settled and inc. 1828; a port city on Chattahouchee R.

Transportation: 1 airport; metro bus system; 2 bus lines; 2 railroads. Communications: 5 TV, 11 radio stations. Medical facilities: 5 hospitals. Educational facilities: 1 college; 53 public schools. Further information: Chamber of Commerce, P.O. Box 1200, Columbus, GA 31902.

## Columbus, Ohio

**Population:** 632,945; **Pop. density:** 3,497 per sq. mi.; **Pop. growth:** 12.0%. **Area:** 181 sq. mi. **Employment:** 338,849 employed, 5.8% unemployed; **Per capita income:** $18,630; % change 1981-91: 77.6.

History: first settlement 1797; laid out as new capital 1812 with current name; became city 1834.

Transportation: 2 airports; 3 railroads; 4 intercity bus lines. Communications: 5 TV, 19 radio stations. Medical facilities: 22 hospitals. Educational facilities: 12 universities and colleges. Further information: Chamber of Commerce, P.O. Box 1527, Columbus, OH 43216.

## Corpus Christi, Texas

**Population:** 257,453; **Pop. density:** 2,476 per sq. mi.; **Pop. growth:** 10.9%. **Area:** 104 sq. mi. **Employment:** 118,026 employed, 9.2% unemployed; **Per capita income:** $15,273; % change 1981-91: 42.6.

History: settled 1839 and inc. 1852.

Transportation: 1 international airport; 2 bus lines, metro bus system; 3 freight railroads. Communications: 6 TV, 17 radio stations. Medical facilities: 14 hospitals including a children's center. Educational facilities: 1 university, 1 college. Further information: Chamber of Commerce, PO Box 640, Corpus Christi, TX 78403.

## Dallas, Texas

**Population:** 1,007,618; **Pop. density:** 3,024 per sq. mi.; **Pop. growth:** 11.3%. **Area:** 333 sq. mi. **Employment:** 520,135 employed, 8.9% unemployed; **Per capita income:** $20,892; % change 1981-91: 60.2.

History: first settled 1841; platted 1846; inc. 1871; developed as the financial and commercial center of Southwest; known for its oil industry and cotton market.

Transportation: 1 international airport; Amtrak; major transit system. Communications: 10 TV, 49 radio stations. Medical facilities: 70 hospitals; major medical center. Educational facilities: 7 universities, 2 colleges. Further information: Chamber of Commerce, 1201 Elm, Dallas, TX 75270.

## Dayton, Ohio

**Population:** 182,005; **Pop. density:** 3,793 per sq. mi.; **Pop. growth:** −5.9%. **Area:** 48 sq. mi. **Employment:** 71,854 employed, 10.9% unemployed; **Per capita income:** $18,302; % change 1981-91: 71.8.

History: settled 1796; inc. 1805; disastrous flood 1913; site where Wright Bros. invented first airplane to sustain flight 1903.

Transportation: 1 international airport, 14 airlines; 3 railroads; 3 bus lines; countywide Dayton Regional Transit Authority. Communications: 5 TV, 17 radio stations. Medical facilities: 14 hospitals including VA facility. Educational facilities: 26 institutions of higher learning. Further information: Dayton Area Chamber of Commerce, Fifth and Main, Chamber Plaza, Dayton, OH 45402.

## Denver, Colorado

**Population:** 467,610; **Pop. density:** 4,213 per sq. mi.; **Pop. growth:** −5.1%. **Area:** 111 sq. mi. **Employment:** 227,968 employed, 7.1% unemployed; **Per capita income:** $21,441; % change 1981-91: 59.4.

History: settled 1858 by gold prospectors and miners; inc. 1861; growth spurred by gold and silver boom; the financial and industrial center of Rocky Mt. region.

Transportation: 1 international airport; 5 major rail freight lines, Amtrak; 2 bus lines. Communications: 7 TV, 35 radio stations. Medical facilities: 34 hospitals. Educational facilities: 5 universities, 2 colleges. Further information: Greater Denver Chamber of Commerce, 1445 Market St., Denver, CO 80202.

## Des Moines, Iowa

**Population:** 193,189; **Pop. density:** 2,927 per sq. mi.; **Pop. growth:** 1.1%. **Area:** 66 sq. mi. **Employment:** 113,241 employed, 5.0% unemployed; **Per capita income:** $20,570; % change 1981-91: 69.6.

History: Fort Des Moines built 1843; settled and inc. 1851; chartered as city 1857.

Transportation: 1 international airport; 3 bus lines; 4 railroads; metro bus system. Communications: 5 TV, 18 radio stations. Medical facilities: 8 hospitals. Educational facilities: 1 university, 2 colleges. Further information: Chamber of Commerce, 601 Locust St., Ste. 100, Des Moines, IA 50309.

## Detroit, Michigan

**Population:** 1,027,974; **Pop. density:** 7,559 per sq. mi.; **Pop. growth:** −14.6%. **Area:** 136 sq. mi. **Employment:** 328,371 employed, 16.5% unemployed; **Per capita income:** $20,585; % change 1981-91: 72.6.

History: founded by French 1701; controlled by British 1760; acquired by U.S. 1796; destroyed by fire 1805; capital of state 1837-47; inc. as city 1824; auto manufacturing began 1899.

**Transportation:** 1 international airport; 10 railroads; major international port; public transit system. **Communications:** 9 TV, 37 radio stations. **Medical facilities:** 28 hospitals, major medical center. **Educational facilities:** 13 universities and colleges. **Further information:** Greater Detroit Chamber of Commerce, 600 W. Lafayette Blvd., Detroit, MI 48226.

## El Paso, Texas

**Population:** 515,342; **Pop. density:** 2,156 per sq. mi. **Pop. growth:** 21.2%. **Area:** 239 sq. mi. **Employment:** 210,618 employed, 10.3% unemployed; **Per capita income:** $11,764; % change 1981-91: 62.2.

**History:** first settled 1827; inc. 1873; arrival of railroad 1881 boosted city's population and industries.

**Transportation:** 1 international airport; 5 major rail lines; 8 bus lines; 9 major highways; gateway to Mexico. **Communications:** 6 TV, 23 radio stations. **Medical facilities:** 16 hospitals; cancer treatment center. **Educational facilities:** 2 colleges and universities. **Further information:** Convention and Visitors Bureau, 5 Civic Center Plaza, El Paso, TX 79901.

## Fort Wayne, Indiana

**Population:** 172,971; **Pop. density:** 3,328 per sq. mi.; **Pop. growth:** 0.4%. **Area:** 52 sq. mi. **Employment:** 86,782 employed, 7.5% unemployed; **Per capita income:** $17,962; % change 1981-91: 71.6.

**History:** French fort 1680; U.S. fort 1794; settled by 1832; inc. 1840 prior to Wabash-Erie canal completion 1843.

**Transportation:** 1 airport, 7 airlines; 3 railroads; 5 bus lines. **Communications:** 5 TV, 13 radio stations. **Medical facilities:** 3 major hospitals; VA hospital. **Educational facilities:** 5 colleges; 82 public schools. **Further information:** Chamber of Commerce, 826 Ewing Street, Fort Wayne, IN 46802-2182.

## Fort Worth, Texas

**Population:** 447,619; **Pop. density:** 1,549 per sq. mi.; **Pop. growth:** 16.2%. **Area:** 289 sq. mi. **Employment:** 213,559 employed, 9.2% unemployed; **Per capita income:** $18,714; % change 1981-91: 55.4.

**History:** est. as military post 1849; inc. 1873; oil discovered 1917.

**Transportation:** 1 international airport; 8 major railroads, Amtrak; local bus service; 2 transcontinental, 2 intrastate bus lines. **Communications:** 9 TV, 37 radio stations. **Medical facilities:** 35 hospitals; 2 children's hospitals; 4 government hospitals. **Educational facilities:** 8 universities and colleges. **Further information:** Chamber of Commerce, 777 Taylor St. #900, Fort Worth, TX 76102.

## Fremont, California

**Population:** 173,339; **Pop. density:** 2,211 per sq. mi.; **Pop. growth:** 31.4%. **Area:** 78.4 sq. mi. **Employment:** 96,255 employed, 4.5% unemployed; **Per capita income:** $23,545; % change 1981-91: 70.0.

**History:** area first settled by Spanish 1769; during 1800s a collection of towns formed the area; inc. 1956.

**Transportation:** intracity bus line; Bay Area Rapid Transit System (southern terminal). **Communications:** NA. **Medical facilities:** 1 hospital. **Educational facilities:** 1 junior college; 43 public schools. **Further information:** Chamber of Commerce, 2201 Walnut Ave., Ste. 110, Fremont, CA 94538.

## Fresno, California

**Population:** 354,091; **Pop. density:** 5,449 per sq. mi.; **Pop. growth:** 62.9%. **Area:** 65 sq. mi. **Employment:** 151,788 employed, 13.0% unemployed; **Per capita income:** $15,994; % change 1981-91: 50.7.

**History:** founded 1872; inc. as city 1885.

**Transportation:** 2 municipal airports; Amtrak; 1 bus line; intracity bus system. **Communications:** 11 TV, 58 radio stations. **Medical facilities:** 6 general hospitals including a VA facility. **Educational facilities:** 8 universities and colleges; 85 public schools. **Further information:** Chamber of Commerce, P.O. Box 1469, Fresno, CA 93716-1469.

## Garland, Texas

**Population:** 180,650; **Pop. density:** 3,226 per sq. mi.; **Pop. growth:** 30.1%. **Area:** 56 sq. mi. **Employment:** 99,852 employed, 5.9% unemployed; **Per capita income:** $20,892; % change 1981-91: 60.2.

**History:** city in Dallas co., 14 mi. NE of Dallas.

**Transportation:** 45 miles from Dallas/Ft. Worth airport; 2 railroads. **Communications:** 3 TV stations (from Dallas). **Medical facilities:** total of 306 hospital beds. **Educational facilities:** 1 university, 2 community colleges; 53 public schools. **Further information:** Chamber of Commerce, 914 S. Garland Ave., Garland, TX 75040.

## Glendale, California

**Population:** 180,038; **Pop. density:** 5,886 per sq. mi.; **Pop. growth:** 29%. **Area:** 30.59 sq. mi. **Employment:** 84,942 employed, 9.1% unemployed; **Per capita income:** $20,967; % change 1981-91: 59.5.

**History:** Township in 1887, incorporated in 1906. Adjacent to Los Angeles.

**Transportation:** 1 airport; 1 railroad; in triangle surrounded by 3 freeways; Southern California Rapid Transit system; Glendale Beeline bus. **Communications:** 2 radio stations. **Medical facilities:** 1,100 beds in three hospitals. **Educational facilities:** 1 community college. **Further information:** Chamber of Commerce, 200 S. Louise, Glendale, CA 91205.

## Grand Rapids, Michigan

**Population:** 189,126; **Pop. density:** 4,358 per sq. mi.; **Pop. growth:** 4.0%. **Area:** 43.4 sq. mi. **Employment:** 90,336 employed, 10.2% unemployed; **Per capita income:** $18,008; % change 1981-91: 75.4.

**History:** originally site of Ottowa Indian village; trading post 1826; became lumbering center and chartered as town 1850.

**Transportation:** 1 international airport; 4 railroads; 5 bus lines; transit bus system. **Communications:** 6 TV, 25 radio stations. **Medical facilities:** 10 hospitals. **Educational facilities:** 8 colleges; 64 public schools. **Further information:** Chamber of Commerce, 17 Fountain St., NW, Grand Rapids, MI 49503.

## Greensboro, North Carolina

**Population:** 183,894; **Pop. density:** 3,059 per sq. mi.; **Pop. growth:** 17.9%. **Area:** 60 sq. mi. **Employment:** 101,263 employed, 5.6% unemployed; **Per capita income:** $18,943; % change 1981-91: 83.7.

**History:** settled 1749; site of Revolutionary War conflict 1781 between Nathanael Greene and Cornwallis; inc. 1807.

**Transportation:** 1 regional airport; 2 railroads; Trailways/Greyhound bus service. **Communications:** all cable TV stations; 11 radio stations. **Medical facilities:** 4 hospitals. **Educational facilities:** 2 universities, 3 colleges; 38 public schools. **Further information:** Chamber of Commerce, P.O. Box 3246, Greensboro, NC 27402.

## Hialeah, Florida

**Population:** 188,008; **Pop. density:** 8,545 per sq. mi.; **Pop. growth:** 29.4%. **Area:** 22 sq. mi. **Employment:** 87,733 employed, 10.4% unemployed; **Per capita income:** $18,252; % change 1981-91: 65.5.

**History:** inc. 1925; built over drained swamplands NW of Miami.

**Transportation:** Miami Int'l. airport is 5 miles away; Amtrak; 2 rail freight lines. **Communications:** NA. **Medical facilities:** 4 hospitals. **Educational facilities:** 5 universities and colleges. **Further information:** Hialeah Dept. of Eco. Development, Office of the Mayor, 501 Palm Ave., Hialeah, FL 33010.

## Honolulu, Hawaii

**Population:** 365,272; **Pop. density:** 613 per sq. mi.; **Pop. growth:** 0.1%. **Area:** 596 sq. mi. **Employment (MSA):** 394,028 employed, 3.5% unemployed; **Per capita income:** $22,102; % change 1981-91: 84.0.

**History:** harbor entered by Europeans 1794; declared capital of kingdom by King Kamehameha III 1850; Pearl Harbor naval base attacked by Japanese Dec. 7, 1941.

**Transportation:** 1 major airport; large, active port for passengers and cargo. **Communications:** 10 TV, 30 radio stations. **Medical facilities:** 36 hospitals. **Educational facilities:** 4 universities, 1 college; 165 public schools, 98 private schools. **Further information:** Visitors Bureau, 2270 Kalakaua Avenue, Honolulu, HI 96815.

## Houston, Texas

**Population:** 1,630,864; **Pop. density:** 2,933 per sq. mi.; **Pop. growth:** 2.2%. **Area:** 556 sq. mi. **Employment:** 806,617 employed; 8.7% unemployed; **Per capita income:** $20,169; % change 1981-91: 42.2.

**History:** founded 1836; inc. 1837; capital of Republic of Texas 1837-39; developed rapidly after completion of canal to Gulf of Mexico 1914; important oil and natural gas center.

**Transportation:** 3 commercial airports; 4 mainline railroads; major bus transit system; major international port. **Communications:** 11 TV, 53 radio stations. **Medical facilities:** 66 hospitals; major medical center. **Educational facilities:** 26 universities and colleges. **Further information:** Greater Houston Partnership, 1100 Milam, Houston, TX 77002-5507.

## Huntington Beach, California

**Population:** 181,519; **Pop. density:** 6,723 per sq. mi.; **Pop. growth:** 6.5%. **Area:** 27 sq. mi. **Employment:** 108,192 employed, 4.7% unemployed; **Per capita income:** $20,967; % change 1981-91: 59.5.

**History:** settled in early 1880s; inc. 1909; oil discovered 1920, led to city's development.

**Transportation:** 1 railroad; 2 bus lines. **Communications:** 1 TV station. **Medical facilities:** 2 hospitals. **Educational facilities:** 1 junior college; 45 public schools. **Further information:** Chamber of Commerce, Seacliff Office Park, 2100 Main #200, Huntington Beach, CA 92648.

## Indianapolis, Indiana

**Population:** 731,327; **Pop. density:** 2,108 per sq. mi.; **Pop. growth:** 4.3%. **Area:** 352 sq. mi. **Employment:** 375,706 employed, 6.0% unemployed; **Per capita income:** $19,844; % change 1981-91: 79.0.

**History:** settled in 1820, made into capital 1825.

**Transportation:** 1 international airport; 5 railroads; 3 interstate bus lines. **Communications:** 10 TV, 26 radio stations. **Medical facilities:** 17 hospitals; 1 major medical and research center. **Educational facilities:** 8 universities and colleges; major public library system. **Further information:** Chamber of Commerce, 320 N. Meridian Street, Indianapolis, IN 46204.

## Jackson, Mississippi

**Population:** 196,637; **Pop. density:** 1,852 per sq. mi.; **Pop. growth:** −3.1%. **Area:** 106.2 sq. mi. **Employment:** 90,756 employed, 6.2% unemployed; **Per capita income:** $15,991; % change 1981-91: 66.0.

**History:** originally known as Le Fleur's Bluff, selected as capital 1822 and named for Andrew Jackson; inc. 1823; scene of secession convention 1861; captured by Sherman 1863.

**Transportation:** 6 airlines; 2 bus lines; 3 railroads. **Communications:** 5 TV, 26 radio stations. **Medical facilities:** 14 hospitals including a VA facility. **Educational facilities:** 2 universities, 4 colleges; 7 public school districts. **Further information:** Metro Jackson Chamber of Commerce, P.O. Box 22548, Jackson, MS 39225-2548.

## Jacksonville, Florida

**Population:** 635,230; **Pop. density:** 885 per sq. mi.; **Pop. growth:** 17.9%. **Area:** 760 sq. mi. **Employment:** 304,160 employed, 7.3% unemployed; **Per capita income:** $17,937; % change 1981-91: 75.8.

**History:** settled 1816 as Cowford; renamed after Andrew Jackson 1822; inc. 1832; rechartered 1851; scene of conflicts in Seminole and Civil wars.

**Transportation:** 1 international airport; 3 railroads; 2 interstate bus lines. **Communications:** 6 TV, 21 radio stations. **Medical facilities:** 14 hospitals. **Educational facilities:** 5 universities and colleges. **Further information:** Chamber of Commerce, 3 Independent Drive, P.O. Box 329, Jacksonville, FL 32201.

## Jersey City, New Jersey

**Population:** 228,517; **Pop. density:** 17,313 per sq. mi.; **Pop. growth:** 2.2%. **Area:** 13.2 sq. mi. **Employment:** 91,801 employed, 14.4% unemployed; **Per capita income:** $25,583; % change 1981-91: 92.1.

**History:** bought from Indians 1630; chartered as town by British 1668; scene of Revolutionary War conflict 1779; chartered under present name 1838; important station on Underground Railroad.

**Transportation:** bus and subway system. **Medical facilities:** 10 hospitals. **Educational facilities:** 3 colleges. **Further information:** Chamber of Commerce & Industry of Hudson County, 911 Bergen Ave., Jersey City, NJ 07303.

## Kansas City, Missouri

**Population:** 434,829; **Pop. density:** 1,377 per sq. mi.; **Pop. growth:** −2.9%. **Area:** 316 sq. mi. **Employment:** 221,485 employed, 6.5% unemployed; **Per capita income:** $19,963; % change 1981-91: 70.0.

**History:** settled by 1838 at confluence of the Missouri and Kansas rivers; inc. 1851.

**Transportation:** 1 international airport; a major rail center; 191 trunk lines; several barge companies. **Communications:** 7 TV, 29 radio stations. **Medical facilities:** 14 hospitals; VA facility. **Educational facilities:** 9 universities and colleges. **Further information:** Greater Kansas City Chamber of Commerce, 911 Main St., Ste. 2600, Kansas City, MO 64105.

## Las Vegas, Nevada

**Population:** 258,204; **Pop. density:** 4,696 per sq. mi.; **Pop. growth:** 56.9%. **Area:** 55 sq. mi. **Employment:** 139,269 employed, 6.7% unemployed; **Per capita income:** $18,474; % change 1981-91: 58.7.

**History:** occupied by Mormons 1855-57; bought by railroad 1903; city of Las Vegas inc. 1911; gambling legalized 1931.

**Transportation:** 1 international airport; 2 railroads; bus system. **Communcations:** 7 TV, 33 radio stations. **Medical facilities:** 8 hospitals. **Educational facilities:** 1 university, 1 college; 170 public schools. **Further information:** Chamber of Commerce, 711 E. Desert Inn Rd., Las Vegas, NV 89109.

## Lexington–Fayette, Kentucky

**Population:** 225,366; **Pop. density:** 794 per sq. mi.; **Pop. growth:** 10.4%. **Area:** 284 sq. mi. **Employment:** 123,985 employed, 4.1% unemployed; **Per capita income:** $18,142; % change 1981-91: 77.9.

**History:** site was founded and named 1775 by hunters who heard of the Revolutionary War battle at Lexington, Mass.; settled 1779; inc. 1832.

**Transportation:** 8 airlines; 2 railroads; city buses. **Communications:** 5 TV, 9 radio stations. **Medical facilities:** 5 general, 5 specialized hospitals. **Educational facilities:** 2 universities, 2 colleges. **Further information:** Chamber of Commerce, 330 East Main, Lexington, KY 40507.

## Lincoln, Nebraska

**Population:** 191,972; **Pop. density:** 3,200 per sq. mi.; **Pop. growth:** 11.7%. **Area:** 60 sq. mi. **Employment:** 117,678 employed, 2.5% unemployed; **Per capita income:** $18,429; % change 1981-91: 70.5.

**History:** originally called Lancaster, chosen state capital 1867 and renamed after Abraham Lincoln; inc. 1869.

**Transportation:** 1 airport; Greyhound; Amtrak, 2 railroads. **Communications:** 1 TV, 13 radio stations. **Medical facilities:** 4 hospitals including a VA facility. **Educational facilities:** 2 universities, 1 college; 46 public, 15 private schools. **Further information:** Chamber of Commerce, 1221 N St., Lincoln, NE 68508.

## Little Rock, Arkansas

**Population:** 175,727; **Pop. density:** 2,225 per sq. mi.; **Pop. growth:** 10.5%. **Area:** 79 sq. mi. **Employment:** 92,612 employed, 5.8% unemployed; **Per capita income:** $17,610; % change 1981-91: 77.0.

**History:** founded 1821; inc. as city 1835.

**Transportation:** 1 airport, 9 airlines; 3 railroads; 1 bus line. **Communications:** 7 TV, 34 radio stations. **Medical facilities:** 16 hospitals; veterans' medical center. **Educational facilities:** 8 universities and colleges, Univ. of Arkansas; 49 public schools. **Further information:** Chamber of Commerce, One Spring St., Little Rock, AR 72201.

## Long Beach, California

**Population:** 429,321; **Pop. density:** 8,589 per sq. mi.; **Pop. growth:** 18.8%. **Area:** 50 sq. mi. **Employment:** 192,208 employed, 9.0% unemployed; **Per capita income:** $20,967; % change 1981-91: 59.5.

**History:** settled as early as 1769 by Spanish; by 1884 present site developed due to its harbor; inc. 1888; oil discovered 1921.

**Transportation:** 1 airport; 3 railroads; major international port; 6 bus lines, "lite" rail service. **Communications:** 4 radio stations. **Medical facilities:** 10 hospitals. **Educational facilities:** 1 university, 1 college; 78 public

schools. **Further information:** Chamber of Commerce, One World Trade Center, Long Beach, CA 90831.

## Los Angeles, California

**Population:** 3,485,398; **Pop. density:** 7,495 per sq. mi.; **Pop. growth:** 17.4%. **Area:** 465 sq. mi. **Employment:** 1,628,879 employed, 10.9% unemployed; **Per capita income:** $20,967; % change 1981-91: 59.5.

**History:** founded by Spanish 1781; captured by U.S. 1846; inc. 1850; Hollywood a district of L.A.

**Transportation:** 1 international airport; 4 railroads; major freeway system; intracity transit system. **Communications:** 19 TV, 71 radio stations. **Medical facilities:** 822 hospitals and clinics. **Educational facilities:** 11 universities and colleges; 1,642 public schools; 800 private schools. **Further information:** Chamber of Commerce, 404 S. Bixel St., P.O. Box 3696, Los Angeles, CA 90051.

## Louisville, Kentucky

**Population:** 269,555; **Pop. density:** 4,484 per sq. mi.; **Pop. growth:** −9.9%. **Area:** 60 sq. mi. **Employment:** 122,272 employed, 7.2% unemployed. **Per capita income:** $18,912; % change 1981-91: 78.5.

**History:** settled 1778; named for Louis XVI of France; inc. 1828; base for Union forces in Civil War.

**Transportation:** 2 municipal airports; 1 terminal, 6 trunk-line railroads; 2 bus lines; 5 barge lines. **Communications:** 4 TV, 21 radio stations, 2 educational. **Medical facilities:** 21 hospitals. **Educational facilities:** 10 universities and colleges, 9 business colleges and technical schools. **Further information:** Louisville Area Chamber of Commerce, 600 W. Main, Louisville, KY 40202.

## Lubbock, Texas

**Population:** 186,206; **Pop. density:** 2,069 per sq. mi.; **Pop. growth:** 6.8%. **Area:** 90 sq. mi. **Employment:** 92,047 employed, 6.6% unemployed; **Per capita income:** $15,577; % change 1981-91: 55.0.

**History:** settled 1879; inc. 1909 through merger of two towns.

**Transportation:** 1 international airport; 2 railroads, bus line. **Communications:** 5 TV, 18 radio stations. **Medical facilities:** 7 hospitals. **Educational facilities:** 2 universities, 1 college; 51 public schools. **Further information:** Chamber of Commerce, P.O. Box 561, Lubbock, TX 79408.

## Madison, Wisconsin

**Population:** 190,766; **Pop. density:** 3,188 per sq. mi.; **Pop. growth:** 12.1%. **Area:** 60 sq. mi. **Employment:** 121,973 employed, 2.9% unemployed; **Per capita income:** $20,629; % change 1981-91: 76.7.

**History:** first white settlement 1832; named after James Madison who died in 1836; chartered 1856.

**Transportation:** 1 airport, 10 airlines; 2 railroads; intercity and intracity bus systems. **Communications:** 6 TV, 18 radio stations. **Medical facilities:** 5 hospitals. **Educational facilities:** 3 colleges and universities, Univ. of Wisconsin; 39 public schools. **Further information:** Chamber of Commerce, P.O. Box 71, Madison, WI 53701.

## Memphis, Tennessee

**Population:** 610,337; **Pop. density:** 2,312 per sq. mi.; **Pop. growth:** −5.5%. **Area:** 264 sq. mi. **Employment:** 264,752 employed, 6.7% unemployed; **Per capita income:** $18,331; % change 1981-91: 87.1.

**History:** French, Spanish, and U.S. forts by 1797; settled by 1819; inc. as town 1826, as city 1840; surrendered charter to state 1879 after yellow fever epidemics; re-chartered as city 1893.

**Transportation:** 1 international airport; 6 railroads; bus system. **Communications:** 6 TV, 29 radio stations. **Medical facilities:** 21 hospitals. **Educational facilities:** 12 universities and colleges; 205 public, 76 private schools. **Further information:** Memphis Area Chamber of Commerce, 22 N. Front St., Box 224, Memphis TN 38101.

## Mesa, Arizona

**Population:** 288,104; **Pop. density:** 4,237 per sq. mi.; **Pop. growth:** 89.0%. **Area:** 68 sq. mi. **Employment:** 133,357 employed, 5.4% unemployed; **Per capita income:** $22,014; % change 1981-91: 61.6.

**History:** founded by Mormons 1878; inc. 1883; 15 mi. from Phoenix; population boomed fivefold from 1960-80.

**Transportation:** 1 international airport; 2 railroads; trolley and bus lines. **Medical facilities:** 4 major hospitals. **Educational facilities:** 1 university, 1 college; 49 public schools. **Further information:** Convention and Visitor's Bureau, 120 N. Center, Mesa, AZ 85201.

## Miami, Florida

**Population:** 358,648; **Pop. density:** 10,546 per sq. mi.; **Pop. growth:** 3.4%. **Area:** 34 sq. mi. **Employment:** 148,041 employed, 14.2% unemployed; **Per capita income:** $18,252; % change 1981-91: 65.5.

**History:** site of fort 1836; settlement began 1870; inc. 1896 and modern city developed into resort and recreation center; land speculation 1920s added to city's growth, as did Cuban immigration in 1970s and 1980s.

**Transportation:** 1 international airport; 2 passenger railroads, 1 all-freight; 2 bus lines; 65 truck lines. **Communications:** 6 commercial, 5 educational TV stations; 31 radio stations. **Medical facilities:** 41 hospitals, VA Hospital. **Educational facilities:** 6 universities and colleges. **Further information:** Metro-Dade Department of Tourism, 234 W. Flagler St., Miami, FL 33130.

## Milwaukee, Wisconsin

**Population:** 628,088; **Pop. density:** 6,543 per sq. mi.; **Pop. growth:** -1.3%. **Area:** 96 sq. mi. **Employment:** 258,525 employed, 5.8% unemployed; **Per capita income:** $20,325; % change 1981-91: 67.6.

**History:** Indian trading post by 1674; settlement began 1835; inc. as city 1848; famous beer industry.

**Transportation:** 1 international airport; 2 railroads; major port; 4 bus lines. **Communications:** 12 TV, 34 radio stations. **Medical facilities:** 24 hospitals; major medical center. **Educational facilities:** 12 universities and colleges. **Further information:** Association of Commerce, 756 N. Milwaukee Street, Milwaukee, WI 53202.

## Minneapolis, Minnesota

**Population:** 368,383; **Pop. density:** 6,698 per sq. mi.; **Pop. growth:** -0.7%. **Area:** 55 sq. mi. **Employment:** 194,572 employed, 4.8% unemployed; **Per capita income:** $21,665; % change 1981-91: 72.7.

**History:** site visited by Hennepin 1680; included in area of military reservations 1819; inc. 1867.

**Transportation:** 1 international airport; 6 railroads; mass transit systems; 5 major barge lines. **Communications:** 10 TV, 39 radio stations. **Medical facilities:** 36 hospitals, including leading heart hospital at Univ. of Minnesota. **Educational facilities:** 13 universities and colleges. 48 public school districts. **Further information:** Greater Minneapolis Chamber of Commerce, 81 S. 9th St., Ste. 200, Minneapolis, MN 55402.

## Mobile, Alabama

**Population:** 196,278; **Pop. density:** 1,596 per sq. mi.; **Pop. growth:** -2.1%. **Area:** 123 sq. mi. **Employment:** 85,454 employed, 8.7% unemployed; **Per capita income:** $15,134; % change 1981-91: 68.8.

**History:** settled by French 1711; later occupied by U.S. 1813; inc. as town 1814, as city 1819; only seaport of Alabama.

**Transportation:** 4 rail freight lines, Amtrak; 5 major airlines; 65 truck lines; leading river system. **Communications:** 8 TV, 20 radio stations. **Medical facilities:** 7 hospitals. **Educational facilities:** 1 university, 3 colleges. **Further information:** Chamber of Commerce, P.O. Box 2187, Mobile, AL 36652.

## Montgomery, Alabama

**Population:** 187,543; **Pop. density:** 1,462 per sq. mi.; **Pop. growth:** 5.2%. **Area:** 128 sq. mi. **Employment:** 84,637 employed, 6.5% unemployed; **Per capita income:** $17,158; % change 1981-91: 86.7.

**History:** inc. as town 1819, as city 1837; first capital of Confederacy 1861.

**Transportation:** 5 airlines; 2 railroads; 4 bus lines; Alabama River is navigable to Gulf of Mexico. **Communications:** 7 TV, 16 radio stations. **Medical facilities:** 10 hospitals; VA and 32 clinics. **Educational facilities:** 5 universities; 49 public, 31 private schools. **Further information:** Chamber of Commerce, P.O. Box 79, Montgomery, AL 36101.

## Nashville-Davidson, Tennessee

**Population:** 516,880; **Pop. density:** 984 per sq. mi.; **Pop. growth:** 6.9%. **Area:** 525 sq. mi. **Employment:** 254,831 employed, 4.8% unemployed; **Per capita income:** $19,059; % change 1981-91: 87.4.

**History:** settled 1779; first chartered 1806; home of the Grand Ole Opry.

**Transportation:** 1 airport; 1 railroad; bus line; transit system of buses and trolleys. **Communications:** 7 TV, 30 radio stations. **Medical facilities:** 14 hospitals; VA Hospital, speech-hearing center. **Educational facilities:** 16 universities and colleges. **Further information:** Chamber of Commerce, 161 4th Ave., Nashville, TN 37219.

## Newark, New Jersey

**Population:** 275,221; **Pop. density:** 11,468 per sq. mi.; **Pop. growth:** -16.4%. **Area:** 24 sq. mi. **Employment:** 96,361 employed, 16.8% unemployed; **Per capita income:** $25,583; % change 1981-91: 92.1.

**History:** settled by Puritans 1666; used as supply base by Washington 1776; inc. as town 1833, as city 1836.

**Transportation:** 1 international airport; 2 railroads; bus system; 2 subways. **Communications:** 3 TV, 5 radio stations. **Medical facilities:** 6 hospitals. **Educational facilities:** 5 universities and colleges; 71 public schools. **Further information:** Metro Newark Chamber of Commerce, 40 Clinton St., Newark, NJ 07102.

## New Orleans, Louisiana

**Population:** 496,938; **Pop. density:** 2,497 per sq. mi.; **Pop. growth:** -10.9%. **Area:** 199 sq. mi. **Employment:** 190,555 employed, 7.3% unemployed; **Per capita income:** $16,959; % change 1981-91: 53.3.

**History:** founded by French 1718, became major seaport on Mississippi R.; acquired by U.S. as part of La. Purchase 1803; inc. as city 1805; 29-day Battle of New Orleans fought during War of 1812.

**Transportation:** 2 airports; major railroad center; major international port. **Communications:** 7 TV, 18 radio stations. **Medical facilities:** numerous hospitals; major medical research center. **Educational facilities:** 13 universities and colleges. **Further information:** Chamber of Commerce, 301 Camp Street, New Orleans, LA 70130.

## Newport News, Virginia

**Population:** 171,439; **Pop. density:** 2,464 per sq. mi.; **Pop. growth:** 17.4%. **Area:** 69 sq. mi. **Employment:** 76,373 employed, 7.6% unemployed; **Per capita income:** $17,030; % change 1981-91: 68.4.

**History:** the cities of Warwick and Newport News consolidated in 1958 into the larger city of Newport News; one of the world's major shipbuilding centers.

**Transportation:** 1 international airport; 2 railroads; Greyhound buses; local bus system. **Communications:** 7 TV, 20 radio stations received in area. **Medical facilities:** 3 hospitals; adolescent psychiatry hospital. **Educational facilities:** 33 public schools. **Further information:** Peninsula Chamber of Commerce, A-12, Coliseum Mall, 1800 West Mercury Blvd., Hampton, VA 23666.

## New York City, New York

**Population:** 7,322,564; **Pop. density:** 24,327 per sq. mi.; **Pop. growth:** 3.5%. **Area:** 301 sq. mi. **Employment:** 2,952,000 employed, 10.8% unemployed; **Per capita income:** $25,583; % change 1981-91: 92.1.

**History:** trading post established by H. Hudson 1609; British took control from Dutch 1664 and named New York; briefly capital of U.S.; Washington inaugurated as president 1789; comprised of 5 boroughs: The Bronx, Brooklyn, Manhattan, Queens, Staten Island.

**Transportation:** 2 airports; 2 rail terminals; major subway network; ferry system; 4 underwater tunnels. **Communications:** 13 TV, 117 radio stations. **Medical facilities:** 100 hospitals; 5 medical research centers. **Educational facilities:** 94 universities and colleges; 976 public schools, 914 private schools. **Further information:** Convention and Visitors Bureau, 2 Columbus Circle, New York, NY 10019.

## Norfolk, Virginia

**Population:** 261,250; **Pop. density:** 4,929 per sq. mi.; **Pop. growth:** −2.2%. **Area:** 53 sq. mi. **Employment:** 89,091 employed, 7.8% unemployed; **Per capita income:** $17,030; % change 1981-91: 68.4.

**History:** founded 1682; burned by patriots to prevent capture by British during Revolutionary War; rebuilt and inc. as town 1805, as city 1845; location of world's largest naval base.

**Transportation:** 1 international airport; 4 major railroad systems in area. **Communications:** 7 TV, 38 radio stations. **Medical facilities:** 11 hospitals. **Educational facilities:** 2 universities, 1 college; 53 public schools. **Further information:** Hampton Roads Chamber of Commerce, 480 Bank St., Norfolk, VA 23510.

## Oakland, California

**Population:** 372,242; **Pop. density:** 6,893 per sq. mi.; **Pop. growth:** 9.7%. **Area:** 54 sq. mi. **Employment:** 162,476 employed, 10.0% unemployed; **Per capita income:** $23,545; % change 1981-91: 70.0.

**History:** area settled by Spanish 1820; inc. as city under present name 1854.

**Transportation:** 1 international airport; western terminus for 3 railroads; underground, underwater 75-mile subway. **Communications:** 1 TV, 3 radio stations. **Medical facilities:** 7 hospitals, including Children's Hospital Medical Center, VA hospital. **Educational facilities:** 8 "eastbay" colleges and universities; 94 public schools. **Further information:** Chamber of Commerce, 475 14th St., Oakland, CA 94612-1903.

## Oklahoma City, Oklahoma

**Population:** 444,719; **Pop. density:** 736 per sq. mi.; **Pop. growth:** 10.1%. **Area:** 604 sq. mi. **Employment:** 217,167 employed, 5.7% unemployed; **Per capita income:** $16,799; % change 1981-91: 39.8.

**History:** settled during landrush in Midwest 1889; inc. 1890; oil discovered 1928.

**Transportation:** 1 international airport; 3 railroads; public transit system; 5 major bus lines. **Communications:** 8 TV, 24 radio stations. **Medical facilities:** 12 hospitals, VA hospital. **Educational facilities:** 17 universities and colleges; 87 public schools. **Further information:** Chamber of Commerce, One Santa Fe Plaza, Oklahoma City, OK 73102.

## Omaha, Nebraska

**Population:** 335,719; **Pop. density:** 3,690 per sq. mi.; **Pop. growth:** 7.0%. **Area:** 91 sq. mi. **Employment:** 181,986 employed, 3.7% unemployed; **Per capita income:** $19,037; % change 1981-91: 70.8.

**History:** founded 1854; inc. 1857; large livestock market; home for U.S. Strategic Command.

**Transportation:** 8 major airlines; 4 major railroads; intercity bus line. **Communications:** 8 TV, 22 radio stations. **Medical facilities:** 17 hospitals; institute for cancer research. **Educational facilities:** 3 universities, 6 colleges; 216 public, 82 private schools. **Further information:** Chamber of Commerce, 1301 Harney St., Omaha, NE 68102.

## Philadelphia, Pennsylvania

**Population:** 1,585,577; **Pop. density:** 11,659 per sq. mi.; **Pop. growth:** −6.1%. **Area:** 136 sq. mi. **Employment:** 637,988 employed, 8.8% unemployed; **Per capita income:** $22,014; % change 1981-91: 87.2.

**History:** first settled by Swedes 1636; by English 1681; named Philadelphia 1682; chartered 1701; Continental Congress met 1774, 1775; Dec. of Independence signed 1776; national capital 1790-1800; cap. of Penn. 1683-1799.

**Transportation:** 1 major airport; 3 railroads; major freshwater port; subway, el, rail commuter, bus, and streetcar system. **Communications:** 6 TV, 53 radio stations. **Medical facilities:** 124 hospitals. **Educational facilities:** 88 degree-granting institutions. **Further information:** Office of City Representative, 1660 Municipal Services Bldg., Philadelphia, PA 19107.

## Phoenix, Arizona

**Population:** 983,392; **Pop. density:** 3,035 per sq. mi.; **Pop. growth:** 24.5%. **Area:** 324 sq. mi. **Employment:** 473,232 employed, 7.0% unemployed; **Per capita income:** $18,156; % change 1981-91: 61.6.

**History:** settled in 1870; inc. as city 1881.

**Transportation:** 1 international airport; 2 railroads; 2 transcontinental bus lines; public transit system. **Communications:** 11 TV, 40 radio stations. **Medical facilities:** 42 hospitals, 1 medical research center. **Educational facilities:** 12 institutions of higher learning; 161 public schools. **Further information:** Chamber of Commerce, 201 N. Central Ave. #2700, Phoenix, AZ 85004.

## Pittsburgh, Pennsylvania

**Population:** 369,879; **Pop. density:** 6,725 per sq. mi.; **Pop. growth:** −12.8%. **Area:** 55 sq. mi. **Employment:** 165,141 employed, 6.6% unemployed; **Per capita income:** $19,579; % change 1981-91: 69.6.

**History:** settled around Ft. Pitt 1758; inc. as city 1816; has one of largest inland ports; by Civil War, already a center for iron production.

**Transportation:** 1 international airport; 20 railroads; 2 bus lines; trolley/subway system. **Communications:** 6 TV, 25 radio stations. **Medical facilities:** 32 hospitals; VA installation. **Educational facilities:** 3 universities, 6 colleges; 86 public schools. **Further information:** Chamber of Commerce, 3 Gateway Ctr., Pittsburgh, PA 15222.

## Portland, Oregon

**Population:** 438,802; **Pop. density:** 4,246 per sq. mi.; **Pop. growth:** 18.8%. **Area:** 103 sq. mi. **Employment:** 230,352 employed, 7.4% unemployed; **Per capita income:** $19,235; % change 1981-91: 63.8.

**History:** settled by pioneers 1845, developed as trading center, aided by California Gold Rush 1849; chartered as city 1851.

**Transportation:** 1 international airport; 3 major rail freight lines, Amtrak; 2 intercity bus lines; 27-mi. frontage freshwater port; mass transit bus and rail system. **Communications:** 6 TV, 27 radio stations. **Medical facilities:** 40 hospitals; VA hospital. **Educational facilities:** 21 universities and colleges, 3 community colleges. **Further information:** Portland Metropolitan Chamber of Commerce, 221 N.W. 2nd Ave., Portland, OR 97209-3999.

## Raleigh, North Carolina

**Population:** 212,050; **Pop. density:** 3,851 per sq. mi.; **Pop. growth:** 38.4%. **Area:** 54 sq. mi. **Employment:** 126,429 employed, 4.4% unemployed; **Per capita income:** $20,170; % change 1981-91: 99.7.

**History:** named after Sir Walter Raleigh, site chosen for capital 1788; laid out 1792; inc. 1795; occupied by Gen. Sherman 1865.

**Transportation:** 1 airport, 6 airlines; 3 railroads; 1 bus line. **Communications:** 6 TV, 20 radio stations. **Medical facilities:** 11 hospitals. **Educational facilities:** 4 universities and colleges, 4 junior colleges; 82 public schools. **Further information:** Chamber of Commerce, 800 S. Salisbury St., P.O. Box 2978, Raleigh, NC 27602.

## Richmond, Virginia

**Population:** 202,798; **Pop. density:** 3,384 per sq. mi.; **Pop. growth:** −7.4%. **Area:** 60 sq. mi. **Employment:** 95,866 employed, 8.5% unemployed; **Per capita income:** $21,416; % change 1981-91: 81.9.

**History:** first settled 1607; attacked by British under Benedict Arnold 1781; inc. as city 1782; capital of Confederate States of America, 1861.

**Transportation:** 1 international airport; 4 railroads; 3 intracity bus lines; deepwater terminal accessible to oceangoing ships. **Communications:** 6 TV, 26 radio stations. **Medical facilities:** Medical Coll. of Virginia renowned for heart and kidney transplants; 19 other hospitals including VA facility. **Educational facilities:** 9 universities and colleges; 173 public, 45 private schools. **Further information:** Chamber of Commerce, P.O. Box 12324, Richmond, VA 23241.

## Riverside, California

**Population:** 226,546; **Pop. density:** 3,190 per sq. mi.; **Pop. growth:** 32.8%. **Area:** 71 sq. mi. **Employment:** 97,842 employed, 12.2% unemployed; **Per capita income:** $16,707; % change 1981-91: 51.9.

**History:** founded 1870; inc. 1886; known for its citrus industry.

**Communications:** 11 TV, 13 radio stations. **Educational facilities:** 3 universities, 1 community college. **Further information:** Chamber of Commerce, 4261 Main St., Riverside, CA 92501.

## Rochester, New York

**Population:** 230,356; **Pop. density:** 6,813 per sq. mi.; **Pop. growth:** −4.2%. **Area:** 34 sq. mi. **Employment:** 100,056 employed, 8.4% unemployed; **Per capita income:** $20,784; % change 1981-91: 77.2.

**History:** first permanent white settlement 1812; inc. as village 1817, as city 1834; developed as Erie Canal town.

**Transportation:** 1 airport; Amtrak; 3 bus lines; intracity transit service; Port of Rochester. **Communications:** 5 TV, 18 radio stations. **Medical facilities:** 8 general hospitals. **Educational facilities:** 10 colleges, 3 community colleges. **Further information:** Chamber of Commerce, 55 St. Paul St., Rochester, NY 14604.

## Sacramento, California

**Population:** 369,365; **Pop. density:** 3,848 per sq. mi.; **Pop. growth:** 34.0%. **Area:** 96 sq. mi. **Employment:** 168,401 employed, 9.4% unemployed; **Per capita income:** $19,540; % change 1981-91: 70.1.

**History:** settled 1839; important trading center during California Gold Rush 1840s.

**Transportation:** metropolitan airport; 2 mainline transcontinental rail carriers; bus and light rail system. **Communications:** 7 TV, 25 radio stations. **Medical facilities:** 8 hospitals. **Educational facilities:** 2 universities, 4 community colleges. **Further information:** Chamber of Commerce, 917 7th St., P.O. Box 1017, Sacramento, CA 95805.

## St. Louis, Missouri

**Population:** 396,685; **Pop. density:** 6,503 per sq. mi.; **Pop. growth:** −12.4%. **Area:** 61 sq. mi. **Employment:** 164,899 employed, 8.0% unemployed; **Per capita income:** $20,507; % change 1981-91: 75.9.

**History:** founded 1764 as a fur trading post by French; acquired by U.S. 1803; chartered as city 1822; lies on Mississippi R., near confluence with Missouri R.

**Transportation:** 1 international airport; major rail center, 17 trunk-line railroads; major inland port; 14 bus lines; 14 barge lines. **Communications:** 7 TV, 35 radio stations. **Medical facilities:** 65 hospitals. **Educational facilities:** 6 universities, 25 colleges and seminaries. **Further information:** Regional Commerce and Growth Assoc., 100 S. 4th St., Ste. 500, St. Louis, MO 63102.

## St. Paul, Minnesota

**Population:** 272,235; **Pop. density:** 5,235 per sq. mi.; **Pop. growth:** 0.7%. **Area:** 52 sq. mi. **Employment:** 134,231 employed, 5.2% unemployed; **Per capita income:** $21,665; % change 1981-91: 72.7.

**History:** founded in early 1840s as "Pig's Eye Landing;" became capital of the Minnesota territory 1849 and chartered as St. Paul.

**Transportation:** 1 international airport; 6 major rail lines; 3 interstate bus lines; public transit system. **Communications:** 6 TV, 35 radio stations. **Medical facilities:** 7 hospitals. **Educational facilities:** 2 universities, 5 colleges. **Further information:** Chamber of Commerce, 600 N. Central Tower, 445 Minnesota St., St. Paul, MN 55101.

## St. Petersburg, Florida

**Population:** 240,318; **Pop. density:** 4,056 per sq. mi.; **Pop. growth:** 0.0%. **Area:** 59 sq. mi. **Employment:** 114,287 employed, 7.5% unemployed; **Per capita income:** $18,445; % change 1981-91: 72.4.

**History:** settled 1888; inc. 1892.

**Transportation:** 1 international airport; bus system; 1 full-service port. **Communications:** 12 TV, 22 radio stations. **Medical facilities:** 9 hospitals. **Educational facilities:** 6 colleges; 120 public schools. **Further information:**

Chamber of Commerce, P.O. Box 1371, St. Petersburg, FL 33731.

## San Antonio, Texas

**Population:** 935,933; **Pop. density:** 2,681 per sq. mi.; **Pop. growth:** 19.1%. **Area:** 349 sq. mi. **Employment:** 416,566 employed, 7.4% unemployed; **Per capita income:** $15,950; % change 1981-91: 64.2.

**History:** first Spanish garrison 1718; Battle at the Alamo fought here 1836; city subsequently captured by Texans; inc. 1837.

**Transportation:** 1 international airport; 4 railroads; 4 bus lines; public transit system. **Communications:** 8 TV, 33 radio stations. **Medical facilities:** 34 hospitals; major medical center. **Educational facilities:** 14 universities and colleges. **Further information:** Chamber of Commerce, 602 E. Commerce, P.O. Box 1628, San Antonio, TX 78296.

## San Diego, California

**Population:** 1,110,554; **Pop. density:** 3,470 per sq. mi.; **Pop. growth:** 26.8%. **Area:** 320 sq. mi. **Employment:** 507,386 employed, 7.5% unemployed; **Per capita income:** $19,799; % change 1981-91: 68.3.

**History:** claimed by the Spanish 1542, first mission est. 1769; scene of conflict during Mexican-American War 1846; inc. 1850.

**Transportation:** 1 major airport; 1 railroad; major freeway system; bus system; trolley system. **Communications:** 8 TV, 22 radio stations. **Medical facilities:** 28 hospitals. **Educational facilities:** 5 universities, 7 colleges. **Further information:** Greater SD Chamber of Commerce, 402 W. Broadway, Suite 1000, San Diego, CA 92101-3585.

## San Francisco, California

**Population:** 723,959; **Pop. density:** 15,403 per sq. mi.; **Pop. growth:** 6.6%. **Area:** 47 sq. mi. **Employment:** 368,789 employed, 7.0% unemployed; **Per capita income:** $30,555; % change 1981-91: 77.5.

**History:** nearby Farallon Islands sighted by Spanish 1542, city settled by 1776; claimed by U.S. 1846; became a major city during California Gold Rush 1849; inc. as city 1850; earthquake devastated city 1906.

**Transportation:** 1 major airport; intracity railway system; 2 railway transit systems; bus and railroad service; ferry system; 1 underwater tunnel. **Communications:** 14 TV and cable stations; 69 radio stations. **Medical facilities:** 23 hospitals; 1 major medical center. **Educational facilities:** 4 universities and colleges. **Further information:** Chamber of Commerce, 465 California Street, San Francisco, CA 94104.

## San Jose, California

**Population:** 782,248; **Pop. density:** 4,951 per sq. mi.; **Pop. growth:** 24.3%. **Area:** 158 sq. mi. **Employment:** 387,202 employed, 8.0% unemployed; **Per capita income:** $25,955; % change 1981-91: 78.6.

**History:** founded by the Spanish 1777 between San Francisco and Monterey; briefly capital of Calif. 1849-51; inc. 1850.

**Transportation:** 1 international airport; 2 railroads; bus system. **Communications:** 4 TV, 14 radio stations. **Medical facilities:** 6 hospitals. **Educational facilities:** 3 universities and colleges. **Further information:** Chamber of Commerce, 180 S. Market St., San Jose, CA 95113.

## Santa Ana, California

**Population:** 293,827; **Pop. density:** 10,879 per sq. mi.; **Pop. growth:** 44.0%. **Area:** 27 sq. mi. **Employment:** 140,515 employed, 10.8% unemployed; **Per capita income:** $24,077; % change 1981-91: 65.4.

**History:** founded 1869; inc. as city 1886.

**Transportation:** 1 airport; 5 major freeways including main Los Angeles-San Diego artery; Amtrak. **Communications:** CATV system. **Medical facilities:** 4 hospitals. **Educational facilities:** 1 community college. **Further information:** Chamber of Commerce, 801 Civic Center Dr. W., Ste. 110, Santa Ana, CA 92701.

## Seattle, Washington

**Population:** 516,259; **Pop. density:** 6,146 per sq. mi.; **Pop. growth:** 4.5%. **Area:** 84 sq. mi. **Employment:** 289,247 employed, 7.1% unemployed; **Per capita income:** $23,329; % change 1981-91: 71.3.

**History:** settled 1851; inc. 1869; suffered severe fire 1889; played prominent role during Alaska Gold Rush 1897; growth followed opening of Panama Canal 1914; center of aircraft industry WWII.

**Transportation:** 1 international airport; 2 railroads; ferries serve Puget Sound, Alaska, Canada. **Communications:** 7 TV, 39 radio stations. **Medical facilities:** 40 hospitals. **Educational facilities:** 7 universities, 6 colleges, 11 community colleges. **Further information:** Greater Seattle Chamber of Commerce, 600 University St., Ste. 1200, Seattle, WA 98101-3186.

## Shreveport, Louisiana

**Population:** 198,525; **Pop. density:** 2,482 per sq. mi.; **Pop. growth:** -4.1%. **Area:** 80 sq. mi. **Employment:** 86,056 employed, 7.6% unemployed; **Per capita income:** $15,897; % change 1981-91: 54.7.

**History:** founded 1833 near site of a 160-mile log jam cleared by Capt. Henry Shreve; inc. 1839; oil discovered 1906.

**Transportation:** 2 airports; 2 bus lines. **Communications:** 5 TV, 16 radio stations. **Medical facilities:** 13 hospitals. **Educational facilities:** 4 universities, 3 colleges. **Further information:** Chamber of Commerce, P.O. Box 20074, Shreveport, LA 71120.

## Spokane, Washington

**Population:** 177,165; **Pop. density:** 3,408 per sq. mi.; **Pop. growth:** 3.4%. **Area:** 52 sq. mi. **Employment:** 80,676 employed, 7.7% unemployed; **Per capita income:** $16,857; % change 1981-91: 63.7.

**History:** settled 1872; inc. as village of Spokane Falls 1881 but destroyed in fire 1889; reinc. as city of Spokane 1891.

**Transportation:** 1 international airport; 2 railroads; bus system. **Communications:** 5 TV, 25 radio stations. **Medical facilities:** 5 major hospitals. **Educational facilities:** 8 universities and colleges; 14 public school districts, 11 high schools. **Further information:** Chamber of Commerce, W. 1020 Riverside Ave., P.O. Box 2147, Spokane, WA 99210.

## Stockton, California

**Population:** 210,943; **Pop. density:** 5,274 per sq. mi.; **Pop. growth:** 42.3%. **Area:** 40 sq. mi. **Employment:** 73,854 employed, 16.7% unemployed; **Per capita income:** $15,582; % change 1981-91: 41.9.

**History:** site purchased 1842; settled 1847; inc. 1850; chief distributing point for agricultural products of San Joaquin Valley.

**Transportation:** 1 airport, 7 railroads; 2 bus lines, city bus system. **Communications:** 5 TV stations. **Medical**

**facilities:** 4 hospitals; regional burn and heart centers. **Educational facilities:** 5 universities and colleges; 45 public schools. **Further information:** Chamber of Commerce, 445 W. Weber Ave., Suite 220, Stockton, CA 95203.

## Tacoma, Washington

**Population:** 176,664; **Pop. density:** 3,696 per sq. mi.; **Pop. growth:** 11.5%. **Area:** 47.8 sq. mi. **Employment:** 71,768 employed, 9.1% unemployed; **Per capita income:** $17,184; % change 1981-91: 60.9.
**History:** area explored 1792 by the British; first permanent settlement 1864; terminus for the Northern Pacific Railroad; inc. 1884.
**Transportation:** 1 airport; 2 railroads; transit system; Port of Tacoma. **Communications:** NA. **Medical facilities:** 6 hospitals, VA facility. **Educational facilities:** 3 universities, 2 colleges. **Further information:** Chamber of Commerce, P.O. Box 1933, Tacoma, WA 98401-1933.

## Tampa, Florida

**Population:** 280,015; **Pop. density:** 3,334 per sq. mi.; **Pop. growth:** 3.1%. **Area:** 84 sq. mi. **Employment:** 135,431 employed, 8.8% unemployed; **Per capita income:** $18,445; % change 1981-91: 72.4.
**History:** U.S. army fort on site 1824; inc. 1855.
**Transportation:** 1 international airport; Port of Tampa; bus system. **Communications:** 7 TV, 27 radio stations. **Medical facilities:** 17 hospitals. **Educational facilities:** 4 universities and colleges; 183 public schools. **Further information:** Chamber of Commerce, 801 E. Kennedy Blvd., P.O. Box 420, Tampa, FL 33601.

## Toledo, Ohio

**Population:** 332,943; **Pop. density:** 3,964 per sq. mi.; **Pop. growth:** −6.1%. **Area:** 84 sq. mi. **Employment:** 145,508 employed, 9.7% unemployed; **Per capita income:** $17,713; % change 1981-91: 62.7.
**History:** site of Ft. Industry, 1794; settled 1817; figured in "Toledo War" 1835-36 between Ohio and Michigan over their borders; inc. 1837.
**Transportation:** 3 major airlines; 5 railroads; 100 motor freight lines; 2 interstate bus lines. **Communications:** 4 TV, 17 radio stations. **Medical facilities:** 9 major hospital complexes. **Educational facilities:** 4 universities and colleges. **Further information:** Office of Tourism and Conventions, 401 Jefferson Ave., Toledo, OH 43604.

## Tucson, Arizona

**Population:** 405,371; **Pop. density:** 4,095 per sq. mi.; **Pop. growth:** 22.6%. **Area:** 99 sq. mi. **Employment:** 188,721 employed, 5.8% unemployed; **Per capita income:** $16,087; % change 1981-91: 59.6.
**History:** settled 1775 by Spanish as a presidio; acquired by U.S. in Gadsden Purchase 1853; inc. 1877.
**Transportation:** 1 international airport; 3 railroads; bus system. **Communications:** 10 TV, 27 radio stations. **Medical facilities:** 13 hospitals. **Educational facilities:** 2 universities, 1 college; 165 public schools. **Further information:** Chamber of Commerce, P.O. Box 991, Tucson, AZ 85702.

## Tulsa, Oklahoma

**Population:** 367,302; **Pop. density:** 1,979 per sq. mi.; **Pop. growth:** 1.8%. **Area:** 185.6 sq. mi. **Employment:**

173,362 employed, 5.9% unemployed; **Per capita income:** $17,837; % change 1981-91: 41.8.
**History:** settled in 1830s by Creek Indians; modern town founded 1882 and inc. 1898; oil discovered early 20th century.
**Transportation:** 1 international airport; 5 rail lines; 2 bus lines; transit bus system. **Communications:** 7 TV, 23 radio stations. **Medical facilities:** 6 hospitals. **Educational facilities:** 6 universities and colleges; 57 public, 23 private schools. **Further information:** Chamber of Commerce, 616 S. Boston Ave., Tulsa, OK 74119.

## Virginia Beach, Virginia

**Population:** 393,089; **Pop. density:** 1,541 per sq. mi.; **Pop. growth:** 49.9%. **Area:** 255 sq. mi. **Employment:** 183,038 employed, 5.9% unemployed; **Per capita income:** $17,030; % change 1981-91: 68.4.
**History:** area founded by Capt. John Smith 1607; formed by merger with Princess Anne co. 1963.
**Transportation:** 1 airport; 2 railroads; 2 bus lines; public transit system. **Communications:** 6 TV, 40 radio stations. **Medical facilities:** 2 hospitals. **Educational facilities:** 1 university, 2 colleges; 62 public schools. **Further information:** Chamber of Commerce, 4512 Virginia Beach Blvd., Virginia Beach, VA 23462.

## Washington, District of Columbia

**Population:** 606,900; **Pop. density:** 9,633 per sq. mi.; **Pop. growth:** −4.9%. **Area:** 63 sq. mi. **Employment:** 253,000 employed, 8.4% unemployed; **Per capita income:** $25,338; % change 1981-91: 84.2.
**History:** capital of the U.S.; 10-mile-square diamond at Potomac R. chosen by George Washington 1790 on land ceded from Va. and Md.; Congress first met 1800; inc. 1802; sacked by British, War of 1812.
**Transportation:** 3 airports; rail transit system; extensive local bus service; 1 bus, 3 rail lines. **Communications:** 5 TV, 61 radio stations. **Medical facilities:** 43 hospitals; major medical research center. **Educational facilities:** 10 universities and colleges. **Further information:** Convention and Visitors Association, 1301 Pennsylvania Ave. NW, Suite 309, Washington, DC 20004.

## Wichita, Kansas

**Population:** 304,017; **Pop. density:** 3,010 per sq. mi.; **Pop. growth:** 8.6%. **Area:** 101 sq. mi. **Employment:** 160,010 employed, 4.9% unemployed; **Per capita income:** $19,206; % change 1981-91: 54.8.
**History:** founded 1864; inc. 1871.
**Transportation:** 2 airports; 3 major rail freight lines; 2 bus lines. **Communications:** 5 TV, 26 radio stations. **Medical facilities:** 7 hospitals, 2 psychiatric rehab. centers. **Educational facilities:** 2 universities, 2 colleges; 96 public schools. **Further information:** Chamber of Commerce, 350 W. Douglas, Wichita, KS 67202.

## Yonkers, New York

**Population:** 188,082; **Pop. density:** 10,449 per sq. mi.; **Pop. growth:** −3.7%. **Area:** 18 sq. mi. **Employment:** 83,898 employed, 8.4% unemployed; **Per capita income:** $25,583; % change 1981-91: 92.1.
**History:** founded 1641 by the Dutch; inc. as town 1855; chartered as city 1872; borders NYC to the North.
**Transportation:** intracity bus system; rail service. **Communications:** see New York City. **Medical facilities:** 3 hospitals. **Educational facilities:** 3 colleges; 30 public schools. **Further information:** Chamber of Commerce, 480 N. Broadway, Yonkers, NY 10701.

## Notable Tall Buildings in North American Cities

Height from sidewalk to roof, including penthouse and tower if enclosed as integral part of structure; actual number of stories beginning at street level. Asterisks (*) denote buildings still under construction Jan. 1994. Year is date of completion.

| City | Hgt. ft. | Stories |
|---|---|---|
| **Albany, N.Y.** | | |
| Erastus Corning II Tower . . . . . . . . . | 589 | 44 |
| State Office Building . . . . . . . . . . . | 388 | 34 |
| Agency (4 bldgs.), So. Mall. . . . . . . . | 310 | 23 |
| **Atlanta, Ga.** | | |
| Nation's Bank Tower (1992) . . . . . . . | 1,050 | 57 |
| One Peachtree Center (1992) . . . . . . | 880 | 63 |
| Atlantic Center/IBM (1988). . . . . . . | 828 | 52 |
| 191 Peachtree (1990). . . . . . . . . . . | 770 | 54 |
| Westin Peachtree Plaza (1973) . . . . . | 723 | 71 |
| Georgia Pacific Tower (1981) . . . . . . | 697 | 51 |
| Promenade II/AT&T (1989) . . . . . . . | 691 | 40 |
| Southern Bell Telephone (1980). . . . . | 677 | 47 |
| GLG Grand/Occidental Hotel (1992) . . . | 629 | 53 |
| Concourse Tower #5 (1988) . . . . . . . | 570 | 32 |
| State of Georgia Tower (1968) . . . . . . | 556 | 44 |
| Marriott Marquis (1985). . . . . . . . . | 554 | 52 |
| Concourse Tower #6 (1991) . . . . . . . | 553 | 32 |
| Equitable Building, 100 Peachtree (1967). | 453 | 34 |
| 101 Marietta Tower, 101 Marietta (1975). | 446 | 36 |
| Ravinia #3 (1991). . . . . . . . . . . . | 444 | 34 |
| AT&T Long Line Bldg (1975). . . . . . . | 433 | |
| Bell South Enterprises (1990) . . . . . . | 428 | 28 |
| Atlanta Plaza I (1986). . . . . . . . . . | 425 | 32 |
| Park Place, 2660 Peachtree (1986). . . . | 420 | 40 |
| Club Towers Apts. (1989) . . . . . . . . | 410 | 38 |
| South Trust Bank (1961) . . . . . . . . . | 409 | 32 |
| Peachtree Summit/Federal Bldg. (1975) . | 406 | 31 |
| North Avenue Tower (1979) . . . . . . . | 403 | 26 |
| Tower Place, 3361 Piedmont Rd. (1974) . | 401 | 29 |
| First Union Bank (1987). . . . . . . . . | 396 | 30 |
| Richard B. Russell, Federal Bldg. (1978) . | 383 | 26 |
| Atlanta Hilton Hotel (1974) . . . . . . . | 383 | 32 |
| Peachtree Center, Harris Bldg. (1975) . . | 382 | 31 |
| Marquis One (1985). . . . . . . . . . . | 378 | 30 |
| Marquis Two (1987). . . . . . . . . . . | 378 | 30 |
| Trust Company Bank (1968) . . . . . . . | 377 | 28 |
| 260 Peachtree (1971). . . . . . . . . . | 377 | 27 |
| Peachtree Center Cain Building (1972) . . | 376 | 30 |
| Peachtree Center Building (1966) . . . . . | 374 | 31 |
| One Georgia Center (1966) . . . . . . . | 371 | 29 |
| Mayfair Apts. Tower (1990) . . . . . . . | 370 | 34 |
| The Campanile, 1145 Peachtree (1987) . | 367 | 25 |
| Riverwood Tower/Barnett Bank (1989). . . | 362 | 34 |
| **Austin, Tex.** | | |
| One American Center (1982) . . . . . . . | 395 | 32 |
| One Congress Plaza (1987) . . . . . . . | 391 | 30 |
| NCNB Tower (1975) . . . . . . . . . . . | 328 | 26 |
| **Baltimore, Md.** | | |
| U.S. Fidelity & Guaranty Co. . . . . . . . | 529 | 40 |
| Maryland National Bank Bldg. . . . . . . | 509 | 34 |
| 6 St. Paul Place . . . . . . . . . . . . . | 493 | 37 |
| World Trade Center Bldg. . . . . . . . . | 395 | 32 |
| Tremont Plaza Hotel . . . . . . . . . . . | 395 | 37 |
| 250 W. Pratt St. . . . . . . . . . . . . . | 360 | 26 |
| Harbor Court. . . . . . . . . . . . . . . | 356 | 28 |
| Blaustein Bldg. . . . . . . . . . . . . . | 342 | 30 |
| Union Trust Tower. . . . . . . . . . . . | 335 | 24 |
| Central Savings Bank Bldg. . . . . . . . | 330 | 28 |
| Charles Center South. . . . . . . . . . . | 330 | 26 |
| **Baton Rouge, La.** | | |
| State Capitol (1932). . . . . . . . . . . | 460 | 34 |
| Hancock Bank Bldg. (1974) . . . . . . . | 315 | 24 |
| **Birmingham, Ala.** | | |
| Southtrust Tower (1986) . . . . . . . . . | 454 | 34 |
| AmSouth/Harbert Plaza (1989) . . . . . . | 390 | 30 |
| AmSouth/Sonat Tower (1972). . . . . . . | 390 | 30 |
| South Central Bell Hdqts. Bldg. . . . . . | 390 | 30 |
| City Federal Bldg. (1913). . . . . . . . . | 325 | 27 |
| **Boston, Mass.** | | |
| John Hancock Tower . . . . . . . . . . . | 790 | 60 |
| Prudential Center . . . . . . . . . . . . | 750 | 52 |
| Boston Co. Bldg., Court St. . . . . . . . | 605 | 41 |
| Federal Reserve Bldg. . . . . . . . . . . | 604 | 32 |
| International Place, 100 Oliver St. . . . . . | 600 | 46 |

| City | Hgt. ft. | Stories |
|---|---|---|
| First National Bank of Boston . . . . . . | 591 | 37 |
| One Financial Center . . . . . . . . . . | 590 | 46 |
| Shawmut Bank Bldg. . . . . . . . . . . | 520 | 38 |
| Exchange Place, 53 State St. . . . . . . | 510 | 39 |
| Sixty State St. . . . . . . . . . . . . . . | 509 | 38 |
| One Post Office Sq. . . . . . . . . . . . | 507 | 40 |
| One Beacon St. . . . . . . . . . . . . . | 507 | 40 |
| New England Merch. Bank Bldg.. . . . . | 500 | 40 |
| U.S. Custom House . . . . . . . . . . . | 496 | 32 |
| John Hancock Bldg. . . . . . . . . . . . | 495 | 26 |
| State St. Bank Bldg.. . . . . . . . . . . | 477 | 34 |
| 125 High St. (1990) . . . . . . . . . . . | 455 | 30 |
| One Hundred Summer St. . . . . . . . . | 450 | 33 |
| McCormack Bldg. . . . . . . . . . . . . | 401 | 22 |
| Keystone Custodian Funds. . . . . . . . | 400 | 32 |
| Saltonstall Office Bldg. . . . . . . . . . | 396 | 22 |
| Devonshire, 250 Wash. St. . . . . . . . | 396 | 40 |
| Harbor Towers (2 bldgs.). . . . . . . . . | 396 | 40 |
| Westin Hotel, Copley Place . . . . . . . | 395 | 36 |
| Federal Center (1988) . . . . . . . . . . | 393 | 28 |
| 75 State St. (1988) . . . . . . . . . . . | 390 | 31 |
| John F. Kennedy Bldg. . . . . . . . . . | 387 | 24 |
| Marriott Hotel, Copley Place . . . . . . . | 383 | 39 |
| 101 Federal St. (1988) . . . . . . . . . | 382 | 31 |
| Longfellow Towers (2 bldgs.) . . . . . . . | 380 | 38 |
| **Buffalo, N.Y.** | | |
| Marine Midland Center (1971) . . . . . . | 529 | 40 |
| City Hall (1926) . . . . . . . . . . . . . | 378 | 32 |
| Rand Bldg., not incl. 40-ft. beacon (1929) | 351 | ... |
| Main Place Tower (1969). . . . . . . . . | 350 | 26 |
| **Calgary, Alta.** | | |
| Petro-Canada Centre, W. Tower (1984) . | 689 | 52 |
| Bankers Hall (1989). . . . . . . . . . . | 645 | 50 |
| Calgary Tower (1988). . . . . . . . . . . | 626 | ... |
| Canterra Tower (1988) . . . . . . . . . . | 580 | 46 |
| First Canadian Centre (1983) . . . . . . | 547 | 44 |
| Scotia Centre (1976) . . . . . . . . . . | 504 | 38 |
| Nova Bldg., 801 7th Ave. SW . . . . . . | 500 | 37 |
| Petro-Canada Centre, E. Tower (1984). . | 469 | 33 |
| Two Bow Valley Square (1974) . . . . . . | 468 | 39 |
| Fifth & Fifth Bldg. . . . . . . . . . . . . | 460 | 35 |
| Home Oil Tower . . . . . . . . . . . . . | 463 | 34 |
| Canada Trust Tower (1991) . . . . . . . | 462 | 40 |
| Shell Tower . . . . . . . . . . . . . . . | 460 | 34 |
| Dome Oil Tower . . . . . . . . . . . . . | 449 | 33 |
| Four Bow Valley Square (1982) . . . . . | 441 | 37 |
| Esso Plaza (twin towers) . . . . . . . . | 435 | 34 |
| Oxford Square. . . . . . . . . . . . . . | 421 | 33 |
| Family Life Bldg. . . . . . . . . . . . . | 410 | 33 |
| Pan Canadian Bldg., 150 9th Ave. SW . | 410 | 28 |
| Norcen Tower . . . . . . . . . . . . . . | 408 | 33 |
| Alberta Stock Exchange Bldg. . . . . . . | 407 | 33 |
| Amoco Centre (1988). . . . . . . . . . . | 396 | 30 |
| Western Centre . . . . . . . . . . . . . | 385 | 40 |
| Calgary Place . . . . . . . . . . . . . . | 385 | 30 |
| Three Bow Valley Square . . . . . . . . | 382 | 33 |
| **Charlotte, N.C.** | | |
| NationsBank Corp. Center (1992) . . . . . | 871 | 60 |
| One First Union Center (1988) . . . . . . | 580 | 42 |
| NationsBank Plaza (1974) . . . . . . . . | 503 | 40 |
| Interstate Tower (1990). . . . . . . . . . | 462 | 32 |
| Two First Union Center (1971). . . . . . . | 433 | 32 |
| Wachovia Center (1974) . . . . . . . . . | 420 | 32 |
| Carillon (1991). . . . . . . . . . . . . . | 394 | 24 |
| Charlotte Plaza (1982) . . . . . . . . . . | 388 | 27 |
| **Chicago, Ill.** | | |
| Sears Tower (world's tallest) (1974) . . . | 1,454 | 110 |
| Amoco (1974) . . . . . . . . . . . . . . | 1,136 | 80 |
| John Hancock Center (1969) . . . . . . . | 1,127 | 100 |
| 311 S. Wacker (1990). . . . . . . . . . . | 970 | 65 |
| Two Prudential Plaza (1990) . . . . . . . | 901 | 64 |
| AT&T Corporate Center (1989) . . . . . . | 891 | 60 |
| 900 N. Michigan (1989). . . . . . . . . . | 871 | 66 |
| Water Tower Place (1976) . . . . . . . . | 859 | 74 |
| First Natl. Bank (1969) . . . . . . . . . . | 852 | 60 |
| Three First National Plaza (1981) . . . . . | 775 | 57 |
| Olympia Centre (1984) . . . . . . . . . . | 727 | 63 |
| Leo Burnett Bldg. (1989) . . . . . . . . . | 700 | 46 |

| City | Hgt. ft. | Stories |
|---|---|---|
| IBM Plaza (1991) | 695 | 52 |
| One Magnificent Mile (1983) | 673 | 58 |
| Paine Webber Bldg., 181 W. Madison | 644 | 50 |
| Daley Center (1965) | 662 | 31 |
| 1,000 Lake Shore Plaza (1964) | 648 | 55 |
| Lake Point Tower (1968) | 645 | 70 |
| Board of Trade, incl. 81 ft. statue (1930) | 605 | 44 |
| Prudential Bldg., 130 E. Randolph (1955). | 601 | 41 |
| Antenna tower, 311 ft., makes total. | 912 | ... |
| CNA Plaza (1972) | 600 | 44 |
| Huron Apts. | 599 | 56 |
| Marina City Apts., 2 buildings | 588 | 61 |
| Mid Continental Plaza (1972) | 580 | 50 |
| Associates Center (1983) | 575 | 41 |
| Pittsfield, 55 E. Washington St. (1927) | 572 | 38 |
| Onterie Center (1985) | 570 | 58 |
| Civic Opera Bldg. (1929) | 555 | 45 |
| Lincoln Tower, 75 E. Wacker Dr. (1928) | 554 | 42 |
| Newberry Plaza, State & Oak (1974) | 553 | 56 |
| One South Wacker Dr. (1983) | 550 | 40 |
| Harbor Point (1975) | 550 | 54 |
| Madison Plaza (1982) | 551 | 45 |
| 190 S. LaSalle (1986) | 550 | 40 |
| LaSalle Natl. Bank (1934) | 535 | 44 |
| One N. LaSalle Street (1930) | 530 | 49 |
| 111 E. Chestnut St. (1972) | 529 | 56 |
| Chicago Mercantile Exchange (2 bldgs) | 525 | 40 |
| River Plaza, Rush & Hubbard (1988) | 524 | 56 |
| 35 E. Wacker Drive (1926) | 523 | 40 |
| United Ins. Bldg., 1 E. Wacker Dr. (1962) | 522 | 41 |
| Quaker Tower (1987) | 518 | 35 |
| Carbide & Carbon, 230 N. Mich. (1929). | 503 | 37 |
| Walton Colonnade (1972) | 500 | 44 |
| Xerox Center (1980) | 500 | 40 |
| One Financial Place (1985) | 498 | 40 |
| LaSalle-Wacker, 221 N. LaSalle St. | 491 | 41 |
| Amer. Nat'l. Bank, 33 N. LaSalle St. | 479 | 40 |
| Bankers, 105 W. Adams St. (1927) | 476 | 41 |
| Brunswick Bldg. (1965) | 475 | 37 |
| 310 Center (1924) | 475 | 37 |

### Cincinnati, Oh.

| City | Hgt. ft. | Stories |
|---|---|---|
| Carew Tower (1931) | 568 | 49 |
| Central Trust Tower (1979) | 504 | 33 |
| 312 Walnut St. | 500 | 35 |
| Dubois Tower, 5th & Walnut (1969) | 423 | 32 |
| Cincinnati Commerce Center (1984) | 418 | 29 |
| Chemed Center | 411 | 31 |
| Chiquita Center | 391 | 29 |
| Star Bank Center (1981) | 351 | 26 |

### Cleveland, Oh.

| City | Hgt. ft. | Stories |
|---|---|---|
| Society Center (1991) | 948 | 57 |
| Terminal Tower (1930) | 708 | 52 |
| BP America (1985) | 658 | 46 |
| Plaza Tower at Erieview (1964) | 529 | 40 |
| One Cleveland Center (1983) | 450 | 31 |
| Bank One Center (1991) | 446 | 28 |
| Justice Center, 1250 Ontario (1976) | 420 | 26 |
| Federal Bldg. (1967) | 419 | 32 |
| National City Center (1980) | 410 | 35 |
| 900 Euclid (1971) | 383 | 29 |
| Cleveland St. J. F. Rhodes Tower (1971). | 373 | 20 |
| Eaton Center (1983) | 360 | 28 |
| Ohio-Bell. (1927) | 360 | 22 |

### Columbus, Oh.

| City | Hgt. ft. | Stories |
|---|---|---|
| James A. Rhodes (State Office Tower). | 629 | 41 |
| LeVeque Tower, 50 W. Broad | 555 | 47 |
| Ohio Bureau of Worker's Compensation & Ind. Comm. (1990) | 530 | 33 |
| Huntington Center, 41 S. High St. | 512 | 37 |
| Verne-Riffe State Office Tower | 503 | 33 |
| One Nationwide Plaza | 482 | 40 |
| One Riverside Plaza | 456 | 31 |
| Borden Bldg., 180 E. Broad | 438 | 34 |
| Three Nationwide Plaza (1989) | 408 | 27 |
| One Columbus. | 366 | 26 |
| Columbus Center, 100 E. Broad. | 357 | 24 |

### Dallas, Tex.

| City | Hgt. ft. | Stories |
|---|---|---|
| National Bank Plaza (1985) | 939 | 72 |
| Bank One Center (1987) | 787 | 60 |
| Texas Commerce Tower (1987). | 738 | 55 |
| First Interstate Bank Tower (1986) | 721 | 60 |
| Renaissance Tower (1987). | 710 | 56 |
| Trammell Crow Center (1984) | 686 | 50 |
| First City Center (1984). | 655 | 50 |
| Thanksgiving Tower (1982). | 645 | 50 |

| City | Hgt. ft. | Stories |
|---|---|---|
| First National Bank | 625 | 52 |
| Republic Bank Tower | 598 | 50 |
| SW Bell Admin. Tower | 580 | 37 |
| Lincoln Plaza (1984) | 579 | 45 |
| Olympia York Tower (1982) | 562 | 36 |
| Cityplace Center East (1988) | 560 | 50 |
| Southland Center Tower (1959) | 550 | 42 |
| Maxus Energy (1980) | 550 | 34 |
| 2001 Bryan St. (1973) | 512 | 40 |
| San Jacinto Tower (1982) | 456 | 33 |
| NationsBank Center Tower 1 (1954) | 452 | 36 |
| Stouffer Hotel | 451 | 29 |
| Skyway Tower (1981). | 448 | 31 |
| One Main Place (1968) | 445 | 34 |
| 1600 Pacific Bldg. (1964) | 434 | 32 |
| Magnolia Bldg. (1923). | 430 | 27 |
| Mart Hotel | 400 | 29 |
| Complex Union Tower | 400 | 33 |

### Dayton, Oh.

| City | Hgt. ft. | Stories |
|---|---|---|
| Kettering Tower, 2d & Main (1970) | 405 | 30 |
| Mead World Hqtrs, 10 W. 2d St. (1976). | 385 | 28 |

### Denver, Col.

| City | Hgt. ft. | Stories |
|---|---|---|
| Republic Plaza. | 714 | 56 |
| Mountain Bell Center | 709 | 54 |
| United Bank of Denver | 698 | 52 |
| 1999 Broadway | 544 | 43 |
| Arco Tower. | 527 | 41 |
| Anaconda Tower | 507 | 40 |
| Amoco Bldg., 17th Ave. & Broadway | 448 | 36 |
| 17th Street Plaza | 438 | 35 |
| Stellar Plaza | 437 | 31 |
| First Interstate Tower North | 434 | 32 |
| One Denver Place. | 428 | 34 |
| Brooks Towers, 1020 15th St. | 420 | 42 |
| Tabor Center, #1. | 408 | 32 |
| Manville Plaza | 404 | 29 |
| Colorado Nat'l. Bank, 17th & Curtis | 389 | 26 |
| First Interstate Tower South | 385 | 28 |
| Security Life Bldg. | 384 | 33 |
| Mellon Financial Center. | 374 | 31 |
| Dominion Plaza | 368 | 30 |
| Lincoln Center | 366 | 30 |
| Denver Natl. Bank Plaza | 363 | 29 |
| Bank Western | 357 | 27 |
| Colorado State Bank | 352 | 26 |

### Des Moines, Ia.

| City | Hgt. ft. | Stories |
|---|---|---|
| Principal Financial Group Bldg. (1990) | 630 | 44 |
| Ruan Center (1974) | 457 | 35 |
| Financial Center, 7th & Walnut (1973) | 345 | 25 |
| Marriott Hotel, 700 Grand Ave. (1981) | 340 | 33 |
| Plaza, 3d & Walnut (1984) | 340 | 25 |

### Detroit, Mich.

| City | Hgt. ft. | Stories |
|---|---|---|
| Westin Hotel | 720 | 71 |
| Penobscot Bldg. | 557 | 47 |
| 1 Detroit Center | 491 | 44 |
| Guardian | 485 | 40 |
| Renaissance Center (4 bldgs.). | 479 | 39 |
| Book Tower | 472 | 35 |
| 150 W. Jefferson Bldg. | 470 | 29 |
| Prudential 3000 Town Center | 448 | 32 |
| Cadillac Tower. | 437 | 40 |
| David Stott | 436 | 38 |
| ANR Bldg. | 430 | 32 |
| Fisher. | 420 | 28 |
| J. L. Hudson Bldg. | 397 | 28 |
| McNamara Federal Office Bldg. | 393 | 27 |
| 2000 Prudential Town Ctr. | 392 | 28 |
| American Center | 374 | 27 |
| Top of Troy Bldg. | 374 | 27 |
| Comerica Bldg., 211 N. Fort | 370 | 28 |
| Edison Plaza | 365 | 25 |
| David Broderick Tower | 358 | 34 |
| 1st National Bldg. | 350 | 25 |
| Buhl, 535 Griswold | 350 | 26 |

### Edmonton, Alta.

| City | Hgt. ft. | Stories |
|---|---|---|
| Manulife Place (1983) | 479 | 36 |
| AGT Tower (1971) | 441 | 33 |
| Canada Trust Tower (1982) | 440 | 31 |
| City Centre (1990). | 409 | 30 |
| Metropolitan Place (1980) | 397 | 31 |
| Oxford Tower (1978) | 390 | 27 |
| TD Tower (1975) | 386 | 27 |
| Scotia Place (1983) | 366 | 28 |
| CN Tower (1966) | 365 | 27 |

| City | Hgt. ft. | Stories |
|---|---|---|
| Phipps McKinnon (1977) | 359 | 20 |

## Fort Wayne, Ind.

| | | |
|---|---|---|
| One Summit Square (1981) | 442 | 26 |
| Ft. Wayne Natl. Bank (1970) | 339 | 26 |

## Fort Worth, Tex.

| | | |
|---|---|---|
| City Center Tower II (1984) | 546 | 38 |
| Burnett Plaza (1983) | 538 | 40 |
| Continental Plaza (1982) | 520 | 40 |
| 1st City Bank Tower (1982) | 475 | 33 |
| Team Bank-Ft. Worth (1974) | 457 | 37 |
| Texas Bldg. (1955) | 420 | 31 |

## Hartford, Conn.

| | | |
|---|---|---|
| City Place (1983) | 535 | 38 |
| Travelers Ins. Co. Bldg. (1919) | 527 | 34 |
| Goodwin Square (1990) | 522 | 30 |
| Hartford Plaza (1967) | 420 | 22 |
| Shawmut Bank (1960) | 360 | 26 |
| One Commercial Plaza (1984) | 349 | 28 |
| Bushnell Tower (1969) | 349 | 27 |

## Honolulu, Hi.

| | | |
|---|---|---|
| Imperial Plaza (1992) | 400 | 40 |
| Waterfront Towers (1990) | 400 | 46 |
| Nauru Tower (1991) | 400 | 45 |
| Ala Moana Hotel | 396 | 38 |
| Pacific Tower | 350 | 30 |
| Franklin Towers | 350 | 41 |
| Honolulu Tower | 350 | 40 |
| Discovery Bay | 350 | 42 |
| Hyatt Regency Waikiki | 350 | 39 |
| Maile Court Hotel | 350 | 43 |
| Regency Tower, 2525 Date St. | 350 | 42 |
| Pearlridge Square | 350 | 43 |
| Yacht Harbor Towers | 350 | 40 |
| Canterbury Place | 350 | 40 |
| Royal Iolani | 350 | 38 |
| Island Colony | 350 | 44 |
| Century Center | 350 | 41 |
| Pacific Beach Hotel | 350 | 43 |
| Hawaiian Monarch Hotel | 350 | 43 |
| Waikiki Hobron | 350 | 43 |
| Honolulu Tower 2 | 350 | 40 |
| Tapa Tower, 2005 Kalia Rd. | 350 | 36 |
| Executive Center, 1088 Bishop St. | 350 | 41 |
| 1001 Bishop | 350 | 28 |

## Houston, Tex.

| | | |
|---|---|---|
| Texas Commerce Tower (1981) | 1,002 | 75 |
| First Interstate Plaza (1983) | 992 | 71 |
| Transco Tower (1983) | 901 | 64 |
| NationsBank Center (1983) | 780 | 56 |
| Heritage Plaza, 1111 Bagby | 762 | 53 |
| InterFirst Plaza (1980) | 744 | 55 |
| 1600 Smith St. (1984) | 729 | 54 |
| Chevron Tower, 1301 McKinney (1982) | 725 | 52 |
| One Shell Plaza (not incl. 285 ft. TV tower) (1970) | 714 | 50 |
| Enron Bldg. (1983) | 692 | 50 |
| Capital Natl. Bank Plaza | 685 | 50 |
| One Houston Center (1978) | 678 | 47 |
| First City, Tex. Financial Center (1984) | 662 | 47 |
| 1100 Milam Bldg. (1973) | 651 | 47 |
| San Felipe Plaza (1984) | 620 | 45 |
| Exxon Bldg. (1962) | 606 | 44 |
| The America Tower | 577 | 42 |
| Marathon Oil Tower (1983) | 572 | 41 |
| Two Houston Center (1974) | 570 | 40 |
| Kellogg Tower (1973) | 550 | 40 |
| 1415 Louisiana Tower (1983) | 550 | 44 |
| Pennzoil, 700 Milam (2 bldgs.) (1975) | 523 | 36 |
| Two Allen Center (1978) | 521 | 36 |
| 1201 Louisiana Bldg. (1971) | 518 | 35 |
| Huntington | 506 | 34 |
| Tenneco Bldg. (1962) | 502 | 33 |
| Conoco Tower (1973) | 465 | 32 |
| One Allen Center (1974) | 452 | 34 |
| Summit Tower West (1979) | 441 | 31 |
| Coastal Tower (1978) | 441 | 31 |
| Four Leafs Towers (2 bldgs.) | 439 | 40 |
| Phoenix Tower (1984) | 434 | 34 |
| Chevron Bldg. | 428 | 37 |
| The Spires | 426 | 41 |
| Central Tower (4 Oaks Place) | 420 | 30 |
| First City Natl. Bank (1960) | 410 | 32 |

| City | Hgt. ft. | Stories |
|---|---|---|
| Houston Lighting & Power (1968) | 410 | 27 |
| Niels Esperson Bldg. (1927) | 409 | 31 |
| Hyatt Regency Houston (1972) | 401 | 34 |

## Indianapolis, Ind.

| | | |
|---|---|---|
| Bank One Tower (1989) | 728 | 51 |
| AUL Tower (1981) | 533 | 38 |
| Market Tower (1988) | 515 | 32 |
| Indiana Natl. Bank Tower (1969) | 504 | 35 |
| Riley Towers (2 bldgs.) (1963) | 427 | 30 |
| 300 N. Meridian Bldg. (1988) | 408 | 28 |

## Jacksonville, Fla.

| | | |
|---|---|---|
| Barnett Center (1990) | 617 | 42 |
| Independent Life Bldg. (1975) | 535 | 37 |
| Southern Bell (1983) | 447 | 32 |
| Gulf Life Tower (1967) | 432 | 28 |
| American Heritage Life (1989) | 357 | 23 |

## Kansas City, Mo.

| | | |
|---|---|---|
| One Kansas City Place | 626 | 42 |
| AT&T Town Pavilion | 590 | 38 |
| Hyatt Regency | 504 | 40 |
| Kansas City Power and Light Bldg. | 476 | 32 |
| City Hall | 443 | 29 |
| Federal Office Bldg. | 413 | 35 |
| Commerce Tower | 402 | 32 |
| City Center Sq. | 402 | 30 |
| Southwest Bell Telephone Bldg. | 394 | 27 |
| Pershing Road Associates | 352 | 28 |

## Las Vegas, Nev.

| | | |
|---|---|---|
| *Vegas World Tower | 1,012 | ... |
| Fitzgerald Casino-Hotel | 400 | 34 |
| Landmark Hotel | 356 | 31 |
| Las Vegas Hilton | 345 | 30 |

## Lexington, Ky.

| | | |
|---|---|---|
| Lexington Financial Center (1986) | 410 | 30 |
| Kincaid Tower (1980) | 333 | 22 |

## Little Rock, Ark.

| | | |
|---|---|---|
| TCBY Towers (1986) | 546 | 40 |
| First Commercial Bank (1975) | 454 | 30 |
| Worthen Bank & Trust (1969) | 375 | 24 |
| Stephens Bldg. (1985) | 365 | 25 |
| Tower Bldg. (1960) | 350 | 18 |
| Union National Bank (1968) | 331 | 21 |

## Los Angeles, Cal.

| | | |
|---|---|---|
| First Interstate World Center (1989) | 1,017 | 73 |
| First Interstate Bank | 858 | 62 |
| Cal. Plaza 11A | 750 | 57 |
| Wells Fargo Tower | 750 | 54 |
| Security Pacific Plaza | 735 | 55 |
| So. Cal. Gas Center (1990) | 733 | 55 |
| 777 Tower | 725 | 52 |
| Mitsui Fudoson (1990) | 716 | 52 |
| Atlantic Richfield Tower | 699 | 52 |
| Bank of America Tower | 699 | 52 |
| 444 S. Flower St. | 625 | 48 |
| AT&T Bldg. | 620 | 42 |
| One California Plaza | 578 | 42 |
| Century Plaza Towers (2 bldgs.) | 571 | 44 |
| IBM Tower | 560 | 45 |
| Citicorp Plaza | 534 | 42 |
| 1999 Ave. of the Stars (1989) | 533 | 39 |
| Manulife Tower (1990) | 517 | 37 |
| Union Bank Square | 516 | 41 |
| MCA-Getty | 506 | 36 |
| WTC Bldg. | 496 | 36 |
| Fox Plaza | 492 | 34 |
| ARCO Center | 462 | 33 |
| City Hall | 454 | 32 |
| Equitable Life Bldg. | 454 | 34 |
| Transamerica Center | 452 | 32 |
| Mutual Benefit Life Ins. Bldg. | 435 | 31 |
| Warner Center Plaza III | 415 | 25 |
| Broadway Plaza | 414 | 33 |
| 1900 Ave. of Stars | 398 | 28 |
| 1 Wilshire Bldg. | 395 | 27 |
| The Evian | 390 | 31 |
| 400 S. Hope St. | 375 | 28 |
| Westin Bonaventure Hotel | 367 | 35 |
| Beaudry Center | 365 | 29 |
| Cal. Fed. Savings & Loan Bldg. | 363 | 28 |
| Century City North | 363 | 26 |
| Home Savings Tower | 356 | 25 |

## Louisville, Ky.

| City | Hgt. ft. | Stories |
|---|---|---|
| First Natl. Bank (1972) | 512 | 40 |
| Citizen's Plaza (1971) | 420 | 30 |
| Humana Bldg. | 350 | 27 |
| Meindinger Tower (1982) | 338 | 26 |
| Brown & Williamson Tower (1982) | 338 | 26 |

## Memphis, Tenn.

| | | |
|---|---|---|
| 100 N. Main Bldg. | 430 | 37 |
| Commerce Square | 396 | 31 |
| Sterick Bldg. | 365 | 31 |
| Clark, 5100 Poplar | 365 | 32 |
| Morgan Keegan Tower, 50 Front St. | 341 | 23 |
| First Natl. Bank Bldg. | 332 | 25 |

## Miami, Fla.

| | | |
|---|---|---|
| Southeast Financial Center (1983) | 764 | 55 |
| Centrust Tower (1987) | 562 | 35 |
| Metro-Dade Administration Bldg. | 510 | 30 |
| Florida National Tower (1986) | 484 | 35 |
| One Biscayne Corp. | 456 | 40 |
| Amerifirst Bldg. (1973) | 375 | 32 |
| Hotel Inter-Continental Miami | 366 | 35 |
| Venitia, 1635 Bayshore Dr. | 365 | 42 |
| Dade County Court House | 357 | 28 |

## Milwaukee, Wis.

| | | |
|---|---|---|
| Firstar Center | 625 | 42 |
| 100 E. Wisconsin (1989) | 549 | 37 |
| Milwaukee Center | 425 | 29 |
| 411 E. Wisconsin | 385 | 30 |
| Northwestern Mutual Tower (1989) | 350 | 19 |
| City Hall | 350 | 9 |

## Minneapolis, Minn.

| | | |
|---|---|---|
| IDS Center (1973) | 787 | 51 |
| Norwest (1988) | 777 | 57 |
| *First Bank Place | 774 | 53 |
| Multifoods Tower (1983) | 651 | 52 |
| Piper Jaffray Tower (1984) | 627 | 42 |
| *Dain Bosworth Plaza | 550 | 40 |
| Pillsbury Center, 200 S. 6th St. (1981) | 545 | 40 |
| Lincoln Centre, 333 S. 7th (1987) | 496 | 31 |
| Foshay Tower, not including 163-ft. antenna tower (1929) | 496 | 32 |
| Plaza VII, 45 S. 7th (1987) | 494 | 36 |
| 100 South Fifth (1987) | 490 | 36 |
| Telephone Bldg. (1931) | 423 | 27 |
| Hennepin Co. Govt. Center (1974) | 413 | 24 |
| First Bank Place West (1960) | 386 | 26 |
| Marriott Hotel (1983) | 379 | 31 |

## Montreal, Que.

| | | |
|---|---|---|
| 1100 Rue de la Gauchetiere | 669 | 45 |
| 1250 Boulevard Rene Levesque | 640 | 45 |
| Place Victoria (1963) | 624 | 47 |
| Place Ville Marie (1962) | 620 | 45 |
| Canadian Imperial Bank of Commerce (1962) | 590 | 45 |
| Le Complexe Desjardins | | |
| La Tour du Sud | 498 | 40 |
| La Tour du L'Est | 428 | 32 |
| La Tour du Nord | 355 | 27 |
| Les Cooperants (1987) | 479 | 34 |
| Place Montreal Trust (1988) | 449 | 32 |
| Chateau Champlain Hotel (1967) | 420 | 38 |
| Port Royal Apts. | 400 | 33 |
| Royal Bank Tower | 397 | 22 |
| Sun Life Bldg. | 390 | 26 |
| 500 Place d'Armes | 390 | 32 |

## Nashville, Tenn.

| | | |
|---|---|---|
| Third National Financial Center | 490 | 30 |
| American General Center | 452 | 31 |
| Landmark Center | 409 | 30 |
| Nashville City Center (1987) | 402 | 27 |
| James K. Polk State Office Bldg. | 392 | 32 |
| Stouffer Hotel (1987) | 385 | 35 |
| First American Center | 354 | 28 |
| One Nashville Plaza | 346 | 23 |

## Newark, N.J.

| | | |
|---|---|---|
| Natl. Newark & Essex Bldg. | 465 | 36 |
| Raymond-Commerce | 448 | 37 |
| Park Plaza Bldg. | 400 | 26 |
| Prudential Plaza | 370 | 24 |
| Public Service Elec. & Gas | 360 | 26 |
| Prudential Ins. Co., 753 Broad St. | 360 | 26 |
| AT&T Bldg. | 359 | 31 |

| | | |
|---|---|---|
| Gateway 1 | 355 | 28 |

## New Orleans, La.

| City | Hgt. ft. | Stories |
|---|---|---|
| One Shell Square (1972) | 697 | 51 |
| Place St. Charles (1985) | 645 | 53 |
| Plaza Tower (1969) | 531 | 45 |
| Energy Centre (1984) | 530 | 39 |
| LL&E Tower (1987) | 481 | 36 |
| Sheraton Hotel (1985) | 478 | 47 |
| Marriott Hotel (1972) | 450 | 42 |
| Texaco Bldg. (1983) | 442 | 33 |
| Canal Place One (1979) | 439 | 32 |
| 1010 Common (1971) | 438 | 31 |
| Int'l. Trade Mart Bldg. | 407 | 33 |
| 225 Baronne St. (1965) | 362 | 28 |
| One Poydras Plaza (1983) | 360 | 28 |
| Hyatt-Regency Hotel (1976) | 360 | 25 |
| Hibernia Bank Bldg. (1920) | 355 | 23 |

## New York, N.Y.

| | | |
|---|---|---|
| World Trade Center (2 towers) (1973) | 1,368/ 1,362 | 110/110 |
| Empire State, 34th St. & 5th Ave. | 1,250 | 102 |
| TV tower, 164 ft., makes total (1931) | 1,414 | ... |
| Chrysler, Lexington & 43d (1930) | 1,046 | 77 |
| Amer. International, 70 Pine (1932) | 950 | 67 |
| 40 Wall Tower (1929) | 927 | 71 |
| Citicorp Center (1977) | 914 | 46 |
| G.E. Bldg., Rockefeller Center (1933) | 850 | 70 |
| Chase Manhattan Plaza (1960) | 813 | 60 |
| MetLife Bldg. (1963) | 808 | 59 |
| Cityspire (1989) | 802 | 72 |
| Woolworth, 233 Broadway (1913) | 792 | 60 |
| 1 Worldwide Plaza | 778 | 47 |
| 1 Penn Plaza (1972) | 764 | 57 |
| Carnegie Tower | 756 | 59 |
| Exxon, 1251 Ave. of Americas (1971) | 750 | 54 |
| Equitable Center Tower West (1985) | 750 | 58 |
| 60 Wall St. (1989) | 745 | 50 |
| 1 Liberty Plaza (1972) | 743 | 50 |
| Citibank (1907) | 741 | 57 |
| World Financial Center, Tower C (1988) | 739 | 54 |
| One Astor Plaza (1969) | 730 | 54 |
| Solow Bldg. (1979) | 725 | 50 |
| Marine Midland | 724 | 52 |
| Metropolitan Tower (1988) | 716 | 66 |
| Union Carbide Bldg. (1960) | 707 | 52 |
| General Motors Bldg. (1968) | 705 | 50 |
| Metropolitan Life (1909) | 700 | 50 |
| 500 5th Ave. (1928) | 697 | 58 |
| Chem. Bank, N.Y. Trust Bldg. (1963) | 687 | 50 |
| 55 Water St. | 687 | 53 |
| 1585 Broadway | 685 | 42 |
| Four Seasons Hotel (1993) | 682 | 52 |
| Chanin, Lexington & 42d (1929) | 680 | 56 |
| 15 Columbus Circle (1970) | 679 | 44 |
| McGraw Hill, 1221 Ave. of Am. (1972) | 674 | 51 |
| Citicorp (Queens) (1990) | 673 | 50 |
| Lincoln, 60 E. 42d Street (1939) | 673 | 53 |
| 1633 Broadway | 670 | 48 |
| Trump Tower, 725 5th Ave. (1983) | 664 | 68 |
| 599 Lexington Ave. (1988) | 653 | 47 |
| Museum Tower Apts. (1985) | 650 | 58 |
| 712 5th Ave. (1990) | 650 | 56 |
| American Brands, 245 Park Ave. | 648 | 40 |
| A. T. & T. Tower (1983) | 648 | 37 |
| World Financial Center Tower B (1986) | 645 | 50 |
| General Electric, 570 Lexington (1931) | 640 | 50 |
| Irving Trust, 1 Wall St. (1932) | 640 | 50 |
| 345 Park Ave. | 634 | 44 |
| Grace Plaza, 1114 Ave. of Am. | 630 | 50 |
| 1 New York Plaza (1969) | 630 | 50 |
| Home Insurance Co. Bldg. | 630 | 44 |
| N.Y. Telephone, 1095 Ave. of Am. | 630 | 40 |
| Central Park Place (1988) | 628 | 56 |
| 888 7th Ave. | 628 | 42 |
| 1 Hammarskjold Plaza | 628 | 50 |
| Waldorf-Astoria, 301 Park Ave. (1931) | 625 | 47 |
| Burlington House (1970) | 625 | 50 |
| Olympic Tower, 645 5th Ave. (1976) | 620 | 51 |
| 10 E. 40th St. | 620 | 48 |
| 101 Park Ave. | 618 | 50 |
| 750 7th Ave. | 615 | 35 |
| New York Life, 51 Madison Ave. (1928) | 615 | 40 |
| Rihga Royal Hotel | 610 | 54 |
| 17 State St. | 610 | 41 |
| Penney Bldg., 1301 Ave. of Am. | 609 | 46 |
| IBM, 590 Madison Ave. (1983) | 603 | 41 |

| City | Hgt. ft. | Stories |
|---|---|---|
| 780 3rd Ave. | 600 | 50 |
| Celanese Bldg. (1973) | 592 | 45 |
| U.S. Court House, 505 Pearl St. (1976). | 590 | 37 |
| Kalikow Hotel | 588 | 58 |
| Federal Bldg., Foley Square | 587 | 41 |
| Time & Life, 1271 Ave. of Am. (1959) | 587 | 47 |
| Cooper Bregstein Bldg., 1250 Bway. | 580 | 40 |
| Stevens Tower, 1185 Ave. of Am. | 580 | 42 |
| Municipal, Bldg. (1919) | 580 | 34 |
| 520 Madison Ave. (1983) | 577 | 42 |
| 1 Madison Square Plaza (1968) | 576 | 42 |
| World Financial Center Tower A (1986) | 575 | 42 |
| One Financial Sq. (1987) | 575 | 37 |
| Park Ave. Plaza (1981) | 575 | 44 |
| Westvaco Bldg. 299 Park Ave. | 574 | 42 |
| Marriott Marquis Hotel (1985) | 574 | 42 |
| Socony Mobil Bldg., East 42d St. | 572 | 45 |
| Sperry Rand Bldg., 1290 Ave. of Am. | 570 | 43 |
| 600 3d Ave. | 570 | 42 |
| Helmsley Bldg., 230 Park (1929) | 565 | 35 |
| 1 Bankers Trust Plaza | 565 | 40 |
| Hemsley Palace Hotel (1980) | 563 | 51 |
| 30 Broad St. | 562 | 48 |
| Park Ave Tower (1986) | 561 | 36 |
| Sherry-Netherland, 5th Ave. & 59th St. | 560 | 40 |
| Continental Can, 633 3d Ave. (1983) | 557 | 39 |
| Sperry & Hutchinson, 330 Madison | 555 | 39 |
| Continental Corp., 180 Maiden Lane | 555 | 41 |
| Galleria, 117 E. 57th St. (1975) | 552 | 57 |
| Interchem Bldg., 1133 Ave. of Am. | 552 | 45 |
| 151 E. 44th St. | 550 | 44 |
| N.Y. Telephone, 323 Bway. (1979) | 550 | 45 |
| 919 3d Ave. | 550 | 47 |
| Burroughs Bldg., 605 3d Ave. | 550 | 44 |
| Bankers Trust, 33 E. 48 St. (1963) | 547 | 41 |
| Transportation Bldg., 225 Bway. | 546 | 45 |
| Equitable, 120 Broadway (1915). | 545 | 42 |
| 1 Brooklyn Bridge Plaza (1976) | 540 | 42 |
| Paine Webber Bldg. (1961). | 540 | 42 |
| Ritz Tower, Park Ave. & 57th St. | 540 | 41 |
| Bankers Trust, 6 Wall St. | 540 | 39 |
| 1166 Ave. of Americas | 540 | 44 |
| 1700 Broadway | 533 | 41 |
| Downtown Athletic Club, 19 West St. | 530 | 45 |
| Nelson Towers, 7th Ave. & 34th St. | 525 | 45 |
| 767 3d Ave. | 525 | 39 |
| Hotel Pierre, 5th Ave. & 61st St. (1928). | 525 | 44 |
| House of Seagram (1958) | 525 | 38 |
| 7 World Trade Center (1985) | 525 | 44 |
| Random House, 825 3d Ave. | 522 | 40 |
| 3 Park Ave. | 522 | 42 |
| North American Plywood, 800 3d Ave. | 520 | 41 |
| Du Mont Bldg., 515 Madison Ave. | 520 | 42 |
| 26 Broadway | 520 | 31 |
| Newsweek Bldg., 444 Madison Ave. | 518 | 43 |
| Sterling Drug Bldg., 90 Park Ave. | 515 | 41 |
| First National City Bank. | 515 | 41 |
| Bank of New York, 48 Wall St. | 513 | 32 |
| Navarre, 512 7th Ave. | 513 | 43 |
| Manhattan Savings Bank, Bklyn. | 512 | 42 |
| ITT—American, 437 Madison Ave. | 512 | 40 |
| International, Rockefeller Ctr. | 512 | 41 |
| 1407 Broadway Realty Corp. | 512 | 44 |
| United Nations, 405 E. 42 St. (1953) | 505 | 39 |

### Oakland, Cal.

| City | Hgt. ft. | Stories |
|---|---|---|
| Ordway Bldg., 2150 Valdez St. | 404 | 28 |
| Kaiser Bldg. | 390 | 28 |
| Lake Merritt Plaza | 371 | 27 |
| Federal Bldg. (2 Bldgs.). | 368 | 19 |
| American President Lines (1990) | 360 | 29 |
| Raymond Kaiser Engineer Bldg. | 336 | 25 |
| Clorox Bldg. | 330 | 24 |

### Oklahoma City, Okla.

| City | Hgt. ft. | Stories |
|---|---|---|
| Liberty Tower (1971) | 500 | 36 |
| First National Center (1974) | 493 | 33 |
| City Place (1985) | 440 | 32 |
| First Oklahoma Tower (1982) | 425 | 31 |
| Kerr-McGee Center (1973). | 393 | 30 |
| Mid America Tower (1981) | 362 | 19 |

### Omaha, Neb.

| City | Hgt. ft. | Stories |
|---|---|---|
| Woodmen Tower (1969) | 469 | 30 |
| Northwestern Bell Telephone (1980) | 334 | 16 |
| Masonic Manor (1963) | 320 | 22 |
| First Natl. Center (1971) | 320 | 22 |

### Orlando, Fla.

| City | Hgt. ft. | Stories |
|---|---|---|
| Sun Bank Center Tower (1988) | 441 | 31 |
| DuPont Center Bldg. (1988) | 409 | 28 |

### Ottawa, Ont.

| City | Hgt. ft. | Stories |
|---|---|---|
| Place de Ville, Tower C. | 368 | 29 |
| R.H. Coats Bldg.. | 326 | 27 |

### Philadelphia, Pa.

| City | Hgt. ft. | Stories |
|---|---|---|
| One Liberty Place (1987). | 960 | 61 |
| Two Liberty Place (1989). | 845 | 52 |
| Mellon Bank Center (1989). | 795 | 54 |
| Bell Atlantic Tower (1991) | 739 | 53 |
| Blue Cross Tower (1990). | 700 | 50 |
| Commerce Sq., #1 (1990). | 572 | 40 |
| Commerce Sq., #2 (1992). | 572 | 40 |
| City Hall Tower, incl. 37-ft. statue of Wm. Penn. (1901) | 548 | 7 |
| 1818 Market St. (1974). | 500 | 40 |
| Provident Mutual Life (1983) | 491 | 40 |
| Meridan Bank (1972) | 492 | 38 |
| Phila. Saving Fund Society (1932). | 492 | 39 |
| Central Penn Natl. Bank (1970) | 490 | 36 |
| Centre Square (2 towers) (1973) | 490/416 | 38/32 |
| Industrial Valley Bank (1968). | 482 | 32 |
| Philadelphia National Bank (1930). | 475 | 25 |
| Two Mellon Plaza (1930). | 450 | 27 |
| 2000 Market St. (1973). | 435 | 29 |
| Two Logan Square (1987) | 435 | 34 |
| 2 Girard Plaza (1930) | 412 | 30 |
| Fidelity Bank Bldg. (1927) | 405 | 30 |
| Lewis Tower, 15th & Locust (1929) | 400 | 33 |
| One Logan Square (1982) | 400 | 32 |
| 1500 Locust St. (1973) | 390 | 44 |
| Philadelphia Electric Co. (1970). | 384 | 29 |
| Academy House, 1420 Locust St. | 377 | 37 |
| Penn Mutual Life (1931) | 375 | 20 |
| The Drake, 15th & Spruce (1928) | 375 | 33 |
| INA Annex | 369 | 27 |
| Medical Tower, 255 So. 17th (1931) | 364 | 33 |
| United Engineers, 17th & Ludlow (1976) | 344 | 22 |
| Inquirer Building (1924) | 340 | 18 |

### Phoenix, Ariz.

| City | Hgt. ft. | Stories |
|---|---|---|
| Valley National Bank (1972) | 483 | 40 |
| Arizona Bank Downtown(1976) | 407 | 31 |
| Phoenix Plaza (1990) | 397 | 25 |
| First Interstate Bank Plaza (1971). | 372 | 27 |
| Phoenix Center (1979) | 361 | 28 |
| Citibank Plaza (1980) | 356 | 27 |
| One Renaissance Sq. (1987) | 347 | 26 |
| Two Renaissance Sq. (1989) | 347 | 26 |
| Merabank Tower | 341 | 26 |

### Pittsburgh, Pa.

| City | Hgt. ft. | Stories |
|---|---|---|
| USX Towers | 841 | 64 |
| One Mellon Bank Center | 725 | 54 |
| One PPG Place | 635 | 40 |
| Fifth Avenue Place (1987) | 616 | 32 |
| One Oxford Centre | 615 | 46 |
| Gulf, 7th Ave. and Grant St. | 582 | 44 |
| University of Pittsburgh | 535 | 42 |
| Mellon Bank Bldg. | 520 | 41 |
| 1 Oliver Plaza | 511 | 39 |
| Grant, Grant St. at 3rd Ave. | 485 | 40 |
| Koppers, 7th Ave. and Grant | 475 | 34 |
| Equibank Bldg. | 445 | 34 |
| CNG Tower (1987) | 430 | 32 |
| Pittsburgh National Bldg. | 424 | 30 |
| Alcoa Bldg., 425 Sixth Ave.. | 410 | 30 |
| Liberty Tower | 358 | 29 |
| Westinghouse Bldg. | 355 | 23 |
| Oliver, 535 Smithfield St. | 347 | 25 |
| Gateway Bldg. No. 3 | 344 | 24 |
| Centre City Tower. | 341 | 26 |
| Federal Bldg., 1000 Liberty Ave.. | 340 | 23 |
| Bell Telephone, 416 7th Ave.. | 339 | 21 |
| Hilton Hotel. | 333 | 22 |
| Frick, 437 Grant St. | 330 | 20 |

### Portland, Ore.

| City | Hgt. ft. | Stories |
|---|---|---|
| First Interstate Tower | 546 | 41 |
| U.S. Bancorp Tower. | 536 | 39 |
| Koin Tower Plaza | 509 | 35 |
| Standard Insurance Center. | 367 | 27 |
| Pacwest Center | 356 | 31 |

### Providence, R.I.

| City | Hgt. ft. | Stories |
|---|---|---|
| Fleet National Bank | 420 | 26 |

| City | Hgt. ft. | Stories |
|---|---|---|
| Rhode Island Hospital Trust Tower | 410 | 30 |
| 40 Westminster Bldg. | 301 | 24 |

### Raleigh, N.C.

| City | Hgt. ft. | Stories |
|---|---|---|
| BB & T/2 Hanover Sq. (1991) | 431 | 29 |
| First Union Capitol Center (1991) | 390 | 29 |

### Richmond, Va.

| | Hgt. ft. | Stories |
|---|---|---|
| James Monroe Bldg. | 450 | 29 |
| City Hall (incl. penthouse) | 425 | 17 |
| Crestar Bank Hdqt. Bldg. | 400 | 24 |
| Federal Reserve Bank | 393 | 26 |
| Sovran Center | 333 | 25 |

### Rochester, N.Y.

| | Hgt. ft. | Stories |
|---|---|---|
| Xerox Tower (1967) | 443 | 30 |
| Lincoln First Tower (1973) | 392 | 27 |
| Eastman Kodak Bldg. (1914) | 340 | 19 |

### Sacramento, Cal.

| | Hgt. ft. | Stories |
|---|---|---|
| Wells Fargo Center | 405 | 30 |
| Park Plaza Tower | 373 | 26 |
| Renaissance Tower | 372 | 28 |

### St. Louis, Mo.

| | Hgt. ft. | Stories |
|---|---|---|
| Gateway Arch | 630 | ... |
| Metropolitan Square Tower | 591 | 42 |
| S.W. Bell Telephone Bldg. | 587 | 44 |
| Mercantile Center Tower | 550 | 37 |
| Centerre Plaza | 433 | 31 |
| Laclede Gas. Bldg., 8th & Olive | 400 | 31 |
| S.W. Bell Telephone Bldg. | 398 | 31 |
| Civil Courts | 387 | 13 |

### St. Paul, Minn.

| | Hgt. ft. | Stories |
|---|---|---|
| First Natl. Bank Bldg., incl. 100-ft. sign. | 517 | 32 |
| Minn. World Trade Center | 471 | 36 |
| Galtier Plaza's Jackson Tower. | 440 | 46 |
| Osborn Bldg., 320 Wabasha | 368 | 20 |
| Kellogg Square Apts. | 366 | 32 |
| Northwestern Bell Telephone (2 bldgs.). | 340 | 16 |
| Pointe of St. Paul | 340 | 34 |
| American National Bank Bldg. | 335 | 25 |
| North Central Tower, 445 Minn. | 328 | 27 |
| Amhoist/Park Tower | 324 | 26 |

### Salt Lake City, Ut.

| | Hgt. ft. | Stories |
|---|---|---|
| L.D.S. Church Office Bldg. | 420 | 30 |
| Beneficial Life Tower | 351 | 21 |
| Utah One Center (1992) | 350 | 24 |

### San Antonio, Tex.

| | Hgt. ft. | Stories |
|---|---|---|
| Tower of the Americas (1968) | 622 | ... |
| Marriott Rivercenter (1988). | 546 | 38 |
| NBC Bank (1988) | 444 | 32 |
| Tower Life (1929) | 404 | 30 |
| NCNB Plaza (1983) | 387 | 28 |
| Nix Professional Bldg. (1931) | 375 | 23 |

### San Diego, Cal.

| | Hgt. ft. | Stories |
|---|---|---|
| One American Plaza (1991) | 500 | 34 |
| Symphony Tower (1989) | 499 | 34 |
| Hyatt Regency San Diego (1992) | 495 | 39 |
| Emerald-Shapery Center (1991). | 450 | 30 |
| One Harbor Drive (1992) | 424 | 41 |
| First Interstate Bank (1985) | 398 | 23 |
| Meridian Condominiums (1985) | 395 | 27 |
| Union Bank (1969). | 388 | 27 |
| First National Bank (1982) | 379 | 27 |
| Imperial Bank | 355 | 24 |
| Executive Complex (1963) | 350 | 25 |
| Wells Fargo Bldg. (1982) | 348 | 20 |
| Great American Bldg. (1974). | 333 | 24 |

### San Francisco, Cal.

| | Hgt. ft. | Stories |
|---|---|---|
| Transamerica Pyramid (1972) | 853 | 48 |
| Bank of America (1969) | 778 | 52 |
| 101 California St. (1986) | 600 | 48 |
| 5 Fremont Center (1983) | 600 | 43 |
| Embarcadero Center, No. 4 (1982) | 570 | 45 |
| Security Pacific Bank | 569 | 45 |
| One Market Plaza, Spear St. (1976) | 565 | 43 |
| Wells Fargo Bldg. | 561 | 43 |
| Standard Oil, 575 Market St. (1975) | 551 | 39 |
| One Sansome-Citicorp | 550 | 39 |
| Shaklee Bldg., 444 Market | 537 | 38 |
| Aetna Life | 529 | 38 |

| City | Hgt. ft. | Stories |
|---|---|---|
| First & Market Bldg. (1973). | 529 | 38 |
| Metropolitan Life (1973) | 524 | 38 |
| Crocker National Bank | 500 | 38 |
| Hilton Hotel. | 493 | 46 |
| Pacific Gas & Electric (1970). | 492 | 34 |
| Union Bank (1972). | 487 | 37 |
| Pacific Insurance (1972) | 476 | 34 |
| Bechtel Bldg., Fremont St. (1977) | 475 | 33 |
| 333 Market Bldg. (1979) | 474 | 33 |
| Hartford Bldg. (1965) | 465 | 33 |
| Mutual Benefit Life (1969) | 438 | 32 |
| Russ Bldg. (1928) | 435 | 31 |
| Pacific Telephone Bldg. (1925) | 435 | 26 |
| Pacific Gateway (1983) | 416 | 30 |
| Embarcadero Center, No. 3 (1976) | 412 | 31 |
| Embarcadero Center, No. 2 (1974) | 412 | 31 |
| 595 Market Bldg. (1979) | 410 | 31 |
| 101 Montgomery St. | 405 | 28 |
| Cal. State Automobile Assn. (1974) | 399 | 29 |
| Alcoa Bldg. | 398 | 27 |
| St. Francis Hotel (1970) | 395 | 32 |
| Shell Bldg. (1928) | 386 | 29 |
| Del Monte | 378 | 28 |
| Meridien Hotel (1984). | 374 | 34 |

### Seattle, Wash.

| | Hgt. ft. | Stories |
|---|---|---|
| Columbia Seafirst Center (1985) | 954 | 76 |
| Two Union Square (1989) | 740 | 56 |
| Washington Mutual Tower (1988) | 730 | 55 |
| AT&T Gateway Tower (1990) | 722 | 62 |
| 1001 4th Pl. (1969) | 609 | 50 |
| Space Needle (1962) | 605 | ... |
| Pacific First Center (1989) | 580 | 44 |
| First Interstate Center (1983) | 574 | 48 |
| Seafirst 5th Ave. Plaza (1981) | 543 | 42 |
| Security Pacific Bank Tower (1977) | 514 | 42 |
| Smith Tower (1914) | 500 | 42 |
| 520 Pike Tower (1984) | 498 | 29 |
| Key Tower (1986) | 493 | 40 |
| Federal Office Bldg. | 487 | 37 |
| US West Communications | 466 | 33 |
| One Union Square (1981) | 456 | 38 |
| 1111 3d Ave. Bldg. (1980) | 454 | 35 |
| Westin Bldg., 2001 6th Ave. (1981) | 409 | 34 |
| Westin Hotel | 397 | 40 |
| Unigard Financial Center (1973) | 389 | 27 |
| Century Square (1986) | 379 | 30 |
| Sheraton Seattle Hotel | 371 | 34 |

### Tampa, Fla.

| | Hgt. ft. | Stories |
|---|---|---|
| 100 N. Tampa (1992) | 579 | 42 |
| Barnett Plaza (1986) | 577 | 42 |
| Tampa City Center (1981) | 537 | 39 |
| Landmark Centre (1992) | 525 | 36 |
| First Financial Tower (1973) | 458 | 36 |
| NCNB Plaza (1988) | 454 | 33 |

### Toledo, Oh.

| | Hgt. ft. | Stories |
|---|---|---|
| Owens-Illinois Corp. Headquarters | 411 | 32 |
| Owens-Corning Fiberglas Tower | 400 | 30 |
| Ohio Citizens Bank Bldg. | 368 | 27 |
| Toledo Govt. Center. | 327 | 22 |

### Toronto, Ont.

| | Hgt. ft. | Stories |
|---|---|---|
| CN Tower, World's tallest self-supporting structure (1975) | 1,821 | ... |
| First Canadian Place (1979) | 952 | 72 |
| Bay/Adelaide Project (1991). | 951 | 57 |
| Scotia Plaza (1988) | 902 | 68 |
| Canada Trust Tower (1990) | 869 | 52 |
| Bay-Wellington Tower (1990) | 705 | 47 |
| Commerce Court West (1972). | 784 | 57 |
| Toronto-Dominion Tower (TD Centre) (1967) | 758 | 56 |
| Royal Trust Tower (TD Centre) (1969) | 600 | 46 |
| Royal Bank Plaza—South Tower (1977) | 589 | 41 |
| Manulife Centre (1975) | 545 | 53 |
| IBM Tower (TD Centre) (1986). | 520 | 36 |
| Two Bloor West (1974) | 488 | 34 |
| Exchange Tower (1981) | 480 | 36 |
| Commerce Court North (1930) | 476 | 34 |
| Simpson Tower (1968) | 473 | 33 |
| Eaton Tower (1990) | 471 | 34 |
| Cadillac-Fairview Tower (1982) | 466 | 36 |
| Palace Point (1991) | 455 | 46 |
| Palace Pier (1978). | 453 | 46 |
| Continental Bank Bldg. (1980) | 450 | 35 |
| Sheraton Centre (1972) | 443 | 43 |
| Hudson's Bay Centre (1974). | 442 | 35 |

| City | Hgt. ft. | Stories |
|---|---|---|
| Royal York Hotel (1929) | 439 | 26 |
| Ernst & Yonge Tower (1990) | 438 | 31 |
| Old Toronto Exchange Bldg. (1990) | 436 | 31 |
| Leaside Towers (2 bldgs.) (1970) | 423 | 44 |
| Metro Hall (1991) | 420 | 27 |
| Commercial Union Tower (1974) | 420 | 32 |
| Maple Leaf Mills Tower | 419 | 30 |
| Plaza 2 Hotel | 415 | 41 |
| Sun Life Bldg. (1981) | 410 | 28 |

### Tulsa, Okla.

| City | Hgt. ft. | Stories |
|---|---|---|
| Bank of Oklahoma Tower | 667 | 52 |
| City of Faith Clinic Tower | 640 | 60 |
| 1st National Tower | 516 | 41 |
| Mid-Continent Tower | 513 | 36 |
| 4th Natl. Bank of Tulsa | 412 | 33 |
| 320 South Boston Bldg. | 400 | 24 |
| Occidental Place | 388 | 28 |
| Univ. Club Tower | 377 | 32 |
| City of Faith Hospital | 348 | 30 |
| Philtower | 343 | 24 |

### Vancouver, B.C.

| City | Hgt. ft. | Stories |
|---|---|---|
| Royal Centre Tower (1973) | 460 | 36 |
| Canada Trust Tower, 1055 Melville | 454 | 35 |
| Scotiabank Tower | 451 | 36 |
| Bentall IV (1981) | 450 | 35 |
| Vancouver Center (1977) | 450 | 36 |
| Park Place (1984) | 450 | 35 |
| T-D Bank Tower (1978) | 440 | 30 |
| 200 Granville Square (1973) | 438 | 28 |
| Harbour Centre (1977) | 428 | 21 |
| Bentall III (1974) | 399 | 31 |

### Winnipeg, Man.

| City | Hgt. ft. | Stories |
|---|---|---|
| Toronto Dominion Center (1989) | 407 | 31 |
| Richardson Bldg. (1969) | 390 | 32 |
| Commodity Exchange Tower (1980) | 384 | 31 |

### Winston-Salem, N.C.

| City | Hgt. ft. | Stories |
|---|---|---|
| Wachovia Bldg. (1965) | 410 | 30 |
| One Triad Park (1987) | 340 | 20 |
| Reynolds Bldg. (1929) | 315 | 21 |

## Other Notable Tall Buildings in U.S.

Cape Canaveral, Fla., Vehicle Assembly Bldg., 40 (552); Amarillo, Tex., American Natl. Bank, 33 (374); Atlantic City, N.J., Taj Mahal, 51 (429); Charleston, W. Va., Kanawha Valley Bldg., 20 (384); Galveston, Tex., American National Ins., 20 (358); Hamilton, Ont., Century Twenty One, 43 (418); Harrisburg, PA., State Office Tower #2, 21 (334); Knoxville, Tenn., United American Bank, 30 (400); Lincoln, Neb., State Capitol (432); Mobile, Ala., First Natl. Bank, 33 (420); Niagara Falls, Ont., Skylon, (520); Shreveport La., Commercial National Tower, 24 (365); Springfield, Mass., Valley Bank Tower, 29 (370); Tallahassee, Fla., State Capitol Tower, 22 (345).

## Some Notable Foreign Structures

| Structure | Hgt. ft. | Stories |
|---|---|---|
| Central Plaza, Hong Kong (1992) | 1,028 | 78 |
| Bank of China, Hong Kong (1989) | 1,001 | 70 |
| Eiffel Tower, Paris (1889) | 984 | - |
| Landmark Tower, Yokohama (1993) | 971 | 70 |
| Overseas Union Bank, Singapore (1984) | 919 | 63 |
| MesseTurm. Bldg, Frankfurt (1990) | 841 | 70 |
| One Canada Sq, London (1991) | 800 | 59 |
| Tokyo City Hall (1992) | 797 | 59 |
| Metropolitan Tower, Tokyo (1992) | 796 | 50 |
| Rialto Tower, Melbourne (1985) | 794 | 60 |
| Palace of Science & Culture, Warsaw | 790 | 42 |
| Moscow State Univ (incl. spire) | 787 | 39 |
| Treasury Bldg., Singapore (1986) | 770 | 52 |
| Seoul Tower, S. Korea (1988) | 764 | 63 |
| Maine Montparnasse, Paris (1973) | 751 | 64 |
| MLC Center, Sydney (1977) | 748 | 60 |
| Governor Philip Tower, Sydney (1993) | 745 | 54 |

| Structure | Hgt. ft. | Stories |
|---|---|---|
| Raffles City Hotel, Singapore (1986) | 742 | 73 |
| Ikebukuro Office Tower, Tokyo (1978) | 742 | 60 |
| Bourke Place, Melbourne (1991) | 735 | 48 |
| Central Park, Perth (1992) | 733 | 51 |
| Carlton Centre, Johannesburg (1973) | 722 | 50 |
| Shinjuku Center, Tokyo (1979) | 709 | 55 |
| Shinjuku Mitsui, Tokyo | 696 | 55 |
| Shinjuku Nomura, Tokyo | 666 | 53 |
| Overseas-Chinese Banking Corp., Singapore | 660 | 52 |
| Shinjuku Sumitomo, Tokyo | 656 | 52 |
| Parque Central Torre Oficinas, Caracas | 656 | 56 |
| Ukraine Hotel, Moscow | 650 | 60 |
| Natwest Tower, London | 600 | 50 |
| Tour Elf Aquitaine, Paris | 578 | 48 |
| Ulm Cathedral, Germany | 530 | - |
| Cologne Cathedral, Germany | 515 | - |
| Tour du Cite Administrative, Brussels | 492 | 36 |

## Notable Bridges in North America

Source: Survey of State Highway Engineers (1993)

Asterisk (*) designates railroad bridge. Span of a bridge is distance (in feet) between its supports.

### Suspension

| Year | Bridge | Location | Longest span |
|---|---|---|---|
| 1964 | Verrazano-Narrows | New York, N.Y. | 4,260 |
| 1937 | Golden Gate | San Fran. Bay, Cal. | 4,200 |
| 1957 | Mackinac | Sts. of Mackinac | 3,800 |
| 1931 | Geo. Washington | Hudson R., N.Y.- N.J. | 3,500 |
| 1950 | Tacoma Narrows | Washington | 2,800 |
| 1936 | [1]Transbay | San Fran. Bay, Cal. | 2,310 |
| 1939 | Bronx-Whitestone | East R., N.Y.C. | 2,300 |
| 1970 | Pierre Laporte | Quebec | 2,190 |
| 1951 | Del. Memorial | Wilmington, Del. | 2,150 |
| 1968 | Del. Mem. (new) | Wilmington, Del. | 2,150 |
| 1957 | Walt Whitman | Phila., Pa. | 2,000 |
| 1929 | Ambassador | Detroit-Canada | 1,850 |
| 1961 | Throgs Neck | Long Is. Sound, N.Y. | 1,800 |
| 1926 | Benjamin Franklin | Philadelphia, Pa. | 1,750 |
| 1924 | Bear Mt., N.Y. | Hudson R. | 1,632 |
| 1952 | [2]Wm. Preston Lane Mem. | Sandy Point, Md. | 1,600 |
| 1903 | Williamsburg | East R., N.Y.C. | 1,600 |
| 1969 | Newport | Narragansett Bay, R.I. | 1,600 |
| 1883 | Brooklyn | East R., N.Y.C. | 1,595 |
| 1939 | Lion's Gate | Burrard Inlet, B.C. | 1,550 |
| 1930 | Mid-Hudson | Poughkeepsie, N.Y. | 1,500 |

| Year | Bridge | Location | Longest span |
|---|---|---|---|
| 1964 | Vincent Thomas | Los Angeles Harbor | 1,500 |
| 1909 | Manhattan | East R., N.Y.C. | 1,470 |
| 1936 | Triboro | East R., N.Y.C. | 1,380 |
| 1931 | St. Johns | Portland, Ore. | 1,207 |
| 1929 | Mount Hope | Rhode Island | 1,200 |
| 1960 | Ogdensburg, N.Y. | St. Lawrence R. | 1,150 |
| 1939 | Deer Isle | Maine | 1,080 |
| 1931 | Maysville (Ky.) | Ohio R. | 1,060 |
| 1867 | Cincinnati | Ohio R. | 1,057 |
| 1971 | Dent | Clearwater Co., Ida. | 1,050 |
| 1900 | Miampimi | Mexico | 1,030 |
| 1849 | Wheeling, W. Va. | Ohio R. | 1,010 |

### Cantilever

| Year | Bridge | Location | Longest span |
|---|---|---|---|
| 1917 | Quebec | Quebec | 1,800 |
| 1981 | Ravenswood | W. Va. | 1,723 |
| 1974 | Commodore Barry | Chester, Pa. | 1,622 |
| 1958 | Mississippi R. | New Orleans, La. | 1,575 |
| 1988 | Mississippi R. | New Orleans, La | 1,575 |
| 1936 | Transbay | San Fran. Bay | 1,400 |
| 1968 | W. 17th St. | Huntington, W. Va. | 1,312 |
| 1968 | Mississippi R. | Baton Rouge, La. | 1,235 |
| 1955 | Tappan Zee | Hudson R. | 1,212 |
| 1930 | Lewis and Clark | Longview, Wash. | 1,200 |

| Year | Bridge | Location | Longest span |
|---|---|---|---|
| 1909 | Queensboro | East R., N.Y.C. | 1,182 |
| 1927 | Carquinez Strait | California | 1,100 |
| 1958 | Parallel Span | " | 1,100 |
| 1930 | Jacques Cartier | Montreal, Can. | 1,097 |
| 1968 | Isaiah D. Hart | Jacksonville, Fla. | 1,088 |
| 1957 | [3]Richmond | San Fran. Bay, Cal. | 1,070 |
| 1929 | Grace Memorial | Charleston, S.C. | 1,050 |
| 1980 | Newburgh-Beacon | Hudson R., N.Y. | 1,000 |
| 1963 | Newburgh-Beacon | Hudson R., N.Y. | 1,000 |
| 1949 | Martin Luther King | St. Louis, Mo. | 962 |
| 1982 | Yeager | Charleston, W. Va. | 947 |
| 1975 | Caruthersville, Mo. | Mississippi R. | 920 |
| 1977 | Saint Marys | Saint Marys, W. Va. | 900 |
| 1969 | Silver Memorial | Pt. Pleasant, W. Va. | 900 |
| 1987 | Carl Perkins | Ohio R., Ky. | 900 |
| 1986 | Mississippi R. | Natchez, Miss. | 875 |
| 1940 | Mississippi R. | Natchez, Miss. | 875 |
| 1938 | Blue Water | Pt. Huron, Mich. | 871 |
| 1972 | Mississippi R. | Vicksburg, Miss | 870 |
| 1972 | N. Fork American R. | Auburn, Cal. | 862 |
| 1940 | *Baton Rouge | Mississippi R. | 848 |
| 1899 | *Cornwall | St. Lawrence R. | 843 |
| 1940 | Mississippi R. | Greenville, Miss. | 840 |
| 1961 | Helena, Ark. | Mississippi R. | 840 |
| 1963 | Brent Spence | Covington, Ky. | 831 |
| 1963 | Cincinnati | Ohio R. | 830 |
| 1963 | Mississippi R. | Donaldsonville, La. | 825 |
| 1940 | Mississippi R. | Vicksburg, Miss. | 825 |
| 1929 | Louisville | Ohio R. | 820 |
| 1961 | Campbellton-Cross Point | New Brunswick-Quebec. | 815 |
| 1950 | Maurice J. Tobin | Boston, Mass. | 800 |
| 1935 | Rip Van Winkle | Catskill, N.Y. | 800 |
| 1938 | Cairo | Ohio R., Ill.-Ky. | 800 |
| 1932 | Washington Mem. | Seattle, Wash. | 800 |
| 1936 | McCullough | Coos Bay, Ore. | 793 |
| 1935 | [4]Huey P Long | New Orleans | 790 |
| 1916 | *Memphis (Harahan) | Mississippi R. | 790 |
| 1892 | *Memphis | Mississippi R. | 790 |
| 1949 | Memphis-Arkansas | Mississippi R. | 790 |
| 1904 | *Mingo Jct., W. Va. | Ohio R. | 769 |
| 1910 | *Beaver, Pa. | Ohio R. | 767 |
| 1941 | Columbia R. | Kettle Falls, Wash. | 600 |
| 1954 | Columbia R. | Umatilla, Ore. | 600 |
| 1954 | Columbia R. | The Dalles, Ore. | 573 |

## Simple Truss

| Year | Bridge | Location | Longest span |
|---|---|---|---|
| 1976 | Chester | Chester, W. Va. | 745 |
| 1917 | *Metropolis | Ohio R. | 720 |
| 1929 | Irvin S. Cobb | Ohio R.-Ill.-Ky. | 716 |
| 1922 | *Tanana R. | Nenana, Alaska | 700 |
| 1933 | *Henderson | Ohio R.-Ind.-Ky. | 665 |
| 1967 | I-77, Ohio R. | Williamstown, W. Va. | 650 |
| 1917 | 4 MacArthur, Ill.-Mo. | St. Louis | 647 |
| 1919 | Louisville | Ohio R. | 644 |
| 1989 | St. Charles | Missouri R. | 625 |
| 1933 | Atchafalaya | Morgan City, La. | 608 |
| 1924 | *Castleton | Hudson R. | 598 |
| 1937 | Delaware R. | Easton, Pa. | 550 |
| 1930 | Swindell Bridge | Pittsburgh, Pa. | 545 |
| 1889 | *Cincinnati | Ohio R. | 542 |
| 1952 | Allegheny R., Tpk. | Pittsburgh, Pa. | 534 |
| 1930 | *Martinez | California | 528 |
| 1951 | Rankin | Pittsburgh, Pa. | 525 |
| 1914 | Old Brownsville | Brownsville, Pa. | 520 |
| 1906 | Donora-Webster | Donora-Webster, Pa. | 515 |
| 1909 | Hulton | Pittsburgh, Pa. | 505 |
| 1967 | Tanana R. | Alaska | 500 |

## Steel Truss

| Year | Bridge | Location | Longest span |
|---|---|---|---|
| 1988 | Glade Creek | Raleigh Co., W.Va. | 784 |
| 1973 | Atchafalaya R. | Krotz Springs, La. | 780 |
| 1972 | Piscataqua R. | N.H., Me. | 756 |
| 1972 | Atchafalaya R. | Simmesport, La. | 720 |
| 1957 | SR-3, Rappahannock R. | Middlesex Co., Va. | 648 |
| 1940 | Jamestown | Jamestown, R.I. | 640 |
| 1949 | Memphis | Mississippi R., Ark. | 621 |
| 1978 | Atchafalaya R. | Morgan City, La. | 607 |
| 1938 | US-22 | Delaware R., N.J. | 540 |
| 1955 | Interstate (I-5) | Columbia R., Ore.-Wash. | 531 |
| 1910 | [4]McKinley, St. Louis | Mississippi R. | 517 |
| 1972 | Mississippi R. | Muscatine, Ia. | 512 |
| 1896 | Newport | Ohio R., Ky. | 511 |
| 1970 | Lake Koocanusa | Lincoln Co., Mon. | 500 |
| 1931 | US-60 | Cumberland R., Ky. | 500 |
| 1958 | Lake Oahe | Mobridge, S.D. | 500 |

| Year | Bridge | Location | Longest span |
|---|---|---|---|
| 1958 | Lake Oahe | Gettysburg, S.D. | 500 |

## Continuous Truss

| Year | Bridge | Location | Longest span |
|---|---|---|---|
| 1966 | Columbia R. (Astoria) | Ore.-Wash. | 1,232 |
| 1977 | Francis Scott Key | Baltimore, Md. | 1,200 |
| 1943 | Dubuque, Ia. | Mississippi R. | 845 |
| 1956 | [7]Earl C. Clements | Ohio R., Ill-Ky. | 825 |
| 1953 | John E. Mathews | Jacksonville, Fla. | 810 |
| 1940 | Gov. Nice Mem. | Potomac River, Md. | 800 |
| 1957 | Kingston-Rhinecliff | Hudson R., N.Y. | 800 |
| 1986 | Rochester-Monaca | Rochester-Monaca, Pa. | 780 |
| 1918 | *Sciotoville | Ohio R. | 775 |
| 1976 | I-275, Lawrenceburg | Ohio R., Ind.-Ky. | 750 |
| 1981 | Sewickley | Sewickley, Pa. | 750 |
| 1984 | 13th St. Bridge, Ohio R. | Ashland, Ky. | 740 |
| 1959 | Monaca-E. Rochester | Monaca-East Rochester, Pa. | 730 |
| 1976 | Betsy Ross | Philadelphia, Pa. | 729 |
| 1929 | Madison-Milton | Ohio R., Ind.-Ky. | 727 |
| 1966 | [5]Matthew E. Welsh | Mauckport, Ind. | 725 |
| 1977 | I-275, Brent | Ohio R. | 720 |
| 1970 | Vanport | Vanport, Pa. | 715 |
| 1962 | Champlain | Montreal, P.Q. | 707 |
| 1973 | Girard Point | Philadelphia, Pa. | 700 |
| 1954 | Pa. Tpk., Delaware R. | Philadelphia, Pa. | 682 |
| 1949 | George Platt. | Philadelphia, Pa. | 680 |
| 1938 | Port Arthur-Orange. | Tex. | 680 |
| 1929 | *Cincinnati | Ohio R. | 675 |
| 1928 | Cape Girardeau, Mo. | Mississippi R. | 672 |
| 1946 | Chester, Ill. | Mississippi R. | 670 |
| 1970 | Gulfgate | Port Arthur, Tex. | 664 |
| 1953 | Jefferson City | Missouri R. | 640 |
| 1930 | Quincy, Ill. | Mississippi R. | 628 |
| 1961 | Shippingport | Shippingport, Pa. | 620 |
| 1959 | US 181, over harbor | Corpus Christi, Tex. | 620 |
| 1934 | Bourne | Cape Cod Canal | 616 |
| 1935 | Sagamore | Cape Cod Canal | 616 |
| 1965 | Clarion R. (I-80) | Clarion, Pa. | 612 |
| 1975 | Donora-Monesson | Donora-Monesson, Pa. | 608 |
| 1957 | Blatnik | Duluth, Minn. | 600 |
| 1965 | Rio Grande Gorge | Taos, N.M. | 600 |
| 1987 | Jefferson City | Missouri R. | 596 |
| 1962 | W. Br. Feather R. | Oroville, Cal. | 576 |
| 1967 | Glenwood | Pittsburgh, Pa. | 567 |
| 1936 | Meredosia | Illinois R. | 567 |
| 1936 | Mark Twain Mem. | Hannibal, Mo. | 562 |
| 1957 | Mackinac | Mackinac Straits, Mich. | 560 |

## Continuous Box and Plate Girder

| Year | Bridge | Location | Longest span |
|---|---|---|---|
| 1988 | Piney Creek-US19 | Beckley, W. Va. | 1,760 |
| 1973 | Danville-US119 | Danville, W. Va. | 1,545 |
| 1983 | Mississippi R. | Luling, La. | 1,222 |
| 1974 | Dunbar-S. Charleston | S. Charleston, W. Va. | 842 |
| 1988 | Beaver Creek-I-64 | Beckley, W. Va. | 764 |
| 1982 | Houston Ship Chan. | Houston, Tex. | 750 |
| 1967 | San Mateo-Hayward No. 2 | San Fran. Bay, Cal. | 750 |
| 1977 | Intracoastal Canal | Gibbstown, La. | 750 |
| 1976 | Intracoastal Canal | Forked Is., La. | 750 |
| 1969 | [6]San Diego-Coronado | San Diego Bay, Cal. | 660 |
| 1987 | Columbia R. | Umatilla, Ore. | 660 |
| 1981 | Douglas | Juneau, Alaska | 620 |
| 1976 | Wax L. Outlet | Calumet, La. | 618 |
| 1975 | S. Charleston-I-64 | S. Charleston, W. Va. | 612 |
| 1981 | Glenn Jackson (I-205) | Columbia R., Ore.-Wash. | 600 |
| 1967 | Poplar St. | St. Louis, Mo. | 600 |
| 1982 | Illinois R. | Pekin, Ill. | 550 |
| 1982 | I-440 | Arkansas R. | 540 |
| 1977 | US-64, Tennessee R. | Savannah, Tenn. | 525 |
| 1988 | Mon City | Monongahela, Pa. | 520 |
| 1965 | McDonald-Cartier | Ottawa, Ont. | 520 |
| 1984 | Columbia R. | Richland, Wash. | 450 |
| 1986 | Veterans | Pittsburgh, Pa. | 440 |
| 1986 | SR 76, Cumberland R. | Dover, Tenn. | 440 |
| 1985 | SR 20, Tennessee R. | Perryville, Tenn. | 440 |
| 1970 | Willamette R., I-205. | West Linn, Ore. | 430 |
| 1974 | I-430 | Arkansas R. | 430 |
| 1985 | FAU 3456, Tenn. R. | Chattanooga, Tenn. | 420 |
| 1967 | I-24, Tennessee R. | Marion Co., Tenn. | 420 |
| 1978 | Snake R. | Clarkston, Wash. | 420 |
| 1975 | 36th St. | Charleston, W.Va. | 420 |

## Continuous Plate

| Year | Bridge | Location | Longest span |
|---|---|---|---|
| 1973 | Ship Channel (I-610) | Houston, Tex. | 630 |
| 1971 | W. Atchafalaya | Henderson, La. | 573 |

| Year | Bridge | Location | Longest span |
|------|--------|----------|------|
| 1981 | Illinois 23 | Illinois R., Ill. | 510 |
| 1968 | Trinity R. | Dallas, Tex. | 480 |
| 1978 | San Joaquin R. | Antioch, Cal. | 460 |
| 1977 | Thomas Johnson Mem. | Solomons, Md. | 451 |
| 1975 | Lewis | St. Louis, Mo. | 450 |
| 1975 | I-129 | Missouri R., Ia. | 450 |
| 1967 | Mississippi R. | LaCrescent, Minn. | 450 |
| 1972 | Whiskey Bay Pilot Channel | Ramah, La. | 425 |
| 1966 | I-480 | Missouri R., Ia.-Neb. | 425 |
| 1970 | I-435 | Missouri R., Mo. | 425 |
| 1972 | I-80 | Missouri R., Ia.-Neb. | 425 |
| 1985 | I-435 | Missouri R., Ks.-Mo. | 425 |
| 1984 | US-36 | Missouri R., Ks.-Mo. | 425 |
| 1972 | I-635, Kansas City | Missouri R., Ks.-Mo. | 425 |
| 1978 | I-24 | Cumberland R., Ky. | 420 |

### Cable-Stayed

| Year | Bridge | Location | Longest span |
|------|--------|----------|------|
| 1987 | Sunshine Skyway | Tampa Bay, Fla. | 1,200 |
| 1991 | Talmadge Mem. | Savannah, Ga. | 1,100 |
| 1979 | Intercity | Pasco-Kennewick, Wash. | 970 |
| 1985 | E. Huntington | Huntington, W. Va. | 900 |
| 1985 | Mississippi R. | Quincy, Ill. | 900 |
| 1980 | Veterans Mem'l | W. Va.-Oh. | 820 |
| 1991 | Neches R. | Port Arthur - Orange, Tex. | 640 |
| 1990 | James R. | Henrico Co., Va. | 630 |
| 1972 | Sitka Harbor. | Sitka, Alaska | 450 |

### I-Beam Girder

| Year | Bridge | Location | Longest span |
|------|--------|----------|------|
| 1980 | Shreveport Int. | Louisiana | 438 |
| 1948 | US-27 | Licking R., Ky. | 316 |
| 1947 | US-31E | Green R., Ky. | 316 |
| 1941 | US-62 | Rolling Fork, Ky. | 240 |
| 1942 | Licking R. | Owingsville, Ky. | 240 |
| 1954 | Fuller Warren | Jacksonville, Fla. | 224 |

### Steel Arch

| Year | Bridge | Location | Longest span |
|------|--------|----------|------|
| 1977 | New R. Gorge. | Fayetteville, W. Va. | 1,700 |
| 1931 | Bayonne, N.J. | Kill Van Kull | 1,652 |
| 1973 | Fremont | Portland, Ore. | 1,255 |
| 1964 | Port Mann | British Columbia. | 1,200 |
| 1916 | *Hell Gate | East R., N.Y.C. | 1,038 |
| 1959 | Glen Canyon | Colorado R. | 1,028 |
| 1967 | Trois-Rivieres | St. Lawrence R., P.Q. | 1,100 |
| 1990 | Roosevelt Lake | Arizona. | 1,080 |
| 1962 | Lewiston-Queenston | Niagara R., Ont. | 1,000 |
| 1976 | Perrine | Twin Falls, Ida. | 993 |
| 1941 | Rainbow | Niagara Falls | 984 |
| 1986 | Moundsville | Ohio R., W. Va. | 912 |
| 1984 | I-255 | Mississippi R., Mo. | 909 |
| 1972 | [9]I-40, Mississippi R. | Memphis, Tenn. | 900 |
| 1970 | Lake Quinsigamond | Worcester, Mass. | 849 |
| 1966 | Charles Braga. | Somerset, Mass. | 840 |
| 1936 | Henry Hudson | Harlem R., N.Y.C. | 840 |
| 1967 | Lincoln Trail | Ohio R., Ind.-Ky. | 825 |
| 1978 | I-57, Cairo, Ill. | Mississippi R. | 821 |
| 1980 | I-65 Mobile R. | Mobile, Ala. | 800 |
| 1961 | Sherman Minton | Louisville, Ky. | 800 |
| 1936 | French King | Conn. R. (Rt. 2, Mass.) | 782 |
| 1978 | I-470 Bridge, Ohio R. | Wheeling, W. Va. | 760 |
| 1930 | West End | Pittsburgh, Pa. | 780 |

### Concrete Arch

| Year | Bridge | Location | Longest span |
|------|--------|----------|------|
| 1971 | Selah Creek (twin) | Selah, Wash. | 549 |
| 1968 | Cowlitz R. | Mossyrock, Wash. | 520 |
| 1931 | Westinghouse | Pittsburgh, Pa. | 460 |
| 1923 | Cappelen | Minneapolis, Minn. | 435 |

### Twin Concrete Trestle

| Year | Bridge | Location | Longest span |
|------|--------|----------|------|
| 1979 | I-55/I-10 | Manchae, La. | 181,157 |
| 1969 | L. Pontchartrain Cswy. | Mandeville, La. | 126,720 |

| Year | Bridge | Location | Longest span |
|------|--------|----------|------|
| 1972 | Atchafalaya Flwy. | Baton Rouge, La. | 93,984 |
| 1963 | [6]L. Pontchartrain | Slidell, La. | 28,547 |

### Concrete Slab Dam

| Year | Bridge | Location | Longest span |
|------|--------|----------|------|
| 1927 | Conowingo Dam | Maryland. | 4,611 |
| 1952 | SR-4, Roanoke R. | Mecklenburg Co., Va. | 2,785 |
| 1936 | Hoover Dam. | Boulder City, Nev. | 1,324 |

## Drawbridges

### Vertical Lift

| Year | Bridge | Location | Longest span |
|------|--------|----------|------|
| 1959 | *Arthur Kill. | N.Y.-N.J. | 558 |
| 1965 | Pennsylvania Railroad | Kirkwood-Mt. Pleasant, Del. | 548 |
| 1935 | *Cape Cod Canal. | Massachusetts | 544 |
| 1960 | *Delair, N.J. | Delaware R. | 542 |
| 1937 | Marine Parkway | Jamaica Bay, N.Y.C. | 540 |
| 1931 | Burlington, N.J. | Delaware R. | 534 |
| 1908 | *Willamette R. | Portland, Ore. | 521 |
| 1968 | Second Narrows | Vancouver, B.C. | 493 |
| 1912 | *A-S-B Fratt. | Kansas City | 428 |
| 1945 | *Harry S. Truman. | Kansas City | 427 |
| 1955 | Roosevelt Island | East R., N.Y.C. | 418 |
| 1980 | US-17, James R. | Isle of Wight, Co., Va. | 415 |
| 1932 | *M-K-T R.R. | Missouri R. | 414 |
| 1969 | Cape Fear Mem. | Wilmington, N.C. | 408 |
| 1930 | Aerial. | Duluth, Minn. | 386 |
| 1941 | Main St. | Jacksonville, Fla. | 386 |
| 1962 | Burlington | Ontario. | 370 |
| 1941 | Acosta | St. Johns R., Fla. | 365 |
| 1922 | *Cincinnati. | Ohio R. | 365 |
| 1967 | SR-156, James R. | Prince George Co., Va. | 364 |
| 1964 | Red R. | Alexandria, La. | 360 |
| 1957 | Industrial Canal | New Orleans, La. | 360 |
| 1950 | Red R. | Moncla, La. | 360 |
| 1936 | Tribo | Harlem R., N.Y.C. | 344 |
| 1961 | *Corpus Christi Harbor. | Corpus Christi, Tex. | 344 |
| 1939 | U.S. 1&9, Passaic R. | Newark, N.J. | 333 |
| 1929 | Carlton. | Bath-Woolwich, Me. | 328 |
| 1930 | *Martinez | California. | 328 |
| 1960 | St. Andrews Bay | Panama City, Fla. | 327 |
| 1929 | *Penn-Lehigh | Newark Bay | 322 |
| 1987 | Industrial Canal | New Orleans, La. | 320 |
| 1920 | *Chattanooga. | Tennessee R. | 310 |

### Bascule

| Year | Bridge | Location | Longest span |
|------|--------|----------|------|
| 1969 | E. Pearl R. | Slidell, La. | 482 |
| 1940 | Lorain, Oh. | Black R. | 330 |
| 1917 | SR-8, Tennessee R. | Chattanooga, Tenn. | 306 |
| 1956 | Duwamish R. | Seattle, Wash. | 300 |
| 1955 | Chehalis R. | Aberdeen, Wash. | 288 |
| 1968 | Elizabeth R. | Chesapeake, Va. | 280 |
| 1913 | Broadway | Portland, Ore. | 278 |

### Swing Bridges

| Year | Bridge | Location | Longest span |
|------|--------|----------|------|
| 1926 | [4]Fort Madison | Mississippi R. | 525 |
| 1991 | SW Spokane St. | Seattle, Wash. | 480 |
| 1930 | Rigolets Pass | New Orleans, La. | 400 |
| 1950 | Douglass Memorial | Wash. D.C. | 386 |
| 1945 | Lord Delaware | Mattaponi R., Va. | 252 |
| 1957 | Eltham | Pamunkey R., Va. | 237 |

### Swing Span

| Year | Bridge | Location | Longest span |
|------|--------|----------|------|
| 1903 | *East Omaha | Missouri R. | 519 |
| 1952 | US-17 | York R., Va. | 500 |
| 1897 | *Duluth, Minn. | St. Louis Bay | 486 |
| 1899 | *C.M.&N.R.R. | Chicago | 474 |
| 1913 | Rt. 82, Conn-R. | E. Haddam, Ct. | 465 |
| 1914 | *Coos Bay. | Oregon. | 458 |

### Floating Pontoon

| Year | Bridge | Location | Longest span |
|------|--------|----------|------|
| 1963 | Evergreen Pt. | Seattle, Wash. | 7,518 |
| 1961 | Hood Canal | Pt. Gamble, Wash. | 6,471 |
| 1989 | 3rd Lake Washington. | Seattle, Wash. | 6,130 |

(1) The Transbay Bridge has 2 spans of 2,310 ft. each. (2) A second bridge in parallel was completed in 1973. (3) The Richmond Bridge has twin spans 1,070 ft. each. (4) Railroad and vehicular bridge. (5) Two spans each 707 ft. (6) Two spans each 660 ft. (7) Two spans each 825 ft. (8) Total length of bridge. (9) Two spans each 900 ft.

## Notable International Bridges

**Angostura,** suspension type, span 2,336 feet, 1967 at Ciudad Bolivar, Venezuela. Total length, 5,507.

**Bendorf Bridge** on the Rhine River, 5 mi. n. of Coblenz, completed 1965, is a 3-span cement girder bridge, 3,378 ft. overall length, 101 ft. wide, with the main span 682 ft.

**Bosporus Bridge** linking Europe and Asia opened at Istanbul in 1973, at 3,524 ft. is the fifth longest suspension bridge in the world.

*(continued)*

Gladesville Bridge at Sydney, Australia, has the longest concrete arch in the world (1,000 ft. span).

Humber Bridge, with a suspension span of 4,626 ft., the longest in the world, crosses the Humber estuary 5 miles west of the city of Kingston upon Hull, England. Unique in a large suspension bridge are the towers of reinforced concrete instead of steel.

Second Narrow's Bridge, Canada's longest railway lift span connecting Vancouver and North Vancouver over Burrard Inlet.

Oland Island Bridge in Sweden was completed in 1972. It is 19,882 feet long, Europe's longest.

Oosterscheldebrug, opened Dec. 15, 1965, is a 3.125-mile causeway for automobiles over a sea arm in Zeeland, the Netherlands. It completes a direct connection between Flushing and Rotterdam.

Rio-Niteroi, Guanabara Bay, Brazil, completed in 1972, is world's longest continuous box and plate girder bridge, 8 miles, 3,363 feet long, with a center span of 984 feet and a span on each side of 656 feet.

Tagus River Bridge near Lisbon, Portugal, has a 3,323-ft. main span. Opened Aug. 6, 1966, it was named Salazar Bridge for the former premier.

Zoo Bridge across the Rhine at Cologne, with steel box girders, has a main span of 850 ft.

### Oldest U.S. Bridge in Continuous Use

Completed in 1841, the 178 ft. long, wood truss (with orthotropic steel deck) covered bridge spans the Housatonic River on Rt. 128 in West Cornwall, Conn.

## Underwater Vehicular Tunnels in North America

(over 5,000 feet in length)

| Name | Location | Waterway | Feet |
|---|---|---|---|
| Bart Trans-Bay Tubes (Rapid Transit) | San Francisco, Cal. | S.F. Bay | 3.6 miles |
| Brooklyn-Battery | New York, N.Y. | East River | 9,117 |
| Holland Tunnel | New York, N.Y. | Hudson River | 8,557 |
| Lincoln Tunnel | New York, N.Y. | Hudson River | 8,216 |
| Thimble Shoal Channel | Northampton Co., Va. | Chesapeake Bay | 8,187 |
| Chesapeake Channel | Northampton Co., Va. | Chesapeake Bay | 7,941 |
| Baltimore Harbor Tunnel | Baltimore, Md. | Patapsco River | 7,650 |
| Hampton Roads (twin) | Hampton, Va. | Hampton Roads. | 7,479 |
| Fort McHenry Tunnel (2) | Baltimore, Md. | Baltimore Harbor | 7,200 |
| Queens Midtown | New York, N.Y. | East River | 6,414 |
| Sumner Tunnel | Boston, Mass. | Boston Harbor | 5,650 |
| Louis-Hippolyte Lafontaine Tunnel | Montreal, Que. | St. Lawrence River | 5,280 |
| Detroit-Windsor | Detroit, Mich. | Detroit River | 5,160 |
| Callahan Tunnel | Boston, Mass. | Boston Harbor. | 5,046 |

## Land Vehicular Tunnels in U.S.

(over 3,000 feet in length.)

| Name | Location | Feet | Name | Location | Feet |
|---|---|---|---|---|---|
| E. Johnson Memorial | I-70, Col. | 8,959 | Lehigh | Penn. Turnpike. | 4,379 |
| Eisenhower Memorial | I-70, Col. | 8,941 | Wawona | Yosemite Natl. Park | 4,233 |
| Allegheny (twin) | Penn. Turnpike | 6,072 | Big Walker Mt. | Bland Co., Va. | 4,229 |
| Liberty Tubes | Pittsburgh, Pa. | 5,920 | Hanging Lake (twin) | Glenwood Canyon, Col. | 4,000 |
| Zion Natl. Park | Rte. 9, Utah. | 5,766 | Fort Pitt | Pittsburgh, Pa. | 3,560 |
| East River Mt. (twin) | Bland Co., Va. | 5,412 | Dingess Tunnel | Mingo Co., W.Va. | 3,400 |
| Tuscarora (twin) | Penn. Turnpike | 5,400 | Mall Tunnel | Dist. of Columbia. | 3,400 |
| Trans-Koolau | H-3, Hawaii | 5,165 | Caldecott | Oakland, Cal. | 3,371 |
| Kittatinny (twin) | Penn. Turnpike | 4,660 | Cody No. 1 | U.S. 14, 16, 20, Wyo. | 3,202 |
| Blue Mountain (twin) | Penn. Turnpike | 4,435 | | | |

## World's Longest Railway Tunnels

Source: Railway Directory & Year Book. Tunnels over 8 miles in length.

| Tunnel | Date | Miles | Operating railway | Country |
|---|---|---|---|---|
| Seikan | 1985 | 33.5 | Japanese Railway | Japan |
| Dai-shimizu | 1979 | 14 | Japanese Railway | Japan |
| Simplon No. 1 and 2 | 1906, 1922 | 12 | Swiss Fed. & Italian St. | Switz.-Italy |
| Kanmon | 1975 | 12 | Japanese Railway | Japan |
| Apennine | 1934 | 11 | Italian State | Italy |
| Rokko | 1972 | 10 | Japanese Railway | Japan |
| Mt. MacDonald | 1989 | 9.1 | Canadian Pacific | Canada |
| Gotthard | 1882 | 9 | Swiss Federal | Switzerland |
| Lotschberg | 1913 | 9 | Bern-Lotschberg-Simplon. | Switzerland |
| Hokuriku | 1962 | 9 | Japanese Railway | Japan |
| Mont Cenis (Frejus) | 1871 | 8 | Italian State. | France-Italy |
| Shin-Shimizu | 1961 | 8 | Japanese Railway. | Japan |
| Aki | 1975 | 8 | Japanese Railway. | Japan |
| Cascade | 1929 | 8 | Burlington Northern | U.S. |
| Flathead | 1970 | 8 | Burlington Northern | U.S. |

# SOCIAL SECURITY

## Social Security Programs

Source: Social Security Administration, U.S. Dept. of Health and Human Services

## Old-Age, Survivors, and Disability Insurance; Medicare; Supplemental Security Income

### Social Security Benefits

Social Security benefits are based on a worker's primary insurance amount (PIA), which is related by law to the average indexed monthly earnings (AIME) on which social security contributions have been paid. The full PIA is payable to a retired worker who becomes entitled to benefits at age 65 and to an entitled disabled worker at any age. Spouses and children of retired or disabled workers and survivors of deceased workers receive set proportions of the PIA subject to a family maximum amount. The PIA is calculated by applying varying percentages to succeeding parts of the AIME. The formula is adjusted annually to reflect changes in average annual wages.

Automatic increases in Social Security benefits are initiated for December of a year whenever the Consumer Price Index (CPI) of the Bureau of Labor Statistics for the third calendar quarter of a year increases relative to the CPI for the base quarter, which is either the third calendar quarter of the preceding year or the quarter in which an increase legislated by Congress becomes effective. The size of the benefit increase is determined by the actual percentage rise of the CPI between the quarters measured.

The average monthly benefit payable to all retired workers was $653.00 in December 1992. The average amount for disabled workers in that month was $627.00.

### Minimum and maximum monthly retired-worker benefits payable to individuals who retired at age 65[1]

| Year of attainment of age 65[2] | Minimum benefit Payable at time of retirement | Payable effective Dec. 1992 | Maximum benefit Payable at time of retirement Men[3] | Women | Payable effective Dec. 1992 Men[3] | Women |
|---|---|---|---|---|---|---|
| 1965 | $44.00 | $261.00 | $131.70 | $135.90 | $697.70 | $720.00 |
| 1970 | 64.00 | 261.00 | 189.80 | 196.40 | 773.20 | 800.70 |
| 1980 | 133.90 | 261.00 | 572.00 | ... | 1,115.40 | ... |
| 1990 | (4) | (4) | 975.00 | ... | 1,097.50 | ... |
| 1993 | (4) | (4) | 1,128.80 | ... | ... | ... |

(1) Assumes retirement at beginning of year. (2) The final benefit amount payable after Supplementary Medical Insurance (SMI) premium or any other deductions is rounded to next lower $1 (if not already a multiple of $1). (3) Benefit for both men and women are shown in men's columns except where women's benefit appears separately. (4) Minimum eliminated for workers who reach age 62 after 1981.

### Amount of Work Required

To qualify for benefits, the worker must have worked in covered employment long enough to become insured. Just how long depends on when the worker reaches age 62 or, if earlier, when he or she dies or becomes disabled.

A person is fully insured if he or she has one quarter of coverage for every year after 1950 (or year age 21 is reached, if later) up to but not including the year in which the worker reaches age 62, dies, or becomes disabled. In 1993, a person earns one quarter of coverage for each $590 of annual earnings in covered employment, up to a maximum of 4 quarters per year.

The law permits special monthly payments under the Social Security program to certain very old persons who are not eligible for regular social security benefits since they had little or no opportunity to earn social security work credits during their working lifetime.

To get disability benefits, in addition to being fully insured, the worker must also have credit for 20 quarters of coverage out of the 40 calendar quarters before he or she becomes disabled. A disabled blind worker need meet only the fully insured requirement. Persons disabled before age 31 can qualify with a briefer period of coverage. Certain survivor benefits are payable if the deceased worker had 6 quarters of coverage in the 13 quarters preceding death.

### Work credit for fully insured status for benefits

Born after 1929; die, become disabled, or reach age 62 in:

| Year | Years needed |
|---|---|
| 1983 | 8 |
| 1984 | 8¼ |
| 1985 | 8½ |
| 1986 | 8¾ |
| 1987 | 9 |
| 1988 | 9¼ |
| 1989 | 9½ |
| 1990 | 9¾ |
| 1991 and after | 10 |

### Contribution and benefit base

| Calendar year | OASDI[1] Base | HI[2] Base |
|---|---|---|
| 1984 | $37,800 | — |
| 1985 | 39,600 | — |
| 1986 | 42,000 | — |
| 1987 | 43,800 | — |
| 1988 | 45,000 | — |
| 1989 | 48,000 | — |
| 1990 | 51,300 | — |
| 1991 | 53,400 | $125,000[3] |
| 1992 | 55,500 | 130,200 |
| 1993 | 57,600 | 135,000 |

(1) Old-Age, Survivors, and Disability Insurance. (2) Hospital Insurance. (3) Although the OASDI and HI bases were the same prior to 1991, they have differed since that time.

### Tax-rate schedule
[Percent of covered earnings]

| Year | Total Employees and employers, each | OASDI | HI |
|---|---|---|---|
| 1979-80 | 6.13 | 5.08 | 1.05 |
| 1981 | 6.65 | 5.35 | 1.30 |
| 1982-83 | 6.70 | 5.40 | 1.30 |
| 1984 | 7.00 | 5.70 | 1.30 |
| 1985 | 7.05 | 5.70 | 1.35 |
| 1986-87 | 7.15 | 5.70 | 1.45 |
| 1988-89 | 7.51 | 6.06 | 1.45 |
| 1990 and after | 7.65 | 6.20 | 1.45 |
| | Self-employed | | |
| 1979-80 | 8.10 | 7.05 | 1.05 |
| 1981 | 9.30 | 8.00 | 1.30 |
| 1982-83 | 9.35 | 8.05 | 1.30 |
| 1984 | 14.00 | 11.40 | 2.60 |
| 1985 | 14.10 | 11.40 | 2.70 |
| 1986-87 | 14.30 | 11.40 | 2.90 |
| 1988-89 | 15.02 | 12.12 | 2.90 |
| 1990 and after | 15.30 | 12.40 | 2.90 |

### What Aged Workers Get

When a person has enough work in covered employment and reaches retirement age (currently 65 for full benefit, 62 for reduced benefit), he or she may retire and get monthly old-age benefits. The age at which unreduced benefits are payable will be increased gradually from 65 to 67 over a 21-year period beginning with workers age 62 in the year 2000; (reduced benefits will still be available as early as age 62 but with a larger reduction at age 62.) If a person aged 65 or older continues to work and has earnings of more than $10,560 in 1993, $1 in benefits will be withheld for every $3 above $10,560. The annual exempt amount for people under age 65 is $7,680 in 1993, and $1 in benefits is withheld for every $2 in earnings above the exempt amount for them. The annual exempt amount is raised automatically as the general earnings level rises. The eligible worker who is 70 receives the full benefit regardless of earnings.

For workers who reach age 65 from 1982 through 1989, the worker's benefit is raised by 3% for each year for which the worker between 65 and 70 (72 before 1984) did not receive benefits because of earnings from work or because the worker had not applied for benefits. The delayed retirement credit is 1 percent a year for workers reaching age 65 before 1982. The delayed retirement credit will gradually rise to 8% per year from 1990 through 2008. The rate for workers reaching age 65 in 1992-93 is 4%.

Effective December 1992, the special benefit for persons aged 72 or over who do not meet the regular coverage requirements is $178.80 a month. Like the monthly benefits, these payments are subject to cost-of-living increases. The special payment is not made to persons on the public assistance or supplemental security income rolls.

Workers retiring before age 65 have their benefits permanently reduced by 5/9 of 1% for each month they receive benefits before age 65. Thus, workers entitled to benefits in the month they reach age 62 receive 80% of the PIA, while a worker retiring at age 65 receives a benefit equal to 100% of the PIA. The nearer to age 65 the worker is when he or she begins collecting a benefit, the larger the benefit will be.

### Benefits for Worker's Spouse

The spouse of a worker who is getting Social Security retirement or disability payments may become entitled to a spouse's insurance benefit when he or she reaches 65 of one-half of the worker's PIA. Reduced spouse's benefits are available at age 62 (25/36 of 1% reduction for each month of entitlement before age 65). Benefits are also payable to the aged-divorced spouse of an insured worker if he or she was married to the worker for at least 10 years.

### Benefits for Children of Retired or Disabled Workers

If a retired or disabled worker has a child under 18 the child will get a benefit that is half of the worker's unreduced benefit, and so will the worker's spouse, even if he or she is under 62 if he or she is caring for an entitled child of the worker who is under 16 or who became disabled before age 22. Total benefits paid on a worker's earnings record are subject to a maximum and if the total that would be paid to a family exceeds that maximum, the individual dependents' benefits are adjusted downward. (Total benefits paid to the family of a worker who retired in January 1993 at age 65 and who always had the maximum amount of earnings creditable under Social Security can be no higher than $1,974.70.)

When entitled children reach 18, their benefits will generally stop, except that a child disabled before age 22 may get a benefit as long as his or her disability meets the definition in the law. Additionally, benefits will be paid to a child until age 19 if the child is in full-time attendance at an elementary or secondary school.

Benefits may also be paid to a grandchild or step-grandchild of a worker or of his or her spouse, in special circumstances.

| OASDI | May 1993 | May 1992 | May 1991 |
|---|---|---|---|
| **Monthly beneficiaries, total (in thousands)** . . . . . . . . . . | 41,784 | 40,956 | 40,119 |
| Aged 65 and over, total . . . . . . | 30,484 | 30,030 | 29,516 |
| Retired workers . . . . . . . . . | 23,303 | 22,889 | 22,432 |
| Survivors and dependents . . . | 7,178 | 7,137 | 7,078 |
| Special age-72 beneficiaries . . | 3 | 4 | 6 |
| Under age 65, total . . . . . . . . | 11,300 | 10,926 | 10,603 |
| Retired workers . . . . . . . . . | 2,529 | 2,536 | 2,539 |
| Disabled workers . . . . . . . . | 3,571 | 3,306 | 3,076 |
| Survivors and dependents . . . | 5,200 | 5,084 | 4,988 |
| **Total monthly benefits (in millions)** . . . . . . . . . . . . | $24,623 | $23,307 | $21,880 |

### What Disabled Workers Get

If a worker becomes so severely disabled that he or she is unable to work, he or she may be eligible to receive a monthly disability benefit. Benefits continue until it is determined that the individual is no longer disabled. Each beneficiary's eligibility is reviewed periodically. When a disabled-worker beneficiary reaches 65, the disability benefit becomes a retired-worker benefit.

Benefits generally like those provided for dependents of retired-worker beneficiaries may be paid to dependents of disabled beneficiaries. However, the maximum family benefit in disability cases is generally lower than in retirement cases.

### Survivor Benefits

If an insured worker should die, one or more types of benefits may be payable to survivors, again subject to a maximum family benefit as described above.

1. If claiming benefits at 65, the surviving spouse will receive a benefit that is 100% of the deceased worker's PIA. The surviving spouse may choose to get the benefit as early as age 60, but the benefit is then reduced by 19/40 of 1% for each month it is paid before age 65. However, for those whose spouses claimed their benefits before 65, the benefit is limited to the reduced amount the worker would be getting if alive but not less than 82 1/2% of the worker's PIA. Marriage after the worker's death ends the surviving spouses benefit rights. However, if he or she marries and the marriage is ended, he or she regains benefit rights (A marriage after age 60, 50 if disabled, is deemed not to have occurred for benefit purposes.). This benefit may also be paid to the divorced spouse, if the marriage lasted for at least 10 years.

Disabled widows and widowers may under certain circumstances qualify for benefits after attaining age 50 at the rate of 71.5% of the deceased worker's PIA. The widow or widower must have become totally disabled before or within 7 years after the spouse's death, the last month in which he or she received mother's or father's insurance benefits, or the last month he or she previously received surviving spouse's benefits.

2. A benefit for each child until the child reaches 18. The monthly benefit of each child of a worker who has died is three-quarters of the amount the worker would have received if he or she had lived and drawn full retirement benefits. A child with a disability that began before age 22 may receive benefits. Also, a child may receive benefits until age 19 if he or she is in full-time attendance at an elementary or secondary school.

3. A mother's or father's benefit for the widow(er), if children of the worker under 16 are in his or her care. The benefit is 75% of the PIA and he or she draws it until the youngest child reaches 16, at which time payments stop even if the child's benefit continues. They may start again when he or she is 60 (50 if disabled) unless he or she is married. If he or she has a disabled child beneficiary aged 16 or over in care, benefits also continue.

4. Dependent parents may be eligible for benefits, if they have been receiving at least half their support from the worker before his or her death, have reached age 62, and (except in certain circumstances) have not remarried since the worker's death. Each parent gets 75% of the worker's PIA; if only one parent survives the benefit is 82 1/2%.

5. A lump sum cash payment of $255. Payment is made only when there is a spouse who was living with the worker or a spouse or child eligible for immediate monthly survivor benefits.

### Self-Employed

A self-employed person who has net earnings of $400 or more in a year must report such earnings for social security tax and credit purposes. The person reports net returns from the business. Income from real estate, savings, dividends, loans, pensions, or insurance policies may not be included unless they are part of the business.

A self-employed person gets a quarter of coverage for each $590 (for 1993), up to a maximum of 4 quarters of coverage.

The nonfarm self-employed have the option of reporting their earnings as 2/3 of their gross income from self-employment but not more than $1,600 a year and not less than their actual net earnings. This option can be used only if actual net earnings from self-employment income is less than $1,600 and may be used only 5 times. Also, the self-employed person must have actual net earnings of $400 or more in 2 of the 3 taxable years immediately preceding the year in which he or she uses the option.

When a person has both taxable wages and earnings from self-employment, the wages are credited for Social Security purposes first; only as much of the self-employment income as will bring total earnings up to the current taxable maximum is subject to the self-employment tax.

## Farm Owners and Workers

Self-employed farmers whose gross annual earnings from farming are $2,400 or less may report ²/₃ of their gross earnings instead of net earnings for social security purposes. Farmers whose gross income is over $2,400 and whose net earnings are less than $1,600 can report $1,600. Cash or crop shares received from a tenant or share farmer count if the owner participated materially in production or management. The self-employed farmer pays contributions at the same rate as other self-employed persons.

**Agricultural employees.** A worker's earnings from farm work count toward benefits (1) if the employer pays him $150 or more in cash during the year; or (2) if the employer spends $2,500 or more in the year for agricultural labor. Under these rules a person gets credit for one calendar quarter for each $590 in cash pay in 1993 up to four quarters.

Foreign farm workers admitted to the United States on a temporary basis are not covered.

## Household Workers

Anyone working as maid, cook, laundress, nursemaid, baby-sitter, chauffeur, gardener and at other household tasks in the house of another is covered by Social Security if he or she is paid $50 or more in cash in a calendar quarter by any one employer. Room and board do not count, but carfare counts if paid in cash. The job does not have to be regular or full time. The employee should get a Social Security card at the social security office and show it to the employer.

The employer deducts the amount of the employee's social security tax from the worker's pay, adds an identical amount as the employer's social security tax and sends the total amount to the federal government, with the employee's social security number.

## Medicare

The Medicare health insurance program provides acute-care coverage for Social Security and Railroad Retirement beneficiaries aged 65 and over and, for persons entitled to 24 months to receive a social security disability benefit, and certain persons with end-stage kidney disease. The Medicare program cost $129 billion in 1992 and served more than 35 million people.

Persons eligible for Medicare may choose to have their covered services provided through a Health Maintenance Organization.

**Hospital insurance.** The hospital insurance program pays the cost of covered services for hospital and posthospital care as follows:

- Medicare pays for all necessary inpatient hospital care for the first 60 days of each benefit period, except for a deductible ($676 in 1993). For days 61-90, Medicare pays for covered services except for a coinsurance amount ($169 per day in 1993). After 90 days, the beneficiary has 60 reserve days for which Medicare helps pay. The coinsurance amount for reserve days was $338 in 1993.
- Up to 100 days' care in a skilled-nursing facility (skilled-nursing home) in each benefit period. Hospital insurance pays for all covered services for the first 20 days; for the 21-100th day, the beneficiary pays coinsurance ($84.50 in 1993).
- Visits by nurses or other health workers (not doctors) from a home health agency.
- Hospice care for terminally ill individuals.

**Medical insurance.** Aged persons can receive benefits under this supplementary program only if they sign up for them and agree to a monthly premium ($36.60 in 1993). The Federal Government pays the rest of the cost.

The medical insurance program pays 80% of the approval amount (after the first $100 in each calendar year) for the following services:

Medicare helps pay for covered services you receive from your doctor in his or her office, in a hospital, in a skilled nursing facility, in your home, or any other location.

Doctors' services covered by Medicare include:

- Medical and surgical services, including anesthesia.
- Diagnostic tests and procedures that are part of your treatment.

- Radiology and pathology services by doctors while you are a hospital inpatient or outpatient.
- Treatment of mental illness. Medicare payments for nonhospital treatment are limited—you may get the services from doctors, comprehensive outpatient rehabilitation facilities (CORFs), physician assistants, psychologists, and clinical social workers.

These services for nonhospital treatment of a mental illness are subject to a special payment rule. In effect, once the annual deductible is met, Medicare pays only 50% (not 80%) of approved charges for these services. On assigned claims, beneficiaries are responsible for paying the remaining 50%. For unassigned claims, beneficiaries may have to pay more.

Partial hospitalization services for treatment of mental illness are not subject to this special payment rule. Also, brief office visits for the sole purpose of monitoring or changing drug prescriptions used in the treatment of mental illness are not subject to this special payment rule.

- Other services such as:
  - X-rays.
  - Services of your doctor's office nurse.
  - Drugs and biologicals that cannot be self-administered.
  - Transfusions of blood and blood components.
  - Medical supplies.
  - Physical/occupational therapy and speech pathology services.

To get medical insurance protection, persons approaching age 65 may enroll in the 7-month period that includes 3 months before the 65th birthday, the month of the birthday, and 3 months after the birthday, but if they wish coverage to begin in the month they reach 65 they must enroll in the 3 months before their birthday. Persons not enrolling within their first enrollment period may enroll later, during the first 3 months of each year, but their premium is 10% higher for each 12-month period elapsed since they first could have enrolled.

The monthly premium is deducted from the cash benefit for persons receiving Social Security, Railroad Retirement, or Civil Service retirement benefits. Income from the medical premiums and the federal matching payments are put in a Supplementary Medical Insurance Trust Fund, from which benefits and administrative expenses are paid.

**Medicare card.** Persons qualifying for hospital insurance under Social Security receive a health insurance card similar to cards now used by Blue Cross and other health insurers. The card indicates whether the individual has taken out medical insurance protection. It is to be shown to the hospital, skilled-nursing facility, home health agency, doctor, or whoever provides the covered services.

Payments are made only in the 50 states, Puerto Rico, the Virgin Islands, Guam, and American Samoa, except that hospital services may be provided in border areas immediately outside the U.S. if comparable services are not accessible in the U.S. for a beneficiary who becomes ill or is injured in the U.S.

## Social Security Financing

Social Security is paid for by a tax on earnings (for 1993, up to $57,600 for Old Age, Survivors, and Disability Insurance and up to $135,000 for Hospital Insurance with the Medicare Program; the taxable earnings bases have been adjusted annually to reflect increases in average wages). The employed worker and his or her employer share the tax equally. Beginning in 1994, there will be no ceiling on earnings subject to the Medicare tax.

Employers remit amounts withheld from employee wages for Social Security and income taxes to the Internal Revenue Service; employer Social Security taxes are also payable at the same time. (Self-employed workers pay their Social Security taxes along with their regular income tax forms.) The Social Security taxes (along with revenues arising from partial taxation of the Social Security benefits of certain high-income people) are transferred to the Social Security Trust Funds—the Federal Old-Age and Survivors Insurance (OASI) Trust Fund, the Federal Disability Insurance (DI) Trust Fund, and the Federal Hospital Insurance (HI) Trust Fund; they can be used only to pay benefits, the cost of rehabilitation services, and administrative expenses. Money not immediately needed for these purposes is by law invested in obligations of the Federal Government, which must pay interest on the money borrowed and must repay the principal when the obligations are redeemed or mature.

## Supplemental Security Income

On Jan. 1, 1974, the Supplemental Security Income (SSI) program established by the 1972 Social Security Act amendments replaced the former federal grants to states for aid to the needy aged, blind, and disabled in the 50 states and the District of Columbia. The program provides both for federal payments based on uniform national standards and eligibility requirements and for state supplementary payments varying from state to state. The Social Security Administra-

tion administers the federal payments financed from general funds of the Treasury—and the state supplements as well, if the state elects to have its supplementary program federally administered. The states may supplement the federal payment for all recipients and must supplement it for persons otherwise adversely affected by the transition from the former public assistance programs. In May 1993, the number of persons receiving federal payments and federally administered state payments was 5,786,998 and the amount of these payments was $2.14 billion.

The maximum monthly federal SSI payment for individuals with no other countable income, living in their own household, was $434.00 in 1993. For couples it was $652.00.

## Examples of monthly cash benefit awards for selected beneficiary families with first entitlement in 1993, effective January 1993

| Beneficiary Family | Low Earnings ($10,544 in 1993) (45% of average) | Career Earnings Level Average Earnings ($23,432 in 1993)[1] | Maximum Earnings ($57,600 in 1993) |
|---|---|---|---|
| Primary Insurance amount (worker retiring at 65) | $496.70 | $819.90 | $1,128.80 |
| Maximum family benefit (worker retiring at 65) | 744.40 | 1,492.90 | 1,973.90 |
| Disability maximum family benefit (worker disabled at 55; in 1992) * | 694.40 | 1,221.00 | 1,722.31 |
| Disabled worker: (worker disabled at 55) | | | |
| Worker alone | 494.00 | 814.00 | 1,148.50 |
| Worker, spouse, and 1 child | 693.00 | 1,220.00 | 1,721.00 |
| Retired worker claiming benefits at age 62: | | | |
| Worker alone[2] | 398.00 | 656.00 | 899.00 |
| Worker with spouse claiming benefits at— | | | |
| Age 65 or over | 645.00 | 1,063.00 | 1,457.00 |
| Age 62[2] | 587.00 | 984.00 | 1,312.00 |
| Widow or widower claiming benefits at— | | | |
| Age 65 or over[3] | 496.00 | 819.00 | 1,128.00 |
| Age 60 | 355.00 | 586.00 | 807.00 |
| Disabled widow or widower claiming benefits at age 50-59[4] | 355.00 | 586.00 | 807.00 |
| 1 surviving child | 372.00 | 614.00 | 846.00 |
| Widow or widower age 65 or over and 1 child[5] | 744.00 | 1,433.00 | 1,972.00 |
| Widowed mother or father and 1 child[5] | 744.00 | 1,228.00 | 1,692.00 |
| Widowed mother or father and 2 children[5] | 744.00 | 1,491.00 | 1,974.00 |

* Assumes work beginning at age 22. (1) Estimate. (2) Assumes maximum reduction. (3) A widow(er)'s benefit amount is limited to the amount the spouse would have been receiving if still living but not less than 82.5 percent of the PIA. (4) Effective January 1984, disabled widow(er)s claiming benefit at ages 50-59 will receive benefit equal to 71.5 percent of the PIA (based on 1983 Social Security Amendment provision). (5) Based on worker dying at age 65.

## Social Security Trust Funds
### Old-Age and Survivors Insurance Trust Fund, 1940-1992

(In millions)

| | | Income | | | | Disbursements | | | | | |
|---|---|---|---|---|---|---|---|---|---|---|---|
| Fiscal year[1] | Total | Net contributions[2] | Income from taxation of benefits | Payments from the general fund of the Treasury[3] | Net interest[4] | Total | Benefit payments[5] | Administrative expenses | Transfers to Railroad Retirement program | Interfund borrowing transfers[6] | Net increase in fund | Fund at end of period |
| 1940 | $592 | $550 | — | — | $42 | $28 | $16 | $12 | — | — | $564 | $1,745 |
| 1950 | 2,367 | 2,106 | — | $4 | 257 | 784 | 727 | 57 | — | — | 1,583 | 12,893 |
| 1960 | 10,360 | 9,843 | — | — | 517 | 11,073 | 10,270 | 202 | $600 | — | −713 | 20,829 |
| 1970 | 31,746 | 29,955 | — | 442 | 1,350 | 27,321 | 26,268 | 474 | 579 | — | 4,425 | 32,616 |
| 1980 | 100,051 | 97,608 | — | 557 | 1,886 | 103,228 | 100,626 | 1,160 | 1,442 | — | −3,177 | 24,566 |
| 1985 | 179,881 | 175,305 | $3,151 | 105 | 1,321 | 169,210 | 165,310 | 1,589 | 2,310 | $−4,364 | 6,308 | 33,877 |
| 1990 | 278,607 | 261,506 | 2,924 | 34 | 14,143 | 223,481 | 218,948 | 1,564 | 2,969 | — | 55,126 | 203,445 |
| 1991 | 293,288 | 270,841 | 5,790 | −2,089 | 18,746 | 241,316 | 236,195 | 1,746 | 3,375 | — | 51,972 | 255,417 |
| 1992 | 307,102 | 278,506 | 6,019 | 19 | 22,557 | 256,239 | 251,268 | 1,823 | 3,148 | — | 50,862 | 306,280 |

(1) Under the Congressional Budget Act of 1974 (Public Law 93-344), fiscal years 1977 and later consist of the 12 months ending on September 30 of each year. Fiscal years prior to 1977 consisted of the 12 months ending on June 30 of each year.
(2) Beginning in 1983, includes transfers from general fund of Treasury representing contributions that would have been paid on deemed wage credits for military service in 1957 and later, if such credits were considered to be covered wages.
(3) Includes payments (a) in 1947-52 and in 1967 and later, for costs of noncontributory wage credits for military service performed before 1957; (b) in 1972-83, for costs of deemed wage credits for military service performed after 1956; and (c) in 1969 and later, for costs of benefits to certain uninsured persons who attained age 72 before 1968.
(4) Net interest includes net profits or losses on marketable investments. Beginning in 1967, administrative expenses are charged currently to the trust fund on an estimated basis, with a final adjustment, including interest, made in the following fiscal year. The amounts of these interest adjustments are included in net interest. For years prior to 1967, a description of the method of accounting for administrative expenses is contained in the 1970 Annual Report. Beginning in October 1973, the figures shown include relatively small amounts of gifts to the fund. Figures for 1983-86 reflect payments from a borrowing trust fund to a lending trust fund for interest on amounts owed under the interfund borrowing provisions. During 1983-91, interest paid from the trust fund to the general fund on advance tax transfers is reflected. The amounts shown for 1985 and 1986 include interest adjustments of $76.5 million and $11.5 million, respectively, on unnegotiated checks issued before April 1985.
(5) Beginning in 1967, includes payments for vocational rehabilitation services furnished to disabled persons receiving benefits because of their disabilities. Beginning in 1983, amounts are reduced by amount of reimbursement for unnegotiated benefit checks.
(6) Negative figures represent amounts repaid from the OASI Trust Fund to the DI and HI Trust Funds.

## Disability Insurance Trust Fund, 1960-1992

(In millions)

| Fiscal year[1] | Income | | | | | Disbursements | | | | | Net increase in fund | Fund at end of period |
|---|---|---|---|---|---|---|---|---|---|---|---|---|
| | Total | Net contributions[2] | Income from taxation of benefits | Payments from the general fund of the Treasury[3] | Net interest[4] | Total | Benefit payments[5] | Administrative expenses | Transfers to Railroad Retirement program | Interfund borrowing transfers[6] | | |
| 1960 | $1,034 | $987 | — | — | $47 | $533 | $528 | $32 | −$27 | — | $501 | $2,167 |
| 1970 | 4,380 | 4,141 | — | $16 | 223 | 2,954 | 2,795 | 149 | 10 | — | 1,426 | 5,104 |
| 1980 | 17,376 | 16,805 | — | 118 | 453 | 15,320 | 14,998 | 334 | −12 | — | 2,056 | 7,680 |
| 1985 | 17,984 | 16,876 | $217 | — | 891 | 19,294 | 18,648 | 603 | 43 | $2,540 | 1,230 | 5,873 |
| 1990 | 28,215 | 27,291 | 158 | — | 766 | 25,124 | 24,327 | 717 | 80 | — | 3,091 | 11,455 |
| 1991 | 29,322 | 28,953 | 131 | −775 | 1,014 | 27,780 | 26,909 | 789 | 82 | — | 1,543 | 12,997 |
| 1992 | 31,168 | 29,871 | 218 | — | 1,080 | 31,285 | 30,382 | 845 | 58 | — | −116 | 12,881 |

(1) Under the Congressional Budget Act of 1974 (Public Law 93-344), fiscal years 1977 and later consist of the 12 months ending on September 30 of each year. The act further provides that the calendar quarter July-September 1976 is a period of transition from fiscal year 1976, which ended on June 30, 1976, to fiscal year 1977, which began on October 1, 1976.
(2) Beginning in 1983, includes government contributions on deemed wage credits for military service in 1957 and later.
(3) Includes payments (a) in 1967 and later, for costs of noncontributory wage credits for military service performed before 1957; and (b) in 1972-83, for costs of deemed wage credits for military service performed after 1956.
(4) Net interest includes net profits or losses on marketable investments. Beginning in 1967, administrative expenses are charged currently to the trust fund on an estimated basis, with a final adjustment, including interest, made in the following fiscal year. The amounts of these interest adjustments are included in net interest. For years prior to 1967, a description of the method of accounting for administrative expenses is contained in the 1970 Annual Report of the Board of Trustees of the Federal Old-Age and Survivors Insurance and Disability Insurance Trust Funds. Beginning in 1983, these figures reflect payments from a borrowing trust fund to a lending trust fund for interest on amounts owed under the interfund borrowing provisions. Also, beginning in 1983, interest paid from the trust fund to the general fund on advance tax transfers is reflected. The amount shown for 1985 includes an interest adjustment of $14.8 million on unnegotiated checks issued before April 1985.
(5) Beginning in 1967, includes payments for vocational rehabilitation services furnished to disabled persons receiving benefits because of their disabilities. Beginning in 1983, amounts are reduced by amount of reimbursement for unnegotiated benefit checks. The amount shown for 1983 is reduced by $48 million for all unnegotiated checks issued before 1983; reductions in subsequent years are relatively small.
(6) Negative figure represents amounts lent by the DI Trust Fund to the OASI Trust Fund. Positive figures represent repayment of these amounts.

## Supplementary Medical Insurance Trust Fund, 1970-1992

(In millions)

| Fiscal year[1] | Income | | | | Disbursements | | | Balance in fund at end of year[4] |
|---|---|---|---|---|---|---|---|---|
| | Premium from participants | Government contributions[2] | Interest and other income[3] | Total income | Benefit payments | Administrative expenses | Total disbursements | |
| 1970 | $936 | $928 | $12 | $1,876 | $1,979 | $217 | $2,196 | $57 |
| 1975 | 1,887 | 2,330 | 105 | 4,322 | 3,765 | 405 | 4,170 | 1,424 |
| 1980 | 2,928 | 6,932 | 415 | 10,275 | 10,144 | 593 | 10,737 | 4,532 |
| 1985 | 5,524 | 17,898 | 1,155 | 24,577 | 21,808 | 922 | 22,730 | 10,646 |
| 1990 | 11,494[5] | 33,210 | 1,434[5] | 46,138[5] | 41,498 | 1,524[5] | 43,022[5] | 14,527[5] |
| 1991 | 11,807 | 34,730 | 1,629 | 48,166 | 45,514 | 1,505 | 47,019 | 15,675 |
| 1992 | 12,748 | 38,684 | 1,717 | 53,149 | 48,627 | 1,661 | 50,288 | 18,535 |

(1) For 1967 through 1976, fiscal years cover the interval from July 1 through June 30; fiscal years 1977 and later cover the interval from October 1 through September 30. (2) The payments shown as being from the general fund of the Treasury include certain interest-adjustment items. (3) Other income includes recoveries of amounts reimbursed from the trust fund that are not obligations of the trust fund and other miscellaneous income. (4) The financial status of the program depends on both the total net assets and the liabilities of the program. (5) Includes the impact of the Medicare Catastrophic Coverage Act of 1988 (Public Law 100-360).

## Hospital Insurance Trust Fund, 1970-1992

(In millions)

| Fiscal Year[1] | Income | | | | | | | Disbursements | | | Trust Fund | |
|---|---|---|---|---|---|---|---|---|---|---|---|---|
| | Payroll taxes | Transfers from railroad retirement account | Reimbursement for uninsured persons | Premiums from voluntary enrollees | Payments for military wage credits | Interest on investments and other income[2] | Total income | Benefit payments[3] | Administrative expense[4] | Total disbursements | Net increase fund | Fund at end of year |
| 1970 | $4,785 | $64 | 617 | — | $11 | $137 | $5,614 | $4,804 | $149 | $4,953 | $661 | $2,677 |
| 1975 | 11,291 | 132 | 481 | 6 | 48 | 609 | 12,568 | 10,353 | 259 | 10,612 | 1,956 | 9,870 |
| 1980 | 23,244 | 244 | 697 | 17 | 141 | 1,072 | 25,415 | 23,790 | 497 | 24,288 | 1,127 | 14,490 |
| 1985 | 46,490 | 371 | 766 | 38 | 86 | 3,182 | 50,933 | 47,841 | 813 | 48,654 | 4,103[5] | 21,277[5] |
| 1990 | 70,655 | 367 | 413 | 113 | 107 | 7,908 | 79,563 | 65,912 | 774 | 66,687 | 12,876 | 95,631 |
| 1991 | 74,655 | 352 | 605 | 367 | −1,011[6] | 8,969 | 83,938 | 68,705 | 934 | 69,638 | 14,299 | 109,930 |
| 1992 | 80,978 | 374 | 621 | 484 | 86 | 10,133 | 92,677 | 80,784 | 1,191 | 81,974 | 10,703 | 120,633 |

(1) Fiscal years 1976 and earlier consist of the 12 months ending on June 30 of each year; fiscal years 1977 and later consist of the 12 months ending on September 30 of each year. (2) Other income includes recoveries of amounts reimbursed from the trust fund that are not obligations of the trust fund and a small amount of miscellaneous income. (3) Includes costs of Peer Review Organizations (beginning with the implementation of the Prospective Payment System on October 1, 1983). (4) Includes costs of experiments and demonstration projects. (5) In fiscal year 1983, $12,437 million was loaned to the Old-Age and Survivors Insurance Trust Fund under the interfund borrowing provisions of the Social Security Act. Repayments of $1,824 million and $10,613 million were made in fiscal years 1985 and 1986, respectively. (6) Includes the lump sum general revenue adjustment of $-1,100 million, as provided for by section 151 of P.L. 98-21. NOTE: Totals do not necessarily equal the sum of rounded components.

# HEALTH
## Ethics Regarding Care of the Terminally Ill

Physician-assisted suicide for the terminally ill remained a prominent issue. On Aug. 4, 1993, Dr. Jack Kevorkian, a retired Michigan pathologist, assisted a suicide for the 17th time since beginning such procedures in June 1990; in most cases he employed an apparatus—which must be activated by the patient—consisting of a face mask attached by a tube to a container of carbon monoxide. A new Michigan law that went into effect in Feb. 1993 made it a felony to assist in a suicide. A county judge struck down the law in May on a technicality, but an appellate court stayed that decision, leaving the law in effect while court challenges continued. On Aug. 17, Kevorkian was indicted for his role in the Aug. death. On Sept. 10, the same day he was ordered to stand trial, Kevorkian assisted a suicide for the 18th time. In Nov. 1992, California voters defeated a ballot measure that would have legalized in that state physician-assisted suicide for the terminally ill.

In a 1992 survey conducted by the American Society of Internal Medicine, one in five physicians said they had deliberately taken action to cause a patient's death. Another survey of medical practitioners, published in 1993, found that nearly half the attending physicians and nurses and 70 percent of the resident physicians surveyed said they had acted against their own convictions by ignoring requests from terminally ill patients to withhold life support.

Another prominent ethical issue in recent years has involved the questions of whether and under what circumstances life-support for comatose patients with no apparent hope of recovery could be discontinued. The Supreme Court heard its first ever "right-to-die" case on Dec. 6, 1989. *Cruzan v. Missouri Dept. of Health* concerned Nancy Beth Cruzan, 32, who had been unconscious since Jan. 1983, after a car accident. Her parents and a guardian appointed to represent her sought to stop the medical treatment sustaining her in a "persistent vegetative state." On June 25, 1990, the Supreme Court, in a 5-4 ruling, interpreted the 14th Amendment as conferring on patients a right to refuse life-sustaining treatment, but it held that in the case of comatose patients a state could, as Missouri did, require that "clear and convincing" evidence about the patient's previous wishes regarding life-sustaining treatment be presented before such care could be withdrawn. (Since the state courts had found that there was not "clear and convincing" evidence, the Cruzans' request to withdraw their daughter's feeding tube was denied. However, after the family presented further evidence in a new state court proceeding, removal of the feeding tube was permitted, and Nancy Cruzan died in Dec. 1990.)

As of Jan. 1988, hospitals are required by the Joint Commission on Accreditation of Health Care Organizations to have formal policies specifying when doctors and nurses can refrain from trying to resuscitate terminally ill patients. The policy must be developed in consultation with the medical staff and the nursing staff, adopted by the medical staff, and then approved by the hospital's governing body. The policy must define the roles of physicians, nursing personnel, and members of the patient's family in any decision to withhold resuscitation. It must also include "provisions designed to assure that a patient's rights are respected."

In March 1986, the American Medical Association announced that it would be ethical for doctors to withhold "all means of life prolonging medical treatment," including food and water, from permanently unconscious patients even if death was not imminent. The withholding of such therapy should occur only when a patient's unconscious state "is beyond doubt irreversible and there are adequate safeguards to confirm the accuracy of the diagnosis," the association's judicial council said.

In June 1991, the AMA adopted 2 reports of its Council on Ethical and Judicial Affairs dealing with refusal of life-prolonging treatment when patients are incurably ill. The first, "Decisions Near the End of Life," concluded: "the principle of patient autonomy requires that physicians must respect the decision to forego life-sustaining treatment of a patient who possesses decisionmaking capacity." Life-sustaining treatment was defined as "any treatment that serves to prolong life without reversing the underlying medical condition," including "mechanical ventilation, renal dialysis, chemotherapy, antibiotics and artificial nutrition and hydration." The Council also reaffirmed its position that "physicians must not perform euthanasia or participate in assisted suicide." The second report, "Decisions to Forego Life-Sustaining Treatment for Incompetent Patients," encouraged the use of advance directives (living wills and the designation of durable power of attorney) by persons to ensure that their interests will be promoted in the event that they become incompetent. When there is no advance directive designating a proxy decisionmaker, the Council concluded, the patient's family should become the surrogate decisionmaker. Family was defined as "persons with whom the patient is closely associated." Surrogate decisionmakers should consider the patient's previous values and preferences and base decisions on what the patient would have likely decided had he or she been competent. When this is not possible, decisions should be based on what would objectively be in the best interests of the patient. The Council encouraged the establishment and use of ethics committees designed to facilitate sound decisionmaking.

A number of states have "living will" statutes that set out a procedure for a mentally competent person to declare that he or she does not wish to be subjected to a "death-prolonging" procedure. In Oct. 1990, Congress passed the Patient Self-Determination Act, which took effect in December 1991. The Act requires health care facilities that receive funds from Medicare or Medicaid to provide written information to all patients about advance directives and patients' rights under their state laws and document whether or not a patient has an advance directive. Information on living wills and health-care powers of attorney can be obtained from the American Bar Association's Commission on Legal Problems of the Elderly.

## Estimated New Cancer Cases and Deaths by Sex for Leading Sites, 1993*

Source: American Cancer Society

### Estimated New Cases

| Total | | Women | | Men | |
|---|---|---|---|---|---|
| All Sites | 1,170,000 | All Sites | 570,000 | All Sites | 600,000 |
| Breast | 183,000 | Breast | 182,000 | Prostate | 165,000 |
| Lung | 170,000 | Colorectal | 75,000 | Lung | 100,000 |
| Prostate | 165,000 | Lung | 70,000 | Colorectal | 77,000 |
| Colorectal | 152,000 | Uterus | 44,500 | Bladder | 39,000 |
| Bladder | 52,300 | Lymphoma | 22,400 | Lymphoma | 28,500 |

### Estimated Deaths

| Total | | Women | | Men | |
|---|---|---|---|---|---|
| All Sites | 526,000 | All Sites | 249,000 | All Sites | 277,000 |
| Lung | 149,000 | Lung | 56,000 | Lung | 93,000 |
| Colorectal | 57,000 | Breast | 46,000 | Prostate | 35,000 |
| Breast | 46,300 | Colorectal | 28,200 | Colorectal | 28,800 |
| Prostate | 35,000 | Ovary | 13,300 | Pancreas | 12,000 |
| Pancreas | 25,000 | Pancreas | 13,000 | Lymphoma | 11,500 |

*Note: The estimates of new cancer cases are offered as a rough guide and should not be regarded as definitive. About 700,000 basal and squamous cell skin cancers and 100,000 carcinoma in situ cases are not included in the totals.

## Cancer Prevention

Source: American Cancer Society

**PRIMARY PREVENTION:** steps that can be taken to avoid those factors that might lead to the development of cancer.

**Smoking**
Cigarette smoking is responsible for 90% of lung cancer cases among men, 79% among women—about 87% overall. Smoking accounts for about 30% of all cancer deaths. Those who smoke two or more packs of cigarettes a day have lung cancer mortality rates 15-25 times greater than nonsmokers.

**Nutrition**
Risk for colon, breast, and uterine cancers increases in obese people. High-fat diets may contribute to the development of cancers of the breast, colon, and prostate. High-fiber foods may help reduce risk of colon cancer. A varied diet containing plenty of vegetables and fruits rich in vitamins A and C may reduce risk for many cancers. Salt-cured, smoked, and nitrite-cured foods have been linked to esophageal and stomach cancer.

**Sunlight**
Almost all of the more than 700,000 cases of non-melanoma skin cancer diagnosed each year in the U.S. are sun-related. Epidemiological evidence shows that sun exposure is a major factor in the development of melanoma, and the incidence increases for those living near the equator.

**Alcohol**
Oral cancer and cancers of the larynx, throat, esophagus, and liver occur more frequently among heavy drinkers of alcohol, especially when accompanied by cigarette smoking or use of chewing tobacco.

**Smokeless Tobacco**
Use of chewing tobacco or snuff increases risk of cancers of the mouth, larynx, throat, and esophagus.

**Estrogen**
Estrogen treatment to control menopausal symptoms can increase risk of endometrial cancer. However, including progesterone in estrogen replacement therapy helps to minimize this risk. Use of estrogen by menopausal women needs careful discussion by the woman and her physician, while research continues.

**Radiation**
Excessive exposure to ionizing radiation can increase cancer risk. Most medical and dental X rays are adjusted to deliver the lowest dose possible without sacrificing image quality. Excessive radon exposure in the home may increase lung cancer risk, especially in cigarette smokers. If levels are found to be too high, remedial actions should be taken.

**Occupational Hazards**
Exposure to several different industrial agents (including nickel, chromate, asbestos, and vinyl chloride) increases risk of various cancers. Risk of lung cancer from asbestos is greatly increased when combined with smoking.

**SECONDARY PREVENTION:** steps to be taken to diagnose a cancer or precursor as early as possible after it has developed.

**Colorectal Tests**
The ACS recommends 3 tests for the early detection of colon and rectum cancer in people without symptoms: The digital rectal examination performed by a physician during an office visit, every year after the age of 40; the stool blood test, every year after 50; and the proctosigmoidoscopy examination, every 3 to 5 years, based on the advice of a physician.

**Pap Test**
For cervical cancer, women who are or have been sexually active, or have reached 18 years, should have an annual Pap test and pelvic examination. After a woman has had 3 or more consecutive satisfactory normal exams, the Pap test may be performed less frequently at the discretion of her physician.

**Breast Cancer Detection**
The ACS recommends monthly breast self-examination by women 20 years and older. Examination of the breast by a health care professional should be done every 3 years from ages 20 to 40 and then every year. The ACS recommends a mammogram every year for asymptomatic women age 50 and over. Women age 40-49 should have mammography every 1-2 years, depending on physical and mammographic findings.

## Some Benefits of Quitting Smoking

Source: American Cancer Society; U.S. Centers for Disease Control and Prevention

**Within 20 Minutes**
- Blood pressure drops to normal
- Pulse rate drops to normal
- Body temperature of hands and feet increases to normal

**Within 8 Hours**
- Carbon monoxide level in blood drops to normal
- Oxygen level in blood increases to normal

**Within 24 Hours**
- Chance of heart attack decreases

**Within 48 Hours**
- Nerve endings start regrowing
- Ability to smell and taste is enhanced

**Within 2 Weeks to 3 Months**
- Circulation improves
- Walking becomes easier
- Lung function increases up to 30 percent

**Within 1 to 9 Months**
- Coughing, sinus congestion, fatigue, shortness of breath decrease

- Cilia regrow in lungs, increasing ability to handle mucus, clean the lungs, reduce infection
- Body's overall energy increases

**Within 1 Year**
- Excess risk of coronary heart disease is half that of a smoker

**Within 5 Years**
- Lung cancer death rate for average former smoker (one pack a day) decreases by almost half
- Stroke risk is reduced to that of a nonsmoker 5-15 years after quitting
- Risk of cancer of the mouth, throat, and esophagus is half that of a smoker's

**Within 10 Years**
- Lung cancer death rate similar to that of nonsmokers
- Precancerous cells are replaced
- Risk of cancer of the mouth, throat, esophagus, bladder, kidney, and pancreas decreases

**Within 15 Years**
- Risk of coronary heart disease is that of a nonsmoker

## Cancer Death Rates by Site, U.S., 1930-1989
Source: American Cancer Society; rates adjusted to 1970 population

**Females**

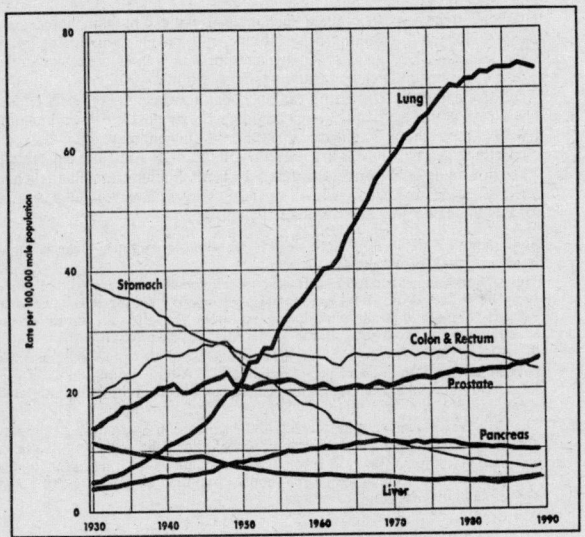

**Males**

## Cancer's 7 Warning Signals*
Source: American Cancer Society

1. A change in bowel or bladder habits.
2. A sore that does not heal.
3. Unusual bleeding or discharge.
4. Thickening or lump in breast or elsewhere.
5. Indigestion or difficulty in swallowing.
6. Obvious change in wart or mole.
7. Nagging cough or hoarseness.
* If you have a warning signal, see your doctor.

## Heart and Blood Vessel Disease
Source: American Heart Association, Dallas
### Warning Signs

**Of Heart Attack**
- Uncomfortable pressure, fullness, squeezing, or pain in the center of the chest lasting two minutes or longer
- Pain may radiate to the shoulder, arm, neck, or jaw
- Sweating may accompany pain or discomfort
- Nausea and vomiting may also occur
- Shortness of breath, dizziness, or fainting may accompany other signs

The American Heart Association advises immediate action at the onset of these symptoms. The Association points out that more than half of heart attack victims die before they reach the hospital and that the average victim waits 2 hours before seeking help.

**Of Stroke**
- Sudden temporary weakness or numbness of face or limbs on one side of the body
- Temporary loss of speech, or trouble speaking or understanding speech
- Temporary dim or lost vision, especially in one eye
- Unexplained dizziness, unsteadiness, or sudden falls

## Some Major Risk Factors

**Blood pressure**—High blood pressure increases the risk of stroke, heart attack, kidney failure, and congestive heart failure.

**Cholesterol**—A blood cholesterol level over 240 mg/dl (milligrams of cholesterol per deciliter of blood) approximately doubles the risk of coronary heart disease; about 25% of the U.S. adult population falls into this category. Blood cholesterol levels between 200 and 240 mg/dl are in a zone of moderate and increasing risk. An estimated 26.1 mln. (36%) of youths age 19 and under have levels of 170 mg/dl or higher, comparable to a level of 200 mg/dl in adults.

**Cigarettes**—Cigarette smokers have more than twice the risk of heart attack and 2-4 times the risk of sudden cardiac death as nonsmokers. Young smokers have a higher risk for early death from stroke.

**Obesity**—47 mln. adults are 20% or more over their desirable weight. (24.4% of white males, 25.7% of black males, 25.1% of white females, 43.8% of black females.)

## Cardiovascular Diseases Statistical Summary, 1991

**Prevalence** — 56,450,000 Americans had one or more forms of heart and blood vessel disease.
- high blood pressure — 50,000,000
- coronary heart disease — 6,300,000
- stroke — 3,020,000
- rheumatic heart disease — 1,340,000

**Mortality** — 923,422 in 1991 (42.7% of all deaths).
- Someone died from cardiovascular disease every 34 seconds in the U.S. in 1991.

**Congenital or inborn heart defects** —
- postnatal mortality from heart defects 5,800 in 1991.

**Coronary heart disease (heart attack)** — caused 478,530 deaths in 1991.

- 6,300,000 alive today have history of heart attack and/or angina pectoris.
- As many as 1,500,000 Americans had a heart attack in 1991, about one-third of them fatal.

**Stroke** — killed about 144,070 in 1991; afflicted 3,060,000.

**Hypertension (high blood pressure)** — afflicts 50,000,000 Americans age 6 and above.

**Rheumatic heart disease** — afflicted 1,340,000 in 1991.
- killed 6,020 in 1991.

Note: 1991 mortality data are estimates based on 1991 provisional data published by the National Center for Health Statistics.

## Immunization Schedule for Children

Source: American Academy of Pediatrics, Aug. 3, 1993

By ensuring that your child gets immunized on schedule, you can provide the best defense against dangerous childhood diseases. Childhood immunization means protection from nine major diseases: hepatitis B, polio, measles, mumps, rubella (German measles), pertussis (whooping cough), diphtheria, tetanus (lockjaw), and *Haemophilus influenzae* type b (a bacterium that can cause such serious infections as meningitis and pneumonia).

For the best possible protection against diphtheria, tetanus, and pertussis, your child needs a series of five shots of the combination diphtheria-tetanus-pertussis (DTP) vaccine. The first four doses should be given at 2, 4, 6, and 15 to 18 months of age, with a final booster dose given before school entry (4 to 6 years). For the fourth and fifth dose, the acellular (DTaP) vaccine may be substituted for the DTP vaccine.

For protection against polio, your child needs a series of four oral polio vaccine doses, the first three at 2, 4, and 15 to 18 months and the final dose before school entry (4 to 6 years).

To be completely protected against hepatitis B, your child needs to be vaccinated with a series of three hepatitis B virus (HBV) vaccine shots. The American Academy of Pediatrics recommends that these immunizations be given at birth, at 1 to 2 months, and at 6 to 18 months of age. In some cases your pediatrician may decide to begin the 3-dose schedule after your baby has left the hospital.

Several vaccines are available for protection against *Haemophilus influenzae* type b (Hib). However, only two vaccines—HbOC and PRP-OMP—are approved for children under 15 months of age. The Academy recommends that your child receive either the HbOC vaccine at 2, 4, and 6 months of age, with a final dose at 12 to 15 months or the PRP-OMP vaccine at 2 and 4 months, with a final dose at 12 to 15 months.

At 15 months, your child should have an immunization for measles, mumps, and rubella (MMR). A second MMR vaccination, primarily to boost measles and mumps immunity, should be given to children 11 to 12 years or older who have not had measles. If there is a measles outbreak in your community or if you live in a high-risk area, the MMR booster may be given just before kindergarten or at an earlier age.

If you do not have a pediatrician, call your local public health department. It usually has supplies of vaccine and may give immunizations free.

| | DTP[1] | Polio | Hepatitis B[2] | Measles[3] | Mumps[3] | Rubella[3] | Hib[4] | Tetanus-Diphtheria |
|---|---|---|---|---|---|---|---|---|
| Birth | | | X | | | | | |
| 1-2 months | | | X | | | | | |
| 2 months | X | X | | | | | X | |
| 4 months | X | X | | | | | X | |
| 6 months | X | | | | | | X | |
| 6-18 months | | | X | | | | | |
| 12-15 months | | | | | | | X | |
| 15 months | | | | X | X | X | | |
| 15-18 months | X | X | | | | | | |
| 4-6 years | X | X | | | | | | |
| 11-12 years | | | | X | X | X | | |
| 14-16 years | | | | | | | | X |

(1) For the fourth and fifth doses, the acellular (DTaP) pertussis vaccine may be substituted for the DTP vaccine. (2) Infants of mothers with positive blood tests for hepatitis B must receive hepatitis B immune globulin (HBIG) at or shortly after the first dose. These infants will also require a second hepatitis B vaccine dose at 1 month and a third hepatitis B vaccine injection at 6 months of age. (3) Combined MMR vaccine. Second dose at 11-12 years except where public health authorities require otherwise. (4) The 6-month dose depends on the type of *Haemophilus influenzae* type b vaccine given previously.

## Drug Use: America's Students

Source: National Institute on Drug Abuse/Univ. of Michigan Inst. for Social Research

The long-term decline in the use of a number of drugs among 12th-graders continued in 1992, according to the report of the 18th national survey of American high school seniors. However, some results of the 2nd annual national survey of 8th-graders and 10th-graders were interpreted as warning signals: there were modest but statistically significant increases in 8th-graders' use of marijuana, cocaine, crack, LSD, other hallucinogens, stimulants, and inhalants. Researchers expressed concern that the newest wave of adolescents entering the teen years could be at the vanguard of a reversal of previously improving conditions, with LSD possibly a prime example of "generational forgetting."

Cigarette smoking remained quite high among all 3 grade levels in 1992: 16 percent of 8th-graders, 22 percent of 10th-graders, and 28 percent of 12th-graders reported having smoked during the 30 days before they responded to the survey. Eighth-graders showed some modest, but not statistically significant, increases in alcohol use.

Although the surveys missed the 15 to 20 percent of a class group that drops out of school early, investigators said there was little reason to believe trends would differ among this group, although it would undoubtedly have higher rates of use overall.

In 1992, around 17,000 seniors in 135 public and private high schools participated in the survey, along with 15,000 10th-graders in 125 schools and 18,000 8th-graders in 160 schools.

A separate 1992 survey of 1,500 college students found that the long-term decline in illicit drug use by such students had halted. It was found that 30.6 percent of the college students used some illicit drugs at least once in the prior 12 months—a slight increase over the 29.2 percent figure for 1991. The change was attributed largely to an increase in the percentage of college students using marijuana, for which use rose from 26 percent to 27 percent. One in every eight college students (13 percent) reported using an illicit drug other than marijuana, representing virtually no change from 1991. However, the use of one class of illicit drugs did rise: hallucinogen use rose among college students for the third year in a row. In 1989, 5.1 percent reported using a hallucinogen; by 1992, 6.8 percent reported such use. LSD use accounted for most or all of this increase, rising from 3.4 percent to 5.7 percent between 1989 and 1992. Cocaine's popularity continued to decline, with use dropping from 3.6 percent of college students surveyed in 1991 to 3 percent of the 1992 students. Crack, stimulants, barbiturates, tranquilizers, inhalants, heroin, opiates other than heroine, and other illicitly used drugs showed little or no further decline in active use among college students in 1992, although a number of them had been declining previously.

## Drug Use: America's High School Seniors

| | Class of 1975 | Class of 1980 | Class of 1985 | Class of 1986 | Percent ever used Class of 1987 | Class of 1988 | Class of 1989 | Class of 1990 | Class of 1991 | Class of 1992 | '91-'92 change |
|---|---|---|---|---|---|---|---|---|---|---|---|
| Marijuana/Hashish | 47.3 | 60.3 | 54.2 | 50.9 | 50.2 | 47.2 | 43.7 | 40.7 | 36.7 | 32.6 | −4.1sss |
| Inhalants | NA | 11.9 | 15.4 | 15.9 | 17.0 | 16.7 | 17.6 | 18.0 | 17.6 | 16.6 | −1.0 |
| Inhalants Adjusted[1] | NA | 17.6 | 18.1 | 20.1 | 18.6 | 17.5 | 18.6 | 18.5 | 18.0 | 17.0 | −1.0 |
| Amyl & Butyl Nitrites | NA | 11.1 | 7.9 | 8.6 | 4.7 | 3.2 | 3.3 | 2.1 | 1.6 | 1.5 | −0.1 |
| Hallucinogens | 16.3 | 13.3 | 10.3 | 9.7 | 10.3 | 8.9 | 9.4 | 9.4 | 9.6 | 9.2 | −0.4 |
| Hallucinogens Adjusted[2] | NA | 15.7 | 12.1 | 11.9 | 10.6 | 9.2 | 9.9 | 9.7 | 10.0 | 9.4 | −0.6 |
| LSD | 11.3 | 9.3 | 7.5 | 7.2 | 8.4 | 7.7 | 8.3 | 8.7 | 8.8 | 8.6 | −0.2 |
| PCP | NA | 9.6 | 4.9 | 4.8 | 3.0 | 2.9 | 3.9 | 2.8 | 2.9 | 2.4 | −0.5 |
| Cocaine | 9.0 | 15.7 | 17.3 | 16.9[5] | 15.2 | 12.1 | 10.3 | 9.4 | 7.8 | 6.1 | −1.7ss |
| "Crack" | NA | NA | NA | NA | 5.6 | 4.8 | 4.7 | 3.5 | 3.1 | 2.6 | −0.5 |
| Heroin | 2.2 | 1.1 | 1.2 | 1.1 | 1.2 | 1.1 | 1.3 | 1.3 | 0.9 | 1.2 | +0.3 |
| Other opiates[3] | 9.0 | 9.8 | 10.2 | 9.0 | 9.2 | 8.6 | 8.3 | 8.3 | 6.6 | 6.1 | −0.5 |
| Stimulants Adjusted[3,4] | NA | NA | 26.2 | 23.4 | 21.6 | 19.8 | 19.1 | 17.5 | 15.4 | 13.9 | −1.5s |
| Sedatives[3] | 18.2 | 14.9 | 11.8 | 10.4 | 8.7 | 7.8 | 7.4 | 5.3 | 6.7 | 6.1 | −0.6 |
| Barbiturates[3] | 16.9 | 11.0 | 9.2 | 8.4 | 7.4 | 6.7 | 6.5 | 6.8 | 6.2 | 5.5 | −0.7 |
| Methaqualone[3] | 8.1 | 9.5 | 6.7 | 5.2 | 4.0 | 3.3 | 2.7 | 2.3 | 1.3 | 1.6 | +0.3 |
| Tranquilizers[3] | 17.0 | 15.2 | 11.9 | 10.9 | 10.9 | 9.4 | 7.6 | 7.2 | 7.2 | 6.0 | −1.2s |
| Alcohol | 90.4 | 93.2 | 92.2 | 91.3 | 92.2 | 92.0 | 90.7 | 89.5 | 88.0 | 87.5 | −0.5 |
| Cigarettes | 73.6 | 71.0 | 68.8 | 67.6 | 67.2 | 66.4 | 65.7 | 64.4 | 63.1 | 61.8 | −1.3 |

NA=Not available. Level of significance between the two most recent classes: s=.05, ss=.01, sss=.001. (1) Adjusted for under-reporting of amyl and butyl nitrites. (2) Adjusted for underreporting of PCP. (3) Only drug use that was not under a doctor's orders. (4) Adjusted for overreporting of the nonprescription stimulants. (5) In 1986, three-fourths of those who used cocaine used it in powder form; the remainder used the "crack" form.

## Drug Use in the General U.S. Population

According to the National Institute on Drug Abuse (NIDA) 1991 National Household Survey on Drug Abuse, 75.4 million (37% of) Americans age 12 and older reported some use of an illicit drug at least once during their lifetimes, 12.8% reported use during the previous year, and 6.2% reported use in the month before the survey was conducted.

For those age 25 and under, an estimated 2.5 million reported using cocaine (including crack), and 9 million reported using marijuana at least once within the previous year. For those age 26 and over, 3.9 million reported using cocaine (including crack), and 10.5 million reported using marijuana at least once within the previous year.

The NIDA Drug Abuse Warning Network reported an estimated 400,000 admissions to hospital emergency rooms nationwide that involved drug abuse in 1991. A total of 6,601 drug-abuse related deaths were reported in 1991 by 130 medical examiners in 27 metropolitan areas.

## Federal Drug Control Budget

Federal spending on drug control programs increased from $1.7 billion in fiscal 1982 to $12 billion in fiscal 1992, according to the Office of Natl. Drug Control Policy.

# Basic First Aid

First aid experts stress that knowing what to do for an injured person until a doctor or trained person gets to an accident scene can save a life, especially in cases of stoppage of breath, severe bleeding, and shock.

People with special medical problems, such as diabetes, cardiovascular disease, epilepsy, or allergy, are also urged to wear some sort of emblem identifying it, as a safeguard against use of medication that might be injurious or fatal in an emergency. Emblems may be obtained from Medic Alert Foundation, Turlock, CA 95380.

Most accidents occur in homes. National Safety Council figures show that home accidents exceed those in other locations, such as in cars, at work, or in public places.

In all cases, get medical assistance as soon as possible.

**Animal bite** — Wound should be washed with soap under running water and animal should be caught alive for rabies test.

**Asphyxiation** — Start mouth-to-mouth resuscitation immediately after getting patient to fresh air.

**Bleeding** — Elevate the wound above the heart if possible. Press hard on wound with sterile compress until bleeding stops. Send for doctor if it is severe.

**Burn** — If mild, with skin unbroken and no blisters, plunge into ice water until pain subsides. Apply a dry dressing if necessary. Send for physician if burn is severe. Apply sterile compresses and keep patient quiet and comfortably warm until doctor's arrival. Do not try to clean burn, or to break blisters.

**Chemical in eye** — With patient lying down, pour cupsful of water immediately into corner of eye, letting it run to other side to remove chemicals thoroughly. Cover with sterile compress. Get medical attention immediately .

**Choking** — Do not use back slaps to dislodge obstruction. (See Abdominal Thrust)

**Convulsions** — Place person on back on bed or rug. Loosen clothing. Turn head to side. Do not place a blunt object between the victim's teeth. If convulsions do not stop, get medical attention immediately.

**Cut (minor)** — Apply mild antiseptic and sterile compress after washing with soap under warm running water.

**Drowning** — (See Mouth-to-Mouth Resuscitation) Artificial breathing must be started at once, before victim is out of the water, if possible. If the victim's stomach is bloated with water, put victim on stomach, place hands under stomach, and lift. If no pulse is felt, begin cardio-pulmonary resuscitation. This should only be done by those professionally trained. If necessary, treat for shock. (See Shock)

**Electric shock** — If possible, turn off power. Don't touch victim until contact is broken; pull him from contact with electrical source using rope, wooden pole, or loop of dry cloth. Start mouth-to-mouth resuscitation if breathing has stopped.

**Foreign body in eye** — Touch object with moistened corner of handkerchief if it can be seen. If it cannot be seen or does not come out after a few attempts, take patient to doctor. Do not rub eye.

**Fainting** — If victim feels faint, lower head to knees. Lay him down with head turned to side if he becomes unconscious. Loosen clothing and open windows. Keep patient lying quietly for at least 15 minutes after he regains consciousness. Call doctor if faint lasts for more than a few minutes.

**Fall** — Send for physician if patient has continued pain. Cover wound with sterile dressing and stop any severe bleeding. Do not move patient unless absolutely necessary — as in case of fire — if broken bone is suspected. Keep patient warm and comfortable.

**Loss of Limb** — If a limb is severed, it is important to properly protect the limb so that it can possibly be reattached to the victim. After the victim is cared for, the limb should be placed in a clean plastic bag, garbage can, or other suitable container. Pack ice around the limb on the OUTSIDE of the bag to keep the limb cold. Call ahead to the hospital to alert them of the situation.

**Poisoning** — Call doctor. Use antidote listed on label if container is found. Call local Poison Control Center if possible. Except for lye, other caustics, and petroleum products, induce vomiting unless victim is unconscious. Give milk if poison or antidote is unknown.

**Shock (injury-related)** — Keep the victim lying down; if uncertain as to his injuries, keep him flat on his back. Maintain the victim's normal body temperature; if the weather is cold or damp, place blankets or extra clothing over and under the victim; if weather is hot, provide shade.

**Snakebite** — Immediately get victim to a hospital. If there is mild swelling or pain, apply a constricting band 2 to 4 inches above the bite.

**Sting from insect** — If possible, remove stinger and apply solution of ammonia and water, or paste of baking soda. Call physician immediately if body swells or patient collapses.

**Unconsciousness** — Send for doctor and place person on his back. Start resuscitation if he stops breathing. Never give food or liquids to an unconscious person.

## Abdominal Thrust

The American Red Cross and the American Heart Association both agree that the recommended first aid for choking victims is the abdominal thrust, also known as the Heimlich maneuver, after its creator, Dr. Henry Heimlich. Slaps on the back are no longer advised and may even prove detrimental in an attempt to assist a choking victim.

- Get behind the victim and wrap your arms around him above his waist.
- Make a fist with one hand and place it, with the thumb knuckle pressing inward, just below the point of the "v" of the rib cage.
- Grasp the wrist with the other hand and give one or more upward thrusts or hugs.
- Start mouth-to-mouth resuscitation if breathing stops.

## Mouth-to-Mouth Resuscitation

Stressing that your breath can save a life, the American Red Cross gives the following directions for mouth-to-mouth resuscitation if the victim is not breathing:

- Determine consciousness by tapping the victim on the shoulder and asking loudly, "Are you okay?"
- Tilt the victim's head back so that his chin is pointing upward. Do not press on the soft tissue under the chin, as this might obstruct the airway. If you suspect that an accident victim might have neck or back injuries, open the airway by placing the tips of your index and middle fingers on the corners of the victim's jaw to lift it forward without tilting the head.
- Place your cheek and ear close to the victim's mouth and nose. Look at the victim's chest to see if it rises and falls. Listen and feel for air to be exhaled for about 5 seconds.
- If there is no breathing, pinch the victim's nostrils shut with the thumb and index finger of your hand that is pressing on the victim's forehead. Another way to prevent leakage of air when the lungs are inflated is to press your cheek against the victim's nose.
- Blow air into victim's mouth by taking a deep breath and then sealing your mouth tightly around the victim's mouth. Initially, give two, quick (approx. 1.5 seconds each), full breaths without allowing the lungs to deflate completely between each breath.
- Watch the victim's chest to see if it rises.
- Stop blowing when the victim's chest is expanded. Raise your mouth; turn your head to the side and listen for exhalation.
- Watch the chest to see if it falls.
- Repeat the blowing cycle until the victim starts breathing.

  Note: Infants (up to one year) and children (1 to 8 years) should be administered mouth-to-mouth resuscitation as described above, except for the following:
- Do not tilt the head as far back as an adult's head.
- Both the mouth and nose of the infant should be sealed by the mouth.
- Give breaths to a child once every four seconds.
- Blow into the infant's mouth and nose once every three seconds with less pressure and volume than for a child.

## Nutritive Value of Food (Calories, Proteins, etc.)

Source: Home and Garden Bulletin No. 72; available from Supt. of Documents, U. S. Government Printing Office, Washington, DC 20402

| Food | Measure | Grams | Food Energy (calories) | Protein (grams) | Fat (grams) | Saturated fats (grams) | Carbohydrate (grams) | Calcium (milligrams) | Iron (milligrams) | Vitamin A (I.U.) | Thiamin (milligrams) | Riboflavin (milligrams) |
|---|---|---|---|---|---|---|---|---|---|---|---|---|
| **Dairy products** | | | | | | | | | | | | |
| Cheese, cheddar | 1 oz. | 28 | 115 | 7 | 9 | 6.1 | T | 204 | .2 | 300 | .01 | .11 |
| Cheese, cottage, small curd | 1 cup | 210 | 220 | 26 | 9 | 6.0 | 6 | 126 | .3 | 340 | .04 | .34 |
| Cheese, cream | 1 oz. | 28 | 100 | 2 | 10 | 6.2 | 1 | 23 | .3 | 400 | T | .06 |
| Cheese, Swiss | 1 oz. | 28 | 105 | 8 | 8 | 5.0 | 1 | 272 | T | 240 | .01 | .10 |
| Half-and-Half | 1 tbsp. | 15 | 20 | T | 2 | 1.1 | 1 | 16 | T | 20 | .01 | .02 |
| Cream, sour | 1 tbsp. | 15 | 25 | T | 3 | 1.6 | 1 | 14 | T | 90 | T | .02 |
| Milk, whole | 1 cup | 244 | 150 | 8 | 8 | 5.1 | 11 | 291 | .1 | 310 | .09 | .40 |
| Milk, nonfat (skim) | 1 cup | 244 | 85 | 8 | T | .3 | 12 | 302 | .1 | 500 | .09 | .37 |
| Milkshake, chocolate | 10.6 oz. | 300 | 355 | 9 | 8 | 5.0 | 63 | 396 | .9 | 260 | .14 | .67 |
| Ice Cream, hardened | 1 cup | 133 | 270 | 5 | 14 | 8.9 | 32 | 176 | .1 | 540 | .05 | .33 |
| Sherbet | 1 cup | 193 | 270 | 2 | 4 | 2.4 | 59 | 103 | .3 | 190 | .03 | .09 |
| Yogurt, fruit-flavored | 8 oz. | 227 | 230 | 10 | 3 | 1.8 | 42 | 343 | .2 | 120 | .08 | .40 |
| **Eggs** | | | | | | | | | | | | |
| Fried in butter | 1 | 46 | 85 | 5 | 6 | 2.4 | 1 | 26 | .9 | 290 | .03 | .13 |
| Hard-cooked | 1 | 50 | 80 | 6 | 6 | 1.7 | 1 | 28 | 1.0 | 260 | .04 | .14 |
| Scrambled in butter (milk added) | 1 | 64 | 95 | 6 | 7 | 2.8 | 1 | 47 | .9 | 310 | .04 | .16 |
| **Fats & oils** | | | | | | | | | | | | |
| Butter | 1 tbsp. | 14 | 100 | T | 12 | 7.2 | T | 3 | T | 430 | T | T |
| Margarine | 1 tbsp. | 14 | 100 | T | 12 | 2.1 | T | 3 | T | 470 | T | T |
| Salad dressing, blue cheese | 1 tbsp. | 15 | 75 | 1 | 8 | 1.6 | 1 | 12 | T | 30 | T | .02 |
| Salad dressing, French | 1 tbsp. | 16 | 65 | T | 6 | 1.1 | 3 | 2 | 1 | — | — | — |
| Salad dressing, Italian | 1 tbsp. | 15 | 85 | T | 9 | 1.6 | 1 | 2 | T | T | T | T |
| Mayonnaise | 1 tbsp. | 14 | 100 | T | 11 | 2.0 | T | 3 | .1 | 40 | T | .01 |
| **Meat, poultry, fish** | | | | | | | | | | | | |
| Bluefish, baked with butter or margarine | 3 oz. | 85 | 135 | 22 | 4 | — | 0 | 25 | 0.6 | 40 | .09 | .08 |
| Clams, raw, meat only | 3 oz. | 85 | 65 | 11 | 1 | — | 2 | 59 | 5.2 | 90 | .08 | .15 |
| Crabmeat, white or king, canned | 1 cup | 135 | 135 | 24 | 3 | .6 | 1 | 61 | 1.1 | — | .11 | .11 |
| Fish sticks, breaded, cooked, frozen | 1 oz. | 28 | 50 | 5 | 3 | — | 2 | 3 | .1 | 0 | .01 | .02 |
| Salmon, pink, canned | 3 oz. | 85 | 120 | 17 | 5 | .9 | 0 | 167 | .7 | 60 | .03 | .16 |
| Sardines, Atlantic, canned in oil | 3 oz. | 85 | 175 | 20 | 9 | 3.0 | 0 | 372 | 2.5 | 190 | .02 | .17 |
| Shrimp, French fried | 3 oz. | 85 | 190 | 17 | 9 | 2.3 | 9 | 61 | 1.7 | — | .03 | .07 |
| Tuna, canned in oil | 3 oz. | 85 | 170 | 24 | 7 | 1.7 | 0 | 7 | 1.6 | 70 | .04 | .10 |
| Bacon, broiled or fried crisp | 2 slices | 15 | 85 | 4 | 8 | 2.5 | T | 2 | .5 | 0 | .08 | .05 |
| Ground beef, broiled, 10% fat | 3 oz. | 85 | 185 | 23 | 10 | 4.0 | 0 | 10 | 3.0 | 20 | .08 | .20 |
| Roast beef, relatively lean | 3 oz. | 85 | 165 | 25 | 7 | 2.8 | 0 | 11 | 3.2 | 10 | .06 | .19 |
| Beef steak, lean and fat | 3 oz. | 85 | 330 | 20 | 27 | 11.3 | 0 | 9 | 2.5 | 50 | .05 | .15 |
| Beef & vegetable stew | 1 cup | 245 | 220 | 16 | 11 | 4.9 | 15 | 29 | 2.9 | 2,400 | .15 | .17 |
| Lamb, chop, lean and fat | 3.1 oz. | 89 | 360 | 18 | 32 | 14.8 | 0 | 8 | 1.0 | — | .11 | .19 |
| Liver, beef | 3 oz. | 85 | 195 | 22 | 9 | 2.5 | 5 | 9 | 7.5 | 45,390 | .22 | 3.56 |
| Ham, light cure, lean and fat | 3 oz. | 85 | 245 | 18 | 19 | 6.8 | 0 | 8 | 2.2 | 0 | .40 | .15 |
| Pork, chop, lean and fat | 2.7 oz. | 78 | 305 | 19 | 25 | 8.9 | 0 | 9 | 2.7 | 0 | .75 | .22 |
| Bologna | 1 slice | 28 | 85 | 3 | 8 | 3.0 | T | 2 | .5 | — | .05 | .06 |
| Frankfurter, cooked | 1 | 56 | 170 | 7 | 15 | 5.6 | 1 | 3 | .8 | — | .08 | .11 |
| Sausage, pork link, cooked | 1 link | 13 | 60 | 2 | 6 | 2.1 | T | 1 | .3 | 0 | .10 | .04 |
| Veal, cutlet, braised or boiled | 3 oz. | 85 | 185 | 23 | 9 | 4.0 | 0 | 9 | 2.7 | — | .06 | .21 |
| Chicken, drumstick, fried, bones removed | 1.3 oz. | 38 | 90 | 12 | 4 | 1.1 | T | 6 | .9 | 50 | .03 | .15 |
| Chicken, half broiler, broiled, bones removed | 6.2 oz. | 176 | 240 | 42 | 7 | 2.2 | 0 | 16 | 3.0 | 160 | .09 | .34 |
| **Fruits & products** | | | | | | | | | | | | |
| Apple, raw, 2-3/4 in. diam. | 1 | 138 | 80 | T | T | — | 20 | 10 | .4 | 120 | .04 | .03 |
| Applejuice | 1 cup | 248 | 120 | T | T | — | 30 | 15 | 1.5 | — | .02 | .05 |
| Apricots, raw | 3 | 107 | 55 | 1 | T | — | 14 | 18 | .5 | 2,890 | .03 | .04 |
| Banana, raw | 1 | 119 | 100 | 1 | T | — | 26 | 10 | .8 | 230 | .06 | .07 |
| Cherries, sweet, raw | 10 | 68 | 45 | 1 | T | — | 12 | 15 | .3 | 70 | .03 | .04 |
| Fruit cocktail, canned in heavy syrup | 1 cup | 255 | 195 | 1 | T | — | 50 | 23 | 1.0 | 360 | .05 | .03 |
| Grapefruit, raw, medium, white | 1/2 | 241 | 45 | 1 | T | — | 12 | 19 | .5 | 10 | .05 | .02 |
| Grapes, Thompson seedless | 10 | 50 | 35 | T | T | — | 9 | 6 | .2 | 50 | .03 | .02 |
| Lemonade, frozen, diluted | 1 cup | 248 | 105 | T | T | — | 28 | 2 | .1 | 10 | .01 | .02 |
| Cantaloupe, 5-in. diam. | 1/2 | 477 | 80 | 2 | T | — | 20 | 38 | 1.1 | 9,240 | .11 | .08 |
| Orange, 2-5/8 in. diam. | 1 | 131 | 65 | 1 | T | — | 16 | 54 | .5 | 260 | .13 | .05 |
| Orange juice, frozen, diluted | 1 cup | 249 | 120 | 2 | T | — | 29 | 25 | .2 | 540 | .23 | .03 |
| Peach, raw, 2-1/2 in. diam. | 1 | 100 | 40 | 1 | T | — | 10 | 9 | .5 | 1,330 | .02 | .05 |
| Raisins, seedless | 1 cup | 145 | 420 | 4 | T | — | 112 | 90 | 5.1 | 30 | .16 | .12 |
| Strawberries, whole | 1 cup | 149 | 55 | 1 | 1 | — | 13 | 31 | 1.5 | 90 | .04 | .10 |
| Watermelon, 4 by 8 in. wedge | 1 wedge | 926 | 110 | 2 | 1 | — | 27 | 30 | 2.1 | 2,510 | .13 | .13 |
| **Grain products** | | | | | | | | | | | | |
| Bagel, egg | 1 | 55 | 165 | 6 | 2 | .5 | 28 | 9 | 1.2 | 30 | .14 | .10 |
| Biscuit, 2 in. diam., from home recipe | 1 | 28 | 105 | 2 | 5 | 1.2 | 13 | 34 | .4 | T | .08 | .08 |
| Bread, white, enriched, soft-crumb | 1 slice | 25 | 70 | 2 | 1 | .2 | 13 | 21 | .6 | T | .10 | .06 |
| Bread, whole wheat, soft-crumb | 1 slice | 28 | 65 | 3 | 1 | .1 | 14 | 24 | .8 | T | .09 | .03 |
| Oatmeal or rolled oats | 1 cup | 240 | 130 | 5 | 2 | .4 | 23 | 22 | 1.4 | 0 | .19 | .05 |
| Bran flakes (40% bran), added sugar, salt, iron, vitamins | 1 cup | 35 | 105 | 4 | 1 | — | 28 | 19 | 12.4 | 1,650 | .41 | .49 |
| Corn flakes, added sugar, salt, iron, vitamins | 1 cup | 25 | 95 | 2 | T | — | 21 | * | 0.6 | 1,180 | .29 | .35 |
| Rice, puffed, added iron, thiamin, niacin | 1 cup | 15 | 60 | 1 | T | — | 13 | 3 | .3 | 0 | .07 | .01 |
| Wheat, shredded, plain, 1 biscuit or 1/2 cup | 1 serving | 25 | 90 | 2 | 1 | — | 20 | 11 | .9 | 0 | .06 | .03 |
| Cake, angel food, 1/12 of cake | 1 | 53 | 135 | 3 | T | — | 32 | 50 | .2 | 0 | .03 | .08 |
| Cupcake, 2-1/2 in. diam., with chocolate icing | 1 | 36 | 130 | 2 | 5 | 2.0 | 21 | 47 | .4 | 60 | .05 | .06 |
| Boston cream pie with custard filling, 1/12 of cake | 1 | 69 | 210 | 3 | 6 | 1.9 | 34 | 46 | .7 | 140 | .09 | .11 |
| Fruitcake, dark, 1/30 of loaf | 1 | 15 | 55 | 1 | 2 | .5 | 9 | 11 | .4 | 20 | .02 | .02 |
| Cake, pound, 1/17 of loaf | 1 | 33 | 160 | 2 | 10 | 2.5 | 16 | 6 | .5 | 80 | .05 | .06 |
| Brownies, with nuts, from commercial recipe | 1 | 20 | 85 | 1 | 4 | .9 | 13 | 9 | .4 | 20 | .03 | .02 |
| Cookies, chocolate chip, from home recipe | 4 | 40 | 205 | 2 | 12 | 3.5 | 24 | 14 | .8 | 40 | .06 | .06 |
| Crackers, graham | 2 | 14 | 55 | 1 | 1 | .3 | 10 | 6 | .5 | 0 | .02 | .08 |

| Food | Measure | Grams | Food Energy (calories) | Protein (grams) | Fat (grams) | Saturated fats (grams) | Carbohydrate (grams) | Calcium (milligrams) | Iron (milligrams) | Vitamin A (I.U.) | Thiamin (milligrams) | Riboflavin (milligrams) |
|---|---|---|---|---|---|---|---|---|---|---|---|---|
| Crackers, saltines. | 4 | 11 | 50 | 1 | 1 | .3 | 8 | 2 | .5 | 0 | .05 | .05 |
| Danish pastry, round piece. | 1 | 65 | 275 | 5 | 15 | 4.7 | 30 | 33 | 1.2 | 200 | .18 | .19 |
| Doughnut, cake type | 1 | 25 | 100 | 1 | 5 | 1.2 | 13 | 10 | .4 | 20 | .05 | .05 |
| Macaroni and cheese, from home recipe. | 1 cup | 200 | 430 | 17 | 22 | 8.9 | 40 | 362 | 1.8 | 860 | .20 | .40 |
| Muffin, corn | 1 | 40 | 125 | 3 | 4 | 1.2 | 19 | 42 | .7 | 120 | .10 | .10 |
| Noodles, enriched, cooked. | 1 cup | 160 | 200 | 7 | 2 | — | 37 | 16 | 1.4 | 110 | .22 | .13 |
| Pie, apple, 1/7 of pie. | 1 | 135 | 345 | 3 | 15 | 3.9 | 51 | 11 | .9 | 40 | .15 | .11 |
| Pie, cherry, 1/7 of pie | 1 | 135 | 350 | 4 | 15 | 4.0 | 52 | 19 | .9 | 590 | .16 | .12 |
| Pie, lemon meringue, 1/7 of pie. | 1 | 120 | 305 | 4 | 12 | 3.7 | 45 | 17 | 1.0 | 200 | .09 | .12 |
| Pie, pecan, 1/7 of pie. | 1 | 118 | 495 | 6 | 27 | 4.0 | 61 | 55 | 3.7 | 190 | .26 | .14 |
| Pizza, cheese, 1/8 of 12 in. diam. pie. | 1 | 60 | 145 | 6 | 4 | 1.7 | 22 | 86 | 1.1 | 230 | .16 | .18 |
| Popcorn, popped, plain. | 1 cup | 6 | 25 | 1 | T | T | 5 | 1 | .2 | — | — | .01 |
| Pretzels, stick | 10 | 3 | 10 | T | T | — | 2 | 1 | T | 0 | .01 | .01 |
| Rolls, enriched, brown & serve | 1 | 26 | 85 | 2 | 2 | .4 | 14 | 20 | .5 | T | .10 | .06 |
| Rolls, frankfurter & hamburger | 1 | 40 | 120 | 3 | 2 | .5 | 21 | 30 | .8 | T | .16 | .10 |
| Spaghetti with meat balls & tomato sauce | 1 cup | 248 | 330 | 19 | 12 | 3.3 | 39 | 124 | 3.7 | 1,590 | .25 | .30 |
| **Legumes, nuts, seeds** | | | | | | | | | | | | |
| Beans, Great Northern, cooked | 1 cup | 180 | 210 | 14 | 1 | — | 38 | 90 | 4.9 | 0 | .25 | .13 |
| Peanuts, roasted in oil, salted | 1 cup | 144 | 840 | 37 | 72 | 13.7 | 27 | 107 | 3.0 | — | .46 | .19 |
| Peanut butter | 1 tbsp. | 16 | 95 | 4 | 8 | 1.5 | 3 | 9 | .3 | — | .02 | .02 |
| Sunflower seeds | 1 cup | 145 | 810 | 35 | 69 | 8.2 | 29 | 174 | 10.3 | 70 | 2.84 | .33 |
| **Sugars & sweets** | | | | | | | | | | | | |
| Candy, caramels | 1 oz. | 28 | 115 | 1 | 3 | 1.6 | 22 | 42 | .4 | T | .01 | .05 |
| Candy, milk chocolate | 1 oz. | 28 | 145 | 2 | 9 | 5.5 | 16 | 65 | .3 | 80 | .02 | .10 |
| Fudge, chocolate | 1 oz. | 28 | 115 | 1 | 3 | 1.3 | 21 | 22 | .3 | T | .01 | .03 |
| Candy, hard | 1 oz. | 28 | 110 | 0 | T | — | 28 | 6 | .5 | 0 | 0 | 0 |
| Honey | 1 tbsp. | 21 | 65 | T | 0 | 0 | 17 | 1 | .1 | 0 | T | .01 |
| Jams & Preserves | 1 tbsp. | 20 | 55 | T | T | — | 14 | 4 | .2 | T | T | .01 |
| Sugar, white, granulated | 1 tbsp. | 12 | 45 | 0 | 0 | 0 | 12 | 0 | T | 0 | 0 | 0 |
| **Vegetables** | | | | | | | | | | | | |
| Asparagus, canned, spears | 4 spears | 80 | 15 | 2 | T | — | 3 | 15 | 1.5 | 640 | .05 | .08 |
| Beans, green, from frozen, cuts. | 1 cup | 135 | 35 | 2 | T | — | 8 | 54 | .9 | 780 | .09 | .12 |
| Broccoli, cooked | 1 stalk | 180 | 45 | 6 | 1 | — | 8 | 158 | 1.4 | 4,500 | .16 | .36 |
| Cabbage, raw, coarsely shredded or sliced | 1 cup | 70 | 15 | 1 | T | — | 4 | 34 | .3 | 90 | .04 | .04 |
| Carrots, raw, 7-1/2 by 1-1/8 in. | 1 | 72 | 30 | 1 | T | — | 7 | 27 | .5 | 7,930 | .04 | .04 |
| Celery, raw | 1 stalk | 40 | 5 | T | T | — | 2 | 16 | .1 | 110 | .01 | .01 |
| Collards, cooked | 1 cup | 190 | 65 | 7 | 1 | — | 10 | 357 | 1.5 | 14,820 | .21 | .38 |
| Corn, sweet, cooked | 1 ear | 140 | 70 | 2 | 1 | — | 16 | 2 | .5 | 310 | .09 | .08 |
| Lettuce, iceberg, chopped | 1 cup | 55 | 5 | T | T | — | 2 | 11 | .3 | 180 | .03 | .03 |
| Mushrooms, raw | 1 cup | 70 | 20 | 2 | T | — | 3 | 4 | .6 | T | .07 | .32 |
| Onions, raw, chopped | 1 cup | 170 | 65 | 3 | T | — | 15 | 46 | .9 | T | .05 | .07 |
| Peas, frozen, cooked. | 1 cup | 160 | 110 | 8 | T | — | 19 | 30 | 3.0 | 960 | .43 | .14 |
| Potatoes, baked, peeled | 1 | 156 | 145 | 4 | T | — | 33 | 14 | 1.1 | T | .15 | .07 |
| Potatoes, frozen, French fried. | 10 | 50 | 110 | 2 | 4 | 1.1 | 17 | 5 | .9 | T | .07 | .01 |
| Potatoes, mashed, milk added. | 1 cup | 210 | 135 | 4 | 2 | .7 | 27 | 50 | .8 | 40 | .17 | .11 |
| Potato chips | 10 | 20 | 115 | 1 | 8 | 2.1 | 10 | 8 | .4 | T | .04 | .01 |
| Potato salad | 1 cup | 250 | 250 | 7 | 7 | 2.0 | 41 | 80 | 1.5 | 350 | .20 | .18 |
| Spinach, chopped, from frozen | 1 cup | 205 | 45 | 6 | 1 | — | 8 | 232 | 4.3 | 16,200 | .14 | .31 |
| Sweet potatoes, baked in skin, peeled | 1 | 114 | 160 | 2 | 1 | — | 37 | 46 | 1.0 | 9,230 | .10 | .08 |
| Tomatoes, raw | 1 | 135 | 25 | 1 | T | — | 6 | 16 | .6 | 1,110 | .07 | .05 |
| **Miscellaneous** | | | | | | | | | | | | |
| Beer | 12 fl. oz. | 360 | 150 | 1 | 0 | 0 | 14 | 18 | T | — | .01 | .11 |
| Gin, rum, vodka, whisky, 86 proof. | 1-1/2 fl. oz. | 42 | 105 | — | 0 | 0 | T | — | — | — | — | — |
| Wine, table. | 3-1/2 fl. oz. | 102 | 85 | T | 0 | 0 | 4 | 9 | .4 | — | T | .01 |
| Cola-type beverage. | 12 fl. oz. | 369 | 145 | 0 | 0 | 0 | 37 | — | — | 0 | 0 | 0 |
| Ginger ale. | 12 fl. oz | 366 | 115 | 0 | 0 | 0 | 29 | — | — | 0 | 0 | 0 |
| Gelatin dessert | 1 cup | 240 | 140 | 4 | 0 | 0 | 34 | — | — | — | — | — |
| Olives, pickled, green. | 4 medium | 16 | 15 | T | 2 | .2 | T | 8 | .2 | 40 | — | — |
| Pickles, dill, whole. | 1 | 65 | 5 | T | T | — | 1 | 17 | .7 | 70 | T | .01 |
| Popsicle, 3 fl. oz. | 1 | 95 | 70 | 0 | 0 | 0 | 18 | 0 | T | 0 | 0 | 0 |
| Soup, tomato, prepared with water | 1 cup | 245 | 90 | 2 | 3 | .5 | 16 | 15 | .7 | 1,000 | .05 | .05 |

T — indicates trace  * — Varies by brand

## Recommended Weight Tables

Source: Metropolitan Life Insurance Co., 1983

Weights for people age 25-59 based on lowest mortality. Weight in lbs. according to frame (in indoor clothing weighing 5 lbs. for men, 3 lbs. for women). Heights include shoes with 1-inch heels.

| | | Men | | | | | Women | | |
|---|---|---|---|---|---|---|---|---|---|
| **Height** | | Small Frame | Medium Frame | Large Frame | **Height** | | Small Frame | Medium Frame | Large Frame |
| Feet | Inches | | | | Feet | Inches | | | |
| 5 | 2 | 128-134 | 131-141 | 138-150 | 4 | 10 | 102-111 | 109-121 | 118-131 |
| 5 | 3 | 130-136 | 133-143 | 140-153 | 4 | 11 | 103-113 | 111-123 | 120-134 |
| 5 | 4 | 132-138 | 135-145 | 142-156 | 5 | 0 | 104-115 | 113-126 | 122-137 |
| 5 | 5 | 134-140 | 137-148 | 144-160 | 5 | 1 | 106-118 | 115-129 | 125-140 |
| 5 | 6 | 136-142 | 139-151 | 146-164 | 5 | 2 | 108-121 | 118-132 | 128-143 |
| 5 | 7 | 138-145 | 142-154 | 149-168 | 5 | 3 | 111-124 | 121-135 | 131-147 |
| 5 | 8 | 140-148 | 145-157 | 152-172 | 5 | 4 | 114-127 | 124-138 | 134-151 |
| 5 | 9 | 142-151 | 148-160 | 155-176 | 5 | 5 | 117-130 | 127-141 | 137-155 |
| 5 | 10 | 144-154 | 151-163 | 158-180 | 5 | 6 | 120-133 | 130-144 | 140-159 |
| 5 | 11 | 146-157 | 154-166 | 161-184 | 5 | 7 | 123-136 | 133-147 | 143-163 |
| 6 | 0 | 149-160 | 157-170 | 164-188 | 5 | 8 | 126-139 | 136-150 | 146-167 |
| 6 | 1 | 152-164 | 160-174 | 168-192 | 5 | 9 | 129-142 | 139-153 | 149-170 |
| 6 | 2 | 155-168 | 164-178 | 172-197 | 5 | 10 | 132-145 | 142-156 | 152-173 |
| 6 | 3 | 158-172 | 167-182 | 176-202 | 5 | 11 | 135-148 | 145-159 | 155-176 |
| 6 | 4 | 162-176 | 171-187 | 181-207 | 6 | 0 | 138-151 | 148-162 | 158-179 |

# Food and Nutrition

Food contains proteins, carbohydrates, fats, water, vitamins and minerals. Nutrition is the way your body takes in and uses these ingredients to maintain proper functioning.

The U.S. Dept. of Health and Human Services and the Dept. of Agriculture issued dietary guidelines Nov. 5, 1990 that were the most specific ever, and covered children from age 2 as well as adults. Recommended were: (1) no more than 30 percent of calories from fat, or about 67 grams of fat in a 2,000-calorie daily diet; and no more than 10 percent or 22 grams of that from saturated fats high in cholesterol; (2) maximum alcohol consumption of about 1 drink a day for women, 2 for men; (3) daily consumption of vegetables of 3-5 servings; fruits, 2-4; pastas, cereals or breads, 6-11; milk, 2-3; meat, poultry, fish and eggs, 2-3. (For vegetables, 1 serving=about 1 cup raw leafy greens or one-half cup other kinds; fruit, 1 medium apple, banana, or orange; grains, 1 slice of bread or 1 oz. cereal; milk, 1 cup or 1.5 oz. of cheese; meat and poultry, 2-3 oz. cooked lean beef or chicken without skin.)

## Protein

Proteins, composed of amino acids, are indispensable in the diet. They build, maintain, and repair the body. Best sources: eggs, milk, fish, meat, poultry, soybeans, nuts. High quality proteins such as eggs, meat, or fish supply all 8 amino acids needed in the diet.

## Fats

Fats provide energy by furnishing calories to the body, and by carrying vitamins A, D, E, and K. They are the most concentrated source of energy in the diet. Best sources: butter, margarine, salad oils, nuts, cream, egg yolks, most cheeses, lard, meat.

## Carbohydrates

Carbohydrates provide energy for body function and activity by supplying immediate calories. The carbohydrate group includes sugars, starches, fiber, and starchy vegetables. Best sources: grains, legumes, nuts, potatoes, fruits.

## Water

Water dissolves and transports other nutrients throughout the body, aiding the processes of digestion, absorption, circulation, and excretion. It helps regulate body temperature.

## Vitamins

Vitamin A—promotes good eyesight and helps keep the skin and mucous membranes resistant to infection. Best sources: liver, carrots, sweet potatoes, kale, collard greens, turnips, fortified milk.

Vitamin B1 (thiamine)—prevents beriberi. Essential to carbohydrate metabolism and health of nervous system.

Vitamin B2 (riboflavin)—protects skin, mouth, eye, eyelids, and mucous membranes. Essential to protein and energy metabolism. Best sources: liver, milk, meat, poultry, broccoli, mushrooms.

Vitamin B6 (pyridoxine)—important in the regulation of the central nervous system and in protein metabolism. Best sources: whole grains, meats, nuts, brewers' yeast.

Vitamin B12 (cobalamin)—needed to form red blood cells. Best sources: liver, meat, fish, eggs, soybeans.

Niacin—maintains the health of skin, tongue, and digestive system. Best sources: poultry, peanuts, fish, organ meats, enriched flour and bread.

Other B vitamins—biotin, choline, folic acid (folacin), inositol, PABA (para-aminobenzoic acid), pantothenic acid.

Vitamin C (ascorbic acid)—maintains collagen, a protein necessary for the formation of skin, ligaments, and bones. It helps heal wounds and mend fractures, and aids in resisting some types of virus and bacterial infections. Best sources: citrus fruits and juices, turnips, broccoli, Brussels sprouts, potatoes and sweet potatoes, tomatoes, cabbage.

Vitamin D—important for bone development. Best sources: sunlight, fortified milk and milk products, fish-liver oils, egg yolks, organ meats.

Vitamin E (tocopherol)—helps protect red blood cells. Best sources: vegetable oils, wheat germ, whole grains, eggs, peanuts, organ meats, margarine, green leafy vegetables.

Vitamin K—necessary for formation of prothrombin, which helps blood to clot. Also made by intestinal bacteria. Best dietary sources: green leafy vegetables, tomatoes.

## Minerals

Calcium—the most abundant mineral in the body, works with phosphorus in building and maintaining bones and teeth. Best sources: milk and milk products, cheese, and blackstrap molasses.

Phosphorus—the 2d most abundant mineral, performs more functions than any other mineral, and plays a part in nearly every chemical reaction in the body. Best source: whole grains, cheese, milk.

Iron—Necessary for the formation of myoglobin, which transports oxygen to muscle tissue, and hemoglobin, which transports oxygen in the blood. Best sources: organ meats, beans, green leafy vegetables, and shellfish.

Other minerals—chromium, cobalt, copper, fluorine, iodine, magnesium, manganese, molybdenum, potassium, selenium, sodium, sulfur, and zinc.

# Recommended Daily Dietary Allowances

Source: Food and Nutrition Board, Natl. Academy of Sciences—Natl. Research Council; 1989

| Age (years) and sex group | Weight (lbs.) | Protein (grams) | Fat soluble vitamins | | | | Water soluble vitamins | | | | | | | | Minerals | | | | | | |
|---|---|---|---|---|---|---|---|---|---|---|---|---|---|---|---|---|---|---|---|---|---|
| | | | Vitamin A[1] | Vitamin D[2] | Vitamin E[3] | Vitamin K | Vitamin C | Thiamin (mg.) | Riboflavin (mg.) | Niacin (mg.)[4] | Vitamin B6 (mg.) | Folate (micrograms) | Vitamin B12 (micrograms) | Calcium (mg.) | Phosphorus (mg.) | Magnesium (mg.) | Iron (mg.) | Zinc (mg.) | Iodine (micrograms) | Selenium (micrograms) |
| Infants... to 5 mos. | 13 | 13 | 375 | 7.5 | 3 | 5 | 30 | 0.3 | 0.4 | 5 | 0.3 | 25 | 0.3 | 400 | 300 | 40 | 6 | 5 | 40 | 10 |
| to 1 yr. | 20 | 14 | 375 | 10 | 4 | 10 | 35 | 0.4 | 0.5 | 6 | 0.6 | 35 | 0.5 | 600 | 500 | 60 | 10 | 5 | 50 | 15 |
| Children. 1-3 | 29 | 16 | 400 | 10 | 6 | 15 | 40 | 0.7 | 0.8 | 9 | 1.0 | 50 | 0.7 | 800 | 800 | 80 | 10 | 10 | 70 | 20 |
| 4-6 | 44 | 24 | 500 | 10 | 7 | 20 | 45 | 0.9 | 1.1 | 12 | 1.1 | 75 | 1.0 | 800 | 800 | 120 | 10 | 10 | 90 | 20 |
| 7-10 | 62 | 28 | 700 | 10 | 7 | 30 | 45 | 1.0 | 1.2 | 13 | 1.4 | 100 | 1.4 | 800 | 800 | 170 | 10 | 10 | 120 | 30 |
| Males... 11-14 | 99 | 45 | 1000 | 10 | 10 | 45 | 50 | 1.3 | 1.5 | 17 | 1.7 | 150 | 2.0 | 1200 | 1200 | 270 | 12 | 15 | 150 | 40 |
| 15-18 | 145 | 59 | 1000 | 10 | 10 | 65 | 60 | 1.5 | 1.8 | 20 | 2.0 | 200 | 2.0 | 1200 | 1200 | 400 | 12 | 15 | 150 | 50 |
| 19-24 | 160 | 58 | 1000 | 10 | 10 | 70 | 60 | 1.5 | 1.7 | 19 | 2.0 | 200 | 2.0 | 1200 | 1200 | 350 | 10 | 15 | 150 | 70 |
| 25-50 | 174 | 63 | 1000 | 5 | 10 | 80 | 60 | 1.5 | 1.7 | 19 | 2.0 | 200 | 2.0 | 800 | 800 | 350 | 10 | 15 | 150 | 70 |
| 51+ | 170 | 63 | 1000 | 5 | 10 | 80 | 60 | 1.2 | 1.4 | 15 | 2.0 | 200 | 2.0 | 800 | 800 | 350 | 10 | 15 | 150 | 70 |
| Females. 11-14 | 101 | 46 | 800 | 10 | 8 | 45 | 50 | 1.1 | 1.3 | 15 | 1.4 | 150 | 2.0 | 1200 | 1200 | 280 | 15 | 12 | 150 | 45 |
| 15-18 | 120 | 44 | 800 | 10 | 8 | 55 | 60 | 1.1 | 1.3 | 15 | 1.5 | 180 | 2.0 | 1200 | 1200 | 300 | 15 | 12 | 150 | 50 |
| 19-24 | 128 | 46 | 800 | 10 | 8 | 60 | 60 | 1.1 | 1.3 | 15 | 1.6 | 180 | 2.0 | 1200 | 1200 | 280 | 15 | 12 | 150 | 55 |
| 25-50 | 138 | 50 | 800 | 5 | 8 | 65 | 60 | 1.1 | 1.3 | 15 | 1.6 | 180 | 2.0 | 800 | 800 | 280 | 15 | 12 | 150 | 55 |
| 51+ | 143 | 50 | 800 | 5 | 8 | 65 | 60 | 1.0 | 1.2 | 13 | 1.6 | 180 | 2.0 | 800 | 800 | 280 | 10 | 12 | 150 | 55 |

(1) Retinol equivalents. (2) Micrograms of cholecalciferol. (3) Milligrams alpha-tocopherol equivalents. (4) Niacin equivalents.

# The New Food Labels

Source: Food Labeling Education Information Center, Beltville, Md.

The federal Nutrition Labeling and Education Act of 1990 established new requirements regarding what information must appear on the labels of processed foods. The effective date of the new regulations is the middle of 1994, although some products may carry the new labels earlier, and products with old labels may still be sold after the effective date as long as they were labeled earlier. Consumers should be aware that new labels use the words "Nutrition Facts" on the back or side panel, while the old ones use "Nutrition Information Per Serving." The new labels offer four basic improvements, according to the U.S. government's Food Labeling Education Information Center:

(1) **You can believe the claims on the package.** You will be able to believe the descriptive terms that say a food is "low in fat" or the health claims that link a certain nutrient to a specific disease because government regulations now define and regulate use of the terms and claims.

(2) **You can more easily compare products because serving sizes will be more comparable for similar food products.** For the first time, virtually all processed and packaged products will have to contain nutrition information. The information on the label will reflect an average serving in amounts customarily consumed. Since the serving size for each product is defined in the regulations, product comparisons will be easier and more meaningful than previously.

(3) **By using the "% Daily Value," you can quickly determine if a product is high or low in a nutrient.** You can use the % Daily Value column to easily compare one product to another. If you want to lower the fat in your diet, you can compare products and select the ones with the lower percentage. You can also use the % Daily Value to make dietary tradeoffs with other foods throughout the day. This means you don't have to deprive yourself of a favorite food that might be high in fat, if you watch what else they eat the rest of the day.

(4) **By consulting the Daily Values, you can determine how much (or how little) of the major nutrients you should eat on a daily basis.** Daily Values serve as a reference for dietary guidance. They help consumers understand how much of a nutrient they should eat at a minimum (say for fiber or calcium) or maximum (fat and cholesterol). The Daily Values are listed for people who take in approximately 2,000 calories a day (many older adults, children, and sedentary women) or 2,500 calories a day (active men, teenage boys, and very active women).
Note: The new labeling requirements do not cover restaurant menus. Nor do they cover fresh produce, meat and poultry, and fish.

## Sample of the New Nutrition Labels

Source: Food Labeling Education Information Center, Beltville, Md.

New heading signals new label.

More consistent serving sizes, in both household and metric measures, replace those that used to be set by manufacturers.

Nutrients required on nutrition panel are those most important to the health of today's consumers, most of whom need to worry about getting too much of certain items (fat, for example), rather than too few vitamins or minerals, as in the past.

Conversion guide helps consumers learn caloric value of the energy-producing nutrients.

New mandatory component helps consumers meet dietary guidelines recommending no more than 30 percent of calories from fat.

%Daily Value shows how a food fits into the overall daily diet.

Reference values help consumers learn good diet basics. They can be adjusted, depending on a person's calorie needs.

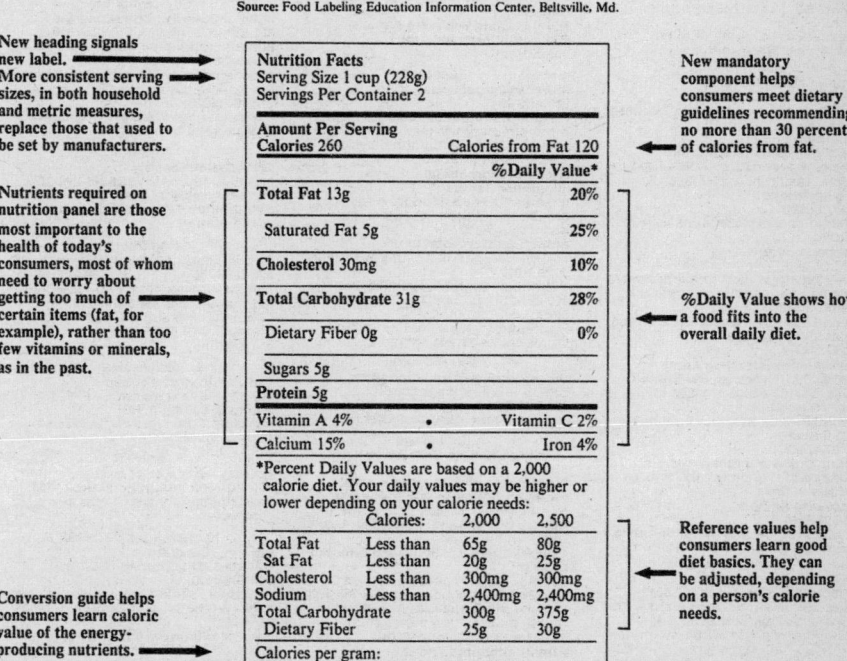

| Nutrition Facts | | |
|---|---|---|
| Serving Size 1 cup (228g) | | |
| Servings Per Container 2 | | |
| **Amount Per Serving** | | |
| Calories 260 | | Calories from Fat 120 |
| | | %Daily Value* |
| **Total Fat** 13g | | 20% |
| Saturated Fat 5g | | 25% |
| **Cholesterol** 30mg | | 10% |
| **Total Carbohydrate** 31g | | 28% |
| Dietary Fiber 0g | | 0% |
| Sugars 5g | | |
| **Protein** 5g | | |
| Vitamin A 4% | • | Vitamin C 2% |
| Calcium 15% | • | Iron 4% |

*Percent Daily Values are based on a 2,000 calorie diet. Your daily values may be higher or lower depending on your calorie needs:

| | | Calories: 2,000 | 2,500 |
|---|---|---|---|
| Total Fat | Less than | 65g | 80g |
| Sat Fat | Less than | 20g | 25g |
| Cholesterol | Less than | 300mg | 300mg |
| Sodium | Less than | 2,400mg | 2,400mg |
| Total Carbohydrate | | 300g | 375g |
| Dietary Fiber | | 25g | 30g |

Calories per gram:
Fat 9 • Carbohydrate 4 • Protein 4

# Where to Get Help

Source: Reprinted from Health & Medical Year Book 1993, "Where to Get Help," pp. 278-283.
Copyright ©1993 by P.F. Collier, Inc. Reprinted by permission of the publisher.

Listed below are some of the major U.S. organizations providing information about good health practices generally or about specific conditions and how to deal with them. Where a toll-free number is not available, an address is given when possible.

## General Sources

**Centers for Disease Control Voice Information System**
404-332-4555
Tape-recorded information about public health topics, such as AIDS, Lyme disease, and chronic fatigue syndrome. Also, you can request to talk with a CDC expert.

**National Health Information Center**
800-336-4797; in Maryland, 301-565-4167
Provides phone numbers for more than 1,000 health-related organizations and offers various printed materials.

**National Institutes of Health**
Bethesda, MD 20892
301-496-4000
Free information, including the latest research findings, on a wide range of diseases.

**Tel-Med**
Check the phone book for local listings or call Tel-Med headquarters at 714-825-6034
Tape-recorded information on over 600 health topics. Sponsored by local medical societies, health organizations, or hospitals.

## Aging

**National Council on the Aging**
800-424-9046
Provides information and publications on all aspects of aging.

**National Institute on Aging**
Public Information Office
Federal Building, Room 6C12
Bethesda, MD 20892
410-496-1752
Provides information about disabling conditions, support groups, and community resources.

## AIDS

**National AIDS Hotline**
800-342-AIDS 24 hours; in Spanish, 800-344-SIDA; for the hearing impaired, 800-AIDS-TTY
Provides recorded information on the prevention and spread of AIDS.

## Alcoholism and Drug Abuse

**Alcohol Abuse Emergency**
800-ALCOHOL

**Alcoholism and Drug Addiction Treatment Center**
800-382-4357
Offers referrals to local facilities for adolescents and adults; operates 24 hours.

**National Clearinghouse for Alcohol and Drug Information**
800-729-6686
Provides federal publications and literature searches.

**National Cocaine Hotline**
800-COCAINE
Answers questions about cocaine and other drugs; provides referral to drug treatment centers. Operates 24 hours.

**National Council on Alcoholism and Drug Dependence Hopeline**
800-475-HOPE

**National Institute for Drug Abuse**
800-662-HELP; in Spanish, 800-66-AYUDA
Makes referrals to support groups and treatment programs.

**National Parents' Resource Institute for Drug Education**
800-677-7433
Recording gives telephone numbers to call and an address to write to for drug information. Operates 24 hours.

**Recovering Network**
800-527-5344
Provides treatment referrals and counseling for recovering alcoholics; operates 24 hours.

## Alzheimer's Disease

**Alzheimer's Association**
800-621-0379; in Illinois, 800-572-6037
Makes referrals to local chapters and support groups; offers information on publications available from the association.

## Anemia

**National Association for Sickle Cell Disease**
800-421-8453; in California, 213-736-5455

Offers genetic counseling and information packet.

## Arthritis

**Arthritis Foundation**
800-283-7800
Provides information, publications, and referrals to local groups.

## Asthma and Allergies

**Asthma and Allergy Foundation Patient Information Line**
800-7-ASTHMA
Provides general information, publications and videos, and referrals to physicians.

**Asthma Information Line**
800-822-ASMA
Provides written materials on asthma and allergies. Operates 24 hours.

## Blindness and Eye Care

**American Council of the Blind**
800-424-8666; in Washington, D.C., 202-467-5081
Offers information on blindness; provides referrals to clinics and other organizations.

**American Foundation for the Blind**
800-AF-BLIND; in New York State, 212-620-2147
Gives information on visual impairments and on AFB services, products, and publications.

**Blind Children's Center**
800-222-3566; in California, 800-222-3567

**National Association for Parents of the Visually Impaired**
800-562-6265
Offers support and information for parents of individuals who are visually impaired.

**National Retinitis Pigmentosa Foundation**
800-638-2300; in Maryland, 301-225-9400; for the hearing impaired, 301-225-9409
Answers questions and provides written materials.

**NSPB (National Society to Prevent Blindness) Center for Sight**
800-221-3004

## Cancer

**American Cancer Society**
800-ACS-2345
Provides publications and information about cancer and coping with cancer; makes referrals to local chapters of the American Cancer Society for support services.

**National Cancer Institute's Cancer Information Service**
800-4-CANCER; 800-638-6070 in Alaska; 808-524-1234 in Oahu, Ha. (neighboring islands call collect)
Answers questions about cancer; Spanish-speaking staff members available in some areas.

**Y-Me Breast Cancer Support Program**
800-221-2141; in Illinois, 708-799-8228, 24 hours
Provides information and literature on breast cancer, counseling, and referrals.

## Cerebral Palsy

**United Cerebral Palsy Associations**
800-USA-5UCP; in Washington, D.C., 202-842-1266
Provides literature about cerebral palsy.

## Child Abuse

**Childhelp's National Child Abuse Hotline**
800-4-A-CHILD
Provides crisis intervention, professional counseling, referrals to local groups offering counseling and to shelters for runaways, and literature in English and Spanish. Operates 24 hours.

**National Center for Missing and Exploited Children**
800-843-5678; for the hearing impaired, 800-826-7653; in Arlington, Va., 703-235-3900
Operates a hotline for reporting missing children and sightings of missing children. Assists law enforcement agencies.

**Parents Anonymous Hotline**
800-421-0353; in California, 800-352-0386
Provides information on self-help groups for parents. Operates 24 hours.

## Crisis

**National Adolescent Suicide Hotline**
800-621-4000; in California, 800-352-0386
Provides crisis intervention and referrals for runaways. Operates 24 hours.

**National Youth Crisis Hotline**
800-HIT-HOME
Provides counseling for youths dealing with drug abuse, pregnancy, molestation, suicide, and child abuse; makes referrals to local drug treatment centers, shelters, and counseling services. Operates 24 hours.

## Cystic Fibrosis

**Cystic Fibrosis Foundation**
800-FIGHT-CF; in Maryland, 301-951-4422
Answers questions and offers literature and referrals to local clinics.

## Diabetes

**American Diabetes Association**
800-ADA-DISC; in Virginia and Washington, D.C., 703-549-1500
Provides literature and referrals to local affiliates for information on support groups.

**Juvenile Diabetes Foundation Hotline**
800-223-1138 or 800-533-2873; in New York City, 212-889-7575
Answers questions, provides literature (some in Spanish), and refers to local chapters, physicians, and clinics.

## Digestive Diseases

**National Digestive Diseases Information Clearinghouse**
Box NDDIC, Bethesda, MD 20892
301-468-6344

**National Foundation for Ileitis and Colitis**
800-343-3637; in New York, 212-679-1570
Provides educational materials, refers to local support groups and physicians.

## Down Syndrome

**National Down Syndrome Congress**
800-232-6372; in Illinois, 312-823-7550
Answers questions and makes referrals to local organizations.

**National Down Syndrome Society Hotline**
800-221-4602; in New York City, 212-460-9330
Provides information and gives referrals for local programs for newborn.

## Dyslexia

**Orton Dyslexia Society**
800-ABCD-123; in Maryland, 301-296-0232
Provides information on testing, tutoring, and computers to aid people with dyslexia and related disorders.

## Eating Disorders

**Bulimia/Anorexia Self-Help Hotline**
800-227-4785
Provides information on bulimia and anorexia.

**National Anorexic Aid Society**
1925 East Dublin-Granville Road
Columbus, Ohio 43229-3517
614-436-1112

## Endometriosis

**Endometriosis Association**
800-992-ENDO; in Wisconsin, 414-962-8972; in Canada, 800-426-2END
Provides a 24-hour recording for callers to request information.

## Epilepsy

**Epilepsy Foundation of America**
800-332-1000; in Maryland, 301-459-3700
Provides information and referrals to local chapters.

## Handicaps and Disabilities

**Library of Congress**
800-424-9100; in Washington, D.C., 202-707-5100
Lends braille and audio-recorded books; refers callers to state and local libraries with these services.

**National Information Center for Children and Youth With Handicaps**
800-999-5599 or 703-893-6061
Offers information and referrals for disabled and handicapped children.

**National Information System for Health Related Services**
800-922-9234; in South Carolina, 800-922-1107
Makes referrals to support groups and to sources of financial, medical, and legal assistance for developmentally disabled and chronically ill children.

## Headaches

**National Headache Foundation**
800-843-2256; in Illinois, 800-523-8858
Offers literature on headaches and treatment.

**National Institute of Neurological Disorders and Stroke**
P.O. Box 5801
Bethesda, MD 20824
800-352-9424

## Hearing

**American Speech-Language-Hearing Association Helpline**
800-638-8255; in Maryland call collect, 301-897-0039
Offers materials on hearing aids and on pathologists and audiologists certified by the association.

**Dial A Hearing Screening Test**
800-222-EARS; in Pennsylvania, 800-345-EARS
Answers questions on hearing problems, makes referrals to local numbers for a two-minute hearing test, as well as to ear, nose, and throat specialists and to organizations with specialized ear and hearing aid information.

**Hearing Helpline**
800-EAR-WELL; in Virginia, 703-642-0580
Provides information on better hearing and preventing deafness.

**National Hearing Aid Helpline**
800-521-5247
Provides information and distributes a directory of hearing aid specialists certified by the National Hearing AID Society.

## Heart Disease

**American Heart Association**
7272 Greenville Avenue
Dallas, TX 75231
800-242-1793; 214-373-6300

**National Heart, Lung, and Blood Institute Information Office**
9000 Rockville Pike
Building 31-4A21
Bethesda, MD 20892
301-496-4236

## Hospices

**Children's Hospice International**
800-242-4453; in Virginia, 703-684-0330
Provides information on and referrals to children's hospices.

**Hospice Education Institute Hospicelink**
800-331-1620; in Connecticut, 203-767-1620
Offers general information about hospice care and makes referrals to local programs.

## Huntington's Disease

**Huntington's Disease Society of America**
800-345-4372; in New York, 212-242-1968
Provides information and referrals to physicians and support groups.

## Hysterectomy

**Hysterectomy Resources and Services Foundation**
422 Bryn Mawr Ave.
Bala-Cynwyd, PA 19004
215-667-7757
Offers peer support for women considering hysterectomy, referrals for second opinions, legal referrals.

## Impotence

**Impotence Information Center**
800-843-4315
Provides information on the causes and treatment of impotence.

**Impotence Institute of America Hotline**
800-669-1603
Offers literature, physician referrals, and phone numbers of local Impotents Anonymous chapters.

## Kidney Diseases

**National Kidney Foundation**
800-622-9010
Provides information and referrals.

**National Kidney and Urologic Diseases Information Clearinghouse**
P.O. Box NKUDIC
Bethesda, MD 20892
301-468-6345

## Lead Exposure

**National Lead Information Center Hotline**
800-LEAD-FYI
Makes recommendations for reducing a child's exposure to lead, in the home and elsewhere.

## Liver Diseases

**American Liver Foundation**
800-223-0179; in New Jersey, 201-256-2550
Provides information and physician and support group referrals.

## Lung Diseases

**American Lung Association**
Check the phone book for local listings or call the national office at 212-315-8700

**National Jewish Center for Immunology and Respiratory Medicine Information Service**
800-222-LUNG; in Denver, 303-355-LUNG
Answers questions on asthma, emphysema, allergies, smoking, and other respiratory and immune system disorders.

## Lupus

**American Lupus Society**
800-331-1802
Provides literature on lupus research and referrals to physicians and local chapters.

**Lupus Foundation of America**
800-558-0121; in Rockville, Md., 301-670-9292; in Washington, D.C., 202-328-4550.
Answers basic questions and provides literature about lupus; refers to local affiliates.

## Mental Health

**American Mental Health Fund**
800-433-5959; in Illinois, 800-826-2336
Provides a 24-hour recorded message for callers to request a pamphlet on mental health.

**American Schizophrenic Association**
800-847-3802
Provides information about mental illness, physician referrals, and book lists.

**National Depressive and Manic Depressive Association**
800-826-3632
Offers support for patients and families, provides emergency assistance, and helps patients seek qualified treatment.

**National Foundation for Depressive Illness**
800-248-4344
Provides a 24-hour recorded message describing the symptoms of depression and offering an address for more information and physician referral.

**National Mental Health Association**
800-969-6642
Makes referrals to mental health groups.

**OCD (Obsessive-Compulsive Disorder) Foundation**
P.O. Box 9573
New Haven, CT 06535
203-772-0565

## Multiple Sclerosis

**National Multiple Sclerosis Society**
800-624-8236
A 24-hour recording allows callers to request information and leave name and address; to speak to a staff member, call 800-227-3166.

## Nutrition

**National Center for Nutrition and Dietetics Hotline**
800-366-1655
Offers general information on nutrition, answers questions, and provides literature.

**USDA Food, Safety, and Inspection Service Meat and Poultry Hotline**
800-535-4555
Provides information on proper handling, preparation, storage, and cooking of meat, poultry, and eggs.

**University of Alabama at Birmingham Nutrition Information Service**
800-231-DIET
Answers questions on healthful eating and food handling.

## Pain

**National Chronic Pain Outreach Association**
7979 Old Georgetown Road
Suite 100
Bethesda, MD 20814-2429
301-652-4948
Provides information clearinghouse, makes referrals, and publishes newsletters.

## Parkinson's Disease

**National Parkinson's Foundation**
800-327-4545; in Florida, 800-433-7022; in Miami, 305-547-6666
Answers questions, makes physician referrals, and provides written information.

**Parkinson's Educational Program**
800-344-7872; in California, 714-250-2975
Provides written materials as well as information on support groups and physician referrals. Operates 24 hours.

## Prostate Problems

**Prostate Information Line**
800-543-9632

## Sexually Transmitted Diseases

**American Social Health Association's National STD Hotline**
800-227-8922
Provides information and confidential referrals for treatment.

## Skin Problems

**National Psoriasis Foundation**
6443 W.W. Beaverton Hwy., Suite 210
Portland, OR 97221
503-297-1545
Offers information and referrals.

## Sleep Disorders

**American Narcolepsy Association**
800-222-6085; in California, 415-591-7979
Provides literature on narcolepsy, a condition marked by brief attacks of deep sleep.

## Speech Disorders

**National Center for Stuttering**
800-221-2483; in New York City, 212-532-1460
Provides information on stuttering in young children, as well as older children and adults.

**Stuttering Foundation of America**
800-992-9392
Provides referrals to speech pathologists, resource lists, and other publications. Operates 24 hours.

## Spina Bifida

**Spina Bifida Information and Referral**
800-621-3141; in Maryland, 301-770-7222
Offers information and referrals to local chapters.

## Spinal Injuries

**American Paralysis Association's Spinal Cord Injury Hotline**
800-526-3456
Provides literature on spinal cord injuries and makes referrals to organizations and support groups.

**National Spinal Cord Injury Association**
800-962-9629; in Massachusetts, 617-935-2722
Offers peer counseling and makes referrals to local chapters and other organizations.

## Stroke

**National Stroke Association**
800-787-6537
Provides written and referral information.

## Sudden Infant Death Syndrome

**American Sudden Infant Death Syndrome Institute**
800-232-SIDS; in Georgia, 800-847-7437
Answers questions, distributes literature, and makes referrals to other organizations. Operates 24 hours.

**National SIDS Foundation**
800-221-SIDS; in Maryland, 301-964-8000
Provides literature on medical information, referrals, and support groups.

## Tourette Syndrome

**Tourette Syndrome Association**
800-237-0717; in New York, 718-224-2999
Provides a 24-hour recording for callers to request information, published in English and Spanish.

## Urinary Incontinence

**Help for Incontinent People**
800-BLADDER
Offers information on bladder control, services available for incontinence, and assistive devices.

**Simon Foundation**
800-23-SIMON
Offers support and literature on incontinence.

## Women's Health

**National Women's Health Network**
1325 G St. NW
Washington, D.C. 20005
202-347-1140

**National Women's Health Resource Center**
2440 M St. NW
Washington, D.C.
202-293-6045

# NATIONAL DEFENSE

Data as of mid-1993
**Chairman, Joint Chiefs of Staff**
Gen. Colin L. Powell (until Sept. 30, 1993)
Gen. John Shalikashvili (as of Oct. 1, 1993)

**Vice Chairman**
Adm. David E. Jeremiah

The Joint Chiefs of Staff consists of the Chairman and Vice Chairman of the Joint Chiefs of Staff; the Chief of Staff, U.S. Army; the Chief of Naval Operations; the Chief of Staff, U.S. Air Force; and the Commandant of the Marine Corps.

## Army

**Date of Rank**
Chief of Staff—Gordon R. Sullivan
**Generals**

| | | |
|---|---|---|
| Burba, Edwin H. Jr. | Sept. | 27, 1989 |
| Franks, Frederick M. Jr. | Aug. | 23, 1991 |
| Galvin, John R. | Feb. | 25, 1985 |
| Joulwan, George A. | Nov. | 21, 1990 |
| Powell, Colin L. | Apr. | 4, 1989 |
| Reimer, Dennis J. | June | 21, 1991 |
| RisCassi, Robert W. | Jan. | 17, 1989 |
| Ross, Jimmy D. | Feb. | 1, 1992 |
| Saint, Crosbie E. | June | 24, 1988 |
| Stiner, Carl W. | July | 1, 1990 |

## Air Force

Chief of Staff—Merrill A. McPeak
**Generals**

| | | |
|---|---|---|
| Boyd, Charles G. | Dec. | 1, 1992 |
| Butler, George L. | Jan. | 25, 1991 |
| Carns, Michael P.C. | May | 16, 1991 |
| Davis, James B. | June | 1, 1992 |
| Fogleman, Ronald R. | Sept. | 1, 1992 |
| Horner, Charles A. | June | 1, 1992 |
| Loh, John M. | June | 1, 1990 |
| Oaks, Robert C. | July | 1, 1990 |
| Rutherford, Robert L. | Feb. | 1, 1993 |
| Viccellio Jr., Henry | Dec. | 10, 1992 |
| Yates, Ronald W. | Apr. | 1, 1990 |

## Navy

**Date of Rank**
Chief of Naval Operations
Adm. Frank B. Kelso II (submariner)
**Admirals**

| | | |
|---|---|---|
| Arthur, Stanley R. (aviator) | July | 6, 1992 |
| Boorda, Jeremy M. (surface warfare) | Mar. | 2, 1992 |
| DeMars, Bruce (submariner) | Nov. | 1, 1988 |
| Jeremiah, David E. (surface warfare) | Oct. | 1, 1987 |
| Kelly, Robert J. (aviator) | Mar. | 1, 1991 |
| Larson, Charles R. (submariner) | Mar. | 1, 1990 |
| Mauz, Henry N. Jr. (surface warfare) | Aug. | 1, 1992 |
| Miller, Paul D. (surface warfare) | Feb. | 1, 1991 |
| Smith, William D. (submariner) | Feb. | 22, 1991 |

## Marine Corps

Corps Commandant, with rank of General

| | | |
|---|---|---|
| Carl E. Mundy Jr. | July | 1, 1991 |

**ACMC/Chief of Staff, with rank of Gen.**

| | | |
|---|---|---|
| Walter E. Boomer | Sept. | 1, 1992 |
| Joseph P. Hoar | Sept. | 1, 1991 |

## Coast Guard

Commandant, with rank of Admiral

| | | |
|---|---|---|
| J. William Kime | June | 1, 1990 |

Vice Commandant, with rank of Vice Admiral

| | | |
|---|---|---|
| Robert T. Nelson | June | 5, 1992 |

## Unified Defense Commands Commanders in Chief
(as of mid-1993)

**U.S. European Command,** Brussels, Belgium — Maj. Gen. John Shalikashvili* (USA) (concurrently NATO Supreme Allied Commander, Europe)

**U.S. Southern Command,** Quarry Heights, Panama Canal Zone — Gen. George A. Joulwan (USA)

**U.S. Atlantic Command,** Norfolk, Virginia — Adm. Paul D. Miller (USN) (concurrently NATO Supreme Allied Commander, Atlantic)

**U.S. Pacific Command,** Honolulu, Hawaii — Adm. Charles R. Larson (USN)

**U.S. Space Command,** Peterson AFB, Colo. — Gen. Charles A. Horner (USAF)

**U.S. Strategic Command,** Omaha, Neb. — Gen. George L. Butler (USAF)

**U.S. Forces Command,** Fort McPherson, Ga. — Gen. Dennis J. Reimer (USA)

**U.S. Transportation Command,** Scott AFB, Ill. — Gen. Ronald R. Fogleman (USAF)

**U.S. Special Operations Command,** Fort Walton Beach, Fla. — Gen. Wayne A. Dowling (USA)

**U.S. Central Command,** MacDill AFB, Fla. — Gen. Joseph P. Hoar (USMC)

## North Atlantic Treaty Organization International Commands
(as of mid-1993)

**Supreme Allied Commander, Europe (SACEUR)** — Gen. John Shalikashvili* (USA)

**Deputy Supreme Allied Commander, Europe (DSACEUR)** — Gen. Sir John Waters (UKA)

**Commander in Chief Allied Forces Northern Europe** — Gen. Sir Garry Johnson (UKA)

**Commander in Chief Allied Forces Central Europe** — Gen. Henning von Ondarva (GEA)

**Commander in Chief Allied Forces Southern Europe** — Adm. Jeremy M. Boorda

**Commander in Chief United Kingdom Air Forces** — Gen. John Thomson (UKAF)

**Chairman, NATO Military Committee** — Field Marshall Sir Richard Vincent (UKA)

* Named by Pres. Bill Clinton, Aug. 11, 1993, to become Chairman of the Joint Chiefs of Staff, effective Oct. 1, 1993.

## Principal U.S. Military Training Centers
### Army

| Name, P.O. address | Zip | Nearest city | Name, P.O. address | Zip | Nearest city |
|---|---|---|---|---|---|
| Aberdeen Proving Ground, MD | 21005 | Aberdeen | Fort Devens, MA | 01433 | Ayer |
| Carlisle Barracks, PA | 17013 | Carlisle | Fort Dix, NJ | 08640 | Trenton |
| Fort Benning, GA | 31905 | Columbus | Fort Eustis, VA | 23604 | Newport News |
| Fort Bliss, TX | 79916 | El Paso | Fort Gordon, GA | 30905 | Augusta |
| Fort Bragg, NC | 28307 | Fayetteville | Fort Benjamin Harrison, IN | 46216 | Indianapolis |

| Name, P.O. address | Zip | Nearest city | Name, P.O. address | Zip | Nearest city |
|---|---|---|---|---|---|
| Fort Sam Houston, TX | 78234 | San Antonio | Fort Rucker, AL. | 36362 | Dothan |
| Fort Huachuca, AZ | 85613 | Sierra Vista | Fort Sill, OK. | 73503 | Lawton |
| Fort Jackson, SC. | 29207 | Columbia | Fort Leonard Wood, MO. | 65473 | Rolla |
| Fort Knox, KY. | 40121 | Louisville | Joint Readiness, Ft. Chaffee, AR. | 72905 | Fort Smith |
| Fort Leavenworth, KS | 66027 | Leavenworth | National Training Center. | 92311 | Barstow, CA |
| Fort Lee, VA. | 23801 | Petersburg | The Judge Advocate | | Charlottes- |
| Fort McClellan, AL. | 36205 | Anniston | General School, VA | 22901 | ville |
| Fort Monmouth, NJ. | 07703 | Red Bank | U.S. Military Acad., NY. | 10996 | West Point |

## Navy

| | | | | | |
|---|---|---|---|---|---|
| Great Lakes, IL | 60088 | North Chicago | Annapolis, MD | 21402 | Annapolis |

## Marine Corps

| Name, P.O. address | Zip | Nearest city | Name, P.O. address | Zip | Nearest city |
|---|---|---|---|---|---|
| MCB Camp Lejeune, NC. | 28542 | Jacksonville | MCAS Kaneohe Bay, | | |
| MCB Camp Pendleton, CA. | 92055 | Oceanside | Oahu, HI. | San | |
| MCAGCC Twentynine Palms, CA. | 92278 | Palm Springs | | Francisco | Kailua |
| MCCDC Quantico, VA. | 22134 | Quantico | | 96863 | |
| MCRD Parris Island, SC. | 29905 | Beaufort | MCAS Beaufort, SC. | 29904 | Beaufort |
| MCAS Cherry Point, NC. | 28533 | Havelock | MCAS Yuma, AZ. | 85369 | Yuma |
| MCAS Tustin, CA. | 92780 | Santa Ana | MCMWTC Bridgeport, CA. | 93517 | Bridgeport |
| MCAS New River, NC | 28545 | Jacksonville | | | |

MCB = Marine Corps Base. MCCDC = Marine Corps Combat Development Command. MCAS = Marine Corps Air Station. MCRD = Marine Corps Recruit Depot. MCAGCC = Marine Corps Air-Ground Combat Center. MCMWTC = Marine Corps Mountain Warfare Training Center.

## Air Force

| | | | | | |
|---|---|---|---|---|---|
| Chanute AFB, IL | 61868 | Rantoul | Lackland AFB, TX | 78236 | San Antonio |
| Goodfellow AFB, TX | 76908 | San Angelo | Lowry AFB, CO. | 80230 | Denver |
| Gunter AFB, AL* | 36114 | Montgomery | Maxwell AFB, AL* | 36112 | Montgomery |
| Keesler AFB, MS | 39534 | Biloxi | Sheppard AFB, TX. | 76311 | Wichita Falls |

\* Air University Bases. All others are Air Training Command Bases.

## Personal Salutes and Honors

The United States national salute, 21 guns, is also the salute to a national flag. The independence of the United States is commemorated by the salute to the Union — one gun for each state — fired at noon on July 4 at all military posts provided with suitable artillery.

A 21-gun salute on arrival and departure, with 4 ruffles and flourishes, is rendered to the President of the United States, to an ex-President and to a President-elect. The national anthem or *Hail to the Chief*, as appropriate, is played for the President, and the national anthem for the others. A 21-gun salute on arrival and departure, with 4 ruffles and flourishes, also is rendered to the sovereign or chief of state of a foreign country or a member of a reigning royal family; the national anthem of his or her country is played. The music is considered an inseparable part of the salute and will immediately follow the ruffles and flourishes without pause.

| Rank | Salute—guns Arrive—Leave | | Ruffles, flour- ishes | Music |
|---|---|---|---|---|
| Vice President of United States | 19 | | 4 | Hail Columbia |
| Speaker of the House | 19 | | 4 | March |
| American or foreign ambassador. | 19 | | 4 | Nat. anthem of official |
| Premier or prime minister | 19 | | 4 | Nat. anthem of official |
| Secretary of Defense, Army, Navy or Air Force | 19 | 19 | 4 | Honors March |
| Other Cabinet members, Senate President pro tempore, Governor, or Chief Justice of U.S. | 19 | | 4 | Honors March |
| Chairman, Joint Chiefs of Staff. | 19 | 19 | 4 | |
| Army Chief of Staff, Chief of Naval Operations, Air Force Chief of Staff, Marine Commandant | 19 | 19 | 4 | General's or Admiral's March |
| General of the Army, General of the Air Force, Fleet Admiral. | 19 | 19 | 4 | |
| Generals, Admirals. | 17 | 17 | 4 | |
| Assistant secretaries of Defense, Army, Navy or Air Force | 17 | 17 | 4 | Honors March |
| Chairman of a committee of Congress. | 17 | | 4 | Honors March |

Other salutes (on arrival only) include 15 guns for U.S. envoys or ministers and foreign envoys or ministers accredited to the U.S.; 15 guns for a lieutenant general or vice admiral; 13 guns for a major general or rear admiral (upper half); 13 guns for U.S. ministers resident and ministers resident accredited to the U.S.; 11 guns for a brigadier general or rear admiral (lower half); 11 guns for U.S. charges d'affaires and like officials accredited to the U.S.; and 11 guns for consuls general accredited to the U.S.

## Military Units, U.S. Army and Air Force

**Army Units. Squad.** In infantry usually ten enlisted personnel under a staff sergeant. **Platoon.** In infantry 4 squads under a lieutenant. **Company.** Headquarters section and 4 platoons under a captain. (Company-size unit in the artillery is a battery; in the cavalry, a troop.) **Battalion.** Hdqts. and 4 or more companies under a lieutenant colonel. (Battalion-size unit in the cavalry is a squadron.) **Brigade.** Hdqts. and 3 or more battalions under a colonel. **Division.** Hdqts. and 3 brigades with artillery, combat support, and combat service support units under a major general. **Army Corps.** Two or more divisions with corps troops under a lieutenant general. **Field Army.** Hdqts. and two or more corps with field Army troops under a general.

**Air Force Units. Flight.** Numerically designated flights are the lowest level unit in the Air Force. They are used primarily where there is a need for small mission elements to be incorporated into an organized unit. **Squadron.** A squadron is the basic unit in the Air Force. It is used to designate the mission units in operational commands. **Group.** The group is a flexible unit composed of two or more squadrons whose functions may be either tactical, support or administrative in nature. **Wing.** An operational wing normally has two or more assigned mission squadrons in an area such as combat, flying training or airlift. **Air Division.** The organization of the air division may be similar to that of the numbered air force, though on a much smaller scale. Functions are usually limited to operations and logistics. **Numbered Air Forces.** Normally an operationally oriented agency, the numbered air force is designed for the control of two or more air divisions or units of comparable strength. It is a flexible organization and may be of any size. Its wings may be assigned to air divisions or directly under the numbered air force. **Major Command.** A major subdivision of the Air Force that is assigned a major segment of the USAF mission.

## The Federal Service Academies

**U.S. Military Academy, West Point, N.Y.** Founded 1802. Awards B.S. degree and Army commission for a 5-year service obligation. For admissions information, write Admissions Office, USMA, West Point, NY 10996.

**U.S. Naval Academy, Annapolis, Md.** Founded 1845. Awards B.S. degree and Navy or Marine Corps commission for a 5-year service obligation. For admissions information, write Dean of Admissions, Naval Academy, Annapolis, MD 21402.

**U.S. Air Force Academy, Colorado Springs, Col.** Founded 1954. Awards B.S. degree and Air Force commission for a 5-year service obligation. For admissions information, write Registrar, U.S. Air Force Academy, CO 80840.

**U.S. Coast Guard Academy, New London, Conn.** Founded 1876. Awards B.S. degree and Coast Guard commission for a 5-year service obligation. For admissions information, write Director of Admissions, Coast Guard Academy, New London, CT 06320.

**U.S. Merchant Marine Academy, Kings Point, N.Y.** Founded 1943. Awards B.S. degree, a license as a deck, engineer, or dual officer, and a U.S. Naval Reserve commission. Service obligations vary according to options taken by the graduate. For admissions information, write Admission Office, U.S. Merchant Marine Academy, Kings Point, NY 11024.

## U.S. Army Insignia and Chevrons

Source: Department of the Army, U.S. Dept. of Defense

### Grade          Insignia

**General of the Armies**
General John J. Pershing, the only person to have held this rank, was authorized to prescribe his own insignia, but never wore in excess of four stars. The rank originally was established by Congress for George Washington in 1799, and he was promoted to the rank by joint resolution of Congress, approved by Pres. Ford Oct. 19, 1976.

**General of Army** . . . Five silver stars fastened together in a circle and the coat of arms of the United States in gold color metal with shield and crest enameled.

| | |
|---|---|
| General . . . . . . . . . . . | Four silver stars |
| Lieutenant General . . . . . | Three silver stars |
| Major General . . . . . . . . | Two silver stars |
| Brigadier General . . . . . . | One silver star |
| Colonel . . . . . . . . . . . | Silver eagle |
| Lieutenant Colonel . . . . . | Silver oak leaf |
| Major . . . . . . . . . . . . | Gold oak leaf |
| Captain . . . . . . . . . . . | Two silver bars |
| First Lieutenant . . . . . . . | One silver bar |
| Second Lieutenant . . . . . . | One gold bar |

### Warrant Officers
Grade Four—Silver bar with 4 enamel black squares.
Grade Three—Silver bar with 3 enamel black squares.
Grade Two—Silver bar with 2 enamel black squares.

Grade One—Silver bar with 1 enamel black squares.

### Noncommissioned Officers
**Sergeant Major of the Army (E-9).** Same as Command Sergeant Major (below) but with 2 stars. Also wears distinctive red and white shield on lapel.

**Command Sergeant Major (E-9).** Three chevrons above three arcs with a 5-pointed star with a wreath around the star between the chevrons and arcs.

**Sergeant Major (E-9).** Three chevrons above three arcs with a five-pointed star between the chevrons and arcs.

**First Sergeant (E-8).** Three chevrons above three arcs with a lozenge between the chevrons and arcs.

**Master Sergeant (E-8).** Three chevrons above three arcs.

**Sergeant First Class (E-7).** Three chevrons above two arcs.

**Staff Sergeant (E-6).** Three chevrons above one arc.

**Sergeant (E-5).** Three chevrons.

**Corporal (E-4).** Two chevrons.

### Specialists
**Specialist (E-4).** Eagle device only.

### Other enlisted
**Private First Class (E-3).** One chevron above one arc.

**Private (E-2).** One chevron.

**Private (E-1).** None.

## U.S. Navy Insignia

Source: Dept. of the Navy, U.S. Dept. of Defense

### Navy
Stripes and corps device are of gold embroidery.

### Stripes

| | |
|---|---|
| Fleet Admiral . . . . . | 1 two inch with 4 one-half inch. |
| Admiral . . . . . . . . | 1 two inch with 3 one-half inch. |
| Vice Admiral . . . . . . | 1 two inch with 2 one-half inch. |
| Rear Admiral (upper half) . . . . . . . . | 1 two inch with 1 one-half inch. |
| Rear Admiral (lower half) . . . . . . . . | 1 two inch. |
| Captain . . . . . . . . . | 4 one-half inch. |
| Commander . . . . . . | 3 one-half inch. |
| Lieut. Commander . . | 2 one-half inch, with 1 one-quarter inch between. |
| Lieutenant . . . . . . . | 2 one-half inch. |
| Lieutenant (j.g.) . . . . | 1 one-half inch with one-quarter inch above. |
| Ensign . . . . . . . . . | 1 one-half inch. |

Warrant Officers—One 1/2" broken with 1/2" intervals of blue as follows:

Warrant Officer W-4—1 break

Warrant Officer W-3—2 breaks, 2" apart
Warrant Officer W-2—3 breaks, 2" apart

The breaks are symmetrically centered on outer face of the sleeve.

Enlisted personnel (noncommissioned petty officers) . . . A rating badge worn on the upper left arm, consisting of a spread eagle, appropriate number of chevrons, and centered specialty mark.

### Marine Corps
Marine Corps and Army officer insignia are similar. Marine Corps and Army enlisted insignia, although basically similar, differ in color, design, and fewer Marine Corps subdivisions. The Marine Corps' distinctive cap and collar ornament is a combination of the American eagle, globe, and anchor.

### Coast Guard
Coast Guard insignia follow Navy custom, with certain minor changes such as the officer cap insignia. The Coast Guard shield is worn on both sleeves of officers and on the right sleeve of all enlisted personnel.

# U.S. Army Personnel on Active Duty[1]

Source: Department of the Army, U.S. Dept. of Defense

| June 30[2] | Total strength | Commissioned officers | | | Warrant officers | | Enlisted personnel | | |
|---|---|---|---|---|---|---|---|---|---|
| | | Total | Male | Female[3] | Male[4] | Female | Total | Male | Female |
| 1940 . . . . . . | 267,767 | 17,563 | 16,624 | 939 | 763 | — | 249,441 | 249,441 | — |
| 1942 . . . . . . | 3,074,184 | 203,137 | 190,662 | 12,475 | 3,285 | — | 2,867,762 | 2,867,762 | — |
| 1943 . . . . . . | 6,993,102 | 557,657 | 521,435 | 36,222 | 21,919 | 0 | 6,413,526 | 6,358,200 | 55,325 |
| 1944 . . . . . . | 7,992,868 | 740,077 | 692,351 | 47,726 | 36,893 | 10 | 7,215,888 | 7,144,601 | 71,287 |
| 1945 . . . . . . | 8,266,373 | 835,403 | 772,511 | 62,892 | 56,216 | 44 | 7,374,710 | 7,283,930 | 90,780 |
| 1946 . . . . . . | 1,889,690 | 257,300 | 240,643 | 16,657 | 9,826 | 18 | 1,622,546 | 1,605,847 | 16,699 |
| 1950 . . . . . . | 591,487 | 67,784 | 63,375 | 4,409 | 4,760 | 22 | 518,921 | 512,370 | 6,551 |
| 1955 . . . . . . | 1,107,606 | 111,347 | 106,173 | 5,174 | 10,552 | 48 | 985,659 | 977,943 | 7,716 |
| 1960 . . . . . . | 871,348 | 91,056 | 86,832 | 4,224 | 10,141 | 39 | 770,112 | 761,833 | 8,279 |
| 1965 . . . . . . | 967,049 | 101,812 | 98,029 | 3,783 | 10,285 | 23 | 854,929 | 846,409 | 8,520 |
| 1970 . . . . . . | 1,319,735 | 143,704 | 138,469 | 5,235 | 23,005 | 13 | 1,153,013 | 1,141,537 | 11,476 |
| 1975 . . . . . . | 781,316 | 89,756 | 85,184 | 4,572 | 13,214 | 22 | 678,324 | 640,621 | 37,703 |
| 1980 (Sept 30) . . . | 772,661 | 85,339 | 77,843 | 7,496 | 13,265 | 113 | 673,944 | 612,593 | 61,351 |
| 1985 (Sept. 30) | 776,244 | 94,103 | 83,563 | 10,540 | 15,296 | 288 | 666,557 | 598,639 | 67,918 |
| 1990 (Mar. 31) | 746,220 | 91,330 | 79,520 | 11,810 | 15,177 | 470 | 639,713 | 567,015 | 72,698 |
| 1991 (Mar. 31) | 740,023 | 89,448 | 77,489 | 11,959 | 14,771 | 505 | 635,299 | 564,180 | 71,119 |
| 1992 (Mar. 31) | 661,391 | 85,953 | 74,326 | 11,627 | 13,840 | 494 | 561,104 | 496,335 | 64,769 |
| 1993 (Mar. 31) | 590,324 | 76,714 | 66,336 | 10,378 | 12,359 | 441 | 500,810 | 443,942 | 56,868 |

(1) Represents strength of the active Army, including Philippine Scouts, retired Regular Army personnel on extended active duty, and National Guard and Reserve personnel on extended active duty; excludes U.S. Military Academy cadets, contract surgeons, and National Guard and Reserve personnel not on extended active duty.
(2) Data for 1940 to 1946 include personnel in the Army Air Forces and its predecessors (Air Service and Air Corps).
(3) Includes: women doctors, dentists, and Medical Service Corps officers for 1946 and subsequent years, women in the Army Nurse Corps for all years, and the Women's Army Corps and Women's Medical Specialists Corps (dietitians, physical therapists, and occupational specialists) for 1943 and subsequent years.
(4) Act of Congress approved April 27, 1926, directed the appointment as warrant officers of field clerks still in active service. Includes flight officers as follows: 1943, 5,700; 1944, 13,615; 1945, 31,117; 1946, 2,580.

# U.S. Navy Personnel on Active Duty

| June 30 | Officers | Nurses | Enlisted | Off. Cand. | Total |
|---|---|---|---|---|---|
| 1940 (June) . . . . . . . . . . . | 13,162 | 442 | 144,824 | 2,569 | 160,997 |
| 1945 (June) . . . . . . . . . . . | 320,293 | 11,086 | 2,988,207 | 61,231 | 3,380,817 |
| 1950 (June) . . . . . . . . . . . | 42,687 | 1,964 | 331,860 | 5,037 | 381,538 |
| 1960 (June) . . . . . . . . . . . | 67,456 | 2,103 | 544,040 | 4,385 | 617,984 |
| 1970 (June) . . . . . . . . . . . | 78,488 | 2,273 | 605,899 | 6,000 | 692,660 |
| 1980 (June) . . . . . . . . . . . | 63,100[1] | — | 464,100[2] | — | 527,200 |
| 1990 (Sept.) . . . . . . . . . . . | 74,429[1] | — | 530,133[2] | — | 604,562 |
| 1992 (Mar.) . . . . . . . . . . . | 71,826[1] | — | 500,459[2] | — | 572,285 |
| 1993 (Mar.) . . . . . . . . . . . | 66,787[1] | — | 445,409[2] | — | 512,196 |

(1) Nurses are included. (2) Officer candidates are included.

# U.S. Marine Corps Personnel On Active Duty

(midyear personnel figures)

| Year | Officers | Enlisted | Total | Year | Officers | Enlisted | Total | Year | Officers | Enlisted | Total |
|---|---|---|---|---|---|---|---|---|---|---|---|
| 1955 . . | 18,417 | 186,753 | 205,170 | 1980 . . | 18,198 | 170,271 | 188,469 | 1991 . . | 19,753 | 174,297 | 194,050 |
| 1960 . . | 16,203 | 154,418 | 170,621 | 1985 . . | 20,175 | 177,850 | 198,025 | 1992 . . | 19,132 | 165,397 | 184,529 |
| 1965 . . | 17,258 | 172,955 | 190,213 | 1990 . . | 19,958 | 176,694 | 196,652 | 1993 . . | 18,878 | 161,205 | 180,083 |
| 1970 . . | 24,941 | 234,796 | 259,737 | | | | | | | | |

# U.S. Air Force Personnel on Active Duty

| Year[1] | Strength | Year[1] | Strength | Year[1] | Strength | Year[1] | Strength |
|---|---|---|---|---|---|---|---|
| 1907 . . . . . . . . . . . . | 3 | 1941 . . . . . . . . . . | 152,125 | 1950 . . . . . . . | 411,277 | 1988 . . . . . . . | 575,603 |
| 1918 . . . . . . . . . | 195,023 | 1942 . . . . . . . . . | 764,415 | 1960 . . . . . . . | 814,213 | 1989 . . . . . . . | 570,965 |
| 1920 . . . . . . . . . | 9,050 | 1943 . . . . . . . . . | 2,197,114 | 1970 . . . . . . . | 791,078 | 1990 . . . . . . . | 535,200 |
| 1930 . . . . . . . . . | 13,531 | 1944 . . . . . . . . . | 2,372,292 | 1980 . . . . . . . | 557,969 | 1991 . . . . . . . | 508,500 |
| 1940 . . . . . . . . . | 51,165 | 1945 . . . . . . . . . | 2,282,259 | 1986 . . . . . . . | 608,200 | 1992 . . . . . . . | 486,800 |

(1) Prior to 1947, data are for U.S. Army Air Corps and Air Service of the Signal Corps.

# U.S. Coast Guard Personnel on Active Duty

Source: U.S. Dept. of Transportation

| Year | Total | Officers | Cadets | Enlisted | Year | Total | Officers | Cadets | Enlisted |
|---|---|---|---|---|---|---|---|---|---|
| 1970 . . . . . . . . | 37,689 | 5,512 | 653 | 31,524 | 1985 . . . . . . . . | 38,595 | 6,775 | 733 | 31,087 |
| 1975 . . . . . . . . | 36,788 | 5,630 | 1,177 | 29,981 | 1986 . . . . . . . . | 37,284 | 6,577 | 754 | 29,953 |
| 1980 . . . . . . . . | 39,381 | 6,463 | 877 | 32,041 | 1987 . . . . . . . . | 38,576 | 6,644 | 859 | 31,073 |
| 1981 . . . . . . . . | 39,760 | 6,519 | 981 | 32,260 | 1988 . . . . . . . . | 37,723 | 6,530 | 887 | 30,306 |
| 1982 . . . . . . . . | 38,248 | 6,431 | 902 | 30,915 | 1990 . . . . . . . . | 37,308 | 6,475 | 820 | 29,860 |
| 1983 . . . . . . . . | 39,708 | 6,535 | 811 | 32,362 | 1991 . . . . . . . . | 38,280 | 7,095 | 900 | 30,285 |
| 1984 . . . . . . . . | 38,705 | 6,790 | 759 | 31,156 | 1992 . . . . . . . . | 39,185 | 7,348 | 919 | 30,918 |

# Defense Contracts

Source: U.S. Dept. of Defense; thousands of dollars

The 50 companies (including their subsidiaries) receiving the largest dollar volume of prime contract awards from the Department of Defense during fiscal 1992.

| Company | Amount | Company | Amount | Company | Amount |
|---|---|---|---|---|---|
| McDonnell Douglas | $5,311,151 | TRW | 1,012,521 | FMC | 447,616 |
| Northrop | 4,851,015 | IBM | 931,776 | Dyncorp | 446,517 |
| Lockheed | 4,659,404 | Unisys | 834,011 | Mitre | 434,253 |
| General Dynamics | 4,463,771 | ITT | 797,273 | Johns Hopkins University | 406,267 |
| General Electric | 4,007,764 | Foundation Health | 751,262 | Teledyne | 401,602 |
| General Motors | 3,694,122 | Texas Instruments | 730,601 | MIT | 389,144 |
| Raytheon | 2,840,686 | GTE | 724,489 | Johnson Controls | 373,738 |
| United Technologies | 2,802,878 | Science Applications | | Oshkosh Trucking | 372,228 |
| Boeing | 2,495,191 | International | 685,606 | Hercules | 364,165 |
| Martin Marietta | 2,356,077 | Alliant Techsystems | 609,676 | Motorola | 353,384 |
| Litton Industries | 2,334,436 | Tenneco | 584,822 | Royal Dutch Shell Group | 344,473 |
| Grumman | 2,182,739 | Olin | 573,331 | Gencorp | 339,079 |
| Loral | 1,815,445 | E-Systems | 500,880 | Harris | 307,604 |
| AT&T | 1,337,587 | Computer Sciences | 495,419 | Coastal | 306,543 |
| Rockwell International | 1,233,435 | Renco Group | 462,143 | Exxon | 306,116 |
| Textron | 1,161,072 | Allied Signal | 458,869 | | |
| Bath Holding | 1,148,372 | Sikorsky | $458,619 | | |
| Westinghouse Electric | $1,147,210 | CFM International | 447,648 | | |

# Women in the Armed Forces

Source: U.S. Dept. of Defense

Women in the Army, Navy, Air Force, Marines, and Coast Guard are all fully integrated with male personnel. Expansion of military women's programs began in the Department of Defense in fiscal year 1973.

As of 1992, women made up 11.5 percent of the armed forces. Almost 25 percent of medical and dental specialists were women; of active duty women personnel, fewer than 1 percent served in the infantry, gun crews, or aboard ship.

### Women Active Duty Troops in 1992

| Service | Pct. Women |
|---|---|
| Army | 12.2 |
| Navy | 10.4 |
| Marines | 4.5 |
| Air Force | 14.7 |
| Coast Guard | 7.7 |

### Women on Active Duty, All Services: 1973-1992

| Year | Pct. Women | Year | Pct. Women |
|---|---|---|---|
| 1973 | 2.5 | 1983 | 9.3 |
| 1975 | 4.6 | 1987 | 10.2 |
| 1981 | 8.9 | 1992 | 11.5 |

In Apr. 1993, the Defense Dept. ordered the military to drop most of its restrictions on women in aerial and naval combat. The Clinton administration in 1993 announced that it would ask Congress to repeal a law barring women from serving on many warships. In addition, each service was directed to justify all remaining jobs that were off limits to women, including service in ground combat units.

Admission of women to the service academies began in the fall of 1976.

**Army** — Information: Chief, Office of Public Affairs, Dept. of the Army, Wash., DC 20310.

**Army Nurse Corps** — Chief, Army Nurse Corps, Office of the Surgeon General, Dept. of the Army, 5109 Leesburg Pike, Falls Church, VA 22041.

**Navy** — Information: Chief of Information, Dept. of the Navy, Wash., DC 20350-1200.

**Navy Nurse Corps** — Dir., Navy Nurse Corps, Dept. of the Navy, Wash., DC 20372-2000.

**Air Force** — Information: Office of Public Affairs, Dept. of the Air Force, Wash., DC 20330.

**Air Force Nurse Corps** — Chief, Air Force Nurse Corps, Office of the Surgeon General, USAF, Bolling AFB, Wash., DC 20332.

**Marine Corps** — Information: Commandant of the Marine Corps (Code PA), Headquarters, Marine Corps, Wash., DC 20380-0001.

**Coast Guard** — Information: Commandant (G-PDP), U.S. Coast Guard, 2100 Second St., SW, Wash., DC 20593-0001.

# Veteran Population

Source: U.S. Dept. of Veterans Affairs; as of July 1992; in thousands

| | |
|---|---|
| **Total veterans in civilian life[a,b]** | 26,981 |
| **Total wartime veterans** | 20,828 |
| Total Persian Gulf War | 730 |
| Persian Gulf War with service in Vietnam era | 111 |
| Persian Gulf War with no prior wartime service | 618 |
| Total Vietnam era | 8,278 |
| Vietnam era with service in Korean conflict | 560 |
| Vietnam era with no prior wartime service | 7,718 |
| Total Korean conflict | 4,782 |
| Korean conflict with service in WWII | 823 |
| Korean conflict with no prior wartime service | 3,958 |
| World War II | 8,500 |
| World War I | 34 |
| **Total peacetime veterans** | 6,153 |
| Total post-Vietnam era | 3,060 |
| Service between Korean conflict and Vietnam era only | 2,911 |
| Other peacetime | 181 |

NOTE: Detail may not add to total shown due to rounding. (a) The category "Wartime veterans" equals the sum of Persian Gulf War (no service in Vietnam era), Vietnam era (no service in Korean conflict), Korean conflict (no service in World War II), World War II and World War I. The data refer only to veterans living in the U.S. and Puerto Rico since data on veterans living elsewhere are not available. (b) There are an indeterminate number of Mexican Border period veterans, 42 of whom were receiving benefits in March 1993.

## Veterans Compensation and Pension Case Payments

| Fiscal year | Living veteran cases (no.) | Deceased veteran cases (no.) | Total cases (no.) | Total dis-bursement (dollars) | Fiscal year | Living veteran cases (no.) | Deceased veteran cases (no.) | Total cases (no.) | Total dis-bursement (dollars) |
|---|---|---|---|---|---|---|---|---|---|
| 1900... | 752,510 | 241,019 | 993,529 | 138,462,130 | 1960... | 3,008,935 | 950,802 | 3,959,737 | 3,314,761,383 |
| 1910... | 602,622 | 318,461 | 921,083 | 159,974,056 | 1970... | 3,127,338 | 1,487,176 | 4,614,514 | 5,113,649,490 |
| 1920... | 419,627 | 349,916 | 769,543 | 316,418,029 | 1980... | 3,195,395 | 1,450,785 | 4,646,180 | 11,045,412,000 |
| 1930... | 542,610 | 298,223 | 840,833 | 418,432,808 | 1990... | 2,746,329 | 837,596 | 3,583,925 | 15,535,069,000 |
| 1940... | 610,122 | 239,176 | 849,298 | 429,138,465 | 1991.. | 2,709,500 | 799,677 | 3,509,177 | 15,975,440,000 |
| 1950... | 2,368,238 | 658,123 | 3,026,361 | 2,009,462,298 | 1992 .. | 2,673,833 | 753,981 | 3,427,814 | 16,145,203,000 |

## Active Duty U.S. Military Personnel Strengths, Worldwide

(As of Sept. 30, 1992)

Source: U.S. Dept. of Defense

**U.S. Territories & Special Locations**
| | |
|---|---|
| U.S., 48 contiguous states | 1,171,208 |
| Alaska | 22,208 |
| Hawaii | 44,864 |
| Guam | 7,844 |
| Johnston Atoll | 238 |
| Puerto Rico | 3,518 |
| Transients | 42,379 |
| Afloat | 170,731 |
| **Total[1]** | **1,463,112** |

**Western & Southern Europe**
| | |
|---|---|
| Belgium | 2,151 |
| Germany | 134,483 |
| Greece | 1,260 |
| Greenland | 137 |
| Iceland | 3,094 |
| Italy | 13,246 |
| Netherlands | 2,384 |

| | |
|---|---|
| Norway | 218 |
| Portugal | 1,523 |
| Spain | 3,863 |
| Turkey | 4,824 |
| United Kingdom | 20,048 |
| Afloat | 17,464 |
| **Total[1]** | **205,052** |

**East Asia & Pacific**
| | |
|---|---|
| Australia | 518 |
| Japan | 45,964 |
| Philippines | 1,929 |
| Rep. of Korea | 35,743 |
| Singapore | 145 |
| Thailand | 105 |
| Afloat | 12,990 |
| **Total[1]** | **97,609** |

**Africa, Near East & South Asia**
| | |
|---|---|
| Bahrain | 305 |

| | |
|---|---|
| Diego Garcia | 1,253 |
| Egypt | 1,120 |
| Kuwait | 1,980 |
| Saudi Arabia | 1,801 |
| Afloat | 14,438 |
| **Total[1]** | **21,243** |
| **Sub-Saharan Africa** | **547** |

**Other Western Hemisphere**
| | |
|---|---|
| Bermuda | 891 |
| Canada | 513 |
| Cuba (Guantánamo) | 2,392 |
| Honduras | 853 |
| Panama | 10,447 |
| Afloat | 2,407 |
| **Total[1]** | **18,113** |
| **Total Worldwide** | **1,807,177** |

(1) Area totals include countries with fewer than 100 assigned U.S. military members.

## Estimates of Total Dollar Costs of American Wars

(millions of dollars, except percent)

Source: *The Military Budget and National Economic Priorities,* revised and updated by James L. Clayton.

| Item | World War II | Vietnam Conflict | Korean Conflict | World War I | Civil War: Union | Civil War: Confed-eracy | Spanish Ameri-can War | American Revolution | War of 1812 | Mexi-can War |
|---|---|---|---|---|---|---|---|---|---|---|
| **Original increment, direct costs:[1]** | | | | | | | | | | |
| Current dollars...... | 360,000 | 140,600 | 50,000 | 32,700 | 2,300 | 1,000 | 270 | 100-140 | 89 | 82 |
| Constant (1967) dollars. | 816,300 | 148,800 | 69,300 | 100,000 | 8,500 | 3,700 | 1,100 | 400-680 | 170 | 300 |
| Percent 1 year's GNP.. | 188 | 14 | 15 | 43 | 74 | 123 | 2 | 104 | 14 | 4 |
| Service-connected veterans' benefits[2].... | 96,666 | 32,288 | 19,512 | 19,580 | 3,290 | — | 2,111 | 28 | 20 | 26 |
| Interest, pmts. on war loans[3]........ | (5) | (5) | (5) | 11,000 | 1,200 | (5) | 60 | 20 | 14 | 10 |
| Current cost to 1990[4] ... | 466,000 | 179,000 | 72,000 | 63,500 | 6,790 | (5) | 2,441 | 170 | 120 | 120 |

(1) Figures are rounded and taken from Claudia D. Goldin, *Encyclopedia of American Economic History.* (2) Total cost to Oct. 1, 1990. For World War I and later wars, benefits are actual service-connected figures from *Annual Report* of Veterans Administration. For earlier wars, service-connected veterans' benefits are estimated at 40 percent of total, the approximate ratio of service-connected to total benefits since World War I. (3) Total cost to 1990. Interest payments are a very rough approximation based on the percentage of the original costs of each war financed by money creation and debt, the difference between the level of public debt at the beginning of the war and at its end, and the approximate time required to pay off the war debts. (4) Figures are rounded estimates. (5) Unknown.

## The Medal of Honor

The Medal of Honor is the highest military award for bravery that can be given to any individual in the United States. The first Army Medals were awarded on March 25, 1863, and the first Navy Medals went to sailors and Marines on April 3, 1863.

The Medal of Honor, established by Joint Resolution of Congress, July 12, 1862 (amended by Acts of Congress, July 9, 1918, and July 25, 1963), is awarded in the name of Congress to a person who, while a member of the Armed Forces, distinguishes himself or herself conspicuously by gallantry and intrepidity at the risk of life above and beyond the call of duty while engaged in an action against any enemy of the United States; while engaged in military operations involving conflict with an opposing foreign force; or while serving with friendly foreign forces engaged in an armed conflict against an opposing armed force in which the United States is not a belligerent party. The deed performed must have been one of personal bravery or self-sacrifice so conspicuous as to clearly distinguish the individual above his or her comrades and must have involved risk of life. Incontestable proof of the performance of service is required, and each recommendation for award of this decoration is considered on the standard of extraordinary merit.

Prior to World War I, the 2,625 Army Medal of Honor awards up to that time were reviewed to determine which past awards met new stringent criteria. The Army removed 911 names from the list, most of them former members of a volunteer infantry group during the Civil War who had been induced to extend their enlistments when they were promised the Medal.

Since that review Medals of Honor have been awarded in the following numbers:

| | | | |
|---|---|---|---|
| World War I . . . . . . . | 96 | Korean War. . . . . . . | 131 |
| World War II . . . . . . | 432 | Vietnam War . . . . . . | 238 |

## Armed Services Senior Enlisted Advisers

The U.S. Army, Navy, and Air Force in 1966-1967 each created a new position of senior enlisted adviser, whose primary job is to represent the point of view of the services' enlisted men and women on matters of welfare, morale, and any problems concerning enlisted personnel. The senior adviser has direct access to the military chief of the service and policy-making bodies. The senior enlisted adviser for each service as of mid-1993 is:

**Army**—Sgt. Major of the Army Richard A. Kidd.

**Navy**—Master Chief Petty Officer of the Navy John Hagan.

**Air Force**—Chief Master Sgt. of the Air Force Gary R. Pfingston.

**Marines**—Sgt. Major of the Marine Corps Harold G. Overstreet.

## Armed Forces Per 1,000 Persons, 1992[1]

Source: U.S. Arms Control and Disarmament Agency

| | | | | | |
|---|---|---|---|---|---|
| Argentina | 2.0 | India | 1.4 | Pakistan | 4.5 |
| Australia | 3.9 | Indonesia | 1.5 | Philippines | 1.7 |
| Austria | 6.6 | Iran | 8.9 | Poland | 7.7 |
| Belgium | 8.1 | Iraq | 20.3 | Portugal | 5.6 |
| Bolivia | 4.1 | Israel | 33.4 | Romania | 8.6 |
| Brazil | 2.0 | Italy | 6.2 | Russia | 18.2 |
| Bulgaria | 11.9 | Japan | 2.0 | Singapore | 19.9 |
| Canada | 3.0 | Jordan | 27.3 | South Africa | 1.9 |
| Chile | 6.8 | Korea, North | 50.9 | Spain | 5.6 |
| China | 2.6 | Korea, South | 14.5 | Sweden | 8.8 |
| Colombia | 4.1 | Kuwait | 9.8 | Switzerland | 0.2 |
| Cuba | 16.1 | Lebanon | 13.1 | Syria | 32.4 |
| Denmark | 5.7 | Libya | 19.1 | Taiwan | 17.4 |
| Egypt | 7.3 | Mexico | 2.1 | Thailand | 5.0 |
| El Salvador | 8.0 | Mongolia | 7.1 | Turkey | 9.6 |
| Finland | 6.5 | Morocco | 7.5 | United Kingdom | 5.1 |
| France | 7.5 | Netherlands | 6.1 | United States | 7.5 |
| Germany | 5.6 | Nicaragua | 3.6 | Venezuela | 3.7 |
| Greece | 15.5 | Norway | 7.6 | Vietnam | 12.4 |
| Hungary | 7.8 | Oman | 21.8 | | |

(1) Includes active-duty personnel performing national security functions. Does not include reserves or paramilitary forces.

## Monthly Military Pay Scale

Source: U.S. Dept. of Defense

(effective Jan. 1, 1993)

| Rank/Grade | Years of Service | | | | | | |
|---|---|---|---|---|---|---|---|
| | 2 | 4 | 8 | 12 | 16 | 20 | 26 |
| General—O-10 . . . . . | $6,889.20 | $6,889.20 | $7,153.50 | $7,549.80 | $8,089.80 | $8,631.60 | $9,169.50 |
| Lt. General—O-9 . . . . . | 6,052.50 | 6,181.50 | 6,338.70 | 6,602.40 | 7,153.50 | 7,549.80 | 8,089.80 |
| Major General—O-8 . . . . | 5,502.30 | 5,632.80 | 6,052.50 | 6,338.70 | 6,602.40 | 7,153.50 | 7,329.90 |
| Brig. General—O-7 . . . . | 4,740.60 | 4,740.60 | 4,953.30 | 5,240.40 | 6,052.50 | 6,468.90 | 6,468.90 |
| Colonel—O-6 . . . . . . . | 3,614.70 | 3,851.70 | 3,851.70 | 3,851.70 | 4,612.20 | 4,953.30 | 5,683.50 |
| Lt. Colonel—O-5 . . . . . | 3,089.40 | 3,303.30 | 3,303.30 | 3,586.50 | 4,113.30 | 4,480.80 | 4,637.40 |
| Major—O-4 . . . . . . . . | 2,700.90 | 2,881.20 | 3,063.90 | 3,456.90 | 3,773.40 | 3,877.50 | 3,877.50 |
| Captain—O-3 . . . . . . . | 2,304.60 | 2,725.80 | 2,958.60 | 3,273.00 | 3,353.40 | 3,353.40 | 3,353.40 |
| 1st Lt.—O-2 . . . . . . . . | 1,962.60 | 2,437.50 | 2,488.20 | 2,488.20 | 2,488.20 | 2,488.20 | 2,488.20 |
| 2d Lt.—O-1 . . . . . . . . | 1,624.20 | 1,962.60 | 1,962.60 | 1,962.60 | 1,962.60 | 1,962.60 | 1,962.60 |
| Chief Warrant—W-4 . . . | 2,253.00 | 2,304.60 | 2,515.50 | 2,804.40 | 3,037.50 | 3,219.60 | 3,586.50 |
| Warrant Officer—W-1 . . . | 1,596.90 | 1,730.10 | 1,886.10 | 2,043.90 | 2,200.50 | 2,358.30 | 2,358.30 |
| Sgt. Major—E-9 . . . . . | 0.00 | 0.00 | 0.00 | 2,497.80 | 2,613.00 | 2,723.40 | 3,144.90 |
| Master Sgt.—E-8 . . . . . | 0.00 | 0.00 | 2,048.70 | 2,162.70 | 2,277.60 | 2,387.10 | 2,808.60 |
| Sgt. 1st class—E-7 . . . . | 1,544.10 | 1,657.20 | 1,768.20 | 1,881.90 | 2,022.90 | 2,106.00 | 2,527.20 |
| Staff Sgt.—E-6 . . . . . . | 1,341.30 | 1,456.50 | 1,565.40 | 1,706.70 | 1,817.10 | 1,844.70 | 1,844.70 |
| Sergeant—E-5 . . . . . . | 1,175.40 | 1,286.10 | 1,426.50 | 1,537.50 | 1,565.40 | 1,565.40 | 1,565.40 |
| Corporal—E-4 . . . . . . | 1,063.80 | 1,213.20 | 1,261.20 | 1,261.20 | 1,261.20 | 1,261.20 | 1,261.20 |
| Pvt. 1st class—E-3 . . . . | 1,001.10 | 1,082.10 | 1,082.10 | 1,082.10 | 1,082.10 | 1,082.10 | 1,082.10 |
| Private—E-2 . . . . . . . . | 913.20 | 913.20 | 913.20 | 913.20 | 913.20 | 913.20 | 913.20 |
| Recruit—E-1 . . . . . . . | 814.80 | 814.80 | 814.80 | 814.80 | 814.80 | 814.80 | 814.80 |

## Chairmen of the Joint Chiefs of Staff

| | |
|---|---|
| Gen. of the Army Omar N. Bradley, USA . . . . . . . . . . . . . . . . | Aug. 16, 1949 – Aug. 14, 1953 |
| Adm. Arthur W. Radford, USN . . . . | Aug. 15, 1953 – Aug. 14, 1957 |
| Gen. Nathan F. Twining, USAF . . . . | Aug. 15, 1957 – Sept. 30, 1960 |
| Gen. Lyman L. Lemnitzer, USA . . . . | Oct. 1, 1960 – Sept. 30, 1962 |
| Gen. Maxwell D. Taylor, USA . . . . . | Oct. 1, 1962 – July 3, 1964 |
| Gen. Earle G. Wheeler, USA . . . . . . | July 3, 1964 – July 2, 1970 |
| Adm. Thomas H. Moorer, USN . . . . | July 3, 1970 – June 30, 1974 |
| Gen. George S. Brown, USAF . . . . . | July 1, 1974 – June 20, 1978 |
| Gen. David C. Jones, USAF . . . . . . . | June 21, 1978 – June 18, 1982 |
| Gen. John W. Vessey Jr., USA . . . . | June 18, 1982 – Sept. 30, 1985 |
| Adm. William J. Crowe, Jr., USN . . . . | Oct. 1, 1985 – Sept. 30, 1989 |
| Gen. Colin L. Powell, USA . . . . . . . | Oct. 1, 1989 – Sept. 30, 1993 |
| Gen. John Shalikashvili, USA . . . . . . | Oct. 1, 1993 – |

## Nuclear Arms Treaties and Negotiations: An Historical Overview

**Aug. 4, 1963—Nuclear Test Ban Treaty** signed in Moscow by the U.S., USSR, and Great Britain; prohibited testing of nuclear weapons in space, above ground, and under water.

**Jan. 1967—Outer Space Treaty** banned the introduction of nuclear weapons into space.

**1968—Nuclear Nonproliferation Treaty,** with U.S., USSR, and Great Britain as major signers, limited the spread of military nuclear technology by agreement not to assist nonnuclear nations in getting or making nuclear weapons.

**May 26, 1972—Strategic Arms Limitation Treaty (SALT I)** signed in Moscow by U.S. and USSR. In the area of defensive nuclear weapons, the treaty limited antiballistic missiles to 2 sites of 100 antiballistic missile launchers in each country (amended in 1974 to one site in each country). The treaty also imposed a 5-year freeze on testing and deployment of intercontinental ballistic missiles and submarine-launched ballistic missiles. An interim short-term agreement putting a ceiling on numbers of offensive nuclear weapons was also signed. SALT I was in effect until Oct. 3, 1977.

**July 3, 1974—Protocol on antiballistic missile systems** and a treaty and protocol on limiting underground testing of nuclear weapons were signed by U.S. and USSR in Moscow.

**Sept. 1977—U.S. and USSR** agreed to continue to abide by SALT I, despite its expiration date.

**June 18, 1979—SALT II,** signed in Vienna by the U.S. and USSR, constrained offensive nuclear weapons, limiting each side to 2,400 missile launchers and heavy bombers with that ceiling to apply Jan. 1, 1985. The treaty also set a subceiling of 1,320 ICBMs and SLBMs with multiple warheads on each side. Although approved by the U.S. Senate Foreign Relations Committee, the treaty never reached the Senate floor for ratification because Pres. Jimmy Carter withdrew his support for the treaty following the December 1979 invasion of Afghanistan by Soviet troops.

**Dec. 8, 1987—Intermediate-Range Nuclear Forces (INF) Treaty** signed in Washington, D.C., by USSR leader Mikhail Gorbachev and U.S. Pres. Ronald Reagan, eliminating all medium- and shorter-range nuclear missiles; ratified with conditions by U.S. Senate on May 27, 1988.

**July 31, 1991—Strategic Arms Reduction Treaty (START I)** signed in Moscow by Soviet Pres. Mikhail Gorbachev and U.S. Pres. George Bush to reduce strategic offensive arms by approximately 30 percent in three phases over seven years. START I was the first treaty to mandate reductions by the superpowers. The treaty was approved by the U.S. Senate Oct. 1, 1992. With the breakup of the Soviet Union in December 1991, four former Soviet republics became independent nations with strategic nuclear weapons on their territory—Russia, Ukraine, Kazakhstan, and Belarus. The last 3 agreed in principle in 1992 to transfer their nuclear weapons to Russia and ratify START I. The Russian Supreme Soviet voted to ratify Nov. 4, 1992, but Russia decided not to provide the instruments of ratification until Ukraine, Kazakhstan, and Belarus each ratified START I and acceded to the Nuclear Nonproliferation Treaty as nonnuclear nations. By late 1993, Belarus and Kazakhstan had ratified START I and acceded to the nonproliferation treaty. In September 1993, Ukrainian President Leonid Kravchuk agreed to a plan that could restart stalled negotiations on the transfer of nuclear weapons to Russia.

**Jan. 3, 1993—START II** signed in Moscow by U.S. Pres. George Bush and Russian Pres. Boris Yeltsin. Potentially the broadest disarmament pact in history, it called for both sides to reduce their long-range nuclear arsenals to about one-third of their then-current levels within a decade and would entirely eliminate land-based multiple-warhead missiles. Action will not be taken on START II until START I is fully ratified. START II will require ratification only by the U.S. Senate and the legislature of Russia, which would, under the guidelines for START I finalization, be the only remaining nuclear republic of the former Soviet Union.

## Leading Arms Importers, 1989

Source: U.S. Arms Control and Disarmament Agency

| | Principal supplier[1] | Imports (millions of dollars) | | Principal supplier[1] | Imports (millions of dollars) |
|---|---|---|---|---|---|
| 1. Saudi Arabia . . . . . | United Kingdom | $4,200 | 11. Turkey . . . . . . . . . | United States | $1,100 |
| 2. Afghanistan . . . . . . | Soviet Union | 3,800 | 12. Syria . . . . . . . . . . | Soviet Union | 1,000 |
| 3. India . . . . . . . . . | Soviet Union | 3,500 | 13. Libya . . . . . . . . | Soviet Union | 975 |
| 4. Greece . . . . . . . . | United States | 2,000 | 14. Ethiopia . . . . . . . . | Soviet Union | 925 |
| 5. Iraq . . . . . . . . . | Soviet Union | 1,900 | 15. Soviet Union . . . . . | Czechoslovakia | 900 |
| 6. United States . . . . . | — | 1,600 | 16. W. Germany . . . . . | United States | 875 |
| 7. Japan . . . . . . . . . | United States | 1,400 | 17. United Arab Emirates | France | 850 |
| 8. Iran . . . . . . . . . . | — | 1,300 | 18. E. Germany . . . . . . | Soviet Union | 825 |
| 9. Vietnam . . . . . . . . | Soviet Union | 1,300 | 19. Angola . . . . . . . . | Soviet Union | 750 |
| 10. Cuba . . . . . . . . . | Soviet Union | 1,200 | 20. Spain . . . . . . . . . | United States | 750 |

(1) Supplies more than 50 percent of total value of imports.

## Policy Guidelines on Homosexual Conduct in the Armed Forces

Source: U.S. Dept. of Defense

On July 19, 1993, Secretary of Defense Les Aspin directed the implementation of President Bill Clinton's new policy on homosexual conduct in the U.S. armed forces. The move followed months of controversy and marked a compromise between the Clinton administration and those in the Pentagon and Congress opposed to lifting an unqualified ban on homosexuals in the military that had stood for 50 years. The following are excerpts from the Department of Defense's official policy guidelines, effective October 1, 1993.

**Accession Policy:** Applicants for military service will no longer be asked or required to reveal if they are homosexual or bisexual, but applicants will be informed of the conduct that is proscribed for members of the armed forces, including homosexual conduct.

**Discharge Policy:** Sexual orientation will not be a bar to service unless manifested by homosexual conduct. The military will discharge members who engage in homosexual conduct, which is defined as a homosexual act, a statement that the member is homosexual or bisexual, or a marriage or attempted marriage to someone of the same gender.

**Investigations Policy:** No investigations or inquiries will be conducted solely to determine a servicemember's sexual orientation. Commanders will initiate inquiries or investigations when there is credible information that a basis for discharge or disciplinary action exists. Sexual orientation, absent credible information that a crime has been committed, will not be the subject of a criminal investigation. An allegation or statement by another that a servicemember is a homosexual, alone, is not grounds for either a criminal investigation or a commander's inquiry.

**Credible Information:** Credible information of homosexual conduct exists when the information, considered in light of its source and all attendant circumstances, supports a reasonable belief that a servicemember has engaged in such conduct. It requires a determination based on articulable facts, not just a belief or suspicion.

**Off-Base Conduct:** No distinction will be made between off-base and on-base conduct.

## Casualties in Principal Wars of the U.S.

Source: U.S. Dept. of Defense

Data prior to World War I are based on incomplete records in many cases. Casualty data are confined to dead and wounded personnel and therefore exclude personnel captured or missing in action who were subsequently returned to military control. Dash (—) indicates information is not available.

| Wars | Branch of service | Number serving | Battle deaths | Other deaths | Wounds not mortal[7] | Total |
|---|---|---|---|---|---|---|
| Revolutionary War | Total | — | 4,435 | — | 6,188 | — |
| 1775-1783 | Army | 184,000 | 4,044 | — | 6,004 | — |
| | Navy | to | 342 | — | 114 | — |
| | Marines | 250,000 | 49 | — | 70 | — |
| War of 1812 | Total | 286,730[8] | 2,260 | — | 4,505 | 6,765 |
| 1812-1815 | Army | — | 1,950 | — | 4,000 | 5,950 |
| | Navy | — | 265 | — | 439 | 704 |
| | Marines | — | 45 | — | 66 | 111 |
| Mexican War | Total | 78,718[8] | 1,733 | 11,550 | 4,152 | 17,435 |
| 1846-1848 | Army | — | 1,721 | 11,500 | 4,102 | 17,373 |
| | Navy | — | 1 | — | 3 | 4 |
| | Marines | — | 11 | — | 47 | 58 |
| Civil War | Total | 2,213,363[8] | 140,414 | 224,097 | 281,881 | 646,392 |
| (Union forces) | Army | 2,128,948 | 138,154 | 221,374 | 280,040 | 639,568 |
| 1861-1865 | Navy | — | 2,112 | 2,411 | 1,710 | 6,233 |
| | Marines | 84,415 | 148 | 312 | 131 | 591 |
| Confederate forces | Total | — | 74,524 | 59,297 | — | 133,821 |
| (estimate)[1] | Army | 600,000 | — | — | — | — |
| 1863-1866 | Navy | to | — | — | — | — |
| | Marines | 1,500,000 | — | — | — | — |
| Spanish-American | Total | 306,760 | 385 | 2,061 | 1,662 | 4,108 |
| War | Army[3] | 280,564 | 369 | 2,061 | 1,594 | 4,024 |
| 1898 | Navy | 22,875 | 10 | 0 | 47 | 57 |
| | Marines | 3,321 | 6 | 0 | 21 | 27 |
| World War I | Total | 4,743,826 | 53,513 | 63,195 | 204,002 | 320,710 |
| April 6, 1917- | Army[4] | 4,057,101 | 50,510 | 55,868 | 193,663 | 300,041 |
| Nov. 11, 1918 | Navy | 599,051 | 431 | 6,856 | 819 | 8,106 |
| | Marines | 78,839 | 2,461 | 390 | 9,520 | 12,371 |
| | Coast Guard | 8,835 | 111 | 81 | — | 192 |
| World War II | Total | 16,353,659 | 292,131 | 115,185 | 670,846 | 1,078,162 |
| Dec. 7, 1941- | Army[5] | 11,260,000 | 234,874 | 83,400 | 565,861 | 884,135 |
| Dec. 31, 1946[2] | Navy[6] | 4,183,466 | 36,950 | 25,664 | 37,778 | 100,392 |
| | Marines | 669,100 | 19,733 | 4,778 | 67,207 | 91,718 |
| | Coast Guard | 241,093 | 574 | 1,343 | — | 1,917 |
| Korean War[9] | Total | 5,764,143 | 33,651 | — | 103,284 | — |
| June 25, 1950- | Army | 2,834,000 | 27,709 | — | 77,596 | — |
| July 27, 1953 | Navy | 1,177,000 | 474 | 176 | 1,576 | 2,226 |
| | Marines | 424,000 | 4,270 | 339 | 23,744 | 28,353 |
| | Air Force | 1,285,000 | 1,198 | 298 | 368 | 1,864 |
| | Coast Guard | 44,143 | — | — | — | — |
| Vietnam War[10] | Total | 8,744,000 | 47,369 | 10,799 | 153,303 | 211,471 |
| Aug. 4, 1964- | Army | 4,368,000 | 30,911 | 7,274 | 96,802 | 134,987 |
| Jan. 27, 1973 | Navy | 1,842,000 | 1,631 | 927 | 4,178 | 6,736 |
| | Marines | 794,000 | 13,083 | 1,754 | 51,392 | 66,229 |
| | Air Force | 1,740,000 | 1,739 | 842 | 931 | 3,512 |
| | Coast Guard | — | 5 | 2 | — | 7 |
| Persian Gulf War | Total | 467,539[11] | 148 | 145 | 467 | 760 |
| 1991 | Army | 246,682 | 98 | 105 | — | — |
| | Navy | 98,852 | 6 | 8 | — | — |
| | Marines | 71,254 | 24 | 26 | — | — |
| | Air Force | 50,751 | 20 | 6 | — | — |

(1) Authoritative statistics for the Confederate forces are not available. An estimated 26,000-31,000 Confederate personnel died in Union prisons.

(2) Data are for the period Dec. 1, 1941 through Dec. 31, 1946 when hostilities were officially terminated by Presidential Proclamation, but few battle deaths or wounds not mortal were incurred after the Japanese acceptance of Allied peace terms on Aug. 14, 1945. Numbers serving from Dec. 1, 1941-Aug. 31, 1945 were: Total—14,903,213; Army—10,420,000; Navy—3,883,520; and Marine Corps—599,693.

(3) Number serving covers the period April 21-Aug. 13, 1898, while dead and wounded data are for the period May 1-Aug. 31, 1898. Active hostilities ceased on Aug. 13, 1898, but ratifications of the treaty of peace were not exchanged between the United States and Spain until April 11, 1899.

(4) Includes Army Air Forces battle deaths and wounds not mortal, as well as casualties suffered by American forces in Northern Russia to Aug. 25, 1919, and in Siberia to April 1, 1920. Other deaths covered the period April 1, 1917-Dec. 31, 1918.

(5) Includes Army Air Forces.

(6) Battle deaths and wounds not mortal include casualties incurred in Oct. 1941 due to hostile action.

(7) Marine Corps data for World War II, the Spanish-American War and prior wars represent the number of individuals wounded, whereas all other data in this column represent the total number (incidence) of wounds.

(8) As reported by the Commissioner of Pensions in his Annual Report for Fiscal Year 1903.

(9) Battle deaths and other deaths associated with the conflict differ from previously reported figures due to a reexamination of individual files by the U.S. Dept. of Defense.

(10) Number serving covers the period Aug. 4, 1964-Jan. 27, 1973 (date of ceasefire). Number of casualties incurred in connection with the conflict in Vietnam covers the period Jan. 1, 1961-Sept. 30, 1977. Includes casualties incurred in Mayaguez Incident. Wounds not mortal exclude 150,375 persons not requiring hospital care.

(11) Estimated because of continual changing deployment figures.

# CONSUMER INFORMATION

## Consumer Information Catalog

Source: Consumer Information Center, U.S. General Services Administration

The *Consumer Information Catalog* is a free listing of about 200 of the best federal consumer publications. They range from booklets on financial planning to planning a diet, from learning about federal benefits to getting an education, from fixing a car to dealing effectively with consumer problems or getting a passport or a birth certificate. Many of these booklets are free.

The *Consumer Information Catalog* is published quarterly by the Consumer Information Center of the U.S. General Services Administration. For a free copy of the most current *Consumer Information Catalog*, send your name and address to: Consumer Information Catalog, Pueblo, CO 81009. Educators, libraries, and other nonprofit groups who are able to distribute 25 or more copies of the *Consumer Information Catalog* on a quarterly basis should write to the same address for an application to be placed on the mailing list. Costs prevent the Consumer Information Center from maintaining a mailing list for individuals.

The booklets listed below are available *free* from the *Consumer Information Catalog* as of fall 1993. Quantities of some may be limited. There is a $1 fee for handling. To order, please send your name and address, the item numbers of the booklets you want, and the $1 fee to: S. James, Consumer Information Center, Pueblo, CO 81009.

## Some Free Publications

### Children

**Feeding Baby: Nature and Nurture.** Explains why breast milk is best for babies. Compares milk-based and soy-based formulas and discusses the dangers of confusing soy beverages with soy-based formulas. 4 pp. (1990) 506Z.

**Growing up Drug Free.** Shows parents what children should understand about drugs, including alcohol and tobacco; identifies classes and types of drugs and resource contacts. 55 pp. (1989) 507Z.

**Preparing Your Child for College: A Resource Book for Parents.** Worksheets and checklists to help you and your child plan for college academically and financially. Gives examples and charts of typical college costs; suggests ways to save and invest; discusses financial assistance. 49 pp. (1992) 596Z.

### Unemployment and Health Insurance

**Health Benefits Under COBRA (Consolidated Omnibus Budget Reconciliation Act).** Helps you keep or buy coverage for yourself and your family after a job loss, reduced work hours, divorce, or death of employed family member. 18 pp. (1990) 509Z.

**How to File a Claim for Your COBRA Benefits.** An outline of what to do if your COBRA claim or appeal is denied. Covers what the law does for you, waiting period, and more. 2 pp. (1991) 510Z.

### Federal Benefits

**Guide to Health Insurance for People with Medicare.** Provides guidance on filling in gaps in Medicare coverage while avoiding paying for duplicate benefits. 24 pp. (1992) 515Z.

**Medicare and Advance Directives.** Explains how to set up a living will or durable power of attorney to help you receive the medical treatment you want if you become physically or mentally unable to communicate. 4 pp. (1992) 516Z.

**Medicare Q & A.** Answers 60 frequently asked questions about Medicare, including eligibility, enrollment, deductibles, services, and benefits. 16 pp. (1991) 517Z.

**Request for Earnings and Benefit Estimate Statement.** A form to complete and return to the Social Security Administration to get your earnings history and an estimate of future benefits. 3 pp. (1989) 519Z.

**Understanding Social Security.** Explains retirement, disability, and survivor's benefits, Medicare coverage, Supplemental Security Income, and more. 41 pp. (1991) 521Z.

### Health

**Cancer Tests You Should Know About: A Guide for People 65 and Over.** Describes six tests that can help detect cancer early. Checklists included. 16 pp. (1992) 619Z.

**Clearing the Air.** Tips on how to quit smoking for keeps. 24 pp. (1991) 529Z.

**Contact Lenses: The Better the Care the Safer the Wear.** Discusses infection risks and charts proper care for hard, gas-permeable, and extended-wear soft lenses. 3 pp. (1991) 530Z.

**Cosmetic Safety.** Describes which cosmetic products are regulated and explains terms such as "hypoallergenic" and "natural." 8 pp. (1992) 614Z.

**Facing Forward: A Guide for Cancer Survivors.** Advice on coping with the many effects of this illness. Practical information on health care, insurance, job concerns, and more. 45 pp. (1990) 513Z.

**Guide to Choosing a Nursing Home.** Help for evaluating your need, with information on services. Medicare/Medicaid coverage, insurance, contracts, and more. 199 pp. (1991) 533Z.

**Hocus-Pocus as Applied to Arthritis.** Discusses fraudulent cures and medically sound treatments for arthritis, rheumatism, and gout. 7 pp. (1989) 355Z.

**Silicone Breast Implants.** Where to get more information or report problems, and what to do if you already have gel-filled or saline implants. 4 pp. (1992) 598Z.

**Surviving Cold and Flu Season.** Discusses symptoms of different cold and flu viruses, when to consider vaccines, and treatments. 8 pp. (1993) 599Z.

**Who Donates Better Blood for You Than You Do?** Discusses the advantages of donating blood to yourself before undergoing surgery. (1991) 538Z.

### Mental Health

**Bipolar Disorder (Manic-Depressive Illness).** Discusses signs and symptoms, available treatments, and how to get help. 5 pp. (1989) 621Z.

**A Consumer's Guide to Mental Health Services.** Answers common questions, identifies warning signs, discusses treatments, and lists resources for help and information. 28 pp. (1987) 556Z.

**Depression.** Describes symptoms and causes, diagnosis and treatment, and how to help someone suffering from depression. 4 pp. (1989) 557Z.

**Eating Disorders.** Describes the dangers of these disorders, symptoms, treatments, how to help a victim, and resources for more information. (Anorexia and bulimia afflict at least 3% of girls and young adult women in the U.S.) 17 pp. (1993) **613Z.**

**Obsessive-Compulsive Disorder.** Covers how to identify and get help for this disorder, as well as treatments. 11 pp. (1991) **559Z.**

**You Are Not Alone.** Facts about mental health and illness, behavior that may indicate a problem, and how to find help. 12 pp. (1992) **566Z.**

## Housing

**Fair Housing: It's Your Right.** Outlines how you are protected against discrimination when buying, selling, or renting a home or apartment and when applying for a mortgage. Includes a form to use if you think your rights have been violated. 9 pp. (1993) **567Z.**

**A Home of Your Own.** Advice on choosing and buying a home. Answers questions about FHA-insured homes that have been foreclosed and reverted to government ownership. 30 pp. (1990) **568Z.**

**How to Buy a Home with a Low Down Payment.** Describes private and federal options for obtaining a low-down-payment mortgage, how to qualify, and how to determine what you can afford. 8 pp. (1993) **631Z.**

**Tips for Energy Savers.** How to save energy and money through conservation measures relating to transportation, home heating and cooling, lighting, cooking, and running appliances. 29 pp. (1991) **604Z.**

## Money Management

**Building Your Future with Annuities.** An annuity is tax-deferred money set aside for future use, typically at retirement. Discusses various types—their features and costs—and answers questions. 13 pp. (1992) **571Z.**

**Buying Treasury Securities.** Information about bills, notes, and bonds issued by the U.S. government. 16 pp. (1993) **572Z.**

**Investment Swindles: How They Work and How to Avoid Them.** How to protect yourself against illegal, yet legitimate-sounding telemarketing and direct mail offers. 20 pp. (1987) **573Z.**

**Investors' Bill of Rights.** Tips to help make an informed decision when making investments. 7 pp. (1987) **574Z.**

# Business Directory

Listed below are major U.S. corporations, and major foreign corporations, whose operations—products and services—directly concern the American consumer. At the end of each listing is a representative sample of the company's products.

Company...Address...Phone Number...Chief executive officer...Business.

**A & W Brands Inc....**709 Westchester Ave., White Plains, NY 10604...(914) 397-1700...M.L. Lowenkron...soft drinks.

**AMR Corp....**PO Box 619616, Dallas/Ft. Worth Airport, TX 75261...(817) 355-1234...Robert Crandall...Air transportation (American Airlines).

**Abbott Laboratories...**One Abbott Park Rd., Abbott Park, IL 60064...(708) 937-6100...D.L. Burnham...health care prods.

**Aetna Life & Casualty Co....**151 Farmington Ave., Hartford, CT 06156...(203) 273-0123...Ronald E. Compton...insurance, financial services.

**H.F. Ahmanson & Co....**4900 Rivergrade Rd., Irwindale, CA 91706...(818) 814-7986...R.H. Deihi...operates largest S&L assn. in U.S. (Home Savings of America).

**Alberto-Culver Co....**2525 Armitage Ave., Melrose Park, IL 60160...(708) 450-3000...Leonard H. Lavin...hair care preparations, feminine hygiene products, household and grocery items.

**Albertson's Inc....**250 Parkcenter Blvd., Boise, ID 83726...(208) 385-6200...Gary Michael...supermarkets.

**Alcan Aluminium Ltd....**1188 Sherbrooke St. W., Montreal, Que., Canada H3A 3G2...(514) 848-8000...David Morton...aluminum producer.

**Alexander & Alexander Services Inc....**1211 Ave. of the Americas, New York, NY 10036...(212) 840-8500...T.H. Irvin...insurance & financial services.

**AlliedSignal Inc....**Box 4000, Morristown, NJ 07962...(201) 455-2000...Lawrence Bossidy...aerospace, engineered materials, automotive prods.

**Alltel Corp....**One Allied Dr., Little Rock, AR 72202...(501) 661-8000...J.T. Ford...telephone service in Midwest, South, and Eastern U.S.

**Aluminum Co. of America...**1501 Alcoa Bldg., Pittsburgh, PA 15219...(412) 553-4545...Paul O'Neill...mining, refining, & processing of aluminum.

**Amerada Hess Corp....**1185 Ave. of the Americas, N.Y., NY 10036...(212) 997-8500...L. Hess...integrated petroleum co.

**American Brands, Inc....**1700 E. Putnam Ave., Old Greenwich, CT 06870...(203) 698-5000...W.J. Alley...tobacco (Pall Mall, Carlton, Half and Half, Paleden pipe tobacco), whiskey (Jim Beam), snack foods, life insurance, office prods., food, financial services, toiletries.

**American Cyanamid Co....**One Cyanamid Plaza, Wayne, NJ 07470...(201) 831-2000...A.J. Costello...medical, agricultural, chemical, and consumer prods.

**American Express Co....**World Financial Center, N.Y., NY 10285...(212) 640-2000...H. Golub...travelers checks, credit card services, insurance, investment services (Shearson Lehman).

**American Greetings Corp....**10500 American Rd., Cleveland, OH 44144...(216) 252-7300...M. Weiss...greeting cards, stationery, gift items.

**American Home Products Corp....**685 3d Ave., N.Y., NY 10017...(212) 986-1000...J.R. Stafford...prescription and ethical drugs (Advil, Anacin, Robitussin), household prods. (Woolite, Easy-Off oven cleaner, Black Flag, Wizard air fresheners), food (Chef Boy-ar-dee).

**American Stores Co....**709 E. South Temple, Salt Lake City, Utah 84102...(801) 539-0112...Victor Lund...retail food markets, dept. & drug stores.

**American Telephone & Telegraph Co....**32 Ave. of the Americas, N.Y., NY 10013...(212) 605-5500...Robert Allen...communications, financial services.

**Amoco Corp....**200 E. Randolph Dr., Chicago, IL 60601...(312) 856-6111...H.L. Fuller...oil and gas exploration, production, and marketing.

**Anheuser-Busch, Inc....**One Busch Place, St. Louis, MO 63118...(314) 577-2000...August A. Busch 3d...brewing (Budweiser, Michelob, Bud Light, Natural Light, Busch), theme parks, snack foods (Eagle).

**Apple Computer, Inc....**10260 Bandley Dr., Cupertino, CA 95014...(408) 996-1010...Michael Spindler...manuf. personal computers.

**Armstrong World Industries...**P.O. Box 3001, 313 W. Liberty St., Lancaster, PA 17604...(717) 397-0611...W.W. Adams...interior furnishings.

**Arvin Industries, Inc....**Box 3000, Columbus, IN 47202...(812) 379-3000...J.K. Baker...auto emission & noise control systems.

**Ashland Oil, Inc....**P.O. Box 391, Ashland, KY 41114...(606) 329-3333...J.R. Hall...petroleum refiner, chemicals.

**Atlantic Richfield Co....**515 S. Flower St., Los Angeles, CA 90071...(213) 486-3511...L.M. Cook...petroleum, chemicals, other natural resources.

**Avery Denison Corp....**150 N. Orange Grove Blvd., Pasadena, CA 91103...(818) 304-2000...Charles D. Miller...self-adhesive labels, office products, specialty chemicals.

**Avon Products, Inc....**9 West 57th St., N.Y., NY 10019...(212) 546-6015...J. E. Preston...cosmetics, fragrances, toiletries, health care.

**Bausch & Lomb...**One Lincoln First Square, Rochester, NY 14601...(716) 338-6000...D.E. Gill...manuf. of vision care products, accessories.

**Baxter International Inc....**One Baxter Pky., Deerfield, IL 60015...(708) 948-2000...Vernon R. Loucks Jr....health care prods. & services.

**Bell Atlantic Corp.**...1717 Arch St., Philadelphia, PA 19103...(215) 963-6000...R.W. Smith...telephone service in mid-Atlantic region.

**BellSouth Corp.**...1155 Peachtree St. NE, Atlanta, GA 30367...(404) 249-2000...J.L. Clendenin...telephone service in the South.

**Bethlehem Steel Corp.**...8th & Eaton Ave., Bethlehem, PA 18016...(215) 694-2424...C.H. Barnette...steel & steel prods.

**Bic Corporation**...500 Bic Dr., Milford, CT 06400...(203) 783-2000...Bruno Bich...writing instruments, disposable lighters, shavers, and correction fluid (Wite-Out).

**Black & Decker Corp.**...701 E. Joppa Rd., Towson, MD 21286...(410) 583-3900...N.D. Archibald...manuf. power tools, household prods., small appliances.

**H & R Block, Inc.**...4410 Main St., Kansas City, MO 64111...(816) 753-6900...Henry W. Bloch...tax preparation.

**Blockbuster Entertainment Corp.**...One Blockbuster Plaza, Ft. Lauderdale, FL 33301...(305) 832-3000...H. Wayne Huizenga...video rental superstores.

**Boeing Company**...7755 E. Marginal Way So., Seattle, WA 98108...(206) 655-6123...F.A. Shrontz...aircraft manuf.

**Boise Cascade Corp.**...One Jefferson Square, Boise, ID 83728...(208) 384-6161...J.B. Fery...timber, paper, wood prod.

**Borden, Inc.**...277 Park Ave., N.Y., NY 10172...(212) 573-4000...A.S. D'Amato...food, cheese and cheese products, snacks (Cracker Jack), beverages, adhesives (Elmer's, Krazy Glue), pasta (Prince, Creamette), pasta sauce (Aunt Millie's, Classico).

**Bristol-Myers Squibb Co.**...345 Park Ave., N.Y., NY 10154...(212) 546-4000...Richard L. Gelb...toiletries (Ban antiperspirant), hair items (Clairol), drugs (Bufferin, Comtrex, Excedrin), household prods. (Drano, Windex), infant formula (Enfamil).

**Brown-Forman Inc.**...850 Dixie Highway, Louisville, KY 40210...(502) 585-1100...Owsley Brown 2d...distilled spirits (Jack Daniel's, Early Times), wines (Bolla, Fontana Candita), champagne (Korbel), liquor (Southern Comfort), Lenox china and crystal.

**Brown Group, Inc.**...8400 Maryland Ave., St. Louis, MO 63166...(314) 854-4000...B.A. Brightwater Jr....manuf. and wholesaler of women's and children's shoes (Buster Brown, Naturalizer); specialty retailing.

**Brunswick Corp.**...One N. Field Ct., Lake Forest, IL 60045...(708) 735-4700...J.F. Reichert...marine, recreation prods., bowling centers & equip., fishing equip.

**Burlington Coat Factory Warehouse Corp.**...1830 Route 130 North, Burlington, NJ 08016...(609) 387-7800...M.G. Milstein...discount apparel stores.

**Burlington Northern Inc.**...777 Main St., Ft. Worth, TX 76102...(817) 878-2000...G. Grinstein...rail transportation.

**CBS Inc.**...51 W. 52d St., N.Y., NY 10019...(212) 975-4321...L.A. Tisch...broadcasting.

**CPC International, Inc.**...International Plaza, Englewood Cliffs, NJ 07632...(201) 894-4000...Charles Shoemate...branded food items (Hellman's mayonnaise, Best Foods, Mazola corn oil, Skippy peanut butter, Knorr soups, Thomas' English muffins, Mueller pasta prods., Arnold breads).

**Caesar's World, Inc.**...1801 Century Park East, Los Angeles, CA 90067...(310) 552-2711...H. Gluck...hotels & casinos, resort hotels.

**Caldor Corp.**...20 Glover Ave., Norwalk, CT 06856...(203) 849-2000...D.R. Clarke...discount retailer.

**Callaway Golf Co.**...2285 Rutherford Rd., Carlsbad, CA 92008...(619) 931-1771...E. Callaway...manuf. & markets golf clubs.

**Campbell Soup Co.**...Campbell Pl., Camden, NJ 08103...(609) 342-4800...D.W. Johnson...canned soups, spaghetti (Franco-American), vegetable juice (V-8), pork and beans, pet foods, confections, Swanson frozen dinners, Prego spaghetti sauce, Mrs. Paul's frozen fish, Pepperidge Farm breads.

**Capital Cities/ABC, Inc.**...77 W. 66th Street, New York, NY 10023...(212) 456-7777...D.B. Burke...operates television and radio stations, newspapers, cable TV (ESPN); newspapers, specialized business and consumer periodicals.

**Carnival Cruise Lines Inc.**...3655 NW 87th St., Miami, FL 33138...(305) 599-2600...M. Arison...cruise line.

**Carter-Wallace, Inc.**...1345 Ave. of the Americas, New York, NY 10105...(212) 339-5000...H.H. Hoyt Jr....personal care items, antiperspirant (Arrid), shave lathers (Rise), tooth polish (Pearl Drops), condoms (Trojan), laxative (Carter's Pills), pet prods. (Victory flea collars).

**Caterpillar Inc.**...100 N.E. Adams St., Peoria, IL 61629...(309) 675-1000...Donald Fites...heavy duty earth-moving equip.

**Chase Manhattan Corp.**...1 Chase Manhattan Plaza, New York, NY 10081...(212) 552-2222...Thomas Labrecque...bank holding co.

**Chevron Corp.**...225 Bush St., San Francisco, CA 94104...(415) 894-7700...K.T. Derr...integrated oil co.

**Chrysler Corp.**...12000 Chrysler Dr., Highland Pk., MI 48288...(313) 956-5741...R.J. Eaton...cars, trucks.

**Church & Dwight Co., Inc.**...469 N. Harrison St., Princeton, NJ 08543...(609) 683-5900...D.C. Minton...consumer prods. (Arm & Hammer).

**Circuit City Stores, Inc.**...9950 Maryland Dr., Richmond, VA 23233...(804) 527-4000...R.L. Sharp...retailer of electronic equip., consumer appliances.

**Circus Circus Enterprises, Inc.**...2880 Las Vegas Blvd. S., Las Vegas, NV 89109...(702) 734-0410...W.G. Bennett...casino operator.

**Citicorp**...399 Park Ave., N.Y., NY 10043...(212) 559-1000...J.S. Reed...largest U.S. commercial bank.

**Clayton Homes**...P.O. Box 15169, Knoxville, TN 37901...(615) 970-7200...J.L. Clayton...produces & sells manufactured homes.

**Clorox Co.**...1221 Broadway, Oakland, CA 94612...(510) 271-7000...C.R. Weaver...retail consumer prods. (Formula 409, Pine-Sol, Kingsford charcoal briquets, Deer Park bottled water, Combat insecticides, Hidden Valley Ranch salad dressing, Soft Scrub cleanser).

**Coachman Industries Inc.**...601 E. Beardsley Ave., Elkhart, IN 46515...(219) 262-0123...T.H. Corson...manuf. recreational vehicles.

**Coca-Cola Co.**...One Coca-Cola Plaza N.W., Atlanta, GA 30313...(404) 676-2121...R.C. Goizueta...soft drinks (Coca-Cola, Sprite, Nestea), syrups, citrus and fruit juices (Minute Maid, Hi-C).

**Colgate-Palmolive Co.**...300 Park Ave., N.Y., NY 10022...(212) 310-2000...R. Mark...soaps (Palmolive, Irish Spring), detergents (Fab, Ajax, Fresh Start), toothpaste (Colgate, Ultra Brite), household prods. (Handy Wipes, Curad bandages).

**Commodore International Ltd.**...1200 Wilson Dr., West Chester, PA 19380...(215) 431-9100...I. Gould...microcomputer systems, semiconductors component, consumer electronics, office equipment.

**Compaq Computer Corp.**...20555 SH 149, Houston, TX 77070...(713) 370-0670...E. Pfeiffer...portable, desktop computers.

**Adolph Coors Co.**...Golden, CO 80401...(303) 279-6565...W. K. Coors...brewery.

**Corning Inc.**...Houghton Park, Corning, NY 14831...(607) 974-9000...J.R. Houghton...glass mfg.

**Crane Co.**...100 First Stamford Place, Stamford, CT 06902...(203) 363-7300...R.S. Evans...manuf. engineered industrial prods.

**A.T. Cross Co.**...One Albion Rd., Lincoln, RI 02865...(401) 333-1200...B.R. Boss...writing instruments.

**Crystal Brands, Inc.**...Crystal Brands Rd., Southport, CT 06490...(203) 254-6200...G.E. Allen...apparel, accessories (Evan Picone, Izod).

**Culbro Corp.**...387 Park Avenue South, New York, NY 10016...(212) 561-8700...E. M. Cullman...cigars (Corina, Robert Burns, White Owl, Tiparillo's), snack foods.

**Dana Corp.**...4500 Dorr St., Toledo, OH 43615...(419) 535-4500...S.J. Morcott...truck and auto parts supplies.

**Data General Corp.**...4400 Computer Dr., Westboro, MA 01580...(508) 366-8911...R.L. Skates...computer & communications sytems manuf.

**Dayton Hudson Corp.**...777 Nicollet Mall, Minneapolis, MN 55402...(612) 370-6948...K.A. Macke...department, specialty stores, Mervyn's, Target.

**Deere & Co.**...John Deere Rd., Moline, IL 61265...(309) 765-8000...H.W. Becherer...farm, industrial, and outdoor power equip.

**Delta Air Lines, Inc.**...Hartsfield Atlanta Intl. Airport, Atlanta, GA 30320...(404) 765-2600...Ronald W. Allen...air transportation.

**Dial Corp.**...Dial Tower, Phoenix, AZ 85077-2346...(602) 207-4000...J.W. Teets...consumer prods. (Dial, Purex detergents, Armour Star meats, Breck shampoo), contract and fast food services, manuf. buses.

**Diebold, Inc.**...P.O. Box 8230, Canton, OH 44711...(216) 489-4000...R.W. Mahoney...manuf. equip. for financial insts.

**Digital Equipment Corp.**...146 Main St., Maynard, MA 01754...(508) 493-5111...R.B. Palmer...computer systems manuf.

**Walt Disney Co.**...500 S. Buena Vista St., Burbank, CA 91521...(818) 560-1000...M.D. Eisner...motion pictures, cable television, theme parks (Walt Disney World, Disneyland) and resorts, publishing, recordings, retailing (Disney stores).

**Dole Food Co.** . . .31355 Oak Crest Drive, Westlake Village, CA 91361 . . .(818) 879-6600 . . .David Murdock . . .food products, fresh fruits and vegetables, real estate.

**R.R. Donnelley & Sons Co.** . . .77 W. Wacker Rd., Chicago, IL 60616 . . .(312) 326-8000 . . .J.R. Walter . . .largest commercial printer.

**Dow Chemical Co.** . . .2030 Dow Center, Midland, MI 48674 . . .(517) 636-1000 . . .F.P. Popoff . . .chemicals, plastics, metals, consumer prods. (Ziploc, Saran Wrap, Fantastik).

**Dow Jones & Co.** . . .200 Liberty St., New York, NY 10281 . . .(212) 416-2000 . . .P. R. Kann . . .financial news service, publishing (Wall Street Journal, Barron's, Ottaway Newspapers).

**Dun & Bradstreet Corp.** . . .299 Park Ave., New York, NY 10171 . . .(212) 593-6800 . . .C.W. Moritz . . .business information and computer services, publishing, broadcasting.

**E.I. du Pont de Nemours & Co.** . . .1007 Market St., Wilmington, DE 19898 . . .(302) 774-1000 . . .Edgar Woolard Jr. . . .chemicals, petroleum, consumer prods., coal.

**Duracell Intl. Co.** . . .Berkshire Corporate Park, Bethel, CT 06801 . . .(203) 796-4000 . . .C.R. Kidder . . .manuf. batteries.

**Eastman Kodak Co.** . . .343 State St., Rochester, NY 14650 . . .(716) 724-4000 . . .K.R. Whitmore . . .photographic prods., chemicals, health care.

**Eaton Corp.** . . .Eaton Center, Cleveland, OH 44114 . . .(216) 523-5000 . . .W.E. Butler . . .manuf. of electronic, electrical prods., vehicle components.

**Emerson Electric Co.** . . .8000 W. Florissant Ave., St. Louis, MO 63136 . . .(314) 553-2000 . . .C.F. Knight . . .electrical/electronics products & systems.

**Ethyl Corp.** . . .330 S. 4th St., Richmond, VA 23217 . . .(804) 788-5000 . . .B.C. Gottwald . . .petroleum and industrial chemicals.

**Exxon Corp.** . . .225 E. John W. Carpenter Freeway, Irving, TX 75062 . . .(214) 444-1000 . . .L.G. Rawl . . .oil, natural gas, coal, chemicals.

**Fabri-Centers of America, Inc** . . .5555 Darrow Rd., Hudson, OH 44236 . . .(216) 656-2600 . . .Alan Rosskamm . . .specialty fabric stores.

**Family Dollar Stores, Inc.** . . .P.O. Box 1017, Charlotte, NC 28201 . . .(704) 847-6961 . . .L. Levine . . .discount variety stores.

**Fedders Corp.** . . .158 Highway 206, P.O. Box 265, Peapack, NJ 07977 . . .(908) 234-2100 . . .S. Giordano Jr. . . .manuf. of room air conditioners.

**Federal Express Corp.** . . .2005 Corporate Ave., Memphis, TN 38132 . . .(901) 369-3600 . . .F.W. Smith . . .express delivery service.

**Fieldcrest Cannon, Inc.** . . .One Lake Dr., Kannapolis, NC 28081 . . .(704) 939-2000 . . .J.M. Fitzgibbons . . .household textile prods., rugs (Karastan).

**First Brands Corp.** . . .83 Wooster Hts. Rd., Danbury, CT 06813 . . .(203) 731- 2300 . . .A.E. Dudley . . .consumer prods. (Glad plastic bags, Scoop-Away cat litter, Prestone auto prods.).

**Fleetwood Enterprises, Inc.** . . .P.O. Box 7638, Riverside, CA 92523 . . .(714) 351-3500 . . .John C. Crean . . .manufactured homes, recreational vehicles.

**Fluor Corp.** . . .3333 Michelson Dr., Irvine, CA 92730 . . .(714) 975-2000 . . .L.G. McGraw . . .engineering and construction, natural resources.

**Ford Motor Co.** . . .The American Rd., Dearborn, MI 48121 . . .(313) 322-3000 . . .H.A. Poling . . .motor vehicles, Ford Tractor, Lincoln-Mercury.

**Fruit of The Loom, Inc.** . . .6300 Sears Tower, Chicago, IL 60606 . . .(312) 876-1724 . . .W. Farley . . .manuf. of men's and boy's underwear.

**GTE Corp.** . . .One Stamford Forum, Stamford, CT 06904 . . .(203) 965-2000 . . .C.E. Lee . . .largest U.S. local exchange telephone co., cellular telephone operator.

**Gannett Co., Inc.** . . .1100 Wilson Blvd., Arlington, VA 22234 . . .(703) 284-6000 . . .J.J. Curley . . .newspaper publishing (USA Today), TV stations, outdoor advertising.

**The GAP, Inc.** . . .1 Harrison, San Francisco, CA 94105 . . .(415) 952-4400 . . .D.G. Fisher . . .casual and activewear retailer.

**Gencorp** . . .175 Ghent Rd., Fairlawn, OH 44313 . . .(216) 869-4200 . . .A.W. Reynolds . . .aerospace, auto prods., polymer prods.

**General Dynamics Corp.** . . .3190 Fairview Park Dr., Falls Church, VA 22042 . . .(703) 876-3000 . . .William Anders . . .military and commercial aircraft, tactical missiles.

**General Electric Co.** . . .3135 Easton Ave., Fairfield, CT 06431 . . .(203) 373-2211 . . .J. F. Welch Jr. . . .electrical, electronic equip., radio, television (NBC), plastics manuf.

**General Host Corp.** . . .1 Station Place, Stamford, CT 06902 . . .(203) 357-9900 . . .H.J. Ashton . . .crafts, lawn and garden retail stores (Frank's Nursery & Crafts).

**General Mills, Inc.** . . .One General Mills Blvd., Minneapolis, MN 55426 . . .(612) 540-2311 . . .H.B. Atwater Jr. . . .foods (Total, Bisquick, Wheaties, Cheerios, Hamburger Helper, Gorton's, Betty Crocker), restaurants (Red Lobster, Olive Garden).

**General Motors Corp.** . . .3044 W. Grand Rapids, Detroit, MI 48202 . . .(313) 556-5000 . . .J.F. Smith Jr. . . .world's largest auto manuf.

**Genesco Inc.** . . .Genesco Park, Nashville, TN 37202 . . .(615) 367-7000 . . .W.S. Wire 2d . . .footwear and men's clothing manuf. and retailer.

**Genuine Parts Co.** . . .2999 Circle 75 Pkwy., Atlanta, GA 30339 . . .(404) 953-1700 . . .L. L. Prince . . .distributes auto replacement parts (NAPA).

**Georgia-Pacific Corp.** . . .133 Peachtree St., NE, Atlanta, GA 30303 . . .(404) 521-4000 . . .T.M. Hahn Jr. . . .building prods., pulp, paper, chemicals.

**Gerber Products Co.** . . .445 State St., Fremont, MI 49413 . . .(616) 928-2718 . . .A.A. Piergallini . . .baby foods, clothing, nursery accessories.

**Giant Food Inc.** . . .P.O. Box 1804, Washington, DC 20013 . . .(301) 341-4100 . . .I. Cohen . . .supermarkets.

**Gillette Co.** . . .Prudential Tower Bldg., Boston, MA 02199 . . .(617) 421-7000 . . .Alfred Zeier . . .razors, pens (Paper Mate), toiletries (Right Guard deodorants, Foamy shaving cream, Earth Born shampoo), hair products (Toni, Adorn).

**Goodyear Tire & Rubber Co.** . . .1144 E. Market St., Akron, OH 44316 . . .(216) 796-2121 . . .Stanley Gault . . .tires, rubber prods.

**W.R. Grace & Co.** . . .One Town Center Rd., Boca Raton, FL 33486 . . .(407) 362-2000 . . .J.P. Bolduc . . .chemicals, natural resources, health care.

**Great Atlantic & Pacific Tea Co.** . . .2 Paragon Dr., Montvale, NJ 07645 . . .(201) 573-9700 . . .James Wood . . .supermarket chain.

**Grumman Corp.** . . .1111 Stewart Ave., Bethpage, NY 11714 . . .(516) 575-0574 . . .Renso Caporali . . .aerospace, truck bodies, electronics.

**Hannaford Bros. Co.** . . .145 Pleasant Hill Rd., Scarborough, ME 04074 . . .(207) 883-2911 . . .Hugh G. Farrington . . .operates supermarkets, drug stores.

**Harley-Davidson, Inc.** . . .3700 W. Juneau Ave., Milwaukee, WI 53201 . . .(414) 342-4680 . . .R.F. Terrlink . . .manuf. of motorcycles, parts & accessories.

**Hartmarx** . . .101 N. Wacker Dr., Chicago, IL 60606 . . .(312) 372-6300 . . .E.O. Hand . . .apparel manufacturer and retailer (Hickey-Freeman, Hart Schaffner & Marx).

**Hasbro Inc.** . . .1027 Newport Ave., Pawtucket, RI 02862 . . .(401) 431-8400 . . .A.G. Hassenfeld . . .toy manuf. & marketer (Milton Bradley, Playskool, G.I. Joe, Parker Bros. games, Tonka trucks, Play-Doh).

**H.J. Heinz Co.** . . .P.O. Box 57, Pittsburgh, PA 15230 . . .(412) 456-3700 . . .Anthony J.F. O'Reilly . . .foods (Star-Kist, Ore-Ida, '57 Varieties), 9-Lives cat food, Weight Watchers.

**Helene Curtis** . . .325 N. Wells St., Chicago, IL 60610 . . .(312) 661-0222 . . .R.J. Gidwitz . . .hair care prods. (Finesse, Suave, Salon Selectives), antiperspirant (Degree).

**Hershey Foods Corp.** . . .100 Crystal A Dr., Hershey, PA 17033 . . .(717) 534-7552 . . .R.A. Zimmerman . . .chocolate & confectionery prods. (Reese's peanut butter cups, Kit Kat, Peter Paul Mounds, Almond Joy), pasta (San Giorgio, Ronzoni).

**Hewlett-Packard Co.** . . .P.O. Box 10301, Palo Alto, CA 94304 . . .(415) 857-1501 . . .L.E. Platt . . .manuf. electronic prods. and systems.

**Hillenbrand Industries, Inc.** . . .Highway 46, Batesville, IN 47006 . . .(812) 934-7000 . . .W.A. Hillenbrand . . .manuf. burial caskets, electronically operated hospital beds, luggage.

**Home Depot, Inc.** . . .2727 Paces Ferry Rd., Atlanta, GA 30339 . . .(404) 433-8211 . . .Bernard Marcus . . .retailer of building materials & home improvement prods.

**Honda Motor Co., LTD** . . .1290 Ave. of the Americas, N.Y., NY 10104 . . .(212) 765-3804 . . .N. Kawamoto . . .manuf. autos, motorcycles.

**Honeywell, Inc.** . . .Honeywell Plaza, Minneapolis, MN 55408 . . .(612) 951-1000 . . .J.J. Renier . . .industrial systems & controls, aerospace guidance systems, information systems.

**Geo. A. Hormel & Co.** . . .501 16th Ave. N.E., Austin, MN 55912 . . .(507) 437-5611 . . .R.L. Knowlton . . .meat packaging, pork and beef prods. (Spam, Dinty Moore, Mary Kitchen).

**Houghton Mifflin Co.** . . .One Beacon St., Boston, MA 02108 . . .(617) 351-5000 . . .Nader F. Darehshori . . .book publishing.

**Household International Inc.** . . .2700 Sanders Rd., Prospect Heights, IL 60070 . . .(708) 564-5000 . . .D.C. Clark . . .financial and insurance services.

**Huffy Corp.** . . .7701 Byers Rd., Miamisburg, OH 45342 . . .(513) 866-6251 . . .H.A. Shaw 3d . . .bicycles, sports and hardware equip. manuf.

**Humana, Inc.** . . .500 W. Main St., Louisville, KY 40201 . . .(502) 580-1000 . . .D. A. Jones . . .operates hospitals, provides health care plans.

**ITT Corp.** . . .1330 Ave. of the Americas, N.Y., NY 10022 . . .(212) 258-1000 . . .R.V. Araskog . . .manuf., installs communication and electronic equip., auto equip., insurance, financial services, hotels, educational services.

**Imperial Oil Ltd.** . . .111 St. Clair Ave. W., Toronto, Ont., Canada M5W 1K3 . . .(416) 968-5076 . . .R.B. Peterson . . . Canada's largest oil co.

**International Business Machines Corp.** . . .Old Orchard Rd., Armonk, NY 10504 . . .(914) 765-7777 . . .Louis Gerstner Jr. . . .information processing systems, equip., and services.

**International Paper Co.** . . .2 Manhattanville Rd., Purchase, NY 10577 . . .(914) 397-1500 . . .J.A. Georges . . .paper, wood prods.

**Johnson & Johnson** . . .One Johnson & Johnson Plaza, New Brunswick, NJ 08933 . . .(201) 524-0400 . . .R.S. Larsen . . . surgical dressings, pharmaceuticals (Tylenol), consumer prods.

**Jostens, Inc.** . . .5501 Norman Center Dr., Minneapolis, MN 55437 . . .(612) 830-3300 . . .H. W. Lurton . . .school rings, yearbooks.

**Kmart Corp.** . . .3100 W. Big Beaver Rd., Troy, MI 48084 . . .(313) 643-1000 . . .J. E. Antonini . . .largest U.S. chain of discount stores, book stores (Waldenbooks), cafeterias, drug stores (Pay Less Drug Stores), home improvement retail stores.

**Kellogg Co.** . . .One Kellogg Sq., Battle Creek, MI 49016 . . .(616) 961-6122 . . .Arnold G. Laugbo . . .ready to eat cereals & other food prods., Mrs. Smith's Pie Co., Eggo.

**Kimberly-Clark Corp.** . . .P.O. Box 619100, Dallas, TX 75261 . . .(214) 830-1200 . . .Wayne R. Sanders . . .paper and lumber prods., consumer prods. (Kleenex, Huggies, Depend).

**King World Productions, Inc.** . . .1700 Broadway, N.Y., NY 10019 . . .(212) 315-4000 . . .M. King . . .syndicator of TV programs (Oprah Winfrey Show, Wheel of Fortune, Jeopardy, Inside Edition).

**Knight-Ridder, Inc.** . . .One Herold Plaza, Miami, FL 33132 . . .(305) 376-3800 . . .J.K. Batten . . .newspaper publishing, TV broadcasting, book publishing, information services.

**Kroger Co.** . . .1014 Vine St., Cincinnati, OH 45202 . . .(513) 762-4000 . . .Joseph Pichler . . .grocery chain.

**L.A. Gear, Inc.** . . .2850 Ocean Park Blvd., Santa Monica, CA 90405 . . .(213) 822-1995 . . .Stanley P. Gold . . .athletic & leisure footwear, casual apparel.

**La-Z-Boy Chair Co.** . . .1284 N. Telegraph Rd., Monroe, MI 48161 . . .(313) 242-1444 . . .C. T. Knabusch . . .reclining chair mfg.

**Lands' End, Inc.** . . .One Lands' End Lane, Dodgeville, WI 53595 . . .(608) 935-9341 . . .R.C. Anderson . . .direct-mail catalog co.

**Eli Lilly & Company** . . .Lilly Corp. Center, Indianapolis, IN 46285 . . .(317) 276-2000 . . .Vaughn D. Bryson . . .mfg. human health and agricultural products.

**The Limited, Inc.** . . .Two Limited Pkwy., Columbus, OH 43216 . . .(614) 479-7000 . . .L.H. Wexner . . .women's apparel stores (Lane Bryant, Lerner, Victoria's Secret), Abercrombie & Fitch.

**Litton Industries, Inc.** . . .360 N. Crescent Dr., Beverly Hills, CA 90210 . . .(310) 859-5000 . . .A.J. Brann . . .industrial systems & services, advanced electronic systems, electronic & electrical prods., marine engineering.

**Lockheed Corp.** . . .4500 Park Granada Blvd., Calabasas, CA 91399 . . .(818) 876-2380 . . .D.M. Tellep . . .commercial and military aircraft, missiles.

**Loews Corp.** . . .667 Madison Ave., N.Y., NY 10021 . . .(212) 545-2000 . . .Laurence A. Tisch . . .tobacco prods. (Kent, Newport, True), watches, hotels, real estate, insurance.

**Long's Drug Stores Corp.** . . .141 North Civic Dr., Walnut Creek, CA 94596 . . .(510) 937-1170 . . .R.M. Long . . .drug store chain.

**Lowe's Cos., Inc.** . . .Hwy. 268 East, N. Wilkesboro, NC 28659 . . .(919) 651-4000 . . .L.G. Herring . . .retailer of building materials & related prods.

**Luby's Cafeterias, Inc.** . . .2211 Northeast Loop 410, San Antonio, TX 78265 . . .(512) 654-9000 . . .R. Erben . . .operates cafeterias in SW U.S.

**Manor Care, Inc.** . . .10750 Columbia Pike, Silver Spring, MD 20901 . . .(301) 681-9400 . . .S. Bainum Jr. . . .operates nursing homes.

**Marriott Corp.** . . .Marriott Dr., Wash., DC 20058 . . .(301) 380-9000 . . .J. Willard Marriott Jr. . . .hotels, food service.

**Martin Marietta Corp.** . . .6801 Rockledge Dr., Bethesda, MD 20817 . . .(301) 897-6000 . . .N.R. Augustine . . .electronics, aerospace.

**Mattel, Inc.** . . .333 Continental Blvd., El Segundo, CA 90245 . . .(213) 524-2000 . . .J.W. Amerman . . .toy & hobby prods. (Barbie doll, Hot Wheels).

**May Department Stores Co.** . . .611 Olive Street, St. Louis, MO 63101 . . .(314) 342-6300 . . .D.C. Farrell . . .department stores (Hecht's, Lord & Taylor, Foley's).

**Maytag Corp.** . . .403 W. 4th St. North, Newton, IA 50208 . . .(515) 792-8000 . . .L.A. Handley . . .manuf. home laundry equip., appliances (Magic Chef, Admiral).

**McDonald's Corp.** . . .McDonald's Plaza, Oak Brook, IL 60521 . . .(708) 575-3000 . . .M.R. Quinlan . . .fast food restaurants.

**McDonnell Douglas Corp.** . . .P.O. Box 516, St. Louis, MO 63166 . . .(314) 232-0232 . . .J. F. McDonnell . . .commercial & military aircraft, space systems & missiles.

**McGraw-Hill, Inc.** . . .1221 Ave. of the Americas, New York, NY 10020 . . .(212) 512-2000 . . .J.L. Dionne . . .book, magazine publishing (Business Week), information & financial services (Standard and Poor's), TV stations.

**Mead Corporation** . . .Courthouse Plaza Northeast, Dayton, OH 45463 . . .(513) 495-6323 . . .S.C. Mason . . .printing and writing paper, paperboard, packaging, shipping containers, pulp and lumber.

**Media General, Inc.** . . .333 E. Grace St., Richmond, VA 23219 . . .(804) 649-6000 . . .J.S. Bryan 3d . . .broadcasting, newspaper publishing.

**Medtronic, Inc.** . . .7000 Central Ave. N.E., Minneapolis, MN 55432 . . .(612) 574-4000 . . .W.W. George . . .manuf. prosthetic and therapeutic devices.

**Melville Corp.** . . .1 Theall Rd., Rye, NY 10580 . . .(914) 925-4000 . . .S.P. Goldstein . . .shoe stores (Thom McAn), apparel (Marshalls, Chess King), drug stores.

**Merck & Co., Inc.** . . .P.O. Box 2000, Rahway, NJ 07065 . . .(908) 594-4000 . . .P. Roy Vagelos . . .human & animal health care prods.

**Meredith Corp.** . . .1716 Locust St., Des Moines, IA 50336 . . .(515) 284-3000 . . .J.D. Rehm . . .magazine publishing (Better Homes and Gardens, Ladies Home Journal), book publishing, broadcasting.

**Merrill Lynch & Co., Inc.** . . .World Financial Center, N. Tower, N.Y., NY 10281 . . .(212) 449-1000 . . .Daniel P. Tully . . .securities broker, financial services.

**Microsoft Corp.** . . .16011 Northeast 36th Way, Redmond, WA 98073-9717 . . .(206) 882-8080 . . .William H. Gates . . .the world's largest computer software company.

**Minnesota Mining & Manuf. Co.** . . .3M Center, St. Paul, MN 55144 . . .(612) 733-1110 . . .L.D. DeSimone . . .abrasives, adhesives, building services & chemicals, electrical, health care, photographic, printing, recording materials, consumer prods. (Scotch Tape, Post-It).

**Mirage Resorts, Inc.** . . .3400 Las Vegas Blvd. S., Las Vegas, NV 89109 . . .(702) 791-7111 . . .S.A. Wynn . . .hotel-casino operator (Mirage, Treasure Island, Golden Nugget).

**Mobil Corp.** . . .3225 Gallows Rd., Fairfax, VA 22037 . . .(703) 846-3000 . . .A.E. Murray . . .international oil co., chemicals.

**Monsanto Company** . . .800 N. Lindbergh Blvd., St. Louis, MO 63167 . . .(314) 694-1000 . . .R. J. Mahoney . . .chemicals, agricultural prods., pharmaceuticals, consumer prods. (Nutra-Sweet).

**Motorola, Inc.** . . .1303 E. Algonquin Rd., Schaumburg, IL 60196 . . .(708) 576-5000 . . .G. Fisher . . .electronic equipment and components.

**National Medical Enterprises, Inc.** . . .P.O. Box 4070, Santa Monica, CA 90404 . . .(310) 315-8000 . . .J.C. Barbakow . . .operates hospitals.

**National Semiconductor Corp.** . . .2900 Semiconductor Dr., Santa Clara, CA 95052 . . .(408) 721-5000 . . .P. Sprague . . .manuf. of semiconductors.

**Navistar Intl. Corp.** . . .455 N. Cityfront Plaza Dr., Chicago, IL 60611 . . .(312) 836-2000 . . .J.C. Cotting . . .manuf. heavy duty trucks, parts.

**New York Times Co.** . . .229 W. 43rd St., N.Y., NY 10036 . . .(212) 556-4317 . . .A. O. Sulzberger . . .newspapers, radio, CATV stations, magazines (Family Circle, Golf Digest).

**Nike, Inc.** . . .One Bowerman Dr., Beaverton, OR 97005 . . .(503) 671-6453 . . .Philip Knight . . .athletic & leisure footware.

**Norfolk Southern Corp.** . . .3 Commercial Place, Norfolk, VA 23510 . . .(804) 629-2600 . . .D.R. Goode . . .operates Norfolk & Southern railways, freight carrier (North American Van Lines).

**Northrop Corp.** . . .1840 Century Park E., Los Angeles, CA 90067 . . .(213) 553-6262 . . .K. Kresa . . .aircraft, electronics, communications.

**Nynex Corp.** . . .335 Madison Ave., N.Y., NY 10017 . . .(212) 370-7400 . . .W.C. Ferguson . . .telephone co. in northeast U.S.

**Occidental Petroleum Corp.** . . .10889 Wilshire Blvd., Los Angeles, CA 90024 . . .(310) 208-2880 . . .Ray Irani . . .oil, gas, chemicals, coal, agriculture.

**Office Depot, Inc....**2200 Old Germantown Rd., Delray Beach, FL 33445...(407) 278-4800...D.I. Fuente...retail office supply stores.

**Ogden Corp....**2 Pennsylvania Plaza, New York, NY 10121...(212) 868-6100...R.R. Ablon...transportation, foods, metals, financial services.

**Olin Corp....**120 Long Ridge Rd., Stamford, CT 06904...(203) 356-2000...J.W. Johnstone Jr....chemicals, water treatment prods., aerospace.

**Olsten Corp....**One Merrick Ave., Westbury, NY 11590...(516) 832-8200...F. N. Liguori...provides temporary workers.

**Outboard Marine Corp....**100 Sea Horse Dr., Waukegan, IL 60085...(708) 689-6200...J.C. Chapman...outboard motors (Evinrude, Johnson), boats.

**'Owens-Corning Fiberglas Corp....**Fiberglas Tower, Toledo, OH 43659...(419) 248-8000...G.H. Minor...glass fiber and related prods.

**Oxford Industries, Inc....**222 Piedmont Ave., N.E., Atlanta, GA 30308...(404) 659-2424...J.H. Lanier...manuf. men's and women's apparel.

**Pacific Telesis Group...**130 Kearny St., San Francisco, CA 94108...(415) 394-3000...S. L. Ginn...telephone service.

**Paramount Communications Inc....**15 Columbus Circle, N.Y., NY 10023...(212) 373-8000...M.S. Davis...entertainment (Paramount Pictures, Madison Square Garden), publishing (Simon & Schuster, Prentice Hall).

**J.C. Penney Co....**14841 N. Dallas Pkwy., P.O. Box 659000, Dallas, TX 75240...(214) 591-1000...W. R. Howell...dept. stores, catalog sales, drug stores, insurance.

**Pennzoil Co....**P.O. Box 2967, Houston, TX 77252...(713) 546-4000...J.L. Pate...integrated oil and gas co.

**Pep Boys—Manny, Moe & Jack...**3111 W. Allegheny Ave., Philadelphia, Pa. 19132...(215) 229-9000...M. G. Leibovitz...automotive parts and accessories, retail stores.

**PepsiCo, Inc....**PepsiCo. World HQ, Purchase, NY 10577...(914) 253-2000...W. Calloway...soft drinks (Pepsi-Cola, Slice), snack foods (Ruffles, Lays, Sunchips, Doritos), restaurants (Pizza Hut, KFC, Taco Bell).

**Perry Drug Stores, Inc....**5400 Perry Dr., P.O. Box 436021, Pontiac, MI 48343...(313) 334-1300...J.A. Robinson...drug stores, health care.

**Petrie Stores Corp....**70 Enterprise Ave., Secaucus, NJ 07094...(201) 866-3600...M.J. Petrie...operates chain of women's specialty stores.

**Pfizer Inc....**235 E. 42d St., N.Y., NY 10017...(212) 573-2323...W.C. Steere Jr....pharmaceutical, hospital, agricultural, chemical prods., consumer prods. (Visine eye drops, Ben-Gay pain relief).

**Philip Morris Cos., Inc....**120 Park Ave., N.Y., NY 10017...(212) 880-5000...Michael A. Miles...cigarettes (Marlboro, Virginia Slims), beer (Miller High Life, Lowenbrau brands), packaged foods (Jell-o, Entenmann baked goods, Maxwell House coffee, Kool Aid, Oscar Mayer meats, Tang, Cheez Whiz & Velveeta cheese prods.).

**Phillips-Van Heusen Corp....**1290 Ave. of the Americas, New York, NY 10104...(212) 541-5200...L. S. Phillips...manuf. apparel for men & women; operates retail stores.

**Pitney Bowes, Inc....**One Elmcroft Rd., Stamford, CT 06926...(203) 356-5000...G. B. Harvey...postage meters, mail handling equip., office equipment.

**Playboy Enterprises, Inc....**680 N. Lake Shore Dr., Chicago, IL 60611...(312) 751-8000...C. Hefner...magazine publishing, CATV, merchandising.

**Polaroid Corp....**549 Technology Sq., Cambridge, MA 02139...(617) 577-2000...I.M. Booth...photographic equip., supplies, and optical goods.

**Premark Intl., Inc....**1717 Deerfield Rd., Deerfield, IL 60015...(708) 405-6000...W.L. Batts...consumer prods. (Tupperware, Hobart, West Bend).

**Primerica, Corp....**65 E. 55th St., N.Y., NY 10022...(212) 891-8900...S. I. Weill...insurance, financial services (Smith Barney, Shearson).

**Procter & Gamble Co....**One Procter & Gamble Plaza, Cincinnati, OH 45202...(513) 983-1100...E. L. Artzt...soap & detergent (Ivory, Cheer, Tide, Mr. Clean, Comet, Spic and Span, Zest), toiletries (Crest toothpaste, Prell, Head and Shoulders shampoos, Noxzema, Oil of Olay, Old Spice), pharmaceuticals (Pepto-Bismol); Pampers disposable diapers, Folgers coffee, Hawaiian Punch, Ultra Charmin toilet tissues, Bounty towels, Vicks cough medicines, Duncan Hines cakes, Crisco shortening.

**Promus Cos. Inc....**1023 Cherry Rd., Memphis, TN 38117...(901) 762-8600...M.D. Rose...casinos (Harrah), lodging (Hampton Inn, Embassy Suites).

**Quaker Oats Co....**321 N. Clark St., Chicago, IL 60604...(312) 222-7111...William D. Smithburg...foods, cereal (Quaker Oat Bran, Life, Cap'n Crunch, Puffed Wheat, Puffed Rice), foods (Aunt Jemima, Celeste pizza, Van Camp's pork and beans, Gatorade), pet foods (Ken-L-Ration, Gaines).

**Quaker State Corp....**255 Elm St., Oil City, PA 16301...(814) 676-7676...H.M. Baum...refining, marketing petroleum prods., filters, mining & marketing coal.

**Ralston Purina Co....**Checkerboard Sq., St. Louis, MO 63164...(314) 982-2161...W. P. Stiritz...pet and livestock food (Purina), consumer prods. (Chex cereal, Beech-Nut baby food, Wonder bread, Hostess baked goods, Eveready and Energizer batteries).

**Raytheon Company...**141 Spring St., Lexington, MA 02173...(617) 862-6600...Dennis J. Picard...electronics, aviation, appliances; Amana Refrigeration, Beech Aircraft.

**Reader's Digest Assn....**Pleasantville, NY 10570...(914) 238-1000...George V. Grune...magazines, books.

**Reebok Intl. Ltd....**100 Technology Ctr. Dr., Stoughton, MA 02072...(617) 341-5000...P.B. Fireman...athletic & casual footwear, sportswear.

**Reynolds Metals Co....**6601 W. Broad St., Richmond, VA 23230...(804) 281-2000...Richard G. Holder...aluminum prods.

**Rite Aid Corp....**30 Hunter Lane, Camp Hill, PA 17011...(717) 761-2633...A. Grass...discount drug stores, beauty aid stores, auto parts stores.

**RJR Nabisco Holdings Corp....**1301 Ave. of the Americas, N.Y., NY 10019...(212) 258-5600...C.M. Harper...cigarettes (Winston, Salem, Camel), foods (Oreos, Ritz crackers).

**Rockwell Intl. Corp....**2201 Seal Beach Blvd., Seal Beach, CA 90740...(213) 647-5000...D. R. Beall...aerospace, electronic, automotive prods.

**Rubbermaid Inc....**1147 Akron Rd., Wooster, OH 44691...(216) 264-6464...W.R. Schmidt...rubber and plastic consumer prods.

**Russell Corp....**1 Lee St., Alexander City, AL 35010...(205) 329-4000...J.C. Adams...manuf. leisure apparel, athletic uniforms.

**Ryder System, Inc....**3600 NW 82d Ave., Miami, FL 33166...(305) 593-3726...M. A. Burns...truck leasing service.

**Santa Fe Pacific Corp....**1700 E. Golf Rd., Schaumburg, IL 60173...(708) 995-6000...Robert D. Krebs...railroad, real estate, construction, natural resources.

**Sara Lee Corp....**3 First National Plaza, Chicago, IL 60602...(312) 726-2600...J.H. Bryan...baked goods, fresh and processed meats, fresh and frozen fruits and vegetables and other packaged foods, beverages, tobacco products, hosiery, intimate apparel and knitwear, Hanes, Kiwi, Shasta, Hillshire Farm, L'eggs, Isotoner.

**Schering-Plough Corp....**One Giralda Farms, Madison, NJ 07940...(201) 822-7000...R. P. Luciano...pharmaceuticals, consumer prods.

**Schlumberger Ltd....**277 Park Ave., New York, NY 10172...(212) 350-9400...D.E. Baird...oilfield services, electronics, measurement and control devices.

**Scott Paper Co....**Scott Plaza, Phila., PA 19113...(215) 522-5000...P. E. Lippincott...toilet tissue, paper towels, napkins.

**Seagram Co. Ltd....**1430 Peel St., Montreal, Que., Canada H3A 1S9...(514) 849-5271...E.M. Bronfman...distilled spirits & wine (Crown Royal, Chivas Regal, Calvert, Wolfschmidt Vodka, Paul Masson, Christian Brothers, Martell, Myer's Jamaica Rum), juice (Tropicana).

**Sears, Roebuck & Co....**Sears Tower, Chicago, IL 60684...(312) 875-2500...E.A. Brennan...merchandising, insurance (Allstate).

**Service Merchandise, Inc....**7100 Service Merchandise Dr., Brentwood, TN 37027...(615) 660-6000...R. Zimmerman...operates catalog showrooms.

**Shaw Industries, Inc....**616 E. Walnut Ave., Dalton, GA 30722...(404) 278-3812...R.E. Shaw...manuf. tufted carpeting (Magee, Philadelphia).

**Sherwin-Williams Co....**101 Prospect Ave. N.W., Cleveland, OH 44115...(216) 566-2000...John G. Breen...paint manuf. (Dutch Boy, Kem-Tone).

**Sizzler Intl., Inc....**12655 W. Jefferson Blvd., Los Angeles, CA 90060...(310) 827-2300...B.P. Bermington...quick service restaurants.

**Skyline Corp....**2520 By-Pass Rd., Elkhart, IN 46515...(219) 294-6521...Arthur J. Decio...mfg. housing and recreational vehicles.

**Smucker (J.M.) Co....**Strawberry Lane, Orrville, OH 44667...(216) 682-3000...R.K. Smucker...preserves, jams, jellies, toppings.

**Snap-on Tools Corp....**2801 80th St., Kenosha, WI 53141...(414) 656-5200...R. A. Cornog...manuf. mechanic's tools, equip.

**Sony Corp.**...9 W. 57th St., New York, NY 10019...(212) 371-5800...N. Ohga...manuf. televisions, radios, tape recorders, audio equip. (Walkman), videotape recorders; entertainment (Sony Pictures).

**Southwest Airlines Co.**...P.O. Box 36611, Dallas, TX 75235...(214) 904-4000...H.D. Kelleher...air transportation.

**Southwestern Bell Corp.**...P.O. Box 2933, San Antonio, TX 78299...(210) 821-4105...E.E. Whitacre Jr....telephone services.

**Sprint Corp.**...2330 Shawnee Mission Pkwy., Westwood, KS 66025...(913) 624-3000...W.T. Esrey...long-distance telecommunications.

**Stanley Works.**...1000 Stanley Drive, P.O. Box 7000, New Britain CT 06050...(203) 225-5111...R.H. Ayers...hand tools, hardware, door opening equip.

**Stride Rite Corp.**...5 Cambridge Center, Cambridge, MA 02142...(617) 491-8800...Erwin Shames...manuf. & retailer children's footwear.

**Sun Company, Inc.**...1801 Market St., Philadelphia, PA 19103...(215) 977-3000...R.H. Campbell...energy resources co.

**Syms Corp.**...Syms Way, Secaucus, NJ 07094...(201) 902-9600...S. Syms...operates off-price apparel stores.

**Tambrands Inc.**...777 Westchester Ave., White Plains, NY 10604...(914) 696-6000...C. Chapman...feminine hygiene products (Tampax, Maxithins).

**Tandem Computers**...19333 Vallco Pkwy., Cupertino, CA 95014...(408) 285-6000...T. G. Treybig...supplier of computer systems and networks.

**Tandy Corp.**...1800 One Tandy Center, Fort Worth, TX 76102...(817) 390-3700...J.F. Roach...consumer electronics retailing (Computer City, Radio Shack).

**Teledyne, Inc.**...1901 Ave. of the Stars, Los Angeles, CA 90067...(310) 277-3311...William Rutledge...electronics, aerospace prods., industrial prods., insurance, finance.

**Tenneco, Inc.**...P.O. Box 2511, Houston, TX 77252...(713) 757-2131...M. H. Walsh...oil, natural gas pipelines, shipbuilding, farm equip.

**Texaco Inc.**...2000 Westchester Ave., White Plains, NY 10650...(914) 253-4000...J.W. Kinnear...petroleum and petroleum prods.

**Texas Instruments Inc.**...13500 N. Central Expressway, Dallas, TX 75265...(214) 995-2011...Jerry Junkins...electrical & electronics prods.

**Textron Inc.**...40 Westminster St., Providence, RI 02903...(401) 421-2800...J.F. Handyman...aerospace, consumer, industrial, metal prods., consumer finance, insurance, management services.

**Tiffany & Co.**...727 5th Ave., New York, NY 10022...(212) 755-8000...W.R. Chaney...designs, manuf., and distributes jewelry & gift items.

**Time Warner Inc.**...Time & Life Bldg., Rockefeller Center, New York, NY 10020...(212) 522-1212...G.M. Levin...magazine publisher (Time, Sports Illustrated, Fortune, Money, People), CATV (HBO, Cinemax), book publishing (Little, Brown, Warner Books), motion pictures (Warner Bros.).

**Tootsie Roll Industries, Inc.**...7401 S. Cicero Ave., Chicago, IL 60629...(312) 838-3400...M.J. Gordon...candy (Tootsie Roll, Mason Dots, Charms).

**Toro Co.**...8111 Lyndale Ave. South, Bloomington, MN 55420...(612) 887-8801...K. B. Melrose...lawn and turf maintenance (Lawn Boy); snow removal equipment.

**Toys "R" Us**...461 From Rd., Paramus, NJ 07652...(201) 262-7800...Charles Lazarus...toy retailer, clothing stores (Kids "R" Us).

**Transamerica Corp.**...600 Montgomery St., San Francisco, CA 94111...(415) 983-4000...Frank C. Herringer...insurance, financial, business services.

**Travelers Corp.**...One Tower Sq., Hartford, CT 06183...(203) 277-0111...E. H. Budd...insurance.

**Tribune Co.**...435 N. Michigan Ave., Chicago, IL 60611...(312) 222-9100...C.T. Brumback...newpaper publishing, broadcasting, entertainment (Chicago Cubs baseball team).

**Trinity Industries, Inc.**...2525 Stemmons Freeway, Dallas, TX 75356...(214) 631-4420...W.R. Wallace...manufactures variety of metal products.

**TRW Inc.**...1900 Richmond Rd., Cleveland, OH 44124...(216) 291-7000...J.T. Gorman...car and truck operations, electronics, and space systems.

**Turner Broadcasting System, Inc.**...1 CNN Center, Atlanta, GA 30303...(404) 827-1700...R.E. Turner...operates cable TV networks: CNN, TBS, TNT; owns MGM film library; owns Atlanta Braves, Hawks.

**USAIR Group, Inc.**...1911 Jefferson Davis Hwy., Arlington, VA 22202...(703) 418-7000...Seth E. Schofield...air carrier of passengers, property, and mail.

**UST Inc.**...100 W. Putnam Ave., Greenwich, CT 06830...(203) 661-1100...L.F. Bantle...smokeless tobacco (Copenhagen, Skoal, Happy Days), pipes, pipe tobacco.

**USX-U.S. Steel Group**...600 Grant St., Pittsburgh, PA 15230...(412) 433-1121...C.A. Corry...steel manuf.

**Unilever, PLC**...390 Park Ave., New York, NY 10022...(212) 906-3398...Michael Perry, chmn....soap, detergent, margarine, frozen food, toothpaste, tea, dried soups, ice cream, cosmetics, fragrances (Lever Brothers, Lipton, Pond's Vaseline Intensive Care, Obsession, Q-Tips, Cutex).

**Union Carbide Corp.**...39 Old Ridgebury Rd., Danbury, CT 06817...(203) 794-2000...R.D. Kennedy...chemicals, industrial gases.

**Union Pacific Corp.**...Martin Tower, Bethlehem, PA 18018...(215) 861-3200...D. Lewis...railroad, natural resources.

**Unisys Corp.**...P.O. Box 500, Blue Bell, PA 19424...(215) 986-6999...James Unruh...computer based information systems.

**U.S. Shoe Corp.**...One Eastwood Dr., Cincinnati, OH 45227...(513) 527-7459...B.B. Hudson...apparel, retailer (Casual Corner), shoes (Red Cross, Joyce), eye-care stores (LensCrafters).

**United Technologies Corp.**...United Technologies Bldg., Hartford, CT 06101...(203) 728-7000...R.F. Daniell...aerospace, industrial prods. & services, Carrier Corp., Otis Elevator, Pratt & Whitney, Sikorsky Aircraft.

**Univar Corp.**...6100 Carillon Pt., Kirkland, WA 98033...(206) 899-3400...J.W. Bernard...industrial and agricultural chemicals, laboratory and graphic arts products distributor, home furnishing supplies and fabrics distributors.

**Universal Foods Corp.**...433 East Michigan St., Milwaukee, WI 53202...(414) 271-6755...G.A. Osborn...yeast products, cheese products, dehydrated seasonings, food colors and flavors, imported gourmet foods.

**Upjohn Co.**...7000 Portage Rd., Kalamazoo, MI 49001...(616) 323-4000...W.U. Parfet...pharmaceuticals (Motrin, Nuprin, Halcion), chemicals, agricultural and health care prods.

**VF Corp.**...1047 No. Park Rd., Wyomissing, PA 19610...(215) 378-1151...L.R. Pugh...apparel, Vanity Fair, Lee, Wrangler jeans, Jantzen.

**Wal-Mart Stores Inc.**...Box 116, Bentonville, AR 72716...(501) 273-4000...D.D. Glass...retail dept. stores (Sam's Wholesale Clubs).

**Walgreen Co.**...200 Wilmot Rd., Deerfield, IL 60015...(312) 940-2500...Charles R. Walgreen 3d...retail drug chain.

**Warner-Lambert Co.**...201 Tabor Rd., Morris Plains, NJ 07950...(201) 540-2000...M.R. Goodes, chmn....health care prods. (Benadryl), consumer prods. (Efferdent dental cleanser, Hall cough tablets, Schick razors, Rolaids antacid, Listerine mouthwash).

**Washington Post Co.**...1150 15th St., N.W., Washington, DC 20071...(202) 334-6000...D.E. Graham...newspapers, magazines (Newsweek), TV stations.

**Weis Markets, Inc.**...1000 South Second Street, Sunbury, PA 17801...(717) 286-4571...S. Weis...operates supermarkets, distributes frozen foods and grocery items.

**Wells Fargo & Co.**...420 Montgomery St., San Francisco, CA 94163...(415) 477-1000...C.E. Reichardt...banking.

**Wendy's Intl., Inc.**...4288 W. Dublin-Granville Rd., Dublin, OH 43017...(614) 764-3100...J.W. Near...quick service restaurants.

**Westinghouse Electric Corp.**...Westinghouse Bldg., Gateway Center, Pittsburgh, PA 15222...(412) 244-2000...Michael H. Jordan...manuf. electrical, mechanical equip.; radio and television stations.

**Westvaco Corp.**...299 Park Avenue, New York, NY 10171...(212) 688-5000...J.A. Luke Jr....manufactures paper for graphic reproduction, communications, and packaging.

**Weyerhaeuser Co.**...Tacoma, WA 98477...(206) 924-2345...George H. Weyerhaeuser...manuf., distribution of forest prods.

**Whirlpool Corp.**...Benton Harbor, MI 49022...(616) 926-5000...D.R. Whitwam...major home appliances.

**Whitman Corp.**...111 Crossroads of Commerce, 3501 Algonquin Rd., Rolling Meadows, IL 60008...(708) 818-5000...Bruce S. Chelberg...diversified prods. and services, consumer prods., food, auto prods. (Midas).

**Winn-Dixie Stores, Inc.**...5050 Edgewood Ct., Jacksonville, FL 32205...(904) 783-5000...A.D. Davis, chmn....supermarket chain.

**Winnebago Industries, Inc.**...P.O. Box 152, Forest City, IA 50436...(515) 582-3535...J.K. Hanson, chmn....manuf. of motor homes, recreation vehicles.

**Wolverine World Wide Corp.**...9341 Courtland Dr., Rockford, MI 49351...(616) 866-5500...T.D. Gleason...manuf. footwear (Hush Puppies).

**Woolworth Corp.**....233 Broadway, N.Y., NY 10279...(212) 553-2000...W.K. Lavin...variety stores, shoe stores (Kinney), men's clothing (Richman Brothers), children's apparel (Kid's Mart), athletic footwear (Foot Locker).

**Wm. Wrigley Jr. Co.**....410 N. Michigan Ave., Chicago, IL 60611...(312) 644-2121...William Wrigley...chewing gum.

**Xerox Corp.**....P.O. Box 1600, Stamford, CT 06904...(203) 968-3000...Paul Allaire...equip. for reproduction, reduction, and transmission of business prods. & systems.

**Zenith Electronics Corp.**....1000 Milwaukee Ave., Glenview, IL 60025...(708) 391-7000...Jerry K. Pearlman...consumer electronic prods.

## Who Owns What: Familiar Consumer Products

Listed below are familiar consumer products and their parent companies. The parent company address can be found on pages 710-716.

Admiral appliances: Maytag
Advil: American Home Products
Ajax cleanser: Colgate-Palmolive
Almond Joy candy: Hershey
Anacin: American Home Products
Arrid antiperspirant: Carter-Wallace
Arnold breads: CPC International
Aunt Millie's pasta sauce: Borden
Ban antiperspirant: Bristol-Myers
Beech Aircraft: Raytheon
Beech-Nut babyfood: Ralston Purina
Ben-Gay: Pfizer
Betty Crocker products: General Mills
Breck shampoo: Dial
Budweiser beer: Anheuser-Busch
Bufferin: Bristol-Myers Squibb
Business Week magazine: McGraw-Hill
Buster Brown shoes: Brown Group
Cap'n Crunch cereal: Quaker Oats
Carrier air conditioners: United Technologies
Celeste Pizza: Quaker Oats
Charmin toilet tissues: Procter & Gamble
Chef Boy-ar-dee products: American Home Products
Cheer detergent: Procter & Gamble
Cheerios cereal: General Mills
Clairol hair products: Bristol-Myers Squibb
Clorets mints: Warner-Lambert
Combat insecticides: Clorox
Comet cleanser: Procter & Gamble
Copenhagen snuff: UST
Cracker Jacks: Borden
Crest toothpaste: Procter & Gamble
Crisco shortening: Procter & Gamble
Deer Park bottled water: Clorox
Degree antiperspirant: Helene Curtis
Doritos chips: PepsiCo
Drano: Bristol-Myers Squibb
Dristan: American Home Products
Duncan Hines cakes: Procter & Gamble
Easy-Off oven cleaner: American Home Products
Efferdent dental cleanser: Warner-Lambert
ESPN: Capital Cities/ABC
Eveready batteries: Ralston Purina
Excedrin: Bristol-Myers
Fab detergent: Colgate-Palmolive
Family Circle magazine: New York Times
Foamy shaving cream: Gillette
Folgers coffee: Procter & Gamble
Formula 409 spray cleaner: Clorox
Franco-American foods: Campbell Soup
Frito-Lay snacks: PepsiCo
Gatorade: Quaker Oats
Gleem toothpaste: Procter & Gamble
Handy Wipes: Colgate-Palmolive
Hanes hosiery: Sara Lee
Hawaiian Punch: Procter & Gamble
Head and Shoulders shampoo: Procter & Gamble
Hellman's mayonnaise: CPC International
Hi-C fruit drinks: Coca-Cola
Hillshire Farm meats: Sara Lee
Home Box Office: Time Warner
Hostess baked goods: Ralston Purina
Hush Puppies shoes: Wolverine World Wide
Ivory soap products: Procter & Gamble
Jack Daniel bourbon: Brown-Forman
Jell-o: Philip Morris
Jim Beam whiskey: American Brands
Ken-L-Ration pet foods: Quaker Oats
Kent cigarettes: Loews
Kinney shoe stores: Woolworth
Knorr soups: CPC International
Kool Aid: Philip Morris
Ladies Home Journal magazine: Meredith
Lee jeans: VF Corp.
Lenox china: Brown-Forman
Lens Crafters: U.S. Shoe
Lerner stores: The Limited

Lipton tea: Unilever
Listerine mouthwash: Warner-Lambert
Log Cabin syrup: Philip Morris
Lord & Taylor dept. stores: May Dept. Stores
Marlboro cigarettes: Philip Morris
Mazola oil: CPC International
Maxwell House coffee: Philip Morris
Michelob beer: Anheuser-Busch
Midas automotive centers: Whitman
Miller beer: Philip Morris
Milton Bradley games: Hasbro
Minute Rice: Philip Morris
Mrs. Paul's frozen fish: Campbell Soup
NBC Broadcasting: General Electric
Newsweek magazine: Washington Post
9-Lives cat food: H.J. Heinz
North American Van Lines: Norfolk Southern
Obsession fragrance: Unilever
Old Spice: Procter & Gamble
Olive Garden restaurants: General Mills
Ore-Ida frozen foods: H.J. Heinz
Oreo cookies: RJR Nabisco
Pampers: Procter & Gamble
Paper Mate pens: Gillette
People magazine: Time Warner
Pepto-Bismol: Procter & Gamble
Pepperidge Farm products: Campbell Soup
Pizza Hut restaurants: PepsiCo
Playskool toys: Hasbro
Prego spaghetti sauce: Campbell Soup
Prell shampoo: Procter & Gamble
Prentice-Hall publishing: Paramount
Prestone auto products: First Brands
Post-It stickers: Minn. Min. & Manuf.
Purex detergent: Dial
Q-Tips: Unilever
Radio Shack retail outlets: Tandy
Red Lobster Inns: General Mills
Reese's peanut butter cups: Hershey
Right Guard deodorant: Gillette
Rise shave lathers: Carter-Wallace
Ritz crackers: RJR Nabisco
Robitussin: American Home Products
Rolaids antacid: Warner-Lambert
Ruffles chips: PepsiCo
San Giorgio pasta: Hershey
Saran Wrap: Dow Chemical
Scotch tape: Minn. Min. & Manuf.
Skippy peanut butter: CPC International
Simon & Schuster publishing: Paramount
Southern Comfort liquor: Brown-Forman
Sports Illustrated magazine: Time Warner
Sprite soda: Coca-Cola
Sugartwin: Alberto Culver
Swanson frozen dinners: Campbell Soup
Taco Bell restaurants: PepsiCo
Thomas' English muffins: CPC International
Tide detergent: Procter & Gamble
Tonka trucks: Hasbro
Trojan condoms: Carter-Wallace
Tropicana juices: Seagram
Tupperware: Premark
Tylenol: Johnson & Johnson
Ultra Brite toothpaste: Colgate-Palmolive
V-8 vegetable juice: Campbell Soup
Vanity Fair apparel: VF Corp.
Velveeta cheese prods.: Philip Morris
Vicks cough medicines: Procter & Gamble
Victory flea collars: Carter-Wallace
Virginia Slims cigarettes: Philip Morris
Walkman: Sony
Wall Street Journal: Dow Jones
Weight Watchers: H.J. Heinz
Wheaties cereal: General Mills
White Owl cigars: Culbro
Wizard air freshener: American Home Products
Wyler's drink mixes: Borden

## Interest Laws and Consumer Finance Loan Rates

Source: Revised by Christian T. Jones. Editor, Consumer Finance Law Bulletin. San Diego, CA

All states have laws regulating interest rates. These laws fix a legal or conventional rate, which applies when there is no contract for interest. They also fix a general maximum contract rate, but there are so many exceptions that the general contract maximum actually applies only to exceptional cases. Also, federal law has preempted state limits on first home mortgages, subject to each state's right to reinstate its own law, and given depository institutions parity with other state lenders.

**Legal rate of interest.** The legal or conventional rate of interest applies to money obligations when no interest rate is contracted for and also to judgments. The rate is usually somewhat below the general interest rate.

**General maximum contract rates.** General interest laws in most states set the maximum rate between 8% and 16% per year. The general maximum is fixed by the state constitution at 5% over the Federal Reserve discount rate in Arkansas. Loans to corporations are frequently exempted or subject to a higher maximum. In recent years, it has also been common to provide special rates for home mortgage loans and variable usury rates that are indexed to market rates.

**Specific enabling acts.** In many states special statutes permit industrial loan companies, second mortgage lenders, and banks to charge 1.5% a month or more. Laws regulating revolving loans, charge accounts, and credit cards generally limit rates to between 1.5% and 2% per month plus annual fees for credit cards. Rates for installment sales contracts in most states are somewhat higher. Credit unions may generally charge 1% to 1.5% a month. Pawnbrokers' rates vary widely. Savings and loan associations, and loans insured by federal agencies, are also specially regulated. A number of states allow regulated lenders to charge any rate agreed to with the customer either for all credit or over a certain dollar amount.

**Consumer finance loan statutes.** Most consumer finance loan statutes are based on early models drafted by the Russell Sage Foundation (1916-42) to provide small loans to wage earners under license and other protective regulations. Since 1969 the model has frequently been the Uniform Consumer Credit Code, which applies to credit sales and loans for consumer purposes. In general, licensed lenders may charge 3% a month and reduced rates for additional amounts. An add-on of 17% ($17 per $100) per year yields about 2.5% per month if paid in equal monthly installments. Discount rates produce higher yields than add-on rates of the same amount. In the table below, unless otherwise stated, monthly and annual rates are based on reducing principal balances, annual add-on rates are based on the original principal for the full term, and two or more rates apply to different portions of the balance or original principal.

### States with consumer finance loan laws and the rates of charge as of Aug. 1, 1993

Maximum monthly rates computed on unpaid balances, unless otherwise stated.

Ala.. . . Annual add-on: 15% to $750, 10% to $2,000 (min. 1.5% on unpaid balances). Higher rates for loans up to $749. Over $2,000, any agreed rate. Fee: 4% (max. $25); 5% real estate.

Alas. . . 3% to $850, 2% to $10,000. Over $10,000, any agreed rate.

Ariz. . . To $1,000: 3%. Over $1,000: 3% to $500, 2% to $10,000. Over $10,000, any agreed rate.

Cal. . . 2.5% to $225, 2% to $900, 1.5% to $1,650, 1% to $2,500 (1.6% min.). Over $2,500, any agreed rate. 5% fee (max. $50) to $2,500

Col. . . 36% per year to $630, 21% to $2,100, 15% to $25,000 (21% min.).

Conn. . Annual add-on: 17% to $600, 11% to $5,000; 11% over $1,800 to $5,000 for certain secured loans. Any agreed rate for second mortgages.

Del.. . . Any agreed rate.

D.C. . . 24% per year.

Fla.. . . 30% per year to $1,000, 24% to $2,000, 18% to $25,000.

Ga.. . . 10% per year discount to 18 months, add-on to 36½ months; 8% fee to $600, 4% on excess plus $2 per month. Over $3,000, any agreed rate.

Ha.. . . 3.5% to $100, 2.5% to $300; 2% on entire balance over $300 or discount rates.

Ida.. . . Any agreed rate.

Ill.. . . Any agreed rate.

Ind.. . . 36% per year to $840, 21% to $2,800, 15% to $25,000 (21% min.).

Ia. . . . 3% to $1,000, 2% to $2,800, 1.5% to $10,000; or equivalent flat rate. Over $10,000, 21% per year.

Kan.. . 36% per year to $780, 21% to $2,600, 14.45% to $25,000 (18% min.). Fee: 2% (max. $100); 3% real estate.

Ky.. . . 3% to $1,000, 2% to $3,000. Over $3,000, 2%.

La. . . . 36% per year to $1,400, 27% to $4,000, 24% to $7,000, 21% over $7,000, plus $25 fee.

Me.. . . 30% per year to $700, 21% to $2,000, 15% to $25,000 (18% min.).

Md.. . . 2.75% to $1,000, 2% to $2,000. Over $2,000, 2%.

Mass. . 23% per year plus $20 annual fee to $6,000; any agreed rate over $6,000.

Mich.. . 22% per year to $8,000; 18% for second mortgages, plus 2% fee (max. $200).

Minn.. . 33% per year to $750, 19% over $750 (21.75% min.).

Miss.. . 36% per year to $1,000, 33% to $1,800, 24% to $5,000, 14% over $5,000. Over $25,000, 18%. 2% fee (max. $50).

Mo.. . . 2.218% to $1,200, 1.67% over $1,200, plus 5% fee (max. $15); 1.67% plus 2% for second mortgages.

Mon.. . Any agreed rate.

Neb.. . 24% per year to $1,000. 21% over, plus fee of 7% to $2,000 and 5% over (max. $500).

Nev.. . Any agreed rate.

N.H. . . 2% to $600, 1.5% to $1,500; any agreed rate over $1,500 or for real estate mortgages.

N.J.. . . 30% per year to $5,000 or for second mortgages.

N.M. . . Any agreed rate.

N.Y. . . 25% per year.

N.C. . . 2.5% to $1,000, 1.5% to $7,500; 1.5% on entire amount to $10,000. 1.5% or variable plus 2% fee for second mortgages.

N.D. . . 2.5% to $250, 2% to $500, 1.75% to $750, 1.5% to $1,000; any agreed rate over $1,000.

Oh.. . . 28% per year to $1,000, 22% to $5,000; 25% on entire amount over $5,000; plus fee.

Okla.. . 30% per annum to $900, 21% to $3,000, 15% to $45,000 (21% min.). Special rates to $500.

Ore. . . Any agreed rate.

Pa. . . . 9.5% per year discount to 48 months, 6% for remaining time plus 2% fee (max. $100); or 2% on unpaid balances; 1.85% for second mortgages over $5,000, plus 2% fee.

P.R. . . Variable: 25% max., 19% min.

R.I. . . . 3% to $300, 2.5% for loans between $300 and $800; 2% for larger loans to $5,000. 1.75% over $5,000.

S.C. . . Any agreed and posted rate.

S.D. . . Any agreed rate.

Tenn.. . Over $100, 24% per year or discount rates plus fees.

Tex.. . . Annual add-on: 18% to $1,200, 8% to $10,000 or formula rate (18% to 24% per year on unpaid balances.)

Ut.. . . Any agreed rate.

Vt.. . . 2% to $1,000, 1% to $3,000 (min. 1.5%); 1.5% for second mortgages.

Va.. . . 2.56% to $800, 1.9% to $2,000, 1.4% to $3,500; or annual add-on of 17% to $800, 15% to $2,000, 11% to $3,500; 2% fee. Any agreed rate over $3,500 for second mortgages, plus 2% fee.

Wash. . 25% per year plus fees.

W.Va. . 36% per year to $500, 24% to $1,500, 18% to $2,000. Over $2,000, 27% per year to $2,000, 25% to $10,000, 18% on remainder, plus 2% fee.

Wis. . . Any agreed rate.

Wyo.. . 36% per year to $1,000, 21% to $25,000. No limit over $25,000.

## How to Check Your Credit File

Any individual can investigate the contents of his or her credit file by directly contacting one or more of the approximately 2,000 credit bureaus, or consumer credit clearinghouses, in the United States. The nearest ones can be found by calling a local Better Business Bureau or by looking in the telephone Yellow Pages under "Credit Rating or Reporting Agencies."

Although the Fair Credit Reporting Act requires that a bureau give a person no more than an oral or written credit history review, many bureaus will go beyond the technical requirements of the law and furnish the same computer-generated compilation of facts that they give the banks, retailers and other companies that subscribe to their service. An individual who has been denied credit on the basis of negative information from a credit bureau can obtain this review without charge within 30 days of the denial. Sometimes there is a small fee for such a credit check.

After inspecting this record of past credit behavior, a consumer can question any item believed to be inaccurate, misleading or vague. The credit bureau must then investigate and remove any item that cannot be substantiated.

When a bureau affirms, rather than removes, a questionable item, an individual can present a 100-word explanation that must be placed in his or her file. And whenever an adverse item is deleted from the file or an explantory statement is added to one, a consumer may request that the credit bureau inform every credit grantor who received a report within the last six months.

## Credit Card Rates

(As of Aug. 1, 1993)

(Prepared by Christian T. Jones, San Diego, CA)

Nearly all states have special laws dealing with rates charged for credit cards issued by state banks and other financial institutions. Although some state laws apply only to banks, under federal parity law, the same charges can be made by other financial institutions. A national bank can charge the highest rates allowed for revolving credit extended by any other creditor in the state where the bank is located for similar types of credit, and such rates may also be charged to residents of any other state. Maximum rates and fees shown below; rates are yearly unless otherwise stated.

| | | | | | |
|---|---|---|---|---|---|
| Ala. | No limit. | | annual fee. | Okla. | 30-21-15% @ $870, $2,900; or |
| Alas. | 17% plus fee. | Me. | 18%; $12 annual fee. | | 21%. |
| Ariz. | No limit. | Md. | 24%; 2% fee. | Ore. | No limit. |
| Ark. | 5% over FRB discount rate | Mass. | 18% or formula rate. | Pa. | 12% loans; 15% purchases; $15 |
| | (max. 17%). | Mich. | 18%; no limit on annual fee. | | annual fee. |
| Cal. | No limit. | Minn. | 18%; $50 annual fee. | P.R. | 2.17% per mo. |
| Col. | 21%. | Miss. | 21%; or 18% plus $12 annual | R.I. | 18%. |
| Conn. | 18%. | | fee. | S.C. | No limit. |
| D.C. | 24%. | Mo. | 22-10% @ $1,000. | S.D. | No limit. |
| Del. | No limit. | Mon. | No limit. | Tenn. | 24%. |
| Fla. | No limit. | Neb. | 18% plus fee. | Tex. | Set by rule (max. 24%, min. |
| Ga. | No limit on rate or fee. | Nev. | No limit. | | 18%.) |
| Ha. | 24%. | N.H. | No limit. | Ut. | No limit. |
| Ida. | No limit. | N.J. | 30%; $15 annual fee or $50 | Vt. | 18%; no limit on annual fee. |
| Ill. | No limit; plus fee. | | over $5,000. | Va. | No limit. |
| Ind. | 36-21-15%, @ $840, $2,800; or | N.M. | No limit. | Wash. | 12% or 4% over U.S. T-bill rate. |
| | 21%. | N.Y. | 25% plus annual fee. | W.Va. | 18%. |
| Ia. | No limit. | N.C. | 18%; $24 annual fee. | Wis. | No limit. |
| Kan. | 18-14.45% @ $1,000. | N.D. | No limit. | Wyo. | 36-21% @ $1,000; no limit over |
| Ky. | 21%; $20 annual fee. | Oh. | 25% to 1/1/96. | | $25,000. |
| La. | 18%; 4% cash advance and $12 | | | | |

## The Cost of Raising a Child

**Source:** Family Economics Research Group, U.S. Dept. of Agriculture

Projected annual expenditures in current dollars on a child born in 1990, by income group for married-couple families.

| Year | Age of child | Income group[1] Low | Medium | High | Year | Age of child | Income group[1] Low | Medium | High |
|---|---|---|---|---|---|---|---|---|---|
| 1990 | under 1 . . . . | $4,330 | $6,140 | $8,770 | 1999 | 9 . . . . . . . | 7,570 | 10,690 | 15,120 |
| 1991 | 1 . . . . . . . . | 4,590 | 6,510 | 9,300 | 2000 | 10 . . . . . . . | 8,020 | 11,340 | 16,030 |
| 1992 | 2 . . . . . . . . | 4,870 | 6,900 | 9,850 | 2001 | 11 . . . . . . . | 8,500 | 12,020 | 16,990 |
| 1993 | 3 . . . . . . . . | 5,510 | 7,790 | 11,030 | 2002 | 12 . . . . . . . | 10,360 | 14,190 | 19,680 |
| 1994 | 4 . . . . . . . . | 5,850 | 8,260 | 11,690 | 2003 | 13 . . . . . . . | 10,980 | 15,040 | 20,860 |
| 1995 | 5 . . . . . . . . | 6,200 | 8,750 | 12,390 | 2004 | 14 . . . . . . . | 11,640 | 15,940 | 22,110 |
| 1996 | 6 . . . . . . . . | 6,550 | 9,220 | 12,950 | 2005 | 15 . . . . . . . | 13,160 | 17,950 | 24,610 |
| 1997 | 7 . . . . . . . . | 6,950 | 9,770 | 13,730 | 2006 | 16 . . . . . . . | 13,950 | 19,030 | 26,090 |
| 1998 | 8 . . . . . . . . | 7,360 | 10,360 | 14,550 | 2007 | 17 . . . . . . . | 14,780 | 20,170 | 27,650 |
| | | | | | **Total** | | **$151,170** | **$210,070** | **$293,400** |

(1) Low income is under $29,900 in 1990; middle is $29,900 to $48,299; high is $48,300 or more. Projection assumes 6 percent annual inflation.

## Tourism: Foreign Visitors to the U.S., 1990

**Source:** U.S. Travel & Tourism Admin.; Bureau of Economic Analysis

| Country of origin | Visitors (millions) | Expenditures (millions) | Expenditures per visitor | Country of origin | Visitors (millions) | Expenditures (millions) | Expenditures per visitor |
|---|---|---|---|---|---|---|---|
| Japan . . . . . . . | 3.2 | $7,694 | $2,381 | France . . . . . . . | 0.7 | $1,219 | $1,703 |
| Canada . . . . . . | 17.3 | 5,690 | 330 | Australia . . . . . . | 0.5 | 1,061 | 2,279 |
| Mexico . . . . . . . | 6.8 | 4,004 | 592 | Italy . . . . . . . | 0.4 | 781 | 1,973 |
| United | | | | Netherlands . . . . | 0.3 | 404 | 1,422 |
| Kingdom . . . | 2.2 | 3,581 | 1,596 | New Zealand . . . | 0.2 | 379 | 2,181 |
| Germany . . . . . | 1.2 | 2,139 | 1,778 | All countries . . . | 39.1 | $40,579 | $1,038 |

Note: Excludes international passenger fare payments and cruise travel. Numbers may not add up due to rounding.

# U.S. Passport, Visa, and Health Requirements

Source: Bureau of Consular Affairs, U.S. Dept. of State as of mid-1993

Passports are issued by the U.S. Department of State to citizens and nationals of the United States for the purpose of documenting them for foreign travel and identifying them as Americans.

## How to Obtain a Passport

Applicants who have never been issued a passport in their own name must execute an application in person before (1) a passport agent; (2) a clerk of any federal court or state court of record or a judge or clerk of any probate court accepting applications; (3) a postal employee designated by the postmaster at a post office that has been selected to accept passport applications; or (4) a U.S. diplomatic or consular officer abroad. A DSP-11 is the correct form to use for applicants who must apply in person. All persons are required to obtain individual passports in their own name. An applicant who is 13 years of age or older is required to appear in person before the clerk or agent executing the application. A parent or legal guardian may execute the application for children under 13.

A full validity passport previously issued to the applicant, or one in which he or she was included, will be accepted as proof of U.S. citizenship. If the applicant has no prior passport and was born in the U.S., a certified copy of his/her birth certificate shall be presented to the agent accepting the passport application. To be acceptable, the certificate must show the given name and surname, the date and place of birth, and that the birth record was filed shortly after birth. A delayed birth certificate (a record filed more than one year after the date of birth) is acceptable provided that it shows acceptable secondary evidence was used for creating this record. Contact the nearest Dept. of State passport office for more information concerning acceptable secondary evidence.

If a birth certificate is not obtainable, a notice from a state registrar shall be submitted stating that no birth record exists. The notice shall be accompanied by the best obtainable secondary evidence, such as a baptismal certificate or a hospital birth record.

A naturalized citizen with no previous passport must present a Certificate of Naturalization. A person born abroad claiming U.S. citizenship through either a native-born or naturalized citizen parent must submit a Certificate of Citizenship issued by the Immigration and Naturalization Service; or a Consular Report of Birth or Certification of Birth Abroad issued by the Dept. of State. If one of the above documents has not been obtained, evidence of citizenship of the parent(s) through whom citizenship is claimed and evidence that would establish the parent/child relationship must be submitted. Additionally, if citizenship is derived through birth to citizen parent(s), the following documents will be required: parents' marriage certificate plus an affidavit from parent(s) showing periods and places of residence or physical presence in the U.S. and abroad, specifying periods spent abroad in the employment of the U.S. government, including the armed forces, or with certain international organizations. If citizenship is derived through naturalization of parents, evidence of admission to the U.S. for permanent residence also will be required.

Persons who possess the most recent passport issued within the last 12 years and after their 16th birthday may be eligible to apply for a new passport by mail. A form DSP-82, Application for Passport by Mail must be filled out and mailed to the address shown on the form, together with the previous passport, 2 recent identical photographs and $55.00. The DSP-82 may not be used if the most recent passport has been altered or mutilated.

## Photographs, Fees and Identity

**Photographs** — Submit 2 identical photographs that are sufficiently recent (normally not more than 6 months old) to be a good likeness of and satisfactorily identify the applicant. Photographs should be $2 \times 2$ inches in size. The image size measured from the bottom of the chin to the top of the head (including hair) should be not less than one inch nor more than 1 3/8 inches. Photographs should be portrait-type prints. They must be clear, front view, full face, with a plain, white or off-white background. Photographs that depict the applicant as relaxed and smiling are encouraged.

**Fees** — The passport fee is $30.00 for passports issued to persons under 18 years of age. These passports are valid for 5 years from the date of issue. The passport fee is $55.00 for passports issued to persons 18 and older. These passports are valid for 10 years from the date of issuance. An additional fee of $10.00 is charged for the execution of the application. There is no execution fee when using DSP-82, Application for Passport by Mail. Applicants eligible to use this form pay only the $55.00 passport fee.

**Identity**—Applicants must also establish their identity to the satisfaction of the person accepting the application and to Passport Services. Generally acceptable documents of identity include a previous U.S. passport, a Certificate of Naturalization, a Certificate of Citizenship, a valid driver's license, or a government identification card. Applicants may not use a Social Security card, learner's or temporary driver's license, credit card, or expired identity card. Extremely old documents cannot be used by themselves. Applicants unable to establish identity must present some documentation in their own name (e.g., Social Security card) and must be accompanied by a person who has known the applicant for at least 2 years and who is a U.S. citizen or legal U.S. permanent resident alien. That person must sign an affidavit before the individual who executes the passport application. The witness will be required to establish his or her own identity.

The loss or theft of a valid passport is a serious matter and should be reported immediately to Passport Services, 1425 K Street, N.W., Dept. of State, Wash., D.C. 20524, tel: (202) 647-0518 or to the nearest passport agency, or the nearest U.S. embassy or consulate when abroad.

## Foreign Regulations

A visa, usually rubber stamped in a passport by a representative of the country to be visited, indicates that the bearer of the passport is permitted to enter that country for a certain purpose and length of time. In most instances, you must obtain necessary visas before you leave the U.S. Apply directly to the embassy or nearest consulate of each country you plan to visit, or consult a travel agent.

The State Dept.'s "Foreign Entry Requirements" contains entry requirements and application instructions for most foreign countries and is available for 50¢ from the Consumer Information Center, Dept. 438T, Pueblo, CO 81009.

The process may take several weeks, so it is important to apply well in advance and verify requirements with the embassy or nearest consulate of each country before applying.

# How to Obtain Birth, Marriage, Death Records

The pamphlet "Where to Write for Vital Records: Births, Deaths, Marriages, and Divorces" (Pub. #93-1142, Stock # 017-022-01196-4) is available from the Superintendent of Documents, Government Printing Office, Washington, DC 20402; advance payment of $2.25 is required. "How You May Save Time Proving Your Age and Other Birth Facts" is available from the U.S. Dept. of Health and Human Services, National Center for Health Statistics, Rockville, MD 20852. "Geneological Research in the National Archives" is sold by the National Archives Trust Fund Board, P.O. Box 100793, Atlanta, GA 30384.

# Copyright Law of The United States

Source: Copyright Office, Library of Congress

## What Copyright Is

Copyright is a form of protection provided by the laws of the United States (title 17, U.S. Code) to the authors of "original works of authorship" including literary, dramatic, musical, artistic, and certain other intellectual works. This protection is available to both published and unpublished works. Section 106 of the Copyright Act generally gives the owner of copyright the exclusive right to do and to authorize others to do the following:

• *To reproduce* the copyrighted work in copies or phonorecords;

• *To prepare derivative works* based upon the copyrighted work;

• *To distribute copies or phonorecords* of the copyrighted work to the public by sale or other transfer of ownership, or by rental, lease, or lending;

• *To perform the copyrighted work publicly,* in the case of literary, musical, dramatic, and choreographic works, pantomimes, and motion pictures and other audiovisual works; and

• *To display the copyrighted work publicly,* in the case of literary, musical, dramatic, and choreographic works, pantomimes, and pictorial, graphic, or sculptural works, including the individual images of a motion picture or other audiovisual work.

It is illegal for anyone to violate any of the rights provided by the Act to the owner of copyright. These rights, however, are not unlimited in scope. Sections 107 through 119 of the Copyright Act establish limitations on these rights. In some cases, these limitations are specified exemptions from copyright liability. One major limitation is the doctrine of "fair use," which is given a statutory basis by section 107 of the Act. In other instances, the limitation takes the form of a "compulsory license" under which certain limited uses of copyrighted works are permitted upon payment of specified royalties and compliance with statutory conditions.

Copyright protection subsists from the time the work is created in fixed form; that is, it is an incident of the process of authorship. The copyright in the work of authorship *immediately* becomes the property of the author who created it. Only the author or those deriving their rights from the author can rightfully claim copyright.

In the case of works made for hire, the employer and not the employee is presumptively considered the author. Section 101 of the copyright statute defines a "work made for hire" as:

(1) a work prepared by an employee within the scope of his or her employment; or

(2) a work specially ordered or commissioned for use as a contribution to a collective work, as a part of a motion picture or other audiovisual work, as a translation, as a supplementary work, as a compilation, as an instructional text, as a test, as answer material for a test, or as an atlas, if the parties expressly agree in a written instrument signed by them that the work shall be considered a work made for hire.

The authors of a joint work are co-owners of the copyright in the work, unless there is an agreement to the contrary.

Copyright in each separate contribution to a periodical or other collective work is distinct from copyright in the collective work as a whole and vests initially with the author of the contribution.

Works published on or after January 1, 1978, are subject to protection under the copyright statute if, on the date of first publication, one or more of the authors is a national or domiciliary of the U.S., or is a national, domiciliary, or sovereign authority of a foreign nation that is a party to a copyright treaty to which the U.S. is also a party, or is a stateless person, regardless of domicile, or if the work is first published either in the U.S. or in a foreign nation that on the date of first publication is a party to the Universal Copyright Convention or the Berne Union.

## What Works Are Protected

Copyright protects "original works of authorship" that are fixed in a tangible form of expression. The fixation need not be directly perceptible, so long as it may be communicated with the aid of a machine or device. Copyrightable works include the following categories:

(1) literary works;

(2) musical works, including any accompanying words;

(3) dramatic works, including any accompanying music;

(4) pantomimes and choreographic works;

(5) pictorial, graphic, and sculptural works;

(6) motion pictures and other audiovisual works;

(7) sound recordings; and

(8) architectural works.

These categories should be viewed quite broadly: for example, computer programs and most "compilations" are registrable as "literary works"; maps and architectural plans are registrable as "pictorial, graphic, and sculptural works."

## What Is Not Protected by Copyright

Several categories of material are generally not eligible for statutory copyright protection. These include among others:

• Works that have *not* been fixed in a tangible form of expression. For example: choreographic works that have not been notated or recorded, or improvisational speeches or performances that have not been written or recorded.

• Titles, names, short phrases, and slogans; familiar symbols or designs; mere variations of typographic ornamentation, lettering, or coloring; mere listings of ingredients or contents.

• Ideas, procedures, methods, systems, processes, concepts, principles, discoveries, or devices, as distinguished from a description, explanation, or illustration.

• Works consisting *entirely* of information that is common property and containing no original authorship. For example: standard calendars, height and weight charts, tape measures and rulers, and lists or tables taken from public documents or other common sources.

## Notice of Copyright

For works first published on and after March 1, 1989, use of the copyright notice is optional, though highly recommended. Before March 1, 1989, the use of the notice was mandatory on all published works, and any work first published before that date *must* bear a notice or risk loss of copyright protection.

Use of the notice is recommended because it informs the public that the work is protected by copyright, identifies the copyright owner, and shows the year of first publication. Furthermore, in the event that a work is infringed, if the work carries a proper notice, the court will not allow a defendant to claim "innocent infringement"—that is, that he or she did not realize that the work is protected. (A successful innocent infringement claim may result in a reduction in damages that the copyright owner would otherwise receive.)

The use of the copyright notice is the responsibility of the copyright owner and does not require advance permission from, or registration with, the Copyright Office.

For visually perceptible copies, the form of the notice consists of the following: © (the letter C in a circle), the word "Copyright," or "Copr.," and the year of first publication, and the name of the owner of copyright in the work. Example: © 1993 Judy Smith. The notice must be affixed in such manner and location as to give reasonable notice of the claim of copyright.

The notice of copyright prescribed for all published phonorecords of sound recordings consists of the symbol ℗ (the letter P in a circle), the year of first publication of the sound recording, and the name of the owner of copyright in the sound recording. Example ℗ 1993 XYZ Records, Inc. The notice on phonorecords may appear on the surface of the phonorecord or on the phonorecord label or container, provided the manner of placement and location give reasonable notice of the claim.

## How Long Copyright Protection Endures

### Works Originally Copyrighted on or After January 1, 1978

A work that is created (fixed in tangible form for the first time) on or after January 1, 1978, is automatically protected from the moment of its creation, and is ordinarily given a term enduring for the author's life, plus an additional 50 years after the author's death. In the case of "a joint work prepared by two or more authors who did not work for hire," the term lasts for 50 years after the last surviving author's death. For works made for hire, and for anonymous and pseudonymous works (unless the author's identity is revealed in Copyright Office records), the duration of copyright will be 75 years from publication or 100 years from creation, whichever is shorter.

Works that were created but not published or registered for copyright before January 1, 1978, have been automatically brought under the statute and are now given Federal copyright protection. The duration of copyright in these works will generally be computed in the same way as for works created on or after January 1, 1978: the life-plus-50 or 75/100-year terms will apply to them as well. The law provides that in no case will the term of copyright for works in this category expire before December 31, 2002, and for works published on or before December 31, 2002, the term of copyright will not expire before December 31, 2027.

### Works Copyrighted Before January 1, 1978

Under the law in effect before 1978, copyright was secured either on the date a work was published or on the date of registration if the work was registered in unpublished form. In either case, the copyright endured for a first term of 28 years from the date it was secured. During the last (28th) year of the first term, the copyright was eligible for renewal. The current copyright law has extended the renewal term from 28 to 47 years for copyrights that were subsisting on January 1, 1978, making these works eligible for a total term of protection of 75 years. On June 26, 1992, President Bush signed Public Law 102-307, which amends the Copyright Law to extend automatically the term of copyrights secured between January 1, 1964, and December 31, 1977, to a further term of 47 years and increases the filing fee from $12.00 to $20.00. This fee increase applies to all renewal applications filed on or after June 29, 1992.

P.L. 102-307 makes renewal registration optional. There is no need to make the renewal filing in order to extend the original 28-year copyright term to the full 75 years.

## International Copyright Protection

There is no such thing as an "international copyright" that will automatically protect an author's writings throughout the entire world. Protection against unauthorized use in a particular country depends, basically, on the national laws of that country. However, most countries do offer protection to foreign works under certain conditions, and these conditions have been greatly simplified by international copyright treaties and conventions. The U.S. belongs to both global, multilateral copyright treaties—the Universal Copyright Convention (UCC) and the Berne Convention for the Protection of Literary and Artistic Works.

A U.S. author may obtain copyright protection in all countries that are members of the Berne Union and the Universal Copyright Convention. A work first published in the U.S. or another Berne Union country (or first published in a non-Berne Union country, followed by publication within 30 days in a Berne Union country) is eligible for protection in all Berne member countries. There are no special requirements. In UCC member countries, where no formalities are required, the works of U.S. authors are also automatically protected. Member countries whose laws impose formalities protect U.S. works if all published copies bear a Convention notice, which consists of the symbol ©, together with the name of the copyright owner and the year of publication. Example: © JOHN DOE 1993.

For a list of countries that maintain copyright relations with the U.S., write or call the Copyright Office and ask for Circular 38a.

## Copyright Registration

Copyright registration is a legal formality intended to make a public record of the basic facts of a particular copyright. Except in specific situations, registration is not a condition for protection, but the copyright law provides several inducements or advantages to encourage copyright owners to register. Among these advantages are the following:

• Registration establishes a public record of the copyright claim;

• Before an infringement suit may be filed in court, registration is necessary for works of U.S. origin and for foreign works not originating in a Berne Union country. (For more information on when a work is of U.S. origin, request Circular 93 from the Copyright Office);

• If made before or within 5 years of publication, registration will establish prima facie evidence in court of the validity of the copyright and of the facts stated in the certificate; and

• If registration is made within 3 months after publication of the work or prior to an infringement of the work, statutory damages and attorney's fees will be available to the copyright owner in court actions. Otherwise, only an award of actual damages and profits is available to the copyright owner.

Copyright registration allows the owner of the copyright to record the registration with the U.S. Customs Service for protection against the importation of infringing copies. For additional information, request Publication No. 563 from:

Commissioner of Customs
ATTN: IPR Branch,
Room 2104
U.S. Customs Service
1301 Constitution Avenue, N.W.
Washington, D.C. 20229

Registration may be made at any time within the life of the copyright. When a work has been registered in unpublished form, it is not necessary to make another registration when the work becomes published (although the copyright owner may register the published edition, if desired).

The process of registration is quite simple. An appropriate form is requested from the Copyright Office and completed. It is returned to the Copyright Office along with a $20 nonrefundable filing fee and the appropriate deposit(s) of the work for which registration is sought. In a common example—a published book—the deposit is two copies of the best edition of the book. A certificate of registration is sent once the paperwork is completed, a process that usually takes 12

to 16 weeks due to the large volume of registrations the Office must handle.

Although a copyright registration is not required, the Copyright Act establishes a mandatory deposit requirement for works published in the U.S. In general, the owner of copyright, or the owner of the exclusive right of publication in the work, has a legal obligation to deposit in the Copyright Office, within three months of publication in the U.S., two copies (or, in the case of sound recordings, two phonorecords) for the use of the Library of Congress. Failure to make the deposit can result in fines and other penalties, but does not affect copyright protection. Certain categories of works are *exempt entirely* from the mandatory deposit requirements, and the obligation is reduced for certain other categories.

Information on registration and application forms may be obtained free of charge by writing the Copyright Office, Information Section, LM-401, Library of Congress, Washington, DC 20559. Registration application forms and circulars may be ordered on a 24-hour basis by calling (202) 707-9100. Request Circular 1 for additional general information on copyright, including a list of which application forms to use when registering specific types of works.

## Birthstones

Source: Jewelry Industry Council

| Month | Ancient | Modern |
|---|---|---|
| January | Garnet | Garnet |
| February | Amethyst | Amethyst |
| March | Jasper | Bloodstone or Aquamarine |
| April | Sapphire | Diamond |
| May | Agate | Emerald |
| June | Emerald | Pearl, Moonstone, or Alexandrite |

| Month | Ancient | Modern |
|---|---|---|
| July | Onyx | Ruby |
| August | Carnelian | Sardonyx or Peridot |
| September | Chrysolite | Sapphire |
| October | Aquamarine | Opal or Tourmaline |
| November | Topaz | Topaz |
| December | Ruby | Turquoise or Zircon |

## Mortgage Payment Tables

Source: *The Mortgage Money Guide.* Federal Trade Commission

### 8% Annual Percentage Rate
Monthly Payments (Principal and Interest)

| Amount Financed | 10 Years | 15 Years | 20 Years | 25 Years | 30 Years |
|---|---|---|---|---|---|
| $ 25,000 | 303.32 | 238.91 | 209.11 | 192.95 | 183.44 |
| 35,000 | 424.65 | 334.48 | 292.75 | 270.14 | 256.82 |
| 45,000 | 545.97 | 430.04 | 376.40 | 347.32 | 330.19 |
| 50,000 | 606.64 | 477.83 | 418.22 | 385.91 | 366.88 |
| 60,000 | 727.97 | 573.39 | 501.86 | 463.09 | 440.26 |
| 70,000 | 849.29 | 668.96 | 585.51 | 540.27 | 513.64 |
| 80,000 | 970.62 | 764.52 | 669.15 | 617.45 | 587.01 |
| 90,000 | 1091.95 | 860.09 | 752.80 | 694.63 | 660.39 |
| 100,000 | 1213.28 | 955.65 | 836.44 | 771.82 | 733.76 |
| 120,000 | 1455.94 | 1146.78 | 1003.72 | 926.18 | 880.52 |
| 140,000 | 1698.58 | 1337.92 | 1171.02 | 1080.54 | 1027.28 |
| 160,000 | 1941.24 | 1529.04 | 1338.30 | 1234.90 | 1174.02 |
| 180,000 | 2183.90 | 1720.18 | 1505.60 | 1389.26 | 1320.78 |
| 200,000 | 2426.56 | 1911.30 | 1672.88 | 1543.64 | 1467.52 |

### 12% Annual Percentage Rate
Monthly Payments (Principal and Interest)

| Amount Financed | 10 Years | 15 Years | 20 Years | 25 Years | 30 Years |
|---|---|---|---|---|---|
| $ 25,000 | 358.68 | 300.05 | 275.28 | 263.31 | 257.16 |
| 35,000 | 502.15 | 420.06 | 385.39 | 368.63 | 360.02 |
| 45,000 | 645.62 | 540.08 | 495.49 | 473.96 | 462.88 |
| 50,000 | 717.36 | 600.09 | 550.55 | 526.62 | 514.31 |
| 60,000 | 860.83 | 720.11 | 660.66 | 631.93 | 617.17 |
| 70,000 | 1004.30 | 840.12 | 770.77 | 737.26 | 720.03 |
| 80,000 | 1147.77 | 960.14 | 880.87 | 842.58 | 822.90 |
| 90,000 | 1291.24 | 1080.15 | 990.98 | 947.90 | 925.75 |
| 100,000 | 1434.71 | 1200.17 | 1101.09 | 1053.23 | 1028.62 |
| 120,000 | 1721.66 | 1440.22 | 1321.32 | 1263.86 | 1234.34 |
| 140,000 | 2008.60 | 1680.24 | 1541.54 | 1474.52 | 1440.06 |
| 160,000 | 2295.54 | 1920.28 | 1761.74 | 1685.16 | 1645.80 |
| 180,000 | 2582.48 | 2160.30 | 1981.96 | 1895.80 | 1851.50 |
| 200,000 | 2869.42 | 2400.34 | 2202.18 | 2106.46 | 2057.24 |

### 10% Annual Percentage Rate
Monthly Payments (Principal and Interest)

| Amount Financed | 10 Years | 15 Years | 20 Years | 25 Years | 30 Years |
|---|---|---|---|---|---|
| $ 25,000 | 330.38 | 268.65 | 241.26 | 227.18 | 219.39 |
| 35,000 | 462.53 | 376.11 | 337.76 | 318.05 | 307.15 |
| 45,000 | 594.68 | 483.57 | 434.26 | 408.92 | 394.91 |
| 50,000 | 660.75 | 537.30 | 482.51 | 454.35 | 438.79 |
| 60,000 | 792.90 | 644.76 | 579.01 | 545.22 | 526.54 |
| 70,000 | 925.06 | 752.22 | 675.52 | 636.09 | 614.30 |
| 80,000 | 1057.20 | 859.68 | 772.02 | 726.96 | 702.06 |
| 90,000 | 1189.36 | 967.14 | 868.52 | 817.83 | 789.81 |
| 100,000 | 1321.51 | 1074.61 | 965.02 | 908.70 | 877.57 |
| 120,000 | 1585.80 | 1289.52 | 1158.02 | 1090.44 | 1053.08 |
| 140,000 | 1850.12 | 1504.44 | 1351.04 | 1272.18 | 1228.60 |
| 160,000 | 2114.40 | 1719.36 | 1544.04 | 1453.92 | 1404.12 |
| 180,000 | 2378.72 | 1934.28 | 1737.04 | 1635.66 | 1579.62 |
| 200,000 | 2643.02 | 2149.22 | 1930.04 | 1817.40 | 1755.14 |

### 14% Annual Percentage Rate
Monthly Payments (Principal and Interest)

| Amount Financed | 10 Years | 15 Years | 20 Years | 25 Years | 30 Years |
|---|---|---|---|---|---|
| $ 25,000 | 388.17 | 332.94 | 310.89 | 300.95 | 296.22 |
| 35,000 | 543.44 | 466.11 | 435.24 | 421.32 | 414.71 |
| 45,000 | 698.70 | 599.29 | 559.59 | 541.70 | 533.20 |
| 50,000 | 776.34 | 665.88 | 621.77 | 601.89 | 592.44 |
| 60,000 | 931.60 | 799.05 | 746.12 | 722.26 | 710.93 |
| 70,000 | 1086.87 | 932.22 | 870.47 | 842.64 | 829.42 |
| 80,000 | 1242.14 | 1065.40 | 994.82 | 963.01 | 947.90 |
| 90,000 | 1397.40 | 1198.57 | 1119.17 | 1083.38 | 1066.38 |
| 100,000 | 1552.67 | 1331.75 | 1243.53 | 1203.77 | 1184.88 |
| 120,000 | 1863.20 | 1598.10 | 1492.24 | 1444.52 | 1421.86 |
| 140,000 | 2173.74 | 1864.44 | 1740.94 | 1685.28 | 1658.84 |
| 160,000 | 2484.28 | 2130.80 | 1989.64 | 1926.02 | 1895.80 |
| 180,000 | 2794.80 | 2397.14 | 2238.34 | 2166.76 | 2132.76 |
| 200,000 | 3105.34 | 2663.50 | 2487.06 | 2407.54 | 2369.76 |

# Median Price of Existing Single-Family Homes

Source: National Association of Realtors

| City[1] | Apr. 1990 | Apr. 1992 | Apr. 1993 | City[1] | Apr. 1990 | Apr. 1992 | Apr. 1993 |
|---|---|---|---|---|---|---|---|
| Akron, Oh. | $67,700 | $75,500 | $77,400 | Louisville, Ky. | $60,800 | $69,700 | $69,900 |
| Albuquerque, N.M. | 84,500 | 86,700 | 94,400 | Madison, Wis. | 82,300 | 89,400 | 97,700 |
| Anaheim/Santa Ana, Cal. | 242,400 | 235,100 | 222,200 | Memphis, Tenn. | 78,100 | 83,600 | 84,200 |
| Atlanta, Ga. | 86,400 | 85,800 | NA | Miami, Fla. | 89,300 | 97,300 | 98,000 |
| Baltimore, Md. | 105,900 | 111,500 | 113,200 | Milwaukee, Wis. | 84,400 | 96,100 | 98,400 |
| Baton Rouge, La. | 64,900 | 71,800 | 72,800 | Minneapolis, Minn. | 88,700 | 94,800 | 96,400 |
| Birmingham, Ala. | 80,800 | 89,500 | 89,000 | Mobile, Ala. | 59,100 | 63,300 | 66,200 |
| Boston, Mass. | 174,200 | 168,200 | 165,200 | Nashville, Tenn. | 81,800 | 89,000 | 87,000 |
| Bradenton, Fla. | 69,600 | 80,400 | 84,300 | New Haven, Conn. | 153,300 | 142,400 | 142,600 |
| Buffalo, N.Y. | 77,200 | 79,700 | 84,200 | New Orleans, La. | 67,800 | 68,400 | 73,000 |
| Charleston, S.C. | 76,200 | 82,000 | 86,200 | New York, N.Y. | 174,900 | 169,300 | 168,000 |
| Chicago, Ill. | 116,800 | 131,100 | 131,200 | Oklahoma City, Okla. | 53,200 | 59,800 | 61,100 |
| Cincinnati, Oh. | 79,800 | 87,500 | 85,600 | Omaha, Neb. | 63,000 | 67,400 | 64,300 |
| Cleveland, Oh. | 80,600 | 88,100 | 89,200 | Orlando, Fla. | 62,800 | 86,200 | 86,900 |
| Columbia, S.C. | 77,100 | 85,100 | 82,300 | Philadelphia, Pa. | 108,700 | 119,800 | 108,900 |
| Columbus, Oh. | 81,600 | 90,300 | 89,300 | Phoenix, Ariz. | 84,000 | 84,700 | 86,300 |
| Corpus Christi, Tex. | 63,200 | 62,500 | 66,600 | Pittsburgh, Pa. | 70,100 | 74,800 | 75,900 |
| Dallas, Tex. | 89,500 | 90,500 | 89,600 | Portland, Ore. | 79,500 | 92,300 | 99,600 |
| Daytona Beach, Fla. | 64,100 | 63,600 | 67,600 | Providence, R.I. | 127,900 | 120,300 | 112,500 |
| Denver, Col. | 86,400 | 91,300 | 96,300 | Sacramento, Cal. | 137,100 | 135,600 | 130,400 |
| Des Moines, Ia. | 60,500 | 71,200 | 71,600 | St. Louis, Mo. | 75,700 | 81,600 | 80,900 |
| Detroit, Mich. | 76,700 | 77,500 | 92,200 | Salt Lake City, Ut. | 69,400 | 73,000 | 79,000 |
| El Paso, Tex. | 63,600 | 65,900 | 67,900 | San Antonio, Tex. | 63,600 | 68,000 | 72,600 |
| Grand Rapids, Mich. | 68,300 | 73,000 | 73,900 | San Diego, Cal. | 183,600 | 182,700 | 175,500 |
| Hartford, Conn. | 157,300 | 141,500 | 135,500 | San Francisco, Cal. | 259,300 | 243,900 | 249,300 |
| Honolulu, Hi. | 352,000 | 342,000 | 347,000 | Seattle, Wash. | 142,000 | 141,300 | 145,000 |
| Houston, Tex. | 70,700 | 78,200 | 78,000 | Spokane, Wash. | 55,500 | 71,300 | 79,100 |
| Indianapolis, Ind. | 74,800 | 80,100 | 83,800 | Syracuse, N.Y. | 80,700 | 77,400 | 86,100 |
| Jacksonville, Fla. | 72,400 | 75,100 | 74,100 | Tampa, Fla. | 71,400 | 70,100 | 69,900 |
| Kansas City, Mo. | 74,100 | 76,100 | 79,100 | Toledo, Oh. | 62,800 | 74,000 | 65,700 |
| Knoxville, Tenn. | 75,400 | 78,300 | 82,400 | Tulsa, Okla. | 63,900 | 68,500 | 68,200 |
| Las Vegas, Nev. | 93,000 | 101,400 | 105,200 | Washington, D.C. | 150,200 | 152,500 | 153,500 |
| Los Angeles, Cal. | 212,800 | 218,000 | 199,700 | | | | |

(1) All areas are metropolitan statistical areas as defined by the U.S. Office of Management and Budget. They include the named central city and surrounding suburban areas. NA=not available.

# Housing Affordability

Source: National Association of Realtors; data as of midyear

| | Median-priced existing home | Average mortgage rate | Monthly principal and interest payment | Payment as percentage of median income | | Median-priced existing home | Average mortgage rate | Monthly principal and interest payment | Payment as percentage of median income |
|---|---|---|---|---|---|---|---|---|---|
| 1982 | $67,800 | 15.38% | $702 | 35.9% | 1988 | $90,600 | 9.31% | $591 | 22.0% |
| 1983 | 70,300 | 12.85 | 616 | 30.1 | 1989 | 93,100 | 10.11 | 660 | 23.1 |
| 1984 | 72,400 | 12.49 | 618 | 28.2 | 1990 | 97,500 | 10.04 | 673 | 22.7 |
| 1985 | 75,500 | 11.74 | 609 | 26.2 | 1991 | 99,700 | 9.51 | 671 | 22.3 |
| 1986 | 80,300 | 10.25 | 563 | 23.0 | 1992 | 100,900 | 8.48 | 620 | 20.0 |
| 1987 | 85,600 | 9.28 | 565 | 21.9 | 1993 | 106,100 | 7.30 | 582 | 18.8 |

Note: The average mortgage rate is based on the effective rate of loans closed on existing homes monitored by the Federal Home Loan Bank Board.

# Income Needed to Get a Mortgage

Source: National Association of Realtors

The following shows the minimum annual gross income needed for various size home loans at different rates. The figures are based on a 30-year loan and assume that the borrower's monthly payments can't exceed 28% of gross income, the ceiling most lenders use. The figures do not include property taxes and insurance as part of the monthly payment.

| Interest rate (Percent) | $50,000 | $75,000 | Loan amount $100,000 income needed | $150,000 | $200,000 |
|---|---|---|---|---|---|
| 8 | $15,724 | $23,586 | $31,447 | $47,171 | $62,895 |
| 8½ | 16,477 | 24,715 | 32,954 | 49,430 | 65,907 |
| 9 | 17,242 | 25,863 | 34,484 | 51,726 | 68,968 |
| 9½ | 18,018 | 27,028 | 36,037 | 54,055 | 72,074 |
| 10 | 18,085 | 28,208 | 37,611 | 56,415 | 75,221 |
| 10½ | 19,602 | 29,403 | 39,203 | 58,805 | 78,406 |
| 11 | 20,407 | 30,611 | 40,814 | 61,221 | 81,628 |
| 11½ | 21,221 | 31,531 | 42,441 | 63,662 | 84,883 |
| 12 | 22,042 | 33,063 | 44,084 | 66,125 | 88,167 |
| 12½ | 22,870 | 34,305 | 45,740 | 68,610 | 91,479 |
| 13 | 23,704 | 35,556 | 47,409 | 71,113 | 94,817 |

# Marriage Laws

Source: Gary N. Skoloff, Skoloff & Wolfe, Livingston, N.J.; as of May 1, 1993.

| State | Age with parental consent Male | Female | Age without consent Male | Female | Physical exam & blood test for male and female Maximum period between exam and license | Scope of medical exam | Waiting period Before license | After license |
|---|---|---|---|---|---|---|---|---|
| Alabama* | 14a | 14a | 18 | 18 | — | b | — | s |
| Alaska | 16z | 16z | 18 | 18 | — | b | 3 da., w | — |
| Arizona | 16z | 16z | 18 | 18 | — | — | — | — |
| Arkansas | 17c | 16c | 18 | 18 | — | — | v | — |
| California | aa | aa | 18 | 18 | 30 da., w | zz | — | h |
| Colorado* | 16z | 16z | 18 | 18 | — | bb | — | s |
| Connecticut | 16z | 16z | 18 | 18 | — | bb | 4 da., w | ttt |
| Delaware | 18c | 16c | 18 | 18 | — | — | — | e, s |
| Florida | 16a, c | 16a, c | 18 | 18 | — | b | 3 da. | s |
| Georgia* | aa | aa | 18 | 18 | — | b | 3 da., g | s* |
| Hawaii | 16d | 16d | 18 | 18 | — | b | — | — |
| Idaho* | 16z | 16z | 18 | 18 | — | bb | — | — |
| Illinois | 16 | 16 | 18 | 18 | 30 da. | b, n | — | ee |
| Indiana | 17c | 17c | 18 | 18 | — | bb | 72 hrs. | t |
| Iowa* | 18z | 18z | 18 | 18 | — | — | 3 da., v | tt |
| Kansas*y | 18z | 18z | 18 | 18 | — | — | 3 da., w | — |
| Kentucky | 18c, z | 18c, z | 18 | 18 | — | — | — | — |
| Louisiana | 18z | 18z | 18 | 18 | 10 da. | b | 72 hrs., w | — |
| Maine | 16z | 16z | 18 | 18 | — | b | 3 da., v, w | h |
| Maryland | 16c, f | 16c, f | 18 | 18 | — | — | 48 hrs., w | ff |
| Massachusetts | 14j | 12j | 18 | 18 | 60 da. | bb | 3 da., v | — |
| Michigan | 16c, d | 16c | 18 | 18 | 30 da. | b | 3 da., w | — |
| Minnesota | 16z | 16z | 18 | 18 | — | — | 5 da., w | — |
| Mississippi | 17 | 15 | 21 | 21 | 30 da. | b | 3 da., w | — |
| Missouri | 15d, 18z | 15d, 18z | 18 | 18 | — | — | — | — |
| Montana*yy | 16 | 16 | 18 | 18 | — | b | — | ff |
| Nebraskayy | 17 | 17 | 19 | 19 | — | bb | — | — |
| Nevada | 16z | 16z | 18 | 18 | — | — | — | — |
| New Hampshire | 14j | 13j | 18 | 18 | — | l,zz | 3 da., v | h |
| New Jersey | 16z, c | 16z, c | 18 | 18 | 30 da. | b | 72 hrs., w | s |
| New Mexicoy | 16d | 16d | 18 | 18 | 30 da. | b | — | — |
| New York | 14j | 14j | 18 | 18 | — | nn | — | 24 hrs., w, t |
| North Carolina | 16c, g | 16c, g | 18 | 18 | — | m | — | t |
| North Dakota | 16 | 16 | 18 | 18 | — | — | — | t |
| Ohio* | 18c, z | 16c, z | 18 | 18 | 30 da. | b | 5 da.,w | t |
| Oklahoma* | 16c | 16c | 18 | 18 | 30 da., w | b | — | s |
| Oregon | 17 | 17 | 18 | 18 | — | — | 3 da., w | — |
| Pennsylvania* | 16d | 16d | 18 | 18 | 30 da. | b | 3 da., w | t |
| Puerto Ricoy | 18c, d, z | 16c, d, z | 21 | 21 | — | b | — | — |
| Rhode Island* | 18d | 16d | 18 | 18 | — | bb | — | — |
| South Carolina* | 16c | 14c | 18 | 18 | — | — | 1 da. | — |
| South Dakota | 16c | 16c | 18 | 18 | — | — | — | tt |
| Tennessee | 16d | 16d | 18 | 18 | — | — | 3 da., cc | s |
| Texas*y | 14j, k | 14j, k | 18 | 18 | — | — | — | s |
| Utah* | 14 | 14 | 18x | 18x | 30 da. | b | — | s |
| Vermont | 16z | 16z | 18 | 18 | 30 da. | b | 1 da., w | — |
| Virginia | 16a, c | 16a, c | 18 | 18 | — | b | — | t |
| Washington | 17d | 17d | 18 | 18 | — | bbb | 3 da. | t |
| West Virginia | 18c | 18c | 18 | 18 | — | b | 3 da., w | — |
| Wisconsin | 16d | 16d | 18 | 18 | — | b | 5 da., w | s |
| Wyoming | 16d | 16d | 18 | 18 | — | bb | — | — |
| Dist. of Columbia* | 16a | 16a | 18 | 18 | 30 da. | b | 3 da. w | |

* Indicates 1987 common-law marriage recognized; in many states, such marriages are only recognized if entered into many years before. (a) Parental consent not required if minor was previously married. (aa) No age limits. (b) Venereal diseases. (bb) Venereal diseases and Rubella (for female). In Colorado and Wyoming, Rubella for female under 45 and Rh type. (bbb) No medical exam required; however, applicants must file affidavit showing non-affliction of contagious venereal disease. (c) Younger parties may obtain license in case of pregnancy or birth of child. (cc) Unless parties are over 18 years of age. (d) Younger parties may obtain license in special circumstances. (e) Residents before expiration of 24-hour waiting period; non-residents formerly residents, before expiration of 96-hour waiting period; others 96 hours. (ee) License effective 1 day after issuance, unless court orders otherwise, valid for 60 days only. (f) If parties are at least 16 years of age, proof of age and the consent of parents in person is required. If a parent is ill, an affidavit by the incapacitated parent and a physician's affidavit to that effect required. (ff) License valid for 180 days only. (g) Unless parties are 18 years of age or more, or female is pregnant, or applicants are the parents of a living child born out of wedlock. (h) License valid for 90 days only. (j) Parental consent and/or permission of judge required. (k) Below age of consent parties need parental consent and permission of judge. (l) With each certificate issued to couples, a list of family planning agencies and services available to them is provided. (m) Mental incompetence, infectious tuberculosis, venereal diseases and Rubella (certain counties only). (n) Venereal diseases; test for sickle cell anemia given at request of examining physician. (nn) Tests for sickle cell anemia may be required for certain applicants. Marriage prohibited unless it is established that procreation is not possible. (s) License valid for 30 days only. (t) License valid for 60 days only. (tt) License valid for 20 days only. (ttt) License valid for 65 days. (v) Parties must file notice of intention to marry with local clerk. (w) Waiting period may be avoided. (x) Authorizes counties to provide for premarital counseling as a requisite to issuance of license to persons under 19 and persons previously divorced. (y) Marriages by proxy are valid. (yy) Proxy marriages are valid under certain conditions. (z) Younger parties may marry with parental consent and/or permission of judge. In Connecticut, judicial approval. (zz) Required offer of HIV test, and/or must be provided with information on AIDS.

# Divorce Laws

**Source:** Gary N. Skoloff, Skoloff & Wolfe, Livingston, N.J.; as of May 1, 1993. Important: almost all states also have other laws, as well as qualifications of the laws shown below and proposed divorce-reform laws pending. It would be wise to consult a lawyer in conjunction with the use of this chart.

### Some grounds for absolute divorce

| | Residence | Adultery | Cruelty | Desertion | Alcoholism | Impotency | Non-support | Insanity | Pregnancy at marriage | Bigamy | Separation | Felony conviction or imprisonment | Drug addiction | Fraud, force, duress |
|---|---|---|---|---|---|---|---|---|---|---|---|---|---|---|
| PR | 1 yr. | Yes | Yes | 1 yr. | Yes | Yes | No | Yes | No | A | 2 yrs. | Yes* | Yes | No |
| AL | 6 mos.* | Yes | Phys. only | 1 yr. | Yes | Yes* | 2 yrs. | 5 yrs. | Yes | A | 2 yrs.* | 2 yrs* | Yes | A |
| AK | * | Yes | Yes | 1 yr. | 1 yr. | Yes | No | 18 mos. | No | A | No | Yes | Yes | A |
| AZ | 90 da. | No | No | No | No | No | No | No | No | No | No | No | No | No |
| AR | 60 da. | Yes | Yes | No | 1 yr. | Yes | Yes | 3 yrs. | No | No | 18 mos. | Yes | No | A |
| CA | 6 mos. | No | No | No | No | A | No | Yes, A | No | A | No | No | No | A |
| CO | 90 da. | No | No | No | No | No | No | No | No | A | No | No | No | A |
| CT | 1 yr.* | Yes | Yes | 1 yr. | Yes | No | No | 5 yrs. | No | A | 18 mos.* | life* | No | Yes |
| DE | 6 mos. | Yes | Yes | Yes | Yes | A | No | A | No | Yes | 6 mos. | Yes | Yes | A |
| FL | 6 mos. | No | No | No | No | No | No | 3 yrs. | No | No | No | No | No | No |
| GA | 6 mos. | Yes | Yes | 1 yr. | Yes | Yes | No | 2 yrs. | Yes | A | No | Yes* | Yes | Yes |
| HI | 6 mos.* | No | No | No | No | No | No | A | No | A | 2 yrs.* | No | No | A |
| ID | 6 wks. | Yes | Yes | Yes | Yes | A | No | 3 yrs. | Yes | A | 5 yrs. | Yes | No | A |
| IL | 90 da. | Yes | Yes | 1 yr. | 2 yrs. | Yes | No | No | No | Yes | 2 yrs.* | Yes | 2 yrs. | No |
| IN | 6 mos.* | No | No | No | No | Yes | No | 2 yrs. | No | A | No | Yes | No | A |
| IA | 1 yr.* | No | No | No | No | A | No | A | No | A | No | No | No | No |
| KS | 60 da. | No | No | No | No | No | Yes | 2 yrs. | A | A | No | No | No | A |
| KY | 180 da. | No | No | No | No | A | No | No | No | A | No | No | No | A |
| LA | 1 yr.* | Yes | No | No | No | No | No | No | No | A | 6 mos. | Yes* | No | A |
| ME | 6 mos.* | Yes | Yes | 3 yrs. | Yes | Yes | Yes | A | No | A | No | No | Yes | No |
| MD | 1 yr.* | Yes | Yes | 1 yr.* | No | No | No | 3 yrs. | No | A | 1 yr.* | 1 yr.* | Yes | No |
| MA | 1 yr.* | Yes | Yes | 1 yr. | Yes | Yes | Yes | No | No | A | No | 5 yrs. | Yes | No |
| MI | 180 da. | No | No | No | No | No | No | No | No | No | No | No | No | A |
| MN | 180 da. | No | No | No | No | No | No | No | No | No | No | No | No | A |
| MS | 6 mos. | Yes | Yes | 1 yr. | Yes | Yes | No | 3 yrs. | Yes | Yes | No | Yes* | Yes | A |
| MO | 90 da. | No | No | No | No | A | No | No | No | A | No | No | No | A |
| MT | 90 da. | No | No | No | No | A | No | No | No | A | 180 da.* | No | No | A |
| NE | 1 yr.* | No | No | No | No | A | No | No | No | A | No | No | No | A |
| NV | 6 wks. | No | No | No | No | No | No | 2 yrs. | No | A | 1 yr. | No | No | A |
| NH | 1 yr.* | Yes | Yes | 2 yrs. | 2 yrs. | Yes | 2 yrs. | No | No | A | Yes | 1 yr.* | No | No |
| NJ | 1 yr.* | Yes | Yes | 1 yr. | 1 yr. | A | No | 2 yrs. | No | A | 18 mos. | 18 mos. | 1 yr. | A |
| NM | 6 mos. | Yes | Yes | Yes* | No | No | No | No | No | No | No | No | No | A |
| NY | 1 yr.* | Yes | Yes | 1 yr. | No | No | No | No | No | A | 1 yr. | 3 yrs. | No | A |
| NC | 6 mos. | No | No | No | No | No | No | 3 yrs. | No | A | 1 yr. | No | No | No |
| ND | 6 mos. | Yes | Yes | 1 yr. | 1 yr. | A | 1 yr. | 5 yrs.* | No | A | No | Yes | 1 yr. | A |
| OH | 6 mos. | Yes | Yes | 1 yr. | Yes | Yes | Yes | No | No | Yes, A | 1 yr. | Yes | No | Yes, A |
| OK | 6 mos. | Yes | Yes | 1 yr. | Yes | Yes | Yes | 5 yrs. | Yes | Yes | No | Yes | No | Yes |
| OR | 6 mos.* | No | No | No | No | No | No | No | No | No | No | No | No | A |
| PA | 6 mos. | Yes | Yes | 1 yr. | No | No | No | 18 mos.* | No | Yes | 2 yrs.* | Yes | No | No |
| RI | 1 yr. | Yes | Yes | 5 yrs.* | Yes | Yes | 1 yr. | No | No | Yes | 3 yrs. | Yes | Yes | No |
| SC | 1 yr.* | Yes | Phys. only | 1 yr. | Yes | No | No | No | No | No | 1 yr. | No | Yes | No |
| SD | none* | Yes | Yes | 1 yr. | 1 yr. | A | 1 yr. | 5 yrs. | No | A | No | Yes | No | A* |
| TN | 6 mos.* | Yes | Yes | 1 yr. | Yes | Yes | Yes | No | Yes | Yes | 2 yrs. | Yes | Yes | A |
| TX | 6 mos.* | Yes | Yes | 1 yr. | * | A | No | 3 yrs. | No | No | 3 yrs. | 1 yr. | No | No |
| UT | 3 mos.* | Yes | Yes | 1 yr. | Yes | Yes | Yes | Yes | No | A | 3 yrs.* | Yes | No | No |
| VT | 6 mos.* | Yes | Yes | 7 yrs.* | No | No | Yes | 5 yrs. | No | A | 6 mos. | 3 yrs. | No | A |
| VA | 6 mos.* | Yes | Yes* | 1 yr. | No | A | No | No | A | A | 1 yr.* | 1 yr.* | No | A |
| WA | bona fide res. | No | No | No | No | No | No | No | No | No | No | No | No | A |
| WV | 1 yr.* | Yes | Yes | 6 mos. | Yes | A | No | 3 yrs. | A | A | 1 yr. | Yes | Yes | No |
| WI | 6 mos. | No | No | No | No | A | No | No | No | A | 1 yr. | No | No | A |
| WY | 60 da.* | No | No | No | No | No | No | 2 yrs. | No | A | No | No | No | A |
| DC | 6 mos. | No | No | No | No | A | No | A* | No | A | 6 mos.-1 yr. | No | No | A |

(*) indicates qualification-check local statutes; (A) indicates grounds for annulment.

# Wedding Anniversaries

The traditional names for wedding anniversaries go back many years in social usage. As such names as wooden, crystal, silver, and golden were applied it was considered proper to present the married pair with gifts made of these products or of something related. The list of traditional gifts, with a few allowable revisions in parentheses, is presented below, followed by modern gifts in bold face.

1st-Paper, **clocks**
2d-Cotton, **china**
3d-Leather, **crystal & glass**
4th-Linen (silk), **electrical appliances**
5th-Wood, **silverware**
6th-Iron, **wood**
7th-Wool (copper), **desk sets**
8th-Bronze, **linens & lace**
9th-Pottery (china), **leather**

10th-Tin (aluminum), **diamond jewelry**
11th-Steel, **fashion jewelry, accessories**
12th-Silk, **pearls or colored gems**
13th-Lace, **textiles & furs**
14th-Ivory, **gold jewelry**
15th-Crystal, **watches**
20th-China, **platinum**

25th-Silver, **sterling silver jubliee**
30th-Pearl, **diamond**
35th-Coral (jade), **jade**
40th-Ruby, **ruby**
45th-Sapphire, **sapphire**
50th-Gold, **gold**
55th-Emerald, **emerald**
60th-Diamond, **diamond**

# RELIGIOUS INFORMATION

## Census of Religious Groups in the U.S.

Source: 1993 Yearbook of American and Canadian Churches

Comparisons of membership statistics from group to group are not necessarily meaningful. Membership definitions vary—e.g., Roman Catholics count members from infancy, but some Protestant groups count only "adult" members, usually 13 years or older; some groups compile data carefully, but others estimate; not all groups report annually.

The number of churches appears in parentheses. Asterisk (*) indicates church declines to publish membership figures; denominations that are not listed have not provided data for at least 10 years.

| Group | Members |
|---|---|
| **Adventist churches:** | |
| Advent Christian Ch. (335) | 28,000 |
| Church of God General Conf. (Oregon, IL) (89) | 5,526 |
| Primitive Advent Christian Ch. (10) | 343 |
| Seventh-day Adventists (4,229) | 733,026 |
| **American Rescue Workers (20)** | 2,700 |
| **Anglican Orthodox Church (40)** | 6,000 |
| **Apostolic Christian Ch. (Nazarene) (48)** | 2,799 |
| **Apostolic Christian Churches of America (80)** | 11,450 |
| **Baha'i Faith (1,700)** | 110,000 |
| **Baptist churches:** | |
| Amer. Baptist Assn. (1,705) | 250,000 |
| Amer. Baptist Chs. in U.S.A. (5,862) | 1,527,840 |
| Baptist Bible Fellowship Intl. (3,500) | * |
| Baptist General Conference (821) | 134,658 |
| Baptist Missionary Assn. of America (1,312) | 230,127 |
| Conservative Baptist Assn. of America (1,126) | 210,000 |
| Free Will Baptists, Natl. Assn. of (2,495) | 209,223 |
| Gen. Assn. of Regular Baptist Chs. (1,532) | 160,123 |
| Gen. Baptists, Gen. Assn. of (876) | 74,156 |
| Liberty Baptist Fellowship (100) | * |
| Natl. Baptist Convention of America (2,500) | 3,500,000 |
| Natl. Baptist Convention, U.S.A. (36,000) | 8,000,000 |
| Natl. Missionary Baptist Convention of America (*) | 2,500,000 |
| No. Amer. Baptist Conference (265) | 43,087 |
| Progressive National Baptist Convention (1,400) | 2,500,000 |
| Separate Baptists in Christ (101) | 10,000 |
| Seventh Day Baptist General Conference (90) | 5,250 |
| Southern Baptist Convention (36,168) | 15,232,347 |
| Sovereign Grace Baptists (300) | 3,000 |
| **Brethren (German Baptists):** | |
| Brethren Ch. (Ashland, Ohio) (124) | 13,322 |
| Fellowship of Grace Brethren (322) | 39,237 |
| Old German Baptist Brethren (55) | 5,475 |
| **Brethren, River:** | |
| Brethren in Christ Ch. (194) | 17,454 |
| United Zion Ch. (13) | 850 |
| **Buddhist Churches of America (67)** | 19,441 |
| **Christian Brethren (1,150)** | 98,000 |
| **Christian Catholic Church (6)** | 2,500 |
| **Christian Church (Disciples of Christ) (4,031)** | 1,022,926 |
| **Christian Churches and Churches of Christ (5,579)** | 1,070,616 |
| **Christian Congregation (1,447)** | 110,716 |
| **Christian Nation Church U.S.A. (5)** | 200 |
| **Christian Union (114)** | 6,000 |
| **Churches of Christ:** | |
| Church of the Living God (170) | 42,000 |
| Churches of Christ (13,200) | 1,690,000 |
| Churches of Christ in Christian Union (240) | 10,349 |
| **Churches of God:** | |
| Chs. of God, General Conference (354) | 33,584 |
| Ch. of God (Anderson, Ind.) (2,330) | 214,743 |
| Ch. of God (Seventh Day), Denver, Col. (153) | 5,749 |
| Church of God by Faith (145) | 8,235 |
| Church of God in Christ Which He Purchased With His Own Blood (7) | 800 |
| **Church of Christ, Scientist (3,000)** | * |
| **Church of the Nazarene (5,172)** | 573,834 |
| **Community Churches, Intl. Council of (398)** | * |
| **Congregational Christian Chs. (405)** | 90,000 |
| **Conservative Congregational Christian Conference (176)** | 28,035 |
| **Eastern Orthodox churches:** | |
| Albanian Orth. Diocese of America (2) | 1,873 |
| American Carpatho-Russian Orth. Greek Catholic Ch. (72) | 17,981 |
| Antiochian Orth. Christian Archdiocese of No. Amer. (170) | 350,000 |
| Apostolic Catholic Assyrian Ch. of the East, N.A. Diocese (22) | 120,000 |
| Armenian Apostolic Ch. of America (30) | 150,000 |
| Armenian Church of Amer., Diocese of the (72) | * |
| Bulgarian Eastern Orth. Ch. (9) | 10,000 |
| Coptic Orthodox Ch. (55) | 260,000 |
| Orthodox Ch. in America (1,000) | 1,030,000 |
| Patriarchal Parishes of the Russian Orth. Ch. in the U.S.A. (38) | 9,780 |
| Romanian Orth. Episcopate of America (37) | 65,000 |
| Serbian Orthodox Ch. of U.S.A. & Canada (68) | 67,000 |
| Syrian Orth. Ch. of Antioch (Archdiocese of the U.S.A. and Canada) (28) | 30,000 |
| True Orthodox Church of Greece (8) | 900 |
| Ukrainian Orth. Ch. in America (Ecumenical Patriarchate) (27) | 5,000 |
| **Episcopal Church (7,367)** | 2,471,880 |
| **American Ethical Union (Ethical Culture Movement) (21)** | 3,212 |
| **Evangelical Church (185)** | 16,398 |
| **Evangelical Congregational Church (155)** | 24,437 |
| **The Evangelical Covenant Church (590)** | 89,735 |
| **Evangelical Free Church of America (1,113)** | 187,775 |
| **Fellowship of Fundamental Bible Churches (26)** | 2,087 |
| **Fire Baptized Holiness Church (Wesleyan) (49)** | 695 |
| **Friends:** | |
| Evangelical Friends International, No. Amer. (246) | 26,322 |
| Friends General Conference (520) | 30,902 |
| Friends United Meeting (526) | 50,803 |
| Religious Society of Friends (Conservative) (28) | 1,744 |
| **Grace Gospel Fellowship (50)** | 4,500 |
| **Independent Fundamental Churches of America (700)** | 78,174 |
| **Jehovah's Witnesses (9,890)** | 914,079 |
| **Jewish organizations:** | |
| Union of Amer. Hebrew Congregations (Reform) (848) | 1,300,000 |
| Union of Orthodox Jewish Congregations of America (1,200) | 1,000,000 |
| United Synagogue of America (Conservative) (800) | 2,000,000 |
| **Latter-day Saints:** | |
| Ch. of Jesus Christ (Bickertonites) (63) | 2,707 |
| Ch. of Jesus Christ of Latter-day Saints (Mormon) (9,468) | 4,336,000 |
| Reorganized Ch. of Jesus Christ of Latter Day Saints (1,001) | 150,143 |
| **Liberal Catholic Ch.-Province of the U.S.A. (34)** | 2,800 |
| **Lutheran churches:** | |
| Apostolic Lutheran Ch. of America (53) | 7,583 |
| Ch. of the Lutheran Brethren of America (111) | 22,478 |
| Ch. of the Lutheran Confession (70) | 8,722 |
| Conservative Lutheran Assn. (12) | 1,530 |
| Estonian Evangelical Lutheran Ch. (24) | 7,298 |
| Evangelical Lutheran Ch. in America (11,074) | 5,245,177 |
| Evangelical Lutheran Synod (126) | 21,347 |
| Free Lutheran Congregations, Assn. of (210) | 27,650 |
| Latvian Evangelical Lutheran Church of America (56) | 12,553 |
| Lutheran Ch.-Missouri Synod (5,364) | 2,607,309 |
| Lutheran Chs., Amer. Assn. of (78) | 15,150 |
| Protestant Conference (Lutheran) (7) | 1,150 |
| Wisconsin Evangelical Lutheran Synod (1,211) | 420,039 |
| **Mennonite churches:** | |
| Beachy Amish Mennonite Chs. (99) | 6,872 |
| Church of God in Christ (Mennonite) (78) | 9,999 |
| Evangelical Mennonite Ch. (27) | 4,059 |
| Fellowship of Evangelical Bible Churches (14) | 1,925 |
| Hutterian Brethren (95) | 6,700 |
| Mennonite Brethren Chs., The Conf. of (144) | 16,843 |
| Mennonite Church (1,053) | 99,431 |
| Mennonite Ch., The General Conference (229) | 33,937 |
| Old Order Amish Ch. (876) | 78,840 |
| **Methodist churches:** | |
| African Methodist Episcopal Ch. (*) | 3,500,000 |
| African Methodist Episcopal Zion Ch. (3,000) | 1,200,000 |
| Allegheny Wesleyan Methodist Connection (117) | 2,130 |
| Christian Methodist Episcopal Church (2,340) | 718,922 |
| Evangelical Methodist Ch. (126) | 8,514 |

(continued)

| Group | Members | Group | Members |
|---|---|---|---|
| Free Methodist Ch. of North America (1,063)... | 73,572 | National Gay Pentecostal Alliance (2)....... | * |
| Fundamental Methodist Ch. (12)........... | 1,075 | Open Bible Standard Chs. (368)........... | 40,000 |
| Primitive Methodist Ch., U.S.A. (85)........ | 8,244 | Pentecostal Assemblies of the World (1,005)... | 500,000 |
| Reformed Methodist Union Episcopal Ch. (18).. | 3,800 | Pentecostal Church of God (1,160)......... | 92,060 |
| Southern Methodist Ch. (133)............ | 7,745 | Pentecostal Free-Will Baptist Ch. (148)...... | 11,757 |
| United Methodist Ch. (37,100)........... | 8,785,135 | United Pentecostal Ch. Intl. (3,500)........ | 550,000 |
| The Wesleyan Church (U.S.A.) (1,211)...... | 316,813 | **Presbyterian churches:** | |
| **Metropolitan Community Churches, Univ.** | | Associate Reformed Presbyterian Ch. (Gen. | |
| **Fellowship of (195).** | 25,076 | Synod) (189)................... | 38,552 |
| **Moravian churches:** | | Cumberland Presbyterian Ch. (784)........ | 92,433 |
| Moravian Ch. Northern Province (98)...... | 29,805 | Evangelical Presbyterian Ch. (180)........ | 56,000 |
| Moravian Ch. in America Southern Province (56) | 21,513 | Korean Presbyterian Church in America (203)... | 26,988 |
| Unity of the Brethren (26)............. | 3,615 | Orthodox Presbyterian Ch. (170).......... | 18,137 |
| **Moslems** .................... | **6,000,000** | Presbyterian Ch. in America (*)......... | 233,770 |
| **Natl. Organization of the New Apostolic Ch. of** | | Presbyterian Ch. (U.S.A.) (11,468)........ | 3,778,358 |
| **N.A. (523).** | **39,816** | Reformed Presbyterian Ch. of No. Amer. (68).. | 5,174 |
| **Natl. Spiritualist Assn. of Churches (137).....** | **3,883** | **Reformed churches:** | |
| **Old Catholic churches:** | | Christian Reformed Ch. in N. America (739)... | 224,921 |
| Christ Catholic Ch. (10)............. | 1,435 | Hungarian Reformed Ch. in America (27)..... | 9,780 |
| North American Old Roman Catholic Church-N.Y. | | Netherlands Reformed Congregations (15).... | 5,250 |
| Archdiocese (5)................ | 400 | Reformed Ch. in America (967)........... | 340,991 |
| **Pentecostal churches:** | | Reformed Ch. in the U.S. (34).......... | 3,778 |
| Apostolic Faith Mission (Portland, Ore.) (50)... | 4,100 | United Church of Christ (6,301).......... | 1,583,830 |
| Apostolic Faith Mission Ch. of God (18)...... | 6,200 | **Reformed Episcopal Church (83)..........** | **6,565** |
| Apostolic Overcoming Holy Church of God (12). | 479 | **The Roman Catholic Church (19,971).......** | **58,267,424** |
| Assemblies of God (11,536)........... | 2,234,708 | **The Salvation Army (1,151)............** | **446,403** |
| Bible Church of Christ (6)............ | 6,700 | **The Schwenkfelder Church (5)...........** | **2,489** |
| Christian Church of N.A., Gen. Council (104)... | 13,500 | **The Swedenborgian Church (50).........** | **2,423** |
| Church of God (Cleveland, Tenn.) (5,841).... | 620,393 | **Unitarian Universalist Assn. (1,020).......** | **141,315** |
| Church of God in Christ (15,300)........ | 5,499,875 | **United Brethren:** | |
| Church of God in Christ, Intl. (300)......... | 200,000 | United Brethren in Christ (260).......... | 25,775 |
| Church of God of Prophecy (2,072)........ | 72,465 | United Christian Ch. (12)............. | 420 |
| Congregational Holiness Ch. (176)......... | 7,116 | **Vedanta Societies (13)................** | **2,500** |
| Elim Fellowship (177)............... | 20,000 | | |
| Gen. Council, Christian Ch. of No. Amer. (104).. | 13,500 | | |
| Intl. Ch. of the Foursquare Gospel (1,516).... | 208,150 | | |

## Women and Blacks Enrolled in Seminaries, 1972-1992[1]

Source: *1993 Yearbook of American and Canadian Churches*

| | Women | | | Blacks | | |
|---|---|---|---|---|---|---|
| Year | Number of Students | Percentage Annual Change | Percentage of Total Enrollment | Number of Students | Percentage Annual Change | Percentage of Total Enrollment |
| 1972 | 3,358 | NA | 10.2 | 1,061 | + 16.9 | 3.2 |
| 1973 | 4,021 | + 19.7 | 11.8 | 1,210 | + 14.0 | 3.6 |
| 1974 | 5,255 | + 30.7 | 14.3 | 1,246 | + 3.0 | 3.4 |
| 1975 | 6,505 | + 23.8 | 15.9 | 1,365 | + 9.6 | 3.3 |
| 1976 | 7,349 | + 13.0 | 17.1 | 1,524 | + 11.6 | 3.5 |
| 1977 | 8,371 | + 13.9 | 18.5 | 1,759 | + 15.4 | 3.9 |
| 1978 | 8,972 | + 7.2 | 19.3 | 1,919 | + 9.1 | 4.1 |
| 1979 | 10,204 | + 13.7 | 21.1 | 2,043 | + 6.5 | 4.2 |
| 1980 | 10,830 | + 6.1 | 21.8 | 2,205 | + 7.9 | 4.4 |
| 1981 | 11,683 | + 7.9 | 23.1 | 2,371 | + 7.5 | 4.7 |
| 1982 | 12,473 | + 6.8 | 23.7 | 2,576 | + 8.6 | 4.9 |
| 1983 | 13,451 | + 7.8 | 24.4 | 2,881 | + 11.8 | 5.2 |
| 1984 | 14,142 | + 5.1 | 25.0 | 2,917 | + 1.2 | 5.2 |
| 1985 | 14,572 | + 3.0 | 25.8 | 3,046 | + 4.4 | 5.4 |
| 1986 | 14,864 | + 2.0 | 26.4 | 3,277 | + 7.6 | 5.8 |
| 1987 | 15,310 | + 3.0 | 27.0 | 3,379 | + 3.1 | 6.0 |
| 1988 | 16,344 | + 6.8 | 29.3 | 3,662 | + 8.4 | 6.6 |
| 1989 | 16,461 | + 0.7 | 29.3 | 3,961 | + 8.2 | 7.1 |
| 1990 | 17,571 | + 6.7 | 29.7 | 4,303 | + 8.6 | 7.3 |
| 1991 | 18,384 | + 4.6 | 30.6 | 4,671 | + 8.6 | 7.8 |
| 1992 | 19,653 | + 6.9 | 31.1 | 5,554 | + 18.9 | 8.8 |

(1) Data cover U.S. and Canadian seminaries that are members of the Assn. of Theological Schools. NA=not available.

## Adherents of All Religions by Continental Areas, Mid-1992

Source: *1993 Encyclopedia Britannica Book of the Year*

| | Africa | Asia | Europe | Latin America | Northern America | Oceania | Former U.S.S.R. | World |
|---|---|---|---|---|---|---|---|---|
| Christians | 327,204,000 | 285,365,000 | 413,756,000 | 435,811,000 | 239,004,000 | 22,628,000 | 109,254,000 | 1,833,022,000 |
| Roman Catholics | 122,907,000 | 123,597,000 | 262,638,000 | 405,623,000 | 97,022,000 | 8,208,000 | 5,590,000 | 1,025,585,000 |
| Protestants | 87,332,000 | 81,476,000 | 73,939,000 | 17,263,000 | 96,312,000 | 7,518,000 | 9,858,000 | 373,698,000 |
| Orthodox | 28,549,000 | 3,655,000 | 36,165,000 | 1,764,000 | 6,008,000 | 576,000 | 93,705,000 | 170,422,000 |
| Anglicans | 26,863,000 | 707,000 | 32,956,000 | 1,300,000 | 7,338,000 | 5,719,000 | 400 | 74,883,400 |
| Other Christians | 61,553,000 | 75,930,000 | 8,058,000 | 9,861,000 | 32,324,000 | 607,000 | 100,600 | 188,433,600 |
| Moslems | 278,250,800 | 636,976,000 | 12,574,500 | 1,350,500 | 2,847,000* | 100,500 | 39,229,400 | 971,328,700 |
| Nonreligious | 1,896,000 | 691,144,000 | 52,411,000 | 17,159,000 | 25,265,000 | 3,291,000 | 85,066,000 | 876,232,000 |
| Hindus | 1,475,000 | 728,118,000 | 704,000 | 884,000 | 1,269,000 | 360,000 | 2,000 | 732,812,000 |
| Buddhists | 21,000 | 313,114,000 | 272,000 | 541,000 | 558,000 | 26,000 | 407,000 | 314,939,000 |
| Atheists | 316,000 | 161,414,000 | 17,604,000 | 3,224,000 | 1,319,000 | 535,000 | 55,898,000 | 240,310,000 |

| | Africa | Asia | Europe | Latin America | Northern America | Oceania | Former U.S.S.R. | World |
|---|---|---|---|---|---|---|---|---|
| Chinese folk religionists | 13,000 | 186,817,000 | 60,000 | 73,000 | 122,000 | 21,000 | 1,000 | 187,107,000 |
| New-Religionists | 21,000 | 141,382,000 | 50,000 | 530,000 | 1,421,000 | 10,000 | 1,000 | 143,415,000 |
| Tribal religionists | 70,588,000 | 24,948,000 | 1,000 | 936,000 | 41,000 | 67,000 | 0 | 96,581,000 |
| Sikhs | 26,000 | 18,272,000 | 231,000 | 8,000 | 254,000 | 9,000 | 500 | 18,800,500 |
| Jews | 337,000 | 5,587,000 | 1,469,000 | 1,092,000 | 7,003,000 | 98,000 | 2,236,000 | 17,822,000 |
| Shamanists | 1,000 | 10,233,000 | 2,000 | 1,000 | 1,000 | 1,000 | 254,000 | 10,493,000 |
| Confucians | 1,000 | 5,994,000 | 2,000 | 2,000 | 26,000 | 1,000 | 2,000 | 6,028,000 |
| Baha'is | 1,496,000 | 2,680,000 | 91,000 | 801,000 | 365,000 | 77,000 | 7,000 | 5,517,000 |
| Jains | 53,000 | 3,717,000 | 15,000 | 4,000 | 4,000 | 1,000 | 0 | 3,794,000 |
| Shintoists | 200 | 3,220,000 | 500 | 500 | 1,000 | 500 | 100 | 3,222,800 |
| Other religionists | 433,000 | 12,292,000 | 1,469,000 | 3,570,000 | 485,000 | 4,000 | 333,000 | 18,586,000 |
| **Total Population** | **682,132,200** | **3,231,273,000** | **500,712,000** | **465,987,000** | **279,985,000** | **27,230,000** | **292,691,000** | **5,480,010,000** |

**Notes:** *This figure is disputed by the U.S. Moslem community, who claim 6 million adherents in the U.S. alone.

**Adherents:** As defined and enumerated for each of the world's countries in *World Christian Encyclopedia* (1982), projected to mid-1992, adjusted for recent data.

**Christians:** Followers of Jesus Christ affiliated with churches (church members, including children: 1,692,466,000) plus persons professing in censuses or polls though not so affiliated.

**Other Christians:** Catholics (non-Roman), marginal Protestants, crypto-Christians, and adherents of African, Asian, black, and Latin-American indigenous churches.

**Moslems:** 83% Sunnites, 16% Shi'ites, 1% other schools. The definition excludes former ethnic Moslems who have now abandoned Islam, also followers of syncretistic religions combining Islam with other belief systems. In the U.S., a recent detailed survey showed that most Asian immigrants previously thought to be Moslems are now in fact Christians.

**Nonreligious:** Persons professing no religion, nonbelievers, agnostics, freethinkers, dereligionized secularists indifferent to all religion.

**Hindus:** 70% Vaishnavites, 25% Shaivites, 2% neo-Hindus and reform Hindus.

**Buddhists:** 56% Mahayana, 38% Theravada, 6% Tantrism.

**Atheists:** Persons professing atheism, skepticism, disbelief, or irreligion, including antireligious (opposed to all religion).

**Chinese folk religionists:** Followers of traditional Chinese religion (local deities, ancestor veneration, Confucian ethics, Taoism, universism, divination, some Buddhist elements).

**New-Religionists:** Followers of Asian 20th-century New Religions, New Religious movements, radical new crisis religions, and non-Christian syncretistic mass religions, all founded since 1800 and mostly since 1945.

**Jews:** 84% Ashkenazis, 10% Orientals, 4% Sephardis. The definition includes nonpracticing Jews, underground Jews, and crypto-Jews in Moslem countries.

**Confucians:** Non-Chinese followers of Confucius and Confucianism, mostly Koreans in Korea.

**Other religionists:** Including 50 minor world religions and a large number of spiritist religions, New Age religions, quasi religions, pseudoreligions, parareligions, religious or mystic systems, and religious and semireligious brotherhoods.

**Total Population:** UN medium variant figures for mid-1992, as given in *World Population Prospects 1990* (UN, 1991).

## Change in Membership of Some U.S. Denominations, 1980–1990

Source: *1993 Yearbook of American and Canadian Churches*

| Denomination | 1980–1990 % Change in Adherents |
|---|---|
| Advent Christian Church | −32.9% |
| African Methodist Episcopal Zion | 4.5% |
| American Baptist Churches USA | −2.5% |
| Apostolic Christian Church (Nazarene) | 20.6% |
| Apostolic Lutheran Church of America | 0.1% |
| Armenian Apostolic Ch. Amer., E.Prelacy | 619.1% |
| Assemblies of God | 34.0% |
| Assoc. Reformed Presbyterian Church | 18.8% |
| Baptist General Conference | 11.0% |
| Baptist Missionary Association of Amer. | 5.6% |
| Beachy Amish Mennonite Churches | 39.6% |
| Berean Fundamental Church | 46.6% |
| Bible Church of Christ, Inc. | 119.6% |
| Brethren Church (Ashland, Ohio) | −11.1% |
| Brethren in Christ Church | 7.2% |
| Catholic Church | 12.4% |
| Christ Catholic Church | −40.2% |
| Christian & Missionary Alliance | 59.3% |
| Christian Brethren | 29.1% |
| Christian Church (Disciples of Christ) | −14.4% |
| Christian Churches & Churches of Christ | 7.6% |
| Christian Reformed Church | 6.7% |
| Church of God (Anderson, Indiana)** | −56.5% |
| Church of God (Cleveland, Tennessee) | 46.5% |
| Church of God (Seventh Day), Denver, Colo. | 89.8% |
| Church of God Gen. Conf. (Abrahamic Faith) | −14.1% |
| Church of God in Christ (Mennonite) | 68.2% |
| Church of Jesus Christ of Latter-day Saints | 31.9% |
| Church of the Brethren | −10.3% |
| Church of the Lutheran Brethren of Amer. | 62.7% |
| Church of the Lutheran Confession | −6.4% |
| Church of the Nazarene | 0.3% |
| Churches of Christ | 5.1% |
| Congr. Christian Churches, Nat'l Assoc. of | −17.3% |
| Conservative Congregational Christian Conf. | 28.0% |

| Denomination | 1980–1990 % Change in Adherents |
|---|---|
| Cumberland Presbyterian Church | 0.4% |
| Episcopal Church | −13.4% |
| Estonian Evangelical Lutheran Church | −43.1% |
| Evangelical Bible Churches, Fellowship of | −24.0% |
| Evangelical Congregational Church | −2.7% |
| Evangelical Free Church of America | 155.4% |
| Evangelical Lutheran Church in America* | −2.8% |
| Evangelical Lutheran Synod | 7.4% |
| Evangelical Mennonite Church, Inc. | 11.5% |
| Evangelical Methodist Church | −5.8% |
| Fire Baptized Holiness Church (Wesleyan) | −2.0% |
| Free Lutheran Congregations, The Assoc. of | 88.9% |
| Free Methodist Church of North America** | −59.5% |
| Friends-USA | −5.0% |
| General Conf. of Mennonite Brethren Chs. | 14.7% |
| Internat'l Church of the Foursquare Gospel | 59.4% |
| Jewish (estimate)** | 645.3% |
| Latvian Evang. Lutheran Church in Amer. | 5.0% |
| Lutheran Church—Missouri Synod | −0.7% |
| Mennonite Church | 30.4% |
| Mennonite Church, The General Conference | −12.7% |
| Missionary Church | 26.8% |
| Moravian Church in America, Alaska Prov. | 22.1% |
| Moravian Church in America, Northern Prov. | −4.1% |
| Moravian Church in America, Southern Prov. | 1.0% |
| North American Baptist Conference | 4.4% |
| Old Order Amish Church | 42.1% |
| Pentecostal Holiness Church, Inc. | 29.2% |
| Presbyterian Church (USA)* | −11.5% |
| Presbyterian Church in America* | 95.7% |
| Primitive Advent Christian Church | −21.2% |
| Primitive Methodist Church, U.S.A. | −34.7% |
| Protestant Conference (Lutheran), The | −21.8% |
| Reformed Church in America | −2.2% |
| Reformed Episcopal Church | −10.9% |

| Denomination | 1980–1990 % Change in Adherents | Denomination | 1980–1990 % Change in Adherents |
|---|---|---|---|
| Salvation Army, The** | −64.7% | United Christian Church | −2.3% |
| Seventh Day Baptist General Conference | 4.8% | United Church of Christ | −4.9% |
| Seventh-day Adventists | 35.1% | United Methodist Church, The | −4.0% |
| Southern Baptist Convention | 16.3% | Wisconsin Evangelical Lutheran Synod | 3.8% |
| Syrian Orthodox Church of Antioch | 25.1% | Total | 12.4% |
| Unitarian Universalist Association** | 21.7% | | |

**Notes:** Many Protestant denominations do not include children in membership, and a number of groups could not provide data on adherents; therefore, an estimating formula was used to include children, which made this study's adherent figures higher than the *Yearbook's* membership figures. * 1980 figures include denominations that merged during the decade. ** Methodology for reporting adherents differed in 1980 and 1990.

## Predominant Religious Groups in U.S. Counties

Source: *1993 Yearbook of American and Canadian Churches*

| Religious Group | No. of Counties Where Predominant | Religious Group | No. of Counties Where Predominant |
|---|---|---|---|
| Baptist | 1,322 | Pentecostal | 5 |
| Catholic | 959 | Presbyterian | 5 |
| Lutheran | 266 | Brethren | 2 |
| Methodist | 249 | Jewish | 2 |
| Latter-day Saints | 83 | Moravian | 2 |
| Disciples of Christ | 54 | Adventist | 1 |
| Reformed | 8 | Episcopal | 1 |
| Mennonite | 7 | Friends | 1 |
| United Church of Christ | 6 | | |

## Episcopal Church Calendar and Liturgical Colors

Source: The Episcopal Church Center, New York City

**White**—from Christmas Day through the First Sunday after Epiphany; Maundy Thursday (as an alternative to crimson at the Eucharist); from the Vigil of Easter to the Day of Pentecost (Whitsunday); Trinity Sunday; Feasts of the Lord (except Holy Cross Day); the Confession of St. Peter; the Conversion of St. Paul; St. Joseph; St. Mary Magdalene; St. Mary the Virgin; St. Michael and All Angels; All Saints' Day; St. John the Evangelist; memorials of other saints who were not martyred; Independence Day and Thanksgiving Day; weddings and funerals. **Red**—the Day of Pentecost; Holy Cross Day; feasts of apostles and evangelists (except those listed above); feasts and memorials of martyrs (including Holy Innocents' Day). **Black**—optional alternative for funerals. Alternative colors used in some churches: **Blue**—Advent; **Lenten White**—Ash Wednesday to Palm Sunday. **Violet**—Advent and Lent. **Crimson** (dark red)—Holy Week. **Green**—the seasons after Epiphany and after Pentecost.

In the Episcopal Church the days of fasting are Ash Wednesday and Good Friday. Other days of special devotion (abstinence) are the 40 days of Lent and all Fridays of the year, except those in Christmas and Easter seasons and any Feasts of the Lord that occur on a Friday or during Lent. Ember Days (optional) are days of prayer for the Church's ministry. They fall on the Wednesday, Friday, and Saturday after the first Sunday in Lent, the Day of Pentecost, Holy Cross Day, and the Third Sunday of Advent. Rogation Days (also optional) are the three days before Ascension Day, and are days of prayer for God's blessing on the crops, on commerce and industry, and for the conservation of the earth's resources.

| Days, etc. | 1993 | 1994 | 1995 | 1996 | 1997 |
|---|---|---|---|---|---|
| Golden Number | 18 | 19 | 1 | 2 | 3 |
| Sunday Letter | C | B | A | GF | E |
| Sundays after Epiphany | 7 | 6 | 8 | 7 | 5 |
| Ash Wednesday | Feb. 24 | Feb. 16 | Mar. 1 | Feb. 21 | Feb. 12 |
| First Sunday in Lent | Feb. 28 | Feb. 20 | Mar. 5 | Feb. 25 | Feb. 16 |
| Passion/Palm Sunday | Apr. 4 | Mar. 27 | Apr. 9 | Mar. 31 | Mar. 23 |
| Good Friday | Apr. 9 | Apr. 1 | Apr. 14 | Apr. 5 | Mar. 28 |
| Easter Day | Apr. 11 | Apr. 3 | Apr. 16 | Apr. 7 | Mar. 30 |
| Ascension Day | May 20 | May 12 | May 25 | May 16 | May 8 |
| The Day of Pentecost | May 30 | May 22 | June 4 | May 26 | May 18 |
| Trinity Sunday | June 6 | May 29 | June 11 | June 2 | May 25 |
| Numbered Proper of 2 Pentecost | #6 | #5 | #6 | #5 | #4 |
| First Sunday of Advent | Nov. 28 | Nov. 27 | Dec. 3 | Dec. 1 | Nov. 30 |

## Greek Orthodox Movable Ecclesiastical Dates

| | 1993 | 1994 | 1995 | 1996 | 1997 |
|---|---|---|---|---|---|
| Triódion begins | February 7 | February 20 | February 12 | February 4 | February 16 |
| Sat. of Souls | February 20 | March 5 | February 25 | February 17 | March 1 |
| Meat Fare | February 21 | March 6 | February 26 | February 18 | March 2 |
| 2nd Sat. of Souls | February 27 | March 12 | March 4 | February 24 | March 8 |
| Lent Begins | March 1 | March 14 | March 6 | February 26 | March 10 |
| St. Theodore 3rd Sat. of Souls | March 6 | March 19 | March 11 | March 2 | March 15 |
| Sunday of Orthodoxy | March 7 | March 20 | March 12 | March 3 | March 16 |
| Sat. of Lazarus | April 10 | April 23 | April 15 | April 6 | April 19 |
| Palm Sunday | April 11 | April 24 | April 16 | April 7 | April 20 |
| Holy (Good) Friday | April 16 | April 29 | April 21 | April 12 | April 25 |
| Western Easter | April 11 | April 3 | April 16 | April 7 | March 30 |
| **Orthodox Easter** | April 18 | May 1 | April 23 | April 14 | April 27 |
| Ascension | May 27 | June 9 | June 1 | May 23 | June 5 |
| Sat. of Souls | June 5 | June 18 | June 10 | June 1 | June 14 |
| Pentecost | June 6 | June 19 | June 11 | June 2 | June 15 |
| All Saints | June 13 | June 26 | June 18 | June 9 | June 22 |

## Jewish Holy Days, Festivals, and Fasts

| | 1993 (5753-54) | | 1994 (5754-55) | | 1995 (5755-56) | | 1996 (5756-57) | | 1997 (5757-58) | |
|---|---|---|---|---|---|---|---|---|---|---|
| Tu B'Shvat . . . . . . . . . . . . | Feb. 6 | Sat. | Jan. 27 | Thu. | Jan. 16 | Mon. | Feb. 5 | Mon. | Jan. 23 | Thu. |
| Ta'anis Esther (Fast of Esther) . . . . | Mar. 4 | Thu.* | Feb. 24 | Thu. | Mar. 15 | Wed. | Mar. 4 | Mon. | Mar. 20 | Thu.* |
| Purim . . . . . . . . . . . . . . . | Mar. 7 | Sun. | Feb. 25 | Fri. | Mar. 16 | Thu. | Mar. 5 | Tue. | Mar. 23 | Sun. |
| Passover . . . . . . . . . . . . . | Apr. 6 | Tue. | Mar. 27 | Sun. | Apr. 15 | Sat. | Apr. 4 | Thu. | Apr. 22 | Tue. |
| | Apr. 13 | Tue. | Apr. 3 | Sun. | Apr. 22 | Sat. | Apr. 11 | Thu. | Apr. 29 | Tue. |
| Lag B'Omer . . . . . . . . . . . . | May 9 | Sun. | Apr. 29 | Fri. | May 18 | Thu. | May 7 | Tue. | May 25 | Sun. |
| Shavuot . . . . . . . . . . . . . . | May 26 | Wed. | May 16 | Mon. | June 4 | Sun | May 24 | Fri. | June 11 | Sun. |
| | May 27 | Thu. | May 17 | Tue. | June 5 | Mon. | May 25 | Sat. | June 12 | Mon. |
| Fast of the 17th Day of Tammuz . . | July 6 | Tue. | June 26 | Sun. | July 16 | Sun.* | July 4 | Thu. | July 22 | Tue. |
| Fast of the 9th Day of Ac . . . . . . | July 27 | Tue. | July 17 | Sun. | Aug. 6 | Sun. | July 25 | Thu. | Aug. 12 | Tue. |
| Rosh Hashanah . . . . . . . . . . . | Sept. 16 | Thu. | Sept. 6 | Tue. | Sept. 25 | Mon. | Sept. 14 | Sat. | Oct. 2 | Thu. |
| | Sept. 17 | Fri. | Sept. 7 | Wed. | Sept. 26 | Tue. | Sept. 15 | Sun. | Oct. 3 | Fri. |
| Fast of Gedalya . . . . . . . . . . | Sept. 19 | Sun.* | Sept. 8 | Thu. | Sept. 27 | Wed. | Sept. 16 | Mon. | Oct. 5 | Sun.* |
| Yom Kippur . . . . . . . . . . . . | Sept. 25 | Sat. | Sept. 15 | Thu. | Oct. 4 | Wed. | Sept 23 | Mon. | Oct. 11 | Sat. |
| Sukkot . . . . . . . . . . . . . . | Sept. 30 | Thu. | Sept. 20 | Tue. | Oct. 9 | Mon. | Sept. 28 | Sat. | Oct. 16 | Thu. |
| | Oct. 6 | Wed. | Sept. 26 | Mon. | Oct. 15 | Sun. | Oct. 4 | Fri. | Oct. 22 | Wed. |
| Shmini Atzeret . . . . . . . . . . . | Oct. 7 | Thu. | Sept. 27 | Tue. | Oct. 16 | Mon. | Oct. 5 | Sat. | Oct. 23 | Thu. |
| | Oct. 8 | Fri. | Sept. 28 | Wed. | Oct. 17 | Tue. | Oct. 6 | Sun. | Oct. 24 | Fri. |
| Chanukah . . . . . . . . . . . . . | Dec. 9 | Thu. | Nov. 28 | Mon. | Oct. 18 | Mon. | Dec. 6 | Fri. | Dec. 24 | Wed. |
| | Dec. 16 | Thu. | Dec. 5 | Mon. | Oct. 25 | Mon. | Dec. 13 | Fri. | Dec. 31 | Wed. |
| Fast of the 10th of Tevet . . . . . . | Dec. 24 | Fri. | Dec. 13 | Tue. | Jan. 2 | Tue. | Dec. 21 | Sat. | Jan. 8 | Thu. |

**The months of the Jewish year are:** 1) Tishri; 2) Cheshvan (also Marcheshvan); 3) Kislev; 4) Tebet (also Tebeth); 5) Shebat (also Shebhat); 6) Adar; 6a) Adar Sheni (II) added in leap years; 7) Nisan; 8) Iyar; 9) Sivan; 10) Tammuz; 11) Av (also Abh); 12) Elul. All Jewish holy days, etc., begin at sunset on the day previous. *Date changed to avoid Sabbath.

## Islamic (Moslem) Calendar 1993-1998 (1414-1418)

The Islamic calendar is a lunar reckoning from the year of the *hegira*, 622 A.D., when Muhammed moved from Mecca to Medina. It runs in cycles of 30 years, of which the 2nd, 5th, 7th, 10th, 13th, 16th, 18th, 21st, 24th, 26th, and 29th are leap years; 1414 is the 4th year of the cycle. Common years have 354 days, leap years 355, the extra day being added to the last month, Zu'lhijjah. Except for this case, the 12 months beginning with Muharram have alternately 30 and 29 days.

| Year | Name of month | Month begins | Year | Name of month | Month begins |
|---|---|---|---|---|---|
| 1414 | Muharram (New Year) . . . . . . . . . | June 21, 1993 | 1416 | Rajab . . . . . . . . . . . . . . . . . | Nov. 24, 1995 |
| 1414 | Safar . . . . . . . . . . . . . . . . . | July 21, 1993 | 1416 | Shaban . . . . . . . . . . . . . . . . | Dec. 24, 1995 |
| 1414 | Rabia I . . . . . . . . . . . . . . . . | Aug. 19, 1993 | 1416 | Ramadan . . . . . . . . . . . . . . | Jan. 22, 1996 |
| 1414 | Rabia II . . . . . . . . . . . . . . . . | Sept. 18, 1993 | 1416 | Shawwai . . . . . . . . . . . . . . | Feb. 21, 1996 |
| 1414 | Jamada I . . . . . . . . . . . . . . . | Oct. 17, 1993 | 1416 | Zu'lkadah . . . . . . . . . . . . . | Mar. 21, 1996 |
| 1414 | Jamada II . . . . . . . . . . . . . . . | Nov. 16, 1993 | 1416 | Zu'lhijjah . . . . . . . . . . . . . | Apr. 20, 1996 |
| 1414 | Rajab . . . . . . . . . . . . . . . . . | Dec. 15, 1993 | 1417 | Muharram (New Year) . . . . . . . . . | May 19, 1996 |
| 1414 | Shaban . . . . . . . . . . . . . . . . | Jan. 14, 1994 | 1417 | Safar . . . . . . . . . . . . . . . . . | June 18, 1996 |
| 1414 | Ramadan . . . . . . . . . . . . . . | Feb. 12, 1994 | 1417 | Rabia I . . . . . . . . . . . . . . . . | July 17, 1996 |
| 1414 | Shawwai . . . . . . . . . . . . . . | Mar. 14, 1994 | 1417 | Rabia II . . . . . . . . . . . . . . . . | Aug. 16, 1996 |
| 1414 | Zu'lkadah . . . . . . . . . . . . . | April 12, 1994 | 1417 | Jamada I . . . . . . . . . . . . . . . | Sept. 14, 1996 |
| 1414 | Zu'lhijjah . . . . . . . . . . . . . | May 12, 1994 | 1417 | Jamada II . . . . . . . . . . . . . . . | Oct. 14, 1996 |
| 1415 | Muharram (New Year) . . . . . . . . . | June 10, 1994 | 1417 | Rajab . . . . . . . . . . . . . . . . . | Nov. 12, 1996 |
| 1415 | Safar . . . . . . . . . . . . . . . . . | July 10, 1994 | 1417 | Shaban . . . . . . . . . . . . . . . . | Dec. 12, 1996 |
| 1415 | Rabia I . . . . . . . . . . . . . . . . | Aug. 8, 1994 | 1417 | Ramadan . . . . . . . . . . . . . . | Jan. 10, 1997 |
| 1415 | Rabia II . . . . . . . . . . . . . . . . | Sept. 7, 1994 | 1417 | Shawwai . . . . . . . . . . . . . . | Feb. 9, 1997 |
| 1415 | Jamada I . . . . . . . . . . . . . . . | Oct. 6, 1994 | 1417 | Zu'lkadah . . . . . . . . . . . . . | March 10, 1997 |
| 1415 | Jamada II . . . . . . . . . . . . . . . | Nov. 5, 1994 | 1417 | Zu'lhijjah . . . . . . . . . . . . . | Apr. 9, 1997 |
| 1415 | Rajab . . . . . . . . . . . . . . . . . | Dec. 12, 1994 | 1418 | Muharram (New Year) . . . . . . . . . | May 9, 1997 |
| 1415 | Shaban . . . . . . . . . . . . . . . . | Jan. 3, 1995 | 1418 | Safar . . . . . . . . . . . . . . . . . | June 8, 1997 |
| 1415 | Ramadan . . . . . . . . . . . . . . | Feb. 2, 1995 | 1418 | Rabia I . . . . . . . . . . . . . . . . | July 7, 1997 |
| 1415 | Shawwai . . . . . . . . . . . . . . | Mar. 3, 1995 | 1418 | Rabia II . . . . . . . . . . . . . . . . | Aug. 6, 1997 |
| 1415 | Zu'lkadah . . . . . . . . . . . . . | Apr. 4, 1995 | 1418 | Jamada I . . . . . . . . . . . . . . . | Sept. 4, 1997 |
| 1415 | Zu'lhijjah . . . . . . . . . . . . . | May 1, 1995 | 1418 | Jamada II . . . . . . . . . . . . . . . | Oct. 4, 1997 |
| 1416 | Muharram (New Year) . . . . . . . . . | May 21, 1995 | 1418 | Rajab . . . . . . . . . . . . . . . . . | Nov. 2, 1997 |
| 1416 | Safar . . . . . . . . . . . . . . . . . | June 30, 1995 | 1418 | Shaban . . . . . . . . . . . . . . . . | Dec. 2, 1997 |
| 1416 | Rabia I . . . . . . . . . . . . . . . . | July 29, 1995 | 1418 | Ramadan . . . . . . . . . . . . . . | Dec. 31, 1997 |
| 1416 | Rabia II . . . . . . . . . . . . . . . . | Aug. 28, 1995 | 1418 | Shawwai . . . . . . . . . . . . . . | Jan. 30, 1998 |
| 1416 | Jamada I . . . . . . . . . . . . . . . | Sept. 26, 1995 | 1418 | Zu'lkadah . . . . . . . . . . . . . | Feb. 27, 1998 |
| 1416 | Jamada II . . . . . . . . . . . . . . . | Oct. 26, 1995 | 1418 | Zu'lhijjah . . . . . . . . . . . . . | March 30, 1998 |

## Ash Wednesday and Easter Sunday

| Year | Ash Wed. | Easter Sunday | Year | Ash Wed. | Easter Sunday | Year | Ash Wed. | Easter Sunday | Year | Ash Wed. | Easter Sunday |
|---|---|---|---|---|---|---|---|---|---|---|---|
| 1901 | Feb. 20 | Apr. 7 | 1914 | Feb. 25 | Apr. 12 | 1927 | Mar. 2 | Apr. 17 | 1940 | Feb. 7 | Mar. 24 |
| 1902 | Feb. 12 | Mar. 30 | 1915 | Feb. 17 | Apr. 4 | 1928 | Feb. 22 | Apr. 8 | 1941 | Feb. 26 | Apr. 13 |
| 1903 | Feb. 25 | Apr. 12 | 1916 | Mar. 8 | Apr. 23 | 1929 | Feb. 13 | Mar. 31 | 1942 | Feb. 18 | Apr. 5 |
| 1904 | Feb. 17 | Apr. 3 | 1917 | Feb. 21 | Apr. 8 | 1930 | Mar. 5 | Apr. 20 | 1943 | Mar. 10 | Apr. 25 |
| 1905 | Mar. 8 | Apr. 23 | 1918 | Feb. 13 | Mar. 31 | 1931 | Feb. 18 | Apr. 5 | 1944 | Feb. 23 | Apr. 9 |
| 1906 | Feb. 28 | Apr. 15 | 1919 | Mar. 5 | Apr. 20 | 1932 | Feb. 10 | Mar. 27 | 1945 | Feb. 14 | Apr. 1 |
| 1907 | Feb. 13 | Mar. 31 | 1920 | Feb. 18 | Apr. 4 | 1933 | Mar. 1 | Apr. 16 | 1946 | Mar. 6 | Apr. 21 |
| 1908 | Mar. 4 | Apr. 19 | 1921 | Feb. 9 | Mar. 27 | 1934 | Feb. 14 | Apr. 1 | 1947 | Feb. 19 | Apr. 6 |
| 1909 | Feb. 24 | Apr. 11 | 1922 | Mar. 1 | Apr. 16 | 1935 | Mar. 6 | Apr. 21 | 1948 | Feb. 11 | Mar. 28 |
| 1910 | Feb. 9 | Mar. 27 | 1923 | Feb. 14 | Apr. 1 | 1936 | Feb. 26 | Apr. 12 | 1949 | Mar. 2 | Apr. 17 |
| 1911 | Mar. 1 | Apr. 16 | 1924 | Mar. 5 | Apr. 20 | 1937 | Feb. 10 | Mar. 28 | 1950 | Feb. 22 | Apr. 9 |
| 1912 | Feb. 21 | Apr. 7 | 1925 | Feb. 25 | Apr. 12 | 1938 | Mar. 2 | Apr. 17 | 1951 | Feb. 7 | Mar. 25 |
| 1913 | Feb. 5 | Mar. 23 | 1926 | Feb. 17 | Apr. 4 | 1939 | Feb. 22 | Apr. 9 | 1952 | Feb. 27 | Apr. 13 |

| Year | Ash Wed. | Easter Sunday | Year | Ash Wed. | Easter Sunday | Year | Ash Wed. | Easter Sunday | Year | Ash Wed. | Easter Sunday |
|---|---|---|---|---|---|---|---|---|---|---|---|
| 1953 | Feb. 18 | Apr. 5 | 1990 | Feb. 28 | Apr. 15 | 2027 | Feb. 10 | Mar. 28 | 2064 | Feb. 20 | Apr. 6 |
| 1954 | Mar. 3 | Apr. 18 | 1991 | Feb. 13 | Mar. 31 | 2028 | Mar. 1 | Apr. 16 | 2065 | Feb. 11 | Mar. 29 |
| 1955 | Feb. 23 | Apr. 10 | 1992 | Mar. 4 | Apr. 19 | 2029 | Feb. 14 | Apr. 1 | 2066 | Feb. 24 | Apr. 11 |
| 1956 | Feb. 15 | Apr. 1 | 1993 | Feb. 24 | Apr. 11 | 2030 | Mar. 6 | Apr. 21 | 2067 | Feb. 16 | Apr. 3 |
| 1957 | Mar. 6 | Apr. 21 | 1994 | Feb. 16 | Apr. 3 | 2031 | Feb. 26 | Apr. 13 | 2068 | Mar. 7 | Apr. 22 |
| 1958 | Feb. 19 | Apr. 6 | 1995 | Mar. 1 | Apr. 16 | 2032 | Feb. 11 | Mar. 28 | 2069 | Feb. 27 | Apr. 14 |
| 1959 | Feb. 11 | Mar. 29 | 1996 | Feb. 21 | Apr. 7 | 2033 | Mar. 2 | Apr. 17 | 2070 | Feb. 12 | Mar. 30 |
| 1960 | Mar. 2 | Apr. 17 | 1997 | Feb. 12 | Mar. 30 | 2034 | Feb. 22 | Apr. 9 | 2071 | Mar. 4 | Apr. 19 |
| 1961 | Feb. 15 | Apr. 2 | 1998 | Feb. 25 | Apr. 12 | 2035 | Feb. 7 | Mar. 25 | 2072 | Feb. 24 | Apr. 10 |
| 1962 | Mar. 7 | Apr. 22 | 1999 | Feb. 17 | Apr. 4 | 2036 | Feb. 27 | Apr. 13 | 2073 | Feb. 8 | Mar. 26 |
| 1963 | Feb. 27 | Apr. 14 | 2000 | Mar. 8 | Apr. 23 | 2037 | Feb. 18 | Apr. 5 | 2074 | Feb. 28 | Apr. 15 |
| 1964 | Feb. 12 | Mar. 29 | 2001 | Feb. 28 | Apr. 15 | 2038 | Mar. 10 | Apr. 25 | 2075 | Feb. 20 | Apr. 7 |
| 1965 | Mar. 3 | Apr. 18 | 2002 | Feb. 13 | Mar. 31 | 2039 | Feb. 23 | Apr. 10 | 2076 | Mar. 4 | Apr. 19 |
| 1966 | Feb. 23 | Apr. 10 | 2003 | Mar. 5 | Apr. 20 | 2040 | Feb. 15 | Apr. 1 | 2077 | Feb. 24 | Apr. 11 |
| 1967 | Feb. 8 | Mar. 26 | 2004 | Feb. 25 | Apr. 11 | 2041 | Mar. 6 | Apr. 21 | 2078 | Feb. 16 | Apr. 3 |
| 1968 | Feb. 28 | Apr. 14 | 2005 | Feb. 9 | Mar. 27 | 2042 | Feb. 19 | Apr. 6 | 2079 | Mar. 8 | Apr. 23 |
| 1969 | Feb. 19 | Apr. 6 | 2006 | Mar. 1 | Apr. 16 | 2043 | Feb. 11 | Mar. 29 | 2080 | Feb. 21 | Apr. 7 |
| 1970 | Feb. 11 | Mar. 29 | 2007 | Feb. 21 | Apr. 8 | 2044 | Mar. 2 | Apr. 17 | 2081 | Feb. 12 | Mar. 30 |
| 1971 | Feb. 24 | Apr. 11 | 2008 | Feb. 6 | Mar. 23 | 2045 | Feb. 22 | Apr. 9 | 2082 | Mar. 4 | Apr. 19 |
| 1972 | Feb. 16 | Apr. 2 | 2009 | Feb. 25 | Apr. 12 | 2046 | Feb. 7 | Mar. 25 | 2083 | Feb. 17 | Apr. 4 |
| 1973 | Mar. 7 | Apr. 22 | 2010 | Feb. 17 | Apr. 4 | 2047 | Feb. 27 | Apr. 14 | 2084 | Mar. 9 | Apr. 26 |
| 1974 | Feb. 27 | Apr. 14 | 2011 | Mar. 9 | Apr. 24 | 2048 | Feb. 19 | Apr. 5 | 2085 | Feb. 28 | Apr. 15 |
| 1975 | Feb. 12 | Mar. 30 | 2012 | Feb. 22 | Apr. 8 | 2049 | Mar. 3 | Apr. 18 | 2086 | Feb. 13 | Mar. 31 |
| 1976 | Mar. 3 | Apr. 18 | 2013 | Feb. 13 | Mar. 31 | 2050 | Feb. 23 | Apr. 10 | 2087 | Mar. 5 | Apr. 20 |
| 1977 | Feb. 23 | Apr. 10 | 2014 | Mar. 5 | Apr. 20 | 2051 | Feb. 15 | Apr. 2 | 2088 | Feb. 25 | Apr. 11 |
| 1978 | Feb. 8 | Mar. 26 | 2015 | Feb. 18 | Apr. 5 | 2052 | Mar. 6 | Apr. 21 | 2089 | Feb. 16 | Apr. 3 |
| 1979 | Feb. 28 | Apr. 15 | 2016 | Feb. 10 | Mar. 27 | 2053 | Feb. 19 | Apr. 6 | 2090 | Mar. 1 | Apr. 16 |
| 1980 | Feb. 20 | Apr. 6 | 2017 | Mar. 1 | Apr. 16 | 2054 | Feb. 11 | Mar. 29 | 2091 | Feb. 21 | Apr. 8 |
| 1981 | Mar. 4 | Apr. 19 | 2018 | Feb. 14 | Apr. 1 | 2055 | Mar. 3 | Apr. 18 | 2092 | Feb. 13 | Mar. 30 |
| 1982 | Feb. 24 | Apr. 11 | 2019 | Mar. 6 | Apr. 21 | 2056 | Feb. 16 | Apr. 2 | 2093 | Feb. 25 | Apr. 12 |
| 1983 | Feb. 16 | Apr. 3 | 2020 | Feb. 26 | Apr. 12 | 2057 | Mar. 7 | Apr. 22 | 2094 | Feb. 17 | Apr. 4 |
| 1984 | Mar. 7 | Apr. 22 | 2021 | Feb. 17 | Apr. 4 | 2058 | Feb. 27 | Apr. 14 | 2095 | Mar. 9 | Apr. 24 |
| 1985 | Feb. 20 | Apr. 7 | 2022 | Mar. 2 | Apr. 17 | 2059 | Feb. 12 | Mar. 30 | 2096 | Feb. 29 | Apr. 15 |
| 1986 | Feb. 12 | Mar. 30 | 2023 | Feb. 22 | Apr. 9 | 2060 | Mar. 3 | Apr. 18 | 2097 | Feb. 13 | Mar. 31 |
| 1987 | Mar. 4 | Apr. 19 | 2024 | Feb. 14 | Mar. 31 | 2061 | Feb. 23 | Apr. 10 | 2098 | Mar. 5 | Apr. 20 |
| 1988 | Feb. 17 | Apr. 3 | 2025 | Mar. 5 | Apr. 20 | 2062 | Feb. 8 | Mar. 26 | 2099 | Feb. 25 | Apr. 12 |
| 1989 | Feb. 8 | Mar. 26 | 2026 | Feb. 18 | Apr. 5 | 2063 | Feb. 28 | Apr. 15 | 2100 | Feb. 10 | Mar. 28 |

## The Ten Commandments

According to Judeo-Christian tradition, as related in the Bible, the Ten Commandments were revealed by God to Moses, and form the basic moral component of God's covenant with Israel. The Ten Commandments appear in two different places in the Old Testament—Exodus 20:1-17 and Deuterotomy 5:6-21—the phrasing similar but not identical. Most Protestant, Anglican, and Orthodox Christians enumerate the commandments differently from Roman Catholics and Lutherans. Jewish tradition considers the introduction, "I am the Lord ..." to be the first commandment and makes the prohibition against "other gods" and idolatry the second.

Abridged Text of the Ten Commandments in Exodus 20:1-17.

I. I am the Lord your God, who brought you out of the land of Egypt, out of the house of bondage. You shall have no other gods before me.
II. You shall not make for yourself a graven image. You shall not bow down to them or serve them.
III. You shall not take the name of the Lord your God in vain.
IV. Remember the sabbath day, to keep it holy.
V. Honor your father and your mother.
VI. You shall not kill.
VII. You shall not commit adultery.
VIII. You shall not steal.
IX. You shall not bear false witness against your neighbor.
X. You shall not covet.

## Books of the Bible

### Old Testament—Standard Protestant English Versions

| | | |
|---|---|---|
| Genesis | II Chronicles | Daniel |
| Exodus | Ezra | Hosea |
| Leviticus | Nehemiah | Joel |
| Numbers | Esther | Amos |
| Deuteronomy | Job | Obadiah |
| Joshua | Psalms | Jonah |
| Judges | Proverbs | Micah |
| Ruth | Ecclesiastes | Nahum |
| I Samuel | Song of Solomon | Habakkuk |
| II Samuel | Isaiah | Zephaniah |
| I Kings | Jeremiah | Haggai |
| II Kings | Lamentations | Zechariah |
| I Chronicles | Ezekiel | Malachi |

### New Testament—Standard Protestant English Versions

| | | |
|---|---|---|
| Matthew | Ephesians | Hebrews |
| Mark | Phillippians | James |
| Luke | Colossians | I Peter |
| John | I Thessalonians | II Peter |
| Acts | II Thessalonians | I John |
| Romans | I Timothy | II John |
| I Corinthians | II Timothy | III John |
| II Corinthians | Titus | Jude |
| Galatians | Philemon | Revelation |

### Catholic Versions

All the Catholic books of the Bible (Old Testament and New Testament) have the same names as Protestant Versions. A Catholic Version (and Pre-Reformation Bibles) simply has the books Tobit, Judith, Wisdom, Sirach (Ecclesiasticus), Baruch, I Maccabees, and II Maccabees as part of the Old Testament. The Old Testament books that a Catholic Bible includes and a Protestant Bible does not are called "Deuterocanonical Books."

# Roman Catholic Hierarchy

Source: U.S. Catholic Conference; mid-1993

## Supreme Pontiff

At the head of the Roman Catholic Church is the Supreme Pontiff, Pope John Paul II, Karol Wojtyla, born at Wadowice (Krakow), Poland, May 18, 1920; ordained priest Nov. 1, 1946; appointed bishop July 4, 1958; promoted to archbishop of Krakow Jan. 13, 1964; proclaimed cardinal June 26, 1967; elected pope as successor of Pope John Paul I Oct. 16, 1978; installed as pope Oct. 22, 1978.

## College of Cardinals

Members of the Sacred College of Cardinals are chosen by the Pope to be his chief assistants and advisers in the administration of the church. Among their duties is the election of the Pope when the Holy See becomes vacant.

In its present form, the College of Cardinals dates from the 12th century. The first cardinals, from about the 6th century, were deacons and priests of the leading churches of Rome, and bishops of neighboring diocese. The title of cardinal was limited to members of the college in 1567. The number of cardinals was set at 70 in 1586 by Pope Sixtus V. From 1959 Pope John XXIII began to increase the number. However, the number of cardinals eligible to participate in papal elections was limited to 120. There were lay cardinals until 1918, when the Code of Canon Law specified that all cardinals must be priests. Pope John XXIII in 1962 established that all cardinals must be bishops. The first age limits were set in 1971 by Pope Paul VI, who decreed that at age 80 cardinals must retire from curial departments and offices and from participation in papal elections. They continue as members of the college, with all rights and privileges.

### U.S. Cardinals

| Name | Office | Born | Named Cardinal |
|---|---|---|---|
| Baum, William W. | Major Penitentiary of Apostolic Penitentiary, the Vatican | 1926 | 1976 |
| Bevilacqua, Anthony J. | Archbishop of Philadelphia | 1923 | 1991 |
| Bernardin, Joseph L. | Archbishop of Chicago | 1928 | 1983 |
| Carberry, John J.* | Archbishop emeritus of St. Louis | 1904 | 1969 |
| Hickey, James A. | Archbishop of Washington | 1920 | 1988 |
| Krol, John J.* | Archbishop emeritus of Philadelphia | 1910 | 1967 |
| Law, Bernard F. | Archbishop of Boston | 1931 | 1985 |
| Mahony, Roger | Archbishop of Los Angeles | 1936 | 1991 |
| O'Connor, John J. | Archbishop of New York | 1920 | 1985 |
| Szoka, Edmund C. | Pres. of Prefecture of Economic Affairs of Holy See, the Vatican | 1927 | 1988 |

*Asterisk indicates cardinals ineligible to take part in papal elections.

# Census of Religious Groups in Canada

Source: *1993 Yearbook of American and Canadian Churches*; number of churches in parenthesis; groups with under 1,000 members not included.

| Religious Body | Members |
|---|---|
| Anglican Church of Canada (1,767) | 848,256 |
| Antiochian Orthodox Christian Archdiocese of North America (12) | 20,000 |
| Apostolic Church in Canada (14) | 1,600 |
| Apostolic Church of Pentecost of Canada Inc. (132) | 13,842 |
| Associated Gospel Churches (126) | N.A. |
| Bahá'í Faith (398) | 27,000 |
| Baptist Convention of Ontario and Quebec (372) | 44,713 |
| Baptist General Conference of Canada (70) | 6,066 |
| Baptist Union of Western Canada (172) | 20,719 |
| Brethren in Christ Church, Canadian Conference (36) | 3,069 |
| Canadian and American Reformed Churches (44) | 13,182 |
| Canadian Baptist Federation (1,165) | 129,720 |
| Canadian Convention of Southern Baptists (104) | 6,001 |
| Canadian Yearly Meeting of the Religious Society of Friends (52) | 1,556 |
| Central Canada Baptist Conference (37) | N.A. |
| Christian and Missionary Alliance in Canada (336) | 76,119 |
| Christian Brethren (also known as Plymouth Brethren) (600) | 52,000 |
| Christian Church (Disciples of Christ) in Canada (36) | 4,251 |
| Christian Churches and Churches of Christ in Canada (140) | 7,500 |
| Christian Reformed Church in North America (240) | 86,281 |
| Church of God (Anderson, Ind.) (50) | 3,151 |
| Church of God (Cleveland, Tenn.) (98) | 5,958 |
| Church of God of Prophecy in Canada (50) | 2,915 |
| Church of Jesus Christ of Latter-day Saints in Canada (380) | 126,000 |
| Church of the Nazarene (161) | 10,915 |
| Churches of Christ in Canada (147) | 7,181 |
| Conference of Mennonites in Canada (150) | 28,648 |
| Coptic Church in Canada (12) | N.A. |
| Estonian Evangelical Lutheran Church (13) | 6,478 |
| Evangelical Baptist Churches in Canada, Fellowship of (484) | 57,780 |
| Evangelical Church in Canada (46) | 3,688 |
| Evangelical Covenant Church in Canada (23) | 1,278 |
| Evangelical Free Church of Canada (124) | 13,299 |
| Evangelical Lutheran Church in Canada (656) | 206,187 |
| Evangelical Mennonite Conference (50) | 6,000 |
| Evangelical Mennonite Mission Conference (28) | 3,559 |
| Foursquare Gospel Church of Canada (46) | 2,019 |
| Free Methodist Church in Canada (147) | 7,479 |

| Religious Body | Members |
|---|---|
| Free Will Baptists (17) | 1,125 |
| Greek Orthodox Diocese of Toronto (Canada) (58) | 230,000 |
| Italian Pentecostal Church of Canada (21) | 3,300 |
| Jehovah's Witnesses (1,312) | 105,052 |
| Latvian Evangelical Lutheran Church in America (8) | 2,380 |
| Lutheran Church–Canada (321) | 78,566 |
| Mennonite Brethren Churches, Canadian Conference of (193) | 27,597 |
| Metropolitan Community Churches, Universal Fellowship (12) | 1,500 |
| Missionary Church of Canada (92) | 6,431 |
| Moravian Church in America, Northern Province, Canadian District of (9) | 2,126 |
| Netherlands Reformed Congregations of North America (9) | 4,660 |
| North American Baptist Conference (120) | 18,125 |
| Old Order Amish Church (17) | N.A. |
| Open Bible Standard Churches of Canada (4) | 1,000 |
| Orthodox Church in America (Canada Section) (59) | N.A. |
| Pentecostal Assemblies of Canada (976) | 194,972 |
| Pentecostal Assemblies of Newfoundland (160) | 33,700 |
| Presbyterian Church in Canada (1,023) | 245,883 |
| Reformed Church in Canada (40) | 6,779 |
| Reformed Doukhobors, Christian Community and Brotherhood of (1) | 2,108 |
| Reorganized Church of Jesus Christ of Latter Day Saints (83) | 12,258 |
| Roman Catholic Church in Canada (11,286) | 11,852,350 |
| Romanian Orthodox Episcopate of America (Jackson, MI) (13) | 8,600 |
| Russian Orthodox Church in Canada, Patriarchal Parishes (24) | 7,000 |
| Salvation Army in Canada (402) | 99,658 |
| Serbian Orthodox Church in the U.S.A. and Canada, Diocese of Canada (17) | 18,494 |
| Seventh-day Adventist Church in Canada (320) | 41,085 |
| Ukranian Orthodox Church of Canada (258) | 120,000 |
| Union D'Eglises Baptistes Francaises Au Canada (23) | 1,969 |
| Unitarian Universalist Association (40) | 6,003 |
| United Baptist Convention of the Atlantic Provinces (558) | 64,093 |
| United Church of Canada (4,044) | 2,018,808 |
| United Pentecostal Church in Canada (213) | N.A. |
| Wesleyan Church of Canada (72) | 5,232 |

N.A.=not available

# The Major World Religions

## Buddhism

**Founded:** About 525 BC, reportedly near Benares, India.

**Founder:** Gautama Siddhartha (ca. 563-480), the Buddha, who achieved enlightenment through intense meditation.

**Sacred Texts:** The *Tripitaka*, a collection of the Buddha's teachings, rules of monastic life, and philosophical commentaries on the teachings; also a vast body of Buddhist teachings and commentaries, many of which are called *sutras*.

**Organization:** The basic institution is the *sangha* or monastic order through which the traditions are passed to each generation. Monastic life tends to be democratic and anti-authoritarian. Large lay organizations have developed in some sects.

**Practice:** Varies widely according to the sect and ranges from austere meditation to magical chanting and elaborate temple rites. Many practices, such as exorcism of devils, reflect pre-Buddhist beliefs.

**Divisions:** A wide variety of sects grouped into 3 primary branches: Theravada (sole survivor of the ancient Hinayana schools), which emphasizes the importance of pure thought and deed; Mahayana, which includes Zen and Soka-gakkai, ranges from philosophical schools to belief in the saving grace of higher beings or ritual practices, and to practical meditative disciplines; and Tantrism, an unusual combination of belief in ritual magic and sophisticated philosophy.

**Location:** Throughout Asia, from Sri Lanka to Japan. Zen and Soka-gakkai have several thousand adherents in the U.S.

**Beliefs:** Life is misery and decay, and there is no ultimate reality in it or behind it. The cycle of endless birth and rebirth continues because of desire and attachment to the unreal "self". Right meditation and deeds will end the cycle and achieve Nirvana, the Void, nothingness.

## Hinduism

**Founded:** Ca. 1500 BC by Aryan invaders of India where their Vedic religion intermixed with the practices and beliefs of the natives.

**Sacred texts:** The *Veda*, including the *Upanishads*, a collection of rituals and mythological and philosophical commentaries; a vast number of epic stories about gods, heroes, and saints, including the *Bhagavadgita*, a part of the *Mahabharata*, and the *Ramayana;* and a great variety of other literature.

**Organization:** None, strictly speaking. Generally, rituals should be performed or assisted by Brahmins, the priestly caste, but in practice simpler rituals can be performed by anyone. Brahmins are the final judges of ritual purity, the vital element in Hindu life. Temples and religious organizations are usually presided over by Brahmins.

**Practice:** A variety of private rituals, primarily passage rites (eg. initiation, marriage, death, etc.) and daily devotions, and a similar variety of public rites in temples. Of the latter, the *puja*, a ceremonial dinner for a god, is the most common.

**Divisions:** There is no concept of orthodoxy in Hinduism, which presents a variety of sects, most of them devoted to the worship of one of the many gods. The 3 major living traditions are those devoted to the gods Vishnu and Shiva and to the goddess Shakti; each of them divided into further subsects. Numerous folk beliefs and practices, often in amalgamation with the above groups, exist side-by-side with sophisticated philosophical schools and exotic cults.

**Location:** Mainly India, Nepal, Malaysia, Guyana, Suriname, Sri Lanka.

**Beliefs:** There is only one divine principle; the many gods are only aspects of that unity. Life in all its forms is an aspect of the divine, but it appears as a separation from the divine, a meaningless cycle of birth and rebirth (*samsara* ) determined by the purity or impurity of past deeds (*karma* ). To improve one's *karma* or escape *samsara* by pure acts, thought, and/or devotion is the aim of every Hindu.

## Islam

**Founded:** 622 AD in Medina, Arabian peninsula.

**Founder:** Mohammed (ca. 570-632), the Prophet.

**Sacred texts:** *Koran,* the words of God. *Hadith,* collections of the sayings of the Prophet.

**Organization:** Theoretically the state and religious community are one, administered by a caliph. In practice, Islam is a loose collection of congregations united by a very conservative tradition. Islam is basically egalitarian and non-authoritarian.

**Practice:** Every Moslem has 5 duties: to make the profession of faith ("There is no god but Allah ..."), pray 5 times a day, give a regular portion of his goods to charity, fast during the day in the month of Ramadan, and make at least one pilgrimage to Mecca if possible.

**Divisions:** The 2 major sects of Islam are the Sunni (orthodox) and the Shi'ah. The Shi'ah believe in 12 *imams,* perfect teachers, who still guide the faithful from Paradise. Shi'ah practice tends toward the ecstatic, while the Sunni is staid and simple. The Shi'ah sect affirms man's free will; the Sunni is deterministic. The mystic tradition in Islam is Sufism. A Sufi adept believes he has acquired a special inner knowledge direct from Allah.

**Location:** From the west coast of Africa to the Philippines across a broad band that includes Tanzania, Central Asia and western China, India, Malaysia, and Indonesia. Islam has several million adherents in the U.S.

**Beliefs:** Strictly monotheistic. God is creator of the universe, omnipotent, just, and merciful. Man is God's highest creation, but limited and commits sins. He is misled by Satan, an evil spirit. God revealed the *Koran* to Mohammed to guide men to the truth. Those who repent and sincerely submit to God return to a state of sinlessness. In the end, the sinless go to Paradise, a place of physical and spiritual pleasure, and the wicked burn in Hell.

## Judaism

**Founded:** About 1300 BCE.

**Founder:** Abraham is regarded as the founding patriarch, but the Torah of Moses is the basic source of the teachings.

**Sacred Texts:** The five books of Moses constitute the written Torah. Special sanctity is also assigned other writings of the Hebrew Bible— the teachings of oral Torah are recorded in the Talmud, the Midrash, and various commentaries.

**Organization:** Originally theocratic, Judaism has evolved a congregational polity. The basic institution is the local synagogue, operated by the congregation and led by a rabbi of their choice. Chief Rabbis in France and Great Britain have authority only over those who accept it; in Israel, the 2 Chief Rabbis have civil authority in family law.

**Practice:** Among traditional practitioners, almost all areas of life are governed by strict religious discipline. Sabbath and holidays are marked by special observances, and attendance at public worship is regarded as especially important then. The chief annual observances are Passover, celebrating the liberation of the Israelites from Egypt and marked by the ritual Seder meal in the home, and the 10 days from Rosh Hashana (New Year) to Yom Kippur (Day of Atonement), a period of fasting and penitence.

**Divisions:** Judaism is an unbroken spectrum from ultra conservative to ultra liberal, largely reflecting different points of view regarding the binding character of the prohibitions and duties—particularly the dietary and Sabbath observations—prescribed in the daily life of the Jew.

**Location:** Almost worldwide, with concentrations in Israel and the U.S.

**Beliefs:** Strictly monotheistic. God is the creator and absolute ruler of the universe. Men are free to choose to rebel against God's rule. God established a particular relationship with the Hebrew people: by obeying a divine law God gave them they would be a special witness to God's mercy and justice. The emphasis in Judaism is on ethical behavior (and, among the traditional, careful ritual obedience) as the true worship of God.

*(See following pages for discussion of Christian denominations.)*

## Major Christian Denominations:

*Italics* indicate that area which, generally speaking, most

| Denomination | Origins | Organization | Authority | Special rites |
|---|---|---|---|---|
| Baptists | In radical Reformation objections to infant baptism, demands for church-state separation; John Smyth, English Separatist in 1609; Roger Williams, 1638, Providence, R.I. | Congregational, *i.e.,* each local church is autonomous. | Scripture; some Baptists, particularly in the South, interpret the Bible literally. | Baptism, after about age 12, by total immersion; Lord's Supper. |
| Church of Christ (Disciples) | Among evangelical Presbyterians in Ky. (1804) and Penn. (1809), in distress over Protestant factionalism and decline of fervor. Organized 1832. | Congregational. | *"Where the Scriptures speak, we speak; where the Scriptures are silent, we are silent."* | Adult baptism, Lord's Supper (weekly). |
| Episcopalians | Henry VIII separated English Catholic Church from Rome, 1534, for political reasons. Protestant Episcopal Church in U.S. founded 1789. | *Bishops, in apostolic succession. are elected by diocesan representatives; part of Anglican Communion, symbolically headed by Archbishop of Canterbury.* | Scripture as interpreted by tradition, esp. 39 Articles (1563); not dogmatic. Tri-annual convention of bishops, priests, and laymen. | Infant baptism, Holy Communion, others. Sacrament is symbolic, but has real spiritual effect. |
| Lutherans | Martin Luther in Wittenberg, Germany, 1517, objected to Catholic doctrine of salvation by merit and sale of indulgences; break complete by 1519. | Varies from congregational to episcopal; in U.S. a combination of regional synods and congregational polities is most common. | *Scripture, and tradition as spelled out in Augsburg Confession (1530) and other creeds. These confessions of faith are binding although interpretations vary.* | Infant baptism, Lord's Supper. Christ's true body and blood present "in, with, and under the bread and wine." |
| Methodists | Rev. John Wesley began movement, 1738, within Church of England. First U.S. denomination Baltimore, 1784. | Conference and superintendent system. *In United Methodist Church, general superintendents are bishops—not a priestly order, only an office—who are elected for life.* | Scripture as interpreted by tradition, reason, and experience. | Baptism of infants or adults, Lord's Supper commanded. Other rites, inc. marriage, ordination, solemnize personal commitments. |
| Mormons | In visions of the Angel Moroni by Joseph Smith, 1827, in New York, in which he received a new revelation on golden tablets: *The Book of Mormon.* | Theocratic; all male adults are in priesthood which culminates in Council of 12 Apostles and 1st Presidency (1st President, 2 counselors). | *The Bible, Book of Mormon and other revelations to Smith, and certain pronouncements of the 1st Presidency.* | Baptism, at age 8, laying on of hands (which confers the gift of the Holy Spirit), Lord's Supper. Temple rites: baptism for the dead, marriage for eternity, others. |
| Orthodox | Original Christian proselytizing in 1st century; broke with Rome, 1054, after centuries of doctrinal disputes and diverging traditions. | Synods of bishops in autonomous, usually national, churches elect a patriarch, archbishop or metropolitan. These men, as a group, are the heads of the church. | Scripture, tradition, and the first 7 church councils up to Nicaea II in 787. Bishops in council have authority in doctrine and policy. | Seven sacraments: infant baptism and anointing, Eucharist (both bread and wine), ordination, penance, anointing of the sick, marriage. |
| Pentecostal | In Topeka, Kansas (1901), and Los Angeles (1906) in reaction to loss of evangelical fervor among Methodists and other denominations. | Originally a movement, not a formal organization, Pentecostalism now has a variety of organized forms and continues also as a movement. | Scripture, individual charismatic leaders, the teachings of the Holy Spirit. | *Spirit baptism, esp. as shown in "speaking in tongues"; healing and sometimes exorcism; adult baptism, Lord's Supper.* |
| Presbyterians | In Calvinist Reformation in 1500s; differed with Lutherans over sacraments, church government. John Knox founded Scotch Presbyterian church about 1560. | *Highly structured representational system of ministers and laypersons (presbyters) in local, regional and national bodies. (synods).* | Scripture. | Infant baptism, Lord's Supper; bread and wine symbolize Christ's spiritual presence. |
| Roman Catholics | Traditionally, by Jesus who named St. Peter the 1st Vicar; historically, in early Christian proselytizing and the conversion of imperial Rome in the 4th century. | Hierarchy with supreme power vested in Pope elected by cardinals. Councils of Bishops advise on matters of doctrine and policy. | *The Pope, when speaking for the whole church in matters of faith and morals, and tradition, which is partly recorded in scripture and expressed in church councils.* | Seven sacraments: baptism, contrition and penance, confirmation, Eucharist, marriage, ordination, and anointing of the sick (unction). |
| United Church of Christ | *By ecumenical union, 1957, of Congregationalists and Evangelical & Reformed, representing both Calvinist and Lutheran traditions.* | Congregational; a General Synod, representative of all congregations, sets general policy. | Scripture. | Infant baptism, Lord's Supper. |

# How Do They Differ?

distinguishes that denomination from any other.

| Practice | Ethics | Doctrine | Other | Denomination |
|---|---|---|---|---|
| Worship style varies from staid to evangelistic. Extensive missionary activity. | Usually opposed to alcohol and tobacco; sometimes tends toward a perfectionist ethical standard. | *No creed; true church is of believers only, who are all equal.* | Since no authority can stand between the believer and God, the Baptists are strong supporters of church-state separation. | Baptists |
| Tries to avoid any rite or doctrine not explicitly part of the 1st century church. Some congregations may reject instrumental music. | Some tendency toward perfectionism; increasing interest in social action programs. | Simple New Testament faith; avoids any elaboration not firmly based on Scripture. | Highly tolerant in doctrinal and religious matters; strongly supportive of scholarly education. | Church of Christ (Disciples) |
| Formal, based on *Book of Common Prayer* (1549); services range from austerely simple to highly elaborate. | Tolerant; sometimes permissive; some social action programs. | *Apostles' Creed* is basic; otherwise, considerable variation ranges from rationalist and liberal to acceptance of most Roman Catholic dogma. | Strongly ecumenical, holding talks with all other branches of Christendom. | Episcopalians |
| Relatively simple formal liturgy with emphasis on the sermon. | Generally, conservative in personal and social ethics; doctrine of "2 kingdoms" (worldly and holy) supports conservatism in secular affairs. | Salvation by faith alone through grace. Lutheranism has made major contributions to Protestant theology. | Though still somewhat divided along ethnic lines (German, Swede, etc.), main divisions are between fundamentalists and liberals. | Lutherans |
| Worship style varies widely by denomination, local church, geography. | Originally pietist and perfectionist; always strong social activist elements. | No distinctive theological development; 25 Articles abridged from Church of England's 39 not binding. | In 1968, United Methodist Church joined pioneer English- and German-speaking groups. UMs leaders in ecumenical movement. | Methodists |
| Staid service with hymns, sermon. Secret temple ceremonies may be more elaborate. Strong missionary activity. | Temperance; strict tithing. Combine a strong work ethic with communal self-reliance. | God is a material being; he created the universe out of pre-existing matter; all persons can be saved and many will become divine. Most other beliefs are traditionally Christian. | Mormons regard mainline churches as apostate, corrupt. Reorganized Church (founded 1860) rejects most Mormon doctrine and practice except Book of Mormon. | Mormons |
| *Elaborate liturgy, usually in the vernacular, though extremely traditional. The liturgy is the essence of Orthodoxy. Veneration of icons.* | Tolerant; very little social action; divorce, remarriage permitted in some cases. Priests need not be celibate; bishops are. | Emphasis on Christ's resurrection, rather than crucifixion; the Holy Spirit proceeds from God the Father only. | Orthodox Church in America, originally under Patriarch of Moscow, was granted autonomy in 1970. Greek Orthodox do not recognize this autonomy. | Orthodox |
| Loosely structured service with rousing hymns and sermons, culminating in spirit baptism. | Usually, emphasis on perfectionism with varying degrees of tolerance. | Simple traditional beliefs, usually Protestant, with emphasis on the immediate presence of God in the Holy Spirit. | Once confined to lower-class "holy rollers," Pentecostalism now appears in mainline churches and has established middle-class congregations. | Pentecostal |
| A simple, sober service in which the sermon is central. | Traditionally, a tendency toward strictness with firm church- and self-discipline; otherwise tolerant. | Emphasizes the sovereignty and justice of God; no longer doctrinaire. | While traces of belief in predestination (that God has foreordained salvation for the "elect") remain, this area is no longer a central element in Presbyterianism. | Presbyterians |
| Relatively elaborate ritual; wide variety of public and private rites, eg., mass, rosary recitation, processions, novenas. | Theoretically very strict; tolerant in practice on most issues. Divorce and remarriage not accepted. Celibate clergy, except in Eastern rite. | Highly elaborated. Salvation by merit gained through faith. Unusual development of doctrines surrounding Mary. Dogmatic. | Roman Catholicism went through a period of relatively rapid change as a result of Vatican Council II. | Roman Catholics |
| Usually simple services with emphasis on the sermon. | Tolerant; some social action emphasis. | Standard Protestant; *Statement of Faith* (1959) is not binding. | The 2 main churches in the 1957 union represented earlier unions with small groups of almost every Protestant denomination. | United Church of Christ |

# NATIONS OF THE WORLD

As of mid-1993

The nations of the world are listed in alphabetical order. Initials in the following articles include UN (United Nations), OAS (Org. of American States), NATO (North Atlantic Treaty Org.), EC (European Communities, or Common Market), OAU (Org. of African Unity), ILO (Intl. Labor Org.), FAO (Food & Agriculture Org.), WHO (World Health Org.), IMF (Intl. Monetary Fund), GATT (General Agreement on Tarriffs & Trade), CIS (Commonwealth of Independent States). **Sources:** U.S. Dept. of State; U.S. Census Bureau; The World Factbook; International Monetary Fund; UN Statistical Yearbook; UN Demographic Yearbook; International Iron and Steel Institute; The Statesman's Year-Book; Encyclopaedia Britannica; Funk & Wagnalls New Encyclopedia. All embassy addresses are Wash., DC; area codes (202), unless otherwise noted. Literacy rates are usually based on the ability to read and write on a lower elementary school level. The concept of literacy is changing in the industrialized countries, where literacy is defined as the ability to read instructions necessary for a job or a license. By these standards, illiteracy may be more common than present rates suggest. Per person figures in communications and health sections are post-1988.

*See pages 481-496 for full-color maps and flags.*

## Afghanistan

### Republic of Afghanistan

### De Afghanistan Jamhuriat

**People: Population** (1992 est.): 16,095,000. **Pop. density:** 63 per sq. mi. **Urban** (1990): 18%. **Ethnic groups:** Pushtun 38%; Tajik 25%; Uzbek 6%; Hazara 19%. **Languages:** Pushtu, Dari Persian (spoken by Tajiks, Hazaras), Uzbek (Turkic). **Religions:** Sunni Moslem 74%, Shi'a Moslem 5%.

**Geography: Area:** 251,773 sq. mi., about the size of Texas. **Location:** In SW Asia, NW of the Indian subcontinent. **Neighbors:** Pakistan on E, S, Iran on W, Turkmenistan, Tajikistan, Uzbekistan on N; the NE tip touches China. **Topography:** The country is landlocked and mountainous, much of it over 4,000 ft. above sea level. The Hindu Kush Mts. tower 16,000 ft. above Kabul and reach a height of 25,000 ft. to the E. Trade with Pakistan flows through the 35-mile-long Khyber Pass. The climate is dry, with extreme temperatures, and there are large desert regions, though mountain rivers produce intermittent fertile valleys. **Capital:** Kabul. **Cities** (1988 est.): Kabul 1.4 mln.

**Government: Type:** In transition. **Head of state:** Pres. Burhanuddin Rabbani; in office: June 28, 1992. **Local divisions:** 30 provinces. **Defense:** 15% of GDP (1990).

**Economy: Industries:** Textiles, furniture, cement. **Chief crops:** Nuts, wheat, fruits. **Minerals:** Copper, coal, zinc, iron. **Other resources:** Wool, hides, karacul pelts. **Arable land:** 13%. **Livestock** (1990): cattle: 1.6 mln.; sheep: 13 mln. **Electricity prod.** (1991): 1.4 bln. kWh. **Labor force:** agriculture supports about 80% of the population.

**Finance: Monetary unit:** Afghani (Mar. 1993: 50.60 = $1 US). **Gross domestic product** (1989): $3.1 bln. **Per capita GDP:** $220. **Imports** (1991): $874 mln.; partners: CIS 55%, Jap. 8%. **Exports** (1991): $236 mln.; partners: CIS 72%. **International reserves less gold** (Feb. 1992): $229 mln. **Gold:** 965,000 oz t. **Consumer prices** (change in 1991): 56%.

**Transport: Motor vehicles:** in use (1990): 31,000 passenger cars, 30,000 comm. vehicles. **Civil aviation** (1989): 194 mln. passenger-km.

**Communications: Television sets:** 1 per 169 persons; **Radios:** 1 per 11 persons. **Telephones in use:** 1 per 443 persons. **Daily newspaper circ.** (1988): 10 per 1,000 pop.

**Health: Life expectancy at birth** (1992): 45 male; 43 female. **Births** (per 1,000 pop. 1992): 44. **Deaths** (per 1,000 pop. 1991): 20. **Natural increase:** 2.3%. **Hospital beds:** 1 per 2,054 persons. **Physicians:** 1 per 4,797 persons. **Infant mortality** (per 1,000 live births 1992): 164.

**Education** (1990): Literacy: 29%. Over 88% of adults have no formal schooling.

**Major International Organizations:** UN (World Bank, IMF) **Embassy:** 2341 Wyoming Ave. NW, 20008; 234-3770.

Afghanistan, occupying a favored invasion route since antiquity, has been variously known as Ariana or Bactria (in ancient times) and Khorasan (in the Middle Ages). Foreign empires alternated rule with local emirs and kings until the 18th century, when a unified kingdom was established. In 1973, a military coup ushered in a republic.

Pro-Soviet leftists took power in a bloody 1978 coup, and concluded an economic and military treaty with the USSR.

Late in Dec. 1979, the USSR began a massive military airlift into Kabul. The three-month-old regime of Hafizullah Amin ended with a Soviet-backed coup, Dec. 27. He was replaced by Babrak Karmal, a more pro-Soviet leader. Soviet troops fanned out over Afghanistan, fighting Islamic rebels. Fighting continued for 9 years as the Soviets found themselves engaged in a protracted guerrilla war.

An UN-mediated agreement was signed Apr. 14, 1988 providing for the withdrawal of Soviet troops from Afghanistan, creation of a neutral Afghan state, and repatriation of millions of Afghan refugees. The U.S. and USSR pledged to serve as guarantors of the agreement. Afghan rebels rejected the pact and vowed to continue fighting while the "Soviets and their puppets" remained in Afghanistan.

The Soviets disclosed that during the war some 15,000 soldiers were killed. They completed their troop withdrawal Feb. 15, 1989; fighting between Afghan rebels and government forces ensued.

Communist Pres. Najibullah resigned Apr. 16, 1992 as competing guerrilla forces advanced on Kabul. The rebels achieved power, Apr. 28, ending 14 years of Soviet-backed regimes. Over 2 million Afghans had been killed and 6 million had fled the country since 1979. There were immediate clashes between moderates and Islamac fundamentalist forces. Burhanuddin Rabbani, a guerrilla leader, became president June 28, 1992. Fierce fighting continued around Kabul in 1993.

## Albania

### Republic of Albania

### Republika e Shqipërisë

**People: Population** (1991 est.): 3,285,000. **Pop. density:** 295 per sq. mi. **Urban** (1991): 35%. **Ethnic groups:** Albanians (Gegs in N, Tosks in S) 90%, Greeks 8%. **Languages:** Albanian, Greek. **Religions:** Moslem 70%, Greek Orthodox 20%, Roman Catholic 10%.

**Geography: Area:** 11,100 sq. mi., slightly larger than Maryland. **Location:** On SE coast of Adriatic Sea. **Neighbors:** Greece on S, Yugoslavia on N, Macedonia on E. **Topography:** Apart from a narrow coastal plain, Albania consists of hills and mountains covered with scrub forest, cut by small E-W rivers. **Capital:** Tiranë. **Cities** (1990 est.): Tiranë 243,000; Durres 85,000; Elbasin 84,000.

**Government: Type:** Democracy. **Head of state:** Pres. Sali Berisha; in office: Apr. 9, 1992. **Head of government:** Premier Alexander Meksi; in office: Apr. 13, 1992. **Local divisions:** 26 districts. **Defense:** 4.1% of GNP (1990).

**Economy: Industries:** Cement, textiles, food processing. **Chief crops:** Corn, wheat, cotton, potatoes, tobacco, fruits. **Minerals:** Chromium, coal, oil. **Other resources:** Forests. **Arable land:** 21%. **Livestock** (1991): 650,000 cattle; 1.6 mln. sheep. **Electricity prod.** (1990): 5.0 bln. kWh. **Labor force:** 60% agric; 40% ind. & comm.

**Finance: Monetary unit:** Lek (Nov. 1992: 109 = $1 US). **Gross national product** (1991): $4.0 bln. **Per capita GNP** (1987): $1,300. **Imports** (1991): $147 mln.; partners: Czech., Yugoslavia, Rom. **Exports** (1991): $80 mln.; partners: Czech., Yugoslavia, Italy. **National budget** (1991): $1.4 bln. expenditures.

**Chief ports:** Durres, Vlone, Sarande.

**Communications: Television sets:** 1 per 13 persons. **Radios:** 1 per 6 persons. **Daily newspaper circ.:** 48 per 1,000 pop.

**Health: Life expectancy at birth** (1992): 72.0 yrs. male; 79 yrs. female. **Births** (per 1,000 pop. 1992): 23. **Deaths** (per 1,000 pop. 1992): 5. **Natural increase:** 2.0%. **Hospital beds:** 1 per 176 persons. **Physicians:** 1 per 574 persons. **Infant mortality** (per 1,000 live births 1992): 27.

**Major International Organizations:** UN (FAO, WHO).

**Education** (1990): **Literacy:** 72%. Free and compulsory ages 7-15.

Ancient Illyria was conquered by Romans, Slavs, and Turks (15th century); the latter Islamized the population. Independent Albania was proclaimed in 1912, republic was formed in 1920. King Zog I ruled 1925-39, until Italy invaded.

Communist partisans took over in 1944, allied Albania with USSR, then broke with USSR in 1960 over de-Stalinization. Strong political alliance with China followed, leading to several billion dollars in aid, which was curtailed after 1974. China cut off aid in 1978 when Albania attacked its policies after the death of Chinese ruler Mao Tse-tung.

Large-scale purges of officials occurred during the 1970s. Enver Hoxha, the nation's ruler for 4 decades, died Apr. 11, 1985.

There was some liberalization in 1990, including measures providing for freedom to travel abroad and restoration of the right to practice religion.

In 1991, a general strike and urban opposition forced the communist cabinet to resign; a non-communist caretaker was installed. By March, over 40,000 Albanians had left their country and sailed to Italy. James Baker became the first U.S. secy. of state to visit Albania, June 22.

Albania's former Communists were routed in parliamentary elections Mar. 1992 amid economic collapse and social unrest. Berisha was elected as the first non-Communist president since World War II. Inflation was about 150%, unemployment was estimated at 70% nationwide, and almost all food came from foreign aid.

# Algeria

### Democratic and Popular Republic of Algeria

### al-Jumhuriya al-Jazāiriya ad-Dimuqratiya ash-Shabiya

**People: Population** (1992 est.); 26,666,000. **Age distrib. (%):** 0–14: 43.9; 15–59: 50.3; 60+: 5.8. **Pop. density:** 31 per sq. mi. **Urban** (1990): 51%. **Ethnic groups:** Arabs 75%, Berbers 25%. **Languages:** Arabic (official), Berber (indigenous language). **Religions:** Sunni Moslem (state religion).

**Geography: Area:** 918,497 sq. mi., more than 3 times the size of Texas. **Location:** In NW Africa, from Mediterranean Sea into Sahara Desert. **Neighbors:** Morocco on W, Mauritania, Mali, Niger on S, Libya, Tunisia on E. **Topography:** The Tell, located on the coast, comprises fertile plains 50-100 miles wide, with a moderate climate and adequate rain. Two major chains of the Atlas Mts., running roughly E-W, and reaching 7,000 ft., enclose a dry plateau region. Below lies the Sahara, mostly desert with major mineral resources. **Capital:** Algiers (El Djazair). **Cities** (1987 est.): El Djazair 1,483,000; Wahran 590,000; Qacentina 483,000.

**Government: Type:** Republic. **Head of state:** Pres. Ali Kafi; in office: July 1, 1992. **Head of government:** Prime Min. Redha Malek; in office: Aug. 21, 1993. **Local divisions:** 48 provinces. **Defense:** 1.8% of GDP (1992).

**Economy: Industries:** Oil, light industry, food processing. **Chief crops:** Grains, wine-grapes, potatoes, dates, olives, oranges. **Minerals:** Mercury, iron, zinc, lead. **Crude oil reserves** (1987): 4.8 bln. bbls. **Other resources:** Cork trees. **Arable land:** 3%; **Livestock** (1988): cattle: 1.7 mln.; sheep: 14 mln. **Electricity prod.** (1991): 16.7 bln. kWh. **Crude steel prod.** (1991): 767,000 metric tons. **Labor force:** 24% agric.; 40% ind. and commerce; 24% government, & services.

**Finance: Monetary Unit:** Dinar (Mar. 1993: 23 = $1 US). **Gross domestic product** (1990): $54 bln. **Per capita GDP:** $2,130. **Imports** (1991): $9.2 bln.; partners: EEC 64%. **Exports** (1991): $11.7 bln.; partners: EEC 74%. **National budget** (1990): $17.3 bln. **International reserves less gold** (Mar. 1993): $1.8 bln. **Gold:** 5.5 mln. oz t. **Consumer prices** (change in 1990): 26%

**Transport: Railroads** (1991): **Length:** 2,668 mi. **Motor vehicles:** in use (1990): 750,000 passenger cars, 500,000 comm. vehicles. **Chief ports:** El Djazair.

**Communications: Television sets:** 1 per 15 persons. **Radios:** 1 per 4 persons. **Telephones in use:** 1 per 23 persons. **Daily newspaper circ.** (1990): 53 per 1,000 pop.

**Health: Life expectancy at birth** (1992): 66 male; 68 female. **Births** (per 1,000 pop. 1992): 31 **Deaths** (per 1,000 pop. 1992): 7.0. **Natural increase:** 2.4%. **Hospital beds:** 1 per 393 persons. **Physicians:** 1 per 1,062 persons. **Infant mortality** (per 1,000 live births 1992): 57.

**Education** (1991): **Literacy:** 52%.

**Major International Organizations:** UN (FAO, IMF, WHO), OAU, Arab League, OPEC.

**Embassy:** 2118 Kalorama Rd. NW, 20008; 328-5300.

Earliest known inhabitants were ancestors of Berbers, followed by Phoenicians, Romans, Vandals, and, finally, Arabs. Turkey ruled 1518 to 1830, when France took control.

Large-scale European immigration and French cultural inroads did not prevent an Arab nationalist movement from launching guerrilla war. Peace, and French withdrawal, was negotiated with French Pres. Charles de Gaulle. One million Europeans left. Independence came July 5, 1962.

Ahmed Ben Bella was the victor of infighting and ruled 1962-65, when an army coup installed Col. Houari Boumedienne as leader.

In 1967, Algeria declared war on Israel, broke ties with U.S., and moved toward eventual military and political ties with the USSR. Some 500 died in riots protesting economic hardship in 1988. In 1989, voters approved a new constitution which cleared the way for a multiparty system and guaranteed "fundamental rights and freedoms" of Algerians.

The government canceled Jan. 1992 elections Islamic fundamentalists were expected to win and banned all nonreligious activities at Algeria's 10,000 mosques. Pres. Mohammed Boudiaf was assassinated June 29, 1992. There were several attacks on high-ranking officials by militant Moslem fundamentalists in 1993.

# Andorra

### Principality of Andorra

### Principat d'Andorra

**People: Population** (1992 est.): 54,000. **Age distrib. (%):** 0–14: 17.4; 14–59: 68.8; 60+: 13.8. **Pop. density:** 291 per sq. mi. **Ethnic groups:** Catalan 61%, Spanish 30%, Andorran 6%, French 3%. **Languages:** Catalan (official), Spanish, French. **Religion:** Roman Catholic.

**Geography: Area:** 185 sq. mi., half the size of New York City. **Location:** In Pyrenees Mtns. **Neighbors:** Spain on S, France on N. **Topography:** High mountains and narrow valleys over the country. **Capital:** Andorra la Vella.

**Government: Type:** Parliamentary democracy. **Head of government:** Oscar Ribas Reig; in office: May 4, 1992. **Local divisions:** 7 parishes.

**Economy: Industries:** Tourism, tobacco products. **Labor force:** 20% agric.; 80% ind. and commerce; services; government.

**Finance: Monetary unit:** French franc, Spanish peseta.

**Communications: Television sets:** 1 per 8 persons. **Radios:** 1 per 4 persons. **Telephones in use:** 1 per 2 persons.

**Health: Births** (per 1,000 pop. 1992): 10. **Deaths** (per 1,000 pop. 1992): 4. **Natural increase:** 0.7%.

**Education** (1992): **Literacy:** 99%. School compulsory to age 16.

**Major International Organizations:** UN.

Andorra was a co-principality, with joint sovereignty by France and the bishop of Urgel, from 1278 to 1993.

Tourism, especially skiing, is the economic mainstay. A free port, allowing for an active trading center, draws some 10 million tourists annually. The ensuing economic prosperity, accompanied by Andorra's virtual law-free status, gave rise to calls for reform.

Andorra voters chose to end a feudal system that had been in place for 715 years and adopt a parliamentary system of government Mar. 14, 1993.

# Angola

## Republic of Angola
## República de Angola

**People: Population** (1991 est.): 8,902,000. **Pop. density:** 18 per sq. mi. **Ethnic groups:** Ovimbundu 38%, Kimbundu 25%; Bakongo 13%. **Urban** (1991): 29%. **Languages:** Portuguese (official), various Bantu languages. **Religions:** Roman Catholic 38%, Protestant 15%, indigenous beliefs 47%.

**Geography: Area:** 481,353 sq. mi., larger than Texas and California combined. **Location:** In SW Africa on Atlantic coast. **Neighbors:** Namibia on S, Zambia on E, Zaire on N; Cabinda, an enclave separated from rest of country by short Atlantic coast of Zaire, borders Congo Republic. **Topography:** Most of Angola consists of a plateau elevated 3,000 to 5,000 feet above sea level, rising from a narrow coastal strip. There is also a temperate highland area in the west-central region, a desert in the S, and a tropical rain forest covering Cabinda. **Capital:** Luanda (1988 est.): 1.1 mln.

**Government: Type:** Republic. **Head of state:** Pres. Jose Eduardo dos Santos b. Aug. 28, 1942; in office: Sept. 20, 1979. Prime Min. Marcolino Moco; in office: Dec. 2, 1992. **Local divisions:** 18 provinces. **Defense:** 14.3% of GNP (1984).

**Economy: Industries:** Food processing, textiles, mining, tires, petroleum. **Chief crops:** Coffee, bananas. **Minerals:** Iron, diamonds (over 2 mln. carats a year), copper, phosphates, oil. **Livestock** (1991): cattle: 3.1 mln.; goats: 1 mln. **Crude oil reserves** (1987): 1.9 bln. bbls. **Arable land:** 3%. **Fish catch** (1990): 178,000 metric tons. **Electricity prod.** (1991): 770 mln. kWh. **Labor force:** 85% agric., 15% industry.

**Finance: Monetary unit:** new Kwanza (Nov. 1992: 550 = $1 US). **Gross domestic product** (1991): $8.3 bln. **Per capita GDP:** $950. **Imports** (1991): $1.3 bln.; partners: Portugal 29%, Fra. 9%; U.S. 9%. **Exports** (1991): $3.4 bln.; partners: U.S. 56%.

**Transport: Motor vehicles:** in use (1990): 130,000 passenger cars, 44,000 comm. vehicles. **Chief ports:** Cabinda, Lobito, Luanda.

**Communications: Television sets:** 1 per 200 persons. Radios: 1 per 22 persons. **Telephones in use:** 1 per 132 persons. **Daily newspaper circ.** (1984): 13 per 1,000 pop.

**Health: Life expectancy at birth** (1992): 43 male; 47 female. **Births** (per 1,000 pop. 1992): 46. **Deaths** (per 1,000 pop. 1992): 19. **Natural increase:** 2.7%. **Hospital beds:** 1 per 845 persons. **Physicians:** 1 per 15,136 persons. **Infant mortality** (per 1,000 live births 1992): 151.

**Education** (1992): **Literacy:** 40%.
**Major International Organizations:** UN (ILO, WHO), OAU.

From the early centuries AD to 1500, Bantu tribes penetrated most of the region. Portuguese came in 1583, allied with the Bakongo kingdom in the north, and developed the slave trade. Large-scale colonization did not begin until the 20th century, when 400,000 Portuguese immigrated.

A guerrilla war begun in 1961 lasted until 1975, when Portugal granted independence. Fighting then erupted between three rival rebel groups —the National Front, based in Zaire, the Soviet-backed Popular Movement for the Liberation of Angola (MPLA), and the National Union for the Total Independence of Angola (UNITA), aided by the U.S. and S. Africa. The civil war killed thousands of blacks, drove most whites to emigrate, and completed economic ruin. Cuban troops and Soviet aid helped the MPLA win control of most of the country by 1976 and gain wide recognition as the government of Angola, but UNITA continued fighting.

An agreement was signed in Dec. 1988 between Angola, Cuba, and S. Africa on a timetable for withdrawal of Cuban troops, completed May 25, 1991. The 16-year war ended May 1, 1991, as the government and UNITA signed a peace agreement which would lead to democracy.

Elections were held in Sept. 1992, but fighting again broke out, as UNITA rejected the presidential election results, and continued into 1993, with UNITA forces holding about 50 percent of the nation's territory. The U.S. formally recognized the government of Angola, May 19, 1993, for the first time since independence.

# Antigua and Barbuda

**People: Population** (1992 est.) 64,000 (incl. Redonda). **Urban:** (1990) 32%. **Ethnic groups:** Mostly African. **Language:** English (official). **Religion:** Predominantly Church of England.

**Geography: Area:** 171 sq. mi. **Location:** Eastern Caribbean. **Neighbors:** approx. 30 mi. north of Guadeloupe. **Capital:** St. John's, (1988 est.) 27,000.

**Government: Type:** Constitutional monarchy with British-style parliament. **Head of state:** Queen Elizabeth II; represented by Sir Wilfred E. Jacobs. **Head of government:** Prime Min. Vere Cornwall Bird; b. Dec. 7, 1910; in office Nov. 1, 1981.

**Economy: Industries:** Manufacturing, tourism. **Arable land:** 18%.

**Finance: Monetary unit:** East Caribbean dollar (June 1993): 2.70 = $1 U.S. **Gross domestic product** (1990): $350 mln.

**Health: Infant mortality** (per 1,000 live births 1992): 20.
**Education** (1990): **Literacy:** 90%.
**Major International Organizations:** UN, Commonwealth of Nations.

**Embassy:** 2400 International Dr., NW 20008; 362-5122.

Columbus landed on Antigua in 1493. The British colonized it in 1632.

The British associated state of Antigua achieved independence as Antigua and Barbuda on Nov. 1, 1981. The government maintains close relations with the U.S., United Kingdom, and Venezuela.

# Argentina

## Argentine Republic
## República Argentina

**People: Population** (1992 est.): 32,901,000. **Age distrib.** (%): 0–14: 30.3; 15–59: 56.8; 60+: 12.9. **Pop. density:** 30 per sq. mi. **Urban** (1991): 87%. **Ethnic groups:** Europeans 95% (Spanish, Italian), Indians, Mestizos, Arabs. **Languages:** Spanish (official), Italian. **Religions:** Roman Catholic 92%.

**Geography: Area:** 1,065,189 sq. mi., 4 times the size of Texas, second largest in S. America. **Location:** Occupies most of southern S. America. **Neighbors:** Chile on W, Bolivia, Paraguay on N, Brazil, Uruguay on NE. **Topography:** The mountains in W: the Andean, Central, Misiones, and Southern. Aconcagua is the highest peak in the Western hemisphere, alt. 22,834 ft. E of the Andes are heavily wooded plains, called the Gran Chaco in the N, and the fertile, treeless Pampas in the central region. Patagonia, in the S, is bleak and arid. Rio de la Plata, 170 by 140 mi., is mostly fresh water, from 2,485-mi. Parana and 1,000-mi. Uruguay rivers. **Capital:** Buenos Aires. (The Senate has approved the moving of the capital to the Patagonia Region). **Cities** (1991 est.): Buenos Aires 12,582,000 met.; Cordoba 1.1 mln.; Rosario 1.0 mln. (met.).

**Government: Type:** Republic. **Head of state:** Pres. Carlos Saúl Menem; b. July 2, 1930; in office: July 8, 1989. **Local divisions:** 28 provinces, 1 federal dist. **Defense:** 1.4% of GNP (1991).

**Economy: Industries:** Food processing, flour milling, chemicals, textiles, machinery, autos. **Chief crops:** Grains, corn, grapes, linseed, sugar, tobacco, rice, soybeans, citrus fruits. **Minerals:** Oil, lead, zinc, iron, copper, tin, uranium. **Crude oil reserves** (1987): 2.1 bln. bbls. **Arable land:** 9%. **Livestock** (1991): cattle: 50 mln.; sheep: 27 mln. **Fish catch** (1990): 555,000 metric tons. **Electricity prod.** (1991): 46.0 bln. kWh. **Crude steel prod.** (1991): 2.9 mln. metric tons. **Labor force:** 19% agric.; 36% ind. and comm.; 20% services.

**Finance: Monetary unit:** Peso (July 1993: .99 = $1 US). **Gross domestic product** (1991): $101.2 bln. **Per capita GDP:** $3,100. **Imports** (1991): $8.0 bln.; partners: U.S. 21%, W. Ger. 9%, Braz. 16%, Jap. 7%. **Exports** (1991): $12.3 bln.; partners: CIS 13%, Neth. 9%, U.S. 12%. **Tourists** (1990): receipts: $903 mln. **National budget** (1991): $17.3 bln. expenditures. **International reserves less gold** (Jan. 1992): $6.6 bln. **Gold:** 4.12 mln. oz t. **Consumer prices** (change in 1992): 24.9%.

**Transport: Railroads** (1988): **Length:** 21,198 mi. **Motor vehicles:** in use (1989): 4.0 mln. passenger cars, 1.5 mln. comm. vehicles. **Civil aviation:** (1991) 8.2 mln. passenger-km. 1,473 airports **Chief ports:** Buenos Aires, Bahia Blanca, La Plata.

**Communications: Television sets:** 1 per 4 persons. **Radios:** 1 per 1 person. **Telephones in use:** 1 per 9 persons. **Daily newspaper circ.** (1986): 88 per 1,000 pop.

**Health: Life expectancy at birth** (1992): 67 male; 74 female. **Births** (per 1,000 pop. 1992): 20. **Deaths** (per 1,000 pop. 1992): 9. **Natural increase:** 1.2%. **Hospital beds:** 1 per 150 persons. **Physicians:** 1 per 326 persons. **Infant mortality** (per 1,000 live births 1992): 31.

**Education** (1992): **Literacy:** 95%. **Years compulsory:** 7.

**Major International Organizations:** UN (WHO, IMF, FAO), OAS.

**Embassy:** 1600 New Hampshire Ave. NW 20009; 939-6400.

Nomadic Indians roamed the Pampas when Spaniards arrived, 1515-16, led by Juan Diaz de Solis. Nearly all the Indians were killed by the late 19th century. The colonists won independence, 1816, and a long period of disorders ended in a strong central-ized government.

Large-scale Italian, German, and Spanish immigration in the decades after 1880 spurred modernization, making Argentina the most prosperous, educated, and industrialized of the major Latin American nations. Social reforms were enacted in the 1920s, but military coups prevailed 1930-46, until the election of Gen. Juan Peron as president.

Peron, with his wife Eva Duarte, effected labor reforms, but also suppressed speech and press freedoms, closed religious schools, and ran the country into debt. A 1955 coup exiled Pe-ron, who was followed by a series of military and civilian re-gimes. Peron returned in 1973, and was once more elected president. He died 10 months later, succeeded by his wife, Isa-bel, who had been vice president, and who became the first woman head of state in the Western hemisphere.

A military junta ousted Mrs. Peron in 1976 amid charges of corruption. Under a continuing state of siege, the army battled guerrillas and leftists, killed 5,000 people, and jailed and tortured others. On Dec. 9, 1985, after a trial of 5 months and nearly 1,000 witnesses, 5 former junta members, including ex-presi-dents Jorge Videla and Gen. Roberto Eduardo Viola, were found guilty of murder and human rights abuses.

A severe worsening in economic conditions placed extreme pressure on the military government.

Argentine troops seized control of the British-held Falkland Islands on Apr. 2, 1982. Both countries had claimed sovereignty over the islands, located 250 miles off the Argentine coast, since 1833. The British dispatched a task force and declared a total air and sea blockade around the Falklands. Fighting began May 1; several hundred lost their lives as the result of the destruction of a British destroyer and the sinking of an Argentine cruiser.

British troops landed in force on East Falkland Island May 21. By June 2, the British had surrounded Stanley, the capital city and Argentine stronghold. The Argentine troops surrendered, June 14; Argentine President Leopoldo Galtieri resigned June 17.

Democratic rule returned to Argentina in 1983 as Raul Alfon-sin's Radical Civic Union gained an absolute majority in the pres-idential electoral college and Congress. In 1989 the nation was plagued by severe financial problems as inflation reached crisis levels; over 6,000%. The hyperinflation sparked a week of loot-ing and rioting in several cities; the government declared a 30-day state of siege May 29.

The government unveiled harsh economic measures in an ef-fort to combat spiraling inflation, control government spending, and restructure the foreign debt 1991-92.

## Armenia
### Republic of Armenia
### Haikakan Hanrapetoutioun

**People: Population** (1992 est.): 3,415,000. **Pop. density:** 302 per sq. mi. **Urban** (1991): 70%. **Language:** Armenian. **Eth-nic groups:** Armenian 93%. **Religion:** Mostly Christian.

**Geography: Area:** 11,306 sq. mi., slightly larger than Mary-land. **Neighbors:** Georgia on N., Azerbaijan on E., Iran on S., Turkey on W. **Topography:** Mountainous with many peaks above 10,000 ft. **Capital:** Yerevan.

**Government: Type:** Republic. **Head of state:** Pres. Levon Ter-Petrosyan; in office: Oct. 16, 1991. **Head of government:** Gagik Arutyunyaw.

**Economy: Industries:** Mining, chemicals. **Chief crops:** Cot-ton, figs, grain. **Minerals:** Copper, zinc. **Arable land:** 10%.

**Finance: Monetary unit:** Ruble.

**Transport: Vehicles** (1989): 230,000 passenger cars.

**Communications: Television sets:** 1 per 5 persons. **Radios:** 1 per 5 persons. **Telephones:** 1 per 6 persons. **Newspaper circ.:** 468 per 1,000 pop.

**Health: Life expectancy at birth** (1992): 68 male; 74 female. **Physicians:** 1 per 246 persons. **Hospital beds:** 1 per 117 per-sons. **Infant mortality** (per 1,000 live births 1992): 35.

**Major International Organizations:** UN (IMF), CIS.

**Embassy:** 122 C St. NW 20001; 628-5766.

Armenia is an ancient country, parts of which are now in Tur-key and Iran. Present-day Armenia was set up as a Soviet Re-public Apr. 2, 1921. It joined Georgian and Azerbaijan SSRs Mar. 12, 1922 to form the Transcaucasian SFSR, which became part of the USSR Dec. 30, 1922. Armenia became a constituent republic of the USSR Dec. 5, 1936. An earthquake struck Arme-nia Dec. 7, 1988; over 55,000 were killed and several cities and towns were left in ruins. Armenia declared independence Sept. 23, 1991, and became an independent state when the USSR disbanded Dec. 26, 1991.

Fighting between mostly Christian Armenia and mostly Mos-lem Azerbaijan escalated in 1992 and continued in 1993. Each country claimed Nagorno-Karabakh, an enclave in Azerbaijan that has a majority population of ethnic Armenians.

## Australia
### Commonwealth of Australia

**People: Population** (1992 est.): 17,576,000 (incl. Macquarie Island). **Age distrib.** (%): 0–14: 21.9; 15–59; 62.6; ; 59 +: 15.5. **Pop. density:** 5.9 per sq. mi. **Urban** (1990): 85%. **Ethnic groups:** European 95%, Asian 4%, aborigines (including mixed) 1.5%. **Languages:** English, aboriginal languages. **Religions:** Anglican 26%, other Protestant 25%, Roman Catholic 26%.

**Geography: Area:** 2,966,200 sq. mi., almost as large as the continental U.S. **Location:** SE of Asia, Indian O. is W and S, Pa-cific O. (Coral, Tasman seas) is E; they meet N of Australia in Timor and Arafura seas: Tasmania lies 150 mi. S of Victoria state, across Bass Strait. **Neighbors:** Nearest are Indonesia, Papua New Guinea on N, Solomons, Fiji, and New Zealand on E. **Topography:** An island continent. The Great Dividing Range along the E coast has Mt. Kosciusko, 7,310 ft. The W plateau rises to 2,000 ft., with arid areas in the Great Sandy and Great Victoria deserts. The NW part of Western Australia and Northern Terr. are arid and hot. The NE has heavy rainfall and Cape York Peninsula has jungles. The Murray R. rises in New South Wales and flows 1,600 mi. to the Indian O. **Capital:** Canberra. **Cities** (1991 est.): Sydney 3,600,000; Melbourne 3,000,000; Brisbane 1,200,000; Perth 1,200,000; Adelaide 1,000,000.

**Government: Type:** Democratic, federal state system. **Head of state:** Queen Elizabeth II, represented by Gov.-Gen. William Hayden; in office: Feb. 16, 1989. **Head of government:** Prime Min. Paul Keating; b. Jan. 18, 1944; in office: Dec. 20, 1991. **Lo-cal divisions:** 6 states, 2 territories. **Defense:** 2.3% of GDP (1992).

**Economy: Industries:** Iron, steel, textiles, electrical equip., chemicals, autos, aircraft, ships, machinery. **Chief crops:** Wheat (a leading export), barley, oats, corn, hay, sugar, wine, fruit, veg-etables. **Minerals:** Coal, copper, iron, lead, tin, uranium, zinc. **Crude oil reserves** (1987): 1.6 bln. bbls. **Other resources:** Wool (30% of world output). **Arable land:** 9%. **Livestock** (1991): cattle: 22 mln.; sheep: 162 mln.; pigs: 2.5 mln. **Fish catch** (1990): 175,000 metric tons. **Electricity prod.** (1991): 155 bln. kWh. **Crude steel prod.** (1991): 6.1 mln. metric tons. **Labor force:** 6% agric.; 33% finance & services; 36% trade & manuf.

**Finance: Monetary unit:** Dollar (July 1993: 1.47 = $1.00 US). **Gross domestic product** (1991): $311 bln. **Per capita income:** $18,054. **Imports** (1992): $43.7 bln; partners: U.S. 21%, Jap. 20%, UK 7%. **Exports** (1992): $42.4 bln.; partners: Jap. 27%, U.S. 11%, NZ 5%. **Tourists** (1990): $3.7 bln. re-ceipts. **National budget** (1991): $93 bln. expenditures. **Interna-tional reserves less gold** (Mar. 1993): $9.3 bln. **Gold:** 7.93 mln. oz t. **Consumer prices** (change in 1992): 1.0%.

**Transport: Railroads** (1991): **Length:** 22,051 mi. **Motor ve-hicles:** in use (1990): 7.6 mln. passenger cars, 2.1 mln. comm.

vehicles. **Civil aviation** (1990): 23.0 mln. passenger-km.; 441 airports with scheduled flights. **Chief ports:** Sydney, Melbourne, Newcastle, Port Kembla, Fremantle, Geelong.

**Communications: Television sets:** 1 per 2 persons. **Radios:** 1 per 2 persons. **Telephones in use:** 1 per 2 persons. **Daily newspaper circ.** (1988): 405 per 1,000 pop.

**Health: Life expectancy at birth** (1992): 74 male; 80 female. **Births** (per 1,000 pop. 1992): 15. **Deaths** (per 1,000 pop. 1992): 8. **Natural increase:** .8%. **Hospital beds:** 1 per 199 persons. **Physicians:** 1 per 438 persons. **Infant mortality** (per 1,000 live births 1992): 8.

**Education** (1992): **Literacy:** 99%. **School:** compulsory to age 15; attendance 94%.

**Major International Organizations:** UN and all its specialized agencies, OECD, Commonwealth of Nations.

**Embassy:** 1601 Massachusetts Ave NW 20036; 797-3000.

Capt. James Cook explored the E coast in 1770, when the continent was inhabited by a variety of different tribes. The first settlers, beginning in 1788, were mostly convicts, soldiers, and government officials. By 1830, Britain had claimed the entire continent, and the immigration of free settlers began to accelerate. The commonwealth was proclaimed Jan. 1, 1901. Northern Terr. was granted limited self-rule July 1, 1978.

| States | Area (sq. mi.) | Population (1991 cen.) |
|---|---|---|
| New South Wales, Sydney | 309,500 | 5,731,926 |
| Victoria, Melbourne | 87,900 | 4,243,719 |
| Queensland, Brisbane | 666,990 | 2,976,617 |
| Western Aust., Perth | 975,100 | 1,586,393 |
| South Aust., Adelaide | 379,900 | 1,400,656 |
| Tasmania, Hobart | 26,200 | 452,847 |
| Aust. Capital Terr., Canberra | 900 | 280,085 |
| Northern Terr., Darwin | 519,800 | 175,253 |

Australia's racially discriminatory immigration policies were abandoned in 1973, after 3 million Europeans (half British) had entered since 1945. The 50,000 aborigines and 150,000 part-aborigines are mostly detribalized, but there are several preserves in the Northern Territory. They remain economically disadvantaged.

Australia's agricultural success makes the country among the top exporters of beef, lamb, wool, and wheat. Major mineral deposits have been developed as well, largely for exports. Industrialization has been completed.

Australia harbors many plant and animal species not found elsewhere, including the kangaroo, koalas, platypus, dingo (wild dog), Tasmanian devil (racoon-like marsupial), wombat (bear-like marsupial), and barking and frilled lizards.

The nation suffered through a deep recession 1990-93. Unemployment was 11.1 percent in Feb. 1993.

## Australian External Territories

**Norfolk Is.,** area 13½ sq. mi., pop. (1990) 1,800, was taken over, 1914. The soil is very fertile, suitable for citrus fruits, bananas, and coffee. Many of the inhabitants are descendants of the Bounty mutineers, moved to Norfolk 1856 from Pitcairn Is. Australia offered the island limited home rule, 1978.

**Coral Sea Is. Territory,** 1 sq. mi., is administered from Norfolk Is.

**Territory of Ashmore and Cartier Is.,** area 2 sq. mi., in the Indian O. came under Australian authority 1934 and are administered as part of Northern Territory. **Heard** and **McDonald Is.** are administered by the Dept. of Science.

**Cocos (Keeling) Is.,** 27 small coral islands in the Indian O. 1,750 mi. NW of Australia. Pop. (1990) 600, area: 5½ sq. mi. The residents voted to become part of Australia, Apr. 1984.

**Christmas Is.** 52 sq. mi., pop. 1,700 (1991), 230 mi. S of Java, was transferred by Britain in 1958. It has phosphate deposits.

**Australian Antarctic Territory** was claimed by Australia in 1933, including 2,362,000 sq. mi. of territory S of 60th parallel S Lat. and between 160th-45th meridians E Long. It does not include Adelie Coast.

# Austria
## Republic of Austria
## Republik Österreich

**People: Population** (1992 est.): 7,867,000. **Age distrib. (%):** 0–14: 17.4; 15–59: 62.1; 60+: 20.5. **Pop. density:** 243 per sq. mi. **Urban** (1991): 54%. **Ethnic groups:** German 99%, Slovene, Croatian. **Languages:** German. **Religions:** Roman Catholic 89%.

**Geography: Area:** 32,377 sq. mi., slightly smaller than Maine. **Location:** In S Central Europe. **Neighbors:** Switzerland, Liechtenstein on W, Germany, Czech Rep., Slovakia on N, Hungary on E, Slovenia, Italy on S. **Topography:** Austria is primarily mountainous, with the Alps and foothills covering the western and southern provinces. The eastern provinces and Vienna are located in the Danube River Basin. **Capital:** Vienna. **Cities** (1991 est.): Vienna 1,500,000.

**Government: Type:** Parliamentary democracy. **Head of state:** Pres. Thomas Klestil; in office: July 8, 1992. **Head of government:** Chancellor Franz Vranitzky; b. Oct. 4, 1937; in office: June 16, 1986. **Local divisions:** 9 lander (states), each with a legislature. **Defense:** 1.2% of GDP (1990).

**Economy: Type: Industries:** Steel, machinery, autos, electrical and optical equip., glassware, sport goods, paper, textiles, chemicals, cement. **Chief crops:** Grains, potatoes, beets. **Minerals:** Iron ore, oil, magnesite. **Other resources:** Forests, hydro power. **Arable land:** 17%. **Livestock** (1991): cattle: 2.5 mln.; pigs: 3.6 mln. **Electricity prod.** (1991): 49.5 bln. kWh. **Crude steel prod.** (1991): 4.1 mln. metric tons. **Labor force:** 8% agric.; 35% ind. & comm.; 56% service.

**Finance: Monetary unit:** Schilling (June 1993: 11.90 = $1 US). **Gross domestic product** (1991): $164 bln. **Per capita GDP:** $20,895. **Imports** (1991): $54.1 bln.; partners: EC 70%. **Exports** (1992): $44.4 bln.; partners: EC 68%. **Tourists** (1990): receipts: $13.0 bln. **National budget** (1990): $49.6 bln. expenditures. **International reserves less gold** (Mar. 1993): $12.1 bln. **Gold:** 19.9 mln. oz t. **Consumer prices** (change in 1992): 4.0%.

**Transport: Railroads** (1991): **Length:** 4,041 mi. **Motor vehicles** in use (1991): 2.9 mln. passenger cars, 256,000 comm. **Civil aviation** (1991): 2.9 bln. passenger-km; 6 airports with scheduled flights.

**Communications: Television sets:** 1 per 2.8 persons. **Radios:** 1 per 1.6 persons. **Telephones in use:** 1 per 1.8 persons. **Daily newspaper circ.** (1991): 445 per 1,000 pop.

**Health: Life expectancy at birth** (1991): 74 male; 81 female. **Births** (per 1,000 pop. 1992): 12. **Deaths** (per 1,000 pop. 1992): 11. **Natural increase:** −.1%. **Hospital beds:** 1 per 101 persons. **Physicians:** 1 per 334 persons. **Infant mortality** (per 1,000 live births 1992): 8.

**Education** (1992): **Literacy:** 99%. **School years compulsory:** 9; attendance 95%.

**Major International Organizations:** UN and all of its specialized agencies, EFTA, OECD.

**Embassy:** 3524 International Court NW 20008; 895-6700.

Rome conquered Austrian lands from Celtic tribes around 15 BC. In 788 the territory was incorporated into Charlemagne's empire. By 1300, the House of Hapsburg had gained control; they added vast territories in all parts of Europe to their realm in the next few hundred years.

Austrian dominance of Germany was undermined in the 18th century and ended by Prussia by 1866. But the Congress of Vienna, 1815, confirmed Austrian control of a large empire in southeast Europe consisting of Germans, Hungarians, Slavs, Italians, and others.

The dual Austro-Hungarian monarchy was established in 1867, giving autonomy to Hungary and almost 50 years of peace.

World War I, started after the June 28, 1914 assassination of Archduke Franz Ferdinand, the Hapsburg heir, by a Serbian nationalist, destroyed the empire. By 1918 Austria was reduced to a small republic, with the borders it has today.

Nazi Germany invaded Austria Mar. 13, 1938. The republic was reestablished in 1945, under Allied occupation. Full independence and neutrality were restored in 1955.

Austria produces most of its food, as well as an array of industrial products. A large part of Austria's economy is controlled by state enterprises. Socialists have shared or alternated power with the conservative People's Party.

# Azerbaijan

### Azerbaijani Republic

### Azerbaijchan Respublikasy

**People: Population** (1992 est.): 7,450,000; **Pop. density:** 223 per sq. mi. **Urban** (1991): 54%. **Ethnic groups:** Azerbaijani 82%, Russian 6%, Armenian 6%. **Language:** Azeri, Turkish, Russian. **Religions:** mostly Moslem.

**Geography: Area:** 33,400 sq. mi., slightly larger than Maine. **Neighbors:** Russia, Georgia on N., Iran on S., Armenia on W., Caspian Sea on E. **Capital:** Baku.

**Government: Type:** in transition. **Head of state:** Pres. Geidar A. Aliyev; in office: June 30, 1993. **Head of government:** Prime Min. Surat Huseynov; in office: June 30, 1993.

**Economy: Industries:** Oil refining. **Chief crops:** Grain, cotton, rice, silk. **Minerals:** Iron, copper, lead, zinc. **Livestock** (1989): cattle: 2.1 mln., goats & sheep: 5.7 mln. **Electricity prod.** (1991): 23.3 bln. kWh.

**Finance: Monetary unit:** Manat: (Jan. 1993: 31.68 = $1 US).

**Transport: Vehicles** (1990): 240,000 passenger cars.

**Communications: Newspaper circ.** (1990): 73 per 1,000 pop.

**Health: Life expectancy at birth** (1992): 65 male; 73 female. **Births** (per 1,000 pop. 1992): 26. **Deaths** (per 1,000 pop. 1992): 7. **Natural increase:** 1.9%. **Physicians:** 1 per 255 persons. **Hospital beds:** 1 per 98 persons. **Infant mortality** (per 1,000 live births 1992): 45.

**Major International Organizations:** UN.

Azerbaijan was the home of Scythian tribes and part of the Roman Empire. It was overrun by Turks in the 11th century and conquered by Russia in 1806 and 1813. It joined the USSR Dec. 30, 1922, and became a constituent republic in 1936. Azerbaijan declared independence Aug. 30, 1991 and became an independent state when the Soviet Union disbanded Dec. 26, 1991.

Fighting between mostly Moslem Azerbaijan and mostly Christian Armenia escalated in 1992 and continued in 1993. Each country claimed Nagorno-Karabakh, an enclave in Azerbaijan with a majority population of ethnic Armenians.

A National Council ousted communist Pres. Mutaibov and took power May 19, 1992. Abulfez Elchibey became the nation's first democratically elected president June 7, but was ousted from office by Surat Huseynov, commander of a private militia, June 30, 1993. Huseynov became prime minister with expanded authority over the ministries of defense, interior, and security.

# The Bahamas

### The Commonwealth of the Bahamas

**People: Population** (1992 est.): 255,000. **Age distrib. (%):** 0–14: 38.0; 15–59: 56.3; 60+: 5.7. **Pop. density:** 47 per sq. mi. **Urban** (1990): 60%. **Ethnic groups:** black 85%, white (British, Canadian, U.S.) 15%. **Languages:** English. **Religions:** Baptist 32%, Anglican 20%, Roman Catholic 19%.

**Geography: Area:** 5,380 sq. mi., about the size of Connecticut. **Location:** In Atlantic O., E of Florida. **Neighbors:** Nearest are U.S. on W, Cuba on S. **Topography:** Nearly 700 islands (30 inhabited) and over 2,000 islets in the western Atlantic extend 760 mi. NW to SE. **Capital:** Nassau. **Cities:** (1990 est.) New Providence 171,000; Freeport 25,000.

**Government: Type:** Independent commonwealth. **Head of state:** Queen Elizabeth II, represented by Gov.-Gen. Clifford Darling. **Head of government:** Prime Min. Hubert Ingraham; b. 1947; in office: Aug. 21, 1992. **Local divisions:** 21 districts.

**Economy: Industries:** Tourism (50% of GDP), rum, banking, pharmaceuticals. **Chief crops:** Fruits, vegetables. **Minerals:** Salt. **Other resources:** Lobsters. **Arable land:** 2%. **Electricity prod.** (1991): 857 mln. kWh. **Labor force:** 5% agric.; 25% tourism, 30% government.

**Finance: Monetary unit:** Dollar (Apr. 1993: 1 = $1 US). **Gross domestic product** (1989): $2.4 bln. **Per capita income** (1988): $7,178. **Imports** (1991): $1.1 bln.; partners: U.S. 35%, Nigeria 21%. **Exports** (1991): $306 mln.; partners: U.S. 41%, Norway 30%. **Tourism** (1990): $1.1 bln. **National budget** (1991): $727 mln. expenditures. **International reserves less**

gold (Mar. 1993): $242 mln. **Consumer prices** (change in 1992): 5.7%.

**Transport: Motor vehicles:** in use (1989): 67,000 passenger cars, 14,000 comm. vehicles. **Chief ports:** Nassau, Freeport.

**Communications: Radios:** 1 per 2 persons. **Television sets:** 1 per 4.6 persons. **Telephones in use:** 1 per 2 persons. **Daily newspaper circ.** (1991): 135 per 1,000 pop.

**Health: Life expectancy at birth** (1992): 69 male; 76 female. **Births** (per 1,000 pop. 1992): 19. **Deaths** (per 1,000 pop. 1992): 5. **Natural increase:** 1.4%. **Infant mortality** (per 1,000 live births 1992): 19.

**Education** (1992): **Literacy:** 95%; School compulsory through age 14.

**Major International Organizations:** UN (World Bank, IMF, WHO), OAS.

**Embassy:** 600 New Hampshire Ave. NW 20037; 338-3940.

Christopher Columbus first set foot in the New World on San Salvador (Watling I.) in 1492, when Arawak Indians inhabited the islands. British settlement began in 1647; the islands became a British colony in 1783. Internal self-government was granted in 1964; full independence within the Commonwealth was attained July 10, 1973.

International banking and investment management has become a major industry alongside tourism, despite controversy over financial irregularities.

# Bahrain

### State of Bahrain

### Dawlat al-Bahrayn

**People: Population** (1992 est.): 551,000. **Age distrib. (%):** 0–14: 32.7; 15–59: 64.2; 60+ 3.1. **Pop. density:** 2,055 per sq. mi. **Urban** (1990): 82%. **Ethnic groups:** Bahraini 63%, Asian 13%, other Arab 10%, Iranian 6%. **Languages:** Arabic (official), Farsi, Urdu. **Religions:** Sunni Moslem 30%, Shi'ah Moslem 70%.

**Geography: Area:** 268 sq. mi., smaller than New York City. **Location:** In Persian Gulf. **Neighbors:** Nearest are Saudi Arabia on W, Qatar on E. **Topography:** Bahrain Island, and several adjacent, smaller islands, are flat, hot and humid, with little rain. **Capital:** Manama. **Cities** (1988 est.): Manama 151,000.

**Government: Type:** Traditional monarchy. **Head of state:** Amir Isa bin Sulman al-Khalifa; b. July 3, 1933; in office: Nov. 2, 1961. **Head of government:** Prime Min. Kahlifa ibn Sulman al-Khalifa; b. 1935; in office: Jan. 19, 1970. **Local divisions:** 12 districts. **Defense:** 6.0% of GDP (1990).

**Economy: Industries:** Oil products, aluminum smelting. **Chief crops:** Fruits, vegetables. **Minerals:** Oil, gas. **Crude oil reserves** (1985): 173 mln. bbls. **Arable land:** 5%. **Electricity prod.** (1991): 10.5 bln. kWh. **Labor force:** 5% agric.; 85% ind. and commerce; 5% services; 3% gov.

**Finance: Monetary unit:** Dinar (Mar. 1993: 1.00 = $2.66 US). **Gross domestic product** (1989): $3.4 bln. **Per capita income** (1989): $7,300. **Imports** (1991): $4.0 bln.; partners: Sau. Ar. 60%, UK 6%, U.S. 9%. **Exports** (1991): $3.4 bln.; partners: UAE 18%, Jap. 12%, Sing. 10%, U.S. 6%. **National budget** (1989): $1.3 bln. expenditures. **International reserves less** gold (Mar. 1993): $1.3 bln. **Gold:** 150,000 oz t. **Consumer prices** (change in 1992): -0.2%.

**Transport: Motor vehicles:** in use (1990): 104,000 passenger cars, 23,000 comm. vehicles. **Chief ports:** Sitra.

**Communications: Television sets:** 1 per 2.3 persons. **Radios:** 1 per 1.7 persons. **Telephones in use:** 1 per 3.4 persons.

**Health: Life expectancy at birth** (1992): 70 male; 75 female. **Births** (per 1,000 pop. 1992): 27. **Deaths** (per 1,000 pop. 1992): 3. **Natural increase:** 2.4. Medical services are free. **Infant mortality** (per 1,000 live births 1992): 21.

**Education** (1992): **Literacy:** 77%.

**Major International Organizations:** UN (GATT, IMF, WHO), Arab League.

**Embassy:** 3502 International Dr. NW 20008; 342-0741.

Long ruled by the Khalifa family, Bahrain was a British protectorate from 1861 to Aug. 15, 1971, when it regained independence.

Pearls, shrimp, fruits, and vegetables were the mainstays of the economy until oil was discovered in 1932. By the 1970s, oil reserves were depleted; international banking thrived.

Bahrain took part in the 1973-74 Arab oil embargo against the U.S. and other nations. The government bought controlling interest in the oil industry in 1975.

# Bangladesh

## People's Republic of Bangladesh

## Gama Prajātantrī Bangladesh

**People: Population** (1992 est.): 119,000,000. **Age distrib. (%):** 0-14: 44.3; 15-59: 50.4; 60+: 5.3. **Pop. density:** 2,132 per sq. mi. **Urban** (1990): 24%. **Ethnic groups:** Bengali 98%, Bihari, tribesmen. **Languages:** Bengali (official), Chakma, Magh. **Religions:** Moslem 83%, Hindu 16%.

**Geography: Area:** 55,813 sq. mi. slightly smaller than Wisconsin. **Location:** In S Asia, on N bend of Bay of Bengal. **Neighbors:** India nearly surrounds country on W, N, E; Myanmar on SE. **Topography:** The country is mostly a low plain cut by the Ganges and Brahmaputra rivers and their delta. The land is alluvial and marshy along the coast, with hills only in the extreme SE and NE. A tropical monsoon climate prevails, among the rainiest in the world. **Capital:** Dhaka. **Cities** (1991 est.): Dhaka (met.) 6.1 mln.; Chittagong (met.) 2.1 mln.; Khulna (met.) 877,000.

**Government: Type:** Parliamentary democracy. **Head of state:** Pres. Abdur Rahman Biswas in office: Oct. 10, 1991. **Head of Government:** Prime Min. Khaleda Zia; b. Nov. 1944; in office: Mar. 20, 1991. **Local divisions:** 64 districts. **Defense:** 1.5% of GDP (1992).

**Economy: Industries:** Food processing, jute, textiles, fertilizers, petroleum products. **Chief crops:** Jute (most of world output), rice, tea. **Minerals:** Natural gas, offshore oil, coal. **Arable land:** 67%. **Livestock** (1991): cattle: 23 mln.; goats: 22 mln. **Fish catch** (1990): 847,000 metric tons. **Electricity prod.** (1990): 5.7 bln. kWh. **Labor force:** 74% agric; 11% ind.; 15% services.

**Finance: Monetary unit:** Taka (Mar. 1993: 39 = $1 US). **Gross domestic product** (1991): $23.1 bln. **Per capita GDP:** $200. **Imports** (1991): $3.6 bln.; partners: Jap. 9%, U.S. 6%. **Exports** (1991): $1.6 bln.; partners: U.S. 31%, It. 9%; Pak 5%. **Tourism** (1990): $11.0 mln. receipts. **National budget** (1991): $3.7 bln. expenditures. **International reserves less gold** (Mar. 1993): $2.1 bln. **Gold:** 87,000 oz t. **Consumer prices** (change in 1992): 4.7%.

**Transport: Railroads** (1989): **Length:** 1,750 mi. **Motor vehicles:** in use (1990): 41,000 passenger cars, 53,000 comm. vehicles. **Chief ports:** Chittagong, Chalna.

**Communications: Radios:** 1 per 24 persons. **Television sets:** 1 per 315 persons. **Telephones in use:** 1 per 572 persons. **Daily newspaper circ.** (1988) 8 per 1,000 pop.

**Health: Life expectancy at birth** (1992): 55 male; 54 female. **Births** (per 1,000 pop. 1992): 36. **Deaths** (per 1,000 pop. 1992): 13. **Natural increase:** 2.3%. **Hospital beds:** 1 per 3,195 persons. **Physicians:** 1 per 5,500 persons. **Infant mortality** (per 1,000 live births 1992): 112.

**Education** (1992): **Literacy:** 47%. **Attendance:** 73% primary school; 26% secondary school.

**Major International Organizations:** UN (GATT, IMF, WHO). **Embassy:** 2201 Wisconsin Ave. NW 20007; 342-8372.

Moslem invaders conquered the formerly Hindu area in the 12th century. British rule lasted from the 18th century to 1947, when East Bengal became part of Pakistan.

Charging West Pakistani domination, the Awami League, based in the East, won National Assembly control in 1971. Assembly sessions were postponed; riots broke out. Pakistani troops attacked Mar. 25; Bangladesh independence was proclaimed the next day. In the ensuing civil war, one million died and 10 million fled to India.

War between India and Pakistan broke out Dec. 3, 1971. Pakistan surrendered in the East on Dec. 15. Sheik Mujibur Rahman became prime minister. The country moved into the Indian and Soviet orbits in response to U.S. support of Pakistan, and much of the economy was nationalized. Bangladesh adopted a parliamentary system of government in 1991.

Chronic destitution among the densely crowded population has been worsened by the decline of jute as a major world commodity.

On May 30, 1981, Pres. Ziaur Rahman was shot and killed in an unsuccessful coup attempt by army rivals. Vice President Ab-

dus Sattar assumed the presidency but was ousted in a coup led by army chief of staff Gen. H.M. Ershad, Mar. 1982. Ershad declared Bangladesh an Islamic Republic in 1988. Bangladesh remains one of the world's poorest countries.

In 1988 and 1989 natural disasters and monsoon rains brought devastation to Bangladesh: over 4,000 died, 30 million were made homeless. A cyclone struck Apr. 1991, killing over 131,000 people and causing $2.7 billion in damages. Some 7,500 U.S. military personnel aided in the relief effort.

# Barbados

**People: Population** (1992 est.): 254,000 **Age distrib. (%):** 0-14: 24.8%; 15-59: 60.6; 60+: 14.6. **Pop. density:** 1,530 per sq. mi. **Urban** (1990): 42%. **Ethnic groups:** African 80%, mixed 16%, Caucasian 4%. **Languages:** English. **Religions:** Protestant 67%, Roman Catholic 4%.

**Geography: Area:** 166 sq. mi. **Location:** In Atlantic, farthest E of W. Indies. **Neighbors:** Nearest are Trinidad, Grenada on SW. **Topography:** The island lies alone in the Atlantic almost completely surrounded by coral reefs. Highest point is Mt. Hilaby, 1,115 ft. **Capital:** Bridgetown. **Cities** (1990): Bridgetown 6,700.

**Government: Type:** Parliamentary democracy. **Head of state:** Queen Elizabeth II, represented by Gov.-Gen. Dame Nita Barrow; in office: June 6, 1990. **Head of government:** Prime Min. Erskine Sandiford; b. Mar. 24, 1937; in office: June 1, 1987. **Local divisions:** 11 parishes and Bridgetown.

**Economy: Industries:** Sugar, tourism. **Chief crops:** Sugar, cotton. **Minerals:** Lime. **Other resources:** Fish. **Arable land:** 76%. **Electricity prod.** (1991): 539 mln. kWh. **Labor force:** 5% agric.; 17% ind. and comm.; 37% services and government.

**Finance: Monetary unit:** Dollar (June 1993: 2.01 = $1 US). **Gross domestic product** (1990): $1.7 bln. **Per capita GDP** $6,500. **Imports** (1991): $694 mln.; partners: U.S. 35%, CARACOM 12%. **Exports** (1991): $205 mln.; partners: U.S. 21%, CARACOM 30%. **Tourism** (1990): $502 mln. receipts. **National budget** (1992): $615 mln. expenditures. **International reserves less gold** (Mar. 1993): $172 mln. **Consumer prices** (change in 1992): 6.1%.

**Transport: Motor vehicles:** in use (1991): 38,000 passenger cars; 9,000 comm. vehicles. **Chief ports:** Bridgetown.

**Communications: Television sets:** 1 per 3.9 persons. **Radios:** 1 per 1.1 persons. **Telephones in use:** 1 per 2.4 persons. **Daily newspaper circ.** (1990): 161 per 1,000 pop.

**Health: Life expectancy at birth** (1992): male: 70 female: 76. **Births** (per 1,000 pop. 1992): 16. **Deaths** (per 1,000 pop. 1992): 9. **Natural increase:** 0.7%. **Hospital beds:** 1 per 123 persons. **Physicians:** 1 per 1,042 persons. **Infant mortality** (per 1,000 live births 1992): 23.

**Education** (1992): **Literacy:** 99%. **Years compulsory:** to age 16.

**Major International Organizations:** UN (FAO, GATT, ILO, IMF, WHO), OAS.

**Embassy:** 2144 Wyoming Ave. NW 20008; 939-9200.

Barbados was probably named by Portuguese sailors in reference to bearded fig trees. An English ship visited in 1605, and British settlers arrived on the uninhabited island in 1627. Slaves worked the sugar plantations until slavery was abolished in 1834. Self-rule came gradually, with full independence proclaimed Nov. 30, 1966. British traditions have remained.

# Belarus

## Republic of Belarus

## Respublika Belarus

**People: Population** (1992 est.): 10,373,000. **Pop. density:** 129 per sq. mi. **Urban** (1991): 67%. **Ethnic groups:** Belarus 80%, Russian 13%. **Languages:** Belorussian, Russian.

**Geography: Area:** 80,134 sq. mi. **Neighbors:** Poland on W, Latvia, Lithuania on N, Russia on E, Ukraine on S. **Capital:** Minsk. **Cities** (1991): Minsk 1.6 mln., Homel 503,000.

**Government: Type:** Republic. **Head of state:** Pres. Stanislav Shushkevich; in office: Sept. 1991. **Head of government:** Prime Min. Vyacheslav Kebich. **Local divisions:** 6 regions.

**Economy: Industries:** Food processing, chemicals, machine-tool & agricultural machinery. **Chief crops:** Grain, flax, potatoes, sugar beets. **Livestock** (1991): cattle: 6.3 mln., pigs: 4.7 mln. **Electricity prod.** (1991): 38.7 mln. kWh.

**Finance: Monetary unit:** Belarus ruble.

**Transport: Railroads** (1991): **Length:** 3,472 mi. **Passenger Cars** (1990): 500,000.

**Communications: Television sets:** 1 per 3.3 persons. **Radios:** 1 per 1.3 persons. **Telephones:** 1 per 6.3 persons. **Newspaper circ.** (1990): 260 per 1,000 pop.

**Health: Life expectancy at birth** (1992): 66 male; 76 female. **Birth** (per 1,000 pop. 1992): 15. **Deaths** (per 1,000 pop. 1992): 11. **Physicians:** 1 per 248 persons. **Hospital beds** 1 per 76 persons. **Infant mortality** (per 1,000 live births 1992): 20.

**Major International Organizations:** UN, CIS.

The region was subject to Lithuanians and Poles in medieval times, and was a prize of war between Russia and Poland beginning in 1503. It became part of the USSR in 1922 although the western part of the region was controlled by Poland. Belarus was overrun by German armies in 1941; recovered by Soviet troops in 1944. Following World War II, Belarus increased in area through Soviet annexation of part of NE Poland. Belarus declared independence Aug. 25, 1991. It became an independent state when the Soviet Union disbanded Dec. 26, 1991.

# Belgium

## Kingdom of Belgium

### Koninkrijk België (Dutch)
### Royaume de Belgique (French)

**People: Population** (1992 est.): 10,016,000. **Age distrib.** (%): 0–14: 18.2; 15–59: 61.7; 60+: 20.1 **Pop. density:** 848 per sq. mi. **Urban** (1992): 96%. **Ethnic groups:** Fleming 55%, Walloon 33%. **Languages:** Flemish (Dutch) 57%, French 33%, Italian, German. **Religions:** Roman Catholic 75%.

**Geography: Area:** 11,799 sq. mi., slightly larger than Maryland. **Location:** In NW Europe, on N. Sea. **Neighbors:** France on W, S, Luxembourg on SE, Germany on E, Netherlands on N. **Topography:** Mostly flat, the country is trisected by the Scheldt and Meuse, major commercial rivers. The land becomes hilly and forested in the SE (Ardennes) region. **Capital:** Brussels. **Cities** (1991 est.): Brussels (met.) 970,000; Antwerp (met.) 467,000; Ghent 233,000; Charleroi 209,000; Liege 195,000.

**Government: Type:** Parliamentary democracy under a constitutional monarch. **Head of state:** King Albert; in office: Aug. 1, 1993. **Head of government:** Premier Jean-Luc Dehaene; b. Aug. 7, 1940; in office: Mar. 7, 1992. **Local divisions:** 9 provinces; 3 regions; 3 cultural communities. **Defense:** 2.7% of GDP (1991).

**Economy: Industries:** Steel, glassware, diamond cutting, textiles, chemicals. **Chief crops:** Wheat, potatoes, sugar beets. **Minerals:** Coal. **Other resources:** Forests. **Arable land** (incl. Lux.): 26.5%. **Livestock** (1991): cattle: 3.1 mln; pigs: 6.4 mln. **Fish catch** (1988): 23.3 metric tons. **Electricity prod.** (1991): 67 bln. kWh. **Crude steel prod.** (1991): 11.3 mln. metric tons. **Labor force:** 2% agric.; 26% ind. & comm.; 37% services & transportation; 23% public service.

**Finance: Monetary unit:** Franc (Aug. 1993: 35.50 = $1 US). **Gross domestic product** (1991): $171 bln. **Per capita GDP** $17,300. *Note:* the following trade and tourist data includes Luxembourg. **Imports** (1992): $120 bln.; partners: EC 73%. **Exports** (1992): $118 bln.; partners: EC 74%. **Tourism** (1990): receipts: $3.5 bln. **National budget** (1989): $51 bln. expenditures. **International reserves less gold** (Mar. 1993): $13.2 bln. **Gold:** 23.1 mln. oz t. **Consumer prices** (change in 1992): 2.4%.

**Transport: Railroads** (1990): **Length:** 2,162 mi. **Motor vehicles:** in use (1991): 3.9 mln. passenger cars, 596,000 comm. vehicles. **Civil aviation** (1990): 7.5 bln. passenger-km; 4 airports with scheduled flights. **Chief ports:** Antwerp, Zeebrugge, Ghent.

**Communications: Television sets:** 1 per 4.2 persons. **Radios:** 1 per 2.2 persons; **Telephones: in use** 1 per 1.9 persons. **Daily newspaper circ.** (1990): 213 per 1,000 pop.

**Health: Life expectancy at birth** (1992): 73 male; 80 female. **Births** (per 1,000 pop. 1992): 10. **Deaths** (per 1,000 pop. 1992): 10. **Natural increase** 0.2%. **Hospital beds:** 1 per 108 persons. **Physicians:** 1 per 317 persons. **Infant mortality** (per 1,000 live births 1992): 8.

**Education** (1992): **Literacy:** 98%. School compulsory to age 18.

**Major International Organizations:** UN and all of its specialized agencies, NATO, EC, OECD.

**Embassy:** 3330 Garfield St. NW 20008; 333-6900

Belgium derives its name from the Belgae, the first recorded inhabitants, probably Celts. The land was conquered by Julius Caesar, and was ruled for 1800 years by conquerors, including Rome, the Franks, Burgundy, Spain, Austria, and France. After 1815, Belgium was made a part of the Netherlands, but it became an independent constitutional monarchy in 1830.

Belgian neutrality was violated by Germany in both world wars. King Leopold III surrendered to Germany, May 28, 1940. After the war, he was forced by political pressure to abdicate in favor of his son, King Baudouin.

The Flemings of northern Belgium speak Dutch while French is the language of the Walloons in the south. The language difference has been a perennial source of controversy and led to antagonism between the 2 groups. Parliament has passed measures aimed at transferring power from the central government to 3 regions—Wallonia, Flanders, and Brussels.

Belgium lives by its foreign trade; about 50% of its entire production is sold abroad.

# Belize

**People: Population** (1992 est.): 189,000. **Age distrib. (%):** 0–14: 44.5; 15–59: 47.8; 60+: 7.6. **Pop. density:** 21 per sq. mi. **Ethnic groups:** Mestizo 43%, Creole 29%, Maya 8%. **Languages:** English (official), Spanish, native Creole dialects. **Religions:** Roman Catholic 57%, Protestant 28%.

**Geography: Area:** 8,867 sq. mi. **Location:** eastern coast of Central America. **Neighbors:** Mexico on N, Guatemala on W and S. **Capital:** Belmopan. **Cities** (1991 est.): Belize City 44,000.

**Government: Type:** Parliamentary democracy. **Head of state:** Gov. Gen. Minita Gordon. **Head of government:** Prime Min. George Cadle Price; in office: Sept. 8, 1989. **Local divisions:** 6 districts.

**Economy:** Sugar is the main export.

**Finance: Monetary unit:** Belize dollar (Mar. 1993) 2 = $1 U.S. **Gross domestic product** (1990): $290 mln. **Per capita GDP:** $1,637. **Imports** (1992): $273 mln.; partners: U.S. 55%, UK 8%. **Exports:** (1992): $102 mln.; partners: U.S. 46%, UK 31%. **National budget** (1991): $23 mln. expenditures.

**Health: Life expectancy at birth** (1992): male: 67; female: 72. **Births** (per 1,000 pop. 1992): 31. **Deaths** (per 1,000 pop. 1992): 5. **Hospital beds:** 1 per 309 persons. **Physicians:** 1 per 1,543 persons. **Infant mortality** (per 1,000 live births, 1992): 30.

**Education:** (1991) **Literacy:** 93%.; **Years compulsory:** 9; attendance 55%.

**Major International Organizations:** OAS, UN (IMF, World Bank), Commonwealth of Nations.

**Embassy:** 3400 International Dr., NW 20005; 363-4505.

Belize (formerly called British Honduras) was Great Britain's last colony on the American mainland. The country achieved independence on Sept. 21, 1981. British troops in Belize guarantee security.

# Benin

## Republic of Benin

### République du Benin

**People: Population** (1992 est.): 4,997,000. **Age distrib. (%):** 0–14: 46.5; 15–59: 49.0; 60+: 4.5. **Pop. density:** 114 per sq. mi. **Urban** (1985): 20%. **Ethnic groups:** Fon, Adja, Bariba, Yoruba. **Languages:** French (official), Fon, Yoruba, Somba. **Religions:** Mainly animist with Christian, Moslem minorities.

**Geography: Area:** 43,483 sq. mi., slightly smaller than Pennsylvania. **Location:** In W Africa on Gulf of Guinea. **Neighbors:** Togo on W, Burkina Faso, Niger on N, Nigeria on E. **Topography:** most of Benin is flat and covered with dense vegetation. The coast is hot, humid, and rainy. **Capital:** Porto-Novo. **Cities** (1984 est.): Cotonou 330,000.

**Government: Type:** Democracy. **Head of state:** Nicephore Soglo; in office: Apr. 4, 1991. **Local divisions:** 6 provinces. **Defense:** 2.1% of GDP (1988).

Economy: Chief crops: Palm products, peanuts, cotton, coffee, tobacco. Minerals: Oil. Arable land: 12%. Livestock (1989): sheep: 890,000; goats: 1.1 mln. Fish catch (1990): 39,000 metric tons. Electricity prod. (1991): 24 mln. kWh. Labor force: 60% agric; 38% serv. & comm.

Finance: Monetary unit: CFA franc (Mar. 1993: 273 = $1 US). Gross domestic product (1991): $1.7 bln. Per capita GDP: $400. Imports (1990): $428 mln.; partners: Fr. 34%. Exports (1990): $263 mln.; partners: EC. National budget (1990): $390 bln. expenditures. International reserves less gold (Feb. 1993): $245 mln.

Transport: Railroads (1992): Length: 359 mi. Chief ports: Cotonou.

Communications: Radios: 1 per 14 persons. Televisions: 1 per 281 persons. Daily newspaper circ. (1990): 3 per 1,000 pop.

Health: Life expectancy at birth (1992): 49 male; 52 female. Births (per 1,000 pop. 1992): 49. Deaths (per 1,000 pop. 1992): 16. Natural increase: 3.7%. Hospital beds: 1 per 749 persons. Physicians: 1 per 16,025 persons. Infant mortality (per 1,000 live births 1992): 115.

Education (1991): Literacy: 28%. Years compulsory 6; attendance 43%.

Major International Organizations: UN (GATT, IMF, WHO), OAU.

Embassy: 2737 Cathedral Ave. NW 20008; 232-6656.

The Kingdom of Abomey, rising to power in wars with neighboring kingdoms in the 17th century, came under French domination in the late 19th century and was incorporated into French West Africa by 1904.

Under the name Dahomey, the country became independent Aug. 1, 1960. The name was changed to Benin in 1975. In the fifth coup since independence Col. Ahmed Kerekou took power in 1972; two years later he declared a socialist state with a "Marxist-Leninist" philosophy. In Dec. 1989, Kerekou announced that Marxism-Leninism would no longer be the state ideology. In 1991, Kerekou was defeated in Benin's first free presidential elections in 30 years by Nicephore Soglo.

The economy relies on the development of agriculturally based industries.

## Bhutan
### Kingdom of Bhutan
### Druk-Yul

People: Population (1992 est.): 1,660,000. Age distrib. (%): 0–14: 39.8; 15–59: 53.8; over 60: 6.4 Pop. density: 91 per sq. mi. Ethnic groups: Bhote 60%, Napalese 25%. Languages: Dzongkha (official), Gurung, Assamese. Religions: Buddhist (state religion) 75%, Hindu 25%.

Geography: Area: 18,147 sq. mi., the size of Vermont and New Hampshire combined. Location: In eastern Himalayan Mts. Neighbors: India on W (Sikkim) and S, China on N. Topography: Bhutan is comprised of very high mountains in the N, fertile valleys in the center, and thick forests in the Duar Plain in the S. Capital: Thimphu (Paro Dzong is administrative capital). City (1987 est.): Thimphu 20,000.

Government: Type: Monarchy. Head of state: King Jigme Singye Wangchuk; b. Nov. 11, 1955; in office: July 21, 1972. Local divisions: 18 districts.

Economy: Industries: Handicrafts, chemicals. Chief crops: Rice, corn, wheat. Other resources: Timber. Arable land: 2%. Labor force: 93% agric.

Finance: Monetary unit: Ngultrum (Mar. 1993: 28.29 = $1 US). (Indian Rupee also used). Gross domestic product (1989): $273 mln. Per capita GDP: $199. Tourism (1990): 2.0 mln. Imports (1991): $138 mln.; partners: India 67%. Exports (1989): $70 mln.; partners: India 93%.

Communications: Radios: 1 per 64 persons. Telephones in use: 1 per 675 persons.

Health: Life expectancy at birth (1992): 50 male; 48 female. Births (per 1,000 pop. 1992): 40. Deaths (per 1,000 pop. 1992): 17. Natural increase: 2.3%. Hospital beds: 1 per 1,476 persons. Physicians: 1 per 9,686 persons. Infant mortality (per 1,000 live births 1992): 126.

Education (1989): Literacy: 15%. School attendance: 25%.

Major International Organizations: UN (IMF, World Bank).

The region came under Tibetan rule in the 16th century. British influence grew in the 19th century. A monarchy, set up in 1907, became a British protectorate by a 1910 treaty. The country became independent in 1949, with India guiding foreign relations and supplying aid.

Links to India have been strengthened by airline service and a road network. Most of the population engages in subsistence agriculture.

## Bolivia
### Republic of Bolivia
### República de Bolivia

People: Population (1992 est.): 7,323,000. Age distrib. (%): 0–14: 41.1; 15–59: 52.4; 60+: 5.5. Pop. density: 17 per sq. mi. Urban (1990): 51%. Ethnic groups: Quechua 30%, Aymara 25%, mixed 30%, European 14%. Languages: Spanish, Quechua, Aymara (all official). Religions: Roman Catholic 95%.

Geography: Area: 424,165 sq. mi., the size of Texas and California combined. Location: In central Andes Mtns. Neighbors: Peru, Chile on W, Argentina, Paraguay on S, Brazil on E and N. Topography: The great central plateau, at an altitude of 12,000 ft., over 500 mi. long, lies between two great cordilleras having 3 of the highest peaks in S. America. Lake Titicaca, on Peruvian border, is highest lake in world on which steamboats ply (12,506 ft.). The E central region has semitropical forests; the llanos, or Amazon-Chaco lowlands are in E. Capitals: Sucre, (legal), La Paz (de facto). Cities (1989 est.): La Paz 1,669,000; Santa Cruz 529,000; Cochabamba 403,000.

Government: Type: Republic. Head of state: Pres. Gonzalo Sanchez de Lozada; in office: Aug. 6, 1993. Local divisions: 9 departments. Defense: 1.5% of GDP (1990).

Economy: Industry: Textiles, food processing, mining, clothing. Chief crops: Potatoes, sugar, coffee, corn, coca (sold for cocaine processing). Minerals: Antimony, tin, tungsten, silver, zinc, oil, gas, iron. Crude oil reserves (1985): 157 mln. bbls. Other resources: rubber, cinchona bark. Arable land: 3%. Livestock (1991): cattle: 5.3 mln.; sheep: 12.3 mln.; pigs: 1.6 mln. Electricity prod. (1991): 1.7 bln. kWh. Labor force: 50% agric., 10% ind. & comm, 26% serv. & govt.

Finance: Monetary unit: Bolivianos (Mar. 1993: 4.17 = $1 US). Gross domestic product (1990): $4.8 bln. Per capita GDP: $690. Imports (1991): $760 mln.; partners: U.S. 20%, Jap. 10%, Arg. 14%, Braz. 20%. Exports (1991): $970 mln.; partners: U.S. 19%. National budget (1991): $825 mln. expenditures. International reserves less gold (Mar. 1993): $134 mln. Gold: 894,000 oz t. Consumer prices (change in 1991): 21%.

Transport: Railroads (1991): Length: 2,269 mi. Motor vehicles: in use (1988): 83,000 passenger cars, 150,000 comm. vehicles. Civil aviation (1990): 1.2 bln. passenger-km.; 19 airports with scheduled flights.

Communications: Television sets: 1 per 16 persons. Radios: 1 per 1.8 persons. Telephones in use: 1 per 37 persons. Daily newspaper circ. (1986): 35 per 1,000 pop.

Health: Life expectancy at birth (1992): 59 male; 64 female. Births (per 1,000 pop. 1992): 34. Deaths (per 1,000 pop. 1992): 19. Natural increase: 2.5%. Hospital beds: 1 per 686 persons. Physicians: 1 per 2,124 persons. Infant mortality (per 1,000 live births 1992): 83.

Education (1991): Literacy: 78%. Years compulsory: ages 7-14; attendance 82%.

Major International Organizations: UN (IMF, FAO, WHO), OAS.

Embassy: 3014 Massachusetts Ave. NW 20008; 483-4410.

The Incas conquered the region from earlier Indian inhabitants in the 13th century. Spanish rule began in the 1530s and lasted until Aug. 6, 1825. The country is named after Simon Bolivar, independence fighter.

In a series of wars, Bolivia lost its Pacific coast to Chile, the oil-bearing Chaco to Paraguay, and rubber-growing areas to Brazil, 1879-1935.

Economic unrest, especially among the militant mine workers, has contributed to continuing political instability. A reformist government under Victor Paz Estenssoro, 1951-64, nationalized tin mines and attempted to improve conditions for the Indian majority but was overthrown by a military junta. A series of coups and countercoups continued through 1981, until the military junta elected Gen. Villa as president.

In July 1982, the military junta assumed power amid a growing economic crisis and foreign debt difficulties. The junta resigned in October and allowed the Congress, elected democratically in 1980, to take power.

U.S. pressure on the government to reduce the country's output of coca, the raw material for cocaine, has led to clashes between police and coca growers and increased anti-U.S. feeling among Bolivians.

## Bosnia and Herzegovina

**People: Population** (1992 est.): 4,365,000. **Pop. density:** 221 per sq. mi. **Ethnic groups:** Moslem Slav 43%, Serbian 31%, Croatian 17%. **Languages:** Serbo-Croatian (official). **Religions:** Eastern Orthodox, Catholic, Moslem.

**Geography: Area:** 19,741 sq. mi. **Location:** in SE Europe. **Neighbors:** Yugoslavia, Croatia, Adriatic Sea. **Topography:** Hilly with some mountains. About 50% of the land is forested. **Capital:** Sarajevo.

**Government: Type:** In transition. **Head of state:** Pres. Alija Izetbegovic.

**Economy: Industries:** Textiles, rugs, timber. **Chief crops:** Corn, wheat, oats, barley. **Minerals:** Bauxite, iron ore, coal.

**Finance: Monetary unit:** New Yugoslav Dinar. (Dec. 1992: 225 = $1 US.) **Gross domestic product** (1991): $14 bln.

**Health: Doctors:** 1 per 624 persons; **Hospital beds:** 1 per 219 persons.

**Education:** Literacy (1991): 90%.

**International Organizations:** UN.

Bosnia was ruled by Croatian kings c. 958 A.D., and by Hungary 1000-1200. It became organized c. 1200 and later took control of Herzegovina. The kingdom disintegrated from 1391, with the southern part becoming the independent duchy Herzegovina. It was conquered by Turks in 1463 and made a Turkish province. The area was placed under control of Austria-Hungary in 1878, and made part of the province of **Bosnia and Herzegovina**, which was formally annexed to Austria-Hungary 1908, and it became a province of Yugoslavia in 1918. It was reunited with Herzegovina as a federated republic in the 1946 constitution.

The Bosnia and Herzegovina parliament adopted a declaration of sovereignty Oct. 15, 1991. A referendum for independence was passed Feb. 29, 1992. Ethnic Serbs' opposition to the referendum spurred violent clashes and bombings. The U.S. and EC recognized the republic as independent Apr. 7. Fierce fighting continued—interrupted by 2 cease-fires in June—as Serbs massacred many thousands of Bosnians, most of them civilians. Serb forces launched major offensives, July 13, marking the 100th day of the siege of Sarajevo, Bosnia's capital. By Sept. 1992, Serb nationalist forces occupied some 70% of Bosnia, with a small area under Croatian control.

The U.S. air dropped relief supplies to Moslem towns under siege in E. Bosnia Feb. 28-Mar. 3, 1993. Bosnian Croats, Serbs, and Moslems agreed in principle to the partitioning of the country into autonomous ethnic regions July 30. Despite the accord, fierce fighting continued around Sarajevo and elsewhere in Bosnia. The mostly Moslem Bosnian Parliament rejected a specific partition plan Aug. 29; negotiations resumed in Sept.

## Botswana

### Republic of Botswana

**People: Population** (1992 est.): 1,300,000. **Age distrib. (%):** 0–14: 39.6; 15–64: 48.3; 65+: 3.1. **Pop. density:** 5 per sq. mi. **Urban** (1991): 25%. **Ethnic groups:** Tswana, Kalanga, others. **Languages:** English (official), Setswana. **Religions:** indigenous beliefs 50%, Christian 50%.

**Geography: Area:** 231,804 sq. mi., slightly smaller than Texas. **Location:** In southern Africa. **Neighbors:** Namibia on N and W, S. Africa on S, Zimbabwe on NE; Botswana claims border with Zambia on N. **Topography:** The Kalahari Desert, supporting nomadic Bushmen and wildlife, spreads over SW; there are swamplands and farming areas in N, and rolling plains in E where livestock are grazed. **Capital:** Gaborone. **Cities** (1991): Gaborone 138,000.

**Government: Type:** Parliamentary republic. **Head of state:** Pres. Quett Masire; b. 1925; in office: July 13, 1980. **Local divisions:** 10 district councils and 4 town councils. **Defense:** 4.4% of GDP (1991).

**Economy: Industries:** Livestock processing, mining. **Chief crops:** Corn, sorghum, beans. **Minerals:** Copper, coal, nickel, diamonds. **Other resources:** Big game. **Arable land:** 2%. **Electricity prod.** (1991): 630 mln. kWh. **Labor force:** 70% agric.

**Finance: Monetary unit:** Pula (Mar. 1993: 1.00 = $.42 US). **Gross domestic product** (1990): $3.1 bln. **Imports** (1991): $2.2 bln.; partners: S. Africa 88%. **Exports** (1991): $2.7 bln.; partners: Europe 67%, U.S. 17%, S. Africa 7%. **National budget** (1992): $1.7 bln. expenditures. **International reserves less gold** (Mar. 1992): $3.7 bln. **Consumer prices** (change in 1993): 16.2%

**Transport: Railroads** (1991): **Length:** 443 mi. **Motor vehicles:** in use (1991): 26,000 passenger cars, 47,000 comm. vehicles.

**Communications: Radios:** 1 per 1.2 persons. **Telephones:** 1 per 26 persons. **Daily newspaper circ.** (1989): 22 per 1,000 pop.

**Health: Life expectancy at birth** (1992): male: 59; female: 65. **Births** (1,000 pop. 1992): 36. **Deaths** (per 1,000 pop. 1992): 9. **Natural increase:** 2.7%. **Hospital beds** (1990): 5,022. **Physicians:** 1 per 7,185 persons. **Infant mortality** (per 1,000 live births 1992): 43.

**Education** (1990): Literacy: 23%.

**Major International Organizations:** UN (GATT, IMF, WHO), OAU, Commonwealth of Nations.

**Embassy:** 3400 International Dr. NW 20008; 244-4990.

First inhabited by bushmen, then by Bantus, the region became the British protectorate of Bechuanaland in 1886, halting encroachment by Boers and Germans from the south and southwest. The country became fully independent Sept. 30, 1966, changing its name to Botswana.

Cattle raising and mining (diamonds, copper, nickel) have contributed to the country's economic growth. The economy is closely tied to S. Africa.

## Brazil

### Federative Republic of Brazil
### República Federativa do Brasil

**People: Population** (1992 est.): 158,000,000. **Age distrib. (%):** 0–14: 35.2; 15–59: 57.7; 60+: 7.1. **Pop. density:** 48 per sq. mi. **Urban** (1989): 76%. **Ethnic groups:** Portuguese, Africans, and mulattoes make up the vast majority; Italians, Germans, Japanese, Indians, Jews, Arabs. **Languages:** Portuguese (official), English, German, Italian. **Religions:** Roman Catholic 89%.

**Geography: Area:** 3,286,470 sq. mi., larger than contiguous 48 U.S. states; largest country in S. America. **Location:** Occupies eastern half of S. America. **Neighbors:** French Guiana, Suriname, Guyana, Venezuela on N, Colombia, Peru, Bolivia, Paraguay, Argentina on W, Uruguay on S. **Topography:** Brazil's Atlantic coastline stretches 4,603 miles. In N is the heavily-wooded Amazon basin covering half the country. Its network of rivers navigable for 15,814 mi. The Amazon itself flows 2,093 miles in Brazil, all navigable. The NE region is semiarid scrubland, heavily settled and poor. The S central region, favored by climate and resources, has almost half of the population, produces 75% of farm goods and 80% of industrial output. The narrow coastal belt includes most of the major cities. Almost the entire country has a tropical or semitropical climate. **Capital:** Brasilia. **Cities** (1991 est.): Sao Paulo 15.2 mln.; Rio de Janeiro 6.0 mln.; Belo Horizonte 2.4 mln.; Salvador 2.0 mln.

**Government: Type:** Federal republic. **Head of state:** Pres. Itamar Franco; in office: Dec. 29, 1992. **Local divisions:** 26 states, federal district (Brasilia). **Defense:** 2.6% of GDP (1990).

**Economy: Industries:** Steel, autos, ships, appliances, petrochemicals, machinery. **Chief crops:** Coffee (largest grower), cotton, soybeans, sugar, cocoa, rice, corn, fruits. **Minerals:** Chromium, iron, manganese, diamonds, gold, nickel, gem stones, tin, bauxite, oil. **Crude oil reserves** (1991): 2.8 bln. bbls. **Arable land:** 8%. **Livestock** (1989): cattle: 136 mln.; pigs: 33 mln.; sheep: 20 mln. **Fish catch** (1989): 850,000 metric tons. **Electricity prod.** (1991): 229 bln. kWh. **Crude steel prod.** (1991): 22.6 mln. metric tons. **Labor force:** 42% services, 31% agric.; 25% ind.

**Finance: Monetary unit:** Cruzeiro (June 1992: 3,059 = $1 US). **Gross domestic product** (1990): $388 bln. **Per capita GDP** (1990): $2,540. **Imports** (1992): $23 bln.; partners: U.S.

21%, EC 23%. **Exports** (1992): $36 bln.; partners: U.S. 26%, EC 27%. **Tourism** (1991): receipts: $1.4 bln. **National budget** (1991): $170 bln expenditures. **International reserves less gold** (Jan. 1993): $22.5 bln. **Gold:** 2.2 mln. oz t. **Consumer prices** (change in 1992): 1,100%.

**Transport: Railroads** (1990): **Length:** 18,721 mi. **Motor vehicles:** in use (1988): 14 mln. passenger cars, 1.6 mln. **Civil aviation** (1991): 17.2 bln. passenger-km.; 100 airports with scheduled flights. **Chief ports:** Santos, Rio de Janeiro, Vitoria, Salvador, Rio Grande, Recife.

**Communications: Television sets:** 1 per 5 persons. **Radios:** 1 per 2.5 persons. **Telephones in use:** 1 per 10 persons. **Daily newspaper circ.** (1990): 55 per 1,000 pop.

**Health: Life expectancy at birth** (1992): 62 male; 68 female. **Births** (per 1,000 pop. 1992): 26. **Deaths** (per 1,000 pop. 1992): 7. **Natural increase:** 1.9%. **Hospital beds:** 1 per 285 persons. **Physicians:** 1 per 684 persons. **Infant mortality** (per 1,000 live births 1992): 67.

**Education** (1991): **Literacy:** 81%.

**Major International Organizations:** UN and most of its specialized agencies, OAS.

**Embassy:** 3006 Massachusetts Ave. NW 20008; 745-2700.

Pedro Alvares Cabral, a Portuguese navigator, is generally credited as the first European to reach Brazil, in 1500. The country was thinly settled by various Indian tribes. Only a few have survived to the present, mostly in the Amazon basin.

In the next centuries, Portuguese colonists gradually pushed inland, bringing along large numbers of African slaves. Slavery was not abolished until 1888.

The King of Portugal, fleeing before Napoleon's army, moved the seat of government to Brazil in 1808. Brazil thereupon became a kingdom under Dom Joao VI. After his return to Portugal, his son Pedro proclaimed the independence of Brazil, Sept. 7, 1822, and was acclaimed emperor. The second emperor, Dom Pedro II, was deposed in 1889, and a republic proclaimed, called the United States of Brazil. In 1967 the country was renamed the Federative Republic of Brazil.

A military junta took control in 1930; dictatorial power was assumed by Getulio Vargas, until finally forced out by the military in 1945. A democratic regime prevailed 1945-64, during which time the capital was moved from Rio de Janeiro to Brasilia in the interior.

In 1964, Pres. Joao Belchoir Marques Goulart instituted economic policies that aggravated Brazil's inflation; he was overthrown by an army revolt. The next 5 presidents were all military leaders. Censorship was imposed, and much of the opposition was suppressed amid charges of torture. In 1974 elections, the official opposition party made gains in the chamber of deputies; some relaxation of censorship occurred.

Since 1930, successive governments have pursued industrial and agricultural growth and the development of interior areas. Exploiting vast mineral resources, fertile soil in several regions, and a huge labor force, Brazil became the leading industrial power of Latin America by the 1970s, while agricultural output soared. Democratic presidential elections were held in 1985 as the nation returned to civilian rule. Fernando Collor de Mello was elected president in Dec. 1989.

However, income maldistribution and inflation have led to severe economic recession. Foreign debt is among the largest in the world. Brazil and its principal commercial bank lenders agreed to restructure the nation's $44 billion commercial debts, July 1992. The 1991 census revealed that population growth dipped below 2 percent for the first time in half a century.

Brazil unveiled a comprehensive environmental program for the Amazon region in 1989, amid an international outcry by environmentalists and others concerned about the ongoing destruction of the Amazon ecosystem. The Amazon rain forest was considered a global resource because of its impact on world weather patterns. Brazil hosted delegates from 178 countries at the Earth Summit June 3-14, 1992.

In Sept. 1992, Pres. Collor was impeached for corruption. He resigned on Dec. 29 as his trial was beginning, and Franco, who had been acting president, was sworn in as president.

# Brunei Darussalam
## State of Brunei Darussalam
## Negara Brunei Darussalam

**People: Population** (1992 est.): 369,000. **Pop. density:** 165 per sq. mi. **Ethnic groups:** Malay 65%, Chinese 20%. **Language:** Malay, English, (both official), Chinese. **Religion:** Moslem 60%, Buddhist 14%, Christian 10%.

**Geography: Area:** 2,226 sq. mi.; larger than Delaware. **Location:** on the north coast of the island of Borneo; it is surrounded on its landward side by the Malaysian state of Sarawak. **Capital:** Bandar Seri Begawan. **Cities** (1982 est.): Bandar Seri Begawan 51,000.

**Government: Type:** Independent sultanate. **Head of government:** Sultan Sir Muda Hassanal Bolkiah Mu'izzadin Waddaulah; in office: Jan. 1, 1984. **Local divisions:** 4 districts.

**Economy: Industries:** petroleum (about 90% of revenue is derived from oil exports). **Chief crops:** rice, bananas, cassava.

**Finance: Monetary unit:** Brunei dollar (Dec. 1992: 1.60 = $1). **Gross domestic product** (1989): $3.1 bln. **Per capita GDP:** $9,600.

**Transport: Motor vehicles:** In use (1990): 100,000 passenger cars, 12,000 commercial vehicles.

**Communications: Television sets:** 1 per 2.6 persons. **Radios:** 1 per 3 persons. **Telephones:** 1 per 6 persons.

**Education** (1987): **Literacy:** 95% among young.

**Health: Life expectancy at birth:** (1992): 69 male; 73 female. **Infant mortality** (per 1,000 live births 1992): 26.

**Major International Organizations:** UN and some of its specialized agencies.

The Sultanate of Brunei was a powerful state in the early 16th century, with authority over all of the island of Borneo as well as parts of the Sulu Islands and the Philippines. In 1888, a treaty was signed which placed the state under the protection of Great Britain.

Brunei became a fully sovereign and independent state on Jan. 1, 1984.

The Sultan of Brunei donated $10 million to the Nicaraguan *contras* in 1987; the subsequent misplacement of the funds generated much media attention in the U.S.

# Bulgaria
## Republic of Bulgaria
## Republika Bulgaria

**People: Population** (1992 est.): 8,868,000. **Age distrib.** (%): 0–14: 20.6; 15–59: 60.5; 60+: 18.9. **Pop. density:** 199 per sq. mi. **Urban** (1992): 67%. **Ethnic groups:** Bulgarian 85%, Turk 8.5%. **Languages:** Bulgarian (official), Turkish. **Religions:** Bulgarian Orthodox, 85%, Moslem 13%.

**Geography: Area:** 44,365 sq. mi., about the size of Ohio. **Location:** In eastern Balkan Peninsula on Black Sea. **Neighbors:** Romania on N, Yugoslavia, Macedonia on W, Greece, Turkey on S. **Topography:** The Stara Planina (Balkan) Mts. stretch E-W across the center of the country, with the Danubian plain on N, the Rhodope Mts. on SW, and Thracian Plain on SE. **Capital:** Sofia. **Cities** (1991 est.): Sofia 1,200,000; Plovdiv 379,000; Varna 320,000.

**Government: Type:** Republic. **Head of state:** Pres. Zhelyu Zhelev; b. Mar. 3, 1935; in office: Aug. 1, 1990. **Head of government:** Premier Lyuben Berov; in office: Dec. 30, 1992. **Local divisions:** 9 provinces. **Defense:** 4.4% of GNP (1991).

**Economy: Industries:** Chemicals, machinery, metals, textiles, processed food. **Chief crops:** Grains, fruit, corn, potatoes, tobacco. **Minerals:** Lead, manganese, lignite, coal. **Arable land:** 34%. **Livestock** (1990): cattle: 1.5 mln.; pigs: 4.3 mln.; sheep: 7.9 mln. **Fish catch** (1989): 121,000 metric tons. **Electricity prod.** (1990): 45 bln. kWh. **Crude steel prod.** (1991): 2.3 mln. metric tons. **Labor force:** 20% agric.; 33% ind.

**Finance: Monetary unit:** Leva (Dec. 1992: 25 = $1 US). **Gross national product** (1990): $47.3 bln. **Per capita GNP:** $5,300. **Imports** (1990): $9.6 bln.; partners: CIS 56%. **Exports** (1990): $8.4 bln.; partners: CIS 70%. **Tourism** (1989): revenues: $362 mln. **National budget** (1988): $28 bln. expenditures.

**Transport: Railroads** (1991): **Length:** 4,106 km. **Motor vehicles:** in use (1990): 1.3 mln. passenger cars, 200,000 commercial. **Civil aviation** (1990): 3.7 bln. passenger km.; 3 airports. **Chief ports:** Burgas, Varna.

**Communications: Television sets:** 1 per 3.9 persons. **Radios:** 1 per 4.8 persons. **Telephones in use:** 1 per 4.8 persons. **Daily newspaper circ.** (1988): 316 per 1,000 pop.

**Health: Life expectancy at birth** (1992): 69 male; 76 female. **Births** (per 1,000 pop. 1992): 13. **Deaths** (per 1,000 pop. 1992): 12. **Hospital beds:** 1 per 103 persons. **Physicians:** 1 per 337 persons. **Infant mortality** (per 1,000 live births 1992): 13.

**Education** (1990): **Literacy:** 98%.

**Major International Organizations:** UN.

**Embassy:** 1621-22d St. NW 20008; 387-7969.

Bulgaria was settled by Slavs in the 6th century. Turkic Bulgars arrived in the 7th century, merged with the Slavs, became Christians by the 9th century, and set up powerful empires in the 10th and 12th centuries. The Ottomans prevailed in 1396 and remained for 500 years.

A revolt in 1876 led to an independent kingdom in 1908. Bulgaria expanded after the first Balkan War but lost its Aegean coastline in World War I, when it sided with Germany. Bulgaria joined the Axis in World War II but withdrew in 1944. Communists took power with Soviet aid; the monarchy was abolished Sept. 8, 1946.

On Nov. 10, 1989, Communist party leader and head of state Todor Zhivkov, who had held power for 35 years, resigned. Zhivkov was imprisoned, Jan. 1990, and convicted, Sept. 1992, of corruption and abuse of power. In Jan. 1990, parliament voted to revoke the constitutionally guaranteed dominant role of the Communist Party.

## Burkina Faso

**People: Population** (1992 est.): 9,653,000. **Pop. density:** 91 per sq. mi. **Urban** (1988): 8%. **Ethnic groups:** Voltaic groups (Mossi, Bobo), Mande. **Languages:** French (official), Sudanic tribal languages. **Religions:** animist 65%, Moslem 25%, Christian 10%.

**Geography: Area:** 105,869 sq. mi., the size of Colorado. **Location:** In W. Africa, S of the Sahara. **Neighbors:** Mali on NW, Niger on NE, Benin, Togo, Ghana, Côte d' Ivoire on S. **Topography:** Landlocked Burkina Faso is in the savannah region of W. Africa. The N is arid, hot, and thinly populated. **Capital:** Ouagadougou. **Cities** (1990): Ouagadougou 500,000; Bobo-Dioulasso 250,000.

**Government: Type:** Military. **Head of state:** Pres. Blaise Compaoré; in office: Oct. 15, 1987. **Head of government:** Prime Min. Youssouf Ouedraogo; in office: June 16, 1992. **Local divisions:** 30 provinces. **Defense:** 2.7% of GDP (1988).

**Economy: Chief crops:** Millet, sorghum, rice, peanuts, grain. **Minerals:** Manganese, gold, limestone. **Arable land:** 10%. **Electricity prod.** (1991): 320 mln. kWh. **Labor force:** 82% agric. **Finance: Monetary unit:** CFA Franc (Mar. 1993: 273 = $1 US). **Gross domestic product** (1990): $2.9 bln. **Per capita GDP** (1989): $205. **Imports** (1989): $322 mln.; partners: EC, Côte d' Ivoire. **Exports** (1989): $95 mln.; partners: Côte d' Ivoire, EC, China. **International reserves less gold** (Jan. 1993): $345 mln. **Gold:** 11,000 oz t. **Consumer prices** (change in 1992): −1.4%.

**Transport: Motor vehicles:** in use (1990): 12,000 passenger cars, 13,000 comm. vehicles.

**Communications: Television sets:** 1 per 223 persons. **Radios:** 1 per 44 persons. **Telephones in use:** 1 per 482 persons. **Daily newspaper circ.** (1989): 1 per 1,000 pop.

**Health: Life expectancy at birth** (1992): 52 male; 53 female. **Births** (per 1,000 pop. 1992): 50. **Deaths** (per 1,000 pop. 1992): 16. **Natural increase:** 3.4%. **Hospital beds:** 1 per 1,359 persons. **Physicians:** 1 per 29,914 persons. **Infant mortality** (per 1,000 live births 1992): 117.

**Education** (1991): **Literacy:** 18%. Only 8% attend school. **Major International Organizations:** UN and many of its specialized agencies, OAU.

**Embassy:** 2340 Massachusetts Ave. NW 20008; 332-5577.

The Mossi tribe entered the area in the 11th to 13th centuries. Their kingdoms ruled until defeated by the Mali and Songhai empires.

French control came by 1896, but Upper Volta (name changed to Burkina Faso on Aug. 4, 1984) was not finally established as a separate territory until 1947. Full independence came Aug. 5, 1960, and a pro-French government was elected. The military seized power in 1980. A 1987 coup established the current regime, which restored limited democracy in the early 1990s.

Several hundred thousand farm workers migrate each year to Côte D'Ivoire and Ghana. Burkina Faso is heavily dependent on foreign aid.

## Burma

### (See Myanmar)

## Burundi
### Republic of Burundi
### Republika y'Uburundi

**People: Population** (1992 est.): 6,022,000. **Age distrib. (%):** 0–14: 45.1; 15–59: 50.1; 60+: 4.8. **Pop. density:** 559 per sq. mi. **Urban** (1986): 8%. **Ethnic groups:** Hutu 85%, Tutsi 14%, Twa (pygmy) 1%. **Languages:** French, Rundi (both official). **Religions:** Roman Catholic 62%, traditional African 32%.

**Geography: Area:** 10,759 sq. mi., the size of Maryland. **Location:** In central Africa. **Neighbors:** Rwanda on N, Zaire on W, Tanzania on E. **Topography:** Much of the country is grassy highland, with mountains reaching 8,900 ft. The southernmost source of the White Nile is located in Burundi. Lake Tanganyika is the second deepest lake in the world. **Capital:** Bujumbura. **Cities** (1991 est.): Bujumbura 240,000.

**Government: Type:** Republic. **Head of state:** Pres. Maj. Pierre Buyoya; in office: Sept. 9, 1987. **Head of government:** Pres. Melchior Ndadaye; in office: July 10, 1993. **Local divisions:** 15 provinces. **Defense** (1990): 19% of govt. budget.

**Economy: Chief crops:** Coffee (87% of exports), cotton, tea. **Minerals:** Nickel. **Arable land:** 43%. **Electricity prod.** (1991): 105 mln. kWh. **Labor force:** 93% agric.

**Finance: Monetary unit:** Franc (Apr. 1993: 236 = $1 US). **Gross domestic product** (1990): $1.2 bln. **Per capita GDP:** $200. **Imports** (1991): $248 mln.; partners: Belg.-Lux. 17%; Ger. 18%. **Exports** (1991): $90 mln; partners: Ger. 31%, Belg. 20%. **Tourism** (1990): $4 mln. receipts. **National budget** (1990): $203 mln. expenditures. **International reserves less gold** (Mar. 1993): $196 mln. **Gold:** 17,000 oz t. **Consumer prices** (change in 1992): 4.7%.

**Transport: Motor vehicles:** in use (1990): 12,000 passenger cars, 12,000 comm. vehicles.

**Communications: Radios:** 1 per 11 persons. **Telephones in use:** 1 per 611 persons.

**Health: Life expectancy at birth** (1992): 51 male; 55 female. **Births** (per 1,000 pop. 1992): 46. **Deaths** (per 1,000 pop. 1992): 14. **Natural increase:** 3.2%. **Hospital beds:** 1 per 515 persons. **Physicians:** 1 per 31,777 persons. **Infant mortality** (per 1,000 live births 1992): 106.

**Education** (1991): **Literacy:** 50%. **Years compulsory:** 6; **Attendance:** 45%.

**Major International Organizations:** UN (GATT, IMF, WHO), OAU.

**Embassy:** 2233 Wisconsin Ave. NW 20007; 342-2574.

The pygmy Twa were the first inhabitants, followed by Bantu Hutus, who were conquered in the 16th century by the Tutsi (Watusi), probably from Ethiopia. Under German control in 1899, the area fell to Belgium in 1916, which exercised successively a League of Nations mandate and UN trusteeship over Ruanda-Urundi (now the two countries of Rwanda and Burundi).

Independence came in 1962.

An unsuccessful Hutu rebellion in 1972-73 left 10,000 Tutsi and 150,000 Hutu dead. Over 100,000 Hutu fled to Tanzania and Zaire. In the 1980s, Burundi's Tutsi-dominated regime pledged itself to ethnic reconciliation and democratic reform. In the nation's first democratic presidential election, in June 1993, a Hutu was elected. Burundi remains one of the poorest and most densely populated countries in Africa.

# Cambodia

## State of Cambodia

## Roat Kampuchea

**People: Population** (1992 est.): 7,249,000. **Pop. density:** 103 per sq. mi. **Urban** (1990): 12%. **Ethnic groups:** Cambodian 90%, Vietnamese 4%, Chinese 5%. **Languages:** Khmer (official), French. **Religions:** Theravada Buddhism 95%.

**Geography: Area:** 70,238 sq. mi., the size of Missouri. **Location:** In Indochina Peninsula. **Neighbors:** Thailand on W, N, Laos on NE, Vietnam on E. **Topography:** The central area, formed by the Mekong R. basin and Tonle Sap lake, is level. Hills and mountains are in SE, a long escarpment separates the country from Thailand on NW. 75% of the area is forested. **Capital:** Phnom Penh. **Cities** (1990 est.): Phnom Penh 800,000.

**Government: Type:** Constitutional monarchy. **Head of State:** King Norodom Sihanouk; b. Oct. 31, 1922; in office: Sept. 24, 1993. **Head of Government:** First Prime Min. Prince Norodom Ranariddh; in office: Sept. 24, 1993. **Local divisions:** 19 provinces and 2 cities.

**Economy: Industries:** Rice milling, wood & rubber. **Chief crops:** Rice, corn. **Minerals:** Iron, copper, manganese. **Other resources:** Forests, rubber. **Arable land:** 16%. **Livestock** (1991): cattle: 2.0 mln. pigs: 1.5 mln. **Fish catch** (1991): 105,000 metric tons. **Electricity prod.** (1991): 200 mln. kWh. **Labor force:** 74% agri.

**Finance: Monetary unit:** Riel (Jan. 1993: 1,508 = $1 US). **Gross domestic product** (1991): $930 mln. **Per capita GDP:** $130. **Imports** (1988): $147 mln. **Exports** (1988): $32 mln.

**Transport: Railroads** (1989): Length: 649 mi. **Motor vehicles:** in use (1988): 4,000 passenger cars, 7,000 trucks. **Chief ports:** Kompong Som.

**Communications: Television sets:** 1 per 125 persons. **Radios:** 1 per 10 persons. **Telephones in use:** 1 per 3,300 persons.

**Health: Life expectancy at birth** (1992): 48 male; 51 female. **Births** (per 1,000 pop. 1992): 37. **Deaths** (per 1,000 pop. 1992): 15. **Natural increase:** 2.2. **Hospital beds:** 1 per 632 persons. **Physicians:** 1 per 27,000 persons. **Infant Mortality** (per 1,000 live births 1992): 121.

**Education** (1990): **Literacy:** 50%.

**Major International Organizations:** UN.

Early kingdoms dating from that of Funan in the 1st century AD culminated in the great Khmer empire which flourished from the 9th century to the 13th, encompassing present-day Thailand, Cambodia, Laos, and southern Vietnam. The peripheral areas were lost to invading Siamese and Vietnamese, and France established a protectorate in 1863. Independence came in 1953.

Prince Norodom Sihanouk, king 1941-1955 and head of state from 1960, tried to maintain neutrality. Relations with the U.S. were broken in 1965, after South Vietnam planes attacked Vietcong forces within Cambodia. Relations were restored in 1969, after Sihanouk charged Viet communists with arming Cambodian insurgents.

In 1970, pro-U.S. premier Lon Nol seized power, demanding removal of 40,000 North Viet troops; the monarchy was abolished. Sihanouk formed a government-in-exile in Peking, and open war began between the government and Khmer Rouge. The U.S. provided heavy military and economic aid.

Khmer Rouge forces captured Phnom Penh April 17, 1975. The new government evacuated all cities and towns, and shuffled the rural population, sending virtually the entire population to clear jungle, forest, and scrub, which covered half the country. Over one million people were killed in executions and enforced hardships.

Severe border fighting broke out with Vietnam in 1978; developed into a full-fledged Vietnamese invasion. The Vietnamese-backed Kampuchean National United Front for National Salvation, a Cambodian rebel movement, announced, Jan. 8, 1979, the formation of a government one day after the Vietnamese capture of Phnom Pehn. Thousands of refugees flowed into Thailand and widespread starvation was reported.

On Jan. 10, 1983, Vietnam launched an offensive against rebel forces in the west. They overran a refugee camp, Jan. 31, driving 30,000 residents into Thailand. In March, Vietnam launched a major offensive against camps on the Cambodian-Thailand border, engaged Khmer Rouge guerrillas, and crossed the border instigating clashes with Thai troops. Vietnam announced that it would withdraw all its troops by Sept. 1989.

Following UN-sponsored elections that ended May 28, 1993, the 2 leading parties agreed, June 18, to share power in an interim government until a new constitution was adopted. On Sept. 21, a constitution that created a constitutional monarchy was adopted by the National Assembly. it went into effect on Sept. 24.

# Cameroon

## Republic of Cameroon

**People: Population** (1992 est.): 12,658,000. **Age distrib.** (%): 0–14: 46.1; 15–59: 48.3; 60+: 5.6. **Pop. density:** 70 per sq. mi. **Urban** (1990): 40%. **Ethnic groups:** Some 200 tribes; largest are Bamileke 30%, Fulani 7%. **Languages:** English, French (both official), numerous African groups. **Religions:** Animist 51%, Moslem 16%, Christian 33%.

**Geography: Area:** 179,714 sq. mi., somewhat larger than California. **Location:** Between W and central Africa. **Neighbors:** Nigeria on NW, Chad, Central African Republic on E, Congo, Gabon, Equatorial Guinea on S. **Topography:** A low coastal plain with rain forests is in S; plateaus in center lead to forested mountains in W, including Mt. Cameroon, 13,000 ft.; grasslands in N lead to marshes around Lake Chad. **Capital:** Yaounde. **Cities** (1988 est.): Douala 852,000; Yaounde 700,000.

**Government: Type:** Republic, one party presidential regime. **Head of state:** Pres. Paul Biya; b. Feb. 13, 1933; in office: Nov. 6, 1982. Prime Min. Simon Achidi Achu; in office: Apr. 9, 1992. **Local divisions:** 10 provinces. **Defense:** 1.7% of GDP (1990).

**Economy: Industries:** Aluminum processing, oil prod., palm products. **Chief crops:** Cocoa, coffee, cotton. **Crude oil reserves** (1985): 531 mln. bbls. **Other resources:** Timber. **Arable land:** 14%. **Livestock** (1989): cattle: 4.5 mln.; sheep: 3.1 mln.; pigs: 1.2 mln. **Fish catch** (1990): 77,000 metric tons. **Electricity prod.** (1991): 2.9 bln. kWh. **Labor force:** 74% agric., 11% ind. and commerce.

**Finance: Monetary unit:** CFA franc (Mar. 1993: 274 = $1 US). **Gross domestic product** (1991): $11.6 bln. **Per capita GDP** (1991): $1,010. **Imports** (1990): $2.1 bln.; partners: Fr. 42%. **Exports** (1990): $928 mln.; partners: EC 50%. **National budget** (1990): $2.1 bln. **International reserves less gold** (Jan. 1993): $32.5 mln. **Gold:** 30,000 oz t.

**Transport: Railroads** (1990): Length: 686 mi. **Motor vehicles:** in use (1987): 78,000 passenger cars, 43,000 comm. vehicles. **Chief ports:** Douala.

**Communications: Radios:** 1 per 6 persons. **Telephones in use:** 1 per 185 persons. **Daily newspaper circ.** (1991): 6 per 1,000 pop.

**Health: Life expectancy at birth** (1992): 55 male; 60 female. **Births** (per 1,000 pop. 1992): 44. **Deaths** (per 1,000 pop. 1992): 11. **Natural increase:** 3.1%. **Hospital beds:** 1 per 377 persons. **Physicians:** 1 per 12,540 persons. **Infant mortality** (per 1,000 live births 1992): 81.

**Education** (1991): **Literacy:** 65%. About 70% attend school.

**Major International Organizations:** UN, OAU, EC (Associate).

**Embassy:** 2349 Massachusetts Ave. NW 20008; 265-8790.

Portuguese sailors were the first Europeans to reach Cameroon, in the 15th century. The European and American slave trade was very active in the area. German control lasted from 1884 to 1916, when France and Britain divided the territory, later receiving League of Nations mandates and UN trusteeships. French Cameroon became independent Jan. 1, 1960; one part of British Cameroon joined Nigeria in 1961, the other part joined Cameroon. Stability has allowed for development of roads, railways, agriculture, and petroleum production. Some 3,000 died in 1986 as a result of clouds of toxic gas of volcanic origin emanating from Lake Nyos.

# Canada

**People: Population** (1992 est.): 27,351,000. **Age distrib.** (%): 0–14: 20.9; 15–59: 63.1; 60+: 16.0. **Pop. density:** 7 per sq. mi. **Urban** (1990): 77%. **Ethnic groups:** British 25%; French 24%; other European 16%; mixed 28%. **Language:** English, French (both official). **Religion:** Roman Catholic 46%, Protestant 41%.

**Geography: Area:** 3,849,672 sq. mi., the largest country in land size in the western hemisphere. Canada stretches 3,426 miles from east to west and extends southward from the North Pole to the U.S. border. Its seacoast includes 36,356 miles of mainland and 115,133 miles of islands, including the Arctic islands almost from Greenland to near the Alaskan border. Climate, while generally temperate, varies from freezing winter cold to blistering summer heat. **Capital:** Ottawa. **Cities** (met. 1991 est.): Montreal 3,100,000; Toronto 3,800,000; Vancouver 1,600,000; Ottawa-Hull 920,000; Winnipeg 652,000; Edmonton 839,000, Calgary 754,000, Quebec 645,000.

**Government: Type:** Confederation with parliamentary democracy. **Head of state:** Queen Elizabeth II, represented by Gov.-Gen. Ramon Hnatyshyn; in office: Jan. 29, 1990. **Head of government:** Prime Min. Kim Campbell; b. Mar. 10, 1947; in office: June 25, 1993. **Local divisions:** 10 provinces, 2 territories. **Defense:** 2% of GDP (1991).

**Economy: Minerals:** Nickel, zinc, copper, gold, lead, molybdenum, potash, silver. **Crude oil reserves** (1991): 6.4 bln. barrels. **Arable land:** 5%. **Livestock** (1990): cattle: 12.0 mln.; pigs: 10.8 mln.; sheep: 722,000. **Fish catch** (1989): 1.6 mln. metric tons. **Electricity prod.** (1991): 479 bln. kWh. **Crude steel prod.** (1991): 12.9 mln. metric tons. **Labor force:** 4% agric.; 52% ind. & comm., 28% services.

**Finance: Monetary unit:** Dollar (July 1993: 1.27 = $1 US). **Gross domestic product** (1991): $521 bln. **Per capita GDP:** $19,400. **Imports** (1992): $124 bln.; partners: U.S. 69%, EC 8%, Jap. 5%. **Exports** (1992): $134 bln.; partners: U.S. 75%, EC 9%, Jap. 5%. **Tourism** (1990): receipts: $6.3 bln. **National budget** (1990-91): $127 bln. expenditures. **International reserves less gold** (Mar. 1993): $12.7 bln. **Gold:** 9.1 mln. oz t. **Consumer prices** (change in 1992): 1.5%.

**Transport: Railroads** (1990): Length: 56,771 mi. **Motor vehicles:** in use (1989): 12.0 mln. passenger cars, 3.7 mln. comm. **Civil aviation** (1990): 46 bln. passenger-km: 106 airports with scheduled flights.

**Communications: Television sets:** 1 per 1.7 persons. **Radios:** 1 per 1.2 persons. **Telephones in use:** 1 per 1.3 persons. **Daily newspaper circ.** (1991): 187 per 1,000 pop.

**Health: Life expectancy at birth** (1992): 74 male; 81 female. **Births** (per 1,000 pop. 1992): 14. **Deaths** (per 1,000 pop. 1992): 7. **Natural increase:** .7%. **Hospital beds:** 1 per 148 persons. **Physicians:** 1 per 449 persons. **Infant mortality** (per 1,000 live births 1992): 7.3.

**Education** (1991): **Literacy:** 99%.

**Major International Organizations:** UN and all of its specialized agencies, NATO, OECD, Commonwealth of Nations.

**Embassy:** 501 Pennsylvania Ave. NW 20001; 682-1740.

French explorer Jacques Cartier, who reached the Gulf of St. Lawrence in 1534, is generally regarded as the founder of Canada. But English seaman John Cabot sighted Newfoundland 37 years earlier, in 1497, and Vikings are believed to have reached the Atlantic coast centuries before either explorer.

Canadian settlement was pioneered by the French who established Quebec City (1608) and Montreal (1642) and declared New France a colony in 1663.

Britain, as part of its American expansion, acquired Acadia (later Nova Scotia) in 1717 and, through military victory over French forces in Canada (an extension of a European conflict between the 2 powers), captured Quebec (1759) and obtained control of the rest of New France in 1763. The French, through the Quebec Act of 1774, retained the rights to their own language, religion, and civil law.

The British presence in Canada increased during the American Revolution when many colonials, proudly calling themselves United Empire Loyalists, moved north to Canada.

Fur traders and explorers led Canadians westward across the continent. Sir Alexander Mackenzie reached the Pacific in 1793 and scrawled on a rock by the ocean, "from Canada by land."

In Upper and Lower Canada (later called Ontario and Quebec) and in the Maritimes, legislative assemblies appeared in the 18th century and reformers called for responsible government. But the War of 1812 intervened. The war, a conflict between Great Britain and the United States fought mainly in Upper Canada, ended in a stalemate in 1814.

In 1837 political agitation for more democratic government culminated in rebellions in Upper and Lower Canada. Britain sent Lord Durham to investigate and, in a famous report (1839), he recommended union of the 2 parts into one colony called Canada. The union lasted until Confederation, July 1, 1867, when proclamation of the British North America (BNA) Act launched the Dominion of Canada, consisting of Ontario, Quebec, and the former colonies of Nova Scotia and New Brunswick.

Since 1840 the Canadian colonies had held the right to internal self-government. The BNA act, which became the country's written constitution, established a federal system of government on the model of a British parliament and cabinet structure under the crown. Canada was proclaimed a self-governing Dominion within the British Empire in 1931.

In 1982 Canada severed its last formal legislative link with Britain by obtaining the right to amend its constitution (the British North America Act of 1867).

The Meech Lake Agreement was signed June 3, 1987. The historic accord would have assured constitutional protection for Quebec's efforts to preserve its French language and culture. Critics of the accord charged that it did not make any provision for other minority groups and that it gave Quebec too much power, which might enable it to pass laws that conflicted with the nation's 1982 Charter of Rights and Freedoms. The accord died June 22, 1990.

Its failure sparked a separatist revival in Quebec which culminated in Aug. 1992 in the Charlottetown agreement. This called for changes to the constitution, such as recognition of Quebec as a "distinct society" within the Canadian confederation and self-government for native peoples. The accord was defeated in a national referendum on Oct. 26, 1992.

In May 1992 voters in the Northwest Territories approved the creation of a self-governing homeland for the 17,500 Inuit living in the territories. The area—to be known as Nunavut, "Our Land"—would cover an area of 136,493 sq. mi. and will take effect by 1999.

Canada became the first nation to ratify the North American Free Trade Agreement between Canada, Mexico, and the U.S., June 23, 1993.

## Canadian Provinces

| | Sq. mi. | Population, 1991 cen. |
|---|---|---|
| Alberta | 255,287 | 2,545,553 |
| British Columbia | 365,947 | 3,282,061 |
| Manitoba | 250,947 | 1,091,942 |
| New Brunswick | 28,355 | 723,900 |
| Newfoundland | 156,949 | 568,474 |
| Nova Scotia | 21,425 | 899,942 |
| Ontario | 412,581 | 10,084,885 |
| Prince Edward Island | 2,185 | 129,765 |
| Quebec | 594,860 | 6,895,963 |
| Saskatchewan | 251,866 | 988,928 |
| **Territories** | | |
| Northwest Territories | 1,322,909 | 57,649 |
| Yukon | 186,661 | 27,797 |

## Prime Ministers of Canada

Canada is a constitutional monarchy with a parliamentary system of government. It is also a federal state. Canada's official head of state is the King or Queen of England, represented by a resident Governor-General. However, in practice the nation is governed by the Prime Minister, leader of the party that commands the support of a majority of the House of Commons, dominant chamber of Canada's bicameral Parliament.

| Name | Party | Term | Name | Party | Term |
|---|---|---|---|---|---|
| Sir John A. MacDonald | Conservative | 1867-1873 | Sir John J. C. Abbott | Conservative | 1891-1892 |
| | | 1878-1891 | Sir John S. D. Thompson | Conservative | 1892-1894 |
| Alexander Mackenzie | Liberal | 1873-1878 | Sir Mackenzie Bowell | Conservative | 1894-1896 |

| Name | Party | Term |
|------|-------|------|
| Sir Charles Tupper | Conservative | 1896 |
| Sir Wilfrid Laurier | Liberal | 1896-1911 |
| Sir Robert L. Borden | Cons. Union. | 1911-1920 |
| Arthur Meighen | Cons. Union. | 1920-1921 |
| W.L. Mackenzie King | Liberal | 1921-1926[1] |
| | | 1926-1930 |
| | | 1935-1948 |
| R. B. Bennett | Conservative | 1930-1935 |
| Louis St. Laurent | Liberal | 1948-1957 |

| Name | Party | Term |
|------|-------|------|
| John G. Diefenbaker | Prog. Cons. | 1957-1963 |
| Lester B. Pearson | Liberal | 1963-1968 |
| Pierre Elliott Trudeau | Liberal | 1968-1979 |
| Joe Clark | Prog. Cons. | 1979-1980 |
| Pierre Elliott Trudeau | Liberal | 1980-1984 |
| John Turner | Liberal | 1984 |
| Brian Mulroney | Prog. Cons. | 1984-1993 |
| Kim Campbell | Prog. Cons. | 1993 |

(1) King's term was interrupted from June 26-Sept. 25, 1926, when Arthur Meighen again served as prime minister.

## Cape Verde

### Republic of Cape Verde

### República de Cabo Verde

**People: Population** (1992 est.): 398,000. **Age distrib. (%):** 0–14: 45.6; 15–59: 47.7; 60+: 6.7. **Pop. density:** 255 per sq. mi. **Urban** (1991): 29%. **Ethnic groups:** Creole (mulatto) 71%, African 28%, European 1%. **Languages:** Portuguese (official), Crioulo. **Religions:** 80% Roman Catholic.

**Geography: Area:** 1,557 sq. mi., a bit larger than Rhode Island. **Location:** In Atlantic O., off western tip of Africa. **Neighbors:** Nearest are Mauritania, Senegal. **Topography:** Cape Verde Islands are 15 in number, volcanic in origin (active crater on Fogo). The landscape is eroded and stark, with vegetation mostly in interior valleys. **Capital:** Praia. **Cities** (1990 est.): Mindelo 47,000; Praia 61,000.

**Government: Type:** Republic. **Head of state:** Pres. Antonio Mascarenhas Monteiro; in office: Mar. 17, 1991. **Head of government:** Prime Min. Carlos Veiga; in office: Apr. 4, 1991. **Local divisions:** 14 administrative districts.

**Economy: Chief crops:** Bananas, coffee, beats, corn, beans. **Minerals:** Salt. **Other resources:** Fish. **Arable land:** 10%. **Electricity prod.** (1991): 15 mln. kWh.

**Finance: Monetary unit:** Escudo (Mar. 1993: 77 = $1 US). **Gross domestic product** (1990): $310 mln. **Per capita GDP:** $800. **Imports** (1989): $108 mln.; partners: Port. 33%, Neth. 12%. **Exports** (1989): $10.9 mln.; partners: Port. 32%, Ang. 21%.

**Transport: Motor vehicles:** in use (1988): 13,000 passenger cars, 4,000 comm. vehicles. **Chief ports:** Mindelo, Praia.

**Communications: Radios:** 1 per 6.8 persons. **Telephones in use:** 1 per 76 persons.

**Health: Life expectancy at birth** (1992): 60 male; 64 female. **Births** (per 1,000 pop. 1992): 48. **Deaths** (per 1,000 pop. 1992): 11. **Natural increase:** 3.8%. **Hospital beds:** 1 per 550 persons. **Physicians:** 1 per 4,208 persons. **Infant mortality** (per 1,000 live births 1992): 61.

**Education** (1989): **Literacy:** 37%.

**Major International Organizations:** UN (GATT, IMF, WHO), OAU.

**Embassy:** 3415 Massachusetts Ave. NW 20007; 965-6820.

The uninhabited Cape Verdes were discovered by the Portuguese in 1456 or 1460. The first Portuguese colonists landed in 1462; African slaves were brought soon after, and most Cape Verdeans descend from both groups. Cape Verde independence came July 5, 1975. The islands have suffered from repeated extreme droughts and famines. Emphasis is placed on the development of agriculture and on fishing.

Antonio Mascarenhas Monteiro won the nation's first free presidential election in 1991.

## Central African Republic

### République Centrafricaine

**People: Population** (1992 est.): 3,029,000. **Pop. density:** 12 per sq. mi. **Urban** (1990): 47%. **Ethnic groups:** Banda 27%, Baya 34%, Mandja 21%, Sara 10%. **Languages:** French (official), local dialects. **Religions:** Protestant 25%, Roman Catholic 25%, traditional 24%.

**Geography: Area:** 240,534 sq. mi., slightly smaller than Texas. **Location:** In central Africa. **Neighbors:** Chad on N, Cameroon on W, Congo, Zaire on S, Sudan on E. **Topography:** Mostly rolling plateau, average altitude 2,000 ft., with rivers draining S to the Congo and N to Lake Chad. Open, well-watered savanna covers most of the area, with an arid area in NE, and tropical rainforest in SW. **Capital:** Bangui. **Cities** (1988 est.): Bangui (met.) 596,000.

**Government: Type:** Republic (under military rule). **Head of state:** Gen. Andre Kolingba; in office: Sept. 1, 1981. **Head of government:** Prime Min. Enoch Devant Lakoue; in office: Feb. 1993. **Local divisions:** 16 prefectures. **Defense:** 2% of GDP (1989).

**Economy: Industries:** Textiles, light manuf, mining. **Chief crops:** Cotton, coffee, peanuts, tobacco. **Minerals:** Diamonds (chief export), uranium. **Other resources:** Timber. **Arable land:** 3%. **Electricity prod.** (1991): 93 mln. kWh. **Labor force:** 72% agric.

**Finance: Monetary unit:** CFA Franc (Mar. 1993: 273 = $1 US). **Gross domestic product** (1990): $1.3 bln. **Per capita GDP:** $440. **Imports** (1990): $214 mln.; partners: Fr. 44%. **Exports** (1990): $151 mln.; partners: Fr. 53%, Belg.-Lux. 23%. **National budget** (1991): $193 mln. expenditures. **International reserves less gold** (Jan. 1993): $103 mln. **Gold:** 12,000 oz t.

**Transport: Motor vehicles:** in use (1989): 10,000 passenger cars, 8,000 comm. vehicles.

**Communications: Radios:** 1 per 5 persons. **Telephones:** 1 per 380 persons.

**Health: Life expectancy at birth** (1992): 46 male; 49 female. **Births** (per 1,000 pop. 1992): 44. **Deaths** 1 per 1,000 pop. 1992): 19. **Natural increase:** 2.5%. **Hospital beds:** 1 per 689 persons. **Physicians:** 1 per 17,292 persons. **Infant mortality** (per 1,000 live births 1992): 135.

**Education** (1991): **Literacy:** 27%. **Attendance:** primary school 79%; secondary school 18%.

**Major International Organizations:** UN (GATT, IMF, WHO), OAU.

**Embassy:** 1618 22d St. NW 20008; 483-7800.

Various Bantu tribes migrated through the region for centuries before French control was asserted in the late 19th century, when the region was named Ubangi-Shari. Complete independence was attained Aug. 13, 1960.

All political parties were dissolved in 1960, and the country became a center for Chinese political influence in Africa. Relations with China were severed after 1965. Elizabeth Domitien, premier 1975-76, was the first woman to hold that post in an African country. Pres. Jean-Bedel Bokassa, who seized power in a 1965 military coup, proclaimed himself constitutional emperor of the renamed Central African Empire Dec. 1976.

Bokassa's rule was characterized by ruthless and cruel authority and human rights violations. Bokassa was ousted in a bloodless coup aided by the French government, Sept. 20, 1979, and replaced by his cousin David Dacko, former president from 1960 to 1965. In 1981, the political situation deteriorated amid strikes and economic crisis. Gen. Kolingba replaced Dacko as head of state in a bloodless coup. Multiparty legislative and presidential elections were held in Oct. 1992 but were canceled by the government when Kolingba was losing. New elections were scheduled for Oct. 1993.

## Chad

### Republic of Chad

### République du Tchad

**People: Population** (1992 est.): 5,238,000. **Age distrib. (%):** 0–14: 42.5; 15–59: 51.7; 60+: 5.8. **Pop. density:** 10 per sq. mi. **Urban** (1990): 32%. **Ethnic groups:** 200 distinct groups. **Languages:** French, Arabic, (both official), some 100 other languages. **Religions:** Moslem 44%, animist 23%, Christian 33%.

**Geography: Area:** 495,755 sq. mi., four-fifths the size of Alaska. **Location:** In central N. Africa. **Neighbors:** Libya on N, Niger, Nigeria, Cameroon on W, Central African Republic on S, Sudan on E. **Topography:** Southern wooded savanna, steppe, and desert, part of the Sahara, in the N. Southern rivers flow N to Lake Chad, surrounded by marshland. **Capital:** N'Djamena. **Cities** (1992 est.): N'Djamena 500,000.

**Government: Type:** Republic. **Head of state:** Pres. Idriss Deby; in office: Dec. 4, 1990. **Head of government:** Prime Min. Joseph Yodoyman; in office: May 20, 1992. **Local divisions:** 14 prefectures. **Defense:** 5.6% of GDP (1990).

**Economy: Chief crops:** Cotton. **Minerals:** Uranium, salt. **Arable land:** 2%. **Fish catch** (1990): 115,000 metric tons. **Electricity prod.** (1991): 69 mln. kWh. **Labor force:** 85% agric.

**Finance: Monetary unit:** CFA franc (Mar. 1993: 273 = $1 US). **Gross domestic product** (1992): $1.0 bln. **Per capita GDP:** $190. **Imports** (1990): $264 mln.; partners: Fr. 47%. **Exports** (1990): $174 mln.; partners Fra. **International reserves less gold** (Jan. 1993): $74 mln. **Gold:** 11,000 oz t.

**Transport: Motor vehicles:** in use (1989): 8,000 passenger cars, 6,000 comm. vehicles.

**Communications: Radios:** 1 per 4.3 persons. **Telephones in use:** 1 per 555 persons.

**Health: Life expectancy at birth** (1992): 39 male; 41 female. **Births** (per 1,000 pop. 1992): 42. **Deaths** (per 1,000 pop. 1992): 22. **Natural increase:** 2.0%. **Hospital beds** (1980): 3.500. **Physicians** (1980): 94. **Infant mortality** (per 1,000 live births 1992): 136.

**Education** (1991): **Literacy:** 30%.

**Major International Organizations:** UN, (GATT, IMF, WHO), OAU, EEC.

**Embassy:** 2002 R St. NW 20009; 462-4009.

Chad was the site of paleolithic and neolithic cultures before the Sahara Desert formed. A succession of kingdoms and Arab slave traders dominated Chad until France took control around 1900. Independence came Aug. 11, 1960.

Northern Moslem rebels have fought animist and Christian southern government and French troops from 1966, despite numerous cease-fires and peace pacts.

Libyan troops entered the country at the request of the Chad government, December 1980. On Jan. 6, 1981, Libya and Chad announced their intention to unite. France together with several African nations condemned the agreement as a menace to African security. The Libyan troops were withdrawn from Chad in November 1981.

Rebel forces, led by Hissene Habre, captured the capital and forced Pres. Goukouni Oueddei to flee the country in June 1982.

In 1983, France sent some 3,000 troops to Chad to assist Habre in opposing Libyan-backed rebels. France and Libya agreed to a simultaneous withdrawal of troops from Chad in September 1984, but Libyan forces remained in the north until Mar. 1987 when Chad forces drove them from their last major stronghold. In Dec. 1990, Pres. Hissene Habre was overthrown by a Libyan-supported insurgent group, the Patriotic Salvation Movement. The group's leader, Idriss Deby, assumed the presidency.

# Chile

## Republic of Chile
### República de Chile

**People: Population** (1992 est.): 13,528,000. **Age distrib.** (%): 0–14: 30.9 15–59: 60.4; 60+: 7.7. **Pop. density:** 44 per sq. mi. **Urban** (1990): 84%. **Ethnic groups:** Mestizo 66%, Spanish 25%, Indian 5%. **Languages:** Spanish. **Religions:** Roman Catholic 89%, Protestant 11%.

**Geography: Area:** 302,779 sq. mi., twice the size of California. **Location:** Occupies western coast of southern S. America. **Neighbors:** Peru on N, Bolivia on NE, Argentina on E. **Topography:** Andes Mtns. are on E border including some of the world's highest peaks; on W is 2,650-mile Pacific Coast. Width varies between 100 and 250 miles. In N is Atacama Desert, in center are agricultural regions, in S are forests and grazing lands. **Capital:** Santiago. **Cities** (1992 metro est.) Santiago 5,300,000.

**Government: Type:** Republic. **Head of state:** Pres. Patricio Aylwin Ozocar; b. Nov. 26, 1918; in office: Mar. 11, 1990. **Local divisions:** 13 regions. **Defense:** 3.4% of GNP (1991).

**Economy: Industries:** Fish processing, wood products, iron, steel. **Chief crops:** Grain, onions, beans, potatoes, peas, fruits. **Minerals:** Copper (about half of export revenues), molybdenum, nitrates, iodine (half world output), iron, coal, oil, gas, gold, cobalt, zinc, manganese, borate, mica, mercury, salt, sulphur, marble, onyx. **Other resources:** Water, forests. **Arable land:** 7%. **Livestock** (1990): cattle: 3.3 mln.; sheep: 6.5 mln.; pigs: 1.1 mln. **Fish catch** (1991): 6.1 mln. metric tons. **Electricity prod.** (1991): 21.4 bln. kWh. **Labor force:** 19% agric., forestry, fishing; 34% ind & comm., 30% serv.

**Finance: Monetary unit:** Peso (July 1993: 392 = $1 US). **Gross domestic product** (1991): $29.2 bln. **Per capita GDP** (1990): $2,200. **Imports** (1991): $7.6 bln.; partners: U.S. 19%, EC 23%. **Exports** (1991): $9.0 bln.; partners: EC 34%, U.S. 18%. **Tourism** (1990): $548 mln. receipts. **National budget** (1991): $8.3 bln. expenditures. **International reserves less gold** (Mar. 1993): $9.7 bln. **Gold:** 1.86 mln. oz. t. **Consumer prices** (change in 1992): 15.4%.

**Transport: Railroads** (1990): **Length:** 4,470 mi. **Motor vehicles:** in use (1989): 690,000 passenger cars, 300,000 comm. vehicles. **Civil aviation** (1990): 2.9 bln. passenger-km.; 17 airports with scheduled flights. **Chief ports:** Valparaiso, Arica, Antofagasta.

**Communications: Television sets:** 1 per 4.1 persons. **Radios:** 1 per 3.3 persons. **Telephones in use:** 1 per 16 persons.

**Health: Life expectancy at birth** (1992): 71 male; 77 female. **Births** (per 1,000 pop. 1992): 21. **Deaths** (per 1,000 pop. 1992): 6. **Natural increase:** 1.5%. **Hospital beds:** 1 per 304 persons. **Physicians:** 1 per 919 persons. **Infant mortality** (per 1,000 live births 1992): 18.

**Education** (1991): **Literacy:** 92%. Compulsory ages 6-14.

**Major International Organizations:** UN and all of its specialized agencies, OAS.

**Embassy:** 1732 Massachusetts Ave. NW 20036; 785-1746.

Northern Chile was under Inca rule before the Spanish conquest, 1536-40. The southern Araucanian Indians resisted until the late 19th century. Independence was gained 1810-18, under Jose de San Martin and Bernardo O'Higgins; the latter, as supreme director 1817-23, sought social and economic reforms until deposed. Chile defeated Peru and Bolivia in 1836-39 and 1879-84, gaining mineral-rich northern land.

Eduardo Frei Montalva came into office in 1964, instituting social programs and gradual nationalization of foreign-owned mining companies. In 1970, Salvador Allende Gossens, a Marxist, became president with a third of the national vote.

The Allende government furthered nationalizations and improved conditions for the poor. But illegal and violent actions by extremist supporters of the government, the regime's failure to attain majority support, and poorly planned socialist economic programs led to political and financial chaos.

A military junta seized power Sept. 11, 1973, and said Allende killed himself. The junta named a mostly military cabinet and announced plans to "exterminate Marxism."

Repression continued during the 1980s with little sign of any political liberalization. In a plebiscite held Oct. 5, 1988, voters rejected junta-candidate Gen. Augusto Pinochet Ugarte who, if victorious, would have governed Chile until 1997. Pinochet accepted the rejection and called for presidential elections. In Dec. 1989 voters removed Pinochet from office and elected Patricio Aylwin as president. A 1991 report documented more than 2,200 deaths that were a result of human rights violoations during Pinochet's rule.

**Tierra del Fuego** is the largest (18,800 sq. mi.) island in the archipelago of the same name at the southern tip of South America, an area of majestic mountains, tortuous channels, and high winds. It was discovered 1520 by Magellan and named the Land of Fire because of its many Indian bonfires. Part of the island is in Chile, part in Argentina. Punta Arenas, on a mainland peninsula, is a center of sheep raising and the world's southernmost city (pop. about 70,000); Puerto Williams is the southernmost settlement.

# China

## People's Republic of China
### Zhonghua Renmin Gonghe Guo

**People: Population** (1992 est.): 1,169,619,000. **Pop. density:** 315 per sq. mi. **Urban** (1990): 27%. **Ethnic groups:** Han

Chinese 94%, Mongol, Korean, Manchu, others. **Languages:** Mandarin (official), Yue, Wu Hakka, Xiang, Gan, Min, Zhuang, Hui, Yi. **Religions:** officially atheist; Confucianism, Buddhism, Taoism are traditional.

**Geography: Area:** 3,696,100 sq. mi., slightly larger than the U.S. **Location:** Occupies most of the habitable mainland of E. Asia. **Neighbors:** Mongolia on N, Russia on NE and NW, Afghanistan, Pakistan, Tajikistan, Kazakhstan on W, India, Nepal, Bhutan, Myanmar, Laos, Vietnam on S, N. Korea on NE. **Topography:** Two-thirds of the vast territory is mountainous or desert, and only one-tenth is cultivated. Rolling topography rises to high elevations in the N in the Daxinganlingshanmai separating Manchuria and Mongolia; the Tienshan in Xinjiang; the Himalayan and Kunlunshanmai in the SW and in Tibet. Length is 1,860 mi. from N to S, width E to W is more than 2,000 mi. The eastern half of China is one of the best-watered lands in the world. Three great river systems, the Changjiang, the Huanghe, and the Xijiang provide water for vast farmlands. **Capital:** Beijing. **Cities** (1990 est.): Shanghai 7.7 mln.; Beijing 6.9 mln.; Tianjin 5.7 mln.; Canton 3.5 mln.; Shenyang 4.5 mln.; Wuhan 3.7 mln.

**Government: Type:** Communist Party led state. **Head of state:** Pres. Jiang Zemin; in office: Mar. 27, 1993. **Head of government:** Premier Li Peng; in office: Apr. 9, 1989. **Local divisions:** 22 provinces, 5 autonomous regions, and 3 cities. **Defense:** 3.0% of GNP (1992).

**Economy: Industries:** Iron and steel, textiles, agriculture implements, trucks. **Chief crops:** Grain, rice, cotton, tea. **Minerals:** tungsten, antimony, coal, iron, lead, manganese, molybdenum, tin. **Crude oil reserves** (1991): 30.8 bln. barrels. **Other resources:** Silk. **Arable land:** 11%. **Livestock** (1991): cattle: 81 mln.; pigs: 369 mln.; sheep: 112 mln. **Fish catch** (1990): 12.0 mln. metric tons. **Electricity prod.** (1991): 670 bln. kWh. **Crude steel prod.** (1991): 70.4 mln. metric tons. **Labor force:** 60% agric.; 25% ind. & comm.

**Finance: Monetary unit:** Yuan (July 1993): 5.71 = $1 US). **Gross national product** (1989): $393 bln. **Per capita GNP:** $360. **Imports** (1992): $76.3 bln.; partners: Jap. 20%, U.S. 11%, Hong Kong 20%. **Exports** (1992): $80.5 bln.; partners: Hong Kong 38%, Jap. 16%, U.S. 7%. **Tourism** (1991): $2.8 bln. receipts. **National budget** (1987): $66.1 bln. expenditures. **International reserves less gold** (Feb. 1993): $42.8 bln. **Gold:** 12.7 mln. oz t. **Consumer prices** (change in 1991): 2.1%.

**Transport: Railroads** (1990): **Length:** 41,973 mi. **Motor vehicles:** in use (1990): 1.6 mln. passenger cars, 4.1 mln. comm. vehicles. **Civil aviation** (1991): 30.1 bln. passenger km, 90 airports with scheduled flights. **Chief ports:** Shanghai, Qinhuangdao, Dalian, Canton.

**Communications: Television sets:** 1 per 8 persons. **Radios:** 1 per 9.1 persons. **Telephones:** 1 per 89 persons. **Daily newspaper circ.** (1989): 37 per 1,000 pop.

**Health: Life expectancy at birth** (1992): 69 male; 72 female. **Births** (per 1,000 pop. 1992): 22. **Deaths** (per 1,000 pop. 1992): 7. **Natural increase:** 1.5%. **Infant mortality** (per 1,000 live births 1992): 33. **Hospital beds:** 1 per 428 persons. **Physicians:** 1 per 646 persons.

**Education** (1987): **Literacy:** 70%. Years compulsory 9; first grade enrollment 93%.

**Major International Organizations:** UN (IMF, FAO, WHO). **Embassy:** 2300 Conn. Ave. NW 20008; 328-2500.

**History.** Remains of various man-like creatures who lived as early as several hundred thousand years ago have been found in many parts of China. Neolithic agricultural settlements dotted the Huanghe basin from about 5,000 BC. Their language, religion, and art were the sources of later Chinese civilization.

Bronze metallurgy reached a peak and Chinese pictographic writing, similar to today's, was in use in the more developed culture of the Shang Dynasty (c. 1500 BC-c. 1000 BC) which ruled much of North China.

A succession of dynasties and interdynastic warring kingdoms ruled China for the next 3,000 years. They expanded Chinese political and cultural domination to the south and west, and developed a brilliant technologically and culturally advanced society. Rule by foreigners (Mongols in the Yuan Dynasty, 1271-1368, and Manchus in the Ch'ing Dynasty, 1644-1911) did not alter the underlying culture.

A period of relative stagnation left China vulnerable to internal and external pressures in the 19th century. Rebellions left tens of millions dead, and Russia, Japan, Britain, and other powers exercised political and economic control in large parts of the country. China became a republic Jan. 1, 1912, following the Wuchang Uprising inspired by Dr. Sun Yat-sen.

For a period of 50 years, 1894-1945, China was involved in conflicts with Japan. In 1895, China ceded Korea, Taiwan, and other areas. On Sept. 18, 1931, Japan seized the Northeastern Provinces (Manchuria) and set up a puppet state called Manchukuo. The border province of Jehol was cut off as a buffer state in 1933. Japan invaded China proper July 7, 1937. After its defeat in World War II, Japan gave up all seized land.

Following World War II, internal disturbances arose involving the Kuomintang, communists, and other factions. China came under domination of communist armies, 1949-1950. The Kuomintang government moved to Taiwan, 90 mi. off the mainland, Dec. 8, 1949.

The People's Republic of China was proclaimed in Peking Sept. 21, 1949, by the Chinese People's Political Consultative Conference under Mao Zedong.

China and the USSR signed a 30-year treaty of "friendship, alliance and mutual assistance," Feb. 15, 1950.

The U.S. refused recognition of the new regime. On Nov. 26, 1950, the People's Republic sent armies into Korea against U.S. troops and forced a stalemate.

By the 1960s, relations with the USSR deteriorated, with disagreements on borders, ideology and leadership of world communism. The USSR cancelled aid accords, and China, with Albania, launched anti-Soviet propaganda drives.

On Oct. 25, 1971, the UN General Assembly ousted the Taiwan government from the UN and seated the People's Republic in its place. The U.S. had supported the mainland's admission but opposed Taiwan's expulsion.

U.S. Pres. Nixon visited China Feb. 21-28, 1972, on invitation from Premier Zhou Enlai, ending years of antipathy between the 2 nations. China and the U.S. opened liaison offices in each other's capitals, May-June 1973. The U.S., Dec. 15, 1978, formally recognized the People's Republic of China as the sole legal government of China; diplomatic relations between the 2 nations were established, Jan. 1, 1979.

**Internal developments.** After an initial period of consolidation, 1949-52, industry, agriculture, and social and economic institutions were forcibly molded according to Maoist ideals. However, frequent drastic changes in policy and violent factionalism interfered with economic development.

In 1957, Mao Tse-tung admitted an estimated 800,000 people had been executed 1949-54; opponents claimed much higher figures.

The Great Leap Forward, 1958-60, tried to force the pace of economic development through intensive labor on huge new rural communes, and through emphasis on ideological purity and enthusiasm. The program caused resistance and was largely abandoned. Serious food shortages developed, and the government was forced to buy grain from the West.

The Great Proletarian Cultural Revolution, 1965, was an attempt to oppose pragmatism and bureaucratic power and instruct a new generation in revolutionary principles. Massive purges took place. A program of forcibly relocating millions of urban teenagers into the countryside was launched.

By 1968 the movement had run its course; many purged officials returned to office in subsequent years, and reforms in education and industry that had placed ideology above expertise were gradually weakened.

In a continuing "reassessment" of the policies of Mao Zedong, Mao's widow, Jiang Quing, and other Gang of Four members were convicted of "committing crimes during the 'Cultural Revolution,' " Jan. 25, 1981.

In the mid-1970s, factional and ideological fighting increased, and emerged into the open after the 1976 deaths of Mao and Premier Zhou Enlai. Mao's widow and 3 other leading leftists were purged and placed under arrest, after reportedly trying to seize power. The new ruling group modified Maoist policies in education, culture, and industry, and sought better ties with non-communist countries.

Relations with Vietnam deteriorated in 1978 as China charged persecution of ethnic Chinese. In retaliation for Vietnam's invasion of Cambodia, China attacked 4 Vietnamese border provinces Feb. 17, 1979; heavy border fighting ensued.

By the mid 1980's, China had enacted far-reaching economic reforms highlighted by the departure from rigid central planning and the stressing of market-oriented socialism.

Some 100,000 students and workers mounted a march in Beijing to demand democratic reforms, May 4, 1989. The demonstrations continued during a visit to Beijing by Soviet leader Mikhail Gorbachev May 15-18. It was the first Sino-Soviet summit since 1959. A million people gathered in Beijing to demand democratic reforms and the removal of Deng and other leaders. There were protests in at least 20 other Chinese cities. Martial law was imposed, May 20, but was mostly ignored by the protesters.

Chinese army troops entered Beijing, June 3-4, and crushed the pro-democracy protests. Tanks and armored personnel carriers attacked Tiananmen Square, outside the Great Hall of the People, which was the main scene of the demonstrations and hunger strikes. It is estimated that 5,000 died, 10,000 were injured, and hundreds of students and workers arrested.

China's population, the world's largest, is still increasing, but with more couples following the government's one-child policy some experts predict that the nation's population will actually decline after peaking in the early 21st century.

**Manchuria.** Home of the Manchus, rulers of China 1644-1911, Manchuria has accommodated millions of Chinese settlers in the 20th century. Under Japanese rule 1931-45, the area became industrialized. China no longer uses the name Manchuria for the region, which is divided into the 3 NE provinces of Heilongjiang, Jilin, and Liaoning.

**Guangxi** is in SE China, bounded on N by Kweichow and Hunan provinces, E and S by Kwangtung, on SW by North Vietnam, and on W by Yunnan. It produces rice in the river valleys and has valuable forest products.

**Inner Mongolia** was organized by the People's Republic in 1947. Its boundaries have undergone frequent changes, reaching its greatest extent (and restored in 1979) in 1956, with an area of 454,000 sq. mi., allegedly in order to dilute the minority Mongol population. Chinese settlers outnumber the Mongols more than 10 to 1. Pop. (1990 cen.): 21.4 mln. Capital: Hohhot.

**Xinjiang,** in Central Asia, is 633,802 sq. mi., pop. (1990 cen.): 15.1 mln. (75% Uygurs, a Turkic Moslem group, with a heavy Chinese increase in recent years). Capital: Urumqi. It is China's richest region in strategic minerals.

**Tibet,** 470,000 sq. mi., is a thinly populated region of high plateaus and massive mountains, the Himalayas on the S, the Kunluns on the N. High passes connect with India and Nepal; roads lead into China proper. Capital: Lhasa. Average altitude is 15,000 ft. Jiachan, 15,870 ft., is believed to be the highest inhabited town on earth. Agriculture is primitive. Pop. (1990 cen.): 2.1 mln. (of whom about 500,000 are Chinese). Another 4 million Tibetans form the majority of the population of vast adjacent areas that have long been incorporated into China.

China ruled all of Tibet from the 18th century, but independence came in 1911. China reasserted control in 1951, and a communist government was installed in 1953, revising the theocratic Lamaist Buddhist rule. Serfdom was abolished, but all land remained collectivized.

A Tibetan uprising within China in 1956 spread to Tibet in 1959. The rebellion was crushed with Chinese troops, and Buddhism was almost totally suppressed. The Dalai Lama and 100,000 Tibetans fled to India.

# Colombia

## Republic of Colombia
## República de Colombia

**People: Population** (1992 est.): 34,296,000. **Age distrib. (%):** 0-14: 36.1; 15-59: 57.8; 60+: 6.1. **Pop. density:** 77 per sq. mi. **Urban** (1983): 65.4%. **Ethnic groups:** Mestizo 58%, Caucasian 20%, Mulatto 14%. **Languages:** Spanish. **Religions:** Roman Catholic 95%.

**Geography: Area:** 439,735 sq. mi., about the size of Texas, and New Mexico combined. **Location:** At the NW corner of S. America. **Neighbors:** Panama on NW, Ecuador, Peru on S, Brazil, Venezuela on E. **Topography:** Three ranges of Andes, the Western, Central, and Eastern Cordilleras, run through the country from N to S. The eastern range consists mostly of high table lands, densely populated. The Magdalena R. rises in Andes, flows N to Carribean, through a rich alluvial plain. Sparsely-settled plains in E are drained by Orinoco and Amazon systems. **Capital:** Bogota. **Cities** (1992 est.): Bogota 4,921,000; Medellin 1,581,000; Cali 1,624,000; Barranquilla 1,018,000.

**Government: Type:** Republic. **Head of state:** Pres. Cesar Gaviria Trujillo; b. Mar. 31, 1947; in office: Aug. 7, 1990. **Local divisions:** 23 departments, 8 national territories, and special district of Bogota. **Defense:** 1.4% of GDP (1991).

**Economy: Industries:** Textiles, processed goods, hides, steel, cement, chemicals. **Chief crops:** Coffee (50% of exports), rice, corn, cotton, sugar, bananas. **Minerals:** Oil, gas, emeralds (90% world output), gold, copper, lead, coal, iron, nickel, salt. **Crude oil reserves** (1991): 1.8 bln. bbls. **Other resources:** Rubber, balsam, dye-woods, copaiba, hydro power. **Arable land:** 5%. **Livestock** (1990): cattle: 24.6 mln.; pigs: 2.6 mln.; sheep: 2.6 mln. **Fish catch** (1990): 101,000 metric tons. **Electricity prod.** (1991): 38 bln. kWh. **Labor force:** 30% agric.; 24% ind.; 46% services.

**Finance: Currency:** Peso (July 1993: 678 = $1 US). **Gross domestic product** (1990): $43 bln. **Per capita GDP:** $1,300. **Imports** (1991): $6.1 bln.; partners: U.S. 36%, EC 16%. **Exports** (1991): $7.5 bln.; partners: U.S. 40%, EC 21%. **Tourism** (1990): $362 mln. receipts. **National budget** (1989): $3.9 bln. expenditures. **International reserves less gold** (Mar. 1993): $7.3 bln. **Gold:** 539,000 oz t. **Consumer prices** (change in 1992): 27.0.

**Transport: Railway traffic** (1991): 179 mln. passenger-km. **Motor vehicles:** in use (1989): 936,000 passenger cars, 364,000. **Civil aviation** (1991): 4.5 bln. passenger-km; airports with scheduled flights: 63. **Chief ports:** Buena Ventura, Santa Marta, Barranquilla, Cartagena.

**Communications: Television sets:** 1 per 5.6 persons. **Radios:** 1 per 7.3 persons. **Telephones:** 1 per 13 persons. **Daily newspaper circ.** (1992): 23 per 1,000 pop.

**Health: Life expectancy at birth** (1992): 69 male; 74 female. **Births** (per 1,000 pop. 1992): 24. **Deaths** (per 1,000 pop. 1992): 5. **Natural increase:** 1.9%. **Physicians:** 1 per 1,079 persons. **Infant mortality** (per 1,000 live births 1991): 37%.

**Education** (1990): **Literacy:** 80%. Only 28% finish primary school.

**Major International Organizations:** UN (World Bank, GATT), OAS.

**Embassy:** 2118 Leroy Pl. NW, 20008; 387-8338.

Spain subdued the local Indian kingdoms (Funza, Tunja) by the 1530s and ruled Colombia and neighboring areas as New Granada for 300 years. Independence was won by 1819. Venezuela and Ecuador broke away in 1829-30, and Panama withdrew in 1903.

One of the Latin American democracies, Colombia is plagued by rural and urban violence, though scaled down from "La Violencia" of 1948-58, which claimed 200,000 lives. Attempts at land and social reform and progress in industrialization have not succeeded in reducing massive social problems aggravated by a very high birth rate. In 1989, the government's increased activity against local drug traffickers sparked a series of retaliation killings. On Aug. 18, Luis Carlos Galán, the ruling party's presidential hopeful in the 1990 election, was assassinated. In 1990, 2 other presidential candidates were slain as the drug traffickers carried on a campaign of intimidation to stop the presidential election. Cesar Gaviria Trujillo, a strong advocate of maintaining the government's war against the nation's drug cartels, was elected president in May. His popularity greatly declined in 1992 when a drug boss escaped from prison in July, allegedly with aid from the military and prison officials, and the drug industry continued to grow.

# Comoros

## Federal Islamic Republic of the Comoros
## Jumhurīyat al-Qumur al-Itthādīyah al-Islāmīyah

**People: Population** (1992 est.): 493,000. **Pop. density:** 588 per sq. mi. **Ethnic groups:** Arabs, Africans, East Indians. **Languages:** Arabic, French (both official). **Religions:** Sunni Moslem 86%, Roman Catholic 14%.

**Geography: Area:** 838 sq. mi., half the size of Delaware. **Location:** 3 islands (Grande Comore, Anjouan, and Moheli) in the Mozambique Channel between NW Madagascar and SE Africa. **Neighbors:** Nearest are Mozambique on W, Madagascar on E. **Topography:** The islands are of volcanic origin, with an active volcano on Grand Comoro. **Capital:** Moroni. **Cities** (1992 est.): Moroni (met.) 30,000.

**Government: Type:** Republic. **Head of state:** Pres. Said Mohammed Djohar; in office: Nov. 26, 1989. **Local divisions:** each of the 3 main islands is a prefecture.

**Economy: Industries:** Perfume. **Chief crops:** Vanilla, copra, perfume plants, fruits. **Arable land:** 35%. **Electricity prod.** (1991): 24 mln. kWh. **Labor force:** 80% agric.

**Finance: Monetary unit:** CFA franc (Mar. 1993: 273 = $1 US). **Gross domestic product** (1991): $260 mln. **Per capita GDP:** $540. **Imports** (1990): $41 mln.; partners: Fr. 22%. **Exports** (1990): $16 mln.; partners: Fr. 41%, U.S. 53%.

**Transport: Chief ports:** Dzaoudzi.

**Communications: Radios:** 1 per 9 persons. **Telephones in use:** 1 per 132 persons.

**Health: Life expectancy at birth** (1992): 55 male; 59 female. **Births** (per 1,000 pop. 1992): 47. **Deaths** (per 1,000 pop. 1992): 13. **Natural increase:** 3.5%. **Infant mortality** (per 1,000 live births 1992): 84.

**Education:** (1989): **Literacy:** 15%; less than 20% attend secondary school.

**Major International Organizations:** UN (IMF, World Bank); OAU.

**Embassy:** 336 E. 45th St., New York, NY 10017; (212) 972-8010.

The islands were controlled by Moslem sultans until the French acquired them 1841-1909. They became a French overseas territory in 1947. A 1974 referendum favored independence, with only the Christian island of Mayotte preferring association with France. The French National Assembly decided to allow each of the islands to decide its own fate. The Comoro Chamber of Deputies declared independence July 6, 1975, with Ahmed Abdallah as president. In a referendum in 1976, Mayotte voted to remain French. A leftist regime that seized power from Abdallah in 1975 was deposed in a pro-French 1978 coup in which he regained the presidency.

In Nov. 1989, Pres. Abdallah was assassinated.

# Congo

## Republic of Congo

## République du Congo

**People: Population** (1992 est.): 2,376,000. **Pop. density:** 17 per sq. mi. **Urban** (1990): 41%. **Ethnic groups:** Bakongo 45%, Bateke 20%, others. **Languages:** French (official), Kongo, Teke. **Religions:** Christians 50% (two-thirds Roman Catholic), animists 47%, Moslem 2%.

**Geography: Area:** 132,046 sq. mi., slightly smaller than Montana. **Location:** In western central Africa. **Neighbors:** Gabon, Cameroon on W, Central African Republic on N, Zaire on E, Angola on SW. **Topography:** Much of the Congo is covered by thick forests. A coastal plain leads to the fertile Niari Valley. The center is a plateau; the Congo R. basin consists of flood plains in the lower and savanna in the upper portion. **Capital:** Brazzaville. **Cities** (1992 est.): Brazzaville (met.) 937,000; Pointe-Noire 576,000; Loubomo 83,000.

**Government: Type:** Democracy. **Head of state:** Pres. Pascal Lissouba; in office: Aug. 20, 1992. **Head of government:** Prime Min. Claude Antoine Dacosta; in office: Dec. 6, 1992. **Local divisions:** 9 regions and capital district. **Defense:** 4.6% of GNP (1987).

**Economy: Chief crops:** Palm oil and kernels, cocoa, coffee, tobacco. **Minerals:** Gold, lead, copper, zinc. **Crude oil reserves** (1988): 750 mln. bbls. **Arable land:** 2%. **Fish catch** (1989): 19,000 metric tons. **Electricity prod.** (1991): 315 mln. kWh. **Labor force:** 90% agric.

**Finance: Monetary unit:** CFA franc (Mar. 1993: 273 = $1 US). **Gross domestic product** (1990): $2.4 bln. **Per capita GDP:** $1,070. **Imports** (1990): $621 mln.; partners: Fr. 52%. **Exports** (1990): $981 mln.; partners: U.S. 45%, Fr. 15%. **Tourism** (1990): $7 mln. receipts. **International reserves less gold** (Jan. 1993): $4.1 mln. **Gold:** 11,000 oz t.

**Transport: Railroads** (1989): **Length:** 494 mi. **Motor vehicles:** in use (1989): 26,000 passenger cars, 20,000 comm. vehicles. **Chief ports:** Pointe-Noire, Brazzaville.

**Communications: Television sets:** 1 per 402 persons. **Radios:** 1 per 9.4 persons. **Telephones in use:** 1 per 111 persons.

**Health: Life expectancy at birth** (1992): 52 male; 56 female. **Births** (per 1,000 pop. 1992): 43. **Deaths** (per 1,000 pop. 1992): 13. **Natural increase:** 3.0%. **Hospital beds:** 1 per 456 persons. **Physicians:** 1 per 3,873 persons. **Infant mortality** (per 1,000 live births 1992): 110.

**Education** (1991): **Literacy:** 57%. Years compulsory 10; attendance 80%.

**Major International Organizations:** UN (GATT, IMF, WHO), OAU.

**Embassy:** 4891 Colorado Ave. NW 20011; 726-5500.

The Loango Kingdom flourished in the 15th century, as did the Anzico Kingdom of the Batekes; by the late 17th century they had become weakened. France established control by 1885. Independence came Aug. 15, 1960.

After a 1963 coup sparked by trade unions, the country adopted a Marxist-Leninist stance, with the USSR and China vying for influence. France remained a dominant trade partner and source of technical assistance, and French-owned private enterprise retained a major economic role. However, the government of Pres. Denis Sassou-Nguesso favored a strengthening of relations with the USSR; a socialist constitution was adopted, 1979.

In 1990, Marxism was renounced and opposition parties legalized. In 1991 the country's name was changed to Republic of Congo, and a new constitution was approved.

# Costa Rica

## Republic of Costa Rica

## República de Costa Rica

**People: Population** (1992 est.): 3,187,000. **Age distrib. (%):** 0–14: 36.2; 15–49: 57.4; 50+: 6.4. **Pop. density:** 162 per sq. mi. **Urban** (1991): 50%. **Ethnic groups:** Spanish (with Mestizo minority). **Language:** Spanish (official). **Religions:** Roman Catholic 95%.

**Geography: Area:** 19,652 sq. mi., smaller than W. Virginia. **Location:** In central America. **Neighbors:** Nicaragua on N, Panama on S. **Topography:** Lowlands by the Caribbean are tropical. The interior plateau, with an altitude of about 4,000 ft., is temperate. **Capital:** San Jose. **Cities** (1992 met. est.): San Jose 890,000.

**Government: Type:** Democratic republic. **Head of state:** Pres. Rafael Angel Calderon; b. 1949; in office May 8, 1990. **Local divisions:** 7 provinces.

**Economy: Industries:** Furniture, food processing, aluminum, textiles, fertilizers, roofing, cement. **Chief crops:** Coffee (chief export), bananas, sugar, cocoa, cotton, hemp. **Minerals:** Gold, salt, sulphur, iron. **Other resources:** Fish, forests. **Arable land:** 12%. **Livestock** (1991): cattle: 1.7. mln. **Fish catch** (1990): 20,000 metric tons. **Electricity prod.** (1990): 2.9 bln. kWh. **Labor force:** 32% agric.; 25% ind. & comm.; 38% service and government.

**Finance: Monetary unit:** Colones (Mar. 1993: 138 = $1 US). **Gross domestic product** (1992): $5.6 bln. **Per capita GDP:** $1,810. **Imports** (1992): $2.5 bln.; partners: U.S. 38%, CACM 10%, Jap. 10%. **Exports** (1992): $1.8 bln.; partners: U.S. 45%, CACM 18%. **Tourism** (1989): receipts: $206 mln. **National budget** (1990): $1.0 bln. expenditures. **International reserves less gold** (Mar. 1993): $1.0 bln. **Gold:** 35,000 oz t. **Consumer prices** (change in 1992): 28.7%.

**Transport: Motor vehicles:** in use (1990): 168,000 passenger cars, 94,000 comm. vehicles. **Civil aviation** (1991): 1.0 bln. passenger-km; 9 airports with scheduled flights. **Chief ports:** Limon, Puntarenas, Golfito.

**Communications: Television sets:** 1 per 4.9 persons. **Radios:** 1 per 11 persons. **Telephones:** 1 per 6.9 persons. **Daily newspaper circ.** (1990): 110 per 1,000 pop.

**Health: Life expectancy at birth** (1992): 75 male; 79 female. **Births** (per 1,000 pop. 1992): 27. **Deaths** (per 1,000 pop. 1992): 4. **Natural increase:** 2.3%. **Hospital beds:** 1 per 454 persons. **Physicians:** 1 per 798 persons. **Infant mortality** (per 1,000 live births 1992): 12.

**Education** (1992): **Literacy:** 93%. Years compulsory 6; attendance 99%.

**Major International Organizations:** UN (FAO, ILO, IMF, WHO), OAS.

**Embassy:** 1825 Connecticut Ave. NW, 20009; 234-2945.

Guaymi Indians inhabited the area when Spaniards arrived, 1502. Independence came in 1821. Costa Rica seceded from the Central American Federation in 1838. Since the civil war of 1948-49, there has been little violent social conflict, and free political institutions have been preserved.

An earthquake in Apr. 1991 damaged the banana industry and shut down the port of Limon, adding pressure to a floundering economy.

Costa Rica, though still a largely agricultural country, has achieved a relatively high standard of living and social services, and land ownership is widespread, despite a troubled economy.

# Côte d'Ivoire

## Ivory Coast

## République de la Côte d'Ivoire

**People: Population** (1992 est.): 13,497,000. **Age distrib. (%):** 0–14: 48.2; 15–59: 45.2; 60+: 6.6. **Pop. density:** 104 per sq. mi. **Urban** (1990): 40%. **Ethnic groups:** Baule 23%, Bete 18%, Senufo 15%, Malinke 11%, over 60 tribes. **Languages:** French (official), Akan, Kru, Voltaic, Malinke. **Religions:** Moslem 25%, Christian 12%, indigenous 63%.

**Geography: Area:** 124,503 sq. mi., slightly larger than New Mexico. **Location:** On S. coast of W. Africa. **Neighbors:** Liberia, Guinea on W, Mali, Burkina Faso on N, Ghana on E. **Topography:** Forests cover the W half of the country, and range from a coastal strip to halfway to the N on the E. A sparse inland plain leads to low mountains in NW. **Capital:** Yamoussoukro (official); Abidjan (de facto). **Cities** (1990 est.): Abidjan 2.7 mln.

**Government: Type:** Republic. **Head of state:** Pres. Felix Houphouet-Boigny; b. Oct. 18, 1905; in office: Aug. 7, 1960. **Head of government:** Prime Min. Alassane Ouattara. **Local divisions:** 49 departments.

**Economy: Chief crops:** Coffee, cocoa. **Minerals:** Diamonds, manganese. **Other resources:** Timber, rubber, petroleum. **Arable land:** 9%. **Livestock** (1990): goats: 1.5 mln.; sheep: 1.5 mln.; cattle: 991,000. **Fish catch** (1990): 108,000 metric tons. **Electricity prod.** (1991): 2.6 bln. kWh. **Labor force:** 85% agric., forestry.

**Finance: Monetary unit:** CFA franc (Mar. 1993: 273 = $1 US). **Gross domestic product** (1990): $10 bln. **Per capita GDP:** $800. **Imports** (1989): $2.1 bln.; partners: Fr. 31%, Jap. 5%, U.S. 5%. **Exports** (1989): $2.8 bln.; partners: Fr. 14%, Neth. 19%, U.S. 11%, It. 8%. **Tourism** (1990): $48 mln. receipts; **International reserves less gold** (Jan. 1993): $6.9 mln. **Gold:** 45,000 oz t. **Consumer prices** (changed in 1992): 3.5%.

**Transport: Railroads** (1990): **Length:** 600 km. **Motor vehicles:** in use (1989): 168,000 passenger cars, 90,000 comm. vehicles. **Chief ports:** Abidjan, Sassandra.

**Communications: Television sets:** 1 per 15 persons. **Radios:** 1 per 8.1 persons. **Telephones:** 1 per 143 persons. **Daily newspaper circ.** (1990): 12 per 1,000 pop.

**Health: Life expectancy at birth** (1992): 53 male; 57 female. **Births** (per 1,000 pop. 1992): 48. **Deaths** (per 1,000 pop. 1992): 12. **Natural increase:** 3.6%. **Hospital beds** (1982): 10,062. **Physicians** (1982): 502. **Infant mortality** (per 1,000 live births 1992): 94.

**Education** (1990): **Literacy:** 45%. **Years compulsory:** none; attendance 75%.

**Major International Organizations:** UN and all of its specialized agencies, OAU.

**Embassy:** 2424 Massachusetts Ave. NW 20008; 483-2400.

A French protectorate from 1842, Côte D'Ivoire became independent in 1960. It is the most prosperous of the tropical African nations, due to diversification of agriculture for export, close ties to France, and encouragement of foreign investment. About 20% of the population are workers from neighboring countries. Côte D'Ivoire officially changed its name from Ivory Coast in Oct. 1985.

Students and workers protested, Feb. 1990, demanding the ouster of Pres. Houphouet-Boigny and multiparty democracy. Côte D'Ivoire held its first multiparty presidential election in Oct. 1990.

# Croatia

## Republic of Croatia

## Republika Hrvatska

**People: Population** (1992 est.): 4,784,000. **Pop. density:** 219 per sq. mi. **Ethnic groups:** Croatian 78%, Serbian 12%. **Language:** Croatian. **Religion:** Roman Catholic 77%.

**Geography: Area:** 21,829 sq. mi., slightly smaller than W. Virginia. **Location:** in SE Europe. **Neighbors:** Slovenia, Bosnia and Herzegovina, Hungary, Yugoslavia, and the Adriatic Sea. Over 33 percent is forested. **Capital:** Zagreb.

**Government: Type:** Parliamentary democracy. **Head of state:** Pres. Franjo Tudjman; b. 1922; in office: May 1990. **Head of government:** Prime Min. Hryoje Sarinic; in office: Sept. 8, 1992. **Local divisions:** 102 districts.

**Economy: Industries:** Textiles, chemicals, aluminum prods., paper. **Chief crops:** Olives, wine. **Minerals:** Bauxite, copper, coal. **Arable land:** 32%. **Electricity prod.** (1991): 8.8 mln. kWh.

**Finance: Monetary unit:** Croatian Dinar (Jan. 1993: 365 = $1 US). **Gross domestic product** (1991): $26.3 bln. **Per capita GDP:** $5,600. **Imports** (1990): $4.4 bln. **Exports** (1990): 2.9 bln.

**Transport: Motor vehicles:** in use (1990): 865,000 passenger cars, 72,000 commercial vehicles.

**Communications: Television sets:** 1 per 4 persons. **Radios:** 1 per 4 persons. **Telephones:** 1 per 4 persons. **Newspaper circ.** (1990): 150 per 1,000 pop.

**Health: Life expectancy at birth** (1990): 67 male; 74 female. **Births** (per 1,000 pop. 1992): 12. **Deaths** (per 1,000 pop. 1992): 11. **Physicians:** 1 per 466 persons. **Hospital beds:** 1 per 133 persons. **Infant mortality** (per 1,000 live births 1990): 10.

**Education** (1991): **Literacy:** 96%.

**International Organizations:** UN.

From the 7th century the area was inhabited by Croats, a south Slavic people. It was formed into a kingdom under Tomislav in 924, and joined with Hungary in 1102. The Croats became westernized and separated from Slavs under Serbian influence. The Croats retained autonomy under the Hungarian crown. Slavonia was taken by Turks in the 16th century, the northern part was restored by the Treaty of Karlowitz in 1699. Croatia helped Austria put down the Hungarian revolution 1848-49 and as a result was set up with Slavonia as the separate Austrian crownland of Croatia and Slavonia, which was reunited to Hungary as part of *Ausgleich* in 1867. It united with other Yugoslav areas to proclaim the kingdom of Serbs, Croats, and Slovenes in 1918. At the reorganization of Yugoslavia in 1929, Croatia and Slavonia became Savska co., which in 1939 was united with Primorje co. to form the county of Croatia. A nominally independent state between 1941-45, it became a constituent republic in the 1946 constitution.

On June 25, 1991, Croatia declared independence from Yugoslavia. Fighting began between ethnic Serbs and Croats. There were clashes between Croats and Yugoslavian army units and their Serb supporters. Croatia was granted EC recognition Jan. 15, 1992. Fighting continued in 1992 and 1993 as some 30% of Croatia's territory remained under Serbian control.

# Cuba

## Republic of Cuba

## República de Cuba

**People: Population** (1992 est.): 10,846,000. **Age distrib. (%):** 0-under 15: 23.3; 15–59: 64.9; 60+: 11.8. **Pop. density:** 245 per sq. mi. **Urban** (1991): 72%. **Ethnic groups:** Spanish, African. **Languages:** Spanish. **Religions:** Roman Catholic 42%, none 49%.

**Geography: Area:** 44,218 sq. mi., nearly as large as Pennsylvania. **Location:** Westernmost of West Indies. **Neighbors:** Bahamas, U.S., on N, Mexico on W, Jamaica on S, Haiti on E. **Topography:** The coastline is about 2,500 miles. The N coast is steep and rocky, the S coast low and marshy. Low hills and fertile valleys cover more than half the country. Sierra Maestra, in the E is the highest of 3 mountain ranges. **Capital:** Havana. **Cities** (1989 est.): Havana 2,077,000; Santiago de Cuba 397,000; Camaguey 274,000.

**Government: Type:** Communist state. **Head of state:** Pres. Fidel Castro Ruz; b. Aug. 13, 1926; in office: Dec. 3, 1976 (formerly Prime Min. since Feb. 16, 1959). **Local divisions:** 14 provinces, Havana. **Defense:** 6.0% of GNP (1989).

**Economy: Industries:** Cement, food processing, sugar. **Chief crops:** Sugar (75% of exports), tobacco, rice, coffee, tropical fruit. **Minerals:** Cobalt, nickel, iron, copper, manganese, salt. **Other resources:** Forests. **Arable land:** 29%. **Livestock** (1991): cattle: 4.9 mln.; pigs: 1.9 mln. **Fish catch** (1991): 188,000 metric tons. **Electricity prod.** (1991): 16.2 bln. kWh. **Labor force:** 20% agric.; 33% ind. & comm.; 30% services & govt.

**Finance: Monetary unit:** Peso (Dec. 1992: .76 peso = $1.00 US). **Gross social product:** economic measure not convertible to GNP. **Per capita income** (1990): $2,644. **Imports** (1991): $3.7 bln. **Exports** (1991): $3.6 bln. **Tourism** (1990): $250 mln. revenues. **National budget** (1990): $14.4 bln. expenditures.

**Transport: Railroads (1989): Length:** 3,009 mi. **Motor vehicles:** in use (1988): 241,000 passenger cars, 208,000 comm. vehicles. **Civil aviation** (1991): 3.1 bln. passenger-km.; 11 airports with scheduled flights. **Chief ports:** Havana, Matanzas, Cienfuegos, Santiago de Cuba.

**Communications: Television sets:** 1 per 5 persons. **Radios:** 1 per 3 persons. **Telephones in use:** 1 per 19 persons. **Daily newspaper circ.** (1988): 155 per 1,000 pop.

**Health: Life expectancy at birth:** (1992): 74 male; 79 female. **Births** (per 1,000 pop. 1992): 18. **Deaths** (per 1,000 pop. 1992): 7. **Natural increase:** 1.1%. **Hospital beds:** 1 per 141 persons. **Physicians:** 1 per 303 persons. **Infant mortality** (per 1,000 live births 1992): 12.

**Education** (1992): **Literacy:** 99%. 92% of those between ages 6–14 attend school.

**Major International Organizations:** UN (UNESCO, WHO).

Some 50,000 Indians lived in Cuba when it was reached by Columbus in 1492. Its name derives from the Indian Cubanacan. Except for British occupation of Havana, 1762-63, Cuba remained Spanish until 1898. A slave-based sugar plantation economy developed from the 18th century, aided by early mechanization of milling. Sugar remains the chief product and chief export despite government attempts to diversify.

A ten-year uprising ended in 1878 with guarantees of rights by Spain, which Spain failed to carry out. A full-scale movement under Jose Marti began Feb. 24, 1895.

The U.S. declared war on Spain in April, 1898, after the sinking of the U.S.S. Maine in Havana harbor, and defeated it in the Spanish-American War. Spain gave up all claims to Cuba. U.S. troops withdrew in 1902, but under 1903 and 1934 agreements, the U.S. leases a site at Guantanamo Bay in the SE as a naval base. U.S. and other foreign investments acquired a dominant role in the economy. In 1952, former president Fulgencio Batista seized control and established a dictatorship, which grew increasingly harsh and corrupt. Fidel Castro assembled a rebel band in 1956; guerrilla fighting intensified in 1958. Batista fled Jan. 1, 1959, and in the resulting political vacuum Castro took power, becoming premier Feb. 16.

The government began a program of sweeping economic and social changes, without restoring promised liberties. Opponents were imprisoned and some were executed. Some 700,000 Cubans emigrated in the years after the Castro takeover, mostly to the U.S.

Cattle and tobacco lands were nationalized, while a system of cooperatives was instituted. By 1960 all banks and industrial companies had been nationalized, including over $1 billion worth of U.S.-owned properties, mostly without compensation.

Poor sugar crops resulted in collectivization of farms, stringent labor controls, and rationing, despite continued aid from the USSR and other communist countries.

The U.S. imposed an export embargo in 1962, severely damaging the economy. In 1961, some 1,400 Cubans, trained and backed by the U.S. Central Intelligence Agency, unsuccessfully tried to invade and overthrow the regime.

In the fall of 1962, the U.S. learned that the USSR had brought nuclear missiles to Cuba. After an Oct. 22 warning from Pres. Kennedy, the missiles were removed.

In 1977, Cuba and the U.S. signed agreements to exchange diplomats, without restoring full ties, and to regulate offshore fishing. In 1978, and again in 1980, the U.S. agreed to accept political prisoners released by Cuba some of whom, it was later discovered, were criminals and mental patients. A 1987 agreement provided for 20,000 Cubans to immigrate to the U.S. each year; Cuba agreed to take back some 2,500 jailed in the U.S. since the 1980 Mariel boat lift.

In 1975-78, Cuba sent troops to aid one faction in the Angola civil war. All Cuban troops were withdrawn by May 1991. Cuba's involvement in Central America, Africa, and the Caribbean contributed to poor relations with the U.S.

In 1983, 24 Cubans died and over 700 were captured, later repatriated, as a result of the U.S.-led invasion of Grenada.

Cuba resisted the social and economic reforms that took place in the late 1980s and 1990s in the Soviet Union and its successor states and in Eastern Europe. The nation, whose economy had been heavily dependent on the Soviet Union, suffered severe economic difficulties in the 1990s. A mystery illness of epidemic proportions struck Cuba in 1993. Over 43,000 people were diagnosed with the illness which caused vision loss and impaired coordination.

# Cyprus
## Republic of Cyprus
### Kypriaki Dimokratia (Greek)
### Kibris Cumhuriyeti (Turkish)

**People: Population** (1992 est.): 716,000. **Age distrib.** (%): 0–14: 25.4; 15–59: 60.4; 60+: 14.2. **Pop. density:** 200 per sq. mi. **Urban** (1991): 69%. **Ethnic groups:** Greeks 78%, Turks 18.7%, Armenians, Maronites. **Languages:** Greek, Turkish (both official), English. **Religions:** Orthodox 77%, Moslems 18%.

**Geography: Area:** 3,572 sq. mi., smaller than Connecticut. **Location:** In eastern Mediterranean Sea, off Turkish coast. **Neighbors:** Nearest are Turkey on N, Syria, Lebanon on E. **Topography:** Two mountain ranges run E-W, separated by a wide, fertile plain. **Capital:** Nicosia. **Cities** (1992 est.): Nicosia 166,000.

**Government: Type:** Republic. **Head of state:** Pres. Glafcos Clerides; in office: Mar. 1, 1993. **Local divisions:** 6 districts. **Defense:** 5.0% of GDP (1990).

**Economy: Industries:** Light manuf. **Chief crops:** Grains, grapes, carobs, citrus fruits, potatoes, olives. **Minerals:** Copper, pyrites, asbetos. **Arable land:** 40%. **Electricity prod.** (1990): 1.6 mln. kWh. **Labor force:** 21% agric.; 20% ind., 18% comm., 19% serv.

**Finance: Monetary unit:** Pound (Mar. 1993: 1.00 = $2.05 US). **Gross domestic product** (1990): $5.3 bln. **Per capita GDP:** $7,585. **Imports** (1991): $2.2 bln.; partners: UK 13%, Itl. 12%. **Exports** (1991): $838 mln.; partners: UK 21%, Libya 9%. **Tourism** (1991): receipts: $990 mln. **National budget** (1991): $2.0 bln. expenditures. **International reserves less gold** (Mar. 1993): $1.1 bln. **Gold:** 459,000 oz. t. **Consumer prices** (change in 1992): 6.5%.

**Transport: Motor vehicles:** in use (1989): 159,000 passenger cars, 54,000 comm. vehicles. **Civil aviation** (1991): 2.2 bln. passenger-km; one airport. **Chief ports:** Famagusta, Limassol.

**Communications: Television sets:** 1 per 3.4 persons. **Radios:** 1 per 2.7 persons. **Telephones:** 1 per 2.0 persons. **Daily newspaper circ.** (1991): 161 per 1,000 pop.

**Health: Life expectancy at birth** (1992): 74 male; 78 female. **Births** (per 1,000 pop. 1992): 18. **Deaths** (per 1,000 pop. 1992): 8. **Natural increase:** 1.0%. **Hospital beds:** 1 per 165 persons. **Physicians:** 1 per 480 persons. **Infant mortality** (per 1,000 live births 1992): 10.

**Education** (1991): **Literacy:** 95%. **Years compulsory:** 9; attendance 99%.

**Major International Organizations:** UN (GATT, IMF, WHO), Commonwealth of Nations, EC (Assoc.).

**Embassy:** 2211 R St. NW, 20008; 462-5772.

Agitation for enosis (union) with Greece increased after World War II, with the Turkish minority opposed, and broke into violence in 1955-56. In 1959, Britain, Greece, Turkey, and Cypriot leaders approved a plan for an independent republic, with constitutional guarantees for the Turkish minority and permanent division of offices on an ethnic basis. Greek and Turkish Communal Chambers dealt with religion, education, and other matters.

Archbishop Makarios III, formerly the leader of the enosis movement, was elected president, and full independence became final Aug. 16, 1960. Makarios was reelected in 1968 and 1973.

Further communal strife led the United Nations to send a peacekeeping force in 1964; its mandate has been repeatedly renewed.

The Cypriot National Guard, led by officers from the army of Greece, seized the government July 15, 1974. Makarios fled the country. On July 20, Turkey invaded the island; Greece mobilized its forces but did not intervene. A cease-fire was arranged July 22. A peace conference collapsed Aug. 14; fighting resumed. By Aug. 16, Turkish forces had occupied the NE 40% of the island, despite the presence of UN peacekeeping forces. Makarios resumed the presidency in Dec., until his death in 1977.

Turkish Cypriots voted overwhelmingly, June 8, 1975, to form a separate Turkish Cypriot federated state. A president and assembly were elected in 1976. Some 200,000 Greeks have been expelled from the Turkish-controlled area, replaced by thousands of Turks, some from the mainland.

## Turkish Republic of Northern Cyprus

A declaration of independence was announced by Turkish-Cypriot leader Rauf Denktash, Nov. 15, 1983. The new state is not internationally recognized although it does have trade relations with some countries. TRNC contains 1,295 sq mi., pop. (1992 est.): 176,000, 99% Turkish.

# Czech Republic

*(Figures prior to 1992 are for the Czech and Slovak Federal Republic)*

**People: Population** (1992 est.): 10,400,000. **Age distrib.** (1990) (%): 0–14: 22.5; 15–59: 60.8; 60+: 16.7. **Pop. density:** 342 per sq. mi. **Urban** (1990): 73%. **Ethnic groups:** Czechs 94%, Slovaks 4%. **Language:** Czech.

**Geography: Area:** 30,449 sq. mi. **Location:** In E central Europe. **Neighbors:** Poland on N, Germany on N, W, Austria on S, Slovakia on E, SE. **Topography:** Bohemia, in W, is a plateau surrounded by mountains; Moravia is hilly. **Capital:** Prague. **Cities** (1992 est.): Prague 1.2 mln.; Brno 391,000; Ostrava 331,000.

**Government: Type:** Republic. **Head of state:** Vaclav Havel; b. Oct. 5, 1936; in office: Feb. 15, 1993. **Head of government:** Prime Min. Jan Strasky; in office: July 3, 1992. **Defense:** 6.8% of GNP (1987).

**Economy: Industries:** Machinery, oil products, iron and steel, glass, chemicals, motor vehicles, cement. **Chief crops:** Wheat, sugar beets, potatoes, rye, corn, barley. **Minerals:** coke, coal, iron. **Livestock:** (1989): cattle: 5 mln.; pigs: 7 mln.; sheep: 1 mln. **Electricity prod.** (1991): 89.0 bln. kWh. **Crude steel prod.** (1991): 12.0 mln. metric tons. **Labor force:** 12% agric.; 37% ind.; 22% service, govt.

**Finance: Monetary unit:** Koruna (Aug. 1993: 29.43 = $1 US). **Gross domestic product** (1990): $120 bln. **Per capita GDP:** $7,700. **Imports** (1991): $10.4 bln.; partners: USSR 31%, Ger. 19%, Pol. 6%. **Exports** (1991): $10.8 bln.; partners: USSR 35%, Ger. 7%, Pol. 7%. **Tourism** (1989): $689 mln. receipts. **National budget** (1991): $16.8 bln. expenditures. **International reserves less gold** (Mar. 1993): $1.1 bln. **Gold:** 3.2 mln. oz t. **Consumer prices** (change in 1992): 8.2%.

**Transport: Railroads** (1990): **Length:** 8,142 mi. **Motor vehicles:** in use (1989): 3.1 mln. passenger cars, 327,000 comm. **Civil aviation** (1989): 2.2 bln. passenger-km.; 8 airports.

**Communications: Television sets:** 1 per 2.7 persons. **Radios:** 1 per 3.3 persons. **Telephones:** 1 per 3.9 persons. **Daily newspaper circ.** (1990): 327 per 1,000 pop.

**Health: Life expectancy at birth** (1992): 69 male; 77 female. **Births** (per 1,000 pop. 1991): 14. **Deaths** (per 1,000 pop. 1991): 12. **Natural increase:** .2%. **Hospital beds:** 1 per 99 persons; **Physicians:** 1 per 317 persons. **Infant mortality** (per 1,000 live births 1991): 11.

**Education** (1992): **Literacy:** 99%.

**Major International Organizations:** UN (GATT, WHO). **Embassy:** 3900 Linnean Ave. NW 20008; 263-6315.

Bohemia and Moravia were part of the Great Moravian Empire in the 9th century and later became part of the Holy Roman Empire. Under the kings of Bohemia, Prague in the 14th century was the cultural center of Central Europe. Bohemia and Hungary became part of Austria-Hungary.

In 1914-18 Thomas G. Masaryk and Eduard Benes formed a provisional government with the support of Slovak leaders including Milan Stefanik. They proclaimed the Republic of Czechoslovakia Oct. 28, 1918.

## Czechoslovakia

By 1938 Nazi Germany had worked up disaffection among German-speaking citizens in Sudetenland and demanded its cession. Prime Min. Neville Chamberlain of Britain, with the acquiescence of France, signed with Hitler at Munich, Sept. 30, 1938, an agreement to the cession, with a guarantee of peace by Hitler and Mussolini. Germany occupied Sudetenland Oct. 1-2.

Hitler on Mar. 15, 1939, dissolved Czechoslovakia, made protectorates of Bohemia and Moravia, and supported the auton-

omy of Slovakia, which was proclaimed independent Mar. 14, 1939.

Soviet troops with some Czechoslovak contingents entered eastern Czechoslovakia in 1944 and reached Prague in May 1945; Benes returned as president. In May 1946 elections, the Communist Party won 38% of the votes, and Benes accepted Klement Gottwald, a communist, as prime minister.

In February 1948, the communists seized power in advance of scheduled elections. In May 1948 a new constitution was approved. Benes refused to sign it. On May 30 the voters were offered a one-slate ballot and the communists won full control. Benes resigned June 7 and Gottwald became president. A harsh Stalinist period followed, with complete and violent suppression of all opposition.

In Jan. 1968 a liberalization movement spread explosively through Czechoslovakia. Antonin Novotny, long the Stalinist ruler of the nation, was deposed as party leader and succeeded by Alexander Dubcek, a Slovak, who declared he intended to make communism democratic. On Mar. 22 Novotny resigned as president and was succeeded by Gen. Ludvik Svoboda. On Apr. 6, Premier Joseph Lenart resigned and was succeeded by Oldrich Cernik, whose new cabinet was pledged to carry out democratization and economic reforms.

In July 1968 the USSR and 4 Warsaw Pact nations demanded an end to liberalization. On Aug. 20, the Soviet, Polish, East German, Hungarian, and Bulgarian armies invaded Czechoslovakia.

Despite demonstrations and riots by students and workers, press censorship was imposed, liberal leaders were ousted from office and promises of loyalty to Soviet policies were made by some old-line Communist Party leaders.

On Apr. 17, 1969, Dubcek resigned as leader of the Communist Party and was succeeded by Gustav Husak. In Jan. 1970, Premier Cernik was ousted. Censorship was tightened, and the Communist Party expelled a third of its members. In 1973, amnesty was offered to some of the 40,000 who fled the country after the 1968 invasion, but repressive policies remained in force.

More than 700 leading Czechoslovak intellectuals and former party leaders signed a human rights manifesto in 1977, called Charter 77, prompting a renewed crackdown by the regime.

The police crushed the largest anti-government protests since 1968, when tens of thousands of demonstrators took to the streets of Prague, Nov. 17, 1989. As protesters demanded free elections, the Communist Party leadership resigned Nov. 24; millions went on strike Nov. 27.

On Dec. 10, 1989 the first Cabinet in 41 years without a communist majority took power; Vaclav Havel, playwright and human rights campaigner, was chosen president, Dec. 29. Havel failed to win reelection July 3, 1992; his bid was blocked by a Slovak-led coalition.

Slovakia declared sovereignty, July 17. Czech and Slovak leaders agreed, July 23, on a basic plan for a peaceful division of Czechoslovakia into 2 independent states.

## Czech Republic

Czechoslovakia split into 2 separate states—the Czech Republic and Slovakia—on Jan. 1, 1993.

# Denmark

## Kingdom of Denmark

## Kongeriget Danmark

**People: Population** (1992 est.): 5,163,000. **Age distrib.** (%): 0–14: 17.1; 15–59: 62.5; 60+: 20.4. **Pop. density:** 310 per sq. mi. **Urban** (1990): 86%. **Ethnic groups:** Almost all Scandinavian. **Languages:** Danish. **Religions:** Evangelical Lutheran 90%.

**Geography: Area:** 16,633 sq. mi., the size of Massachusetts and New Hampshire combined. **Location:** In northern Europe, separating the North and Baltic seas. **Neighbors:** Germany on S, Norway on NW, Sweden on NE. **Topography:** Denmark consists of the Jutland Peninsula and about 500 islands, 100 inhabited. The land is flat or gently rolling, and is almost all in productive use. **Capital:** Copenhagen. **Cities** (1991, met.): Copenhagen 1.3 mln. (met.).

**Government: Type:** Constitutional monarchy. **Head of state:** Queen Margrethe II; b. Apr. 16, 1940; in office: Jan. 14, 1972. **Head of government:** Prime Min. Poul Schluter; b. 1929; in office: Sept. 10, 1982. **Local divisions:** 14 counties and one city (Copenhagen). **Defense:** 2.0% of GDP (1991).

**Economy: Industries:** Machinery, textiles, furniture, electronics. **Chief crops:** Dairy products. **Arable land:** 62%. **Livestock** (1987): cattle: 2.3 mln.; pigs: 9.2 mln. **Fish catch** (1989): 1.9 mln. metric tons. **Electricity prod.** (1991): 31 bln. kWh. **Labor force:** 6% agric.; 50% ind. & comm.; 11% serv.; 27% govt.

**Finance: Monetary unit:** Krone (July 1993: 6.56 = $1 US). **Gross domestic product** (1991): $91 bln. **Per capita GDP:** $17,700. **Imports** (1992): $32.3 bln.; partners: EC 52%, Swe. 10%. **Exports** (1992): $39.6 bln.; partners: EC 54%, Swe. 11%. **Tourism** (1991): $3.4 bln. receipts. **International reserves less gold** (Mar. 1993): $12.6 bln. **Gold:** 2.0 mln. oz t. **Consumer prices** (change in 1992): 2.1%.

**Transport: Railroads** (1990): **Length:** 1,763 km. **Motor vehicles:** in use (1990): 1.5 mln. passenger cars, 294,000 comm. vehicles. **Civil aviation** (1990): 4.2 bln. passenger-km; 12 airports with scheduled flights. **Chief ports:** Copenhagen, Alborg, Arhus, Odense.

**Communications: Television sets:** 1 per 2.7 persons. **Radios:** 1 per 2.4 persons. **Telephones:** 1 per 1.2 persons. **Daily newspaper circ.** (1991): 361 per 1,000 pop.

**Health: Life expectancy at birth** (1992): 72 male; 78 female. **Births** (per 1,000 pop. 1992): 12. **Deaths** (per 1,000 pop. 1992): 11. **Hospital beds:** 1 per 177 persons. **Physicians:** 1 per 360 persons. **Infant mortality** (per 1,000 live births 1992): 7.

**Education** (1991): **Literacy:** 99%. Years compulsory 9; attendance 100%.

**Major International Organizations:** UN and all of its specialized agencies, OECD, EC, NATO.

**Embassy:** 3200 Whitehaven St. NW 20008; 234-4300.

The origin of Copenhagen dates back to ancient times, when the fishing and trading place named Havn (port) grew up on a cluster of islets, but Bishop Absalon (1128-1201) is regarded as the actual founder of the city.

Danes formed a large component of the Viking raiders in the early Middle Ages. The Danish kingdom was a major north European power until the 17th century, when it lost its land in southern Sweden. Norway was separated in 1815, and Schleswig-Holstein in 1864. Northern Schleswig was returned in 1920.

Voters ratified the Maastricht Treaty on greater European Community unity, May 1993, after having rejected it in 1992.

The **Faeroe Islands** in the N. Atlantic, about 300 mi. NE of the Shetlands, and 850 mi. from Denmark proper, 18 inhabited, have an area of 540 sq. mi. and pop. (1987) of 46,000. They are self-governing in most matters.

### Greenland

#### (Kalaallit Nunaat)

Greenland, a huge island between the N. Atlantic and the Polar Sea, is separated from the North American continent by Davis Strait and Baffin Bay. Its total area is 840,000 sq. mi., 84% of which is ice-capped. Most of the island is a lofty plateau 9,000 to 10,000 ft. in altitude. The average thickness of the cap is 1,000 ft. The population (1992) is 57,000. Under the 1953 Danish constitution the colony became an integral part of the realm with representatives in the Folketing. The Danish parliament, 1978, approved home rule for Greenland, effective May 1, 1979. Accepting home rule the islanders elected a socialist-dominated legislature, Apr. 4th. With home rule, Greenlandic place names came into official use. The technically correct name for Greenland is now Kalaallit Nunaat; its capital is Nuuk, rather than Gothab. Fish is the principal export.

### Djibouti

#### Republic of Djibouti

#### Jumhouriyya Djibouti

**People: Population** (1992 est.): 390,000. **Pop. density:** 43. **Urban** (1991): 81%. **Ethnic groups:** Somali 60%; Afar 35%. **Languages:** French, Arabic (both official); Afar, Somali. **Religions:** Sunni Moslem 94%.

**Geography: Area:** 8,950 sq. mi., about the size of New Hampshire. **Location:** On E coast of Africa, separated from Arabian Peninsula by the strategically vital strait of Bab el-Mandeb.

**Neighbors:** Ethiopia on W, NW, Eritrea on NW, Somalia on S. **Topography:** The territory, divided into a low coastal plain, mountains behind, and an interior plateau, is arid, sandy, and desolate. The climate is generally hot and dry. **Capital:** Djibouti. **Cities** (1988): Djibouti (met.) 290,000.

**Government: Type:** Republic. **Head of state:** Pres. Hassan Gouled Aptidon b. 1916; in office: June 24, 1977; **Head of government:** Prem. Barkat Gourad Hamadou; in office: Sept. 30, 1978. **Local divisions:** 5 districts.

**Economy: Minerals:** Salt. **Electricity prod.** (1991): 200 mln. kWh.

**Finance: Monetary unit:** Franc (Mar. 1993: 177=$1 US). **Gross domestic product:** (1989): $344 mln. **Per capita GDP:** $1,030. **Imports** (1990): $311 mln.; partners: EC 36%. **Exports** (1990): $190 mln.; partners: Middle East 50%.

**Transport: Motor vehicles:** in use (1989): 13,000 passenger cars, 13,000 commercial vehicles. **Chief ports:** Djibouti.

**Communications: Television sets:** 1 per 38 persons. **Radios:** 1 per 18 persons. **Telephones:** 1 per 55 persons.

**Health: Life expectancy at birth** (1992): 47 male; 50 female. **Births** (per 1,000 pop. 1992): 43. **Deaths** (per 1,000 pop. 1992): 17. **Natural increase:** 2.6%. **Infant mortality** (per 1,000 live births 1992): 115.

**Education** (1991): **Literacy:** 48%.

**Major International Organizations:** UN, OAU, Arab League.

**Embassy:** 866 United Nations Plaza, New York, NY 10017; (212) 753-3163.

France gained control of the territory in stages between 1862 and 1900.

Ethiopia and Somalia have renounced their claims to the area, but each has accused the other of trying to gain control. There were clashes between Afars (ethnically related to Ethiopians) and Issas (related to Somalis) in 1976. Immigrants from both countries continued to enter the country up to independence, which came June 27, 1977.

Unemployment is high and there are few natural resources. French aid is the mainstay of the economy, as well as assistance from the U.S.

### Dominica

#### Commonwealth of Dominica

**People: Population** (1992 est.): 86,000. **Pop. density:** 296 per sq. mi. **Ethnic groups:** nearly all African or mulatto, Caribs. **Languages:** English (official), French creole. **Religions:** Roman Catholic 77%.

**Geography: Area:** 290 sq. mi., about one-fourth the size of Rhode Island. **Location:** In Eastern Caribbean, most northerly Windward Is. **Neighbors:** Guadeloupe to N, Martinique to S. **Topography:** Mountainous, a central ridge running from N to S, terminating in cliffs; volcanic in origin, with numerous thermal springs; rich deep topsoil on leeward side, red tropical clay on windward coast. **Capital** (1987 est.) Roseau 22,000.

**Government: Type:** Parliamentary democracy. **Head of state:** Pres. Clarence Augustus Seignoret; in office: 1984. **Head of government:** Prime Min. Mary Eugenia Charles; b. 1919; in office: July 21, 1980. **Local divisions:** 10 parishes.

**Economy: Industries:** Agriculture, tourism. **Chief crops:** Bananas, citrus fruits, coconuts. **Minerals:** Pumice. **Other resources:** Forests. **Arable land:** 23%. **Electricity prod.** (1991): 16 mln. kWh. **Labor force:** 37% agric.; 20% ind & comm.; 30% services.

**Finance: Monetary unit:** East Caribbean dollar (May 1993: 2.70 = $1 US). **Gross domestic product** (1990): $170 mln. **Imports** (1992): $111 mln.; partners: UK 17%, U.S. 23%. **Exports** (1992): $56 mln.; partners: UK 70%. **Tourism** (1989): $19 mln. receipts. **Consumer prices** (change in 1991): 6.0%.

**Transport: Chief ports:** Roseau.

**Communications: Telephones:** 1 per 11 persons.

**Health: Life expectancy at birth** (1992): 74 male; 79 female. **Births** (per 1,000 pop. 1992): 24. **Deaths** (per 1,000 pop. 1992): 5. **Natural increase:** 1.9%. **Hospital beds:** 1 per 247 persons. **Physicians:** 1 per 1,947 persons. **Infant mortality** (per 1,000 live births 1992): 11.

**Education: Literacy:** 90%.

**Major International Organizations:** UN, OAS.

A British colony since 1805, Dominica was granted self government in 1967. Independence was achieved Nov. 3, 1978.

Hurricane David struck, Aug. 30, 1979, devastating the island and destroying the banana plantations, Dominica's economic mainstay. Coups were attempted in 1980 and 1981.

Dominica took a leading role in the instigation of the 1983 U.S.-led invasion of Grenada.

In 1992 the government instituted a controversial program that offered passports to people from the Far East who agreed to invest large sums of money in the country.

## Dominican Republic

### República Dominicana

**People: Population** (1992 est.): 7,515,000. **Age distrib. (%):** 0–14: 37.9; 15–59: 56.6; 60+: 5.5. **Pop. density:** 401 per sq. mi. **Urban** (1990): 60%. **Ethnic groups:** Caucasian 16%, mixed 73%, black 11%. **Languages:** Spanish. **Religions:** Roman Catholic 95%.

**Geography: Area:** 18,704 sq. mi., the size of Vermont and New Hampshire combined. **Location:** In West Indies, sharing I. of Hispaniola with Haiti. **Neighbors:** Haiti on W. **Topography:** The Cordillera Central range crosses the center of the country, rising to over 10,000 ft., highest in the Caribbean. The Cibao valley to the N is major agricultural area. **Capital:** Santo Domingo. **Cities** (1991 est.): Santo Domingo 2,400,000; Santiago de Los Caballeros 490,000.

**Government: Type:** Representative democracy. **Head of state:** Pres. Joaquin Balaguer; in office: Aug. 16, 1986. **Local divisions:** 29 provinces and Santo Domingo. **Defense:** 1.0% of GDP. (1990).

**Economy: Industries:** Sugar refining, cement, pharmaceuticals. **Chief crops:** sugar, cocoa, coffee, tobacco, rice. **Minerals:** Nickel, gold, silver. **Other resources:** Timber. **Arable land:** 23%. **Livestock.** (1991): cattle: 2.2 mln.; pigs: 431,000. **Electricity prod.** (1991): 4.4 bln. kWh. **Labor force:** 35% agric.; 13% ind.; 23% serv. & govt.

**Finance: Monetary unit:** Peso (Mar. 1993: 12.59 = $1 US). **Gross domestic product** (1991): $7.1 bln. **Per capita GDP:** $950. **Imports** (1991): $1.8 bln.; partners: U.S. 50%. **Exports** (1991): $775 mln.; partners: U.S. 59% EC 19%. **Tourists** (1990): $750 mln. receipts. **National budget** (1990): $938 mln. expenditures. **International reserves less gold** (Mar. 1993): $508 mln. **Gold:** 18,000 oz t. **Consumer prices** (change in 1991): 53.9%

**Transport: Motor vehicles:** in use (1989): 114,000 passenger cars, 72,000 comm. vehicles. **Civil Aviation** (1988): 247 mln. passenger km.; 5 airports. **Chief ports:** Santo Domingo, San Pedro de Macoris, Puerto Plata.

**Communications: Television sets:** 1 per 10 persons. **Radios:** 1 per 6 persons. **Telephones:** 1 per 24 persons. **Daily newspaper circ.** (1990): 37 per 1,000 pop.

**Health: Life expectancy at birth** (1992): 66 male; 70 female. **Births** (per 1,000 pop. 1992): 27. **Deaths** (per 1,000 pop. 1992): 7. **Natural increase:** 2.0%. **Hospital beds:** 1 per 1,508 persons. **Physicians:** 1 per 934 persons. **Infant mortality** (per 1,000 live births 1992): 56.

**Education** (1991): **Literacy:** 83%. Years compulsory 6; attendance 70%.

**Major International Organizations:** UN (World Bank, IMF, GATT), OAS.

**Embassy:** 1715 22d St. NW 20008; 332-6280.

Carib and Arawak Indians inhabited the island of Hispaniola when Columbus landed in 1492. The city of Santo Domingo, founded 1496, is the oldest settlement by Europeans in the hemisphere and has the supposed ashes of Columbus in an elaborate tomb in its ancient cathedral.

The western third of the island was ceded to France in 1697. Santo Domingo itself was ceded to France in 1795. Haitian leader Toussaint L'Ouverture seized it, 1801. Spain returned intermittently 1803-21, as several native republics came and went. Haiti ruled again, 1822-44, and Spanish occupation occurred 1861-63.

The country was occupied by U.S. Marines from 1916 to 1924, when a constitutionally elected government was installed.

In 1930, Gen. Rafael Leonidas Trujillo Molina was elected president. Trujillo ruled brutally until his assassination in 1961. Pres. Balaguer, appointed by Trujillo in 1960, resigned under pressure in 1962. Juan Bosch, elected president in the first free elections in 38 years, was overthrown in 1963.

On April 24, 1965, a revolt was launched by followers of Bosch and others, including a few communists. Four days later U.S. Marines intervened against the pro-Bosch forces. Token units were later sent by 5 So. American countries as a peacekeeping force.

A provisional government supervised a June 1966 election, in which Balaguer defeated Bosch by a 3-2 margin. The Inter-American Peace Force completed its departure Sept. 20, 1966.

Continued depressed world prices have affected the main export commodity, sugar.

## Ecuador

### Republic of Ecuador

### República del Ecuador

**People: Population** (1992 est.): 10,933,000. **Age distrib. (%):** 0–14: 41.3; 15–64: 55.0; 65+: 3.7. **Pop. density:** 99 per sq. mi. **Urban** (1990): 54% **Ethnic groups:** Indians 25%, Mestizo 55%, Spanish 10%, African 10%. **Languages:** Spanish (official), Quechuan, Jivaroan. **Religions:** Roman Catholic 95%.

**Geography: Area:** 109,483 sq. mi., the size of Colorado. **Location:** In NW S. America, on Pacific coast, astride Equator. **Neighbors:** Colombia to N, Peru to E and S. **Topography:** Two ranges of Andes run N and S, splitting the country into 3 zones: hot, humid lowlands on the coast; temperate highlands between the ranges, and rainy, tropical lowlands to the E. **Capital:** Quito. **Cities** (1991 est.): Guayaquil 2,000,000; Quito 1,500,000.

**Government: Type:** Republic. **Head of state:** Pres. Sixto Duran Ballen; b. 1922; in office: Aug. 10, 1992. **Local divisions:** 21 provinces. **Defense:** 1.6% of GDP (1990).

**Economy: Industries:** Food processing, wood prods., textiles. **Chief crops:** Bananas (largest exporter), coffee, rice, sugar, corn. **Minerals:** Oil, copper, iron, lead, silver, sulphur. **Crude oil reserves** (1991): 1.8 bln. bbls. **Other resources:** Rubber, bark. **Arable land:** 6%. **Livestock** (1990): cattle: 3.8 mln.; pigs: 4.1 mln.; sheep: 2.1 mln. **Fish catch** (1989): 767,000 metric tons. **Electricity prod.** (1991): 6.4 bln. kWh. **Labor force:** 39% agric., 12% ind., 42% services.

**Finance: Monetary unit:** Sucre (July 1993: 1,875 = $1 US). **Gross domestic product** (1991): $11.5 bln. **Per capita GDP:** $1,070. **Imports** (1992): $2.4 bln.; partners: U.S. 34%. **Exports** (1992): $3.0 bln.; partners: U.S. 60%. **Tourism** (1990): $193 mln. receipts. **National budget** (1991): $2.2 bln. expenditures. **International reserves less gold** (Mar. 1993): $831 mln. **Gold:** 443,000 oz t. **Consumer prices** (change in 1992): 54.6%.

**Transport: Railroads** (1987): **Length:** 965 km. of **Motor vehicles:** in use (1987): 272,000 passenger cars, 41,000 comm. vehicles. **Civil aviation** (1990): 1.2 bln. passenger-km. **Chief ports:** Guayaquil, Manta, Esmeraldas, Puerto Bolivar.

**Communications: Television sets:** 1 per 17 persons. **Radios:** 1 per 3.4 persons. **Telephones:** 1 per 28 persons. **Daily newspaper circ.** (1989): 87 per 1,000 pop.

**Health: Life expectancy at birth** (1992): 67 male, 72 female. **Births** (per 1,000 pop. 1992): 28. **Deaths** (per 1,000 pop. 1992): 6. **Natural increase:** 2.2%. **Hospital beds:** 1 per 610 persons. **Physicians** (1984): 11,000. **Infant mortality** (per 1,000 live births 1991): 60.

**Education** (1991): **Literacy:** 88%. Attendance through 6th grade—76% urban, 33% rural.

**Major International Organizations:** UN (IMF, WHO), OAS. **Embassy:** 2535 15th St. NW 20009; 234-7200.

Spain conquered the region, which was the northern Inca empire, in 1633. Liberation forces defeated the Spanish May 24, 1822, near Quito. Ecuador became part of the Great Colombia Republic but seceded, May 13, 1830.

Ecuador had been ruled by civilian and military dictatorships since 1968. A peaceful transfer of power from the military junta to the democratic civilian government took place, 1979.

Since 1972, the economy has revolved around its petroleum exports, which have declined since 1982 causing severe economic problems. Ecuador suspended interest payments for 1987 on its estimated $8.2 billion foreign debt following a Mar. 5-6 earthquake which left 20,000 homeless, and destroyed a stretch of the country's main oil pipeline.

Ecuadoran Indians staged a number of protests in 1991 to demand greater rights.

Ecuador and Peru have long disputed their Amazon Valley boundary.

The **Galapagos Islands**, 600 mi. to the W, are the home of huge tortoises and other unusual animals.

# Egypt

## Arab Republic of Egypt

## Jumhūrīyah Misr al-Arabiya

**People: Population** (1992 est.): 56,386,000. **Age distrib** (%) 0-14: 41.8; 15-59: 52.7; 60+: 5.5. **Pop. density:** 146 per sq. mi. **Urban** (1986): 44%. **Ethnic groups:** Eastern Hamitic stock 90%, Bedouin, Nubian. **Languages:** Arabic (official), English. **Religions:** 94% Sunni Moslem.
**Geography: Area:** 386,650 sq. mi, about the size of Texas, Oklahoma, and Arkansas combined. **Location:** NE corner of Africa. **Neighbors:** Libya on W, Sudan on S, Israel on E. **Topography:** Almost entirely desolate and barren, with hills and mountains in E and along Nile. The Nile Valley, where most of the people live, stretches 550 miles. **Capital:** Cairo. **Cities** (1990 est.): Cairo 6,452,000; Alexandria 3,170,000; al-Jizah 2,156,000.
**Government: Type:** Republic. **Head of state:** Pres. Hosni Mubarak; b. 1929; in office: Oct. 14, 1981. **Head of Government:** Atef Sedki in office: Nov. 10, 1986. **Local divisions:** 26 governorates. **Defense:** 7.3% of GDP (1991).
**Economy: Industries:** Textiles, chemicals, petrochemicals, food processing, cement. **Chief crops:** Cotton (one of largest producers), rice, beans, fruits, grains, vegetables, sugar, corn. **Minerals:** Oil, phosphates, gypsum, iron, manganese, limestone. **Crude oil reserves** (1991): 6.2 bln. bbls. **Arable land:** 4%. **Livestock** (1990): cattle: 1.9 mln.; sheep: 1.3 mln. **Fish catch** (1990): 312,000 metric tons. **Electricity prod.** (1991): 45 bln. kWh. **Labor force:** 44% agric.; 22% services; 14% industry.
**Finance: Monetary unit:** Pound (June 1992: 3.32 = $1 US). **Gross domestic product** (1991): $39.2 bln. **Per capita GDP:** $720. **Imports** (1991): $11.5 bln.; partners: U.S. 19%, Ger. 10%, It. 8%, France 8%. **Exports** (1991): $4.5 bln.; partners: It. 22%, Rom. 12%. **Tourism** (1990): $1.9 bln. receipts. **National budget** (1991): $16.7 bln. expenditures. **International reserves less gold** (Jan. 1993): $10.8 bln. **Gold:** 2.43 mln. oz t. **Consumer prices** (change in 1992): 13.6%.
**Transport: Railroads** (1991): **Length:** 5,489 mi. **Motor vehicles:** in use (1989): 826,000 passenger cars, 550,000 comm. vehicles. **Civil aviation** (1991): 5.2 bln. passenger-km.; 10 airports. **Chief ports:** Alexandria, Port Said, Suez.
**Communications: Television sets:** 1 per 15 persons. **Radios:** 1 per 3.9 persons. **Telephones:** 1 per 34 persons. **Daily newspaper circ.** (1991): 62 per 1,000 pop.
**Health: Life expectancy at birth** (1992): 58 male; 62 female. **Births** (per 1,000 pop. 1992): 33. **Deaths** (per 1,000 pop. 1992): 10. **Natural increase:** 2.3%. **Hospital beds:** 1 per 505 persons. **Physicians:** 1 per 616 persons. **Infant mortality** (per 1,000 live births 1992): 80.
**Education** (1990): **Literacy:** 44%. Compulsory ages 6-12.
**Major International Organizations:** UN (IMF, World Bank, GATT), OAU.
**Embassy:** 2310 Decatur Pl. NW 20008; 232-5400.

Archeological records of ancient Egyptian civilization date back to 4000 BC. A unified kingdom arose around 3200 BC, and extended its way south into Nubia and north as far as Syria. A high culture of rulers and priests was built on an economic base of serfdom, fertile soil, and annual flooding of the Nile banks.

Imperial decline facilitated conquest by Asian invaders (Hyksos, Assyrians). The last native dynasty fell in 341 BC to the Persians, who were in turn replaced by Greeks (Alexander and the Ptolemies), Romans, Byzantines, and Arabs, who introduced Islam and the Arabic language. The ancient Egyptian language is preserved only in the liturgy of the Coptic Christians.

Egypt was ruled as part of larger Islamic empires for several centuries. The Mamluks, a military caste of Caucasian origin, ruled Egypt from 1250 until defeat by the Ottoman Turks in 1517. Under Turkish sultans the khedive as hereditary viceroy had wide authority. Britain intervened in 1882 and took control of administration, though nominal allegiance to the Ottoman Empire continued until 1914.

The country was a British protectorate from 1914 to 1922. A 1936 treaty strengthened Egyptian autonomy, but Britain retained bases in Egypt and a condominium over the Sudan. Brit-

ain fought German and Italian armies from Egypt, 1940-42. In 1951 Egypt abrogated the 1936 treaty. The Sudan became independent in 1956.

The uprising of July 23, 1952, led by the Society of Free Officers, named Maj. Gen. Mohammed Naguib commander in chief and forced King Farouk to abdicate. When the republic was proclaimed June 18, 1953, Naguib became its first president and premier. Lt. Col. Gamal Abdel Nasser removed Naguib and became premier in 1954. In 1956, he was voted president. Nasser died in 1970 and was replaced by Vice Pres. Anwar Sadat.

The Aswan High Dam, completed 1971, provides irrigation for more than a million acres of land. Artesian wells, drilled in the Western Desert, reclaimed 43,000 acres, 1960-66.

When the state of Israel was proclaimed in 1948, Egypt joined other Arab nations invading Israel and was defeated.

After terrorist raids across its border, Israel invaded Egypt's Sinai Peninsula, Oct. 29, 1956. Egypt rejected a cease-fire demand by Britain and France; on Oct. 31 the 2 nations dropped bombs and on Nov. 5-6 landed forces. Egypt and Israel accepted a UN cease-fire; fighting ended Nov. 7.

A UN Emergency Force guarded the 117-mile long border between Egypt and Israel until May 19, 1967, when it was withdrawn at Nasser's demand. Egyptian troops entered the Gaza Strip and the heights of Sharm el Sheikh and 3 days later closed the Strait of Tiran to all Israeli shipping. Full-scale war broke out June 5 and before it ended under a UN cease-fire June 10, Israel had captured Gaza and the Sinai Peninsula, controlled the east bank of the Suez Canal and reopened the gulf.

Sporadic fighting with Israel continued almost daily, 1968-70. Israel and Egypt agreed, Aug. 7, 1970, to a cease-fire and peace negotiations proposed by the U.S. Negotiations failed to achieve results, but the cease-fire continued.

In a surprise attack Oct. 6, 1973, Egyptian forces crossed the Suez Canal into the Sinai. (At the same time, Syrian forces attacked Israelis on the Golan Heights.) Egypt was supplied by a USSR military airlift; the U.S. responded with an airlift to Israel. Israel counter-attacked, crossed the canal, surrounded Suez City. A UN cease-fire took effect Oct. 24.

A disengagement agreement was signed Jan. 18, 1974. Under it, Israeli forces withdrew from the canal's W bank; limited numbers of Egyptian forces occupied a strip along the E bank. A second accord was signed in 1975, with Israel yielding Sinai oil fields. Pres. Sadat's surprise visit to Jerusalem, Nov. 1977, opened the prospect of peace with Israel. On Mar. 26, 1979, Egypt and Israel signed a formal peace treaty, ending 30 years of war, and establishing diplomatic relations. Israel returned control of the Sinai to Egypt in April 1982.

Tension between Moslem fundamentalists and Christians in 1981 caused street riots and culminated in a nationwide security crackdown in Sept. Pres Sadat was assassinated on Oct. 6.

Egypt was a political and military supporter of the Allied forces in their defeat of Iraq in the Persian Gulf War, 1991.

Egypt saw a rising tide of Islamic fundamentalist violence in 1992 and 1993. Egyptian security forces conducted raids against Islamic militants Mar. 1993. Seven Islamic militants convicted of participating in 6 separate attacks on tourists were hanged June 8.

The **Suez Canal**, 103 mi. long, links the Mediterranean and Red seas. It was built by a French corporation 1859-69, but Britain obtained controlling interest in 1875. The last British troops were removed June 13, 1956. On July 26, Egypt nationalized the canal.

# El Salvador

## Republic of El Salvador

## República de El Salvador

**People: Population** (1992 est.): 5,574,000. **Age distrib.** (%): 0-14; 44.4; 15-59: 49.9; 60+: 5.7. **Pop. density:** 686 per sq. mi. **Urban** (1991): 45%. **Ethnic groups:** Mestizo 89%, Indian 10%. **Languages:** Spanish (official). **Religions:** Roman Catholic 75%.
**Geography: Area:** 8,124 sq. mi., the size of Massachusetts. **Location:** In Central America. **Neighbors:** Guatemala on W, Honduras on N. **Topography:** A hot Pacific coastal plain in the south rises to a cooler plateau and valley region, densely populated. The N is mountainous, including many volcanoes. **Capital:** San Salvador. **Cities** (1993 est.): San Salvador 1.4 mln.

**Government: Type:** Republic. **Head of state:** Pres., Alfredo Cristiani; b. Nov, 22, 1947; in office: June 1, 1989. **Local divisions:** 14 departments. **Defense:** 3.6% of GDP (1991).

**Economy: Industries:** Food and beverages, textiles, petroleum products. **Chief crops:** Coffee (21% of GNP), cotton, corn, sugar. **Other resources:** Rubber, forests. **Arable land:** 27%. **Livestock** (1990): cattle: 1.1 mln.; pigs: 440,000. **Electricity prod.** (1991): 1.9 bln. kWh. **Labor force:** 40% agric.; 16% ind.; 27% services.

**Finance: Monetary unit:** Colon (Mar. 1993: 8.73 = $1 US). **Gross domestic product** (1992): $5.5 bln. **Per capita GDP:** $1,010. **Imports** (1992): $1.5 bln.; partners: U.S. 41%, CACM 22%. **Exports** (1992): $683 mln.; partners: U.S. 41%, EC 30%, CACM 10%. **Tourism** (1990): $70 mln. receipts. National budget (1990): $790 mln. expenditures. **International reserves less gold**. Mar. 1993): $458 mln. **Gold:** 469,000 oz t. **Consumer prices** (change in 1992): 20%.

**Transport: Railroads** (1991): **Length:** 374 mi. **Motor vehicles:** in use (1990): 80,000 passenger cars, 80,000 comm. vehicles. **Chief ports:** La Union, Acajutla.

**Communications: Television sets:** 1 per 12 persons. **Radios:** 1 per 2.6 persons. **Telephones:** 1 per 36 persons. **Daily newspaper circ.** (1991): 47 per 1,000 pop.

**Health: Life expectancy at birth** (1992): 68 male; 75 female. **Births** (per 1,000 pop. 1992): 33. **Deaths** (per 1,000 pop. 1992): 5. **Natural increase:** 2.8%. **Hospital beds:** 1 per 973 persons. **Physicians:** 1 per 1,322 persons. **Infant mortality** (per 1,000 live births 1992): 26.

**Education** (1991): **Literacy:** 75%. Years compulsory 6; attendance 82%.

**Major International Organizations:** UN (IMF, WHO, ILO), OAS, CACM.

**Embassy:** 2308 California St. NW 20008; 265-9671.

El Salvador became independent of Spain in 1821, and of the Central American Federation in 1839.

A fight with Honduras in 1969 over the presence of 300,000 Salvadorean workers left 2,000 dead. Clashes were renewed 1970 and 1974.

A military coup overthrew the government of Pres. Carlos Humberto Romero in 1979, and the ruling military-civilian junta failed to quell a rebellion by leftist insurgents, armed by Cuba and Nicaragua. Extreme right-wing death squads organized to eliminate suspected leftists were blamed for thousands of deaths in the 1980s. The Reagan administration staunchly supported the government with military aid.

Voters turned out in large numbers in the May 1984 presidential election. Christian Democrat Jose Napoleon Duarte, a moderate, was victorious with 54% of the vote.

The 12-year civil war ended Jan. 16, 1992, as the government and leftist rebels signed a formal peace treaty. The civil war had taken the lives of some 75,000 people. The treaty provided for military and political reforms.

Nine soldiers, including 3 officers, were indicted Jan. 1990 in the Nov. 1989 slaying of 6 Jesuit priests at a university in San Salvador. Two of the officers received maximum 30-year jail sentences. They were released after serving 15 months of their sentences, Mar. 20, 1993, when the National Assembly passed a sweeping amnesty for those who had committed atrocities during the civil war.

## Equatorial Guinea
### Republic of Equatorial Guinea
### República de Guinea Ecuatorial

**People: Population** (1992 est.): 388,000. **Age distrib. (%):** 0–14: 38.1; 15–59: 55.2; 60+: 6.7. **Pop. density:** 35 per sq. mi. **Ethnic groups:** Fangs 80%, Bubi 15%. **Languages:** Spanish (official), Fang, Bubi. **Religions:** Mostly Roman Catholic.

**Geography: Area:** 10,832 sq. mi., the size of Maryland. **Location:** Bioko Is. off W. Africa coast in Gulf of Guinea, and Rio Muni, mainland enclave. **Neighbors:** Gabon on S, Cameroon on E, N. **Topography:** Bioko Is. consists of 2 volcanic mountains and a connecting valley. Rio Muni, with over 90% of the area, has a coastal plain and low hills beyond. **Capital:** Malabo. **Cities** (1989 est.): Malabo 38,000.

**Government: Type:** in transition. **Head of state:** Pres., Supreme Military Council Teodoro Obiang Nguema Mbasogo; b. June 5, 1942; in office: Oct. 10, 1979. **Head of government:** Prime Min. Silvestre Siale Bileka; In office: Mar. 4, 1992. **Local divisions:** 7 provinces.

**Economy: Chief crops:** Cocoa, coffee, bananas, sweet potatoes. **Other resources:** Timber. **Arable land:** 8%. **Electricity prod.** (1991): 60 mln. kWh. **Labor force:** agric. 50%; public sector 40%.

**Finance: Monetary unit:** CFA franc (Mar. 1993: 278 = $1 US). **Gross domestic product** (1990): $136 mln. **Per capita GDP:** $430. **Imports** (1990): 68 mln.; partners: Fra. 26%, Sp. 21%. **Exports** (1990): $37 mln.; partners: Sp. 38%, Neth. 12%.

**Transport: Chief ports:** Malabo, Bata.

**Communications: Radios:** 1 per 3.5 persons.

**Health: Life expectancy at birth** (1992): 49 male; 53 female. **Births** (per 1,000 pop. 1992): 42. **Deaths** (per 1,000 pop. 1992): 15. **Natural increase:** 2.7% **Hospital beds** (1982): 3,200. **Physicians:** 1 per 3,622 persons. **Infant mortality** (per 1,000 live births 1992): 107.

**Education** (1991): **Literacy:** 55%. About 65% attend primary school.

**Major International Organizations:** UN (IMF, World Bank), OAU.

**Embassy:** 801 2d Ave., New York, NY 10017; (212) 599-1523.

Fernando Po (now Bioko) Island was reached by Portugal in the late 15th century and ceded to Spain in 1778. Independence came Oct. 12, 1968. Riots occurred in 1969 over disputes between the island and the more backward Rio Muni province on the mainland. Masie Nguema Biyogo, himself from the mainland, became president for life in 1972.

Masie's 11-year reign was one of the most brutal in Africa, resulting in a bankrupted nation. Most of the nation's 7,000 Europeans emigrated. In 1976, 45,000 Nigerian workers were evacuated amid charges of a reign of terror. Masie was ousted in a military coup, Aug. 1979. Mbasogo, leader of the coup, became president.

The nation is heavily dependent on external aid.

## Eritrea
### State of Eritrea

**People: Population** (1993 est.): 3,200,000. **Pop. density:** 88 per sq. mi. **Ethnic groups:** 9 different ethnic groups. **Languages:** 7 native languages. **Religions:** about evenly split between Moslem and Christian.

**Geography: Area:** 36,170 sq. mi., slightly larger than Maine. **Location:** in E. Africa. **Neighbors:** Ethiopia on S, Djibouti on E, Sudan on W, Red Sea on N. **Topography:** includes many islands of the Dahlak Archipelago, low coastal plains in S., mountain range with peaks to 9,000 ft. in N. **Capital:** Asmera.

**Government: Type:** in transition. **Head of state:** Issaias Afwerki; in office: May 24, 1993.

**Economy:** no industry. **Chief crops:** Cotton, coffee, tobacco. **Transport: Chief ports:** Masewa, Aseb.

**Communications:** no telephones outside the capital.

**Major International Organizations:** UN.

Eritrea was part of the Ethiopian kingdom of Aksum. It was an Italian colony from 1890 to 1941, when it was captured by the British. Following a period of British and UN supervision, Eritrea was awarded to Ethiopia as part of a federation in 1952. Ethiopia annexed Eritrea as a province in 1962. This led to a 31-year struggle for independence, which ended when Eritrea formally declared itself an independent nation May 24, 1993.

## Estonia
### Republic of Estonia
### Eesti Vabariik

**People: Population** (1992 est.): 1,607,000. **Pop. density:** 92 per sq. mi. **Urban** (1991): 72%. **Ethnic groups:** Estonian 65%, Russian 30%. **Languages:** Estonian (official), Russian. **Religion:** Mostly Evangelical Lutheran.

**Geography: Area:** 17,413 sq. mi. **Neighbors:** bounded on N., W. by the Baltic Sea, E. by Russia, S. by Latvia. **Capital:** Tallinn. **Cities** (1991 est.): Tallinn 502,000.

**Government: Type:** Republic. **Head of state:** Pres. Lennart Meri; in office: Oct. 5, 1992. **Head of government:** Prime Min.

Mart Laar; in Office; Oct. 8, 1992. **Local divisions:** 15 districts, 33 towns, 26 urban settlements.
**Economy: Industries:** Agricultural machinery, electric motors. **Chief crops:** Grain, vegetables. **Arable Land:** 22%. **Livestock** (1990): cattle: 823,000, sheep: 138,000. **Electricity prod.** (1990): 17.2 kWh. **Labor force:** Ind. & const. 42%, agric. 13%.
**Finance: Monetary unit:** Kroon (Jan. 1993: 11.26 = $1 US).
**Transport: Railroads** (1991): **Length:** 640 mi. **Motor vehicles:** in use (1989): 198,000 passenger cars. **Chief port:** Tallinn.
**Communications: Television sets:** 1 per 2.7 persons. **Radios:** 1 per 1.7 persons. **Telephones:** 1 per 5.1 persons.
**Health: Life expectancy at birth** (1992): 65 male, 75 female. **Hospital beds:** 1 per 83 persons. **Physicians:** 1
**Education:** 11 year school curriculum.
**Major International Organizations:** UN, IMF.

Estonia was a province of imperial Russia before World War I, was independent between World Wars I and II, but was conquered by the USSR in 1940. Estonia declared itself an "occupied territory," and proclaimed itself a free nation Mar. 1990. During an abortive Soviet coup, Estonia declared immediate full independence, Aug. 20, 1991; the Soviet Union recognized its independence in Sept. 1991. The first free elections in over 50 years were held Sept. 20, 1992.

# Ethiopia

*(Figures prior to 1993 include Eritrea)*

**People: Population** (1993 est.): 51,070,000. **Age distrib.** (%): 0–14: 46.5; 15–59: 47.3; 60+: 6.2. **Pop. density:** 117 per sq. mi. **Urban** (1992): 11%. **Ethnic groups:** Oromo 40%, Amhara 25%, Tigre 12%, Sidama 9%. **Languages:** Amharic (official), Tigre (Semitic languages); Galla (Hamitic). **Religions:** Orthodox Christian 40%, Moslem 40%.
**Geography: Area:** 435,606 sq. mi., about three-quarters the size of Alaska. **Location:** In E. Africa. **Neighbors:** Sudan on W, Kenya on S, Somalia, Djibouti on E, Eritrea on N. **Topography:** A high central plateau, between 6,000 and 10,000 ft. high, rises to higher mountains near the Great Rift Valley, cutting in from the SW. The Blue Nile and other rivers cross the plateau, which descends to plains on both W and SE. **Capital:** Addis Ababa. **Cities** (1984 est.): Addis Ababa 1,412,000.
**Government: Type:** In transition. **Head of state:** Pres. Meles Zenawi; in office: May 28, 1991. **Head of Government:** Prime Min. Timirat Laynie; in office: June 6, 1991. **Local divisions:** 13 provinces. **Defense:** 8% of GDP (1989).
**Economy: Industries:** Food processing, cement, textiles. **Chief crops:** Coffee (over 50% export earnings), grains. **Minerals:** Platinum, gold, copper, potash. **Arable Land:** 13%. **Livestock** (1990): cattle: 30 mln.; sheep: 23 mln. **Electricity prod.** (1991): 650 mln. kWh. **Labor force:** 80% agric.
**Finance: Monetary unit:** Birr (Mar. 1993: 5.00 = $1 US). **Gross domestic product** (1991): $6.6 bln. **Per capita GDP:** $130. **Imports** (1991): $472 mln.; partners: USSR 22%, U.S. 15%, Italy 10%, Jap. 6%, Ger. 10%. **Exports** (1991): $189 mln.; partners: U.S. 20%, Ger. 18%, Italy 7%. **National budget** (1989): $1.7 bln. expenditures. **International reserves less gold** (Mar. 1993): $252 mln. **Gold:** 113,000 oz t. **Consumer prices** (change in 1992): 10.5%.
**Transport: Railroads** (1989): **Length:** 486 mi. **Motor vehicles:** in use (1991): 38,000 passenger cars, 15,000 comm. vehicles. **Civil aviation** (1989): 1.6 bln. passenger-km; 29 airports with scheduled flights.
**Communications: Television sets:** 1 per 503 persons. **Radios:** 1 per 5.5 persons. **Telephones:** 1 per 320 persons. **Daily newspaper circ.** (1990): 1 per 1,000 pop.
**Health: Life expectancy at birth** (1992): 50 male; 53 female. **Births** (per 1,000 pop. 1992): 45. **Deaths** (per 1,000 pop. 1992): 15. **Natural increase:** 3.1%. **Hospital beds:** 1 per 3,873 persons. **Physicians:** 1 per 36,660 persons. **Infant mortality** (per 1,000 live births 1992): 113.
**Education** (1985): **Literacy:** 18%.
**Major International Organizations:** UN (IMF, WHO), OAU.
**Embassy:** 2134 Kalorama Rd. NW 20008; 234-2281.

Ethiopian culture was influenced by Egypt and Greece. The ancient monarchy was invaded by Italy in 1880 but maintained its independence until another Italian invasion in 1936. British forces freed the country in 1941.
The last emperor, Haile Selassie I, established a parliament and judiciary system in 1931 but barred all political parties.

A series of droughts in the 1970s killed hundreds of thousands. An army mutiny, strikes, and student demonstrations led to the dethronement of Selassie in 1974. The ruling junta pledged to form a one-party socialist state and instituted a successful land reform; opposition was violently suppressed. The influence of the Coptic Church, embraced in 330 AD, was curbed, and the monarchy was abolished in 1975.
The regime, torn by bloody coups, faced uprisings by tribal and political groups in part aided by Sudan and Somalia. Ties with the U.S., once a major arms and aid source, deteriorated, while cooperation accords were signed with the USSR in 1977. In 1978, Soviet advisors and Cuban troops helped defeat Somalia forces. Ethiopia and Somalia signed a peace agreement in 1988.
A worldwide relief effort began in 1984, as an extended drought caused millions to face starvation and death. In 1988, victories by Eritrean guerrillas forced the government to curtail the work of foreign aid workers in drought-stricken regions.
The Ethiopian People's Revolutionary Democratic Front (EPRDF), an umbrella group of 6 rebel armies, launched a major push against government forces, Feb. 1991. In May, Pres. Mengistu Haile Mariam resigned and left the country. The EPRDF took posession of the capital and announced plans for a coalition government.
Eritrea, a province on the Red Sea, declared its independence May 24, 1993.

# Fiji
## Republic of Fiji

**People: Population** (1992 est.): 744,000. **Age distrib. (%):** 0–14: 38.2; 15–59: 56.9; 60+: 4.9. **Pop. density:** 105 per sq. mi. **Urban** (1986): 39%. **Ethnic groups:** Indian 48%, Fijian (Melanesian-Polynesian) 46%, Europeans 2%. **Languages:** English (official), Fijian, Hindi. **Religions:** Christian 52%, Hindu 38%, Moslem 8%.
**Geography: Area:** 7,056 sq. mi., the size of Massachusetts. **Location:** In western S. Pacific O. **Neighbors:** Nearest are Solomons on NW, Tonga on E. **Topography:** 322 islands (106 inhabited), many mountainous, with tropical forests and large fertile areas. Viti Levu, the largest island, has over half the total land area. **Capital:** Suva. **Cities** (1986 est.): Suva 69,000.
**Government: Type:** Republic. **Head of state:** Pres. Penaia Ganilau; in office: Dec. 5, 1987. **Head of government:** Prime Min. Sitiveni Rabuka; in office: June 2, 1992. **Local divisions:** 4 divisions, 1 dependency.
**Economy: Industries:** Sugar refining, light industry, tourism. **Chief crops:** Sugar, bananas, ginger. **Minerals:** Gold. **Other resources:** Timber. **Arable land:** 8%. **Electricity prod.** (1990): 325 mln. kWh. **Labor force:** 44% agric.
**Finance: Monetary unit:** Dollar (Mar. 1993: 1.53 = $1.00 US). **Gross domestic product** (1991): $1.3 bln. **Per capita GDP:** $1,700. **Imports** (1991): $840 mln.; partners: Austral. 29%, Jap. 12%, N.Z. 19%. **Exports** (1991): $646 mln.; partners: EC 32%, Aust. 21%. **Tourism** (1990): $320 mln. receipts. **National budget** (1992): $464 mln. expenditures. **International reserves less gold** (Mar. 1993): $283 mln. **Gold:** 10,000 oz t. **Consumer prices** (change in 1992): 4.9%.
**Transport: Motor vehicles:** in use (1990): 40,000 passenger cars, 28,000 comm. vehicles. **Civil aviation** (1990): 882 mln. passenger-km; 17 airports with scheduled flights. **Chief ports:** Suva, Lautoka.
**Communications: Televisions:** 1 per 73 persons. **Radios:** 1 per 1.7 persons. **Telephones:** 1 per 10 persons. **Daily newspaper circ.** (1988): 56 per 1,000 pop.
**Health: Life expectancy at birth** (1992): 62 male; 67 female. **Births** (per 1,000 pop. 1992): 26. **Deaths** (per 1,000 pop. 1992): 7. **Natural increase:** 1.9%. **Hospital beds:** 1 per 413 persons. **Physicians:** 1 per 2,438 persons. **Infant mortality** (per 1,000 live births 1992): 19.
**Education** (1990): **Literacy:** 85%. 95% attend school.
**Major International Organizations:** UN (IMF, WHO).
**Embassy:** 2233 Wisconsin Ave. NW 20007; 337-8320.

A British colony since 1874, Fiji became an independent parliamentary democracy Oct. 10, 1970.
Cultural differences between the majority Indian community, descendants of contract laborers brought to the islands in the 19th century, and the less modernized native Fijians, who by law

own 83% of the land in communal villages, have led to political polarization.

In 1987, a military coup ousted the government; order was restored May 21 when a compromise was reached granting Lt. Col. Rabuka, the coup's leader, increased power. Rabuka staged a second coup Sept. 25 and in Oct. declared Fiji a republic. A civilian government was restored to power in Dec., and a new constitution was drafted which protected the rights of all citizens.

# Finland
## Republic of Finland
## Suomen Tasavalta

**People: Population** (1992 est.): 5,004,000. **Age distrib. (%):** 0–14: 19.3; 15–59: 62.9; 60+: 17.8. **Pop. density:** 38 per sq. mi. **Urban** (1990): 61%. **Ethnic groups:** Finns 94%, Swedes, Lapps. **Languages:** Finnish, Swedish (both official). **Religions:** Lutheran 97%.

**Geography: Area:** 130,119 sq. mi., slightly smaller than Montana. **Location:** In northern Europe. **Neighbors:** Norway on N, Sweden on W, Russia on E. **Topography:** South and central Finland are mostly flat areas with low hills and many lakes. The N has mountainous areas, 3,000–4,000 ft. **Capital:** Helsinki. **Cities** (1992 est.): Helsinki 490,000; Tampere 170,000; Turku 160,000.

**Government: Type:** Constitutional republic. **Head of state:** Pres. Mauno Koivisto; b. Nov. 25, 1923; in office: Jan. 27, 1982. **Head of government:** Prime Min. Esko Aho: b. 1954; in office: Apr. 26, 1991. **Local divisions:** 12 laanit (provinces). **Defense:** 1.4% of GDP (1989).

**Economy: Industries:** Machinery, metal, shipbuilding, textiles, clothing. **Chief crops:** Grains, potatoes, dairy prods. **Minerals:** Copper, iron, zinc. **Other resources:** Forests (40% of exports). **Arable land:** 8%. **Livestock** (1990): cattle; 1.3 mln. pigs: 1.3 mln. **Fish catch** (1989): 160,000 metric tons. **Electricity prod.** (1991): 49.3 bln. kWh. **Crude steel prod.** (1991): 2.8 mln. metric tons. **Labor force:** 9% agric.; 54% ind., comm. & finance; 25% services.

**Finance: Monetary unit:** Markka (June 1993: 5.62 = $1 US). **Gross domestic product** (1991): $80 bln. **Per capita GDP:** $16,200. **Imports** (1992): $21.2 bln.; partners: EC 45%. **Exports** (1992): $23.8 bln.; partners: EC 50%. **Tourism** (1991): $1.2 bln. receipts. **National budget** (1991): $41.5 bln. expenditures. **International reserves less gold** (Mar. 1993): $4.3 bln. **Gold** 2.0 mln. oz t. **Consumer prices** (change in 1992): 2.6%.

**Transport: Railroads** (1991): **Length:** 3,656 mi. **Motor vehicles:** in use (1991): 1.9 mln. passenger cars, 271,000 comm. vehicles; **Civil aviation** (1991): 9.8 bln. passenger-km; 25 airports. **Chief ports:** Helsinki, Turku.

**Communications: Television sets:** 1 per 2.7 persons. **Radios:** 1 per person. **Telephones:** 1 per 2.1 persons. **Daily newspaper circ.** (1990): 521 per 1,000 pop.

**Health: Life expectancy at birth** (1992): 72 male; 80 female. **Births** (per 1,000 pop. 1992): 12. **Deaths** (per 1,000 pop. 1992): 10. **Natural increase:** .02%. **Hospital beds:** 1 per 74 persons. **Physicians:** 1 per 503 persons. **Infant mortality** (per 1,000 live births 1992): 6.

**Education** (1991): **Literacy:** 99%. Years compulsory 9; attendance 99%.

**Major International Organizations:** UN (IMF, GATT), EFTA, OECD.

**Embassy:** 3216 New Mexico Ave. NW 20016; 363-2430.

The early Finns probably migrated from the Ural area at about the beginning of the Christian era. Swedish settlers brought the country into Sweden, 1154 to 1809, when Finland became an autonomous grand duchy of the Russian empire. Russian exactions created a strong national spirit; on Dec. 6, 1917, Finland declared its independence and in 1919 became a republic. On Nov. 30, 1939, the Soviet Union invaded, and the Finns were forced to cede 16,173 sq. mi., including the Karelian Isthmus, Viipuri, and an area on Lake Ladoga. After World War II, in which Finland tried to recover its lost territory, further cessions were exacted. In 1948, Finland signed a treaty of mutual assistance with the USSR; Finland and Russia nullified this treaty with a new pact in Jan. 1992. In 1956, Russia returned Porkkala, which had been ceded as a military base. In 1992 Finland's economy

suffered because of changes in the former Soviet Union and Eastern Europe.

**Aland,** constituting an autonomous department, is a group of small islands, 590 sq. mi., in the Gulf of Bothnia, 25 mi. from Sweden, 15 mi. from Finland. Mariehamn is the principal port.

# France
## French Republic
## République Française

**People: Population** (1992 est.): 57,287,000. **Age distrib. (%):** 0–14: 19.1; 15–60: 61.0; 60+: 19.9. **Pop. density:** 259 per sq. mi. **Urban** (1990): 74%. **Ethnic groups:** A mixture of various European and Mediterranean groups. **Languages:** French (official); minorities speak Breton, Alsatian German, Flemish, Italian, Basque, Catalan. **Religions:** Mostly Roman Catholic.

**Geography: Area:** 220,668 sq. mi., four-fifths the size of Texas. **Location:** In western Europe, between Atlantic O. and Mediterranean Sea. **Neighbors:** Spain on S, Italy, Switzerland, Germany on E, Luxembourg, Belgium on N. **Topography:** A wide plain covers more than half of the country, in N and W, drained to W by Seine, Loire, Garonne rivers. The Massif Central is a mountainous plateau in center. In E are Alps (Mt. Blanc is tallest in W. Europe, 15,771 ft.), the lower Jura range, and the forested Vosges. The Rhone flows from Lake Geneva to Mediterranean. Pyrenees are in SW, on border with Spain. **Capital:** Paris. **Cities** (1990 est.): Paris 2,152,000; Marseille 801,000; Lyon 415,000; Toulouse 359,000; Nice 342,000; Strasbourg 252,000; Nantes 245,000; Bordeaux 201,000.

**Government: Type:** Republic. **Head of state:** Pres. François Mitterrand; b. Oct. 26, 1916; in office: May 21, 1981. **Head of government:** Prime Min. Edouard Balladur; in office: Mar. 29, 1993. **Local divisions:** 22 administrative regions containing 95 departments. **Defense:** 3.6% of GDP (1991).

**Economy: Industries:** Steel, chemicals, textiles, wine, perfume, aircraft, electronic equipment. **Chief crops:** Grains, corn, rice, fruits, vegetables. France is largest food producer, exporter, in W. Eur. **Minerals:** Bauxite, iron, coal. **Crude oil reserves** (1985): 221 mln. bbls. **Other resources:** Forests. **Arable land:** 32%. **Livestock** (1990): cattle: 21.1 mln.; pigs: 12.2 mln.; sheep: 10.3 mln. **Fish catch** (1990): 896,000 metric tons. **Electricity prod.** (1991): 399 bln. kWh. **Crude steel prod.** (1991): 18.4 mln. metric tons. **Labor force:** 9% agric.; 45% ind. & comm.; 46% services.

**Finance: Monetary unit:** Franc (July 1993: 5.79 = $1 US). **Gross domestic product** (1991): $1 trl. **Per capita GDP:** $18,300. **Imports** (1992): $239 bln.; partners: EC 51%. **Exports** (1992): $235 bln.; partners: EC 50%, U.S. 6%. **Tourism** (1990): $21.6 bln. receipts. **National budget** (1992): $246 bln. expenditures. **International reserves less gold** (Feb. 1993): $33.0 bln. **Gold:** 81.85 mln. oz t. **Consumer prices** (change in 1992): 2.4%.

**Transport: Railroads** (1991): **Length:** 21,173 mi. **Motor vehicles:** in use (1991): 23.8 mln. passenger cars, 5.1 mln. **Civil aviation** (1991): 32.5 bln. passenger-km; 64 airports with scheduled flights. **Chief ports:** Marseille, LeHavre, Nantes, Bordeaux, Rouen.

**Communications: Television sets:** 1 per 2.6 persons. **Radios:** 1 per 1.1 persons. **Telephones:** 1 per 1.7 persons. **Daily newspaper circ.** (1990): 176 per 1,000 pop.

**Health: Life expectancy at birth** (1992): 74 male; 82 female. **Births** (per 1,000 pop. 1992): 13. **Deaths** (per 1,000 pop. 1992): 9. **Natural increase:** .4%. **Hospital beds:** 1 per 80 persons. **Physicians:** 1 per 374 persons. **Infant mortality** (per 1,000 live births 1992): 7.

**Education** (1991): **Literacy:** 99%. Years compulsory 10. **Major International Organizations:** UN and most of its specialized agencies, OECD, EC, NATO.

**Embassy:** 4101 Reservoir Rd. NW 20007; 944-6000.

Celtic Gaul was conquered by Julius Caesar 58-51 BC; Romans ruled for 500 years. Under Charlemagne, Frankish rule extended over much of Europe. After his death France emerged as one of the successor kingdoms.

The monarchy was overthrown by the French Revolution (1789-93) and succeeded by the First Republic; followed by the First Empire under Napoleon (1804-15), a monarchy (1814-48), the Second Republic (1848-52), the Second Empire (1852-70), the Third Republic (1871-1946), the Fourth Republic (1946-58), and the Fifth Republic (1958 to present).

France suffered severe losses in manpower and wealth in the first World War, 1914-18, when it was invaded by Germany. By the Treaty of Versailles, French exacted return of Alsace and Lorraine, French provinces seized by Germany in 1871. Germany invaded France again in May, 1940, and signed an armistice with a government based in Vichy. After France was liberated by the Allies Sept. 1944, Gen. Charles de Gaulle became head of the provisional government, serving until 1946.

De Gaulle again became premier in 1958, during a crisis over Algeria, and obtained voter approval for a new constitution, ushering in the Fifth Republic. Using strong executive powers, he promoted French economic and technological advances in the context of the European Economic Community and guarded French foreign policy independence.

France had withdrawn from Indochina in 1954, and from Morocco and Tunisia in 1956. Most of its remaining African territories were freed 1958-62.

In 1966, France withdrew all its troops from the integrated military command of NATO, though 60,000 remained stationed in Germany. France continued to attend political meetings of NATO.

In May 1968 rebellious students in Paris and other centers rioted, battled police, and were joined by workers who launched nationwide strikes. The government awarded pay increases to the strikers May 26. In elections to the Assembly in June, de Gaulle's backers won a landslide victory. Nevertheless, he resigned from office in April, 1969, after losing a nationwide referendum on constitutional reform.

On May 10, 1981, France elected François Mitterrand, a Socialist candidate, president. In September, the government nationalized 5 major industries and most private banks. In 1986, France began a privatization program in which many state-owned companies were sold. In 1993 the government completed the privatization program by selling stakes in 21 companies for about $54 billion. Mitterrand was elected to a 2d 7-year term in 1988.

France set tighter rules for entry into the country and made it easier for the government to expel foreigners in 1993.

The island of **Corsica**, in the Mediterranean W of Italy and N of Sardinia, is an official region of France comprising 2 departments. Area: 3,369 sq. mi.; pop. (1990 cen.): 249,700. The capital is Ajaccio, birthplace of Napoleon.

## Overseas Departments

**French Guiana** is on the NE coast of South America with Suriname on the W and Brazil on the E and S. Its area is 43,740 sq. mi.; pop. (1991): 101,000. Guiana sends one senator and one deputy to the French Parliament. Guiana is administered by a prefect and has a Council General of 16 elected members; capital is Cayenne.

The famous penal colony, Devil's Island, was phased out between 1938 and 1951.

Immense forests of rich timber cover 90% of the land. Placer gold mining is the most important industry. Exports are shrimp, timber, and machinery.

**Guadeloupe**, in the West Indies' Leeward Islands, consists of 2 large islands, Basse-Terre and Grande-Terre, separated by the Salt River, plus Marie Galante and the Saintes group to the S and, to the N, Desirade, St. Barthelemy, and over half of St. Martin (the Netherlands portion is St. Maarten). A French possession since 1635, the department is represented in the French Parliament by 2 senators and 3 deputies; administration consists of a prefect (governor) and an elected general and regional councils.

Area of the islands is 660 sq. mi.; pop. (1991 est.) 395,000, mainly descendants of slaves; capital is Basse-Terre on Basse-Terre Is. The land is fertile; sugar, rum, and bananas are exported; tourism is an important industry.

**Martinique**, the northernmost of the Windward Islands, in the West Indies, has been a possession since 1635, and a department since March 1946. It is represented in the French Parliament by 2 senators and 3 deputies. The island was the birthplace of Napoleon's Empress Josephine.

It has an area of 425 sq. mi.; pop. (1991 est.) 365,000, mostly descendants of slaves. The capital is Fort-de-France (pop. 1991: 101,000). It is a popular tourist stop. The chief exports are rum, bananas, and petroleum products.

**Reunion** is a volcanic island in the Indian O. about 420 mi. E of Madagascar, and has belonged to France since 1665. Area, 969 sq. mi.; pop. (1992 est.) 626,000, 30% of French extraction. Capital: Saint-Denis. The chief export is sugar. It elects 3 deputies, 2 senators to the French Parliament.

## Territorial Collectivities

**Mayotte**, claimed by Comoros and administered by France, voted in 1976 to become a territorial collectivity of France. An island NW of Madagascar, area is 144 sq. mi., pop. (1992 est.) 86,000.

**St. Pierre and Miquelon**, formerly an Overseas Territory (1816-1976) and department (1976-85), made the transition to territorial collectivity in 1985. It consists of 2 groups of rocky islands near the SW coast of Newfoundland, inhabited by fishermen. The exports are chiefly fish products. The St. Pierre group has an area of 10 sq. mi.; Miquelon, 83 sq. mi. Total pop. (1992 est.) 6,513. The capital is St. Pierre. A deputy and a senator are elected to the French Parliament.

## Overseas Territories

**French Polynesia** Overseas Territory, comprises 130 islands widely scattered among 5 archipelagos in the South Pacific; administered by a governor. Territorial Assembly and a Council with headquarters at Papeete, Tahiti, one of the **Society Islands** (which include the **Windward** and **Leeward** islands). A deputy and a senator are elected to the French Parliament.

Other groups are the **Marquesas Islands**, the **Tuamotu Archipelago**, including the **Gambier Islands**, and the **Austral Islands**.

Total area of the islands administered from Tahiti is 1,544 sq. mi.; pop. (1991 est.), 195,000, more than half on Tahiti. Tahiti is picturesque and mountainous with a productive coastline bearing coconut, banana and orange trees, sugar cane and vanilla.

Tahiti was visited by Capt. James Cook in 1769 and by Capt. Bligh in the Bounty, 1788-89. Its beauty impressed Herman Melville, Paul Gauguin, and Charles Darwin.

**French Southern and Antarctic Lands** Overseas Territory comprises **Adelie Land**, on Antarctica, and 4 island groups in the Indian O. Adelie, reached 1840, has a research station, a coastline of 185 mi. and tapers 1,240 mi. inland to the South Pole. The U.S. does not recognize national claims in Antarctica. There are 2 huge glaciers, Ninnis, 22 mi. wide, 99 mi. long, and Mentz, 11 mi. wide, 140 mi. long. The Indian O. groups are:

**Kerguelen Archipelago**, visited 1772, consists of one large and 300 small islands. The chief is 87 mi. long, 74 mi. wide, and has Mt. Ross, 6,429 ft. tall. Principal research station is Port-aux-Francais. Seals often weigh 2 tons; there are blue whales, coal, peat, semi-precious stones. **Crozet Archipelago**, reached 1772, covers 195 sq. mi. Eastern Island rises to 6,560 ft. **Saint Paul**, in southern Indian O., has warm springs with earth at places heating to 120° to 390° F. **Amsterdam** is nearby; both produce cod and rock lobster.

**New Caledonia** and its dependencies, an overseas territory, are a group of islands in the Pacific O. about 1,115 mi. E of Australia and approx. the same distance NW of New Zealand. Dependencies are the **Loyalty Islands**, the **Isle of Pines**, **Huon Islands** and the **Chesterfield Islands**.

New Caledonia, the largest, has 6,530 sq. mi. Total area of the territory is 8,548 sq. mi.; population (1991 est.) 172,000. The group was acquired by France in 1853.

The territory is administered by a governor and government council. There is a popularly elected Territorial Assembly. A deputy and a senator are elected to the French Parliament. Capital: Noumea.

Mining is the chief industry. New Caledonia is one of the world's largest nickel producers. Other minerals found are chrome, iron, cobalt, manganese, silver, gold, lead, and copper. Agricultural products include coffee, copra, cotton, manioc (cassava), corn, tobacco, bananas and pineapples.

In 1987, New Caledonian voters chose by referendum to remain within the French Republic. There were clashes between French and Melanesians (Kanaks) in 1988.

**Wallis and Futuna Islands**, 2 archipelagos raised to status of overseas territory July 29, 1961, are in the SW Pacific S of the Equator between Fiji and Samoa. The islands have a total area of 106 sq. mi. and population (1988 est.) of 15,400. Alofi, attached to Futuna, is uninhabited. Capital: Mata-Utu. Chief products are copra, yams, taro roots, bananas. A senator and a deputy are elected to the French Parliament.

# Gabon

## Gabonese Republic

## République Gabonaise

**People: Population** (1992 est.): 1,106,000. **Pop. density:** 10 per sq. mi. **Urban** (1990): 45%. **Ethnic groups:** Fang 25%, Bapounon 10%, others. **Languages:** French (official), Bantu dialects. **Religions:** Mostly Christian, minority follow traditional beliefs.

**Geography: Area:** 103,346 sq. mi., the size of Colorado. **Location:** On Atlantic coast of central Africa. **Neighbors:** Equatorial Guinea, Cameroon on N, Congo on E, S. **Topography:** Heavily forested, the country consists of coastal lowlands plateaus in N, E, and S, mountains in N, SE, and center. The Ogooue R. system covers most of Gabon. **Capital:** Libreville. **Cities** (1991 est.): Libreville 275,000.

**Government: Type:** Republic. **Head of state:** Pres. Omar Bongo; b. Dec. 30, 1935; in office: Dec. 2, 1967. **Head of government:** Prime Min. Casimir Oye Mba; in office: May 3, 1990. **Local divisions:** 9 provinces. **Defense:** 3.2% of GDP (1990).

**Economy: Industries:** Oil products. **Chief crops:** Cocoa, coffee, rice, peanuts, palm products, cassava, bananas. **Minerals:** Manganese, uranium, oil, iron, gas. **Crude oil reserves** (1985): 623 mln. bbls. **Other resources:** Timber. **Arable land:** 2%. **Electricity prod.** (1991): 995 mln. kWh. **Labor force:** 65% agric.; 30% ind. & comm.

**Finance: Monetary unit:** CFA franc (Mar. 1993: 273 = $1 US). **Gross domestic product** (1991) $5.3 bln. **Per capita income** (1991): $4,400. **Imports** (1990): $780 mln.; partners: Fr. 51%. **Exports** (1990): $1.1 bln.; partners: Fr. 53%, U.S. 22%. **Tourism receipts** (1990): $4 mln. **National budget** (1991): $1.8 bln. **International reserves less gold** (Jan. 1993): $167 mln. **Gold:** 13,000 oz t. **Consumer prices** (change in 1990): 8.0%.

**Transport: Motor vehicles:** in use (1989): 19,000 passenger cars, 15,000 comm. vehicles. **Civil aviation** (1990): 445 mln. passengers-km. **Chief ports:** Port-Gentil, Owendo, Mayumba.

**Communications: Television sets:** 1 per 29 persons. **Radios:** 1 per 5 persons. **Telephones:** 1 per 64 persons.

**Health: Life expectancy at birth** (1992): 51 male; 56 female. **Births** (per 1,000 pop. 1992): 28. **Deaths** (per 1,000 pop. 1992): 15. **Natural increase:** 1.4%. **Hospital beds** (1985): 4,617. **Physicians** (1985): 265. **Infant mortality** (per 1,000 live births 1992): 100.

**Education** (1991): **Literacy:** 70%. Compulsory to age 16; attendance: 100% primary, 14% secondary.

**Major International Organizations:** UN (World Bank), OAU, OPEC.

**Embassy:** 2034 20th St NW 20009; 797-1000.

France established control over the region in the second half of the 19th century. Gabon became independent Aug. 17, 1960. A multiparty political system was introduced in 1990, and a new constitution was enacted in 1991. It is one of the most prosperous black African countries, thanks to abundant natural resources, foreign private investment, and government development programs.

# The Gambia

## Republic of The Gambia

**People: Population** (1992 est.): 902,000. **Age distrib. (%):** 0–14: 45.9; 15–59: 54.4; 60+: 3.8. **Pop. density:** 218 per sq. mi. **Urban** (1990): 21%. **Ethnic groups:** Mandinka 42%, Fula 8%, Wolof 16%, others. **Languages:** English (official), Mandinka, Wolof. **Religions:** Moslem 95%.

**Geography: Area:** 4,127 sq. mi., smaller than Connecticut. **Location:** On Atlantic coast near western tip of Africa. **Neighbors:** Surrounded on 3 sides by Senegal. **Topography:** A narrow strip of land on each side of the lower Gambia. **Capital:** Banjul. **Cities** (1993 est.): Banjul 40,000.

**Government: Type:** Republic. **Head of state:** Pres. Dawda Kairaba Jawara; b. May 16, 1924; in office: Apr. 24, 1970 (prime min. from June 12, 1962). **Local divisions:** 5 divisions and Banjul.

**Economy: Industries:** Tourism, peanut processing. **Chief crops:** Peanuts (main export), rice. **Arable land:** 16%. **Fish

catch** (1989): 17,000 metric tons. **Electricity prod.** (1991): 65 mln. kWh. **Labor force:** 75% agric.; 18% ind. & comm.

**Finance: Monetary unit:** Daiasi (Mar. 1993: 9.14 = $1.00 US). **Gross domestic product** (1991): $207 mln. **Per capita GDP:** $235. **Imports** (1991): $167 mln.; partners: EC 53%. **Exports** (1991): $122 mln.; partners: Japan 60%. **Tourism** (1990): $26 mln. receipts. **National budget** (1990): $95 mln. expenditures. **International reserves less gold** (Jan. 1993): $64 mln. **Consumer prices** (change in 1992): 9.5%.

**Transport: Motor vehicles:** in use (1989): 5,200 passenger cars, 1,000 comm. vehicles. **Chief ports:** Banjul.

**Communications: Radios:** 1 per 6.1 persons. **Telephones:** 1 per 80 persons.

**Health: Life expectancy at birth** (1992): 47 male; 51 female. **Births** (per 1,000 pop. 1992): 47. **Deaths** (per 1,000 pop. 1992): 17. **Natural increase:** 3.0%. **Physicians:** 1 per 17,604 persons. **Infant mortality** (per 100,000 live births 1992): 129.

**Education** (1993): **Literacy:** 30%.

**Major International Organizations:** UN (GATT, IMF, WHO), OAU.

**Embassy:** 1155 15th St. 20005; 785-1399.

The tribes of Gambia were at one time associated with the West African empires of Ghana, Mali, and Songhay. The area became Britain's first African possession in 1588.

Independence came Feb. 18, 1965; republic status within the Commonwealth was achieved in 1970. After a coup attempt in 1981, The Gambia formed the confederation of Senegambia with Senegal that lasted until 1989. The country suffered from severe famine in the 1970s.

# Georgia

## Republic of Georgia

## Sakartvelos Respublica

**People: Population** (1992 est.): 5,570,000. **Pop. density:** 206 per sq. mi. **Urban** (1991): 57%. **Ethnic groups:** Georgian 70%, Armenian 7%, Russian 6%. **Languages:** Georgian (official), Russian. **Religions:** Georgia Orthodox 65%, Russian Orthodox 10%.

**Geography: Area:** 26,911 sq. mi., slightly larger than S.C. **Neighbors:** Black Sea on W, Russia on N, NE, Turkey, Armenia on S, Azerbaijan on SE. **Topography:** Separated from Russia on NE by main range of the Caucasus mts. **Capital:** Tbilisi. **Cities** (1991): Tbilisi 1.2 mln.

**Government: Type:** Republic. **Head of state:** Pres. Eduard A. Shevardnadze; b. Jan. 25, 1928; in office: Nov. 6, 1992. **Head of government:** Prime Min. Otar Patsatsia; in office: Aug. 1993.

**Economy: Industries:** Manganse mining. **Chief crops:** Citrus fruits, wheat, grapes. **Livestock** (1990): cattle: 1.5 mln., sheep: 1.9 mln.

**Finance: Monetary unit:** Ruble. **Imports** (1990): $1.5 bln. **Exports** (1990): $176 mln.

**Transport: Railroads: Length:** 976 mi. **Motor vehicles:** in use: 427,000 passenger cars.

**Communications:** Newspaper circ. (1990): 671 per 1,000 pop.

**Health: Life expectancy at birth:** 67 male; 73 female. **Births** (per 1,000 pop. 1992): 17. **Deaths** (per 1,000 pop. 1992): 9. **Infant mortality** (per 1,000 live births 1992): 34. **Physicians:** 1 per 170 persons; **Hospital beds:** 1 per 90 persons.

The region contained the ancient kingdoms of Colchis and Iberia. It was Christianized in the 4th century and conquered by Arabs in the 8th century. The region expanded to include area from the Black Sea to Caspian and parts of Armenia and Persia before its disintegration under the impact of Mongol and Turkish invasions. The annexation to Russia in 1801 caused the Russian war with Persia, 1804-1813. Georgia entered the USSR in 1922 and became a constituent republic in 1936.

In 1989, strong nationalist feelings led the USSR to attempts at repression; Soviet troops attacked nationalist demonstrators in April, killing some 20 persons. Georgia declared independence Apr. 9, 1991. It became an independent state when the Soviet Union disbanded Dec. 26, 1991, although it did not join the Commonwealth of Independent States.

There was fighting during 1991 between rebel forces and loyalists of Pres. Zviad Gamsakhurdia, whom the rebels accused of aspiring to establish a dictatorship. Gamsakhurdia fled the capital Jan. 6, 1992. The ruling Military Council picked former Soviet Foreign Minister Eduard A. Shevardnadze to chair a newly created State Council. An attempted coup by forces loyal to ousted Pres. Gamsakhurdia was crushed June 24. Shevardnadze was elected president Nov. 1992.

Georgia accused Russia of aiding rebels in Abkhazia, an autonomous region within Georgia, in 1993. The ethnic Abkhazis were in armed revolt to secure independence. Martial law was declared in parts of the region July 6.

# Germany
## Federal Republic of Germany
## Bundesrepublik Deutschland
### (Figures prior to 1990 for original 11 states)

**People: Population** (1992 est.): 80,387,000. **Age distrib. (%):** 0–14: 14.7; 15–59: 64.7; 60+: 20.6. **Pop. density:** 583 per sq. mi. **Urban** (1990): 86% **Ethnic groups:** German 93%. **Languages:** German. **Religions:** Protestant 44%, Roman Catholic 37%.

**Geography: Area:** 137,838 sq. mi. **Location:** In central Europe. **Neighbors:** Denmark on N, Netherlands, Belgium, Luxembourg, France on W, Switzerland, Austria on S, Czech Rep., Poland on E. **Topography:** Germany is flat in N, hilly in center and W, and mountainous in Bavaria. Chief rivers are Elbe, Weser, Ems, Rhine, and Main, all flowing toward North Sea, and Danube, flowing toward Black Sea. **Capital:** Berlin. **Cities** (1991 est.): Berlin 3.0 mln.; Hamburg 1.6 mln.; Munich 1.3 mln.; Cologne 946,000; Essen 622,000; Frankfurt 635,000; Dortmund 575,000; Dusseldorf 593,000; Stuttgart 561,000; Leipzig 549,000; Dresden 521,000.

**Government: Type:** Federal republic. **Head of state:** Pres. Richard von Weizsacker; b. Apr. 15, 1920; in office: May 23, 1984. **Head of government:** Chan. Helmut Kohl; b. Apr. 3, 1930; in office: Oct. 1, 1982. **Local divisions:** 16 laender (states) with substantial powers. **Defense:** 2.5% of GDP (1991).

**Economy: Industries:** Steel, ships, vehicles, machinery, electronics, coal, chemicals. **Chief crops:** Grains, potatoes, sugar beets. **Minerals:** Coal, potash, lignite, iron, uranium. **Arable land:** 35%. **Livestock** (1990): cattle: 15.3 mln.; pigs: 10.0 mln.; sheep: 1.2 mln. **Fish catch** (1990): 390,000 metric tons. **Electricity prod.** (1991): 580 bln. kWh. **Crude steel prod.** (1991): 42.1 mln. metric tons. **Labor force:** 5% agric.; 40% ind. & comm.; 54% services.

**Finance: Monetary unit:** Mark (Aug. 1993: 1.71 = $1 US). **Gross domestic product** (1991): $1,331 bln. **Per capita GDP:** $14,600. **Imports** (1992): $402 bln.; partners: EC 52%; other European 16%. **Exports** (1992): $422 bln.; partners: EC 55%; other European 19%. **Tourists** (1989): receipts $8.6 bln. **National budget** (1990): $245 bln. expenditures. **International reserves less gold** (Mar. 1993): $70 bln. **Gold:** 95.18 mln. oz t. **Consumer prices** (change in 1992): 4.0%.

**Transport: Railroads** (1991): **Length:** 56,397 mi. **Motor vehicles:** in use (1990): 35.5 mln. passenger cars, 2.7 mln. comm. **Civil aviation** (1988): 34.0 bln. passenger-km; 27 airports with scheduled flights. **Chief ports:** Hamburg, Bremen, Bremerhaven, Lubeck.

**Communications: Television sets:** 1 per 2.6 persons. **Radios:** 1 per 2.3 persons. **Telephones:** 1 per 1.5 persons. **Daily newspaper circ.** (1990): 401 per 1,000 pop.

**Health: Life expectancy at birth** (1992): 73 male; 79 female. **Births** (per 1,000 pop. 1992): 11. **Deaths** (per 1,000 pop. 1992): 11. **Hospital beds:** 1 per 95 persons. **Physicians:** 1 per 324 persons. **Infant mortality** (per 1,000 live births 1992): 7.

**Education** (1991): **Literacy:** 99%. **Years compulsory:** 10; attendance 100%.

**Major International Organizations:** UN and all of its specialized agencies, EC, OECD, NATO.

**Embassy:** 4645 Reservoir Rd. NW 20007; 298-4000.

Germany, prior to World War II, was a central European nation composed of numerous states which had a common language and traditions and which had been united in one country since 1871; since World War II until 1990, had been split in 2 parts.

**History and government.** Germanic tribes were defeated by Julius Caesar, 55 and 53 BC, but Roman expansion N of the Rhine was stopped in 9 AD. Charlemagne, ruler of the Franks,

consolidated Saxon, Bavarian, Rhenish, Frankish, and other lands; after him the eastern part became the German Empire. The Thirty Years' War, 1618-1648, split Germany into small principalities and kingdoms. After Napoleon, Austria contended with Prussia for dominance, but lost the Seven Weeks' War to Prussia, 1866. Otto von Bismarck, Prussian chancellor, formed the North German Confederation, 1867.

In 1870 Bismarck maneuvered Napoleon III into declaring war. After the quick defeat of France, Bismarck formed the **German Empire** and on Jan. 18, 1871, in Versailles, proclaimed King Wilhelm I of Prussia German emperor (Deutscher kaiser).

The German Empire reached its peak before World War I in 1914, with 208,780 sq. mi., plus a colonial empire. After that war Germany ceded Alsace-Lorraine to France; West Prussia and Posen (Poznan) province to Poland; part of Schleswig to Denmark; lost all of its colonies and the ports of Memel and Danzig.

**Republic of Germany,** 1919-1933, adopted the Weimar constitution; met reparation payments and elected Friedrich Ebert and Gen. Paul von Hindenburg presidents.

**Third Reich,** 1933-1945, Adolf Hitler led the National Socialist German Workers' (Nazi) party after World War I. In 1923 he attempted to unseat the Bavarian government and was imprisoned. Pres. von Hindenburg named Hitler chancellor Jan. 30, 1933; on Aug. 3, 1934, the day after Hindenburg's death, the cabinet joined the offices of president and chancellor and made Hitler fuehrer (leader). Hitler abolished freedom of speech and assembly, and began a long series of persecutions climaxed by the murder of millions of Jews and opponents.

Hitler repudiated the Versailles treaty and reparations agreements. He remilitarized the Rhineland 1936 and annexed Austria (Anschluss, 1938). At Munich he made an agreement with Neville Chamberlain, British prime minister, which permitted Hitler to annex part of Czechoslovakia. He signed a non-aggression treaty with the USSR, 1939. He declared war on Poland Sept. 1, 1939, precipitating World War II.

With total defeat near, Hitler committed suicide in Berlin Apr. 1945. The victorious Allies voided all acts and annexations of Hitler's Reich.

**Postwar changes.** The zones of occupation administered by the Allied Powers and later relinquished gave the USSR Saxony, Saxony-Anhalt, Thuringia, and Mecklenburg, and the former Prussian provinces of Saxony and Brandenburg.

The territory E of the Oder-Neisse line within 1937 boundaries comprising the provinces of Silesia, Pomerania, and the southern part of East Prussia, totaling about 41,220 sq. mi., was taken by Poland. Northern East Prussia was taken by the USSR.

The Western Allies ended the state of war with Germany in 1951. The USSR did so in 1955.

There was also created the area of Greater Berlin, within but not part of the Soviet zone, administered by the 4 occupying powers under the Allied Command. In 1948 the USSR withdrew, established its single command in East Berlin, and cut off supplies. The Allies utilized a gigantic airlift to bring food to West Berlin, 1948-49. In Aug. 1961 the East Germans built a wall dividing Berlin, after over 3 million E. Germans had emigrated.

On Nov. 9, 1989 the E. German government announced the decision to open the border with the West signaling the end of the infamous Berlin Wall.

**A New Era:** As communism was being rejected in E. Germany, talks began concerning German reunification. At a meeting in Ottawa, Feb. 1990, the foreign ministers of the World War II "Big Four" Allied nations—U.S., USSR, UK, and France—as well as the foreign ministers of E. Germany and W. Germany reached agreement on a format for high-level talks on German reunification.

In May, NATO ministers adopted a package of proposals on reunification, including the inclusion of the united Germany as a full member of NATO and the barring of the new Germany from having its own nuclear, chemical, or biological weapons. In July, the USSR agreed to conditions that would allow Germany to become a member of NATO.

The 2 nations agreed to monetary unification under the W. German mark beginning in July. The merger of the 2 Germanys took place on Oct. 3, 1990, and the first all-German elections since 1932 were held Dec. 2, 1990.

In 1992, neo-Nazi groups intensified their campaign against refugees. The Constitutional Protection Office reported 2,285 violent attacks by right-wingers in 1992. Parliament approved constitutional changes to restrict foreigners' rights to seek asylum in Germany, May 1993.

## East Germany

The German Democratic Republic was proclaimed in the Soviet sector of Berlin Oct. 7, 1949. It was proclaimed fully sovereign in 1954, but Soviet troops remained on grounds of security and the 4-power Potsdam agreement.

Coincident with the entrance of W. Germany into the European Defense community in 1952, the East German government decreed a prohibited zone 3 miles deep along its 600-mile border with W. Germany and cut Berlin's telephone system in two. Berlin was further divided by erection of a fortified wall in 1961, but the exodus of refugees to the West continued, though on a smaller scale.

E. Germany suffered severe economic problems until the mid-1960s. A "new economic system" was introduced, easing the former central planning controls and allowing factories to make profits provided they were reinvested in operations or redistributed to workers as bonuses. By the early 1970s, the economy was highly industrialized. In May 1972 the few remaining private firms were ordered sold to the government. The nation was credited with the highest standard of living among Warsaw Pact countries. But growth slowed in the late 1970s, due to shortages of natural resources and labor, and a huge debt to lenders in the West. Comparison with the lifestyle in the West caused many of the young to leave the country.

The government firmly resisted following the USSR's policy of *glasnost*, but by Oct. 1989, was faced with nationwide demonstrations demanding reform. Pres. Erich Honecker, in office since 1976, was forced to resign, Oct. 18. On Nov. 4, the border with Czechoslovakia was opened and permission granted for refugees to travel on to the West, On Nov. 9, the decision was made to open the border with the West, signaling the end of the "Berlin Wall," which separated the 2 Germanys and was the supreme emblem of the cold war.

On Aug. 23, 1990, the E. German Parliament agreed to formal unification with W. Germany; this took place on Oct. 3.

## West Germany

The Federal Republic of Germany was proclaimed May 23, 1949, in Bonn, after a constitution had been drawn up by a consultative assembly formed by representatives of the 11 laender (states) in the French, British, and American zones. Later reorganized into 9 units, the laender numbered 10 with the addition of the Saar, 1957. Berlin also was granted land (state) status, but the 1945 occupation agreements placed restrictions on it.

The occupying powers, the U.S., Britain, and France, restored the civil status, Sept. 21, 1949. The U. S. resumed diplomatic relations July 2, 1951. The powers lifted controls and the republic became fully independent May 5, 1955.

Dr. Konrad Adenauer, Christian Democrat, was made chancellor Sept. 15, 1949, re-elected 1953, 1957, 1961. Willy Brandt, heading a coalition of Social Democrats and Free Democrats, became chancellor Oct. 21, 1969.

In 1970 Brandt signed friendship treaties with the USSR and Poland. In 1971, the U.S., Britain, France, and the USSR signed an agreement on Western access to West Berlin. In 1972 the Bundestag approved the USSR and Polish treaties and East and West Germany signed their first formal treaty, implementing the agreement easing access to West Berlin. In 1973 a West Germany-Czechoslovakia pact normalized relations and nullified the 1938 "Munich Agreement."

In May 1974 Brandt resigned, saying he took full responsibility for "negligence" for allowing an East German spy to become a member of his staff.

West Germany experienced economic growth since the 1950s. The country led Europe in provisions for worker participation in the management of industry.

The NATO decision to deploy medium-range nuclear missiles in Western Europe sparked a demonstration by some 400,000 protesters in 1983. In 1989, Chancellor Kohl's call for early negotiations with the Soviets on reducing short-range missiles caused a rift with the NATO allies, especially the U.S. and Great Britain.

In 1989, the changes in the E. German government and the opening of the Berlin Wall sparked talk of reunification of the 2 Germanys. In 1990, under the leadership of Chancellor Kohl, W. Germany moved rapidly to reunite with E. Germany.

**Helgoland,** an island of 130 acres in the North Sea, was taken from Denmark by a British Naval Force in 1807 and later ceded to Germany to become a part of Schleswig-Holstein province in return for rights in East Africa. The heavily fortified island was surrendered to UK, May 23, 1945, demilitarized in 1947, and returned to W. Germany, Mar 1, 1952. It is a free port.

# Ghana
## Republic of Ghana

**People: Population** (1992 est.): 16,185,000. **Age distrib.** (%): 0–14: 46.6; 15-59: 48.9; 60+: 4.5. **Pop. density:** 175 per sq. mi. **Urban** (1990): 33%. **Ethnic groups:** Akan 44%, Moshi-Dagomba 16%, Ewe 13%, Ga 8%, others. **Languages:** English (official), Akan, Mossi, Ewe, Ga-Adangme. **Religions:** Christian 24%, traditional beliefs 38%, Moslem 30%.

**Geography: Type:** Area: 92,098 sq. mi., slightly smaller than Oregon. **Location:** On southern coast of W. Africa. **Neighbors:** Côte D'Ivoire on W, Burkina Faso on N, Togo on E. **Topography:** Most of Ghana consists of low fertile plains and scrubland, cut by rivers and by the artificial Lake Volta. **Capital:** Accra. **Cities** (1988 est.): Accra 949,000.

**Government: Type:** Military. **Head of government:** Pres. Jerry Rawlings; b. 1947; in office: Dec. 31, 1981. **Local divisions:** 10 regions.

**Economy: Industries:** Aluminum, light industry. **Chief crops:** Cocoa, coffee. **Minerals:** Gold, manganese, industrial diamonds, bauxite. **Crude oil reserves** (1980): 7 mln. bbls. **Other resources:** Timber, rubber. **Arable land:** 5%. **Livestock** (1990): cattle: 1.1 mln.; sheep: 2.2 mln. **Fish catch** (1990): 360,000 metric tons. **Electricity prod.** (1991): 4.1 bln. kWh. **Labor force:** 55% agric.; 19% ind.

**Finance: Monetary unit:** Cedi (Mar. 1993: 555 = $1.00 US). **Gross domestic product** (1991): $6.2 bln. **Per capita GDP:** $400. **Imports** (1991): $1.2 bln.; partners: UK 10%, Ger. 12%, Nigeria 12%. **Exports** (1991): $843 mln.; partners: U.S. 23%, Neth. 9%, Ger. 9%. **International reserves less gold** (Mar. 1993): 399 mln. **Gold:** 275,000 oz t. **Consumer prices** (change in 1991): 18%.

**Transport: Railroads** (1991): Length: 592 mi. **Motor vehicles:** in use (1986): 26,000 passenger cars, 28,000 comm. vehicles. **Civil aviation** (1990): 407 mln. passenger-km; 3 airports with scheduled flights. **Chief ports:** Tema, Takoradi.

**Communications: Television sets:** 1 per 83 persons. **Radios:** 1 per 4.7 persons. **Telephones:** 1 per 191 persons.

**Health: Life expectancy at birth** (1992): 53 male; 56 female. **Births** (per 1,000 pop. 1992): 46. **Deaths** (per 1,000 pop. 1992): 13. **Natural increase:** 3.3%. **Physicians:** 1 per 22,127 persons. **Infant mortality** (per 1,000 live births 1992): 86.

**Education** (1991): Literacy: 60%.

**Major International Organizations:** UN and all of its specialized agencies, OAU.

**Embassy:** 3512 International Dr., 20008; 686-4500.

Named for an African empire along the Niger River, 400-1240 AD, Ghana was ruled by Britain for 113 years as the Gold Coast. The UN in 1956 approved merger with the British Togoland trust territory. Independence came March 6, 1957. Republic status within the Commonwealth was attained in 1960.

Pres. Kwame Nkrumah built hospitals and schools, promoted development projects like the Volta R. hydroelectric and aluminum plants but ran the country into debt, jailed opponents, and was accused of corruption. A 1964 referendum gave Nkrumah dictatorial powers and set up a one-party socialist state.

Nkrumah was overthrown in 1966 by a police-army coup, which expelled Chinese and East German teachers and technicians. Elections were held in 1969, but 4 further coups occurred in 1972, 1978, 1979, and 1981. The 1979 and 1981 coups, led by Flight Lieut. Jerry Rawlings, were followed by suspension of the constitution and banning of political parties. A new constitution, which allowed for multiparty politics, was approved in April 1992.

# Greece
## Hellenic Republic
### Elliniki Dimokratia

**People: Population** (1992 est.): 10,064,000. **Age distrib.** (%): 0–14: 20.5; 15-59: 61.1; 60+: 20.4. **Pop. density:** 196 per sq. mi. **Urban** (1990): 63.0%. **Ethnic groups:** Greeks 98.5%. **Languages:** Greek. **Religions:** Greek Orthodox 97% (official).

**Geography: Area:** 51,146 sq. mi., the size of Alabama. **Location:** Occupies southern end of Balkan Peninsula in SE Europe. **Neighbors:** Albania, Macedonia, Bulgaria on N, Turkey on E. **Topography:** About 75% of Greece is non-arable, with mountains in all areas. Pindus Mts. run through the country N to S. The heavily indented coastline is 9,385 mi. long. Of over 2,000 islands, only 169 are inhabited, among them Crete, Rhodes, Milos, Kerkira (Corfu), Chios, Lesbos, Samos, Euboea, Delos, Mykonos. **Capital:** Athens. **Cities** (1991 est.): Athens 748,110; Thessaloniki 377,000; Patras 169,000.

**Government: Type:** Presidential parliamentary republic. **Head of state:** Pres. Konstantinos Karamanlis; in office: May, 1990. **Head of government:** Prime Min. Konstantinos Mitsotakis; b. Oct. 18, 1918, in office: Apr. 11, 1990. **Local divisions:** 51 prefectures. **Defense:** 5.5% of GDP (1991).

**Economy: Industries:** Textiles, chemicals, metals, wine, food processng, cement. **Chief crops:** Grains, corn, rice, cotton, tobacco, olives, citrus fruits, raisins, figs. **Minerals:** Bauxite, lignite, oil, manganese. **Crude oil reserves** (1985): 35 mln. bbls. **Arable land:** 23%. **Livestock** (1990): sheep: 11.0 mln.; goats: 5.6 mln. **Fish catch** (1990): 128,000 metric tons. **Electricity prod.** (1991): 36.4 bln. kWh. **Labor force:** 28% agric.; 29% ind., 42% service.

**Finance: Monetary unit:** Drachma (Aug. 1993: 239.00 = $1 US). **Gross domestic product** (1991): $77 bln. **Per capita GDP:** $7,730. **Imports** (1991): $21.5 bln.; partners: Ger. 21%, It. 15%, Fr. 7%. **Exports** (1991): $8.6 bln.; partners: Ger. 20%, It. 17%, Fra. 10%. **Tourism** (1990): $2.5 bln. receipts. **National budget** (1991): $33 bln. expenditures. **International reserves less gold** (Mar. 1993): $4.7 bln. **Gold:** 3.4 mln. oz t. **Consumer prices** (change in 1992): 15.8%.

**Transport: Railroads** (1991): **Length:** 1,540 mi. **Motor vehicles:** in use (1990): 1.6 mln. passenger cars, 781,000 comm. vehicles. **Civil aviation** (1990): 7.7 bln. passenger-km; 33 airports with scheduled flights. **Chief ports:** Piraeus, Thessaloniki, Patrai.

**Communications: Television sets:** 1 per 4.5 persons. **Radios:** 1 per 2.4 persons. **Telephones:** 1 per 2.2 persons. **Daily newspaper circ.** (1986): 88 per 1,000 pop.

**Health: Life expectancy at birth** (1992): 75 male; 80 female. **Births** (per 1,000 pop. 1992): 11. **Deaths** (per 1,000 pop. 1992): 9. **Natural increase:** .2%. **Hospital beds:** 1 per 193 persons. **Physicians:** 1 per 327 persons. **Infant mortality** (per 1,000 live birth 1992): 10.

**Education** (1991): **Literacy:** men 96%, women 89%. **Years compulsory:** 9.

**Major International Organizations:** UN (GATT, IMF, WHO, ILO), EC, NATO, OECD.

**Embassy:** 2221 Massachusetts Ave. NW 20008; 667-3168.

The achievements of ancient Greece in art, architecture, science, mathematics, philosophy, drama, literature, and democracy became legacies for succeeding ages. Greece reached the height of its glory and power, particularly in the Athenian city-state, in the 5th century BC.

Greece fell under Roman rule in the 2d and 1st centuries BC. In the 4th century AD it became part of the Byzantine Empire and, after the fall of Constantinople to the Turks in 1453, part of the Ottoman Empire.

Greece won its war of independence from Turkey 1821-1829, and became a kingdom. A republic was established 1924; the monarchy was restored, 1935, and George II, King of the Hellenes, resumed the throne. In Oct. 1940, Greece rejected an ultimatum from Italy. Nazi support resulted in its defeat and occupation by Germans, Italians, and Bulgarians. By the end of 1944 the invaders withdrew. Communist resistance forces were defeated by Royalist and British troops. A plebiscite recalled King George II. He died Apr. 1, 1947 and was succeeded by his brother, Paul I.

Communists waged guerrilla war 1947-49 against the government but were defeated with the aid of the U.S.

A period of reconstruction and rapid development followed, mainly with conservative governments under Premier Constantine Karamanlis. The Center Union led by George Papandreou won elections in 1963 and 1964. King Constantine, who acceded in 1964, forced Papandreou to resign. A period of political maneuvers ended in the military takeover of April 21, 1967, by Col. George Papadopoulos. King Constantine tried to reverse the consolidation of the harsh dictatorship Dec. 13, 1967, but failed and fled to Italy. Papadopoulos was ousted Nov. 25, 1973.

Greek army officers serving in the National Guard of Cyprus staged a coup on the island July 15, 1974. Turkey invaded Cyprus a week later, precipitating the collapse of the Greek junta, which was implicated in the Cyprus coup.

The 1981 victory of the Panhellenic Socialist Movement (Pasok) of Andreas Papandreou has brought about substantial changes in the internal and external policies that Greece has pursued for the past 5 decades. Greece was victimized in the 1980s by incidents of international terrorism.

A scandal centered on George Kostokas, a banker and publisher, led to the arrest or investigation of about a dozen leading Socialists, implicated Papandreou, and led to the defeat of the Socialists at the polls in 1989.

# Grenada

**People: Population** (1992 est.): 84,000. **Pop. density:** 631 per sq. mi. **Ethnic groups:** Mostly African descent. **Languages:** English (official), French patois. **Religions:** Roman Catholic 64%, Anglican 22%.

**Geography: Area:** 133 sq. mi., twice the size of Washington, D.C. **Location:** 90 mi. N. of Venezuela. **Topography:** Main island is mountainous; country includes Carriacon and Petit Martinique islands. **Capital:** St. George's. **Cities** (1991 est.): St. George's 30,000.

**Government: Type:** Parliamentary democracy. **Head of state:** Queen Elizabeth II, represented by Gov.-Gen. Reginald Palmer. **Head of government:** Prime Minister: Nicholas Brathwaite; in office: Mar. 13, 1990. **Local divisions:** 6 parishes and one dependency.

**Economy: Industries:** Rum. **Chief crops:** Nutmegs, bananas, cocoa, mace. **Arable land:** 15%. **Electricity prod.** (1991): 26 mln. kWh. **Labor force:** 33% agric.; 31% services.

**Finance: Monetary unit:** East Caribbean dollar (Apr. 1993: 2.70 = $1 US). **Gross domestic product** (1989): $238 mln. **Per capita GDP:** $2,800. **Imports** (1989): $200 mln.; partners: UK 19%, Trin./Tob. 12%, U.S. 24%. **Exports** (1990): $26 mln.; partners: UK 23%, CARICOM countries 38%. **Tourism** (1991): $38 mln. receipts. **National budget** (1990): $77 mln. expenditures. **International reserves less gold** (Jan. 1993): $25 mln.

**Transport: Chief ports:** Saint George's.

**Communications: Radios:** 1 per 2.4 persons. **Telephones:** 1 per 9 persons.

**Health: Life expectancy at birth** (1992): 69 male; 74 female. **Births** (per 1,000 pop. 1992): 35. **Deaths** (per 1,000 pop. 1992): 7. **Natural increase:** 2.8%. **Infant mortality** (per 1,000 live births 1992): 28.

**Education** (1991): **Literacy:** 95%; **Years compulsory:** 6. **Major International Organizations:** UN (IMF, WHO), OAS. **Embassy:** 1701 New Hampshire Ave. NW 20009; 265-2561.

Columbus sighted the island 1498. First European settlers were French, 1650. The island was held alternately by France and England until final British occupation, 1784. Grenada became fully independent Feb. 7, 1974 during a general strike. It is the smallest independent nation in the Western Hemisphere.

On Oct. 14, 1983, a military coup ousted Prime Minister Maurice Bishop, who was put under house arrest, later freed by supporters, rearrested, and, finally, on Oct. 19, executed. U.S. forces, with a token force from 6 area nations, invaded Grenada, Oct. 25. Resistance from the Grenadian army and Cuban advisors was quickly overcome as most of the population welcomed the invading forces as liberators. U.S. troops left Grenada in June 1985.

# Guatemala
## Republic of Guatemala
## República de Guatemala

**People: Population** (1992 est.): 9,784,000. **Age distrib. (%):** 0–14: 45.4; 15–59: 49.5; 60+: 5.1. **Pop. density:** 232 per sq. mi. **Urban** (1992): 39%. **Ethnic groups:** Maya 55%, Mestizos 44%. **Languages:** Spanish (official), Mayan languages. **Religions:** Mostly Roman Catholics.

**Geography: Area:** 42,042 sq. mi., the size of Tennessee. **Location:** In Central America. **Neighbors:** Mexico N, W, El Salvador on S, Honduras, Belize on E. **Topography:** The central highland and mountain areas are bordered by the narrow Pacific coast and the lowlands and fertile river valleys on the Caribbean. There are numerous volcanoes in S, more than half a dozen over 11,000 ft. **Capital:** Guatemala City. **Cities** (1992 est.): Guatemala City 1,115,000.

**Government: Type:** Republic. **Head of state:** Pres. Ramiro de Leon Carpio; in office: June 6, 1993. **Local divisions:** Guatemala City and 22 departments. **Defense:** 1.0% of GDP (1990).

**Economy: Industries:** Prepared foods, tires, textiles. **Chief crops:** Coffee (one third of exports), sugar, bananas, cotton, corn. **Minerals:** Oil, nickel. **Crude oil reserves** (1985): 500 mln. bbls. **Other resources:** Rare woods, fish, chicle. **Arable land:** 12%. **Electricity prod.** (1991): 2.5 bln. kWh. **Labor force:** 36% agric.; 24% ind. & comm., 34% services.

**Finance: Monetary unit:** Quetzal (Apr. 1993: 5.47 = $1 US). **Gross domestic product** (1991): $11.7 bln. **Per capita GDP:** $1,260. **Imports** (1992): $2.4 bln.; partners: U.S. 37%, CACM 8%. **Exports** (1992): $1.0 bln.; partners: U.S. 28%, CACM 20%. **Tourism** (1990): $185 mln. **National budget** (1990): $1.1 bln. expenditures. **International reserves** less gold (Mar. 1993): $807 mln. **Gold:** 122,000 oz t. **Consumer prices** (change in 1992): 10.0%.

**Transport: Motor vehicles:** in use (1990): 130,000 passenger cars, 100,000 comm. vehicles. **Civil aviation** (1990): 213 mln. passenger-km; 2 airports with scheduled flights. **Chief ports:** Puerto Barrios, San Jose.

**Communications: Television sets:** 1 per 18 persons. **Radios:** 1 per 22 persons. **Telephones:** 1 per 36 persons. **Daily newspaper circ.** (1989): 22 per 1,000 pop.

**Health: Life expectancy at birth** (1992): 61 male; 66 female. **Births** (per 1,000 pop. 1992): 34. **Deaths** (per 1,000 pop. 1992): 8. **Natural increase:** 2.6%. **Physicians:** 1 per 2,356 persons. **Infant mortality** (per 1,000 live births 1992): 56.

**Education** (1991): **Literacy:** 55%. **Years compulsory:** 6; **Attendance:** 35%.

**Major International Organizations:** UN (IMF, World Bank), OAS.

**Embassy:** 2220 R St. NW 20008; 745-4952.

The old Mayan Indian empire flourished in what is today Guatemala for over 1,000 years before the Spanish.

Guatemala was a Spanish colony 1524-1821; briefly a part of Mexico and then of the U.S. of Central America, the republic was established in 1839.

Since 1945 when a liberal government was elected to replace the long-term dictatorship of Jorge Ubico, the country has seen a swing toward socialism, an armed revolt, renewed attempts at social reform, a military coup, and, in 1986, civilian rule. The Guerrilla Army of the Poor, an insurgent group founded 1975, led a military offensive by attacking army posts and succeeded in incorporating segments of the large Indian population in its struggle against the government.

Dissident army officers seized power, Mar. 23, 1982, denouncing the Mar. 7 presidential election as fraudulent and pledging to restore "authentic democracy" to the nation. Political violence has caused some 200,000 Guatemalans to seek refuge in Mexico. A second military coup occurred Oct. 8, 1983. The nation returned to civilian rule in 1986.

Pres. Jorge Serrano Elias was ousted by the military June 1, 1993. Ramiro de Leon Carpio was elected president by Congress June 6. De Leon fired the defense minister and reassigned several military commanders.

## Guinea
### Republic of Guinea
### République de Guinée

**People: Population** (1992 est.): 7,783,000. **Pop. density:** 81 per sq. mi. **Urban** (1991): 26%. **Ethnic groups:** Foulah 35%, Malinké 30%, Soussous 20%, 15 other tribes. **Languages:** French (official), Peul, Mande. **Religions:** Moslem 85%, Christian 10%.

**Geography: Area:** 94,964 sq. mi., slightly smaller than Oregon. **Location:** On Atlantic coast of W. Africa. **Neighbors:** Guinea-Bissau, Senegal, Mali on N, Côte d'Ivoire on E, Liberia on S. **Topography:** A narrow coastal belt leads to the mountainous middle region, the source of the Gambia, Senegal, and Niger rivers. Upper Guinea, farther inland, is a cooler upland. The SE is forested. **Capital:** Conakry. **Cities** (1989 est.): Conakry 705,000; Labe 273,000; N'Zerekore 250,000; Kankan 278,000.

**Government: Type:** Republic. **Head of state:** Pres. Brig. Gen. Lansana Conte; b. 1944; in office: Apr. 5, 1984. **Local divisions:** 33 administrative regions. **Defense:** 1.2% of GDP (1988).

**Economy: Chief crops:** Bananas, pineapples, rice, corn, palm nuts, coffee, honey. **Minerals:** Bauxite, iron, diamonds. **Arable land:** 6%. **Electricity prod.** (1991) 300 mln. kWh. **Labor force:** 82% agric.; 9% ind. & comm.

**Finance: Monetary unit:** Franc (Jan. 1993: 811 = $1 US). **Gross domestic product** (1990): $3.0 bln. **Per capita GDP:** $410. **Imports** (1990): $692 mln.; partners: U.S. 16%. **Exports** (1990): $788 mln.; partners: U.S. 33%. **National budget** (1990): 708 mln.

**Transport: Motor vehicles:** in use (1989): 13,000 passenger cars, 13,000 comm. vehicles. **Chief ports:** Conakry.

**Communications: Radios:** 1 per 34 persons. **Telephones:** 1 per 355 persons.

**Health: Life expectancy at birth** (1992): 41 male; 45 female. **Births** (per 1,000 pop. 1992): 46. **Deaths** (per 1,000 pop. 1992): 21. **Natural increase:** 2.5%. **Physicians:** 1 per 9,732 persons. **Infant mortality** per 1,000 live births 1992): 144.

**Education** (1989): **Literacy:** 35% (in French). **Years compulsory:** 8; **attendance:** 36% primary, 15% secondary.

**Major International Organizations:** UN and most specialized agencies, OAU.

**Embassy:** 2112 Leroy Pl. NW 20008; 483-9420.

Part of the ancient West African empires, Guinea fell under French control 1849-98. Under Sekou Toure, it opted for full independence in 1958, and France withdrew all aid.

Toure turned to communist nations for support and set up a militant one-party state.

Thousands of opponents were jailed in the 1970s, in the aftermath of an unsuccessful Portuguese invasion. Many were tortured and killed.

The military took control of the government in a bloodless coup after the March 1984 death of Toure. A new constitution was approved in 1991, which promised full democracy by 1996. In 1992, movement toward democracy was slow; although political parties were made legal, political demonstrations were banned.

## Guinea-Bissau
### Republic of Guinea-Bissau
### Republica da Guiné-Bissau

**People: Population** (1992 est.): 1,074,000. **Pop. density:** 77 per sq. mi. **Ethnic groups:** Balante 27%, Fula 23%, Manjaca 11%, Mandinka 12%. **Languages:** Portuguese (official), Crioulo, tribal languages. **Religions:** Traditional 54%, Moslem 38%, Christian 8%.

**Geography: Area:** 13,948 sq. mi. about the size of Connecticut and New Hampshire combined. **Location:** On Atlantic coast of W. Africa. **Neighbors:** Senegal on N, Guinea on E, S. **Topography:** A swampy coastal plain covers most of the country; to the east is a low savanna region. **Capital:** Bissau. **Cities** (1988 est.): Bissau 138,000.

**Government: Type:** Republic. **Head of state:** Brig.-Gen. Joao Bernardo Vieira; b. 1939; in office: Nov. 14, 1980. **Head of government:** Prime Min. Carlos Correia; in office: Dec. 27, 1991. **Local divisions:** 9 regions. **Defense:** 3.3% of GDP (1987).

**Economy: Chief crops:** Peanuts, cotton, rice. **Minerals:** Bauxite. **Arable land:** 10%. **Electricity prod.** (1991): 30 mln. kWh. **Labor force:** 90% agric.

**Finance: Monetary unit:** Peso (Jan. 1993: 4,491 = $1 US). **Gross domestic product** (1989): $154 mln. **Per capita GDP** (1991): $160. **Imports** (1989): $69 mln.; partners: Port. 20%, It. 27%. **Exports** (1989): $14 mln.; partners: Port. 35%. **National Budget** (1989): $30 mln. expenditures.

**Transport: Motor vehicles:** in use (1990): 3,000 passenger cars, 2,500 commercial vehicles.

**Communications: Radios:** 1 per 27 persons. **Daily newspaper circ.** (1990): 12 per 1,000 pop.

**Health: Life expectancy at birth** (1992): 45 male; 48 female. **Births** (per 1,000 pop. 1992): 42. **Deaths** (per 1,000 pop. 1992): 18. **Natural increase:** 2.4%. **Infant mortality** (per 1,000 live births 1992): 125.

**Education** (1991): **Literacy:** 36%. **Years compulsory:** 4. **Major International Organizations:** UN, OAU.

**Embassy:** 211 E 43d St., New York, NY 10017; (212) 611-3977.

Portuguese mariners explored the area in the mid-15th century; the slave trade flourished in the 17th and 18th centuries, and colonization began in the 19th.

Beginning in the 1960s, an independence movement waged a guerrilla war and formed a government in the interior that achieved international support. Full independence came Sept. 10, 1974, after the Portuguese regime was overthrown.

The November 1980 coup gave Vieira absolute power. Vieira initiated political liberalization.

## Guyana

### Co-operative Republic of Guyana

**People: Population** (1992 est.): 739,000. **Age distrib. (%):** 0–14: 33.4; 5–59: 60.7; 60+: 5.9. **Pop. density:** 9 per sq. mi. **Urban** (1990): 35%. **Ethnic groups:** East Indians 51%, African 30%; mixed 14%. **Languages:** English (official), Amerindian dialects. **Religions:** Christian 46%, Hindu 37%; Moslem 9%.

**Geography: Area:** 83,000 sq. mi., the size of Idaho. **Location:** On N coast of S. America. **Neighbors:** Venezuela on W, Brazil on S, Suriname on E. **Topography:** Dense tropical forests cover much of the land, although a flat coastal area up to 40 mi. wide, where 90% of the population lives, provides rich alluvial soil for agriculture. A grassy savanna divides the 2 zones. **Capital:** Georgetown. **Cities** (1985 est.): Georgetown 170,000.

**Government: Type:** Republic. **Head of state:** President Cheddi Jagan; in office: Oct. 9, 1992. **Head of Government:** Prime Min. Sam Hinds; in office: Oct. 9, 1992. **Local divisions:** 10 regions. **Defense:** 6% of GDP (1989).

**Economy: Industries:** Mining, textiles. **Chief crops:** Sugar, rice, citrus and other fruits. **Minerals:** Bauxite, diamonds. **Other resources:** Timber, shrimp. **Arable land:** 2%. **Electricity prod.** (1991): 647 bln. kWh. **Labor force:** 33% agric.; 45% ind. & comm.; 22% services.

**Finance: Monetary unit:** Dollar (Mar. 1993: 126 = $1 US). **Gross domestic product** (1991): $250 mln. **Per capita GDP:** $300. **Imports** (1991): $246 mln.; partners: U.S. 33%, CARICOM 10%. **Exports** (1991): $189 mln.; partners: UK 31%, U.S. 23%. **National budget** (1990): $250 mln. **International reserves less gold** (Feb. 1993): $185 mln. **Consumer prices** (change in 1992): 10.9%.

**Transport: Motor vehicles:** in use (1990): 24,000 passenger cars, 9,000 comm. vehicles. **Chief ports:** Georgetown.

**Communications: Radios:** 1 per 2.5 persons. **Telephones:** 1 per 47 persons. **Daily newspaper circ.** (1991): 53 per 1,000 pop.

**Health: Life expectancy at birth** (1992): 61 male; 68 female. **Births** (per 1,000 pop. 1992): 21. **Deaths** (per 1,000 pop. 1992): 7. **Natural increase:** 1.4% **Hospital beds:** 1 per 341 persons. **Physicians:** 1 per 6,809 persons. **Infant mortality** (per 1,000 live births 1992): 51.

**Education** (1991): Literacy: 95%. **Years compulsory:** ages 5-14.

**Major International Organizations:** UN (GATT, ILO, IMF, World Bank), Commonwealth of Nations, OAS.

**Embassy:** 2490 Tracy Pl. NW 20008; 276-6900.

Guyana became a Dutch possession in the 17th century, but sovereignty passed to Britain in 1815. Indentured servants from India soon outnumbered African slaves. Ethnic tension has affected political life.

Guyana became independent May 26, 1966. A Venezuelan claim to the western half of Guyana was suspended in 1970 but renewed in 1982. The Suriname border is also disputed. The government has nationalized most of the economy which has remained severely depressed.

The Port Kaituma ambush of U.S. Rep. Leo J. Ryan and others investigating mistreatment of American followers of the Rev. Jim Jones' People's Temple cult triggered a mass suicide-execution of 911 cultists at Jonestown in the Guyana jungle, Nov. 18, 1978.

The People's National Congress, the party in power since Guyana became independent, was voted out of office with the election of Cheddi Jagan in Oct. 1992.

## Haiti

### Republic of Haiti

### République d'Haiti

**People: Population** (1992 est.): 6,431,000. **Age distrib. (%):** 4–14: 40.2; 15–59: 53.6; 60+: 6.2. **Pop. density:** 607 per sq. mi. **Urban** (1990): 29%. **Ethnic groups:** African descent 95%. **Languages:** French, Creole (both official). **Religions:** Roman Catholic 80%, Protestant 10%; Voodoo widely practiced.

**Geography: Area:** 10,579 sq. mi., the size of Maryland. **Location:** In West Indies, occupies western third of I. of Hispaniola. **Neighbors:** Dominican Republic on E, Cuba on W. **Topography:** About two-thirds of Haiti is mountainous. Much of the rest is semiarid. Coastal areas are warm and moist. **Capital:** Port-au-Prince. **Cities** (1992 est.): Port-au-Prince 752,000.

**Government: Type:** In transition. **Head of state:** ———. **Head of government:** Prime Min. Robert Malval; in office: Aug. 30, 1993. **Local divisions:** 9 departments. **Defense:** 1.5% of GDP (1990).

**Economy: Industries:** Sugar refining, textiles. **Chief crops:** Coffee, sugar, bananas, cocoa, tobacco, rice. **Minerals:** Bauxite. **Other resources:** Timber. **Arable land:** 20%. **Livestock** (1989): cattle: 1.5 mln.; goats: 1.2 mln. **Electricity prod.** (1991): 468 mln. kWh. **Labor force:** 66% agric.; 9% ind. & comm.; 25% services.

**Finance: Monetary unit:** Gourde (Dec. 1992: 5.00 = $1 US). **Gross domestic product** (1990): $2.7 bln. **Per capita GDP** (1991): $440. **Imports** (1991): $347 mln.; partners: U.S. 64%. **Exports** (1991): $103 mln.; partners: U.S. 84%. **Tourism** (1991): receipts $66 mln. **National budget** (1990): $416 mln. expenditures. **International reserves less gold** (Mar. 1993): $17.3 mln. **Gold:** 18,000 oz t. **Consumer prices** (change in 1991): 15.4%.

**Transport: Motor vehicles:** in use (1989): 32,000 passenger cars, 21,000 comm. vehicles. **Chief ports:** Port-au-Prince, Les Cayes.

**Communications: Television sets:** 1 per 265 persons. **Radios:** 1 per 2.2 persons. **Telephones in use:** 1 per 79 persons. **Daily newspaper circ.** (1990): 8 per 1,000 pop.

**Health: Life expectancy at birth** (1992): 53 male; 55 female. **Births** (per 1,000 pop. 1992): 43. **Deaths** (per 1,000 pop. 1992): 15. **Natural increase:** 2.8% **Hospital beds:** 1 per 1,258 persons. **Physicians:** 1 per 6,039 persons. **Infant mortality rate** (per 1,000 live births, 1992): 104.

**Education** (1991): Literacy: 53%.

**Major International Organizations:** UN and some of its specialized agencies, OAS.

**Embassy:** 2311 Massachusetts Ave. NW 20008; 332-4090.

Haiti, visited by Columbus, 1492, and a French colony from 1677, attained its independence, 1804, following the rebellion led by former slave Toussaint L'Ouverture. Following a period of political violence, the U.S. occupied the country 1915-34.

Dr. Francois Duvalier was voted president in 1957; in 1964 he was named president for life. Upon his death in 1971, he was succeeded by his son, Jean-Claude. Drought in 1975-77 brought famine, and Hurricane Allen in 1980 destroyed most of the rice, bean, and coffee crops.

Following several weeks of unrest, President Jean Claude Duvalier fled Haiti aboard a U.S. Air Force jet Feb. 7, 1986, ending the 28-year dictatorship by the Duvalier family. A military-civilian council headed by Gen. Henri Namphy assumed control. In 1987, voters approved a new constitution.

The Jan. 17, 1988 elections led to Leslie Manigat being named president; opposition leaders charged widespread fraud. Gen. Namphy seized control, June 20, and named himself president of a military government. Namphy was ousted by a military coup in Sept. By mid-1990, there had been 5 governments since Duvalier fled. Father Jean-Bertrand Aristide was elected President Dec. 1990.

A coup led by leaders of the Tonton Macoutes, the private militia of the Duvalier family, was crushed by loyalist army forces, Jan. 1991. The attempted coup sparked riots that left some 70 dead. In Sept. 1991, Aristide was arrested by the military and expelled from the country.

Some 35,000 Haitian refugees were intercepted by the U.S. Coast Guard as they tried to enter the U.S., 1991-92. Most were returned to Haiti despite protests by U.S. human rights and legal organizations.

The UN imposed a worldwide oil, arms, and financial embargo on Haiti June 23, 1993. The embargo was later suspended when the military agreed to Aristide's return to power on Oct. 30.

# Honduras
## Republic of Honduras
## República de Honduras

**People: Population** (1991 est.): 4,949,000. **Age distrib. (%):** 0–14: 44.6; 15–59: 50.5; 60+: 4.9. **Pop. density:** 114 per sq. mi. **Urban** (1990): 40.0%. **Ethnic groups:** Mestizo 90%, Indian 7%. **Languages:** Spanish (official). **Religions:** Roman Catholic 95%.
**Geography: Area:** 43,277 sq. mi., slightly larger than Tennessee. **Location:** In Central America. **Neighbors:** Guatemala on W, El Salvador, Nicaragua on S. **Topography:** The Caribbean coast is 500 mi. long. Pacific coast, on Gulf of Fonseca, is 40 mi. long. Honduras is mountainous, with wide fertile valleys and rich forests. **Capital:** Tegucigalpa. **Cities** (1989 est.): Tegucigalpa 550,000; San Pedro Sula 399,000.
**Government: Type:** Democratic constitutional republic. **Head of State:** Pres. Rafael Leonardo Callejas; in office: Jan. 27, 1990. **Local divisions:** 18 departments. **Defense:** 1.9% of GDP (1990).
**Economy: Industries:** Textiles, wood prods. **Chief crops:** Bananas (chief export), coffee, corn, beans. **Minerals:** Gold, silver, copper, lead, zinc, iron, antimony, coal. **Other resources:** Timber. **Arable land:** 16%. **Livestock** (1989): cattle: 2.8 mln. **Electricity prod.** (1990): 2.0 bln. kWh. **Labor force:** 62% agric.; 20% services; 9% manuf.
**Finance: Monetary unit:** Lempira (Apr. 1992): 5.40 = $1 US). **Gross domestic product** (1990): $4.9 bln. **Per capita GDP** (1989): $960. **Imports** (1989): $981 mln.; partners: U.S. 39%, Jap. 8%. **Exports** (1989): $940 mln.; partners: U.S. 54%, Europe 34%. **Tourists** (1989): $28 mln. receipts. **International reserves less gold** (Mar. 1992): $180 mln. **Gold:** 21,000 oz t. **Consumer prices** (change in 1991): 35.0%.
**Transport: Motor vehicles:** in use (1989) 77,000 passenger cars, 24,000 comm. vehicles. **Civil aviation** (1988): 446 mln. passenger-km; 9 airports with scheduled flights. **Chief ports:** Puerto Cortes, La Ceiba.
**Communications: Television sets:** 1 per 25 persons. **Radios:** 1 per 2.4 persons. **Telephones:** 1 per 58 persons. **Daily newspaper circ.** (1989): 51 per 1,000 pop.
**Health: Life expectancy at birth** (1991): 64 male; 68 female. **Births** (per 1,000 pop. 1991): 38. **Deaths** (per 1,000 pop. 1991): 7. **Natural increase:** 3.0%. **Hospital beds:** 1 per 821 persons. **Physicians:** 1 per 1,586 persons. **Infant mortality** (per 1,000 live births 1991): 56.
**Education** (1991): **Literacy:** 73%. **Years compulsory:** 6; attendance 70%.
**Major International Organizations:** UN, (IMF, WHO, ILO), OAS.
**Embassy:** 4301 Connecticut Ave. NW 20008; 966-7700.

Mayan civilization flourished in Honduras in the 1st millenium AD. Columbus arrived in 1502. Honduras became independent after freeing itself from Spain, 1821 and from the Fed. of Central America, 1838.

Gen. Oswaldo Lopez Arellano, president for most of the period 1963-75 by virtue of one election and 2 coups, was ousted by the army in 1975 over charges of pervasive bribery by United Brands Co. of the U.S.

The government has resumed land distribution, raised minimum wages, and started a literacy campaign. An elected civilian government took power in 1982.

Some 3,200 U.S. troops were sent to Honduras after the Honduran border was violated by Nicaraguan forces, Mar. 1988.

Honduras is one of the poorest countries in the Western Hemisphere.

# Hungary
## Republic of Hungary
## Magyar Köztársaság

**People: Population** (1992 est.): 10,333,000. **Age distrib. (%):** 0–14: 20.8; 15–59: 60.5; 60+: 18.7. **Pop. density:** 287 per sq. mi. **Urban** (1990): 62%. **Ethnic groups:** Magyar 92%, Gypsy 3%, German 2.5%. **Languages:** Hungarian (Magyar). **Religions:** Roman Catholic 67%, Protestant 25%.
**Geography: Area:** 35,919 sq. mi., slightly smaller than Indiana. **Location:** In East Central Europe. **Neighbors:** Slovakia, Ukraine on N, Austria on W, Slovenia, Yugoslavia, Croatia on S, Romania, on E. **Topography:** The Danube R. forms the Slovak border in the NW, then swings S to bisect the country. The eastern half of Hungary is mainly a great fertile plain, the Alfold; the W and N are hilly. **Capital:** Budapest. **Cities** (1991 est.): Budapest 2,016,000; Miskolc 196,000; Debrecen 212,000.
**Government: Type:** Parliamentary democracy. **Head of state:** Pres. Arpad Goncz; in office: May 2, 1990. **Head of government:** Prime Min. Jozsef Antall; in office: May 3, 1990. **Local divisions:** 19 counties, 1 capital. **Defense:** 1.7% of GDP (1992).
**Economy: Industries:** Iron and steel, machinery, pharmaceuticals, vehicles, communications equip., milling, distilling. **Chief crops:** Grains, vegetables, fruits, grapes. **Minerals:** Bauxite, coal, natural gas. **Arable land:** 54%. **Livestock** (1990): cattle: 1.6 mln.; pigs: 7.6 mln.; sheep: 2.0 mln. **Electricity prod.** (1990): 30.4 bln. kWh. **Crude steel prod.** (1991): 1.8 mln. metric tons. **Labor force:** 19% agric.; 48% ind. & comm.; 27% services.
**Finance: Monetary unit:** Forint (Mar. 1993: 88 = $1 US). **Gross domestic product** (1991): $60.1 bln. **Per capita GDP:** $5,700. **Imports** (1991): $11.7 bln.; partners: CIS 34%, EC 21%. **Exports** (1991): $10.2 bln.; partners: CIS 30%, EC 32%. **National budget** (1992): $13.6 bln. **Tourism** (1990): $1 bln. receipts. **Consumer prices** (change in 1991): 34.0%.
**Transport: Railroads** (1990): **Length:** 8,221 mi. **Motor vehicles:** in use (1990): 1.9 mln. passenger cars, 223,000 comm. vehicles. **Civil aviation** (1990): 1.5 bln. passenger-km; 1 airport with scheduled flights.
**Communications: Television sets:** 1 per 2.5 persons. **Radios:** 1 per 1.7 persons. **Telephones:** 1 per 5.5 persons. **Daily newspaper circ.** (1990): 237 per 1,000 pop.
**Health: Life expectancy at birth** (1992): 66 male; 75 female. **Births** (per 1,000 pop. 1992): 12. **Deaths** (per 1,000 pop. 1992): 14. **Natural increase:** −.2%. **Hospital beds:** 1 per 99 persons. **Physicians:** 1 per 306 persons. **Infant mortality** (per 1,000 live births 1992): 14.
**Education** (1992): **Literacy:** 98%. **Years compulsory:** to age 16; attendance 96%.
**Major International Organizations:** UN (IMF, World Bank, GATT).
**Embassy:** 3910 Shoemaker St. NW 20008.

Earliest settlers, chiefly Slav and Germanic, were overrun by Magyars from the east. Stephen I (997-1038) was made king by Pope Sylvester II in 1000 AD. The country suffered repeated Turkish invasions in the 15th-17th centuries. After the defeats of the Turks, 1686-1697, Austria dominated, but Hungary obtained concessions until it regained internal independence in 1867, with the emperor of Austria as king of Hungary in a dual monarchy with a single diplomatic service. Defeated with the Central Powers in 1918, Hungary lost Transylvania to Romania, Croatia and Bacska to Yugoslavia, Slovakia and Carpatho-Ruthenia, all of which had large Hungarian minorities. A republic under Michael Karolyi and a bolshevist revolt under Bela Kun were followed by a vote for a monarchy in 1920 with Admiral Nicholas Horthy as regent.

Hungary joined Germany in World War II, and was allowed to annex most of its lost territories. Russian troops captured the country, 1944-1945. By terms of an armistice with the Allied powers Hungary agreed to give up territory acquired by the 1938 dismemberment of Czechoslovakia and to return to its borders of 1937.

A republic was declared Feb. 1, 1946; Zoltan Tildy was elected president. In 1947 the communists forced Tildy out. Premier Imre Nagy, in office since mid-1953, was ousted for his moderate policy of favoring agriculture and consumer production, April 18, 1955.

In 1956, popular demands for the ousting of Erno Gero, Communist Party secretary, and for formation of a government by Nagy, resulted in the latter's appointment Oct. 23; demonstrations against communist rule developed into open revolt. On Nov. 4 Soviet forces launched a massive attack against Budapest with 200,000 troops, 2,500 tanks and armored cars.

About 200,000 persons fled the country. Nagy was executed, and thousands were arrested. In the spring of 1963 the regime freed many anti-communists and captives from the 1956 revolt in a sweeping amnesty.

Hungarian troops participated in the 1968 Warsaw Pact invasion of Czechoslovakia. Major economic reforms were launched early in 1968, switching from a central planning system to one in which market forces and profit control much of production.

In 1989 parliament passed legislation legalizing freedom of assembly and association as Hungary shifted away from communism toward democracy. In Oct., the Communist Party was formally dissolved. The last Soviet troops left Hungary June 19, 1991.

# Iceland

## Republic of Iceland

## Lýoveldio Island

**People: Population** (1992 est.): 259,000. **Age distrib. (%):** 0–14: 25.5; 15–59: 60.1; 60+: 14.4. **Pop. density:** 6 per sq. mi. **Urban** (1991): 90% **Ethnic groups:** Homogeneous, descendants of Norwegians, Celts. **Language:** Icelandic (Islenska). **Religion:** Evangelical Lutheran 95%.

**Geography: Area:** 39,769 sq. mi., the size of Virginia. **Location:** At N end of Atlantic O. **Neighbors:** Nearest is Greenland. **Topography:** Iceland is of recent volcanic origin. Three-quarters of the surface is wasteland: glaciers, lakes, a lava desert. There are geysers and hot springs, and the climate is moderated by the Gulf Stream. **Capital:** Reykjavik. **Cities** (1991 est.): Reykjavik 97,000.

**Government: Type:** Constitutional republic. **Head of state:** Pres. Vigdis Finnbogadottir; b. Apr. 15, 1930; in office: Aug. 1, 1980. **Head of government:** Prime Min. David Oddsson; in office: Apr. 30, 1991. **Local divisions:** 23 counties, 14 ind. towns.

**Economy: Industries:** Fish products (some 80% of exports), aluminum. **Chief crops:** Potatoes, turnips, hay. **Arable land:** 0.5%. **Livestock** (1991): sheep: 549,000. **Fish catch** (1991): 991,000. metric tons. **Electricity prod.** (1991): 5.1 bln. kWh. **Labor force:** 11% agric.; 55% comm. & services, 14% fisheries.

**Finance: Monetary unit:** Kronur (Mar. 1993: 64.12 = $1 US). **Gross domestic product** (1991): $4.2 bln. **Per capita GDP:** $16,300. **Imports** (1992): $1.7 bln.; partners: EC 50%. **Exports** (1992): $1.6 bln.; partners: EC 67%. **Tourism** (1991): receipts: $223 mln. **National budget** (1991): $1.9 bln. expenditures. **International reserves less gold** (Mar. 1993): $443 mln. **Gold:** 49,000 oz t. **Consumer prices** (change in 1992): 4.0%.

**Transport: Motor vehicles:** in use (1991): 121,000 passenger cars, 16,000 comm. vehicles. **Civil aviation** (1991): 1.8 bln. passenger-km; 21 airports with scheduled flights. **Chief ports:** Reykjavik.

**Communications: Television sets:** 1 per 3.3 persons. **Radios:** 1 per 1.6 persons. **Telephones:** 1 per 2.2 persons. **Daily newspaper circ.** (1990): 518 per 1,000 pop.

**Health: Life expectancy at birth** (1992): 76 male; 81 female. **Births** (per 1,000 pop. 1992): 17. **Deaths** (per 1,000 pop. 1992): 7. **Natural increase:** 1.0%. **Hospital beds:** 1 per 73 persons. **Physicians:** 1 per 373 persons. **Infant mortality** per (1,000 live births 1992): 4.

**Education** (1992): **Literacy:** 99%. **Years compulsory:** 8; **Attendance:** 99%.

**Major International Organizations:** UN (GATT), NATO, OECD.

**Embassy:** 2022 Connecticut Ave. NW 20008; 265-6653.

Iceland was an independent republic from 930 to 1262, when it joined with Norway. Its language has maintained its purity for 1,000 years. Danish rule lasted from 1380-1918; the last ties with the Danish crown were severed in 1941. The Althing, or assembly, is the world's oldest surviving parliament.

# India

## Republic of India

## Bharat

**People: Population** (1992 est.): 886,362,000. **Age distrib. (%):** 0–14: 36.8; 15–59: 56.4; 60+: 5.8. **Pop. density:** 700 per sq. mi. **Urban** (1991): 28%. **Ethnic groups:** Indo-Aryan groups 72%, Dravidians 25%, Mongoloids 3%. **Languages:** 16 languages, including Hindi (official) and English (associate official). **Religions:** Hindu 83%, Moslem 11%, Christian 3%, Sikh 2%.

**Geography: Area:** 1,266,595 sq. mi., one-third the size of the U.S. **Location:** Occupies most of the Indian subcontinent in S. Asia. **Neighbors:** Pakistan on W, China, Nepal, Bhutan on N, Myanmar, Bangladesh on E. **Topography:** The Himalaya Mts., highest in world, stretch across India's northern borders. Below, the Ganges Plain is wide, fertile, and among the most densely populated regions of the world. The area below includes the Deccan Peninsula. Close to one quarter the area is forested. The climate varies from tropical heat in S to near-Arctic cold in N. Rajasthan Desert is in NW; NE Assam Hills get 400 in. of rain a year. **Capital:** New Delhi. **Cities** (1991 est.): Calcutta 10.8 mln.; Bombay 12.5 mln.; New Delhi 8.3 mln.; Madras 5.3 mln.; Bangalore 4.1 mln.; Hyderabad 4.2 mln.

**Government: Type:** Federal republic. **Head of state:** Pres. Ramaswamy Venkataraman; b. Dec. 4, 1910; in office: July 25, 1987. **Head of government:** Prime Min. P. V. Narasimha Rao; b. June 28, 1921; in office: June 21, 1991. **Local divisions:** 25 states, 7 union territories. **Defense:** 3.5% of GNP (1991).

**Economy: Industries:** Textiles, steel, processed foods, cement, machinery, chemicals, fertilizers, consumer appliances, autos. **Chief crops:** Rice, grains, coffee, sugar cane, spices, tea, cashews, cotton, copra, coir, juta, linseed. **Minerals:** Chromium, coal, iron, manganese, mica salt, bauxite, gypsum, oil. **Crude oil reserves** (1991): 4.2 bln. bbls. **Other resources:** Rubber, timber. **Arable land:** 57%. **Livestock** (1989): cattle: 195 mln.; sheep: 55 mln. **Fish catch** (1990): 3.6 mln. metric tons. **Electricity prod.** (1991): 290 bln. kWh. **Crude steel prod.** (1991): 16.3 mln. metric tons. **Labor force:** 70% agric.; 19% ind. & comm.

**Finance: Monetary unit:** Rupee (Aug. 1993: 31.03 = $1 US). **Gross domestic product** (1992): $328 bln. **Per capita GDP:** $380. **Imports** (1991): $25.2 bln.; partners: Jap. 8%, U.S. 12%, EC 33%. **Exports** (1991): $20.2 bln.; partners: U.S. 16%, EC 25%, CIS 19%. **Tourism** (1991): receipts: $1.4 bln. **National budget** (1992): $53.4 bln. expenditures. **International reserves less gold** (Mar. 1993): $6.7 bln. **Gold:** 11.3 mln. oz. t. **Consumer prices** (change in 1992): 11.8%.

**Transport: Railroads** (1991): **Length:** 38,752 mi. **Motor vehicles:** in use (1990): 2.3 mln. passenger cars, 1.4 mln. comm. vehicles. **Civil aviation** (1990): 16.5 bln. passenger-km; 98 airports with scheduled flights. **Chief ports:** Calcutta, Bombay, Madras, Cochin, Vishakhapatnam.

**Communications: Television sets:** 1 per 44 persons. **Radios:** 1 per 15 persons. **Telephones:** 1 per 200 persons. **Daily newspaper circ.** (1988): 21 per. 1,000 pop.

**Health: Life expectancy at birth** (1992): 57 male; 58 female. **Births** (per 1,000 pop. 1992): 30. **Deaths** (per 1,000 pop. 1992): 11. **Natural increase:** 1.9%. **Hospital beds:** 1 per 1,314 persons. **Physicians:** 1 per 2,337 persons. **Infant mortality** (per 1,000 live births 1992): 81.

**Education** (1991): **Literacy:** 48%. **Years Compulsory:** to age 14.

**Major International Organizations:** UN (IMF, World Bank). **Embassy:** 2107 Massachusetts Ave. NW 20008; 939-7000.

India has one of the oldest civilizations in the world. Excavations trace the Indus Valley civilization back for at least 5,000 years. Paintings in the mountain caves of Ajanta, richly carved temples, the Taj Mahal in Agra, and the Kutab Minar in Delhi are among relics of the past.

Aryan tribes, speaking Sanskrit, invaded from the NW around 1500 BC, and merged with the earlier inhabitants to create classical Indian civilization.

Asoka ruled most of the Indian subcontinent in the 3d century BC, and established Buddhism. But Hinduism revived and eventually predominated. During the Gupta kingdom, 4th-6th century AD, science, literature, and the arts enjoyed a "golden age."

Arab invaders established a Moslem foothold in the W in the 8th century, and Turkish Moslems gained control of North India by 1200. The Mogul emperors ruled 1526-1857.

Vasco de Gama established Portuguese trading posts 1498-1503. The Dutch followed. The British East India Co. sent Capt. William Hawkins, 1609, to get concessions from the Mogul emperor for spices and textiles. Operating as the East India Co. the British gained control of most of India. The British parliament assumed political direction; under Lord Bentinck, 1828-35, rule by rajahs was curbed. After the Sepoy troops mutinied, 1857-58, the British supported the native rulers.

Nationalism grew rapidly after World War I. The Indian National Congress and the Moslem League demanded constitutional reform. A leader emerged in Mohandas K. Gandhi (called Mahatma, or Great Soul), born Oct. 2, 1869, assassinated Jan. 30, 1948. He advocated self-rule, non-violence, removal of untouchability. In 1930 he launched "civil disobedience," including boycott of British goods and rejection of taxes without representation.

In 1935 Britain gave India a constitution providing a bicameral federal congress. Mohammed Ali Jinnah, head of the Moslem League, sought creation of a Moslem nation, Pakistan.

The British government partitioned British India into the dominions of India and Pakistan. India became a self-governing member of the Commonwealth and a member of the UN. It became a democratic republic, Jan. 26, 1950.

More than 12 million Hindu & Moslem refugees crossed the India-Pakistan borders in a mass transferral of some of the 2 peoples during 1947; about 200,000 were killed in communal fighting.

After Pakistan troops began attacks on Bengali separatists in East Pakistan, Mar. 25, 1971, some 10 million refugees fled into India. India and Pakistan went to war Dec. 3, 1971, on both the East and West fronts. Pakistan troops in the east surrendered Dec. 16; Pakistan agreed to a cease-fire in the west Dec. 17. In Aug. 1973 India released 93,000 Pakistanis held prisoner since 1971. The 2 countries resumed full relations in 1976.

In 2 days of carnage, the Bengali population of the village of Mandai, Tripura State, 700 people, were massacred in a raid by indigenous tribal residents of the area, June 8-9, 1980. A similar year-long campaign against Bengali immigrants had been going on in Assam State.

Mrs. Indira Gandhi, was named prime minister Jan. 19, 1966. Threatened with adverse court rulings in a voting law case, and opposition protest campaign and strikes, Gandhi invoked emergency provisions of the constitution June, 1975. Thousands of opponents were arrested and press censorship imposed. Measures to control prices, protect small farmers, and improve productivity were adopted.

The emergency, especially enforcement of coercive birth control measures in some areas, and the prominent extra-constitutional role of Indira Gandhi's son Sanjay, was widely resented. Opposition parties, united in the Janata coalition, scored massive victories in federal and state parliamentary elections in 1977, turning Gandhi's New Congress Party from power.

Gandhi became prime minister for the second time, Jan. 14, 1980. She was assassinated by 2 of her Sikh bodyguards Oct. 31, 1984. Widespread rioting followed. Thousands of Sikhs were killed and some 50,000 left homeless. The assassination was in response to the government supression of a Sikh uprising in Punjab in June 1984 which included an assault on the Golden Temple, the holiest Sikh shrine. Rajiv, her son, replaced her as prime minister. He was swept from office in 1989 amid charges of incompetence and corruption. He was assassinated May 21, 1991 during an election campaign to regain the prime ministership.

Sikhs ignited several violent clashes during the 1980s. The government's May 1987 decision to bring the state of Punjab under the rule of the central government led to violence. Many died during a government siege of the Golden Temple at Amritsar, May 1988.

In the biggest wave of criminal violence in Indian history, a series of bombings jolted Bombay and Calcutta, Mar. 12-19, 1993, leaving over 300 dead and some 1,200 injured. The explosions came in the wake of nationwide riots prompted by the destruction of a 16th- century mosque by Hindu militants in Dec. 1992.

Sikkim, bordered by Tibet, Bhutan and Nepal, formerly British protected, became a protectorate of India in 1950. Area, 2,740 sq. mi.; pop. 1991 cen. 405,000; capital, Gangtok. In Sept. 1974 India's parliament voted to make Sikkim an associate Indian state, absorbing it into India.

Kashmir, a predominantly Moslem region in the NW, has been in dispute between India and Pakistan since 1947. A cease-fire was negotiated by the UN Jan. 1, 1949; it gave Pakistan control of one-third of the area, in the west and northwest, and India the remaining two-thirds, the Indian state of Jammu and Kashmir, which enjoys internal autonomy.

In 1990 and 1991, there were repeated clashes between Indian army troops and pro-independence demonstrators triggered by India's decision to impose central government rule. The clashes strained relations between India and Pakistan which India charged was aiding the Moslem separatists.

France, 1952-54, peacefully yielded to India its 5 colonies, former French India, comprising Pondicherry, Karikal, Mahe, Yanaon (which became the Pondicherry Union Territory, area 185 sq. mi., pop. 1991, 807,000) and Chandernagor (which was incorporated into the state of West Bengal).

# Indonesia
## Republic of Indonesia
## Republik Indonesia

**People: Population** (1992 est.): 195,000,000. **Age distrib.** (%): 0–14: 39.2; 15–59: 56.5; 60+: 5.3. **Pop. density:** 262 per sq. mi. **Urban** (1991): 31%. **Ethnic groups:** Malay, Chinese, Irianese. **Languages:** Bahasa Indonesian (Malay) (official), Javanese, other Austronesian languages. **Religions:** Moslem 88%.

**Geography: Area:** 735,268 sq. mi. **Location:** Archipelago SE of Asia along the Equator. **Neighbors:** Malaysia on N, Papua New Guinea on E. **Topography:** Indonesia comprises some 17,000 islands, including Java (one of the most densely populated areas in the world with 1,500 persons to the sq. mi.), Sumatra, Kalimantan (most of Borneo), Sulawesi (Celebes), and West Irian (Irian Jaya, the W. half of New Guinea). Also: Bangka, Billiton, Madura, Bali, Timor. The mountains and plateaus on the major islands have a cooler climate than the tropical lowlands. **Capital:** Jakarta. **Cities** (1988 est.): Jakarta 8,800,000; Surabaya 2,500,000; Bandung 1,400,000; Medan 1,700,000.

**Government: Type:** Republic. **Head of state:** Pres. Suharto; b. June 8, 1921; in office: Mar. 6, 1967. **Local divisions:** 24 provinces, 3 special regions. **Defense:** 2.0% of GDP (1992).

**Economy: Industries:** Food processing, textiles, cement, light industry. **Chief crops:** Rice, coffee, sugar. **Minerals:** Nickel, tin, oil, bauxite, copper, natural gas. **Crude oil reserves** (1991): 10.7 bln. bbls. **Other resources:** Rubber. **Arable land:** 8%. **Livestock** (1989): cattle: 6.5 mln.; sheep: 5.4 mln. **Fish catch** (1990): 3.1 mln. metric tons. **Electricity prod.** (1991): 38 bln. kWh. **Crude steel prod.** (1991): 3 mln. metric tons. **Labor force:** 56% agric.; 23% ind. & comm.; 16% services.

**Finance: Monetary unit:** Rupiah (Aug. 1993: 2,096 = $1 US). **Gross domestic product** (1991): $122 bln. **Per capita GDP:** $630. **Imports** (1991): $25.8 bln.; partners: Jap. 23%, U.S. 12%, Sing. 6%. **Exports** (1991): $29.5 bln.; partners: Jap. 41%, U.S. 16%, Sing. 10%. **Tourism** (1990): $1.8 bln. receipts. **National budget** (1991): $23.4 bln. **International reserves less gold** (Feb. 1993): $10.8 bln. **Gold:** 3.11 mln. oz t. **Consumer prices** (change in 1992): 7.5%.

**Transport: Railway traffic** (1989): 7.8 bln. passenger-km. **Motor vehicles:** in use (1991): 1.3 mln. passenger cars, 1.5 mln. comm. vehicles **Civil aviation** (1991): 12.7 bln. passenger-km; 116 airports. **Chief ports:** Jakarta, Surabaya, Medan, Palembang, Semarang.

**Communications: Television sets:** 1 per 24 persons. **Radios:** 1 per 8 persons. **Telephones:** 1 per 172 persons.

**Health: Life expectancy at birth** (1992): male: 59; female 64 years. **Births** (per 1,000 pop. 1992): 26. **Deaths** (per 1,000 pop. 1992): 8. **Natural increase:** 1.8%. **Hospital beds:** 1 per 1,485 persons. **Physicians:** 1 per 7,427 persons. **Infant mortality** (per 1,000 live births 1992): 70.

**Education** (1990): **Literacy:** 85%. 84% attend primary school.

**Major International Organizations:** UN and all of its specialized agencies, ASEAN, OPEC.

**Embassy:** 2020 Massachusetts Ave. NW 20036; 775-5200.

Hindu and Buddhist civilization from India reached the peoples of Indonesia nearly 2,000 years ago, taking root especially in Java. Islam spread along the maritime trade routes in the 15th century, and became predominant by the 16th century. The Dutch replaced the Portuguese as the most important European trade power in the area in the 17th century. They secured territorial control over Java by 1750. The outer islands were not finally subdued until the early 20th century, when the full area of present-day Indonesia was united under one rule for the first time.

Following Japanese occupation, 1942-45, nationalists led by Sukarno and Hatta proclaimed a republic. The Netherlands ceded sovereignty Dec. 27, 1949, after 4 years of fighting. West Irian, on New Guinea, remained under Dutch control.

After the Dutch in 1957 rejected proposals for new negotiations over West Irian, Indonesia stepped up the seizure of Dutch property. A U.S. mediator's plan was adopted in 1962. In 1963 the UN turned the area over to Indonesia, which promised a plebiscite. In 1969, voting by tribal chiefs favored staying with Indonesia, despite an uprising and widespread opposition.

Sukarno suspended Parliament in 1960, and was named president for life in 1963. Russian-armed Indonesian troops staged raids in 1964 and 1965 into Malaysia, whose formation Sukarno had opposed.

Indonesia's Communist Party tried to seize control in 1965; the army smashed the coup. In parts of Java, communists seized several districts before being defeated; over 300,000 communists were executed.

Gen. Suharto, head of the army, was named president in 1968 and was reelected for a 6th consecutive 5-year term in 1993. A coalition his supporters won a strong majority in House elections in 1971. Moslem opposition parties made gains in 1977 elections but lost ground in the 1982 elections. The military retains a predominant political role.

In 1966 Indonesia and Malaysia signed an agreement ending hostility.

Oil export earnings, and political stability have made Indonesia's economy stable.

# Iran

## Islamic Republic of Iran

## Jomhori-e-Islami-e-Irân

**People: Population** (1992 est.): 61,183,000. **Age distrib. (%):** 0–14: 43.8; 15–59: 50.4; 60+: 5.8. **Pop. density:** 96 per sq. mi. **Urban** (1990): 57%. **Ethnic groups:** Persian 51%, Azerbaijani 25%, Kurd 9%. **Languages:** Farsi (official), Turk, Kurdish, Arabic. **Religions:** Shi'a Moslem 95%.

**Geography: Area:** 636,293 sq. mi. slightly larger than Alaska. **Location:** Between the Middle East and S. Asia. **Neighbors:** Turkey, Iraq on W, Armenia, Azerbaijan, Turkmenistan on N, Afghanistan, Pakistan on E. **Topography:** Interior highlands and plains are surrounded by high mountains, up to 18,000 ft. Large salt deserts cover much of the area, but there are many oases and forest areas. Most of the population inhabits the N and NW. **Capital:** Tehran. **Cities** (1986 cen.): Tehran 6,022,000; Esfahan 1,001,000; Mashhad 1,466,000; Tabriz 994,000; Shiraz 848,000.

**Government: Type:** Islamic republic. **Religious head:** Ayatollah Sayyed Ali Khamenei; b. 1939; in office: June 4, 1989. **Head of state:** Pres. Hashemi Rafsanjani; in office: Aug 3, 1989. **Local divisions:** 24 provinces. **Defense:** 15% of GNP (1991).

**Economy: Industries:** Cement, sugar refining, carpets. **Chief crops:** Grains, rice, fruits, sugar beets, cotton, grapes. **Minerals:** Chromium, oil, gas. **Crude oil reserves** (1991): 63 bln. barrels. **Other resources:** Gums, wool, silk, caviar. **Arable land:** 9%. **Livestock** (1990): cattle: 8.3 mln.; sheep: 34.0 mln. **Electricity prod.** (1990): 40.2 bln. kWh. **Labor force:** 33% agric.; 21% ind. & comm; 27% services.

**Finance: Monetary unit:** Rial (Mar. 1993: 67.07 = $1 US). **Gross national product** (1991): $90 bln. **Per capita GNP:** $1,500. **Imports** (1991): $21.6 bln.; partners: Ger. 20%, Jap. 10%, UK 6%. **Exports** (1991): $15.9 bln.; partners: Jap. 13%, Neth. 12%. **National budget** (1990): $80 bln. expenditures.

**Transport: Motor vehicles:** in use (1990): 2.0 mln. passenger cars, 472,000 comm. vehicles. **Civil Aviation** (1990): 5.5 bln. passenger km.; 17 airports. **Chief ports:** Bandar Abbas.

**Communications: Television sets:** 1 per 23 persons. **Radios:** 1 per 4.7 persons. **Telephones:** 1 per 25 persons. **Daily newspaper circ.** (1990): 13 per 1,000 pop.

**Health: Life expectancy at birth** (1992): 64 male; 66 female. **Births** (per 1,000 pop. 1992): 44. **Deaths** (per 1,000 pop. 1992): 10. **Natural increase:** 3.4%. **Hospital beds:** 1 per 653 persons. **Physicians:** 1 per 2,882 persons. **Infant mortality** (per 1,000 live births 1992): 66.

**Education** (1990): **Literacy:** 54%.

**Major International Organizations:** UN (IMF, WHO), OPEC.

Iran was once called Persia. The Iranians, who supplanted an earlier agricultural civilization, came from the E during the 2d millenium BC; they were an Indo-European group related to the Aryans of India.

In 549 BC Cyrus the Great united the Medes and Persians in the Persian Empire, conquered Babylonia in 538 BC, restored Jerusalem to the Jews. Alexander the Great conquered Persia in 333 BC, but Persians regained their independence in the next century under the Parthians, themselves succeeded by Sassanian Persians in 226 AD. Arabs brought Islam to Persia in the 7th century, replacing the indigenous Zoroastrian faith. After Persian cultural and political autonomy was reasserted in the 9th century, the arts and sciences flourished for several centuries.

Turks and Mongols ruled Persia in turn from the 11th century to 1502, when a native dynasty reasserted full independence. The British and Russian empires vied for influence in the 19th century, and Afghanistan was severed from Iran by Britain in 1857.

Reza Khan abdicated as Shah, 1941, and was succeeded by his son, Mohammad Reza Pahlavi. Under his rule, Iran underwent economic and social change but political opposition was not tolerated.

Conservative Moslem protests led to 1978 violence. Martial law in 12 cities was declared Sept. 8. A military government was appointed Nov. 6 to deal with striking oil workers. Prime Min. Shahpur Bakhtiar was designated by the shah to head a regency council in his absence. The shah left Iran Jan. 16, 1979.

Exiled religious leader Ayatollah Ruhollah Khomeini named a provisional government council in preparation for his return to Iran, Jan. 31. Clashes between Khomeini's supporters and government troops culminated in a rout of Iran's elite Imperial Guard Feb. 11, leading to the fall of Bakhtiar's government.

The Iranian revolution was marked by revolts among the ethnic minorities and by a continuing struggle between the clerical forces and westernized intellectuals and liberals. The Islamic Constitution established final authority to be vested in a Faghi, the Ayatollah Khomeini.

Iranian militants seized the U.S. embassy, Nov. 4, 1979, and took hostages including 62 Americans. Despite international condemnations and U.S. efforts, including an abortive Apr., 1980, rescue attempt, the crisis continued. The U.S. broke diplomatic relations with Iran, Apr. 7th. The shah died in Egypt, July 27th. The hostage drama finally ended Jan. 21, 1981 when an accord, involving the release of frozen Iranian assets, was reached.

A dispute over the Shatt al-Arab waterway that divides the two countries brought Iran and Iraq, Sept. 22, 1980, into open warfare. Iraqi planes attacked Iranian air fields including Teheran airport. Iranian planes bombed Iraqi bases. Iraqi troops occupied Iranian territory including the port city of Khorramshahr in October. Iranian troops recaptured the city and drove Iraqi troops back across the border, May 1982. Iraq, and later Iran, attacked several oil tankers in the Persian Gulf during 1984. Saudi Arabian war planes shot down 2 Iranian jets, June 5, which they felt were threatening Saudi shipping. In Aug. 1988, Iran agreed to accept a UN resolution calling for a cease fire.

In Nov. 1986, senior U.S. officials secretly visited Iran and exchanged arms for Iran's help in obtaining the release of U.S. hostages held by terrorists in Lebanon. The exchange sparked a major scandal in the Reagan administration.

A U.S. Navy warship shot down an Iranian commercial airliner, July 3, 1988, after mistaking it for an F-14 fighter jet; all 290 aboard the plane died.

A major earthquake struck northern Iran June 21, 1990, killing over 45,000, injuring 100,000, and leaving 400,000 homeless. A U.S. offer of assistance was accepted by the Iranian government.

Some one million Kurdish refugees crossed Iran's border to escape Iraqi forces following the Persian Gulf War.

# Iraq

## Republic of Iraq

## al Jumhouriya al 'Iraqia

**People: Population** (1992 est.): 18,445,000. **Age distrib. (%):** 0–14: 44.5; 15–59: 50.3; 60+: 5.2. **Pop. density:** 109 per sq. mi. **Urban** (1991): 70%. **Ethnic groups:** Arabs, 75% Kurds, 15% Turks. **Languages:** Arabic (official), Kurdish. **Religions:** Moslem 95% (Shiites 60%, Sunnis 35%), Christian 5%.

**Geography: Area:** 167,924 sq. mi., larger than California. **Location:** In the Middle East, occupying most of historic Mesopotamia. **Neighbors:** Jordan, Syria on W, Turkey on N, Iran on E, Kuwait, Saudi Arabia on S. **Topography:** Mostly an alluvial plain, including the Tigris and Euphrates rivers, descending from mountains in N to desert in SW. Persian Gulf region is marshland. **Capital:** Baghdad. **Cities** (1985 est.): Baghdad (met.) 3,400,000, Basra 616,000, Mosul 570,000.

**Government: Type:** Republic. **Head of state:** Pres. Saddam Hussein At-Takriti, b. Apr. 29, 1937; in office: July 16, 1979. **Local divisions:** 18 provinces. **Defense:** 18% of GNP (1990).

**Economy: Industries:** Textiles, petrochemicals, oil refining, cement. **Chief crops:** Grains, rice, dates, cotton. **Minerals:** Oil, gas. **Crude oil reserves** (1991): 100 bln. barrels. **Other resources:** Wool, hides. **Arable land:** 13%. **Livestock** (1991): cattle: 1.5 mln.; sheep: 9.6 mln.; goats: 1.4 mln. **Electricity prod.** (1991): 3.8 bln. kWh. **Labor force:** 30% agric.; 48% services; 22% ind.

**Finance: Monetary unit:** Dinar (Mar. 1993: 1.00 = $3.21 US). **Gross national product** (1989): $35 bln. **Per capita GNP** (1989): $1,950. **Imports** (1990): $6.6 bln.; partners: Tur. 2%, U.S. **Exports** (1990): $10.4 bln.; partners: U.S., Tur., Jap. **National budget** (1990): $35 bln. expenditures.

**Transport: Railroads: Length** (1991): **1,484 mi. Motor vehicles:** in use (1991): 744,000 passenger cars, 295,000 comm. vehicles. **Chief ports:** Basra.

**Communications: Television sets:** 1 per 18 persons. **Radios:** 1 per 5 persons. **Telephones:** 1 per 25 persons. **Daily newspaper circ.** (1990): 32 per 1,000 pop.

**Health: Life expectancy at birth** (1992): 62 male; 64 female. **Births** (per 1,000 pop. 1992): 45. **Deaths** (per 1,000 pop. 1992): 8. **Natural increase:** 3.8%. **Hospital beds:** 1 per 586 persons. **Physicians:** 1 per 1,922 persons. **Infant mortality** (per 1,000 live births 1992): 84.

**Major International Organizations:** UN (IMF, ILO), Arab League, OPEC.

**Education** (1991): **Literacy:** 60%. Compulsory age 6 to grade 6.

**Embassy:** 1801 P St. NW 20036; 483-7500.

The Tigris-Euphrates valley, formerly called Mesopotamia, was the site of one of the earliest civilizations in the world. The Sumerian city-states of 3,000 BC originated the culture later developed by the Semitic Akkadians, Babylonians, and Assyrians.

Mesopotamia ceased to be a separate entity after the conquests of the Persians, Greeks, and Arabs. The latter founded Baghdad, from where the caliph ruled a vast empire in the 8th and 9th centuries. Mongol and Turkish conquests led to a decline in population, the economy, cultural life, and the irrigation system.

Britain secured a League of Nations mandate over Iraq after World War I. Independence under a king came in 1932. A leftist, pan-Arab revolution established a republic in 1958, which oriented foreign policy toward the USSR. Most industry has been nationalized, and large land holdings broken up.

A local faction of the international Baath Arab Socialist party has ruled by decree since 1968. Russia and Iraq signed an aid pact in 1972, and arms were sent along with several thousand advisers. The 1978 execution of 21 communists and a shift of trade to the West signalled a more neutral policy, straining relations with the USSR. In the 1973 Arab-Israeli war Iraq sent forces to aid Syria. Within a month of assuming power, Saddam Hussein instituted a bloody purge in the wake of a reported coup attempt against the new regime.

Years of battling with the Kurdish minority resulted in total defeat for the Kurds in 1975, when Iran withdrew support. The fighting led to Iraqi bombing of Kurdish villages in Iran, causing relations with Iran to deteriorate.

After skirmishing intermittently for 10 months over the sovereignty of the disputed Shatt al-Arab waterway that divides the two countries, Iraq and Iran, Sept. 22, 1980, entered into open warfare when Iraqi fighter-bombers attacked 10 Iranian airfields, including Teheran airport, and Iranian planes retaliated with strikes on 2 Iraqi bases. In the following days, there was heavy ground fighting around Abadan and the adjacent port of Khorramshahr as Iraq pressed its attack on Iran's oil-rich province of Khuzistan. In May 1982, Iraqi troops were driven back across the border.

Israeli airplanes destroyed a nuclear reactor near Baghdad on June 7, 1981, claiming that it could be used to produce nuclear weapons.

Iraq and Iran expanded their war to the Persian Gulf in Apr. 1984. There were several attacks on oil tankers. An Iraqi warplane launched a missile attack on the U.S.S. Stark, a U.S. Navy frigate on patrol in the Persian Gulf, May 17, 1987; 37 U.S. sailors died. Iraq apologized for the attack, claiming it was inadvertent. The fierce war ended Aug. 1988, when Iraq accepted a UN resolution for a ceasefire.

Iraq attacked and overran Kuwait Aug. 2, 1990, sparking an international crisis. The United Nations, Aug. 6, imposed a ban on all trade with Iraq and called on member countries to protect the assets of the legitimate government of Kuwait. Iraq declared Kuwait its 19th province, Aug. 28. A campaign of looting, murder, and pillage was mounted against Kuwaiti civilians. Westerners

caught in Iraq and Kuwait were initially held as hostages, but by the end of 1990, all were released.

A U.S.-led coalition launched air and missile attacks on Iraq, Jan. 16, 1991, after the expiration of a UN Security Council deadline for Iraq to withdraw from Kuwait. Iraq retaliated by firing scud missiles at Saudi Arabia and Israel. The coalition began a ground attack to retake Kuwait Feb. 23. Iraqi forces showed little resistance and were soundly defeated in 4 days. Some 175,000 Iraqis were taken prisoner, and casualties were estimated at over 85,000. As part of the cease-fire agreement, Iraq agreed to scrap all poison gas and germ weapons and allow UN observers to inspect the sites. UN trade sanctions would remain in effect until Iraq complied.

In the aftermath of the war, there were revolts against Pres. Saddam Hussein throughout Iraq. In Feb., Iraqi troops drove Kurdish insurgents and civilians to the Iran and Turkey borders, causing a refugee crisis. The U.S. and allies established havens inside Iraq for the Kurds.

Tensions heightened over the UN's efforts to dismantle Iraq's arms-production program, July 5, 1992, when a UN inspection team was denied entrance to a ministry building in Baghdad. Iraq allowed the inspection team access to the building July 26; the team found no arms-related evidence.

The U.S. launched a missile attack aimed at Iraq's intelligence headquarters in Baghdad June 26, 1993. The U.S. justified the attack by citing evidence that Iraq had sponsored a plot to assassinate former Pres. George Bush during his visit to Kuwait in April.

# Ireland

## Eire

**People: Population** (1992 est.): 3,521,000. **Age distrib. (%):** 0–14: 30.5; 15–59: 54.5; 60+:15.0. **Pop. density:** 129 per sq. mi. **Urban** (1990): 57%. **Ethnic groups:** Celtic, English minority. **Languages:** English predominates, Irish (Gaelic) spoken by minority. **Religions:** Roman Catholic 95%, Anglican 3%.

**Geography: Area:** 27,137 sq. mi. slightly larger than W. Va. **Location:** In the Atlantic O. just W of Great Britain. **Neighbors:** United Kingdom (Northern Ireland). **Topography:** Ireland consists of a central plateau surrounded by isolated groups of hills and mountains. The coastline is heavily indented by the Atlantic O. **Capital:** Dublin. **Cities** (1991 est.): Dublin 502,000; Cork (met.) 133,000.

**Government: Type:** Parliamentary republic. **Head of State:** Pres. Mary Robinson; in office: Dec. 3, 1990. **Head of government:** Prime Min. Albert Reynolds; b. 1935; in office: Feb. 11, 1992. **Local divisions:** 26 counties. **Defense:** 1.6% of GDP (1992).

**Economy: Industries:** Food processing, textiles, chemicals, brewing, machinery, tourism. **Chief crops:** Potatoes, grain, sugar beets, fruits, vegetables. **Minerals:** Zinc, lead, silver, gas. **Arable land:** 14%. **Livestock** (1990): cattle: 5.6 mln.; pigs: 961,000; sheep: 4.9 mln. **Fish catch** (1990): 247,000 metric tons. **Electricity prod.** (1991): 14.4 bln. kWh. **Labor force:** 15% agric.; 29% ind. 57% services.

**Finance: Monetary unit:** Punt (June 1993: 0.69 = $1 US). **Gross domestic product** (1991): $39.2 bln. **Per capita GDP:** $11,200. **Imports** (1991): $24.5 bln.; partners: UK 41%, U.S. 14%, other EC 25%. **Exports** (1991): $27.8 bln.; partners: UK 34%, other EC 40%, U.S. 8%. **Tourism** (1990): receipts: $1.4 bln. **National budget** (1992): $12.6 bln. expenditures. **International reserves less gold** (Mar. 1993): $5.0 bln. **Gold:** 360,000 oz. t. **Consumer prices** (change in 1992): 3.2%.

**Transport: Railroads** (1991): **Length:** 2,814 km. **Motor vehicles:** in use (1990): 796,000 passenger cars, 147,000 comm. vehicles. **Civil aviation:** (1990): 3.8 bln. passenger-km; 11 airports. **Chief ports:** Dublin, Cork.

**Communications: Television sets:** 1 per 3.8 persons. **Radios:** 1 per 1.7 persons. **Telephones:** 1 per 3.8 persons. **Daily newspaper circ.** (1991): 179 per 1,000 pop.

**Health: Life expectancy at birth** (1992): 72 male; 78 female. **Births** (per 1,000 pop. 1992): 15. **Deaths** (per 1,000 pop. 1992): 9. **Natural increase:** .6%. **Hospital beds:** 1 per 257 persons. **Physicians:** 1 per 681 persons. **Infant mortality** (per 1,000 live births 1992): 8.

**Education** (1991): **Literacy:** 99%. **Years compulsory:** 9; attendance 91%.

**Major International Organizations:** UN (GATT, IMF, World Bank), EC, OECD.

**Embassy:** 2234 Massachusetts Ave. NW 20008; 462-3939.

Celtic tribes invaded the islands about the 4th century BC; their Gaelic culture and literature flourished and spread to Scotland and elsewhere in the 5th century AD, the same century in which St. Patrick converted the Irish to Christianity. Invasions by Norsemen began in the 8th century, ended with defeat of the Danes by the Irish King Brian Boru in 1014. English invasions started in the 12th century; for over 700 years the Anglo-Irish struggle continued with bitter rebellions and savage repressions.

The Easter Monday Rebellion (1916) failed but was followed by guerrilla warfare and harsh reprisals by British troops, the "Black and Tans." The Dail Eireann, or Irish parliament, reaffirmed independence in Jan. 1919. The British offered dominion status to Ulster (6 counties) and southern Ireland (26 counties) Dec. 1921. The constitution of the Irish Free State, a British dominion, was adopted Dec. 11, 1922. Northern Ireland remained part of the United Kingdom.

A new constitution adopted by plebiscite came into operation Dec. 29, 1937. It declared the name of the state Eire in the Irish language (Ireland in the English) and declared it a sovereign democratic state.

On Dec. 21, 1948, an Irish law declared the country a republic rather than a dominion and withdrew it from the Commonwealth. The British Parliament recognized both actions, 1949, but reasserted its claim to incorporate the 6 northeastern counties in the United Kingdom. This claim has not been recognized by Ireland. *(See United Kingdom — Northern Ireland.)*

Irish governments have favored peaceful unification of all Ireland. Ireland cooperated with Britain against terrorist groups.

Ireland suffered economic hardship in the 1980's; unemployment was over 20% in 1992.

# Israel

## State of Israel

## Medinat Israel

**People: Population** (1992 est.): 4,748,000. **Age distrib.** (%): 0–14: 32.4; 15–59: 55.3; 60+: 13.3. **Pop. density:** 605 per sq. mi. **Urban** (1990): 89%. **Ethnic groups:** Jewish 83%, Arab 16%. **Languages:** Hebrew and Arabic (official). **Religions:** Jewish 83%, Moslem 13%.

**Geography: Area:** 7,847 sq. mi. about the size of New Jersey. **Location:** On eastern end of Mediterranean Sea. **Neighbors:** Lebanon on N, Syria, Jordan on E, Egypt on W. **Topography:** The Mediterranean coastal plain is fertile and well-watered. In the center is the Judean Plateau. A triangular-shaped semidesert region, the Negev, extends from south of Beersheba to an apex at the head of the Gulf of Aqaba. The eastern border drops sharply into the Jordan Rift Valley, including Lake Tiberias (Sea of Galilee) and the Dead Sea, which is 1,312 ft. below sea level, lowest point on the earth's surface. **Capital:** Jerusalem. Most countries maintain their embassy in Tel Aviv. **Cities** (1990 est.): Jerusalem 504,000; Tel Aviv-Yafo 321,000; Haifa 222,000.

**Government: Type:** Republic. **Head of state:** Pres. Chaim Herzog; b. Sept. 17, 1918; in office: May 5, 1983. **Head of government:** Prime Min. Yitzhak Rabin; b. Mar. 1, 1922; in office: July 13, 1992. **Local divisions:** 6 districts. **Defense:** 12.1% of GDP (1992).

**Economy: Industries:** Diamond cutting, textiles, electronics, machinery, food processing. **Chief crops:** Citrus fruit, vegetables. **Minerals:** Potash, copper, phosphate, manganese, sulphur. **Arable land:** 17%. **Livestock** (1991): cattle: 331,000; sheep: 375,000. **Fish catch** (1991): 26,000 metric tons. **Electricity prod.** (1991): 21.0 bln. kWh. **Labor force:** 6% agric.; 23% ind., 30% public services.

**Finance: Monetary unit:** New Sheqalim (Aug. 1993: 2.81 = $1 US). **Gross domestic prod.** (1991): $54.6 bln. **Per capita GDP:** $12,500. **Imports** (1991): $18.1 bln.; partners: U.S. 16%, W. Ger. 13%, UK 9%. **Exports** (1991): $12.1 bln.; partners: U.S. 30%, W. Ger. 5%, UK 7%. **Tourists** (1990): receipts $1.4 bln. **National budget** (1992): $47.6 bln. expenditures. **International reserves less gold** (Jan. 1993): $4.6 bln. **Gold:** 9,000 oz t. **Consumer prices** (change in 1992): 11.6%.

**Transport: Railroads:** (1990): **Length:** 323 mi. **Motor vehicles:** in use (1990): 786,000 passenger cars, 157,000 comm. vehicles. **Civil aviation** (1990): 7.0 mln. passenger-km; 7 airports with scheduled flights. **Chief ports:** Haifa, Ashdod, Eilat.

**Communications: Television sets:** 1 per 4.1 persons. **Radios:** 1 per 2.2 persons. **Telephones:** 1 per 2.1 persons. **Daily newspaper circ.** (1989): 357 per 1,000 pop.

**Health: Life expectancy at birth** (1992) Jewish pop. only: 76 male; 79 female. **Births** (per 1,000 pop. 1992): 21. **Deaths** (per 1,000 pop. 1992): 6%. **Natural increase:** 1.5%. **Hospital beds:** 1 per 161 persons. **Physicians:** 1 per 345 persons. **Infant mortality** (per 1,000 live births 1992): 9.

**Education** (1991): **Literacy:** 92% (Jewish), 70% (Arab). **Major International Organizations:** UN (GATT). **Embassy:** 3514 International Dr. NW 20008; 364-5500.

Occupying the SW corner of the ancient Fertile Crescent, Israel contains some of the oldest known evidence of agriculture and of primitive town life. A more advanced civilization emerged in the 3d millennium BC. The Hebrews probably arrived early in the 2d millennium BC. Under King David and his successors (c.1000 BC-597 BC), Judaism was developed and secured. After conquest by Babylonians, Persians, and Greeks, an independent Jewish kingdom was revived, 168 BC, but Rome took effective control in the next century, suppressed Jewish revolts in 70 AD and 135 AD, and renamed Judea Palestine, after the earlier coastal inhabitants, the Philistines.

Arab invaders conquered Palestine in 636. The Arabic language and Islam prevailed within a few centuries, but a Jewish minority remained. The land was ruled from the 11th century as a part of non-Arab empires by Seljuks, Mamluks, and Ottomans (with a crusader interval, 1098-1291).

After 4 centuries of Ottoman rule, during which the population declined to a low of 350,000 (1785), the land was taken in 1917 by Britain, which in the Balfour Declaration that year pledged to support a Jewish national homeland there, as foreseen by the Zionists. In 1920 a British Palestine Mandate was recognized; in 1922 the land east of the Jordan was detached.

Jewish immigration, begun in the late 19th century, swelled in the 1930s with refugees from the Nazis; heavy Arab immigration from Syria and Lebanon also occurred. Arab opposition to Jewish immigration turned violent in 1920, 1921, 1929, and 1936. The UN General Assembly voted in 1947 to partition Palestine into an Arab and a Jewish state. Britain withdrew in May 1948.

Israel was declared an independent state May 14, 1948; the Arabs rejected partition. Egypt, Jordan, Syria, Lebanon, Iraq, and Saudi Arabia invaded, but failed to destroy the Jewish state, which gained territory. Separate armistices with the Arab nations were signed in 1949; Jordan occupied the West Bank, Egypt occupied Gaza, but neither granted Palestinian autonomy.

After persistent terrorist raids, Israel invaded Egypt's Sinai, Oct. 29, 1956, aided briefly by British and French forces. A UN cease-fire was arranged Nov. 6.

An uneasy truce between Israel and the Arab countries, supervised by a UN Emergency Force, prevailed until May 19, 1967, when the UN force withdrew at the demand of Egypt's Pres. Gamal Abdel Nasser. Egyptian forces reoccupied the Gaza Strip and closed the Gulf of Aqaba to Israeli shipping. In a 6-day war that started June 5, the Israelis took the Gaza Strip, occupied the Sinai Peninsula to the Suez Canal, and captured East Jerusalem, Syria's Golan Heights, and Jordan's West Bank. The fighting was halted June 10 by UN-arranged cease-fire agreements.

Egypt and Syria attacked Israel, Oct. 6, 1973 (Yom Kippur, most solemn day on the Jewish calendar). Israel counter-attacked, driving the Syrians back, and crossed the Suez Canal.

A cease fire took effect Oct. 24; a UN peace-keeping force went to the area. A disengagement agreement was signed Jan. 18, 1974. Israel withdrew from the canal's W bank. A second withdrawal was completed in 1976; Israel returned the Sinai to Egypt in 1982.

Israeli forces raided Entebbe, Uganda, July 3, 1976, and rescued 103 hostages seized by Arab and German terrorists.

In 1977, the conservative opposition, led by Menachem Begin, was voted into office for the first time. Egypt's Pres. Anwar al-Sadat visited Jerusalem Nov. 1977 and on Mar. 26, 1979, Egypt and Israel signed a formal peace treaty, ending 30 years of war and establishing diplomatic relations.

Israel invaded S. Lebanon, March 1978, following a Lebanon-based terrorist attack in Israel. Israel withdrew in favor of a 6,000-man UN force, but continued to aid Christian militiamen. Violence on the Israeli-occupied West Bank rose in 1982 when Israel announced plans to build new Jewish settlements. Israel affirmed the entire city of Jerusalem as its capital, July 1980, encompassing the annexed East Jerusalem.

On June 7, 1981, Israeli jets destroyed an Iraqi atomic reactor near Baghdad that, Israel claimed, would have enabled Iraq to manufacture nuclear weapons.

Israeli jets bombed Palestine Liberation Organization (PLO) strongholds in Lebanon April, May 1982. In reaction to the wounding of the Israeli ambassador to Great Britain, Israeli forces in a coordinated land, sea, and air attack invaded Lebanon, June 6, to destroy PLO strongholds in that country. Israeli forces encircled Beirut June 14. Following massive Israeli bombing of West Beirut, the PLO agreed to evacuate the city.

Israeli troops entered West Beirut after newly elected Lebanese president Bashir Gemayel was assassinated on Sept. 14. Israel received widespread condemnation when Lebanese Christian forces, Sept. 16, entered 2 West Beirut refugee camps and slaughtered hundreds of Palestinian refugees.

In 1989, violence escalated over the Israeli military occupation of the West Bank and Gaza Strip; Palestinian protesters and Israeli troops clashed frequently. Israeli police and stone-throwing Palestinians clashed, Oct. 8, 1990, around the al-Aqsa mosque on the Temple Mount in Jerusalem. Some 20 Palestinians died and 150 were injured.

The Knesset approved a new right-wing coalition government led by Prime Minister Yitzhak Shamir, June 11, 1990, following a 3-month political crisis that began with the fall of the previous "National Unity" government of Shamir and the Labor Party of Shimon Peres.

During the Persian Gulf War, Iraq fired a series of scud missiles at Israel; most were intercepted by U.S. Patriot missiles. Israel agreed in Aug. 1991 to take part in a U.S.-Soviet sponsored Middle East peace conference.

The Labor Party of Yitzhak Rabin won a clear victory in elections held June 23, 1992. Rabin called for peace and reconciliation with Israel's Arab neighbors.

Israeli forces conducted air raids and artillery strikes against guerrilla bases and villages in S. Lebanon, July 25-29, 1993, in retaliation for attacks by a pro-Iranian group on N. Israel.

Ongoing peace talks produced historic agreements between Israel and the Palestine Liberation Organization in Sept. 1993. The latter recognized Israel's right to exist, and Israel recognized the PLO as the representative of the Palestinians; the two sides then signed, Sept. 13, an agreement for limited Palestinian self-rule in Gaza and in the West Bank, beginning with the city of Jericho. The next day, Israel and Jordan signed a framework accord intended to pave the way for a future peace treaty.

# Italy

## Italian Republic

### Repubblica Italiana

**People: Population** (1992 est.): 57,904,000. **Age distrib.** (%): 0-14: 17.8; 15-59: 62.8; 60+: 19.4. **Pop. density:** 497 per sq. mi. **Urban** (1991): 67%. **Ethnic groups:** Italians, small minorities of Germans, Slovenes, Albanians. **Languages:** Italian. **Religions:** Predominantly Roman Catholic.

**Geography: Area:** 116,303 sq. mi., about the size of Florida and Georgia combined. **Location:** In S Europe, jutting into Mediterranean S. **Neighbors:** France on W, Switzerland, Austria on N, Slovenia on E. **Topography:** Occupies a long boot-shaped peninsula, extending SE from the Alps into the Mediterranean, with the islands of Sicily and Sardinia offshore. The alluvial Po Valley drains most of N. The rest of the country is rugged and mountainous, except for intermittent coastal plains, like the Campania, S of Rome. Apennine Mts. run down through center of peninsula. **Capital:** Rome. **Cities** (1991 est.): Rome 2.8 mln.; Milan 1.4 mln.; Naples 1.2 mln.; Turin 1.0 mln.

**Government: Type:** Republic. **Head of state:** Pres. Oscar Luigi Scalfaro; in office: May 28, 1992. **Head of government:** Prime Min. Carlo Azeglio Ciampi; in office: April 22, 1993. **Local divisions:** 20 regions with some autonomy, 94 provinces. **Defense:** 2.2% of GDP (1991).

**Economy: Industries:** Steel, machinery, autos, textiles, shoes, machine tools, chemicals. **Chief crops:** Grapes, olives, citrus fruits, vegetables, wheat, rice. **Minerals:** Mercury, potash, sulphur. **Crude oil reserves** (1991): 700 mln. bbls. **Arable land:** 32%. **Livestock** (1991): cattle: 8.7 mln.; pigs: 9.5 mln.; sheep: 11.6 mln. **Fish catch** (1990): 360,000 metric tons. **Electricity prod.** (1991): 235 bln. kWh. **Crude steel prod.** (1991): 25.4

mln. metric tons. **Labor force:** 10% agric.; 32% ind. and comm.; 58% services and govt.

**Finance: Monetary unit:** Lira (June 1992: 1,202 = $1 US). **Gross domestic product** (1991): $965 bln. **Per capita GDP:** $16,700. **Imports** (1991): $181 bln.; partners: EC 58%, Fr. 15%, U.S. 7%. **Exports** (1991): $170 bln.; partners: EC 58%. **Tourism** (1990): receipts $19.7 bln. **National budget** (1991): $565 bln. expenditures. **International reserves less gold** (Apr. 1993): $26 bln. **Gold:** 66.67 mln. oz t. **Consumer prices** (change in 1992): 5.4%.

**Transport: Railroads** (1990): **Length:** 12,158 mi. **Motor vehicles:** in use (1989): 24.3 mln. passenger cars, 2.0 mln. comm. vehicles. **Civil aviation** (1990): 22.7 bln. passenger-km; 30 airports. **Chief ports:** Genoa, Venice, Trieste, Taranto, Naples, La Spezia.

**Communications: Television sets:** 1 per 3.8 persons. **Radios:** 1 per 3.4 persons. **Telephones:** 1 per 1.8 persons. **Daily newspaper circ.** (1989): 142 per 1,000 pop.

**Health: Life expectancy at birth** (1992): 74 male; 81 female. **Births** (per 1,000 pop. 1992): 11. **Deaths** (per 1,000 pop. 1992): 10. **Natural increase:** .1%. **Hospital beds:** 1 per 135 persons. **Physicians:** 1 per 233 persons. **Infant mortality** (per 1,000 live births 1992): 8.

**Education** (1991): **Literacy:** 98%. **Years compulsory:** 8.

**Major International Organizations:** UN and all of its specialized agencies, NATO, OECD, EC.

**Embassy:** 1601 Fuller St. NW 20009; 328-5500.

Rome emerged as the major power in Italy after 500 BC, dominating the more civilized Etruscans to the N and Greeks to the S. Under the Empire, which lasted until the 5th century AD, Rome ruled most of Western Europe, the Balkans, the Near East, and North Africa. In 1988, archeologists unearthed evidence showing Rome as a dynamic society in the 6th and 7th centuries B.C.

After the Germanic invasions, lasting several centuries, a high civilization arose in the city-states of the N, culminating in the Renaissance. But German, French, Spanish, and Austrian intervention prevented the unification of the country. In 1859 Lombardy came under the crown of King Victor Emmanuel II of Sardinia. By plebiscite in 1860, Parma, Modena, Romagna, and Tuscany joined, followed by Sicily and Naples, and by the Marches and Umbria. The first Italian parliament declared Victor Emmanuel king of Italy Mar. 17, 1861. Mantua and Venetia were added in 1866 as an outcome of the Austro-Prussian war. The Papal States were taken by Italian troops Sept. 20, 1870, on the withdrawal of the French garrison. The states were annexed to the kingdom by plebiscite. Italy recognized the State of Vatican City as independent Feb. 11, 1929.

Fascism appeared in Italy Mar. 23, 1919, led by Benito Mussolini, who took over the government at the invitation of the king Oct. 28, 1922. Mussolini acquired dictatorial powers. He made war on Ethiopia and proclaimed Victor Emmanuel III emperor, defied the sanctions of the League of Nations, sent troops to fight for Franco against the Republic of Spain and joined Germany in World War II.

After Fascism was overthrown in 1943, Italy declared war on Germany and Japan and contributed to the Allied victory. It surrendered conquered lands and lost its colonies. Mussolini was killed by partisans Apr. 28, 1945.

Victor Emmanuel III abdicated May 9, 1946; his son Humbert II was king until June 10, when Italy became a republic after a referendum, June 2-3. Reorganization of the Fascist party is forbidden.

Italy has enjoyed growth in industry and living standards since World War II, in part due to membership in the European Community. A wave of left-wing political violence began in the late 1970s with kidnappings and assassinations and continued into the 1980s. Christian Democratic leader and former Prime Min. Aldo Moro was murdered May 1978 by Red Brigade terrorists.

The Cabinet of Prime Min. Arnaldo Forlani resigned, May 26, 1981, in the wake of revelations that numerous high-ranking officials were members of an illegally secret Masonic lodge. The June 1983 elections saw Bettino Craxi chosen the nation's first Socialist premier. Craxi ended the longest tenure of an Italian leader since World War II by resigning Mar. 1987.

By mid-1991, some 20,000 Albanian refugees had entered Italy as the result of political unrest in their homeland. In Aug. an additional wave of 18,000 Albanians reached Italy. They were rounded up and sent back to Albania.

Italian voters in a referendum and Italy's parliament approved, in 1993, electoral reforms, amid growing political corruption scandals. Under the reforms, most members of parliament would be elected from single districts, rather than in a proportional representation system that fragmented power among several major parties.

**Sicily,** 9,926 sq. mi., pop. (1990) 5,172,000, is an island 180 by 120 mi., seat of a region that embraces the island of **Pantelleria,** 32 sq. mi., and the **Lipari** group, 44 sq. mi., 63 14,000, including 2 active volcanoes: **Vulcano,** 1,637 ft. and **Stromboli,** 3,038 ft. From prehistoric times Sicily has been settled by various peoples; a Greek state had its capital at Syracuse. Rome took Sicily from Carthage 215 BC. **Mt. Etna,** 11,053 ft. active volcano, is tallest peak.

**Sardinia,** 9,301 sq. mi., pop. (1990) 1,657,000, lies in the Mediterranean, 115 mi. W of Italy and 7-½ mi. S of Corsica. It is 160 mi. long, 68 mi. wide, and mountainous, with mining of coal, zinc, lead, copper. In 1720 Sardinia was added to the possessions of the Dukes of Savoy in Piedmont and Savoy to form the Kingdom of Sardinia. Giuseppe Garibaldi is buried on the nearby isle of Caprera. **Elba,** 86 sq. mi., lies 6 mi. W of Tuscany. Napoleon I lived in exile on Elba 1814-1815.

**Trieste.** An agreement, signed Oct. 5, 1954, by Italy and Yugoslavia, confirmed, Nov. 10, 1975, gave Italy provisional administration over the northern section and the seaport of Trieste, and Yugoslavia the part of Istrian peninsula it has occupied.

## Jamaica

**People: Population** (1992 est.): 2,506,000. **Age distrib.** (%): 0–14: 33.7; 15–59: 56.4; 60+: 9.9. **Pop. density:** 592 per sq. mi. **Urban** (1990): 52%. **Ethnic groups:** African 76%, mixed 15%, Chinese, Caucasians, East Indians. **Languages:** English, (official), Jamaican Creole. **Religions:** Protestant 60%.

**Geography: Area:** 4,232 sq. mi., slightly smaller than Connecticut. **Location:** In West Indies. **Neighbors:** Nearest are Cuba on N, Haiti on E. **Topography:** The country is four-fifths covered by mountains. **Capital:** Kingston. **Cities** (1991 est.): St. Andrew 393,000, Kingston 100,000.

**Government: Type:** Parliamentary democracy. **Head of state:** Queen Elizabeth II, represented by Gov.-Gen. Howard Cooke; in office: Aug. 1, 1991. **Head of government:** Prime Min. Percival J. Patterson; in office: Mar. 30, 1992. **Local divisions:** 14 parishes; Kingston and St. Andrew corporate area. **Defense:** 1.0% of GDP (1991).

**Economy: Industries:** Rum, molasses, mining, tourism. **Chief crops:** Sugar cane, coffee, bananas, coconuts, citrus fruits. **Minerals:** Bauxite, limestone, gypsum. **Arable land:** 19%. **Livestock** (1991): cattle: 250,000; goats: 440,000. **Electricity prod.** (1991): 2.5 bln. kWh. **Labor force:** 31% agric.; 27% services; 41% ind.

**Finance: Monetary unit:** Dollar (Apr. 1993: 22.81 = $1 US). **Gross domestic product** (1991): $3.6 bln. **Per capita GDP:** $1,400. **Imports** (1991): $1.8 bln.; partners: U.S. 48%. **Exports** (1991): $1.2 bln.; partners: U.S. 36%. **Tourism** (1990): receipts: $740 mln. **National budget** (1991): $736 mln. **International reserves less gold** (Feb. 1993): $106 mln. **Consumer prices** (change in 1992): 49.9%.

**Transport: Railroads** (1989): **Length:** 211 mi. **Motor vehicles:** in use (1989): 93,000 passenger cars, 16,000 comm. vehicles. **Civil aviation** (1991): 1.3 bln. passenger km.; 6 airports with scheduled flights. **Chief ports:** Kingston, Montego Bay.

**Communications: Television sets:** 1 per 5.9 persons. **Radios:** 1 per 2.6 persons. **Telephones:** 1 per 13 persons. **Daily newspaper circ.** (1991): 51 per 1,000 pop.

**Health: Life expectancy at birth** (1992): 72 male; 76 female. **Births** (per 1,000 pop. 1992): 24. **Deaths:** (per 1,000 pop. 1992): 6. **Natural increase:** 1.8%. **Hospital beds:** 1 per 468 persons. **Physicians:** 1 per 5,904 persons. **Infant mortality** (per 1,000 live births 1992): 17.

**Education** (1990): **Literacy:** 98%. Compulsory to age 14. **Major International Organizations:** UN (World Bank, GATT), OAS.

**Embassy:** 1850 K St. NW 20008; 452-0660.

Jamaica was visited by Columbus, 1494, and ruled by Spain (under whom Arawak Indians died out) until seized by Britain, 1655. Jamaica won independence Aug. 6, 1962.

In 1974 Jamaica sought an increase in taxes paid by U.S. and Canadian companies which mine bauxite on the island. The socialist government acquired 50% ownership of the companies' Jamaican interests in 1976, and was reelected that year. Rudi-

mentary welfare state measures were passed. Relations with the U.S. improved greatly in the 1980s following the election of Edward Seaga.

Hurricane Gilbert struck Jamaica Sept. 12, 1988, killing some 45 and causing extensive damage including half the nation's houses.

## Japan
### Nippon

**People: Population** (1992 est.): 124,460,000. **Age distrib.** (%): 0–14: 17.3; 15–59: 64.1; 60+: 17.3. **Pop. density:** 830 per sq. mi. **Urban** (1990): 77%. **Language:** Japanese. **Ethnic groups:** Japanese 99.4%, Korean 0.5%. **Religions:** Buddhism, Shintoism shared by large majority.

**Geography: Area:** 145,856 sq. mi., slightly smaller than California. **Location:** Archipelago off E. coast of Asia. **Neighbors:** USSR on N, S. Korea on W. **Topography:** Japan consists of 4 main islands: Honshu ("mainland"), 87,805 sq. mi.; Hokkaido, 30,144 sq. mi.; Kyushu, 14,114 sq. mi.; and Shikoku, 7,049 sq. mi. The coast, deeply indented, measures 16,654 mi. The northern islands are a continuation of the Sakhalin Mts. The Kunlun range of China continues into southern islands, the ranges meeting in the Japanese Alps. In a vast transverse fissure crossing Honshu E-W rises a group of volcanoes, mostly extinct or inactive, including 12,388 ft. Fuji-San (Fujiyama) near Tokyo. **Capital:** Tokyo. **Cities** (1991 est.): Tokyo 8.1 mln.; Osaka 2.6 mln.; Yokohama 3.2 mln.; Nagoya 2.1 mln.; Kyoto 1.4 mln.; Kobe 1.4 mln.; Sapporo 1.6 mln.; Kitakyushu 1 mln.; Kawasaki 1.1 mln; Fukuoka 1.2 mln.

**Government: Type:** Parliamentary democracy. **Head of state:** Emp. Akihito; b. Dec. 23, 1933; in office: Jan. 7, 1989. **Head of government:** Prime Min. Morihiro Hosokawa; b. Jan. 14, 1938; in office: Aug. 6, 1993. **Local divisions:** 47 prefectures. **Defense:** Less than 1% of GNP (1992).

**Economy: Industries:** Electrical & electronic equip., autos, machinery, chemicals. **Chief crops:** Rice, grains, vegetables, fruits. **Minerals:** negligible. **Arable land:** 13%. **Livestock** (1991): cattle: 4.8 mln.; pigs: 11.3 mln. **Fish catch** (1990): 10.3 mln. metric tons. **Electricity prod.** (1991): 823 bln. kWh. **Crude steel prod.** (1991): 109 mln. metric tons. **Labor force:** 8% agric.; 32% manuf. & mining; 43% services & trade.

**Finance: Monetary unit:** Yen (June 1992: 127 = $1 US). **Gross domestic product** (1991): $2.3 trl. **Per capita GDP:** $19,100. **Imports** (1991): $233 bln.; partners: U.S. 22%, Middle East 26%, SE Asia 22%, EC 6%. **Exports** (1992): $339 bln.; partners: U.S. 33%, EC 20%, SE Asia 23%. **Tourism** (1990): $3.6 bln. receipts. **National budget** (1991): $532 bln. expenditures. **International reserves less gold** (Mar. 1993): $73 bln. **Gold:** 24.23 mln. oz. t. **Consumer prices** (change in 1992): 1.7%.

**Transport: Railroads** (1991): **Length:** 23,690 mi. **Motor vehicles:** in use (1991): 37.0 mln. passenger cars, 22.6 mln. comm. vehicles. **Civil aviation** (1990): 95.3 bln. passenger-km; 71 airports with scheduled flights. **Chief ports:** Yokohama, Tokyo, Kobe, Osaka, Nagoya, Chiba, Kawasaki, Hakodate.

**Communications: Television sets:** 1 per 1.8 persons. **Radios:** 1 per 1.3 persons. **Telephones:** 1 per 2.3 persons. **Daily newspaper circ.** (1991): 585 per 1,000 pop.

**Health: Life expectancy at birth** (1992): 77 male; 82 female. **Births** (per 1,000 pop. 1992): 10. **Deaths** (per 1,000 pop. 1992): 7. **Natural increase:** 0.3%. **Hospital beds:** 1 per 74 persons. **Physicians:** 1 per 588 persons. **Infant mortality** (per 1,000 live births 1992): 4.

**Education** (1991): **Literacy:** 99%. Most attend school for 12 years.

**Major International Organizations:** UN (IMF, GATT, ILO), OECD.

**Embassy:** 2520 Massachusetts Ave. NW 20008; 939-6700.

According to Japanese legend, the empire was founded by Emperor Jimmu, 660 BC, but earliest records of a unified Japan date from 1,000 years later. Chinese influence was strong in the formation of Japanese civilization. Buddhism was introduced before the 6th century.

A feudal system, with locally powerful noble families and their samurai warrior retainers, dominated from 1192. Central power was held by successive families of shoguns (military dictators), 1192-1867, until recovered by the Emperor Meiji, 1868. The Portuguese and Dutch had minor trade with Japan in the 16th and 17th centuries; U.S. Commodore Matthew C. Perry opened it to U.S. trade in a treaty ratified 1854. Japan fought China, 1894-95, gaining Taiwan. After war with Russia, 1904-05, Russia ceded S half of Sakhalin and gave concessions in China. Japan annexed Korea 1910. In World War I Japan ousted Germany from Shantung, took over German Pacific islands. Japan took Manchuria 1931, started war with China 1932. Japan launched war against the U.S. by attack on Pearl Harbor Dec. 7, 1941. Japan surrendered Aug. 14, 1945.

In a new constitution adopted May 3, 1947, Japan renounced the right to wage war; the emperor gave up claims to divinity; the Diet became the sole law-making authority.

The U.S. and 48 other non-communist nations signed a peace treaty and the U.S. a bilateral defense agreement with Japan, in San Francisco Sept. 8, 1951, restoring Japan's sovereignty as of April 28, 1952.

On June 26, 1968, the U.S. returned to Japanese control the Bonin Is., the Volcano Is. (including Iwo Jima) and Marcus Is. On May 15, 1972, Okinawa, the other Ryukyu Is. and the Daito Is. were returned to Japan by the U.S.; it was agreed the U.S. would continue to maintain military bases on Okinawa.

Industrialization was begun in the late 19th century. After World War II, Japan emerged as one of the most powerful economies in the world, and as a leader in technology.

The U.S. and EC member nations have criticized Japan for its restrictive policy on imports which has given Japan a substantial trade surplus.

Pres. Bush visted Japan, Jan. 1992; he won trade concessions in the areas of auto parts and sales, computers, paper, and glass.

The Recruit scandal, the nation's worst political scandal since World War II, which involved illegal political donations and stock trading, led to the resignation of Premier Noboru Takeshita in May 1989. A series of scandals rocked Japan's financial sector in 1991; one involved the largest bank, another the 4 largest securities firms.

Following a series of political scandals, the Liberal Democratic Party was denied a majority in general elections held July 18, 1993. The LDP had held power in Japan since the party was founded in 1955. Morihiro Hosokawa, a reformer, was chosen prime minister Aug. 6.

## Jordan

### Hashemite Kingdom of Jordan

### al Mamlaka al Urduniya al Hashemiyah

**Population** (1992 est.): 3,557,000. **Age distrib.** (%): 0–14: 48.1; 15–59: 46.9; 60+: 4.0. **Pop. density:** 94 per sq. mi. **Urban** (1990): 68%. **Ethnic groups:** Arab 98%. **Languages:** Arabic (official). **Religions:** Sunni Moslem 92%, Christian 8%.

**Geography: Area:** 37,737 sq. mi., slightly larger than Indiana. **Location:** In W Asia. **Neighbors:** Israel on W, Saudi Arabia on S, Iraq on E, Syria on N. **Topography:** About 88% of Jordan is arid. Fertile areas are in W. Only port is on short Aqaba Gulf coast. Country shares Dead Sea (1,296 ft. below sea level) with Israel. **Capital:** Amman. **Cities** (1989 est.): Amman 936,000; az-Zarqa 318,000; Irbid 161,000.

**Government: Type:** Constitutional monarchy. **Head of state:** King Hussein I; b. Nov. 14, 1935; in office: Aug. 11, 1952. **Head of government:** Prime Min. Sharif Zaid ibn Shaker; in office: Nov. 16, 1991. **Local divisions:** 8 governorates. **Defense:** 9.5% of GDP (1990).

**Economy: Industries:** Textiles, cement, food processing. **Chief crops:** Grains, olives, vegetables, fruits. **Minerals:** Phosphate, potash. **Arable land:** 5%. **Electricity prod.** (1991): 3.9 bln. kWh. **Labor force:** 20% agric. 20% manuf. & mining.

**Finance: Monetary unit:** Dinar (Mar. 1993: 1.00 = $1.43 US). **Gross domestic product** (1991): $3.6 bln. **Imports** (1991): $2.3 bln.; partners: Saudi Ar. 6%, U.S. 11%, Jap. 8%. **Exports** (1991): $1.0 bln.; partners: Saudi Ar. 12%, Ind. 13%, Iraq. 18%. **Tourism** (1989): receipts: $546 mln. **National budget** (1992): $1.8 bln. expenditures. **International reserves less gold** (Mar. 1993): $680 mln. **Gold:** 789,000 oz t. **Consumer prices** (change in 1992): 4.2%.

**Transport: Motor vehicles:** in use (1990): 173,000 passenger cars, 68,000 comm. vehicles. **Civil aviation** (1990): 2.7 bln. passenger-km; 2 airports with scheduled flights. **Chief ports:** Aqaba.

**Communications: Television sets:** 1 per 12 persons. **Radios:** 1 per 4.5 persons. **Telephones:** 1 per 10 persons. **Daily newspaper circ.** (1990): 73 per 1,000 pop.

**Health: Life expectancy at birth** (1991): 70 male; 73 female. **Births** (per 1,000 pop. 1991): 46.7. **Deaths** (per 1,000 pop. 1991): 5. **Natural increase:** 4.1%. **Hospital beds:** 1 per 502 persons. **Physicians:** 1 per 813 persons. **Infant mortality** (per 1,000 live births 1991): 38.

**Education** (1989): **Literacy:** 71%.

**Major International Organizations:** UN (WHO, IMF), Arab League.

**Embassy:** 3504 International Dr. NW 20008; 966-2664.

From ancient times to 1922 the lands to the E of the Jordan River were culturally and politically united with the lands to the W. Arabs conquered the area in the 7th century; the Ottomans took control in the 16th. Britain's 1920 Palestine Mandate covered both sides of the Jordan. In 1921, Abdullah, son of the ruler of Hejaz in Arabia, was installed by Britain as emir of an autonomous Transjordan, covering two-thirds of Palestine. An independent kingdom was proclaimed, 1946.

During the 1948 Arab-Israeli war the West Bank and East Jerusalem were added to the kingdom, which changed its name to Jordan. All these territories were lost to Israel in the 1967 war, which swelled the number of Arab refugees on the East Bank. A 1974 Arab summit conference designated the Palestine Liberation Organization as the sole representative of Arabs on the West Bank. In 1988 Jordan cut legal and administrative ties with the Israeli-occupied West Bank. Jordan and Israel signed, Sept. 14, 1993, a framework accord, intended to lead to a peace treaty.

Some 700,000 refugees entered Jordan following Iraq's invasion of Kuwait, Aug. 1990. Jordan was viewed as supporting Iraq during the 1990-1991 Persian Gulf crisis.

## Kazakhstan

### Republic of Kazakhstan

### Kazak Respublikasy

**People: Population** (1992 est.): 17,101,000. **Pop. density:** 16 per sq. mi. **Urban** (1991): 58%. **Ethnic groups:** Kazakh 40%, Russian 37%, German 6%, Ukrainian 5%. **Languages:** Kazakh, Russian, German. **Religion:** Moslem 47%.

**Geography: Area:** 1,049,200 sq. mi. **Neighbors:** Russia on N, China on E, Kyrgyzstan, Uzbekistan, Turkmenistan on S, Caspian Sea on W. **Topography:** Extends from the lower reaches of Volga in Europe to the Altai Mtns. on the Chinese border. **Capital:** Alma-Ata. **Cities** (1991): Alma-Ata 1.1 mln., Qaraghandy 608,000.

**Government: Type:** Republic. **Head of state:** Pres. Nursultan A. Nazarbayev. **Head of government:** Prime Min. Sergei Tereshchenko.

**Economy: Industries:** Steel, cement, footwear, textiles. **Chief crops:** Grain, cotton. **Minerals:** Coal, tungsten, copper, lead, zinc. **Livestock** (1989): cattle: 9.7 mln., sheep: 36.5 mln., pigs: 3.2 mln.

**Finance: Monetary unit:** Ruble.

**Transport: Railroads** (1991): **Length** (1991): 9,040 mi. **Motor vehicles** (1989): 734,000 passenger cars. **Civil aviation** (1990): 13.3 bln. passenger km.; airports with sched. flights: 5.

**Communications: Telephones:** 1 per 8.5 persons.

**Health: Life expectancy at birth** (1992): 63 male; 72 female. **Birth rate** (per 1,000 pop. 1992): 23. **Death rate** (per 1,000 pop. 1992): 8. **Hospital beds:** 1 per 74 persons. **Physicians:** 1 per 224 persons. **Infant mortality** (per 1,000 live births 1992): 26.

**Major International Organizations:** UN, CIS.

The region came under the Mongols in the 13th century and gradually came under Russian rule, 1730-1853. It was admitted to the USSR as a constituent republic 1936. Kazakhstan declared independence Dec. 16, 1991. It became an independent state when the Soviet Union dissolved Dec. 26, 1991.

# Kenya

### Republic of Kenya

### Jamhuri ya Kenya

**People: Population** (1992 est.): 26,164,000. **Age distrib.** (%): 0–14: 49.6; 15–59: 50.0; 60+: 3.4. **Pop. density:** 116 per sq. mi. **Urban** (1991): 26%. **Ethnic groups:** Kikuyu 21%, Luo 13%, Luhya 14%, Kelenjin 11%, Kamba 11%, others, including Asians, Arabs, Europeans. **Languages:** Swahili (official), Kikuyu, Luhya, Luo, Meru. **Religions:** Protestant 38%, Roman Catholic 28%, Moslem 6%, others.

**Geography: Area:** 224,960 sq. mi., slightly smaller than Texas. **Location:** On Indian O. coast of E. Africa. **Neighbors:** Uganda on W, Tanzania on S, Somalia on E, Ethopia, Sudan on N. **Topography:** The northern three-fifths of Kenya is arid. To the S, a low coastal area and a plateau varying from 3,000 to 10,000 ft. The Great Rift Valley enters the country N-S, flanked by high mountains. **Capital:** Nairobi. **Cities** (1987 est.): Nairobi 959,000; Mombasa 401,000.

**Government: Type:** Republic. **Head of state:** Pres. Daniel arap Moi, b. Sept., 1924; in office: Aug. 22, 1978. **Local divisions:** Nairobi and 7 provinces. **Defense:** 1.0% of GDP (1989).

**Economy: Industries:** Tourism, light industry, petroleum prods. **Chief crops:** Coffee, corn, tea, cereals, cotton, sisal. **Minerals:** Gold, limestone, diatomite, salt, barytes, magnesite, felspar, sapphires, fluospar, garnets. **Other resources:** Timber, hides. **Arable land:** 4%. **Livestock** (1991): cattle: 13.7 mln. **Fish catch** (1990): 144,000 metric tons. **Electricity prod.** (1991): 2.8 bln. kWh. **Labor force:** 78% agric.

**Finance: Monetary unit:** Shilling (Mar. 1993: 45.52 = $1 US). **Gross domestic product** (1991): $9.7 bln. **Per capita GDP:** $385. **Imports** (1991): $1.9 bln.; partners: EC 45%. **Exports** (1991): $1.0 bln.; partners: EC 44%. **Tourism** (1992): receipts: $295 mln. **National budget** (1990): $2.8 bln expenditures. **International reserves less gold** (Mar. 1993): $77 mln. **Gold:** 80,000 oz t. **Consumer prices** (change in 1992): 35.5%.

**Transport: Motor vehicles:** in use (1989): 133,000 passenger cars, 149,000 comm. vehicles. **Civil Aviation** (1991): 1.4 bln. passenger-km; 16 airports with scheduled flights. **Chief ports:** Mombasa.

**Communications: Television sets:** 1 per 100 persons. **Radios:** 1 per 6 persons. **Telephones:** 1 per 67 persons. **Daily newspaper circ.** (1991): 13 per 1,000 pop.

**Health: Life expectancy at birth** (1992): 60 male; 64 female. **Births** (per 1,000 pop. 1992): 44. **Deaths** (per 1,000 pop. 1992): 8. **Natural increase:** 3.6%. **Hospital beds:** 1 per 737 persons. **Physicians:** 1 per 7,313 persons. **Infant mortality** (per 1,000 live births 1992): 68.

**Education** (1989): **Literacy:** 50%. 86% attend primary school.

**Major International Organizations:** UN and all of its specialized agencies, OAU, Commonwealth of Nations.

**Embassy:** 2249 R St. NW 20008; 387-6101.

Arab colonies exported spices and slaves from the Kenya coast as early as the 8th century. Britain obtained control in the 19th century. Kenya won independence Dec. 12, 1963, 4 years after the end of the violent Mau Mau uprising.

Kenya had steady growth in industry and agriculture under a modified private enterprise system, and enjoyed a relatively free political life. But stability was shaken in 1974-5, with opposition charges of corruption and oppression.

Tribal clashes in the western provinces claimed some 2,000 lives and left 50,000 homeless in 1992. The unrest was the worst since independence in 1963. Several western nations issued travel advisories for Kenya.

In the 1990s, Kenya suffered from widespread unemployment and high inflation. Pres. Moi suspended parliament, Jan. 27, 1993, one day after it opened with its first opposition members since the early 1960s.

# Kiribati

### Republic of Kiribati

**People: Population** (1992 est.): 74,000. **Pop. density:** 278 per sq. mi. **Ethnic groups:** nearly all Micronesian, some Polynesians. **Languages:** Gilbertese and English (official). **Religions:** evenly divided between Protestant and Roman Catholic.

**Geography: Area:** 266 sq. mi., slightly smaller than New York City. **Location:** 33 Micronesian islands (the Gilbert, Line, and Phoenix groups) in the mid-Pacific scattered in a 2-mln. sq. mi. chain around the point where the International Date Line cuts the Equator. **Neighbors:** Nearest are Nauru to SW, Tuvalu and Tokelau Is. to S. **Topography:** except Banaba (Ocean) I., all are low-lying, with soil of coral sand and rock fragments, subject to erratic rainfall. **Capital** (1990): Tarawa 25,000.

**Government: Type:** Republic. **Head of state and of government:** Pres. Teateo Teannaki; in office: July 3, 1991.

**Economy: Industries:** Copra. **Chief crops:** Coconuts, breadfruit, pandanus, bananas, paw paw. **Other resources:** Fish. **Electricity prod.** (1990): 13 mln. kWh.

**Finance: Monetary unit:** Australian dollar. **Gross domestic product** (1990): $36 mln.

**Transport: Chief port:** Tarawa.

**Communications: Radios:** 1 per 7 persons. **Telephones:** 1 per 53 persons.

**Health: Hospital beds:** 1 per 231 persons. **Physicians:** 1 per 4,104 persons.

**Education: Literacy** (1985): 90%.

A British protectorate since 1892, the Gilbert and Ellice Islands colony was completed with the inclusion of the Phoenix Islands, 1937. Self-rule was granted 1971; the Ellice Islands separated from the colony 1975 and became independent Tuvalu, 1978. Kiribati (pronounced *Kiribass*) independence was attained July 12, 1979. Under a Treaty of Friendship the U.S. relinquished its claims to several of the Line and Phoenix islands, including Christmas (Kiritimati), Canton, and Enderbury.

Tarawa Atoll was the scene of some of the bloodiest fighting in the Pacific during WW II.

# Korea, North

### Democratic People's Republic of Korea

### Chosun Minchu-chui Inmin Konghwa-guk

**People: Population** (1992 est.): 22,227,000. **Pop. density:** 477 per sq. mi. **Urban** (1990): 60%. **Ethnic groups:** Korean. **Languages:** Korean. **Religions:** activities almost nonexistent; traditionally Buddhism, Confucianism, Chondokyo.

**Geography: Area:** 46,540 sq. mi., slightly smaller than Mississippi. **Location:** In northern E. Asia. **Neighbors:** China, Russia on N, S. Korea on S. **Topography:** Mountains and hills cover nearly all the country, with narrow valleys and small plains in between. The N and the E coast are the most rugged areas. **Capital:** Pyongyang. **Cities** (1987 est.): Pyongyang 2,355,000.

**Government: Type:** Communist state. **Head of state:** Pres. Kim Il-Sung; b. Apr. 15, 1912; in office: Dec. 28, 1972. **Head of government:** Premier Kang Song San; in office: Dec. 11, 1992. **Head of Communist Party:** Gen. Sec. Kim Il-Sung; in office: 1945. **Local divisions:** 9 provinces, 3 special cities. **Defense** (1991): 24% of GNP.

**Economy: Industries:** Textiles, petrochemicals, food processing. **Chief crops:** Corn, potatoes, fruits, vegetables, rice. **Minerals:** Coal, lead tungsten, graphite, magnesite, iron, copper, gold, phosphate, salt, fluorspar. **Arable land:** 19%. **Livestock** (1990): cattle: 1.2 mln; pigs: 3.1 mln. **Fish catch** (1990): 1.7 mln. metric tons. **Crude steel prod.** (1991) 7.0 mln. metric tons. **Electricity prod.** (1991): 36 bln. kWh. **Labor force:** 48% agric.

**Finance: Monetary unit:** Won (Mar. 1993): 2.15 = $1 US). **Gross national product** (1991): $23 bln. **Imports** (1990): $2.6 bln.; partners: China 17%, USSR 36%, Jap. 19%. **Exports** (1990): $2.0 bln.; partners: USSR 43% China 13%, Jap. 15%. **National budget** (1990): $17.7 bln. expenditures.

**Communications: Television sets:** 1 per 90 persons. **Radios:** 1 per 6 persons.

**Transport: Chief ports:** Chonglin, Hamhung, Nampo.

**Health: Life expectancy at birth** (1992): 66 male; 72 female. **Births** (per 1,000 pop. 1992): 24. **Deaths** (per 1,000 pop. 1992): 6. **Natural increase:** 1.8%. **Hospital beds:** 1 per 74 persons. **Physicians:** 1 per 370 persons. **Infant mortality** (per 1,000 live births, 1992): 30.

**Education** (1991): **Literacy:** 99%. **Years compulsory:** 11.

**Major International Organizations:** UN.

The Democratic People's Republic of Korea was founded May 1, 1948, in the zone occupied by Russian troops after World War II. Its armies tried to conquer the south, 1950. After 3 years of fighting, with Chinese and U.S. intervention, a cease-fire was proclaimed.

Industry, begun by the Japanese during their 1910-45 occupation, and nationalized in the 1940s, had grown substantially, using N. Korea's abundant mineral and hydroelectric resources.

In Mar. 1993, N. Korea became the first nation to formally withdraw from the Nuclear Nonproliferation Treaty, the international pact designed to limit the spread of nuclear weapons; the nation suspended its withdrawal in June in reaction to threats of UN economic sanctions.

# Korea, South

## Republic of Korea

## Taehan Min'guk

**People: Population** (1992 est.): 44,149,000. **Age distrib.** (%): 0–14: 27.3; 15–59: 65.5; 60+: 7.2. **Pop. density:** 1,161 per sq. mi. **Urban** (1990): 74%. **Ethnic groups:** Korean. **Languages:** Korean. **Religions:** Christian 43%, Buddhist 18%.

**Geography: Area:** 38,025 sq. mi., slightly larger than Indiana. **Location:** In Northern E. Asia. **Neighbors:** N. Korea on N. **Topography:** The country is mountainous, with a rugged east coast. The western and southern coasts are deeply indented, with many islands and harbors. **Capital:** Seoul. **Cities** (1990 est.): Seoul 10.7 mln.; Pusan 3,800,000; Taegu 2,200,000; Inchon 1,600,000; Kwangju 1,200,000; Taejon 1,000,000.

**Government: Type:** Republic, with power centralized in a strong executive. **Head of state:** Pres. Kim Young Sam; in office: Feb. 25, 1993. **Head of government:** Prime Min. Hwang In Sung; in office: Feb. 22, 1993. **Local divisions:** 9 provinces and 6 special cities. **Defense:** 4.5% of GNP (1992).

**Economy: Industries:** Electronics, ships, textiles, clothing, motor vehicles. **Chief crops:** Rice, barley, vegetables, wheat. **Minerals:** Tungsten, coal, graphite. **Arable land:** 22%. **Livestock** (1990): cattle: 2.0 mln.; pigs: 4.8 mln. **Fish catch** (1990): 3.2 mln. metric tons. **Electricity prod.** (1991): 106 bln. kWh. **Crude steel prod.** (1991): 26.0 mln. metric tons. **Labor force:** 21% agric.; 27% manuf. & mining; 52% services.

**Finance: Monetary unit:** Won (Aug. 1993: 805 = $1 US). **Gross national product** (1991): $273 bln. **Per capita GNP:** $6,300. **Imports** (1992): $81 bln.; partners: Jap. 26%, U.S. 21%. **Exports** (1992): $72 bln.; partners: U.S. 26%, Jap. 18%. **Tourism** (1991): receipts: $3.5 bln. **National budget** (1992): $44 bln. expenditures. **International reserves less gold** (Mar. 1993): $18 bln. **Gold:** 323,000 oz t. **Consumer prices** (change in 1992): 6.2%.

**Transport: Railroads** (1990): **Length:** 4,000 mi. **Motor vehicles:** in use (1990): 2.0 mln. passenger cars, 1.3 mln. comm. vehicles. **Civil aviation** (1990): 18.7 bln. passenger-km; 12 airlines with scheduled flights. **Chief ports:** Pusan, Inchon.

**Communications: Television sets:** 1 per 4.9 persons. **Radios:** 1 per 1.0 persons. **Telephones:** 1 per 3.3 persons. **Daily newspaper circ.** (1990): 309 per 1,000 pop.

**Health: Life expectancy at birth** (1992): 67 male; 73 female. **Births** (per 1,000 pop. 1992): 15. **Deaths** (per 1,000 pop. 1992): 6. **Natural increase:** 0.9%. **Hospital beds:** 1 per 429 persons. **Physicians:** 1 per 1,007 persons. **Infant mortality** (per 1,000 live births 1992): 23.

**Education** (1991): **Literacy:** 96%. **Attendance:** High school 90%, college 14%.

**Embassy:** 2320 Massachusetts Ave. NW 20008; 939-5600. **Major International Organizations:** UN.

Korea, once called the Hermit Kingdom, has a recorded history since the 1st century BC. It was united in a kingdom under the Silla Dynasty, 668 AD. It was at times associated with the Chinese empire; the treaty that concluded the Sino-Japanese war of 1894-95 recognized Korea's complete independence. In 1910 Japan forcibly annexed Korea as Chosun.

At the Potsdam conference, July, 1945, the 38th parallel was designated as the line dividing the Soviet and the American occupation. Russian troops entered Korea Aug. 10, 1945, U.S. troops entered Sept. 8, 1945. The Soviet military organized socialists and communists and blocked efforts to let the Koreans unite their country. *(See Index for Korean War.)*

The South Koreans formed the Republic of Korea in May 1948 with Seoul as the capital. Dr. Syngman Rhee was chosen president but a movement spearheaded by college students forced his resignation Apr. 26, 1960.

In an army coup May 16, 1961, Gen. Park Chung Hee became chairman of the ruling junta. He was elected president, 1963; a 1972 referendum allowed him to be reelected for 6 year terms unlimited times. Park was assassinated by the chief of the Korean CIA, Oct. 26, 1979. The calm of the new government was halted by the rise of Gen. Chun Doo Hwan, head of the military intelligence, who reinstated martial law, and reverted South Korea to the police state it was under Park.

In July 1972 South and North Korea agreed on a common goal of reunifying the 2 nations by peaceful means. But there was no sign of a thaw in relations between the two regimes until 1985 when they agreed to discuss economic issues. In 1988, radical students demanding reunification clashed with police.

On June 10, 1987, middle class office workers, shopkeepers, and business executives joined students in antigovernment protests in Seoul. They were protesting President Chun's decision to choose his successor and not allow the next president to be chosen by direct vote of the people. Following weeks of rioting and violence, Chun, July 1, agreed to permit election of the next president by direct popular vote and other constitutional reforms. In Dec., Roh Tae Woo was elected president. In 1990, the nation's 3 largest political parties merged; some 100,000 students demonstrated, charging that the merger was undemocratic.

Kim Young Sam took office in 1993 as the first civilian president since 1961.

# Kuwait

## State of Kuwait

## Dowlat al-Kuwait

**People: Population** (1992 est.): 1,318,000. **Age distrib.** (%): 0–14: 35.5; 15–59: 62.1; 60+: 2.4. **Pop. density:** 191 per sq. mi. **Urban** (1990): 95%. **Ethnic groups:** Kuwaiti 50%, other Arab 35%, Iranians, Indians, Pakistanis. **Languages:** Arabic, (official). **Religions:** Moslem 85%.

**Geography: Area:** 6,880 sq. mi., slightly smaller than New Jersey. **Location:** In Middle East, at N end of Persian Gulf. **Neighbors:** Iraq on N, Saudi Arabia on S. **Topography:** The country is flat, very dry, and extremely hot. **Capital:** Kuwait. **Cities** (1985 est.): Hawalli 145,000; as-Salimiyah 153,000.

**Government: Type:** Constitutional monarchy. **Head of state:** Emir Shaikh Jabir al-Ahmad al-Jabir as-Sabah; b. 1928; in office: Jan. 1, 1978. **Head of government:** Prime Min. Shaikh Saad Abdulla as-Salim as-Sabah; in office: Feb. 8, 1978. **Local divisions:** 5 governorates. **Defense:** 21% of GDP (1991).

**Economy: Industries:** Oil products. **Minerals:** Oil, gas. **Crude oil reserves** (1990): 94 bln. barrels. **Cultivated land:** 1%. **Electricity prod.** (1991): 3.1 bln. kWh. **Labor force:** social services 45%; construction 20%.

**Finance: Monetary unit:** Dinar (Mar. 1993: 1.00 = $3.30 US). **Gross domestic product** (1991): $8.7 bln. **Per capita GDP:** $6,200. **Imports** (1991): $4.7 bln.; partners: Jap. 21%, U.S. 9%. **Exports** (1989): $11.4 bln.; partners: Jap. 16%, It. 10%. **Tourism** (1990): $180 mln. receipts. **National budget** (1992): $21 bln. expenditures. **International reserves less gold** (Mar. 1993): $4.2 bln. **Gold:** 2.53 mln. oz t.

**Transport: Motor vehicles:** in use (1990): 500,000 passenger cars, 114,000 comm. vehicles. **Civil aviation** (1991): 1.8 mln. passenger-km. 1 airport with scheduled flight. **Chief ports:** Mina al-Ahmadi.

**Communications: Television sets:** 1 per 2.6 persons. **Radios:** 1 per 1.8 persons. **Telephones:** 1 per 6.9 persons. **Daily newspaper circ.** (1992): 550 per 1,000 pop.

**Health: Life expectancy at birth** (1992): 72 male; 76 female. **Births** (per 1,000 pop. 1992): 32. **Deaths** (per 1,000 pop. 1992): 2. **Natural increase:** 3.0%. **Hospital beds:** 1 per 336 persons. **Physician:** 1 per 695 persons. **Infant mortality** (per 1,000 live births 1992): 15.

**Education** (1989): **Literacy:** 71%. **Years compulsory:** 8. **Major International Organizations:** UN (World Bank, IMF, GATT), Arab League, OPEC. **Embassy:** 2940 Tilden St. NW 20008; 966-0702.

Kuwait is ruled by the Al-Sabah dynasty, founded 1759. Britain ran foreign relations and defense from 1899 until independence in 1961. The majority of the population is non-Kuwaiti, with many Palestinians, and cannot vote.

Oil, first exported in 1946, is the fiscal mainstay, providing most of Kuwait's income. Oil pays for free medical care, education, and social security. There are no taxes, except customs duties.

Kuwaiti oil tankers have come under frequent attack by Iran because of Kuwait's support of Iraq in the Iran-Iraq War. In July 1987, U.S. Navy warships began escorting Kuwaiti tankers in the Persian Gulf.

In 1988, a Kuwaiti Airways jet was hijacked by pro-Iranian Shiite Moslem terrorists who demanded the release of 17 Shiite terrorists. The ordeal lasted 16 days as Kuwait refused to release the terrorists.

Kuwait was attacked and overrun by Iraqian forces Aug. 2, 1990. The Emir and senior members of the ruling family fled to Saudi Arabia to establish a government in exile. On Aug. 28, Iraq announced that Kuwait was its 19th province. Following several weeks of aerial attacks on Iraq and Iraqi forces in Kuwait, a U.S.-led coalition began a ground attack Feb. 23, 1991. By Feb. 27, Iraqi forces were routed and Kuwait liberated.

Following liberation, there were reports of abuse of Palestinians and others suspected of collaborating with Iraqi occupiers.

Former U.S. President George Bush visited Kuwait, Apr. 14-16, 1993, and was honored as the leader of the Persian Gulf War alliance that expelled Iraqi troops in 1991. Prior to the visit, Kuwait authorities arrested a group of Iraqis who had planned to assassinate Bush during his visit. An inquiry by the FBI substantiated accusations that Iraq was involved in the plot.

# Kyrgyzstan

## Republic of Kyrgyzstan

### Kyrgyz Respublikasy

**People: Population** (1992 est.): 4,567,000. **Pop density:** 59 per sq. mi. **Urban** (1991): 38%. **Ethnic groups:** Kyrghiz 52%, Russian 22%, Uzbec 13%.

**Geography: Area:** 76,642 sq. mi. **Neighbors:** Kazakhstan on N., China on E., Uzbekistan on W., Tajikistan on S. **Capital:** Bishkek. **Cities** (1991): Bishkek 631,000; Osh 218,000.

**Government: Type:** Republic. **Head of state:** Pres. Askar Akayev. **Head of government:** Prime Min. Tursunbek Chyng Yshev. **Local divisions:** 6 oblasts.

**Economy: Industries:** Tanning, tobacco, textiles, mining. **Chief crops:** Wheat, sugar beets, tobacco. **Livestock** (1989): cattle: 1.2 mln., sheep: 10.4 mln.

**Finance: Monetary unit:** Som (May 1993): 1.00 = $.24 US.

**Transport: Railroads** (1991): **Length:** 490 mi. **Motor vehicles:** in use (1990): 173,000 passenger cars. **Civil aviation** (1990): 3.7 bln. passenger-km; 1 airport.

**Communications: Telephones:** 1 per 14 persons. **Newspaper circ.** (1990): 367 per 1,000 pop.

**Health: Life expectancy at birth** (1992): 62 male; 71 female. **Birth rate** (per 1,000 pop. 1992): 31. **Death rate** (per 1,000 pop. 1992): 8. **Hospital beds:** 1 per 84 persons. **Physicians:** 1 per 275 persons. **Infant mortality** (per 1,000 live births 1992): 56. **Major International Organizations:** UN (IMF), CIS.

The region was inhabited around the 13th century by the Kirghiz. It was annexed to Russia 1864. After 1917, it was nominally a Kara-Kirghiz autonomous area, which was reorganized 1926, and made a constituent republic of the USSR in 1936. Kyrgyzstan declared independence Aug. 31, 1991. It became an independent state when the USSR disbanded Dec. 26, 1991.

# Laos

## Lao People's Democratic Republic

### Sathalanalat Paxathipatai Paxaxōn Lao

**People: Population** (1992 est.): 4,440,000. **Pop. density:** 48 per sq. mi. **Urban** (1990): 19%. **Ethnic groups:** Lao 50%, Mon-Khmer tribes 25%, Thai 14%, Meo and Yao 13%, others. **Languages:** Lao (official), Palaung-Wa, Tai. **Religions:** Buddhists 80%, tribal 20%.

**Geography: Area:** 91,428 sq. mi., slightly larger than Utah. **Location:** In Indochina Peninsula in SE Asia. **Neighbors:** Myan-

mar, China on N, Vietnam on E, Cambodia on S, Thailand on W. **Topography:** Landlocked, dominated by jungle. High mountains along the eastern border are the source of the E-W rivers slicing across the country to the Mekong R., which defines most of the western border. **Capital:** Vientiane. **Cities** (1985 cen.): Vientiane 377,000.

**Government: Type:** Communist. **Head of state:** Pres. Nouhak Phoumsavan; in office: Nov. 25, 1992. **Head of government:** Prime Min. Khamtai Siphandon; in office: Aug. 15 1991. **Local divisions:** 17 provinces, 1 municipality. **Armed forces: Defense:** 3.8% of GDP (1988).

**Economy: Industries:** Wood products, mining. **Chief crops:** Rice, corn, tobacco, cotton, opium, citrus fruits, coffee. **Minerals:** Tin. **Other resources:** Forests. **Arable land:** 4%. **Livestock** (1990): pigs: 1.3 mln. **Fish catch** (1990): 20,000 metric tons. **Electricity prod.** (1991): 1.1 bln. kWh. **Labor force:** 85% agric.; 6% ind.

**Finance: Monetary unit:** New kip (Dec. 1992): 714 = $1 US). **Gross domestic product** (1991): $800 mln. **Per capita GDP:** $200. **Imports** (1990): $240 mln.; partners: Thai. 45%, Jap. 20%. **Exports** (1990): $72 mln.; partners: Thai, Viet, USSR.

**Transport: Motor vehicles:** in use (1989): 17,000 passenger cars, 3,500 comm. vehicles. **Civil Aviation** (1987): 18 mln. passenger km; 4 airports with scheduled flights.

**Communications: Radios:** 1 per 9 persons.

**Health: Life expectancy at birth** (1992): 49 male; 52 female. **Births** (per 1,000 pop. 1992): 44. **Deaths** (per 1,000 pop. 1992): 16. **Natural increase:** 2.8%. **Hospital beds:** 1 per 369 persons. **Physicians:** 1 per 6,495 persons. **Infant mortality** (per 1,000 live births, 1992): 107.

**Education:** (1991): **Literacy:** 45%. **Major International Organizations:** UN (FAO, IMF, WHO). **Embassy:** 2222 S St. NW 20008; 332-6416.

Laos became a French protectorate in 1893, but regained independence as a constitutional monarchy July 19, 1949.

Conflicts among neutralist, communist and conservative factions created a chaotic political situation. Armed conflict increased after 1960.

The 3 factions formed a coalition government in June 1962, with neutralist Prince Souvanna Phouma as premier. A 14-nation conference in Geneva signed agreements, 1962, guaranteeing neutrality and independence. By 1964 the Pathet Lao had withdrawn from the coalition, and, with aid from N. Vietnamese troops, renewed sporadic attacks. U.S. planes bombed the Ho Chi Minh trail, supply line from N. Vietnam to communist forces in Laos and S. Vietnam.

In 1970 the U.S. stepped up air support and military aid. After Pathet Lao military gains, Souvanna Phouma in May 1975 ordered government troops to cease fighting; the Pathet Lao took control. A Lao People's Democratic Republic was proclaimed Dec. 3, 1975.

# Latvia

## Republic of Latvia

### Latvijas Republika

**People: Population** (1992 est.): 2,728,000. **Pop density:** 109 per sq. mi. **Urban** (1991): 71%. **Language:** Latvian. **Religion:** Mostly Evangelical Lutheran. **Ethnic groups:** Latvian 54%, Russian 33%.

**Geography: Area:** 24,900 sq. mi., slightly larger than W. Va. **Neighbors:** Estonia & Baltic Sea on N., Baltic Sea on W., Lithuania & Belarus on S., Russia on E. **Capital:** Riga. **Cities** (1991): Riga 910,000.

**Government: Type:** Republic. **Head of state:** Anatolijs Gorbunovs. **Head of government:** Prime Min. Ivars Godmanis. **Local divisions:** 26 districts, 56 towns, 37 urban settlements.

**Economy: Industries:** Electric railway passenger cars, paper. **Chief crops:** oats, barley, potatoes. **Livestock** (1989): cattle 1.5 mln. **Arable land:** 27%. **Electricity prod.** (1991): 6.5 bln. kWh. **Labor force:** 16% agric. & forestry; 41% ind. & comm.

**Finance: Monetary unit:** Latvian ruble. **Imports** (1990): $9.0 bln. **Exports** (1990): $239 mln.

**Transport: Railroads: Length** (1991): 1,489 mi. **Motor vehicles:** in use (1990): 271,000 passenger cars, 14,000 comm. vehicles. **Civil aviation** (1990): 3.7 bln. passenger-km; 1 airport.

**Communications: Telephones:** 1 per 3.7 persons. **Newspaper circ.** (1990): 1,637 per 1,000 pop.

**Health: Life expectancy at birth** (1992): 64 male, 75 female. **Births** (per 1,000 pop. 1992): 15. **Deaths** (per 1,000 pop. 1992): 12. **Hospital beds:** 1 per 60 persons. **Physicians:** 1 per 200 persons. **Infant mortality rates** (per 1,000 live births 1992): 19.

**Transport: Motor vehicles:** in use (1988): 241,000 passenger cars. **Chief port:** Riga.

**Communications: Television sets** (1990): 1.2 per household, **Radios:** 1.4 per household. **Telephones:** 1 per 4.3 persons.

Prior to 1918, Latvia was occupied by the Russians and Germans. It was an independent republic, 1918-39. The Aug. 1939 Soviet-German agreement assigned it to the Soviet sphere of influence. It was officially accepted as part of the USSR on Aug. 5, 1940. It was overrun by the German army, but retaken in 1945. It attempted to establish independence 1990.

During an abortive Soviet coup, Latvia declared independence, Aug. 21, 1991. The Soviet Union recognized Latvia's independence in Sept. 1991.

# Lebanon

### Republic of Lebanon

### al-Jumhouriya al-Lubnaniya

**People: Population** (1992 est.): 3,439,000. **Age distrib. (%):** 0–14: 37.0; 15–59: 55.1; 60+: 7.9. **Pop. density:** 856 per sq. mi. **Urban** (1990): 84%. **Ethnic groups:** Arab 95%, Armenian 4%, Palestinian 9%. **Languages:** Arabic (official), French. **Religions:** Moslem 75%; Christian 25%.

**Geography: Area:** 4,015 sq. mi., smaller than Connecticut. **Location:** On Eastern end of Mediterranean Sea. **Neighbors:** Syria on E Israel on S. **Topography:** There is a narrow coastal strip, and 2 mountain ranges running N-S enclosing the fertile Beqaa Valley. The Litani R. runs S through the valley, turning W to empty into the Mediterranean. **Capital:** Beirut. **Cities** (1991 est.): Beirut 1,100,000; Tripoli 240,000.

**Government: Type:** Republic. **Head of state:** Pres. Elias Hrawi; in office: Nov. 24, 1989. **Head of government:** Prime Min. Rafiq al-Hariri; in office: Oct. 31, 1992. **Local divisions:** 5 governorates. **Defense:** 8.2% of GDP (1992).

**Economy: Industries:** Trade, food products, textiles, cement, oil products. **Chief crops:** Fruits, olives, tobacco, grapes, vegetables, grains. **Minerals:** Iron. **Arable land:** 21%. **Livestock** (1991): goats: 400,000; sheep: 205,000. **Electricity prod.** (1991): 3.8 bln. kWh. **Labor force:** 11% agric.; 79% ind., comm., services.

**Finance: Monetary unit:** Pound (Aug. 1993: 1,728 = $1 US). **Gross domestic product** (1991): $4.8 bln. **Per capita GDP:** $1,400. **Imports** (1990): $1.9 bln.; partners: It. 15%, Fr. 10%, U.S. 6%. **Exports** (1990): $700 mln.; partners: Saudi Ar. 16%, Jor. 6%, Kuw. 8%. **National budget** (1991): $1.3 bln. expenditures. **International reserves less gold** (Mar. 1993): $1.2 bln. **Gold:** 9.22 mln. oz t.

**Transport: Motor vehicles:** in use (1985): 300,000 passenger cars, 50,000 comm. vehicles. **Civil aviation** (1990): 1.5 bln. passenger-km. **Chief ports:** Beirut, Tripoli, Sidon.

**Communications: Television sets:** 1 per 3.4 persons. **Radios:** 1 per 1.3 persons. **Telephones:** 1 per 18.4 persons. **Daily newspaper circ.** (1986): 211 per 1,000 pop.

**Health: Life expectancy at birth** (1992): 66 male; 71 female. **Births** (per 1,000 pop. 1992): 28. **Deaths** (per 1,000 pop. 1992): 7. **Natural increase:** 2.1%. **Hospital beds:** 1 per 263 persons. **Physicians:** 1 per 771 persons. **Infant mortality** (per 1,000 live births 1992): 43.

**Education:** (1991): **Literacy:** 75%. **Years compulsory:** 5; attendance 93%.

**Major International Organizations:** UN (IMF, ILO, WHO). **Embassy:** 2560 28th St. NW 20008; 939-6300.

Formed from 5 former Turkish Empire districts, Lebanon became an independent state Sept. 1, 1920, administered under French mandate 1920-41. French troops withdrew in 1946.

Under the 1943 National Covenant, all public positions were divided among the various religious communities, with Christians in the majority. By the 1970s, Moslems became the majority and demanded a larger political and economic role.

U.S. Marines intervened, May-Oct. 1958, during a Syrian-aided revolt. Continued raids against Israeli civilians, 1970-75, brought Israeli attacks against guerrilla camps and villages. Is-

raeli troops occupied S. Lebanon, March 1978, and again in Apr. 1980.

An estimated 60,000 were killed and billions of dollars in damage inflicted in a 1975-76 civil war. Palestinian units and leftist Moslems fought against the Maronite militia, the Phalange, and other Christians. Several Arab countries provided political and arms support to the various factions, while Israel aided Christian forces. Up to 15,000 Syrian troops intervened in 1976, and fought Palestinian groups. Arab League troops from several nations tried to impose a cease-fire.

Clashes between Syrian troops and Christian forces erupted, Apr. 1, 1981, bringing to an end the cease-fire. By Apr. 22, fighting had also broken out between two Moslem factions. In July, Israeli air raids on Beirut killed or wounded some 800 persons.

Israeli forces invaded Lebanon June 6, 1982, in a coordinated land, sea, and air attack aimed at crushing strongholds of the Palestine Liberation Organization (PLO). Israeli and Syrian forces engaged in the Bekaa Valley. By June 14, Israeli troops had encircled Beirut. On Aug. 21, the PLO evacuated west Beirut following massive Israeli bombings of the city. Israeli troops entered west Beirut following the Sept. 14 assassination of newly elected Lebanese Pres. Bashir Gemayel. On Sept. 16, Lebanese Christian troops entered 2 refugee camps and massacred hundreds of Palestinian refugees. Israeli troops withdrew from Lebanon in June 1985.

In 1983, terrorist bombings became a way of life in Beirut as some 50 people were killed in an explosion at the U.S. Embassy, Apr. 18; 241 U.S. servicemen and 58 French soldiers died in separate Moslem suicide attacks, Oct. 23.

On Apr. 26, 1984, pro-Syrian Rashid Karami was appointed premier. The appointment failed to end virtual civil war in Beirut between Christian forces and Druse and Shiite Moslem militias. There was heavy fighting between Shiite militiamen and Palestinian guerrillas in May 1985. In June, Beirut Airport was the scene of a hostage crisis where Shiite terrorists held U.S. citizens for 17 days. Fierce artillery duels between Christian east Beirut and Moslem west Beirut, Mar.-Apr. 1989, left some 200 dead and 700 wounded.

Kidnapping of foreign nationals by Islamic militants became common in the 1980s. U.S., British, French, and Soviet citizens were victims. All were released by 1992.

A treaty signed May 22, 1991, between Lebanon and Syria recognized Lebanon as a separate and independent state for the first time since the 2 countries gained independence in 1943.

Israeli forces conducted air raids and artillery strikes against guerrilla bases and villages in S Lebanon, causing over 200,000 to flee their homes July 25-29, 1993.

# Lesotho

### Kingdom of Lesotho

**People: Population** (1992 est.): 1,848,000. **Age distrib. (%):** 0–14: 42.3; 15–59: 52.2; 60+: 5.7. **Pop. density:** 157 per sq. mi. **Ethnic groups:** Sotho 99%. **Languages:** English, Sotho (both official). **Religions:** Roman Catholic 38%, Protestant 42%.

**Geography: Area:** 11,716 sq. mi., slightly larger than Maryland. **Location:** In Southern Africa. **Neighbors:** Completely surrounded by Republic of South Africa. **Topography:** Landlocked and mountainous, with altitudes ranging from 5,000 to 11,000 ft. **Capital:** Maseru. **Cities** (1990 est.): Maseru 109,000.

**Government: Type:** Parliamentary democracy & constitutional monarchy. **Head of state:** King Letsie 3d; in office: Nov. 12, 1990. **Head of government:** Prime Min. Ntsu Mokhehle; in office: Apr. 1, 1993. **Local divisions:** 10 districts. **Defense:** 8.6% of GDP (1990).

**Economy: Industries:** Food processing. **Chief crops:** Corn, grains, peas, beans. **Other resources:** Diamonds. **Arable land:** 13%. **Labor force:** 40% agric.

**Finance: Monetary unit:** Maloti (Mar. 1993: 1.00 = $.31 US). **Gross domestic product** (1990): $420 mln. **Per capita GDP** (1990): $240. **Imports** (1990): $600 mln.; partners: Mostly So. Afr. **Exports** (1990): $60 mln.; partners: Mostly So. Afr. **National budget** (1991): $288 mln.

**Transport: Motor vehicles:** in use (1987): 6,000 passenger cars, 15,000 comm. vehicles.

**Communications: Radios:** 1 per 5 persons. **Daily newspaper circ.** (1990): 5 per 1,000 pop.

**Health: Life expectancy at birth** (1992): 60 male; 63 female. **Births** (per 1,000 pop. 1992): 35. **Deaths** (per 1,000 pop. 1992):

10. **Natural increase:** 2.5%. **Hospital beds:** 1 per 672 persons. **Physicians:** 1 per 15,728 persons. **Infant mortality** (per 1,000 live births 1992): 74.

**Education** (1990): **Literacy:** 59%.

**Major International Organizations:** UN (IMF, UNESCO, WHO), OAU.

**Embassy:** 2511 Massachusetts Ave. NW 20008; 797-5533.

Lesotho (once called Basutoland) became a British protectorate in 1868 when Chief Moshesh sought protection against the Boers. Independence came Oct. 4, 1966. Elections were suspended in 1970. Most of Lesotho's GNP is provided by citizens working in S. Africa. Livestock raising is the chief industry; diamonds are the chief export.

S. Africa imposed a blockade, Jan. 1, 1986, because of Lesotho's giving sanctuary to rebel groups fighting to overthrow the S. African Government. The blockade sparked a Jan. 20 military coup, and was lifted, Jan. 25, when the new leaders agreed to expel the rebels.

In 1990, King Moshoeshoe was sent into exile by the military government. In Mar. 1993, Ntsu Mokhehle, a civilian, was elected prime minister ending 23 years of military rule.

## Liberia

### Republic of Liberia

**People: Population** (1992 est.): 2,462,000. **Age distrib. (%):** 0–14: 46.8; 15–59: 48.3; 60+: 4.9. **Pop. density:** 64 per sq. mi. **Urban** (1990): 46%. **Ethnic groups:** Americo-Liberians 5%, indigenous tribes 95% **Languages:** English (official), tribal dialects. **Religions:** Moslem 20%, Christian 10%, traditional beliefs 70%.

**Geography: Area:** 38,250 sq. mi., slightly smaller than Pennsylvania. **Location:** On SW coast of W. Africa. **Neighbors:** Sierra Leone on W, Guinea on N, Côte d'Ivoire on E. **Topography:** Marshy Atlantic coastline rises to low mountains and plateaus in the forested interior; 6 major rivers flow in parallel courses to the ocean. **Capital:** Monrovia. **Cities** (1987 est.): Monrovia 400,000.

**Government: Type:** Civilian republic. **Head of state:** Pres. Amos Sawyer, act.; in office: Nov. 22, 1990. **Local divisions:** 13 counties. **Defense:** 3.8% of GDP (1987).

**Economy: Industries:** Food processing, mining. **Chief crops:** Rice, cassava, coffee, cocoa, sugar. **Minerals:** Iron, diamonds, gold. **Other resources:** Rubber, timber. **Arable land:** 1%. **Fish catch** (1990): 16,000 metric tons. **Electricity prod.** (1991): 750 mln. kWh. **Labor force:** 82% agric.

**Finance: Monetary unit:** Dollar (May 1993: 1.00 = $1 US). **Gross national product** (1989): $1.0 bln. **Per capita GNP** (1989): $440. **Imports** (1989): $394 mln.; partners: U.S. 32%, W. Ger. 10%, Jap. 6%, Neth. 7%. **Exports** (1989): $505 mln.; partners: W. Ger. 31%, U.S. 20%, It. 14%, Fr. 9%. **National budget** (1989): $435 mln. **International reserves less gold** (Feb. 1991): $7,000. **Consumer prices** (change in 1990): 5.8%.

**Transport: Motor vehicles:** in use (1990): 8,000 passenger cars, 4,000 comm. vehicles. **Chief ports:** Monrovia, Buchanan, Greenville.

**Communications: Television sets:** 1 per 60 persons. **Radios:** 1 per 4.4 persons. **Telephones:** 1 per 278 persons. **Daily newspaper circ.** (1990): 11 per 1,000 pop.

**Health: Life expectancy at birth** (1992): 54 male; 59 female. **Births** (per 1,000 pop. 1992): 45. **Deaths** (per 1,000 pop. 1992): 13. **Natural increase:** 3%. **Hospital beds** (1981): 3,000. **Physicians** (1981): 236. **Infant mortality** (per 1,000 live births 1992): 119.

**Education** (1990): **Literacy:** 40%; 35% attend primary school.

**Major International Organizations:** UN and most specialized agencies, OAU.

**Embassy:** 5201 16th St. NW 20011; 723-0437.

Liberia was founded in 1822 by U.S. black freedmen who settled at Monrovia with the aid of colonization societies. It became a republic July 26, 1847, with a constitution modeled on that of the U.S. Descendants of freedmen dominated politics.

Charging rampant corruption, an Army Redemption Council of enlisted men staged a bloody predawn coup, April 12, 1980, in which Pres. Tolbert was killed and replaced as head of state by Sgt. Samuel Doe. Doe was chosen president in a disputed election, and survived a subsequent coup, in 1985.

A civil war began Dec. 1989. Rebel forces seeking to depose Pres. Doe made major territorial gains and advanced on the capital, June 1990. In Sept., Doe was captured and put to death. A cease-fire was declared Feb. 13, 1991. More than half of the nation's population became refugees as a result of the civil war.

## Libya

### Socialist People's Libyan Arab Jamahiriya

### al-Jamahiriyah al-Arabiya al-Libya al-Shabiya al-Ishtirakiya

**People: Population:** (1992 est.): 4,485,000. **Age distrib. (%):** 0–14: 45.0; 15–59: 51.2; 60+: 3.8. **Pop. density:** 6 per sq. mi. **Urban** (1990): 70%. **Ethnic groups:** Arab-Berber 97%. **Languages:** Arabic. **Religions:** Sunni Moslem 97%.

**Geography: Area:** 679,359 sq. mi., larger than Alaska. **Location:** On Mediterranean coast of N. Africa. **Neighbors:** Tunisia, Algeria on W, Niger, Chad on S, Sudan, Egypt on E. **Topography:** Desert and semidesert regions cover 92% of the land, with low mountains in N, higher mountains in S, and a narrow coastal zone. **Capital:** Tripoli. **Cities** (1988 est.): Tripoli 591,000.

**Government: Type:** Islamic Arabic Socialist "Mass-State." **Head of state:** Col. Muammar al-Qaddafi; b. Sept. 1942; in office: Sept. 1969. **Head of government:** Premier Abu Zaid Umar Dourda; in office: Oct. 7, 1990. **Local divisions:** 25 municipalities. **Defense:** 11.1% of GNP (1987).

**Economy: Industries:** Carpets, textiles, petroleum. **Chief crops:** Dates, olives, citrus and other fruits, grapes, wheat. **Minerals:** Gypsum, oil, gas. **Crude oil reserves** (1987): 22 bln. bbls. **Arable land:** 2%. **Livestock** (1991): sheep: 5.5 mln.; goats: 1.0 mln. **Electricity prod.** (1991): 13.6 bln. kWh. **Labor force:** 18% agric.; 31% ind.; 27% services; 24% govt.

**Finance: Monetary unit:** Dinar (Feb. 1993: 1.00 = $3.37 US). **Gross domestic product** (1990): $28.9 bln. **Per capita GDP:** $6,800. **Imports** (1990): $7.6 bln.; partners: It. 21%, W. Ger. 11%, Fr. 6%. **Exports** (1990): $11.0 bln.; partners: It. 57%, W. Ger. 27%, Sp. 13%. **National budget** (1989): $9.8 bln. expenditures. **International reserves less gold** (Mar. 1993): $6.1 bln. **Gold:** 3.6 mln. oz t.

**Transport: Motor vehicles:** in use (1989): 448,000 passenger cars, 322,000 comm. vehicles. **Chief ports:** Tripoli, Benghazi.

**Communications: Television sets:** 1 per 8 persons. **Radios:** 1 per 4 persons. **Daily newspaper circ.** (1990): 10 per 1,000 pop.

**Health: Life expectancy at birth** (1992): 66 male; 71 female. **Births** (per 1,000 pop. 1992): 36. **Deaths** (per 1,000 pop. 1992): 6. **Natural increase:** 3.0%. **Hospital beds** (1982): 16,051. **Physicians** (1982): 5,200. **Infant mortality** (per 1,000 live births 1992): 60.

**Education** (1991): **Literacy:** 64%. **Years compulsory:** 7; **Attendance:** 90%.

**Major International Organizations:** UN, Arab League, OAU, OPEC.

First settled by Berbers, Libya was ruled by Carthage, Rome, and Vandals, the Ottomans, Italy from 1912, and Britain and France after WW II. It became an independent constitutional monarchy Jan. 2, 1952. In 1969 a junta lead by Col. Muammar al-Qaddafi seized power.

In the mid-1970s, Libya helped arm violent revolutionary groups in Egypt and Sudan, and had aided terrorists of various nationalities.

Libya and Egypt fought several air and land battles along their border in July, 1977. Chad charged Libya with military occupation of its uranium-rich northern region in 1977. Libyan troops were driven from their last major stronghold by Chad forces in 1987, leaving over $1 billion in military equipment behind.

On Jan. 7, 1986, the U.S. imposed economic sanctions against Libya, ordered all Americans to leave that country and froze all Libyan assets in the U.S. The U.S. commenced flight operations over the Gulf of Sidra, Jan. 27, and a U.S. Navy task force began conducting exercises in the Gulf, Mar. 23. When Libya fired antiaircraft missiles at American warplanes, the U.S. responded by sinking 2 Libyan ships and bombing a missile installation in Libya. The U.S. withdrew from the Gulf, Mar. 27.

The U.S. accused Libyan leader Qaddafi of having ordered the April 5 bombing of a West Berlin discotheque which killed 3, including a U.S. serviceman. After failing to get their European allies to join them in imposing economic sanctions against Libya, the U.S. sent warplanes to attack terrorist-related targets in Tripoli and Benghazi, Libya, Apr. 14.

The UN imposed limited sanctions, Apr. 15, 1992, for Libya's failure to extradite 2 intelligence agents linked to the 1988 bombing of Pan American World Airways Flight 103 over Lockerbie, Scotland, and 4 others linked to an airplane bombing over Niger.

# Liechtenstein
## Principality of Liechtenstein
## Fürstentum Liechtenstein

**People: Population** (1992 est.): 28,642. **Age distrib. (%):** 0–14: 20.1; 15–59: 66.3; 60+: 11.6. **Pop. density:** 461 per sq. mi. **Ethnic groups:** Alemannic 95%, Italian 5%. **Languages:** German (official), Alemannic dialect. **Religions:** Roman Catholic 87%, Protestant 8%.

**Geography: Area:** 62 sq. mi., the size of Washington, D.C. **Location:** In the Alps. **Neighbors:** Switzerland on W, Austria on E. **Topography:** The Rhine Valley occupies one-third of the country, the Alps cover the rest. **Capital:** Vaduz. **Cities** (1991 cen.): Vaduz 4,874, Schaan 4,930.

**Government: Type:** Hereditary constitutional monarchy. **Head of state:** Prince Hans Adam; in office: Nov. 13, 1989. **Head of government:** Hans Brunhart; b. Mar. 28, 1945; in office: Apr. 26, 1978. **Local divisions:** 2 districts, 11 communities.

**Economy: Industries:** Machines, instruments, chemicals, furniture, ceramics. **Arable land:** 25%. **Labor force:** 54% industry, trade and building; 41% services; 4% agric., fishing, forestry.

**Finance: Monetary unit:** Swiss Franc. **Gross domestic product** (1990): $630 mln.

**Communications: Radios:** 1 per 2.9 persons. **Telephones:** 1 per 1.0 persons. **Daily newspaper circ.** (1990): 598 per 1,000 pop.

**Health: Births** (per 1,000 pop. 1992): 13. **Deaths** (per 1,000 pop. 1992): 7. **Natural increase:** .6%. **Infant mortality** (per 1,000 live births 1992): 5.

**Education** (1992): **Literacy:** 100%. **Years compulsory** 9; attendance 100%.

Liechtenstein became sovereign in 1866. Austria administered Liechtenstein's ports up to 1920; Switzerland has administered its postal services since 1921. Liechtenstein is united with Switzerland by a customs and monetary union. Taxes are low; many international corporations have headquarters there. Foreign workers comprise a third of the population.

The 1986 general elections were the first in which women were allowed to vote.

# Lithuania
## Republic of Lithuania
## Lietuvos Respublika

**People: Population** (1992 est.): 3,788,000. **Pop. density:** 150 per sq. mi. **Urban** (1992): 68%. **Ethnic groups:** Lithuanian 80%, Russian 9%, Polish 7%. **Religion:** mostly Roman Catholic.

**Geography: Area:** 25,170 sq. mi. **Neighbors:** Latvia on N., Belarus on E., S., Poland, Russia, & Baltic Sea on W. **Capital:** Vilnius. **Cities** (1992): Vilnius 597,000; Kaunas 433,000.

**Government: Type:** Republic. **Head of state:** Pres. Algirdas Brazauskas; in office: Nov. 25, 1992. **Head of government:** Prime Min. Bronislovas Lubys; in office: Dec. 2, 1992.

**Economy: Industries:** Engineering, shipbuilding. **Chief crops:** grain, potatoes, vegetables. **Arable land:** 49%. **Livestock** (1991): cattle: 2.4 mln., pigs: 2.7 mln. **Electricity prod.** (1991): 25 mln. kWh. **Labor force:** 29% agric., 25% ind.

**Finance: Monetary unit:** Lit.

**Transport: Railroads** (1989): **Length:** 1,951 mi. **Civil aviation:** (1991): 2.3 mln. passenger km.; 3 airports. **Chief Port:** Klaipeda.

**Communications: Television sets:** 1 per 2.9 persons. **Radios:** 1 per 1.2 persons. **Telephones:** 1 per 4.5 persons.

**Health: Life expectancy at birth:** (1992); 66 male, 76 female. **Births** (per 1,000 pop. 1992): 15. **Deaths** (per 1,000 pop. 1992): 11. **Hospital beds:** 1 per 81 persons. **Physicians:** 1 per 262 persons. **Infant mortality rate** (per 1,000 live births): 18.

**Major international organizations:** UN

Lithuania, was occupied by the German Army, 1914-18. It was annexed by the USSR, but the Soviets were overthrown, 1919. Lithuania was a democratic republic until 1926 when the regime was ousted by a coup. In 1939, the Soviet-German treaty assigned most of Lithuania to the Soviet sphere of influence. It became part of the USSR Aug. 3, 1940. Lithuania formally declared its independence from the Soviet Union Mar. 11, 1990. Soviet forces began large-scale maneuvers Mar. 18; border controls were tightened Mar. 21. The Soviets cut off oil and gas supplies Apr. 19.

Soviet troops killed 15 protesters in Vilnius, Jan. 13, 1991, in an attempted coup. During an abortive Soviet coup in Aug., the Western nations recognized Lithuania's independence, which was recognized by the Soviet Union in Sept. 1991.

In 1992 elections, former communists won an absolute majority in the legislature.

# Luxembourg
## Grand Duchy of Luxembourg
## Grand-Duché de Luxembourg

**People: Population:** (1992 est.): 392,000. **Age distrib. (%):** 0–14: 17.3; 15–59: 64.5; 60+: 18.2. **Pop. density:** 400 per sq. mi. **Urban** (1991): 91%. **Ethnic groups:** Mixture of French and Germans predominate. **Languages:** French, German (both official), Luxembourgish. **Religions:** Roman Catholic 97%.

**Geography: Area:** 998 sq. mi., smaller than Rhode Island. **Location:** In W. Europe. **Neighbors:** Belgium on W, France on S, Germany on E. **Topography:** Heavy forests (Ardennes) cover N, S is a low, open plateau. **Capital:** Luxembourg. **Cities** (1991 est.): Luxembourg 75,000.

**Government: Type:** Constitutional monarchy. **Head of state:** Grand Duke Jean; b. Jan. 5, 1921; in office: Nov. 12, 1964. **Head of government:** Prime Min. Jacques Santer; in office: July 21, 1984. **Local divisions:** 3 districts. **Defense:** 1.2% of GDP (1991).

**Economy: Industries:** Steel, chemicals, beer, tires, tobacco, metal products, cement. **Chief crops:** Corn, wine. **Minerals:** Iron. **Arable land:** 25%. **Electricity prod.** (1991): 1.1 bln. kWh. **Labor force:** 1% agric.; 42% ind. & comm.; 45% services.

**Finance: Monetary unit:** Franc (Mar. 1993: 33.24 = $1 US). **Gross domestic product** (1991): $7.8 bln. **Per capita GDP:** $20,200. **Note:** trade and tourism data included in Belgian statistics. **Tourism** (1989): $286 mln. receipts. **Consumer prices** (change in 1992): 3.2%.

**Transport: Railroads** (1991): **Length:** 169 mi. **Motor vehicles:** in use (1991): 192,000 passenger cars, 18,000 comm. vehicles.

**Communications: Television sets:** 1 per 4.0 persons. **Radios:** 1 per 1.6 persons. **Telephones:** 1 per 2.3 persons. **Daily newspaper circ.** (1990): 340 per 1,000 pop.

**Health: Life expectancy at birth** (1992): 73 male; 80 female. **Births** (per 1,000 pop. 1992): 12. **Deaths** (per 1,000 pop. 1992): 11. **Hospital beds:** 1 per 85 persons. **Physicians:** 1 per 498 persons. **Infant mortality** (per 1,000 live births 1992): 7.

**Education** (1989): **Literacy:** 100%. **Years compulsory** 9; attendance 100%.

**Major International Organizations:** UN, OECD, EC, NATO. **Embassy:** 2200 Massachusetts Ave. NW 20008; 265-4171.

Luxembourg, founded about 963, was ruled by Burgundy, Spain, Austria, and France from 1448 to 1815. It left the Germanic Confederation in 1866. Overrun by Germany in 2 world wars, Luxembourg ended its neutrality in 1948, when a customs union with Belgium and Netherlands was adopted.

# Macedonia

## Republic of Macedonia

**People: Population** (1992 est.): 2,050,000. **Pop. density:** 206 per sq. mi. **Ethnic groups:** Macedonian 68%, Albanian 20%. **Languages:** Macedonian, Albanian, Bulgarian, Greek. **Religions:** mostly Eastern Orthodox; Moslem.

**Geography: Area:** 9,928 sq. mi., slightly larger than Vermont. **Location:** In SE Europe. **Neighbors:** Bulgaria on E., Greece on S, Albania on W, Yugoslavia on N. **Capital:** Skopje. **Cities** (1991 met. est.): Skopje 563,000, Tetova 180,000.

**Government: Type:** Republic. **Head of state:** Pres. Kiro Gliforov. **Head of government:** Prime Min. Branko Crenkovski. **Local divisions:** 30 districts.

**Economy: Industries:** Steel, cement. **Chief crops:** Wheat, cotton, tobacco. **Livestock** (1992): 2.2 mln. sheep. **Electricity prod.** (1990): 5.7 bln. kWh.

**Finance: Monetary unit:** Denar **Gross domestic product** (1990): $4.8 bln. **Per capita GDP:** $2,399.

**Transport: Railroads** (1990): **Length:** 431 mi. **Vehicles:** in use (1990): 230,000 passenger cars, 23,000 comm. vehicles. **Civil aviation:** 1 airport.

**Communications: Television sets:** 1 per 5.2 persons. **Radios:** 1 per 4.5 persons. **Telephones:** 1 per 5.7 persons. **Newspaper circ.** (1990): 26 per 1,000 pop.

**Health: Hospital beds:** 1 per 171 persons. **Physicians:** 1 per 464 persons. **Infant mortality** (per 1,000 live births 1990): 35.3.

**Education** (1990): **Literacy:** 90%.

**Major International Organizations:** UN.

Macedonia, as part of a larger region also called Macedonia, was ruled by Moslem Turks from 1389 to 1912, when native Greeks, Bulgarians, and Slavs won independence. Serbia received the largest part of the territory with the rest going to Greece and Bulgaria. The area was incorporated in Serbia in 1918.

Macedonia declared its independence from Yugoslavia, Sept. 8, 1991. At the request of Greece, the U.S. and most European nations have not recognized Macedonia as an independent nation until it changes its name and flag, which it has refused to do.

Macedonia was admitted to the UN under a provisional name in 1993. A UN force, which included 300 U.S. troops, was deployed in Macedonia in 1993 to deter the warring factions in Bosnia from carrying their dispute into other areas of the Balkans.

# Madagascar

## Democratic Republic of Madagascar
## Repoblika Demokratika Malagasy

**People: Population** (1992 est.): 12,596,000. **Pop. density:** 55 per sq. mi. **Urban** (1990): 22%. **Ethnic groups:** 18 Malayan-Indonesian tribes (Merina 26%), with Arab and African presence. **Languages:** Malagasy, French (both official). **Religions:** animists 52%, Christian 41%, Moslem 7%.

**Geography: Area:** 226,657 sq. mi., slightly smaller than Texas. **Location:** In the Indian O., off the SE coast of Africa. **Neighbors:** Comoro Is., Mozambique (across Mozambique Channel). **Topography:** Humid coastal strip in the E, fertile valleys in the mountainous center plateau region, and a wider coastal strip on the W. **Capital:** Antananarivo. **Cities** (1990 est.): Antananarivo 802,000.

**Government: Type:** Republic. **Head of state:** Pres. Albert Zafy; in office: Feb. 10, 1993. **Head of government:** Prime Min. Guy Razanamasy; in office: Aug. 8, 1991. **Local divisions:** 6 provinces. **Defense:** 2.2% of GDP (1989).

**Economy: Industries:** Food processing, textiles. **Chief crops:** Coffee (over 50% of exports), cloves, vanilla, rice, sugar, sisal, tobacco, peanuts. **Minerals:** Chromium, graphite, coal, bauxite. **Arable land:** 5%. **Livestock** (1990): cattle: 10.4 mln.; pigs: 1.3 mln. **Fish catch** (1990): 99,000 metric tons. **Electricity prod.** (1991): 450 mln. kWh. **Labor force:** 90% agric.

**Finance: Monetary unit:** Franc (Mar. 1993: 1,920 = $1 US). **Gross domestic product** (1991): $2.4 bln. **Per capita GDP:** $200. **Imports** (1991): $442 mln.; partners: Fr. 32%, U.S. 15%. **Exports** (1991): $305 mln.; partners: Fr. 34%, U.S. 14%. **Tourism** (1990): $28 mln. receipts. **National budget** (1990): $525

mln. **International reserves less gold** (Jan. 1993): $89 mln. **Consumer prices** (change in 1992): 14.5%.

**Transport: Railroads** (1990): **Length:** 655 mi. **Motor vehicles:** in use (1990): 46,000 passenger cars, 33,000 comm. vehicles. **Civil aviation:** (1990): 512 mln. passenger-km; 50 airports with scheduled flights. **Chief ports:** Tamatave, Diego-Suarez, Majunga, Tulear.

**Communications: Television sets:** 1 per 95 persons. **Radios:** 1 per 8 persons. **Telephones in use:** 1 per 239 persons.

**Health: Life expectancy at birth** (1992): 51 male; 55 female. **Births** (per 1,000 pop. 1991): 47. **Deaths** (per 1,000 pop. 1991): 15. **Natural increase:** 3.2%. **Hospital beds** (1982): 20,800. **Physicians** (1982): 940. **Infant mortality** (per 1,000 live births 1992): 93.

**Education** (1987): **Literacy:** 53%. **Years compulsory:** 5; attendance 83%.

**Major International Organizations:** UN (GATT, WHO, IMF), OAU.

**Embassy:** 2374 Massachusetts Ave. NW 20008; 265-5525.

Madagascar was settled 2,000 years ago by Malayan-Indonesian people, whose descendants still predominate. A unified kingdom ruled the 18th and 19th centuries. The island became a French protectorate, 1885, and a colony 1896. Independence came June 26, 1960.

Discontent with inflation and French domination led to a coup in 1972. The new regime nationalized French-owned financial interests, closed French bases and a U.S. space tracking station, and obtained Chinese aid. The government conducted a program of arrests, expulsion of foreigners, and repression of strikes, 1979.

In 1990, Madagascar ended a ban on multiparty politics that had been in place since 1975. Albert Zafy was elected president of Madagascar in 1993, ending the 17-year rule of Didier Ratsiraka, whose rule was marked by a blend of socialism and authoritarianism.

# Malawi

## Republic of Malawi

**People: Population** (1992 est.): 9,605,000. **Age distrib. (%):** 0–14: 47.8; 15–59: 48.0; 60+: 4.2. **Pop. density:** 209 per sq. mi. **Urban** (1990): 15%. **Ethnic groups:** Chewa, 90%, Nyanja, Lomwe, other Bantu tribes. **Languages:** English, Chewa (both official), Lomwe, Yao. **Religions:** Christian 75%, Moslem 20%.

**Geography: Area:** 45,747 sq. mi., the size of Pennsylvania. **Location:** In SE Africa. **Neighbors:** Zambia on W, Mozambique on SE, Tanzania on N. **Topography:** Malawi stretches 560 mi. N-S along Lake Malawi (Lake Nyasa), most of which belongs to Malawi. High plateaus and mountains line the Rift Valley the length of the nation. **Capital:** Lilongwe. **Cities** (1987 est.): Blantyre 402,000; Lilongwe 220,000.

**Government: Type:** One-party state. **Head of state:** Pres. Hastings Kamuzu Banda, b. May 14, 1906; in office: July 6, 1966. **Local divisions:** 24 districts. **Defense:** 1.6% of GDP (1989).

**Economy: Industries:** Textiles, sugar, cement. **Chief crops:** Tea, tobacco, sugar, coffee. **Other resources:** Rubber. **Arable land:** 25%. **Fish catch** (1990): 68 metric tons. **Electricity prod.** (1991): 535 mln. kWh. **Labor force:** 43% agric.; 23% ind. and comm.; 17% services.

**Finance: Monetary unit:** Kwacha (Mar. 1993: 4.40 = $1 US). **Gross domestic product** (1991): $1.9 bln. **Per capita GDP:** $200. **Imports** (1992): $720 mln.; partners: So. Afr. 29%, UK 24%, Jap. 6%. **Exports** (1992): $392 mln.; partners: UK 27%, S. Afr. 8%., Ger. 10%. **National budget** (1991): $510 mln. **International reserves less gold** (Mar. 1993): $45 mln. **Gold:** 13,000 oz t. **Consumer prices** (change in 1992): 12.4%.

**Transport: Railroads** (1987): **Length:** 495 mi. **Motor vehicles:** in use (1990): 16,000 passenger cars, 17,000 comm. vehicles. **Civil aviation** (1990) 86 mln. passenger-km; 5 airports with scheduled flights.

**Communications: Radios:** 1 per 4.3 persons. **Telephones:** 1 per 176 persons. **Daily newspaper circ.** (1991): 3 per 1,000 pop.

**Health: Life expectancy at birth** (1992): 48 male; 51 female. **Births** (per 1,000 pop. 1992): 52. **Deaths** (per 1,000 pop. 1992): 18. **Natural increase:** 3.4%. **Hospital beds:** 1 per 627 persons. **Physicians:** 1 per 27,094 persons. **Infant mortality** (per 1,000 live births 1992): 136.

**Education** (1989): **Literacy:** 25%. About 45% attend school.
**Major International Organizations:** UN (World Bank, IMF), OAU, Commonwealth of Nations.
**Embassy:** 2408 Massachusetts Ave. NW 20008; 797-1007.

Bantus came in the 16th century, Arab slavers in the 19th. The area became the British protectorate Nyasaland, in 1891. It became independent July 6, 1964, and a republic in 1966.

## Malaysia

**People: Population** (1992 est.): 18,410,000. **Age distrib. (%):** 0–14: 37.8; 15–59: 56.5; 60+: 5.7. **Pop. density:** 144 per sq. mi. **Urban** (1985): 38%. **Ethnic groups:** Malays 59%, Chinese 32%, Indian 9%. **Languages:** Malay (official), English, Chinese, Indian languages. **Religions:** Moslem, Hindu, Buddhist, Confucian, Taoist, local religions.

**Geography: Area:** 127,316 sq. mi., slightly larger than New Mexico. **Location:** On the SE tip of Asia, plus the N. coast of the island of Borneo. **Neighbors:** Thailand on N, Indonesia on S. **Topography:** Most of W. Malaysia is covered by tropical jungle, including the central mountain range that runs N-S through the peninsula. The western coast is marshy, the eastern, sandy. E. Malaysia has a wide, swampy coastal plain, with interior jungles and mountains. **Capital:** Kuala Lumpur. **Cities** (1991 est.): Kuala Lumpur 1 mln.

**Government: Type:** Federal parliamentary democracy with a constitutional monarch. **Head of state:** Paramount Ruler Sultan Azlan Shah; in office: Apr. 26, 1989. **Head of government:** Prime Min. Datuk Seri Mahathir bin Mohamad; b. Dec. 20, 1925; in office: July 16, 1981. **Local divisions:** 13 states and 2 federal terr. **Defense:** 5.0% of GDP (1992).

**Economy: Industries:** Rubber goods, steel, electronics. **Chief crops:** Palm oil, copra, rice, pepper. **Minerals:** Tin (35% world output), iron. **Crude oil reserves** (1987): 3.2 bln. bbls. **Other resources:** Rubber (35% world output). **Arable land:** 13%. **Livestock** (1990): pigs: 2.2 mln. **Fish catch** (1990): 604,000 metric tons. **Electricity prod.** (1991): 16.5 bln. kWh. **Labor force:** 18% agric.; 11% tourism & trade; 10% govt.

**Finance: Monetary unit:** Ringgit (June 1993: 2.58 = $1 US). **Gross domestic product** (1991): $48 bln. **Per capita GDP:** $2,670. **Imports** (1991): $38.7 bln.; partners: Jap. 21%, U.S. 18%, Sing. 14%. **Exports** (1991): $35.4 bln.; partners: Jap. 20%, U.S. 17% Sing. 19%, Neth. 6%. **Tourism** (1990): $1.6 bln. receipts. **National budget** (1991): $11.8 bln. **International reserves less gold** (Mar. 1993): $19.4 bln. **Gold:** 2.22 mln. oz t. **Consumer prices** (change in 1992): 4.4%.

**Transport: Railroads** (incl. Singapore) (1991): **Length:** 1,381 mi. **Motor vehicles:** in use (1990): 1.8 mln. passenger cars, 407,000 comm. vehicles. **Civil aviation:** (1990): 11.9 bln. passenger-km; 38 airports with scheduled flights. **Chief ports:** George Town, Kelang, Melaka, Kuching.

**Communications: Television sets:** 1 per 9 persons. **Radios:** 1 per 2.4 persons. **Telephones:** 1 per 8 persons. **Daily newspaper circ.** (1989): 145 per 1,000 pop.

**Health: Life expectancy at birth** (1992): 66 male; 71 female. **Births** (per 1,000 pop. 1992): 30. **Deaths** (per 1,000 pop. 1992): 6. **Natural increase:** 2.4%. **Hospital beds:** 1 per 457 persons. **Physicians:** 1 per 2,638 persons. **Infant mortality** (per 1,000 live births 1992): 27.

**Education** (1991): **Literacy:** 80%; 96% attend primary school, 65% attend secondary.
**Major International Organizations:** UN (World Bank, IMF, GATT), ASEAN.
**Embassy:** 2401 Massachusetts Ave. NW 20008; 328-2700.

European traders appeared in the 16th century; Britain established control in 1867. Malaysia was created Sept. 16, 1963. It included Malaya (which had become independent in 1957 after the suppression of Communist rebels), plus the formerly-British Singapore, Sabah (N Borneo), and Sarawak (NW Borneo). Singapore was separated in 1965, in order to end tensions between Chinese, the majority in Singapore, and Malays in control of the Malaysian government.

A monarch is elected by a council of hereditary rulers of the Malayan states every 5 years.

Abundant natural resources have assured prosperity, and foreign investment has aided industrialization.

## Maldives
### Republic of Maldives
### Divehi Jumhuriya

**People: Population** (1992 est.): 226,000. **Age distrib. (%):** 0–14: 44.4; 15–59: 51.7; 60+: 3.9. **Pop. density:** 1,965 per sq. mi. **Urban** (1990): 26%. **Ethnic groups:** Sinhalese, Dravidian, Arab mixture. **Languages:** Divehi (Sinhalese dialect). **Religions:** Sunni Moslem.

**Geography: Area:** 115 sq. mi., twice the size of Washington, D.C. **Location:** In the Indian O. SW of India. **Neighbors:** Nearest is India on N. **Topography:** 19 atolls with 1,087 islands, about 200 inhabited. None of the islands are over 5 sq. mi. in area, and all are nearly flat. **Capital:** Male. **Cities** (1991 est.): Male 55,000.

**Government: Type:** Republic. **Head of state:** Pres. Maumoon Abdul Gayoom; b. Dec. 29, 1939; in office: Nov. 11, 1978. **Local divisions:** 19 districts.

**Economy: Industries:** Fish processing, tourism. **Chief crops:** Coconuts, fruit, millet. **Other resources:** Shells. **Arable land:** 10%. **Fish catch** (1990): 76,000 metric tons. **Electricity prod.** (1991): 11.0 mln. kWh. **Labor force:** 80% fishing, agriculture, & manufacturing.

**Finance: Monetary unit:** Rufiyaa (Mar. 1993: 10.48 = $1 US). **Gross domestic product** (1990): $174 mln. **Per capita GDP:** $770. **Imports** (1990): $128 mln.; partners: Sing., Ger., Sri Lan. **Exports** (1990): $52 mln.; partners: U.S., U.K.. **Tourism** (1990): $142 mln. receipts.

**Transport: Chief ports:** Male Atoll.

**Communications: Radios:** 1 per 8 persons. **Telephones:** 1 per 60 persons.

**Health: Life expectancy at birth** (1992): 62 male; 64 female. **Births** (per 1,000 pop. 1992): 45. **Deaths** (per 1,000 pop. 1992): 8. **Natural increase:** 3.7%. **Infant morality** (per 1,000 live births 1992): 61.

**Education** (1989): **Literacy:** 93%. Only 6% of those aged 11-15 attend school.
**Major International Organizations:** UN.

The islands had been a British protectorate since 1887. The country became independent July 26, 1965. Long a sultanate, the Maldives became a republic in 1968. Natural resources and tourism are being developed; however, it remains one of the world's poorest countries.

## Mali
### Republic of Mali
### République du Mali

**People: Population** (1992 est.): 8,641,000. **Age distrib. (%):** 0–14: 46.0; 15–59: 49.4; 60+: 4.6. **Pop. density:** 18 per sq. mi. **Urban** (1992): 25%. **Ethnic groups:** Mande (Bambara, Malinke, Sarakole) 50%, Peul 17%, Voltaic 12%, Songhai 6%, Tuareg and Moor, 5%. **Languages:** French (official), Bambara, Senufo. **Religions:** Moslem 90%.

**Geography: Area:** 478,764 sq. mi., about the size of Texas and California combined. **Location:** In the interior of W. Africa. **Neighbors:** Mauritania, Senegal on W, Guinea, Côte d'Ivoire, Burkina Faso on S, Niger on E, Algeria on N. **Topography:** A landlocked grassy plain in the upper basins of the Senegal and Niger rivers, extending N into the Sahara. **Capital:** Bamako. **Cities** (1989 est.): Bamako (met.) 800,000.

**Government: Type:** Republic. **Head of state:** Pres. Alpha Oumar Konare; in office: June 8, 1992. **Local divisions:** 8 regions. **Defense:** 2.4% of GDP (1989).

**Economy: Chief crops:** Millet, rice, peanuts, cotton. **Other resources:** Bauxite, iron, gold. **Arable land:** 2%. **Livestock** (1989): sheep: 5.7 mln.; cattle: 4.8 mln. **Fish catch** (1990): 71,000 metric tons. **Electricity prod.** (1991): 750 mln. kWh. **Labor force:** 72% agric.; 12% ind. & comm.; 16% services.

**Finance: Monetary unit:** Franc (Mar. 1993: 273 = $1 US). **Gross domestic product** (1990): $2.2 bln. **Per capita GDP:** $265. **Imports** (1989): $513 mln.; partners: Fr. 22%, Ivory Coast 25%. **Exports** (1989): $285 mln.; partners: Belg.-Lux. 25%, Fr. 15%. **Tourism** (1990): $37 mln. receipts. **National budget** (1989): $519 mln. expenditures. **International reserves less gold** (Feb. 1993): $307 mln. **Gold:** 19,000 oz t.

**Transport: Railroads** (1991): **Length:** 401 mi. **Motor vehicles:** in use (1987): 29,000 passenger cars, 7,500 comm. vehicles.

**Communications: Radios:** 1 per 53 persons. **Telephones:** 1 per 730 persons.

**Health: Life expectancy at birth** (1992): 43 male; 47 female. **Births** (per 1,000 pop. 1992): 51. **Deaths** (per 1,000 pop. 1992): 21. **Natural increase:** 3.0%. **Hospital beds** (1983): 4,215. **Physicians** (1983): 283. **Infant mortality** (per 1,000 live births 1992): 110.

**Education** (1991): **Literacy:** 25%. **Attendance:** 21% attend primary school.

**Major International Organizations:** UN and all of its specialized agencies, OAU, EC.

**Embassy:** 2130 R St. NW 20008; 332-2249.

Until the 15th century the area was part of the great Mali Empire. Timbuktu was a center of Islamic study. French rule was secured, 1898. The Sudanese Rep. and Senegal became independent as the Mali Federation June 20, 1960, but Senegal withdrew, and the Sudanese Rep. was renamed Mali.

Mali signed economic agreements with France and, in 1963, with Senegal. In 1968, a coup ended the socialist regime. Famine struck in 1973-74, killing as many as 100,000 people. Drought conditions returned in the 1980s.

The military, Mar. 26, 1991, overthrew the government of Pres. Amadou Toumani Traore, who had been in power since 1968. A multiparty democracy was promised.

## Malta

### Repubblika Ta' Malta

**People: Population** (1992 est.): 354,000. **Age distrib. (%):** 0–14: 23.6; 15–59: 61.8; 60+: 14.6. **Pop. density:** 2,901 per sq. mi. **Ethnic groups:** Italian, Arab, French. **Languages:** Maltese, English (both official). **Religions:** Mainly Roman Catholic.

**Geography: Area:** 122 sq. mi., twice the size of Washington, D.C. **Location:** In center of Mediterranean Sea. **Neighbors:** Nearest is Italy on N. **Topography:** Island of Malta is 95 sq. mi.; other islands in the group: Gozo, 26 sq. mi., Comino, 1 sq. mi. The coastline is heavily indented. Low hills cover the interior. **Capital:** Valletta. **Cities** (1990 est.): Birkirkara 21,000, Qormi 19,000.

**Government: Type:** Parliamentary democracy. **Head of state:** Pres. Censu Tabone; in office: Apr. 4, 1989. **Head of government:** Prime Min. Edward Fenech-Adami; b. Feb. 7, 1934; in office: May 12, 1987. **Local Divisions:** 13 electoral districts. **Defense:** 1.3% of GNP (1990).

**Economy: Industries:** Textiles, machinery, food & beverages, tourism. **Chief crops:** Potatoes, tomatoes. **Arable land:** 38%. **Electricity prod.** (1991): $1.1 bln. kWh. **Labor force:** 2% agric.; 24% manuf.; 43% services; 29% gov.

**Finance: Monetary unit:** Maltese Lera (Mar. 1993: 1.00 = $2.64 US). **Gross domestic product** (1990): $2.5 bln. **Per capita GDP:** $7,000. **Imports** (1991): $2.1 bln.; partners: UK 16%, It. 30%, Ger. 14%, U.S. 4%. **Exports** (1991): $1.2 bln.; partners: Ger. 23%, UK 11%, It. 30%. **Tourism** (1989): receipts: $475 mln. **National budget** (1992): $1.3 bln. expenditures. **International reserves less gold** (Mar. 1992): 1.1 bln. **Gold:** 126,000 oz t. **Consumer prices** (change in 1992): 2.2%.

**Transport: Motor vehicles:** in use (1990): 104,000 passenger cars, 19,000 comm. vehicles. **Civil aviation** (1990): 903 mln. passenger-km; 1 airport. **Chief ports:** Valletta.

**Communications: Television sets:** 1 per 2.6 persons. **Radios:** 1 per 3.3 persons. **Telephones in use:** 1 per 2.1 persons.

**Health: Life expectancy at birth** (1992): 74 male; 79 female. **Births** (per 1,000 pop. 1992): 14. **Deaths** (per 1,000 pop. 1992): 8. **Natural increase:** .6%. **Hospital beds:** 1 per 108 persons. **Physicians:** 1 per 444 persons. **Infant mortality** (per 1,000 live births 1992): 7.

**Education** (1988): **Literacy:** 90%. **Compulsory:** until age 16. **Major International Organizations:** UN (GATT, WHO, IMF), Commonwealth of Nations.

**Embassy:** 2017 Connecticut Ave. NW 20008; 462-3611.

Malta was ruled by Phoenicians, Romans, Arabs, Normans, the Knights of Malta, France, and Britain (since 1814). It became independent Sept. 21, 1964. Malta became a republic in 1974. The withdrawal of the last of its sailors, Apr. 1, 1979, ended 179 years of British military presence on the island.

## Marshall Islands

### Republic of the Marshall Islands

**People: Population** (1992 est.): 50,000. **Pop. density:** 714 per sq. mi. **Ethnic groups:** Marshallese 97%. **Languages:** English (official), Marshallese, Japanese. **Religions:** Protestant 90%.

**Geography: Area:** 70 sq. mi. **Location:** In central Pacific Ocean; comprised of 2 800-mi-long parallel chains of coral atolls. **Capital:** Majuro.

**Government: Type:** Republic. **Head of state:** Pres. Amata Kabua.

**Economy:** Agriculture and tourism are mainstays of the economy. **Electricity prod.** (1990): 80 mln. kwh.

**Finance: Monetary unit:** U.S. dollar. **Gross domestic product** (1989): $63 mln. **Per capita GDP** (1989): $1,500. **Imports** (1988): 34 mln. **Exports** (1988): $2 mln.

**Transport:** 24 airports with scheduled flights. **Port:** Majuro.

**Communications: Telephones:** 1 per 53 persons.

**Health: Life expectancy at birth** (1992): 61 male; 64 female. **Births** (per 1,000 pop. 1992): 47. **Deaths** (per 1,000 pop. 1992): 8. **Infant mortality** (per 1,000 live births 1992): 53.

**Education** (1990): **Literacy:** 86%.

**Major International Organizations:** UN.

The Marshall Islands were a German possession until World War 1 and were administered by Japan between the World Wars. After WW2, they were administered as part of the UN Trust Territory of the Pacific Islands by the U.S.

The Marshall Islands secured international recognition as an independent nation on Sept. 17, 1991.

## Mauritania

### Islamic Republic of Mauritania

### République Islamique de Mauritanie

**People: Population** (1992 est.): 2,059,000. **Age distrib. (%):** 0–14: 46.4; 15–59: 49.0; 60+: 4.6. **Pop. density:** 5 per sq. mi. **Urban** (1987): 34%. **Ethnic groups:** Arab-Berber 80%, Negroes 20%. **Languages:** Arabic, French (both official), Hassanya Arabic (national). **Religion:** Nearly 100% Moslem.

**Geography: Area:** 419,212 sq. mi., the size of Texas and California combined. **Location:** In W. Africa. **Neighbors:** Morocco on N, Algeria, Mali on E, Senegal on S. **Topography:** The fertile Senegal R. valley in the S gives way to a wide central region of sandy plains and scrub trees. The N is arid and extends into the Sahara. **Capital:** Nouakchott. **Cities** (1992 est.): Nouakchott 550,000; Nouadhibou 70,000; Kaedi 74,000.

**Government: Type:** Islamic republic. **Head of state:** Pres. Maaouya Ould Sidi Ahmed Taya; in office: Apr. 18, 1992. **Head of government:** Prime Min. Sidi Mohamed Ould Boubacar; in office: Apr. 18, 1992 **Local divisions:** 12 regions, one capital district. **Defense:** 4.2% of GDP (1990).

**Economy: Chief crops:** Dates, grain. **Industries:** iron mining. **Minerals:** Iron, ore, gypsum. **Livestock** (1988): sheep: 4.1 mln.; goats: 3.9 mln.; cattle: 1.2 mln. **Fish catch** (1991): 92,000 metric tons. **Electricity prod.** (1991): 136 mln. kWh. **Labor force:** 47% agric., 14% ind. & comm., 29% services.

**Finance: Monetary unit:** Ouguiya (Mar. 1993: 116 = $1 US). **Gross domestic product** (1990): $1.0 bln. **Per capita GDP:** $520. **Imports** (1990): $639 mln.; partners: EC 60%. **Exports** (1990): $437 mln.; partners: EC 43%, Jap. 27%. **International reserves less gold** (Feb. 1993): $35 mln.

**Transport: Motor vehicles:** in use (1990): 10,000 passenger cars, 5,000 comm. vehicles. **Chief ports:** Nouakchott, Nouadhibou.

**Communications: Radios:** 1 per 7.8 persons. **Television sets:** 1 per 1,100 persons.

**Health: Life expectancy at birth** (1992): 44 male; 50 female. **Births** (per 1,000 pop. 1992): 49. **Deaths** (per 1,000 pop. 1992): 19. **Natural increase:** 3.0%. **Hospital beds:** 1 per 1,217 persons. **Physicians:** 1 per 10,128 persons. **Infant mortality** (per 1,000 live births 1992): 89.

**Education** (1991): **Literacy:** 30%. **Attendance:** 79% in primary school, 18% in secondary school.

**Major International Organizations:** UN (GATT, IMF, WHO), OAU, Arab League.

**Embassy:** 2129 Leroy Pl. NW 20008; 232-5700.

Mauritania was a French protectorate from 1903. It became independent Nov. 28, 1960. It annexed the south of former Spanish Sahara in 1976. Saharan guerrillas stepped up attacks in 1977; 8,000 Moroccan troops and French bomber raids aided the government. Mauritania signed a peace treaty with the Polisario Front, 1980, resumed diplomatic relations with Algeria while breaking a defense treaty with Morocco, and renounced sovereignty over its share of former Spanish Sahara. Morocco annexed the territory.

## Mauritius

**People: Population** (1992 est.): 1,081,900. **Age distrib. (%):** 0–14: 36.3; 15–59: 57.2; 60+: 6.4. **Pop. density:** 1,313 per sq. mi. **Urban** (1990): 41%. **Ethnic groups:** Indo-Mauritian 68%, Creole 27%, others. **Languages:** English (official), French Creole, Bhojpuri. **Religions:** Hindu 51%, Christian 30%, Moslem 16%.

**Geography: Area:** 720 sq. mi., about the size of Rhode Island. **Location:** In the Indian O., 500 mi. E of Madagascar. **Neighbors:** Nearest is Madagascar on W. **Topography:** A volcanic island nearly surrounded by coral reefs. A central plateau is encircled by mountain peaks. **Capital:** Port Louis. **Cities** (1991 est.): Port Louis 142,000.

**Government: Type:** Republic. **Head of state:** Pres. Cassam Uteem; in office: June 30, 1992. **Head of government:** Prime Min. Aneerood Jugnauth; in office: June 12, 1982. **Local divisions:** 9 districts, 3 dependencies.

**Economy: Industries:** Tourism, food processing. **Chief crops:** Sugar cane, tea. **Arable land:** 54%. **Electricity prod.** (1990): 423 mln. kWh. **Labor force:** 17% agric. & fishing; 32% manuf.; 14% govt. services.

**Finance: Monetary unit:** Rupee (Mar. 1993: 17.17 = $1 US). **Gross domestic product** (1991): $2.5 bln. **Per capita GDP:** $2,300. **Imports** (1991): $1.5 bln.; partners: UK 9%, Fr. 12%, So. Afr. 9%. **Exports** (1991): $1.1 bln.; partners: UK 50%, Fr. 22%, U.S. 8%. **Tourists** (1992): $264 mln. receipts. **National budget** (1989): $540 mln. **International reserves less gold** (Feb. 1993): $859 mln. **Gold:** 61,000 oz t. **Consumer prices** (change in 1992): 4.6%.

**Transport: Motor vehicles:** in use (1990): 29,000 passenger cars, 6,000 comm. vehicles. **Chief ports:** Port Louis.

**Communications: Television sets:** 1 per 8.2 persons. **Radios:** 1 per 4.2 persons. **Telephones:** 1 per 15 persons. **Daily newspaper circ.** (1989): 75 per 1,000 pop.

**Health: Life expectancy at birth** (1992): 66 male; 74 female. **Births** (per 1,000 pop. 1992): 19. **Deaths** (per 1,000 pop. 1992): 6. **Natural increase:** 1.3%. **Hospital beds:** 1 per 364 persons. **Physicians:** 1 per 1,118 persons. **Infant mortality** (per 1,000 live births 1992): 22.

**Education** (1989): **Literacy:** 94%. **Attendance:** almost all children attend school.

**Major International Organizations:** UN and all of its specialized agencies, OAU, Commonwealth of Nations.

**Embassy:** 4301 Connecticut Ave. NW 20008; 244-1491.

Mauritius was uninhabited when settled in 1638 by the Dutch, who introduced sugar cane. France took over in 1721, bringing African slaves. Britain ruled from 1810 to Mar. 12, 1968, bringing Indian workers for the sugar plantations.

Mauritius formally severed its association with the British crown Mar. 12, 1992.

## Mexico
### United Mexican States
### Estados Unidos Mexicanos

**People: Population** (1992 est.): 92,380,000. **Age distrib. (%):** 0–14: 36.5; 15–59: 57.8; 60+: 5.7. **Pop. density:** 121 per sq. mi. **Urban** (1990): 72%. **Ethnic groups:** Mestizo 60%, American Indian 29%, Caucasian 9%. **Languages:** Spanish (official), Ameridian languages. **Religions:** Roman Catholic 97%.

**Geography: Area:** 761,604 sq. mi., three times the size of Texas. **Location:** In southern N. America. **Neighbors:** U.S. on N, Guatemala, Belize on S. **Topography:** The Sierra Madre Occidental Mts. run NW-SE near the west coast; the Sierra Madre Oriental Mts., run near the Gulf of Mexico. They join S of Mexico City. Between the 2 ranges lies the dry central plateau, 5,000 to 8,000 ft. alt., rising toward the S, with temperate vegetation. Coastal lowlands are tropical. About 45% of land is arid. **Capital:** Mexico City. **Cities** (1991 est.): Mexico City (metro) 20 mln.; Guadalajara (metro) 3 mln.; Monterrey (metro) 2.7 mln.

**Government: Type:** Federal republic. **Head of state:** Pres. Carlos Salinas de Gortari; b. Apr. 3, 1948; in office: Dec. 1, 1988. **Local divisions:** Federal district and 31 states. **Defense:** 1.0% of GDP (1988).

**Economy: Industries:** Steel, chemicals, electric goods, textiles, rubber, petroleum, tourism. **Chief crops:** Cotton, coffee, wheat, rice, sugar cane, vegetables, corn. **Minerals:** Silver, lead, zinc, gold, oil, natural gas. **Crude oil reserves** (1991): 51 bln. barrels. **Arable land:** 13%. **Livestock** (1991): cattle: 31 mln.; pigs: 15 mln.; sheep: 6 mln. **Fish catch** (1991): 1.1 mln. metric tons. **Electricity prod.** (1991): 114 bln. kWh. **Crude steel prod.** (1991): 7.8 mln. metric tons. **Labor force:** 24% agric.; 19% manuf.; 31% services; 14% comm.

**Finance: Monetary unit:** New peso (July 1993: 3,122 = $1 US). **Gross domestic product** (1991): $289 bln. **Per capita GDP:** $3,200. **Imports** (1991): $36.7 bln.; partners: U.S. 69%, EC 13%. **Exports** (1991): $27 bln.; partners: U.S. 68%, EC 14%. **Tourism** (1992): receipts: $6.6 bln. **National budget** (1990): $47.9 bln. expenditures. **International reserves less gold** (Jan. 1993): $18.9 bln. **Gold:** 685,000 oz t. **Consumer prices** (change in 1992): 15.5%.

**Transport: Railroads** (1992): **Length:** 16,363 mi. **Motor vehicles:** in use (1990): 6.8 mln. passenger cars, 3.0 mln. comm. **Civil aviation** (1991): 17.4 bln. passenger-km; 54 airports. **Chief ports:** Veracruz, Tampico, Mazatlan, Coatzacoalcos.

**Communications: Television sets:** 1 in 6.6 persons. **Radios:** 1 in 5.1 persons. **Telephones:** 1 in 7.6 persons. **Daily newspaper circ.** (1986): 142 per 1,000 pop.

**Health: Life expectancy at birth** (1992): 69 male; 76 female. **Births** (per 1,000 pop. 1992): 29. **Deaths** (per 1,000 pop. 1992): 5. **Natural increase:** 2.4%. **Hospital beds:** 1 per 1,298 persons. **Physicians:** 1 per 600 persons. **Infant mortality** (per 1,000 live births 1992): 29.

**Education** (1993): **Literacy:** 90%. **Years compulsory:** 8.

**Major International Organizations:** UN (IMF, GATT), OAS.

**Embassy:** 1911 Pennsylvania Ave. NW 20006; 728-1600.

Mexico was the site of advanced Indian civilizations. The Mayas, an agricultural people, moved up from Yucatan, built immense stone pyramids, invented a calendar. The Toltecs were overcome by the Aztecs, who founded Tenochtitlan 1325 AD, now Mexico City. Hernando Cortes, Spanish conquistador, destroyed the Aztec empire, 1519-1521.

After 3 centuries of Spanish rule the people rose, under Fr. Miguel Hidalgo y Costilla, 1810, Fr. Morelos y Payon, 1812, and Gen. Agustin Iturbide, who made himself emperor as Agustin I, 1821. A republic was declared in 1823.

Mexican territory extended into the present American Southwest and California until Texas revolted and established a republic in 1836; the Mexican legislature refused recognition but was unable to enforce its authority there. After numerous clashes, the U.S.-Mexican War, 1846-48, resulted in the loss by Mexico of the lands north of the Rio Grande.

French arms supported an Austrian archduke on the throne of Mexico as Maximilian I, 1864-67, but pressure from the U.S. forced France to withdraw. A dictatorial rule by Porfirio Diaz, president 1877-80, 1884-1911, led to fighting by rival forces until the new constitution of Feb. 5, 1917 provided social reform. Since then Mexico has developed large-scale programs of social security, labor protection, and school improvement. A constitutional provision requires management to share profits with labor.

The Institutional Revolutionary Party has been dominant in politics since 1929. Radical opposition, including some guerrilla activity, has been contained by strong measures.

The presidency of Luis Echeverria, 1970-76, was marked by a more leftist foreign policy and domestic rhetoric. Some land redistribution begun in 1976 was reversed under the succeeding administration.

Some gains in agriculture, industry, and social services have been achieved. The land is rich, but the rugged topography and lack of sufficient rainfall are major obstacles. Crops and farm prices are controlled, as are export and import. Economic prospects brightened with the discovery of vast oil reserves, perhaps the world's greatest. But much of the work force is jobless or underemployed.

Inflation and the drop in world oil prices caused economic problems in the 1980s. The peso was devalued and private banks were nationalized to restore financial stability.

Mexico reached agreement with the U.S. and Canada on the North American Free Trade Agreement Aug. 12, 1992. The agreement required ratification by the 3 governments.

## Micronesia
### Federated States of Micronesia

**People: Population:** (1992 est.) 111,000. **Pop. density:** 411 per sq. mi. **Ethnic groups:** Trukese 41%, Pohnpeian 26%. **Languages:** English (official). **Religions:** Mostly Christian.

**Geography: Area:** 270 sq. mi. The Federation consists of 607 islands in the W. Pacific Ocean. **Capital:** Palikir.

**Government: Type:** Republic. **Head of state:** Bailey Olter; in office: May 21, 1991. **Local divisions:** 4 states.

**Economy: Chief crops:** Tropical fruits, vegetables, coconuts. **Finance: Monetary unit:** U.S. dollar. **Gross national product (1989):** $150 million. **Imports** (1988): 67 mln. **Exports** (1988): 3 mln.

**Transport:** 4 airports with scheduled flights.

**Communications: Television sets:** 1 per 16 persons. **Radios:** 1 per 1.6 persons. **Telephones:** 1 per 61 persons.

**Health: Life expectancy at birth** (1992): 65 male; 69 female. **Births** (per 1,000 pop. 1992): 34. **Deaths** (per 1,000 pop. 1992): 5. **Hospital beds:** 1 per 280 persons. **Physicians:** 1 per 2,540 persons. **Infant mortality** (per 1,000 live births 1992): 39.

**Education** (1991): **Literacy:** 90%.

**Major International Organizations:** UN.

The Federated States of Micronesia, formerly known as the Caroline Islands, was ruled successively by Spain, Germany, Japan, and the U.S. It was internationally recognized as an independent nation Sept. 17, 1991.

## Moldova
### Republic of Moldova
### Republica Moldoveneasca

**People: Population** (1992 est.): 4,458,000. **Pop. density:** 342 per sq. mi. **Urban** (1991): **48%. Ethnic groups:** Moldovan 65%, Ukrainian 14%, Russian 13%. **Languages:** Romanian, Ukrainian. **Religion:** E. Orthodox 98%.

**Geography: Area:** 13,012 sq. mi. **Neighbors:** Romania on W, Ukraine on N, E, and S. **Capital:** Kishinev. **Cities** (1991): Kishinev 753,000, Tiraspol 186,000.

**Government: Type:** Republic. **Head of state:** Pres. Mircea Snegur. **Head of government:** Prime Min. Andre Sang Heli; in office: July 1, 1992.

**Economy: Industries:** Canning, wine making, textiles. **Chief crops:** Grain, grapes. **Minerals:** Lignite, gypsum. **Livestock** (1989): cattle: 1.1 mln., pigs: 1.9 mln., sheep: 1.3 mln. **Electricity prod.** (1991): 13 mln. kWh.

**Finance: Monetary unit:** Ruble.

**Transport: Railroads** (1991): **Length:** 715 mi. **Motor vehicles:** in use (1990): 177,000 passenger cars. **Civil aviation** (1990): 2.3 bln. passenger-km. 1 airport.

**Communications: Telephones:** 1 per 8 persons. **Newspaper circ.** (1990): 71 per 1,000 pop.

**Health: Life expectancy at birth** (1992): 64 male; 71 female. **Births** (per 1,000 pop. 1992): 19. **Deaths** (per 1,000 pop. 1992): 10. **Hospital beds:** 1 per 77 persons. **Physicians:** 1 per 251 persons. **Infant mortality** (per 1,000 live births 1992): 35.

**Major International Organizations:** UN, CIS.

In 1918, Romania annexed all of Bessarabia which Russia had acquired from Turkey in 1812 by the Treaty of Bucharest. In 1924, the Soviet Union established the Moldavian Autonomous Soviet Socialist Republic on the eastern bank of the Dniester. It was merged with the Romanian-speaking districts of Bessarabia in 1940 to form the Moldavian SSR.

During World War II, Romania, allied with Germany, occupied the area. It was recaptured by the USSR in 1944. Moldova declared independence Aug. 27, 1991. It became an independent state when the Soviet Union disbanded Dec. 26, 1991. Fighting erupted between Moldovan security forces and Slavic separat-

ists—ethnic Russians and ethnic Ukrainians—Mar. 1992. The Slavs feared that Moldovans, who are Romanian in language and culture, would merge with neighboring Romania.

## Monaco
### Principality of Monaco

**People: Population** (1992 est.): 29,712. **Age distrib.** (%): 0–14: 12.7; 15–59: 56.3 60+: 30.7. **Pop. density:** 49,520 per sq. mi. **Ethnic groups:** French 47%, Italian 16%, Monegasque 16%. **Languages:** French (official). **Religions:** Predominantly Roman Catholic.

**Geography: Area:** 0.6 sq. mi. **Location:** On the NW Mediterranean coast. **Neighbors:** France to W, N, E. **Topography:** Monaco-Ville sits atop a high promontory, the rest of the principality rises from the port up the hillside. **Capital:** Monaco.

**Government: Type:** Constitutional monarchy. **Head of state:** Prince Rainier III; b. May 31, 1923; in office: May 9, 1949. **Head of government:** Min. of State Jacques Dupont.

**Economy: Industries:** Tourism, gambling, chemicals, precision instruments, plastics.

**Finance: Monetary unit:** French franc or Monégasque franc. **Transport: Chief ports:** La Condamine.

**Communications: Television sets:** 17,000 in use (1984). **Telephones in use** (1984): 18,000.

**Health: Births** (per 1,000 pop. 1992): 7. **Deaths** (per 1,000 pop. 1992): 7. **Infant mortality** (per 1,000 live births 1992): 8.

**Education:** (1989): **Literacy:** 99%. **Years compulsory:** 10; attendance 99%.

**Major International Organizations:** UN.

An independent principality for over 300 years, Monaco has belonged to the House of Grimaldi since 1297 except during the French Revolution. It was placed under the protectorate of Sardinia in 1815, and under that of France, 1861. The Prince of Monaco was an absolute ruler until a 1911 constitution.

Monaco's fame as a tourist resort is widespread. It is noted for its mild climate and magnificent scenery. The area has been extended by land reclamation.

## Mongolia

**People: Population** (1992 est.): 2,305,000. **Pop. density:** 3 per sq. mi. **Urban** (1991): 58%. **Ethnic groups:** Mongol 90%. **Languages:** Mongolian (official). **Religion:** traditionally Lama Buddhism.

**Geography: Area:** 604,247 sq. mi., more than twice the size of Texas. **Location:** In E Central Asia. **Neighbors:** Russia N, China on S. **Topography:** Mostly a high plateau with mountains, salt lakes, and vast grasslands. Arid lands in the S are part of the Gobi Desert. **Capital:** Ulaanbaatar. **Cities** (1991 est.): Ulaanbaatar 575,000, Darhan 90,000.

**Government: Type:** In transition. **Head of state:** Pres. Punsalmaagiyn Ochirbat; b. 1942; in office: Mar. 21, 1990. **Head of government:** Prime Min. Puntsagiyn Jasray; in office: July 21, 1992. **Local divisions:** 18 provinces, 3 municipalities. **Defense:** 11.5% of GNP (1984).

**Economy: Industries:** Food processing, textiles, chemicals, cement. **Chief crops:** Grain. **Minerals:** Coal, tungsten, copper, molybdenum, gold, tin. **Arable land:** 1%. **Livestock** (1990): sheep: 14.8 mln.; cattle 2.2 mln. **Electricity prod.** (1991): 3.7 bln. kWh. **Labor force:** 52% agric.; 10% manuf.

**Finance: Monetary unit:** Tugrik (Jan. 1993: 120 = $1 US). **Gross domestic product** (1991): $2.1 bln. **Per capita GDP:** $900. **Imports** (1991): $360 mln.; partners: CIS 91%. **Exports** (1991): $279 mln.; partners: CIS 80%.

**Transport: Railroads** (1991): **Length:** 1,445 mi.

**Communications: Television sets:** 1 per 18 persons. **Radios:** 1 per 7.5 persons. **Telephones:** 1 per 32 persons. **Daily newspaper circ.** (1990): 106 per 1,000 pop.

**Health: Life expectancy at birth** (1992): 63 male; 68 female. **Births** (per 1,000 pop. 1992): 34. **Deaths** (per 1,000 pop. 1992): 8. **Natural increase:** 2.6%. **Hospital beds:** 1 per 79 persons. **Physicians:** 1 per 345 persons. **Infant mortality** (per 1,000 live births 1992): 47.

**Major International Organizations:** UN (ILO, WHO). **Education** (1990): **Literacy:** 89%.

One of the world's oldest countries, Mongolia reached the zenith of its power in the 13th century when Genghis Khan and his successors conquered all of China and extended their influence as far west as Hungary and Poland. In later centuries, the empire dissolved and Mongolia became a province of China.

With the advent of the 1911 Chinese revolution, Mongolia, with Russian backing, declared its independence. A Mongolian Communist regime was established July 11, 1921.

Mongolia has been changed from a nomadic culture to one of settled agriculture and growing industries with aid from the USSR and East European nations.

In 1990, the Mongolian Communist Party surrendered its monopoly on power. Free elections were held July 1990; the communists were victorious.

# Morocco
## Kingdom of Morocco
## al-Mamlaka al-Maghrebia

**People: Population** (1992 est.): 26,708,000. **Age distrib. (%):** 0–14: 41.2; 15–59: 53.7; 60+: 5.1. **Pop. density:** 154 per sq. mi. **Urban** (1992): 50%. **Ethnic groups:** Arab-Berber 99%. **Languages:** Arabic (official), Berber. **Religions:** Sunni Moslems 99%.

**Geography: Area:** 172,413 sq. mi., larger than California. **Location:** on NW coast of Africa. **Neighbors:** W. Sahara on S, Algeria on E. **Topography:** Consists of 5 natural regions: mountain ranges (Riff in the N, Middle Atlas, Upper Atlas, and Anti-Atlas); rich plains in the W; alluvial plains in SW; well-cultivated plateaus in the center; a pre-Sahara arid zone extending from SE. **Capital:** Rabat. **Cities** (1984): Casablanca 2,600,000; Rabat 556,000, Fes 852,000.

**Government: Type:** Constitutional monarchy. **Head of state:** King Hassan II; b. July 9, 1929; in office: Mar. 3, 1961. **Head of government:** Prime Min. Mohammed Karim Lamrani; in office: Aug. 11, 1992. **Local divisions:** 37 provinces, 5 municipalities. **Defense:** 4.2% of GDP (1992).

**Economy: Industries:** Carpets, clothing, leather goods, mining, tourism. **Chief crops:** Grain, fruits, dates, grapes. **Minerals:** Copper, cobalt, manganese, phosphates, lead, oil. **Crude oil reserves** (1980): 100 mln. bbls. **Arable land:** 18%. **Livestock** (1990): cattle: 3.5 mln.; sheep; 17 mln.; goats: 5.9 mln. **Fish catch** (1989): 551,000 metric tons. **Electricity prod.** (1991): 8.1 bln. kWh. **Labor force:** 50% agric., 26% services; 15% ind.

**Finance: Monetary unit:** Dirham (Mar. 1993: 9.09 = $1 US). **Gross domestic product** (1991): $27.3 bln. **Per capita GDP:** $1,060. **Imports** (1991): $6.0 bln.; partners: EC 53%, U.S. 11%. **Exports** (1991): $4.1 bln.; partners: EC 58%. **Tourism** (1990): $1.2 bln. receipts. **National budget** (1992): $7.7 bln. expenditures. **International reserves less gold** (Mar. 1993): $3.2 bln. **Gold:** 704,000 oz t. **Consumer prices** (change in 1992): 4.9%.

**Transport: Railroads** (1990): **Length:** 1,893 km. **Motor vehicles:** in use (1992): 666,000 passenger cars, 280,000 comm. vehicles. **Civil aviation** (1989): 2.7 bln. passenger-km; 15 airports. **Chief ports:** Tangier, Casablanca, Kenitra.

**Communications: Television sets:** 1 per 21 persons. **Radios:** 1 per 5.4 persons. **Telephones in use:** 1 per 62 persons. **Daily newspaper circ.** (1990): 15 per 1,000 pop.

**Health: Life expectancy at birth** (1992): 63 male; 67 female. **Births** (per 1,000 pop. 1992): 30. **Deaths** (per 1,000 pop. 1992): 8. **Natural increase:** 2.2%. **Hospital beds:** 1 per 959 persons. **Physicians:** 1 per 4,415 persons. **Infant mortality** (per 1,000 live births 1992): 56.

**Education** (1990): **Literacy:** 50%.

**Major International Organizations:** UN (ILO, IMF, WHO), OAU, Arab League.

**Embassy:** 1601 21st St. NW 20009; 462-7979.

Berbers were the original inhabitants, followed by Carthaginians and Romans. Arabs conquered in 683. In the 11th and 12th centuries, a Berber empire ruled all NW Africa and most of Spain from Morocco.

Part of Morocco came under Spanish rule in the 19th century; France controlled the rest in the early 20th. Tribal uprisings lasted from 1911 to 1933. The country became independent Mar. 2, 1956. Tangier, an internationalized seaport, was turned over to Morocco, 1956. Ifni, a Spanish enclave, was ceded in 1969.

Morocco annexed over 70,000 sq. mi. of phosphate-rich land Apr. 14, 1976, two-thirds of former Spanish Sahara, with the remainder annexed by Mauritania. Spain had withdrawn in Febru-

ary. Polisario, a guerrilla movement, proclaimed the region independent Feb. 27, and launched attacks with Algerian support. Morocco accepted U.S. military and economic aid. When Mauritania signed a treaty with the Polisario Front and gave up its portion of the former Spanish Sahara, Morocco occupied the area, 1980. Morocco accused Algeria of instigating Polisario attacks.

After years of bitter fighting, Morocco controlled the main urban areas, but the Polisario Front's guerrillas moved freely in the vast, sparsely populated deserts. The 2 sides signed a ceasefire agreement in 1990. The UN will conduct a referendum in Western Sahara on whether the territory should become independent or remain part of Morocco.

# Mozambique
## Republic of Mozambique
## República de Moçambique

**People: Population** (1992 est.): 15,469,000. **Age distrib. (%):** 0–14: 45.3; 15–59: 50.6; 60+: 4.1. **Pop. density:** 50 per sq. mi. **Ethnic groups:** Bantu tribes. **Languages:** Portuguese (official), Makua, Malawi, Shona, Tsonga. **Religions:** Traditional beliefs 60%, Christian 30%, Moslem 10%.

**Geography: Area:** 303,769 sq. mi., about the size of Texas. **Location:** On SE coast of Africa. **Neighbors:** Tanzania on N, Malawi, Zambia, Zimbabwe on W, South Africa, Swaziland on S. **Topography:** Coastal lowlands comprise nearly half the country with plateaus rising in steps to the mountains along the western border. **Capital:** Maputo. **Cities:** (1991 est.): Maputo 931,000, Beira 298,000.

**Government: Type:** Republic. **Head of state:** Pres. Joaquim Chissano; b. Oct. 22, 1939; in office: Oct. 19, 1986. **Head of Government:** Mario de Graca Machungo; in office: July 17, 1986. **Local divisions:** 10 provinces. **Defense:** 8.4% of GNP (1987).

**Economy: Industries:** Cement, alcohol, textiles. **Chief crops:** Cashews, cotton, sugar, copra, tea. **Minerals:** Coal, titanium. **Arable land:** 4%. **Livestock** (1991): cattle: 1.3 mln. **Fish catch** (1990): 35,000 metric tons. **Electricity prod.** (1991): 1.7 bln. kWh. **Labor force:** 85% agric., 9% ind. & comm., 2% services.

**Finance: Monetary unit:** Metical (Mar. 1993: 2,982 = $1 US). **Gross domestic product** (1991): $1.7 bln. **Per capita GDP:** $120. **Imports** (1990): $870 mln.; partners: So. Afr. 11%, U.S. 8%, USSR 12%, It. 10%. **Exports** (1990): $117 mln.; partners: Sp. 21%, U.S. 16%, Jap. 15%. **National budget** (1989): $208 mln.

**Transport: Railroads** (1990): Length: 2,033 mi. **Motor vehicles:** in use (1990): 87,000 passenger cars, 24,000 comm. vehicles. **Chief ports:** Maputo, Beira, Nacala, Quelimane.

**Communications: Television sets:** 1 per 418 persons. **Radios:** 1 per 29 persons. **Telephones:** 1 per 217 persons. **Daily newspaper circ.** (1991): 3 per 1,000 pop.

**Health: Life expectancy at birth** (1992): 46 male; 49 female. **Births** (per 1,000 pop. 1992): 46. **Deaths** (per 1,000 pop. 1992): 17. **Natural increase:** 2.9%. **Hospital beds:** 1 per 1,227 persons. **Physicians:** 1 per 43,536 persons. **Infant mortality** (per 1,000 live births 1992): 134.

**Education** (1989): **Literacy:** 14%.

**Major International Organization:** UN (IMF, World Bank), OAU.

The first Portuguese post on the Mozambique coast was established in 1505, on the trade route to the East. Mozambique became independent June 25, 1975, after a ten-year war against Portuguese colonial domination. The 1974 revolution in Portugal paved the way for the orderly transfer of power to Frelimo (Front for the Liberation of Mozambique). Frelimo took over local administration Sept. 20, 1974, over the opposition, in part violent, of some blacks and whites. The new government, led by Maoist Pres. Samora Machel, promised a gradual transition to a communist system. Private schools were closed, rural collective farms organized, and private homes nationalized. Economic problems included the emigration of most of the country's whites, a politically untenable economic dependence on white-ruled South Africa, and a large external debt.

In the 1980s, severe drought and civil war caused famine and heavy loss of life.

# Myanmar (Formerly Burma)

## Union of Myanmar

## Pyidaungzu Myanma Naingngandaw

**People: Population** (1992 est.): 42,642,000. **Age distrib.** (%): 0–14: 41.2; 15–59: 52.8; 60+: 6.0. **Pop. density:** 162 per sq. mi. **Urban** (1991): 25%. **Ethnic groups:** Burmans (related to Tibetans) 68%; Karen 4%, Shan 7%, Rakhine 3%. **Languages:** Burmese (official), Karen, Shan. **Religions:** Buddhist 85%; animist, Christian.

**Geography: Area:** 261,789 sq. mi., nearly as large as Texas. **Location:** Between S. and S.E. Asia, on Bay of Bengal. **Neighbors:** Bangladesh, India on W, China, Laos, Thailand on E. **Topography:** Mountains surround Myanmar on W, N, and E, and dense forests cover much of the nation. N-S rivers provide habitable valleys and communications, especially the Irrawaddy, navigable for 900 miles. The country has a tropical monsoon climate. **Capital:** Yangon. **Cities** (1983 est.): Yangon 2,458,712; Mandalay 458,000; Karbe ('73 cen.): 253,600; Moulmein 188,000.

**Government: Type:** Military. **Head of state and head of government:** Prime Min. Gen. Than Shwe; in office: Apr. 24, 1992. **Local divisions:** 7 states and 7 divisions. **Defense:** 3.0% of GDP (1989).

**Economy: Industries:** mining, textiles, footwear, petroleum, refining. **Chief crops:** Rice, sugarcane, peanuts, beans. **Minerals:** Oil, lead, silver, tin, tungsten, precious stones. **Crude oil reserves** (1985): 733 mln. bbls. **Other resources:** Rubber, teakwood. **Arable land:** 15%. **Livestock.** (1991): cattle: 9.3 mln.; pigs: 2.2 mln. **Fish catch** (1990): 743,000 metric tons. **Electricity prod.** (1991): 2.9 bln. kWh. **Labor force:** 66% agric.; 12% ind.

**Finance: Monetary unit:** Kyat (Mar. 1993: 6.19 = $1 US). **Gross domestic product** (1991): $22.2 bln. **Per capita GDP:** $530. **Imports** (1991): $1.1 bln.; partners: Jap. 50%, EC 20%. **Exports** (1991): $568 mln.; partners: SE Asian countries 30%; EC 12%. **Tourism** (1990): $5 mln. receipts. **National budget** (1991): $9.3 bln. **International reserves less gold** (Mar. 1993): $294 mln. **Gold:** 251,000 oz t. **Consumer prices** (change in 1992): 23.5%.

**Transport: Railroads** (1990): **Length: 1,949 mi. Motor vehicles:** in use (1989): 27,000 passenger cars, 42,000 comm. vehicles. **Civil aviation** (1988): 214 mln. passenger-km.; 21 airports with scheduled flights. **Chief ports:** Yangon, Bassein, Moulmein.

**Communications: Television sets:** 1 per 592 persons. **Radios:** 1 per 13 persons. **Telephones:** 1 per 501 persons. **Daily newspaper circ.** (1989): 14 per 1,000 pop.

**Health: Life expectancy at birth** (1992): 57 male; 61 female. **Births** (per 1,000 pop. 1992): 29. **Deaths** (per 1,000 pop. 1992): 10. **Natural increase:** 1.9%. **Hospital beds:** 1 per 1,602 persons. **Physicians:** 1 per 3,389 persons. **Infant mortality** (per 1,000 live births 1992): 68.

**Education** (1990): **Literacy:** 81%. **Years compulsory:** 4; **Attendance:** 84%.

**Major International Organizations:** UN (World Bank, IMF, GATT).

**Embassy:** 2300 S St. NW 20008; 332-9044.

The Burmese arrived from Tibet before the 9th century, displacing earlier cultures, and a Buddhist monarchy was established by the 11th. Burma was conquered by the Mongol dynasty of China in 1272, then ruled by Shans as a Chinese tributary, until the 16th century.

Britain subjugated Burma in 3 wars, 1824-84, and ruled the country as part of India until 1937, when it became self-governing. Independence outside the Commonwealth was achieved Jan. 4, 1948.

Gen. Ne Win dominated politics from 1962 to 1988, when he abdicated power, following waves of anti-government demonstrations. He led a Revolutionary Council which drove Indians from the civil service and Chinese from commerce. Socialization of the economy was advanced, isolation from foreign countries enforced.

In 1987 Burma, once the richest nation in SE Asia, was granted less developed country status by the UN. Following Ne Win's resignation, Sein Lwin and later Maung Maung, a civilian, took power but rioting and street violence continued. In Sept., Gen. Saw Maung, a close associate of Ne Win, seized power.

In 1989 the country's name was changed to Myanmar.

The first free, multiparty elections in 30 years took place May 27, 1990, with the main opposition party winning a decisive victory, but the military rulers refused to hand over power.

# Namibia

## Republic of Namibia

**People: Population** (1992 est.): 1,574,000. **Pop density:** 4 per sq. mi. **Urban** (1991): 33%. **Ethnic groups:** Ovambo 50%, Kavango 10%, Herero 7%, Damara 7%. **Languages:** Afrikaans, English, (official), several indigenous languages. **Religion:** Lutheran 50%, other Christian 30%.

**Geography: Area:** 317,818 sq. mi., slightly more than half the size of Alaska. **Location:** In S. Africa on the coast of the Atlantic Ocean. Angola on the N, Botswana on the E, and South Africa on the S. **Capital:** Windhoek. **Cities** (1990 est.): Windhoek, 114,000.

**Government: Type:** Republic. **Head of state:** Pres. Sam Nujoma; in office: Feb. 16, 1990. **Head of government:** Prime Min. Hage Geingob. **Local divisions:** 14 regions.

**Economy:** Mining accounts for over 40% of GDP. **Minerals:** Diamonds. **Fish catch** (1990): 289,000. **Electricity prod.** (1991): 1.2 mln. kWh.

**Finance: Monetary unit:** South African Rand. **Gross domestic product** (1991): $2.0 bln. **Per capital GDP:** $1,400. **Imports** (1989): $894 mln. **Exports** (1989): $1.0 bln. **National budget** (1992): $1.1 bln. expenditures.

**Transport: Railroads:** (1990): **Length:** 1,480 mi.

**Communications: Television sets:** 1 per 42 persons. **Radios:** 1 per 5.8 persons. **Telephones:** 1 per 17 persons.

**Health: Life Expectancy at Birth** (1992): 58 male; 63 female. **Births** (per 1,000 pop. 1992): 45. **Deaths** (per 1,000 pop 1992): 10. **Natural increase:** 3.5. **Hospital beds:** 1 per 166 persons. **Physicians:** 1 per 4,450 persons. **Infant mortality** (per 1,000 live births 1992): 66.

**Education** (1989): **Literacy:** 16% nonwhite. **Embassy:** 1413 K St. NW 20005; 289-3871.

Namibia was declared a protectorate by Germany in 1890 and officially called South-West Africa. South Africa seized the territory from Germany in 1915 during World War I; the League of Nations gave South Africa a mandate over the territory in 1920. In 1966, the Marxist South-West Africa People's Organization (SWAPO) launched a guerrilla war for independence.

In 1968 the UN General Assembly gave the area the name Namibia.

In a 1977 referendum, white voters backed a plan for a multiracial interim government to lead to independence. SWAPO rejected the plan. Both S. Africa and Namibian rebels agreed to a UN plan for independence by the end of 1978. S. Africa rejected the plan, Sept. 20, 1978, and held elections for Namibia's constituent assembly, Dec., that were ignored by the major black opposition parties.

In 1982, So. Africa and SWAPO agreed in principle on a cease-fire and the holding of UN-supervised elections. So. Africa, however, insisted on the withdrawal of Cuban forces from Angola as a precondition to Namibian independence. On Jan. 18, 1983, South Africa dissolved the Namibian National Assembly and resumed direct control of the territory.

In 1988, A U.S.-mediated plan was agreed upon by So. Africa, Angola, and Cuba, which called for withdrawal of Cuban troops from Angola and black majority rule in Namibia.

Namibia became an independent nation March 21, 1990.

Walvis Bay, the principal deepwater port in the country, was turned over to South African administration in 1922. So. Africa said in 1978 it would discuss sovereignty only after Namibian independence. In Aug. 1993, So. Africa agreed to turn over control of the port to Namibia, with the transfer likely to occur in 1994.

# Nauru

## Republic of Nauru

## Naoero

**People: Population** (1992): 9,460. **Pop density:** 1,182 per sq. mi. **Ethnic groups:** Nauruans 57%, Pacific Islanders 26%, Chinese 8%, European 8%. **Languages:** Nauruan (official). **Religions:** Predominately Christian.

**Geography: Area:** 8 sq. mi. **Location:** In Western Pacific O. just S of Equator. **Neighbors:** Nearest are Solomon Is. **Topography:** Mostly a plateau bearing high grade phosphate deposits, surrounded by a coral cliff and a sandy shore in concentric rings. **Capital:** Yaren.

**Government: Type:** Republic. **Head of state:** Pres. Bernard Dowiyogo; in office: Dec. 12, 1989. **Local divisions:** 14 districts.

**Economy:** Phosphate mining. **Electricity prod.** (1990): 48 mln. kWh.

**Finance: Monetary unit:** Australian dollar. **Gross national product** (1989): $60 mln.

**Communications: Radios:** 4,000 in use (1985). **Telephones in use** (1980): 1,500.

**Health: Births** (per 1,000 pop. 1992): 19. **Deaths** (per 1,000 pop. 1992): 5. **Natural increase:** 1.4%. **Infant mortality** (per 1,000 live births 1992): 41.

**Education** (1988): **Literacy:** 99%; compulsory ages 6-16.

The island was discovered in 1798 by the British but was formally annexed to the German Empire in 1886. After World War I, Nauru became a League of Nations mandate administered by Australia. During World War II the Japanese occupied the island and shipped 1,200 Nauruans to the fortress island of Truk as slave laborers.

In 1947 Nauru was made a UN trust territory, administered by Australia. Nauru became an independent republic Jan. 31, 1968.

Phosphate exports provide one of the world's highest per capita revenues for the Nauru people.

# Nepal
## Kingdom of Nepal
## Nepal Adhirajya

**People: Population** (1992 est.): 20,086,000. **Age distrib.** (%): 0–14: 42.2; 15–59: 52.9; 60+: 4.9. **Pop. density:** 357 per sq. mi. **Urban** (1987): 8%. **Ethnic groups:** The many tribes are descendants of Indian, Tibetan, and Central Asian migrants. **Languages:** Nepali (official) (an Indic language), many others. **Religions:** Hindu (official) 90%, Buddhist 7%.

**Geography: Area:** 56,136 sq. mi., the size of North Carolina. **Location:** Astride the Himalaya Mts. **Neighbors:** China on N, India on S. **Topography:** The Himalayas stretch across the N, the hill country with its fertile valleys extends across the center, while the southern border region is part of the flat, subtropical Ganges Plain. **Capital:** Kathmandu. **Cities** (1987 est.): Kathmandu 422,000, Pokhara, Biratnagar, Birganj.

**Government: Type:** Parliamentary democracy. **Head of state:** King Birendra Bir Bikram Shah Dev; b. Dec. 28, 1945; in office: Jan. 31, 1972. **Head of government:** Prime Min. Giriga Prasad Koirala; in office: May 26, 1991. **Local divisions:** 14 zones. **Defense:** 2.0% of GDP (1992).

**Economy: Industries:** Sugar, jute mills, tourism. **Chief crops:** Jute, rice, grain. **Minerals:** Quartz. **Other resources:** Forests. **Arable land:** 17%. **Livestock** (1991): cattle: 6.3 mln. **Electricity prod.** (1990): 530 mln. kWh. **Labor force:** 93% agric.

**Finance: Monetary unit:** Rupee (Mar. 1993: 49 = $1 US). **Gross domestic product** (1991): $3.2 bln. **Per capita GDP:** $165. **Imports** (1991): $545 mln.; partners: India 47%, Jap. 25%. **Exports** (1991): $180 mln.; partners: India 68%. **Tourism** (1990): receipts: $57 mln. **National budget** (1991): $624 mln. **International reserves less gold** (Mar. 1993): $480 mln. **Gold:** 152,000 oz t. **Consumer prices** (change in 1992): 17.1%.

**Transport: Civil aviation** (1989): 408 mln. passenger-km.

**Communications: Radios:** 1 per 32 persons. **Telephones:** 1 per 415 persons.

**Health: Life expectancy at birth** (1992): 51 male; 51 female. **Births** (per 1,000 pop. 1992): 38. **Deaths** (per 1,000 pop. 1992): 14. **Natural increase:** 2.4%. **Hospital beds:** 1 per 3,960 persons. **Physicians:** 1 per 19,644 persons. **Infant mortality** (per 1,000 live births 1992): 90.

**Education** (1989): **Literacy:** 29%. **Years compulsory:** 3; Attendance: 79% primary, 22% secondary.

**Major International Organizations:** UN (IMF).

**Embassy:** 2131 Leroy Pl. NW 20008; 667-4550.

Nepal was originally a group of petty principalities, the inhabitants of one of which, the Gurkhas, became dominant about 1769. In 1951 King Tribhubana Bir Bikram, member of the Shah

family, ended the system of rule by hereditary premiers of the Ranas family, who had kept the kings virtual prisoners, and established a cabinet system of government.

Virtually closed to the outside world for centuries, Nepal is now linked to India and Pakistan by roads and air service and to Tibet by road. Polygamy, child marriage, and the caste system were officially abolished in 1963.

In response to numerous pro-democracy protests, the government, which had banned all political parties since 1960, announced the legalization of political parties in 1990. Multi-party elections were held in 1991.

# Netherlands
## Kingdom of the Netherlands
## Koninkrijk der Nederlanden

**People: Population** (1992 est.) 15,112,000. **Age distrib.** (%): 0–14: 18.8; 15–60: 64.2; 60+: 17.0. **Pop. density:** 958 per sq. mi. **Urban** (1990): 88.3%. **Ethnic groups:** Dutch 97%. **Languages:** Dutch. **Religions:** Roman Catholic 40%, Dutch Reformed 19.3%.

**Geography: Area:** 15,770 sq. mi., the size of Mass., Conn., and R.I. combined. **Location:** In NW Europe on North Sea. **Topography:** The land is flat, an average alt. of 37 ft. above sea level, with much land below sea level reclaimed and protected by some 1,500 miles of dikes. Since 1920 the government has been draining the IJsselmeer, formerly the Zuider Zee. **Capital:** Amsterdam. **Cities** (1990): Amsterdam 694,000; Rotterdam 576,100; Hague 441,000.

**Government: Type:** Parliamentary democracy under a constitutional monarch. **Head of state:** Queen Beatrix; b. Jan. 31, 1938; in office: Apr. 30, 1980. **Head of government:** Prime Min. Ruud Lubbers; in office: Nov. 4, 1982. **Seat of govt.:** The Hague. **Local divisions:** 12 provinces. **Defense:** 2.7% of GDP (1991).

**Economy: Industries:** Metals, machinery, chemicals, oil refinery, diamond cutting, electronics, tourism. **Chief crops:** Grains, potatoes, sugar beets, vegetables, fruits, flowers. **Minerals:** Natural gas, oil. **Crude oil reserves** (1987): 195 mln. bbls. **Arable land:** 26%. **Livestock** (1990): cattle: 4.9 mln.; pigs: 13.9 mln. **Fish catch** (1989): 421,000 metric tons. **Electricity prod.** (1991): 63.0 bln. kWh. **Crude steel prod.** (1991): 5.1 mln. metric tons. **Labor force:** 1% agric.; 30% ind., 44% services, 23% govt.

**Finance: Monetary unit:** Guilder (June 1993: 1.90 = $1 US). **Gross domestic product** (1991): $249 bln. **Per capita GDP:** $16,600. **Imports** (1992): $156 bln.; partners: Ger. 26%, Belg. 14%, U.S. 9%, U.K. 9%. **Exports** (1992): $160 bln.; partners: Ger. 26%, Belg. 14%, Fr. 10%, UK 9%. **Tourism** (1990): receipts: $3.6 bln. **National budget** (1991): $110 bln. expenditures. **International reserves less gold** (Mar. 1993): $27.2 bln. **Gold:** 31.09 mln. oz t. **Consumer prices** (change in 1992): 3.7%.

**Transport: Railroads** (1990): **Length:** 2,828 km. **Motor vehicles:** in use (1990): 5.5 mln. passenger cars, 555,000 comm. vehicles. **Civil aviation** (1990): 28.3 bln. passenger-km; 5 airports. **Chief ports:** Rotterdam, Amsterdam, IJmuiden.

**Communications: Television sets:** 1 per 3.2 persons. **Radios:** 1 per 1.2 persons. **Telephones:** 1 per 1.6 persons. **Daily newspaper circ.** (1987): 312 per 1,000 pop.

**Health: Life expectancy at birth** (1992): 75 male; 81 female. **Births** (per 1,000 pop. 1992): 13 **Deaths** (per 1,000 pop. 1992): 9. **Natural increase:** .4%. **Hospital beds:** 1 per 164 persons. **Physicians:** 1 per 414 persons. **Infant mortality** (per 1,000 live births 1992): 7

**Education** (1991): **Literacy:** 99%. **Years compulsory:** 10; attendance: 100%.

**Major International Organizations:** UN and all of its specialized agencies, NATO, EC, OECD.

**Embassy:** 4200 Linnean Ave. NW 20008; 244-5300.

Julius Caesar conquered the region in 55 BC, when it was inhabited by Celtic and Germanic tribes.

After the empire of Charlemagne fell apart, the Netherlands (Holland, Belgium, Flanders) split among counts, dukes and bishops, passed to Burgundy and thence to Charles V of Spain. His son, Philip II, tried to check the Dutch drive toward political freedom and Protestantism (1568-1573). William the Silent, prince of Orange, led a confederation of the northern provinces, called Estates, in the Union of Utrecht, 1579. The Estates retained individual sovereignty, but were represented jointly in the States-General, a body that had control of foreign affairs and defense. In 1581 they repudiated allegiance to Spain. The rise of the Dutch republic to naval, economic, and artistic eminence came in the 17th century.

The United Dutch Republic ended 1795 when the French formed the Batavian Republic. Napoleon made his brother Louis king of Holland, 1806; Louis abdicated 1810 when Napoleon annexed Holland. In 1813 the French were expelled. In 1815 the Congress of Vienna formed a kingdom of the Netherlands, including Belgium, under William I. In 1830, the Belgians seceded and formed a separate kingdom.

The constitution, promulgated 1814, and subsequently revised, assures a hereditary constitutional monarchy.

The Netherlands maintained its neutrality in World War I, but was invaded and brutally occupied by Germany, 1940-45.

In 1949, after several years of fighting, the Netherlands granted independence to Indonesia, where it had ruled since the 17th century. In 1963, West New Guinea was turned over to Indonesia.

The independence of former Dutch colonies has instigated mass emigrations to the Netherlands.

Though the Netherlands has been heavily industrialized, its productive small farms export large quantities of pork and dairy foods. Rotterdam, located along the principal mouth of the Rhine, handles the most cargo of any ocean port in the world. Canals, of which there over 3,400 miles, are important in transportation.

### Netherlands Antilles

The **Netherlands Antilles**, constitutionally on a level of equality with the Netherlands homeland within the kingdom, consist of 2 groups of islands in the West Indies. **Curacao, Aruba,** and **Bonaire** are near the South American coast; **St. Eustatius, Saba,** and the southern part of **St. Maarten** are SE of Puerto Rico. Northern two-thirds of St. Maarten belong to French Guadeloupe; the French call the island St. Martin. Total area of the 2 groups is 385 sq. mi., including: Aruba 75, Bonaire 111, Curacao 171, St. Eustatius 11, Saba 5, St. Maarten (Dutch part) 13.

**Aruba** was separated from The Netherlands Antilles on Jan. 1, 1986; it is an autonomous member of The Netherlands, the same status as the Netherland Antilles.

Total pop. (est. 1992) was 184,000. Willemstad, on Curacao, is the capital. Principal industry is the refining of crude oil from Venezuela. Tourism is an important industry, as is shipbuilding.

## New Zealand

**People: Population:** (1991 est.): 3,347,000. **Age distrib.** (%): 0–14: 23.1, 15–59: 61.9; 60+: 15.0 **Pop. density:** 32 per sq. mi. **Urban** (1991): 76%. **Ethnic groups:** European (mostly British) 87%, Polynesian (mostly Maori) 9%. **Languages:** English, Maori (both official). **Religions:** Anglican 22%, Presbyterian 16%, Roman Catholic 15%, others.

**Geography: Area:** 103,736 sq. mi., the size of Colorado. **Location:** In SW Pacific O. **Neighbors:** Nearest are Australia on W, Fiji, Tonga on N. **Topography:** Each of the 2 main islands (North and South Is.) is mainly hilly and mountainous. The east coasts consist of fertile plains, especially the broad Canterbury Plains on South Is. A volcanic plateau is in center of North Is. South Is. has glaciers and 15 peaks over 10,000 ft. **Capital:** Wellington. **Cities** (1991 est.): Auckland 315,000; Christchurch 292,000; Wellington 148,000; Manukau 224,000.

**Government: Type:** Parliamentary democracy. **Head of state:** Queen Elizabeth II, represented by Gov.-Gen. Dame Catherine Tizard. **Head of government:** Prime Min. Jim Bolger; b. 1935; in office: Oct. 27, 1990. **Local divisions:** 93 counties, 12 towns & districts. **Defense:** 2.0% of GDP (1992).

**Economy: Industries:** Food processing, textiles, machinery, fish, forest prods. **Chief crops:** Grains, fruits. **Minerals:** Oil, gas, iron, coal **Crude oil reserves** (1987): 182 mln. bbls. **Other resources:** Wool, timber. **Arable land:** 2%. **Livestock** (1991): cattle: 8.0 mln.; sheep: 55 mln. **Fish catch** (1989): 509,000 metric tons. **Electricity prod.** (1991): 28.0 bln. kWh. **Labor force:** 11% agric. & mining; 41% ind. and commerce, 47% services and gov.

**Finance: Monetary unit:** Dollar (June 1993: 1.85 = $1 US). **Gross domestic product** (1991): $46 bln. **Per capita GDP:** $14,000. **Imports** (1992): $9.2 bln.; partners: Austral. 22%, U.S.

16%, Jap. 20%. **Exports** (1992): $9.8 bln.; partners: UK 9%, U.S. 15%, Jap. 15%, Austral. 16%. **Tourism** (1990): receipts $900,000 mln. **National budget** (1991): $18.3 bln. **International reserves less gold** (Feb. 1993): $3.0 bln. **Gold:** 1,000 oz t. **Consumer prices** (change in 1992): 1.0%.

**Transport: Railroads** (1990): **Length:** 2,627 mi. **Motor vehicles:** in use (1990): 1.5 mln. passenger cars; 310,000 comm. vehicles. **Civil aviation:** (1990): 10.5 bln. passenger-km, 36 airports. **Chief ports:** Auckland, Wellington, Lyttleton, Tauranga.

**Communications: Television sets:** 1 per 3.1 persons. **Radios:** 1 per 1.1 persons. **Telephones:** 1 per 1.4 persons. **Daily newspaper circ.** (1989): 306 per 1,000 pop.

**Health: Life expectancy at birth** (1992): 72 male; 80 female. **Births** (per 1,000 pop. 1992): 15. **Deaths** (per 1,000 pop. 1992): 8. **Natural increase:** .8%. **Hospital beds:** 1 per 111 persons. **Physicians:** 1 per 359 persons. **Infant mortality** (per 1,000 live births 1992): 10.

**Education** (1991): **Literacy:** 99%. Compulsory ages 6-15; attendance: 100%.

**Major International Organizations:** UN (GATT, World Bank, IMF), Commonwealth of Nations, OECD.

**Embassy:** 37 Observatory Cir. NW 20008; 328-4800.

The Maoris, a Polynesian group from the eastern Pacific, reached New Zealand before and during the 14th century. The first European to sight New Zealand was Dutch navigator Abel Janszoon Tasman, but Maoris refused to allow him to land. British Capt. James Cook explored the coasts, 1769-1770.

British sovereignty was proclaimed in 1840, with organized settlement beginning in the same year. Representative institutions were granted in 1853. Maori Wars ended in 1870 with British victory. The colony became a dominion in 1907, and is an independent member of the Commonwealth.

In July 1985, the *Rainbow Warrior*, flagship of the Greenpeace organization, was bombed and sunk in Auckland harbour by French secret service agents.

A labor tradition in politics dates back to the 19th century. Private ownership is basic to the economy, but state ownership or regulation affects many industries. Transportation, broadcasting, mining, and forestry are largely state-owned.

The native Maoris number about 325,000. Four of 97 members of the House of Representatives are elected directly by the Maori people.

New Zealand comprises **North Island,** 44,035 sq. mi.; **South Island,** 58,304 sq. mi.; **Stewart Island,** 674 sq. mi.; **Chatham Islands,** 372 sq. mi.

In 1965, the **Cook Islands** (pop. 1986 est., 17,185; area 93 sq. mi.) became self-governing although New Zealand retains responsibility for defense and foreign affairs. **Niue** attained the same status in 1974; it lies 400 mi. to W (pop. 1987 est., 2,500; area 100 sq. mi.). **Tokelau Is.,** (pop. 1987 est., 1,600; area 4 sq. mi.) are 300 mi. N of Samoa.

**Ross Dependency,** administered by New Zealand since 1923, comprises 160,000 sq. mi. of Antarctic territory.

## Nicaragua
### Republic of Nicaragua
### República de Nicaragua

**People: Population** (1992 est.): 3,878,000. **Age distrib.** (%): 0–14: 45.8; 15–59: 49.9; 60+: 4.3. **Pop. density:** 77 per sq. mi. **Urban** (1990): 60%. **Ethnic groups:** Mestizo 69%, Caucasian 17%, black 9%, Indian 5%. **Languages:** Spanish, (official). **Religion:** Roman Catholic 88%.

**Geography: Area:** 50,193 sq. mi., about the size of Iowa. **Location:** In Central America. **Neighbors:** Honduras on N, Costa Rica on S. **Topography:** Both Atlantic and Pacific coasts are over 200 mi. long. The Cordillera Mtns., with many volcanic peaks, runs NW-SE through the middle of the country. Between this and a volcanic range to the E lie Lakes Managua and Nicaragua. **Capital:** Managua. **Cities** (1986): Managua 1 mln.

**Government: Type:** Republic. **Head of Government:** Violeta Barrios de Chamorro; b. 1929; in office Apr. 25, 1990. **Local divisions:** 16 departments. **Defense:** 3.8% of GDP (1991).

**Economy: Industries:** Oil refining, food processing, chemicals, textiles. **Chief crops:** Bananas, cotton, fruit, yucca, coffee, sugar, corn, beans, cocoa, rice, sesame, tobacco, wheat. **Minerals:** Gold, silver, copper, tungsten. **Other resources:** Forests, shrimp. **Arable land:** 10%. **Livestock** (1991): cattle: 1.6 mln.;

pigs: 709,000. **Electricity prod.** (1991): 1.4 bln. kWh. **Labor force:** 44% agric.; 13% Ind.; 43% services.

**Finance: Monetary unit:** Cordoba oro (May 1993: 5.00 = $1 US). **Gross domestic product** (1991): $1.7 bln. **Per capita GDP:** $425. **Imports** (1991): $738 mln.; partners: U.S. 25%, Latin Amer. 30%, EC 20%. **Exports** (1991): $342 mln.; partners: OECD 75%. **National budget** (1991): $499 mln. expenditures. **Consumer prices** (change in 1990): 11,000%.

**Transport: Railroads** (1991): **Length:** 186 mi. **Motor vehicles:** in use (1990): 31,000 passenger cars, 42,000 comm. vehicles. **Chief ports:** Corinto, Puerto Somoza, San Juan del Sur.

**Communications: Television sets:** 1 per 18 persons. **Radios:** 1 per 4.3 persons. **Telephones:** 1 per 82 persons. **Daily newspaper circ.** (1991): 28 per 1,000 pop.

**Health: Life expectancy at birth** (1992): 61 male; 66 female. **Births** (per 1,000 pop. 1992): 37. **Deaths** (per 1,000 pop. 1992): 8. **Natural increase:** 2.9%. **Hospital beds:** 1 per 761 persons. **Physicians:** 1 per 1,678 persons. **Infant mortality** (per 1,000 live births 1992): 57.

**Education** (1991): **Literacy:** 57%. **Years compulsory:** 11 years or 16 years old.

**Major International Organizations:** UN and all of its specialized agencies, OAS.

**Embassy:** 1627 New Hampshire Ave. NW 20009; 387-4371.

Nicaragua, inhabited by various Indian tribes, was conquered by Spain in 1552. After gaining independence from Spain, 1821, Nicaragua was united for a short period with Mexico, then with the United Provinces of Central America, finally becoming an independent republic, 1838.

U.S. Marines occupied the country at times in the early 20th century, the last time from 1926 to 1933.

Gen. Anastasio Somoza Debayle was elected president 1967. He resigned 1972, but was elected president again in 1974. Martial law was imposed in Dec. 1974, after officials were kidnapped by the Marxist Sandinista guerrillas. Violent opposition spread to nearly all classes in 1978; nationwide strikes called against the government touched off a state of civil war. Months of simmering civil war ended when Somoza fled, July 19, 1979.

Relations with the U.S. were strained due to Nicaragua's aid to leftist guerrillas in El Salvador and the U.S. backing anti-Sandinista contra guerrilla groups.

In 1983, the contras launched their first major offensive; the Sandinistas imposed rule by decree. In 1985, the U.S. House rejected Pres. Reagan's request for military aid to the contras.

The diversion of funds to the contras from the proceeds of a secret arms sale to Iran caused a major scandal in the U.S. The plan, masterminded by the administration's national security advisor and his deputy, took place at a time when military aid to the contras was forbidden by law.

In a stunning upset, Violeta Barrios de Chamorro defeat Ortega in national elections, Feb. 25, 1990.

## Niger
### Republic of Niger
### République du Niger

**People: Population** (1992 est.): 8,052,000. **Age distrib. (%):** 0–14: 46.7; 15–59: 48.5; 60+: 4.8. **Pop. density:** 16 per sq. mi. **Urban** (1988): 21%. **Ethnic groups:** Hausa 56%, Djerma 22%, Fulani 8%, Tuareg 8%. **Languages:** French (official), Hausa, Fulani. **Religions:** Sunni Moslem 98%.

**Geography: Area:** 489,189 sq. mi., almost 3 times the size of California. **Location:** In the interior of N. Africa. **Neighbors:** Libya, Algeria on N, Mali, Burkina Faso on W, Benin, Nigeria on S, Chad on E. **Topography:** Mostly arid desert and mountains. A narrow savanna in the S and the Niger R. basin in the SW contain most of the population. **Capital:** Niamey. **Cities** (1987 est.): Niamey 350,000.

**Government: Type:** Republic. **Head of government:** Pres. Ali Seibou; in office: Dec. 20, 1989. **Prime Min.** Amadou Cheiffou; in office: Oct. 27, 1991. **Local divisions:** 7 departments. **Defense:** 0.8% of GDP (1989).

**Economy: Chief crops:** Peanuts, cotton. **Minerals:** Uranium, coal, iron. **Arable land:** 3%. **Livestock** (1991): cattle: 2.2 mln.; sheep: 3.5 mln.; goats: 4.8 mln. **Electricity prod.** (1991): 230 mln. kWh. **Labor force:** 90% agric.

**Finance: Monetary unit:** CFA franc (Mar. 1993: 273 = $1 US). **Gross domestic product** (1991): $2.4 bln. **Per capita**

**GDP:** $300. **Imports** (1990): $439 mln.; partners: Fr. 32%. **Exports** (1990): $320 mln.; partners: Fr. 65%, Nig. 11%. **National budget** (1989): $452 mln. expenditures. **International reserves less gold** (Jan. 1993): $225 mln. **Gold:** 11,000 oz t. **Consumer prices** (change in 1991): −7.8%.

**Transport: Motor vehicles:** in use (1989): 16,000 passenger cars, 18,000 comm. vehicles.

**Communications: Television sets:** 1 per 321 persons. **Radios:** 1 per 19 persons. **Telephones:** 1 per 563 persons. **Daily newspaper circ.** (1991): 1 per 1,000 pop.

**Health: Life expectancy at birth** (1992): 42 male; 45 female. **Births** (per 1,000 pop. 1992): 58. **Deaths** (per 1,000 pop. 1992): 23. **Natural increase:** 3.5%. **Infant mortality** (per 1,000 live births 1992): 125.

**Education** (1991): **Literacy:** 28%. **Years compulsory:** 6; attendance: 15%.

**Major International Organizations:** UN (GATT, IMF, WHO, FAO), OAU.

**Embassy:** 2204 R St. NW 20008; 483-4224.

Niger was part of ancient and medieval African empires. European explorers reached the area in the late 18th century. The French colony of Niger was established 1900-22, after the defeat of Tuareg fighters, who had invaded the area from the N a century before. The country became independent Aug. 3, 1960. The next year it signed a bilateral agreement with France retaining close economic and cultural ties.

## Nigeria
### Federal Republic of Nigeria

**People: Population** (1991 cen.): 88,500,000. **Pop. density:** 248 per sq. mi. **Urban** (1990): 35%. **Ethnic groups:** Hausa 21%, Yoruba 20%, Ibo 17%, Fulani 9%, others. **Languages:** English (official), Hausa, Yoruba, Ibo. **Religions:** Moslem 50% (in N), Christian 40% (in S), others.

**Geography: Area:** 356,667 sq. mi., more than twice the size of California. **Location:** On the S coast of W. Africa. **Neighbors:** Benin on W, Niger on N, Chad, Cameroon on E. **Topography:** 4 E-W regions divide Nigeria: a coastal mangrove swamp 10-60 mi. wide, a tropical rain forest 50-100 mi. wide, a plateau of savanna and open woodland, and semidesert in the N. **Capital:** Abuja. **Cities:** (1992): Lagos 1,347,000; Ibadan 1,295,000.

**Government: Type:** In transition. **Head of state:** Pres. Ernest Shonekan; in office: Aug. 26, 1993. **Local divisions:** 30 states plus federal capital territory. **Defense:** 1.0% of GNP (1990).

**Economy: Industries:** Crude oil (95% of export), food processing, assembly of vehicles, textiles. **Chief crops:** Cocoa (main export crop), tobacco, palm products, peanuts, cotton, soybeans. **Minerals:** Oil, gas, coal, iron, limestone, columbium, tin. **Crude oil reserves** (1991): 17.4 bln. bbls. **Other resources:** Timber, rubber, hides. **Arable land:** 31%. **Livestock** (1991): cattle: 14.5 mln.; goats: 36 mln.; sheep: 24 mln. **Fish catch** (1989): 315,000 metric tons. **Electricity prod.** (1991): 11.2 bln. kWh. **Labor force:** 54% agric., 19% ind., comm. and serv.

**Finance: Monetary unit:** Naira (Feb. 1993: 24.86 = $1 US). **Gross domestic product** (1991): $28 bln. **Per capita GDP:** $230. **Imports** (1990): $9.5 bln.; partners: U.S., EC. **Exports** (1990): $13.0 bln.; partners: U.S., EC. **Tourism receipts** (1990): $21 mln. **National budget** (1992): $10.0 bln. expenditures. **International reserves less gold** (Jan. 1993): $966 mln. **Gold:** 687,000 oz t. **Consumer prices** (change in 1992): 53.9%.

**Transport: Motor vehicles:** in use (1990): 785,000 passenger cars, 625,000 comm. vehicles. **Civil aviation** (1991): 774 mln. passenger-km; 14 airports. **Chief ports:** Port Harcourt, Lagos, Warri, Calabar.

**Communications: Television sets:** 1 per 30 persons. **Radios:** 1 per 12 persons. **Telephones:** 1 per 240 persons. **Daily newspaper circ.** (1990): 12 per 1,000 pop.

**Health: Life expectancy at birth** (1992): 48 male; 50 female. **Births** (per 1,000 pop. 1992): 46. **Deaths** (per 1,000 pop. 1992): 17. **Natural increase:** 2.9%. **Hospital beds:** 1 per 1,142 persons. **Physicians:** 1 per 6,900 persons. **Infant mortality** (per 1,000 live births 1992): 110.

**Education** (1991): **Literacy:** 51%. **Primary school attendance:** 42%.

**Major International Organizations:** UN (GATT, IMO, WHO), OPEC, OAU, Commonwealth of Nations.

**Embassy:** 2201 M St. NW 20037; 822-1500.

Early cultures in Nigeria date back to at least 700 BC. From the 12th to the 14th centuries, more advanced cultures developed in the Yoruba area, at Ife, and in the north, where Moslem influence prevailed.

Portuguese and British slavers appeared from the 15th-16th centuries. Britain seized Lagos, 1861, during an anti-slave trade campaign, and gradually extended control inland until 1900. Nigeria became independent Oct. 1, 1960, and a republic Oct. 1, 1963.

On May 30, 1967, the Eastern Region seceded, proclaiming itself the Republic of Biafra, plunging the country into civil war. Casualties in the war were est. at over 1 million, including many "Biafrans" (mostly Ibos) who died of starvation despite international efforts to provide relief. The secessionists, after steadily losing ground, capitulated Jan. 12, 1970. Within a few years, the ibos were reintegrated into national life.

Oil revenues have made possible a massive economic development program, largely using private enterprise, but agriculture has lagged.

After 13 years of military rule, the nation experienced a peaceful return to civilian government, Oct., 1979.

Military rule returned to Nigeria, Dec. 31, 1983 as a coup ousted the democratically elected government. The government had promised a return to civilian rule. However, the June 23, 1993, presidential election was voided by the incumbent president, Gen. Ibrahim Babangida, who rescinded his promise to surrender power to an elected civilian government. Babangida resigned and appointed a civilian to head an interim government Aug. 26.

# Norway

## Kingdom of Norway

## Kongeriket Norge

**People: Population** (1992 est.): 4,294,000. **Age distrib. (%):** 0–14: 19.0; 15–59: 59.9; 60+: 21.1. **Pop. density:** 34 per sq. mi. **Urban** (1990): 75%. **Ethnic groups:** Germanic (Nordic, Alpine, Baltic), minority Lapps. **Languages:** Norwegian (official). **Religions:** Evangelical Lutheran 94%.

**Geography: Area:** 125,181 sq. mi., slightly larger than New Mexico. **Location:** Occupies the W part of Scandinavian peninsula in NW Europe (extends farther north than any European land). **Neighbors:** Sweden, Finland, Russia on E. **Topography:** A highly indented coast is lined with tens of thousands of islands. Mountains and plateaus cover most of the country, which is only 25% forested. **Capital:** Oslo. **Cities** (1991): Oslo 467,000; Bergen 215,000.

**Government: Type:** Hereditary constitutional monarchy. **Head of state:** King Harald V; b. Feb. 21, 1937; in office: Jan. 17, 1991. **Head of government:** Prime Min. Gro Harlem Brundtland; in office: Nov. 3, 1990. **Local divisions:** Oslo, Svalbard and 18 fylker (counties). **Defense:** 3.2% of GDP (1991).

**Economy: Industries:** Paper, shipbuilding, engineering, metals, chemicals, food processing oil, gas. **Chief crops:** Grains, potatoes, fruits. **Minerals:** Oil, copper, pyrites, nickel, iron, zinc, lead. **Crude oil reserves** (1987): 11.1 bln. bbls. **Other resources:** Timber. **Arable land:** 3%. **Livestock** (1991): sheep: 1.0 mln.; cattle: 967,000; pigs: 721,000. **Fish catch** (1991): 1.9 mln. metric tons. **Electricity prod.** (1991): 121 bln. kWh. **Labor force:** 7% agric.; 47% ind., banking, comm.; 18% services, 26% govt.

**Finance: Monetary unit:** Kroner (July 1993: 7.18 = $1 US). **Gross domestic product** (1991): $72.9 bln. **Per capita GDP:** $17,100. **Imports** (1992): $25.9 bln.; partners: EC 47%. **Exports** (1992): $35.1 bln.; partners: EC 65%. **Tourism** (1990): receipts: $1.5 bln. **National budget** (1991): $52 bln. expenditures. **International reserves less gold** (Mar. 1993): $11.9 bln. **Gold:** 1.18 mln. oz t. **Consumer prices** (change in 1992): 2.3%.

**Transport: Railroads** (1990): **Length:** 2,600 mi. **Motor vehicles:** in use (1991): 1.6 mln. passenger cars, 383,000 comm. vehicles. **Civil aviation:** (1990): 7.6 bln. passenger-km; 47 airports. **Chief ports:** Bergen, Stavanger, Oslo, Tonsberg.

**Communications: Television sets:** 1 per 2.9 persons. **Radios:** 1 per 1.3 persons. **Telephones:** 1 per 1.6 persons. **Daily newspaper circ.** (1991): 510 per 1,000 pop.

**Health: Life expectancy at birth** (1992): 74 male; 81 female. **Births** (per 1,000 pop. 1992): 14. **Deaths** (per 1,000 pop. 1992):

**11. Natural increase:** .3%. **Hospital beds:** 1 per 168 persons. **Physicians:** 1 per 309 persons. **Infant mortality** (per 1,000 live births 1992): 7.1.

**Education** (1991): **Literacy:** 99%. **Years Compulsory:** 9. **Major International Organizations:** UN and all of its specialized agencies, NATO, OECD.

**Embassy:** 2720 34th St. NW 20008; 888-6000.

The first supreme ruler of Norway was Harald the Fairhaired who came to power in 872 AD. Between 800 and 1000, Norway's Vikings raided and occupied widely dispersed parts of Europe.

The country was united with Denmark 1381-1814, and with Sweden, 1814-1905. In 1905, the country became independent with Prince Charles of Denmark as king.

Norway remained neutral during World War I. Germany attacked Norway Apr. 9, 1940, and held it until liberation May 8, 1945. The country abandoned its neutrality after the war, and joined the NATO alliance.

Abundant hydroelectric resources provided the base for Norway's industrialization, producing one of the highest living standards in the world.

Norway's merchant marine is one of the world's largest.

Svalbard is a group of mountainous islands in the Arctic O., c. 23,957 sq. mi., pop. varying seasonally from 1,500 to 3,600. The largest, Spitsbergen (formerly called West Spitsbergen), 15,060 sq. mi., seat of governor, is about 370 mi. N of Norway. By a treaty signed in Paris, 1920, major European powers recognized the sovereignty of Norway, which incorporated it in 1925.

# Oman

## Sultanate of Oman

## Saltanat 'Uman

**People: Population** (1992 est.): 1,587,000. **Pop. density:** 19 per sq. mi. **Urban** (1990): 10%. **Ethnic groups:** Omani Arab 74%, Pakistani 21%. **Languages:** Arabic (official). **Religions:** Ibadhi Moslem 75%, Sunni Moslem.

**Geography: Area:** 82,030 sq. mi., about the size of New Mexico. **Location:** On SE coast of Arabian peninsula. **Neighbors:** United Arab Emirates, Saudi Arabia, Yemen on W. **Topography:** Oman has a narrow coastal plain up to 10 mi. wide, a range of barren mountains reaching 9,900 ft., and a wide, stony, mostly waterless plateau, avg. alt. 1,000 ft. Also the tip of the Ruus-al-Jebal peninsula controls access to the Persian Gulf. **Capital:** Muscat. **Cities** (1990 est.): Muscat 85,000.

**Government: Type:** Absolute monarchy. **Head of state:** Sultan Qabus bin Said; b. Nov. 18, 1942; in office: July 23, 1970. **Defense:** 16% of GDP (1992).

**Economy: Chief crops:** Dates, fruits, vegetables, wheat, bananas. **Minerals:** Oil (95% of exports). **Crude oil reserves** (1987): 4.5 bln. bbls. **Fish catch** (1990): 110,000 metric tons. **Electricity prod.** (1991): 5.0 bln. kWh. **Labor force:** 60% agric. & fishing.

**Finance: Monetary unit:** Rial Omani (Mar. 1993: .38 = $1 US). **Gross domestic product** (1989): $7.7 bln. **Imports** (1990): $2.6 bln.; partners: Jap. 21%, UAE 17%, UK 14%. **Exports** (1990): $2.6 bln.; partners: Jap. 58%, Europe 30%. **National budget** (1990): $4.9 bln. revenues; $5.4 bln. expenditures. **International reserves less gold** (Mar. 1993): $1.6 bln. **Gold:** 289,000 oz t.

**Transport: Motor vehicles:** in use (1990): 96,000 passenger cars, 70,000 comm. vehicles. **Civil aviation** (1990): 1.6 bln. passenger-km. 6 airports. **Chief ports:** Matrah, Muscat.

**Communications: Television sets:** 1 per 1.4 persons. **Radios:** 1 per 1.6 persons. **Telephones:** 1 per 14 persons.

**Health: Life expectancy at birth** (1992): 65 male; 69 female. **Hospital beds:** 1 per 380 persons. **Physicians:** 1 per 1,071 persons. **Infant mortality** (per 1,000 live births 1992): 40.

**Education** (1989): **Literacy:** 20%. **Attendance:** 80% primary, 30% secondary.

**Major International Organizations:** UN (World Bank, IMF), Arab League.

**Embassy:** 2342 Massachusetts Ave. NW 20008; 387-1980.

A long history of rule by other lands, including Portugal in the 16th century, ended with the ouster of the Persians in 1744. By the early 19th century, Muscat and Oman was one of the most important countries in the region, controlling much of the Persian and Pakistan coasts, and ruling far-away Zanzibar, which was separated in 1861 under British mediation.

British influence was confirmed in a 1951 treaty, and Britain helped suppress an uprising by traditionally rebellious interior tribes against control by Muscat in the 1950s.

On July 23, 1970, Sultan Said bin Taimur was overthrown by his son who changed the nation's name to Sultanate of Oman.

Oil is the major source of income.

Oman opened its air bases to Western forces following the Iraqi invasion of Kuwait on Aug. 2, 1990.

# Pakistan

## Islamic Republic of Pakistan
## Islam-i Jamhuriya-e Pakistan

**People: Population** (1992 est.): 121,664,000. **Pop. density:** 391 per sq. mi. **Urban** (1988): 32%. **Ethnic groups:** Punjabi 66%, Sindhi 13%, Pathan 8.5%, Urdu 7.6%, Baluchi 2.5%, others. **Languages:** Urdu, (official), Punjabi, Sindhi, Pushtu, Baluchi, Brahvi. **Religions:** Moslem 97%.

**Geography: Area:** 310,403 sq. mi., about the size of Texas. **Location:** In W part of South Asia. **Neighbors:** Iran on W, Afghanistan, China on N, India on E. **Topography:** The Indus R. rises in the Hindu Kush and Himalaya mtns. in the N (highest is K2, or Godwin Austen, 28,250 ft., 2nd highest in world), then flows over 1,000 mi. through fertile valley and empties into Arabian Sea. Thar Desert, Eastern Plains flank Indus Valley. **Capital:** Islamabad. **Cities** (1992 est.): Karachi 7.0 mln.; Lahore 3.5 mln.; Faisalabad 2.0 mln.; Hyderabad 795,000; Rawalpindi 928,000.

**Government: Type:** Parliamentary democracy in a federal setting. **Head of state:** Pres. Ghulam Ishaq Khan; in office: Dec. 12, 1988. **Head of government:** Prime Min. Nawaz Sharif; in office: Nov. 6, 1990. **Local divisions:** Federal capital, 4 provinces, tribal areas. **Defense:** 6.4% of GDP (1992).

**Economy: Industries:** Textiles, food processing, chemicals, petroleum prods. **Chief crops:** Rice, wheat. **Minerals:** Natural gas, iron ore. **Crude oil reserves** (1987): 116 mln. bbls. **Other resources:** Wool. **Arable land:** 26%. **Livestock** (1990): cattle: 17.2 mln.; sheep: 28.3 mln.; goats: 34.2 mln. **Fish catch** (1990): 479,000 metric tons. **Electricity prod.** (1991): 35 bln. kWh. **Labor force:** 53% agric.; 13% ind; 33% services.

**Finance: Monetary unit:** Rupee (Aug. 1993: 29.75 = $1 US). **Gross domestic product** (1991): $45 bln. **Per capita GDP** (1991): $380. **Imports** (1991): $7.9 bln.; partners: EC 21%, Jap. 13%, U.S. 16%. **Exports** (1991): $6.0 bln.; partners: EC 31%, Jap. 10%, U.S. 10%. **Tourism** (1990): $156 mln. receipts. **National budget** (1992): $10.0 bln. expenditures. **International reserves less gold** (Mar. 1993): $797 mln. **Gold:** 2.0 mln. oz t. **Consumer prices** (change in 1992): 9.5%.

**Transport: Railroads** (1990): **Length:** 5,453 mi. **Motor vehicles:** in use (1989): 738,000 passenger cars, 171,000 comm. vehicles. **Civil aviation** (1990): 9.3 bln. passenger-km; 35 airports with scheduled flights. **Chief ports:** Karachi.

**Communications: Television sets:** 1 per 61 persons. **Radios:** 1 per 13 persons. **Telephones:** 1 per 131 persons. **Daily newspaper circ.** (1990): 9 per 1,000 pop.

**Health: Life expectancy at birth** (1992): 56 male; 57 female. **Births** (per 1,000 pop. 1992): 43 **Deaths** (per 1,000 pop. 1992): 14. **Natural increase:** 2.9%. **Hospital beds:** 1 per 1,706 persons. **Physicians:** 1 per 2,364 persons. **Infant mortality** (per 1,000 live births 1992): 105.

**Education** (1991): **Literacy:** 35%.

**Major International Organizations:** UN (GATT, ILO, IMF, WHO).

**Embassy:** 2315 Massachusetts Ave. NW 20008; 939-6200.

Present-day Pakistan shares the 5,000-year history of the India-Pakistan sub-continent. At present day Harappa and Mohenjo Daro, the Indus Valley Civilization, with large cities and elaborate irrigation systems, flourished c. 4,000-2,500 BC.

Aryan invaders from the NW conquered the region around 1,500 BC, forging a Hindu civilization that dominated Pakistan as well as India for 2,000 years.

Beginning with the Persians in the 6th century BC, and continuing with Alexander the Great and with the Sassanians, successive nations to the west ruled or influenced Pakistan, eventually separating the area from the Indian cultural sphere.

The first Arab invasion, 712 AD, introduced Islam. Under the Mogul empire (1526-1857), Moslems ruled most of India, yielding to British encroachment and resurgent Hindus.

After World War I the Moslems of British India began agitation for minority rights in elections. Mohammad Ali Jinnah (1876-1948) was the principal architect of Pakistan. A leader of the Moslem League from 1916, he worked for dominion status for India; from 1940 he advocated a separate Moslem state.

When the British withdrew Aug. 14, 1947, the Islamic majority areas of India acquired self-government as Pakistan, with dominion status in the Commonwealth. Pakistan was divided into 2 sections, West Pakistan and East Pakistan. The 2 areas were nearly 1,000 mi. apart on opposite sides of India.

Pakistan became a republic in 1956. Pakistan had a National Assembly (legislature) with equal membership from East and West Pakistan, and 2 Provincial Assemblies. In Oct. 1958, Gen. Mohammad Ayub Khan took power in a coup. He was elected president in 1960, reelected in 1965.

Ayub resigned Mar. 25, 1969, after several months of violent rioting and unrest, most of it in East Pakistan, which demanded autonomy. The government was turned over to Gen. Agha Mohammad Yahya Khan and martial law was declared.

The Awami League, which sought regional autonomy for East Pakistan, won a majority in Dec. 1970 elections to a National Assembly which was to write a new constitution. In March, 1971 Yahya postponed the Assembly. Rioting and strikes broke out in the East.

On Mar. 25, 1971, government troops launched attacks in the East. The Easterners, aided by India, proclaimed the independent nation of Bangladesh. In months of widespread fighting, countless thousands were killed. Some 10 million Easterners fled into India.

Full scale war between India and Pakistan had spread to both the East and West fronts by Dec. 3. Pakistan troops in the East surrendered Dec. 16; Pakistan agreed to a cease-fire in the West Dec. 17. On July 3, 1972, Pakistan and India signed a pact agreeing to withdraw troops from their borders and seek peaceful solutions to all problems.

Zulfikar Ali Bhutto, leader of the Pakistan People's Party, which had won the most West Pakistan votes in the Dec. 1970 elections, became president Dec. 20.

Bhutto was overthrown in a military coup July, 1977. Convicted of complicity in a 1974 political murder, Bhutto was executed Apr.4, 1979. Benazir Bhutto, his daughter, returned to Pakistan from exile in Europe in 1986. Her efforts to relaunch the Pakistan People's Party sparked violence and antigovernment riots.

Pres. Mohammad Zia ul-Haq was killed when his plane exploded in Aug. 1988. Following Nov. elections, Benazir Bhutto was named Prime Minister, the first woman leader of a Moslem nation. Her party was soundly defeated in the Oct. 1990 elections; there were charges of corruption against Bhutto.

Legislation was submitted in 1991 to adopt Islamic law in place of the current secular code.

Prime Min. Nawaz Sharif was ousted from office by Pres. Khan, Apr. 18, 1993; he was reinstated by Pakistan's Supreme Court on May 26.

# Panama

## Republic of Panama
## República de Panamá

**People: Population** (1992 est.): 2,529,000. **Age distrib. (%):** 0–14: 35.5; 15–59: 57.6; 60+: 6.9. **Pop. density:** 84 per sq. mi. **Urban** (1990): 53%. **Ethnic groups:** Mestizo 70%, West Indian 14%, Caucasian 10%, Indian 6%. **Languages:** Spanish (official), English. **Religions:** Roman Catholic 93%, Protestant 6%.

**Geography: Area:** 29,762 sq. mi., slightly larger than West Virginia. **Location:** In Central America. **Neighbors:** Costa Rica on W., Colombia on E. **Topography:** 2 mountain ranges run the length of the isthmus. Tropical rain forests cover the Caribbean coast and eastern Panama. **Capital:** Panama. **Cities** (1990 est.): Panama City 411,000.

**Government: Type:** Constitutional democracy. **Head of state and head of government:** Pres. Guillermo Endara Galimany; in office: Dec. 20, 1989. **Local divisions:** 9 provinces, 1 territory. **Defense:** 1.5% of GDP (1990).

**Economy: Industries:** Oil refining, international banking. **Chief crops:** Bananas, pineapples, cocoa, corn, coconuts, sugar. **Minerals:** Copper. **Other resources:** Forests (mahogany), shrimp. **Arable land:** 6%. **Livestock** (1990): cattle: 1.5 mln.; pigs: 240,000. **Electricity prod.** (1991): 3.3 mln. kWh. **Labor force:** 26% agric., 28%, govt. & community services.

**Finance: Monetary unit:** Balboa (Apr. 1993: 1.00 = $1 US). **Gross domestic product** (1991): $5.2 bln. **Per capita GDP:** $1,150. **Imports** (1991): $1.5 bln.; partners: U.S. 37%. **Exports** (1991): $380 mln.; partners: U.S. 44%. **Tourism** (1990): $167 mln. receipts. **National budget** (1992): $1.7 mln. **International reserves less gold** (Jan. 1993): $553 mln. **Consumer prices** (change in 1992): 1.8%.

**Transport: Motor vehicles:** in use (1990): 186,000 passenger cars, 49,000 comm. vehicles. **Civil aviation** (1990): 195 mln. passenger-km; 8 airports with scheduled flights. **Chief ports:** Balboa, Cristobal.

**Communications: Television sets:** 1 per 12 persons. **Radios:** 1 per 2.5 persons. **Telephones:** 1 per 9.3 persons. **Daily newspaper circ.** (1990): 60 per 1,000 pop.

**Health: Life expectancy at birth** (1992): 73 male; 77 female. **Births** (per 1,000 pop. 1992): 26. **Deaths** (per 1,000 pop. 1992): 5. **Natural increase:** 2.1%. **Hospital beds:** 1 per 330 persons. **Physicians:** 1 per 880 persons. **Infant mortality** (per 1,000 live births 1992): 17.

**Education** (1991): **Literacy:** 87%. **Primary school attendance:** almost 100%.

**Major international Organizations:** UN (IMF, IMO, World Bank), OAS.

**Embassy:** 2862 McGill Terrace NW 20008; 483-1407.

The coast of Panama was sighted by Rodrigo de Bastidas, sailing with Columbus for Spain in 1501, and was visited by Columbus in 1502. Vasco Nunez de Balboa crossed the isthmus and "discovered" the Pacific O. Sept. 13, 1513. Spanish colonies were ravaged by Francis Drake, 1572-95, and Henry Morgan, 1668-71. Morgan destroyed the old city of Panama which had been founded in 1519. Freed from Spain, Panama joined Colombia in 1821.

Panama declared its independence from Colombia Nov. 3, 1903, with U.S. recognition. U.S. naval forces deterred action by Colombia. On Nov. 18, 1903, Panama granted use, occupation and control of the Canal Zone to the U.S. by treaty, ratified Feb. 26, 1904.

In 1978, a new treaty provided for a gradual takeover by Panama of the canal, and withdrawal of U.S. troops, to be completed by 1999. U.S. payments were substantially increased in the interim. The permanent neutrality of the canal was also guaranteed.

President Delvalle was ousted by the National Assembly, Feb. 26, 1988, after he tried to fire the head of the Panama Defense Forces, Gen. Manuel Antonio Noriega. Noriega had been indicted by 2 U.S. federal grand juries on drug charges. A general strike followed. Despite U.S.-imposed economic sanctions Noriega remained in power. Voters went to the polls to elect a new president May 7, 1989. Noriega claimed victory but foreign observers said that the opposition had won overwhelmingly and that Noriega was trying to steal the election. The government voided the election May 10, charging foreign interference. There was an attempted coup against Noriega Oct. 3.

U.S. troops invaded Panama Dec. 20 following a series of incidents, including the killing of a U.S. Marine by Panamanian soldiers. The operation had as its chief objective the capture of Noriega, who was wanted in the U.S. on drug trafficking charges. Noriega took refuge in the Vatican diplomatic mission, but surrendered after 10 days to U.S. officials Jan. 3, 1990. He was convicted on 8 counts of racketeering and drug trafficking in a U.S. District Court in Miami, Fla., Apr. 9, 1992.

## Papua New Guinea

**People: Population** (1992 est.): 4,006,000. **Age distrib.** (%): 0-14: 41.6; 15-59: 52.8; 60+: 5.6. **Pop. density:** 22 per sq. mi. **Urban** (1990): 15%. **Ethnic groups:** Papuans (in S and interior), Melanesian (N,E), pygmies, minorities of Chinese, Australians, Polynesians. **Languages:** English (official), Melanesian languages, Papuan languages. **Religions:** Protestant 63%, Roman Catholic 31%, local religions.

**Geography: Area:** 178,260 sq. mi., slightly larger than California. **Location:** Occupies eastern half of island of New Guinea.

**Neighbors:** Indonesia (West Irian) on W, Australia on S. **Topography:** Thickly forested mtns. cover much of the center of the country, with lowlands along the coasts. Included are some of the nearby islands of Bismarck and Solomon groups, including Admiralty Is., New Ireland, New Britain, and Bougainville. **Capital:** Port Moresby. **Cities** (1991): Port Moresby 193,000; Lae 80,000.

**Government: Type:** Parliamentary democracy. **Head of state:** Queen Elizabeth II, represented by Gov. Gen. Wiwa Korowi; in office: Oct. 4, 1991. **Head of government:** Prime Min. Paias Wingti; in office: July 17, 1992. **Local divisions:** 20 provinces. **Defense:** approx. 1.5% of GDP (1989).

**Economy: Chief crops:** Coffee, coconuts, cocoa. **Minerals:** Gold, copper, silver. **Arable land:** 1%. **Livestock** (1990): pigs: 1.7 mln. **Electricity prod.** (1991): 1.5 bln. kWh. **Labor force:** 82% agric., 3% ind. and commerce, 8% services.

**Finance: Monetary unit:** Kina (Mar. 1993: 1.00 = $1.02 US). **Gross domestic product** (1991): $3.1 bln. **Per capita GDP:** $800. **Imports** (1992): $1.5 bln.; partners: Austral. 40%, Jap. 17%; U.S. 9%. **Exports** (1992): $1.8 bln.; partners: Jap. 26%, W. Ger. 36%, Austral. 8%. **National budget** (1992): $1.4 bln. **International reserves less gold** (Mar. 1993): $180 mln. **Gold:** 63,000 oz t. **Consumer prices** (change in 1992): 3.6%.

**Transport: Motor vehicles:** in use (1989): 17,000 passenger cars, 26,000 comm. vehicles. **Chief ports:** Port Moresby, Lae.

**Communications: Television sets:** 1 per 375 persons. **Radios:** 1 per 15 persons. **Telephones:** 1 per 48 persons. **Daily newspaper circ.** (1988): 8 per 1,000 pop.

**Health: Life expectancy at birth** (1992): 55 male; 56 female. **Births** (per 1,000 pop. 1992): 34. **Deaths** (per 1,000 pop. 1992): 11. **Natural increase:** 2.3%. **Hospital beds:** 1 per 222 persons. **Physicians:** 1 per 11,904 persons. **Infant mortality** (per 1,000 live births 1992): 55.

**Education** (1991): **Literacy:** 52%. **Attendance:** 65% primary school; 13% secondary school.

**Major international Organizations:** UN (GATT), Commonwealth of Nations.

**Embassy:** 1330 Connecticut Ave., NW 20036; 659-0856

Human remains have been found in the interior of New Guinea dating back at least 10,000 years and possibly much earlier. Successive waves of peoples probably entered the country from Asia through Indonesia. Europeans visited in the 15th century, but land claims did not begin until the 19th century, when the Dutch took control of the western half of the island.

The southern half of eastern New Guinea was first claimed by Britain in 1884, and transferred to Australia in 1905. The northern half was claimed by Germany in 1884, but captured in World War I by Australia, which was granted a League of Nations mandate and then a UN trusteeship over the area. The 2 territories were administered jointly after 1949, given self-government Dec. 1, 1973, and became independent Sept. 16, 1975.

The indigenous population consists of a huge number of tribes, many living in almost complete isolation with mutually unintelligible languages.

## Paraguay
### Republic of Paraguay
### República del Paraguay

**People: Population** (1992 est.): 4,929,000. **Age distrib.** (%): 0-14: 41.0; 15-59: 52.0; 60+: 7.0. **Pop. density:** 31 per sq. mi. **Urban** (1990): 46%. **Ethnic groups:** Mestizo 95%, small Caucasian, Indian, black minorities. **Languages:** Spanish (official), Guarani. **Religions:** Roman Catholic (official) 97%.

**Geography: Area:** 157,047 sq. mi., the size of California. **Location:** One of the 2 landlocked countries of S. America. **Neighbors:** Bolivia on N, Argentina on S, Brazil on E. **Topography:** Paraguay R. bisects the country. To E are fertile plains, wooded slopes, grasslands. To W is the Chaco plain, with marshes and scrub trees. Extreme W is arid. **Capital:** Asunción. **Cities** (1990 est.): Asunción 607,000.

**Government: Type:** Republic. **Head of state:** Pres. Juan Carlos Wasmosy; in office: Aug. 15, 1993. **Local divisions:** 19 departments. **Defense:** 1.0% of GDP (1988).

**Economy: Industries:** Food processing, wood products, textiles, cement. **Chief crops:** Corn, cotton, beans, sugarcane. **Minerals:** Iron, manganese, limestone. **Other resources:** Forests. **Arable land:** 20%. **Livestock** (1991): cattle: 8.2 mln.; pigs:

2.4 mln. **Electricity prod.** (1991): 15.4 bln. kWh. **Labor force:** 44% agric., 34% ind. and commerce, 18% services.

**Finance: Monetary unit:** Guarani (Mar. 1993: 1,631 = $1 US). **Gross domestic product** (1991): $7.0 bln. **Per capita GDP:** $1,460. **Imports** (1991): $1.8 bln.; partners: Braz. 32%, EC 20%. **Exports** (1991): $642 mln.; partners: EC 37%, Braz. 25%. **Tourism** (1990): $113 mln. receipts. **National budget** (1991): $1.2 bln. expenditures. **International reserves less gold** (Mar. 1993): $561 mln. **Gold:** 35,000 oz t. **Consumer prices** (change in 1991): 27.3%.

**Transport: Motor vehicles:** in use (1990): 117,000 passenger cars, 5,000 comm. vehicles. **Civil aviation** (1990): 571 mln. passenger-km; 1 airport with scheduled flights. **Chief ports:** Asuncion.

**Communications: Television sets:** 1 per 12 persons. **Radios:** 1 per 5.4 persons. **Telephones:** 1 per 42 persons. **Daily newspaper circ.** (1990): 29 per 1,000 pop.

**Health: Life expectancy at birth** (1992): 71 male; 74 female. **Births** (per 1,000 pop. 1992): 33. **Deaths** (per 1,000 pop. 1992): 5. **Natural increase:** 2.8%. **Hospital beds:** 1 per 931 persons. **Physicians:** 1 per 1,008 persons. **Infant mortality** (per 1,000 live births 1992): 28.

**Education** (1991): **Literacy:** 90%. **Years compulsory:** 7. **Attendance:** 83%.

**Major International Organizations:** UN (IMF, WHO, ILO), OAS.

**Embassy:** 2400 Massachusetts Ave. NW 20008; 483-6960.

The Guarani Indians were settled farmers speaking a common language before the arrival of Europeans.

Visited by Sebastian Cabot in 1527 and settled as a Spanish possession in 1535, Paraguay gained its independence from Spain in 1811. It lost much of its territory to Brazil, Uruguay, and Argentina in the War of the Triple Alliance, 1865-1870. Large areas were won from Bolivia in the Chaco War, 1932-35.

Gen. Alfredo Stroessner, who ruled since 1954, was ousted in a military coup led by Gen. Andres Rodriguez on Feb. 3, 1989. Rodriguez was elected president May 1. Juan Carlos Wasmosy was elected the nation's first civilian head of state in 1993.

## Peru

### Republic of Peru
### República del Peru

**People: Population** (1992 est.): 22,767,000. **Age distrib.** (%): 0-14: 37.2; 15-59: 56.8; 60+: 6.0. **Pop. density:** 45 per sq. mi. **Urban** (1992): 70%. **Ethnic groups:** Indians 45%, Mestizos 37%, Caucasians 15%, blacks, Asians. **Languages:** Spanish, Quechua (both official), Aymara. **Religions:** Roman Catholic 90%.

**Geography: Area:** 496,222 sq. mi., slightly larger than Alaska. **Location:** On the Pacific coast of S. America. **Neighbors:** Ecuador, Colombia on N, Brazil, Bolivia on E, Chile on S. **Topography:** An arid coastal strip, 10 to 100 mi. wide, supports much of the population thanks to widespread irrigation. The Andes cover 27% of land area. The uplands are well-watered, as are the eastern slopes reaching the Amazon basin, which covers half the country with its forests and jungles. **Capital:** Lima. **Cities** (1990 est.): Lima 5,826,000; Arequipa 634,000; Callao 589,000.

**Government: Type:** in transition. **Head of state:** Pres. Alberto Fujimori; b. July 28, 1938; in office: July 28, 1990. **Head of government:** Prime Min. Oscar de la Puente Raygada; in office: Apr. 6, 1992. **Local divisions:** 24 departments, 1 province. **Defense:** 2.4% of GDP (1991).

**Economy: Industries:** Fish meal, mineral processing, light industry, textiles. **Chief crops:** Cotton, sugar, coffee, corn. **Minerals:** Copper, lead, molybdenum, silver, zinc, iron, oil. **Crude oil reserves** (1987): 535 mln. bbls. **Other resources:** Wool, sardines. **Arable land:** 3%. **Livestock** (1991): cattle: 3.6 mln.; pigs: 2.3 mln.; sheep: 11.2 mln. **Fish catch** (1990): 6.1 mln. metric tons. **Electricity prod.** (1991): 15.8 bln. kWh. **Labor force:** 38% agric.; 17% ind. and mining; 45% govt. and other services.

**Finance: Monetary unit:** Nuevo Sol (July 1993: 2.01 = $1 US). **Gross domestic product** (1991): $20.6 bln. **Per capita GDP:** $920. **Imports** (1991): $3.5 bln.; partners: U.S. 32%, EC 17%. **Exports** (1991): $3.3 bln.; partners: U.S. 20%, EC 28%, Jap. 13%. **Tourism** (1990): $353 mln. receipts. **National budget** (1991): $1.8 bln. **International reserves less gold** (Mar.

1993): $2.9 bln. **Gold:** 1.8 mln. oz t. **Consumer prices** (change in 1992): 73.5%.

**Transport: Railroads** (1991): **Length:** 2,157 mi. **Motor vehicles:** in use (1990): 368,000 passenger cars, 237,000 comm. vehicles. **Civil aviation** (1990): 2.0 bln. passenger-km; 22 airports. **Chief ports:** Callao, Chimbate, Mollendo.

**Communications: Television sets:** 1 per 11 persons. **Radios:** 1 per 5.2 persons. **Telephones:** 1 per 28 persons. **Daily newspaper circ.** (1987): 57 per 1,000 pop.

**Health: Life expectancy at birth** (1992): 63 male; 67 female. **Births** (per 1,000 pop. 1992): 28. **Deaths** (per 1,000 pop. 1992): 8. **Natural increase:** 2.0%. **Hospital beds:** 1 per 625 persons. **Physicians:** 1 per 997 persons. **Infant mortality** (per 1,000 live births 1992): 59.

**Education** (1991): **Literacy:** 85%. **Years compulsory:** 10.

**Major International Organizations:** UN and all of its specialized agencies, OAS.

**Embassy:** 1700 Massachusetts Ave. NW 20036; 833-9860.

The powerful Inca empire had its seat at Cuzco in the Andes covering most of Peru, Bolivia, and Ecuador, as well as parts of Colombia, Chile, and Argentina. Building on the achievements of 800 years of Andean civilization, the Incas had a high level of skill in architecture, engineering, textiles, and social organization.

A civil war had weakened the empire when Francisco Pizarro, Spanish conquistador, began raiding Peru for its wealth, 1532. In 1533 he had the seized ruling Inca, Atahualpa, fill a room with gold as a ransom, then executed him and enslaved the natives.

Lima was the seat of Spanish viceroys until the Argentine liberator, Jose de San Martin, captured it in 1821; Spain was defeated by Simon Bolivar and Antonio J. de Sucre; recognized Peruvian independence, 1824.

On Oct. 3, 1968, a military coup ousted Pres. Fernando Belaunde Terry. In 1968-74, the military government put through sweeping agrarian changes, and nationalized oil, mining, fishmeal, and banking industries.

Food shortages, escalating foreign debt, and strikes led to another coup, Aug. 29, 1976, and to a slowdown of socialist programs.

After 12 years of military rule, Peru returned to democratic leadership under former Pres. Fernando Belaunde Terry, July 1980.

Pres. Fujimori dissolved the National Congress, suspended parts of the constitution, and instituted press censorship, Apr. 5, 1992.

## Philippines

### Republic of the Philippines

**People: Population** (1992 est.): 67,114,000. **Age distrib.** (%): 0-14: 39.0; 15-59: 56.2; 60+: 4.8. **Pop. density:** 579 per sq. mi. **Urban** (1991): 43%. **Ethnic groups:** Malays the large majority, Chinese, Americans, Spanish are minorities. **Languages:** Pilipino (based on Tagalog), English (both official), Cebuano, Bicol, Ilocano, Pampango, many others. **Religions:** Roman Catholics 83%, Protestants 9%, Moslems 5%.

**Geography: Area:** 115,831 sq. mi., slightly larger than Arizona. **Location:** An archipelago off the SE coast of Asia. **Neighbors:** Nearest are Malaysia, Indonesia on S, Taiwan on N. **Topography:** The country consists of some 7,100 islands stretching 1,100 mi. N-S. About 95% of area and population are on 11 largest islands, which are mountainous, except for the heavily indented coastlines and for the central plain on Luzon. **Capital:** Quezon City (Manila is de facto capital). **Cities** (1990 est.): Manila 1.8 mln.; Quezon City 1.5 mln.; Cebu 552,000.

**Government: Type:** Republic. **Head of state:** Pres. Fidel V. Ramos; b. 1928; in office: June 30, 1992. **Local divisions:** 72 provinces, 61 cities. **Defense:** 2.1% of GNP (1991).

**Economy: Industries:** Food processing, textiles, clothing, drugs, wood prods., appliances. **Chief crops:** Sugar, rice, corn, pineapple, coconut. **Minerals:** Cobalt, copper, gold, nickel, silver, iron, petroleum. **Other resources:** Forests (42% of area). **Arable land:** 26%. **Livestock** (1990): cattle: 1.4 mln.; pigs: 7.8 mln. **Fish catch** (1990): 2.0 mln. metric tons. **Electricity prod.** (1991): 31 bln. kWh. **Labor force:** 47% agric., 20% ind. and comm., 13% services.

**Finance: Monetary unit:** Peso (May 1993: 25.51 = $1 US). **Gross national product** (1991): $47 bln. **Per capita GNP:** $720. **Imports** (1991): $12.3 bln.; partners: U.S. 25%, Jap. 16%. **Exports** (1991): $8.7 bln.; partners: U.S. 35%, Jap. 17%,

EC 19%. **Tourism** (1990): $1.3 bln. receipts. **National budget** (1991): $9.3 bln. expenditures. **International reserves less gold** (Mar. 1993): $5.7 bln. **Gold:** 2.8 mln. oz t. **Consumer prices** (change in 1992): 8.9%.

**Transport: Railroads** (1991): **Length:** 658 mi. **Motor vehicles:** in use (1990): 454,000 passenger cars, 783,000 comm. vehicles. **Civil aviation** (1991): 9.3 bln. passenger-km; 31 airports with scheduled flights. **Chief ports:** Cebu, Manila, Iloilo, Davao.

**Communications: Television sets:** 1 per 8.8 persons. **Radios:** 1 per 16 persons. **Telephones:** 1 per 60 persons. **Daily newspaper circ.** (1988): 44 per 1,000 pop.

**Health: Life expectancy at birth** (1992): 62 male; 68 female. **Births** (per 1,000 pop. 1992): 29. **Deaths** (per 1,000 pop. 1992): 7. **Natural increase:** 2.2%. **Hospital beds:** 1 per 683 persons. **Physicians:** 1 per 1,062 persons. **Infant mortality** (per 1,000 live births 1992): 54.

**Education** (1989): **Literacy:** 88%. **Attendance:** 97% in elementary, 55% secondary.

**Major International Organizations:** UN (World Bank, IMF, GATT), ASEAN.

**Embassy:** 1617 Massachusetts Ave. NW 20036; 483-1414

The Malay peoples of the Philippine islands, whose ancestors probably migrated from Southeast Asia, were mostly hunters, fishers, and unsettled cultivators when first visited by Europeans.

The archipelago was visited by Magellan, 1521. The Spanish founded Manila, 1571. The islands, named for King Philip II of Spain, were ceded by Spain to the U.S. for $20 million, 1898, following the Spanish-American War. U.S. troops suppressed a guerrilla uprising in a brutal 6-year war, 1899-1905.

Japan attacked the Philippines Dec. 8, 1941 and occupied the islands during WW II.

On July 4, 1946, independence was proclaimed in accordance with an act passed by the U.S. Congress in 1934. A republic was established.

Riots by radical youth groups and terrorism by leftist guerrillas and outlaws, increased from 1970. On Sept. 21, 1972, President Marcos declared martial law. Ruling by decree, he ordered some land reform and stabilized prices. But opposition was suppressed, and a high population growth rate aggravated poverty and unemployment. Political corruption was widespread. On Jan. 17, 1973, Marcos proclaimed a new constitution with himself as president. His wife received wide powers in 1978 to supervise planning and development.

Government troops battled Moslem (Moro) secessionists, 1973-76, in southern Mindanao. Fighting resumed, 1977, after a Libyan-mediated agreement on autonomy was rejected by the region's mainly Christian voters.

Martial law was lifted Jan. 17, 1981. Marcos turned over legislative power to the National Assembly, released political prisoners, and said he would no longer rule by decree. He was re-elected to a new 6-year term as president.

The assassination of prominent opposition leader Benigno S. Aquino Jr, Aug. 21, 1983, sparked demonstrations calling for the resignation of Marcos.

A bitter presidential election campaign ended Feb. 7, 1986 as elections were held amid allegations of widespread fraud. On Feb. 16, Marcos was declared the victor over Corazon Aquino, widow of slain opposition leader Benigno Aquino. Aquino declared herself president and announced a nonviolent "active resistance" to overthrow the Marcos government.

On Feb. 22, 2 leading military allies of Marcos quit their posts to protest the rigged elections. Marcos, Feb. 24, declared a state of emergency as his military and religious support continued to erode. That same day U.S. President Ronald Reagan urged Marcos to resign. Marcos ended his 20-year tenure as president Feb. 26 as he fled the country. Aquino was recognized immediately as president by the U.S. and other nations.

In 1987, Aquino announced the start of land reforms. Candidates endorsed by Aquino won large majorities in legislative elections held in May, attesting to her popularity. She was plagued, however, by a weak economy, widespread poverty, communist insurgents, and lukewarm support from the military.

Rebel troops seized military bases, TV stations, and bombed the presidential palace, Dec. 1, 1989. Government forces defeated the attempted coup with the aid of air cover provided by U.S. F-4s.

The U.S. vacated the Subic Bay Naval Station at the end of 1992; the Philippine government served a notice of eviction following the collapse of talks on a gradual 3-year pull out.

The archipelago has a coastline of 10,850 mi. Manila Bay, with an area of 770 sq. mi., and a circumference of 120 mi., is the finest harbor in the Far East.

All natural resources of the Philippines belong to the state.

# Poland

## Republic of Poland

## Rzeczpospolita Polska

**People: Population** (1992 est.): 38,385,000. **Age distrib. (%):** 0–14: 25.7; 15–59: 60.2; 60+: 14.1. **Pop. density:** 317 per sq. mi. **Urban** (1992): 62%. **Ethnic groups:** Polish 98%, Germans, Ukrainians, Belorussians. **Language:** Polish. **Religion:** Roman Catholic 94%.

**Geography: Area:** 120,727 sq. mi., slightly smaller than New Mexico. **Location:** On the Baltic Sea in E Central Europe. **Neighbors:** Germany on W, Czech Rep., Slovakia on S, Lithuania, Belarus, Ukraine on E. **Topography:** Mostly lowlands forming part of the Northern European Plain. The Carpathian Mts. along the southern border rise to 8,200 ft. **Capital:** Warsaw. **Cities** (1991 est.): Warsaw 1.6 mln., Lodz 851,000, Kracow 748,000, Wroclaw 631,000, Poznan 570,000.

**Government: Type:** Democratic state. **Head of state:** Pres. Lech Walesa; in office: Dec. 22, 1990. **Head of government:** Prime Min. Hanna Suchocka (prior to Sept. 1993 elections). **Local divisions:** 49 provinces.

**Economy: Industries:** Shipbuilding, chemicals, metals, autos, food processing. **Chief crops:** Grains, potatoes, sugar beets, tobacco, flax. **Minerals:** Coal, copper, zinc, silver, zinc, sulphur, natural gas. **Arable land:** 46%. **Livestock** (1991): cattle: 10.0 mln.; pigs: 19.4 mln. **Fish catch** (1990): 473,000 metric tons. **Electricity prod.** (1991): 136 bln. kWh. **Crude steel prod.** (1991): 10.4 mln. metric tons. **Labor force:** 27% agric.; 36% ind. & comm.; 21% services.

**Finance: Monetary unit:** Zloty (July 1993: 17,225 = $1 US). **Gross domestic product** (1991): $162.7 bln. **Per capita GDP:** $4,300. **Imports** (1991): $15.7 bln.; partners: CIS 18%, Ger. 15%, Czech. 5%. **Exports** (1991): $14.9 bln.; partners: CIS 25%, E. Ger. 14%, Czech. 6%. **National budget** (1991): $22.4 bln. expenditures. **Tourism** (1990): $266 mln. receipts. **International reserves less gold** (Mar. 1993): $3.5 bln. **Gold:** 473,000. **Consumer prices** (change in 1992): 43.0%.

**Transport: Railroads** (1991): **Length:** 25,848 km. **Motor vehicles:** in use (1991): 5.2 mln. passenger cars, 1.1 mln. comm. vehicles. **Civil aviation** (1991): 3.4 bln. passenger-km; 12 airports. **Chief ports:** Gdansk, Gdynia, Szczecin.

**Communications: Television sets:** 1 per 3.9 persons. **Radios:** 1 per 3.6 persons. **Telephones:** 1 per 7.5 persons. **Daily newspaper circ.** (1991): 217 per 1,000 pop.

**Health: Life expectancy at birth** (1992): 68 male; 76 female. **Births** (per 1,000 pop. 1992): 14. **Deaths** (per 1,000 pop. 1992): 9. **Natural increase:** .5%. **Hospital beds:** 1 per 154 persons. **Physicians:** 1 per 471 persons. **Infant mortality** (per 1,000 live births 1992): 14.

**Education** (1991): **Literacy:** 98%. **Years compulsory:** 8; attendance 97%.

**Major International Organizations:** UN (GATT, WHO).

**Embassy:** 2640 16th St. NW 20009; 234-3800.

Slavic tribes in the area were converted to Latin Christianity in the 10th century. Poland was a great power from the 14th to the 17th centuries. In 3 partitions (1772, 1793, 1795) it was apportioned among Prussia, Russia, and Austria. Overrun by the Austro-German armies in World War I, its independence, self-declared on Nov.11, 1918, was recognized by the Treaty of Versailles, June 28, 1919. Large territories to the east were taken in a war with Russia, 1921.

Germany and the USSR invaded Poland Sept. 1-27, 1939, and divided the country. During the war, some 6 million Polish citizens were killed by the Nazis, half of them Jews. With Germany's defeat, a Polish government-in-exile in London was recognized by the U.S., but the USSR pressed the claims of a rival group. The election of 1947 was completely dominated by the Communists.

In compensation for 69,860 sq. mi. ceded to the USSR, 1945, Poland received approx. 40,000 sq. mi. of German territory E of the Oder-Neisse line comprising Silesia, Pomerania, West Prussia, and part of East Prussia.

In 12 years of rule by Stalinists, large estates were abolished, industries nationalized, schools secularized, and Roman Catholic prelates jailed. Farm production fell off. Harsh working conditions caused a riot in Poznan, June 28-29, 1956.

A new Politburo, committed to development of a more independent Polish Communism, was named Oct. 1956, with Wladyslaw Gomulka as first secretary of the Communist Party. Collectivization of farms was ended and many collectives were abolished.

In Dec. 1970 workers in port cities rioted because of price rises and new incentive wage rules. On Dec. 20 Gomulka resigned as party leader; he was succeeded by Edward Gierek; the incentive rules were dropped, price rises were revoked.

A law promulgated Feb. 13, 1953, required government consent to high Roman Catholic church appointments. In 1956 Gomulka agreed to permit religious liberty and religious publications, provided the church kept out of politics. In 1961 religious studies in public schools were halted.

After 2 months of labor turmoil had crippled the country, the Polish government, Aug. 30, 1980, met the demands of striking workers at the Lenin Shipyard, Gdansk. Among the 21 concessions granted were the right to form independent trade unions and the right to strike — unprecedented political developments in the Soviet bloc. By 1981, 9.5 mln. workers had joined the independent trade union (Solidarity). Farmers won official recognition for their independent trade union in May. Solidarity leaders proposed, Dec. 12, a nationwide referendum on establishing a non-Communist government if the government failed to agree to a series of demands which included access to the mass media and free elections to local councils in the provinces.

Spurred by the fear of Soviet intervention, the government, Dec. 13, imposed martial law. Public gatherings, demonstrations, and strikes were banned and an internal and external blackout was imposed. Solidarity leaders called for a nationwide strike, but there were only scattered work stoppages. Lech Walesa and other Solidarity leaders were arrested. The U.S. imposed economic sanctions which were lifted when martial law was suspended Dec. 1982.

On Apr. 5, 1989, an accord was reached between the government and opposition factions on a broad range of political and economic reforms incl. free elections. In the first free elections in over 40 years, candidates endorsed by Solidarity swept the parliamentary elections, June 4. On Aug. 19, Tadeusz Mazowiecki became the first non-Communist to head an Eastern bloc nation, when he became prime minister. Lech Walesa became president, 1990.

A radical economic program designed to transform the economy into a free-market system drew protests from unions, farmers, and miners because it resulted in inflation and unemployment. In Sept. 1993 elections former Communists and other leftists won a majority of seats in the lower house of parliament.

# Portugal

## Republic of Portugal

### República Portuguesa

**People: Population** (1992 est.): 10,448,000 (incl. Azores & Madeira Islands). **Age distrib.** (%): 0-14: 22.7; 15-59: 59.9; 60+: 17.4. **Pop. density:** 287 per sq. mi. **Urban** (1990): 34%. **Ethnic groups:** Homogeneous Mediterranean stock with small African minority. **Languages:** Portuguese. **Religions:** Roman Catholics 97%.

**Geography: Area:** 36,390 sq. mi., incl. the Azores and Madeira Islands, slightly smaller than Indiana. **Location:** At SW extreme of Europe. **Neighbors:** Spain on N, E. **Topography:** Portugal N of Tajus R, which bisects the country NE-SW, is mountainous, cool and rainy. To the S there are drier, rolling plains, and a warm climate. **Capital:** Lisbon. **Cities** (1987 est.): Lisbon 2 mln. (met.), Oporto, 1.5 mln. (met.).

**Government: Type:** Parliamentary democracy. **Head of state:** Pres. Mario Soares; b. Dec. 7, 1924; in office: Mar. 9, 1986. **Head of government:** Prime Min. Anibal Cavaco Silva; in office: Nov. 6, 1985. **Local divisions:** 18 districts, 2 autonomous regions, one dependency. **Defense:** 2.8% of GDP (1991).

**Economy: Industries:** Textiles, footwear, cork, chemicals, fish canning, wine, paper. **Chief crops:** Grains, potatoes, rice, grapes, olives, fruits. **Minerals:** Tungsten, uranium, copper, iron. **Other resources:** Forests (world leader in cork production). **Ar-**

**able land:** 32%. **Livestock** (1991): sheep: 5.6 mln.; pigs: 2.6 mln; cattle: 1.3 mln. **Fish catch** (1990): 321,000 metric tons. **Electricity prod.** (1991): 16 bln. kWh. **Labor force:** 19% agric.; 34% ind. and comm.; 46% services and govt.

**Finance: Monetary unit:** Escudo (July 1993: 166 = $1 US). **Gross domestic product** (1991): $87 bln. **Per capita GDP:** $8,400. **Imports** (1992): $30.0 bln.; partners: Ger. 12%, UK 8%, Fr. 11%. **Exports** (1992): $18.2 bln.; partners: UK 15%, Ger. 13%, Fr. 13%. **Tourism** (1990): $3.5 bln. receipts. **National budget** (1991): $33.9 bln. expenditures. **International reserves less gold** (Mar. 1993): $19.4 bln. **Gold:** 16.0 mln. oz t. **Consumer prices** (change in 1992): 8.9%.

**Transport: Railroads** (1991): **Length:** 2,229 mi. **Motor vehicles:** in use (1990): 3.2 mln. passenger cars, 189,000 comm. vehicles. **Civil aviation** (1990): 6.8 bln. passenger-km; 13 airports. **Chief ports:** Lisbon, Setubal, Leixoes.

**Communications: Television sets:** 1 per 5.8 persons. **Radios:** 1 per 4.2 persons. **Telephones:** 1 per 3.6 persons. **Daily newspaper circ.** (1991): 50 per 1,000 pop.

**Health: Life expectancy at birth** (1992): 71 male; 78 female. **Births** (per 1,000 pop. 1992): 12. **Deaths** (per 1,000 pop. 1992): 10. **Natural increase:** .2%. **Hospital beds:** 1 per 230 persons. **Physicians:** 1 per 352 persons. **Infant mortality** (per 1,000 live births 1992): 10.

**Education** (1990): **Literacy:** 83%. **Years compulsory:** 6; attendance 60%.

**Major International Organizations:** UN (GATT, IMF, WHO), NATO, EC, OECD.

**Embassy:** 2125 Kalorama Rd. NW 20008; 328-8610.

Portugal, an independent state since the 12th century, was a kingdom until a revolution in 1910 drove out King Manoel II and a republic was proclaimed.

From 1932 a strong, repressive government was headed by Premier Antonio de Oliveira Salazar. Illness forced his retirement in Sept. 1968.

On Apr. 25, 1974, the government was seized by a military junta led by Gen. Antonio de Spinola, who was named president.

The new government reached agreements providing independence for Guinea-Bissau, Mozambique, Cape Verde Islands, Angola, and Sao Tome and Principe. Despite a 64% victory for democratic parties in April 1975, the Soviet-supported Communist party increased its influence. Banks, insurance companies, and other industries were nationalized.

Parliament approved, June 1, 1989, a package of reforms that did away with the socialist economy and created a "democratic" economy and the denationalization of industries.

**Azores Islands,** in the Atlantic, 740 mi. W. of Portugal, have an area of 868 sq. mi. and a pop. (1992) of 236,000. A 1951 agreement gave the U.S. rights to use defense facilities in the Azores. The **Madeira Islands,** 350 mi. off the NW coast of Africa, have an area of 307 sq. mi. and a pop. (1992) of 253,000. Both groups were offered partial autonomy in 1976.

**Macau,** area of 6 sq. mi., is an enclave, a peninsula and 2 small islands, at the mouth of the Canton R. in China. Portugal granted broad autonomy in 1976. In 1987, Portugal and China agreed that Macau would revert to China in 1999. Macao, like Hong Kong, was guaranteed 50 years of noninterference in its way of life and capitalist system. Pop. (1992 est.): 367,000.

# Qatar

## State of Qatar

### Dawlet al-Qatar

**People: Population** (1992 est.): 484,000. **Pop. density:** 113 per sq. mi. **Ethnic groups:** Arab 40%, Pakistani 18%, Indian 10%, Iranian 14%, others. **Languages:** Arabic (official), English. **Religions:** Moslem 95%.

**Geography: Area:** 4,247 sq. mi., smaller than Connecticut and Rhode Island combined. **Location:** Occupies peninsula on W coast of Persian Gulf. **Neighbors:** Saudi Arabia on W, United Arab Emirates on S. **Topography:** Mostly a flat desert, with some limestone ridges, vegetation of any kind is scarce. **Capital:** Doha. **Cities** (1987 est.): Doha 250,000.

**Government: Type:** Traditional monarchy. **Head of state and head of government:** Emir & Prime Min. Khalifah ibn Hamad ath-Thani; b. 1932; in office: Feb. 22, 1972 (amir), 1970 (prime min.) **Defense:** 8.0% of GDP (1989).

**Economy: Arable land:** 2.9%. **Electricity prod.** (1991): 4.2 bln. kWh. **Labor force:** 10% agric., 70% ind., services and commerce.

**Finance: Monetary unit:** Riyal (Mar. 1993: 3.64 = $1.00 US). **Gross domestic product** (1990): $7.4 bln. **Per capita GDP:** $15,000. **Imports** (1990): $1.4 bln.; partners: Jap. 11%, UK 13%, U.S. 9%. **Exports** (1990): $3.2 bln.; partners: Jap. 61%. **National budget** (1991): $3.2 bln. expenditures.

**Transport: Chief ports:** Doha, Musayid.

**Communications: Television sets:** 1 per 2.5 persons. **Radios:** 1 per 2.5 persons. **Telephones:** 1 per 3.4 persons.

**Health: Life expectancy at birth** (1992): 69 male; 74 female. **Hospital beds:** 1 per 399 persons. **Physicians:** 1 per 568 persons. **Infant mortality** (per 1,000 live births 1992): 24.

**Education** (1991): **Literacy:** 76%. **Compulsory:** ages 6-16; attendance: 98%.

**Major International Organizations:** UN (FAO, GATT, IMF, World Bank), Arab League, OPEC.

**Embassy:** 600 New Hampshire Ave. NW 20037; 338-0111.

Qatar was under Bahrain's control until the Ottoman Turks took power, 1872 to 1915. In a treaty signed 1916, Qatar gave Great Britain responsibility for its defense and foreign relations. After Britain announced it would remove its military forces from the Persian Gulf area by the end of 1971, Qatar sought a federation with other British protected states in the area; this failed and Qatar declared itself independent, Sept. 1 1971.

Oil revenues give Qatar a per capita income among the highest in the world, but lack of skilled labor hampers development plans.

# Romania

**People: Population** (1992 est.): 23,169,000. **Age distrib. (%):** 0–14: 24.7; 15–59: 60.9; 60+: 14.4. **Pop. density:** 252 per sq. mi. **Urban** (1992): 55%. **Ethnic groups:** Romanians 78%, Hungarians 11%. **Languages:** Romanian (official), Hungarian, German. **Religions:** Orthodox 80%, Roman Catholic 6%.

**Geography: Area:** 91,699 sq. mi., slightly smaller than Oregon. **Location:** In SE Europe on the Black Sea. **Neighbors:** Moldova on E, Ukraine on N, Hungary, Yugoslavia on W, Bulgaria on S. **Topography:** The Carpathian Mts. encase the north-central Transylvanian plateau. There are wide plains S and E of the mountains, through which flow the lower reaches of the rivers of the Danube system. **Capital:** Bucharest. **Cities** (1992 est.): Bucharest 2,064,000, Constanta 350,000, Iasi 342,000, Timisoara 333,000.

**Government: Type:** Republic. **Head of state:** Pres. Ion Iliescu; in office; Dec. 25, 1989. **Head of government:** Prime Min. Nicolae Vacaroiu; in office; Nov. 4, 1992. **Local divisions:** Bucharest and 40 counties. **Defense:** 4.3% of GNP (1985).

**Economy: Industries:** Steel, metals, machinery, oil products, chemicals, textiles, shoes, tourism. **Chief crops:** Grains, sunflower, vegetables, potatoes. **Minerals:** Oil, gas, coal. **Other resources:** Timber. **Arable land:** 45%. **Livestock** (1991): cattle: 6.2 mln.; pigs: 11.6 mln.; sheep: 15.4 mln. **Fish catch** (1990): 127,000 metric tons. **Electricity prod.** (1990): 64 bln. kWh. **Crude steel prod.** (1991): 7 mln. metric tons. **Labor force:** 28% agric.; 34% ind. & comm.

**Finance: Monetary unit:** Lei (Mar. 1993: 598 = $1 US). **Gross domestic product** (1991): $71.9 bln. **Per capita GDP:** $3,100. **Imports** (1991): $15.4 bln.; partners: CIS 50%. **Exports** (1991): $14.0 bln.; partners: CIS 30%. **Tourism** (1990): $106 mln. receipts. **National budget** (1991): $20 bln. expenditures.

**Transport: Railroads** (1991): **Length:** 6,887 mi. **Motor vehicles:** in use (1992): 1.3 mln. passenger cars; 332,000 comm. vehicles. **Civil aviation** (1991): 1.6 bln. passenger-km; 14 airports. **Chief ports:** Constanta, Galati, Braila.

**Communications: Television sets:** 1 per 6.0 persons. **Radios:** 1 per 7.3 persons. **Telephones:** 1 per 7.7 persons. **Daily newspaper circ.** (1991): 134 per 1,000 pop.

**Health: Life expectancy at birth** (1992): 68 male; 74 female. **Births** (per 1,000 pop. 1992): 14. **Deaths** (per 1,000 pop. 1992): 10. **Hospital beds:** 1 per 107 persons. **Physicians:** 1 per 472 persons. **Infant mortality** (per 1,000 live births 1992): 22.

**Education** (1991): **Literacy:** 96%. **Years compulsory:** 10; attendance 98%.

**Major International Organizations:** UN (World Bank, IMF, GATT).

**Embassy:** 1607 23d St. NW 20008; 232-4747.

Romania's earliest known people merged with invading Proto-Thracians, preceding by centuries the Dacians. The Dacian kingdom was occupied by Rome, 106 AD-271 AD; people and language were Romanized. The principalities of Wallachia and Moldavia, dominated by Turkey, were united in 1859, became Romania in 1861. In 1877 Romania proclaimed independence from Turkey, became an independent state by the Treaty of Berlin, 1878, a kingdom, 1881, under Carol I. In 1886 Romania became a constitutional monarchy with a bicameral legislature.

Romania helped Russia in its war with Turkey, 1877-78. After World War I it acquired Bessarabia, Bukovina, Transylvania, and Banat. In 1940 it ceded Bessarabia and Northern Bukovina to the USSR, part of southern Dobrudja to Bulgaria, and northern Transylvania to Hungary.

In 1941, Romanian premier Marshal Ion Antonescu led his country in support of Germany against the USSR. In 1944 Antonescu was overthrown by King Michael and Romania joined the Allies.

With occupation by Soviet troops the communist-headed National Democratic Front displaced the National Peasant party. A People's Republic was proclaimed, Dec. 30, 1947; Michael was forced to abdicate. Land owners were dispossessed; most banks, factories and transportation units were nationalized.

On Aug. 22, 1965, a new constitution proclaimed Romania a Socialist, rather than a People's Republic.

Internal policies were oppressive. Ethnic Hungarians protested cultural and job discrimination, which has led to strained relations with Hungary.

Romania became industrialized, but lagged in consumer goods and in personal freedoms. All industry was state owned, and state farms and cooperatives owned almost all the arable land.

On Dec. 16, 1989, security forces opened fire on demonstrators in Timisoara; hundreds were buried in mass graves. President Nicolae Ceausescu declared a state of emergency as protests spread to other cities. By Dec. 21, the protests had spread to Bucharest where security forces fired on protestors. Army units joined the rebellion, Dec. 22, and a group known as the "Council of National Salvation" announced that it had overthrown the government. Fierce fighting took place between the army, which backed the new government, and forces loyal to Ceausescu.

Ceausescu was captured, Dec. 23 and, following a trial in which he and his wife were found guilty of genocide, was executed Dec. 25. The U.S. and USSR quickly recognized the new government.

# Russia

## Russian Federation

*(Figures prior to 1990 are for the former USSR)*

**People: Population** (1992 est.): 149,527,000. **Age distrib. (%):** –14: 23.1; 15 –59: 61.5; 60+: 15.4. **Pop. density:** 22 per sq. mi. **Urban** (1991): 74%. **Ethnic groups:** Russians 82%, Tatar 3%. **Languages:** Russian (official), Ukrainian, Belorussian, Uzbek, Armenian, Azerbaijani, Georgian, many others. **Religions:** Russian Orthodox 25%, non-religious 60%.

**Geography: Area:** 6,592,800 sq. mi., over 76% of the total area of the former USSR and is the largest country in the world. **Location:** Stretches from E. Europe across N Asia to the Pacific O. **Neighbors:** Finland, Poland, Norway, Estonia, Belarus, Ukraine on W, Georgia, Azerbaijan, Kazakhstan, China, Mongolia, N. Korea on S. **Topography:** Russia contains every type of climate except the distinctly tropical, and has a varied topography.

The European portion is a low plain, grassy in S, wooded in N, with Ural Mtns. on the E, and Caucasus Mts. on the S. Urals stretch N-S for 2,500 mi. The Asiatic portion is also a vast plain, with mountains on the S and in the E; tundra covers extreme N, with forest belt below; plains, marshes are in W, desert in SW. **Capital:** Moscow. **Cities** (1991 est.): Moscow 8.8 mln.; St. Petersburg 4.4 mln.; Samara 1.2 mln.; Nizhniy Novgorod 1.4 mln.

**Government: Type:** Federation. **Head of state:** Pres. Boris Yeltsin; b. Feb. 1, 1931; in office: July 10, 1991. **Head of government:** Prime Min. Viktor Chernomyrdin; in office: Dec. 14, 1992. **Local divisions:** 20 autonomous republics, 49 oblasts, 6 krays. **Defense:** 8% of GNP (1991).

**Economy: Industries:** Steel, machinery, machine tools, vehicles, chemicals, cement, textiles, appliances, paper. **Chief crops:** Grain, cotton, sugar beets, potatoes, vegetables, sunflowers. **Minerals:** Manganese, mercury, potash, bauxite, cobalt, chromium, copper, coal, gold, lead, molybdenum, nickel, phosphates, silver, tin, tungsten, zinc, oil, potassium salts. **Other resources:** Forests. **Arable land:** 11%. **Livestock** (1990): cattle: 118 mln.; sheep: 142 mln.; pigs: 77 mln.; goats 142 mln. **Fish catch** (1989): 10.9 mln. metric tons. **Electricity prod.** (1991): 1,100 bln. kwh. **Crude steel prod.** (1988): 164 mln. metric tons. **Labor force:** 22% agric.; 29% industry, 26% services.

**Finance: Monetary unit:** Ruble. (Aug. 1993: 987 = $1 US). **Gross domestic product** (1988): $2.5 trl. **Imports** (1991): $43.5 bln.; partners: EC, CIS. **Exports** (1991): $58.7 bln.; partners: EC, CIS. **National budget** (1989): $310 bln. expenditures. **Tourism** (1988): receipts: $216 mln.

**Transport: Motor vehicles:** in use (1991): 8.9 mln. passenger cars. **Civil aviation** (1990): 153 bln. passenger-km; 58 airports with scheduled flights. **Chief ports:** St. Petersburg, Murmansk, Tver, Archangelsk.

**Communications:** Television sets: 1 per 3.2 persons. **Radios:** 1 per 1.5 persons. **Telephones:** 1 per 6.7 persons. **Daily newspaper circ.** (1990): 112 per 1,000 pop.

**Health:** Life expectancy at birth (1992): 63 male; 74 female. **Births** (per 1,000 pop. 1992): 15. **Deaths** (per 1,000 pop. 1992): 11. **Natural increase:** .4%. **Hospital beds:** 1 per 77 persons. **Physicians:** 1 per 221 persons. **Infant mortality** (per 1,000 live births 1992): 31.

**Education** (1993): **Literacy:** 99%. Most receive 11 years of schooling.

**Major International Organizations:** UN (ILO, IMF, UNESCO, WHO), CIS.

**Embassy:** 1125 16th St. NW 20036; 628-7551.

**History.** Slavic tribes began migrating into Russia from the W in the 5th century AD. The first Russian state, founded by Scandinavian chieftains, was established in the 9th century, centering in Novgorod and Kiev.

In the 13th century the Mongols overran the country. It recovered under the grand dukes and princes of Muscovy, or Moscow, and by 1480 freed itself from the Mongols. Ivan the Terrible was the first to be formally proclaimed Tsar (1547). Peter the Great (1682-1725), extended the domain and in 1721, founded the Russian Empire.

Western ideas and the beginnings of modernization spread through the huge Russian empire in the 19th and early 20th centuries. But political evolution failed to keep pace.

Military reverses in the 1905 war with Japan and in World War I led to the breakdown of the Tsarist regime. The 1917 Revolution began in March with a series of sporadic strikes for higher wages by factory workers. A provisional democratic government under Prince Georgi Lvov was established but was quickly followed in May by the second provisional government, led by Alexander Kerensky. The Kerensky government and the freely-elected Constituent Assembly were overthrown in a communist coup led by Vladimir Ilyich Lenin Nov. 7.

## Soviet Union

Lenin's death Jan. 21, 1924, resulted in an internal power struggle from which Joseph Stalin eventually emerged the absolute ruler of Russia. Stalin secured his position at first by exiling opponents, but from the 1930s to 1953, he resorted to a series of "purge" trials, mass executions, and mass exiles to work camps. These measures resulted in millions of deaths, according to most estimates.

Germany and the Soviet Union signed a non-aggression pact Aug. 1939; Germany launched a massive invasion of the Soviet Union, June 1941. Notable heroic episode was the "900 days" siege of Leningrad, lasting to Jan. 1944, and causing a million deaths; the city was never taken. Russian winter counterthrusts, 1941 to '42 and 1942 to '43, stopped the German advance. Turning point was the failure of German troops to take and hold Stalingrad, Sept. 1942 to Feb. 1943. With British and U.S. Lend-Lease aid and sustaining great casualties, the Russians drove the German forces from eastern Europe and the Balkans in the next 2 years.

After Stalin died, Mar. 5, 1953, Nikita Khrushchev was elected first secretary of the Central Committee. In 1956 he condemned Stalin. "De-Stalinization" of the country on all levels was effected after Stalin's body was removed from the Lenin-Stalin tomb in Moscow.

Under Khrushchev the open antagonism of Poles and Hungarians toward domination by Moscow was brutally suppressed in 1956. He advocated peaceful co-existence with the capitalist countries, but continued arming the Soviet Union with nuclear weapons. He aided the Cuban revolution under Fidel Castro but withdrew Soviet missiles from Cuba during confrontation by U.S. Pres. Kennedy, Sept.-Oct. 1962.

Khrushchev was suddenly deposed, Oct. 1964, and replaced as party first secretary by Leonid I. Brezhnev.

In Aug. 1968 Russian, Polish, East German, Hungarian, and Bulgarian military forces invaded Czechoslovakia to put a curb on liberalization policies of the Czech government.

Massive Soviet military aid to North Vietnam in the late 1960s and early 1970s helped assure communist victories throughout Indo-China. Soviet arms aid and advisers were sent to several African countries in the 1970s, including Algeria, Angola, Somalia, and Ethiopia.

In 1979, Soviet forces entered Afghanistan to support that government against rebels. In 1988, the Soviets announced withdrawal of their troops, ending a futile 8-year war.

Mikhail Gorbachev was chosen Gen. Secy. of the Communist Party, Mar. 1985. He was the youngest member of the Politburo and signaled a change in Soviet leadership from those whose attitudes were shaped by Stalinism and World War II.

He held 4 summit meetings with U.S. Pres. Reagan. In 1987, in Washington, an INF treaty was signed.

In 1987, Gorbachev initiated a program of reforms, including expanded freedoms and the democratization of the political process, through openness (*glasnost*) and restructuring (*perestroika*). The reforms were opposed by some Eastern bloc countries and many old-line communists in the USSR. In 1989, the first Soviet Parliament was held since 1918.

Gorbachev faced economic problems as well as ethnic and nationalist unrest in the republics in 1990; the economy was in its worst state since WWII.

On Aug. 19, 1991, it was announced that the vice president had taken over the country due to Gorbachev's illness. A state of emergency was imposed for 6 months with all power resting with the State Committee on the State of Emergency. The Russian republic's pres. Boris Yeltsin denounced the coup and called for a general strike. Some 50,000 demonstrated at the Russian parliament in support of Yeltsin. By Aug. 21, the coup had failed and Gorbachev was restored as pres. On Aug. 24, Gorbachev resigned as leader of the Communist Party and recommended that its central committee be disbanded. Several republics declared their independence including Russia, Ukraine, and Kazakhstan. On Aug. 29, the Soviet parliament voted to suspend all activities of the Communist Party.

On Sept. 2, Gorbachev declared that the nation was "on the brink of catastrophe," and proposed to transfer all central authority to himself, the leaders of 10 republics, and an appointed legislative council in order to form a new kind of Soviet Union.

The Soviet Union officially broke up Dec. 26, 1991, one day after Gorbachev resigned. The Soviet hammer and sickle flying over the Kremlin was lowered and replaced by the flag of Russia, ending the domination of the Communist Party over all areas of national life since 1917.

## Russian Federation

In the first major step in radical economic reform, Russia eliminated state subsidies of most goods and services, Jan. 1992. The effect was to allow prices to soar far beyond the means of ordinary workers. Pres. Yeltsin met with Pres. Bush in Washington, D.C., June 16-17. The two leaders agreed to massive arms reductions. Yeltsin addressed a joint session of Congress and appealed for economic aid for the CIS.

Russia launched a drive to privatize thousands of large and medium-sized state-owned enterprises in 1993. Pres. Yeltsin narrowly survived an impeachment vote by the Congress of People's Deputies, Mar. 28. Yeltsin received strong support from voters in a countrywide referendum Apr. 25, but he continued to feud with a legislature dominated by conservatives and former Communists.

# Rwanda

### Republic of Rwanda

### Republika y'u Rwanda

**People: Population** (1992 est.): 8,206,000. **Age distrib. (%):** 0–14: 48.7; 15–59: 47.1; 60+: 4.2. **Pop. density:** 806 per sq. mi. **Urban** (1991): 5%. **Ethnic groups:** Hutu 90%, Tutsi 9%, Twa (pygmies) 1%. **Languages:** French, Rwanda (both official). **Religions:** Christian 74%, traditional 25%, Moslem 1%.

**Geography: Area:** 10,169 sq. mi., the size of Maryland. **Location:** In E central Africa. **Neighbors:** Uganda on N, Zaire on W, Burundi on S, Tanzania on E. **Topography:** Grassy uplands and hills cover most of the country, with a chain of volcanoes in the NW. The source of the Nile R. has been located in the headwaters of the Kagera (Akagera) R., SW of Kigali. **Capital:** Kigali. **Cities** (1991 est.): Kigali 232,000.

**Government: Type:** Republic. **Head of state:** Pres. Juvenal Habyarimana; b. Mar. 8, 1937; in office: July 5, 1973. **Head of government:** Prime Min. Dismas Nsengiyaremye; in office: Apr. 2, 1992. **Local divisions:** 10 prefectures. **Defense:** 1.6% of GDP (1989).

**Economy: Chief crops:** Coffee, tea. **Minerals:** Tin, gold, wolframite. **Arable land:** 29%. **Electricity prod.** (1991): 130 mln. kWh. **Labor force:** 91% agric.

**Finance: Monetary unit:** Franc (Apr. 1993: 145 = $1 US). **Gross domestic product** (1990): $2.1 bln. **Per capita GDP:** $310. **Imports** (1990): $279.2 mln.; partners: Ken. 21%, Belg. 16%, Jap. 12%, W. Ger. 9%. **Exports** (1990): $111.7 mln.; partners: EC, Ugan. **National budget** (1989): $491 million expenditures. **International reserves less gold** (Mar. 1993): $64 mln. **Consumer prices** (change in 1992): 9.5%.

**Transport: Motor vehicles:** in use (1990): 8,000 passenger cars, 10,000 comm. vehicles.

**Communications: Radios:** 1 per 11 persons. **Telephones:** 1 per 497 persons.

**Health: Life expectancy at birth** (1992): 51 male; 55 female. **Births** (per 1,000 pop. 1992): 52. **Deaths** (per 1,000 pop. 1992): 15. **Natural increase:** 3.7%. **Hospital beds** (1984): 9,000. **Physicians** (1984): 177. **Infant mortality** (per 1,000 live births 1992): 108.

**Education** (1991): **Literacy:** 50%. **Years compulsory:** 8; **attendance:** 70%.

**Major International Organizations:** UN (GATT, IMF, WHO), OAU.

**Embassy:** 1714 New Hampshire Ave. NW 20009; 232-2882.

For centuries, the Tutsi (an extremely tall people) dominated the Hutus (90% of the population). A civil war broke out in 1959 and Tutsi power was ended. A referendum in 1961 abolished the monarchic system. Some 8,000 exiled Tutsi invaded Rwanda from Uganda, Sept. 1990. A new constitution was signed into effect in 1991 calling for multiparty politics, freedom of the press, and a limited presidential term. A peace accord between the government and the Tutsi rebels was signed in Aug. 1993.

Rwanda, which had been part of the Belgian UN trusteeship of Rwanda-Urundi, became independent July 1, 1962. The government was overthrown in a 1973 military coup. Rwanda is one of the most densely populated countries in Africa. All available arable land is being used, and is being subject to erosion.

# Saint Kitts and Nevis

### Federation of Saint Kitts & Nevis

**People: Population** (1992 est.): 40,293. **Pop. density:** 398 per sq. mi. **Ethnic groups:** black African 95%. **Language:** English. **Religion:** Protestant 76%.

**Geography: Area:** 101 sq. mi. in the northern part of the Leeward group of the Lesser Antilles in the eastern Caribbean Sea. **Capitol:** Basseterre. (1989): 15,000.

**Government:** Constitutional monarchy. **Head of state:** Queen Elizabeth represented by Sir Clement Arrindell. **Head of government:** Prime Minister Kennedy A. Simmonds; b. Apr. 12, 1936; in office: Sept. 19, 1983.

**Economy:** Sugar is the principal industry.

**Finance: Monetary unit:** E. Caribbean Dollar (Mar. 1993): 2.70 = $1 U.S. **Gross domestic product** (1990): $146 mln. **Tourism** (1990): $63 mln. receipts.

**Communications: Telephones:** 1 per 6 persons. **Health: Infant mortality** (per 1,000 live births, 1992): 22. **Education: Literacy** (1991): 98%.

St. Kitts (known by the natives as Liamuiga) and Nevis were reached (and named) by Columbus in 1493. They were settled by Britain in 1623, but ownership was disputed with France until 1713. They were part of the Leeward Islands Federation, 1871-1956, and the Federation of the W. Indies, 1958-62. The colony achieved self-government as an Associated State of the UK in 1967, and became fully independent Sept. 19, 1983.

# Saint Lucia

**People: Population** (1992 est.): 151,000. **Age distrib. (%):** 0–20: 44.5; 21–64: 47.5; 65+: 8.0. **Pop. density:** 634 per sq. mi. **Ethnic groups:** Predominantly African descent. **Languages:** English (official), French patois. **Religions:** Roman Catholic 90%.

**Geography: Area:** 238 sq. mi., about one-fifth the size of Rhode Island. **Location:** In Eastern Caribbean, 2d largest of the Windward Is. **Neighbors:** Martinique to N, St. Vincent to SW. **Topography:** Mountainous, volcanic in origin; Soufriere, a volcanic crater, in the S. Wooded mountains run N-S to Mt. Gimie, 3,145 ft., with streams through fertile valleys. **Capital:** Castries. **City:** Castries (1989 est.): 55,000.

**Government: Type:** Parliamentary democracy. **Head of state:** Queen Elizabeth II, represented by Gov.-Gen. S.A. James; **Head of government:** Prime Min. John Compton; in office: May 3, 1982. **Local divisions:** 11 quarters

**Economy: Industries:** Agriculture, tourism, manufacturing. **Chief crops:** Bananas, coconuts, cocoa, citrus fruits. **Other resources:** Forests. **Arable land:** 8%. **Electricity prod.** (1991): 112 mln. kWh. **Labor force:** 36% agric., 20% ind. & commerce, 18% services.

**Finance: Monetary unit:** East Caribbean dollar (Mar. 1993: 2.70 = $1 US). **Gross domestic product** (1990): $295 mln. **Per capita GDP:** $1,930. **Imports** (1990): $270 mln.; partners: U.S. 36%, UK 12%, Trin./Tob. 11%. **Exports** (1990): $127 mln.; partners: U.S. 19%, UK 51%. **Tourism** (1990): receipts $155 mln.

**Transport: Motor vehicles:** in use (1989): 7,000 passenger cars, 4,000 comm. vehicles. **Chief ports:** Castries, Vieux Fort.

**Communications: Television sets:** 1 per 6 persons. **Radios:** 1 per 1.5 persons. **Telephones:** 1 per 10 persons.

**Health: Life expectancy at birth** (1992): 70 male; 75 female. **Births** (per 1,000 pop. 1992): 26. **Deaths** (per 1,000 pop. 1992): 5. **Natural increase:** 2.1%. **Hospital beds:** 1 per 283 persons. **Physicians:** 1 per 2,521 persons. **Infant mortality** (per 1,000 live births 1992): 18.

**Education: Literacy** (1989): 78%; **Years compulsory:** ages 5-15; **Attendance:** 80%.

**Major International Organizations:** UN (IMF, ILO), CARICOM, OAS.

St. Lucia was ceded to Britain by France at the Treaty of Paris, 1814. Self government was granted with the West Indies Act, 1967. Independence was attained Feb. 22, 1979.

# Saint Vincent and the Grenadines

**People: Population** (1992 est.): 114,000. **Pop. density:** 760 per sq. mi. **Ethnic groups:** Mainly of African descent. **Languages:** English. **Religions:** Methodists, Anglicans, Roman Catholics.

**Geography: Area:** 150 sq. mi., about twice the size of Washington, D.C. **Location:** In the eastern Caribbean, St. Vincent (133 sq. mi.) and the northern islets of the Grenadines form a part of the Windward chain. **Neighbors:** St. Lucia to N, Barbados to E, Grenada to S. **Topography:** St. Vincent is volcanic, with a ridge of thickly wooded mountains running its length. **Capital:** Kingstown. **Cities** (1991 est.): Kingstown 15,000.

**Government: Type:** Constitutional monarchy. **Head of state:** Queen Elizabeth II, represented by Gov.-Gen. David Jack; in office: Sept. 20 1989. **Head of government:** James Mitchell; in office: July 30, 1984.

**Economy: Industries:** Agriculture, tourism. **Chief crops:** Bananas (62% of exports), arrowroot, coconuts. **Arable land:** 50%. **Electricity prod.** (1991): 63 mln. kWh. **Labor force:** 30% agric.

**Finance: Monetary unit:** East Caribbean dollar (Mar. 1993: 2.70 = $1 US). **Gross domestic product** (1989): $146 mln. **Per capita GDP** (1989): $1,315. **Tourism** (1991): $53 mln. receipts. **National budget** (1990): $67 mln. expenditures.

**Transport: Motor vehicles:** in use (1991): 5,000 passenger cars, 2,800 comm. vehicles. **Chief port:** Kingstown.

**Communications: Telephones:** 1 per 6 persons.

**Health: Life expectancy at birth** (1992): 71 male; 74 female. **Births** (per 1,000 pop. 1992): 23. **Deaths** (per 1,000 pop. 1992): 5. **Natural increase:** 1.7%. **Infant mortality** (per 1,000 live births 1992): 19.

**Education** (1989): **Literacy:** 85%.

Columbus landed on St. Vincent on Jan. 22, 1498 (St. Vincent's Day). Britain and France both laid claim to the island in the 17th and 18th centuries; the Treaty of Versailles, 1783, finally ceded it to Britain. Associated State status was granted 1969; independence was attained Oct. 27, 1979.

The entire economic life of St. Vincent is dependent upon agriculture and tourism.

# San Marino

## Most Serene Republic of San Marino

## Serenissima Repubblica di San Marino

**People: Population** (1992 est.): 23,000. **Age distrib.** (%): 0–14: 16.1; 15–59: 65.3; 60+: 16.1. **Pop. density:** 958 per sq. mi. **Urban** (1992): 90.5%. **Ethnic groups:** Sanmarinese 80%, Italian 18%. **Languages:** Italian. **Religion:** mostly Roman Catholic.

**Geography: Area:** 24 sq. mi. **Location:** In N central Italy near Adriatic coast. **Neighbors:** Completely surrounded by Italy. **Topography:** The country lies on the slopes of Mt. Titano. **Capital:** San Marino. **Cities** (1991 est.): San Marino 4,643.

**Government: Type:** Republic. **Head of state:** Two co-regents appt. every 6 months. **Local divisions:** 9 municipalities.

**Economy: Industries:** Postage stamps, tourism, woolen goods, paper, cement, ceramics. **Arable land:** 17%.

**Finance: Monetary unit:** Italian lira. **Gross domestic product** (1991): $400 mln. **Tourism** (1991): 3.1 mln. arrivals.

**Communications: Television sets:** 1 per 3.4 persons. **Radios:** 1 per 1.8 persons. **Telephones:** 1 per 1.6 persons.

**Births** (per 1,000 pop. 1992): 8. **Deaths** (per 1,000 pop. 1992): 7. **Natural increase:** 0.1%. **Infant mortality** (per 1,000 live births 1992): 8.

**Education** (1991): **Literacy:** 97%. **Years compulsory:** 8. **Attendance:** 93%.

**Major International Organizations:** UN.

San Marino claims to be the oldest state in Europe and to have been founded in the 4th century. A communist-led coalition ruled 1947-57; a similar coalition ruled 1978-86. It has had a treaty of friendship with Italy since 1862.

# São Tomé and Príncipe

## Democratic Republic of São Tomé and Príncipe

## República Democrática de São Tomé e Príncipe

**People: Population** (1992 est.): 132,000. **Pop. density:** 354 per sq. mi. **Ethnic groups:** Portuguese-African mixture, African minority (Angola, Mozambique immigrants). **Languages:** Portuguese. **Religions:** Christian 80%.

**Geography: Area:** 372 sq. mi., slightly larger than New York City. **Location:** In the Gulf of Guinea about 125 miles off W Central Africa. **Neighbors:** Gabon, Equatorial Guinea on E. **Topography:** São Tomé and Príncipe islands, part of an extinct volcano chain, are both covered by lush forests and croplands. **Capital:** São Tomé. **Cities** (1988 est.): São Tomé 40,000.

**Government: Type:** Republic. **Head of state:** Pres. Miguel Trovoada; in office: Apr. 3, 1991. **Head of government:** Prime Min. Norberto Jose D'Alva Costa Alegre Daio; in office: May 16, 1992. **Local divisions:** 2 districts.

**Economy: Chief crops:** Cocoa (82% of exports), coconut products. **Arable land:** 38%. **Electricity prod.** (1991): 10 mln. kWh.

**Finance: Monetary unit:** Dobra (Jan. 1993: 240 = $1 US). **Gross domestic product** (1989): $46 mln. **Per capita GDP:** $384. **Imports** (1990): $21.3 mln.; partners: Port. 61%, Angola 13%. **Exports** (1990): $4.4 mln.; partners: Neth. 52%, Port. 33%, Ger. 8%.

**Transport: Chief ports:** São Tomé, Santo Antonio.

**Communications: Radios:** 1 per 3.9 persons.

**Health: Births** (per 1,000 pop. 1992): 38. **Deaths** (per 1,000 pop. 1992): 7. **Natural increase:** 3.0%. **Physicians:** 1 per 2,819 persons. **Infant mortality** (per 1,000 live births 1992): 58.

**Education** (1988): **Literacy:** 50%.

**Major International Organizations:** UN, OAU.

**Embassy:** 801 2d Ave., New York, NY 10017; 212-697-4211.

The islands were uninhabited when discovered in 1471 by the Portuguese, who brought the first settlers — convicts and exiled Jews. Sugar planting was replaced by the slave trade as the chief economic activity until coffee and cocoa were introduced in the 19th century.

Portugal agreed, 1974, to turn the colony over to the Gabon-based Movement for the Liberation of São Tomé and Príncipe, which proclaimed as first president its East German-trained leader Manuel Pinto da Costa. Independence came July 12, 1975. Democratic reforms were instituted in 1987. In 1991 Miguel Trovoada won the first free presidential election following the withdrawal of Pres. Manuel Pinto da Costa. Da Costa had ruled the country since independence.

Agriculture and fishing are the mainstays of the economy.

# Saudi Arabia

## Kingdom of Saudi Arabia

## al-Mamlaka al-'Arabiya as-Sa'udiya

**People: Population** (1992 cen.): 16,900,000. **Pop. density:** 20 per sq. mi. **Urban** (1990): 78%. **Ethnic groups:** Arab tribes, immigrants from other Arab and Moslem countries. **Language:** Arabic. **Religion:** Moslem 99%.

**Geography: Area:** 839,996 sq. mi., one-third the size of the U.S. **Location:** Occupies most of Arabian Peninsula in Middle East. **Neighbors:** Kuwait, Iraq, Jordan on N, Yemen, Oman on S, United Arab Emirates, Qatar on E. **Topography:** The highlands on W, up to 9,000 ft., slope as an arid, barren desert to the Persian Gulf. **Capital:** Riyadh. **Cities** (1986 est.): Riyadh 1,380,000; Jidda 1,210,000; Mecca 463,000.

**Government: Type:** Monarchy with council of ministers. **Head of state and head of government:** King Fahd; b. 1922; in office: June 13, 1982. **Local divisions:** 14 emirates. **Defense:** 13% of GDP (1992).

**Economy: Industries:** Oil products. **Chief crops:** Dates, wheat, barley, fruit. **Minerals:** Oil, gas, gold, copper, iron. **Crude oil reserves** (1990): 255 bln. barrels. **Arable land:** 2%. **Livestock** (1991): sheep: 5.6 mln.; goats: 3.5 mln. **Electricity prod.** (1991): 60 bln. kWh. **Labor force:** 14% agric.; 11% ind.; 53% serv., comm., & govt.; 20% construction.

**Finance: Monetary unit:** Riyal (July 1993: 3.70 = $1 US). **Gross domestic product** (1991): $104 bln. **Per capita GDP:** $5,800. **Imports** (1990): $21.5 bln.; partners: US 15%, Jap. 12%, UK 14%. **Exports** (1990): $28.3 bln.; partners: U.S. 22%, Jap. 20%. **National budget** (1990): $38 bln. expenditures. **International reserves less gold** (Mar. 1992): $11.6 bln. **Gold:** 4.59 mln. oz t. **Consumer prices** (change in 1991): 4.1%.

**Transport: Railroads** (1989): **Length:** 555 mi. **Motor vehicles:** in use (1989): 2.2 mln. passenger cars, 2.0 mln. comm. vehicles. **Civil aviation** (1990): 16.0 bln.; passenger-km.; 25 airports. **Chief ports:** Jidda, Ad-Dammam, Ras Tannurah.

**Communications: Television sets:** 1 per 3.5 persons. **Radios:** 1 per 3.3 persons. **Telephones:** 1 per 13 persons. **Daily newspaper circ.** (1989): 49 per 1,000 pop.

**Health: Life expectancy at birth** (1991): 65 male; 68 female. **Births** (per 1,000 pop. 1991): 38. **Deaths** (per 1,000 pop. 1991): 7. **Natural increase:** 3.1%. **Hospital beds:** 1 per 406 persons. **Physicians:** 1 per 852 persons. **Infant mortality** (per 1,000 live births 1991): 69.

**Education** (1990): **Literacy:** 62%.

**Major International Organizations:** UN (IMF, WHO, FAO), Arab League, OPEC.

**Embassy:** 601 New Hampshire Ave. NW 20037; 342-3800.

Arabia was united for the first time by Mohammed, in the early 7th century. His successors conquered the entire Near East and North Africa, bringing Islam and the Arabic language. But Arabia itself soon returned to its former status.

Nejd, long an independent state and center of the Wahhabi sect, fell under Turkish rule in the 18th century, but in 1913 Ibn Saud, founder of the Saudi dynasty, overthrew the Turks and captured the Turkish province of Hasa; took the Hejaz in 1925 and by 1926, most of Asir. The discovery of oil in the 1930s transformed the new country.

Crown Prince Khalid was proclaimed king on Mar. 25, 1975, after the assassination of King Faisal. Fahd became king on June 13, 1982 following Khalid's death. There is no constitution and no parliament. The king exercises authority together with a Council of Ministers. The Islamic religious code is the law of the land. Alcohol and public entertainments are restricted, and women have an inferior legal status.

Saudi units fought against Israel in the 1948 and 1973 Arab-Israeli wars. Many billions of dollars of advanced arms have been purchased from Britain, France, and the U.S., including jet fighters, missiles, and, in 1981, 5 airborne warning and control system (AWACS) aircraft from the U.S., despite strong opposition from Israel. Beginning with the 1967 Arab-Israeli war, Saudi Arabia provided large annual financial gifts to Egypt; aid was later extended to Syria, Jordan, and Palestinian guerrilla groups, as well as to other Moslem countries.

Faisal played a leading role in the 1973-74 Arab oil embargo against the U.S. and other nations in an attempt to force them to adopt an anti-Israel policy. Saudi Arabia joined most other Arab states, 1979, in condemning Egypt's peace treaty with Israel.

In the 1980s, Saudi Arabia's moderate position on crude oil prices often prevailed at OPEC meetings.

The Hejaz contains the holy cities of Islam — Medina where the Mosque of the Prophet enshrines the tomb of Mohammed, who died in the city June 7, 632, and Mecca, his birthplace. More than 600,000 Moslems from 60 nations pilgrimage to Mecca annually.

Two Saudi oil tankers were attacked May 1984, as Iran and Iraq began air attacks against shipping in the Persian Gulf. On May 29, the U.S., citing grave concern over the growing escalation of the Iran-Iraq war in the Persian Gulf, authorized the sale of 400 Stinger antiaircraft missiles.

In 1987, Iranians making a pilgrimage to Mecca clashed with anti-Iranian pilgrims and Saudi police; over 400 were killed. Saudi Arabia broke diplomatic relations with Iran in 1988. Some 1,426 Moslem pilgrims died July 2, 1990 when a stampede occurred in a pedestrian tunnel leading to Mecca.

Following Iraq's attack on Kuwait, Aug. 2, 1990, Saudi Arabia accepted the Kuwait royal family and over 400,000 Kuwaiti refugees. King Fahd invited Western and Arab troops to deploy on its soil in support of Saudi defense forces. During the Persian Gulf war, Iraq fired a series of Scud missiles at Saudi Arabia; most were intercepted by U.S. Patriot missiles, although 28 U.S. soldiers were killed when a scud hit their barracks in Dhahran, Feb. 25. The nation's northern Gulf coastline suffered severe pollution as a result of Iraqi sabotage of the Kuwaiti oil fields.

# Senegal

## Republic of Senegal
## République du Sénégal

**People: Population** (1992 est.): 8,205,000. **Age distrib. (%):** 0–14: 47.5; 15–59: 47.5; 60+: 5.0. **Pop. density:** 108 per sq. mi. **Urban** (1986): 30%. **Ethnic groups:** Wolof 36%, Serer 17%, Fulani 17%, Diola 9%, Toucouleur 9%, Mandingo 6%. **Languages:** French (official), Wolof, Serer, Peul, Tukulor, others. **Religions:** Moslem 92%, Christian 2%.

**Geography: Area:** 75,750 sq. mi., the size of South Dakota. **Location:** At western extreme of Africa. **Neighbors:** Mauritania on N, Mali on E, Guinea, Guinea-Bissau on S, Gambia surrounded on three sides. **Topography:** Low rolling plains cover most of Senegal, rising somewhat in the SE. Swamp and jungles are in SW. **Capital:** Dakar. **Cities** (1992): Dakar 1.7 mln.; Thies 201,000; Kaolack 179,000.

**Government: Type:** Republic. **Head of state:** Pres. Abdou Diouf; b. Sept. 7, 1935; in office: Jan. 1, 1981. **Head of government:** Habib Thiam; in office: Apr. 8, 1991. **Local divisions:** 10 regions. **Defense:** 2.0% of GDP (1989).

**Economy: Industries:** Food processing, fishing. **Chief crops:** Peanuts are chief export; millet, rice. **Minerals:** Phosphates. **Arable land:** 27%. **Livestock** (1991): cattle: 2.8 mln.; sheep: 4.0 mln.; goats: 1.2 mln. **Fish catch** (1989): 255,000 metric tons. **Electricity prod.** (1991): 758 mln. kWh. **Labor force:** 77% agric.

**Finance: Monetary unit:** CFA franc (Mar. 1993: 273 = $1 US). **Gross domestic product** (1990): $5.0 bln. **Per capita GDP:** $615. **Imports** (1990): $1.0 bln.; partners Fr. 37%, U.S. 6%. **Exports** (1990): $814 mln.; partners Fr. 25%, UK 6%. **Tourism** (1990): $152 mln. receipts. **National budget** (1989): $1.0 bln. expenditures. **International reserves less gold** (Jan. 1993): $12.4 mln. **Gold:** 29,000 oz t. **Consumer prices** (change in 1991): 1.8%.

**Transport: Railroads** (1992): **Length:** 562 mi. **Motor vehicles:** in use (1989): 90,000 passenger cars, 36,000 comm. vehicles. **Chief ports:** Dakar, Saint-Louis.

**Communications: Television sets:** 1 per 125 persons. **Radios:** 1 per 8.7 persons. **Telephones:** 1 per 150 persons. **Daily newspaper circ.** (1990): 7 per 1,000 pop.

**Health: Life expectancy at birth** (1992): 54 male, 57 female. **Births** (per 1,000 pop. 1992): 44. **Deaths** (per 1,000 pop. 1992): 13. **Natural increase:** 2.9%. **Hospital beds:** 1 per 1,134 persons. **Physicians:** 1 per 17,072 persons. **Infant mortality** (per 1,000 live births 1992): 80.

**Education** (1988): **Literacy:** 10%. **Attendance:** 48% primary, 11% secondary.

**Major International Organizations:** UN and all of its specialized agencies, OAU.

**Embassy:** 2112 Wyoming Ave. NW 20008; 234-0540.

Portuguese settlers arrived in the 15th century, but French control grew from the 17th century. The last independent Moslem state was subdued in 1893. Dakar became the capital of French West Africa.

Independence as part, along with the Sudanese Rep., of the Mali Federation, came June 20, 1960. Senegal withdrew Aug. 20. French political and economic influence is strong.

Senegal, Dec. 17, 1981, signed an agreement with The Gambia for confederation of the 2 countries under the name of Senegambia. The confederation began Feb. 1, 1982. The 2 nations retained their individual sovereignty but adopted joint defense and monetary policies. The confederation collapsed in 1989, although in 1991 the 2 nations signed a friendship and cooperation treaty.

In 1989, a border incident sparked ethnic violence against Senegalese in Mauritania and, in retaliation, against Mauritanians in Senegal.

# Seychelles

## Republic of Seychelles

**People: Population** (1992 est.): 68,000. **Age distrib. (%):** 0–14: 36.3; 15–64: 57.3; 65+: 6.4. **Pop. density:** 397 per sq. mi. **Urban** (1990): 60% **Ethnic groups:** Creoles (mixture of Asians, Africans, and French) predominate. **Languages:** English, French, (both official). **Religions:** Roman Catholic 90%.

**Geography: Area:** 171 sq. mi. **Location:** In the Indian O. 700 miles NE of Madagascar. **Neighbors:** Nearest are Madagascar on SW, Somalia on NW. **Topography:** A group of 86 islands, about half of them composed of coral, the other half granite, the latter predominantly mountainous. **Capital:** Victoria. **Cities** (1986): Victoria 23,000.

**Government: Type:** Single party republic. **Head of state:** Pres. France-Albert Rene, b. Nov. 16, 1935; in office: June 5, 1977. **Local divisions:** 23 districts. **Defense:** 6.0% of GDP (1990).

**Economy: Industries:** Food processing. **Chief crops:** Coconut products, cinnamon, vanilla, patchouli. **Electricity prod.** (1991): 80 mln. kWh. **Labor force:** 12% agric.; 19.4% tourism, comm.; 32% serv.; 40% govt.

**Finance: Monetary unit:** Rupee (Mar. 1993: 5.21 = $1 US). **Gross domestic product** (1991): $350 mln. **Per capita GDP:** $5,200. **Imports** (1991): $172 mln.; partners: UK 20%, So. Afr. 13%. **Exports** (1991): $48 mln.; partners: Pak. 38%; Jap. 26%. **National Budget** (1989): $168 mln. **Tourism** (1991): $97 mln. receipts. **International reserves less gold** (Mar. 1993): $26.5 mln. **Consumer prices** (change in 1992): 3.3%.

**Transport: Motor vehicles:** in use (1989): 4,000 passenger cars, 1,300 comm. vehicles. **Port:** Victoria.

**Communications: Radios:** 1 per 3 persons. **Telephones:** 1 per 5 persons. **Daily newspaper circ.** (1990): 47 per 1,000 pop.

**Health: Life expectancy at birth** (1992): 65 male; 75 female. **Births** (per 1,000 pop. 1992): 23. **Deaths** (per 1,000 pop. 1992): 7. **Natural increase:** 1.6%. **Hospital beds:** 1 per 171 persons. **Physicians:** 1 per 992 persons. **Infant mortality** (per 1,000 live births 1992): 15.

**Education** (1991): **Literacy:** 85%. **Years compulsory** 9; attendance 98%.

**Major International Organizations:** UN, OAU, Commonwealth of Nations.

The islands were occupied by France in 1768, and seized by Britain in 1794. Ruled as part of Mauritius from 1814, the Seychelles became a separate colony in 1903. The ruling party had opposed independence as impractical, but pressure from the OAU and the UN became irresistible, and independence was declared June 29, 1976. The first president was ousted in a coup a year later by a socialist leader.

A new constitution, announced Mar. 1979, turned the country into a one-party state.

# Sierra Leone
## Republic of Sierra Leone

**People: Population** (1992 est.): 4,456,000. **Age distrib. (%):** 0–14: 41.4; 15–59: 53.5; 60+: 5.1. **Pop. density:** 159 per sq. mi. **Urban** (1991): 33%. **Ethnic groups:** Temne 30%, Mende 29%, others. **Languages:** English (official), tribal languages. **Religions:** animist 30%, Moslem 30%, Christian 10%.

**Geography: Area:** 27,925 sq. mi., slightly smaller than South Carolina. **Location:** On W coast of W. Africa. **Neighbors:** Guinea on N, E, Liberia on S. **Topography:** The heavily-indented, 210-mi. coastline has mangrove swamps. Behind are wooded hills, rising to a plateau and mountains in the E. **Capital:** Freetown. **Cities** (1985 est.): Freetown 469,000; Bo, Kenema, Makeni.

**Government: Type:** Military. **Head of government:** Capt. Valentine E. M. Strasser; in office: May 7, 1992. **Local divisions:** 4 provinces.

**Economy: Industries:** Mining, tourism. **Chief crops:** Cocoa, coffee, palm kernels, rice, ginger. **Minerals:** Diamonds, bauxite. **Arable land:** 25%. **Fish catch** (1990): 52,000 metric tons. **Electricity prod.** (1991): 185 mln. kWh. **Labor force:** 75% agric.; 15% ind. & serv.

**Finance: Monetary unit:** Leone (Mar. 1993): 561 = $1.00 US). **Gross domestic product** (1991): $1.4 bln. **Per capita GDP:** $330. **Imports** (1992): $131 mln.; partners: UK 22%, Fr. 11%. **Exports** (1992): $145 mln.; partners: Neth. 31%; UK 15%, U.S. 9%. **National budget** (1991): $181 mln. expenditures. **International reserves less gold** (Mar. 1993): $23 mln. **Consumer prices** (change in 1992): 65.5%.

**Transport: Motor Vehicles:** in use (1989): 29,000 passenger cars, 10,000 comm. vehicles. **Chief ports:** Freetown, Bonthe.

**Communications: Television sets:** 1 per 170 persons. **Radios:** 1 per 4.2 persons. **Telephones:** 1 per 160 persons. **Daily newspaper circ.** (1991): 3 per 1,000 pop.

**Health: Life expectancy at birth** (1992): 43 male; 48 female. **Births** (per 1,000 pop. 1992): 46. **Deaths** (per 1,000 pop. 1992): 21. **Natural increase:** 2.5%. **Hospital beds:** 1 per 980 persons. **Physicians:** 1 per 13,150 persons. **Infant mortality** (per 1,000 live births 1992): 148.

**Education** (1991): **Literacy:** 21%.

**Major International Organizations:** UN (GATT, IMF, WHO), Commonwealth of Nations, OAU.

**Embassy:** 1701 19th St. NW 20009; 939-9261.

Freetown was founded in 1787 by the British government as a haven for freed slaves. Their descendants, known as Creoles, number more than 60,000.

Successive steps toward independence followed the 1951 constitution. Full independence arrived Apr. 27, 1961. Sierra Leone became a republic Apr. 19, 1971. A one-party state approved by referendum 1978, brought political stability, but the economy has been plagued by inflation, corruption, and dependence upon the International Monetary Fund and creditors.

Mutinous soldiers ousted Pres. Momoh Apr. 30, 1992.

# Singapore
## Republic of Singapore

**People: Population** (1992 est.): 2,792,000. **Age distrib. (%):** 0–14: 23.4; 15–59: 68.4; 60+: 8.2. **Pop. density:** 12,464 per sq. mi. **Ethnic groups:** Chinese 77%, Malays 15%, Indians 6%. **Languages:** Chinese, Malay, Tamil, English all official. **Religions:** Buddhism 29%, Taoism 13%, Moslem 16%, Christian 19%.

**Geography: Area:** 224 sq. mi., smaller than New York City. **Location:** Off tip of Malayan Peninsula in S.E. Asia. **Neighbors:** Nearest are Malaysia on N, Indonesia on S. **Topography:** Singapore is a flat, formerly swampy island. The nation includes 40 nearby islets. **Capital:** Singapore.

**Government: Type:** Republic. **Head of state:** Pres. Ong Teng Cheong; in office: Sept. 2, 1993. **Head of government:** Prime Min. Goh Chok Tong; b. May 20, 1941; in office: Nov. 28, 1990. **Defense:** 4% of GDP (1990).

**Economy: Industries:** Shipbuilding, oil refining, electronics, banking, textiles, food, rubber, lumber processing, tourism. **Arable land:** 11%. **Livestock** (1989): pigs: 321,000. **Electricity prod.** (1990): 14.4 bln. kWh. **Labor force:** 1% agric.; 58% ind. & comm.; 35% services.

**Finance: Monetary unit:** Dollar (May 1993: 1.64 = $1 US). **Gross domestic product** (1991): $38.3 bln. **Per capita GDP:** $13,900. **Imports** (1992): $72.1 bln.; partners: Jap. 18%, Malay. 13%, U.S. 17%, Sau. Ar. 9%. **Exports** (1992): $63.4 bln., partners: U.S. 20%, Malay. 16%, Jap. 11%, HK 6%. **Tourism** (1990): $4.3 bln. receipts. **National budget** (1991): $9.0 bln. expenditures. **Consumer prices** (change in 1992): 2.3%.

**Transport: Motor vehicles:** in use (1991): 300,000 passenger cars, 127,000 comm. vehicles. **Civil aviation:** (1991) 33.4 bln. passenger-km; 1 airport.

**Communications: Television sets:** 1 per 4.9 persons. **Radios:** 1 per 4.2 persons. **Telephones:** 1 per 2.1 persons. **Daily newspaper circ.** (1990): 289 per 1,000 pop.

**Health: Life expectancy at birth** (1992): 73 male; 78 female. **Births** (per 1,000 pop. 1992): 18. **Deaths** (per 1,000 pop. 1992): 5. **Natural increase:** 1.3%. **Hospital beds:** 1 per 272 persons. **Physicians:** 1 per 779 persons. **Infant mortality** (per 1,000 live births 1992): 6.

**Education** (1990): **Literacy:** 87%. **Years compulsory:** none; attendance 94%.

**Major International Organizations:** UN (GATT, IMF, WHO), ASEAN.

**Embassy:** 1824 R St. NW 20009; 667-7555.

Founded in 1819 by Sir Thomas Stamford Raffles, Singapore was a British colony until 1959 when it became autonomous within the Commonwealth. On Sept. 16, 1963, it joined with Malaya, Sarawak and Sabah to form the Federation of Malaysia.

Tensions between Malayans, dominant in the federation, and ethnic Chinese, dominant in Singapore, led to an agreement under which Singapore became a separate nation, Aug. 9, 1965.

Singapore is one of the world's largest ports. Standards in health, education, and housing are high. International banking has grown.

# Slovakia
## Slovensko

**People: Population** (1993 est.): 5,300,000. **Pop. density:** 279 per sq. mi. **Ethnic groups:** Slovak 87%, Hungarian 10%.

**Geography: Area:** 18,932 sq. mi. **Location:** In E central Europe. **Neighbors:** Poland on N., Hungary on S, Austria, Czech Rep. on W, Ukraine on E. **Topography:** mountains (Carpathians) in N, fertile Danube plane in S. **Capital:** Bratislava. **Cities** (1991 est.): Bratislava 440,000, Kosice 236,000.

**Government: Type:** Republic. **Head of state:** Pres. Michal Kovac; b. 1931; in office: Feb. 2, 1993. **Head of government:** Prime Min. Vladimir Meciar; in office: Jan. 1, 1993.

**Economy: Industries:** Iron and steel, glass, chemicals, cement. **Chief crops:** Wheat potatoes, rye, corn.

**Finance: Monetary unit:** new Koruna (Feb. 1993: 29.00 = $1 US).

**Education** (1993): **Literacy:** 99%.

**Major International Organizations:** UN.

Slovakia was originally settled by Illyrian, Celtic, and Germanic tribes and was incorporated into Great Moravia in the 9th century. It became part of Hungary in the 11th century. Overrun by Czech Hussites in the 15th century, it was restored to Hungarian rule in 1526. The Slovaks disassociated themselves from Hungary following World War I and joined the Czechs of Bohemia to form the Republic of Czechoslovakia, Oct. 28, 1918.

Germany invaded Czechoslovakia, 1939, and declared Slovakia an independent state. Slovakia rejoined Czechoslovakia in 1945.

Czechoslovakia split into 2 seperate states—the Czech Republic and Slovakia—on Jan. 1, 1993.

## Slovenia

### Republic of Slovenia
### Republica of Slovenija

**People: Population** (1992 est.): 1,974,000. **Pop. density:** 252 per sq. mi. **Ethnic groups:** Slovenes 91%. **Language:** Slovenian, Serbo-Croatian. **Religions:** Mostly Roman Catholic.

**Geography: Area:** 7,819 sq. mi., slightly larger than New Jersey. **Location:** in SE Europe. **Neighbors:** Italy, Austria, Hungary, Croatia. **Topography:** mostly hilly; 42% of the land is forested. **Capital:** Ljubljana. **Cities** (1991): Ljubljana 323,000.

**Government: Type:** Republic. **Head of state:** Pres. Milan Kucan. **Head of government:** Janez Drnovsek; in office: May 14, 1992.

**Economy: Industries:** Steel, textiles. **Minerals:** Coal, mercury. **Chief crops:** Wheat, potatoes. **Livestock** (1991): cattle: 546,000; pigs: 576,000. **Electricity prod.** (1991): 12.2 bln. kWh.

**Finance: Monetary unit:** Tolar. **Gross domestic product** (1991): $21 bln. **Per capita GDP:** $10,700. **Imports** (1990): $4.6 bln. **Exports** (1990): $4.1 bln.

**Transport: Motor vehicles:** in use (1990): 581,000 passenger cars.

**Communications: Television sets:** 1 per 3.7 persons. **Telephones:** 1 per 3 persons. **Newspaper circ.** (1990): 112 per 1,000 pop.

**Health: Life expectancy at birth** (1992): 70 male; 78 female. **Hospital beds:** 1 per 143 persons. **Physicians:** 1 per 481 persons. **Infant mortality:** (per 1,000 live births 1991): 9.

**Education:** Literacy (1991): 90%.

**Major International Organizations:** UN.

The Slovenes settled in their current territory in the period from the 6th to the 8th centuries. They fell under German domination as early as the 9th century. Modern Slovenian political history began after 1848 when the Slovenes, who were divided among several Austrian provinces, began their struggle for political and national unification. With the establishment of Yugoslavia in 1918, this unification was largely achieved when the majority of the Slovenes entered the new state, which became the Kingdom of the Serbs, Croats, and Slovenes.

Slovenia declared independence June 25, 1991.

## Solomon Islands

**People: Population** (1992 est.): 360,000. **Age distrib. (%):** 0–14: 49; 15–59: 45.5; 60+: 5.5. **Pop. density:** 33 per sq. mi. **Urban** (1986): 15%. **Ethnic groups:** Melanesian 93%, Polynesian 4%. **Languages:** English (official), Papuan, Melanesian, Polynesian languages. **Religions:** Anglican 34%, Roman Catholic 19%, Evangelical 24%, traditional religions.

**Geography: Area:** 10,640 sq. mi., slightly larger than Maryland. **Location:** Melanesian archipelago in the western Pacific O. **Neighbors:** Nearest is Papua New Guinea on W. **Topography:** 10 large volcanic and rugged islands and 4 groups of smaller ones. **Capital:** Honiara. **Cities:** (1988): Honiara 30,000.

**Government: Type:** Parliamentary democracy within the Commonwealth of Nations. **Head of state:** Queen Elizabeth II, represented by Gov.-Gen. George Lepping. **Head of government:** Prime Min. Solomon Mamaloni; in office: Mar. 28, 1989. **Local divisions:** 7 provinces and Honiara.

**Economy: Industries:** Fish canning. **Chief crops:** Coconuts, rice, bananas, yams. **Other resources:** Forests, marine shell. **Arable land:** 2%. **Fish catch** (1990): 25,000 metric tons. **Electricity prod.** (1991): 39 mln. kWh. **Labor force:** 32% agric., 32% services, 18% ind. & comm.

**Finance: Monetary unit:** Dollar (Mar. 1993: 3.16 = $1 US). **Gross domestic product** (1990): $200 mln. **Per capita GDP:** $600. **Imports** (1990): $92 mln.; partners: Austral. 31%, Jap. 14%, Sing. 18%. **Exports** (1990): $70 mln.; partners: Jap. 37%, UK 11%.

**Communications: Radios:** 1 per 4.6 persons. **Telephones:** 1 per 44 persons.

**Health: Life expectancy at birth** (1992): 67 male; 72 female. **Births:** (per 1,000 pop. 1992): 41. **Deaths** (per 1,000 pop. 1992): 5. **Natural increase:** 3.6%. **Infant mortality** (per 1,000 live births 1992): 30.

**Education** (1989): **Literacy:** 60%. **Primary school** 78%. **Secondary school:** 21%.

**Major International Organizations:** UN, Commonwealth of Nations.

The Solomon Islands were sighted in 1568 by an expedition from Peru. Britain established a protectorate in the 1890s over most of the group, inhabited by Melanesians. The islands saw major World War II battles. Self-government came Jan. 2, 1976, and independence was formally attained July 7, 1978.

## Somalia

### Somali Democratic Republic
### Jamhuriyadda Dimugradiga Somaliya

**People: Population** (1992 est.): 7,235,000. **Pop. density:** 29 per sq. mi. **Urban** (1990): 36%. **Ethnic groups:** mainly Hamitic, others. **Languages:** Somali, Arabic (both official). **Religions:** Sunni Moslems 99%.

**Geography: Area:** 246,300 sq. mi., slightly smaller than Texas. **Location:** Occupies the eastern horn of Africa. **Neighbors:** Djibouti, Ethiopia, Kenya on W. **Topography:** The coastline extends for 1,700 mi. Hills cover the N; the center and S are flat. **Capital:** Mogadishu. **Cities** (1986 est.): Mogadishu 700,000.

**Government: Type:** In transition. **Local divisions:** 16 regions.

**Economy: Chief crops:** Incense, sugar, bananas, sorghum, corn, gum. **Minerals:** Iron, tin, gypsum, bauxite, uranium. **Arable land:** 2%. **Livestock** (1991): cattle: 4.9 mln.; goats: 20 mln.; sheep: 14 mln. **Fish catch** (1990): 18,000 metric tons. **Electricity prod.** (1991): 60 mln. kWh. **Labor force:** 82% agric.

**Finance: Monetary unit:** Shilling (Dec. 1992: 2,615 = $1 US). **Gross domestic product** (1989): $1.7 bln. **Per capita GDP** (1989): $170. **Imports** (1990): $249 mln.; partners: It. 29%, Fra. 18%. **Exports** (1990): $58 mln.; partners: It. 17%. **Consumer prices** (change in 1990): 102%.

**Transport: Motor vehicles:** in use (1990): 20,000 passenger cars, 12,000 comm. vehicles. **Chief ports:** Mogadishu, Berbera.

**Communications: Radios:** 1 per 20 persons.

**Health: Life expectancy at birth** (1992): 56 male; 56 female. **Births** (per 1,000 pop. 1992): 46. **Deaths** (per 1,000 pop. 1992): 13. **Natural increase:** 3.3%. **Hospital beds:** 1 per 1,053 persons. **Physicians:** 1 per 19,071 persons. **Infant mortality** (per 1,000 live births 1992): 116.

**Education** (1990): **Literacy:** 24%. 50% attend primary school, 7% attend secondary school.

**Major International Organizations:** UN, OAU, Arab League. **Embassy:** 600 New Hampshire Ave. NW 20037; 342-1575.

The UN in 1949 approved eventual creation of Somalia as a sovereign state and in 1950 Italy took over the trusteeship held by Great Britain since World War II.

British Somaliland was formed in the 19th century in the NW. Britain gave it independence June 26, 1960; on July 1 it joined with the former Italian part to create the independent Somali Republic.

On Oct. 21, 1969, a Supreme Revolutionary Council seized power in a bloodless coup, named a Council of Secretaries of State, and abolished the Assembly. In May, 1970, several foreign companies were nationalized.

Somalia has laid claim to Ogaden, the huge eastern region of Ethiopia, peopled mostly by Somalis. Ethiopia battled Somali rebels in 1977. Some 11,000 Cuban troops with Soviet arms defeated Somali army troops and ethnic Somali rebels in Ethiopia, 1978. As many as 1.5 mln. refugees entered Somalia. Guerrilla fighting in Ogaden continued until 1988 when a peace agreement was reached with Ethiopia.

Twenty-one years of one-man rule ended in Jan. 1991 with the flight of Gen. Muhammad Siyad Barrah from the capital. Fighting between rival factions caused 40,000 casualties in 1991 and 1992, and by mid-1992 the civil war, drought, and banditry combined to produce a famine that threatened some 1.5 million people with starvation. In July 1992 the UN secretary general declared Somalia to be a country without a government. In Dec. 1992 the UN accepted a U.S. offer of troops to safeguard the delivery of food to the starving. The UN took control of the multinational relief effort from the U.S. May 4, 1993, and sponsored negotiations among rival factions aimed at establishing an interim government. U.S. and UN forces carried out attacks against the forces of and sought the capture of Gen. Mohammed Farah Aidid, the strongest Somali warlord, who opposed the UN role in Somalia.

# South Africa

## Republic of South Africa

## Republiek van Suid-Afrika

**People: Population** (1992 est.): 41,688,000. **Age distrib.** (%): 0–14: 32.1; 15–59: 60.6; 60+: 7.3. **Pop. density:** 88 per sq. mi. **Urban** (1991): 60%. **Ethnic groups:** black 70%, white 16%, Coloured 8%, Asian 3%. **Religions:** Mainly Christian, Hindu, Moslem minorities. **Languages:** Afrikaans, English (both official), Nguni, Sotho languages.

**Geography: Area:** 472,359 sq. mi., about twice the size of Texas. **Location:** At the southern extreme of Africa. **Neighbors:** Namibia, Botswana, Zimbabwe on N, Mozambique, Swaziland on E; surrounds Lesotho. **Topography:** The large interior plateau reaches close to the country's 2,700-mi. coastline. There are few major rivers or lakes; rainfall is sparse in W, more plentiful in E. **Capitals:** Cape Town (legislative), Pretoria (administrative), and Bloemfontein (judicial). **Cities** (1990 met.): Durban 1 mln. Cape Town 1.9 mln. Johannesburg 1.7 mln. Pretoria 850,000.

**Government: Type:** Republic with tricameral parliament, with one chamber each for whites, Coloureds (people of mixed race), and Asians; no franchise or parliamentary representation for blacks. **Head of State:** State Pres. Frederik W. de Klerk; b. Mar. 18, 1936; in office: Sept. 20, 1989. **Local divisions:** 4 provinces, 10 "homelands" for black Africans. **Defense:** 3% of GDP (1992).

**Economy: Industries:** Steel, tires, motors, textiles, plastics. **Chief crops:** Corn, wool, dairy products, grain, tobacco, sugar, fruit, peanuts, grapes. **Minerals:** Gold (largest producer), chromium, antimony, coal, iron, manganese, nickel, phosphates, tin, uranium, gem diamonds, platinum, copper, vanadium. **Other resources:** Wool. **Arable land:** 12%. **Livestock** (1989): cattle: 11.8 mln.; sheep: 30.3 mln. **Fish catch** (1989): 878,000 metric tons. **Electricity prod.** (1991): 180 bln. kWh. **Crude steel prod.** (1991): 9.3 mln. metric tons. **Labor force:** 25% agric.; 32% ind. and commerce; 34% serv.; 7% mining.

**Finance: Monetary unit:** Rand (Aug. 1993: 3.38 = $1 US). **Gross domestic product** (1991): $104 bln. **Per capita GDP** $2,600. **Imports** (1992): $21.2 bln.; partners: Ger. 19%, U.S. 68%, UK. 12%. **Exports** (1992): $23.8 bln.; partners: U.S. 43%, Jap. 9%. **Tourism** (1990): $1.0 bln. receipts. **National budget** (1993): $35.0 bln. **International reserves less gold** (Mar. 1993): $1.5 bln. **Gold:** 5.6 mln. oz t. **Consumer prices** (change in 1992): 13.9%.

**Transport: Railroads** (1990): **Length:** 15,793 mi. **Motor vehicles:** in use (1990): 3.3 mln. passenger cars, 1.4 mln. comm. vehicles. **Civil aviation:** (1991): 8.3 bln. passenger-km: 41 airports. **Chief ports:** Durban, Cape Town, East London, Port Elizabeth.

**Communications: Television sets:** 1 per 11 persons. **Radios:** 1 per 3.0 persons. **Telephones:** 1 per 6.1 persons. **Daily newspaper circ.** (1990): 48 per 1,000 pop.

**Health: Life expectancy at birth** (1992): 62 Male; 67 Female. **Births** (per 1,000 pop. 1992): 35. **Deaths** (per 1,000 pop. 1992): 8. **Natural increase:** 2.7%. **Physicians:** 1 per 1,320 persons. **Infant mortality** (per 1,000 live births 1992) 51.

**Education** (1990): Literacy: 99% (whites), 69% (Asians), 62% (Coloureds), 50% (Africans).

**Major International Organizations:** UN (GATT).
**Embassy:** 3051 Massachusetts Ave. NW 20008; 232-4400.

Bushmen and Hottentots were the original inhabitants. Bantus, including Zulu, Xhosa, Swazi, and Sotho, had occupied the area from Transvaal to south of Transkei before the 17th century.

The Cape of Good Hope area was settled by Dutch, beginning in the 17th century. Britain seized the Cape in 1806. Many Dutch trekked north and founded 2 republics, the Transvaal and the Orange Free State. Diamonds were discovered, 1867, and gold, 1886. The Dutch (Boers) resented encroachments by the British and others; the Anglo-Boer War followed, 1899-1902. Britain won and, effective May 31, 1910, created the Union of South Africa, incorporating the British colonies of the Cape and Natal, the Transvaal and the Orange Free State. After a referendum, the Union became the Republic of South Africa, May 31, 1961, and withdrew from the Commonwealth.

With the election victory of Daniel Malan's National party in 1948, the policy of separate development of the races, or apartheid, already existing unofficially, became official. This called for separate development, separate residential areas, and ultimate political independence for the whites, Bantus, Asians, and Coloureds. In 1959 the government passed acts providing the eventual creation of several Bantu nations or Bantustans on 13% of the country's land area, though most black leaders opposed the plan.

Under apartheid, blacks were severely restricted to certain occupations, and paid far lower wages than whites for similar work. Only whites could vote or run for public office. There is an advisory Indian Council, partly elected, partly appointed. In 1969, a Coloured People's Representative Council was created.

At least 600 persons, mostly Bantus, were killed in 1976 riots protesting apartheid. Black protests continued through the 1980s as violence broke out in several black townships. A new constitution was approved by referendum, Nov. 1983, which extended the parliamentary franchise to the Coloured and Asian minorities. Laws banning interracial sex and marriage were repealed in 1985.

In 1963, the Transkei, an area in the SE, became the first of these partially self-governing territories or "Homelands." Transkei became independent on Oct. 26, 1976, Bophuthatswana on Dec. 6, 1977, and Venda on Sept. 13, 1979; none received international recognition.

In 1981, So. Africa launched military operations in Angola and Mozambique to combat terrorists groups; So. African troops attacked the South West African People's Organization (SWAPO) guerrillas in Angola, March, 1982. South Africa and Mozambique signed a non-aggression pact in 1984.

In 1986, Nobel Peace Prize winner Bishop Desmond Tutu called for Western nations to apply sanctions against So. Africa to force an end to apartheid. President Botha announced in Apr. the end to the nation's system of racial pass laws and offered blacks an advisory role in government.

On May 19, So. Africa attacked 3 neighboring countries—Zimbabwe, Botswana, Zambia—to strike at guerrilla strongholds of the African National Congress.

A nationwide state of emergency was declared June 12, giving almost unlimited power to the security forces. On Apr. 22, 1987, a 6-week-old walkout by railway workers erupted into violence after the dismissal of 16,000 strikers. As confrontation between blacks and government increased, there was widespread support in Western nations for a complete trade embargo on So. Africa.

Some 2 million South African black workers staged a massive strike, June 6-8, 1988, to protest the government's new labor laws and the banning of political activity by trade unions and antiapartheid groups. P.W. Botha, head of the government since 1978, resigned Aug. 14, 1989, and was replaced by Frederik W. de Klerk.

In 1990, the government lifted its bar on the African National Congress, the primary black group fighting to end white minority rule. On Feb. 11, black nationalist leader Nelson Mandela was freed after more than 27 years in prison. In Oct. the Separate Amenities Act was repealed, ending the legal basis of segregation in public places. In Feb. 1991 Pres. de Klerk announced plans to end all apartheid laws. In June the race registration law was repealed.

A band of marauders swept through the township of Boipatong, June 17, 1992, killing some 40 blacks and prompting the African National Congress to temporarily break off constitutional talks with the white-minority government. Violence involving rival black groups continued later in the year. Violence flared in several black townships following the assassination of Chris Hani, head of the South African Communist Party, Apr. 10, 1993. The nation's negotiating parties, June 3, settled upon Apr. 27, 1994, as the tentative date for South Africa's first elections, in which all races can vote, which would choose multiracial constituent assembly that would serve as an interim legislature and write a new constitution. Negotiators agreed, Sept. 7, on the creation of a multiracial transition committee to oversee government operations prior to the elections.

**Bophuthatswana: Population** (1992 est.): 2,056,000. **Area:** 16,988 sq. mi., 6 discontinuous geographic units. **Capital:** Mmabatho. **Head of state:** Pres. Kgosi Lucas Manyane Mangope, b. Dec. 27, 1923; in office: Dec. 6, 1977.

**Ciskei: Population** (1992 est.): 854,000. **Area:** 2,996 sq. mi. **Capitol:** Bisho. **Head of State:** Brig. Joshua Oupa Gqozo.

**Transkei: Population** (1992 est.): 3,301,000. **Area:** 16,855 sq. mi., 3 discontinuous geographic units. **Capital:** Umtata. **Head of government:** Gen. Bantu Holomisa; in office: Dec. 30, 1987.

**Venda: Population** (1992 est.): 567,000. **Area:** 2,771 sq. mi., 2 discontinuous geographic units. **Capital:** Thohoyandou. **Head of state:** Gabriel Ramushwana; in office: Apr. 5, 1990.

# Spain
## España

**People: Population** (1992 est.): 39,118,000 (incl. Balearic & Canary Islands). **Age distrib.** (%): 0–14: 18.4; 15–59: 62.2; 60+: 19.4. **Pop. density:** 200 per sq. mi. **Urban** (1990): 79%. **Ethnic groups:** Spanish (Castilian, Valencian, Andalusian, Asturian) 72.8%, Catalan 16.4%, Galician 8.2%, Basque 2.3%. **Languages:** Spanish (official), Catalan, Galician, Basque. **Religions:** Roman Catholic 90%.

**Geography: Area:** 194,896 sq. mi., the size of Arizona and Utah combined. **Location:** In SW Europe. **Neighbors:** Portugal on W. France on N. **Topography:** The interior is a high, arid plateau broken by mountain ranges and river valleys. The NW is heavily watered, the south has lowlands and a Mediterranean climate. **Capital:** Madrid. **Cities** (1991 est.): Madrid 2,909,000; Barcelona 1,623,000; Valencia 752,000; Seville 659,000.

**Government: Type:** Constitutional monarchy. **Head of state:** King Juan Carlos I de Borbon y Borbon, b. Jan. 5, 1938; in office: Nov. 22, 1975. **Head of government:** Prime Min. Felipe Gonzalez Marquez; in office: Dec. 2, 1982. **Local divisions:** 17 autonomous communities. **Defense:** 2.0% of GDP (1991).

**Economy: Industries:** Machinery, steel, textiles, shoes, autos, processed foods. **Chief crops:** Grains, olives, grapes, citrus fruits, vegetables, olives. **Minerals:** Lignite, uranium, lead, iron, copper, zinc, coal. **Other resources:** Forests (cork). **Arable land:** 31%. **Livestock** (1990): cattle: 4.9 mln.; pigs: 16.9 mln.; sheep: 23.7 mln. **Fish catch** (1989): 974,000 tons. **Electricity prod.** (1991): 157 bln. kWh. **Crude steel prod.** (1991): 12.7 mln. metric tons. **Labor force:** 16% agric.; 24% ind. and comm.; 52% serv.

**Finance: Monetary unit:** Peseta (July 1993: 133.29 = $1 US). **Gross domestic product** (1991): $487 bln. **Per capita GDP:** $12,400. **Imports** (1992): $99.7 bln.; partners: U.S. 8%, EC 57%. **Exports** (1992): $64.3 bln.; partners: EC 71%, U.S. 6%. **Tourism** (1990): $18.5 bln. receipts. **National budget** (1991): $115 bln. expenditures. **International reserves less gold** (Mar. 1993): $44.4 bln. **Gold:** 15.6 mln. oz t. **Consumer prices** (change in 1992): 5.8%.

**Transport: Railroads** (1991): **Length:** 12,563 km. **Motor vehicles:** in use (1990): 11.9 mln. passenger cars, 2.4 mln. comm. **Civil aviation:** (1990): 22.1 bln. passenger-km; 25 airports with scheduled flights. **Chief ports:** Barcelona, Bilbao, Valencia, Cartagena, Gijon.

**Communications: Television sets:** 1 per 2.6 persons. **Radios:** 1 per 3.4 persons. **Telephones:** 1 per 2.5 persons. **Daily newspaper circ.** (1991): 76 per 1,000 pop.

**Health: Life expectancy at birth** (1992): 75 male; 82 female. **Births** (per 1,000 pop. 1992): 11. **Deaths** (per 1,000 pop. 1992): 8. **Natural increase:** .3%. **Hospital beds:** 1 per 198 persons. **Physicians:** 1 per 275 persons. **Infant mortality** (per 1,000 live births 1992): 6.

**Education** (1991): **Literacy:** 97%. **School compulsory:** to age 16.

**Major International Organizations:** UN and all of its specialized agencies, NATO, OECD, EC.

**Embassy:** 2700 15th St. NW 20009; 265-0190.

Spain was settled by Iberians, Basques, and Celts, partly overrun by Carthaginians, conquered by Rome c.200 BC. The

Visigoths, in power by the 5th century AD, adopted Christianity but by 711 AD lost to the Islamic invasion from Africa. Christian reconquest from the N led to a Spanish nationalism. In 1469 the kingdoms of Aragon and Castile were united by the marriage of Ferdinand II and Isabella I, and the last Moorish power was broken by the fall of the kingdom of Granada, 1492. Spain became a bulwark of Roman Catholicism.

Spain obtained a colonial empire with the discovery of America by Columbus, 1492, the conquest of Mexico by Cortes, and Peru by Pizarro. It also controlled the Netherlands and parts of Italy and Germany. Spain lost its American colonies in the early 19th century. It lost Cuba, the Philippines, and Puerto Rico during the Spanish-American War, 1898.

Primo de Rivera became dictator in 1923. King Alfonso XIII revoked the dictatorship, 1930, but was forced to leave the country 1931. A republic was proclaimed which disestablished the church, curtailed its privileges, and secularized education. A conservative reaction occurred 1933 but was followed by a Popular Front (1936-1939) composed of socialists, communists, republicans, and anarchists.

Army officers under Francisco Franco revolted against the government, 1936. In a destructive 3-year war, in which some one million died, Franco received massive help and troops from Italy and Germany, while the USSR, France, and Mexico supported the republic. War ended Mar. 28, 1939. Franco was named caudillo, leader of the nation. Spain was neutral in World War II but its relations with fascist countries caused its exclusion from the UN until 1955.

In July 1969, Franco and the Cortes designated Prince Juan Carlos as the future king and chief of state. After Franco's death, Nov. 20, 1975, Juan Carlos was sworn in as king. He presided over the formal dissolution of the institutions of the Franco regime. In free elections June 1977, moderates and democratic socialists emerged as the largest parties.

Catalonia and the Basque country were granted autonomy, Jan. 1980, following overwhelming approval in home-rule referendums. Basque extremists, however, have continued their campaign for independence.

The **Balearic Islands** in the western Mediterranean, 1,935 sq. mi., are a province of Spain; they include **Majorca** (Mallorca), with the capital, Palma; **Minorca, Cabrera, Ibiza** and **Formentera.** The **Canary Islands,** 2,807 sq. mi., in the Atlantic W of Morocco, form 2 provinces, including the islands of **Tenerife, Palma, Gomera, Hierro, Grand Canary, Fuerteventura,** and **Lanzarote** with Las Palmas and Santa Cruz thriving ports. **Ceuta** and **Melilla,** small enclaves on Morocco's Mediterranean coast, are part of Metropolitan Spain.

Spain has sought the return of Gibraltar, in British hands since 1704.

# Sri Lanka
## Democratic Socialist Republic of Sri Lanka
### Sri Lanka Prajathanthrika Samajavadi Janarajaya

**People: Population** (1992 est.): 17,631,000. **Age distrib.** (%): 0–14: 35.3; 15–59: 58.1; 60+: 6.6. **Pop. density:** 695 per sq. mi. **Urban** (1991): 26%. **Ethnic groups:** Sinhalese 74%, Tamils 17%, Moors 7%. **Languages:** Sinhalese, and Tamil, (both official). **Religions:** Buddhist 69%, Hindu 15%, Christian 8%, Moslem 7%.

**Geography: Area:** 25,332 sq. mi. about the size of W. Va. **Location:** in Indian O. off SE coast of India. **Neighbors:** India on NW. **Topography:** The coastal area and the northern half are flat; the S-central area is hilly and mountainous. **Capital:** Colombo. **Cities** (1990): Colombo 615,000.

**Government: Type:** Republic. **Head of state:** Pres. Dingiri Banda Wijetungle; b. 1923; in office: May 7, 1993. **Head of government:** Prime Minister Ranil Wickremasinghe; in office: May 7, 1993. **Local divisions:** 9 provinces, 24 districts. **Defense:** 5% of GDP (1991).

**Economy: Industries:** Plywood, paper, milling, chemicals, textiles. **Chief crops:** Tea, coconuts, rice. **Minerals:** Graphite, limestone, gems, phosphate. **Other resources:** Forests, rubber. **Arable land:** 16%. **Livestock** (1991): cattle: 1.8 mln. **Fish catch** (1990): 165,000 metric tons. **Electricity prod.** (1991): 4.2 bln. kWh. **Labor force:** 46% agric.; 27% ind. and comm.; 26% serv.

**Finance: Monetary unit:** Rupee (Mar. 1993: 47 = $1 US). **Gross domestic product** (1991): $7.2 bln. **Per capita GDP:** $410. **Imports** (1991): $3.0 bln.; partners: Jap. 15%, UK 7%. **Exports** (1991): $2.3 bln.; partners: U.S. 22%, UK 7%. **Tourism** (1990): $125 mln. receipts. **National budget** (1992): $3.7 bln. expenditures. **International reserves less gold** (Mar. 1993): $1.0 bln. **Gold:** 160,000 oz t. **Consumer prices** (change in 1992): 11.4%.

**Transport: Railroads** (1990): **Length:** 1,453 km. **Motor vehicles:** in use (1990): 173,000 passenger cars, 146,000 comm. vehicles. **Civil aviation** (1991): 3.4 bln. passenger-km; 1 airport. **Chief ports:** Colombo, Trincomalee, Galle.

**Communications: Television sets:** 1 per 25 persons. **Radios:** 1 per 8 persons. **Telephones:** 1 per 102 persons.

**Health: Life expectancy at birth** (1992): 69 male; 74 female. **Births** (per 1,000 pop. 1992): 21. **Deaths** (per 1,000 pop. 1992): 6. **Natural increase:** 1.5%. **Hospital beds:** 1 per 356 persons. **Physicians:** 1 per 6,609 persons. **Infant mortality** (per 1,000 live births 1992): 21.

**Education** (1990): **Literacy:** 90%. **Years compulsory:** To age 12; attendance 98%.

**Major International Organizations:** UN (World Bank, IMF), Commonwealth of Nations.

**Embassy:** 2148 Wyoming Ave. NW 20008; 483-4025.

The island was known to the ancient world as Taprobane (Greek for copper-colored) and later as Serendip (from Arabic). Colonists from northern India subdued the indigenous Veddahs about 543 BC; their descendants, the Buddhist Sinhalese, still form most of the population. Hindu descendants of Tamil immigrants from southern India account for one-fifth of the population. Parts were occupied by the Portuguese in 1505 and by the Dutch in 1658. The British seized the island in 1796. As Ceylon it became an independent member of the Commonwealth in 1948. On May 22, 1972, Ceylon became the Republic of Sri Lanka.

Prime Min. W. R. D. Bandaranaike was assassinated Sept. 25, 1959. In new elections, the Freedom Party was victorious under Mrs. Sirimavo Bandaranaike, widow of the former prime minister.

After May 1970 elections, Mrs. Bandaranaike became prime minister again. In 1971 the nation suffered economic problems and terrorist activities by ultra-leftists, thousands of whom were executed. Massive land reform and nationalization of foreign-owned plantations were undertaken in the mid-1970s. Mrs. Bandaranaike was ousted in 1977 elections. A presidential form of government was installed in 1978 to restore stability.

Tension between the Sinhalese and Tamil separatists erupted into violence repeatedly in the 1980s. In 1987, hundreds died in an attack by Tamil rebels Apr. 17. Sri Lanka forces retaliated in June with attacks on the rebel-held Jaffna peninsula. Over 20,000 have died in the civil war, which continued into the 1990s. Pres. Ranasinghe Premadasa was assassinated May 1, 1993, by a Tamil rebel.

# Sudan

### Republic of the Sudan

### Jamhuryat as-Sudan

**People: Population** (1992 est.): 28,305,000. **Pop. density:** 29 per sq. mi. **Urban** (1990): 22%. **Ethnic groups:** black 52%, Arab 39%, Beja 6%. **Languages:** Arabic (official), Dinka, Nubian, Nuer, Beja, others. **Religions:** Sunni Moslem 70%, animist 18%, Christians 5%.

**Geography: Area:** 966,757 sq. mi., the largest country in Africa, over one-fourth the size of the U.S. **Location:** At the E end of Sahara desert zone. **Neighbors:** Egypt on N, Libya, Chad, Central African Republic on W, Zaire, Uganda, Kenya on S, Ethiopia and Eritrea on E. **Topography:** The N consists of the Libyan Desert in the W, and the mountainous Nubia desert in E, with narrow Nile valley between. The center contains large, fertile, rainy areas with fields, pasture, and forest. The S has rich soil, heavy rain. **Capital:** Khartoum. **Cities** (1983 est.): Khartoum 476,000; Omdurman 526,000; North Khartoum 341,000; Port Sudan 206,000.

**Government: Type:** Military. **Head of government:** Prime Min. Gen. Omar Al-Bashir; in office: June 30, 1989. **Local divisions:** 9 states. **Defense:** 7% of GDP (1990).

**Economy: Industries:** Textiles, food processing. **Chief crops:** Gum arabic (principal world source), durra (sorghum), cotton (main export), sesame, peanuts, rice, coffee, sugar cane,

wheat, dates. **Minerals:** Chrome, copper, **Other resources:** Mahogany. **Arable land:** 5%. **Livestock** (1991): cattle: 20 mln.; sheep: 15 mln.; goats: 15 mln. **Electricity prod.** (1991): 905 mln. kWh. **Labor force:** 78% agric.; 9% ind., comm.

**Finance: Monetary unit:** Dinar (Mar. 1993: 1.00 = $2.74 US). **Gross domestic product** (1991): $12.1 bln. **Per capita GDP:** $450. **Imports** (1991): $1.4 bln.; partners: EC 32%, U.S. 13%. **Exports** (1991): $325 mln.; partners: EC 46%. **National budget** (1991): $2.1 bln. expenditures. **International reserves less gold** (Mar. 1993): $3.7 mln. **Consumer prices** (change in 1992): 112.6%.

**Transport: Railroads** (1988): **Length:** 5,503 km. **Motor vehicles:** in use (1990): 116,000 passenger cars, 56,000 comm. vehicles. **Civil aviation:** (1991): 425 mln. passenger-km; 12 airports with scheduled flights. **Chief ports:** Port Sudan.

**Communications: Television sets:** 1 per 117 persons. **Radios:** 1 per 4.6 persons. **Telephones:** 1 per 338 persons. **Daily newspaper circ.** (1990): 21 per 1,000 pop.

**Health: Life expectancy at birth** (1992): 53 male; 54 female. **Births** (per 1,000 pop. 1992): 44. **Deaths** (per 1,000 pop. 1992): 14. **Natural increase:** 3.0%. **Hospital beds:** 1 per 1,110 persons. **Physicians** (1983): 2,169. **Infant mortality** (per 1,000 live births 1992): 85.

**Education** (1991): **Literacy:** 27%. **Years compulsory:** 9; attendance 50%.

**Major International Organizations:** UN (IMF, WHO, FAO), Arab League, OAU.

Northern Sudan, ancient Nubia, was settled by Egyptians in antiquity, and was converted to Coptic Christianity in the 6th century. Arab conquests brought Islam in the 15th century.

In the 1820s Egypt took over the Sudan, defeating the last of earlier empires, including the Fung. In the 1880s a revolution was led by Mohammed Ahmed who called himself the Mahdi (leader of the faithful) and his followers, the dervishes.

In 1898 an Anglo-Egyptian force crushed the Mahdi's successors. In 1951 the Egyptian Parliament abrogated its 1899 and 1936 treaties with Great Britain, and amended its constitution, to provide for a separate Sudanese constitution.

Sudan voted for complete independence as a parliamentary government effective Jan. 1, 1956.

In 1969, a Revolutionary Council took power, but a civilian premier and cabinet were appointed; the government announced it would create a socialist state. The northern 12 provinces are predominantly Arab-Moslem and have been dominant in the central government. The 3 southern provinces are black Christians and animists. A 1972 peace agreement gave the South regional autonomy. The 2 halves of the nation began a civil war in 1988. Some 50,000 government soldiers launched a massive offensive against the southern rebels in 1992.

Economic problems plagued the nation in the 1980s, aggravated by a huge influx of refugees from neighboring countries. After 16 years in power, Pres. Nimeiry was overthrown in a bloodless military coup, Apr. 6, 1985. The Sudan held its first democratic parliamentary elections in 18 years in 1986. The elected government was overthrown in a bloodless coup June 30, 1989.

Sudan agreed to allow large-scale UN relief efforts in 1991, as some 7 million people were threatened with famine. The UN suspended aid to southern Sudan in 1992 because of the fighting. In 1993, Amnesty International accused Sudan of practicing "ethnic cleansing" against the Nuba people of southern Sudan and of gross human rights violations in other war zones in the south.

# Suriname

### Republic of Suriname

**People: Population** (1992 est.): 410,000. **Pop. density:** 6 per sq. mi. **Ethnic groups** Hindustanis 37%, Creole 31%, Javanese 15%. **Languages:** Dutch (official), Sranantonga, English. **Religions:** Moslem 19%, Hindu 27%, Christian 47%.

**Geography: Area:** 63,037 sq. mi., slightly larger than Georgia. **Location:** On N shore of S. America. **Neighbors:** Guyana on W, Brazil on S, French Guiana on E. **Topography:** A flat Atlantic coast, where dikes permit agriculture. Inland is a forest belt; to the S, largely unexplored hills cover 75% of the country. **Capital:** Paramaribo. **Cities** (1989): Paramaribo 192,000.

**Government: Type:** Republic. **Head of state:** Pres. Roland Venetiaan; in office: Sept. 16, 1991. **Head of government:**

Prime Min. Jules Adjodhia; in office: Sept. 16, 1991. **Local divisions:** 10 districts.

**Economy: Industries:** Aluminum. **Chief crops:** Rice, sugar, fruits. **Minerals:** Bauxite. **Other resources:** Forests, shrimp. **Arable land:** 1%. **Electricity prod.** (1991): 2.0 bln. kWh. **Labor force:** 29% agric.; 15% ind. and commerce; 42% govt.

**Finance: Monetary unit:** Guilder (Mar. 1993: 1.78 = $1 US). **Gross domestic product** (1990): $472 mln. **Per capita GDP:** $3,400. **Imports** (1990): $370 mln.; partners: U.S. 37%, Neth. 15%, Trin./Tob. 9%. **Exports** (1990): $472 mln.; partners: Nor. 33%, U.S. 13%, Neth. 26%. **Tourism** (1990): receipts: $11 mln. **National budget** (1990): $716 mln. expenditures. **International reserves less gold** (Mar. 1993): $12.9 mln. **Gold:** 54,000 oz t.

**Transport: Motor vehicles:** in use (1990): 36,000 passenger cars, 14,000 comm. vehicles. **Chief ports:** Paramaribo, Nieuw-Nickerie.

**Communications: Television sets:** 1 per 10 persons. **Radios:** 1 per 1.6 persons. **Telephones:** 1 per 8 persons. **Daily newspaper circ.** (1991): 43 per 1,000 pop.

**Health: Life expectancy at birth** (1992): 66 male; 71 female. **Births** (per 1,000 pop. 1992): 27. **Deaths** (per 1,000 pop. 1992): 5. **Natural increase:** 2.1%. **Infant mortality** (per 1,000 live births 1992): 34.

**Education** (1989): Literacy: 65%; compulsory ages 6–12.

**Major International Organizations:** UN (WHO, ILO, FAO, World Bank, IMF), OAS.

**Embassy:** 2600 Virginia Ave. NW 20037; 338-6980.

The Netherlands acquired Suriname in 1667 from Britain, in exchange for New Netherlands (New York). The 1954 Dutch constitution raised the colony to a level of equality with the Netherlands and the Netherlands Antilles. In the 1970s the Dutch government pressured for Suriname independence, which came Nov. 25, 1975, despite objections from East Indians. Some 40% of the population (mostly East Indians) emigrated to the Netherlands in the months before independence.

The National Military Council took over control of the government, Feb. 1982. The government came under democratic leadership in 1988.

## Swaziland
### Kingdom of Swaziland

**People: Population** (1992 est.): 913,000. **Age distrib.** (%): 0–14: 47.3; 15–59: 47.4; 60+: 5.3. **Pop. density:** 136 per sq. mi. **Urban** (1990): 30%. **Ethnic groups:** Swazi 90%, Zulu 2.3%, European 2.1%, other African, non-African groups. **Languages:** Swazi, English, (both official). **Religions:** Christians 60%, indigenous beliefs 40%.

**Geography: Area:** 6,704 sq. mi., slightly smaller than New Jersey. **Location:** in southern Africa, near Indian O. coast. **Neighbors:** South Africa on N, W, S, Mozambique on E. **Topography:** The country descends from W-E in broad belts, becoming more arid in the lowveld region, then rising to a plateau in the E. **Capital:** Mbabane. **Cities** (1990 est.): Mbabane 46,000; Manzini 53,000.

**Government: Type:** Monarchy. **Head of state:** King Mswati 3d; as of: Apr. 25, 1986. **Head of government:** Prime Min. Obed Dlamini; in office: July 12, 1989. **Local divisions:** 4 districts, 2 municipalities, 40 regions.

**Economy: Industries:** Wood pulp. **Chief crops:** Sugar, corn, cotton, rice, pineapples, sugar, citrus fruits. **Minerals:** Asbestos, iron, coal. **Other resources:** Forests. **Arable land:** 8%. **Electricity prod.** (1991): 155 mln. kWh. **Labor force:** 53% agric.; 9% ind. and commerce; 9% serv.

**Finance: Monetary unit:** Lilangeni (Mar. 1993: 1.00 = $.31 US). **Gross domestic product** (1990): $563 mln. **Per capita GDP:** $752. **Imports** (1992): $746 mln.; partners: So. Afr., 92%. **Exports** (1990): $543 mln.; partners: So. Afr. 40%. **National budget** (1993): $360 mln. expenditures. **International reserves less gold** (Feb. 1993): $256 mln. **Consumer prices** (change in 1991): 12.1%.

**Transport: Motor vehicles:** in use (1991): 25,000 passenger cars, 28,000 comm. vehicles.

**Communications: Radios:** 1 per 6.3 persons. **Telephones:** 1 per 34 persons. **Daily newspaper circ.** (1990): 24 per 1,000 pop.

**Health: Life expectancy at birth** (1992): 52 male; 60 female. **Births** (per 1,000 pop. 1992): 44. **Deaths** (per 1,000 pop. 1992): 12. **Natural increase:** 3.2%. **Hospital beds** (1984): 1,608. **Phy-**

sicians (1984): 80. **Infant mortality rate** (per 1,000 live births 1992): 98.

**Education** (1990): **Literacy:** 65%. 82% attend primary school.

**Major International Organizations:** UN (IMF, WHO, FAO), OAU, Commonwealth of Nations.

**Embassy:** 3400 International Dr. NW 20008; 362-6683.

The royal house of Swaziland traces back 400 years, and is one of Africa's last ruling dynasties. The Swazis, a Bantu people, were driven to Swaziland from lands to the N by the Zulus in 1820. Their autonomy was later guaranteed by Britain and Transvaal, with Britain assuming control after 1903. Independence came Sept. 6, 1968. In 1973 the king repealed the constitution and assumed full powers.

Under the constitution political parties are forbidden; parliament's role in government is limited to debate and advice.

## Sweden
### Kingdom of Sweden
### Konungariket Sverige

**People: Population** (1992 est.): 8,602,000. **Age distrib.** (%): 0–14: 17.9; 15–59: 59.0; 60+: 23.1. **Pop. density:** 49 per sq. mi. **Urban** (1985): 85%. **Ethnic groups:** Swedish 91%, Finnish 3%, Lapps, European immigrants. **Languages:** Swedish. **Religion:** Lutheran (official) 95%.

**Geography: Area:** 173,731 sq. mi., larger than California. **Location:** On Scandinavian Peninsula in N. Europe. **Neighbors:** Norway on W, Denmark on S (across Kattegat), Finland on E. **Topography:** Mountains along NW border cover 25% of Sweden, flat or rolling terrain covers the central and southern areas, which includes several large lakes. **Capital:** Stockholm. **Cities** (1992): Stockholm 679,000; Goteborg 433,000; Malmo 234,000.

**Government: Type:** Constitutional monarchy. **Head of state:** King Carl XVI Gustaf; b. Apr. 30, 1946; in office: Sept. 19, 1973. **Head of government:** Prime Min. Carl Bildt; b. July 15, 1949; in office: Oct. 3, 1991. **Local divisions:** 24 provinces. **Defense:** 3.9% of GDP (1991).

**Economy: Industries:** Steel, machinery, instruments, autos, shipbuilding, shipping, paper. **Chief crops:** Grains, potatoes, sugar beets. **Minerals:** Zinc, iron, lead, copper, gold, silver. **Other resources:** Forests (half the country); yield one fourth exports. **Arable land:** 7%. **Livestock** (1990): cattle: 1.7 mln.; pigs: 2.2 mln. **Fish catch** (1990): 240,000 metric tons. **Electricity prod.** (1991): 142 bln. kWh. **Crude steel prod.** (1991): 4.2 mln. metric tons. **Labor force:** 5% agric.; 24% manuf. & mining; 37% social services.

**Finance: Monetary unit:** Krona (July 1993: 7.97 = $1 US). **Gross domestic product** (1991): $147 bln. **Per capita GDP:** $17,200. **Imports** (1992): $49.7 bln.; partners: EC 56%. **Exports** (1992): $56.1 bln.; partners: EC 55%. **Tourism** (1990): $2.8 bln. receipts. **National budget** (1991): $78.7 bln. expenditures. **International reserves less gold** (Mar. 1993): $19.7 bln. **Gold:** 6.06 mln. oz t. **Consumer prices** (change in 1992): 2.3%.

**Transport: Railroads** (1990): Length: 6,960 mi. **Motor vehicles:** in use (1991): 3.6 mln. passenger cars, 324,000 comm. vehicles. **Civil aviation** (1990): 7.2 bln. passenger-km; 42 airports. **Chief ports:** Goteborg, Stockholm, Malmo.

**Communications: Television sets:** 1 per 2.4 persons. **Radios:** 1 per 1.2 persons. **Telephones:** 1 per 1.1 persons. **Daily newspaper circ.** (1990): 572 per 1,000 pop.

**Health: Life expectancy at birth** (1992): 75 male; 81 female. **Births** (per 1,000 pop. 1992): 13. **Deaths** (per 1,000 pop. 1992): 11. **Hospital beds:** 1 per 148 persons. **Physicians:** 1 per 320 persons. **Infant mortality** (per 1,000 live births 1992): 6.

**Education** (1991): Literacy: 99%. **Years compulsory:** 12; attendance 100%.

**Major International Organizations:** UN and all of its specialized agencies, EFTA, OECD.

**Embassy:** 600 New Hampshire Ave. NW 20037; 944-5600.

The Swedes have lived in present-day Sweden for at least 5,000 years, longer than nearly any other European people. Gothic tribes from Sweden played a major role in the disintegration of the Roman Empire. Other Swedes helped create the first Russian state in the 9th century.

The Swedes were Christianized from the 11th century, and a strong centralized monarchy developed. A parliament, the Riksdag, was first called in 1435, the earliest parliament on the European continent, with all classes of society represented.

Swedish independence from rule by Danish kings (dating from 1397) was secured by Gustavus I in a revolt, 1521-23; he built up the government and military and established the Lutheran Church. In the 17th century Sweden was a major European power, gaining most of the Baltic seacoast, but its international position subsequently declined.

The Napoleonic wars, in which Sweden acquired Norway (it became independent 1905), were the last in which Sweden participated. Armed neutrality was maintained in both world wars.

Over 4 decades of Social Democratic rule was ended in 1976 parliamentary elections but the party was returned to power in the 1982 elections. Although 90% of the economy is in private hands, the government holds a large interest in water power production and the railroads are operated by a public agency.

Carl Bildt, a non-Socialist, became prime minister Oct. 1991. His coalition government promised to turn the nation away from long-established economic and social programs.

## Switzerland
### Swiss Confederation

**People: Population** (1992 est.): 6,828,000. **Age distrib.** (%): 0–14: 17.0; 15–59: 63.7; 60+: 19.3. **Pop. density:** 428 per sq. mi. **Urban** (1991): 60%. **Ethnic groups:** Mixed European stock. **Languages:** German, French, Italian (all official). **Religions:** Roman Catholic 49%, Protestant 48%.

**Geography: Area:** 15,941 sq. mi., as large as Mass., Conn., and R.I., combined. **Location:** In the Alps Mts. in Central Europe. **Neighbors:** France on W, Italy on S, Austria on E, Germany on N. **Topography:** The Alps cover 60% of the land area, the Jura, near France, 10%. Running between, from NE to SW, are midlands, 30%. **Capital:** Bern. **Cities** (1991): Zurich 342,000; Basel 171,200; Geneva 161,000; Bern 135,000.

**Government: Type:** Federal republic. **Head of government:** Pres. Adolf Ogi; in office: Jan. 1, 1993. **Local divisions:** 20 full cantons, 6 half cantons. **Defense:** 2.2% of GDP (1990).

**Economy: Industries:** Machinery, machine tools, steel, instruments, watches, textiles, foodstuffs (cheese, chocolate), banking, tourism. **Chief crops:** Grains, potatoes, sugar beets, vegetables, tobacco. **Minerals:** Salt. **Other resources:** Hydro power potential. **Arable land:** 10%. **Livestock** (1991): cattle: 1.8 mln.; pigs: 1.9 mln. **Electricity prod.** (1991): 59 bln. kWh. **Crude steel prod.** (1988): 825,000 metric tons. **Labor force:** 39% ind. and commerce, 7% agric., 50% serv.

**Finance: Monetary unit:** Franc (July 1993: 1.49 = $1 US). **Gross domestic product** (1991): $147 bln. **Per capita GDP:** $21,700. **Imports** (1992): $61.7 bln.; partners: EC 71%. **Exports** (1992): $61.3 bln.; partners: EC 56%. **Tourism** (1991): receipts: $6.8 bln. **National budget** (1990): $23.8 bln. **International reserves less gold** (Mar. 1993): $31.3 bln. **Gold:** 83.28 mln. oz t. **Consumer prices** (change in 1992): 4.0%.

**Transport: Railroads** (1989): **Length:** 3,119 mi. **Motor vehicles:** in use (1990): 3.0 mln. passenger cars, 285,000 comm. vehicles. **Civil aviation:** (1991): 15.1 bln. passenger-km; 6 airports with scheduled flights.

**Communications: Television sets:** 1 per 2.9 persons. **Radios:** 1 per 2.6 persons. **Telephones:** 1 per 1.2 persons. **Daily newspaper circ.** (1990): 471 per 1,000 pop.

**Health: Life expectancy at birth** (1992): 76 male; 83 female. **Births** (per 1,000 pop. 1992): 12 **Deaths** (per 1,000 pop. 1992): 10 **Natural increase:** .2%. **Physicians:** 1 per 317 persons. **Infant mortality** (per 1,000 live births 1992): 5.

**Education** (1991): **Literacy:** 99%. **Years compulsory:** 9; attendance 100%.

**Major International Organizations:** Many UN specialized agencies (though not a member). **Embassy:** 2900 Cathedral Ave. NW 20008; 745-7900.

Switzerland, the Roman province of Helvetia, is a federation of 23 cantons (20 full cantons and 6 half cantons), 3 of which in 1291 created a defensive league and later were joined by other districts. Voters in the French-speaking part of Canton Bern voted for self-government, 1978; Canton Jura was created Jan. 1, 1979.

In 1648 the Swiss Confederation obtained its independence from the Holy Roman Empire. The cantons were joined under a federal constitution in 1848, with large powers of local control retained by each canton.

Switzerland has maintained an armed neutrality since 1815, and has not been involved in a foreign war since 1515. It is the seat of many UN and other international agencies.

Switzerland is a leading world banking center; stability of the currency brings funds from many quarters. The nation's famed secret bank accounts were phased out in 1992.

## Syria
### Syrian Arab Republic
### al-Jumhuriyah al-Arabiyah

**People: Population** (1992 est.): 13,730,000. **Age distrib.** (%): 0–14: 49.3; 15–59: 44.2; 60+: 6.5. **Pop. density:** 192 per sq. mi. **Urban** (1990): 50%. **Ethnic groups:** Arab 90%, Kurd, Armenian, others. **Languages:** Arabic (official), Kurdish, Armenian. **Religions:** Sunni Moslem 74%, other Moslem 16%, Christian 10%.

**Geography: Area:** 71,498 sq. mi., slightly larger than North Dakota. **Location:** At eastern end of Mediterranean Sea. **Neighbors:** Lebanon, Israel on W, Jordan on S, Iraq on E, Turkey on N. **Topography:** Syria has a short Mediterranean coastline, then stretches E and S with fertile lowlands and plains, alternating with mountains and large desert areas. **Capital:** Damascus. **Cities** (1992 est.): Damascus 1,451,000; Aleppo 1,445,000; Homs 518,000.

**Government: Type:** Republic (under military regime). **Head of state:** Pres. Hafez al-Assad; b. Mar. 1930; in office: Feb. 22, 1971. **Head of government:** Prime Min. Mahmoud Zuabi; in office: Nov. 1, 1987. **Local divisions:** Damascus and 13 provinces. **Defense:** 10.9% of GDP (1989).

**Economy: Industries:** Oil products, textiles, tobacco, glassware, brassware. **Chief crops:** Cotton, grain, olives, fruits, vegetables. **Minerals:** Oil, phosphate, gypsum. **Crude oil reserves** (1987): 1.4 bln. bbls. **Other resources:** Wool. **Arable land:** 28%. **Livestock** (1990): sheep: 13 mln., goats: 1 mln. **Electricity prod.** (1991): 8 bln. kWh. **Labor force:** 32% agric.; 29% ind. & comm.; 39% services.

**Finance: Monetary unit:** Pound (Mar. 1993: 11.22 = $1 US). **Gross domestic product** (1991): $30.0 bln. **Per capita GDP:** $2,300.1. **Imports** (1991): $2.7 bln.; partners: EC 42%. **Exports** (1991): $3.6 bln.; partners: E. Europe 42%, EC 31%. **Tourism** (1990): receipts: $244 mln. **National budget** (1991): $7.5 bln. expenditures. **Consumer prices** (change in 1991): 7.7%.

**Transport: Railroads** (1991): **Length:** 948 mi. **Motor vehicles:** in use (1990): 117,000 passenger cars, 138,000 comm. vehicles. **Civil aviation** (1989): 833 mln. passenger-km; 5 airports with scheduled flights. **Chief ports:** Latakia, Tartus.

**Communications: Television sets:** 1 per 17 persons. **Radios:** 1 per 4.1 persons. **Telephones:** 1 per 17 persons. **Daily newspaper circ.** (1990): 21 per 1,000 pop.

**Health: Life expectancy at birth** (1992): 65 male; 67 female. **Births** (per 1,000 pop. 1992): 44. **Deaths** (per 1,000 1992): 7. **Natural increase:** 3.7%. **Hospital beds:** 1 per 840 persons. **Physicians:** 1 per 1,347 persons. **Infant mortality** (per 1,000 live births 1992): 45.

**Education** (1990): **Literacy:** 64%. **Years compulsory:** 6; attendance: 94%.

**Major International Organizations:** UN (IMF, WHO, FAO), Arab League.

**Embassy:** 2215 Wyoming Ave. NW 20008; 232-6313.

Syria contains some of the most ancient remains of civilization. It was the center of the Seleucid empire, but later became absorbed in the Roman and Arab empires. Ottoman rule prevailed for 4 centuries, until the end of World War I.

The state of Syria was formed from former Turkish districts, made a separate entity by the Treaty of Sevres 1920 and divided into the states of Syria and Greater Lebanon. Both were administered under a French League of Nations mandate 1920-1941.

Syria was proclaimed a republic by the occupying French Sept. 16, 1941, and exercised full independence effective Apr. 17, 1946. Syria joined in the Arab invasion of Israel in 1948.

Syria joined with Egypt in Feb. 1958 in the United Arab Republic but seceded Sept. 30, 1961. The Socialist Baath party and military leaders seized power in Mar. 1963. The Baath, a pan-Arab organization, became the only legal party. The government has been dominated by members of the minority Alawite sect.

In the Arab-Israeli war of June 1967, Israel seized and occupied the Golan Heights area inside Syria, from which Israeli settlements had for years been shelled by Syria.

On Oct. 6, 1973, Syria joined Egypt in an attack on Israel. Arab oil states agreed in 1974 to give Syria $1 billion a year to aid anti-Israel moves. Some 30,000 Syrian troops entered Lebanon in 1976 to mediate in a civil war. They fought Palestinian guerrillas and, later, Christian militiamen. Syrian troops again battled Christian forces in Lebanon, Apr. 1981, ending a ceasefire that had been in place.

Following the June 6, 1982 Israeli invasion of Lebanon, Israeli planes destroyed 17 Syrian antiaircraft missile batteries in the Bekka Valley, June 9. Some 25 Syrian planes were downed during the engagement. Israel and Syria agreed to a cease fire June 11. In 1983, Syria backed the PLO rebels who ousted Yasir Arafat's forces from Tripoli.

Syria's role in promoting acts of international terrorism led to the breaking of diplomatic relations with Great Britain and the implementation of limited sanctions by the European Communities in 1986.

Syria condemned the Aug. 1990 Iraqi invasion on Kuwait and sent troops to help Allied Forces in the Gulf War.

In 1991, Syria accepted U.S. proposals for the terms of an Arab-Israeli peace conference.

# Taiwan

## Republic of China

## Chung-hua Min-kuo

**People: Population** (1992 est.): 20,878,000. **Age distrib. (%):** 0–14: 27.1; 15–59: 63.2; 60+: 9.7. **Pop. density:** 1,503 per sq. mi. **Urban** (1990): 75%. **Ethnic groups:** Taiwanese 85%, Chinese 14%. **Languages:** Mandarin Chinese (official), Taiwan, Hakka dialects. **Religions:** Buddhism, Taoism, Confucianism prevail.

**Geography: Area:** 13,885 sq. mi., about the size of Connecticut & New Hampshire combined. **Location:** Off SE coast of China, between E. and S. China Seas. **Neighbors:** Nearest is China. **Topography:** A mountain range forms the backbone of the island; the eastern half is very steep and craggy, the western slope is flat, fertile, and well-cultivated. **Capital:** Taipei. **Cities** (1991): Taipei (met.) 2,716,000; Kaohsiung 1,398,000; Taichung 777,000; Tainan 685,000.

**Government: Type:** Democracy. **Head of state and Nationalist Party chmn.:** Pres. Lee Teng-hui; b. Jan. 15, 1923; in office: Jan. 13, 1988. **Head of government:** Prime Min. Lien Chan; in office: Feb. 10, 1993. **Local divisions:** 16 counties, 5 cities, Taipei & Kao-Hsiung. **Defense:** 4.6% of GNP (1991).

**Economy: Industries:** Textiles, clothing, electronics, processed foods, chemicals, plastics. **Chief crops:** Rice, bananas, pineapples, sugarcane, sweet potatoes, peanuts. **Minerals:** Coal, limestone, marble. **Crude oil reserves** (1987): 10 mln. bbls. **Arable land:** 25%. **Livestock** (1989): pigs: 6.9 mln. **Fish catch** (1989): 1.2 mln. metric tons. **Electricity prod.** (1991): 76 bln. kWh. **Crude steel prod.** (1991): 10.9 mln. metric tons. **Labor force:** 15% agric.; 53% ind. & comm.; 22% services.

**Finance: Monetary unit:** New Taiwan dollar (July 1993: 26.28 = $1 US). **Gross national product** (1991): $180.1 bln. **Per capita GNP:** $8,790. **Imports** (1992): $72 bln.; partners: U.S. 23%, Jap. 30%. **Exports** (1992): $81 bln.; partners: U.S. 39%, Jap. 13%, Hong Kong 8%. **Tourists** (1990): $1.7 bln. receipts. **National budget** (1991): $30.1 bln.

**Transport: Motor vehicles:** in use (1991): 2.6 mln. passenger cars, 653,000 commercial vehicles. **Civil Aviation** (1991): 29.0 bln. passenger-km; 12 airports. **Chief ports:** Kaohsiung, Keelung, Hualien, Taichung.

**Communications: Television sets:** 1 per 3.2 persons. **Radios:** 1 per 1.5 persons. **Telephones:** 1 per 3.0 persons. **Daily newspaper circ.** (1989): 202 per 1,000 pop.

**Health: Life expectancy at birth** (1992): 72 male; 78 female. **Births** (per 1,000 pop. 1992): 16. **Deaths** (per 1,000 pop. 1992): 5. **Natural increase:** 1.1%. **Physicians:** 1 per 910 persons. **Hospital beds:** 1 per 227 persons. **Infant mortality** (per 1,000 live births 1992): 6.

**Education** (1991): **Literacy:** 90%. **Years compulsory:** 9; attendance 99%.

Large-scale Chinese immigration began in the 17th century. The island came under mainland control after an interval of

Dutch rule, 1620-62. Taiwan (also called Formosa) was ruled by Japan 1895-1945. Two million Kuomintang supporters fled to Taiwan in 1949. Both the Taipei and Peking governments consider Taiwan an integral part of China. Taiwan has rejected Peking's efforts at reunification, but unofficial dealings with the mainland have grown more flexible in the 1980s.

The U.S. upon its recognition of the People's Republic of China, Dec. 15, 1978, severed diplomatic ties with Taiwan. It maintains the unofficial American Institute in Taiwan, while Taiwan has established the Coordination Council for North American Affairs in Washington, D.C.

Land reform, government planning, U.S. aid and investment, and free universal education have brought huge advances in industry, agriculture, and mass living standards. In 1987, martial law was lifted after 38 years and in 1991, the 43-year period of emergency rule ended.

Taiwan has one of the world's strongest economies and is among the 10 leading capital exporters.

The **Penghu** (Pescadores), 50 sq. mi., pop. 120,000, lie between Taiwan and the mainland. **Quemoy** and **Matsu,** pop. (1990) 70,000 lie just off the mainland.

# Tajikistan

## Republic of Tajikistan

## Respubliki i Tojikiston

**People: Population** (1992 est.): 5,680,000. **Pop. density:** 105 per sq. mi. **Urban** (1991): 32%. **Ethnic groups:** Tajik 62%, Uzbek 23%, Russian 8%. **Languages:** Tadzhik, Russian. **Religion:** Mostly Sunni Moslem.

**Geography: Area:** 54,019 sq. mi., slightly smaller than Wisconsin. **Neighbors:** Uzbekistan and Kyrgyzstan on N and W, China on E, Afghanistan on S and E. **Topography:** Mountainous region which contains the Pamirs, Trans Alai mountain system. **Capital:** Dushanbe.

**Government: Type:** Parliamentary republic. **Head of state:** Pres. Imomali Rakhmonov; in office: Nov. 20, 1992. **Head of government:** vacant.

**Economy: Industries:** Cement, knitwear, footwear. **Chief crops:** Barley, cotton, wheat, vegetables. **Minerals:** Coal, lead, zinc. **Livestock** (1990): cattle: 1.3 mln., sheep: 3.3 mln. **Electricity prod.** (1991): 17 bln. kWh.

**Finance: Monetary Unit:** Ruble. **Imports** (1990): 1.3 bln. **Exports** (1990): $706 mln.

**Transportation: Railroads** (1990): **Length:** 554 mi. **Civil aviation** (1990): 5.1 bln. passenger-km.; 1 airport.

**Communications: Television sets:** 1 per 6 persons. **Telephones:** 1 per 10 persons. **Newspaper circ.** (1990): 298 per 1,000 pop.

**Health: Life expectancy at birth** (1992): 64 male; 70 female. **Births** (per 1,000 pop. 1992): 40. **Deaths** (per 1,000 pop. 1992): 8. **Hospital beds:** 1 per 93 persons. **Physicians:** 1 per 362 persons. **Infant mortality** (per 1,000 live births 1992): 74.

**Major International Organizations:** UN, CIS.

There were settled societies in the region from about 3000 B.C. Throughout history, the region has undergone invasions by Iranians (Arabs who converted the population to Islam), Mongols, Uzbeks, Afghans, and Russians. In 1924, the Tadzhik ASSR was created within the Uzbek SSR. The Tadzhik SSR was proclaimed in 1929. Tajikistan declared independence Sept. 9, 1991. It became an independent state when the Soviet Union disbanded Dec. 26, 1991. The ruling Communist Party has retained power in Tajikistan. There were demonstrations by opposition forces—anti-communists and Islamic fundamentalists—in 1992.

# Tanzania

## United Republic of Tanzania

## Jamhuri ya Mwungano wa Tanzania

**People: Population** (1992 est.) 27,791,000. **Pop. density:** 76 per sq. mi. **Urban** (1990): 32%. **Ethnic groups:** African. **Languages:** Swahili, English (both official), many others. **Religions:** Moslems 33%, Christians 33%, traditional beliefs 33%.

**Geography: Area:** 364,886 sq. mi., more than twice the size of California. **Location:** On coast of E. Africa. **Neighbors:** Kenya, Uganda on N, Rwanda, Burundi, Zaire on W, Zambia, Malawi, Mozambique on S. **Topography:** Hot, arid central plateau, surrounded by the lake region in the W, temperate highlands in N and S, the coastal plains. Mt. Kilimanjaro, 19,340 ft., is highest in Africa. **Capital:** Dar-es-Salaam. **Cities** (1992): Dar-es-Salaam 1.4 mln.

**Government: Type:** Republic. **Head of state:** Pres. Ali Hassan Mwinyi; b. May 8, 1925; in office: Nov. 5, 1985. **Head of government:** Prime Min. John Malecela; in office: Nov. 9, 1990. **Local divisions:** 25 regions. **Defense:** 3.9% of GDP (1992).

**Economy: Industries:** Food processing, clothing. **Chief crops:** Sisal, cotton, coffee, tea, tobacco. **Minerals:** Diamonds, gold, nickel. **Other resources:** Hides. **Arable land:** 6%. **Livestock** (1991): cattle: 14 mln.; goats: 8.8 mln.; sheep: 3.5 mln. **Fish catch** (1989): 340,000 metric tons. **Electricity prod.** (1991): 905 mln. kWh. **Labor force:** 90% agric., 10% ind., comm. & govt.

**Finance: Monetary unit:** Shilling (Mar. 1993: 350 = $1 US). **Gross domestic product** (1991): $6.9 bln. **Per capita GDP:** $260. **Imports** (1991): $1.5 bln.; partners: UK 14%, Jap. 12%, Ger. 10%. **Exports** (1991): $418 mln.; partners: Ger. 15%, UK 13%. **Tourism** (1990): $63 mln. receipts. **National budget** (1990): $631 mln. expenditures. **International reserves less gold** (Jan. 1993): $204 mln. **Consumer prices** (change in 1992): 21.1%.

**Transport: Motor vehicles:** in use (1990): 44,000 passenger cars; 52,000 comm. vehicles. **Civil aviation** (1991): $280 mln. passenger-km; 19 airports. **Chief ports:** Dar-es-Salaam, Mtwara, Tanga.

**Communications: Radios:** 1 per 6 persons. **Telephones:** 1 per 174 persons. **Daily newspaper circ.** (1989): 8 per 1,000 pop.

**Health: Life expectancy at birth** (1992): 50 male; 55 female. **Births** (per 1,000 pop. 1992): 50. **Deaths** (per 1,000 pop. 1992): 16. **Natural increase:** 3.4%. **Hospital beds** (1984): 22,800. **Physicians** (1984): 1,065. **Infant mortality** (per 1,000 live births 1992): 103.

**Education** (1987): **Literacy:** 85%. **Attendance:** 87% attend primary school.

**Major International Organizations:** UN and all of its specialized agencies, OAU, Commonwealth of Nations.

**Embassy:** 2139 R. St. NW 20008; 939-6125.

The Republic of Tanganyika in E. Africa and the island Republic of Zanzibar, off the coast of Tanganyika, joined into a single nation, the United Republic of Tanzania, Apr. 26, 1964. Zanzibar retains internal self-government.

**Tanganyika.** Arab colonization and slaving began in the 8th century AD; Portuguese sailors explored the coast by about 1500. Other Europeans followed.

In 1885 Germany established German East Africa of which Tanganyika formed the bulk. It became a League of Nations mandate and, after 1946, a UN trust territory, both under Britain. It became independent Dec. 9, 1961, and a republic within the Commonwealth a year later.

In 1967 the government set on a socialist course; it nationalized all banks and many industries. The government also ordered that Swahili, not English, be used in all official business. Tanzanian forces drove Idi Amin from Uganda, Mar., 1979.

**Zanzibar,** the Isle of Cloves, lies 23 mi. off the coast of Tanganyika; its area is 621 sq. mi. The island of **Pemba,** 25 mi. to the NE, area 380 sq. mi., is included in the administration. The total population (1990 est.) is 375,000.

Chief industry is the production of cloves and clove oil of which Zanzibar and Pemba produce the bulk of the world's supply.

Zanzibar was for centuries the center for Arab slave-traders. Portugal ruled for 2 centuries until ousted by Arabs around 1700. Zanzibar became a British Protectorate in 1890; independence came Dec. 10, 1963. Revolutionary forces overthrew the Sultan Jan. 12, 1964. The new government ousted Western diplomats and newsmen, slaughtered thousands of Arabs, and nationalized farms. Union with Tanganyika followed, 1964. The ruling parties of Tanganyika and Zanzibar were united in 1977, as political tension eased.

# Thailand

## Kingdom of Thailand

## Muang Thai or Prathet Thai

**People: Population** (1992 est.): 57,624,000. **Age distrib. (%):** 0–14: 45.0; 15–59: 49.0; 60+: 6.0. **Pop. density:** 290 per sq. mi. **Urban** (1990): 20%. **Ethnic groups:** Thai 75%, Chinese 14%, others 11%. **Languages:** Thai, (official), Chinese, Malay, regional dialects. **Religions:** Buddhist 95%, Moslem 4%.

**Geography: Area:** 198,456 sq. mi., about the size of Texas. **Location:** On Indochinese and Malayan Peninsulas in S.E. Asia. **Neighbors:** Myanmar on W. Laos on N, Cambodia on E, Malaysia on S. **Topography:** A plateau dominates the NE third of Thailand, dropping to the fertile alluvial valley of the Chao Phraya R. in the center. Forested mountains are in N, with narrow fertile valleys. The southern peninsula region is covered by rain forests. **Capital:** Bangkok. **Cities** (1991 est.): Bangkok (met.): 6.0 mln.

**Government: Type:** Constitutional monarchy. **Head of state:** King Bhumibol Adulyadej; b. Dec. 5, 1927; in office: June 9, 1946. **Head of government:** Prime Min. Chuan Leekpai; in office: Sept. 23, 1992. **Local divisions:** 72 provinces. **Defense:** 3.0% of GNP (1992).

**Economy: Industries:** Textiles, mining, wood prods., tourism. **Chief crops:** Rice (a major export), corn tapioca, sugarcane. **Minerals:** Antimony, tin (among largest producers), tungsten, iron, gas. **Other resources:** Forests (teak is exported), rubber. **Arable land:** 34%. **Livestock** (1991): cattle: 5.6 mln.; pigs: 4.9 mln. **Fish catch** (1989): 2.3 mln. metric tons. **Electricity prod.** (1991): 37.5 bln. kWh. **Labor force:** 59% agric.; 26% ind. & comm.; 10% serv.; 8% govt.

**Finance: Monetary unit:** Baht (Mar. 1993: 25.36 = $1 US). **Gross national product** (1991): $92.6 bln. **Per capita GNP:** $1,630. **Imports** (1991): $39.0 bln.; partners: Jap. 30%, U.S. 11%. **Exports** (1991): $27.5 bln.; partners: Jap. 17%, U.S. 22%. **Tourism** (1990): $4.3 mln. receipts. **National budget** (1992): $17.9 bln. **International reserves less gold** (Mar. 1993): $21.4 bln. **Gold:** 2.47 mln. oz t. **Consumer prices** (change in 1991): 5.7%.

**Transport: Railroads** (1990): **Length:** 2,399 mi. **Motor vehicles:** in use (1990): 655,000 passenger cars, 1.5 mln. comm. vehicles. **Civil aviation** (1991): 18.2 bln. passenger-km; 24 airports with scheduled flights. **Chief ports:** Bangkok, Sattahip.

**Communication: Television sets:** 1 per 17 persons. **Radios:** 1 per 5.7 persons. **Telephones:** 1 per 41 persons. **Daily newspaper circ.** (1989): 50 per 1,000 pop.

**Health: Life expectancy at birth** (1992): 67 male; 71 female. **Births** (per 1,000 pop. 1992): 20 **Deaths** (per 1,000 pop. 1992): 7. **Natural increase:** 1.3%. **Hospital beds:** 1 per 597 persons. **Physicians:** 1 per 4,227 persons. **Infant mortality** (per 1,000 live births 1992): 35.

**Education** (1991): **Literacy:** 89%. **Years compulsory:** 6; attendance 96%.

**Major International Organizations:** UN (GATT, World Bank). **Embassy:** 2300 Kalorama Rd. NW 20008; 483-7200.

Thais began migrating from southern China in the 11th century. Thailand is the only country in SE Asia never taken over by a European power, thanks to King Mongkut and his son King Chulalongkorn who ruled from 1851 to 1910, modernized the country, and signed trade treaties with both Britain and France. A bloodless revolution in 1932 limited the monarchy.

Japan occupied the country in 1941.

The military took over the government in a bloody 1976 coup. Kriangsak Chomanan, prime minister resigned, Feb. 1980, under opposition over soaring inflation, oil price increases, labor unrest and growing crime. Chatichai Choonhavan was chosen prime minister in a democratic election, Aug. 1988. In Feb. 1991, the military ousted Choonhavan in a bloodless coup. Elections were held Sept. 1992; Chuan Leekpai was chosen prime minister.

Vietnamese troops had crossed the border and been repulsed by Thai forces in the 1980s.

# Togo

## Republic of Togo

## République Togolaise

**People: Population** (1992 est.): 3,958,000. **Age distrib. (%):** 0–14: 45.3; 15–59: 49.7; 60+:5.0.**Pop. density:** 176 per sq. mi. **Urban** (1990): 25%. **Ethnic groups:** Ewe 35%, Mina 6%, Kabye 22%. **Languages:** French (official), Gur & Kwa languages. **Religions:** Traditional 50%, Christian 30%, Moslem 20%.

**Geography: Area:** 21,622 sq. mi., slightly smaller than West Virginia. **Location:** On S coast of W. Africa. **Neighbors:** Ghana on W, Burkina Faso on N, Benin on E. **Topography:** A range of hills running SW-NE splits Togo into 2 savanna plains regions. **Capital:** Lomé. **Cities** (1989 est.): Lomé 600,000.

**Government: Type:** in transition. **Head of state:** Pres. Gnassingbe Eyadema; b. Dec. 26, 1937; in office: Apr. 14, 1967. **Head of government:** Prime Min. Joseph Kokou Koffgoh. In office: Aug. 27, 1991. **Local divisions:** 21 prefectures.

**Economy: Industries:** Textiles, shoes. **Chief crops:** Coffee, cocoa, yams, manioc, millet, rice. **Minerals:** Phosphates. **Arable land:** 26%. **Electricity prod.** (1991): 209 mln. kWh. **Labor force:** 75% agric.; 20% industry.

**Finance: Monetary unit:** CFA franc (Mar. 1993: 273 = $1 US). **Gross domestic product** (1990): $1.5 bln. **Per capita GDP:** $400. **Imports** (1990): $502 mln.; partners: EC 61%. **Exports** (1990): $363 mln.; partners: EC 70%. **Tourism** (1990): $23 mln. receipts. **International reserves less gold** (Jan. 1993): $272 mln. **Gold:** 13,000 oz t. **Consumer prices** (change in 1991): 1.0%.

**Transport: Railroads** (1991): **Length:** 326 mi. **Motor vehicles:** in use (1990): 45,000 passenger cars. **Chief ports:** Lome. **Communications: Television sets:** 1 per 156 persons. **Radios:** 1 per 5.0 persons. **Telephones:** 1 per 169 persons. **Daily newspaper circ.** (1991): 3 per 1,000 pop.

**Health: Life expectancy at birth** (1992): 54 male; 58 female. **Births** (per 1,000 pop. 1992): 48. **Deaths** (per 1,000 pop. 1992): 12. **Natural increase:** 3.6%. **Hospital beds:** 1 per 752 persons. **Physicians:** 1 per 12,992 persons. **Infant mortality** (per 1,000 live births 1992): 94.

**Education** (1990): **Literacy:** 45%.

**Major International Organizations:** UN (GATT, IMF), OAU. **Embassy:** 2208 Massachusetts Ave. NW 20008; 234-4212.

The Ewe arrived in southern Togo several centuries ago. The country later became a major source of slaves. Germany took control in 1884. France and Britain administered Togoland as UN trusteeships. The French sector became the republic of Togo Apr. 27, 1960.

The population is divided between Bantus in the S and Hamitic tribes in the N. Togo has actively promoted regional integration, as a means of stimulating the economy.

Some 25,000 people fled Togo to the neighboring countries of Ghana and Benin as a result of civil unrest in 1993.

# Tonga

## Kingdom of Tonga

## Pule 'anga Tonga

**People: Population** (1992 est.): 102,000. **Age distrib. (%):** 0–14: 44.4; 15–59: 50.5; 60+: 5.1. **Pop. density:** 377 per sq. mi. **Ethnic groups:** Tongans 98%, other Polynesian, European. **Languages:** Tongan, English (both official). **Religions:** Free Wesleyan 47%, Roman Catholics 14%, Free Church of Tonga 14%, Mormons 9%, Church of Tonga 9%.

**Geography: Area:** 270 sq. mi., smaller than New York City. **Location:** In western S. Pacific O. **Neighbors:** Nearest is Fiji, on W, New Zealand, on S. **Topography:** Tonga comprises 169 volcanic and coral islands, 45 inhabited. **Capital:** Nuku'alofa. **Cities** (1986): Nuku'alofa (met.) 29,000.

**Government: Type:** Constitutional monarchy. **Head of state:** King Taufa'ahau Tupou IV; b. July 4, 1918; in office: Dec. 16, 1965. **Head of government:** Prime Min. Baron Vaea; in office: Aug. 21, 1991. **Local divisions:** 3 main island groups.

**Economy: Industries:** Tourism. **Chief crops:** Coconut products, bananas are exported. **Other resources:** Fish. **Arable**

land: 25%. **Electricity prod.** (1991): 8 mln. kWh. **Labor force:** 45% agric, 27% services.

**Finance: Monetary unit:** Pa'anga (Apr. 1993: 1.36 = $1 US). **Gross domestic product** (1990): $92 mln. **Imports** (1991): $59 mln.; partners: N Z 39%, Aust. 25%. **Exports** (1991): $13 mln.; partners: Aust. 29%, N Z 56%. **Tourism** (1991): $7.6 mln. receipts.

**Transport: Motor vehicles:** in use (1989): 1,400 passenger cars, 2,700 comm. vehicles. **Chief ports:** Nuku'alofa.

**Communications: Radios:** 1 per 1.2 persons. **Telephones:** 1 per 18 persons.

**Health: Life expectancy at birth** (1992): 65 male; 70 female. **Births** (per 1,000 pop. 1992): 27. **Deaths** (per 1,000 pop. 1992): 5. **Natural increase:** 2.2%. **Infant mortality** (per 1,000 live births 1992): 23.

**Education** (1988): **Literacy:** 99%. **Years compulsory:** 8. **Attendance:** 77%.

The islands were first visited by the Dutch in the early 17th century. A series of civil wars ended in 1845 with establishment of the Tupou dynasty. In 1900 Tonga became a British protectorate. On June 4, 1970, Tonga became independent and a member of the Commonwealth.

# Trinidad and Tobago

## Republic of Trinidad and Tobago

**People: Population** (1992 est.): 1,285,000. **Age distrib. (%):** 0–14: 32.9; 15–59: 58.7; 60+: 8.4. **Pop. density:** 648 per sq. mi. **Ethnic groups:** Africans 43%, East Indians 40%, mixed 14%. **Languages:** English (official). **Religions:** Roman Catholic 32%, Protestant 29%, Hindu 25%, Moslem 6%.

**Geography: Area:** 1,980 sq. mi., the size of Delaware. **Location:** Off eastern coast of Venezuela. **Neighbors:** Nearest is Venezuela on SW. **Topography:** Three low mountain ranges cross Trinidad E-W, with a well-watered plain between N and Central Ranges. Parts of E and W coasts are swamps. Tobago, 116 sq. mi., lies 20 mi. NE. **Capital:** Port-of-Spain. **Cities** (1990 met. est.): Port-of-Spain 300,000; San Fernando 50,000.

**Government: Type:** Parliamentary democracy. **Head of state:** Pres. Noor Hassanali; in office: Mar. 19, 1987. **Head of government:** Prime Min. Patrick Manning; in office: Dec. 17, 1991. **Local divisions:** 8 counties, 3 municipalities.

**Economy: Industries:** Oil products, rum, cement, tourism. **Chief crops:** Sugar, cocoa, coffee, citrus fruits, bananas. **Minerals:** Asphalt, oil, **Crude oil reserves** (1987): 567 mln. bbls. **Arable land:** 14%. **Electricity prod.** (1991): 3.4 bln. kWh. **Labor force:** 18% construction-utilities, 14% manuf., mining, commerce, 47% services.

**Finance: Monetary unit:** Dollar (Mar. 1993: 4.25 = $1 US). **Gross domestic product** (1990): $4.9 bln. **Per capita GDP:** $3,600. **Imports** (1991): $1.6 bln.; partners: U.S. 51%, UK 8%. **Exports** (1991): $1.9 bln.; partners: U.S. 53%. **Tourism** (1990): $122 mln. receipts. **National budget** (1991): $1.7 bln. expenditures. **International reserves less gold** (Mar. 1993): $172 mln. **Gold:** 54,000 oz t. **Consumer prices** (change in 1992): 6.5%.

**Transport: Motor vehicles:** in use (1989): 269,000 passenger cars, 68,000 comm. vehicles. **Civil aviation** (1990): 2.7 bln. passenger-km; 2 airports. **Chief ports:** Port-of-Spain.

**Communications: Television sets:** 1 per 5 persons. **Radios:** 1 per 3.1 persons. **Telephones:** 1 per 5 persons. **Daily newspaper circ.** (1990): 140 per 1,000 pop.

**Health: Life expectancy at birth** (1992): 68 male; 73 female. **Births** (per 1,000 pop. 1992): 21. **Deaths** (per 1,000 pop. 1992): 6. **Natural increase:** 1.5%. **Hospital beds:** 1 per 318 persons. **Physicians:** 1 per 1,543 persons. **Infant mortality** (per 1,000 pop. 1992): 18.

**Education** (1988): **Literacy:** 97%. **Years compulsory:** 8. **Major International Organizations:** UN (GATT, IMF, WHO), Commonwealth of Nations, OAS. **Embassy:** 1708 Massachusetts Ave. NW 20036; 467-6490.

Columbus sighted Trinidad in 1498. A British possession since 1802, Trinidad and Tobago won independence Aug. 31, 1962. It became a republic in 1976. The People's National Movement party has held control of the government since 1956.

The nation is one of the most prosperous in the Caribbean. Oil production has increased with offshore finds. Middle Eastern oil is refined and exported, mostly to the U.S.

In July 1990, some 120 Moslem extremists captured the parliament building and TV station and took about 50 hostages including Prime Minister Arthur Robinson, who was beaten, shot in the legs, and tied to explosives. After a 6-day siege, the rebels surrendered.

# Tunisia

## Republic of Tunisia

## al Jumhuriyah at-Tunisiyah

**People: Population** (1992 est.): 8,445,000. **Age distrib. (%)** 0–14: 39.0; 15–59: 54.2; 60+: 6.8. **Pop. density:** 133 per sq. mi. **Ethnic groups:** Arab 98%. **Languages:** Arabic (official), French. **Religions:** Moslem 99%.

**Geography: Area:** 63,170 sq. mi., about the size of Missouri. **Location:** On N coast of Africa. **Neighbors:** Algeria on W, Libya on E. **Topography:** The N is wooded and fertile. The central coastal plains are given to grazing and orchards. The S is arid, approaching Sahara Desert. **Capital:** Tunis. **Cities** (1984 est.): Tunis 1,000,000, Sfax 475,000.

**Government: Type:** Republic. **Head of state:** Pres. Gen. Zine al-Abidine Ben Ali; b. Sept 3, 1936; in office: Nov. 7, 1987. **Head of government:** Prime Min. Hamed Karoui; in office: Sept. 27, 1989. **Local divisions:** 23 governorates. **Defense:** 5.0% of GDP (1992).

**Economy: Industries:** Food processing, textiles, oil products, mining, construction materials. **Chief crops:** Grains, dates, olives, citrus fruits, figs, vegetables, grapes. **Minerals:** Phosphates, iron, oil, lead, zinc. **Crude oil reserves** (1987): 1.7 bln. bbls. **Arable land:** 20%. **Livestock** (1990): sheep: 5.0 mln.; goats: 1 mln. **Fish catch** (1990): 95,000 metric tons. **Electricity prod.** (1991): 4.2 bln. kWh. **Labor force:** 25% agric.; 34% industry; 40% serv.

**Finance: Monetary unit:** Dinar (Mar. 1993: 1.00 = $1 US). **Gross domestic product** (1991): $10.9 bln. **Per capita GDP:** $1,320. **Imports** (1992): $6.4 bln.; partners: EC 68%. **Exports** (1992): $4.0 bln.; partners: EC 73%. **Tourism** (1990): $953 mln. receipts. **National budget** (1992): $5.4 bln. expenditures. **International reserves less gold** (Mar. 1993): $730 mln. **Gold:** 215,000 oz t. **Consumer prices** (change in 1992): 5.4%.

**Transport: Railroads** (1990): **Length:** 1,343 mi. **Motor vehicles:** in use (1989): 321,000 passenger cars, 208,000 comm. vehicles; **Civil aviation:** (1991): 1.5 bln. passenger-km; 5 airports. **Chief ports:** Tunis, Sfax, Bizerte.

**Communications: Television sets:** 1 per 13 persons. **Radios:** 1 per 4.7 persons. **Telephones:** 1 per 24 persons. **Daily newspaper circ.** (1991): 28 per 1,000 pop.

**Health: Life expectancy at birth** (1992): 70 male; 74 female. **Births** (per 1,000 pop. 1992): 26. **Deaths** (per 1,000 pop. 1992): 5. **Natural increase:** 2.1%. **Hospital beds:** 1 per 506 persons. **Physicians:** 1 per 1,834 persons. **Infant mortality** (per 1,000 pop. live births 1992): 38.

**Education** (1990): **Literacy:** 62%. **Years compulsory:** 8; attendance 85%.

**Major International Organizations:** UN, Arab League, OAU. **Embassy:** 1515 Massachusetts Ave. NW 20005; 862-1850.

Site of ancient Carthage and a former Barbary state under the suzerainty of Turkey, Tunisia became a protectorate of France under a treaty signed May 12, 1881. The nation became independent Mar. 20, 1956, and ended the monarchy the following year.

Tunisia has actively repressed Islamic fundamentalism.

# Turkey

## Republic of Turkey

## Turkiye Cumhuriyeti

**People: Population** (1992 est.): 59,640,000. **Age distrib. (%):** 0–14: 38.5; 15–59: 54.9; 60+: 6.6. **Pop. density:** 197 per sq. mi. **Urban** (1990): 61%. **Ethnic groups:** Turks 80%, Kurds 17%. **Languages:** Turkish (official), Kurdish, Arabic. **Religions:** Moslem 98%.

**Geography: Area:** 301,381 sq. mi., twice the size of California. **Location:** Occupies Asia Minor, between Mediterranean and Black Seas. **Neighbors:** Bulgaria, Greece on W, Georgia, Armenia on N, Iran on E, Iraq, Syria on S. **Topography:** Central Turkey has wide plateaus, with hot, dry summers and cold winters. High mountains ring the interior on all but W, with more than 20 peaks over 10,000 ft. Rolling plains are in W; mild, fertile coastal plains are in S, W. **Capital:** Ankara. **Cities** (1990 est.): Istanbul 6,700,000; Ankara 2,553,000; Izmir 1,700,000; Adana 931,000.

**Government: Type:** Republic. **Head of state:** Pres. Suleyman Demirel; in office: May 16, 1993. **Head of government:** Prime Min. Tansu Ciller; in office: July 5, 1993. **Local divisions:** 73 provinces. **Defense:** 3.5% of GDP (1992).

**Economy: Industries:** Iron, steel, machinery, metal prods., cars, processed foods. **Chief crops:** Tobacco, cereals, cotton, barley, corn, fruits, potatoes, sugar beets. **Minerals:** Chromium, mercury, boron, copper, coal. **Crude oil reserves** (1987): 139 mln. bbls. **Other resources:** Wool, silk, forests. **Arable land:** 30%. **Livestock** (1991): cattle: 12.0 mln.; sheep: 31 mln. **Fish catch** (1989): 457,000 metric tons. **Electricity prod.** (1991): 44 bln. kWh. **Crude steel prod.** (1991): 9.2 mln. metric tons. **Labor force:** 56% agric.; 14% ind. and comm.; 29% serv.

**Finance: Monetary unit:** Lira (Aug. 1993: 11,366= $1 US). **Gross domestic product** (1991): $198 bln. **Per capita GDP:** $3,400. **Imports** (1991): $21.0 bln.; partners: EC 49%, U.S. 7%. **Exports** (1991): $13.5 bln.; partners: EC 49%. **Tourism** (1991): $2.5 bln. receipts. **National budget** (1992): $49.7 bln. expenditures. **International reserves less gold** (Feb. 1993): $6.4 bln. **Gold:** 4.0 mln. oz t. **Consumer prices** (change in 1992): 70.1%.

**Transport: Railroads** (1991): **Length:** 5,238 mi. **Motor vehicles:** in use (1990): 1.6 mln. passenger cars, 584,000 comm. vehicles. **Civil aviation** (1991): 4.2 bln. passenger-km; 12 airports with scheduled flights. **Chief ports:** Istanbul, Izmir, Mersin, Samsun.

**Communications: Television sets:** 1 per 5 persons. **Radios:** 1 per 7.8 persons. **Telephones:** 1 per 7 persons.

**Health: Life expectancy at birth** (1992): 68 male; 72 female. **Births** (per 1,000 pop. 1992): 28. **Deaths** (per 1,000 pop. 1992): 6. **Natural increase:** 2.2%. **Hospital beds:** 1 per 465 persons. **Physicians:** 1 per 1,108 persons. **Infant mortality** (per 1,000 live births 1992): 54.

**Education** (1990): **Literacy:** 81%. **Years compulsory:** 6; attendance 95%.

**Major International Organizations:** UN (GATT, WHO, IMF), NATO, OECD, EC.

**Embassy:** 1714 Massachusetts Ave. NW 20036.

Ancient inhabitants of Turkey were among the worlds first agriculturalists. Such civilizations as the Hittite, Phrygian, and Lydian flourished in Asiatic Turkey (Asia Minor), as did much of Greek civilization. After the fall of Rome in the 5th century, Constantinople was the capital of the Byzantine Empire for 1,000 years. It fell in 1453 to Ottoman Turks, who ruled a vast empire for over 400 years.

Just before World War I, Turkey, or the Ottoman Empire, ruled what is now Syria, Lebanon, Iraq, Jordan, Israel, Saudi Arabia, Yemen, and islands in the Aegean Sea.

Turkey joined Germany and Austria in World War I and its defeat resulted in loss of much territory and fall of the sultanate. A republic was declared Oct. 29, 1923. The Caliphate (spiritual leadership of Islam) was renounced 1924.

Long embroiled with Greece over Cyprus, off Turkey's south coast, Turkey invaded the island July 20, 1974, after Greek officers seized the Cypriot government as a step toward unification with Greece. Turkey sought a new government for Cyprus, with Greek Cypriot and Turkish Cypriot zones. In reaction to Turkey's moves, the U.S. cut off military aid in 1975. Turkey, in turn, suspended the use of most U.S. bases. Aid was restored in 1978. There was a military takeover, Sept. 12, 1980.

Religious and ethnic tensions and active left and right extremists have caused endemic violence. Martial law, imposed in 1978, was lifted in 1984. The military formally transferred power to an elected parliament in 1983.

Turkey was a member of the Allied forces which ousted Iraq from Kuwait, 1991. In the aftermath of the war, millions of Kurdish refugees fled to Turkey's border to escape Iraqi forces.

Kurdish militants raided Turkish diplomatic missions in some 25 Western European cities June 24, 1993. The militants were demanding an independent state for the Kurds.

# Turkmenistan

## Republic of Turkmenistan

**People: Population** (1992 est.): 3,838,000. **Pop. density:** 20 per sq. mi. **Urban** (1991): 46%. **Ethnic groups:** Turkmen 72%, Russian 9%, Uzbek 9%. **Languages:** Turkmen, Russian. **Religion:** Moslem 85%.

**Geography: Area:** 188,417 sq. mi., slightly larger than California. **Neighbors:** Uzbekistan, Kazakhstan on N, NE, Afghanistan and Iran on S. The Kara Kum desert occupies 80% of the area. **Capital:** Ashkhabad. **Cities** (1991): Ashkhabad 416,000.

**Government: Type:** Republic. **Head of state:** Pres. Saparmurad Niyazov. **Head of government:** Prime Min. Khan A. Akhmedov. **Local divisions:** 5 regions.

**Economy: Industries:** Mining, textiles. **Chief crops:** Grain, cotton, grapes. **Minerals:** Coal, sulfur, salt. **Livestock** (1990): sheep: 5.0 mln. **Electricity prod.** (1991): 14.9 bln. kWh.

**Finance: Monetary unit:** Ruble. **Imports** (1990): $970 mln. **Exports** (1990): $239 mln.

**Transportation: Railroads:** (1990): **Length:** 1,317 mi.

**Communications: Telephones:** 1 per 15 persons.

**Health: Life expectancy at birth** (1992): 59 male; 66 female. **Births** (per 1,000 pop. 1992): 36. **Deaths** (per 1,000 pop. 1992): 9. **Hospital beds:** 1 per 86 persons. **Physicians:** 1 per 274 persons. **Infant mortality** (1 per 1,000 live births 1992): 94.

**Major International Organizations:** UN, CIS.

The region has been inhabited by Turki tribes since the 10th century. It became part of Russian Turkistan 1881, and a constituent republic of the USSR 1925. Turkmenistan declared independence Oct. 27, 1991, and became an independent state when the Soviet Union disbanded Dec. 25, 1991.

Power rests mostly with the former Communist Party apparatus.

# Tuvalu

**People: Population** (1992 est.): 9,494. **Pop. density:** 949 per sq. mi. **Ethnic group:** Polynesian. **Languages:** Tuvaluan, English. **Religions:** mainly Protestant.

**Geography: Area:** 10 sq. mi., less than one-half the size of Manhattan. **Location:** 9 islands forming a NW-SE chain 360 mi. long in the SW Pacific O. **Neighbors:** Nearest are Samoa on SE, Fiji on S. **Topography:** The islands are all low-lying atolls, nowhere rising more than 15 ft. above sea level, composed of coral reefs. **Capital:** Funafuti (pop. 1985): 2,800.

**Government: Head of state:** Queen Elizabeth II, represented by Gov.-Gen. Toaripi Lauti; in office: Oct. 1, 1990. **Head of government:** Prime Min. Bikenibeu Paeniu; in office: Oct. 16, 1989. **Local divisions:** 8 island councils on the permanently inhabited islands.

**Economy: Industries:** Copra. **Chief crops:** Coconuts. **Labor force:** Approx. 1,500 Tuvaluans work overseas in the Gilberts' phosphate industry, or as overseas labor.

**Finance: Monetary unit:** Australian dollar.

**Transport: Chief port:** Funafuti.

**Health:** (including former Gilbert Is.) **Life expectancy at birth** (1992): 61 male; 64 female. **Births** (per 1,000 pop. 1992): 29. **Deaths** (per 1,000 pop. 1992): 10. **Natural increase:** 1.9%. **Infant mortality** (per 1,000 live births 1992): 33.

**Education: Literacy** (1990): 96%.

The Ellice Islands separated from the British Gilbert and Ellice Islands colony in 1975 and became independent Tuvalu, Oct. 1, 1978.

# Uganda

## Republic of Uganda

**People: Population** (1992 est.): 19,386,000. **Age distrib. (%):** 0–14: 48.5; 15–59: 47.3; 60+: 4.2. **Pop. density:** 207 per sq. mi. **Urban** (1991): 11%. **Ethnic groups:** Bantu, Nilotic, Nilo-Hamitic, Sudanic tribes. **Languages:** English (official), Luganda, Swahili. **Religions:** Christian 63%, Moslem 6%, traditional beliefs.

**Geography: Area:** 93,354 sq. mi., slightly smaller than Oregon. **Location:** In E. Central Africa. **Neighbors:** Sudan on N, Zaire on W, Rwanda, Tanzania on S, Kenya on E. **Topography:** Most of Uganda is a high plateau 3,000-6,000 ft. high, with high Ruwenzori range in W (Mt. Margherita 16,750 ft.), volcanoes in SW, NE is arid, W and SW rainy. Lakes Victoria, Edward, Albert form much of borders. **Capital:** Kampala. **Cities** (1991): Kampala 773,000.

**Government: Type:** Republic. **Head of state:** Pres. Yoweri Kaguta Museveni; b. 1944; in office: Jan. 29, 1986. **Head of government:** Prime Min. George Cosmas Adyebo; in office: Jan. 22, 1991. **Local divisions:** 10 provinces. **Defense:** 1.5% of GDP (1989).

**Economy: Chief Crops:** Coffee, cotton, tea, corn, bananas, sugar. **Minerals:** Copper, cobalt. **Arable land:** 23%. **Livestock** (1991): cattle: 5.2 mln.; goats: 3.3 mln.; sheep: 1.9 mln. **Fish catch** (1990): 245,000 metric tons. **Electricity prod.** (1991): 312 mln. kWh. **Labor force:** 90% agric.

**Finance: Monetary unit:** Shilling (Mar. 1993: 1,217 = $1 US). **Gross domestic product** (1991): $5.6 bln. **Per capita GDP:** $300. **Imports** (1991): $196 mln.; partners: Kenya 24%, U.K. 17%. **Exports** (1991): $200 mln.; partners: U.S. 14%, U.K. 12%, Neth. 15%. **National budget** (1989): $790 mln. expenditures. **International reserves less gold** (Jan. 1993): $59 mln. **Consumer prices** (change in 1992): 52.4%.

**Transport: Motor vehicles:** in use (1990): 35,000 passenger cars, 6,000 comm. vehicles.

**Communications: Television sets:** 1 per 191 persons. **Radios:** 1 per 5.1 persons. **Telephones:** 1 per 286 persons. **Daily newspaper circ.** (1990): 2 per 1,000 pop.

**Health: Life expectancy at birth** (1992): 50 male; 52 female. **Births** (per 1,000 pop. 1992): 51. **Deaths** (per 1,000 pop. 1992): 15. **Natural increase:** 3.6%. **Hospital beds:** 1 per 817 persons. **Physicians:** 1 per 20,000 persons. **Infant mortality** (per 1,000 live births 1992): 91.

**Education** (1989): **Literacy:** 52%. About 50% attend primary school.

**Major International Organizations:** UN (GATT, WHO, IMF), OAU, Commonwealth of Nations.

**Embassy:** 5909 16th St. NW 20011; 726-7100.

Britain obtained a protectorate over Uganda in 1894. The country became independent Oct. 9, 1962, and a republic within the Commonwealth a year later. In 1967, the traditional kingdoms, including the powerful Buganda state, were abolished and the central government strengthened.

Gen. Idi Amin seized power from Prime Min. Milton Obote in 1971. As many as 300,000 of his opponents were reported killed in subsequent years. Amin was named president for life in 1976.

In 1972 Amin expelled nearly all of Uganda's 45,000 Asians. In 1973 the U.S. withdrew all diplomatic personnel.

Amid worsening economic and domestic crises, Uganda's troops exchanged invasion attacks with long-standing foe Tanzania, 1978 to 1979. Tanzanian forces, coupled with Ugandan exiles and rebels, ended the dictatorial rule of Amin, Apr. 11, 1979.

# Ukraine

## Ukrayina

**People: Population** (1992 est.): 51,994,000. **Age distrib. (%):** 0-19: 24.8; 20-59: 62.1; 60+: 13.0. **Pop. density:** 223 per sq. mi. **Urban** (1991): 68%. **Official language:** Ukrainian. **Ethnic groups:** Ukrainian 73%, Russian 22%. **Religion:** Orthodox 76%, Ukrainian Catholic 13.5%, Moslem 8.2%.

**Geography: Area:** 233,100 sq. mi. **Location:** In SE Europe. **Neighbors:** Belarus on N, Russia on NE and E, Moldova and Romania on SW, Hungary, Slovakia, and Poland on W. **Topography:** Part of the E. European plain. Mountainous areas include the Carpathians in the SW and the Crimean chain in the S. Arable black soil constitutes a large part of the country. **Climate:** Average temperature range from 21F in Jan. to 66F in July. Annual precipitation averages 27.5 in. in the W. part of the country and less than 11 in. in the East. **Capital:** Kiev. **Cities** (1991 est.): Kiev 2,637,000; Kharkiv 1,622,000; Donetsk 1,121,000; Dnipropetrovsk 1,100,000; Odessa 1,104,000.

**Government: Type:** Constitutional republic. **Head of state:** Pres. Leonid M. Kravchuk; b. 1934; in office: December 5, 1991. **Local divisions:** 24 provinces (oblasts), 1 autonomous province.

**Economy: Industries:** Steel, chemicals, machinery, vehicles, cement. **Chief crops:** Grains, sugar beets, potatoes. **Minerals:** Iron, manganese, chromium, copper, coal, lead, gold, nickel, potassium salts. **Other resources:** Forests. **Arable land:** 56%. **Fish catch** (1990): 550,000 metric tons. **Electricity prod.**

(1990): 76.2 bln. kWh. **Crude steel prod.** (1990): 43.1 mln. metric tons. **Labor force:** 19% agric.; 41% ind. & comm.; 28% services.

**Finance: Monetary unit:** Karbovanet (May 1993: 3,000 = $1 US). **Gross national product** (1990): $47.6 bln. **Per capita income** (1987): $2,500. **Imports** (1990): $16.7 bln. **Exports** (1990): $13.5 bln. **National budget** (1990): $8 bln. expenditures.

**Transport: Railway traffic** (1990): 75.8 bln. passenger-km.; 484.1 bln. net ton-km. **Civil aviation** (1990): 16.1 bln. passenger-km., 20 airports. **Chief ports:** Odessa, Kherson, Zhdanov, Sevastopil, Berdiansk.

**Communications: Television sets:** 1 per 3 persons. **Radios:** 1 per 4 persons. **Daily newspaper circ.** (1990): 202 per 1,000 pop.

**Health: Life expectancy at birth** (1992): 65 male; 75 female. **Births** (per 1,000 pop. 1992): 14. **Deaths** (per 1,000 pop. 1992): 12. **Hospital beds:** 1 per 74 persons. **Physicians:** 1 per 229 persons. **Infant mortality** (per 1,000 live births 1992): 22.

**Education** (1990): **Literacy:** 99%.

**Major International Organizations:** UN, CIS.

The ancient ancestors of Ukrainians, the Trypilians, flourished along the Dnipro River, Ukraine's main artery, from 6000-1000 BC. The Slavic ancestors of the Ukrainians inhabited modern Ukrainian territory well before the first century AD.

The princes of Kyyiv established a strong state called Kyyivan Rus in the 9th century. A strong dynasty was established, with ties to virtually all major European royal families. St. Volodymyr the Great, ruler of Kyyivan Ukraine, accepted Christianity as the national faith in 988. At the crossroads of major European trade routes, Kyyivan Rus reached its zenith during the reign of Iaroslav the Wise (1019-1054). While directly absorbing most of the Asian invasion of Europe in the 13th century, the Ukrainian state slowly disintegrated and was divided mainly between Russia and Poland.

The Ukrainian Cossack State, founded in the late 16th century, waged numerous wars of liberation against the occupiers of Ukraine: Russia, Poland, and Turkey. By the late 18th century, Ukrainian independence was lost. Ukraine's neighbors once again divided its territory. At the turn of the last century, Ukraine was occupied by 2 colonial powers, Russia and Austria-Hungary.

An independent Ukrainian National Republic was proclaimed on January 22, 1918. In 1921, Ukraine's neighbors occupied and divided Ukrainian territory. In 1932-33, the Soviet government engineered a man-made famine in eastern Ukraine, resulting in the deaths of 7-10 million Ukrainians.

In March 1939, independent Carpatho-Ukraine was the first European state to wage war against Nazi-led aggression in the region. During WW2 the Ukrainian nationalist underground and its Ukrainian Insurgent Army (UPA) fought both Nazi German and Soviet forces. The restoration of Ukrainian independence was declared on June 30, 1941. Over 5 million Ukrainians lost their lives during the War. With the reoccupation of Ukraine by Soviet troops in 1944 came a renewed wave of mass arrests, executions, and deportations of Ukrainians.

The world's worst nuclear power plant disaster occurred in Chernobyl, Ukraine, in April 1986.

Ukrainian independence was restored in 1991 with the dissolution of the Soviet Union. In a landslide national referendum, over 90% of Ukraine's population voted for independence on Dec. 1, 1991.

Ukraine suffered economic hardships in 1993; inflation hit 170% in the first quarter, and the GDP fell 10 percent from the previous year.

## United Arab Emirates
### Ittihād al-Imarat al-Arabiyah

**People: Population** (1992 est.): 2,522,000. **Pop. density:** 78 per sq. mi. **Ethnic groups:** Arab, Iranian, Pakistani, Indian. **Languages:** Arabic (official), several others. **Religions:** Moslem 96%, Christian, Hindu.

**Geography: Area:** 32,000 sq. mi., the size of Maine. **Location:** On the S shore of the Persian Gulf. **Neighbors:** Qatar on N, Saudi Ar. on W, S, Oman on E. **Topography:** A barren, flat coastal plain gives way to uninhabited sand dunes on the S. Hajar Mtns. are on E. **Capital:** Abu Dhabi. **Cities** (1990 est.): Abu Dhabi 722,000; Dubayy 266,000.

**Government: Type:** Federation of emirates. **Head of state:** Pres. Zaid ibn Sultan an-Nahayan b. 1923; in office: Dec. 2, 1971. **Head of government:** Prime Min. Sheikh Maktum ibn Rashid al-Maktum; in office: Nov. 20, 1990. **Local divisions:** 7 autonomous emirates: Abu Dhabi, Ajman, Dubai, Fujaira, Ras al-Khaimah, Sharjah, Umm al-Qaiwain. **Defense:** 6.8% of GDP (1989).

**Economy: Chief crops:** Vegetables, dates, limes. **Minerals:** Oil. **Crude oil reserves** (1991): 66 bln. barrels. **Arable land:** 1%. **Electricity prod.** (1991): 17.0 bln. kWh. **Labor force:** 5% agric.; 85% ind. and commerce; 5% serv.; 5% gvt.

**Finance: Monetary unit:** Dirham (July 1993: 3.67 = $1 US). **Gross domestic product** (1989): $28.4 bln. **Per capita GDP:** $12,100. **Imports** (1992): $13.7 bln.; partners: Jap. 14%, UK 11%, Ger. 6%. **Exports** (1990): $21.3 bln.; partners: Jap. 36%. **International reserves less gold** (Feb. 1993): $5.5 bln. **Gold:** 797,000 oz t.

**Transport: Motor Vehicles** (1990): 302,000 passenger cars; 157,000 commercial vehicles. **Civil aviation** (1991): 3.8 bln. passenger-km., 4 airports with scheduled flights. **Chief ports:** Dubavy, Abu Dhabi.

**Communications: Television sets:** 1 per 12 persons. **Radios:** 1 per 4.7 persons. **Telephones:** 1 per 4.3 persons.

**Health: Life expectancy at birth** (1992): 70 male, 74 female. **Hospital beds:** 1 per 442 persons. **Physicians:** 1 per 1,057 persons. **Infant mortality** (per 1,000 live births 1992): 23%.

**Education** (1989): **Literacy:** 68%. **Years Compulsory:** ages 6-12.

**Major International Organizations:** UN (World Bank, IMF, ILO), Arab League, OPEC.

**Embassy:** 600 New Hampshire Ave. NW 20037; 338-6500.

The 7 "Trucial Sheikdoms" gave Britain control of defense and foreign relations in the 19th century. They merged to become an independent state Dec. 2, 1971.

The Abu Dhabi Petroleum Co. was fully nationalized in 1975. Oil revenues have given the UAE one of the highest per capita GDPs in the world. International banking has grown in recent years.

## United Kingdom of Great Britain and Northern Ireland

**People: Population** (1992 est.): 57,797,800. **Age distrib.** (%): 0-14: 19.2; 15-59: 60.1; 60+: 20.7. **Pop. density:** 613 per sq. mi. **Urban** (1990): 90%. **Ethnic groups:** English 81.5%, Scottish 9.6%, Irish 2.4%, Welsh 1.9%, Ulster 1.8%; West Indian, Indian, Pakistani over 2%; others. **Languages:** English, Welsh spoken in western Wales. **Religions:** Church of England, Roman Catholic.

**Geography: Area:** 94,226 sq. mi., slightly smaller than Oregon. **Location:** Off the NW coast of Europe, across English Channel, Strait of Dover, and North Sea. **Neighbors:** Ireland to W, France to SE. **Topography:** England is mostly rolling land, rising to Uplands of southern Scotland; Lowlands are in center of Scotland, granite Highlands are in N. Coast is heavily indented, especially on W. British Isles have milder climate than N Europe, due to the Gulf Stream, and ample rainfall. Severn, 220 mi., and Thames, 215 mi., are longest rivers. **Capital:** London. **Cities** (1988 est.): London 6,735,000; Birmingham 993,000; Glasgow 703,000; Leeds 710,000; Sheffield 532,000; Liverpool 469,000; Manchester 445,000; Edinburgh 433,000; Bradford 463,000; Bristol 377,000.

**Government: Type:** Constitutional monarchy. **Head of state:** Queen Elizabeth II; b. Apr. 21, 1926; in office: Feb. 6, 1952. **Head of government:** Prime Min. John Major; b. Mar. 29, 1943; in office: Nov. 28, 1990. **Local divisions:** England and Wales: 47 non-metro counties, 7 metro counties, Greater London; Scotland: 9 regions, 3 island areas; N. Ireland: 26 districts. **Defense:** 4.3% of GDP.

**Economy: Industries:** Steel, metals, vehicles, shipbuilding, banking, textiles, chemicals, electronics, aircraft, machinery, distilling. **Chief crops:** Grains, sugar beets, fruits, vegetables. **Minerals:** Coal, tin, oil, gas, limestone, iron, salt, clay. **Crude oil reserves** (1991): 4.0 bln. bbls. **Arable land:** 30%. **Livestock** (1991): cattle: 11.8 mln.; pigs: 7.3 mln.; sheep: 29.9 mln. **Fish catch** (1991): 803,000 metric tons. **Electricity prod.** (1991): 316 bln. kWh. **Crude steel prod.** (1991): 16.4 mln. metric tons. **Labor force:** 2% agric.; 26% manuf. & eng., 60% services.

**Finance: Monetary unit:** Pound (June 1992: .54 = $1 US). **Gross domestic product** (1991): $915 bln. **Per capita GDP:** $15,900. **Imports** (1992): $221 bln.; partners: EC 52%, U.S. 10%. **Exports** (1992): $190 bln.; partners: EC 53%, U.S. 13%. **Tourism** (1991): receipts: $18.8 bln. **National budget** (1992): $469 bln. expenditures. **International reserves less gold** (Mar. 1993): $38 bln. **Gold:** 19.0 mln. oz t. **Consumer prices** (change in 1992): 3.7%.

**Transport: Railroads** (1991): **Length:** 23,518 mi. **Motor vehicles:** in use (1991): 19.7 mln. passenger cars, 2.7 mln. comm. vehicles. **Civil aviation** (1990): 79.5 bln. passenger-km: 56 airports with scheduled flights. **Chief ports:** London, Liverpool, Glasgow, Southampton, Cardiff, Belfast.

**Communications: Television sets:** 1 per 3 persons. **Radios:** 1 per 1 person. **Telephones:** 1 per 1.9 persons. **Daily newspaper circ.** (1990): 388 per 1,000 pop.

**Health: Life expectancy at birth:** (1992): 73 male; 79 female. **Births:** (per 1,000 pop. 1992): 14. **Deaths:** (per 1,000 pop. 1992): 11. **Natural increase:** 0.3%. **Hospital beds:** 1 per 138 persons. **Physicians:** 1 per 611 persons. **Infant mortality:** (per 1,000 live births 1992): 8.

**Education** (1991): **Literacy:** 99%. **Years compulsory:** 12; attendance 99%.

**Major International Organizations:** UN all of and its specialized agencies, NATO, EC, OECD.

**Embassy:** 3100 Massachusetts Ave. NW 20008; 462-1340.

The United Kingdom of Great Britain and Northern Ireland comprises England, Wales, Scotland, and Northern Ireland.

**Queen and Royal Family.** The ruling sovereign is Elizabeth II of the House of Windsor, born Apr. 21, 1926, elder daughter of King George VI. She succeeded to the throne Feb. 6, 1952, and was crowned June 2, 1953. She was married Nov. 20, 1947, to Lt. Philip Mountbatten, born June 10, 1921, former Prince of Greece. He was created Duke of Edinburgh, Earl of Merioneth, and Baron Greenwich, and given the style H.R.H., Nov. 19, 1947; he was given the title Prince of the United Kingdom and Northern Ireland Feb. 22, 1957. Prince Charles Philip Arthur George, born Nov. 14, 1948, is the Prince of Wales and heir apparent. His son, William Philip Arthur Louis, born June 21, 1982, is second in line to the throne.

**Parliament** is the legislative governing body for the United Kingdom, with certain powers over dependent units. It consists of 2 houses: The **House of Lords** includes 763 hereditary and 314 life peers and peeresses, certain judges, 2 archbishops and 24 bishops of the Church of England. Total membership is over 1,000. The **House of Commons** has 650 members, who are elected by direct ballot and divided as follows: England 516; Wales 36; Scotland 71; Northern Ireland 12.

**Resources and Industries.** Great Britain's major occupations are manufacturing and trade. Metals and metal-using industries contribute more than 50% of the exports. Of about 60 million acres of land in England, Wales and Scotland, 46 million are farmed, of which 17 million are arable, the rest pastures.

Large oil and gas fields have been found in the North Sea. Commercial oil production began in 1975. There are large deposits of coal.

Britain imports all of its cotton, rubber, sulphur, about 80% of its wool, half of its food and iron ore, also certain amounts of paper, tobacco, chemicals. Manufactured goods made from these basic materials have been exported since the industrial age began. Main exports are machinery, chemicals, woolen and synthetic textiles, clothing, autos and trucks, iron and steel, locomotives, ships, jet aircraft, farm machinery, drugs, radio, TV, radar and navigation equipment, scientific instruments, arms, whisky.

**Religion and Education.** The Church of England is Protestant Episcopal. The queen is its temporal head, with rights of appointments to archbishoprics, bishoprics, and other offices. There are 2 provinces, Canterbury and York, each headed by an archbishop. The most famous church is Westminster Abbey (1050-1760), site of coronations, tombs of Elizabeth I, Mary of Scots, kings, poets, and of the Unknown Warrior.

The most celebrated British universities are Oxford and Cambridge, each dating to the 13th century. There are about 40 other universities.

**History.** Britain was part of the continent of Europe until about 6,000 BC, but migration of peoples across the English Channel continued long afterward. Celts arrived 2,500 to 3,000 years ago. Their language survives in Welsh, and Gaelic enclaves.

England was added to the Roman Empire in 43 AD. After the withdrawal of Roman legions in 410, waves of Jutes, Angles, and Saxons arrived from German lands. They contended with Danish raiders for control from the 8th through 11th centuries.

The last successful invasion was by French speaking Normans in 1066, who united the country with their dominions in France.

Opposition by nobles to royal authority forced King John to sign the Magna Carta in 1215, a guarantee of rights and the rule of law. In the ensuing decades, the foundations of the parliamentary system were laid.

English dynastic claims to large parts of France led to the Hundred Years War, 1338-1453, and the defeat of England. A long civil war, the War of the Roses, lasted 1455-85, and ended with the establishment of the powerful Tudor monarchy. A distinct English civilization flourished. The economy prospered over long periods of domestic peace unmatched in continental Europe. Religious independence was secured when the Church of England was separated from the authority of the Pope in 1534.

Under Queen Elizabeth I, England became a major naval power, leading to the founding of colonies in the new world and the expansion of trade with Europe and the Orient. Scotland was united with England when James VI of Scotland was crowned James I of England in 1603.

A struggle between Parliament and the Stuart kings led to a bloody civil war, 1642-49, and the establishment of a republic under the Puritan Oliver Cromwell. The monarchy was restored in 1660, but the "Glorious Revolution" of 1688 confirmed the sovereignty of Parliament: a Bill of Rights was granted 1689.

In the 18th century, parliamentary rule was strengthened. Technological and entrepreneurial innovations led to the Industrial Revolution. The 13 North American colonies were lost, but replaced by growing empires in Canada and India. Britain's role in the defeat of Napoleon, 1815, strengthened its position as the leading world power.

The extension of the franchise in 1832 and 1867, the formation of trade unions, and the development of universal public education were among the drastic social changes which accompanied the spread of industrialization and urbanization in the 19th century. Large parts of Africa and Asia were added to the empire during the reign of Queen Victoria, 1837-1901.

Though victorious in World War I, Britain suffered huge casualties and economic dislocation. Ireland became independent in 1921, and independence movements became active in India and other colonies.

The country suffered major bombing damage in World War II, but held out against Germany singlehandedly for a year after the fall of France in 1940.

Industrial growth continued in the postwar period, but Britain lost its leadership position to other powers. Labor governments passed socialist programs nationalizing some basic industries and expanding social security. The Thatcher government has however, tried to increase the role of private enterprise. In 1987, Margaret Thatcher became the first British leader in 160 years to be elected to a 3d consecutive term as prime minister. She resigned as prime minister in Nov. 1990.

The UK supported the UN resolutions against Iraq and sent military forces to the Persian Gulf war.

## Wales

The Principality of Wales in western Britain has an area of 8,019 sq. mi. and a population (1991 cen.) of 2,798,000. Cardiff is the capital, pop. (1981 est.) 273,856.

England and Wales are administered as a unit. Less than 20% of the population of Wales speak both English and Welsh; about 32,000 speak Welsh solely. A 1979 referendum rejected, 4-1, the creation of an elected Welsh Assembly.

Early Anglo-Saxon invaders drove Celtic peoples into the mountains of Wales, terming them Waelise (Welsh, or foreign). There they developed a distinct nationality. Members of the ruling house of Gwynedd in the 13th century fought England but were crushed, 1283. Edward of Caernarvon, son of Edward I of England, was created Prince of Wales, 1301.

## Scotland

Scotland, a kingdom now united with England and Wales in Great Britain, occupies the northern 37% of the main British island, and the Hebrides, Orkney, Shetland and smaller islands. Length, 275 mi., breadth approx. 150 mi., area, 30,405 sq. mi., population (1991 cen.) 4,957,000.

The Lowlands, a belt of land approximately 60 mi. wide from the Firth of Clyde to the Firth of Forth, divide the farming region of the Southern Uplands from the granite Highlands of the North, contain 75% of the population and most of the industry. The Highlands, famous for hunting and fishing, have been opened to industry by many hydroelectric power stations.

Edinburgh, pop. (1986 est.) 439,000, is the capital. Glasgow, pop. (1986 est.) 733,000, is Britain's greatest industrial center. It is a shipbuilding complex on the Clyde and an ocean port. Aberdeen, pop. (1986 est.) 215,000, NE of Edinburgh, is a major port, center of granite industry, fish processing, and North Sea oil exploitation. Dundee, pop. (1986 est.) 177,000, NE of Edinburgh, is an industrial and fish processing center. About 90,000 persons speak Gaelic as well as English.

**History.** Scotland was called Caledonia by the Romans who battled early Celtic tribes and occupied southern areas from the 1st to the 4th centuries. Missionaries from Britain introduced Christianity in the 4th century; St. Columba, an Irish monk, converted most of Scotland in the 6th century.

The Kingdom of Scotland was founded in 1018. William Wallace and Robert Bruce both defeated English armies 1297 and 1314, respectively.

In 1603 James VI of Scotland, son of Mary, Queen of Scots, succeeded to the throne of England as James I, and effected the Union of the Crowns. In 1707 Scotland received representation in the British Parliament, resulting from the union of former separate Parliaments. Its executive in the British cabinet is the Secretary of State for Scotland. The growing Scottish National Party urges independence. A 1979 referendum on the creation of an elected Scotland Assembly was defeated.

Memorials of Robert Burns, Sir Walter Scott, John Knox, Mary, Queen of Scots draw many tourists, as do the beauties of the Trossachs, Loch Katrine, Loch Lomond and abbey ruins.

**Industries.** Engineering products are the most important industry, with growing emphasis on office machinery, autos, electronics and other consumer goods. Oil has been discovered offshore in the North Sea, stimulating on-shore support industries.

Scotland produces fine woolens, worsteds, tweeds, silks, fine linens and jute. It is known for its special breeds of cattle and sheep. Fisheries have large hauls of herring, cod, whiting. Whisky is the biggest export.

**The Hebrides** are a group of c. 500 islands, 100 inhabited, off the W coast. The Inner Hebrides include **Skye, Mull,** and **Iona,** the last famous for the arrival of St. Columba, 563 AD. The Outer Hebrides include **Lewis** and **Harris.** Industries include sheep raising and weaving. The **Orkney Islands,** c. 90, are to the NE. The capital is Kirkwall, on Pomona Is. Fish curing, sheep raising and weaving are occupations. NE of the Orkneys are the 200 **Shetland Islands,** 24 inhabited, home of Shetland pony. The Orkneys and Shetlands have become centers for the North Sea oil industry.

## Northern Ireland

Six of the 9 counties of Ulster, the NE corner of Ireland, constitute Northern Ireland, with the parliamentary boroughs of Belfast and Londonderry. Area 5,463 sq. mi., 1991 cen. pop. 1,570,000, capital and chief industrial center, Belfast, (1990 est.) 297,000.

**Industries.** Shipbuilding, including large tankers, has long been an important industry, centered in Belfast, the largest port. Linen manufacture is also important, along with apparel, rope, and twine. Growing diversification has added engineering products, synthetic fibers, and electronics. They are large numbers of cattle, hogs, and sheep, potatoes, poultry, and dairy foods are also produced.

**Government.** An act of the British Parliament, 1920, divided Northern from Southern Ireland, each with a parliament and government. When Ireland became a dominion, 1921, and later a republic, Northern Ireland chose to remain a part of the United Kingdom. It elects 12 members to the British House of Commons.

During 1968-69, large demonstrations were conducted by Roman Catholics who charged they were discriminated against in voting rights, housing, and employment. The Catholics, a minority comprising about a third of the population, demanded abolition of property qualifications for voting in local elections. Violence and terrorism intensified, involving branches of the Irish Republican Army (outlawed in the Irish Republic), Protestant groups, police, and British troops.

A succession of Northern Ireland prime ministers pressed reform programs but failed to satisfy extremists on both sides. Over 2,000 were killed in over 15 years of bombings and shootings through 1990, many in England itself. Britain suspended the Northern Ireland parliament Mar. 30, 1972, and imposed direct

British rule. A coalition government was formed in 1973 when moderates won election to a new one-house Assembly. But a Protestant general strike overthrew the government in 1974 and direct rule was resumed.

The turmoil and agony of Northern Ireland was dramatized in 1981 by the deaths of 10 imprisoned Irish nationalist hunger strikers in Maze Prison near Belfast. The inmates had starved themselves to death in an attempt to achieve status as political prisoners, but the British government refused to yield to their demands. In 1985, the Hillsborough agreement gave the Rep. of Ireland a voice in the governing of Northern Ireland; the accord was strongly opposed by Ulster loyalists.

**Education and Religion.** Northern Ireland is 2/3 Protestant, 1/3 Roman Catholic. Education is compulsory through age 15.

## Channel Islands

The Channel Islands, area 75 sq. mi., est. pop. 1986 145,000, off the NW coast of France, the only parts of the one-time Dukedom of Normandy belonging to England, are **Jersey, Guernsey** and the dependencies of Guernsey — **Alderney, Brechou, Great Sark, Little Sark, Herm, Jethou** and **Lihou.** Jersey and Guernsey have separate legal existences and lieutenant governors named by the Crown. The islands were the only British soil occupied by German troops in World War II.

## Isle of Man

The Isle of Man, area 227 sq. mi., 1991 cen. pop. 69,788, is in the Irish Sea, 20 mi. from Scotland, 30 mi. from Cumberland. It is rich in lead and iron. The island has its own laws and a lieutenant governor appointed by the Crown. The Tynwald (legislature) consists of the Legislative Council, partly elected, and House of Keys, elected. Capital: Douglas. Farming, tourism, fishing (kippers, scallops) are chief occupations. Man is famous for the Manx tailless cat.

## Gibraltar

Gibraltar, a dependency on the southern coast of Spain, guards the entrance to the Mediterranean. The Rock has been in British possession since 1704. The Rock is 2.75 mi. long, 3/4 of a mi. wide and 1,396 ft. in height; a narrow isthmus connects it with the mainland. Est. pop. 1992, 29,651.

In 1966 Spain called on Britain to give "substantial sovereignty" of Gibraltar to Spain and imposed a partial blockade. In 1967, residents voted for remaining under Britain. A new constitution, May 30, 1996, gave an elected House of Assembly more control in domestic affairs. A UN General Assembly resolution requested Britain to end Gibraltar's colonial status by Oct. 1, 1996. No settlement has been reached.

## British West Indies

Swinging in a vast arc from the coast of Venezuela NE, then N and NW toward Puerto Rico are the Leeward Islands, forming a coral and volcanic barrier sheltering the Caribbean from the open Atlantic. Many of the islands are self-governing British possessions. Universal suffrage was instituted 1951-54; ministerial systems were set up 1956-1960.

The **Leeward Islands,** still associated with the UK are **Montserrat** (1987 pop. 11,600, area 32 sq. mi., capital Plymouth), the small **British Virgin Islands** (pop. 1991 cen.: 16,749), and **Anguilla** (pop. 1990 est.: 7,000), the most northerly of the Leeward Islands.

The three **Cayman Islands,** a dependency, lie S of Cuba, NW of Jamaica. Pop. 23,000 (1987), most of it on Grand Cayman. It is a free port; in the 1970s Grand Cayman became a tax-free refuge for foreign funds and branches of many Western banks were opened there. Total area 102 sq. mi., capital Georgetown.

The **Turks and Caicos Islands,** at the SE end of the Bahama Islands, are a separate possession. There are about 30 islands, only 6 inhabited (pop. 1990 cen.: 11,696; area 193 sq. mi.; capital Grand Turk). Salt, crayfish and conch shells are the main exports.

## Bermuda

**Bermuda** is a British dependency governed by a royal governor and an assembly, dating from 1620, the oldest legislative body among British dependencies. Capital is Hamilton.

It is a group of 360 small islands of coral formation, 20 inhabited, comprising 20.6 sq. mi. in the western Atlantic, 580 mi. E of North Carolina. Pop., 1992 est., was 60,213 (about 61% of African descent). Density is high.

The U.S. has air and naval bases under long-term lease, and a NASA tracking facility.

Bermuda boasts many resort hotels. The government raises most revenue from import duties. Exports: petroleum products, medicine.

## South Atlantic

**Falkland Islands and Dependencies,** a British dependency, lies 300 mi. E of the Strait of Magellan at the southern end of South America.

The Falklands or Islas Malvinas include about 200 islands, area 4,700 sq. mi., pop. (1991 cen.) 2,121. Sheep-grazing is the main industry; wool is the principal export. There are indications of large oil and gas deposits. The islands are also claimed by Argentina though 97% of inhabitants are of British origin. Argentina invaded the islands Apr. 2, 1982. The British responded by sending a task force to the area, landing their main force on the Falklands, May 21, and forcing an Argentine surrender at Port Stanley, June 14.

**British Antarctic Territory,** south of 60° S lat., was made a separate colony in 1962 and comprises mainly the **South Shetland Islands,** the **South Orkneys** and **Graham's Land.** A chain of meteorological stations is maintained.

**St. Helena,** an island 1,200 mi. off the W coast of Africa and 1,800 E of South America, has 47 sq. mi. and est. pop., 1985 of 5,400. Flax, lace and rope making are the chief industries. After Napoleon Bonaparte was defeated at Waterloo the Allies exiled him to St. Helena, where he lived from Oct. 16, 1815, to his death, May 5, 1821. Capital is Jamestown.

**Tristan da Cunha** is the principal of a group of islands of volcanic origin, total area 40 sq. mi., half way between the Cape of Good Hope and South America. A volcanic peak 6,760 ft. high erupted in 1961. The 262 inhabitants were removed to England, but most returned in 1963. The islands are dependencies of St. Helena.

**Ascension** is an island of volcanic origin, 34 sq. mi. in area, 700 mi. NW of St. Helena, through which it is administered. It is a communications relay center for Britain, and has a U.S. satellite tracking center. Est. pop., 1985, was 1,500, half of them communications workers. The island is noted for sea turtles.

## Hong Kong

A Crown Colony at the mouth of the Canton R. in China, 90 mi. S of Canton. Its nucleus is Hong Kong Is., 35½ sq. mi., acquired from China 1841, on which is located Victoria, the capital. Opposite is Kowloon Peninsula, 3 sq. mi. and Stonecutters Is., ¼ sq. mi., added, 1860. An additional 355 sq. mi. known as the New Territories, a mainland area and islands, were leased from China, 1898, for 99 years. Britain and China, Dec. 19, 1984, signed an agreement under which Hong Kong would be allowed to keep its capitalist system for 50 years after 1997, the year that the 99-year lease will expire. Total area of the colony is 409 sq. mi., with a population, 1992 est., of 5.8 million including fewer than 20,000 British. From 1949 to 1962 Hong Kong absorbed more than a million refugees from China.

Hong Kong harbor was long an important British naval station and one of the world's great trans-shipment ports.

Principal industries are textiles and apparel; also tourism, $4.9 bln. expenditures (1991), shipbuilding, iron and steel, fishing, cement, and small manufactures.

Spinning mills, among the best in the world, and low wages compete with textiles elsewhere and have resulted in the protective measures in some countries. Hong Kong also has a booming electronics industry.

## British Indian Ocean Territory

Formed Nov. 1965, embracing islands formerly dependencies of Mauritius or Seychelles: the Chagos Archipelago (including Diego Garcia), Aldabra, Farquhar and Des Roches. The latter 3 were transferred to Seychelles, which became independent in 1976. Area 22 sq mi. No civilian population remains.

## Pacific Ocean

**Pitcairn Island** is in the Pacific, halfway between South America and Australia. The island was discovered in 1767 by Carteret but was not inhabited until 23 years later when the mutineers of the Bounty landed there. The area is 1.7 sq. mi. and 1991 pop. was 59. It is a British colony and is administered by a British Representative in New Zealand and a local Council. The uninhabited islands of **Henderson, Ducie** and **Oeno** are in the Pitcairn group.

# United States of America

**People: Population** (1993 est.): 256,561,239 (incl. 50 states & Dist. of Columbia). **Age distrib.(%):** 0–14: 21.7; 15–59: 61.4; 60+: 16.9. **Pop. density:** 70 per sq. mi. **Urban** (1990): 76%.

**Geography:** 3,618,770 sq. mi. (incl. 50 states and D. of C.). Vast central plain, mountains in west, hills and low mountains in east.

**Government:** Federal republic, strong democratic tradition. **Head of state:** Bill Clinton; b. Aug. 19, 1946; in office: Jan. 20, 1993. **Administrative divisions:** 50 states and Dist. of Columbia. **Defense:** 5.7% of GNP (1991).

**Economy: Minerals:** Coal, copper, lead, molybdenum, phosphates, uranium, bauxite, gold, iron, mercury, nickel, potash, silver, tungsten, zinc. **Crude oil reserves** (1991): 26 bln. barrels. **Arable land:** 21%. **Livestock** (1991): cattle: 98 mln.; pigs: 54 mln.; sheep: 11.3 mln. **Fish catch** (1991): 4.3 mln. metric tons. **Electricity prod.** (1991): 2,822 bln. kWh. **Crude steel prod.** (1991): 79.2 mln. metric tons.

**Finance: Gross domestic product** (1991): 5.6 trl. **Per capita GDP:** $22,470. **Imports** (1992): $553 bln.; partners: Can. 17%, Jap. 20%, Mex. 6%. **Exports** (1992): $447 bln.; partners: Can. 22%, Jap. 12%, Mex. 6%, UK 5%. **Tourism** (1991): receipts $45.5 bln. **International reserves less gold** (Mar. 1993): $63.3 bln. **Gold:** 261.8 mln. oz t. **Consumer prices** (change in 1992): 3.0%.

**Transport: Railroads** (1990): **Length:** 144,000 mi. **Motor vehicles:** in use (1990): 143 mln. passenger cars, 45 mln. comm. vehicles. **Civil aviation** (1990): 751 bln. passenger-km; 834 airports with scheduled flights.

**Communications: Television sets:** 1 per 1.3 persons. **Radios:** 1 per 0.5 persons. **Telephones:** 1 per 1.9 persons. **Daily newspaper circ.** (1990): 255 per 1,000 pop.

**Health: Life expectancy at birth** (1992): 72 male; 79 female. **Births** (per 1,000 pop. 1992): 14. **Deaths** (per 1,000 pop. 1992): 9. **Natural increase:** .5%. **Hospital beds:** 1 per 198 persons. **Physicians:** 1 per 404 persons. **Infant mortality** (per 1,000 live births 1992): 10.

**Major International Organizations:** UN (GATT, IMF, WHO, FAO), OAS, NATO, OECD.

**Education** (1991): **Literacy:** 97%.

# Uruguay

## Republic of Uruguay

## República del Uruguay

**People: Population** (1992 est.): 3,121,000. **Age distrib. (%):** 0–14: 26.9; 15–59: 57.7; 60+: 15.4. **Pop. density:** 45 per sq. mi. **Urban** (1990): 86.0%. **Ethnic groups:** Caucasians (Iberians, Italians) 89%, mestizos 10%, mulatto and black. **Languages:** Spanish. **Religions:** Roman Catholic 66%.

**Geography: Area:** 68,037 sq. mi., the size of Washington State. **Location:** In southern S. America, on the Atlantic O. **Neighbors:** Argentina on W, Brazil on N. **Topography:** Uruguay is composed of rolling, grassy plains and hills, well-watered by rivers flowing W to Uruguay R. **Capital:** Montevideo. **Cities** (1991 est.): Montevideo 1,400,000.

**Government: Type:** Republic. **Head of state:** Pres. Luis Alberto Lacalle; in office: Nov. 26, 1989. **Local divisions:** 19 departments. **Defense:** 1.4% of GDP (1989).

**Economy: Industries:** Meat-packing, textiles, wine, cement, oil products. **Chief crops:** Corn, wheat, citrus fruits, rice, oats, linseed. **Arable land:** 8%. **Livestock** (1990): cattle: 8.7 mln.; sheep: 25.2 mln. **Fish catch** (1990): 88,000 metric tons. **Electricity prod.** (1991): 5.6 bln. kWh. **Labor force** 13% agric.; 22% manuf.; 16% serv.; 20% govt., 17% comm.

**Finance: Monetary unit:** New Peso (May 1993: 3,621 = $1 US). **Gross domestic product** (1991): $9.1 bln. **Per capita GDP:** $2,935. **Imports** (1991): $1.3 bln.; partners: EC 27%, Braz. 24%, Arg. 14%, U.S. 8%. **Exports** (1991): $1.6 bln.; partners: Braz. 28%, U.S. 11%, EC 23%. **Tourism** (1990): $261 mln. receipts. **National budget** (1989): $1.5 bln. expenditures. **International reserves less gold** (Jan. 1993): $538 mln. **Gold:** 2.0 mln. oz t. **Consumer prices** (change in 1992): 68.5%

Transport: Railroads (1989): Length: 3,002 km. Motor vehicles: in use (1989): 190,000 passenger cars, 100,000 comm. vehicles. Civil aviation (1990): 471 mln. passenger-km; 7 airports. Chief ports: Montevideo.

Communications: Television sets: 1 per 4.8 persons. Radios: 1 per 1.0 persons. Telephones: 1 per 5.8 persons. Daily newspaper circ. (1989): 227 per 1,000 pop.

Health: Life expectancy at birth (1992): 69 male; 76 female. Births (per 1,000 pop. 1992): 17. Deaths (per 1,000 pop. 1992): 10. Natural increase: .7%. Hospital beds: 1 per 127 persons. Physicians: 1 per 341 persons. Infant mortality (per 1,000 live births 1992): 22.

Education (1990): Literacy: 96%.

Major International Organizations: UN (GATT, IMF, WHO), OAS.

Embassy: 1919 F St. NW 20006; 331-1313.

Spanish settlers did not begin replacing the indigenous Charrua Indians until 1624. Portuguese from Brazil arrived later, but Uruguay was attached to the Spanish Viceroyalty of Rio de la Plata in the 18th century. Rebels fought against Spain beginning in 1810. An independent republic was declared Aug. 25, 1825.

Socialist measures were adopted as far back as 1911. The state owns the power, telephone, railroad, cement, oil-refining and other industries.

Uruguay's standard of living was one of the highest in South America, and political and labor conditions among the freest. Economic stagnation, inflation, floods and drought, and a general strike in the late 1960s brought government attempts to strengthen the economy through devaluation of the peso and wage and price controls.

Terrorist activities led to Pres. Juan Maria Bordaberry agreeing to military control of his administration Feb. 1973. In June he abolished Congress and set up a Council of State in its place. Bordaberry was removed by the military in a 1976 coup. Civilian government was restored to the country in 1985.

## Uzbekistan

### Republic of Uzbekistan

### Ozbekiston Republikasy

People: Population (1992 est.): 21,626,000. Pop. density: 125 per sq. mi. Urban (1991): 40%. Ethnic groups: Uzbek 70%, Russian 11%. Religion: Mostly Sunni Moslem.

Geography: Area: 172,700 sq. mi., slightly larger than California. Neighbors: Kazakhstan on N and W, Kyrgyzstan and Tajikistan on E, Afghanistan and Turkmenistan on S. Topography: mostly plains and desert. Capital: Tashkent.

Government: Type: Republic. Head of state: Pres. Islam A. Karimov. Head of government: Prime Min. Abdulkhashim Mutalov; in office: Jan. 8, 1992. Local divisions: 11 oblasts, 1 autonomous republic.

Economy: Industries: Steel, tractors, cars, textiles. Chief crops: Cotton, rice. Minerals: Coal, copper. Livestock (1990): cattle: 4.1 mln., sheep: 8.7 mln. Electricity prod. (1991): 54 bln. kWh. Labor force: 39% agric. & forestry; 39% ind. & comm.

Finance: Monetary unit: Ruble. Imports (1990): $3.5 bln. Exports (1990): $1.5 bln.

Transportation: Railroads: (1990): Length: 4,225 mi. Civil aviation (1990): 11.0 bln. passenger-km; 1 airport.

Communications: Television sets: 1 per 6 persons. Telephones: 1 per 15 persons.

Health: Life expectancy at birth (1992): 64 male; 70 female. Births (per 1,000 pop. 1992): 34. Deaths (per 1,000 pop. 1992): 7. Hospital beds: 1 per 82 persons. Physicians: 1 per 281 persons. Infant mortality rate (per 1,000 live births 1992): 65.

Major International Organizations: UN, CIS.

The region was overrun by the Mongols under Genghis Khan in 1220. In the 14th century, Uzbekistan became the center of a native empire—that of the Timurids. In later centuries Moslem feudal states emerged. Russian military conquest began in the 19th century.

The Uzbek SSR became a Soviet Union republic in 1925. Uzbekistan declared independence Aug. 29, 1991. It became an independent republic when the Soviet Union disbanded Dec. 26, 1991.

## Vanuatu

### Republic of Vanuatu

### Ripablik Blong Vanuatu

People: Population (1992 est.): 174,000. Pop. density: 30 per sq. mi. Ethnic groups: Mainly Melanesian, some European, Polynesian, Micronesian. Languages: Bislama, French, and English all official. Religions: Presbyterian 40%, Anglican 14%, Roman Catholic 16%, animist 15%.

Geography: Area: 5,700 sq. mi., slightly larger than Connecticut. Location: SW Pacific, 1,200 mi. NE of Brisbane, Australia. Topography: dense forest with narrow coastal strips of cultivated land. Capital: Port-Vila. Cities: Vila (1990): 19,000.

Government: Type: Republic. Head of state: Pres. Fred Timakata; in office: Jan. 12, 1989. Head of gov't: Prime Min. Maxime Carlot Korman; in office: Dec. 16, 1991.

Economy: Industries: Fish-freezing, meat canneries, tourism. Chief crops: Copra (38% of export), cocoa, coffee. Minerals: Manganese. Other resources: Forests, cattle. Fish catch (1990): 3.3 metric tons.

Finance: Monetary unit: Vatu (Mar. 1993): 120 = $1 US). Gross domestic product (1990): $142 mln. Imports (1990): $60 mln.; partners: Aus. 36%, Fr. 8%, Japan 13%. Exports (1990): $15 mln.; partners: Neth. 34%, Jap. 17%, Fr. 27%.

Health: Life expectancy at birth (1992): 67 male, 72 female. Infant mortality (per 1,000 live births 1992): 30.

Education: Literacy (1990): 90%. Education not compulsory, but 85-90% of children of primary school age attend primary schools.

The Anglo-French condominium of the New Hebrides, administered jointly by France and Great Britain since 1906, became the independent Republic of Vanuatu on July 30, 1980.

## Vatican City

### The Holy See

People: Population (1992 est.): 802. Ethnic groups: Italians, Swiss. Languages: Italian, Latin.

Geography: Area: 108.7 acres. Location: In Rome, Italy. Neighbors: Completely surrounded by Italy.

Monetary unit: Lira.

Apostolic Nunciature in U.S.: 3339 Massachusetts Ave. NW 20008; 333-7121.

The popes for many centuries, with brief interruptions, held temporal sovereignty over mid-Italy (the so-called Papal States), comprising an area of some 16,000 sq. mi., with a population in the 19th century of more than 3 million. This territory was incorporated in the new Kingdom of Italy, the sovereignty of the pope being confined to the palaces of the Vatican and the Lateran in Rome and the villa of Castel Gandolfo, by an Italian law, May 13, 1871. This law also guaranteed to the pope and his successors a yearly indemnity of over $620,000. The allowance, however, remained unclaimed.

A Treaty of Conciliation, a concordat and a financial convention were signed Feb. 11, 1929, by Cardinal Gasparri and Premier Mussolini. The documents established the independent state of Vatican City, and gave the Catholic religion special status in Italy. The treaty (Lateran Agreement) was made part of the Constitution of Italy (Article 7) in 1947. Italy and the Vatican reached preliminary agreement in 1976 on revisions of the concordat, that would eliminate Roman Catholicism as the state religion and end required religious education in Italian schools.

Vatican City includes St. Peter's, the Vatican Palace and Museum covering over 13 acres, the Vatican gardens, and neighboring buildings between Viale Vaticano and the Church. Thirteen buildings in Rome, outside the boundaries, enjoy extraterritorial rights; these buildings house congregations or officers necessary for the administration of the Holy See.

The legal system is based on the code of canon law, the apostolic constitutions and the laws especially promulgated for the Vatican City by the pope. The Secretariat of State represents the Holy See in its diplomatic relations. By the Treaty of Conciliation the pope is pledged to a perpetual neutrality unless his mediation is specifically requested. This, however, does not prevent the defense of the Church whenever it is persecuted.

The present sovereign of the State of Vatican City is the Supreme Pontiff John Paul II, Karol Wojtyla, born in Wadowice, Poland, May 18, 1920, elected Oct. 16, 1978 (the first non-Italian to be elected Pope in 456 years).

The U.S. restored formal relations in 1984 after the U.S. Congress repealed an 1867 ban on diplomatic relations with the Vatican.

# Venezuela

### Republic of Venezuela

### Republica de Venezuela

**People: Population** (1992 est.): 20,675,000. **Age distrib.** (%): 0–14: 38.3; 15–59: 56.0; 60+: 5.7. **Pop. density:** 58 per sq. mi. **Urban** (1990): 83%. **Ethnic groups:** Mestizo 69%, white (Spanish, Portuguese, Italian) 20%, black 9%, Indian 2%. **Languages:** Spanish (official). **Religions:** Roman Catholic 92%.

**Geography: Area:** 352,143 sq. mi., more than twice the size of California. **Location:** On the Caribbean coast of S. America. **Neighbors:** Colombia on W, Brazil on S, Guyana on E. **Topography:** Flat coastal plain and Orinoco Delta are bordered by Andes Mtns. and hills. Plains, called llanos, extend between mountains and Orinoco. Guyana Highlands and plains are S of Orinoco, which stretches 1,600 mi. and drains 80% of Venezuela. **Capital:** Caracas. **Cities** (1990 est.): Caracas 1,290,000; Maracaibo 1,206,000; Barquisimeto 723,000; Valencia 955,000.

**Government: Type:** Federal republic. **Head of state:** Pres. Ramon Jose Velaquez; in office June 5, 1993. **Local divisions:** 21 states, territory, federal district, federal dependency. **Defense:** 4.3% of GDP (1991).

**Economy: Industries:** Steel, oil products, textiles, containers, paper. **Chief crops:** Coffee, rice, fruits, sugar. **Minerals:** Oil, iron (extensive reserves and production), gold. **Crude oil reserves** (1991): 60 bln. barrels. **Arable land:** 4%. **Livestock** (1990): cattle: 13.8 mln. **Fish catch** (1990): 327,000 metric tons. **Electricity prod.** (1991): 55.7 bln. kWh. **Crude steel prod.** (1991): 3.2 mln. metric tons. **Labor force:** 6% agric.; 35% ind.; 26% services.

**Finance: Monetary unit:** Bolivar (Apr. 1993: 84 = $1 US). **Gross domestic product** (1991): $52.3 bln. **Per capita GDP:** $2,590. **Imports** (1991): $10.2 bln.; partners: U.S. 44%. **Exports** (1991): $15.1 bln.; partners: U.S. 50%. **Tourism** (1990): $359 mln. receipts. **National budget** (1991): $13 bln. expenditures. **International reserves less gold** (Mar. 1993): $8.5 bln. **Gold:** 11.46 mln. oz t. **Consumer prices** (change in 1992): 31.4%.

**Transport: Railroads** (1990): **Length:** 226 mi. **Motor vehicles:** in use (1990): 1.6 mln. passenger cars, 459 mln. mln. vehicles. **Civil aviation** (1990): 4.0 mln. passenger-km; 32 airports with scheduled flights. **Chief ports:** Maracaibo, La Guaira, Puerto Cabello.

**Communications: Television sets:** 1 per 5.6 persons. **Radios:** 1 per 2.4 persons. **Telephones:** 1 per 11 persons. **Daily newspaper circ.** (1989): 111 per 1,000 pop.

**Health: Life expectancy at birth** (1992): 71 male; 78 female. **Births** (per 1,000 pop. 1992): 28. **Deaths** (per 1,000 pop. 1992): 4. **Natural increase:** 2.4%. **Hospital beds:** 1 per 370 persons. **Physicians:** 1 per 576 persons. **Infant mortality** (per 1,000 live births 1992): 23.

**Education** (1991): **Literacy:** 88%. **Years compulsory:** 8; attendance 83%.

**Major International Organizations:** UN (IMF, WHO, FAO), OAS, OPEC.

**Embassy:** 1099 30th St. NW 20007; 342-2214.

Columbus first set foot on the South American continent on the peninsula of Paria, Aug. 1498. Alonso de Ojeda, 1499, found Lake Maracaibo, called the land Venezuela, or Little Venice, because natives had houses on stilts. Venezuela was under Spanish domination until 1821. The republic was formed after secession from the Colombian Federation in 1830.

Military strongmen ruled Venezuela for most of the 20th century. They promoted the oil industry; some social reforms were implemented. Since 1959, the country has had democratically-elected governments.

Venezuela helped found the Organization of Petroleum Exporting Countries (OPEC). The government, Jan. 1, 1976, nationalized the oil industry with compensation. Oil accounts for much of total export earnings and the economy suffered a severe cash crisis in the 1980s as the result of falling oil revenues. The government has attempted to reduce dependence on oil.

A coup attempt, led by mid-level military officers, was thwarted by loyalist troops Feb. 4, 1992. Pres. Perez announced a series of economic and political reforms Mar. 5.

A second coup attempt was thwarted in Nov. Perez was suspended from office and charged with misappropriating government funds, May 1993.

# Vietnam

### Socialist Republic of Vietnam

### Cong Hoa Xa Hoi Chu Nghia Viet Nam

**People: Population** (1992 est.): 68,964,000. **Age distrib.** (%): 0–14: 40.8; 15–59: 53.6; 60+: 5.6 **Pop. density:** 541 per sq. mi. **Urban** (1989): 20%. **Ethnic groups:** Vietnamese 84%, Chinese 2%, remainder Muong, Thai, Meo, Khmer, Man, Cham. **Languages:** Vietnamese (official), Chinese. **Religions:** Buddhists, Confucians, and Taoists most numerous, Roman Catholics, animists, Muslims, Protestants.

**Geography: Area:** 127,330 sq. mi., the size of New Mexico. **Location:** On the E coast of the Indochinese Peninsula in SE Asia. **Neighbors:** China on N, Laos, Cambodia on W. **Topography:** Vietnam is long and narrow, with a 1,400-mi. coast. About 24% of country is readily arable, including the densely settled Red R. valley in the N, narrow coastal plains in center, and the wide, often marshy Mekong R. Delta in the S. The rest consists of semi-arid plateaus and barren mountains, with some stretches of tropical rain forest. **Capital:** Hanoi. **Cities** (1992): Ho Chi Minh City 4.0 mln.; Hanoi 2.0 mln.

**Government: Type:** Communist. **Head of state:** Pres. Lee Duc Anh; in office: Sept. 23, 1992. **Head of government:** Prime Min. Vo Van Kiet; in office: Aug. 8, 1991. **Local divisions:** 50 provinces, 3 municipalities. **Defense:** 19.4% of GNP (1986).

**Economy: Industries:** Food processing, textiles, cement, chemical fertilizers. **Chief crops:** Rice, rubber, fruits and vegetables, corn, manioc, sugarcane. **Minerals:** Phosphates, coal, iron, manganese, bauxite, apatite, chromate. **Other resources:** Forests. **Arable land:** 23%. **Livestock** (1991): cattle: 3.2 mln.; pigs: 12.5 mln. **Fish catch** (1990): 850,000 metric tons. **Electricity prod.** (1991): 9.2 bln. kWh. **Labor force:** 65% agric.; 35% ind. and service.

**Finance: Monetary unit:** Dong (Jan. 1993: 10,881 = $1 US). **Gross national product** (1991): $15.2 bln. **Per capita GNP:** $230. **Imports** (1991): $1.9 bln.; partners: CIS, Jap. **Exports** (1991): $1.8 bln.; partners: CIS. **National budget** (1990): $1.3 bln. expenditures.

**Transport: Motor vehicles:** in use (1976): 100,000 passenger cars, 200,000 comm. vehicles. **Civil Aviation** (1988): 10.3 bln. passenger km; 3 airports with scheduled flights. **Chief ports:** Ho Chi Minh City, Haiphong, Da Nang.

**Communications: Television sets:** 1 per 31 persons. **Radios:** 1 per 10 persons. **Telephones:** 1 per 544 persons. **Daily newspaper circ.** (1990): 38 per 1,000 pop.

**Health: Life expectancy at birth** (1992): 63 male; 67 female. **Births** (per 1,000 pop. 1992): 29. **Deaths** (per 1,000 pop. 1992): 8. **Natural increase:** 2.1%. **Hospital beds:** 1 per 292 persons. **Physicians:** 1 per 3,096 persons. **Infant mortality** (per 1,000 live births 1992): 48.

**Education** (1989): **Literacy:** 88%.

**Major International Organizations:** UN (IMF, WHO).

Vietnam's recorded history began in Tonkin before the Christian era. Settled by Viets from central China, Vietnam was held by China, 111 BC-939 AD, and was a vassal state during subsequent periods. Vietnam defeated the armies of Kublai Khan, 1288. Conquest by France began in 1858 and ended in 1884 with the protectorates of Tonkin and Annam in the N. and the colony of Cochin-China in the S.

In 1940 Vietnam was occupied by Japan; nationalist aims gathered force. A number of groups formed the Vietminh (Independence) League, headed by Ho Chi Minh, communist guerrilla leader. In Aug. 1945 the Vietminh forced out Bao Dai, former emperor of Annam, head of a Japan-sponsored regime. France, seeking to reestablish colonial control, battled communist and nationalist forces, 1946-1954, and was finally defeated at Dien-bienphu, May 8, 1954. Meanwhile, on July 1, 1949, Bao Dai had formed a State of Vietnam, with himself as chief of state, with French approval. China backed Ho Chi Minh.

A cease-fire accord signed in Geneva July 21, 1954, divided Vietnam along the Ben Hai R. It provided for a buffer zone, withdrawal of French troops from the North and elections to determine the country's future. Under the agreement the communists gained control of territory north of the 17th parallel, with its capital at Hanoi and Ho Chi Minh as president. South Vietnam came to comprise the 39 southern provinces. Some 900,000 North Vietnamese fled to South Vietnam.

On Oct. 26, 1955, Ngo Dinh Diem, premier of the interim government of South Vietnam, proclaimed the Republic of Vietnam and became its first president.

The North, adopted a constitution Dec. 31, 1959, based on communist principles and calling for reunification of all Vietnam. North Vietnam sought to take over South Vietnam beginning in 1954. Fighting persisted from 1956, with the communist Vietcong, aided by North Vietnam, pressing war in the South. Northern aid to Vietcong guerrillas was intensified in 1959, and large-scale troop infiltration began in 1964, with Soviet and Chinese arms assistance. Large Northern forces were stationed in border areas of Laos and Cambodia.

A serious political conflict arose in the South in 1963 when Buddhists denounced authoritarianism and brutality. This paved the way for a military coup Nov. 1-2, 1963, which overthrew Diem. Several military coups followed.

In 1964, the U.S. began air strikes against North Vietnam. Beginning in 1965, the raids were stepped up and U.S. troops became combatants. U.S. troop strength in Vietnam, which reached a high of 543,400 in Apr. 1969, was ordered reduced by President Nixon in a series of withdrawals, beginning in June 1969. U.S. bombings were resumed in 1972-73.

A cease-fire agreement was signed in Paris Jan. 27, 1973 by the U.S., North and South Vietnam, and the Vietcong. It was never implemented.

North Vietnamese forces launched attacks against remaining government outposts in the Central Highlands in the first months of 1975. Government retreats turned into a rout, and the Saigon regime surrendered April 30. North Vietnam assumed control, and began transforming society along communist lines. All businesses and farms were collectivized.

The war's toll included — Combat deaths: U.S. 47,369; South Vietnam over 200,000; other allied forces 5,225. Civilian casualties were over a million. Displaced war refugees in South Vietnam totaled over 6.5 million.

The first National Assembly of both parts of the country met and the country was officially reunited July 2, 1976. The Northern capital, flag, anthem, emblem, and currency were applied to the new state. Nearly all major government posts went to officials of the former Northern government.

Heavy fighting with Cambodia took place, 1977-80, amid mutual charges of aggression and atrocities against civilians. Increasing numbers of Vietnamese civilians, ethnic Chinese, escaped the country, via the sea, or the overland route across Cambodia. Vietnam launched an offensive against Cambodian refugee strongholds along the Thai-Cambodian border in 1985; they also engaged Thai troops.

Relations with China soured as 140,000 ethnic Chinese left Vietnam charging discrimination; China cut off economic aid. Reacting to Vietnam's invasion of Cambodia, China attacked 4 Vietnamese border provinces, Feb., 1979, instigating heavy fighting.

Vietnam announced a package of reforms aimed at reducing central control of the economy in 1987, as many of the old revolutionary followers of Ho Chi Minh were removed from office.

Progress has been made with the U.S. over the repatriating of "Amerasians," the children fathered by U.S. servicemen.

## Western Samoa

### Independent State of Western Samoa

### Malotuto'atasi o Samoa i Sisifo

**People: Population** (1992 est.): 190,000. **Age distrib. (%):** 0–14: 50.4; 15–59: 45.4; 60+: 4.3. **Pop. density:** 167 per sq. mi. **Urban** (1981): 21.2%. **Ethnic groups:** Samoan (Polynesian) 88%, Euronesian (mixed) 10%, European, other Pacific Islanders. **Languages:** Samoan, English both official. **Religions:** Protestant 70%, Roman Catholic 20%.

**Geography: Area:** 1,133 sq. mi., the size of Rhode Island. **Location:** In the S. Pacific O. **Neighbors:** Nearest are Fiji on W, Tonga on S. **Topography:** Main islands, Savai'i (670 sq. mi.) and Upolu (429 sq. mi.), both ruggedly mountainous, and small islands Manono and Apolima. **Capital:** Apia. **Cities** (1983 est.): Apia 35,000.

**Government: Type:** Constitutional monarchy. **Head of state:** Malietoa Tanumafili II; b. Jan. 4, 1913; in office: Jan. 1, 1962. **Head of government:** Prime Min. Toflau Eti Alesana; in office: Apr. 11, 1988. **Local divisions:** 11 districts.

**Economy: Chief crops:** Cocoa, copra, bananas. **Other resources:** Hardwoods, fish. **Arable land:** 43%. **Electricity prod.** (1991): 45 mln. kWh. **Labor force:** 67% agric.

**Finance: Monetary unit:** Tala (Mar. 1993: 1.00 = $.39 US). **Gross domestic product** (1990): $114 mln. **Per capita GDP** (1990): $690. **Imports** (1992): $113 mln.; partners: NZ 28% Austral. 20%, Jap. 13%, U.S. 5%. **Exports** (1992): $6.0 mln.; partners: EC 28%. **International reserves less gold** (Mar. 1993): $57 mln. **Consumer prices** (change in 1992): 8.5%.

**Transport: Motor vehicles:** in use (1990): 2,500 passenger cars, 3,000 comm. vehicles. **Chief ports:** Apia, Asau.

**Communications: Radios:** 1 per 2.3 persons. **Telephones:** 1 per 29 persons.

**Health: Life expectancy at birth** (1992): 65 male; 70 female. **Births** (per 1,000 pop. 1992): 34. **Deaths** (per 1,000 pop. 1992): 7. **Natural increase:** 2.8%. **Hospital beds:** 1 per 255 persons. **Physicians:** 1 per 3,584 persons. **Infant mortality** (per 1,000 live births 1992): 40.

**Education** (1989): **Literacy:** 90%. 95% attend elementary school.

**Major International Organizations:** UN (IMF, World Bank), Commonwealth of Nations.

Western Samoa was a German colony, 1899 to 1914, when New Zealand landed troops and took over. It became a New Zealand mandate under the League of Nations and, in 1945, a New Zealand UN Trusteeship.

An elected local government took office in Oct. 1959 and the country became fully independent Jan. 1, 1962.

## Yemen

### Republic of Yemen

### al-Jumhūrīyah al-Yamanīyah

**People: Population** (1992 est.): 10,394,000. **Pop. density:** 51 per sq. mi. **Urban** (1991): 29%. **Ethnic groups:** Arabs, Indians, some Negroids. **Languages:** Arabic. **Religions:** Sunni Moslem 53%; Shute Moslem 46%.

**Geography: Area:** 203,796 sq. mi., slightly smaller than France. **Location:** On the southern coast of the Arabian Peninsula. **Neighbors:** Saudi Arabia on NE, Oman on the E. **Topography:** A sandy coastal strip leads to well-watered fertile mountains in interior. **Capital:** Sanaa. **Cities** (1986 est.): Sanaa 427,000; Aden 250,000.

**Government: Type:** Republic. **Head of state:** Pres. Ali Abdullah Saleh, b. 1942; in office: July 17, 1978. **Head of government:** Prime Min. Haydar Abu Bakr-al Attas; in office: May 22, 1990. **Local divisions:** 17 provinces. **Defense:** 20% of GDP (1990).

**Economy: Industries:** Food processing, mining, petroleum refining. **Chief crops:** Wheat, sorghum, fruits, coffee, cotton. **Minerals:** Salt. **Crude oil reserves** (1984): 600 mln. bbls. **Arable land:** 6%. **Livestock** (1990): goats: 3.1 mln.; sheep: 3.6 mln. **Fish catch** (1990): 89,000 metric tons. **Electricity prod.** (1990): 1 bln. kWh. **Labor force:** 64% agric.; 11% ind. and commerce; 25% serv.

**Finance: Monetary unit:** Rial (Jan. 1993: 16.50 = $1 US). **Gross domestic product** (1990): $5.3 bln. **Per capita GDP:** $545. **Imports** (1990): $2.1 bln.; partners: Saudi Ar. 20%, Fr. 8%, Jap. 16%. **Exports** (1990): $908 mln.; partners: S. Yemen 23%, Saudi Ar. 8%, Pak. 19%.

**Transport: Motor vehicles** in use (1990): 150,000 passenger cars, 220,000 commercial vehicles. **Civil aviation** (1990): 1.0 bln. passenger-km.; 12 airports with scheduled flights. **Chief ports:** Al-Hudaydah, Al-Mukha, Aden.

**Communications: Television sets:** 1 per 38 persons. **Radios:** 1 per 35 persons. **Telephones:** 1 per 157 persons.

**Health: Life expectancy at birth** (1992): 49 male; 51 female. **Births** (per 1,000 pop. 1992): 51. **Deaths** (per 1,000 pop. 1992): 16. **Natural increase:** 3.5%. **Hospital beds:** 1 per 995 persons.

**Physicians:** 1 per 5,531 persons. **Infant mortality** (per 1,000 live births 1992): 118.
**Education** (1990): **Literacy:** 38%. **Primary school attendance:** 59%.
**Major International Organizations:** UN (IMF, WHO), Arab League.
**Embassy:** 2600 Virginia Ave. NW 20037; 965-4760.

Yemen's territory once was part of the ancient kindgom of Sheba, or Saba, a prosperous link in trade between Africa and India. A Biblical reference speaks of its gold, spices and precious stones as gifts borne by the Queen of Sheba to King Solomon.

Yemen became independent in 1918, after years of Ottoman Turkish rule, but remained politically and economically backward. Imam Ahmed ruled 1948-1962. Army officers headed by Brig. Gen. Abdullah al-Salal declared the country to be the Yemen Arab Republic.

The Imam Ahmed's heir, the Imam Mohamad al-Badr, fled to the mountains where tribesmen joined royalist forces; internal warfare between them and the republican forces continued. About 150,000 people died in the fighting.

There was a bloodless coup Nov. 5, 1967. In April 1970 hostilities ended with an agreement between Yemen and Saudi Arabia.

On June 13, 1974, an army group, led by Col. Ibrahim al-Hamidi, seized the government. He was assassinated in 1977.

Meanwhile, South Yemen won independence from Britain in 1967, formed out of the British colony of Aden and the British protectorate of South Arabia. It became the Arab world's only Marxist state, taking the name People's Democratic Republic of Yemen in 1970 and signing a 20-year friendship treaty with the USSR in 1979 that allowed for the stationing of Soviet troops in the south.

More than 300,000 Yemenis fled from the south to the north after independence, contributing to 2 decades of hostility between the 2 states that flared into warfare twice in the 1970's.

An Arab League-sponsored agreement between North and South Yemen on unification of the 2 countries was signed Mar. 29, 1979. An agreement providing for widespread political and economic cooperation was signed in 1988.

The 2 countries were formally united on May 21, 1990.

# Yugoslavia

## Federal Republic of Yugoslavia

## Federativna Republika Jugoslavija

*(Data prior to 1992 include former republics Croatia, Slovenia, Bosnia and Herzegovina, and Macedonia)*

**People: Population** (1992 est.): 10,337,000. **Age distrib.** (%): 0-14: 23.5; 15-59: 63.7; 60+: 12.8. **Pop. density:** 262 per sq. mi. **Urban** (1990): 50%. **Ethnic groups** (1992): Serbs 80%, Albanians 15%. **Languages:** Serbian (official), Macedonian, Hungarian, Albanian. **Religions:** Serbian Orthodox 80%, Roman Catholic, Moslem.

**Geography: Area:** 39,449 sq. mi. **Location:** On the Balkan Peninsula in SE Europe. Present-day Yugoslavia consists of the former republics of Serbia and Montenegro. **Neighbors:** Croatia, Bosnia and Herzegovina on W., Hungary on N, Romania, Bulgaria on E, Greece, Albania, Macedonia on S. **Capital:** Belgrade. **Cities** (1992 est.): Belgrade 1,553,000.

**Government: Type:** Republic. **Head of state:** Pres. Zoran Lilic; in office: June 1993. **Local divisions:** 2 republics. **Defense:** 4.6% of GDP (1991).

**Economy: Industries:** Steel, wood products. **Chief crops:** Corn, grains, tobacco, sugar beets. **Minerals:** Antimony, bauxite, lead, mercury, coal, iron, copper, chrome, zinc, salt. **Arable land:** 28%. **Livestock** (1991): cattle: 2.0 mln.; pigs: 4.5 mln.; sheep: 3.0 mln. **Fish catch:** (1990): 8,000 metric tons. **Electricity prod.** (1990): 83.4 bln. kWh. **Crude steel prod.** (1990): 3.6 mln. metric tons. **Labor force:** 22% agric.; 70% ind.

**Finance: Monetary unit:** Dinar (Feb. 1993: 225 = $1 US). **Gross national product** (1990): $120.1 bln. **Per capita GNP:** $5,040. **Imports** (1990): $19.1 bln.; partners: EC 54%, USSR 15%. **Exports** (1990): $14.6 bln.; partners: EC 54%, USSR 17%. **Tourism** (1990): $2.7 bln. receipts. **National budget** (1990): $6.4 bln. expenditures. **International reserves less gold** (Mar. 1993): $1.4 bln. **Gold:** 1.90 mln. oz t. **Consumer prices** (change in 1991): 117.4%.

**Transport: Motor vehicles:** in use (1990): 1.4 mln. passenger cars, 132,000 comm. vehicles. **Civil aviation** (1992): 7 airports.
**Communications: Television sets:** 1 per 3.6 persons. **Radios:** 1 per 6 persons. **Telephones:** 1 per 4.9 persons. **Daily newspaper circ.** (1990): 88 per 1,000 pop.
**Health: Life expectancy at birth** (1991): 70 male; 76 female. **Births** (per 1,000 pop. 1991): 14. **Deaths** (per 1,000 pop. 1991): 9. **Natural increase:** .5%. **Hospital beds:** 1 per 163 persons. **Physicians:** 1 per 490 persons. **Infant mortality** (per 1,000 live births 1991): 21.
**Education** (1991): **Literacy:** 90%. Almost all attend primary school.
**Major International Organizations:** UN (IMF, World Bank).
**Embassy:** 2410 California St. NW 20008; 462-6566.

Serbia, which had since 1389 been a vassal principality of Turkey, was established as an independent kingdom by the Treaty of Berlin, 1878. Montenegro, independent since 1389, also obtained international recognition in 1878. After the Balkan wars Serbia's boundaries were enlarged by the annexation of Old Serbia and Macedonia, 1913.

When the Austro-Hungarian empire collapsed after World War I, the Kingdom of the Serbs, Croats, and Slovenes was formed from the former provinces of Croatia, Dalmatia, Bosnia, Herzegovina, Slovenia, Voyvodina and the independent state of Montenegro. The name was later changed to Yugoslavia.

Nazi Germany invaded in 1941. Many Yugoslav partisan troops continued to operate. Among these were the Chetniks led by Draja Mikhailovich, who fought other partisans led by Josip Broz, known as Marshal Tito. Tito, backed by the USSR and Britain from 1943, was in control by the time the Germans had been driven from Yugoslavia in 1945. Mikhailovich was executed July 17, 1946, by the Tito regime.

A constituent assembly proclaimed Yugoslavia a republic Nov. 29, 1945. It became a federated republic Jan. 31, 1946, and Marshal Tito, a communist, became head of the government.

The Stalin policy of dictating to all communist nations was rejected by Tito. He accepted economic aid and military equipment from the U.S. and received aid in foreign trade also from France and Great Britain. Tito also supported the liberal government of Czechoslovakia in 1968 before the Soviet invasion.

A separatist movement among Croatians brought arrests and a change of leaders in the Croatian Republic in Jan. 1972. Violence by Croatian nationalists and fears of Soviet political intervention led to restrictions on political and intellectual dissent.

Beginning in 1965, reforms designed to decentralize the administration of economic development and to force industries to produce more efficiently in competition with foreign producers were introduced, and considerable trade with the West was developed.

Pres. Tito died May 4, 1980; with his death, the post as head of the Collective Presidency and also that as head of the League of Communists became a rotating system of succession among the members representing each republic.

On Jan. 22, 1990, a Communist Party conference renounced its constitutionally guaranteed leading role in society and called on parliament to enact "political pluralism, including a multiparty system."

Croatia and Slovenia formally declared independence June 25, 1991. In Croatia, fighting began between Croats and ethnic Serbs. Serbia sent arms and medical supplies to the Serb rebels in Croatia. In Aug., there were numerous clashes between Croatian forces and Yugoslavian army units and their Serb supporters.

The republics of Serbia and Montenegro proclaimed a new "Federal Republic of Yugoslavia" Apr. 17, 1992. Serbia was the main supplier of arms to the ethnic Serb fighters in Bosnia and Herzegovina. The UN imposed sweeping international sanctions on Yugoslavia as a means of ending the bloodshed in Bosnia, May 30. Some 100,000 protesters in Belgrade called for the ouster of Serbian President Milosevic, June 28. As the result of UN trade sanctions and the nation's continued printing of money to support Serb forces in the Bosnian and Croatian conflicts, inflation was over 200 percent and unemployment at 40 percent, Feb. 1993.

**Kosovo:** An area in southern Serbia (4,203 sq. mi.), with a population of about 2,000,000, mostly Albanians. The capital is Pristina. The Albanian majority has declared its independence, which Serbia has not recognized.

**Vojvodina:** An area in northern Serbia (3,304 sq. mi.), with a population of about 2,000,000, mostly Serbian. The capital is Novi Sad.

# Zaire

## Republic of Zaire

## République du Zaïre

**People: Population** (1992 est.): 39,084,000. **Pop. density:** 43 per sq. mi. **Urban** (1988): 44.2%. **Ethnic groups:** Bantu tribes 80%, over 200 other tribes. **Languages:** French (official), Kongo, Luba, Mongo, Rwanda, others. **Religions:** Christian 70%, Moslem 10%.

**Geography: Area:** 905,563 sq. mi., one-fourth the size of the U.S. **Location:** In central Africa. **Neighbors:** Congo on W, Central African Republic, Sudan on N, Uganda, Rwanda, Burundi, Tanzania on E, Zambia, Angola on S. **Topography:** Zaire includes the bulk of the Zaire (Congo) R. Basin. The vast central region is a low-lying plateau covered by rain forest. Mountainous terraces in the W, savannas in the S and SE, grasslands toward the N, and the high Ruwenzori Mtns. on the E surround the central region. A short strip of territory borders the Atlantic O. The Zaire R. is 2,718 mi. long. **Capital:** Kinshasa. **Cities** (1991 est.): Kinshasa 3,741,000; Lubumbashi 709,000.

**Government: Type:** Republic with strong presidential authority (in transition). **Head of state:** Pres. Mobutu Sese Seko; b. Oct. 14, 1930; in office: Nov. 25, 1965. **Head of government:** Prime Min. Etienne Tshisekedi wa Mulumba; in office: Aug. 15, 1992. **Local divisions:** 10 regions, Kinshasa. **Defense:** 1% of GDP (1988).

**Economy: Chief crops:** Coffee, rice, sugar cane, bananas, plantains, manioc, mangoes, tea, cocoa, palm oil. **Minerals:** Cobalt (60% of world reserves), copper, cadmium, gold, silver, tin, germanium, zinc, iron, manganese, uranium, radium. **Crude oil reserves** (1987): 111 mln. bbls. **Other resources:** Forests, rubber, ivory. **Arable land:** 3%. **Livestock** (1991): cattle: 1.6 mln.; goats: 2.9 mln. **Fish catch** (1990): 162,000 metric tons. **Electricity prod.** (1991): 6.0 bln. kWh. **Labor force:** 75% agric.

**Finance: Monetary unit:** Zaire (Mar. 1993: 2,652 = $1 US). **Gross domestic product** (1990): $6.6 bln. **Per capita GDP:** $180. **Imports** (1991): $710 mln.; partners: Chi. 38%, Belg. 16%, Ger. 7%, Fra. 7%. **Exports** (1991): $828 mln.; partners: Belg.-Lux. 36%, U.S. 19%. **National budget** (1991): $1.1 bln. expenditures. **International reserves less gold** (Mar. 1993): $156 mln. **Gold:** 27,000 oz t. **Consumer prices** (change in 1992): 6,921.

**Transport: Railroads** (1989): **Length:** 3,193 mi. **Motor vehicles:** in use (1985): 24,000 passenger cars, 60,000 comm. vehicles. **Civil aviation** (1990): 487 mln. passenger-km; 26 airports with scheduled flights. **Chief ports:** Matadi, Boma.

**Communications: Television sets:** 1 per 1,707 persons. **Radios:** 1 per 9.7 persons. **Telephones:** 1 per 1,026 persons. **Daily newspaper circ.** (1988): 1 per 1,000 pop.

**Health: Life expectancy at birth** (1992): 52 male; 56 female. **Births** (per 1,000 pop. 1992): 45. **Deaths** (per 1,000 pop. 1992): 14. **Natural increase:** 3.1%. **Hospital beds:** 1 per 476 persons. **Physicians:** 1 per 23,193 persons. **Infant mortality** (per 1,000 live births 1992): 97.

**Education** (1990): **Literacy:** 72%.

**Major International Organizations:** UN and all of its specialized agencies, OAU.

**Embassy:** 1800 New Hampshire Ave. NW 20008; 234-7690.

The earliest inhabitants of Zaire may have been the pygmies, followed by Bantus from the E and Nilotic tribes from the N. The large Bantu Bakongo kingdom ruled much of Zaire and Angola when Portuguese explorers visited in the 15th century.

Leopold II, king of the Belgians, formed an international group to exploit the Congo in 1876. In 1877 Henry M. Stanley explored the Congo and in 1878 the king's group sent him back to organize the region and win over the native chiefs. The Conference of Berlin, 1884-85, organized the Congo Free State with Leopold as king and chief owner. Exploitation of native laborers on the rubber plantations caused international criticism and led to granting of a colonial charter, 1908.

Belgian and Congolese leaders agreed Jan. 27, 1960, that the Congo would become independent June 30. In the first general elections, May 31, the National Congolese movement of Patrice Lumumba won 35 of 137 seats in the National Assembly. He was appointed premier June 21, and formed a coalition cabinet.

Widespread violence caused Europeans and others to flee. The UN Security Council Aug. 9, 1960, called on Belgium to withdraw its troops and sent a UN contingent. President Kasavubu removed Lumumba as premier; he was murdered in 1961.

The last UN troops left the Congo June 30, 1964, and Moise Tshombe became president.

On Sept. 7, 1964, leftist rebels set up a "People's Republic" in Stanleyville. Tshombe hired foreign mercenaries and sought to rebuild the Congolese Army. In Nov. and Dec. 1964 rebels slew scores of white hostages and thousands of Congolese; Belgian paratroops, dropped from U.S. transport planes, rescued hundreds. By July 1965 the rebels had lost their effectiveness.

In 1965 Gen. Joseph D. Mobutu was named president. He later changed his name to Mobutu Sese Seko. The country changed its name to Republic of Zaire on Oct. 27, 1971; in 1972 Zairians with Christian names were ordered to change them to African names.

Serious economic difficulties, amid charges of corruption by government officials, plagued Zaire in the 1980s. In 1990, Pres. Mobutu announced an end to a 20-year ban on multiparty politics. In 1993, Prime Min. Etienne Tshisekedi wa Mulumba called for foreign military assistance in toppling Pres. Mobuto Sese Soto, who had held office for almost 28 years.

# Zambia

## Republic of Zambia

**People: Population** (1992 est.): 8,745,000. **Age distrib. (%):** 0–14: 48.2; 15–59: 47.8; 60+: 4.0. **Pop. density:** 30 per sq. mi. **Urban** (1990): 49%. **Ethnic groups:** Mostly Bantu tribes. **Languages:** English (official), Bantu dialects. **Religions:** Predominantly animist, Roman Catholic 21%, Protestant, Hindu, Moslem minorities.

**Geography: Area:** 290,586 sq. mi., larger than Texas. **Location:** In southern central Africa. **Neighbors:** Zaire on N, Tanzania, Malawi, Mozambique on E, Zimbabwe, Namibia on S, Angola on W. **Topography:** Zambia is mostly high plateau country covered with thick forests, and drained by several important rivers, including the Zambezi. **Capital:** Lusaka. **Cities** (1992): Lusaka 982,000; Kitwe 348,000; Ndola 376,000.

**Government: Type:** Republic. **Head of state:** Pres. Frederick Chiluba; b. 1943; in office: Nov. 2, 1991. **Local divisions:** 9 provinces. **Defense:** 6.8% of GDP (1985).

**Economy: Chief crops:** Corn, tobacco, peanuts, cotton, sugar. **Minerals:** Cobalt, copper, zinc, gold, lead, vanadium, manganese, coal. **Other resources:** Rubber, ivory. **Arable land:** 7%. **Livestock** (1990): cattle: 2.8 mln. **Fish catch** (1989): 68,000 metric tons. **Electricity prod.** (1991): 12 bln. kWh. **Labor force:** 60% agric.; 40% ind. and commerce.

**Finance: Monetary unit:** Kwacha (Mar. 1993: 1.00 = $.01 US). **Gross domestic product** (1991): $4.2 bln. **Per capita GDP:** $380. **Imports** (1991): $1.3 bln.; S. Af. 13%, Ger. 6%, U.S. 7%. **Exports** (1991): $1.1 bln.; partners: Jap. 4%, UK 3%, U.S. 10%, Ger. 9%. **National budget** (1991): $1.5 bln. expenditures. **International reserves less gold** (Jan. 1992): $184 mln. **Gold:** 15,000 oz t. **Consumer prices** (change in 1991): 92%.

**Transport: Motor vehicles:** in use (1982): 105,000 passenger cars, 97,000 comm. vehicles. **Civil aviation** (1991): 322 mln. passenger-km; 8 airports with scheduled flights.

**Communications: Television sets:** 1 per 44 persons. **Radios:** 1 per 14 persons. **Telephones:** 1 per 78 persons. **Daily newspaper circ.** (1989): 15 per 1,000 pop.

**Health: Life expectancy at birth** (1992): 55 male; 59 female. **Births** (per 1,000 pop. 1992): 48. **Deaths** (per 1,000 pop. 1992): 11. **Natural increase:** 3.7%. **Hospital beds:** 1 per 311 persons. **Physicians:** 1 per 8,437 persons. **Infant mortality** (per 1,000 live births 1992): 77.

**Education** (1991): **Literacy:** 54%. **Attendance:** less than 50% in grades 1–7.

**Major International Organizations:** UN (GATT, IMF, WHO), OAU, Commonwealth of Nations.

**Embassy:** 2419 Massachusetts Ave. NW 20008; 265-9717.

As Northern Rhodesia, the country was under the administration of the South Africa Company, 1889 until 1924, when the office of governor was established, and, subsequently, a legislature. The country became an independent republic within the Commonwealth Oct. 24, 1964.

After the white government of Rhodesia declared its independence from Britain Nov. 11, 1965, relations between Zambia and Rhodesia became strained.

As part of a program of government participation in major industries, a government corporation in 1970 took over 51% of the ownership of 2 foreign-owned copper mining companies. Privately-held land and other enterprises were nationalized in 1975, as were all newspapers. In the 1980s, decline in copper prices hurt the economy and severe drought caused famine.

Food riots erupted in June 1990, as the nation suffered its worst violence since independence.

Elections held Oct. 1991, resulted in an end to one-party rule.

## Zimbabwe

### Republic of Zimbabwe

**People: Population** (1992 est.): 11,033,000. **Age distrib. (%):** 0–14: 44.9; 15–59: 51.1; 60+: 4.0. **Pop. density:** 73 per sq. mi. **Urban** (1990): 25%. **Ethnic groups:** Shona 80%, Ndebele 19%. **Languages:** English (official), Shona, Sinde bele. **Religions:** Predominantly traditional tribal beliefs, Christian minority.

**Geography: Area:** 150,803 sq. mi., slightly larger than Montana. **Location:** In southern Africa. **Neighbors:** Zambia on N, Botswana on W, S. Africa on S, Mozambique on E. **Topography:** Zimbabwe is high plateau country, rising to mountains on eastern border, sloping down on the other borders. **Capital:** Harare. **Cities** (1988 est.): Harare 730,000; Bulawayo (met.) 415,000.

**Government: Type:** Parliamentary democracy. **Head of state:** Pres. Robert Mugabe; b. Feb. 21, 1924; in office: Jan. 1, 1988. **Local divisions:** 8 provinces. **Defense:** 6.0% of GDP (1991).

**Economy: Industries:** Clothing, chemicals, light industries. **Chief crops:** Tobacco, sugar, cotton, corn, wheat. **Minerals:** Chromium, gold, nickel, asbestos, copper, iron, coal. **Arable land:** 7%. **Livestock** (1991): cattle: 5.9 mln.; goats: 2.4 mln. **Electricity prod.** (1991): 7.5 bln. kWh. **Labor force:** 74% agric.; 16% serv.

**Finance: Monetary unit:** Dollar (Mar. 1993: 1.00 = $.15 US). **Gross domestic product** (1991): $7.1 bln. **Per capita GDP:** $660. **Imports** (1991): $1.6 bln. partners: EC 31%, So. Afr. 21%. **Exports** (1991): $1.8 bln.; partners: EC 40%. **National budget** (1991): $3.3 bln. expenditures. **Total reserves less**

gold (Mar. 1992): $278 mln. **Consumer prices** (change in 1992): 46.3%.

**Transport: Motor vehicles:** in use (1990): 178,000 passenger cars, 82,000 comm. vehicles. **Civil aviation** (1989): 709 mln. passenger-km. 8 airports with scheduled flights.

**Communications: Television sets:** 1 per 70 persons. **Radios:** 1 per 18 persons. **Telephones:** 1 per 31 persons. **Daily newspaper circ.** (1990): 23 per 1,000 pop.

**Health: Life expectancy at birth** (1992): 60 male; 64 female. **Births** (per 1,000 pop. 1992): 41. **Deaths** (per 1,000 pop. 1992): 8. **Natural increase:** 3.3%. **Physicians:** 1 per 6,951 persons. **Infant mortality** (per 1,000 live births 1992): 59.

**Education** (1990): **Literacy:** 67%. **Attendance:** 90% primary, 15% secondary for Africans; higher for whites, Asians.

**Major International Organizations:** UN (IMF, World Bank), OAU, Commonwealth of Nations.

**Embassy:** 2852 McGill Terrace NW 20008; 332-7100.

Britain took over the area as Southern Rhodesia in 1923 from the British South Africa Co. (which, under Cecil Rhodes, had conquered the area by 1897) and granted internal self-government. Under a 1961 constitution, voting was restricted to maintain whites in power. On Nov. 11, 1965, Prime Min. Ian D. Smith announced his country's unilateral declaration of independence. Britain termed the act illegal, and demanded Zimbabwe (known as Rhodesia until 1980) broaden voting rights to provide for eventual rule by the majority Africans.

Urged by Britain, the UN imposed sanctions, including embargoes on oil shipments to Zimbabwe. Some oil and gasoline reached Zimbabwe, however, from South Africa and Mozambique, before the latter became independent in 1975. In May 1968, the UN Security Council ordered a trade embargo.

A new constitution came into effect, Mar. 2, 1970. The election law effectively prevented full black representation through income tax requirements.

Intermittent negotiations between the government and various black nationalist groups failed to prevent increasing skirmishes. An "internal settlement" signed Mar. 1978 in which Smith and 3 popular black leaders share control until transfer of power to the black majority was rejected by guerrilla leaders.

In the country's first universal-franchise election, Apr. 21, 1979, Bishop Abel Muzorewa's United African National Council gained a bare majority control of the black-dominated parliament. Britain, 1979, began efforts to normalize its relationship with Zimbabwe. A British cease-fire was accepted by all parties, Dec. 5th. Independence was finally achieved Apr. 18, 1980.

Pres. Mugabe declared Zimbabwe's drought a national disaster and appealed to foreign donors for food, money, and medicine, Mar. 6, 1992.

## Area and Population of the World

Source: Bureau of the Census, U.S. Dept. of Commerce; prior to 1950, Rand McNally & Co.

| Continent | Area (1,000 sq. mi.) | % of Earth | Population (est., thousands) | | | | | | | % World Total, 1991[1] |
|---|---|---|---|---|---|---|---|---|---|---|
| | | | 1650 | 1750 | 1850 | 1900 | 1950[1] | 1980[1] | 1991[1] | |
| North America | 9,400 | 16.2 | 5,000 | 5,000 | 39,000 | 106,000 | 166,000 | 252,000 | 279,000 | 5.1 |
| South America | 6,900 | 11.9 | 8,000 | 7,000 | 20,000 | 38,000 | — | — | — | — |
| Latin America, Caribbean | — | — | — | — | — | — | 166,000 | 364,000 | 458,000 | 8.4 |
| Europe | 3,800 | 6.6 | 100,000 | 140,000 | 265,000 | 400,000 | 392,000 | 484,000 | 502,000 | 9.2 |
| Asia | 17,400 | 30.1 | 335,000 | 476,000 | 754,000 | 932,000 | 1,368,000 | 2,494,000 | 3,046,000 | 56.2 |
| Africa | 11,700 | 20.2 | 100,000 | 95,000 | 95,000 | 118,000 | 281,000 | 594,000 | 817,000 | 15.0 |
| Former USSR | — | — | — | — | — | — | 180,000 | 266,000 | 293,000 | 5.4 |
| Oceania, incl. Australia | 3,300 | 5.7 | 2,000 | 2,000 | 2,000 | 6,000 | 12,000 | 23,000 | 27,000 | 0.4 |
| Antarctica | 5,400 | 9.3 | Uninhabited . . . . . . . . . . . . . . . . . . . . . . . . . . . . . . . | | | | | | | |
| World | 57,900 | — | 550,000 | 725,000 | 1,175,000 | 1,600,000 | 2,564,000 | 4,478,000 | 5,423,000 | — |

(1) Figures do not add to total because of independent rounding.

## Leading Countries in Population and Area in 1992

China has the highest population in the world, with 1.17 billion inhabitants, which is more than one-fifth of the world's population. India has almost 900 million people and is expected to reach 1 billion by the end of the decade. The United States has the third largest population, with over 250 million, followed by Indonesia, Brazil, and Russia. Russia is the largest country in area, with over 6.5 million square miles, followed by Canada, China, the United States, and Brazil.

## Population of World's Largest Cities

Source: Bureau of the Census, U.S. Dept. of Commerce

The table below represents one attempt at comparing the world's largest cities. The cities are defined as population clusters of continuous built-up areas with a population density of a least 5,000 persons per square mile. The boundary of the city was determined by examining detailed maps of each city in conjunction with the most recent official population statistics. Exclaves of areas exceeding the minimum population density were added to the city if the intervening gap was less than one mile. To the extent practical, nonresidential areas such as parks, airports, industrial complexes, and water were excluded from the area reported for each city, thus making the population density reflective of the concentrations in the residential portions of the city. By using a consistent definition for the city, it is possible to make comparisons of the cities on the basis of total population, area, and population density.

The population of each city was projected based on projected country populations and the proportion of each city population to the total population of the country at the time of the last 2 censuses. Figures in the table below may differ from city population figures elsewhere in The World Almanac because of different methods of determining population.

| City, Country | 1991 (thou-sands) | 2000 (thou-sands projected) | Area (sq. mi.) | Density 1991 (pop per sq. mi.) | City, Country | 1991 (thou-sands) | 2000 (thou-sands projected) | Area (sq. mi.) | Density 1991 (pop per sq. mi.) |
|---|---|---|---|---|---|---|---|---|---|
| Tokyo-Yokohama, Japan | 27,245 | 29,971 | 1,089 | 25,019 | Manchester, U.K. | 4,030 | 3,827 | 357 | 11,287 |
| Mexico City, Mexico | 20,899 | 27,872 | 522 | 40,037 | Philadelphia, U.S. | 4,003 | 3,979 | 471 | 8,499 |
| São Paulo, Brazil | 18,701 | 25,354 | 451 | 41,466 | San Francisco, U.S. | 3,986 | 4,214 | 428 | 9,315 |
| Seoul, South Korea | 16,792 | 21,976 | 342 | 49,101 | Belo Horizonte, Brazil | 3,812 | 5,125 | 79 | 48,249 |
| New York, U.S. | 14,625 | 14,648 | 1,274 | 11,480 | Kinshasa, Zaire | 3,747 | 5,646 | 57 | 65,732 |
| Osaka-Kobe-Kyoto, Japan | 13,872 | 14,287 | 495 | 28,025 | Ho Chi Minh City, Vietnam | 3,725 | 4,481 | 31 | 120,168 |
| Bombay, India | 12,101 | 15,357 | 95 | 127,461 | Ahmadabad, India | 3,709 | 4,837 | 32 | 115,893 |
| Calcutta, India | 11,898 | 14,088 | 209 | 56,927 | Hyderabad, India | 3,673 | 4,765 | 88 | 41,741 |
| Rio de Janeiro, Brazil | 11,688 | 14,169 | 260 | 44,952 | Sydney, Australia | 3,536 | 3,708 | 338 | 10,460 |
| Buenos Aires, Argentina | 11,657 | 12,911 | 535 | 21,790 | Athens, Greece | 3,507 | 3,866 | 116 | 30,237 |
| Moscow, Russia | 10,446 | 11,121 | 379 | 27,562 | Miami, U.S. | 3,471 | 3,894 | 448 | 7,748 |
| Manila, Philippines | 10,156 | 12,846 | 188 | 54,024 | Guadalajara, Mexico | 3,370 | 4,451 | 78 | 43,205 |
| Los Angeles, U.S. | 10,130 | 10,714 | 1,110 | 9,126 | Guangzhou, China | 3,360 | 3,652 | 79 | 42,537 |
| Cairo, Egypt | 10,099 | 12,512 | 104 | 97,106 | Surabaya, Indonesia | 3,248 | 3,632 | 43 | 75,544 |
| Jakarta, Indonesia | 9,882 | 12,804 | 76 | 130,026 | Caracas, Venezuela | 3,217 | 3,435 | 54 | 59,582 |
| Teheran, Iran | 9,779 | 14,251 | 112 | 87,312 | Wuhan, China | 3,200 | 3,495 | 65 | 49,225 |
| London, U.K. | 9,115 | 8,574 | 874 | 10,429 | Toronto, Canada | 3,145 | 3,296 | 154 | 20,420 |
| Delhi, India | 8,778 | 11,849 | 138 | 63,612 | Porto Alegre, Brazil | 3,114 | 4,109 | 231 | 13,479 |
| Paris, France | 8,720 | 8,803 | 432 | 20,185 | Rome, Italy | 3,033 | 3,129 | 69 | 43,949 |
| Karachi, Pakistan | 8,014 | 11,299 | 190 | 42,179 | Berlin, Germany | 3,021 | 3,006 | 274 | 11,026 |
| Lagos, Nigeria | 7,998 | 12,528 | 56 | 142,821 | Naples, Italy | 2,978 | 3,134 | 62 | 48,032 |
| Essen, Germany | 7,452 | 7,239 | 704 | 10,585 | Casablanca, Morocco | 2,973 | 3,795 | 35 | 84,953 |
| Shanghai, China | 6,936 | 7,540 | 78 | 88,924 | Detroit, U.S. | 2,969 | 2,735 | 468 | 6,343 |
| Lima, Peru | 6,815 | 9,241 | 120 | 56,794 | Alexandria, Egypt | 2,941 | 3,304 | 35 | 84,022 |
| Taipei, Taiwan | 6,695 | 8,516 | 138 | 48,517 | Monterrey, Mexico | 2,939 | 3,974 | 77 | 38,169 |
| Istanbul, Turkey | 6,678 | 8,875 | 165 | 40,476 | Montreal, Canada | 2,916 | 3,071 | 164 | 17,779 |
| Chicago, U.S. | 6,529 | 6,568 | 762 | 8,568 | Melbourne, Australia | 2,915 | 2,968 | 327 | 8,914 |
| Bangkok, Thailand | 5,955 | 7,587 | 102 | 58,379 | Ankara, Turkey | 2,872 | 3,777 | 55 | 52,221 |
| Bogotá, Colombia | 5,913 | 7,935 | 79 | 74,851 | Yangon, Myanmar | 2,864 | 3,332 | 47 | 60,927 |
| Madras, India | 5,896 | 7,384 | 115 | 51,270 | Kiev, Ukraine | 2,796 | 3,237 | 62 | 45,095 |
| Beijing, China | 5,762 | 5,993 | 151 | 38,156 | Dallas, U.S. | 2,787 | 3,257 | 419 | 6,652 |
| Hong Kong | 5,693 | 5,956 | 23 | 247,501 | Singapore, Singapore | 2,719 | 2,913 | 78 | 34,856 |
| Santiago, Chile | 5,378 | 6,294 | 128 | 40,018 | Taegu, South Korea | 2,651 | 4,051 | NA | NA |
| Pusan, South Korea | 5,008 | 6,700 | 54 | 92,735 | Harbin, China | 2,643 | 2,887 | 30 | 88,110 |
| Tianjin, China | 4,850 | 5,298 | 49 | 98,990 | Washington, U.S. | 2,565 | 2,707 | 357 | 7,184 |
| Bangalore, India | 4,802 | 6,764 | 50 | 96,041 | Poona, India | 2,547 | 3,647 | NA | NA |
| Nagoya, Japan | 4,791 | 5,303 | 307 | 15,606 | Boston, U.S. | 2,476 | 2,485 | 303 | 8,172 |
| Milan, Italy | 4,749 | 4,839 | 344 | 13,806 | Lisbon, Portugal | 2,426 | 2,717 | NA | NA |
| St. Petersburg, Russia | 4,672 | 4,738 | 139 | 33,614 | Tashkent, Uzbekistan | 2,418 | 2,947 | NA | NA |
| Madrid, Spain | 4,513 | 5,104 | 66 | 68,385 | Chongqing, China | 2,395 | 2,961 | NA | NA |
| Dhaka, Bangladesh | 4,419 | 6,492 | 32 | 138,108 | Chengdu, China | 2,372 | 2,591 | 25 | 94,870 |
| Lahore, Pakistan | 4,376 | 5,864 | 57 | 76,779 | Vienna, Austria | 2,344 | 2,647 | NA | NA |
| Shenyang, China | 4,289 | 4,684 | 39 | 109,974 | Houston, U.S. | 2,329 | 2,651 | 310 | 7,512 |
| Barcelona, Spain | 4,227 | 4,834 | 87 | 48,584 | Budapest, Hungary | 2,303 | 2,335 | 138 | 16,691 |
| Baghdad, Iraq | 4,059 | 5,239 | 97 | 41,843 | Salvador, Brazil | 2,298 | 3,286 | NA | NA |

## Population Projections, by Region and for Selected Countries: 2000 and 2020

Source: Bureau of the Census, U.S. Dept. of Commerce

(in thousands)

| Region and Country | 2000 | 2020 | Region and Country | 2000 | 2020 |
|---|---|---|---|---|---|
| Sub-Saharan Africa[1] | 736,325 | 1,279,014 | Guinea-Bissau | 1,265 | 1,926 |
| Angola | 11,424 | 19,153 | Kenya | 34,259 | 57,265 |
| Benin | 6,509 | 11,990 | Liberia | 3,674 | 6,534 |
| Botswana | 1,554 | 2,181 | Madagascar | 16,185 | 29,183 |
| Burkina Faso | 12,464 | 23,016 | Malawi | 11,892 | 22,235 |
| Burundi | 7,731 | 13,725 | Mali | 10,667 | 19,169 |
| Cameroon | 14,453 | 23,487 | Mauritania | 2,652 | 4,849 |
| Central African Republic | 3,702 | 5,944 | Mozambique | 20,936 | 35,443 |
| Chad | 6,204 | 9,361 | Namibia | 2,081 | 3,925 |
| Congo | 2,995 | 4,955 | Niger | 11,056 | 20,606 |
| Côte d'Ivoire | 18,144 | 33,581 | Nigeria | 160,751 | 273,197 |
| Ethiopia[2] | 69,374 | 123,584 | Rwanda | 11,047 | 21,948 |
| Ghana | 20,527 | 35,579 | Senegal | 10,482 | 18,466 |
| Guinea | 9,232 | 14,419 | Sierra Leone | 5,399 | 8,919 |

| Region and Country | 2000 | 2020 |
|---|---|---|
| Somalia | 9,409 | 17,190 |
| South Africa | 51,375 | 82,882 |
| Sudan | 35,870 | 59,307 |
| Tanzania | 36,489 | 68,772 |
| Togo | 5,248 | 9,900 |
| Uganda | 25,802 | 48,393 |
| Zaire | 50,043 | 89,164 |
| Zambia | 11,572 | 21,973 |
| Zimbabwe | 13,806 | 21,338 |
| | | |
| **Near East and North Africa[1]** | **327,119** | **506,134** |
| Algeria | 32,024 | 46,007 |
| Cyprus | 768 | 889 |
| Egypt | 66,498 | 97,505 |
| Iraq | 27,205 | 50,943 |
| Israel | 5,321 | 6,850 |
| Jordan | 4,880 | 8,987 |
| Kuwait | 2,879 | 4,564 |
| Lebanon | 4,058 | 5,755 |
| Libya | 5,599 | 8,549 |
| Morocco | 31,392 | 43,324 |
| Oman | 2,099 | 4,163 |
| Saudi Arabia | 25,003 | 45,836 |
| Syria | 18,212 | 35,761 |
| Tunisia | 9,713 | 12,597 |
| Turkey | 70,368 | 96,514 |
| United Arab Emirates | 3,598 | 6,182 |
| Yemen | 13,603 | 25,907 |
| | | |
| **Asia[1]** | **3,528,307** | **4,500,233** |
| Afghanistan | 24,935 | 39,915 |
| Bangladesh | 143,226 | 209,898 |
| Cambodia | 8,498 | 11,947 |
| China | 1,303,342 | 1,541,143 |
| India | 1,018,092 | 1,316,989 |
| Indonesia | 223,820 | 287,289 |
| Iran | 78,246 | 143,230 |
| Japan | 128,144 | 127,716 |
| Korea, North | 25,491 | 30,969 |
| Korea, South | 45,962 | 48,649 |
| Laos | 4,964 | 6,923 |
| Malaysia | 21,950 | 31,598 |
| Mongolia | 2,836 | 4,390 |
| Nepal | 24,340 | 37,488 |
| Myanmar (Burma) | 49,787 | 67,689 |
| Pakistan | 149,147 | 251,305 |
| Philippines | 77,734 | 101,387 |
| Singapore | 3,021 | 3,401 |
| Sri Lanka | 19,296 | 23,283 |
| Taiwan | 22,441 | 25,059 |
| Thailand | 63,832 | 76,108 |
| Vietnam | 79,801 | 102,948 |

(1) Includes countries not shown separately.
(2) Includes Eritrea.

| Region and Country | 2000 | 2020 |
|---|---|---|
| **Latin America and the Caribbean[1]** | **537,168** | **704,930** |
| Argentina | 36,036 | 43,462 |
| Belize | 301 | 451 |
| Bolivia | 8,721 | 12,435 |
| Brazil | 180,536 | 231,672 |
| Chile | 15,025 | 18,484 |
| Colombia | 39,745 | 51,443 |
| Costa Rica | 3,803 | 5,294 |
| Cuba | 11,613 | 12,795 |
| Dominican Republic | 8,676 | 11,439 |
| Ecuador | 12,997 | 18,029 |
| El Salvador | 6,471 | 8,811 |
| Guatemala | 11,315 | 15,632 |
| Haiti | 7,649 | 11,374 |
| Honduras | 6,243 | 9,064 |
| Jamaica | 2,762 | 3,533 |
| Mexico | 108,754 | 147,911 |
| Nicaragua | 4,729 | 7,013 |
| Panama | 2,937 | 3,908 |
| Paraguay | 6,023 | 8,812 |
| Peru | 26,435 | 35,055 |
| Trinidad and Tobago | 1,425 | 1,761 |
| Uruguay | 3,289 | 3,620 |
| Venezuela | 24,596 | 34,357 |
| **North America, Europe, and the former USSR[1]** | **1,125,095** | **1,204,719** |
| Albania | 3,824 | 4,677 |
| Austria | 7,762 | 7,488 |
| Belgium | 9,989 | 9,692 |
| Bulgaria | 9,004 | 9,071 |
| Canada | 29,301 | 33,128 |
| Czechoslovakia (Former) | 16,303 | 16,995 |
| Denmark | 5,147 | 4,980 |
| Finland | 5,075 | 5,024 |
| France | 58,548 | 60,149 |
| Germany | 81,532 | 81,883 |
| Greece | 10,166 | 9,902 |
| Hungary | 10,604 | 10,393 |
| Ireland | 3,509 | 3,837 |
| Italy | 58,592 | 56,068 |
| Netherlands | 15,642 | 15,698 |
| Norway | 4,411 | 4,497 |
| Poland | 38,889 | 41,698 |
| Portugal | 10,652 | 10,671 |
| Romania | 24,534 | 25,981 |
| Spain | 40,456 | 40,428 |
| Sweden | 8,761 | 8,645 |
| Switzerland | 7,018 | 6,843 |
| USSR (Former) | 311,637 | 355,092 |
| United Kingdom | 58,719 | 59,431 |
| United States | 268,266 | 294,364 |
| Yugoslavia (Former) | 25,112 | 26,349 |

# Customs Exemptions and Advice to Travelers

**Source: U.S. Customs Service**

U.S. residents returning after a stay abroad of at least 48 hours are usually granted customs exemptions of $400 each. The duty-free articles must accompany the traveler at the time of his or her return, be for personal or household use, have been acquired as an incident of the trip, and be properly declared to Customs. Not more than one liter of alcoholic beverages may be included in the $400 exemption.

If a U.S. resident arrives directly or indirectly from the U.S. Virgin Islands, or a contiguous country that maintains a free zone or a free port, the purchase may be valued up to $800 fair retail value, but not more than $400 of the exemption may be applied to the value of articles acquired elsewhere than in such insular possessions, and 5 liters of alcoholic beverages may be included in the exemption, but not more than one liter of such beverages may have been acquired elsewhere than in the designated islands.

The exemption for alcoholic beverages is accorded only when the returning resident has attained 21 years of age at the time of arrival. One hundred cigars and 200 cigarettes may be included in either exemption. Cuban cigars may be included if obtained in Cuba and all articles acquired there do not exceed $100 in retail value.

The $400 or $800 exemption may be granted only if the exemption, or any part of it, has not been used within the preceding 30-day period and the stay abroad was for at least 48 hours. The 48-hour absence requirement does not apply to travelers returning from Mexico or the U.S. Virgin Islands.

Gifts costing no more than $50 fair retail value or $100 from American Samoa, Guam, or the Virgin Islands may be mailed duty-free.

Most items—including alcoholic beverages, cigars, cigarettes and perfume—made in designated Caribbean and Central American countries may enter the U.S. duty-free under the Caribbean Basin Economic Recovery Act. Countries currently designated for such duty-free treatment are: Aruba, Antigua and Barbuda, Bahamas, Barbados, Belize, British Virgin Islands, Costa Rica, Dominica, Dominican Republic, El Salvador, Grenada, Guatemala, Guyana, Honduras, Jamaica, Montserrat, Netherlands Antilles, Nicaragua, Panama, Saint Kitts and Nevis, Saint Lucia, Saint Vincent and the Grenadines, and Trinidad and Tobago. Exceptions are: most textiles (incl. clothing), footwear, handbags, luggage, flat goods, work gloves and leather wearing apparel, and certain watches and watch parts. Alcoholic beverages and perfumes remain subject to IRS tax.

# The World's Refugees

(as of Dec. 31, 1992)

**Source:** *World Refugee Survey 1993.* U.S. Committee for Refugees, a nonprofit corp. The refugees in this table include only those who are in need of protection and/or assistance and do not include refugees who have resettled.

| Country of Asylum | Mostly From | Number |
|---|---|---|
| **Total Africa** | | **5,698,540** |
| Algeria | W. Sahara, Mali | 165,000[1] |
| Angola | Zaire | 9,000 |
| Benin | Togo | 4,300 |
| Botswana | S. Africa, Angola | 5,000 |
| Burkina Faso | Mali | 6,300 |
| Burundi | Rwanda, Zaire | 107,350[1] |
| Cameroon | Chad | 1,500 |
| Central African Rep. | Chad, Sudan | 18,000 |
| Congo | Chad, Angola | 9,400 |
| Côte d'Ivoire | Liberia | 195,500 |
| Djibouti | Ethiopia, Somalia | 96,000 |
| Egypt | Palestinians, Somalia | 10,650 |
| Ethiopia/Eritrea | Sudan, Somalia | 416,000[1] |
| Gabon | various | 200 |
| Gambia, The | Senegal, Liberia | 3,300 |
| Ghana | Liberia, Togo | 12,100 |
| Guinea | Liberia, Sierra Leone | 485,000[1] |
| Guinea-Bissau | Senegal | 12,000 |
| Kenya | Ethiopia, Sudan, Somalia | 422,900[1] |
| Lesotho | South Africa | 200 |
| Liberia | Sierra Leone | 100,000 |
| Malawi | Mozambique | 1,070,000 |
| Mali | Mauritania | 10,000 |
| Mauritania | Mali | 40,000 |
| Morocco | various | 800 |
| Mozambique[2] | various | 250 |
| Namibia | various | 150 |
| Niger | Chad | 3,600 |
| Nigeria | Chad, Liberia | 2,900 |
| Rwanda | Burundi | 24,500 |
| Senegal | Mauritania | 55,100 |
| Sierra Leone | Liberia | 7,600 |
| Somalia | Ethiopia/Eritrea | 10,000[1] |
| S. Africa | Mozambique | 250,000[1] |
| Sudan | Ethiopia/Eritrea, Chad | 750,500[1] |
| Swaziland | South Africa, Mozambique | 52,000 |
| Tanzania | Burundi, Mozambique | 257,800 |
| Togo | various | 350 |
| Uganda | Sudan, Rwanda | 179,600[1] |
| Zaire | Angola, Burundi, Sudan | 442,400 |
| Zambia | Angola, Mozambique, Zaire | 155,700 |
| Zimbabwe | Mozambique | 265,000 1[1] |
| **Total East Asia/Pacific** | | **398,600** |
| Australia | various | 24,000 |
| China | Myanmar | 12,500[1] |
| Hong Kong | Vietnam | 45,300 |
| Indonesia | Vietnam, Cambodia | 15,600 |
| Japan | Vietnam | 700 |
| Korea | Vietnam | 150 |
| Malaysia | Vietnam, Myanmar | 16,700 |
| Papua New Guinea | Indonesia | 3,800 |
| Philippines | Vietnam | 5,600 |
| Singapore | Vietnam | 100 |
| Taiwan | Vietnam | 150 |
| Thailand | Myanmar, Laos, Cambodia | 255,000 |
| Vietnam | Cambodia | 19,000 |
| **Total Europe & No. America** | | **3,423,600** |
| Armenia | Azerbaijan | 300,000[1] |
| Austria | Former Yugoslavia | 82,100 |
| Azerbaijan | Armenia | 246,000[1] |

| Country of Asylum | Mostly From | Number |
|---|---|---|
| Belarus | various | 3,700 |
| Belgium | various | 19,100 |
| Bosnia and Herzegovina | Former Yugoslavia | 70,000[1] |
| Canada | various | 37,700 |
| Croatia | Former Yugoslavia | 420,000[1] |
| Czech Rep./Slovakia | Former Yugoslavia | 2,200 |
| Denmark | Former Yugoslavia | 13,900 |
| Finland | various | 3,500 |
| France | various | 29,400 |
| Germany | Former Yugoslavia | 536,000 |
| Greece | various | 1,900 |
| Hungary | Former Yugoslavia | 40,000 |
| Italy | Former Yugoslavia | 19,100 |
| Luxembourg | Former Yugoslavia | 1,800 |
| Macedonia | Former Yugoslavia | 32,700[1] |
| Netherlands | various | 24,600 |
| Norway | various | 5,700 |
| Poland | Former Yugoslavia | 1,500 |
| Russia | various | 460,000[1] |
| Slovenia | Former Yugoslavia | 68,900[1] |
| Spain | various | 12,700 |
| Sweden | Former Yugoslavia | 88,400 |
| Switzerland | Former Yugoslavia | 81,700 |
| Turkey | Iraq, Former Yugoslavia | 31,700 |
| Ukraine | various | 40,000[1] |
| United Kingdom | various | 24,600 |
| United States | various | 103,700 |
| Yugoslavia[2] | Former Yugoslavia | 621,000[1] |
| **Total Latin America/Caribbean** | | **107,700** |
| Belize | El Salvador, Guatemala | 6,100 |
| Brazil | various | 200 |
| Colombia | various | 400 |
| Costa Rica | El Salvador, Nicaragua | 34,350 |
| Cuba | Haiti | 1,100 |
| Ecuador | various | 200 |
| El Salvador | various | 250 |
| French Guiana | Suriname | 1,600 |
| Guatemala | El Salvador, Nicaragua | 4,900 |
| Honduras | various | 150 |
| Mexico | Guatemala, El Salvador | 47,300 |
| Nicaragua | El Salvador | 5,850 |
| Panama | various | 850 |
| Peru | Cuba | 400 |
| Uruguay | various | 100 |
| Venezuela | Cuba, Haiti | 1,350 |
| **Total Middle East/South & Central Asia** | | **7,938,550** |
| Afghanistan | Tajikistan | 52,000 |
| Bangladesh | Myanmar | 245,000 |
| India | Bangladesh, Tibet, Sri Lanka | 378,000[1] |
| Iran | Afghanistan, Iraq | 2,781,800[1] |
| Iraq | Iran | 64,000 |
| Nepal | Tibet, Bhutan | 89,400 |
| Pakistan | Afghanistan | 1,577,000 |
| Saudi Arabia | Iraq | 27,400 |
| Yemen | Somalia | 52,500 |
| Palestinians | | |
| Gaza Strip | | 560,200 |
| Jordan | | 1,010,850[3] |
| Lebanon | | 322,900[3] |
| Syria | | 307,400[3] |
| West Bank | | 459,100 |
| **Total Refugees** | | **17,556,900** |

(1) Significant variance among sources in number reported. (2) Incl. Serbia/Montenegro. (3) Incl. some non-Palestinians.

## Principal Sources of Refugees

| | | | | | |
|---|---|---|---|---|---|
| Afghanistan | 4,286,000[1] | Angola | 404,200 | Rwanda | 201,500[1] |
| Palestinians | 2,658,000 | Croatia | 350,000 | Sierra Leone | 200,000 |
| Mozambique | 1,725,000[1] | Azerbaijan | 350,000[1] | Burundi | 184,000 |
| Bosnia and Herzegovina | 940,000 | Myanmar | 333,700[1] | Sri Lanka | 181,000 |
| Somalia | 864,800[1] | Sudan | 263,000 | Western Sahara | 165,000[1] |
| Ethiopia/Eritrea | 834,800[1] | Armenia | 202,000[1] | Cambodia | 148,600 |
| Liberia | 599,200[1] | | | | |

(1) Significant variance among sources in number reported.

# U.S. Immigration Law

Source: Immigration and Naturalization Service, U.S. Dept. of Justice

The Immigration Act of 1990 became law when it was signed by President Bush on Nov. 29, 1990. Bush called the bill the "most comprehensive reform of U.S. immigration laws in 66 years." Most of its provisions amend the Immigration and Nationality Act which remains the basic law. The new law raised the total number of numerically limited immigrants entering the U.S. annually in FY 1992-94 to 700,000 (excluding refugees whose admission numbers are announced annually and some others not subject to limitation). The visas would be distributed as follows:

- 465,000 for family immigrants;
- 55,000 for the spouses and children of aliens legalized under IRCA;
- 140,000 for employment-based immigrants;
- 40,000 for nationals from "adversely affected" countries.

Beginning in FY 1995 the number drops to a minimum of 675,000. These visas would be distributed as follows:

- 480,000 for family immigrants;
- 140,000 for employment based immigrants;
- 55,000 for "diversity immigrants."

## Family Immigrants

Fiscal year 1992-94: 465,000 minus the number of "immediate relatives" admitted the previous fiscal year, *plus* any numbers unused by the employment-based preference system. During this period, the number of family-sponsored visas cannot fall below 226,000 (10,000 visas higher than the current allocation). If visa availability dips below this new floor, the shortfall will be made up from the category below.

During this period, 55,000 additional visas will be made available to the spouses and children of aliens legalized under the Immigration Reform and Control Act (IRCA) of 1986.

Fiscal year 1995 and beyond: 480,000 minus the number of "immediate relatives" admitted during the previous fiscal year, plus any unused numbers under the employment-based preference system. That number may not drop below a floor of 226,000. If it does (*as it is certain to*), the "cap" simply gets pierced.

## New Family Preference System

First preference—unmarried sons and daughters of U.S. citizens: 23,400 visas plus unused visas from the 4th preference.

Second preference—spouses and unmarried children of Lawful Permanent Residents (LPRs): 114,200 visas, plus any visas available above the floor of 226,000 family preference visas, plus any unused visas from the previous preference.

The category is subdivided as follows: A minimum of 77 percent of the visas allocated to the category goes to the spouses and minor children of LPRs; 75 percent of the visas are issued without regard to per country ceilings; these visas will be distributed in the order in which the petitions were filed; a maximum of 23 percent of the category visa allocation goes to the unmarried sons and daughters of LPRs. This group of visas will continue to be subject to per country ceilings.

Third preference—married sons and daughters of U.S. citizens; 23,400 visas plus unused visas from all earlier preferences.

Fourth preference—brothers and sisters of U.S. citizens: 65,000 plus unused visas from all earlier preferences.

## Employment-Based Immigrants

A total of 140,000 plus, beginning in 1994, any unused numbers under the family-sponsored system. These visas would be distributed as follows:

First preference—Priority Workers—28.6 percent of the employment-based limit; 40,040 visas in 1992 plus visas unused by the fourth and fifth employment-based preferences "investors" and "special immigrants". The category is subdivided as follows: extraordinary ability, demonstrated by sustained national or international acclaim, in the sciences, arts, education, business, and athletics. No U.S. employer required;

Outstanding, internationally recognized and with at least 3 years of experience, professors and researchers seeking to enter in senior positions. U.S. employer required; executives and managers of multinationals—requires one year of prior service with the firm during the preceding 3 years. The terms are extensively defined. U.S. employer required.

Second preference—Professionals with advanced degrees and aliens of exceptional ability—28.6 percent of the employment-based limit; 40,040 visas in 1992 plus any unused "priority worker" visas. A U.S. employer and labor certification are required—although the Attorney General can waive both requirements. Members of the professions with advanced degrees or exceptional ability in the sciences, arts, or business. The possession of a degree, certificate, or license is not by itself considered sufficient evidence of exceptional ability.

Third preference—Skilled workers, professionals, and "Other" Workers—40,000 visas plus any visas unused by the 2 previous categories. Requires a U.S. employer and labor certification. Skilled workers must be in an occupation that requires at least 2 years training or experience. Professionals need a Bachelor's degree. "Other" workers refers to unskilled workers. Their numbers are limited to no more than 10,000 visas per year.

Fourth preference—Special immigrants—7.1 percent of the employment-based limit; 9,040 visas in 1992. This category includes ministers of religion and persons working for religious organizations for at least 2 years, foreign medical graduates, employees of the U.S. government abroad including certain employees of the U.S. mission in Hong Kong who file for admission as special immigrants before Jan. 1, 2002, retired employees of international organizations, etc.

Fifth preference—7.1 percent of the employment-based limit; 9,040 employment creation (investor) visas in 1992—7,000 for investors of $1 million in urban areas and 3,000 for investors of no less than $500,000 in rural or high-unemployment areas. The Attorney General may increase the required investment amount up to $3 million for high employment areas. Investment must create employment for at least 10 U.S. workers.

## Labor Certification

A pilot program is created for FY 1992-94 giving Dept. of Labor the authority to identify up to 10 "shortage" or "surplus" occupations and make certifications for these occupations. If the occupation is in "shortage," automatic certification would be offered; if the occupation is in "surplus," the employer may still petition for the immigrant but will be required to demonstrate that he/she has undertaken extensive recruitment.

## Student Visas

A 3-year program (FY 1992-94) allows foreign students to be employed off-campus for up to 20 hours per week during the school year, and without restrictions when school is out of session. The employment can only come after their first year of school but may be unrelated to their studies.

The employer must attest that he has recruited for U.S. workers for at least 60 days and that he offers both foreign and U.S. workers the actual wage level for the occupation at the place of employment or, if greater, the prevailing wage level for the occupation in the area of employment. If the Secretary of Labor finds the attestation to be a misrepresentation, the employer can be disqualified from employing a foreign student.

# Major International Organizations

As of mid-1993

Association of Southeast Asian Nations (ASEAN), formed in 1967 to promote economic, social, and cultural cooperation and development among the non-communist states of the region. Members in 1993 are Brunei Darussalam, Indonesia, Malaysia, Philippines, Singapore, Thailand. Annual ministerial meetings set policy; a central Secretariat in Jakarta and specialized intergovernmental committees work in trade, transportation, communications, agriculture, science, finance, and culture.

Caribbean Community and Common Market (Caricom), established July 4, 1973. Its function is to further cooperation in economics, health, education, culture, science and technology, and tax administration, as well as the coordination of foreign policy. Members in 1993 are Antigua and Barbuda, Bahamas, Barbados, Belize, Dominica, Grenada, Guyana, Jamaica, Montserrat, Saint Kitts and Nevis, Saint Lucia, Saint Vincent and the Grenadines, Trinidad and Tobago.

Commonwealth of Independent States (CIS), created Dec. 1991 upon the disbanding of the Soviet Union. It is made up of 10 of the 15 former Soviet constituent republics. Members are Armenia, Belarus, Kazakhstan, Kyrgyzstan, Moldova, Russia, Tajikistan, Turkmenistan, Ukraine, and Uzbekistan. The commonwealth is not in itself a state, but an alliance of fully independent states. Commonwealth policy is set through coordinating bodies such as a Council of Heads of State and Council of Heads of Government. The capital of the commonwealth is Minsk, Belarus.

Commonwealth of Nations, originally called the British Commonwealth of Nations, an association of nations and dependencies loosely joined by a common interest based on having been parts of the old British Empire. The British monarch is the symbolic head of the Commonwealth.

There are 50 self-governing independent nations in the Commonwealth, plus various colonies and protectorates. As of 1993, the members were the United Kingdom of Great Britain and Northern Ireland and 15 other nations recognizing the British monarch, represented by a governor-general, as their head of state: Antigua and Barbuda, Australia, The Bahamas, Barbados, Belize, Canada, Grenada, Jamaica, New Zealand, Papua New Guinea, Saint Kitts and Nevis, Saint Lucia, Saint Vincent and the Grenadines, Solomon Islands, and Tuvalu (a special member); and 34 countries with their own heads of state: Bangladesh, Botswana, Brunei Darussalam, Cyprus, Dominica, The Gambia, Ghana, Guyana, India, Kenya, Kiribati, Lesotho, Malawi, Malaysia, The Maldives, Malta, Mauritius, Namibia, Nauru (a special member), Nigeria, Pakistan, Seychelles, Sierra Leone, Singapore, Sri Lanka, Swaziland, Tanzania, Tonga, Trinidad and Tobago, Uganda, Vanuatu, Western Samoa, Zambia, and Zimbabwe.

The Commonwealth facilitates consultation among member states through meetings of prime ministers and finance ministers, and through a permanent Secretariat. Members consult on economic, scientific, educational, financial, legal, and military matters, and try to coordinate policies.

European Community (EC)—officially, the European Communities—the collective designation of three organizations with common membership: the European Economic Community (Common Market), the European Coal and Steel Community, and the European Atomic Energy Community (Euratom). The 12 full members are: Belgium, Denmark, France, Germany, Greece, Ireland, Italy, Luxembourg, Netherlands, Portugal, Spain, United Kingdom. Some 60 nations in Africa, the Caribbean, and the Pacific are affiliated under the Lomé Convention.

A merger of the 3 communities' executives went into effect July 1, 1967, though the component organizations date back to 1951 and 1958. The Council of Ministers, the Commission of the European Communities, the European Parliament, and the European Court of Justice comprise the permanent structure. The EC aims to integrate the economies, coordinate social developments, and bring about political union of the democratic states of Europe. Effective Dec. 31, 1992, there are no restrictions on the movement of goods,

services, capital, workers, and tourists within the community. There are also common agricultural, fisheries, and nuclear research policies.

Leaders of the 12 European Community nations met Dec. 9–11, 1991, in Maastricht, the Netherlands. Treaties on monetary union and political union and accompanying protocols agreed upon by the leaders:

- Committed the EC to launching a common currency for at least some nations by 1999. Britain and, later, Denmark were allowed to "opt out" of joining.
- Sought to establish common foreign policies for the 12 members.
- Laid the groundwork for a common defense policy under the Western European Union.
- Expanded the policy issues in which the EC would have a voice.
- Gave the EC a leading role in social policy. Britain was not included in this plan.
- Pledged increased aid for the community's four poorest nations—Ireland, Greece, Spain, and Portugal.
- Slightly increased the powers of the 518-member European Parliament.

The treaties require ratification by all 12 members before they can go into effect.

European Free Trade Association (EFTA), created May 3, 1960, to promote expansion of free trade. Current members are Austria, Finland, Iceland, Liechtenstein, Norway, Sweden, and Switzerland. By Dec. 31, 1966, tariffs and quotas between members nations had been eliminated. Members of the association entered into free trade agreements with the EC in 1972 and 1973. In 1992 the EFTA and EC concluded an agreement to create a single market—with free flow of goods, services, capital, and labor—encompassing the 19 nations of the two organizations.

Group of Seven (G-7), organization of seven major industrial democracies who meet periodically to discuss world economic and other issues. Established Sept. 22, 1985. Members are Canada, France, Germany, Italy, Japan, United Kingdom, and United States.

International Criminal Police Organization (Interpol), created June 13, 1956, to ensure and promote the widest possible mutual assistance between all police authorities within the limits of the law existing in the different countries and in the spirit of the Universal Declaration of Human Rights. There are 152 members in 1993.

League of Arab States (The Arab League), created Mar. 22, 1945. Members in 1993 are Algeria, Bahrain, Djibouti, Egypt, Iraq, Jordan, Kuwait, Lebanon, Libya, Mauritania, Morocco, Oman, The Palestine Liberation Org., Qatar, Saudi Arabia, Somalia, Sudan, Syria, Tunisia, United Arab Emirates, Yemen. The League promotes economic, social, political, and military cooperation and mediates disputes among the Arab states; it represents Arab states in certain international negotiations. The league's headquarters is in Cairo.

North Atlantic Treaty Organization (NATO), created by treaty (signed Apr. 4, 1949; in effect Aug. 24, 1949). Members in 1993 are Belgium, Canada, Denmark, France, Germany, Greece, Iceland, Italy, Luxembourg, Netherlands, Norway, Portugal, Spain, Turkey, United Kingdom, and United States. The members agreed to settle disputes by peaceful means; to develop their individual and collective capacity to resist armed attack; to regard an attack on one as an attack on all; and to take necessary action to repel an attack under Article 51 of the United Nations Charter.

The NATO structure consists of a Council and a Military Committee of 3 commands (Allied Command Europe, Allied Command Atlantic, Allied Command Channel) and the Canada-U.S. Regional Planning Group.

With the dissolution of the Soviet Union and end of the cold war in the early 1990's, NATO members sought to modify the organization's mission, putting greater stress on political action and creating a rapid deployment force to react to local crises. Former Warsaw Pact members were no longer considered adversaries, and Hungary gained associate membership in 1991.

**Organization of African Unity (OAU),** formed May 25, 1963, by 32 African countries (51 members in 1993) to promote peace and security as well as economic and social development. It holds annual conferences of heads of state. Headquarters is in Addis Ababa, Ethiopia.

**Organization of American States (OAS),** formed in Bogotá, Colombia, Apr. 30, 1948. Headquarters is in Washington, D.C. It has a Permanent Council, Inter-American Economic and Social Council, Inter-American Council for Education, Science, and Culture, Juridical Committee, and Commission on Human Rights. The Permanent Council can call meetings of foreign ministers to deal with urgent security matters. A General Assembly meets annually. A secretary general and assistant are elected for 5-year terms. There are 35 members, each with one vote in the various organizations: Antigua and Barbuda, Argentina, The Bahamas, Barbados, Belize, Bolivia, Brazil, Canada, Chile, Colombia, Costa Rica, Cuba, Dominica, Dominican Republic, Ecuador, El Salvador, Grenada, Guatemala, Guyana, Haiti, Honduras, Jamaica, Mexico, Nicaragua, Panama, Paraguay, Peru, Saint Kitts and Nevis, Saint Lucia, Saint Vincent and

the Grenadines, Suriname, Trinidad and Tobago, United States, Uruguay, Venezuela. In 1962, the OAS excluded Cuba from OAS activities but not from membership.

**Organization for Economic Cooperation and Development (OECD),** established Sept. 30, 1961, to promote economic and social welfare in member countries, and to stimulate and harmonize efforts on behalf of developing nations. The OECD collects and disseminates economic and environmental information. Members in 1993 are: Australia, Austria, Belgium, Canada, Denmark, Finland, France, Germany, Greece, Iceland, Ireland, Italy, Japan, Luxembourg, Netherlands, New Zealand, Norway, Portugal, Spain, Sweden, Switzerland, Turkey, United Kingdom, United States. Headquarters is in Paris.

**Organization of Petroleum Exporting Countries (OPEC),** created Sept. 14, 1960. The group attempts to set world oil prices by controlling oil production. It is also involved in advancing members' interests in trade and development dealings with industrialized oil-consuming nations. Members in 1993 are Algeria, Gabon, Indonesia, Iran, Iraq, Kuwait, Libya, Nigeria, Qatar, Saudi Arabia, United Arab Emirates, Venezuela.

# United Nations

The 48th regular session of United Nations General Assembly opened in September 1993.

UN headquarters is in New York, N.Y., between First Ave. and Roosevelt Drive and E. 42d St. and E. 48th St. The General Assembly Bldg., Secretariat, Conference and Library bldgs. are interconnected.

A European office at Geneva includes Secretariat and agency staff members. Other offices of UN bodies and related organizations with a staff of some 23,000 from some 150 countries are scattered throughout the world.

The UN has a post office originating its own stamps.

Proposals to establish an organization of nations for maintenance of world peace led to the United Nations Conference on International Organization at San Francisco, Apr. 25-June 26, 1945, where the charter of the United Nations was drawn up. It was signed June 26 by 50 nations, and by Poland, one of the original 51 UN members, on Oct. 15, 1945. The charter came into effect Oct. 24, 1945, upon

ratification by the permanent members of the Security Council and a majority of other signatories.

**Purposes:** To maintain international peace and security; to develop friendly relations among nations; to achieve international cooperation in solving economic, social, cultural, and humanitarian problems and in promoting respect for human rights and fundamental freedoms; to be a center for harmonizing the actions of nations in attaining these common ends.

**Visitors to the UN:** Headquarters is open to the public every day of the year except Christmas and New Year's Day. Guided tours are given approximately every half hour from 9:15 a.m. to 4:45 p.m. daily. Groups of 15 or more persons should write to the Group Program Unit, Visitors' Service, Room GA-56, United Nations, New York, NY 10017, or telephone (212) 963-4440. Children under 5 are not permitted on tours.

## Roster of the United Nations

The 184 members of the United Nations, with the years in which they became members; as of Sept. 1993

| Member | Year | Member | Year | Member | Year | Member | Year |
|---|---|---|---|---|---|---|---|
| Afghanistan | 1946 | Cambodia | 1955 | Finland | 1955 | Korea, N. | 1991 |
| Albania | 1955 | Cameroon | 1960 | France | 1945 | Korea, S. | 1991 |
| Algeria | 1962 | Canada | 1945 | Gabon | 1960 | Kuwait | 1963 |
| Andorra | 1993 | Cape Verde | 1975 | Gambia, The | 1965 | Kyrgyzstan | 1992 |
| Angola | 1976 | Central Afr. Rep. | 1960 | Georgia | 1992 | Laos | 1955 |
| Antigua and Barbuda | 1981 | Chad | 1960 | Germany | 1973 | Latvia | 1991 |
| Argentina | 1945 | Chile | 1945 | Ghana | 1957 | Lebanon | 1945 |
| Armenia | 1992 | China[1] | 1945 | Greece | 1945 | Lesotho | 1966 |
| Australia | 1945 | Colombia | 1945 | Grenada | 1974 | Liberia | 1945 |
| Austria | 1955 | Comoros | 1975 | Guatemala | 1945 | Libya | 1955 |
| Azerbaijan | 1992 | Congo | 1960 | Guinea | 1958 | Liechtenstein | 1990 |
| Bahamas | 1973 | Costa Rica | 1945 | Guinea-Bissau | 1974 | Lithuania | 1991 |
| Bahrain | 1971 | Côte d'Ivoire | 1960 | Guyana | 1966 | Luxembourg | 1945 |
| Bangladesh | 1974 | Croatia | 1992 | Haiti | 1945 | Macedonia[5] | 1993 |
| Barbados | 1966 | Cuba | 1945 | Honduras | 1945 | Madagascar | 1960 |
| Belarus | 1945 | Cyprus | 1960 | Hungary | 1955 | Malawi | 1964 |
| Belgium | 1945 | Czech Rep.[2] | 1993 | Iceland | 1946 | Malaysia[6] | 1957 |
| Belize | 1981 | Denmark | 1945 | India | 1945 | Maldives | 1965 |
| Benin | 1960 | Djibouti | 1977 | Indonesia[4] | 1950 | Mali | 1960 |
| Bhutan | 1971 | Dominica | 1978 | Iran | 1945 | Malta | 1964 |
| Bolivia | 1945 | Dominican Rep. | 1945 | Iraq | 1945 | Marshall Islands | 1991 |
| Bosnia and | | Ecuador | 1945 | Ireland | 1955 | Mauritania | 1961 |
| Herzegovina | 1992 | Egypt[3] | 1945 | Israel | 1949 | Mauritius | 1968 |
| Botswana | 1966 | El Salvador | 1945 | Italy | 1955 | Mexico | 1945 |
| Brazil | 1945 | Equatorial Guinea | 1968 | Jamaica | 1962 | Micronesia | 1991 |
| Brunei Darussalam | 1984 | Eritrea | 1993 | Japan | 1956 | Moldova | 1992 |
| Bulgaria | 1955 | Estonia | 1991 | Jordan | 1955 | Monaco | 1993 |
| Burkina Faso | 1960 | Ethiopia | 1945 | Kazakhstan | 1992 | Mongolia | 1961 |
| Burundi | 1962 | Fiji | 1970 | Kenya | 1963 | Morocco | 1956 |

| Member | Year | Member | Year | Member | Year | Member | Year |
|---|---|---|---|---|---|---|---|
| Mozambique | 1975 | Portugal | 1955 | Slovakia[2] | 1993 | Turkey | 1945 |
| Myanmar (Burma) | 1948 | Qatar | 1971 | Slovenia | 1992 | Turkmenistan | 1992 |
| Namibia | 1990 | Romania | 1955 | Solomon Islands | 1978 | Uganda | 1962 |
| Nepal | 1955 | Russia | 1945 | Somalia | 1960 | Ukraine | 1945 |
| Netherlands | 1945 | Rwanda | 1962 | South Africa[7] | 1945 | United Arab Emirates | 1971 |
| New Zealand | 1945 | Saint Kitts | | Spain | 1955 | United Kingdom | 1945 |
| Nicaragua | 1945 | and Nevis | 1983 | Sri Lanka | 1955 | United States | 1945 |
| Niger | 1960 | Saint Lucia | 1979 | Sudan | 1956 | Uruguay | 1945 |
| Nigeria | 1960 | Saint Vincent and | | Suriname | 1975 | Uzbekistan | 1992 |
| Norway | 1945 | the Grenadines | 1980 | Swaziland | 1968 | Vanuatu | 1981 |
| Oman | 1971 | Samoa (Western) | 1976 | Sweden | 1946 | Venezuela | 1945 |
| Pakistan | 1947 | San Marino | 1992 | Syria[3] | 1945 | Vietnam | 1977 |
| Panama | 1945 | São Tomé and Príncipe | 1975 | Tajikistan | 1992 | Yemen[9] | 1947 |
| Papua New Guinea | 1975 | Saudi Arabia | 1945 | Tanzania[8] | 1961 | Yugoslavia[10] | 1945 |
| Paraguay | 1945 | Senegal | 1960 | Thailand | 1946 | Zaire | 1960 |
| Peru | 1945 | Seychelles | 1976 | Togo | 1960 | Zambia | 1964 |
| Philippines | 1945 | Sierra Leone | 1961 | Trinidad and Tobago | 1962 | Zimbabwe | 1980 |
| Poland | 1945 | Singapore[6] | 1965 | Tunisia | 1956 | | |

(1) The General Assembly voted in 1971 to expel the Chinese government on Taiwan and admit the Beijing government in its place. (2) Czechoslovakia, which split into the separate nations of the Czech Republic and Slovakia on Jan. 1, 1993, was a UN member from 1945 to 1992. (3) Egypt and Syria were original members of the UN. In 1958, the United Arab Republic was established by a union of Egypt and Syria and continued as a single member of the UN. In 1961, Syria resumed its separate membership. (4) Indonesia withdrew from the UN in 1965 and rejoined in 1966. (5) Admitted under the provisional name of The Former Yugoslav Republic of Macedonia. (6) Malaya joined the UN in 1957. In 1963, its name was changed to Malaysia following the accession of Singapore, Sabah, and Sarawak. Singapore became an independent UN member in 1965. (7) The General Assembly rejected the credentials of the South African delegates in 1974 and suspended the country from the Assembly. (8) Tanganyika was a member of the United Nations from 1961 and Zanzibar was a member from 1963. Following the ratification in 1964 of Articles of Union between Tanganyika and Zanzibar, the United Republic of Tanganyika and Zanzibar continued as a single member of the United Nations, later changing its name to United Republic of Tanzania. (9) The Yemen Arab Republic was admitted in 1947; the People's Republic of Yemen, in 1967. The two nations merged in 1990. (10) The Socialist Federal Republic of Yugoslavia became a member in 1945. After four of its six republics (Bosnia and Herzegovina, Croatia, Macedonia, and Slovenia) declared independence in 1991-1992, the two remaining republics, Montenegro and Serbia, reconstituted themselves as the Federal Republic of Yugoslavia, which assumed Yugoslavia's UN seat Apr. 8, 1992. The General Assembly suspended Yugoslavia in September 1992 for violating UN resolutions relating to the civil wars in the former Yugoslav republics.

## United Nations Secretaries General

| Year | Secretary, Nation | Year | Secretary, Nation | Year | Secretary, Nation |
|---|---|---|---|---|---|
| 1946 | Trygve Lie, Norway | 1961 | U Thant, Burma | 1982 | Javier Perez de Cuellar, Peru |
| 1953 | Dag Hammarskjold, Sweden | 1972 | Kurt Waldheim, Austria | 1992 | Boutros Boutros-Ghali, Egypt |

## U.S. Representatives to the United Nations

The U.S. Representative to the United Nations is the Chief of the U.S. Mission to the United Nations in New York and holds the rank and status of Ambassador Extraordinary and Plenipotentiary.

| Year | Representative | Year | Representative | Year | Representative |
|---|---|---|---|---|---|
| 1946 | Edward R. Stettinius Jr. | 1968 | George W. Ball | 1977 | Andrew Young |
| 1946 | Herschel V. Johnson (act.) | 1968 | James Russell Wiggins | 1979 | Donald McHenry |
| 1947 | Warren R. Austin | 1969 | Charles W. Yost | 1981 | Jeane J. Kirkpatrick |
| 1953 | Henry Cabot Lodge Jr. | 1971 | George Bush | 1985 | Vernon A. Walters |
| 1960 | James J. Wadsworth | 1973 | John A. Scali | 1989 | Thomas R. Pickering |
| 1961 | Adlai E. Stevenson | 1975 | Daniel P. Moynihan | 1992 | Edward J. Perkins |
| 1965 | Arthur J. Goldberg | 1976 | William W. Scranton | 1993 | Madeleine K. Albright |

## Organization of the United Nations

The text of the UN Charter may be obtained from the Office of Public Information, United Nations, New York, NY 10017.

**General Assembly.** The General Assembly is composed of representatives of all the member nations. Each nation is entitled to one vote.

The General Assembly meets in regular annual sessions and in special session when necessary. Special sessions are convoked by the Secretary General at the request of the Security Council or of a majority of the members of the UN.

On important questions a two-thirds majority of members present and voting is required; on other questions a simple majority is sufficient.

The General Assembly must approve the budget and apportion expenses among members. A member in arrears will have no vote if the amount of arrears equals or exceeds the amount of the contributions due for the preceding two full years.

**Security Council.** The Security Council consists of 15 members, 5 with permanent seats. The remaining 10 are elected for 2-year terms by the General Assembly; they are not eligible for immediate reelection.

Permanent members of the Council are: China, France, Russia, United Kingdom, United States.

Nonpermanent members are: Cape Verde, Hungary, Japan, Morocco, Venezuela (until Dec. 31, 1993); Brazil, Djibouti, New Zealand, Pakistan, Spain (until Dec. 31, 1994).

The Security Council has the primary responsibility within the UN for maintaining international peace and security. The Council may investigate any dispute that threatens international peace and security.

Any member of the UN at UN headquarters may participate in its discussions and a nation not a member of UN may appear if it is a party to a dispute.

Decisions on procedural questions are made by an affirmative vote of 9 members. On all other matters the affirmative vote of 9 members must include the concurring votes of all permanent members; it is this clause which gives rise to the so-called veto power of permanent members. A party to a dispute must refrain from voting.

The Security Council directs the various peacekeeping forces deployed throughout the world.

**Economic and Social Council.** The Economic and Social Council consists of 54 members elected by the General Assembly for 3-year terms of office. The council is responsible under the General Assembly for carrying out the functions of the United Nations with regard to international economic, social, cultural, educational, health, and related matters. The council usually meets twice a year.

**Trusteeship Council.** The administration of trust territories is under UN supervision. The only remaining trust territory is Palau, administered by the U.S.

**Secretariat.** The Secretary General is the chief administrative officer of the UN. He may bring to the attention of the Security Council any matter that threatens international peace. He reports to the General Assembly.

**Budget:** The General Assembly approved a total budget for 1992-93 of $2.36 billion.

**International Court of Justice (World Court).** The International Court of Justice is the principal judicial organ of the United Nations. All members are *ipso facto* parties to the statute of the Court. Other states may become parties to the Court's statute.

The jurisdiction of the Court comprises cases which the parties submit to it and matters especially provided for in the charter or in treaties. The Court gives advisory opinions and renders judgments. Its decisions are binding only between the parties concerned and in respect to a particular dispute. If any party to a case fails to heed a judgment, the other party may have recourse to the Security Council.

The 15 judges are elected for 9-year terms by the General Assembly and the Security Council. Retiring judges are eligible for reelection. The Court remains permanently in session, except during vacations. All questions are decided by majority. The Court sits in The Hague, Netherlands.

## Selected Specialized and Related Agencies

These agencies are autonomous, with their own memberships and organs, which have a functional relationship or working agreement with the UN (headquarters.)

**Food and Agriculture Organization (FAO),** aims to increase production from farms, forests, and fisheries; improve food distribution and marketing, nutrition, and the living conditions of rural people. (Viale delle Terme di Caracalla, 00100 Rome, Italy.)

**General Agreement on Tariffs and Trade (GATT),** the only treaty setting rules for world trade, provides a forum for settling trade disputes and negotiating trade liberalization. (Centre William Rappard, 154 rue de Lausanne, 1211 Geneva 21, Switzerland.)

**International Atomic Energy Agency (IAEA),** aims to promote the safe, peaceful uses of atomic energy. (Vienna International Centre, PO Box 100, A-1400, Vienna, Austria.)

**International Bank for Reconstruction and Development (IBRD) (World Bank),** provides loans and technical assistance for economic development projects in developing member countries; encourages cofinancing for projects from other public and private sources. The **International Development Association (IDA),** an affiliate of the Bank, provides funds for development projects on concessionary terms to the poorer developing member countries. The **International Finance Corporation (IFC),** an affiliate of the Bank, promotes the growth of the private sector in developing member countries; encourages the development of local capital markets; stimulates the international flow of private capital. (1818 H St., NW, Washington, DC 20433.)

**International Civil Aviation Organization (ICAO),** promotes international civil aviation standards and regulations. (1000 Sherbrooke St. W., Montreal, Quebec, Canada H3A 2R2.)

**International Fund for Agricultural Development (IFAD),** aims to mobilize funds for agricultural and rural projects in developing countries. (107 Via del Serafico, Rome, Italy.)

**International Labor Organization (ILO),** aims to promote employment; improve labor conditions and living standards. (4 route de Morillons, CH-1211 Geneva 22, Switzerland.)

**International Maritime Organization (IMO),** aims to promote cooperation on technical matters affecting international shipping. (4 Albert Embankment, London SE1 7SR, England.)

**International Monetary Fund (IMF),** aims to promote international monetary cooperation and currency stabilization and expansion of international trade. (700 19th St., NW, Washington, DC 20431.)

**International Telecommunication Union (ITU),** establishes international regulations for radio, telegraph, telephone, and space radio-communications, allocates radio frequencies. (Place des Nations, 1211 Geneva 20, Switzerland.)

**United Nations Children's Fund (UNICEF),** provides aid and development assistance to programs for children and mothers in developing countries. (1 UN Plaza, New York, NY 10017.)

**United Nations Development Fund For Women (INIFEM),** aims to assist poor women in their economic roles in Africa, Asia, and Latin America. (304 E. 45th St., New York, NY 10017.)

**United Nations Educational, Scientific, and Cultural Organization (UNESCO),** aims to promote collaboration among nations through education, science, and culture. (7 Place de Fontenoy, 75352 Paris 07SP, France.)

**United Nations High Commissioner for Refugees (UNHCR),** provides essential assistance for refugees. (Place des Nations, 1211 Geneva 10, Switzerland.)

**Universal Postal Union (UPU)** aims to perfect postal services and promote international collaboration. (Weltpoststrasse 4, 3000 Berne, 15 Switzerland.)

**World Health Org. (WHO)** aims to aid the attainment of the highest possible level of health. (1211 Geneva 27, Switzerland.)

**World Intellectual Property Organization (WIPO)** seeks to protect, through international cooperation, literary, industrial, scientific, and artistic works. (34, Chemin des Colom Bettes, 1211 Geneva, Switzerland.)

**World Meteorological Org. (WMO)** aims to co-ordinate and improve world meteorological work. (Case Postale 5, CH-1211 Geneva 20, Switzerland.)

# Geneva Conventions
### As of mid-1992

The Geneva Conventions are 4 international treaties governing the protection of civilians in time of war, the treatment of prisoners of war, and the care of the wounded and sick in the armed forces. The first convention, covering the sick and wounded, was concluded in Geneva, Switzerland, in 1864; it was amended and expanded in 1906. A third convention, in 1929, covered prisoners of war. Outrage at the treatment of prisoners and civilians during World War II by some belligerents, notably Germany and Japan, prompted the conclusion, in August 1949, of 4 new conventions. Three of these restated and strengthened the previous conventions, and the fourth codified general principles of international law governing the treatment of civilians in wartime.

The 1949 convention for civilians provided for special safeguards for the wounded, children under 15, pregnant women, and the elderly. Discrimination was forbidden on racial, religious, national, or political grounds. Torture, collective punishment, reprisals, the unwarrented destruction of property, and the forced use of civilians for an occupier's armed forces were also prohibited.

Also included in the new 1949 treaties was a pledge to treat prisoners humanely, feed them adequately, and deliver relief supplies to them. They were not to be forced to disclose more than minimal information.

Most countries have formally accepted all or most of the humanitarian conventions as binding. A nation is not free to withdraw its ratification of the conventions during wartime. However, there is no permanent machinery in place to apprehend, try, or punish violators.

# Ambassadors and Envoys

As of mid-1993

The address of U.S. embassies abroad is the appropriate foreign capital. The U.S. does not have diplomatic relations with the following countries: Liechtenstein, Maldives, Cambodia,[1] Taiwan,[2] Cuba,[3] Iran,[4] Libya,[5] Vietnam,[1] N. Korea, Iraq,[6] Somalia.[7] There are informal relations with Bhutan and Vanuatu.

| Countries | Envoys from United States | Envoys to United States |
|---|---|---|
| Afghanistan | Vacancy | Abdul Ghafoor Jawshan, Chargé |
| Albania | William E. Ryerson, Amb. | Roland Bimo, Amb. |
| Algeria | Mary Ann Casey, Amb. | Vacancy |
| Angola | Vacancy | Vacancy |
| Antigua & Barbuda | Bryant J. Salter, Amb. | Patrick A. Lewis, Amb. |
| Argentina | Terence A. Todman, Amb. | Carlos Ortiz de Rosas, Amb. |
| Armenia | Thomas L. Price, Chargé | Alexandre Arzoumanian, Chargé |
| Australia | Marilyn A. Meyers, Chargé | Michael J. Cook, Amb. |
| Austria | James W. Swihart Jr., Chargé | Helmut Turk |
| Azerbaijan | Richard Miles, Amb. | D. N. Molla-Zade, Chargé |
| Bahamas | Lino Gutierrez, Chargé | Timothy B. Donaldson |
| Bahrain | David S. Robins, Chargé | Abdul Al-Khalifa, Amb. |
| Bangladesh | William B. Milam, Amb. | Abdul Ahsan, Amb. |
| Barbados | C. Philip Hughes, Amb. | Rudi V. Webster, Amb. |
| Belarus | David Swartz, Amb. | Serguei Martynov, Chargé |
| Belgium | Bruce S. Gelb, Amb. | Jean Cassiers, Amb. |
| Belize | Eugene L. Scassa, Amb. | James V. Hyde, Amb. |
| Benin | Ruth A. Davis, Amb. | Candide Pierre Ahouansou, Amb. |
| Bolivia | Charles R. Bowers, Amb. | Jose Crespo-Velasco, Amb. |
| Bosnia and Herzegovina | Victor Jackovich, Chargé | Vacancy |
| Botswana | David Passage, Amb. | Botsweletse K. Sebele, Amb. |
| Brazil | Richard H. Melton, Amb. | Rubens Ricupero, Amb. |
| Brunei | Donald B. Ensanet, Amb. | D.H. Mohammad Kassim, Amb. |
| Bulgaria | H. Kenneth Hill, Amb. | Ognian R. Pishev, Amb. |
| Burkina Faso | Edward P. Byrnn, Amb. | Thomas Kambou, Chargé |
| Burundi | Franklin P. Huddle Jr., Chargé | Julien Kavakure, Amb. |
| Cameroon | Tibor P. Nagy Jr., Chargé | Paul Pondi, Amb. |
| Canada | James J. Blanchard, Amb. | John G. D. de Chastelain, Amb. |
| Cape Verde | Joseph M. Segars, Amb. | Carlos Silva, Amb. |
| Central African Rep. | Robert E. Gribbon 3d, Amb. | Jean-Pierre Sohahong-Kombet, Amb. |
| Chad | William W. Bogosian, Amb. | E. Acheikh ibn Oumar, Amb. |
| Chile | Curtis W. Kamman, Amb. | Patricio Silva, Amb. |
| China | J. Stapleton Roy, Amb. | Zhu Qizhen, Amb. |
| Colombia | Morris D. Busby, Amb. | Jamie Garcia-Parra, Amb. |
| Comoros | Kenneth N. Peltier, Amb. | Amini Ali Moumin, Amb. |
| Congo | James D. Phillips, Amb. | Roger Issombo, Amb. |
| Costa Rica | Luis Guinot Jr., Amb. | Gonzalo Facio, Amb. |
| Côte d'Ivoire | Hume A. Horan, Amb. | Charles Gomis, Amb. |
| Croatia | Peter W. Galbraith, Amb. | Peter A. Sarcevic, Amb. |
| Cyprus | Robert E. Lamb, Amb. | Michael E. Sherifis, Amb. |
| Czech Rep. | Adrian A. Basora, Amb. | Michael Zantovsky, Amb. |
| Denmark | Richard B. Stone, Amb. | Peter P. Dyvig, Amb. |
| Djibouti | Charles Baquet 3d, Amb. | Roble Olhale, Amb. |
| Dominica | C. Philip Hughes, Amb. | Edward I. Watty, Amb. |
| Dominican Republic | Robert S. Pastorino, Amb. | Jose del Carmen Ariza, Amb. |
| Ecuador | James F. Mack, Chargé | Edgar Teran-Teran, Amb. |
| Egypt | Robert H. Pelletreau Jr., Amb. | Ahmed Maher El Sayed, Amb. |
| El Salvador | Alan H. Flanigan, Amb. | Miguel A. Salaverria, Amb. |
| Equatorial Guinea | John E. Bennett, Amb. | Damaso Obiang Ndong, Amb. |
| Estonia | Robert C. Frasure, Amb. | Ernst Jaakson, Amb. |
| Ethiopia | Marc Baas, Amb. | Berhane Gebre-Chirstos, Amb. |
| Fiji | Evelyn I.H. Teegen, Amb. | Pita Kewa Nacuva, Amb. |
| Finland | John H. Kelly, Amb. | Jukka Valtasaari, Amb. |
| France | Pamela C. Herriman, Amb. | Jacques Andreani, Amb. |
| Gabon | Joseph C. Wilson, Amb. | Guy M. Eboumi, Chargé |
| Gambia, The | Arlene Render, Amb. | Ousman A. Sallah, Amb. |
| Georgia | Kent N. Brown, Amb. | Vacancy |
| Germany | Richard C. Holbrooke, Amb. | Immo Stabreit, Amb. |
| Ghana | Kenneth L. Brown, Amb. | Joseph Abbey, Amb. |
| Greece | James A. Williams, Chargé | Christos Zacharakis, Amb. |
| Grenada | C. Annette T. Veler, Chargé | Denneth Modeste, Amb. |
| Guatemala | James F. Keane, Chargé | Magdalena Toriello, Chargé |
| Guinea | Dane F. Smith, Amb. | Elhadj B. Barry, Amb. |
| Guinea-Bissau | Rogert A. McGuire, Amb. | Alfredo Lopes Cabral, Amb. |
| Guyana | George F. Jones, Amb. | June Persaud, Chargé |
| Haiti | Charles E. Redman, Chargé | Jean Casimir, Amb. |
| Honduras | Cresencio S. Arcos, Amb. | R. E. Bendana-Valenzuela, Amb. |
| Hungary | Charles H. Thomas, Amb. | Pal Tar, Amb. |
| Iceland | Jon Gundersen, Chargé | Tomas Tomasson, Amb. |
| India | Kenneth C. Brill, Chargé | Siddhartha S. Ray, Amb. |
| Indonesia | Robert L. Barry, Amb. | Abdul Rachman Ramly, Amb. |
| Ireland | Thomas M. Tonkin, Chargé | Dermot A. Gallagher, Amb. |
| Israel | Vacancy | Zalman Shoval, Amb. |
| Italy | Daniel P. Serwer, Chargé | Boris Biancheri, Amb. |
| Jamaica | Shirley Chisholm | Richard L. Bernal, Amb. |
| Japan | Walter F. Mondale, Amb. | Takakazu Kuriyama, Amb. |
| Jordan | Roger G. Harrison, Amb. | Fayez A. Tarawneh, Amb. |
| Kazakhstan | William Courtney, Amb. | Alim S. Djambourchine, Amb. |
| Kenya | E. Michael Southwick, Chargé | Denis D. Afande, Amb. |

| Countries | Envoys from United States | Envoys to United States |
| --- | --- | --- |
| Kiribati | Evelyn I.H. Teegen, Amb. | Vacancy |
| Korea, South | Raymond F. Burghardt Jr., Chargé | Hong-Choo Hyun, Amb. |
| Kuwait | Edward Gnehm, Amb. | Shaikh S. N. Al-Sabah, Amb. |
| Kyrgyzstan | Edward Hurwitz, Amb. | Roza Otumbayeva, Amb. |
| Laos | Charles B. Salmon Jr., Amb. | Hiem Phommachanh, Amb. |
| Latvia | Ints M. Silins, Amb. | Ojars E. Kalnins, Amb. |
| Lebanon | Ryan C. Crocker, Amb. | Simon M. Karam, Amb. |
| Lesotho | Karl Hoffman, Chargé | Teboho E. Kitleli, Amb. |
| Liberia | William P. Twaddell, Chargé | Konah Blackett, Chargé |
| Lithuania | Darryl N. Johnson, Amb. | Stasys Lozoraitis Jr., Amb. |
| Luxembourg | Edward M. Rowell, Amb. | Alphonse Berns, Amb. |
| Madagascar | Dennis P. Barrett, Amb. | Pierrot J. Rajaonarivelo, Amb. |
| Malawi | Michael T. F. Pistor, Amb. | Robert Mbaya, Amb. |
| Malaysia | John S. Wolf, Amb. | Dato Abdul Majid, Amb. |
| Maldives | Teresita C. Schaffer, Amb. | Vacancy |
| Mali | Herbert D. Gelber, Amb. | Siragatou I. Cisse, Amb. |
| Malta | William A. Moffitt, Chargé | Borg Olivier de Puget, Amb. |
| Marshall Islands | David C. Fields, Amb. | Wilfred Kendall, Amb. |
| Mauritania | Gordon S. Brown, Amb. | Mohammed Fall Ainini, Amb. |
| Mauritius | David B. Dunn, Chargé | Chitmansing Jesseramsing, Amb. |
| Mexico | Jim Jones, Amb. | Jorge Montoya, Amb. |
| Micronesia | Aurelia E. Brazeal, Amb. | Jesse B. Marehalau, Amb. |
| Moldova | Mary C. Pendleton, Amb. | Vacancy |
| Mongolia | Donald C. Johnson, Amb. | Luvsandort Dawagiv, Amb. |
| Morocco | Joan M. Plaisted, Chargé | Mohamed Belkhayat, Amb. |
| Mozambique | Townsend B. Friedman Jr., Amb. | Hipolito Patricio, Amb. |
| Myanmar | Franklin P. Huddle Jr., Chargé | U Thaung, Amb. |
| Namibia | Howard J. Jeter, Chargé | Tuliameni Kalomoh, Amb. |
| Nauru | Marilyn A. Meyers, Chargé | Vacancy |
| Nepal | Julia Chang Bloch, Amb. | Yog Prasad Upadhyay, Amb. |
| Netherlands | Thomas H. Gewecke, Chargé | Johan H. Meesman, Amb. |
| New Zealand | David M. Walker, Chargé | Denis B.G. McLean, Amb. |
| Nicaragua | John Maisto, Amb. | Ernesto Palizio, Amb. |
| Niger | Jennifer C. Ward, Amb. | Adamou Seydou, Amb. |
| Nigeria | William L. Swing, Amb. | Zubair Kazaure, Amb. |
| Norway | William C. McCahill, Chargé | Kjeld Vibe, Amb. |
| Oman | David J. Dunford, Amb. | Awadh Bader Al-Shanfari, Amb. |
| Pakistan | John C. Monjo, Amb. | Syeda A. Hussain, Amb. |
| Panama | Deane R. Hinton, Amb. | Jaime F. Boyd, Amb. |
| Papua New Guinea | Robert W. Farrand, Amb. | Margaret Taylor, Amb. |
| Paraguay | Jon David Glassman, Amb. | Juan E. Aguirre, Amb. |
| Peru | Charles H. Brayshaw, Chargé | Ricardo V. Luna, Amb. |
| Philippines | Vacancy | Franklin M. Ebdalin, Amb. |
| Poland | Michael M. Hornblow, Chargé | Kazimierz Dziewanowski, Amb. |
| Portugal | Edward Ellis Briggs, Amb. | Francisco Knopfli, Amb. |
| Qatar | Kenneth W. Keith, Amb. | Ali Saad Al-Kharji, Amb. |
| Romania | John R. Davis Jr., Amb. | Aurel-Dragos Munteanu, Amb. |
| Russia | Thomas Pickering, Amb. | Vladimir P. Lukin |
| Rwanda | Robert A. Flaten, Amb. | Aloys Uwimana, Amb. |
| St. Kitts & Nevis | C. Philip Hughes, Amb. | Aubrey Hart, Chargé |
| St. Lucia | C. Philip Hughes, Amb. | Joseph E. Edmunds, Amb. |
| St. Vincent and The Grenadines | C. Philip Hughes, Amb. | Kingsley C.A. Layne, Amb. |
| Sao Tome and Principe | Joseph C. Wilson, Amb. | Vacancy |
| Saudi Arabia | C. David Welch, Chargé | Bandar Bin Sultan, Amb. |
| Senegal | Robert J. Kott, Chargé | Ibra Deguene Ka, Amb. |
| Seychelles | F. Stephen Malott, Chargé | Marc Marengo, Chargé |
| Sierra Leone | Lauralee M. Peters, Amb. | William Wright, Chargé |
| Singapore | John M. Huntsman, Amb. | S.R. Nathan, Amb. |
| Slovakia | Vacancy | Milan Erban, Chargé |
| Slovenia | Allan Wendt, Amb. | Ernest Petric, Amb. |
| Solomon Islands | Robert W. Farrand, Amb. | Vacancy |
| South Africa | Princeton N. Lyman, Amb. | Harry H. Schwarz, Amb. |
| Spain | David N. Greenlee, Chargé | Jaime de Ojeda, Amb. |
| Sri Lanka | Teresita C. Schaffer, Amb. | Anada W. P. Guruge, Amb. |
| Sudan | David K. Petterson, Amb. | Abdalla Ahmed Abdalla, Amb. |
| Suriname | John P. Leonard, Amb. | Willem A. Udenhout, Amb. |
| Swaziland | Stephen H. Rogers, Amb. | Absalom V. Mamba, Amb. |
| Sweden | Michael Klosson, Chargé | Carl Sihver Liljegren, Amb. |
| Switzerland | John Hall, Chargé | Edouard Brunner, Amb. |
| Syria | Christopher W. S. Ross, Amb. | Walid Al-Moualem, Amb. |
| Tajikistan | Stanley Escudero, Amb. | Vacancy |
| Tanzania | Peter Jon de Vos, Amb. | Charles M. Nyirabu, Amb. |
| Thailand | David F. Lambertson, Amb. | M. L. B. Kasemeri, Amb. |
| Togo | Harmon E. Kirby, Amb. | Edem F. Hegbe, Chargé |
| Tonga | Evelyn I.H. Teegen, Amb. | Sione Kite, Amb. |
| Trinidad and Tobago | Sally G. Cowal, Amb. | Corinne A. McKnight, Amb. |
| Tunisia | John T. McCarthy, Amb. | Ismail Khelil, Amb. |
| Turkey | Richard C. Barkley, Amb. | Nuzhet Kandemir, Amb. |
| Turkmenistan | Joseph S Hulings 3d, Amb. | Vacancy |
| Tuvalu | Evelyn I.H. Teegen, Amb. | Vacancy |
| Uganda | Johnnie Carson, Amb. | Stephen K. Katenta-Apuli, Amb. |
| Ukraine | Roman Popadiuk, Amb. | Oleh H. Bilorus, Amb. |
| United Arab Emirates | William A. Rugh, Amb. | Mohammad ben Hussein Al-Shaali, Amb. |
| United Kingdom | William J. Crowe Jr., Amb. | Robin R. Renwick, Amb. |
| Uruguay | Thomas J. Dodd, Amb. | Eduardo MacGillycuddy |
| Uzbekistan | Henry L. Clarke, Amb. | Vacancy |
| Vatican | Cameron Hume, Chargé | Agostino Cacciavillan, Pro-Nuncio |

| Countries | Envoys from United States | Envoys to United States |
|---|---|---|
| Venezuela | Jeffrey Davidow, Amb. | Simon A. Consalvi, Amb. |
| Western Samoa | Eric D. Tunis, Chargé | Terry Toomata, Chargé |
| Yemen | Arthur H. Hughes, Amb. | Mohsin A. Alaini, Amb. |
| Yugoslavia | Robert Rackmales, Chargé | Ivan Zivkovic, Chargé |
| Zaire | John M. Yates, Chargé | Tatanee Manata, Amb. |
| Zambia | Gordon L. Streeb, Amb. | Dustin W. Kamana, Amb. |
| Zimbabwe | Edward G. Lanpher, Amb. | Mark Marongwe, Chargé |

**Special Missions**

U.S. Mission to North Atlantic Treaty Organization, Brussels—Vacancy 4th
U.S. Mission to the European Communities, Brussels—Stuart E. Eizenstat
U.S. Mission to the United Nations, New York—Madeleine K. Albright, Amb.
U.S. Mission to the European Office of the UN, Geneva—Morris B. Abram, Amb.
U.S. Mission to the Organization for Economic Cooperation and Development, Paris—David L. Aaron
U.S. Mission to the Organization of American States, Washington—Luigi R. Einaudi, Amb.

(1) U.S. embassy closed in 1975. (2) U.S. severed relations in 1978; unofficial relations are maintained. (3) Relations severed in 1961; limited ties restored in 1977. (4) U.S. severed relations on Apr. 7, 1980. (5) Embassy closed on May 2, 1980. U.S. closed the Libyan mission on May 6, 1981. (6) Operations temporarily suspended. (7) Embassy evacuated Jan. 5, 1991.

# Codes for International Direct Dial Calling From the U.S.

**Station-to-station:** 011+country code (below)+city code+local number.
**Person-to-person** (operator assisted, collect calls, credit card calls, and calls billed to another number): 01+country code (below)+city code+local number.

| Country | Code | Country | Code | Country | Code |
|---|---|---|---|---|---|
| Algeria | 213 | Greenland | 299 | Oman | 968 |
| American Samoa | 684 | Grenada | 809* | Pakistan | 92 |
| Andorra | 33 | Guadeloupe | 590 | Panama | 507 |
| Anguilla | 809* | Guam | 671 | Papua New Guinea | 675 |
| Antigua | 809* | Guantanamo | 53 | Paraguay | 595 |
| Argentina | 54 | Guatemala | 502 | Peru | 51 |
| Aruba | 297 | Guinea | 224 | Philippines | 63 |
| Ascension Island | 247 | Guyana | 592 | Poland | 48 |
| Australia | 61 | Haiti | 509 | Portugal | 351 |
| Austria | 43 | Honduras | 504 | Qatar | 974 |
| Bahamas | 809* | Hong Kong | 852 | Reunion Island | 262 |
| Bahrain | 973 | Hungary | 36 | Romania | 40 |
| Bangladesh | 880 | Iceland | 354 | Russia (Moscow) | 7 |
| Barbados | 809* | India | 91 | Rwanda | 250 |
| Belgium | 32 | Indonesia | 62 | Saipan | 670 |
| Belize | 501 | Iran | 98 | San Marino | 39 |
| Benin | 229 | Iraq | 964 | Saudi Arabia | 966 |
| Bermuda | 809* | Ireland | 353 | Senegal | 221 |
| Bolivia | 591 | Israel | 972 | Seychelles Islands | 248 |
| Botswana | 267 | Italy | 39 | Sierra Leone | 232 |
| Brazil | 55 | Jamaica | 809* | Singapore | 65 |
| British Virgin Islands | 809* | Japan | 81 | Slovakia | 42 |
| Brunei | 673 | Jordan | 962 | Solomon Island | 677 |
| Bulgaria | 359 | Kenya | 254 | South Africa | 27 |
| Burkina Faso | 226 | Kiribati | 686 | Spain | 34 |
| Cameroon | 237 | Korea | 82 | Sri Lanka | 94 |
| Canada | Use Area Codes | Kuwait | 965 | St. Kitts | 809* |
| Cape Verde Islands | 238 | Lebanon | 961 | St. Lucia | 809* |
| Cayman Islands | 809* | Lesotho | 266 | St. Pierre & Miquelon | 508 |
| Chile | 56 | Liberia | 231 | St. Vincent | 809* |
| China | 86 | Libya | 218 | Suriname | 597 |
| Colombia | 57 | Liechtenstein | 41 | Swaziland | 268 |
| Congo | 242 | Luxembourg | 352 | Sweden | 46 |
| Costa Rica | 506 | Macao | 853 | Switzerland | 41 |
| Cote d'Ivoire | 225 | Malawi | 265 | Syria | 963 |
| Cyprus | 357 | Malaysia | 60 | Taiwan | 886 |
| Czech. Rep. | 42 | Maldives | 960 | Tanzania | 255 |
| Denmark | 45 | Mali Republic | 223 | Thailand | 66 |
| Djibouti | 253 | Malta | 356 | Togo | 228 |
| Dominica | 809* | Marshall Islands | 692 | Tonga | 676 |
| Dominican Republic | 809* | Mauritius | 230 | Trinidad & Tobago | 809* |
| Ecuador | 593 | Mexico | 52 | Tunisia | 216 |
| Egypt | 20 | Micronesia | 691 | Turkey | 90 |
| El Salvador | 503 | Monaco | 33 | Turks & Caicos | |
| Ethiopia | 251 | Montserrat | 809* | Islands | 809* |
| Faeroe Islands | 298 | Morocco | 212 | Uganda | 256 |
| Fiji Islands | 679 | Namibia | 264 | United Arab | |
| Finland | 358 | Nauru | 674 | Emirates | 971 |
| France | 33 | Nepal | 977 | United Kingdom | 44 |
| French Antilles | 596 | Netherlands | 31 | Uruguay | 598 |
| French Guiana | 594 | Netherlands Antilles | 599 | Vatican City | 39 |
| French Polynesia | 689 | Nevis | 809* | Venezuela | 58 |
| Gabon | 241 | New Caledonia | 687 | Western Samoa | 685 |
| Gambia | 220 | New Zealand | 64 | Yemen Arab Republic | 967 |
| Germany | 49 | Nicaragua | 505 | Yugoslavia | 38 |
| Ghana | 233 | Niger | 227 | Zaire | 243 |
| Gibraltar | 350 | Nigeria | 234 | Zambia | 260 |
| Greece | 30 | Norway | 47 | Zimbabwe | 263 |

* Follow Domestic Dialing instructions: dial "1" + 809 + number you're calling.

## U.S. Aid to Foreign Nations in 1992

Source: Bureau of Economic Analysis, U.S. Dept. of Commerce

Figures are in millions of dollars. (*Less than $500,000.) Data include military supplies and services furnished under the Foreign Assistance Act and direct Defense Department appropriations, and include credits extended to private entities.

Net grants and credits take into account all known returns to the U.S., including reverse grants, returns of grants, and payments of principal. Also included are contributions received from coalition partners for Persian Gulf operations. A minus sign (−) indicates that the total of the returns is greater than the total grants or credits. Nations with net grants or credits under $2 million are included with "Other and Unspecified." Other Assistance represents the transfer of U.S. farm products in exchange for foreign currencies, less the government's disbursements of such currencies as grants or credits or for purchases.

Amounts do not include investments in the following: Asian Development Bank, $86 mln.; Inter-American Development Bank, $128 mln.; International Development Assn., $835 mln.; International Bank for Reconstruction and Development, $94 mln.; African Development Fund, $131 mln.; International Finance Corp., $25 mln; European Bank for Reconstruction and Development, $99 mln.; Inter-American Investment Corporation, $12 mln.; African Development Bank, $9 mln.

| | Total | Net grants | Net credits | Net other |
|---|---|---|---|---|
| Total | 14,784 | 14,614 | 170 | (*) |
| **Western Europe** | 131 | 484 | −353 | (*) |
| Austria | −1 | (*) | −1 | — |
| Finland | −5 | — | −5 | — |
| France | −2 | (*) | −1 | — |
| Ireland | −6 | — | −6 | — |
| Norway | −15 | — | −15 | — |
| Portugal | 158 | 223 | −64 | — |
| Spain | −123 | 1 | −124 | (*) |
| United Kingdom | −115 | (*) | −115 | — |
| Yugoslavia | −21 | (*) | −21 | — |
| Other & Unspecified | 260 | 260 | (*) | — |
| **Eastern Europe** | 577 | 479 | 100 | −2 |
| Albania | 29 | 29 | — | — |
| Armenia | 16 | 16 | — | — |
| Belarus | 22 | (*) | 22 | — |
| Bulgaria | 29 | 29 | — | — |
| Czechoslovakia | 46 | 46 | — | — |
| Estonia | 24 | 14 | 10 | — |
| Hungary | 38 | 38 | — | — |
| Kazakhstan | 2 | 2 | — | — |
| Latvia | 25 | 15 | 9 | — |
| Lithuania | 25 | 16 | 9 | — |
| Moldova | 9 | (*) | 9 | — |
| Poland | 112 | 115 | — | −2 |
| Romania | 25 | 15 | 10 | — |
| Russia | 47 | 26 | 21 | — |
| Tajikistan | 10 | (*) | 10 | — |
| Turkmenistan | 5 | 5 | — | — |
| Ukraine | 8 | 8 | — | — |
| Other & unspecified | 106 | 106 | — | — |
| **Near East & South Asia** | 7,241 | 7,467 | −228 | 2 |
| Afghanistan | 70 | 70 | (*) | — |
| Bangladesh | 136 | 165 | −29 | — |
| Cyprus | 10 | 10 | (*) | (*) |
| Egypt | 2,539 | 2,494 | 37 | 7 |
| Greece | 388 | 55 | 334 | −1 |
| India | 17 | 127 | −110 | (*) |
| Iraq | 9 | 9 | — | — |
| Israel | 4,746 | 4,989 | −243 | — |
| Jordan | 118 | 50 | 67 | (*) |
| Kuwait | −2 | −2 | — | — |
| Lebanon | 11 | 14 | −3 | (*) |
| Nepal | 19 | 20 | (*) | (*) |
| Oman | 13 | 11 | 2 | — |
| Pakistan | 89 | 240 | −148 | −3 |
| Saudi Arabia | −1,328 | −1,328 | — | — |
| Sri Lanka | 53 | 49 | 4 | −1 |
| Turkey | 231 | 372 | −141 | (*) |
| Yemen | 14 | 14 | (*) | — |
| Other & unspecified | 109 | 109 | — | — |
| **East Asia & Pacific** | 583 | 552 | 32 | (*) |
| Australia | −18 | — | −18 | — |
| Cambodia | 54 | 54 | (*) | — |
| China | 31 | — | 31 | — |
| Indonesia | 81 | 72 | 9 | (*) |
| Japan | −30 | −30 | — | — |
| Korea, South | −132 | (*) | −133 | — |
| Mongolia | 2 | 2 | — | — |
| New Zealand | −1 | — | −1 | — |
| Papua New Guinea | 9 | 1 | 9 | — |
| Philippines | 503 | 383 | 120 | (*) |
| Singapore | 3 | 3 | — | — |
| Taiwan | −7 | — | −7 | (*) |
| Thailand | 43 | 21 | 22 | — |
| Other & unspecified | 46 | 45 | 1 | — |
| **Africa** | 1,363 | 1,983 | −620 | −1 |
| Algeria | −13 | (*) | −14 | — |
| Angola | −30 | 5 | −35 | — |
| Benin | 16 | 16 | — | — |
| Botswana | 8 | 10 | −2 | — |
| Burkina Faso | 14 | 14 | — | (*) |
| Burundi | 16 | 16 | — | — |
| Cameroon | 34 | 28 | 6 | — |
| Cape Verde | 8 | 8 | — | — |
| Central African Rep. | 3 | 3 | — | — |
| Chad | 32 | 32 | — | — |
| Comoros | 2 | 2 | — | — |
| Congo | 4 | 1 | 3 | — |
| Côte d'Ivoire | 46 | 13 | 33 | — |
| Djibouti | 6 | 6 | — | — |
| Ethiopia | 62 | 68 | −6 | — |
| Gambia, The | 11 | 11 | — | — |
| Ghana | 28 | 28 | (*) | (*) |
| Guinea | 16 | 15 | (*) | 1 |
| Guinea Bissau | 5 | 5 | — | — |
| Kenya | 75 | 53 | 22 | — |
| Lesotho | 14 | 14 | — | — |
| Liberia | 19 | 18 | (*) | — |
| Madagascar | 12 | 12 | — | — |
| Malawi | 38 | 38 | — | (*) |
| Mali | 31 | 31 | — | (*) |
| Mauritania | 2 | 2 | — | — |
| Morocco | 13 | 56 | −43 | (*) |
| Mozambique | 61 | 61 | 1 | — |
| Namibia | 5 | 5 | — | — |
| Niger | 34 | 34 | (*) | — |
| Nigeria | 31 | 20 | 11 | — |
| Rwanda | 7 | 7 | — | — |
| São Tomé and Príncipe | 2 | 2 | — | — |
| Senegal | 37 | 37 | (*) | — |
| Seychelles | 5 | 5 | — | — |
| Sierra Leone | 14 | 5 | 8 | — |
| Somalia | 307 | 307 | (*) | — |
| South Africa | 44 | 44 | — | — |
| Sudan | 11 | 10 | 1 | — |
| Swaziland | 12 | 12 | (*) | — |
| Tanzania | 28 | 28 | — | — |
| Togo | 11 | 11 | (*) | — |
| Tunisia | 16 | 23 | −7 | (*) |
| Uganda | 22 | 22 | — | — |
| Zaire | 33 | 33 | (*) | 3 |
| Zambia | 76 | 106 | −30 | — |
| Zimbabwe | 72 | 52 | 20 | — |
| Other & Unspecified | 98 | 100 | −3 | — |
| **Western Hemisphere** | 2,244 | 1,590 | 655 | −1 |
| Argentina | 90 | 6 | 83 | — |
| Belize | 10 | 8 | 2 | — |
| Bolivia | 174 | 171 | 3 | — |
| Brazil | 494 | 4 | 490 | — |
| Canada | −38 | — | −38 | — |
| Chile | −56 | 7 | −63 | — |
| Colombia | −77 | 137 | −214 | — |
| Costa Rica | 23 | 40 | −17 | — |
| Dominican Republic | 3 | 23 | −20 | — |
| Ecuador | 26 | 31 | −6 | — |
| El Salvador | 288 | 272 | 17 | — |
| Guatemala | 105 | 95 | 9 | (*) |
| Guyana | 9 | 2 | 7 | — |
| Haiti | 40 | 40 | 1 | −1 |
| Honduras | 126 | 126 | 1 | (*) |
| Jamaica | 83 | 50 | 33 | — |
| Mexico | −172 | 16 | −188 | — |
| Nicaragua | 205 | 155 | 50 | — |
| Panama | 193 | 185 | 8 | — |
| Peru | 607 | 84 | 524 | — |
| Suriname | 5 | (*) | 5 | — |
| Trinidad and Tobago | −10 | (*) | −10 | — |
| Uruguay | −3 | 2 | −4 | — |
| Venezuela | −13 | (*) | −3 | — |
| Other & Unspecified | 119 | 136 | −16 | — |
| **Intl. orgs. & unspecified** | 2,612 | 2,612 | (*) | — |

# SPORTS IN 1993

## Summer Olympic Games Records

The modern Olympic Games, first held in Athens, Greece in 1896, were the result of efforts by Baron Pierre de Coubertin, a French educator, to promote interest in education and culture, also to foster better international understanding through the universal medium of youth's love of athletics.

His source of inspiration for the Olympic Games was the ancient Greek Olympic Games, most notable of the four Panhellenic celebrations. The games were combined patriotic, religious, and athletic festivals held every four years. The first such recorded festival was held in 776 B.C., the date from which the Greeks began to keep their calendar by "Olympiads," or four-year spans between the games.

The first Olympiad is said to have consisted merely of a 200-yard foot race near the small city of Olympia, but the games gained in scope and became demonstrations of national pride. Only Greek citizens — amateurs — were permitted to participate. Winners received laurel, wild olive, and palm wreaths and were accorded many special privileges. Under the Roman emperors, the games deteriorated into professional carnivals and circuses. Emperor Theodosius banned them in 394 A.D.

Baron de Coubertin enlisted 9 nations to send athletes to the first modern Olympics in 1896; now more than 100 nations compete. Winter Olympic Games were started in 1924.

### Sites of Olympic Games

| | | |
|---|---|---|
| 1896 Athens, Greece | 1920 Antwerp, Belgium | 1952 Helsinki, Finland | 1976 Montreal, Canada |
| 1900 Paris, France | 1924 Paris, France | 1956 Melbourne, Australia | 1980 Moscow, USSR |
| 1904 St. Louis, U.S. | 1928 Amsterdam, Netherlands | 1960 Rome, Italy | 1984 Los Angeles, U.S. |
| 1906 Athens*, Greece | 1932 Los Angeles, U.S. | 1964 Tokyo, Japan | 1988 Seoul, S. Korea |
| 1908 London, England | 1936 Berlin, Germany | 1968 Mexico City, Mexico | 1992 Barcelona, Spain |
| 1912 Stockholm, Sweden | 1948 London, England | 1972 Munich, W. Germany | 1996 Atlanta, U.S. |

* Games not recognized by International Olympic Committee. Games 6 (1916), 12 (1940), and 13 (1944) were not celebrated. The 1980 games were boycotted by 62 nations, including the U.S. The 1984 games were boycotted by the USSR and most eastern bloc nations. East and West Germany competed separately 1968-88. The 1992 Unified Team consisted of 12 former Soviet republics. The 1992 Independent Olympic Participants (I.O.C.) were athletes from Serbia, Montenegro, and Macedonia.

## Olympic Games Champions, 1896—1992

(*Indicates Gold Medal-Winning Record)

### Track and Field — Men

#### 100-Meter Run

| | | |
|---|---|---|
| 1896 | Thomas Burke, United States | 12s |
| 1900 | Francis W. Jarvis, United States | 11.0s |
| 1904 | Archie Hahn, United States | 11s |
| 1908 | Reginald Walker, South Africa | 10.8s |
| 1912 | Ralph Craig, United States | 10.8s |
| 1920 | Charles Paddock, United States | 10.8s |
| 1924 | Harold Abrahams, Great Britain | 10.6s |
| 1928 | Percy Williams, Canada | 10.8s |
| 1932 | Eddie Tolan, United States | 10.3s |
| 1936 | Jesse Owens, United States | 10.3s |
| 1948 | Harrison Dillard, United States | 10.3s |
| 1952 | Lindy Remigino, United States | 10.4s |
| 1956 | Bobby Morrow, United States | 10.5s |
| 1960 | Armin Hary, Germany | 10.2s |
| 1964 | Bob Hayes, United States | 10.0s |
| 1968 | Jim Hines, United States | 9.95s |
| 1972 | Valery Borzov, USSR | 10.14s |
| 1976 | Hasely Crawford, Trinidad | 10.06s |
| 1980 | Allan Wells, Great Britain | 10.25s |
| 1984 | Carl Lewis, United States | 9.99s |
| 1988 | Carl Lewis, United States | 9.92s* |
| 1992 | Linford Christie, Great Britain | 9.96s |

#### 200-Meter Run

| | | |
|---|---|---|
| 1900 | Walter Tewksbury, United States | 22.2s |
| 1904 | Archie Hahn, United States | 21.6s |
| 1908 | Robert Kerr, Canada | 22.6s |
| 1912 | Ralph Craig, United States | 21.7s |
| 1920 | Allan Woodring, United States | 22s |
| 1924 | Jackson Scholz, United States | 21.6s |
| 1928 | Percy Williams, Canada | 21.8s |
| 1932 | Eddie Tolan, United States | 21.2s |
| 1936 | Jesse Owens, United States | 20.7s |
| 1948 | Mel Patton, United States | 21.1s |
| 1952 | Andrew Stanfield, United States | 20.7s |
| 1956 | Bobby Morrow, United States | 20.6s |
| 1960 | Livio Berruti, Italy | 20.5s |
| 1964 | Henry Carr, United States | 20.3s |
| 1968 | Tommie Smith, United States | 19.83s |
| 1972 | Valeri Borzov, USSR | 20.00s |
| 1976 | Donald Quarrie, Jamaica | 20.23s |
| 1980 | Pietro Mennea, Italy | 20.19s |
| 1984 | Carl Lewis, United States | 19.80s |

| | | |
|---|---|---|
| 1988 | Joe DeLoach, United States | 19.75s* |
| 1992 | Mike Marsh, United States | 20.01s |

#### 400-Meter Run

| | | |
|---|---|---|
| 1896 | Thomas Burke, United States | 54.2s |
| 1900 | Maxey Long, United States | 49.4s |
| 1904 | Harry Hillman, United States | 49.2s |
| 1908 | Wyndham Halswelle, Great Britain, walkover | 50s |
| 1912 | Charles Reidpath, United States | 48.2s |
| 1920 | Bevil Rudd, South Africa | 49.6s |
| 1924 | Eric Liddell, Great Britain | 47.6s |
| 1928 | Ray Barbuti, United States | 47.8s |
| 1932 | William Carr, United States | 46.2s |
| 1936 | Archie Williams, United States | 46.5s |
| 1948 | Arthur Wint, Jamaica | 46.2s |
| 1952 | George Rhoden, Jamaica | 45.9s |
| 1956 | Charles Jenkins, United States | 46.7s |
| 1960 | Otis Davis, United States | 44.9s |
| 1964 | Michael Larrabee, United States | 45.1s |
| 1968 | Lee Evans, United States | 43.8s |
| 1972 | Vincent Matthews, United States | 44.66s |
| 1976 | Alberto Juantorena, Cuba | 44.26s |
| 1980 | Viktor Markin, USSR | 44.60s |
| 1984 | Alonzo Babers, United States | 44.27s |
| 1988 | Steven Lewis, United States | 43.87s |
| 1992 | Quincy Watts, United States | 43.50s* |

#### 800-Meter Run

| | | |
|---|---|---|
| 1896 | Edwin Flack, Australia | 2m. 11s |
| 1900 | Alfred Tysoe, Great Britain | 2m. 1.2s |
| 1904 | James Lightbody, United States | 1m. 56s |
| 1908 | Mel Sheppard, United States | 1m. 52.8s |
| 1912 | James Meredith, United States | 1m. 51.9s |
| 1920 | Albert Hill, Great Britain | 1m. 53.4s |
| 1924 | Douglas Lowe, Great Britain | 1m. 52.4s |
| 1928 | Douglas Lowe, Great Britain | 1m. 51.8s |
| 1932 | Thomas Hampson, Great Britain | 1m. 49.8s |
| 1936 | John Woodruff, United States | 1m. 52.9s |
| 1948 | Mal Whitfield, United States | 1m. 49.2s |
| 1952 | Mal Whitfield, United States | 1m. 49.2s |
| 1956 | Thomas Courtney, United States | 1m. 47.7s |
| 1960 | Peter Snell, New Zealand | 1m. 46.3s |
| 1964 | Peter Snell, New Zealand | 1m. 45.1s |
| 1968 | Ralph Doubell, Australia | 1m. 44.3s |

| 1972 | Dave Wottle, United States | 1m. 45.9s |
|------|---------------------------|-----------|
| 1976 | Alberto Juantorena, Cuba | 1m. 43.50s |
| 1980 | Steve Ovett, Great Britain | 1m. 45.40s |
| 1984 | Joaquim Cruz, Brazil | 1m. 43.00s* |
| 1988 | Paul Ereng, Kenya | 1m. 43.45s |
| 1992 | William Tanui, Kenya | 1m. 43.66s |

### 1,500-Meter Run

| 1896 | Edwin Flack, Australia | 4m. 33.2s |
|------|------------------------|-----------|
| 1900 | Charles Bennett, Great Britain | 4m. 6.2s |
| 1904 | James Lightbody, United States | 4m. 5.4s |
| 1908 | Mel Sheppard, United States | 4m. 3.4s |
| 1912 | Arnold Jackson, Great Britain | 3m. 56.8s |
| 1920 | Albert Hill, Great Britain | 4m. 1.8s |
| 1924 | Paavo Nurmi, Finland | 3m. 53.6s |
| 1928 | Harry Larva, Finland | 3m. 53.2s |
| 1932 | Luigi Beccali, Italy | 3m. 51.2s |
| 1936 | Jack Lovelock, New Zealand | 3m. 47.8s |
| 1948 | Henri Eriksson, Sweden | 3m. 49.8s |
| 1952 | Joseph Barthel, Luxemburg | 3m. 45.2s |
| 1956 | Ron Delany, Ireland | 3m. 41.2s |
| 1960 | Herb Elliott, Australia | 3m. 35.6s |
| 1964 | Peter Snell, New Zealand | 3m. 38.1s |
| 1968 | Kipchoge Keino, Kenya | 3m. 34.9s |
| 1972 | Pekka Vasala, Finland | 3m. 36.3s |
| 1976 | John Walker, New Zealand | 3m. 39.17s |
| 1980 | Sebastian Coe, Great Britain | 3m. 38.4s |
| 1984 | Sebastian Coe, Great Britain | 3m. 32.53s* |
| 1988 | Peter Rono, Kenya | 3m. 35.96s |
| 1992 | Fermin Cacho Ruiz, Spain | 3m. 40.12s |

### 3,000-Meter Steeplechase

| 1920 | Percy Hodge, Great Britain | 10m. 0.4s |
|------|----------------------------|-----------|
| 1924 | Willie Ritola, Finland | 9m. 33.6s |
| 1928 | Toivo Loukola, Finland | 9m. 21.8s |
| 1932 | Volmari Iso-Hollo, Finland | 10m. 33.4s |
| | (About 3,450 mtrs. extra lap by error) | |
| 1936 | Volmari Iso-Hollo, Finland | 9m. 3.8s |
| 1948 | Thore Sjoestrand, Sweden | 9m. 4.6s |
| 1952 | Horace Ashenfelter, United States | 8m. 45.4s |
| 1956 | Chris Brasher, Great Britain | 8m. 41.2s |
| 1960 | Zdzislaw Krzyszkowiak, Poland | 8m. 34.2s |
| 1964 | Gaston Roelants, Belgium | 8m. 30.8s |
| 1968 | Amos Biwott, Kenya | 8m. 51s |
| 1972 | Kipchoge Keino, Kenya | 8m. 23.6s |
| 1976 | Anders Garderud, Sweden | 8m. 08.2s |
| 1980 | Bronislaw Malinowski, Poland | 8m. 09.7s |
| 1984 | Julius Korir, Kenya | 8m. 11.8s |
| 1988 | Julius Kariuki, Kenya | 8m. 05.51s* |
| 1992 | Matthew Birir, Kenya | 8m. 08.84s |

### 5,000-Meter Run

| 1912 | Hannes Kolehmainen, Finland | 14m. 36.6s |
|------|-----------------------------|-----------|
| 1920 | Joseph Guillemot, France | 14m. 55.6s |
| 1924 | Paavo Nurmi, Finland | 14m. 31.2s |
| 1928 | Willie Ritola, Finland | 14m. 38s |
| 1932 | Lauri Lehtinen, Finland | 14m. 30s |
| 1936 | Gunnar Hockert, Finland | 14m. 22.2s |
| 1948 | Gaston Reiff, Belgium | 14m. 17.6s |
| 1952 | Emil Zatopek, Czechoslovakia | 14m. 6.6s |
| 1956 | Vladimir Kuts, USSR | 13m. 39.6s |
| 1960 | Murray Halberg, New Zealand | 13m. 43.4s |
| 1964 | Bob Schul, United States | 13m. 48.8s |
| 1968 | Mohamed Gammoudi, Tunisia | 14m. 05.0s |
| 1972 | Lasse Viren, Finland | 13m. 26.4s |
| 1976 | Lasse Viren, Finland | 13m. 24.76s |
| 1980 | Miruts Yifter, Ethiopia | 13m. 21.0s |
| 1984 | Said Aouita, Morocco | 13m. 05.59s* |
| 1988 | John Ngugi, Kenya | 13m. 11.70s |
| 1992 | Dieter Baumann, Germany | 13m. 12.52s |

### 10,000-Meter Run

| 1912 | Hannes Kolehmainen, Finland | 31m. 20.8s |
|------|-----------------------------|-----------|
| 1920 | Paavo Nurmi, Finland | 31m. 45.8s |
| 1924 | Willie Ritola, Finland | 30m. 23.2s |
| 1928 | Paavo Nurmi, Finland | 30m. 18.8s |
| 1932 | Janusz Kusocinski, Poland | 30m. 11.4s |
| 1936 | Ilmari Salminen, Finland | 30m. 15.4s |
| 1948 | Emil Zatopek, Czechoslovakia | 29m. 59.6s |
| 1952 | Emil Zatopek, Czechoslovakia | 29m. 17.0s |
| 1956 | Vladimir Kuts, USSR | 28m. 45.6s |
| 1960 | Pyotr Bolotnikov, USSR | 28m. 32.2s |
| 1964 | Billy Mills, United States | 28m. 24.4s |
| 1968 | Naftali Temu, Kenya | 29m. 27.4s |
| 1972 | Lasse Viren, Finland | 27m. 38.4s |

| 1976 | Lasse Viren, Finland | 27m. 40.38s |
|------|----------------------|-------------|
| 1980 | Miruts Yifter, Ethiopia | 27m. 42.7s |
| 1984 | Alberto Cova, Italy | 27m. 47.54s |
| 1988 | Brahim Boutaib, Morocco | 27m. 21.46s* |
| 1992 | Khalid Skah, Morocco | 27m. 46.70s |

### Marathon

| 1896 | Spiridon Loues, Greece | 2h. 58m. 50s |
|------|------------------------|--------------|
| 1900 | Michel Theato, France | 2h. 59m. 45s |
| 1904 | Thomas Hicks, United States | 3h. 28m. 63s |
| 1908 | John J. Hayes, United States | 2h. 55m. 18.4s |
| 1912 | Kenneth McArthur, South Africa | 2h. 36m. 54.8s |
| 1920 | Hannes Kolehmainen, Finland | 2h. 32m. 35.8s |
| 1924 | Albin Stenroos, Finland | 2h. 41m. 22.6s |
| 1928 | A.B. El Ouafi, France | 2h. 32m. 57s |
| 1932 | Juan Zabala, Argentina | 2h. 31m. 36s |
| 1936 | Kijung Son, Japan (Korean) | 2h. 29m. 19.2s |
| 1948 | Delfo Cabrera, Argentina | 2h. 34m. 51.6s |
| 1952 | Emil Zatopek, Czechoslovakia | 2h. 23m. 03.2s |
| 1956 | Alain Mimoun, France | 2h. 25m. |
| 1960 | Abebe Bikila, Ethiopia | 2h. 15m. 16.2s |
| 1964 | Abebe Bikila, Ethiopia | 2h. 12m. 11.2s |
| 1968 | Mamo Wolde, Ethiopia | 2h. 20m. 26.4s |
| 1972 | Frank Shorter, United States | 2h. 12m. 19.8s |
| 1976 | Waldemar Cierpinski, E. Germany | 2h. 09m. 55s |
| 1980 | Waldemar Cierpinski, E. Germany | 2h. 11m. 03s |
| 1984 | Carlos Lopes, Portugal | 2h. 09m. 21 s* |
| 1988 | Gelindo Bordin, Italy | 2h. 10m. 32s |
| 1992 | Hwang Young-Cho, S. Korea | 2h. 13m. 23s |

### 20-Kilometer Walk

| 1956 | Leonid Spirin, USSR | 1h. 31m. 27.4s |
|------|---------------------|----------------|
| 1960 | Vladimir Golubnichy, USSR | 1h. 33m. 7.2s |
| 1964 | Kenneth Mathews, Great Britain | 1h. 29m. 34.0s |
| 1968 | Vladimir Golubnichy, USSR | 1h. 33m. 58.4s |
| 1972 | Peter Frenkel, E. Germany | 1h. 26m. 42.4s |
| 1976 | Daniel Bautista, Mexico | 1h. 24m. 40.6s |
| 1980 | Maurizio Damilano, Italy | 1h. 23m. 35.5s |
| 1984 | Ernesto Canto, Mexico | 1h. 23m. 13.0s |
| 1988 | Josef Pribilinec, Czech. | 1h. 19m. 57.0s* |
| 1992 | Daniel Plaza Montero, Spain | 1h. 21m. 45.0s |

### 50-Kilometer Walk

| 1932 | Thomas W. Green, Great Britain | 4h. 50m. 10s |
|------|--------------------------------|--------------|
| 1936 | Harold Whitlock, Great Britain | 4h. 30m. 41.4s |
| 1948 | John Ljunggren, Sweden | 4h. 41m. 52s |
| 1952 | Giuseppe Dordoni, Italy | 4h. 28m. 07.8s |
| 1956 | Norman Read, New Zealand | 4h. 30m. 42.8s |
| 1960 | Donald Thompson, Great Britain | 4h. 25m. 30s |
| 1964 | Abdon Pamich, Italy | 4h. 11m. 12.4s |
| 1968 | Christoph Hohne, E. Germany | 4h. 11m. 12.4s |
| 1972 | Bern Kannenberg, W. Germany | 3h. 56m. 11.6s |
| 1980 | Hartwig Gauter, E. Germany | 3h. 49m. 24.0s |
| 1984 | Raul Gonzalez, Mexico | 3h. 47m. 26.0s |
| 1988 | Vayachselav Ivanenko, USSR | 3h. 38m. 29.0s* |
| 1992 | Andrei Perlov, Unified Team | 3h 50m. 13.0s |

### 110-Meter Hurdles

| 1896 | Thomas Curtis, United States | 17.6s |
|------|------------------------------|-------|
| 1900 | Alvin Kraenzlein, United States | 15.4s |
| 1904 | Frederick Schule, United States | 16s |
| 1908 | Forrest Smithson, United States | 15s |
| 1912 | Frederick Kelly, United States | 15.1s |
| 1920 | Earl Thomson, Canada | 14.8s |
| 1924 | Daniel Kinsey, United States | 15s |
| 1928 | Sydney Atkinson, South Africa | 14.8s |
| 1932 | George Saling, United States | 14.6s |
| 1936 | Forrest Towns, United States | 14.2s |
| 1948 | William Porter, United States | 13.9s |
| 1952 | Harrison Dillard, United States | 13.7s |
| 1956 | Lee Calhoun, United States | 13.5s |
| 1960 | Lee Calhoun, United States | 13.8s |
| 1964 | Hayes Jones, United States | 13.6s |
| 1968 | Willie Davenport, United States | 13.3s |
| 1972 | Rod Milburn, United States | 13.24s |
| 1976 | Guy Drut, France | 13.30s |
| 1980 | Thomas Munkelt, E. Germany | 13.39s |
| 1984 | Roger Kingdom, United States | 13.20s |
| 1988 | Roger Kingdom, United States | 12.98s* |
| 1992 | Mark McCoy, Canada | 13.12s |

### 400-Meter Hurdles

| 1900 | J.W.B. Tewksbury, United States | 57.6s |
|------|---------------------------------|-------|
| 1904 | Harry Hillman, United States | 53s |

| 1908 | Charles Bacon, United States | 55s |
|---|---|---|
| 1920 | Frank Loomis, United States | 54s |
| 1924 | F. Morgan Taylor, United States | 52.6s |
| 1928 | Lord Burghley, Great Britain | 53.4s |
| 1932 | Robert Tisdall, Ireland | 51.7s |
| 1936 | Glenn Hardin, United States | 52.4s |
| 1948 | Roy Cochran, United States | 51.1s |
| 1952 | Charles Moore, United States | 50.8s |
| 1956 | Glenn Davis, United States | 50.1s |
| 1960 | Glenn Davis, United States | 49.3s |
| 1964 | Rex Cawley, United States | 49.6s |
| 1968 | Dave Hemery, Great Britain | 48.12s |
| 1972 | John Akii-Bua, Uganda | 47.82s |
| 1976 | Edwin Moses, United States | 47.64s |
| 1980 | Volker Beck, E. Germany | 48.70s |
| 1984 | Edwin Moses, United States | 47.75s |
| 1988 | Andre Phillips, United States | 47.19s |
| 1992 | Kevin Young, United States | 46.78s* |

### High Jump

| 1896 | Ellery Clark, United States | 5ft. 11 1-4 in. |
|---|---|---|
| 1900 | Irving Baxter, United States | 6ft. 2 4-5 in. |
| 1904 | Samuel Jones, United States | 5ft. 11 in. |
| 1908 | Harry Porter, United States | 6ft. 3 in. |
| 1912 | Alma Richards, United States | 6ft. 4 in. |
| 1920 | Richmond Landon, United States | 6ft. 4 in. |
| 1924 | Harold Osborn, United States | 6ft. 6 in. |
| 1928 | Robert W. King, United States | 6ft. 4 1-2 in. |
| 1932 | Duncan McNaughton, Canada | 6ft. 5 5-8 in. |
| 1936 | Cornelius Johnson, United States | 6ft. 8 in. |
| 1948 | John L. Winter, Australia | 6ft. 6 in. |
| 1952 | Walter Davis, United States | 6ft. 8.32 in. |
| 1956 | Charles Dumas, United States | 6ft. 11 1-2 in. |
| 1960 | Robert Shavlakadze, USSR | 7ft. 1 in. |
| 1964 | Valery Brumel, USSR | 7ft. 1 3-4 in. |
| 1968 | Dick Fosbury, United States | 7ft. 4 1-4 in. |
| 1972 | Yuri Tarmak, USSR | 7ft. 3 3-4 in. |
| 1976 | Jacek Wszola, Poland | 7ft. 4 1-2 in. |
| 1980 | Gerd Wessig, E. Germany | 7ft. 8 3-4 in. |
| 1984 | Dietmar Mogenburg, W. Germany | 7ft. 8 1-2 in. |
| 1988 | Guennadi Avdeenko, USSR | 7ft. 9 1-2 in.* |
| 1992 | Javier Sotomayor, Cuba | 7ft. 8 in. |

### Long Jump

| 1896 | Ellery Clark, United States | 20ft. 10 in. |
|---|---|---|
| 1900 | Alvin Kraenzlein, United States | 23ft. 6 3-4 in. |
| 1904 | Myer Prinstein, United States | 24ft. 1 in. |
| 1908 | Frank Irons, United States | 24ft. 6 1-2 in. |
| 1912 | Albert Gutterson, United States | 24ft. 11 1-4 in. |
| 1920 | William Petterssen, Sweden | 23ft. 5 1-2 in. |
| 1924 | DeHart Hubbard, United States | 24ft. 5 in. |
| 1928 | Edward B. Hamm, United States | 25ft. 4 1-2 in. |
| 1932 | Edward Gordon, United States | 25ft. 3-4 in. |
| 1936 | Jesse Owens, United States | 26ft. 5 1-2 in. |
| 1948 | William Steele, United States | 25ft. 8 in. |
| 1952 | Jerome Biffle, United States | 24ft. 10 in. |
| 1956 | Gregory Bell, United States | 25ft. 8 1-4 in. |
| 1960 | Ralph Boston, United States | 26ft. 7 3-4 in. |
| 1964 | Lynn Davies, Great Britain | 26ft. 5 3-4 in. |
| 1968 | Bob Beamon, United States | 29ft. 2 1-2 in.* |
| 1972 | Randy Williams, United States | 27ft. 1-2 in. |
| 1976 | Arnie Robinson, United States | 27ft. 4 1-2 in. |
| 1980 | Lutz Dombrowski, E. Germany | 28ft. 1-4 in. |
| 1984 | Carl Lewis, United States | 28ft. 1-4 in. |
| 1988 | Carl Lewis, United States | 28ft. 7 1-4 in. |
| 1992 | Carl Lewis, United States | 28ft. 5 1-2 in. |

### 400-Meter Relay

| 1912 | Great Britain | 42.4s |
|---|---|---|
| 1920 | United States | 42.2s |
| 1924 | United States | 41s |
| 1928 | United States | 41s |
| 1932 | United States | 40s |
| 1936 | United States | 39.8s |
| 1948 | United States | 40.6s |
| 1952 | United States | 40.1s |
| 1956 | United States | 39.5s |
| 1960 | Germany (U.S. disqualified) | 39.5s |
| 1964 | United States | 39.0s |
| 1968 | United States | 38.2s |
| 1972 | United States | 38.19s |
| 1976 | United States | 38.33s |
| 1980 | USSR | 38.26s |
| 1984 | United States | 37.83s |
| 1988 | USSR (U.S. disqualified) | 38.19s |
| 1992 | United States | 37.40s* |

### 1,600-Meter Relay

| 1908 | United States | 3m. 29.4s |
|---|---|---|
| 1912 | United States | 3m. 16.6s |
| 1920 | Great Britain | 3m. 22.2s |
| 1924 | United States | 3m. 16s |
| 1928 | United States | 3m. 14.2s |
| 1932 | United States | 3m. 8.2s |
| 1936 | Great Britain | 3m. 9s |
| 1948 | United States | 3m. 10.4s |
| 1952 | Jamaica | 3m. 03.9s |
| 1956 | United States | 3m. 04.8s |
| 1960 | United States | 3m. 02.2s |
| 1964 | United States | 3m. 00.7s |
| 1968 | United States | 2m. 56.16s |
| 1972 | Kenya | 2m. 59.8s |
| 1976 | United States | 2m. 58.65s |
| 1980 | USSR | 3m. 01.1s |
| 1984 | United States | 2m. 57.91s |
| 1988 | United States | 2m. 56.16s |
| 1992 | United States | 2m. 55.74s* |

### Pole Vault

| 1896 | William Hoyt, United States | 10ft. 10 in. |
|---|---|---|
| 1900 | Irving Baxter, United States | 10ft. 10 in. |
| 1904 | Charles Dvorak, United States | 11ft. 5 3-4 in. |
| 1908 | A. C. Gilbert, United States | |
| | Edward Cook Jr., United States | 12ft. 2 in. |
| 1912 | Harry Babcock, United States | 12ft. 11 1-2 in. |
| 1920 | Frank Foss, United States | 13ft. 5 in. |
| 1924 | Lee Barnes, United States | 12ft. 11 1-2 in. |
| 1928 | Sabin W. Carr, United States | 13ft. 9 1-4 in. |
| 1932 | William Miller, United States | 14ft. 1 3-4 in. |
| 1936 | Earle Meadows, United States | 14ft. 3 1-4 in. |
| 1948 | Guinn Smith, United States | 14ft. 1 1-4 in. |
| 1952 | Robert Richards, United States | 14ft. 11 in. |
| 1956 | Robert Richards, United States | 14ft. 11 1-2 in. |
| 1960 | Don Bragg, United States | 15ft. 5 in. |
| 1964 | Fred Hansen, United States | 16ft. 8 3-4 in. |
| 1968 | Bob Seagren, United States | 17ft. 8 1-2 in. |
| 1972 | Wolfgang Nordwig, E. Germany | 18ft. 1-2 in. |
| 1976 | Tadeusz Slusarski, Poland | 18ft. 1-2 in. |
| 1980 | Wladyslaw Kozakiewicz, Poland | 18ft. 11 1-2 in. |
| 1984 | Pierre Quinon, France | 18ft. 10 1-4 in. |
| 1988 | Sergei Bubka, USSR | 19ft. 9 1-4 in.* |
| 1992 | Maksim Tarassov, Unified Team | 19ft. 1-4 in. |

### Hammer Throw

| 1900 | John Flanagan, United States | 163ft. 1 in. |
|---|---|---|
| 1904 | John Flanagan, United States | 168ft. 1 in. |
| 1908 | John Flanagan, United States | 170ft. 4 1-4 in. |
| 1912 | Matt McGrath, United States | 179ft. 7 1-8 in. |
| 1920 | Pat Ryan, United States | 173ft. 5 5-8 in. |
| 1924 | Fred Tootell, United States | 174ft. 10 1-8 in. |
| 1928 | Patrick O'Callaghan, Ireland | 168ft. 7 1-2 in. |
| 1932 | Patrick O'Callaghan, Ireland | 176ft. 11 1-8 in. |
| 1936 | Karl Hein, Germany | 185ft. 4 in. |
| 1948 | Imre Nemeth, Hungary | 183ft. 11 1-2 in. |
| 1952 | Jozsef Csermak, Hungary | 197ft. 11 9-16 in. |
| 1956 | Harold Connolly, United States | 207ft. 3 1-2 in. |
| 1960 | Vasily Rudenkov, USSR | 220ft. 1 5-8 in. |
| 1964 | Romuald Klim, USSR | 228ft. 9 1-2 in. |
| 1968 | Gyula Zsivotsky, Hungary | 240ft. 8 in. |
| 1972 | Anatoli Bondarchuk, USSR | 247ft. 8 in. |
| 1976 | Yuri Syedykh, USSR | 254ft. 4 in. |
| 1980 | Yuri Syedykh, USSR | 268ft. 4 1-2 in. |
| 1984 | Juha Tiainen, Finland | 256ft. 2 in. |
| 1988 | Sergei Litinov, USSR | 278ft. 2 1-2 in.* |
| 1992 | Andrey Abduvaliyev, Unified Team | 270ft. 9 1-2 in. |

### Discus Throw

| 1896 | Robert Garrett, United States | 95ft. 7 1-2 in. |
|---|---|---|
| 1900 | Rudolf Bauer, Hungary | 118ft. 3 in. |
| 1904 | Martin Sheridan, United States | 128ft. 10 1-2 in. |
| 1908 | Martin Sheridan, United States | 134ft. 2 in. |
| 1912 | Armas Taipale, Finland | 148ft. 3 in. |
| | Both hands—Armas Taipale, Finland | 271ft. 10 1-4 in. |
| 1920 | Elmer Niklander, Finland | 146ft. 7 in. |
| 1924 | Clarence Houser, United States | 151ft. 4 in. |
| 1928 | Clarence Houser, United States | 155ft. 3 in. |
| 1932 | John Anderson, United States | 162ft. 4 in. |
| 1936 | Ken Carpenter, United States | 165ft. 7 in. |
| 1948 | Adolfo Consolini, Italy | 173ft. 2 in. |
| 1952 | Sim Iness, United States | 180ft. 6.85 in. |
| 1956 | Al Oerter, United States | 184ft. 10 1-2 in. |
| 1960 | Al Oerter, United States | 194ft. 2 in. |
| 1964 | Al Oerter, United States | 200ft. 1 1-2 in. |

| | | |
|---|---|---|
| 1968 | Al Oerter, United States | 212ft. 6 1-2 in. |
| 1972 | Ludvik Danek, Czechoslovakia | 211ft. 3 in. |
| 1976 | Mac Wilkins, United States | 221ft. 5.4 in. |
| 1980 | Viktor Rashchupkin, USSR | 218ft. 8 in. |
| 1984 | Rolf Dannenberg, W. Germany | 218ft. 6 in. |
| 1988 | Jurgen Schult, E. Germany | 225ft. 9 1-4 in.* |
| 1992 | Romas Ubartas, Lithuania | 213ft. 7 3-4 in. |

### Triple Jump

| | | |
|---|---|---|
| 1896 | James Connolly, United States | 44ft. 11 3-4 in. |
| 1900 | Myer Prinstein, United States | 47ft. 5 3-4 in. |
| 1904 | Myer Prinstein, United States | 47 ft. |
| 1908 | Timothy Ahearne, Great Britain, Ireland | 48ft. 11 1-4 in. |
| 1912 | Gustaf Lindblom, Sweden | 48ft. 5 1-4 in. |
| 1920 | Vilho Tuulos, Finland | 47ft. 7 in. |
| 1924 | Anthony Winter, Australia | 50ft. 11 1-4 in. |
| 1928 | Mikio Oda, Japan | 49ft. 11 in. |
| 1932 | Chuhei Nambu, Japan | 51ft. 7 in. |
| 1936 | Naoto Tajima, Japan | 52ft. 6 in. |
| 1948 | Arne Ahman, Sweden | 50ft. 6 1-4 in. |
| 1952 | Adhemar da Silva, Brazil | 53ft. 2 3-4 in. |
| 1956 | Adhemar da Silva, Brazil | 53ft. 7 3-4 in. |
| 1960 | Jozef Schmidt, Poland | 55ft. 2 in. |
| 1964 | Jozef Schmidt, Poland | 55ft. 3 1-2 in. |
| 1968 | Viktor Saneev, USSR | 57ft. 3-4 in. |
| 1972 | Viktor Saneev, USSR | 56ft. 11 in. |
| 1976 | Viktor Saneev, USSR | 56ft. 8 3-4 in. |
| 1980 | Jaak Uudmae, USSR | 56ft. 11 1-4 in. |
| 1984 | Al Joyner, United States | 56ft. 7 1-2 in. |
| 1988 | Hristo Markov, Bulgaria | 57ft. 9 1-4 in. |
| 1992 | Mike Conley, United States | 59ft. 7 1-2 in.* |

### 16-lb. Shot Put

| | | |
|---|---|---|
| 1896 | Robert Garrett, United States | 36ft. 9 3-4 in. |
| 1900 | Richard Sheldon, United States | 46ft. 3 1-4 in. |
| 1904 | Ralph Rose, United States | 48ft. 7 in. |
| 1908 | Ralph Rose, United States | 46ft. 7 1-2 in. |
| 1912 | Pat McDonald, United States | 50ft. 4 in. |
| | Both hands—Ralph Rose, United States | 90ft. 5 1-2 in. |
| 1920 | Ville Porhola, Finland | 48ft. 7 1-4 in. |
| 1924 | Clarence Houser, United States | 49ft. 2 1-4 in. |
| 1928 | John Kuck, United States | 52ft. 3-4 in. |
| 1932 | Leo Sexton, United States | 52ft. 6 in. |
| 1936 | Hans Woellke, Germany | 53ft. 1 3-4 in. |
| 1948 | Wilbur Thompson, United States | 56ft. 2 in. |
| 1952 | Parry O'Brien, United States | 57ft. 1 1-2 in. |
| 1956 | Parry O'Brien, United States | 60ft. 11 1-4 in. |
| 1960 | William Nieder, United States | 64ft. 6 3-4 in. |
| 1964 | Dallas Long, United States | 66ft. 8 1-2 in. |
| 1968 | Randy Matson, United States | 67ft. 4 3-4 in. |
| 1972 | Wladyslaw Komar, Poland | 69ft. 6 in. |
| 1976 | Udo Beyer, E. Germany | 69ft. 3-4 in. |
| 1980 | Vladimir Kiselyov, USSR | 70ft. 1-2 in. |

| | | |
|---|---|---|
| 1984 | Alessandro Andrei, Italy | 69ft. 9 in. |
| 1988 | Ulf Timmermann, E. Germany | 73ft. 8 3-4 in.* |
| 1992 | Michael Stulce, United States | 71ft. 2 1-4 in. |

### Javelin

| | | |
|---|---|---|
| 1908 | Erik Lemming, Sweden | 178ft. 7 1-2 in. |
| | Held in middle—Erik Lemming, Sweden | 179ft. 10 1-2 in. |
| 1912 | Erik Lemming, Sweden | 198ft. 11 1-4 in. |
| | Both hands, Julius Saaristo, Finland | 358ft. 11 7-8 in. |
| 1920 | Jonni Myyra, Finland | 215ft. 9 3-4 in. |
| 1924 | Jonni Myyra, Finland | 206ft. 6 3-4 in. |
| 1928 | Eric Lundkvist, Sweden | 218ft. 6 1-8 in. |
| 1932 | Matti Jarvinen, Finland | 238ft. 6 in. |
| 1936 | Gerhard Stoeck, Germany | 235ft. 8 5-16 in. |
| 1948 | Tapio Rautavaara, Finland | 228ft. 10 1-2 in. |
| 1952 | Cy Young, United States | 242ft. 0.79 in. |
| 1956 | Egil Danielson, Norway | 281ft. 2 1-4 in. |
| 1960 | Viktor Tsibulenko, USSR | 277ft. 8 3-8 in. |
| 1964 | Pauli Nevala, Finland | 271ft. 2 1-2 in. |
| 1968 | Janis Lusis, USSR | 295ft. 7 1-4 in. |
| 1972 | Klaus Wolfermann, W. Germany | 296ft. 10 in. |
| 1976 | Miklos Nemeth, Hungary | 310ft. 4 in.* |
| 1980 | Dainis Kula, USSR | 299ft. 2 3-8 in. |
| 1984 | Arto Haerkoenen, Finland | 284ft. 8 in. |
| 1988 | Tapio Korjus, Finland | 276ft. 6 in. |
| 1992 | Jan Zelezny, Czech. | 294ft. 2 in. |

### Decathlon

| | | |
|---|---|---|
| 1912 | Hugo Wieslander, Sweden | 7,724.49 pts.(a) |
| 1920 | Helge Lovland, Norway | 6,804.35 pts. |
| 1924 | Harold Osborn, United States | 7,710.77 pts. |
| 1928 | Paavo Yrjola, Finland | 8,053.29 pts. |
| 1932 | James Bausch, United States | 8,462.23 pts. |
| 1936 | Glenn Morris, United States | 7,900 pts. |
| 1948 | Robert Mathias, United States | 7,139 pts. |
| 1952 | Robert Mathias, United States | 7,887 pts. |
| 1956 | Milton Campbell, United States | 7,937 pts. |
| 1960 | Rafer Johnson, United States | 8,392 pts. |
| 1964 | Willi Holdorf, Germany | 7,887 pts.(c) |
| 1968 | Bill Toomey, United States | 8,193 pts. |
| 1972 | Nikolai Avilov, USSR | 8,454 pts. |
| 1976 | Bruce Jenner, United States | 8,617 pts. |
| 1980 | Daley Thompson, Great Britain | 8,495 pts. |
| 1984 | Daley Thompson, Great Britain | 8,798 pts.*(b) |
| 1988 | Christian Schenk, E. Germany | 8,488 pts. |
| 1992 | Robert Zmelik, Czech. | 8,611 pts. |

(a) Jim Thorpe of the U.S. won the 1912 Decathlon with 8,413 pts. but was disqualified and had to return his medals because he had played professional baseball prior to the Olympic games. The medals were restored posthumously in 1982. (b) Scoring change effective Apr., 1985. (c) Former point systems used prior to 1964.

## Track and Field—Women

### 100-Meter Run

| | | |
|---|---|---|
| 1928 | Elizabeth Robinson, United States | 12.2s |
| 1932 | Stella Walsh, Poland | 11.9s |
| 1936 | Helen Stephens, United States | 11.5s |
| 1948 | Francina Blankers-Koen, Netherlands | 11.9s |
| 1952 | Marjorie Jackson, Australia | 11.5s |
| 1956 | Betty Cuthbert, Australia | 11.5s |
| 1960 | Wilma Rudolph, United States | 11.0s |
| 1964 | Wyomia Tyus, United States | 11.4s |
| 1968 | Wyomia Tyus, United States | 11.0s |
| 1972 | Renate Stecher, E. Germany | 11.07s |
| 1976 | Annegret Richter, W. Germany | 11.08s |
| 1980 | Lyudmila Kondratyeva, USSR | 11.6s |
| 1984 | Evelyn Ashford, United States | 10.97s |
| 1988 | Florence Griffith-Joyner, United States | 10.54s* |
| 1992 | Gail Devers, United States | 10.82s |

### 200-Meter Run

| | | |
|---|---|---|
| 1948 | Francina Blankers-Koen, Netherlands | 24.4s |
| 1952 | Marjorie Jackson, Australia | 23.7s |
| 1956 | Betty Cuthbert, Australia | 23.4s |
| 1960 | Wilma Rudolph, United States | 24.0s |
| 1964 | Edith McGuire, United States | 23.0s |
| 1968 | Irena Szewinska, Poland | 22.5s |
| 1972 | Renate Stecher, E. Germany | 22.40s |
| 1976 | Barbel Eckert, E. Germany | 22.37s |

| | | |
|---|---|---|
| 1980 | Barbel Wockel, E. Germany | 22.03s |
| 1984 | Valerie Brisco-Hooks, United States | 21.81s |
| 1988 | Florence Griffith-Joyner, United States | 21.34s* |
| 1992 | Gwen Torrence, United States | 21.81s |

### 400-Meter Run

| | | |
|---|---|---|
| 1964 | Betty Cuthbert, Australia | 52s |
| 1968 | Colette Besson, France | 52s |
| 1972 | Monika Zehrt, E. Germany | 51.08s |
| 1976 | Irena Szewinska, Poland | 49.29s |
| 1980 | Marita Koch, E. Germany | 48.88s |
| 1984 | Valerie Brisco-Hooks, United States | 48.83s |
| 1988 | Olga Bryzgina, USSR | 48.65s* |
| 1992 | Marie-Jose Perec, France | 48.83s |

### 800-Meter Run

| | | |
|---|---|---|
| 1928 | Lina Radke, Germany | 2m. 16.8s |
| 1960 | Ludmila Shevtsova, USSR | 2m. 4.3s |
| 1964 | Ann Packer, Great Britain | 2m. 1.1s |
| 1968 | Madeline Manning, United States | 2m. 0.9s |
| 1972 | Hildegard Falck, W. Germany | 1m. 58.6s |
| 1976 | Tatyana Kazankina, USSR | 1m. 54.94s |
| 1980 | Nadezhda Olizayrenko, USSR | 1m. 53.5s* |
| 1984 | Doina Melinte, Romania | 1m. 57.6s |
| 1988 | Sigrun Wodars, E. Germany | 1m. 56.10s |
| 1992 | Ellen Van Langen, Netherlands | 1m. 55.54s |

## 1,500-Meter Run

| 1972 | Lyudmila Bragina, USSR | 4m. 01.4s |
|------|------------------------|-----------|
| 1976 | Tatyana Kazankina, USSR | 4m. 05.48s |
| 1980 | Tatyana Kazankina, USSR | 3m. 56.6s |
| 1984 | Gabriella Dorio, Italy | 4m. 03.25s |
| 1988 | Paula Ivan, Romania | 3m. 53.96s* |
| 1992 | Hassiba Boulmerka, Algeria | 3m. 55.30s |

## 3,000-Meter Run

| 1984 | Maricica Puica, Romania | 8:35.96s |
|------|-------------------------|----------|
| 1988 | Tatyana Samolenko, USSR | 8:26.53s* |
| 1992 | Elena Romanova, Unified Team | 8:46.04s |

## 10,000-Meter Run

| 1988 | Olga Boldarenko, USSR | 31m. 44.69s |
|------|-----------------------|-------------|
| 1992 | Derartu Tulu, Ethiopia | 31m. 06.02s* |

## 400-Meter Relay

| 1928 | Canada | 48.4s |
|------|--------|-------|
| 1932 | United States | 46.9s |
| 1936 | United States | 46.9s |
| 1948 | Netherlands | 47.5s |
| 1952 | United States | 45.9s |
| 1956 | Australia | 44.5s |
| 1960 | United States | 44.5s |
| 1964 | Poland | 43.6s |
| 1968 | United States | 42.8s |
| 1972 | West Germany | 42.81s |
| 1976 | East Germany | 42.55s |
| 1980 | East Germany | 41.60s* |
| 1984 | United States | 41.65s |
| 1988 | United States | 41.98s |
| 1992 | United States | 42.11s |

## 1,600-Meter Relay

| 1972 | East Germany | 3m. 23s |
|------|--------------|---------|
| 1976 | East Germany | 3m. 19.23s |
| 1980 | USSR | 3m. 20.02s |
| 1984 | United States | 3m. 18.29s |
| 1988 | USSR | 3 m. 15.18s* |
| 1992 | Unified Team | 3m. 20.20s |

## 100-Meter Hurdles

| 1972 | Annelie Ehrhardt, E. Germany | 12.59s |
|------|------------------------------|--------|
| 1976 | Johanna Schaller, E. Germany | 12.77s |
| 1980 | Vera Komisova, USSR | 12.56s |
| 1984 | Benita Brown-Fitzgerald, United States | 12.84s |
| 1988 | Jordanka Donkova, Bulgaria | 12.38s* |
| 1992 | Paraskevi Patoulidou, Greece | 12.64s |

## 400-Meter Hurdles

| 1984 | Nawal el Moutawakii, Morocco | 54.61s |
|------|------------------------------|--------|
| 1988 | Debra Flintoff-King, Australia | 53.17s* |
| 1992 | Sally Gunnell, Great Britain | 53.23s |

## Heptathlon

| 1984 | Glynis Nunn, Australia | 6,390 pts. |
|------|------------------------|------------|
| 1988 | Jackie Joyner-Kersee, United States | 7,215 pts.* |
| 1992 | Jackie Joyner-Kersee, United States | 7,044 pts. |

## High Jump

| 1928 | Ethel Catherwood, Canada | 5ft. 2 1-2 in. |
|------|--------------------------|----------------|
| 1932 | Jean Shiley, United States | 5ft. 5 1-4 in. |
| 1936 | Ibolya Csak, Hungary | 5ft. 3 in. |
| 1948 | Alice Coachman, United States | 5ft. 6 1-8 in. |
| 1952 | Esther Brand, South Africa | 5ft. 5 3-4 in. |
| 1956 | Mildred L. McDaniel, United States | 5ft. 9 1-4 in. |

| 1960 | Iolanda Balas, Romania | 6ft. 3-4 in. |
|------|------------------------|--------------|
| 1964 | Iolanda Balas, Romania | 6ft. 2 3-4 in. |
| 1968 | Miloslava Reskova, Czechoslovakia | 5ft. 11 1-2 in. |
| 1972 | Ulrike Meyfarth, W. Germany | 6ft. 4 in. |
| 1976 | Rosemarie Ackermann, E. Germany | 6ft. 3 3-4 in. |
| 1980 | Sara Simeoni, Italy | 6ft. 5 1-2 in. |
| 1984 | Ulrike Meyfarth, W. Germany | 6ft. 7 1-2 in. |
| 1988 | Louise Ritter, United States | 6ft. 8 in.* |
| 1992 | Heike Henkel, Germany | 6ft. 7 1-2 in. |

## Discus Throw

| 1928 | Helena Konopacka, Poland | 129ft. 11 3-4 in. |
|------|--------------------------|-------------------|
| 1932 | Lillian Copeland, United States | 133ft. 2 in. |
| 1936 | Gisela Mauermayer, Germany | 156ft. 3 in. |
| 1948 | Micheline Ostermeyer, France | 137ft. 6 1-2 in. |
| 1952 | Nina Romaschkova, USSR | 168ft. 8 in. |
| 1956 | Olga Fikotova, Czechoslovakia | 176ft. 1 in. |
| 1960 | Nina Ponomareva, USSR | 180ft. 8 1-4 in. |
| 1964 | Tamara Press, USSR | 187ft. 10 in. |
| 1968 | Lia Manoliu, Romania | 191ft. 2 in. |
| 1972 | Faina Melnik, USSR | 218ft. 7 in. |
| 1976 | Evelin Schlaak, E. Germany | 226ft. 4 in. |
| 1980 | Evelin Jahl, E. Germany | 229ft. 6 in. |
| 1984 | Ria Stalman, Netherlands | 214ft. 5 in. |
| 1988 | Martina Hellmann, E. Germany | 237ft. 2 1-4 in.* |
| 1992 | Maritza Marten Garcia, Cuba | 222ft. 10 in. |

## Javelin Throw

| 1932 | "Babe" Didrikson, United States | 143ft. 4 in. |
|------|----------------------------------|--------------|
| 1936 | Tilly Fleischer, Germany | 148ft. 2 3-4 in. |
| 1948 | Herma Bauma, Austria | 149ft. 6 in. |
| 1952 | Dana Zatopkova, Czechoslovakia | 165ft. 7 in. |
| 1956 | Inese Jaunzeme, USSR | 176ft. 8 in. |
| 1960 | Elvira Ozolina, USSR | 183ft. 8 in. |
| 1964 | Mihaela Penes, Romania | 198ft. 7 1-2 in. |
| 1968 | Angela Nemeth, Hungary | 198ft. 1-2 in. |
| 1972 | Ruth Fuchs, E. Germany | 209ft. 7 in. |
| 1976 | Ruth Fuchs, E. Germany | 216ft. 4 in. |
| 1980 | Maria Colon, Cuba | 224ft. 5 in. |
| 1984 | Tessa Sanderson, Great Britain | 228ft. 2 in. |
| 1988 | Petra Felke, E. Germany | 245ft.* |
| 1992 | Silke Renke, Germany | 224ft. 2 1-2 in. |

## Shot Put (8lb., 13oz.)

| 1948 | Micheline Ostermeyer, France | 45ft. 1 1-2 in. |
|------|-------------------------------|-----------------|
| 1952 | Galina Zybina, USSR | 50ft. 1 3-4 in. |
| 1956 | Tamara Tishkyevich, USSR | 54ft. 5 in. |
| 1960 | Tamara Press, USSR | 56ft. 10 in. |
| 1964 | Tamara Press, USSR | 59ft. 6 1-4 in. |
| 1968 | Margitta Gummel, E. Germany | 64ft. 4 in. |
| 1972 | Nadezhda Chizova, USSR | 69ft. |
| 1976 | Ivanka Hristova, Bulgaria | 69ft. 5 1-4 in. |
| 1980 | Ilona Slupianek, E. Germany | 73ft. 6 1-4 in.* |
| 1984 | Claudia Losch, W. Germany | 67ft. 2 1-4 in. |
| 1988 | Natalya Lisovskaya, USSR | 72ft. 11 1-2 in. |
| 1992 | Svetlana Kriveleva, Unified Team | 69ft. 1 1-2in. |

## Long Jump

| 1948 | Olga Gyarmati, Hungary | 18ft. 8 1-4 in. |
|------|------------------------|-----------------|
| 1952 | Yvette Williams, New Zealand | 20ft. 5 3-4 in. |
| 1956 | Elzbieta Krzeskinska, Poland | 20ft. 9 3-4 in. |
| 1960 | Vyera Krepkina, USSR | 20ft. 10 3-4 in. |
| 1964 | Mary Rand, Great Britain | 22ft. 2 1-4 in. |
| 1968 | Viorica Viscopoleanu, Romania | 22ft. 4 1-2 in. |
| 1972 | Heidemarie Rosendahl, W. Germany | 22ft. 3 in. |
| 1976 | Angela Voigt, E. Germany | 22ft. 3-4 in. |
| 1980 | Tatyana Kolpakova, USSR | 23ft. 2 in. |
| 1984 | Anisoara Stanciu, Romania | 22ft. 10 in. |
| 1988 | Jackie Joyner-Kersee, United States | 24ft. 3 1-2 in. |
| 1992 | Helke Drechsler, Germany | 23ft. 5 1-4 in.* |

## Marathon

| 1984 | Joan Benoit, United States | 2h. 24m. 52s* |
|------|----------------------------|---------------|
| 1988 | Rosa Mota, Portugal | 2h. 25m. 40s |
| 1992 | Valentina Yegorova, Unified Team | 2h. 32m. 41s |

## Swimming and Diving—Men

### 50-Meter Freestyle

| | | |
|---|---|---|
| 1988 | Matt Biondi, U.S.. | 22.14 |
| 1992 | Alexandre Popov, Unified Team | 21.91* |

### 100-Meter Freestyle

| | | |
|---|---|---|
| 1896 | Alfred Hajos, Hungary | 1:22.2 |
| 1904 | Zoltan de Halmay, Hungary (100 yards) | 1:02.8 |
| 1908 | Charles Daniels, U.S.. | 1:05.6 |
| 1912 | Duke P. Kahanamoku, U.S.. | 1:03.4 |
| 1920 | Duke P. Kahanamoku, U.S.. | 1:01.4 |
| 1924 | John Weissmuller, U.S.. | 59.0 |
| 1928 | John Weissmuller, U.S.. | 58.6 |
| 1932 | Yasuji Miyazaki, Japan. | 58.2 |
| 1936 | Ferenc Csik, Hungary. | 57.6 |
| 1948 | Wally Ris, U.S.. | 57.3 |
| 1952 | Clark Scholes, U.S.. | 57.4 |
| 1956 | Jon Henricks, Australia. | 55.4 |
| 1960 | John Devitt, Australia. | 55.2 |
| 1964 | Don Schollander, U.S.. | 53.4 |
| 1968 | Mike Wenden, Australia | 52.2 |
| 1972 | Mark Spitz, U.S.. | 51.22 |
| 1976 | Jim Montgomery, U.S.. | 49.99 |
| 1980 | Jorg Woithe, E. Germany. | 50.40 |
| 1984 | Rowdy Gaines, U.S.. | 49.80 |
| 1988 | Matt Biondi, United States. | 48.63* |
| 1992 | Alexandre Popov, Unified Team | 49.02 |

### 200-Meter Freestyle

| | | |
|---|---|---|
| 1968 | Mike Wenden, Australia | 1:55.2 |
| 1972 | Mark Spitz, U.S.. | 1:52.78 |
| 1976 | Bruce Furniss, U.S.. | 1:50.29 |
| 1980 | Sergei Kopliakov, USSR | 1:49.81 |
| 1984 | Michael Gross, W. Germany | 1:47.44 |
| 1988 | Duncan Armstrong, Australia. | 1:47.25 |
| 1992 | Yevgeny Sadovyi, Unified Team | 1:46.70* |

### 400-Meter Freestyle

| | | |
|---|---|---|
| 1904 | C. M. Daniels, U.S. (440 yards) | 6:16.2 |
| 1908 | Henry Taylor, Great Britain. | 5:36.8 |
| 1912 | George Hodgson, Canada. | 5:24.4 |
| 1920 | Norman Ross, U.S.. | 5:26.8 |
| 1924 | John Weissmuller, U.S.. | 5:04.2 |
| 1928 | Albert Zorilla, Argentina. | 5:01.6 |
| 1932 | Clarence Crabbe, U.S.. | 4:48.4 |
| 1936 | Jack Medica, U.S.. | 4:44.5 |
| 1948 | William Smith, U.S.. | 4:41.0 |
| 1952 | Jean Boiteux, France. | 4:30.7 |
| 1956 | Murray Rose, Australia. | 4:27.3 |
| 1960 | Murray Rose, Australia. | 4:18.3 |
| 1964 | Don Schollander, U.S.. | 4:12.2 |
| 1968 | Mike Burton, U.S.. | 4:09.0 |
| 1972 | Brad Cooper, Australia | 4:00.27 |
| 1976 | Brian Goodell, U.S.. | 3:51.93 |
| 1980 | Vladimir Salnikov, USSR | 3:51.31 |
| 1984 | George DiCarlo, U.S.. | 3:51.23 |
| 1988 | Ewe Dassler, E. Germany | 3:46.95 |
| 1992 | Yevgeny Sadovyi, Unified Team | 3:45.00* |

### 1,500-Meter Freestyle

| | | |
|---|---|---|
| 1908 | Henry Taylor, Great Britain. | 22:48.4 |
| 1912 | George Hodgson, Canada. | 22:00.0 |
| 1920 | Norman Ross, U.S.. | 22:23.2 |
| 1924 | Andrew Charlton, Australia. | 20:06.6 |
| 1928 | Arne Borg, Sweden. | 19:51.8 |
| 1932 | Kusuo Kitamura, Japan. | 19:12.4 |
| 1936 | Noboru Terada, Japan. | 19:13.7 |
| 1948 | James McLane, U.S.. | 19:18.5 |
| 1952 | Ford Konno, U.S.. | 18:30.3 |
| 1956 | Murray Rose, Australia. | 17:58.9 |
| 1960 | Jon Konrads, Australia. | 17:19.6 |
| 1964 | Robert Windle, Australia. | 17:01.7 |
| 1968 | Mike Burton, U.S.. | 16:38.9 |
| 1972 | Mike Burton, U.S.. | 15:52.58 |
| 1976 | Brian Goodell, U.S.. | 15:02.40 |
| 1980 | Vladimir Salnikov, USSR | 14:58.27 |
| 1984 | Michael O'Brien, U.S.. | 15:05.20 |
| 1988 | Vladimir Salnikov, USSR | 15:00.40 |
| 1992 | Kieren Perkins, Australia. | 14:43.48* |

### 400-Meter Medley Relay

| | | |
|---|---|---|
| 1960 | United States. | 4:05.4 |
| 1964 | United States. | 3:58.4 |
| 1968 | United States. | 3:54.9 |
| 1972 | United States. | 3:48.16 |
| 1976 | United States. | 3:42.22 |
| 1980 | Australia | 3:45.70 |
| 1984 | United States. | 3:39.30 |
| 1988 | United States. | 3:36.93* |
| 1992 | United States. | 3:36.93* |

### 400-Meter Freestyle Relay

| | | |
|---|---|---|
| 1964 | United States. | 3:31.2 |
| 1968 | United States. | 3:31.7 |
| 1972 | United States. | 3:26.42 |
| 1984 | United States. | 3:19.03 |
| 1988 | United States. | 3:16.53* |
| 1992 | United States. | 3:16.74 |

### 800-Meter Freestyle Relay

| | | |
|---|---|---|
| 1908 | Great Britain. | 10:55.6 |
| 1912 | Australia | 10:11.6 |
| 1920 | United States. | 10:04.4 |
| 1924 | United States. | 9:53.4 |
| 1928 | United States. | 9:36.2 |
| 1932 | Japan. | 8:58.4 |
| 1936 | Japan. | 8:51.5 |
| 1948 | United States. | 8:46.0 |
| 1952 | United States. | 8:31.1 |
| 1956 | Australia. | 8:23.6 |
| 1960 | United States. | 8:10.2 |
| 1964 | United States. | 7:52.1 |
| 1968 | United States. | 7:52.33 |
| 1972 | United States. | 7:35.78 |
| 1976 | United States. | 7:23.22 |
| 1980 | USSR. | 7:23.50 |
| 1984 | United States. | 7:15.69 |
| 1988 | United States. | 7:12.51 |
| 1992 | Unified Team. | 7:11.95* |

### 100-Meter Backstroke

| | | |
|---|---|---|
| 1904 | Walter Brack, Germany (100 yds.) | 1:16.8 |
| 1908 | Arno Bieberstein, Germany | 1:24.6 |
| 1912 | Harry Hebner, U.S.. | 1:21.2 |
| 1920 | Warren Kealoha, U.S.. | 1:15.2 |
| 1924 | Warren Kealoha, U.S.. | 1:13.2 |
| 1928 | George Kojac, U.S.. | 1:08.2 |
| 1932 | Masaji Kiyokawa, Japan. | 1:08.6 |
| 1936 | Adolph Kiefer, U.S.. | 1:05.9 |
| 1948 | Allen Stack, U.S.. | 1:06.4 |
| 1952 | Yoshi Oyakawa, U.S.. | 1:05.4 |
| 1956 | David Thiele, Australia. | 1:02.2 |
| 1960 | David Thiele, Australia. | 1:01.9 |
| 1968 | Roland Matthes, E. Germany. | 58.7 |
| 1972 | Roland Matthes, E. Germany. | 56.58 |
| 1976 | John Naber, U.S.. | 55.49 |
| 1980 | Bengt Baron, Sweden. | 56.33 |
| 1984 | Rick Carey, U.S.. | 55.79 |
| 1988 | Daichi Suzuki, Japan. | 55.05 |
| 1992 | Mark Tewksbury, Canada. | 53.98* |

### 200-Meter Backstroke

| | | |
|---|---|---|
| 1964 | Jed Graef, U.S.. | 2:10.3 |
| 1968 | Roland Matthes, E. Germany. | 2:09.6 |
| 1972 | Roland Matthes, E. Germany. | 2:02.82 |
| 1976 | John Naber, U.S.. | 1:59.19 |
| 1980 | Sandor Wladar, Hungary. | 2:01.93 |
| 1984 | Rick Carey, U.S.. | 2:00.23 |
| 1988 | Igor Polianski, USSR | 1:59.37 |
| 1992 | Martin Lopez-Zubero, Spain. | 1:58.47* |

### 100-Meter Breaststroke

| | | |
|---|---|---|
| 1968 | Don McKenzie, U.S.. | 1:07.7 |
| 1972 | Nobutaka Taguchi, Japan. | 1:04.94 |
| 1976 | John Hencken, U.S.. | 1:03.11 |
| 1980 | Duncan Goodhew, Great Britain. | 1:03.44 |
| 1984 | Steve Lundquist, U.S.. | 1:01.65 |
| 1988 | Adrian Moorhouse, Great Britain. | 1:02.04 |
| 1992 | Nelson Diebel, U.S.. | 1:01.50* |

## 200-Meter Breaststroke

| 1908 | Frederick Holman, Great Britain | 3:09.2 |
|---|---|---|
| 1912 | Walter Bathe, Germany | 3:01.8 |
| 1920 | Haken Malmroth, Sweden | 3:04.4 |
| 1924 | Robert Skelton, U.S. | 2:56.6 |
| 1928 | Yoshiyuki Tsuruta, Japan | 2:48.8 |
| 1932 | Yoshiyuki Tsuruta, Japan | 2:45.4 |
| 1936 | Tetsuo Hamuro, Japan | 2:41.5 |
| 1948 | Joseph Verdeur, U.S. | 2:39.3 |
| 1952 | John Davies, Australia | 2:34.4 |
| 1956 | Masura Furukawa, Japan | 2:34.7 |
| 1960 | William Mulliken, U.S. | 2:37.4 |
| 1964 | Ian O'Brien, Australia | 2:27.8 |
| 1968 | Felipe Munoz, Mexico | 2:28.7 |
| 1972 | John Hencken, U.S. | 2:21.55 |
| 1976 | David Wilkie, Great Britain | 2:15.11 |
| 1980 | Robertas Zhulpa, USSR | 2:15.85 |
| 1984 | Victor Davis, Canada | 2:13.34 |
| 1988 | Jozsef Szabo, Hungary | 2:13.52 |
| 1992 | Mike Barrowman, U.S. | 2:10.16* |

## 100-Meter Butterfly

| 1968 | Doug Russell, U.S. | 55.9 |
|---|---|---|
| 1972 | Mark Spitz, U.S. | 54.27 |
| 1976 | Matt Vogel, U.S. | 54.35 |
| 1980 | Par Arvidsson, Sweden | 54.92 |
| 1984 | Michael Gross, W. Germany | 53.08 |
| 1988 | Anthony Nesty, Suriname | 53.00* |
| 1992 | Pablo Morales, U.S. | 53.32 |

## 200-Meter Butterfly

| 1956 | William Yorzyk, U.S. | 2:19.3 |
|---|---|---|
| 1960 | Michael Troy, U.S. | 2:12.8 |
| 1964 | Kevin J. Berry, Australia | 2:06.6 |
| 1968 | Carl Robie, U.S. | 2:08.7 |
| 1972 | Mark Spitz, U.S. | 2:00.70 |
| 1976 | Mike Bruner, U.S. | 1:59.23 |
| 1980 | Sergei Fesenko, USSR | 1:59.76 |
| 1984 | Jon Sieben, Australia | 1:57.04 |
| 1988 | Michael Gross, W. Germany | 1:56.94 |
| 1992 | Mel Stewart, U.S. | 1:56.26* |

## 200-Meter Individual Medley

| 1968 | Charles Hickcox, U.S. | 2:12.0 |
|---|---|---|
| 1972 | Gunnar Larsson, Sweden | 2:07.17 |
| 1984 | Alex Baumann, Canada | 2:01.42 |
| 1988 | Tamas Darnyi, Hungary | 2:00.17* |
| 1992 | Tamas Darnyi, Hungary | 2:00.76 |

## 400-Meter Individual Medley

| 1964 | Dick Roth, U.S. | 4:45.4 |
|---|---|---|
| 1968 | Charles Hickcox, U.S. | 4:48.4 |
| 1972 | Gunnar Larsson, Sweden | 4:31.98 |
| 1976 | Rod Strachan, U.S. | 4:23.68 |
| 1980 | Aleksandr Sidorenko, USSR | 4:22.89 |
| 1984 | Alex Baumann, Canada | 4:17.41 |
| 1988 | Tamas Darnyi, Hungary | 4:14.75 |
| 1992 | Tamas Darnyi, Hungary | 4:14.23* |

## Springboard Diving — Points

| 1908 | Albert Zurner, Germany | 85.5 |
|---|---|---|
| 1912 | Paul Guenther, Germany | 79.23 |
| 1920 | Louis Kuehn, U.S. | 675.40 |
| 1924 | Albert White, U.S. | 97.46 |
| 1928 | Pete Desjardins, U.S. | 185.04 |
| 1932 | Michael Galitzen, U.S. | 161.38 |
| 1936 | Richard Degener, U.S. | 163.57 |
| 1948 | Bruce Harlan, U.S. | 163.64 |
| 1952 | David Browning, U.S. | 205.29 |
| 1956 | Robert Clotworthy, U.S. | 159.56 |
| 1960 | Gary Tobian, U.S. | 170.00 |
| 1964 | Kenneth Sitzberger, U.S. | 159.90 |
| 1968 | Bernie Wrightson, U.S. | 170.15 |
| 1972 | Vladimir Vasin, USSR | 594.09 |
| 1976 | Phil Boggs, U.S. | 619.52 |
| 1980 | Aleksandr Portnov, USSR | 905.02 |
| 1984 | Greg Louganis, U.S. | 754.41 |
| 1988 | Greg Louganis, U.S. | 730.80 |
| 1992 | Mark Lenzi, U.S. | 676.530 |

## Platform Diving — Points

| 1904 | Dr. G.E. Sheldon, U.S. | 12.75 |
|---|---|---|
| 1908 | Hjalmar Johansson, Sweden | 83.75 |
| 1912 | Erik Adlerz, Sweden | 73.94 |
| 1920 | Clarence Pinkston, U.S. | 100.67 |
| 1924 | Albert White, U.S. | 97.46 |
| 1928 | Pete Desjardins, U.S. | 98.74 |
| 1932 | Harold Smith, U.S. | 124.80 |
| 1936 | Marshall Wayne, U.S. | 113.58 |
| 1948 | Sammy Lee, U.S. | 130.05 |
| 1952 | Sammy Lee, U.S. | 156.28 |
| 1956 | Joaquin Capilla, Mexico | 152.44 |
| 1960 | Robert Webster, U.S. | 165.56 |
| 1964 | Robert Webster, U.S. | 148.58 |
| 1968 | Klaus Dibiasi, Italy | 164.18 |
| 1972 | Klaus Dibiasi, Italy | 504.12 |
| 1976 | Klaus Dibiasi, Italy | 600.51 |
| 1980 | Falk Hoffmann, E. Germany | 835.65 |
| 1984 | Greg Louganis, U.S. | 710.91 |
| 1988 | Greg Louganis, U.S. | 638.61 |
| 1992 | Sun Shuwei, China | 677.310 |

# Swimming and Diving—Women

## 50-Meter Freestyle

| 1988 | Kristin Otto, E. Germany | 25.49 |
|---|---|---|
| 1992 | Yang Wenyi, China | 24.76* |

## 100-Meter Freestyle

| 1912 | Fanny Durack, Australia | 1:22.2 |
|---|---|---|
| 1920 | Ethelda Bleibtrey, U.S. | 1:13.6 |
| 1924 | Ethel Lackie, U.S. | 1:12.4 |
| 1928 | Albina Osipowich, U.S. | 1:11.0 |
| 1932 | Helene Madison, U.S. | 1:06.8 |
| 1936 | Hendrika Mastenbroek, Holland | 1:05.9 |
| 1948 | Greta Andersen, Denmark | 1:06.3 |
| 1952 | Katalin Szoke, Hungary | 1:06.8 |
| 1956 | Dawn Fraser, Australia | 1:02.0 |
| 1960 | Dawn Fraser, Australia | 1:01.2 |
| 1964 | Dawn Fraser, Australia | 59.5 |
| 1968 | Jan Henne, U.S. | 1:00.0 |
| 1972 | Sandra Neilson, U.S. | 58.59 |
| 1976 | Kornelia Ender, E. Germany | 55.65 |
| 1980 | Barbara Krause, E. Germany | 54.79 |
| 1984 | (tie) Carrie Steinseifer, U.S. | 55.92 |
|  | Nancy Hogshead, U.S. | 55.92 |
| 1988 | Kristin Otto, E. Germany | 54.93 |
| 1992 | Zhuang Yong, China | 54.64* |

## 200-Meter Freestyle

| 1968 | Debbie Meyer, U.S. | 2:10.5 |
|---|---|---|
| 1972 | Shane Gould, Australia | 2:03.56 |
| 1976 | Kornelia Ender, E. Germany | 1:59.26 |
| 1980 | Barbara Krause, E. Germany | 1:58.33 |
| 1984 | Mary Wayte, U.S. | 1:59.23 |
| 1988 | Heike Friedrich, E. Germany | 1:57.65* |
| 1992 | Nicole Haislett, U.S. | 1:57.90 |

## 400-Meter Freestyle

| 1924 | Martha Norelius, U.S. | 6:02.2 |
|---|---|---|
| 1928 | Martha Norelius, U.S. | 5:42.8 |
| 1932 | Helene Madison, U.S. | 5:28.5 |
| 1936 | Hendrika Mastenbroek, Netherlands | 5:26.4 |
| 1948 | Ann Curtis, U.S. | 5:17.8 |
| 1952 | Valerie Gyenge, Hungary | 5:12.1 |
| 1956 | Lorraine Crapp, Australia | 4:54.6 |
| 1960 | Susan Chris von Saltza, U.S. | 4:50.6 |
| 1964 | Virginia Duenkel, U.S. | 4:43.3 |
| 1968 | Debbie Meyer, U.S. | 4:31.8 |
| 1972 | Shane Gould, Australia | 4:19.44 |
| 1976 | Petra Thuemer E. Germany | 4:09.89 |
| 1980 | Ines Diers, E. Germany | 4:08.76 |
| 1984 | Tiffany Cohen, U.S. | 4:07.10 |
| 1988 | Janet Evans, U.S. | 4:03.85* |
| 1992 | Dagmar Hase, Germany | 4:07.18 |

## 800-Meter Freestyle

| | | |
|---|---|---|
| 1968 | Debbie Meyer, U.S. | 9:24.0 |
| 1972 | Keena Rothhammer, U.S. | 8:53.68 |
| 1976 | Petra Thuemer, E. Germany | 8:37.14 |
| 1980 | Michelle Ford, Australia | 8:28.90 |
| 1984 | Tiffany Cohen, U.S. | 8:24.95 |
| 1988 | Janet Evans, U.S. | 8:20.20* |
| 1992 | Janet Evans, U.S. | 8:25.52 |

## 100-Meter Backstroke

| | | |
|---|---|---|
| 1924 | Sybil Bauer, U.S. | 1:23.2 |
| 1928 | Marie Braun, Netherlands | 1:22.0 |
| 1932 | Eleanor Holm, U.S. | 1:19.4 |
| 1936 | Dina Senff, Netherlands | 1:18.9 |
| 1948 | Karen Harup, Denmark | 1:14.4 |
| 1952 | Joan Harrison, South Africa | 1:14.3 |
| 1956 | Judy Grinham, Great Britain | 1:12.9 |
| 1960 | Lynn Burke, U.S. | 1:09.3 |
| 1964 | Cathy Ferguson, U.S. | 1:07.7 |
| 1968 | Kaye Hall, U.S. | 1:06.2 |
| 1972 | Melissa Belote, U.S. | 1:05.78 |
| 1976 | Ulrike Richter, E. Germany | 1:01.83 |
| 1980 | Rica Reinisch, E. Germany | 1:00.86 |
| 1984 | Theresa Andrews, U.S. | 1:02.55 |
| 1988 | Kristin Otto, E. Germany | 1:00.89 |
| 1992 | Krisztina Egerszegi, Hungary | 1:00.68* |

## 200-Meter Backstroke

| | | |
|---|---|---|
| 1968 | Pokey Watson, U.S. | 2:24.8 |
| 1972 | Melissa Belote, U.S. | 2:19.19 |
| 1976 | Ulrike Richter, E. Germany | 2:13.43 |
| 1980 | Rica Reinisch, E. Germany | 2:11.77 |
| 1984 | Jolanda De Rover, Netherlands | 2:12.38 |
| 1988 | Krisztina Egerszegi, Hungary | 2:09.29 |
| 1992 | Krisztina Egerszegi, Hungary | 2:07.06* |

## 100-Meter Breaststroke

| | | |
|---|---|---|
| 1968 | Djurdjica Bjedov, Yugoslavia | 1:15.8 |
| 1972 | Cathy Carr, U.S. | 1:13.58 |
| 1976 | Hannelore Anke, E. Germany | 1:11:16 |
| 1980 | Ute Geweniger, E. Germany | 1:10.22 |
| 1984 | Petra Van Staveren, Netherlands | 1:09.88 |
| 1988 | Tania Dangalakova, Bulgaria | 1:07.95* |
| 1992 | Elena Roudkovskaia, Unified Team | 1:08.00 |

## 200-Meter Breaststroke

| | | |
|---|---|---|
| 1924 | Lucy Morton, Great Britain | 3:33.2 |
| 1928 | Hilde Schrader, Germany | 3:12.6 |
| 1932 | Clare Dennis, Australia | 3:06.3 |
| 1936 | Hideko Maehata, Japan | 3:03.6 |
| 1948 | Nelly Van Vliet, Netherlands | 2:57.2 |
| 1952 | Eva Szekely, Hungary | 2:51.7 |
| 1956 | Ursula Happe, Germany | 2:53.1 |
| 1960 | Anita Lonsbrough, Great Britain | 2:49.5 |
| 1964 | Galina Prozumenschikova, USSR | 2:46.4 |
| 1968 | Sharon Wichman, U.S. | 2:44.4 |
| 1972 | Beverly Whitfield, Australia | 2:41.71 |
| 1976 | Marina Koshevaia, USSR | 2:33.35 |
| 1980 | Lina Kachushite, USSR | 2:29.54 |
| 1984 | Anne Ottenbrite, Canada | 2:30.38 |
| 1988 | Silke Hoerner, E. Germany | 2:26.71 |
| 1992 | Kyoko Iwasaki, Japan | 2:26.65* |

## 200-Meter Individual Medley

| | | |
|---|---|---|
| 1968 | Claudia Kolb, U.S. | 2:24.7 |
| 1972 | Shane Gould, Australia | 2:23.07 |
| 1984 | Tracy Caulkins, U.S. | 2:12.64 |
| 1988 | Daniela Hunger, E. Germany | 2:12.59 |
| 1992 | Lin Li, China | 2:11.65* |

## 400-Meter Individual Medley

| | | |
|---|---|---|
| 1964 | Donna de Varona, U.S. | 5:18.7 |
| 1968 | Claudia Kolb, U.S. | 5:08.5 |
| 1972 | Gail Neall, Australia | 5:02.97 |
| 1976 | Ulrike Tauber, E. Germany | 4:42.77 |
| 1980 | Petra Schneider, E. Germany | 4:36.29* |
| 1984 | Tracy Caulkins, U.S. | 4:39.24 |

| | | |
|---|---|---|
| 1988 | Janet Evans, U.S. | 4:37.76 |
| 1992 | Krisztina Egerszegi, Hungary | 4:36.54 |

## 100-Meter Butterfly

| | | |
|---|---|---|
| 1956 | Shelley Mann, U.S. | 1:11.0 |
| 1960 | Carolyn Schuler, U.S. | 1:09.5 |
| 1964 | Sharon Stouder, U.S. | 1:04.7 |
| 1968 | Lynn McClements, Australia | 1:05.5 |
| 1972 | Mayumi Aoki, Japan | 1:03.34 |
| 1976 | Kornelia Ender, E. Germany | 1:00.13 |
| 1980 | Caren Metschuck, E. Germany | 1:00.42 |
| 1984 | Mary T. Meagher, U.S. | 59.26 |
| 1988 | Kristin Otto, E. Germany | 59.00 |
| 1992 | Qian Hong, China | 58.62* |

## 200-Meter Butterfly

| | | |
|---|---|---|
| 1968 | Ada Kok, Netherlands | 2:24.7 |
| 1972 | Karen Moe, U.S. | 2:15.57 |
| 1976 | Andrea Pollack, E. Germany | 2:11.41 |
| 1980 | Ines Geissler, E. Germany | 2:10.44 |
| 1984 | Mary T. Meagher, U.S. | 2:06.90* |
| 1988 | Kathleen Nord, E. Germany | 2:09.51 |
| 1992 | Summer Sanders, U.S. | 2:08.67 |

## 400-Meter Medley Relay

| | | |
|---|---|---|
| 1960 | United States | 4:41.1 |
| 1960 | United States | 4:33.9 |
| 1968 | United States | 4:28.3 |
| 1972 | United States | 4:20.75 |
| 1976 | East Germany | 4:07.95 |
| 1980 | East Germany | 4:06.67 |
| 1984 | United States | 4:08.34 |
| 1988 | E. Germany | 4:03.74 |
| 1992 | United States | 4:02.54* |

## 400-Meter Freestyle Relay

| | | |
|---|---|---|
| 1912 | Great Britain | 5:52.8 |
| 1920 | United States | 5:11.6 |
| 1924 | United States | 4:58.8 |
| 1928 | United States | 4:47.6 |
| 1932 | United States | 4:38.0 |
| 1936 | Netherlands | 4:36.0 |
| 1948 | United States | 4:29.2 |
| 1952 | Hungary | 4:24.4 |
| 1956 | Australia | 4:17.1 |
| 1960 | United States | 4:08.9 |
| 1964 | United States | 4:03.8 |
| 1968 | United States | 4:02.5 |
| 1972 | United States | 3:55.19 |
| 1976 | United States | 3:44.82 |
| 1980 | East Germany | 3:42.71 |
| 1984 | United States | 3:43.43 |
| 1988 | E. Germany | 3:40.63 |
| 1992 | United States | 3:39.46* |

## Springboard Diving — Points

| | | |
|---|---|---|
| 1920 | Aileen Riggin, U.S. | 539.90 |
| 1924 | Elizabeth Becker, U.S. | 474.50 |
| 1928 | Helen Meany, U.S. | 78.62 |
| 1932 | Georgia Coleman U.S. | 87.52 |
| 1936 | Marjorie Gestring, U.S. | 89.27 |
| 1948 | Victoria M. Draves, U.S. | 108.74 |
| 1952 | Patricia McCormick, U.S. | 147.30 |
| 1956 | Patricia McCormick, U.S. | 142.36 |
| 1960 | Ingrid Kramer, Germany | 155.81 |
| 1964 | Ingrid Engel-Kramer, Germany | 145.00 |
| 1968 | Sue Gossick, U.S. | 150.77 |
| 1972 | Micki King, U.S. | 450.03 |
| 1976 | Jenni Chandler, U.S. | 506.19 |
| 1980 | Irina Kalinina, USSR | 725.91 |
| 1984 | Sylvie Bernier, Canada | 530.70 |
| 1988 | Gao Min, China | 580.23 |
| 1992 | Gao Min, China | 572.400 |

## Platform Diving — Points

| | | |
|---|---|---|
| 1912 | Greta Johansson, Sweden | 39.90 |
| 1920 | Stefani Fryland-Clausen, Denmark | 34.60 |
| 1924 | Caroline Smith, U.S. | 33.20 |
| 1928 | Elizabeth B. Pinkston, U.S. | 31.60 |
| 1932 | Dorothy Poynton, U.S. | 40.26 |

| 1936 | Dorothy Poynton Hill, U.S. | 33.93 | 1972 | Ulrika Knape, Sweden | 390.00 |
|------|----------------------------|-------|------|----------------------------|--------|
| 1948 | Victoria M. Draves, U.S. | 68.87 | 1976 | Elena Vaytsekhouskaya, USSR | 406.59 |
| 1952 | Patricia McCormick, U.S. | 79.37 | 1980 | Martina Jaschke, E. Germany | 596.25 |
| 1956 | Patricia McCormick, U.S. | 84.85 | 1984 | Zhou Jihong, China | 435.51 |
| 1960 | Ingrid Kramer, Germany | 91.28 | 1988 | Xu Yanmei, China | 445.20 |
| 1964 | Lesley Bush, U.S. | 99.80 | 1992 | Fu Mingxia, China | 461.430 |
| 1968 | Milena Duchkova, Czech | 109.59 | | | |

# Boxing

## Light Flyweight (106 lbs)

| 1968 | Francisco Rodriguez, Venezuela |
|------|--------------------------------|
| 1972 | Gyorgy Gedo, Hungary |
| 1976 | Jorge Hernandez, Cuba |
| 1980 | Shamil Sabyrov, USSR |
| 1984 | Paul Gonzalez, U.S. |
| 1988 | Ivailo Hristov, Bulgaria |
| 1992 | Rogelio Marcelo, Cuba |

## Flyweight (112 lbs)

| 1904 | George Finnegan, U.S. |
|------|-----------------------|
| 1920 | William Di Gennara, U.S. |
| 1924 | Fidel LaBarba, U.S. |
| 1928 | Antal Kocsis, Hungary |
| 1932 | Istvan Enekes, Hungary |
| 1936 | Willi Kaiser, Germany |
| 1948 | Pascual Perez, Argentina |
| 1952 | Nathan Brooks, U.S. |
| 1956 | Terence Spinks, Great Britain |
| 1960 | Gyula Torok, Hungary |
| 1964 | Fernando Atzori, Italy |
| 1968 | Ricardo Delgado, Mexico |
| 1972 | Georgi Kostadinov, Bulgaria |
| 1976 | Leo Randolph, U.S. |
| 1980 | Peter Lessov, Bulgaria |
| 1984 | Steve McCrory, U.S. |
| 1988 | Kim Kwang Sun, S. Korea |
| 1992 | Su Choi Choi, N. Korea |

## Bantamweight (119 lbs)

| 1904 | Oliver Kirk, U.S. |
|------|-------------------|
| 1908 | A Henry Thomas, Great Britain |
| 1920 | Clarence Walker, South Africa |
| 1924 | William Smith, South Africa |
| 1928 | Vittorio Tamagnini, Italy |
| 1932 | Horace Gwynne, Canada |
| 1936 | Ulderico Sergo, Italy |
| 1948 | Tibor Csik, Hungary |
| 1952 | Pentti Hamalainen, Finland |
| 1956 | Wolfgang Behrendt, E. Germany |
| 1960 | Oleg Grigoryev, USSR |
| 1964 | Takao Sakurai, Japan |
| 1968 | Valery Sokolov, USSR |
| 1972 | Orlando Martinez, Cuba |
| 1976 | Yong-Jo Gu, N. Korea |
| 1980 | Juan Hernandez, Cuba |
| 1984 | Maurizio Stecca, Italy |
| 1988 | Kennedy McKinney, U.S. |
| 1992 | Joel Casamayor, Cuba |

## Featherweight (126 lbs)

| 1904 | Oliver Kirk, U.S. |
|------|-------------------|
| 1908 | Richard Gunn, Great Britain |
| 1920 | Paul Fritsch, France |
| 1924 | John Fields, U.S. |
| 1928 | Lambertus van Klaveren, Netherlands |
| 1932 | Carmelo Robledo, Argentina |
| 1936 | Oscar Casanovas, Argentina |
| 1948 | Ernesto Formenti, Italy |
| 1952 | Jan Zachara, Czech. |
| 1956 | Vladimir Safronov, USSR |
| 1960 | Francesco Musso, Italy |
| 1964 | Stanislav Stephashkin, USSR |
| 1968 | Antonin Roldan, Mexico |
| 1972 | Boris Kousnetsov, USSR |
| 1976 | Angel Herrera, Cuba |
| 1980 | Rudi Fink, E. Germany |
| 1984 | Meldrick Taylor, U.S. |
| 1988 | Giovanni Parisi, Italy |
| 1992 | Andreas Tews, Germany |

## Lightweight (132 lbs)

| 1904 | Harry Spanger, U.S. |
|------|---------------------|
| 1908 | Frederick Grace, Great Britain |
| 1920 | Samuel Mosberg, U.S. |
| 1924 | Hans Nielsen, Denmark |
| 1928 | Carlo Orlandi, Italy |
| 1932 | Lawrence Stevens, South Africa |
| 1936 | Imre Harangi, Hungary |
| 1948 | Gerald Dreyer, South Africa |
| 1952 | Aureliano Bolognesi, Italy |
| 1956 | Richard McTaggart, Great Britain |
| 1960 | Kazimierz Pazdzior, Poland |
| 1964 | Jozef Grudzien, Poland |
| 1968 | Ronald Harris, U.S. |
| 1972 | Jan Szczepanski, Poland |
| 1976 | Howard Davis, U.S. |
| 1980 | Angel Herrera, Cuba |
| 1984 | Pernell Whitaker, U.S. |
| 1988 | Andreas Zuelow, E. Germany |
| 1992 | Oscar De La Hoya, U.S. |

## Light Welterweight (140 lbs)

| 1952 | Charles Adkins, U.S. |
|------|----------------------|
| 1956 | Vladimir Yengibaryan, USSR |
| 1960 | Bohumil Nemecek, Czech. |
| 1964 | Jerzy Kulej, Poland |
| 1968 | Jerzy Kulej, Poland |
| 1972 | Ray Seales, U.S. |
| 1976 | Ray Leonard, U.S. |
| 1980 | Patrizio Oliva, Italy |
| 1984 | Jerry Page, U.S. |
| 1988 | Viatcheslav Janovski, USSR |
| 1992 | Hector Vinent, Cuba |

## Welterweight (147 lbs)

| 1904 | Albert Young, U.S. |
|------|--------------------|
| 1920 | Albert Schneider, Canada |
| 1924 | Jean Delarge, Belgium |
| 1928 | Edward Morgan, New Zealand |
| 1932 | Edward Flynn, U.S. |
| 1936 | Sten Suvio, Finland |
| 1948 | Julius Torma, Czech. |
| 1952 | Zygmunt Chychla, Poland |
| 1956 | Nicolae Linca, Romania |
| 1960 | Giovanni Benvenuti, Italy |
| 1964 | Marian Kasprzyk, Poland |
| 1968 | Manfred Wolke, E. Germany |
| 1972 | Emilio Correa, Cuba |
| 1976 | Jochen Bachfeld, E. Germany |
| 1980 | Andres Aldama, Cuba |
| 1984 | Mark Breland, U.S. |
| 1988 | Robert Wangila, Kenya |
| 1992 | Michael Carruth, Ireland |

## Light Middleweight (157 lbs)

| 1952 | Laszlo Papp, Hungary |
|------|----------------------|
| 1956 | Laszlo Papp, Hungary |
| 1960 | Wilbert McClure, U.S. |
| 1964 | Boris Lagutin, USSR |
| 1968 | Boris Lagutin, USSR |
| 1972 | Dieter Kottysch, W. Germany |
| 1976 | Jerzy Rybicki, Poland |
| 1980 | Armando Martinez, Cuba |
| 1984 | Frank Tate, U.S. |
| 1988 | Park Si Hun, S. Korea |
| 1992 | Juan Lemus, Cuba |

## Middleweight (165 lbs)

| 1904 | Charles Mayer, U.S. |
|------|---------------------|
| 1908 | John Douglas, Great Britain |
| 1920 | Harry Mallin, Great Britain |
| 1924 | Harry Mallin, Great Britain |
| 1928 | Piero Toscani, Italy |
| 1932 | Carmen Barth, U.S. |
| 1936 | Jean Despeaux, France |
| 1948 | Laszio Papp, Hungary |
| 1952 | Floyd Patterson, U.S. |
| 1956 | Gennady Schatkov, USSR |
| 1960 | Edward Crook, U.S. |
| 1964 | Valery Popenchenko, USSR |
| 1968 | Christopher Finnegan, Great Britain |
| 1972 | Vyacheslav Lemechev, USSR |
| 1976 | Michael Spinks, U.S. |
| 1980 | Jose Gomez, Cuba |
| 1984 | Joon-Sup Shin, S. Korea |
| 1988 | Henry Maske, E. Germany |
| 1992 | Ariel Hernandez, Cuba |

## Light Heavyweight (179 lbs)

| 1920 | Edward Eagan, U.S. |
|------|--------------------|
| 1924 | Harry Mitchell, Great Britain |
| 1928 | Victor Avendano, Argentina |
| 1932 | David Carstens, South Africa |
| 1936 | Roger Michelot, France |
| 1948 | George Hunter, South Africa |
| 1952 | Norvel Lee, U.S. |
| 1956 | James Boyd, U.S. |
| 1960 | Cassius Clay, U.S. |
| 1964 | Cosimo Pinto, Italy |
| 1968 | Dan Poznyak, USSR |
| 1972 | Mate Parlov, Yugoslavia |
| 1976 | Leon Spinks, U.S. |
| 1980 | Siobodan Kacar, Yugoslavia |
| 1984 | Anton Josipovic, Yugoslavia |
| 1988 | Andrew Maynard, U.S. |
| 1992 | Torsten May, Germany |

## Heavyweight (201 lbs)

| 1984 | Henry Tillman, U.S. |
|------|---------------------|
| 1988 | Ray Mercer, U.S. |
| 1992 | Felix Savon, Cuba |

## Super Heavyweight (Unlimited)
### (known as heavyweight from 1904-1980)

| 1904 | Samuel Berger, U.S. |
|------|---------------------|
| 1908 | Albert Oldham, Great Britain |
| 1920 | Ronald Rawson, Great Britain |
| 1924 | Otto von Porat, Norway |
| 1928 | Arturo Rodriguez Jurado, Argentina |
| 1932 | Santiago Lovell, Argentina |
| 1936 | Herbert Runge, Germany |
| 1948 | Rafael Inglesias, Argentina |
| 1952 | H. Edward Sanders, U.S. |
| 1956 | T. Peter Rademacher, U.S. |
| 1960 | Franco De Piccoli, Italy |
| 1964 | Joe Frazier, U.S. |
| 1968 | George Foreman, U.S. |
| 1972 | Teofilo Stevenson, Cuba |
| 1976 | Teofilo Stevenson, Cuba |
| 1980 | Teofilo Stevenson, Cuba |
| 1984 | Tyrell Biggs, U.S. |
| 1988 | Lennox Lewis, Canada |
| 1992 | Roberto Balado, Cuba |

# 25th Summer Olympics

Barcelona, Spain, July 25–Aug. 9, 1992

Over 14,000 athletes gathered in Barcelona, Spain in July and August for 16 days to compete in the Games of the XXV Olympiad. The athletes represented a record 172 nations, 11 more than had participated in any previous Olympics, and competed for medals in 257 events.

The 1992 games will be remembered mostly for the appearance of the Dream Team—the United States basketball team—featuring, for the first time, the stars of the National Basketball Association. As expected, the team crushed all its opponents on the way to a gold medal. Other notable events at the games were the victory in the long jump for Carl Lewis, his third consecutive gold medal in the event; the successful defense in the heptathlon by Jackie Joyner-Kersee; and the domination in men's gymnastics by Vitaly Shcherbo of the Unified Team. Perhaps the biggest surprise was the failure of world-record holder Sergei Bubka (Ukraine) to win a medal in the pole vault. Also notable was the appearance of South African athletes after missing 7 consecutive Olympiads.

The Unified Team made up of athletes of 12 republics of the former Soviet Union won the most gold medals, 45, and the most medals, 112. The United States finished second with 37 gold medals and 108 medals overall.

## Final Medal Standings

### Medals Standing

| | Gold | Silver | Bronze | Total | | Gold | Silver | Bronze | Total |
|---|---|---|---|---|---|---|---|---|---|
| Unified Team[1] | 45 | 38 | 29 | 112 | Ethiopia | 1 | 0 | 2 | 3 |
| United States | 37 | 34 | 37 | 108 | Latvia | 0 | 2 | 1 | 3 |
| Germany | 33 | 21 | 28 | 82 | Croatia | 0 | 1 | 2 | 3 |
| China | 16 | 22 | 16 | 54 | Belgium | 0 | 1 | 2 | 3 |
| Cuba | 14 | 6 | 11 | 31 | Iran | 0 | 1 | 2 | 3 |
| Hungary | 11 | 12 | 7 | 30 | I.O.P.[2] | 0 | 1 | 2 | 3 |
| South Korea | 12 | 5 | 12 | 29 | Greece | 2 | 0 | 0 | 2 |
| France | 8 | 5 | 16 | 29 | Ireland | 1 | 1 | 0 | 2 |
| Australia | 7 | 9 | 11 | 27 | Algeria | 1 | 0 | 1 | 2 |
| Spain | 13 | 7 | 2 | 22 | Estonia | 1 | 0 | 1 | 2 |
| Japan | 3 | 8 | 11 | 22 | Lithuania | 1 | 0 | 1 | 2 |
| Britain | 5 | 3 | 12 | 20 | Austria | 0 | 2 | 0 | 2 |
| Italy | 6 | 5 | 8 | 19 | Namibia | 0 | 2 | 0 | 2 |
| Poland | 3 | 6 | 10 | 19 | South Africa | 0 | 2 | 0 | 2 |
| Canada | 6 | 5 | 7 | 18 | Israel | 0 | 1 | 1 | 2 |
| Romania | 4 | 6 | 8 | 18 | Mongolia | 0 | 0 | 2 | 2 |
| Bulgaria | 3 | 7 | 6 | 16 | Slovenia | 0 | 0 | 2 | 2 |
| Netherlands | 2 | 6 | 7 | 15 | Switzerland | 1 | 0 | 0 | 1 |
| Sweden | 1 | 7 | 4 | 12 | Mexico | 0 | 1 | 0 | 1 |
| New Zealand | 1 | 4 | 5 | 10 | Peru | 0 | 1 | 0 | 1 |
| North Korea | 4 | 0 | 5 | 9 | Taiwan | 0 | 1 | 0 | 1 |
| Kenya | 2 | 4 | 2 | 8 | Argentina | 0 | 0 | 1 | 1 |
| Czechoslovakia | 4 | 2 | 1 | 7 | Bahamas | 0 | 0 | 1 | 1 |
| Norway | 2 | 4 | 1 | 7 | Colombia | 0 | 0 | 1 | 1 |
| Turkey | 2 | 2 | 2 | 6 | Ghana | 0 | 0 | 1 | 1 |
| Denmark | 1 | 1 | 4 | 6 | Malaysia | 0 | 0 | 1 | 1 |
| Indonesia | 2 | 2 | 1 | 5 | Pakistan | 0 | 0 | 1 | 1 |
| Finland | 1 | 2 | 2 | 5 | Philippines | 0 | 0 | 1 | 1 |
| Jamaica | 0 | 3 | 1 | 4 | Puerto Rico | 0 | 0 | 1 | 1 |
| Nigeria | 0 | 3 | 1 | 4 | Qatar | 0 | 0 | 1 | 1 |
| Brazil | 2 | 1 | 0 | 3 | Suriname | 0 | 0 | 1 | 1 |
| Morocco | 1 | 1 | 1 | 3 | Thailand | 0 | 0 | 1 | 1 |

(1) Athletes from 12 former Soviet republics. (2) Independent Olympic Participants (athletes from Serbia, Montenegro, Macedonia).

## Other Summer Olympics Gold Medalists in 1992

### Archery

**Men's 70-Meter Individual**—Sebastien Flute, France.
**Men's Team**—Spain.
**Women's 70-Meter Individual**—Cho Youn Jeong, S. Korea.
**Women's Team**—S. Korea.

### Badminton

**Men's Singles**—Alan Budi Kusuma, Indonesia.
**Men's Doubles**—Kim Moon Soo and Park Joo Bong, S. Korea.
**Women's Singles**—Susi Susanti, Indonesia.
**Women's Doubles**—Hwang Hye Young and Chung So-Young, S. Korea.

### Baseball

G-Cuba; S-Taiwan; B-Japan.

### Basketball

**Men**—G-U.S.; S-Croatia; B-Lithuania.
**Women**—G-Cuba; S-China; B-U.S.

### Canoe/Kayak

#### Men

**Single Kayak Slalom**—Pierpaolo Ferrazzi, Italy.
**Kayak 500M Singles**—Mikko Yrjoe Kolehmainen, Finland.
**Kayak 500M Doubles**—Germany.
**Kayak 1,000M Singles**—Clint Robinson, Australia.
**Kayak 1,000M Doubles**—Germany.
**Kayak 1,000M Fours**—Germany.
**Double Canoe Slalom**—U.S.
**Canoe Slalom**—Lukas Pollert, Czechoslovakia.
**Canoe 500M Singles**—Nikolai Boukhalov, Bulgaria.
**Canoe 500M Doubles**—Unified Team.
**Canoe 1,000M Singles**—Nikolai Boukhalov, Bulgaria.
**Canoe 1,000M Doubles**—Germany.

#### Women

**Kayak Slalom**—Elisabeth Micheler, Germany.
**Kayak 500M Singles**—Birgit Schmidt, Germany.
**Kayak 500M Doubles**—Germany.
**Kayak 500M Fours**—Hungary.

## Cycling

### Men

**Individual Road Race**—Fabio Casartelli, Italy.
**Sprint**—Jens Fiedler, Germany.
**Individual Points Race**—Giovanni Lombardi, Italy.
**4,000 Team Pursuit**—Germany.
**4K Individual Pursuit**—Chris Boardman, Great Britain.
**1 KM Time Trial**—Jose Moreno, Spain.
**Road Race**—Germany.

### Women

**Sprint**—Erika Salumae, Estonia.
**Individual Pursuit**—Petra Rossner, Germany.
**Individual Road Race**—Kathryn Watt, Australia.

## Diving

**Men's Platform**—Sun Shuwei, China.
**Men's Springboard**—Mark Lenzi, U.S.
**Women's Platform**—Fu Mingxia, China.
**Women's Springboard**—Gao Min, China.

## Equestrian

**Ind. Three-Day Event**—Matthew Ryan, Australia.
**Team Three-Day Event**—Australia.
**Individual Dressage**—Nicole Uphoff, Germany.
**Team Dressage**—Germany.
**Individual Jumping**—Ludger Beerbaum, Germany.
**Team Jumping**—Netherlands.

## Fencing

### Men

**Individual Foil**—Philippe Omnes, France.
**Team Foil**—Germany.
**Individual Saber**—Bence Szabo, Hungary.
**Team Saber**—Unified Team.
**Individual Épée**—Eric Srecki, France.
**Team Épée**—Germany.

### Women

**Individual Foil**—Giovanna Trillini, Italy.
**Team Foil**—Italy.

## Field Hockey

**Men**—G-Germany; S-Australia; B-Pakistan.
**Women**—G-Spain; S-Germany; B-Great Britain.

## Gymnastics

### Men

**Floor Exercise**—Li Xiaosahuang, China.
**Horizontal Bar**—Trent Dimas, U.S.
**Parallel Bars**—Vitaly Shcherbo, Unified Team.
**Pommel Horse**—(tie) Vitaly Shcherbo, Unified Team; Pae Gil Su, N. Korea.
**Rings**—Vitaly Shcherbo, Unified Team.
**Vault**—Vitaly Shcherbo, Unified Team.
**Individual All-Around**—Vitaly Shcherbo, Unified Team.
**Team**—Unified Team.

### Women

**Balance Beam**—Tatiana Lisenko, Unified Team.
**Floor Exercise**—Lavinia Corina Milosovici, Romania.
**Uneven Bars**—Lu Li, China.
**Vault**—(tie) Henrietta Onodi, Hungary; Lavinia Corina Milosovici, Romania.
**All - Around**—Tatiana Gutsu, Unified Team.
**Team Artistic**—Unified Team.

## Rhythmic Gymnastics

Alexandra Timoshenko, Unified Team.

## Judo

### Men

**132 Pounds**—Nazim Gousseinov, Unified Team.
**143 Pounds**—Rogerio Sampalo Cardoso, Brazil.
**157 Pounds**—Toshihiko Koga, Japan.
**172 Pounds**—Hidehiko Yoshida, Japan.

**198 Pounds**—Waldemar Legien, Poland.
**209 Pounds**—Antal Kovacs, Hungary.
**Heavyweight**—David Khakhaleichvili, Unified Team.

### Women

**106 Pounds**—Cecile Nowak, France.
**115 Pounds**—Almudena Munoz Martinez, Spain.
**123 Pounds**—Miriam Blasco Soto, Spain.
**134 Pounds**—Catherine Fleury, France.
**146 Pounds**—Odalis Reve Jimenez, Cuba.
**159 Pounds**—Kim Mi Jung, S. Korea.
**Over 159 Pounds**—Zhuang Xiaoyan, China.

## Modern Pentathlon

**Individual**—Arkadiusz Skrzypaszek, Poland.
**Team**—Poland.

## Rowing

### Men

**Single Sculls**—Thomas Lange, Germany.
**Double Sculls**—Australia.
**Coxless Pairs**—Great Britain.
**Coxed Pairs**—Great Britain.
**Coxed Fours**—Romania.
**Coxless Fours**—Australia.
**Quadruple Sculls**—Germany.
**Coxed Eights**—Canada.

### Women

**Single Sculls**—Elisabeta Lipa, Romania.
**Double Sculls**—Germany.
**Coxless Pairs**—Canada.
**Coxless Fours**—Canada.
**Quadruple Sculls**—Germany.
**Coxed Eights**—Canada.

## Shooting

### Men

**Running Game Target**—Michael Jakosits, Germany.
**Rapid Fire Pistol**—Ralf Schumann, Germany.
**Three-Position Rifle**—Gratchia Petikiane, Unified Team.
**Free Rifle**—Lee Eun Chul, S. Korea.
**Air Pistol**—Wang Yifu, China.
**Air Rifle**—Iouri Fedkine, Unified Team.
**Free Pistol**—Konstantine Loukachik, Unified Team.

### Women

**Air Pistol**—Marina Logvinenko, Unified Team.
**Three-Position Rifle**—Launi Meili, U.S.
**Sport Pistol**—Marina Logvinenko, Unified Team.
**Air Rifle**—Yeo Kab Soon, S. Korea.

### Mixed

**Trap**—Petr Hrdlicka, Czechoslovakia.
**Skeet**—Zhang Shan, China.

## Soccer

G-Spain; S-Poland; B-Ghana.

## Synchronized Swimming

**Solo**—Kristen Babb-Sprague, U.S.
**Duet**—Karen Josephson and Sarah Josephson, U.S.

## Table Tennis

**Men's Singles**—Jan Waldner, Sweden.
**Men's Doubles**—Lu Lin and Wang Tao, China.
**Women's Singles**—Deng Yaping, China.
**Women's Doubles**—Deng Yaping and Qiao Hong, China.

## Team Handball

**Men**—G-Unified Team; S-Sweden; B-France.
**Women**—G-S. Korea; S-Norway; B-Unified Team.

## Tennis

**Men's Singles**—Marc Rosset, Switzerland.
**Men's Doubles**—Boris Becker and Michael Stich, Germany.
**Women's Singles**—Jennifer Capriati, U.S.
**Women's Doubles**—Gigi Fernandez and Mary Joe Fernandez, U.S.

## Volleyball

**Men**—G-Brazil; S-Netherlands; B-U.S.
**Women**—G-Cuba; S-Unified Team; B-U.S.

## Water Polo

G-Italy; S-Spain; B-Unified Team.

## Weight Lifting

**115 Pounds**—Ivan Ivanov, Bulgaria.
**123 Pounds**—Chun Byung Kwan, S. Korea.
**132 Pounds**—Naim Suleymanoglu, Turkey.
**148 Pounds**—Israel Militossian, Unified Team.
**165 Pounds**—Fedor Kassapu, Unified Team.
**180 Pounds**—Pyrros Dimas, Greece.
**198 Pounds**—Kakhi Kakhiachvili, Unified Team.
**220 Pounds**—Victor Tregoubov, Unified Team.
**243 Pounds**—Ronny Weller, Germany.
**Over 243 Pounds**—Aleksandr Kourlovitch, Unified Team.

## Wrestling

### Freestyle

**106 Pounds**—Kim Il, N. Korea.
**115 Pounds**—Li Hak Son, S. Korea.
**126 Pounds**—Alejandro Puerto Diaz, Cuba.
**137 Pounds**—John Smith, U.S.
**150 Pounds**—Arsen Fadzaev, Unified Team.
**163 Pounds**—Park Jang Soon, S. Korea.
**182 Pounds**—Kevin Jackson, U.S.
**198 Pounds**—Makharbek Khadartsev, Unified Team.
**220 Pounds**—Leri Khabelov, Unified Team.
**286 Pounds**—Bruce Baumgartner, U.S.

### Greco-Roman

**106 Pounds**—Oleg Koutherenko, Unified Team.
**115 Pounds**—Jon Ronningen, Norway.
**126 Pounds**—An Han Bong, S. Korea.
**137 Pounds**—M. Akif Pirim, Turkey.
**150 Pounds**—Attila Repka, Hungary.
**163 Pounds**—Mnatsakan Iskandarian, Unified Team.
**181 Pounds**—Peter Farkas, Hungary.
**198 Pounds**—Maik Bullmann, Germany.
**220 Pounds**—Hector Milian Perez, Cuba.
**286 Pounds**—Aleksandr Karelin, Unified Team.

## Yachting

**Soling**—Denmark.
**Finn**—Jose Van Der Ploeg, Spain.
**Tornado**—France.
**Europe**—Linda Anderson, Norway.
**Flying Dutchman**—Spain.
**Star**—U.S.
**Men's Sailboard**—Franck David, France.
**Women's Sailboard**—Barbara Kendall, New Zealand.
**Men's 470**—Spain.
**Women's 470**—Spain.

# Olympic Information

**Symbol:** Five rings or circles, linked together to represent the sporting friendship of all peoples. The rings also symbolize 5 geographic areas—Europe, Asia, Africa, Australia, and America. Each ring is a different color—blue, yellow, black, green, and red.

**Flag:** The symbol of the 5 rings on a plain white background.

**Motto:** "Citius, Altius, Fortius." Latin meaning "faster, higher, braver," or the modern interpretation "swifter, higher, stronger." The motto was coined by Father Didon, a French educator, in 1895.

**Creed:** "The most important thing in the Olympic Games is not to win but to take part, just as the most important thing in life is not the triumph but the struggle. The essential thing is not to have conquered but to have fought well."

**Oath:** An athlete of the host country recites the following at the opening ceremony. "In the name of all competitors I promise that we will take part in these Olympic Games, respecting and abiding by the rules which govern them, in the true spirit of sportsmanship for the glory of sport and the honor of our teams." Both the oath and the creed were composed by Pierre de Coubertin, the founder of the modern Games.

**Flame:** Symbolizes the continuity between the ancient and modern Games. The modern version of the flame was adopted in 1936. The torch used to kindle the flame is first lit by the sun's rays at Olympia, Greece, and then carried to the site of the Games by relays of runners. Ships and planes are used when necessary.

# Winter Olympic Games Champions, 1924-1992

## Sites of Games

| | | |
|---|---|---|
| 1924 Chamonix, France | 1956 Cortina d'Ampezzo, Italy | 1980 Lake Placid, N.Y. |
| 1928 St. Moritz, Switzerland | 1960 Squaw Valley, Cal. | 1984 Sarajevo, Yugoslavia |
| 1932 Lake Placid, N.Y. | 1964 Innsbruck, Austria | 1988 Calgary, Alberta |
| 1936 Garmisch-Partenkirchen, Germany | 1968 Grenoble, France | 1992 Albertville, France |
| 1948 St. Moritz, Switzerland | 1972 Sapporo, Japan | 1994 Lillehammer, Norway |
| 1952 Oslo, Norway | 1976 Innsbruck, Austria | |

In 1992, the Unified Team represented the former Soviet republics of Russia, Ukraine, Belarus, Kazakhstan, and Uzbekistan.

## Bobsledding

### 4-Man Bob

| (Driver in parentheses) | Time |
|---|---|
| 1924 Switzerland (Eduard Scherrer) | 5:45.54 |
| 1928 United States (William Fiske) (5-man) | 3:20.50 |
| 1932 United States (William Fiske) | 7:53.68 |
| 1936 Switzerland (Pierre Musy) | 5:19.85 |
| 1948 United States (Francis Tyler) | 5:20.10 |
| 1952 Germany (Andreas Ostler) | 5:07.84 |
| 1956 Switzerland (Franz Kapus) | 5:10.44 |
| 1964 Canada (Victor Emery) | 4:14.46 |
| 1968 Italy (Eugenio Monti) (2 races) | 2:17.39 |
| 1972 Switzerland (Jean Wicki) | 4:43.07 |
| 1976 E. Germany (Meinhard Nehmer) | 3:40.43 |
| 1980 E. Germany (Meinhard Nehmer) | 3:59.92 |
| 1984 E. Germany (Wolfgang Hoppe) | 3:20.22 |

| | Time |
|---|---|
| 1988 Switzerland (Ekkehard Fasser) | 3:47.51 |
| 1992 Austria (Ingo Appelt) | 3:53.90 |

### 2-Man Bob

| | Time |
|---|---|
| 1932 United States (Hubert Stevens) | 8:14.74 |
| 1936 United States (Ivan Brown) | 5:29.29 |
| 1948 Switzerland (F. Endrich) | 5:29.20 |
| 1952 Germany (Andreas Ostler) | 5:24.54 |
| 1956 Italy (Dalla Costa) | 5:30.14 |
| 1964 Great Britain (Anthony Nash) | 4:21.90 |
| 1968 Italy (Eugenio Monti) | 4:41.54 |
| 1972 W. Germany (Wolfgang Zimmerer) | 4:57.07 |
| 1976 E. Germany (Meinhard Nehmer) | 3:44.42 |
| 1980 Switzerland (Erich Schaerer) | 4:09.36 |
| 1984 E.Germany (Wolfgang Hoppe) | 3:25.56 |
| 1988 USSR (Janis Kipours) | 3:54.19 |
| 1992 Switzerland (Gustav Weber) | 4:03.26 |

## Luge

### Men's Singles

| | | Time |
|---|---|---|
| 1964 | Thomas Keohler, Germany | 3:26.77 |
| 1968 | Manfred Schmid, Austria | 2:52.48 |
| 1972 | Wolfgang Scheidel, E. Germany | 3:27.58 |
| 1976 | Detlef Guenther, E. Germany | 3:27.688 |
| 1980 | Bernhard Glass, E. Germany | 2:54.796 |
| 1984 | Paul Hildgartner, Italy | 3:04.258 |
| 1988 | Jens Mueller, E. Germany | 3:05.548 |
| 1992 | Georg Hackl, Germany | 3:02.363 |

### Men's Pairs

| | | Time |
|---|---|---|
| 1964 | Austria | 1:41.62 |
| 1968 | E. Germany | 1:35.85 |
| 1972 | Italy, E. Germany (tie) | 1:28.35 |
| 1976 | E. Germany | 1:25.604 |
| 1980 | E. Germany | 1:19.331 |
| 1984 | W. Germany | 1:23.620 |
| 1988 | E. Germany | 1:31.940 |
| 1992 | Germany | 1:32.053 |

### Women's Singles

| | | Time |
|---|---|---|
| 1964 | Ortun Enderlein, Germany | 3:24.67 |
| 1968 | Erica Lechner, Italy | 2:28.66 |
| 1972 | Anna M. Muller, E. Germany | 2:59.18 |
| 1976 | Margit Schumann, E. Germany | 2:50.621 |
| 1980 | Vera Zozulya, USSR | 2:36.537 |
| 1984 | Steffi Martin, E. Germany | 2:46.570 |
| 1988 | Steffi Walter, E. Germany | 3:03.973 |
| 1992 | Doris Neuner, Austria | 3:06.696 |

## Biathlon

### Men's 10 Kilometers

| | | Time |
|---|---|---|
| 1980 | Frank Ullrich, E. Germany | 32:10.69 |
| 1984 | Eirik Kvalfoss, Norway | 30:53.80 |
| 1988 | Frank-Peter Roetsch, E. Germany | 25:08.10 |
| 1992 | Mark Kirchner, Germany | 26:02.30 |

### Men's 20 Kilometers

| | | Time |
|---|---|---|
| 1960 | Klas Lestander, Sweden | 1:33:21.6 |
| 1964 | Vladimir Melanin, USSR | 1:20:26.8 |
| 1968 | Magnar Solberg, Norway | 1:13:45.9 |
| 1972 | Magnar Solberg, Norway | 1:15:55.50 |
| 1976 | Nikolai Kruglov, USSR | 1:14:12.26 |
| 1980 | Anatoly Aljabiev, USSR | 1:08:16.31 |
| 1984 | Peter Angerer, W. Germany | 1:11:52.7 |
| 1988 | Frank-Peter Roetsch, E. Germany | 0:56:33.33 |
| 1992 | Yevgeny Redkine, Unified Team | 0:57:34.4 |

### Men's 30-Kilometer Relay

| | | Time |
|---|---|---|
| 1968 | USSR, Norway, Sweden | 2:13:02.4 |
| 1972 | USSR, Finland, E. Germany | 1:51:44.92 |
| 1976 | USSR, Finland, E. Germany | 1:57:55.64 |
| 1980 | USSR, E. Germany, W. Germany (30 km.) | 1:34:03.27 |
| 1984 | USSR, Norway, W. Germany | 1:38:51.70 |
| 1988 | USSR, W. Germany, Italy | 1:22:30.00 |
| 1992 | Germany, Unified Team, Sweden | 1:24:43.50 |

### Women's 7.5 Kilometers

| | | Time |
|---|---|---|
| 1992 | Anfissa Restsova, Unified Team | 24:29.20 |

### Women's 22.5 Kilometer Relay

| | | Time |
|---|---|---|
| 1992 | France, Germany, Unified Team | 1:15:55.6 |

### Women's 15 Kilometers

| | | Time |
|---|---|---|
| 1992 | Antje Misersky, Germany | 51:47.2 |

## Figure Skating

### Men's Singles

| | |
|---|---|
| 1908 | Ulrich Salchow, Sweden |
| 1920 | Gillis Grafstrom, Sweden |
| 1924 | Gillis Grafstrom, Sweden |
| 1928 | Gillis Grafstrom, Sweden |
| 1932 | Karl Schaefer, Austria |
| 1936 | Karl Schaefer, Austria |
| 1948 | Richard Button, U.S. |
| 1952 | Richard Button, U.S. |
| 1956 | Hayes Alan Jenkins, U.S. |
| 1960 | David W. Jenkins, U.S. |
| 1964 | Manfred Schnelldorfer, Germany |
| 1968 | Wolfgang Schwartz, Austria |
| 1972 | Ondrej Nepela, Czechoslovakia |
| 1976 | John Curry, Great Britain |
| 1980 | Robin Cousins, Great Britain |
| 1984 | Scott Hamilton, U.S. |
| 1988 | Brian Boitano, U.S. |
| 1992 | Viktor Petrenko, Unified Team |

### Women's Singles

| | |
|---|---|
| 1908 | Madge Syers, Great Britain |
| 1920 | Magda Julin-Mauroy, Sweden |
| 1924 | Herma von Szabo-Planck, Austria |
| 1928 | Sonja Henie, Norway |
| 1932 | Sonja Henie, Norway |
| 1936 | Sonja Henie, Norway |
| 1948 | Barbara Ann Scott, Canada |
| 1952 | Jeanette Altwegg, Great Britain |
| 1956 | Tenley Albright, U.S. |
| 1960 | Carol Heiss, U.S. |
| 1964 | Sjoukje Dijkstra, Netherlands |
| 1968 | Peggy Fleming, U.S. |
| 1972 | Beatrix Schuba, Austria |
| 1976 | Dorothy Hamill, U.S. |
| 1980 | Anett Poetzsch, E. Germany |
| 1984 | Katarina Witt, E. Germany |
| 1988 | Katarina Witt, E. Germany |
| 1992 | Kristi Yamaguchi, U.S. |

### Pairs

| | |
|---|---|
| 1908 | Anna Hubler & Heinrich Burger, Germany |
| 1920 | Ludovika & Walter Jakobsson, Finland |
| 1924 | Helene Engelman & Alfred Berger, Austria |
| 1928 | Andree Joly & Pierre Brunet, France |
| 1932 | Andree Joly & Pierre Brunet, France |
| 1936 | Maxi Herber & Ernst Baier, Germany |
| 1948 | Micheline Lannoy & Pierre Baugniet, Belgium |
| 1952 | Ria and Paul Falk, Germany |
| 1956 | Elisabeth Schwartz & Kurt Oppelt, Austria |
| 1960 | Barbara Wagner & Robert Paul, Canada |
| 1964 | Ludmila Beloussova & Oleg Protopopov, USSR |
| 1968 | Ludmila Beloussova & Oleg Protopopov, USSR |
| 1972 | Irina Rodnina & Alexei Ulanov, USSR |
| 1976 | Irina Rodnina & Aleksandr Zaitzev, USSR |
| 1980 | Irina Rodnina & Aleksandr Zaitzev, USSR |
| 1984 | Elena Valova & Oleg Vassiliev, USSR |
| 1988 | Ekaterina Gordeeva & Sergei Grinkov, USSR |
| 1992 | Natalia Mishkutienok & Artur Dimitriev, Unified Team |

### Ice Dancing

| | |
|---|---|
| 1976 | Ludmila Pakhomova & Aleksandr Gorschkov, USSR |
| 1980 | Natalya Linichuk & Gennadi Karponosov, USSR |
| 1984 | Jayne Torvill & Christopher Dean, Great Britain |
| 1988 | Natalia Bestemianova & Andrei Bukin, USSR |
| 1992 | Marina Klimova & Sergei Ponomarenko, Unified Team |

## Ice Hockey

| | |
|---|---|
| 1920 | Canada, U.S., Czechoslovakia |
| 1924 | Canada, U.S., Great Britain |
| 1928 | Canada, Sweden, Switzerland |
| 1932 | Canada, U.S., Germany |
| 1936 | Great Britain, Canada, U.S. |
| 1948 | Canada, Czechoslovakia, Switzerland |
| 1952 | Canada, U.S., Sweden |
| 1956 | USSR, U.S., Canada |
| 1960 | U.S., Canada, USSR |
| 1964 | USSR, Sweden, Czechoslovakia |
| 1968 | USSR, Czechoslovakia, Canada |
| 1972 | USSR, U.S., Czechoslovakia, |
| 1976 | USSR, Czechoslovakia, W. Germany |
| 1980 | U.S., USSR, Sweden |
| 1984 | USSR, Czechoslovakia, Sweden |
| 1988 | USSR, Finland, Sweden |
| 1992 | Unified Team, Canada, Czechlosovakia |

## Alpine Skiing

### Men's Downhill

| | | Time |
|---|---|---|
| 1948 | Henri Oreiller, France | 2:55.0 |
| 1952 | Zeno Colo, Italy | 2:30.8 |
| 1956 | Anton Sailer, Austria | 2:52.2 |
| 1960 | Jean Vuarnet, France | 2:06.0 |
| 1964 | Egon Zimmermann, Austria | 2:18.16 |
| 1968 | Jean-Claude Killy, France | 1:59.85 |
| 1972 | Bernhard Russi, Switzerland | 1:51.43 |
| 1976 | Franz Klammer, Austria | 1:45.73 |
| 1980 | Leonhard Stock, Austria | 1:45.50 |
| 1984 | Bill Johnson, U.S. | 1:45:59 |

| | | |
|---|---|---|
| 1988 | Pirmin Zurbriggen, Switzerland | 1:59.63 |
| 1992 | Patrick Ortlieb, Austria | 1:50.37 |

### Men's Super Giant Slalom — Time

| | | |
|---|---|---|
| 1988 | Franck Piccard, France | 1:39.66 |
| 1992 | Kjetil-Andre Aamodt, Norway | 1:13.04 |

### Men's Giant Slalom — Time

| | | |
|---|---|---|
| 1952 | Stein Eriksen, Norway | 2:25.0 |
| 1956 | Anton Sailer, Austria | 3:00.1 |
| 1960 | Roger Staub, Switzerland | 1:48.3 |
| 1964 | Francois Bonlieu, France | 1:46.71 |
| 1968 | Jean-Claude Killy, France | 3:29.28 |
| 1972 | Gustavo Thoeni, Italy | 3:09.62 |
| 1976 | Heini Hemmi, Switzerland | 3:26.97 |
| 1980 | Ingemar Stenmark, Sweden | 2:40.74 |
| 1984 | Max Julen, Switzerland | 2:41.18 |
| 1988 | Alberto Tomba, Italy | 2:06.37 |
| 1992 | Alberto Tomba, Italy | 2:06.98 |

### Men's Slalom — Time

| | | |
|---|---|---|
| 1948 | Edi Reinalter, Switzerland | 2:10.3 |
| 1952 | Othmar Schneider, Austria | 2:00.0 |
| 1956 | Anton Sailer, Austria | 194.7 pts. |
| 1960 | Ernst Hinterseer, Austria | 2:08.9 |
| 1964 | Josef Stiegler, Austria | 2:11.13 |
| 1968 | Jean-Claude Killy, France | 1:39.73 |
| 1972 | Francisco Fernandez Ochoa, Spain | 1:49.27 |
| 1976 | Piero Gros, Italy | 2:03.29 |
| 1980 | Ingemar Stenmark, Sweden | 1:44.26 |
| 1984 | Phil Mahre, U.S. | 1:39.41 |
| 1988 | Alberto Tomba, Italy | 1:39.47 |
| 1992 | Finn Christian Jagge, Norway | 1:44.39 |

### Men's Combined — Points

| | | |
|---|---|---|
| 1988 | Hubert Strolz, Austria | 36.55 |
| 1992 | Josef Polig, Italy | 14.58 |

### Women's Downhill — Time

| | | |
|---|---|---|
| 1948 | Hedi Schlunegger, Switzerland | 2:28.3 |
| 1952 | Trude Jochum-Beiser, Austria | 1:47.1 |
| 1956 | Madeleine Berthod, Switzerland | 1:40.7 |
| 1960 | Heidi Biebl, Germany | 1:37.6 |
| 1964 | Christl Haas, Austria | 1:55.39 |
| 1968 | Olga Pall, Austria | 1:40.87 |
| 1972 | Marie Therese Nadig, Switzerland | 1:36.68 |
| 1976 | Rosi Mittermaier, W. Germany | 1:46.16 |
| 1980 | Annemarie Proell Moser, Austria | 1:37.52 |
| 1984 | Michela Figini, Switzerland | 1:13.36 |
| 1988 | Marina Kiehl, W. Germany | 1:25.86 |
| 1992 | Kerrin Lee-Gartner, Canada | 1:52.55 |

### Women's Super Giant Slalom — Time

| | | |
|---|---|---|
| 1988 | Sigrid Wolf, Austria | 1:19.03 |
| 1992 | Deborah Compagnoni, Italy | 1:21.22 |

### Women's Giant Slalom — Time

| | | |
|---|---|---|
| 1952 | Andrea Mead Lawrence, U.S. | 2:06.8 |
| 1956 | Ossi Reichert, Germany | 1:56.5 |
| 1960 | Yvonne Ruegg, Switzerland | 1:39.9 |
| 1964 | Marielle Goitschel, France | 1:52.24 |
| 1968 | Nancy Greene, Canada | 1:51.97 |
| 1972 | Marie Therese Nadig, Switzerland | 1:29.90 |
| 1976 | Kathy Kreiner, Canada | 1:29.13 |
| 1980 | Hanni Wenzel, Liechtenstein (2 runs) | 2:41.66 |
| 1984 | Debbie Armstrong, U.S. | 2:20.98 |
| 1988 | Vreni Schneider, Switzerland | 2:06.49 |
| 1992 | Pernilla Wiberg, Sweden | 2:12.74 |

### Women's Slalom — Time

| | | |
|---|---|---|
| 1948 | Gretchen Fraser, U.S. | 1:57.2 |
| 1952 | Andrea Mead Lawrence, U.S. | 2:10.6 |
| 1956 | Renee Colliard, Switzerland | 112.3 pts. |
| 1960 | Anne Heggtveigt, Canada | 1:49.6 |
| 1964 | Christine Goitschel, France | 1:29.86 |
| 1968 | Marielle Goitschel, France | 1:25.86 |
| 1972 | Barbara Cochran, U.S. | 1:31.24 |
| 1976 | Rosi Mittermaier, W. Germany | 1:30.54 |
| 1980 | Hanni Wenzel, Liechtenstein | 1:25.09 |
| 1984 | Paoletta Magoni, Italy | 1:36.47 |
| 1988 | Vreni Schneider, Switzerland | 1:36.69 |
| 1992 | Petra Kronberger, Austria | 1:32.68 |

### Women's Combined — Points

| | | |
|---|---|---|
| 1988 | Anita Wachter, Austria | 29.25 |
| 1992 | Petra Kronberger, Austria | 2.55 |

## Freestyle Skiing

### Men's Moguls — Points

| | | |
|---|---|---|
| 1992 | Edgar Grospiron, France | 25.81 |

### Women's Moguls — Points

| | | |
|---|---|---|
| 1992 | Donna Weinbrecht, U.S. | 23.69 |

## Cross-Country Skiing

### Men's 10 kilometers (6.2 miles) — Time

| | | |
|---|---|---|
| 1992 | Vegard Ulvang, Norway | 27:36.0 |

### Men's 15 kilometers (9.3 miles) — Time

| | | |
|---|---|---|
| 1924 | Thorleif Haug, Norway | 1:14:31 |
| 1928 | Johan Grottumsbraaten, Norway | 1:37:01 |
| 1932 | Sven Utterstrom, Sweden | 1:23:07 |
| 1936 | Erik-August Larsson, Sweden | 1:14:38 |
| 1948 | Martin Lundstrom, Sweden | 1:13:50 |
| 1952 | Hallgeir Brenden, Norway | 1:01:34 |
| 1956 | Hallgeir Brenden, Norway | 49:39.0 |
| 1960 | Haakon Brusveen, Norway | 51:55.5 |
| 1964 | Eero Maentyranta, Finland | 50:54.1 |
| 1968 | Harald Groenningen, Norway | 47:54.2 |
| 1972 | Sven-Ake Lundback, Sweden | 45:28.24 |
| 1976 | Nikolai Balukov, USSR | 43:58.47 |
| 1980 | Thomas Wassberg, Sweden | 41:57.63 |
| 1984 | Gunde Svan, Sweden | 41:25.6 |
| 1988 | Mikhail Deviatiarov, USSR | 41:18.9 |
| 1992 | Bjorn Dahlie, Norway | 38:01.9 |

(Note: approx. 18-km. course 1924-1952)

### 30 kilometers (18.6 miles) — Time

| | | |
|---|---|---|
| 1956 | Veikko Hakulinen, Finland | 1:44:06.0 |
| 1960 | Sixten Jernberg, Sweden | 1:51:03.9 |
| 1964 | Eero Maentyranta, Finland | 1:30:50.7 |
| 1968 | Franco Nones, Italy | 1:35:39.2 |
| 1972 | Vyacheslav Vedenine, USSR | 1:36:31.15 |
| 1976 | Sergei Saveliev, USSR | 1:30:29.38 |
| 1980 | Nikolai Zimyatov, USSR | 1:27:02.80 |
| 1984 | Nikolai Zimyatov, USSR | 1:28:56.3 |
| 1988 | Aleksei Prokourorov, USSR | 1:24:26.3 |
| 1992 | Vegard Ulvang, Norway | 1:22:27.8 |

### 50 kilometers (31.2 miles) — Time

| | | |
|---|---|---|
| 1924 | Thorleif Haug, Norway | 3:44:32.0 |
| 1928 | Per Erik Hedlund, Sweden | 4:52:03.0 |
| 1932 | Veli Saarinen, Finland | 4:28:00.0 |
| 1936 | Elis Wiklund, Sweden | 3:30:11.0 |
| 1948 | Nils Karlsson, Sweden | 3:47:48.0 |
| 1952 | Veikko Hakulinen, Finland | 3:33:33.0 |
| 1956 | Sixten Jernberg, Sweden | 2:50:27.0 |
| 1960 | Kalevi Hamalainen, Finland | 2:59:06.3 |
| 1964 | Sixten Jernberg, Sweden | 2:43:52.6 |
| 1968 | Ole Ellefsaeter, Norway | 2:28:45.8 |
| 1972 | Paal Tyldum, Norway | 2:43:14.75 |
| 1976 | Ivar Formo, Norway | 2:37:30.05 |
| 1980 | Nikolai Zimyatov, USSR | 2:27:24.60 |
| 1984 | Thomas Wassberg, Sweden | 2:15:55.8 |
| 1988 | Gunde Svan, Sweden | 2:04:30.9 |
| 1992 | Bjorn Dahlie, Norway | 2:03:41.5 |

### 40-km. Relay — Time

| | | |
|---|---|---|
| 1936 | Finland, Norway, Sweden | 2:41:33.0 |
| 1948 | Sweden, Finland, Norway | 2:32:08.0 |
| 1952 | Finland, Norway, Sweden | 2:20:16.0 |
| 1956 | USSR, Finland, Sweden | 2:15:30.0 |
| 1960 | Finland, Norway, USSR | 2:18:45.6 |
| 1964 | Sweden, Finland, USSR | 2:18:34.6 |
| 1968 | Norway, Sweden, Finland | 2:08:33.5 |
| 1972 | USSR, Norway, Switzerland | 2:04:47.94 |
| 1976 | Finland, Norway, USSR | 2:07:59.72 |
| 1980 | USSR, Norway, Finland | 1:57:03.46 |
| 1984 | Sweden, USSR, Finland | 1:55:06.30 |
| 1988 | Sweden, USSR, Czechoslovakia | 1:43:58.60 |
| 1992 | Norway, Italy, Finland | 1:39:26.00 |

### Combined Cross-Country & Jumping — Points

| | | |
|---|---|---|
| 1924 | Thorleif Haug, Norway | 453.800 |
| 1928 | Johan Grottumsbraaten, Norway | 427.800 |
| 1932 | Johan Grottumsbraaten, Norway | 446.000 |
| 1936 | Oddbjorn Hagen, Norway | 430.300 |
| 1948 | Heikki Hasu, Finland | 448.800 |
| 1952 | Simon Slattvik, Norway | 451.621 |
| 1956 | Sverre Stenersen, Norway | 455.000 |
| 1960 | Georg Thoma, Germany | 457.952 |
| 1964 | Tormod Knutsen, Norway | 469.280 |

| 1968 | Franz Keller, W. Germany | 449.040 |
|---|---|---|
| 1972 | Ulrich Wehling, E. Germany | 413.340 |
| 1976 | Ulrich Wehling, E. Germany | 423.390 |
| 1980 | Ulrich Wehling, E. Germany | 432.200 |
| 1984 | Tom Sandberg, Norway | 422.595 |
| 1988 | Hippolyt Kempf, Switzerland | 235.8 |
| 1992 | Fabrice Guy, France | 426.470 |

### Men's Team Ski Jumping (90 meters)    Points

| 1988 | Finland, Yugoslavia, Norway | 634.4 |
|---|---|---|
| 1992 | Finland, Austria, Czechoslovakia | 644.4 |

### Ski Jumping (90 meters)    Points

| 1924 | Jacob Thams, Norway | 227.5 |
|---|---|---|
| 1928 | Alfred Andersen, Norway | 230.5 |
| 1932 | Birger Ruud, Norway | 228.1 |
| 1936 | Birger Ruud, Norway | 232.0 |
| 1948 | Petter Hugsted, Norway | 228.1 |
| 1952 | Arnfinn Bergmann, Norway | 226.0 |
| 1956 | Antti Hyvarinen, Finland | 227.0 |
| 1960 | Helmut Recknagel, Germany | 227.2 |
| 1964 | Toralf Engan, Norway | 230.7 |
| 1968 | Vladimir Beloussov, USSR | 231.3 |
| 1972 | Wojiech Fortuna, Poland | 219.9 |
| 1976 | Karl Schnabl, Austria | 234.8 |
| 1980 | Jouko Tormanen, Finland | 271.0 |
| 1984 | Matti Nykaenen, Finland | 231.2 |
| 1988 | Matti Nykaenen, Finland | 224.0 |
| 1992 | Ernst Vettori, Austria | 222.8 |

### Ski Jumping (120 meters)    Points

| 1992 | Toni Nicminen, Finland | 239.5 |
|---|---|---|

### Men's Nordic Team Combined    Time

| 1988 | W. Germany, Switzerland, Austria | 1:20:46.0 |
|---|---|---|
| 1992 | Japan, Norway, Austria | 1:23:36.5 |

### Women's Events
### 5 kilometers (approx. 3.1 miles)    Time

| 1964 | Claudia Boyarskikh, USSR | 17:50.5 |
|---|---|---|
| 1968 | Toini Gustafsson, Sweden | 16:45.2 |
| 1972 | Galina Koulacova, USSR | 17:00.50 |
| 1976 | Helena Takalo, Norway | 15:48.69 |
| 1980 | Raisa Smetanina, USSR | 15:06.92 |
| 1984 | Marja-Liisa Haemaelainen, Finland | 17:04.0 |
| 1988 | Marjo Matikainen, Finland | 15:04.0 |
| 1992 | Marjut Lukkarinen, Finland | 14:13.8 |

### 10 kilometers (6.2 miles)    Time

| 1952 | Lydia Wideman, Finland | 41:40.0 |
|---|---|---|
| 1956 | Lyubov Kosyreva, USSR | 38:11.0 |
| 1960 | Maria Gusakova, USSR | 39:46.6 |
| 1964 | Claudia Boyarskikh, USSR | 40:24.3 |
| 1968 | Toini Gustafsson, Sweden | 36:46.5 |
| 1972 | Galina Koulacova, USSR | 34:17.82 |
| 1976 | Raisa Smetanina, USSR | 30:13.41 |
| 1980 | Barbara Petzold, E. Germany | 30:31.54 |
| 1984 | Marja-Liisa Haemaelainen, Finland | 31:44.2 |
| 1988 | Vida Ventsene, USSR | 30:08.3 |
| 1992 | Lyubov Yegorova, Unified Team | 25:53.7 |

### 15 kilometers (9.3 miles)    Time

| 1992 | Lyubov Yegorova, Unified Team | 42:20.8 |
|---|---|---|

### 30 kilometers (18.6 miles)    Time

| 1992 | Stefania Belmondo, Italy | 1:22:30.1 |
|---|---|---|

### 20-km. Relay    Time

| 1956 | Finland, USSR, Sweden (15 km.) | 1:09:01.0 |
|---|---|---|
| 1960 | Sweden, USSR, Finland (15 km.) | 1:04:21.4 |
| 1964 | USSR, Sweden, Finland (15 km.) | 59:20.2 |
| 1968 | Norway, Sweden, USSR (15 km.) | 57:30.0 |
| 1972 | USSR, Finland, Norway (15 km.) | 48:46.15 |
| 1976 | USSR, Finland, E. Germany | 1:07:49.75 |
| 1980 | E. Germany, USSR, Norway | 1:02:11.10 |
| 1984 | Norway, Czechoslovakia, Finland | 1:06:49.70 |
| 1988 | USSR, Norway, Finland | 59:51.1 |
| 1992 | United Team, Norway, Italy | 59:34.8 |

## Speed Skating

### Men's 500 meters    Time

| 1924 | Charles Jewtraw, U.S. | 0:44.0 |
|---|---|---|
| 1928 | Thunberg, Finland & Evensen, Norway (tie) | 0:43.4 |
| 1932 | John A. Shea, U.S. | 0:43.4 |
| 1936 | Ivar Ballangrud, Norway | 0:43.4 |
| 1948 | Finn Helgesen, Norway | 0:43.1 |
| 1952 | Kenneth Henry, U.S. | 0:43.2 |

| 1956 | Evgeniy Grishin, USSR | 0:40.2 |
|---|---|---|
| 1960 | Evgeniy Grishin, USSR | 0:40.2 |
| 1964 | Terry McDermott, U.S. | 0:40.1 |
| 1968 | Erhard Keller, W. Germany | 0:40.3 |
| 1972 | Erhard Keller, W. Germany | 0:39.44 |
| 1976 | Evgeny Kulikov, USSR | 0:39.17 |
| 1980 | Eric Heiden, U.S. | 0:38.03 |
| 1984 | Sergei Fokichev, USSR | 0:38.19 |
| 1988 | Uwe-Jens Mey, E. Germany | 0:36.45 |
| 1992 | Uwe-Jens Mey, Germany | 0:37.14 |

### Men's 1,000 meters    Time

| 1976 | Peter Mueller, U.S. | 1:19.32 |
|---|---|---|
| 1980 | Eric Heiden, U.S. | 1:15.18 |
| 1984 | Gaetan Boucher, Canada | 1:15.80 |
| 1988 | Nikolai Guiliaev, USSR | 1:13.03 |
| 1992 | Olaf Zinke, Germany | 1:14.85 |

### Men's 1,500 meters    Time

| 1924 | Clas Thunberg, Finland | 2:20.8 |
|---|---|---|
| 1928 | Clas Thunberg, Finland | 2:21.1 |
| 1932 | John A. Shea, U.S. | 2:57.5 |
| 1936 | Charles Mathiesen, Norway | 2:19.2 |
| 1948 | Sverre Farstad, Norway | 2:17.6 |
| 1952 | Hjalmar Andersen, Norway | 2:20.4 |
| 1956 | Grishin, & Mikhailov, both USSR (tie) | 2:08.6 |
| 1960 | Aas, Norway & Grishin, USSR (tie) | 2:10.4 |
| 1964 | Ants Anston, USSR | 2:10.3 |
| 1968 | Cornelis Verkerk, Netherlands | 2:03.4 |
| 1972 | Ard Schenk, Netherlands | 2:02.96 |
| 1976 | Jan Egil Storholt, Norway | 1:59.38 |
| 1980 | Eric Heiden, U.S. | 1:55.44 |
| 1984 | Gaetan Boucher, Canada | 1:58.36 |
| 1988 | Andre Hoffmann, E. Germany | 1:52.06 |
| 1992 | Johann Koss, Norway | 1:54.81 |

### Men's 5,000 meters    Time

| 1924 | Clas Thunberg, Finland | 8:39.0 |
|---|---|---|
| 1928 | Ivar Ballangrud, Norway | 8:50.5 |
| 1932 | Irving Jaffee, U.S. | 9:40.8 |
| 1936 | Ivar Ballangrud, Norway | 8:19.6 |
| 1948 | Reidar Liaklev, Norway | 8:29.4 |
| 1952 | Hjalmar Andersen, Norway | 8:10.6 |
| 1956 | Boris Shilkov, USSR | 7:48.7 |
| 1960 | Viktor Kosichkin, USSR | 7:51.3 |
| 1964 | Knut Johannesen, Norway | 7:38.4 |
| 1968 | F. Anton Maier, Norway | 7:22.4 |
| 1972 | Ard Schenk, Netherlands | 7:23.61 |
| 1976 | Sten Stensen, Norway | 7:24.48 |
| 1980 | Eric Heiden, U.S. | 7:02.29 |
| 1984 | Sven Tomas Gustafson, Sweden | 7:12.28 |
| 1988 | Tomas Gustafson, Sweden | 6:44.63 |
| 1992 | Geir Karlstad, Norway | 6:59.97 |

### Men's 10,000 meters    Time

| 1924 | Julius Skutnabb, Finland | 18:04.8 |
|---|---|---|
| 1928 | Event not held, thawing of ice | |
| 1932 | Irving Jaffee, U.S. | 19:13.6 |
| 1936 | Ivar Ballangrud, Norway | 17:24.3 |
| 1948 | Ake Seyffarth, Sweden | 17:26.3 |
| 1952 | Hjalmar Andersen, Norway | 16:45.8 |
| 1956 | Sigvard Ericsson, Sweden | 16:35.9 |
| 1960 | Knut Johannesen, Norway | 15:46.6 |
| 1964 | Jonny Nilsson, Sweden | 15:50.1 |
| 1968 | Jonny Hoeglin, Sweden | 15:23.6 |
| 1972 | Ard Schenk, Netherlands | 15:01.35 |
| 1976 | Piet Kleine, Netherlands | 14:50.59 |
| 1980 | Eric Heiden, U.S. | 14:28.13 |
| 1984 | Igor Malkov, USSR | 14:39.90 |
| 1988 | Tomas Gustafson, Sweden | 13:48.20 |
| 1992 | Bart Veldkamp, Netherlands | 14:12.12 |

### Women's 500 meters    Time

| 1960 | Helga Haase, Germany | 0:45.9 |
|---|---|---|
| 1964 | Lydia Skoblikova, USSR | 0:45.0 |
| 1968 | Ludmila Titova, USSR | 0:46.1 |
| 1972 | Anne Henning, U.S. | 0:43.33 |
| 1976 | Sheila Young, U.S. | 0:42.76 |
| 1980 | Karin Enke, E. Germany | 0:41.78 |
| 1984 | Christa Rothenburger, E. Germany | 0:41.02 |
| 1988 | Bonnie Blair, U.S. | 0:39.10 |
| 1992 | Bonnie Blair, U.S. | 0:40.33 |

### Women's 1,000 meters    Time

| 1960 | Klara Guseva, USSR | 1:34.1 |
|---|---|---|
| 1964 | Lydia Skoblikova, USSR | 1:33.2 |
| 1968 | Carolina Geijssen, Netherlands | 1:32.6 |
| 1972 | Monika Pflug, W. Germany | 1:31.40 |
| 1976 | Tatiana Averina, USSR | 1:28.43 |

| 1980 | Natalya Petruseva, USSR | 1:24.10 |
|---|---|---|
| 1984 | Karin Enke, E. Germany | 1:21.61 |
| 1988 | Christa Rothenburger, E. Germany | 1:17.65 |
| 1992 | Bonnie Blair, U.S. | 1:21.90 |

| Women's 1,500 meters | | Time |
|---|---|---|
| 1960 | Lydia Skoblikova, USSR | 2:52.2 |
| 1964 | Lydia Skoblikova, USSR | 2:22.6 |
| 1968 | Kaija Mustonen, Finland | 2:22.4 |
| 1972 | Dianne Holum, U.S. | 2:20.85 |
| 1976 | Galina Stepanskaya, USSR | 2:16.58 |
| 1980 | Anne Borckink, Netherlands | 2:10.95 |
| 1984 | Karin Enke, E. Germany | 2:03.42 |
| 1988 | Yvonne van Gennip, Netherlands | 2:00.68 |
| 1992 | Jacqueline Boerner, Germany | 2:05.87 |

| Women's 3,000 meters | | Time |
|---|---|---|
| 1960 | Lydia Skoblikova, USSR | 5:14.3 |
| 1964 | Lydia Skoblikova, USSR | 5:14.9 |
| 1968 | Johanna Schut, Netherlands | 4:56.2 |
| 1972 | Christina Baas-Kaiser, Netherlands | 4:52.14 |
| 1976 | Tatiana Averina, USSR | 4:45.19 |
| 1980 | Bjoerg Eva Jensen, Norway | 4:32.13 |

| 1984 | Andrea Schoene, E. Germany | 4:24.79 |
|---|---|---|
| 1988 | Yvonne van Gennip, Netherlands | 4:11.94 |
| 1992 | Gunda Niemann, Germany | 4:19.90 |

| Women's 5,000 meters | | Time |
|---|---|---|
| 1988 | Yvonne van Gennip, Netherlands | 7:14:13 |
| 1992 | Gunda Niemann, Germany | 7:31.57 |

### Short Track Speed Skating

| Men's 1,000 meters | | Time |
|---|---|---|
| 1992 | Kim Ki-Hoon, S. Korea | 1:30.76 |

| Men's 5,000-meter relay | | Time |
|---|---|---|
| 1992 | S. Korea, Canada, Japan | 7:14.02 |

| Women's 500 meters | | Time |
|---|---|---|
| 1992 | Cathy Turner, U.S. | 47:04 |

| Women's 3,000-meter relay | | Time |
|---|---|---|
| 1992 | Canada, U.S., Unified Team | 4:36.62 |

## Winter Olympic Games in 1992

Albertville, France, Feb. 8-23, 1992

The 16th Olympics winter games in Albertville, France featured a record 2,174 athletes from 63 countries competing for medals. Germany, whose athletes won a games-high 26 medals, competed as a single team for the first time since 1964. The Unified Team, made up of some former Soviet republics, finished second with 23 medals.

### Medal Winners

| | Gold | Silver | Bronze | Total |
|---|---|---|---|---|
| Germany | 10 | 10 | 6 | 26 |
| Unified Team | 9 | 6 | 8 | 23 |
| Austria | 6 | 7 | 8 | 21 |
| Norway | 9 | 6 | 5 | 20 |
| Italy | 4 | 6 | 4 | 14 |
| United States | 5 | 4 | 2 | 11 |
| France | 3 | 5 | 1 | 9 |
| Canada | 2 | 3 | 2 | 7 |
| Finland | 3 | 1 | 3 | 7 |
| Japan | 1 | 2 | 4 | 7 |

| | Gold | Silver | Bronze | Total |
|---|---|---|---|---|
| Netherlands | 1 | 1 | 2 | 4 |
| South Korea | 2 | 1 | 1 | 4 |
| Sweden | 1 | 0 | 3 | 4 |
| China | 0 | 3 | 0 | 3 |
| Czechoslovakia | 0 | 0 | 3 | 3 |
| Switzerland | 1 | 0 | 2 | 3 |
| Luxembourg | 0 | 2 | 0 | 2 |
| New Zealand | 0 | 1 | 0 | 1 |
| North Korea | 0 | 0 | 1 | 1 |
| Spain | 0 | 0 | 1 | 1 |

## HOCKEY

### National Hockey League, 1992-1993

Final Standings

### Wales Conference

#### Adams Division

| | W | L | T | GF | GA | PTS |
|---|---|---|---|---|---|---|
| Boston | 51 | 26 | 7 | 332 | 268 | 109 |
| Quebec | 47 | 27 | 10 | 351 | 300 | 104 |
| Montreal | 48 | 30 | 6 | 326 | 280 | 102 |
| Buffalo | 38 | 36 | 10 | 335 | 297 | 86 |
| Hartford | 26 | 52 | 6 | 284 | 369 | 58 |
| Ottawa | 10 | 70 | 4 | 202 | 395 | 24 |

#### Patrick Division

| | W | L | T | GF | GA | PTS |
|---|---|---|---|---|---|---|
| Pittsburgh | 56 | 21 | 7 | 367 | 268 | 119 |
| Washington | 43 | 34 | 7 | 325 | 286 | 93 |
| N.Y. Islanders | 40 | 37 | 7 | 335 | 297 | 87 |
| New Jersey | 40 | 37 | 7 | 308 | 299 | 87 |
| Philadelphia | 36 | 37 | 11 | 319 | 319 | 83 |
| N.Y. Rangers | 34 | 39 | 11 | 304 | 308 | 79 |

### Campbell Conference

#### Norris Division

| | W | L | T | GF | GA | PTS |
|---|---|---|---|---|---|---|
| Chicago | 47 | 25 | 12 | 279 | 230 | 106 |
| Detroit | 47 | 28 | 9 | 369 | 280 | 103 |
| Toronto | 44 | 29 | 11 | 288 | 241 | 99 |
| St. Louis | 37 | 36 | 11 | 282 | 278 | 85 |
| Minnesota | 36 | 38 | 10 | 272 | 293 | 82 |
| Tampa Bay | 23 | 54 | 7 | 245 | 332 | 53 |

#### Smythe Division

| | W | L | T | GF | GA | PTS |
|---|---|---|---|---|---|---|
| Vancouver | 46 | 29 | 9 | 346 | 278 | 101 |
| Calgary | 43 | 30 | 11 | 322 | 282 | 97 |
| Los Angeles | 39 | 35 | 10 | 338 | 340 | 88 |
| Winnipeg | 40 | 37 | 7 | 322 | 320 | 87 |
| Edmonton | 26 | 50 | 8 | 242 | 337 | 60 |
| San Jose | 11 | 71 | 2 | 218 | 414 | 24 |

### Montreal Wins Stanley Cup Championship

The Montreal Canadiens won the 1993 Stanley Cup by defeating the Los Angeles Kings in five games. It was the 24th Stanley Cup championship for the Canadiens. Montreal goalie Patrick Roy won the Conn Smythe Trophy as the most valuable player in the playoffs.

# Stanley Cup Playoff Results

**Wales Conference**

Buffalo defeated Boston 4-0
Pittsburgh defeated New Jersey 4-1
N.Y. Islanders defeated Washington 4-2
Montreal defeated Quebec 4-2
Montreal defeated Buffalo 4-0
N.Y. Islanders defeated Pittsburgh 4-3
Montreal defeated N.Y. Islanders 4-1

**Campbell Conference**

St. Louis defeated Chicago 4-0
Vancouver defeated Winnipeg 4-2
Los Angeles defeated Calgary 4-2
Toronto defeated Detroit 4-3
Los Angeles defeated Vancouver 4-2
Toronto defeated St. Louis 4-3
Los Angeles defeated Toronto 4-3

## Finals

Montreal defeated Los Angeles 4-1

# Stanley Cup Champions Since 1927

| Year | Champion | Coach | Final opponent | Year | Champion | Coach | Final opponent |
|------|----------|-------|----------------|------|----------|-------|----------------|
| 1927 | Ottawa | Dave Gill | Boston | 1961 | Chicago | Rudy Pilous | Detroit |
| 1928 | N.Y. Rangers | Lester Patrick | Montreal | 1962 | Toronto | Punch Imlach | Chicago |
| 1929 | Boston | Cy Denneny | N.Y. Rangers | 1963 | Toronto | Punch Imlach | Detroit |
| 1930 | Montreal | Cecil Hart | Boston | 1964 | Toronto | Punch Imlach | Detroit |
| 1931 | Montreal | Cecil Hart | Chicago | 1965 | Montreal | Toe Blake | Chicago |
| 1932 | Toronto | Dick Irvin | N.Y. Rangers | 1966 | Montreal | Toe Blake | Detroit |
| 1933 | N.Y. Rangers | Lester Patrick | Toronto | 1967 | Toronto | Punch Imlach | Montreal |
| 1934 | Chicago | Tommy Gorman | Detroit | 1968 | Montreal | Toe Blake | St. Louis |
| 1935 | Montreal Maroons | Tommy Gorman | Toronto | 1969 | Montreal | Claude Ruel | St. Louis |
| 1936 | Detroit | Jack Adams | Toronto | 1970 | Boston | Harry Sinden | St. Louis |
| 1937 | Detroit | Jack Adams | N.Y. Rangers | 1971 | Montreal | Al MacNeil | Chicago |
| 1938 | Chicago | Bill Stewart | Toronto | 1972 | Boston | Tom Johnson | N.Y. Rangers |
| 1939 | Boston | Art Ross | Toronto | 1973 | Montreal | Scotty Bowman | Chicago |
| 1940 | N.Y. Rangers | Frank Boucher | Toronto | 1974 | Philadelphia | Fred Shero | Boston |
| 1941 | Boston | Cooney Weiland | Detroit | 1975 | Philadelphia | Fred Shero | Buffalo |
| 1942 | Toronto | Hap Day | Detroit | 1976 | Montreal | Scotty Bowman | Philadelphia |
| 1943 | Detroit | Jack Adams | Boston | 1977 | Montreal | Scotty Bowman | Boston |
| 1944 | Montreal | Dick Irvin | Chicago | 1978 | Montreal | Scotty Bowman | Boston |
| 1945 | Toronto | Hap Day | Detroit | 1979 | Montreal | Scotty Bowman | N.Y. Rangers |
| 1946 | Montreal | Dick Irvin | Boston | 1980 | N.Y. Islanders | Al Arbour | Philadelphia |
| 1947 | Toronto | Hap Day | Montreal | 1981 | N.Y. Islanders | Al Arbour | Minnesota |
| 1948 | Toronto | Hap Day | Detroit | 1982 | N.Y. Islanders | Al Arbour | Vancouver |
| 1949 | Toronto | Hap Day | Detroit | 1983 | N.Y. Islanders | Al Arbour | Edmonton |
| 1950 | Detroit | Tommy Ivan | N.Y. Rangers | 1984 | Edmonton | Glen Sather | N.Y. Islanders |
| 1951 | Toronto | Joe Primeau | Montreal | 1985 | Edmonton | Glen Sather | Philadelphia |
| 1952 | Detroit | Tommy Ivan | Montreal | 1986 | Montreal | Jean Perron | Calgary |
| 1953 | Montreal | Dick Irvin | Boston | 1987 | Edmonton | Glen Sather | Philadelphia |
| 1954 | Detroit | Tommy Ivan | Montreal | 1988 | Edmonton | Glen Sather | Boston |
| 1955 | Detroit | Jimmy Skinner | Montreal | 1989 | Calgary | Terry Crisp | Montreal |
| 1956 | Montreal | Toe Blake | Detroit | 1990 | Edmonton | John Muckler | Boston |
| 1957 | Montreal | Toe Blake | Boston | 1991 | Pittsburgh | Bob Johnson | Minnesota |
| 1958 | Montreal | Toe Blake | Boston | 1992 | Pittsburgh | Scotty Bowman | Chicago |
| 1959 | Montreal | Toe Blake | Toronto | 1993 | Montreal | Jacques Demers | Los Angeles |
| 1960 | Montreal | Toe Blake | Toronto | | | | |

# Individual Leaders

### Points

Mario Lemieux, Pittsburgh, 160; Pat Lafontaine, Buffalo, 148; Adam Oates, Boston, 142; Steve Yzerman, Detroit, 137; Teemu Selanne, Winnipeg, 132; Pierre Turgeon, N.Y. Islanders, 132.

### Goals

Alexander Mogilny, Buffalo, 76; Teemu Selanne, Winnipeg, 76; Mario Lemieux, Pittsburgh, 69; Luc Robitaille, Los Angeles, 63; Pavel Bure, Vancouver, 60.

### Assists

Adam Oates, Boston, 97; Doug Gilmour, Toronto, 95; Pat Lafontaine, Buffalo, 95; Mario Lemieux, Pittsburgh, 91; Craig Janney, St. Louis, 82.

### Power-play goals

Dave Andreychuk, Buff.-Tor., 32; Brett Hull, St. Louis, 29; Alexander Mogilny, Buffalo, 27; Kevin Stevens, Pittsburgh, 26.

### Shorthanded goals

Pavel Bure, Vancouver, 7; Steve Yzerman, Detroit, 7; Mario Lemieux, Pittsburgh, 6; Scott Young, Quebec, 6.

### Shooting percentage

(minimum 80 shots)

Craig Simpson, Edmonton, 26.4; Petr Nedved, Vancouver, 25.5; Dimitri Khristich, Washington, 24.4; Mario Lemieux, Pittsburgh, 24.1; Luc Robitaille, Los Angeles, 23.8.

### Plus/Minus

Mario Lemieux, Pittsburgh, 55; Larry Murphy, Pittsburgh, 45; Ray Bourque, Boston, 38; Ulf Samuelsson, Pittsburgh, 36; Lyle Odelein, Montreal, 35; Pavel Bure, Vancouver, 35.

## GOALTENDING LEADERS

(minimum 25 games)

### Goals against average

Felix Potvin, Toronto, 2.50; Ed Belfour, Chicago, 2.59; Tom Barrasso, Pittsburgh, 3.01; Curtis Joseph, St. Louis, 3.02; Kay Whitmore, Vancouver, 3.10.

### Wins

Tom Barrasso, Pittsburgh, 43; Ed Belfour, Chicago, 41; Andy Moog, Boston, 37; Tim Cheveldae, Detroit, 34; Bob Essensa, Winnipeg, 33.

### Save percentage

Curtis Joseph, St. Louis, .911; Felix Potvin, Toronto, .910; Ed Belfour, Chicago; .906; Tom Barrasso, Pittsburgh, .901; John Vanbiesbrouck, N.Y. Rangers, .900.

### Shutouts

Ed Belfour, Chicago, 7; Tommy Soderstrom, Philadelphia, 5; John Vanbiesbrouck, N.Y. Rangers, 4; Tom Barrasso, Pittsburgh, 4; Tim Cheveldae, Detroit, 4.

# Individual Scoring

(40 or more games played)

## Boston Bruins

| | GP | G | A | Pts | +/- | PIM |
|---|---|---|---|---|---|---|
| Adam Oates | 84 | 45 | 97 | 142 | 15 | 32 |
| Joe Juneau | 84 | 32 | 70 | 102 | 23 | 33 |
| Ray Bourque | 78 | 19 | 63 | 82 | 38 | 40 |
| Dmitri Kvartalnov | 73 | 30 | 42 | 72 | 9 | 16 |
| Stephen Leach | 79 | 26 | 25 | 51 | 6- | 126 |
| Dave Poulin | 84 | 16 | 33 | 49 | 29 | 62 |
| Vladimir Ruzicka | 60 | 19 | 22 | 41 | 6- | 38 |
| Dave Reid | 65 | 20 | 16 | 36 | 12 | 10 |
| Ted Donato | 82 | 15 | 20 | 35 | 2 | 61 |
| Don Sweeney | 84 | 7 | 27 | 34 | 34 | 68 |
| Glen Wesley | 64 | 8 | 25 | 33 | 2- | 47 |
| Stephen Heinze | 73 | 18 | 13 | 31 | 20 | 24 |
| David Shaw | 77 | 10 | 14 | 24 | 10 | 108 |
| Gord Murphy | 49 | 5 | 12 | 17 | 13- | 62 |
| Gordie Roberts | 65 | 5 | 12 | 17 | 23 | 105 |
| C.J. Young | 43 | 7 | 7 | 14 | 6- | 32 |
| Darin Kimble | 55 | 7 | 3 | 10 | 4 | 177 |
| Brent Hughes | 62 | 5 | 4 | 9 | 4- | 191 |
| Andy Moog | 55 | 0 | 1 | 1 | 0 | 14 |

Coach—Brian Sutter

## Buffalo Sabres

| | GP | G | A | Pts | +/- | PIM |
|---|---|---|---|---|---|---|
| Pat Lafontaine | 84 | 53 | 95 | 148 | 11 | 63 |
| Alexander Mogilny | 77 | 76 | 51 | 127 | 7 | 40 |
| Dale Hawerchuk | 81 | 16 | 80 | 96 | 17- | 52 |
| Doug Bodger | 81 | 9 | 45 | 54 | 14 | 87 |
| Bob Sweeney | 80 | 21 | 26 | 47 | 2 | 118 |
| Randy Wood | 82 | 18 | 25 | 43 | 6 | 77 |
| Yuri Khmylev | 68 | 20 | 19 | 39 | 6 | 28 |
| Wayne Presley | 79 | 15 | 17 | 32 | 5 | 96 |
| Richard Smehlik | 80 | 4 | 27 | 31 | 9 | 59 |
| Brad May | 82 | 13 | 13 | 26 | 3 | 242 |
| Petr Svoboda | 40 | 2 | 24 | 26 | 3 | 59 |
| Ken Sutton | 63 | 8 | 14 | 22 | 3- | 30 |
| Dave Hannan | 55 | 5 | 15 | 20 | 8 | 43 |
| Donald Audette | 44 | 12 | 7 | 19 | 8- | 51 |
| Bob Errey | 62 | 9 | 9 | 18 | 0 | 80 |
| Grant Ledyard | 50 | 2 | 14 | 16 | 2- | 45 |
| Gord Donnelly | 60 | 3 | 8 | 11 | 5 | 221 |
| Bob Corkum | 68 | 6 | 4 | 10 | 3- | 38 |
| Rob Ray | 68 | 3 | 2 | 5 | 3- | 211 |
| Grant Fuhr | 58 | 0 | 0 | 0 | 0 | 10 |

Coach—John Muckler

## Calgary Flames

| | GP | G | A | Pts | +/- | PIM |
|---|---|---|---|---|---|---|
| Theoren Fleury | 83 | 34 | 66 | 100 | 14 | 88 |
| Robert Reichel | 80 | 40 | 48 | 88 | 25 | 54 |
| Gary Suter | 81 | 23 | 58 | 81 | 1- | 112 |
| Gary Roberts | 58 | 38 | 41 | 79 | 32 | 172 |
| Joe Nieuwendyk | 79 | 38 | 37 | 75 | 9 | 52 |
| Sergei Makarov | 71 | 18 | 39 | 57 | 0 | 40 |
| Al Macinnis | 50 | 11 | 43 | 54 | 15 | 61 |
| Joel Otto | 75 | 19 | 33 | 52 | 2 | 150 |
| Paul Ranheim | 83 | 21 | 22 | 43 | 4- | 26 |
| Greg Paslawski | 73 | 18 | 24 | 42 | 3 | 12 |
| Ronnie Stern | 70 | 10 | 15 | 25 | 4 | 207 |
| Brent Ashton | 58 | 10 | 13 | 23 | 11 | 52 |
| Chris Lindberg | 62 | 9 | 12 | 21 | 3- | 18 |
| Roger Johansson | 77 | 4 | 16 | 20 | 13 | 62 |
| Trent Yawney | 63 | 1 | 16 | 17 | 9 | 67 |
| Frank Musil | 80 | 6 | 10 | 16 | 28 | 131 |
| Craig Berube | 77 | 4 | 8 | 12 | 6- | 209 |
| Kevin Dahl | 61 | 2 | 9 | 11 | 9 | 56 |
| Chris Dahlquist | 74 | 3 | 7 | 10 | 0 | 66 |
| Mike Vernon | 64 | 0 | 2 | 2 | 0 | 42 |

Coach—Dave King

## Chicago Blackhawks

| | GP | G | A | Pts | +/- | PIM |
|---|---|---|---|---|---|---|
| Jeremy Roenick | 84 | 50 | 57 | 107 | 15 | 86 |
| Chris Chelios | 84 | 15 | 58 | 73 | 14 | 282 |
| Steve Larmer | 84 | 35 | 35 | 70 | 23 | 48 |
| Steve Smith | 78 | 10 | 47 | 57 | 12 | 214 |
| Brent Sutter | 65 | 20 | 34 | 54 | 10 | 67 |
| Christian Ruuttu | 84 | 17 | 37 | 54 | 14 | 134 |
| Michel Goulet | 63 | 23 | 21 | 44 | 10 | 41 |
| Dirk Graham | 84 | 20 | 17 | 37 | 0 | 141 |
| Stephane Matteau | 79 | 15 | 18 | 33 | 6 | 98 |
| Greg Gilbert | 77 | 13 | 19 | 32 | 5 | 57 |
| Jocelyn Lemieux | 81 | 10 | 21 | 31 | 5 | 111 |
| Brian Noonan | 63 | 16 | 14 | 30 | 3 | 82 |
| Bryan Marchment | 78 | 5 | 15 | 20 | 15 | 313 |
| Frantisek Kucera | 71 | 5 | 14 | 19 | 7 | 59 |
| Dave Christian | 60 | 4 | 14 | 18 | 6 | 12 |
| Troy Murray | 51 | 4 | 7 | 11 | 15- | 59 |
| Craig Muni | 81 | 0 | 11 | 11 | 14- | 75 |
| Cam Russell | 67 | 2 | 4 | 6 | 5 | 151 |
| Ed Belfour | 71 | 0 | 3 | 3 | 0 | 28 |
| Stu Grimson | 78 | 1 | 1 | 2 | 2 | 193 |

Coach—Darryl Sutter

## Detroit Red Wings

| | GP | G | A | Pts | +/- | PIM |
|---|---|---|---|---|---|---|
| Steve Yzerman | 84 | 58 | 79 | 137 | 33 | 44 |
| Dino Ciccarelli | 82 | 41 | 56 | 97 | 12 | 81 |
| Sergei Fedorov | 73 | 34 | 53 | 87 | 33 | 72 |
| Paul Coffey | 80 | 12 | 75 | 87 | 16 | 77 |
| Ray Sheppard | 70 | 32 | 34 | 66 | 7 | 29 |
| Paul Ysebaert | 80 | 34 | 28 | 62 | 19 | 42 |
| Steve Chiasson | 79 | 12 | 50 | 62 | 14 | 155 |
| Dallas Drake | 72 | 18 | 26 | 44 | 15 | 93 |
| Bob Probert | 80 | 14 | 29 | 43 | 9- | 292 |
| Nicklas Lidstrom | 84 | 7 | 34 | 41 | 7 | 28 |
| Yves Racine | 80 | 9 | 31 | 40 | 10 | 80 |
| Shawn Burr | 80 | 10 | 25 | 35 | 18 | 74 |
| Mark Howe | 60 | 3 | 31 | 34 | 22 | 22 |
| Keith Primeau | 73 | 15 | 17 | 32 | 6- | 152 |
| Sheldon Kennedy | 68 | 19 | 11 | 30 | 1- | 46 |
| Gerard Gallant | 67 | 10 | 20 | 30 | 20 | 188 |
| Vlad. Konstantinov | 82 | 5 | 17 | 22 | 22 | 137 |
| Mike Sillinger | 51 | 4 | 17 | 21 | 0 | 16 |
| Jim Hiller | 61 | 8 | 12 | 20 | 7 | 109 |
| Steve Konroyd | 65 | 3 | 12 | 15 | 15- | 67 |
| Brad McCrimmon | 60 | 1 | 14 | 15 | 21 | 71 |
| Tim Cheveldae | 67 | 0 | 4 | 4 | 0 | 4 |

Coach—Bryan Murray

## Edmonton Oilers

| | GP | G | A | Pts | +/- | PIM |
|---|---|---|---|---|---|---|
| Petr Klima | 68 | 32 | 16 | 48 | 15- | 100 |
| Doug Weight | 78 | 17 | 31 | 48 | 2 | 65 |
| Shayne Corson | 80 | 16 | 31 | 47 | 19- | 209 |
| Craig Simpson | 60 | 24 | 22 | 46 | 14- | 36 |
| Dave Manson | 83 | 15 | 30 | 45 | 28- | 210 |
| Todd Elik | 60 | 14 | 27 | 41 | 4 | 56 |
| Zdeno Ciger | 64 | 13 | 23 | 36 | 13- | 8 |
| Brian Benning | 55 | 10 | 24 | 34 | 1- | 152 |
| Scott Mellanby | 69 | 15 | 17 | 32 | 4- | 147 |
| Kelly Buchberger | 83 | 12 | 18 | 30 | 27- | 133 |
| Craig MacTavish | 82 | 10 | 20 | 30 | 16- | 110 |
| Igor Kravchuk | 55 | 10 | 17 | 27 | 3 | 32 |
| Martin Gelinas | 65 | 11 | 12 | 23 | 3 | 30 |
| Kevin Todd | 55 | 9 | 14 | 23 | 9- | 26 |
| Shjon Podein | 40 | 13 | 6 | 19 | 2- | 25 |
| Geoff Smith | 78 | 4 | 14 | 18 | 11- | 30 |
| Brian Glynn | 64 | 4 | 12 | 16 | 13- | 60 |
| Luke Richardson | 82 | 3 | 10 | 13 | 18- | 142 |
| Louie Debrusk | 51 | 8 | 2 | 10 | 16- | 205 |
| Mike Hudson | 41 | 1 | 7 | 8 | 7- | 46 |
| Bill Ranford | 67 | 0 | 3 | 3 | 0 | 10 |

Coach—Ted Green

## Hartford Whalers

| | GP | G | A | Pts | +/- | PIM |
|---|---|---|---|---|---|---|
| Geoff Sanderson | 82 | 46 | 43 | 89 | 21- | 28 |
| Andrew Cassels | 84 | 21 | 64 | 85 | 11- | 62 |
| Pat Verbeek | 84 | 39 | 43 | 82 | 7- | 197 |
| Zarley Zalapski | 83 | 14 | 51 | 65 | 34- | 94 |
| Terry Yake | 66 | 22 | 31 | 53 | 3 | 46 |
| Patrick Poulin | 81 | 20 | 31 | 51 | 19- | 37 |
| Eric Weinrich | 79 | 7 | 29 | 36 | 11- | 76 |
| Michael Nylander | 59 | 11 | 22 | 33 | 7- | 36 |
| Mark Janssens | 76 | 12 | 17 | 29 | 15- | 237 |
| Nick Kypreos | 75 | 17 | 10 | 27 | 5- | 325 |
| Robert Kron | 45 | 14 | 13 | 27 | 5 | 14 |
| Yvon Corriveau | 57 | 4 | 8 | 12 | 20- | 14 |
| Adam Burt | 65 | 6 | 14 | 20 | 11- | 116 |
| Robert Petrovicky | 42 | 3 | 6 | 9 | 10- | 45 |
| Jim McKenzie | 64 | 3 | 6 | 9 | 10- | 202 |
| Doug Houda | 60 | 2 | 6 | 8 | 19- | 167 |
| Randy Ladouceur | 62 | 2 | 4 | 6 | 18- | 109 |

| | GP | G | A | Pts | +/− | PIM |
|---|---|---|---|---|---|---|
| Allen Pedersen | 59 | 1 | 4 | 5 | 0 | 60 |
| Sean Burke | 50 | 0 | 2 | 2 | 0 | 25 |

**Coach—Paul Holmgren**

## Los Angeles Kings

| | GP | G | A | Pts | +/− | PIM |
|---|---|---|---|---|---|---|
| Luc Robitaille | 84 | 63 | 62 | 125 | 18 | 100 |
| Jari Kurri | 82 | 27 | 60 | 87 | 19 | 38 |
| Tony Granato | 81 | 37 | 45 | 82 | 1− | 171 |
| Jimmy Carson | 86 | 37 | 36 | 73 | 2− | 32 |
| Mike Donnelly | 84 | 29 | 40 | 69 | 17 | 45 |
| Wayne Gretzky | 45 | 16 | 49 | 65 | 6 | 6 |
| Rob Blake | 76 | 16 | 43 | 59 | 18 | 152 |
| Alexei Zhitnik | 78 | 12 | 36 | 48 | 3− | 80 |
| Marty McSorley | 81 | 15 | 26 | 41 | 1 | 399 |
| Corey Millen | 42 | 23 | 16 | 39 | 16 | 42 |
| Darryl Sydor | 80 | 6 | 23 | 29 | 2− | 63 |
| Charlie Huddy | 82 | 2 | 25 | 27 | 16 | 64 |
| Lonnie Loach | 53 | 10 | 13 | 23 | 3 | 27 |
| Pat Conacher | 81 | 9 | 8 | 17 | 16− | 20 |
| Dave Taylor | 48 | 6 | 9 | 15 | 1 | 49 |
| Mark Hardy | 55 | 1 | 13 | 14 | 2− | 89 |
| Warren Rychel | 70 | 6 | 7 | 13 | 15− | 314 |
| Kelly Hrudey | 50 | 0 | 4 | 4 | 0 | 10 |

**Coach—Barry Melrose**

## Minnesota North Stars

| | GP | G | A | Pts | +/− | PIM |
|---|---|---|---|---|---|---|
| Mike Modano | 82 | 33 | 60 | 93 | 7− | 83 |
| Russ Courtnall | 84 | 36 | 43 | 79 | 1 | 49 |
| Dave Gagner | 84 | 33 | 43 | 76 | 13− | 141 |
| Ulf Dahlen | 83 | 35 | 39 | 74 | 20− | 6 |
| Mark Tinordi | 69 | 15 | 27 | 42 | 1− | 157 |
| Mike McPhee | 84 | 18 | 22 | 40 | 2− | 44 |
| Mike Craig | 70 | 15 | 23 | 38 | 11− | 106 |
| Tommy Sjodin | 77 | 7 | 29 | 36 | 25− | 30 |
| Neal Broten | 82 | 12 | 21 | 33 | 7 | 22 |
| Gaetan Duchesne | 84 | 16 | 13 | 29 | 6 | 32 |
| Trent Klatt | 47 | 4 | 19 | 23 | 2 | 38 |
| Jim Johnson | 79 | 3 | 20 | 23 | 9 | 105 |
| Brent Gilchrist | 68 | 10 | 11 | 21 | 12− | 49 |
| Shane Churla | 73 | 5 | 16 | 21 | 8− | 286 |
| Derian Hatcher | 67 | 4 | 15 | 19 | 27− | 178 |
| Stewart Gavin | 63 | 10 | 8 | 18 | 4− | 59 |
| Bobby Smith | 45 | 5 | 7 | 12 | 9− | 10 |
| Craig Ludwig | 78 | 1 | 10 | 11 | 1 | 153 |
| Richard Matvichuk | 53 | 2 | 3 | 5 | 8− | 26 |
| Mark Osiecki | 43 | 1 | 4 | 5 | 20− | 19 |
| Jon Casey | 60 | 0 | 3 | 3 | 0 | 28 |
| Brad Berry | 63 | 0 | 3 | 3 | 2 | 109 |

**Coach—Bob Gainey**

## Montreal Canadiens

| | GP | G | A | Pts | +/− | PIM |
|---|---|---|---|---|---|---|
| Vincent Damphousse | 84 | 39 | 58 | 97 | 5 | 98 |
| Kirk Muller | 80 | 37 | 57 | 94 | 8 | 77 |
| Brian Bellows | 82 | 40 | 48 | 88 | 4 | 44 |
| Stephan Lebeau | 71 | 31 | 49 | 80 | 23 | 20 |
| Mike Keane | 77 | 15 | 45 | 60 | 29 | 95 |
| Denis Savard | 63 | 16 | 34 | 50 | 1 | 90 |
| Gilbert Dionne | 75 | 20 | 28 | 48 | 5 | 63 |
| Eric Desjardins | 82 | 13 | 32 | 45 | 20 | 98 |
| John Leclair | 72 | 19 | 25 | 44 | 11 | 33 |
| Matt Schneider | 60 | 13 | 31 | 44 | 8 | 91 |
| Gary Leeman | 50 | 15 | 17 | 32 | 14 | 24 |
| Patrice Brisebois | 70 | 10 | 21 | 31 | 6 | 79 |
| Kevin Haller | 73 | 11 | 14 | 25 | 7 | 117 |
| Benoit Brunet | 47 | 10 | 15 | 25 | 13 | 19 |
| J. J. Daigneault | 66 | 8 | 10 | 18 | 25 | 57 |
| Rob Ramage | 74 | 5 | 13 | 18 | 24− | 146 |
| Guy Carbonneau | 61 | 4 | 13 | 17 | 9− | 20 |
| Lyle Odelein | 83 | 2 | 14 | 16 | 35 | 205 |
| Todd Ewen | 75 | 5 | 9 | 14 | 6 | 193 |
| Ed Ronan | 53 | 5 | 7 | 12 | 6 | 20 |
| Mario Roberge | 50 | 4 | 4 | 8 | 2 | 142 |
| Patrick Roy | 62 | 0 | 2 | 2 | 0 | 16 |

**Coach—Jacques Demers**

## New Jersey Devils

| | GP | G | A | Pts | +/− | PIM |
|---|---|---|---|---|---|---|
| Claude Lemieux | 77 | 30 | 51 | 81 | 3 | 155 |
| Alexander Semak | 82 | 37 | 42 | 79 | 24 | 70 |
| Stephane Richer | 78 | 38 | 35 | 73 | 1− | 44 |
| Valeri Zelepukin | 78 | 23 | 41 | 64 | 19 | 70 |
| Bernie Nicholls | 69 | 13 | 47 | 60 | 13− | 80 |
| Scott Stevens | 81 | 12 | 45 | 57 | 14 | 120 |

| | GP | G | A | Pts | +/− | PIM |
|---|---|---|---|---|---|---|
| Bruce Driver | 83 | 14 | 40 | 54 | 10− | 66 |
| John Maclean | 80 | 24 | 24 | 48 | 6 | 102 |
| Peter Stastny | 62 | 17 | 23 | 40 | 5− | 22 |
| Scott Niedermayer | 80 | 11 | 29 | 40 | 8 | 47 |
| Bobby Holik | 61 | 20 | 19 | 39 | 6− | 76 |
| Bill Guerin | 65 | 14 | 20 | 34 | 14 | 63 |
| Viacheslav Fetisov | 76 | 4 | 23 | 27 | 7 | 158 |
| Randy McKay | 73 | 11 | 11 | 22 | 0 | 206 |
| Scott Pellerin | 45 | 10 | 11 | 21 | 1− | 41 |
| Tom Chorske | 50 | 7 | 12 | 19 | 1− | 25 |
| Alexei Kasatonov | 64 | 3 | 14 | 17 | 4 | 57 |
| Dave Barr | 62 | 6 | 8 | 14 | 1 | 61 |
| Ken Daneyko | 84 | 2 | 11 | 13 | 4 | 236 |
| Craig Billington | 42 | 0 | 1 | 1 | 0 | 8 |
| Chris Terreri | 48 | 0 | 0 | 0 | 0 | 6 |

**Coach—Herb Brooks**

## New York Islanders

| | GP | G | A | Pts | +/− | PIM |
|---|---|---|---|---|---|---|
| Pierre Turgeon | 83 | 58 | 74 | 132 | 1− | 26 |
| Steve Thomas | 79 | 37 | 50 | 87 | 3 | 111 |
| Derek King | 77 | 38 | 38 | 76 | 3− | 47 |
| Benoit Hogue | 70 | 33 | 42 | 75 | 13 | 108 |
| Patrick Flatley | 80 | 13 | 47 | 60 | 4 | 63 |
| Vladimir Malakhov | 64 | 14 | 38 | 52 | 14 | 59 |
| Jeff Norton | 66 | 12 | 38 | 50 | 3− | 45 |
| Uwe Krupp | 80 | 9 | 29 | 38 | 7 | 67 |
| Tom Kurvers | 52 | 8 | 30 | 38 | 8 | 38 |
| Brian Mullen | 81 | 18 | 14 | 32 | 5 | 28 |
| Brad Dalgarno | 57 | 15 | 17 | 32 | 17 | 62 |
| Marty McInnis | 56 | 10 | 20 | 30 | 7 | 24 |
| Ray Ferraro | 46 | 14 | 13 | 27 | 0 | 40 |
| Tom Fitzgerald | 77 | 9 | 18 | 27 | 2− | 34 |
| Travis Green | 61 | 7 | 18 | 25 | 4 | 43 |
| Scott Lachance | 75 | 7 | 17 | 24 | 1− | 67 |
| Dave Volek | 56 | 8 | 13 | 21 | 1− | 34 |
| Darius Kasparaitis | 79 | 4 | 17 | 21 | 15 | 166 |
| Claude Loiselle | 41 | 5 | 3 | 8 | 5− | 90 |
| Mick Vukota | 74 | 2 | 5 | 7 | 3 | 216 |
| Richard Pilon | 44 | 1 | 3 | 4 | 4− | 164 |
| Glenn Healy | 47 | 0 | 2 | 2 | 0 | 2 |

**Coach—Al Arbour**

## New York Rangers

| | GP | G | A | Pts | +/− | PIM |
|---|---|---|---|---|---|---|
| Mark Messier | 75 | 25 | 66 | 91 | 6− | 72 |
| Tony Amonte | 83 | 33 | 43 | 76 | 0 | 49 |
| Mike Gartner | 84 | 45 | 23 | 68 | 4− | 59 |
| Adam Graves | 84 | 36 | 29 | 65 | 4− | 148 |
| Sergei Nemchinov | 81 | 23 | 31 | 54 | 15 | 34 |
| Darren Turcotte | 71 | 25 | 28 | 53 | 3− | 40 |
| Ed Olczyk | 71 | 21 | 28 | 49 | 2− | 52 |
| Esa Tikkanen | 81 | 16 | 24 | 40 | 24− | 94 |
| Alexei Kovalev | 65 | 20 | 18 | 38 | 10− | 79 |
| Sergei Zubov | 49 | 8 | 23 | 31 | 1− | 4 |
| James Patrick | 60 | 5 | 21 | 26 | 1 | 61 |
| Phil Bourque | 55 | 6 | 14 | 20 | 9− | 39 |
| Jeff Beukeboom | 82 | 2 | 17 | 19 | 9 | 153 |
| Jan Erixon | 45 | 5 | 11 | 16 | 11 | 10 |
| Kevin Lowe | 49 | 3 | 12 | 15 | 2− | 58 |
| Paul Broten | 60 | 5 | 9 | 14 | 6− | 48 |
| Jay Wells | 53 | 1 | 9 | 10 | 2− | 107 |
| Joe Cirella | 55 | 3 | 6 | 9 | 1 | 85 |
| Joey Kocur | 65 | 3 | 6 | 9 | 9− | 131 |
| Mike Hartman | 61 | 4 | 4 | 8 | 7− | 160 |
| John McIntyre | 60 | 3 | 5 | 8 | 14− | 84 |
| John Vanbiesbrouck | 48 | 0 | 1 | 1 | 0 | 18 |

**Coach—Roger Neilson; Ron Smith**

## Ottawa Senators

| | GP | G | A | Pts | +/− | PIM |
|---|---|---|---|---|---|---|
| Norm Maciver | 80 | 17 | 46 | 63 | 46− | 84 |
| Jamie Baker | 76 | 19 | 29 | 48 | 20− | 54 |
| Sylvain Turgeon | 72 | 25 | 18 | 43 | 29− | 104 |
| Bob Kudelski | 63 | 24 | 17 | 41 | 25− | 30 |
| Brad Shaw | 81 | 7 | 34 | 41 | 47− | 34 |
| Jody Hull | 69 | 13 | 21 | 34 | 24− | 14 |
| Mark Lamb | 71 | 7 | 19 | 26 | 40− | 64 |
| Mike Peluso | 81 | 15 | 10 | 25 | 35− | 318 |
| Mark Freer | 63 | 10 | 14 | 24 | 35− | 39 |
| Neil Brady | 55 | 7 | 17 | 24 | 25− | 57 |
| Andrew McBain | 59 | 7 | 16 | 23 | 37− | 43 |
| Laurie Boschman | 70 | 9 | 7 | 16 | 26− | 101 |
| Darren Rumble | 69 | 3 | 13 | 16 | 24− | 61 |
| David Archibald | 44 | 9 | 6 | 15 | 16− | 32 |
| Doug Smail | 51 | 4 | 10 | 14 | 34− | 51 |
| Tomas Jelinek | 49 | 7 | 6 | 13 | 21− | 52 |

| | | | | | |
|---|---|---|---|---|---|
| Chris Luongo | 76 | 3 | 9 | 12 47— | 68 |
| Rob Murphy | 44 | 3 | 7 | 10 23— | 30 |
| Darcy Loewen | 79 | 4 | 5 | 9 26— | 145 |
| Ken Hammond | 62 | 4 | 4 | 8 42— | 104 |
| Brad Marsh | 59 | 0 | 3 | 3 29— | 30 |
| Peter Sidorkiewicz | 64 | 0 | ·0 | 0 0 | 8 |

**Coach**—Rick Bowness

## Philadelphia Flyers

| | GP | G | A | Pts +/— | PIM |
|---|---|---|---|---|---|
| Mark Recchi | 84 | 53 | 70 | 123 1 | 95 |
| Rod Brind'Amour | 81 | 37 | 49 | 86 8— | 89 |
| Eric Lindros | 61 | 41 | 34 | 75 28 | 147 |
| Kevin Dineen | 83 | 35 | 28 | 63 14 | 201 |
| Garry Galley | 83 | 13 | 49 | 62 18 | 115 |
| Brent Fedyk | 74 | 21 | 38 | 59 14 | 48 |
| Per-Erik Eklund | 55 | 11 | 38 | 49 12 | 16 |
| Greg Hawgood | 69 | 11 | 35 | 46 8— | 74 |
| Josef Beranek | 66 | 15 | 18 | 33 8— | 78 |
| Dimitri Yushkevich | 82 | 5 | 27 | 32 12 | 71 |
| Keith Acton | 83 | 8 | 15 | 23 10— | 51 |
| Doug Evans | 65 | 8 | 13 | 21 9— | 70 |
| Andrei Lomakin | 51 | 8 | 12 | 20 15 | 34 |
| Terry Carkner | 83 | 3 | 16 | 19 18 | 150 |
| Ric Nattress | 44 | 7 | 10 | 17 1 | 29 |
| V. Butsayev | 52 | 2 | 14 | 16 3 | 61 |
| Ryan McGill | 72 | 3 | 10 | 13 9 | 238 |
| Tommy Soderstrom | 44 | 0 | 2 | 2 0 | 4 |
| Dave Brown | 70 | 0 | 2 | 2 5— | 78 |

**Coach**—Bill Dineen

## Pittsburgh Penguins

| | GP | G | A | Pts +/— | PIM |
|---|---|---|---|---|---|
| Mario Lemieux | 60 | 69 | 91 | 160 55 | 38 |
| Kevin Stevens | 72 | 55 | 56 | 111 17 | 177 |
| Rick Tocchet | 80 | 48 | 61 | 109 28 | 252 |
| Ron Francis | 84 | 24 | 76 | 100 6 | 68 |
| Jaromir Jagr | 81 | 34 | 60 | 94 30 | 61 |
| Larry Murphy | 83 | 22 | 63 | 85 45 | 73 |
| Joe Mullen | 72 | 33 | 37 | 70 19 | 14 |
| Shawn McEachern | 84 | 28 | 33 | 61 21 | 46 |
| Ulf Samuelsson | 77 | 3 | 26 | 29 36 | 249 |
| Dave Tippett | 74 | 6 | 19 | 25 5 | 56 |
| Troy Loney | 82 | 5 | 16 | 21 1 | 99 |
| Jim Paek | 77 | 3 | 15 | 18 13 | 64 |
| Paul Stanton | 77 | 4 | 12 | 16 7 | 97 |
| Martin Straka | 42 | 3 | 13 | 16 2 | 29 |
| Peter Taglianetti | 72 | 2 | 12 | 14 12 | 184 |
| Mike Needham | 56 | 8 | 5 | 13 1— | 14 |
| Mike Stapleton | 78 | 4 | 9 | 13 8— | 10 |
| Mike Ramsey | 45 | 3 | 10 | 13 17 | 28 |
| Jeff Daniels | 58 | 5 | 4 | 9 5— | 14 |
| Kjell Samuelsson | 63 | 3 | 6 | 9 25 | 106 |
| Tom Barrasso | 63 | 0 | 8 | 8 0 | 24 |
| Grant Jennings | 58 | 0 | 5 | 5 6 | 65 |

**Coach**—Scotty Bowman

## Quebec Nordiques

| | GP | G | A | Pts +/— | PIM |
|---|---|---|---|---|---|
| Mats Sundin | 80 | 47 | 67 | 114 21 | 96 |
| Joe Sakic | 78 | 48 | 57 | 105 3— | 40 |
| Steve Duchesne | 82 | 20 | 62 | 82 15 | 57 |
| Mike Ricci | 77 | 27 | 51 | 78 8 | 123 |
| Owen Nolan | 73 | 36 | 41 | 77 1— | 185 |
| Andrei Kovalenko | 81 | 27 | 41 | 68 13 | 57 |
| Scott Young | 82 | 30 | 30 | 60 5 | 20 |
| Martin Rucinsky | 77 | 18 | 30 | 48 16 | 51 |
| Claude LaPointe | 74 | 10 | 26 | 36 5 | 98 |
| Curtis Leschyshyn | 82 | 9 | 23 | 32 25 | 61 |
| Mike Hough | 77 | 8 | 22 | 30 11— | 69 |
| Alexei Gusarov | 79 | 8 | 22 | 30 18 | 57 |
| Gino Cavallini | 67 | 9 | 15 | 24 10 | 34 |
| Kerry Huffman | 52 | 4 | 18 | 22 0 | 54 |
| Adam Foote | 81 | 4 | 12 | 16 6 | 168 |
| Scott Pearson | 41 | 13 | 1 | 14 3 | 95 |
| Steven Finn | 80 | 5 | 9 | 14 3— | 160 |
| Bill Lindsay | 44 | 4 | 9 | 13 0 | 16 |
| Ron Hextall | 54 | 0 | 2 | 2 0 | 56 |

**Coach**—Pierre Page

## St. Louis Blues

| | GP | G | A | Pts +/— | PIM |
|---|---|---|---|---|---|
| Craig Janney | 84 | 24 | 82 | 106 4— | 12 |
| Brett Hull | 80 | 54 | 47 | 101 27— | 41 |
| Brendan Shanahan | 71 | 51 | 43 | 94 10 | 174 |
| Jeff Brown | 71 | 25 | 53 | 78 6— | 58 |

| | | | | | |
|---|---|---|---|---|---|
| Nelson Emerson | 82 | 22 | 51 | 73 2 | 62 |
| Kevin Miller | 82 | 24 | 25 | 49 2 | 100 |
| Doug Crossman | 59 | 10 | 28 | 38 7— | 28 |
| Rich Sutter | 84 | 13 | 14 | 27 4— | 100 |
| Ron Sutter | 59 | 12 | 15 | 27 11— | 99 |
| Igor Korolev | 74 | 4 | 23 | 27 1— | 20 |
| Bob Bassen | 53 | 9 | 10 | 19 0 | 63 |
| Ron Wilson | 78 | 8 | 11 | 19 8— | 44 |
| Garth Butcher | 84 | 5 | 10 | 15 0 | 211 |
| Rick Zombo | 71 | 0 | 15 | 15 2— | 78 |
| Dave Lowry | 58 | 5 | 8 | 13 18— | 101 |
| Philippe Bozon | 54 | 6 | 6 | 12 3— | 55 |
| Stephane Quintal | 75 | 1 | 10 | 11 6— | 100 |
| Basil McRae | 47 | 3 | 6 | 9 16— | 169 |
| Bret Hedican | 42 | 0 | 8 | 8 2— | 30 |
| Kelly Chase | 49 | 2 | 5 | 7 9— | 204 |
| Murray Baron | 53 | 2 | 2 | 4 5— | 59 |
| Curt Giles | 48 | 0 | 4 | 4 2— | 40 |
| Curtis Joseph | 68 | 0 | 2 | 2 0 | 8 |

**Coach**—Bob Plager; Bob Berry

## San Jose Sharks

| | GP | G | A | Pts +/— | PIM |
|---|---|---|---|---|---|
| Kelly Kisio | 78 | 26 | 52 | 78 15— | 90 |
| Johan Garpenlov | 79 | 22 | 44 | 66 26— | 56 |
| Rob Gaudreau | 59 | 23 | 20 | 43 18— | 18 |
| Dean Evason | 84 | 12 | 19 | 31 35— | 132 |
| Pat Falloon | 41 | 14 | 14 | 28 25— | 12 |
| Jeff Odgers | 66 | 12 | 15 | 27 26— | 253 |
| Tom Pederson | 44 | 7 | 13 | 20 16— | 31 |
| Doug Wilson | 42 | 3 | 17 | 20 28— | 40 |
| Mark Pederson | 41 | 10 | 7 | 17 22— | 28 |
| John Carter | 55 | 7 | 9 | 16 25— | 81 |
| Doug Zmolek | 84 | 5 | 10 | 15 50— | 229 |
| Mike Sullivan | 81 | 6 | 8 | 14 42— | 30 |
| David Williams | 40 | 1 | 11 | 12 27— | 49 |
| Jay More | 73 | 5 | 6 | 11 35— | 179 |
| David Maley | 56 | 2 | 7 | 9 28— | 155 |
| Peter Ahola | 50 | 3 | 5 | 8 10— | 36 |
| Neil Wilkinson | 59 | 1 | 7 | 8 50— | 96 |
| Rob Zettler | 80 | 0 | 7 | 7 50— | 150 |
| Robin Bawa | 42 | 5 | 0 | 5 25— | 47 |

**Coach**—George Kingston

## Tampa Bay Lightning

| | GP | G | A | Pts +/— | PIM |
|---|---|---|---|---|---|
| Brian Bradley | 80 | 42 | 44 | 86 24— | 92 |
| John Tucker | 78 | 17 | 39 | 56 12— | 69 |
| Chris Kontos | 66 | 27 | 24 | 51 7— | 12 |
| Rob Zamuner | 84 | 15 | 28 | 43 25— | 74 |
| Adam Creighton | 83 | 19 | 20 | 39 19— | 110 |
| Shawn Chambers | 55 | 10 | 29 | 39 21— | 36 |
| Bob Beers | 64 | 12 | 24 | 36 25— | 70 |
| Marc Bureau | 63 | 10 | 21 | 31 12— | 111 |
| Mikael Andersson | 77 | 16 | 11 | 27 14— | 14 |
| Danton Cole | 67 | 12 | 15 | 27 2— | 23 |
| Rob DiMaio | 54 | 9 | 15 | 24 0 | 62 |
| Roman Hamrlik | 67 | 6 | 15 | 21 21— | 71 |
| Steve Maltais | 63 | 7 | 13 | 20 20— | 35 |
| Marc Bergevin | 78 | 2 | 12 | 14 16— | 66 |
| Joe Reekie | 42 | 2 | 11 | 13 2 | 69 |
| Steve Kasper | 68 | 4 | 7 | 11 17— | 20 |
| Randy Gilhen | 44 | 3 | 4 | 7 14— | 14 |
| Pat Jablonski | 43 | 0 | 2 | 2 0 | 7 |

**Coach**—Terry Crisp

## Toronto Maple Leafs

| | GP | G | A | Pts +/— | PIM |
|---|---|---|---|---|---|
| Doug Gilmour | 83 | 32 | 95 | 127 32 | 100 |
| Dave Andreychuk | 83 | 54 | 45 | 99 4 | 56 |
| Nikolai Borschevsky | 78 | 34 | 40 | 74 33 | 28 |
| Glenn Anderson | 76 | 22 | 43 | 65 19 | 117 |
| John Cullen | 66 | 18 | 32 | 50 23— | 111 |
| Todd Gill | 69 | 11 | 32 | 43 4 | 66 |
| Dave Ellett | 70 | 6 | 34 | 40 19 | 46 |
| Mike Krushelnyski | 84 | 19 | 20 | 39 3 | 62 |
| Wendel Clark | 66 | 17 | 22 | 39 2 | 193 |
| Rob Pearson | 78 | 23 | 14 | 37 2— | 211 |
| Peter Zezel | 70 | 12 | 23 | 35 0 | 24 |
| Dimitri Mironov | 59 | 7 | 24 | 31 1— | 40 |
| Mark Osborne | 76 | 12 | 14 | 26 7— | 89 |
| Bill Berg | 80 | 13 | 11 | 24 3 | 103 |
| Drake Berehowsky | 41 | 4 | 15 | 19 1 | 61 |
| Jamie Macoun | 77 | 4 | 15 | 19 3 | 55 |
| Dave McIlwain | 66 | 14 | 4 | 18 18— | 30 |
| Mike Foligno | 55 | 13 | 5 | 18 2 | 84 |
| Bob Rouse | 82 | 3 | 11 | 14 7 | 130 |

| | | | | | |
|---|---|---|---|---|---|
| Sylvain LeFebvre | 81 | 2 | 12 | 14 | 8 | 90 |
| Ken Baumgartner | 63 | 1 | 0 | 1 | 11— | 155 |
| Felix Potvin | 48 | 0 | 1 | 1 | 0 | 4 |

**Coach—Pat Burns**

## Vancouver Canucks

| | GP | G | A | Pts | +/− | PIM |
|---|---|---|---|---|---|---|
| Pavel Bure | 83 | 60 | 50 | 110 | 35 | 69 |
| Cliff Ronning | 79 | 29 | 56 | 85 | 19 | 30 |
| Geoff Courtnall | 84 | 31 | 46 | 77 | 27 | 167 |
| Murray Craven | 77 | 25 | 52 | 77 | 1— | 32 |
| Trevor Linden | 84 | 33 | 39 | 72 | 19 | 64 |
| Petr Nedved | 84 | 38 | 33 | 71 | 20 | 96 |
| Greg Adams | 53 | 25 | 31 | 56 | 31 | 14 |
| Dixon Ward | 70 | 22 | 30 | 52 | 34 | 82 |
| Anatoli Semenov | 75 | 12 | 37 | 49 | 16 | 32 |
| Jyrki Lumme | 74 | 8 | 36 | 44 | 30 | 55 |
| Sergio Momesso | 84 | 18 | 20 | 38 | 11 | 200 |
| Jim Sandlak | 59 | 10 | 18 | 28 | 2 | 122 |
| Adrien Plavsic | 57 | 6 | 21 | 27 | 28 | 53 |
| Jiri Slegr | 41 | 4 | 22 | 26 | 16 | 109 |
| Doug Lidster | 71 | 6 | 19 | 25 | 9 | 36 |
| Gerald Diduck | 80 | 6 | 14 | 20 | 32 | 171 |
| Dave Babych | 43 | 3 | 16 | 19 | 6 | 44 |
| Gino Odjick | 75 | 4 | 13 | 17 | 3 | 370 |
| Dana Murzyn | 79 | 5 | 11 | 16 | 34 | 196 |
| Garry Valk | 48 | 6 | 7 | 13 | 6 | 77 |
| Tim Hunter | 74 | 5 | 7 | 12 | 3— | 193 |
| Robert Dirk | 69 | 4 | 8 | 12 | 25 | 150 |
| Kirk McLean | 54 | 0 | 1 | 1 | 0 | 16 |

**Coach—Pat Quinn**

## Washington Capitals

| | GP | G | A | Pts | +/− | PIM |
|---|---|---|---|---|---|---|
| Peter Bondra | 83 | 37 | 48 | 85 | 8 | 70 |
| Mike Ridley | 84 | 26 | 56 | 82 | 5 | 44 |
| Kevin Hatcher | 83 | 34 | 45 | 79 | 7— | 114 |
| Dale Hunter | 84 | 20 | 59 | 79 | 3 | 198 |

| | | | | | |
|---|---|---|---|---|---|
| Michal Pivonka | 69 | 21 | 53 | 74 | 14 | 66 |
| Dimitri Khristich | 64 | 31 | 36 | 67 | 29 | 66 |
| Al Iafrate | 81 | 25 | 41 | 66 | 15 | 169 |
| Pat Elynuik | 80 | 22 | 35 | 57 | 3 | 66 |
| Sylvain Cote | 77 | 21 | 29 | 50 | 28 | 34 |
| Kelly Miller | 84 | 18 | 27 | 45 | 2— | 32 |
| Calle Johansson | 77 | 7 | 38 | 45 | 3 | 56 |
| Bob Carpenter | 68 | 11 | 17 | 28 | 16— | 65 |
| Keith Jones | 71 | 12 | 14 | 26 | 18 | 124 |
| Todd Krygier | 77 | 11 | 12 | 23 | 13— | 60 |
| Paul MacDermid | 72 | 9 | 8 | 17 | 13— | 80 |
| Paul Cavallini | 82 | 6 | 11 | 17 | 6 | 56 |
| Alan May | 83 | 6 | 10 | 16 | 1 | 268 |
| Shawn Anderson | 60 | 2 | 6 | 8 | 2— | 18 |
| Don Beaupre | 58 | 0 | 1 | 1 | 0 | 20 |

**Coach—Terry Murray**

## Winnipeg Jets

| | GP | G | A | Pts | +/− | PIM |
|---|---|---|---|---|---|---|
| Teemu Selanne | 84 | 76 | 56 | 132 | 8 | 45 |
| Phil Housley | 80 | 18 | 79 | 97 | 14— | 52 |
| Alexei Zhamnov | 68 | 25 | 47 | 72 | 7 | 58 |
| Thomas Steen | 80 | 22 | 50 | 72 | 8— | 75 |
| Darrin Shannon | 84 | 20 | 40 | 60 | 4— | 91 |
| Fredrik Olausson | 68 | 16 | 41 | 57 | 4— | 22 |
| Keith Tkachuk | 83 | 28 | 23 | 51 | 13— | 201 |
| Evgeny Davydov | 79 | 28 | 21 | 49 | 2— | 66 |
| Teppo Numminen | 66 | 7 | 30 | 37 | 4 | 33 |
| Luciano Borsato | 67 | 15 | 20 | 35 | 1— | 38 |
| Mike Eagles | 84 | 8 | 18 | 26 | 1— | 131 |
| Sergei Bautin | 71 | 5 | 18 | 23 | 2— | 96 |
| John Druce | 50 | 6 | 14 | 20 | 4— | 37 |
| Kris King | 78 | 8 | 11 | 19 | 4 | 203 |
| Bryan Erickson | 41 | 4 | 12 | 16 | 2 | 14 |
| Igor Ulanov | 56 | 2 | 14 | 16 | 6 | 124 |
| Tie Domi | 61 | 5 | 10 | 15 | 1 | 344 |
| Mike Lalor | 64 | 1 | 8 | 9 | 10— | 76 |
| Dean Kennedy | 78 | 1 | 7 | 8 | 3— | 105 |
| Bob Essensa | 67 | 0 | 5 | 5 | 0 | 2 |

**Coach—John Paddock**

## Ross Trophy (Leading Scorer)

| | | | | | |
|---|---|---|---|---|---|
| 1927 | Bill Cook, N.Y. Rangers | 1950 | Ted Lindsay, Detroit | 1972 | Phil Esposito, Boston |
| 1928 | Howie Morenz, Montreal | 1951 | Gordie Howe, Detroit | 1973 | Phil Esposito, Boston |
| 1929 | Ace Bailey, Toronto | 1952 | Gordie Howe, Detroit | 1974 | Phil Esposito, Boston |
| 1930 | Cooney Weiland, Boston | 1953 | Gordie Howe, Detroit | 1975 | Bobby Orr, Boston |
| 1931 | Howie Morenz, Montreal | 1954 | Gordie Howe, Detroit | 1976 | Guy Lafleur, Montreal |
| 1932 | Harvey Jackson, Toronto | 1955 | Bernie Geoffrion, Montreal | 1977 | Guy Lafleur, Montreal |
| 1933 | Bill Cook, N.Y. Rangers | 1956 | Jean Beliveau, Montreal | 1978 | Guy Lafleur, Montreal |
| 1934 | Charlie Conacher, Toronto | 1957 | Gordie Howe, Detroit | 1979 | Bryan Trottier, N.Y. Islanders |
| 1935 | Charlie Conacher, Toronto | 1958 | Dickie Moore, Montreal | 1980 | Marcel Dionne, Los Angeles |
| 1936 | Dave Schriner, N.Y. Americans | 1959 | Dickie Moore, Montreal | 1981 | Wayne Gretzky, Edmonton |
| 1937 | Dave Schriner, N.Y. Americans | 1960 | Bobby Hull, Chicago | 1982 | Wayne Gretzky, Edmonton |
| 1938 | Gordie Drillon, Toronto | 1961 | Bernie Geoffrion, Montreal | 1983 | Wayne Gretzky, Edmonton |
| 1939 | Toe Blake, Montreal | 1962 | Bobby Hull, Chicago | 1984 | Wayne Gretzky, Edmonton |
| 1940 | Milt Schmidt, Boston | 1963 | Gordie Howe, Detroit | 1985 | Wayne Gretzky, Edmonton |
| 1941 | Bill Cowley, Boston | 1964 | Stan Mikita, Chicago | 1986 | Wayne Gretzky, Edmonton |
| 1942 | Bryan Hextall, N.Y. Rangers | 1965 | Stan Mikita, Chicago | 1987 | Wayne Gretzky, Edmonton |
| 1943 | Doug Bentley, Chicago | 1966 | Bobby Hull, Chicago | 1988 | Mario Lemieux, Pittsburgh |
| 1944 | Herbie Cain, Boston | 1967 | Stan Mikita, Chicago | 1989 | Mario Lemieux, Pittsburgh |
| 1945 | Elmer Lach, Montreal | 1968 | Stan Mikita, Chicago | 1990 | Wayne Gretzky, Los Angeles |
| 1946 | Max Bentley, Chicago | 1969 | Phil Esposito, Boston | 1991 | Wayne Gretzky, Los Angeles |
| 1947 | Max Bentley, Chicago | 1970 | Bobby Orr, Boston | 1992 | Mario Lemieux, Pittsburgh |
| 1948 | Elmer Lach, Montreal | 1971 | Phil Esposito, Boston | 1993 | Mario Lemieux, Pittsburgh |
| 1949 | Roy Conacher, Chicago | | | | |

## James Norris Memorial Trophy (Outstanding Defenseman)

| | | | | | |
|---|---|---|---|---|---|
| 1954 | Red Kelly, Detroit | 1968 | Bobby Orr, Boston | 1981 | Randy Carlyle, Pittsburgh |
| 1955 | Doug Harvey, Montreal | 1969 | Bobby Orr, Boston | 1982 | Doug Wilson, Chicago |
| 1956 | Doug Harvey, Montreal | 1970 | Bobby Orr, Boston | 1983 | Rod Langway, Washington |
| 1957 | Doug Harvey, Montreal | 1971 | Bobby Orr, Boston | 1984 | Rod Langway, Washington |
| 1958 | Doug Harvey, Montreal | 1972 | Bobby Orr, Boston | 1985 | Paul Coffey, Edmonton |
| 1959 | Tom Johnson, Montreal | 1973 | Bobby Orr, Boston | 1986 | Paul Coffey, Edmonton |
| 1960 | Doug Harvey, Montreal | 1974 | Bobby Orr, Boston | 1987 | Ray Bourque, Boston |
| 1961 | Doug Harvey, Montreal | 1975 | Bobby Orr, Boston | 1988 | Ray Bourque, Boston |
| 1962 | Doug Harvey, N.Y. Rangers | 1976 | Denis Potvin, N.Y. Islanders | 1989 | Chris Chelios, Montreal |
| 1963 | Pierre Pilote, Chicago | 1977 | Larry Robinson, Montreal | 1990 | Ray Bourque, Boston |
| 1964 | Pierre Pilote, Chicago | 1978 | Denis Potvin, N.Y. Islanders | 1991 | Ray Bourque, Boston |
| 1965 | Pierre Pilote, Chicago | 1979 | Denis Potvin, N.Y. Islanders | 1992 | Brian Leetch, N.Y. Rangers |
| 1966 | Jacques Laperriere, Montreal | 1980 | Larry Robinson, Montreal | 1993 | Chris Chelios, Chicago |
| 1967 | Harry Howell, N.Y. Rangers | | | | |

## *Vezina Trophy (Leading Goalie)

| | | | | | |
|---|---|---|---|---|---|
| 1927 | George Hainsworth, Montreal | 1951 | Al Rollins, Toronto | 1974 | Bernie Parent, Philadelphia; |
| 1928 | George Hainsworth, Montreal | 1952 | Terry Sawchuk, Detroit | | Tony Esposito, Chicago |
| 1929 | George Hainsworth, Montreal | 1953 | Terry Sawchuk, Detroit | 1975 | Bernie Parent, Philadelphia |
| 1930 | Tiny Thompson, Boston | 1954 | Harry Lumley, Toronto | 1976 | Ken Dryden, Montreal |
| 1931 | Roy Worters, N.Y. Americans | 1955 | Terry Sawchuk, Detroit | 1977 | Dryden, Larocque, Montreal |
| 1932 | Charlie Gardiner, Chicago | 1956 | Jacques Plante, Montreal | 1978 | Dryden, Larocque, Montreal |
| 1933 | Tiny Thompson, Boston | 1957 | Jacques Plante, Montreal | 1979 | Dryden, Larocque, Montreal |
| 1934 | Charlie Gardiner, Chicago | 1958 | Jacques Plante, Montreal | 1980 | Sauve, Edwards, Buffalo |
| 1935 | Lorne Chabot, Chicago | 1959 | Jacques Plante, Montreal | 1981 | Sevigny, Larocque, Herron, |
| 1936 | Tiny Thompson, Boston | 1960 | Jacques Plante, Montreal | | Montreal |
| 1937 | Normie Smith, Detroit | 1961 | John Bower, Toronto | 1982 | Bill Smith, N.Y. Islanders |
| 1938 | Tiny Thompson, Boston | 1962 | Jacques Plante, Montreal | 1983 | Pete Peeters, Boston |
| 1939 | Frank Brimsek, Boston | 1963 | Glenn Hall, Chicago | 1984 | Tom Barrasso, Buffalo |
| 1940 | Dave Kerr, N.Y. Rangers | 1964 | Charlie Hodge, Montreal | 1985 | Pelle Lindbergh, Philadelphia |
| 1941 | Turk Broda, Toronto | 1965 | Sawchuk, Bower, Toronto | 1986 | John Vanbiesbrouck, N.Y. |
| 1942 | Frank Brimsek, Boston | 1966 | Worsley, Hodge, Montreal | | Rangers |
| 1943 | Johnny Mowers, Detroit | 1967 | Hall, DeJordy, Chicago | 1987 | Ron Hextall, Philadelphia |
| 1944 | Bill Durnan, Montreal | 1968 | Worsley, Vachon, Montreal | 1988 | Grant Fuhr, Edmonton |
| 1945 | Bill Durnan, Montreal | 1969 | Hall, Plante, St. Louis | 1989 | Patrick Roy, Montreal |
| 1946 | Bill Durnan, Montreal | 1970 | Tony Esposito, Chicago | 1990 | Patrick Roy, Montreal |
| 1947 | Bill Durnan, Montreal | 1971 | Giacomin, Villemure, N.Y. | 1991 | Ed Belfour, Chicago |
| 1948 | Turk Broda, Toronto | | Rangers | 1992 | Patrick Roy, Montreal |
| 1949 | Bill Durnan, Montreal | 1972 | Esposito, Smith, Chicago | 1993 | Ed Belfour, Chicago |
| 1950 | Bill Durnan, Montreal | 1973 | Ken Dryden, Montreal | | |

* Awarded to goalie who played a minimum 25 games for the team which allowed the fewest goals; since 1982, awarded to outstanding goalie.

## Calder Memorial Trophy (Rookie of the Year)

| | | | | | |
|---|---|---|---|---|---|
| 1933 | Carl Voss, Detroit | 1952 | Bernie Geoffrion, Montreal | 1973 | Steve Vickers, N.Y. Rangers |
| 1934 | Russ Blinco, Montreal | 1953 | Gump Worsley, N.Y. Rangers | 1974 | Denis Potvin, N.Y. Islanders |
| | Maroons | 1954 | Camille Henry, N.Y. Rangers | 1975 | Eric Vail, Atlanta |
| 1935 | Dave Schriner, N.Y. Americans | 1955 | Ed Litzenberger, Chicago | 1976 | Bryan Trottier, N.Y. Islanders |
| 1936 | Mike Karakas, Chicago | 1956 | Glenn Hall, Detroit | 1977 | Willi Plett, Atlanta |
| 1937 | Syl Apps, Toronto | 1957 | Larry Regan, Boston | 1978 | Mike Bossy, N.Y. Islanders |
| 1938 | Cully Dahlstrom, Chicago | 1958 | Frank Mahovlich, Toronto | 1979 | Bobby Smith, Minnesota |
| 1939 | Frank Brimsek, Boston | 1959 | Ralph Backstrom, Montreal | 1980 | Ray Bourque, Boston |
| 1940 | Kilby Macdonald, N.Y. | 1960 | Bill Hay, Chicago | 1981 | Peter Stastny, Quebec |
| | Rangers | 1961 | Dave Keon, Toronto | 1982 | Dale Hawerchuk, Winnipeg |
| 1941 | John Quilty, Montreal | 1962 | Bobby Rousseau, Montreal | 1983 | Steve Larmer, Chicago |
| 1942 | Grant Warwick, N.Y. Rangers | 1963 | Kent Douglas, Toronto | 1984 | Tom Barrasso, Buffalo |
| 1943 | Gaye Stewart, Toronto | 1964 | Jacques Laperriere, Montreal | 1985 | Mario Lemieux, Pittsburgh |
| 1944 | Gus Bodnar, Toronto | 1965 | Roger Crozier, Detroit | 1986 | Gary Suter, Calgary |
| 1945 | Frank McCool, Toronto | 1966 | Brit Selby, Toronto | 1987 | Luc Robitaille, Los Angeles |
| 1946 | Edgar Laprade, N.Y. Rangers | 1967 | Bobby Orr, Boston | 1988 | Joe Nieuwendyk, Calgary |
| 1947 | Howie Meeker, Toronto | 1968 | Derek Sanderson, Boston | 1989 | Brian Leetch, N.Y. Rangers |
| 1948 | Jim McFadden, Detroit | 1969 | Danny Grant, Minnesota | 1990 | Sergei Makarov, Calgary |
| 1949 | Pentti Lund, N.Y. Rangers | 1970 | Tony Esposito, Chicago | 1991 | Ed Belfour, Chicago |
| 1950 | Jack Gelineau, Boston | 1971 | Gilbert Perreault, Buffalo | 1992 | Pavel Bure, Vancouver |
| 1951 | Terry Sawchuk, Detroit | 1972 | Ken Dryden, Montreal | 1993 | Teemu Selanne, Winnipeg |

## Lady Byng Memorial Trophy (Most Gentlemanly Player)

| | | | | | |
|---|---|---|---|---|---|
| 1925 | Frank Nighbor, Ottawa | 1948 | Buddy O'Connor, N.Y. | 1971 | John Bucyk, Boston |
| 1926 | Frank Nighbor, Ottawa | | Rangers | 1972 | Jean Ratelle, N.Y. Rangers |
| 1927 | Billy Burch, N.Y. Americans | 1949 | Bill Quackenbush, Detroit | 1973 | Gil Perreault, Buffalo |
| 1928 | Frank Boucher, N.Y. Rangers | 1950 | Edgar Laprade, N.Y. Rangers | 1974 | John Bucyk, Boston |
| 1929 | Frank Boucher, N.Y. Rangers | 1951 | Red Kelly, Detroit | 1975 | Marcel Dionne, Detroit |
| 1930 | Frank Boucher, N.Y. Rangers | 1952 | Sid Smith, Toronto | 1976 | Jean Ratelle, N.Y. R.-Boston |
| 1931 | Frank Boucher, N.Y. Rangers | 1953 | Red Kelly, Detroit | 1977 | Marcel Dionne, Los Angeles |
| 1932 | Joe Primeau, Toronto | 1954 | Red Kelly, Detroit | 1978 | Butch Goring, Los Angeles |
| 1933 | Frank Boucher, N.Y. Rangers | 1955 | Sid Smith, Toronto | 1979 | Bob MacMillan, Atlanta |
| 1934 | Frank Boucher, N.Y. Rangers | 1956 | Earl Reibel, Detroit | 1980 | Wayne Gretzky, Edmonton |
| 1935 | Frank Boucher, N.Y. Rangers | 1957 | Andy Hebenton, N.Y. Rangers | 1981 | Rick Kehoe, Pittsburgh |
| 1936 | Doc Romnes, Chicago | 1958 | Camille Henry, N.Y. Rangers | 1982 | Rick Middleton, Boston |
| 1937 | Marty Barry, Detroit | 1959 | Alex Delvecchio, Detroit | 1983 | Mike Bossy, N.Y. Islanders |
| 1938 | Gordie Drillon, Toronto | 1960 | Don McKenney, Boston | 1984 | Mike Bossy, N.Y. Islanders |
| 1939 | Clint Smith, N.Y. Rangers | 1961 | Red Kelly, Toronto | 1985 | Jari Kurri, Edmonton |
| 1940 | Bobby Bauer, Boston | 1962 | Dave Keon, Toronto | 1986 | Mike Bossy, N.Y. Islanders |
| 1941 | Bobby Bauer, Boston | 1963 | Dave Keon, Toronto | 1987 | Joe Mullen, Calgary |
| 1942 | Syl Apps, Toronto | 1964 | Ken Wharram, Chicago | 1988 | Mats Naslund, Montreal |
| 1943 | Max Bentley, Chicago | 1965 | Bobby Hull, Chicago | 1989 | Joe Mullen, Calgary |
| 1944 | Clint Smith, Chicago | 1966 | Alex Delvecchio, Detroit | 1990 | Brett Hull, St. Louis |
| 1945 | Bill Mosienko, Chicago | 1967 | Stan Mikita, Chicago | 1991 | Wayne Gretzky, Los Angeles |
| 1946 | Toe Blake, Montreal | 1968 | Stan Mikita, Chicago | 1992 | Wayne Gretzky, Los Angeles |
| 1947 | Bobby Bauer, Boston | 1969 | Alex Delvecchio, Detroit | 1993 | Pierre Turgeon, N.Y. Islanders |
| | | 1970 | Phil Goyette, St. Louis | | |

## Frank J. Selke Trophy (Best Defensive Forward)

| | | | | | |
|---|---|---|---|---|---|
| 1978 | Bob Gainey, Montreal | 1984 | Doug Jarvis, Washington | 1989 | Guy Carbonneau, Montreal |
| 1979 | Bob Gainey, Montreal | 1985 | Craig Ramsay, Buffalo | 1990 | Rick Meagher, St. Louis |
| 1980 | Bob Gainey, Montreal | 1986 | Troy Murray, Chicago | 1991 | Dirk Graham, Chicago |
| 1981 | Bob Gainey, Montreal | 1987 | Dave Poulin, Philadelphia | 1992 | Guy Carbonneau, Montreal |
| 1982 | Steve Kasper, Boston | 1988 | Guy Carbonneau, Montreal | 1993 | Doug Gilmour, Toronto |
| 1983 | Bobby Clarke, Philadelphia | | | | |

## Hart Memorial Trophy (MVP)

| | | | | | |
|---|---|---|---|---|---|
| 1927 | Herb Gardiner, Montreal | 1948 | Buddy O'Connor, N.Y. | 1971 | Bobby Orr, Boston |
| 1928 | Howie Morenz, Montreal | | Rangers | 1972 | Bobby Orr, Boston |
| 1929 | Roy Worters, N.Y. Americans | 1949 | Sid Abel, Detroit | 1973 | Bobby Clarke, Philadelphia |
| 1930 | Nels Stewart, Montreal | 1950 | Chuck Rayner, N.Y. Rangers | 1974 | Phil Esposito, Boston |
| | Maroons | 1951 | Milt Schmidt, Boston | 1975 | Bobby Clarke, Philadelphia |
| 1931 | Howie Morenz, Montreal | 1952 | Gordie Howe, Detroit | 1976 | Bobby Clarke, Philadelphia |
| 1932 | Howie Morenz, Montreal | 1953 | Gordie Howe, Detroit | 1977 | Guy Lafleur, Montreal |
| 1933 | Eddie Shore, Boston | 1954 | Al Rollins, Chicago | 1978 | Guy Lafleur, Montreal |
| 1934 | Aurel Joliat, Montreal | 1955 | Ted Kennedy, Toronto | 1979 | Bryan Trottier, N.Y. Islanders |
| 1935 | Eddie Shore, Boston | 1956 | Jean Beliveau, Montreal | 1980 | Wayne Gretzky, Edmonton |
| 1936 | Eddie Shore, Boston | 1957 | Gordie Howe, Detroit | 1981 | Wayne Gretzky, Edmonton |
| 1937 | Babe Siebert, Montreal | 1958 | Gordie Howe, Detroit | 1982 | Wayne Gretzky, Edmonton |
| 1938 | Eddie Shore, Boston | 1959 | Andy Bathgate, N.Y. Rangers | 1983 | Wayne Gretzky, Edmonton |
| 1939 | Toe Blake, Montreal | 1960 | Gordie Howe, Detroit | 1984 | Wayne Gretzky, Edmonton |
| 1940 | Ebbie Goodfellow, Detroit | 1961 | Bernie Geoffrion, Montreal | 1985 | Wayne Gretzky, Edmonton |
| 1941 | Bill Cowley, Boston | 1962 | Jacques Plante, Montreal | 1986 | Wayne Gretzky, Edmonton |
| 1942 | Tom Anderson, N.Y. | 1963 | Gordie Howe, Detroit | 1987 | Wayne Gretzky, Edmonton |
| | Americans | 1964 | Jean Beliveau, Montreal | 1988 | Mario Lemieux, Pittsburgh |
| 1943 | Bill Cowley, Boston | 1965 | Bobby Hull, Chicago | 1989 | Wayne Gretzky, Los Angeles |
| 1944 | Babe Pratt, Toronto | 1966 | Bobby Hull, Chicago | 1990 | Mark Messier, Edmonton |
| 1945 | Elmer Lach, Montreal | 1967 | Stan Mikita, Chicago | 1991 | Brett Hull, St. Louis |
| 1946 | Max Bentley, Chicago | 1968 | Stan Mikita, Chicago | 1992 | Mark Messier, N.Y. Rangers |
| 1947 | Maurice Richard, Montreal | 1969 | Phil Esposito, Boston | 1993 | Mario Lemieux, Pittsburgh |
| | | 1970 | Bobby Orr, Boston | | |

## Conn Smythe Trophy (MVP in Playoffs)

| | | | | | |
|---|---|---|---|---|---|
| 1965 | Jean Beliveau, Montreal | 1975 | Bernie Parent, Philadelphia | 1985 | Wayne Gretzky, Edmonton |
| 1966 | Roger Crozier, Detroit | 1976 | Reg Leach, Philadelphia | 1986 | Patrick Roy, Montreal |
| 1967 | Dave Keon, Toronto | 1977 | Guy Lafleur, Montreal | 1987 | Ron Hextall, Philadelphia |
| 1968 | Glenn Hall, St. Louis | 1978 | Larry Robinson, Montreal | 1988 | Wayne Gretzky, Edmonton |
| 1969 | Serge Savard, Montreal | 1979 | Bob Gainey, Montreal | 1989 | Al MacInnis, Calgary |
| 1970 | Bobby Orr, Boston | 1980 | Bryan Trottier, N.Y. Islanders | 1990 | Bill Ranford, Edmonton |
| 1971 | Ken Dryden, Montreal | 1981 | Butch Goring, N.Y. Islanders | 1991 | Mario Lemieux, Pittsburgh |
| 1972 | Bobby Orr, Boston | 1982 | Mike Bossy, N.Y. Islanders | 1992 | Mario Lemieux, Pittsburgh |
| 1973 | Yvan Cournoyer, Montreal | 1983 | Billy Smith, N.Y. Islanders | 1993 | Patrick Roy, Montreal |
| 1974 | Bernie Parent, Philadelphia | 1984 | Mark Messier, Edmonton | | |

## Most NHL Goals in a Season

| Player | Team | Season | Goals | Player | Team | Season | Goals |
|---|---|---|---|---|---|---|---|
| Wayne Gretzky | Edmonton | 1981-82 | 92 | Mike Bossy | N.Y. Islanders | 1980-81 | 68 |
| Wayne Gretzky | Edmonton | 1983-84 | 87 | Jari Kurri | Edmonton | 1985-86 | 68 |
| Brett Hull | St. Louis | 1990-91 | 86 | Phil Esposito | Boston | 1971-72 | 66 |
| Mario Lemieux | Pittsburgh | 1988-89 | 85 | Lanny McDonald | Calgary | 1982-83 | 66 |
| Phil Esposito | Boston | 1970-71 | 76 | Steve Yzerman | Detroit | 1988-89 | 65 |
| Alexander Mogilny | Buffalo | 1992-93 | 76 | Mike Bossy | N.Y. Islanders | 1981-82 | 64 |
| Teemu Selanne | Winnipeg | 1992-93 | 76 | Luc Robitaille | Los Angeles | 1992-93 | 63 |
| Wayne Gretzky | Edmonton | 1984-85 | 73 | Wayne Gretzky | Edmonton | 1986-87 | 62 |
| Brett Hull | St. Louis | 1989-90 | 72 | Steve Yzerman | Detroit | 1989-90 | 62 |
| Wayne Gretzky | Edmonton | 1982-83 | 71 | Mike Bossy | N.Y. Islanders | 1985-86 | 61 |
| Jari Kurri | Edmonton | 1984-85 | 71 | Phil Esposito | Boston | 1974-75 | 61 |
| Mario Lemieux | Pittsburgh | 1987-88 | 70 | Reggie Leach | Philadelphia | 1975-76 | 61 |
| Bernie Nicholls | Los Angeles | 1988-89 | 70 | Mike Bossy | N.Y. Islanders | 1982-83 | 60 |
| Bret Hull | St. Louis | 1991-92 | 70 | Guy Lafleur | Montreal | 1977-78 | 60 |
| Mike Bossy | N.Y. Islanders | 1978-79 | 69 | Steve Shutt | Montreal | 1976-77 | 60 |
| Mario Lemieux | Pittsburgh | 1992-93 | 69 | Dennis Maruk | Washington | 1981-82 | 60 |
| Phil Esposito | Boston | 1973-74 | 68 | Pavel Bure | Vancouver | 1992-93 | 60 |

## NCAA Hockey Champions

| | | | | | | | |
|---|---|---|---|---|---|---|---|
| 1948 | Michigan | 1960 | Denver | 1972 | Boston Univ. | 1983 | Wisconsin |
| 1949 | Boston College | 1961 | Denver | 1973 | Wisconsin | 1984 | Bowling Green |
| 1950 | Colorado College | 1962 | Michigan Tech | 1974 | Minnesota | 1985 | RPI |
| 1951 | Michigan | 1963 | North Dakota | 1975 | Michigan Tech | 1986 | Michigan State |
| 1952 | Michigan | 1964 | Michigan | 1976 | Minnesota | 1987 | North Dakota |
| 1953 | Michigan | 1965 | Michigan Tech | 1977 | Wisconsin | 1988 | Lake Superior St. |
| 1954 | RPI | 1966 | Michigan State | 1978 | Boston Univ. | 1989 | Harvard |
| 1955 | Michigan | 1967 | Cornell | 1979 | Minnesota | 1990 | Wisconsin |
| 1956 | Michigan | 1968 | Denver | 1980 | North Dakota | 1991 | N. Michigan |
| 1957 | Colorado College | 1969 | Denver | 1981 | Wisconsin | 1992 | Lake Superior St. |
| 1958 | Denver | 1970 | Cornell | 1982 | North Dakota | 1993 | Maine |
| 1959 | North Dakota | 1971 | Boston Univ. | | | | |

## THOROUGHBRED RACING

### Triple Crown Winners

Since 1920, colts have carried 126 lbs. in triple crown events; fillies 121 lbs.

(Kentucky Derby, Preakness, and Belmont Stakes)

| Year | Horse | Jockey | Trainer | Year | Horse | Jockey | Trainer |
|------|-------|--------|---------|------|-------|--------|---------|
| 1919 | Sir Barton | J. Loftus | H. G. Bedwell | 1946 | Assault | W. Mehrtens | M. Hirsch |
| 1930 | Gallant Fox | E. Sande | J. Fitzsimmons | 1948 | Citation | E. Arcaro | H.A. Jones |
| 1935 | Omaha | W. Sanders | J. Fitzsimmons | 1973 | Secretariat | R. Turcotte | L. Laurin |
| 1937 | War Admiral | C. Kurtsinger | G. Conway | 1977 | Seattle Slew | J. Cruguet | W.H. Turner Jr. |
| 1941 | Whirlaway | E. Arcaro | B.A. Jones | 1978 | Affirmed | S. Cauthen | L.S. Barrera |
| 1943 | Count Fleet | J. Longden | G.D. Cameron | | | | |

### Kentucky Derby

Churchill Downs, Louisville, Ky.; inaugurated 1875; distance 1-1/4 miles; 1-1/2 miles until 1896. 3-year olds.
Best time: 1:59.2, Secretariat, 1973

| Year | Winner | Jockey | Year | Winner | Jockey | Year | Winner | Jockey |
|------|--------|--------|------|--------|--------|------|--------|--------|
| 1875 | Aristides | O. Lewis | 1915 | Regret* | J. Notter | 1955 | Swaps | W. Shoemaker |
| 1876 | Vagrant | R. Swim | 1916 | George Smith | J. Loftus | 1956 | Needles | D. Erb |
| 1877 | Baden Baden | W. Walker | 1917 | Omar Khayyam | C. Borel | 1957 | Iron Liege | W. Hartack |
| 1878 | Day Star | J. Carter | 1918 | Exterminator | W. Knapp | 1958 | Tim Tam | I. Valenzuela |
| 1879 | Lord Murphy | C. Schauer | 1919 | Sir Barton | J. Loftus | 1960 | Tomy Lee | W. Shoemaker |
| 1880 | Fonso | G. Lewis | 1920 | Paul Jones | T. Rice | 1960 | Venetian Way | W. Hartack |
| 1881 | Hindoo | J. McLaughlin | 1921 | Behave Yourself | C. Thompson | 1961 | Carry Back | J. Sellers |
| 1882 | Apollo | B. Hurd | 1922 | Morvich | A. Johnson | 1962 | Decidedly | W. Hartack |
| 1883 | Leonatus | W. Donohue | 1923 | Zev | E. Sande | 1963 | Chateaugay | B. Baeza |
| 1884 | Buchanan | I. Murphy | 1924 | Black Gold | J. D. Mooney | 1964 | Northern Dancer | W. Hartack |
| 1885 | Joe Cotton | E. Henderson | 1925 | Flying Ebony | E. Sande | 1965 | Lucky Debonair | W. Shoemaker |
| 1886 | Ben Ali | P. Duffy | 1926 | Bubbling Over | A. Johnson | 1966 | Kauai King | D. Brumfield |
| 1887 | Montrose | I. Lewis | 1927 | Whiskery | L. McAtee | 1967 | Proud Clarion | R. Ussery |
| 1888 | Macbeth II | G. Covington | 1928 | Reigh Count | C. Lang | 1968 | Dancer's Image (a) | R. Ussery |
| 1889 | Spokane | T. Kiley | 1929 | Clyde Van Dusen | L. McAtee | 1969 | Majestic Prince | W. Hartack |
| 1890 | Riley | I. Murphy | 1930 | Gallant Fox | E. Sande | 1970 | Dust Commander | M. Manganello |
| 1891 | Kingman | I. Murphy | 1931 | Twenty Grand | C. Kurtsinger | 1971 | Canonero II | G. Avila |
| 1892 | Azra | A. Clayton | 1932 | Burgoo King | E. James | 1972 | Riva Ridge | R. Turcotte |
| 1893 | Lookout | E. Kunze | 1933 | Brokers Tip | D. Meade | 1973 | Secretariat | R. Turcotte |
| 1894 | Chant | F. Goodale | 1934 | Cavalcade | M. Garner | 1974 | Cannonade | A. Cordero |
| 1895 | Halma | J. Perkins | 1935 | Omaha | W. Saunders | 1975 | Foolish Pleasure | J. Vasquez |
| 1896 | Ben Brush | W. Simms | 1936 | Bold Venture | I. Hanford | 1976 | Bold Forbes | A. Cordero |
| 1897 | Typhoon II | F. Garner | 1937 | War Admiral | C. Kurtsinger | 1977 | Seattle Slew | J. Cruguet |
| 1898 | Plaudit | W. Simms | 1938 | Lawrin | E. Arcaro | 1978 | Affirmed | S. Cauthen |
| 1899 | Manuel | F. Taral | 1939 | Johnstown | J. Stout | 1979 | Spectacular Bid | R. Franklin |
| 1900 | Lieut. Gibson | J. Boland | 1940 | Gallahadion | C. Bierman | 1980 | Genuine Risk* | J. Vasquez |
| 1901 | His Eminence | J. Winkfield | 1941 | Whirlaway | E. Arcaro | 1981 | Pleasant Colony | J. Velasquez |
| 1902 | Alan-a-Dale | J. Winkfield | 1942 | Shut Out | W. D. Wright | 1982 | Gato del Sol | E. Delahoussaye |
| 1903 | Judge Himes | H. Booker | 1943 | Count Fleet | J. Longden | 1983 | Sunny's Halo | E. Delahoussaye |
| 1904 | Elwood | F. Prior | 1944 | Pensive | C. McCreary | 1984 | Swale | L. Pincay |
| 1905 | Agile | J. Martin | 1945 | Hoop, Jr. | E. Arcaro | 1985 | Spend a Buck | A. Cordero |
| 1906 | Sir Huon | R. Troxler | 1946 | Assault | W. Mehrtens | 1986 | Ferdinand | W. Shoemaker |
| 1907 | Pink Star | A. Minder | 1947 | Jet Pilot | E. Guerin | 1987 | Alysheba | C. McCarron |
| 1908 | Stone Street | A. Pickens | 1948 | Citation | E. Arcaro | 1988 | Winning Colors* | G. Stevens |
| 1909 | Wintergreen | V. Powers | 1949 | Ponder | S. Brooks | 1989 | Sunday Silence | P. Valenzuela |
| 1910 | Donau | F. Herbert | 1950 | Middleground | W. Boland | 1990 | Unbridled | C. Perret |
| 1911 | Meridian | G. Archibald | 1951 | Count Turf | C. McCreary | 1991 | Strike The Gold | C. Antley |
| 1912 | Worth | C.H. Shilling | 1952 | Hill Gail | E. Arcaro | 1992 | Lil E. Tee | P. Day |
| 1913 | Donerail | R. Goose | 1953 | Dark Star | H. Moreno | 1993 | Sea Hero | J. Bailey |
| 1914 | Old Rosebud | J. McCabe | 1954 | Determine | R. York | | | |

(a) Dancer's Image was disqualified from purse money after tests disclosed that he had run with a pain-killing drug, phenylbutazone, in his system. All wagers were paid on Dancer's Image. Forward Pass was awarded first place money.

The Kentucky Derby has been won five times by two jockeys, Eddie Arcaro, 1938, 1941, 1945, 1948, and 1952; and Bill Hartack, 1957, 1960, 1962, 1964, and 1969; four times by Willie Shoemaker, 1955, 1959, 1965, and 1986; and three times by each of three jockeys, Isaac Murphy, 1884, 1890, and 1891; Earle Sande, 1923, 1925, and 1930, and Angel Cordero in 1974, 1976, and 1985. * Regret, Genuine Risk, and Winning Colors are the only fillies to win the Derby.

### Preakness

Pimlico, Baltimore, Md.; inaugurated 1873; 1-3/16 miles. 3 yr. olds. Best time: 1:53.2, Tank's Prospect, 1985

| Year | Winner | Jockey | Year | Winner | Jockey | Year | Winner | Jockey |
|------|--------|--------|------|--------|--------|------|--------|--------|
| 1873 | Survivor | G. Barbee | 1887 | Dunboyne | W. Donohue | 1904 | Bryn Mawr | E. Hildebrand |
| 1874 | Culpepper | M. Donohue | 1888 | Refund | F. Littlefield | 1905 | Cairngorm | W. Davis |
| 1875 | Tom Ochiltree | L. Hughes | 1889 | Buddhist | G. Anderson | 1906 | Whimsical | W. Miller |
| 1876 | Shirley | G. Barbee | 1890 | Montague | W. Martin | 1907 | Don Enrique | G. Mountain |
| 1877 | Cloverbrook | C. Holloway | 1894 | Assignee | F. Taral | 1908 | Royal Tourist | E. Dugan |
| 1878 | Duke of Magenta | C. Holloway | 1895 | Belmar | F. Taral | 1909 | Effendi | W. Doyle |
| 1879 | Harold | L. Hughes | 1896 | Margrave | H. Griffin | 1910 | Layminster | R. Estep |
| 1880 | Grenada | L. Hughes | 1897 | Paul Kauvar | C. Thorpe | 1911 | Watervale | E. Dugan |
| 1881 | Saunterer | W. Costello | 1898 | Sly Fox | W. Simms | 1912 | Colonel Holloway | C. Turner |
| 1882 | Vanguard | W. Costello | 1899 | Half Time | R. Clawson | 1913 | Buskin | J. Butwell |
| 1883 | Jacobus | G. Barbee | 1900 | Hindus | H. Spencer | 1914 | Holiday | A. Schuttinger |
| 1884 | Knight of Ellerslie | S. H. Fisher | 1901 | The Parader | F. Landry | 1915 | Rhine Maiden | D. Hoffman |
| 1885 | Tecumseh | J. McLaughlin | 1902 | Old England | L. Jackson | 1916 | Damrosch | L. McAtee |
| 1886 | The Bard | S. H. Fisher | 1903 | Flocarline | W. Gannon | 1917 | Kalitan | E. Haynes |

| Year | Winner | Jockey | Year | Winner | Jockey | Year | Winner | Jockey |
|---|---|---|---|---|---|---|---|---|
| 1918 | War Cloud | J. Loftus | 1943 | Count Fleet | J. Longden | 1969 | Majestic Prince | W. Hartack |
|  | Jack Hare Jr. | C. Peak | 1944 | Pensive | C. McCreary | 1970 | Personality | E. Belmonte |
| 1919 | Sir Barton | J. Loftus | 1945 | Polynesian | W.D. Wright | 1971 | Canonero II | G. Avila |
| 1920 | Man o' War | C. Kummer | 1946 | Assault | W. Mehrtens | 1972 | Bee Bee Bee | E. Nelson |
| 1921 | Broomspun | F. Coltiletti | 1947 | Faultless | D. Dodson | 1973 | Secretariat | R. Turcotte |
| 1922 | Pillory | L. Morris | 1948 | Citation | E. Arcaro | 1974 | Little Current | M. Rivera |
| 1923 | Vigil | B. Marinelli | 1949 | Capot | T. Atkinson | 1975 | Master Derby | D. McHargue |
| 1924 | Nellie Morse | J. Merimee | 1950 | Hill Prince | E. Arcaro | 1976 | Elocutionist | J. Lively |
| 1925 | Coventry | C. Kummer | 1951 | Bold | E. Arcaro | 1977 | Seattle Slew | J. Cruguet |
| 1926 | Display | J. Malben | 1952 | Blue Man | C. McCreary | 1978 | Affirmed | S. Cauthen |
| 1927 | Bostonian | A. Abel | 1953 | Native Dancer | E. Guerin | 1979 | Spectacular Bid | R. Franklin |
| 1928 | Victorian | R. Workman | 1954 | Hasty Road | J. Adams | 1980 | Codex | A. Cordero |
| 1929 | Dr. Freeland | L. Schaefer | 1955 | Nashua | E. Arcaro | 1981 | Pleasant Colony | J. Velasquez |
| 1930 | Gallant Fox | E. Sande | 1956 | Fabius | W. Hartack | 1982 | Aloma's Ruler | J. Kaenel |
| 1931 | Mate | G. Ellis | 1957 | Bold Ruler | E. Arcaro | 1983 | Deputed Testamony | D. Miller |
| 1932 | Burgoo King | E. James | 1958 | Tim Tam | I. Valenzuela | 1984 | Gate Dancer | A. Cordero |
| 1933 | Head Play | C. Kurtsinger | 1959 | Royal Orbit | W. Hartack | 1985 | Tank's Prospect | P. Day |
| 1934 | High Quest | R. Jones | 1960 | Bally Ache | R. Ussery | 1986 | Snow Chief | A. Solis |
| 1935 | Omaha | W. Saunders | 1961 | Carry Back | J. Sellers | 1987 | Alysheba | C. McCarron |
| 1936 | Bold Venture | G. Woolf | 1962 | Greek Money | J.L. Rotz | 1988 | Risen Star | E. Delahoussaye |
| 1937 | War Admiral | C. Kurtsinger | 1963 | Candy Spots | W. Shoemaker | 1989 | Sunday Silence | P. Valenzuela |
| 1938 | Dauber | M. Peters | 1964 | Northern Dancer | W. Hartack | 1990 | Summer Squall | P. Day |
| 1939 | Challedon | G. Seabo | 1965 | Tom Rolfe | R. Turcotte | 1991 | Hansel | J. Bailey |
| 1940 | Bimelech | F.A. Smith | 1966 | Kauai King | D. Brumfield | 1992 | Pine Bluff | C. McCarron |
| 1941 | Whirlaway | E. Arcaro | 1967 | Damascus | W. Shoemaker | 1993 | Prairie Bayou | M. Smith |
| 1942 | Alsab | B. James | 1968 | Forward Pass | I. Valenzuela |  |  |  |

## Belmont Stakes

Elmont, N.Y.; inaugurated 1867; 1-1/2 miles. 3 year olds. Fastest time: 2:24, Secretariat, 1973

| Year | Winner | Jockey | Year | Winner | Jockey | Year | Winner | Jockey |
|---|---|---|---|---|---|---|---|---|
| 1867 | Ruthless | J. Gilpatrick | 1909 | Joe Madden | E. Dugan | 1953 | Native Dancer | E. Guerin |
| 1868 | General Duke | R. Swim | 1910 | Sweep | J. Butwell | 1954 | High Gun | E. Guerin |
| 1869 | Fenian | C. Miller | 1913 | Prince Eugene | R. Troxler | 1955 | Nashua | E. Arcaro |
| 1870 | Kingfisher | W. Dick | 1914 | Luke McLuke | M. Buxton | 1956 | Needles | D. Erb |
| 1871 | Harry Bassett | W. Miller | 1915 | The Finn | G. Byrne | 1957 | Gallant Man | W. Shoemaker |
| 1872 | Joe Daniels | J. Rowe | 1916 | Friar Rock | E. Haynes | 1958 | Cavan | P. Anderson |
| 1873 | Springbok | J. Rowe | 1917 | Hourless | J. Butwell | 1959 | Sword Dancer | W. Shoemaker |
| 1874 | Saxon | G. Barbee | 1918 | Johren | F. Robinson | 1960 | Celtic Ash | W. Hartack |
| 1875 | Calvin | R. Swim | 1919 | Sir Barton | J. Loftus | 1961 | Sherluck | B. Baeza |
| 1876 | Algerine | W. Donohue | 1920 | Man o' War | C. Kummer | 1962 | Jaipur | W. Shoemaker |
| 1877 | Cloverbrook | C. Holloway | 1921 | Grey Lag | E. Sande | 1963 | Chateaugay | B. Baeza |
| 1878 | Duke of Magenta | L. Hughes | 1922 | Pillory | C.H. Miller | 1964 | Quadrangle | M. Ycaza |
| 1879 | Spendthrift | S. Evans | 1923 | Zev | E. Sande | 1965 | Hail to All | J. Sellers |
| 1880 | Grenada | L. Hughes | 1924 | Mad Play | E. Sande | 1966 | Amberoid | W. Boland |
| 1881 | Saunterer | T. Costello | 1925 | American Flag | A. Johnson | 1967 | Damascus | W. Shoemaker |
| 1882 | Forester | J. McLaughlin | 1926 | Crusader | A. Johnson | 1968 | Stage Door Johnny | H. Gustines |
| 1883 | George Kinney | J. McLaughlin | 1927 | Chance Shot | E. Sande | 1969 | Arts and Letters | B. Baeza |
| 1884 | Panique | J. McLaughlin | 1928 | Vito | C. Kummer | 1970 | High Echelon | J.L. Rotz |
| 1885 | Tyrant | P. Duffy | 1929 | Blue Larkspur | M. Garner | 1971 | Pass Catcher | W. Blum |
| 1886 | Inspector B. | J. McLaughlin | 1930 | Gallant Fox | E. Sande | 1972 | Riva Ridge | R. Turcotte |
| 1887 | Hanover | J. McLaughlin | 1931 | Twenty Grand | C. Kurtsinger | 1973 | Secretariat | R. Turcotte |
| 1888 | Sir Dixon | J. McLaughlin | 1932 | Faireno | T. Malley | 1974 | Little Current | M. Rivera |
| 1889 | Eric | W. Hayward | 1933 | Hurryoff | M. Garner | 1975 | Avatar | W. Shoemaker |
| 1890 | Burlington | S. Barnes | 1934 | Peace Chance | W.D. Wright | 1976 | Bold Forbes | A. Cordero |
| 1891 | Foxford | E. Garrison | 1935 | Omaha | W. Saunders | 1977 | Seattle Slew | J. Cruguet |
| 1892 | Patron | W. Hayward | 1936 | Granville | J. Stout | 1978 | Affirmed | S. Cauthen |
| 1893 | Comanche | W. Simms | 1937 | War Admiral | C. Kurtsinger | 1979 | Coastal | R. Hernandez |
| 1894 | Henry of Navarre | W. Simms | 1938 | Pasteurized | J. Stout | 1980 | Temperence Hill | E. Maple |
| 1895 | Belmar | F. Taral | 1939 | Johnstown | J. Stout | 1981 | Summing | G. Martens |
| 1896 | Hastings | H. Griffin | 1940 | Bimelech | F.A. Smith | 1982 | Conquistador Cielo | L. Pincay |
| 1897 | Scottish Chieftain | J. Scherrer | 1941 | Whirlaway | E. Arcaro | 1983 | Caveat | L. Pincay |
| 1898 | Bowling Brook | F. Littlefield | 1942 | Shut Out | E. Arcaro | 1984 | Swale | L. Pincay |
| 1899 | Jean Bereaud | R.R. Clawson | 1943 | Count Fleet | J. Longden | 1985 | Creme Fraiche | E. Maple |
| 1900 | Ildrim | N. Turner | 1944 | Bounding Home | G.L. Smith | 1986 | Danzig Connection | C. McCarron |
| 1901 | Commando | H. Spencer | 1945 | Pavot | E. Arcaro | 1987 | Bet Twice | C. Perret |
| 1902 | Masterman | J. Bullman | 1946 | Assault | W. Mehrtens | 1988 | Risen Star | E. Delahoussaye |
| 1903 | Africander | J. Bullman | 1947 | Phalanx | R. Donoso | 1989 | Easy Goer | P. Day |
| 1904 | Delhi | G. Odom | 1948 | Citation | E. Arcaro | 1990 | Go and Go | M. Kinane |
| 1905 | Tanya | E. Hildebrand | 1949 | Capot | T. Atkinson | 1991 | Hansel | J. Bailey |
| 1906 | Burgomaster | L. Lyne | 1950 | Middleground | W. Boland | 1992 | A.P. Indy | E. Delahoussaye |
| 1907 | Peter Pan | G. Mountain | 1951 | Counterpoint | D. Gorman | 1993 | Colonial Affair | J. Krone |
| 1908 | Colin | J. Notter | 1952 | One Count | E. Arcaro |  |  |  |

## Annual Leading Jockey—Money Won

| Year | Jockey | Dollars | Year | Jockey | Dollars | Year | Jockey | Dollars |
|---|---|---|---|---|---|---|---|---|
| 1957 | Bill Hartack | 3,060,501 | 1969 | Jorge Velasquez | 2,542,315 | 1981 | Chris McCarron | 8,397,604 |
| 1958 | Willie Shoemaker | 2,961,693 | 1970 | Laffit Pincay Jr. | 2,626,526 | 1982 | Angel Cordero Jr. | 9,483,590 |
| 1959 | Willie Shoemaker | 2,843,133 | 1971 | Laffit Pincay Jr. | 3,784,377 | 1983 | Angel Cordero Jr. | 10,116,697 |
| 1960 | Willie Shoemaker | 2,123,961 | 1972 | Laffit Pincay Jr. | 3,225,827 | 1984 | Chris McCarron | 12,045,813 |
| 1961 | Willie Shoemaker | 2,690,819 | 1973 | Laffit Pincay Jr. | 4,093,492 | 1985 | Laffit Pincay Jr. | 13,353,299 |
| 1962 | Willie Shoemaker | 2,916,844 | 1974 | Laffit Pincay Jr. | 4,251,060 | 1986 | Jose Santos | 11,329,297 |
| 1963 | Willie Shoemaker | 2,526,925 | 1975 | Braulio Baeza | 3,695,198 | 1987 | Jose Santos | 12,375,433 |
| 1964 | Willie Shoemaker | 2,649,553 | 1976 | Angel Cordero Jr. | 4,709,500 | 1988 | Jose Santos | 14,877,298 |
| 1965 | Braulio Baeza | 2,582,702 | 1977 | Steve Cauthen | 6,151,750 | 1989 | Jose Santos | 13,838,389 |
| 1966 | Braulio Baeza | 2,951,022 | 1978 | Darrel McHargue | 6,029,885 | 1990 | Gary Stevens | 13,881,198 |
| 1967 | Braulio Baeza | 3,088,888 | 1979 | Laffit Pincay Jr. | 8,193,535 | 1991 | Chris McCarron | 14,441,083 |
| 1968 | Braulio Baeza | 2,835,108 | 1980 | Chris McCarron | 7,663,300 | 1992 | Kent Desormeaux | 14,193,006 |

# Breeders' Cup

The Breeders' Cup was inaugurated in 1984 and consists of seven races at one track on one day late in the year to determine thoroughbred racing's champion contenders.

## Juvenile

### Distances: one mile 1984-85, 87; 1 1/16 miles 1986 and since 1988

| Year | Jockey | Year | Jockey | Year | Jockey |
|---|---|---|---|---|---|
| 1984 Chief's Crown | Don MacBeth | 1987 Success | | | |
| 1985 Tasso | Laffit Pincay Jr. | Express | Jose Santos | 1990 Fly So Free | Jose Santos |
| 1986 Capote | Laffit Pincay Jr. | 1988 Is It True | Laffit Pincay Jr. | 1991 Arazi | Pat Valenzuela |
| | | 1989 Rhythm | Craig Perret | 1992 Gilded Time | Chris McCarron |

## Juvenile Fillies

### Distances: one mile 1984-85, 87; 1 1/16 miles 1986 and since 1988

| Year | Jockey | Year | Jockey | Year | Jockey |
|---|---|---|---|---|---|
| 1984 *Outstandingly | Walter Guerra | 1988 Open Mind | Angel Cordero Jr. | 1991 Pleasant | |
| 1985 Twilight Ridge | Jorge Velasquez | 1989 Go for Wand | Randy Romero | Stage | Eddie Delahoussaye |
| 1986 Brave Raj | Pat Valenzuela | 1990 Meadow Star | Jose Santos | 1992 Eliza | Pat Valenzuela |
| 1987 Epitome | Pat Day | | | | |
| *By disqualification. | | | | | |

## Sprint

### Distance: six furlongs

| Year | Jockey | Year | Jockey | Year | Jockey |
|---|---|---|---|---|---|
| 1984 Eillo | Craig Perret | 1988 Gulch | Angel Cordero Jr. | 1991 Sheikh | |
| 1985 Precisionist | Chris McCarron | 1989 Dancing Spree | Angel Cordero Jr. | Albadou | Pat Eddery |
| 1986 Smile | Jacinto Vasquez | 1990 Safely Kept | Craig Perret | 1992 Thirty Slews | Eddie Delahoussaye |
| 1987 Very Subtle | Pat Valenzuela | | | | |

## Mile

| Year | Jockey | Year | Jockey | Year | Jockey |
|---|---|---|---|---|---|
| 1984 Royal Heroine | Fernando Toro | 1988 Miesque | Freddie Head | 1991 Opening Verse | Pat Valenzuela |
| 1985 Cozzene | Walter Guerra | 1989 Steinlen | Jose Santos | 1992 Lure | Mike Smith |
| 1986 Last Tycoon | Yves St.-Martin | 1990 Royal | | | |
| 1987 Miesque | Freddie Head | Academy | Lester Piggott | | |

## Distaff

### Distances: 1 1/4 miles 1984-87; 1 1/8 miles since 1988

| Year | Jockey | Year | Jockey | Year | Jockey |
|---|---|---|---|---|---|
| 1984 Princess | | 1987 Sacahuista | Randy Romero | 1990 Bayakoa | Laffit Pincay Jr. |
| Rooney | Eddie Delahoussaye | 1988 Personal | | 1991 Dance Smartly | Pat Day |
| 1985 Life's Magic | Angel Cordero Jr. | Ensign | Randy Romero | 1992 Paseana | Chris McCarron |
| 1986 Lady's Secret | Pat Day | 1989 Bayakoa | Laffit Pincay Jr. | | |

## Turf

### Distance: 1 1/2 miles

| Year | Jockey | Year | Jockey | Year | Jockey |
|---|---|---|---|---|---|
| 1984 Lashkari | Yves St.-Martin | 1988 Great | | 1990 In The Wings | Gary Stevens |
| 1985 Pebbles | Pat Eddery | Communicator | Ray Sibille | 1991 Miss Alleged | Eric Legrix |
| 1986 Manila | Jose Santos | 1989 Prized | Eddie Delahoussaye | 1992 Fraise | Pat Valenzuela |
| 1987 Theatrical | Pat Day | | | | |

## Classic

### Distance: 1 1/4 miles

| Year | Jockey | Year | Jockey | Year | Jockey |
|---|---|---|---|---|---|
| 1984 Wild Again | Pat Day | 1988 Alysheba | Chris McCarron | 1991 Black Tie | |
| 1985 Proud Truth | Jorge Velasquez | 1989 Sunday | | Affair | Jerry Bailey |
| 1986 Skywalker | Laffit Pincay Jr. | Silence | Chris McCarron | 1992 A.P. Indy | Eddie Delahoussaye |
| 1987 Ferdinand | Bill Shoemaker | 1990 Unbridled | Pat Day | | |

# Eclipse Awards

The Eclipse Awards, honoring the Horse of the Year and other champions of the sport, began in 1971, and are sponsored by the *Daily Racing Form*, the Thoroughbred Racing Associations and the National Turf Writers Assn. Prior to 1971, the DRF (1936-70) and the TRA (1950-70) issued separate selections for horse of the year.

## Eclipse Awards in 1992

Horse of the Year—A.P. Indy
2-year-old colt—Gilded Time
2-year-old filly—Eliza
3-year-old colt—A.P. Indy
3-year-old filly—Saratoga Dew
Colt, horse, or gelding (4-year-olds & up)—Pleasant Tap
Filly or mare (4-year-olds & up)—Paseana
Male turf horse—Sky Classic

Turf filly or mare—Flawlessly
Sprinter—Rubiano
Steeplechase horse—Lonesome Glory
Trainer—Ron McNally
Jockey—Kent Desormeaux
Apprentice jockey—Mickey Walls
Breeder—William S. Farish 3d

## Horse of the Year

| Year | Horse | Year | Horse | Year | Horse | Year | Horse |
|------|-------|------|-------|------|-------|------|-------|
| 1936 | Granville | 1952 | One Count (DRF) | 1965 | Roman Brother (DRF) | 1978 | Affirmed |
| 1937 | War Admiral | | Native Dancer (TRA) | | Moccasin (TRA) | 1979 | Affirmed |
| 1938 | Seabiscuit | 1953 | Tom Fool | 1966 | Buckpasser | 1980 | Spectacular Bid |
| 1939 | Challedon | 1954 | Native Dancer | 1967 | Damascus | 1981 | John Henry |
| 1940 | Chaliedon | 1955 | Nashua | 1968 | Dr. Fager | 1982 | Conquistador Cielo |
| 1941 | Whirlaway | 1956 | Swaps | 1969 | Arts and Letters | 1983 | All Along |
| 1942 | Whirlaway | 1957 | Bold Ruler (DRF) | 1970 | Fort Marcy (DRF) | 1984 | John Henry |
| 1943 | Count Fleet | | Dedicate (TRA) | | Personality (TRA) | 1985 | Spend A Buck |
| 1944 | Twilight Tear | 1958 | Round Table | 1971 | Ack Ack | 1986 | Lady's Secret |
| 1945 | Busher | 1959 | Sword Dancer | 1972 | Secretariat | 1987 | Ferdinand |
| 1946 | Assault | 1960 | Kelso | 1973 | Secretariat | 1988 | Alysheba |
| 1947 | Armed | 1961 | Kelso | 1974 | Forego | 1989 | Sunday Silence |
| 1948 | Citation | 1962 | Kelso | 1975 | Forego | 1990 | Criminal Type |
| 1949 | Capot | 1963 | Kelso | 1976 | Forego | 1991 | Black Tie Affair |
| 1950 | Hill Prince | 1964 | Kelso | 1977 | Seattle Slew | 1992 | A.P. Indy |
| 1951 | Counterpoint | | | | | | |

# NATIONAL BASKETBALL ASSOCIATION

## Final Standings, 1992-1993 Season

### Eastern Conference

#### Atlantic Division

| | W | L | Pct | GB |
|---|---|---|-----|-----|
| New York | 60 | 22 | .732 | — |
| Boston | 48 | 34 | .585 | 12 |
| New Jersey | 43 | 39 | .524 | 17 |
| Orlando | 41 | 41 | .500 | 19 |
| Miami | 36 | 46 | .439 | 24 |
| Philadelphia | 26 | 56 | .317 | 34 |
| Washington | 22 | 60 | .268 | 38 |

#### Central Division

| | W | L | Pct | GB |
|---|---|---|-----|-----|
| Chicago | 57 | 25 | .695 | — |
| Cleveland | 54 | 28 | .659 | 3 |
| Charlotte | 44 | 38 | .537 | 13 |
| Atlanta | 43 | 39 | .524 | 14 |
| Indiana | 41 | 41 | .500 | 16 |
| Detroit | 40 | 42 | .488 | 17 |
| Milwaukee | 28 | 54 | .341 | 29 |

### Western Conference

#### Midwest Division

| | W | L | Pct | GB |
|---|---|---|-----|-----|
| Houston | 55 | 27 | .671 | — |
| San Antonio | 49 | 33 | .598 | 6 |
| Utah | 47 | 35 | .573 | 8 |
| Denver | 36 | 46 | .439 | 19 |
| Minnesota | 19 | 63 | .232 | 36 |
| Dallas | 11 | 71 | .134 | 44 |

#### Pacific Division

| | W | L | Pct | GB |
|---|---|---|-----|-----|
| Phoenix | 62 | 20 | .756 | — |
| Seattle | 55 | 27 | .671 | 7 |
| Portland | 51 | 31 | .622 | 11 |
| L.A. Clippers | 41 | 41 | .500 | 21 |
| L.A. Lakers | 39 | 43 | .476 | 23 |
| Golden State | 34 | 48 | .415 | 28 |
| Sacramento | 25 | 57 | .305 | 37 |

## NBA Regular Season Individual Highs in 1992-1993

**Most minutes played, season** — 3,323: Larry Johnson, Charlotte.

**Most points, game** — 64: Michael Jordan, Chicago vs. Orlando, Jan. 16 (OT).

**Most field goals made, game** — 27: Michael Jordan, Chicago vs. Orlando, Jan. 16 (OT).

**Most field goal attempts, game** — 49: Michael Jordan, Chicago vs. Orlando, Jan. 16 (OT).

**Most 3-point field goals made, game** — 10: Brian Shaw, Miami vs. Milwaukee, April 8.

**Most 3-point field goal attempts, game** — 19: Dennis Scott, Orlando vs. Milwaukee, April 13.

**Most free throws made, game** — 23: Dominique Wilkins, Atlanta vs. Chicago, Dec. 8.

**Most rebounds, game** — 34: Rony Seikaly, Miami vs. Washington, March 3.

**Most offensive rebounds, season** — 367: Dennis Rodman, Detroit.

**Most defensive rebounds, season** — 789: Patrick Ewing, New York.

**Most assists, game** — 23: Mookie Blaylock, Atlanta vs. Utah, March 6.

**Most personal fouls, season** — 332: Stanley Roberts, L.A. Clippers.

**Most games disqualified, season** — 15: Stanley Roberts, L.A. Clippers.

### Bulls Win Third Straight Championship by Beating Phoenix Suns in Six Games

The Chicago Bulls won their third consecutive National Basketball Association championship by defeating the Phoenix Suns 4 games to 2. It was the first time a team had won more than two straight titles since the Boston Celtics ran off eight in a row, 1959-1966. Michael Jordan was chosen the most valuable player in the finals for the third consecutive year.

#### Chicago Bulls

| | FG M-A | FT M-A | Reb | Ast | Avg |
|---|--------|--------|-----|-----|-----|
| Jordan | 101-199 | 34-39 | 15-51 | 38 | 41.0 |
| Pippen | 54-123 | 19-35 | 16-55 | 46 | 21.2 |
| Armstrong | 32-63 | 7-7 | 2-11 | 30 | 13.5 |
| Grant | 28-53 | 11-19 | 25-62 | 14 | 11.2 |
| Paxson | 13-21 | 0-0 | 4-9 | 5 | 5.8 |
| S. Williams | 13-32 | 2-7 | 12-38 | 10 | 4.7 |
| Cartwright | 12-30 | 2-4 | 7-19 | 10 | 4.3 |
| Tucker | 7-10 | 0-0 | 1-2 | 4 | 2.8 |
| King | 3-11 | 7-8 | 3-8 | 3 | 2.2 |
| Walker | 0-0 | 0-1 | 0-0 | 1 | 0.0 |
| McCray | 0-0 | 0-0 | 0-1 | 0 | 0.0 |
| Perdue | 0-2 | 0-0 | 1-3 | 0 | 0.0 |
| Totals | 263-544 | 82-130 | 86-321 | 161 | 106.7 |

#### Phoenix Suns

| | FG M-A | FT M-A | Reb | Ast | Avg |
|---|--------|--------|-----|-----|-----|
| Barkley | 60-126 | 42-56 | 22-78 | 33 | 27.3 |
| K. Johnson | 40-95 | 23-25 | 2-18 | 39 | 17.2 |
| Majerle | 35-79 | 16-20 | 12-49 | 22 | 17.2 |
| Dumas | 44-77 | 7-9 | 15-26 | 6 | 15.8 |
| Ainge | 19-40 | 7-9 | 7-18 | 15 | 8.8 |
| Chambers | 14-39 | 12-15 | 5-18 | 3 | 6.7 |
| West | 13-21 | 8-15 | 12-26 | 4 | 5.7 |
| Miller | 12-27 | 6-8 | 10-25 | 8 | 5.0 |
| F. Johnson | 7-17 | 4-4 | 1-2 | 5 | 3.6 |
| Mustaf | 0-0 | 0-0 | 0-0 | 0 | 0.0 |
| Totals | 244-521 | 125-161 | 86-260 | 135 | 106.7 |

## 1993 NBA Playoff Results

### Eastern Division

New York defeated Indiana 3 games to 1
Chicago defeated Atlanta 3 games to 0
Charlotte defeated Boston 3 games to 1
Cleveland defeated New Jersey 3 games to 2
Chicago defeated Cleveland 4 games to 0
New York defeated Charlotte 4 games to 1
Chicago defeated New York 4 games to 2

### Western Division

Phoenix defeated L.A. Lakers 3 games to 2
San Antonio defeated Portland 3 games to 1
Houston defeated L.A. Clippers 3 games to 2
Seattle defeated Utah 3 games to 2
Phoenix defeated San Antonio 4 games to 2
Seattle defeated Houston 4 games to 3
Phoenix defeated Seattle 4 games to 3

### Championship

Chicago defeated Phoenix 4 games to 2

## MVP in Playoffs

| | | | | | | |
|---|---|---|---|---|---|---|
| 1969 | Jerry West, Los Angeles | 1978 | Wes Unseld, Washington | 1986 | Larry Bird, Boston |
| 1970 | Willis Reed, New York | 1979 | Dennis Johnson, Seattle | 1987 | Magic Johnson, L.A. Lakers |
| 1971 | Lew Alcindor, Milwaukee | 1980 | Magic Johnson, Los Angeles | 1988 | James Worthy, L.A. Lakers |
| 1972 | Wilt Chamberlain, Los Angeles | 1981 | Cedric Maxwell, Boston | 1989 | Joe Dumars, Detroit |
| 1973 | Willis Reed, New York | 1982 | Magic Johnson, Los Angeles | 1990 | Isiah Thomas, Detroit |
| 1974 | John Havlicek, Boston | 1983 | Moses Malone, Philadelphia | 1991 | Michael Jordan, Chicago |
| 1975 | Rick Barry, Golden State | 1984 | Larry Bird, Boston | 1992 | Michael Jordan, Chicago |
| 1976 | Jo Jo White, Boston | 1985 | Kareem Abdul-Jabbar, L.A. | 1993 | Michael Jordan, Chicago |
| 1977 | Bill Walton, Portland | | Lakers | | |

## NBA Scoring Leaders

| Year | Scoring champion | Pts | Avg | Year | Scoring champion | Pts | Avg |
|---|---|---|---|---|---|---|---|
| 1947 | Joe Fulks, Philadelphia | 1,389 | 23.2 | 1971 | Lew Alcindor, Milwaukee | 2,596 | 31.7 |
| 1948 | Max Zaslofsky, Chicago | 1,007 | 21.0 | 1972 | Kareem Abdul-Jabbar (Alcindor), | | |
| 1949 | George Mikan, Minneapolis | 1,698 | 28.3 | | Milwaukee | 2,822 | 34.8 |
| 1950 | George Mikan, Minneapolis | 1,865 | 27.4 | 1973 | Nate Archibald, Kansas City-Omaha | 2,719 | 34.0 |
| 1951 | George Mikan, Minneapolis | 1,932 | 28.4 | 1974 | Bob McAdoo, Buffalo | 2,261 | 30.6 |
| 1952 | Paul Arizin, Philadelphia | 1,674 | 25.4 | 1975 | Bob McAdoo, Buffalo | 2,831 | 34.5 |
| 1953 | Neil Johnston, Philadelphia | 1,564 | 22.3 | 1976 | Bob McAdoo, Buffalo | 2,427 | 31.1 |
| 1954 | Neil Johnston, Philadelphia | 1,759 | 24.4 | 1977 | Pete Maravich, New Orleans | 2,273 | 31.1 |
| 1955 | Neil Johnston, Philadelphia | 1,631 | 22.7 | 1978 | George Gervin, San Antonio | 2,232 | 27.2 |
| 1956 | Bob Pettit, St. Louis | 1,849 | 25.7 | 1979 | George Gervin, San Antonio | 2,365 | 29.6 |
| 1957 | Paul Arizin, Philadelphia | 1,817 | 25.6 | 1980 | George Gervin, San Antonio | 2,585 | 33.1 |
| 1958 | George Yardley, Detroit | 2,001 | 27.8 | 1981 | Adrian Dantley, Utah | 2,452 | 30.7 |
| 1959 | Bob Pettit, St. Louis | 2,105 | 29.2 | 1982 | George Gervin, San Antonio | 2,551 | 32.3 |
| 1960 | Wilt Chamberlain, Philadelphia | 2,707 | 37.9 | 1983 | Alex English, Denver | 2,326 | 28.4 |
| 1961 | Wilt Chamberlain, Philadelphia | 3,033 | 38.4 | 1984 | Adrian Dantley, Utah | 2,418 | 30.6 |
| 1962 | Wilt Chamberlain, Philadelphia | 4,029 | 50.4 | 1985 | Bernard King, New York | 1,809 | 32.9 |
| 1963 | Wilt Chamberlain, San Francisco | 3,586 | 44.8 | 1986 | Dominique Wilkins, Atlanta | 2,366 | 30.3 |
| 1964 | Wilt Chamberlain, San Francisco | 2,948 | 36.5 | 1987 | Michael Jordan, Chicago | 3,041 | 37.1 |
| 1965 | Wilt Chamberlain, San Fran., Phila. | 2,534 | 34.7 | 1988 | Michael Jordan, Chicago | 2,868 | 35.0 |
| 1966 | Wilt Chamberlain, Philadelphia | 2,649 | 33.5 | 1989 | Michael Jordan, Chicago | 2,633 | 32.5 |
| 1967 | Rick Barry, San Francisco | 2,775 | 35.6 | 1990 | Michael Jordan, Chicago | 2,753 | 33.6 |
| 1968 | Dave Bing, Detroit | 2,142 | 27.1 | 1991 | Michael Jordan, Chicago | 2,580 | 31.5 |
| 1969 | Elvin Hayes, San Diego | 2,327 | 28.4 | 1992 | Michael Jordan, Chicago | 2,404 | 30.1 |
| 1970 | Jerry West, Los Angeles | 2,309 | 31.2 | 1993 | Michael Jordan, Chicago | 2,541 | 32.6 |

## NBA Most Valuable Player

| | | | |
|---|---|---|---|
| 1956 | Bob Pettit, St. Louis | 1975 | Bob McAdoo, Buffalo |
| 1957 | Bob Cousy, Boston | 1976 | Kareem Abdul-Jabbar, Los Angeles |
| 1958 | Bill Russell, Boston | 1977 | Kareem Abdul-Jabbar, Los Angeles |
| 1959 | Bob Pettit, St. Louis | 1978 | Bill Walton, Portland |
| 1960 | Wilt Chamberlain, Philadelphia | 1979 | Moses Malone, Houston |
| 1961 | Bill Russell, Boston | 1980 | Kareem Abdul-Jabbar, Los Angeles |
| 1962 | Bill Russell, Boston | 1981 | Julius Erving, Philadelphia |
| 1963 | Bill Russell, Boston | 1982 | Moses Malone, Houston |
| 1964 | Oscar Robertson, Cincinnati | 1983 | Moses Malone, Philadelphia |
| 1965 | Bill Russell, Boston | 1984 | Larry Bird, Boston |
| 1966 | Wilt Chamberlain, Philadelphia | 1985 | Larry Bird, Boston |
| 1967 | Wilt Chamberlain, Philadelphia | 1986 | Larry Bird, Boston |
| 1968 | Wilt Chamberlain, Philadelphia | 1987 | Magic Johnson, L.A. Lakers |
| 1969 | Wes Unseld, Baltimore | 1988 | Michael Jordan, Chicago |
| 1970 | Willis Reed, New York | 1989 | Magic Johnson, L.A. Lakers |
| 1971 | Lew Alcindor, Milwaukee | 1990 | Magic Johnson, L.A. Lakers |
| 1972 | Kareem Abdul-Jabbar (Alcindor), Milwaukee | 1991 | Michael Jordan, Chicago |
| 1973 | Dave Cowens, Boston | 1992 | Michael Jordan, Chicago |
| 1974 | Kareem Abdul-Jabbar, Milwaukee | 1993 | Charles Barkley, Phoenix |

## NBA Champions 1947-1993

| | Regular season | | | Playoffs | |
|---|---|---|---|---|---|
| Year | Eastern Conference | Western Conference | Winner | Coach | Runner-up |
| 1947 | Washington | Chicago | Philadelphia | Ed Gottlieb | Chicago |
| 1948 | Philadelphia | St. Louis | Baltimore | Buddy Jeannette | Philadelphia |
| 1949 | Washington | Rochester | Minneapolis | John Kundla | Washington |
| 1950 | Syracuse | Minneapolis | Minneapolis | John Kundla | Syracuse |
| 1951 | Philadelphia | Minneapolis | Rochester | Lester Harrison | New York |
| 1952 | Syracuse | Rochester | Minneapolis | John Kundla | New York |
| 1953 | New York | Minneapolis | Minneapolis | John Kundla | New York |
| 1954 | New York | Minneapolis | Minneapolis | John Kundla | Syracuse |
| 1955 | Syracuse | Ft. Wayne | Syracuse | Al Cervi | Ft. Wayne |
| 1956 | Philadelphia | Ft. Wayne | Philadelphia | George Senesky | Ft. Wayne |
| 1957 | Boston | St. Louis | Boston | Red Auerbach | St. Louis |
| 1958 | Boston | St. Louis | St. Louis | Alex Hannum | Boston |
| 1959 | Boston | St. Louis | Boston | Red Auerbach | Minneapolis |
| 1960 | Boston | St. Louis | Boston | Red Auerbach | St. Louis |
| 1961 | Boston | St. Louis | Boston | Red Auerbach | St. Louis |
| 1962 | Boston | Los Angeles | Boston | Red Auerbach | Los Angeles |
| 1963 | Boston | Los Angeles | Boston | Red Auerbach | Los Angeles |
| 1964 | Boston | San Francisco | Boston | Red Auerbach | San Francisco |
| 1965 | Boston | Los Angeles | Boston | Red Auerbach | Los Angeles |
| 1966 | Philadelphia | Los Angeles | Boston | Red Auerbach | Los Angeles |
| 1967 | Philadelphia | San Francisco | Philadelphia | Alex Hannum | San Francisco |
| 1968 | Philadelphia | St. Louis | Boston | Bill Russell | Los Angeles |
| 1969 | Baltimore | Los Angeles | Boston | Bill Russell | Los Angeles |
| 1970 | New York | Atlanta | New York | Red Holzman | Los Angeles |

| | Atlantic | Central | Midwest | Pacific | Winner | Coach | Runner-up |
|---|---|---|---|---|---|---|---|
| 1971 | New York | Baltimore | Milwaukee | Los Angeles | Milwaukee | Larry Costello | Baltimore |
| 1972 | Boston | Baltimore | Milwaukee | Los Angeles | Los Angeles | Bill Sharman | New York |
| 1973 | Boston | Baltimore | Milwaukee | Los Angeles | New York | Red Holzman | Los Angeles |
| 1974 | Boston | Capital | Milwaukee | Los Angeles | Boston | Tom Heinsohn | Milwaukee |
| 1975 | Boston | Washington | Chicago | Golden State | Golden State | Al Attles | Washington |
| 1976 | Boston | Cleveland | Milwaukee | Golden State | Boston | Tom Heinsohn | Phoenix |
| 1977 | Philadelphia | Houston | Denver | Los Angeles | Portland | Jack Ramsay | Philadelphia |
| 1978 | Philadelphia | San Antonio | Denver | Portland | Washington | Dick Motta | Seattle |
| 1979 | Washington | San Antonio | Kansas City | Seattle | Seattle | Len Wilkens | Washington |
| 1980 | Boston | Atlanta | Milwaukee | Los Angeles | Los Angeles | Paul Westhead | Philadelphia |
| 1981 | Boston | Milwaukee | San Antonio | Phoenix | Boston | Bill Fitch | Houston |
| 1982 | Boston | Milwaukee | San Antonio | Los Angeles | Los Angeles | Pat Riley | Philadelphia |
| 1983 | Philadelphia | Milwaukee | San Antonio | Los Angeles | Philadelphia | Billy Cunningham | Los Angeles |
| 1984 | Boston | Milwaukee | Utah | Los Angeles | Boston | K.C. Jones | Los Angeles |
| 1985 | Boston | Milwaukee | Denver | L.A. Lakers | L.A. Lakers | Pat Riley | Boston |
| 1986 | Boston | Milwaukee | Houston | L.A. Lakers | Boston | K.C. Jones | Houston |
| 1987 | Boston | Atlanta | Dallas | L.A. Lakers | L.A. Lakers | Pat Riley | Boston |
| 1988 | Boston | Detroit | Denver | L.A. Lakers | L.A. Lakers | Pat Riley | Detroit |
| 1989 | New York | Detroit | Utah | L.A. Lakers | Detroit | Chuck Daly | L.A. Lakers |
| 1990 | Philadelphia | Detroit | San Antonio | L.A. Lakers | Detroit | Chuck Daly | Portland |
| 1991 | Boston | Chicago | San Antonio | Portland | Chicago | Phil Jackson | L.A. Lakers |
| 1992 | Boston | Chicago | Utah | Portland | Chicago | Phil Jackson | Portland |
| 1993 | New York | Chicago | Houston | Phoenix | Chicago | Phil Jackson | Phoenix |

## NBA Coach of the Year, 1963-1993

1963 Harry Gallatin, St. Louis Hawks
1964 Alex Hannum, San Francisco Warriors
1965 Red Auerbach, Boston Celtics
1966 Dolph Schayes, Philadelphia 76ers
1967 Johnny Kerr, Chicago Bulls
1968 Richie Guerin, St. Louis Hawks
1969 Gene Shue, Baltimore Bullets
1970 Red Holzman, New York Knicks
1971 Dick Motta, Chicago Bulls
1972 Bill Sharman, Los Angeles Lakers
1973 Tom Heinsohn, Boston Celtics

1974 Ray Scott, Detroit Pistons
1975 Phil Johnson, Kansas City-Omaha Kings
1976 Bill Fitch, Cleveland Cavaliers
1977 Tom Nissalke, Houston Rockets
1978 Hubie Brown, Atlanta Hawks
1979 Cotton Fitzsimmons, Kansas City Kings
1980 Bill Fitch, Boston Celtics
1981 Jack McKinney, Indiana Pacers
1982 Gene Shue, Washington Bullets
1983 Don Nelson, Milwaukee Bucks
1984 Frank Layden, Utah Jazz

1985 Don Nelson, Milwaukee Bucks
1986 Mike Fratello, Atlanta Hawks
1987 Mike Schuler, Portland Trail Blazers
1988 Doug Moe, Denver Nuggets
1989 Cotton Fitzsimmons, Phoenix Suns
1990 Pat Riley, Los Angeles Lakers
1991 Don Chaney, Houston Rockets
1992 Don Nelson, Golden State Warriors
1993 Pat Riley, New York Knicks

## NBA All-League Team in 1993

| First team | Position | Second team |
|---|---|---|
| Karl Malone, Utah | Forward | Dominique Wilkins, Atlanta |
| Charles Barkley, Phoenix | Forward | Larry Johnson, Charlotte |
| Hakeem Olajuwon, Houston | Center | Patrick Ewing, New York |
| Mark Price, Cleveland | Guard | Joe Dumars, Detroit |
| Michael Jordan, Chicago | Guard | John Stockton, Utah |

## NBA Statistical Leaders, 1992-1993

### Scoring
(70 Games or 1,400 Pts.)

| | G | FG | Pts | Avg |
|---|---|---|---|---|
| Jordan, Chicago | 78 | 992 | 2541 | 32.6 |
| Wilkins, Atlanta | 71 | 741 | 2121 | 29.9 |
| K. Malone, Utah | 82 | 797 | 2217 | 27.0 |
| Olajuwon, Houston | 82 | 848 | 2140 | 26.1 |
| Barkley, Phoenix | 76 | 716 | 1944 | 25.6 |
| Ewing, New York | 81 | 779 | 1959 | 24.2 |
| Dumars, Detroit | 77 | 677 | 1809 | 23.5 |
| O'Neal, Orlando | 81 | 733 | 1893 | 23.4 |
| Robinson, San Antonio | 82 | 676 | 1916 | 23.4 |
| Manning, L.A. Clippers | 79 | 702 | 1800 | 22.8 |
| Petrovic, New Jersey | 70 | 587 | 1564 | 22.3 |
| Johnson, Charlotte | 82 | 728 | 1810 | 22.1 |
| Hardaway, Golden St. | 66 | 522 | 1419 | 21.5 |
| Miller, Indiana | 82 | 571 | 1736 | 21.2 |
| Mourning, Charlotte | 78 | 572 | 1639 | 21.0 |
| Lewis, Boston | 80 | 663 | 1666 | 20.8 |
| Coleman, New Jersey | 76 | 564 | 1572 | 20.7 |
| Hawkins, Philadelphia | 81 | 551 | 1643 | 20.3 |
| Daugherty, Cleveland | 71 | 520 | 1432 | 20.2 |
| Anderson, Orlando | 79 | 594 | 1574 | 19.9 |

### Rebounds Per Game
(70 Games or 800 Rebounds)

| | G | Def | Tot | Avg |
|---|---|---|---|---|
| Rodman, Detroit | 62 | 765 | 1132 | 18.3 |
| O'Neal, Orlando | 81 | 780 | 1122 | 13.9 |
| Mutombo, Denver | 82 | 726 | 1070 | 13.0 |
| Olajuwon, Houston | 82 | 785 | 1068 | 13.0 |
| Willis, Atlanta | 80 | 693 | 1028 | 12.9 |
| Barkley, Phoenix | 76 | 691 | 928 | 12.2 |
| Ewing, New York | 81 | 789 | 980 | 12.1 |
| Seikaly, Miami | 72 | 587 | 846 | 11.8 |
| Robinson, San Antonio | 82 | 727 | 956 | 11.7 |
| Coleman, New Jersey | 76 | 605 | 852 | 11.2 |
| K. Malone, Utah | 82 | 692 | 919 | 11.2 |

### Field Goal Percentage
(300 Field Goals)

| | FG | FGA | Pct |
|---|---|---|---|
| Ceballos, Phoenix | 381 | 662 | .576 |
| Daugherty, Cleveland | 520 | 911 | .571 |
| Davis, Indiana | 304 | 535 | .568 |
| O'Neal, Orlando | 733 | 1304 | .562 |
| Thorpe, Houston | 385 | 690 | .558 |
| K. Malone, Utah | 797 | 1443 | .552 |
| Nance, Cleveland | 533 | 971 | .549 |
| Brickowski, Milwaukee | 456 | 836 | .545 |
| Stewart, Washington | 306 | 564 | .543 |
| Carr, San Antonio | 379 | 705 | .538 |

### Free Throw Percentage
(125 Free Throws Made)

| | FT | FTA | Pct |
|---|---|---|---|
| Price, Cleveland | 289 | 305 | .948 |
| Jackson, Denver | 217 | 232 | .935 |
| Johnson, Seattle | 234 | 257 | .911 |
| Williams, Minnesota | 419 | 462 | .907 |
| Skiles, Orlando | 289 | 324 | .892 |
| Pierce, Seattle | 313 | 352 | .889 |

| | FT | FTA | Pct |
|---|---|---|---|
| Miller, Indiana | 427 | 485 | .880 |
| Smith, Houston | 195 | 222 | .878 |
| Petrovic, New Jersey | 315 | 362 | .870 |
| Lewis, Boston | 326 | 376 | .867 |

### 3-Point Field Goal Percentage
(50 3-Point Field Goals)

| | FG | FGA | Pct |
|---|---|---|---|
| Armstrong, Chicago | 63 | 139 | .453 |
| Mullin, Golden St. | 60 | 133 | .451 |
| Petrovic, New Jersey | 75 | 167 | .449 |
| Smith, Houston | 96 | 219 | .438 |
| Les, Sacramento | 66 | 154 | .429 |
| Price, Cleveland | 122 | 293 | .416 |
| Porter, Portland | 143 | 345 | .414 |
| Ainge, Phoenix | 150 | 372 | .403 |
| Scott, Orlando | 108 | 268 | .403 |
| Smith, Miami | 53 | 132 | .402 |

### Assists
(70 Games or 400 Assists)

| | G | Ast | Avg |
|---|---|---|---|
| Stockton, Utah | 82 | 987 | 12.0 |
| Hardaway, Golden St. | 66 | 699 | 10.6 |
| Skiles, Orlando | 78 | 735 | 9.4 |
| M. Jackson, L.A. Clippers | 82 | 724 | 8.8 |
| Bogues, Charlotte | 81 | 711 | 8.8 |
| Williams, Minnesota | 76 | 661 | 8.7 |
| Thomas, Detroit | 79 | 671 | 8.5 |
| Blaylock, Atlanta | 80 | 671 | 8.4 |
| Anderson, New Jersey | 55 | 449 | 8.2 |
| Price, Cleveland | 75 | 602 | 8.0 |

### Steals
(70 Games or 125 Steals)

| | G | Stl | Avg |
|---|---|---|---|
| Jordan, Chicago | 78 | 221 | 2.83 |
| Blaylock, Atlanta | 80 | 203 | 2.54 |
| Stockton, Utah | 82 | 199 | 2.43 |
| McMillan, Seattle | 73 | 173 | 2.37 |
| Robertson, Mil.-Det. | 69 | 155 | 2.25 |
| Harper, L.A. Clippers | 80 | 177 | 2.21 |
| Murdock, Milwaukee | 79 | 174 | 2.20 |
| Williams, Minnesota | 76 | 165 | 2.17 |
| Payton, Seattle | 82 | 177 | 2.16 |
| Pippen, Chicago | 81 | 173 | 2.14 |

### Blocked Shots
(70 Games or 100 Blocked Shots)

| | G | Blk | Avg |
|---|---|---|---|
| Olajuwon, Houston | 82 | 342 | 4.17 |
| O'Neal, Orlando | 81 | 286 | 3.53 |
| Mutombo, Denver | 82 | 287 | 3.50 |
| Mourning, Charlotte | 78 | 271 | 3.47 |
| Robinson, San Antonio | 82 | 264 | 3.22 |
| Nance, Cleveland | 77 | 198 | 2.57 |
| Ellison, Washington | 49 | 108 | 2.20 |
| Bol, Philadelphia | 58 | 119 | 2.05 |
| Robinson, Portland | 82 | 163 | 1.99 |
| Ewing, New York | 81 | 161 | 1.99 |

## NBA Rookie of the Year

| Year | Player | Year | Player | Year | Player |
|---|---|---|---|---|---|
| 1953 | Don Meineke, Ft. Wayne | 1967 | Dave Bing, Detroit | 1980 | Larry Bird, Boston |
| 1954 | Ray Felix, Baltimore | 1968 | Earl Monroe, Baltimore | 1981 | Darrell Griffith, Utah |
| 1955 | Bob Pettit, Milwaukee | 1969 | Wes Unseld, Baltimore | 1982 | Buck Williams, New Jersey |
| 1956 | Maurice Stokes, Rochester | 1970 | Lew Alcindor, Milwaukee | 1983 | Terry Cummings, San Diego |
| 1957 | Tom Heinsohn, Boston | 1971 | Dave Cowens, Boston; | 1984 | Ralph Sampson, Houston |
| 1958 | Woody Sauldsberry, Philadelphia | | Geoff Petrie, Portland (tie) | 1985 | Michael Jordan, Chicago |
| 1959 | Elgin Baylor, Minneapolis | 1972 | Sidney Wicks, Portland | 1986 | Patrick Ewing, New York |
| 1960 | Wilt Chamberlain, Philadelphia | 1973 | Bob McAdoo, Buffalo | 1987 | Chuck Person, Indiana |
| 1961 | Oscar Robertson, Cincinnati | 1974 | Ernie DiGregorio, Buffalo | 1988 | Mark Jackson, New York |
| 1962 | Walt Bellamy, Chicago | 1975 | Keith Wilkes, Golden State | 1989 | Mitch Richmond, Golden State |
| 1963 | Terry Dischinger, Chicago | 1976 | Alvan Adams, Phoenix | 1990 | David Robinson, San Antonio |
| 1964 | Jerry Lucas, Cincinnati | 1977 | Adrian Dantley, Buffalo | 1991 | Derrick Coleman, New Jersey |
| 1965 | Willis Reed, New York | 1978 | Walter Davis, Phoenix | 1992 | Larry Johnson, Charlotte |
| 1966 | Rick Barry, San Francisco | 1979 | Phil Ford, Kansas City | 1993 | Shaquille O'Neal, Orlando |

## Individual Statistics, 1992-1993
(Over 600 Minutes Played)

### Atlanta Hawks

| | Min | FG% | FT% | Reb | Ast | Pts | Avg |
|---|---|---|---|---|---|---|---|
| Wilkins. . . . . . . | 2647 | .468 | .828 | 482 | 227 | 2121 | 29.9 |
| Willis. . . . . . . | 2878 | .506 | .653 | 1028 | 165 | 1435 | 17.9 |
| Augmon. . . . . . | 2112 | .501 | .739 | 287 | 170 | 1021 | 14.0 |
| Blaylock. . . . . . | 2820 | .429 | .728 | 280 | 671 | 1069 | 13.4 |
| Ferrell. . . . . . | 1736 | .470 | .779 | 191 | 132 | 839 | 10.2 |
| Graham . . . . . | 1508 | .457 | .733 | 190 | 164 | 650 | 8.1 |
| Mays . . . . . . | 787 | .417 | .659 | 53 | 72 | 341 | 7.0 |
| Keefe . . . . . . | 1549 | .500 | .700 | 432 | 80 | 542 | 6.6 |
| Henson . . . . . | 719 | .390 | .360 | 55 | 155 | 213 | 4.0 |
| Koncak . . . . . | 1975 | .464 | .480 | 427 | 140 | 275 | 3.5 |

**Coach**—Bob Weiss

### Boston Celtics

| | Min | FG% | FT% | Reb | Ast | Pts | Avg |
|---|---|---|---|---|---|---|---|
| Lewis . . . . . . | 3144 | .470 | .867 | 347 | 298 | 1666 | 20.8 |
| McDaniel . . . . | 2215 | .495 | .793 | 489 | 163 | 1111 | 13.5 |
| Gamble . . . . . | 2541 | .507 | .826 | 246 | 226 | 1093 | 13.3 |
| Parish . . . . . . | 2146 | .535 | .689 | 740 | 61 | 994 | 12.6 |
| Brown . . . . . . | 2254 | .468 | .793 | 246 | 461 | 874 | 10.9 |
| McHale . . . . . | 1656 | .459 | .841 | 358 | 73 | 762 | 10.7 |
| Douglas . . . . . | 1932 | .498 | .560 | 162 | 508 | 618 | 7.8 |
| Abdelnaby . . . . | 1311 | .518 | .759 | 337 | 27 | 578 | 7.7 |
| Fox . . . . . . . | 1082 | .484 | .802 | 159 | 113 | 453 | 6.4 |
| Kleine . . . . . . | 1129 | .404 | .707 | 346 | 39 | 257 | 3.3 |

**Coach**—Chris Ford

### Charlotte Hornets

| | Min | FG% | FT% | Reb | Ast | Pts | Avg |
|---|---|---|---|---|---|---|---|
| Johnson. . . . . . | 3323 | .526 | .767 | 864 | 353 | 1810 | 22.1 |
| Mourning . . . . | 2644 | .511 | .781 | 805 | 76 | 1639 | 21.0 |
| Gill . . . . . . . | 2430 | .449 | .772 | 340 | 268 | 1167 | 16.9 |
| Curry . . . . . . | 2094 | .452 | .866 | 286 | 180 | 1227 | 15.3 |
| Newman . . . . . | 1471 | .522 | .808 | 143 | 117 | 764 | 11.9 |
| Bogues . . . . . | 2833 | .453 | .833 | 298 | 711 | 808 | 10.0 |
| Gattison . . . . . | 1475 | .529 | .604 | 353 | 68 | 508 | 6.8 |
| Wingate . . . . . | 1471 | .536 | .738 | 174 | 183 | 440 | 6.1 |
| Bennett . . . . . | 857 | .423 | .732 | 63 | 136 | 276 | 3.7 |

**Coach**—Allan Bristow

### Chicago Bulls

| | Min | FG% | FT% | Reb | Ast | Pts | Avg |
|---|---|---|---|---|---|---|---|
| Jordan. . . . . . | 3067 | .495 | .837 | 522 | 428 | 2541 | 32.6 |
| Pippen . . . . . | 3123 | .473 | .663 | 621 | 507 | 1510 | 18.6 |
| Grant . . . . . . | 2745 | .508 | .619 | 729 | 201 | 1017 | 13.2 |
| Armstrong . . . . | 2492 | .499 | .861 | 149 | 330 | 1009 | 12.3 |
| S. Williams . . . | 1369 | .466 | .714 | 451 | 68 | 422 | 5.9 |
| Cartwright . . . . | 1253 | .411 | .735 | 233 | 83 | 354 | 5.6 |
| King . . . . . . . | 1059 | .471 | .705 | 207 | 71 | 408 | 5.4 |
| Tucker. . . . . . | 909 | .485 | .818 | 71 | 82 | 356 | 5.2 |
| Perdue . . . . . | 998 | .557 | .604 | 287 | 74 | 341 | 4.7 |
| Paxson . . . . . | 1030 | .451 | .850 | 48 | 136 | 246 | 4.2 |
| McCray . . . . . | 1019 | .451 | .692 | 158 | 81 | 222 | 3.5 |

**Coach**—Phil Jackson

### Cleveland Cavaliers

| | Min | FG% | FT% | Reb | Ast | Pts | Avg |
|---|---|---|---|---|---|---|---|
| Daugherty. . . . . | 2691 | .571 | .795 | 726 | 312 | 1432 | 20.2 |
| Price. . . . . . . | 2380 | .484 | .948 | 201 | 602 | 1365 | 18.2 |
| Nance . . . . . . | 2753 | .549 | .818 | 668 | 223 | 1268 | 16.5 |
| Ehlo . . . . . . . | 2559 | .490 | .717 | 403 | 254 | 949 | 11.6 |
| Wilkins. . . . . . | 2079 | .453 | .840 | 214 | 183 | 890 | 11.1 |
| Williams . . . . . | 2055 | .470 | .716 | 415 | 152 | 738 | 11.0 |
| Brandon . . . . . | 1622 | .478 | .825 | 179 | 302 | 725 | 8.8 |
| Sanders. . . . . . | 1189 | .497 | .756 | 170 | 75 | 454 | 8.6 |
| Ferry . . . . . . | 1461 | .479 | .876 | 279 | 137 | 573 | 7.5 |

**Coach**—Lenny Wilkins

### Dallas Mavericks

| | Min | FG% | FT% | Reb | Ast | Pts | Avg |
|---|---|---|---|---|---|---|---|
| Harper. . . . . . | 2108 | .419 | .756 | 123 | 334 | 1126 | 18.2 |
| Jackson . . . . . | 938 | .395 | .739 | 122 | 131 | 457 | 16.3 |
| Rooks . . . . . . | 2087 | .493 | .602 | 536 | 95 | 970 | 13.5 |
| Davis . . . . . . | 2462 | .455 | .594 | 701 | 68 | 955 | 12.7 |
| Smith . . . . . . | 1524 | .434 | .757 | 328 | 104 | 634 | 10.4 |
| White . . . . . . | 1433 | .435 | .750 | 370 | 49 | 618 | 9.7 |
| Legler . . . . . . | 635 | .436 | .803 | 59 | 46 | 289 | 8.8 |
| Iuzzolino. . . . . | 1769 | .462 | .765 | 140 | 328 | 610 | 8.7 |
| Bond. . . . . . . | 1578 | .402 | .772 | 196 | 122 | 590 | 8.0 |
| Cambridge . . . . | 885 | .484 | .687 | 167 | 58 | 370 | 7.0 |
| Howard . . . . . | 1295 | .442 | .766 | 212 | 67 | 439 | 6.5 |
| Hodge . . . . . . | 1267 | .450 | .683 | 294 | 75 | 393 | 5.0 |

|  | Min | FG% | FT% | Reb | Ast | Pts | Avg |
|---|---|---|---|---|---|---|---|
| Wiley . . . . . . | 995 | .378 | .654 | 91 | 181 | 263 | 4.5 |

**Coach**—Richie Adubato; Garfield Heard

### Denver Nuggets

| | Min | FG% | FT% | Reb | Ast | Pts | Avg |
|---|---|---|---|---|---|---|---|
| Jackson . . . . . | 2710 | .450 | .935 | 225 | 344 | 1553 | 19.2 |
| Williams . . . . . | 2722 | .458 | .804 | 428 | 295 | 1341 | 17.0 |
| Ellis . . . . . . . | 2749 | .504 | .748 | 744 | 151 | 1205 | 14.7 |
| Mutombo . . . . . | 3029 | .510 | .681 | 1070 | 147 | 1131 | 13.8 |
| Pack. . . . . . . | 1579 | .470 | .768 | 160 | 335 | 810 | 10.5 |
| Stith . . . . . . . | 865 | .446 | .832 | 124 | 49 | 347 | 8.9 |
| Liberty . . . . . . | 1585 | .406 | .654 | 335 | 105 | 628 | 8.1 |
| Macon . . . . . . | 1141 | .451 | .700 | 103 | 126 | 358 | 7.5 |
| Lichti. . . . . . . | 752 | .449 | .794 | 102 | 52 | 331 | 6.9 |
| Plummer . . . . . | 737 | .465 | .726 | 173 | 40 | 281 | 4.7 |
| Hammonds . . . . | 713 | .475 | .613 | 127 | 24 | 248 | 4.6 |
| Hastings. . . . . . | 670 | .509 | .727 | 137 | 34 | 156 | 2.1 |

**Coach**—Dan Issel

### Detroit Pistons

| | Min | FG% | FT% | Reb | Ast | Pts | Avg |
|---|---|---|---|---|---|---|---|
| Dumars . . . . . | 3094 | .466 | .864 | 148 | 308 | 1809 | 23.5 |
| Thomas . . . . . | 2922 | .418 | .737 | 232 | 671 | 1391 | 17.6 |
| Mills . . . . . . . | 2183 | .461 | .791 | 472 | 111 | 1199 | 14.8 |
| Woolridge . . . . | 1477 | .479 | .673 | 176 | 112 | 655 | 13.1 |
| Aguirre . . . . . | 1056 | .443 | .767 | 152 | 105 | 503 | 9.9 |
| Robertson . . . . | 2006 | .458 | .656 | 269 | 263 | 618 | 9.0 |
| Laimbeer . . . . . | 1933 | .509 | .894 | 419 | 127 | 687 | 8.7 |
| Rodman. . . . . . | 2410 | .427 | .534 | 1132 | 102 | 468 | 7.5 |
| Polynice. . . . . . | 1299 | .490 | .465 | 418 | 29 | 486 | 7.3 |
| Glass . . . . . . | 848 | .419 | .641 | 142 | 77 | 316 | 5.3 |
| Young . . . . . . | 836 | .413 | .875 | 47 | 119 | 188 | 2.9 |

**Coach**—Ron Rothstein

### Golden State Warriors

| | Min | FG% | FT% | Reb | Ast | Pts | Avg |
|---|---|---|---|---|---|---|---|
| Mullin. . . . . . . | 1902 | .510 | .810 | 232 | 166 | 1191 | 25.9 |
| Hardaway . . . . | 2609 | .447 | .744 | 263 | 699 | 1419 | 21.5 |
| Marciulionis . . . | 836 | .543 | .761 | 97 | 105 | 521 | 17.4 |
| Owens . . . . . . | 1201 | .501 | .639 | 264 | 144 | 612 | 16.5 |
| Sprewell . . . . . | 2741 | .464 | .746 | 271 | 295 | 1182 | 15.4 |
| Alexander . . . . | 1753 | .516 | .685 | 420 | 93 | 809 | 11.2 |
| Gatling . . . . . . | 1248 | .539 | .725 | 320 | 40 | 648 | 9.3 |
| Grayer. . . . . . | 1025 | .467 | .669 | 157 | 70 | 423 | 8.8 |
| Hill . . . . . . . | 2070 | .508 | .624 | 754 | 68 | 640 | 8.6 |
| Buechler . . . . . | 1287 | .437 | .747 | 195 | 94 | 437 | 6.2 |
| Houston . . . . . | 1274 | .446 | .665 | 315 | 69 | 421 | 5.3 |

**Coach**—Don Nelson

### Houston Rockets

| | Min | FG% | FT% | Reb | Ast | Pts | Avg |
|---|---|---|---|---|---|---|---|
| Olajuwon . . . . . | 3242 | .529 | .779 | 1068 | 291 | 2140 | 26.1 |
| Maxwell . . . . . | 2251 | .407 | .719 | 221 | 297 | 982 | 13.8 |
| Smith . . . . . . | 2422 | .520 | .878 | 160 | 446 | 1065 | 13.0 |
| Thorpe . . . . . . | 2357 | .558 | .598 | 589 | 181 | 923 | 12.8 |
| Horry . . . . . . | 2330 | .474 | .715 | 392 | 191 | 801 | 10.1 |
| Herrara . . . . . | 1800 | .541 | .710 | 454 | 61 | 605 | 7.5 |
| Bullard . . . . . | 1356 | .431 | .784 | 222 | 110 | 575 | 7.3 |
| Floyd . . . . . . | 867 | .407 | .794 | 86 | 132 | 345 | 6.6 |
| Brooks . . . . . . | 1516 | .475 | .830 | 99 | 243 | 519 | 6.3 |
| Garland . . . . . | 1004 | .443 | .910 | 108 | 138 | 391 | 5.9 |

**Coach**—Rudy Tomjanovich

### Indiana Pacers

| | Min | FG% | FT% | Reb | Ast | Pts | Avg |
|---|---|---|---|---|---|---|---|
| Miller . . . . . . | 2954 | .479 | .880 | 258 | 262 | 1736 | 21.2 |
| Schrempf . . . . . | 3098 | .476 | .804 | 780 | 493 | 1567 | 19.1 |
| Smits . . . . . . | 2072 | .486 | .732 | 432 | 121 | 1155 | 14.3 |
| Richardson . . . . | 2396 | .479 | .742 | 267 | 573 | 769 | 10.4 |
| Fleming . . . . . | 1503 | .505 | .726 | 169 | 224 | 710 | 9.5 |
| Davis . . . . . . | 2264 | .568 | .529 | 723 | 69 | 727 | 8.9 |
| McCloud . . . . . | 1500 | .411 | .735 | 205 | 192 | 565 | 7.2 |
| Mitchell . . . . . | 1402 | .445 | .811 | 248 | 76 | 584 | 7.2 |
| Williams . . . . . | 844 | .532 | .706 | 228 | 38 | 348 | 6.1 |
| Sealy . . . . . . | 672 | .426 | .689 | 112 | 47 | 330 | 5.7 |
| Thompson . . . . | 730 | .488 | .744 | 178 | 34 | 237 | 3.8 |

**Coach**—Bob Hill

### Los Angeles Clippers

| | Min | FG% | FT% | Reb | Ast | Pts | Avg |
|---|---|---|---|---|---|---|---|
| Manning . . . . . | 2761 | .509 | .802 | 520 | 207 | 1800 | 22.8 |
| Harper. . . . . . | 2970 | .451 | .769 | 425 | 360 | 1443 | 18.0 |

| | Min | FG% | FT% | Reb | Ast | Pts | Avg |
|---|---|---|---|---|---|---|---|
| Norman | 2477 | .511 | .595 | 571 | 165 | 1137 | 15.0 |
| M. Jackson | 3117 | .486 | .803 | 388 | 724 | 1181 | 14.4 |
| Roberts | 1816 | .527 | .488 | 478 | 59 | 870 | 11.3 |
| Vaught | 1653 | .508 | .748 | 492 | 54 | 743 | 9.4 |
| Williams | 1638 | .430 | .543 | 316 | 142 | 492 | 6.6 |
| Grant | 1624 | .441 | .743 | 139 | 353 | 486 | 6.6 |

**Coach—Larry Brown**

## Los Angeles Lakers

| | Min | FG% | FT% | Reb | Ast | Pts | Avg |
|---|---|---|---|---|---|---|---|
| Threatt | 2893 | .508 | .823 | 273 | 564 | 1235 | 15.1 |
| Worthy | 2359 | .447 | .810 | 247 | 278 | 1221 | 14.9 |
| Perkins | 1589 | .459 | .829 | 379 | 128 | 673 | 13.7 |
| Scott | 1677 | .449 | .848 | 134 | 157 | 792 | 13.7 |
| Green | 2819 | .537 | .739 | 711 | 116 | 1051 | 12.8 |
| Divac | 2525 | .485 | .689 | 729 | 232 | 1050 | 12.8 |
| Peeler | 1656 | .468 | .786 | 179 | 166 | 802 | 10.4 |
| Campbell | 1551 | .458 | .637 | 332 | 48 | 606 | 7.7 |
| Edwards | 617 | .452 | .712 | 100 | 41 | 328 | 6.3 |
| Smith | 752 | .484 | .756 | 87 | 63 | 330 | 6.0 |
| Benjamin | 754 | .491 | .663 | 209 | 22 | 335 | 5.7 |
| Cooper | 645 | .392 | .714 | 50 | 150 | 156 | 2.4 |

**Coach—Randy Pfund**

## Miami Heat

| | Min | FG% | FT% | Reb | Ast | Pts | Avg |
|---|---|---|---|---|---|---|---|
| Rice | 3082 | .440 | .820 | 424 | 180 | 1554 | 19.0 |
| Seikaly | 2456 | .480 | .735 | 846 | 100 | 1232 | 17.1 |
| Smith | 1610 | .451 | .787 | 197 | 267 | 766 | 16.0 |
| Long | 2728 | .469 | .765 | 568 | 182 | 1061 | 14.0 |
| Edwards | 1134 | .468 | .844 | 121 | 120 | 556 | 13.9 |
| Coles | 2232 | .464 | .805 | 166 | 373 | 855 | 10.6 |
| Miner | 1383 | .475 | .762 | 147 | 73 | 750 | 10.3 |
| Salley | 1422 | .502 | .799 | 313 | 83 | 423 | 8.3 |
| Shaw | 1603 | .393 | .782 | 257 | 235 | 498 | 7.3 |
| Askins | 935 | .413 | .725 | 196 | 31 | 227 | 3.3 |

**Coach—Kevin Loughery**

## Milwaukee Bucks

| | Min | FG% | FT% | Reb | Ast | Pts | Avg |
|---|---|---|---|---|---|---|---|
| Brickowski | 2075 | .545 | .728 | 405 | 196 | 1115 | 16.9 |
| Edwards | 2729 | .512 | .790 | 382 | 214 | 1382 | 16.9 |
| Murdock | 2437 | .468 | .780 | 284 | 603 | 1138 | 14.4 |
| Day | 1931 | .432 | .717 | 291 | 117 | 983 | 13.8 |
| Woolridge | 1555 | .482 | .678 | 185 | 115 | 698 | 12.0 |
| Avent | 2285 | .433 | .651 | 512 | 91 | 806 | 9.8 |
| Lohaus | 1766 | .461 | .723 | 276 | 127 | 724 | 9.1 |
| Robertson | 1065 | .479 | .629 | 137 | 156 | 339 | 8.7 |
| Roberts | 1488 | .528 | .799 | 237 | 118 | 599 | 7.6 |
| Mayberry | 1503 | .456 | .574 | 118 | 273 | 424 | 5.2 |
| Schayes | 1124 | .399 | .818 | 249 | 78 | 322 | 4.6 |

**Coach—Mike Dunleavy**

## Minnesota Timberwolves

| | Min | FG% | FT% | Reb | Ast | Pts | Avg |
|---|---|---|---|---|---|---|---|
| West | 3104 | .517 | .841 | 247 | 235 | 1543 | 19.3 |
| Laettner | 2823 | .474 | .835 | 708 | 223 | 1472 | 18.2 |
| Person | 2985 | .433 | .649 | 433 | 343 | 1309 | 16.8 |
| Williams | 2661 | .446 | .907 | 273 | 661 | 1151 | 15.1 |
| Bailey | 1276 | .455 | .838 | 215 | 61 | 525 | 7.5 |
| McCann | 1536 | .488 | .625 | 282 | 68 | 495 | 6.3 |
| Longley | 1045 | .455 | .716 | 240 | 51 | 319 | 5.8 |
| Smith | 1266 | .433 | .792 | 96 | 196 | 347 | 4.3 |
| Spencer | 1296 | .465 | .654 | 324 | 17 | 293 | 4.1 |
| Blanks | 642 | .433 | .625 | 68 | 72 | 161 | 2.6 |

**Coach—Jimmy Rodgers; Sidney Lowe**

## New Jersey Nets

| | Min | FG% | FT% | Reb | Ast | Pts | Avg |
|---|---|---|---|---|---|---|---|
| Petrovic | 2660 | .518 | .870 | 190 | 247 | 1564 | 22.3 |
| Coleman | 2759 | .460 | .808 | 852 | 276 | 1572 | 20.7 |
| Anderson | 2010 | .435 | .776 | 226 | 449 | 927 | 16.9 |
| Morris | 2302 | .481 | .794 | 454 | 106 | 1086 | 14.1 |
| Bowie | 2092 | .450 | .779 | 556 | 127 | 717 | 9.1 |
| Robinson | 1585 | .423 | .574 | 159 | 323 | 672 | 8.4 |
| Addison | 1164 | .443 | .814 | 132 | 53 | 428 | 6.3 |
| Brown | 1186 | .483 | .724 | 232 | 51 | 391 | 5.1 |
| Mahorn | 1077 | .472 | .800 | 279 | 33 | 291 | 3.9 |
| Dudley | 1398 | .353 | .518 | 513 | 16 | 245 | 3.5 |

**Coach—Chuck Daly**

## New York Knickerbockers

| | Min | FG% | FT% | Reb | Ast | Pts | Avg |
|---|---|---|---|---|---|---|---|
| Ewing | 3003 | .503 | .719 | 980 | 151 | 1959 | 24.2 |
| Starks | 2477 | .428 | .795 | 204 | 404 | 1397 | 17.5 |
| Smith | 2172 | .469 | .782 | 432 | 142 | 1003 | 12.4 |

| | Min | FG% | FT% | Reb | Ast | Pts | Avg |
|---|---|---|---|---|---|---|---|
| Mason | 2482 | .502 | .682 | 640 | 170 | 831 | 10.3 |
| Blackman | 1434 | .443 | .789 | 102 | 157 | 580 | 9.7 |
| Rivers | 1886 | .437 | .821 | 192 | 405 | 604 | 7.8 |
| Campbell | 1062 | .490 | .678 | 155 | 62 | 449 | 7.7 |
| Oakley | 2230 | .508 | .722 | 708 | 126 | 565 | 6.9 |
| Anthony | 1699 | .415 | .673 | 170 | 398 | 459 | 6.6 |
| Davis | 815 | .438 | .796 | 56 | 83 | 269 | 5.4 |

**Coach—Pat Riley**

## Orlando Magic

| | Min | FG% | FT% | Reb | Ast | Pts | Avg |
|---|---|---|---|---|---|---|---|
| O'Neal | 3071 | .562 | .592 | 1122 | 152 | 1893 | 23.4 |
| Anderson | 2920 | .449 | .741 | 477 | 265 | 1574 | 19.9 |
| Scott | 1759 | .431 | .786 | 186 | 136 | 858 | 15.9 |
| Skiles | 3086 | .467 | .892 | 290 | 735 | 1201 | 15.4 |
| Royal | 1636 | .496 | .815 | 295 | 80 | 706 | 9.2 |
| Tolbert | 1838 | .498 | .726 | 412 | 91 | 583 | 8.1 |
| Bowie | 1761 | .471 | .798 | 194 | 175 | 618 | 8.0 |
| Turner | 1479 | .529 | .800 | 252 | 107 | 528 | 7.0 |
| Green | 626 | .439 | .625 | 34 | 116 | 235 | 4.5 |
| Kite | 640 | .452 | .542 | 193 | 10 | 89 | 1.4 |

**Coach—Matt Guokas**

## Philadelphia 76ers

| | Min | FG% | FT% | Reb | Ast | Pts | Avg |
|---|---|---|---|---|---|---|---|
| Hawkins | 2977 | .470 | .860 | 346 | 317 | 1643 | 20.3 |
| Hornacek | 2860 | .470 | .865 | 342 | 548 | 1511 | 19.1 |
| Weatherspoon | 2654 | .469 | .713 | 589 | 147 | 1280 | 15.6 |
| Gilliam | 1742 | .464 | .843 | 472 | 116 | 992 | 12.4 |
| Perry | 2104 | .468 | .710 | 409 | 126 | 731 | 9.0 |
| Dawkins | 1598 | .437 | .796 | 136 | 339 | 655 | 8.9 |
| Anderson | 1263 | .414 | .809 | 184 | 93 | 561 | 8.1 |
| Lang | 1861 | .425 | .763 | 436 | 79 | 386 | 5.3 |
| Grant | 996 | .350 | .645 | 67 | 206 | 194 | 2.7 |
| Bol | 855 | .409 | .632 | 193 | 18 | 126 | 2.2 |

**Coach—Doug Moe; Fred Carter**

## Phoenix Suns

| | Min | FG% | FT% | Reb | Ast | Pts | Avg |
|---|---|---|---|---|---|---|---|
| Barkley | 2859 | .520 | .765 | 928 | 385 | 1944 | 25.6 |
| Majerle | 3199 | .464 | .778 | 383 | 311 | 1388 | 16.9 |
| K. Johnson | 1643 | .499 | .819 | 104 | 384 | 791 | 16.1 |
| Dumas | 1320 | .524 | .707 | 223 | 60 | 757 | 15.8 |
| Ceballos | 1607 | .576 | .725 | 408 | 77 | 949 | 12.8 |
| Chambers | 1723 | .447 | .837 | 345 | 101 | 892 | 12.2 |
| Ainge | 2163 | .462 | .848 | 214 | 260 | 947 | 11.8 |
| Knight | 888 | .391 | .779 | 64 | 145 | 315 | 6.1 |
| Miller | 1069 | .475 | .710 | 275 | 118 | 313 | 5.6 |
| West | 1558 | .614 | .518 | 458 | 29 | 436 | 5.3 |
| F. Johnson | 1122 | .436 | .776 | 113 | 186 | 332 | 4.3 |

**Coach—Paul Westphal**

## Portland Trail Blazers

| | Min | FG% | FT% | Reb | Ast | Pts | Avg |
|---|---|---|---|---|---|---|---|
| Drexler | 1671 | .429 | .839 | 309 | 278 | 976 | 19.9 |
| Robinson | 2575 | .473 | .690 | 542 | 182 | 1570 | 19.1 |
| Porter | 2883 | .454 | .843 | 116 | 419 | 1476 | 18.2 |
| Strickland | 2474 | .485 | .717 | 337 | 559 | 1069 | 13.7 |
| Kersey | 1719 | .438 | .634 | 406 | 121 | 686 | 10.6 |
| Duckworth | 1762 | .438 | .730 | 387 | 70 | 729 | 9.9 |
| Elie | 1757 | .458 | .855 | 216 | 177 | 708 | 8.6 |
| Williams | 2498 | .511 | .645 | 690 | 75 | 678 | 8.3 |
| Bryant | 1396 | .503 | .703 | 324 | 41 | 476 | 6.0 |

**Coach—Rick Adelman**

## Sacramento Kings

| | Min | FG% | FT% | Reb | Ast | Pts | Avg |
|---|---|---|---|---|---|---|---|
| Richmond | 1728 | .474 | .845 | 154 | 221 | 987 | 21.9 |
| Simmons | 2502 | .444 | .819 | 495 | 312 | 1235 | 17.9 |
| Williams | 1673 | .435 | .742 | 265 | 178 | 1001 | 17.0 |
| Tisdale | 2283 | .509 | .758 | 500 | 108 | 1263 | 16.6 |
| Webb | 2335 | .433 | .851 | 193 | 481 | 1000 | 14.5 |
| Bonner | 1764 | .461 | .593 | 455 | 96 | 601 | 8.6 |
| Higgins | 1425 | .412 | .861 | 193 | 119 | 571 | 8.3 |
| Causwell | 1211 | .545 | .624 | 303 | 35 | 453 | 8.2 |
| Brown | 1726 | .463 | .732 | 212 | 196 | 567 | 7.6 |
| Chilcutt | 834 | .485 | .696 | 194 | 64 | 362 | 6.1 |
| Les | 881 | .425 | .840 | 89 | 169 | 328 | 4.5 |
| Rambis | 822 | .519 | .662 | 227 | 53 | 177 | 2.5 |

**Coach—Garry St. Jean**

## San Antonio Spurs

| | Min | FG% | FT% | Reb | Ast | Pts | Avg |
|---|---|---|---|---|---|---|---|
| Robinson | 3211 | .501 | .732 | 956 | 301 | 1916 | 23.4 |
| Elliott | 2604 | .491 | .795 | 322 | 265 | 1207 | 17.2 |
| Ellis | 2731 | .499 | .797 | 312 | 107 | 1366 | 16.7 |

| | Min | FG% | FT% | Reb | Ast | Pts | Avg |
|---|---|---|---|---|---|---|---|
| Carr | 1947 | .538 | .777 | 388 | 97 | 932 | 13.1 |
| Reid | 1887 | .476 | .764 | 456 | 80 | 780 | 9.4 |
| Daniels | 1573 | .443 | .727 | 216 | 148 | 701 | 9.1 |
| Johnson | 2030 | .502 | .791 | 146 | 561 | 656 | 8.7 |
| Del Negro | 1526 | .507 | .863 | 163 | 291 | 543 | 7.4 |
| Smith | 833 | .437 | .409 | 268 | 28 | 85 | 1.3 |

**Coach**—Jerry Tarkanian; John Lucas

### Seattle SuperSonics

| | Min | FG% | FT% | Reb | Ast | Pts | Avg |
|---|---|---|---|---|---|---|---|
| Pierce | 2218 | .489 | .889 | 192 | 220 | 1403 | 18.2 |
| Kemp | 2582 | .492 | .712 | 833 | 155 | 1388 | 17.8 |
| Johnson | 1869 | .494 | .911 | 272 | 135 | 1177 | 14.4 |
| Payton | 2548 | .494 | .770 | 281 | 399 | 1110 | 13.5 |
| McKey | 2439 | .466 | .741 | 327 | 197 | 1034 | 13.4 |
| Perkins | 2351 | .477 | .820 | 524 | 156 | 1036 | 13.1 |
| Barros | 1243 | .451 | .831 | 107 | 151 | 541 | 7.8 |
| McMillan | 1977 | .464 | .709 | 306 | 384 | 546 | 7.5 |
| Cage | 2156 | .526 | .469 | 659 | 69 | 499 | 6.1 |
| Askew | 1129 | .492 | .705 | 161 | 122 | 411 | 5.6 |

**Coach**—George Karl

### Utah Jazz

| | Min | FG% | FT% | Reb | Ast | Pts | Avg |
|---|---|---|---|---|---|---|---|
| K. Malone | 3099 | .552 | .740 | 919 | 308 | 2217 | 27.0 |

| | Min | FG% | FT% | Reb | Ast | Pts | Avg |
|---|---|---|---|---|---|---|---|
| J. Malone | 2558 | .494 | .852 | 173 | 128 | 1429 | 18.1 |
| Stockton | 2863 | .486 | .798 | 237 | 987 | 1239 | 15.1 |
| Corbin | 2555 | .503 | .826 | 519 | 173 | 950 | 11.6 |
| Humphries | 2034 | .436 | .777 | 143 | 317 | 690 | 8.8 |
| Benoit | 1712 | .436 | .750 | 392 | 43 | 664 | 8.1 |
| Krystkowiak | 1362 | .466 | .796 | 279 | 68 | 513 | 7.2 |
| Brown | 1551 | .430 | .689 | 391 | 64 | 465 | 5.7 |
| Eaton | 1104 | .546 | .700 | 264 | 17 | 177 | 2.8 |

**Coach**—Jerry Sloan

### Washington Bullets

| | Min | FG% | FT% | Reb | Ast | Pts | Avg |
|---|---|---|---|---|---|---|---|
| Grant | 2667 | .487 | .727 | 412 | 205 | 1339 | 18.6 |
| Ellison | 1701 | .521 | .702 | 433 | 117 | 852 | 17.4 |
| Adams | 2499 | .439 | .856 | 240 | 526 | 1035 | 14.8 |
| Gugliotta | 2795 | .426 | .644 | 781 | 306 | 1187 | 14.7 |
| Chapman | 1300 | .477 | .810 | 88 | 116 | 749 | 12.5 |
| Stewart | 1823 | .543 | .727 | 383 | 146 | 796 | 9.8 |
| Smith | 1546 | .458 | .859 | 106 | 186 | 639 | 9.3 |
| Overton | 990 | .471 | .728 | 106 | 157 | 366 | 8.1 |
| MacLean | 674 | .435 | .811 | 122 | 39 | 407 | 6.6 |
| Johnson | 1287 | .479 | .730 | 195 | 89 | 478 | 6.5 |
| Price | 859 | .358 | .794 | 103 | 154 | 262 | 3.9 |

**Coach**—Wes Unseld

## Michael Jordan's Career Scoring Statistics With the Chicago Bulls

| | | Regular Season | | | | | | Playoffs | | | |
|---|---|---|---|---|---|---|---|---|---|---|---|
| Year | G | FG% | FT% | PTS | PPG | | G | FG% | FT% | PTS | PPG |
| 84-85 | 82 | .515 | .845 | 2,313 | 28.2 | | 4 | .436 | .828 | 117 | 29.3 |
| 85-86 | 18 | .457 | .840 | 408 | 22.7 | | 3 | .505 | .872 | 131 | 43.7 |
| 86-87 | 82 | .482 | .857 | 3,041 | 37.1 | | 3 | .417 | .897 | 107 | 35.7 |
| 87-88 | 82 | .535 | .841 | 2,868 | 35.0 | | 10 | .530 | .869 | 363 | 36.3 |
| 88-89 | 81 | .538 | .850 | 2,633 | 32.5 | | 17 | .510 | .799 | 591 | 34.8 |
| 89-90 | 82 | .526 | .848 | 2,753 | 33.6 | | 16 | .514 | .836 | 587 | 36.7 |
| 90-91 | 82 | .539 | .851 | 2,580 | 31.5 | | 17 | .524 | .845 | 529 | 31.1 |
| 91-92 | 80 | .519 | .832 | 2,404 | 30.1 | | 22 | .499 | .857 | 759 | 34.5 |
| 92-93 | 78 | .495 | .837 | 2,541 | 32.6 | | 19 | .475 | .805 | 666 | 35.1 |
| Totals | 667 | .516 | .846 | 21,541 | 32.3 | | 111 | .501 | .834 | 3,820 | 34.7 |

## 1993 NBA Player Draft, First Round Picks

Orlando—Chris Webber,* Michigan
Philadelphia—Shawn Bradley, Brigham Young
Golden State—Anfernee Hardaway,* Memphis St.
Dallas—Jamal Mashburn, Kentucky
Minnesota—J.R. Rider, UNLV
Washington—Calbert Cheaney, Indiana
Sacramento—Bobby Hurley, Duke
Milwaukee—Vin Baker, Hartford
Denver—Rodney Rogers, Wake Forest
Detroit—Lindsey Hunter, Jackson St.
Detroit—Allan Houston, Tennessee
L.A. Lakers—George Lynch, North Carolina
L.A. Clippers—Terry Dehere, Seton Hall
Indiana—Scott Haskin, Oregon St.

Atlanta—Doug Edwards, Florida St.
New Jersey—Rex Walters, Kansas
Charlotte—Greg Graham, Indiana
Utah—Luther Wright, Seton Hall
Boston—Acie Earl, Iowa
Charlotte—Scott Burrell, Connecticut
Portland—James Robinson, Alabama
Cleveland—Chris Mills, Arizona
Seattle—Ervin Johnson, New Orleans
Houston—Sam Cassell, Florida St.
Chicago—Corie Blount, Cincinnati
Orlando—Geert Hammink, LSU
Phoenix—Malcolm Mackey, Georgia Tech

* Webber traded to Golden State for Hardaway and future draft choices.

## Number One First Round NBA Draft Picks, 1966-1993

| Year | Team | Player, college | Year | Team | Player, college |
|---|---|---|---|---|---|
| 1966 | New York | Cazzie Russell, Michigan | 1980 | Golden State | Joe Barry Carroll, Purdue |
| 1967 | Detroit | Jimmy Walker, Providence | 1981 | Dallas | Mark Aguirre, DePaul |
| 1968 | Houston | Elvin Hayes, Houston | 1982 | L.A. Lakers | James Worthy, N. Carolina |
| 1969 | Milwaukee | Lew Alcindor[1], UCLA | 1983 | Houston | Ralph Sampson, Virginia |
| 1970 | Detroit | Bob Lanier, St. Bonaventure | 1984 | Houston | Akeem Olajuwon, Houston |
| 1971 | Cleveland | Austin Carr, Notre Dame | 1985 | New York | Patrick Ewing, Georgetown |
| 1972 | Portland | LaRue Martin, Loyola-Chicago | 1986 | Cleveland | Brad Daugherty, N. Carolina |
| 1973 | Philadelphia | Doug Collins, Illinois St. | 1987 | San Antonio | David Robinson, Navy |
| 1974 | Portland | Bill Walton, UCLA | 1988 | L.A. Clippers | Danny Manning, Kansas |
| 1975 | Atlanta | David Thompson[2], N.C. State | 1989 | Sacramento | Pervis Ellison, Louisville |
| 1976 | Houston | John Lucas, Maryland | 1990 | New Jersey | Derrick Coleman, Syracuse |
| 1977 | Milwaukee | Kent Benson, Indiana | 1991 | Charlotte | Larry Johnson, UNLV |
| 1978 | Portland | Mychal Thompson, Minnesota | 1992 | Orlando | Shaquille O'Neal, LSU |
| 1979 | L.A. Lakers | Magic Johnson, Michigan St. | 1993 | Orlando | Chris Webber[3], Michigan |

(1) Later Kareem Abdul-Jabbar. (2) Signed with Denver of the ABA. (3) Traded to Golden State.

## NBA All-Defensive Team in 1993

| First team | Position | Second team |
|---|---|---|
| Dennis Rodman, Detroit | Forward | Larry Nance, Cleveland |
| Scottie Pippen, Chicago | Forward | Horace Grant, Chicago |
| Hakeem Olajuwon, Houston | Center | David Robinson, San Antonio |
| Michael Jordan, Chicago | Guard | Dan Majerle, Phoenix |
| Joe Dumars, Detroit | Guard | John Starks, New York |

## All-Time NBA Statistical Leaders

(At the start of the 1992-93 season. *Includes 1992-93 season)

### Scoring Average
(400 games or 10,000 Points Minimum)

| | G | Pts. | Avg |
|---|---|---|---|
| *Michael Jordan | 667 | 21,541 | 32.2 |
| Wilt Chamberlain | 1,045 | 31,419 | 30.1 |
| Elgin Baylor | 846 | 23,149 | 27.4 |
| Jerry West | 932 | 25,192 | 27.0 |
| *Dominique Wilkins | 833 | 22,096 | 26.5 |
| Bob Pettit | 792 | 20,880 | 26.4 |
| George Gervin | 791 | 20,708 | 26.2 |
| *Karl Malone | 652 | 16,987 | 26.0 |
| Oscar Robertson | 1,040 | 26,710 | 25.7 |
| Kareem Abdul-Jabbar | 1,560 | 38,387 | 24.6 |

### Field Goal Percentage
(2,000 FGM Minimum)

| | FGA | FGM | Pct. |
|---|---|---|---|
| Artis Gilmore | 9,570 | 5,732 | .599 |
| James Donaldson | 5,109 | 2,941 | .576 |
| Charles Barkley | 7,596 | 4,403 | .580 |
| Steve Johnson | 4,965 | 2,841 | .572 |
| Darryl Dawkins | 6,060 | 3,468 | .572 |
| Jeff Ruland | 3,685 | 2,080 | .564 |
| Kevin McHale | 11,051 | 6,209 | .562 |
| Kareem Abdul-Jabbar | 28,307 | 15,837 | .559 |
| Buck Williams | 8,583 | 4,752 | .554 |
| Bobby Jones | 6,199 | 3,412 | .550 |

### Free Throw Percentage
(1,200 FTM Minimum)

| | FTA | FTM | Pct. |
|---|---|---|---|
| Rick Barry | 4,243 | 3,818 | .900 |
| Calvin Murphy | 3,864 | 3,445 | .892 |
| Larry Bird | 4,126 | 3,647 | .884 |
| Bill Sharman | 3,357 | 3,143 | .884 |
| Chris Mullen | 1,928 | 1,695 | .879 |
| Kiki Vandeweghe | 2,562 | 3,102 | .871 |
| Mike Newlin | 3,456 | 3,005 | .870 |
| Jeff Malone | 2,231 | 1,939 | .869 |
| John Long | 2,051 | 1,765 | .861 |

### Points

| | Pts. |
|---|---|
| Kareem Abdul-Jabbar | 38,387 |
| Wilt Chamberlain | 31,419 |
| Elvin Hayes | 27,313 |
| *Moses Malone | 27,066 |
| Oscar Robertson | 26,710 |
| John Havlicek | 26,395 |
| Alex English | 25,643 |
| Jerry West | 25,192 |
| Adrian Dantley | 23,177 |

### Games Played

| | |
|---|---|
| Kareem Abdul-Jabbar | 1,560 |
| *Robert Parish | 1,339 |
| Elvin Hayes | 1,303 |
| John Havlicek | 1,270 |
| *Moses Malone | 1,257 |
| Paul Silas | 1,254 |
| Alex English | 1,193 |
| Hal Greer | 1,122 |
| Dennis Johnson | 1,100 |

### Assists

| | |
|---|---|
| Magic Johnson | 9,921 |
| Oscar Robertson | 9,887 |
| *Isiah Thomas | 8,662 |
| *John Stockton | 8,352 |
| *Maurice Cheeks | 7,392 |
| Len Wilkens | 7,211 |
| Bob Cousy | 6,955 |
| Guy Rodgers | 6,917 |
| Nate Archibald | 6,476 |

### Field Goals Made

| | |
|---|---|
| Kareem Abdul-Jabbar | 15,837 |
| Wilt Chamberlain | 12,681 |
| Elvin Hayes | 10,976 |
| Alex English | 10,659 |
| John Havlicek | 10,513 |
| Oscar Robertson | 9,508 |
| *Moses Malone | 9,320 |
| Jerry West | 9,016 |
| Elgin Baylor | 8,693 |

### Rebounds

| | |
|---|---|
| Wilt Chamberlain | 23,924 |
| Bill Russell | 21,620 |
| Kareem Addul-Jabbar | 17,440 |
| Elvin Hayes | 16,279 |
| *Moses Malone | 15,940 |
| Nate Thurmond | 14,464 |
| Walt Bellamy | 14,241 |
| Wes Unseld | 13,769 |
| Jerry Lucas | 12,942 |

## Individuals in the Basketball Hall of Fame

Springfield, Mass.

**Players**

Archibald, Nate
Arizin, Paul
Barlow, Thomas
Barry, Rick
Baylor, Elgin
Beckman, John
Bellamy, Walt
Belov, Sergei
Bing, Dave
Borgmann, Bennie
Bradley, Bill
Brennan, Joseph
Cervi, Al
Chamberlain, Wilt
Cooper, Charles
Cousy, Bob
Cowens, Dave
Cunningham, Billy
Davies, Bob
DeBernardi, Forrest
DeBusschere, Dave
Dehnert, Dutch
Endacott, Paul
Erving, Julius
Foster, Bud
Frazier, Walt
Friedman, Max
Fulks, Joe
Gale, Lauren
Gallatin, Harry
Gates, Pop
Gola, Tom
Greer, Hal
Gruenig, Ace
Hagan, Cliff
Hanson, Victor
Harris, Luisa
Havlicek, John
Hawkins, Connie

Hayes, Elvin
Heinsohn, Tom
Holman, Nat
Houbregs, Bob
Hyatt, Chuck
Issel, Dan
Johnson, William
Johnston, Neil
Jones, K.C.
Jones, Sam
Krause, Moose
Kurland, Bob
Lanier, Bob
Lapchick, Joe
Lovellette, Clyde
Lucas, Jerry
Luisetti, Hank
Macauley, Ed
Maravich, Pete
Martin, Slater
McCracken, Branch
McCracken, Jack
McDermott, Bobby
McGuire, Dick
Meyers, Ann
Mikan, George
Monroe, Earl
Murphy, Calvin
Murphy, Stretch
Page, Pat
Pettit, Bob
Phillip, Andy
Pollard, Jim
Ramsay, Frank
Reed, Willis
Robertson, Oscar
Roosma, John S.
Russell, Honey
Russell, Bill
Schayes, Adolph

Schmidt, Ernest
Schommer, John
Sedran, Barney
Semyonova, Ulyona
Sharman, Bill
Steinmetz, Christian
Thompson, Cat
Thurmond, Nate
Twyman, Jack
Unseld, Wes
Vandivier, Fuzzy
Wachter, Edward
Walton, Bill
Wanzer, Bobby
West, Jerry
White, Nera
Wilkins, Lenny
Wooden, John
**Coaches**
Auerbach, Red
Barry, Sam
Blood, Ernest
Cann, Howard
Carlson, Dr. H. C.
Carnesecca, Lou
Carnevale, Ben
Case, Everett
Dean, Everett
Diddle, Edgar
Drake, Bruce
Gaines, Clarence
Gardner, Jack
Gill, Slats
Hickey, Edgar
Hobson, Howard
Holzman, Red
Iba, Hank
Julian, Alvin
Keaney, Frank
Keogan, George

Knight, Bob
Lambert, Ward
Litwack, Harry
Loeffler, Kenneth
Lonborg, Dutch
McCutchan, Arad
McGuire, Al
McGuire, Frank
McLendon, John
Meyer, Ray
Meanwell, Dr. W.E.
Miller, Ralph
Newell, Pete
Ramsay, Jack
Rupp, Adolph
Sachs, Leonard
Shelton, Everett
Smith, Dean
Taylor, Fred
Teague, Bertha
Wade, Margaret
Watts, Stan
Wooden, John
Woolpert, Phil
**Referees**
Enright, James
Hepburn, George
Hoyt, George
Kennedy, Matthew
Leith, Lloyd
Mihalik, Red
Nucatola, John
Quigley, Ernest
Shirley, J. Dallas
Tobey, David
Walsh, David
**Contributors**
Abbott, Sendra B.
Allen, Phog
Bee, Clair

Brown, Walter
Bunn, John
Douglas, Bob
Duer, Al O.
Fagan, Cliff
Fisher, Harry
Fleisher, Larry
Gottlieb, Edward
Gulick, Dr. L. H.
Harrison, Lester
Hepp, Dr. Ferenc
Hickox, Edward
Hinkle, Tony
Irish, Ned
Jones, R. W.
Kennedy, Walter
Liston, Emil
Mokray, Bill
Morgan, Ralph
Morgenweck, Frank
Naismith, Dr. James
O'Brien, John
O'Brien, Larry
Olsen, Harold
Podoloff, Maurice
Porter, H. V.
Reis, William
Ripley, Elmer
St. John, Lynn
Saperstein, Abe
Schabinger, Arthur
Stagg, Amos Alonzo
Steitz, Edward
Taylor, Chuck
Tower, Oswald
Trester, Arthur
Wells, Clifford
Wilke, Lou

# Skiing

## World Cup Alpine Champions

### Men

| | | | | | | | | |
|---|---|---|---|---|---|---|---|---|
| 1967 | Jean Claude Killy, France | 1976 | Ingemar Stenmark, Sweden | 1985 | Marc Girardelli, Luxembourg |
| 1968 | Jean Claude Killy, France | 1977 | Ingemar Stenmark, Sweden | 1986 | Marc Girardelli, Luxembourg |
| 1969 | Karl Schranz, Austria | 1978 | Ingemar Stenmark, Sweden | 1987 | Pirmin Zurbriggen, Switzerland |
| 1970 | Karl Schranz, Austria | 1979 | Peter Luescher, Switzerland | 1988 | Pirmin Zurbriggen, Switzerland |
| 1971 | Gustavo Thoeni, Italy | 1980 | Andreas Wenzel, Liechtenstein | 1989 | Marc Girardelli, Luxembourg |
| 1972 | Gustavo Thoeni, Italy | 1981 | Phil Mahre, U.S. | 1990 | Pirmin Zurbriggen, Switzerland |
| 1973 | Gustavo Thoeni, Italy | 1982 | Phil Mahre, U.S. | 1991 | Marc Girardelli, Luxembourg |
| 1974 | Piero Gros, Italy | 1983 | Phil Mahre, U.S. | 1992 | Paul Accola, Switzerland |
| 1975 | Gustavo Thoeni, Italy | 1984 | Pirmin Zurbriggen, Switzerland | 1993 | Marc Girardelli, Luxembourg |

### Women

| | | | | | |
|---|---|---|---|---|---|
| 1967 | Nancy Greene, Canada | 1976 | Rose Mittermaier, W. Germany | 1985 | Michela Figini, Switzerland |
| 1968 | Nancy Greene, Canada | 1977 | Lise-Marie Morerod, Switzerland | 1986 | Maria Walliser, Switzerland |
| 1969 | Gertrud Gabl, Austria | 1978 | Hanni Wenzel, Liechtenstein | 1987 | Maria Walliser, Switzerland |
| 1970 | Michele Jacot, France | 1979 | Annemarie Proell Moser, Austria | 1988 | Michela Figini, Switzerland |
| 1971 | Annemarie Proell, Austria | 1980 | Hanni Wenzel, Liechtenstein | 1989 | Vreni Schneider, Switzerland |
| 1972 | Annemarie Proell, Austria | 1981 | Marie-Theres Nadig, Switzerland | 1990 | Petra Kronberger, Austria |
| 1973 | Annemarie Proell, Austria | 1982 | Erika Hess, Switzerland | 1991 | Petra Kronberger, Austria |
| 1974 | Annemarie Proell, Austria | 1983 | Tamara McKinney, U.S. | 1992 | Petra Kronberger, Austria |
| 1975 | Annemarie Proell, Austria | 1984 | Erika Hess, Switzerland | 1993 | Anita Wachter, Austria |

# Curling Champions

Source: U.S. Curling News

## World Champions

| Year | Country, skip | Year | Country, skip | Year | Country, skip |
|---|---|---|---|---|---|
| 1979 | Norway, Kristian Soerum | 1984 | Norway, Eigil Ramsfjell | 1989 | Canada, Pat Ryan |
| 1980 | Canada, Rich Folk | 1985 | Canada, Al Hackner | 1990 | Canada, Ed Werenich |
| 1981 | Switzerland, Jurg Tanner | 1986 | Canada, Ed Luckowich | 1991 | Scotland, David Smith |
| 1982 | Canada, Al Hackner | 1987 | Canada, Russ Howard | 1992 | Switzerland, Marcus Eggler |
| 1983 | Canada, Ed Werenich | 1988 | Norway, Eigil Ramsfjell | 1993 | Canada, Russ Howard |

## U.S. Men's Champions

| Year | State, skip | Year | State, skip | Year | State, skip |
|---|---|---|---|---|---|
| 1979 | Minnesota, Scott Baird | 1984 | Minnesota, Bruce Roberts | 1989 | Washington, Jim Vukich |
| 1980 | Minnesota, Paul Pustover | 1985 | Illinois, Tim Wright | 1990 | Washington, Doug Jones |
| 1981 | Wisconsin, Somerville-Nichols | 1986 | Wisconsin, Steve Brown | 1991 | Wisconsin, Steve Brown |
| 1982 | Wisconsin, Steve Brown | 1987 | Washington, Jim Vukich | 1992 | Washington, Doug Jones |
| 1983 | Colorado, Don Cooper | 1988 | Washington, Doug Jones | 1993 | Minnesota, Scott Baird |

## U.S. Women's Champions

| Year | State, skip | Year | State, skip | Year | State, skip |
|---|---|---|---|---|---|
| 1982 | Illinois, Ruth Schwenker | 1986 | Minnesota, Gerri Tilden | 1990 | Colorado, Bev Behnke |
| 1983 | Washington, Nancy Langley | 1987 | Washington, Sharon Good | 1991 | Texas, Maymar Gemmell |
| 1984 | Minnesota, Amy Hatten | 1988 | Washington, Nancy Langey | 1992 | Wisconsin, Lisa Schoeneberg |
| 1985 | Alaska, Bev Birklid | 1989 | North Dakota, Jan Lagasse | 1993 | Colorado, Bev Behnke |

# Westminster Kennel Club

| Year | Best-in-show | Breed | Owner |
|---|---|---|---|
| 1984 | Ch. Seaward's Blackbeard | Newfoundland | Elinor Ayers |
| 1985 | Ch. Braeburn's Close Encounter | Scottish terrier | Sonnie Novick |
| 1986 | Ch. Marjetta National Acclaim | Pointer | Mrs. Alan Robson & Michael Zollo |
| 1987 | Ch. Covy Tucker Hill's Manhattan | German shepherd | Shirley Braunstein & Jane Firestone |
| 1988 | Ch. Great Elms Prince Charming II | Pomeranian | Skip Piazza & Olga Baker |
| 1989 | Ch. Royal Tudor's Wild As The Wind | Doberman | Sue & Art Kemp, Richard & Carolyn Vida, Beth Wilhite |
| 1990 | Ch. Wendessa Crown Prince | Pekingese | Ed Jenner |
| 1991 | Ch. Whisperwind on a Carousel | Poodle | Joan & Frederick Hartsock |
| 1992 | Ch. Registry's Lonesome Dove | Fox terrier | Marion & Sam Lawrence |
| 1993 | Ch. Salilyn's Condor | English springer spaniel | Donna & Roger Herzig |

# Iditarod Trail Sled Dog Race in 1993

Jeff King won the 1993 Iditarod Trail Sled Dog Race on March 17, 1993, in a record time of 10 days 15 hours and 38 minutes. By winning the 1,159-mile race from Anchorage to Nome, King received $50,000 in prize money and a pickup truck valued at about $25,000. DeeDee Jonrowe finished second and Rick Mackey finished third.

# IGFA Freshwater & Saltwater All-Tackle World Records

Source: International Game Fish Association. Records confirmed to May 1993

## Saltwater Fish

| Species | Weight | Where caught | Date | Angler |
|---|---|---|---|---|
| Albacore | 88 lbs. 2 oz. | Pt. Mogan, Canary Islands | Nov. 19, 1977 | Siegfried Dickemann |
| Amberjack, greater | 155 lbs. 10 oz. | Bermuda | June 24, 1981 | Joseph Dawson |
| Barracuda, great | 85 lbs. | Christmas Island | Apr. 11, 1992 | John Helfrich |
| Barracuda, Mexican | 21 lbs. | Costa Rica | Mar. 27, 1987 | E. Greg Kent |
| Barracuda, Pacific | 6 lbs. 3 oz. | Pt. Loma, San Diego, Cal. | Apr. 4, 1992 | James Seibert |
| Bass, barred sand | 13 lbs. 3 oz. | Huntington Beach, Cal. | Aug. 29, 1988 | Joe Mizelle Jr. |
| Bass, black sea | 9 lbs. 8 oz. | Virginia Beach, Va. | Jan. 9, 1987 | Robert Halal |
| | | Virginia Beach, Va. | Dec. 22, 1990 | Jack Stallings, Jr. |
| Bass, giant sea | 563 lbs. 8 oz. | Anacaba Island, Cal. | Aug. 20, 1968 | James D. McAdam Jr. |
| Bass, striped | 78 lbs. 8 oz. | Atlantic City, N.J. | Sept. 21, 1982 | Albert McReynolds |
| Bass, white | 6 lbs. 3 oz. | L. Orange, Va. | July 31, 1989 | Ronald Sprouse |
| Bluefish | 31 lbs. 12 oz. | Hatteras Inlet, N.C. | Jan. 30, 1972 | James M. Hussey |
| Bonefish | 19 lbs. | Zululand, S. Africa | May 26, 1962 | Brian W. Batchelor |
| Bonito, Atlantic | 18 lbs. 14 oz. | Fayal I., Azores | July 8, 1953 | D. G. Higgs |
| Bonito, Pacific | 14 lbs. 12 oz. | San Benitos Is., Mexico | Oct. 12, 1980 | Jerome Rilling |
| Cabezon | 23 lbs. | Juan De Fuca Strait, Wash. | Aug. 4, 1990 | Wesley Hunter |
| Cobia | 135 lbs. 9 oz. | Shark Bay, Australia | July 9, 1985 | Peter W. Goulding |
| Cod, Atlantic | 98 lbs. 12 oz. | Isle of Shoals, N.H. | June 8, 1969 | Alphonse Bielevich |
| Cod, Pacific | 30 lbs. | Andrew Bay, Alaska | June 7, 1984 | Donald Vaughn |
| Conger | 110 lbs. 8 oz. | Plymouth, England | Aug. 20, 1991 | Hans Clausen |
| Dolphin | 87 lbs. | Papagallo Gulf, Costa Rica | Sept. 25, 1976 | Manual Salazar |
| Drum, black | 113 lbs. 1 oz. | Lewes, Del. | Sept. 15, 1975 | Gerald Townsend |
| Drum, red | 94 lbs. 2 oz. | Avon, N.C. | Nov. 7, 1984 | David Deuel |
| Eel, American | 8 lbs. 8 oz. | Brewster, Mass. | May 17, 1992 | Gerald LaPierre |
| Eel, marbled | 36 lbs. 1 oz. | Hazelmere Dam, S. Africa | June 10, 1984 | Ferdie van Nooten |
| Flounder, southern | 20 lbs. 9 oz. | Nassau Sound, Fla. | Dec. 23, 1983 | Larenza Mungin |
| Flounder, summer | 22 lbs. 7 oz. | Montauk, N.Y. | Sept. 15, 1975 | Charles Nappi |
| Grouper, Warsaw | 436 lbs. 12 oz. | Gulf of Mexico, Destin, Fla. | Dec. 22, 1985 | Steve Haeusler |
| Halibut, Atlantic | 255 lbs. 4 oz. | Gloucester, Mass. | July 28, 1989 | Sonny Manley |
| Halibut, California | 53 lbs. 4 oz. | Santa Rosa Is., Cal. | July 7, 1988 | Russell Harmon |
| Halibut, Pacific | 368 lbs. | Gustavus, Alaska | July 5, 1991 | Celia Deuitt |
| Jack, crevalle | 54 lbs. 7 oz. | Pt. Michel, Gabon | Jan. 15, 1982 | Thomas Gibson Jr. |
| Jack, horse-eye | 24 lbs. 8 oz. | Miami, Fla. | Dec. 20, 1982 | Tito Schnau |
| Jack, Pacific crevalle | 26 lbs. 12 oz. | Golfito, Costa Rica | Aug. 2, 1992 | Jerome Matthews |
| Jewfish | 680 lbs. | Fernandina Beach, Fla. | May 20, 1961 | Lynn Joyner |
| Kawakawa | 29 lbs. | Clarion Is., Mexico | Dec. 17, 1986 | Ronald Nakamura |
| Lingcod | 69 lbs. | Langara Is., B.C. | June 16, 1992 | Murray Romer |
| Mackerel, cero | 17 lbs. 2 oz. | Islamorada, Fla. | Apr. 5, 1986 | G. Michael Mills |
| Mackerel, king | 90 lbs. | Key West, Fla. | Feb. 16, 1976 | Norton Thomton |
| Mackerel, Spanish | 13 lbs. | Ocracoke Inlet, N.C. | Nov. 4, 1987 | Robert Cranton |
| Marlin, Atlantic blue | 1,402 lbs. 2 oz. | Vitoria, Brazil | Feb. 29, 1992 | Paulo Amorim |
| Marlin, black | 1,560 lbs. | Cabo Blanco, Peru | Aug. 4, 1953 | A. C. Glassell Jr. |
| Marlin, Pacific blue | 1,376 lbs. | Kaaiwa Pt., Hawaii | May 31, 1982 | J.W. deBeaubien |
| Marlin, striped | 494 lbs. | Tutukaka, New Zealand | Jan. 16, 1986 | Bill Boniface |
| Marlin, white | 181 lbs. 14 oz. | Vitoria, Brazil | Dec. 8, 1979 | Evandro Luiz Caser |
| Permit | 51 lbs. 8 oz. | Lake Worth, Fla. | Apr. 28, 1978 | William M. Kenney |
| Pollack | 27 lbs. 6 oz. | Devon, England | Jan. 16, 1986 | Robert Milkins |
| Pollock | 46 lbs. 10 oz. | Perkins Cove, Me. | Oct. 24, 1990 | Linda Paul |
| Pompano, African | 50 lbs. 8 oz. | Daytona Beach, Fla. | Apr. 21, 1990 | Tom Sargent |
| Roosterfish | 114 lbs. | La Paz, Mexico | June 1, 1960 | Abe Sackheim |
| Runner, blue | 8 lbs. 4 oz. | Bimini, Bahamas | Sept. 9, 1990 | Brent Rowland |
| Runner, rainbow | 37 lbs. 9 oz. | Clarion Is., Mexico | Nov. 21, 1991 | Tom Pfleger |
| Sailfish, Atlantic | 135 lbs. 5 oz. | Lagos, Nigeria | Nov. 10, 1991 | Ron King |
| Sailfish, Pacific | 221 lbs. | Santa Cruz Is., Ecuador | Feb. 12, 1947 | C. W. Stewart |
| Seabass, white | 83 lbs. 12 oz. | San Felipe, Mexico | Mar. 31, 1953 | L.C. Baumgardner |
| Seatrout, spotted | 16 lbs. | Mason's Beach, Va. | May 28, 1977 | William Katko |
| Shark, bigeye thresher | 802 lbs. | Tutukaka, New Zealand | Feb. 8, 1981 | Dianne North |
| Shark, blue | 437 lbs. | Catherine Bay, N.S.W. Australia | Oct. 2, 1976 | Peter Hyde |
| Shark, great hammerhead | 991 lbs. | Sarasota, Fla. | May 30, 1982 | Allen Ogle |
| Shark, Greenland | 1,708 lbs. 9 oz. | Trondheim, Norway | Oct. 18, 1987 | Terje Nordtvedt |
| Shark, man-eater or white | 2,664 lbs. | Ceduna, Australia | Apr. 21, 1959 | Alfred Dean |
| Shark, porbeagle | 465 lbs. | Cornwall, England | July 23, 1976 | Jorge Potier |
| Shark, shortfin mako | 1,115 lbs. | Black R., Mauritius | Nov. 16, 1988 | Patrick Guillanton |
| Shark, tiger | 1,780 lbs. | Cherry Grove, S.C. | June 14, 1964 | Walter Maxwell |
| Skipjack, black | 26 lbs. | Baja, Mexico | Oct. 23, 1991 | Clifford Hamishi |
| Snapper, cubera | 121 lbs. 8 oz. | Cameron, La. | July 5, 1982 | Mike Hebert |
| Snook | 53 lbs. 10 oz. | Costa Rica | Oct. 18, 1978 | Gilbert Ponzi |
| Spearfish, Mediterranean | 90 lbs. 13 oz. | Madeira Island, Portugal | June 2, 1980 | Joseph Larkin |
| Swordfish | 1,182 lbs. | Iquique, Chile | May 7, 1953 | L. Marron |
| Tarpon | 283 lbs. 4 oz. | Sierra Leone | Apr. 16, 1991 | Yvon Sebag |
| Tautog | 24 lbs. | Wachapreagee, Va. | Aug. 25, 1987 | Gregory Bell |
| Tope | 72 lbs. 12 oz. | Parengarenga Harbor, New Zealand | Dec. 19, 1986 | Melanie Feldman |
| Trevally, bigeye | 15 lbs. 8 oz. | Waianae, Hawaii | Mar. 6, 1992 | Darryl Bailey |
| Trevally, giant | 145 lbs. 8 oz. | Makena, Hawaii | Mar. 28, 1991 | Russell Mori |
| Tuna, Atlantic bigeye | 375 lbs. 8 oz. | Ocean City, Md. | Aug. 26, 1977 | Cecil Browne |
| Tuna, blackfin | 42 lbs. | Bermuda | June 2, 1978 | Alan J. Card |
| | | Bermuda | July 18, 1989 | Gilbert Pearman |
| Tuna, bluefin | 1,496 lbs. | Aulds Cove, Nova Scotia | Oct. 26, 1979 | Ken Fraser |
| Tuna, longtail | 79 lbs. 2 oz. | Montague Is., N.S.W., Australia | Apr. 12, 1982 | Tim Simpson |
| Tuna, Pacific bigeye | 435 lbs. | Cabo Blanco, Peru | Apr. 17, 1957 | Dr. Russel Lee |

| Species | Weight | Where caught | Date | Angler |
|---|---|---|---|---|
| Tuna, skipjack | 41 lbs. 14 oz. | Mauritius | Nov. 12, 1985 | Edmund Heinzen |
| Tuna, southern bluefin | 348 lbs. 5 oz. | Whakatane, New Zealand | Jan. 16, 1981 | Rex Wood |
| Tuna, yellowfin | 388 lbs. 12 oz. | San Benedicto Island, Mexico | Apr. 1, 1977 | Curt Wiesenhutter |
| Tunny, little | 35 lbs. 2 oz. | Cap de Garde, Algeria | Dec. 14, 1988 | Jean Yves Chatard |
| Wahoo | 155 lbs. 8 oz. | Bahamas | Apr. 3, 1990 | William Bourne |
| Weakfish | 19 lbs. 2 oz. | Jones Beach Inlet, N.Y. | Oct. 11, 1984 | Dennis Rooney |
|  |  | Delaware Bay, Delaware | May 20, 1989 | William Thomas |
| Yellowtail, California | 79 lbs. 4 oz. | Alijos Rocks, Mexico | July 2, 1991 | Robert Walker |
| Yellowtail, southern | 114 lbs. 10 oz. | Tauranga, New Zealand | Feb. 5, 1984 | Mike Godfrey |

### Freshwater Fish

| Species | Weight | Where caught | Date | Angler |
|---|---|---|---|---|
| Barramundi | 63 lbs. 2 oz. | Normah R., Australia | Apr. 28, 1991 | Scott Barnsley |
| Bass, largemouth | 22 lbs. 4 oz. | Montgomery Lake, Ga. | June 2, 1932 | George W. Perry |
| Bass, peacock | 26 lbs. 8 oz. | Matevini R., Colombia | Jan. 26, 1982 | Rod Neubert |
| Bass, redeye | 8 lbs. 3 oz. | Flint River, Ga. | Oct. 23, 1977 | David A. Hubbard |
| Bass, rock | 3 lbs. | York River, Ont. | Aug. 1, 1974 | Peter Gulgin |
| Bass, smallmouth | 11 lbs. 15 oz. | Dale Hollow Lake, Ky. | July 9, 1955 | David L. Hayes |
| Bass, Suwannee | 3 lbs. 14 oz. | Suwannee River, Fla. | Mar. 2, 1985 | Ronnie Everett |
| Bass, white | 6 lbs. 13 oz. | L. Orange, Va. | July 31, 1989 | Ronald Sprouse |
| Bass, whiterock | 24 lbs. 3 oz. | Leesville L., Va. | May 12, 1989 | David Lambert |
| Bass, yellow | 2 lbs. 4 oz. | Lake Monroe, Ind. | Mar. 27, 1977 | Donald L. Stalker |
| Bluegill | 4 lbs. 12 oz. | Ketona Lake, Ala. | Apr. 9, 1950 | T.S. Hudson |
| Bowfin | 21 lbs. 8 oz. | Florence, S.C. | Jan. 29, 1980 | Robert Harmon |
| Buffalo, bigmouth | 70 lbs. 5 oz. | Bastrop, La. | Apr. 21, 1980 | Delbert Sisk |
| Buffalo, black | 55 lbs. 8 oz. | Cherokee L., Tenn. | May 3, 1984 | Edward McLain |
| Buffalo, smallmouth | 68 lbs. 8 oz. | L. Hamilton, Ark. | May 16, 1984 | Jerry Dolezal |
| Bullhead, brown | 5 lbs. 8 oz. | Veal Pond, Ga. | May 22, 1975 | Jimmy Andrews |
| Bullhead, yellow | 4 lbs. 4 oz. | Mormon Lake, Ariz. | May 11, 1984 | Emily Williams |
| Burbot | 18 lbs. 4 oz. | Pickford, Mich. | Jan. 31, 1980 | Thomas Courtemanche |
| Carp | 75 lbs. 11 oz. | Lac de St. Cassien, France | May 21, 1987 | Leo van der Gugten |
| Catfish, blue | 109 lbs. 4 oz. | Cooper R., S.C. | Mar. 14, 1991 | George Lijewski |
| Catfish, channel | 58 lbs. | Santee-Cooper Res., S.C. | July 7, 1964 | W.B. Whaley |
| Catfish, flathead | 91 lbs. 4 oz. | L. Lewisville, Tex. | Mar. 28, 1982 | Mike Rogers |
| Catfish, white | 18 lbs. 14 oz. | Withlacoochee R., Fla. | Sept. 21, 1991 | Jim Miller |
| Char, Arctic | 32 lbs. 9 oz. | Tree River, Canada | July 30, 1981 | Jeffrey Ward |
| Crappie, white | 5 lbs. 3 oz. | Enid Dam, Miss. | July 31, 1957 | Fred L. Bright |
| Dolly Varden | 16 lbs. 12 oz. | Mashutuk R., Alaska | July 21, 1991 | Gary King Jr. |
| Dorado | 51 lbs. 5 oz. | Corrientes, Argentina | Sept. 27, 1984 | Armando Giudice |
| Drum, freshwater | 54 lbs. 8 oz. | Nickajack Lake, Tenn. | Apr. 20, 1972 | Benny E. Hull |
| Gar, alligator | 279 lbs. | Rio Grande River, Tex. | Dec. 2, 1951 | Bill Valverde |
| Gar, Florida | 21 lbs. 3 oz. | Boca Raton, Fla. | June 3, 1981 | Jeff Sabol |
| Gar, longnose | 50 lbs. 5 oz. | Trinity River, Tex. | July 30, 1954 | Townsend Miller |
| Gar, shortnose | 5 lbs. | Sally Jones L., Oklahoma | Apr. 26, 1985 | Buddy Croslin |
| Gar, spotted | 8 lbs. 12 oz. | Tennessee R., Ala. | Aug. 26, 1987 | Winston Baker |
| Grayling, Arctic | 5 lbs. 15 oz. | Katseyedie River, N.W.T. | Aug. 16, 1967 | Jeanne P. Branson |
| Inconnu | 53 lbs. | Pah R., Alaska | Aug. 20, 1986 | Lawrence Hudnall |
| Kokanee | 9 lbs. 6 oz. | Okanagan Lake, Vernon, B.C. | June 18, 1988 | Norm Kuhn |
| Muskellunge | 65 lbs. | Blackstone Harbor, Ont. | Oct. 16, 1988 | Kenneth O'Brien |
| Muskellunge, tiger | 51 lbs. 3 oz. | Lac Vieux-Desert, Wis., Mich. | July 16, 1919 | John Knobla |
| Perch, Nile | 191 lbs. 8 oz. | L. Victoria, Kenya | Sept. 5, 1991 | Andy Davison |
| Perch, white | 4 lbs. 12 oz. | Messalonskee Lake, Me. | June 4, 1949 | Mrs. Earl Small |
| Perch, yellow | 4 lbs. 3 oz. | Bordentown, N.J. | May, 1865 | Dr. C.C. Abbot |
| Pickerel, chain | 9 lbs. 6 oz. | Homerville, Ga. | Feb. 17, 1961 | Baxley McQuaig Jr. |
| Pike, northern | 55 lbs. 1 oz. | Lake of Grefeern, W. Germany | Oct. 16, 1986 | Lothar Louis |
| Redhorse, greater | 9 lbs. 3 oz. | Salmon R., Pulaski, N.Y. | May 11, 1985 | Jason Wilson |
| Redhorse, silver | 11 lbs. 7 oz. | Plum Creek, Wis. | May 29, 1985 | Neal Long |
| Salmon, Atlantic | 79 lbs. 2 oz. | Tana River, Norway | 1928 | Henrik Henriksen |
| Salmon, chinook | 97 lbs. 4 oz. | Kenai R., Alas. | May 17, 1985 | Les Anderson |
| Salmon, chum | 32 lbs. | Behm Canal, Alas. | June 7, 1985 | Fredrick Thynes |
| Salmon, coho | 33 lbs. 4 oz. | Salmon R., Pulaski, N.Y. | Sept. 27, 1989 | Jerry Lifton |
| Salmon, pink | 13 lbs. 1 oz. | St. Mary's R., Ontario | Sept. 23, 1992 | Ray Higaki |
| Salmon, sockeye | 15 lbs. 3 oz. | Kenai R., Alaska | Aug. 9, 1987 | Stan Roach |
| Sauger | 8 lbs. 12 oz. | Lake Sakakawea, N.D. | Oct. 6, 1971 | Mike Fischer |
| Shad, American | 11 lbs. 4 oz. | Connecticut R., Mass. | May 19, 1986 | Bob Thibodo |
| Sturgeon, white | 468 lbs. | Benicia, Cal. | July 9, 1983 | Joey Pallotta 3d |
| Sunfish, green | 2 lbs. 2 oz. | Stockton Lake, Mo. | June 18, 1971 | Paul M. Dilley |
| Sunfish, redbreast | 1 lb. 12 oz. | Suwannee R., Fla. | May 29, 1984 | Alvin Buchanan |
| Sunfish, redear | 4 lbs. 13 oz. | Marianna, Fla. | Mar. 13, 1986 | Joey Floyd |
| Tigerfish, giant | 97 lbs. | Zaire R., Kinshasa, Zaire | July 9, 1988 | Raymond Houtmans |
| Tilapia | 6 lbs. | L. Okeechobee, Fla. | June 24, 1989 | Joseph M. Tucker |
| Trout, Apache | 5 lbs. 3 oz. | Apache Res., Ariz. | May 29, 1991 | John Baldwin |
| Trout, brook | 14 lbs. 8 oz. | Nipigon River, Ont. | July 1916 | Dr. W.J. Cook |
| Trout, brown | 40 lbs. 4 oz. | Little Red R., Ark. | May 9, 1992 | Howard Collins |
| Trout, bull | 32 lbs. | L. Pend Oreille, Ida. | Oct. 27, 1949 | N.L. Higgins |
| Trout, cutthroat | 41 lbs. | Pyramid Lake, Nev. | Dec. 1925 | J. Skimmerhorn |
| Trout, golden | 11 lbs. | Cook's Lake, Wyo. | Aug. 5, 1948 | Charles S. Reed |
| Trout, lake | 66 lbs. 8 oz. | Great Bear Lake, N.W.T. | July 19, 1991 | Rodney Harback |
| Trout, rainbow | 42 lbs. 2 oz. | Bell Island, Alas. | June 22, 1970 | David Robert White |
| Trout, tiger | 20 lbs. 13 oz. | Lake Michigan, Wis. | Aug. 12, 1978 | Pete Friedland |
| Walleye | 25 lbs. | Old Hickory Lake, Tenn. | Aug. 1, 1960 | Mabry Harper |
| Warmouth | 2 lbs. 7 oz. | Yellow R., Holt, Fla. | Oct. 19, 1985 | Tony D. Dempsey |
| Whitefish, lake | 14 lbs. 6 oz. | Meaford, Ont. | May 21, 1984 | Dennis Laycock |
| Whitefish, mountain | 5 lbs. 6 oz. | Rioh R., Sask. | June 15, 1988 | John Bell |
| Whitefish, river | 11 lbs. 2 oz. | Nymoua, Sweden | Dec. 9, 1984 | Jorgen Larsson |
| Whitefish, round | 6 lbs. | Putahow R., Manitoba | June 14, 1984 | Allen Ristori |
| Zander | 22 lbs. 2 oz. | Trosa, Sweden | June 12, 1986 | Harry Lee Tennison |

# COLLEGE BASKETBALL

## Final Division I Conference Standing, 1992–1993

### Atlantic Coast

| | Conference W L | | Overall W L | |
|---|---|---|---|---|
| North Carolina | 14 | 2 | 34 | 4 |
| Florida St. | 12 | 4 | 25 | 10 |
| Duke | 10 | 6 | 24 | 8 |
| Wake Forest | 10 | 6 | 21 | 9 |
| Virginia | 9 | 7 | 21 | 10 |
| Georgia Tech | 8 | 8 | 19 | 11 |
| Clemson | 5 | 11 | 17 | 13 |
| Maryland | 2 | 14 | 12 | 16 |
| North Carolina St. | 2 | 14 | 8 | 19 |

Tournament Champion—Georgia Tech.

### Atlantic 10

| North Carolina | | | | |
|---|---|---|---|---|
| Massachusetts | 11 | 3 | 24 | 7 |
| George Washington | 8 | 6 | 21 | 9 |
| Rhode Island | 8 | 6 | 19 | 11 |
| St. Joseph's (Pa.) | 8 | 6 | 18 | 11 |
| Temple | 8 | 6 | 20 | 13 |
| West Virginia | 7 | 7 | 17 | 12 |
| Rutgers | 6 | 8 | 13 | 15 |
| St. Bonaventure | 0 | 14 | 10 | 17 |

Tournament Champion—Massachusetts.

### Big East

| Seton Hall | 14 | 4 | 28 | 7 |
|---|---|---|---|---|
| St. John's (N.Y.) | 12 | 6 | 19 | 11 |
| Syracuse | 10 | 8 | 20 | 9 |
| Pittsburgh | 9 | 9 | 17 | 11 |
| Providence | 9 | 9 | 20 | 13 |
| Boston College | 9 | 9 | 18 | 13 |
| Connecticut | 9 | 9 | 15 | 13 |
| Georgetown | 8 | 10 | 20 | 13 |
| Miami (Fla.) | 7 | 11 | 10 | 17 |
| Villanova | 3 | 15 | 8 | 19 |

Tournament Champion—Seton Hall.

### Big Eight

| Kansas | 11 | 3 | 29 | 7 |
|---|---|---|---|---|
| Oklahoma St. | 8 | 6 | 20 | 9 |
| Iowa St. | 8 | 6 | 20 | 11 |
| Nebraska | 8 | 6 | 20 | 11 |
| Kansas St. | 7 | 7 | 19 | 11 |
| Oklahoma | 7 | 7 | 20 | 12 |
| Missouri | 5 | 9 | 19 | 14 |
| Colorado | 2 | 12 | 10 | 17 |

Tournament Champion—Missouri.

### Big Sky

| Idaho | 11 | 3 | 24 | 8 |
|---|---|---|---|---|
| Boise St. | 10 | 4 | 21 | 8 |
| Weber St. | 10 | 4 | 20 | 8 |
| Montana | 8 | 6 | 17 | 11 |
| Idaho St. | 5 | 9 | 10 | 18 |
| Montana St. | 5 | 9 | 9 | 18 |
| Northern Arizona | 4 | 10 | 10 | 16 |
| E. Washington | 3 | 11 | 6 | 20 |

Tournament Champion—Boise St.

### Big South

| Towson St. | 14 | 2 | 18 | 9 |
|---|---|---|---|---|
| Coastal Carolina | 12 | 4 | 22 | 10 |
| Campbell | 10 | 6 | 12 | 15 |
| Liberty | 9 | 7 | 16 | 14 |
| Radford | 8 | 8 | 15 | 16 |
| Md.-Baltimore County | 7 | 9 | 12 | 16 |
| Winthrop | 5 | 11 | 14 | 14 |
| Charleston So. | 5 | 11 | 9 | 18 |
| N.C.-Asheville | 2 | 14 | 4 | 23 |

Tournament Champion—Coastal Carolina.

### Big Ten

| Indiana | 17 | 1 | 31 | 4 |
|---|---|---|---|---|
| Michigan | 15 | 3 | 31 | 5 |
| Iowa | 11 | 7 | 23 | 9 |
| Illinois | 11 | 7 | 19 | 13 |
| Minnesota | 9 | 9 | 22 | 10 |
| Purdue | 9 | 9 | 18 | 10 |
| Ohio St. | 8 | 10 | 15 | 13 |
| Michigan St. | 7 | 11 | 15 | 13 |
| Wisconsin | 7 | 11 | 14 | 14 |
| Northwestern | 3 | 15 | 8 | 19 |
| Penn St. | 2 | 16 | 7 | 20 |

### Big West

| New Mexico St. | 15 | 3 | 26 | 8 |
|---|---|---|---|---|
| UNLV | 13 | 5 | 21 | 8 |
| Pacific | 12 | 6 | 16 | 11 |
| Long Beach St. | 11 | 7 | 22 | 10 |
| UC Santa Barbara | 10 | 8 | 18 | 11 |
| Cal St. Fullerton | 10 | 8 | 15 | 12 |
| Utah St. | 7 | 11 | 10 | 17 |
| Nevada | 4 | 14 | 9 | 17 |
| San Jose St. | 4 | 14 | 7 | 18 |
| UC Irvine | 4 | 14 | 6 | 21 |

Tournament Champion—Long Beach St.

### Colonial Athletic

| Old Dominion | 11 | 3 | 21 | 8 |
|---|---|---|---|---|
| James Madison | 11 | 3 | 21 | 9 |
| Richmond | 10 | 4 | 15 | 12 |
| N.C.-Wilmington | 6 | 8 | 17 | 11 |
| William & Mary | 6 | 8 | 14 | 13 |
| American | 6 | 8 | 11 | 17 |
| East Carolina | 4 | 10 | 13 | 17 |
| George Mason | 2 | 12 | 7 | 21 |

Tournament Champion—East Carolina.

### Great Midwest

| Cincinnati | 8 | 2 | 27 | 5 |
|---|---|---|---|---|
| Memphis St. | 7 | 3 | 20 | 12 |
| Marquette | 6 | 4 | 20 | 8 |
| Ala.-Birmingham | 5 | 5 | 21 | 14 |
| DePaul | 3 | 7 | 16 | 15 |
| St. Louis | 1 | 9 | 12 | 17 |

Tournament Champion—Cincinnati.

### Ivy League

| Pennsylvania | 14 | 0 | 22 | 5 |
|---|---|---|---|---|
| Cornell | 10 | 4 | 16 | 10 |
| Columbia | 9 | 5 | 16 | 10 |
| Princeton | 7 | 7 | 15 | 11 |
| Yale | 6 | 8 | 10 | 16 |
| Dartmouth | 5 | 9 | 11 | 15 |
| Harvard | 3 | 11 | 6 | 20 |
| Brown | 2 | 12 | 7 | 19 |

### Metropolitan

| Louisville | 11 | 1 | 22 | 9 |
|---|---|---|---|---|
| Tulane | 9 | 3 | 22 | 9 |
| Va. Commonwealth | 7 | 5 | 20 | 10 |
| N.C.-Charlotte | 6 | 6 | 15 | 13 |
| Southern Mississippi | 6 | 6 | 10 | 17 |
| South Florida | 2 | 10 | 8 | 19 |
| Virginia Tech | 1 | 11 | 10 | 18 |

Tournament Champion—Louisville.

### Metro Atlantic Athletic

| Manhattan | 12 | 2 | 23 | 7 |
|---|---|---|---|---|
| Niagara | 11 | 3 | 23 | 7 |
| Iona | 9 | 5 | 16 | 11 |
| Siena | 8 | 6 | 16 | 13 |
| Fairfield | 7 | 7 | 14 | 13 |
| Canisius | 5 | 9 | 10 | 18 |
| St. Peter's | 3 | 11 | 9 | 18 |
| Loyola (Md.) | 1 | 13 | 2 | 25 |

Tournament Champion—Manhattan.

### Mid-American

| Ball St. | 14 | 4 | 26 | 8 |
|---|---|---|---|---|
| Miami (Ohio) | 14 | 4 | 22 | 9 |
| Western Michigan | 12 | 6 | 17 | 12 |
| Ohio | 11 | 7 | 14 | 13 |
| Toledo | 9 | 9 | 12 | 16 |
| Eastern Michigan | 8 | 10 | 13 | 17 |
| Bowling Green | 8 | 10 | 11 | 16 |
| Kent | 7 | 11 | 10 | 17 |
| Central Michigan | 4 | 14 | 8 | 18 |
| Akron | 3 | 15 | 8 | 18 |

Tournament Champion—Ball St.

### Mid-Continent

| Cleveland St. | 15 | 1 | 22 | 6 |
|---|---|---|---|---|
| Wright St. | 10 | 6 | 20 | 10 |
| Northern Illinois | 10 | 6 | 15 | 12 |
| Illinois-Chicago | 9 | 7 | 17 | 15 |

| | Conference W L | | Overall W L | |
|---|---|---|---|---|
| Wisconsin-Green Bay | 9 | 7 | 13 | 14 |
| Valparaiso | 7 | 9 | 12 | 16 |
| Eastern Illinois | 7 | 9 | 10 | 17 |
| Western Illinois | 4 | 12 | 7 | 20 |
| Youngstown St. | 1 | 15 | 3 | 23 |

Tournament Champion—Wright St.

### Mid-Eastern Athletic

| Coppin St. | 16 | 0 | 22 | 8 |
|---|---|---|---|---|
| South Carolina St. | 9 | 7 | 16 | 13 |
| North Carolina A&T | 9 | 7 | 14 | 13 |
| Morgan St. | 9 | 7 | 9 | 17 |
| Florida A&M | 8 | 8 | 10 | 18 |
| Md.-East Shore | 7 | 9 | 12 | 15 |
| Delaware St. | 6 | 10 | 13 | 16 |
| Howard | 6 | 10 | 10 | 18 |
| Bethune-Cookman | 2 | 14 | 3 | 24 |

Tournament Champion—Coppin St.

### Midwestern Collegiate

| Xavier (Ohio) | 12 | 2 | 24 | 6 |
|---|---|---|---|---|
| Evansville | 12 | 2 | 23 | 7 |
| La Salle | 9 | 5 | 14 | 13 |
| Detroit Mercy | 7 | 7 | 15 | 12 |
| Duquesne | 5 | 9 | 13 | 15 |
| Butler | 5 | 9 | 11 | 17 |
| Loyola (Ill.) | 3 | 11 | 7 | 20 |
| Dayton | 3 | 11 | 4 | 26 |

Tournament Champion—Evansville.

### Missouri Valley

| Illinois St. | 13 | 5 | 19 | 10 |
|---|---|---|---|---|
| Southern Illinois | 12 | 6 | 23 | 10 |
| Southwest Missouri St. | 11 | 7 | 20 | 11 |
| Tulsa | 10 | 8 | 15 | 14 |
| Drake | 9 | 9 | 14 | 14 |
| Northern Iowa | 8 | 10 | 12 | 15 |
| Bradley | 7 | 11 | 16 | 16 |
| Indiana St. | 7 | 11 | 11 | 17 |
| Wichita St. | 7 | 11 | 10 | 17 |
| Creighton | 6 | 12 | 8 | 18 |

Tournament Champion—S. Illinois.

### North Atlantic

| Drexel | 12 | 2 | 22 | 7 |
|---|---|---|---|---|
| Northeastern | 12 | 2 | 20 | 8 |
| Delaware | 10 | 4 | 22 | 8 |
| Hartford | 7 | 7 | 14 | 14 |
| Maine | 4 | 10 | 10 | 17 |
| Vermont | 4 | 10 | 10 | 17 |
| New Hampshire | 4 | 10 | 6 | 21 |
| Boston Univ. | 3 | 11 | 6 | 21 |

Tournament Champion—Drexel.

### Northeast

| Rider | 14 | 4 | 19 | 11 |
|---|---|---|---|---|
| Wagner | 12 | 6 | 18 | 12 |
| Marist | 10 | 8 | 14 | 16 |
| Mt. St. Mary's (Md.) | 10 | 8 | 13 | 15 |
| FDU-Teaneck | 8 | 10 | 11 | 17 |
| St. Francis (N.Y.) | 8 | 10 | 9 | 18 |
| LIU-Brooklyn | 7 | 11 | 11 | 17 |
| Monmouth (N.J.) | 7 | 11 | 11 | 17 |
| Robert Morris | 7 | 11 | 9 | 18 |
| St. Francis (Pa.) | 7 | 11 | 9 | 18 |

Tournament Champion—Rider.

### Ohio Valley

| Tennessee St. | 13 | 3 | 19 | 10 |
|---|---|---|---|---|
| Murray St. | 11 | 5 | 18 | 12 |
| Eastern Kentucky | 11 | 5 | 15 | 12 |
| Southeast Mo. St. | 9 | 7 | 16 | 11 |
| Tennessee Tech | 7 | 9 | 13 | 13 |
| Morehead St. | 6 | 10 | 6 | 21 |
| Middle Tenn. St. | 5 | 11 | 10 | 16 |
| Tenn.-Martin | 4 | 12 | 7 | 19 |
| Austin Peay | 4 | 12 | 7 | 20 |

Tournament Champion—Tennessee St.

## Pacific-10

| | Confer-ence | | Overall Record | |
|---|---|---|---|---|
| | W | L | W | L |
| Arizona | 17 | 1 | 24 | 4 |
| California | 12 | 6 | 21 | 9 |
| UCLA | 11 | 7 | 22 | 11 |
| Arizona St. | 11 | 7 | 18 | 10 |
| USC | 9 | 9 | 18 | 12 |
| Washington St. | 9 | 9 | 15 | 12 |
| Oregon St. | 9 | 9 | 13 | 14 |
| Washington | 7 | 11 | 13 | 14 |
| Oregon | 3 | 15 | 10 | 20 |
| Stanford | 2 | 16 | 7 | 23 |

## Patriot

| | W | L | W | L |
|---|---|---|---|---|
| Bucknell | 13 | 1 | 23 | 6 |
| Holy Cross | 12 | 2 | 23 | 7 |
| Colgate | 9 | 5 | 18 | 10 |
| Fordham | 9 | 5 | 15 | 16 |
| Navy | 5 | 9 | 18 | 12 |
| Lafayette | 4 | 10 | 7 | 20 |
| Army | 2 | 12 | 4 | 22 |
| Lehigh | 2 | 12 | 4 | 23 |

Tournament Champion—Holy Cross.

## Southeastern
### Eastern Division

| | W | L | W | L |
|---|---|---|---|---|
| Vanderbilt | 14 | 2 | 28 | 6 |
| Kentucky | 13 | 3 | 30 | 4 |
| Florida | 9 | 7 | 16 | 12 |
| Georgia | 8 | 8 | 15 | 14 |
| South Carolina | 5 | 11 | 9 | 18 |
| Tennessee | 4 | 12 | 13 | 17 |

### Western Division

| | W | L | W | L |
|---|---|---|---|---|
| Arkansas | 10 | 6 | 22 | 9 |
| Louisiana St. | 9 | 7 | 22 | 11 |
| Auburn | 8 | 8 | 15 | 12 |
| Alabama | 7 | 9 | 16 | 13 |
| Mississippi St. | 5 | 11 | 13 | 16 |
| Mississippi | 4 | 12 | 10 | 18 |

Tournament Champion—Kentucky.

## Southern

| | W | L | W | L |
|---|---|---|---|---|
| Tenn.-Chattanooga | 16 | 2 | 26 | 7 |
| Ga. Southern | 12 | 6 | 19 | 9 |
| East Tenn. St. | 12 | 6 | 19 | 10 |
| Marshall | 11 | 7 | 16 | 11 |
| Davidson | 10 | 8 | 14 | 14 |
| Appalachian St. | 8 | 10 | 13 | 15 |
| Furman | 8 | 10 | 11 | 17 |
| Citadel | 8 | 10 | 10 | 17 |
| Va. Military | 3 | 15 | 5 | 22 |
| Western Carolina | 2 | 16 | 6 | 21 |

Tournament
Champion—Tenn.-Chattanooga.

## Southland

| | W | L | W | L |
|---|---|---|---|---|
| Northeast La. | 17 | 1 | 26 | 5 |
| Nicholls St. | 11 | 7 | 14 | 12 |
| Texas-Arlington | 10 | 8 | 16 | 12 |
| Texas-San Antonio | 10 | 8 | 15 | 14 |
| Southwest Tex. St. | 9 | 9 | 14 | 13 |
| McNeese St. | 9 | 9 | 12 | 16 |
| Stephen F. Austin | 8 | 10 | 12 | 14 |
| Northwestern La. | 7 | 11 | 13 | 13 |
| North Texas | 5 | 13 | 5 | 21 |
| Sam Houston St. | 4 | 14 | 6 | 19 |

Tournament Champion—Northeast La.

## Southwest

| | W | L | W | L |
|---|---|---|---|---|
| SMU | 12 | 2 | 20 | 8 |
| Rice | 11 | 3 | 18 | 10 |
| Houston | 9 | 5 | 21 | 9 |
| Baylor | 7 | 7 | 16 | 11 |
| Texas Tech | 6 | 8 | 18 | 12 |
| Texas A&M | 5 | 9 | 10 | 17 |
| Texas | 4 | 10 | 11 | 17 |
| Texas Christian | 2 | 12 | 6 | 22 |

Tournament Champion—Texas Tech.

## Southwestern Athletic

| | W | L | W | L |
|---|---|---|---|---|
| Jackson St. | 13 | 1 | 25 | 9 |
| Southern-B.R. | 9 | 5 | 21 | 10 |
| Alabama St. | 9 | 5 | 14 | 13 |
| Texas Southern | 8 | 6 | 12 | 15 |
| Mississippi Valley | 7 | 7 | 13 | 15 |
| Grambling | 5 | 9 | 13 | 14 |
| Alcorn St. | 5 | 9 | 7 | 20 |
| Prairie View | 0 | 14 | 1 | 26 |

Tournament Champion—Southern-B.R.

## Sun Belt

| | W | L | W | L |
|---|---|---|---|---|
| New Orleans | 18 | 0 | 26 | 4 |
| Western Kentucky | 14 | 4 | 26 | 6 |
| Arkansas St. | 11 | 7 | 16 | 12 |
| Southwestern La. | 11 | 7 | 17 | 13 |
| Arkansas-Little Rock | 10 | 8 | 15 | 13 |
| Lamar | 9 | 9 | 15 | 12 |
| South Ala. | 9 | 9 | 15 | 13 |
| Louisiana Tech | 3 | 15 | 7 | 21 |
| Jacksonville | 3 | 15 | 5 | 22 |
| Texas-Pan American | 2 | 16 | 2 | 20 |

Tournament Champion—Western Ky.

## Trans America Athletic

| | W | L | W | L |
|---|---|---|---|---|
| Florida International | 9 | 3 | 20 | 10 |
| Samford | 7 | 5 | 17 | 10 |
| Mercer | 7 | 5 | 13 | 14 |
| Stetson | 6 | 6 | 13 | 14 |
| Georgia St. | 5 | 7 | 13 | 14 |
| Southeastern La. | 4 | 8 | 12 | 15 |
| Centenary | 4 | 8 | 9 | 18 |

## West Coast

| | W | L | W | L |
|---|---|---|---|---|
| Pepperdine | 11 | 3 | 23 | 8 |
| Gonzaga | 10 | 4 | 19 | 9 |
| Santa Clara | 9 | 5 | 19 | 12 |
| San Francisco | 8 | 6 | 19 | 12 |
| San Diego | 7 | 7 | 13 | 14 |
| St. Mary's (Cal.) | 6 | 8 | 11 | 16 |
| Portland | 3 | 11 | 9 | 18 |
| Loyola (Cal.) | 2 | 12 | 7 | 20 |

Tournament Champion—Santa Clara.

## Western Athletic

| | W | L | W | L |
|---|---|---|---|---|
| Utah | 15 | 3 | 24 | 7 |
| Brigham Young | 15 | 3 | 25 | 9 |
| New Mexico | 13 | 5 | 24 | 7 |
| UTEP | 10 | 8 | 21 | 13 |
| Colorado St. | 9 | 9 | 17 | 12 |
| Fresno St. | 8 | 10 | 13 | 15 |
| Wyoming | 7 | 11 | 13 | 15 |
| Hawaii | 7 | 11 | 12 | 16 |
| Air Force | 3 | 15 | 9 | 19 |
| San Diego St. | 3 | 15 | 8 | 21 |

Tournament Champion—New Mexico.

## Independents

| | W | L |
|---|---|---|
| Wis.-Milwaukee | 23 | 4 |
| Charleston | 19 | 8 |
| Mo.-Kansas City | 15 | 12 |
| Southern Utah St. | 14 | 13 |
| Northeastern III. | 11 | 16 |
| Cal St. Northridge | 10 | 17 |
| Central Florida | 10 | 17 |
| N.C.-Greensboro | 10 | 17 |
| Hofstra | 9 | 18 |
| Notre Dame | 9 | 18 |
| Central Conn. St. | 8 | 19 |
| Buffalo | 5 | 22 |
| Chicago St. | 4 | 23 |
| Cal St. Sacramento | 3 | 24 |

# Major College Basketball Tournaments

The National Invitation Tournament (NIT), first played in 1938, is the nation's oldest basketball tournament. The National Collegiate Athletic Association's (NCAA) national championship tournament was first played a year later. Selections for both tournaments are made in March, with the NCAA selecting first from among the top Division I teams.

## National Invitation Tournament Champions

| Year | Champion | Year | Champion | Year | Champion | Year | Champion |
|---|---|---|---|---|---|---|---|
| 1938 | Temple | 1952 | LaSalle | 1966 | Brigham Young | 1980 | Virginia |
| 1939 | Long Island Univ. | 1953 | Seton Hall | 1967 | Southern Illinois | 1981 | Tulsa |
| 1940 | Colorado | 1954 | Holy Cross | 1968 | Dayton | 1982 | Bradley |
| 1941 | Long Island Univ. | 1955 | Duquesne | 1969 | Temple | 1983 | Fresno State |
| 1942 | West Virginia | 1956 | Louisville | 1970 | Marquette | 1984 | Michigan |
| 1943 | St. John's | 1957 | Bradley | 1971 | North Carolina | 1985 | UCLA |
| 1944 | St. John's | 1958 | Xavier (Ohio) | 1972 | Maryland | 1986 | Ohio State |
| 1945 | De Paul | 1959 | St. John's | 1973 | Virginia Tech | 1987 | Southern Mississippi |
| 1946 | Kentucky | 1960 | Bradley | 1974 | Purdue | 1988 | Connecticut |
| 1947 | Utah | 1961 | Providence | 1975 | Princeton | 1989 | St. John's |
| 1948 | St. Louis | 1962 | Dayton | 1976 | Kentucky | 1990 | Vanderbilt |
| 1949 | San Francisco | 1963 | Providence | 1977 | St. Bonaventure | 1991 | Stanford |
| 1950 | CCNY | 1964 | Bradley | 1978 | Texas | 1992 | Virginia |
| 1951 | Brigham Young | 1965 | St. John's | 1979 | Indiana | 1993 | Minnesota |

# EAST

1993 NCAA BASKETBALL TOURNAMENT

**EAST**

(1) N. Carolina 85
(16) E. Carolina 65
    N. Carolina 112
    Rhode Island 67
(8) Rhode Island 74
(9) Purdue 68
        N. Carolina 80

(5) St. John's 85
(12) Texas Tech 67
    St. John's 74
    Arkansas 80
(4) Arkansas 94
(13) Holy Cross 64
        Arkansas 74
            N. Carolina 75 (OT)

(6) Virginia 78
(11) Manhattan 66
    Virginia 71
    Massachusetts 56
(3) Massachusetts 54
(14) Pennsylvania 50
        Virginia 54
            N. Carolina 78

(7) New Mexico St. 93
(10) Nebraska 79
    New Mexico St. 55
    Cincinnati 92
(2) Cincinnati 93
(15) Coppin St. 66
        Cincinnati 71
        Cincinnati 68

**MIDWEST**

(1) Indiana 97
(16) Wright St. 54
    Indiana 73
    Xavier Oh. 70
(8) New Orleans 55
(9) Xavier, Oh. 73
        Indiana 82

(5) Oklahoma St. 74
(12) Marquette 62
    Oklahoma St. 63
    Louisville 78
(4) Louisville 76
(13) Delaware 70
        Louisville 69
            Indiana 77

(6) California 66
(11) LSU 64
    California 82
    Duke 77
(3) Duke 105
(14) Southern Ill. 70
        California 76
            Kansas 68

(7) BYU 80
(10) SMU 71
    BYU 76
    Kansas 90
(2) Kansas 94
(15) Ball State 72
        Kansas 93
        Kansas 83

**N. Carolina 78**
**Kansas 68**

**SOUTHEAST**

(1) Kentucky 96
(16) Rider 52
    Kentucky 83
    Utah 62
(8) Utah 86
(9) Pittsburgh 65
        Kentucky 103

(5) Wake Forest 81
(12) Tenn.-Chatt. 58
    Wake Forest 84
    Iowa 78
(4) Iowa 82
(13) NE La. 69
        Wake Forest 69
            Kentucky 106

(6) Kansas St. 53
(11) Tulane 55
    Tulane 63
    Florida St. 94
(3) Florida St. 82
(14) Evansville 70
        Florida St. 81 (OT)
            Kentucky 79

(7) W. Kentucky 55
(10) Memphis St. 52
    W. Kentucky 72
    Seton Hall 68
(2) Seton Hall 81
(15) Tennessee St. 59
        W. Kentucky 78
        Florida St. 81

**WEST**

(1) Michigan 84
(16) Coastal Carolina 53
    Michigan 86 (OT)
    UCLA 84
(8) Iowa St. 70
(9) UCLA 81
        Michigan 72

(5) New Mexico 68
(12) Geo. Washington 82
    Geo. Washington 90
    Southern-B-R 80
(4) Ga. Tech 78
(13) Southern-B-R 93
        Geo. Washington 64
            Michigan 77

(6) Illinois 75
(11) Long Beach St. 72
    Illinois 68
    Vanderbilt 85
(3) Vanderbilt 92
(14) Boise St. 72
        Vanderbilt 59
            Michigan 81

(7) Temple 75
(10) Missouri 61
    Temple 68
    Santa Clara 57
(2) Arizona 61
(15) Santa Clara 64
        Temple 67
        Temple 72

**N. Carolina 77**
**Michigan 71**

## NCAA Division I Champions

| Year | Champion | Coach | Final opponent | Score | Outstanding player | Site |
|------|----------|-------|----------------|-------|--------------------|------|
| 1939 | Oregon | Howard Hobson | Ohio St. | 46-33 | None | Evanston, Ill. |
| 1940 | Indiana | Branch McCracken | Kansas | 60-42 | Marvin Huffman, Indiana | Kansas City, Mo. |
| 1941 | Wisconsin | Harold Foster | Washington St. | 39-34 | John Kotz, Wisconsin | Kansas City, Mo. |
| 1942 | Stanford | Everett Dean | Dartmouth | 53-38 | Howard Dallmar, Stanford | Kansas City, Mo. |
| 1943 | Wyoming | Everett Shelton | Georgetown | 46-34 | Ken Sailors, Wyoming | New York, N.Y. |
| 1944 | Utah | Vadal Peterson | Dartmouth | 42-40(1) | Arnold Ferrin, Utah | New York, N.Y. |
| 1945 | Oklahoma St.(2) | Henry Iba | NYU | 49-45 | Bob Kurland, Oklahoma St. | New York, N.Y. |
| 1946 | Oklahoma St.(2) | Henry Iba | N. Carolina | 43-40 | Bob Kurland, Oklahoma St. | New York, N.Y. |
| 1947 | Holy Cross | Alvin Julian | Oklahoma | 58-47 | George Kaftan, Holy Cross | New York, N.Y. |
| 1948 | Kentucky | Adolph Rupp | Baylor | 58-42 | Alex Groza, Kentucky | New York, N.Y. |
| 1949 | Kentucky | Adolph Rupp | Oklahoma St. | 46-36 | Alex Groza, Kentucky | Seattle, Wash. |
| 1950 | CCNY | Nat Holman | Bradley | 71-68 | Irwin Dambrot, CCNY | New York, N.Y. |
| 1951 | Kentucky | Adolph Rupp | Kansas St. | 68-58 | None | Minneapolis, Minn. |
| 1952 | Kansas | Forrest Allen | St. John's | 80-63 | Clyde Lovellette, Kansas | Seattle, Wash. |
| 1953 | Indiana | Branch McCracken | Kansas | 69-68 | B.H. Born, Kansas | Kansas City, Mo. |
| 1954 | La Salle | Kenneth Loeffler | Bradley | 92-76 | Tom Gola, La Salle | Kansas City, Mo. |
| 1955 | San Francisco | Phil Woolpert | LaSalle | 77-63 | Bill Russell, San Francisco | Kansas City, Mo. |
| 1956 | San Francisco | Phil Woolpert | Iowa | 83-71 | Hal Lear, Temple | Evanston, Ill. |
| 1957 | N. Carolina | Frank McGuire | Kansas | 54-53(1) | Wilt Chamberlain, Kansas | Kansas City, Mo. |
| 1958 | Kentucky | Adolph Rupp | Seattle | 84-72 | Elgin Baylor, Seattle | Louisville, Ky. |
| 1959 | California | Pete Newell | W. Virginia | 71-70 | Jerry West, W. Virginia | Louisville, Ky. |
| 1960 | Ohio St. | Fred Taylor | California | 75-55 | Jerry Lucas, Ohio St. | San Francisco, Cal. |
| 1961 | Cincinnati | Edwin Jucker | Ohio St. | 70-65(1) | Jerry Lucas, Ohio St. | Kansas City, Mo. |
| 1962 | Cincinnati | Edwin Jucker | Ohio St. | 71-59 | Paul Hogue, Cincinnati | Louisville, Ky. |
| 1963 | Loyola (Ill.) | George Ireland | Cincinnati | 60-58(1) | Art Heyman, Duke | Louisville, Ky. |
| 1964 | UCLA | John Wooden | Duke | 98-83 | Walt Hazzard, UCLA | Kansas City, Mo. |
| 1965 | UCLA | John Wooden | Michigan | 91-80 | Bill Bradley, Princeton | Portland, Ore. |
| 1966 | Texas-El Paso(3) | Don Haskins | Kentucky | 72-65 | Jerry Chambers, Utah | College Park, Md. |
| 1967 | UCLA | John Wooden | Dayton | 79-64 | Lew Alcindor, UCLA | Louisville, Ky. |
| 1968 | UCLA | John Wooden | N. Carolina | 78-55 | Lew Alcindor, UCLA | Los Angeles, Cal. |
| 1969 | UCLA | John Wooden | Purdue | 92-72 | Lew Alcindor, UCLA | Louisville, Ky. |
| 1970 | UCLA | John Wooden | Jacksonville | 80-69 | Sidney Wicks, UCLA | College Park, Md. |
| 1971 | UCLA | John Wooden | Villanova* | 68-62 | Howard Porter, Villanova* | Houston, Tex. |
| 1972 | UCLA | John Wooden | Florida St. | 81-76 | Bill Walton, UCLA | Los Angeles, Cal. |
| 1973 | UCLA | John Wooden | Memphis St. | 87-66 | Bill Walton, UCLA | St. Louis, Mo. |
| 1974 | N. Carolina St. | Norm Sloan | Marquette | 76-64 | David Thompson, N.C. St. | Greensboro, N.C. |
| 1975 | UCLA | John Wooden | Kentucky | 92-85 | Richard Washington, UCLA | San Diego, Cal. |
| 1976 | Indiana | Bob Knight | Michigan | 86-68 | Kent Benson, Indiana | Philadelphia, Pa. |
| 1977 | Marquette | Al McGuire | N. Carolina | 67-59 | Butch Lee, Marquette | Atlanta, Ga. |
| 1978 | Kentucky | Joe Hall | Duke | 94-88 | Jack Givens, Kentucky | St. Louis, Mo. |
| 1979 | Michigan St. | Jud Heathcote | Indiana St. | 75-64 | Magic Johnson, Michigan St. | Salt Lake City, Ut. |
| 1980 | Louisville | Denny Crum | UCLA* | 59-54 | Darrell Griffith, Louisville | Indianapolis, Ind. |
| 1981 | Indiana | Bob Knight | N. Carolina | 63-50 | Isiah Thomas, Indiana | Philadelphia, Pa. |
| 1982 | N. Carolina | Dean Smith | Georgetown | 63-62 | James Worthy, N. Carolina | New Orleans, La. |
| 1983 | N. Carolina St. | Jim Valvano | Houston | 54-52 | Hakeem Olajuwon, Houston | Albuquerque, N.M. |
| 1984 | Georgetown | John Thompson | Houston | 84-75 | Patrick Ewing, Georgetown | Seattle, Wash. |
| 1985 | Villanova | Rollie Massimino | Georgetown | 66-64 | Ed Pinckney, Villanova | Lexington, Ky. |
| 1986 | Louisville | Denny Crum | Duke | 72-69 | Pervis Ellison, Louisville | Dallas, Tex. |
| 1987 | Indiana | Bob Knight | Syracuse | 74-73 | Keith Smart, Indiana | New Orleans, La. |
| 1988 | Kansas | Larry Brown | Oklahoma | 83-79 | Danny Manning, Kansas | Kansas City, Mo. |
| 1989 | Michigan | Steve Fisher | Seton Hall | 80-79(1) | Glen Rice, Michigan | Seattle, Wash. |
| 1990 | UNLV | Jerry Tarkanian | Duke | 103-73 | Anderson Hunt, UNLV | Denver, Col. |
| 1991 | Duke | Mike Krzyzewski | Kansas | 72-65 | Christian Laettner, Duke | Indianapolis, Ind. |
| 1992 | Duke | Mike Krzyzewski | Michigan | 71-51 | Bobby Hurley, Duke | Minneapolis, Minn. |
| 1993 | N. Carolina | Dean Smith | Michigan | 77-71 | Donald Williams, N. Carolina | New Orleans, La. |

* Declared ineligible subsequent to the tournament. (1) Overtime. (2) Known as Oklahoma A&M at that time. (3) Known as Texas Western at that time.

## John R. Wooden Award

Awarded annually to the nation's outstanding college basketball player by the United States Basketball Writers Assn.

| | | | | | |
|---|---|---|---|---|---|
| 1977 | Marques Johnson, UCLA | 1984 | Michael Jordan, North Carolina | 1990 | Lionel Simmons, La Salle |
| 1978 | Phil Ford, North Carolina | 1985 | Chris Mullin, St. John's | 1991 | Larry Johnson, UNLV |
| 1979 | Larry Bird, Indiana State | 1986 | Walter Berry, St. John's | 1992 | Christian Laettner, Duke |
| 1980 | Darrell Griffith, Louisville | 1987 | David Robinson, Navy | 1993 | Calbert Cheaney, Indiana |
| 1981 | Danny Ainge, Brigham Young | 1988 | Danny Manning, Kansas | | |
| 1982 | Ralph Sampson, Virginia | 1989 | Sean Elliott, Arizona | | |
| 1983 | Ralph Sampson, Virginia | | | | |

## NCAA Division I Women's Champions

| Year | Champion | Coach | Final opponent | Year | Champion | Coach | Final opponent |
|------|----------|-------|----------------|------|----------|-------|----------------|
| 1982 | Louisiana Tech | Sonja Hogg | Cheyney | 1988 | Louisiana Tech | Leon Barmore | Auburn |
| 1983 | USC | Linda Sharp | Louisiana Tech | 1989 | Tennessee | Pat Summitt | Auburn |
| 1984 | USC | Linda Sharp | Tennessee | 1990 | Stanford | Tara VanDerveer | Auburn |
| 1985 | Old Dominion | Marianne Stanley | Georgia | 1991 | Tennessee | Pat Summitt | Virginia |
| 1986 | Texas | Jody Conradt | USC | 1992 | Stanford | Tara VanDerveer | W. Kentucky |
| 1987 | Tennessee | Pat Summitt | Louisiana Tech | 1993 | Texas Tech | Marsha Sharp | Ohio St. |

## Selected Division I Basketball Coaches in 1993

| College | Coach | College | Coach | College | Coach |
|---|---|---|---|---|---|
| Akron | Coleman Crawford | Iowa | Tom Davis | Rutgers | Bob Wenzel |
| Alabama | David Hobbs | Iowa St. | Johnny Orr | St. Bonaventure | Jim Baron |
| Ala-Birmingham | Gene Barton | James Madison | Lefty Driesell | St. John's (N.Y.) | Brian Mahoney |
| American | Chris Knoche | Kansas | Roy Williams | St. Joseph's (Pa.) | John Griffin |
| Arizona | Lute Olson | Kansas St. | Dana Altman | St. Louis | Charlie Spoonhour |
| Arizona St. | Bill Frieder | Kent | Dave Grube | St. Mary's (Cal.) | Ernie Kent |
| Arkansas | Nolan Richardson | Kentucky | Rick Pitino | San Diego | Hank Egan |
| Army | Dino Gaudio | Long Beach St. | Seth Greenberg | San Diego St. | Tony Fuller |
| Auburn | Tommy Joe Eagles | LSU | Dale Brown | San Francisco | Jim Brovelli |
| Austin Peay | Dave Loos | Louisville | Denny Crum | San Jose St. | Stan Morrison |
| Ball St. | Dick Hunsaker | Loyola (Cal.) | John Olive | Santa Clara | Dick Dewey |
| Baylor | Darrel Johnson | Loyola (Ill.) | Will Rey | Seton Hall | P. J. Carlesimo |
| Boise St. | Bobby Dye | Marquette | Kevin O'Neill | S. Carolina | Eddie Folger |
| Boston Coll. | Jim O'Brien | Maryland | Gary Williams | S. Florida | Bobby Paschal |
| Bowling Green | Jim Larrange | Massachusetts | John Calipari | SE Mo. St. | Ron Shumate |
| Bradley | Jim Molinari | Memphis St. | Larry Finch | USC | George Raveling |
| BYU | Roger Reid | Miami (Fla.) | Leonard Hamilton | So. Illinois | Rick Herrin |
| Brown | Frank Dobbs | Miami (Oh.) | Joby Wright | SMU | John Shumate |
| Butler | Barry Collier | Michigan | Steve Fisher | So. Mississippi | M. K. Turk |
| California | Todd Bozeman | Michigan St. | Jud Heathcote | SW Mo. St. | Mark Bernsen |
| Cal. St. Fullerton | Brad Holland | Middle Tenn. St. | David Farrar | Stanford | Mike Montgomery |
| UC Irvine | Rod Baker | Minnesota | Clem Haskins | Syracuse | Jim Boeheim |
| UC Santa Barbara | Jerry Pimm | Mississippi | Rob Evans | Temple | John Chaney |
| Central Mich. | Keith Dambrot | Mississippi St. | Richard Williams | Tennessee | Wade Houston |
| Cincinnati | Bob Huggins | Missouri | Norm Stewart | Tennessee St. | Frankie Allen |
| Clemson | Cliff Ellis | Montana | Blaine Taylor | Tennessee Tech | Frank Harrell |
| Cleveland St. | Mike Boyd | Montana St. | Mick Durham | Tennessee-Chatt. | Mark McCarthy |
| Colorado | Joe Harrington | Morehead St. | Dick Fick | Tennessee-Martin | Calvin C. Luther |
| Colorado St. | Stew Morrill | Murray St. | Scott Edgar | Texas | Tom Penders |
| Columbia | Jack Rohan | Nebraska | Danny Nee | Texas A&M | Tony Barone |
| Connecticut | Jim Calhoun | Nevada-Reno | Len Stevens | Tex. Christian | Moe Iba |
| Cornell | Al Walker | UNLV | Rollie Massimino | Tex.-Arlington | Mark Nixon |
| Creighton | Rick Johnson | New Mexico | Dave Bliss | UTEP | Don Haskins |
| Dartmouth | Dave Faucher | New Mexico St. | Neil McCarthy | Toledo | Larry Gipson |
| Dayton | Jim O'Brien | North Carolina | Dean Smith | Tulane | Perry Clark |
| DePaul | Joey Meyer | N.C. A&T | Don Corbett | Tulsa | Tubby Smith |
| Detroit Mercy | Ricky Byrdsong | N.C. State | Les Robinson | UCLA | Jim Harrick |
| Drake | Rudy Washington | N.C.-Charlotte | Jeff Mullins | Utah | Rick Mejerus |
| Duke | Mike Trzyzewski | N.C.-Wilmington | Kevin Eastman | Utah St. | Kohn Smith |
| E. Carolina | Eddie Payne | N. Arizona | Harold Merritt | Valparaiso | Homer Drew |
| E. Illinois | Rick Samuels | N. Illinois | Brian Hammel | Vanderbilt | Jan van Breda Kolff |
| E. Kentucky | Mike Calhoun | N. Iowa | Eldon Miller | Villanova | Steve Lappas |
| E. Michigan | Ben Braun | Northwestern | Ricky Byrdsong | Virginia | Jeff Jones |
| E. Washington | John Wade | Notre Dame | John MacLeod | Va. Commonwealth | Sonny Smith |
| Evansville | Jim Crews | Ohio | Larry Hunter | Va. Tech | Bill Foster |
| Florida | Lon Kruger | Ohio St. | Randy Ayers | Wake Forest | Dave Odom |
| Florida St. | Pat Kennedy | Oklahoma | Billy Tubbs | Washington | Lynn Nance |
| Fresno St. | Gary Colson | Oklahoma St. | Eddie Sutton | Washington St. | Kelvin Sampson |
| George Mason | Paul Westhead | Old Dominion | Oliver Purnell | Weber St. | Ron Abegglen |
| Geo. Washington | Mike Jarvis | Oregon | Jerry Green | W. Virginia | Gale Catlett |
| Georgetown | John Thompson | Oregon St. | Jim Anderson | W. Illinois | Jim Kerwin |
| Georgia | Hugh Durham | Pacific (Cal.) | Bob Thomason | W. Kentucky | Ralph Willard |
| Georgia Tech | Bobby Cremins | Pennsylvania | Fran Dunphy | W. Michigan | Bob Donewald |
| Gonzaga | Dan Fitzgerald | Penn St. | Bruce Parkhill | Wichita St. | Scott Thompson |
| Harvard | Frank Sullivan | Pepperdine | Tom Asbury | William & Mary | Chuck Swenson |
| Hawaii | Riley Wallace | Pittsburgh | Paul Evans | Wisconsin | Stu Jackson |
| Houston | Pat Foster | Portland | Larry Steele | Wis.-Green Bay | Dick Bennett |
| Idaho | Larry Eustachy | Princeton | Pete Carril | Wright St. | Tom Moore |
| Idaho St. | Herb Williams | Providence | Rick Barnes | Wyoming | Benny Dees |
| Illinois | Lou Henson | Purdue | Gene Keady | Xavier (Oh.) | Pete Gillen |
| Illinois St. | Bob Bender | Rhode Island | Al Skinner | Yale | Dick Kuchen |
| Illinois-Chi. | Bob Hallberg | Rice | Willis Wilson | | |
| Indiana | Bob Knight | Richmond | Dick Tarrant | | |
| Indiana St. | Tates Locke | | | | |

## Most Coaching Victories in the NCAA Tournament Through 1993

| Coach, school, years | Wins | Tournaments | Coach, school, years | Wins | Tournaments |
|---|---|---|---|---|---|
| Dean Smith, North Carolina, 1967-93 | 55 | 23 | Adolph Rupp, Kentucky, 1942-72 | 30 | 20 |
| John Wooden, UCLA, 1950-75 | 47 | 16 | John Thompson, Georgetown, 1975-92 | 28 | 16 |
| Bob Knight, Indiana, 1973-93 | 38 | 17 | Guy Lewis, Houston, 1961-84 | 26 | 14 |
| Jerry Tarkanian, Long Beach State and UNLV, 1970-91 | 37 | 16 | Joe Hall, Kentucky, 1973-85 | 20 | 10 |
| Denny Crum, Louisville, 1972-93 | 35 | 17 | Rollie Massimino, Villanova, 1978-91 | 20 | 11 |
| Mike Krzyzewski, Duke, 1984-93 | 34 | 10 | Al McGuire, Marquette, 1968-77 | 20 | 9 |

## NCAA Division I Basketball Statistical Trends

Averages and percentages are for both teams, per game.

| Year | Games | FG Made | FG Att. | Pct. | FT Made | FT Att. | Pct. | PF | Pts. |
|------|-------|---------|---------|------|---------|---------|------|-----|------|
| 1948 | 3945  | 40.6 | 138.7 | 29.3 | 25.3 | 42.2 | 59.8 | 36.9 | 106.5 |
| 1950 | 3659  | 43.2 | 136.8 | 31.6 | 28.7 | 46.5 | 61.8 | 39.0 | 115.1 |
| 1952 | 4009  | 47.5 | 140.6* | 33.7 | 31.6 | 50.5 | 62.6 | 44.9* | 126.6 |
| 1953 | 3754  | 48.0 | 138.1 | 34.7 | 42.1 | 65.8* | 64.0 | 42.5 | 138.1 |
| 1955 | 3829  | 51.1 | 138.6 | 36.9 | 43.1* | 64.7 | 66.5 | 37.9 | 145.3 |
| 1958 | 4153  | 51.6 | 134.2 | 38.4 | 33.6 | 50.5 | 66.4 | 36.4 | 136.8 |
| 1960 | 4295  | 52.6 | 132.3 | 39.8 | 34.7 | 51.5 | 67.4 | 36.7 | 139.9 |
| 1963 | 4180  | 53.2 | 127.6 | 41.7 | 32.6 | 47.8 | 68.2 | 36.4 | 139.0 |
| 1965 | 4520  | 58.3 | 135.4 | 43.1 | 34.7 | 50.3 | 69.0 | 38.5 | 151.4 |
| 1971 | 5232  | 60.2 | 135.6 | 44.4 | 35.0 | 51.3 | 68.1 | 38.5 | 155.4* |
| 1973 | 5582  | 62.3* | 139.2 | 44.8 | 26.2 | 38.3 | 68.4 | 38.4 | 150.9 |
| 1975 | 6147  | 62.9 | 136.7 | 46.0 | 27.4 | 39.7 | 69.0 | 40.3 | 153.1 |
| 1979 | 7131  | 59.2 | 124.1 | 47.7 | 29.5 | 42.2 | 69.7* | 41.1 | 147.9 |
| 1983 | 7957  | 54.3 | 114.0 | 47.7 | 29.0 | 42.3 | 68.5 | 39.7 | 138.7 |
| 1985 | 8269  | 54.5 | 113.9 | 47.9* | 29.3 | 42.5 | 68.9 | 39.3 | 138.3 |
| 1986 | 8360  | 54.7 | 114.6 | 47.7 | 29.4 | 42.5 | 69.1 | 39.1 | 138.7 |
| 1987 | 8580  | 54.4 | 117.3 | 46.6 | 29.7 | 43.0 | 69.1 | 39.3 | 145.5 |
| 1988 | 8587  | 54.8 | 116.6 | 47.0 | 30.2 | 43.8 | 68.9 | 39.4 | 147.8 |
| 1989 | 8677  | 55.7 | 118.5 | 47.0 | 31.1 | 45.0 | 69.1 | 40.2 | 151.4 |
| 1990 | 8646  | 54.7 | 118.9 | 46.0 | 31.1 | 45.1 | 68.9 | 39.6 | 149.8 |
| 1991 | 8720  | 55.6 | 121.3 | 45.8 | 31.7 | 46.3 | 68.5 | 39.2 | 152.9 |
| 1992 | 8803* | 53.0 | 116.6 | 45.5 | 31.6 | 46.4 | 68.1 | 40.0 | 147.6 |

*All-time high.

# HARNESS RACING

## Harness Horse of the Year
(Chosen by the U.S. Trotting Assn. and the U.S. Harness Writers Assn.)

| | | | |
|---|---|---|---|
| 1951 | Pronto Don | 1962 | Su Mac Lad |
| 1952 | Good Time | 1963 | Speedy Scot |
| 1953 | Hi Lo's Forbes | 1964 | Bret Hanover |
| 1954 | Stenographer | 1965 | Bret Hanover |
| 1955 | Scott Frost | 1966 | Bret Hanover |
| 1956 | Scott Frost | 1967 | Nevele Pride |
| 1957 | Torpid | 1968 | Nevele Pride |
| 1958 | Emily's Pride | 1969 | Nevele Pride |
| 1959 | Bye Bye Byrd | 1970 | Fresh Yankee |
| 1960 | Adios Butler | 1971 | Albatross |
| 1961 | Adios Butler | 1972 | Albatross |

| | |
|---|---|
| 1973 | Sir Dalrae |
| 1974 | Delmonica Hanover |
| 1975 | Savior |
| 1976 | Keystone Ore |
| 1977 | Green Speed |
| 1978 | Abercrombie |
| 1979 | Niatross |
| 1980 | Niatross |
| 1981 | Fan Hanover |
| 1982 | Cam Fella |

| | |
|---|---|
| 1983 | Cam Fella |
| 1984 | Fancy Crown |
| 1985 | Nihilator |
| 1986 | Forrest Skipper |
| 1987 | Mack Lobell |
| 1988 | Mack Lobell |
| 1989 | Matt's Scooter |
| 1990 | Beach Towel |
| 1991 | Precious Bunny |
| 1992 | Artsplace |

## The Hambletonian (3-year-old trotters)

| Year | Winner | Driver | Year | Winner | Driver |
|------|--------|--------|------|--------|--------|
| 1965 | Egyptian Candor | Del Cameron | 1980 | Burgomeister | Bill Haughton |
| 1966 | Kerry Way | Frank Ervin | 1981 | Shiaway St. Pat | Ray Remmen |
| 1967 | Speedy Streak | Del Cameron | 1982 | Speed Bowl | Tommy Haughton |
| 1968 | Nevele Pride | Stanley Dancer | 1983 | Duenna | Stanley Dancer |
| 1969 | Lindy's Pride | Howard Beissinger | 1984 | Historic Freight | Ben Webster |
| 1970 | Timothy T | John Simpson Sr. | 1985 | Prakas | Bill O'Donnell |
| 1971 | Speedy Crown | Howard Beissinger | 1986 | Nuclear Kosmos | Ulf Thoresen |
| 1972 | Super Bowl | Stanley Dancer | 1987 | Mack Lobell | John Campbell |
| 1973 | Flirth | Ralph Baldwin | 1988 | Armbro Goal | John Campbell |
| 1974 | Christopher T | Bill Haughton | 1989 | Park Avenue Joe | Ron Waples |
| 1975 | Bonefish | Stanley Dancer | 1990 | Harmonious | John Campbell |
| 1976 | Steve Lobell | Bill Haughton | 1991 | Giant Victory | Jack Moiseyev |
| 1977 | Green Speed | Bill Haughton | 1992 | Alf Palema | Mickey McNicholl |
| 1978 | Speedy Somolli | Howard Beissinger | 1993 | American Winner | Ron Pierce |
| 1979 | Legend Hanover | George Sholty | | | |

# BOWLING

## Professional Bowlers Association
### Hall of Fame

| Performance | | | Meritorious service | |
|---|---|---|---|---|
| Bill Allen | Buzz Fazio | Dick Ritger | Joe Antenora | John Jowdy |
| Glenn Allison | Skee Foremsky | Mark Roth | John Archibald | Joe Kelley |
| Earl Anthony | Jim Godman | Jim St. John | Eddie Elias | Steve Nagy |
| Barry Asher | Johnny Guenther | Carmen Salvino | Frank Esposito | Chuck Pezzano |
| Ray Bluth | Billy Hardwick | Bob Strampe | Dick Evans | Jack Reichert |
| Roy Buckley | Tommy Hudson | Harry Smith | Raymond Firestone | Joe Richards |
| Nelson Burton Jr. | Don Johnson | Dave Soutar | E.A. "Bud" Fisher | Chris Schenkel |
| Don Carter | Joe Joseph | Jim Stefanich | Lou Frantz | Lorraine Stilzlein |
| Pat Colwell | Larry Laub | Wayne Webb | Harry Golden | Al Thompson |
| Steve Cook | Don McCune | Dick Weber | Ted Hoffman Jr. | |
| Dave Davis | Mike McGrath | Billy Welu | | |
| Gary Dickinson | George Pappas | Wayne Zahn | | |
| Mike Durbin | Johnny Petraglia | | | |

## Tournament of Champions

| Year | Winner | Year | Winner | Year | Winner | Year | Winner |
|------|--------|------|--------|------|--------|------|--------|
| 1965 | Billy Hardwick | 1973 | Jim Godman | 1981 | Steve Cook | 1989 | Del Ballard Jr. |
| 1966 | Wayne Zahn | 1974 | Earl Anthony | 1982 | Mike Durbin | 1990 | Dave Ferraro |
| 1967 | Jim Stefanich | 1975 | Dave Davis | 1983 | Joe Berardi | 1991 | David Ozio |
| 1968 | Dave Davis | 1976 | Marshall Holman | 1984 | Mike Durbin | 1992 | Marc McDowell |
| 1969 | Jim Godman | 1977 | Mike Berlin | 1985 | Mark Williams | 1993 | George Branham 3d |
| 1970 | Don Johnson | 1978 | Earl Anthony | 1986 | Marshall Holman | | |
| 1971 | Johnny Petraglia | 1979 | George Pappas | 1987 | Pete Weber | | |
| 1972 | Mike Durbin | 1980 | Wayne Webb | 1988 | Mark Williams | | |

## PBA Leading Money Winners

Total winnings are from PBA, ABC Masters, and BPAA All-Star tournaments only, and do not include numerous other tournaments or earnings from special television shows and matches.

| Year | Bowler | Amount | Year | Bowler | Amount | Year | Bowler | Amount |
|------|--------|--------|------|--------|--------|------|--------|--------|
| 1962 | Don Carter | $49,972 | 1973 | Don McCune | $69,000 | 1984 | Mark Roth | $158,712 |
| 1963 | Dick Weber | 46,333 | 1974 | Earl Anthony | 99,585 | 1985 | Mike Aulby | 201,200 |
| 1964 | Bob Strampe | 33,592 | 1975 | Earl Anthony | 107,585 | 1986 | Walter Ray Williams Jr. | 145,550 |
| 1965 | Dick Weber | 47,674 | 1976 | Earl Anthony | 110,833 | 1987 | Pete Weber | 175,491 |
| 1966 | Wayne Zahn | 54,720 | 1977 | Mark Roth | 105,583 | 1988 | Brian Voss | 225,485 |
| 1967 | Dave Davis | 54,165 | 1978 | Mark Roth | 134,500 | 1989 | Mike Aulby | 298,237 |
| 1968 | Jim Stefanich | 67,377 | 1979 | Mark Roth | 124,517 | 1990 | Amieto Monacelli | 204,775 |
| 1969 | Billy Hardwick | 64,160 | 1980 | Wayne Webb | 116,700 | 1991 | David Ozio | 225,585 |
| 1970 | Mike McGrath | 52,049 | 1981 | Earl Anthony | 164,735 | 1992 | Marc McDowell | 174,215 |
| 1971 | Johnny Petraglia | 85,065 | 1982 | Earl Anthony | 134,760 | | | |
| 1972 | Don Johnson | 56,648 | 1983 | Earl Anthony | 135,605 | | | |

## Leading PBA Averages by Year

| Year | Bowler | Average | Year | Bowler | Average | Year | Bowler | Average |
|------|--------|---------|------|--------|---------|------|--------|---------|
| 1962 | Don Carter | 212.844 | 1973 | Earl Anthony | 215.799 | 1984 | Marshall Holman | 213.911 |
| 1963 | Billy Hardwick | 210.346 | 1974 | Earl Anthony | 219.394 | 1985 | Mark Baker | 213.718 |
| 1964 | Ray Bluth | 210.512 | 1975 | Earl Anthony | 219.060 | 1986 | John Gant | 214.378 |
| 1965 | Dick Weber | 211.895 | 1976 | Mark Roth | 215.970 | 1987 | Marshall Holman | 216.801 |
| 1966 | Wayne Zahn | 208.663 | 1977 | Mark Roth | 218.174 | 1988 | Mark Roth | 218.036 |
| 1967 | Wayne Zahn | 212.342 | 1978 | Mark Roth | 219.834 | 1989 | Pete Weber | 215.432 |
| 1968 | Jim Stefanich | 211.895 | 1979 | Mark Roth | 221.662 | 1990 | Amieto Monacelli | 218.158 |
| 1969 | Bill Hardwick | 212.957 | 1980 | Earl Anthony | 218.535 | 1991 | Norm Duke | 218.208 |
| 1970 | Nelson Burton Jr. | 214.908 | 1981 | Mark Roth | 216.699 | 1992 | Dave Ferraro | 219.702 |
| 1971 | Don Johnson | 213.977 | 1982 | Marshall Holman | 212.844 | | | |
| 1972 | Don Johnson | 215.290 | 1983 | Earl Anthony | 216.645 | | | |

## American Bowling Congress Masters Tournament Champions

| Year | Winner | Year | Winner | Year | Winner |
|------|--------|------|--------|------|--------|
| 1980 | Neil Burton, St. Louis, Mo. | 1985 | Steve Wunderlich, St. Louis, Mo. | 1991 | Doug Kent, Canandaigua, N.Y. |
| 1981 | Randy Lightfoot, St. Charles, Mo. | 1986 | Mark Fahy, Chicago, Ill. | 1992 | Ken Johnson, N. Richmond Hills, Tex. |
| 1982 | Joe Berardi, Brooklyn, N.Y. | 1987 | Rick Steelsmith, Wichita, Kan. | | |
| 1983 | Mike Lastowski, Havre de Grace, Md. | 1988 | Del Ballard Jr., Richardson, Tex. | 1993 | Norm Duke, Oklahoma City, Okla. |
| | | 1989 | Mike Aulby, Indianapolis, Ind. | | |
| 1984 | Earl Anthony, Dublin, Cal. | 1990 | Chris Warren, Dallas, Tex. | | |

## Most Sanctioned 300 Games

| | | | | | |
|---|---|---|---|---|---|
| Bob Learn Jr., Erie, Pa. | 43 | Tony Torrice, Wolcott, Conn. | 24 | Jeff Jensen, Wichita, Kan. | 20 |
| Mike Whalin, Cincinnati, Oh. | 41 | Jerry Kessler, Dayton, Oh. | 23 | Dave Soutar, Kansas City, Mo. | 20 |
| Jim Johnson Jr., Wilmington, Del. | 38 | Teata Semiz, Fairfield, N.J. | 23 | Joe Vito Buenrostro, San Antonio, Tex. | 19 |
| Ron Woolet, Louisville, Ky. | 33 | Don Anthony, Columbus, Oh. | 22 | Paul Cannon, Binghamton, N.Y. | 19 |
| John Wilcox Jr., Shavertown, Pa. | 32 | Mitch Jabczenski, Detroit, Mich. | 22 | Randy Choat, Granite City, Ill. | 19 |
| Elvin Mesger, Sullivan, Mo. | 27 | Jerome Penxa, Detroit, Mich. | 22 | Steve Wilson, Ft. Lauderdale, Fla. | 19 |
| Ralph Burley Jr., Dayton, Oh. | 26 | Steve Carson, Oklahoma City, Okla. | 21 | Jim Doherty, Oklahoma City, Okla. | 18 |
| Steve Gehringer, Reading, Pa. | 26 | Dave Heller, Highland Falls, N.Y. | 21 | Frank May Jr., Reading, Pa. | 18 |
| Alan Hulsizer, Reading, Pa. | 25 | Mark Stibora, Cleveland, Oh. | 21 | Dick Weber, St. Louis, Mo. | 18 |

# Women's International Bowling Congress

## Champions in 1993

**Queens Tournament**—Jan Schmidt, Rochelle, Ill.
**Singles Event**—(tie) Karen Collura, Toronto, Ont., and Kari Murph, Dayton, Oh.
**All Events**—Anne Marie Duggan, Edmond, Okla.

**Doubles Event**—Gloria Collura and Karen Collura, Toronto, Ont.
**Team**—Strike Zone Pro Shop, Rolling, Ill.

## Most Sanctioned 300 Games

| | | |
|---|---|---|
| Jeanne Maiden-Naccarato, Tacoma, Wash. 20 | Tish Johnson, Panorama City, Cal. 13 | Cindy Coburn-Carroll, Tonawanda, N.Y. 10 |
| Vicki Fischel, Wheat Ridge, Col. 15 | Leanne Barrette, Youkon, Okla. 12 | Robin Romeo, Van Nuys, Cal. 9 |
| Aleta Sill, Dearborn, Mich. 14 | Betty Morris, Stockton, Cal. 12 | Cheryl Daniels, Detroit, Mich. 9 |
| | Donna Adamek, Apple Valley, Cal. 11 | |

# Figure Skating Champions

## U.S. Champions

|  |  |  | World Champions | |
|---|---|---|---|---|
| **Men** | **Women** | **Year** | **Men** | **Women** |
| Dick Button | Tenley Albright | 1952 | Dick Button, U.S. | Jacqueline du Bief, France |
| Hayes Jenkins | Tenley Albright | 1953 | Hayes Jenkins, U.S. | Tenley Albright, U.S. |
| Hayes Jenkins | Tenley Albright | 1954 | Hayes Jenkins, U.S. | Gundi Busch, W. Germany |
| Hayes Jenkins | Tenley Albright | 1955 | Hayes Jenkins, U.S. | Tenley Albright, U.S. |
| Hayes Jenkins | Tenley Albright | 1956 | Hayes Jenkins, U.S. | Carol Heiss, U.S. |
| Dave Jenkins | Carol Heiss | 1957 | Dave Jenkins, U.S. | Carol Heiss, U.S. |
| Dave Jenkins | Carol Heiss | 1958 | Dave Jenkins, U.S. | Carol Heiss, U.S. |
| Dave Jenkins | Carol Heiss | 1959 | Dave Jenkins, U.S. | Carol Heiss, U.S. |
| Dave Jenkins | Carol Heiss | 1960 | Alain Giletti, France | Carol Heiss, U.S. |
| Bradley Lord | Laurence Owen | 1961 | none | none |
| Monty Hoyt | Barbara Roles Pursley | 1962 | Don Jackson, Canada | Sjoukje Dijkstra, Neth. |
| Tommy Litz | Lorraine Hanlon | 1963 | Don McPherson, Canada | Sjoukje Dijkstra, Neth. |
| Scott Allen | Peggy Fleming | 1964 | Manfred Schnelldorfer, W. Germany | Sjoukje Dijkstra, Neth. |
| Gary Visconti | Peggy Fleming | 1965 | Alain Calmat, France | Petra Burka, Canada |
| Scott Allen | Peggy Fleming | 1966 | Emmerich Danzer, Austria | Peggy Fleming, U.S. |
| Gary Visconti | Peggy Fleming | 1967 | Emmerich Danzer, Austria | Peggy Fleming, U.S. |
| Tim Wood | Peggy Fleming | 1968 | Emmerich Danzer, Austria | Peggy Fleming, U.S. |
| Tim Wood | Janet Lynn | 1969 | Tim Wood, U.S. | Gabriele Seyfert, E. Germany |
| Tim Wood | Janet Lynn | 1970 | Tim Wood, U.S. | Gabriele Seyfert, E. Germany |
| John Misha Petkevich | Janet Lynn | 1971 | Ondrej Nepela, Czech. | Beatrix Schuba, Austria |
| Ken Shelley | Janet Lynn | 1972 | Ondrej Nepela, Czech. | Beatrix Schuba, Austria |
| Gordon McKellen Jr. | Janet Lynn | 1973 | Ondrej Nepela, Czech. | Karen Magnussen, Canada |
| Gordon McKellen Jr. | Dorothy Hamill | 1974 | Jan Hoffmann, E. Germany | Christine Errath, E. Germany |
| Gordon McKellen Jr. | Dorothy Hamill | 1975 | Sergei Volkov, USSR | Dianne de Leeuw, Neth.-U.S. |
| Terry Kubicka | Dorothy Hamill | 1976 | John Curry, Gt. Britain | Dorothy Hamill, U.S. |
| Charles Tickner | Linda Fratianne | 1977 | Vladimir Kovalev, USSR | Linda Fratianne, U.S. |
| Charles Tickner | Linda Fratianne | 1978 | Charles Tickner, U.S. | Anett Potzsch, E. Germany |
| Charles Tickner | Linda Fratianne | 1979 | Vladimir Kovalev, USSR | Linda Fratianne, U.S. |
| Charles Tickner | Linda Fratianne | 1980 | Jan Hoffmann, E. Germany | Anett Potzsch, E. Germany |
| Scott Hamilton | Elaine Zayak | 1981 | Scott Hamilton, U.S. | Denise Biellmann, Switzerland |
| Scott Hamilton | Rosalynn Sumners | 1982 | Scott Hamilton, U.S. | Elaine Zayak, U.S. |
| Scott Hamilton | Rosalynn Sumners | 1983 | Scott Hamilton, U.S. | Rosalynn Sumners, U.S. |
| Scott Hamilton | Rosalynn Sumners | 1984 | Scott Hamilton, U.S. | Katarina Witt, E. Germany |
| Brian Boitano | Tiffany Chin | 1985 | Aleksandr Fadeev, USSR | Katarina Witt, E. Germany |
| Brian Boitano | Debi Thomas | 1986 | Brian Boitano, U.S. | Debi Thomas, U.S. |
| Brian Boitano | Jill Trenary | 1987 | Brian Orser, Canada | Katarina Witt, E. Germany |
| Brian Boitano | Debi Thomas | 1988 | Brian Boitano, U.S. | Katarina Witt, E. Germany |
| Christopher Bowman | Jill Trenary | 1989 | Kurt Browning, Canada | Midori Ito, Japan |
| Todd Eldredge | Jill Trenary | 1990 | Kurt Browning, Canada | Jill Trenary, U.S. |
| Todd Eldredge | Tonya Harding | 1991 | Kurt Browning, Canada | Kristi Yamaguchi, U.S. |
| Christopher Bowman | Kristi Yamaguchi | 1992 | Viktor Petrenko, Ukraine | Kristi Yamaguchi, U.S. |
| Scott Davis | Nancy Kerrigan | 1993 | Kurt Browning, Canada | Oksana Baiul, Ukraine |

# James E. Sullivan Memorial Trophy Winners

The James E. Sullivan Memorial Trophy, named after the former president of the AAU and inaugurated in 1930, is awarded annually by the AAU to the athlete who "by his or her performance, example and influence as an amateur, has done the most during the year to advance the cause of sportsmanship."

| Year | Winner | Sport | Year | Winner | Sport | Year | Winner | Sport |
|---|---|---|---|---|---|---|---|---|
| 1930 | Bobby Jones | Golf | 1952 | Horace Ashenfelter | Track | 1974 | Rick Wohlhuter | Track |
| 1931 | Barney Berlinger | Track | 1953 | Dr. Sammy Lee | Diving | 1975 | Tim Shaw | Swimming |
| 1932 | Jim Bausch | Track | 1954 | Mal Whitfield | Track | 1976 | Bruce Jenner | Track |
| 1933 | Glenn Cunningham | Track | 1955 | Harrison Dillard | Track | 1977 | John Naber | Swimming |
| 1934 | Bill Bonthron | Track | 1956 | Patricia McCormick | Diving | 1978 | Tracy Caulkins | Swimming |
| 1935 | Lawson Little | Golf | 1957 | Bobby Joe Morrow | Track | 1979 | Kurt Thomas | Gymnastics |
| 1936 | Glenn Morris | Track | 1958 | Glenn Davis | Track | 1980 | Eric Heiden | Speed Skating |
| 1937 | Don Budge | Tennis | 1959 | Parry O'Brien | Track | 1981 | Carl Lewis | Track |
| 1938 | Don Lash | Track | 1960 | Rafer Johnson | Track | 1982 | Mary Decker | Track |
| 1939 | Joe Burk | Rowing | 1961 | Wilma Rudolph Ward | Track | 1983 | Edwin Moses | Track |
| 1940 | Greg Rice | Track | 1962 | James Beatty | Track | 1984 | Greg Louganis | Diving |
| 1941 | Leslie MacMitchell | Track | 1963 | John Pennel | Track | 1985 | Joan Benoit Samuelson | Marathon |
| 1942 | Cornelius Warmerdam | Track | 1964 | Don Schollander | Swimming |  |  |  |
| 1943 | Gilbert Dodds | Track | 1965 | Bill Bradley | Basketball | 1986 | Jackie Joyner-Kersee | Track |
| 1944 | Ann Curtis | Swimming | 1966 | Jim Ryun | Track | 1987 | Jim Abbott | Baseball |
| 1945 | Doc Blanchard | Football | 1967 | Randy Matson | Track | 1988 | Florence Griffith Joyner | Track |
| 1946 | Arnold Tucker | Football | 1968 | Debbie Meyer | Swimming |  |  |  |
| 1947 | John Kelly Jr. | Rowing | 1969 | Bill Toomey | Track | 1989 | Janet Evans | Swimming |
| 1948 | Robert Mathias | Track | 1970 | John Kinsella | Swimming | 1990 | John Smith | Wrestling |
| 1949 | Dick Button | Skating | 1971 | Mark Spitz | Swimming | 1991 | Mike Powell | Track |
| 1950 | Fred Wilt | Track | 1972 | Frank Shorter | Track | 1992 | Bonnie Blair | Speed Skating |
| 1951 | Rev. Robert Richards | Track | 1973 | Bill Walton | Basketball |  |  |  |

# Professional Sports Directory

## Major League Baseball

Commissioner's Office
350 Park Ave.
New York, NY 10022

**National League**

National League Office
350 Park Ave.
New York, NY 10022

Atlanta Braves
PO Box 4064
Atlanta, GA 30302

Chicago Cubs
Wrigley Field
Chicago, IL 60613

Cincinnati Reds
100 Riverfront Stadium
Cincinnati, OH 45202

Colorado Rockies
1700 Broadway
Denver, CO 80290

Florida Marlins
100 NE 3d Ave.
Ft. Lauderdale, FL 33301

Houston Astros
PO Box 288
Houston, TX 77001

Los Angeles Dodgers
Dodger Stadium
Los Angeles, CA 90012

Montreal Expos
PO Box 500, Station M
Montreal, Que. H1V 3P2

New York Mets
Shea Stadium
Flushing, NY 11368

Philadelphia Phillies
PO Box 7575
Philadelphia, PA 19101

Pittsburgh Pirates
Three Rivers Stadium
Pittsburgh, PA 15212

St. Louis Cardinals
Busch Stadium
St. Louis, MO 63102

San Diego Padres
PO Box 2000
San Diego, CA 92112

San Francisco Giants
Candlestick Park
San Francisco, CA 94124

**American League**

American League Office
350 Park Ave.
New York, NY 10022

Baltimore Orioles
333 W. Camden St.
Baltimore, MD 21202

Boston Red Sox
24 Yawkey Way
Boston, MA 02215

California Angels
Anaheim Stadium
Anaheim, CA 92803

Chicago White Sox
333 W. 35th St.
Chicago, IL 60616

Cleveland Indians
Cleveland Stadium
Cleveland, OH 44114

Detroit Tigers
Tiger Stadium
Detroit, MI 48216

Kansas City Royals
P.O. Box 419969
Kansas City, MO 64141

Milwaukee Brewers
Milwaukee County Stadium
Milwaukee, WI 53214

Minnesota Twins
501 Chicago Ave. South
Minneapolis, MN 55415

New York Yankees
Yankee Stadium
Bronx, NY 10451

Oakland A's
Oakland Coliseum
Oakland, CA 94621

Seattle Mariners
P.O. Box 4100
Seattle, WA 98104

Texas Rangers
PO Box 90111
Arlington, TX 76004

Toronto Blue Jays
300 Bremner Blvd.
Toronto, Ont. M5V 3B3

## National Basketball Association

League Office
645 5th Ave.
New York, NY 10022

Atlanta Hawks
1 CNN Center
Atlanta, GA 30303

Boston Celtics
151 Merrimac St.
Boston, MA 02114

Charlotte Hornets
Hive Drive
Charlotte, NC 28217

Chicago Bulls
980 North Michigan Ave.
Chicago, IL 60611

Cleveland Cavaliers
2923 Statesboro Rd.
Richfield, OH 44286

Dallas Mavericks
777 Sports St.
Dallas, TX 75207

Denver Nuggets
1635 Clay St.
Denver, CO 80204

Detroit Pistons
2 Championship Dr.
Auburn Hills, MI 48326

Golden State Warriors
Oakland Coliseum
Oakland, CA 94621

Houston Rockets
The Summit
Houston, TX 77277

Indiana Pacers
300 E. Market St.
Indianapolis, IN 46204

Los Angeles Clippers
3939 S. Figueroa
Los Angeles, CA 90037

Los Angeles Lakers
Great Western Forum
Inglewood, CA 90306

Miami Heat
Miami Arena
Miami, FL 33136

Milwaukee Bucks
1001 N. 4th St.
Milwaukee, WI 53203

Minnesota Timberwolves
600 First Ave. N.
Minneapolis, MN 55403

New Jersey Nets
Meadowlands Arena
E. Rutherford, NJ 07073

New York Knickerbockers
4 Pennsylvania Plaza
New York, NY 10001

Orlando Magic
1 Magic Place
Orlando, FL 32801

Philadelphia 76ers
Veterans Stadium
Philadelphia, PA 19148

Phoenix Suns
P.O. Box 1369
Phoenix, AZ 85001

Portland Trail Blazers
700 NE Multnomah St.
Portland, OR 97232

Sacramento Kings
One Sports Pkwy.
Sacramento, CA 95834

San Antonio Spurs
600 E. Market St.
San Antonio, TX 78205

Seattle SuperSonics
190 Queen Ann Ave. N.
Seattle, WA 98109

Utah Jazz
5 Delta Center
Salt Lake City, UT 84101

Washington Bullets
1 Harry S. Truman Dr.
Landover, MD 20785

## National Hockey League

League Headquarters
Sun Life Bldg.
Montreal, Quebec H3B 2W2

Mighty Ducks of Anaheim
500 Buena Vista St.
Burbank, CA 91521

Boston Bruins
150 Causeway St.
Boston, MA 02114

Buffalo Sabres
Memorial Auditorium
Buffalo, NY 14202

Calgary Flames
P.O. Box 1540
Calgary, Alta. T2P 3B9

Chicago Blackhawks
1800 W. Madison St.
Chicago, IL 60612

Detroit Red Wings
600 Civic Center Drive
Detroit, MI 48226

Edmonton Oilers
Northlands Coliseum
Edmonton, Alta. T5B 4M9

Florida Panthers
200 S. Andrews Ave.
Ft. Lauderdale, FL 33301

Hartford Whalers
242 Trumbull St.
Hartford, CT 06103

Los Angeles Kings
3900 W. Manchester Blvd.
Inglewood, CA 90306

Minnesota North Stars
7901 Cedar Ave. S.
Bloomington, MN 55425

Montreal Canadiens
2313 St. Catherine St., West
Montreal, Quebec H3H 1N2

New Jersey Devils
Meadowlands Arena
E. Rutherford, NJ 07073

New York Islanders
Nassau Coliseum
Uniondale, NY 11553

New York Rangers
4 Pennsylvania Plaza
New York, NY 10121

Ottawa Senators
301 Moodie Dr.
Ottawa, Ont. K2H 9C4

Philadelphia Flyers
Pattison Place
Philadelphia, PA 19148

Pittsburgh Penguins
Civic Arena
Pittsburgh, PA 15219

Quebec Nordiques
2205 Ave. du Colisee
Quebec, Que. G1L 4W7

St. Louis Blues
5700 Oakland Ave.
St. Louis, MO 63110

San Jose Sharks
10 Almaden Blvd.
San Jose, CA 95113

Tampa Bay Lightning
501 E. Kennedy Blvd.
Tampa, FL 33602

Toronto Maple Leafs
60 Carlton St.
Toronto, Ont. M5B 1L1

Vancouver Canucks
100 North Renfrew St.
Vancouver, B.C. V5K 3N7

Washington Capitals
Capital Centre
Landover, MD 20785

Winnipeg Jets
15-1430 Maroons Road
Winnipeg, Man. R3G 0L5

## National Football League

League Office
410 Park Avenue
New York, NY 10022

Atlanta Falcons
2745 Burnett Road
Suwanee, GA 30174

Buffalo Bills
1 Bills Drive
Orchard Park, NY 14127

Chicago Bears
250 N. Washington Rd.
Lake Forest, IL 60045

Cincinnati Bengals
200 Riverfront Stadium
Cincinnati, OH 45202

Cleveland Browns
80 1st Ave.
Berea, OH 44017

Dallas Cowboys
One Cowboys Pkwy.
Irving, TX 75063

Denver Broncos
13655 E. Dove Valley Pkwy.
Englewood, CO 80112

Detroit Lions
1200 Featherstone Rd.
Pontiac, MI 48342

Green Bay Packers
PO Box 10628
Green Bay, WI 54307

Houston Oilers
6910 Fannin St.
Houston, TX 77030

Indianapolis Colts
P.O. Box 53500
Indianapolis, IN 46253

Kansas City Chiefs
1 Arrowhead Drive
Kansas City, MO 64129

Los Angeles Raiders
332 Center St.
El Segundo, CA 90245

Los Angeles Rams
2327 W. Lincoln Ave.
Anaheim, CA 92801

Miami Dolphins
2269 NW 199 St.
Miami, FL 33056

Minnesota Vikings
9520 Viking Dr.
Eden Prairie, MN 55344

New England Patriots
Foxboro Stadium
Foxboro, MA 02035

New Orleans Saints
6928 Saints Dr.
Metairie, LA 70003

New York Giants
Giants Stadium
E. Rutherford, NJ 07073

New York Jets
1000 Fulton Ave.
Hempstead, NY 11550

Philadelphia Eagles
Veterans Stadium
Philadelphia, PA 19148

Phoenix Cardinals
PO Box 888
Phoenix, AZ 85001

Pittsburgh Steelers
Three Rivers Stadium
Pittsburgh, PA 15212

San Diego Chargers
P.O. Box 609609
San Diego, CA 92160

San Francisco 49ers
4949 Centennial Blvd.
Santa Clara, CA 95054

Seattle Seahawks
11220 NE 53d St.
Kirkland, WA 98033

Tampa Bay Buccaneers
1 Buccaneer Place
Tampa, FL 33607

Washington Redskins
21300 Redskin Park Dr.
Ashburn, VA 22011

## Other Sports Organizations

Amateur Athletic Union
3400 W. 86th St.
Indianapolis, IN 46268

Amateur Softball Assn.
2801 NE 50th St.
Oklahoma City, OK 73111

American Horse Show Assn.
220 E. 42d St.
New York, NY 10017

American Kennel Club
51 Madison Ave.
New York, NY 10010

American Water Ski Assn.
799 Overlook Dr. SE
Winter Haven, FL 33884

Canadian Football League
CFL Bldg.
Toronto, Ont. M4R 1A3

Indy-Car
390 Enterprise Court
Bloomfield, MI 48302

Intl. Game Fish Assn.
1301 E. Atlantic Blvd.
Pompano Beach, FL 33060

LPGA
2570 Volusra Ave.
Daytona Beach, FL 32114

Little League Baseball
PO Box 3485
S. Williamsport, PA 17701

National Archery Assn.
One Olympic Plaza
Colorado Springs, CO 80909

NASCAR
PO Box 2875
Daytona Beach, FL 32120

NCAA
6201 College Blvd.
Overland Park, KS 66211

National Rifle Assn.
1600 Rhode Island Ave. NW
Washington, DC 20036

Pro Bowlers Assn.
1720 Merriman Rd.
Akron, OH 44334

Pro Rodeo Cowboys Assn.
101 Pro Rodeo Dr.
Colorado Springs, CO 80919

Special Olympics
1350 New York Ave. NW
Washington, DC 20005

Thoroughbred Racing Assns.
420 Fair Hill Dr.
Elkton, MD 21921

USA Track & Field
P.O. Box 120
Indianapolis, IN 46206

U.S. Auto Club
4910 W. 16th St.
Speedway, IN 46224

U.S. Figure Skating Assn.
20 1st St.
Colorado Springs, CO 80906

U.S. Olympic Committee
1750 E. Boulder St.
Colorado Springs, CO 80909

U.S. Skiing Assn.
1500 Kearns
Park City, UT 84060

U.S. Tennis Assn.
1212 Ave. of the Americas
New York, NY 10036

U.S. Trotting Assn.
750 Michigan Ave.
Columbus, OH 43215

## NCAA Wrestling Champions

| Year | Champion | Year | Champion | Year | Champion | Year | Champion | Year | Champion |
|------|----------|------|----------|------|----------|------|----------|------|----------|
| 1964 | Oklahoma State | 1970 | Iowa State | 1976 | Iowa | 1982 | Iowa | 1988 | Arizona State |
| 1965 | Iowa State | 1971 | Oklahoma State | 1977 | Iowa State | 1983 | Iowa | 1989 | Oklahoma State |
| 1966 | Oklahoma State | 1972 | Iowa State | 1978 | Iowa | 1984 | Iowa | 1990 | Oklahoma State |
| 1967 | Michigan State | 1973 | Iowa State | 1979 | Iowa | 1985 | Iowa | 1991 | Iowa |
| 1968 | Oklahoma State | 1974 | Oklahoma | 1980 | Iowa | 1986 | Iowa | 1992 | Iowa |
| 1969 | Iowa State | 1975 | Iowa | 1981 | Iowa | 1987 | Iowa State | 1993 | Iowa |

# World Swimming Records

As of Aug. 1993

## Men's Records

### Freestyle

| Distance | Time | Holder | Country | Where made | Date |
|---|---|---|---|---|---|
| 50 Meters | 0:21.81 | Tom Jager | U.S. | Nashville, Tenn. | Mar. 24, 1990 |
| 100 Meters | 0:48.42 | Matt Biondi | U.S. | Austin, Tex. | Aug. 10, 1988 |
| 200 Meters | 1:46.69 | Giorgio Lamberti | Italy | Bonn | Aug. 15, 1989 |
| 400 Meters | 3:45.00 | Evgeny Sadovyi | Unified Team | Barcelona | July 29, 1992 |
| 800 Meters | 7:47.85 | Kieren Perkins | Australia | Edmonton | Aug. 25, 1991 |
| 1,500 Meters | 14:43.48 | Kieren Perkins | Australia | Barcelona | July 31, 1992 |

### Breaststroke

| | | | | | |
|---|---|---|---|---|---|
| 100 Meters | 1:01.29 | Norbert Rosza | Hungary | Athens | Aug. 20, 1991 |
| 200 Meters | 2:10.16 | Mike Barrowman | U.S. | Barcelona | July 29, 1992 |

### Butterfly

| | | | | | |
|---|---|---|---|---|---|
| 100 Meters | 0:52.84 | Pablo Morales | U.S. | Orlando, Fla. | June 23, 1986 |
| 200 Meters | 1:55.69 | Melvin Stewart | U.S. | Perth, Australia | Jan. 12, 1991 |

### Backstroke

| | | | | | |
|---|---|---|---|---|---|
| 100 Meters | 0:53.86 | Jeff Rouse | U.S. | Barcelona | July 29, 1992 |
| 200 Meters | 1:56.57 | Martin Lopez-Zubero | Spain | Tuscaloosa, Ala. | Nov. 23, 1991 |

### Individual Medley

| | | | | | |
|---|---|---|---|---|---|
| 200 Meters | 1:56.62 | Jani Sievinen | Finland | Paris | Feb. 6, 1993 |
| 400 Meters | 4:12.36 | Tamas Darnyi | Hungary | Perth, Australia | Jan. 8, 1991 |

### Freestyle Relays

| | | | | | |
|---|---|---|---|---|---|
| 400 M. (4×100) | 3:16.53 | (Jacobs, Dalbey, Jager, Biondi) | U.S. | Seoul | Sept. 23, 1988 |
| 800 M. (4×200) | 7:11.95 | (Lepikov, Pychnenko, Taianovitch, Sadovyi) | Unified Team | Barcelona | July 27, 1992 |

### Medley Relays

| | | | | | |
|---|---|---|---|---|---|
| 400 M. (4×100) | 3:36.93 | (Berkoff, Schroeder, Jacobs, Biondi) | U.S. | Seoul | Sept. 25, 1988 |
| | | (Rouse, Diebel, Morales, Olsen) | U.S. | Barcelona | July 31, 1992 |

## Women's Records

### Freestyle

| | | | | | |
|---|---|---|---|---|---|
| 50 Meters | 0:24.79 | Yang Wenyi | China | Barcelona | Aug. 31, 1992 |
| 100 Meters | 0:54.48 | Jenny Thompson | U.S. | Indianapolis | Mar. 1, 1992 |
| 200 Meters | 1:57.55 | Heike Friedrich | E. Germany | Berlin | June 18, 1986 |
| 400 Meters | 4:03.85 | Janet Evans | U.S. | Seoul | Sept. 22, 1988 |
| 800 Meters | 8:16.22 | Janet Evans | U.S. | Tokyo | Aug. 20, 1989 |
| 1,500 Meters | 15:52.10 | Janet Evans | U.S. | Orlando, Fla. | Mar. 26, 1988 |

### Breaststroke

| | | | | | |
|---|---|---|---|---|---|
| 100 Meters | 1:07.91 | Silke Hoerner | E. Germany | Strasbourg, France | Aug. 21, 1987 |
| 200 Meters | 2:25.35 | Anita Nall | U.S. | Indianapolis | Mar. 2, 1992 |

### Butterfly

| | | | | | |
|---|---|---|---|---|---|
| 100 Meters | 0:57.93 | Mary T. Meagher | U.S. | Brown Deer, Wis. | Aug. 16, 1981 |
| 200 Meters | 2:05.96 | Mary T. Meagher | U.S. | Brown Deer, Wis. | Aug. 13, 1981 |

### Backstroke

| | | | | | |
|---|---|---|---|---|---|
| 100 Meters | 1:00.31 | Krisztina Egerszegi | Hungary | Athens | Aug. 22, 1991 |
| 200 Meters | 2:06.62 | Krisztina Egerszegi | Hungary | Athens | Aug. 25, 1991 |

### Individual Medley

| | | | | | |
|---|---|---|---|---|---|
| 200 Meters | 2:11.65 | Lin Li | China | Barcelona | July 30, 1992 |
| 400 Meters | 4:36.10 | Petra Schneider | E. Germany | Ecuador | Aug. 1, 1982 |

### Freestyle Relays

| | | | | | |
|---|---|---|---|---|---|
| 400 M. (4×100) | 3:39.46 | (Haislett, Torres, Martino, Thompson) | U.S. | Barcelona | July 28, 1992 |

### Medley Relays

| | | | | | |
|---|---|---|---|---|---|
| 400 M. (4×100) | 4:02.54 | (Loveless, Nall, Ahmann-Leighton, Thompson) | U.S. | Barcelona | July 30, 1992 |

# COLLEGE FOOTBALL
## Annual Results of Major Bowl Games
(Note: Dates indicate the year that the game was played.)

### Rose Bowl, Pasadena

| | | |
|---|---|---|
| 1902 Michigan 49, Stanford 0 | 1943 Georgia 9, UCLA 0 | 1970 Southern Cal 10, Michigan 3 |
| 1916 Wash. State 14, Brown 0 | 1944 So. California 29, Washington 0 | 1971 Stanford 27, Ohio State 17 |
| 1917 Oregon 14, Pennsylvania 0 | 1945 So. California 25, Tennessee 0 | 1972 Stanford 13, Michigan 12 |
| 1918-19 Service teams | 1946 Alabama 34, So. California 14 | 1973 So. California 42, Ohio State 17 |
| 1920 Harvard 7, Oregon 6 | 1947 Illinois 45, UCLA 14 | 1974 Ohio State 42, So. California 21 |
| 1921 California 28, Ohio State 0 | 1948 Michigan 49, So. California 0 | 1975 So. California 18, Ohio State 17 |
| 1922 Wash. & Jeff. 0, California 0 | 1949 Northwestern 20, California 14 | 1976 UCLA 23, Ohio State 10 |
| 1923 So. California 14, Penn State 3 | 1950 Ohio State 17, California 14 | 1977 So. California 14, Michigan 6 |
| 1924 Navy 14, Washington 14 | 1951 Michigan 14, California 6 | 1978 Washington 27, Michigan 20 |
| 1925 Notre Dame 27, Stanford 10 | 1952 Illinois 40, Stanford 7 | 1979 So. California 17, Michigan 10 |
| 1926 Alabama 20, Washington 19 | 1953 So. California 7, Wisconsin 0 | 1980 So. California 17, Ohio State 16 |
| 1927 Alabama 7, Stanford 7 | 1954 Mich. State 28, UCLA 20 | 1981 Michigan 23, Washington 6 |
| 1928 Stanford 7, Pittsburgh 6 | 1955 Ohio State 20, So. California 7 | 1982 Washington 28, Iowa 0 |
| 1929 Georgia Tech 8, California 7 | 1956 Mich. State 17, UCLA 14 | 1983 UCLA 24, Michigan 14 |
| 1930 So. California 47, Pittsburgh 14 | 1957 Iowa 35, Oregon St. 19 | 1984 UCLA 45, Illinois 9 |
| 1931 Alabama 24, Wash. State 0 | 1958 Ohio State 10, Oregon 7 | 1985 So. California 20, Ohio State 17 |
| 1932 So. California 21, Tulane 12 | 1959 Iowa 38, California 12 | 1986 UCLA 45, Iowa 28 |
| 1933 So. California 35, Pittsburgh 0 | 1960 Washington 44, Wisconsin 8 | 1987 Arizona St. 22, Michigan 15 |
| 1934 Columbia 7, Stanford 0 | 1961 Washington 17, Minnesota 7 | 1988 Mich. State 20, Southern Cal. 17 |
| 1935 Alabama 29, Stanford 13 | 1962 Minnesota 21, UCLA 3 | 1989 Michigan 22, Southern Cal. 14 |
| 1936 Stanford 7, So. Methodist 0 | 1963 So. California 42, Wisconsin 37 | 1990 Southern Cal. 17, Michigan 10 |
| 1937 Pittsburgh 21, Washington 0 | 1964 Illinois 17, Washington 7 | 1991 Washington 46, Iowa 34 |
| 1938 California 13, Alabama 0 | 1965 Michigan 34, Oregon St. 7 | 1992 Washington 34, Michigan 14 |
| 1939 So. California 7, Duke 3 | 1966 UCLA 14, Mich. State 12 | 1993 Michigan 38, Washington 31 |
| 1940 So. California 14, Tennessee 0 | 1967 Purdue 14, So. California 13 | *Played at Durham, N.C. |
| 1941 Stanford 21, Nebraska 13 | 1968 Southern Cal. 14, Indiana 3 | |
| *1942 Oregon St. 20, Duke 16 | 1969 Ohio State 27, Southern Cal 16 | |

### Orange Bowl, Miami

| | | |
|---|---|---|
| 1935 Bucknell 26, Miami (Fla.) 0 | 1955 Duke 34, Nebraska 7 | 1975 Notre Dame 13, Alabama 11 |
| 1936 Catholic U. 20, Mississippi 19 | 1956 Oklahoma 20, Maryland 6 | 1976 Oklahoma 14, Michigan 6 |
| 1937 Duquesne 13, Miss. State 12 | 1957 Colorado 27, Clemson 21 | 1977 Ohio State 27, Colorado 10 |
| 1938 Auburn 6, Mich. State 0 | 1958 Oklahoma 48, Duke 21 | 1978 Arkansas 31, Oklahoma 6 |
| 1939 Tennessee 17, Oklahoma 0 | 1959 Oklahoma 21, Syracuse 6 | 1979 Oklahoma 31, Nebraska 24 |
| 1940 Georgia Tech 21, Missouri 7 | 1960 Georgia 14, Missouri 0 | 1980 Oklahoma 24, Florida St. 7 |
| 1941 Miss. State 14, Georgetown 7 | 1961 Missouri 21, Navy 14 | 1981 Oklahoma 18, Florida St. 17 |
| 1942 Georgia 40, TCU 26 | 1962 LSU 25, Colorado 7 | 1982 Clemson 22, Nebraska 15 |
| 1943 Alabama 37, Boston Col. 21 | 1963 Alabama 17, Oklahoma 0 | 1983 Nebraska 21, Louisiana St. 20 |
| 1944 LSU 19, Texas A&M 14 | 1964 Nebraska 13, Auburn 7 | 1984 Miami (Fla.) 31, Nebraska 30 |
| 1945 Tulsa 26, Georgia Tech 12 | 1965 Texas 21, Alabama 17 | 1985 Washington 28, Oklahoma 17 |
| 1946 Miami (Fla.) 13, Holy Cross 6 | 1966 Alabama 39, Nebraska 28 | 1986 Oklahoma 25, Penn State 10 |
| 1947 Rice 8, Tennessee 0 | 1967 Florida 27, Georgia Tech 12 | 1987 Oklahoma 42, Arkansas 8 |
| 1948 Georgia Tech 20, Kansas 14 | 1968 Oklahoma 26, Tennessee 24 | 1988 Miami (Fla.) 20, Oklahoma 14 |
| 1949 Texas 41, Georgia 28 | 1969 Penn State 15, Kansas 14 | 1989 Miami (Fla.) 23, Nebraska 3 |
| 1950 Santa Clara 21, Kentucky 13 | 1970 Penn State 10, Missouri 3 | 1990 Notre Dame 21, Colorado 6 |
| 1951 Clemson 15, Miami (Fla.) 14 | 1971 Nebraska 17, Louisiana St. 12 | 1991 Colorado 10, Notre Dame 9 |
| 1952 Georgia Tech 17, Baylor 14 | 1972 Nebraska 38, Alabama 6 | 1992 Miami (Fla.) 22, Nebraska 0 |
| 1953 Alabama 61, Syracuse 6 | 1973 Nebraska 40, Notre Dame 6 | 1993 Florida St. 27, Nebraska 14 |
| 1954 Oklahoma 7, Maryland 0 | 1974 Penn State 16, Louisiana St. 9 | |

### Sugar Bowl, New Orleans

| | | |
|---|---|---|
| 1935 Tulane 20, Temple 14 | 1955 Navy 21, Mississippi 0 | 1974 Nebraska 13, Florida 10 |
| 1936 TCU 3, LSU 2 | 1956 Georgia Tech 7, Pittsburgh 0 | 1975 Alabama 13, Penn State 6 |
| 1937 Santa Clara 21, LSU 14 | 1957 Baylor 13, Tennessee 7 | 1977 (Jan.) Pittsburgh 27, Georgia 3 |
| 1938 Santa Clara 6, LSU 0 | 1958 Mississippi 39, Texas 7 | 1978 Alabama 35, Ohio State 6 |
| 1939 TCU 15, Carnegie Tech 7 | 1959 LSU 7, Clemson 0 | 1979 Alabama 14, Penn State 7 |
| 1940 Texas A&M 14, Tulane 13 | 1960 Mississippi 21, LSU 0 | 1980 Alabama 24, Arkansas 9 |
| 1941 Boston Col. 19, Tennessee 13 | 1961 Mississippi 14, Rice 6 | 1981 Georgia 17, Notre Dame 10 |
| 1942 Fordham 2, Missouri 0 | 1962 Alabama 10, Arkansas 3 | 1982 Pittsburgh 24, Georgia 20 |
| 1943 Tennessee 14, Tulsa 7 | 1963 Mississippi 17, Arkansas 13 | 1983 Penn State 27, Georgia 23 |
| 1944 Georgia Tech 20, Tulsa 18 | 1964 Alabama 12, Mississippi 7 | 1984 Auburn 9, Michigan 7 |
| 1945 Duke 29, Alabama 26 | 1965 LSU 13, Syracuse 10 | 1985 Nebraska 28, Louisiana St. 10 |
| 1946 Oklahoma A&M 33, St. Mary's 13 | 1966 Missouri 20, Florida 18 | 1986 Tennessee 35, Miami (Fla.) 7 |
| 1947 Georgia 20, No. Carolina 10 | 1967 Alabama 34, Nebraska 7 | 1987 Nebraska 30, Louisiana St. 15 |
| 1948 Texas 27, Alabama 7 | 1968 LSU 20, Wyoming 13 | 1988 Syracuse 16, Auburn 16 |
| 1949 Oklahoma 14, No. Carolina 6 | 1969 Arkansas 16, Georgia 2 | 1989 Florida St. 13, Auburn 7 |
| 1950 Oklahoma 35, LSU 0 | 1970 Mississippi 27, Arkansas 22 | 1990 Miami 33, Alabama 25 |
| 1951 Kentucky 13, Oklahoma 7 | 1971 Tennessee 34, Air Force 13 | 1991 Tennessee 23, Virginia 22 |
| 1952 Maryland 28, Tennessee 13 | 1972 Oklahoma 40, Auburn 22 | 1992 Notre Dame 39, Florida 28 |
| 1953 Georgia Tech. 24, Mississippi 7 | *1972 (Dec.) Okla. 14, Penn State 0 | 1993 Alabama 34, Miami (Fla.) 13 |
| 1954 Georgia Tech 42, West Virginia 19 | 1973 Notre Dame 24, Alabama 23 | * Penn St. awarded game by forfeit |

### Fiesta Bowl, Tempe

| | | |
|---|---|---|
| 1971 Arizona St. 45, Florida St. 38 | 1979 Pittsburgh 16, Arizona 10 | 1987 Penn St. 14, Miami (Fla.) 10 |
| 1972 Arizona St. 49, Missouri 35 | 1980 Penn St. 31, Ohio St. 19 | 1988 Florida St. 31, Nebraska 28 |
| 1973 Arizona St. 28, Pittsburgh 7 | 1982 (Jan.) Penn St. 26, USC 10 | 1989 Notre Dame 34, W. Virginia 21 |
| 1974 Okla. St. 16, Brigham Young 6 | 1983 Arizona St. 32, Oklahoma 21 | 1990 Florida St. 41, Nebraska 17 |
| 1975 Arizona St. 17, Nebraska 14 | 1984 Ohio State 28, Pittsburgh 23 | 1991 Louisville 34, Alabama 7 |
| 1976 Oklahoma 41, Wyoming 7 | 1985 UCLA 39, Miami 37 | 1992 Penn St. 42, Tennessee 17 |
| 1977 Penn St. 42, Arizona St. 30 | 1986 Michigan 27, Nebraska 23 | 1993 Syracuse 26, Colorado 22 |
| 1978 UCLA 10, Arkansas 10 | | |

## Hall of Fame Bowl, Tampa

1986 (Dec.) Boston Coll. 27, Georgia 24
1988 (Jan.) Michigan 28, Alabama 24
1989 Syracuse 23, LSU 10

1990 Auburn 31, Ohio St. 14
1991 Clemson 30, Illinois 0

1992 Syracuse 24, Ohio St. 17
1993 Tennessee 38, Boston College 23

## Cotton Bowl, Dallas

1937 TCU 16, Marquette 6
1938 Rice 28, Colorado 14
1939 St. Mary's 20, Texas Tech 13
1940 Clemson 6, Boston Col. 3
1941 Texas A&M 13, Fordham 12
1942 Alabama 29, Texas A&M 21
1943 Texas 14, Georgia Tech 7
1944 Randolph Field 7, Texas 7
1945 Oklahoma A&M 34, TCU 0
1946 Texas 40, Missouri 27
1947 Arkansas 0, LSU 0
1948 So. Methodist 13, Penn State 13
1949 So. Methodist 21, Oregon 13
1950 Rice 27, No. Carolina 13
1951 Tennessee 20, Texas 14
1952 Kentucky 20, TCU 7
1953 Texas 16, Tennessee 0
1954 Rice 28, Alabama 6
1955 Georgia Tech 14, Arkansas 6

1956 Mississippi 14, TCU 13
1957 TCU 28, Syracuse 27
1958 Navy 20, Rice 7
1959 TCU 0, Air Force 0
1960 Syracuse 23, Texas 14
1961 Duke 7, Arkansas 6
1962 Texas 12, Mississippi 7
1963 LSU 13, Texas 0
1964 Texas 28, Navy 6
1965 Arkansas 10, Nebraska 7
1966 LSU 14, Arkansas 7
1967 Georgia 24, So. Methodist 9
1968 Texas A&M 20, Alabama 16
1969 Texas 36, Tennessee 13
1970 Texas 21, Notre Dame 17
1971 Notre Dame 24, Texas 11
1972 Penn State 30, Texas 6
1973 Texas 17, Alabama 13
1974 Nebraska 19, Texas 3

1975 Penn State 41, Baylor 20
1976 Arkansas 31, Georgia 10
1977 Houston 30, Maryland 21
1978 Notre Dame 38, Texas 10
1979 Notre Dame 35, Houston 34
1980 Houston 17, Nebraska 14
1981 Alabama 30, Baylor 2
1982 Texas 14, Alabama 12
1983 SMU 7, Pittsburgh 3
1984 Georgia 10, Texas 9
1985 Boston Coll. 45, Houston 28
1986 Texas A&M 36, Auburn 16
1987 Ohio St. 28, Texas A&M 12
1988 Texas A&M 35, Notre Dame 10
1989 UCLA 17, Arkansas 3
1990 Tennessee 31, Arkansas 27
1991 Miami (Fla.) 46, Texas 3
1992 Florida St. 10, Texas A&M 2
1993 Notre Dame 28, Texas A&M 3

## John Hancock Bowl, El Paso (Sun Bowl until 1989)

1936 Hardin Simmons 14, New Mex. St. 14
1937 Hardin-Simmons 34, Texas Mines 6
1938 West Virginia 7, Texas Tech 6
1939 Utah 26, New Mexico 0
1940 Catholic U. 0, Arizona St. 0
1941 Western Reserve 26, Arizona St. 13
1942 Tulsa 6, Texas Tech 0
1943 2d Air Force 13, Hardin-Simmons 7
1944 Southwestern (Tex.) 7, New Mexico 0
1945 Southwestern (Tex.) 35, U. of Mex. 0
1946 New Mexico 34, Denver 24
1947 Cincinnati 18, Virginia Tech 6
1948 Miami (O.) 13, Texas Tech 12
1949 West Virginia 21, Texas Mines 12
1950 Texas Western 33, Georgetown 20
1951 West Texas St. 14, Cincinnati 13
1952 Texas St. 25, Col. Pacific 14
1953 Col. Pacific 26, Miss. Southern 7

1954 Texas Western 37, Miss. Southern 14
1955 Texas Western 47, Florida St. 20
1956 Wyoming 21, Texas Tech 14
1957 Geo. Washington 13, Tex. Western 0
1958 Louisville 34, Drake 20
1959 Wyoming 14, Hardin-Simmons 6
1960 New Mexico St. 28, No. Texas St. 8
1961 New Mexico St. 20, Utah State 13
1962 Villanova 17, Wichita 9
1963 West Texas St. 15, Ohio U. 14
1964 Oregon 21, So. Methodist 14
1965 Georgia 7, Texas Tech 0
1966 Texas Western 13, TCU 12
1967 Wyoming 28, Florida St. 20
1968 UTex El Paso 14, Mississippi 7
1969 Auburn 34, Arizona 10
1969 (Dec.) Nebraska 45, Georgia 6
1970 Georgia Tech. 17, Texas Tech. 9
1971 LSU 33, Iowa State 15

1972 North Carolina 32, Texas Tech 28
1973 Missouri 34, Auburn 17
1974 Mississippi St. 26, No. Carolina 24
1975 Pittsburgh 33, Kansas 19
1977 (Jan.) Texas A&M 37, Florida 14
1977 (Dec.) Stanford 24, Louisiana St. 14
1978 Texas 42, Maryland 0
1979 Washington 14, Texas 7
1980 Nebraska 31, Mississippi St. 17
1981 Oklahoma 40, Houston 14
1982 North Carolina 26, Texas 10
1983 Alabama 28, SMU 7
1984 Maryland 28, Tennessee 27
1985 Georgia 13, Arizona 13
1986 Alabama 28, Washington 6
1987 Oklahoma St. 35, West Virginia 33
1988 Alabama 29, Army 28
1989 Pittsburgh 31, Texas A&M 28
1990 Michigan St. 17, USC 16
1991 UCLA 6, Illinois 3
1992 Baylor 20, Arizona 15

## Gator Bowl, Jacksonville

1946 Wake Forest 26, So. Carolina 14
1947 Oklahoma 34, N.C. State 13
1948 Maryland 20, Georgia 20
1949 Clemson 24, Missouri 23
1950 Maryland 20, Missouri 7
1951 Wyoming 20, Wash. & Lee 7
1952 Miami (Fla.) 14, Clemson 0
1953 Florida 14, Tulsa 13
1954 Texas Tech 35, Auburn 13
1955 Auburn 33, Baylor 13
1956 Vanderbilt 25, Auburn 13
1957 Georgia St. 21, Pittsburgh 14
1958 Tennessee 3, Texas A&M 0
1959 Mississippi 7, Florida 3
1960 Arkansas 14, Georgia Tech 7
1961 Florida 13, Baylor 12

1962 Penn State 30, Georgia Tech 15
1963 Florida 17, Penn State 7
1964 No. Carolina 35, Air Force 0
1965 Florida St. 36, Oklahoma 19
1966 Georgia Tech 31, Texas Tech 21
1967 Tennessee 18, Syracuse 12
1968 Penn State 17, Florida St. 17
1969 Missouri 35, Alabama 10
1969 (Dec.) Florida 14, Tenn. 13
1971 (Jan.) Auburn 35, Mississippi 28
1972 Georgia 7, N. Carolina 3
1973 Auburn 24, Colorado 3
1973 (Dec.) Tex. Tech. 28, Tenn. 19
1974 Auburn 27, Texas 3
1975 Maryland 13, Florida 0
1976 Notre Dame 20, Penn State 9

1977 Pittsburgh 34, Clemson 3
1978 Clemson 17, Ohio State 15
1979 No. Carolina 17, Michigan 15
1980 Pittsburgh 37, So. Carolina 9
1981 No. Carolina 31, Arkansas 27
1982 Florida St. 31, West Va. 12
1983 Florida 14, Iowa 6
1984 Oklahoma St. 21, So. Carolina 14
1985 Florida St. 34, Oklahoma St. 23
1986 Clemson 27, Stanford 21
1987 LSU 30, So. Carolina 13
1989 (Jan.) Georgia 34, Michigan St. 27
1989 (Dec.) Clemson 27, W. Va. 7
1991 (Jan.) Michigan 35, Mississippi 3
1991 (Dec.) Oklahoma 48, Virginia 14
1992 Florida 27, N.C. State 10

## Liberty Bowl, Memphis

1959 Penn State 7, Alabama 0
1960 Penn State 41, Oregon 12
1961 Syracuse 15, Miami 14
1962 Oregon State 6, Villanova 0
1963 Miss. State 16, N.C. State 12
1964 Utah 32, West Virginia 6
1965 Mississippi 13, Auburn 7
1966 Miami (Fla.) 14, Va. Tech 7
1967 N.C. State 14, Georgia 7
1968 Mississippi 34, Va. Tech 17
1969 Colorado 47, Alabama 33
1970 Tulane 17, Colorado 3

1971 Tennessee 14, Arkansas 13
1972 Georgia Tech 31, Iowa State 30
1973 No. Carolina St. 31, Kansas 18
1974 Tennessee 7, Maryland 3
1975 USC 20, Texas A&M 0
1976 Alabama 36, UCLA 6
1977 Nebraska 21, N. Carolina 17
1978 Missouri 20, Louisiana St. 15
1979 Penn St. 9, Tulane 6
1980 Purdue 28, Missouri 25
1981 Ohio State 31, Navy 28

1982 Alabama 21, Illinois 15
1983 Notre Dame 19, Boston Coll. 18
1984 Auburn 21, Arkansas 15
1985 Baylor 21, Louisiana St. 7
1986 Tennessee 21, Minnesota 14
1987 Georgia 20, Arkansas 17
1988 Indiana 34, S. Carolina 10
1989 Mississippi 42, Air Force 29
1990 Air Force 23, Ohio State 11
1991 Air Force 38, Mississippi St. 15
1992 Mississippi 13, Air Force 0

## Freedom Bowl, Anaheim

1984 Iowa 55, Texas 17
1985 Washington 20, Colorado 17
1986 UCLA 31, Brigham Young 10

1987 Arizona St. 33, Air Force 28
1988 Brigham Young 20, Colorado 17
1989 Washington 34, Florida 7

1990 Colorado St. 32, Oregon 31
1991 Tulsa 28, San Diego St. 17
1992 Fresno St. 24, USC 7

## Copper Bowl, Tucson

1989 Arizona 17, N.C. St. 10
1990 California 17, Wyoming 15

1991 Indiana 24, Baylor 0

1992 Washington St. 31, Utah 28

## Independence Bowl, Shreveport

1976 McNeese St. 20, Tulsa 16
1977 Louisiana Tech 24, Louisville 14
1978 E. Carolina 35, La. Tech 13
1979 Syracuse 31, McNeese St. 7
1980 So. Miss. 16, McNeese St. 14
1981 Texas A&M 33, Oklahoma St. 16

1982 Wisconsin 14, Kansas St. 3
1983 Air Force 9, Mississippi 3
1984 Air Force 23, Virginia Tech 7
1985 Minnesota 20, Clemson 13
1986 Mississippi 20, Texas Tech 17
1987 Washington 24, Tulane 12

1988 S. Mississippi 38, UTEP 18
1989 Oregon 27, Tulsa 24
1990 Louisiana Tech 34, Maryland 34
1991 Georgia 24, Arkansas 15
1992 Wake Forest 39, Oregon 35

## Citrus Bowl, Orlando

1947 Catawba 31, Maryville 6
1948 Catawba 7, Marshall 0
1949 Murray State 21, Sul Ross St. 21
1950 St. Vincent 7, Emory & Henry 6
1951 Morris Harvey 35, Emory & Henry 14
1952 Stetson 35, Arkansas St. 20
1953 East Texas St. 33, Tenn. Tech 0
1954 East Texas St. 7, Arkansas St. 7
1955 Neb.-Omaha 7, Eastern Kentucky 6
1956 Juniata 6, Missouri Valley 6
1957 West Texas St. 20, So. Miss. 13
1958 East Texas St. 10, So. Miss. 9
1958 (Dec.) East Texas St. 26, Missouri Valley 7
1960 (Jan.) Middle Tenn. 21, Presbyterian 12

1960 (Dec.) Citadel 27, Tenn. Tech 0
1961 Lamar 21, Middle Tennessee 14
1962 Houston 49, Miami (O.) 21
1963 Western Ky. 27, Coast Guard 0
1964 E. Carolina 14, Massachusetts 13
1965 East Carolina 31, Maine 0
1966 Morgan State 14, West Chester 6
1967 Tenn.-Martin 25, West Chester 8
1968 Richmond 49, Ohio U. 42
1969 Toledo 56, Davidson 33
1970 Toledo 40, William & Mary 12
1971 Toledo 28, Richmond 3
1972 Tampa 21, Kent State 18
1973 Miami (O.) 16, Florida 7
1974 Miami (O.) 21, Georgia 10
1975 Miami (O.) 20, South Carolina 7
1976 Okla. St. 49, Brigham Young 21

1977 Florida St. 40, Texas Tech 17
1978 N.C. State 30, Pittsburgh 17
1979 LSU 34, Wake Forest 10
1980 Florida 35, Maryland 20
1981 Missouri 19, Southern Miss. 17
1982 Auburn 33, Boston College 26
1983 Tennessee 30, Maryland 23
1984 Georgia 17, Florida St. 17
1985 Ohio St. 10, Brigham Young 7
1987 (Jan.) Auburn 16, USC 7
1988 Clemson 35, Penn St. 10
1989 Clemson 13, Oklahoma 6
1990 Illinois 31, Virginia 21
1991 Georgia Tech 45, Nebraska 21
1992 California 37, Clemson 13
1993 Georgia 21, Ohio St. 14

## Peach Bowl, Atlanta

1968 LSU 31, Florida St. 27
1969 West Virginia 14, S. Carolina 3
1970 Arizona St. 48, N. Carolina 26
1971 Mississippi 41, Georgia Tech. 18
1972 N. Carolina St. 49, W. Va. 13
1973 Georgia 17, Maryland 16
1974 Vanderbilt 6, Texas Tech. 6
1975 W. Virginia 13, No. Carolina St. 10
1976 Kentucky 21, North Carolina 0

1977 N. Carolina St. 24, Iowa St. 14
1978 Purdue 41, Georgia Tech. 21
1979 Baylor 24, Clemson 18
1981 (Jan.) Miami (Fla.) 20, Virginia Tech. 10
1981 (Dec.) West Virginia 26, Florida 6
1982 Iowa 28, Tennessee 22
1983 Florida St. 28, North Carolina 3
1984 Virginia 27, Purdue 24

1985 Army 31, Illinois 29
1986 Va. Tech 25, N.C. State 24
1988 (Jan.) Tennessee 28, Indiana 22
1988 (Dec.) N.C. State 28, Iowa 23
1989 Syracuse 19, Georgia 18
1990 Auburn 27, Indiana 23
1992 (Jan.) E. Carolina 37, N.C. State 34
1993 North Carolina 21, Mississippi St. 17

## Holiday Bowl, San Diego

1978 Navy 23, Brigham Young 16
1979 Indiana 38, Brigham Young 37
1980 Brigham Young 46, SMU 45
1981 Brigham Young 38, Wash. St. 36
1982 Ohio State 47, Brigham Young 17

1983 Brigham Young 21, Missouri 17
1984 Brigham Young 24, Michigan 17
1985 Arkansas 18, Arizona St. 17
1986 Iowa 39, San Diego St. 38
1987 Iowa 20, Wyoming 19

1988 Oklahoma St. 62, Wyoming 14
1989 Penn St. 50, Brigham Young 39
1990 Texas A&M 65, Brigham Young 14
1991 Iowa 13, Brigham Young 13
1992 Hawaii 27, Illinois 17

## Aloha Bowl, Honolulu

1982 Washington 21, Maryland 20
1983 Penn State 13, Washington 10
1984 SMU 27, Notre Dame 20
1985 Alabama 24, USC 3

1986 Arizona 30, North Carolina 21
1987 UCLA 20, Florida 16
1988 Washington St. 24, Houston 22
1989 Michigan St. 33, Hawaii 13

1990 Syracuse 28, Arizona 0
1991 Georgia Tech 18, Stanford 17
1992 Kansas 23, Brigham Young 20

## Blockbuster Bowl, Miami

1990 Florida St. 24, Penn St. 17

1991 Alabama 30, Colorado 25

1993 (Jan.) Stanford 24, Penn St. 3

## Las Vegas Bowl, Las Vegas

1992 Bowling Green 35, Nevada 34

## Outland Award

Honoring the outstanding interior lineman selected by the Football Writers' Association of America.

1946 George Connor, Notre Dame, T
1947 Joe Steffy, Army, G
1948 Bill Fischer, Notre Dame, G
1949 Ed Bagdon, Michigan St., G
1950 Bob Gain, Kentucky, T
1951 Jim Weatherall, Oklahoma, T
1952 Dick Modzelewski, Maryland, T
1953 J. D. Roberts, Oklahoma, G
1954 Bill Brooks, Arkansas, G
1955 Calvin Jones, Iowa, G
1956 Jim Parker, Ohio State, G
1957 Alex Karras, Iowa, T
1958 Zeke Smith, Auburn, G
1959 Mike McGee, Duke, T
1960 Tom Brown, Minnesota, G
1961 Merlin Olsen, Utah State, T

1962 Bobby Bell, Minnesota, T
1963 Scott Appleton, Texas, T
1964 Steve Delong, Tennessee, T
1965 Tommy Nobis, Texas, G
1966 Loyd Phillips, Arkansas, T
1967 Ron Yary, Southern Cal, T
1968 Bill Stanfill, Georgia, T
1969 Mike Reid, Penn State, DT
1970 Jim Stillwagon, Ohio State, LB
1971 Larry Jacobson, Nebraska, DT
1972 Rich Glover, Nebraska, MG
1973 John Hicks, Ohio State, G
1974 Randy White, Maryland, DE
1975 Lee Roy Selmon, Oklahoma, DT
1976 Ross Browner, Notre Dame, DE
1977 Brad Shearer, Texas, DT

1978 Greg Roberts, Oklahoma, G
1979 Jim Ritcher, No. Carolina St., C
1980 Mark May, Pittsburgh, OT
1981 Dave Rimington, Nebraska, C
1982 Dave Rimington, Nebraska, C
1983 Dean Steinkuhler, Nebraska, G
1984 Bruce Smith, Virginia Tech, DT
1985 Mike Ruth, Boston College, DT
1986 Jason Buck, BYU, DT
1987 Chad Hennings, Air Force, DT
1988 Tracy Rocker, Auburn, DT
1989 Mohammed Elewonibi, BYU, G
1990 Russell Maryland, Miami (Fla.), DT
1991 Steve Emtman, Washington, DL
1992 Will Shields, Nebraska, G

## Selected College Division I Football Teams

| Team | Nickname | Team colors | Conference | Coach | 1992 record (W-L-T) |
|---|---|---|---|---|---|
| Air Force | Falcons | Blue & silver | Western Athletic | Fisher De Berry | 7-5-0 |
| Akron | Zips | Blue & gold | Mid-American | Gerry Faust | 7-3-1 |
| Alabama | Crimson Tide | Crimson & white | Southeastern | Gene Stallings | 13-0-0 |
| Arizona | Wildcats | Red & blue | Pacific Ten | Dick Tomey | 6-5-1 |
| Arizona State | Sun Devils | Maroon & gold | Pacific Ten | Bruce Snyder | 6-5-0 |
| Arkansas | Razorbacks | Cardinal & white | Southeastern | Danny Ford | 3-7-1 |
| Arkansas State | Indians | Scarlet & black | Big West | John Bobo | 2-9-0 |
| Army | Cadets | Black, gold, gray | Independent | Bob Sutton | 5-6-0 |
| Auburn | Tigers | Orange & blue | Southeastern | Terry Bowden | 5-5-1 |
| Ball State | Cardinals | Cardinal & white | Mid-American | Paul Schudel | 5-6-0 |
| Baylor | Bears | Green & gold | Southwest | Chuck Reedy | 7-5-0 |
| Boston College | Eagles | Maroon & gold | Big East | Tom Coughlin | 8-3-1 |
| Boston Univ. | Terriers | Scarlet & white | Yankee | Dan Allen | 3-8-1 |
| Bowling Green | Falcons | Orange & brown | Mid-American | Gary Blackney | 10-2-0 |
| Brigham Young | Cougars | Royal blue & white | Western Athletic | LaVell Edwards | 8-5-0 |
| Brown | Bears | Brown, cardinal, white | Ivy | Mickey Kwiatowski | 0-10-0 |
| California | Golden Bears | Blue & gold | Pacific Ten | Keith Gilbertson | 4-7-0 |
| Central Michigan | Chippewas | Maroon & gold | Mid-American | Herb Deromedi | 5-6-0 |
| Cincinnati | Bearcats | Red & black | Independent | Tim Murphy | 3-8-0 |
| Citadel | Bulldogs | Blue & white | Southern | Charles Taaffe | 11-2-0 |
| Clemson | Tigers | Purple & orange | Atlantic Coast | Ken Hatfield | 5-6-0 |
| Colgate | Red Raiders | Maroon | Patriot | Mike Foley | 4-7-0 |
| Colorado State | Rams | Green & gold | Western Athletic | Sonny Lubick | 5-7-0 |
| Colorado | Buffaloes | Silver, gold & black | Big Eight | Bill McCartney | 9-2-1 |
| Cornell | Big Red | Carnelian & white | Ivy | Jim Hofher | 7-3-0 |
| Dartmouth | Big Green | Dartmouth green & white | Ivy | John Lyons | 8-2-0 |
| Delaware | Fightin' Blue Hens | Blue & gold | Yankee | Harold Raymond | 11-3-0 |
| Delaware State | Hornets | Red & blue | Mid-Eastern | William Collick | 6-5-0 |
| Duke | Blue Devils | Royal blue & white | Atlantic Coast | Barry Wilson | 2-9-0 |
| East Carolina | Pirates | Purple & gold | Independent | Steve Logan | 5-6-0 |
| East Tennessee St. | Buccaneers | Blue & gold | Southern | Mike Cavan | 5-6-0 |
| Eastern Illinois | Panthers | Blue & gray | Gateway | Bob Spoo | 9-3-0 |
| Eastern Kentucky | Colonels | Maroon & white | Ohio Valley | Roy Kidd | 1-10-0 |
| Eastern Michigan | Eagles | Green & white | Mid-American | Ron Cooper | 7-4-0 |
| Eastern Washington | Eagles | Red & white | Big Sky | Dick Zornes | 9-4-0 |
| Florida | Gators | Orange & blue | Southeastern | Steve Spurrier | 9-4-0 |
| Florida A&M. | Rattlers | Orange & green | Mid-Eastern | Ken Riley | 7-5-0 |
| Florida State | Seminoles | Garnet & gold | Atlantic Coast | Bobby Bowden | 11-1-0 |
| Fresno State | Bulldogs | Cardinal & blue | Western Athletic | Jim Sweeney | 9-4-0 |
| Furman | Paladins | Purple & white | Southern | Jimmy Satterfield | 6-5-0 |
| Georgia | Bulldogs | Red & black | Southeastern | Ray Goff | 10-2-0 |
| Georgia Southern | Eagles | Blue & white | Southern | Tim Stowers | 7-4-0 |
| Georgia Tech | Yellow Jackets | Old gold & white | Atlantic Coast | Bill Lewis | 5-6-0 |
| Grambling | Tigers | Black & gold | Southwestern | Eddie Robinson | 10-2-0 |
| Harvard | Crimson | Crimson | Ivy | Joe Restic | 3-7-0 |
| Hawaii | Rainbow Warriors | Green & white | Western Athletic | Bob Wagner | 11-2-0 |
| Holy Cross | Crusaders | Royal purple | Patriot | Peter Vaas | 6-5-0 |
| Houston | Cougars | Scarlet & white | Southwest | Kim Helton | 4-7-0 |
| Howard | Bison | Blue & white | Mid-Eastern | Steve Wilson | 7-4-0 |
| Idaho | Vandals | Silver & gold | Big Sky | John L. Smith | 9-3-0 |
| Idaho State | Bengals | Orange & black | Big Sky | Brian McNeely | 3-8-0 |
| Illinois | Fighting Illini | Orange & blue | Big Ten | Lou Tepper | 6-5-1 |
| Illinois State | Redbirds | Red & white | Gateway | Jim Heacock | 5-6-0 |
| Indiana | Hoosiers | Cream & crimson | Big Ten | Bill Mallory | 5-6-0 |
| Indiana State | Sycamores | Blue & white | Gateway | Dennis Raetz | 4-7-0 |
| Iowa | Hawkeyes | Old gold & black | Big Ten | Hayden Fry | 5-7-0 |
| Iowa State | Cyclones | Cardinal & gold | Big Eight | Jim Walden | 4-7-0 |
| Jackson State | Tigers | Blue & white | Southwestern | James Carson | 7-4-0 |
| James Madison | Dukes | Purple & gold | Yankee | Rip Scherer | 4-7-0 |
| Kansas | Jayhawks | Crimson & blue | Big Eight | Glen Mason | 8-4-0 |
| Kansas State | Wildcats | Purple & white | Big Eight | Bill Snyder | 5-6-0 |
| Kent | Golden Flashes | Blue & gold | Mid-American | Pete Cordelli | 2-9-0 |
| Kentucky | Wildcats | Blue & white | Southeastern | Bill Curry | 4-7-0 |
| Lafayette | Leopards | Maroon & white | Patriot | Bill Russo | 8-3-0 |
| Lehigh | Engineers | Brown & white | Patriot | Hank Small | 3-8-0 |
| Liberty | Flames | Red, white, blue | Independent | Sam Rutigliano | 7-4-0 |
| Louisiana State | Fighting Tigers | Purple & gold | Southeastern | Curley Hallman | 2-9-0 |
| Louisiana Tech | Bulldogs | Red & blue | Big West | Joe Raymond Peace | 5-6-0 |
| Louisville | Cardinals | Red, black, white | Independent | Howard Schnellenberger | 5-6-0 |
| Maine | Black Bears | Blue & white | Yankee | Jack Cosgrove | 6-5-0 |
| Marshall | Thundering Herd | Green & white | Southern | Jim Donnan | 11-4-0 |
| Maryland | Terps | Red, white, black & gold | Atlantic Coast | Mark Duffner | 3-8-0 |
| Massachusetts | Minutemen | Maroon & white | Yankee | Mike Hodges | 7-3-0 |
| McNeese State | Cowboys | Blue & gold | Southland | Bobby Keasler | 9-4-0 |
| Memphis State | Tigers | Blue & gray | Independent | Chuck Stobart | 6-5-0 |
| Miami (Fla.) | Hurricanes | Orange, green, white | Big East | Dennis Erickson | 11-1-0 |
| Miami (Ohio) | Redskins | Red & white | Mid-American | Randy Walker | 6-4-1 |
| Michigan | Wolverines | Maize & blue | Big Ten | Gary Moeller | 9-0-3 |
| Michigan State | Spartans | Green & white | Big Ten | George Perles | 5-6-0 |
| Middle Tennessee St. | Blue Raiders | Blue & white | Ohio Valley | Boots Donnelly | 10-3-0 |
| Minnesota | Golden Gophers | Maroon & gold | Big Ten | Jim Wacker | 2-9-0 |

| Team | Nickname | Team colors | Conference | Coach | 1992 record (W-L-T) |
|---|---|---|---|---|---|
| Mississippi | Rebels | Red & blue | Southeastern | Billy Brewer | 9-3-0 |
| Mississippi State | Bulldogs | Maroon & white | Southeastern | Jackie Sherrill | 7-5-0 |
| Miss. Valley | Delta Devils | Green & white | Southwestern | Larry Dorsey | 4-5-0 |
| Missouri | Tigers | Old gold & black | Big Eight | Bob Stull | 3-8-0 |
| Montana | Grizzlies | Copper, silver, gold | Big Sky | Don Read | 6-5-0 |
| Montana State | Bobcats | Blue & gold | Big Sky | Cliff Hyself | 4-7-0 |
| Morehead State | Eagles | Blue & gold | Ohio Valley | Cole Proctor | 3-8-0 |
| Morgan State | Bears | Blue & orange | Mid-Eastern | Ricky Diggs | 2-8-0 |
| Murray State | Racers | Blue & gold | Ohio Valley | Houston Nutt | 2-9-0 |
| Navy | Midshipmen | Navy blue & gold | Independent | George Chaump | 1-10-0 |
| Nebraska | Cornhuskers | Scarlet & cream | Big Eight | Tom Osborne | 9-3-0 |
| Nevada-Las Vegas | Rebels | Scarlet & gray | Big West | Jim Strong | 6-5-0 |
| Nevada-Reno | Wolf Pack | Silver & blue | Big West | Jeff Horton | 7-5-0 |
| New Hampshire | Wildcats | Blue & white | Yankee | Bill Bowes | 5-5-1 |
| New Mexico | Lobos | Cherry & silver | Western Athletic | Dennis Franchione | 3-8-0 |
| New Mexico State | Aggies | Crimson & white | Big West | Jim Hess | 6-5-0 |
| Nicholls St. | Colonels | Red & grey | Southland | Rick Rhoades | 1-9-1 |
| North Carolina | Tar Heels | Blue & white | Atlantic Coast | Mack Brown | 9-3-0 |
| North Carolina A & T. | Aggies | Blue & gold | Mid-Eastern | Bill Hayes | 9-3-0 |
| North Carolina State | Wolfpack | Red & white | Atlantic Coast | Dick Sheridan | 9-3-1 |
| North Texas | Mean Green, Eagles | Green & white | Southland | Dennis Parker | 4-7-0 |
| Northeast Louisiana | Indians | Maroon & gold | Southland | Dave Roberts | 10-3-0 |
| Northeastern | Huskies | Red & black | Yankee | Barry Gallup | 5-5-1 |
| Northern Arizona | Lumberjacks | Blue & gold | Big Sky | Steve Axman | 4-7-0 |
| Northern Illinois | Huskies | Cardinal & black | Big West | Charlie Sadler | 5-6-0 |
| Northern Iowa | Panthers | Purple & old gold | Gateway | Terry Allen | 12-2-0 |
| Northwestern | Wildcats | Purple & white | Big Ten | Gary Barnett | 3-8-0 |
| Northwestern State | Demons | Purple & white | Southland | Sam Goodwin | 7-4-0 |
| Notre Dame | Fighting Irish | Gold & blue | Independent | Lou Holtz | 10-1-1 |
| Ohio State | Buckeyes | Scarlet & gray | Big Ten | John Cooper | 8-3-1 |
| Ohio Univ | Bobcats | Green & white | Mid-American | Tom Lichtenberg | 1-10-0 |
| Oklahoma | Sooners | Crimson & cream | Big Eight | Gary Gibbs | 5-4-2 |
| Oklahoma State | Cowboys | Orange & black | Big Eight | Pat Jones | 4-6-1 |
| Oregon | Ducks | Green & yellow | Pacific Ten | Rich Brooks | 6-6-0 |
| Oregon State | Beavers | Orange & black | Pacific Ten | Jerry Pettibone | 1-9-1 |
| Pacific | Tigers | Orange & black | Big West | Chuck Shelton | 3-8-0 |
| Penn State | Nittany Lions | Blue & white | Big Ten | Joe Paterno | 7-5-0 |
| Pennsylvania | Red & Blue, Quakers | Red & blue | Ivy | Al Bagnoli | 7-3-0 |
| Pittsburgh | Panthers | Gold & blue | Big East | Johnny Majors | 3-9-0 |
| Princeton | Tigers | Orange & black | Ivy | Steve Tosches | 8-2-0 |
| Purdue | Boilermakers | Old gold & black | Big Ten | Jim Colletto | 4-7-0 |
| Rhode Island | Rams | Blue & white | Yankee | Floyd Keith | 1-10-0 |
| Rice | Owls | Blue & gray | Southwest | Fred Goldsmith | 6-5-0 |
| Richmond | Spiders | Red & blue | Yankee | Jim Marshall | 7-4-0 |
| Rutgers | Scarlet Knights | Scarlet | Big East | Doug Graber | 7-4-0 |
| Sam Houston State | Bearkats | Orange & white | Southland | Ron Randleman | 6-3-2 |
| Samford | Bulldogs | Crimson & blue | Independent | Chan Galley | 9-3-0 |
| San Diego State | Aztecs | Scarlet & black | Western Athletic | Al Luginbill | 5-5-1 |
| San Jose State | Spartans | Gold & white | Big West | John Ralston | 7-4-0 |
| South Carolina | Fighting Gamecocks | Garnet & black | Southeastern | Sparky Woods | 5-6-0 |
| South Carolina State | Bulldogs | Garnet & blue | Mid-Eastern | Willie Jeffries | 7-4-0 |
| SE Missouri St. | Indians | Red & black | Ohio Valley | John Mumford | 2-9-0 |
| Southern-Baton Rouge | Jaguars | Blue & gold | Southwestern | Pete Richardson | 5-6-0 |
| Southern California | Trojans | Cardinal & gold | Pacific Ten | John Robinson | 6-5-1 |
| Southern Illinois | Salukis | Maroon & white | Gateway | Bob Smith | 4-7-0 |
| Southern Methodist | Mustangs | Red & blue | Southwest | Tom Rossley | 5-6-0 |
| Southern Mississippi | Golden Eagles | Black & gold | Independent | Jeff Bower | 7-4-0 |
| SW Missouri St | Bears | Maroon & white | Gateway | Jesse Branch | 6-5-0 |
| SW Texas St. | Bobcats | Maroon & gold | Southland | Jim Bob Helduser | 5-5-1 |
| Southwestern La. | Ragin' Cajuns | Vermillion & white | Big West | Nelson Stokley | 2-9-0 |
| Stanford | Cardinal | Cardinal & white | Pacific Ten | Bill Walsh | 10-3-0 |
| Stephen F. Austin St. | Lumberjacks | Purple & white | Southland | John Pearce | 3-8-0 |
| Syracuse | Orangemen | Orange | Big East | Paul Pasqualoni | 10-2-0 |
| Temple | Owls | Cherry & white | Big East | Ron Dickerson | 1-10-0 |
| Tennessee | Volunteers | Orange & white | Southeastern | Philip Fulmer | 9-3-0 |
| Tenn.-Chattanooga | Moccasins | Navy blue & gold | Southern | Tommy West | 2-9-0 |
| Tenn.-Martin | Pacers | Orange, white, blue | Ohio Valley | Don McLeary | 3-8-0 |
| Tennessee State | Tigers | Blue & white | Ohio Valley | Bill Davis | 5-6-0 |
| Tennessee Tech | Golden Eagles | Purple & gold | Ohio Valley | Jim Ragland | 5-6-0 |
| Texas | Longhorns | Orange & white | Southwest | John Mackovic | 6-5-0 |
| Texas A & M | Aggies | Maroon & white | Southwest | R.C. Slocum | 12-1-0 |
| Texas Christian | Horned Frogs | Purple & white | Southwest | Pat Sullivan | 2-8-1 |
| Texas Southern | Tigers | Maroon & gray | Southwestern | Walter Highsmith | 5-6-0 |
| Texas Tech | Red Raiders | Scarlet & black | Southwest | Spike Dykes | 5-6-0 |
| Toledo | Rockets | Blue & gold | Mid-American | Gary Pinkel | 8-3-0 |
| Towson St. | Tigers | Gold & white | Independent | Gordy Combs | 5-5-0 |
| Tulane | Green Wave | Olive green & sky blue | Independent | Buddy Teevens | 2-9-0 |
| Tulsa | Golden Hurricane | Blue & gold | Independent | Dave Rader | 4-7-0 |
| UCLA | Bruins | Blue & gold | Pacific Ten | Terry Donahue | 6-5-0 |
| Utah | Utes | Crimson & white | Western Athletic | Ron McBride | 6-6-0 |
| Utah State | Aggies | Navy blue & white | Big West | Charlie Weatherbie | 5-6-0 |
| UTEP | Miners | Orange, blue, white | Western Athletic | David Lee | 1-10-0 |
| Vanderbilt | Commodores | Black & gold | Southeastern | Gerry DiNardo | 4-7-0 |
| Villanova | Wildcats | Blue & white | Yankee | Andy Talley | 9-3-0 |
| Virginia | Cavaliers | Orange & blue | Atlantic Coast | George Welsh | 7-4-0 |

| Team | Nickname | Team colors | Conference | Coach | 1992 record (W-L-T) |
|------|----------|-------------|------------|-------|---------------------|
| VMI | Keydets | Red, white & yellow | Southern | Jim Shuck | 3-8-0 |
| Virginia Tech | Gobblers, Hokies | Orange & maroon | Big East | Frank Beamer | 2-8-1 |
| Wake Forest | Demon Deacons | Old gold & black | Atlantic Coast | Jim Caldwell | 8-4-0 |
| Washington | Huskies | Purple & gold | Pacific Ten | Jim Lambright | 9-3-0 |
| Washington State | Cougars | Crimson & gray | Pacific Ten | Mike Price | 9-3-0 |
| Weber State | Wildcats | Purple & white | Big Sky | Dave Arsianian | 6-5-0 |
| West Virginia | Mountaineers | Old gold & blue | Big East | Don Nehlen | 5-4-2 |
| Western Carolina | Catamounts | Purple & gold | Southern | Steve Hodgin | 7-4-0 |
| Western Illinois | Leathernecks | Purple & gold | Gateway | Randy Ball | 7-4-0 |
| Western Kentucky | Hilltoppers | Red & white | Independent | Jack Harbaugh | 4-6-0 |
| Western Michigan | Broncos | Brown & gold | Mid-American | Al Molde | 7-3-1 |
| William & Mary | Tribe | Green, gold & silver | Yankee | Jimmye Laycock | 9-2-0 |
| Wisconsin | Badgers | Cardinal & white | Big Ten | Barry Alvarez | 5-6-0 |
| Wyoming | Cowboys | Brown & yellow | Western Athletic | Joe Tiller | 5-7-0 |
| Yale | Bulldogs, Elis | Yale blue & white | Ivy | Carmen Cozza | 4-6-0 |
| Youngstown St. | Penguins | Scarlet & white | Independent | Jim Tressel | 11-3-1 |

## Heisman Trophy Winners

Awarded annually to the nation's outstanding college football player.

| | | | | | |
|---|---|---|---|---|---|
| 1935 | Jay Berwanger, Chicago, HB | 1955 | Howard Cassady, Ohio St., HB | 1974 | Archie Griffin, Ohio State, RB |
| 1936 | Larry Kelley, Yale, E | 1956 | Paul Hornung, Notre Dame, QB | 1975 | Archie Griffin, Ohio State, RB |
| 1937 | Clinton Frank, Yale, HB | 1957 | John Crow, Texas A & M, HB | 1976 | Tony Dorsett, Pittsburgh, RB |
| 1938 | David O'Brien, Tex. Christian, QB | 1958 | Pete Dawkins, Army, HB | 1977 | Earl Campbell, Texas, RB |
| 1939 | Nile Kinnick, Iowa, HB | 1959 | Billy Cannon, La. State, HB | 1978 | Billy Sims, Oklahoma, RB |
| 1940 | Tom Harmon, Michigan, HB | 1960 | Joe Bellino, Navy, HB | 1979 | Charles White, USC, RB |
| 1941 | Bruce Smith, Minnesota, HB | 1961 | Ernest Davis, Syracuse, HB | 1980 | George Rogers, So. Carolina, RB |
| 1942 | Frank Sinkwich, Georgia, HB | 1962 | Terry Baker, Oregon State, QB | 1981 | Marcus Allen, USC, RB |
| 1943 | Angelo Bertelli, Notre Dame, QB | 1963 | Roger Staubach, Navy, QB | 1982 | Herschel Walker, Georgia, RB |
| 1944 | Leslie Horvath, Ohio State, QB | 1964 | John Huarte, Notre Dame, QB | 1983 | Mike Rozier, Nebraska, RB |
| 1945 | Felix Blanchard, Army, FB | 1965 | Mike Garrett, USC, HB | 1984 | Doug Flutie, Boston College, QB |
| 1946 | Glenn Davis, Army, HB | 1966 | Steve Spurrier, Florida, QB | 1985 | Bo Jackson, Auburn, RB |
| 1947 | John Lujack, Notre Dame, QB | 1967 | Gary Beban, UCLA, QB | 1986 | Vinny Testaverde, Miami, QB |
| 1948 | Doak Walker, SMU, HB | 1968 | O. J. Simpson, USC, RB | 1987 | Tim Brown, Notre Dame, WR |
| 1949 | Leon Hart, Notre Dame, E | 1969 | Steve Owens, Oklahoma, RB | 1988 | Barry Sanders, Oklahoma St., RB |
| 1950 | Vic Janowicz, Ohio State, HB | 1970 | Jim Plunkett, Stanford, QB | 1989 | Andre Ware, Houston, QB |
| 1951 | Richard Kazmaier, Princeton, HB | 1971 | Pat Sullivan, Auburn, QB | 1990 | Ty Detmer, BYU, QB |
| 1952 | Billy Vessels, Oklahoma, HB | 1972 | Johnny Rodgers, Nebraska, RB-R | 1991 | Desmond Howard, Michigan, WR |
| 1953 | John Lattner, Notre Dame, HB | 1973 | John Cappelletti, Penn State, RB | 1992 | Gino Torretta, Miami, QB |
| 1954 | Alan Ameche, Wisconsin, FB | | | | |

## All-Time Division I-A Percentage Leaders

(Classified as Division I-A for the last 10 years; record includes bowl games; ties computed as half won and half lost)

| | Years | Won | Lost | Tied | Pct. | Bowl Games W | L | T |
|---|-------|-----|------|------|------|------|---|---|
| Notre Dame | 104 | 712 | 210 | 41 | .761 | 11 | 6 | 0 |
| Michigan | 113 | 731 | 238 | 36 | .745 | 11 | 13 | 0 |
| Alabama | 98 | 682 | 234 | 43 | .734 | 25 | 17 | 3 |
| Oklahoma | 98 | 650 | 237 | 52 | .720 | 19 | 10 | 1 |
| Texas | 100 | 682 | 268 | 31 | .711 | 16 | 16 | 2 |
| USC | 100 | 622 | 249 | 52 | .702 | 22 | 13 | 0 |
| Ohio St. | 103 | 649 | 264 | 52 | .699 | 12 | 13 | 0 |
| Penn St. | 106 | 664 | 289 | 41 | .689 | 17 | 10 | 2 |
| Nebraska | 103 | 662 | 289 | 40 | .688 | 14 | 17 | 0 |
| Tennessee | 96 | 627 | 274 | 52 | .685 | 18 | 15 | 0 |
| Central Michigan | 92 | 475 | 249 | 36 | .649 | 3 | 1 | 0 |
| Washington | 103 | 555 | 306 | 49 | .637 | 12 | 8 | 1 |
| Army | 104 | 582 | 322 | 50 | .636 | 2 | 1 | 0 |
| Miami (Ohio) | 99 | 542 | 301 | 42 | .636 | 5 | 2 | 0 |
| Louisiana St. | 99 | 568 | 319 | 46 | .633 | 11 | 16 | 1 |
| Georgia | 99 | 584 | 327 | 53 | .633 | 15 | 13 | 3 |
| Arizona St. | 80 | 438 | 250 | 24 | .632 | 9 | 5 | 1 |
| Florida St. | 46 | 304 | 175 | 16 | .630 | 13 | 7 | 2 |
| Auburn | 100 | 547 | 335 | 46 | .614 | 12 | 9 | 2 |
| Colorado | 103 | 549 | 345 | 35 | .610 | 5 | 12 | 0 |
| Michigan St. | 96 | 515 | 322 | 43 | .610 | 5 | 5 | 0 |
| Miami (Fla.) | 66 | 402 | 257 | 19 | .607 | 10 | 9 | 0 |
| Bowling Green | 74 | 383 | 240 | 50 | .606 | 2 | 3 | 0 |
| Minnesota | 109 | 551 | 352 | 43 | .605 | 2 | 3 | 0 |
| UCLA | 74 | 429 | 276 | 37 | .603 | 10 | 7 | 1 |

## All-Time Division I-A Coaching Victories (Incl. Bowl Games)

| | | | | | |
|---|---|---|---|---|---|
| Paul "Bear" Bryant | 323 | Eddie Anderson | 201 | John Vaught | 190 |
| Amos Alonzo Stagg | 314 | Vince Dooley | 201 | John Heisman | 185 |
| Glenn "Pop" Warner | 313 | Dana Bible | 198 | Darrell Royal | 184 |
| Joe Paterno | 247 | Dan McGugin | 197 | Lou Holtz | 182 |
| Woody Hayes | 238 | Fielding Yost | 196 | Carl Snavely | 180 |
| Bo Schembechler | 234 | Tom Osborne | 195 | Gil Dobie | 180 |
| Bobby Bowden | 227 | Howard Jones | 194 | Jerry Claiborne | 179 |
| Jess Neely | 207 | Hayden Fry | 194 | Ben Schwartzwalder | 178 |
| Warren Woodson | 203 | LaVell Edwards | 191 | Jim Sweeney | 178 |

Eddie Robinson of Grambling State Univ. holds the record for most college football victories with 381 at the start of the 1993 season.

## National College Football Champions

The unofficial national champion as selected each year by the AP poll of writers and the USA Today-CNN (until 1992 the UPI) poll of coaches. When the polls disagree both teams are listed. The AP poll originated in 1936 and the UPI poll in 1950.

| | | | |
|---|---|---|---|
| 1936 Minnesota | 1951 Tennessee | 1965 Alabama, Mich. State | 1979 Alabama |
| 1937 Pittsburgh | 1952 Michigan State | 1966 Notre Dame | 1980 Georgia |
| 1938 Texas Christian | 1953 Maryland | 1967 Southern Cal. | 1981 Clemson |
| 1939 Texas A&M | 1954 Ohio State, UCLA | 1968 Ohio State | 1982 Penn State |
| 1940 Minnesota | 1955 Oklahoma | 1969 Texas | 1983 Miami (Fla.) |
| 1941 Minnesota | 1956 Oklahoma | 1970 Nebraska, Texas | 1984 Brigham Young |
| 1942 Ohio State | 1957 Auburn, Ohio State | 1971 Nebraska | 1985 Oklahoma |
| 1943 Notre Dame | 1958 Louisiana State | 1972 Southern Cal. | 1986 Penn State |
| 1944 Army | 1959 Syracuse | 1973 Notre Dame, Alabama | 1987 Miami (Fla.) |
| 1945 Army | 1960 Minnesota | 1974 Oklahoma, So. Cal. | 1988 Notre Dame |
| 1946 Notre Dame | 1961 Alabama | 1975 Oklahoma | 1989 Miami (Fla.) |
| 1947 Notre Dame | 1962 Southern Cal. | 1976 Pittsburgh | 1990 Colorado, Georgia Tech |
| 1948 Michigan | 1963 Texas | 1977 Notre Dame | 1991 Miami (Fla.), Washington |
| 1949 Notre Dame | 1964 Alabama | 1978 Alabama, So. Cal. | 1992 Alabama |
| 1950 Oklahoma | | | |

## College Football Coach of the Year

(Selected by the American Football Coaches Assn. & the Football Writers Assn. of America)

| AFCA | | FWAA | | AFCA |
|---|---|---|---|---|
| 1935 | Lynn Waldorf, Northwestern | 1957 | Woody Hayes, Ohio St. | Woody Hayes, Ohio St. |
| 1936 | Dick Harlow, Harvard | 1958 | Paul Dietzel, LSU | Paul Dietzel, LSU |
| 1937 | Edward Mylin, Lafayette | 1959 | Ben Schwartzwalder, Syracuse | Ben Schwartzwalder, Syracuse |
| 1938 | Bill Kern, Carnegie Tech | 1960 | Murray Warmath, Minnesota | Murray Warmath, Minnesota |
| 1939 | Eddie Anderson, Iowa | 1961 | Darrell Royal, Texas | Paul "Bear" Bryant, Alabama |
| 1940 | Clark Shaughnessy, Stanford | 1962 | John McKay, USC | John McKay, USC |
| 1941 | Frank Leahy, Notre Dame | 1963 | Darrell Royal, Texas | Darrell Royal, Texas |
| 1942 | Bill Alexander, Georgia Tech | 1964 | Ara Parseghian, Notre Dame | Frank Broyles, Arkansas; |
| | | | | Ara Paraseghian, Notre Dame |
| 1943 | Amos Alonzo Stagg, Pacific | 1965 | Duffy Daugherty, Michigan St. | Tommy Prothro, UCLA |
| 1944 | Carroll Widdoes, Ohio St. | 1966 | Tom Cahill, Army | Tom Cahill, Army |
| 1945 | Bo McMillin, Indiana | 1967 | John Pont, Indiana | John Pont, Indiana |
| 1946 | Earl "Red" Blaik, Army | 1968 | Woody Hayes, Ohio St. | Joe Paterno, Penn St. |
| 1947 | Fritz Crisler, Michigan | 1969 | Bo Schembechler, Michigan | Bo Schembechler, Michigan |
| 1948 | Bennie Oosterbaan, Michigan | 1970 | Alex Agase, Northwestern | Charles McClendon, LSU; |
| | | | | Darrell Royal, Texas |
| 1949 | Bud Wilkinson, Oklahoma | 1971 | Bob Devaney, Nebraska | Paul "Bear" Bryant, Alabama |
| 1950 | Charlie Caldwell, Princeton | 1972 | John McKay, USC | John McKay, USC |
| 1951 | Chuck Taylor, Stanford | 1973 | Johnny Majors, Pittsburgh | Paul "Bear" Bryant, Alabama |
| 1952 | Biggie Munn, Michigan St. | 1974 | Grant Teaff, Baylor | Grant Teaff, Baylor |
| 1953 | Jim Tatum, Maryland | 1975 | Woody Hayes, Ohio St. | Frank Kush, Arizona St. |
| 1954 | Henry "Red" Sanders, UCLA | 1976 | Johnny Majors, Pittsburgh | Johnny Majors, Pittsburgh |
| 1955 | Duffy Daugherty, Michigan St. | 1977 | Lou Holtz, Arkansas | Don James, Washington |
| 1956 | Bowden Wyatt, Tennessee | 1978 | Joe Paterno, Penn St. | Joe Paterno, Penn St. |
| | | 1979 | Earle Bruce, Ohio St. | Earle Bruce, Ohio St. |
| | | 1980 | Vince Dooley, Georgia | Vince Dooley, Georgia |
| | | 1981 | Danny Ford, Clemson | Danny Ford, Clemson |
| | | 1982 | Joe Paterno, Penn St. | Joe Paterno, Penn St. |
| | | 1983 | Howard Schnellenberger, Miami (Fla.) | Ken Hatfield, Air Force |
| | | 1984 | LaVell Edwards, Brigham Young | LaVell Edwards, Brigham Young |
| | | 1985 | Fisher De Berry, Air Force | Fisher De Berry, Air Force |
| | | 1986 | Joe Paterno, Penn St. | Joe Paterno, Penn St. |
| | | 1987 | Dick MacPherson, Syracuse | Dick MacPherson, Syracuse |
| | | 1988 | Lou Holtz, Notre Dame | Don Nehlen, W. Virginia |
| | | 1989 | Bill McCartney, Colorado | Bill McCartney, Colorado |
| | | 1990 | Bobby Ross, Georgia Tech | Bobby Ross, Georgia Tech |
| | | 1991 | Don James, Washington | Don James, Washington |
| | | 1992 | Gene Stallings, Alabama | Gene Stallings, Alabama |

## Longest Division I-A Winning Streaks

### (Includes Bowl Games)

| Wins | Team | Years | Ended by | Score |
|---|---|---|---|---|
| 47 | Oklahoma | 1953-57 | Notre Dame | 7-0 |
| 39 | Washington | 1908-14 | Oregon State | 0-0 |
| 37 | Yale | 1890-93 | Princeton | 6-0 |
| 37 | Yale | 1887-89 | Princeton | 10-0 |
| 35 | Toledo | 1969-71 | Tampa | 21-0 |
| 34 | Pennsylvania | 1894-96 | Lafayette | 6-4 |
| 31 | Oklahoma | 1948-50 | Kentucky | 13-7 |
| 31 | Pittsburgh | 1914-18 | Cleveland Naval Reserve | 10-9 |
| 31 | Pennsylvania | 1896-98 | Harvard | 10-0 |
| 30 | Texas | 1968-70 | Notre Dame | 24-11 |
| 29 | Michigan | 1901-03 | Minnesota | 6-6 |
| 29 | Miami (Fla.) | 1990-93 | Alabama | 34-13 |
| 28 | Alabama | 1978-80 | Mississippi State | 6-3 |
| 28 | Oklahoma | 1973-75 | Kansas | 23-3 |
| 28 | Michigan State | 1950-53 | Purdue | 6-0 |
| 27 | Nebraska | 1901-04 | Colorado | 6-0 |
| 26 | Cornell | 1921-24 | Williams | 14-7 |
| 26 | Michigan | 1903-05 | Chicago | 2-0 |
| 25 | Michigan | 1946-49 | Army | 21-7 |
| 25 | Army | 1944-46 | Notre Dame | 0-0 |
| 25 | Southern Cal | 1931-33 | Oregon State | 0-0 |
| 25 | Brigham Young | 1983-85 | UCLA | 27-24 |

# College Football Conference Champions

| | Atlantic Coast | | Ivy | | Big Eight | | Big Ten |
|---|---|---|---|---|---|---|---|
| 1979 | No. Carolina St. | 1979 | Yale | 1979 | Oklahoma | 1979 | Ohio State |
| 1980 | North Carolina | 1980 | Yale | 1980 | Oklahoma | 1980 | Michigan |
| 1981 | Clemson | 1981 | Yale, Dartmouth | 1981 | Nebraska | 1981 | Iowa, Ohio State |
| 1982 | Clemson | 1982 | Harvard, Dartmouth, Penn | 1982 | Nebraska | 1982 | Michigan |
| 1983 | Maryland | 1983 | Harvard, Penn | 1983 | Nebraska | 1983 | Illinois |
| 1984 | Maryland | 1984 | Penn | 1984 | Nebraska, Oklahoma | 1984 | Ohio State |
| 1985 | Maryland | 1985 | Penn | 1985 | Oklahoma | 1985 | Iowa |
| 1986 | Clemson | 1986 | Penn | 1986 | Oklahoma | 1986 | Michigan, Ohio State |
| 1987 | Clemson | 1987 | Harvard | 1987 | Oklahoma | 1987 | Michigan St. |
| 1988 | Clemson | 1988 | Penn, Cornell | 1988 | Nebraska | 1988 | Michigan |
| 1989 | Virginia, Duke | 1989 | Yale, Princeton | 1989 | Colorado | 1989 | Michigan |
| 1990 | Georgia Tech | 1990 | Dartmouth | 1990 | Colorado | 1990 | Iowa, Illinois, Michigan, Michigan St. |
| 1991 | Clemson | 1991 | Dartmouth | 1991 | Nebraska, Colorado | 1991 | Michigan |
| 1992 | Florida St. | 1992 | Dartmouth, Princeton | 1992 | Nebraska | 1992 | Michigan |

| | Mid-America | | Southern | | Southeastern | | Southwest |
|---|---|---|---|---|---|---|---|
| 1979 | Central Michigan | 1979 | Tenn.-Chattanooga | 1979 | Alabama | 1979 | Houston, Arkansas |
| 1980 | Central Michigan | 1980 | Furman | 1980 | Georgia | 1980 | Baylor |
| 1981 | Toledo | 1981 | Furman | 1981 | Georgia, Alabama | 1981 | SMU |
| 1982 | Bowling Green | 1982 | Furman | 1982 | Georgia | 1982 | SMU |
| 1983 | Northern Illinois | 1983 | Furman | 1983 | Auburn | 1983 | Texas |
| 1984 | Toledo | 1984 | Tenn.-Chattanooga | 1984 | Florida (title vacated) | 1984 | SMU, Houston |
| 1985 | Bowling Green | 1985 | Furman | 1985 | Tennessee | 1985 | Texas A&M |
| 1986 | Miami | 1986 | Appalachian St. | 1986 | LSU | 1986 | Texas A&M |
| 1987 | E. Michigan | 1987 | Appalachian St. | 1987 | Auburn | 1987 | Texas A&M |
| 1988 | W. Michigan | 1988 | Marshall, Furman | 1988 | Auburn, LSU | 1988 | Arkansas |
| 1989 | Ball State | 1989 | Furman | 1989 | Alabama, Tennessee, Auburn | 1989 | Arkansas |
| 1990 | Central Michigan | 1990 | Furman | 1990 | Tennessee | 1990 | Texas |
| 1991 | Bowling Green | 1991 | Appalachian St. | 1991 | Florida | 1991 | Texas A&M |
| 1992 | Bowling Green | 1992 | Citadel | 1992 | Alabama | 1992 | Texas A&M |

| | Pacific Ten | | Western Athletic | | Big West |
|---|---|---|---|---|---|
| 1979 | USC | 1979 | Brigham Young | 1979 | San Jose St. |
| 1980 | Washington | 1980 | Brigham Young | 1980 | Long Beach State |
| 1981 | Washington | 1981 | Brigham Young | 1981 | San Jose State |
| 1982 | UCLA | 1982 | Brigham Young | 1982 | Fresno State |
| 1983 | UCLA | 1983 | Brigham Young | 1983 | Cal State-Fullerton |
| 1984 | USC | 1984 | Brigham Young | 1984 | Nevada-Las Vegas |
| 1985 | UCLA | 1985 | Brigham Young, Air Force | 1985 | Fresno State |
| 1986 | Arizona State | 1986 | San Diego State | 1986 | San Jose State |
| 1987 | UCLA, USC | 1987 | Wyoming | 1987 | San Jose State |
| 1988 | USC | 1988 | Wyoming | 1988 | Fresno State |
| 1989 | USC | 1989 | Brigham Young | 1989 | Fresno State |
| 1990 | Washington | 1990 | Brigham Young | 1990 | San Jose State |
| 1991 | Washington | 1991 | Brigham Young | 1991 | San Jose St., Fresno St. |
| 1992 | Washington, Stanford | 1992 | Hawaii, Brigham Young | 1992 | Nevada-Reno |

# Canadian Football League

## Grey Cup Championship Game

| | | | |
|---|---|---|---|
| 1956 | Edmonton Eskimos 50, Montreal Alouettes 27 | 1975 | Edmonton Eskimos 9, Montreal Alouettes 8 |
| 1957 | Hamilton Tiger-Cats 32, Winnipeg Blue Bombers 7 | 1976 | Ottawa Rough Riders 23, Saskatchewan Roughriders 20 |
| 1958 | Winnipeg Blue Bombers 35, Hamilton Tiger-Cats 28 | 1977 | Montreal Alouettes 41, Edmonton Eskimos 6 |
| 1959 | Winnipeg Blue Bombers 21, Hamilton Tiger-Cats 7 | 1978 | Edmonton Eskimos 20, Montreal Alouettes 13 |
| 1960 | Ottawa Rough Riders 16, Edmonton Eskimos 6 | 1979 | Edmonton Eskimos 17, Montreal Alouettes 9 |
| 1961 | Winnipeg Blue Bombers 21, Hamilton Tiger-Cats 14 | 1980 | Edmonton Eskimos 48, Hamilton Tiger-Cats 10 |
| 1962 | Winnipeg Blue Bombers 28, Hamilton Tiger-Cats 27 | 1981 | Edmonton Eskimos 26, Ottawa Rough Riders 23 |
| 1963 | Hamilton Tiger-Cats 21, British Columbia Lions 10 | 1982 | Edmonton Eskimos 32, Toronto Argonauts 16 |
| 1964 | British Columbia Lions 34, Hamilton Tiger-Cats 24 | 1983 | Toronto Argonauts 18, B.C. Lions 17 |
| 1965 | Hamilton Tiger-Cats 22, Winnipeg Blue Bombers 16 | 1984 | Winnipeg Blue Bombers 47, Hamilton Tiger-Cats 17 |
| 1966 | Saskatchewan Roughriders 29, Ottawa Rough Riders 14 | 1985 | B.C. Lions 37, Hamilton Tiger-Cats 24 |
| 1967 | Hamilton Tiger-Cats 24, Saskatchewan Roughriders 1 | 1986 | Hamilton Tiger-Cats 39, Edmonton Eskimos 15 |
| 1968 | Ottawa Rough Riders 24, Calgary Stampeders 21 | 1987 | Edmonton Eskimos 38, Toronto Argonauts 36 |
| 1969 | Ottawa Rough Riders 29, Saskatchewan Roughriders 11 | 1988 | Winnipeg Blue Bombers 22, B.C. Lions 21 |
| 1970 | Montreal Alouettes 23, Calgary Stampeders 10 | 1989 | Saskatchewan Roughriders 43, Hamilton Tiger-Cats 40 |
| 1971 | Calgary Stampeders 14, Toronto Argonauts 11 | 1990 | Winnipeg Blue Bombers 50, Edmonton Eskimos 11 |
| 1972 | Hamilton Tiger-Cats 13, Saskatchewan Roughriders 10 | 1991 | Toronto Argonauts 36, Calgary Stampeders 21 |
| 1973 | Ottawa Rough Riders 22, Edmonton Eskimos 18 | 1992 | Calgary Stampeders 24, Winnipeg Blue Bombers 10 |
| 1974 | Montreal Alouettes 20, Edmonton Eskimos 7 | | |

## CFL Teams, Divisions

(at start of 1993 season)

| Western Division | Eastern Division |
|---|---|
| British Columbia Lions | Hamilton Tiger-Cats |
| Calgary Stampeders | Ottawa Rough Riders |
| Edmonton Eskimos | Toronto Argonauts |
| Sacramento Gold Miners | Winnipeg Blue Bombers |
| Saskatchewan Roughriders | |

# NATIONAL FOOTBALL LEAGUE
## Final 1992 Standings

### National Conference

#### Eastern Division

| | W | L | T | Pct | Pts | Opp |
|---|---|---|---|---|---|---|
| Dallas | 13 | 3 | 0 | .813 | 409 | 243 |
| Philadelphia | 11 | 5 | 0 | .688 | 354 | 245 |
| Washington | 9 | 7 | 0 | .563 | 300 | 255 |
| N.Y. Giants | 6 | 10 | 0 | .375 | 306 | 367 |
| Phoenix | 4 | 12 | 0 | .250 | 243 | 332 |

#### Central Division

| | W | L | T | Pct | Pts | Opp |
|---|---|---|---|---|---|---|
| Minnesota | 11 | 5 | 0 | .688 | 374 | 249 |
| Green Bay | 9 | 7 | 0 | .563 | 276 | 296 |
| Tampa Bay | 5 | 11 | 0 | .313 | 267 | 365 |
| Chicago | 5 | 11 | 0 | .313 | 295 | 361 |
| Detroit | 5 | 11 | 0 | .313 | 273 | 332 |

#### Western Division

| | W | L | T | Pct | Pts | Opp |
|---|---|---|---|---|---|---|
| San Francisco | 14 | 2 | 0 | .875 | 431 | 236 |
| New Orleans | 12 | 4 | 0 | .750 | 330 | 202 |
| Atlanta | 6 | 10 | 0 | .375 | 327 | 414 |
| L.A. Rams | 6 | 10 | 0 | .375 | 313 | 383 |

### American Conference

#### Eastern Division

| | W | L | T | Pct | Pts | Opp |
|---|---|---|---|---|---|---|
| Miami | 11 | 5 | 0 | .688 | 340 | 281 |
| Buffalo | 11 | 5 | 0 | .688 | 381 | 283 |
| Indianapolis | 9 | 7 | 0 | .563 | 216 | 302 |
| N.Y. Jets | 4 | 12 | 0 | .250 | 220 | 315 |
| New England | 2 | 14 | 0 | .125 | 205 | 363 |

#### Central Division

| | W | L | T | Pct | Pts | Opp |
|---|---|---|---|---|---|---|
| Pittsburgh | 11 | 5 | 0 | .688 | 299 | 225 |
| Houston | 10 | 6 | 0 | .625 | 352 | 258 |
| Cleveland | 7 | 9 | 0 | .438 | 272 | 275 |
| Cincinnati | 5 | 11 | 0 | .313 | 274 | 364 |

#### Western Division

| | W | L | T | Pct | Pts | Opp |
|---|---|---|---|---|---|---|
| San Diego | 11 | 5 | 0 | .688 | 335 | 241 |
| Kansas City | 10 | 6 | 0 | .625 | 348 | 282 |
| Denver | 8 | 8 | 0 | .500 | 262 | 329 |
| L.A. Raiders | 7 | 9 | 0 | .438 | 249 | 281 |
| Seattle | 2 | 14 | 0 | .125 | 140 | 312 |

**NFC Playoffs**—Washington 24, Minnesota 7; Philadelphia 36, New Orleans 20; Dallas 34, Philadelphia 10; San Francisco 20, Washington 13; Dallas 30, San Francisco 20.

**AFC Playoffs**—San Diego 17, Kansas City 0; Buffalo 41, Houston 38; Miami 31, San Diego 0; Buffalo 24, Pittsburgh 3; Buffalo 29, Miami 10.

## National Football League Champions

| Year | East Winner (W-L-T) | West Winner (W-L-T) | Playoff |
|---|---|---|---|
| 1933 | New York Giants (11-3-0) | Chicago Bears (10-2-1) | Chicago Bears 23, New York 21 |
| 1934 | New York Giants (8-5-0) | Chicago Bears (13-0-0) | New York 30, Chicago Bears 13 |
| 1935 | New York Giants (9-3-0) | Detroit Lions (7-3-2) | Detroit 26, New York 7 |
| 1936 | Boston Redskins (7-5-0) | Green Bay Packers (10-1-1) | Green Bay 21, Boston 6 |
| 1937 | Washington Redskins (8-3-0) | Chicago Bears (9-1-1) | Washington 28, Chicago Bears 21 |
| 1938 | New York Giants (8-2-1) | Green Bay Packers (8-3-0) | New York 23, Green Bay 17 |
| 1939 | New York Giants (9-1-1) | Green Bay Packers (9-2-0) | Green Bay 27, New York 0 |
| 1940 | Washington Redskins (9-2-0) | Chicago Bears (8-3-0) | Chicago Bears 73, Washington 0 |
| 1941 | New York Giants (8-3-0) | Chicago Bears (10-1-1)(a) | Chicago Bears 37, New York 9 |
| 1942 | Wash. Redskins (10-1-1) | Chicago Bears (11-0-0) | Washington 14, Chicago Bears 6 |
| 1943 | Wash. Redskins (6-3-1)(a) | Chicago Bears (8-1-1) | Chicago Bears, 41, Washington 21 |
| 1944 | New York Giants (8-1-1) | Green Bay Packers (8-2-0) | Green Bay 14, New York 7 |
| 1945 | Wash. Redskins (8-2-0) | Cleveland Rams (9-1-0) | Cleveland 15, Washington 14 |
| 1946 | New York Giants (7-3-1) | Chicago Bears (8-2-1) | Chicago Bears 24, New York 14 |
| 1947 | Philadelphia Eagles (8-4-0)(a) | Chicago Cardinals (9-3-0) | Chicago Cardinals 28, Philadelphia 21 |
| 1948 | Philadelphia Eagles (9-2-1) | Chicago Cardinals (11-1-0) | Philadelphia 7, Chicago Cardinals 0 |
| 1949 | Philadelphia Eagles (11-1-0) | Los Angeles Rams (8-2-2) | Philadelphia 14, Los Angeles 0 |
| 1950 | Cleveland Browns (10-2-0)(a) | Los Angeles Rams (9-3-0)(a) | Cleveland 30, Los Angeles 28 |
| 1951 | Cleveland Browns (11-1-0) | Los Angeles Rams (8-4-0) | Los Angeles 24, Cleveland 17 |
| 1952 | Cleveland Browns (8-4-0) | Detroit Lions (9-3-0)(a) | Detroit 17, Cleveland 7 |
| 1953 | Cleveland Browns (11-1-0) | Detroit Lions (10-2-0) | Detroit 17, Cleveland 16 |
| 1954 | Cleveland Browns (9-3-0) | Detroit Lions (9-2-1) | Cleveland 56, Detroit 10 |
| 1955 | Cleveland Browns (9-2-1) | Los Angeles Rams (8-3-1) | Cleveland 38, Los Angeles 14 |
| 1956 | New York Giants (8-3-1) | Chicago Bears (9-2-1) | New York 47, Chicago Bears 7 |
| 1957 | Cleveland Browns (9-2-1) | Detroit Lions (8-4-0)(a) | Detroit 59, Cleveland 14 |
| 1958 | New York Giants (9-3-0)(a) | Baltimore Colts (9-3-0) | Baltimore 23, New York 17(b) |
| 1959 | New York Giants (10-2-0) | Baltimore Colts (9-3-0) | Baltimore 31, New York 16 |
| 1960 | Philadelphia Eagles (10-2-0) | Green Bay Packers (8-4-0) | Philadelphia 17, Green Bay 13 |
| 1961 | New York Giants (10-3-1) | Green Bay Packers (11-3-0) | Green Bay 37, New York 0 |
| 1962 | New York Giants (12-2-0) | Green Bay Packers (13-1-0) | Green Bay 16, New York 7 |
| 1963 | New York Giants (11-3-0) | Chicago Bears (11-1-2) | Chicago 14, New York 10 |
| 1964 | Cleveland Browns (10-3-1) | Baltimore Colts (12-2-0) | Cleveland 27, Baltimore 0 |
| 1965 | Cleveland Browns (11-3-0) | Green Bay Packers (10-3-1)(a) | Green Bay 23, Cleveland 12 |
| 1966 | Dallas Cowboys (10-3-1) | Green Bay Packers (12-2-0) | Green Bay 34, Dallas 27 |

(a) Won divisional playoff. (b) Won at 8:15 sudden death overtime period.

| Year | Conference | Division | Winner (W-L-T) | Playoff |
|---|---|---|---|---|
| 1967 | East | Century | Cleveland (9-5-0) | Dallas 52, Cleveland 14 |
| | | Capitol | Dallas (9-5-0) | |
| | West | Central | Green Bay (9-4-1) | Green Bay 28, Los Angeles 7 |
| | | Coastal | Los Angeles (11-1-2)(a) | Green Bay 21, Dallas 17 |
| 1968 | East | Century | Cleveland (10-4-0) | Cleveland 31, Dallas 20 |
| | | Capitol | Dallas (12-2-0) | |
| | West | Central | Minnesota (8-6-0) | Baltimore 24, Minnesota 14 |
| | | Coastal | Baltimore (13-1-0) | Baltimore 34, Cleveland 0 |

(continued )

| Year | Conference | Division | Winner (W-L-T) | Playoff |
|---|---|---|---|---|
| 1969 | East | Century | Cleveland (10-3-1) | Cleveland 38, Dallas 14 |
| | | Capitol | Dallas (11-2-1) | |
| | West. | Central | Minnesota (12-2-0) | Minnesota 23, Los Angeles 20 |
| | | Coastal | Los Angeles (11-3-0) | Minnesota 27, Cleveland 7 |
| 1970 | American | Eastern | Baltimore (11-2-1) | Baltimore 17, Cincinnati 0 |
| | | Central | Cincinnati (8-6-0) | Oakland 21, Miami 14 |
| | | Western | Oakland (8-4-2) | Baltimore 27, Oakland 17 |
| | National | Eastern | Dallas (10-4-0) | Dallas 5, Detroit 0 |
| | | Central | Minnesota (12-2-0) | San Francisco 17, Minnesota 14 |
| | | Western | San Francisco (10-3-1) | Dallas 17, San Francisco 10 |
| 1971 | American | Eastern | Miami (10-3-1) | Miami 27, Kansas City 24 |
| | | Central | Cleveland (9-5-0) | Baltimore 20, Cleveland 3 |
| | | Western | Kansas City (10-3-1) | Miami 21, Baltimore 0 |
| | National | Eastern | Dallas (11-3-0) | Dallas 20, Minnesota 12 |
| | | Central | Minnesota (11-3-0) | San Francisco 24, Washington 20 |
| | | Western | San Francisco (9-5-0) | Dallas 14, San Francisco 3 |
| 1972 | American | Eastern | Miami (14-0-0) | Miami 20, Cleveland 14 |
| | | Central | Pittsburgh (11-3-0) | Pittsburgh 13, Oakland 7 |
| | | Western | Oakland (10-3-1) | Miami 21, Pittsburgh 17 |
| | National | Eastern | Washington (11-3-0) | Washington 16, Green Bay 3 |
| | | Central | Green Bay (10-4-0) | Dallas 30, San Francisco 28 |
| | | Western | San Francisco (8-5-1) | Washington 26, Dallas 3 |
| 1973 | American | Eastern | Miami (12-2-0) | Miami 34, Cincinnati 16 |
| | | Central | Cincinnati (10-4-0) | Oakland 33, Pittsburgh 14 |
| | | Western | Oakland (9-4-1) | Miami 27, Oakland 10 |
| | National | Eastern | Dallas (10-4-0) | Dallas 27, Los Angeles 16 |
| | | Central | Minnesota (12-2-0) | Minnesota 27, Washington 20 |
| | | Western | Los Angeles (12-2-0) | Minnesota 27, Dallas 10 |
| 1974 | American | Eastern | Miami (11-3-0) | Oakland 28, Miami 26 |
| | | Central | Pittsburgh (10-3-1) | Pittsburgh 32, Buffalo 14 |
| | | Western | Oakland (12-2-0) | Pittsburgh 24, Oakland 13 |
| | National | Eastern | St. Louis (10-4-0) | Minnesota 30, St. Louis 14 |
| | | Central | Minnesota (10-4-0) | Los Angeles 19, Washington 10 |
| | | Western | Los Angeles (10-4-0) | Minnesota 14, Los Angeles 10 |
| 1975 | American | Eastern | Baltimore (10-4-0) | Pittsburgh 28, Baltimore 10 |
| | | Central | Pittsburgh (12-2-0) | Oakland 31, Cincinnati 28 |
| | | Western | Oakland (11-3-0) | Pittsburgh 16, Oakland 10 |
| | National | Eastern | St. Louis (11-3-0) | Dallas 17, Minnesota 14 |
| | | Central | Minnesota (12-2-0) | Los Angeles 35, St. Louis 23 |
| | | Western | Los Angeles (12-2-0) | Dallas 37, Los Angeles 7 |
| 1976 | American | Eastern | Baltimore (11-3-0) | Pittsburgh 40, Baltimore 14 |
| | | Central | Pittsburgh (10-4-0) | Oakland 24, New England 21 |
| | | Western | Oakland (13-1-0) | Oakland 24, Pittsburgh 7 |
| | National | Eastern | Dallas (11-3-0) | Minnesota 35, Washington 20 |
| | | Central | Minnesota (11-2-1) | Los Angeles 14, Dallas 12 |
| | | Western | Los Angeles (10-3-1) | Minnesota 24, Los Angeles 13 |
| 1977 | American | Eastern | Baltimore (10-4-0) | Oakland 37, Baltimore 31 |
| | | Central | Pittsburgh (9-5-0) | Denver 34, Pittsburgh 21 |
| | | Western | Denver (12-2-0) | Dallas 37, Chicago 7 |
| | National | Eastern | Dallas (12-2-0) | Minnesota 14, Los Angeles 7 |
| | | Central | Minnesota (9-5-0) | Denver 20, Oakland 17 |
| | | Western | Los Angeles (10-4-0) | Dallas 23, Minnesota 6 |
| 1978 | American | Eastern | New England (11-5-0) | Pittsburgh 33, Denver 10 |
| | | Central | Pittsburgh (14-2-0) | Houston 31, New England 14 |
| | | Western | Denver (10-6-0) | Pittsburgh 34, Houston 5 |
| | National | Eastern | Dallas (12-4-0) | Dallas 27, Atlanta 20 |
| | | Central | Minnesota (8-7-1) | Los Angeles 34, Minnesota 10 |
| | | Western | Los Angeles (12-4-0) | Dallas 28, Los Angeles 0 |
| 1979 | American | Eastern | Miami (10-6-0) | Houston 17, San Diego 14 |
| | | Central | Pittsburgh (12-4-0) | Pittsburgh 34, Miami 14 |
| | | Western | San Diego (12-4-0) | Pittsburgh 27, Houston 13 |
| | National | Eastern | Dallas (11-5-0) | Tampa Bay 24, Philadelphia 17 |
| | | Central | Tampa Bay (10-6-0) | Los Angeles 21, Dallas 19 |
| | | Western | Los Angeles (9-7-0) | Los Angeles 9, Tampa Bay 0 |
| 1980 | American | Eastern | Buffalo (11-5-0) | San Diego 20, Buffalo 14 |
| | | Central | Cleveland (11-5-0) | Oakland 14, Cleveland 12 |
| | | Western | San Diego (11-5-0) | Oakland 34, San Diego 27 |
| | National | Eastern | Philadelphia (12-4-0) | Philadelphia 31, Minnesota 16 |
| | | Central | Minnesota (9-7-0) | Dallas 30, Atlanta 27 |
| | | Western | Atlanta (12-4-0) | Philadelphia 20, Dallas 7 |
| 1981 | American | Eastern | Miami (11-4-1) | San Diego 41, Miami 38 |
| | | Central | Cincinnati (12-4-0) | Cincinnati 28, Buffalo 21 |
| | | Western | San Diego (10-6-0) | Cincinnati 27, San Diego 7 |
| | National | Eastern | Dallas (12-4-0) | Dallas 38, Tampa Bay 0 |
| | | Central | Tampa Bay (9-7-0) | San Francisco 38, N.Y. Giants 24 |
| | | Western | San Francisco (13-3-0) | San Francisco 28, Dallas 27 |
| 1982 | American | | L.A. Raiders (8-1-0) | |
| | National | | Washington (8-1-0) | Strike-shortened season |

**AFC playoffs**—Miami 28, New England 13; L.A. Raiders 27, Cleveland 10; N.Y. Jets 44, Cincinnati 17; San Diego 31, Pittsburgh 28; N.Y. Jets 17, L.A. Raiders 14; Miami 34, San Diego 13; Miami 14, N.Y. Jets 0. **NFC playoffs**—Washington 31, Detroit 7; Green Bay 41, St. Louis 16; Dallas 30, Tampa Bay 17; Minnesota 30, Atlanta 24; Washington 21, Minnesota 7; Dallas 37, Green Bay 26; Washington 31, Dallas 17.

| 1983 | American | Eastern | Miami (12-4-0) | Seattle 27, Miami 20 |
|---|---|---|---|---|
| | | Central | Pittsburgh (10-6-0) | L.A. Raiders 38, Pittsburgh 10 |
| | | Western | L.A. Raiders (12-4-0) | L.A. Raiders 30, Seattle 14 |
| | National | Eastern | Washington (14-2-0) | Washington 51, L.A. Rams 7 |

| Year | Conference | Division | Winner (W-L-T) | Playoff |
|---|---|---|---|---|
| | | Central | Detroit (9-7-0) | San Francisco 24, Detroit 23 |
| | | Western | San Francisco (10-6-0) | Washington 24, San Francisco 21 |
| 1984 | American | Eastern | Miami (14-2-0) | Miami 31, Seattle 10 |
| | | Central | Pittsburgh (9-7-0) | Pittsburgh 24, Denver 17 |
| | | Western | Denver (13-3-0) | Miami 45, Pittsburgh 28 |
| | National | Eastern | Washington (11-5-0) | Chicago 23, Washington 19 |
| | | Central | Chicago (10-6-0) | San Francisco 21, N.Y. Giants 10 |
| | | Western | San Francisco (15-1-0) | San Francisco 23, Chicago 0 |
| 1985 | American | Eastern | Miami (12-4-0) | New England 27, L.A. Raiders 20 |
| | | Central | Cleveland (8-8-0) | Miami 24, Cleveland 21 |
| | | Western | L.A. Raiders (12-4-0) | New England 31, Miami 14 |
| | National | Eastern | Dallas (10-6-0) | Chicago 21, N.Y. Giants 0 |
| | | Central | Chicago (15-1-0) | L.A. Rams 20, Dallas 0 |
| | | Western | L.A. Rams (11-5-0) | Chicago 24, L.A. Rams 0 |
| 1986 | American | Eastern | New England (11-5-0) | Denver 22, New England 17 |
| | | Central | Cleveland (12-4-0) | Cleveland 23, N.Y. Jets 20 |
| | | Western | Denver (11-5-0) | Denver 23, Cleveland 20 |
| | National | Eastern | N.Y. Giants (14-2-0) | N.Y. Giants 49, San Francisco 3 |
| | | Central | Chicago (14-2-0) | Washington 27, Chicago 13 |
| | | Western | San Francisco (10-5-1) | N.Y. Giants 17, Washington 0 |
| 1987 | American | Eastern | Indianapolis (9-6-0) | Cleveland 38, Indianapolis 21 |
| | | Central | Cleveland (10-5-0) | Denver 34, Houston 10 |
| | | Western | Denver (10-4-1) | Denver 38, Cleveland 33 |
| | National | Eastern | Washington (11-4-0) | Washington 21, Chicago 17 |
| | | Central | Chicago (11-4-0) | Minnesota 36, San Francisco 24 |
| | | Western | San Francisco (13-2-0) | Washington 17, Minnesota 10 |
| 1988 | American | Eastern | Buffalo (12-4-0) | Buffalo 17, Houston 10 |
| | | Central | Cincinnati (12-4-0) | Cincinnati 21, Seattle 13 |
| | | Western | Seattle (9-7-0) | Cincinnati 21, Buffalo 10 |
| | National | Eastern | Philadelphia (10-6-0) | Chicago 20, Philadelphia 12 |
| | | Central | Chicago (12-4-0) | San Francisco 34, Minnesota 9 |
| | | Western | San Francisco (10-6-0) | San Francisco 28, Chicago 3 |
| 1989 | American | Eastern | Buffalo (9-7-0) | Cleveland 34, Buffalo 30 |
| | | Central | Cleveland (9-6-1) | Denver 24, Pittsburgh 23 |
| | | Western | Denver (11-5-0) | Denver 37, Cleveland 21 |
| | National | Eastern | N.Y. Giants (12-4-0) | San Francisco 41, Minnesota 13 |
| | | Central | Minnesota (10-6-0) | L.A. Rams 19, N.Y. Giants 13 |
| | | Western | San Francisco (14-2-0) | San Francisco 30, L.A. Rams 3 |
| 1990 | American | Eastern | Buffalo (13-3-0) | L.A. Raiders 20, Cincinnati 10 |
| | | Central | Cincinnati (9-7-0) | Buffalo 44, Miami 34 |
| | | Western | L.A. Raiders (12-4-0) | Buffalo 51, L.A. Raiders 3 |
| | National | Eastern | N.Y. Giants (13-3-0) | San Francisco 28, Washington 10 |
| | | Central | Chicago (11-5-0) | N.Y. Giants 31, Chicago 3 |
| | | Western | San Francisco (14-2-0) | N.Y. Giants 15, San Francisco 13 |
| 1991 | American | Eastern | Buffalo (13-3-0) | Denver 26, Houston 24 |
| | | Central | Houston (11-5-0) | Buffalo 37, Kansas City 14 |
| | | Western | Denver (12-4-0) | Buffalo 10, Denver 7 |
| | National | Eastern | Washington (14-2-0) | Washington 24, Atlanta 7 |
| | | Central | Detroit (12-4-0) | Detroit 38, Dallas 6 |
| | | Western | New Orleans (11-5-0) | Washington 41, Detroit 10 |
| 1992 | American | Eastern | Miami (11-5-0) | Miami 31, San Diego 0 |
| | | Central | Pittsburgh (11-5-0) | Buffalo 24, Pittsburgh 3 |
| | | Western | San Diego (11-5-0) | Buffalo 29, Miami 10 |
| | National | Eastern | Dallas (13-3-0) | Dallas 34, Philadelphia 10 |
| | | Central | Minnesota (11-5-0) | San Francisco 20, Washington 13 |
| | | Western | San Francisco (14-2-0) | Dallas 30, San Francisco 20 |

## NFL Head Coaches at Start of 1993 Season

**AFC**

Buffalo—Marv Levy
Cincinnati—David Shula
Cleveland—Bill Belichick
Denver—Wade Phillips
Houston—Jack Pardee
Indianapolis—Ted Marchibroda
Kansas City—Marty Schottenheimer
L.A. Raiders—Art Shell
Miami—Don Shula

New England—Bill Parcells
N.Y. Jets—Bruce Coslet
Pittsburgh—Bill Cowher
San Diego—Bobby Ross
Seattle—Tom Flores

**NFC**

Atlanta—Jerry Glanville
Chicago—Dave Wannstedt
Dallas—Jimmy Johnson

Detroit—Wayne Fontes
Green Bay—Mike Holmgren
L.A. Rams—Chuck Knox
Minnesota—Dennis Green
New Orleans—Jim Mora
N.Y. Giants—Dan Reeves
Philadelphia—Rich Kotite
Phoenix—Joe Bugel
San Francisco—George Seifert
Tampa Bay—Sam Wyche
Washington—Joe Gibbs

## George Halas Trophy Winners

The George Halas Trophy is awarded annually to the outstanding defensive player in the NFL as chosen by a panel of sports experts.

| | | | | | |
|---|---|---|---|---|---|
| 1966 | Larry Wilson, St. Louis | 1976 | Jerry Sherk, Cleveland | 1985 | Howie Long, L.A. Raiders |
| 1967 | Deacon Jones, Los Angeles | 1977 | Harvey Martin, Dallas | | Andre Tippett, New England |
| 1968 | Deacon Jones, Los Angeles | 1978 | Randy Gradishar, Denver | 1986 | Lawrence Taylor, N.Y. Giants |
| 1969 | Dick Butkus, Chicago | 1979 | Lee Roy Selmon, Tampa Bay | 1987 | Reggie White, Philadelphia |
| 1970 | Dick Butkus, Chicago | 1980 | Lester Hayes, Oakland | 1988 | Mike Singletary, Chicago |
| 1971 | Carl Eller, Minnesota | 1981 | Joe Klecko, N.Y. Jets | 1989 | Tim Harris, Green Bay |
| 1972 | Joe Greene, Pittsburgh | 1982 | Mark Gastineau, N.Y. Jets | 1990 | Bruce Smith, Buffalo |
| 1973 | Alan Page, Minnesota | 1983 | Jack Lambert, Pittsburgh | 1991 | Pat Swilling, New Orleans |
| 1974 | Joe Greene, Pittsburgh | 1984 | Mike Haynes, L.A. Raiders | 1992 | Junior Seau, San Diego |
| 1975 | Curley Culp, Houston | | | | |

## Cowboys Defeat Bills in Super Bowl

The Dallas Cowboys dominated throughout the game and defeated the Buffalo Bills 52-17 to win Super Bowl XXVII on January 31, 1993. It was the third Super Bowl victory for the Cowboys, who were champions in 1972 and 1978. Troy Aikman, quarterback for the Cowboys, was chosen the game's most valuable player.

### Score by Quarters

| | | | | |
|---|---|---|---|---|
| Buffalo | 7 | 3 | 7 | 0—17 |
| Dallas | 14 | 14 | 3 | 21—52 |

### Scoring

Buffalo—Thomas 2 yd. run (Christie kick)
Dallas—Novacek 23 yd. pass from Aikman (Elliott kick)
Dallas—J. Jones 2 yd. fumble return (Elliott kick)
Buffalo—Christie 21 yd. field goal
Dallas—Irvin 19 yd. pass from Aikman (Elliott kick)
Dallas—Irvin 18 yd. pass from Aikman (Elliott kick)
Dallas—Elliott 20 yd. field goal
Buffalo—Beebe 40 yd. pass from Reich (Christie kick)
Dallas—Harper 45 yd. pass from Aikman (Elliott kick)
Dallas—E. Smith 10 yd. run (Elliott kick)
Dallas—Norton 9 yd. fumble return (Elliott kick)

### Individual Statistics

**Rushing** — Buffalo, K. Davis 15-86, Thomas 11-19, Gardner 1-3, Reich 2-0. Dallas, E. Smith 22-108, Aikman 3-28, Gainer 2-1, Johnston 1-0, Beuerlein 1-0.

**Passing** — Buffalo, Kelly 4-7-2-82, Reich 18-31-2-194. Dallas, Aikman 22-30-0-273.

**Receiving** — Buffalo, Reed 8-152, Thomas 4-10, K. Davis 3-16, Beebe 2-50, Tasker 2-30, Metzelaars 2-12, McKeller 1-6. Dallas, Novacek 7-72, Irvin 6-114, E. Smith 6-27, Johnston 2-15, Harper 1-45.

### Team Statistics

| | Buffalo | Dallas |
|---|---|---|
| First downs | 22 | 20 |
| Total net yards | 362 | 408 |
| Rushing yards | 108 | 137 |
| Passing yards | 254 | 271 |
| Completed-Attempted | 22-38 | 22-30 |
| Yards per pass | 6.0 | 8.7 |
| Punts-average | 3-45 | 4-33 |
| Total return yards | 90 | 149 |
| Penalties-yards | 4-30 | 8-53 |
| Fumbles-lost | 8-5 | 4-2 |
| Time of possession | 28:48 | 31:12 |

## Super Bowl

| Year | Winner | Loser | Winning coach | Site |
|---|---|---|---|---|
| 1967 | Green Bay Packers, 35 | Kansas City Chiefs, 10 | Vince Lombardi | Los Angeles Coliseum |
| 1968 | Green Bay Packers, 33 | Oakland Raiders, 14 | Vince Lombardi | Orange Bowl, Miami |
| 1969 | New York Jets, 16 | Baltimore Colts, 7 | Weeb Ewbank | Orange Bowl, Miami |
| 1970 | Kansas City Chiefs, 23 | Minnesota Vikings, 7 | Hank Stram | Tulane Stadium, New Orleans |
| 1971 | Baltimore Colts, 16 | Dallas Cowboys, 13 | Don McCafferty | Orange Bowl, Miami |
| 1972 | Dallas Cowboys, 24 | Miami Dolphins, 3 | Tom Landry | Tulane Stadium, New Orleans |
| 1973 | Miami Dolphins, 14 | Washington Redskins, 7 | Don Shula | Los Angeles Coliseum |
| 1974 | Miami Dolphins, 24 | Minnesota Vikings, 7 | Don Shula | Rice Stadium, Houston |
| 1975 | Pittsburgh Steelers, 16 | Minnesota Vikings, 6 | Chuck Noll | Tulane Stadium, New Orleans |
| 1976 | Pittsburgh Steelers, 21 | Dallas Cowboys, 17 | Chuck Noll | Orange Bowl, Miami |
| 1977 | Oakland Raiders, 32 | Minnesota Vikings, 14 | John Madden | Rose Bowl, Pasadena |
| 1978 | Dallas Cowboys, 27 | Denver Broncos, 10 | Tom Landry | Superdome, New Orleans |
| 1979 | Pittsburgh Steelers, 35 | Dallas Cowboys, 31 | Chuck Noll | Orange Bowl, Miami |
| 1980 | Pittsburgh Steelers, 31 | Los Angeles Rams, 19 | Chuck Noll | Rose Bowl, Pasadena |
| 1981 | Oakland Raiders, 27 | Philadelphia Eagles, 10 | Tom Flores | Superdome, New Orleans |
| 1982 | San Francisco 49ers, 26 | Cincinnati Bengals, 21 | Bill Walsh | Silverdome, Pontiac, Mich. |
| 1983 | Washington Redskins, 27 | Miami Dolphins, 17 | Joe Gibbs | Rose Bowl, Pasadena |
| 1984 | Los Angeles Raiders, 38 | Washington Redskins, 9 | Tom Flores | Tampa Stadium |
| 1985 | San Francisco 49ers, 38 | Miami Dolphins, 16 | Bill Walsh | Stanford Stadium, Palo Alto, Cal. |
| 1986 | Chicago Bears, 46 | New England Patriots, 10 | Mike Ditka | Superdome, New Orleans |
| 1987 | New York Giants, 39 | Denver Broncos, 20 | Bill Parcells | Rose Bowl, Pasadena |
| 1988 | Washington Redskins, 42 | Denver Broncos, 10 | Joe Gibbs | San Diego Stadium |
| 1989 | San Francisco 49ers, 20 | Cincinnati Bengals, 16 | Bill Walsh | Joe Robbie Stadium, Miami |
| 1990 | San Francisco 49ers, 55 | Denver Broncos, 10 | George Seifert | Superdome, New Orleans |
| 1991 | New York Giants, 20 | Buffalo Bills, 19 | Bill Parcells | Tampa Stadium |
| 1992 | Washington Redskins, 37 | Buffalo Bills, 24 | Joe Gibbs | Metrodome, Minneapolis |
| 1993 | Dallas Cowboys, 52 | Buffalo Bills, 17 | Jimmy Johnson | Rose Bowl, Pasadena |

## Super Bowl MVPs

| | | |
|---|---|---|
| 1967 Bart Starr, Green Bay | 1976 Lynn Swann, Pittsburgh | 1985 Joe Montana, San Francisco |
| 1968 Bart Starr, Green Bay | 1977 Fred Biletnikoff, Oakland | 1986 Richard Dent, Chicago |
| 1969 Joe Namath, N.Y. Jets | 1978 Randy White, Harvey Martin, Dallas | 1987 Phil Simms, N.Y. Giants |
| 1970 Len Dawson, Kansas City | 1979 Terry Bradshaw, Pittsburgh | 1988 Doug Williams, Washington |
| 1971 Chuck Howley, Dallas | 1980 Terry Bradshaw, Pittsburgh | 1989 Jerry Rice, San Francisco |
| 1972 Roger Staubach, Dallas | 1981 Jim Plunkett, Oakland | 1990 Joe Montana, San Francisco |
| 1973 Jake Scott, Miami | 1982 Joe Montana, San Francisco | 1991 Ottis Anderson, N.Y. Giants |
| 1974 Larry Csonka, Miami | 1983 John Riggins, Washington | 1992 Mark Rypien, Washington |
| 1975 Franco Harris, Pittsburgh | 1984 Marcus Allen, L.A. Raiders | 1993 Troy Aikman, Dallas |

## American Football League

| Year | Eastern Division | Western Division | Playoff |
|---|---|---|---|
| 1960 | Houston Oilers (10-4-0) | L. A. Chargers (10-4-0) | Houston 24, Los Angeles 16 |
| 1961 | Houston Oilers (10-3-1) | San Diego Chargers (12-2-0) | Houston 10, San Diego 3 |
| 1962 | Houston Oilers (11-3-0) | Dallas Texans (11-3-0) | Dallas 20, Houston 17(b) |
| 1963 | Boston Patriots (8-6-1)(a) | San Diego Chargers (11-3-0) | San Diego 51, Boston 10 |
| 1964 | Buffalo Bills (12-2-0) | San Diego Chargers (8-5-1) | Buffalo 20, San Diego 7 |
| 1965 | Buffalo Bills (10-3-1) | San Diego Chargers (9-2-3) | Buffalo 23, San Diego 0 |
| 1966 | Buffalo Bills (9-4-1) | Kansas City Chiefs (11-2-1) | Kansas City 31, Buffalo 7 |
| 1967 | Houston Oilers (9-4-1) | Oakland Raiders (13-1-0) | Oakland 40, Houston 7 |
| 1968 | New York Jets (11-3-0) | Oakland Raiders (12-2-0)(a) | New York 27, Oakland 23 |
| 1969 | New York Jets (10-4-0) | Oakland Raiders (12-1-1) | Kansas City 17, Oakland 7(c) |

(a) won divisional playoff (b) won at 2:45 of second overtime. (c) Kansas City defeated Jets to make playoffs.

## National Football Conference Leaders

(National Football League, 1960-69)

### Passing

| Player, team | Atts | Com | YG | TD | Year |
|---|---|---|---|---|---|
| Milt Plum, Cleveland | 250 | 151 | 2,297 | 21 | 1960 |
| Milt Plum, Cleveland | 302 | 177 | 2,416 | 18 | 1961 |
| Bart Starr, Green Bay | 285 | 178 | 2,438 | 12 | 1962 |
| Y.A. Tittle, N.Y. Giants | 367 | 221 | 3,145 | 36 | 1963 |
| Bart Starr, Green Bay | 272 | 163 | 2,144 | 15 | 1964 |
| Rudy Bukich, Chicago | 312 | 176 | 2,641 | 20 | 1965 |
| Bart Starr, Green Bay | 251 | 156 | 2,257 | 14 | 1966 |
| Sonny Jurgensen, Washington | 508 | 288 | 3,747 | 31 | 1967 |
| Earl Morrall, Baltimore | 317 | 182 | 2,909 | 26 | 1968 |
| Sonny Jurgensen, Washington | 442 | 274 | 3,102 | 22 | 1969 |
| John Brodie, San Francisco | 378 | 223 | 2,941 | 24 | 1970 |
| Roger Staubach, Dallas | 211 | 126 | 1,882 | 15 | 1971 |
| Norm Snead, N.Y. Giants | 325 | 196 | 2,307 | 17 | 1972 |
| Roger Staubach, Dallas | 286 | 179 | 2,428 | 23 | 1973 |
| Sonny Jurgensen, Washington | 167 | 107 | 1,185 | 11 | 1974 |
| Fran Tarkenton, Minnesota | 425 | 273 | 2,294 | 25 | 1975 |
| James Harris, Los Angeles | 158 | 91 | 1,460 | 8 | 1976 |
| Roger Staubach, Dallas | 361 | 210 | 2,620 | 18 | 1977 |
| Roger Staubach, Dallas | 413 | 231 | 3,190 | 25 | 1978 |
| Roger Staubach, Dallas | 461 | 267 | 3,586 | 27 | 1979 |
| Ron Jaworski, Philadelphia | 451 | 257 | 3,529 | 27 | 1980 |
| Joe Montana, San Francisco | 488 | 311 | 3,565 | 19 | 1981 |
| Joe Thiesmann, Washington | 252 | 161 | 2,033 | 13 | 1982 |
| Steve Bartkowski, Atlanta | 423 | 274 | 3,167 | 22 | 1983 |
| Joe Montana, San Francisco | 432 | 279 | 3,630 | 28 | 1984 |
| Joe Montana, San Francisco | 494 | 303 | 3,653 | 27 | 1985 |
| Tommy Kramer, Minnesota | 372 | 208 | 3,000 | 24 | 1986 |
| Joe Montana, San Francisco | 398 | 266 | 3,054 | 31 | 1987 |
| Wade Wilson, Minnesota | 332 | 204 | 2,746 | 15 | 1988 |
| Joe Montana, San Francisco | 386 | 271 | 3,521 | 26 | 1989 |
| Phil Simms, N.Y. Giants | 311 | 184 | 2,284 | 15 | 1990 |
| Steve Young, San Francisco | 279 | 180 | 2,517 | 17 | 1991 |
| Steve Young, San Francisco | 402 | 268 | 3,465 | 25 | 1992 |

### Pass-Receiving

| Player, team | Ct | YG | TD | Year |
|---|---|---|---|---|
| Raymond Berry, Baltimore | 74 | 1,298 | 10 | 1960 |
| Jim Phillips, L.A. Rams | 78 | 1,092 | 5 | 1961 |
| Bobby Mitchell, Washington | 72 | 1,384 | 11 | 1962 |
| Bobby Joe Conrad, St. Louis | 73 | 967 | 10 | 1963 |
| Johnny Morris, Chicago | 93 | 1,200 | 10 | 1964 |
| Dave Parks, San Francisco | 80 | 1,344 | 12 | 1965 |
| Charley Taylor, Washington | 72 | 1,119 | 12 | 1966 |
| Charley Taylor, Washington | 70 | 990 | 9 | 1967 |
| Clifton McNeil, San Francisco | 71 | 994 | 7 | 1968 |
| Dan Abramowicz, New Orleans | 73 | 1,015 | 7 | 1969 |
| Dick Gordon, Chicago | 71 | 1,026 | 13 | 1970 |
| Bob Tucker, Giants | 59 | 791 | 4 | 1971 |
| Harold Jackson, Philadelphia | 62 | 1,048 | 4 | 1972 |
| Harold Carmichael, Philadelphia | 67 | 1,116 | 9 | 1973 |
| Charles Young, Philadelphia | 63 | 696 | 3 | 1974 |
| Chuck Foreman, Minnesota | 73 | 691 | 9 | 1975 |
| Drew Pearson, Dallas | 58 | 806 | 6 | 1976 |
| Ahmad Rashad, Minnesota | 51 | 681 | 2 | 1977 |
| Rickey Young, Minnesota | 88 | 704 | 5 | 1978 |
| Ahmad Rashad, Minnesota | 80 | 1,156 | 9 | 1979 |
| Earl Cooper, San Francisco | 83 | 567 | 4 | 1980 |
| Dwight Clark, San Francisco | 85 | 1,105 | 4 | 1981 |
| Dwight Clark, San Francisco | 60 | 913 | 5 | 1982 |
| Roy Green, St. Louis | 78 | 1,227 | 14 | 1983 |
| Charlie Brown, Washington | 78 | 1,225 | 8 | |
| Earnest Gray, N.Y. Giants | 78 | 1,139 | 5 | |
| Art Monk, Washington | 106 | 1,372 | 7 | 1984 |
| Roger Craig, San Francisco | 92 | 1,016 | 6 | 1985 |
| Jerry Rice, San Francisco | 86 | 1,570 | 15 | 1986 |
| J.T. Smith, St. Louis | 91 | 1,117 | 8 | 1987 |
| Henry Ellard, L.A. Rams | 86 | 1,414 | 10 | 1988 |
| Sterling Sharpe, Green Bay | 90 | 1,423 | 12 | 1989 |
| Jerry Rice, San Francisco | 100 | 1,502 | 13 | 1990 |
| Michael Irvin, Dallas | 93 | 1,523 | 8 | 1991 |
| Sterling Sharpe, Green Bay | 108 | 1,461 | 13 | 1992 |

### Scoring

| Player, team | TD | PAT | FG | Pts | Year |
|---|---|---|---|---|---|
| Paul Hornung, Green Bay | 15 | 41 | 15 | 176 | 1960 |
| Paul Hornung, Green Bay | 10 | 41 | 15 | 146 | 1961 |
| Jim Taylor, Green Bay | 19 | 0 | 0 | 114 | 1962 |
| Don Chandler, N.Y. Giants | 0 | 52 | 18 | 106 | 1963 |
| Lenny Moore, Baltimore | 20 | 0 | 0 | 120 | 1964 |
| Gale Sayers, Chicago | 22 | 0 | 0 | 132 | 1965 |
| Bruce Gossett, L.A. Rams | 0 | 29 | 28 | 113 | 1966 |
| Jim Bakken, St. Louis | 0 | 36 | 27 | 117 | 1967 |
| Leroy Kelly, Cleveland | 20 | 0 | 0 | 120 | 1968 |
| Fred Cox, Minnesota | 0 | 43 | 26 | 121 | 1969 |
| Fred Cox, Minnesota | 0 | 35 | 30 | 125 | 1970 |
| Curt Knight, Washington | 0 | 27 | 29 | 114 | 1971 |
| Chester Marcol, Green Bay | 0 | 29 | 33 | 128 | 1972 |
| David Ray, Los Angeles | 0 | 40 | 30 | 130 | 1973 |
| Chester Marcol, Green Bay | 0 | 19 | 25 | 94 | 1974 |
| Chuck Foreman, Minnesota | 22 | 0 | 0 | 132 | 1975 |
| Mark Moseley, Washington | 0 | 31 | 22 | 97 | 1976 |
| Walter Payton, Chicago | 16 | 0 | 0 | 96 | 1977 |
| Frank Corrall, Los Angeles | 0 | 31 | 29 | 118 | 1978 |
| Mark Moseley, Washington | 0 | 39 | 25 | 114 | 1979 |
| Ed Murray, Detroit | 0 | 35 | 27 | 116 | 1980 |
| Ed Murray, Detroit | 0 | 46 | 25 | 121 | 1981 |
| Wendell Tyler, L.A. Rams | 13 | 0 | 0 | 78 | 1982 |
| Mark Moseley, Washington | 0 | 62 | 33 | 161 | 1983 |
| Ray Wersching, San Francisco | 0 | 56 | 25 | 131 | 1984 |
| Kevin Butler, Chicago | 0 | 51 | 31 | 144 | 1985 |
| Kevin Butler, Chicago | 0 | 36 | 28 | 120 | 1986 |
| Jerry Rice, San Francisco | 23 | 0 | 0 | 138 | 1987 |
| Mike Cofer, San Francisco | 0 | 40 | 27 | 121 | 1988 |
| Mike Cofer, San Francisco | 0 | 49 | 29 | 136 | 1989 |
| Chip Lohmiller, Washington | 0 | 41 | 30 | 131 | 1990 |
| Chip Lohmiller, Washington | 0 | 56 | 31 | 149 | 1991 |
| Morten Andersen, New Orleans | 0 | 33 | 29 | 120 | 1992 |

### Rushing

| Player, team | Yds | Atts | TD | Year |
|---|---|---|---|---|
| Jim Brown, Cleveland | 1,257 | 215 | 9 | 1960 |
| Jim Brown, Cleveland | 1,408 | 305 | 8 | 1961 |
| Jim Taylor, Green Bay | 1,474 | 272 | 19 | 1962 |
| Jim Brown, Cleveland | 1,863 | 291 | 12 | 1963 |
| Jim Brown, Cleveland | 1,446 | 280 | 7 | 1964 |
| Jim Brown, Cleveland | 1,544 | 289 | 17 | 1965 |
| Gale Sayers, Chicago | 1,231 | 229 | 8 | 1966 |
| Leroy Kelly, Cleveland | 1,205 | 235 | 11 | 1967 |
| Leroy Kelly, Cleveland | 1,239 | 248 | 16 | 1968 |
| Gale Sayers, Chicago | 1,032 | 236 | 8 | 1969 |
| Larry Brown, Washington | 1,125 | 237 | 5 | 1970 |
| John Brockington, Green Bay | 1,105 | 216 | 4 | 1971 |
| Larry Brown, Washington | 1,216 | 285 | 8 | 1972 |
| John Brockington, Green Bay | 1,144 | 265 | 3 | 1973 |
| Lawrence McCutcheon, Los Angeles | 1,109 | 236 | 3 | 1974 |
| Jim Otis, St. Louis | 1,076 | 269 | 5 | 1975 |
| Walter Payton, Chicago | 1,390 | 311 | 13 | 1976 |
| Walter Payton, Chicago | 1,852 | 339 | 14 | 1977 |
| Walter Payton, Chicago | 1,395 | 333 | 11 | 1978 |
| Walter Payton, Chicago | 1,610 | 369 | 14 | 1979 |
| Walter Payton, Chicago | 1,460 | 317 | 15 | 1980 |
| George Rogers, New Orleans | 1,674 | 378 | 13 | 1981 |
| Tony Dorsett, Dallas | 745 | 177 | 5 | 1982 |
| Eric Dickerson, L.A. Rams | 1,808 | 390 | 18 | 1983 |
| Eric Dickerson, L.A. Rams | 2,105 | 379 | 14 | 1984 |
| Gerald Riggs, Atlanta | 1,719 | 397 | 10 | 1985 |
| Eric Dickerson, L.A. Rams | 1,821 | 404 | 11 | 1986 |
| Charles White, L.A. Rams | 1,374 | 324 | 11 | 1987 |
| Herschel Walker, Dallas | 1,514 | 361 | 5 | 1988 |
| Barry Sanders, Detroit | 1,470 | 280 | 14 | 1989 |
| Barry Sanders, Detroit | 1,304 | 255 | 13 | 1990 |
| Emmitt Smith, Dallas | 1,563 | 365 | 12 | 1991 |
| Emmitt Smith, Dallas | 1,713 | 373 | 18 | 1992 |

## American Football Conference Leaders

### (American Football League, 1960-1969)

### Passing

| Player, team | Atts | Com | YG | TD | Year |
|---|---|---|---|---|---|
| Jack Kemp, Los Angeles | 406 | 211 | 3,018 | 20 | 1960 |
| George Blanda, Houston | 362 | 187 | 3,330 | 36 | 1961 |
| Len Dawson, Dallas | 310 | 189 | 2,759 | 29 | 1962 |
| Tobin Rote, Kansas City | 286 | 170 | 2,510 | 20 | 1963 |
| Len Dawson, Kansas City | 354 | 199 | 2,879 | 30 | 1964 |
| John Hadl, San Diego | 348 | 174 | 2,798 | 20 | 1965 |
| Len Dawson, Kansas City | 284 | 159 | 2,527 | 26 | 1966 |
| Daryle Lamonica, Oakland | 425 | 220 | 3,228 | 30 | 1967 |
| Len Dawson, Kansas City | 224 | 131 | 2,109 | 17 | 1968 |
| Greg Cook, Cincinnati | 197 | 106 | 1,854 | 15 | 1969 |
| Daryle Lamonica, Oakland | 356 | 179 | 2,516 | 22 | 1970 |
| Bob Griese, Miami | 263 | 145 | 2,089 | 19 | 1971 |
| Earl Morrall, Miami | 150 | 83 | 1,360 | 11 | 1972 |
| Ken Stabler, Oakland | 260 | 163 | 1,997 | 14 | 1973 |
| Ken Anderson, Cincinnati | 328 | 213 | 2,667 | 18 | 1974 |
| Ken Anderson, Cincinnati | 377 | 228 | 3,169 | 21 | 1975 |
| Ken Stabler, Oakland | 291 | 194 | 2,737 | 27 | 1976 |
| Bob Griese, Miami | 307 | 180 | 2,252 | 22 | 1977 |
| Terry Bradshaw, Pittsburgh | 368 | 207 | 2,915 | 28 | 1978 |
| Dan Fouts, San Diego | 530 | 332 | 4,082 | 24 | 1979 |
| Brian Sipe, Cleveland | 554 | 337 | 4,132 | 30 | 1980 |
| Ken Anderson, Cincinnati | 479 | 300 | 3,754 | 29 | 1981 |
| Ken Anderson, Cincinnati | 309 | 218 | 2,495 | 12 | 1982 |
| Dan Marino, Miami | 296 | 173 | 2,210 | 20 | 1983 |
| Dan Marino, Miami | 564 | 362 | 5,084 | 48 | 1984 |
| Ken O'Brien, N.Y. Jets | 488 | 297 | 3,888 | 25 | 1985 |
| Dan Marino, Miami | 623 | 378 | 4,746 | 44 | 1986 |
| Bernie Kosar, Cleveland | 389 | 241 | 3,033 | 22 | 1987 |
| Boomer Esiason, Cincinnati | 388 | 223 | 3,572 | 28 | 1988 |
| Boomer Esiason, Cincinnati | 455 | 258 | 3,525 | 28 | 1989 |
| Jim Kelly, Buffalo | 346 | 219 | 2,829 | 24 | 1990 |
| Jim Kelly, Buffalo | 474 | 304 | 3,844 | 33 | 1991 |
| Warren Moon, Houston | 346 | 224 | 2,521 | 18 | 1992 |

### Pass-Receiving

| Player, team | Ct | YG | TD |
|---|---|---|---|
| Lionel Taylor, Denver | 92 | 1,235 | 12 |
| Lionel Taylor, Denver | 100 | 1,176 | 4 |
| Lionel Taylor, Denver | 77 | 908 | 4 |
| Lionel Taylor, Denver | 78 | 1,101 | 10 |
| Charley Hennigan, Houston | 101 | 1,546 | 8 |
| Lionel Taylor, Denver | 85 | 1,131 | 6 |
| Lance Alworth, San Diego | 73 | 1,383 | 13 |
| George Sauer, N.Y. Jets | 75 | 1,189 | 6 |
| Lance Alworth, San Diego | 68 | 1,312 | 10 |
| Lance Alworth, San Diego | 64 | 1,003 | 4 |
| Marlin Briscoe, Buffalo | 57 | 1,036 | 8 |
| Fred Biletnikoff, Oakland | 61 | 929 | 9 |
| Fred Biletnikoff, Oakland | 58 | 802 | 7 |
| Fred Willis, Houston | 57 | 371 | 1 |
| Lydell Mitchell, Baltimore | 72 | 544 | 2 |
| Reggie Rucker, Cleveland | 60 | 770 | 2 |
| Lydell Mitchell, Baltimore | 60 | 554 | 4 |
| MacArthur Lane, Kansas City | 66 | 686 | 1 |
| Lydell Mitchell, Baltimore | 71 | 620 | 4 |
| Steve Largent, Seattle | 71 | 1,168 | 8 |
| Joe Washington, Baltimore | 82 | 750 | 3 |
| Kellen Winslow, San Diego | 89 | 1,290 | 9 |
| Kellen Winslow, San Diego | 88 | 1,075 | 10 |
| Kellen Winslow, San Diego | 54 | 721 | 6 |
| Todd Christensen, L.A. Raiders | 92 | 1,247 | 12 |
| Ozzie Newsome, Cleveland | 89 | 1,001 | 5 |
| Lionel James, San Diego | 86 | 1,027 | 6 |
| Todd Christensen, L.A. Raiders | 95 | 1,153 | 8 |
| Al Toon, N.Y. Jets | 68 | 976 | 5 |
| Al Toon, N.Y. Jets | 93 | 1,067 | 5 |
| Andre Reed, Buffalo | 88 | 1,312 | 9 |
| Haywood Jeffires, Houston | 74 | 1,048 | 8 |
| Drew Hill, Houston | 74 | 1,019 | 5 |
| Haywood Jeffires, Houston | 100 | 1,181 | 7 |
| Haywood Jeffires, Houston | 90 | 913 | 9 |

### Scoring

| Player, team | TD | PAT | FG | Pts | Year |
|---|---|---|---|---|---|
| Gene Mingo, Denver | 6 | 33 | 18 | 123 | 1960 |
| Gino Cappelletti, Boston | 8 | 48 | 17 | 147 | 1961 |
| Gene Mingo, Denver | 4 | 32 | 27 | 137 | 1962 |
| Gino Cappelletti, Boston | 2 | 35 | 22 | 113 | 1963 |
| Gino Cappelletti, Boston | 7 | 36 | 25 | 155 | 1964 |
| Gino Cappelletti, Boston | 9 | 27 | 17 | 132 | 1965 |
| Gino Cappelletti, Boston | 6 | 35 | 16 | 119 | 1966 |
| George Blanda, Oakland | 0 | 56 | 20 | 116 | 1967 |
| Jim Turner, N.Y. Jets | 0 | 43 | 34 | 145 | 1968 |
| Jim Turner, N.Y. Jets | 0 | 33 | 32 | 129 | 1969 |
| Jan Stenerud, Kansas City | 0 | 26 | 30 | 116 | 1970 |
| Garo Yepremian, Miami | 0 | 33 | 28 | 117 | 1971 |
| Bobby Howfield, N.Y. Jets | 0 | 40 | 27 | 121 | 1972 |
| Roy Gerela, Pittsburgh | 0 | 36 | 29 | 123 | 1973 |
| Roy Gerela, Pittsburgh | 0 | 33 | 20 | 93 | 1974 |
| O.J. Simpson, Buffalo | 23 | 0 | 0 | 138 | 1975 |
| Toni Linhart, Baltimore | 0 | 49 | 20 | 109 | 1976 |
| Errol Mann, Oakland | 0 | 39 | 20 | 99 | 1977 |
| Pat Leahy, N.Y. Jets | 0 | 41 | 22 | 107 | 1978 |
| John Smith, New England | 0 | 46 | 23 | 115 | 1979 |
| John Smith, New England | 0 | 51 | 26 | 129 | 1980 |
| Jim Breech, Cincinnati | 0 | 49 | 22 | 115 | 1981 |
| Marcus Allen, L.A. Raiders | 14 | 0 | 0 | 84 | 1982 |
| Gary Anderson, Pittsburgh | 0 | 38 | 27 | 119 | 1983 |
| Gary Anderson, Pittsburgh | 0 | 45 | 24 | 117 | 1984 |
| Gary Anderson, Pittsburgh | 0 | 40 | 33 | 139 | 1985 |
| Tony Franklin, New England | 0 | 44 | 32 | 140 | 1986 |
| Jim Breech, Cincinnati | 0 | 25 | 24 | 97 | 1987 |
| Scott Norwood, Buffalo | 0 | 33 | 32 | 129 | 1988 |
| David Treadwell, Denver | 0 | 39 | 27 | 120 | 1989 |
| Nick Lowery, Kansas City | 0 | 37 | 34 | 139 | 1990 |
| Pete Stoyanovich, Miami | 0 | 28 | 31 | 121 | 1991 |
| Pete Stoyanovich, Miami | 0 | 34 | 30 | 124 | 1992 |

### Rushing

| Player, team | Yds | Atts | TD | Year |
|---|---|---|---|---|
| Abner Haynes, Dallas | 875 | 156 | 9 | 1960 |
| Billy Cannon, Houston | 948 | 200 | 6 | 1961 |
| Cookie Gilchrist, Buffalo | 1,096 | 214 | 13 | 1962 |
| Clem Daniels, Oakland | 1,099 | 215 | 3 | 1963 |
| Cookie Gilchrist, Buffalo | 981 | 230 | 6 | 1964 |
| Paul Lowe, San Diego | 1,121 | 222 | 7 | 1965 |
| Jim Nance, Boston | 1,458 | 299 | 11 | 1966 |
| Jim Nance, Boston | 1,216 | 269 | 7 | 1967 |
| Paul Robinson, Cincinnati | 1,023 | 238 | 8 | 1968 |
| Dick Post, San Diego | 873 | 182 | 6 | 1969 |
| Floyd Little, Denver | 901 | 209 | 3 | 1970 |
| Floyd Little, Denver | 1,133 | 284 | 6 | 1971 |
| O.J. Simpson, Buffalo | 1,251 | 292 | 6 | 1972 |
| O.J. Simpson, Buffalo | 2,003 | 332 | 12 | 1973 |
| Otis Armstrong, Denver | 1,407 | 263 | 9 | 1974 |
| O.J. Simpson, Buffalo | 1,817 | 329 | 16 | 1975 |
| O.J. Simpson, Buffalo | 1,503 | 290 | 8 | 1976 |
| Mark van Eeghen, Oakland | 1,273 | 324 | 7 | 1977 |
| Earl Campbell, Houston | 1,450 | 302 | 13 | 1978 |
| Earl Campbell, Houston | 1,697 | 368 | 19 | 1979 |
| Earl Campbell, Houston | 1,934 | 373 | 13 | 1980 |
| Earl Campbell, Houston | 1,376 | 361 | 10 | 1981 |
| Freeman McNeil, N.Y. Jets | 786 | 151 | 6 | 1982 |
| Curt Warner, Seattle | 1,446 | 335 | 13 | 1983 |
| Earnest Jackson, San Diego | 1,179 | 296 | 8 | 1984 |
| Marcus Allen, L.A. Raiders | 1,759 | 380 | 11 | 1985 |
| Curt Warner, Seattle | 1,481 | 319 | 13 | 1986 |
| Eric Dickerson, L.A. Rams, Indianapolis | 1,288* | 283 | 6 | 1987 |
| Eric Dickerson, Indianapolis | 1,659 | 388 | 14 | 1988 |
| Christian Okoye, Kansas City | 1,480 | 370 | 12 | 1989 |
| Thurman Thomas, Buffalo | 1,297 | 271 | 11 | 1990 |
| Thurman Thomas, Buffalo | 1,407 | 288 | 7 | 1991 |
| Barry Foster, Pittsburgh | 1,690 | 390 | 11 | 1992 |

* 1,011 AFC yards led conference.

# 1992 NFL Individual Leaders

## National Football Conference

### Passing

| | Att | Comp | Pct comp | Yds | Avg gain | TD | Pct TD | Int | Rating points |
|---|---|---|---|---|---|---|---|---|---|
| Young, Steve, San Francisco | 402 | 268 | 66.7 | 3465 | 8.62 | 25 | 6.2 | 7 | 107.0 |
| Miller, Chris, Atlanta | 253 | 152 | 60.1 | 1739 | 6.87 | 15 | 5.9 | 6 | 90.7 |
| Aikman, Troy, Dallas | 473 | 302 | 63.8 | 3445 | 7.28 | 23 | 4.9 | 14 | 89.5 |
| Cunningham, Randall, Philadelphia | 384 | 233 | 60.7 | 2775 | 7.23 | 19 | 4.9 | 11 | 87.3 |
| Favre, Brett, Green Bay | 471 | 302 | 64.1 | 3227 | 6.85 | 18 | 3.8 | 13 | 85.3 |
| Hebert, Bobby, New Orleans | 422 | 249 | 59.0 | 3287 | 7.79 | 19 | 4.5 | 16 | 82.9 |
| Everett, Jim, L.A. Rams | 475 | 281 | 59.2 | 3323 | 7.00 | 22 | 4.6 | 18 | 80.2 |
| Chandler, Chris, Phoenix | 413 | 245 | 59.3 | 2832 | 6.86 | 15 | 3.6 | 15 | 77.1 |
| Harbaugh, Jim, Chicago | 358 | 202 | 56.4 | 2486 | 6.94 | 13 | 3.6 | 12 | 76.2 |
| Testaverde, Vinny, Tampa Bay | 358 | 206 | 57.5 | 2554 | 7.13 | 14 | 3.9 | 16 | 74.2 |
| Gannon, Rich, Minnesota | 279 | 159 | 57.0 | 1905 | 6.83 | 12 | 4.3 | 13 | 72.9 |
| Rypien, Mark, Washington | 479 | 269 | 56.2 | 3282 | 6.85 | 13 | 2.7 | 17 | 71.7 |

### Rushing

| | Att | Yds | Avg | TD |
|---|---|---|---|---|
| Smith, Emmitt, Dallas | 373 | 1713 | 4.6 | 18 |
| Sanders, Barry, Detroit | 312 | 1352 | 4.3 | 9 |
| Allen, Terry, Minnesota | 266 | 1201 | 4.5 | 13 |
| Cobb, Reggie, Tampa Bay | 310 | 1171 | 3.8 | 9 |
| Hampton, Rodney, N.Y. Giants | 257 | 1141 | 4.4 | 14 |
| Gary, Cleveland, L.A. Rams | 279 | 1125 | 4.0 | 7 |
| Walker, Herschel, Philadelphia | 267 | 1070 | 4.0 | 8 |
| Watters, Ricky, San Francisco | 206 | 1013 | 4.9 | 9 |
| Byner, Earnest, Washington | 262 | 998 | 3.8 | 6 |
| Johnson, Johnny, Phoenix | 178 | 734 | 4.1 | 6 |

### Interceptions

| | No | Yds | Long | TD |
|---|---|---|---|---|
| McMillian, Audray, Minnesota | 8 | 157 | 51 | 2 |
| Woolford, Donnell, Chicago | 7 | 67 | 32 | 0 |
| Edwards, Brad, Washington | 6 | 157 | 53 | 1 |
| Cook, Toi, New Orleans | 6 | 90 | 48 | 1 |
| Massey, Robert, Phoenix | 5 | 147 | 46 | 3 |
| Scott, Todd, Minnesota | 5 | 79 | 35 | 1 |
| Glenn, Vencie, Minnesota | 5 | 65 | 39 | 0 |
| Griffin, Don, San Francisco | 5 | 4 | 2 | 0 |

### Pass Receiving

| | No | Yds | Avg | TD |
|---|---|---|---|---|
| Sharpe, Sterling, Green Bay | 108 | 1461 | 13.5 | 13 |
| Rison, Andre, Atlanta | 93 | 1119 | 12.0 | 11 |
| Rice, Jerry, San Francisco | 84 | 1201 | 14.3 | 10 |
| Irvin, Michael, Dallas | 78 | 1396 | 17.9 | 7 |
| Pritchard, Mike, Atlanta | 77 | 827 | 10.7 | 5 |
| Perriman, Brett, Detroit | 69 | 810 | 11.7 | 4 |
| Martin, Eric, New Orleans | 68 | 1041 | 15.3 | 5 |
| Novacek, Jay, Dallas | 68 | 630 | 9.3 | 6 |
| Barnett, Fred, Philadelphia | 67 | 1083 | 16.2 | 6 |
| Clark, Gary, Washington | 64 | 912 | 14.3 | 5 |

### Kickoff Returns

| | No | Yds | Avg | TD |
|---|---|---|---|---|
| Sanders, Deion, Atlanta | 40 | 1067 | 26.7 | 2 |
| Bailey, Johnny, Phoenix | 28 | 690 | 24.6 | 0 |
| Gray, Mel, Detroit | 42 | 1006 | 24.0 | 1 |
| Meggett, Dave, N.Y. Giants | 20 | 455 | 22.8 | 1 |
| Lewis, Darren, Chicago | 23 | 511 | 22.2 | 1 |

### Punt Returns

| | No | Yds | Avg | TD |
|---|---|---|---|---|
| Bailey, Johnny, Phoenix | 20 | 263 | 13.2 | 0 |
| Martin, Kelvin, Dallas | 42 | 532 | 12.7 | 2 |
| Sikahema, Vai, Philadelphia | 40 | 503 | 12.6 | 1 |
| Parker, Anthony, Minnesota | 33 | 336 | 10.2 | 0 |
| Buckley, Terrell, Green Bay | 21 | 211 | 10.0 | 1 |

### Scoring-Touchdowns

| | TD | Rush | Pass | Pts |
|---|---|---|---|---|
| Smith, Emmitt, Dallas | 19 | 18 | 1 | 114 |
| Allen, Terry, Minnesota | 15 | 13 | 2 | 90 |
| Hampton, Rodney, N.Y. Giants | 14 | 14 | 0 | 84 |
| Sharpe, Sterling, Green Bay | 13 | 0 | 13 | 78 |

### Punters

| | No | Yds | Long | Avg |
|---|---|---|---|---|
| Newsome, Harry, Minnesota | 72 | 3243 | 84 | 45.0 |
| Barnhardt, Tommy, New Orleans | 67 | 2947 | 62 | 44.0 |
| Arnold, Jim, Detroit | 65 | 2846 | 71 | 43.8 |
| Landeta, Sean, N.Y. Giants | 53 | 2317 | 71 | 43.7 |
| Saxon, Mike, Dallas | 61 | 2620 | 58 | 43.0 |

### Scoring-Kicking

| | PAT | FG | Pts |
|---|---|---|---|
| Andersen, Morten, New Orleans | 33/34 | 29/34 | 120 |
| Lohmiller, Chip, Washington | 30/30 | 30/40 | 120 |
| Elliott, Lin, Dallas | 47/48 | 24/35 | 119 |
| Cofer, Mike, San Francisco | 53/54 | 18/27 | 107 |
| Reveiz, Fuad, Minnesota | 45/45 | 19/25 | 102 |

### Sacks

| | No |
|---|---|
| Simmons, Clyde, Philadelphia | 19.0 |
| Harris, Tim, San Francisco | 17.0 |
| Martin, Wayne, New Orleans | 15.5 |
| Doleman, Chris, Minnesota | 14.5 |
| White, Reggie, Philadelphia | 14.0 |

## American Football Conference

### Passing

| | Att | Comp | Pct comp | Yds | Avg gain | TD | Pct TD | Int | Rating points |
|---|---|---|---|---|---|---|---|---|---|
| Moon, Warren, Houston | 346 | 224 | 64.7 | 2521 | 7.29 | 18 | 5.2 | 12 | 89.3 |
| Marino, Dan, Miami | 554 | 330 | 59.6 | 4116 | 7.43 | 24 | 4.3 | 16 | 85.1 |
| O'Donnell, Neil, Pittsburgh | 313 | 185 | 59.1 | 2283 | 7.29 | 13 | 4.2 | 9 | 83.6 |
| Kelly, Jim, Buffalo | 462 | 269 | 58.2 | 3457 | 7.48 | 23 | 5.0 | 19 | 81.2 |
| Carlson, Cody, Houston | 227 | 149 | 65.6 | 1710 | 7.53 | 9 | 4.0 | 11 | 81.2 |
| Krieg, Dave, Kansas City | 413 | 230 | 55.7 | 3115 | 7.54 | 15 | 3.6 | 12 | 79.9 |
| Humphries, Stan, San Diego | 454 | 263 | 57.9 | 3356 | 7.39 | 16 | 3.5 | 18 | 76.4 |
| Elway, John, Denver | 316 | 174 | 55.1 | 2242 | 7.09 | 10 | 3.2 | 17 | 65.7 |
| Schroeder, Jay, L.A. Raiders | 253 | 123 | 48.6 | 1476 | 5.83 | 11 | 4.3 | 11 | 63.3 |
| George, Jeff, Indianapolis | 306 | 167 | 54.6 | 1963 | 6.42 | 7 | 2.3 | 15 | 61.5 |
| Esiason, Boomer, Cincinnati | 278 | 144 | 51.8 | 1407 | 5.06 | 11 | 4.0 | 15 | 57.0 |
| Nagle, Browning, N.Y. Jets | 387 | 192 | 49.6 | 2280 | 5.89 | 7 | 1.8 | 17 | 55.7 |
| Gelbaugh, Stan, Seattle | 255 | 121 | 47.5 | 1307 | 5.13 | 6 | 2.4 | 11 | 52.9 |

## Rushing

| | Att | Yds | Avg | TD |
|---|---|---|---|---|
| Foster, Barry, Pittsburgh | 390 | 1690 | 4.3 | 11 |
| Thomas, Thurman, Buffalo | 312 | 1487 | 4.8 | 9 |
| White, Lorenzo, Houston | 265 | 1226 | 4.6 | 7 |
| Green, Harold, Cincinnati | 265 | 1170 | 4.4 | 2 |
| Warren, Chris, Seattle | 223 | 1017 | 4.6 | 3 |
| Higgs, Mark, Miami | 256 | 915 | 3.6 | 7 |
| Butts, Marion, San Diego | 218 | 809 | 3.7 | 4 |
| Dickerson, Eric, L.A. Raiders | 187 | 729 | 3.9 | 2 |
| Baxter, Brad, N.Y. Jets | 152 | 698 | 4.6 | 6 |
| Green, Gaston, Denver | 161 | 648 | 4.0 | 2 |

## Pass Receiving

| | No | Yds | Avg | TD |
|---|---|---|---|---|
| Jeffires, Haywood, Houston | 90 | 913 | 10.1 | 9 |
| Duncan, Curtis, Houston | 82 | 954 | 11.6 | 1 |
| Harmon, Ronnie, San Diego | 79 | 914 | 11.6 | 1 |
| Williams, John L., Seattle | 74 | 556 | 7.5 | 2 |
| Miller, Anthony, San Diego | 72 | 1060 | 14.7 | 7 |
| Givins, Earnest, Houston | 67 | 787 | 11.7 | 10 |
| Reed, Andre, Buffalo | 65 | 913 | 14.0 | 3 |
| Langhorne, Reggie, Indianapolis | 65 | 811 | 12.5 | 1 |
| Thomas, Thurman, Buffalo | 58 | 626 | 10.8 | 3 |
| Burkett, Chris, N.Y. Jets | 57 | 724 | 12.7 | 1 |
| White, Lorenzo, Houston | 57 | 641 | 11.2 | 1 |

## Scoring-Touchdowns

| | TD | Rush | Pass | Pts |
|---|---|---|---|---|
| Thomas, Thurman, Buffalo | 12 | 9 | 3 | 72 |
| Foster, Barry, Pittsburgh | 11 | 11 | 0 | 66 |
| Givins, Earnest, Houston | 10 | 0 | 10 | 60 |
| Culver, Rodney, Indianapolis | 9 | 7 | 2 | 54 |
| Jeffires, Haywood, Houston | 9 | 0 | 9 | 54 |

## Scoring-Kicking

| | PAT | FG | Pts |
|---|---|---|---|
| Stoyanovich, Pete, Miami | 34/36 | 30/37 | 124 |
| Christie, Steve, Buffalo | 43/44 | 24/30 | 115 |
| Anderson, Gary, Pittsburgh | 29/31 | 28/36 | 113 |
| Carney, John, San Diego | 35/35 | 26/32 | 113 |
| Lowery, Nick, Kansas City | 39/39 | 22/24 | 105 |

## interceptions

| | No | Yds | Long | TD |
|---|---|---|---|---|
| Jones, Henry, Buffalo | 8 | 263 | 82 | 2 |
| Robinson, Eugene, Seattle | 7 | 126 | 49 | 0 |
| Carter, Dale, Kansas City | 7 | 65 | 36 | 1 |
| Kelso, Mark, Buffalo | 7 | 21 | 13 | 0 |

## Kickoff Returns

| | No | Yds | Avg | TD |
|---|---|---|---|---|
| Vaughn, Jon, New England | 20 | 564 | 28.2 | 1 |
| Baldwin, Randy, Cleveland | 30 | 675 | 22.5 | 0 |
| Montgomery, Alton, Denver | 21 | 466 | 22.2 | 0 |
| Verdin, Clarence, Indianapolis | 39 | 815 | 20.9 | 0 |
| Ball, Eric, Cincinnati | 20 | 411 | 20.6 | 0 |

## Punt Returns

| | No | Yds | Avg | TD |
|---|---|---|---|---|
| Woodson, Rod, Pittsburgh | 32 | 364 | 11.4 | 1 |
| Verdin, Clarence, Indianapolis | 24 | 268 | 11.2 | 2 |
| Marshall, Arthur, Denver | 33 | 349 | 10.6 | 0 |
| Carter, Dale, Kansas City | 38 | 398 | 10.5 | 2 |
| Brown, Tim, L.A. Raiders | 37 | 383 | 10.4 | 0 |

## Punters

| | No | Yds | Long | Avg |
|---|---|---|---|---|
| Montgomery, Greg, Houston | 53 | 2487 | 66 | 46.9 |
| Stark, Rohn, Indianapolis | 83 | 3716 | 64 | 44.8 |
| Tuten, Rick, Seattle | 108 | 4760 | 65 | 44.1 |
| Barker, Bryan, Kansas City | 75 | 3245 | 65 | 43.3 |
| Royals, Mark, Pittsburgh | 73 | 3119 | 58 | 42.7 |

## Sacks

| | No |
|---|---|
| O'Neal, Leslie, San Diego | 17.0 |
| Fletcher, Simon, Denver | 16.0 |
| Smith, Neil, Kansas City | 14.5 |
| Thomas, Derrick, Kansas City | 14.5 |
| Cox, Bryan, Miami | 14.0 |
| Kennedy, Cortez, Seattle | 14.0 |
| Smith, Bruce, Buffalo | 14.0 |

## Jim Thorpe Trophy Winners

The Jim Thorpe Trophy goes to the most valuable player as chosen by the NFL Players Association.

| | | | |
|---|---|---|---|
| 1955 | Harlon Hill, Chicago Bears | 1974 | Ken Stabler, Oakland Raiders |
| 1956 | Frank Gifford, N.Y. Giants | 1975 | Fran Tarkenton, Minnesota Vikings |
| 1957 | John Unitas, Baltimore Colts | 1976 | Bert Jones, Baltimore Colts |
| 1958 | Jim Brown, Cleveland Browns | 1977 | Walter Payton, Chicago Bears |
| 1959 | Charley Conerly, N.Y. Giants | 1978 | Earl Campbell, Houston Oilers |
| 1960 | Norm Van Brocklin, Philadelphia Eagles | 1979 | Earl Campbell, Houston Oilers |
| 1961 | Y.A. Tittle, N.Y. Giants | 1980 | Earl Campbell, Houston Oilers |
| 1962 | Jim Taylor, Green Bay Packers | 1981 | Ken Anderson, Cincinnati Bengals |
| 1963 | Jim Brown, Cleveland Browns; Y.A. Tittle, N.Y. Giants | 1982 | Dan Fouts, San Diego Chargers |
| 1964 | Lenny Moore, Baltimore Colts | 1983 | Joe Theismann, Washington Redskins |
| 1965 | Jim Brown, Cleveland Browns | 1984 | Dan Marino, Miami Dolphins |
| 1966 | Bart Starr, Green Bay Packers | 1985 | Walter Payton, Chicago Bears |
| 1967 | John Unitas, Baltimore Colts | 1986 | Phil Simms, N.Y. Giants |
| 1968 | Earl Morrall, Baltimore Colts | 1987 | Jerry Rice, San Francisco |
| 1969 | Roman Gabriel, Los Angeles Rams | 1988 | Roger Craig, San Francisco |
| 1970 | John Brodie, San Francisco 49ers | 1989 | Joe Montana, San Francisco |
| 1971 | Bob Griese, Miami Dolphins | 1990 | Warren Moon, Houston |
| 1972 | Larry Brown, Washington Redskins | 1991 | Thurman Thomas, Buffalo |
| 1973 | O.J. Simpson, Buffalo Bills | 1992 | Steve Young, San Francisco |

## NFL Stadiums

| Name, location (built) | Capacity | Name, location (built) | Capacity |
|---|---|---|---|
| Anaheim Stadium, Anaheim, Cal. (1966) | 69,007 | Metrodome, Minneapolis (1982) | 63,000 |
| Arrowhead Stadium, Kansas City, Mo. (1972) | 78,067 | Mile High Stadium, Denver, Col. (1948) | 76,273 |
| Astrodome, Houston, Tex. (1965) | 60,502 | Milwaukee County Stadium (1953) | 56,051 |
| Candlestick Park, San Francisco, Cal. (1960) | 66,455 | Pontiac Silverdome, Mich. (1975) | 80,500 |
| Cleveland Stadium (1931) | 80,098 | Rich Stadium, Buffalo, N.Y. (1973) | 80,290 |
| Foxboro Stadium, Mass. (1971) | 60,794 | Riverfront Stadium, Cincinnati, Oh. (1970) | 60,389 |
| Georgia Dome, Atlanta (1992) | 71,594 | Joe Robbie Stadium, Miami, Fla. (1987) | 73,000 |
| Giants Stadium, E. Rutherford, N.J. (1976) | 76,891 | San Diego Jack Murphy Stadium (1967) | 60,835 |
| Hoosier Dome, Indianapolis, Ind. (1984) | 60,127 | Soldier Field, Chicago, Ill. (1924) | 66,949 |
| Robert F. Kennedy Stadium, Wash., D.C. (1961) | 55,683 | Sun Devil Stadium, Tempe, Ariz. (1958) | 72,608 |
| Kingdome, Seattle, Wash. (1976) | 64,984 | Tampa Stadium, Tampa, Fla. (1967) | 74,314 |
| Lambeau Field, Green Bay, Wis. (1957) | 59,543 | Texas Stadium, Irving, Tex. (1971) | 65,024 |
| Los Angeles Memorial Coliseum (1923) | 92,488 | Three Rivers Stadium, Pittsburgh, Pa. (1970) | 60,750 |
| Louisiana Superdome, New Orleans (1975) | 69,065 | Veterans Stadium, Philadelphia, Pa. (1971) | 65,356 |

# THE BULLS "THREEPEAT"

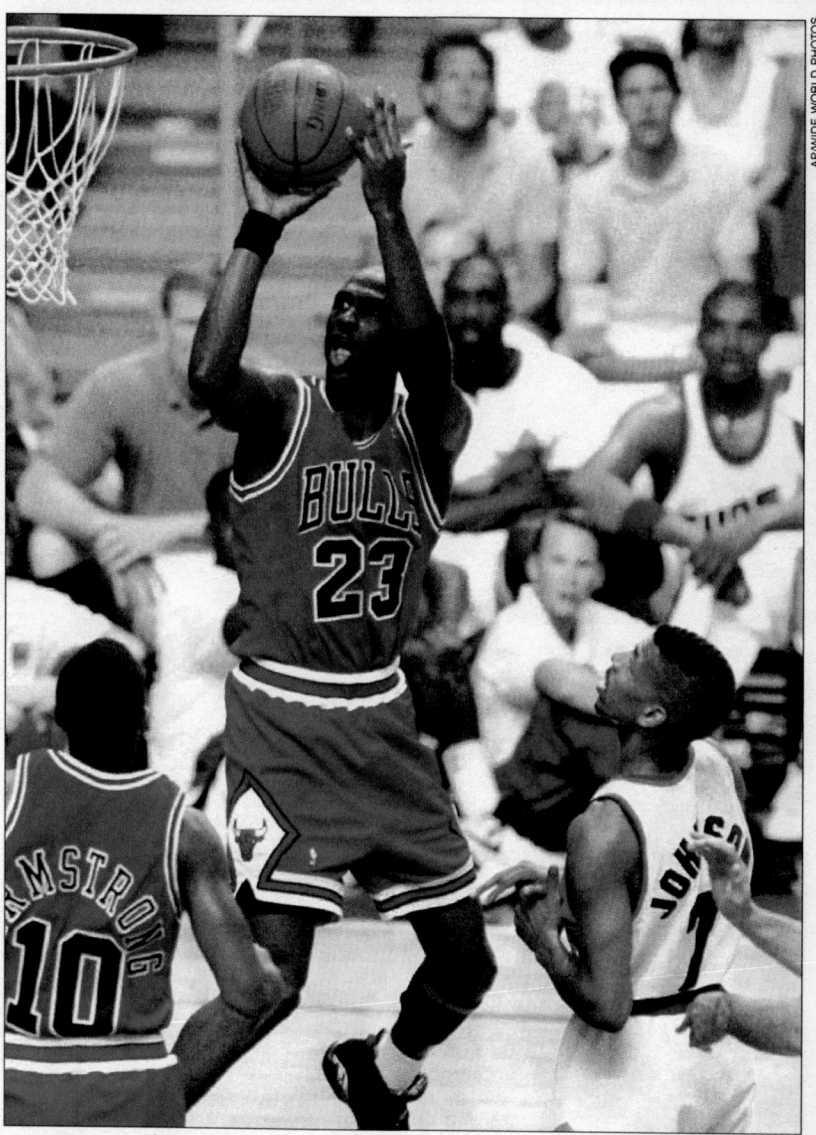

*Michael Jordan—who soon after announced his retirement—
leads the Chicago Bulls to their third straight NBA title.*

# SPORTS HIGHLIGHTS

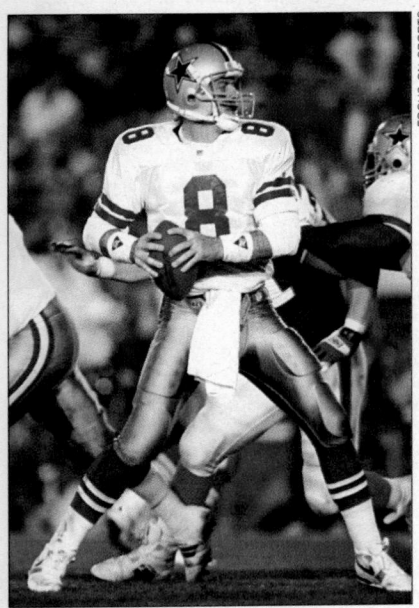

*Eric Montross helps North Carolina defeat Michigan for the NCAA college basketball championship.*

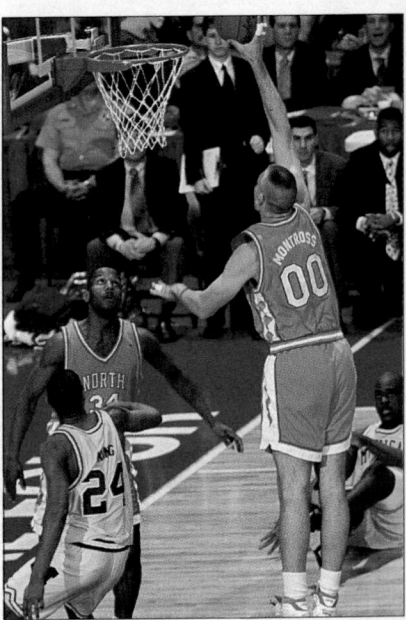

*Most Valuable Player Troy Aikman of the Dallas Cowboys, during their Super Bowl win over the Buffalo Bills.*

*Goaltender Patrick Roy, the playoffs MVP, in action, as the Montreal Canadiens win the NHL finals.*

*Australian Greg Norman raises his arms in triumph after winning the British Open golf tournament.*

*Tennis star Monica Seles after being stabbed at courtside in a Hamburg, Germany, tournament April 30.*

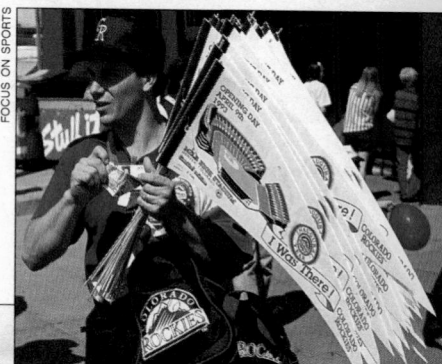

*Over 80,000 fans—and a host of souvenir sellers—pack Mile High Stadium in Denver for the first home opener, April 9, of the Colorado Rockies.*

# PEOPLE IN THE NEWS

*AP/WIDE WORLD PHOTOS*

*Rock veteran Eric Clapton with the six Grammy Awards he received in Los Angeles February 24.*

*Connie Chung joins Dan Rather as co-anchor of the CBS Evening News on June 1.*

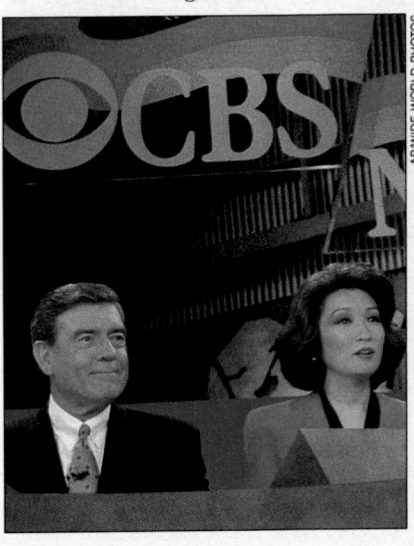

*AP/WIDE WORLD PHOTOS*

*BRIAN SMALE/ONYX*

*Author John Grisham, who at one point had four books on the best-seller lists (left). Below: Louis V. Gerstner is named, March 26, as the new chairman of troubled corporate giant IBM.*

*RICK MAIMAN/SYGMA*

Kim Campbell, selected in June as Canada's first female prime minister.

Dr. Jack Kevorkian, proponent and practitioner of doctor-assisted suicides, leaves a Michigan court.

Maintaining his presence on the talk-show circuit, Ross Perot chats with Tonight Show host Jay Leno.

# ON STAGE AND SCREEN

The T. rex in action in Jurassic Park, a summer blockbuster directed by Steven Spielberg.

AP/WIDE WORLD PHOTOS

Russian-born ballet great Rudolf Nureyev, who died of AIDS January 6.

REUTERS/BETTMANN

PIERRE VAUTHEY/SYGMA

Reclusive pop star Michael Jackson grants a rare interview February 10 to talk-show host Oprah Winfrey.

*Clint Eastwood in* Unforgiven, *which won four Oscars (below). A scene from* Angels in America: Millennium Approaches, *a Pulitzer Prize-winning play dramatizing the AIDS crisis (right).*

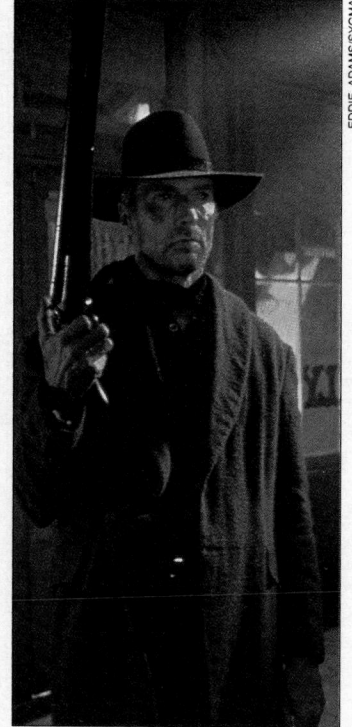

*Comedian David Letterman announces his move from NBC to CBS (below).*

*May 20: curtain call for the final episode of the long-running NBC comedy* Cheers.

# ROYAL FAMILIES

Charles and Diana in a rare post-separation appearance together May 30 (below). Tourists line up August 7 for the first public tours of Buckingham Palace (right).

Japanese Crown Prince Naruhito and new Crown Princess Masako following their June wedding.

## Number One NFL Draft Choices, 1936-1993

| Year | Team | Player, Pos., College | Year | Team | Player, Pos., College |
|------|------|----------------------|------|------|----------------------|
| 1936 | Philadelphia | Jay Berwanger, HB, Chicago | 1966 | Atlanta | Tommy Nobis, LB, Texas |
| 1937 | Philadelphia | Sam Francis, FB, Nebraska | 1967 | Baltimore | Bubba Smith, DT, Michigan St. |
| 1938 | Cleve.Rams | Corbett Davis, FB, Indiana | 1968 | Minnesota | Ron Yary, T, USC |
| 1939 | Chi.Cards | Ki Aldrich, C, TCU | 1969 | Buffalo | O.J. Simpson, RB, USC |
| 1940 | Chi.Cards | George Cafego, HB, Tennessee | 1970 | Pittsburgh | Terry Bradshaw, QB, La.Tech |
| 1941 | Chi.Bears | Tom Harmon, HB, Michigan | 1971 | New England | Jim Plunkett, QB, Stanford |
| 1942 | Pittsburgh | Bill Dudley, HB, Virginia | 1972 | Buffalo | Walt Patulski, DE, Notre Dame |
| 1943 | Detroit | Frank Sinkwich, HB, Georgia | 1973 | Houston | John Matuszak, DE, Tampa |
| 1944 | Boston Yanks | Angelo Bertelli, QB, Notre Dame | 1974 | Dallas | Ed "Too Tall" Jones, Tenn.St. |
| 1945 | Chi.Cards | Charley Trippi, HB, Georgia | 1975 | Atlanta | Steve Bartkowski, QB, Cal. |
| 1946 | Boston Yanks | Frank Dancewicz, QB, Notre Dame | 1976 | Tampa Bay | Lee Roy Selmon, DE, Oklahoma |
| | | | 1977 | Tampa Bay | Ricky Bell, RB, USC |
| 1947 | Chi.Bears | Bob Fenimore, HB, Okla. A&M | 1978 | Houston | Earl Campbell, RB, Texas |
| 1948 | Washington | Harry Gilmer, QB, Alabama | 1979 | Buffalo | Tom Cousineau, LB, Ohio St. |
| 1949 | Philadelphia | Chuck Bednarik, C, Penn | 1980 | Detroit | Billy Sims, RB, Oklahoma |
| 1950 | Detroit | Leon Hart, E, Notre Dame | 1981 | New Orleans | George Rogers, RB, S.Carolina |
| 1951 | N.Y. Giants | Kyle Rote, HB, SMU | 1982 | New England | Kenneth Sims, DT, Texas |
| 1952 | L.A. Rams | Bill Wade, QB, Vanderbilt | 1983 | Baltimore | John Elway, QB, Stanford |
| 1953 | San Francisco | Harry Babcock, E, Georgia | 1984 | New England | Irving Fryar, WR, Nebraska |
| 1954 | Cleveland | Bobby Garrett, QB, Stanford | 1985 | Buffalo | Bruce Smith, DE, Va.Tech |
| 1955 | Baltimore | George Shaw, QB, Oregon | 1986 | Tampa Bay | Bo Jackson, RB, Auburn |
| 1956 | Pittsburgh | Gary Glick, DB, Col. A&M | 1987 | Tampa Bay | Vinny Testaverde, QB, Miami, (Fla.) |
| 1957 | Green Bay | Paul Hornung, QB, Notre Dame | | | |
| 1958 | Chi.Cards | King Hill, QB, Rice | | | |
| 1959 | Green Bay | Randy Duncan, QB, Iowa | 1988 | Atlanta | Aundray Bruce, LB, Auburn |
| 1960 | L.A. Rams | Billy Cannon, HB, LSU | 1989 | Dallas | Troy Aikman, QB, UCLA |
| 1961 | Minnesota | Tommy Mason, HB, Tulane | 1990 | Indianapolis | Jeff George, QB, Illinois |
| 1962 | Washington | Ernie Davis, HB, Syracuse | 1991 | Dallas | Russell Maryland, DL, Miami |
| 1963 | L.A. Rams | Terry Baker, QB, Oregon St. | 1992 | Indianapolis | Steve Emtman, DL, Washington |
| 1964 | San Francisco | Dave Parks, E, Texas Tech | 1993 | New England | Drew Bledsoe, QB, Washington St. |
| 1965 | N.Y. Giants | Tucker Frederickson, HB, Auburn | | | |

## First-Round Selections in the 1993 NFL Draft

| Team | Player | Pos. | College | Team | Player | Pos. | College |
|------|--------|------|---------|------|--------|------|---------|
| 1—New England | Drew Bledsoe* | QB | Washington St. | 16—Indianapolis | Sean Dawkins* | WR | California |
| 2—Seattle | Rick Mirer | QB | Notre Dame | 17—Washington | Tom Carter* | DB | Notre Dame |
| 3—Phoenix | Garrison Hearst* | RB | Georgia | 18—Phoenix | Ernest Dye | OT | S. Carolina |
| 4—N.Y. Jets | Marvin Jones* | LB | Florida St. | 19—Philadelphia | Lester Holmes | OT | Jackson St. |
| 5—Cincinnati | John Copeland | DT | Alabama | 20—New Orleans | Irv Smith | TE | Notre Dame |
| 6—Tampa Bay | Eric Curry | DE | Alabama | 21—Minnesota | Robert Smith* | RB | Ohio St. |
| 7—Chicago | Curtis Conway* | WR | USC | 22—San Diego | Darrien Gordon | DB | Stanford |
| 8—New Orleans | Willie Roaf | OT | La. Tech | 23—Pittsburgh | Deon Figures | DB | Colorado |
| 9—Atlanta | Lincoln Kennedy | OT | Washington | 24—Philadelphia | Leonard Renfroe* | DE | Colorado |
| 10—L.A. Rams | Jerome Bettis* | RB | Notre Dame | 25—Miami | O.J. McDuffie | WR | Penn St. |
| 11—Denver | Dan Williams | DE | Toledo | 26—San Francisco | Dana Stubblefield | DE | Kansas |
| 12—L.A. Raiders | Patrick Bates* | DB | Texas A&M | 27—San Francisco | Todd Kelly | DE | Tennessee |
| 13—Houston | Brad Hopkins | OG | Illinois | 28—Buffalo | Thomas Smith | DB | N. Carolina |
| 14—Cleveland | Steve Everitt | C | Michigan | 29—Green Bay | George Teague | DB | Alabama |
| 15—Green Bay | Wayne Simmons | LB | Clemson | | * Under classmen who chose to enter the NFL draft. | | |

## Pro Football Hall of Fame, Canton, Ohio

| | | | | |
|---|---|---|---|---|
| Herb Adderley | Mike Ditka | Paul Hornung | Mike McCormack | Gale Sayers |
| Lance Alworth | Art Donovan | Ken Houston | Hugh McElhenny | Joe Schmidt |
| Doug Atkins | Paddy Driscoll | Cal Hubbard | John (Blood) McNally | Tex Schramm |
| Morris (Red) Badgro | Bill Dudley | Sam Huff | Mike Michalske | Art Shell |
| Lem Barney | Turk Edwards | Lamar Hunt | Wayne Millner | O.J. Simpson |
| Cliff Battles | Weeb Ewbank | Don Hutson | Bobby Mitchell | Bart Starr |
| Sammy Baugh | Tom Fears | John Henry Johnson | Ron Mix | Roger Staubach |
| Chuck Bednarik | Ray Flaherty | Deacon Jones | Lenny Moore | Ernie Stautner |
| Bert Bell | Len Ford | Stan Jones | Marion Motley | Jan Stenerud |
| Bobby Bell | Dr. Daniel Fortmann | Sonny Jurgensen | George Musso | Ken Strong |
| Raymond Berry | Dan Fouts | Walt Kiesling | Bronko Nagurski | Joe Stydahar |
| Charles Bidwell | Frank Gatski | Frank (Bruiser) Kinard | Joe Namath | Fran Tarkenton |
| Fred Biletnikoff | Bill George | Curly Lambeau | Greasy Neale | Charlie Taylor |
| George Blanda | Frank Gifford | Jack Lambert | Ernie Nevers | Jim Taylor |
| Mel Blount | Sid Gillman | Tom Landry | Ray Nitschke | Jim Thorpe |
| Terry Bradshaw | Otto Graham | Dick (Night Train) Lane | Chuck Noll | Y.A. Tittle |
| Jim Brown | Red Grange | Jim Langer | Leo Nomellini | George Trafton |
| Paul Brown | Joe Greene | Willie Lanier | Merlin Olsen | Charlie Trippi |
| Roosevelt Brown | Forrest Gregg | Yale Lary | Jim Otto | Emlen Tunnell |
| Willie Brown | Bob Griese | Dante Lavelli | Steve Owen | Clyde (Bulldog) Turner |
| Buck Buchanan | Lou Groza | Bobby Layne | Alan Page | Johnny Unitas |
| Dick Butkus | Joe Guyon | Tuffy Leemans | Clarence (Ace) Parker | Gene Upshaw |
| Earl Campbell | George Halas | Bob Lilly | Jim Parker | Norm Van Brocklin |
| Tony Canadeo | Jack Ham | Larry Little | Walter Payton | Steve Van Buren |
| Joe Carr | John Hannah | Vince Lombardi | Joe Perry | Doak Walker |
| Guy Chamberlin | Franco Harris | Sid Luckman | Pete Pihos | Bill Walsh |
| Jack Christiansen | Ed Healey | Link Lyman | Hugh (Shorty) Ray | Paul Warfield |
| Dutch Clark | Mel Hein | John Mackey | Dan Reeves | Bob Waterfield |
| George Connor | Ted Hendricks | Tim Mara | John Riggins | Arnie Weinmeister |
| Jim Conzelman | Pete Henry | Gino Marchetti | Jim Ringo | Bill Willis |
| Larry Csonka | Arnold Herber | George Marshall | Andy Robustelli | Larry Wilson |
| Al Davis | Bill Hewitt | Ollie Matson | Art Rooney | Alex Wojciechowicz |
| Willie Davis | Clarke Hinkle | Don Maynard | Pete Rozelle | Willie Wood |
| Len Dawson | Elroy (Crazy Legs) Hirsch | George McAfee | Bob St. Clair | |

## All-Time NFL Coaching Victories

### (at start of 1993 season)

| Coach | Years | Teams | Regular Season W | L | T | Pct | Career W | L | T | Pct |
|---|---|---|---|---|---|---|---|---|---|---|
| George Halas | 40 | Bears | 319 | 148 | 31 | .672 | 325 | 151 | 31 | .672 |
| Don Shula | 30 | Colts, Dolphins | 300 | 136 | 6 | .685 | 318 | 151 | 6 | .676 |
| Tom Landry | 29 | Cowboys | 250 | 162 | 6 | .605 | 270 | 178 | 6 | .601 |
| Curly Lambeau | 33 | Packers, Cardinals, Redskins | 226 | 132 | 22 | .623 | 229 | 134 | 22 | .623 |
| Chuck Noll | 23 | Steelers | 193 | 148 | 1 | .566 | 209 | 156 | 1 | .572 |
| Chuck Knox | 20 | Rams, Bills, Seahawks | 177 | 124 | 1 | .588 | 184 | 135 | 1 | .577 |
| Paul Brown | 21 | Browns, Bengals | 166 | 100 | 6 | .621 | 170 | 108 | 6 | .609 |
| Bud Grant | 18 | Vikings | 158 | 96 | 5 | .620 | 168 | 108 | 5 | .607 |
| Steve Owen | 23 | Giants | 151 | 100 | 17 | .595 | 153 | 108 | 17 | .582 |
| Joe Gibbs | 12 | Redskins | 124 | 60 | 0 | .674 | 140 | 65 | 0 | .683 |
| Hank Stram | 17 | Chiefs, Saints | 131 | 97 | 10 | .571 | 136 | 100 | 10 | .573 |
| Weeb Ewbank | 20 | Colts, Jets | 130 | 129 | 7 | .502 | 134 | 130 | 7 | .507 |
| Sid Gillman | 18 | Rams, Chargers, Oilers | 122 | 99 | 7 | .550 | 123 | 104 | 7 | .541 |
| George Allen | 12 | Rams, Redskins | 116 | 47 | 5 | .705 | 118 | 54 | 5 | .681 |
| Dan Reeves | 12 | Broncos | 110 | 73 | 1 | .601 | 117 | 79 | 1 | .596 |
| Don Coryell | 14 | Cardinals, Chargers | 111 | 83 | 1 | .572 | 114 | 89 | 1 | .561 |
| John Madden | 10 | Raiders | 103 | 32 | 7 | .750 | 112 | 39 | 7 | .731 |
| Mike Ditka | 11 | Bears | 106 | 62 | 0 | .631 | 112 | 68 | 0 | .622 |
| Buddy Parker | 15 | Cardinals, Lions, Steelers | 104 | 75 | 9 | .577 | 107 | 76 | 9 | .581 |
| Marv Levy | 12 | Chiefs, Bills | 98 | 77 | 0 | .560 | 106 | 82 | 0 | .564 |

## All-Time Professional Football Records

### NFL and AFL

### (at start of 1993 season)

### Leading Lifetime Rushers

| Player | League | Yrs | Att | Yards | Avg | Player | League | Yrs | Att | Yards | Avg |
|---|---|---|---|---|---|---|---|---|---|---|---|
| Walter Payton | NFL | 13 | 3,838 | 16,726 | 4.4 | Marcus Allen | NFL | 11 | 2,090 | 8,545 | 4.1 |
| Eric Dickerson | NFL | 10 | 2,970 | 13,168 | 4.4 | Joe Perry | NFL | 14 | 1,737 | 8,378 | 4.8 |
| Tony Dorsett | NFL | 12 | 2,936 | 12,739 | 4.3 | Gerald Riggs | NFL | 10 | 1,989 | 8,188 | 4.1 |
| Jim Brown | NFL | 9 | 2,359 | 12,312 | 5.2 | Larry Csonka | AFL-NFL | 11 | 1,891 | 8,081 | 4.3 |
| Franco Harris | NFL | 13 | 2,949 | 12,120 | 4.1 | Freeman McNeil | NFL | 12 | 1,798 | 8,074 | 4.5 |
| John Riggins | NFL | 14 | 2,916 | 11,352 | 3.9 | Roger Craig | NFL | 10 | 1,953 | 8,070 | 4.1 |
| O.J. Simpson | AFL-NFL | 11 | 2,404 | 11,236 | 4.7 | James Brooks | NFL | 12 | 1,685 | 7,962 | 4.7 |
| Ottis Anderson | NFL | 14 | 2,562 | 10,273 | 4.0 | Mike Pruitt | NFL | 11 | 1,844 | 7,378 | 4.0 |
| Earl Campbell | NFL | 8 | 2,187 | 9,407 | 4.3 | Leroy Kelly | NFL | 10 | 1,727 | 7,274 | 4.2 |
| Jim Taylor | NFL | 10 | 1,941 | 8,597 | 4.4 | | | | | | |

**Most Yards Gained, Season** — 2,105, Eric Dickerson, Los Angeles Rams, 1984.
**Most Yards Gained, Game** — 275, Walter Payton, Chicago Bears vs. Minnesota Vikings, Nov. 20, 1977.
**Most Touchdowns Rushing, Career** — 110, Walter Payton, Chicago Bears, 1975-1987.
**Most Touchdowns Rushing, Season** — 24, John Riggins, Washington Redskins, 1983.
**Most Touchdowns Rushing, Game** — 6, Ernie Nevers, Chicago Cardinals vs. Chicago Bears, Nov. 8, 1929.
**Most Rushing Attempts, Game** — 45, Jamie Morris, Washington Redskins vs. Cincinnati Bengals, Dec. 17, 1988.
**Longest run from Scrimmage** — 99 yds., Tony Dorsett, Dallas vs. Minnesota, Jan. 3, 1983 (scored touchdown).

### Leading Lifetime Passers

### (Minimum 1,500 attempts)

| Player | League | Yrs | Att | Comp | Yds | Pts* | Player | League | Yrs | Att | Comp | Yds | Pts* |
|---|---|---|---|---|---|---|---|---|---|---|---|---|---|
| Joe Montana | NFL | 13 | 4,600 | 2,929 | 35,124 | 93.5 | Ken Anderson | NFL | 16 | 4,475 | 2,654 | 32,838 | 81.9 |
| Steve Young | NFL | 8 | 1,506 | 908 | 11,877 | 90.4 | Boomer Esiason | NFL | 9 | 3,378 | 1,897 | 25,671 | 81.8 |
| Dan Marino | NFL | 10 | 5,284 | 3,128 | 39,502 | 87.8 | Bernie Kosar | NFL | 8 | 3,012 | 1,174 | 21,097 | 81.8 |
| Jim Kelly | NFL | 7 | 3,024 | 1,824 | 23,031 | 86.9 | Danny White | NFL | 13 | 2,950 | 1,761 | 21,959 | 81.7 |
| Mark Rypien | NFL | 5 | 1,888 | 1,078 | 14,414 | 84.3 | Ken O'Brien | NFL | 9 | 3,465 | 2,039 | 34,386 | 81.0 |
| Roger Staubach | NFL | 11 | 2,958 | 1,685 | 22,700 | 83.4 | Warren Moon | NFL | 9 | 4,026 | 2,329 | 30,200 | 81.0 |
| Neil Lomax | NFL | 8 | 3,153 | 1,817 | 22,771 | 82.7 | Bart Starr | NFL | 16 | 3,149 | 1,808 | 24,718 | 80.5 |
| Sonny Jurgensen | NFL | 18 | 4,262 | 2,433 | 32,224 | 82.6 | Fran Tarkenton | NFL | 18 | 6,467 | 3,686 | 47,003 | 80.4 |
| Len Dawson | NFL-AFL | 19 | 3,741 | 2,136 | 28,711 | 82.6 | Dan Fouts | NFL | 15 | 5,604 | 3,294 | 43,040 | 80.2 |
| Dave Krieg | NFL | 13 | 3,989 | 2,326 | 29,247 | 82.1 | | | | | | | |

* Rating points based on performances in the following categories: Percentage of completions, percentage of touchdown passes, percentage of interceptions, and average gain per pass attempt.

**Most Yards Gained, Season** — 5,084, Dan Marino, Miami Dolphins, 1984.
**Most Yards Gained, Game** — 554, Norm Van Brocklin, Los Angeles Rams vs. New York Yankees, Sept. 18, 1951 (27 completions in 41 attempts).
**Most Touchdowns Passing, Career** — 342, Fran Tarkenton, Minnesota Vikings, 1961-66; N.Y. Giants, 1967-71; Vikings, 1972-78.
**Most Touchdowns Passing, Season** — 48, Dan Marino, Miami Dolphins, 1984.
**Most Touchdowns Passing, Game** — 7, Sid Luckman, Chicago Bears vs. New York Giants, Nov. 14, 1943; Adrian Burk, Philadelphia Eagles vs. Washington Redskins, Oct. 17, 1954; George Blanda, Houston Oilers vs. New York Titans, Nov. 19, 1961; Y.A. Tittle, New York Giants vs. Washington Redskins, Oct. 28, 1962; Joe Kapp, Minnesota Vikings vs. Baltimore Colts, Sept. 28, 1969.
**Most Passes Completed, Season** — 404, Warren Moon, Houston Oilers, 1991.
**Most Passes Completed, Game** — 42, Richard Todd, N.Y. Jets vs. San Francisco 49ers, Sept. 21, 1980.

## Leading Lifetime Receivers

| Player | League | Yrs | No | Yds | Avg | Player | League | Yrs | No | Yds | Avg |
|---|---|---|---|---|---|---|---|---|---|---|---|
| Art Monk | NFL | 13 | 847 | 11,628 | 13.7 | Harold Carmichael | NFL | 14 | 590 | 8,985 | 15.2 |
| Steve Largent | NFL | 14 | 819 | 13,089 | 16.0 | Fred Biletnikoff | AFL-NFL | 14 | 589 | 8,974 | 15.2 |
| Charlie Joiner | NFL | 18 | 750 | 12,146 | 16.2 | Harold Jackson | NFL | 16 | 579 | 10,372 | 17.9 |
| James Lofton | NFL | 15 | 750 | 13,821 | 18.4 | Lionel Taylor | AFL | 10 | 567 | 7,195 | 12.7 |
| Ozzie Newsome | NFL | 13 | 662 | 7,980 | 12.1 | Wes Chandler | NFL | 11 | 559 | 8,966 | 16.0 |
| Charley Taylor | NFL | 13 | 649 | 9,110 | 14.0 | Stanley Morgan | NFL | 14 | 557 | 10,716 | 19.2 |
| Don Maynard | AFL-NFL | 15 | 633 | 11,834 | 18.7 | Roy Green | NFL | 14 | 559 | 8,965 | 16.0 |
| Raymond Berry | NFL | 13 | 631 | 9,275 | 14.7 | Mark Clayton | NFL | 10 | 550 | 8,643 | 15.7 |
| Jerry Rice | NFL | 8 | 610 | 10,273 | 16.8 | Roger Craig | NFL | 10 | 547 | 4,742 | 8.7 |
| Drew Hill | NFL | 13 | 600 | 9,447 | 15.7 | J.T. Smith | NFL | 13 | 544 | 6,974 | 12.8 |

**Most Yards Gained, Season** — 1,746, Charley Hennigan, Houston Oilers, 1961.
**Most Yards Gained, Game** — 336, Flipper Anderson, L.A. Rams vs. New Orleans, Nov. 26, 1989.
**Most Pass Receptions, Season** — 108, Sterling Sharpe, Green Bay Packers, 1992.
**Most Pass Receptions, Game** — 18, Tom Fears, Los Angeles Rams vs. Green Bay Packers, Dec. 3, 1950 (189 yards).
**Most Touchdown Passes, Season** — 22, Jerry Rice, San Francisco 49ers, 1987.
**Most Touchdown Passes, Game** — 5, Bob Shaw, Chicago Cardinals vs. Baltimore Colts, Oct. 2, 1950; Kellen Winslow, San Diego vs. Oakland, Nov. 22, 1981; Jerry Rice, San Francisco vs. Atlanta, Oct. 14, 1990.

## Leading Lifetime Scorers

| Player | League | Yrs | TD | PAT | FG | Total | Player | League | Yrs | TD | PAT | FG | Total |
|---|---|---|---|---|---|---|---|---|---|---|---|---|---|
| George Blanda | NFL-AFL | 26 | 9 | 943 | 335 | 2,002 | Matt Bahr | NFL | 14 | 0 | 431 | 237 | 1,142 |
| Jan Stenerud | AFL-NFL | 19 | 0 | 580 | 373 | 1,699 | Gino Cappelletti | AFL | 11 | 42 | 350 | 176 | 1,130 |
| Pat Leahy | NFL | 18 | 0 | 558 | 304 | 1,470 | Gary Anderson | NFL | 11 | 0 | 356 | 258 | 1,130 |
| Jim Turner | AFL-NFL | 16 | 1 | 521 | 304 | 1,439 | Ray Wersching | NFL | 15 | 0 | 456 | 222 | 1,122 |
| Mark Moseley | NFL | 16 | 0 | 482 | 300 | 1,382 | Eddie Murray | NFL | 12 | 0 | 381 | 244 | 1,113 |
| Jim Bakken | NFL | 17 | 0 | 534 | 282 | 1,380 | Don Cockroft | NFL | 13 | 0 | 432 | 216 | 1,080 |
| Nick Lowery | NFL | 14 | 0 | 449 | 306 | 1,367 | Garo Yepremian | AFL-NFL | 14 | 0 | 444 | 210 | 1,074 |
| Fred Cox | NFL | 15 | 0 | 519 | 282 | 1,365 | Morten Anderson | NFL | 11 | 0 | 347 | 246 | 1,085 |
| Lou Groza | NFL | 17 | 1 | 641 | 234 | 1,349 | Bruce Gossett | NFL | 11 | 0 | 374 | 219 | 1,031 |
| Jim Breech | NFL | 14 | 0 | 517 | 243 | 1,246 | Sam Baker | NFL | 15 | 2 | 428 | 179 | 977 |
| Chris Bahr | NFL | 14 | 0 | 490 | 241 | 1,213 | | | | | | | |

**Most Points, Season** — 176, Paul Hornung, Green Bay Packers, 1960 (15 TD's, 41 PAT's, 15 FG's).
**Most Points, Game** — 40, Ernie Nevers, Chicago Cardinals vs. Chicago Bears, Nov. 28, 1929 (6 TD's, 4 PAT's).
**Most Touchdowns, Season** — 24, John Riggins, Washington Redskins, 1984 (24 rushing).
**Most Touchdowns, Game** — 6, Ernie Nevers, Chicago Cardinals vs. Chicago Bears, Nov. 28, 1929 (6 rushing); Dub Jones, Cleveland Browns vs. Chicago Bears, Nov. 25, 1951 (4 rushing, 2 pass receptions); Gale Sayers, Chicago Bears vs. San Francisco 49ers, Dec. 12, 1965 (4 rushing, 1 pass reception, 1 punt return).
**Most Points After Touchdown, Season** — 66, Uwe von Schamann, Miami Dolphins, 1984.
**Most Consecutive Points After Touchdown** — 234, Tommy Davis, San Francisco 49ers, 1959-1969.
**Most Field Goals, Game** — 7, Jim Bakken, St. Louis Cardinals vs. Pittsburgh Steelers, Sept. 24, 1967; Rich Karlis, Minn. Vikings vs. L.A. Rams, Nov. 5, 1989.
**Longest Field Goal** — 63 yds., Tom Dempsey, New Orleans Saints vs. Detroit Lions, Nov. 8, 1970.

## Bert Bell Memorial Trophy Winners

The Bert Bell Memorial Trophy, named after the former NFL commissioner, is awarded annually to the outstanding NFL rookie.

| 1964 | Charlie Taylor, Washington, WR | | 1977 | Tony Dorsett, Dallas, RB |
|---|---|---|---|---|
| 1965 | Gale Sayers, Chicago, RB | | 1978 | Earl Campbell, Houston, RB |
| 1966 | Tommy Nobis, Atlanta, LB | | 1979 | Ottis Anderson, St. Louis, RB |
| 1967 | Mel Farr, Detroit, RB | | 1980 | Billy Sims, Detroit, RB |
| 1968 | Earl McCullouch, Detroit, WR | | 1981 | Lawrence Taylor, N.Y. Giants, LB |
| 1969 | Calvin Hill, Dallas, RB | | 1982 | Marcus Allen, L.A. Raiders, RB |
| 1970 | Raymond Chester, Oakland, TE | | 1983 | Eric Dickerson, L.A. Rams, RB |
| 1971 | AFC: Jim Plunkett, New England, QB | | 1984 | Louis Lipps, Pittsburgh, WR |
| | NFC: John Brockington, Green Bay, RB | | 1985 | Eddie Brown, Cincinnati, WR |
| 1972 | AFC: Franco Harris, Pittsburgh, RB | | 1986 | Rueben Mayes, New Orleans, RB |
| | NFC: Willie Buchanon, Green Bay, DB | | 1987 | Bo Jackson, L.A. Raiders, RB |
| 1973 | AFC: Boobie Clark, Cincinnati, RB | | 1988 | John Stephens, New England, RB |
| | NFC: Chuck Foreman, Minnesota, RB | | 1989 | Barry Sanders, Detroit, RB |
| 1974 | Don Woods, San Diego, RB | | 1990 | Eric Green, Pittsburgh, TE |
| 1975 | AFC: Robert Brazile, Houston, LB | | 1991 | Mike Croel, Denver, LB |
| | NFC: Steve Bartkowski, Atlanta, QB | | 1992 | Dale Carter, Kansas City, CB |
| 1976 | AFC: Mike Haynes, New England, CB | | | |
| | NFC: Sammy White, Minnesota, WR | | | |

## Boston Marathon in 1993

Cosmos N'Deti of Kenya won the 1993 Boston Marathon with a time of 2 hours 9 minutes 33 seconds. Kim Jae-Yong of South Korea finished second. Olga Markova of Russia was the first woman to cross the finish line.

# GOLF

## United States Open Winners

| Year | Winner | Year | Winner | Year | Winner | Year | Winner |
|------|--------|------|--------|------|--------|------|--------|
| 1903 | Willie Anderson | 1926 | Bobby Jones* | 1951 | Ben Hogan | 1973 | Johnny Miller |
| 1904 | Willie Anderson | 1927 | Tommy Armour | 1952 | Julius Boros | 1974 | Hale Irwin |
| 1905 | Willie Anderson | 1928 | John Farrell | 1953 | Ben Hogan | 1975 | Lou Graham |
| 1906 | Alex Smith | 1929 | Bobby Jones* | 1954 | Ed Furgol | 1976 | Jerry Pate |
| 1907 | Alex Ross | 1930 | Bobby Jones* | 1955 | Jack Fleck | 1977 | Hubert Green |
| 1908 | Fred McLeod | 1931 | Wm. Burke | 1956 | Cary Middlecoff | 1978 | Andy North |
| 1909 | George Sargent | 1932 | Gene Sarazen | 1957 | Dick Mayer | 1979 | Hale Irwin |
| 1910 | Alex Smith | 1933 | John Goodman* | 1958 | Tommy Bolt | 1980 | Jack Nicklaus |
| 1911 | John McDermott | 1934 | Olin Dutra | 1959 | Billy Casper | 1981 | David Graham |
| 1912 | John McDermott | 1935 | Sam Parks Jr. | 1960 | Arnold Palmer | 1982 | Tom Watson |
| 1913 | Francis Ouimet* | 1936 | Tony Manero | 1961 | Gene Littler | 1983 | Larry Nelson |
| 1914 | Walter Hagen | 1937 | Ralph Guldahl | 1962 | Jack Nicklaus | 1984 | Fuzzy Zoeller |
| 1915 | Jerome Travers* | 1938 | Ralph Guldahl | 1963 | Julius Boros | 1985 | Andy North |
| 1916 | Chick Evans* | 1939 | Byron Nelson | 1964 | Ken Venturi | 1986 | Ray Floyd |
| 1917-18 | (Not played) | 1940 | Lawson Little | 1965 | Gary Player | 1987 | Scott Simpson |
| 1919 | Walter Hagen | 1941 | Craig Wood | 1966 | Billy Casper | 1988 | Curtis Strange |
| 1920 | Edward Ray | 1942-45 | (Not played) | 1967 | Jack Nicklaus | 1989 | Curtis Strange |
| 1921 | Jim Barnes | 1946 | Lloyd Mangrum | 1968 | Lee Trevino | 1990 | Hale Irwin |
| 1922 | Gene Sarazen | 1947 | L. Worsham | 1969 | Orville Moody | 1991 | Payne Stewart |
| 1923 | Bobby Jones* | 1948 | Ben Hogan | 1970 | Tony Jacklin | 1992 | Tom Kite |
| 1924 | Cyril Walker | 1949 | Cary Middlecoff | 1971 | Lee Trevino | 1993 | Lee Janzen |
| 1925 | Willie MacFarlane | 1950 | Ben Hogan | 1972 | Jack Nicklaus | | |

\* Amateur

## Professional Golfer's Association Championship Winners

| Year | Winner | Year | Winner | Year | Winner | Year | Winner |
|------|--------|------|--------|------|--------|------|--------|
| 1922 | Gene Sarazen | 1940 | Byron Nelson | 1959 | Bob Rosburg | 1977 | Lanny Wadkins |
| 1923 | Gene Sarazen | 1941 | Victor Ghezzi | 1960 | Jay Hebert | 1978 | John Mahaffey |
| 1924 | Walter Hagen | 1942 | Sam Snead | 1961 | Jerry Barber | 1979 | David Graham |
| 1925 | Walter Hagen | 1944 | Bob Hamilton | 1962 | Gary Player | 1980 | Jack Nicklaus |
| 1926 | Walter Hagen | 1945 | Byron Nelson | 1963 | Jack Nicklaus | 1981 | Larry Nelson |
| 1927 | Walter Hagen | 1946 | Ben Hogan | 1964 | Bob Nichols | 1982 | Ray Floyd |
| 1928 | Leo Diegel | 1947 | Jim Ferrier | 1965 | Dave Marr | 1983 | Hal Sutton |
| 1929 | Leo Diegel | 1948 | Ben Hogan | 1966 | Al Geiberger | 1984 | Lee Trevino |
| 1930 | Tommy Armour | 1949 | Sam Snead | 1967 | Don January | 1985 | Hubert Green |
| 1931 | Tom Creavy | 1950 | Chandler Harper | 1968 | Julius Boros | 1986 | Bob Tway |
| 1932 | Olin Dutra | 1951 | Sam Snead | 1969 | Ray Floyd | 1987 | Larry Nelson |
| 1933 | Gene Sarazen | 1952 | James Turnesa | 1970 | Dave Stockton | 1988 | Jeff Sluman |
| 1934 | Paul Runyan | 1953 | Walter Burkemo | 1971 | Jack Nicklaus | 1989 | Payne Stewart |
| 1935 | Johnny Revolta | 1954 | Melvin Harbert | 1972 | Gary Player | 1990 | Wayne Grady |
| 1936 | Denny Shute | 1955 | Doug Ford | 1973 | Jack Nicklaus | 1991 | John Daly |
| 1937 | Denny Shute | 1956 | Jack Burke | 1974 | Lee Trevino | 1992 | Nick Price |
| 1938 | Paul Runyan | 1957 | Lionel Hebert | 1975 | Jack Nicklaus | 1993 | Paul Azinger |
| 1939 | Henry Picard | 1958 | Dow Finsterwald | 1976 | Dave Stockton | | |

## Masters Golf Tournament Winners

| Year | Winner | Year | Winner | Year | Winner | Year | Winner |
|------|--------|------|--------|------|--------|------|--------|
| 1934 | Horton Smith | 1951 | Ben Hogan | 1966 | Jack Nicklaus | 1980 | Severiano Ballesteros |
| 1935 | Gene Sarazen | 1952 | Sam Snead | 1967 | Gay Brewer Jr. | 1981 | Tom Watson |
| 1936 | Horton Smith | 1953 | Ben Hogan | 1968 | Bob Goalby | 1982 | Craig Stadler |
| 1937 | Byron Nelson | 1954 | Sam Snead | 1969 | George Archer | 1983 | Severiano Ballesteros |
| 1938 | Henry Picard | 1955 | Cary Middlecoff | 1970 | Billy Casper | 1984 | Ben Crenshaw |
| 1939 | Ralph Guldahl | 1956 | Jack Burke | 1971 | Charles Coody | 1985 | Bernhard Langer |
| 1940 | Jimmy Demaret | 1957 | Doug Ford | 1972 | Jack Nicklaus | 1986 | Jack Nicklaus |
| 1941 | Craig Wood | 1958 | Arnold Palmer | 1973 | Tommy Aaron | 1987 | Larry Mize |
| 1942 | Byron Nelson | 1959 | Art Wall Jr. | 1974 | Gary Player | 1988 | Sandy Lyle |
| 1943-1945 | (Not played) | 1960 | Arnold Palmer | 1975 | Jack Nicklaus | 1989 | Nick Faldo |
| 1946 | Herman Keiser | 1961 | Gary Player | 1976 | Ray Floyd | 1990 | Nick Faldo |
| 1947 | Jimmy Demaret | 1962 | Arnold Palmer | 1977 | Tom Watson | 1991 | Ian Woosnam |
| 1948 | Claude Harmon | 1963 | Jack Nicklaus | 1978 | Gary Player | 1992 | Fred Couples |
| 1949 | Sam Snead | 1964 | Arnold Palmer | 1979 | Fuzzy Zoeller | 1993 | Bernhard Langer |
| 1950 | Jimmy Demaret | 1965 | Jack Nicklaus | | | | |

## British Open Winners

| Year | Winner | Year | Winner | Year | Winner | Year | Winner |
|------|--------|------|--------|------|--------|------|--------|
| 1931 | Tommy Armour | 1951 | Max Faulkner | 1966 | Jack Nicklaus | 1980 | Tom Watson |
| 1932 | Gene Sarazen | 1952 | Bobby Locke | 1967 | Roberto de Vicenzo | 1981 | Bill Rogers |
| 1933 | Denny Shute | 1953 | Ben Hogan | 1968 | Gary Player | 1982 | Tom Watson |
| 1934 | Henry Cotton | 1954 | Peter Thomson | 1969 | Tony Jacklin | 1983 | Tom Watson |
| 1935 | Alf Perry | 1955 | Peter Thomson | 1970 | Jack Nicklaus | 1984 | Seve Ballesteros |
| 1936 | Alf Padgham | 1956 | Peter Thomson | 1971 | Lee Trevino | 1985 | Sandy Lyle |
| 1937 | T.H. Cotton | 1957 | Bobby Locke | 1972 | Lee Trevino | 1986 | Greg Norman |
| 1938 | R.A. Whitcombe | 1958 | Peter Thomson | 1973 | Tom Weiskopf | 1987 | Nick Faldo |
| 1939 | Richard Burton | 1959 | Gary Player | 1974 | Gary Player | 1988 | Seve Ballesteros |
| 1940-45 | (Not played) | 1960 | Kel Nagle | 1975 | Tom Watson | 1989 | Mark Calcavecchia |
| 1946 | Sam Snead | 1961 | Arnold Palmer | 1976 | Johnny Miller | 1990 | Nick Faldo |
| 1947 | Fred Daly | 1962 | Arnold Palmer | 1977 | Tom Watson | 1991 | Ian Baker-Finch |
| 1948 | Henry Cotton | 1963 | Bob Charles | 1978 | Jack Nicklaus | 1992 | Nick Faldo |
| 1949 | Bobby Locke | 1964 | Tony Lema | 1979 | Seve Ballesteros | 1993 | Greg Norman |
| 1950 | Bobby Locke | 1965 | Peter Thomson | | | | |

# Professional Golf Tournaments in 1993

## Men

| Date | Event | Winner | Score | Prize |
|------|-------|--------|-------|-------|
| Jan. 10 | Tournament of Champions, Carlsbad, Cal. | Davis Love 3d | 272 | $144,000 |
| Jan. 17 | Hawaiian Open, Honolulu | Howard Twitty | 269 | 216,000 |
| Jan. 24 | Northern Telecom Open, Tucson, Ariz. | Larry Mize | 271 | 198,000 |
| Jan. 31 | Phoenix Open, Ariz. | Lee Janzen | 273 | 180,000 |
| Feb. 7 | A.T.&T. National Pro-Am, Pebble Beach, Cal. | Bret Ogle | 276 | 225,000 |
| Feb. 14 | Bob Hope Classic, La Quinta, Cal. | Tom Kite | 325 | 198,000 |
| Feb. 21 | Buick Invitational, La Jolla, Cal. | Phil Mickelson | 278 | 180,000 |
| Feb. 28 | Los Angeles Open | Tom Kite | 206 | 180,000 |
| Mar. 8 | Doral Open, Miami, Fla. | Greg Norman | 265 | 252,000 |
| Mar. 14 | Honda Classic, Ft. Lauderdale, Fla. | Fred Couples | 207 | 198,000 |
| Mar. 21 | Nestle Invitational, Orlando, Fla. | Ben Crenshaw | 280 | 180,000 |
| Mar. 27 | Tournament Players Championship, Ponte Vedra, Fla. | Nick Price | 270 | 450,000 |
| Apr. 11 | Masters Tournament, Augusta, Ga. | David Frost | 266 | 180,000 |
| Apr. 18 | Heritage Classic, Hilton Head, S.C. | David Edwards | 269 | 180,000 |
| Apr. 25 | Greater Greensboro Open, N.C. | Rocco Mediate | *281 | 270,000 |
| May 9 | Atlanta Classic, Marietta, Ga. | Nolan Henke | 271 | 216,000 |
| May 16 | Byron Nelson Classic, Irving, Tex. | Scott Simpson | 270 | 216,000 |
| May 23 | Kemper Open, Potomac, Md. | Grant Waite | 275 | 234,000 |
| June 6 | Memorial Tournament, Dublin, Oh. | Paul Azinger | 274 | 252,000 |
| June 13 | Buick Classic, Harrison, N.Y. | Vijay Singh | *280 | 180,000 |
| June 20 | U.S. Open, Springfield, N.J. | Lee Janzen | 272 | 290,000 |
| June 27 | Greater Hartford Open, Cromwell, Conn. | Nick Price | 271 | 180,000 |
| July 4 | Western Open, Lemont, Ill. | Nick Price | 269 | 216,000 |
| July 11 | Anheuser-Busch Classic, Williamsburg, Va. | Jim Gallagher | 269 | 198,000 |
| July 25 | New England Classic, Sutton, Mass. | Paul Azinger | 268 | 180,000 |
| Aug. 1 | St. Jude Classic, Memphis, Tenn. | Nick Price | 266 | 198,000 |
| Aug. 8 | Buick Open, Grand Blanc, Mich. | Larry Mize | 272 | 180,000 |
| Aug. 15 | PGA Championship, St. Louis | Paul Azinger | *272 | 280,000 |
| Aug. 22 | The International, Castle Rock, Col. | Phil Mickelson | 45 pts. | 234,000 |
| Aug. 29 | World Series of Golf, Akron, Oh. | Fulton Allem | 270 | 252,000 |
| Sept. 5 | Greater Milwaukee Open | Billy Mayfair | *270 | 180,000 |
| Sept. 12 | Canadian Open, Oakville, Ont. | David Frost | 279 | 180,000 |
| Sept. 19 | Hardee's Classic, Coal Valley, Ill. | David Frost | 259 | 180,000 |
| Sept. 26 | B.C. Open, Endicott, N.Y. | Blaine McCallister | 271 | 144,000 |

## Women

| Date | Event | Winner | Score | Prize |
|------|-------|--------|-------|-------|
| Feb. 21 | Hawaiian Open, Honolulu | Lisa Walters | 210 | $67,000 |
| Mar. 2 | Sprint Classic, Tallahassee, Fla. | Kristi Albers | 279 | 180,000 |
| Mar. 14 | Ping Championship, Tucson, Ariz. | Meg Mallon | 272 | 60,000 |
| Mar. 21 | Standard Register Classic, Phoenix, Ariz. | Patty Sheehan | 275 | 105,000 |
| Mar. 27 | Dinah Shore Invitational, Rancho Mirage, Cal. | Helen Alfredsson | 284 | 105,000 |
| May 9 | Sara Lee Classic, Nashville, Tenn. | Meg Mallon | *205 | 78,000 |
| May 16 | McDonald's Championship, Wilmington, Del. | Laura Davies | 277 | 135,000 |
| May 30 | Corning Classic, Corning, N.Y. | Kelly Robbins | 277 | 75,000 |
| June 6 | Oldsmobile Classic, E. Lansing, Mich. | Jane Geddes | 277 | 82,000 |
| June 13 | Mazda Championship, Bethesda, Md. | Patty Sheehan | 275 | 150,000 |
| June 20 | Rochester International, Pittsford, N.Y. | Tammy Green | 276 | 75,000 |
| June 27 | ShopRite Classic, Somers Pt., N.J. | Shelley Hamlin | 204 | 67,000 |
| July 4 | Jamie Farr Toledo Classic, Oh. | Brandie Burton | 201 | 67,000 |
| July 11 | Warren Classic, Warren, Oh. | Nancy Lopez | 203 | 75,000 |
| July 18 | Big Apple Classic, New Rochelle, N.Y. | Hiromi Kobayashi | 278 | 90,000 |
| July 25 | U.S. Women's Open, Carmel, Ind. | Lauri Merten | 280 | 144,000 |
| Aug. 1 | Ping-Welch Championship, Canton, Mass. | Missie Berteotti | 276 | 67,000 |
| Aug. 8 | McCall's Classic, Vt. | Dana Lofland-Dormann | 275 | 75,000 |
| Aug. 16 | Chicago Sun-Times Challenge, Naperville, Ill. | Cindy Schreyer | 272 | 71,000 |
| Aug. 23 | Minnesota Classic, Brooklyn Park, Minn. | Hiromi Kobayashi | 205 | 67,000 |
| Sept. 5 | Rail Charity Classic, Springfield, Ill. | Helen Dobson | *203 | 75,000 |
| Sept. 12 | Ping Championship, Portland, Ore. | Donna Andrews | 208 | 67,000 |
| Sept. 19 | Safeco Classic, Kent, Wash. | Brandie Burton | 274 | 67,000 |
| Sept. 26 | Inamori Classic, San Diego, Cal. | Kris Monaghan | 275 | 63,000 |

* Won playoff.

## U.S. Women's Open Golf Champions

| Year | Winner | Year | Winner | Year | Winner | Year | Winner |
|------|--------|------|--------|------|--------|------|--------|
| 1948 | "Babe" Zaharias | 1960 | Betsy Rawls | 1972 | Susie Maxwell Berning | 1983 | Jan Stephenson |
| 1949 | Louise Suggs | 1961 | Mickey Wright | 1973 | Susie Maxwell Berning | 1984 | Hollis Stacy |
| 1950 | "Babe" Zaharias | 1962 | Murle Lindstrom | 1974 | Sandra Haynie | 1985 | Kathy Baker |
| 1951 | Betsy Rawls | 1963 | Mary Mills | 1975 | Sandra Palmer | 1986 | Jane Geddes |
| 1952 | Louise Suggs | 1964 | Mickey Wright | 1976 | JoAnne Carner | 1987 | Laura Davies |
| 1953 | Betsy Rawls | 1965 | Carol Mann | 1977 | Hollis Stacy | 1988 | Liselotte Neumann |
| 1954 | "Babe" Zaharias | 1966 | Sandra Spuzich | 1978 | Hollis Stacy | 1989 | Betsy King |
| 1955 | Fay Crocker | 1967 | Catherine Lacoste* | 1979 | Jerilyn Britz | 1990 | Betsy King |
| 1956 | Mrs. K. Cornelius | 1968 | Susie Maxwell Berning | 1980 | Amy Alcott | 1991 | Meg Mallon |
| 1957 | Betsy Rawls | 1969 | Donna Caponi | 1981 | Pat Bradley | 1992 | Patty Sheehan |
| 1958 | Mickey Wright | 1970 | Donna Caponi | 1982 | Janet Alex | 1993 | Lauri Merten |
| 1959 | Mickey Wright | 1971 | JoAnne Carner | | | | |

* Amateur

## PGA Leading Money Winners

| Year | Player | Dollars | Year | Player | Dollars | Year | Player | Dollars |
|---|---|---|---|---|---|---|---|---|
| 1946 | Ben Hogan | $42,556 | 1962 | Arnold Palmer | $81,448 | 1978 | Tom Watson | $362,429 |
| 1947 | Jimmy Demaret | 27,936 | 1963 | Arnold Palmer | 128,230 | 1979 | Tom Watson | 462,636 |
| 1948 | Ben Hogan | 36,812 | 1964 | Jack Nicklaus | 113,284 | 1980 | Tom Watson | 530,808 |
| 1949 | Sam Snead | 31,593 | 1965 | Jack Nicklaus | 140,752 | 1981 | Tom Kite | 375,699 |
| 1950 | Sam Snead | 35,758 | 1966 | Billy Casper | 121,944 | 1982 | Craig Stadler | 446,462 |
| 1951 | Lloyd Mangrum | 26,088 | 1967 | Jack Nicklaus | 188,988 | 1983 | Hal Sutton | 426,668 |
| 1952 | Julius Boros | 37,032 | 1968 | Billy Casper | 205,168 | 1984 | Tom Watson | 476,260 |
| 1953 | Lew Worsham | 34,002 | 1969 | Frank Beard | 175,223 | 1985 | Curtis Strange | 542,321 |
| 1954 | Bob Toski | 65,819 | 1970 | Lee Trevino | 157,037 | 1986 | Greg Norman | 653,296 |
| 1955 | Julius Boros | 65,121 | 1971 | Jack Nicklaus | 244,490 | 1987 | Curtis Strange | 925,941 |
| 1956 | Ted Kroll | 72,835 | 1972 | Jack Nicklaus | 320,542 | 1988 | Curtis Strange | 1,147,644 |
| 1957 | Dick Mayer | 65,835 | 1973 | Jack Nicklaus | 308,362 | 1989 | Tom Kite | 1,395,278 |
| 1958 | Arnold Palmer | 42,407 | 1974 | Johnny Miller | 353,201 | 1990 | Greg Norman | 1,165,477 |
| 1959 | Art Wall Jr. | 53,167 | 1975 | Jack Nicklaus | 323,149 | 1991 | Corey Pavin | 979,430 |
| 1960 | Arnold Palmer | 75,262 | 1976 | Jack Nicklaus | 266,438 | 1992 | Fred Couples | 1,344,188 |
| 1961 | Gary Player | 64,540 | 1977 | Tom Watson | 310,653 | | | |

## LPGA Leading Money Winners

| Year | Player | Dollars | Year | Player | Dollars | Year | Player | Dollars |
|---|---|---|---|---|---|---|---|---|
| 1954 | Patty Berg | $16,011 | 1967 | Kathy Whitworth | $32,937 | 1980 | Beth Daniel | $231,000 |
| 1955 | Patty Berg | 16,492 | 1968 | Kathy Whitworth | 48,379 | 1981 | Beth Daniel | 206,977 |
| 1956 | Marlene Hagge | 20,235 | 1969 | Carol Mann | 49,152 | 1982 | JoAnne Carner | 310,399 |
| 1957 | Patty Berg | 16,272 | 1970 | Kathy Whitworth | 30,235 | 1983 | JoAnne Carner | 291,404 |
| 1958 | Beverly Hanson | 12,629 | 1971 | Kathy Whitworth | 41,181 | 1984 | Betsy King | 266,771 |
| 1959 | Betsy Rawls | 26,774 | 1972 | Kathy Whitworth | 65,063 | 1985 | Nancy Lopez | 416,472 |
| 1960 | Louise Suggs | 16,892 | 1973 | Kathy Whitworth | 82,854 | 1986 | Pat Bradley | 492,021 |
| 1961 | Mickey Wright | 22,236 | 1974 | JoAnne Carner | 87,094 | 1987 | Ayako Okamoto | 466,034 |
| 1962 | Mickey Wright | 21,641 | 1975 | Sandra Palmer | 94,805 | 1988 | Sherri Turner | 347,255 |
| 1963 | Mickey Wright | 31,269 | 1976 | Judy Rankin | 150,734 | 1989 | Betsy King | 654,132 |
| 1964 | Mickey Wright | 29,800 | 1977 | Judy Rankin | 122,890 | 1990 | Beth Daniel | 863,578 |
| 1965 | Kathy Whitworth | 28,658 | 1978 | Nancy Lopez | 189,813 | 1991 | Pat Bradley | 763,118 |
| 1966 | Kathy Whitworth | 33,517 | 1979 | Nancy Lopez | 215,987 | 1992 | Dottie Mochrie | 693,335 |

# Rifle and Pistol Individual Championships in 1993

Source: National Rifle Association

## National Outdoor Rifle and Pistol Championships

**Pistol**—Steve Reiter, Daly City, Cal., 2660-123X.
**Civilian Pistol**—Richard Rodriquez, Stafford, Va., 2647-125X.
**Woman Pistol**—Delores J. Williams, Summersville, W.Va., 2567-63X.
**Smallbore Rifle Prone**—Carolyn D. Millard-Sparks, Atlanta, Ga., 6370-442X.
**Smallbore Rifle NRA 3-Position**—James Meredith, Columbus, Ga., 2267-82X.
**Civilian Smallbore Rifle NRA 3-Position**—Kenneth M. Benyo, New Tripoli, Pa., 2254-82X.
**Woman Smallbore Rifle NRA 3-Position**—Kristin Ann Peterson, Ft. Benning, Ga., 2178-69X.
**High Power Rifle**—G. David Tubb, Canandian, Tex., 2383-110X.
**Woman High Power Rifle**—Nancy H. Tompkins-Gallagher, Prescott, Ariz., 2368-105X.

## National Indoor Rifle and Pistol Championships

**Smallbore Rifle 4-Position**—Karen E. Monez, Colorado Springs, Col., 800.
**Smallbore Rifle NRA 3-Position**—Glenn Dubis, Ft. Benning, Ga., 1190.
**Woman Smallbore Rifle NRA 3-Position**—Tammie Deangelis, Colorado Springs, Col., 1176.
**Smallbore Rifle International**—Michael E. Anti, Columbus, Ga., 1185.
**Woman Smallbore Rifle International**—Kristin Ann Peterson, Columbus, Ga., 1174.
**Air Rifle**—Ann Pfiffner, Dubuque, Ia., 593.
**Conventional Pistol**—Gregory J. Derr, Marshfield, Mass., 888.
**Woman Conventional Pistol**—Kathy S. Chatterton, Millburn, N.J., 864.
**International Free Pistol**—Donald Carl, Ft. Benning, Ga., 547.
**Woman International Free Pistol**—Dorothea Martin, Detroit, Mich., 473.
**International Standard Pistol**—Christopher Alvarez, Woodinville, Wash., 572.
**Woman International Standard Pistol**—Kathie Woolard, Point Richnnond, Cal., 534.
**Air Pistol**—James Henderson, Ft. Benning, Ga., 574.
**Woman Air Pistol**—Rhonda Barush, Columbus, Ga., 559.

## NRA Bianchi Cup National Action Pistol Championships

**Action Pistol**—Bruce Piatt, Montvale, N.J., 1920-170X.
**Woman Action Pistol**—Judith Woolley, Plains, Mont., 1898-148X.
**Junior Action Pistol**—Chad Dietrich, Bismarck, N.D., 1908-154X.

# American Power Boat Assn. Gold Cup Champions

| Year | Boat | Driver | Year | Boat | Driver |
|---|---|---|---|---|---|
| 1975 | Pay 'N Pak | George Henley | 1984 | Atlas Van Lines | Chip Hanauer |
| 1976 | Miss U.S. | Tom D'Eath | 1985 | Miller American | Chip Hanauer |
| 1977 | Atlas Van Lines | Bill Muncey | 1986 | Miller American | Chip Hanauer |
| 1978 | Atlas Van Lines | Bill Muncey | 1987 | Miller American | Chip Hanauer |
| 1979 | Atlas Van Lines | Bill Muncey | 1988 | Miller American | Chip Hanauer |
| 1980 | Miss Budweiser | Dean Chenoweth | 1989 | Miss Budweiser | Tom D'Eath |
| 1981 | Miss Budweiser | Dean Chenoweth | 1990 | Miss Budweiser | Tom D'Eath |
| 1982 | Atlas Van Lines | Chip Hanauer | 1991 | Winston Eagle | Mark Tate |
| 1983 | Atlas Van Lines | Chip Hanauer | 1992 | Miss Budweiser | Chip Hanauer |
| | | | 1993 | Miss Budweiser | Chip Hanauer |

# Notable Sports Personalities

**Henry Aaron,** b. 1934: Milwaukee-Atlanta outfielder hit record 755 home runs; led NL 4 times.

**Kareem Abdul-Jabbar,** b. 1947: Milwaukee, L.A. Lakers center; MVP 6 times; leading scorer twice; playoff MVP, 1971, 1985; all-time leading NBA scorer.

**Grover Cleveland Alexander,** (1887-1950): pitcher won 374 NL games; pitched 16 shutouts, 1916.

**Muhammad Ali,** b. 1942: 3-time heavyweight champion.

**Ken Anderson,** b. 1949: Cinn. Bengals quarterback led AFC in passing 4 times.

**Mario Andretti,** b. 1940; won Indy 500, 1969; Grand Prix champ, 1978.

**Eddie Arcaro,** b. 1916: jockey rode 4,779 winners including the Kentucky Derby 5 times; the Preakness and Belmont Stakes 6 times each.

**Henry Armstrong,** (1912-1988): boxer held feather-, welter-, light-weight titles simultaneously, 1937-38.

**Arthur Ashe,** (1943-1993): U.S. singles champ, 1968, Wimbledon champ, 1975.

**Red Auerbach,** b. 1917: coached Boston Celtics to 9 NBA championships.

**Ernie Banks,** b. 1931: Chicago Cubs slugger hit 512 NL homers; twice MVP.

**Roger Bannister,** b. 1929: Briton ran first sub 4-minute mile, May 6, 1954.

**Rick Barry,** b. 1944: NBA scoring leader, 1967; ABA, 1969.

**Sammy Baugh,** b. 1914: Washington Redskins quarterback held numerous records upon retirement after 16 pro seasons.

**Elgin Baylor,** b. 1934: L.A. Lakers forward; 1st team all-star 10 times.

**Boris Becker,** b. 1967: German tennis star; won U.S. Open 1989; Wimbledon champ 3 times.

**Jean Beliveau,** b. 1931: Montreal Canadiens center scored 507 goals; twice MVP.

**Johnny Bench,** b. 1947: Cincinnati Reds catcher; MVP twice; led league in home runs twice, RBIs 3 times.

**Patty Berg,** b. 1918: won over 80 golf tournaments: AP Woman Athlete-of-the-Year 3 times.

**Yogi Berra,** b. 1925: N.Y. Yankees catcher; MVP 3 times; played in 14 World Series.

**Raymond Berry,** b. 1933: Baltimore Colts receiver caught 631 passes.

**Matt Biondi,** b. 1965: swimmer won 5 gold medals at 1988 Olympics.

**Larry Bird,** b. 1956: Boston Celtics forward; chosen MVP 1984-86, playoff MVP, 1984, 1986.

**George Blanda,** b. 1927: quarterback, kicker; 26 years as active player, scoring record 2,002 points.

**Wade Boggs,** b. 1958: AL batting champ, 1983, 1985-88.

**Bjorn Borg,** b. 1956: led Sweden to first Davis Cup, 1975; Wimbledon champion, 5 times.

**Mike Bossy,** b.1957; N.Y. Islanders right wing scored over 50 goals 8 times.

**Ray Bourque,** b. 1960: Boston Bruins defenseman won Norris Trophy 4 times.

**Terry Bradshaw,** b. 1948: Pittsburgh Steelers quarterback led team to 4 Super Bowl titles.

**George Brett,** b. 1953: Kansas City Royals infielder led AL in batting, 1976, 1980, 1990; MVP, 1980.

**Lou Brock,** b. 1939: St. Louis Cardinals outfielder stole record 118 bases, 1974; led NL 8 times.

**Jimmy Brown,** b. 1936: Cleveland Browns fullback ran for 12,312 career yards; MVP 3 times.

**Paul Brown,** (1908-1991), football owner, coach; led Cleveland Browns to 4 NFL championships.

**Paul "Bear" Bryant,** (1913-1983), college football coach with 323 victories.

**Sergei Bubka,** b. 1963: Ukrainian pole vaulter; first to clear 20 feet both indoors and outdoors.

**Maria Bueno,** b. 1939: U.S. singles champ 4 times; Wimbledon champ 3 times.

**Dick Butkus,** b. 1942: Chicago Bears linebacker twice chosen best NFL defensive player.

**Dick Button,** b. 1929: figure skater won 1948, 1952 Olympic gold medals; world titlist, 1948-52.

**Walter Camp,** (1859-1925): Yale football player, coach, athletic director; established many rules; promoted All-America designations.

**Roy Campanella,** (1921-1993): Brooklyn Dodgers catcher; MVP 3 times.

**Earl Campbell,** b. 1955: NFL running back; NFL MVP 1978-1980.

**Rod Carew,** b. 1945: AL infielder won 7 batting titles; MVP, 1977.

**Steve Carlton,** b. 1944: NL pitcher won 20 games 5 times, Cy Young award 4 times.

**Billy Casper,** b. 1931: PGA Player-of-the-Year 3 times; U.S. Open champ twice.

**Wilt Chamberlain,** b. 1936: center was NBA leading scorer 7 times; MVP 4 times.

**Bobby Clarke,** b. 1949: Philadelphia Flyers center led team to 2 Stanley Cup championships; MVP, 1966.

**Roger Clemens,** b. 1962: Boston Red Sox pitcher; AL MVP 1986; Cy Young Award 1986, 1987, 1991.

**Roberto Clemente,** (1934-1972): Pittsburgh Pirates outfielder won 4 batting titles; MVP, 1966.

**Ty Cobb,** (1886-1961): Detroit Tigers outfielder had record .367 lifetime batting average, 12 batting titles.

**Sebastian Coe,** b. 1956: Briton won Olympic 1,500-meter run, 1980, 1984.

**Nadia Comaneci,** b. 1961: Romanian gymnast won 3 gold medals, achieved 7 perfect scores, 1976 Olympics.

**Maureen Connolly,** (1934-1969): won tennis "grand slam," 1953; AP Woman-Athlete-of-the-Year 3 times.

**Jimmy Connors,** b. 1952: U.S. singles champ 5 times; Wimbledon champ twice.

**James J. Corbett,** (1866-1933): heavyweight champion, 1892-97; credited with being the first "scientific" boxer.

**Angel Cordero,** b. 1942: leading money winner, 1976, 1982-83; rode 3 Kentucky Derby winners.

**Margaret Smith Court,** b. 1942: Australian won U.S. singles championship 5 times; Wimbledon champ 3 times.

**Bob Cousy,** b. 1928: Boston Celtics guard led team to 6 NBA championships: MVP, 1957.

**Andre Dawson,** b. 1954: slugger led NL in home runs, MVP, 1987.

**Dizzy Dean,** (1911-1974): colorful pitcher for St. Louis Cardinals "Gashouse Gang" in the 30s; MVP, 1934.

**Jack Dempsey,** (1895-1983); heavyweight champion, 1919-26.

**Eric Dickerson,** b. 1960: running back ran for NFL record 2,105 yds., 1984; led NFC 3 times, AFC twice.

**Joe DiMaggio,** b. 1914: N.Y. Yankees outfielder hit safely in record 56 consecutive games, 1941; MVP 3 times.

**Leo Durocher,** (1906-1991): manager won 3 NL pennants.

**Stefan Edberg,** b. 1966: U.S. singles champ 1991, 1992; Wimbledon champ 1988, 1990.

**Gertrude Ederle,** b. 1906: first woman to swim English Channel, broke existing men's record, 1926.

**Julius Erving,** b. 1950: MVP and leading scorer in ABA 3 times; NBA MVP, 1981.

**Phil Esposito,** b. 1942: NHL scoring leader 5 times.

**Chris Evert,** b. 1954: U.S. singles champ 6 times, Wimbledon champ 3 times.

**Patrick Ewing,** b. 1962: center led Georgetown Univ. to 1984 NCAA championship.

**Ray Ewry,** (1873-1937): track and field star won 8 gold medals, 1900, 1904, and 1908 Olympics.

**Nick Faldo,** 1957: British golfer won Masters, 1989-90; British Open 3 times.

**Juan Fangio,** b. 1911: World Grand Prix champion 5 times.

**Bob Feller,** b. 1918: Cleveland Indians pitcher won 266 games; pitched 3 no-hitters, 12 one-hitters.

**Peggy Fleming,** b. 1948: world figure skating champion, 1966-68; gold medalist 1968 Olympics.

**Whitey Ford,** b. 1928: N.Y. Yankees pitcher won record 10 World Series games.

**Dick Fosbury,** b. 1947: high jumper won 1968 Olympic gold medal; developed the "Fosbury Flop."

**Jimmie Foxx,** (1907-1967): Red Sox, Athletics slugger; MVP 3 times; triple crown, 1933.

**A.J. Foyt,** b. 1935: won Indy 500 4 times; U.S. Auto Club champ 7 times.

**Joe Frazier,** b. 1944: heavyweight champion, 1970-73.

**Lou Gehrig,** (1903-1941): N.Y. Yankees 1st baseman played record 2,130 consecutive games; MVP, 1936.

**George Gervin,** b. 1952: leading NBA scorer, 1978-80, 1982.

**Althea Gibson,** b. 1927: twice U.S. and Wimbledon singles champ.

**Bob Gibson,** b. 1935: St. Louis Cardinals pitcher won Cy Young award twice; struck out 3,117 batters.

**Frank Gifford,** b. 1930: N.Y. Giants back; MVP, 1956.

**Dwight Gooden,** b. 1964: N.Y. Mets pitcher was NL Rookie of Year, 1984; Cy Young award, 1985.

**Steffi Graf,** b. 1969: German won tennis "grand slam," 1988; U.S. champ 1988, 1989, 1993; Wimbledon champ 3 times.

**Otto Graham,** b. 1921: Cleveland Browns quarterback; all-pro 44 times.

**Red Grange,** (1903-1991): All-America at Univ. of Illinois 1923-25; played for Chicago Bears, 1925-35.

**Joe Greene,** b. 1946: Pittsburgh Steelers lineman; twice NFL outstanding defensive player.

**Wayne Gretzky,** b. 1961: Edmonton Oilers center scored record 92 goals, 212 pts., 1982; MVP, 1980-87, 1989.
**Florence Griffith Joyner,** b. 1959: sprinter won 3 gold medals at 1988 Olympics.
**Lefty Grove,** (1900-1975): pitcher won 300 AL games; 20-game winner 8 times.
**Tony Gwynn,** b. 1960: NL batting champ, 1984, 1987-1989.
**Walter Hagen,** (1892-1969): won PGA championship 5 times. British Open 4 times.
**George Halas,** (1895-1983): founder-coach of Chicago Bears; won 5 NFL championships.
**Bill Hartack,** b. 1932: jockey rode 5 Kentucky Derby winners.
**John Havlicek,** b. 1940: Boston Celtics forward scored over 26,000 NBA points.
**Rickey Henderson,** b. 1958: AL outfielder stole record 130 bases, 1982, record lifetime steals; AL MVP, 1990.
**Sonja Henie,** (1912-1969): world champion figure skater, 1927-36; Olympic gold medalist, 1928, 1932, 1936.
**Ben Hogan,** b. 1912: won 4 U.S. Open championships, 2 PGA, 2 Masters.
**Rogers Hornsby,** (1896-1963): NL 2d baseman batted record .424 in 1924; twice won triple crown; batting leader, 1920-25.
**Paul Hornung,** b. 1935: Green Bay Packers runner-placekicker scored record 176 points, 1960.
**Gordie Howe,** b. 1928: hockey forward; NHL MVP 6 times.
**Carl Hubbell,** (1903-1988): N.Y. Giants pitcher; 20-game winner 5 consecutive years, 1933-37.
**Bobby Hull,** b. 1939: NHL all-star 10 times.
**Brett Hull,** b. 1964: St. Louis Blues forward led NHL in goals, 1990-92; MVP 1991.
**Catfish Hunter,** b. 1946: pitched perfect game, 1968; 20-game winner 5 times.
**Don Hutson,** b. 1913: Green Bay Packers receiver caught 99 NFL touchdown passes.
**Reggie Jackson,** b. 1946: slugger led AL in home runs 4 times; MVP, 1973; hit 5 World Series home runs, 1977.
**Jack Johnson,** (1878-1946): heavyweight champion, 1910-15.
**Magic Johnson,** b. 1959: NBA MVP 1987, 1989, 1990. Playoff MVP 1980, 1982, 1987.
**Walter Johnson,** (1887-1946): Washington Senators pitcher won 413 games.
**Bobby Jones,** (1902-1971): won "grand slam of golf" 1930; U.S. Amateur champ 5 times, U.S. Open champ 4 times.
**Deacon Jones,** b. 1938: L.A. Rams lineman; twice NFL outstanding defensive player.
**Michael Jordan,** b. 1963: NBA leading scorer, 1987-93; MVP, 1988, 1991, 1992; Playoff MVP, 1991, 1992, 1993.
**Jackie Joyner-Kersee,** b. 1962: Olympic gold medalist in heptathlon, 1988, 1992.
**Sonny Jurgensen,** b. 1934: quarterback named all-pro 5 times.
**Duke Kahanamoku,** (1890-1968): swimmer won 1912, 1920 Olympic gold medals in 100-meter freestyle.
**Harmon Killebrew,** b. 1936: Minnesota Twins slugger led AL in home runs 6 times.
**Jean Claude Killy,** b. 1943: French skier won 3 1968 Olympic gold medals.
**Ralph Kiner,** b. 1922: Pittsburgh Pirates slugger led NL in home runs 7 consecutive years, 1946-52.
**Billie Jean King,** b. 1943: U.S. singles champ 4 times; Wimbledon champ 6 times.
**Bob Knight,** b. 1940: Indiana U. basketball coach lead team to NCAA championships, 1976, 1981, 1987.
**Olga Korbut,** b. 1955: Soviet gymnast won 3 1972 Olympic gold medals.
**Sandy Koufax,** b. 1935: Dodgers pitcher won Cy Young award 3 times; lowest ERA in NL, 1962-66; pitched 4 no-hitters, one a perfect game.
**Guy Lafleur,** b. 1951: forward led NHL in scoring 3 times; MVP, 1977, 1978.
**Tom Landry,** b. 1924: Dallas Cowboys head coach 1960-88.
**Rod Laver,** b. 1938: Australian won tennis "grand slam," 1962, 1969; Wimbledon champ 4 times.
**Mario Lemieux,** b. 1965: NHL leading scorer, 1988-89, 1992-93; MVP, 1988, 1993; Playoff MVP, 1991, 1992.
**Ivan Lendl,** b. 1960: U.S. singles champ, 1985-87.
**Sugar Ray Leonard,** b. 1956: former world welterweight champ.
**Carl Lewis,** b. 1961: track and field star won 8 Olympic gold medals in sprinting and the long jump.
**Vince Lombardi,** (1913-1970): Green Bay Packers coach led team to 5 NFL championships and 2 Super Bowl victories.
**Joe Louis,** (1914-1981): heavyweight champion, 1937-49.
**Sid Luckman,** b. 1916: Chicago Bears quarterback led team to 4 NFL championships; MVP, 1943.
**Connie Mack,** (1862-1956): Philadelphia Athletics manager, 1901-50; won 9 pennants, 5 championships.
**Bill Madlock,** b. 1951: NL batting leader 4 times.
**Moses Malone,** b. 1955: NBA center was MVP 1979, 1982, 1983.

**Mickey Mantle,** b. 1931: N.Y. Yankees outfielder; triple crown, 1956; 18 World Series home runs.
**Pete Maravich** (1948-1988): guard scored NCAA record 44.2 ppg during collegiate career; led NBA in scoring, 1977.
**Rocky Marciano,** (1923-1969): heavyweight champion, 1952-56; retired undefeated.
**Dan Marino,** b. 1961: Miami Dolphins quarterback passed for NFL record 5,084 yds, 1984.
**Roger Maris,** (1934-1985): N.Y. Yankees outfielder hit record 61 home runs, 1961; MVP, 1960 and 1961.
**Eddie Mathews,** b. 1931: Milwaukee-Atlanta 3d baseman hit 512 career home runs.
**Christy Mathewson,** (1880-1925): N.Y. Giants pitcher won 373 games.
**Bob Mathias,** b. 1930: decathlon gold medalist, 1948, 1952.
**Don Mattingly,** b. 1961: N.Y. Yankees 1st baseman won 1984 AL batting title; MVP, 1985.
**Willie Mays,** b. 1931: N.Y.-S.F. Giants center fielder hit 660 home runs; twice MVP.
**Willie McCovey,** b. 1938: S.F. Giants slugger hit 521 home runs; led NL 3 times.
**John McEnroe,** b. 1959: U.S. singles champ, 1979-81, 1984; Wimbledon champ, 1981, 1983-84.
**John McGraw,** (1873-1934): N.Y. Giants manager led team to 10 pennants, 3 championships.
**Mark Messier,** center chosen NHL MVP, 1990; Conn Smythe Trophy, 1984.
**George Mikan,** b. 1924: Minn. Lakers center considered the best basketball player of the first half of the century.
**Stan Mikita,** b. 1940: Chicago Black Hawks center led NHL in scoring 4 times; MVP twice.
**Joe Montana,** b. 1956: QB was Super Bowl MVP, 1982, 1985, 1990.
**Archie Moore,** b. 1913: world light-heavyweight champion, 1952-62.
**Howie Morenz,** (1902-1937): Montreal Canadiens forward considered the best hockey player of the first half of the century.
**Joe Morgan,** b. 1943: National League MVP, 1975, 1976.
**Thurman Munson,** (1947-1979): N.Y. Yankees catcher; MVP, 1976.
**Dale Murphy,** b. 1956: outfielder chosen NL MVP 1982, 1983.
**Stan Musial,** b. 1920: St. Louis Cardinals star won 7 NL batting titles; MVP 3 times.
**Bronko Nagurski,** (1908-1990): Chicago Bears fullback and tackle; gained over 4,000 yds. rushing.
**Joe Namath,** b. 1943: quarterback led N.Y. Jets to 1969 Super Bowl title.
**Martina Navratilova,** b. 1956: Wimbledon champ 8 times, U.S. champ 1983-1984; 1986-87.
**Byron Nelson,** b. 1912: won 11 consecutive golf tournaments in 1945; twice Masters and PGA titlist.
**Ernie Nevers,** (1903-1976): Stanford star selected the best college fullback to play between 1919-1969.
**John Newcombe,** b. 1943: Australian twice U.S. singles champ; Wimbledon titlist 3 times.
**Jack Nicklaus,** b. 1940: PGA Player-of-the-Year, 1967, 1972; leading money winner 8 times; won Masters 6 times.
**Chuck Noll,** b. 1931: coach led Pittsburgh Steelers to 4 Super Bowl titles.
**Paavo Nurmi,** (1897-1973): Finnish distance runner won 6 Olympic gold medals, 1920, 1924, 1928.
**Al Oerter,** b. 1936: discus thrower won gold medal at 4 consecutive Olympics, 1956-68.
**Bobby Orr,** b. 1948: Boston Bruins defenseman; Norris Trophy 8 times; led NHL in scoring twice, assists 5 times.
**Mel Ott,** (1909-1958): N.Y. Giants outfielder hit 511 home runs; led NL 6 times.
**Jesse Owens,** (1913-1980): track and field star won 4 1936 Olympic gold medals.
**Satchel Paige,** (1906-1982): pitcher starred in Negro leagues, 1924-48; entered major leagues at age 42.
**Arnold Palmer,** b. 1929: golf's first $1 million winner; won 4 Masters, 2 British Opens.
**Jim Palmer,** b. 1945: Baltimore Orioles pitcher; Cy Young award 3 times; 20-game winner 7 times.
**Floyd Patterson,** b. 1935: twice heavyweight champion.
**Walter Payton,** b. 1954: Chicago Bears running back has most rushing yards in NFL history; leading NFC rusher, 1976-80.
**Pele,** b. 1940: Brazilian soccer star scored 1,281 goals during 22-year career.
**Bob Pettit,** b. 1932: first NBA player to score 20,000 points; twice NBA scoring leader.
**Richard Petty,** b. 1937: NASCAR national champ 7 times; 7-times Daytona 500 winner.
**Laffit Pincay Jr.,** b. 1946: leading money-winning jockey, 1970-74, 1979.
**Jacques Plante,** (1929-1986): goalie, 7 Vezina trophies; first goalie to wear a mask in a game.

**Kirby Puckett,** b. 1961: Minn. Twins outfielder won AL Batting Title, 1989; led AI in hits, 1987-89, 1992.

**Willis Reed,** b. 1942: N.Y. Knicks center; MVP, 1970; playoff MVP, 1970, 1973.

**Jerry Rice,** b. 1962: S.F. 49ers receiver chosen 1989 Super Bowl MVP.

**Jim Rice,** b. 1953: Boston Red Sox outfielder led AL in home runs, 1977-78, 1983; MVP 1978.

**Maurice Richard,** b. 1921: Montreal Canadiens forward scored 544 regular season goals, 82 playoff goals.

**Branch Rickey,** (1881-1965): executive instrumental in breaking baseball's color barrier, 1947; initiated farm system, 1919.

**Pat Riley,** b. 1945: coached L.A. Lakers to 4 NBA championships.

**Cal Ripken Jr.,** b. 1961: Baltimore Orioles shortstop; AL MVP 1983, 1991.

**Oscar Robertson,** b. 1938: guard averaged career 25.7 points per game; record 9,887 career assists; MVP, 1964.

**Brooks Robinson,** b. 1937: Baltimore Orioles 3d baseman played in 4 World Series; MVP, 1964.

**Frank Robinson,** b. 1935: slugger MVP in both NL and AL; triple crown winner, 1966; first black manager in majors.

**Jackie Robinson,** (1919-1972): broke baseball's color barrier with Brooklyn Dodgers, 1947; MVP, 1949.

**Larry Robinson,** b. 1951: NHL defenseman won Norris trophy, 1977, 1980.

**Sugar Ray Robinson,** (1920-1989): middleweight champion 5 times, welterweight champion.

**Knute Rockne,** (1888-1931): Notre Dame football coach, 1918-31; revolutionized game by stressing forward pass.

**Pete Rose,** b. 1941: won 3 NL batting titles; hit safely in 44 consecutive games, 1978; has most major league hits.

**Wilma Rudolph,** b. 1940: sprinter won 3 1960 Olympic gold medals.

**Bill Russell,** b. 1934: Boston Celtics center led team to 11 NBA titles; MVP 5 times; first black coach of major pro sports team.

**Babe Ruth,** (1895-1948): N.Y. Yankees outfielder hit 60 home runs, 1927; 714 lifetime; led AL 11 times.

**Johnny Rutherford,** b. 1938: auto racer won Indy 500 3 times.

**Nolan Ryan,** b. 1947: pitcher struck out record 383 batters, 1973; record 5,714 career; pitched record 7 no-hitters; won 324 ML games.

**Bret Saberhagen,** b. 1964: Pitcher won AL Cy Young award, 1985, 1989; WS MVP, 1985.

**Gene Sarazen,** b. 1902: won PGA championship 3 times, U.S. Open twice; developer of sand wedge.

**Gale Sayers,** b. 1943: Chicago Bears back twice led NFC in rushing.

**Mike Schmidt,** b. 1949: Phillies 3d baseman led NL in home runs, 1974-76, 1980-81, 1983-84, 1986; NL MVP, 1980, 1981, 1986.

**Tom Seaver,** b. 1944: pitcher won NL Cy Young award 3 times, won 311 major league games.

**Monica Seles,** b. 1973: U.S. Open champ 1991, 1992.

**Bill Shoemaker,** b. 1931: jockey rode 3 Kentucky Derby and 5 Belmont Stakes winners; leading career money winner.

**Eddie Shore,** (1902-1985): Boston Bruins defenseman; MVP 4 times, first-team all-star 7 times.

**Al Simmons,** (1902-1956): AL outfielder had lifetime .334 batting average.

**O.J. Simpson,** b. 1947: running back rushed for 2,003 yds., 1973; AFC leading rusher 4 times.

**George Sisler,** (1893-1973): St. Louis Browns 1st baseman had record 257 hits, 1920; batted .340 lifetime.

**Billy Smith,** b. 1950: N.Y. Islanders goalie led team to 4 Stanley Cup championships.

**Sam Snead,** b. 1912: PGA and Masters champ 3 times each.

**Warren Spahn,** b. 1921: pitcher won 363 NL games; 20-game winner 13 times; Cy Young award, 1957.

**Tris Speaker,** (1885-1958): AL outfielder batted .344 over 22 seasons; hit record 793 career doubles.

**Mark Spitz,** b. 1950: swimmer won 7 1972 Olympic gold medals.

**Amos Alonzo Stagg,** (1862-1965): coached Univ. of Chicago football team for 41 years, including 5 undefeated seasons; introduced huddle, man-in-motion, and end-around play.

**Bart Starr,** b. 1934: Green Bay Packers quarterback led team to 5 NFL titles and 2 Super Bowl victories.

**Roger Staubach,** b. 1942: Dallas Cowboys quarterback; leading NFC passer 5 times.

**Casey Stengel,** (1890-1975): managed Yankees to 10 pennants, 7 championships, 1949-60.

**Jackie Stewart,** b. 1939: Scot auto racer retired with 27 Grand Prix victories.

**John L. Sullivan,** (1858-1918): last bareknuckle heavyweight champion, 1882-1892.

**Fran Tarkenton,** b. 1940: quarterback holds career passing records for touchdowns, completions, yardage.

**Lawrence Taylor,** b. 1959: linebacker led N.Y. Giants to 2 Super Bowl titles; played in 10 Pro Bowls.

**Gustavo Thoeni,** b. 1951: Italian 4-time world alpine ski champ.

**Jim Thorpe,** (1888-1953): football All-America, 1911, 1912; won pentathlon and decathlon, 1912 Olympics.

**Bill Tilden,** (1893-1953): U.S. singles champ 7 times; played on 11 Davis Cup teams.

**Y.A. Tittle,** b. 1926: N.Y. Giants quarterback; MVP, 1961, 1963.

**Lee Trevino,** b. 1939: won the U.S. and British Open championships twice.

**Bryan Trottier,** b. 1956: center played on 6 Stanley Cup championship teams.

**Wyomia Tyus,** b. 1945: sprinter won 1964, 1968 Olympic 100-meter dash.

**Johnny Unitas,** b. 1933: Baltimore Colts quarterback passed for over 40,000 yds.; MVP, 1957, 1967.

**Al Unser,** b. 1939: Indy 500 winner, 4 times.

**Bobby Unser,** b. 1934: Indy 500 winner 3 times.

**Norm Van Brocklin,** (1926-1983): quarterback passed for game record 554 yds., 1951; MVP, 1960.

**Honus Wagner,** (1874-1955): Pittsburgh Pirates shortstop won 8 NL batting titles.

**Tom Watson,** b. 1949: golfer won British Open 5 times.

**Johnny Weissmuller,** (1903-1984): swimmer won 52 national championships, 5 Olympic gold medals; set 67 world records.

**Jerry West,** b. 1938: L.A. Lakers guard had career average 27 points per game; first team all-star 10 times.

**Kathy Whitworth,** b. 1939: women's golf leading money winner 8 times: first woman to earn over $300,000.

**Ted Williams,** b. 1918: Boston Red Sox outfielder won 6 batting titles; last major leaguer to hit over .400: .406 in 1941; .344 lifetime batting average.

**Katarina Witt,** b. 1965: German figure skater; won Olympic gold medal, 1984, 1988.

**John Wooden,** b. 1910: coached UCLA basketball team to 10 national championships.

**Mickey Wright,** b. 1935: won LPGA championship 4 times, Vare Trophy 5 times; twice AP Woman-Athlete-of-the-Year.

**Carl Yastrzemski,** b. 1939: Boston Red Sox slugger won 3 batting titles, triple crown, 1967.

**Cy Young,** (1867-1955): pitcher won record 511 major league games.

**Babe Didrikson Zaharias,** (1914-1956): track star won 2 1932 Olympic gold medals; won numerous golf tournaments.

## Tour de France in 1993

On July 25, Miguel Indurain of Spain won the Tour de France, the world's most prestigious bicycle race, for the third consecutive year. His margin of victory in the 80th Tour de France was 4 minutes 59 seconds, and he completed the 21-day, 2,312-mile race in a total time of 95 hours, 57 minutes, 9 seconds. Tony Rominger of Switzerland finished second.

## World Gymnastics Championships in 1993

Vitali Scherbo of Belarus won the men's all-around title at the World Gymnastics Championship in Birmingham, England. Scherbo also won the vault and parallel bars titles. Shannon Miller of Edmond, Okla., won the women's all-around title.

# TRACK AND FIELD
## World Track and Field Records
### As of Sept. 1993

*Indicates pending record; some new records await confirmation. The International Amateur Athletic Federation, the world body of track and field, recognizes only records in metric distances except for the mile.

## Men's Records
### Running

| Event | Record | Holder | Country | Date | Where made |
|---|---|---|---|---|---|
| 100 meters | 9.86 s. | Carl Lewis | U.S. | Aug. 25, 1991 | Tokyo |
| 200 meters | 19.72 s. | Pietro Mennea | Italy | Sept. 12, 1979 | Mexico City |
| 400 meters | 43.29 s. | Butch Reynolds | U.S. | Aug. 16, 1988 | Zurich |
| 800 meters | 1 m., 41.73 s. | Sebastian Coe | Gr. Britain | June 10, 1981 | Florence, Italy |
| 1,000 meters | 2 m., 12.18 s. | Sebastian Coe | Gr. Britain | July 11, 1981 | Oslo |
| 1,500 meters | 3 m., 28.86 s. | Noureddine Morceli | Algeria | Sept. 6, 1992 | Rieti, Italy |
| 1 mile | *3 m., 44.39 s. | Noureddine Morceli | Algeria | Sept. 5, 1993 | Rieti, Italy |
| 2,000 meters | 4 m., 50.81 s. | Said Aouita | Morocco | July 16, 1987 | Paris |
| 3,000 meters | 7 m., 28.96 s. | Moses Kiptanui | Kenya | Aug. 16, 1992 | Cologne |
| 5,000 meters | 12 m., 58.39 s. | Said Aouita | Morocco | July 22, 1987 | Rome |
| 10,000 meters | *26 m., 58.38 s. | Yobes Ondieki | Kenya | July 10, 1993 | Oslo |
| 20,000 meters | 56 m., 55.6 s. | Arturo Barrios | Mexico | May 30, 1991 | France |
| 25,000 meters | 1 hr., 13 m., 55.8 s. | Toshihiko Seko | Japan | Mar. 22, 1981 | New Zealand |
| 3,000 meter stpl | 8 m., 02.08 s. | Moses Kiptanui | Kenya | Aug. 19, 1992 | Zurich |
| Marathon | 2 hr., 6 m., 50 s. | Belayneh Densimo | Ethiopia | Apr. 17, 1988 | Rotterdam |

### Hurdles

| | | | | | |
|---|---|---|---|---|---|
| 110 meters | *12.91 s. | Colin Jackson | U.K. | Aug. 20, 1993 | Stuttgart |
| 400 meters | 46.78 s. | Kevin Young | U.S. | Aug. 6, 1992 | Barcelona |

### Relay Races

| | | | | | |
|---|---|---|---|---|---|
| 400 mtrs. | 37.40 s. | (Marsh, Burrell, Mitchell, Lewis) | U.S. | Aug. 8, 1992 | Barcelona |
| | | (Drummond, Cason, Mitchell, Burrell) | U.S. | Aug. 22, 1993 | Sheffield, Eng. |
| 800 mtrs. (4×200) | 1m., 19.11 s. | (Marsh, Burrell, Heard Lewis) | U.S. | Apr. 25, 1992 | Philadelphia |
| 1,600 mtrs. (4×400) | *2 m., 54.29 s. | (Valmon, Watts, Johnson, Reynolds) | U.S. | Aug. 22, 1993 | Sheffield, Eng. |
| 3,200 mtrs. (4×800) | 7 m., 03.89 s. | (Elliott, Cook, Cram, Coe) | Gr. Britain | Aug. 30, 1982 | London |

### Field Events

| | | | | | |
|---|---|---|---|---|---|
| High jump | *8 ft., ½ in. | Javier Sotomayor | Cuba | July 27, 1993 | Salamanca, Spain |
| Long jump | 29 ft., 4½ in. | Mike Powell | U.S. | Aug. 30, 1992 | Tokyo |
| Triple jump | 58 ft., 11½ in. | Willie Banks | U.S. | June 16, 1985 | Indianapolis |
| Pole vault | 20 ft., 1½ in. | Sergei Bubka | Ukraine | Sept. 19, 1992 | Tokyo |
| 16 lb. shot put | 75 ft., 10¼ in. | Randy Barnes | U.S. | May 20, 1990 | Los Angeles |
| Discus | 243 ft. | Juergen Schult | E. Germany | June 6, 1986 | E. Germany |
| Javelin | *313 ft., 10 in. | Jan Zelezny | Czech Rep. | Aug. 29, 1993 | Sheffield, Eng. |
| 16 lb. hammer | 284 ft., 7 in. | Yuri Sedykh | USSR | Aug. 30, 1986 | Stuttgart |
| Decathlon | 8,891 pts. | Dave O'Brien | U.S. | Sept. 4-5, 1992 | Talence, France |

## Women's Records
### Running

| | | | | | |
|---|---|---|---|---|---|
| 100 meters | 10.49 s. | Florence Griffith Joyner | U.S. | July 16, 1988 | Indianapolis |
| 200 meters | 21.34 s. | Florence Griffith Joyner | U.S. | Sept. 29, 1988 | Seoul |
| 400 meters | 47.60 s. | Marita Koch | E. Germany | Oct. 6, 1985 | Canberra |
| 800 meters | 1 m., 53.28 s. | Jarmila Kratochvilova | Czech. | July 26, 1983 | Munich |
| 1,000 meters | 2 m., 30.60 s. | Tatyana Providokhina | USSR | Aug. 20, 1978 | USSR |
| 1,500 meters | *3 m., 50.56 s. | Qu Yunxia | China | Sept. 11, 1993 | Beijing |
| 1 mile | 4 m., 15.61 s. | Paula Ivan | Romania | July 10, 1989 | Nice |
| 2,000 meters | 5 m., 28.69 s. | Maricica Puica | Romania | July 11, 1986 | London |
| 3,000 meters | *8 m., 06.11 s. | Wang Junxia | China | Sept. 13, 1993 | Beijing |
| 5,000 meters | 14 m., 37.33 s. | Ingrid Kristiansen | Norway | Aug. 5, 1986 | Stockholm |
| 10,000 meters | *29 m., 31.78 s. | Wang Junxia | China | Sept. 8, 1993 | Beijing |
| Marathon | 2 h., 21 m., 06 s. | Ingrid Kristiansen | Norway | Apr. 21, 1985 | London |

### Hurdles

| | | | | | |
|---|---|---|---|---|---|
| 100 meters | 12.21 s. | Yordanka Donkova | Bulgaria | Aug. 21, 1988 | Bulgaria |
| 400 meters | *52.74 s. | Sally Gunnell | U.K. | Aug. 19, 1993 | Sheffield, Eng. |

### Field Events

| | | | | | |
|---|---|---|---|---|---|
| High jump | 6 ft., 10¼ in. | Stefka Kostadinova | Bulgaria | Aug. 30, 1987 | Rome |
| Shot put | 74 ft., 3 in. | Natalya Lisouskaya | USSR | June 7, 1987 | Moscow |
| Long jump | 24 ft., 8¼ in. | Galina Chistyakova | USSR | June 11, 1988 | Leningrad |
| Triple Jump | *49 ft., 6¼ in. | Ana Biryukova | Russia | Aug. 21, 1993 | Sheffield, Eng. |
| Discus | 252 ft. | Gabriele Reinsch | E. Germany | July 9, 1988 | E. Germany |
| Javelin | 262 ft., 5 in. | Petra Felke | E. Germany | Sept. 9, 1988 | Potsdam |
| Heptathlon | 7,291 pts. | Jackie Joyner-Kersee | U.S. | Sept. 23-24, 1988 | Seoul |

## Relay Races

| Event | Record | Team | Country | Date | Where |
|---|---|---|---|---|---|
| 400 mtrs. (4×100) | 41.37 s. | National team | E. Germany | Oct. 6, 1985 | Canberra |
| 800 mtrs. (4×200) | 1 m., 28.15 s. | National team | E. Germany | Aug. 9, 1980 | E. Germany |
| 1,600 mtrs. (4×400) | 3 m., 15.18 s. | National team | USSR | Oct. 1, 1988 | Seoul |
| 3,200 mtrs. (4×800) | 7 m., 50.17 s. | National team | USSR | Aug. 5, 1984 | Moscow |

# World Track and Field Indoor Records

### As of Sept. 1993

The International Amateur Athletic Federation began recognizing world indoor track and field records as official on January 1, 1987. Prior to that, there were only unofficial world indoor bests. World indoor bests set prior to January 1, 1987, are subject to approval as world records providing they meet the prescribed IAAF world records criteria, including drug testing. To be accepted as a world indoor record, a performance must meet the same criteria as a world record outdoors except that a track performance can not be set on an indoor track larger than 200 meters. *Record pending.

## Men

| Event | Record | Holder | Country | Date | Where made |
|---|---|---|---|---|---|
| 50 meters | 5.61 | Manfred Kokot | E. Germany | Feb. 4, 1973 | E. Berlin |
| 60 meters | 6.41 | Andre Cason | U.S. | Feb. 14, 1992 | Madrid |
| 200 meters | 20.36 | Bruno Marie-Rose | France | Feb. 22, 1987 | Lievin, France |
| 400 meters | 45.02 | Danny Everett | U.S. | Feb. 2, 1992 | Germany |
| 800 meters | 1:44.84 | Paul Ereng | Kenya | Mar. 4, 1989 | Budapest |
| 1,000 meters | 2:15.26 | Noureddine Morceli | Algeria | Feb. 22, 1992 | Birmingham, England |
| 1,500 meters | 3:34.16 | Noureddine Morceli | Algeria | Feb. 28, 1991 | Seville, Spain |
| 1 Mile | 3:49.78 | Eamonn Coghlan | Ireland | Feb. 27, 1983 | E. Rutherford, N.J. |
| 3,000 meters | 7:37.31 | Moses Kiptanui | Kenya | Feb. 20, 1992 | Seville, Spain |
| 5,000 meters | 13:20.40 | Suleiman Nyambui | Tanzania | Feb. 6, 1981 | New York |
| 50-meter hurdles | 6.25 | Mark McKoy | Canada | Jan. 27, 1985 | Rosemont, Ill. |
| 60-meter hurdles | 7.36 | Greg Foster | U.S. | Jan. 16, 1987 | Los Angeles |
| High Jump | 7 ft. 11½ in. | Javier Sotomayor | Cuba | Mar. 4, 1989 | Budapest |
| Pole Vault | *20 ft. 2 in. | Sergei Bubka | Ukraine | Feb. 21, 1993 | Ukraine |
| Long Jump | 28 ft. 10¼ in. | Carl Lewis | U.S. | Feb. 27, 1984 | New York |
| Triple Jump | 58 ft. 3¼ in. | Mike Conley | U.S. | Feb. 27, 1987 | New York |
| Shot Put | 74 ft. 4¼ in. | Randy Barnes | U.S. | Jan. 20, 1989 | Los Angeles |

## Women

| Event | Record | Holder | Country | Date | Where made |
|---|---|---|---|---|---|
| 50 meters | *6.00 | Irina Privalova | Russia | Feb. 2, 1993 | Moscow |
| 60 meters | *6.95 | Gail Devers | U.S. | Mar. 12, 1993 | Toronto |
| 200 meters | 21.87 | Merlene Ottey | Jamaica | Feb. 13, 1993 | Lievin, France |
| 400 meters | 49.59 | Jarmila Kratochvilova | Czechoslovakia | Mar. 7, 1982 | Milan |
| 800 meters | 1:56.40 | Christine Wachtel | E. Germany | Feb. 13, 1988 | Vienna |
| 1,000 meters | 2:34.67 | Lilia Nurutdinova | Russia | Feb. 7, 1992 | Moscow |
| 1,500 meters | 4:00.27 | Doina Melinte | Romania | Feb. 9, 1990 | E. Rutherford, N.J. |
| 1 Mile | 4:17.13 | Doina Melinte | Romania | Feb. 9, 1990 | E. Rutherford, N.J. |
| 3,000 meters | 8:33.82 | Elly Van Hulst | Netherlands | Feb. 8, 1986 | England |
| 5,000 meters | 15:03.17 | Liz McColgan | Scotland | Feb. 22, 1992 | Birmingham, England |
| 50-meter hurdles | 6:58 | Cornelia Oschkenat | E. Germany | Feb. 20, 1988 | Berlin |
| 60-meter hurdles | *7.63 | Lyudmila Narozhilenko | Russia | Mar. 4, 1993 | Seville, Spain |
| High Jump | 6 ft. 9½ in. | Heike Henkel | Germany | Feb. 8, 1992 | Germany |
| Long Jump | 24 ft. 2¼ in. | Heike Dreschler | E. Germany | Feb. 13, 1988 | Vienna |
| Triple Jump | 47 ft. 4½ in. | Inessa Kravets | USSR | Mar. 9, 1991 | Seville, Spain |
| Shot Put | 73 ft. 10 in. | Helena Fibingerova | Czechoslovakia | Feb. 19, 1977 | Czech. |

# World Track & Field Championships in 1993

### Stuttgart, Germany, Aug. 14-22, 1993

## Men

**100 Meters**—Linford Christie, Gt. Britain. Time—0:09.87.
**200 Meters**—Frank Fredericks, Namibia. Time—0:19.85.
**400 Meters**—Michael Johnson, U.S. Time—0:43.65.
**800 Meters**—Paul Ruto, Kenya. Time—1:44.71.
**1,500 Meters**—Noureddine Morceli, Algeria. Time—3:34.24.
**3,000-Meter Steeplechase**—Moses Kiptanui, Kenya. Time — 8:06.36.
**5,000 Meters**—Ismael Kirui, Kenya. Time—13:02.75.
**10,000 Meters**—Haile Gebresilasie, Ethiopia. Time—27:46.02.
**Marathon**—Mark Plaatjes, U.S. Time—2:13.57.
**400-Meter Relay**—U.S. Time—0:37.48.
**1,600-Meter Relay**—U.S. Time—2:54.29.
**110-Meter Hurdles**—Colin Jackson, Gt. Britain. Time—0:12.91.
**400-Meter Hurdles**—Kevin Young, U.S. Time—0:47.18.
**High Jump**—Javier Sotomayor, Cuba. 7 Ft. 10½ in.
**Pole Vault**—Sergei Bubka, Ukraine. 19 Ft. 8¼ in.
**Long Jump**—Mike Powell, U.S. 28 Ft. 2¼ in.
**Triple Jump**—Mike Conley, U.S. 58 Ft. 7¼ in.
**Shot Put**—Werner Guenthor, Switzerland. 72 Ft. 1 in.
**Discus**—Lars Riedel, Germany. 222 Ft. 2 in.
**Javelin**—Jan Zelezny, Czech Rep. 282 Ft. 1 in.
**Decathlon**—Dan O'Brien, U.S. 8,817 Pts.

## Women

**100 Meters**—Gail Devers, U.S. Time—0:10.82.
**200 Meters**—Merlene Ottey, Jamaica. Time—0:21.98.
**400 Meters**—Jearl Miles, U.S. Time—0:49.82.
**800 Meters**—Maria Mutola, Mozambique. Time—1:55.43.
**1,500 Meters**—Dong Liu, China. Time—4:00.50.
**3,000 Meters**—Yunxia Qu, China. Time—8:28.71.
**400-Meter Relay**—Russia. Time—0:41.49.
**1,600-Meter Relay**—U.S. Time—3:16.71.
**100-Meter Hurdles**—Gail Devers, U.S. Time—0:12.46.
**400-Meter Hurdles**—Sally Gunnell, Gt. Britain. Time—0:52.74.
**High Jump**—Ioamnet Quintero, Cuba. 6 Ft. 6¼ in.
**Long Jump**—Heike Drechsler, Germany. 23 Ft. 4 in.
**Triple Jump**—Ana Biryukova, Russia. 49 Ft. 6¼ in.
**Shot Put**—Zhihong Huang, China. 67 Ft. 6 in.
**Discus**—Olga Burova, Russia. 221 Ft. 1 in.
**Javelin**—Trine Hattestad, Norway. 227 Ft.
**Heptathlon**—Jackie Joyner-Kersee, U.S. 6,837 Pts.

# TENNIS
## U.S. Open Champions
### Men's Singles

| Year | Champion | Final opponent | Year | Champion | Final opponent |
|------|----------|----------------|------|----------|----------------|
| 1910 | William Larned | T. C. Bundy | 1952 | Frank Sedgman | Gardnar Mulloy |
| 1911 | William Larned | Maurice McLoughlin | 1953 | Tony Trabert | E. Victor Seixas Jr. |
| 1912 | Maurice McLoughlin | Wallace Johnson | 1954 | E. Victor Seixas Jr. | Rex Hartwig |
| 1913 | Maurice McLoughlin | Richard Williams | 1955 | Tony Trabert | Ken Rosewall |
| 1914 | Richard Williams | Maurice McLoughlin | 1956 | Ken Rosewall | Lewis Hoad |
| 1915 | William Johnston | Maurice McLoughlin | 1957 | Malcolm Anderson | Ashley Cooper |
| 1916 | Richard Williams | William Johnston | 1958 | Ashley Cooper | Malcolm Anderson |
| 1917 | R. L. Murray | N. W. Niles | 1959 | Neale A. Fraser | Alejandro Olmedo |
| 1918 | R. L. Murray | Bill Tilden | 1960 | Neale A. Fraser | Rod Laver |
| 1919 | William Johnston | Bill Tilden | 1961 | Roy Emerson | Rod Laver |
| 1920 | Bill Tilden | William Johnston | 1962 | Rod Laver | Roy Emerson |
| 1921 | Bill Tilden | Wallace Johnson | 1963 | Rafael Osuna | F. A. Froehling 3d |
| 1922 | Bill Tilden | William Johnston | 1964 | Roy Emerson | Fred Stolle |
| 1923 | Bill Tilden | William Johnston | 1965 | Manuel Santana | Cliff Drysdale |
| 1924 | Bill Tilden | William Johnston | 1966 | Fred Stolle | John Newcombe |
| 1925 | Bill Tilden | William Johnston | 1967 | John Newcombe | Clark Graebner |
| 1926 | Rene Lacoste | Jean Borotra | 1968 | Arthur Ashe | Tom Okker |
| 1927 | Rene Lacoste | Bill Tilden | 1969 | Rod Laver | Tony Roche |
| 1928 | Henri Cochet | Francis Hunter | 1970 | Ken Rosewall | Tony Roche |
| 1929 | Bill Tilden | Francis Hunter | 1971 | Stan Smith | Jan Kodes |
| 1930 | John Doeg | Francis Shields | 1972 | Ilie Nastase | Arthur Ashe |
| 1931 | H. Ellsworth Vines | George Lott | 1973 | John Newcombe | Jan Kodes |
| 1932 | H. Ellsworth Vines | Henri Cochet | 1974 | Jimmy Connors | Ken Rosewall |
| 1933 | Fred Perry | John Crawford | 1975 | Manuel Orantes | Jimmy Connors |
| 1934 | Fred Perry | Wilmer Allison | 1976 | Jimmy Connors | Bjorn Borg |
| 1935 | Wilmer Allison | Sidney Wood | 1977 | Guillermo Vilas | Jimmy Connors |
| 1936 | Fred Perry | Don Budge | 1978 | Jimmy Connors | Bjorn Borg |
| 1937 | Don Budge | Baron G. von Cramm | 1979 | John McEnroe | Vitas Gerulaitis |
| 1938 | Don Budge | C. Gene Mako | 1980 | John McEnroe | Bjorn Borg |
| 1939 | Robert Riggs | S. Welby Van Horn | 1981 | John McEnroe | Bjorn Borg |
| 1940 | Don McNeill | Robert Riggs | 1982 | Jimmy Connors | Ivan Lendl |
| 1941 | Robert Riggs | F. L. Kovacs | 1983 | Jimmy Connors | Ivan Lendl |
| 1942 | F. R. Schroeder Jr. | Frank Parker | 1984 | John McEnroe | Ivan Lendl |
| 1943 | Joseph Hunt | Jack Kramer | 1985 | Ivan Lendl | John McEnroe |
| 1944 | Frank Parker | William Talbert | 1986 | Ivan Lendl | Miloslav Mecir |
| 1945 | Frank Parker | William Talbert | 1987 | Ivan Lendl | Mats Wilander |
| 1946 | Jack Kramer | Thomas Brown Jr. | 1988 | Mats Wilander | Ivan Lendl |
| 1947 | Jack Kramer | Frank Parker | 1989 | Boris Becker | Ivan Lendl |
| 1948 | Pancho Gonzales | Eric Sturgess | 1990 | Pete Sampras | Andre Agassi |
| 1949 | Pancho Gonzales | F. R. Schroeder Jr. | 1991 | Stefan Edberg | Jim Courier |
| 1950 | Arthur Larsen | Herbert Flam | 1992 | Stefan Edberg | Pete Sampras |
| 1951 | Frank Sedgman | E. Victor Seixas Jr. | 1993 | Pete Sampras | Cedric Pioline |

### Women's Singles

| Year | Champion | Final opponent | Year | Champion | Final opponent |
|------|----------|----------------|------|----------|----------------|
| 1926 | Molla B. Mallory | Elizabeth Ryan | 1960 | Darlene Hard | Maria Bueno |
| 1927 | Helen Wills | Betty Nuthall | 1961 | Darlene Hard | Ann Haydon |
| 1928 | Helen Wills | Helen Jacobs | 1962 | Margaret Smith | Darlene Hard |
| 1929 | Helen Wills | M. Watson | 1963 | Maria Bueno | Margaret Smith |
| 1930 | Betty Nuthall | L. A. Harper | 1964 | Maria Bueno | Carole Graebner |
| 1931 | Helen Wills Moody | E. B. Whittingstall | 1965 | Margaret Smith | Billie Jean Moffitt |
| 1932 | Helen Jacobs | Carolin A. Babcock | 1966 | Maria Bueno | Nancy Richey |
| 1933 | Helen Jacobs | Helen Wills Moody | 1967 | Billie Jean King | Ann Haydon Jones |
| 1934 | Helen Jacobs | Sarah H. Palfrey | 1968 | Virginia Wade | Billie Jean King |
| 1935 | Helen Jacobs | Sarah P. Fabyan | 1969 | Margaret Court | Nancy Richey |
| 1936 | Alice Marble | Helen Jacobs | 1970 | Margaret Court | Rosemary Casals |
| 1937 | Anita Lizana | Jadwiga Jedrzejowska | 1971 | Billie Jean King | Rosemary Casals |
| 1938 | Alice Marble | Nancye Wynne | 1972 | Billie Jean King | Kerry Melville |
| 1939 | Alice Marble | Helen Jacobs | 1973 | Margaret Court | Evonne Goolagong |
| 1940 | Alice Marble | Helen Jacobs | 1974 | Billie Jean King | Evonne Goolagong |
| 1941 | Sarah Palfrey Cooke | Pauline Betz | 1975 | Chris Evert | Evonne Goolagong |
| 1942 | Pauline Betz | Louise Brough | 1976 | Chris Evert | Evonne Goolagong |
| 1943 | Pauline Betz | Louise Brough | 1977 | Chris Evert | Wendy Turnbull |
| 1944 | Pauline Betz | Margaret Osborne | 1978 | Chris Evert | Pam Shriver |
| 1945 | Sarah P. Cooke | Pauline Betz | 1979 | Tracy Austin | Chris Evert Lloyd |
| 1946 | Pauline Betz | Doris Hart | 1980 | Chris Evert Lloyd | Hana Mandlikova |
| 1947 | Louise Brough | Margaret Osborne | 1981 | Tracy Austin | Martina Navratilova |
| 1948 | Margaret Osborne duPont | Louise Brough | 1982 | Chris Evert Lloyd | Hana Mandlikova |
| 1949 | Margaret Osborne duPont | Doris Hart | 1983 | Martina Navratilova | Chris Evert Lloyd |
| 1950 | Margaret Osborne duPont | Doris Hart | 1984 | Martina Navratilova | Chris Evert Lloyd |
| 1951 | Maureen Connolly | Shirley Fry | 1985 | Hana Mandlikova | Martina Navratilova |
| 1952 | Maureen Connolly | Doris Hart | 1986 | Martina Navratilova | Helena Sukova |
| 1953 | Maureen Connolly | Doris Hart | 1987 | Martina Navratilova | Steffi Graf |
| 1954 | Doris Hart | Louise Brough | 1988 | Steffi Graf | Gabriela Sabatini |
| 1955 | Doris Hart | Patricia Ward | 1989 | Steffi Graf | Martina Navratilova |
| 1956 | Shirley Fry | Althea Gibson | 1990 | Gabriela Sabatini | Steffi Graf |
| 1957 | Althea Gibson | Louise Brough | 1991 | Monica Seles | Martina Navratilova |
| 1958 | Althea Gibson | Darlene Hard | 1992 | Monica Seles | Arantxa Sanchez Vicario |
| 1959 | Maria Bueno | Christine Truman | 1993 | Steffi Graf | Helena Sukova |

# All-England Champions, Wimbledon

## Men's Singles

| Year | Champion | Final opponent | Year | Champion | Final opponent |
|------|----------|----------------|------|----------|----------------|
| 1933 | Jack Crawford | Ellsworth Vines | 1966 | Manuel Santana | Dennis Ralston |
| 1934 | Fred Perry | Jack Crawford | 1967 | John Newcombe | Wilhelm Bungert |
| 1935 | Fred Perry | Gottfried von Cramm | 1968 | Rod Laver | Tony Roche |
| 1936 | Fred Perry | Gottfried von Cramm | 1969 | Rod Laver | John Newcombe |
| 1937 | Donald Budge | Gottfried von Cramm | 1970 | John Newcombe | Ken Rosewall |
| 1938 | Donald Budge | Wilfred Austin | 1971 | John Newcombe | Stan Smith |
| 1939 | Bobby Riggs | Elwood Cooke | 1972 | Stan Smith | Ilie Nastase |
| 1940-45 | not held | | 1973 | Jan Kodes | Alex Metreveli |
| 1946 | Yvon Petra | Geoff E. Brown | 1974 | Jimmy Connors | Ken Rosewall |
| 1947 | Jack Kramer | Tom P. Brown | 1975 | Arthur Ashe | Jimmy Connors |
| 1948 | Bob Falkenburg | John Bromwich | 1976 | Bjorn Borg | Ilie Nastase |
| 1949 | Ted Schroeder | Jaroslav Drobny | 1977 | Bjorn Borg | Jimmy Connors |
| 1950 | Budge Patty | Frank Sedgman | 1978 | Bjorn Borg | Jimmy Connors |
| 1951 | Dick Savitt | Ken McGregor | 1979 | Bjorn Borg | Roscoe Tanner |
| 1952 | Frank Sedgman | Jaroslav Drobny | 1980 | Bjorn Borg | John McEnroe |
| 1953 | Vic Seixas | Kurt Nielsen | 1981 | John McEnroe | Bjorn Borg |
| 1954 | Jaroslav Drobny | Ken Rosewall | 1982 | Jimmy Connors | John McEnroe |
| 1955 | Tony Trabert | Kurt Nielsen | 1983 | John McEnroe | Chris Lewis |
| 1956 | Lew Hoad | Ken Rosewall | 1984 | John McEnroe | Jimmy Connors |
| 1957 | Lew Hoad | Ashley Cooper | 1985 | Boris Becker | Kevin Curren |
| 1958 | Ashley Cooper | Neale Fraser | 1986 | Boris Becker | Ivan Lendl |
| 1959 | Alex Olmedo | Rod Laver | 1987 | Pat Cash | Ivan Lendl |
| 1960 | Neale Fraser | Rod Laver | 1988 | Stefan Edberg | Boris Becker |
| 1961 | Rod Laver | Chuck McKinley | 1989 | Boris Becker | Stefan Edberg |
| 1962 | Rod Laver | Martin Mulligan | 1990 | Stefan Edberg | Boris Becker |
| 1963 | Chuck McKinley | Fred Stolle | 1991 | Michael Stich | Boris Becker |
| 1964 | Roy Emerson | Fred Stolle | 1992 | Andre Agassi | Goran Ivanisevic |
| 1965 | Roy Emerson | Fred Stolle | 1993 | Pete Sampras | Jim Courier |

## Women's Singles

| Year | Champion | Year | Champion | Year | Champion | Year | Champion |
|------|----------|------|----------|------|----------|------|----------|
| 1946 | Pauline Betz | 1958 | Althea Gibson | 1970 | Margaret Smith Court | 1982 | Martina Navratilova |
| 1947 | Margaret Osborne | 1959 | Maria Bueno | 1971 | Evonne Goolagong | 1983 | Martina Navratilova |
| 1948 | Louise Brough | 1960 | Maria Bueno | 1972 | Billie Jean King | 1984 | Martina Navratilova |
| 1949 | Louise Brough | 1961 | Angela Mortimer | 1973 | Billie Jean King | 1985 | Martina Navratilova |
| 1950 | Louise Brough | 1962 | Karen Hantze-Susman | 1974 | Chris Evert | 1986 | Martina Navratilova |
| 1951 | Doris Hart | 1963 | Margaret Smith | 1975 | Billie Jean King | 1987 | Martina Navratilova |
| 1952 | Maureen Connolly | 1964 | Maria Bueno | 1976 | Chris Evert | 1988 | Steffi Graf |
| 1953 | Maureen Connolly | 1965 | Margaret Smith | 1977 | Virginia Wade | 1989 | Steffi Graf |
| 1954 | Maureen Connolly | 1966 | Billie Jean King | 1978 | Martina Navratilova | 1990 | Martina Navratilova |
| 1955 | Louise Brough | 1967 | Billie Jean King | 1979 | Martina Navratilova | 1991 | Steffi Graf |
| 1956 | Shirley Fry | 1968 | Billie Jean King | 1980 | Evonne Goolagong | 1992 | Steffi Graf |
| 1957 | Althea Gibson | 1969 | Ann Haydon-Jones | 1981 | Chris Evert Lloyd | 1993 | Steffi Graf |

## Davis Cup Challenge Round

| Year | Result | Year | Result | Year | Result |
|------|--------|------|--------|------|--------|
| 1900 | United States 5, British Isles 0 | 1932 | France 3, United States 2 | 1965 | Australia 4, Spain 1 |
| 1901 | (not played) | 1933 | Great Britain 3, France 2 | 1966 | Australia 4, India 1 |
| 1902 | United States 3, British Isles 2 | 1934 | Great Britain 4, United States 1 | 1967 | Australia 4, Spain 1 |
| 1903 | British Isles 4, United States 1 | 1935 | Great Britain 5, United States 0 | 1968 | United States 4, Australia 1 |
| 1904 | British Isles 5, Belgium 0 | 1936 | Great Britain 3, Australia 2 | 1969 | United States 5, Romania 0 |
| 1905 | British Isles 5, United States 0 | 1937 | United States 4, Great Britain 1 | 1970 | United States 5, W. Germany 0 |
| 1906 | British Isles 5, United States 0 | 1938 | United States 3, Australia 2 | 1971 | United States 3, Romania 2 |
| 1907 | Australia 3, British Isles 2 | 1939 | Australia 3, United States 2 | 1972 | United States 3, Romania 2 |
| 1908 | Australasia 3, United States 2 | 1940-45 | (not played) | 1973 | Australia 5, United States 0 |
| 1909 | Australasia 5, United States 0 | 1946 | United States 5, Australia 0 | 1974 | South Africa (default by India) |
| 1910 | (not played) | 1947 | United States 4, Australia 1 | 1975 | Sweden 3, Czech. 2 |
| 1911 | Australasia 5, United States 0 | 1948 | United States 5, Australia 0 | 1976 | Italy 4, Chile 1 |
| 1912 | British Isles 3, Australasia 2 | 1949 | United States 4, Australia 1 | 1977 | Australia 3, Italy 1 |
| 1913 | United States 3, British Isles 2 | 1950 | Australia 4, United States 1 | 1978 | United States 4, Great Britain 1 |
| 1914 | Australasia 3, United States 2 | 1951 | Australia 3, United States 2 | 1979 | United States 5, Italy 0 |
| 1915-18 | (not played) | 1952 | Australia 4, United States 1 | 1980 | Czechoslovakia 4, Italy 1 |
| 1919 | Australasia 4, British Isles 1 | 1953 | Australia 3, United States 2 | 1981 | United States 3, Argentina 1 |
| 1920 | United States 5, Australasia 0 | 1954 | United States 3, Australia 2 | 1982 | United States 3, France, 0 |
| 1921 | United States 5, Japan 0 | 1955 | Australia 5, United States 0 | 1983 | Australia 3, Sweden 1 |
| 1922 | United States 4, Australasia 1 | 1956 | Australia 5, United States 0 | 1984 | Sweden 3, United States 2 |
| 1923 | United States 4, Australasia 1 | 1957 | Australia 3, United States 2 | 1985 | Sweden 3, W. Germany 2 |
| 1924 | United States 5, Australasia 0 | 1958 | United States 3, Australia 2 | 1986 | Australia 3, Sweden 2 |
| 1925 | United States 5, France 0 | 1959 | Australia 3, United States 2 | 1987 | Sweden 5, India 0 |
| 1926 | United States 4, France 1 | 1960 | Australia 4, Italy 1 | 1988 | W. Germany 4, Sweden 1 |
| 1927 | France 3, United States 2 | 1961 | Australia 5, Italy 0 | 1989 | W. Germany 3, Sweden 2 |
| 1928 | France 4, United States 1 | 1962 | Australia 5, Mexico 0 | 1990 | United States 3, Australia 2 |
| 1929 | France 3, United States 2 | 1963 | United States 3, Australia 2 | 1991 | France 3, United States 1 |
| 1930 | France 4, United States 1 | 1964 | Australia 3, United States 2 | 1992 | United States 3, Switzerland 1 |
| 1931 | France 3, Great Britain 2 | | | | |

## French Open Champions

| Year | Men | Women | Year | Men | Women |
|------|-----|-------|------|-----|-------|
| 1969 | Rod Laver | Margaret Smith Court | 1982 | Mats Wilander | Martina Navratilova |
| 1970 | Jan Kodes | Margaret Smith Court | 1983 | Yannick Noah | Chris Evert Lloyd |
| 1971 | Jan Kodes | Evonne Goolagong | 1984 | Ivan Lendl | Martina Navratilova |
| 1972 | Andres Gimeno | Billie Jean King | 1985 | Mats Wilander | Chris Evert Lloyd |
| 1973 | Ilie Nastase | Margaret Smith Court | 1986 | Ivan Lendl | Chris Evert Lloyd |
| 1974 | Bjorn Borg | Chris Evert | 1987 | Ivan Lendl | Steffi Graf |
| 1975 | Bjorn Borg | Chris Evert | 1988 | Mats Wilander | Steffi Graf |
| 1976 | Adriano Panatta | Sue Barker | 1989 | Michael Chang | Arantxa Sanchez |
| 1977 | Guillermo Vilas | Mima Jausovec | 1990 | Andres Gomez | Monica Seles |
| 1978 | Bjorn Borg | Virginia Ruzici | 1991 | Jim Courier | Monica Seles |
| 1979 | Bjorn Borg | Chris Evert Lloyd | 1992 | Jim Courier | Monica Seles |
| 1980 | Bjorn Borg | Chris Evert Lloyd | 1993 | Sergi Bruguera | Steffi Graf |
| 1981 | Bjorn Borg | Hana Mandlikova | | | |

## Australian Open Champions

| Year* | Men | Women | Year* | Men | Women |
|-------|-----|-------|-------|-----|-------|
| 1969 | Rod Laver | Margaret Smith Court | 1981 | Johan Kriek | Martina Navratilova |
| 1970 | Arthur Ashe | Margaret Smith Court | 1982 | Johan Kriek | Chris Evert Lloyd |
| 1971 | Ken Rosewall | Margaret Smith Court | 1983 | Mats Wilander | Martina Navratilova |
| 1972 | Ken Rosewall | Virginia Wade | 1984 | Mats Wilander | Chris Evert Lloyd |
| 1973 | John Newcombe | Margaret Smith Court | 1985 | Stefan Edberg | Martina Navratilova |
| 1974 | Jimmy Connors | Evonne Goolagong | 1986 | Not held | Not held |
| 1975 | John Newcombe | Evonne Goolagong | 1987 | Stefan Edberg | Hana Mandlikova |
| 1976 | Mark Edmondson | Evonne Goolagong | 1988 | Mats Wilander | Steffi Graf |
| 1977 | Roscoe Tanner | Kerry Reid | 1989 | Ivan Lendl | Steffi Graf |
| | Vitas Gerulaitis | Evonne Goolagong | 1990 | Ivan Lendl | Steffi Graf |
| 1978 | Guillermo Vilas | Chris O'Neill | 1991 | Boris Becker | Monica Seles |
| 1979 | Guillermo Vilas | Barbara Jordan | 1992 | Jim Courier | Monica Seles |
| 1980 | Brian Teacher | Hana Mandlikova | 1993 | Jim Courier | Monica Seles |

* Two tournaments were held in 1977 (Jan. & Dec.). Tournament moved back to Jan. in 1987, so no championship was decided in 1986.

# AUTO RACING

## Indianapolis 500 Winners

| Year | Winner, Car | MPH | Year | Winner, Car | MPH |
|------|-------------|-----|------|-------------|-----|
| 1911 | Ray Harroun, Marmon Wasp | 74.59 | 1955 | Bob Sweikert, John Zink Special | 128.209 |
| 1912 | Joe Dawson, National | 78.72 | 1956 | Pat Flaherty, John Zink Special | 128.490 |
| 1913 | Jules Goux, Peugeot | 75.933 | 1957 | Sam Hanks, Belond Exhaust | 135.601 |
| 1914 | Rene Thomas, Delage | 82.47 | 1958 | Jimmy Bryan, Belond A.P. | 133.791 |
| 1915 | Ralph DePalma, Mercedes | 89.84 | 1959 | Rodger Ward, Leader Card Special | 135.857 |
| 1916 | Dario Resta, Peugeot | 84.00 | 1960 | Jim Rathmann, Ken Paul Special | 138.767 |
| 1917-18 | race not held | | 1961 | A.J. Foyt, Bowes Seal Fast | 139.130 |
| 1919 | Howdy Wilcox, Peugeot | 88.05 | 1962 | Rodger Ward, Leader Card Special | 140.293 |
| 1920 | Gaston Chevrolet, Monroe | 88.16 | 1963 | Parnelli Jones, Agajanian Special | 143.137 |
| 1921 | Tommy Milton, Frontenac | 89.62 | 1964 | A.J. Foyt, Sheraton-Thompson Special | 147.350 |
| 1922 | Jimmy Murphy, Murphy Special | 94.48 | 1965 | Jim Clark, Lotus-Ford | 150.686 |
| 1923 | Tommy Milton, H.C.S. | 90.95 | 1966 | Graham Hill, American Red Ball | 144.317 |
| 1924 | L.L. Corum-Joe Boyer, Duesenberg | 98.23 | 1967 | A.J. Foyt, Sheraton-Thompson Special | 151.207 |
| 1925 | Pete DePaolo, Duesenberg | 101.13 | 1968 | Bobby Unser, Rislone Special | 152.882 |
| 1926 | Frank Lockhart, Miller | 95.904 | 1969 | Mario Andretti, STP Oil Treatment Special | 156.867 |
| 1927 | George Souders, Duesenberg | 97.545 | | | |
| 1928 | Louis Meyer, Miller | 99.482 | 1970 | Al Unser, Johnny Lightning Special | 155.749 |
| 1929 | Ray Keech, Simplex | 97.585 | 1971 | Al Unser, Johnny Lightning Special | 157.735 |
| 1930 | Billy Arnold, Miller-Hartz | 100.448 | 1972 | Mark Donohue, Sunoco McLaren | 162.962 |
| 1931 | Louis Schneider, Bowes Seal Fast | 96.629 | 1973 | Gordon Johncock, STP Double Oil Filter | 159.036 |
| 1932 | Fred Frame, Miller-Hartz | 104.144 | 1974 | Johnny Rutherford, McLaren | 158.589 |
| 1933 | Louis Meyer, Tydol | 104.162 | 1975 | Bobby Unser, Jorgensen Eagle | 149.213 |
| 1934 | Bill Cummings, Boyle Products | 104.863 | 1976 | Johnny Rutherford, Hygain McLaren | 148.725 |
| 1935 | Kelly Petillo, Gilmore Speedway | 106.240 | 1977 | A.J. Foyt, Gilmore Coyote-Ford | 161.331 |
| 1936 | Louis Meyer, Ring Free | 109.069 | 1978 | Al Unser, Lola Cosworth | 161.363 |
| 1937 | Wilbur Shaw, Shaw-Gilmore | 113.580 | 1979 | Rick Mears, Penske-Cosworth | 158.899 |
| 1938 | Floyd Roberts, Burd Piston Ring | 117.200 | 1980 | Johnny Rutherford, Chaparral-Cosworth | 142.862 |
| 1939 | Wilbur Shaw, Boyle | 115.035 | 1981 | Bobby Unser, Penske-Cosworth | 139.085 |
| 1940 | Wilbur Shaw, Boyle | 114.277 | 1982 | Gordon Johncock, Wildcat-Cosworth | 162.026 |
| 1941 | Floyd Davis-Mauri Rose, Knock-Out-Hose Clip | 115.117 | 1983 | Tom Sneva, March-Cosworth | 162.117 |
| | | | 1984 | Rick Mears, March-Cosworth | 163.621 |
| 1942-45 | race not held | | 1985 | Danny Sullivan, March-Cosworth | 152.982 |
| 1946 | George Robson, Thorne Engineering | 114.820 | 1986 | Bobby Rahal, March-Cosworth | 170.722 |
| 1947 | Mauri Rose, Blue Crown Special | 116.338 | 1987 | Al Unser, March-Cosworth | 162.175 |
| 1948 | Mauri Rose, Blue Crown Special | 119.814 | 1988 | Rick Mears, Penske-Chevy V8 | 144.809 |
| 1949 | Bill Holland, Blue Crown Special | 121.327 | 1989 | Emerson Fittipaldi, Penske PC 18-Chevy | 167.581 |
| 1950 | Johnny Parsons, Wynn Kurtis Kraft | 124.002 | 1990 | Arie Luyendyk, Lola-Chevy | 185.984 |
| 1951 | Lee Wallard, Belanger | 126.224 | 1991 | Rick Mears, Penske-Chevy | 176.457 |
| 1952 | Troy Ruttman, Agajanian | 128.922 | 1992 | Al Unser Jr., Galmer-Chevy A | 134.477 |
| 1953 | Bill Vukovich, Fuel Injection | 128.740 | 1993 | Emerson Fittipaldi, Penske-Chevy C | 157.207 |
| 1954 | Bill Vukovich, Fuel Injection | 130.840 | | | |

The race was less than 500 miles in the following years: 1916 (300 mi.), 1926 (400 mi.), 1950 (345 mi.), 1973 (332.5 mi.), 1975 (435 mi.), 1976 (255 mi.). Race record—185.984 MPH, Arie Luyendyk, 1990.

## Notable One-Mile Speed Records

| Date | Driver | Car | MPH | Date | Driver | Car | MPH |
|------|--------|-----|-----|------|--------|-----|-----|
| 1/26/06 | Marriott. . . . . . | Stanley (Steam) | 127.659 | 9/ 3/35 | Campbell. . . . . | Bluebird Special | 301.13 |
| 3/16/10 | Oldfield. . . . . . | Benz | 131.724 | 11/19/37 | Eyston . . . . . . | Thunderbolt 1 | 311.42 |
| 4/23/11 | Burman. . . . . . | Benz | 141.732 | 9/16/38 | Eyston . . . . . . | Thunderbolt 1 | 357.5 |
| 2/12/19 | DePalma. . . . . | Packard | 149.875 | 8/23/39 | Cobb . . . . . . . | Railton | 368.9 |
| 4/27/20 | Milton. . . . . . . | Dusenberg | 155.046 | 9/16/47 | Cobb . . . . . . . | Railton-Mobil | 394.2 |
| 4/28/26 | Parry-Thomas . . | Thomas Spl. | 170.624 | 8/ 5/63 | Breedlove . . . . | Spirit of America | 407.45 |
| 3/29/27 | Seagrave . . . . | Sunbeam | 203.790 | 10/27/64 | Arfons . . . . . . | Green Monster | 536.71 |
| 4/22/28 | Keech . . . . . . | White Triplex | 207.552 | 11/15/65 | Breedlove . . . . | Spirit of America | 600.601 |
| 3/11/29 | Seagrave . . . . | Irving-Napier | 231.446 | 10/23/70 | Gabelich . . . . . | Blue Flame | 622.407 |
| 2/ 5/31 | Campbell. . . . . | Napier-Campbell | 246.086 | 10/9/79 | Barrett . . . . . . | Budweiser Rocket | 638.637* |
| 2/24/32 | Campbell. . . . . | Napier-Campbell | 253.96 | 10/4/83 | Noble. . . . . . . | Thrust 2 | 633.6 |
| 2/22/33 | Campbell. . . . . | Napier-Campbell | 272.109 | *not recognized as official by sanctioning bodies. | | | |

## IndyCar Champions

(U.S. Auto Club Champions prior to 1979; Cart Champions, 1979-93)

| Year | Driver | Year | Driver | Year | Driver | Year | Driver |
|------|--------|------|--------|------|--------|------|--------|
| 1960 | A. J. Foyt | 1969 | Mario Andretti | 1978 | Tom Sneva | 1986 | Bobby Rahal |
| 1961 | A. J. Foyt | 1970 | Al Unser | 1979 | Rick Mears | 1987 | Bobby Rahal |
| 1962 | Rodger Ward | 1971 | Joe Leonard | 1980 | Johnny Rutherford | 1988 | Danny Sullivan |
| 1963 | A. J. Foyt | 1972 | Joe Leonard | 1981 | Rick Mears | 1989 | Emerson Fittipaldi |
| 1964 | A. J. Foyt | 1973 | Roger McCluskey | 1982 | Rick Mears | 1990 | Al Unser Jr. |
| 1965 | Mario Andretti | 1974 | Bobby Unser | 1983 | Al Unser | 1991 | Michael Andretti |
| 1966 | Mario Andretti | 1975 | A. J. Foyt | 1984 | Mario Andretti | 1992 | Bobby Rahal |
| 1967 | A. J. Foyt | 1976 | Gordon Johncock | 1985 | Al Unser | 1993 | Nigel Mansell |
| 1968 | Bobby Unser | 1977 | Tom Sneva | | | | |

## Le Mans 24-Hour Race in 1993

Christophe Bouchut and Eric Helary of France and Geoff Brabham of Australia drove their Peugeot 905 to victory in the 1993 Le Mans 24-hour race. They traveled the 2,779 miles at an average of 133.34 mph.

## World Grand Prix Champions

| Year | Driver | Year | Driver | Year | Driver |
|------|--------|------|--------|------|--------|
| 1951 | Jan Fangio, Argentina | 1965 | Jim Clark, Scotland | 1979 | Jody Scheckter, So. Africa |
| 1952 | Alberto Ascari, Italy | 1966 | Jack Brabham, Australia | 1980 | Alan Jones, Australia |
| 1953 | Alberto Ascari, Italy | 1967 | Denis Hulme, New Zealand | 1981 | Nelson Piquet, Brazil |
| 1954 | Juan Fangio, Argentina | 1968 | Graham Hill, England | 1982 | Keke Rosberg, Finland |
| 1955 | Juan Fangio, Argentina | 1969 | Jackie Stewart, Scotland | 1983 | Nelson Piquet, Brazil |
| 1956 | Juan Fangio, Argentina | 1970 | Jochen Rindt, Austria | 1984 | Niki Lauda, Austria |
| 1957 | Juan Fangio, Argentina | 1971 | Jackie Stewart, Scotland | 1985 | Alain Prost, France |
| 1958 | Mike Hawthorne, England | 1972 | Emerson Fittipaldi, Brazil | 1986 | Alain Prost, France |
| 1959 | Jack Brabham, Australia | 1973 | Jackie Stewart, Scotland | 1987 | Nelson Piquet, Brazil |
| 1960 | Jack Brabham, Australia | 1974 | Emerson Fittipaldi, Brazil | 1988 | Ayrton Senna, Brazil |
| 1961 | Phil Hill, United States | 1975 | Niki Lauda, Austria | 1989 | Alain Prost, France |
| 1962 | Graham Hill, England | 1976 | James Hunt, England | 1990 | Ayrton Senna, Brazil |
| 1963 | Jim Clark, Scotland | 1977 | Niki Lauda, Austria | 1991 | Ayrton Senna, Brazil |
| 1964 | John Surtees, England | 1978 | Mario Andretti, U.S. | 1992 | Nigel Mansell, Britain |

## Grand Prix for Formula 1 Cars in 1993

| Grand Prix | Winner, car | Grand Prix | Winner, car |
|------------|-------------|------------|-------------|
| Belgian . . . . . . . . | Damon Hill, Williams-Renault | Hungarian . . . . . . . . | Damon Hill, Williams-Renault |
| Brazilian . . . . . . . . | Ayrton Senna, McLaren-Ford | Italian . . . . . . . . | Damon Hill, Williams-Renault |
| British . . . . . . . . | Alain Prost, Williams-Renault | Monaco. . . . . . . . . | Ayrton Senna, McLaren-Honda |
| Canadian. . . . . . . . | Alain Prost, Williams-Renault | San Marino. . . . . . . | Alain Prost, Williams-Renault |
| European. . . . . . . . | Ayrton Senna, McLaren-Ford | South Africa . . . . . . | Alain Prost, Williams-Renault |
| French . . . . . . . . | Alain Prost, Williams-Renault | Spanish. . . . . . . . . | Alain Prost, Williams-Renault |
| German. . . . . . . . . | Alain Prost, Williams-Renault | | |

## Winston Cup Champions (NASCAR)

| Year | Driver | Year | Driver | Year | Driver | Year | Driver |
|------|--------|------|--------|------|--------|------|--------|
| 1949 | Red Byron | 1960 | Rex White | 1971 | Richard Petty | 1982 | Darrell Waltrip |
| 1950 | Bill Rexford | 1961 | Ned Jarrett | 1972 | Richard Petty | 1983 | Bobby Allison |
| 1951 | Herb Thomas | 1962 | Joe Weatherly | 1973 | Benny Parsons | 1984 | Terry Labonte |
| 1952 | Tim Flock | 1963 | Joe Weatherly | 1974 | Richard Petty | 1985 | Darrell Waltrip |
| 1953 | Herb Thomas | 1964 | Richard Petty | 1975 | Richard Petty | 1986 | Dale Earnhardt |
| 1954 | Lee Petty | 1965 | Ned Jarrett | 1976 | Cale Yarborough | 1987 | Dale Earnhardt |
| 1955 | Tim Flock | 1966 | David Pearson | 1977 | Cale Yarborough | 1988 | Bill Elliott |
| 1956 | Buck Baker | 1967 | Richard Petty | 1978 | Cale Yarborough | 1989 | Rusty Wallace |
| 1957 | Buck Baker | 1968 | David Pearson | 1979 | Richard Petty | 1990 | Dale Earnhardt |
| 1958 | Lee Petty | 1969 | David Pearson | 1980 | Dale Earnhardt | 1991 | Dale Earnhardt |
| 1959 | Lee Petty | 1970 | Bobby Isaac | 1981 | Darrell Waltrip | 1992 | Alan Kulwicki |

## Daytona 500 Winners

| Year | Driver, car | Avg. MPH | Year | Driver, car | Avg. MPH |
|------|-------------|----------|------|-------------|----------|
| 1959 | Lee Petty, Oldsmobile | 135.521 | 1977 | Cale Yarborough, Chevrolet | 153.218 |
| 1960 | Junior Johnson, Chevrolet | 124.740 | 1978 | Bobby Allison, Ford | 159.730 |
| 1961 | Marvin Panch, Pontiac | 149.601 | 1979 | Richard Petty, Oldsmobile | 143.977 |
| 1962 | Fireball Roberts, Pontiac | 152.529 | 1980 | Buddy Baker, Oldsmobile | 177.602 |
| 1963 | Tiny Lund, Ford | 151.566 | 1981 | Richard Petty, Buick | 169.651 |
| 1964 | Richard Petty, Plymouth | 154.334 | 1982 | Bobby Allison, Buick | 153.991 |
| 1965 | Fred Lorenzen, Ford (a) | 141.539 | 1983 | Cale Yarborough, Pontiac | 155.979 |
| 1966 | Richard Petty, Plymouth (b) | 160.627 | 1984 | Cale Yarborough, Chevrolet | 150.994 |
| 1967 | Mario Andretti, Ford | 146.926 | 1985 | Bill Elliott, Ford | 172.265 |
| 1968 | Cale Yarborough, Mercury | 143.251 | 1986 | Geoff Bodine, Chevrolet | 148.124 |
| 1969 | Lee Roy Yarborough, Ford | 160.875 | 1987 | Bill Elliott, Ford | 176.263 |
| 1970 | Pete Hamilton, Plymouth | 149.601 | 1988 | Bobby Allison, Buick | 137.531 |
| 1971 | Richard Petty, Plymouth | 144.456 | 1989 | Darrell Waltrip, Chevrolet | 148.466 |
| 1972 | A. J. Foyt, Mercury | 161.550 | 1990 | Derrike Cope, Chevrolet | 165.761 |
| 1973 | Richard Petty, Dodge | 157.205 | 1991 | Ernie Irvin, Chevrolet | 148.148 |
| 1974 | Richard Petty, Dodge (c) | 140.894 | 1992 | Davey Allison, Ford | 160.256 |
| 1975 | Benny Parsons, Chevrolet | 153.649 | 1993 | Dale Jarrett, Chevrolet | 154.972 |
| 1976 | David Pearson, Mercury | 152.181 | | | |

(a) 322.5 miles. (b) 495 miles. (c) 450 miles.

## NASCAR Racing in 1993

### Winston Cup Races

| Date | Race, site | Winner | Car |
|------|-----------|--------|-----|
| Feb. 14 | Daytona 500, Daytona Beach, Fla. | Dale Jarrett | Chevrolet |
| Feb. 28 | Goodwrench 500, Rockingham, N.C. | Rusty Wallace | Pontiac |
| Mar. 8 | Pontiac Excitement 400, Richmond, Va. | Davey Allison | Ford |
| Mar. 20 | Motorcraft 500, Hampton, Ga. | Morgan Shepherd | Ford |
| Mar. 28 | Transouth 500, Darlington, S.C. | Dale Earnhardt | Chevrolet |
| Apr. 4 | Food City 500, Bristol, Tenn. | Rusty Wallace | Pontiac |
| Apr. 18 | First Union 400, N. Wilkesboro, N.C. | Rusty Wallace | Pontiac |
| Apr. 25 | Hanes 500, Martinsville, Va. | Rusty Wallace | Pontiac |
| May 2 | Winston 500, Talladega, Ala. | Ernie Irvan | Chevrolet |
| May 30 | Coca Cola 600, Concord, N.C. | Dale Earnhardt | Chevrolet |
| June 6 | Budweiser 500, Dover, Del. | Dale Earnhardt | Chevrolet |
| June 13 | Champion Spark Plug 500, Pocono, Pa. | Kyle Petty | Pontiac |
| June 20 | Miller Genuine Draft 400, Brooklyn, Mich. | Ricky Rudd | Chevrolet |
| July 3 | Pepsi 400, Daytona Beach, Fla. | Dale Earnhardt | Chevrolet |
| July 18 | Miller Genuine Draft 500, Pocono, Pa. | Dale Earnhardt | Chevrolet |
| July 25 | Die-Hard 500, Talladega, Ala. | Dale Earnhardt | Chevrolet |
| Aug. 8 | Budweiser at The Glen, Watkins Glen, N.Y. | Mark Martin | Ford |
| Aug. 15 | Champion Spark Plug 400, Brooklyn, Mich. | Mark Martin | Ford |
| Aug. 27 | Bud 500, Bristol, Tenn. | Mark Martin | Ford |
| Sept. 5 | Southern 500, Darlington, S.C. | Mark Martin | Ford |
| Sept. 11 | Miller Genuine Draft 400, Richmond, Va. | Rusty Wallace | Pontiac |
| Sept. 19 | Spitfire Spark Plug 500, Dover, Del. | Rusty Wallace | Pontiac |
| Sept. 26 | Goody's 500, Martinsville, Va. | Ernie Irvan | Ford |

# LACROSSE

## Lacrosse Champions in 1993

U.S. Club Lacrosse Association Championship—Baltimore, Md., June 19: Mount Washington 18, Brine L.C. 16.

NCAA Division I Championship—College Park, Md., May 31: Syracuse 13, North Carolina 12.

NCAA Division II Championship—Brookville, N.Y., May 15: Adelphi 11, C. W. Post 7.

NCAA Division III Championship—College Park, Md., May 30: Hobart 16, Ohio Wesleyan 10.

USILA Division I All-Star Game—Baltimore, Md., June 18: North 28, South 16.

USILA Division III All-Star Game—Baltimore, Md., June 18: South 16, North 12.

National Junior College Championship—Corning, N.Y., May 9: Herkimer (N.Y.) C.C. 17, Essex (Md.) C.C. 11.

NCAA Women's Division I Championship—College Park, Md., May 16: Virginia 8, Princeton 6 (Double O.T.).

NCAA Women's Division III Championship—College Park, Md., May 16: Trenton State 10, William Smith 9.

### USILA Division I All America Team

Attack: Brian Piccola, Johns Hopkins; Mark Millon, Massachusetts; Matt Riter, Syracuse.

Midfield: Andy Towers, Brown; Dom Fin, Syracuse; Ryan Wade, North Carolina; Roy Colsey, Syracuse.

Defense: David Morrow, Princeton; Alex Martin, North Carolina; Greg Paradine, North Carolina.

Goal: Scott Bacigalupo, Princeton.

Coach of the Year: John Danowski, Hofstra.

Note: 4 midfielders selected for the 3 midfield positions

## NCAA Division I Champions

| Year | Champion | Year | Champion | Year | Champion | Year | Champion |
|------|----------|------|----------|------|----------|------|----------|
| 1972 | Virginia | 1978 | Johns Hopkins | 1984 | Johns Hopkins | 1989 | Syracuse |
| 1973 | Maryland | 1979 | Johns Hopkins | 1985 | Johns Hopkins | 1990 | Syracuse |
| 1974 | Johns Hopkins | 1980 | Johns Hopkins | 1986 | North Carolina | 1991 | North Carolina |
| 1975 | Maryland | 1981 | North Carolina | 1987 | Johns Hopkins | 1992 | Princeton |
| 1976 | Cornell | 1982 | North Carolina | 1988 | Syracuse | 1993 | Syracuse |
| 1977 | Cornell | 1983 | Syracuse | | | | |

# BOXING
## Champions by Classes

There are numerous governing bodies in boxing including the World Boxing Council, the World Boxing Assn., the International Boxing Federation, the United States Boxing Assn., the North American Boxing Federation, and the European Boxing Union. Other organizations are recognized by TV networks and the print media. All the governing bodies have their own champions and assorted boxing divisions. The following are the recognized champions, as of mid-1993, in the principal divisions of the World Boxing Association, the World Boxing Council, and the International Boxing Federation.

| Class, Weight limit | WBA | WBC | IBF |
|---|---|---|---|
| Heavyweight . . . . . . . . . . . | Riddick Bowe, U.S. | Lennox Lewis, U.K. | Riddick Bowe, U.S. |
| Cruiserweight (195 lbs.). . . . . | Bobby Cruz, U.S. | Anaclet Wamba, France | Al Cole, U.S. |
| Light Heavyweight (175 lbs.) . . . | Virgil Hill, U.S. | Jeff Harding, Australia | Henry Maske, Germany |
| Super Middleweight (168 lbs.) . . | Michael Nunn, U.S. | Nigel Benn, U.K. | Chris Eubank, U.K. |
| Middleweight (160 lbs.) . . . . . . | Reggie Johnson, U.S. | Gerald McClellan, U.S. | Roy Jones, U.S. |
| Jr. Middleweight (154 lbs.) . . . . | Julio Cesar Vasquez, Argentina | Terry Norris, U.S. | Gianfranco Rosi, Italy |
| Welterweight (147 lbs.) . . . . . . | Crisanto Espana, N. Ireland | Pernell Whitaker, U.S. | Felix Trinidad, Puerto Rico |
| Jr. Welterweight (140 lbs.) . . . . | Juan Coggi, Argentina | Julio Cesar Chavez, Mexico | Charles Murray, U.S. |
| Lightweight (135 lbs.) . . . . . . . | Dingaan Thobela, S. Africa | Miguel Angel Gonzalez, Mexico | Freddie Pendleton, U.S. |
| Jr. Lightweight (130 lbs.) . . . . . | Genaro Hernandez, U.S. | Azumah Nelson, Ghana | John-John Molina, Puerto Rico |
| Featherweight (126 lbs.) . . . . . | Yung Kyun Park, S. Korea | Goyo Vargas, Mexico | Tom Johnson, U.S. |
| Jr. Featherweight (122 lbs.) . . . | Wilfredo Vasquez, Puerto Rico | Tracy Patterson, U.S. | Kennedy McKinney, U.S. |
| Bantamweight (118 lbs.) . . . . . | Eliecer Julio, Colombia | Jung Il Byun, S. Korea | Orlando Canizales, U.S. |
| Flyweight (112 lbs.) . . . . . . . . | David Griman, Venezuela | Yuri Arbachakov, Japan | Phichit Sithbang Prachan, Thailand |
| Jr. Flyweight (108 lbs.) . . . . . . | Myung Woo Yuh, S. Korea | Michael Carbajal, U.S. | Michael Carbajal, U.S. |

## Ring Champions by Years

*Abandoned title

### Heavyweights

| | |
|---|---|
| 1882-1892 | John L. Sullivan (a) |
| 1892-1897 | James J. Corbett (b) |
| 1897-1899 | Robert Fitzsimmons |
| 1899-1905 | James J. Jeffries (c) |
| 1905-1906 | Marvin Hart |
| 1906-1908 | Tommy Burns |
| 1908-1915 | Jack Johnson |
| 1915-1919 | Jess Willard |
| 1919-1926 | Jack Dempsey |
| 1926-1928 | Gene Tunney* |
| 1928-1930 | vacant |
| 1930-1932 | Max Schmeling |
| 1932-1933 | Jack Sharkey |
| 1933-1934 | Primo Carnera |
| 1934-1935 | Max Baer |
| 1935-1937 | James J. Braddock |
| 1937-1949 | Joe Louis* |
| 1949-1951 | Ezzard Charles |
| 1951-1952 | Joe Walcott |
| 1952-1956 | Rocky Marciano* |
| 1956-1959 | Floyd Patterson |
| 1959-1960 | Ingemar Johansson |
| 1960-1962 | Floyd Patterson |
| 1962-1964 | Sonny Liston |
| 1964-1967 | Cassius Clay* (Muhammad Ali) (d) |
| 1970-1973 | Joe Frazier |
| 1973-1974 | George Foreman |
| 1974-1978 | Muhammad Ali |
| 1978-1979 | Leon Spinks (e), Muhammad Ali* |
| 1978 | Ken Norton (WBC), Larry Holmes (WBC) (f) |
| 1979 | John Tate (WBA) |
| 1980 | Mike Weaver (WBA) |
| 1982 | Michael Dokes (WBA) |
| 1983 | Gerrie Coetzee (WBA) |
| 1984 | Tim Witherspoon (WBC); Pinklon Thomas (WBC); Greg Page (WBA) |
| 1985 | Tony Tubbs (WBA); Michael Spinks (IBF) |
| 1986 | Tim Witherspoon (WBA); Trevor Berbick (WBC); Mike Tyson (WBC); James (Bone-crusher) Smith (WBA). |
| 1987 | Mike Tyson (WBA, 1988—IBF). |
| 1990 | James "Buster" Douglas (WBA, WBC, IBF) |
| 1990 | Evander Holyfield (WBA, WBC, IBF) |
| 1992 | Riddick Bowe (WBA, IBF, WBC); Lennox Lewis (WBC) (g) |

(a) London Prize Ring (bare knuckle champion).
(b) First Marquis of Queensberry champion.
(c) Jeffries abandoned the title (1905) and designated Marvin Hart and Jack Root as logical contenders. Hart defeated Root in 12 rounds (1905) and in turn was defeated by Tommy Burns (1906) who laid claim to the title. Jack Johnson defeated Burns (1908) and was recognized as champion. He clinched the title by defeating Jeffries in an attempted comeback (1910).

(d) Title declared vacant by the WBA and other groups in 1967 after Clay's refusal to fulfill his military obligation. Joe Frazier was recognized as champion by 6 states, Mexico, and So. America. Jimmy Ellis was declared champion by the WBA. Frazier KOd Ellis, Feb. 16, 1970.
(e) After Spinks defeated Ali, the WBC recognized Ken Norton as champion. Norton subsequently lost his title to Larry Holmes.
(f) Holmes was stripped of his WBC title in 1984. He was the IBF champion when he lost to Michael Spinks.
(g) Lewis was named WBC champion when Bowe refused to fight him.

### Light Heavyweights

| | |
|---|---|
| 1903 | Jack Root, George Gardner |
| 1903-1905 | Bob Fitzsimmons |
| 1905-1912 | Philadelphia Jack O'Brien* |
| 1912-1916 | Jack Dillon |
| 1916-1920 | Battling Levinsky |
| 1920-1922 | George Carpentier |
| 1922-1923 | Battling Siki |
| 1923-1925 | Mike McTigue |
| 1925-1926 | Paul Berlenbach |
| 1926-1927 | Jack Delaney* |
| 1927-1929 | Tommy Loughran* |
| 1930-1934 | Maxey Rosenbloom |
| 1934-1935 | Bob Olin |
| 1935-1939 | John Henry Lewis* |
| 1939 | Melio Bettina |
| 1939-1941 | Billy Conn* |
| 1941 | Anton Christoforidis (won NBA title) |
| 1941-1948 | Gus Lesnevich, Freddie Mills |
| 1948-1950 | Freddie Mills |
| 1950-1952 | Joey Maxim |
| 1952-1960 | Archie Moore |
| 1961-1962 | vacant |
| 1962-1963 | Harold Johnson |
| 1963-1965 | Willie Pastrano |
| 1965-1966 | Jose Torres |
| 1966-1968 | Dick Tiger |
| 1968-1974 | Bob Foster*, John Conteh (WBA) |
| 1975-1977 | John Conteh (WBC), Miguel Cuello (WBC), Victor Galindez (WBA) |
| 1978 | Mike Rossman (WBA), Mate Parlov (WBC), Marvin Johnson (WBC) |
| 1979 | Matthew Saad Muhammad (WBC), Victor Galindez (WBA), Marvin Johnson (WBA) |
| 1980 | Eddie Mustafa Muhammad (WBA) |
| 1981 | Michael Spinks (WBA), Dwight Braxton (WBC) |
| 1983-1985 | Michael Spinks* |
| 1985 | J. B. Williamson (WBC) |
| 1986 | Marvin Johnson (WBA); Dennis Andries (WBC) |
| 1987 | Thomas Hearns (WBC); Leslie Stewart (WBA); Virgil Hill (WBA); Don Lalonde (WBC) |
| 1988 | Ray Leonard* (WBC) |
| 1989 | Jeff Harding (WBC) |
| 1990 | Dennis Andries (WBC) |

| | |
|---|---|
| 1991 | Thomas Hearns (WBA); Jeff Harding (WBC) |
| 1992 | Iran Barkley* (WBA); Virgil Hill (WBA) |

## Middleweights

| | |
|---|---|
| 1884-1891 | Jack "Nonpareil" Dempsey |
| 1891-1897 | Bob Fitzsimmons* |
| 1897-1907 | Tommy Ryan* |
| 1907-1908 | Stanley Ketchel, Billy Papke |
| 1908-1910 | Stanley Ketchel |
| 1911-1913 | vacant |
| 1913 | Frank Klaus, George Chip |
| 1914-1917 | Al McCoy |
| 1917-1920 | Mike O'Dowd |
| 1920-1923 | Johnny Wilson |
| 1923-1926 | Harry Greb |
| 1926-1931 | Tiger Flowers, Mickey Walker |
| 1931-1932 | Gorilla Jones (NBA) |
| 1932-1937 | Marcel Thil |
| 1938 | Al Hostak (NBA), Solly Krieger (NBA) |
| 1939-1940 | Al Hostak (NBA) |
| 1941-1947 | Tony Zale |
| 1947-1948 | Rocky Graziano |
| 1948 | Tony Zale, Marcel Cerdan |
| 1949-1951 | Jake LaMotta |
| 1951 | Ray Robinson, Randy Turpin, Ray Robinson* |
| 1953-1955 | Carl (Bobo) Olson |
| 1955-1957 | Ray Robinson |
| 1957 | Gene Fullmer, Ray Robinson, Carmen Basilio |
| 1958 | Ray Robinson |
| 1959 | Gene Fullmer (NBA); Ray Robinson (N.Y.) |
| 1960 | Gene Fullmer (NBA); Paul Pender (New York and Mass.) |
| 1961 | Gene Fullmer (NBA); Terry Downes (New York, Mass., Europe) |
| 1962 | Gene Fullmer, Dick Tiger (NBA), Paul Pender (New York and Mass.)* |
| 1963 | Dick Tiger (universal). |
| 1963-1965 | Joey Giardello |
| 1965-1966 | Dick Tiger |
| 1966-1967 | Emile Griffith |
| 1967 | Nino Benvenuti |
| 1967-1968 | Emile Griffith |
| 1968-1970 | Nino Benvenuti |
| 1970-1977 | Carlos Monzon* |
| 1977-1978 | Rodrigo Valdez |
| 1978-1979 | Hugo Corro |
| 1979-1980 | Vito Antuofermo |
| 1980 | Alan Minter, Marvin Hagler |
| 1987 | Ray Leonard* (WBC); Thomas Hearns (WBC); Sumbu Kalambay (WBA). |
| 1988 | Iran Barkley (WBC) |
| 1989 | Mike McCallum (WBA); Roberto Duran (WBC) |
| 1991 | Julian Jackson (WBC) |
| 1992 | Reggie Johnson (WBA) |
| 1993 | Gerald McClellan (WBC) |

## Welterweights

| | |
|---|---|
| 1892-1894 | Mysterious Billy Smith |
| 1894-1896 | Tommy Ryan |
| 1896 | Kid McCoy* |
| 1900 | Rube Ferns, Matty Matthews |
| 1901 | Rube Ferns |
| 1901-1904 | Joe Walcott |
| 1904-1906 | Dixie Kid, Joe Walcott, Honey Mellody |
| 1907-1911 | Mike Sullivan |
| 1911-1915 | vacant |
| 1915-1919 | Ted Lewis |
| 1919-1922 | Jack Britton |
| 1922-1926 | Mickey Walker |
| 1926 | Pete Latzo |
| 1927-1929 | Joe Dundee |
| 1929 | Jackie Fields |
| 1930 | Jack Thompson, Tommy Freeman |
| 1931 | Freeman, Thompson, Lou Brouillard |
| 1932 | Jackie Fields |
| 1933 | Young Corbett, Jimmy McLarnin |
| 1934 | Barney Ross, Jimmy McLarnin |
| 1935-1938 | Barney Ross |
| 1938-1940 | Henry Armstrong |
| 1940-1941 | Fritzie Zivic |
| 1941-1946 | Fred Cochrane |
| 1946-1946 | Marty Servo*; Ray Robinson (a) |
| 1946-1950 | Ray Robinson* |
| 1951 | Johnny Bratton (NBA) |
| 1951-1954 | Kid Gavilan |
| 1954-1955 | Johnny Saxton |
| 1955 | Tony De Marco, Carmen Basilio |
| 1956 | Carmen Basilio, Johnny Saxton, Basilio |
| 1957 | Carmen Basilio* |
| 1958-1960 | Virgil Akins, Don Jordan |
| 1960 | Benny Paret |
| 1961 | Emile Griffith, Benny Paret |
| 1962 | Emile Griffith |
| 1963 | Luis Rodriguez, Emile Griffith |
| 1964-1966 | Emile Griffith* |
| 1966-1969 | Curtis Cokes |
| 1969-1970 | Jose Napoles, Billy Backus |
| 1971-1975 | Jose Napoles |
| 1975-1976 | John Stracey (WBC), Angel Espada (WBA) |
| 1976-1979 | Carlos Palomino (WBC), Jose Cuevas (WBA) |
| 1979 | Wilfredo Benitez (WBC), Sugar Ray Leonard (WBC) |
| 1980 | Roberto Duran (WBC), Thomas Hearns (WBA), Sugar Ray Leonard (WBC) |
| 1981-1982 | Sugar Ray Leonard* |
| 1983 | Donald Curry (WBA); Milton McCrory (WBC) |
| 1985 | Donald Curry |
| 1986 | Lloyd Honeyghan (WBC) |
| 1987 | Mark Breland (WBA); Marlon Starling (WBA); Jorge Vaca (WBC). |
| 1988 | Tomas Molinares (WBA); Lloyd Honeyghan (WBC). |
| 1989 | Marlon Starling (WBC); Mark Breland (WBA) |
| 1990 | Maurice Blocker (WBC); Aaron Davis (WBA) |
| 1991 | Meldrick Taylor (WBA); Simon Brown (WBC); Buddy McGirt (WBC) |
| 1992 | Crisanto Espana (WBA) |
| 1993 | Pernell Whitaker (WBC) |

(a) Robinson gained the title by defeating Tommy Bell in an elimination agreed to by the NY Commission and the NBA. Both claimed Robinson waived his title when he won the middleweight crown from LaMotta in 1951.

## Lightweights

| | |
|---|---|
| 1896-1899 | Kid Lavigne |
| 1899-1902 | Frank Erne |
| 1902-1908 | Joe Gans |
| 1908-1910 | Battling Nelson |
| 1910-1912 | Ad Wolgast |
| 1912-1914 | Willie Ritchie |
| 1914-1917 | Freddie Welsh |
| 1917-1925 | Benny Leonard* |
| 1925 | Jimmy Goodrich, Rocky Kansas |
| 1926-1930 | Sammy Mandell |
| 1930 | Al Singer, Tony Canzoneri |
| 1930-1933 | Tony Canzoneri |
| 1933-1935 | Barney Ross* |
| 1935-1936 | Tony Canzoneri |
| 1936-1938 | Lou Ambers |
| 1938 | Henry Armstrong |
| 1939 | Lou Ambers |
| 1940 | Lew Jenkins |
| 1941-1943 | Sammy Angott |
| 1944 | S. Angott (NBA), J. Zurita (NBA) |
| 1945-1951 | Ike Williams (NBA: later universal) |
| 1951-1952 | James Carter |
| 1952 | Lauro Salas, James Carter |
| 1953-1954 | James Carter |
| 1954 | Paddy De Marco; James Carter |
| 1955 | James Carter; Bud Smith |
| 1956 | Bud Smith, Joe Brown |
| 1956-1962 | Joe Brown |
| 1962-1965 | Carlos Ortiz |
| 1965 | Ismael Laguna |
| 1965-1968 | Carlos Ortiz |
| 1968-1969 | Teo Cruz |
| 1969-1970 | Mando Ramos |
| 1970 | Ismael Laguna, Ken Buchanan (WBA) |
| 1971 | Mando Ramos (WBC), Pedro Carrasco (WBC) |
| 1972-1979 | Roberto Duran* (WBA) |
| 1972 | Pedro Carrasco, Mando Ramos, Chango Carmona, Rodolfo Gonzalez (all WBC) |
| 1974-1976 | Guts Ishimatsu (WBC) |
| 1976-1977 | Esteban De Jesus (WBC) |
| 1979 | Jim Watt (WBC), Ernesto Espana (WBA) |
| 1980 | Hilmer Kenty (WBA) |
| 1981 | Alexis Arguello (WBC), Sean O'Grady (WBA), Arturo Frias (WBA) |
| 1982-1984 | Ray Mancini (WBA) |
| 1983 | Edwin Rosario (WBC) |
| 1984 | Livingstone Bramble (WBA); Jose Luis Ramirez (WBC) |
| 1985 | Hector (Macho) Camacho (WBC) |
| 1986 | Edwin Rosario (WBA); Jose Luis Ramirez (WBC). |
| 1987 | Julio Cesar Chavez (WBA). |

| 1989 | Edwin Rosario (WBA); Pernell Whitaker (WBC) |
|---|---|
| 1990 | Juan Nazario (WBA); Pernell Whitaker (WBA) |
| 1992 | Joey Gamache (WBA) |
| 1992 | Tony Lopez (WBA); Miguel Angel Gonzalez (WBC) |
| 1993 | Dingaan Thobela (WBA) |

### Featherweights

| 1892-1900 | George Dixon (disputed) |
|---|---|
| 1900-1901 | Terry McGovern, Young Corbett* |
| 1901-1912 | Abe Attell |
| 1912-1923 | Johnny Kilbane |
| 1923 | Eugene Criqui, Johnny Dundee |
| 1923-1925 | Johnny Dundee* |
| 1925-1927 | Kid Kaplan* |
| 1927-1928 | Benny Bass, Tony Canzoneri |
| 1928-1929 | Andre Routis |
| 1929-1932 | Battling Battalino* |
| 1932-1934 | Tommy Paul (NBA) |
| 1933-1936 | Freddie Miller |
| 1936-1937 | Petey Sarron |
| 1937-1938 | Henry Armstrong* |
| 1938-1940 | Joey Archibald (b) |
| 1940-41 | Harry Jeffra |
| 1942-1948 | Willie Pep |
| 1948-1949 | Sandy Saddler |
| 1949-1950 | Willie Pep |
| 1950-1957 | Sandy Saddler* |
| 1957-1959 | Hogan (Kid) Bassey |
| 1959-1963 | Davey Moore |
| 1963-1964 | Sugar Ramos |

| 1964-1967 | Vicente Saldivar* |
|---|---|
| 1968-1971 | Paul Rojas (WBA), Sho Saijo (WBA) |
| 1971 | Antonio Gomez (WBA), Kuniaki Shibada (WBC) |
| 1972 | Ernesto Marcel* (WBA), Clemente Sanchez* (WBC), Jose Legra (WBC) |
| 1973 | Eder Jofre (WBC) |
| 1974 | Ruben Olivares (WBA), Alexis Arguello (WBA), Bobby Chacon (WBC) |
| 1975 | Ruben Olivares (WBC), David Kotey (WBC) |
| 1976 | Danny Lopez (WBC) |
| 1977 | Rafael Ortega (WBA) |
| 1978 | Cecilio Lastra (WBA), Eusebio Pedrosa (WBA) |
| 1980 | Salvador Sanchez (WBC) |
| 1982 | Juan LaPorte (WBC) |
| 1984 | Wilfredo Gomez (WBC); Azumah Nelson (WBC) |
| 1985 | Barry McGuigan (WBA) |
| 1986 | Steve Cruz (WBA) |
| 1987 | Antonio Esparragoza (WBA) |
| 1988 | Jeff Fenech (WBC) |
| 1990 | Marcos Villasana (WBC) |
| 1991 | Park Yung Kyun (WBA) |
| 1991 | Paul Hodkinson (WBC) |
| 1993 | Goyo Vargas (WBC) |

(b) After Petey Scalzo knocked out Archibald in an overweight match and was refused a title bout, the NBA named Scalzo champion. The NBA title succession: Scalzo, 1938-1941; Richard Lemos, 1941; Jackie Wilson, 1941-1943; Jackie Callura, 1943; Phil Terranova, 1943-1944; Sal Bartolo, 1944-1946.

## History of Heavyweight Championship Bouts

*Title Changed Hands

1889—July 8—John L. Sullivan def. Jake Kilrain, 75, Richburg, Miss. Last championship bare knuckles bout.

*1892—Sept. 7—James J. Corbett def. John L. Sullivan, 21, New Orleans. Big gloves used for first time.

1894—Jan. 25—James J. Corbett KOd Charley Mitchell, 3, Jacksonville, Fla.

*1897—Bob Fitzsimmons def. James J. Corbett, 14, Carson City, Nev.

*1899—June 9—James J. Jeffries def. Bob Fitzsimmons, 11, Coney Island, N.Y.

1899—Nov. 3—James J. Jeffries def. Tom Sharkey, 25, Coney Island, N.Y.

1900—May 11—James J. Jeffries KOd James J. Corbett, 23, Coney Island, N.Y.

1901—Nov. 15—James J. Jeffries KOd Gus Ruhlin, 5, San Francisco.

1902—July 25—James J. Jeffries KOd Bob Fitzsimmons, 8, San Francisco.

1903—Aug. 14—James J. Jeffries def. James J. Corbett, 10, San Francisco.

1904—Aug. 26—James J. Jeffries KOd Jack Monroe, 2, San Francisco.

*1905—James J. Jeffries retired, July 3—Marvin Hart KOd Jack Root, 12, Reno. Jeffries refereed and presented the title to the victor. Jack O'Brien also claimed the title.

*1906—Feb. 23—Tommy Burns def. Marvin Hart, 20, Los Angeles.

1906—Nov. 28—Philadelphia Jack O'Brien and Tommy Burns, 20, draw, Los Angeles.

1907—May 8—Tommy Burns def. Jack O'Brien, 20, Los Angeles.

1907—July 4—Tommy Burns KOd Bill Squires, 1, Colma, Cal.

1907—Dec. 2—Tommy Burns KOd Gunner Moir, 10, London.

1908—Feb. 10—Tommy Burns KOd Jack Palmer, 4, London.

1908—March 17—Tommy Burns KOd Jem Roche, 1, Dublin.

1908—April 18—Tommy Burns KOd Jewey Smith, 5, Paris.

1908—June 13—Tommy Burns KOd Bill Squires, 8, Paris.

1908—Aug. 24—Tommy Burns KOd Bill Squires, 13, Sydney, New South Wales.

1908—Sept. 2—Tommy Burns KOd Bill Lang, 2, Melbourne, Australia.

*1908—Dec. 26—Jack Johnson KOd Tommy Burns, 14, Sydney, Australia. Police halted contest.

1909—May 19—Jack Johnson and Jack O'Brien, 6, draw, Philadelphia.

1909—June 30—Jack Johnson and Tony Ross, 6, draw, Pittsburgh.

1909—Sept. 9—Jack Johnson and Al Kaufman, 10, draw, San Francisco.

1909—Oct. 16—Jack Johnson KOd Stanley Ketchel, 12, Colma, Cal.

1910—July 4—Jack Johnson KOd Jim Jeffries, 15, Reno, Nev. Jeffries came back from retirement.

1912—July 4—Jack Johnson def. Jim Flynn, 9, Las Vegas, N.M. Contest stopped by police.

1913—Nov. 28—Jack Johnson KOd Andre Spaul, 2, Paris.

1913—Dec. 9—Jack Johnson and Jim Johnson, 10, draw, Paris. Bout called a draw when Jack Johnson declared he had broken his arm.

1914—June 27—Jack Johnson def. Frank Moran, 20, Paris.

*1915—April 5—Jess Willard KOd Jack Johnson, 26, Havana, Cuba.

1916—March 25—Jess Willard and Frank Moran, 10, draw, New York.

*1919—July 4—Jack Dempsey KOd Jess Willard, Toledo, Oh. Willard failed to answer bell for 4th round.

1920—Sept. 6—Jack Dempsey KOd Billy Miske, 3, Benton Harbor, Mich.

1920—Dec. 14—Jack Dempsey KOd Bill Brennan, 12, New York.

1921—July 2—Jack Dempsey KOd George Carpentier, 4, Boyle's Thirty Acres, Jersey City, N.J. Carpentier had held the so-called white heavyweight title since July 16, 1914, in a series established in 1913, after Jack Johnson's exile in Europe late in 1912.

1923—July 4—Jack Dempsey def. Tom Gibbons, 15, Shelby, Mont.

1923—Sept. 14—Jack Dempsey KOd Luis Firpo, 2, New York.

*1926—Sept. 23—Gene Tunney def. Jack Dempsey, 10, Philadelphia.

1927—Sept. 22—Gene Tunney def. Jack Dempsey, 10, Chicago.

1928—July 26—Gene Tunney KOd Tom Heeney, 11, New York; soon afterward he announced his retirement.

*1930—June 12—Max Schmeling def. Jack Sharkey, 4, New York. Sharkey fouled Schmeling in a bout which was generally considered to have resulted in the election of a successor to Gene Tunney, New York.

1931—July 3—Max Schmeling KOd Young Stribling, 15, Cleveland.

*1932—June 21—Jack Sharkey def. Max Schmeling, 15, New York.

*1933—June 29—Primo Carnera KOd Jack Sharkey, 6, New York.

1933—Oct. 22—Primo Carnera def. Paulino Uzcudun, 15, Rome.

1934—March 1—Primo Carnera def. Tommy Loughran, 15, Miami.

*1934—June 14—Max Baer KOd Primo Carnera, 11, New York.

*1935—June 13—James J. Braddock def. Max Baer, 15, New York.

*1937—June 22—Joe Louis KOd James J. Braddock, 8, Chicago.

1937—Aug. 30—Joe Louis def. Tommy Farr, 15, New York.

**1938**—Feb. 23—Joe Louis KOd Nathan Mann, 3, New York.
**1938**—April 1—Joe Louis KOd Harry Thomas, 5, Chicago.
**1938**—June 22—Joe Louis KOd Max Schmeling, 1, New York.
**1939**—Jan. 25—Joe Louis KOd John H. Lewis, 1, New York.
**1939**—April 17—Joe Louis KOd Jack Roper, 1, Los Angeles.
**1939**—June 28—Joe Louis KOd Tony Galento, 4, New York.
**1939**—Sept. 20—Joe Louis KOd Bob Pastor, 11, Detroit.
**1940**—February 9—Joe Louis def. Arturo Godoy, 15, New York.
**1940**—March 29—Joe Louis KOd Johnny Paycheck, 2, New York.
**1940**—June 20—Joe Louis KOd Arturo Godoy, 8, New York.
**1940**—Dec. 16—Joe Louis KOd Al McCoy, 6, Boston.
**1941**—Jan. 31—Joe Louis KOd Red Burman, 5, New York.
**1941**—Feb. 17—Joe Louis KOd Gus Dorzaio, 2, Philadelphia.
**1941**—March 21—Joe Louis KOd Abe Simon, 13, Detroit.
**1941**—April 8—Joe Louis KOd Tony Musto, 9, St. Louis.
**1941**—May 23—Joe Louis def. Buddy Baer, 7, Washington, D.C., on a disqualification.
**1941**—June 18—Joe Louis KOd Billy Conn, 13, New York.
**1941**—Sept. 29—Joe Louis KOd Lou Nova, 6, New York.
**1942**—Jan. 9—Joe Louis KOd Buddy Baer, 1, New York.
**1942**—March 27—Joe Louis KOd Abe Simon, 6, New York.
**1946**—June 19—Joe Louis KOd Billy Conn, 8, New York.
**1946**—Sept. 18—Joe Louis KOd Tami Mauriello, 1, New York.
**1947**—Dec. 5—Joe Louis def. Joe Walcott, 15, New York.
**1948**—June 25—Joe Louis KOd Joe Walcott, 11, New York.
**\*1949**—June 22—Following Joe Louis' retirement Ezzard Charles def. Joe Walcott, 15, Chicago, NBA recognition only.
**1949**—Aug. 10—Ezzard Charles KOd Gus Lesnevich, 7, New York.
**1949**—Oct. 14—Ezzard Charles KOd Pat Valentino, 8, San Francisco; clinched American title.
**1950**—Aug. 15—Ezzard Charles KOd Freddy Beshore, 14, Buffalo.
**1950**—Sept. 27—Ezzard Charles def. Joe Louis in latter's attempted comeback, 15, New York; universal recognition.
**1950**—Dec. 5—Ezzard Charles KOd Nick Barone, 11, Cincinnati.
**1951**—Jan. 12—Ezzard Charles KOd Lee Oma, 10, New York.
**1951**—March 7—Ezzard Charles def. Joe Walcott, 15, Detroit.
**1951**—May 30—Ezzard Charles def. Joey Maxim, light heavyweight champion, 15, Chicago.
**\*1951**—July 18—Joe Walcott KOd Ezzard Charles, 7, Pittsburgh.
**1952**—June 5—Joe Walcott def. Ezzard Charles, 15, Philadelphia.
**\*1952**—Sept. 23—Rocky Marciano KOd Joe Walcott, 13, Philadelphia.
**1953**—May 15—Rocky Marciano KOd Joe Walcott, 1, Chicago.
**1953**—Sept. 24—Rocky Marciano KOd Roland LaStarza, 11, New York.
**1954**—June 17—Rocky Marciano def. Ezzard Charles, 15, New York.
**1954**—Sept. 17—Rocky Marciano KOd Ezzard Charles, 8, New York.
**1955**—May 16—Rocky Marciano KOd Don Cockell, 9, San Francisco.
**1955**—Sept. 21—Rocky Marciano KOd Archie Moore, 9, New York. Marciano retired undefeated, Apr. 27, 1956.
**\*1956**—Nov. 30—Floyd Patterson KOd Archie Moore, 5, Chicago.
**1957**—July 29—Floyd Patterson KOd Hurricane Jackson, 10, New York.
**1957**—Aug. 22—Floyd Patterson KOd Pete Rademacher, 6, Seattle.
**1958**—Aug. 18—Floyd Patterson KOd Roy Harris, 12, Los Angeles.
**1959**—May 1—Floyd Patterson KOd Brian London, 11, Indianapolis.
**\*1959**—June 26—Ingemar Johansson KOd Floyd Patterson, 3, New York.
**\*1960**—June 20—Floyd Patterson KOd Ingemar Johansson, 5, New York. First heavyweight in boxing history to regain title.
**1961**—Mar. 13—Floyd Patterson KOd Ingemar Johansson, 6, Miami Beach.
**1961**—Dec. 4—Floyd Patterson KOd Tom McNeeley, 4, Toronto.
**\*1962**—Sept. 25—Sonny Liston KOd Floyd Patterson, 1, Chicago.
**1963**—July 22—Sonny Liston KOd Floyd Patterson, 1, Las Vegas.
**\*1964**—Feb. 25—Cassius Clay KOd Sonny Liston, 7, Miami Beach.
**1965**—May 25—Cassius Clay KOd Sonny Liston, 1, Lewiston, Maine.

**1965**—Nov. 11—Cassius Clay KOd Floyd Patterson, 12, Las Vegas.
**1966**—Mar. 29—Cassius Clay def. George Chuvalo, 15, Toronto.
**1966**—May 21—Cassius Clay KOd Henry Cooper, 6, London.
**1966**—Aug. 6—Cassius Clay KOd Brian London, 3, London.
**1966**—Sept. 10—Cassius Clay KOd Karl Mildenberger, 12, Frankfurt, Germany.
**1966**—Nov. 14—Cassius Clay KOd Cleveland Williams, 3, Houston.
**1967**—Feb. 6—Cassius Clay def. Ernie Terrell, 15, Houston.
**1967**—Mar. 22—Cassius Clay KOd Zora Folley, 7, New York. Clay was stripped of his title by the WBA and others for refusing military service.
**\*1970**—Feb. 16—Joe Frazier KOd Jimmy Ellis, 5, New York.
**1970**—Nov. 18—Joe Frazier KOd Bob Foster, 2, Detroit.
**1971**—Mar. 8—Joe Frazier def. Cassius Clay (Muhammad Ali), 15, New York.
**1972**—Jan. 15—Joe Frazier KOd Terry Daniels, 4, New Orleans.
**1972**—May 25—Joe Frazier KOd Ron Stander, 5, Omaha.
**\*1973**—Jan. 22—George Foreman KOd Joe Frazier, 2, Kingston, Jamaica.
**1973**—Sept. 1—George Foreman KOd Joe Roman, 1, Tokyo.
**1974**—Mar. 3—George Foreman KOd Ken Norton, 2, Caracas.
**\*1974**—Oct. 30—Muhammad Ali KOd George Foreman, 8, Zaire.
**1975**—Mar. 24—Muhammad Ali KOd Chuck Wepner, 15, Cleveland.
**1975**—May 16—Muhammad Ali KOd Ron Lyle, 11, Las Vegas.
**1975**—June 30—Muhammad Ali def. Joe Bugner, 15, Malaysia.
**1975**—Oct. 1—Muhammad Ali KOd Joe Frazier, 14, Manila.
**1976**—Feb. 20—Muhammad Ali KOd Jean-Pierre Coopman, 5, San Juan.
**1976**—Apr. 30—Muhammad Ali def. Jimmy Young, 15, Landover, Md.
**1976**—May 25—Muhammad Ali KOd Richard Dunn, 5, Munich.
**1976**—Sept. 28—Muhammad Ali def. Ken Norton, 15, New York.
**1977**—May 16—Muhammad Ali def. Alfredo Evangelista, 15, Landover, Md.
**1977**—Sept. 29—Muhammad Ali def. Earnie Shavers, 15, New York.
**\*1978**—Feb. 15—Leon Spinks def. Muhammad Ali, 15, Las Vegas.
**\*1978**—Sept. 15—Muhammad Ali def. Leon Spinks, 15, New Orleans. Ali retired in 1979.

(Bouts when title changed hands only)

**\*1978**—June 9—(WBC) Larry Holmes def. Ken Norton, 15, Las Vegas.
**\*1980**—Mar. 31—(WBA) Mike Weaver KOd John Tate, 15, Knoxville.
**\*1982**—Dec. 10—(WBA) Michael Dokes KOd Mike Weaver, 1, Las Vegas.
**\*1983**—Sept. 23—(WBA) Gerrie Coetzee KOd Michael Dokes, 10, Richfield, Oh.
**\*1984**—Mar. 10—(WBC) Tim Witherspoon def. Greg Page, 12, Las Vegas, Nev.
**\*1984**—Aug. 31—(WBC) Pinklon Thomas def. Tim Witherspoon, 12, Las Vegas, Nev.
**\*1984**—Dec. 2—(WBA) Greg Page KOd Gerrie Coetzee, 8, Sun City, Bophuthatswana
**\*1985**—Apr. 29—(WBA) Tony Tubbs def. Greg Page, 15, Buffalo, N.Y.
**\*1985**—Sept. 21—(IBF) Michael Spinks def. Larry Holmes, 15, Las Vegas, Nev.
**\*1986**—Jan. 17—(WBA) Tim Witherspoon def. Tony Tubbs, 15, Atlanta, Ga.
**\*1986**—Mar. 23—(WBC) Trevor Berbick def. Pinklon Thomas, 12, Miami, Fla.
**\*1986**—Nov. 22—(WBC) Mike Tyson KOd Trevor Berbick, 2, Las Vegas.
**\*1986**—Dec. 12—(WBA) James (Bonecrusher) Smith KOd Tim Witherspoon, 1, New York.
**\*1987**—Mar. 7—(WBA) Mike Tyson def. James (Bonecrusher) Smith, 12, Las Vegas.
**\*1988**—June 27—(IBF) Mike Tyson KOd Michael Spinks, 1, Atlantic City.
**\*1990**—Feb. 11—(WBA, WBC, IBF) James "Buster" Douglas KOd Mike Tyson, 10, Tokyo.
**\*1990**—Oct. 25—(WBA, WBC, IBF) Evander Holyfield KOd James "Buster" Douglas, 3, Las Vegas.
**\*1992**—Nov. 13—(WBA, WBC, IBF) Riddick Bowe def. Evander Holyfield, 12, Las Vegas.

## Pro Rodeo Championship Standings in 1992

| Event | Winner | Money won | Event | Winner | Money won |
|---|---|---|---|---|---|
| All Around | Ty Murray, Stephenville, Tex. | $225,992 | Steer Wrestling | Mark Roy, Dalemead, Alta. | $112,103 |
| Saddle Bronc | Robert Etbauer, Ree Heights, S.D. | 184,675 | Steer Roping | Guy Allen, Vinita, Okla. | 44,729 |
| Bareback | Wayne Herman, Dickinson, N.D. | 122,949 | Women's Barrel | | |
| Bull Riding | Cody Custer, Wickenburg, Ariz. | 149,814 | Racing | Charmayne Rodman, Galt, Cal. | 110,868 |
| Calf Roping | Joe Beaver, Huntsville, Tex. | 124,525 | | | |

## Pro Rodeo Cowboy All Around Champions

| Year | Winner | Money won | Year | Winner | Money won |
|---|---|---|---|---|---|
| 1972 | Phil Lyne, George West, Tex. | $60,852 | 1982 | Chris Lybbert, Coyote, Cal. | $123,709 |
| 1973 | Larry Mahan, Dallas, Tex. | 64,447 | 1983 | Roy Cooper, Durant, Okla. | 153,391 |
| 1974 | Tom Ferguson, Miami, Okla. | 66,929 | 1984 | Dee Pickett, Caldwell, Ida. | 122,618 |
| 1975 | Leo Camarillo, Oakdale, Cal. | 50,300 | 1985 | Lewis Feild, Elk Ridge, Ut. | 130,347 |
| | Tom Ferguson, Miami, Okla. | 50,300 | 1986 | Lewis Feild, Elk Ridge, Ut. | 166,042 |
| 1976 | Tom Ferguson, Miami, Okla. | 87,908 | 1987 | Lewis Feild, Elk Ridge, Ut. | 144,335 |
| 1977 | Tom Ferguson, Miami, Okla. | 76,730 | 1988 | Dave Appleton, Arlington, Tex. | 121,546 |
| 1978 | Tom Ferguson, Miami, Okla. | 103,734 | 1989 | Ty Murray, Odessa, Tex. | 134,806 |
| 1979 | Tom Ferguson, Miami, Okla. | 96,272 | 1990 | Ty Murray, Stephenville, Tex. | 213,772 |
| 1980 | Paul Tierney, Rapid City, S.D. | 105,568 | 1991 | Ty Murray, Stephenville, Tex. | 244,230 |
| 1981 | Jimmie Cooper, Monument, N.M. | 105,862 | 1992 | Ty Murray, Stephenville, Tex. | 225,992 |

## The America's Cup

In the 1992 America's Cup match the United States yacht *America* [3] defeated the Italian yacht *Il Moro di Venezia* 4-1 in the waters off San Diego, Cal. *America* [3] was skippered by Bill Koch. The next America's Cup competition is scheduled for 1995 in San Diego.

Competition for the America's Cup grew out of the first contest to establish a world yachting championship, one of the carnival features of the London Exposition of 1851. The race, open to all classes of yachts from all over the world, covered a 60-mile course around the Isle of Wight; the prize was a cup worth about $500, donated by the Royal Yacht Squadron of England, known as the "America's Cup" because it was first won by the United States yacht *America*.

### Winners of the America's Cup

| | |
|---|---|
| 1851 | America |
| 1870 | Magic defeated Cambria, England, (1-0) |
| 1871 | Columbia (first three races) and Sappho (last two races) defeated Livonia, England, (4-1) |
| 1876 | Madeline defeated Countess of Dufferin, Canada, (2-0) |
| 1881 | Mischief defeated Atalanta, Canada, (2-0) |
| 1885 | Puritan defeated Genesta, England, (2-0) |
| 1886 | Mayflower defeated Galatea, England, (2-0) |
| 1887 | Volunteer defeated Thistle, Scotland, (2-0) |
| 1893 | Vigilant defeated Valkyrie II, England, (3-0) |
| 1895 | Defender defeated Valkyrie III, England, (3-0) |
| 1899 | Columbia defeated Shamrock, England, (3-0) |
| 1901 | Columbia defeated Shamrock II, England, (3-0) |
| 1903 | Reliance defeated Shamrock III, England, (3-0) |
| 1920 | Resolute defeated Shamrock IV, England, (3-2) |
| 1930 | Enterprise defeated Shamrock V, England, (4-0) |
| 1934 | Rainbow defeated Endeavour, England, (4-2) |
| 1937 | Ranger defeated Endeavour II, England, (4-0) |
| 1958 | Columbia defeated Sceptre, England, (4-0) |
| 1962 | Weatherly defeated Gretel, Australia, (4-1) |
| 1964 | Constellation defeated Sovereign, England, (4-0) |
| 1967 | Intrepid defeated Dame Pattie, Australia, (4-0) |
| 1970 | Intrepid defeated Gretel II, Australia, (4-1) |
| 1974 | Courageous defeated Southern Cross, Australia, (4-0) |
| 1977 | Courageous defeated Australia, Australia, (4-0) |
| 1980 | Freedom defeated Australia, Australia, (4-1) |
| 1983 | Australia II, Australia defeated Liberty, (4-3) |
| 1987 | Stars & Stripes defeated Kookaburra III, Australia, (4-0) |
| 1988 | Stars & Stripes defeated New Zealand, New Zealand, (2-0) |
| 1992 | America[3] defeated Il Moro di Venezia, Italy, (4-1) |

## The World Cup

The World Cup, emblematic of international soccer supremacy, was won by West Germany on July 8, 1990, with a 1-0 victory over defending champion Argentina on a penalty shot in the 84th minute. It was the lowest-scoring final in the 60 years of World Cup play. It was the 3d World Cup title for West Germany, equaling Brazil and Italy. In 1994 the U.S. will host the tournament for the first time. Winners and sites of previous World Cup play follow:

| Year | Winner | Final opponent | Site | Year | Winner | Final opponent | Site |
|---|---|---|---|---|---|---|---|
| 1930 | Uruguay | Argentina | Uruguay | 1966 | England | W. Germany | England |
| 1934 | Italy | Czechoslovakia | Italy | 1970 | Brazil | Italy | Mexico |
| 1938 | Italy | Hungary | France | 1974 | W. Germany | Netherlands | W. Germany |
| 1950 | Uruguay | Brazil | Brazil | 1978 | Argentina | Netherlands | Argentina |
| 1954 | W. Germany | Hungary | Switzerland | 1982 | Italy | W. Germany | Spain |
| 1958 | Brazil | Sweden | Sweden | 1986 | Argentina | W. Germany | Mexico |
| 1962 | Brazil | Czechoslovakia | Chile | 1990 | W. Germany | Argentina | Italy |

# BASEBALL
## Major League Pennant Winners, 1901–1993

**National League**             **American League**

| Year | Winner | Won | Lost | Pct | Manager | Year | Winner | Won | Lost | Pct | Manager |
|------|--------|-----|------|-----|---------|------|--------|-----|------|-----|---------|
| 1901 | Pittsburgh | 90 | 49 | .647 | Clarke | 1901 | Chicago | 83 | 53 | .610 | Griffith |
| 1902 | Pittsburgh | 103 | 36 | .741 | Clarke | 1902 | Philadelphia | 83 | 53 | .610 | Mack |
| 1903 | Pittsburgh | 91 | 49 | .650 | Clarke | 1903 | Boston | 91 | 47 | .659 | Collins |
| 1904 | New York | 106 | 47 | .693 | McGraw | 1904 | Boston | 95 | 59 | .617 | Collins |
| 1905 | New York | 105 | 48 | .686 | McGraw | 1905 | Philadelphia | 92 | 56 | .622 | Mack |
| 1906 | Chicago | 116 | 36 | .763 | Chance | 1906 | Chicago | 93 | 58 | .616 | Jones |
| 1907 | Chicago | 107 | 45 | .704 | Chance | 1907 | Detroit | 92 | 58 | .613 | Jennings |
| 1908 | Chicago | 99 | 55 | .643 | Chance | 1908 | Detroit | 90 | 63 | .588 | Jennings |
| 1909 | Pittsburgh | 110 | 42 | .724 | Clarke | 1909 | Detroit | 98 | 54 | .645 | Jennings |
| 1910 | Chicago | 104 | 50 | .675 | Chance | 1910 | Philadelphia | 102 | 48 | .680 | Mack |
| 1911 | New York | 99 | 54 | .647 | McGraw | 1911 | Philadelphia | 101 | 50 | .669 | Mack |
| 1912 | New York | 103 | 48 | .682 | McGraw | 1912 | Boston | 105 | 47 | .691 | Stahl |
| 1913 | New York | 101 | 51 | .664 | McGraw | 1913 | Philadelphia | 96 | 57 | .627 | Mack |
| 1914 | Boston | 94 | 59 | .614 | Stallings | 1914 | Philadelphia | 99 | 53 | .651 | Mack |
| 1915 | Philadelphia | 90 | 62 | .592 | Moran | 1915 | Boston | 101 | 50 | .669 | Carrigan |
| 1916 | Brooklyn | 94 | 60 | .610 | Robinson | 1916 | Boston | 91 | 63 | .591 | Carrigan |
| 1917 | New York | 98 | 56 | .636 | McGraw | 1917 | Chicago | 100 | 54 | .649 | Rowland |
| 1918 | Chicago | 84 | 45 | .651 | Mitchell | 1918 | Boston | 75 | 51 | .595 | Barrow |
| 1919 | Cincinnati | 96 | 44 | .686 | Moran | 1919 | Chicago | 88 | 52 | .629 | Gleason |
| 1920 | Brooklyn | 93 | 60 | .604 | Robinson | 1920 | Cleveland | 98 | 56 | .636 | Speaker |
| 1921 | New York | 94 | 59 | .614 | McGraw | 1921 | New York | 98 | 55 | .641 | Huggins |
| 1922 | New York | 93 | 61 | .604 | McGraw | 1922 | New York | 94 | 60 | .610 | Huggins |
| 1923 | New York | 95 | 58 | .621 | McGraw | 1923 | New York | 98 | 54 | .645 | Huggins |
| 1924 | New York | 93 | 60 | .608 | McGraw | 1924 | Washington | 92 | 62 | .597 | Harris |
| 1925 | Pittsburgh | 95 | 58 | .621 | McKechnie | 1925 | Washington | 96 | 55 | .636 | Harris |
| 1926 | St. Louis | 89 | 65 | .578 | Hornsby | 1926 | New York | 91 | 63 | .591 | Huggins |
| 1927 | Pittsburgh | 94 | 60 | .610 | Bush | 1927 | New York | 110 | 44 | .714 | Huggins |
| 1928 | St. Louis | 95 | 59 | .617 | McKechnie | 1928 | New York | 101 | 53 | .656 | Huggins |
| 1929 | Chicago | 98 | 54 | .645 | McCarthy | 1929 | Philadelphia | 104 | 46 | .693 | Mack |
| 1930 | St. Louis | 92 | 62 | .597 | Street | 1930 | Philadelphia | 102 | 52 | .662 | Mack |
| 1931 | St. Louis | 101 | 53 | .656 | Street | 1931 | Philadelphia | 107 | 45 | .704 | Mack |
| 1932 | Chicago | 90 | 64 | .584 | Grimm | 1932 | New York | 107 | 47 | .695 | McCarthy |
| 1933 | New York | 91 | 61 | .599 | Terry | 1933 | Washington | 99 | 53 | .651 | Cronin |
| 1934 | St. Louis | 95 | 58 | .621 | Frisch | 1934 | Detroit | 101 | 53 | .656 | Cochrane |
| 1935 | Chicago | 100 | 54 | .649 | Grimm | 1935 | Detroit | 93 | 58 | .616 | Cochrane |
| 1936 | New York | 91 | 62 | .597 | Terry | 1936 | New York | 102 | 51 | .667 | McCarthy |
| 1937 | New York | 95 | 57 | .625 | Terry | 1937 | New York | 102 | 52 | .662 | McCarthy |
| 1938 | Chicago | 89 | 63 | .586 | Hartnett | 1938 | New York | 99 | 53 | .651 | McCarthy |
| 1939 | Cincinnati | 97 | 57 | .630 | McKechnie | 1939 | New York | 106 | 45 | .702 | McCarthy |
| 1940 | Cincinnati | 100 | 53 | .654 | McKechnie | 1940 | Detroit | 90 | 64 | .584 | Baker |
| 1941 | Brooklyn | 100 | 54 | .649 | Durocher | 1941 | New York | 101 | 53 | .656 | McCarthy |
| 1942 | St. Louis | 106 | 48 | .688 | Southworth | 1942 | New York | 103 | 51 | .669 | McCarthy |
| 1943 | St. Louis | 105 | 49 | .682 | Southworth | 1943 | New York | 98 | 56 | .636 | McCarthy |
| 1944 | St. Louis | 105 | 49 | .682 | Southworth | 1944 | St. Louis | 89 | 65 | .578 | Sewell |
| 1945 | Chicago | 98 | 56 | .636 | Grimm | 1945 | Detroit | 88 | 65 | .575 | O'Neill |
| 1946 | St. Louis | 98 | 58 | .628 | Dyer | 1946 | Boston | 104 | 50 | .675 | Cronin |
| 1947 | Brooklyn | 94 | 60 | .610 | Shotton | 1947 | New York | 97 | 57 | .630 | Harris |
| 1948 | Boston | 91 | 62 | .595 | Southworth | 1948 | Cleveland | 97 | 58 | .626 | Boudreau |
| 1949 | Brooklyn | 97 | 57 | .630 | Shotton | 1949 | New York | 97 | 57 | .630 | Stengel |
| 1950 | Philadelphia | 91 | 63 | .591 | Sawyer | 1950 | New York | 98 | 56 | .636 | Stengel |
| 1951 | New York | 98 | 59 | .624 | Durocher | 1951 | New York | 98 | 56 | .636 | Stengel |
| 1952 | Brooklyn | 96 | 57 | .627 | Dressen | 1952 | New York | 95 | 59 | .617 | Stengel |
| 1953 | Brooklyn | 105 | 49 | .682 | Dressen | 1953 | New York | 99 | 52 | .656 | Stengel |
| 1954 | New York | 97 | 57 | .630 | Durocher | 1954 | Cleveland | 111 | 43 | .721 | Lopez |
| 1955 | Brooklyn | 98 | 55 | .641 | Alston | 1955 | New York | 96 | 58 | .623 | Stengel |
| 1956 | Brooklyn | 93 | 61 | .604 | Alston | 1956 | New York | 97 | 57 | .630 | Stengel |
| 1957 | Milwaukee | 95 | 59 | .617 | Haney | 1957 | New York | 98 | 56 | .636 | Stengel |
| 1958 | Milwaukee | 92 | 62 | .597 | Haney | 1958 | New York | 92 | 62 | .597 | Stengel |
| 1959 | Los Angeles | 88 | 68 | .564 | Alston | 1959 | Chicago | 94 | 60 | .610 | Lopez |
| 1960 | Pittsburgh | 95 | 59 | .617 | Murtaugh | 1960 | New York | 97 | 57 | .630 | Stengel |
| 1961 | Cincinnati | 93 | 61 | .604 | Hutchinson | 1961 | New York | 109 | 53 | .673 | Houk |
| 1962 | San Francisco | 103 | 62 | .624 | Dark | 1962 | New York | 96 | 66 | .593 | Houk |
| 1963 | Los Angeles | 99 | 63 | .611 | Alston | 1963 | New York | 104 | 57 | .646 | Houk |
| 1964 | St. Louis | 93 | 69 | .574 | Keane | 1964 | New York | 99 | 63 | .611 | Berra |
| 1965 | Los Angeles | 97 | 65 | .599 | Alston | 1965 | Minnesota | 102 | 60 | .630 | Mele |
| 1966 | Los Angeles | 95 | 67 | .586 | Alston | 1966 | Baltimore | 97 | 63 | .606 | Bauer |
| 1967 | St. Louis | 101 | 60 | .627 | Schoendienst | 1967 | Boston | 92 | 70 | .568 | Williams |
| 1968 | St. Louis | 97 | 65 | .599 | Schoendienst | 1968 | Detroit | 103 | 59 | .636 | Smith |

## National League

| Year | East | | | | West | | | | Playoff |
|------|------|---|---|---|------|---|---|---|---------|
| | Winner | W | L | Pct | Manager | Winner | W | L | Pct | Manager | winner |

| Year | Winner | W | L | Pct | Manager | Winner | W | L | Pct | Manager | Playoff winner |
|------|--------|---|---|-----|---------|--------|---|---|-----|---------|----------------|
| 1969 | N.Y. Mets | 100 | 62 | .617 | Hodges | Atlanta | 93 | 69 | .574 | Harris | New York |
| 1970 | Pittsburgh | 89 | 73 | .549 | Murtaugh | Cincinnati | 102 | 60 | .630 | Anderson | Cincinnati |
| 1971 | Pittsburgh | 97 | 65 | .599 | Murtaugh | San Francisco | 90 | 72 | .556 | Fox | Pittsburgh |
| 1972 | Pittsburgh | 96 | 59 | .619 | Virdon | Cincinnati | 95 | 59 | .617 | Anderson | Cincinnati |
| 1973 | N.Y. Mets | 82 | 79 | .509 | Berra | Cincinnati | 99 | 63 | .611 | Anderson | New York |
| 1974 | Pittsburgh | 88 | 74 | .543 | Murtaugh | Los Angeles | 102 | 60 | .630 | Alston | Los Angeles |
| 1975 | Pittsburgh | 92 | 69 | .571 | Murtaugh | Cincinnati | 108 | 54 | .667 | Anderson | Cincinnati |
| 1976 | Philadelphia | 101 | 61 | .623 | Ozark | Cincinnati | 102 | 60 | .630 | Anderson | Cincinnati |

| Year | East Winner | W | L | Pct | Manager | West Winner | W | L | Pct | Manager | Playoff winner |
|---|---|---|---|---|---|---|---|---|---|---|---|
| 1977 | Philadelphia | 101 | 61 | .623 | Ozark | Los Angeles | 98 | 64 | .605 | Lasorda | Los Angeles |
| 1978 | Philadelphia | 90 | 72 | .556 | Ozark | Los Angeles | 95 | 67 | .586 | Lasorda | Los Angeles |
| 1979 | Pittsburgh | 98 | 64 | .605 | Tanner | Cincinnati | 90 | 71 | .559 | McNamara | Pittsburgh |
| 1980 | Philadelphia | 91 | 71 | .562 | Green | Houston | 93 | 70 | .571 | Virdon | Philadelphia |
| 1981(a) | Philadelphia | 34 | 21 | .618 | Green | Los Angeles | 36 | 21 | .632 | Lasorda | (c) |
| 1981(b) | Montreal | 30 | 23 | .566 | Williams, Fanning | Houston | 33 | 20 | .623 | Virdon | Los Angeles |
| 1982 | St. Louis | 92 | 70 | .568 | Herzog | Atlanta | 89 | 73 | .549 | Torre | St. Louis |
| 1983 | Philadelphia | 90 | 72 | .556 | Corrales, Owens | Los Angeles | 91 | 71 | .562 | Lasorda | Philadelphia |
| 1984 | Chicago | 96 | 65 | .596 | Frey | San Diego | 92 | 70 | .568 | Williams | San Diego |
| 1985 | St. Louis | 101 | 61 | .623 | Herzog | Los Angeles | 95 | 67 | .586 | Lasorda | St. Louis |
| 1986 | N.Y. Mets | 108 | 54 | .667 | Johnson | Houston | 96 | 66 | .593 | Lanier | New York |
| 1987 | St. Louis | 95 | 67 | .586 | Herzog | San Francisco | 90 | 72 | .556 | Craig | St. Louis |
| 1988 | N.Y. Mets | 100 | 60 | .625 | Johnson | Los Angeles | 94 | 67 | .584 | Lasorda | Los Angeles |
| 1989 | Chicago | 93 | 69 | .571 | Zimmer | San Francisco | 92 | 70 | .568 | Craig | San Francisco |
| 1990 | Pittsburgh | 95 | 67 | .586 | Leyland | Cincinnati | 91 | 71 | .562 | Piniella | Cincinnati |
| 1991 | Pittsburgh | 98 | 64 | .605 | Leyland | Atlanta | 94 | 68 | .580 | Cox | Atlanta |
| 1992 | Pittsburgh | 96 | 66 | .593 | Leyland | Atlanta | 98 | 64 | .605 | Cox | Atlanta |
| 1993 | Philadelphia | 97 | 65 | .599 | Fregosi | Atlanta | 104 | 58 | .642 | Cox | Philadelphia |

## American League

| Year | East Winner | W | L | Pct | Manager | West Winner | W | L | Pct | Manager | Playoff winner |
|---|---|---|---|---|---|---|---|---|---|---|---|
| 1969 | Baltimore | 109 | 53 | .673 | Weaver | Minnesota | 97 | 65 | .599 | Martin | Baltimore |
| 1970 | Baltimore | 108 | 54 | .667 | Weaver | Minnesota | 98 | 64 | .605 | Rigney | Baltimore |
| 1971 | Baltimore | 101 | 57 | .639 | Weaver | Oakland | 101 | 60 | .627 | Williams | Baltimore |
| 1972 | Detroit | 86 | 70 | .551 | Martin | Oakland | 93 | 62 | .600 | Williams | Oakland |
| 1973 | Baltimore | 97 | 65 | .599 | Weaver | Oakland | 94 | 68 | .580 | Williams | Oakland |
| 1974 | Baltimore | 91 | 71 | .562 | Weaver | Oakland | 90 | 72 | .556 | Dark | Oakland |
| 1975 | Boston | 95 | 65 | .594 | Johnson | Oakland | 98 | 64 | .605 | Dark | Boston |
| 1976 | New York | 97 | 62 | .610 | Martin | Kansas City | 90 | 72 | .556 | Herzog | New York |
| 1977 | New York | 100 | 62 | .617 | Martin | Kansas City | 102 | 60 | .630 | Herzog | New York |
| 1978 | New York | 100 | 63 | .613 | Martin, Lemon | Kansas City | 92 | 70 | .568 | Herzog | New York |
| 1979 | Baltimore | 102 | 57 | .642 | Weaver | California | 88 | 74 | .543 | Fregosi | Baltimore |
| 1980 | New York | 103 | 59 | .636 | Howser | Kansas City | 97 | 65 | .599 | Frey | Kansas City |
| 1981(a) | New York | 34 | 22 | .607 | Michael | Oakland | 37 | 23 | .617 | Martin | (d) |
| 1981(b) | Milwaukee | 31 | 22 | .585 | Rodgers | Kansas City | 30 | 23 | .566 | Frey, Howser | New York |
| 1982 | Milwaukee | 95 | 67 | .586 | Rodgers, Kuenn | California | 93 | 69 | .574 | Mauch | Milwaukee |
| 1983 | Baltimore | 98 | 64 | .605 | Altobelli | Chicago | 99 | 63 | .611 | LaRussa | Baltimore |
| 1984 | Detroit | 104 | 58 | .642 | Anderson | Kansas City | 84 | 78 | .519 | Howser | Detroit |
| 1985 | Toronto | 99 | 62 | .615 | Cox | Kansas City | 91 | 71 | .562 | Howser | Kansas City |
| 1986 | Boston | 95 | 66 | .590 | McNamara | California | 92 | 70 | .568 | Mauch | Boston |
| 1987 | Detroit | 98 | 64 | .605 | Anderson | Minnesota | 85 | 77 | .525 | Kelly | Minnesota |
| 1988 | Boston | 89 | 73 | .549 | McNamara, Morgan | Oakland | 104 | 58 | .642 | LaRussa | Oakland |
| 1989 | Toronto | 89 | 73 | .549 | Williams, Gaston | Oakland | 99 | 63 | .611 | LaRussa | Oakland |
| 1990 | Boston | 88 | 74 | .543 | Morgan | Oakland | 103 | 59 | .636 | LaRussa | Oakland |
| 1991 | Toronto | 91 | 71 | .562 | Gaston | Minnesota | 95 | 67 | .586 | Kelly | Minnesota |
| 1992 | Toronto | 96 | 66 | .593 | Gaston | Oakland | 96 | 66 | .593 | LaRussa | Toronto |
| 1993 | Toronto | 95 | 67 | .586 | Gaston | Chicago | 94 | 68 | .580 | Lamont | Toronto |

(a) First half; (b) Second half; (c) Montreal and L.A. won the divisional playoffs; (d) N.Y. and Oakland won the divisional playoffs.

## The Sporting News Gold Glove Awards in 1992

### National League

Mark Grace, Chicago, first base
Jose Lind, Pittsburgh, second base
Terry Pendleton, Atlanta, third base
Ozzie Smith, St. Louis, shortstop
Larry Walker, Montreal, outfield
Andy Van Slyke, Pittsburgh, outfield
Barry Bonds, Pittsburgh, outfield
Tom Pagnozzi, St. Louis, catcher
Greg Maddux, Chicago, pitcher

### American League

Don Mattingly, New York, first base
Roberto Alomar, Toronto, second base
Robin Ventura, Chicago, third base
Cal Ripken Jr., Baltimore, shortstop
Devon White, Toronto, outfield
Kirby Puckett, Minnesota, outfield
Ken Griffey Jr., Seattle, outfield
Ivan Rodriguez, Texas, catcher
Mark Langston, California, pitcher

The following are the players at each position who have won the most Gold Gloves since the award was instituted in 1957.

| First base: | Keith Hernandez | 11 | Shortstop: | Ozzie Smith | 13 | | Dwight Evans | 8 |
|---|---|---|---|---|---|---|---|---|
| | George Scott | 8 | | Luis Aparicio | 9 | | Garry Maddox | 8 |
| Second base: | Ryne Sandberg | 9 | Outfield: | Roberto Clemente | 12 | Catcher: | Johnny Bench | 10 |
| | Bill Mazeroski | 8 | | Willie Mays | 12 | | Bob Boone | 7 |
| | Frank White | 8 | | Al Kaline | 10 | Pitcher: | Jim Kaat | 16 |
| Third base: | Brooks Robinson | 16 | | Paul Blair | 8 | | Bob Gibson | 9 |
| | Mike Schmidt | 10 | | | | | | |

## Home Run Leaders

| National League | | | American League | | |
|---|---|---|---|---|---|
| **Year** | **Player, Club** | **HR** | **Year** | **Player, Club** | **HR** |
| 1901 | Sam Crawford, Cincinnati | 16 | 1901 | Napoleon Lajoie, Philadelphia | 14 |
| 1902 | Thomas Leach, Pittsburgh | 6 | 1902 | Socks Seybold, Philadelphia | 16 |
| 1903 | James Sheckard, Brooklyn | 9 | 1903 | Buck Freeman, Boston | 13 |
| 1904 | Harry Lumley, Brooklyn | 9 | 1904 | Harry Davis, Philadelphia | 10 |
| 1905 | Fred Odwell, Cincinnati | 9 | 1905 | Harry Davis, Philadelphia | 8 |
| 1906 | Timothy Jordan, Brooklyn | 12 | 1906 | Harry Davis, Philadelphia | 12 |
| 1907 | David Brain, Boston | 10 | 1907 | Harry Davis, Philadelphia | 8 |
| 1908 | Timothy Jordan, Brooklyn | 12 | 1908 | Sam Crawford, Detroit | 7 |
| 1909 | Red Murray, New York | 7 | 1909 | Ty Cobb, Detroit | 9 |
| 1910 | Fred Beck, Bos., Frank Schulte, Chi. | 10 | 1910 | Jake Stahl, Boston | 10 |
| 1911 | Frank Schulte, Chicago | 21 | 1911 | J. Franklin Baker, Philadelphia | 11 |
| 1912 | Henry Zimmerman, Chicago | 14 | 1912 | J. Franklin Baker, Philadelphia, Tris Speaker, Boston | 10 |
| 1913 | Gavvy Cravath, Philadelphia | 19 | 1913 | J. Franklin, Baker, Philadelphia | 12 |
| 1914 | Gavvy Cravath, Philadelphia | 19 | 1914 | J. Franklin, Baker, Philadelphia | 9 |
| 1915 | Gavvy Cravath, Philadelphia | 24 | 1915 | Robert Roth, Chicago-Cleveland | 7 |
| 1916 | Dave Robertson, N.Y., Fred (Cy) Williams, Chi. | 12 | 1916 | Wally Pipp, New York | 12 |
| 1917 | Dave Robertson, N.Y., Gavvy Cravath, Phil. | 12 | 1917 | Wally Pipp, New York | 9 |
| 1918 | Gavvy Cravath, Philadelphia | 8 | 1918 | Babe Ruth, Bos., Tilly Walker, Phil. | 11 |
| 1919 | Gavvy Cravath, Philadelphia | 12 | 1919 | Babe Ruth, Boston | 29 |
| 1920 | Cy Williams, Philadelphia | 15 | 1920 | Babe Ruth, New York | 54 |
| 1921 | George Kelly, New York | 23 | 1921 | Babe Ruth, New York | 59 |
| 1922 | Rogers Hornsby, St. Louis | 42 | 1922 | Ken Williams, St. Louis | 39 |
| 1923 | Cy Williams, Chicago | 41 | 1923 | Babe Ruth, New York | 41 |
| 1924 | Jacques Fournier, Brooklyn | 27 | 1924 | Babe Ruth, New York | 46 |
| 1925 | Rogers Hornsby, St. Louis | 39 | 1925 | Bob Meusel, New York | 33 |
| 1926 | Hack Wilson, Chicago | 21 | 1926 | Babe Ruth, New York | 47 |
| 1927 | Hack Wilson, Chicago; Cy Williams, Philadelphia | 30 | 1927 | Babe Ruth, New York | 60 |
| 1928 | Hack Wilson, Chicago; Jim Bottomley, St. Louis | 31 | 1928 | Babe Ruth, New York | 54 |
| 1929 | Chuck Klein, Philadelphia | 43 | 1929 | Babe Ruth, New York | 46 |
| 1930 | Hack Wilson, Chicago | 56 | 1930 | Babe Ruth, New York | 49 |
| 1931 | Chuck Klein, Philadelphia | 31 | 1931 | Babe Ruth, Lou Gehrig, New York | 46 |
| 1932 | Chuck Klein, Philadelphia, Mel Ott, New York | 38 | 1932 | Jimmie Foxx, Philadelphia | 58 |
| 1933 | Chuck Klein, Philadelphia | 28 | 1933 | Jimmie Foxx, Philadelphia | 48 |
| 1934 | Rip Collins, St. Louis; Mel Ott, New York | 35 | 1934 | Lou Gehrig, New York | 49 |
| 1935 | Walter Berger, Boston | 34 | 1935 | Jimmie Foxx, Philadelphia, Hank Greenberg, Detroit | 36 |
| 1936 | Mel Ott, New York | 33 | 1936 | Lou Gehrig, New York | 49 |
| 1937 | Mel Ott, New York; Joe Medwick, St. Louis | 31 | 1937 | Joe DiMaggio, New York | 46 |
| 1938 | Mel Ott, New York | 36 | 1938 | Hank Greenberg, Detroit | 58 |
| 1939 | John Mize, St. Louis | 28 | 1939 | Jimmie Foxx, Boston | 35 |
| 1940 | John Mize, St. Louis | 43 | 1940 | Hank Greenberg, Detroit | 41 |
| 1941 | Dolph Camilli, Brooklyn | 34 | 1941 | Ted Williams, Boston | 37 |
| 1942 | Mel Ott, New York | 30 | 1942 | Ted Williams, Boston | 36 |
| 1943 | Bill Nicholson, Chicago | 29 | 1943 | Rudy York, Detroit | 34 |
| 1944 | Bill Nicholson, Chicago | 33 | 1944 | Nick Etten, New York | 22 |
| 1945 | Tommy Holmes, Boston | 28 | 1945 | Vern Stephens, St. Louis | 24 |
| 1946 | Ralph Kiner, Pittsburgh | 23 | 1946 | Hank Greenberg, Detroit | 44 |
| 1947 | Ralph Kiner, Pittsburgh; John Mize, New York | 51 | 1947 | Ted Williams, Boston | 32 |
| 1948 | Ralph Kiner, Pittsburgh; John Mize, New York | 40 | 1948 | Joe DiMaggio, New York | 39 |
| 1949 | Ralph Kiner, Pittsburgh | 54 | 1949 | Ted Williams, Boston | 43 |
| 1950 | Ralph Kiner, Pittsburgh | 47 | 1950 | Al Rosen, Cleveland | 37 |
| 1951 | Ralph Kiner, Pittsburgh | 42 | 1951 | Gus Zernial, Chicago-Philadelphia | 33 |
| 1952 | Ralph Kiner, Pittsburgh; Hank Sauer, Chicago | 37 | 1952 | Larry Doby, Cleveland | 32 |
| 1953 | Ed Mathews, Milwaukee | 47 | 1953 | Al Rosen, Cleveland | 43 |
| 1954 | Ted Kluszewski, Cincinnati | 49 | 1954 | Larry Doby, Cleveland | 32 |
| 1955 | Willie Mays, New York | 51 | 1955 | Mickey Mantle, New York | 37 |
| 1956 | Duke Snider, Brooklyn | 43 | 1956 | Mickey Mantle, New York | 52 |
| 1957 | Hank Aaron, Milwaukee | 44 | 1957 | Roy Sievers, Washington | 42 |
| 1958 | Ernie Banks, Chicago | 47 | 1958 | Mickey Mantle, New York | 42 |
| 1959 | Ed Mathews, Milwaukee | 46 | 1959 | Rocky Colavito, Cleve., Harmon Killebrew, Wash. | 42 |
| 1960 | Ernie Banks, Chicago | 41 | 1960 | Mickey Mantle, New York | 40 |
| 1961 | Orlando Cepeda, San Francisco | 46 | 1961 | Roger Maris, New York | 61 |
| 1962 | Willie Mays, San Francisco | 49 | 1962 | Harmon Killebrew, Minnesota | 48 |
| 1963 | Hank Aaron, Milwaukee, Willie McCovey, S.F. | 44 | 1963 | Harmon Killebrew, Minnesota | 45 |
| 1964 | Willie Mays, San Francisco | 47 | 1964 | Harmon Killebrew, Minnesota | 49 |
| 1965 | Willie Mays, San Francisco | 52 | 1965 | Tony Conigliaro, Boston | 32 |
| 1966 | Hank Aaron, Atlanta | 44 | 1966 | Frank Robinson, Baltimore | 49 |
| 1967 | Hank Aaron, Atlanta | 39 | 1967 | Carl Yastrzemski, Boston, Harmon Killebrew, Minn. | 44 |
| 1968 | Willie McCovey, San Francisco | 36 | 1968 | Frank Howard, Washington | 44 |
| 1969 | Willie McCovey, San Francisco | 45 | 1969 | Harmon Killebrew, Minnesota | 49 |
| 1970 | Johnny Bench, Cincinnati | 45 | 1970 | Frank Howard, Washington | 44 |
| 1971 | Willie Stargell, Pittsburgh | 48 | 1971 | Bill Melton, Chicago | 33 |
| 1972 | Johnny Bench, Cincinnati | 40 | 1972 | Dick Allen, Chicago | 37 |
| 1973 | Willie Stargell, Pittsburgh | 44 | 1973 | Reggie Jackson, Oakland | 32 |
| 1974 | Mike Schmidt, Philadelphia | 36 | 1974 | Dick Allen, Chicago | 32 |
| 1975 | Mike Schmidt, Philadelphia | 38 | 1975 | George Scott, Milwaukee; Reggie Jackson, Oakland | 36 |
| 1976 | Mike Schmidt, Philadelphia | 38 | 1976 | Graig Nettles, New York | 32 |
| 1977 | George Foster, Cincinnati | 52 | 1977 | Jim Rice, Boston | 39 |
| 1978 | George Foster, Cincinnati | 40 | 1978 | Jim Rice, Boston | 46 |
| 1979 | Dave Kingman, Chicago | 48 | 1979 | Gorman Thomas, Milwaukee | 45 |
| 1980 | Mike Schmidt, Philadelphia | 48 | 1980 | Reggie Jackson, New York; Ben Oglivie, Milwaukee | 41 |
| 1981 | Mike Schmidt, Philadelphia | 31 | 1981 | Bobby Grich, California; Tony Armas, Oakland; Dwight Evans, Boston; Eddie Murray, Baltimore | 22 |
| 1982 | Dave Kingman, New York | 37 | 1982 | Gorman Thomas, Milwaukee; Reggie Jackson, Cal. | 39 |

| Year | Player, Club | HR | Year | Player, Club | HR |
|---|---|---|---|---|---|
| 1983 | Mike Schmidt, Philadelphia | 40 | 1983 | Jim Rice, Boston | 39 |
| 1984 | Mike Schmidt, Phil.; Dale Murphy, Atlanta | 36 | 1984 | Tony Armas, Boston | 43 |
| 1985 | Dale Murphy, Atlanta | 37 | 1985 | Darrell Evans, Detroit | 40 |
| 1986 | Mike Schmidt, Philadelphia | 37 | 1986 | Jesse Barfield, Toronto | 40 |
| 1987 | Andre Dawson, Chicago | 49 | 1987 | Mark McGwire, Oakland | 49 |
| 1988 | Darryl Strawberry, New York | 39 | 1988 | Jose Canseco, Oakland | 42 |
| 1989 | Kevin Mitchell, San Francisco | 47 | 1989 | Fred McGriff, Toronto | 36 |
| 1990 | Ryne Sandberg, Chicago | 40 | 1990 | Cecil Fielder, Detroit | 51 |
| 1991 | Howard Johnson, New York | 38 | 1991 | Cecil Fielder, Detroit; Jose Canseco, Oakland | 44 |
| 1992 | Fred McGriff, San Diego | 35 | 1992 | Juan Gonzalez, Texas | 43 |
| 1993 | Barry Bonds, San Francisco | 46 | 1993 | Juan Gonzalez, Texas | 46 |

## Runs Batted In Leaders

### National League

### American League

| Year | Player, Club | RBI | Year | Player, Club | RBI |
|---|---|---|---|---|---|
| 1907 | Honus Wagner, Pittsburgh | 91 | 1907 | Ty Cobb, Detroit | 116 |
| 1908 | Honus Wagner, Pittsburgh | 106 | 1908 | Ty Cobb, Detroit | 101 |
| 1909 | Honus Wagner, Pittsburgh | 102 | 1909 | Ty Cobb, Detroit | 115 |
| 1910 | Sherwood Magee, Philadelphia | 116 | 1910 | Sam Crawford, Detroit | 115 |
| 1911 | Frank Schulte, Chicago | 121 | 1911 | Ty Cobb, Detroit | 144 |
| 1912 | Henry Zimmerman, Chicago | 98 | 1912 | J. Franklin Baker, Philadelphia | 133 |
| 1913 | Gavvy Cravath, Philadelphia | 118 | 1913 | J. Franklin Baker, Philadelphia | 126 |
| 1914 | Sherwood Magee, Philadelphia | 101 | 1914 | Sam Crawford, Detroit | 112 |
| 1915 | Gavvy Cravath, Philadelphia | 118 | 1915 | Sam Crawford, Detroit | 116 |
| 1916 | Hal Chase, Cincinnati | 94 | 1916 | Wally Pipp, New York | 99 |
| 1917 | Henry Zimmerman, New York | 100 | 1917 | Robert Veach, Detroit | 115 |
| 1918 | Frederick Merkle, Chicago | 71 | 1918 | George Burns, Phila., Robert Veach, Detroit | 74 |
| 1919 | Hi Myers, Boston | 72 | 1919 | Babe Ruth, Boston | 112 |
| 1920 | George Kelly, N.Y., Rogers Hornsby, St. Louis | 94 | 1920 | Babe Ruth, New York | 137 |
| 1921 | Rogers Hornsby, St. Louis | 126 | 1921 | Babe Ruth, New York | 171 |
| 1922 | Rogers Hornsby, St. Louis | 152 | 1922 | Ken Williams, St. Louis | 155 |
| 1923 | Emil Meusel, New York | 125 | 1923 | Babe Ruth, New York | 131 |
| 1924 | George Kelly, New York | 136 | 1924 | Goose Goslin, Washington | 129 |
| 1925 | Rogers Hornsby, St. Louis | 143 | 1925 | Bob Meusel, New York | 138 |
| 1926 | Jim Bottomley, St. Louis | 120 | 1926 | Babe Ruth, New York | 145 |
| 1927 | Paul Waner, Pittsburgh | 131 | 1927 | Lou Gehrig, New York | 175 |
| 1928 | Jim Bottomley, St. Louis | 136 | 1928 | Babe Ruth, N.Y., Lou Gehrig, N.Y. | 142 |
| 1929 | Hack Wilson, Chicago | 159 | 1929 | Al Simmons, Philadelphia | 157 |
| 1930 | Hack Wilson, Chicago | 190 | 1930 | Lou Gehrig, New York | 174 |
| 1931 | Chuck Klein, Philadelphia | 121 | 1931 | Lou Gehrig, New York | 184 |
| 1932 | Don Hurst, Philadelphia | 143 | 1932 | Jimmie Foxx, Philadelphia | 169 |
| 1933 | Chuck Klein, Philadelphia | 120 | 1933 | Jimmie Foxx, Philadelphia | 163 |
| 1934 | Mel Ott, New York | 135 | 1934 | Lou Gehrig, New York | 165 |
| 1935 | Walter Berger, Boston | 130 | 1935 | Hank Greenberg, Detroit | 170 |
| 1936 | Joe Medwick, St. Louis | 138 | 1936 | Hal Trosky, Cleveland | 162 |
| 1937 | Joe Medwick, St. Louis | 154 | 1937 | Hank Greenberg, Detroit | 183 |
| 1938 | Joe Medwick, St. Louis | 122 | 1938 | Jimmie Foxx, Boston | 175 |
| 1939 | Frank McCormick, Cincinnati | 128 | 1939 | Ted Williams, Boston | 145 |
| 1940 | John Mize, St. Louis | 137 | 1940 | Hank Greenberg, Detroit | 150 |
| 1941 | Adolph Camilli, Brooklyn | 120 | 1941 | Joe DiMaggio, New York | 125 |
| 1942 | John Mize, New York | 110 | 1942 | Ted Williams, Boston | 137 |
| 1943 | Bill Nicholson, Chicago | 128 | 1943 | Rudy York, Detroit | 118 |
| 1944 | Bill Nicholson, Chicago | 122 | 1944 | Vern Stephens, St. Louis | 109 |
| 1945 | Dixie Walker, Brooklyn | 124 | 1945 | Nick Etten, New York | 111 |
| 1946 | Enos Slaughter, St. Louis | 130 | 1946 | Hank Greenberg, Detroit | 127 |
| 1947 | John Mize, New York | 138 | 1947 | Ted Williams, Boston | 114 |
| 1948 | Stan Musial, St. Louis | 131 | 1948 | Joe DiMaggio, New York | 155 |
| 1949 | Ralph Kiner, Pittsburgh | 127 | 1949 | Ted Williams, Bos., Vern Stephens, Bos. | 159 |
| 1950 | Del Ennis, Philadelphia | 126 | 1950 | Walt Dropo, Bos., Vern Stephens, Bos. | 144 |
| 1951 | Monte Irvin, New York | 121 | 1951 | Gus Zernial, Chicago-Philadelphia | 129 |
| 1952 | Hank Sauer, Chicago | 121 | 1952 | Al Rosen, Cleveland | 105 |
| 1953 | Roy Campanella, Brooklyn | 142 | 1953 | Al Rosen, Cleveland | 145 |
| 1954 | Ted Kluszewski, Cincinnati | 141 | 1954 | Larry Doby, Cleveland | 126 |
| 1955 | Duke Snider, Brooklyn | 136 | 1955 | Ray Boone, Detroit, Jackie Jensen, Boston | 116 |
| 1956 | Stan Musial, St. Louis | 109 | 1956 | Mickey Mantle, New York | 130 |
| 1957 | Hank Aaron, Milwaukee | 132 | 1957 | Roy Sievers, Washington | 114 |
| 1958 | Ernie Banks, Chicago | 129 | 1958 | Jackie Jensen, Boston | 122 |
| 1959 | Ernie Banks, Chicago | 143 | 1959 | Jackie Jensen, Boston | 112 |
| 1960 | Hank Aaron, Milwaukee | 126 | 1960 | Roger Maris, New York | 112 |
| 1961 | Orlando Cepeda, San Francisco | 142 | 1961 | Roger Maris, New York | 142 |
| 1962 | Tommy Davis, Los Angeles | 153 | 1962 | Harmon Killebrew, Minnesota | 126 |
| 1963 | Hank Aaron, Milwaukee | 130 | 1963 | Dick Stuart, Boston | 118 |
| 1964 | Ken Boyer, St. Louis | 119 | 1964 | Brooks Robinson, Baltimore | 118 |
| 1965 | Deron Johnson, Cincinnati | 130 | 1965 | Rocky Colavito, Cleveland | 108 |
| 1966 | Hank Aaron, Atlanta | 127 | 1966 | Frank Robinson, Baltimore | 122 |
| 1967 | Orlando Cepeda, St. Louis | 111 | 1967 | Carl Yastrzemski, Boston | 121 |
| 1968 | Willie McCovey, San Francisco | 105 | 1968 | Ken Harrelson, Boston | 109 |
| 1969 | Willie McCovey, San Francisco | 126 | 1969 | Harmon Killebrew, Minnesota | 140 |
| 1970 | Johnny Bench, Cincinnati | 148 | 1970 | Frank Howard, Washington | 126 |
| 1971 | Joe Torre, St. Louis | 137 | 1971 | Harmon Killebrew, Minnesota | 119 |
| 1972 | Johnny Bench, Cincinnati | 125 | 1972 | Dick Allen, Chicago | 113 |
| 1973 | Willie Stargell, Pittsburgh | 119 | 1973 | Reggie Jackson, Oakland | 117 |
| 1974 | Johnny Bench, Cincinnati | 129 | 1974 | Jeff Burroughs, Texas | 118 |
| 1975 | Greg Luzinski, Philadelphia | 120 | 1975 | George Scott, Milwaukee | 109 |

| Year | Player, Club | RBI |
|------|-------------|-----|
| 1976 | George Foster, Cincinnati | 121 |
| 1977 | George Foster, Cincinnati | 149 |
| 1978 | George Foster, Cincinnati | 120 |
| 1979 | Dave Winfield, San Diego | 118 |
| 1980 | Mike Schmidt, Philadelphia | 121 |
| 1981 | Mike Schmidt, Philadelphia | 91 |
| 1982 | Dale Murphy, Atlanta; Al Oliver, Montreal | 109 |
| 1983 | Dale Murphy, Atlanta | 121 |
| 1984 | Mike Schmidt, Phil.; Gary Carter, Montreal | 106 |
| 1985 | Dave Parker, Cincinnati | 125 |
| 1986 | Mike Schmidt, Philadelphia | 119 |
| 1987 | Andre Dawson, Chicago | 137 |
| 1988 | Will Clark, San Francisco | 109 |
| 1989 | Kevin Mitchell, San Francisco | 125 |
| 1990 | Matt Williams, San Francisco | 122 |
| 1991 | Howard Johnson, New York | 117 |
| 1992 | Darren Daulton, Philadelphia | 109 |
| 1993 | Barry Bonds, San Francisco | 123 |

| Year | Player, Club | RBI |
|------|-------------|-----|
| 1976 | Lee May, Baltimore | 109 |
| 1977 | Larry Hisle, Minnesota | 119 |
| 1978 | Jim Rice, Boston | 139 |
| 1979 | Don Baylor, California | 139 |
| 1980 | Cecil Cooper, Milwaukee | 122 |
| 1981 | Eddie Murray, Baltimore | 78 |
| 1982 | Hal McRae, Kansas City | 133 |
| 1983 | Cecil Cooper, Milwaukee; Jim Rice, Boston | 126 |
| 1984 | Tony Armas, Boston | 123 |
| 1985 | Don Mattingly, New York | 145 |
| 1986 | Joe Carter, Cleveland | 121 |
| 1987 | George Bell, Toronto | 134 |
| 1988 | Jose Canseco, Oakland | 124 |
| 1989 | Ruben Sierra, Texas | 119 |
| 1990 | Cecil Fielder, Detroit | 132 |
| 1991 | Cecil Fielder, Detroit | 133 |
| 1992 | Cecil Fielder, Detroit | 124 |
| 1993 | Albert Belle, Cleveland | 129 |

## Batting Champions

### National League

| Year | Player | Club | Pct. |
|------|--------|------|------|
| 1901 | Jesse C. Burkett | St. Louis | .382 |
| 1902 | Clarence Beaumont | Pittsburgh | .357 |
| 1903 | Honus Wagner | Pittsburgh | .355 |
| 1904 | Honus Wagner | Pittsburgh | .349 |
| 1905 | James Seymour | Cincinnati | .377 |
| 1906 | Honus Wagner | Pittsburgh | .339 |
| 1907 | Honus Wagner | Pittsburgh | .350 |
| 1908 | Honus Wagner | Pittsburgh | .354 |
| 1909 | Honus Wagner | Pittsburgh | .339 |
| 1910 | Sherwood Magee | Philadelphia | .331 |
| 1911 | Honus Wagner | Pittsburgh | .334 |
| 1912 | Henry Zimmerman | Chicago | .372 |
| 1913 | Jacob Daubert | Brooklyn | .350 |
| 1914 | Jacob Daubert | Brooklyn | .329 |
| 1915 | Larry Doyle | New York | .320 |
| 1916 | Hal Chase | Cincinnati | .339 |
| 1917 | Edd Roush | Cleveland | .341 |
| 1918 | Zach Wheat | Brooklyn | .335 |
| 1919 | Edd Roush | Cincinnati | .321 |
| 1920 | Rogers Hornsby | St. Louis | .370 |
| 1921 | Rogers Hornsby | St. Louis | .397 |
| 1922 | Rogers Hornsby | St. Louis | .401 |
| 1923 | Rogers Hornsby | St. Louis | .384 |
| 1924 | Rogers Hornsby | St. Louis | .424 |
| 1925 | Rogers Hornsby | St. Louis | .403 |
| 1926 | Eugene Hargrave | Cincinnati | .353 |
| 1927 | Paul Waner | Pittsburgh | .380 |
| 1928 | Rogers Hornsby | Boston | .387 |
| 1929 | Lefty O'Doul | Philadelphia | .398 |
| 1930 | Bill Terry | New York | .401 |
| 1931 | Chick Hafey | St. Louis | .349 |
| 1932 | Lefty O'Doul | Brooklyn | .368 |
| 1933 | Chuck Klein | Philadelphia | .368 |
| 1934 | Paul Waner | Pittsburgh | .362 |
| 1935 | Arky Vaughan | Pittsburgh | .385 |
| 1936 | Paul Waner | Pittsburgh | .373 |
| 1937 | Joe Medwick | St. Louis | .374 |
| 1938 | Ernie Lombardi | Cincinnati | .342 |
| 1939 | John Mize | St. Louis | .349 |
| 1940 | Debs Garms | Pittsburgh | .355 |
| 1941 | Pete Reiser | Brooklyn | .343 |
| 1942 | Ernie Lombardi | Boston | .330 |
| 1943 | Stan Musial | St. Louis | .357 |
| 1944 | Dixie Walker | Brooklyn | .357 |
| 1945 | Phil Cavarretta | Chicago | .355 |
| 1946 | Stan Musial | St. Louis | .365 |
| 1947 | Harry Walker | Philadelphia | .363 |
| 1948 | Stan Musial | St. Louis | .376 |
| 1949 | Jackie Robinson | Brooklyn | .342 |
| 1950 | Stan Musial | St. Louis | .346 |
| 1951 | Stan Musial | St. Louis | .355 |
| 1952 | Stan Musial | St. Louis | .336 |
| 1953 | Carl Furillo | Brooklyn | .344 |
| 1954 | Willie Mays | New York | .345 |
| 1955 | Richie Ashburn | Philadelphia | .338 |
| 1956 | Hank Aaron | Milwaukee | .328 |
| 1957 | Stan Musial | St. Louis | .351 |
| 1958 | Richie Ashburn | Philadelphia | .350 |
| 1959 | Hank Aaron | Milwaukee | .355 |
| 1960 | Dick Groat | Pittsburgh | .325 |
| 1961 | Roberto Clemente | Pittsburgh | .351 |
| 1962 | Tommy Davis | Los Angeles | .346 |
| 1963 | Tommy Davis | Los Angeles | .326 |
| 1964 | Roberto Clemente | Pittsburgh | .339 |

### American League

| Year | Player | Club | Pct. |
|------|--------|------|------|
| 1901 | Napoleon Lajoie | Philadelphia | .422 |
| 1902 | Ed Delahanty | Washington | .376 |
| 1903 | Napoleon Lajoie | Cleveland | .355 |
| 1904 | Napoleon Lajoie | Cleveland | .381 |
| 1905 | Elmer Flick | Cleveland | .308 |
| 1906 | George Stone | St. Louis | .358 |
| 1907 | Ty Cobb | Detroit | .350 |
| 1908 | Ty Cobb | Detroit | .324 |
| 1909 | Ty Cobb | Detroit | .377 |
| 1910 | Ty Cobb | Detroit | .385 |
| 1911 | Ty Cobb | Detroit | .420 |
| 1912 | Ty Cobb | Detroit | .410 |
| 1913 | Ty Cobb | Detroit | .390 |
| 1914 | Ty Cobb | Detroit | .368 |
| 1915 | Ty Cobb | Detroit | .369 |
| 1916 | Tris Speaker | Cleveland | .386 |
| 1917 | Ty Cobb | Detroit | .383 |
| 1918 | Ty Cobb | Detroit | .382 |
| 1919 | Ty Cobb | Detroit | .384 |
| 1920 | George Sisler | St. Louis | .407 |
| 1921 | Harry Heilmann | Detroit | .394 |
| 1922 | George Sisler | St. Louis | .420 |
| 1923 | Harry Heilmann | Detroit | .403 |
| 1924 | Babe Ruth | New York | .378 |
| 1925 | Harry Heilmann | Detroit | .393 |
| 1926 | Henry Manush | Detroit | .378 |
| 1927 | Harry Heilmann | Detroit | .398 |
| 1928 | Goose Goslin | Washington | .379 |
| 1929 | Lew Fonseca | Cleveland | .369 |
| 1930 | Al Simmons | Philadelphia | .381 |
| 1931 | Al Simmons | Philadelphia | .390 |
| 1932 | Dale Alexander | Detroit-Boston | .367 |
| 1933 | Jimmie Foxx | Philadelphia | .356 |
| 1934 | Lou Gehrig | New York | .363 |
| 1935 | Buddy Myer | Washington | .349 |
| 1936 | Luke Appling | Chicago | .388 |
| 1937 | Charlie Gehringer | Detroit | .371 |
| 1938 | Jimmie Foxx | Boston | .349 |
| 1939 | Joe DiMaggio | New York | .381 |
| 1940 | Joe DiMaggio | New York | .352 |
| 1941 | Ted Williams | Boston | .406 |
| 1942 | Ted Williams | Boston | .356 |
| 1943 | Luke Appling | Chicago | .328 |
| 1944 | Lou Boudreau | Cleveland | .327 |
| 1945 | George Stirnweiss | New York | .309 |
| 1946 | Mickey Vernon | Washington | .353 |
| 1947 | Ted Williams | Boston | .343 |
| 1948 | Ted Williams | Boston | .369 |
| 1949 | George Kell | Detroit | .343 |
| 1950 | Billy Goodman | Boston | .354 |
| 1951 | Ferris Fain | Philadelphia | .344 |
| 1952 | Ferris Fain | Philadelphia | .327 |
| 1953 | Mickey Vernon | Washington | .337 |
| 1954 | Roberto Avila | Cleveland | .341 |
| 1955 | Al Kaline | Detroit | .340 |
| 1956 | Mickey Mantle | New York | .353 |
| 1957 | Ted Williams | Boston | .388 |
| 1958 | Ted Williams | Boston | .328 |
| 1959 | Harvey Kuenn | Detroit | .353 |
| 1960 | Pete Runnels | Boston | .320 |
| 1961 | Norm Cash | Detroit | .361 |
| 1962 | Pete Runnels | Boston | .326 |
| 1963 | Carl Yastrzemski | Boston | .321 |
| 1964 | Tony Oliva | Minnesota | .323 |

| Year | Player | Club | Pct. | Year | Player | Club | Pct. |
|------|--------|------|------|------|--------|------|------|
| 1965 | Roberto Clemente | Pittsburgh | .329 | 1965 | Tony Oliva | Minnesota | .321 |
| 1966 | Matty Alou | Pittsburgh | .342 | 1966 | Frank Robinson | Baltimore | .316 |
| 1967 | Roberto Clemente | Pittsburgh | .357 | 1967 | Carl Yastrzemski | Boston | .326 |
| 1968 | Pete Rose | Cincinnati | .335 | 1968 | Carl Yastrzemski | Boston | .301 |
| 1969 | Pete Rose | Cincinnati | .348 | 1969 | Rod Carew | Minnesota | .332 |
| 1970 | Rico Carty | Atlanta | .366 | 1970 | Alex Johnson | California | .328 |
| 1971 | Joe Torre | St. Louis | .363 | 1971 | Tony Oliva | Minnesota | .337 |
| 1972 | Billy Williams | Chicago | .333 | 1972 | Rod Carew | Minnesota | .318 |
| 1973 | Pete Rose | Cincinnati | .338 | 1973 | Rod Carew | Minnesota | .350 |
| 1974 | Ralph Garr | Atlanta | .353 | 1974 | Rod Carew | Minnesota | .364 |
| 1975 | Bill Madlock | Chicago | .354 | 1975 | Rod Carew | Minnesota | .359 |
| 1976 | Bill Madlock | Chicago | .339 | 1976 | George Brett | Kansas City | .333 |
| 1977 | Dave Parker | Pittsburgh | .338 | 1977 | Rod Carew | Minnesota | .388 |
| 1978 | Dave Parker | Pittsburgh | .334 | 1978 | Rod Carew | Minnesota | .333 |
| 1979 | Keith Hernandez | St. Louis | .344 | 1979 | Fred Lynn | Boston | .333 |
| 1980 | Bill Buckner | Chicago | .324 | 1980 | George Brett | Kansas City | .390 |
| 1981 | Bill Madlock | Pittsburgh | .341 | 1981 | Carney Lansford | Boston | .336 |
| 1982 | Al Oliver | Montreal | .331 | 1982 | Willie Wilson | Kansas City | .332 |
| 1983 | Bill Madlock | Pittsburgh | .323 | 1983 | Wade Boggs | Boston | .361 |
| 1984 | Tony Gwynn | San Diego | .351 | 1984 | Don Mattingly | New York | .343 |
| 1985 | Willie McGee | St. Louis | .353 | 1985 | Wade Boggs | Boston | .368 |
| 1986 | Tim Raines | Montreal | .334 | 1986 | Wade Boggs | Boston | .357 |
| 1987 | Tony Gwynn | San Diego | .369 | 1987 | Wade Boggs | Boston | .363 |
| 1988 | Tony Gwynn | San Diego | .313 | 1988 | Wade Boggs | Boston | .366 |
| 1989 | Tony Gwynn | San Diego | .336 | 1989 | Kirby Puckett | Minnesota | .339 |
| 1990 | Willie McGee | St. Louis | .335 | 1990 | George Brett | Kansas City | .329 |
| 1991 | Terry Pendleton | Atlanta | .319 | 1991 | Julio Franco | Texas | .342 |
| 1992 | Gary Sheffield | San Diego | .330 | 1992 | Edgar Martinez | Seattle | .343 |
| 1993 | Andres Galarraga | Colorado | .370 | 1993 | John Olerud | Toronto | .363 |

## Cy Young Award Winners

| Year | Player, club | Year | Player, club | Year | Player, club |
|------|--------------|------|--------------|------|--------------|
| 1956 | Don Newcombe, Dodgers | 1972 | (NL) Steve Carlton, Phillies | 1983 | (AL) Pete Vuckovich, Brewers |
| 1957 | Warren Spahn, Braves | | (AL) Gaylord Perry, Indians | | (NL) John Denny, Phillies |
| 1958 | Bob Turley, Yankees | 1973 | (NL) Tom Seaver, Mets | | (AL) LaMarr Hoyt, White Sox |
| 1959 | Early Wynn, White Sox | | (AL) Jim Palmer, Orioles | 1984 | (NL) Rick Sutcliffe, Cubs |
| 1960 | Vernon Law, Pirates | 1974 | (NL) Mike Marshall, Dodgers | | (AL) Willie Hernandez, Tigers |
| 1961 | Whitey Ford, Yankees | | (AL) Jim (Catfish) Hunter, A's | 1985 | (NL) Dwight Gooden, Mets |
| 1962 | Don Drysdale, Dodgers | 1975 | (NL) Tom Seaver, Mets | | (AL) Bret Saberhagen, Royals |
| 1963 | Sandy Koufax, Dodgers | | (AL) Jim Palmer, Orioles | 1986 | (NL) Mike Scott, Astros |
| 1964 | Dean Chance, Angels | 1976 | (NL) Randy Jones, Padres | | (AL) Roger Clemens, Red Sox |
| 1965 | Sandy Koufax, Dodgers | | (AL) Jim Palmer, Orioles | 1987 | (NL) Steve Bedrosian, Phillies |
| 1966 | Sandy Koufax, Dodgers | 1977 | (NL) Steve Carlton, Phillies | | (AL) Roger Clemens, Red Sox |
| 1967 | (NL) Mike McCormick, Giants | | (AL) Sparky Lyle, Yankees | 1988 | (NL) Orel Hershiser, Dodgers |
| | (AL) Jim Lonborg, Red Sox | 1978 | (NL) Gaylord Perry, Padres | | (AL) Frank Viola, Twins |
| 1968 | (NL) Bob Gibson, Cardinals | | (AL) Ron Guidry, Yankees | 1989 | (NL) Mark Davis, Padres |
| | (AL) Dennis McLain, Tigers | 1979 | (NL) Bruce Sutter, Cubs | | (AL) Bret Saberhagen, Royals |
| 1969 | (NL) Tom Seaver, Mets | | (AL) Mike Flanagan, Orioles | 1990 | (NL) Doug Drabek, Pirates |
| | (AL) (tie) Dennis McLain, Tigers | 1980 | (NL) Steve Carlton, Phillies | | (AL) Bob Welch, A's |
| | Mike Cuellar, Orioles | | (AL) Steve Stone, Orioles | 1991 | (NL) Tom Glavine, Braves |
| 1970 | (NL) Bob Gibson, Cardinals | 1981 | (NL) Fernando Valenzuela, | | (AL) Roger Clemens, Red Sox |
| | (AL) Jim Perry, Twins | | Dodgers | 1992 | (NL) Greg Maddux, Cubs |
| 1971 | (NL) Ferguson Jenkins, Cubs | | (AL) Rollie Fingers, Brewers | | (AL) Dennis Eckersley, A's |
| | (AL) Vida Blue, A's | 1982 | (NL) Steve Carlton, Phillies | | |

## Pitchers with 300 Major League Wins

| | | | | | | | | | |
|---|---|---|---|---|---|---|---|---|---|
| Cy Young | 511 | Warren Spahn | 363 | Steve Carlton | 329 | Nolan Ryan | 324 | Mickey Welch | 311 |
| Walter Johnson | 416 | Pud Galvin | 361 | Eddie Plank | 327 | Phil Niekro | 318 | Old Hoss Radbourn | 308 |
| Christy Mathewson | 373 | Kid Nichols | 360 | John Clarkson | 326 | Gaylord Perry | 314 | Lefty Grove | 300 |
| Grover Alexander | 373 | Tim Keefe | 344 | Don Sutton | 324 | Tom Seaver | 311 | Early Wynn | 300 |

## Division Realignment in 1994

The National and American leagues are expected to switch from a two-division to a three-division alignment for the 1994 season. Postseason play will have an additional playoff series. Four teams in each league will make the playoffs—the three division winners and the non-division winner with the best record (the wild card team). The new format was not official as of Oct. 1993.

### National League

| East | Central | West |
|------|---------|------|
| Atlanta | Chicago | Colorado |
| Florida | Cincinnati | Los Angeles |
| Montreal | Houston | San Diego |
| New York | Pittsburgh | San Francisco |
| Philadelphia | St. Louis | |

### American League

| East | Central | West |
|------|---------|------|
| Baltimore | Chicago | California |
| Boston | Cleveland | Oakland |
| Detroit | Kansas City | Seattle |
| New York | Milwaukee | Texas |
| Toronto | Minnesota | |

## Most Valuable Player
Baseball Writers' Association
### National League

| Year | Player, team | Year | Player, team | Year | Player, team |
|------|-------------|------|-------------|------|-------------|
| 1931 | Frank Frisch, St. Louis | 1952 | Hank Sauer, Chicago | 1973 | Pete Rose, Cincinnati |
| 1932 | Charles Klein, Philadelphia | 1953 | Roy Campanella, Brooklyn | 1974 | Steve Garvey, Los Angeles |
| 1933 | Carl Hubbell, New York | 1954 | Willie Mays, New York | 1975 | Joe Morgan, Cincinnati |
| 1934 | Dizzy Dean, St. Louis | 1955 | Roy Campanella, Brooklyn | 1976 | Joe Morgan, Cincinnati |
| 1935 | Gabby Hartnett, Chicago | 1956 | Don Newcombe, Brooklyn | 1977 | George Foster, Cincinnati |
| 1936 | Carl Hubbell, New York | 1957 | Henry Aaron, Milwaukee | 1978 | Dave Parker, Pittsburgh |
| 1937 | Joe Medwick, St. Louis | 1958 | Ernie Banks, Chicago | 1979 | (tie) Willie Stargell, Pittsburgh |
| 1938 | Ernie Lombardi, Cincinnati | 1959 | Ernie Banks, Chicago | | Keith Hernandez, St. Louis |
| 1939 | Bucky Walters, Cincinnati | 1960 | Dick Groat, Pittsburgh | 1980 | Mike Schmidt, Philadelphia |
| 1940 | Frank McCormick, Cincinnati | 1961 | Frank Robinson, Cincinnati | 1981 | Mike Schmidt, Philadelphia |
| 1941 | Dolph Camilli, Brooklyn | 1962 | Maury Wills, Los Angeles | 1982 | Dale Murphy, Atlanta |
| 1942 | Mort Cooper, St. Louis | 1963 | Sandy Koufax, Los Angeles | 1983 | Dale Murphy, Atlanta |
| 1943 | Stan Musial, St. Louis | 1964 | Ken Boyer, St. Louis | 1984 | Ryne Sandberg, Chicago |
| 1944 | Martin Marion, St. Louis | 1965 | Willie Mays, San Francisco | 1985 | Willie McGee, St. Louis |
| 1945 | Phil Cavarretta, Chicago | 1966 | Roberto Clemente, Pittsburgh | 1986 | Mike Schmidt, Philadelphia |
| 1946 | Stan Musial, St. Louis | 1967 | Orlando Cepeda, St. Louis | 1987 | Andre Dawson, Chicago |
| 1947 | Bob Elliott, Boston | 1968 | Bob Gibson, St. Louis | 1988 | Kirk Gibson, Los Angeles |
| 1948 | Stan Musial, St. Louis | 1969 | Willie McCovey, San Francisco | 1989 | Kevin Mitchell, San Francisco |
| 1949 | Jackie Robinson, Brooklyn | 1970 | Johnny Bench, Cincinnati | 1990 | Barry Bonds, Pittsburgh |
| 1950 | Jim Konstanty, Philadelphia | 1971 | Joe Torre, St. Louis | 1991 | Terry Pendleton, Atlanta |
| 1951 | Roy Campanella, Brooklyn | 1972 | Johnny Bench, Cincinnati | 1992 | Barry Bonds, Pittsburgh |

### American League

| Year | Player, team | Year | Player, team | Year | Player, team |
|------|-------------|------|-------------|------|-------------|
| 1931 | Lefty Grove, Philadelphia | 1952 | Bobby Shantz, Philadelphia | 1973 | Reggie Jackson, Oakland |
| 1932 | Jimmie Foxx, Philadelphia | 1953 | Al Rosen, Cleveland | 1974 | Jeff Burroughs, Texas |
| 1933 | Jimmie Foxx, Philadelphia | 1954 | Yogi Berra, New York | 1975 | Fred Lynn, Boston |
| 1934 | Mickey Cochrane, Detroit | 1955 | Yogi Berra, New York | 1976 | Thurman Munson, New York |
| 1935 | Hank Greenberg, Detroit | 1956 | Mickey Mantle, New York | 1977 | Rod Carew, Minnesota |
| 1936 | Lou Gehrig, New York | 1957 | Mickey Mantle, New York | 1978 | Jim Rice, Boston |
| 1937 | Charley Gehringer, Detroit | 1958 | Jackie Jensen, Boston | 1979 | Don Baylor, California |
| 1938 | Jimmie Foxx, Boston | 1959 | Nellie Fox, Chicago | 1980 | George Brett, Kansas City |
| 1939 | Joe DiMaggio, New York | 1960 | Roger Maris, New York | 1981 | Rollie Fingers, Milwaukee |
| 1940 | Hank Greenberg, Detroit | 1961 | Roger Maris, New York | 1982 | Robin Yount, Milwaukee |
| 1941 | Joe DiMaggio, New York | 1962 | Mickey Mantle, New York | 1983 | Cal Ripken Jr., Baltimore |
| 1942 | Joe Gordon, New York | 1963 | Elston Howard, New York | 1984 | Willie Hernandez, Detroit |
| 1943 | Spurgeon Chandler, New York | 1964 | Brooks Robinson, Baltimore | 1985 | Don Mattingly, New York |
| 1944 | Hal Newhouser, Detroit | 1965 | Zoilo Versalles, Minnesota | 1986 | Roger Clemens, Boston |
| 1945 | Hal Newhouser, Detroit | 1966 | Frank Robinson, Baltimore | 1987 | George Bell, Toronto |
| 1946 | Ted Williams, Boston | 1967 | Carl Yastrzemski, Boston | 1988 | Jose Canseco, Oakland |
| 1947 | Joe DiMaggio, New York | 1968 | Denny McLain, Detroit | 1989 | Robin Yount, Milwaukee |
| 1948 | Lou Boudreau, Cleveland | 1969 | Harmon Killebrew, Minnesota | 1990 | Rickey Henderson |
| 1949 | Ted Williams, Boston | 1970 | John (Boog) Powell, Baltimore | 1991 | Cal Ripken Jr., Baltimore |
| 1950 | Phil Rizzuto, New York | 1971 | Vida Blue, Oakland | 1992 | Dennis Eckersley, Oakland |
| 1951 | Yogi Berra, New York | 1972 | Dick Allen, Chicago | | |

## Rookie of the Year
Baseball Writers' Association
1947—Combined selection—Jackie Robinson, Brooklyn, 1b
1948—Combined selection—Alvin Dark, Boston, N.L. ss
### National League

| Year | Player, team | Year | Player, team | Year | Player, team |
|------|-------------|------|-------------|------|-------------|
| 1949 | Don Newcombe, Brooklyn, p | 1965 | Jim Lefebvre, Los Angeles, 2b | 1979 | Rick Sutcliffe, Los Angeles, p |
| 1950 | Sam Jethroe, Boston, of | 1966 | Tommy Helms, Cincinnati, 2b | 1980 | Steve Howe, Los Angeles, p |
| 1951 | Willie Mays, New York, of | 1967 | Tom Seaver, New York, p | 1981 | Fernando Valenzuela, Los |
| 1952 | Joe Black, Brooklyn, p | 1968 | Johnny Bench, Cincinnati c | | Angeles, p |
| 1953 | Jim Gilliam, Brooklyn, 2b | 1969 | Ted Sizemore, Los Angeles, 2b | 1982 | Steve Sax, Los Angeles, 2b |
| 1954 | Wally Moon, St. Louis, of | 1970 | Carl Morton, Montreal, p | 1983 | Darryl Strawberry, New York, of |
| 1955 | Bill Virdon, St. Louis, of | 1971 | Earl Williams, Atlanta, c | 1984 | Dwight Gooden, New York, p |
| 1956 | Frank Robinson, Cincinnati, of | 1972 | Jon Matlack, New York, p | 1985 | Vince Coleman, St. Louis, of |
| 1957 | Jack Sanford, Philadelphia, p | 1973 | Gary Matthews, S.F., of | 1986 | Todd Worrell, St. Louis, p |
| 1958 | Orlando Cepeda, S.F., 1b | 1974 | Bake McBride, St. Louis, of | 1987 | Benito Santiago, San Diego, c |
| 1959 | Willie McCovey, S.F., 1b | 1975 | John Montefusco, S.F., p | 1988 | Chris Sabo, Cincinnati, 3b |
| 1960 | Frank Howard, Los Angeles, of | 1976 | (tie) Butch Metzger, San Diego, p | 1989 | Jerome Walton, Chicago, of |
| 1961 | Billy Williams, Chicago, of | | Pat Zachry, Cincinnati, p | 1990 | Dave Justice, Atlanta, of |
| 1962 | Ken Hubbs, Chicago, 2b | 1977 | Andre Dawson, Montreal, of | 1991 | Jeff Bagwell, Houston, 1b |
| 1963 | Pete Rose, Cincinnati, 2b | 1978 | Bob Horner, Atlanta, 3b | 1992 | Eric Karros, Los Angeles, 1b |
| 1964 | Richie Allen, Philadelphia, 3b | | | | |

### American League

| Year | Player, team | Year | Player, team | Year | Player, team |
|------|-------------|------|-------------|------|-------------|
| 1949 | Roy Sievers, St. Louis, of | 1964 | Tony Oliva, Minnesota, of | 1979 | (tie) John Castino, Minnesota, 3b |
| 1950 | Walt Dropo, Boston, 1b | 1965 | Curt Blefary, Baltimore, of | | Alfredo Griffin, Toronto, ss |
| 1951 | Gil McDougald, New York, 3b | 1966 | Tommie Agee, Chicago, of | 1980 | Joe Charboneau, Cleveland, of |
| 1952 | Harry Byrd, Philadelphia, p | 1967 | Rod Carew, Minnesota, 2b | 1981 | Dave Righetti, New York, p |
| 1953 | Harvey Kuenn, Detroit, ss | 1968 | Stan Bahnsen, New York, p | 1982 | Cal Ripken Jr., Baltimore, ss |
| 1954 | Bob Grim, New York, p | 1969 | Lou Piniella, Kansas City, of | 1983 | Ron Kittle, Chicago, of |
| 1955 | Herb Score, Cleveland, p | 1970 | Thurman Munson, New York, c | 1984 | Alvin Davis, Seattle, 1b |
| 1956 | Luis Aparicio, Chicago, ss | 1971 | Chris Chambliss, Cleveland, 1b | 1985 | Ozzie Guillen, Chicago, ss |
| 1957 | Tony Kubek, New York, if-of | 1972 | Carlton Fisk, Boston, c | 1986 | Jose Canseco, Oakland, of |
| 1958 | Albie Pearson, Washington, of | 1973 | Al Bumbry, Baltimore, of | 1987 | Mark McGwire, Oakland, 1b |
| 1959 | Bob Allison, Washington, of | 1974 | Mike Hargrove, Texas, 1b | 1988 | Walt Weiss, Oakland, ss |
| 1960 | Ron Hansen, Baltimore, ss | 1975 | Fred Lynn, Boston, of | 1989 | Gregg Olson, Baltimore, p |
| 1961 | Don Schwall, Boston, p | 1976 | Mark Fidrych, Detroit, p | 1990 | Sandy Alomar Jr., Cleveland, c |
| 1962 | Tom Tresh, New York, if-of | 1977 | Eddie Murray, Baltimore, dh | 1991 | Chuck Knoblauch, Minnesota, 2b |
| 1963 | Gary Peters, Chicago, p | 1978 | Lou Whitaker, Detroit, 2b | 1992 | Pat Listach, Milwaukee, ss |

# National League Records, 1993

### Final standings

## Eastern Division

| | W | L | Pct. | GB | Home | vs. RHP | Grass | Night |
|---|---|---|---|---|---|---|---|---|
| Philadelphia | 97 | 65 | .599 | — | 52-29 | 61-46 | 30-19 | 72-45 |
| Montreal | 94 | 68 | .580 | 3 | 55-26 | 65-47 | 24-25 | 72-40 |
| St. Louis | 87 | 75 | .537 | 10 | 49-32 | 62-57 | 27-23 | 56-56 |
| Chicago | 84 | 78 | .519 | 13 | 43-38 | 66-52 | 66-58 | 43-31 |
| Pittsburgh | 75 | 87 | .463 | 22 | 40-41 | 55-59 | 26-24 | 54-65 |
| Florida | 64 | 98 | .395 | 33 | 35-46 | 43-75 | 54-70 | 49-78 |
| New York | 59 | 103 | .364 | 38 | 28-53 | 48-70 | 47-77 | 38-65 |

## Western Division

| | W | L | Pct. | GB | Home | vs. RHP | Grass | Night |
|---|---|---|---|---|---|---|---|---|
| Atlanta | 104 | 58 | .642 | — | 51-30 | 75-43 | 82-43 | 77-43 |
| San Francisco | 103 | 59 | .636 | 1 | 50-31 | 71-38 | 78-47 | 49-33 |
| Houston | 85 | 77 | .525 | 19 | 44-37 | 58-48 | 27-24 | 56-53 |
| Los Angeles | 81 | 81 | .500 | 23 | 41-40 | 60-59 | 64-61 | 60-57 |
| Cincinnati | 73 | 89 | .451 | 31 | 41-40 | 66-66 | 20-30 | 52-63 |
| Colorado | 67 | 95 | .414 | 37 | 39-42 | 54-75 | 53-72 | 41-63 |
| San Diego | 61 | 101 | .377 | 43 | 34-47 | 38-74 | 50-75 | 42-69 |

## National League Championship Series

Philadelphia 4, Atlanta 3 (10 innings)
Atlanta 14, Philadelphia 3

Atlanta 9, Philadelphia 4
Philadelphia 2, Atlanta 1

Philadelphia 4, Atlanta 3 (10 innings)
Philadelphia 6, Atlanta 3

## Team Batting

| | Avg. | AB | R | H | HR | RBI |
|---|---|---|---|---|---|---|
| San Francisco | .276 | 5557 | 808 | 1534 | 168 | 759 |
| Philadelphia | .274 | 5685 | 877 | 1555 | 156 | 811 |
| Colorado | .273 | 5517 | 758 | 1507 | 142 | 704 |
| St. Louis | .272 | 5551 | 758 | 1508 | 118 | 724 |
| Chicago | .270 | 5627 | 738 | 1521 | 161 | 706 |
| Pittsburgh | .267 | 5549 | 707 | 1482 | 110 | 664 |
| Houston | .267 | 5464 | 716 | 1459 | 138 | 656 |
| Cincinnati | .264 | 5517 | 722 | 1457 | 137 | 669 |
| Atlanta | .262 | 5515 | 767 | 1444 | 169 | 712 |
| Los Angeles | .261 | 5588 | 675 | 1458 | 130 | 639 |
| Montreal | .257 | 5493 | 732 | 1410 | 122 | 682 |
| San Diego | .252 | 5503 | 679 | 1386 | 153 | 633 |
| New York | .248 | 5448 | 672 | 1350 | 158 | 632 |
| Florida | .248 | 5475 | 581 | 1356 | 94 | 542 |

## Team Pitching

| | ERA | IP | H | BB | SO | SV |
|---|---|---|---|---|---|---|
| Atlanta | 3.14 | 1455 | 1297 | 480 | 1036 | 46 |
| Houston | 3.49 | 1441⅓ | 1363 | 476 | 1056 | 42 |
| Los Angeles | 3.50 | 1472⅔ | 1406 | 567 | 1043 | 36 |
| Montreal | 3.55 | 1456⅔ | 1369 | 521 | 934 | 61 |
| San Francisco | 3.61 | 1456⅔ | 1385 | 442 | 982 | 50 |
| Philadelphia | 3.95 | 1472⅔ | 1419 | 573 | 1117 | 46 |
| New York | 4.05 | 1438 | 1483 | 434 | 867 | 22 |
| St. Louis | 4.09 | 1453 | 1553 | 383 | 775 | 54 |
| Florida | 4.13 | 1440⅓ | 1437 | 598 | 945 | 48 |
| Chicago | 4.18 | 1449⅔ | 1514 | 470 | 905 | 56 |
| San Diego | 4.23 | 1437⅓ | 1470 | 558 | 957 | 32 |
| Cincinnati | 4.51 | 1434 | 1510 | 508 | 996 | 37 |
| Pittsburgh | 4.77 | 1445⅔ | 1557 | 485 | 832 | 34 |
| Colorado | 5.41 | 1431⅓ | 1664 | 609 | 913 | 35 |

## Individual Batting (at least 175 at-bats); Individual Pitching (at least 75 innings or 10 saves)

### Atlanta Braves

| Batting | Avg | AB | R | H | HR | RBI |
|---|---|---|---|---|---|---|
| Blauser | .305 | 597 | 110 | 182 | 15 | 73 |
| McGriff | .291 | 557 | 111 | 162 | 37 | 101 |
| Sanders | .276 | 272 | 42 | 75 | 6 | 28 |
| Gant | .274 | 606 | 113 | 166 | 36 | 117 |
| Pendleton | .272 | 633 | 81 | 172 | 17 | 84 |
| Justice | .270 | 585 | 90 | 158 | 40 | 120 |
| Nixon | .269 | 461 | 77 | 124 | 1 | 24 |
| Bream | .260 | 277 | 33 | 72 | 9 | 35 |
| Lemke | .252 | 493 | 52 | 124 | 7 | 49 |
| Berryhill | .245 | 335 | 24 | 82 | 8 | 43 |
| Olson | .225 | 262 | 23 | 59 | 4 | 24 |

| Pitching | W | L | ERA | IP | H | BB | SO |
|---|---|---|---|---|---|---|---|
| McMichael | 2 | 3 | 2.06 | 91.2 | 68 | 29 | 89 |
| Maddux | 20 | 10 | 2.36 | 267.0 | 228 | 52 | 197 |
| Avery | 18 | 6 | 2.94 | 223.1 | 216 | 43 | 125 |
| Glavine | 22 | 6 | 3.20 | 239.1 | 236 | 90 | 120 |
| Smoltz | 15 | 11 | 3.62 | 243.2 | 208 | 100 | 208 |
| Smith | 4 | 8 | 4.37 | 90.2 | 92 | 36 | 53 |

Manager—Bobby Cox

### Chicago Cubs

| Batting | Avg | AB | R | H | HR | RBI |
|---|---|---|---|---|---|---|
| Grace | .325 | 594 | 86 | 193 | 14 | 98 |
| Sandberg | .309 | 456 | 67 | 141 | 9 | 45 |
| Wilkins | .303 | 446 | 78 | 135 | 30 | 73 |
| Smith | .300 | 310 | 51 | 93 | 11 | 35 |
| May | .295 | 465 | 62 | 137 | 10 | 77 |
| Vizcaino | .287 | 551 | 74 | 158 | 4 | 54 |
| Sanchez | .282 | 344 | 35 | 97 | 0 | 28 |
| Buechele | .272 | 460 | 53 | 125 | 15 | 65 |
| Sosa | .261 | 598 | 92 | 156 | 33 | 93 |
| Wilson | .258 | 221 | 29 | 57 | 1 | 11 |
| Roberson | .189 | 180 | 23 | 34 | 9 | 27 |

| Pitching | W | L | ERA | IP | H | BB | SO |
|---|---|---|---|---|---|---|---|
| Bautista | 10 | 3 | 2.82 | 111.2 | 105 | 27 | 63 |
| Myers | 2 | 4 | 3.11 | 75.1 | 65 | 26 | 86 |
| Hibbard | 15 | 11 | 3.96 | 191.0 | 209 | 47 | 82 |
| Morgan | 10 | 15 | 4.03 | 207.2 | 206 | 74 | 111 |
| Guzman | 12 | 10 | 4.34 | 191.0 | 188 | 74 | 163 |
| Scanlan | 4 | 5 | 4.54 | 75.1 | 79 | 28 | 44 |
| Castillo | 5 | 8 | 4.84 | 141.1 | 162 | 39 | 84 |
| Harkey | 10 | 10 | 5.26 | 157.1 | 187 | 43 | 67 |

Manager—Jim LeFebvre

## Cincinnati Reds

| Batting | Avg | AB | R | H | HR | RBI |
|---|---|---|---|---|---|---|
| Mitchell | .341 | 323 | 56 | 110 | 19 | 64 |
| Kelly | .319 | 320 | 44 | 102 | 9 | 35 |
| Morris | .317 | 379 | 48 | 120 | 7 | 49 |
| Larkin | .315 | 384 | 57 | 121 | 8 | 51 |
| Sanders | .274 | 496 | 90 | 136 | 20 | 83 |
| Milligan | .274 | 234 | 30 | 64 | 6 | 29 |
| Brumfield | .268 | 272 | 40 | 73 | 6 | 23 |
| Sabo | .259 | 552 | 86 | 143 | 21 | 82 |
| Branson | .241 | 381 | 40 | 92 | 3 | 22 |
| Roberts | .240 | 292 | 46 | 70 | 1 | 18 |
| Oliver | .239 | 482 | 40 | 115 | 14 | 75 |
| Samuel | .230 | 261 | 31 | 60 | 4 | 26 |

| Pitching | W | L | ERA | IP | H | BB | SO |
|---|---|---|---|---|---|---|---|
| Rijo | 14 | 9 | 2.48 | 257.1 | 218 | 62 | 227 |
| Belcher | 9 | 6 | 4.47 | 137.0 | 134 | 47 | 101 |
| Luebbers | 2 | 5 | 4.54 | 77.1 | 74 | 38 | 38 |
| Browning | 7 | 7 | 4.74 | 114.0 | 159 | 20 | 53 |
| Pugh | 10 | 15 | 5.26 | 164.1 | 200 | 59 | 94 |
| Ayala | 7 | 10 | 5.60 | 98.0 | 106 | 45 | 65 |
| Smiley | 3 | 9 | 5.62 | 105.2 | 117 | 31 | 60 |
| Roper | 2 | 5 | 5.63 | 80.0 | 92 | 36 | 54 |

**Manager—Tony Perez; Dave Johnson**

## Houston Astros

| Batting | Avg | AB | R | H | HR | RBI |
|---|---|---|---|---|---|---|
| Bagwell | .320 | 535 | 76 | 171 | 20 | 88 |
| Gonzalez | .300 | 540 | 82 | 162 | 15 | 72 |
| Biggio | .287 | 610 | 98 | 175 | 21 | 64 |
| Bass | .284 | 229 | 31 | 65 | 3 | 37 |
| Cedeno | .283 | 505 | 69 | 143 | 11 | 56 |
| Finley | .266 | 545 | 69 | 145 | 8 | 44 |
| Caminiti | .262 | 543 | 75 | 142 | 13 | 75 |
| Donnels | .257 | 179 | 18 | 46 | 2 | 24 |
| Taubensee | .250 | 288 | 26 | 72 | 9 | 42 |
| Anthony | .249 | 486 | 70 | 121 | 15 | 66 |
| Servais | .244 | 258 | 24 | 63 | 11 | 32 |

| Pitching | W | L | ERA | IP | H | BB | SO |
|---|---|---|---|---|---|---|---|
| Hernandez | 4 | 5 | 2.61 | 96.2 | 75 | 28 | 101 |
| Portugal | 18 | 4 | 2.77 | 208.0 | 194 | 77 | 131 |
| Harnisch | 16 | 9 | 2.98 | 217.2 | 171 | 79 | 185 |
| Kile | 15 | 8 | 3.51 | 171.2 | 152 | 69 | 141 |
| Drabek | 9 | 18 | 3.79 | 237.2 | 242 | 60 | 157 |
| Swindell | 12 | 13 | 4.16 | 190.1 | 215 | 40 | 124 |
| D. Jones | 4 | 10 | 4.54 | 85.1 | 102 | 21 | 66 |
| Williams | 4 | 4 | 4.83 | 82.0 | 76 | 38 | 56 |

**Manager—Art Howe**

## Colorado Rockies

| Batting | Avg | AB | R | H | HR | RBI |
|---|---|---|---|---|---|---|
| Galarraga | .370 | 470 | 71 | 174 | 22 | 98 |
| Bichette | .310 | 538 | 93 | 167 | 21 | 89 |
| Hayes | .305 | 573 | 89 | 175 | 25 | 98 |
| Girardi | .290 | 310 | 35 | 90 | 3 | 31 |
| Benavides | .286 | 213 | 20 | 61 | 3 | 26 |
| Clark | .282 | 478 | 65 | 135 | 13 | 67 |
| Sheaffer | .278 | 216 | 26 | 60 | 4 | 32 |
| Jones | .273 | 209 | 29 | 57 | 6 | 31 |
| E. Young | .269 | 490 | 82 | 132 | 3 | 42 |
| Boston | .261 | 291 | 46 | 76 | 14 | 40 |
| Cole | .256 | 348 | 50 | 89 | 0 | 24 |
| Castilla | .255 | 337 | 36 | 86 | 9 | 30 |
| Mejia | .231 | 229 | 31 | 53 | 5 | 20 |

| Pitching | W | L | ERA | IP | H | BB | SO |
|---|---|---|---|---|---|---|---|
| Ruffin | 6 | 5 | 3.87 | 139.2 | 145 | 69 | 126 |
| Reynoso | 12 | 11 | 4.00 | 189.0 | 206 | 63 | 117 |
| Holmes | 3 | 3 | 4.05 | 66.2 | 56 | 20 | 60 |
| Reed | 9 | 5 | 4.48 | 84.1 | 80 | 30 | 51 |
| Harris | 11 | 17 | 4.59 | 225.1 | 239 | 69 | 123 |
| Blair | 6 | 10 | 4.75 | 146.0 | 184 | 42 | 84 |
| Bottenfield | 5 | 10 | 5.07 | 159.2 | 179 | 71 | 63 |
| Nied | 5 | 9 | 5.17 | 87.0 | 99 | 42 | 46 |

**Manager—Don Baylor**

## Los Angeles Dodgers

| Batting | Avg | AB | R | H | HR | RBI |
|---|---|---|---|---|---|---|
| Piazza | .318 | 547 | 81 | 174 | 35 | 112 |
| Butler | .298 | 607 | 80 | 181 | 1 | 42 |
| Reed | .276 | 445 | 46 | 123 | 2 | 31 |
| Offerman | .269 | 590 | 77 | 159 | 1 | 62 |
| Snyder | .266 | 516 | 61 | 137 | 11 | 56 |
| Karros | .247 | 619 | 74 | 153 | 23 | 80 |
| Davis | .234 | 376 | 57 | 88 | 14 | 53 |
| Wallach | .222 | 477 | 42 | 106 | 12 | 62 |
| Rodriguez | .222 | 176 | 20 | 39 | 8 | 23 |

| Pitching | W | L | ERA | IP | H | BB | SO |
|---|---|---|---|---|---|---|---|
| Gott | 4 | 8 | 2.32 | 77.2 | 71 | 17 | 67 |
| P. Martinez | 10 | 5 | 2.61 | 107.0 | 76 | 57 | 119 |
| Candiotti | 8 | 10 | 3.12 | 213.2 | 192 | 71 | 155 |
| R. Martinez | 10 | 12 | 3.44 | 211.2 | 202 | 104 | 127 |
| Astacio | 14 | 9 | 3.57 | 186.1 | 165 | 68 | 122 |
| Hershiser | 12 | 14 | 3.59 | 215.2 | 201 | 72 | 141 |
| Ke. Gross | 13 | 13 | 4.14 | 202.1 | 224 | 74 | 150 |

**Manager—Tommy Lasorda**

## Florida Marlins

| Batting | Avg | AB | R | H | HR | RBI |
|---|---|---|---|---|---|---|
| Sheffield | .294 | 494 | 67 | 145 | 20 | 73 |
| Conine | .292 | 595 | 75 | 174 | 12 | 79 |
| Magadan | .286 | 227 | 22 | 65 | 4 | 29 |
| Barberie | .277 | 375 | 45 | 104 | 5 | 33 |
| Arias | .269 | 249 | 27 | 67 | 2 | 20 |
| Carr | .267 | 551 | 75 | 147 | 4 | 41 |
| Weiss | .266 | 500 | 50 | 133 | 1 | 39 |
| Destrade | .255 | 569 | 61 | 145 | 20 | 87 |
| Renteria | .255 | 263 | 27 | 67 | 2 | 30 |
| Felix | .238 | 214 | 25 | 51 | 7 | 22 |
| Santiago | .230 | 469 | 49 | 108 | 13 | 50 |
| Whitmore | .204 | 250 | 24 | 51 | 4 | 19 |

| Pitching | W | L | ERA | IP | H | BB | SO |
|---|---|---|---|---|---|---|---|
| Harvey | 1 | 5 | 1.70 | 69.0 | 45 | 13 | 73 |
| Lewis | 6 | 3 | 3.26 | 77.1 | 68 | 43 | 65 |
| Aquino | 6 | 8 | 3.42 | 110.2 | 115 | 40 | 67 |
| Rodriguez | 2 | 4 | 3.79 | 76.0 | 73 | 33 | 43 |
| Rapp | 4 | 6 | 4.02 | 94.0 | 101 | 39 | 57 |
| Hough | 9 | 16 | 4.27 | 204.1 | 202 | 71 | 126 |
| Bowen | 8 | 12 | 4.42 | 156.2 | 156 | 87 | 98 |
| Armstrong | 9 | 17 | 4.49 | 196.1 | 210 | 78 | 118 |
| Hammond | 11 | 12 | 4.66 | 191.0 | 207 | 66 | 108 |

**Manager—Rene Lachemann**

## Montreal Expos

| Batting | Avg | AB | R | H | HR | RBI |
|---|---|---|---|---|---|---|
| Grissom | .298 | 630 | 104 | 188 | 19 | 95 |
| DeShields | .295 | 481 | 75 | 142 | 2 | 29 |
| Lansing | .287 | 491 | 64 | 141 | 3 | 45 |
| Alou | .286 | 482 | 70 | 138 | 18 | 85 |
| Frazier | .286 | 189 | 27 | 54 | 1 | 16 |
| Walker | .265 | 490 | 85 | 130 | 22 | 86 |
| Berry | .261 | 299 | 50 | 78 | 14 | 49 |
| Fletcher | .255 | 396 | 33 | 101 | 9 | 60 |
| Cordero | .248 | 475 | 56 | 118 | 10 | 58 |
| Vanderwal | .233 | 215 | 34 | 50 | 5 | 30 |
| Bolick | .211 | 213 | 25 | 45 | 4 | 24 |

| Pitching | W | L | ERA | IP | H | BB | SO |
|---|---|---|---|---|---|---|---|
| Wetteland | 9 | 3 | 1.37 | 85.1 | 58 | 28 | 113 |
| Fassero | 12 | 5 | 2.29 | 149.2 | 119 | 54 | 140 |
| Rueter | 8 | 0 | 2.73 | 85.2 | 85 | 18 | 31 |
| Rojas | 5 | 8 | 2.95 | 88.1 | 80 | 30 | 48 |
| Hill | 9 | 7 | 3.23 | 183.2 | 163 | 74 | 90 |
| Martinez | 15 | 9 | 3.85 | 224.2 | 211 | 64 | 138 |
| Nabholz | 9 | 8 | 4.09 | 116.2 | 100 | 63 | 74 |
| Shaw | 2 | 7 | 4.14 | 95.2 | 91 | 32 | 50 |
| Barnes | 2 | 6 | 4.41 | 100.0 | 105 | 48 | 60 |
| Henry | 3 | 9 | 6.12 | 103.0 | 135 | 28 | 47 |

**Manager—Felipe Alou**

## New York Mets

| Batting | Avg | AB | R | H | HR | RBI |
|---|---|---|---|---|---|---|
| Murray | .285 | 610 | 77 | 174 | 27 | 100 |
| Orsulak | .284 | 409 | 59 | 116 | 8 | 35 |
| Coleman | .279 | 373 | 64 | 104 | 2 | 25 |
| Gallagher | .274 | 201 | 34 | 55 | 6 | 28 |
| Kent | .270 | 496 | 65 | 134 | 21 | 80 |
| Bonilla | .265 | 502 | 81 | 133 | 34 | 87 |
| O'Brien | .255 | 188 | 15 | 48 | 4 | 23 |
| Thompson | .250 | 288 | 34 | 72 | 11 | 26 |
| Bogar | .244 | 205 | 19 | 50 | 3 | 25 |
| Burnitz | .243 | 263 | 49 | 64 | 13 | 38 |
| Johnson | .238 | 235 | 32 | 56 | 7 | 26 |
| Hundley | .228 | 417 | 40 | 95 | 11 | 53 |
| Walker | .225 | 213 | 18 | 48 | 5 | 19 |

| Pitching | W | L | ERA | IP | H | BB | SO |
|---|---|---|---|---|---|---|---|
| S. Fernandez | 5 | 6 | 2.93 | 119.2 | 82 | 36 | 81 |
| Saberhagen | 7 | 7 | 3.29 | 139.1 | 131 | 17 | 93 |
| Gooden | 12 | 15 | 3.45 | 208.2 | 188 | 61 | 149 |
| Maddux | 3 | 8 | 3.60 | 75.0 | 67 | 27 | 57 |
| Young | 1 | 16 | 3.77 | 100.1 | 103 | 42 | 62 |
| Hillman | 2 | 9 | 3.97 | 145.0 | 173 | 24 | 60 |
| Innis | 2 | 3 | 4.11 | 76.2 | 81 | 38 | 36 |
| Tanana | 7 | 15 | 4.48 | 183.0 | 198 | 48 | 104 |
| Telgheder | 6 | 2 | 4.76 | 75.2 | 82 | 21 | 35 |
| Franco | 4 | 3 | 5.20 | 36.1 | 46 | 19 | 29 |
| Schourek | 5 | 12 | 5.96 | 128.1 | 168 | 45 | 72 |

**Manager**—Jeff Torborg; Dallas Green

## Philadelphia Phillies

| Batting | Avg | AB | R | H | HR | RBI |
|---|---|---|---|---|---|---|
| Stocker | .324 | 259 | 46 | 84 | 2 | 31 |
| Eisenreich | .318 | 362 | 51 | 115 | 7 | 54 |
| Kruk | .316 | 535 | 100 | 169 | 14 | 85 |
| Dykstra | .305 | 637 | 143 | 194 | 19 | 66 |
| Duncan | .282 | 496 | 68 | 140 | 11 | 73 |
| Chamberlain | .282 | 284 | 34 | 80 | 12 | 45 |
| Incaviglia | .274 | 368 | 60 | 101 | 24 | 89 |
| Hollins | .273 | 543 | 104 | 148 | 18 | 93 |
| Thompson | .262 | 340 | 42 | 89 | 4 | 44 |
| Daulton | .257 | 510 | 90 | 131 | 24 | 105 |
| Morandini | .247 | 425 | 57 | 105 | 3 | 33 |

| Pitching | W | L | ERA | IP | H | BB | SO |
|---|---|---|---|---|---|---|---|
| West | 6 | 4 | 2.92 | 86.1 | 60 | 51 | 87 |
| Mulholland | 12 | 9 | 3.25 | 191.0 | 177 | 40 | 116 |
| Williams | 3 | 7 | 3.34 | 62.0 | 56 | 44 | 60 |
| Greene | 16 | 4 | 3.42 | 200.0 | 175 | 62 | 167 |
| Jackson | 12 | 11 | 3.77 | 210.1 | 214 | 80 | 120 |
| Schilling | 16 | 7 | 4.02 | 235.1 | 234 | 57 | 186 |
| Mason | 5 | 12 | 4.06 | 99.2 | 90 | 34 | 71 |
| Rivera | 13 | 9 | 5.02 | 163.0 | 175 | 85 | 123 |

**Manager**—Jim Fregosi

## Pittsburgh Pirates

| Batting | Avg | AB | R | H | HR | RBI |
|---|---|---|---|---|---|---|
| Merced | .313 | 447 | 68 | 140 | 8 | 70 |
| Bell | .310 | 604 | 102 | 187 | 9 | 51 |
| Van Slyke | .310 | 323 | 42 | 100 | 8 | 50 |
| Slaught | .300 | 377 | 34 | 113 | 10 | 55 |
| King | .295 | 611 | 82 | 180 | 9 | 98 |
| L. Smith | .286 | 199 | 35 | 57 | 6 | 24 |
| Martin | .281 | 480 | 85 | 135 | 18 | 64 |
| Clark | .271 | 277 | 43 | 75 | 11 | 46 |
| Garcia | .269 | 546 | 77 | 147 | 12 | 47 |
| Foley | .253 | 194 | 18 | 49 | 3 | 22 |
| Young | .236 | 449 | 38 | 106 | 6 | 47 |
| McClendon | .221 | 181 | 21 | 40 | 2 | 19 |
| Prince | .196 | 179 | 14 | 35 | 2 | 24 |

| Pitching | W | L | ERA | IP | H | BB | SO |
|---|---|---|---|---|---|---|---|
| Belinda | 3 | 1 | 3.61 | 42.1 | 35 | 11 | 30 |
| Cooke | 10 | 10 | 3.89 | 210.2 | 207 | 59 | 132 |
| Minor | 8 | 6 | 4.10 | 94.1 | 94 | 26 | 84 |
| Wagner | 8 | 8 | 4.27 | 141.1 | 143 | 42 | 114 |
| Z. Smith | 3 | 7 | 4.55 | 83.0 | 97 | 22 | 32 |
| Tomlin | 4 | 8 | 4.85 | 98.1 | 109 | 15 | 44 |

| | | | | IP | H | BB | SO |
|---|---|---|---|---|---|---|---|
| Neagle | 3 | 5 | 5.31 | 81.1 | 82 | 37 | 73 |
| Wakefield | 6 | 11 | 5.61 | 128.1 | 145 | 75 | 59 |
| Walk | 13 | 14 | 5.68 | 187.0 | 214 | 70 | 80 |

**Manager**—Jim Leyland

## St. Louis Cardinals

| Batting | Avg | AB | R | H | HR | RBI |
|---|---|---|---|---|---|---|
| Jefferies | .342 | 544 | 89 | 186 | 16 | 83 |
| Jordan | .309 | 223 | 33 | 69 | 10 | 44 |
| Gilkey | .305 | 557 | 99 | 170 | 16 | 70 |
| O. Smith | .288 | 545 | 75 | 157 | 1 | 53 |
| Alicea | .279 | 362 | 50 | 101 | 3 | 46 |
| Zeile | .277 | 571 | 82 | 158 | 17 | 103 |
| Pappas | .276 | 228 | 25 | 63 | 1 | 28 |
| Pagnozzi | .258 | 330 | 31 | 85 | 7 | 41 |
| Pena | .256 | 254 | 34 | 65 | 5 | 30 |
| Whiten | .253 | 562 | 81 | 142 | 25 | 99 |
| Lankford | .238 | 407 | 64 | 97 | 7 | 45 |

| Pitching | W | L | ERA | IP | H | BB | SO |
|---|---|---|---|---|---|---|---|
| Osborne | 10 | 7 | 3.76 | 155.2 | 153 | 47 | 83 |
| Arocha | 11 | 8 | 3.78 | 188.0 | 197 | 31 | 96 |
| Tewksbury | 17 | 10 | 3.83 | 213.2 | 258 | 20 | 97 |
| Olivares | 5 | 3 | 4.17 | 118.2 | 134 | 54 | 63 |
| Cormier | 7 | 6 | 4.33 | 145.1 | 163 | 27 | 75 |
| L. Smith | 2 | 4 | 4.50 | 50.0 | 49 | 9 | 49 |
| Watson | 6 | 7 | 4.60 | 86.0 | 90 | 28 | 49 |
| Magrane | 8 | 10 | 4.97 | 116.0 | 127 | 37 | 38 |

**Manager**—Joe Torre

## San Diego Padres

| Batting | Avg | AB | R | H | HR | RBI |
|---|---|---|---|---|---|---|
| Gwynn | .358 | 489 | 70 | 175 | 7 | 59 |
| Clark | .313 | 240 | 33 | 75 | 9 | 33 |
| Gardner | .262 | 404 | 53 | 106 | 1 | 24 |
| Bell | .262 | 542 | 73 | 142 | 21 | 72 |
| Bean | .260 | 177 | 19 | 46 | 5 | 32 |
| Gutierrez | .251 | 438 | 76 | 110 | 5 | 26 |
| Teufel | .250 | 200 | 26 | 50 | 7 | 31 |
| Cianfrocco | .243 | 296 | 30 | 72 | 12 | 48 |
| Plantier | .240 | 462 | 67 | 111 | 34 | 100 |
| Shipley | .235 | 230 | 25 | 54 | 4 | 22 |
| Higgins | .221 | 181 | 17 | 40 | 0 | 13 |

| Pitching | W | L | ERA | IP | H | BB | SO |
|---|---|---|---|---|---|---|---|
| Ge. Harris | 6 | 6 | 3.03 | 59.1 | 57 | 37 | 39 |
| Benes | 15 | 15 | 3.78 | 230.2 | 200 | 86 | 179 |
| Whitehurst | 4 | 7 | 3.83 | 105.2 | 109 | 30 | 57 |
| Hoffman | 4 | 6 | 3.90 | 90.0 | 80 | 39 | 79 |
| Brocail | 4 | 13 | 4.56 | 128.1 | 143 | 42 | 70 |
| Worrell | 2 | 7 | 4.92 | 100.2 | 104 | 43 | 52 |
| Ashby | 3 | 10 | 6.80 | 123.0 | 168 | 56 | 77 |

**Manager**—Jim Riggleman

## San Francisco Giants

| Batting | Avg | AB | R | H | HR | RBI |
|---|---|---|---|---|---|---|
| Bonds | .336 | 539 | 129 | 181 | 46 | 123 |
| Thompson | .312 | 494 | 85 | 154 | 19 | 65 |
| McGee | .301 | 475 | 53 | 143 | 4 | 46 |
| Williams | .294 | 579 | 105 | 170 | 38 | 110 |
| Benzinger | .288 | 177 | 25 | 51 | 6 | 26 |
| Clark | .283 | 491 | 82 | 139 | 14 | 73 |
| Clayton | .282 | 549 | 54 | 155 | 6 | 70 |
| Manwaring | .275 | 432 | 48 | 119 | 5 | 49 |
| Lewis | .253 | 522 | 84 | 132 | 2 | 48 |
| Martinez | .241 | 241 | 28 | 58 | 5 | 27 |

| Pitching | W | L | ERA | IP | H | BB | SO |
|---|---|---|---|---|---|---|---|
| Beck | 3 | 1 | 2.16 | 79.1 | 57 | 13 | 86 |
| Rogers | 2 | 2 | 2.68 | 80.2 | 71 | 28 | 62 |
| Swift | 21 | 8 | 2.82 | 232.2 | 195 | 55 | 157 |
| Jackson | 6 | 6 | 3.03 | 77.1 | 58 | 24 | 70 |
| Black | 8 | 2 | 3.56 | 93.2 | 89 | 33 | 45 |
| Wilson | 7 | 5 | 3.60 | 110.0 | 110 | 40 | 57 |
| Burkett | 22 | 7 | 3.65 | 231.2 | 224 | 40 | 145 |
| Burba | 10 | 3 | 4.25 | 95.1 | 95 | 37 | 88 |
| Hickerson | 7 | 5 | 4.26 | 120.1 | 137 | 39 | 69 |
| Brantley | 5 | 6 | 4.28 | 113.2 | 112 | 46 | 76 |

**Manager**—Dusty Baker

# American League Records, 1993

Final standings

## Eastern Division

| | W | L | Pct. | GB | Home | vs. RHP | Grass | Night |
|---|---|---|---|---|---|---|---|---|
| Toronto | 95 | 67 | .586 | — | 48-33 | 72-40 | 39-24 | 57-51 |
| New York | 88 | 74 | .543 | 7 | 50-31 | 55-50 | 77-61 | 54-56 |
| Baltimore | 85 | 77 | .525 | 10 | 48-33 | 61-55 | 75-63 | 63-53 |
| Detroit | 85 | 77 | .525 | 10 | 44-37 | 59-59 | 72-65 | 53-50 |
| Boston | 80 | 82 | .494 | 15 | 43-38 | 58-61 | 67-70 | 50-56 |
| Cleveland | 76 | 86 | .469 | 19 | 46-35 | 55-62 | 69-69 | 52-54 |
| Milwaukee | 69 | 93 | .426 | 26 | 38-43 | 45-61 | 58-79 | 44-58 |

## Western Division

| | W | L | Pct. | GB | Home | vs. RHP | Grass | Night |
|---|---|---|---|---|---|---|---|---|
| Chicago | 94 | 68 | .580 | — | 45-36 | 68-44 | 77-61 | 68-47 |
| Texas | 86 | 76 | .531 | 8 | 50-31 | 70-56 | 76-61 | 65-60 |
| Kansas City | 84 | 78 | .519 | 10 | 43-38 | 62-56 | 31-31 | 57-55 |
| Seattle | 82 | 80 | .506 | 12 | 46-35 | 51-58 | 26-36 | 61-56 |
| California | 71 | 91 | .438 | 23 | 44-37 | 54-68 | 63-72 | 52-63 |
| Minnesota | 71 | 91 | .438 | 23 | 36-45 | 53-69 | 28-34 | 47-61 |
| Oakland | 68 | 94 | .420 | 26 | 38-43 | 48-66 | 52-84 | 45-48 |

## American League Championship Series

| | | |
|---|---|---|
| Toronto 7, Chicago 3 | Chicago 6, Toronto 1 | Toronto 5, Chicago 3 |
| Toronto 3, Chicago 1 | Chicago 7, Toronto 4 | Toronto 6, Chicago 3 |

## Team Batting

| | Avg. | AB | R | H | HR | RBI |
|---|---|---|---|---|---|---|
| New York | .279 | 5615 | 821 | 1568 | 178 | 793 |
| Toronto | .279 | 5579 | 847 | 1556 | 159 | 796 |
| Cleveland | .275 | 5619 | 790 | 1547 | 141 | 747 |
| Detroit | .275 | 5620 | 899 | 1546 | 178 | 853 |
| Texas | .267 | 5510 | 835 | 1472 | 181 | 780 |
| Baltimore | .267 | 5508 | 786 | 1470 | 157 | 744 |
| Chicago | .265 | 5483 | 776 | 1454 | 162 | 731 |
| Minnesota | .264 | 5601 | 693 | 1480 | 121 | 642 |
| Boston | .264 | 5496 | 686 | 1451 | 114 | 644 |
| Kansas City | .263 | 5522 | 675 | 1455 | 125 | 641 |
| Seattle | .260 | 5494 | 734 | 1429 | 161 | 681 |
| California | .260 | 5391 | 684 | 1399 | 114 | 644 |
| Milwaukee | .258 | 5525 | 733 | 1426 | 125 | 688 |
| Oakland | .254 | 5543 | 715 | 1408 | 158 | 679 |

## Team Pitching

| | ERA | IP | H | BB | SO | Sv |
|---|---|---|---|---|---|---|
| Chicago | 3.70 | 1454 | 1398 | 566 | 974 | 48 |
| Boston | 3.77 | 1452⅓ | 1379 | 552 | 997 | 44 |
| Kansas City | 4.04 | 1445⅓ | 1379 | 547 | 985 | 48 |
| Seattle | 4.20 | 1453⅔ | 1421 | 605 | 1083 | 41 |
| Toronto | 4.21 | 1441⅓ | 1441 | 620 | 1023 | 50 |
| Texas | 4.28 | 1438⅓ | 1476 | 562 | 957 | 45 |
| Baltimore | 4.31 | 1442⅔ | 1427 | 579 | 900 | 42 |
| California | 4.34 | 1447 | 1482 | 550 | 843 | 41 |
| New York | 4.35 | 1438⅓ | 1467 | 552 | 899 | 38 |
| Milwaukee | 4.45 | 1447 | 1511 | 522 | 810 | 29 |
| Cleveland | 4.58 | 1445⅓ | 1591 | 591 | 888 | 45 |
| Detroit | 4.65 | 1436⅔ | 1547 | 542 | 828 | 36 |
| Minnesota | 4.71 | 1444⅓ | 1591 | 514 | 901 | 44 |
| Oakland | 4.90 | 1452⅓ | 1551 | 680 | 864 | 42 |

## Individual Batting (at least 175 at-bats); Individual Pitching (at least 75 innings or 10 saves)

### Baltimore Orioles

| Batting | Avg | AB | R | H | HR | RBI |
|---|---|---|---|---|---|---|
| Baines | .313 | 416 | 64 | 130 | 20 | 78 |
| Hoiles | .310 | 419 | 80 | 130 | 29 | 82 |
| Pagliarulo | .303 | 370 | 55 | 112 | 9 | 44 |
| Hulett | .300 | 260 | 40 | 78 | 2 | 23 |
| McLemore | .284 | 581 | 81 | 165 | 4 | 72 |
| Segui | .273 | 450 | 54 | 123 | 10 | 60 |
| Anderson | .263 | 560 | 87 | 147 | 13 | 66 |
| Ripkin | .257 | 641 | 87 | 165 | 24 | 90 |
| Reynolds | .252 | 485 | 64 | 122 | 4 | 47 |
| Devereaux | .250 | 527 | 72 | 132 | 14 | 75 |
| Gomez | .197 | 244 | 30 | 48 | 10 | 25 |

| Pitching | W | L | ERA | IP | H | BB | SO |
|---|---|---|---|---|---|---|---|
| Olson | 0 | 2 | 1.60 | 45.0 | 37 | 18 | 44 |
| Mills | 5 | 4 | 3.23 | 100.1 | 80 | 51 | 68 |
| McDonald | 13 | 14 | 3.39 | 220.1 | 185 | 86 | 171 |
| Moyer | 12 | 9 | 3.43 | 152.0 | 154 | 38 | 90 |
| Frohwirth | 6 | 7 | 3.83 | 96.1 | 91 | 44 | 50 |
| Mussina | 14 | 6 | 4.46 | 167.2 | 163 | 44 | 117 |
| Williamson | 7 | 5 | 4.91 | 88.0 | 106 | 25 | 45 |
| Valenzuela | 8 | 10 | 4.94 | 178.2 | 179 | 79 | 78 |
| Sutcliffe | 10 | 10 | 5.75 | 166.0 | 212 | 74 | 80 |
| Rhodes | 5 | 6 | 6.51 | 85.2 | 91 | 49 | 49 |

Manager—John Oates

### Boston Red Sox

| Batting | Avg | AB | R | H | HR | RBI |
|---|---|---|---|---|---|---|
| Greenwell | .315 | 540 | 77 | 170 | 13 | 72 |
| Vaughn | .297 | 539 | 86 | 160 | 29 | 101 |
| Hatcher | .287 | 508 | 71 | 146 | 9 | 57 |
| Fletcher | .285 | 480 | 81 | 137 | 5 | 45 |
| Cooper | .279 | 526 | 67 | 147 | 9 | 63 |
| Valentin | .278 | 468 | 50 | 130 | 11 | 66 |
| Dawson | .273 | 461 | 44 | 126 | 13 | 67 |
| Quintana | .244 | 303 | 31 | 74 | 1 | 19 |
| Zupcic | .241 | 286 | 40 | 69 | 2 | 26 |
| Melvin | .222 | 176 | 13 | 39 | 3 | 23 |
| Deer | .210 | 466 | 66 | 98 | 21 | 55 |
| Pena | .181 | 304 | 20 | 55 | 4 | 19 |

| Pitching | W | L | ERA | IP | H | BB | SO |
|---|---|---|---|---|---|---|---|
| Russell | 1 | 4 | 2.70 | 46.2 | 39 | 14 | 45 |
| Sele | 7 | 2 | 2.74 | 111.2 | 100 | 48 | 93 |
| Viola | 11 | 8 | 3.14 | 183.2 | 180 | 72 | 91 |
| Darwin | 15 | 11 | 3.26 | 229.1 | 196 | 49 | 130 |
| Harris | 6 | 7 | 3.77 | 112.1 | 95 | 60 | 103 |
| Quantrill | 6 | 12 | 3.91 | 138.0 | 151 | 44 | 66 |
| Clemens | 11 | 14 | 4.46 | 191.2 | 175 | 67 | 160 |
| Dopson | 7 | 11 | 4.97 | 155.2 | 170 | 59 | 89 |

Manager—Butch Hobson

## California Angels

| Batting | Avg | AB | R | H | HR | RBI |
|---|---|---|---|---|---|---|
| Easley | .313 | 230 | 33 | 72 | 2 | 22 |
| Javier | .291 | 237 | 33 | 69 | 3 | 28 |
| Curtis | .285 | 583 | 94 | 166 | 6 | 59 |
| Salmon | .283 | 515 | 93 | 146 | 31 | 95 |
| Polonia | .271 | 576 | 75 | 156 | 1 | 32 |
| Myers | .255 | 290 | 27 | 74 | 7 | 40 |
| R. Gonzales | .251 | 335 | 34 | 84 | 2 | 31 |
| Lovullo | .251 | 367 | 42 | 92 | 6 | 30 |
| Perez | .250 | 180 | 16 | 45 | 4 | 30 |
| Davis | .243 | 573 | 74 | 139 | 27 | 112 |
| Snow | .241 | 419 | 60 | 101 | 16 | 57 |
| DiSarcina | .238 | 416 | 44 | 99 | 3 | 45 |

| Pitching | W | L | ERA | IP | H | BB | SO |
|---|---|---|---|---|---|---|---|
| Grahe | 4 | 1 | 2.86 | 56.2 | 54 | 25 | 31 |
| Frey | 2 | 3 | 2.98 | 48.1 | 41 | 26 | 22 |
| Finley | 16 | 14 | 3.15 | 251.1 | 243 | 82 | 187 |
| Langston | 16 | 11 | 3.20 | 256.1 | 220 | 85 | 196 |
| Leftwich | 4 | 6 | 3.79 | 80.2 | 81 | 27 | 31 |
| Sanderson | 7 | 11 | 4.46 | 135.1 | 153 | 27 | 66 |
| Farrell | 3 | 12 | 7.35 | 90.2 | 110 | 44 | 45 |

**Manager—Buck Rodgers**

## Chicago White Sox

| Batting | Avg | AB | R | H | HR | RBI |
|---|---|---|---|---|---|---|
| Thomas | .317 | 549 | 106 | 174 | 41 | 128 |
| Johnson | .311 | 540 | 75 | 168 | 0 | 47 |
| Raines | .306 | 415 | 75 | 127 | 16 | 54 |
| Guillen | .280 | 457 | 44 | 128 | 4 | 50 |
| Burks | .275 | 499 | 75 | 137 | 17 | 74 |
| Cora | .268 | 579 | 95 | 155 | 2 | 51 |
| Ventura | .262 | 554 | 85 | 145 | 22 | 94 |
| Jackson | .232 | 284 | 32 | 66 | 16 | 45 |
| Karkovice | .228 | 403 | 60 | 92 | 20 | 54 |
| Grebeck | .226 | 190 | 25 | 43 | 1 | 12 |
| Bell | .217 | 410 | 36 | 89 | 13 | 64 |
| Calderon | .209 | 239 | 26 | 50 | 1 | 22 |
| Pasqua | .205 | 176 | 22 | 36 | 5 | 20 |

| Pitching | W | L | ERA | IP | H | BB | SO |
|---|---|---|---|---|---|---|---|
| Hernandez | 3 | 4 | 2.29 | 78.2 | 66 | 20 | 71 |
| Alvarez | 15 | 8 | 2.95 | 207.2 | 168 | 122 | 155 |
| Fernandez | 18 | 9 | 3.13 | 247.1 | 221 | 67 | 169 |
| McDowell | 22 | 10 | 3.37 | 256.2 | 261 | 69 | 158 |
| Bere | 12 | 5 | 3.47 | 142.2 | 109 | 81 | 129 |
| McCaskill | 4 | 8 | 5.23 | 113.2 | 144 | 36 | 65 |

**Manager—Gene Lamont**

## Cleveland Indians

| Batting | Avg | AB | R | H | HR | RBI |
|---|---|---|---|---|---|---|
| Lofton | .325 | 569 | 116 | 185 | 1 | 42 |
| Baerga | .321 | 624 | 105 | 200 | 21 | 114 |
| Treadway | .303 | 221 | 25 | 67 | 2 | 27 |
| Belle | .290 | 594 | 93 | 172 | 38 | 129 |
| Espinoza | .278 | 263 | 34 | 73 | 4 | 27 |
| Alomar | .270 | 215 | 24 | 58 | 6 | 32 |
| Kirby | .269 | 458 | 71 | 123 | 6 | 60 |
| Fermin | .263 | 480 | 48 | 126 | 2 | 45 |
| Sorrento | .257 | 463 | 75 | 119 | 18 | 65 |
| Jefferson | .249 | 366 | 35 | 91 | 10 | 34 |
| Martinez | .244 | 262 | 26 | 64 | 5 | 31 |
| Howard | .236 | 178 | 26 | 42 | 3 | 23 |
| Ortiz | .221 | 249 | 19 | 55 | 0 | 20 |

| Pitching | W | L | ERA | IP | H | BB | SO |
|---|---|---|---|---|---|---|---|
| Lilliquist | 4 | 4 | 2.25 | 64.0 | 64 | 19 | 40 |
| DiPoto | 4 | 4 | 2.40 | 56.1 | 57 | 30 | 41 |
| Plunk | 4 | 5 | 2.79 | 71.0 | 57 | 30 | 77 |
| Hernandez | 6 | 5 | 3.14 | 77.1 | 75 | 27 | 44 |
| Kramer | 7 | 3 | 4.02 | 121.0 | 126 | 59 | 71 |
| Clark | 7 | 5 | 4.28 | 109.1 | 119 | 25 | 57 |
| Mesa | 10 | 12 | 4.92 | 208.2 | 232 | 62 | 118 |
| Mutis | 3 | 6 | 5.78 | 81.0 | 93 | 33 | 29 |

**Manager—Mike Hargrove**

## Detroit Tigers

| Batting | Avg | AB | R | H | HR | RBI |
|---|---|---|---|---|---|---|
| Trammell | .329 | 401 | 72 | 132 | 12 | 60 |
| Phillips | .313 | 566 | 113 | 177 | 7 | 57 |
| Fryman | .300 | 607 | 98 | 182 | 22 | 97 |
| Livingstone | .293 | 304 | 39 | 89 | 2 | 39 |
| Whitaker | .290 | 383 | 72 | 111 | 9 | 67 |
| Kreuter | .286 | 374 | 59 | 107 | 15 | 51 |
| Fielder | .267 | 573 | 80 | 153 | 30 | 117 |
| Gladden | .267 | 356 | 52 | 95 | 13 | 56 |
| Gibson | .261 | 403 | 62 | 105 | 13 | 62 |
| Tettleton | .245 | 522 | 79 | 128 | 32 | 110 |
| Cuyler | .213 | 249 | 46 | 53 | 0 | 19 |

| Pitching | W | L | ERA | IP | H | BB | SO |
|---|---|---|---|---|---|---|---|
| Henneman | 5 | 3 | 2.64 | 71.2 | 69 | 32 | 58 |
| Krueger | 6 | 4 | 3.40 | 82.0 | 90 | 30 | 60 |
| Boever | 6 | 3 | 3.61 | 102.1 | 101 | 44 | 63 |
| Wells | 11 | 9 | 4.19 | 187.0 | 183 | 42 | 139 |
| Doherty | 14 | 11 | 4.44 | 184.2 | 205 | 48 | 63 |
| Bolton | 6 | 6 | 4.47 | 102.2 | 113 | 45 | 66 |
| Leiter | 6 | 6 | 4.73 | 106.2 | 111 | 44 | 70 |
| S. Davis | 2 | 8 | 5.05 | 98.0 | 93 | 48 | 73 |
| Moore | 13 | 9 | 5.22 | 213.2 | 227 | 89 | 89 |
| Gullickson | 13 | 9 | 5.37 | 159.1 | 186 | 44 | 70 |

**Manager—Sparky Anderson**

## Kansas City Royals

| Batting | Avg | AB | R | H | HR | RBI |
|---|---|---|---|---|---|---|
| Gwynn | .300 | 287 | 36 | 86 | 1 | 25 |
| Joyner | .292 | 497 | 83 | 145 | 15 | 65 |
| McRae | .282 | 627 | 78 | 177 | 12 | 69 |
| Gagne | .280 | 540 | 66 | 151 | 10 | 57 |
| Macfarlane | .273 | 388 | 55 | 106 | 20 | 67 |
| Brett | .266 | 560 | 69 | 149 | 19 | 75 |
| Mayne | .254 | 205 | 22 | 52 | 2 | 22 |
| Jose | .253 | 499 | 64 | 126 | 6 | 43 |
| Lind | .248 | 431 | 33 | 107 | 0 | 37 |
| McReynolds | .245 | 351 | 44 | 86 | 11 | 42 |
| Gaetti | .245 | 331 | 40 | 81 | 14 | 50 |
| Hiatt | .218 | 238 | 30 | 52 | 7 | 36 |

| Pitching | W | L | ERA | IP | H | BB | SO |
|---|---|---|---|---|---|---|---|
| Montgomery | 7 | 5 | 2.27 | 87.1 | 65 | 23 | 66 |
| Appier | 18 | 8 | 2.56 | 238.2 | 183 | 81 | 186 |
| Cone | 11 | 14 | 3.33 | 254.0 | 205 | 114 | 191 |
| Gordon | 12 | 6 | 3.58 | 155.2 | 125 | 77 | 143 |
| Pichardo | 7 | 8 | 4.04 | 165.0 | 183 | 53 | 70 |
| Gubicza | 5 | 8 | 4.66 | 104.1 | 128 | 43 | 80 |
| Haney | 9 | 9 | 6.02 | 124.0 | 141 | 53 | 65 |
| Gardner | 4 | 6 | 6.19 | 91.2 | 92 | 36 | 54 |

**Manager—Hal McRae**

## Milwaukee Brewers

| Batting | Avg | AB | R | H | HR | RBI |
|---|---|---|---|---|---|---|
| Hamilton | .310 | 520 | 74 | 161 | 9 | 48 |
| Surhoff | .274 | 552 | 66 | 151 | 7 | 79 |
| Thon | .269 | 245 | 23 | 66 | 1 | 33 |
| Seitzer | .269 | 417 | 45 | 112 | 11 | 57 |
| Vaughn | .267 | 569 | 97 | 152 | 30 | 97 |
| Jaha | .264 | 515 | 78 | 136 | 19 | 70 |
| Yount | .258 | 454 | 62 | 117 | 8 | 51 |
| Nilsson | .257 | 296 | 35 | 76 | 7 | 40 |
| Reimer | .249 | 437 | 53 | 109 | 13 | 60 |
| Listach | .244 | 356 | 50 | 87 | 3 | 30 |
| Spiers | .238 | 340 | 43 | 81 | 2 | 36 |
| Bell | .234 | 286 | 42 | 67 | 5 | 29 |
| Brunansky | .183 | 224 | 20 | 41 | 6 | 29 |

| Pitching | W | L | ERA | IP | H | BB | SO |
|---|---|---|---|---|---|---|---|
| Miranda | 4 | 5 | 3.30 | 120.0 | 100 | 52 | 88 |
| Eldred | 16 | 16 | 4.01 | 258.0 | 232 | 91 | 180 |
| Wegman | 4 | 14 | 4.48 | 120.2 | 135 | 34 | 50 |
| Bones | 11 | 11 | 4.86 | 203.2 | 222 | 63 | 63 |
| Navarro | 11 | 12 | 5.33 | 214.1 | 254 | 73 | 114 |

**Manager—Phil Garner**

## Minnesota Twins

| Batting | Avg | AB | R | H | HR | RBI |
|---|---|---|---|---|---|---|
| Hale | .333 | 186 | 25 | 62 | 3 | 27 |
| Harper | .304 | 530 | 52 | 161 | 12 | 73 |
| Puckett | .296 | 622 | 89 | 184 | 22 | 89 |
| Knoblauch | .277 | 602 | 82 | 167 | 2 | 41 |
| Mack | .276 | 503 | 66 | 139 | 10 | 61 |
| Winfield | .271 | 547 | 72 | 148 | 21 | 76 |
| Reboulet | .258 | 240 | 33 | 62 | 1 | 15 |
| Meares | .251 | 346 | 33 | 87 | 0 | 33 |
| Hrbek | .242 | 392 | 60 | 95 | 25 | 83 |
| Munoz | .233 | 326 | 34 | 76 | 13 | 38 |
| McCarty | .214 | 350 | 36 | 75 | 2 | 21 |

| Pitching | W | L | ERA | IP | H | BB | SO |
|---|---|---|---|---|---|---|---|
| Aquilera | 4 | 3 | 3.11 | 72.1 | 60 | 14 | 59 |
| Hartley | 1 | 2 | 4.00 | 81.0 | 86 | 36 | 57 |
| Banks | 11 | 12 | 4.04 | 171.1 | 186 | 78 | 138 |
| Deshaies | 11 | 13 | 4.41 | 167.1 | 159 | 51 | 80 |
| Tapani | 12 | 15 | 4.43 | 225.2 | 243 | 57 | 150 |
| Trombley | 6 | 6 | 4.88 | 114.1 | 131 | 41 | 85 |
| Erickson | 8 | 19 | 5.19 | 218.2 | 266 | 71 | 116 |
| Guardado | 3 | 8 | 6.18 | 94.2 | 123 | 36 | 46 |

Manager—Tom Kelly

## Seattle Mariners

| Batting | Avg | AB | R | H | HR | RBI |
|---|---|---|---|---|---|---|
| Griffey | .309 | 582 | 113 | 180 | 45 | 109 |
| Amaral | .290 | 373 | 53 | 108 | 1 | 44 |
| Blowers | .280 | 379 | 55 | 106 | 15 | 57 |
| Buhner | .272 | 563 | 91 | 153 | 27 | 98 |
| T. Martinez | .265 | 408 | 48 | 108 | 17 | 60 |
| Magadan | .259 | 228 | 27 | 59 | 1 | 21 |
| Valle | .258 | 423 | 48 | 109 | 13 | 63 |
| O'Brien | .257 | 210 | 30 | 54 | 7 | 27 |
| Vizquel | .255 | 560 | 68 | 143 | 2 | 31 |
| Boone | .251 | 271 | 31 | 68 | 12 | 38 |
| Sasser | .218 | 188 | 18 | 41 | 1 | 21 |
| Felder | .211 | 342 | 31 | 72 | 1 | 20 |

| Pitching | W | L | ERA | IP | H | BB | SO |
|---|---|---|---|---|---|---|---|
| Charlton | 1 | 3 | 2.34 | 34.2 | 22 | 17 | 48 |
| Johnson | 19 | 8 | 3.24 | 255.1 | 185 | 99 | 308 |
| Bosio | 9 | 9 | 3.45 | 164.1 | 138 | 59 | 119 |
| Hanson | 11 | 12 | 3.47 | 215.0 | 215 | 60 | 163 |
| Fleming | 12 | 5 | 4.36 | 167.1 | 189 | 67 | 75 |
| Leary | 11 | 9 | 5.05 | 169.1 | 202 | 58 | 68 |

Manager—Lou Piniella

## New York Yankees

| Batting | Avg | AB | R | H | HR | RBI |
|---|---|---|---|---|---|---|
| James | .332 | 343 | 62 | 114 | 7 | 36 |
| O'Neill | .311 | 498 | 71 | 155 | 20 | 75 |
| Leyritz | .309 | 259 | 43 | 80 | 14 | 53 |
| Stanley | .305 | 423 | 70 | 129 | 26 | 84 |
| Boggs | .302 | 560 | 83 | 169 | 2 | 59 |
| Velarde | .301 | 226 | 28 | 68 | 7 | 24 |
| Mattingly | .291 | 530 | 78 | 154 | 17 | 86 |
| Gallego | .283 | 403 | 63 | 114 | 10 | 54 |
| Kelly | .273 | 406 | 49 | 111 | 7 | 51 |
| B. Williams | .268 | 567 | 67 | 152 | 12 | 68 |
| Tartabull | .250 | 513 | 87 | 128 | 31 | 102 |
| Nokes | .249 | 217 | 25 | 54 | 10 | 35 |
| Owen | .234 | 334 | 41 | 78 | 2 | 20 |

| Pitching | W | L | ERA | IP | H | BB | SO |
|---|---|---|---|---|---|---|---|
| Key | 18 | 6 | 3.00 | 236.2 | 219 | 43 | 173 |
| Kamieniecki | 10 | 7 | 4.08 | 154.1 | 163 | 59 | 72 |
| Farr | 2 | 2 | 4.21 | 47.0 | 44 | 28 | 39 |
| Abbott | 11 | 14 | 4.37 | 214.0 | 221 | 73 | 95 |
| Wickman | 14 | 4 | 4.63 | 140.0 | 156 | 69 | 70 |
| Monteleone | 7 | 4 | 4.94 | 85.2 | 85 | 35 | 50 |
| Perez | 6 | 14 | 5.19 | 163.0 | 173 | 64 | 148 |

Manager—Buck Showalter

## Texas Rangers

| Batting | Avg | AB | R | H | HR | RBI |
|---|---|---|---|---|---|---|
| Gonzalez | .310 | 536 | 105 | 166 | 46 | 118 |
| Palmeiro | .295 | 597 | 124 | 176 | 37 | 105 |
| Hulse | .290 | 407 | 71 | 118 | 1 | 29 |
| Franco | .289 | 532 | 85 | 154 | 14 | 84 |
| Redus | .288 | 222 | 28 | 64 | 6 | 31 |
| Diaz | .273 | 205 | 24 | 56 | 2 | 24 |
| Rodriguez | .273 | 473 | 56 | 129 | 10 | 66 |
| Strange | .256 | 484 | 58 | 124 | 7 | 60 |
| Canseco | .255 | 231 | 30 | 59 | 10 | 46 |
| Palmer | .245 | 519 | 88 | 127 | 33 | 96 |
| Lee | .220 | 205 | 31 | 45 | 1 | 12 |

| Pitching | W | L | ERA | IP | H | BB | SO |
|---|---|---|---|---|---|---|---|
| Henke | 5 | 5 | 2.91 | 74.1 | 55 | 27 | 79 |
| Pavlik | 12 | 6 | 3.41 | 166.1 | 151 | 80 | 131 |
| Brown | 15 | 12 | 3.59 | 233.0 | 228 | 74 | 142 |
| Rogers | 16 | 10 | 4.10 | 208.1 | 210 | 71 | 140 |
| Leibrandt | 9 | 10 | 4.55 | 150.1 | 169 | 45 | 89 |
| Bohanon | 4 | 4 | 4.76 | 92.2 | 107 | 46 | 45 |
| Lefferts | 3 | 9 | 6.05 | 83.1 | 102 | 28 | 58 |

Manager—Kevin Kennedy

## Oakland Athletics

| Batting | Avg | AB | R | H | HR | RBI |
|---|---|---|---|---|---|---|
| Neel | .290 | 427 | 59 | 124 | 19 | 63 |
| Gates | .290 | 535 | 64 | 155 | 7 | 69 |
| Steinbach | .285 | 389 | 47 | 111 | 10 | 43 |
| Aldrete | .267 | 255 | 40 | 68 | 10 | 33 |
| Hemond | .256 | 215 | 31 | 55 | 6 | 26 |
| Browne | .250 | 260 | 27 | 65 | 2 | 19 |
| Bordick | .249 | 546 | 60 | 136 | 3 | 48 |
| Brosius | .249 | 213 | 26 | 53 | 6 | 25 |
| Sierra | .233 | 630 | 77 | 147 | 22 | 101 |
| D. Henderson | .220 | 382 | 37 | 84 | 20 | 53 |
| Paquette | .219 | 393 | 35 | 86 | 12 | 46 |
| Blankenship | .190 | 252 | 43 | 48 | 2 | 23 |

| Pitching | W | L | ERA | IP | H | BB | SO |
|---|---|---|---|---|---|---|---|
| Nunez | 3 | 6 | 3.81 | 75.2 | 89 | 29 | 58 |
| Eckersley | 2 | 4 | 4.16 | 67.0 | 67 | 13 | 80 |
| Witt | 14 | 13 | 4.21 | 220.0 | 226 | 91 | 131 |
| Van Poppel | 6 | 6 | 5.04 | 84.0 | 76 | 62 | 47 |
| Darling | 5 | 9 | 5.16 | 178.0 | 198 | 72 | 95 |
| Welch | 9 | 11 | 5.29 | 166.2 | 208 | 56 | 63 |
| Downs | 5 | 10 | 5.64 | 119.2 | 135 | 60 | 66 |

Manager—Tony LaRussa

## Toronto Blue Jays

| Batting | Avg | AB | R | H | HR | RBI |
|---|---|---|---|---|---|---|
| Olerud | .363 | 551 | 109 | 200 | 24 | 107 |
| Molitar | .332 | 636 | 121 | 211 | 22 | 111 |
| Alomar | .326 | 589 | 109 | 192 | 17 | 93 |
| Fernandez | .306 | 353 | 45 | 108 | 4 | 50 |
| Henderson | .289 | 481 | 114 | 139 | 21 | 59 |
| White | .273 | 598 | 116 | 163 | 15 | 52 |
| Sprague | .260 | 546 | 50 | 142 | 12 | 73 |
| Borders | .254 | 488 | 38 | 124 | 9 | 55 |
| Carter | .254 | 603 | 92 | 153 | 33 | 121 |
| Coles | .253 | 194 | 26 | 49 | 4 | 26 |
| Jackson | .216 | 176 | 15 | 38 | 5 | 19 |

| Pitching | W | L | ERA | IP | H | BB | SO |
|---|---|---|---|---|---|---|---|
| D. Ward | 2 | 3 | 2.13 | 71.2 | 49 | 25 | 97 |
| Cox | 7 | 6 | 3.12 | 83.2 | 73 | 29 | 84 |
| Hentgen | 19 | 9 | 3.87 | 216.1 | 215 | 74 | 122 |
| Guzman | 14 | 3 | 3.99 | 221.0 | 211 | 110 | 194 |
| Leiter | 9 | 6 | 4.11 | 105.0 | 93 | 56 | 66 |
| Stewart | 12 | 8 | 4.44 | 162.0 | 146 | 72 | 96 |
| Stottlemyre | 11 | 12 | 4.84 | 176.2 | 204 | 69 | 98 |
| Morris | 7 | 12 | 6.19 | 152.2 | 189 | 65 | 103 |

Manager—Cito Gaston

## National Baseball Hall of Fame and Museum, Cooperstown, N.Y.

| | | | | |
|---|---|---|---|---|
| Aaron, Hank | Connolly, Thomas H. | Hamilton, Bill | Lyons, Ted | Rusie, Amos |
| Alexander, Grover Cleveland | Connor, Roger | Harridge, Will | Mack, Connie | Ruth, Babe |
| Alston, Walt | Coveleski, Stan | Harris, Bucky | MacPhail, Larry | Schalk, Ray |
| Anson, Cap | Crawford, Sam | Hartnett, Gabby | Mantle, Mickey | Schoendienst, Red |
| Aparicio, Luis | Cronin, Joe | Heilmann, Harry | Manush, Henry | Seaver, Tom |
| Appling, Luke | Cummings, Candy | Herman, Billy | Maranville, Rabbit | Sewell, Joe |
| Averill, Earl | Cuyler, Kiki | Hooper, Harry | Marichal, Juan | Simmons, Al |
| Baker, Home Run | Dandridge, Ray | Hornsby, Rogers | Marquard, Rube | Sisler, George |
| Bancroft, Dave | Dean, Dizzy | Hoyt, Waite | Mathews, Eddie | Slaughter, Enos |
| Banks, Ernie | Delahanty, Ed | Hubbard, Cal | Mathewson, Christy | Snider, Duke |
| Barlick, Al | Dickey, Bill | Hubbell, Carl | Mays, Willie | Spahn, Warren |
| Barrow, Edward G. | DiHigo, Martin | Huggins, Miller | McCarthy, Joe | Spalding, Albert |
| Beckley, Jake | DiMaggio, Joe | Hunter, Catfish | McCarthy, Thomas | Speaker, Tris |
| Bell, Cool Papa | Doerr, Bobby | Irvin, Monte | McCovey, Willie | Stargell, Willie |
| Bench, Johnny | Drysdale, Don | Jackson, Reggie | McGinnity, Joe | Stengel, Casey |
| Bender, Chief | Duffy, Hugh | Jackson, Travis | McGowan, Bill | Terry, Bill |
| Berra, Yogi | Evans, Billy | Jenkins, Ferguson | McGraw, John | Thompson, Sam |
| Bottomley, Jim | Evers, John | Jennings, Hugh | McKechnie, Bill | Tinker, Joe |
| Boudreau, Lou | Ewing, Buck | Johnson, Byron | Medwick, Joe | Traynor, Pie |
| Bresnahan, Roger | Faber, Urban | Johnson, William (Judy) | Mize, Johnny | Vance, Dazzy |
| Brock, Lou | Feller, Bob | Johnson, Walter | Morgan, Joe | Vaughan, Arky |
| Brouthers, Dan | Ferrell, Rick | Joss, Addie | Musial, Stan | Veeck, Bill |
| Brown, Mordecai (Three Finger) | Fingers, Rollie | Kaline, Al | Newhouser, Hal | Waddell, Rube |
| Bulkeley, Morgan C. | Flick, Elmer H. | Keefe, Timothy | Nichols, Kid | Wagner, Honus |
| Burkett, Jesse C. | Ford, Whitey | Keeler, William | O'Rourke, James | Wallace, Roderick |
| Campanella, Roy | Foster, Andrew | Kell, George | Ott, Mel | Walsh, Ed |
| Carew, Rod | Foxx, Jimmie | Kelley, Joe | Paige, Satchel | Waner, Lloyd |
| Carey, Max | Frick, Ford | Kelly, George | Palmer, Jim | Waner, Paul |
| Cartwright, Alexander | Frisch, Frank | Kelly, King | Pennock, Herb | Ward, John |
| Chadwick, Henry | Galvin, Pud | Killebrew, Harmon | Perry, Gaylord | Weiss, George |
| Chance, Frank | Gehrig, Lou | Kiner, Ralph | Plank, Ed | Welch, Mickey |
| Chandler, Happy | Gehringer, Charles | Klein, Chuck | Radbourn, Charlie | Wheat, Zach |
| Charleston, Oscar | Gibson, Bob | Klem, Bill | Reese, Pee Wee | Wilhelm, Hoyt |
| Chesbro, John | Gibson, Josh | Koufax, Sandy | Rice, Sam | Williams, Billy |
| Clarke, Fred | Giles, Warren | Lajoie, Napoleon | Rickey, Branch | Williams, Ted |
| Clarkson, John | Gomez, Lefty | Landis, Kenesaw M. | Rixey, Eppa | Wilson, Hack |
| Clemente, Roberto | Goslin, Goose | Lazzeri, Tony | Roberts, Robin | Wright, George |
| Cobb, Ty | Greenberg, Hank | Lemon, Bob | Robinson, Brooks | Wright, Harry |
| Cochrane, Mickey | Griffith, Clark | Leonard, Buck | Robinson, Frank | Wynn, Early |
| Collins, Eddie | Grimes, Burleigh | Lindstrom, Fred | Robinson, Jackie | Yastrzemski, Carl |
| Collins, James | Grove, Lefty | Lloyd, Pop | Robinson, Wilbert | Yawkey, Tom |
| Combs, Earle | Hafey, Chick | Lombardi, Ernie | Roush, Edd | Young, Cy |
| Comiskey, Charles A. | Haines, Jesee | Lopez, Al | Ruffing, Red | Youngs, Ross |
| Conlan, Jocko | | | | |

## Hall of Famers Chosen in First Year of Eligibility

| Year | | Year | | Year | |
|---|---|---|---|---|---|
| 1962 | Jackie Robinson, Bob Feller | 1974 | Mickey Mantle | 1982 | Hank Aaron, Frank Robinson |
| 1966 | Ted Williams | 1977 | Ernie Banks | 1983 | Brooks Robinson |
| 1969 | Stan Musial | 1979 | Willie Mays | 1985 | Lou Brock |
| 1972 | Sandy Koufax | 1980 | Al Kaline | 1986 | Willie McCovey |
| 1973 | Warren Spahn | 1981 | Bob Gibson | 1988 | Willie Stargell |
| | | | | 1989 | Johnny Bench, Carl Yastrzemski |
| | | | | 1990 | Jim Palmer, Joe Morgan |
| | | | | 1992 | Tom Seaver |
| | | | | 1993 | Reggie Jackson |

## All-Star Baseball Games, 1933-1993

| Year | Winner | Score | Location | Year | Winner | Score | Location |
|---|---|---|---|---|---|---|---|
| 1933 | American | 4-2 | Chicago | 1962 | American | 9-4 | Chicago |
| 1934 | American | 9-7 | New York | 1963 | National | 5-3 | Cleveland |
| 1935 | American | 4-1 | Cleveland | 1964 | National | 7-4 | New York |
| 1936 | National | 4-3 | Boston | 1965 | National | 6-5 | Minnesota |
| 1937 | American | 8-3 | Washington | 1966 | National (3) | 2-1 | St. Louis |
| 1938 | National | 4-1 | Cincinnati | 1967 | National (4) | 2-1 | Anaheim |
| 1939 | American | 3-1 | New York | 1968* | National | 1-0 | Houston |
| 1940 | National | 4-0 | St. Louis | 1969 | National | 9-3 | Washington |
| 1941 | American | 7-5 | Detroit | 1970* | National (2) | 5-4 | Cincinnati |
| 1942 | American | 3-1 | New York | 1971* | American | 6-4 | Detroit |
| 1943* | American | 5-3 | Philadelphia | 1972* | National | 4-3 | Atlanta |
| 1944* | National | 7-1 | Pittsburgh | 1973* | National | 7-1 | Kansas City |
| 1945 | (not played) | | | 1974* | National | 7-2 | Pittsburgh |
| 1946 | American | 12-0 | Boston | 1975* | National | 6-3 | Milwaukee |
| 1947 | American | 2-1 | Chicago | 1976* | National | 7-1 | Philadelphia |
| 1948 | American | 5-2 | St. Louis | 1977* | National | 7-5 | New York |
| 1949 | American | 11-7 | New York | 1978* | National | 7-3 | San Diego |
| 1950 | National (1) | 4-3 | Chicago | 1979* | National | 7-6 | Seattle |
| 1951 | National | 8-3 | Detroit | 1980* | National | 4-2 | Los Angeles |
| 1952 | National | 3-2 | Philadelphia | 1981* | National | 5-4 | Cleveland |
| 1953 | National | 5-1 | Cincinnati | 1982* | National | 4-1 | Montreal |
| 1954 | American | 11-9 | Cleveland | 1983* | American | 13-3 | Chicago |
| 1955 | National (2) | 6-5 | Milwaukee | 1984* | National | 3-1 | San Francisco |
| 1956 | National | 7-3 | Washington | 1985* | National | 6-1 | Minneapolis |
| 1957 | American | 6-5 | St. Louis | 1986* | American | 3-2 | Houston |
| 1958 | American | 4-3 | Baltimore | 1987* | National (5) | 2-0 | Oakland |
| 1959 | National | 5-4 | Pittsburgh | 1988* | American | 2-1 | Cincinnati |
| 1959 | American | 5-3 | Los Angeles | 1989* | American | 5-3 | Anaheim |
| 1960 | National | 5-3 | Kansas City | 1990* | American | 2-0 | Chicago |
| 1960 | National | 6-0 | New York | 1991* | American | 4-2 | Toronto |
| 1961 | National (3) | 5-4 | San Francisco | 1992* | American | 13-6 | San Diego |
| 1961 | Called-rain | 1-1 | Boston | 1993* | American | 9-3 | Baltimore |
| 1962 | National (3) | 3-1 | Washington | | | | |

(1) 14 innings, (2) 12 innings, (3) 10 innings, (4) 15 innings; (5) 13 innings. * Night game.

# Major League Leaders in 1993

## American League

### Batting

Olerud, Toronto, .363; Molitor, Toronto, .332; Alomar, Toronto, .326; Lofton, Cleveland, .325; Baerga, Cleveland, .321.

### Runs

Palmeiro, Texas, 124; Molitor, Toronto, 121; Lofton, Cleveland, 116; White, Toronto, 116; Henderson, Toronto, 114.

### Runs Batted In

Belle, Cleveland, 129; Thomas, Chicago, 128; Carter, Toronto, 121; Gonzalez, Texas, 118; Fielder, Detroit, 117.

### Hits

Molitor, Toronto, 211; Baerga, Cleveland, 200; Olerud, Toronto, 200; Alomar, Toronto, 192; Lofton, Cleveland, 185.

### Doubles

Olerud, Toronto, 54; White, Toronto, 42; Valentin, Boston, 40; Palmeiro, Texas, 40; Puckett, Minnesota, 39.

### Triples

L. Johnson, Chicago, 14; Cora, Chicago, 13; Hulse, Texas, 10; McRae, Kansas City, 9; Fernandez, Toronto, 9.

### Home Runs

Gonzalez, Texas, 46; Griffey Jr, Seattle, 45; Thomas, Chicago, 41; Belle, Cleveland, 38; Palmeiro, Texas, 37.

### Stolen Bases

Lofton, Cleveland, 70; Alomar, Toronto, 55; Polonia, California, 55; Henderson, Toronto, 53; Curtis, California, 48.

### Pitching (17 Decisions)

Guzman, Toronto, 14-3, .824; Wickman, New York, 14-4, .778, 4.63; Key, New York, 18-6, .750, 3.00; Bere, Chicago, 12-5, .706, 3.47; Fleming, Seattle, 12-5, .706, 4.36.

### Strikeouts

R. Johnson, Seattle, 308; Langston, California, 196; Guzman, Toronto, 194; Cone, Kansas City, 191; Finley, California, 187.

### Saves

Montgomery, Kansas City, 45; Ward, Toronto, 45; Henke, Texas, 40; Hernandez, Chicago, 38; Eckersley, Oakland, 36.

## National League

### Batting

Galarraga, Colorado, .370; Gwynn, San Diego, .358; Jefferies, St. Louis, .342; Bonds, San Francisco, .336; Grace, Chicago, .325.

### Runs

Dykstra, Philadelphia, 143; Bonds, San Francisco, 129; Gant, Atlanta, 113; McGriff, Atlanta, 111; Blauser, Atlanta, 110.

### Runs Batted In

Bonds, San Francisco, 123; Justice, Atlanta, 120; Gant, Atlanta, 117; Piazza, Los Angeles, 112; Williams, San Francisco, 110.

### Hits

Dykstra, Philadelphia, 193; Grace, Chicago, 193; Grissom, Montreal, 188; Bell, Pittsburgh, 187; Jefferies, St. Louis, 186.

### Doubles

Hayes, Colorado, 45; Dykstra, Philadelphia, 44; Bichette, Colorado, 43; Biggio, Houston, 41; Gwynn, San Diego, 41.

### Triples

Finley, Houston, 13; Butler, Los Angeles, 10; Morandini, Philadelphia, 9; Bell, Pittsburgh, 9; Young, Colorado, 8; Martin, Pittsburgh, 8; Coleman, New York, 8.

### Home Runs

Bonds, San Francisco, 46; Justice, Atlanta, 40; Williams, San Francisco, 38; McGriff, Atlanta, 37; Gant, Atlanta, 36.

### Stolen Bases

Carr, Florida, 58; Grissom, Montreal, 53; Nixon, Atlanta, 47; Lewis, San Francisco, 46; Jefferies, St. Louis, 46.

### Pitching (17 Decisions)

Portugal, Houston, 18-4, .818, 2.77; Greene, Philadelphia, 16-4, .800, 3.42; Glavine, Atlanta, 22-6, .786, 3.20; Burkett, San Francisco, 22-7, .759, 3.65; Avery, Atlanta, 18-6, .750, 2.94.

### Strikeouts

Rijo, Cincinnati, 227; Smoltz, Atlanta, 208; Maddux, Atlanta, 197; Schilling, Philadelphia, 186; Harnisch, Houston, 185.

### Saves

Myers, Chicago, 53; Beck, San Francisco, 48; Harvey, Florida, 45; Wetteland, Montreal, 43; Williams, Philadelphia, 43; Smith, St. Louis, 43.

## Earned-Run Average Leaders

### National League

| Year | Player, club | G | IP | ERA |
|---|---|---|---|---|
| 1972 | Steve Carlton, Philadelphia . . . | 41 | 346 | 1.98 |
| 1973 | Tom Seaver, New York . . . . . | 36 | 290 | 2.07 |
| 1974 | Buzz Capra, Atlanta . . . . . . . | 39 | 217 | 2.28 |
| 1975 | Randy Jones, San Diego . . . . | 37 | 285 | 2.24 |
| 1976 | John Denny, St. Louis . . . . . . | 30 | 207 | 2.52 |
| 1977 | John Candelaria, Pittsburgh . . | 33 | 231 | 2.34 |
| 1978 | Craig Swan, New York . . . . . | 29 | 207 | 2.43 |
| 1979 | J. R. Richard, Houston . . . . . | 38 | 292 | 2.71 |
| 1980 | Don Sutton, Los Angeles . . . . | 32 | 212 | 2.21 |
| 1981 | Nolan Ryan, Houston . . . . . . | 21 | 149 | 1.69 |
| 1982 | Steve Rogers, Montreal . . . . | 35 | 277 | 2.40 |
| 1983 | Atlee Hammaker, San Fran. . . | 23 | 172 | 2.25 |
| 1984 | Alejandro Pena, Los Angeles . | 28 | 199 | 2.48 |
| 1985 | Dwight Gooden, New York . . . | 35 | 276 | 1.53 |
| 1986 | Mike Scott, Houston . . . . . . . | 37 | 275 | 2.22 |
| 1987 | Nolan Ryan, Houston . . . . . . | 34 | 211 | 2.76 |
| 1988 | Joe Magrane, St. Louis . . . . . | 24 | 165 | 2.18 |
| 1989 | Scott Garrelts, San Francisco . | 30 | 193 | 2.28 |
| 1990 | Danny Darwin, Houston. . . . . | 48 | 162 | 2.21 |
| 1991 | Dennis Martinez, Montreal . . . | 31 | 222 | 2.39 |
| 1992 | Bill Swift, San Francisco . . . . | 30 | 164 | 2.08 |
| 1993 | Greg Maddux, Atlanta . . . . . . | 36 | 267 | 2.36 |

### American League

| Year | Player, club | G | IP | ERA |
|---|---|---|---|---|
| 1972 | Luis Tiant, Boston. . . . . . . | 43 | 179 | 1.91 |
| 1973 | Jim Palmer, Baltimore . . . . . . | 38 | 296 | 2.40 |
| 1974 | Catfish Hunter, Oakland . . . . | 41 | 318 | 2.49 |
| 1975 | Jim Palmer, Baltimore . . . . . . | 39 | 323 | 2.09 |
| 1976 | Mark Fidrych, Detroit. . . . . . . | 31 | 250 | 2.34 |
| 1977 | Frank Tanana, California. . . . | 31 | 241 | 2.54 |
| 1978 | Ron Guidry, New York . . . . . | 35 | 274 | 1.74 |
| 1979 | Ron Guidry, New York . . . . . | 33 | 236 | 2.78 |
| 1980 | Rudy May, New York. . . . . . | 41 | 175 | 2.47 |
| 1981 | Steve McCatty, Oakland. . . . . | 22 | 186 | 2.32 |
| 1982 | Rick Sutcliffe, Cleveland . . . . | 34 | 216 | 2.96 |
| 1983 | Rick Honeycutt, Texas . . . . . | 25 | 174 | 2.42 |
| 1984 | Mike Boddicker, Baltimore . . . . | 34 | 261 | 2.79 |
| 1985 | Dave Stieb, Toronto . . . . . . | 36 | 265 | 2.48 |
| 1986 | Roger Clemens, Boston . . . . . | 33 | 254 | 2.48 |
| 1987 | Jimmy Key, Toronto . . . . . . | 36 | 261 | 2.76 |
| 1988 | Allan Anderson, Minnesota . . . | 30 | 202 | 2.45 |
| 1989 | Bret Saberhagen, Kansas City . | 36 | 262 | 2.16 |
| 1990 | Roger Clemens, Boston . . . . . | 31 | 228 | 1.93 |
| 1991 | Roger Clemens, Boston . . . . . | 35 | 271 | 2.62 |
| 1992 | Roger Clemens, Boston . . . . . | 32 | 246 | 2.41 |
| 1993 | Kevin Appier, Kansas City . . . . | 34 | 238 | 2.56 |

ERA is computed by multiplying earned runs allowed by 9, then dividing by innings pitched.

## Nolan Ryan's No-Hit Games

**May 15, 1973:** California (AL), at Kansas City, 3-0.
**July 15, 1973:** California (AL), at Detroit, 6-0.
**Sept. 28, 1974:** California (AL), vs. Minnesota, 4-0.
**June 1, 1975:** California (AL), vs. Baltimore, 1-0.

**Sept. 26, 1981:** Houston (NL), vs. Los Angeles, 5-0.
**June 11, 1990:** Texas (AL), at Oakland, 5-0.
**May 1, 1991:** Texas (AL), vs. Toronto, 3-0.

## All-Time Major League Leaders
(Includes 1993 season)

| Games | | At Bats | | Runs Batted In | | Stolen Bases (since 1898) | |
|---|---|---|---|---|---|---|---|
| Pete Rose | 3562 | Pete Rose | 14,043 | Hank Aaron | 2297 | Rickey Henderson | 1095 |
| Carl Yastrzemski | 3308 | Hank Aaron | 12,364 | Babe Ruth | 2204 | Lou Brock | 938 |
| Hank Aaron | 3298 | Carl Yastrzemski | 11,988 | Lou Gehrig | 1990 | Ty Cobb | 892 |
| Ty Cobb | 3033 | Ty Cobb | 11,429 | Ty Cobb | 1961 | Tim Raines | 751 |
| Stan Musial | 3026 | Robin Yount | 11,008 | Stan Musial | 1951 | Eddie Collins | 742 |
| Willie Mays | 2992 | Stan Musial | 10,972 | Jimmie Foxx | 1922 | Max Carey | 738 |
| Rusty Staub | 2951 | Willie Mays | 10,881 | Willie Mays | 1903 | Honus Wagner | 703 |
| Brooks Robinson | 2896 | Brooks Robinson | 10,654 | Mel Ott | 1860 | Joe Morgan | 689 |
| Robin Yount | 2856 | Dave Winfield | 10,594 | Carl Yastrzemski | 1844 | Willie Wilson | 667 |
| Dave Winfield | 2850 | Honus Wagner | 10,427 | Ted Williams | 1839 | Bert Campaneris | 649 |
| **Runs** | | **Hits** | | **Strikeouts** | | **Shutouts** | |
| Ty Cobb | 2245 | Pete Rose | 4256 | Nolan Ryan | 5714 | Walter Johnson | 110 |
| Hank Aaron | 2174 | Ty Cobb | 4191 | Steve Carlton | 4136 | Grover C. Alexander | 90 |
| Babe Ruth | 2174 | Hank Aaron | 3771 | Bert Blyleven | 3701 | Christy Mathewson | 83 |
| Pete Rose | 2165 | Stan Musial | 3630 | Tom Seaver | 3640 | Cy Young | 77 |
| Willie Mays | 2062 | Tris Speaker | 3515 | Don Sutton | 3574 | Eddie Plank | 69 |
| Stan Musial | 1949 | Honus Wagner | 3430 | Gaylord Perry | 3534 | Warren Spahn | 63 |
| Lou Gehrig | 1888 | Carl Yastrzemski | 3419 | Walter Johnson | 3508 | Mordecai Brown | 63 |
| Tris Speaker | 1881 | Eddie Collins | 3309 | Phil Niekro | 3340 | Tom Seaver | 61 |
| Mel Ott | 1859 | Willie Mays | 3283 | Ferguson Jenkins | 3192 | Nolan Ryan | 61 |
| Frank Robinson | 1829 | Nap Lajoie | 3252 | Bob Gibson | 3117 | Bert Blyleven | 60 |

## All-Time Home Run Leaders

| Player | HR | Player | HR | Player | HR | Player | HR |
|---|---|---|---|---|---|---|---|
| Hank Aaron | 755 | Ted Williams | 521 | Carl Yastrzemski | 452 | Graig Nettles | 390 |
| Babe Ruth | 714 | Willie McCovey | 521 | Dave Kingman | 442 | Johnny Bench | 389 |
| Willie Mays | 660 | Ed Mathews | 512 | Eddie Murray | 441 | Dwight Evans | 385 |
| Frank Robinson | 586 | Ernie Banks | 512 | Billy Williams | 426 | Frank Howard | 382 |
| Harmon Killebrew | 573 | Mel Ott | 511 | Darrell Evans | 414 | Jim Rice | 382 |
| Reggie Jackson | 563 | Lou Gehrig | 493 | Andre Dawson | 412 | Orlando Cepeda | 379 |
| Mike Schmidt | 548 | Stan Musial | 475 | Duke Snider | 407 | Tony Perez | 379 |
| Mickey Mantle | 536 | Willie Stargell | 475 | Al Kaline | 399 | | |
| Jimmy Foxx | 534 | Dave Winfield | 453 | Dale Murphy | 398 | | |

## Players With 3,000 Major League Hits

In 1993, Dave Winfield of the Minnesota Twins became the 19th player to record 3,000 major league hits.

| Player | Hits | Player | Hits | Player | Hits |
|---|---|---|---|---|---|
| Pete Rose | 4,256 | Eddie Collins | 3,309 | Rod Carew | 3,053 |
| Ty Cobb | 4,191 | Willie Mays | 3,283 | Lou Brock | 3,023 |
| Hank Aaron | 3,771 | Nap Lajoie | 3,252 | Dave Winfield | 3,014 |
| Stan Musial | 3,630 | George Brett | 3,154 | Al Kaline | 3,007 |
| Tris Speaker | 3,515 | Paul Waner | 3,152 | Roberto Clemente | 3,000 |
| Honus Wagner | 3,430 | Robin Yount | 3,142 | | |
| Carl Yastrzemski | 3,419 | Cap Anson | 3,081 | | |

## Baseball Stadiums

### National League

| Team | Stadium (built) | Surface | Home run distances (ft.) | | | Seating capacity |
|---|---|---|---|---|---|---|
| | | | LF | Center | RF | |
| Atlanta Braves | Atlanta-Fulton County Stadium (1965) | Grass | 330 | 402 | 330 | 52,003 |
| Chicago Cubs | Wrigley Field (1914) | Grass | 355 | 400 | 353 | 38,710 |
| Cincinnati Reds | Riverfront Stadium (1970) | Artificial | 330 | 404 | 330 | 52,952 |
| Colorado Rockies | Mile High Stadium (1948) | Artificial | 335 | 423 | 370 | 76,100 |
| Florida Marlins | Joe Robbie Stadium (1987) | Grass | 335 | 410 | 345 | 48,000 |
| Houston Astros | Astrodome (1965) | Artificial | 325 | 400 | 325 | 54,816 |
| Los Angeles Dodgers | Dodger Stadium (1962) | Grass | 330 | 395 | 330 | 56,000 |
| Montreal Expos | Olympic Stadium (1976) | Artificial | 325 | 404 | 325 | 43,739 |
| New York Mets | Shea Stadium (1964) | Grass | 338 | 410 | 338 | 55,601 |
| Philadelphia Phillies | Veterans Stadium (1971) | Artificial | 330 | 408 | 330 | 62,382 |
| Pittsburgh Pirates | Three Rivers Stadium (1970) | Artificial | 335 | 400 | 335 | 58,727 |
| St. Louis Cardinals | Busch Stadium (1966) | Artificial | 330 | 402 | 330 | 56,227 |
| San Diego Padres | Jack Murphy Stadium (1967) | Grass | 327 | 405 | 327 | 59,022 |
| San Francisco Giants | Candlestick Park (1960) | Grass | 335 | 400 | 330 | 62,000 |

### American League

| Team | Stadium (built) | Surface | Home run distances (ft.) | | | Seating capacity |
|---|---|---|---|---|---|---|
| | | | LF | Center | RF | |
| Baltimore Orioles | Camden Yards (1992) | Grass | 333 | 400 | 318 | 48,041 |
| Boston Red Sox | Fenway Park (1912) | Grass | 315 | 390 | 302 | 34,142 |
| California Angels | Anaheim Stadium (1966) | Grass | 333 | 404 | 333 | 64,593 |
| Chicago White Sox | Comiskey Park (1991) | Grass | 347 | 400 | 347 | 44,702 |
| Cleveland Indians | Cleveland Stadium (1931) | Grass | 320 | 404 | 320 | 74,483 |
| Detroit Tigers | Tiger Stadium (1912) | Grass | 340 | 440 | 325 | 52,416 |
| Kansas City Royals | Kauffman Stadium (1973) | Artificial | 330 | 410 | 330 | 40,625 |
| Milwaukee Brewers | Milwaukee County Stadium (1953) | Grass | 315 | 402* | 315 | 53,192 |
| Minnesota Twins | Hubert H. Humphrey Metrodome (1982) | Artificial | 343 | 408 | 327 | 55,883 |
| New York Yankees | Yankee Stadium (1923) | Grass | 318 | 408 | 314 | 57,545 |
| Oakland A's | Oakland Alameda County Coliseum (1968) | Grass | 330 | 400 | 330 | 47,313 |
| Seattle Mariners | Kingdome (1976) | Artificial | 331 | 405 | 312 | 59,702 |
| Texas Rangers | Arlington Stadium (1972) | Grass | 330 | 400 | 330 | 43,521 |
| Toronto Blue Jays | Sky-Dome (1989) | Artificial | 328 | 400 | 328 | 50,516 |

# 1993 World Series

Joe Carter hit a three-run home run in the bottom of the ninth of game 6, Oct. 23, to give the Toronto Blue Jays a come-from-behind 8-6 victory over the Philadelphia Phillies and their second consecutive World Series triumph, 4 games to 2. It was the first time in 15 years that a team had won back-to-back championships. The Blue Jays' designated hitter, Paul Molitor, who had 2 doubles, 2 triples, 2 homers, and 8 RBIs in the 6 games, was named the Series' most valuable player.

## First Game

| Philadelphia | ab | r | h | bi | Toronto | ab | r | h | bi |
|---|---|---|---|---|---|---|---|---|---|
| Dykstra, cf | 4 | 1 | 1 | 0 | Henderson, lf | 3 | 1 | 1 | 0 |
| Duncan, 2b | 5 | 2 | 3 | 0 | White, cf | 4 | 3 | 2 | 2 |
| Kruk, 1b | 4 | 2 | 3 | 2 | Alomar, 2b | 4 | 0 | 1 | 2 |
| Hollins, 3b | 4 | 0 | 0 | 0 | Carter, rf | 3 | 1 | 1 | 1 |
| Daulton, c | 4 | 0 | 1 | 1 | Olerud, 1b | 3 | 2 | 2 | 1 |
| Eisenreich, rf | 5 | 0 | 1 | 1 | Molitor, dh | 4 | 0 | 1 | 1 |
| Jordan, dh | 5 | 0 | 1 | 0 | Fernandez, ss | 3 | 0 | 0 | 1 |
| Thompson, lf | 3 | 0 | 0 | 0 | Sprague, 3b | 4 | 0 | 1 | 0 |
| Incaviglia, ph-lf | 1 | 0 | 0 | 0 | Borders, c | 4 | 1 | 1 | 0 |
| Stocker, ss | 3 | 0 | 1 | 0 | Totals | 32 | 8 | 10 | 8 |
| Totals | 38 | 5 | 11 | 4 | | | | | |

| | | | | | | | | | | |
|---|---|---|---|---|---|---|---|---|---|---|
| Philadelphia | 2 | 0 | 1 | 0 | 1 | 0 | 0 | 0 | 1—5 |
| Toronto | 0 | 2 | 1 | 0 | 1 | 1 | 3 | 0 | x—8 |

| | ip | h | r | er | bb | so |
|---|---|---|---|---|---|---|
| Philadelphia | | | | | | |
| Schilling L, 0-1 | 6⅓ | 8 | 7 | 6 | 2 | 3 |
| West | 0 | 2 | 1 | 1 | 0 | 0 |
| Andersen | ⅔ | 0 | 0 | 0 | 1 | 1 |
| Mason | 1 | 0 | 0 | 0 | 0 | 1 |
| Toronto | | | | | | |
| Guzman | 5 | 5 | 4 | 4 | 4 | 6 |
| Leiter W, 1-0 | 2⅔ | 4 | 0 | 0 | 1 | 2 |
| Ward S, 1 | 1⅓ | 2 | 1 | 0 | 0 | 3 |

E - Thompson (1), Alomar (1), Carter (1), Sprague (1). LOB - Philadelphia 11, Toronto 4. 2B - White (1), Alomar (1). 3B - Duncan (1). HR - White (1), Olerud (1). RBI - Kruk 2 (2), Daulton (1), Eisenreich (1), White 2 (2), Alomar 2 (2), Carter (1), Olerud (1), Molitor (1), Fernandez (1). SB - Dykstra (1), Duncan (1), Alomar (1). SF - Carter.

**How runs were scored**—Two in Phillies first: Dykstra walked and stole second. Kruk singled scoring Dykstra. Hollins walked. Daulton singled scoring Kruk.

Two in Blue Jays second: Carter and Olerud singled. Molitor singled scoring Carter. Fernandez grounded out scoring Olerud.

One in Phillies third: Duncan singled and stole second. Kruk singled scoring Duncan.

One in Blue Jays third: White reached third on an error. Carter hit a sacrifice fly scoring White.

One in Phillies fifth: Duncan tripled and scored on a wild pitch.

One in Blue Jays fifth: White hit a home run.

One in Blue Jays sixth: Olerud hit a home run.

Three in Blue Jays seventh: Borders and Henderson singled. White doubled scoring Borders. Alomar doubled scoring Henderson and White.

One in Phillies ninth: Kruk singled and went to second on an error. Eisenreich singled scoring Kruk.

## Second Game

| Philadelphia | ab | r | h | bi | Toronto | ab | r | h | bi |
|---|---|---|---|---|---|---|---|---|---|
| Dykstra, cf | 4 | 2 | 2 | 1 | Henderson, lf | 3 | 0 | 0 | 0 |
| Duncan, 2b | 4 | 1 | 1 | 0 | White, cf | 4 | 0 | 1 | 0 |
| Kruk, 1b | 5 | 1 | 2 | 1 | Molitor, dh | 3 | 2 | 2 | 0 |
| Hollins, 3b | 4 | 1 | 2 | 1 | Carter, rf | 4 | 1 | 1 | 2 |
| Batiste, 3b | 0 | 0 | 0 | 0 | Olerud, 1b | 3 | 0 | 0 | 1 |
| Daulton, c | 5 | 0 | 1 | 0 | Alomar, 2b | 3 | 1 | 1 | 0 |
| Eisenreich, rf | 4 | 1 | 1 | 3 | Fernandez, ss | 3 | 0 | 2 | 1 |
| Incaviglia, lf | 4 | 0 | 1 | 0 | Sprague, 3b | 3 | 0 | 1 | 0 |
| Thompson, pr-lf | 0 | 0 | 0 | 0 | Griffin, pr | 0 | 0 | 0 | 0 |
| Jordan, dh | 4 | 0 | 1 | 0 | Borders, c | 4 | 0 | 1 | 0 |
| Stocker, ss | 3 | 0 | 1 | 0 | Totals | 31 | 4 | 8 | 4 |
| Totals | 37 | 6 | 12 | 6 | | | | | |

| | | | | | | | | | | |
|---|---|---|---|---|---|---|---|---|---|---|
| Philadelphia | 0 | 0 | 5 | 0 | 0 | 0 | 1 | 0 | 0—6 |
| Toronto | 0 | 0 | 0 | 2 | 0 | 1 | 0 | 1 | 0—4 |

| | ip | h | r | er | bb | so |
|---|---|---|---|---|---|---|
| Philadelphia | | | | | | |
| Mulholland W, 1-0 | 5⅔ | 7 | 3 | 3 | 2 | 4 |
| Mason H, 1 | 1⅔ | 1 | 1 | 1 | 0 | 2 |
| Williams S, 1 | 1⅔ | 0 | 0 | 0 | 2 | 0 |
| Toronto | | | | | | |
| Stewart L, 0-1 | 6 | 6 | 5 | 5 | 4 | 6 |

| Castillo | 1 | 3 | 1 | 1 | 0 | 0 |
|---|---|---|---|---|---|---|
| Eichhorn | ⅓ | 1 | 0 | 0 | 1 | 0 |
| Timlin | 1⅔ | 2 | 0 | 0 | 0 | 2 |

LOB - Philadelphia 9, Toronto 5. 2B - White (2), Molitor (1), Fernandez (1), Dykstra (1), Eisenreich (1). RBI - Dykstra (1), Kruk (3), Hollins (1), Eisenreich 3 (4), Carter 2 (3), Olerud (2), Fernandez (2). SB - Molitor (1), Alomar (2). SF - Olerud.

**How runs were scored**—Five in Phillies third: Dykstra and Duncan walked. Kruk singled scoring Dykstra. Hollins singled scoring Duncan. Eisenreich hit a home run scoring Kruk and Hollins.

Two in Blue Jays fourth: Molitor singled. Carter hit a home run scoring Molitor.

One in Blue Jays sixth: Alomar singled. Fernandez doubled scoring Alomar.

One in Phillies seventh: Dykstra hit a home run.

One in Blue Jays eighth: Molitor doubled and stole third. Olerud hit a sacrifice fly scoring Molitor.

## Third Game

| Toronto | ab | r | h | bi | Philadelphia | ab | r | h | bi |
|---|---|---|---|---|---|---|---|---|---|
| Henderson, lf | 4 | 2 | 2 | 0 | Dykstra, cf | 5 | 0 | 1 | 0 |
| White, cf | 4 | 2 | 1 | 1 | Duncan, 2b | 5 | 0 | 2 | 1 |
| Molitor, 1b | 4 | 3 | 3 | 3 | Kruk, 1b | 3 | 1 | 2 | 0 |
| Carter, rf | 4 | 1 | 1 | 1 | Hollins, 3b | 3 | 0 | 0 | 0 |
| Alomar, 2b | 5 | 2 | 4 | 2 | Daulton, c | 3 | 0 | 0 | 0 |
| Fernandez, ss | 3 | 0 | 2 | 2 | Eisenreich, rf | 4 | 0 | 1 | 1 |
| Sprague, 3b | 4 | 0 | 0 | 1 | Incaviglia, lf | 3 | 0 | 0 | 0 |
| Borders, c | 4 | 0 | 0 | 0 | Thigpen, p | 0 | 0 | 0 | 0 |
| Hentgen, p | 3 | 0 | 0 | 0 | Morandini, ph | 0 | 0 | 0 | 0 |
| Cox, p | 1 | 0 | 0 | 0 | Andersen, p | 0 | 0 | 0 | 0 |
| Ward, p | 0 | 0 | 0 | 0 | Stocker, ss | 4 | 0 | 1 | 0 |
| Totals | 36 | 10 | 13 | 10 | Jackson, p | 1 | 0 | 0 | 0 |
| | | | | | Chamberlain, ph | 1 | 0 | 0 | 0 |
| | | | | | Rivera, p | 0 | 0 | 0 | 0 |
| | | | | | Thompson, lf | 2 | 2 | 2 | 1 |
| | | | | | Totals | 34 | 3 | 9 | 3 |

| | | | | | | | | | | |
|---|---|---|---|---|---|---|---|---|---|---|
| Toronto | 3 | 0 | 1 | 0 | 0 | 1 | 3 | 0 | 2—10 |
| Philadelphia | 0 | 0 | 0 | 0 | 1 | 1 | 0 | 1— 3 |

| | ip | h | r | er | bb | so |
|---|---|---|---|---|---|---|
| Toronto | | | | | | |
| Hentgen W, 1-0 | 6 | 5 | 1 | 1 | 3 | 6 |
| Cox | 2 | 3 | 1 | 1 | 2 | 2 |
| Ward | 1 | 1 | 1 | 1 | 0 | 2 |
| Philadelphia | | | | | | |
| Jackson L, 0-1 | 5 | 6 | 4 | 4 | 1 | 4 |
| Rivera | 1⅓ | 4 | 4 | 4 | 2 | 3 |
| Thigpen | 1⅔ | 0 | 0 | 0 | 1 | 0 |
| Andersen | 1 | 3 | 2 | 2 | 0 | 0 |

E - Carter (2). LOB - Toronto 7, Philadelphia 9. 2B - Henderson (1), Kruk (1). 3B - White (1), Molitor (1). HR - Thompson (1), Molitor (1). RBI - White (3), Molitor 3 (4), Carter (4), Alomar 2 (4), Fernandez 2 (4), Sprague (1), Duncan (1), Eisenreich (5), Thompson (1). SB - Alomar 2 (4). SF - Carter, Fernandez, Sprague.

**How runs were scored**—Three in Blue Jays first: Henderson singled. White walked. Molitor tripled scoring Henderson and White. Carter hit a sacrifice fly scoring Molitor.

One in Blue Jays third: Molitor hit a home run.

One in Blue Jays sixth: Alomar singled and stole second and third. Fernandez hit a sacrifice fly scoring Alomar.

One in Phillies sixth: Kruk and Daulton walked. Eisenreich singled scoring Kruk.

Three in Blue Jays seventh: Henderson doubled. White tripled scoring Henderson. Molitor walked. Alomar singled scoring White and moving Molitor to third. Sprague hit a sacrifice fly scoring Molitor.

One in Phillies seventh: Thompson and Dykstra singled. Duncan singled scoring Thompson.

Two in Blue Jays ninth: Molitor singled. Carter hit into a force play. Alomar tripled scoring Carter. Fernandez singled scoring Alomar.

One in Phillies ninth: Thompson hit a home run.

## Fourth Game

| Toronto | ab | r | h | bi | Philadelphia | ab | r | h | bi |
|---|---|---|---|---|---|---|---|---|---|
| Henderson, lf | 5 | 2 | 2 | 2 | Dykstra, cf | 5 | 4 | 3 | 4 |
| White, cf | 5 | 2 | 3 | 2 | Duncan, 2b | 6 | 1 | 3 | 1 |
| Alomar, 2b | 6 | 1 | 2 | 1 | Kruk, 1b | 5 | 0 | 0 | 0 |
| Carter, rf | 6 | 2 | 3 | 0 | Hollins, 3b | 4 | 3 | 2 | 0 |
| Olerud, 1b | 4 | 2 | 1 | 0 | Daulton, c | 3 | 2 | 1 | 2 |
| Molitor, 3b | 4 | 2 | 2 | 2 | Eisenreich, rf | 4 | 2 | 1 | 1 |
| Griffin, 3b | 0 | 0 | 0 | 0 | Thompson, lf | 5 | 1 | 3 | 5 |
| Fernandez, ss | 6 | 2 | 3 | 5 | Stocker, ss | 4 | 0 | 0 | 0 |
| Borders, c | 4 | 1 | 1 | 1 | Greene, p | 1 | 1 | 1 | 0 |
| Stottlemyre, p | 0 | 0 | 0 | 0 | Mason, p | 1 | 0 | 0 | 0 |
| Butler, ph | 1 | 1 | 0 | 0 | Jordan, ph | 1 | 0 | 0 | 0 |
| Leiter, p | 1 | 0 | 1 | 0 | West, p | 0 | 0 | 0 | 0 |
| Castillo, p | 0 | 0 | 0 | 0 | Chamberlain, ph | 1 | 0 | 0 | 0 |
| Sprague, ph | 1 | 0 | 0 | 0 | Andersen, p | 0 | 0 | 0 | 0 |
| Timlin, p | 0 | 0 | 0 | 0 | Williams, p | 0 | 0 | 0 | 0 |
| Ward, p | 0 | 0 | 0 | 0 | Morandini, ph | 1 | 0 | 0 | 0 |
| Totals | 44 | 15 | 18 | 15 | Thigpen, p | 0 | 0 | 0 | 0 |
|  |  |  |  |  | Totals | 41 | 14 | 14 | 14 |

```
Toronto ..........  3 0 4 0 0 2 0 6 0—15
Philadelphia ......  4 2 0 1 5 1 1 0—14
```

| Toronto | ip | h | r | er | bb | so |
|---|---|---|---|---|---|---|
| Stottlemyre | 2 | 3 | 6 | 6 | 4 | 1 |
| Leiter | 2⅔ | 8 | 6 | 6 | 0 | 1 |
| Castillo W, 1-0 | 2⅓ | 3 | 2 | 2 | 3 | 1 |
| Timlin | ⅔ | 0 | 0 | 0 | 0 | 0 |
| Ward S, 2 | 1⅓ | 0 | 0 | 0 | 0 | 0 |
| **Philadelphia** | | | | | | |
| Greene | 2⅓ | 7 | 7 | 7 | 4 | 1 |
| Mason | 2⅔ | 2 | 0 | 0 | 1 | 2 |
| West | 1 | 3 | 2 | 2 | 0 | 0 |
| Andersen | 1⅓ | 2 | 3 | 3 | 1 | 2 |
| Williams L, 0-1 | ⅔ | 3 | 3 | 3 | 1 | 1 |
| Thigpen | 1 | 1 | 0 | 0 | 0 | 0 |

LOB - Toronto 10, Philadelphia 8. 2B - Henderson (2), White (3), Molitor (2), Carter (1), Leiter (1), Dykstra (1), Hollins (1), Thompson (1). 3B - White (2), Thompson (1). HR - Dykstra 2 (3), Daulton (1). RBI - Henderson 2 (2), White 4 (7), Alomar (5), Molitor 2 (6), Fernandez 5 (9), Borders (1), Dykstra 4 (5), Duncan (2), Daulton 3 (4), Eisenreich (6), Thompson 5 (6). SB - Henderson (1), White (1), Dykstra (3), Duncan (2).

**How runs were scored**—Three in Blue Jays first: Henderson doubled. White walked. Carter singled. Molitor walked scoring Henderson. Fernandez singled scoring White and Carter.

Four in Phillies first: Dykstra walked and stole second. Hollins and Daulton walked. Eisenreich walked scoring Dykstra. Thompson tripled scoring Hollins, Daulton and Eisenreich.

Two in Phillies second: Greene singled. Dykstra hit a home run scoring Greene.

Four in Blue Jays third: Olerud walked. Molitor singled. Fernandez singled scoring Olerud. Borders singled scoring Molitor. Butler reached on a fielder's choice. Henderson walked. White singled scoring Fernandez and Butler.

One in Phillies fourth: Dykstra doubled. Duncan singled scoring Dykstra.

Five in Phillies fifth: Hollins singled. Daulton hit a home run scoring Hollins. Eisenreich singled. Thompson doubled scoring Eisenreich. Dykstra hit a home run scoring Thompson.

Two in Blue Jays sixth: White doubled. Alomar singled scoring White. Olerud singled. Molitor hit by pitch. Fernandez bounced out scoring Alomar.

One in Phillies sixth: Hollins doubled. Thompson singled scoring Hollins.

One in Phillies seventh: Duncan singled. Kruk and Hollins walked. Daulton hit by pitch scoring Duncan.

Six in Blue Jays eighth: Carter singled. Olerud walked. Fernandez singled scoring Carter. Borders walked. Henderson singled scoring Molitor and Fernandez. White tripled scoring Borders and Henderson.

**World Series Records**—The 29 runs scored in game 4 represented the highest total ever in a World Series game, breaking a 57-year-old record set in game 2 of the 1936 "Subway" Series. In that game, the New York Yankees decisively defeated the Giants, at that time also of New York, by a score of 18-4. Game 4 was also the longest World Series game ever, lasting 4 hours and 14 minutes.

## Fifth Game

| Toronto | ab | r | h | bi | Philadelphia | ab | r | h | bi |
|---|---|---|---|---|---|---|---|---|---|
| Henderson, lf | 3 | 0 | 0 | 0 | Dykstra, cf | 2 | 1 | 0 | 0 |
| White, cf | 3 | 0 | 0 | 0 | Duncan, 2b | 4 | 0 | 0 | 0 |
| Alomar, 2b | 3 | 0 | 1 | 0 | Kruk, 1b | 3 | 0 | 1 | 1 |
| Carter, rf | 4 | 0 | 0 | 0 | Hollins, 3b | 3 | 0 | 1 | 0 |
| Olerud, 1b | 4 | 0 | 1 | 0 | Batiste, 3b | 0 | 0 | 0 | 0 |
| Molitor, 3b | 4 | 0 | 1 | 0 | Daulton, c | 4 | 1 | 1 | 0 |
| Fernandez, ss | 3 | 0 | 0 | 0 | Eisenreich, rf | 4 | 0 | 0 | 0 |
| Borders, c | 3 | 0 | 2 | 0 | Thompson, lf | 3 | 0 | 0 | 0 |
| Canate, pr | 0 | 0 | 0 | 0 | Stocker, ss | 2 | 0 | 1 | 1 |
| Knorr, c | 0 | 0 | 0 | 0 | Schilling, p | 2 | 0 | 1 | 0 |
| Guzman, p | 2 | 0 | 0 | 0 | Totals | 27 | 2 | 5 | 2 |
| Butler, ph | 1 | 0 | 1 | 0 |  |  |  |  |  |
| Cox, p | 0 | 0 | 0 | 0 |  |  |  |  |  |
| Totals | 30 | 0 | 5 | 0 |  |  |  |  |  |

```
Toronto ...........  0 0 0 0 0 0 0 0 0—0
Philadelphia ......  1 1 0 0 0 0 0 0 x—2
```

|  | ip | h | r | er | bb | so |
|---|---|---|---|---|---|---|
| **Toronto** | | | | | | |
| Guzman L, 0-1 | 7 | 5 | 2 | 1 | 4 | 6 |
| Cox | 1 | 0 | 0 | 0 | 2 | 3 |
| **Philadelphia** | | | | | | |
| Schilling W, 1-1 | 9 | 5 | 0 | 0 | 3 | 6 |

E - Borders (1), Duncan (1). LOB - Toronto 6, Philadelphia 8. 2B - Daulton (1), Stocker (1), Dykstra (3). RBI - Kruk (4), Stocker (1). SB - Dykstra (3). CS - Alomar (2). S - Schilling.

**How runs were scored**—One in Phillies first: Dykstra walked. Dykstra stole second and advanced to third on catcher Borders' throwing error. Kruk grounded out scoring Dykstra.

One in Phillies second: Daulton doubled. Eisenreich grounded out moving Daulton to third. Stocker doubled scoring Daulton.

## Sixth Game

| Philadelphia | ab | r | h | bi | Toronto | ab | r | h | bi |
|---|---|---|---|---|---|---|---|---|---|
| Dykstra, cf | 3 | 1 | 1 | 3 | Henderson, lf | 4 | 1 | 0 | 0 |
| Duncan, dh | 5 | 1 | 1 | 0 | White, cf | 4 | 1 | 0 | 0 |
| Kruk, 1b | 3 | 0 | 0 | 0 | Molitor, dh | 5 | 3 | 3 | 2 |
| Hollins, 3b | 5 | 1 | 1 | 1 | Carter, rf | 4 | 1 | 1 | 4 |
| Batiste, 3b | 0 | 0 | 0 | 0 | Olerud, 1b | 3 | 1 | 1 | 0 |
| Daulton, c | 4 | 1 | 1 | 0 | Griffin, pr-3b | 0 | 0 | 0 | 0 |
| Eisenreich, rf | 5 | 0 | 2 | 1 | Alomar, 2b | 4 | 1 | 3 | 1 |
| Thompson, lf | 3 | 0 | 0 | 0 | Fernandez, ss | 3 | 0 | 0 | 0 |
| Incaviglia, ph-lf | 0 | 0 | 0 | 0 | Sprague, 3b-1b | 3 | 0 | 0 | 1 |
| Stocker, ss | 3 | 1 | 0 | 0 | Borders, c | 4 | 0 | 2 | 0 |
| Morandini, 2b | 4 | 1 | 1 | 0 | Totals | 33 | 8 | 10 | 8 |
| Totals | 35 | 6 | 7 | 6 |  |  |  |  |  |

```
Philadelphia ......  0 0 0 1 0 0 5 0 0—6
Toronto ...........  3 0 0 1 1 0 0 0 3—8
```

|  | ip | h | r | er | bb | so |
|---|---|---|---|---|---|---|
| **Philadelphia** | | | | | | |
| Mulholland | 5 | 7 | 5 | 5 | 1 | 1 |
| Mason | 2⅓ | 1 | 0 | 0 | 0 | 2 |
| West | 0 | 1 | 0 | 0 | 1 | 0 |
| Andersen | ⅔ | 0 | 0 | 0 | 1 | 0 |
| Williams L, 0-2 | ⅓ | 2 | 3 | 3 | 1 | 0 |
| **Toronto** | | | | | | |
| Stewart | 6 | 4 | 4 | 4 | 4 | 2 |
| Cox | ⅓ | 3 | 2 | 2 | 1 | 1 |
| Leiter | 1⅔ | 0 | 0 | 0 | 1 | 2 |
| Ward W, 1-0 | 1 | 0 | 0 | 0 | 0 | 0 |

E - Alomar (2), Sprague (2). LOB - Philadelphia 9, Toronto 7. 2B - Daulton (2), Olerud (1), Alomar (2). 3B - Molitor (2). HR - Molitor (2), Carter (2), Dykstra (4). RBI - Dykstra 3 (8), Hollins (2), Eisenreich (7), Incaviglia (1), Molitor 2 (8), Carter 4 (8), Alomar (6), Sprague (2). SB - Dykstra (4), Duncan (3). SF - Incaviglia, Carter, Sprague.

**How runs were scored**—Three in Blue Jays first: White walked. Molitor tripled scoring White. Carter hit a sacrifice fly scoring Molitor. Olerud doubled. Alomar singled scoring Olerud.

One in Phillies fourth: Daulton doubled. Eisenreich singled scoring Daulton.

One in Blue Jays fourth: Alomar doubled. Fernandez grounded out moving Alomar to third. Sprague hit a sacrifice fly scoring Alomar.

One in Blue Jays fifth: Molitor hit a home run.

Five in Phillies seventh: Stocker walked. Morandini singled moving Stocker to third. Dykstra hit a home run scoring Stocker and Morandini. Duncan singled and stole second. Hollins singled scoring Duncan. Daulton walked. Eisenreich singled to load the bases. Incaviglia hit a sacrifice fly scoring Hollins.

Three in Blue Jays ninth: Henderson walked. Molitor singled. Carter hit a home run scoring Henderson and Molitor.

# 1993 World Series Composite Box Score

## Philadelphia Phillies Batting

| | g | ab | r | h | 2b | 3b | hr | rbi | so | bb | avg | po | a | e | pct |
|---|---|---|---|---|---|---|---|---|---|---|---|---|---|---|---|
| Tommy Greene p | 1 | 1 | 1 | 1 | 0 | 0 | 0 | 0 | 0 | 0 | 1.000 | 0 | 0 | 0 | — |
| Curt Schilling p | 2 | 2 | 0 | 1 | 0 | 0 | 0 | 0 | 1 | 0 | .500 | 0 | 3 | 0 | 1.000 |
| Lenny Dykstra cf | 6 | 23 | 9 | 8 | 1 | 0 | 4 | 8 | 4 | 7 | .348 | 19 | 1 | 0 | 1.000 |
| John Kruk 1b | 6 | 23 | 4 | 8 | 1 | 0 | 0 | 4 | 7 | 7 | .348 | 42 | 3 | 0 | 1.000 |
| Mariano Duncan 2b-dh | 6 | 29 | 5 | 10 | 4 | 1 | 0 | 2 | 7 | 1 | .345 | 10 | 17 | 1 | .964 |
| Milt Thompson lf-pr | 6 | 16 | 3 | 5 | 1 | 1 | 1 | 6 | 2 | 1 | .313 | 10 | 0 | 1 | .909 |
| Dave Hollins 3b | 6 | 23 | 5 | 6 | 1 | 0 | 0 | 2 | 5 | 6 | .261 | 9 | 9 | 0 | 1.000 |
| Jim Eisenreich rf | 6 | 26 | 3 | 6 | 0 | 0 | 1 | 7 | 4 | 2 | .231 | 18 | 0 | 0 | 1.000 |
| Darren Daulton c | 6 | 23 | 4 | 5 | 2 | 0 | 1 | 4 | 5 | 5 | .217 | 31 | 4 | 0 | 1.000 |
| Kevin Stocker ss | 6 | 19 | 1 | 4 | 1 | 0 | 0 | 0 | 0 | 5 | .211 | 8 | 13 | 0 | 1.000 |
| Ricky Jordan dh-ph | 3 | 10 | 0 | 2 | 0 | 0 | 0 | 0 | 2 | 1 | .200 | 0 | 0 | 0 | — |
| Mickey Morandini ph-2b | 3 | 5 | 1 | 1 | 0 | 0 | 0 | 1 | 0 | 0 | .200 | 2 | 0 | 0 | 1.000 |
| Pete Incaviglia ph-lf | 4 | 8 | 0 | 1 | 0 | 0 | 0 | 1 | 4 | 0 | .125 | 7 | 0 | 0 | 1.000 |
| Wes Chamberlain ph | 2 | 2 | 0 | 0 | 0 | 0 | 0 | 0 | 1 | 0 | .000 | 0 | 0 | 0 | — |
| Danny Jackson p | 1 | 1 | 0 | 0 | 0 | 0 | 0 | 0 | 0 | 0 | .000 | 0 | 0 | 0 | — |
| Roger Mason p | 4 | 1 | 0 | 0 | 0 | 0 | 0 | 0 | 0 | 0 | .000 | 0 | 0 | 0 | — |
| Larry Andersen p | 4 | 0 | 0 | 0 | 0 | 0 | 0 | 0 | 0 | 0 | — | 0 | 1 | 0 | 1.000 |
| Kim Batiste 3b | 2 | 0 | 0 | 0 | 0 | 0 | 0 | 0 | 0 | 0 | — | 1 | 1 | 0 | 1.000 |
| Terry Mulholland p | 2 | 0 | 0 | 0 | 0 | 0 | 0 | 0 | 0 | 0 | — | 0 | 0 | 0 | — |
| Ben Rivera p | 1 | 0 | 0 | 0 | 0 | 0 | 0 | 0 | 0 | 0 | — | 0 | 1 | 0 | 1.000 |
| Bobby Thigpen p | 2 | 0 | 0 | 0 | 0 | 0 | 0 | 0 | 0 | 0 | — | 0 | 0 | 0 | — |
| David West p | 3 | 0 | 0 | 0 | 0 | 0 | 0 | 0 | 0 | 0 | — | 0 | 1 | 0 | 1.000 |
| Mitch Williams p | 3 | 0 | 0 | 0 | 0 | 0 | 0 | 0 | 0 | 0 | — | 0 | 0 | 0 | — |
| **Totals** | 6 | 212 | 36 | 58 | 7 | 2 | 7 | 35 | 50 | 34 | .274 | 157 | 54 | 2 | .991 |

## Toronto Blue Jays Batting

| | g | ab | r | h | 2b | 3b | hr | rbi | so | bb | avg | po | a | e | pct |
|---|---|---|---|---|---|---|---|---|---|---|---|---|---|---|---|
| Al Leiter p | 3 | 1 | 0 | 1 | 1 | 0 | 0 | 0 | 0 | 0 | 1.000 | 0 | 0 | 0 | — |
| Paul Molitor dh-1b-3b | 6 | 24 | 10 | 12 | 2 | 2 | 2 | 8 | 0 | 3 | .500 | 7 | 3 | 0 | 1.000 |
| Rob Butler ph | 2 | 2 | 1 | 1 | 0 | 0 | 0 | 0 | 0 | 0 | .500 | 0 | 0 | 0 | — |
| Roberto Alomar 2b | 6 | 25 | 5 | 12 | 2 | 1 | 0 | 6 | 3 | 2 | .480 | 10 | 21 | 2 | .939 |
| Tony Fernandez ss | 6 | 21 | 2 | 7 | 1 | 0 | 0 | 9 | 3 | 2 | .333 | 11 | 8 | 0 | 1.000 |
| Pat Borders c | 6 | 23 | 2 | 7 | 1 | 0 | 1 | 1 | 3 | 1 | .304 | 50 | 2 | 1 | .981 |
| Devon White cf | 6 | 24 | 8 | 7 | 3 | 2 | 1 | 7 | 7 | 4 | .292 | 16 | 0 | 0 | 1.000 |
| Joe Carter rf | 6 | 25 | 5 | 7 | 1 | 0 | 2 | 8 | 4 | 1 | .280 | 12 | 0 | 2 | .857 |
| John Olerud 1b | 6 | 17 | 5 | 4 | 1 | 0 | 1 | 2 | 2 | 5 | .235 | 36 | 0 | 0 | 1.000 |
| Rickey Henderson lf | 6 | 22 | 6 | 5 | 0 | 0 | 0 | 2 | 6 | 1 | .227 | 8 | 0 | 0 | 1.000 |
| Ed Sprague 3b-ph-1b | 6 | 15 | 0 | 1 | 0 | 0 | 0 | 0 | 1 | 0 | .067 | 4 | 9 | 2 | .867 |
| Pat Hentgen p | 1 | 3 | 0 | 0 | 0 | 0 | 0 | 0 | 1 | 0 | .000 | 0 | 1 | 0 | 1.000 |
| Juan Guzman p | 2 | 2 | 0 | 0 | 0 | 0 | 0 | 0 | 1 | 0 | .000 | 0 | 0 | 0 | — |
| Tony Castillo p | 2 | 1 | 0 | 0 | 0 | 0 | 0 | 0 | 0 | 0 | .000 | 1 | 0 | 0 | 1.000 |
| Danny Cox p | 3 | 1 | 0 | 0 | 0 | 0 | 0 | 0 | 0 | 0 | — | 0 | 0 | 0 | — |
| Alfredo Griffin pr-3b | 3 | 0 | 0 | 0 | 0 | 0 | 0 | 0 | 0 | 0 | — | 0 | 0 | 0 | — |
| Willie Canate pr | 1 | 0 | 0 | 0 | 0 | 0 | 0 | 0 | 0 | 0 | — | 0 | 0 | 0 | — |
| Mark Eichhorn p | 1 | 0 | 0 | 0 | 0 | 0 | 0 | 0 | 0 | 0 | — | 3 | 0 | 0 | 1.000 |
| Randy Knorr c | 1 | 0 | 0 | 0 | 0 | 0 | 0 | 0 | 0 | 0 | — | 1 | 1 | 0 | 1.000 |
| Dave Stewart p | 2 | 0 | 0 | 0 | 0 | 0 | 0 | 0 | 0 | 1 | — | 0 | 0 | 0 | — |
| Todd Stottlemyre p | 1 | 0 | 0 | 0 | 0 | 0 | 0 | 0 | 0 | 0 | — | 0 | 0 | 0 | — |
| Mike Timlin p | 2 | 0 | 0 | 0 | 0 | 0 | 0 | 0 | 0 | 0 | — | 0 | 0 | 0 | — |
| Duane Ward p | 4 | 0 | 0 | 0 | 0 | 0 | 0 | 0 | 0 | 0 | — | 0 | 0 | 0 | — |
| **Totals** | 6 | 206 | 45 | 64 | 13 | 5 | 6 | 45 | 30 | 25 | .311 | 159 | 45 | 7 | .967 |

## Philadelphia Phillies Pitching

| | g | cg | ip | h | r | bb | so | hb | wp | w | l | sv | pct | er | era |
|---|---|---|---|---|---|---|---|---|---|---|---|---|---|---|---|
| Bobby Thigpen | 2 | 0 | 2⅔ | 1 | 0 | 0 | 0 | 1 | 0 | 0 | 0 | 0 | — | 0 | 0.00 |
| Roger Mason | 4 | 0 | 7⅔ | 4 | 1 | 1 | 7 | 0 | 0 | 0 | 0 | 0 | — | 1 | 1.17 |
| Curt Schilling | 2 | 1 | 15⅓ | 13 | 7 | 5 | 9 | 0 | 0 | 1 | 1 | 0 | .500 | 6 | 3.52 |
| Terry Mulholland | 2 | 0 | 10⅔ | 14 | 8 | 3 | 5 | 1 | 0 | 1 | 1 | 0 | .000 | 8 | 7.20 |
| Danny Jackson | 1 | 0 | 5 | 6 | 4 | 1 | 3 | 1 | 0 | 0 | 0 | 0 | — | 5 | 12.27 |
| Larry Andersen | 4 | 0 | 3⅔ | 5 | 6 | 4 | 1 | 0 | 0 | 0 | 2 | 1 | .000 | 6 | 20.25 |
| Mitch Williams | 3 | 0 | 2⅔ | 5 | 6 | 4 | 1 | 1 | 0 | 0 | 0 | 0 | — | 7 | 27.00 |
| Tommy Greene | 1 | 0 | 2⅓ | 7 | 7 | 2 | 3 | 0 | 0 | 0 | 0 | 0 | — | 7 | 27.00 |
| Ben Rivera | 1 | 0 | 1⅓ | 4 | 4 | 2 | 0 | 1 | 0 | 0 | 0 | 0 | — | 3 | 27.00 |
| David West | 3 | 0 | 1 | 5 | 3 | 1 | 1 | 0 | 0 | 0 | 0 | 0 | — | 3 | 27.00 |
| **Totals** | 6 | 1 | 52⅓ | 64 | 45 | 25 | 30 | 3 | 0 | 2 | 4 | 1 | .333 | 44 | 7.57 |

## Toronto Blue Jays Pitching

| | g | cg | ip | h | r | bb | so | hb | wp | w | l | sv | pct | er | era |
|---|---|---|---|---|---|---|---|---|---|---|---|---|---|---|---|
| Mike Timlin | 2 | 0 | 2⅓ | 2 | 0 | 0 | 4 | 0 | 0 | 0 | 0 | 0 | — | 0 | 0.00 |
| Mark Eichhorn | 1 | 0 | ⅓ | 1 | 0 | 0 | 1 | 0 | 0 | 0 | 0 | 0 | — | 0 | 0.00 |
| Pat Hentgen | 1 | 0 | 6 | 5 | 1 | 3 | 6 | 0 | 0 | 1 | 0 | 0 | 1.000 | 1 | 1.50 |
| Duane Ward | 4 | 0 | 4⅔ | 3 | 2 | 0 | 7 | 0 | 0 | 1 | 0 | 2 | 1.000 | 1 | 1.93 |
| Juan Guzman | 2 | 0 | 12 | 10 | 6 | 8 | 12 | 0 | 1 | 0 | 1 | 0 | .000 | 5 | 3.75 |
| Dave Stewart | 2 | 0 | 12 | 10 | 9 | 8 | 8 | 0 | 1 | 2 | 0 | 0 | 1.000 | 9 | 6.75 |
| Al Leiter | 3 | 0 | 7 | 12 | 6 | 2 | 5 | 0 | 1 | 0 | 0 | 0 | — | 6 | 7.71 |
| Tony Castillo | 2 | 0 | 3⅓ | 6 | 3 | 3 | 1 | 1 | 0 | 0 | 0 | 0 | — | 3 | 8.10 |
| Danny Cox | 3 | 0 | 3⅓ | 6 | 3 | 6 | 4 | 1 | 0 | 0 | 0 | 0 | — | 3 | 27.00 |
| Todd Stottlemyre | 1 | 0 | 2 | 3 | 6 | 4 | 1 | 0 | 2 | 0 | 1 | 0 | .667 | 34 | 5.77 |
| **Totals** | 6 | 0 | 53 | 58 | 36 | 34 | 50 | 1 | 2 | 4 | 2 | 2 | .667 | 34 | 5.77 |

## Score By Innings

| | | | | | | | | | | | |
|---|---|---|---|---|---|---|---|---|---|---|---|
| Philadelphia | 7 | 3 | 6 | 2 | 6 | 2 | 8 | 0 | 2 | — | 36 |
| Toronto | 9 | 2 | 6 | 3 | 2 | 5 | 6 | 7 | 5 | — | 45 |

## World Series Results, 1903-1993

| | | |
|---|---|---|
| 1903 Boston AL 5, Pittsburgh NL 3 | 1934 St. Louis NL 4, Detroit AL 3 | 1964 St. Louis NL 4, New York AL 3 |
| 1904 No series | 1935 Detroit AL 4, Chicago NL 2 | 1965 Los Angeles NL 4, Minnesota AL 3 |
| 1905 New York NL 4, Philadelphia AL 1 | 1936 New York AL 4, New York NL 2 | 1966 Baltimore AL 4, Los Angeles NL 0 |
| 1906 Chicago AL 4, Chicago NL 2 | 1937 New York AL 4, New York NL 1 | 1967 St. Louis NL 4, Boston AL 3 |
| 1907 Chicago AL 4, Detroit AL 0, 1 tie | 1938 New York AL 4, Chicago NL 0 | 1968 Detroit AL 4, St. Louis NL 3 |
| 1908 Chicago NL 4, Detroit AL 1 | 1939 New York AL 4, Cincinnati NL 0 | 1969 New York NL 4, Baltimore AL 1 |
| 1909 Pittsburgh NL 4, Detroit AL 3 | 1940 Cincinnati NL 4, Detroit AL 3 | 1970 Baltimore AL 4, Cincinnati NL 1 |
| 1910 Philadelphia AL 4, Chicago NL 1 | 1941 New York AL 4, Brooklyn NL 1 | 1971 Pittsburgh NL 4, Baltimore AL 3 |
| 1911 Philadelphia AL 4, New York NL 2 | 1942 St. Louis NL 4, New York AL 1 | 1972 Oakland AL 4, Cincinnati NL 3 |
| 1912 Boston AL 4, New York NL 3, 1 tie | 1943 New York AL 4, St. Louis NL 1 | 1973 Oakland AL 4, New York NL 3 |
| 1913 Philadelphia AL 4, New York NL 1 | 1944 St. Louis NL 4, St. Louis AL 2 | 1974 Oakland AL 4, Los Angeles NL 1 |
| 1914 Boston NL 4, Philadelphia AL 0 | 1945 Detroit AL 4, Chicago NL 3 | 1975 Cincinnati NL 4, Boston AL 3 |
| 1915 Boston AL 4, Philadelphia NL 1 | 1946 St. Louis NL 4, Boston AL 3 | 1976 Cincinnati NL 4, New York AL 0 |
| 1916 Boston AL 4, Brooklyn NL 1 | 1947 New York AL 4, Brooklyn NL 3 | 1977 New York AL 4, Los Angeles NL 2 |
| 1917 Chicago AL 4, New York NL 2 | 1948 Cleveland AL 4, Boston NL 2 | 1978 New York AL 4, Los Angeles NL 2 |
| 1918 Boston AL 4, Chicago NL 2 | 1949 New York AL 4, Brooklyn NL 1 | 1979 Pittsburgh NL 4, Baltimore AL 3 |
| 1919 Cincinnati NL 5, Chicago AL 3 | 1950 New York AL 4, Philadelphia NL 0 | 1980 Philadelphia NL 4, Kansas City AL 2 |
| 1920 Cleveland AL 5, Brooklyn NL 2 | 1951 New York AL 4, New York NL 2 | |
| 1921 New York NL 5, New York AL 3 | 1952 New York AL 4, Brooklyn NL 3 | 1981 Los Angeles NL 4, New York AL 2 |
| 1922 New York NL 4, New York AL 0, 1 tie | 1953 New York AL 4, Brooklyn NL 2 | 1982 St. Louis NL 4, Milwaukee AL 3 |
| 1923 New York AL 4, New York NL 2 | 1954 New York NL 4, Cleveland AL 0 | 1983 Baltimore AL 4, Philadelphia NL 1 |
| 1924 Washington AL 4, New York NL 3 | 1955 Brooklyn NL 4, New York AL 3 | 1984 Detroit AL 4, San Diego NL 1 |
| 1925 Pittsburgh NL 4, Washington AL 3 | 1956 New York AL 4, Brooklyn NL 3 | 1985 Kansas City AL 4, St. Louis NL 3 |
| 1926 St. Louis NL 4, New York AL 3 | 1957 Milwaukee NL 4, New York AL 3 | 1986 New York NL 4, Boston AL 3 |
| 1927 New York AL 4, Pittsburgh NL 0 | 1958 New York AL 4, Milwaukee NL 3 | 1987 Minnesota AL 4, St. Louis NL 3 |
| 1928 New York AL 4, St. Louis NL 0 | 1959 Los Angeles NL 4, Chicago AL 2 | 1988 Los Angeles NL 4, Oakland AL 1 |
| 1929 Philadelphia AL 4, Chicago NL 1 | 1960 Pittsburgh NL 4, New York AL 3 | 1989 Oakland AL 4, San Francisco NL 0 |
| 1930 Philadelphia AL 4, St. Louis NL 2 | 1961 New York AL 4, Cincinnati NL 1 | 1990 Cincinnati NL 4, Oakland AL 0 |
| 1931 St. Louis NL 4, Philadelphia AL 3 | 1962 New York AL 4, San Francisco NL 3 | 1991 Minnesota AL 4, Atlanta NL 3 |
| 1932 New York AL 4, Chicago NL 0 | | 1992 Toronto AL 4, Atlanta NL 2 |
| 1933 New York NL 4, Washington AL 1 | 1963 Los Angeles NL 4, New York AL 0 | 1993 Toronto AL 4, Philadelphia NL 2 |

## Chess

Source: U.S. Chess Federation

Chess dates back to antiquity, its exact origin unknown. The best players of their time, regarded by later generations as world champions, were Francois Philidor, Alexandre Deschappelles, Louis de la Bourdonnais, all France; Howard Staunton, England; Adolph Anderssen, Germany and Paul Morphy, U.S. In 1866 Wilhelm Steinitz defeated Adolph Anderssen and claimed the world champion title. Official world champions since the title was first used follow:

| | | |
|---|---|---|
| 1866-1894 Wilhelm Steinitz, Austria | 1948-1957 Mikhail Botvinnik, USSR | 1969-1972 Boris Spassky, USSR |
| 1894-1921 Emanuel Lasker, Germany | 1957-1958 Vassily Smyslov, USSR | 1972-1975 Bobby Fischer, U.S. (a) |
| 1921-1927 Jose R. Capablanca, Cuba | 1958-1959 Mikhail Botvinnik, USSR | 1975-1985 Anatoly Karpov, USSR |
| 1927-1935 Alexander A. Alekhine, France | 1960-1961 Mikhail Tal, USSR | 1985 Gary Kasparov, |
| 1935-1937 Max Euwe, Netherlands | 1961-1963 Mikhail Botvinnik, USSR | USSR/Russia (b) |
| 1937-1946 Alexander A. Alekhine, France | 1963-1969 Tigran Petrosian, USSR | |

(a) Defaulted championship after refusal to accept International Chess Federation rules for a championship match, April 1975. (b) Kasparov broke with the International Chess Federation (FIDE), Feb. 26, 1993. FIDE stripped Kasparov of his title Mar. 23. Kasparov defeated Nigel Short of Great Britain in a world championship match played Sept.-Oct. 1993 under the auspices of a new organization they two had founded, the Professional Chess Association. FIDE held a championship match between Anatoly Karpov (Russia) and Jan Timman (the Netherlands).

## Ten Most Dramatic Sports Events, Nov. 1992—Oct. 1993

—John Paxson sank a 3-point shot with 3.9 seconds left in the game to give the Chicago Bulls a 99-98 victory over the Phoenix Suns, June 20, and their third consecutive National Basketball Association championship. The Bulls defeated the Suns 4 games to 2.

—The University of Alabama defeated the top-ranked University of Miami in the Sugar Bowl, 34-13, on New Year's Day. The victory broke a 29-game winning streak for Miami and propelled the Crimson Tide into the top spot in the national polls for collegiate champion.

—North Carolina won the NCAA basketball championship, April 5, by defeating Michigan, 77-71. Chris Webber of Michigan called an illegal time-out with 11 seconds left in the game and his team trailing by 2 points, giving the Tar Heels 2 technical foul shots and the ball, which sealed the victory.

—Noureddine Morceli of Algeria broke the world record in the mile, Sept. 5, with a time of 3 minutes 44.39 seconds at a meet in Rieti, Italy. Morceli took nearly 2 seconds off the old record, set by Steve Cram in 1985.

—Mark Whiten of the St. Louis Cardinals hit 4 home runs in a game against the Cincinnati Reds, Sept. 7. He became the 12th major leaguer to hit 4 homers in a game. He also tied the major league record of 12 RBI's in a game, set in 1924.

—In the biggest comeback in NFL history, the Buffalo Bills overcame a 35-3 deficit to beat the Houston Oilers,

41-38, in overtime, Jan. 3, in the first round of the National Football League playoffs. The Bills were eventually defeated in the Super Bowl, Jan. 31, by the Dallas Cowboys, 52-17.

—Welterweights Julio Cesar Chavez and Pernell Whitaker fought to a 12-round draw in San Antonio, Texas, Sept. 10, in a bout billed as a fight to decide who was the world's best boxer "pound for pound." The result was widely criticized, as Whitaker was perceived by most to have won easily.

—With a 4-1 victory on June 9, the Montreal Canadiens won their 24th National Hockey League Stanley Cup championship, defeating the Los Angeles Kings, 4 games to 1. It was the first Stanley Cup title for the Canadiens since 1986.

—Monica Seles, the No. 1-ranked women's tennis player, was seriously injured when she was stabbed in the back by a spectator during a tournament in Hamburg, Germany, April 30. The attacker was apparently a fanatical fan of Seles' rival, Steffi Graf of Germany. Seles, who required lengthy rehabilitation and was unable to play for months, lost her No. 1 ranking to Graf June 3.

—A dramatic ninth-inning home run by Joe Carter in game 6, Oct. 23, gave the Toronto Blue Jays an 8-6 win and their second straight World Series victory, 4 games to 2 over the Philadelphia Phillies. Three days earlier a 6-run eighth inning in game 4 had given the Blue Jays a come-from-behind 15-14 victory in the highest scoring (29 runs) and longest (4 hours, 14 minutes) game in World Series history.

# VITAL STATISTICS

## Births, Deaths, Marriages, and Divorces, First Quarter 1993

Source: National Center for Health Statistics, U.S. Dept. of Health and Human Services

### Births

According to provisional statistics for the first quarter of 1993, there were 991,000 births, a slight decrease from the number reported for the same 3-month period in 1992 (998,000). The birthrate declined by 1 percent, from 15.8 per 1,000 population in the first quarter of 1992 to 15.7 in the first quarter of 1993.

During the 12 months ending with March 1993, there were an estimated 4,078,000 live births, 1 percent less than reported for the comparable period ending a year earlier (4,126,000). The birthrate was 15.9 per 1,000 population, 2 percent below the rate for the 12 months ending with March 1992 (16.3).

### Marriages

The total number of marriages for the first quarter of 1993 was 412,000, a decrease of 3 percent from the number for the comparable period in 1992 (423,000). The marriage rate was 6.6 per 1,000 population, a decrease of 1 percent from the first quarter of 1992.

During the 12 months ending with March 1993, an estimated 2,351,000 couples married, a decrease of 1 percent from the previous 12-month period. The 12-month marriage rate was 9.2, down 2 percent from the rate for the 12 months ending with March 1992.

### Divorces

A total of 292,000 couples divorced during the first quarter of 1993, a 3 percent decrease compared to the first quarter of 1992 (300,000). The divorce rate was 4.6 per 1,000 population, a decrease of 4 percent from the first quarter of 1992 (4.8).

During the 12 months ending with March 1993, an estimated 1,206,000 couples divorced, up slightly from 1,203,000 during the 12 months ending March 1992, and the rate declined from 4.8 to 4.7 per 1,000 population.

### Deaths

According to provisional statistics, there were 600,000 deaths during the first quarter of 1993, 2 percent more than for the first quarter of 1992 (587,000). The death rate was 9.5 per 1,000 population, 2 percent higher than the Jan.-March 1992 rate. Among the deaths for the first quarter of 1993 were 8,700 deaths at ages under 1 year, yielding an infant mortality rate of 8.7 per 1,000 live births, 6 percent lower than the rate of 9.3 for the first quarter of 1992.

The death rate for the 12 months ending with March 1993 (8.6 deaths per 1,000 population) was the same as the rate for the comparable 12-month period a year earlier. The infant mortality rate for this 12-month-period was 8.3 per 1,000 live births, 6 percent lower than the rate of 8.8 for the 12 months ending with March 1992.

### Provisional Statistics
12 months ending with March

| | Number | | Rate* | |
|---|---|---|---|---|
| | 1993 | 1992 | 1993 | 1992 |
| Live births .... | 4,078,000 | 4,126,000 | 15.9 | 16.3 |
| Deaths ...... | 2,190,000 | 2,186,000 | 8.6 | 8.6 |
| Natural increase. | 1,888,000 | 1,940,000 | 7.3 | 7.7 |
| Marriages .... | 2,351,000 | 2,384,000 | 9.2 | 9.4 |
| Divorces ..... | 1,206,000 | 1,203,000 | 4.7 | 4.8 |
| Infant deaths... | 33,700 | 36,300 | 8.3 | 8.8 |

* Per 1,000 population. **Note:** Figures include revisions.

## Annual Report for the Year 1992 (Provisional Statistics)

Source: National Center for Health Statistics, U.S. Dept. of Health and Human Services

### Highlights

Provisional data for 1992 show that both the birthrate and the death rate per 1,000 population were lower than the comparable rates for the previous year. Between 1991 and 1992 a decrease was also observed for the infant mortality rate per 1,000 live births. The marriage rate per 1,000 population decreased in comparison with the rate for 1991. Only the divorce rate increased from 1991 to 1992.

### Births

An estimated 4,084,000 babies were born in the United States in 1992, a decline of 1 percent from the 4,111,000 births in 1991. The birthrate of 16.0 per 1,000 population was 2 percent lower than the rate of 16.3 for the preceding year. The fertility rate (the number of live births per 1,000 women aged 15-44 years) for 1992 was 69.2, 1 percent lower than the rate for 1991 (69.6).

### Deaths

The provisional count of deaths during 1992 was 2,177,000, about 1 percent more than in the previous year (2,165,000). The death rate of 853.3 deaths per 100,000 population was 1 percent lower than the rate of 858.5 for 1991. About 34,400 of these deaths were to infants under 1 year of age. The infant mortality rate was 848.7 per 1,000 live births, 5 percent lower than the rate of 892.8 for 1991.

### Natural Increase

As a result of natural increase, the excess of births over deaths, an estimated 1,907,000 persons were added to the population in 1992. This rate was 7.5, per 1,000 population, 3 percent lower than the rate of 7.7 for 1991. The decline in the rate of natural increase continues to be due to a larger decrease in the birthrate than in the death rate.

### Marriages

An estimated 2,362,000 marriages were performed in 1992, slightly lower than the number in 1991 (2,371,000). The marriage rate was 1 percent lower in 1992 (9.3) than in 1991 (9.4).

### Divorces

The number of divorces granted in 1992 (1,215,000) was 2 percent higher than in 1991 (1,187,000). Although the number was an all-time high, the divorce rate in 1992 (4.8 per 1,000 population) was 9 percent lower than the peak rate of 1981 (5.3) but slightly higher than the rate of 4.7 from 1988 to 1991.

## Births and Deaths in the U.S.

Source: National Center for Health Statistics, U.S. Dept. of Health and Human Services

Refers only to events occurring within the U.S. Excludes fetal deaths. Rates per 1,000 population enumerated as of April 1 for 1960, and 1970; estimated as of July 1 for all other years. Beginning 1970 excludes births and deaths occurring to nonresidents of the U.S.

| | Births | | Deaths | |
|---|---|---|---|---|
| Year | Total number | Rate | Total number | Rate |
| 1960............. | 4,257,850 | 23.7 | 1,711,982 | 9.5 |
| 1970............. | 3,731,386 | 18.4 | 1,921,031 | 9.5 |
| 1970............. | 3,612,258 | 15.9 | 1,986,000 | 8.7 |
| 1980............. | 4,179,000 | 16.7 | 2,162,000 | 8.6 |
| 1990............. | 4,111,000 | 16.3 | 2,165,000 | 8.6 |
| 1991............. | 4,084,000 | 16.0 | 2,177,000 | 8.5 |
| 1992............. | | | | |

## Births and Deaths by States and Regions, 1991-1992

Source: National Center for Health Statistics, U.S. Dept. of Health and Human Services

| Area | Live births 1991 Number | 1991 Rate | 1992 Number | 1992 Rate | Deaths 1991 Number | 1991 Rate | 1992 Number | 1992 Rate |
|---|---|---|---|---|---|---|---|---|
| New England | 189,547 | 14.4 | 189,276 | 14.3 | 112,411 | 8.5 | 116,218 | 8.8 |
| Maine | 16,581 | 13.4 | 15,623 | 12.7 | 10,952 | 8.9 | 10,900 | 8.8 |
| New Hampshire | 16,060 | 14.5 | 15,719 | 14.1 | 8,513 | 7.7 | 8,555 | 7.7 |
| Vermont | 7,712 | 13.6 | 7,625 | 13.4 | 4,541 | 8.0 | 4,732 | 8.3 |
| Massachusetts | 86,321 | 14.4 | 88,185 | 14.7 | 51,366 | 8.6 | 54,292 | 9.1 |
| Rhode Island | 14,591 | 14.5 | 14,789 | 14.7 | 9,294 | 9.2 | 9,444 | 9.4 |
| Connecticut | 48,282 | 14.7 | 47,335 | 14.4 | 27,745 | 8.4 | 28,295 | 8.6 |
| Middle Atlantic | 578,773 | 15.3 | 570,697 | 15.1 | 360,314 | 9.5 | 359,395 | 9.5 |
| New York | 292,400 | 16.2 | 285,568 | 15.8 | 166,795 | 9.2 | 164,869 | 9.1 |
| New Jersey | 117,789 | 15.2 | 119,923 | 15.4 | 69,983 | 9.0 | 71,201 | 9.1 |
| Pennsylvania | 168,584 | 14.1 | 165,206 | 13.8 | 123,536 | 10.3 | 123,325 | 10.3 |
| East North Central | 662,427 | 15.6 | 654,228 | 15.3 | 379,282 | 8.9 | 372,449 | 8.7 |
| Ohio | 158,638 | 14.5 | 169,067 | 15.3 | 99,104 | 9.1 | 99,601 | 9.0 |
| Indiana | 84,707 | 15.1 | 83,832 | 14.8 | 51,780 | 9.2 | 50,144 | 8.9 |
| Illinois | 193,987 | 16.8 | 192,483 | 16.5 | 104,677 | 9.1 | 101,590 | 8.7 |
| Michigan | 153,359 | 16.3 | 138,968 | 14.7 | 79,972 | 8.5 | 79,307 | 8.4 |
| Wisconsin | 71,736 | 14.5 | 69,878 | 14.0 | 43,749 | 8.8 | 41,807 | 8.3 |
| West North Central | 262,368 | 14.7 | 259,737 | 14.5 | 164,055 | 9.2 | 162,094 | 9.0 |
| Minnesota | 67,020 | 15.1 | 65,477 | 14.6 | 35,270 | 8.0 | 34,909 | 7.8 |
| Iowa | 36,011 | 12.9 | 38,120 | 13.6 | 25,906 | 9.3 | 27,002 | 9.6 |
| Missouri | 77,991 | 15.1 | 75,437 | 14.5 | 53,461 | 10.4 | 50,447 | 9.7 |
| North Dakota | 9,071 | 14.3 | 8,935 | 14.0 | 5,648 | 8.9 | 5,797 | 9.1 |
| South Dakota | 11,042 | 15.7 | 11,281 | 15.9 | 6,594 | 9.4 | 6,927 | 9.7 |
| Nebraska | 23,933 | 15.0 | 23,003 | 14.3 | 14,665 | 9.2 | 14,852 | 9.2 |
| Kansas | 37,300 | 14.9 | 37,484 | 14.9 | 22,511 | 9.0 | 22,160 | 8.8 |
| South Atlantic | 689,068 | 15.5 | 680,220 | 15.1 | 396,655 | 8.9 | 403,745 | 9.0 |
| Delaware | 11,175 | 16.4 | 10,902 | 15.8 | 5,880 | 8.6 | 5,937 | 8.6 |
| Maryland | 84,452 | 17.4 | 76,173 | 15.5 | 37,982 | 7.8 | 37,806 | 7.7 |
| District of Columbia | 9,971 | 16.8 | 10,052 | 17.1 | 6,961 | 11.7 | 6,578 | 11.2 |
| Virginia | 96,610 | 15.4 | 97,600 | 15.3 | 49,151 | 7.8 | 49,541 | 7.8 |
| West Virginia | 22,195 | 12.3 | 22,123 | 12.2 | 19,801 | 11.0 | 20,107 | 11.1 |
| North Carolina | 102,442 | 15.2 | 103,047 | 15.1 | 58,909 | 8.7 | 59,478 | 8.7 |
| South Carolina | 57,742 | 16.2 | 56,635 | 15.7 | 29,983 | 8.4 | 30,609 | 8.5 |
| Georgia | 110,024 | 16.6 | 111,397 | 16.5 | 52,708 | 8.0 | 53,288 | 7.9 |
| Florida | 194,457 | 14.7 | 192,291 | 14.3 | 135,280 | 10.2 | 140,401 | 10.4 |
| East South Central | 232,052 | 15.1 | 234,462 | 15.1 | 144,284 | 9.4 | 147,410 | 9.5 |
| Kentucky | 54,931 | 14.8 | 53,906 | 14.4 | 35,281 | 9.5 | 35,341 | 9.4 |
| Tennessee | 73,104 | 14.8 | 74,048 | 14.7 | 45,351 | 9.2 | 47,149 | 9.4 |
| Alabama | 60,513 | 14.8 | 63,021 | 15.2 | 38,027 | 9.3 | 39,630 | 9.6 |
| Mississippi | 43,522 | 16.8 | 43,487 | 16.6 | 25,625 | 9.9 | 25,290 | 9.7 |
| West South Central | 482,024 | 17.8 | 479,421 | 17.4 | 221,795 | 8.2 | 224,221 | 8.1 |
| Arkansas | 34,588 | 14.6 | 34,967 | 14.6 | 24,230 | 10.2 | 25,202 | 10.5 |
| Louisiana | 74,562 | 17.5 | 71,743 | 16.7 | 38,290 | 9.0 | 37,446 | 8.7 |
| Oklahoma | 47,312 | 14.9 | 47,850 | 14.9 | 30,349 | 9.6 | 30,626 | 9.5 |
| Texas | 325,562 | 18.8 | 324,861 | 18.4 | 128,926 | 7.4 | 130,947 | 7.4 |
| Mountain | 243,405 | 17.3 | 245,352 | 17.1 | 99,248 | 7.1 | 103,301 | 7.2 |
| Montana | 11,544 | 14.3 | 11,551 | 14.0 | 7,071 | 8.7 | 7,151 | 8.7 |
| Idaho | 17,233 | 16.6 | 17,475 | 16.4 | 7,789 | 7.5 | 8,063 | 7.6 |
| Wyoming | 6,801 | 14.8 | 6,823 | 14.6 | 3,167 | 6.9 | 3,333 | 7.2 |
| Colorado | 53,968 | 16.0 | 54,586 | 15.7 | 22,334 | 6.6 | 22,528 | 6.5 |
| New Mexico | 28,160 | 18.2 | 28,463 | 18.0 | 11,116 | 7.2 | 11,561 | 7.3 |
| Arizona | 67,656 | 18.1 | 66,698 | 17.4 | 29,329 | 7.8 | 30,659 | 8.0 |
| Utah | 35,070 | 19.8 | 37,411 | 20.6 | 9,199 | 5.2 | 9,904 | 5.5 |
| Nevada | 22,973 | 17.9 | 22,345 | 16.5 | 9,243 | 7.2 | 10,102 | 7.6 |
| Pacific | 759,966 | 19.0 | 753,550 | 18.5 | 290,482 | 7.3 | 287,474 | 7.1 |
| Washington | 75,734 | 15.1 | 79,300 | 15.4 | 37,682 | 7.5 | 37,272 | 7.3 |
| Oregon | 42,807 | 14.6 | 41,606 | 14.0 | 25,205 | 8.6 | 25,862 | 8.7 |
| California | 610,166 | 20.1 | 601,028 | 19.5 | 218,735 | 7.2 | 215,206 | 7.0 |
| Alaska | 11,245 | 19.7 | 11,706 | 19.9 | 2,145 | 3.8 | 2,225 | 3.8 |
| Hawaii | 20,014 | 17.7 | 19,910 | 17.2 | 6,715 | 5.9 | 6,909 | 6.0 |

**Notes:** Data are provisional estimates, reported by state of residence. Figures include revisions, and so may differ from those previously published. Rates for births and deaths are per 1,000 population. Rates for deaths in 1991 have been recomputed based on revised population estimates.

## Deaths Under 1 Year and Infant Mortality Rates, for 10 Selected Causes, 1991-92

Source: National Center for Health Statistics, U.S. Dept. of Health and Human Services

| Age and cause of death | 1991 Number | 1991 Rate | 1992 Number | 1992 Rate | Age and cause of death | 1991 Number | 1991 Rate | 1992 Number | 1992 Rate |
|---|---|---|---|---|---|---|---|---|---|
| Total, under 1 year | 36,500 | 892.8 | 34,400 | 848.7 | Birth trauma | 160 | 3.9 | 170 | 4.2 |
| Under 28 days | 22,640 | 554.2 | 21,860 | 538.6 | Intrauterine hypoxia and birth asphyxia | 730 | 17.9 | 720 | 17.6 |
| 28 days to 11 months | 13,830 | 338.6 | 12,570 | 309.7 | Respiratory distress syndrome | 2,300 | 56.3 | 2,380 | 58.3 |
| Certain gastrointestinal diseases | 320 | 7.8 | 340 | 8.3 | Other conditions originating in the prenatal period | 8,730 | 213.7 | 8,550 | 209.3 |
| Pneumonia and influenza | 610 | 14.9 | 720 | 17.6 | Sudden infant death syndrome | 5,170 | 126.6 | 4,660 | 114.1 |
| Congenital anomalies | 7,600 | 186.0 | 7,500 | 183.6 | All other causes | 6,340 | 155.2 | 5,610 | 137.4 |
| Disorders relating to short gestation and unspecified low birthweight | 4,500 | 110.2 | 3,790 | 92.8 | | | | | |

**Notes:** Data are provisional, estimated from a 10 percent sample of deaths. Rates are on an annual basis per 100,000 live births. Due to rounding of estimates, figures may not add to totals.

## Infant Mortality Rates, by Race and Sex, 1960-1990[1]

Source: National Center for Health Statistics, U.S. Dept. of Health and Human Services

| Year | All races | | | White | | | Black | | |
|---|---|---|---|---|---|---|---|---|---|
| | Both sexes | Male | Female | Both sexes | Male | Female | Both sexes | Male | Female |
| 1960 | 26.0 | 29.3 | 22.6 | 22.9 | 26.0 | 19.6 | 44.3 | 49.1 | 39.4 |
| 1970 | 20.0 | 22.4 | 17.5 | 17.8 | 20.0 | 15.4 | 32.6 | 36.2 | 29.0 |
| 1980 | 12.6 | 13.9 | 11.2 | 11.0 | 12.3 | 9.6 | 21.4 | 23.3 | 19.4 |
| 1981 | 11.9 | 13.1 | 10.7 | 10.5 | 11.7 | 9.2 | 20.0 | 21.7 | 18.3 |
| 1982 | 11.5 | 12.8 | 10.2 | 10.1 | 11.2 | 8.9 | 19.6 | 21.5 | 17.7 |
| 1983 | 11.2 | 12.3 | 10.0 | 9.7 | 10.8 | 8.6 | 19.2 | 21.1 | 17.2 |
| 1984 | 10.8 | 11.9 | 9.6 | 9.4 | 10.5 | 8.3 | 18.4 | 19.8 | 16.9 |
| 1985 | 10.6 | 11.9 | 9.3 | 9.3 | 10.6 | 8.0 | 18.2 | 19.9 | 16.5 |
| 1986 | 10.4 | 11.5 | 9.1 | 8.9 | 10.0 | 7.8 | 18.0 | 20.0 | 16.0 |
| 1987 | 10.1 | 11.2 | 8.9 | 8.6 | 9.6 | 7.6 | 17.9 | 19.6 | 16.0 |
| 1988 | 10.0 | 11.0 | 8.9 | 8.5 | 9.5 | 7.4 | 17.6 | 19.0 | 16.1 |
| 1989 | 9.8 | 10.8 | 8.8 | 8.1 | 9.0 | 7.1 | 18.6 | 20.0 | 17.2 |
| 1990 | 9.2 | 10.3 | 8.1 | 7.6 | 8.5 | 6.6 | 18.0 | 19.6 | 16.2 |

(1) Final data.

## The 10 Leading Causes of Death, 1992[1]

Source: National Center for Health Statistics, U.S. Dept. of Health and Human Services

| Rank | Cause of death | Number | Death rate[2] | Percent of total deaths |
|---|---|---|---|---|
| | All causes | 2,177,000 | 853.3 | 100.0 |
| 1. | Heart Disease | 720,480 | 282.5 | 33.1 |
| 2. | Cancer | 521,090 | 204.3 | 23.9 |
| 3. | Stroke | 143,640 | 56.3 | 6.6 |
| 4. | Chronic obstructive lung diseases and allied conditions | 91,440 | 35.8 | 4.2 |
| 5. | Accidents and adverse effects | 86,310 | 33.8 | 4.0 |
| | Motor vehicle accidents | 41,710 | 16.4 | 1.9 |
| | All other accidents and adverse effects | 44,600 | 17.5 | 2.0 |
| 6. | Pneumonia and influenza | 76,120 | 29.8 | 3.5 |
| 7. | Diabetes mellitus | 50,180 | 19.7 | 2.3 |
| 8. | Human immunodeficiency virus (HIV) infection[3] | 33,590 | 13.2 | 1.5 |
| 9. | Suicide | 29,760 | 11.7 | 1.4 |
| 10. | Homicide and legal intervention | 26,570 | 10.4 | 1.2 |

(1) Data are provisional, estimated from a 10 percent sample of deaths. Figures may not add to totals due to rounding. Rates have been recomputed based on revised population estimates. (2) Per 100,000 population. (3) HIV is the virus that causes AIDS.

## Suicides by Age, Race, and Sex, 1992

Source: National Center for Health Statistics, U.S. Dept. of Health and Human Services

| | All ages | 1-14 yrs. | 15-24 yrs. | 25-34 yrs. | 35-44 yrs. | 45-54 yrs. | 55-64 yrs. | 65-74 yrs. | 75-84 yrs. | 85 yrs. & over | Age not stated |
|---|---|---|---|---|---|---|---|---|---|---|---|
| All races, both sexes | 29,760 | 310 | 6,030 | 5,740 | 3,970 | 3,040 | 2,620 | 2,780 | 600 | 10 | |
| Male | 24,260 | 220 | 3,970 | 4,980 | 4,650 | 2,970 | 2,390 | 2,120 | 2,430 | 520 | 10 |
| Female | 5,500 | 90 | 690 | 1,050 | 1,090 | 650 | 500 | 350 | 80 | — | |
| White, both sexes | 26,980 | 290 | 3,950 | 5,220 | 5,230 | 3,670 | 2,870 | 2,530 | 2,670 | 550 | — |
| Male | 22,050 | 210 | 3,360 | 4,360 | 4,280 | 2,710 | 2,260 | 2,050 | 2,350 | 470 | — |
| Female | 4,930 | 80 | 580 | 860 | 960 | 960 | 600 | 490 | 320 | 80 | — |
| Black, both sexes | 2,000 | 10 | 500 | 630 | 320 | 220 | 160 | 30 | 80 | 40 | 10 |
| Male | 1,670 | 10 | 460 | 500 | 260 | 190 | 110 | 30 | 60 | 40 | 10 |
| Female | 330 | — | 40 | 140 | 60 | 30 | 40 | — | 20 | — | |

Note: Data are provisional, estimated from a 10 percent sample of deaths. Due to rounding of estimates, figures may not add to totals.

## Ownership of Life Insurance in the U.S. and Assets of U.S. Life Insurance Companies

Source: American Council of Life Insurance
(millions of dollars)

| Year | Purchases of life insurance | | | | Insurance in force | | | | | Assets |
|---|---|---|---|---|---|---|---|---|---|---|
| | Ordinary | Group | Industrial | Total | Ordinary | Group | Industrial | Credit | Total | |
| 1940 | 6,689 | 691 | 3,350 | 10,730 | 79,346 | 14,938 | 20,866 | 380 | 115,530 | 30,802 |
| 1950 | 17,326 | 6,068 | 5,402 | 28,796 | 149,116 | 47,793 | 33,415 | 3,844 | 234,168 | 64,020 |
| 1960 | 52,883 | 14,645 | 6,880 | 74,408 | 341,881 | 175,903 | 39,563 | 29,101 | 586,448 | 119,576 |
| 1965 | 83,485 | 51,385* | 7,296 | 142,166* | 499,638 | 308,078 | 39,818 | 53,020 | 900,554 | 158,884 |
| 1970 | 122,820 | 63,690* | 6,612 | 193,122* | 734,730 | 551,357 | 38,644 | 77,392 | 1,402,123 | 207,254 |
| 1975 | 188,003 | 95,190* | 6,729 | 289,922* | 1,083,421 | 904,695 | 39,423 | 112,032 | 2,139,571 | 289,304 |
| 1980 | 385,575 | 183,418 | 3,609 | 572,602 | 1,760,474 | 1,579,355 | 35,994 | 165,215 | 3,541,038 | 479,210 |
| 1985 | 910,944 | 319,503 | 722 | 1,231,169 | 3,247,289 | 2,561,595 | 28,250 | 215,973 | 6,053,107 | 825,901 |
| 1986 | 933,592 | 374,741* | 418 | 1,308,751* | 3,658,203 | 2,801,049 | 27,168 | 233,859 | 6,720,279 | 937,551 |
| 1987 | 986,660 | 365,529 | 324 | 1,352,513 | 4,139,071 | 3,043,782 | 26,668 | 242,977 | 7,452,498 | 1,044,459 |
| 1988 | 995,686 | 410,848 | 320 | 1,406,854 | 4,511,608 | 3,232,080 | 25,456 | 251,015 | 8,020,159 | 1,166,870 |
| 1989 | 1,020,719 | 420,707 | 252 | 1,441,678 | 4,939,964 | 3,469,498 | 24,446 | 260,107 | 8,694,015 | 1,299,756 |
| 1990 | 1,069,660 | 459,271 | 220 | 1,529,151 | 5,366,982 | 3,753,506 | 24,071 | 248,038 | 9,392,597 | 1,408,402 |
| 1991 | 1,041,508 | 573,953* | 198 | 1,615,659* | 5,677,777 | 4,057,606 | 22,475 | 228,478 | 9,986,336 | 1,551,201 |
| 1992 | 1,048,135 | 440,143 | 222 | 1,488,500 | 5,941,810 | 4,240,919 | 20,973 | 202,090 | 10,405,792 | 1,664,531 |

* Includes Servicemen's Group Life Insurance $27.8 billion in 1965, $17.1 billion in 1970, $1.7 billion in 1975, $51.0 billion in 1986, and $166.7 billion in 1991, as well as $10.8 billion of Federal Employees' Group Life Insurance in 1986.

## Marriage and Divorce in the U.S. in 1992

Source: Bureau of the Census, U.S. Dept. of Commerce; Dec. 1992.

• Although 90 percent of current young adult Americans expect to marry at some time, this figure is lower than the historical 95 percent marriage rate for Americans.

• Among young adult Americans, about 90 percent of white women expect to marry at some time, but fewer than 75 percent of black women expect to do so.

• Women are marrying later. In 1990 the proportion of women 20 to 24 years old who had married for the first time was 38 percent, a drop of 25 percentage points from the 1975 rate of 63 percent.

• There are different divorce patterns for women under 30, those between 30 and 44, and those between 45 and 54. Women in the 30 to 44 age group are expected to end up with the highest divorce rates, (an estimated 40 to 42 percent). Women under 30 are expected to have divorce rates of 38 to 39 percent, and women 45 to 54 are expected to have divorce rates of about 30 to 36 percent. The same general pattern holds true across racial and ethnic groups.

• The younger the woman at her first marriage, the greater the likelihood she will divorce.

• Women who complete 16 years of school are the least likely of all ever-married women to be divorced from their first husbands.

• Mothers who conceive or bear a child before their first marriage have a greater likelihood of divorce than mothers whose children are all conceived after marriage.

• The median duration of first marriages that end in divorce is about 6.3 years. However, women in their late 20s and early 30s, the prime ages for divorce, spend a median of 3.4 and 4.9 years, respectively, in their first marriages before divorcing.

• The median duration between a first divorce and remarriage is 2.5 years. Three-quarters of remarriages occur within 5 years of divorce.

• Twenty-one percent of all households containing a married couple and children include at least one stepchild under 18 years of age. This figure compares with about 16 percent of such households in 1980.

## Parenthood in the U.S. in 1992

Source: Bureau of the Census, U.S. Dept. of Commerce

• Increasing proportions of never-married mothers were being found in all regions and most socioeconomic groups across the country in 1992. About 24 percent of single women age 18 to 44 had borne a child (as of June 1992), compared with 15 percent a decade earlier. The proportion of single mothers more than doubled among women with one or more years of college (4.4 percent in 1982; 11.3 percent in 1992) and nearly doubled among women with a high school diploma (17.2 percent in 1982; 32.5 percent in 1992). The proportion of single mothers among women who did not complete high school was also higher in 1992 (48.4 percent) than in 1982 (35.2 percent).

• Out-of-wedlock childbearing increased among all racial and ethnic groups between 1982 and 1992. About two-thirds (67 percent) of births to black women in 1992 were out of wedlock, compared to 27 percent for Hispanic women and 17 percent for white women. Comparable figures in 1982 were 49 percent, 16 percent, and 10 percent, respectively.

• The proportion of dual-employed married couples with children increased between 1976 and 1992. Of the wives 15 to 44 years old in 1992 (30 million), 47 percent were in families with children where both spouses were employed (14 percentage points higher than the figure for 1976). The traditional family, where only the husband worked while the wife remained at home with the children, declined from 43 to 24 percent; there were 7 million such families in 1992.

• Rates of home ownership were significantly higher in 1992 among dual-employed married couples with children (78 percent) than among childless couples (66 percent).

• The majority of women with infants were in the labor force. Among women 18 to 44 years old who had a child in the 12-month period ending in June 1992, 54 percent were in the labor force, compared with 44 percent in June 1982. Women 18 to 44 years old with a graduate or professional degree had a labor force participation rate (72 percent) more than double that of women who had less than four years of high school (31 percent).

• In 1992, about 65 percent of teenage (15 to 19 years old) births were out of wedlock. Ninety-four percent of black American teenage births were out of wedlock, compared to 60 percent of Hispanic and 56 percent of white teenage births.

• Women in their thirties had the largest increases in fertility rates during the 1980s and early 1990s. For women 30 to 34 years old in 1992, the fertility rate was 76.1 births per 1,000 women, up from 60.0 in 1980. And for women 35 to 39 in 1992, the fertility rate was 38 births per 1,000 women, up from 26.9 in 1980.

• In 1992, women 30 to 34 and 35 to 39 years old were nearing completion of their childbearing years with levels of childlessness at 26 and 19 percent, respectively. Each of these rates was 4 percentage points higher than in 1982.

• The average number of lifetime births expected for women 18 to 34 years old in June 1992 was 2,098 per 1,000 women, slightly lower than the 1976 average of 2,160.

## Sixty-Five Plus in the U.S.

Source: Bureau of the Census, U.S. Dept. of Commerce

• America is an aging society. In colonial times, half the population was under age 16; in 1990, fewer than 1 in 4 Americans were under age 16 and half were 33 or older; by 2050, at least half could be 39 or older.

• The 1990 census counted 31.1 million Americans age 65 or older, 12.5 percent of the total population. Among the elderly, 18 million were age 65 to 74, 10 million were age 75 to 84, and 3 million were 85 or older.

• The elderly population increased by 22 percent over the decade of the 1980s. Undramatic growth of the older population from 1990 to 2010 is projected. From 2010 to 2030, however, the Bureau of Census predicts, the elderly population will grow 76 percent while the population under age 65 increases 6.5 percent.

• The United States had 6.9 million persons age 80 or older in 1990, and that population could grow to more than 29 million by 2050. One in 35 Americans were 80 or older in 1990; by 2050, at least 1 in 13 could be 80 or older.

• Centenarians, those who had reached the age of 100 years or older, numbered 35,808 in 1990. The centenarian population more than doubled during the 1980s. This population group is 80 percent white and 79 percent female.

• Nine states had more than 1 million elderly in 1990. California had the largest number of persons age 65 or older (3.1 million). Florida had the largest proportion of elderly (18 percent).

• From 1980 to 1990, America's oldest old population (85 years and over) increased almost 38 percent. Eight states had more than 100,000 persons age 85 or older in 1990.

• There is increasing racial diversity within the elderly population. In 1990, 1 in 10 elderly persons were nonwhite. That could increase to about 2 in 10 by the middle of the next century. Additionally, the Census Bureau expects a greater proportion of the elderly will be persons of Hispanic origin (who may be of any race).

## U.S. Population 65 Years and Over, 1990

Source: Bureau of the Census, U.S. Dept. of Commerce

| Race and sex | Total 65 years and over | 65 to 69 years | 70 to 74 years | Total 75 years and over | 75 to 79 years |
|---|---|---|---|---|---|
| **All Races** | | | | | |
| Total | 31,078,895 | 10,065,835 | 7,979,660 | 13,033,400 | 6,102,929 |
| Male | 12,492,766 | 4,507,539 | 3,399,275 | 4,585,952 | 2,388,895 |
| Female | 18,586,129 | 5,558,296 | 4,580,385 | 8,447,448 | 3,714,034 |
| Males per 100 females | 67.2 | 81.1 | 74.2 | 54.3 | 64.3 |
| **White** | | | | | |
| Total | 28,020,562 | 8,983,978 | 7,191,013 | 11,845,571 | 5,518,341 |
| Male | 11,284,407 | 4,047,535 | 3,079,801 | 4,157,071 | 2,165,061 |
| Female | 16,736,155 | 4,936,443 | 4,111,212 | 7,688,500 | 3,353,280 |
| Males per 100 females | 67.4 | 82.0 | 74.9 | 54.1 | 64.6 |
| **Black** | | | | | |
| Total | 2,492,221 | 859,694 | 638,077 | 994,450 | 483,535 |
| Male | 956,936 | 360,653 | 252,967 | 343,316 | 178,695 |
| Female | 1,535,285 | 499,041 | 385,110 | 651,134 | 304,840 |
| Males per 100 females | 62.3 | 72.3 | 65.7 | 52.7 | 58.6 |
| **American Indian, Eskimo, and Aleut** | | | | | |
| Total | 116,153 | 43,374 | 29,831 | 42,948 | 21,522 |
| Male | 48,874 | 19,658 | 12,759 | 16,457 | 8,552 |
| Female | 67,279 | 23,716 | 17,072 | 26,491 | 12,970 |
| Males per 100 females | 72.6 | 82.9 | 74.7 | 62.1 | 65.9 |
| **Asian and Pacific Islander** | | | | | |
| Total | 449,959 | 178,789 | 120,739 | 150,431 | 79,531 |
| Male | 202,549 | 79,693 | 53,748 | 69,108 | 36,587 |
| Female | 247,410 | 99,096 | 66,991 | 81,323 | 42,944 |
| Males per 100 females | 81.9 | 80.4 | 80.2 | 85.0 | 85.2 |
| **Hispanic Origin[1]** | | | | | |
| Total | 1,146,223 | 431,000 | 284,085 | 431,138 | 211,432 |
| Male | 474,830 | 192,949 | 118,696 | 163,185 | 82,364 |
| Female | 671,393 | 238,051 | 165,389 | 267,953 | 129,068 |
| Males per 100 females | 70.7 | 81.1 | 71.8 | 60.9 | 63.8 |

(1) People of Hispanic origin may be of any race.

## U.S. Population 80 Years and Over, 1990

Source: Bureau of the Census, U.S. Dept. of Commerce

| Race and sex | Total 80 years and over | 80 to 84 years | Total 85 years and over | 85 to 89 years | 90 to 94 years | 95 to 99 years | Total 100 years and over |
|---|---|---|---|---|---|---|---|
| **All Races** | | | | | | | |
| Total | 6,930,471 | 3,909,046 | 3,021,425 | 2,034,661 | 747,979 | 202,977 | 35,808 |
| Male | 2,197,057 | 1,355,830 | 841,227 | 605,936 | 184,048 | 43,544 | 7,699 |
| Female | 4,733,414 | 2,553,216 | 2,180,198 | 1,428,725 | 563,931 | 159,433 | 28,109 |
| Males per 100 females | 46.4 | 53.1 | 38.6 | 42.4 | 32.6 | 27.3 | 27.4 |
| **White** | | | | | | | |
| Total | 6,327,230 | 3,566,268 | 2,760,962 | 1,858,176 | 689,928 | 183,505 | 29,353 |
| Male | 1,992,010 | 1,232,184 | 759,826 | 547,832 | 167,568 | 38,559 | 5,867 |
| Female | 4,335,220 | 2,334,084 | 2,001,136 | 1,310,344 | 522,360 | 144,946 | 23,486 |
| Males per 100 females | 45.9 | 52.8 | 38.0 | 41.8 | 32.1 | 26.6 | 25.0 |
| **Black** | | | | | | | |
| Total | 510,915 | 288,283 | 222,632 | 150,294 | 49,599 | 17,049 | 5,690 |
| Male | 164,621 | 98,351 | 66,270 | 46,949 | 13,485 | 4,277 | 1,559 |
| Female | 346,294 | 189,932 | 156,362 | 103,345 | 36,114 | 12,772 | 4,131 |
| Males per 100 females | 47.5 | 51.8 | 42.4 | 45.4 | 37.3 | 33.5 | 37.7 |
| **American Indian, Eskimo, and Aleut** | | | | | | | |
| Total | 21,426 | 12,236 | 9,190 | 6,287 | 1,982 | 659 | 262 |
| Male | 7,905 | 4,641 | 3,264 | 2,265 | 680 | 222 | 97 |
| Female | 13,521 | 7,595 | 5,926 | 4,022 | 1,302 | 437 | 165 |
| Males per 100 females | 58.5 | 61.1 | 55.1 | 56.3 | 52.2 | 50.8 | 58.8 |
| **Asian and Pacific Islander** | | | | | | | |
| Total | 70,900 | 42,259 | 28,641 | 19,904 | 6,470 | 1,764 | 503 |
| Male | 32,521 | 20,654 | 11,867 | 8,890 | 2,315 | 486 | 176 |
| Female | 38,379 | 21,605 | 16,774 | 11,014 | 4,155 | 1,278 | 327 |
| Males per 100 females | 84.7 | 95.6 | 70.7 | 80.7 | 55.7 | 38.0 | 53.8 |
| **Hispanic Origin[1]** | | | | | | | |
| Total | 219,706 | 128,302 | 91,404 | 64,945 | 19,257 | 5,616 | 1,586 |
| Male | 80,821 | 48,430 | 32,391 | 23,695 | 6,405 | 1,726 | 565 |
| Female | 138,885 | 79,872 | 59,013 | 41,250 | 12,852 | 3,890 | 1,021 |
| Males per 100 females | 58.2 | 60.6 | 54.9 | 57.4 | 49.8 | 44.4 | 55.3 |

(1) People of Hispanic orgin may be of any race.

## Countries With More Than 1 Million Octogenarians in 1991

Source: Bureau of the Census, U.S. Dept. of Commerce; in thousands

| Country | Population 80 and over | Country | Population 80 and over |
|---|---|---|---|
| China | 9,173 | France | 2,170 |
| United States | 7,310 | United Kingdom | 2,130 |
| India | 3,578 | Italy | 1,853 |
| Japan | 3,089 | Spain | 1,164 |
| Germany | 3,081 | | |

## Percent Change of U.S. Population 65 and Over, 1980-1990

Source: Bureau of the Census, U.S. Dept. of Commerce

| Region, division, and state | Percent change 1980 to 1990 | Region, division, and state | Percent change 1980 to 1990 |
|---|---|---|---|
| United States | 22.3 | Nebraska | 8.5 |
| Northeast | 15.2 | Kansas | 11.9 |
| New England | 16.4 | South Atlantic | 33.6 |
| Middle Atlantic | 14.8 | Delaware | 36.4 |
| Midwest | 15.8 | Maryland | 30.8 |
| East North Central | 17.9 | District of Columbia | 4.8 |
| West North Central | 11.4 | Virginia | 31.5 |
| South | 26.3 | West Virginia | 13.0 |
| South Atlantic | 33.6 | North Carolina | 33.3 |
| East South Central | 16.5 | South Carolina | 38.1 |
| West South Central | 20.1 | Georgia | 26.6 |
| West | 34.3 | Florida | 40.4 |
| Mountain | 43.6 | East South Central | 16.5 |
| Pacific | 31.3 | Kentucky | 13.9 |
| New England | | Tennessee | 19.6 |
| Maine | 16.4 | Alabama | 18.9 |
| Vermont | 15.9 | Mississippi | 11.0 |
| New Hampshire | 13.7 | West South Central | 20.1 |
| Massachusetts | 21.4 | Arkansas | 12.0 |
| Rhode Island | 12.8 | Louisiana | 16.0 |
| Connecticut | 18.6 | Oklahoma | 12.8 |
| Middle Atlantic | 22.2 | Texas | 25.2 |
| New York | 14.8 | Mountain | 43.6 |
| New Jersey | 9.4 | Montana | 25.9 |
| Pennsylvania | 20.0 | Idaho | 29.4 |
| East North Central | 19.5 | Wyoming | 27.0 |
| Ohio | 17.9 | Colorado | 33.2 |
| Indiana | 20.3 | New Mexico | 40.7 |
| Illinois | 18.9 | Arizona | 55.8 |
| Michigan | 13.8 | Utah | 37.3 |
| Wisconsin | 21.5 | Nevada | 94.1 |
| West North Central | 15.4 | Pacific | 31.3 |
| Minnesota | 11.4 | Washington | 33.3 |
| Iowa | 14.0 | Oregon | 29.0 |
| Missouri | 9.9 | California | 29.9 |
| North Dakota | 10.7 | Alaska | 93.7 |
| South Dakota | 13.2 | Hawaii | 64.2 |
| | 12.4 | | |

## Countries With More Than 2 Million Elderly Persons in 1991

Source: Bureau of the Census, U.S. Dept. of Commerce; in thousands

| Country | Population 65 and over | Country | Population 65 and over | Country | Population 65 and over |
|---|---|---|---|---|---|
| China | 67,967 | Indonesia | 5,962 | Turkey | 2,789 |
| India | 32,780 | Spain | 5,378 | Nigeria | 2,676 |
| United States | 32,045 | Pakistan | 4,734 | Romania | 2,489 |
| Japan | 15,253 | Poland | 3,851 | Philippines | 2,380 |
| Germany | 12,010 | Mexico | 3,522 | Thailand | 2,350 |
| United Kingdom | 9,025 | Bangladesh | 3,492 | Yugoslavia | 2,328 |
| Italy | 8,665 | Vietnam | 3,196 | South Korea | 2,135 |
| France | 8,074 | Canada | 3,140 | Egypt | 2,077 |
| Brazil | 6,680 | Argentina | 3,012 | Iran | 2,052 |

## Countries Projected to Have More Than 2 Million Elderly Persons in 2020

Source: Bureau of the Census, U.S. Dept. of Commerce; in thousands

| Country | Population 65 and over | Country | Population 65 and over | Country | Population 65 and over |
|---|---|---|---|---|---|
| China | 179,561 | Poland | 7,243 | Burma (Myanmar) | 3,425 |
| India | 88,495 | Vietnam | 6,707 | Czechoslovakia | 3,149 |
| United States | 53,627 | Philippines | 6,646 | Morocco | 2,972 |
| Japan | 33,421 | South Korea | 6,550 | Venezuela | 2,912 |
| Indonesia | 22,183 | Canada | 6,404 | Saudi Arabia | 2,867 |
| Brazil | 18,800 | Egypt | 5,680 | North Korea | 2,734 |
| Germany | 18,396 | Iran | 5,235 | Zaire | 2,643 |
| Italy | 13,078 | Yugoslavia | 4,933 | Peru | 2,580 |
| France | 12,119 | Argentina | 4,862 | Sri Lanka | 2,527 |
| United Kingdom | 12,108 | Romania | 4,588 | Algeria | 2,450 |
| Mexico | 10,857 | Colombia | 4,464 | Greece | 2,237 |
| Pakistan | 9,678 | South Africa | 4,084 | Hungary | 2,186 |
| Nigeria | 9,152 | Australia | 3,956 | Malaysia | 2,139 |
| Bangladesh | 9,057 | Ethiopia | 3,920 | Chile | 2,133 |
| Spain | 8,162 | Taiwan | 3,500 | Belgium | 2,071 |
| Turkey | 7,990 | Netherlands | 3,461 | Portugal | 2,053 |
| Thailand | 7,828 | | | | |

## Living Arrangements of the Elderly, 1980 and 1990

Source: Bureau of the Census, U.S. Dept. of Commerce; in thousands; noninstitutional population.

| Living arrangement and age | 1980 Number | | | 1980 Percent distribution | | | 1990 Number | | | 1990 Percent distribution | | |
|---|---|---|---|---|---|---|---|---|---|---|---|---|
| | Total | Men | Women | Total | Men | Women | Total | Men | Women | Total | Men | Women |
| **65 years and over ..** | 24,157 | 9,889 | 14,268 | 100.0 | 100.0 | 100.0 | 29,566 | 12,334 | 17,232 | 100.0 | 100.0 | 100.0 |
| Living: | | | | | | | | | | | | |
| Alone ......... | 7,067 | 1,447 | 5,620 | 29.3 | 14.6 | 39.4 | 9,176 | 1,942 | 7,233 | 31.0 | 15.7 | 42.0 |
| With spouse ..... | 12,781 | 7,441 | 5,340 | 52.9 | 75.2 | 37.4 | 16,003 | 9,158 | 6,845 | 54.1 | 74.3 | 39.7 |
| With other relatives . | 3,892 | 832 | 3,060 | 16.1 | 8.4 | 21.4 | 3,734 | 953 | 2,782 | 12.6 | 7.7 | 16.1 |
| With nonrelatives only[1] ....... | 417 | 169 | 248 | 1.7 | 1.7 | 1.7 | 653 | 281 | 372 | 2.2 | 2.3 | 2.2 |
| **65 to 74 years ....** | 15,302 | 6,621 | 8,681 | 100.0 | 100.0 | 100.0 | 17,979 | 8,013 | 9,966 | 100.0 | 100.0 | 100.0 |
| Living: | | | | | | | | | | | | |
| Alone ......... | 3,750 | 797 | 2,953 | 24.5 | 12.0 | 34.0 | 4,350 | 1,042 | 3,309 | 24.2 | 13.0 | 33.2 |
| With spouse ..... | 9,436 | 5,285 | 4,151 | 61.7 | 79.8 | 47.8 | 11,353 | 6,265 | 5,089 | 63.1 | 78.2 | 51.1 |
| With other relatives . | 1,890 | 436 | 1,454 | 12.4 | 6.6 | 16.7 | 1,931 | 528 | 1,401 | 10.7 | 6.6 | 14.1 |
| With nonrelatives only[1] ....... | 226 | 103 | 123 | 1.5 | 1.6 | 1.4 | 345 | 178 | 167 | 1.9 | 2.2 | 1.7 |
| **75 to 84 years ....** | 7,172 | 2,708 | 4,464 | 100.0 | 100.0 | 100.0 | 9,354 | 3,562 | 5,792 | 100.0 | 100.0 | 100.0 |
| Living: | | | | | | | | | | | | |
| Alone ......... | 2,664 | 505 | 2,159 | 37.1 | 18.6 | 48.4 | 3,774 | 688 | 3,086 | 40.3 | 19.3 | 53.3 |
| With spouse ..... | 2,977 | 1,882 | 1,095 | 41.5 | 69.5 | 24.5 | 4,145 | 2,537 | 1,607 | 44.3 | 71.2 | 27.7 |
| With other relatives . | 1,394 | 271 | 1,123 | 19.4 | 10.0 | 25.2 | 1,237 | 264 | 974 | 13.2 | 7.4 | 16.8 |
| With nonrelatives only[1] ....... | 137 | 50 | 87 | 1.9 | 1.8 | 1.9 | 198 | 73 | 125 | 2.1 | 2.0 | 2.2 |
| **85 years and over ..** | 1,683 | 560 | 1,123 | 100.0 | 100.0 | 100.0 | 2,233 | 758 | 1,475 | 100.0 | 100.0 | 100.0 |
| Living: | | | | | | | | | | | | |
| Alone ......... | 653 | 145 | 508 | 38.8 | 25.9 | 45.2 | 1,051 | 213 | 838 | 47.1 | 28.1 | 56.8 |
| With spouse ..... | 368 | 274 | 94 | 21.9 | 48.9 | 8.4 | 505 | 356 | 150 | 22.6 | 47.0 | 10.2 |
| With other relatives . | 608 | 125 | 483 | 36.1 | 22.3 | 43.0 | 567 | 160 | 406 | 25.4 | 21.1 | 27.5 |
| With nonrelatives only[1] ....... | 54 | 16 | 38 | 3.2 | 2.9 | 3.4 | 110 | 29 | 81 | 4.9 | 3.8 | 5.5 |

(1) 1980 data include a small number of persons in unrelated subfamilies.

## Persons Living Alone, 1970-1991

Source: Bureau of the Census, U.S. Dept. of Commerce

| Sex and Age | Number of Persons (1,000) | | | | Percent Distribution | | | |
|---|---|---|---|---|---|---|---|---|
| | 1970 | 1980 | 1990 | 1991 | 1970 | 1980 | 1990 | 1991 |
| **Both sexes. ...........** | 10,851 | 18,296 | 22,999 | 23,590 | 100 | 100 | 100 | 100 |
| 15 to 24 years old[1] ....... | 558 | 1,726 | 1,210 | 1,140 | 5 | 9 | 5 | 5 |
| 25 to 34 years old ........ | 1,604[2] | 4,729[2] | 3,972 | 4,116 | 15[2] | 26[2] | 17 | 17 |
| 35 to 44 years old ........ | (2) | (2) | 3,138 | 3,402 | (2) | (2) | 14 | 14 |
| 45 to 64 years old ........ | 3,622 | 4,514 | 5,502 | 5,550 | 33 | 25 | 24 | 24 |
| 65 to 74 years old ........ | 2,815 | 3,851 | 4,350 | 4,494 | 26 | 21 | 19 | 19 |
| 75 years old and over ...... | 2,258 | 3,477 | 4,825 | 4,887 | 21 | 19 | 21 | 21 |
| **Male ...............** | 3,532 | 6,966 | 9,049 | 9,450 | 33 | 38 | 39 | 40 |
| 15 to 24 years old[1] ....... | 274 | 947 | 674 | 622 | 3 | 5 | 3 | 3 |
| 25 to 34 years old ........ | 933[2] | 2,920[2] | 2,395 | 2,491 | 9[2] | 16[2] | 10 | 11 |
| 35 to 44 years old ........ | (2) | (2) | 1,836 | 2,008 | (2) | (2) | 8 | 9 |
| 45 to 64 years old ........ | 1,152 | 1,613 | 2,203 | 2,319 | 11 | 9 | 10 | 10 |
| 65 to 74 years old ........ | 611 | 775 | 1,042 | 1,096 | 6 | 4 | 5 | 5 |
| 75 years old and over ...... | 563 | 711 | 901 | 914 | 5 | 4 | 4 | 4 |
| **Female ...............** | 7,319 | 11,330 | 13,950 | 14,141 | 68 | 62 | 61 | 68 |
| 15 to 24 years old[1] ....... | 282 | 779 | 538 | 518 | 3 | 4 | 2 | 2 |
| 25 to 34 years old ........ | 671[2] | 1,809[2] | 1,578 | 1,626 | 6[2] | 10[2] | 7 | 7 |
| 35 to 44 years old ........ | (2) | (2) | 1,303 | 1,394 | (2) | (2) | 6 | 6 |
| 45 to 64 years old ........ | 2,470 | 2,901 | 3,300 | 3,232 | 23 | 16 | 14 | 14 |
| 65 to 74 years old ........ | 2,204 | 3,076 | 3,309 | 3,397 | 20 | 17 | 14 | 14 |
| 75 years old and over ...... | 1,693 | 2,766 | 3,924 | 3,973 | 16 | 15 | 17 | 15 |

(1) 1970, persons 14 to 24 years old. (2) Data for persons 35 to 44 years old included with persons 25 to 34 years old.

## Female Family Householders With No Spouse Present, 1980-1991

Source: Bureau of the Census, U.S. Dept. of Commerce; as of March; persons 15 years old and over.

| Characteristic | Unit | White 1980 | 1990 | 1991 | Black 1980 | 1990 | 1991 | Hispanic Origin[1] 1980 | 1990 | 1991 |
|---|---|---|---|---|---|---|---|---|---|---|
| **Female family householder ...** | 1,000 ... | 6,052 | 7,306 | 7,512 | 2,495 | 3,275 | 3,430 | 610 | 1,116 | 1,186 |
| Percent of all families ..... | Percent .. | 12 | 13 | 13 | 40 | 44 | 46 | 20 | 23 | 24 |
| Median age ............. | Years ... | 43.7 | 42.5 | 41.9 | 37.4 | 37.6 | 38.5 | 37.0 | 38.8 | 39.0 |
| Marital status: | | | | | | | | | | |
| Single (never married) ...... | Percent .. | 11 | 15 | 17 | 27 | 39 | 41 | 23 | 27 | 27 |
| Married, spouse absent ..... | Percent .. | 17 | 16 | 18 | 29 | 21 | 19 | 32 | 29 | 31 |
| Separated ............. | Percent .. | 14 | 14 | 14 | 27 | 19 | 16 | 29 | 23 | 24 |
| Other ............... | Percent .. | 3 | 3 | 4 | 2 | 2 | 3 | 4 | 6 | 7 |
| Widowed ............. | Percent .. | 33 | 26 | 24 | 22 | 17 | 17 | 15 | 16 | 16 |
| Divorced ............. | Percent .. | 40 | 43 | 42 | 22 | 23 | 23 | 30 | 29 | 27 |
| Presence of children under 18: | | | | | | | | | | |
| No own children .......... | Percent .. | 41 | 43 | 42 | 28 | 32 | 33 | 25 | 33 | 33 |
| With own children ........ | Percent .. | 59 | 58 | 58 | 72 | 68 | 67 | 75 | 67 | 67 |
| 1 child ............. | Percent .. | 28 | 30 | 30 | 26 | 30 | 28 | 28 | 25 | 26 |
| 2 children ........... | Percent .. | 20 | 19 | 19 | 23 | 22 | 21 | 23 | 22 | 23 |
| 3 children ........... | Percent .. | 7 | 7 | 7 | 11 | 9 | 11 | 15 | 13 | 11 |
| 4 or more children ...... | Percent .. | 3 | 2 | 2 | 11 | 7 | 7 | 9 | 6 | 7 |
| Children per family ........ | Number .. | 1.03 | 0.95 | 0.95 | 1.51 | 1.26 | 1.27 | 1.56 | 1.37 | 1.37 |

(1) Person of Hispanic origin may be of any race.

## Living Arrangements of Children, 1970-1991

Source: Bureau of the Census, U.S. Dept. of Commerce; as of March; excludes persons under 18 yrs. who maintained households or family groups.

| Race, Hispanic Origin and Year | Number (1,000) | Both parents | Percent Living With—Mother only | | | | | Father only | Neither parent |
|---|---|---|---|---|---|---|---|---|---|
| | | | Total | Divorced | Married spouse absent | Single[1] | Widowed | | |
| **White** | | | | | | | | | |
| 1970 | 58,790 | 90 | 8 | 3 | 3 | Z | 2 | 1 | 2 |
| 1980 | 52,242 | 83 | 14 | 7 | 4 | 1 | 2 | 2 | 2 |
| 1990 | 51,390 | 79 | 16 | 8 | 4 | 3 | 1 | 2 | 2 |
| 1991 | 51,918 | 79 | 17 | 8 | 4 | 3 | 1 | 3 | 2 |
| **Black** | | | | | | | | | |
| 1970 | 9,422 | 59 | 30 | 5 | 16 | 4 | 4 | 2 | 10 |
| 1980 | 9,375 | 42 | 44 | 11 | 16 | 13 | 4 | 2 | 12 |
| 1990 | 10,018 | 38 | 51 | 10 | 12 | 27 | 2 | 4 | 8 |
| 1991 | 10,209 | 36 | 54 | 10 | 11 | 31 | 2 | 4 | 7 |
| **Hispanic[2]** | | | | | | | | | |
| 1970 | 4,006[3] | 78 | NA | NA | NA | NA | NA | NA | NA |
| 1980 | 5,459 | 75 | 20 | 6 | 8 | 4 | 2 | 2 | 4 |
| 1990 | 7,174 | 67 | 27 | 7 | 10 | 8 | 2 | 3 | 3 |
| 1991 | 7,462 | 66 | 27 | 7 | 10 | 9 | 2 | 3 | 4 |

NA=Not available. Z=Less than .5 percent. (1) Never married. (2) Hispanic persons may be of any race. (3) All persons under 18 years old.

## Living Arrangements of Young Adults, 1960-1990

Source: Bureau of the Census, U.S. Dept. of Commerce; in thousands

| Living arrangement | 1960 | 1970 | 1980 | 1990 | Percent distribution | | | |
|---|---|---|---|---|---|---|---|---|
| | | | | | 1960 | 1970 | 1980 | 1990 |
| **Adults 18-24 Years, Total** | 14,718 | 22,357 | 29,122 | 25,310 | 100.0 | 100.0 | 100.0 | 100.0 |
| Male | 6,842 | 10,398 | 14,278 | 12,450 | 100.0 | 100.0 | 100.0 | 100.0 |
| Child of householder[1] | 3,583 | 5,641 | 7,755 | 7,232 | 52.4 | 54.3 | 54.3 | 58.1 |
| Family householder or spouse | 2,160 | 3,119 | 3,041 | 1,838 | 31.6 | 30.0 | 21.3 | 14.8 |
| Nonfamily householder | 182 | 563 | 1,581 | 1,228 | 2.7 | 5.4 | 11.1 | 9.9 |
| Other | 917 | 1,075 | 1,902 | 2,152 | 13.4 | 10.3 | 13.3 | 17.3 |
| Female | 7,876 | 11,959 | 14,844 | 12,860 | 100.0 | 100.0 | 100.0 | 100.0 |
| Child of householder[1] | 2,750 | 4,941 | 6,336 | 6,135 | 34.9 | 41.3 | 42.7 | 47.7 |
| Family householder or spouse | 4,026 | 5,351 | 5,367 | 3,793 | 51.1 | 44.7 | 36.2 | 29.5 |
| Nonfamily householder | 172 | 503 | 1,195 | 1,024 | 2.2 | 4.2 | 8.1 | 8.0 |
| Other | 928 | 1,164 | 1,946 | 1,908 | 11.8 | 9.7 | 13.1 | 14.8 |
| **Adults 25-34 Years, Total** | 22,483 | 24,556 | 36,796 | 43,240 | 100.0 | 100.0 | 100.0 | 100.0 |
| Male | 10,896 | 11,929 | 18,107 | 21,462 | 100.0 | 100.0 | 100.0 | 100.0 |
| Child of householder | 1,185 | 1,129 | 1,894 | 3,213 | 10.9 | 9.5 | 10.5 | 15.0 |
| Family householder or spouse | 8,557 | 9,455 | 12,024 | 11,998 | 78.5 | 79.3 | 66.4 | 55.9 |
| Nonfamily householder | 398 | 775 | 2,765 | 3,467 | 3.7 | 6.5 | 15.3 | 16.2 |
| Other | 756 | 570 | 1,424 | 2,784 | 6.9 | 4.8 | 7.9 | 13.0 |
| Female | 11,587 | 12,637 | 18,689 | 21,779 | 100.0 | 100.0 | 100.0 | 100.0 |
| Child of householder | 853 | 829 | 1,300 | 1,774 | 7.4 | 6.6 | 7.0 | 8.1 |
| Family householder or spouse | 9,981 | 10,877 | 14,591 | 15,966 | 86.1 | 86.1 | 78.1 | 73.3 |
| Nonfamily householder | 244 | 440 | 1,646 | 2,151 | 2.1 | 3.5 | 8.8 | 9.9 |
| Other | 509 | 491 | 1,153 | 1,888 | 4.4 | 3.9 | 6.2 | 8.7 |

(1) Child of householder includes unmarried college students living in dormitories.

## One-Parent Family Groups in 1970, 1980, and 1991

Source: Bureau of the Census, U.S. Dept. of Commerce; in thousands

| | 1970 | | 1980 | | 1991 | | Average annual change | |
|---|---|---|---|---|---|---|---|---|
| | Number | Percent | Number | Percent | Number | Percent | 1970-80 | 1980-91 |
| **White** | | | | | | | | |
| One-parent family groups | 2,638 | 100.0 | 4,664 | 100.0 | 6,550 | 100.0 | 5.7 | 3.1 |
| Maintained by mother | 2,330 | 88.3 | 4,122 | 88.4 | 5,482 | 83.7 | 5.7 | 2.6 |
| Never married | 73 | 2.8 | 379 | 8.1 | 1,271 | 19.4 | 16.5 | 11.0 |
| Spouse absent | 796 | 30.2 | 1,033 | 22.1 | 1,301 | 19.9 | 2.6 | 2.1 |
| Separated | 477 | 18.1 | 840 | 18.0 | 1,062 | 16.2 | 5.7 | 2.1 |
| Divorced | 930 | 35.3 | 2,201 | 47.2 | 2,565 | 39.2 | 8.6 | 1.4 |
| Widowed | 531 | 20.1 | 511 | 11.0 | 345 | 5.3 | -0.4 | -3.6 |
| Maintained by father | 307 | 11.6 | 542 | 11.6 | 1,068 | 16.3 | 5.7 | 6.2 |
| Never married | 18 | 0.7 | 32 | 0.7 | 255 | 3.9 | (B) | (B) |
| Spouse absent[1] | 196 | 7.4 | 141 | 3.0 | 223 | 3.4 | -3.3 | 4.2 |
| Divorced | (NA) | (NA) | 288 | 6.2 | 531 | 8.1 | (NA) | 5.6 |
| Widowed | 93 | 3.5 | 82 | 1.8 | 59 | 0.9 | -1.3 | -3.0 |
| **Black** | | | | | | | | |
| One-parent family groups | 1,148 | 100.0 | 2,114 | 100.0 | 3,240 | 100.0 | 6.1 | 3.9 |
| Maintained by mother | 1,063 | 92.6 | 1,984 | 93.9 | 3,000 | 92.6 | 6.2 | 3.8 |
| Never married | 173 | 15.1 | 665 | 31.5 | 1,755 | 54.2 | 13.5 | 8.8 |
| Spouse absent | 570 | 49.7 | 667 | 31.6 | 567 | 17.5 | 1.6 | -1.5 |
| Separated | 479 | 41.7 | 616 | 29.1 | 472 | 14.6 | 2.5 | -2.4 |
| Divorced | 172 | 15.0 | 477 | 22.6 | 551 | 17.0 | 10.2 | 1.3 |
| Widowed | 148 | 12.9 | 174 | 8.2 | 128 | 4.0 | 1.6 | -2.8 |
| Maintained by father | 85 | 7.4 | 129 | 6.1 | 239 | 7.4 | 4.2 | 5.6 |
| Never married | 4 | 0.3 | 30 | 1.4 | 99 | 3.1 | (B) | (B) |
| Spouse absent[1] | 50 | 4.4 | 37 | 1.8 | 50 | 1.5 | (B) | (B) |
| Divorced | (NA) | (NA) | 43 | 2.0 | 79 | 2.4 | (NA) | (B) |
| Widowed | 30 | 2.6 | 19 | 0.9 | 11 | 0.3 | (B) | (B) |

NA = Not available. B = Base less than 75,000. (1) Data for 1970 include divorced fathers. Note: Family groups comprise family households, related subfamilies, and unrelated subfamilies.

## Principal Types of Accidental Deaths, 1970-1992

Source: National Safety Council

| Year | Motor vehicle | Falls | Poison (solid, liquid) | Drowning | Fires, Burns | Injestion of Food, Object | Firearms | Poison (gases) |
|------|------|------|------|------|------|------|------|------|
| 1970 .... | 54,633 | 16,926 | 3,679 | 7,860 | 6,718 | 2,753 | 2,406 | 1,620 |
| 1975 .... | 45,853 | 14,896 | 4,694 | 8,000 | 6,071 | 3,106 | 2,380 | 1,577 |
| 1980 .... | 53,172 | 13,294 | 3,089 | 7,257 | 5,822 | 3,249 | 1,955 | 1,242 |
| 1985 .... | 45,901 | 12,001 | 4,091 | 5,316 | 4,938 | 3,551 | 1,649 | 1,079 |
| 1990 .... | 46,300 | 12,400 | 5,700 | 5,200 | 4,300 | 3,200 | 1,400 | 800 |
| 1991 .... | 43,500 | 12,200 | 5,600 | 4,600 | 4,200 | 2,900 | 1,400 | 800 |
| 1992 .... | 40,300 | 12,400 | 5,200 | 4,300 | 4,000 | 2,700 | 1,400 | 700 |
| | | | **Death rates per 100,000 population** | | | | | |
| 1970 .... | 26.8 | 8.3 | 1.8 | 3.9 | 3.3 | 1.4 | 1.2 | 0.8 |
| 1975 .... | 21.3 | 6.9 | 2.2 | 3.7 | 2.8 | 1.4 | 1.1 | 0.7 |
| 1980 .... | 23.4 | 5.9 | 1.4 | 3.2 | 2.6 | 1.4 | 0.9 | 0.5 |
| 1985 .... | 19.2 | 5.0 | 1.7 | 2.2 | 2.1 | 1.5 | 0.7 | 0.5 |
| 1990 .... | 18.8 | 5.0 | 2.3 | 2.1 | 1.7 | 1.3 | 0.6 | 0.3 |
| 1991 .... | 17.2 | 4.8 | 2.2 | 1.8 | 1.7 | 1.1 | 0.6 | 0.3 |
| 1992 .... | 15.8 | 4.9 | 2.0 | 1.7 | 1.6 | 1.1 | 0.5 | 0.3 |

**Note:** There were 12,000 other accidental deaths in 1992; the most frequently occurring types were medical complications, machinery, air transport, water transport, mechanical suffocation, and excessive cold.

## Motor Vehicle Accidents, 1992

Source: National Safety Council

Motor vehicle deaths decreased 7 percent from 1991 to 1992, while mileage increased 3 percent, the number of vehicles increased 1 percent, and the population increased 1 percent. Almost 2 out of 3 deaths in 1992 occurred in places classified as rural. In urban areas, more than one-fourth of the victims were pedestrians; in rural areas, the victims were mostly occupants of motor vehicles. More than one-half of all deaths occurred in night accidents. About 48 percent of all traffic fatalities in 1992 involved an intoxicated or alcohol-impaired driver or nonoccupant. Of these 19,899 alcohol-related traffic fatalities, an estimated 15,944 occurred in accidents in which a driver or nonoccupant was intoxicated, and the remainder involved a driver or nonoccupant who had been drinking but was not legally intoxicated. Alcohol was also a factor in about 19 percent of serious injury accidents and 6 percent of property damage accidents. The estimated cost of all alcohol-related motor vehicle accidents in 1992 was about $32.7 billion.

| | Death Total | % Change from 1991 | Death Rate[1] |
|---|---|---|---|
| **All motor vehicle accidents** | **40,300** | **—7** | **15.8** |
| Urban | 14,400 | —6 | |
| Rural | 25,900 | —8 | |
| **Collision between motor vehicles** | **17,400** | **—6** | **6.8** |
| Urban | 6,300 | —9 | |
| Rural | 11,100 | —5 | |
| **Collision with fixed object** | **10,900** | **—9** | **4.3** |
| Urban | 3,000 | —12 | |
| Rural | 7,900 | —8 | |
| **Pedestrian accidents** | **6,500** | **—3** | **2.5** |
| Urban | 4,100 | +5 | |
| Rural | 2,400 | —14 | |

| | Death Total | % Change from 1991 | Death Rate[1] |
|---|---|---|---|
| **Noncollision accidents** | **4,200** | **—9** | **1.6** |
| Urban | 500 | 0 | |
| Rural | 3,700 | —10 | |
| **Collision with pedalcycle** | **700** | **—22** | **0.3** |
| Urban | 400 | —33 | |
| Rural | 300 | 0 | |
| **Collision with railroad train** | **500** | **—17** | **0.2** |
| Urban | 100 | 0 | |
| Rural | 400 | —20 | |
| **Other collision (animal, animal-drawn vehicles, street cars)** | **100** | **0** | **(2)** |

(1) Deaths per 100,000 population. (2) Death rate was less than 0.05.

## Improper Driving Reported in Accidents, 1992

Source: National Safety Council; in percent

| Kind of Improper Driving | Fatal Accidents Total | Urban | Rural | Injury Accidents Total | Urban | Rural | All Accidents Total | Urban | Rural |
|---|---|---|---|---|---|---|---|---|---|
| Total . . . . . . . . . . . . . . . . . | 100.0% | 100.0% | 100.0% | 100.0% | 100.0% | 100.0% | 100.0% | 100.0% | 100.0% |
| **Improper driving** . . . . . . . . . | **55.5** | **52.3** | **57.3** | **68.6** | **69.7** | **63.5** | **67.2** | **67.0** | **68.5** |
| Speed too fast or unsafe . . . . . . . | 16.5 | 15.9 | 17.2 | 13.2 | 19.5 | 11.7 | 11.7 | 10.8 | 16.0 |
| Right of way . . . . . . . . . . . . . | 12.5 | 14.0 | 10.6 | 24.1 | 27.8 | 14.5 | 20.8 | 22.2 | 15.1 |
| Failed to yield . . . . . . . . . . . | 7.8 | 8.2 | 7.2 | 17.0 | 19.0 | 11.7 | 15.7 | 16.4 | 12.3 |
| Passed stop sign . . . . . . . . | 2.6 | 2.8 | 2.4 | 2.2 | 2.4 | 1.6 | 1.6 | 1.7 | 1.5 |
| Disregarded signal . . . . . . . . | 2.2 | 3.0 | 1.0 | 4.9 | 6.4 | 1.2 | 3.6 | 4.1 | 1.2 |
| Drove left of center . . . . . . . . . | 7.5 | 5.7 | 9.8 | 2.2 | 1.8 | 3.8 | 1.9 | 1.4 | 3.9 |
| Improper overtaking . . . . . . . . . . . | 1.0 | 0.9 | 1.2 | 0.9 | 0.8 | 1.5 | 1.3 | 1.2 | 1.9 |
| Made improper turn . . . . . . . . . | 2.5 | 2.0 | 3.2 | 3.1 | 3.1 | 3.5 | 4.2 | 4.1 | 4.8 |
| Followed too closely . . . . . . . . | 0.6 | 0.7 | 0.5 | 6.9 | 7.4 | 3.4 | 7.2 | 8.0 | 3.8 |
| Other improper driving . . . . . . . | 13.8 | 13.2 | 14.6 | 18.1 | 19.4 | 21.3 | 20.1 | 19.4 | 23.0 |
| **No improper driving stated** . . . | **45.5** | **47.7** | **42.7** | **31.4** | **30.3** | **36.5** | **32.8** | **33.0** | **31.5** |

**Notes:** Based on reports from 14 state traffic authorities. When a driver was under the influence of alcohol or drugs, the accident was considered a result of the driver's physical condition—not a driving error. For this reason, accidents in which the driver was reported to be under the influence are classified under "no improper driving."

## Deaths Involving Firearms

Source: National Safety Council

| | All Ages | Under 5 | 1990 Firearm Deaths by Age | | | | | |
|---|---|---|---|---|---|---|---|---|
| | | | 5-14 | 15-24 | 25-44 | 45-64 | 65-74 | 75 & Over |
| Total Firearm Deaths[1] . . . . . | 36,866 | 103 | 681 | 9,463 | 15,340 | 6,255 | 2,596 | 2,428 |
| Male . . . . . . . . . . . . . | 31,458 | 63 | 516 | 8,382 | 12,880 | 5,175 | 2,232 | 2,210 |
| Female . . . . . . . . . . . . | 5,408 | 40 | 165 | 1,081 | 2,460 | 1,080 | 364 | 218 |
| Accidents . . . . . . . . . . | 1,416 | 34 | 202 | 500 | 442 | 149 | 50 | 39 |
| Male . . . . . . . . . . . . . | 1,255 | 24 | 180 | 457 | 385 | 131 | 42 | 36 |
| Female . . . . . . . . . . . . | 161 | 10 | 22 | 43 | 57 | 18 | 8 | 3 |
| Suicide . . . . . . . . . . . | 18,885 | 0 | 144 | 3,165 | 6,818 | 4,356 | 2,245 | 2,157 |
| Male . . . . . . . . . . . . . | 16,285 | 0 | 106 | 2,778 | 5,721 | 3,671 | 1,976 | 2,033 |
| Female . . . . . . . . . . . . | 2,600 | 0 | 38 | 387 | 1,097 | 685 | 269 | 124 |
| Homicide . . . . . . . . . . | 16,218 | 69 | 321 | 5,679 | 7,951 | 1,703 | 282 | 213 |
| Male . . . . . . . . . . . . . | 13,629 | 39 | 218 | 5,046 | 6,672 | 1,334 | 197 | 123 |
| Female . . . . . . . . . . . . | 2,589 | 30 | 103 | 633 | 1,279 | 369 | 85 | 90 |
| Undetermined[2] . . . . . . . | 347 | 0 | 14 | 119 | 129 | 47 | 19 | 19 |
| Male . . . . . . . . . . . . . | 289 | 0 | 12 | 101 | 102 | 39 | 17 | 18 |
| Female . . . . . . . . . . . . | 58 | 0 | 2 | 18 | 27 | 8 | 2 | 1 |

(1) Excludes firearm deaths by legal intervention. These deaths totaled 318 in 1990. (2) Undetermined means the intentionality of the death (accident, suicide, homicide) cannot be determined.

**Handguns.** Handguns are involved in the majority of firearm deaths and injuries in the U.S. According to the Center to Prevent Handgun Violence, there are an estimated 24,000 handgun-related deaths in America every year. Handguns account for about one-third of all firearms, but account for two-thirds of all firearm-related deaths. In 1989, about 75 percent of firearm homicides were by handguns, according to the FBI. Comparable police data are not available for suicides, but local studies suggest that about two-thirds of firearm suicides are due to handguns. For children 10-14 years of age, handguns account for 73 percent of firearm homicides and 70 per cent of firearm suicides. Of all children ages 16 and under, half of those injured in a handgun accident were shot in their own home.

## Home Accident Deaths, 1950-1992

Source: National Safety Council

| Year | Total | Falls | Poison (solid, liquid) | Fires, burns[2] | Suffo., ingesting object | Firearms | Suffo., mech- anical | Poison (gases) | All Other[4] |
|---|---|---|---|---|---|---|---|---|---|
| 1950 . . . . . . . . . . . . | 29,000 | 14,800 | 1,300 | 5,000 | (1) | 950 | 1,600 | 1,250 | 4,100 |
| 1960 . . . . . . . . . . . . | 28,000 | 12,300 | 1,350 | 6,350 | 1,850 | 1,200 | 1,500 | 900 | 2,550 |
| 1970 . . . . . . . . . . . . | 27,000 | 3,000 | 5,600 | 1,800 | 1,100* | 1,200 | 1,500 | 900 | — |
| 1980 . . . . . . . . . . . . | 22,800 | 7,100 | 2,500 | 1,800 | 1,100 | 1,100 | 1,400 | 3,300 | — |
| 1990 . . . . . . . . . . . . | 21,500 | 6,500 | 4,700 | 4,800 | 2,000 | 1,100 | 500 | 700 | 4,100[3] |
| 1991 . . . . . . . . . . . . | 20,500 | 6,100 | 4,400 | 3,300 | 2,000 | 800 | 800 | 400 | 2,400 |
| 1992 . . . . . . . . . . . . | 19,500 | 6,200 | 4,100 | 3,500 | 1,800 | 800 | 600 | 500 | 2,200 |
| | | | | 3,200 | 1,700 | 500 | 700 | 400 | 2,700 |

* Data for this year and subsequent years not comparable with previous years due to classification changes. (1) Included in All Other. (2) Includes deaths resulting from conflagration, regardless of nature of injury. (3) Includes about 1,000 excessive deaths due to summer heat wave. (4) Includes drowning in swimming pools and bathtubs.

## Worldwide Airline Fatalities

Source: National Safety Council

| Year | Aircraft Accidents[1] | Passenger Deaths | Death Rate[2] | Year | Aircraft Accidents[1] | Passenger Deaths | Death Rate[2] |
|---|---|---|---|---|---|---|---|
| 1980 . . . . . . . | 22 | 814 | 0.14 | 1987 . . . . . . . | 24 | 890 | 0.10 |
| 1981 . . . . . . . | 21 | 362 | 0.06 | 1988 . . . . . . . | 25 | 699 | 0.08 |
| 1982 . . . . . . . | 26 | 764 | 0.13 | 1989 . . . . . . . | 27 | 817 | 0.08 |
| 1983 . . . . . . . | 20 | 809 | 0.13 | 1990 . . . . . . . | 22 | 440 | 0.04 |
| 1984 . . . . . . . | 16 | 223 | 0.03 | 1991 . . . . . . . | 25 | 510 | 0.05 |
| 1985 . . . . . . . | 22 | 1,066 | 0.15 | 1992[3] . . . . . . . | 25 | 990 | 0.09 |
| 1986 . . . . . . . | 17 | 331 | 0.04 | | | | |

(1) Involving a passenger fatality. (2) Passenger deaths per 100 million passenger miles. (3) Preliminary.

## U.S. Civil Aviation Accidents

Source: National Safety Council

| 1992 | Accidents | | Deaths[1] | Accident Rates | | | |
|---|---|---|---|---|---|---|---|
| | | | | Per 100,000 Aircraft-Hours | | Per million Aircraft-Miles | |
| | Total | Fatal | | Total | Fatal | Total | Fatal |
| Large airlines . . . . . | 19 | 4 | 33 | 0.155 | 0.033 | 0.0038 | 0.0008 |
| Commuter airlines. . . | 23 | 7 | 21 | 1.055 | 0.321 | 0.056 | 0.017 |
| On-demand air taxis . . | 74 | 24 | 66 | 3.32 | 1.08 | — | — |
| General aviation . . . . | 1,956 | 408 | 812 | 7.19 | 1.50 | — | — |

(1) Includes passengers, crew members, and others.

## Occupational Injuries for Industries with 100,000 or More Injury Cases, 1990 and 1991

Source: Bureau of Labor Statistics. U.S. Dept. of Labor; total cases in thousands

| Industry | Total cases | | Incidence rate[1] | | Industry | Total cases | | Incidence rate[1] | |
|---|---|---|---|---|---|---|---|---|---|
| | 1990 | 1991 | 1990 | 1991 | | 1990 | 1991 | 1990 | 1991 |
| Eating and drinking places . | 353.6 | 310.0 | 8.4 | 7.4 | Nursing and personal care facilities . . . . . . . . . | 168.2 | 174.1 | 15.4 | 15.0 |
| Hospitals . . . . . . . . . . . | 282.4 | 308.9 | 10.0 | 10.8 | Department stores . . . . . | 165.4 | 154.8 | 11.1 | 11.0 |
| Grocery stores . . . . . . . | 246.4 | 238.4 | 12.1 | 11.7 | Motor vehicles and equipment manufacturing | 148.5 | 139.2 | 18.9 | 18.6 |
| Trucking and courier services, except air . . . . | 203.8 | 200.6 | 14.1 | 14.4 | Hotels and motels . . . . . . | 126.0 | 118.9 | 10.4 | 10.2 |

(1) Per 100,000 full-time workers.

# Crime in the U.S., 1973-1992

Source: 1992 *Uniform Crime Reports*, FBI

| Population[1] | Crime Index total[2] | Violent crime[3] | Property crime[3] | Murder and non- negligent man- slaughter | Forcible rape | Robbery | Burglary | Larceny theft |
|---|---|---|---|---|---|---|---|---|
| **Population by year** | | | | Number of offenses | | | | |
| 1973-209,851,000. . . | 8,718,000 | 875,910 | 7,842,200 | 19,640 | 51,400 | 384,220 | 2,565,500 | 4,347,900 |
| 1974-211,392,000. . . | 10,253,400 | 974,720 | 9,278,700 | 20,710 | 55,400 | 442,400 | 3,039,200 | 5,262,500 |
| 1975-213,124,000. . . | 11,292,400 | 1,039,710 | 10,252,700 | 20,510 | 56,090 | 470,500 | 3,265,300 | 5,977,700 |
| 1976-214,659,000. . . | 11,349,700 | 1,004,210 | 10,345,500 | 18,780 | 57,080 | 427,810 | 3,108,700 | 6,270,800 |
| 1977-216,332,000. . . | 10,984,500 | 1,029,580 | 9,955,000 | 19,120 | 63,500 | 412,610 | 3,071,500 | 5,905,700 |
| 1978-218,059,000. . . | 11,209,000 | 1,085,550 | 10,123,400 | 19,560 | 67,610 | 426,930 | 3,128,300 | 5,991,000 |
| 1979-220,099,000. . . | 12,249,500 | 1,208,030 | 11,041,500 | 21,460 | 76,390 | 480,700 | 3,327,700 | 6,601,000 |
| 1980-225,349,264. . . | 13,408,300 | 1,344,520 | 12,063,700 | 23,040 | 82,990 | 565,840 | 3,795,200 | 7,136,900 |
| 1981-229,146,000. . . | 13,423,800 | 1,361,820 | 12,061,900 | 22,520 | 82,500 | 592,910 | 3,779,700 | 7,194,400 |
| 1982-231,534,000. . . | 12,974,400 | 1,322,390 | 11,652,000 | 21,010 | 78,770 | 553,130 | 3,129,900 | 6,712,800 |
| 1983-233,981,000. . . | 12,108,600 | 1,258,090 | 10,850,500 | 19,310 | 78,920 | 506,570 | 3,129,900 | 6,591,900 |
| 1984-236,158,000. . . | 11,881,800 | 1,273,280 | 10,608,500 | 18,690 | 84,230 | 485,010 | 2,984,400 | 6,591,900 |
| 1985-238,740,000. . . | 12,431,400 | 1,328,800 | 11,102,600 | 18,980 | 88,670 | 497,870 | 3,073,300 | 6,926,400 |
| 1986-241,077,000. . . | 13,211,900 | 1,489,170 | 11,722,700 | 20,610 | 91,460 | 542,780 | 3,241,400 | 7,257,200 |
| 1987-243,400,000. . . | 13,508,700 | 1,484,000 | 12,024,700 | 20,100 | 91,110 | 517,700 | 3,236,200 | 7,499,900 |
| 1988-245,807,000. . . | 13,923,100 | 1,566,220 | 12,356,900 | 20,680 | 92,490 | 542,970 | 3,218,100 | 7,705,900 |
| 1989-248,239,000. . . | 14,251,400 | 1,646,040 | 12,605,400 | 21,500 | 94,500 | 578,330 | 3,168,200 | 7,872,400 |
| 1990-248,709,873. . . | 14,475,600 | 1,820,130 | 12,655,500 | 23,440 | 102,560 | 639,270 | 3,073,900 | 7,945,700 |
| 1991-252,177,000. . . | 14,872,900 | 1,911,770 | 12,961,100 | 24,700 | 106,590 | 687,730 | 3,157,200 | 8,142,200 |
| 1992-255,082,000. . . | 14,438,200 | 1,932,270 | 12,505,900 | 23,760 | 109,060 | 672,480 | 2,979,900 | 7,915,200 |
| **Percent change: number of offenses** | | | | | | | | |
| 1992/1991. . . . . . . | −2.9 | +1.1 | −3.5 | −3.8 | +2.3 | −2.2 | −5.6 | −2.8 |
| 1992/1988. . . . . . . | +3.7 | +23.4 | +1.2 | +14.9 | +17.9 | +23.9 | −7.4 | +2.7 |
| 1992/1983. . . . . . . | +19.2 | +53.6 | +15.3 | +23.0 | +38.2 | +32.8 | −4.8 | +17.9 |
| **Year** | | | | Rate per 100,000 inhabitants | | | | |
| 1973 . . . . . . . . . | 4,154.4 | 417.4 | 3,737.0 | 9.4 | 24.5 | 183.1 | 1,222.5 | 2,071.9 |
| 1974 . . . . . . . . . | 4,850.4 | 461.1 | 4,389.3 | 9.8 | 26.2 | 209.3 | 1,437.7 | 2,489.5 |
| 1975 . . . . . . . . . | 5,298.5 | 487.8 | 4,810.7 | 9.6 | 26.3 | 220.8 | 1,532.1 | 2,804.8 |
| 1976 . . . . . . . . . | 5,287.3 | 467.8 | 4,819.5 | 8.8 | 26.6 | 199.3 | 1,448.2 | 2,921.3 |
| 1977 . . . . . . . . . | 5,077.6 | 475.9 | 4,601.7 | 8.8 | 29.4 | 190.7 | 1,419.8 | 2,729.9 |
| 1978 . . . . . . . . . | 5,140.3 | 497.8 | 4,642.5 | 9.0 | 31.0 | 195.8 | 1,434.6 | 2,747.4 |
| 1979 . . . . . . . . . | 5,565.5 | 548.9 | 5,016.6 | 9.7 | 34.7 | 218.4 | 1,511.9 | 2,999.1 |
| 1980 . . . . . . . . . | 5,950.0 | 596.6 | 5,353.3 | 10.2 | 36.8 | 251.1 | 1,684.1 | 3,167.0 |
| 1981 . . . . . . . . . | 5,858.2 | 594.3 | 5,263.9 | 9.8 | 36.0 | 258.7 | 1,649.5 | 3,139.7 |
| 1982 . . . . . . . . . | 5,603.6 | 571.1 | 5,032.5 | 9.1 | 34.0 | 238.9 | 1,488.8 | 3,084.8 |
| 1983 . . . . . . . . . | 5,175.0 | 537.7 | 4,637.4 | 8.3 | 33.7 | 216.5 | 1,337.7 | 2,868.9 |
| 1984 . . . . . . . . . | 5,031.3 | 539.2 | 4,492.1 | 7.9 | 35.7 | 205.4 | 1,263.7 | 2,791.3 |
| 1985 . . . . . . . . . | 5,207.1 | 556.6 | 4,650.5 | 7.9 | 37.1 | 208.5 | 1,287.3 | 2,901.2 |
| 1986 . . . . . . . . . | 5,480.4 | 617.7 | 4,862.6 | 8.6 | 37.9 | 225.1 | 1,344.6 | 3,010.3 |
| 1987 . . . . . . . . . | 5,550.0 | 609.7 | 4,940.3 | 8.3 | 37.4 | 212.7 | 1,329.6 | 3,081.3 |
| 1988 . . . . . . . . . | 5,664.2 | 637.2 | 5,027.1 | 8.4 | 37.6 | 220.9 | 1,309.2 | 3,134.9 |
| 1989 . . . . . . . . . | 5,741.0 | 663.1 | 5,077.9 | 8.7 | 38.1 | 233.0 | 1,276.3 | 3,171.3 |
| 1990 . . . . . . . . . | 5,820.3 | 731.8 | 5,088.5 | 9.4 | 41.2 | 257.0 | 1,235.9 | 3,194.8 |
| 1991 . . . . . . . . . | 5,897.8 | 758.1 | 5,139.7 | 9.8 | 42.3 | 272.7 | 1,252.0 | 3,228.8 |
| 1992 . . . . . . . . . | 5,660.2 | 757.5 | 4,902.7 | 9.3 | 42.8 | 263.6 | 1,168.2 | 3,103.0 |
| **Percent change: rate per 100,000 inhabitants** | | | | | | | | |
| 1992/1991. . . . . . . | −4.0 | −.1 | −4.6 | −5.1 | +1.2 | −3.3 | −6.7 | −3.9 |
| 1992/1988. . . . . . . | −.1 | +18.9 | −2.5 | +10.7 | +13.8 | +19.3 | −10.8 | −1.0 |
| 1992/1983. . . . . . . | +9.4 | +40.9 | +5.7 | +12.0 | +27.0 | +21.8 | −12.7 | +8.2 |

(1) Populations are Bureau of the Census provisional estimates as of July 1, except 1980 and 1990, which are the decennial census counts. (2) Because of rounding, the offenses may not add to totals. (3) Violent crimes are murder, forcible rape, robbery, and aggravated assault. Property crimes are burglary, larceny-theft, and motor vehicle theft. Data are not included for the property crime of arson. **Note:** All rates were calculated on the offenses before rounding.

## Law Enforcement Officers

Source: 1992 *Uniform Crime Reports*, FBI

The U.S. law enforcement community employed an average of 2.3 full-time officers for every 1,000 inhabitants as of October 31, 1992. Considering full-time civilians, the overall law enforcement employee rate was 3.1 per 1,000 inhabitants according to 13,032 city, county, and state police agencies. These agencies collectively offered law enforcement service to a population of over 241 million, employing 544,309 officers and 204,521 civilians.

The law enforcement employee average for all cities nationwide was 2.8 per 1,000 inhabitants. City law enforcement employee averages ranged from 3.4 per 1,000 inhabitants in those with populations of less than 10,000 to 3.6 for those with populations of 250,000 or more. Rural and suburban counties averaged full-time law enforcement employee rates of 3.9 and 3.6 per 1,000 population, respectively.

Regionally, the highest law enforcement employee rate was in the South, with 3.2, and lowest in the West, 2.4.

Nationally, males comprised 91 percent of all sworn employees. Ninety-three percent of the officers in rural counties and 91 percent of those in cities were males, while in suburban counties males accounted for 89 percent.

Civilians made up 27 percent of the total U.S. law enforcement employee force. They represented 22 percent of the police employees in cities, 34 percent of those in rural counties, and 36 percent in suburban counties.

Sixty-one law enforcement officers were feloniously slain in the line of duty in 1992, 10 fewer than in 1991. Another 66 officers were killed due to accidents occurring while performing official duties.

## Prison Situation Among the States, 1992

Source: *Prisoners in 1992.* Bureau of Justice Statistics, U.S. Dept. of Justice; year-end 1992.

| 10 States with the Largest 1992 Prison Populations | Number of Inmates | 10 States with the Highest Incarceration Rates, 1992* | Prisoners per 100,000 Residents | 10 States with the Largest % Increases in Prison Population | | | |
|---|---|---|---|---|---|---|---|
| | | | | 1991-92 | % Increase | 1987-92* | % Increase |
| California | 109,496 | Louisiana | 478 | Texas | 18.4% | New Hampshire | 105.0% |
| New York | 61,736 | South Carolina | 477 | West Virginia | 16.2 | Rhoda Island | 94.3 |
| Texas | 61,178 | Oklahoma | 463 | New Hampshire | 15.9 | Colorado | 87.1 |
| Florida | 48,302 | Nevada | 461 | Idaho | 15.5 | Idaho | 72.5 |
| Michigan | 39,019 | Arizona | 415 | Wisconsin | 15.4 | Vermont | 66.9 |
| Ohio | 38,378 | Michigan | 414 | Vermont | 13.3 | California | 63.5 |
| Illinois | 31,640 | Alabama | 404 | Oklahoma | 11.1 | Michigan | 63.4 |
| Georgia | 25,290 | Maryland | 380 | Minnesota | 10.1 | Washington | 62.4 |
| Pennsylvania | 24,974 | Delaware | 371 | Nevada | 9.9 | Kentucky | 61.0 |
| New Jersey | 22,653 | Georgia | 366 | Massachusetts | 9.8 | Massachusetts | 60.5 |

**Note:** The District of Columbia as a wholly urban jurisdiction is excluded. * Prisoners with sentences of more than 1 year.

## State and Federal Prison Population; Death Penalty

Source: Prison population: Bureau of Justice Statistics, U.S. Dept. of Justice, Dec. 31, 1992; Death penalty: NAACP Legal Defense and Education Fund; Bureau of Justice Statistics; "Executions" and "Death penalty" as of Dec. 31, 1992; "Under sentence of death" as of April, 1992.

The number of prisoners under the jurisdiction of federal or state correctional authorities at year-end 1992 reached a record high of 883,593. The states and the District of Columbia added 50,809 prisoners; the federal system, 8,651. The increase for 1992 brought total growth in the prison population since 1980 to 553,772—an increase of about 168% in the 12-year period. The 1992 growth rate of 7.2 percent was greater than the percentage increase recorded during 1991 (6.6 percent), and the number of new prisoners added during 1992 was 8,451 more than the number added during the preceding year (51,009). The 1992 increase translated into a nationwide need for approximately 1,143 prison bedspaces per week, compared to the 981 prison bedspaces per week needed in 1991. In 1980, about 1 of every 15 court-committed entries to state prison was an offender convicted of a drug offense. In 1990, drug offenses accounted for about 1 in 3 new commitments to state prisons. During the same period, the percentage of prison admissions entering as violators of probation or parole conditions also increased—from about 17% to about 30%.

| | Sentenced to more than 1 yr. | | % change 1991-92 | Death penalty | | |
|---|---|---|---|---|---|---|
| | Final 1991 | Advance 1992 | | Under sentence of death | Executions | Death penalty |
| **Total** | 789,349 | 846,695 | 7.3% | 2,600 | 31 | — |
| Federal institutions | 56,696 | 65,706 | 15.9 | 6 | 1 | Yes |
| State institutions | 732,653 | 780,989 | 6.6 | 2,594 | 30 | 36 |
| **Northeast** | 127,450 | 133,372 | 4.7 | 152 | 0 | — |
| Connecticut | 8,585 | 8,794 | 2.4 | 4 | 0 | Yes |
| Maine | 1,558 | 1,488 | -4.5 | 0 | 0 | No |
| Massachusetts | 8,561 | 9,382 | 9.6 | 0 | 0 | No |
| New Hampshire | 1,533 | 1,777 | 15.9 | 0 | 0 | Yes |
| New Jersey | 23,483 | 22,653 | -3.5 | 8 | 0 | Yes |
| New York | 57,862 | 61,736 | 6.7 | 0 | 0 | No |
| Pennsylvania | 23,386 | 24,966 | 6.8 | 140 | 0 | Yes |
| Rhode Island | 1,749 | 1,709 | -2.3 | 0 | 0 | No |
| Vermont | 733 | 867 | 18.3 | 0 | 0 | No |
| **Midwest** | 155,573 | 166,042 | 6.7 | 395 | 1 | — |
| Illinois | 29,115 | 31,640 | 8.7 | 145 | 0 | Yes |
| Indiana | 12,865 | 13,012 | 1.1 | 52 | 0 | Yes |
| Iowa | 4,145 | 4,518 | 9.0 | 0 | 0 | No |
| Kansas | 5,903 | 6,028 | 2.1 | 0 | 0 | No |
| Michigan | 36,423 | 39,019 | 7.1 | 0 | 0 | No |
| Minnesota | 3,472 | 3,822 | 10.1 | 0 | 0 | No |
| Missouri | 15,897 | 16,198 | 1.9 | 82 | 1 | Yes |
| Nebraska | 2,375 | 2,492 | 4.9 | 12 | 0 | Yes |
| North Dakota | 441 | 415 | -5.9 | 0 | 0 | No |
| Ohio | 35,744 | 38,378 | 7.4 | 104 | 0 | Yes |
| South Dakota | 1,374 | 1,487 | 8.2 | 0 | 0 | Yes |
| Wisconsin | 7,819 | 9,033 | 15.5 | 0 | 0 | No |
| **South** | 292,542 | 315,280 | 7.8 | 1,488 | 25 | — |
| Alabama | 16,400 | 16,938 | 3.3 | 115 | 2 | Yes |
| Arkansas | 7,722 | 8,129 | 5.3 | 35 | 2 | Yes |
| Delaware | 2,430 | 2,665 | 9.7 | 6 | 1 | Yes |
| District of Columbia | 7,106 | 7,528 | 5.9 | 0 | 0 | No |
| Florida | 46,533 | 48,302 | 3.8 | 315 | 2 | Yes |
| Georgia | 22,910 | 24,848 | 8.5 | 110 | 0 | Yes |
| Kentucky | 9,799 | 10,364 | 5.8 | 29 | 0 | Yes |
| Louisiana | 20,003 | 20,603 | 3.0 | 40 | 0 | Yes |
| Maryland | 17,824 | 18,808 | 5.5 | 14 | 0 | Yes |
| Mississippi | 8,682 | 8,877 | 2.3 | 52 | 0 | Yes |
| North Carolina | 18,272 | 20,024 | 9.6 | 105 | 1 | Yes |
| Oklahoma | 13,340 | 14,821 | 11.1 | 125 | 1 | Yes |
| South Carolina | 17,208 | 17,612 | 2.4 | 46 | 0 | Yes |
| Tennessee | 11,474 | 11,849 | 3.3 | 100 | 0 | Yes |
| Texas | 51,677 | 61,178 | 18.4 | 349 | 12 | Yes |
| Virginia | 19,660 | 20,989 | 6.8 | 47 | 4 | Yes |
| West Virginia | 1,502 | 1,745 | 16.2 | 0 | 0 | No |

(continued)

| | Sentenced to more than 1 yr. | | % change 1991-92 | Under sentence of death | Death penalty | |
|---|---|---|---|---|---|---|
| | Final 1991 | Advance 1992 | | | Executions — | Death penalty — |
| West | 157,088 | 166,295 | 5.9 | 559 | 4 | No |
| Alaska | 1,840 | 1,944 | 5.7 | 0 | 0 | No |
| Arizona | 14,843 | 15,850 | 6.8 | 101 | 1 | Yes |
| California | 98,515 | 105,467 | 7.1 | 328 | 1 | Yes |
| Colorado | 8,392 | 8,997 | 7.2 | 3 | 0 | No |
| Hawaii | 1,766 | 1,922 | 8.8 | 0 | 0 | No |
| Idaho | 2,143 | 2,475 | 15.5 | 21 | 0 | Yes |
| Montana | 1,478 | 1,553 | 5.1 | 8 | 0 | Yes |
| Nevada | 5,503 | 6,049 | 9.9 | 60 | 0 | Yes |
| New Mexico | 3,016 | 3,154 | 4.6 | 1 | 0 | Yes |
| Oregon | 6,732 | 5,216 | —* | 16 | 0 | Yes |
| Utah | 2,605 | 2,687 | 3.2 | 12 | 1 | Yes |
| Washington | 9,156 | 9,959 | 8.8 | 9 | 0 | Yes |
| Wyoming | 1,099 | 1,022 | -7.0 | 0 | 1 | Yes |

**Note:** Prisoner counts for 1991 may differ from those reported previously. Counts for 1992 are subject to revision. *Before 1992, Oregon reported all prisoners as having sentences of more than 1 year.

## Total Estimated Arrests,[1] 1992

Source: 1992 *Uniform Crime Reports,* FBI

| | |
|---|---|
| Total[2] | 14,075,100 |
| Murder and nonnegligent manslaughter | 22,510 |
| Forcible rape | 39,100 |
| Robbery | 173,310 |
| Aggravated assault | 507,210 |
| Burglary | 424,000 |
| Larceny-theft | 1,504,500 |
| Motor vehicle theft | 197,600 |
| Arson | 19,900 |
| **Violent crimes[3]** | **742,130** |
| **Property crime[4]** | **2,146,000** |
| **Crime Index total[5]** | **2,888,200** |
| Other assaults | 1,074,700 |
| Forgery and counterfeiting | 105,400 |
| Fraud | 424,200 |
| Embezzlement | 13,700 |
| Stolen property: buying, receiving, possessing | 161,500 |
| Vandalism | 323,100 |
| Weapons: carrying, possessing, etc. | 239,300 |
| Prostitution and commercialized vice | 96,200 |
| Sex offenses (except forcible rape and prostitution) | 108,400 |
| Drug abuse violations | 1,066,400 |
| Gambling | 17,100 |
| Offenses against family and children | 109,200 |
| Driving under the influence | 1,624,500 |
| Liquor laws | 541,700 |
| Drunkenness | 832,300 |
| Disorderly conduct | 753,100 |
| Vagrancy | 34,300 |
| All other offenses | 3,389,500 |
| Suspicion (not included in totals) | 18,400 |
| Curfew and loitering law violations | 91,100 |
| Runaways | 181,300 |

(1) Arrest totals are based on all reporting agencies and estimates for unreported areas. (2) Because of rounding, figures may not add to totals. (3) Violent crimes are murder, forcible rape, robbery, and aggravated assault. (4) Property crimes are burglary, larceny-theft, motor vehicle theft, and arson. (5) Includes arson.

## Crime, by Type of Area, 1992

Source: 1992 *Uniform Crime Reports,* FBI

| Area | Population[1] | Crime Index total | Violent crime[2] | Property crime[3] | Murder | Forcible rape | Robbery | Aggravated assault | Burglary | Larceny-theft | Motor vehicle theft |
|---|---|---|---|---|---|---|---|---|---|---|---|
| **United States** | | | | | | | | | | | |
| **Total** | 255,082,000 | 14,438,191 | 1,932,274 | 12,505,917 | 23,760 | 109,062 | 672,478 | 1,126,974 | 2,979,884 | 7,915,199 | 1,610,834 |
| Rate per 100,000 inhabitants | | 5,660.2 | 757.5 | 4,902.7 | 9.3 | 42.8 | 263.6 | 441.8 | 1,168.2 | 3,103.0 | 631.5 |
| **Metropolitan Statistical Area** | 201,843,745 | | | | | | | | | | |
| Area actually reporting[4] | 97.0% | 12,425,059 | 1,736,064 | 10,688,995 | 20,712 | 91,248 | 647,785 | 976,319 | 2,503,818 | 6,675,499 | 1,509,678 |
| Estimated totals | 100.0% | 12,660,331 | 1,758,505 | 10,901,826 | 20,943 | 93,114 | 652,364 | 992,084 | 2,553,535 | 6,818,473 | 1,529,818 |
| Rate per 100,000 inhabitants | | 6,272.3 | 871.2 | 5,401.1 | 10.4 | 46.1 | 323.2 | 491.5 | 1,265.1 | 3,378.1 | 757.9 |
| **Cities outside metropolitan areas** | 21,254,000 | | | | | | | | | | |
| Area actually reporting[4] | 90.0% | 1,012,709 | 91,616 | 921,093 | 997 | 7,080 | 13,274 | 70,265 | 191,215 | 688,686 | 41,192 |
| Estimated totals | 100.0% | 1,129,982 | 103,346 | 1,026,636 | 1,147 | 7,912 | 14,904 | 79,383 | 215,062 | 765,446 | 46,128 |
| Rate per 100,000 inhabitants | | 5,316.6 | 486.2 | 4,830.3 | 5.4 | 37.2 | 70.1 | 373.5 | 1,011.9 | 3,601.4 | 217.0 |
| **Rural Counties** | 31,983,255 | | | | | | | | | | |
| Area actually reporting[4] | 86.1% | 571,898 | 60,336 | 511,562 | 1,408 | 7,141 | 4,472 | 47,315 | 186,528 | 294,309 | 30,725 |
| Estimated totals | 100.0% | 647,878 | 70,423 | 577,455 | 1,670 | 8,036 | 5,210 | 55,507 | 211,287 | 331,280 | 34,888 |
| Rate per 100,000 inhabitants | | 2,025.7 | 220.2 | 1,805.5 | 5.2 | 25.1 | 16.3 | 173.6 | 660.6 | 1,035.8 | 109.1 |

(1) Populations are Bureau of the Census provisional estimates as of July 1, 1992, and are subject to change. (2) Violent crimes are murder, forcible rape, robbery, and aggravated assault. (3) Property crimes are burglary, larceny-theft, and motor vehicle theft. Data are not included for the property crime of arson. (4) The percentage representing area actually reporting will not coincide with the ratio between reported and estimated crime totals, since these data represent the sum of the calculations for individual states, which have varying populations, portions reporting, and crime rates.

# Murder Weapons and Circumstances, 1988-1992

Source: 1992 *Uniform Crime Reports*, FBI

| | 1988 | 1990 | 1992 | | 1988 | 1990 | 1992 |
|---|---|---|---|---|---|---|---|
| **Total Murders[1]** | 17,971 | 20,273 | 22,540 | Burglary | 210 | 202 | 206 |
| **Weapon or Method Used** | | | | Larceny-theft | 16 | 28 | 41 |
| Firearms | 10,895 | 13,035 | 15,377 | Motor Vehicle theft | 30 | 55 | 65 |
| Handguns | 8,147 | 10,099 | 12,489 | Arson | 184 | 152 | 148 |
| Rifles | 753 | 746 | 698 | Prostitution and commercialized | | | |
| Shotguns | 1,105 | 1,245 | 1,104 | vice | 16 | 27 | 32 |
| Other guns | 15 | 25 | 42 | Other sex offenses | 61 | 50 | 34 |
| Type not known | 875 | 920 | 1,044 | Narcotic drug laws | 1,003 | 1,367 | 1,291 |
| Knives or cutting instruments | 3,457 | 3,526 | 3,265 | Gambling | 26 | 11 | 20 |
| Blunt objects (clubs, hammers, etc.) | 1,126 | 1,085 | 1,029 | Other—not specified | 230 | 294 | 659 |
| Personal weapons (hands, fists, feet, etc.)[2] | 1,105 | 1,119 | 1,121 | Suspected felony | 225 | 148 | 280 |
| | | | | Other than felony | 9,604 | 10,889 | 11,152 |
| Poison | 15 | 11 | 13 | Romatic triangle | 310 | 407 | 335 |
| Explosives | 34 | 13 | 19 | Child killed by babysitter | 23 | 34 | 36 |
| Fire | 255 | 288 | 203 | Brawl due to alcohol | 418 | 533 | 426 |
| Narcotics | 36 | 29 | 23 | Brawl due to narcotics | 197 | 242 | 249 |
| Drowning | 38 | 36 | 27 | Argument over money or | | | |
| Strangulation | 331 | 312 | 313 | property | 483 | 514 | 481 |
| Asphyxiation | 73 | 96 | 114 | Other arguments | 5,410 | 6,044 | 6,027 |
| Other weapons or weapon not known | 606 | 723 | 1,036 | Gangland killings | 45 | 104 | 137 |
| **Circumstances** | | | | Juvenile gang killings | 327 | 679 | 809 |
| | | | | Institutional killings | 24 | 16 | 18 |
| Felony | 3,417 | 4,209 | 4,887 | Sniper attack | 56 | 41 | 33 |
| Rape | 144 | 152 | 137 | Other—not specified | 2,311 | 2,275 | 2,601 |
| Robbery | 1,497 | 1,871 | 2,254 | Unknown | 4,725 | 5,027 | 6,221 |

(1) Total number of murder victims for whom supplemental homicide information was received. (2) Includes murders in which victim was pushed.

# U.S. Fires, 1991

Source: National Fire Protection Assn.

**Fires**
- Public fire departments responded to 2,041,500 fires in 1991, a 1.1 percent increase from 1990.
- There were 640,500 structure fires in 1991, a 2.6 percent increase from 1990.
- 75 percent of all structure fires, or 478,000 fires, occurred in residential properties.
- There were 428,500 vehicle fires in 1991, virtually no change from 1990.
- The number of fires in outside properties increased by 1.5 percent, to 972,500 fires.
- The South and the Northeast—with 9.6 fires per 1,000 population—had the highest fire incidence rate in the nation.

**Civilian deaths**
- The number of civilian fire deaths decreased significantly in 1991—by 14.1 percent to 4,465.
- About 78 percent of all fire deaths occurred in homes.
- There were 3,500 home fire deaths in 1991, a drop of 13.6 percent from 1990.
- The North Central region had the highest regional death rate, with 22.7 civilian deaths per million population, followed closely by the South, with 21.4 deaths per million.

**Civilian injuries**
- There were 29,375 civilian fire injuries in 1991, a 2.7 percent increase from the year before. This estimate is low because of underreporting of civilian injuries to the fire service.
- 21,850 civilian injuries, or 74.4 percent, occurred in residential properties; 11.6 percent, or 3,125 injuries, occurred in nonresidential structure fires.

- The Northeast had the highest civilian injury rate, with 148.3 civilian injuries per million population.

**Property damage**
- Property damage resulting from fires in 1991 jumped by 21.1 percent, to an estimated $9.467 billion. The increase was due almost entirely to the Oakland, California, fire, which resulted in an estimated $1.5 billion loss.
- Structure fires account for 88 percent of all property damage, or $8.320 billion.
- 67 percent of all structure property loss occurred in residential properties. The cost totaled $5.552 billion.
- The West had the highest property loss rate in the nation: $57.2 per person, which reflects the loss resulting from the Oakland fire.

**Incendiary and suspicious fires**
- 15.3 percent of all structure fires, or an estimated 98,000 fires, were deliberately set or suspected of having been deliberately set. This represents a slight increase from 1990.
- Incendiary or suspicious structure fires resulted in the deaths of 490 people in 1991, a 35.4 percent decrease from the year before. These fires cost $1.531 billion in property damage. This represents 18.4 percent of all structure property loss, an increase of 9.8 percent from 1990.
- Vehicle fires of incendiary or suspicious origin decreased by 3.9 percent, to 49,000. They cost $182 million in property damage, up 9.0 percent from the previous year.

# Physicians by Age, Sex, and Specialty

Source: American Medical Assn., Jan. 1, 1992

| | Total Physicians* | | Under 35 yrs. | | 35–44 yrs. | | 45–54 yrs. | | 55–64 yrs. | |
|---|---|---|---|---|---|---|---|---|---|---|
| | Male | Female | Male | Female | Male | Female | Male | Female | Male | Female |
| **All Specialties** | 534,543 | 118,519 | 93,287 | 40,431 | 153,921 | 44,336 | 110,790 | 18,026 | 80,288 | 7,224 |
| Aerospace Medicine | 650 | 41 | 103 | 15 | 208 | 20 | 151 | 4 | 122 | 2 |
| Allergy & Immunology | 2,889 | 552 | 198 | 96 | 868 | 248 | 813 | 123 | 600 | 48 |
| Anesthesiology | 22,978 | 5,170 | 5,379 | 1,408 | 8,044 | 1,958 | 4,757 | 1,144 | 3,288 | 460 |
| Cardiovascular Disease | 15,563 | 915 | 1,923 | 210 | 6,288 | 469 | 4,024 | 160 | 2,179 | 48 |
| Child Psychiatry | 2,981 | 1,637 | 269 | 245 | 999 | 688 | 889 | 397 | 577 | 204 |
| Colon/Rectal Surgery | 840 | 29 | 47 | 7 | 304 | 18 | 235 | 3 | 135 | 1 |
| Dermatology | 6,006 | 1,906 | 745 | 716 | 1,838 | 805 | 1,777 | 265 | 1,020 | 88 |
| Diagnostic Radiology | 14,354 | 2,899 | 3,628 | 1,165 | 5,389 | 1,296 | 3,690 | 336 | 1,217 | 78 |
| Emergency Medicine | 13,111 | 2,359 | 2,543 | 788 | 6,378 | 1,133 | 2,716 | 331 | 978 | 77 |
| Family Practice | 41,261 | 9,708 | 8,556 | 4,104 | 16,661 | 4,135 | 6,828 | 971 | 5,377 | 314 |

(continued)

| | Total Physicians* | | Under 35 yrs. | | 35–44 yrs. | | 45–54 yrs. | | 55–64 yrs. | |
|---|---|---|---|---|---|---|---|---|---|---|
| | Male | Female | Male | Female | Male | Female | Male | Female | Male | Female |
| Forensic Pathology | 325 | 98 | 15 | 8 | 100 | 46 | 83 | 26 | 83 | 14 |
| Gastroenterology | 7,438 | 508 | 1,040 | 136 | 3,242 | 287 | 2,052 | 72 | 784 | 9 |
| General Practice | 18,391 | 2,328 | 367 | 111 | 1,998 | 625 | 3,170 | 721 | 5,297 | 455 |
| General Preventive Med. | 877 | 299 | 102 | 75 | 254 | 130 | 213 | 48 | 160 | 22 |
| General Surgery | 36,380 | 2,831 | 9,737 | 1,623 | 8,694 | 940 | 7,656 | 179 | 6,147 | 57 |
| Internal Medicine | 67,138 | 18,701 | 22,286 | 9,573 | 21,321 | 6,531 | 10,279 | 1,770 | 7,579 | 558 |
| Neurological Surgery | 4,355 | 146 | 785 | 53 | 1,196 | 73 | 1,139 | 16 | 834 | 3 |
| Neurology | 8,110 | 1,632 | 1,273 | 464 | 3,238 | 784 | 2,141 | 250 | 1,078 | 101 |
| Nuclear Medicine | 1,156 | 216 | 91 | 41 | 349 | 96 | 358 | 58 | 271 | 17 |
| Obstetrics/Gynecology | 23,497 | 8,090 | 3,802 | 3,607 | 6,914 | 3,028 | 6,099 | 1,013 | 4,566 | 302 |
| Occupational Medicine | 2,465 | 322 | 107 | 35 | 539 | 148 | 424 | 61 | 659 | 45 |
| Ophthalmology | 14,691 | 1,742 | 2,245 | 643 | 4,322 | 742 | 4,049 | 219 | 2,670 | 82 |
| Orthopedic Surgery | 20,126 | 514 | 4,056 | 228 | 6,192 | 225 | 5,305 | 40 | 3,241 | 9 |
| Otolaryngology | 7,882 | 491 | 1,425 | 206 | 2,209 | 226 | 2,228 | 35 | 1,388 | 17 |
| Pathology-Anat./Clin. | 12,849 | 4,156 | 1,722 | 1,069 | 3,590 | 1,646 | 3,243 | 934 | 2,966 | 336 |
| Pediatric Cardiology | 829 | 211 | 116 | 59 | 302 | 68 | 219 | 46 | 143 | 25 |
| Pediatrics | 23,842 | 16,573 | 5,191 | 6,761 | 7,415 | 5,824 | 5,410 | 2,625 | 3,649 | 885 |
| Physical Med./Rehab. | 3,124 | 1,345 | 857 | 398 | 1,030 | 494 | 580 | 272 | 397 | 138 |
| Plastic Surgery | 4,354 | 334 | 352 | 59 | 1,532 | 183 | 1,456 | 64 | 754 | 20 |
| Psychiatry | 27,377 | 9,028 | 3,315 | 2,360 | 7,092 | 3,243 | 7,003 | 1,832 | 5,887 | 960 |
| Public Health | 1,505 | 479 | 41 | 24 | 316 | 136 | 350 | 92 | 350 | 103 |
| Pulmonary Diseases | 5,777 | 560 | 746 | 146 | 2,757 | 272 | 1,491 | 82 | 507 | 36 |
| Radiation Oncology | 2,447 | 566 | 501 | 157 | 776 | 237 | 679 | 130 | 344 | 30 |
| Radiology | 7,064 | 784 | 231 | 90 | 962 | 268 | 2,387 | 261 | 2,312 | 119 |
| Thoracic Surgery | 2,090 | 30 | 150 | 7 | 514 | 17 | 571 | 5 | 543 | 1 |
| Urological Surgery | 9,290 | 162 | 1,341 | 70 | 2,490 | 73 | 2,796 | 14 | 1,812 | 5 |
| Other | 6,304 | 991 | 364 | 111 | 1,618 | 372 | 1,345 | 216 | 1,483 | 152 |
| Unspecified | 6,024 | 2,085 | 3,680 | 1,373 | 1,168 | 484 | 446 | 139 | 327 | 53 |

* Includes physicians 65 and over, those living in U.S. possessions, those "Inactive," "Not Classified," and "Address Unknown."

## Patients Receiving Home Health Care or Hospice Care, 1992

Source: National Center for Health Statistics, U.S. Dept. of Health and Human Services

| Patient characteristic | Total | Percent distribution | Home health care Total | Percent distribution | Hospice care Total | Percent distribution |
|---|---|---|---|---|---|---|
| All patients | 1,284,200 | 100.0 | 1,237,100 | 100.0 | 47,200 | 100.0 |
| **Age** | | | | | | |
| Under 45 years | 140,700 | 11.0 | 137,800 | 11.1 | 3,000 | 6.3 |
| 45–54 years | 49,900 | 3.9 | 47,800 | 3.9 | 2,100 | 4.5 |
| 55–64 years | 115,900 | 9.0 | 111,100 | 9.0 | 4,900 | 10.3 |
| 65 years and over | 965,700 | 75.2 | 929,500 | 75.1 | 36,200 | 76.7 |
| 65–69 years | 136,100 | 10.6 | 129,400 | 10.5 | 6,700 | 14.3 |
| 70–74 years | 176,900 | 13.8 | 170,600 | 13.8 | 6,200 | 13.2 |
| 75–79 years | 212,100 | 16.5 | 203,700 | 16.5 | 8,300 | 17.7 |
| 80–84 years | 220,800 | 17.2 | 211,700 | 17.1 | 9,100 | 19.3 |
| 85 years and over | 219,900 | 17.1 | 214,100 | 17.3 | 5,800 | 12.3 |
| Unknown | 12,000 | 0.9 | 10,900 | 0.9 | — | — |
| **Sex** | | | | | | |
| Male | 432,600 | 33.7 | 411,300 | 33.2 | 21,300 | 45.1 |
| Female | 851,600 | 66.3 | 825,800 | 66.8 | 25,900 | 54.9 |
| **Race** | | | | | | |
| White | 879,700 | 68.5 | 840,500 | 67.9 | 39,200 | 83.2 |
| Black | 169,200 | 13.2 | 165,600 | 13.4 | 3,600 | 7.6 |
| Other or unknown | 235,300 | 18.3 | 231,000 | 18.7 | 4,300 | 9.2 |

Note: Figures may not add to totals because of rounding.

## Persons Receiving Care in Nursing Homes, 1980 and 1990

Source: Bureau of the Census, U.S. Dept. of Commerce

| Age | 1980 Number | Percent | 1990 Number | Percent | Percent change, 1980 to 1990 | 1990 Male | 1990 Female |
|---|---|---|---|---|---|---|---|
| Total | 1,426,371 | 100.0 | 1,772,032 | 100.0 | 24.2 | 493,609 | 1,278,423 |
| Under 35 years | 29,418 | 2.1 | 19,362 | 1.1 | −34.2 | 11,880 | 7,482 |
| 35 to 44 years | 20,764 | 1.5 | 27,303 | 1.5 | 31.5 | 16,178 | 11,125 |
| 45 to 54 years | 42,857 | 3.0 | 40,903 | 2.3 | −4.6 | 21,662 | 19,241 |
| 55 to 64 years | 100,374 | 7.0 | 93,701 | 5.3 | −6.6 | 46,844 | 46,857 |
| 65 to 74 years | 238,962 | 16.8 | 244,676 | 13.8 | 2.4 | 97,873 | 146,803 |
| 75 to 79 years | 219,571 | 15.4 | 245,972 | 13.9 | 12.0 | 75,542 | 170,430 |
| 80 to 84 years | 286,679 | 20.1 | 361,330 | 20.4 | 26.0 | 88,362 | 272,968 |
| 85 to 89 years | 276,251 | 19.4 | 378,612 | 21.4 | 37.1 | 135,268 | 603,517 |
| 90 to 94 years | 158,807 | 11.1 | 247,648 | 14.0 | 55.9 | (NA) | (NA) |
| 95 years and over | 52,688 | 3.7 | 112,525 | 6.4 | 113.6 | (NA) | (NA) |
| Under 25 years | 12,902 | 0.9 | 4,231 | 0.2 | −67.2 | 2,399 | 1,832 |
| Under 55 years | 93,039 | 6.5 | 87,568 | 4.9 | −5.9 | 49,720 | 37,848 |
| Under 65 years | 193,413 | 13.6 | 181,269 | 10.2 | −6.3 | 96,564 | 84,705 |
| 65 years and over | 1,232,958 | 86.4 | 1,590,763 | 89.8 | 29.0 | 397,045 | 1,193,718 |
| 85 years and over | 487,746 | 34.2 | 738,785 | 41.7 | 51.5 | 135,268 | 603,517 |

(NA)—Not available; included in previous age group. NOTE: In the 1990 decennial census, "Nursing homes" include skilled-nursing facilities, intermediate-care facilities, long-term care rooms in wards or buildings on the grounds of hospitals, or long-term care room/nursing wings in congregate housing facilities. Also included are nursing, convalescent, and rest homes, such as soldiers', sailors', veterans', and fraternal or religious homes for the aged, with or without nursing care.

## AIDS Deaths and New AIDS Cases in the U.S., 1985-1992

Source: *Health United States 1992*, National Center for Health Statistics, U.S. Dept. of Health and Human Services

| | All years[1] | 1985 | 1986 | 1987 | 1988 | 1989 | 1990 | 1991 | 1992 |
|---|---|---|---|---|---|---|---|---|---|
| TOTAL DEATHS .......... | 166,211 | 6,681 | 11,535 | 15,451 | 19,656 | 26,151 | 28,053 | 30,579 | 22,660 |
| NEW AIDS CASES | | | | | | | | | |
| All races .............. | 244,939 | 8,210 | 13,147 | 21,088 | 30,719 | 33,595 | 41,653 | 43,701 | 45,472 |
| **Male** | | | | | | | | | |
| All males, 13 years and over ... | 214,981 | 7,555 | 12,002 | 19,082 | 27,108 | 29,625 | 36,378 | 37,656 | 38,789 |
| White, not Hispanic .......... | 124,778 | 4,798 | 7,527 | 12,332 | 16,060 | 17,509 | 20,935 | 20,686 | 20,740 |
| Black, not Hispanic .......... | 59,083 | 1,712 | 2,760 | 4,321 | 7,159 | 8,055 | 10,292 | 11,105 | 12,031 |
| Hispanic ................ | 28,809 | 987 | 1,608 | 2,242 | 3,648 | 3,729 | 4,749 | 5,431 | 5,498 |
| American Indian[2]. ......... | 374 | 7 | 19 | 24 | 33 | 57 | 68 | 68 | 94 |
| Asian or Pacific Islander[3] .... | 1,435 | 48 | 78 | 130 | 163 | 213 | 254 | 252 | 276 |
| 13–19 years ............. | 635 | 31 | 44 | 68 | 85 | 89 | 100 | 99 | 95 |
| 20–29 years ............. | 39,959 | 1,470 | 2,490 | 3,798 | 5,464 | 5,719 | 6,845 | 6,478 | 6,292 |
| 30–39 years ............. | 99,956 | 3,620 | 5,654 | 8,868 | 12,612 | 13,904 | 16,844 | 17,414 | 17,795 |
| 40–49 years ............. | 51,837 | 1,663 | 2,576 | 4,290 | 6,112 | 6,823 | 8,914 | 9,642 | 10,317 |
| 50–59 years ............. | 16,367 | 605 | 917 | 1,471 | 1,995 | 2,241 | 2,657 | 2,904 | 3,059 |
| 60 years and over ......... | 6,227 | 166 | 321 | 587 | 840 | 849 | 1,018 | 1,119 | 1,231 |
| **Female** | | | | | | | | | |
| All females, 13 years and over. ... | 25,928 | 526 | 962 | 1,684 | 3,040 | 3,374 | 4,552 | 5,378 | 5,940 |
| White, not Hispanic .......... | 6,924 | 143 | 268 | 545 | 853 | 949 | 1,228 | 1,362 | 1,457 |
| Black, not Hispanic .......... | 14,538 | 286 | 523 | 896 | 1,655 | 1,896 | 2,543 | 3,101 | 3,391 |
| Hispanic ................ | 4,207 | 93 | 160 | 229 | 500 | 493 | 741 | 862 | 1,026 |
| American Indian[2]. ......... | 61 | 3 | 2 | 3 | 5 | 9 | 10 | 12 | 16 |
| Asian or Pacific Islander[3] .... | 141 | 1 | 8 | 11 | 22 | 17 | 19 | 25 | 36 |
| 13–19 years ............. | 259 | 4 | 12 | 11 | 23 | 29 | 63 | 53 | 57 |
| 20–29 years ............. | 6,454 | 175 | 275 | 482 | 771 | 889 | 1,106 | 1,222 | 1,359 |
| 30–39 years ............. | 12,128 | 236 | 446 | 749 | 1,506 | 1,620 | 2,100 | 2,540 | 2,730 |
| 40–49 years ............. | 4,398 | 46 | 127 | 229 | 412 | 506 | 787 | 1,001 | 1,240 |
| 50–59 years ............. | 1,468 | 26 | 47 | 91 | 151 | 172 | 277 | 342 | 344 |
| 60 years and over ......... | 1,221 | 39 | 55 | 122 | 177 | 158 | 219 | 220 | 210 |
| **Children** | | | | | | | | | |
| All children, under 13 years .... | 4,030 | 129 | 183 | 322 | 571 | 596 | 723 | 667 | 743 |
| White, not Hispanic .......... | 871 | 27 | 42 | 85 | 150 | 111 | 162 | 145 | 128 |
| Black, not Hispanic .......... | 2,308 | 83 | 105 | 162 | 304 | 342 | 385 | 403 | 468 |
| Hispanic ................ | 811 | 19 | 35 | 72 | 112 | 136 | 168 | 112 | 138 |
| American Indian[2]. ......... | 13 | — | — | 2 | — | 2 | 4 | 2 | 3 |
| Asian or Pacific Islander[3] .... | 19 | — | 1 | 1 | 4 | 3 | 4 | 2 | 3 |
| Under 1 year ............. | 1,601 | 54 | 78 | 141 | 193 | 239 | 284 | 248 | 305 |
| 1–12 years .............. | 2,429 | 75 | 105 | 181 | 378 | 357 | 439 | 419 | 438 |

(1) Includes cases and deaths prior to 1985. (2) Includes Aleut and Eskimo. (3) Includes Chinese, Japanese, Filipino, Hawaiian and part Hawaiian, and other Asian or Pacific Islander. **Notes:** The AIDS case definition was changed in Sept. 1987 to allow for the presumptive diagnosis of AIDS-associated diseases and conditions and to expand the spectrum of human immunodeficiency virus-associated diseases reportable as AIDS. Excludes residents of U.S. territories. Data are updated periodically because of reporting delays. Data for all years have been updated through Dec. 31, 1992.

## New AIDS Cases in the U.S., 1985-1992, by Transmission Category

Source: *Health United States 1992*, National Center for Health Statistics, U.S. Dept. of Health and Human Services

| Sex and transmission category | All years[1] | 1985 | 1986 | 1987 | 1988 | 1989 | 1990 | 1991 | 1992 |
|---|---|---|---|---|---|---|---|---|---|
| Male ................... | 214,981 | 7,555 | 12,002 | 19,082 | 27,108 | 29,625 | 36,378 | 37,656 | 38,789 |
| Men who have sex with men ... | 141,137 | 5,429 | 8,542 | 13,550 | 17,860 | 19,688 | 23,890 | 23,872 | 23,653 |
| Injecting drug use .......... | 39,865 | 1,111 | 1,767 | 2,708 | 5,296 | 5,441 | 6,992 | 7,664 | 7,879 |
| Men who have sex with men and injecting drug use ............. | 15,244 | 592 | 989 | 1,551 | 2,037 | 2,189 | 2,389 | 2,454 | 2,355 |
| Hemophilia/coagulation disorder . | 1,958 | 73 | 118 | 202 | 293 | 279 | 328 | 303 | 310 |
| Born in Caribbean/African countries | 2,075 | 109 | 160 | 187 | 262 | 236 | 304 | 325 | 283 |
| Heterosexual contact[2] ....... | 3,942 | 28 | 65 | 161 | 326 | 504 | 721 | 881 | 1,243 |
| Sex with injecting drug user . | 2,413 | 25 | 44 | 114 | 228 | 369 | 462 | 521 | 639 |
| Transfusion[3] ............. | 2,952 | 111 | 193 | 399 | 488 | 438 | 467 | 424 | 387 |
| Undetermined[4] ............ | 7,808 | 102 | 168 | 324 | 546 | 850 | 1,287 | 1,733 | 2,679 |
| Female ................. | 25,928 | 526 | 962 | 1,684 | 3,040 | 3,374 | 4,552 | 5,378 | 5,940 |
| Injecting drug use .......... | 12,925 | 284 | 477 | 840 | 1,630 | 1,771 | 2,260 | 2,683 | 2,701 |
| Hemophilia/coagulation disorder . | 43 | 1 | 4 | 4 | 4 | 6 | 9 | 8 | 3 |
| Born in Caribbean/African countries | 885 | 31 | 56 | 74 | 108 | 130 | 111 | 167 | 170 |
| Heterosexual contact[2] ....... | 8,236 | 116 | 276 | 486 | 861 | 1,003 | 1,499 | 1,826 | 2,092 |
| Sex with injecting drug user . | 5,374 | 82 | 193 | 330 | 634 | 694 | 1,019 | 1,160 | 1,207 |
| Transfusion[3] ............. | 1,848 | 60 | 105 | 217 | 322 | 284 | 324 | 239 | 263 |
| Undetermined[4] ............ | 1,991 | 34 | 63 | 115 | 180 | 349 | 455 | 711 |  |

(1) Includes cases prior to 1985. (2) Includes persons who have had heterosexual contact with a person with human immunodeficiency virus (HIV) infection or at risk of HIV infection. (3) Receipt of blood transfusion, blood components, or tissue. (4) Includes persons for whom risk information is incomplete, men reported only to have had heterosexual contact with prostitutes, and interviewed persons for whom no specific risk is identified. **Notes:** The AIDS case definition was changed in Sept. 1987 to allow for the presumptive diagnosis of AIDS-associated diseases and conditions and to expand the spectrum of HIV-associated diseases reportable as AIDS. Excludes residents of U.S. territories. Data are updated periodically because of reporting delays. Data for all years have been updated through Dec. 31, 1992.

# Health Services: Estimated Annual Revenue, 1990-1991

Source: Bureau of the Census, U.S. Dept. of Commerce

| Kind of business | Revenue (millions of dollars) 1990 | 1991 | Percent change 1990-1991 | Kind of business | Revenue (millions of dollars) 1990 | 1991 | Percent change 1990-1991 |
|---|---|---|---|---|---|---|---|
| Health services . . . . | $521,700 | $571,392 | 9.5 | Intermediate care facilities . . . . . . . | 4,382 | 4,910 | 12.0 |
| Offices and clinics of MDs . . . . . . . | 128,763 | 138,048 | 7.2 | Nursing and personal care facilities . . . . . | 2,198 | 2,543 | 15.7 |
| Offices and clinics of dentists . . . . . . . . | 29,202 | 30,488 | 4.4 | Hospitals . . . . . . . . | 276,273 | 305,971 | 10.8 |
| Offices and clinics of osteopaths . . . . . . | 2,513 | 2,599 | 3.5 | General medical and surgical hospitals . . | 247,923 | 275,106 | 11.0 |
| Offices and clinics of other health practitioners . . . . | 14,802 | 15,628 | 5.6 | Psychiatric hospitals . . | 14,639 | 15,368 | 5.0 |
| | | | | Specialty hospitals, except psychiatric . . | 13,711 | 15,496 | 13.0 |
| Offices and clinics of chiropractors . . . | 4,828 | 4,986 | 3.3 | Medical and dental laboratories . . . . . | 9,872 | 10,528 | 6.6 |
| Offices and clinics of optometrists . . . . | 4,275 | 4,430 | 3.6 | Medical laboratories . . | 8,209 | 8,849 | 7.8 |
| | | | | Dental laboratories . . | 1,663 | 1,678 | 0.9 |
| Offices and clinics of podiatrists . . . . . | 1,689 | 1,826 | 8.1 | Home health care services . . . . . . . . | 9,429 | 11,240 | 19.2 |
| Nursing and personal care facilities . . . . . | 35,749 | 39,319 | 10.0 | Miscellaneous health and allied services . . | 15,098 | 17,572 | 16.4 |
| | | | | Kidney dialysis centers | 1,545 | 1,824 | 18.0 |
| Skilled nursing care facilities . . . . . . . . | 29,168 | 31,866 | 9.3 | Specialty outpatient facilities . . . . . . . . | 8,276 | 9,715 | 17.4 |

# Health Insurance Coverage, 1990

Source: Bureau of the Census, U.S. Dept. of Commerce

(monthly average, first through fourth quarters)

| | Quarter 1 | Quarter 2 | Quarter 3 | Quarter 4 | | Quarter 1 | Quarter 2 | Quarter 3 | Quarter 4 |
|---|---|---|---|---|---|---|---|---|---|
| All persons. . . . . . . | 246,194 | 246,818 | 247,492 | 248,195 | Covered by Private Health Insurance Related to Employment of Self or Other Family Member | | | | |
| % Covered by Private or Gvt. Health Insurance | | | | | Total. . . . . . . . . . . | 61.1 | 61.6 | 61.4 | 61.3 |
| Total. . . . . . . . . . . | 86.4 | 87.0 | 87.2 | 87.1 | Age | | | | |
| Age | | | | | Less than 16 years. . . . | 59.6 | 59.5 | 59.1 | 59.0 |
| Less than 16 years. . . . | 85.4 | 86.0 | 86.4 | 86.2 | 16 to 24 years . . . . . . | 54.8 | 54.3 | 54.0 | 53.4 |
| 16 to 24 years . . . . . . | 78.2 | 78.7 | 78.7 | 78.1 | 25 to 34 years . . . . . . | 66.3 | 67.6 | 67.3 | 67.1 |
| 25 to 34 years . . . . . . | 81.3 | 82.8 | 83.1 | 83.0 | 35 to 44 years . . . . . . | 74.1 | 75.0 | 75.7 | 75.3 |
| 35 to 44 years . . . . . . | 86.9 | 87.4 | 88.1 | 87.9 | 45 to 54 years . . . . . . | 72.9 | 73.7 | 73.4 | 73.5 |
| 45 to 54 years . . . . . . | 88.3 | 88.6 | 88.5 | 88.6 | 55 to 64 years . . . . . . | 65.0 | 65.4 | 64.8 | 64.7 |
| 55 to 64 years . . . . . . | 89.9 | 89.9 | 89.9 | 89.5 | 65 years and over . . . . | 34.2 | 34.6 | 34.6 | 35.1 |
| 65 years and over . . . . | 99.6 | 99.7 | 99.7 | 99.7 | Race and Hispanic Origin | | | | |
| Race and Hispanic Origin | | | | | White . . . . . . . . . . . | 63.6 | 64.1 | 64.1 | 64.0 |
| White . . . . . . . . . . . | 87.3 | 87.8 | 88.1 | 88.0 | Black . . . . . . . . . . . | 47.0 | 46.9 | 46.4 | 46.2 |
| Black . . . . . . . . . . . | 81.4 | 82.2 | 82.2 | 82.0 | Hispanic origin[1] . . . . . . | 42.8 | 43.8 | 44.1 | 44.8 |
| Hispanic origin[1] . . . . . . | 68.7 | 70.2 | 71.2 | 71.8 | % Covered by Medicaid | | | | |
| Covered by Private Health Insurance | | | | | Total. . . . . . . . . . . | 7.5 | 7.8 | 7.9 | 8.1 |
| Total. . . . . . . . . . . | 75.6 | 76.3 | 76.5 | 76.1 | Age | | | | |
| Age | | | | | Less than 16 years. . . . | 13.8 | 14.5 | 14.9 | 15.5 |
| Less than 16 years. . . . | 70.8 | 71.2 | 71.1 | 70.7 | 16 to 24 years . . . . . . | 7.4 | 7.8 | 7.7 | 8.0 |
| 16 to 24 years . . . . . . | 69.8 | 70.1 | 70.6 | 70.0 | 25 to 34 years . . . . . . | 6.2 | 6.6 | 6.6 | 6.8 |
| 25 to 34 years . . . . . . | 73.4 | 74.8 | 75.0 | 74.9 | 35 to 44 years . . . . . . | 3.7 | 3.6 | 3.7 | 3.8 |
| 35 to 44 years . . . . . . | 81.4 | 82.1 | 82.9 | 82.7 | 45 to 54 years . . . . . . | 3.2 | 3.3 | 3.2 | 3.4 |
| 45 to 54 years . . . . . . | 83.2 | 83.8 | 83.9 | 83.8 | 55 to 64 years . . . . . . | 4.6 | 4.6 | 4.9 | 5.1 |
| 55 to 64 years . . . . . . | 80.8 | 80.9 | 80.8 | 80.2 | 65 years and over . . . . | 7.6 | 7.5 | 7.6 | 7.4 |
| 65 years and over . . . . | 77.1 | 78.4 | 77.8 | 77.4 | Race and Hispanic Origin | | | | |
| Race and Hispanic Origin | | | | | White . . . . . . . . . . . | 5.2 | 5.4 | 5.4 | 5.7 |
| White . . . . . . . . . . . | 79.0 | 79.7 | 79.9 | 79.5 | Black . . . . . . . . . . . | 21.7 | 22.6 | 22.8 | 23.0 |
| Black . . . . . . . . . . . | 56.0 | 56.9 | 56.2 | 55.9 | Hispanic origin[1] . . . . . . | 15.8 | 15.9 | 16.4 | 16.9 |
| Hispanic origin[1] . . . . . . | 50.4 | 52.3 | 52.9 | 53.0 | | | | | |

(1) Persons of Hispanic origin may be of any race.

# Selected Health Services: Estimated Sources of Revenue, 1991

Source: Bureau of the Census, U.S. Dept. of Commerce; in millions of dollars

| | Kind of business | | | | | | | |
|---|---|---|---|---|---|---|---|---|
| | Health practitioners | | Offices and clinics of MDs | | Offices and clinics of dentists | | Nursing and personal care | |
| Source of revenue | Revenue | Percent of total revenue | Revenue | Percent of total revenue | Revenue | Percent of total revenue | Revenue | Percent of total revenue |
| Total . . . . . . . . | $186,763 | 100.0 | $138,048 | 100.0 | $30,488 | 100.0 | $39,319 | 100.0 |
| Medicare . . . . . . . . | 33,439 | 17.9 | 31,159 | 22.6 | 184 | 0.6 | 3,218 | 8.2 |
| Medicaid . . . . . . . . | 8,778 | 4.7 | 7,580 | 5.5 | 610 | 2.0 | 20,799 | 52.9 |
| Other government . . . | 3,955 | 2.1 | 3,298 | 2.4 | 213 | 0.7 | 1,762 | 4.5 |
| Private insurance . . . . | 80,134 | 42.9 | 58,094 | 42.1 | 14,520 | 47.6 | 10,643 | 27.1 |
| Patient . . . . . . . . . . | 49,428 | 26.5 | 28,655 | 20.7 | 14,623 | 48.0 | 2,061 | 5.2 |
| Other . . . . . . . . . . | 11,028 | 5.9 | 9,262 | 6.7 | 338 | 1.1 | | |

# U.S. Health Expenditures, 1960-1991

Source: Health Care Financing Administration, Office of the Actuary; data from Office of National Health Statistics; in billions of dollars.

| Type of expenditure | 1960 | 1970 | 1980 | 1985 | 1986 | 1987 | 1988 | 1989 | 1990 | 1991 |
|---|---|---|---|---|---|---|---|---|---|---|
| National health expenditures | $27.1 | $74.4 | $250.1 | $422.6 | $454.8 | $494.1 | $546.0 | $604.3 | $675.0 | $751.8 |
| Health services & supplies | 25.4 | 69.1 | 238.9 | 407.2 | 438.9 | 476.9 | 526.2 | 583.6 | 652.4 | 728.6 |
| Personal health care | 23.9 | 64.9 | 219.4 | 369.7 | 400.8 | 439.3 | 482.8 | 530.9 | 591.5 | 660.2 |
| Hospital care | 9.3 | 27.9 | 102.4 | 168.3 | 179.8 | 194.2 | 212.0 | 232.4 | 258.1 | 288.6 |
| Physician services | 5.3 | 13.6 | 41.9 | 74.0 | 82.1 | 93.0 | 105.1 | 116.1 | 128.8 | 142.0 |
| Dental services | 2.0 | 4.7 | 14.4 | 23.3 | 24.7 | 27.1 | 29.4 | 31.6 | 34.1 | 37.1 |
| Other professional services | 0.6 | 1.5 | 8.7 | 16.6 | 18.6 | 21.1 | 23.8 | 27.1 | 30.7 | 35.8 |
| Home health care | 0.0 | 0.1 | 1.3 | 3.8 | 4.0 | 4.1 | 4.5 | 5.6 | 7.6 | 9.8 |
| Drugs & other medical nondurables | 4.2 | 8.8 | 21.6 | 36.2 | 39.7 | 43.2 | 46.3 | 50.5 | 55.6 | 60.7 |
| Vision products & other medical durables | 0.8 | 2.0 | 4.6 | 7.1 | 8.1 | 9.1 | 10.1 | 10.4 | 11.7 | 12.4 |
| Nursing home care | 1.0 | 4.9 | 20.0 | 34.1 | 36.7 | 39.7 | 42.8 | 47.5 | 53.3 | 59.9 |
| Other personal health care | 0.7 | 1.4 | 4.6 | 6.4 | 7.1 | 7.8 | 8.7 | 9.8 | 11.5 | 14.0 |
| Program administration & net cost of private health insurance | 1.2 | 2.8 | 12.2 | 25.2 | 24.6 | 23.0 | 26.9 | 33.8 | 38.9 | 43.9 |
| Government public health activities | 0.4 | 1.4 | 7.2 | 12.3 | 13.5 | 14.6 | 16.6 | 18.9 | 22.0 | 24.5 |
| Research & construction | 1.7 | 5.3 | 11.3 | 15.4 | 16.0 | 17.3 | 19.8 | 20.7 | 22.7 | 23.1 |
| Research[1] | 0.7 | 2.0 | 5.4 | 7.8 | 8.5 | 9.0 | 10.3 | 11.0 | 11.9 | 12.6 |
| Construction | 1.0 | 3.4 | 5.8 | 7.6 | 7.4 | 8.2 | 9.5 | 9.7 | 10.8 | 10.6 |
| | | | Average annual % change from previous year shown | | | | | | | |
| National health expenditures | — | 10.6 | 12.9 | 11.1 | 7.6 | 8.6 | 10.5 | 10.7 | 11.7 | 11.4 |
| Health services & supplies | — | 10.5 | 13.2 | 11.3 | 7.8 | 8.6 | 10.3 | 10.9 | 11.8 | 11.7 |
| Personal health care | — | 10.5 | 13.0 | 11.0 | 8.4 | 9.6 | 9.9 | 10.0 | 11.4 | 11.6 |
| Hospital care | — | 11.7 | 13.9 | 10.4 | 6.8 | 8.0 | 9.2 | 9.6 | 11.1 | 11.8 |
| Physician services | — | 9.9 | 11.9 | 12.1 | 10.9 | 13.3 | 13.1 | 10.4 | 11.0 | 10.2 |
| Dental services | — | 9.1 | 11.9 | 10.1 | 6.4 | 9.6 | 8.5 | 7.5 | 7.7 | 8.8 |
| Other professional services | — | 9.6 | 19.1 | 13.8 | 12.0 | 13.6 | 12.4 | 13.8 | 13.5 | 16.7 |
| Home health care | — | 14.5 | 25.2 | 23.3 | 3.6 | 3.4 | 9.9 | 24.4 | 34.4 | 29.0 |
| Drugs & other medical nondurables | — | 7.6 | 9.4 | 10.8 | 9.9 | 8.6 | 7.2 | 9.1 | 10.3 | 9.0 |
| Vision products & other medical durables | — | 9.6 | 8.5 | 9.4 | 13.0 | 12.3 | 11.8 | 2.8 | 12.6 | 5.4 |
| Nursing home care | — | 17.4 | 15.2 | 11.3 | 7.6 | 8.0 | 7.8 | 11.1 | 12.3 | 12.4 |
| Other personal health care | — | 7.1 | 12.8 | 6.9 | 11.1 | 10.0 | 12.1 | 11.8 | 17.4 | 21.9 |
| Program administration & net cost of private health insurance | — | 9.0 | 16.0 | 15.5 | −2.5 | −6.6 | 16.8 | 25.7 | 15.3 | 12.7 |
| Government public health activities | — | 13.9 | 18.0 | 11.3 | 9.6 | 8.3 | 13.5 | 14.3 | 16.0 | 11.6 |
| Research & construction | — | 12.1 | 7.8 | 6.4 | 3.7 | 8.2 | 14.9 | 4.2 | 9.6 | 2.1 |
| Research[1] | — | 10.9 | 10.8 | 7.4 | 9.5 | 5.7 | 14.5 | 6.2 | 8.0 | 6.1 |
| Construction | — | 12.8 | 5.6 | 5.4 | −2.4 | 11.1 | 15.3 | 1.9 | 11.5 | −2.2 |

(1) Research and development expenditures of drug companies and other manufacturers and providers of medical equipment and supplies are excluded from "research expenditures," but included in the expenditure class in which the product falls. **Note:** Numbers may not add to totals because of rounding.

# The 25 Drugs Most Frequently Prescribed in Physicians' Offices, 1990

Source: National Center for Health Statistics. U.S. Dept. of Health and Human Services; in thousands

| Rank | Name of drug and principal generic substance[1] | Number of times prescribed | Therapeutic use |
|---|---|---|---|
| 1. | Amoxicillin | 17,891 | Antibiotic |
| 2. | Amoxil (amoxicillin) | 13,448 | Antibiotic |
| 3. | Ceclor (cefaclor) | 8,910 | Antibiotic |
| 4. | Lasix (furosemide) | 8,868 | Diuretic, antihypertensive |
| 5. | Prednisone | 7,830 | Steroid replacement therapy, anti-inflammatory agent |
| 6. | Naprosyn (naproxen) | 7,585 | Nonsteroidal anti-inflammatory agent |
| 7. | Seldane (terfenadine) | 7,251 | Antihistaminic |
| 8. | Motrin (ibuprofen) | 6,988 | Nonsteroidal anti-inflammatory agent |
| 9. | Zantac (ranitidine) | 6,501 | Duodenal or gastric ulcer |
| 10. | Premarin (estrogens) | 6,327 | Estrogen replacement therapy |
| 11. | Lanoxin (digoxin) | 6,275 | Cardiotonic/digitalis |
| 12. | Vasotec (enalapril) | 5,991 | Antihypertensive |
| 13. | Aspirin or A.S.A. | 5,896 | Analgesic, anti-inflammatory, antipyretic |
| 14. | Proventil (albuterol) | 5,614 | Bronchodilator |
| 15. | Dyazide (triamterene, hydrochlorothiazide) | 5,584 | Diuretic, antihypertensive |
| 16. | Diphtheria tetanus toxoids pertussis | 5,176 | Immunization |
| 17. | Voltaren (diclofenac sodium) | 5,160 | Nonsteroidal anti-inflammatory agent |
| 18. | Tylenol (acetaminophen) | 5,144 | Analgesic |
| 19. | Synthroid (levothyroxine) | 5,137 | Thyroid hormone therapy |
| 20. | Xanax (alprazolam) | 5,089 | Anxiety disorders |
| 21. | Cardizem (ditiazem) | 4,979 | Cardiotonic/calcium channel blocking agent |
| 22. | Capoten (captopril) | 4,785 | Antihypertensive |
| 23. | Prozac (fluoxetine) | 4,785 | Antidepressant |
| 24. | Calan (verapamil) | 4,755 | Cardiotonic/calcium channel blocking agent |
| 25. | Ventolin (albuterol) | 4,666 | Bronchodilator |

(1) The trade or generic name used by the physician on the prescription or other medical records. The use of trade names is for identification only and does not imply endorsement by the Public Health Service or the U.S. Department of Health and Human Services. Because of its nonspecific nature, the entry "Allergy relief or shots," with 4,184,000 mentions, is omitted.

## Years of Life Expected at Birth

Source: National Center for Health Statistics

| Year | All Races Total | Male | Female | White Total | Male | Female | Black and Other Total | Male | Female |
|---|---|---|---|---|---|---|---|---|---|
| 1920* . . . . . | 54.1 | 53.6 | 54.6 | 54.9 | 54.4 | 55.6 | 45.3 | 45.5 | 45.2 |
| 1930 . . . . . | 59.7 | 58.1 | 61.6 | 61.4 | 59.7 | 63.5 | 48.1 | 47.3 | 49.2 |
| 1940 . . . . . | 62.9 | 60.8 | 65.2 | 64.2 | 62.1 | 66.6 | 53.1 | 51.5 | 54.9 |
| 1950 . . . . . | 68.2 | 65.6 | 71.1 | 69.1 | 66.5 | 72.2 | 60.8 | 59.1 | 62.9 |
| 1960 . . . . . | 69.7 | 66.6 | 73.1 | 70.6 | 67.4 | 74.1 | 63.6 | 61.1 | 66.3 |
| 1965 . . . . . | 70.2 | 66.8 | 73.7 | 71.0 | 67.6 | 74.7 | 64.1 | 61.1 | 67.4 |
| 1970 . . . . . | 70.8 | 67.1 | 74.7 | 71.7 | 68.0 | 75.6 | 65.3 | 61.3 | 69.4 |
| 1971 . . . . . | 71.1 | 67.4 | 75.0 | 72.0 | 68.3 | 75.8 | 65.6 | 61.6 | 69.8 |
| 1972 . . . . . | 71.2 | 67.4 | 75.1 | 72.0 | 68.3 | 75.9 | 65.7 | 61.5 | 70.1 |
| 1973 . . . . . | 71.4 | 67.6 | 75.3 | 72.2 | 68.5 | 76.1 | 66.1 | 62.0 | 70.3 |
| 1974 . . . . . | 72.0 | 68.2 | 75.9 | 72.8 | 69.0 | 76.7 | 67.1 | 62.9 | 71.3 |
| 1975 . . . . . | 72.6 | 68.8 | 76.6 | 73.4 | 69.5 | 77.3 | 68.0 | 63.7 | 72.4 |
| 1976 . . . . . | 72.9 | 69.1 | 76.8 | 73.6 | 69.9 | 77.5 | 68.4 | 64.2 | 72.7 |
| 1977 . . . . . | 73.3 | 69.5 | 77.2 | 74.0 | 70.2 | 77.9 | 68.9 | 64.7 | 73.2 |
| 1978 . . . . . | 73.5 | 69.6 | 77.3 | 74.1 | 70.4 | 78.0 | 68.1 | 63.7 | 72.4 |
| 1979 . . . . . | 73.9 | 70.0 | 77.8 | 74.6 | 70.8 | 78.4 | 69.8 | 65.4 | 74.1 |
| 1980 . . . . . | 73.7 | 70.0 | 77.5 | 74.4 | 70.7 | 78.1 | 69.5 | 65.3 | 73.6 |
| 1981 . . . . . | 74.2 | 70.4 | 77.8 | 74.8 | 71.1 | 78.4 | 70.3 | 66.2ʳ | 74.4 |
| 1982 . . . . . | 74.5 | 70.9 | 78.1 | 75.1 | 71.5 | 78.7 | 70.9ʳ | 66.8 | 74.9ʳ |
| 1983 . . . . . | 74.6 | 71.0 | 78.1 | 75.2 | 71.7 | 78.7 | 70.9ʳ | 67.0ʳ | 74.7ʳ |
| 1984 . . . . . | 74.7 | 71.2 | 78.2 | 75.3 | 71.8 | 78.7 | 71.1ʳ | 67.2ʳ | 74.9ʳ |
| 1985 . . . . . | 74.7 | 71.2 | 78.2 | 75.3 | 71.9 | 78.7 | 67.0ʳ | 64.8ʳ | 69.3ʳ |
| 1986 . . . . . | 74.8 | 71.3 | 78.3 | 75.4 | 72.0 | 78.8 | 70.9ʳ | 66.8ʳ | 74.9ʳ |
| 1987 . . . . . | 75.0 | 71.5 | 78.4 | 75.6 | 72.2 | 78.9 | 69.1ʳ | 65.0ʳ | 74.8ʳ |
| 1988 . . . . . | 74.9 | 71.5 | 78.3 | 75.6 | 72.3 | 78.9 | 70.8ʳ | 66.7ʳ | 74.9ʳ |
| 1989 . . . . . | 75.1 | 71.7 | 78.5 | 75.9 | 72.5 | 79.2 | 70.9ʳ | 67.0ʳ | 74.9ʳ |
| 1990 . . . . . | 75.4 | 71.8 | 78.8 | 76.1 | 72.9 | 79.4 | 71.2ʳ | 67.0ʳ | 75.2ʳ |
| 1992ᵖ . . . . . | 75.7 | 72.3 | 79.0 | 76.5 | 73.2 | 79.7 | 71.8 | 67.8 | 75.6 |

p= preliminary. r= revised. * Data prior to 1940 for death-registration states only.

## Average Height and Weight for Children

Source: *Physicians Handbook*, 1990

| Age Years | Boys ft | Height in | cm | Weight lb | kg | Age Years | Girls ft | Height in | cm | Weight lb | kg |
|---|---|---|---|---|---|---|---|---|---|---|---|
| (Birth) | 1 | 8 | 50.8 | 7½ | 3.4 | (Birth) | 1 | 8 | 50.8 | 7½ | 3.4 |
| ½ | 2 | 2 | 66.0 | 17 | 7.7 | ½ | 2 | 2 | 66.0 | 16 | 7.2 |
| 1 | 2 | 5 | 73.6 | 21 | 9.5 | 1 | 2 | 5 | 73.6 | 20 | 9.1 |
| 2 | 2 | 9 | 83.8 | 26 | 11.8 | 2 | 2 | 9 | 83.8 | 25 | 11.3 |
| 3 | 3 | 0 | 91.4 | 31 | 14.0 | 3 | 3 | 0 | 91.4 | 30 | 13.6 |
| 4 | 3 | 3 | 99.0 | 34 | 15.4 | 4 | 3 | 3 | 99.0 | 33 | 15.0 |
| 5 | 3 | 6 | 106.6 | 39 | 17.7 | 5 | 3 | 5 | 104.1 | 38 | 17.2 |
| 6 | 3 | 9 | 114.2 | 46 | 20.9 | 6 | 3 | 8 | 111.7 | 45 | 20.4 |
| 7 | 3 | 11 | 119.3 | 51 | 23.1 | 7 | 3 | 11 | 119.3 | 49 | 22.2 |
| 8 | 4 | 2 | 127.0 | 57 | 25.9 | 8 | 4 | 2 | 127.0 | 56 | 25.4 |
| 9 | 4 | 4 | 132.0 | 63 | 28.6 | 9 | 4 | 4 | 132.0 | 62 | 28.1 |
| 10 | 4 | 6 | 137.1 | 69 | 31.3 | 10 | 4 | 6 | 137.1 | 69 | 31.3 |
| 11 | 4 | 8 | 142.2 | 77 | 34.9 | 11 | 4 | 8 | 142.2 | 77 | 34.9 |
| 12 | 4 | 10 | 147.3 | 83 | 37.7 | 12 | 4 | 10 | 147.3 | 86 | 39.0 |
| 13 | 5 | 0 | 152.4 | 92 | 41.7 | 13 | 5 | 0 | 152.4 | 98 | 45.5 |
| 14 | 5 | 2 | 157.5 | 107 | 48.5 | 14 | 5 | 2 | 157.5 | 107 | 48.5 |

This table gives a general picture of American children at specific ages. When used as a standard, the individual variation in children's growth should not be overlooked. In most cases the height-weight relationship is probably a more valid index of weight status than a weight-for-age assessment.

## Average Weight of Americans by Height and Age

Source: Society of Actuaries

The figures represent weights in ordinary indoor clothing and shoes, and heights with shoes.

| Men Height | 20-24 | 25-29 | 30-39 | 40-49 | 50-59 | 60-69 | Women Height | 20-24 | 25-29 | 30-39 | 40-49 | 50-59 | 60-69 |
|---|---|---|---|---|---|---|---|---|---|---|---|---|---|
| 5'2" . . . . | 130 | 134 | 138 | 140 | 141 | 140 | 4'10" . . . | 105 | 110 | 113 | 118 | 121 | 123 |
| 5'3" . . . . | 136 | 140 | 143 | 144 | 145 | 144 | 4'11" . . . | 110 | 112 | 115 | 121 | 125 | 127 |
| 5'4" . . . . | 139 | 143 | 147 | 149 | 150 | 149 | 5'0" . . . . | 112 | 114 | 118 | 123 | 127 | 130 |
| 5'5" . . . . | 143 | 147 | 151 | 154 | 155 | 153 | 5'1" . . . . | 116 | 119 | 121 | 127 | 131 | 133 |
| 5'6" . . . . | 148 | 152 | 156 | 158 | 159 | 158 | 5'2" . . . . | 120 | 121 | 124 | 129 | 133 | 136 |
| 5'7" . . . . | 153 | 156 | 160 | 163 | 164 | 163 | 5'3" . . . . | 124 | 125 | 128 | 133 | 137 | 140 |
| 5'8" . . . . | 157 | 161 | 165 | 167 | 168 | 167 | 5'4" . . . . | 127 | 128 | 131 | 136 | 141 | 143 |
| 5'9" . . . . | 163 | 166 | 170 | 172 | 173 | 172 | 5'5" . . . . | 130 | 132 | 134 | 139 | 144 | 147 |
| 5'10" . . . . | 167 | 171 | 174 | 176 | 177 | 176 | 5'6" . . . . | 133 | 134 | 137 | 143 | 147 | 150 |
| 5'11" . . . . | 171 | 175 | 179 | 181 | 182 | 181 | 5'7" . . . . | 137 | 138 | 141 | 147 | 152 | 155 |
| 6'0" . . . . | 176 | 181 | 184 | 186 | 187 | 186 | 5'8" . . . . | 141 | 142 | 145 | 150 | 156 | 158 |
| 6'1" . . . . | 182 | 186 | 190 | 192 | 193 | 191 | 5'9" . . . . | 146 | 148 | 150 | 155 | 159 | 161 |
| 6'2" . . . . | 187 | 191 | 195 | 197 | 198 | 196 | 5'10" . . . | 149 | 150 | 153 | 158 | 162 | 163 |
| 6'3" . . . . | 193 | 197 | 201 | 203 | 204 | 200 | 5'11" . . . | 155 | 156 | 159 | 162 | 166 | 167 |
| 6'4" . . . . | 198 | 202 | 206 | 208 | 209 | 207 | 6'0" . . . . | 157 | 159 | 164 | 168 | 171 | 172 |

# OBITUARIES

## Deaths, Oct. 26, 1992-Oct. 15, 1993

**A**

**Abe, Kobo,** 68; Japanese novelist and poet; Tokyo, Jan. 22.

**Acuff, Roy,** 89; singer and fiddler, star of the Grand Ole Opry for over 50 years; Nashville, Nov. 23.

**Adams, Diana,** 66; a leading ballerina of the 1950s and 1960s; San Andreas, Cal., Jan. 10.

**Adler, Stella,** 91; acting teacher, was a leading exponent of "Method" acting; Los Angeles, Dec. 21.

**Albert, Stephen J.,** 51; composer of symphonic music, won the 1985 Pulitzer Prize; Truro, Mass., Dec. 27.

**Albertson, Joseph A.,** 86; founder of supermarket chain; Boise, Jan. 20.

**Allison, Davey,** 32; stock-car driver; Birmingham, Ala., July 13.

**Ames, Leon,** 91; film and TV actor best-known for his roles as a kind, affectionate father ("Meet Me in St. Louis"); Laguna Beach, Cal., Oct. 12.

**Anderson, Marian,** 96; contralto who shattered racial barriers; Portland, Ore., Apr. 8.

**Andre the Giant,** 46; professional wrestler; Paris, reported Jan. 30.

**Andrews, Dana,** 83; actor, starred in films in the 1940s and 1950s; Los Alamitos, Cal., Dec. 17.

**Ashe, Arthur,** 49; tennis player, won the 1968 U.S. Open; New York, Feb. 6.

**B**

**Baudouin,** 62; king of Belgium for 42 years; Motril, Spain, July 31.

**Boulding, Kenneth,** 83; British-born economist, philosopher, and poet; Boulder, Col., Mar. 19.

**Boyle, Kay,** 90; novelist and short-story writer; Mill Valley, Cal., Dec. 27.

**Brian, David,** 82; actor, appeared in films and TV in the 1940s and 1950s; Sherman Oaks, Cal., July 15.

**Bridges, James,** 57; film writer and director; Los Angeles, June 6.

**Brusati, Franco,** 66; Italian film director, "Bread and Chocolate"; Rome, Feb. 28.

**Buell, Marjorie,** 88; creator of the Little Lulu cartoon character; Elyria, Oh., May 30.

**Burdett, Winston,** 79; radio and TV correspondent for CBS News; Rome, May 19.

**Burr, Raymond,** 76; actor, starred in the "Perry Mason" and "Ironside" TV series; Dry Creek Valley, Cal., Sept. 12.

**Bush, Dorothy Walker,** 91; mother of Pres. George Bush; Greenwich, Conn., Nov. 19.

**Butts, Alfred M.,** 93; inventor of the Scrabble board game; Rhinebeck, N.Y., Apr. 4.

**C**

**Cahn, Sammy,** 79; lyricist, collaborated with Jule Styne, Jimmy Van Heusen for numerous hit songs, "All the Way", "High Hopes"; Los Angeles, Jan. 15.

**Campanella, Roy,** 71; Hall of Fame catcher for the Brooklyn Dodgers; Woodland Hills, Cal., June 26.

**Cantinflas,** 81; Mexican comic actor, "Around the World in 80 Days"; Mexico City, Apr. 20.

**Charteris, Leslie,** 85; mystery writer, created Simon Templar, a hero known as "The Saint"; Windsor, England, Apr. 15.

**Chavez, Cesar,** 66; labor leader, founded the United Farm Workers of America; San Luis, Ariz., Apr. 23.

**Coles, Charles "Honi",** 81; tap dancer known for elegance and speed; New York, Nov. 12.

**Conn, Billy,** 75; boxer famed for 1941 heavyweight title bout against Joe Louis; Pittsburgh, May 29.

**Connally, John B.,** 76; Texas governor shot in the Kennedy assassination, Treasury secretary in the Nixon administration; Houston, June 15.

**Connors, Chuck,** 71; actor, starred in "The Rifleman" TV series, 1958-1963; Los Angeles, Nov. 10.

**Crews, Tim,** 31; pitcher for the Cleveland Indians; Little Lake Nellie, Fla., Mar. 22.

**Crichton, Robert,** 68; author of best-sellers "The Imposter", "The Secret of Santa Vittoria"; New Rochelle, N.Y., Mar. 23.

**Crosby, Bob,** 80; swing-era bandleader; Torrey Pines, Cal., Mar. 9.

**Culliford, Pierre,** 64; creator of the "Smurf" cartoon characters; Brussels, Belgium, Dec. 24.

**Cunningham, Harry,** 85; developer of Kmart, pioneered discount mass-merchandising; North Palm Beach, Fla., Nov. 11.

**Cusack, Cyril,** 82; Irish actor in theater and films; London, Oct. 7.

**D**

**De Mille, Agnes,** 88; noted choreographer of ballets ("Rodeo," "Fall River Legend") and musicals ("Oklahoma," "Carousel") on American themes; New York, Oct. 7.

**DeRita, Curly Joe,** 83; last surviving member of the Three Stooges comedy team; Woodland Hills, Cal., July 3.

**De Vries, Peter,** 83; writer, best known as a contributor to *The New Yorker* magazine; Norwalk, Conn., Sept. 28.

**Diebenkorn, Richard,** 71; artist, was a leading American painter of the postwar era; Berkeley, Cal., Mar. 30.

**Doolittle, James,** 96; aviation pioneer, Air Force general who led daylight air raid on Tokyo 4 months after Pearl Harbor attack; Pebble Beach, Cal., Sept. 27.

**Dopsie, Rockin',** 61; leading player of zydeco music; Opelousas, La., Aug. 26.

**Dorsey, Thomas A.,** 93; pianist known as the father of gospel music; Chicago, Jan. 23.

**Drysdale, Don,** 56; Hall of Fame pitcher for the L.A. Dodgers, sportscaster; Montreal, July 3.

**Dubcek, Alexander,** 70; Czechoslovak leader whose attempt at liberalization was crushed by Warsaw Pact troops in 1968; Prague, Nov. 7.

**E**

**Eckstine, Billy,** 78; singer and bandleader popular in the 1940s and 1950s; Pittsburgh, Mar. 8.

**F**

**Falco, Louis,** 50; Modern dance choreographer; New York, Mar. 26.

**Ford, Constance,** 69; actress, appeared on the "Another World" daytime serial for 25 years; New York, Feb. 26.

**G**

**Gallo, Julio,** 83; winery owner; nr. Tracy, Cal., May 2.

**Gardenia, Vincent,** 71; character actor in theater, films, and TV; Philadelphia, Dec. 9.

**Gehringer, Charlie,** 89; Hall of Fame 2d baseman for the Detroit Tigers, had a .320 career batting average; Bloomfield Hills, Mich., Jan. 21.

**Gesell, Gerhard,** 82; federal judge who presided over high-profile cases in the Watergate scandal; Washington, D.C., Feb. 19.

**Gillespie, Dizzy,** 75; trumpet player and a founding father of modern jazz; Englewood, N.J., Jan. 6.

**Gish, Lillian,** 99; actress, was a major star of silent films; New York, Feb. 27.

**Gleason, Thomas,** 92; labor leader, headed the International Longshoremen's Assn., 1963-1987; New York, Dec. 24.

**Golding, William,** 81; author, "Lord of the Flies"; won 1983 Nobel Prize for literature; Perranarworthal, England, June 19.

**Goodson, Mark,** 77; game show creator, "What's My Line?", "The Price Is Right"; New York, Dec. 18.

**Gould, Jack,** 79; TV and radio critic for the *New York Times*, 1944-1972; Concord, Cal., May 24.

**Granger, Stewart,** 80; leading man in swashbuckler films in the 1950s; Santa Monica, Cal., Aug. 16.

**Grey, Nan,** 75; leading lady in Hollywood films in the 1930s; San Diego, July 25.

**Gwynne, Fred,** 66; actor, best known as Herman Munster in the 1960s TV series "The Munsters"; Taneytown, Md., July 2.

**H**

**Hale, Clara "Mother",** 87; founder of Hale House, nurtured hundreds of abandoned and orphaned babies in New York City; New York, Dec. 18.

**Hamlin, Vincent,** 93; cartoonist, created the Alley Oop cartoon strip; Spring Hill, Fla., June 14.

**Hamner, Granville,** 66; major league shortstop for 17 seasons; Philadelphia, Sept. 12.

**Harken, Dwight,** 83; pioneering heart surgeon; Washington, D.C., Aug. 25.

**Hayes, Helen,** 92; actress, starred in the theater for some 65 years and, from 1931, in films; Nyack, N.Y., Mar. 17.

**Hearst, William Randolph, Jr.,** 85; editor in chief of the Hearst newspaper empire; New York, May 14.

**Henry, Paul,** 51; U.S. representative from Michigan since 1985; Grand Rapids, Mich., July 31.

**Hepburn, Audrey,** 63; actress, starred in numerous films in the 1950s and 1960s, "Roman Holiday," "Breakfast at Tiffany's"; Tolochenaz, Switzerland, Jan. 20.

**Hersey, John,** 78; journalist and novelist; Key West, Fla., Mar. 24.

**Hibbert, Eleanor,** 80s; author of some 200 novels, mostly as Victoria Holt or Jean Plaidy; at sea, Jan. 18.

**Holley, Robert W.,** 71; biologist, won the 1968 Nobel Prize for physiology or medicine; Los Gatos, Cal., Feb. 11.

**Holloway, Sterling,** 87; actor, was the voice of "Winnie-the-Pooh" in several animated films; Los Angeles, Nov. 22.

**Howe, Irving,** 72; literary and social critic, editor; New York, May 5.

**Hunt, James,** 45; British race car driver, won 1976 Formula One world championship; London, June 15.

**I**

**Iba, Henry,** 88; basketball coach, won 767 games, mostly with Oklahoma St.; won 2 national championships, 3 Olympic gold medals; Stillwater, Okla., Jan. 15.

973

**J**

**Janeway, Eliot**, 80; political economist and author; New York, Feb. 8.

**Jordan, James**, 57; father of NBA star Michael Jordan; Fayetteville, N.C., July 23.

**Jordan, Richard**, 56; actor, director, and writer; Los Angeles, Aug. 30.

**K**

**Kanin, Michael**, 83; screenwriter, producer, and director; Los Angeles, Mar. 12.

**Kauffman, Ewing M.**, 76; owner of the Kansas City Royals baseball team; Mission Hills, Kan., Aug. 1.

**Keeler, Ruby**, 82; tap-dancing star of musicals in the 1930s; Palm Springs, Cal., Feb. 28.

**Kemeny, John**, 66; computer pioneer and educator; Lebanon, N.H., Dec. 26.

**King, Albert**, 69; blues guitarist and singer; Memphis, Dec. 21.

**Kirchner, Claude**, 77; pioneer in children's TV, ringmaster of Tarrytown Circus in the 1950s and 1960s; Hawthorne, N.Y., Mar. 8.

**Kirsten, Dorothy**, 82; lyric soprano, sang at the Metropolitan Opera for over 30 years; Los Angeles, Nov. 18.

**Knebel, Fletcher**, 81; coauthor of best-selling novel "Seven Days in May"; Honolulu, Feb. 26.

**Kulwicki, Alan**, 38; auto racer, won the 1992 NASCAR championship; nr. Bristol, Tenn., Apr. 1.

**Kurtzman, Harvey**, 68; cartoonist, created Mad magazine; Mt. Vernon, N.Y., Feb. 21.

**Kusch, Polykarp**, 82; Nobel Prize winner in physics in 1955; Dallas, Mar. 20.

**L**

**Lamborghini, Ferruccio**, 76; founder of Italian sports car company; Perugia, Italy, Feb. 20.

**Lee, Brandon**, 27; actor, starred in martial arts films; Wilmington, N.C., Mar. 31.

**Lee, Pinky**, 85; vaudeville comic, hosted children's TV shows in the 1950s; Mission Viejo, Cal., Apr. 3.

**Lewis, Reggie**, 27; basketball player for the Boston Celtics; Waltham, Mass., July 27.

**Lewis, Reginald F.**, 50; financier, acquired Beatrice Cos. for $1 billion in 1987; New York, Jan. 19.

**M**

**MacMillan, Kenneth**, 62; choreographer, headed the Royal Ballet in Britain, 1970-1977; London, Oct. 29.

**Maglie, Sal**, 75; pitcher for the N.Y. Giants in the 1950s; Niagara Falls, N.Y., Dec. 28.

**Maleska, Eugene T.**, 77; crossword puzzle editor of the New York Times since 1978; Daytona Beach, Fla., Aug. 3.

**Mankiewicz, Joseph L.**, 83; film writer, director, and producer; won 4 Oscars; Mt. Kisco, N.Y., Feb. 5.

**Marshall, Thurgood**, 84; associate justice of the U.S. Supreme Court, 1967-1991; as a civil rights lawyer, won landmark 1954 "Brown vs. Board of Education" decision to desegregate public schools; Bethesda, Md., Jan. 24.

**Maynard, Robert C.**, 56; journalist who was the first black owner and editor of a major daily U.S. newspaper; Oakland, Cal., Aug. 17.

**McCluskey, Roger**, 63; race car driver, was U.S.A.C. national champion 5 times; Indianapolis, Ind., Aug. 29.

**McFarland, Spanky**, 64; child star of the "Our Gang" and "Little Rascals" films; Grapeville, Tex., June 30.

**Mickelson, George S.**, 52; governor of South Dakota; nr. Dubuque, Ia., Apr. 19.

**Milstein, Nathan**, 88; Russian-born violin virtuoso; London, Dec. 21.

**Mize, Johnny**, 80; baseball Hall of Famer, won 4 NL home run titles; Demorest, Ga., June 2.

**Montoya, Carlos**, 89; flamenco guitarist; Wainscott, N.Y., Mar. 3.

**Morgan, Edward P.**, 82; radio and TV journalist; McLean, Va., Jan. 27.

**Mosconi, Willie**, 80; world pocket billiards champion 13 times from 1941 through 1956; Haddon Heights, N.J., Sept. 16.

**Most, Johnny**, 69; radio voice of the Boston Celtics for almost 40 years; Cape Cod, Mass., Jan. 3.

**N**

**Nixon, "Pat"**, 81; wife of former President Richard Nixon; Park Ridge, N.J., June 22.

**Nureyev, Rudolf**, 54; dancer who was a leading ballet star of the 20th century; Paris, Jan. 6.

**O**

**O'Connell, Helen**, 73; big-band singer of the 1940s; San Diego, Cal., Sept. 9.

**Olin, Steve**, 27; pitcher for the Cleveland Indians; Little Lake Nellie, Fla., Mar. 22.

**Oort, Jan H.**, 92; Dutch astronomer; Leiden, the Netherlands, Nov. 5.

**Ozal, Turgut**, 66; president and former premier of Turkey; Ankara, Turkey, Apr. 17.

**P**

**Parish, Mitchell**, 92; lyricist, "Star Dust," "Deep Purple"; New York, Mar. 31.

**Pennel, John**, 53; pole vaulter, was the first to clear 17 feet; Santa Monica, Cal., Sept. 26.

**Petrovic, Drazen**, 28; basketball player for the N.J. Nets; Germany, June 7.

**Philbrick, Herbert**, 78; FBI spy whose book "I Led Three Lives" inspired a 1950s TV series; North Hampton, N.H., Aug. 16.

**Pollard, Jim**, 70; basketball Hall of Famer, played on 5 NBA championship teams; Stockton, Cal., Jan. 22.

**Pulitzer, Joseph, Jr.**, 80; chairman of the Pulitzer Publishing Co.; St. Louis, May 26.

**R**

**Ra, Sun**, 79; jazz pianist and bandleader; Birmingham, Ala., May 30.

**Reid, Kate**, 62; actress who appeared in films, TV, and the theater for some 40 years; Stratford, Ont., Mar. 27.

**Ridgway, Matthew B.**, 98; Army general who led U.S. forces in Normandy and UN troops in Korea; Fox Chapel, Pa., July 27.

**Riegels, Roy**, 84; football player famed for running 69 yards in the wrong direction at the 1929 Rose Bowl game; Woodland, Cal., Mar. 26.

**Roach, Hal**, 100; writer, producer, and director who was a leading pioneer in film comedy; Los Angeles, Nov. 2.

**Ross, Steven J.**, 65; entrepreneur who built and ran Time Warner Inc.; Los Angeles, Dec. 20.

**S**

**Sabin, Albert**, 86; pioneering researcher on viruses and viral diseases; developed oral polio vaccine; Washington, D.C., Mar. 3.

**St. Aubin, Helen**, 69; baseball player whose career inspired the film "A League of Their Own"; Los Angeles, Cal., Dec. 8.

**Salant, Richard S.**, 78; head of CBS News in the 1960s and 1970s; Bridgeport, Conn., Feb. 16.

**Salisbury, Harrison E.**, 84; Pulitzer Prize-winning foreign correspondent and New York Times editor; author of 29 books; Providence, R.I., July 5.

**Schwartzwalder, Ben**, 83; football coach at Syracuse University, 1949-1973; St. Petersburg, Fla., Apr. 28.

**Sharaff, Irene**, 83; costume designer who won 5 Oscars and a Tony award; New York, Aug. 16.

**Sharkey, Ray**, 40; film and TV actor; New York, June 11.

**Shawn, William**, 85; editor of The New Yorker magazine, 1952-1987; New York, Dec. 8.

**Sheaffer, Louis**, 80; biographer of Eugene O'Neill who won the 1974 Pulitzer Prize; New York, Aug. 7.

**Shirley, Anne**, 75; actress, starred in films in the 1930s and 1940s; Los Angeles, July 4.

**Simon, Norton**, 86; industrialist and art collector; Los Angeles, June 2.

**Slayton, Donald "Deke"**, 69; one of the original 7 U.S. astronauts; League City, Tex., June 13.

**Smith, Alexis**, 72; stage and screen actress; Los Angeles, June 9.

**Stegner, Wallace**, 84; novelist and short story writer, won 1972 Pulitzer Prize, "Angle of Repose"; Santa Fe, N.M., Apr. 13.

**Sulzberger, C. L.**, 80; foreign correspondent and foreign affairs columnist for the New York Times for nearly 40 years; Paris, Sept. 20.

**Swift, Kay**, 95; songwriter, "Can't We Be Friends," "Fine and Dandy"; Southington, Conn., Jan. 28.

**T**

**Tajo, Italo**, 77; Italian operatic bass noted for comic roles; Cincinnati, Ohio, Mar. 29.

**Todd, Ann**, 84; British stage and film actress, "The Seventh Veil"; London, May 6.

**Trace, Al**, 92; bandleader and songwriter, "Mairzy Doats"; Sun City West, Ariz., Aug. 31.

**Troyanos, Tatiana**, 54; mezzo-soprano; New York, Aug. 21.

**Twitty, Conway**, 59; country and western singer, had over 50 No. 1 songs on the country charts; Springfield, Mo., June 5.

**V**

**Valvano, Jim**, 47; basketball coach and TV commentator, led North Carolina State to the 1983 national championship; Durham, N.C., Apr. 28.

**Varsi, Diane**, 54; actress, starred in films in the 1950s; Los Angeles, Nov. 19.

**Villechaize, Herve**, 50; actor, best known as Tattoo in the "Fantasy Island" TV series; Los Angeles, Sept. 4.

**W**

**Waymer, David**, 34; NFL defensive back; Mooresville, N.C., Apr. 30.

**Westall, Robert**, 63; author of children's books; Cheshire, England, Apr. 15.

**White, F. Clifton**, 74; political strategist, served 4 Republican presidents; Greenwich, Conn., Jan. 9.

**Whitney, C. V.** 93; prominent figure in horse racing and the arts; Saratoga Springs, N.Y., Dec. 13.

**Wood, Walter A.**, 85; explorer, participated in over 100 mountaineering treks on 4 continents; West Palm Beach, Fla., May 18.

## Offbeat News Stories of 1993

**Hot Streak** — Soccer fans in the Bolivian village of Ixiamas were so excited with their team's 3-1 victory against Uruguay in a World Cup qualifying game that they didn't notice their homes were on fire. By the time the fire was spotted, it had spread to 40 homes. The fire began when firecrackers thrown by fans landed on the thatched roofs of homes.

**Body Shop** — The Los Angeles County Coroner's Office has gone into business. The office opened a shop called Skeletons in the Closet that offers such items as a toe tag like the ones attached to bodies, a tote bag with a skeleton figure (called Sherlock Bones) wearing a trench coat, and a beach towel with a chalk body outline. The profits help pay for a program to educate youths on the dangers of drunken driving.

**Goldberg Variations: A Boy Named Beerhall** — It is against the law in Germany to name a child after Whoopi Goldberg. Parents are forbidden by law from choosing names that blur gender or otherwise "endanger the well-being of the child." Whoopi was rejected by authorities as being too suggestive of the phrase "making whoopee." Other proscribed names included Bierstübl (beerhall) and Störenfried (disturber of the peace).

**Dog Gone** — A dog was suspended from baseball for the 1993 season. Baseball's Executive Council, which had suspended Cincinnati Reds owner Marge Schott for the 1993 season for using racial slurs, shortly afterward suspended her dog, Schottzie 02, from the field of Riverfront Stadium. The dog's suspension was welcomed by Reds players because the dog interfered with workouts at the ballpark and frequently soiled the artificial turf.

**Are You A Marxist?** — About 20 first-term House members were asked, "Do you approve of what we're doing to stop what's going on in Freedonia?" or "Do you approve of what we're doing to stop ethnic cleansing in Freedonia?" Replies included "take action" and "it's a different situation than the Middle East." None of the 20 House freshmen recognized the fictitious nation of Freedonia from the 1933 Marx Brothers movie *Duck Soup*. The joker was *Spy* magazine, whose national editor, Jamie Malanowski, characterized the responses as "completely understandable." "In campaigning," he said of the new lawmakers, "they are asked a lot of dumb questions, and they are all used to supplying answers."

**Too Late** — The Italian cabinet quickly abolished a regulation making people still responsible for the $50 annual health tax in the year in which they had died. Health Minister Maria Pia Garavaglia, who had issued the regulation, conceded that there was no way to enforce it.

**Hang 'Em High School** — Outlaw Tiburcio Vasquez was the hands-down winner in a local contest to name a new high school in Agua Dulce, Cal., winning out over the likes of John Wayne and Magic Johnson. Vasquez, whose reputation for cattle rustling and stagecoach robbing earned him the title Scourge of California, was hanged for murder in 1875.

**Isn't This A Rerun?** — The cable television company that serves Columbia, S.C., aimed a camera full-time at an aquarium to occupy a vacant channel while awaiting the start-up of the Science-Fiction Channel. When the Science-Fiction Channel replaced the "fish channel," complaints were so numerous that the cable company was forced to find another channel for the aquarium, which it ran 14 hours a day.

**Turning On** — A suspected drug dealer in Charles City, Va., tried to elude sheriff's deputies by slipping into the woods, but he was caught because he was wearing the wrong sneakers. He was wearing L.A. Gear's Light Gear sneakers, which feature battery-operated lights that flash when the heel hits the ground. "Every time he took a step, we knew exactly where he was," said a member of the sheriff's department.

## Miscellaneous Facts

—What has been the greatest upset in sports? In a survey of visitors by the Las Vegas Hilton, the most commonly picked event was the U.S. hockey team's defeat of the Soviet team at the 1980 Winter Olympics. Buster Douglas's 1990 knockout of heavyweight champion Mike Tyson was ranked second, and the N.Y. Jets' defeat of the Baltimore Colts in the 1969 Super Bowl ranked third.

—Psychiatric disorders affect 15 percent of American adults in any six-month period, according to the National Institute of Mental Health Advisory Council. The Council also reported that 12 percent of youths under 18 have mental, behavioral, or developmental disorders and that 10.9 percent of the U.S. population seeks mental health treatment annually.

—A survey by the National Opinion Research Center at the Univ. of Chicago found that nine of every ten Americans believe in God and that 78 percent believe in a life after death. Seven of every ten Americans believe in miracles, and four of ten report contact with the dead. About four of every ten attend church at least two or three times a month.

—There are laws against drunken driving and none against drunken walking, yet more than a third of the 5,546 pedestrians killed by cars in the U.S. in 1992 were drunk, according to the National Highway Traffic Safety Administration. The blood-alcohol level of 36 percent of pedestrians over age 14 who were killed by motor vehicles was high enough for them to be cited for drunken driving had they been behind the wheel.

—Have you been wondering whatever happened to the baseball hit by Mookie Wilson of the N.Y. Mets that rolled between Bill Buckner's legs in Game 6 of the 1986 World Series with the Boston Red Sox? In 1992 the ball was purchased at auction by actor Charlie Sheen for $85,000. At that same auction, a jersey used by Tom Seaver in 1969, the year the Mets won their first World Series, sold for $50,000, and Ty Cobb's full Detroit Tigers uniform from 1924 sold for $160,000.

—It cost the U.S. Census Bureau $2.51 billion to conduct the 1990 census. The Bureau counted 248.7 million people, at a cost of some $10 a person.

—Ludwig van Beethoven is the Elvis of classical music lovers, according to a listeners poll conducted by radio station WQXR-FM in New York City. Five of his works placed in the top ten, with his Ninth Symphony voted the most popular. His other works in the top ten were Symphonies no. 5, 6, and 7, and his Piano Concerto no. 5 (*Emperor*). Other works in the top ten were Bach's *Brandenburg Concerti*, Handel's *Messiah*, Dvorak's *New World Symphony*, Vivaldi's *The Four Seasons*, and Mozart's *Eine Kleine Nachtmusik*.

—The risk of a heart attack on Monday is as much as 50 percent greater than on any other day, according to findings by German researchers presented at an American Heart Association meeting.

# QUICK REFERENCE INDEX

For complete Index, see pp. 3-30